Visit classzone.com and get connected

ClassZone resources are linked together and provide instruction, practice, and learning support.

- **Online Examples** offer extra at-home support.
- **Online test practice** prepares students for assessments.
- **Self-scoring quizzes** provide comprehension checks.
- **Flashcards and crosswords** help students review vocabulary.
- **Animated Algebra** activities explore concepts.

MCDE2I49PVAPG
Use this code to create your own user password.

Also visit classzone.com to learn more about these innovative online resources.

eEdition Plus ONLINE
@HomeTutor
eWorkbook
Chapter-Based Support
Easy Planner Plus Online

Now it all clicks!™

McDougal Littell

Illinois 

McDougal Littell

ALGEBRA 1

Built for Illinois

Featuring:

- Illinois Standards Pacing Guide
- Illinois Table of Contents
- Illinois Student Guide
- PSAE Chapter Support
- Additional Standards Based Lessons
- Full Standards Correlation

About the Authors

Ron Larson is a professor of mathematics at Penn State University at Erie, where he has taught since receiving his Ph.D. in mathematics from the University of Colorado. Dr. Larson is well known as the author of a comprehensive program for mathematics that spans middle school, high school, and college courses.Dr. Larson's numerous professional activities keep him in constant touch with the needs of teachers and supervisors. He closely follows developments in mathematics standards and assessment.

Laurie Boswell is a mathematics teacher at The Riverside School in Lyndonville, Vermont, and has taught mathematics at all levels, elementary through college. A recipient of the Presidential Award for Excellence in Mathematics Teaching, she was also a Tandy Technology Scholar. She served on the NILM Board of Directors (2002–2005), and she speaks frequently at regional and national conferences on topics related to instructional strategies and course content.

Timothy D. Kanold is the superintendent of Adlai E. Stevenson High School District 125 in Lincolnshire, Illinois. Dr. Kanold served as a teacher and director of mathematics for 17 years prior to becoming superintendent. He is the recipient of the Presidential Award for Excellence in Mathematics and Science Teaching, and a past president of the Council for Presidential Awardees in Mathematics. Dr. Kanold is a frequent speaker at national and international mathematics meetings.

Lee Stiff is a professor of mathematics education in the College of Education and Psychology of North Carolina State University at Raleigh and has taught mathematics at the high school and middle school levels. He served on the NILM Board of Directors and was elected President of NILM for the years 2000–2002. He is a recipient of the W. W. Rankin Award for Excellence in Mathematics Education presented by the North Carolina Council of Teachers of Mathematics.

Printed in Canada

ISBN-13: 978-0-618-88852-8

ISBN-10: 0-618-88852-7 123456789—TBQ—10 09 08 07

Internet Web Site: http://www.mcdougallittell.com

Great lessons begin when your students are active and involved

Integrated print and technology captures the imagination and helps your students connect to essential math concepts.

Animated Algebra

Animated Algebra helps you answer the why and how of math with interactive, animated problem-solving graphics that capture your students' imagination.

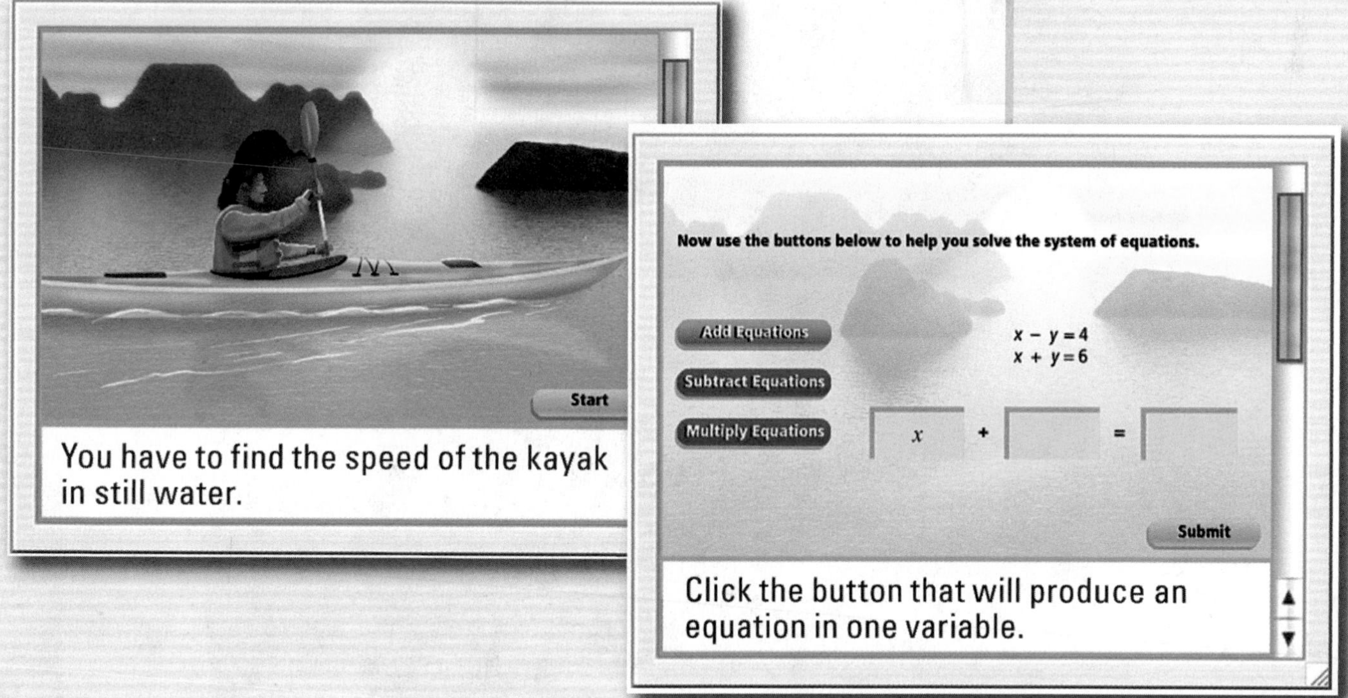
Start
You have to find the speed of the kayak in still water.
Now use the buttons below to help you solve the system of equations.
Add Equations
Subtract Equations
Multiply Equations
x − y = 4
x + y = 6
x + =
Submit
Click the button that will produce an equation in one variable.

Illinois 

McDougal Littell

ALGEBRA 1

GREAT LESSONS BEGIN

- When your students are active and involved
- When you teach the way you want to teach
- When assessment informs your daily instruction

Capture the imagination and provide a vital link to real-life problem solving with hands-on **Investigating Algebra Activities** to motivate the lesson.

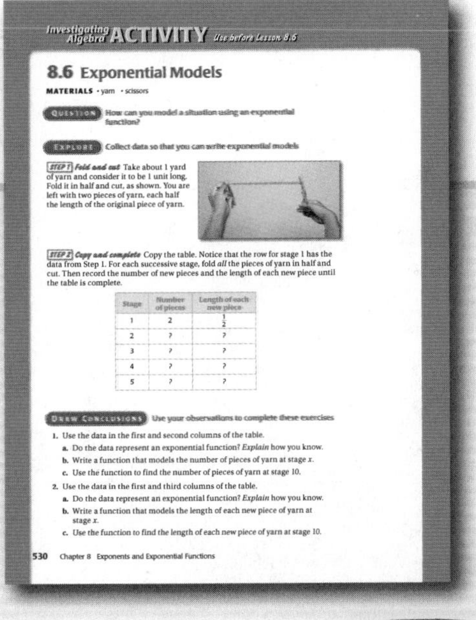

Investigating Algebra **ACTIVITY** *Use before Lesson 8.6*

8.6 Exponential Models

MATERIALS • yarn • scissors

QUESTION How can you model a situation using an exponential function?

EXPLORE Collect data so that you can write exponential models

STEP 1 ***Fold and cut*** Take about 1 yard of yarn and consider it to be 1 unit long. Fold it in half and cut, as shown. You are left with two pieces of yarn, each half the length of the original piece of yarn.

STEP 2 ***Copy and complete*** Copy the table. Notice that the row for stage 1 has the data from Step 1. For each successive stage, fold *all* the pieces of yarn in half and cut. Then record the number of new pieces and the length of each new piece until the table is complete.

Stage	Number of pieces	Length of each new piece
1	2	$\frac{1}{2}$
2	?	?
3	?	?
4	?	?
5	?	?

DRAW CONCLUSIONS Use your observations to complete these exercises

1. Use the data in the first and second columns of the table.
   a. Do the data represent an exponential function? *Explain* how you know.
   b. Write a function that models the number of pieces of yarn at stage x.
   c. Use the function to find the number of pieces of yarn at stage 10.
2. Use the data in the first and third columns of the table.
   a. Do the data represent an exponential function? *Explain* how you know.
   b. Write a function that models the length of each new piece of yarn at stage x.
   c. Use the function to find the length of each new piece of yarn at stage 10.

530 Chapter 8 Exponents and Exponential Functions

The **@Home Tutor CD-ROM** makes it easier than ever for students to focus on the math, enabling them to be more prepared for class.

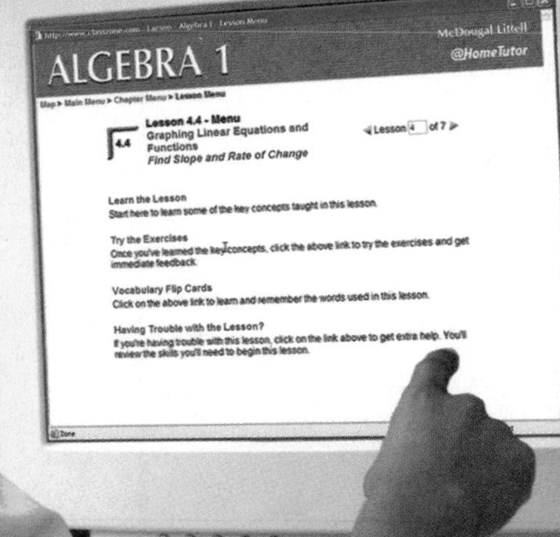

Great lessons begin when
you teach the way you want to teach

Flexible teaching tools help you reduce your preparation time and maximize your goals, while giving you the freedom to teach your way every day.

Power Presentations

The Electronic Classroom CD-ROM is the all-in-one source for dynamic teaching tools that save time and help you deliver the interactive lessons your students will remember.

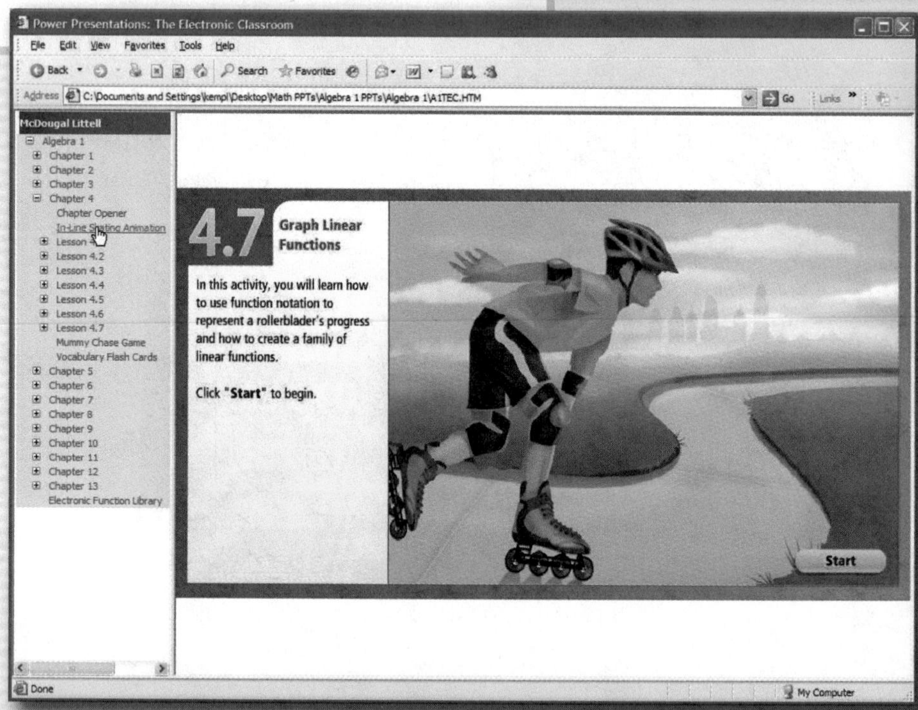

The **Electronic Function Library** is an easy-to-use graphing tool that makes it simple to incorporate everything from dynamic function families to colorful number lines.

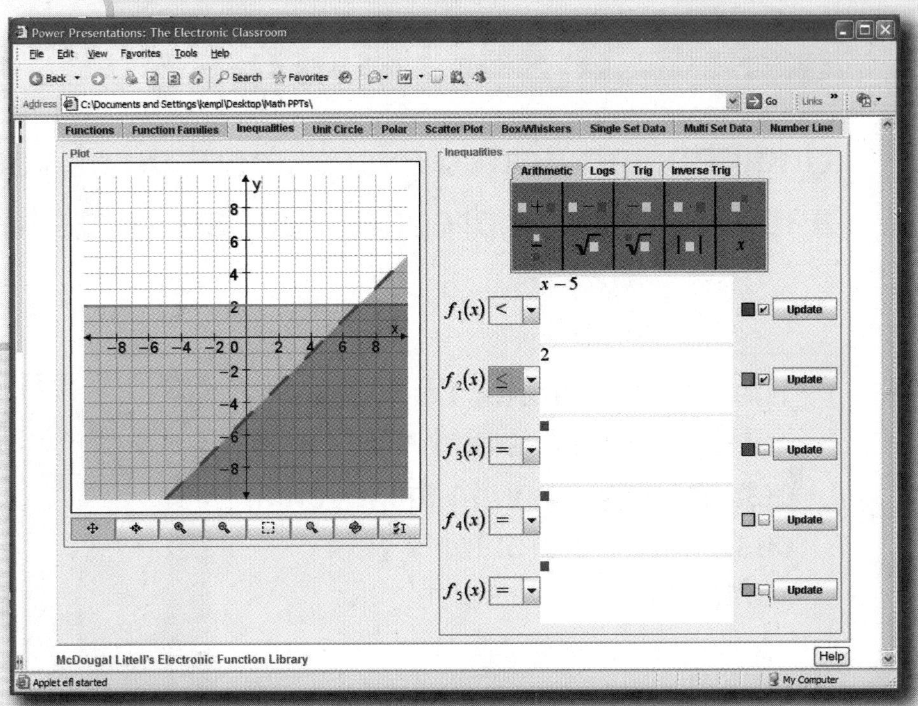

The **Activity Generator CD-ROM** gets students thinking with easily customized and leveled hands-on activities that are aligned to chapter content and to your state standards.

Editable Classroom Activities

High School Activity Generator STATE SPECIFIC

Get students thinking with editable hands-on activities aligned to your state standards.

New Version

This CD contains:

- Over 1000 editable, engaging activities
- Leveled activities designed to meet the needs of ALL students
- Hands-on, concept and calculator activities for every lesson in the program
- Activities correlated to your state standards

McDougal Littell

Great lessons begin when assessment informs your daily instruction

Ongoing, integrated assessment gives you the power, flexibility and feedback to prepare your students for success.

The **Test Generator CD-ROM** helps you assess both skills and comprehension with the leveled, customizable problems your students need to solve.

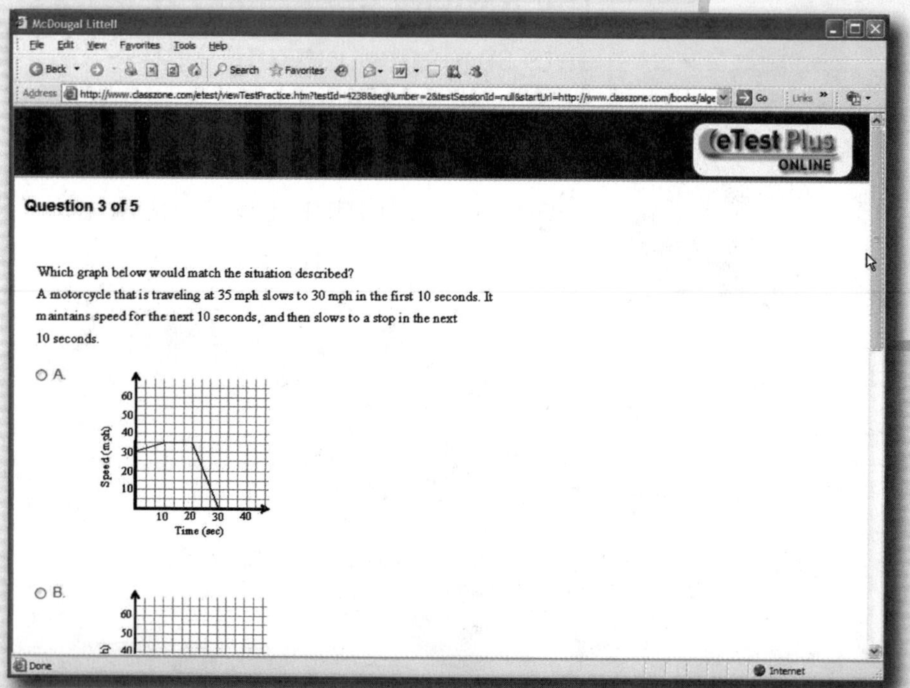

Online support at classzone.com provides online quizzes and chapter tests, instructional test practice, extra examples, and at-home tutorials just a click away.

McDougal Littell Assessment System

The **McDougal Littell Assessment System** is the full-circle assessment and remediation solution that helps you track, record, and accurately address each student's individual progress.

TEST
Unique testing is custom built to Illinois Standards.

REPORT
Diagnostic reports show you what Illinois Standards were missed.

SCORE
Automatic scoring gives you results in minutes.

RETEACH
Personalized remediation helps you target reteaching.

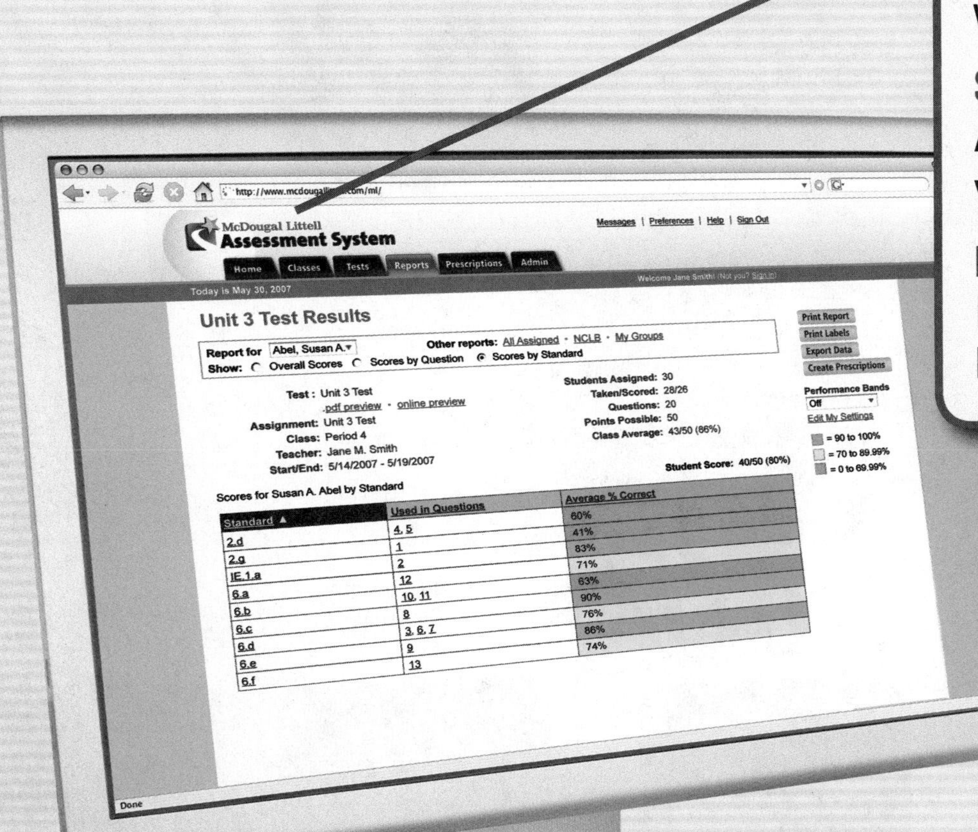

PROGRAM OVERVIEW

ALGEBRA 1 provides a complete set of resources organized for ease of use.

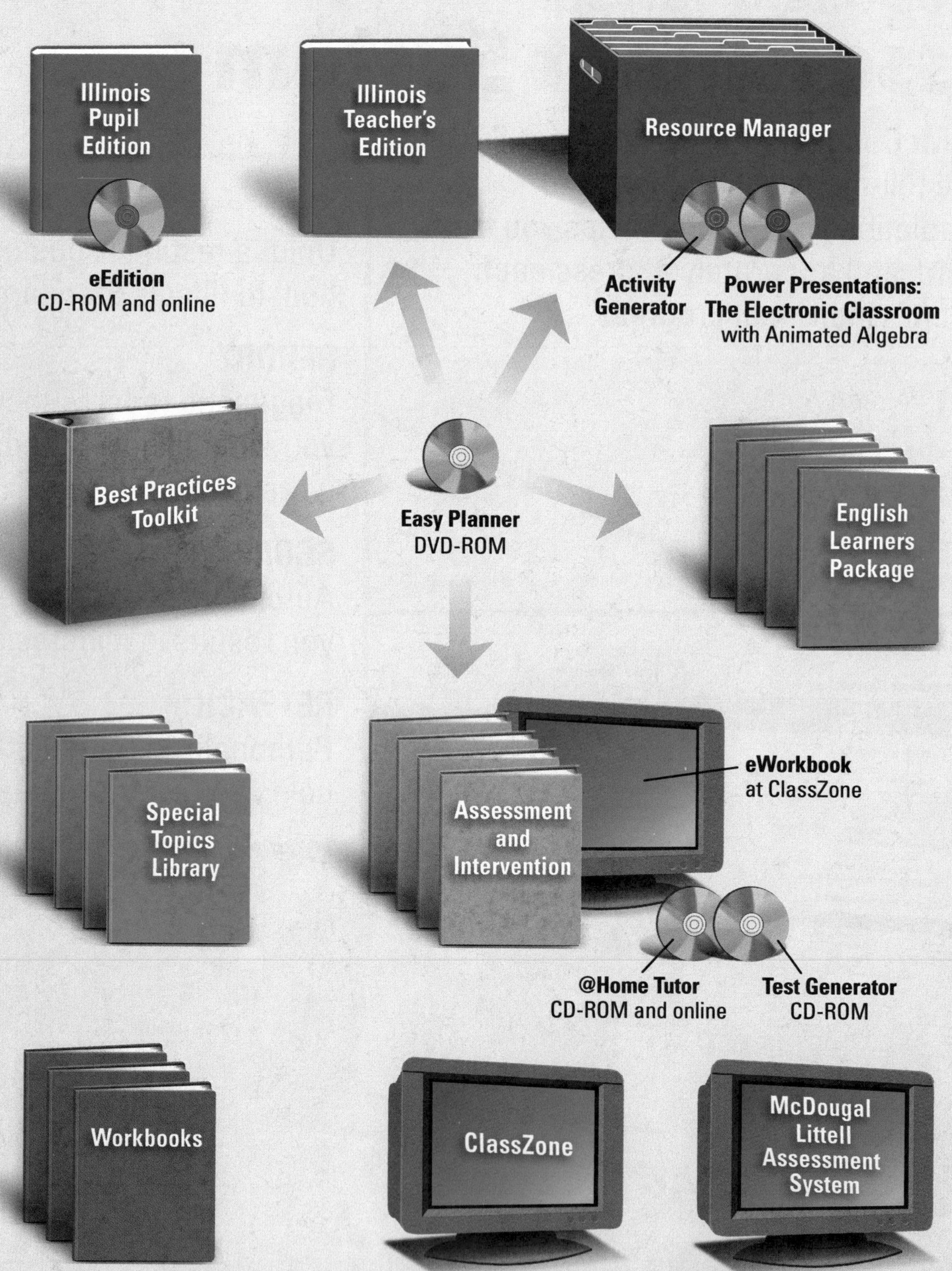

Guide to the Illinois Mathematics Assessment Frameworks

- Daily practice in every lesson
- Weekly practice in the mid-chapter mixed review
- Summative practice in the end-of-chapter assessment

Buckingham Fountain, Chicago, Illinois © Mark Segal/Getty Images

ILLINOIS STANDARDS PACING GUIDE

The following table gives a suggested pacing for presenting the textbook material so that the necessary content is covered for the state test in about 160 instructional days. The Mixed Review for Preparation and Practice material can be distributed throughout the course, as shown below, or you may wish to present it in the weeks immediately before the state test.

Day	Pages	Lesson or Feature	Illinois Standards
1	2–7	1.1 Evaluate Expressions	6.11.05, 6.11.07, 6.11.15, 7.11.03, 7.11.04, 7.11.05, 8.11.06, 8.11.16, 8.11.19, 8.11.22, 9.11.04, 9.11.05, 9.11.07, 9.11.08
2	8–12 13	1.2 Apply Order of Operations 1.2 Graphing Calculator Activity	6.11.04, 6.11.14, 6.11.15, 7.11.01, 7.11.03, 8.11.06 6.11.04, 8.11.06
3	14–20	1.3 Write Expressions	6.11.15, 6.11.17, 7.11.07, 8.11.02, 8.11.06
4	21–26 27	1.4 Write Equations and Inequalities Mixed Review	6.11.15, 7.11.03, 7.11.04, 9.11.05, 9.11.07, 9.11.08 6.11.04, 6.11.07, 6.11.15, 6.11.17, 7.11.03, 8.11.02, 8.11.06, 8.11.16
5	28–33 34	1.5 Use a Problem Solving Plan 1.5 Problem Solving Workshop	6.11.13, 6.11.14, 6.11.15, 6.11.18, 7.11.03, 7.11.04, 8.11.02, 8.11.16, 8.11.19, 8.11.22, 9.11.04, 9.11.05, 9.11.07, 9.11.08 6.11.13
6	35–40 41	1.6 Represent Functions as Rules and Tables 1.6 Graphing Calculator Activity	6.11.15, 8.11.04, 8.11.06, 8.11.11, 8.11.12, 8.11.13, 9.11.11, 10.11.01, 10.11.02, 10.11.04 7.11.04, 8.11.16, 8.11.19, 8.11.22, 9.11.07, 9.11.08, 10.11.01, 10.11.02, 10.11.04
7, 8	42–48 49–50 51	1.7 Represent Functions as Graphs 1.7 Extension: Determine Whether a Relation is a Function Mixed Review	8.11.11, 8.11.12, 8.11.13, 10.11.01, 10.11.02, 10.11.04 8.11.14, 10.11.01, 10.11.02, 10.11.04 6.11.14
9	52–56	Chapter Summary and Review	6.11.04, 7.11.03, 7.11.04, 8.11.04, 8.11.06, 9.11.05, 9.11.07, 9.11.08
10	57	Chapter Test	6.11.04, 6.11.14, 8.11.06
11	58–61	Test Preparation and Practice	6.11.14, 8.11.04
12	64–70 71–72	2.1 Use Integers and Rational Numbers 2.1 Extension: Apply Sets to Numbers and Functions	6.11.01, 6.11.15, 6.11.16, 9.11.05, 9.11.18 8.11.11, 8.11.12, 8.11.13
13	73–79	2.2 Add Real Numbers	6.11.05, 6.11.10, 6.11.13, 6.11.15, 9.11.05
14, 15	80–84 85 86	2.3 Subtract Real Numbers 2.3 Spreadsheet Activity Mixed Review	6.11.05, 6.11.10, 6.11.13, 6.11.15 6.11.10 6.11.01, 6.11.10, 6.11.13
16	87–93 94–95	2.4 Multiply Real Numbers 2.4 Extension: Perform Matrix Addition, Subtraction, Scalar Multiplication	6.11.05, 6.11.07, 6.11.10, 6.11.13, 6.11.15 6.11.03, 6.11.07, 6.11.12
17	96–101 102	2.5 Apply the Distributive Property 2.5 Problem Solving Workshop	6.11.05, 6.11.13, 6.11.14, 6.11.15, 8.11.01, 8.11.06 6.11.13
18	103–108	2.6 Divide Real Numbers	6.11.07, 6.11.10, 6.11.15, 9.11.18
19, 20	109–116 117–118 119	2.7 Find Square Roots and Compare Real Numbers 2.7 Extension: Use Logical Reasoning Mixed Review	6.11.01, 6.11.02, 6.11.07, 6.11.08, 6.11.09, 9.11.18 6.11.02, 8.11.21, 9.11.18 6.11.05, 6.11.07, 6.11.10, 6.11.13
21	120–124	Chapter Summary and Review	6.11.01, 6.11.02, 6.11.05, 6.11.07, 6.11.09, 6.11.14, 8.11.01, 8.11.06
22	125	Chapter Test	6.11.01, 8.11.01, 8.11.06
23	126–129	Test Preparation and Practice	6.11.10, 6.11.13, 8.11.02, 8.11.12, 10.11.01
24	132–140	3.1 Solve One-Step Equations	6.11.05, 6.11.15, 8.11.01, 8.11.02, 8.11.22
25	141–146 147	3.2 Solve Two-Step Equations 3.2 Problem Solving Workshop	6.11.15 6.11.10, 6.11.13, 8.11.02, 10.11.01
26	148–153	3.3 Solve Multi-Step Equations	6.11.05, 6.11.15, 7.11.07
27, 28	154–159 160 161	3.4 Solve Equations with Variables on Both Sides 3.4 Spreadsheet Activity Mixed Review	6.11.15 6.11.05, 6.11.15, 8.11.12 6.11.05, 6.11.15, 8.11.01, 8.11.02
29	162–167	3.5 Write Ratios and Proportions	6.11.15, 6.11.17, 7.11.06, 7.11.07

Day	Pages	Lesson or Feature	Illinois Standards
30	168–173	3.6 Solve Proportions Using Cross Products	6.11.17, 7.11.06, 7.11.07, 9.11.03
	174–175	3.6 Extension: Apply Proportions to Similar Figures	6.11.17, 7.11.04, 7.11.06, 9.11.05, 9.11.07, 9.11.08, 9.11.12, 9.11.16, 9.11.19
31	176–181	3.7 Solve Percent Problems	6.11.17, 6.11.18, 7.11.03, 7.11.04, 9.11.05, 9.11.07, 9.11.08
	182–183	3.7 Extension: Find Percent of Change	6.11.17
32, 33	184–189	3.8 Rewrite Equations and Formulas	6.11.18, 7.11.03, 7.11.04, 8.11.01, 8.11.14, 8.11.16, 8.11.19, 8.11.22, 9.11.04, 9.11.05, 9.11.07, 9.11.08, 9.11.10
	190	Mixed Review	7.11.03, 7.11.04, 8.11.16, 8.11.19, 9.11.04, 9.11.05, 9.11.07, 9.11.08
34	191–196	Chapter Summary and Review	6.11.05, 6.11.17, 6.11.18, 7.11.03
35	197	Chapter Test	6.11.17, 6.11.18
36	198–201	Test Preparation and Practice	6.11.05, 6.11.17, 6.11.18, 8.11.02, 8.11.16, 8.11.22
37	202–203	Cumulative Review	6.11.16, 6.11.17, 7.11.03, 7.11.04, 7.11.06, 7.11.07, 8.11.04, 8.11.14, 9.11.05, 9.11.07, 9.11.08
38	206–212	4.1 Plot Points in a Coordinate Plane	7.11.04, 8.11.01, 8.11.04, 8.11.11, 8.11.12, 8.11.13, 8.11.22, 9.11.09, 9.11.11
	213–214	4.1 Extension: Perform Transformations	9.11.02
39, 40	215–221	4.2 Graph Linear Equations	8.11.03, 8.11.06, 8.11.07, 8.11.08, 8.11.11, 8.11.12, 8.11.13, 8.11.14, 8.11.22, 9.11.11, 10.11.01, 10.11.02, 10.11.04
	222	4.2 Graphing Calculator Activity	8.11.03, 8.11.14, 10.11.01, 10.11.02, 10.11.04
	223–224	4.2 Extension: Identify Discrete and Continuous Functions	8.11.03, 8.11.11, 8.11.14
41	225–232	4.3 Graph Using Intercepts	6.11.17, 8.11.11, 8.11.12, 8.11.13, 8.11.14, 9.11.11, 10.11.01, 10.11.02, 10.11.04
	233	Mixed Review	8.11.03, 8.11.06, 8.11.08, 8.11.11, 8.11.12, 8.11.13, 8.11.14
42	234–242	4.4 Find Slope and Rate of Change	6.11.17, 7.11.07, 8.11.02, 8.11.05, 8.11.09, 8.11.10, 8.11.11, 8.11.12, 8.11.13, 8.11.14, 8.11.22, 9.11.09, 10.11.01, 10.11.02, 10.11.04
43	243–250	4.5 Graph Using Slope-Intercept Form	8.11.09, 8.11.10, 8.11.12, 8.11.13, 8.11.22, 9.11.07, 9.11.08, 9.11.09, 10.11.01, 10.11.02, 10.11.04
	251–252	4.5 Extension: Solve Linear Equations by Graphing	8.11.12, 8.11.13, 8.11.16, 8.11.22, 10.11.01, 10.11.02
44	253–259	4.6 Model Direct Variation	6.11.19, 7.11.07, 8.11.05, 8.11.07, 8.11.09, 8.11.10, 8.11.12, 8.11.13, 8.11.22, 10.11.01, 10.11.02, 10.11.04
	260–261	4.6 Problem Solving Workshop	6.11.13, 6.11.19, 8.11.10, 8.11.12, 8.11.13, 8.11.22
45, 56	262–268	4.7 Graph Linear Functions	6.11.19, 8.11.03, 8.11.06, 8.11.07, 8.11.11, 8.11.12, 8.11.13, 8.11.14, 8.11.16, 8.11.22, 9.11.11, 10.11.01, 10.11.02, 10.11.04
	269	Mixed Review	6.11.19, 8.11.05, 9.11.09
47	270–274	Chapter Summary and Review	6.11.17, 6.11.19, 7.11.07, 8.11.03, 8.11.05, 8.11.08, 8.11.09, 8.11.10, 8.11.11, 8.11.12, 8.11.13, 8.11.14, 8.11.16, 8.11.22, 9.11.09
48	275	Chapter Test	6.11.19, 8.11.16
49	276–279	Test Preparation and Practice	6.11.19
50	282–289	5.1 Write Linear Equations in Slope-Intercept Form	7.11.03, 7.11.04, 7.11.07, 8.11.07, 8.11.08, 8.11.09, 8.11.10, 8.11.11, 8.11.12, 8.11.13, 8.11.14, 8.11.16, 8.11.22, 9.11.05, 9.11.07, 9.11.08, 10.11.01, 10.11.02, 10.11.04
	290–291	5.1 Graphing Calculator Activity	8.11.07, 8.11.10, 8.11.12, 8.11.13, 8.11.22, 10.11.01, 10.11.02, 10.11.04
51	292–299	5.2 Use Linear Equations in Slope-Intercept Form	8.11.05, 8.11.07, 8.11.09, 8.11.10, 8.11.12, 8.11.13, 8.11.16, 8.11.22, 10.11.01, 10.11.02, 10.11.04
	300–301	5.2 Problem Solving Workshop	8.11.09, 8.11.12, 8.11.13, 8.11.16, 8.11.22
52	302–308	5.3 Write Linear Equations in Point-Slope Form	6.11.16, 6.11.17, 7.11.07, 8.11.05, 8.11.07, 8.11.09, 8.11.10, 8.11.11, 8.11.12, 8.11.13, 8.11.16, 8.11.22, 10.11.01, 10.11.02, 10.11.04
	309–310	5.3 Extension: Relate Arithmetic Sequences to Linear Functions	8.11.04, 8.11.12, 8.11.13, 8.11.22, 10.11.01, 10.11.02, 10.11.04
53, 54	311–316	5.4 Write Linear Equations in Standard Form	8.11.07, 8.11.09, 8.11.10, 8.11.12, 8.11.13, 8.11.16, 8.11.22, 10.11.01, 10.11.02, 10.11.04
	317	Mixed Review	8.11.04, 8.11.05, 9.11.09
55	318–324	5.5 Write Equations of Parallel and Perpendicular Lines	6.11.19, 8.11.07, 8.11.09, 8.11.10, 8.11.12, 8.11.13, 8.11.16, 8.11.22, 9.11.07, 9.11.08, 9.11.18, 10.11.01, 10.11.02, 10.11.04
56	325–331	5.6 Fit a Line to Data	8.11.05, 8.11.07, 8.11.09, 8.11.10, 8.11.11, 8.11.12, 8.11.13, 8.11.16, 8.11.22
	332–333	5.6 Graphing Calculator Activity	8.11.07, 8.11.09, 8.11.10, 8.11.12, 8.11.13, 8.11.22
57, 58	334–341	5.7 Predict with Linear Models	8.11.07, 8.11.09, 8.11.10, 8.11.11, 8.11.12, 8.11.13, 8.11.22
	342	5.7 Internet Activity	8.11.07, 8.11.09, 8.11.10, 8.11.11, 8.11.12, 8.11.13, 8.11.22
	343	Mixed Review	8.11.07

Illinois Standards Pacing Guide

Day	Pages	Lesson or Feature	Illinois Standards
59	344–348	Chapter Summary and Review	8.11.07, 8.11.09, 8.11.10, 8.11.12, 8.11.13, 8.11.16, 8.11.22, 9.11.07, 9.11.08
60	349	Chapter Test	8.11.07, 8.11.09, 8.11.10, 8.11.12, 8.11.13, 8.11.22
61	350–353	Test Preparation and Practice	8.11.07
62	356–361	6.1 Solve Inequalities Using Addition and Subtraction	6.11.05, 8.11.16, 8.11.22
63	362–368	6.2 Solve Inequalities Using Multiplication and Division	6.11.05, 7.11.07, 8.11.16, 8.11.22
64, 65	369–374 375–376 377–378	6.3 Solve Multi-Step Inequalities 6.3 Problem Solving Workshop 6.3 Extension: Solve Linear Inequalities by Graphing	8.11.16, 10.11.03 6.11.13 8.11.16
66, 67	379–387 388 389	6.4 Solve Compound Inequalities 6.4 Graphing Calculator Activity Mixed Review	6.11.16, 8.11.02, 8.11.16 8.11.16 8.11.16
68, 69	390–395 396–397 398–403	6.5 Solve Absolute Value Equations 6.5 Extension: Graph Absolute Value Functions 6.6 Extension: Solve Absolute Value Inequalities	6.11.16, 8.11.16 6.11.16, 8.11.08, 8.11.10, 8.11.12, 8.11.13, 8.11.14, 8.11.19, 9.11.02 6.11.16
70, 71	404–412 413	6.7 Graph Linear Inequalities in Two Variables Mixed Review	6.11.16, 8.11.16 8.11.16
72	414–418	Chapter Summary and Review	8.11.16
73	419	Chapter Test	8.11.16
74	420–423	Test Preparation and Practice	8.11.16
75	426–433 434	7.1 Solve Linear Systems by Grap hing 7.1 Graphing Calculator Activity	8.11.02, 8.11.15, 8.11.17, 8.11.22 8.11.15, 8.11.17, 8.11.22
76	435–441 442	7.2 Solve Linear Systems by Substitution 7.2 Problem Solving Works hop	8.11.02, 8.11.17, 8.11.22 6.11.10, 8.11.17, 10.11.01
77	443–450	7.3 Solve Linear Systems by Adding or Subtracting	6.11.06, 8.11.02, 8.11.17, 8.11.22
78	451–457 458	7.4 Solve Linear Systems by Multiplying First Mixed Review	8.11.15, 8.11.17, 8.11.22 8.11.02, 8.11.15, 8.11.17, 8.11.22
79	459–465	7.5 Solve Special Types of Linear Systems	8.11.02, 8.11.15, 8.11.17, 8.11.22, 9.11.18
80, 81	466–472 473	7.6 Solve Systems of Linear Inequalities Mixed Review	8.11.02, 8.11.15, 8.11.17, 8.11.22 8.11.02, 8.11.15, 8.11.17, 8.11.22
82	474–478	Chapter Summary and Review	8.11.02, 8.11.15, 8.11.17, 8.11.22
83	479	Chapter Test	8.11.02, 8.11.15, 8.11.17, 8.11.22
84	480–483	Test Preparation and Practice: Proportional Change Problems	8.11.02, 8.11.15, 8.11.17, 8.11.22
85	484–485	Cumulative Review	6.11.05, 6.11.10, 6.11.13, 6.11.16, 6.11.17, 6.11.19, 8.11.01, 8.11.02, 8.11.07, 8.11.12, 8.11.13, 8.11.14, 8.11.16, 8.11.17, 8.11.22
86	488–494	8.1 Apply Exponent Properties Involving Products	6.11.07, 7.11.03, 7.11.04, 8.11.01, 9.11.05, 9.11.07, 9.11.08
87	495–501	8.2 Apply Exponent Properties Involving Quotients	6.11.07, 8.11.01, 8.11.02
88, 89	502–508 509–510 511	8.3 Define and Use Zero and Negative Exponents 8.3 Extension: Define and Use Fractional Exponents Mixed Review	8.11.04, 8.11.17 6.11.07 6.11.07, 7.11.01, 7.11.03, 8.11.01, 9.11.05
90	512–518 519	8.4 Use Scientific Notation 8.4 Graphing Calculator Activity	6.11.01, 6.11.02, 8.11.02 8.11.02
91, 92	520–527 528–529 530–538	8.5 Write and Graph Exponential Growth Functions 8.5 Problem Solving Workshop 8.6 Write and Graph Exponential Decay Functions	6.11.18, 7.11.07, 8.11.02, 8.11.03, 8.11.04, 8.11.08, 8.11.11, 8.11.12, 8.11.13, 8.11.14, 8.11.19, 10.11.01, 10.11.02, 10.11.04 8.11.02, 8.11.03, 8.11.14, 8.11.19 6.11.18, 8.11.02, 8.11.03, 8.11.04, 8.11.08, 8.11.11, 8.11.12, 8.11.13, 8.11.14, 8.11.19, 10.11.01, 10.11.02, 10.11.04
93	539–540	8.6 Extension: Relate Geometric Sequences to Exponential Functions	6.11.17, 8.11.02, 8.11.03, 8.11.04, 8.11.12, 8.11.13, 8.11.14, 8.11.19, 10.11.01, 10.11.02, 10.11.04
94	541	Mixed Review	8.11.11, 8.11.14
95	542–546	Chapter Summary and Review	8.11.02, 8.11.11, 8.11.14

Day	Pages	Lesson or Feature	Illinois Standards
96	547	Chapter Test	6.11.18, 8.11.02, 8.11.11, 8.11.14
97	548–551	Test Preparation and Practice	8.11.02, 8.11.03, 8.11.04, 8.11.06, 8.11.14
98	554–559 560	9.1 Add and Subtract Polynomials 9.1 Graphing Calculator Activity	8.11.04 8.11.01, 8.11.12, 8.11.13
99	561–568	9.2 Multiply Polynomials	8.11.17
100	569–574	9.3 Find Special Products of Polynomials	6.11.06, 7.11.03, 7.11.04, 9.11.05, 9.11.07, 9.11.08
101	575–580 581	9.4 Solve Polynomial Equations in Factored Form Mixed Review	8.11.01, 8.11.17 8.11.01, 8.11.02, 9.11.05
102	582–589 590–591	9.5 Factor $x^2 + bx + c$ 9.5 Problem Solving Workshop	8.11.01 8.11.01, 8.11.02, 8.11.12, 9.11.05
103	592–599	9.6 Factor $ax^2 + bx + c$	6.11.16, 8.11.01, 8.11.02
104	600–605	9.7 Factor Special Products	8.11.01
105, 106	606–613 614	9.8 Factor Polynomials Completely Mixed Review	7.11.03, 7.11.04, 8.11.01, 9.11.05, 9.11.07, 9.11.08, 9.11.10 7.11.03, 7.11.04, 8.11.01, 8.11.02, 9.11.05
107	615–620	Chapter Summary and Review	8.11.01, 8.11.02
108	621	Chapter Test	8.11.01
109	622–625	Test Preparation and Practice	7.11.03, 7.11.04, 8.11.01, 8.11.02, 8.11.12, 8.11.13, 9.11.05
110	628–634	10.1 Graph $y = ax^2 + c$	8.11.03, 8.11.08, 8.11.10, 8.11.11, 8.11.12, 8.11.13, 8.11.14, 8.11.17, 8.11.18, 8.11.19, 10.11.01, 10.11.02, 10.11.04
111	635–640 641–642	10.2 Graph $y = ax^2 + bx + c$ 10.2 Extension: Graph Quadratic Functions in Intercept Form	8.11.03, 8.11.08, 8.11.10, 8.11.11, 8.11.12, 8.11.13, 8.11.14, 8.11.18, 8.11.19, 10.11.01, 10.11.02, 10.11.04 8.11.03, 8.11.08, 8.11.10, 8.11.11, 8.11.12, 8.11.14, 8.11.18, 8.11.19, 10.11.01, 10.11.02, 10.11.04
112	643–649 650–651	10.3 Solve Quadratic Equations by Graphing 10.3 Graphing Calculator Activity	8.11.03, 8.11.08, 8.11.10, 8.11.11, 8.11.12, 8.11.13, 8.11.14, 8.11.18, 8.11.19, 10.11.01, 10.11.02, 10.11.04 8.11.08, 8.11.10, 8.11.12, 8.11.13, 8.11.14, 8.11.18, 8.11.19, 10.11.01, 10.11.02, 10.11.04
113, 114	652–658 659–660 661	10.4 Use Square Roots to Solve Quadratic Equations 10.4 Problem Solving Workshop Mixed Review	8.11.18, 8.11.19, 10.11.01, 10.11.02, 10.11.04 8.11.19 8.11.03, 8.11.08, 8.11.10, 8.11.11, 8.11.12, 8.11.13, 8.11.14, 8.11.19, 9.11.05, 10.11.01, 10.11.04
115	662–668 669–670	10.5 Solve Quadratic Equations by Completing the Square 10.5 Extension: Graph Quadratic Functions in Vertex Form	8.11.18, 8.11.19, 10.11.01, 10.11.02, 10.11.04 8.11.03, 8.11.08, 8.11.10, 8.11.11, 8.11.12, 8.11.13, 8.11.14, 8.11.18, 8.11.19, 10.11.04
116	671–676	10.6 Solve Quadratic Equations by the Quadratic Formula	8.11.14, 8.11.18, 8.11.19, 10.11.01, 10.11.02, 10.11.04
117	677–683	10.7 Interpret the Discriminant	7.11.04, 8.11.18, 8.11.19, 10.11.01, 10.11.02, 1010.11.04
118	684–691 692–693	10.8 Compose Linear, Exponential, and Quadratic Equations 10.8 Graphing Calculator Activity	8.11.02, 8.11.03, 8.11.08, 8.11.10, 8.11.11, 8.11.12, 8.11.13, 8.11.14, 8.11.18, 8.11.19, 10.11.01, 10.11.02, 10.11.04 8.11.18, 10.11.01, 10.11.02, 10.11.04
119	694	Mixed Review	7.11.05, 8.11.02, 8.11.03, 10.11.02, 10.11.04
120	695–700	Chapter Summary and Review	8.11.03, 8.11.08, 8.11.10, 8.11.11, 8.11.12, 8.11.13, 8.11.14, 8.11.19
121	701	Chapter Test	8.11.14, 8.11.19
122	702–705	Test Preparation and Practice	8.11.02, 8.11.03, 8.11.08, 8.11.10, 8.11.11, 8.11.12, 8.11.13, 8.11.14, 8.11.19
123	706–707	Cumulative Review	6.11.10, 8.11.01, 8.11.02, 8.11.03, 8.11.06, 8.11.08, 8.11.10, 8.11.11, 8.11.12, 8.11.13, 8.11.14, 8.11.16, 8.11.17, 8.11.19, 10.11.01
124	710–716 717	11.1 Graph Square Root Functions 11.1 Graphing Calculator Activity	6.11.07, 8.11.11, 8.11.12, 8.11.13 8.11.12, 8.11.13
125, 236	718 719–726 727–728	11.2 Investigating Algebra Activity 11.2 Simplify Radical Expressions 11.2 Extension: Derive the Quadratic Formula	6.11.07 8.11.01 6.11.07, 8.11.03, 8.11.19

Illinois Standards Pacing Guide

Day	Pages	Lesson or Feature	Illinois Standards
127	729–734	11.3 Solve Radical Equations	**6.11.07, 8.11.02**
128	735	Mixed Review	**6.11.07, 8.11.02, 8.11.12, 8.11.13, 8.11.14, 8.11.19**
129	736–742	11.4 Apply the Pythagorean Theorem and Its Converse	**9.11.01**
130, 131	743–750 751 752	11.5 Apply the Distance and Midpoint Formulas 11.5 Problem Solving Workshop Mixed Review	**9.11.01, 9.11.09** **9.11.01** **9.11.01**
132	753–756	Chapter Summary and Review	**9.11.01, 9.11.09**
133	757	Chapter Test	**9.11.01, 9.11.09**
134	758–761	Test Preparation and Practice: Problems Involving the Pythagorean Theorem	**9.11.01**
135	764–772	12.1 Model Inverse Variation	**6.11.19, 8.11.02, 10.11.01, 10.11.02, 10.11.04**
136	773–782	12.2 Graph Rational Functions	**6.11.19, 7.11.03, 8.11.11, 8.11.12, 8.11.13, 9.11.05, 9.11.07, 9.11.08, 9.11.10, 10.11.01, 10.11.02, 10.11.04**
137	783–791 792–793	12.3 Divide Polynomials 12.3 Graphing Calculator Activity	**8.11.01, 8.11.02, 8.11.06, 8.11.08, 8.11.12, 8.11.13, 8.11.14, 8.11.19** **9.11.18**
138	794–800	12.4 Simplify Rational Expressions	**8.11.01**
139	801	Mixed Review	**6.11.17, 8.11.01, 8.11.02, 8.11.06, 8.11.08, 8.11.12, 8.11.13, 8.11.14, 8.11.19, 9.11.05**
140	802–809 810–811	12.5 Multiply and Divide Rational Expressions 12.5 Extension: Simplify Complex Fractions	**6.11.08, 6.11.09** **7.11.03, 7.11.04, 8.11.18, 9.11.05, 9.11.07, 9.11.08, 9.11.10**
141	812–819	12.6 Add and Subtract Rational Expressions	**6.11.06, 8.11.01, 8.11.02**
142	820–826 827–828	12.7 Solve Rational Equations 12.7 Problem Solving Workshop	**6.11.05, 6.11.06, 8.11.01, 8.11.02** **6.11.05, 6.11.10, 6.11.18, 8.11.02, 8.11.12**
143	829	Mixed Review	**6.11.05, 6.11.10, 6.11.18, 8.11.01, 8.11.02**
144	830–834	Chapter Summary and Review	**6.11.19, 8.11.01**
145	835	Chapter Test	**6.11.19, 8.11.01, 8.11.02, 8.11.06, 8.11.12, 8.11.13, 8.11.14**
146	836–839	Test Preparation and Practice	**8.11.01, 8.11.02, 8.11.06, 8.11.08, 8.11.12, 8.11.13, 8.11.14**
147	842–848 849–850	13.1 Find Probabilities and Odds 13.1 Extension: Perform Simulations	**8.11.02, 10.11.07, 10.11.08** **10.11.07, 10.11.08**
148	851–855	13.2 Find Probabilities Using Permutations	**10.11.07, 10.11.08, 10.11.10**
149	856–859 860	13.3 Find Probabilities Using Combinations 13.3 Graphing Calculator Activity	**10.11.07, 10.11.08, 10.11.10** **10.11.07, 10.11.08, 10.11.10**
150, 151	861–867 868–869 870	13.4 Find Probabilities of Compound Events 13.4 Problem Solving Workshop Mixed Review	**10.11.03, 10.11.07, 10.11.08** **10.11.09** **8.11.02, 10.11.07, 10.11.08, 10.11.10**
152	871–874	13.5 Analyze Surveys and Samples	
153	875–878 879–880	13.6 Use Measures of Central Tendency and Dispersion 13.6 Extension: Calculate Variance and Standard Deviation	**6.11.01, 10.11.04, 10.11.05, 10.11.06** **10.11.04, 10.11.05, 10.11.06**
154	881–885 886	13.7 Interpret Stem-and-Leaf Plots and Histograms 13.7 Graphing Calculator Activity	**10.11.04, 10.11.05, 10.11.06** **10.11.01, 10.11.02**
155, 156	887–892 893 894	13.8 Interpret Box-and-Whisker Plots 13.8 Graphing Calculator Activity Mixed Review	**10.11.04, 10.11.05, 10.11.06** **10.11.04, 10.11.05, 10.11.06** **10.11.04, 10.11.05, 10.11.06**
157	895–900	Chapter Summary and Review	**10.11.04, 10.11.05, 10.11.06, 10.11.10**
158	901	Chapter Test	**8.11.02, 10.11.01, 10.11.02, 10.11.05, 10.11.06, 10.11.07, 10.11.08**
159	902–905	Test Preparation and Practice	**10.11.05, 10.1 1.06**
160	906–907	Cumulative Review	**8.11.17, 9.11.01, 9.11.09, 10.11.05, 10.11.06**

ILLINOIS

ALGEBRA 1

Ron Larson
Laurie Boswell
Timothy D. Kanold
Lee Stiff

McDougal Littell
A DIVISION OF HOUGHTON MIFFLIN COMPANY
Evanston, Illinois • Boston • Dallas

About *Algebra I*

The content of *Algebra 1* is organized around families of functions, with special emphasis on linear and quadratic functions. As you study each family of functions, you will learn to represent them in multiple ways—as verbal descriptions, equations, tables, and graphs. You will also learn to model real-world situations using functions in order to solve problems arising from those situations.

In addition to its algebra content, *Algebra 1* includes lessons on probability and data analysis as well as numerous examples and exercises involving geometry. These math topics often appear on standardized tests, so maintaining your familiarity with them is important. To help you prepare for standardized tests, *Algebra 1* provides instruction and practice on standardized test questions in a variety of formats—multiple choice, short response, extended response, and so on. Technology support for both learning algebra and preparing for standardized tests is available at classzone.com.

ISBN-13: 978-0-618-88763-7
ISBN-10: 0-618-88763-6 123456789—VJM—09 08 07 06 05

Internet Web Site: http://www.mcdougallittell.com

About the Authors

Ron Larson is a professor of mathematics at Penn State University at Erie, where he has taught since receiving his Ph.D. in mathematics from the University of Colorado. Dr. Larson is well known as the author of a comprehensive program for mathematics that spans middle school, high school, and college courses. Dr. Larson's numerous professional activities keep him in constant touch with the needs of teachers and supervisors. He closely follows developments in mathematics standards and assessment.

Laurie Boswell is a mathematics teacher at The Riverside School in Lyndonville, Vermont, and has taught mathematics at all levels, elementary through college. A recipient of the Presidential Award for Excellence in Mathematics Teaching, she was also a Tandy Technology Scholar. She served on the NCTM Board of Directors (2002–2005), and she speaks frequently at regional and national conferences on topics related to instructional strategies and course content.

Timothy D. Kanold is the superintendent of Adlai E. Stevenson High School District 125 in Lincolnshire, Illinois. Dr. Kanold served as a teacher and director of mathematics for 17 years prior to becoming superintendent. He is the recipient of the Presidential Award for Excellence in Mathematics and Science Teaching, and a past president of the Council for Presidential Awardees in Mathematics. Dr. Kanold is a frequent speaker at national and international mathematics meetings.

Lee Stiff is a professor of mathematics education in the College of Education and Psychology of North Carolina State University at Raleigh and has taught mathematics at the high school and middle school levels. He served on the NCTM Board of Directors and was elected President of NCTM for the years 2000–2002. He is a recipient of the W. W. Rankin Award for Excellence in Mathematics Education presented by the North Carolina Council of Teachers of Mathematics.

Advisers and Reviewers

Illinois Advisers and Reviewers

Phyllis Cavalone
Principal / Freelance Mathematics Consultant
St. Therese Chinese Catholic School
Chicago, IL

Laura Lauschke
Mathematics Department Chair
Alton High School
Alton, IL

Sharon Mikula
Algebra Teacher
Niles West High School
Skokie, IL

Marilyn O'Brien
Mathematics Department Chair
Glenwood High School
Chatham, IL

Maria Vlahos
Mathematics Division Head
Barrington High School
Barrington, IL

Kathy Young
Mathematics Department Chair
Lemont High School
Lemont, IL

Curriculum Advisers and Reviewers

Leticia Alvarado
Mathematics Department Chair
Hornedo Middle School
El Paso, TX

Arlene Banks
Mathematics Teacher
Westridge Middle School
Overland Park, KS

Monette Bartel
Associate Adjunct Professor
College of the Canyons
Valencia, CA

Janice Beauchamp
Mathematics Teacher
Buchanan High School
Clovis, CA

Jan Berghaus
Mathematics Teacher
Shawnee Mission West High School
Overland Park, KS

Cindy Branson
Mathematics Teacher
Creekview High School
Carrollton, TX

Dennis Dickson
Mathematics Teacher
Leavenworth High School
Leavenworth, KS

Pauline Embree
Mathematics Department Chair
Rancho San Joaquin Middle School
Irvine, CA

Coleen Floberg
Mathematics Teacher
Highland Park High School
Topeka, KS

Rhonda Foote
Secondary Math Resource Specialist
North Kansas City School District
Kansas City, MO

Alberto Hernandez Galindo
Mathematics Department Chair
San Jose High Academy
San Jose, CA

Phillip Gegen
Mathematics Teacher
Oak Park High School
Kansas City, MO

Jason Godfrey
Mathematics Teacher
Grandview High School
Grandview, MO

IL 4

Curriculum Advisers and Reviewers

Leticia Gonzales-Reynolds
Mathematics Teacher
Crockett High School
Austin, TX

Maria Gossett
Mathematics Department Chair
E.M. Daggett Middle School
Fort Worth, TX

Tom Griffith
Mathematics Department Chair
Scripps Ranch High School
San Diego, CA

Ruth Hadnot
Mathematics Department Chair
Chicago Military Academy-Bronzeville
Chicago, IL

Michael J. Klein
Educational Consultant
Macomb ISD
Clinton Township, MI

Debra Konvalin
Mathematics Teacher
Hiram W. Johnson High School
Sacramento, CA

Ronald J. Labrocca
Mathematics Chairperson
Stimson Middle School
Huntington Station, NY

William Lee Littles
Mathematics Teacher
Central High School
Beaumont, TX

Maria Magdalena Lucio
Mathematics Department Chair
Homer Hanna High School
Brownsville, TX

John McHugh
Mathematics Department Chair
Holbrook Middle School
Lowell, NC

Fizza Munaim
Mathematics Teacher
Eastwood High School
El Paso, TX

Alvin E. Nash, Jr.
Mathematics Teacher
Pasadena High School
Pasadena, CA

Anne Papakonstantinou
Director, School Mathematics Project
Rice University
Houston, TX

Richard Parr
Director of Education Technology, School Mathematics Project
Rice University
Houston, TX

Rebecca S. Poe
Mathematics Teacher
Winnsboro High School
Winnsboro, TX

Lori Rapp
Secondary Mathematics Specialist
Lewisville School District
The Colony, TX

Deborah Reilly
Mathematics Teacher
West Middle School
Leavenworth, KS

Jon Simon
Mathematics Teacher
Casa Grande High School
Petaluma, CA

Karen S. Skinner
Mathematics Teacher
New Mark Middle School
Kansas City, MO

Steve Snider
Mathematics Teacher
Spring Garden Middle School
St. Joseph, MO

Bertha Stimac
Instructional Specialist
Elsik 9th Grade Center
Houston, TX

Karen Stohlmann
Mathematics Teacher
Blue Valley Northwest High School
Overland Park, KS

Deborah Sylvester
Mathematics Teacher
Manhattan High School
Manhattan, KS

Tommie L. Walsh
Mathematics Teacher
Smylie Wilson Junior High School
Lubbock, TX

Mary Warner
Mathematics Teacher
Richard King High School
Corpus Christi, TX

Peggy S. Winfree White
Mathematics Teacher
Caprock High School
Amarillo, TX

Maureen Williams
Mathematics Department Chair
Southwest Junior High School
Lawrence, KS

IL 5

ILLINOIS

Overview
Illinois Student Edition

- Daily practice in every lesson
- Weekly practice in the mid-chapter mixed review
- Summative practice in the end-of-chapter assessment

Buckingham Fountain, Chicago, Illinois © Mark Segal/Getty Images

ILLINOIS TABLE OF CONTENTS

Chapter 1 Summary

Chapter 1 focuses on the basics of algebra, showing how **variables** are used in forming **algebraic expressions** and how expressions are used in forming **equations and inequalities**. Along the way, students evaluate expressions using the **order of operations** and solve equations and inequalities using **mental math**. Students also use equations to solve real-world problems as part of the four-step **problem solving plan**. The chapter concludes by looking at the dependence of one variable on another in the form of **functional relationships**. Students see that functions have **multiple representations**: verbal descriptions, rules, tables, and graphs.

Standards

8.11.06 Evaluate variable expressions and functions.

6.11.04 Apply the rules of order of operations to real-number expressions.

6.11.13 Set up, evaluate, or solve single- and multi-step number sentences and word problems with rational numbers using the four basic operations.

8.11.12 Create and connect representations that are tabular, graphic, numeric, and symbolic from a set of data.

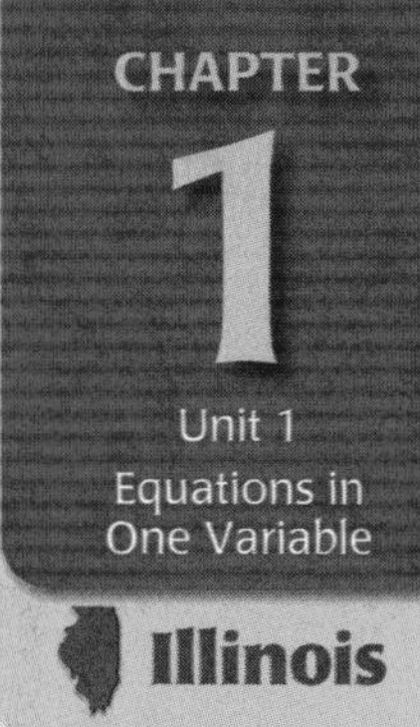

Problem Solving, p. 29
$0.1s + 0.6 = 2$

Expressions, Equations, and Functions

Illinois

ASSESSMENT
- Illinois Practice Examples, 10, 30
- Illinois Daily Practice, 7, 12, 20, 26, 33, 40, 48
- Illinois Preparation and Practice, 5, 6, 7, 11, 12, 17, 18, 19, 20, 23, 24, 25, 26, 31, 32, 33, 38, 39, 40, 46, 48
- Writing, 5, 10, 18, 24, 31, 38, 46, 47, 53

PROBLEM SOLVING
- Illinois Mixed Review, 27, 51
- Multiple Representations, 33, 39
- Multi-Step Problems, 6, 11, 19, 27, 40, 51
- Using Alternative Methods, 34
- Real-World Problem Solving Examples, 4, 10, 17, 23, 28, 30, 35, 37, 45

TECHNOLOGY

At classzone.com:
- Animated Algebra, 1, 7, 9, 14, 21, 29, 34, 37, 50
- @Home Tutor, IL 64, 6, 11, 13, 19, 25, 32, 39, 41, 47, 53
- Online Quiz, 7, 12, 20, 26, 33, 40, 48
- Electronic Function Library, 52
- State Test Practice, 27, 51, 61

IL 8 Contents

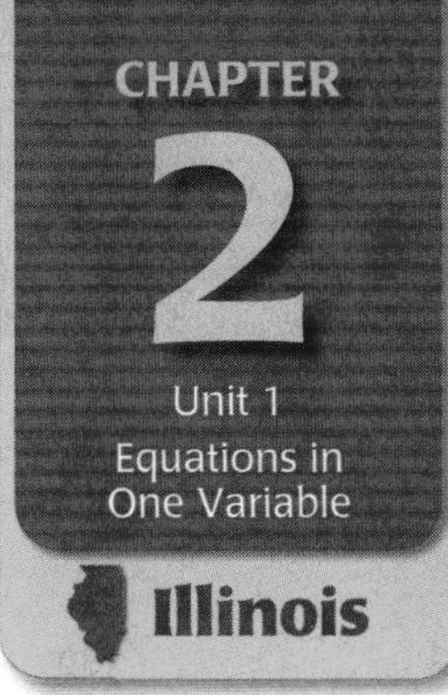

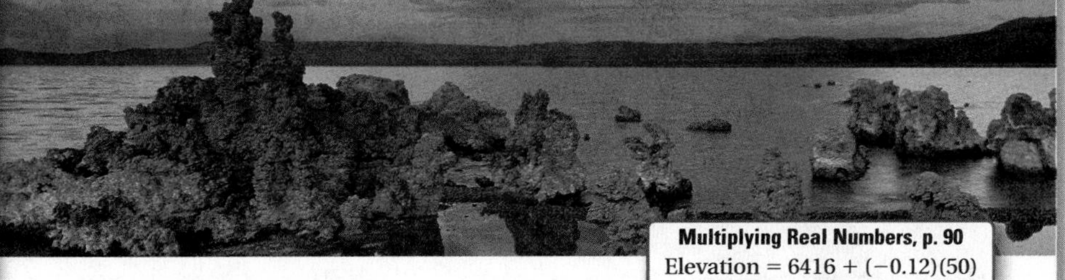

Multiplying Real Numbers, p. 90
Elevation = 6416 + (−0.12)(50)

Illinois

Properties of Real Numbers

Illinois

ASSESSMENT

- Illinois Practice Examples, 98
- Illinois Daily Practice, 70, 79, 84, 93, 101, 108, 116
- Illinois Preparation and Practice, 68, 69, 70, 76, 78, 79, 82, 83, 90, 92, 93, 98, 99, 100, 101, 106, 107, 108, 114, 115
- Writing, 67, 77, 82, 83, 91, 99, 106, 107, 113, 114

PROBLEM SOLVING

- Illinois Mixed Review, 86, 119
- Multiple Representations, 83, 93, 116
- Multi-Step Problems, 69, 78, 86, 107, 115, 119
- Using Alternative Methods, 102
- Real-World Problem Solving Examples, 65, 76, 81, 90, 98, 104, 111

TECHNOLOGY

At classzone.com:

- Animated Algebra, 63, 73, 80, 90, 93, 98
- @Home Tutor, 62, 69, 78, 83, 92, 100, 107, 115, 121
- Online Quiz, 70, 79, 84, 93, 101, 108, 116
- State Test Practice, 86, 119, 129

Chapter 2 Summary

Chapter 2 focuses on the set of **real numbers** and its various subsets, including integers, rational numbers, and irrational numbers. Students become proficient at **comparing and ordering** real numbers and **performing operations** on them. Students also learn the **properties** of real-number addition and multiplication, including the **distributive property,** which students use to simplify expressions. The chapter emphasizes logical reasoning by asking students to write **conditional statements** and to determine whether those statements are true or false. Students learn to provide **justifications** for true statements and **counterexamples** for false statements.

Standards

6.11.01 Recognize, represent, order, compare real numbers, and locate real numbers on a number line (e.g., π, $\sqrt{2}$, $\sqrt{5}$, $\frac{2}{3}$, -1.6).

6.11.10 Perform numerical computations with real numbers.

6.11.05 Simplify or test expressions by applying field properties (commutative, associative, distributive), order properties (transitive, reflexive, symmetric), and properties of equality for the set of real numbers.

Chapter 3 Summary

Chapter 3 focuses on **solving linear equations** in one variable. In the first half of the chapter, students learn the **properties of equality** in the course of solving simple one-step equations, and they employ those properties to solve increasingly complex multi-step equations. In the second half of the chapter, students solve **proportions** using the multiplication property of equality as well as the cross products property, and they solve **percent problems** by using proportions as well as the percent equation. The chapter concludes by asking students to **rewrite functions and formulas** by solving for one variable in terms of the other(s).

Standards

8.11.16 Solve linear equations and inequalities, including selecting and evaluating formulas.

6.11.17 Set up, evaluate, or solve number sentences or word problems involving ratios and proportions with rational numbers (e.g., scale drawing, unit rate, scale factor, rate of change).

6.11.18 Set up, evaluate, or solve common problems involving percent (e.g., sales tax, tip, interest, discount, markup, commission, compound interest).

7.11.03 Determine and calculate to an indicated precision the length, width, height, perimeter/circumference, area, volume, surface area, angle measures, or sums of angle measures of common geometric figures or combinations of common geometric figures.

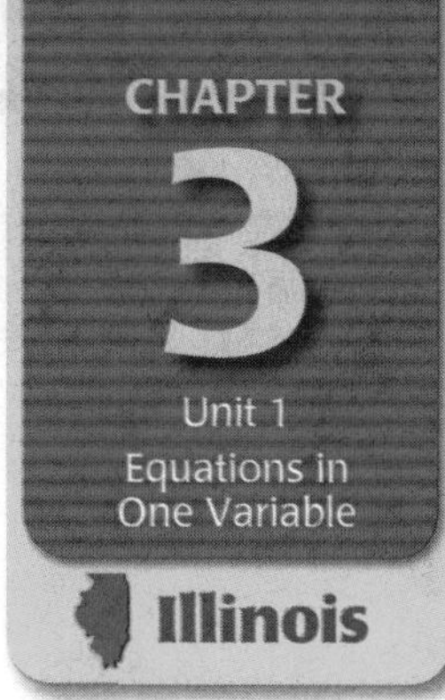

Solving Linear Equations

Illinois

ASSESSMENT

PROBLEM SOLVING

TECHNOLOGY

At classzone.com:

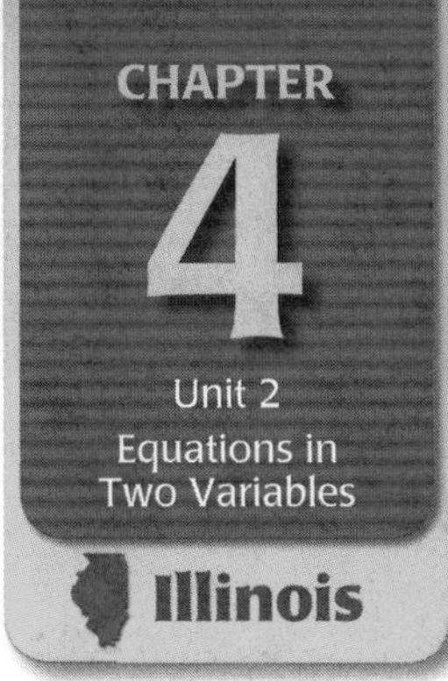

Illinois

Graphing Linear Equations, p. 231
$2x + y = 128$

Graphing Linear Equations and Functions

Chapter 4 Summary

Chapter 4 focuses on **graphing linear equations** in two variables. Students learn a variety of graphing techniques, including making a table of values and plotting points, identifying and using just the ***x*- and *y*-intercepts**, and identifying and using just the **slope** and *y*-intercept. Students recognize that the slope of a line is constant and that slope can be interpreted as a **rate of change** in real-world graphs. Students examine a special type of linear relationship known as **direct variation**, and they use direct variation models to solve real-world problems. The chapter concludes by introducing students to **function notation** while examining the effects of m and b on the graph of $f(x) = mx + b$.

Standards

9.11.11 Graph, locate, and identify points on a coordinate system.

8.11.11 Analyze functions by investigating domain, range, rates of change, intercepts, and zeros.

8.11.09 Identify slope from an equation, table of values, or graph.

6.11.19 Set up, evaluate, or solve problems stated in terms of direct and inverse variation of simple quantities.

Illinois

ASSESSMENT
- Illinois Practice Examples, 215, 262
- Illinois Daily Practice, 212, 221, 232, 242, 250, 259, 268
- Illinois Preparation and Practice, 209, 212, 218, 219, 220, 221, 227, 230, 231, 232, 239, 242, 247, 248, 249, 255, 257, 258, 259, 266, 267, 268
- Writing, 209, 210, 214, 219, 229, 239, 241, 247, 256, 257, 265, 271

PROBLEM SOLVING
- Illinois Mixed Review, 233, 269
- Multiple Representations, 211, 221, 230, 259, 260
- Multi-Step Problems, 211, 220, 231, 233, 241, 269
- Using Alternative Methods, 260, 261
- Real-World Problem Solving Examples, 208, 218, 227, 228, 237, 238, 245, 246, 255, 256, 265

TECHNOLOGY
At classzone.com:
- Animated Algebra, 205, 207, 216, 226, 238, 245, 254
- @Home Tutor, 204, 210, 211, 220, 222, 230, 241, 248, 249, 258, 267, 271
- Online Quiz, 212, 221, 232, 242, 250, 259, 268
- Electronic Function Library, 270
- State Test Practice, 233, 269, 279

Chapter 5 Summary

Chapter 5 focuses on **writing linear equations** in two variables. Students learn to write equations in a various forms: **slope-intercept form**, **point-slope form**, and **standard form**. Students then solve real-world problems using these forms. For instance, given a real-world situation involving a starting value and a constant rate of change, students model the situation using a linear equation in slope-intercept form. Students also examine the relationships among slopes of **parallel and perpendicular lines** and write equations based on those relationships. The chapter concludes by showing students how to **fit lines to data** and **make predictions** from the resulting linear models.

Standards

8.11.07 Identify an equation of a line or an equation of a line of best fit from given information (e.g., from a set of ordered pairs, graphs, tables).

8.11.11 Analyze functions by investigating domain, range, rates of change, intercepts, and zeros.

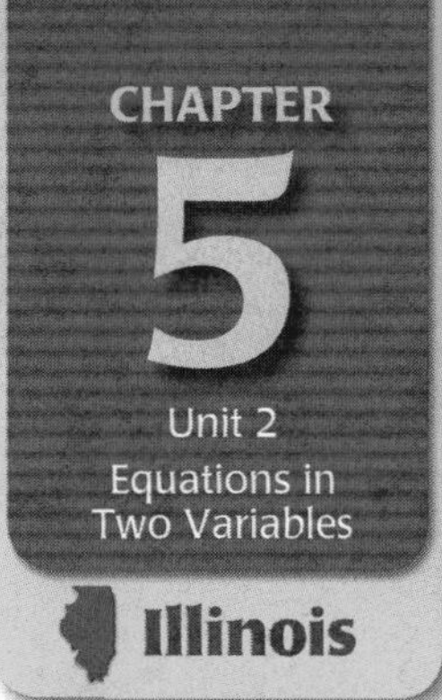

Slopes of Lines, p. 321
$12y = -7x + 42$

Writing Linear Equations

Illinois

ASSESSMENT

- Illinois Practice Examples, 283, 293
- Illinois Daily Practice, 289, 299, 308, 316, 324, 331, 341
- Illinois Preparation and Practice, 285, 286, 287, 288, 289, 294, 295, 297, 298, 304, 305, 306, 307, 313, 314, 315, 322, 323, 324, 329, 330, 339, 340
- Writing, 286, 287, 296, 297, 305, 314, 322, 328, 338, 345

PROBLEM SOLVING

- Illinois Mixed Review, 317, 343
- Multiple Representations, 288, 299, 315, 340
- Multi-Step Problems, 317, 343
- Using Alternative Methods, 300
- Real-World Problem Solving Examples, 285, 294, 295, 304, 313, 321, 326, 327, 337

TECHNOLOGY

At classzone.com:

- Animated Algebra, 281, 283, 303, 307, 311, 327, 335
- @Home Tutor, 280, 288, 291, 298, 307, 315, 323, 330, 333, 339, 340, 342, 345
- Online Quiz, 289, 299, 308, 316, 324, 331, 341
- State Test Practice, 317, 343, 353

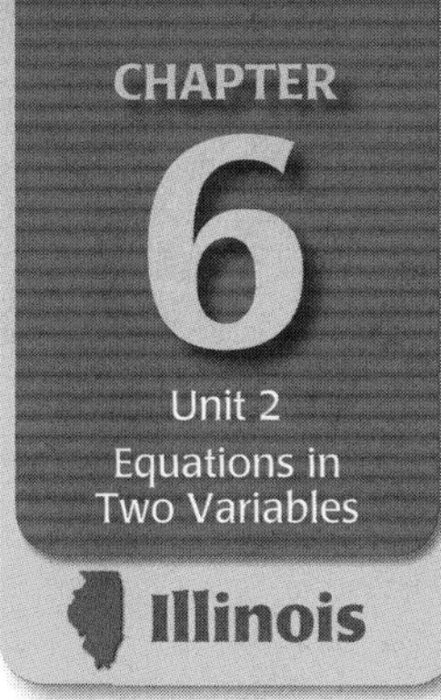

Graphing Inequalities, p. 356
$T \leq 134$

Solving and Graphing Linear Inequalities

Illinois

ASSESSMENT

- Illinois Practice Examples, 365, 405
- Illinois Daily Practice, 361, 368, 374, 387, 395, 403, 412
- Illinois Preparation and Practice, 360, 361, 366, 368, 371, 372, 373, 374, 383, 385, 386, 387, 393, 394, 395, 400, 401, 402, 403, 408, 409, 411, 412
- Writing, 359, 360, 366, 372, 384, 393, 401, 409, 410, 415

PROBLEM SOLVING

- Illinois Mixed Review, 389, 413
- Multiple Representations, 361, 367, 374, 386, 402, 411
- Multi-Step Problems, 360, 389, 403, 411, 413
- Using Alternative Methods, 375, 376
- Real-World Problem Solving Examples, 358, 365, 371, 383, 392, 400, 408

TECHNOLOGY

At classzone.com:

- Animated Algebra, 355, 358, 364, 382, 387, 390, 391, 399, 407
- @Home Tutor, 354, 360, 367, 373, 385, 388, 394, 402, 410, 415
- Online Quiz, 361, 368, 374, 387, 395, 403, 412
- State Test Practice, 389, 413, 423

Chapter 6 Summary

Chapter 6 focuses on **solving linear inequalities** in one variable and **graphing linear inequalities** in two variables. Paralleling the development of Chapter 3, students use the **properties of inequality** to solve inequalities, starting with simple one-step inequalities and progressing to more complicated multi-step inequalities. Students then solve **compound inequalities** involving *and* and *or*, and students extend this skill to solving **absolute value equations and inequalities**. The chapter concludes by showing students how to graph a linear inequality in two variables by graphing the related equation (using techniques from Chapter 4) and shading the appropriate half-plane.

Standards

6.11.08 Determine the appropriate solution, including rounding, from a context (e.g., rounding up, down, to the nearest integer).

8.11.19 Solve problems that include nonlinear functions, including selecting and evaluating formulas (i.e., absolute value, trigonometric, logarithmic, exponential).

Chapter 7 Summary

Chapter 7 focuses on **solving systems of linear equations** and inequalities in two variables. Students learn various methods for solving systems of equations: by graphing and finding the point where the lines intersect (**graphing method**), by solving one equation for one of the variables and substituting into the other equation (**substitution method**), and by combining the equations to eliminate one of the variables (**elimination method**). Students also examine **special cases** where a system has no solution or has infinitely many solutions. The chapter concludes by showing students how to graph a system of inequalities using the method for graphing single inequalities from Chapter 6.

Standards

8.11.17 Solve systems of equations and inequalities.

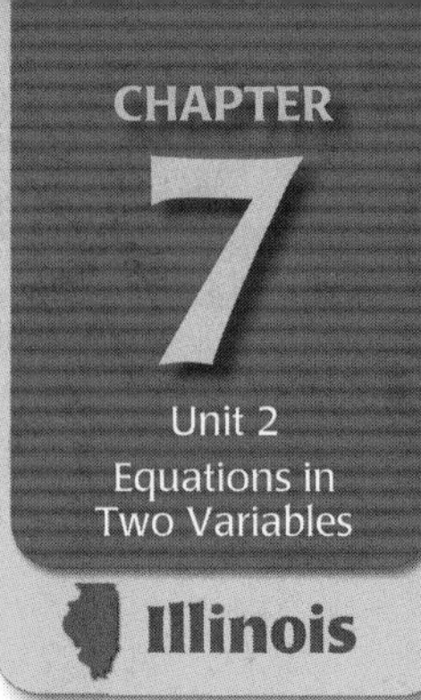

Solving Linear Systems, p. 446
$x - y = 4, x + y = 6$

Systems of Equations and Inequalities

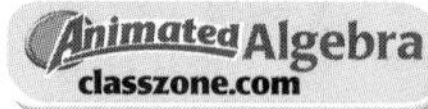

Illinois

ASSESSMENT

- Illinois Practice Examples, 429, 453
- Illinois Daily Practice, 433, 441, 450, 457, 465, 472
- Illinois Preparation and Practice, 430, 431, 432, 437, 439, 440, 441, 447, 448, 450, 455, 456, 463, 464, 465, 469, 470, 471
- Writing, 430, 431, 439, 440, 447, 454, 455, 462, 469

PROBLEM SOLVING

- Illinois Mixed Review, 458, 473
- Multiple Representations, 433, 442, 449, 456
- Multi-Step Problems, 440, 450, 458, 465, 473
- Using Alternative Methods, 442
- Real-World Problem Solving Examples, 430, 438, 446, 453, 461, 468

TECHNOLOGY

At classzone.com:

- Animated Algebra, 425, 428, 435, 441, 446, 452, 459, 466
- @Home Tutor, 424, 432, 434, 440, 449, 456, 464, 471, 475
- Online Quiz, 433, 441, 450, 457, 465, 472
- State Test Practice, 458, 473, 483

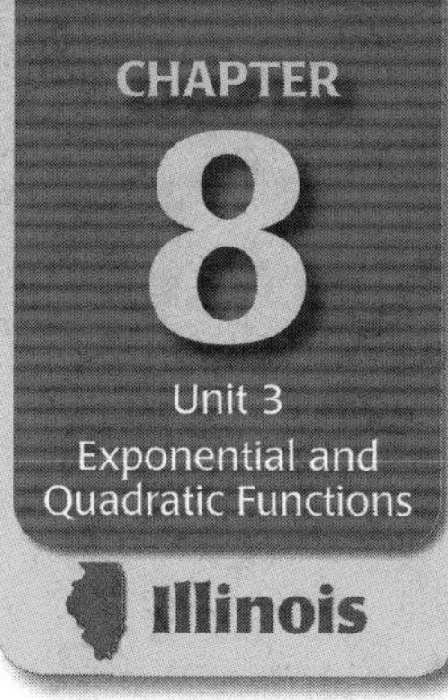

Scientific Notation, p. 516
9.065×10^9 miles

Exponents and Exponential Functions

Illinois

ASSESSMENT

- Illinois Practice Examples, 505, 523
- Illinois Daily Practice, 494, 501, 508, 518, 527, 538
- Illinois Preparation and Practice, 492, 493, 494, 497, 499, 501, 506, 507, 508, 514, 515, 516, 517, 522, 524, 526, 534, 535, 536, 537
- Writing, 492, 498, 506, 515, 523, 524, 527, 535, 536, 543

PROBLEM SOLVING

- Illinois Mixed Review, 511, 541
- Multiple Representations, 493, 500, 507, 517, 525, 528, 537
- Multi-Step Problems, 493, 511, 517, 525, 538, 541
- Using Alternative Methods, 528, 529
- Real-World Problem Solving Examples, 491, 498, 505, 514, 522, 523, 534

TECHNOLOGY

At classzone.com:

- Animated Algebra, 487, 505, 512, 522, 534, 536
- @Home Tutor, 486, 493, 500, 507, 516, 519, 525, 537, 543
- Online Quiz, 494, 501, 508, 518, 527, 538
- State Test Practice, 511, 541, 551

Chapter 8 Summary

Chapter 8 focuses on **working with exponents** and **graphing exponential functions**. Students learn the **properties of exponents** while working with positive exponents, then they extend the properties to **zero and negative exponents**. Students also learn to write numbers in **scientific notation** using positive, negative, and zero exponents and to compare and perform operations with numbers written in scientific notation. With an understanding of exponents, students are prepared to examine exponential functions, their first encounter with **nonlinear functions**. Students write and graph exponential functions and then use **exponential growth and decay models** to solve real-world problems.

Standards

6.11.07 Determine the effects of operations on the magnitudes of quantities (e.g., multiplication, division, powers, roots).

8.11.01 Simplify or identify equivalent algebraic expressions (e.g., exponential, rational, logarithmic, factored, polynomial).

6.11.02 Represent numbers in equivalent forms (e.g., fraction/decimal/percent, exponential/logarithmic, radical/rational exponents, absolute value, scientific notation).

8.11.12 Create and connect representations that are tabular, graphic, numeric, and symbolic from a set of data.

Chapter 9 Summary

Chapter 9 focuses on **working with polynomials** and **solving polynomial equations**. In the first half of the chapter, students learn to **classify polynomials** by degree and by the number of terms and to **add, subtract, and multiply polynomials**, including recognizing patterns for **special products**. In the second half of the chapter, students learn to **factor polynomials** using several techniques: factoring out a common monomial factor, factoring a trinomial into a product of binomials, and factoring special products. Students then use factoring and the **zero product property** to solve polynomial equations, with particular emphasis on solving quadratic equations.

Standards

8.11.01 Simplify or identify equivalent algebraic expressions (e.g., exponential, rational, logarithmic, factored, polynomial).

8.11.19 Solve problems that include nonlinear functions, including selecting and evaluating formulas (i.e., absolute value, trigonometric, logarithmic, exponential).

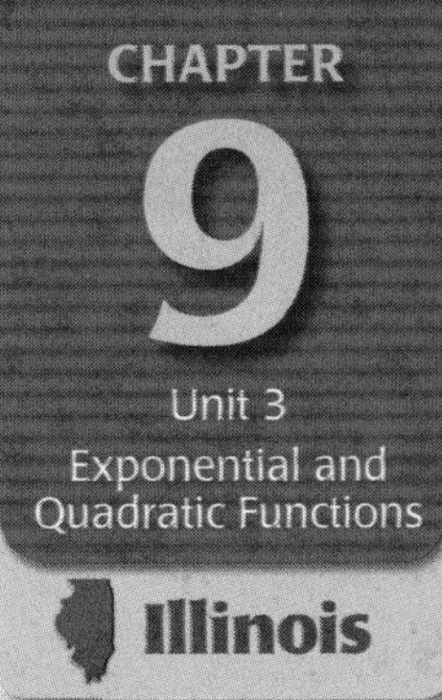

CHAPTER 9

Unit 3 Exponential and Quadratic Functions

Illinois

Subtracting Polynomials, p. 558
$B = -0.0262t^3 + 0.376t^2 - 0.574t + 9.67$

Polynomials and Factoring

Illinois

ASSESSMENT

- Illinois Practice Examples, 564, 596
- Illinois Daily Practice, 559, 568, 574, 580, 589, 599, 605, 613
- Illinois Preparation and Practice, 556, 557, 558, 559, 564, 566, 567, 568, 571, 572, 573, 574, 577, 578, 579, 580, 585, 586, 587, 588, 589, 597, 598, 603, 604, 609, 610, 612
- Writing, 557, 565, 572, 578, 586, 596, 603, 610, 611, 616

PROBLEM SOLVING

- Illinois Mixed Review, 581, 614
- Multiple Representations, 573, 580, 589, 598
- Multi-Step Problems, 581, 614
- Using Alternative Methods, 590
- Real-World Problem Solving Examples, 556, 564, 571, 577, 585, 595, 602, 609

TECHNOLOGY

At classzone.com:

- Animated Algebra, 553, 555, 582, 592, 598, 601
- @Home Tutor, 552, 558, 560, 567, 573, 579, 588, 598, 604, 612, 616
- Online Quiz, 559, 568, 574, 580, 589, 599, 605, 613
- State Test Practice, 581, 614, 625

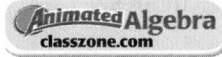

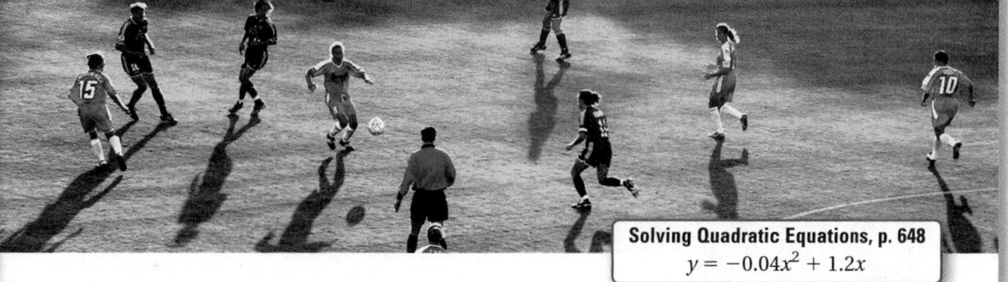

Solving Quadratic Equations, p. 648
$y = -0.04x^2 + 1.2x$

Quadratic Equations and Functions

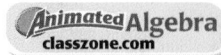

Illinois

ASSESSMENT

- Illinois Practice Examples, 631, 671
- Illinois Daily Practice, 634, 640, 649, 658, 668, 676, 683, 691
- Illinois Preparation and Practice, 632, 633, 634, 638, 640, 646, 647, 648, 649, 654, 655, 656, 657, 665, 666, 668, 674, 676, 680, 681, 682, 687, 688, 690
- Writing, 632, 638, 639, 647, 655, 666, 667, 674, 681, 688

PROBLEM SOLVING

- Illinois Mixed Review, 661, 694
- Multiple Representations, 658, 659, 667, 676, 690
- Multi-Step Problems, 658, 661, 668, 675, 683, 694
- Using Alternative Methods, 659
- Real-World Problem Solving Examples, 631, 637, 646, 654, 665, 672, 680, 687

TECHNOLOGY

At classzone.com:

- Animated Algebra, 627, 634, 636, 642, 662, 668, 672, 684
- @Home Tutor, 626, 633, 639, 648, 651, 657, 667, 675, 682, 689, 690, 692, 696
- Online Quiz, 634, 640, 649, 658, 668, 676, 683, 691
- Electronic Function Library, 695
- State Test Practice, 661, 694, 705

Chapter 10 Summary

Chapter 10 focuses on **graphing quadratic functions** and **solving quadratic equations**. Students learn the effects of *a* and *c* on the graph of $y = ax^2 + c$ and then extend their understanding of quadratic graphs to $y = ax^2 + bx + c$. Students are able to solve quadratic equations graphically by interpreting the solutions as the *x*-intercepts of related graphs. Students also solve quadratic equations by **completing the square**, and this method leads to the **quadratic formula** when applied to the general equation $ax^2 + bx + c = 0$. Students see that the **discriminant** in the quadratic formula determines the number of solutions that a quadratic equation has. The chapter concludes by comparing linear models (from Chapter 5), exponential models (from Chapter 8), and **quadratic models** and asking students to choose an appropriate model for a given set of data.

Standards

8.11.08 Recognize and describe the general shape and properties of functions from graphs, tables, or equations (e.g., linear, absolute value, quadratic, exponential, logarithmic).

8.11.19 Solve problems that include nonlinear functions, including selecting and evaluating formulas (i.e., absolute value, trigonometric, logarithmic, exponential).

8.11.14 Model problems using mathematical functions and relations (e.g., linear, non-linear).

Chapter 11 Summary

Chapter 11 focuses on **working with radicals** and **connections to geometry**. In the first half of the chapter, students learn to **graph square root functions**. Students then **simplify square root expressions** using the properties of radicals and **solve square root equations** by squaring both sides. In the second half of the chapter, students look at geometric situations involving square roots. In particular, students solve right-triangle problems using the **Pythagorean theorem and its converse**, and they solve coordinate-plane problems using the **distance and midpoint formulas**.

Standards

8.11.08 Recognize and describe the general shape and properties of functions from graphs, tables, or equations (e.g., linear, absolute value, quadratic, exponential, logarithmic).

8.11.01 Simplify or identify equivalent algebraic expressions (e.g., exponential, rational, logarithmic, factored, polynomial).

8.11.19 Solve problems that include nonlinear functions, including selecting and evaluating formulas (i.e., absolute value, trigonometric, logarithmic, exponential).

9.11.01 Apply the Pythagorean theorem.

9.11.09 Solve problems that involve calculating distance, midpoint, and slope using coordinate geometry.

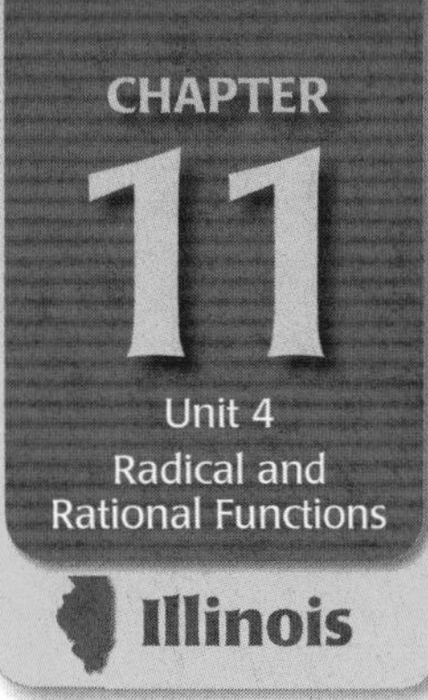

Solving Radical Equations, p. 731
$s = 1.34\sqrt{\ell}$

Radicals and Geometry Connections

Illinois

ASSESSMENT
- Illinois Practice Examples, 738, 746
- Illinois Daily Practice, 716, 726, 734, 742, 750
- Illinois Preparation and Practice, 713, 714, 716, 723, 726, 732, 734, 740, 741, 742, 747, 748, 749
- Writing, 713, 723, 732, 733, 740, 741, 747, 748

PROBLEM SOLVING
- Illinois Mixed Review, 735, 752
- Multiple Representations, 725
- Multi-Step Problems, 715, 725, 733, 735, 748, 752
- Using Alternative Methods, 751
- Real-World Problem Solving Examples, 713, 722, 731, 738, 739, 746

TECHNOLOGY

At classzone.com:
- Animated Algebra, 709, 711, 719, 722, 731, 737, 746
- @Home Tutor, 708, 715, 717, 725, 733, 741, 748, 749, 754, 755
- Online Quiz, 716, 726, 734, 742, 750
- State Test Practice, 735, 752, 761

Dividing Rational Expressions, p. 807

$$T = \frac{100 + 2.2x}{1 - 0.014x}$$

Rational Equations and Functions

Illinois

ASSESSMENT

- Illinois Daily Practice, 772, 782, 791, 800, 809, 819, 826
- Illinois Preparation and Practice, 768, 769, 771, 772, 778, 779, 781, 788, 789, 790, 791, 798, 800, 805, 806, 807, 808, 809, 815, 817, 818, 819, 822, 823, 824, 825
- Writing, 769, 779, 780, 788, 797, 798, 806, 816, 823, 831

PROBLEM SOLVING

- Illinois Mixed Review, 801, 829
- Multiple Representations, 771, 781, 790, 808
- Multi-Step Problems, 801, 818, 825, 829
- Using Alternative Methods, 827
- Real-World Problem Solving Examples, 768, 778, 787, 797, 805, 815, 822

TECHNOLOGY

At classzone.com:

- Animated Algebra, 763, 766, 777, 783, 791, 804, 814
- @Home Tutor, 762, 770, 780, 789, 793, 799, 807, 808, 817, 824, 831
- Online Quiz, 772, 782, 791, 800, 809, 819, 826
- State Test Practice, 801, 829, 839

Chapter 12 Summary

Chapter 12 focuses on **rational expressions and equations**. In the first half of the chapter, students learn to **graph rational functions** whose numerators and denominators have degree 0 or 1, including the special case of **inverse variation**. Students also extend their work with polynomials in Chapter 9 by using **polynomial division** to put rational functions in a form for graphing. In the second half of the chapter, students learn to **simplify and perform operations** on rational expressions, and they use graphs to check their work visually. Students then learn to **solve rational equations** and check for extraneous solutions.

Standards

6.11.19 Set up, evaluate, or solve problems stated in terms of direct and inverse variation of simple quantities.

8.11.08 Recognize and describe the general shape and properties of functions from graphs, tables, or equations (e.g., linear, absolute value, quadratic, exponential, logarithmic).

8.11.01 Simplify or identify equivalent algebraic expressions (e.g., exponential, rational, logarithmic, factored, polynomial).

8.11.19 Solve problems that include nonlinear functions, including selecting and evaluating formulas (i.e., absolute value, trigonometric, logarithmic, exponential).

Chapter 13 Summary

Chapter 13 focuses on **probability and combinatorics** as well as **data analysis**. In the first half of the chapter, students learn to find probabilities of **simple and compound events**. Students also learn to calculate **permutations and combinations**, which are in turn used to find probabilities. In the second half of the chapter, students learn to recognize potential bias in **sampling methods and survey questions**. Students also learn to find **measures of central tendency and dispersion** and to display data using **stem-and-leaf plots, histograms**, and **box-and-whisker plots**.

Standards

10.11.01 Read, interpret, predict, interpolate, extrapolate, and use information from a variety of graphs, charts, and tables.

10.11.10 Apply counting techniques (e.g., permutations, combinations, Fundamental Counting Principle).

10.11.08 Compute probabilities for compound events.

10.11.05 Calculate, interpret, and use measures of central tendency and dispersion.

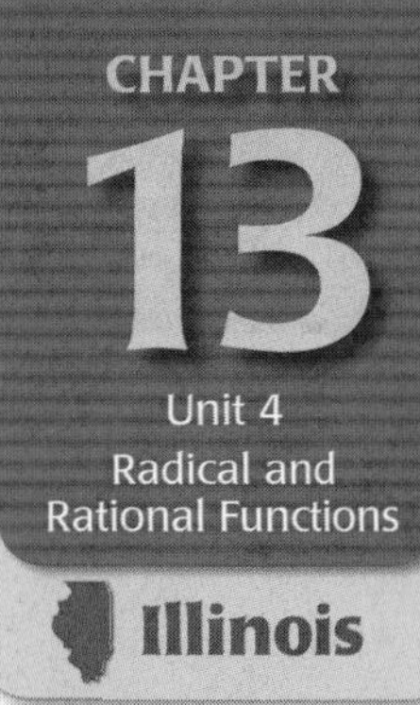

Using Permutations, p. 855

$$\text{Probability} = \frac{{}_5P_5}{{}_7P_7}$$

Probability and Data Analysis

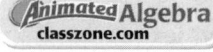

Illinois

ASSESSMENT

- Illinois Practice Examples, 845, 889
- Illinois Daily Practice, 848, 855, 859, 867, 874, 878, 885, 892
- Illinois Preparation and Practice, 846, 847, 848, 853, 854, 855, 858, 859, 864, 865, 866, 873, 874, 877, 878, 883, 885, 890, 891
- Writing, 846, 853, 858, 864, 865, 873, 877, 883, 884, 889, 896

PROBLEM SOLVING

- Illinois Mixed Review, 870, 894
- Multiple Representations, 854, 866
- Multi-Step Problems, 870, 894
- Using Alternative Methods, 868
- Real-World Problem Solving Examples, 844, 852, 853, 857, 863, 871, 872, 876, 882, 888, 889

TECHNOLOGY

At classzone.com:

- Animated Algebra, 841, 845, 848, 856, 875, 887
- @Home Tutor, 840, 847, 854, 859, 860, 866, 874, 877, 878, 884, 886, 890, 891, 893, 896
- Online Quiz, 848, 855, 859, 867, 874, 878, 885, 892
- State Test Practice, 870, 894, 905

Contents of Student Resources

Complete Illinois Mathematics Assessment Frameworks
page S1

IL 22

ILLINOIS

Student Guide to the Standards

The Illinois Mathematics Assessment Frameworks

- The Illinois Mathematics Assessment Frameworks are goals set by the state to ensure that you are being taught a thoughtful, complete curriculum.
- Teachers and other educators use the state goals when developing courses and tests.
- Lessons in your book connects to a state goal, which is listed next to the lesson in the table of contents beginning on IL 8. These state goals are also shown on the first page of each lesson throughout the book.

Complete Illinois Mathematics Assessment Frameworks *page S1*

Buckingham Fountain, Chicago, Illinois © Mark Segal/Getty Images

ILLINOIS STUDENT GUIDE

Guide to the Illinois Mathematics Assessment Frameworks

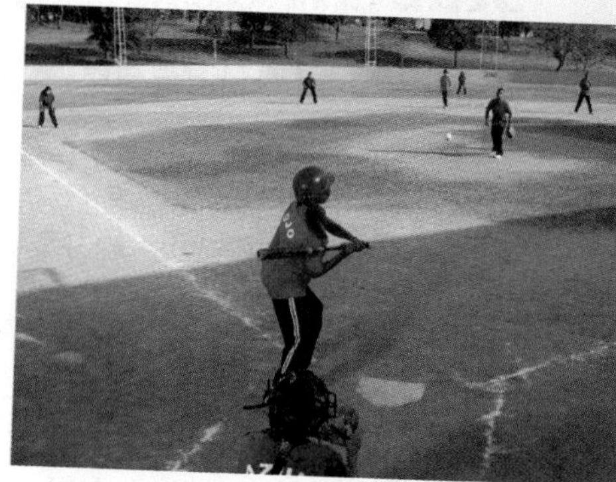

Learning the Illinois Mathematics Assessment Frameworks will help you hit a homerun!

Did you know . . .

. . . that baseball and math standards have some things in common?

. . . and, that your math standards have been written as a commitment to you, the Illinois student?

So . . .

. . . "What are Math Standards and what do they have in common with baseball?"

Compare the standards to a set of rules that must be followed in a sport event. For example, in a baseball game, the batter must move from first base to second base and then third base before proceeding to the home plate to score a run. Learning this rule enables the team to win the game.

Without the knowledge of how a baseball game is played, the team will not have the fundamental concepts to compete.

Math standards, like the rules in baseball, help you focus on a common foundation of mathematical concepts that you will use in everyday life and later in the workplace.

And . . .

. . . How will learning the Illinois Mathematics Assessment Frameworks make a difference for you, the student?

It is important to learn material that is closely aligned to the math standards because they are what you will be tested on when it comes time to take your state test.

The Illinois state standards have been written as a commitment to you, the student, to help you focus on the proper content to achieve both depth and understanding of mathematical knowledge.

Illinois Mathematics Assessment Frameworks Decoder

Part 1 The math standards for Illinois are organized under the following state goals:

6. Number Sense
7. Measurement
8. Algebra
9. Geometry
10. Data Analysis, Statistics, and Probability

Part 2 Each state goal is divided into standards by grade level.

Part 3 Each standard is broken down further into assessment objectives. The information from the 3 parts will help you break the standard code!

Here is an example:

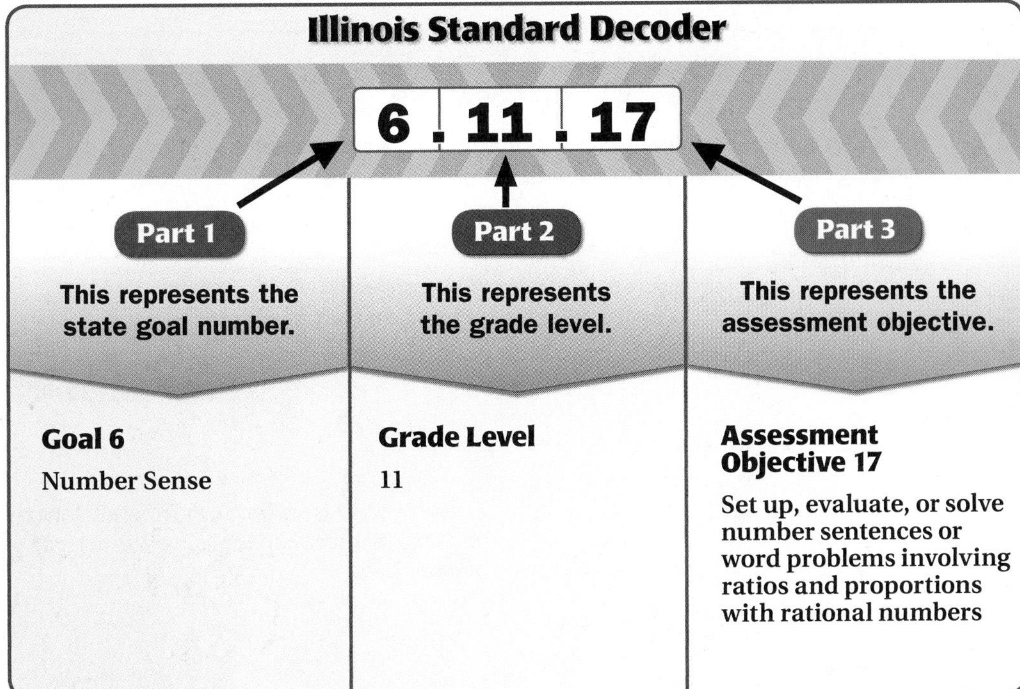

Illinois Standard Decoder
6 . 11 . 17
Part 1
This represents the state goal number.
Goal 6
Number Sense
Part 2
This represents the grade level.
Grade Level
11
Part 3
This represents the assessment objective.
Assessment Objective 17
Set up, evaluate, or solve number sentences or word problems involving ratios and proportions with rational numbers

IL 25

Illinois Mathematics Assessment Frameworks

State Goal 6: Number Sense

Standards

6A. Demonstrate knowledge and use of numbers and their representations in a broad range of theoretical and practical settings.

6B. Investigate, represent, and solve problems using number facts, operations (addition, subtraction, multiplication, division) and their properties, algorithms, and relationships.

6C. Compute and estimate using mental mathematics, paper–and–pencil methods, calculators, and computers.

6D. Solve problems using comparison of quantities, ratios, proportions, and percents.

What It Means To You

All students studying math should develop an understanding of properties of, and relationships among, numbers. Numbers are the cornerstone of any mathematics curriculum and permeate all areas of life.

Here is what a question might look like on the PSAE:

6.11.17. Set up, evaluate, or solve number sentences or word problems involving ratios and proportions with rational numbers

Tara ran 175 feet in 35 seconds. Leslie ran at the same rate for 25 seconds. How much farther did Tara run than Leslie?

A. 25 ft

B. 50 ft

C. 75 ft

D. 125 ft

E. 150 ft

Solution

Write and solve a proportion to find the distance d that Leslie ran.

$$\frac{175}{35} = \frac{d}{25} \quad \begin{matrix} \leftarrow \text{distance} \\ \leftarrow \text{time} \end{matrix}$$

$$175 \cdot 25 = 35 \cdot d$$

$$125 = d$$

Leslie ran 125 feet. Tara ran 175 feet. Tara ran 50 feet farther than Leslie, so the correct answer is B.

IL 26

State Goal 7: Measurement

Standards

7A. Measure and compare quantities using appropriate units, instruments, and methods.

7B. Estimate measurements and determine acceptable levels of accuracy.

7C. Select and use appropriate technology, instruments and formulas to solve problems, interpret results, and communicate findings.

What It Means To You

Measurement is the assignment of a numerical value to a characteristic of an object, such as the length of a football field. Studying about measurement is important in the mathematics curriculum because of its practicality and occurrence in so many aspects of everyday life.

Here is what a question might look like on the PSAE:

7.11.04. Describe the general trends of how the change in one measure affects other measures in the same figure (e.g., length, area, volume)

Hexagon *LMNOPQ* is similar to hexagon *UVWXYZ*. By what scale factor was hexagon *UVWXYZ* dilated to form hexagon *LMNOPQ*?

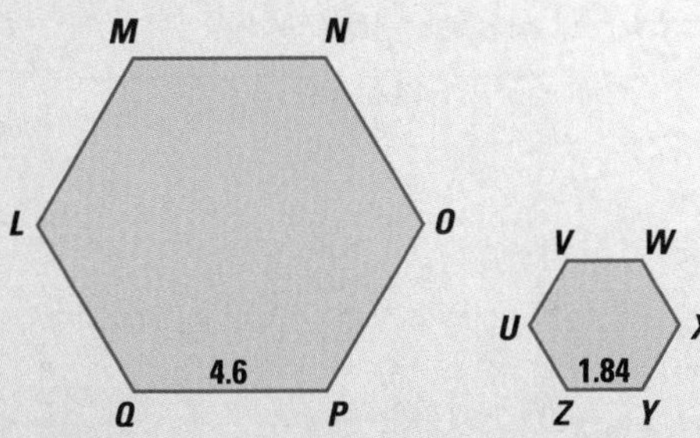

A. 0.4

B. 1.6

C. 2.5

D. 2.8

E. 3.0

Solution

The scale factor of a dilation is the ratio of side lengths after the dilation to corresponding side lengths before the dilation.

Here, the known side length after the dilation is the length of segment *QP*. The known side length before the dilation is the length of segment *ZY*.

To determine the scale factor, *x*, write and simplify the ratio.

$$x = \frac{QP}{ZY}$$

$$x = \frac{4.6}{1.84}$$

$$x = 2.5$$

The scale factor is 2.5. So, the correct answer is C.

STANDARDS

State Goal 8: Algebra

Standards

8A. Describe numerical relationships using variables and patterns.

8B. Interpret and describe numerical relationships using tables, graphs, and symbols

8C. Solve problems using systems of numbers and their properties.

8D. Use algebraic concepts and procedures to represent and solve problems.

What It Means To You

Algebra is the branch of mathematics in which symbols, usually letters, are used to represent numbers and quantities. Thinking algebraically includes recognizing and analyzing patterns, studying and representing relationships, making generalizations, and analyzing how things change.

Here is what a question might look like on the PSAE:

8.11.07. Identify an equation of a line or an equation of a line of best fit from given information

The scatterplot shows the cost for ladders in relation to the length of the ladders.

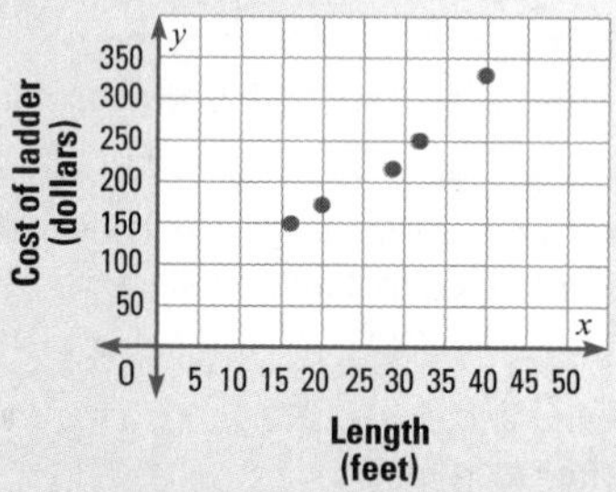

Which statement best describes the relationship on the scatterplot?

A. The price of ladders decreases as the length increases.

B. The price of ladders increases as the length increases.

C. The price of ladders first increases and then decreases as the length increases.

D. The price of ladders shows no relationship with the length.

E. The price of ladders remains constant.

Solution

The y-coordinates increase as the x-coordinates increase. The scatterplot shows a positive relationship, so the price of ladders increases as the length increases.

The correct answer is B.

State Goal 9: Geometry

Standards

9A. Demonstrate and apply geometric concepts involving points, lines, planes, and space.

9B. Identify, describe, classify, and compare relationships using points, lines, planes, and solids.

9C. Construct convincing arguments and proofs to solve problems.

9D. Use trigonometric ratios and circular functions to solve problems.

What It Means To You

Geometry is the study of the properties, measurement, and relationships of points, lines, angles, surfaces, and solids. Also, studying geometry provides an avenue to learn how to use deductive reasoning to formulate convincing explanations for conjectures and solutions. Trigonometry is the branch of mathematics that deals with the relationships between the sides and the angles of triangles and the calculations based on them.

Here is what a question might look like on the PSAE:

9.11.02. Identify and represent transformations (rotations, reflections, translations, dilations) of an object in the plane, and describe the effects of transformations on points in words or coordinates

Describe the effect on the area of a circle when the radius is halved.

A. The area remains constant.

B. The area is squared.

C. The area is 25% of the original area.

D. The area is halved.

E. The area decreases.

Solution for Question 1

The scale factor of the original circle to the new circle is $1 : \frac{1}{2}$. The ratio of the areas is $1^2 : \left(\frac{1}{2}\right)^2$, or $1 : \frac{1}{4}$. So, the area is $\frac{1}{4}$, or 25%, of the original.

The correct answer is C.

The dimensions of a hexagon are doubled to create a larger hexagon. The perimeter of the smaller hexagon is 30 centimeters. What is the perimeter of the larger hexagon?

A. 15 cm

B. 60 cm

C. 150 cm

D. 180 cm

E. 200 cm

Solution for Question 2

The scale factor of the smaller hexagon to the larger one is 1 : 2. Let x be the perimeter of the larger hexagon.

$$\frac{1}{2} = \frac{30}{x}$$

$$1 \cdot x = 2 \cdot 30$$

$$x = 60$$

The correct answer is B.

STANDARDS

IL 29

State Goal 10: Data Analysis, Statistics, and Probability

Standards

10A. Organize, describe, and make predictions from existing data.

10B. Formulate questions, design data collection methods, gather and analyze data, and communicate findings.

10C. Determine, describe, and apply the probabilities of events.

What It Means To You

Data analysis involves using data and statistics to solve problems that come up in work and in life. Probability is the study of the likelihood that a given event will occur. Both topics are important to know about in order to reason statistically.

Here is what a question might look like on the PSAE:

10.11.01. Read, interpret, predict, interpolate, extrapolate, and use information from a variety of graphs, charts, and tables

Steven glanced at the graph below.

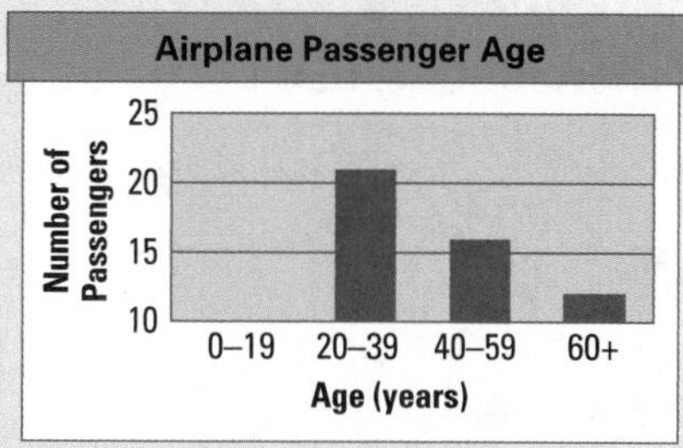

He concluded that there were no passengers under the age of 20 on the plane. Why might he be incorrect?

A. The bars of the graph fall between the numbers shown in the vertical scale.

B. The graph divides the passengers into too few age groups.

C. The vertical scale starts at 10.

D. The vertical scale ends too low.

E. The vertical scale ends too high.

Solution

The vertical scale of the graph starts at 10. So, if there are ten or fewer passengers in an age group this information will not appear on the graph.

It is possible that there are as many as 10 passengers in the 0- to 19-year-old range.

The most likely explanation of Steven's incorrect conclusion is that he failed to notice the vertical scale of the graph starts at 10. The correct answer is **C**.

IL 30

ILLINOIS

Countdown to PSAE

Additional Test Practice @ classzone.com

What is PSAE?

- The Illinois state test is called the Prairie State Achievement Examination (PSAE). The PSAE is given in the spring to students at grade 11.
- The test is made up of multiple-choice questions that evaluate your knowledge of the Illinois Mathematics Assessment Frameworks.

Getting Ready

You can use the questions on the following pages to practice for the PSAE. Each question addresses an assessment objective.

The questions are in the same format as those on the PSAE, and are organized by goals (for example, Goal 6 Strand 1 is Number Sense).

If you need practice with a particular assessment objective, use the chart on the next page to find which questions address that assessment objective. If you need additional preparation, the chart lists lessons you can review.

You will have more opportunities to practice for the PSAE in every lesson and chapter throughout the book.

Buckingham Fountain, Chicago, Illinois © Mark Segal/Getty Images

Countdown Reference Chart

This chart lists which questions address each goal and assessment objective. Lesson support is referenced and the full text of the standards is available on S1.

IL State Goals	Practice Questions for the PSAE	Lesson-by-Lesson PSAE Support
State Goal 6: Demonstrate and apply a knowledge and sense of numbers, including numeration and operations (addition, subtraction, multiplication, division), patterns, ratios and proportions.		
6.11.01	1, 2, 3, 4	Lesson 2.7
6.11.02	5, 6, 7	SRH p. 917
6.11.03	8	Extension 2.4
6.11.04	9, 10	Lesson 1.2
6.11.05	11	Lesson 2.2
6.11.05	12	Lesson 2.5
6.11.05	13	Lesson 2.6
6.11.06	14, 15, 16	SRH p. 911
6.11.07	17, 18	Lesson 2.4
6.11.08	19, 20	Lesson 2.7
6.11.12	21, 22	Extension 2.4
6.11.13	23, 24	Lesson 3.4
6.11.13	25	Lesson 1.4
6.11.16	26, 27, 28	Lesson 6.5
6.11.17	29, 30	Lesson 4.4
6.11.17	31	Lesson 3.6
6.11.18	32, 33	Lesson 3.7
6.11.18	34	Extension 3.7
6.11.19	35, 36, 37	Lesson 12.1
State Goal 7: Estimate, make and use measurements of objects, quantities and relationships and determine acceptable levels of accuracy.		
7.11.01	38, 39, 40	SRH p. 929
7.11.02	41, 42, 43	Additional Lesson B
7.11.05	44, 45, 46	Extension 3.6
7.11.06	47	Lesson 3.5
7.11.06	48	Lesson 3.6
7.11.07	49, 50	Lesson 3.6
State Goal 8: Use algebraic and analytical methods to identify and describe patterns and relationships in data, solve problems and predict results.		
8.11.01	51	Lesson 8.1
8.11.01	52	Lesson 8.2
8.11.01	53	Lesson 9.3
8.11.01	54	Lesson 11.3
8.11.02	55	Lesson 5.1
8.11.02	56	Lesson 7.2
8.11.02	57	Lesson 6.4
8.11.03	58, 59	Lesson 10.2
8.11.03	60	Lesson 4.3
8.11.04	61	Extension 3.7
8.11.04	62	Lesson 5.3
8.11.05	63, 64	Lesson 4.4

IL 32

IL State Goals	Practice Questions for the PSAE	Lesson-by-Lesson PSAE Support
8.11.06	65, 66	Lesson 1.1
8.11.06	67	Lesson 1.6
8.11.07	68, 69	Lesson 5.6
8.11.07	70	Lesson 5.2
8.11.09	71	Lesson 5.4
8.11.09	72	Lesson 4.4
8.11.11	73	Lesson 1.6
8.11.11	74	Lesson 4.2
8.11.11	75	Lesson 10.1
8.11.15	76	Lesson 7.1
8.11.15	77	Lesson 6.7
8.11.17	78, 80	Lesson 7.4
8.11.17	79	Lesson 7.3
8.11.17	81	Lesson 7.6
8.11.18	82, 83, 84	Lesson 9.5
8.11.18	85, 86	Lesson 9.7
8.11.22	87	Lesson 5.4
8.11.22	88	Lesson 5.3
State Goal 9: Use geometric methods to analyze, categorize and draw conclusions about points, lines, planes and space.		
9.11.02	89, 90	Lesson 11.4
9.11.02	91, 92	SRH p. 923
9.11.05	93	SRH p. 925
9.11.05	94	Lesson 11.5
9.11.09	95, 96, 97, 98, 99, 100	Lesson 11.5
9.11.12	101, 102	Extension 3.6
9.11.13	103, 104	SRH p. 925
9.11.17	105, 106, 107	Extension 2.7
9.11.18	108, 109, 110	Lesson 2.1
9.11.19	111, 112	Additional Lesson F
9.11.19	113, 114, 116	Lesson 11.4
9.11.20	115	Additional Lesson C
9.11.22	117	Additional Lesson E
9.11.22	118, 119	Additional Lesson F
State Goal 10: Collect, organize and analyze data using statistical methods; predict results; and interpret uncertainty using concepts of probability.		
10.11.01	120	Lesson 10.8
10.11.01	121, 122	Lesson 5.7
10.11.03	123, 124	SRH p. 930
10.11.04	125, 127	Lesson 4.4, 8.5
10.11.04	126	Lesson 5.5
10.11.04	128, 129, 130, 131	Lesson 13.6
10.11.06	132	Lesson 13.6
10.11.06	133	Lesson 13.8
10.11.07	134, 137, 138	Lesson 13.4
10.11.07	135, 136	Lesson 13.3
10.11.08	139, 140, 141, 142, 144	Lesson 13.2
10.11.08	143	Lesson 13.3

COUNTDOWN *to* PSAE

Countdown to PSAE

1. E
2. H
3. C
4. H
5. D
6. F
7. E

State Goal 6 Number Sense

6.11.01 Recognize, represent, order, compare real numbers, and locate real numbers on a number line (e.g. $\pi, \sqrt{2}, \sqrt{5}, \frac{2}{3}, -1.6$)

1. Which set is in order from least to greatest? *(p. 114, prob. 25)*

A. $\{-3, -\pi, -7.1, \pi, \sqrt{9}\}$
B. $\{-3, -\pi, -7.1, \sqrt{9}, \pi\}$
C. $\{\pi, \sqrt{9}, -3, -\pi, -7.1\}$
D. $\{-7.1, -\pi, -3, \pi, \sqrt{9}\}$
E. $\{-7.1, -\pi, -3, \sqrt{9}, \pi\}$

2. Which statement below is true? *(p. 114, prob. 27)*

F. $\pi > 3.2$
G. $-4 > 3$
H. $\sqrt{5} < 3$
J. $2.35 > 2.354$
K. $4 < \sqrt{3}$

3. Which of the following is true? *(p. 114, prob. 24)*

A. $\sqrt{17} < 4$
B. $\sqrt{\frac{4}{16}} = \frac{1}{4}$
C. $\sqrt{28} > 5$
D. $\sqrt{\frac{10}{20}} = \frac{1}{2}$
E. $\sqrt{\frac{4}{25}} \leq 1$

4. Which point could have the value $\sqrt{2}$? *(p. 114, prob. 15–29)*

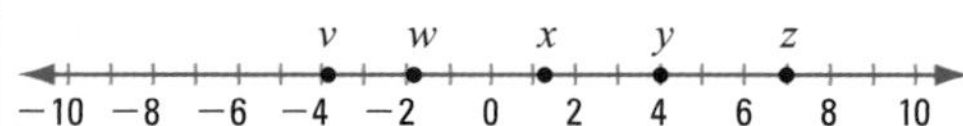

F. Point v
G. Point w
H. Point x
J. Point y
K. Point z

6.11.02 Represent numbers in equivalent forms (e.g., fraction/decimal/percent, exponential/logarithmic, radical/rational exponents, absolute value, scientific notation).

5. Which is the fraction $\frac{3}{4}$ written as a decimal? *(p. 917, prob. 21–30)*

A. 0.25
B. 0.43
C. 0.50
D. 0.75
E. 1.33

6. Which is 30% written as a fraction? *(p. 917, prob. 1–10)*

F. $\frac{3}{10}$
G. $\frac{30}{10}$
H. $\frac{10}{3}$
J. $\frac{10}{30}$
K. $\frac{100}{30}$

7. Which is the decimal 0.42 written as a fraction in lowest terms? *(p. 917, prob. 11–20)*

A. $\frac{10}{7}$
B. $\frac{7}{10}$
C. $\frac{100}{42}$
D. $\frac{50}{21}$
E. $\frac{21}{50}$

Go On

Countdown to PSAE

8. G
9. C
10. H

State Goal 6 Number Sense

6.11.03 Use matrices to organize data.

8. The junior varsity basketball team lost more games than it won during playoffs in 2001 and 2003. Which matrix displays a possible record for the playoffs?
(p. 95, prob. 11)

F. $\begin{array}{c} \\ 2001 \\ 2002 \\ 2003 \end{array} \begin{array}{c} \textit{Wins}\ \textit{Losses} \\ \begin{bmatrix} 4 & 2 \\ 1 & 4 \\ 3 & 4 \end{bmatrix} \end{array}$

G. $\begin{array}{c} \\ 2001 \\ 2002 \\ 2003 \end{array} \begin{array}{c} \textit{Wins}\ \textit{Losses} \\ \begin{bmatrix} 1 & 4 \\ 4 & 2 \\ 3 & 4 \end{bmatrix} \end{array}$

H. $\begin{array}{c} \\ 2001 \\ 2002 \\ 2003 \end{array} \begin{array}{c} \textit{Wins}\ \textit{Losses} \\ \begin{bmatrix} 4 & 2 \\ 3 & 4 \\ 1 & 4 \end{bmatrix} \end{array}$

J. $\begin{array}{c} \\ 2001 \\ 2002 \\ 2003 \end{array} \begin{array}{c} \textit{Wins}\ \textit{Losses} \\ \begin{bmatrix} 2 & 3 \\ 3 & 2 \\ 4 & 3 \end{bmatrix} \end{array}$

K. $\begin{array}{c} \\ 2001 \\ 2002 \\ 2003 \end{array} \begin{array}{c} \textit{Wins}\ \textit{Losses} \\ \begin{bmatrix} 3 & 2 \\ 4 & 1 \\ 1 & 2 \end{bmatrix} \end{array}$

6.11.04 Apply the rules of order of operations to real-number expressions.

9. What is the value of $3^2 + 9 \cdot 6$?
(p. 10, prob. 6)

A. 24

B. 60

C. 63

D. 90

E. 108

10. What is the value of the expression below? *(p. 10, prob. 14)*

$$5 + 2(3 + 4)^2$$

F. 27

G. 37

H. 103

J. 201

K. 343

COUNTDOWN to PSAE

Go On

Countdown to PSAE

11. B
12. K
13. B
14. K
15. D
16. K

State Goal 6 Number Sense

6.11.05 Simplify or test expressions by applying field properties (commutative, associative, distributive), order properties (transitive, reflexive, symmetric), and properties of equality for the set of real numbers.

11. If a, b and c are real numbers and $6a + (2b + 3c) = 10$, then $(6a + 2b) + 3c = 10$. This statement represents which of the following real number properties? *(p. 77, prob. 27)*

A. Commutative Property

B. Associative Property

C. Distributive Property

D. Inverse Property

E. Identity Property

12. If z and w are real numbers, what property of the real numbers is represented by the equation below? *(p. 99, prob. 11)*

$$5(3z + 6w) = 15z + 30w$$

F. Associative Property

G. Commutative Property

H. Inverse Property

J. Identity Property

K. Distributive Property

13. What is the multiplicative inverse of -5? *(p. 106, prob. 3–10)*

A. -5

B. $-\frac{1}{5}$

C. $\frac{1}{5}$

D. 5

E. 10

6.11.06 Apply number theory concepts to the solution of problems (e.g., prime and composite numbers, prime factorization, greatest common factor, least common multiple, divisibility rules).

14. Which is the prime factorization of 36? *(p. 911, prob. 1–12)*

F. 36 is already a prime number

G. 3×12

H. 9×4

J. 4×3^2

K. $2^2 \times 3^2$

15. What is the greatest common factor of 21 and 63? *(p. 911, prob. 13–24)*

A. 3

B. 7

C. 9

D. 21

E. 63

16. What is the least common multiple of 100 and 64? *(p. 911, prob. 25–36)*

F. 4

G. 8

H. 32

J. 64

K. 1600

Go On 

17. A
18. H
19. C
20. J

State Goal 6 Number Sense

6.11.07 Determine the effects of operations on the magnitudes of quantities (e.g., multiplication, division, powers, roots).

17. What is the value of the expression $(-3)x$ when $x = 11$? *(p. 91, prob. 37–42)*

A. -33

B. -3

C. 3

D. 33

E. 111

18. What is the product of $-4r(3r^2)$? *(p. 91, prob. 28–36)*

F. $-12r$

G. $-12r^2$

H. $-12r^3$

J. $12r^2$

K. $12r^3$

6.11.08 Determine the appropriate solution, including rounding, from a context (e.g., rounding up, down, to the nearest integer).

19. What is the value of $-\sqrt{19}$ to the nearest integer? *(p. 114, prob. 15–22)*

A. -19

B. -5

C. -4

D. 4

E. 5

20. What is the value of $\sqrt{37}$ to the nearest integer? *(p. 114, prob. 15–22)*

F. -5

G. -6

H. 5

J. 6

K. 7

COUNTDOWN to PSAE

Go On 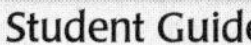

21. E
22. H
23. D
24. G
25. C

State Goal 6 — Number Sense

6.11.12 Solve problems using simple matrix operations (addition, subtraction, multiplication, scalar multiplication).

21. What is the sum of the matrices? *(p. 95, prob. 1)*

$$\begin{bmatrix} 5 & -3 \\ -2 & -1 \\ 0 & 6 \end{bmatrix} + \begin{bmatrix} -4 & -2 \\ 3 & -2 \\ 5 & -4 \end{bmatrix}$$

A. $\begin{bmatrix} 1 & -1 \\ -1 & 3 \\ 5 & 10 \end{bmatrix}$

B. $\begin{bmatrix} 1 & 5 \\ -2 & -3 \\ 0 & -10 \end{bmatrix}$

C. $\begin{bmatrix} 1 & -5 \\ 1 & -3 \\ 5 & -2 \end{bmatrix}$

D. $\begin{bmatrix} -1 & 5 \\ -1 & 3 \\ -5 & -2 \end{bmatrix}$

E. $\begin{bmatrix} 1 & -5 \\ 1 & -3 \\ 5 & 2 \end{bmatrix}$

22. What is the difference of the matrices? *(p. 95, prob. 3–4, 6)*

$$\begin{bmatrix} 7 & 5 \\ 2 & -4 \end{bmatrix} - \begin{bmatrix} -4 & 3 \\ 5 & -2 \end{bmatrix}$$

F. $\begin{bmatrix} 3 & 8 \\ 7 & -6 \end{bmatrix}$

G. $\begin{bmatrix} 3 & 2 \\ -3 & -2 \end{bmatrix}$

H. $\begin{bmatrix} 11 & 2 \\ -3 & -2 \end{bmatrix}$

J. $\begin{bmatrix} 11 & 2 \\ 7 & -2 \end{bmatrix}$

K. $\begin{bmatrix} 11 & 2 \\ -3 & -6 \end{bmatrix}$

6.11.13 Set up, evaluate, or solve single- and multi-step number sentences and word problems with rational numbers using the four basic operations.

23. What is the solution of $5(2x - 1) = 7x + 4$? *(p. 157, prob. 12)*

A. $\frac{5}{17}$

B. 1

C. $1\frac{2}{3}$

D. 3

E. –3

24. What is the solution of $3x + 7 = \frac{1}{2}(x - 6)$? *(p. 157, prob. 14)*

F. -13

G. -4

H. 0

J. 4

K. 13

25. A rope 25 feet long runs from the top of a pole straight to the ground, and then along the ground to a point 12 feet from the base of the pole. What equation can be used to find h, the height of the pole? *(p. 25, prob. 39)*

A. $h = 25 + 12$

B. $h = 25 \times 12$

C. $h = 25 - 12$

D. $h = 12 - 25$

E. $h = \frac{25}{12}$

Go On 

Countdown to PSAE

26. F
27. E
28. F
29. C
30. J
31. E

State Goal 6 Number Sense

6.11.16 Simplify numerical problems involving absolute value.

26. What is the solution to the equation below? *(p. 393, prob. 14)*

$$|x + 3| = 3$$

F. $x = -6$ or $x = 0$

G. $x = 6$

H. $x = 6$ or $x = 0$

J. $x = 0$

K. $x = -6$ or $x = 6$

27. What is the solution to the equation below? *(p. 393, prob. 23–31)*

$$|x - 6| + 6 = 2$$

A. $x = 14$ or $x = -14$

B. $x = 2$ or $x = -2$

C. $x = 0$

D. $x = -14$ or $x = 0$

E. no solution

28. What is the solution to the equation below? *(p. 393, prob. 23–31)*

$$-2|x + 1| - 2 = -14$$

F. $x = 5$ or $x = -7$

G. $x = 6$ or $x = -6$

H. $x = 5$ or $x = 0$

J. $x = 7$ or $x = -8$

K. no solution

6.11.17 Set up, evaluate, or solve number sentences or word problems involving ratios and proportions with rational numbers (e.g., scale drawing, unit rate, scale factor, rate of change).

29. A concert sold out in 4.5 hours. If 7155 tickets were sold, at what rate did the tickets sell? *(p. 241, prob. 36)*

A. 15.9 tickets per hour

B. 159 tickets per hour

C. 1590 tickets per hour

D. 15,900 tickets per hour

E. 32,197.5 tickets per hour

30. You jog $2\frac{2}{5}$ miles in 30 minutes. What is your average speed? *(p. 240, prob. 20)*

F. 0.08 miles per hour

G. $1\frac{1}{5}$ miles per hour

H. $2\frac{2}{5}$ miles per hour

J. $4\frac{4}{5}$ miles per hour

K. 72 miles per hour

31. On a map, 1 cm = 26 km. If the actual distance between two cities is 169 kilometers, what is the distance on the map? *(p. 172, prob. 39)*

A. 65 km

B. 65 cm

C. 65.5 cm

D. 6.5 km

E. 6.5 cm

Go On 

COUNTDOWN to PSAE

32. G
33. D
34. K
35. A
36. F
37. D

State Goal 6 | Number Sense

6.11.18 Set up, evaluate, or solve common problems involving percent (e.g., sales tax, tip, interest, discount, markup, commission, compound interest).

32. Mrs. Howard earns a base salary of \$450 a month plus an 18% commission on sales over \$3,500. Last month, she had sales that totaled \$25,490. What was her salary for the month? Round your answer to the nearest cent. *(p. 177, prob. 5)*

F. \$4,031.00 **J.** \$26,578.20

G. \$4,408.20 **K.** \$30,078.20

H. \$8,088.20

33. Fred's dog weighs 85% more than his cat, and his cat weighs 50% more than Fred's rabbit. How much does Fred's dog weigh if the rabbit weighs 4 pounds? *(p. 181, prob. 40)*

A. 1.7 pounds **D.** 11.1 pounds

B. 6 pounds **E.** 37.1 pounds

C. 10 pounds

34. Jose invests \$5,000 in a 5-year Certificate of Deposit (CD) with an interest rate of 4.5% compounded annually. To the nearest dollar, how much will the CD be worth at the end of five years? *(p. 183, prob. 8)*

F. \$5,046 **J.** \$6,125

G. \$5,225 **K.** \$6,231

H. \$5,450

6.11.19 Set up, evaluate, or solve problems stated in terms of direct and inverse variation of simple quantities.

35. If x and y vary inversely, and $x = \frac{2}{3}$ when $y = 24$, which equation relates x and y? *(p. 769, prob. 28–42)*

A. $y = \frac{16}{x}$ **D.** $y = 16x$

B. $y = \frac{36}{x}$ **E.** $y = 36x$

C. $y = \frac{x}{16}$

36. Your parents give you an allowance bonus for each A you receive on your report card. The number of allowance bonuses, b, they give you varies directly with the number, n, of A's on your report card. Which equation models this situation? *(p. 769, prob. 3)*

F. $b = kn$ **J.** $nb = k$

G. $n = k + b$ **K.** $n = kb$

H. $b = \frac{k}{n}$

37. The percent grade p on an exam varies directly with the number n of correct answers. (There are 25 questions each worth 4 points.) Which equation relates the two variables? *(p. 769, prob. 9)*

A. $p = \frac{1}{4}n$ **D.** $p = 4n$

B. $n = \frac{4}{p}$ **E.** $n = \frac{1}{4}p$

C. $n = 4p$

Go On 

Countdown to PSAE

38. K
39. D
40. G
41. B
42. H
43. C

State Goal 7 | Measurement

7.11.01 Change from one unit to another within the same system of measurement, including calculations with mixed units (e.g., 3 hours plus 4 hours and 20 minutes; 2 feet minus 16 inches).

38. It took 86 hours for Joe Kittinger to cross the Atlantic Ocean, a distance of 3543 miles, in his balloon, *Rosie O'Grady.* What was the average speed of the balloon in yards per day? Round your answer to the nearest yard. *(p. 929, prob. 12)*

F. 41 yd/day

G. 148 yd/day

H. 989 yd/day

J. 304,698 yd/day

K. 1,740,190 yd/day

39. An airplane travels 1200 miles in 180 minutes. What is its average speed in miles per hour? *(p. 929, prob. 8)*

A. 7 mph

B. 20 mph

C. 90 mph

D. 400 mph

E. 72,000 mph

40. A gift comes in a cubical box that is 9 inches on each side. What is the surface area of the gift box, in square feet? *(p. 929, prob. 10)*

F. 2.25 square feet

G. 3.375 square feet

H. 30.375 square feet

J. 486 square feet

K. 729 square feet

7.11.02 Change from one unit in one system of measurement to a unit in another system of measurement, given a conversion factor.

41. The temperature at a certain city is 56°F. What is this temperature in degrees Celsius to the nearest degree? (Use $C = \frac{5}{9}(F - 32)$.) *(Additional Lesson B)*

A. −1°C

B. 13°C

C. 43°C

D. 45°C

E. 49°C

42. A container holds $\frac{2}{5}$ gallon of liquid. How many liters does it hold? Round your answer to the nearest hundredth. (Use 1 gal ≈ 3.79 L.) *(Additional Lesson B)*

F. 0.11 L

G. 0.66 L

H. 1.52 L

J. 4.19 L

K. 9.48 L

43. The distance from your school to the nearest library is 21 kilometers. What is this distance in miles? Round your answer to the nearest hundredth. (Use 1 km ≈ 0.62 mi.) *(Additional Lesson B)*

A. 0.03 miles

B. 6.51 miles

C. 13.02 miles

D. 33.87 miles

E. 26.04 miles

Go On 

COUNTDOWN *to* PSAE

Countdown to PSAE

44. H
45. C
46. J
47. D
48. J

State Goal 7 Measurement

7.11.05 Determine the linear measure, perimeter, area, surface area, and volume of similar figures.

44. In the figure, triangle MRT is similar to triangle SWY. *(p. 175, prob. 1)*

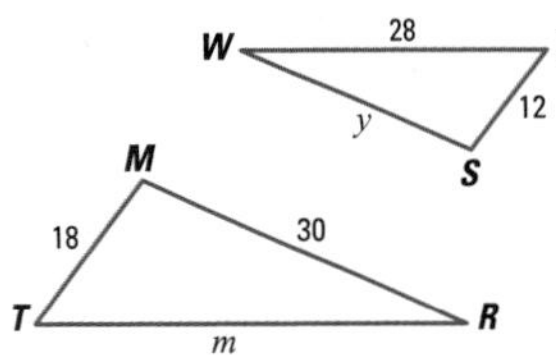

What is the value of m?

F. 20
G. 24
H. 42
J. 48
K. 63

45. In the figure below, triangle DEF is similar to triangle RST. *(p. 175, prob. 2)*

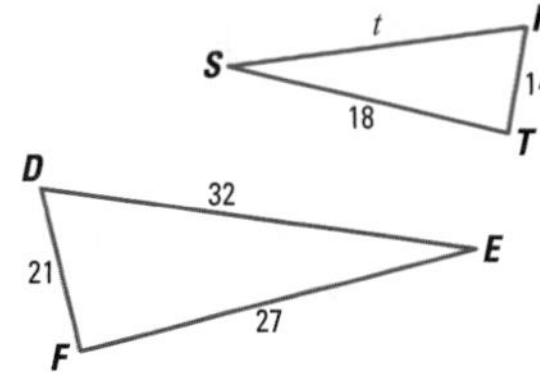

What is the value of t?

A. $9\frac{3}{6}$
B. $12\frac{1}{3}$
C. $21\frac{1}{3}$
D. 41
E. 48

46. A 3-foot tall fence post casts a shadow 8 feet long. A silo next to the post casts a shadow 180 feet long. How tall is the silo? *(p. 175, prob. 5)*

F. 0.13 feet
G. 30 feet
H. 60 feet
J. 67.5 feet
K. 480 feet

7.11.06 Determine the ratio of perimeters, areas, and volumes of figures.

47. A rectangular yard has a ratio of width to length of 4 : 5. If the length of the yard is 25 feet, what is the width? *(p. 166, prob. 45–52)*

A. 2 feet
B. 9 feet
C. 16 feet
D. 20 feet
E. 24 feet

48. Which of the following equations could be used to find the area A of a square with side s that is enlarged by a factor of 3? *(p. 172, prob. 33–41)*

F. $A = 3s$
G. $A = 3s^2$
H. $A = 9s$
J. $A = 9s^2$
K. $A = \frac{9}{s^2}$

Go On 

49. D
50. J
51. D
52. H
53. E
54. J

Strand 7 Measurement

7.11.07 Use measures expressed as rates (e.g., speed, density), measures expressed as products (e.g., person-days), and dimensional analysis (e.g., converting ft/sec to yards/min) to solve problems.

49. It took Molly 45 minutes to reach her home from the library on Saturday. If she traveled at an average speed of 55 miles per hour, how far away is the library from her home? *(p. 172, prob. 34)*

A. 1.22 miles

B. 13.75 miles

C. 18.75 miles

D. 41.25 miles

E. 73.33 miles

50. A certain remote control car travels at a speed of 21 ft/min. What is this speed in yards per minute? *(p. 172, prob. 34)*

F. $\frac{1}{7}$ yd/min

G. $\frac{7}{20}$ yd/min

H. $\frac{20}{7}$ yd/min

J. 7 yd/min

K. 63 yd/min

Strand 8 Algebra

8.11.01 Simplify or identify equivalent algebraic expressions (e.g., exponential, rational, logarithmic, factored, polynomial).

51. Simplify $(r^3s^7t^5)^3(s^2t)^5$ *(p. 492, prob. 37)*

A. $r^6s^{17}t^{13}$ **D.** $r^9s^{31}t^{20}$

B. $r^6s^{17}t^{14}$ **E.** $r^9s^{17}t^{13}$

C. $r^6s^{70}t^{75}$

52. Which of the following is a simplified form of the expression $\frac{-3x^6}{2y^4} \cdot \frac{4xy^5}{2x^3y^4}$? *(p. 499, prob. 43)*

F. $-3x^4y^3$ **J.** $-\frac{6x^4}{y^3}$

G. $-6x^4y^3$ **K.** $\frac{6x^4}{y^3}$

H. $-\frac{3x^4}{y^3}$

53. Which of the following is equal to $(7c - 2d)^2$? *(p. 572, prob. 27)*

A. $7c^2 - 2d^2$

B. $49c^2 - 4d^2$

C. $49c^2 + 4d^2$

D. $49c^2 + 28cd - 4d^2$

E. $49c^2 - 28cd + 4d^2$

54. What is the solution of the equation $\sqrt{x+2} = 9$? *(p. 732, prob. 7)*

F. 7 **J.** 79

G. 11 **K.** 81

H. 49

Go On

COUNTDOWN to PSAE

55. E
56. H
57. C

State Goal 8 | Algebra

8.11.02 Represent mathematical relationships using symbolic algebra.

55. A cellular phone company charges a flat fee of \$10 a month plus \$0.25 per minute. Which equation represents this situation, if y represents the total cost and x represents minutes used? *(p. 288, prob. 47)*

A. $y = 0.25x$

B. $y = 0.25(10)$

C. $10y = 0.25x$

D. $y = 10x + 0.25$

E. $y = 0.25x + 10$

56. Two numbers have a sum of 11 and a product of 24. Which system of equations can be used to find the two numbers? *(p. 439, prob. 11)*

F. $x + y = 24$
$xy = 11$

G. $x + y + xy = 35$
$x + y = 11$

H. $xy = 24$
$x - y = 11$

J. $xy = 24$
$xy = 11$

K. $\frac{x}{y} = 24$

57. On a road in the city of Wilsonville, the maximum driving speed is 55 miles per hour and the minimum speed is 30 miles per hour. If x represents someone's driving speed, which inequality best expresses the speed limits? *(p. 383, prob. 11)*

A. $55 \le x \le 30$

B. $x - 30 \le 55$

C. $55 \ge x \ge 30$

D. $x - 30 \ge 55$

E. $30 \ge x \ge 55$

Go On 

State Goal 8 | Algebra

8.11.03 Identify essential quantitative relationships in a situation, and determine the class or classes of functions (e.g., linear, quadratic, exponential) that model the relationships.

58. Which is the graph of the quadratic equation $y = x^2 - 4x + 4$? *(p. 638, prob. 15)*

F.

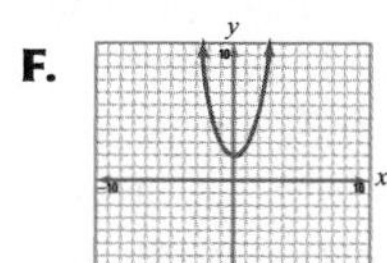

J.

G.

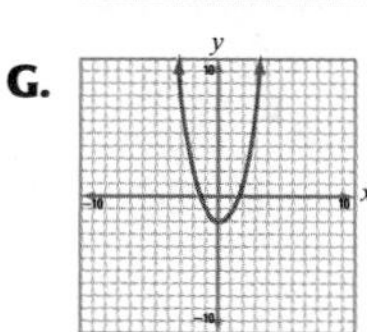

K.

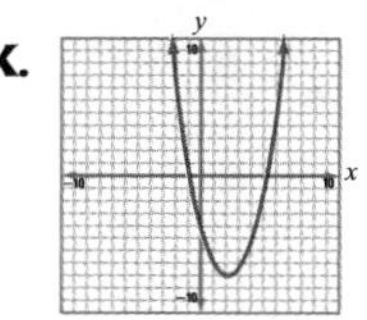

H.

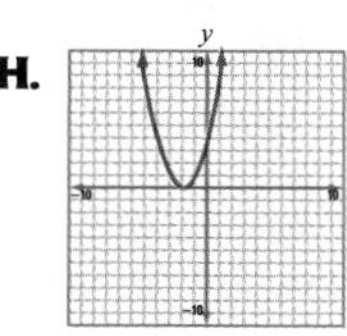

59. Which of the following is the graph of the quadratic equation $y = -x^2 + 4x + 3$? *(p. 638, prob. 22)*

A.

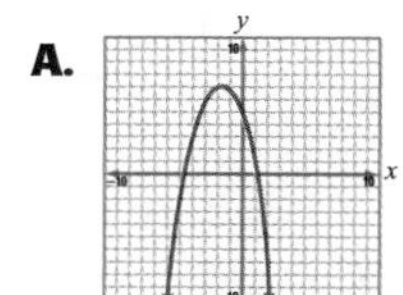

D.

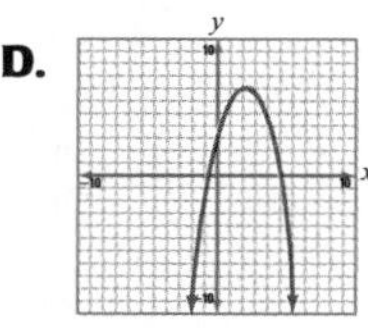

B.

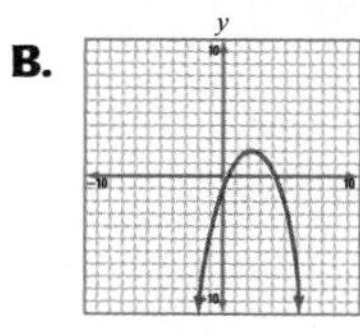

E.

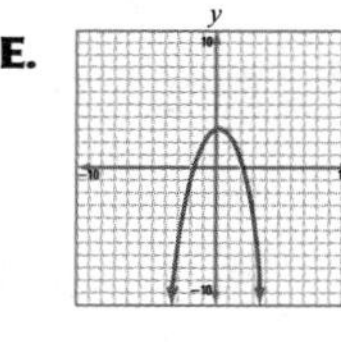

C.

60. Which of the following is the graph of the linear equation $4x + 2y = 8$? *(p. 229, prob. 22)*

F.

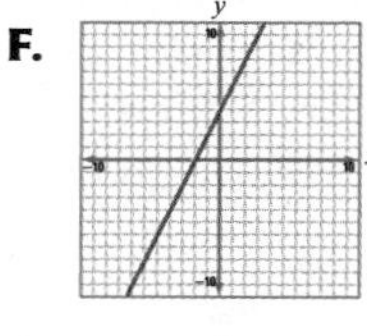

G.

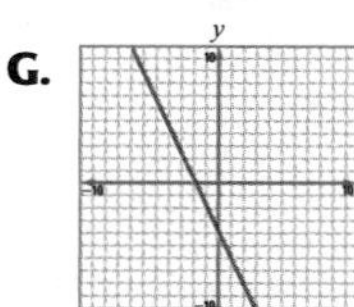

H.

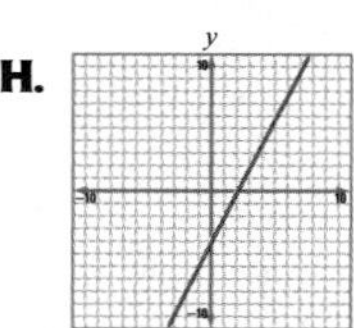

J.

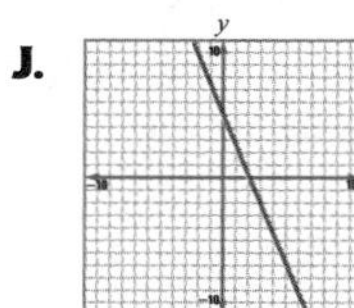

K.

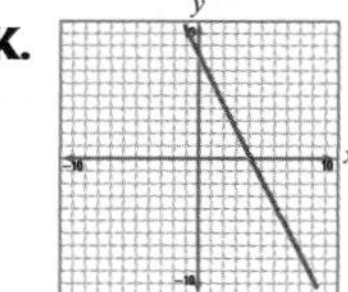

Go On

COUNTDOWN *to* PSAE

Countdown to PSAE

58. J
59. D
60. J

Countdown to PSAE

61. C
62. G
63. D
64. G

State Goal 8 | Algebra

8.11.04 Determine a specific term, a finite sum, or a rule that generates terms of a pattern.

61. In a financial deal, you are promised \$500 the first day. Each day after that, you will receive 45% of the previous day's amount. When one day's amount drops below \$1, you will stop getting paid from that day on. Which day is the first day you would receive no payment? *(p. 183, prob. 14)*

A. 7th day

B. 8th day

C. 9th day

D. 10th day

E. 14th day

62. If $a_n = -6 + 3 \cdot (n - 1)$, what is the value of a_5? *(p. 310, prob. 1)*

F. 3

G. 6

H. 9

J. 12

K. 15

8.11.05 Model and describe slope as a constant rate of change.

63. Geraldine can walk 3 miles in 36 minutes and 5 miles in 60 minutes. If x represents the number of miles she can walk in y minutes, then this information can be represented by plotting the points (3, 36) and (5, 60) in the coordinate plane. What is the slope of the line that contains these two points? *(p. 239, prob. 16)*

A. -12

B. $-\frac{1}{12}$

C. $\frac{1}{12}$

D. 12

E. 24

64. In the graph below, what is the slope of the line and what does it represent? *(p. 239, prob. 6)*

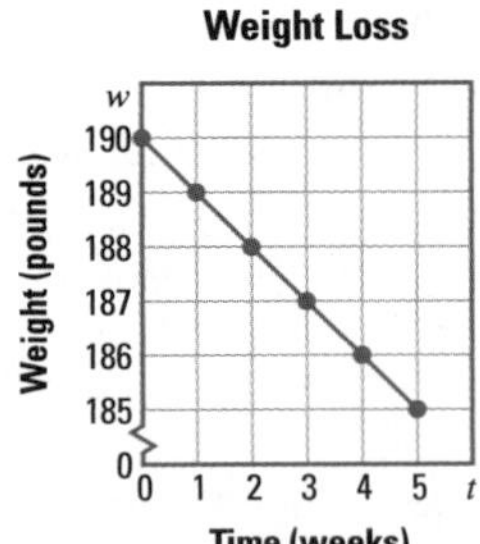

F. -5; pounds per day

G. -1; pounds per week

H. 1; pounds per week

J. 5; pounds per day

K. 5; total weight loss

State Goal 8 Algebra

8.11.06 Evaluate variable expressions and functions.

65. What is the value of the expression $x^3 - y - 8$ when $x = 4$ and $y = 19$? *(p. 5, prob. 41)*

A. -14

B. -11

C. -9

D. 37

E. 38

66. What is the value of $x^2 + x$ when $x = 4$? *(p. 5, prob. 39)*

F. 12

G. 20

H. 21

J. 56

K. 64

67. For the equation $y = -\frac{1}{4}x - 5$, what is the value of y when $x = 8$? *(p. 39, prob. 14)*

A. -7

B. -3

C. 0

D. 3

E. 7

8.11.07 Identify an equation of a line or an equation of a line of best fit from given information (e.g., from a set of ordered pairs, graphs, tables).

68. Which graph shows the best fit line for the scatter plot? *(p. 329, prob. 15)*

F.

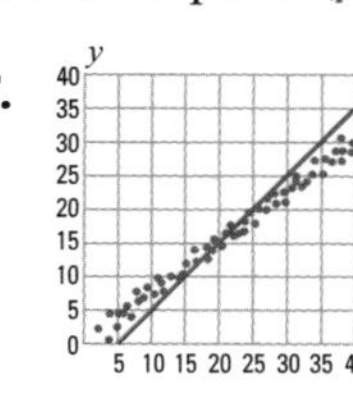

J.

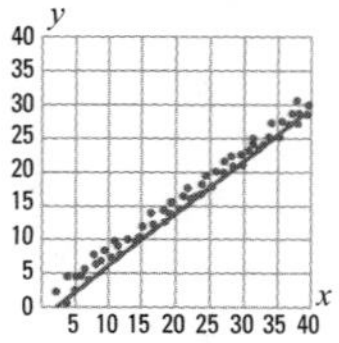

G.

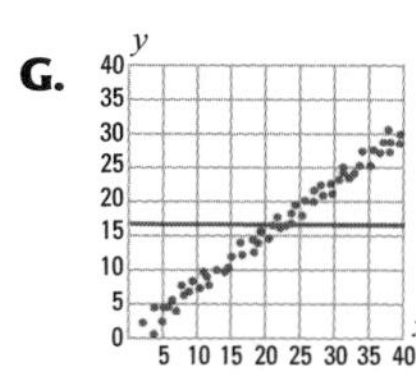

K.

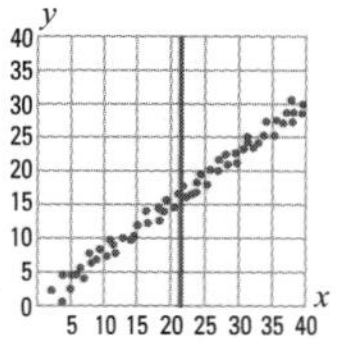

H.

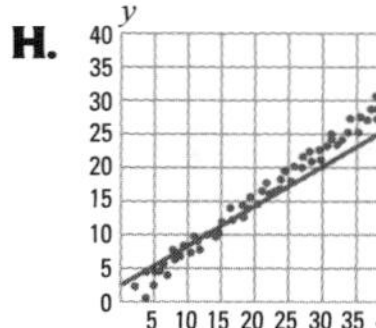

69. Which equation represents the line of best fit for the scatter plot below? *(p. 329, prob. 8)*

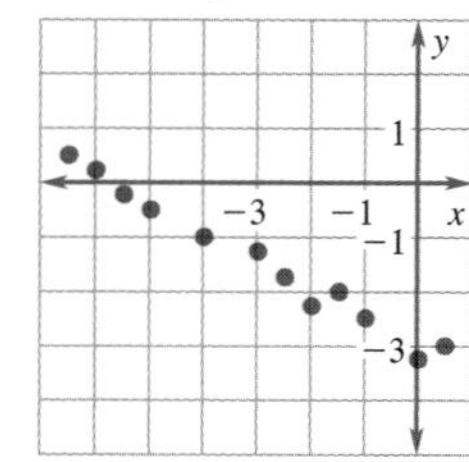

A. $y = -\frac{1}{2}x - 3$

B. $y = 2x - 3$

C. $y = -2x - 3$

D. $y = -2x + 3$

E. $y = \frac{1}{2}x - 3$

Go On

COUNTDOWN to PSAE

Countdown to PSAE

65. D
66. G
67. A
68. J
69. A

Countdown to PSAE

70. G
71. B
72. G
73. C
74. H

State Goal 8 Algebra

8.11.07 Identify an equation of a line or an equation of a line of best fit from given information (e.g., from a set of ordered pairs, graphs, tables).

70. What is the equation of the line that passes through the points $(-2, 1)$ and $(2, 3)$? *(p. 296, prob. 13)*

F. $y = 2x + 2$

G. $y = \frac{1}{2}x + 2$

H. $y = \frac{1}{2}x - 2$

J. $y = 2x - 2$

K. $y = -\frac{1}{2}x + 2$

8.11.09 Identify slope from an equation, table of values, or graph.

71. What is the slope of the line whose equation is $4x + 6y = 18$? *(p. 314, prob. 15)*

A. $-\frac{3}{2}$

B. $-\frac{2}{3}$

C. $\frac{2}{3}$

D. $\frac{3}{2}$

E. $\frac{9}{2}$

72. Find the slope of a line that contains the points $(-9, 0)$ and $(1, -1)$? *(p. 239, prob. 10)*

F. -10

G. $-\frac{1}{10}$

H. 0

J. $\frac{1}{10}$

K. 10

8.11.11 Analyze functions by investigating domain, range, rates of change, intercepts, and zeros.

73. If the domain of the function $f(x) = 2x^2 - 4x - 3$ is $[-3, 3]$, then what is the corresponding range? *(p. 39, prob. 16)*

A. $[-5, 27]$

B. $[-3, 27]$

C. $[3, 27]$

D. $[5, 27]$

E. $[3, -27]$

74. What is the domain and range of the graph below? *(p. 219, prob. 26–31)*

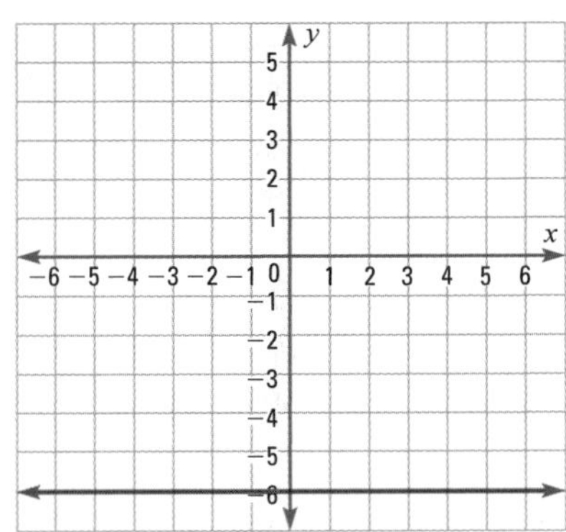

F. $D = \{-6\}, R = \{-6\}$

G. $D = \{\text{All real numbers}\}$, $R = \{\text{All real numbers}\}$

H. $D = \{\text{All real numbers}\}, R = \{-6\}$

J. $D = \{-6\}, R = \{\text{All real numbers}\}$

K. $D = \{\text{All real numbers}\}$, $R = \{\text{All negative numbers}\}$

Go On 

Countdown to PSAE

75. A
76. G
77. B

State Goal 8 Algebra

8.11.11 Analyze functions by investigating domain, range, rates of change, intercepts, and zeros.

75. What is the domain D of the function whose graph is shown below? *(p. 633, prob. 40)*

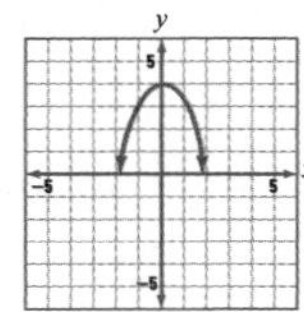

A. $D = \{-2 < x < 2\}$

B. $D = \{-2 \le x \le 2\}$

C. $D = \{0 < x < 4\}$

D. $D = \{0 \le x \le 4\}$

E. $D = \{-2 \le x < 2\}$

8.11.15 Interpret the graph of a system of equations and inequalities, including cases where there are no solutions.

76. The Student Council charged \$2 for students and \$3 for adults to attend a soccer game. If 60 tickets were sold, then \$140 was made. The graph below represents this situation. *(p. 432, prob. 31)*

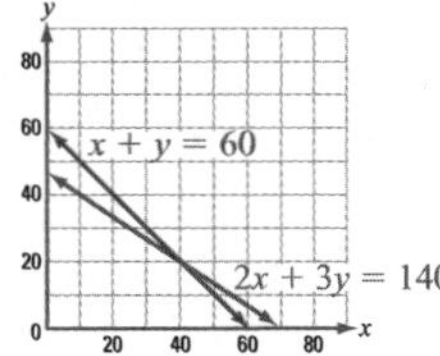

If x represents the number of student tickets sold, and y represents the number of adult tickets sold, how many students and adult tickets were sold?

F. 40 students, 40 adults

G. 40 students, 20 adults

H. 20 students, 40 adults

J. 20 students, 20 adults

K. 30 students, 30 adults

77. The solution set of what inequality is shown below? *(p. 409, prob. 16)*

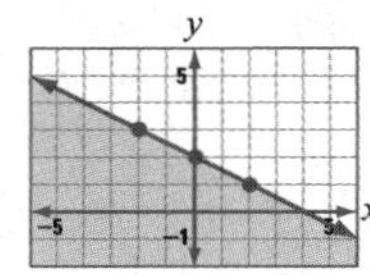

A. $x + 2y \le 2$

B. $x + 2y \le 4$

C. $x + 2y \ge 4$

D. $x - 2y \ge 4$

E. $x - 2y \le 4$

Go On 

COUNTDOWN to PSAE

78. J
79. C
80. J
81. B
82. F
83. C

State Goal 8 | Algebra

8.11.17 Solve systems of equations and inequalities.

78. What is the solution of the system of equations below? *(p. 454, prob. 3)*

$$4x + 3y = 27$$
$$2x - y = 1$$

F. $(-4, 3)$
G. $(1, 1)$
H. $\left(1\frac{1}{2}, 7\right)$
J. $(3, 5)$
K. $(1, 5)$

79. The sum of two numbers is -15. If their difference is 21, what is the larger number? *(p. 447, prob. 9)*

A. -18
B. -3
C. 3
D. 18
E. 36

80. What is the solution of the following system of linear equations? *(p. 457, prob. 11)*

$$2x - 5y = 10$$
$$-3x + 4y = 6$$

F. $(0.5, 1.125)$
G. $(-2, 0)$
H. $(-6, -10)$
J. $(-10, -6)$
K. $(0, -6)$

81. Which system of linear inequalities is defined by the shaded region? *(p. 469, prob. 9–20)*

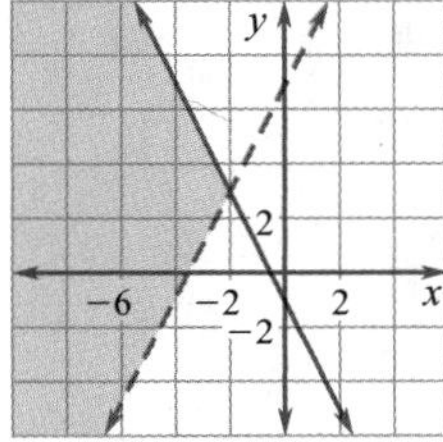

A. $y > 2x - 7; y = -x - 1$
B. $y > 2x + 7; y \le -2x - 1$
C. $y \ge \frac{1}{2}x - 8; y < 2x + 7$
D. $y \ge -2x - 8; y \le 2x + 1$
E. $y \ge -2x - 8; y \le 2x + 7$

8.11.18 Solve quadratic equations over the complex number system, including selecting and evaluating formulas.

82. What are the solutions of the equation $x^2 + 4 = 40$? *(p. 586, prob. 25)*

F. ± 6
G. ± 7
H. ± 11
J. ± 36
K. ± 44

83. What are the solutions of equation $x^2 + 10x = 39$? *(p. 586, prob. 24)*

A. $-3, -13$
B. $-3, 13$
C. $3, -13$
D. $3, 13$
E. there are no solutions

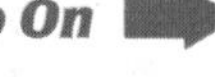

Countdown to PSAE

84. K
85. B
86. F
87. C
88. H

State Goal 8 Algebra

8.11.18 Solve quadratic equations over the complex number system, including selecting and evaluating formulas.

84. What are the solutions of the equation $x^2 - 13x + 36 = 0$? *(p. 586, prob. 21)*

F. 4 and -8

G. -4 and 9

H. 3 and 9

J. -4 and -9

K. 4 and 9

85. What is the solution of the equation $9m^2 + 24m + 16 = 0$? *(p. 603, prob. 26)*

A. $m = -4$

B. $m = -\frac{4}{3}$

C. $m = -\frac{3}{4}$

D. $m = \frac{3}{4}$

E. $m = \frac{4}{3}$

86. What is the product of the solutions of the equation below? *(p. 603, prob. 29)*

$$2x^2 + x - 10 = 0$$

F. -5

G. $-\frac{1}{2}$

H. $\frac{1}{2}$

J. 5

K. $-\frac{5}{2}$

8.11.22 Identify equivalent forms of equations, inequalities, and systems of equations.

87. Rewrite the equation of the line $-4x - 6y = 3$ in slope intercept form. *(p. 314, prob. 18)*

A. $x = -1.5y + 3$

B. $x = -1.5y - \frac{3}{4}$

C. $y = -\frac{2}{3}x - \frac{1}{2}$

D. $y = -\frac{2}{3}x + 3$

E. $y = \frac{2}{3}x + \frac{1}{2}$

88. What is the equation of the line $2(y - x) = 12$ in slope intercept form? *(p. 305, prob. 12)*

F. $y = -x + 12$

G. $y = x - 12$

H. $y = x + 6$

J. $y = x - 6$

K. $y = -x - 6$

COUNTDOWN to PSAE

Go On 

89. B
90. G
91. C
92. F

State Goal 9 | Geometry

9.11.01 Apply the Pythagorean Theorem.

89. A 20-foot ladder is placed 12 feet from the base of a building. How high up the wall does the ladder reach? *(p. 740, prob. 10)*

A. 22 feet

B. 16 feet

C. 8 feet

D. 6 feet

E. 3 feet

90. The lengths of the legs of a right triangle are 8 and 15 units. How long is the hypotenuse of the triangle? *(p. 740, prob. 10)*

F. 12.69 units

G. 17 units

H. 120 units

J. 161 units

K. 289 units

9.11.02 Identify and represent transformations (rotations, reflections, translations, dilations) of an object in the plane, and describe the effects of transformations on points in words or coordinates.

91. The vertices of a rectangle are $(-1, -1)$, $-1, 1)$, $(2, 1)$, and $(2, -1)$. If the rectangle is dilated by a factor of 2, what are the vertices of the new rectangle? *(p. 923, prob. 9–13)*

A. $(1, 1)$, $(1, 3)$, $(3, 2)$, and $(4, 1)$

B. $(-3, -3)$, $(-3, -1)$, $(0, -1)$, and $(0, -3)$

C. $(-2, -2)$, $(-2, 2)$, $(4, 2)$, and $(4, -2)$

D. $(-0.5, -0.5)$, $(-0.5, 0.5)$, $(1, 0.5)$, and $(1, -0.5)$

E. $(-2, -1)$, $(-2, 1)$, $(4, 1)$, and $(4, -1)$

92. The vertices of a triangle are $(2, 3)$, $(4, 3)$, and $(5, 7)$. If the triangle is translated 1 unit to the right and 3 units down, what are the new vertices of the triangle? *(p. 923, prob. 1–5)*

F. $(3, 0)$, $(5, 0)$, and $(6, 4)$

G. $(1, 0)$, $(3, 0)$, and $(4, 4)$

H. $(-1, 4)$, $(1, 4)$, and $(2, 8)$

J. $(5, 2)$, $(7, 2)$, and $(8, 6)$

K. $(-1, 0)$, $(1, 0)$, and $(2, 4)$

Go On

IL 52

Countdown to PSAE

93. D
94. G
95. C
96. G
97. B

State Goal 9 Geometry

9.11.05 Identify, apply, or solve problems that require knowledge of geometric properties of plane figures (e.g., triangles, quadrilaterals, parallel lines cut by a transversal, angles, diagonals, triangle inequality).

93. Parallelogram *DONE* is shown below.

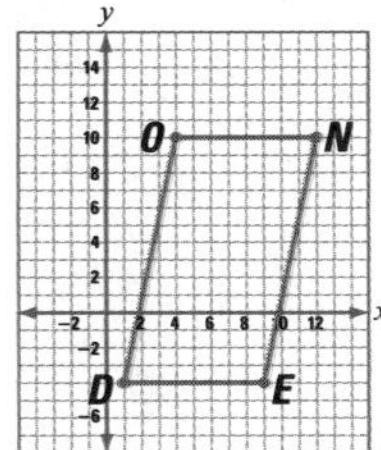

What is the perimeter of the parallelogram? Round your answer to the nearest tenth of a decimal place. *(p. 925, prob. 2)*

A. 12.6 units
B. 15.4 units
C. 30.3 units
D. 44.6 units
E. 60.6 units

94. Triangle *XYZ* is shown below

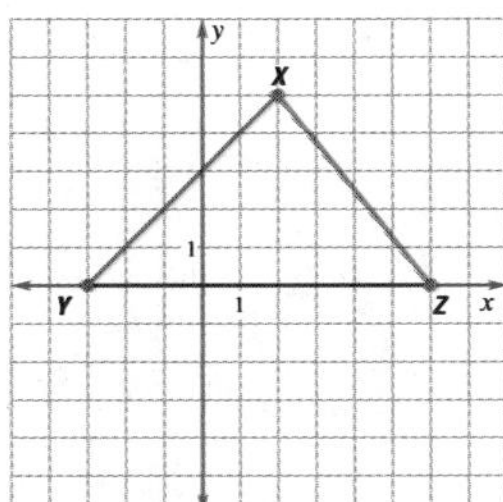

What is the length of line segment *YX*? Round your answer to the nearest whole number. *(p. 747, prob. 6)*

F. 5
G. 7
H. 14
J. 25
K. 50

9.11.09 Solve problems that involve calculating distance, midpoint, and slope using coordinate geometry.

95. The coordinates of the midpoint of line segment *PQ* are (3, 4). If the coordinates of point *P* are (1, 1), what are the coordinates of point *Q*? *(p. 748, prob. 38)*

A. $(-1, 0)$
B. $(-2, -2)$
C. $(5, 7)$
D. $(5, 0)$
E. $(-5, 7)$

96. What are the coordinates of the midpoint of a segment whose endpoints are $(-8, 3)$ and $(-5, -1)$? *(p. 747, prob. 25)*

F. $(-7, 2)$
G. $\left(-6\frac{1}{2}, 1\right)$
H. $\left(6\frac{1}{2}, 1\right)$
J. $\left(1, 6\frac{1}{2}\right)$
K. $\left(1\frac{1}{2}, 2\right)$

97. What is the midpoint of $\overline{PQ}$? *(p. 747, prob. 24)*

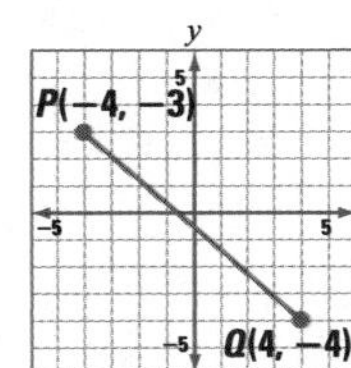

A. $(0, \frac{1}{2})$
B. $(0, -\frac{1}{2})$
C. $(-\frac{1}{2}, 0)$
D. $(-\frac{1}{2}, \frac{1}{4})$
E. $(\frac{1}{4}, -\frac{1}{2})$

Go On

COUNTDOWN to PSAE

98. H
99. B
100. G
101. A

9.11.09 Solve problems that involve calculating distance, midpoint, and slope using coordinate geometry.

98. Westernville and Southbury are located on a coordinate plane, where 1 unit represents 1 km. Westernville is located at (0, −63) and Southbury is located at (0, −26). What is the distance between Westernville and Southbury? *(p. 747, prob. 5)*

F. 89 km **J.** $\sqrt{3293}$ km

G. 63 km **K.** $\sqrt{4645}$ km

H. 37 km

99. What is the distance between the two coordinates (−1, 4) and (7, −8)? Round your answer to the nearest tenth. *(p. 747, prob. 10)*

A. 20.0 **D.** 8.9

B. 14.4 **E.** 7.6

C. 13.4

100. What is the distance between point A and point B? *(p. 747, prob. 11)*

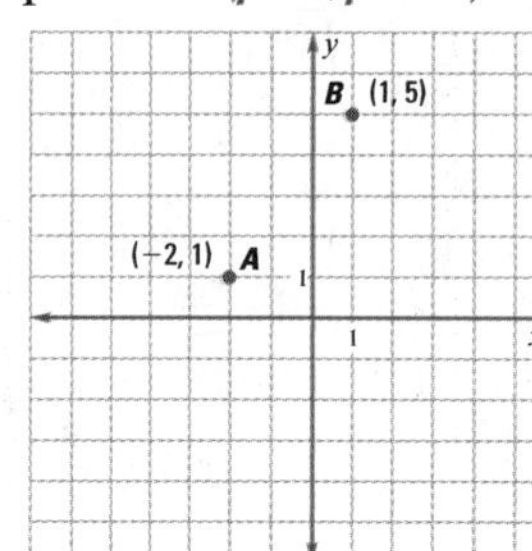

F. 4 **J.** 7

G. 5 **K.** 8

H. 6

9.11.12 Solve problems involving similar figures.

101. A realtor sketches a living room with dimensions shown in the figure.

Realtor's Sketch

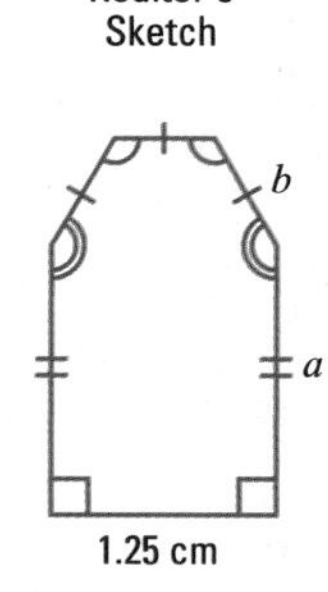

Actual Measurements

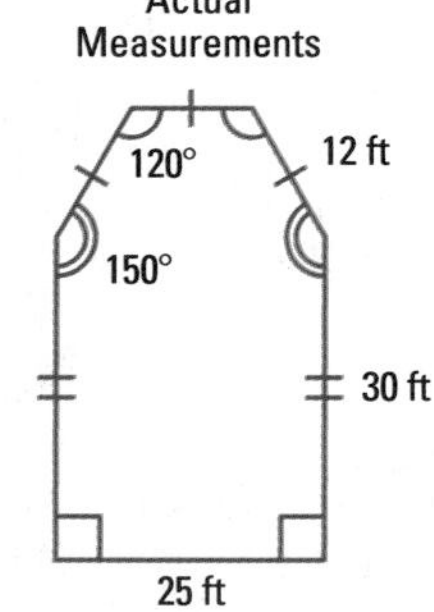

She wrote equations to find the values of the variables and solved them to get $a = 1.5$ and $b = 0.6$. Which of these equations did she use? Were her answers correct? *(p. 175, prob. 1–4)*

A. $\frac{30}{a} = \frac{25}{1.25}; \frac{12}{b} = \frac{25}{1.25}$; Yes

B. $\frac{30}{a} = \frac{25}{1.25}; \frac{12}{b} = \frac{25}{1.25}$; No

C. $\frac{1.25}{a} = \frac{30}{25}; \frac{1.25}{b} = \frac{12}{25}$; Yes

D. $\frac{1.25}{a} = \frac{30}{25}; \frac{1.25}{b} = \frac{12}{25}$; No

E. $\frac{1.25}{a} = \frac{25}{30}; \frac{12}{b} = \frac{25}{1.25}$; Yes

Go On

Countdown to PSAE

102. H
103. C
104. J
105. D
106. F
107. E

State Goal 9 | Geometry

9.11.12 Solve problems involving similar figures.

102. $\triangle ACD$ is similar to $\triangle ABK$. *(p. 175, prob. 1–4)*

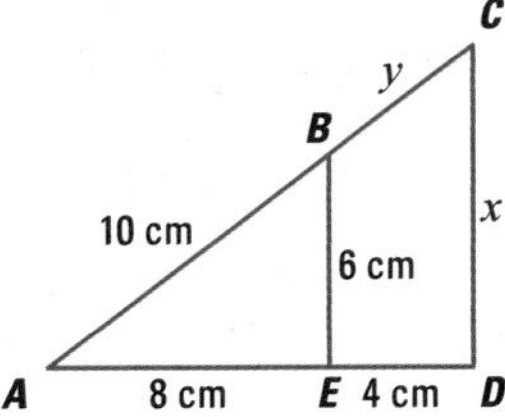

What are the values of x and y?

F. $x = 3$ cm and $y = 5$ cm

G. $x = 3$ cm and $y = 15$ cm

H. $x = 9$ cm and y $= 5$ cm

J. $x = 9$ cm and $y = 15$ cm

K. $x = 9$ cm and $y = 10$ cm

9.11.13 Solve problems using triangle congruence.

103. If $\triangle ABC \cong \triangle DEF$ and the area of $\triangle DEF$ is 24 square inches, and it's height is 6 inches, what is the length of the base of $\triangle ABC$? *(p. 925, prob. 6, 11)*

A. 4 inches

B. 6 inches

C. 8 inches

D. 12 inches

E. 24 inches

104. If triangle PQR and triangle STU are congruent right triangles, which statement below is true? *(p. 925, prob. 6, 11)*

F. $\overline{PQ} \cong \overline{SU}$

G. $\angle R \cong \angle S$

H. $\angle Q \cong \angle P$

J. $\overline{QR} \cong \overline{TU}$

K. $\overline{RP} \cong \overline{TS}$

9.11.17 Recognize and apply mathematical and geometric axioms, fundamental theorems of geometry, and deductive reasoning.

105. Look at the steps shown to solve the equation $3(5 - 2x) + 7x - 15 = x$. Which statement could be used to justify the third step? *(p. 118, prob. 3)*

Step	Justification
$3(5 - 2x) + 7x - 15$	
$= 15 - 6x + 7x - 15$	Distributive Property
$= 15 - 15 - 6x + 7x$	Commutative Property
$= 0 - 6x + 7x$	Identity Property of Addition
$= -6x + 7x$	Addition Property of Equality
$= x$	

A. Identity Property of Multiplication

B. Inverse Property of Multiplication

C. Identity Property of Addition

D. Inverse Property of Addition

E. Commutative Property

106. Which property can be used to show that if $x = y$, then $y = x$? *(p. 118, prob. 3)*

F. Symmetric Property

G. Reflexive Property

H. Transitive Property

J. Inverse Property

K. Commutative Property

107. Which property can be used to show that $a + b + c = a + c + b$? *(p. 118, prob. 3)*

A. Symmetric Property

B. Reflexive Property

C. Transitive Property

D. Inverse Property

E. Commutative Property

Go On 

COUNTDOWN to PSAE

108. J
109. A
110. K
111. A
112. K
113. C

State Goal 9 | Geometry

9.11.18 Identify a counter-example to disprove a conjecture.

108. Read the conjecture below.

The sum of two numbers is always greater than at least one of the numbers.

Which of these is a counterexample to the conjecture? *(p. 68, prob. 35)*

F. $8 + (-4)$
G. $6 + 0$
H. $-2 + 1$
J. $-3 + (-2)$
K. $5 + 2$

109. Tad says that when 5 is multiplied by another number, x, the absolute value of the result is greater than 5. Which values of x provide a counterexample to Tad's statement? *(p. 68, prob. 37)*

A. $0 < x < 1$
B. $3 < x < 5$
C. $x < -10$
D. $x < -1$
E. $x > 1$

110. Given the statement below, determine which answer gives a counterexample. *(p. 68, prob. 35)*

If I am wet, then it is raining outside.

F. If it is raining, then I am wet.
G. If I am wet, then it is not raining.
H. If I am not wet, then it is not raining.
J. If it is not raining, then I am not wet.
K. If I went swimming, then I am wet.

9.11.19 Determine distances and angle measures using indirect measurement (e.g., properties of right triangles, Law of Sines, Law of Cosines).

111. A diagonal skateboarding ramp is 10 feet in length and makes a 35° angle with the ground. How high is the ramp from the ground, to the nearest hundredth of a foot? *(Additional Lesson F)*

A. 5.74 feet
B. 6.00 feet
C. 8.19 feet
D. 12.21 feet
E. 17.43 feet

112. A building casts a shadow of 25 feet. The angle formed between the top of the building and the shadow is 30°. How tall is the building, to the nearest tenth of a foot? *(Additional Lesson F)*

F. 12.5 feet
G. 14.4 feet
H. 21.7 feet
J. 28.0 feet
K. 43.3 feet

113. Mary's garden is in the shape of a right triangle. The lengths of the legs of the triangle are 4 feet and 7 feet. What is the approximate length of the hypotenuse of the garden? *(p. 742, prob. 35–38)*

A. 5.74 feet
B. 7 feet
C. 8.06 feet
D. 33 feet
E. 65 feet

Go On 

Countdown to PSAE

114. J
115. E
116. J
117. B
118. F
119. C

State Goal 9 Geometry

9.11.20 Solve problems using 45°-45°-90° and 30°-60°-90° triangles.

114. The legs of a right triangle both measure 10 centimeters. What is the length of the hypotenuse of the triangle? *(p. 740, prob. 3–14)*

F. 5

G. $5\sqrt{2}$

H. $5\sqrt{3}$

J. $10\sqrt{2}$

K. $10\sqrt{3}$

115. The longer leg in a 30°-60°-90° triangle measures 4 inches. What is the length of the hypotenuse? *(Additional Lesson C)*

A. $\frac{\sqrt{2}}{4}$

B. $2\sqrt{3}$

C. $4\sqrt{2}$

D. $4\sqrt{3}$

E. $8\sqrt{3}$

116. The legs of a 45°-45°-90° triangle measure 3 feet. What is the length of the hypotenuse to the nearest tenth of a foot? *(p. 740, prob. 3–14)*

F. 1.5 feet

G. 2.1 feet

H. 2.6 feet

J. 4.2 feet

K. 5.2 feet

9.11.22 Define, identify, and evaluate trigonometric ratios.

117. Which is the tangent of angle R in the triangle shown below? *(Additional Lesson E)*

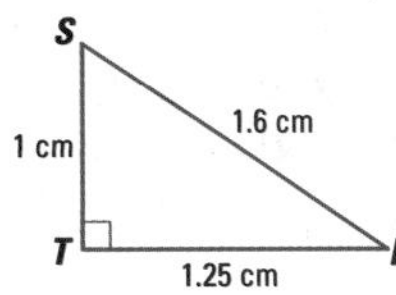

A. 0.625 **D.** 1.28

B. 0.8 **E.** 1.6

C. 1.25

118. Which is the cosine of angle C in the triangle shown below? *(Additional Lesson F)*

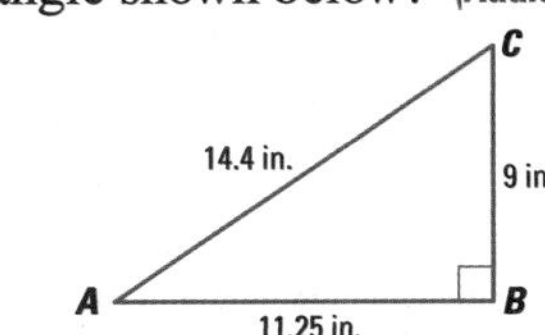

F. $\frac{9}{14.4}$ **J.** $\frac{14.4}{9}$

G. $\frac{9}{11.25}$ **K.** $\frac{14.4}{11.25}$

H. $\frac{11.25}{14.4}$

119. Which is the sine of angle F, to the nearest hundredth, in the triangle shown below? *(Additional Lesson F)*

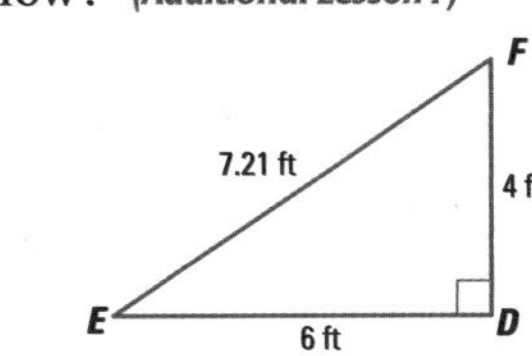

A. 0.55 **D.** 1.20

B. 0.67 **E.** 1.5

C. 0.83

Go On

COUNTDOWN to PSAE

120. F
121. B
122. H

State Goal 10 — Data Analysis, Statistics, and Probability

10.11.01 Read, interpret, predict, interpolate, extrapolate, and use information from a variety of graphs, charts, and tables.

120. The data in the table below is best represented by: *(p. 688, prob. 16)*

x	0	1	2	3	4
y	1	5	25	125	625

F. an exponential function

G. a quadratic function

H. a linear function

J. an inverse variation

K. none of the above

121. The table shows the relationship between time and distance for a bicyclist.

Elapsed Time (minutes)	10	15	20	25	30
Distance (miles)	2.5	3.75	5	6.25	7.5

What is the best estimate of the distance traveled after 50 minutes? *(p. 339, prob. 18)*

A. 11.25 miles

B. 12.5 miles

C. 13.75 miles

D. 15 miles

E. 16.25 miles

122. The increase in Sam's income from 2004 to 2005 is the same as the average yearly increase from 2002 to 2004. *(p. 340, prob. 19)*

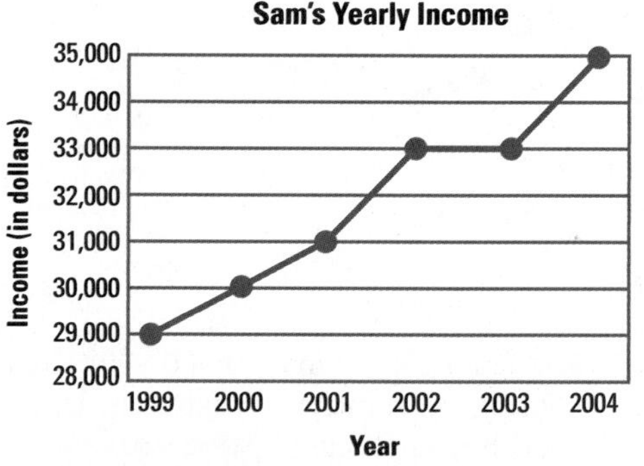

What is the best prediction for Sam's income in 2005?

F. $34,000

G. $35,000

H. $36,000

J. $37,000

K. $38,000

Go On 

Countdown to PSAE

123. C
124. H
125. A

State Goal 10 Data Analysis, Statistics, and Probability

10.11.03 Solve problems involving Venn diagrams.

Use the following Venn diagram to answer questions 123 and 124.

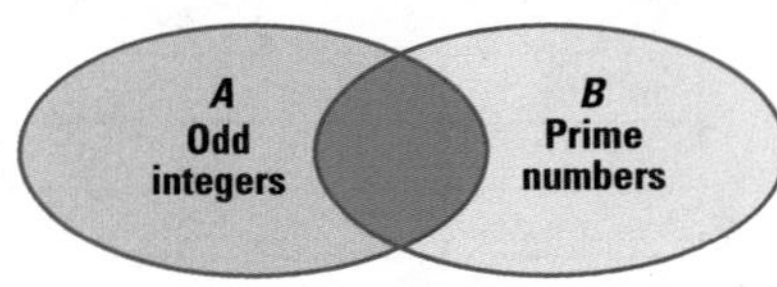

123. What is the intersection of Set A and Set B? *(p. 930, prob. 1–4)*

A. All prime numbers

B. All odd integers

C. All prime numbers except 2

D. All odd integers except 1

E. No intersection

124. What is the union of Set A and Set B? *(p. 930, prob. 1–4)*

F. All prime numbers

G. All odd integers

H. All odd integers and 2

J. All prime numbers and 1

K. All real numbers

10.11.04 Find an unknown value in a data set given information about descriptive statistics.

125. Look at the graph below.

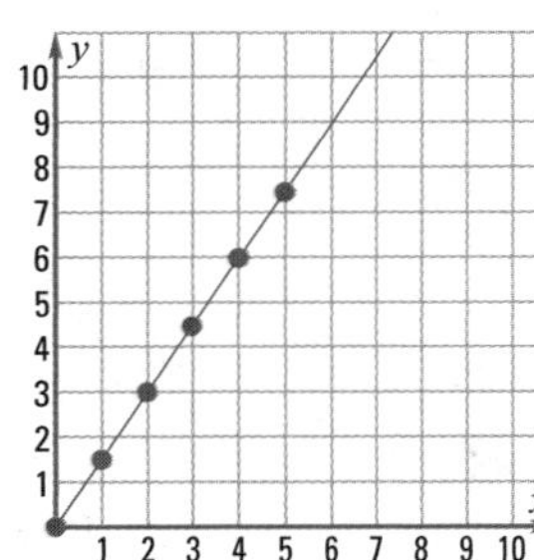

Which scenario can be represented by this graph? *(p. 241, prob. 38)*

A. By doing chores around the house, Chris can earn $1.50 per hour.

B. For each degree Celsius that the temperature falls, 1.5 inches of ice will form on the lake. When the temperature is 0 degrees Celsius, there is one inch of ice on the lake.

C. A potato with a one-inch diameter weighs one ounce. For each inch of diameter, the weight of the potato will increase by 1.5 ounces.

D. Peter is one mile away from his house. He walks at a rate of one mile every one and a half hours.

E. Water is draining from a bucket at a rate of 1.5 inches each hour.

Go On

COUNTDOWN to PSAE

126. J
127. C
128. H
129. A

State Goal 10 Data Analysis, Statistics, and Probability

10.11.04 Find an unknown value in a data set given information about descriptive statistics.

126. The graph of the equation $y = 4x - 2$ is shown below. *(p. 322, prob. 20)*

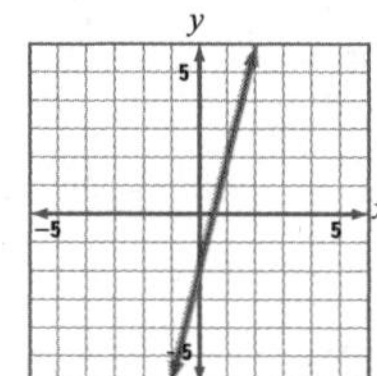

A new equation formed by changing the coefficient of x to $-\frac{1}{4}$. Which best describes the graph of the new equation $y = -\frac{1}{4}x - 2$?

F. Parallel to the given line with a different y-intercept

G. Parallel to the given line with the same y-intercept

H. Perpendicular to the given line with a different y-intercept

J. Perpendicular to the given line with the same y-intercept

K. The line will look the same.

127. Between 1950 and 1980 a town's population decreased at a rate of 0.34% per year. In 1950, the population was 5000. What was the population of the town in 1972? *(p. 525, prob. 38–41)*

A. 2336 **D.** 5388

B. 4514 **E.** 10,433

C. 4639

10.11.05 Calculate, interpret, and use measures of central tendency and dispersion.

128. The following table shows the number of hours that Hannah worked each day for the last two weeks.

Day	Number of Hours Worked
Monday	8
Tuesday	7.5
Wednesday	8.5
Thursday	7
Friday	6.5
Sunday	5
Tuesday	8
Thursday	6.5
Friday	7.5
Saturday	8

What is the mean number of hours Hannah worked in one day? *(p. 877, prob. 8)*

F. 6.75 hr **J.** 7.5 hr

G. 7.125 hr **K.** 7.75 hr

H. 7.25 hr

129. At a small college graduation there were 52 graduates. One was 82 years old, 2 were 42 years old, 3 were 29 years old, 6 were 25 years old, 22 were 22 years old, and 18 were 21 years old. Which of the following measures would not be used to represent the typical age of the 52 graduates? *(p. 877, prob. 19)*

A. mean

B. mode and median

C. mean and mode

D. median and mean

E. mean, median, and mode

Go On

Countdown to PSAE

130. F
131. C
132. K
133. A

State Goal 10 Data Analysis, Statistics, and Probability

10.11.05 Calculate, interpret, and use measures of central tendency and dispersion.

130. The stem-and-leaf plot shows the number of birdies recorded by the top 10 birdie leaders from the 2001 LPGA tour.

5	4 4 5 7 8
6	0 1 6 8 9

Key: 6|0 = 60

What is the mean of the data? *(p. 877, prob. 3–6)*

F. 60.2
G. 59
H. 54.8
J. 54
K. 52.4

131. The stem-and-leaf plot shows the ages of the members of a family at a family picnic.

1	0 0 5 6
2	
3	2
4	0 2 5 6
5	1 2
6	
7	
8	0 1

Key: 3|2 = 32

What was the median age? *(p. 877, prob. 3–8)*

A. 10
B. 40
C. 42
D. 45
E. 85

10.11.06 Compare two or more data sets on measures of central tendency and dispersion.

132. Jeff's first four test scores this semester are 74%, 86%, 79%, and 81%. He wants his average after the fifth test to be an 84%. What will he have to score on the fifth test to accomplish this? *(p. 877, prob. 3)*

F. 80%
G. 84%
H. 90%
J. 94%
K. 100%

133. The box-and-whisker plots show the number of goals scored per soccer game by two players.

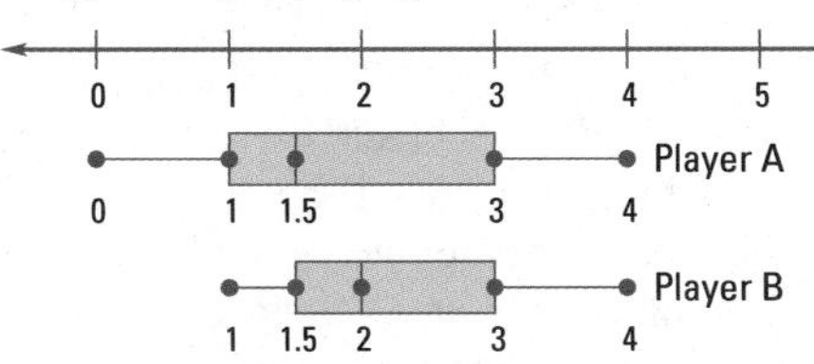

What conclusions can you make about who is the better player? *(p. 891, prob. 19)*

A. Player B is the better player because the player averages more goals per game and is more consistent because the range is smaller.

B. Player A is the better player because the range of scores is larger than the range for Player G.

C. Player A is the better player because the box enclosing the first and third quartiles is larger than that for Player B.

D. They are both equally good players because their maximum is the same.

E. No conclusions can be drawn from the box-and-whisker plots.

Go On

COUNTDOWN *to* PSAE

134. K
135. D
136. H
137. C
138. F

State Goal 10 Data Analysis, Statistics, and Probability

10.11.07 Compute the probability of an event composed of single or repeated trials with or without replacement.

134. A coin bank contains 16 quarters, 14 nickels, and 20 dimes. A quarter is chosen and then returned to the bank. What is the probability that the next coin drawn will also be a quarter? *(p. 864, prob. 8)*

F. $\frac{1}{16}$ **J.** $\frac{15}{49}$

G. $\frac{3}{10}$ **K.** $\frac{8}{25}$

H. $\frac{12}{125}$

135. Josh has a bag of 50 jelly beans. There are 10 yellow, 5 black, 22 red, 8 white, and 5 purple beans. If he draws one jelly bean, does not replace it, and then draws another one, what is the probability that both jelly beans are red? *(p. 857, prob. 3)*

A. $\frac{11}{25}$ **D.** $\frac{33}{175}$

B. $\frac{121}{625}$ **E.** $\frac{231}{1250}$

C. $\frac{242}{1225}$

136. A test has 5 true-false questions. If a student guesses the answers to all five questions, what is the probability that she will answer all questions correctly? *(p. 858, prob. 6)*

F. $\frac{1}{5}$ **J.** $\frac{1}{125}$

G. $\frac{1}{25}$ **K.** $\frac{1}{3125}$

H. $\frac{1}{32}$

137. Two standard 1–6 number cubes are rolled. What is the probability that the sum is 4? *(p. 864, prob. 9–12)*

A. $\frac{1}{36}$

B. $\frac{1}{24}$

C. $\frac{1}{12}$

D. $\frac{1}{11}$

E. $\frac{1}{6}$

10.11.08 Compute probabilities for compound events.

138. Carlos rolls a die and flips a coin. What is the probability that he will roll a two or a four and flip tails? *(p. 864, prob. 7–12)*

F. $\frac{1}{6}$

G. $\frac{1}{5}$

H. $\frac{1}{4}$

J. $\frac{1}{3}$

K. $\frac{1}{2}$

Go On

Countdown to PSAE

139. E
140. J
141. D
142. G
143. E
144. G

State Goal 10 Data Analysis, Statistics, and Probability

10.11.10 Apply counting techniques (e.g., permutations, combinations, Fundamental Counting Principle).

139. A pizzeria has a special on large pizzas that includes your choice of 4 different crusts, 3 different sauces, and 8 different toppings. How many different one-topping pizzas can be made? *(p. 855, prob. 37)*

A. 15 **B.** 20 **C.** 48 **D.** 56 **E.** 96

140. Paul has 2 pairs of pants, 4 shirts, and 3 pairs of shoes. How many different outfits can he make using one pair of pants, one shirt, and one pair of shoes? *(p. 855, prob. 36)*

F. 9 **G.** 12 **H.** 16 **J.** 24 **K.** 36

141. An ice cream shop has 3 flavors of ice cream, 4 flavors of toppings, and 2 choices of sprinkles. How many different combinations can be made with 1 ice cream, 1 topping, and 1 serving of sprinkles? *(p. 854, prob. 32)*

A. 8 **B.** 9 **C.** 12 **D.** 24 **E.** 36

142. A group of 5 figure skaters compete in a regional championship. Awards are given for first, second, and third place. In how many different ways can 3 of the 5 skaters win awards? *(p. 854, prob. 30)*

F. 120 **G.** 60 **H.** 15 **J.** 10 **K.** 6

143. In one season of a basketball league, each team plays every other team twice. If there are five teams in the league, how many games are played in all? *(p. 859, prob. 23)*

A. 8 **B.** 10 **C.** 18 **D.** 19 **E.** 20

144. Alex has three drawers in his dresser. He has to put away T-shirts, shorts, and socks. In how many different ways can he organize his dresser so that he has one drawer for T-shirts, one for shorts, and one for socks? *(p. 854, prob. 30)*

F. 3 **G.** 6 **H.** 9 **J.** 12 **K.** 15

COUNTDOWN to PSAE

Illinois Resources Guide

Pacing and Assignment Guide

REGULAR SCHEDULE

Pre-AP For pacing and assignments for a Pre-AP course, see the *Algebra 1 Toolkit.*

Lesson	Les. Day	BASIC	AVERAGE	ADVANCED
1.1 8.11.06	Day 1	SRH p. 914 Exs. 11–15; pp. 5–7 Exs. 1, 2, 3–13 odd, 15–25, 27–41 odd, 48–52, 56–65	pp. 5–7 Exs. 1, 2, 4–14 even, 15, 16–22 even, 24, 25, 26–44 even, 45, 46, 49–54, 57–65	pp. 5–7 Exs. 1, 2, 10–14, 15–23 odd, 32–44 even*, 45–47, 50–63*
1.2 6.11.04	Day 1	SRH p. 915 Exs. 11–15; pp. 10–12 Exs. 1, 2, 3–17 odd, 19–26, 28–30, 34–38, 41–52	pp. 10–12 Exs. 1, 2, 8–18 even, 20–39, 41–52	pp. 10–12 Exs. 1, 2, 13–19, 25–33*, 36–40*, 43–52
1.3 6.11.13	Day 1	SRH p. 929 Exs. 1–6; pp. 18–20 Exs. 1, 2, 3–11 odd, 13, 14, 15–21 odd, 22–27, 31–35, 38–46 even	pp. 18–20 Exs. 1, 2, 4–12 even, 13–29, 32–37, 41–46	pp. 18–20 Exs. 1, 2, 9–14, 18–25, 28–30*, 33–37*, 44–46
1.4	Day 1	pp. 24–26 Exs. 1, 2, 3–13 odd, 14–16, 17–35 odd, 39–45, 49–57 odd	pp. 24–26 Exs. 1, 2, 7–11, 13–16, 21–28, 32–38, 41–46, 50–56 even	pp. 24–26 Exs. 1, 2, 9–13, 16, 22–28 even, 32–38*, 42–48*, 50, 51, 56, 57
1.5 8.11.13	Day 1	SRH p. 937 Exs. 1–4; pp. 31–33 Exs. 1–10, 14–20, 24–32	pp. 31–33 Exs. 1, 2, 4–13, 16–22, 24–32	pp. 31–33 Exs. 1, 2, 4, 5, 8–13*, 17–23*, 25–31 odd
1.6 8.11.12	Day 1	pp. 38–40 Exs. 1–15	pp. 38–40 Exs. 1, 2, 4, 5, 7–16	pp. 38–40 Exs. 1, 2, 5, 8, 11–13, 18, 19, 22*
	Day 2	pp. 38–40 Exs. 16–20, 23–27, 30–36	pp. 38–40 Exs. 17–28, 30–36	pp. 38–40 Exs. 23–36*
1.7 8.11.12	Day 1	pp. 46–48 Exs. 1–11, 15–19, 21–30	pp. 46–48 Exs. 1, 2, 4–13, 15–19, 21–30	pp. 46–48 Exs. 1, 2, 6–8, 11–20*, 23–30
Review	Day 1	pp. 53–56 Exs. 1–40	pp. 53–56 Exs. 1–40	pp. 53–56 Exs. 1–40
Assess	Day 1	Chapter 1 Test	Chapter 1 Test	Chapter 1 Test
Yearly Pacing		Chapter 1 Total – 10 days	Chapter 1 Total – 10 days	Remaining – 150 days

*Challenge Exercises EP = Extra Practice SRH = Skills Review Handbook

BLOCK SCHEDULE

DAY 1	DAY 2	DAY 3	DAY 4	DAY 5
1.1	**1.3**	**1.5**	**1.6 (CONT.)**	**REVIEW**
pp. 5–7 Exs. 1, 2, 4–14 even, 15, 16–22 even, 24, 25, 26–44 even, 45, 46, 49–54, 57–65	pp. 18–20 Exs. 1, 2, 3–11 odd, 13–29, 32–37, 41–46	pp. 31–33 Exs. 1, 2, 4–13, 16–22, 24–32	pp. 38–40 Exs. 17–28, 30–36	pp. 53–56 Exs. 1–40
1.2	**1.4**	**1.6**	**1.7**	**ASSESS**
pp. 10–12 Exs. 1, 2, 8–18 even, 20–39, 41–52	pp. 24–26 Exs. 1, 2, 7–11, 13–16, 21–28, 32–38, 41–46, 50–56 even	pp. 38–40 Exs. 1, 2, 4, 5, 7–16	pp. 46–48 Exs. 1, 2, 4–13, 15–19, 21–30	Chapter 1 Test
Yearly Pacing	Chapter 1 Total – 5 days	Chapter 1 Total – 5 days	Remaining – 75 days	

Chapter Resource Guide

1

Chapter Resource Book

CHAPTER SUPPORT							
Parents as Partners (Chapter Overview with home involvement exercises and activity)						p. 1	
LESSON SUPPORT **Standard**	1.1 **8.11.06**	1.2 **6.11.04**	1.3 **6.11.13**	1.4	1.5 **6.11.13**	1.6 **8.11.12**	1.7 **8.11.12**
Teaching Guide/Lesson Plan	p. 3	p. 15	p. 27	p. 37	p. 49	p. 59	p. 70
Activity Masters		p. 17		p. 39			
Technology Activities & Keystrokes	p. 5	p. 18				p. 61	
Activity Support Masters							
Practice (3 levels)	p. 7	p. 19	p. 29	p. 40	p. 51	p. 62	p. 72
Study Guide	p. 10	p. 23	p. 32	p. 43	p. 54	p. 65	p. 78
Catch-Up for Absent Students	p. 12	p. 24	p. 34	p. 45	p. 56	p. 67	p. 80
Problem Solving/Application	p. 13	p. 25	p. 35	p. 46	p. 57	p. 68	p. 81
Challenge Practice	p. 14	p. 26	p. 36	p. 48	p. 58	p. 69	p. 82

REVIEW			
Chapter Review Games and Activities	p. 83	Cumulative Practice	p. 86
Project with Rubric	p. 84	Resource Book Answers	A1

Transparencies	1.1	1.2	1.3	1.4	1.5	1.6	1.7
Warm-Up/Daily Homework Quiz	✔	✔	✔	✔	✔	✔	✔
Notetaking Guide	✔	✔	✔	✔	✔	✔	✔
Teacher Support			✔			✔	✔
Answer Transparencies	✔	✔	✔	✔	✔	✔	✔

ASSESSMENT BOOK

Quizzes	p. 1	SAT/ACT Chapter Test	p. 12
Chapter Tests (3 levels)	p. 4	Alternative Assessment with Rubric	p. 14
Standardized Chapter Test	p. 10		

TECHNOLOGY

- Easy Planner
- Test and Practice Generator
- Power Presentations
- @HomeTutor
- Activity Generator
- Animated Algebra
- Classzone.com
- eEdition Plus Online
- eWorkbook Plus Online
- ML Assessment System

ADDITIONAL RESOURCES

Illinois Additional Lessons

- Additional Lesson A
- Estimation and Accuracy of Measurement
- Additional Lesson B
- Metric/customary Conversions
- Worked-Out Solution Key
- Notetaking Guide
- Practice Workbook
- Algebra 1 Toolkit
- Benchmark Tests
- Reteaching and Remediation
- Spanish Study Guide
- Spanish Assessment Book
- Spanish Resources in Spanish
- Multi-Language Visual Glossary

1 Lesson Practice Level B

LESSON 1.1 Practice B
For use with pages 2–7

Evaluate the expression.

1. $y + 12$ when $y = 29$ 41
2. $47 - x$ when $x = 38$ 9
3. $0.8a$ when $a = 7.5$ 6
4. $12.5 + m$ when $m = 7.6$ 20.1
5. $r(4.6)$ when $r = 8.1$ 37.26
6. $6.25 \div g$ when $g = 2.5$ 2.5
7. $\frac{x}{0.9}$ when $x = 54$ 60
8. $\frac{62}{d}$ when $d = 3.1$ 20
9. $\frac{4}{7} \cdot t$ when $t = \frac{7}{8}$ $\frac{1}{2}$
10. $r(8.3)$ when $r = 10.2$ 84.66
11. $w + \frac{2}{5}$ when $w = \frac{1}{2}$ $\frac{9}{10}$
12. $\frac{n}{2.4}$ when $n = 12$ 5

Write the power in words and as a product.

13. 8^7 eight to the seventh power; $8 \cdot 8 \cdot 8 \cdot 8 \cdot 8 \cdot 8 \cdot 8$
14. $(0.1)^4$ one tenth to the fourth power; $0.1 \cdot 0.1 \cdot 0.1 \cdot 0.1$
15. x^5 x to the fifth power; $x \cdot x \cdot x \cdot x \cdot x$

Evaluate the power.

16. 9^2 81
17. 2^6 64
18. $(0.4)^3$ 0.064

Evaluate the expression.

19. x^2 when $x = \frac{1}{5}$ $\frac{1}{25}$
20. m^4 when $m = 0.6$ 0.1296
21. $2y^3$ when $y = 4$ 128

22. **Side Table** A side table has interior storage space in the shape of a cube. What is the volume of the storage space if the interior length is 12 inches? 1728 in.^{3}

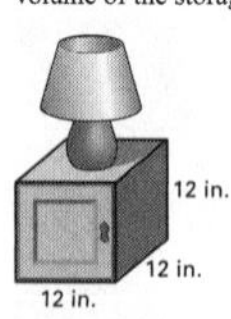

23. **Playing Cards** There are 52 cards in a standard deck of playing cards. You are combining decks of cards so that you can play a game with a large number of people. The expression $52d$ represents the number of cards in d decks. If you combine 4 decks of cards, how many cards will you have altogether? 208 cards

24. **Sales Tax** An item costs c dollars and 6% sales tax is charged. The total cost including sales tax is given by the expression $1.06c$. You are buying a skateboard that costs \$75. What is the cost of the skateboard including sales tax? \$74.50

25. **Flower Arranging** You are creating a flower arrangement for a friend. The total cost (in dollars) for one vase and f flowers is given by the expression $8 + 2.5f$. How much will it cost to make an arrangement with 8 flowers? \$28

LESSON 1.1

LESSON 1.2 Practice B
For use with pages 8–13

Evaluate the expression.

1. $16 \div 8 \cdot 5$ 10
2. $7^2 - 24 \div 3$ 41
3. $5 + 1.2 \div 0.3$ 9
4. $18 \div 6 + 4 \cdot 3$ 15
5. $13 - 15 \div 5 + 9$ 19
6. $\frac{2}{3} \cdot 3^2 - 5$ 1
7. $8(6 - 2) + 4$ 36
8. $28 - 3(4 + 5)$ 1
9. $1.2 \cdot 5 - 6 \div 3$ 4
10. $(11 + 15) \div 13$ 2
11. $35 - 3^2 \cdot 2$ 17
12. $\frac{4}{5}(3 \cdot 20) - 17$ 31

Evaluate the expression.

13. $3x^4 - 5$ when $x = 5$ 1870
14. $8m^3 \div 6$ when $m = 3$ 36
15. $200 - 3y^2$ when $y = 8$ 8
16. $5c^2 - 2c$ when $c = 9$ 387
17. $3 \cdot 18t^2$ when $t = \frac{1}{3}$ 6
18. $\frac{42}{n} + n$ when $n = 6$ 13
19. $7(x + 5)$ when $x = 10$ 105
20. $\frac{5a}{a - 6}$ when $a = 8$ 20
21. $\frac{4d^2}{d + 1}$ when $d = 3$ 9

22. Was the expression evaluated correctly using the order of operations? If not, find and correct the error.

$80 - \frac{1}{3}(15)^2 = 80 - 5^2 = 80 - 25 = 55$ no; $80 - \frac{1}{3}(15)^2 = 80 - \frac{1}{3}(225) = 80 - 75 = 5$

23. **Tournament** During a bowling tournament, you bowled three games with scores of 110, 130, and 129, respectively. Your average bowling score is given by $\frac{110 + 130 + 129}{3}$. What is your average score? 123

24. **Painting** Three weeks ago, an art supply store started selling a paint kit for 75% of the original price. Now the kit is 15% off of the sale price. The expression $0.75x - 0.15(0.75x)$ represents the current price of the paint kit where x is the kit's original price (in dollars). Find the current price of the kit if it originally cost \$48. \$30.60

25. **Crown Molding** You are decorating the perimeter of the ceiling of your living room with crown molding. The expression $2x + 2y$ represents the total amount of molding you need where x is the width of the room (in feet) and y is the length of the room (in feet). Find the total amount of wood you need if the room is 11 feet wide and 10.5 feet long. 43 ft

26. **Core Sample** Before a structure is built on a plot of land, it is sometimes necessary to test the surface beneath the plot of land to determine its integrity. So, it may be necessary to take a core sample which is cylindrical in shape. Find the volume of the core sample shown by using the expression $\pi r^2 h$ where r is the radius (in inches) and h is the height (in inches) of the cylinder. Use 3.14 for π. 1017.36 in.^{3}

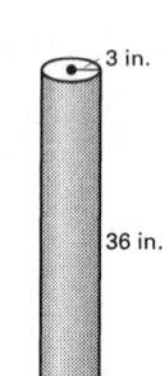

LESSON 1.2

LESSON 1.3 Practice B
For use with pages 14–20

Translate the verbal phrase into an expression.

1. The difference of 9 and a number n $9 - n$
2. The quotient of a number y and 22 $\frac{y}{22}$
3. The sum of 57 and a number b $57 + b$
4. $\frac{2}{3}$ of a number x $\frac{2}{3}x$
5. 18 less than a number c $c - 18$
6. 25 more than twice a number m $25 + 2m$
7. The quotient of 8 and twice a number z $\frac{8}{2z}$
8. The sum of 2 and the square of a number r $2 + r^2$

Write an expression for the situation.

9. The amount of money you spent if you started with \$40 and now have d dollars $40 - d$
10. The total height of a 1-foot tall birdbath if it is placed on a base that is b feet tall $b + 1$
11. Each person's share of baseball cards if 4 people share c cards equally $\frac{c}{4}$
12. Number of minutes in h hours $60h$

Find the unit rate.

13. $\frac{\$75}{\text{5 video games}}$ \$15/video game
14. $\frac{\text{600 students}}{\text{8 classes}}$ 75 students/class
15. $\frac{\text{32 pencils}}{\text{4 boxes}}$ 8 pencils/box

16. **Candle Making** You are making candles for your friends. A mold for the candles costs \$22.50 and wax to make one candle costs \$5. Write an algebraic expression for the total cost of making x candles. You make 8 candles. Find the total cost. $22.5 + 5x$; \$62.50

17. **Baseball** Last season, a baseball player scored 14 runs in 18 games. This season, the baseball player scored 12 runs in 15 games. Find the number of runs scored per game in each season. Round your answers to the nearest hundredth. Then identify the season in which the player scored more runs per game. Last season: 0.78 runs/game; This season: 0.80 runs/game; This season

18. **Car Trip** You are getting ready to make a 640-mile car trip. In general, your car can drive 160 miles on 5 gallons of gasoline. How many gallons of gasoline will you use for the trip? You started out with 4 gallons of gasoline in your car and gasoline is \$2.05 per gallon. How much money will you spend on gasoline on the trip? 20 gal; \$32.80

19. **Plant Trellis** You are building the wood trellis shown in the figure so that you can grow a vine up the side of your home. Write an expression for the total number of feet of wood needed to build the trellis. *Hint:* Write separate expressions for the number of feet of vertical pieces needed and the number of feet of horizontal pieces needed. Then find the total number of feet of wood needed if the trellis is 8 feet tall and 2 feet wide.

$6x + 3y$; 36 ft

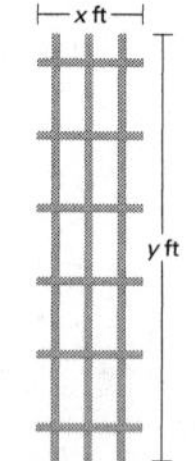

LESSON 1.3

LESSON 1.4 Practice B
For use with pages 21–26

Write an equation or an inequality.

1. The difference of a number c and 17 is more than 33. $c - 17 > 33$
2. The product of 3 and a number x is at most 21. $3x \le 21$
3. The sum of 14 and twice a number y is equal to 78. $14 + 2y = 78$
4. The difference of 22 and the quotient of a number m and 4 is 54. $22 - \frac{m}{4} = 54$
5. The sum of 7 and three times a number b is at least 12. $7 + 3b \ge 12$

Check whether the given number is a solution of the equation or inequality.

6. $6x + 7 = 25; 3$ yes
7. $22 - 5c = 8; 3$ no
8. $\frac{b}{4} - 7 = 1; 36$ no
9. $7a + 4 \ge 20; 2.7$ yes
10. $4y - 3 > 12; 4$ yes
11. $\frac{m}{3} + 14 < 33; 9$ yes

Solve the equation using mental math.

12. $x + 9 = 17$ 8
13. $y - 5 = 12$ 17
14. $8w = 48$ 6
15. $\frac{m}{4} = 16$ 64
16. $2x - 1 = 15$ 8
17. $3x + 2 = 20$ 6

18. **Computers** You are buying a new printer and a new scanner for your computer, and you cannot spend over \$150. The printer you want costs \$80. Write an inequality that describes the most that you can spend on the scanner and still stay within your budget. If you buy a scanner that costs \$75, will you remain within your budget? $80 + x \le 150$; no

19. **Go-Carts** You and three of your friends are going to race go-carts. The last time you went, you had a coupon for \$3 off each admission and paid \$48 for the 4 admissions. What was the total price without the coupon? You pay the regular price this time and share it equally. How much does each person pay? \$60; \$15

20. **Bracelets** You are making beaded bracelets for your friends. You want to use 30 beads for each bracelet and want to use no more than 145 beads. Write an inequality that models this situation. Can you make 4 bracelets? $30x \le 145$; yes

21. **Staircase** When building a staircase, you need to be concerned with the height of the riser and the depth of the tread so that people can go up and down the stairs comfortably. One rule of thumb used to determine proper riser height and tread depth is that the sum of the tread depth (in inches) and twice the riser height (in inches) should equal 26 inches. Write an equation that models this situation. The riser height of a set of steps is 5 inches. What should the depth be? $t + 2r = 26$; 16 in.

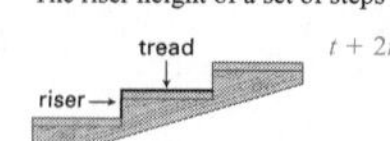

LESSON 1.4

Practice B
For use with pages 28–34

In Exercises 1 and 2, identify what you know and what you need to find out. You do *not* need to solve the problem. See below.

1. You are making cookies for a bake sale and need to make enough cookies to fill 24 boxes containing 6 cookies each. How many dozen cookies do you need to make?
2. The cellular phone plan you signed up for gives you 400 minutes a month for \$35 and charges \$.15 for each additional minute over 400 minutes. How long can you talk on the phone each month and stay within a budget of \$45?

In Exercises 3 and 4, state the formula that is needed to solve the problem. You do *not* need to solve the problem.

3. You invest \$200 into a savings account that earns 2% simple interest. How long will it take to earn \$50 in interest? $I = Prt$
4. It takes you half an hour to travel 26 miles to work. What is your average speed? $d = rt$
5. **Sticker Collection** Your sticker collection consists of 175 stickers. Each sticker is either an animated cartoon character or an animal. There are 42 less stickers that are animated characters than stickers that are animals. Let x be the number of stickers that are animals. Which equation correctly models this situation? c
   a. $x - 42 = 175$
   b. $x + (x + 42) = 175$
   c. $x + (x - 42) = 175$
6. **Bookshelf** You installed a bookshelf on the wall to organize some of your books. The books that you absolutely want on the shelf weigh a total of $6\frac{3}{4}$ pounds. The bookshelf can handle no more than 9 pounds. You plan on filling the rest of the shelf with your paperbacks that each weigh about $\frac{1}{8}$ pound. Assuming you won't run out of room, how many paperback books can you add to the shelf? 18
7. **Camping** You are responsible for buying supplies for an upcoming camping trip. You can buy packages of stew that just need water added and then are heated. Each package costs \$4.95 and contains enough stew for 2 people. You need to buy enough packages so that you can have stew for 3 days of the trip. There will be 8 people on the trip. How many packages do you need? What is the total cost? 12; \$59.40
8. **Banking** You are going to open a certificate of deposit (CD) that earns simple interest. One bank offers a CD in which you must deposit \$500 for 3 years with 2% interest. Another bank offers a CD in which you must deposit \$250 for 4 years with 3% interest. Which CD will earn more interest?
   Neither; they both earn the same amount.

1. Know: Number of boxes and number of cookies in one box; Need to find out: How many dozen cookies need made

2. Know: Charge for 400 minutes of service, charge per minute over 400 minutes, and amount you can spend; Need to find out: How many minutes over 400 you can talk

LESSON 1.5

LESSON 1.6

Practice B
For use with pages 35–41

Complete the sentence.

1. The input variable is called the __?__ variable. independent
2. The output variable is called the __?__ variable. dependent

6.

Domain	1	2	3	4
Range	2	6	10	14

Tell whether the pairing is a function.

3.

Input	Output
1	15
3	20
5	15
7	20

function

4.

Input	Output
5	5
6	5
7	5
8	5

function

5. 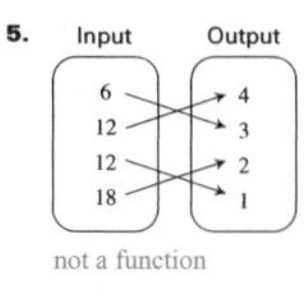

not a function

Make a table for the function. Identify the range of the function.

6. $y = 4x - 2$
   Domain: 1, 2, 3, 4
   See above.
7. $y = 0.1x + 3$
   Domain: 10, 20, 30, 40
   See below.
8. $y = \frac{1}{2}x + 2$
   Domain: 6, 7, 8, 9
   See below.

Write a rule for the function.

9.

Input, x	1	2	3	4
Output, y	5	10	15	20

$y = 5x$

10.

Input, x	10	11	12	13
Output, y	3	4	5	6

$y = x - 7$

11. **Shoe Sizes** The table shows men's shoe sizes in the United States and Australia. Write a rule for the Australian size as a function of the United States' size.

U.S. size	5	6	7	8	9	10
Australian size	3	4	5	6	7	8

$y = x - 2$

7.

Domain	10	20	30	40
Range	4	5	6	7

12. **Balloon Bunches** You are making balloon bunches to attach to tables for a charity event. You plan on using 8 balloons in each bunch. Write a rule for the total number of balloons used as a function of the number of bunches created. Identify the independent and dependent variables. How many balloons will you use if you make 10 bunches? $y = 8x$; independent: number of balloon bunches; dependent: number of balloons; 80 balloons
13. **Baking** A baker has baked 10 loaves of bread so far today and plans on baking 3 loaves more each hour for the rest of his shift. Write a rule for the total number of loaves baked as a function of the number of hours left in the baker's shift. Identify the independent and dependent variables. How many loaves will the baker make if he has 4 hours left in his shift?
    $y = 10 + 3x$; independent: number of hours left in shift; dependent: number of loaves baked; 22 loaves

8. 

Domain	6	7	8	9
Range	5	5.5	6	6.5

LESSON 1.7

Practice B
For use with pages 42–48

Graph the ordered pairs.

1. (3, 4), (4, 7), (5, 10), (6, 13), (7, 16)

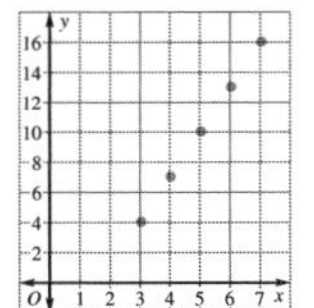

2. (2, 5), (6, 7), (4, 6), (12, 10), (10, 9)

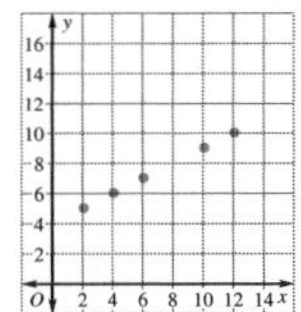

Complete the input-output table for the function.

3. $y = 3x + 2$

x	0	1	2	3
y	2	5	8	11

4. $y = 4x - 1$

x	1	2	3	4
y	3	7	11	15

Graph the function.

5. $y = 6 - x$
   Domain: 6, 5, 4, 3, 2

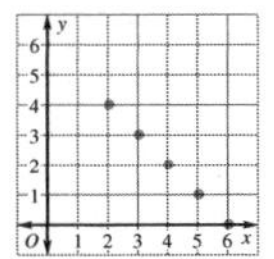

6. $y = \frac{1}{3}x$
   Domain: 6, 9, 12, 15, 18
7. $y = 4x - 3$
   Domain: 1, 2, 3, 4, 5
8. $y = 1.2x$
   Domain: 1, 2, 3, 4, 5

LESSON 1.7

LESSON 1.7

Practice B *continued*
For use with pages 42–48

Write a rule for the function represented by the graph. Identify the domain and range of the function. **10.** $y = 4x - 1$; Domain: 1, 2, 3, 4; Range: 3, 7, 11, 15

9. 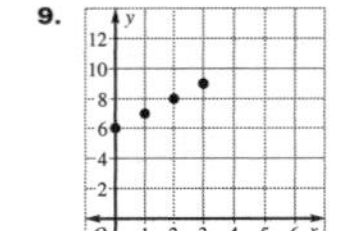
10. 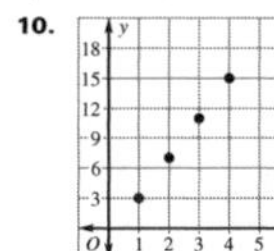
11. 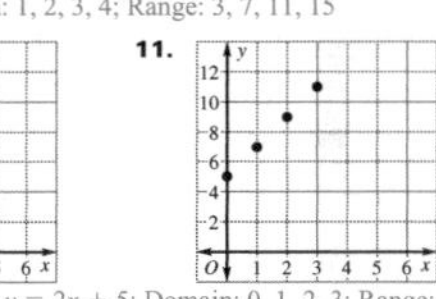

9. $y = x + 6$; Domain: 0, 1, 2, 3; Range: 6, 7, 8, 9 **11.** $y = 2x + 5$; Domain: 0, 1, 2, 3; Range: 5, 7, 9, 11

12.
13. 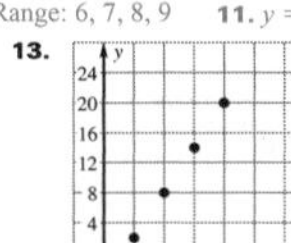
14. 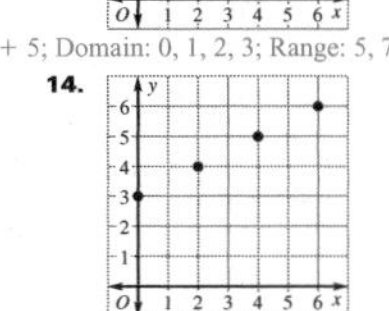

12. $y = \frac{1}{3}x$; Domain: 3, 6, 9, 12; Range: 1, 2, 3, 4 **13.** $y = 6x - 4$; Domain: 1, 2, 3, 4; Range: 2, 8, 14, 20

15. **High Temperatures** The table shows the high temperature H (in degrees Fahrenheit) in a city during the week as a function of the number of days d since Monday. Graph the function. Describe how the high temperatures change as the week progresses. **15.** Answers will vary.

Number of days since Monday, d	0	1	2	3	4	5
High temperature (degrees Fahrenheit), H	24	34	41	39	37	39

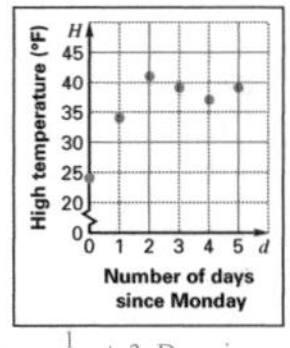

14. $y = \frac{1}{2}x + 3$; Domain: 0, 2, 4, 6; Range: 3, 4, 5, 6

16. **Metal Screws** The table shows the number of threads per inch on a screw as a function of screw size.

Screw size number, x	0	1	2	3	4	5	6
Number of threads per inch, y	80	72	64	56	48	44	40

   a. Graph the function.
   b. Describe how the number of threads per inch changes as the screw size increases.
   c. Would it be reasonable to expect a #8 screw to have 32 threads per inch? *Explain.* **16. c.** Yes. Answers will vary.

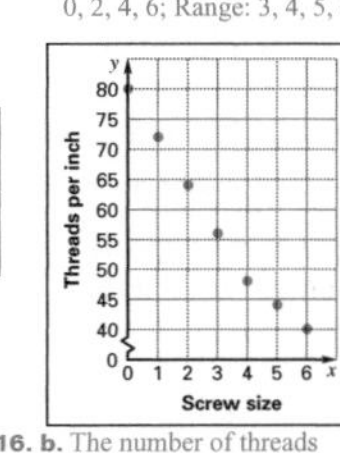

16. b. The number of threads decrease as the screw size increases.

LESSON 1.7

CHAPTER 1 Quiz 1
For use after Lessons 1.1–1.3

Evaluate the expression.

1. $8 + a$ when $a = 5$
2. $27 - h$ when $h = 21$
3. $\frac{p}{4}$ when $p = 16$
4. $7 + y^2$ when $y = 3$
5. $\frac{2m + 9}{m}$ when $m = 2$
6. $\frac{3x}{x - 1}$ when $x = 3$

Translate the verbal phrase into an expression.

7. 10 more than $\frac{1}{2}$ of a number r
8. Twice a number d
9. The difference of 19 and t
10. The sum of a number p and the square of a number b

Answers

1. 13
2. 6
3. 4
4. 16
5. $6\frac{1}{2}$
6. $4\frac{1}{2}$
7. $10 + \frac{1}{2}r$
8. $2d$
9. $19 - t$
10. $p + b^2$

CHAPTER 1 Quiz 2
For use after Lessons 1.4–1.5

Write an equation or an inequality.

1. The sum of twice a number d and 3 is 12.
2. Six less than four times a number j is 18.
3. The product of 8 and a number q is at least 32.
4. The difference of 10 and a number w is no more than 8.

In Exercises 5–8, check whether the given number is a solution of the equation or inequality.

5. $z - 4 = 9$; 12
6. $2x - 9 \geq 11$; 10
7. $k - 8.2 < 10$; 18
8. $4d + 1 < 13$; 3
9. What is the interest on $950 invested for 4 years in an account that earns simple interest at a rate of 3% per year?
10. A car travels 210 miles in 3.5 hours. What is the average speed of the car?

Answers

1. $2d + 3 = 12$
2. $4j - 6 = 18$
3. $8q \geq 32$
4. $10 - w \leq 8$
5. no
6. yes
7. yes
8. no
9. $114
10. 60 mi/h

CHAPTER 1 Quiz 3
For use after Lessons 1.6–1.7

Identify the domain and range of the function.

1.

Input	Output
0	1
2	5
4	9
6	13

2.

Input	Output
1	2
2	5
3	8
4	11

Tell whether the pairing is a function.

3.

Input	Output
2	10
2	3
4	7
6	2
8	2

4.

Input	Output
3	5
4	7
5	9
6	11

Graph the function.

5. $y = x - 2$; Domain: 2, 3, 4, 5, 6

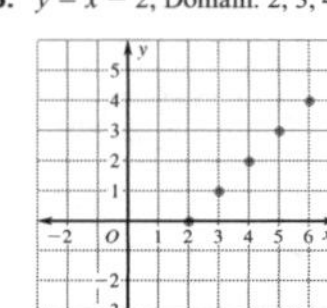

6. $y = \frac{1}{2}x + 3$; Domain: 0, 2, 4, 6, 8

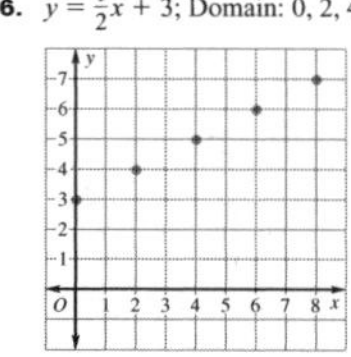

In Exercises 7–9, use the graph at the right.

7. Write a rule for the function represented by the graph.
8. Identify the domain of the function.
9. Identify the range of the function.

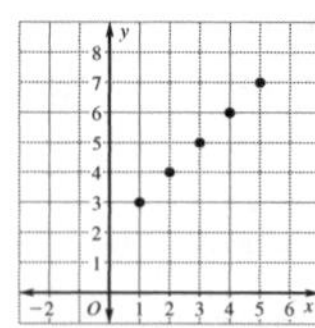

Answers

1. domain: 0, 2, 4, 6;
range: 1, 5, 9, 13
2. domain: 1, 2, 3, 4;
range: 2, 5, 8, 11
3. no
4. yes
5. See left.
6. See left.
7. $y = x + 2$
8. domain: 1, 2, 3, 4, 5
9. range: 3, 4, 5, 6, 7

CHAPTER 1 Chapter Test B
For use after Chapter 1

Evaluate the expression.

1. $34.5x$ when $x = 4$
2. $\frac{1}{3}y$ when $y = \frac{9}{10}$

Evaluate the power.

3. 5^4
4. 1^7
5. $\left(\frac{1}{2}\right)^5$
6. You can convert temperatures in degrees Fahrenheit to degrees Celsius by using the expression $\frac{9}{5}C + 32$, where C is the temperature (in degrees Celsius). Convert 35°C to degrees Fahrenheit.

Evaluate the expression.

7. $16 \div (4 - 2) - 3$
8. $3[15 - (2^3 - 6)^2]$

Evaluate the expression for the given values of the variables.

9. $3m - n$ when $m = 5$ and $n = 4$
10. $2u^2 + v$ when $u = 3$ and $v = 7$
11. A rectangular box is created by cutting out squares of equal sides of lengths x from a piece of cardboard 10 inches by 15 inches and folding up the sides as shown in the figure. The volume of the box is given by $V = x(10 - 2x)(15 - 2x)$. Find the volume of the box when the side length of the square is 3 inches.

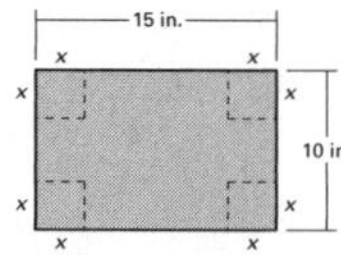

Write an algebraic expression, an equation, or an inequality.

12. The quotient of the square of a number t and 14
13. Amount you earn if you make 6.5 dollars an hour for h hours
14. The product of 6 and the quantity 2 more than a number x is at least 45.
15. The sum of 4 and the quotient of a number k and 9 is 12.

Answers

1. 138
2. $\frac{3}{10}$
3. 625
4. 1
5. $\frac{1}{32}$
6. 95°F
7. 5
8. 33
9. 11
10. 25
11. 108 in.^{3}
12. $\frac{t^2}{14}$
13. $6.5h$
14. $6(2 + x) \geq 45$
15. $4 + \frac{k}{9} = 12$

CHAPTER 1 **Chapter Test B** *continued*

For use after Chapter 1

Check whether the given number is a solution of the equation or the inequality.

16. $7z + 8 > 20$; 2

17. $\frac{r}{5} + 15 = 20$; 25

18. A carpet outlet advertises a price of $470.40 to carpet a 12-foot by 16-foot room. If a customer was given a price of $725.20 for carpeting a room that is 16 feet wide, what is the length of the room?

Write a rule for the function.

19.

Input, x	1	3	5	7
Output, y	2	6	10	14

20.

Input, x	12	15	18	21
Output, y	4	5	6	7

Find the range of the function. Then graph the function.

21. $y = \frac{1}{2}x + 3$

Domain: 0, 1, 2, 3, 4

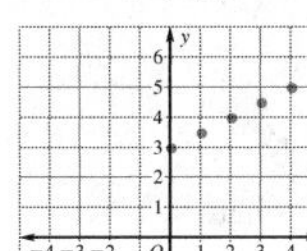

22. $y = x - 6$

Domain: 10, 12, 14, 16, 18

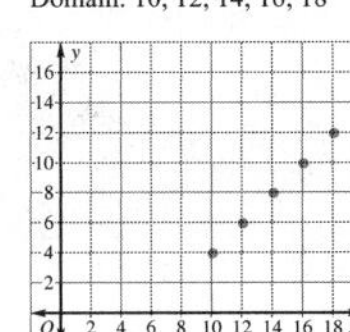

Answers

16. yes

17. yes

18. $18\frac{1}{2}$ ft

19. $y = 2x$

20. $y = \frac{x}{3}$

21. Range: 3, 3.5, 4, 4.5, 5

See left.

22. Range: 4, 6, 8, 10, 12

See left.

CHAPTER 1 **Standardized Test**

For use after Chapter 1

Multiple Choice

1. What is the value of $3.2n$ when $n = 5$? C

Ⓐ 0.16 Ⓑ 1.6 Ⓒ 16 Ⓓ 161

2. What is the value of 5^4? C

Ⓐ 20 Ⓑ 54 Ⓒ 625 Ⓓ 1024

3. Let d be the number of dollars you spent on gas and let g be the number of gallons you purchased. Which expression represents the price you paid per gallon? D

Ⓐ $d + g$ Ⓑ $\frac{g}{d}$

Ⓒ dg Ⓓ $\frac{d}{g}$

4. What is the value of $3[1^2(5 - 3 + 1)^3 \div 9]$? B

Ⓐ $\frac{1}{3}$ Ⓑ 9 Ⓒ 18 Ⓓ 6

5. What is the value of $\frac{108}{x^2} + 4x$ when $x = 6$? A

Ⓐ 27 Ⓑ 33 Ⓒ 42 Ⓓ 55

6. Which expression represents the phrase "twice the quotient of 5 less than a number m and 6"? B

Ⓐ $2\left(\frac{5 - m}{6}\right)$ Ⓑ $2\left(\frac{m - 5}{6}\right)$

Ⓒ $\frac{2m - 5}{6}$ Ⓓ $\frac{2(5) - m}{6}$

7. Which inequality corresponds to the sentence "Five less than the product of a number n and -6 is at least 8."? D

Ⓐ $5 - (-6n) \geq 8$ Ⓑ $-6n - 5 \leq 8$

Ⓒ $-\frac{n}{6} - 5 \geq 8$ Ⓓ $-6n - 5 \geq 8$

8. What is the solution of the equation $\frac{x}{4} - 12 = -4$? C

Ⓐ -64 Ⓑ -32 Ⓒ 32 Ⓓ 64

9. A car travels an average speed of 45 miles per hour. How many hours would it take to travel 540 miles? A

Ⓐ 12 hours Ⓑ 12.5 hours

Ⓒ 13 hours Ⓓ 14 hours

10. The temperature is 77°F. What is the temperature in degrees Celsius? B

Ⓐ 11°C Ⓑ 25°C

Ⓒ 61°C Ⓓ 225°C

11. The range of the function $y = 3x - 2$ is 1, 7, 13, 16, and 19. Which number is in the domain of the function? C

Ⓐ 2 Ⓑ 4 Ⓒ 6 Ⓓ 8

12. Each output of a function is 0.25 greater than the corresponding input. Which equation is a rule for the function? A

Ⓐ $y = x + 0.25$ Ⓑ $y = x - 0.25$

Ⓒ $y = 0.25x$ Ⓓ $y = \frac{x}{0.25}$

13. Which set of numbers represents the domain of the function in the table? D

Input	Output
−2	6
0	0
2	−6
4	−12

Ⓐ −12, −6, 0, 6

Ⓑ −12, −6, −2, 0, 2, 4, 6

Ⓒ −2, 2, 4

Ⓓ −2, 0, 2, 4

CHAPTER 1 **Standardized Test** *continued*

For use after Chapter 1

14. Which ordered pair is a solution of the function $y = 2x + 5$? B

Ⓐ (7, 1) Ⓑ (0, 5)

Ⓒ (−2, 9) Ⓓ (0, 0)

15. The relation in the table is a function. Which ordered pair can be included with this relation to form a new relation that is also a function? D

Input	−5	0	5	10
Output	12	15	18	21

Ⓐ (5, 7) Ⓑ (0, 2)

Ⓒ (−5, 5) Ⓓ (2, 16)

16. The graph of what function is shown? A

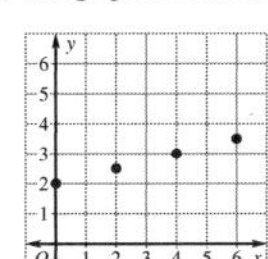

Ⓐ $y = \frac{1}{4}x + 2$ Ⓑ $y = \frac{1}{4}x + 4$

Ⓒ $y = 2x + \frac{1}{4}$ Ⓓ $y = 4x + 2$

Gridded Answer

17. What is the value of the expression $\frac{1}{3}x^2 + 4$ when $x = 9$?

Gridded answer: 31

19. b.

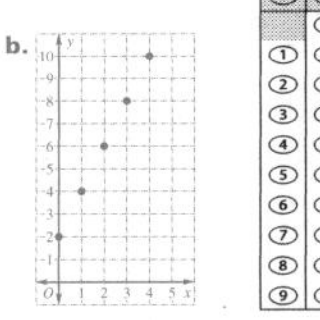

Short Response

18. You need to buy school supplies. Notebooks are $1.95 each and folders are $1.25 each. You only have $7.35 to spend.

a. Write an inequality for this situation. Let n represent the number of notebooks you can buy and let f represent the number of folders you can buy. $1.95n + 1.25f \leq 7.35$

b. What is the maximum number of notebooks you can buy if you want to buy one folder? 3

c. Would you have enough money left to buy a binder for $2.49 if you purchased two notebooks and one folder? *Explain.* See below.

Extended Response

19. Use the table to complete parts a–c.

Input	Output
0	2
1	4
2	6
3	8
4	10

19. a. $y = 2x + 2$; domain: 0, 1, 2, 3, 4; range: 2, 4, 6, 8, 10

a. Write a rule for the function represented by the table. Identify the domain and range of the function.

b. Graph the function. See left.

c. Write a problem that involves a real-world situation that can be solved using the rule for the function you wrote in part a. *Explain.*

Answers will vary.

18. c. No; If you buy 2 notebooks and 1 folder, you only have $2.20 left, which is not enough to buy a binder.

CHAPTER 1 **Alternative Assessment and Math Journal**

For use after Chapter 1

Journal

1. Explain the difference between an algebraic expression and an equation. Write an example of each, and explain what it means to evaluate an algebraic expression.

Multi-Step Problem

2. A local pizza shop offers the following special every Tuesday: buy one large pizza with one topping at regular price, and get as many medium one topping pizza as you would like for $6.25 each.

a. If the cost of a large pizza with one topping is $13.50, how much would it cost to purchase one large and five medium pizzas?

b. Complete the table by calculating the total cost of purchasing one large pizza and the indicated number of medium pizzas.

Number of medium pizzas	0	1	2	3	4
Total cost	?	?	?	?	?

c. Graph the function for total cost using your work in the table above.

d. Write a rule for the function representing the total cost of purchasing one large pizza with one topping and m medium pizzas.

e. You and a group of friends decide to pool your money to have a pizza party. If you have a total of $100 and purchase one large pizza, how many medium pizzas can you buy?

f. Your parents decide to purchase one large pizza and five medium pizzas. Determine the total area (in square inches) of pizza if a large pizza has a radius of 8 inches and a medium pizza has a radius of 5 inches. (*Hint:* $A = \pi r^2$) Use 3.14 for π. Round your answer to the nearest inch.

g. What is the cost per square inch of pizza if one large and five medium pizzas are purchased?

1. Complete answers should include: a clear distinction that an equation contains the equal sign and algebraic expressions do not; one example of an algebraic expression and one example of an equation; a written explanation describing how to replace the variable(s) in the expression with particular values to evaluate the expression.

2. a. $44.75 **b.** $13.50; $19.75; $26.00; $32.25; $38.50

c.

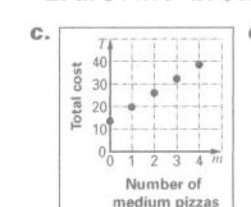

d. $T = 6.25m + 13.50$

e. 13 medium pizzas **f.** about 594 in.² **g.** about $.08 per square inch

PLAN AND PREPARE

Main Ideas

In Chapter 1, students write and evaluate expressions, equations, and inequalities. They learn to apply the order of operations and to use a problem solving plan to solve real-world problems. Students represent functions as rules and as tables. They also graph functions given a rule or table of values.

Prerequisite Skills

- Using fractions and percents
- Finding perimeter and area

Additional resources for reviewing prerequisite skills are:

- Skills Review Handbook, pp. 909–937
- @HomeTutor

1 Expressions, Equations, and Functions

Before

In previous courses, you learned the following skills, which you'll use in Chapter 1: using fractions and percents, and finding perimeter and area.

Prerequisite Skills

VOCABULARY CHECK

Copy and complete the statement.

1. In the fraction $\frac{2}{3}$, _?_ is the numerator and _?_ is the denominator. 2, 3
2. Two fractions that represent the same number are called _?_ fractions. equivalent
3. The word *percent* (%) means "divided by _?_." 100

SKILLS CHECK

Perform the indicated operation. ***(Review pp. 914–915 for 1.1, 1.2.)***

4. $\frac{2}{3}+\frac{3}{5}$ $1\frac{4}{15}$
5. $\frac{5}{6}-\frac{3}{4}$ $\frac{1}{12}$
6. $\frac{3}{5}\times\frac{2}{3}$ $\frac{2}{5}$
7. $\frac{1}{2}\div\frac{5}{8}$ $\frac{4}{5}$

Write the percent as a decimal. ***(Review p. 916 for 1.5.)***

8. 4% 0.04
9. 23% 0.23
10. 1.5% 0.015
11. 2.5% 0.025

12. Find the perimeter and area of the rectangle. ***(Review p. 924 for 1.5.)*** 31 in., $49\frac{1}{2}$ in.^{2}

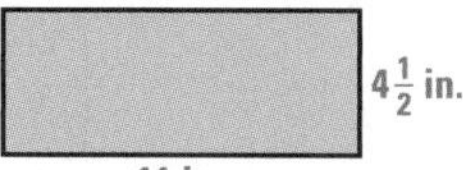

Chapter Planning Guide

Chapter 1 Resource Book
- Teaching Guide/Lesson Plan (pp. 3, 15, 27, 37, 49, 59, 70)
- Project with Rubric (p. 84)

Assessment and Intervention
- Assessment Book (pp. 1–15)
- Benchmark Tests
- Reteaching and Remediation Book

Interactive Technology
- Easy Planner
- Power Presentations CD-ROM
- Activity Generator CD-ROM
- Animated Algebra
- Test Generator CD-ROM
- Online Quizzes
- eWorkbook
- eEdition
- @HomeTutor

Resources for English Learners
- Quick Reference for English Learners
- Spanish Study Guide
- Multi-Language Visual Glossary
- Student Resources in Spanish

Now

In Chapter 1, you will apply the big ideas listed below and reviewed in the Chapter Summary on page 52. You will also use the key vocabulary listed below.

Big Ideas

1. **Writing and evaluating algebraic expressions**
2. **Using expressions to write equations and inequalities**
3. **Representing functions as verbal rules, equations, tables, and graphs**

KEY VOCABULARY

- variable, *p. 2*
- algebraic expression, *p. 2*
- power, exponent, base, *p. 3*
- order of operations, *p. 8*
- verbal model, *p. 16*
- rate, unit rate, *p. 17*
- open sentence, *p. 21*
- equation, inequality, *p. 21*
- solution of an equation or inequality, *p. 22*
- formula, *p. 30*
- function, *p. 35*
- domain, range, *p. 35*
- independent variable, *p. 36*
- dependent variable, *p. 36*

Why?

You can use multiple representations to describe a real-world situation. For example, you can solve an equation, make a table, or draw a diagram to determine a running route.

Animated Algebra

The animation illustrated below for Example 1 on page 28 helps you answer this question: How does the number of blocks you run affect the total distance?

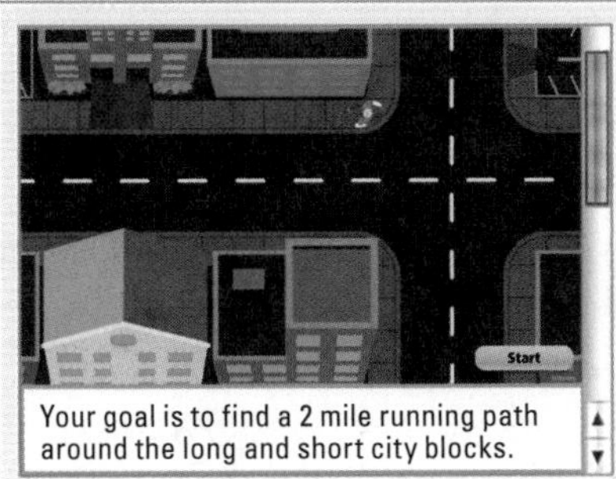

Your goal is to find a 2 mile running path around the long and short city blocks.

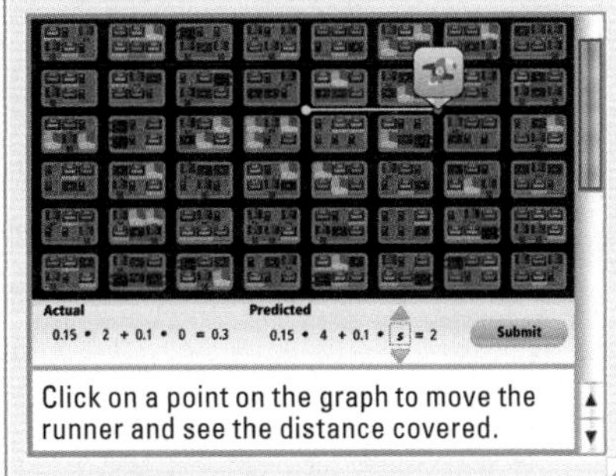

Click on a point on the graph to move the runner and see the distance covered.

Animated Algebra at classzone.com

Other animations for Chapter 1: pages 7, 9, 14, 21, 37, 50, and 52

Algebra 1 Toolkit

- Reading Strategies for Chapter 1, pp. 9–10
- Differentiated Instruction Notes, pp. 41–44
- English Learners Notes, pp. 97–98
- Inclusion Notes, pp. 129–130
- Teaching Strategies with Sample Worksheets, pp. 155–178
- Using Technology in the Classroom, pp. 179–184
- Tips for New Teachers, pp. 185–186
- Math Background Notes, pp. 211–212
- Pre-AP Strategies and Copymasters, pp. 279, 304–312
- Teacher Survival Activities, pp. 555–556, 581–582
- Bulletin Board Idea, p. 607
- Teacher Tool Transparencies, following p. 620

1 PLAN AND PREPARE

Warm-Up Exercises

Transparency Available

Perform the indicated operation.

1. 12 ÷ 1.5 **8**

2. 3.3 × 7 **23.1**

3. 11.6 − 5.9 **5.7**

4. Julia ran $10\frac{2}{3}$ miles last week and $8\frac{5}{6}$ miles this week. How many more miles did she run last week? $1\frac{5}{6}$ **mi**

Notetaking Guide

Transparency Available

Promotes interactive learning and notetaking skills, pp. 1–3.

Pacing

Basic: 1 day

Average: 1 day

Advanced: 1 day

Block: 0.5 block with 1.2

- See *Teaching Guide/Lesson Plan.*

2 FOCUS AND MOTIVATE

Essential Question

Big Idea 1, p. 1

How do you evaluate algebraic expressions and powers? **Tell students they will learn how to answer this question by substituting values for the variables in an expression and then performing the operation.**

1.1 Evaluate Expressions

8.11.06 Evaluate variable expressions and functions.

Before You used whole numbers, fractions, and decimals.

Now You will evaluate algebraic expressions and use exponents.

Why So you can calculate sports statistics, as in Ex. 50.

Key Vocabulary
- variable
- algebraic expression
- power
- base
- exponent

A **variable** is a letter used to represent one or more numbers. The numbers are the values of the variable. An **algebraic expression**, or *variable expression*, consists of numbers, variables, and operations.

Algebraic expression	Meaning	Operation
$5(n)$ $\quad 5 \cdot n \quad 5n$	5 times n	Multiplication
$\frac{14}{y} \quad 14 \div y$	14 divided by y	Division
$6 + c$	6 plus c	Addition
$8 - x$	8 minus x	Subtraction

To **evaluate an algebraic expression**, substitute a number for the variable, perform the operation(s), and simplify the result, if necessary. The resulting number is the value of the expression.

EXAMPLE 1 Evaluate algebraic expressions

AVOID ERRORS
Use the multiplication symbol • instead of × in algebraic expressions to avoid confusing × with the variable *x*.

Evaluate the expression when $n = 3$.

a. $13 \cdot n = 13 \cdot 3$ **Substitute 3 for *n*.**

$= 39$ **Multiply.**

b. $\frac{9}{n} = \frac{9}{3}$ **Substitute 3 for *n*.**

$= 3$ **Divide.**

c. $n - 1 = 3 - 1$ **Substitute 3 for *n*.**

$= 2$ **Subtract.**

d. $n + 8 = 3 + 8$ **Substitute 3 for *n*.**

$= 11$ **Add.**

✓ GUIDED PRACTICE for Example 1

Evaluate the expression when $y = 2$.

1. $6y$ **12** **2.** $\frac{8}{y}$ **4** **3.** $y + 4$ **6** **4.** $11 - y$ **9**

Resource Planning Guide

Chapter Resource Book
- Teaching Guide/Lesson Plan (pp. 3–4)
- Activity Master (p. 5)
- Practice levels A, B, C (pp. 7–9)
- Study Guide (pp. 10–11)
- Catch-up for Absent Students (p. 12)
- Application (p. 13)
- Challenge (p. 14)

Workbooks
- Notetaking Guide (pp. 1–3)
- Practice Workbook (pp. 1–2)

Teaching Options
- **Power Presentations CD-ROM** provides dynamic electronic teaching resources for the classroom.
- **Activity Generator CD-ROM** provides editable activities for all ability levels.

Interactive Technology
- Easy Planner
- Power Presentations CD-ROM
- Activity Generator CD-ROM
- Animated Algebra
- Test Generator CD-ROM
- Online Quiz
- eWorkbook
- eEdition
- @HomeTutor

Resources for English Learners
- Quick Reference for English Learners
- Spanish Study Guide
- Multi-Language Visual Glossary
- Student Resources in Spanish

See also the *Algebra 1 Toolkit* for more strategies for meeting individual needs.

EXAMPLE 2 Evaluate an expression

MOVIES The total cost of seeing a movie at a theater can be represented by the expression $a + r$ where a is the cost (in dollars) of admission and r is the cost (in dollars) of refreshments. Suppose you pay $7.50 for admission and $7.25 for refreshments. Find the total cost.

Solution

Total cost $= a + r$	**Write expression.**
$= 7.50 + 7.25$	**Substitute 7.50 for *a* and 7.25 for *r*.**
$= 14.75$	**Add.**

▶ The total cost is $14.75.

EXPRESSIONS USING EXPONENTS A **power** is an expression that represents repeated multiplication of the same factor. For example, 81 is a power of 3 because $81 = 3 \cdot 3 \cdot 3 \cdot 3$. A power can be written in a form using two numbers, a **base** and an **exponent**. The exponent represents the number of times the base is used as a factor, so 81 can be written as 3^4.

base ↓ ↙ exponent

$$\underbrace{3^4}_{\text{power}} = \underbrace{3 \cdot 3 \cdot 3 \cdot 3}_{\text{4 factors of 3}}$$

EXAMPLE 3 Read and write powers

Write the power in words and as a product.

Power	Words	Product
a. 7^1	seven to the first power	7
b. 5^2	five to the second power, or five *squared*	$5 \cdot 5$
c. $\left(\frac{1}{2}\right)^3$	one half to the third power, or one half *cubed*	$\frac{1}{2} \cdot \frac{1}{2} \cdot \frac{1}{2}$
d. z^5	*z* to the fifth power	$z \cdot z \cdot z \cdot z \cdot z$

WRITE EXPONENTS
For a number raised to the first power, you usually do not write the exponent 1. For instance, you write 7^1 simply as 7.

GUIDED PRACTICE for Examples 2 and 3

5. **WHAT IF?** In Example 2, suppose you go back to the theater with a friend to see an afternoon movie. You pay for both admissions. Your total cost (in dollars) can be represented by the expression $2a$. If each admission costs $4.75, what is your total cost? **$9.50**

Write the power in words and as a product.

6. 9^5 **nine to the fifth power, $9 \cdot 9 \cdot 9 \cdot 9 \cdot 9$**
7. 2^8 **two to the eighth power, $2 \cdot 2 \cdot 2 \cdot 2 \cdot 2 \cdot 2 \cdot 2 \cdot 2$**
8. n^4 ***n* to the fourth power, $n \cdot n \cdot n \cdot n$**

Differentiated Instruction

English Learners Some mathematical terms can be associated with more common English definitions. For example, the *base* is the lower part or bottom of something. Therefore, in any power expression, the base is the number at the bottom (and the exponent is the number at the top).

See also the *Algebra 1 Toolkit* for more strategies.

Motivating the Lesson

You want to save money to buy a digital music player. If you know how much it costs, you can determine how much you need to save each week depending on whether you want to purchase it in 2, 3, 4, or more weeks. You can do this by evaluating an expression that involves a variable.

3 TEACH

Extra Example 1

Evaluate the expression when $c = 4$.

a. $4c$ **16**

b. $\frac{8}{c}$ **2**

c. $15 + c$ **19**

Extra Example 2

You are ordering a skateboard and a helmet from an on-line store. The total weight of the two items can be represented by $s + h$, where s is the weight of the skateboard and h is the weight of the helmet. Find the total weight if the helmet weighs 1.3 kilograms and the skateboard weighs 5.4 kilograms. **6.7 kg**

Key Question to Ask for Example 2

- How are the letters used as variables appropriate for this situation? **The first letter in the word *admission* is *a* and the first letter in the word *refreshments* is *r*.**

Extra Example 3

Write the power in words and as a product.

a. $\left(\frac{1}{5}\right)^1$ **one fifth to the first power; $\frac{1}{5}$**

b. 6^2 **six squared; $6 \cdot 6$**

c. 3^4 **three to the fourth power; $3 \cdot 3 \cdot 3 \cdot 3$**

d. p^3 ***p* to the third power or *p* cubed; $p \cdot p \cdot p$**

Extra Example 4

Evaluate the expression.

a. n^5 when $n = 3$ 243

b. d^2 when $d = \frac{9}{5}$ $\frac{81}{25}$

Extra Example 5

Each side of a square garden measures 22 feet. You are going to buy fertilizer for the garden before you begin planting and you need to determine its area. Find the area of the garden. 484 ft^2

Key Question to Ask for Example 5

- Why is 14 substituted for *s*? The variable *s* represents the length of an edge of the cube, and this length is given as 14 inches.

Avoiding Common Errors

When evaluating a power, students sometimes make the mistake of multiplying the base of the power by the exponent. For example, they would evaluate 14^3 as $14 \times 3 = 42$. Stress that the exponent in a power indicates how many times to multiply the base by itself.

Closing the Lesson

Have students summarize the major points of the lesson and answer the Essential Question: How do you evaluate algebraic expressions and powers?

- Algebraic expressions can be used to represent a situation in which the actual numerical value used may change.
- A power is written using a base and an exponent. The exponent is the number of times you multiply the base by itself.

To evaluate an algebraic expression, substitute the given value for the variable and then perform the operation. To evaluate a power, multiply the base by itself the number of times indicated by exponent.

EXAMPLE 4 Evaluate powers

Evaluate the expression.

a. x^4 when $x = 2$

b. n^3 when $n = 1.5$

Solution

a. $x^4 = 2^4$

$= 2 \cdot 2 \cdot 2 \cdot 2$

$= 16$

b. $n^3 = 1.5^3$

$= (1.5)(1.5)(1.5)$

$= 3.375$

✓ GUIDED PRACTICE for Example 4

Evaluate the expression.

9. x^3 when $x = 8$ 512 **10.** k^2 when $k = 2.5$ 6.25 **11.** d^4 when $d = \frac{1}{3}$ $\frac{1}{81}$

REVIEW AREA AND VOLUME
For help with area and volume, see pp. 924 and 927.

AREA AND VOLUME Exponents are used in the formulas for the area of a square and the volume of a cube. In fact, the words *squared* and *cubed* come from the formula for the area of a square and the formula for the volume of a cube.

$A = s^2$

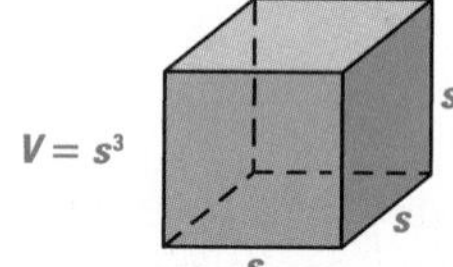

$V = s^3$

EXAMPLE 5 Evaluate a power

STORAGE CUBES Each edge of the medium-sized pop-up storage cube shown is 14 inches long. The storage cube is made so that it can be folded flat when not in use. Find the volume of the storage cube.

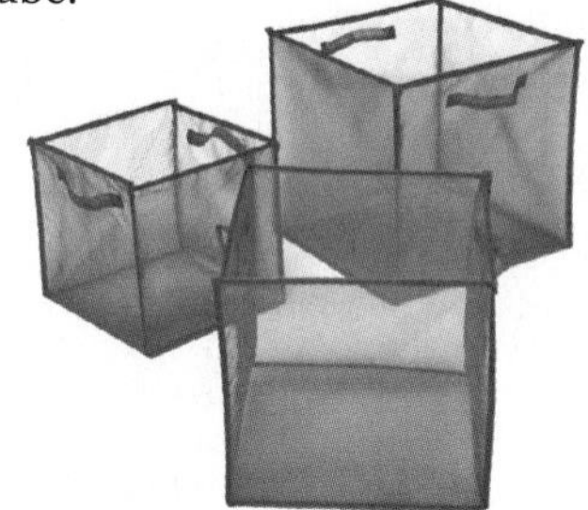

Solution

$V = s^3$ Write formula for volume.

$= 14^3$ Substitute 14 for *s*.

$= 2744$ Evaluate power.

▶ The volume of the storage cube is 2744 cubic inches.

✓ GUIDED PRACTICE for Example 5

12. WHAT IF? In Example 5, suppose the storage cube is folded flat to form a square. Find the area of the square. 196 $in.^2$

1.1 EXERCISES

HOMEWORK KEY
○ = **WORKED-OUT SOLUTIONS** on p. WS1 for Exs. 19, 35, and 51
★ = **STANDARDIZED TEST PRACTICE** Exs. 2, 15, 44, 45, 52, and 54

SKILL PRACTICE

A

1. **VOCABULARY** Identify the exponent and the base in the expression 6^{12}. exponent: 12, base: 6

2. ★ **WRITING** *Describe* the steps you would take to evaluate the expression n^5 when $n = 3$. Then evaluate the expression. Substitute 3 for *n*. Then write 3^5 as the product $3 \cdot 3 \cdot 3 \cdot 3 \cdot 3$ and multiply; 243.

16. twelve to the fifth power, $12 \cdot 12 \cdot 12 \cdot 12 \cdot 12$

EXAMPLE 1 on p. 2 for Exs. 3–15

EVALUATING EXPRESSIONS Evaluate the expression.

3. $15x$ when $x = 4$ 60
4. $0.4r$ when $r = 6$ 2.4
5. $w - 8$ when $w = 20$ 12
6. $1.6 - g$ when $g = 1.2$ 0.4
7. $5 + m$ when $m = 7$ 12
8. $0.8 + h$ when $h = 3.7$ 4.5
9. $\frac{24}{f}$ when $f = 8$ 3
10. $\frac{t}{5}$ when $t = 4.5$ 0.9
11. $2.5m$ when $m = 4$ 10
12. $\frac{1}{2}k$ when $k = \frac{2}{3}$ $\frac{1}{3}$
13. $y - \frac{1}{2}$ when $y = \frac{5}{6}$ $\frac{1}{3}$
14. $h + \frac{1}{3}$ when $h = 1\frac{1}{3}$ $1\frac{2}{3}$

18. three and two tenths squared, $3.2 \cdot 3.2$

19. three tenths to the fourth power, $0.3 \cdot 0.3 \cdot 0.3 \cdot 0.3$

15. ★ **MULTIPLE CHOICE** What is the value of $2.5m$ when $m = 10$? D

Ⓐ 0.25 Ⓑ 2.5 Ⓒ 12.5 Ⓓ 25

EXAMPLE 3 on p. 3 for Exs. 16–25

WRITING POWERS Write the power in words and as a product. 16, 18–20. See margin.

16. 12^5
17. 7^3 seven to the third power, $7 \cdot 7 \cdot 7$
18. $(3.2)^2$
19. $(0.3)^4$
20. $\left(\frac{1}{2}\right)^8$
21. n^7 *n* to the seventh power, $n \cdot n \cdot n \cdot n \cdot n \cdot n \cdot n$
22. y^6 *y* to the sixth power, $y \cdot y \cdot y \cdot y \cdot y \cdot y$
23. t^4 *t* to the fourth power, $t \cdot t \cdot t \cdot t$

20. one half to the eighth power, $\frac{1}{2} \cdot \frac{1}{2} \cdot \frac{1}{2} \cdot \frac{1}{2} \cdot \frac{1}{2} \cdot \frac{1}{2} \cdot \frac{1}{2} \cdot \frac{1}{2}$

ERROR ANALYSIS *Describe* and correct the error in evaluating the power. 24, 25. See margin.

24. $(0.4)^2 = 2(0.4) = 0.8$ 

25. $5^4 = 4 \cdot 4 \cdot 4 \cdot 4 \cdot 4 = 1024$ 

EXAMPLE 4 on p. 4 for Exs. 26–37

EVALUATING POWERS Evaluate the power.

26. 3^2 9
27. 10^2 100
28. 1^5 1
29. 11^3 1331
30. 5^3 125
31. 3^5 243
32. 2^6 64
33. 6^4 1296
34. $\left(\frac{1}{4}\right)^2$ $\frac{1}{16}$
35. $\left(\frac{3}{5}\right)^3$ $\frac{27}{125}$
36. $\left(\frac{2}{3}\right)^4$ $\frac{16}{81}$
37. $\left(\frac{1}{6}\right)^3$ $\frac{1}{216}$

B

EVALUATING EXPRESSIONS Evaluate the expression.

38. x^2 when $x = \frac{3}{4}$ $\frac{9}{16}$
39. p^2 when $p = 1.1$ 1.21
40. $x + y$ when $x = 11$ and $y = 6.4$ 17.4
41. kn when $k = 9$ and $n = 4.5$ 40.5
42. $w - z$ when $w = 9.5$ and $z = 2.8$ 6.7
43. $\frac{b}{c}$ when $b = 24$ and $c = 2.5$ 9.6

24. 0.4 was multiplied by 2 instead of squared; $(0.4)^2 = (0.4)(0.4) = 0.16$.

25. The base was used as the exponent and the exponent was used as the base; $5^4 = 5 \cdot 5 \cdot 5 \cdot 5 = 625$.

44. ★ **MULTIPLE CHOICE** Which expression has the greatest value when $x = 10$ and $y = 0.5$? C

Ⓐ xy Ⓑ $x - y$ Ⓒ $\frac{x}{y}$ Ⓓ $\frac{y}{x}$

4 PRACTICE AND APPLY

Assignment Guide

Answer Transparencies available for all exercises

Basic:
Day 1: SRH p. 914 Exs. 11–15
pp. 5–7
Exs. 1, 2, 3–13 odd, 15–25, 27–41 odd, 48–52, 56–65

Average:
Day 1: pp. 5–7
Exs. 1, 2, 4–14 even, 15, 16–22 even, 24, 25, 26–44 even, 45, 46, 49–54, 57–65

Advanced:
Day 1: pp. 5–7
Exs. 1, 2, 10–14, 15–23 odd, 32–44 even*, 45–47, 50–63*

Block:
pp. 5–7
Exs. 1, 2, 4–14 even, 15, 16–22 even, 24, 25, 26–44 even, 45, 46, 49–54, 57–65 (with 1.2)

Differentiated Instruction

See *Algebra 1 Best Practices Toolkit* for suggestions on addressing the needs of a diverse classroom.

Homework Check

For a quick check of student understanding of key concepts, go over the following exercises:

Basic: 5, 18, 31, 48, 51
Average: 10, 20, 32, 49, 51
Advanced: 12, 21, 34, 50, 52

Extra Practice

- Student Edition, p. 938
- Chapter 1 Resource Book: Practice levels A, B, C, pp. 7–9

Practice Worksheet

An easily-readable reduced practice page (with answers) for this lesson can be found on p. 1C.

Differentiated Instruction

Auditory Learners For students who begin learning algebra, the concept of a variable is a new idea. When saying the word *variable* out loud to students, stress the sounds "vary" and "able" as in "able to vary." Explain that letters such as *x* are called variables because they represent a number that varies, or changes. For example, in **Exercise 3**, $x = 4$; but in **Exercise 38**, $x = \frac{3}{4}$.

See also the *Algebra 1 Toolkit* for more strategies.

Study Strategy

Exercise 45 For students who have difficulty with this problem, suggest that they replace the variables with numbers in order to determine the mathematical operation to be used. For example, *I bought 12 tokens and used 2 of them. What operation should I use to determine how many tokens I have left?*

Reading Strategy

Exercise 47 Suggest that the following might be an alternative reading of the problem. *When is the value of the square of a whole number greater than the value of 2 raised to that whole number power?*

Teaching Strategy

Exercise 53 You may wish to step out this exercise into parts as was done in Exercises 50 and 51. For example, part a might be finding the Patriots' net score, part b would be finding the Panthers' net score, and part c would be the comparison of the net scores. Point out that breaking problems into parts helps to clarify the solution process and can help students avoid incomplete solutions.

An **Animated Algebra** activity is available on-line for **Exercise 54**. This activity is also available on the **Power Presentations CD-ROM**.

Exercise 50 For more information about women's soccer, go to www.wusa.com.

Exercise 53 Additional statistical information about teams in the National Football League can be found at www.nfl.com/stats.

45. ★ **MULTIPLE CHOICE** Let b be the number of tokens you bought at an arcade, and let u be the number you have used. Which expression represents the number of tokens remaining? B

 (A) $b + u$ (B) $b - u$ (C) bu (D) $\frac{b}{u}$

C

46. **COMPARING POWERS** Let x and y be whole numbers greater than 0 with $y > x$. Which has the greater value, 3^x or 3^y? *Explain.* 3^y; if $y > x$, then 3^y is raised to a higher power than 3^x.

47. **CHALLENGE** For which whole number value(s) of x greater than 0 is the value of x^2 greater than the value of 2^x? *Explain.* 3; $3^2 = 9$ and $2^3 = 8$. For $x = 1$ and $x > 4$, $x^2 < 2^x$. For $x = 2$ and $x = 4$, $x^2 = 2^x$.

Problem Solving

EXAMPLE 2 on p. 3 for Exs. 48–50

A

48. **GEOMETRY** The perimeter of a square with a side length of s is given by the expression $4s$. What is the perimeter of the square shown? 30 m

7.5 m

@HomeTutor for problem solving help at classzone.com

49. **LEOPARD FROG** You can estimate the distance (in centimeters) that a leopard frog can jump using the expression 13ℓ where ℓ is the frog's length (in centimeters). What distance can a leopard frog that is 12.5 centimeters long jump? 162.5 cm

@HomeTutor for problem solving help at classzone.com

50. **MULTI-STEP PROBLEM** Jen was the leading scorer on her soccer team. She scored 120 goals and had 20 assists in her high school career.

 a. The number n of points awarded for goals is given by $2g$ where g is the number of goals scored. How many points did Jen earn for goals? 240 points

 b. The point total is given by $n + a$ where a is the number of assists. Use your answer from part (a) to find Jen's point total. 260 points

EXAMPLE 5 on p. 4 for Exs. 51–52

51. **MULTI-STEP PROBLEM** You are buying a tank for three fish. You have a flame angel that is 3.5 inches long, a yellow sailfin tang that is 5.5 inches long, and a coral beauty that is 3 inches long. The area (in square inches) of water surface the fish need is given by the expression $12f$ where f is the sum of the lengths (in inches) of all the fish in the tank.

 a. What is the total length of the three fish? 12 in.

 b. How many square inches of water surface do the fish need? 144 in.^{2}

B

52. ★ **MULTIPLE CHOICE** For a snow sculpture contest, snow is packed into a cube-shaped box with an edge length of 8 feet. The box is frozen and removed, leaving a cube of snow. One cubic foot of the snow weighs about 30 pounds. You can estimate the weight (in pounds) of the cube using the expression $30V$ where V is the volume (in cubic feet) of the snow. About how much does the uncarved cube weigh? C

 (A) 240 pounds (B) 1920 pounds

 (C) 15,360 pounds (D) 216,000 pounds

○ = WORKED-OUT SOLUTIONS on p. WS1 ★ = STANDARDIZED TEST PRACTICE

54d. *Sample answer:* The volume of the cube is multiplied by n^3. The edge length of Bin B is 2 times the edge length of Bin A, so the volume of Bin B is 2^3 or 8 times the volume of Bin A. The edge length of Bin C is 3 times the edge length of Bin A, so the volume of Bin C is 3^3 or 27 times the volume of Bin A.

53. **FOOTBALL** A football team's net score for the regular season is given by the expression $a - b$ where a is the total number of points the team scored and b is the total number of points scored against the team. The table shows the point totals for the 2003 National Football League Conference Champions. Which team's net score was greater? New England Patriots

Team	Points scored, a	Points scored against, b
New England Patriots	336	238
Carolina Panthers	325	304

C 54. ★ **EXTENDED RESPONSE** A manufacturer produces three different sizes of cube-shaped stacking bins with edge lengths as shown.

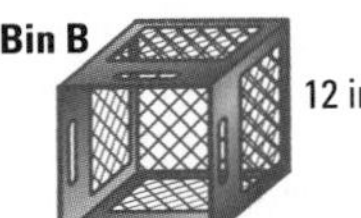

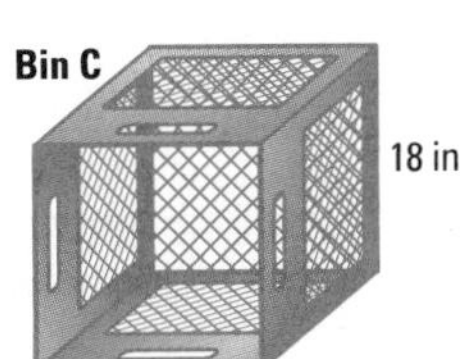

a. **Evaluate** Find the volume of each bin. 216 in.^{3}; 1728 in.^{3}; 5832 in.^{3}

b. **Compare** How many times greater is the edge length of bin B than the edge length of bin A? How many times greater is the volume of bin B than the volume of bin A? 2; 8

c. **Compare** Answer the questions in part (b) for bin A and bin C. 3; 27

d. **CHALLENGE** *Explain* how multiplying the edge length of a cube by a number n affects the volume of the cube. *Justify* your explanation.

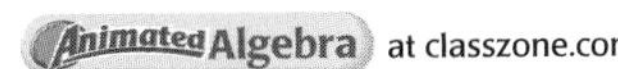

55. **CHALLENGE** You purchase a set of 100 cube-shaped miniature magnets, each with an edge length of $\frac{1}{8}$ inch. You arrange the cubes to form larger cubes, each one with a different edge length. How many cubes can you form? What is their total volume? 3 cubes; about 0.1934 in.^{3}

ILLINOIS MIXED REVIEW

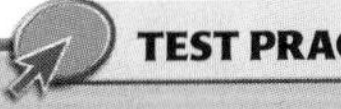

TEST PRACTICE at classzone.com

56. A fence that surrounds a rectangular portion of a field is 32 feet long. If one side of the fence is 10 feet long, which of the following is the length of another side? A

Ⓐ 6 ft Ⓑ 8 ft Ⓒ 11 ft Ⓓ 22 ft

57. Half of the money a company earns is used to pay for workers' wages, and $\frac{1}{4}$ of the earnings is used to pay for supplies. An additional 10% of the **earnings** is used to pay for advertising, and the rest is profit. What percent of the company's earnings is profit? B

Ⓐ 10% Ⓑ 15% Ⓒ 25% Ⓓ 35%

5 ASSESS AND RETEACH

Daily Homework Quiz

Transparency Available

Evaluate the expression or power.

1. $13g$ when $g = 7$ 91
2. $1.65 - a$ when $a = 0.75$ 0.9
3. 5^4 625
4. $\left(\frac{1}{3}\right)^3$ $\frac{1}{27}$
5. Emily is saving for a $300 bicycle. She has saved $128.25. The amount she still needs to save is given by the expression $c - s$, where c is the cost of the bicycle and s is the amount she has saved. How much does she have left to save? $171.75

Available at **classzone.com**

Diagnosis/Remediation

- Practice A, B, C in Chapter 1 Resource Book, pp. 7–9
- Study Guide in Chapter 1 Resource Book, pp. 10–11
- Practice Workbook, pp. 1–2
- @HomeTutor

Challenge

Additional challenge is available in the Chapter 1 Resource Book, p. 14.

1 PLAN AND PREPARE

Warm-Up Exercises

Transparency Available

Evaluate the expression.

1. $a + 5.7$ when $a = 1.3$ 7
2. b^3 when $b = 4$ 64
3. The number of weeks it takes you to read a novel is given by $\frac{n}{p}$, where n is total pages in the novel and p is pages read per week. How long will it take you to read a 340-page novel if you read 85 pages per week? 4 weeks

Notetaking Guide

Transparency Available

Promotes interactive learning and notetaking skills, pp. 4–6.

Pacing

Basic: 1 day
Average: 1 day
Advanced: 1 day
Block: 0.5 block with 1.1

- See *Teaching Guide/Lesson Plan.*

2 FOCUS AND MOTIVATE

Essential Question

Big Idea 1, p. 1

How do you use the order of operations to evaluate an expression? Tell students they will learn how to answer this question by using an algorithm (an ordered series of steps).

1.2 Apply Order of Operations

6.11.04 Apply the rules of order of operations to real-number expressions.

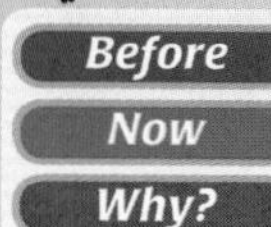

Before You evaluated algebraic expressions and used exponents.
Now You will use the order of operations to evaluate expressions.
Why? So you can determine online music costs, as in Ex. 35.

Key Vocabulary
- order of operations

Mathematicians have established an **order of operations** to evaluate an expression involving more than one operation.

KEY CONCEPT *For Your Notebook*

Order of Operations

STEP 1 **Evaluate** expressions inside grouping symbols.

STEP 2 **Evaluate** powers.

STEP 3 **Multiply** and **divide** from left to right.

STEP 4 **Add** and **subtract** from left to right.

EXAMPLE 1 Evaluate expressions

Evaluate the expression $27 \div 3^2 \times 2 - 3$.

STEP 1 There are no grouping symbols, so go to Step 2.

STEP 2 **Evaluate** powers.

$27 \div 3^2 \times 2 - 3 = 27 \div 9 \times 2 - 3$ **Evaluate power.**

STEP 3 **Multiply** and **divide** from left to right.

$27 \div 9 \times 2 - 3 = 3 \times 2 - 3$ **Divide.**

$3 \times 2 - 3 = 6 - 3$ **Multiply.**

STEP 4 **Add** and **subtract** from left to right.

$6 - 3 = 3$ **Subtract.**

▶ The value of the expression $27 \div 3^2 \times 2 - 3$ is 3.

GUIDED PRACTICE for Example 1

Evaluate the expression.

1. $20 - 4^2$ 4
2. $2 \cdot 3^2 + 4$ 22
3. $32 \div 2^3 + 6$ 10
4. $15 + 6^2 - 4$ 47

Resource Planning Guide

Chapter Resource Book
- Teaching Guide/Lesson Plan (pp. 15–16)
- Activity Master (p. 17)
- Practice levels A, B, C (pp. 19–21)
- Study Guide (pp. 22–23)
- Catch-up for Absent Students (p. 24)
- Application (p. 25)
- Challenge (p. 26)

Workbooks
- Notetaking Guide (pp. 4–6)
- Practice Workbook (pp. 3–4)

Teaching Options
- **Power Presentations CD-ROM** provides dynamic electronic teaching resources for the classroom.
- **Activity Generator CD-ROM** provides editable activities for all ability levels.

Interactive Technology
- Easy Planner
- Power Presentations CD-ROM
- Activity Generator CD-ROM
- Animated Algebra
- Test Generator CD-ROM
- Online Quiz
- eWorkbook
- eEdition
- @HomeTutor

Resources for English Learners
- Quick Reference for English Learners
- Spanish Study Guide
- Multi-Language Visual Glossary
- Student Resources in Spanish

See also the *Algebra 1 Toolkit* for more strategies for meeting individual needs.

GROUPING SYMBOLS Grouping symbols such as parentheses ( ) and brackets [ ] indicate that operations inside the grouping symbols should be performed first. For example, to evaluate $2 \cdot 4 + 6$, you multiply first, then add. To evaluate $2(4 + 6)$, you add first, then multiply.

EXAMPLE 2 Evaluate expressions with grouping symbols

Evaluate the expression.

a. $7(13 - 8) = 7(5)$ — Subtract within parentheses.

$= 35$ — Multiply.

b. $24 - (3^2 + 1) = 24 - (9 + 1)$ — Evaluate power.

$= 24 - 10$ — Add within parentheses.

$= 14$ — Subtract.

c. $2[30 - (8 + 13)] = 2[30 - 21]$ — Add within parentheses.

$= 2[9]$ — Subtract within brackets.

$= 18$ — Multiply.

AVOID ERRORS When grouping symbols appear inside other grouping symbols, work from the innermost grouping symbols outward.

FRACTION BARS A fraction bar can act as a grouping symbol. Evaluate the numerator and denominator before you divide:

$$\frac{8 + 4}{5 - 2} = (8 + 4) \div (5 - 2) = 12 \div 3 = 4$$

EXAMPLE 3 Evaluate an algebraic expression

Evaluate the expression when $x = 4$.

$\frac{9x}{3(x + 2)} = \frac{9 \cdot 4}{3(4 + 2)}$ — Substitute 4 for x.

$= \frac{9 \cdot 4}{3 \cdot 6}$ — Add within parentheses.

$= \frac{36}{18}$ — Multiply.

$= 2$ — Divide.

at classzone.com

✓ GUIDED PRACTICE for Examples 2 and 3

Evaluate the expression.

5. $4(3 + 9)$ 48 **6.** $3(8 - 2^2)$ 12 **7.** $2[(9 + 3) \div 4]$ 6

Evaluate the expression when $y = 8$.

8. $y^2 - 3$ 61 **9.** $12 - y - 1$ 3 **10.** $\frac{10y + 1}{y + 1}$ 9

Motivating the Lesson

On a 3-day trip, the Browns drove 186 miles the first day, 168 miles the second day, and 255 miles the third day. Ask students what series of calculations they would use to find the average number of miles driven each day. Then ask them how they would write a single numerical expression to calculate this average.

3 TEACH

Extra Example 1

Evaluate the expression $6 + 12 \div 3 \times 4^2$. 70

Extra Example 2

Evaluate the expression.

a. $24 \div (4 - 1)$ 8

b. $48 - (6 + 5^2)$ 17

c. $3[32 \div (2 + 6)]$ 12

Key Questions to Ask for Example 2

- How are the expressions in Example 2 different from those in Example 1? The expressions in Example 2 involve grouping symbols.
- In part c, why is the addition done first? You evaluate the expression in the innermost grouping symbols first.

Extra Example 3

Evaluate the expression $\frac{10x}{2(x + 2)}$ when $x = 3$. 3

An **Animated Algebra** activity is available on-line for **Example 3**. This activity is also available on the **Power Presentations CD-ROM**.

Differentiated Instruction

Inclusion Students having difficulty using basic arithmetic operations may be allowed to rely on calculators. Have students work in groups with a variety of calculators. Include a calculator that does *not* follow the order of operations. Present each group with a simple expression to evaluate on the calculator, such as $2 + 3 \cdot 4$. For different calculators, the answer will be 14 or 20. Help students understand how to use their own calculator to evaluate numerical expressions.

See also the *Algebra 1 Toolkit* for more strategies.

Extra Example 4

John had 4 copies of a science report made to give to his lab partners. In each copied report there were 20 black-and-white pages and 5 color pages. He paid a copy center to make and bind the copies. His cost in dollars is given by the expression $4(5c + 20b)$, where c is the cost of a color page and b is the cost of a black-and-white page. What is the total cost if a color page costs \$2 and a black-and-white page costs \$.05? D

 \$23 (B) \$26
(C) \$41 (D) \$44

Key Questions to Ask for Example 4

- Why must the value of the expression inside the parentheses be found first? Parentheses are one type of grouping symbol and evaluating expressions inside grouping symbols is the first step of the order of operations.
- What is the order of operations within the parentheses? Multiply from left to right and then add the products.

Closing the Lesson

Have students summarize the major points of the lesson and answer the Essential Question: How do you use the order of operations to evaluate an expression?

- The order of operations is a series of steps to use when evaluating expressions.
- Parentheses, brackets, and fraction bars act as grouping symbols.

Always evaluate expressions using the following order: evaluate expressions inside grouping symbols, evaluate powers, multiply and divide from left to right, and then add and subtract from left to right.

★  **Standardized Test Practice**

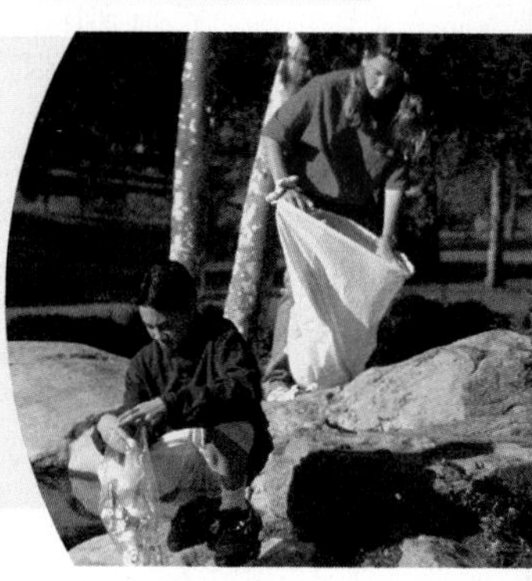

A group of 12 students volunteers to collect litter for one day. A sponsor provides 3 juice drinks and 2 sandwiches for each student and pays \$30 for trash bags. The sponsor's cost (in dollars) is given by the expression $12(3j + 2s) + 30$ where j is the cost of a juice drink and s is the cost of a sandwich. A juice drink costs \$1.25. A sandwich costs \$2. What is the sponsor's cost?

(A) \$79 (B) \$123 (C) \$129 (D) \$210

ELIMINATE CHOICES
You can eliminate choices A and D by estimating. When j is about 1 and s is 2, the value of the expression is about $12(3 + 4) + 30$, or \$114.

Solution

$12(3j + 2s) + 30 = 12(3 \cdot 1.25 + 2 \cdot 2) + 30$	**Substitute 1.25 for j and 2 for s.**
$= 12(3.75 + 4) + 30$	**Multiply within parentheses.**
$= 12(7.75) + 30$	**Add within parentheses.**
$= 93 + 30$	**Multiply.**
$= 123$	**Add.**

▶ The sponsor's cost is \$123. The correct answer is B. (A) (B) (C) (D).

 **GUIDED PRACTICE** for Example 4

11. **WHAT IF?** In Example 4, suppose the number of volunteers doubles. Does the sponsor's cost double as well? *Explain.* No; the total cost of the juice drinks and sandwiches will double, but the cost of the trash bags will not.

1.2 EXERCISES

HOMEWORK KEY
○ = **WORKED-OUT SOLUTIONS** on p. WS1 for Exs. 16 and 35
★ = **STANDARDIZED TEST PRACTICE** Exs. 2, 19, 31, 37, 39, and 40

SKILL PRACTICE

1. **VOCABULARY** According to the order of operations, which operation would you perform first in simplifying $50 - 5 \times 4^2 \div 2$? Square 4.

2. ★ **WRITING** *Describe* the steps you would use to evaluate the expression $2(3x + 1)^2$ when $x = 3$. Substitute 3 for x; multiply $3 \cdot 3$; add $9 + 1$; square 10; multiply $2 \cdot 100$. The result is 200.

EXAMPLES 1 and 2 on pp. 8–9 for Exs. 3–21

EVALUATING EXPRESSIONS **Evaluate the expression.**

3. $13 - 8 + 3$ 8
4. $8 - 2^2$ 4
5. $3 \cdot 6 - 4$ 14
6. $5 \cdot 2^3 + 7$ 47
7. $48 \div 4^2 + \frac{3}{5}$ $3\frac{3}{5}$
8. $1 + 5^2 \div 50$ $1\frac{1}{2}$
9. $2^4 \cdot 4 - 2 \div 8$ $63\frac{3}{4}$
10. $4^3 \div 8 + 8$ 16
11. $(12 + 72) \div 4$ 21
12. $24 + 4(3 + 1)$ 40
13. $12(6 - 3.5)^2 - 1.5$ 73.5
14. $24 \div (8 + 4^2)$ 1
15. $\frac{1}{2}(21 + 2^2)$ $12\frac{1}{2}$
16. $\frac{1}{6}(6 + 18) - 2^2$ 0
17. $\frac{3}{4}[13 - (2 + 3)]^2$ 48
18. $8[20 - (9 - 5)^2]$ 32

19. ★ **MULTIPLE CHOICE** What is the value of $3[20 - (7 - 5)^2]$? A

(A) 48 (B) 56 (C) 192 (D) 972

20.7 + 7 was added before dividing 14 by 7; $(1 + 13) \div 7 + 7 = 14 \div 7 + 7 = 2 + 7 = 9$

ERROR ANALYSIS ***Describe*** **and correct the error in evaluating the expression.** 20, 21. See margin.

20. $(1 + 13) \div 7 + 7 = 14 \div 7 + 7 = 14 \div 14 = 1$ ✗

21. $20 - \frac{1}{2} \cdot 6^2 = 20 - 3^2 = 20 - 9 = 11$ ✗

EXAMPLE 3 B on p. 9 for Exs. 22–31

21. $\frac{1}{2}$ was multiplied by 6 before squaring 6; $20 - \frac{1}{2} \cdot 6^2 = 20 - \frac{1}{2} \cdot 36 = 20 - 18 = 2.$

EVALUATING EXPRESSIONS **Evaluate the expression.**

22. $4n - 12$ when $n = 7$ 16

23. $2 + 3x^2$ when $x = 3$ 29

24. $6t^2 - 13$ when $t = 2$ 11

25. $11 + r^3 - 2r$ when $r = 5$ 126

26. $5(w - 4)$ when $w = 7$ 15

27. $3(m^2 - 2)$ when $m = 1.5$ 0.75

28. $\frac{9x + 4}{3x + 1}$ when $x = 7$ $3\frac{1}{22}$

29. $\frac{k^2 - 1}{k + 3}$ when $k = 5$ 3

30. $\frac{b^3 - 21}{5b + 9}$ when $b = 3$ $\frac{1}{4}$

31. ★ **MULTIPLE CHOICE** What is the value of $\frac{x^2}{25} + 3x$ when $x = 10$? B

(A) 26 (B) 34 (C) 43 (D) 105

C **CHALLENGE** **Insert grouping symbols in the expression so that the value of the expression is 14.**

32. $9 + 39 + 22 \div 11 - 9 + 3$
$(9 + 39 + 22) \div (11 - 9 + 3)$

33. $2 \times 2 + 3^2 - 4 + 3 \times 5$
$(2 \times 2 + 3)^2 - (4 + 3) \times 5$

PROBLEM SOLVING

EXAMPLE 4 A on p. 10 for Exs. 34–37

34. **SALES** Your school's booster club sells school T-shirts. Half the T-shirts come from one supplier at a cost of $5.95 each, and half from another supplier at a cost of $6.15 each. The average cost (in dollars) of a T-shirt is given by the expression $\frac{5.95 + 6.15}{2}$. Find the average cost. $6.05

@HomeTutor for problem solving help at classzone.com

35. **MULTI-STEP PROBLEM** You join an online music service. The total cost (in dollars) of downloading 3 singles at $.99 each and 2 albums at $9.95 each is given by the expression $3 \cdot 0.99 + 2 \cdot 9.95$.

a. Find the total cost. $22.87

b. You have $25 to spend. How much will you have left? $2.13

@HomeTutor for problem solving help at classzone.com

36. **PHYSIOLOGY** If you know how tall you were at the age of 2, you can estimate your adult height (in inches). Girls can use the expression $25 + 1.17h$ where h is the height (in inches) at the age of 2. Boys can use the expression $22.7 + 1.37h$. Estimate the adult height of each person to the nearest inch.

a. A girl who was 34 inches tall at age 2 65 in.

b. A boy who was 33 inches tall at age 2 68 in.

4 PRACTICE AND APPLY

Assignment Guide

Answer Transparencies available for all exercises

Basic:
Day 1: SRH p. 915 Exs. 11–15
pp. 10–12
Exs. 1, 2, 3–17 odd, 19–26, 28–30, 34–38, 41–52

Average:
Day 1: pp. 10–12
Exs. 1, 2, 8–18 even, 20–39, 41–52

Advanced:
Day 1: pp. 10–12
Exs. 1, 2, 13–19, 25–33*, 36–40*, 43–52

Block:
pp. 10–12
Exs. 1, 2, 8–18 even, 20–39, 41–52 (with 1.1)

Differentiated Instruction

See *Algebra 1 Best Practices Toolkit* for suggestions on addressing the needs of a diverse classroom.

Homework Check

For a quick check of student understanding of key concepts, go over the following exercises:

Basic: 5, 10, 22, 34, 35

Average: 10, 16, 24, 35, 36

Advanced: 13, 18, 28, 36, 37

Extra Practice

- Student Edition, p. 938
- Chapter 1 Resource Book: Practice levels A, B, C, pp. 19–21

Practice Worksheet

An easily-readable reduced practice page (with answers) for this lesson can be found on p. 1C.

Differentiated Instruction

Below Level Point out that the fraction bars appearing in **Exercises 28–30** are grouping symbols. To help students evaluate the expressions in these exercises, suggest that they use this algorithm: *evaluate the numerator, then evaluate the denominator, and divide the value of the numerator by the value of the denominator.* You might suggest that they remember *numerator/denominator/divide* as a shortened version of the algorithm.

See also the *Algebra 1 Toolkit* for more strategies.

5 ASSESS AND RETEACH

Daily Homework Quiz

Transparency Available

Evaluate the expression.

1. $3^3 \div 9 + 4 \cdot 3$ 15
2. $12 + (5 - 3)^2$ 16
3. $2(c^2 + 4)$ when $c = 4$ 40
4. $\frac{g^2 - 8}{2g - 5}$ when $g = 6$ 4
5. The cost (in dollars) to buy p posters at the Posters Plus online store is given by the expression $3.5p + 6.75$. At the More Posters online store, the cost is given by $4.25p + 2.55$. Which store has the lower cost for 5 posters? More Posters

Online Quiz

Available at **classzone.com**

Diagnosis/Remediation

- Practice A, B, C in Chapter 1 Resource Book, pp. 19–21
- Study Guide in Chapter 1 Resource Book, pp. 22–23
- Practice Workbook, pp. 3–4
- @HomeTutor

Challenge

Additional challenge is available in the Chapter 1 Resource Book, p. 26.

37. ★ **OPEN-ENDED** Write a numerical expression including parentheses that has the same value when you remove the parentheses. *Sample answer:* $(3 \times 4) + 5$

B

38. ONLINE SHOPPING The regular shipping fee (in dollars) for an online computer store is given by the expression $0.5w + 4.49$ where w is the weight (in pounds) of the item. The fee (in dollars) for rush delivery is given by $0.99w + 6.49$. You purchase a 26.5 pound computer. How much do you save using regular shipping instead of rush delivery? $14.99

39. ★ **SHORT RESPONSE** You make and sell flags for $10 each. Each flag requires $4.50 worth of fabric. You pay $12.99 for a kit to punch holes to hang the flags. Your expenses (in dollars) are given by the expression $4.50m + 12.99$ where m is the number of flags you make. Your income is given by the expression $10s$ where s is the number of flags you sell. Your profit is equal to the difference of your income and your expenses.

a. You make 50 flags and sell 38 of them. Find your income and your expenses. Then find your profit. $380, $237.99; $142.01

b. *Explain* how you could use a single expression to determine your profit. *Sample answer:* You could write an expression showing the difference of your income and expenses as $P = 10s - (4.50m + 12.99)$.

C

40. ★ **EXTENDED RESPONSE** Each year Heisman Trophy voters select the outstanding college football player. Each voter selects three players ranked first to third. A first place vote is worth 3 points, a second place vote is worth 2 points, and a third place vote is worth 1 point. Let f, s, and t be, respectively, the number of first place, second place, and third place votes a player gets. The table shows the votes for the winner and the runner-up in 2003.

Player	First place	Second place	Third place
Jason White	319	204	116
Larry Fitzgerald	253	233	128

a. Analyze *Explain* why the expression $3f + 2s + t$ represents a player's point total. See margin.

b. Calculate Use the expression in part (a) to determine how many more points Jason White got than Larry Fitzgerald got. 128 points

c. CHALLENGE Can you rearrange the order of the votes for each player in such a way that Larry Fitzgerald would have won? *Explain.*

40a. *Sample answer:* First place votes are worth 3 points which is $3f$, second place votes are worth 2 points which is $2s$, third place votes are worth 1 point which is $1t$. A player's point total is $3f + 2s + t$.

40c. Yes. *Sample answer*: Change each of the first place votes to third place votes, change each of the second place votes to first place votes, and change each of the third place votes to second place votes.

ILLINOIS MIXED REVIEW

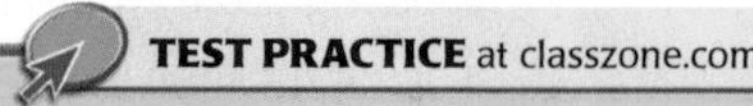

TEST PRACTICE at classzone.com

41. What is the total surface area of a rectangular prism with edge lengths of 3 centimeters, 5 centimeters, and 9 centimeters? D

Ⓐ 17 cm^2 Ⓑ 87 cm^2 Ⓒ 135 cm^2 Ⓓ 174 cm^2

42. A student bikes 1.5 kilometers to school and the same distance home. How many meters does the student bike altogether? D

Ⓐ 3 m Ⓑ 150 m Ⓒ 300 m Ⓓ 3000 m

EXTRA PRACTICE for Lesson 1.2, p. 938

ONLINE QUIZ at classzone.com

@HomeTutor
classzone.com
Keystrokes

1.2 Use Order of Operations

QUESTION How can you use a graphing calculator to evaluate an expression?

You can use a graphing calculator to evaluate an expression. When you enter the expression, it is important to use grouping symbols so that the calculator performs operations in the correct order.

EXAMPLE Evaluate an expression

Use a graphing calculator to evaluate an expression.

Lean body mass is the mass of the skeleton, muscles, and organs. Physicians use lean body mass to determine dosages of medicine.

Scientists have developed separate formulas for the lean body masses of men and women based on their mass m (in kilograms) and height h (in meters). Lean body mass in measured in units called BMI (Body Mass Index) units.

Men: $1.10m - \frac{128m^2}{10,000h^2}$ **Women:** $1.07m - \frac{148m^2}{10,000h^2}$

Find the lean body mass (in BMI units) of a man who is 1.8 meters tall and has a mass of 80 kilograms.

Solution

Enter the expression for men in the calculator. Substitute 80 for m and 1.8 for h. Because the fraction bar is a grouping symbol, enter the denominator using parentheses.

Use the following keystrokes.

1.10 [×] 80 [−] 128 [×] 80 [x^2] [÷] [(] 10000 [×] 1.8 [x^2] [)]

▶ The lean body mass of a man who is 1.8 meters tall and has a mass of 80 kilograms is about 62.7 BMI units.

PRACTICE

Use a calculator to evaluate the expression for $n = 4$. Round to the nearest thousandth.

1. $3 + 5 \cdot n \div 10$ 5

2. $2 + \frac{3n^2}{4}$ 14

3. $\frac{83}{3n^2} - 1.3$ 0.429

4. $\frac{14.2n}{8 + n^3}$ 0.789

5. $\frac{7 - n}{n^2}$ 0.188

6. $5n^2 + \frac{4n^3 + 1}{3}$ 165.667

7. Find the lean body mass (to the nearest tenth of a BMI unit) of a woman who is 1.6 meters tall and has a mass of 54 kilograms. 40.9 BMI units

1 PLAN AND PREPARE

Learn the Method

- Students will learn how to use a graphing calculator to evaluate an algebraic expression.
- After completing the activity, students can use their graphing calculators to check their answers for Exercises 3–19 and 22–31 in Lesson 1.2. They can also use their calculators to test various placements of grouping symbols in the expressions given in Exercises 32 and 33.

Keystroke Help

Keystrokes for several models of calculators are available in blackline format in the *Chapter 1 Resource Book*.

2 TEACH

Tips for Success

In the keystroking shown, point out the use of parentheses around the denominator since the expression involves a fraction bar. Stress that the right parenthesis comes after the second x^2 key.

Extra Example

A person's body mass index (BMI) indicates if they are overweight and at risk for health problems. BMI is calculated using the formula $\frac{w}{h^2} \cdot 703$, where w is the person's weight in pounds and h is their height in inches. Calculate the BMI for a person who weighs 120 pounds and is 64.5 inches tall. about 20.3

3 ASSESS AND RETEACH

Use a calculator to evaluate the expression for $b = 2$. Round to the nearest thousandth.

1. $7 + \frac{9b^2}{3}$ 19

2. $\frac{83}{4b^3 - 7.4}$ 3.374

Investigating Algebra ACTIVITY Use before Lesson 1.3

Animated Algebra classzone.com

1.3 Patterns and Expressions

MATERIALS • graph paper

QUESTION **How can you use an algebraic expression to describe a pattern?**

EXPLORE **Create and describe a pattern**

STEP 1

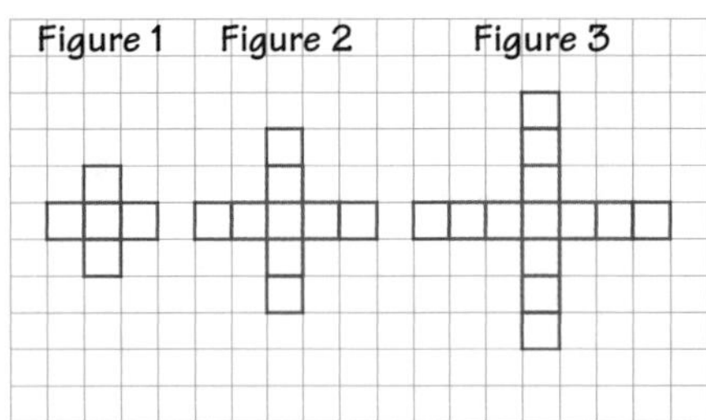

Draw a figure Draw a unit square on graph paper. Then draw a unit square against each side of the first square to form figure 1.

Copy figure 1 and draw a square on each "arm" to form figure 2. Use the same method to form figure 3.

STEP 2

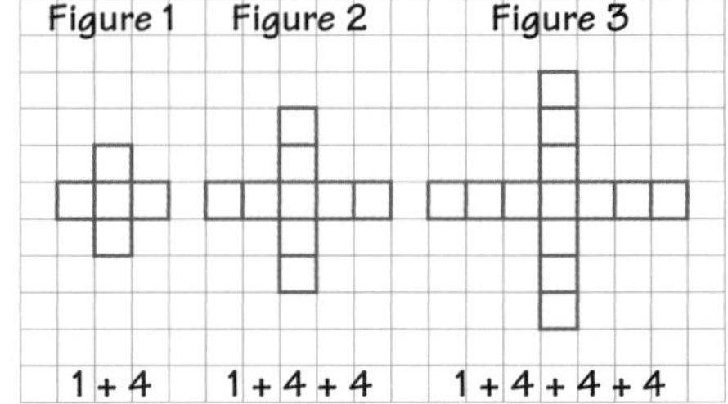

Write expressions For each figure, write a numerical expression that describes the number of squares in the figure.

DRAW CONCLUSIONS **Use your observations to complete these exercises**

In Exercises 1–3, use the pattern in Steps 1 and 2 above.

1. How is the figure number related to the number of times 4 is added in the numerical expression? Predict the number of squares in the fourth figure. Create figure 4 and check your prediction. **The figure number is equal to the number of times 4 is added in the numerical expression; 17 squares; see margin.**
2. *Describe* how to calculate the number of squares in the nth figure. **Find the sum of 1 and the quantity 4 times n.**
3. Write an algebraic expression for the number of squares in the nth figure. (*Hint:* Remember that repeated addition can be written as multiplication.) $1 + 4n$
4. Write an algebraic expression for the number of squares in the nth figure of the pattern shown. $2n$

Figure 1 **Figure 2** **Figure 3** **Figure 4**

1 PLAN AND PREPARE

Explore the Concept

- Students will describe a pattern.
- This activity leads into the study of writing an algebraic expression in Example 2 in Lesson 1.3.

Materials

Each student or pair of students will need graph paper.

Recommended Time

Work activity: 10 min

Discuss results: 5 min

Grouping

Students can work individually or in pairs. If students work in pairs, one student can draw and label the figures and the other can write the numerical expression.

2 TEACH

Tips for Success

To visually reinforce the pattern, in Figures 2 and 3 have students shade those squares that appeared in the previous figure. Students should readily see that four new squares are added at each stage.

An **Animated Algebra** activity is available on-line. This activity is also available on the **Power Presentations CD-ROM**.

Key Discovery

Algebraic expressions can be used to determine the nth number in a pattern.

3 ASSESS AND RETEACH

Without drawing it, how can you find the number of squares in the 15th figure of the pattern? **Multiply 4 × 15 and add 1.**

1.

1.3 Write Expressions

6.11.13 Set up, evaluate, or solve single- and multi-step number sentences and word problems with rational numbers using the four basic operations.

Before You evaluated expressions.

Now You will translate verbal phrases into expressions.

Why? So you can find the time needed to do a job, as in Ex. 36.

Key Vocabulary
- **verbal model**
- **rate**
- **unit rate**

To translate verbal phrases into expressions, look for words that indicate mathematical operations.

KEY CONCEPT *For Your Notebook*

Translating Verbal Phrases

Operation	Verbal Phrase	Expression
Addition: sum, plus, total, more than, increased by	The sum of 2 and a number x	$2 + x$
	A number n plus 7	$n + 7$
Subtraction: difference, less than, minus, decreased by	The difference of a number n and 6	$n - 6$
	A number y minus 5	$y - 5$
Multiplication: times, product, multiplied by, of	12 times a number y	$12y$
	$\frac{1}{3}$ of a number x	$\frac{1}{3}x$
Division: quotient, divided by, divided into	The quotient of a number k and 2	$\frac{k}{2}$

Order is important when writing subtraction and division expressions. For instance, "the difference of a number n and 6" is written $n - 6$, *not* $6 - n$, and "the quotient of a number k and 2" is written $\frac{k}{2}$, *not* $\frac{2}{k}$.

EXAMPLE 1 **Translate verbal phrases into expressions**

AVOID ERRORS
When you translate verbal phrases, the words "the quantity" tell you what to group. In part (a), you write $6n - 4$, *not* $(6 - 4)n$.

	Verbal Phrase	Expression
a.	4 less than the quantity 6 times a number n	$6n - 4$
b.	3 times the sum of 7 and a number y	$3(7 + y)$
c.	The difference of 22 and the square of a number m	$22 - m^2$

GUIDED PRACTICE for Example 1

1. Translate the phrase "the quotient when the quantity 10 plus a number x is divided by 2" into an expression. $\frac{10 + x}{2}$

1 PLAN AND PREPARE

Warm-Up Exercises

Transparency Available

1. Evaluate $2[54 \div (4^2 + 2)]$. 6
2. Evaluate $\frac{5x}{x + 2}$ when $x = 3$. 3
3. Eight students each ordered 2 drawing kits and 4 drawing pencils. The expression $8(2k + 4p)$ gives the total cost, where k is the cost of a kit and p is the cost of a pencil. Find the total cost if a kit costs \$25 and a pencil costs \$1.25. \$440

Notetaking Guide

Transparency Available

Promotes interactive learning and notetaking skills, pp. 7–9.

Pacing

Basic: 1 day
Average: 1 day
Advanced: 1 day
Block: 0.5 block with 1.4
- See *Teaching Guide/Lesson Plan.*

2 FOCUS AND MOTIVATE

Essential Question

Big Idea 1, p. 1

How do you write an expression to represent a real-world situation?
Tell students they will learn how to answer this question by using variables, symbols, and a verbal model to describe the situation.

Resource Planning Guide

Chapter Resource Book
- Teaching Guide/Lesson Plan (pp. 27–28)
- Practice levels A, B, C (pp. 29–31)
- Study Guide (pp. 32–33)
- Catch-up for Absent Students (p. 34)
- Problem Solving Workshop (p. 35)
- Challenge (p. 36)

Workbooks
- Notetaking Guide (pp. 7–9)
- Practice Workbook (pp. 5–6)

Teaching Options
- **Power Presentations CD-ROM** provides dynamic electronic teaching resources for the classroom.
- **Activity Generator CD-ROM** provides editable activities for all ability levels.

Interactive Technology
- Easy Planner
- Power Presentations CD-ROM
- Activity Generator CD-ROM
- Animated Algebra
- Test Generator CD-ROM
- Online Quiz
- eWorkbook
- eEdition
- @HomeTutor

Resources for English Learners
- Quick Reference for English Learners
- Spanish Study Guide
- Multi-Language Visual Glossary
- Student Resources in Spanish

See also the *Algebra 1 Toolkit* for more strategies for meeting individual needs.

Motivating the Lesson

You want to invite some friends to a football game. You know tickets cost $4 each. If you translate the situation into an expression, you can use it to find the cost of inviting different numbers of friends to the game.

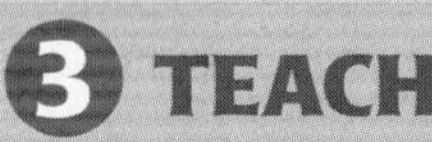

3 TEACH

Extra Example 1

Translate the verbal phrase into an expression.

a. 8 times the quantity 4 plus a number n $8(4 + n)$

b. 12 decreased by a number x $12 - x$

c. The quotient of the square of a number w and 5 $\frac{w^2}{5}$

Extra Example 2

The length of a building is 20 feet more than its width w. Write an expression for the length of the building. $w + 20$

Extra Example 3

You and 4 friends meet to have dinner at a restaurant. Everyone decides to order the nightly special. Write an expression for the total cost of the meals. $5s$, where s is the cost of the nightly special

Key Questions to Ask for Example 3

- Why is the amount of money in the jar represented by a variable? The amount changes each day.
- What phrase in the problem indicates division? "share the amount in the jar equally"
- Why is the number of people given as 6 and not 5? You need to include yourself in the total.

EXAMPLE 2 Write an expression

CHOOSE A VARIABLE
To write an expression for a real-world problem, choose a letter that reminds you of the quantity represented, such as ℓ for length.

CUTTING A RIBBON A piece of ribbon ℓ feet long is cut from a ribbon 8 feet long. Write an expression for the length (in feet) of the remaining piece.

Solution

Draw a diagram and use a specific case to help you write the expression.

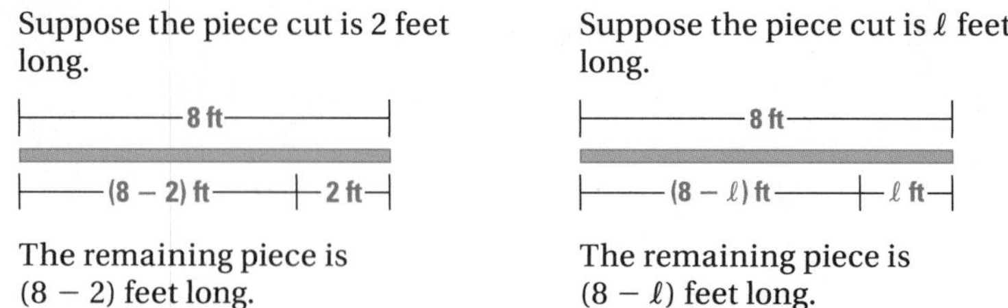

Suppose the piece cut is 2 feet long.
8 ft
(8 – 2) ft
2 ft
The remaining piece is (8 – 2) feet long.
Suppose the piece cut is ℓ feet long.
8 ft
(8 – ℓ) ft
ℓ ft
The remaining piece is (8 – ℓ) feet long.

▶ The expression $8 - \ell$ represents the length (in feet) of the remaining piece.

VERBAL MODEL A **verbal model** describes a real-world situation using words as labels and using math symbols to relate the words. You can replace the words with numbers and variables to create a *mathematical model*, such as an expression, for the real-world situation.

EXAMPLE 3 Use a verbal model to write an expression

TIPS You work with 5 other people at an ice cream stand. All the workers put their tips into a jar and share the amount in the jar equally at the end of the day. Write an expression for each person's share (in dollars) of the tips.

Solution

STEP 1 **Write** a verbal model.

Amount in jar ÷ Number of people

STEP 2 **Translate** the verbal model into an algebraic expression. Let a represent the amount (in dollars) in the jar.

$a \div 6$

AVOID ERRORS
Read the statement of the problem carefully. The number of people sharing tips is 6.

▶ An expression that represents each person's share (in dollars) is $\frac{a}{6}$.

✓ GUIDED PRACTICE for Examples 2 and 3

2. **WHAT IF?** In Example 2, suppose that you cut the original ribbon into p pieces of equal length. Write an expression that represents the length (in feet) of each piece. $\frac{8}{p}$

3. **WHAT IF?** In Example 3, suppose that each of the 6 workers contributes an equal amount for an after-work celebration. Write an expression that represents the total amount (in dollars) contributed. $6d$, where d represents the amount contributed by each worker.

Differentiated Instruction

Inclusion Students with conceptual processing difficulties may have a hard time with the many verbal descriptions and symbolic notations for expressing the same operation. For example, "k divided by 2" or "the quotient of k and 2" can be written as $\frac{k}{2}$, $k/2$, and $k \div 2$. Students with such difficulties should be provided with resource sheets listing as many possible descriptions and notations for each standard operation. See also the *Algebra 1 Toolkit* for more strategies.

RATES A **rate** is a fraction that compares two quantities measured in different units. If the denominator of the fraction is 1 unit, the rate is called a **unit rate**.

EXAMPLE 4 Find a unit rate

READING
Per means "for each" or "for every" and can also be represented using the symbol /, as in mi/h.

A car travels 110 miles in 2 hours. Find the unit rate.

$$\frac{110 \text{ miles}}{2 \text{ hours}} = \frac{110 \text{ miles} \div 2}{2 \text{ hours} \div 2} = \frac{55 \text{ miles}}{1 \text{ hour}}$$

▶ The unit rate is 55 miles per hour, or 55 mi/h.

EXAMPLE 5 Solve a multi-step problem

CELL PHONES Your basic monthly charge for cell phone service is \$30, which includes 300 free minutes. You pay a fee for each extra minute you use. One month you paid \$3.75 for 15 extra minutes. Find your total bill if you use 22 extra minutes.

Solution

STEP 1 **Calculate** the unit rate.

$$\frac{3.75}{15} = \frac{0.25}{1} = \$.25 \text{ per minute}$$

STEP 2 **Write** a verbal model and then an expression. Let m be the number of extra minutes.

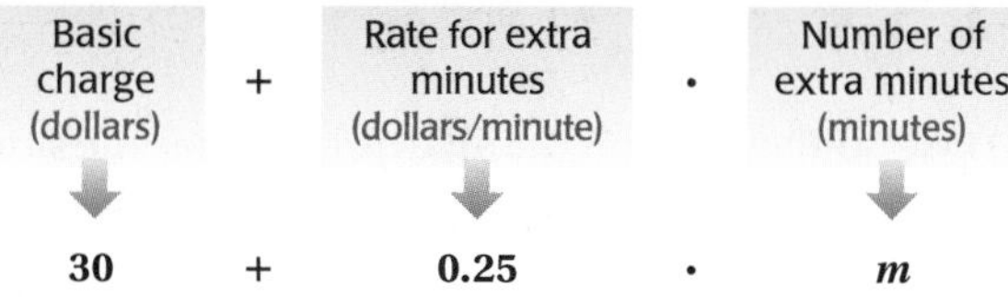

Basic charge (dollars)
+
Rate for extra minutes (dollars/minute)
·
Number of extra minutes (minutes)
30
+
0.25
·
m

USE UNIT ANALYSIS
You expect the answer, which is a cost, to be in dollars. You can use unit analysis to check that the expression produces an answer in dollars.

Use *unit analysis* to check that the expression $30 + 0.25m$ is reasonable.

$$\text{dollars} + \frac{\text{dollars}}{\cancel{\text{minute}}} \cdot \cancel{\text{minutes}} = \text{dollars} + \text{dollars} = \text{dollars}$$

Because the units are dollars, the expression is reasonable.

STEP 3 **Evaluate** the expression when $m = 22$.

$$30 + 0.25(22) = 35.5$$

▶ The total bill is \$35.50.

✓ GUIDED PRACTICE for Examples 4 and 5

4. Suppose your friends share cell phone service. They pay a basic charge of \$35 and \$8.80 for 40 extra minutes. Find their total bill if they use 35 extra minutes. \$42.70

Extra Example 4

A 16-ounce box of cereal costs \$2.99. Find the unit rate to the nearest cent. 19¢/oz

Key Questions to Ask for Example 4

- Why do you divide by 2? So the denominator of the fraction is 1 hour.
- Why do you divide *both* the numerator and the denominator by 2? So the resulting unit rate is equivalent to the original rate.

Extra Example 5

You have a membership in a local ski club. The membership costs you \$40 per month, which includes 10 lift passes. You must pay a fee for each lift pass after the tenth one. Two months ago you paid \$13.50 for 3 extra lift passes. Find your total cost for last month if you bought 7 extra lift passes. \$71.50

Key Question to Ask for Example 5

- Why do you need to know the unit rate? So you can determine the cost to talk for 22 minutes.

Closing the Lesson

Have students summarize the major points of the lesson and answer the Essential Question: How do you write an expression to represent a real-world situation?

- Certain words and phrases indicate the operation(s) to be used in a real-world situation.
- A verbal model can be used to write an expression that models a real-world situation.
- Use division to change a given rate to a unit rate.

Translate the verbal phrases in the problem into operations and variables, create a verbal model, and then translate the verbal model into an expression.

4 PRACTICE AND APPLY

Assignment Guide

Answer Transparencies available for all exercises

Basic:
Day 1: SRH p. 929 Exs. 1–6
pp. 18–20
Exs. 1, 2, 3–11 odd, 13, 14, 15–21 odd, 22–27, 31–35, 38–46 even

Average:
Day 1: pp. 18–20
Exs. 1, 2, 4–12 even, 13–29, 32–37, 41–46

Advanced:
Day 1: pp. 18–20
Exs. 1, 2, 9–14, 18–25, 28–30*, 33–37*, 44–46

Block:
pp. 18–20
Exs. 1, 2, 3–11 odd, 13–29, 32–37, 41–46 (with 1.4)

Differentiated Instruction

See *Algebra 1 Best Practices Toolkit* for suggestions on addressing the needs of a diverse classroom.

Homework Check

For a quick check of student understanding of key concepts, go over the following exercises:

Basic: 7, 15, 19, 23, 31
Average: 9, 17, 20, 24, 32
Advanced: 11, 18, 21, 25, 33

Extra Practice

- Student Edition, p. 938
- Chapter 1 Resource Book: Practice levels A, B, C, pp. 29–31

Practice Worksheet

An easily-readable reduced practice page (with answers) for this lesson can be found on p. 1C.

1.3 EXERCISES

HOMEWORK KEY
○ = **WORKED-OUT SOLUTIONS** on p. WS1 for Exs. 11, 21, and 33
★ = **STANDARDIZED TEST PRACTICE** Exs. 2, 13, 14, 34, and 37

SKILL PRACTICE

A

1. **VOCABULARY** Copy and complete: A(n) __?__ is a fraction that compares two quantities measured in different units. rate

2. ★ **WRITING** *Explain* how to write $\frac{20 \text{ miles}}{4 \text{ hours}}$ as a unit rate. See margin.

2. Divide the numerator and the denominator by 4; $\frac{20 \text{ miles} \div 4}{4 \text{ hours} \div 4} = \frac{5 \text{ mi}}{1 \text{h}}$ or 5 mi/h.

EXAMPLE 1 on p. 15 for Exs. 3–14

TRANSLATING PHRASES **Translate the verbal phrase into an expression.**

3. 8 more than a number x $x + 8$
4. The product of 6 and a number y $6y$
5. $\frac{1}{2}$ of a number m $\frac{1}{2}m$
6. 50 divided by a number h $\frac{50}{h}$
7. The difference of 7 and a number n $7 - n$
8. The sum of 15 and a number x $15 + x$
9. The quotient of twice a number t and 12
10. 3 less than the square of a number p $p^2 - 3$
11. 7 less than twice a number k $2k - 7$
12. 5 more than 3 times a number w $3w + 5$

9. $\frac{2t}{12}$

13. ★ **MULTIPLE CHOICE** Which expression represents the phrase "the product of 15 and the quantity 12 more than a number x"? C

Ⓐ $15 + 12 \cdot x$ Ⓑ $(15 + 12)x$ Ⓒ $15(x + 12)$ Ⓓ $15 \cdot 12 + x$

14. ★ **MULTIPLE CHOICE** Which expression represents the phrase "twice the quotient of 50 and the sum of a number y and 8"? C

Ⓐ $\frac{2 \cdot 50}{y} + 8$ Ⓑ $2\left(\frac{50 + y}{8}\right)$ Ⓒ $2\left(\frac{50}{y + 8}\right)$ Ⓓ $\frac{2}{50} + (y + 8)$

EXAMPLES 2 and 3 on p. 16 for Exs. 15–21

WRITING EXPRESSIONS **Write an expression for the situation.**

15. Number of tokens needed for v video games if each game takes 4 tokens $4v$
16. Number of pages of a 5 page article left to read if you've read p pages $5 - p$
17. Each person's share if p people share 16 slices of pizza equally $\frac{16}{p}$
18. Amount you spend if you buy a shirt for \$20 and jeans for j dollars $20 + j$
19. Number of days left in the week if d days have passed so far $7 - d$
20. Number of hours in m minutes $\frac{m}{60}$
21. Number of months in y years $12y$

EXAMPLE 4 on p. 17 for Exs. 22–27

UNIT RATES **Find the unit rate.**

22. $\frac{32 \text{ students}}{4 \text{ groups}}$ 8 students per group
23. $\frac{4.5 \text{ pints}}{3 \text{ servings}}$ 1.5 pints per serving
24. $\frac{12 \text{ runs}}{5 \text{ innings}}$ 2.4 runs per inning
25. $\frac{\$136}{20 \text{ shares}}$ \$6.80 per share

B

ERROR ANALYSIS ***Describe*** **and correct the error in the units.**

26. $\frac{\$2}{\text{foot}} \cdot 24 \text{ feet} = \frac{\$48}{\text{ft}^2}$ 

Feet should cancel out, not be squared; \$48.

27. $9 \text{ yards} \cdot \frac{3 \text{ feet}}{1 \text{ yard}} \cdot \frac{\$2}{\text{foot}} = \frac{\$54}{\text{ft}}$ 

Feet should cancel out; \$54.

COMPARING RATES In Exercises 28 and 29, tell which rate is greater.

28. $1\frac{1}{4}$ miles in 2 minutes and 4 seconds, or $1\frac{3}{16}$ miles in 1 minute and 55 seconds $1\frac{3}{16}$ **mi in 1 min 55 sec**

29. $1.60 for 5 minutes, or $19.50 for 1 hour **$19.50 for 1 h**

C 30. **CHALLENGE** Look for a pattern in the expressions shown below. Use the pattern to write an expression for the sum of the whole numbers from 1 to n. Then find the sum of the whole numbers from 1 to 50.

$1 + 2 = \frac{2 \cdot 3}{2}$ $\quad 1 + 2 + 3 = \frac{3 \cdot 4}{2}$ $\quad 1 + 2 + 3 + 4 = \frac{4 \cdot 5}{2}$ $\quad$ **$\frac{n \cdot (n+1)}{2}$; 1275**

PROBLEM SOLVING

EXAMPLE 5 A on p. 17 for Exs. 31–34

31. **TICKET PRICES** Tickets to a science museum cost $19.95 each. There is a $3 charge for each order no matter how many tickets are ordered. Write an expression for the cost (in dollars) of ordering tickets. Then find the total cost if you order 5 tickets. **$19.95t + 3$; $102.75**

@HomeTutor for problem solving help at classzone.com

32. **FOSSIL FUELS** Fossil fuels are produced by the decay of organic material over millions of years. To make one gallon of gas, it takes about 98 tons of organic material, roughly the amount of wheat that could be harvested in a 40 acre field. Write an expression for the amount (in tons) of organic material it takes to make g gallons of gas. How many tons would it take to make enough gas to fill a car's 20 gallon gas tank? **$98g$; 1960 tons**

@HomeTutor for problem solving help at classzone.com

33. **MULTI-STEP PROBLEM** A 48 ounce container of juice costs $2.64. A 64 ounce container of the same juice costs $3.84.

a. Find the cost per ounce of each container. **$.055, $.06**

b. Which size container costs less per ounce? **48 oz container**

c. You want to buy 192 ounces of juice. How much do you save using the container size from your answer to part (b)? **$.96**

34. ★ **OPEN-ENDED** *Describe* a real-world situation that can be modeled by the rate $\frac{30}{x}$ where x is a period of time (in hours). Identify the units for 30. Choose a value for x and find the unit rate.

34. *Sample answer:* You earn 30 dollars for shoveling driveways in a certain amount of time. If $x =$ 4 hours, the unit rate is $7.50 per hour.

35. **WILDLIFE EDUCATION** A wildlife center presents a program about birds of prey. The center charges a basic fee of $325 and an additional fee for each bird exhibited. If 5 birds are exhibited, the additional fee is $125. What is the total cost if 7 birds are exhibited? **$500**

B 36. **DIGITAL PHOTOS** Your printer takes 36 seconds to print a small photo and 60 seconds to print a large one. Write an expression for the time (in seconds) your printer would take to print a batch including both small and large photos. Then find the time your printer would take to print 12 small photos and 5 large photos. **$36s + 60\ell$; 732 sec**

Avoiding Common Errors

Exercises 28–29 In Exercise 28, watch for students who convert 2 minutes and 4 seconds to 2.4 minutes, and 1 minute and 55 seconds to 1.55 minutes. Show them that $2.4 \times 60 = 144$ seconds, but the correct calculation is $2(60) + 4 = 124$ seconds. In Exercise 29, point out that one rate involves minutes and the other uses hours.

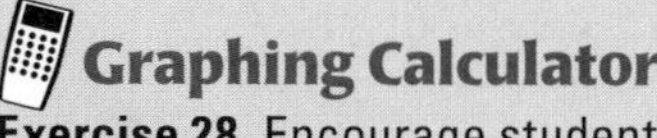

Graphing Calculator

Exercise 28 Encourage students to use their calculators to compare rates. Point out that it will be necessary to convert the fractions $\frac{1}{4}$ and $\frac{3}{16}$ to decimals before calculating the unit rates.

Reading Strategy

Exercise 32 Caution students to read the problem carefully and to use only relevant information to write their expression. If necessary, point out that the information about how much wheat can be harvested from a 40 acre field is not needed to find the answer.

Internet Reference

Exercise 32 For more information on energy sources, including fossil fuels, visit the U.S. Department of Energy's website at www.doe.gov.

Teaching Strategy

Exercise 35 To help students solve this problem, instruct them to write out a detailed solution like the one shown in Example 5.

5 ASSESS AND RETEACH

Daily Homework Quiz

Transparency Available

1. Write an expression for the situation: The number of miles left in a 425-mile trip after m miles have been traveled. $425 - m$
2. Find the unit rate for the rate $\frac{18 \text{ figurines}}{6 \text{ boxes}}$. 3 figurines per box
3. A video store charges $5 per game rental plus $12 to rent the game system. Write an expression for renting the game system and a number of games. Then find the total cost if you rent 6 games. $5g + 12$, where g is the number of games; $42

Online Quiz

Available at **classzone.com**

Diagnosis/Remediation

- Practice A, B, C in Chapter 1 Resource Book, pp. 29–31
- Study Guide in Chapter 1 Resource Book, pp. 32–33
- Practice Workbook, pp. 5–6
- @HomeTutor

Challenge

Additional challenge is available in the Chapter 1 Resource Book, p. 36.

Quiz

An easily-readable reduced copy of the quiz (with answers) on Lessons 1.1–1.3 from the Assessment Book can be found on p. 1E.

C **37.** ★ **EXTENDED RESPONSE** A national survey determines the champion tree in a species. The champion is the tree with the greatest score, based on the tree's girth, its height, and its crown spread as shown.

A tree's score is the sum of the girth in inches, the height in feet, and $\frac{1}{4}$ the crown spread in feet. The data for three champion trees are given. Note that the girth is given in feet.

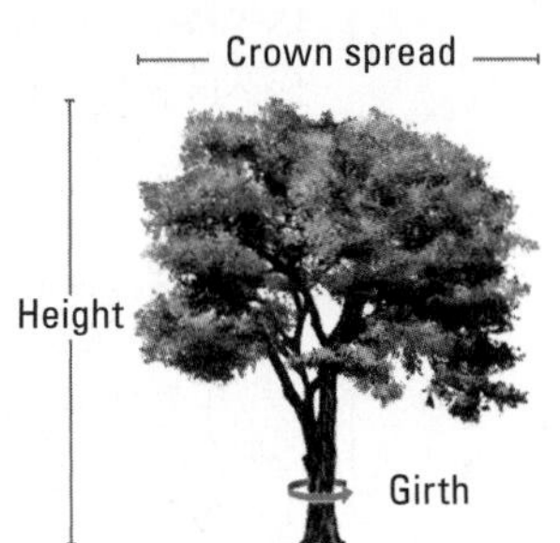

Species	Girth (ft)	Height (ft)	Crown spread (ft)
Narrowleaf cottonwood	12	97	24
Green ash	21.5	95	95
Green buttonwood	14.5	51	68

a. **Write** Write an expression for a tree's score. $12g + h + \frac{1}{4}c$

b. **Evaluate** Find the score for each tree in the table. 247; 376.75; 242

c. **CHALLENGE** Let n be any number greater than 0. Which change would have the greatest effect on a tree's score, an increase of n feet in the girth, in the height, or in the crown spread? *Explain* your reasoning. Girth; because it is multiplied by 12.

ILLINOIS MIXED REVIEW

TEST PRACTICE at classzone.com

38. The cost in dollars of renting a truck is given by $40d + 0.4m$ where d is the number of days for which the truck is rented and m is the number of miles driven. How much does it cost to rent the truck for 2 days and drive it 100 miles? B

Ⓐ $80 Ⓑ $120 Ⓒ $440 Ⓓ $480

39. In a recent election, 2 out of every 5 voters voted for candidate A, 15% voted for candidate B, and the rest voted for candidate C. What percent voted for candidate C? C

Ⓐ 25% Ⓑ 40% Ⓒ 45% Ⓓ 55%

QUIZ for Lessons 1.1–1.3

Evaluate the expression.

1. $y + 10$ when $y = 43$ *(p. 2)* 53
2. $15 - b$ when $b = 9$ *(p. 2)* 6
3. t^2 when $t = 20$ *(p. 2)* 400
4. $3n - 5$ when $n = 8$ *(p. 8)* 19
5. $2y^2 - 1$ when $y = 5$ *(p. 8)* 49
6. $\frac{3x - 6}{8}$ when $x = 8$ *(p. 8)* $2\frac{1}{4}$

Translate the verbal phrase into an expression. *(p. 15)*

7. 7 less than a number y $y - 7$
8. 5 more than a number t $t + 5$
9. Twice a number k $2k$
10. **CAMPING** The rental cost for a campsite is $25 plus $2 per person. Write an expression for the total cost. Then find the total cost for 5 people. *(p. 15)* $25 + 2p$; $35

1.4 Write Equations and Inequalities

Before You translated verbal phrases into expressions.
Now You will translate verbal sentences into equations or inequalities.
Why So you can calculate team competition statistics, as in Ex. 41.

Key Vocabulary
- **open sentence**
- **equation**
- **inequality**
- **solution of an equation**
- **solution of an inequality**

An **open sentence** is a mathematical statement that contains two algebraic expressions and a symbol that compares them.

An **equation** is an open sentence that contains the symbol =. An **inequality** is an open sentence that contains one of the symbols $<$, $\le$, $>$, or $\ge$.

KEY CONCEPT *For Your Notebook*

Symbol	Meaning	Associated Words
$=$	is equal to	the same as
$<$	is less than	fewer than
$\le$	is less than or equal to	at most, no more than
$>$	is greater than	more than
$\ge$	is greater than or equal to	at least, no less than

COMBINING INEQUALITIES Sometimes two inequalities are combined. For example, the inequalities $x > 4$ and $x < 9$ can be combined to form the inequality $4 < x < 9$, which is read "x is greater than 4 and less than 9."

EXAMPLE 1 Write equations and inequalities

	Verbal Sentence	Equation or Inequality
a.	The difference of twice a number k and 8 is 12.	$2k - 8 = 12$
b.	The product of 6 and a number n is at least 24.	$6n \ge 24$
c.	A number y is no less than 5 and no more than 13.	$5 \le y \le 13$

Animated Algebra at classzone.com

GUIDED PRACTICE for Example 1

1. Write an equation or an inequality: The quotient of a number p and 12 is at least 30. $\frac{p}{12} \ge 30$

1 PLAN AND PREPARE

Warm-Up Exercises

Transparency Available

1. Write an expression for the phrase: 4 times the difference of 6 and a number y. $4(6 - y)$
2. A museum charges $50 for an annual membership and then a reduced price of $2 per ticket. Write an expression to represent the situation. Then find the total cost to join the museum and buy 9 tickets. $50 + 2t$, where t is the number of tickets; $68

Notetaking Guide

Transparency Available

Promotes interactive learning and notetaking skills, pp. 10–12.

Pacing

Basic: 1 day
Average: 1 day
Advanced: 1 day
Block: 0.5 block with 1.3
- See *Teaching Guide/Lesson Plan*.

2 FOCUS AND MOTIVATE

Essential Question

Big Idea 2, p. 1

How do you write equations and inequalities? Tell students they will learn how to answer this question by translating sentences into equations or inequalities.

Resource Planning Guide

Chapter Resource Book
- Teaching Guide/Lesson Plan (pp. 37–38)
- Activity Master (p. 39)
- Practice levels A, B, C (pp. 40–42)
- Study Guide (pp. 43–44)
- Catch-up for Absent Students (p. 45)
- Problem Solving Workshop (p. 46)
- Challenge (p. 48)

Workbooks
- Notetaking Guide (pp. 10–12)
- Practice Workbook (pp. 7–8)

Teaching Options
- **Power Presentations CD-ROM** provides dynamic electronic teaching resources for the classroom.
- **Activity Generator CD-ROM** provides editable activities for all ability levels.

Interactive Technology
- Easy Planner
- Power Presentations CD-ROM
- Activity Generator CD-ROM
- Animated Algebra
- Test Generator CD-ROM
- Online Quiz
- eWorkbook
- eEdition
- @HomeTutor

Resources for English Learners
- Quick Reference for English Learners
- Spanish Study Guide
- Multi-Language Visual Glossary
- Student Resources in Spanish

See also the *Algebra 1 Toolkit* for more strategies for meeting individual needs.

Motivating the Lesson

Planning an event, such as a school dance, is a major undertaking. One issue to be decided is the price of a ticket. Do you want to at least break even, or do you want to make at least a specific profit? By writing an inequality, you can represent either of these situations and then find the amount you need to charge for a ticket.

Extra Example 1

Write an equation or an inequality.

a. The sum of twice a number r and 3 is 11. $2r + 3 = 11$

b. The quotient of a number n and 2 is at most 16. $\frac{n}{2} \le 16$

c. A number q is at least 5 and less than 17. $5 \le q < 17$

An **Animated Algebra** activity is available on-line for **Example 1**. This activity is also available on the **Power Presentations CD-ROM**.

Extra Example 2

Check whether 5 is a solution of the equation or inequality.

a. $24 - 3d = 9$ $9 = 9$; 5 is a solution.

b. $3x + 4 = 18$ $19 \ne 18$; 5 is *not* a solution.

c. $2w - 7 \le 3$ $3 \le 3$; 5 is a solution.

d. $4 + 3p > 19$ $19 \not> 19$; 5 is *not* a solution.

Key Question to Ask for Example 2

- In part c, what is the least whole number solution? Explain. 4; $2(4) + 5 = 13$ and 13 is greater than 12.

SOLUTIONS When you substitute a number for the variable in an open sentence like $x + 2 = 5$ or $2y > 6$, the resulting statement is either true or false. If the statement is true, the number is a **solution of the equation** or a **solution of the inequality**.

READING A question mark above a symbol indicates a question. For instance, $8 - 2(3) \stackrel{?}{=} 2$ means "Is $8 - 2(3)$ equal to 2?"

EXAMPLE 2 Check possible solutions

Check whether 3 is a solution of the equation or inequality.

Equation/Inequality	Substitute	Conclusion
a. $8 - 2x = 2$	$8 - 2(3) \stackrel{?}{=} 2$	$2 = 2$ ✓ 3 is a solution.
b. $4x - 5 = 6$	$4(3) - 5 \stackrel{?}{=} 6$	$7 = 6$ ✗ 3 is *not* a solution.
c. $2z + 5 > 12$	$2(3) + 5 \stackrel{?}{>} 12$	$11 > 12$ ✗ 3 is *not* a solution.
d. $5 + 3n \le 20$	$5 + 3(3) \stackrel{?}{\le} 20$	$14 \le 20$ ✓ 3 is a solution.

USING MENTAL MATH Some equations are simple enough to solve using mental math. Think of the equation as a question. Once you answer the question, check the solution.

EXAMPLE 3 Use mental math to solve an equation

Equation	Think	Solution	Check
a. $x + 4 = 10$	What number plus 4 equals 10?	6	$6 + 4 = 10$ ✓
b. $20 - y = 8$	20 minus what number equals 8?	12	$20 - 12 = 8$ ✓
c. $6n = 42$	6 times what number equals 42?	7	$6(7) = 42$ ✓
d. $\frac{a}{5} = 9$	What number divided by 5 equals 9?	45	$\frac{45}{5} = 9$ ✓

✓ GUIDED PRACTICE for Examples 2 and 3

Check whether the given number is a solution of the equation or inequality.

2. $9 - x = 4$; 5 solution **3.** $b + 5 < 15$; 7 solution **4.** $2n + 3 \ge 21$; 9 solution

Solve the equation using mental math.

5. $m + 6 = 11$ 5 **6.** $5x = 40$ 8 **7.** $\frac{r}{4} = 10$ 40

EXAMPLE 4 Solve a multi-step problem

MOUNTAIN BIKING The last time you and 3 friends went to a mountain bike park, you had a coupon for \$10 off and paid \$17 for 4 tickets. What is the regular price of 4 tickets? If you pay the regular price this time and share it equally, how much does each person pay?

Solution

STEP 1 **Write** a verbal model. Let p be the regular price of 4 tickets. Write an equation.

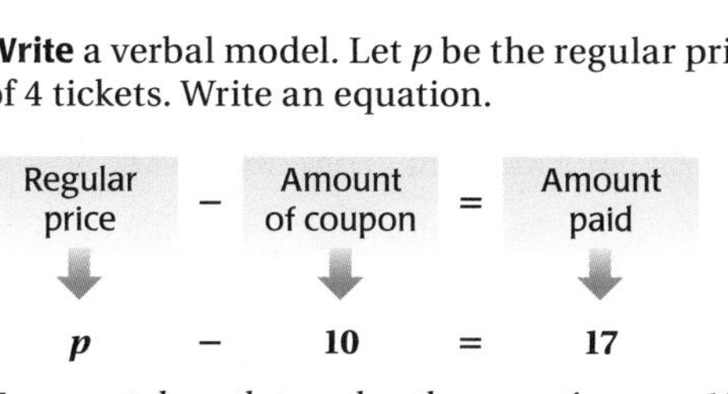

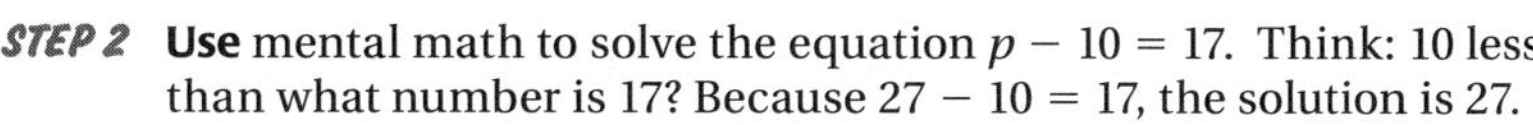

$$p - 10 = 17$$

STEP 2 **Use** mental math to solve the equation $p - 10 = 17$. Think: 10 less than what number is 17? Because $27 - 10 = 17$, the solution is 27.

▶ The regular price for 4 tickets is \$27.

STEP 3 **Find** the cost per person: $\frac{\$27}{4 \text{ people}} = \$6.75$ per person

▶ Each person pays \$6.75.

EXAMPLE 5 Write and check a solution of an inequality

BASKETBALL A basketball player scored 351 points last year. If the player plays 18 games this year, will an average of 20 points per game be enough to beat last year's total?

Solution

STEP 1 **Write** a verbal model. Let p be the average number of points per game. Write an inequality.

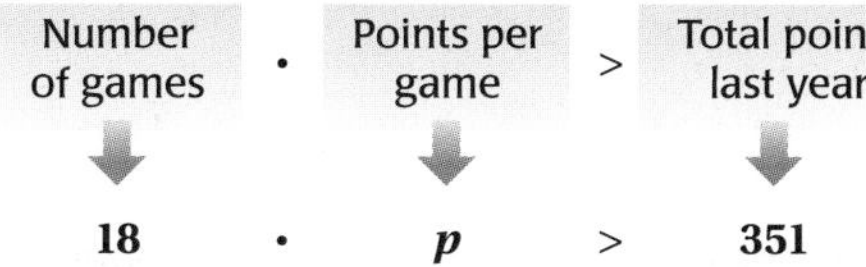

$$18 \cdot p > 351$$

USE UNIT ANALYSIS
Unit analysis shows that games $\cdot \frac{\text{points}}{\text{games}}$ = points, so the inequality is reasonable.

STEP 2 **Check** that 20 is a solution of the inequality $18p > 351$. Because $18(20) = 360$ and $360 > 351$, 20 is a solution. ✓

▶ An average of 20 points per game will be enough.

✓ **GUIDED PRACTICE** for Examples 4 and 5

8. **WHAT IF?** In Example 4, suppose that the price of 4 tickets with a half-off coupon is \$15. What is each person's share if you pay full price? \$7.50

9. **WHAT IF?** In Example 5, suppose that the player plays 16 games. Would an average of 22 points per game be enough to beat last year's total? yes

Extra Example 3

Solve the equation using mental math.

a. $y + 8 = 13$ 5 **b.** $a - 6 = 3$ 9
c. $8c = 32$ 4 **d.** $\frac{h}{7} = 4$ 28

Extra Example 4

Sarah enrolled in a guitar class. The enrollment fee was \$25. She paid a total of \$70 for the enrollment fee and 3 lessons. What is the cost of 3 lessons? How much did each lesson cost? \$45; \$15

Key Questions to Ask for Example 4

- How did you know to subtract 10 in Step 1? **Having a \$10 discount coupon means you subtract \$10.**
- What phrase indicates that you need to divide? **share it equally**

Extra Example 5

Tyler would like to make no less than \$610 selling coffee mugs online. If he sells 28 mugs for \$22 each, will he achieve his goal? yes

Closing the Lesson

Have students summarize the major points of the lesson and answer the Essential Question: How do you write equations and inequalities?

- **An equation is two expressions related by an equal sign, and an inequality is two expressions related by an inequality symbol.**
- **Substitute numbers for the variables and solve to find solutions for equations and inequalities.**

Use the verbal phrases associated with an equal sign and with each type of inequality symbol to determine whether to write an equation or an inequality. Then use the techniques for writing expressions learned in Lesson 1.3 to write the expressions on each side of the equal sign or inequality symbol.

4 PRACTICE AND APPLY

Assignment Guide

Answer Transparencies available for all exercises

Basic:
Day 1: pp. 24–26
Exs. 1, 2, 3–13 odd, 14–16, 17–35 odd, 39–45, 49–57 odd

Average:
Day 1: pp. 24–26
Exs. 1, 2, 7–11, 13–16, 21–28, 32–38, 41–46, 50–56 even

Advanced:
Day 1: pp. 24–26
Exs. 1, 2, 9–13, 16, 22–28 even, 32–38*, 42–48*, 50, 51, 56, 57

Block:
pp. 24–26
Exs. 1, 2, 7–11, 13–16, 21–28, 32–38, 41–46, 50–56 even (with 1.3)

Differentiated Instruction

See *Algebra 1 Best Practices Toolkit* for suggestions on addressing the needs of a diverse classroom.

Homework Check

For a quick check of student understanding of key concepts, go over the following exercises:

Basic: 5, 19, 31, 39, 40
Average: 8, 22, 33, 41, 42
Advanced: 10, 26, 34, 42, 43

Extra Practice

- Student Edition, p. 938
- Chapter 1 Resource Book: Practice levels A, B, C, pp. 40–42

Practice Worksheet

An easily-readable reduced practice page (with answers) for this lesson can be found on p. 1C.

1.4 EXERCISES

HOMEWORK KEY
○ = WORKED-OUT SOLUTIONS on p. WS1 for Exs. 7 and 41
★ = STANDARDIZED TEST PRACTICE Exs. 2, 16, 37, 44, 45, and 46

SKILL PRACTICE

A

1. **VOCABULARY** Give an example of an open sentence. *Sample answer:* $3x + 5 = 20$

2. ★ **WRITING** *Describe* the difference between an expression and an equation. An expression does not contain an equal sign but an equation does.

EXAMPLE 1 on p. 21 for Exs. 3–16

WRITING OPEN SENTENCES Write an equation or an inequality.

3. The sum of 42 and a number n is equal to 51. $42 + n = 51$
4. The difference of a number z and 11 is equal to 35. $z - 11 = 35$
5. The difference of 9 and the quotient of a number t and 6 is 5. $9 - \frac{t}{6} = 5$
6. The sum of 12 and the quantity 8 times a number k is equal to 48. $12 + 8k = 48$
7. The product of 9 and the quantity 5 more than a number t is less than 6. $9(t + 5) < 6$
8. The product of 4 and a number w is at most 51. $4w \le 51$
9. The sum of a number b and 3 is greater than 8 and less than 12. $8 < b + 3 < 12$
10. The product of 8 and a number k is greater than 4 and no more than 16. $4 < 8k \le 16$
11. The difference of a number t and 7 is greater than 10 and less than 20. $10 < t - 7 < 20$

STORE SALES Write an inequality for the price p (in dollars) described.

12. 

$p \le 10$

13. 

$p \ge 12.99$

ERROR ANALYSIS *Describe* and correct the error in writing the verbal sentence as an equation or an inequality.

14. The sum of a number n and 4 is no more than 13.

The wrong inequality symbol is used; $n + 4 \le 13$.

15. The quotient of a number t and 4.2 is at most 15.

The wrong inequality symbol is used; $\frac{t}{4.2} \le 15$.

16. ★ **MULTIPLE CHOICE** Which equation corresponds to the sentence "The product of a number b and 3 is no less than 12"? D

Ⓐ $3b < 12$ Ⓑ $3b \le 12$ Ⓒ $3b > 12$ Ⓓ $3b \ge 12$

EXAMPLE 2 on p. 22 for Exs. 17–28

CHECK POSSIBLE SOLUTIONS Check whether the given number is a solution of the equation or inequality.

17. $x + 9 = 17; 8$ solution
18. $9 + 4y = 17; 1$ not a solution
19. $6f - 7 = 29; 5$ not a solution
20. $\frac{k}{5} + 9 = 11; 10$ solution
21. $\frac{r}{3} - 4 = 4; 12$ not a solution
22. $\frac{x-5}{3} \ge 2.8; 11$ not a solution
23. $15 - 4y > 6; 2$ solution
24. $y - 3.5 < 6; 9$ solution
25. $2 + 3x \le 8; 2$ solution
26. $2p - 1 \ge 7; 3$ not a solution
27. $4z - 5 < 3; 2$ not a solution
28. $3z + 7 > 20; 4$ not a solution

Differentiated Instruction

Kinesthetic Learners To assist students in **Exercises 3–11**, have students associate "less than" with their left hand and "greater than" with their right hand. Then if they open the associated hand as if it is "eating" something, they can identify the correct inequality symbol.

See also the *Algebra 1 Toolkit* for more strategies.

EXAMPLE 3 on p. 22 for Exs. 29–34

MENTAL MATH **Solve the equation using mental math.**

29. $x + 8 = 13$ 5
30. $y + 16 = 25$ 9
31. $z - 11 = 1$ 12
32. $5w = 20$ 4
33. $8b = 72$ 9
34. $\frac{f}{6} = 4$ 24

EQUATIONS AND INEQUALITIES **In Exercises 35 and 36, write an open sentence. Then check whether $3\frac{1}{2}$ is a solution of the open sentence.**

B

35. 2 less than the product of 3 and a number x is equal to the sum of x and 5. $3x - 2 = x + 5$; solution
36. 4 more than twice a number k is no greater than the sum of k and 11. $2k + 4 \le k + 11$; solution
37. ★ **MULTIPLE CHOICE** Which equation has the same solution as $z - 9 = 3$? C

(A) $z - 4 = 16$ (B) $\frac{1}{2}z = 7$ (C) $z + 15 = 27$ (D) $5z = 45$

C

38. **CHALLENGE** Use mental math to solve the equation $3x + 4 = 19$. *Explain* your thinking. 5; ask what number times 3 plus 4 equals 19.

PROBLEM SOLVING

EXAMPLES A **4 and 5** on p. 23 for Exs. 39–43

39. **CHARITY WALK** You are taking part in a charity walk, and you have walked 12.5 miles so far. Your goal is to walk 20 miles. How many more miles do you need to walk to meet your goal? 7.5 mi

@HomeTutor for problem solving help at classzone.com

40. **COMPACT DISCS** You buy a storage rack that holds 40 CDs. You have 27 CDs. Write an inequality that describes how many more CDs you can buy and still have no more CDs than the rack can hold. You buy 15 CDs. Will they all still fit? $27 + c \le 40$; no

@HomeTutor for problem solving help at classzone.com

41. **ECO-CHALLENGE** Eco-Challenge Fiji was a competition that included jungle trekking, ocean swimming, mountain biking, and river kayaking. In 2002, the U.S. team finished second about 6 hours after the winning team from New Zealand. The U.S. team finished in about 173 hours. What was the winning team's time? 167 h
42. **BAKING MEASUREMENTS** You are baking batches of cookies for a bake sale. Each batch takes 2.5 cups of flour. You have 18 cups of flour. Can you bake 8 batches? *Explain.*
43. **EMPLOYMENT** Your friend takes a job cleaning up a neighbor's yard and mowing the grass, and asks you and two other friends to help. Your friend divides the amount the neighbor pays equally among all the members of the group. Each of you got \$25. How much did the neighbor pay? \$100
44. ★ **OPEN-ENDED** Describe a real-world situation you could model using the equation $5x = 50$. Use mental math to solve the equation. *Explain* what the solution means in this situation. See margin.

42. No. *Sample answer*: Since each batch of cookies takes 2.5 cups of flour and you want to make 8 batches, you need to multiply 2.5 by 8, which gives you 20 cups. Since you only have 18 cups, you do not have enough.

Vocabulary

Exercise 35 Some students may be confused by the words "less" and "less than" since they both indicate subtraction. Point out that "less than" means "subtracted from" while "less" means "minus." So, "2 less than the product of 3 and a number x" means 2 subtracted from $3x$, or $3x - 2$.

Mathematical Reasoning

Exercise 38 Point out that $3x$ must have a value of 15 in order for x to be a solution of the equation. Students should then see that the solution of the equation $3x = 15$ is the solution of the given equation.

Reading Strategy

Exercise 40 Students may want to reword the third sentence of this exercise. The following sentence may be easier for students to decipher: *Write an inequality that describes the number of additional CDs you can buy without having too many to fit in the storage rack.*

Avoiding Common Errors

Exercise 43 Watch for students who use 3 as the number of workers in the group. Suggest they give names to each of the persons discussed in the problem as they read it. Then ask them to count the number of workers; they will discover that there are 4 workers.

44. *Sample answer:* You want to buy \$5 gift certificates to a music store for your friends. If you have \$50, how many certificates can you buy? 10 certificates; you can buy 10 \$5 gift certificates for \$50.

5 ASSESS AND RETEACH

Daily Homework Quiz

Transparency Available

Write an equation or an inequality.

1. 3 less than twice a number n is 12. $2n - 3 = 12$
2. The product of 5 and a number k is no more than 30. $5k \le 30$
3. Check whether 2 is a solution of the inequality $3p + 2 > 8$. $8 \not> 8$; 2 is *not* a solution.
4. You need to practice a gymnastic routine for at least 25 hours. You have already practiced 8.5 hours. If you practice for another 16.5 hours, will you reach your goal? Explain. Yes; the inequality $h + 8.5 \ge 25$ represents the situation. If you substitute 16.5 for h, $16.5 + 8.5 = 25$ and $25 \ge 25$.

Available at **classzone.com**

Diagnosis/Remediation

- Practice A, B, C in Chapter 1 Resource Book, pp. 40–42
- Study Guide in Chapter 1 Resource Book, pp. 43–44
- Practice Workbook, pp. 7–8
- @HomeTutor

Challenge

Additional challenge is available in the Chapter 1 Resource Book, p. 48.

B

45. ★ **SHORT RESPONSE** You have two part-time jobs. You earn \$6 per hour running errands and \$5 per hour walking dogs. You can work a total of 10 hours this weekend and hope to earn at least \$55. Let r be the number of hours you spend running errands.

a. Write an inequality that describes the situation. Your inequality should involve only one variable, r. $6r + 5(10 - r) \ge 55$

b. If you spend the same amount of time at each job, will you meet your goal? *Explain.* Yes; you will earn \$30 running errands and \$25 walking dogs; $30 + 25 = 5$

c. Can you meet your goal by working all 10 hours at only one job? *Explain.* Yes; if you work 10 hours running errands, you will earn \$60. You will not meet your goal if you work all 10 hours walking dogs.

46. ★ **EXTENDED RESPONSE** Your school's service club is sponsoring a dance in the school gym to raise money for a local charity. The expenses will be \$600. The club members will sell tickets for \$10. They hope to raise enough money to cover the expenses and have enough left to donate \$1000 to the charity.

a. How many tickets must they sell to cover their expenses? 60 tickets

b. How many tickets must they sell to cover their expenses and meet their goal? 160 tickets

c. The school allows no more than 200 students in the gymnasium for a dance. Can the club members sell enough tickets to exceed their goal? What is the greatest possible amount by which they can exceed their goal? *Explain* your reasoning. Yes; \$400; if they sell 200 tickets they will bring in \$2000, which is \$400 over their goal.

C

47. CHALLENGE You and your friend are reading the same series of science fiction books. You tell your friend, "I've read 3 times as many books as you have." Your friend replies, "You've read only 4 more books than I have." How many books have each of you read? friend: 2 books; you: 6 books

48. CHALLENGE Each of the long sides of a rectangle has a length of x inches. Each of the other sides is 1 inch shorter than the long sides. The perimeter of the rectangle is 22 inches. Find the length and the width of the rectangle. *Justify* your answer. 6 in., 5 in.; $P = 2\ell + 2w$, $2(6) + 2(5) = 12 + 10 = 22$

ILLINOIS MIXED REVIEW

TEST PRACTICE at classzone.com

49. You are buying several birds and a birdcage. The birdcage costs \$25 and the birds cost \$8 each. If you have \$50 altogether to spend on the birds and the birdcage, how many birds can you buy? B

(A) 2 (B) 3 (C) 4 (D) 6

50. A rectangle has a perimeter of 40 inches and an area of 36 square inches. A similar rectangle has a perimeter of 20 inches. What is the area of the smaller rectangle? A

(A) 9 in.^{2} (B) 18 in.^{2} (C) 20 in.^{2} (D) 72 in.^{2}

Illinois Test Practice

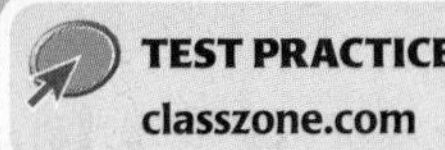

TEST PRACTICE
classzone.com

Lessons 1.1–1.4

1. **PHOTO QUILT** You are making a photo quilt by transferring photos to 48 rectangular pieces of fabric. Each rectangle is 3 inches long and 2 inches wide. The fabric you buy is 24 inches wide. How long a piece of fabric do you need?

   A. 8 in. **C.** 16 in.
   B. 12 in. **D.** 18 in.

2. **STRAWBERRIES** You pay $7.50 for 3 quarts of strawberries. Later, you realize your recipe calls for 5 quarts of strawberries. How much will the additional strawberries cost?

   F. $2.50 **H.** $5.50
   G. $5 **J.** $12.50

3. **CALORIES** The number of calories in one serving of any food is the sum of the calories from fat, protein, and carbohydrate. The table shows the calories in 1 gram of each of the three food components.

Component	Calories in 1 gram
Fat	9
Protein	4
Carbohydrate	4

   A serving of cheddar cheese contains 14 grams of fat, 11 grams of protein, and 1 gram of carbohydrate. How many calories are in a serving of cheddar cheese?

   A. 70 calories **C.** 174 calories
   B. 141 calories **D.** 234 calories

4. **MINIATURE CARS** You collect miniature cars and display them on shelves that hold 20 cars each. Which expression describes the number of shelves needed for any number of miniature cars?

   F. $\frac{x}{20}$ **H.** $20x$
   G. $\frac{20}{x}$ **J.** None of the above

5. **GARDENING** A gardener has a rectangular garden with a length of 10 feet and a width of 5 feet. The gardener plans to increase the length of the garden by 3 feet. What will the area of the enlarged garden be?

   A. 25 ft^2 **C.** 65 ft^2
   B. 26 ft^2 **D.** 80 ft^2

6. **BIKE FRAME** The ideal height (in centimeters) of a mountain bike frame is about 10 centimeters less than two thirds of the bike rider's leg length (in centimeters). Two riders' leg lengths are 80 centimeters and 85 centimeters. To the nearest tenth of a centimeter, how much taller should the taller mountain bike frame be?

   F. 3.3 cm **H.** 13.3 cm
   G. 5 cm **J.** 23.3 cm^2

7. **REFRIGERATORS** You are comparing two dorm-size refrigerators, both with cube-shaped interiors. One model has an interior edge length of 14 inches. Another model has an interior edge length of 16 inches. How many more cubic inches of storage space does the larger model have?

   A. 8 **C.** 1352
   B. 360 **D.** 4096

8. **CHARITY RACE** A runner has three sponsors for a charity race. For each mile the runner completes, one sponsor pays $1.50, another pays $3, and a third pays $2.50. Suppose the runner completes 5 miles. How much (in dollars) do the sponsors pay altogether?

   F. $13 **H.** $56.25
   G. $12.50 **J.** $35

Illinois Mixed Review

1. B
2. G
3. C
4. F
5. C
6. F
7. C
8. J

1.5 Use a Problem Solving Plan

6.11.13 Set up, evaluate, or solve single- and multi-step number sentences and word problems with rational numbers using the four basic operations.

Before You used problem solving strategies.

Now You will use a problem solving plan to solve problems.

Why? So you can determine a route, as in Example 1.

1 PLAN AND PREPARE

Warm-Up Exercises

Transparency Available

1. Mr. Lu is planting trees around the perimeter of a rectangular park. The park measures 72 feet by 48 feet. The trees need to be spaced 12 feet apart. A tree is to be planted in each corner. How many trees are needed? **20 trees**
2. In an aviary, there are three times as many finches as mockingbirds. If there are 48 birds, how many mockingbirds are there? **12 mockingbirds**

Notetaking Guide

Transparency Available

Promotes interactive learning and notetaking skills, pp. 13–15.

Pacing

Basic: 1 day
Average: 1 day
Advanced: 1 day
Block: 0.5 block with 1.6
- See *Teaching Guide/Lesson Plan.*

2 FOCUS AND MOTIVATE

Essential Question

Big Idea 2, p. 1

How can you use a problem solving plan to solve a problem? **Tell students they will learn how to answer this question by working through the steps of a problem solving plan.**

Key Vocabulary
- formula

KEY CONCEPT — *For Your Notebook*

A Problem Solving Plan

STEP 1 **Read and Understand** Read the problem carefully. Identify what you know and what you want to find out.

STEP 2 **Make a Plan** Decide on an approach to solving the problem.

STEP 3 **Solve the Problem** Carry out your plan. Try a new approach if the first one isn't successful.

STEP 4 **Look Back** Once you obtain an answer, check that it is reasonable.

EXAMPLE 1 Read a problem and make a plan

RUNNING You run in a city where the short blocks on north-south streets are 0.1 mile long. The long blocks on east-west streets are 0.15 mile long. You will run 2 long blocks east, a number of short blocks south, 2 long blocks west, then back to your starting point. You want to run 2 miles. How many short blocks should you run?

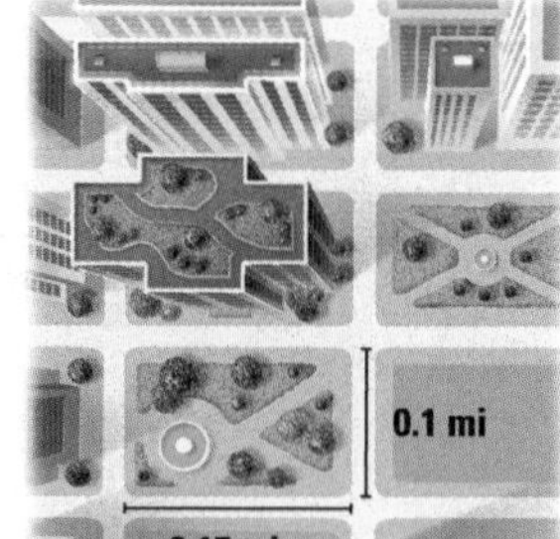

Solution

ANOTHER WAY
For an alternative method for solving the problem in Example 1, turn to page 34 for the **Problem Solving Workshop**.

STEP 1 **Read and Understand**

What do you know?

You know the length of each size block, the number of long blocks you will run, and the total distance you want to run.

You can conclude that you must run an even number of short blocks because you run the same number of short blocks in each direction.

What do you want to find out?

You want to find out the number of short blocks you should run so that, along with the 4 long blocks, you run 2 miles.

STEP 2 **Make a Plan** Use what you know to write a verbal model that represents what you want to find out. Then write an equation and solve it, as in Example 2.

Resource Planning Guide

Chapter Resource Book
- Teaching Guide/Lesson Plan (pp. 49–50)
- Practice levels A, B, C (pp. 51–53)
- Study Guide (pp. 54–55)
- Catch-up for Absent Students (p. 56)
- Problem Solving Workshop (p. 57)
- Challenge (p. 58)

Workbooks
- Notetaking Guide (pp. 13–15)
- Practice Workbook (pp. 9–10)

Teaching Options
- **Power Presentations CD-ROM** provides dynamic electronic teaching resources for the classroom.
- **Activity Generator CD-ROM** provides editable activities for all ability levels.

Interactive Technology
- Easy Planner
- Power Presentations CD-ROM
- Activity Generator CD-ROM
- Animated Algebra
- Test Generator CD-ROM
- Online Quiz
- eWorkbook
- eEdition
- @HomeTutor

Resources for English Learners
- Quick Reference for English Learners
- Spanish Study Guide
- Multi-Language Visual Glossary
- Student Resources in Spanish

See also the *Algebra 1 Toolkit* for more strategies for meeting individual needs.

EXAMPLE 2 Solve a problem and look back

Solve the problem in Example 1 by carrying out the plan. Then check your answer.

Solution

STEP 3 **Solve the Problem** Write a verbal model. Then write an equation. Let s be the number of short blocks you run.

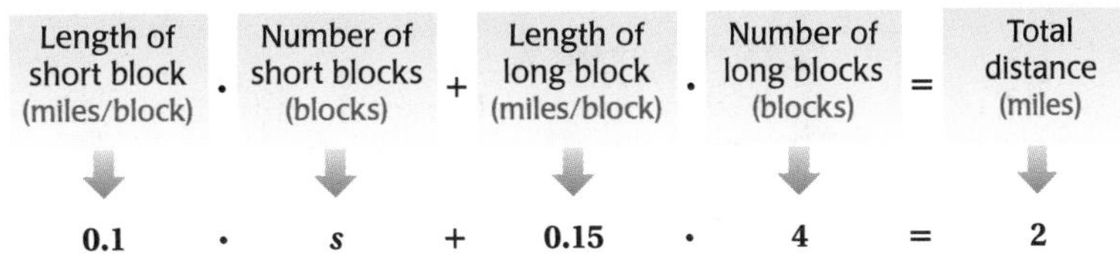

Length of short block (miles/block) · Number of short blocks (blocks) + Length of long block (miles/block) · Number of long blocks (blocks) = Total distance (miles)

$$0.1 \cdot s + 0.15 \cdot 4 = 2$$

The equation is $0.1s + 0.6 = 2$. One way to solve the equation is to use the strategy *guess, check, and revise.*

REVIEW PROBLEM SOLVING
To review problem solving strategies, see p. 936.

Guess an even number that is easily multiplied by 0.1. Try 20.

Check whether 20 is a solution.

$0.1s + 0.6 = 2$ **Write equation.**

$0.1(20) + 0.6 \stackrel{?}{=} 2$ **Substitute 20 for *s*.**

$2.6 = 2$ ✗ **Simplify; 20 does not check.**

Revise. Because $2.6 > 2$, try an even number less than 20. Try 14.

Check whether 14 is a solution.

$0.1s + 0.6 = 2$ **Write equation.**

$0.1(14) + 0.6 \stackrel{?}{=} 2$ **Substitute 14 for *s*.**

$2 = 2$ ✓ **Simplify.**

▶ To run 2 miles, you should run 14 short blocks along with the 4 long blocks you run.

STEP 4 **Look Back** Check your answer by making a table. You run 0.6 mile on long blocks. Each two short blocks add 0.2 mile.

Short blocks	0	2	4	6	8	10	12	14
Total distance	0.6	0.8	1.0	1.2	1.4	1.6	1.8	2.0

The total distance is 2 miles when you run 4 long blocks and 14 short blocks. The answer in Step 3 is correct.

 at classzone.com

GUIDED PRACTICE for Examples 1 and 2

1. **WHAT IF?** In Example 1, suppose that you want to run a total distance of 3 miles. How many short blocks should you run? **24 short blocks**

Motivating the Lesson

Ask students to recount a complex situation they have had to resolve, such as allocating time for homework, activities, and chores after school each day. After they share some problems, tell them that this lesson offers a plan for solving complex math problems.

3 TEACH

Extra Example 1

You are designing the layout for a newspaper about teen issues. The newspaper will be $22\frac{1}{2}$ inches wide. You plan to have 5 columns with $\frac{1}{8}$-inch gaps between them and $\frac{3}{8}$-inch margins on the left and right sides. How wide will each column be? **Step 1: I know the width of the newspaper, the number of columns, the size of the margins, and the size of the gaps between the columns. I want to find out how many gaps there are, so I can determine the width of each column. Step 2: I can use a diagram to find the number of gaps and then use what I know to make a verbal model. Next, I can write an equation and solve it.**

Extra Example 2

Solve the problem in Extra Example 1 by carrying out the plan. Then check your answer. **Step 3: Let w be the width of each column. There are two margins and four gaps. The problem is modeled by $5w + 2\left(\frac{3}{8}\right) + 4\left(\frac{1}{8}\right) = 22\frac{1}{2}$. Using the guess, check, and revise strategy, the width of each column should be $4\frac{1}{4}$ inches. Step 4: Substituting $4\frac{1}{4}$ into the equation for w results in a true statement.**

Differentiated Instruction

Below Level In Step 1 of **Example 1**, some students may not be able to conclude that there must be an even number of short blocks. Have these students draw a diagram of the route and label it using the information in the problem. The diagram should enable them to see that the number of short blocks must be even. Suggest they use the diagram to create a verbal model for the problem.

See also the *Algebra 1 Toolkit* for more strategies.

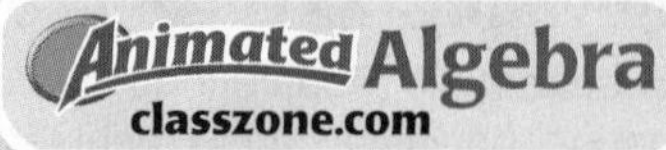

An **Animated Algebra** activity is available on-line for **Example 2** on page 29. This activity is also available on the **Power Presentations CD-ROM**.

Extra Example 3

A builder lays sod on the lawns of new homes. The installed cost for sod is \$.38 per square foot. What is the cost of installing sod on a rectangular lawn that is 32 feet long and 18 feet wide? D

Ⓐ \$19.00 Ⓑ \$38.00
Ⓒ \$184.32 Ⓓ \$218.88

Key Question to Ask for Example 3

- Why do you use the formula $A = \ell w$? **The piece of leather is described as being rectangular and the words *square inches* indicate area, so the formula $A = \ell w$ is needed to solve the problem.**

Closing the Lesson

Have students summarize the major points of the lesson and answer the Essential Question: How can you use a problem solving plan to solve a problem?

- **A problem solving plan is a guide that helps you organize the steps of the work necessary to solve a problem.**
- **Any problem solving strategy can be utilized within the problem solving plan.**

By following the steps in the plan, you can identify what you need to know, decide on a strategy to use, carry out the strategy, and then check that the answer you calculate is reasonable.

FORMULAS A **formula** is an equation that relates two or more quantities. You may find it helpful to use formulas in problem solving.

REVIEW FORMULAS
For additional formulas, see pp. 924–928 and the Table of Formulas on pp. 952–953.

KEY CONCEPT — *For Your Notebook*

Formulas

Temperature

$C = \frac{5}{9}(F - 32)$ where F = degrees Fahrenheit and C = degrees Celsius

Simple interest

$I = Prt$ where I = interest, P = principal, r = interest rate (as a decimal), and t = time

Distance traveled

$d = rt$ where d = distance traveled, r = rate (constant or average speed), and t = time

Profit

$P = I - E$ where P = profit, I = income, and E = expenses

★ EXAMPLE 3 Standardized Test Practice

You are making a leather book cover. You need a rectangular piece of leather as shown. Find the cost of the piece if leather costs \$.25 per square inch.

Ⓐ \$14.50 Ⓑ \$49.50

Ⓒ \$58.00 Ⓓ \$198.00

ELIMINATE CHOICES
You can eliminate choices A and D by estimating. The area of the piece of leather is about 200 square inches, and \$.25(200) is about \$50.

Solution

Use the formula for the area of a rectangle, $A = \ell w$, with ℓ = 18 inches and w = 11 inches.

$A = \ell w$	Write area formula.
$= 18(11)$	Substitute 18 for ℓ and 11 for w.
$= 198$	Simplify.

The area is 198 square inches, so the total cost is \$.25(198) = \$49.50.

▶ The correct answer is B. Ⓐ Ⓑ Ⓒ Ⓓ

GUIDED PRACTICE for Example 3

2. **GARDENING** A gardener determines the cost of planting daffodil bulbs to be \$2.40 per square foot. How much will it cost to plant daffodil bulbs in a rectangular garden that is 12 feet long and 5 feet wide? D

Ⓐ \$40.80 Ⓑ \$60 Ⓒ \$81.60 Ⓓ \$144

Differentiated Instruction

Visual Learners A diagram is often the most helpful way to solve a word problem. If a diagram such as the one in **Example 3** is given, that is a sign to use it. Encourage visual learners to construct diagrams whenever possible. Have them construct a similar diagram for **Guided Practice Exercise 2**.

See also the *Algebra 1 Toolkit* for more strategies.

1.5 EXERCISES

HOMEWORK KEY

○ = **WORKED-OUT SOLUTIONS** on p. WS2 for Exs. 5 and 17

★ = **STANDARDIZED TEST PRACTICE** Exs. 2, 11, 12, 20, and 22

◆ = **MULTIPLE REPRESENTATIONS** Ex. 21

SKILL PRACTICE

A

1. **VOCABULARY** Give an example of a formula. *Sample answer:* $d = rt$

2. ★ **WRITING** *Describe* how you can use a formula to solve the following problem: The inner edges of a cube-shaped pot have a length of 1.5 feet. How much does it cost to fill the planter if soil costs $4 per cubic foot? See margin.

EXAMPLES 1 and 2 on pp. 28–29 for Exs. 3–5

READING AND UNDERSTANDING In Exercises 3–5, identify what you know and what you need to find out. You do *not* need to solve the problem.

3. **CRAFT SHOW** You make 35 dog collars and anticipate selling all of them at a craft show. You spent $85 for materials and hope to make a profit of $90. How much should you charge for each collar? See margin.

4. **DISTANCE RUNNING** A runner ran at a rate of 0.15 mile per minute for 40 minutes. The next day, the runner ran at a rate of 0.16 mile per minute for 50 minutes. How far did the runner run altogether? See margin.

5. **TEMPERATURE** One day, the temperature in Rome, Italy, was 30°C. The temperature in Dallas, Texas, was 83°F. Which temperature was higher? See margin.

ERROR ANALYSIS *Describe* and correct the error in solving the problem.

A town is fencing a rectangular field that is 200 feet long and 150 feet wide. At $10 per foot, how much will it cost to fence the field? 6, 7. See margin.

6.
P = 200 + 150 = 350 ✗
$10(350) = $3500

7.
A = (200)(150) = 30,000 ✗
$10(30,000) = $300,000

EXAMPLE 3 on p. 30 for Exs. 8–12

B

CHOOSING A FORMULA In Exercises 8–10, state the formula that is needed to solve the problem. You do *not* need to solve the problem.

8. The temperature is 68°F. What is the temperature in degrees Celsius? $C = \frac{5}{9}(F - 32)$

9. A store buys a baseball cap for $5 and sells it for $20. What is the profit? $P = I - E$

10. Find the area of a triangle with a base of 25 feet and a height of 8 feet. $A = \frac{1}{2}bh$

11. ★ **MULTIPLE CHOICE** What is the interest on $1200 invested for 2 years in an account that earns simple interest at a rate of 5% per year? C

(A) $12 (B) $60 (C) $120 (D) $240

12. ★ **MULTIPLE CHOICE** A car travels at an average speed of 55 miles per hour. How many miles does the car travel in 2.5 hours? D

(A) 22 miles (B) 57.5 miles (C) 110 miles (D) 137.5 miles

C

13. **CHALLENGE** Write a formula for the length ℓ of a rectangle given its perimeter P and its width w. *Justify* your thinking.
$\ell = \frac{P}{2} - w$. *Sample answer:* Dividing the perimeter by 2 will give the sum of the length and the width. Subtracting the width will give the length.

4 PRACTICE AND APPLY

Assignment Guide

Answer Transparencies available for all exercises

Basic:
Day 1: SRH p. 937 Exs. 1–4
pp. 31–33
Exs. 1–10, 14–20, 24–32

Average:
Day 1: pp. 31–33
Exs. 1, 2, 4–13, 16–22, 24–32

Advanced:
Day 1: pp. 31–33
Exs. 1, 2, 4, 5, 8–13*, 17–23*, 25–31 odd

Block:
pp. 31–33
Exs. 1, 2, 4–13, 16–22, 24–32 (with 1.6)

Differentiated Instruction

See *Algebra 1 Best Practices Toolkit* for suggestions on addressing the needs of a diverse classroom.

Homework Check

For a quick check of student understanding of key concepts, go over the following exercises:

Basic: 3, 4, 8, 14, 16
Average: 4, 5, 9, 16, 17
Advanced: 4, 5, 10, 17, 18

Extra Practice

- Student Edition, p. 938
- Chapter 1 Resource Book: Practice levels A, B, C, pp. 51–53

Practice Worksheet

An easily-readable reduced practice page (with answers) for this lesson can be found on p. 1D.

Differentiated Instruction

Advanced You may wish to pair advanced students with other students who are struggling with the word problems in the exercises of this lesson. Both students will benefit from this interaction—the advanced student must follow the steps of the problem solving plan for each problem when they often might not while working on their own, and the assisted student receives the guidance they need to succeed.

See also the *Algebra 1 Toolkit* for more strategies.

2. *Sample answer:* Since you are filling a cubic container, you need to use the volume formula $V = s^3$ where s is the length of an edge. Substituting 1.5 for s gives $V = 1.5^3 = 3.375$ cubic feet. If the soil costs $4 per cubic foot, $3.375 \cdot 4 =$ $13.50 to fill the planter.

3. You know how many collars you've made, how much you have spent to make them, and how much money you want to make. You need to find what to charge for each collar so you make $90.

5–7. See Additional Answers beginning on p. AA1.

Teaching Strategy

Exercises 14–19 Some students may feel they can solve these problems without needing to follow a plan. Encourage them to use the 4-step plan in order to gain practice using it. Stress that when they encounter a problem they find to be more difficult, they will know how to use the steps to simplify their work.

Study Strategy

Exercises 15, 17 Some students may find it easier to work with decimals than fractions. Suggest they convert the fractions to decimals as part of Step 3 in the problem solving plan.

Exercises 15, 19 For students who find these problems difficult, suggest they draw a diagram to help visualize the problem.

20c. 120; \$382.80; The perimeter of the park is $150 + 200 + 250 =$ 600 feet. A post is placed every 5 feet so divide 600 by 5, which is 120 posts. Multiply 120 by the cost per post, $120 \cdot 3.19 = \$382.80$.

PROBLEM SOLVING

EXAMPLES 1, 2, and 3 on pp. 28–30 for Exs. 14–18

A

14. **DVD STORAGE** A stackable storage rack holds 22 DVDs and costs \$21. How much would it cost to buy enough racks to hold 127 DVDs? \$126

@HomeTutor for problem solving help at classzone.com

15. **FRAMING** For an art project, you make a square print with a side length of 8 inches. You make a frame using strips of wood $1\frac{1}{4}$ inches wide. What is the area of the frame? 46.25 in.^{2}

@HomeTutor for problem solving help at classzone.com

16. **MOUNTAIN BOARDS** You have saved \$70 to buy a mountain board that costs \$250. You plan to save \$10 each week. How many weeks will it take to save for the mountain board? 18 wk

17. **HIKING** You are hiking. The total weight of your backpack and its contents is $13\frac{3}{8}$ pounds. You want to carry no more than 15 pounds. How many extra water bottles can you add to your backpack if each bottle weighs $\frac{3}{4}$ pound? 2 water bottles

18. **PIZZA** Thick crust pizza requires about 0.15 ounce of dough per square inch of surface area. You have two rectangular pans, one that is 16 inches long and 14 inches wide, and one that is 15.5 inches long and 10 inches wide. How much more dough do you need to make a thick crust pizza in the larger pan than in the smaller one? 10.35 oz

19. **SONAR** A diver uses a sonar device to determine the distance to her diving partner. The device sends a sound wave and records the time it takes for the wave to reach the diving partner and return to the device. Suppose the wave travels at a rate of about 4800 feet per second.

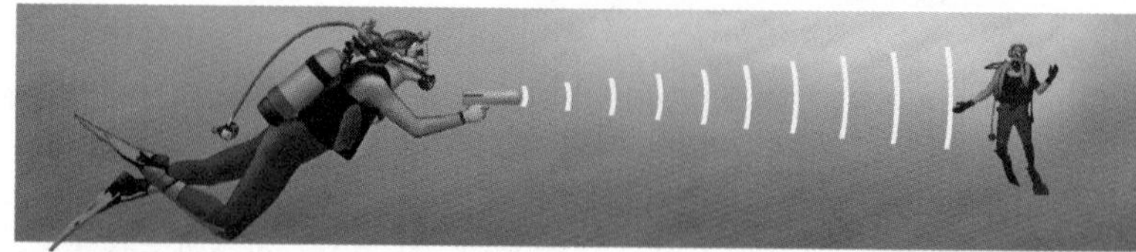

a. The wave returns 0.2 second after it was sent. How far did the wave travel? 960 ft

b. How far away is the diving partner? 480 ft

B

20. ★ **EXTENDED RESPONSE** A gardener is reseeding a city park that has the shape of a right triangle with a base of 150 feet and a height of 200 feet. The third side of the park is 250 feet long.

a. One bag of grass seed covers 3750 square feet and costs \$27.50. How many bags are needed? What is the total cost? 4 bags; \$110

b. Wire fencing costs \$23.19 for each 50 foot roll. How much does it cost to buy fencing to enclose the area? \$278.28

c. Fence posts cost \$3.19 each and should be placed every 5 feet. How many posts are needed, and how much will they cost altogether? *Explain.* See margin.

◯ = WORKED-OUT SOLUTIONS on p. WS1 ★ = STANDARDIZED TEST PRACTICE ◆ = MULTIPLE REPRESENTATIONS

21a.

Room size (feet)	1 by 1	2 by 2	3 by 3	4 by 4	5 by 5
Remaining area (square feet)	431	428	423	416	407

21. ◆ **MULTIPLE REPRESENTATIONS** Homeowners are building a square closet in a rectangular room that is 24 feet long and 18 feet wide. They want the remaining floor area to be at least 400 square feet. Because they don't want to cut any of the 1 foot by 1 foot square floor tiles, the side length of the closet floor should be a whole number of feet.

a. **Making a Table** Make a table showing possible side lengths of the closet floor and the remaining area for each side length. See margin.

b. **Writing an Inequality** Write an inequality to describe the situation. Use your table to find the greatest possible side length of the closet floor. $1 \le s \le 5$; 5 ft

22. ★ **SHORT RESPONSE** A farmer plans to build a fence around a rectangular pen that is 16 feet long. The area of the pen is 80 square feet. Is 40 feet of fencing enough to fence in the pen? *Explain.* No. *Sample answer:* The width of the pen is 5 feet long. The farmer would need $2(5) + 2(16) = 42$ feet of fencing.

C 23. **CHALLENGE** You and your friend live 12 miles apart. You leave home at the same time and travel toward each other. You walk at a rate of 4 miles per hour and your friend bicycles at a rate of 11 miles per hour.

a. How long after you leave home will you meet? How far from home will each of you be? 48 min; you: 3.2 mi, your friend: 8.8 mi

b. Suppose your friend bicycles at a rate of 12 miles per hour. How much sooner will you meet? How far from home will each of you be? 3 min; you: 3 mi, your friend: 9 mi

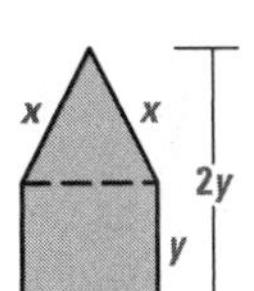

TEST PRACTICE at classzone.com

ILLINOIS MIXED REVIEW

24. The figure shown is made up of a triangle and a square. Which expression gives the area of the figure? D

Ⓐ $2y + \frac{xy}{2}$ Ⓒ $y^2 + \frac{x^2}{2}$

Ⓑ $y^2 + \frac{xy}{2}$ Ⓓ $\frac{3y^2}{2}$

25. Suppose the perimeter of the figure shown is 24 inches and the value of x is 6 inches. Find the value of y. B

Ⓐ 3 in. Ⓑ 4 in. Ⓒ 6 in. Ⓓ 9 in.

QUIZ for Lessons 1.4–1.5

Write an equation or an inequality. *(p. 21)*

1. 4 more than twice a number n is equal to 25. $2n + 4 = 25$

2. The quotient of a number x and 2 is no more than 9. $\frac{x}{2} \le 9$

Check whether the given number is a solution of the equation or inequality. *(p. 21)*

3. $13 - 2x = 5$; 4 solution 4. $5d - 4 \ge 16$; 4 solution 5. $4y + 3 \ge 15$; 3 solution

6. **CAR TRAVEL** One car travels about 28.5 miles on each gallon of gas. Suppose the average price of gas is $2 per gallon. About how much would the gas for a 978 mile trip cost? *(p. 28)* about $68.63

5 ASSESS AND RETEACH

Daily Homework Quiz

Transparency Available

1. Gerry is borrowing money from a friend at a simple interest rate of 4%. If she borrows $2000 and plans to pay it back in 2 years, how much interest will she owe? $160

2. A migrating whale is traveling at an average speed of 5.4 kilometers per hour. How far will the whale travel in 18 hours at this rate? 97.2 km

3. Skye sells baskets that she weaves from sweet grass. She makes a profit of $68 per basket and her expenses are $2.50 per basket. How much does she charge a customer for 3 baskets? $211.50

Online Quiz

Available at **classzone.com**

Diagnosis/Remediation

- Practice A, B, C in Chapter 1 Resource Book, pp. 51–53
- Study Guide in Chapter 1 Resource Book, pp. 54–55
- Practice Workbook, pp. 9–10
- @HomeTutor

Challenge

Additional challenge is available in the Chapter 1 Resource Book, p. 58.

Quiz

An easily-readable reduced copy of the quiz (with answers) on Lessons 1.4–1.5 from the Assessment Book can be found on p. 1E.

Alternative Strategy

Example 1 on page 28 can be solved by drawing a diagram. This method allows students to visualize the solution and will help them to better understand the algebraic solution given in Example 2 on page 29.

Teaching Strategy

Stress that each pair of rectangles represents running 4 long blocks and 2 short blocks. Point out how each figure is labeled to indicate the total distance along its outer edges. Emphasize that carefully drawing an accurate diagram improves one's chances of avoiding errors and solving the problem correctly.

An **Animated Algebra** activity is available on-line for the **Problem**. This activity is also available on the **Power Presentations CD-ROM**.

1. 9 pieces of cake; Draw a diagram of a 9 inch by 11 inch pan and divide it into 3 inch by 3 inch pieces. From the diagram you see that the cake can be divided into 9 pieces of cake.

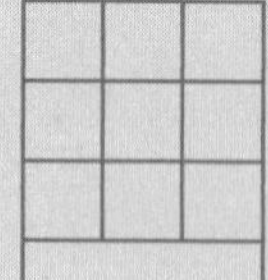

2. 2 ft. *Sample answer:* Method 1: Draw a diagram of the rope showing two of the floats 3 feet from each end. Divide the remaining rope so that the 4 floats are equally spaced. From the diagram you can see that there is 2 feet between consecutive floats.

3 ft | 2 ft | 2 ft | 2 ft | 3 ft

Method 2: Use the equation $3x + 6 = 12$ where 3 is the number of spaces between the floats, x is the length of space in between the floats, 6 is the total space at each end of the rope, and 12 is the total length of the rope. Solving the equation gives $x = 2$.

PROBLEM SOLVING WORKSHOP LESSON 1.5 Using ALTERNATIVE METHODS

Another Way to Solve Example 1, page 28

MULTIPLE REPRESENTATIONS In Example 1 on page 28, you saw how to solve a problem about running using an equation. You can also solve the problem by using the strategy *draw a diagram.*

PROBLEM

RUNNING You run in a city where the short blocks on north-south streets are 0.1 mile long. The long blocks on east-west streets are 0.15 mile long. You will run 2 long blocks east, a number of short blocks south, 2 long blocks west, then back to your starting point. You want to run a total of 2 miles. How many short blocks should you run?

METHOD

Drawing a Diagram You can draw a diagram to solve the problem.

STEP 1 **Read** the problem carefully. It tells you the lengths of a short block and a long block. You plan to run 4 long blocks and a distance of 2 miles.

STEP 2 **Draw** a pair of rectangles to represent running 1 short block in each direction. The total distance is $4(0.15) + 2(0.1) = 0.8$ mile. Continue adding pairs of rectangles until the total distance run is 2 miles.

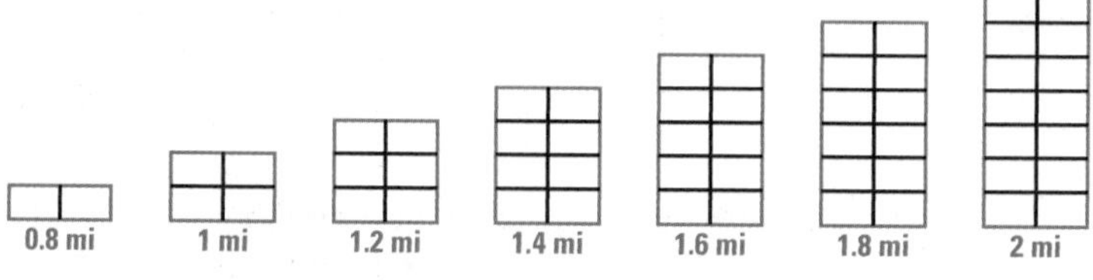

▸ You should run 14 short blocks.

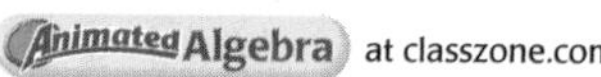

PRACTICE

1–4. See margin.

1. **BAKING** A cake pan is 9 inches wide and 11 inches long. How many 3 inch by 3 inch square pieces can you cut? Solve this problem using an equation. Then draw a diagram. *Explain* why a diagram is useful.

2. **SWIMMING** A 12 foot rope strung through 4 floats marks off the deep end of a pool. Each end of the rope is 3 feet from a float. The floats are equally spaced. How far apart are they? Solve this problem using two different methods.

3. **ERROR ANALYSIS** *Describe* and correct the error in solving Exercise 2.

$$4x + 6 = 12$$
$$4(1.5) + 6 = 12$$

The floats are 1.5 feet apart.

4. **GEOMETRY** The length of a rectangle is twice its width. The perimeter is 72 inches. What is its length? Solve this problem using two different methods.

3. The equation should be $3x + 6 = 12$ because there are only 3 spaces between the 4 floats; $3(2) + 6 = 12$.

4. 24 in. *Sample answer:* Method 1: Use the formula $P = 2\ell + 2w$ to find the length. Substitute 72 for P and $2w$ for ℓ to get the equation $72 = 2(2w) + 2w$. Solving the equation gives $w = 12$. If the length is $2w$, the length is 24 inches. Method 2: Draw a diagram of the rectangle. Label the width, w, and the length, $2w$. If you add up the sides to find the perimeter you will get the equation $6w = 72$. Solving the equation gives $w = 12$, so the length must be 24 inches.

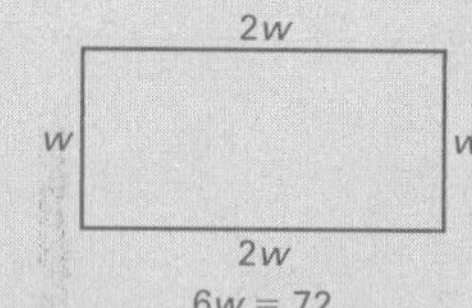

1.6 Represent Functions as Rules and Tables

 **8.11.12** Create and connect representations that are tabular, graphic, numeric, and symbolic from a set of data.

Before You wrote algebraic expressions and equations.

Now You will represent functions as rules and as tables.

Why? So you can describe consumer costs, as in Example 1.

Key Vocabulary
- function
- domain
- range
- independent variable
- dependent variable

When you pump gas, the total cost depends on the number of gallons pumped. The total cost is a *function* of the number of gallons pumped.

A **function** consists of:

- A set called the **domain** containing numbers called **inputs**, and a set called the **range** containing numbers called **outputs**.
- A pairing of inputs with outputs such that each input is paired with exactly one output.

EXAMPLE 1 Identify the domain and range of a function

The input-output table shows the cost of various amounts of regular unleaded gas from the same pump. Identify the domain and range of the function.

Input (gallons)	10	12	13	17
Output (dollars)	19.99	23.99	25.99	33.98

Solution

▶ The domain is the set of inputs: 10, 12, 13, and 17. The range is the set of outputs: 19.99, 23.99, 25.99, and 33.98.

✓ **GUIDED PRACTICE** for Example 1

1. Identify the domain and range of the function.
domain: 0, 1, 2, and 4, range: 1, 2, and 5

Input	0	1	2	4
Output	5	2	2	1

MAPPING DIAGRAMS A function may be represented by a *mapping diagram.* Notice that an output may be paired with more than one input, but no input is paired with more than one output.

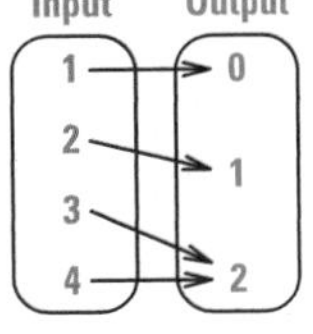

1 PLAN AND PREPARE

Warm-Up Exercises

Transparency Available

1. Write an expression: 7 more than a number x. $x + 7$
2. Determine if 3 is a solution of $2x - 4 = 2$. $2 = 2$; 3 is a solution.
3. Gae spent $4 more than twice as much as Casey at a store. If Casey spent $6, how much did Gae spend? $16

Notetaking Guide

Transparency Available

Promotes interactive learning and notetaking skills, pp. 16–18.

Pacing

Basic: 2 days
Average: 2 days
Advanced: 2 days
Block: 0.5 block with 1.5
0.5 block with 1.7

- See *Teaching Guide/Lesson Plan.*

2 FOCUS AND MOTIVATE

Essential Question

Big Idea 3, p. 1

How do you represent functions as tables and rules? Tell students they will learn how to answer this question by describing the relationships between domain and range, between input and output, and between independent and dependent variables.

Resource Planning Guide

Chapter Resource Book
- Teaching Guide/Lesson Plan (pp. 59–60)
- Activity Master (p. 61)
- Practice levels A, B, C (pp. 62–64)
- Study Guide (pp. 65–66)
- Catch-up for Absent Students (p. 67)
- Application (p. 68)
- Challenge (p. 69)

Workbooks
- Notetaking Guide (pp. 16–18)
- Practice Workbook (pp. 11–12)

Teaching Options
- **Power Presentations CD-ROM** provides dynamic electronic teaching resources for the classroom.
- **Activity Generator CD-ROM** provides editable activities for all ability levels.

Interactive Technology
- Easy Planner
- Power Presentations CD-ROM
- Activity Generator CD-ROM
- Animated Algebra
- Test Generator CD-ROM
- Online Quiz
- eWorkbook
- eEdition
- @HomeTutor

Resources for English Learners
- Quick Reference for English Learners
- Spanish Study Guide
- Multi-Language Visual Glossary
- Student Resources in Spanish

See also the *Algebra 1 Toolkit* for more strategies for meeting individual needs.

Motivating the Lesson

Students have already encountered situations where numerical data is presented in a table, such as the shipping costs for various package weights when ordering from a catalog. Ask them about other real-world situations where they have encountered data given in a table.

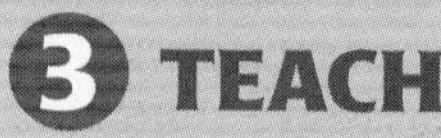

Extra Example 1

The input-output table shows the amount of money Miguel earns at his job for several numbers of hours. Identify the domain and range of the function.

Input (hours)	2	5	7	8
Output (dollars)	14	35	49	56

domain: 2, 5, 7, 8
range: 14, 35, 49, 56

Extra Example 2

Tell whether the pairing is a function.

a.

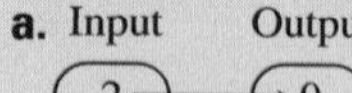

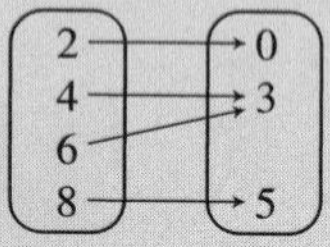

The pairing is a function, because each input is paired with exactly one output.

b.

Input	1	2	2	4
Output	2	3	4	6

The pairing is *not* a function, because the input 2 is paired with both 3 and 4.

Extra Example 3

The domain of the function $y = x + 4$ is 0, 2, 3, 6, and 7. Make a table for the function. Identify the range. range: 4, 6, 7, 10, 11

x	0	2	3	6	7
$y = x + 4$	4	6	7	10	11

EXAMPLE 2 Identify a function

Tell whether the pairing is a function.

a.

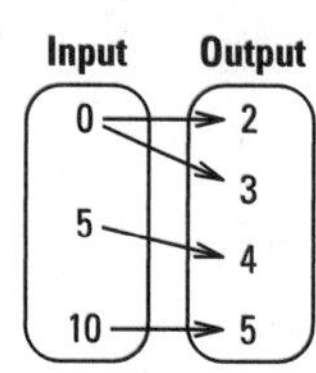

The pairing is *not* a function because the input 0 is paired with both 2 and 3.

b.

Input	Output
0	0
1	2
4	8
6	12

The pairing is a function because each input is paired with exactly one output.

✓ GUIDED PRACTICE for Example 2

Tell whether the pairing is a function.

2.

Input	3	6	9	12
Output	1	2	2	1

function

3.

Input	2	2	4	7
Output	0	1	2	3

not a function

FUNCTION RULES A function may be represented using a rule that relates one variable to another. The input variable is called the **independent variable.** The output variable is called the **dependent variable** because its value depends on the value of the input variable.

READING
Function rules typically give the dependent variable in terms of the independent variable. In an equation like $y = x + 3$, you know that y is the dependent variable.

KEY CONCEPT *For Your Notebook*

Functions

Verbal Rule
The output is 3 more than the input.

Equation
$y = x + 3$

Table

Input, x	0	1	2	3	4
Output, y	3	4	5	6	7

EXAMPLE 3 Make a table for a function

The domain of the function $y = 2x$ is 0, 2, 5, 7, and 8. Make a table for the function, then identify the range of the function.

Solution

x	0	2	5	7	8
$y = 2x$	$2(0) = 0$	$2(2) = 4$	$2(5) = 10$	$2(7) = 14$	$2(8) = 16$

The range of the function is 0, 4, 10, 14, and 16.

Differentiated Instruction

Visual Learners To help students remember that the input is the domain and the output is the range, show that the word pairings (domain, range) and (input, output) are both in alphabetical order. Emphasize that the first words in each pairing are associated with each other, as are the second words. This type of association can also be shown later in Lesson 1.7 with ordered pairs (x, y).

See also the *Algebra 1 Toolkit* for more strategies.

EXAMPLE 4 Write a function rule

Write a rule for the function.

Input	0	1	4	6	10
Output	2	3	6	8	12

Solution

Let x be the input, or independent variable, and let y be the output, or dependent variable. Notice that each output is 2 more than the corresponding input. So, a rule for the function is $y = x + 2$.

EXAMPLE 5 Write a function rule for a real-world situation

CONCERT TICKETS You are buying concert tickets that cost \$15 each. You can buy up to 6 tickets. Write the amount (in dollars) you spend as a function of the number of tickets you buy. Identify the independent and dependent variables. Then identify the domain and the range of the function.

Solution

CHOOSE A VARIABLE
To write a function rule for a real-world situation, choose letters for the variables that remind you of the quantities represented.

Write a verbal model. Then write a function rule. Let n represent the number of tickets purchased and A represent the amount spent (in dollars).

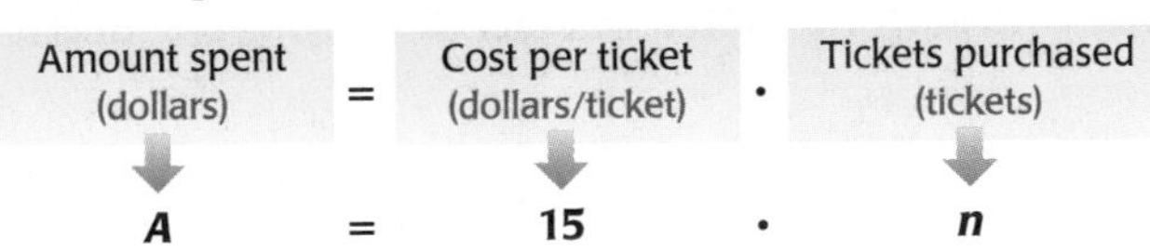

Amount spent (dollars) = Cost per ticket (dollars/ticket) · Tickets purchased (tickets)
A = 15 · n

So, the function rule is $A = 15n$. The amount spent depends on the number of tickets bought, so n is the independent variable and A is the dependent variable.

Because you can buy up to 6 tickets, the domain of the function is 0, 1, 2, 3, 4, 5, and 6. Make a table to identify the range.

Number of tickets, n	0	1	2	3	4	5	6
Amount (dollars), A	0	15	30	45	60	75	90

The range of the function is 0, 15, 30, 45, 60, 75, and 90.

Animated Algebra at classzone.com

✓ GUIDED PRACTICE for Examples 3, 4, and 5

4. Make a table for the function $y = x - 5$ with domain 10, 12, 15, 18, and 29. Then identify the range of the function. See margin.

5. Write a rule for the function. Identify the domain and the range.
$y = 8x$; domain: 1, 2, 3, and 4, range: 8, 16, 24, and 32

Time (hours)	1	2	3	4
Pay (dollars)	8	16	24	32

Extra Example 4

Write a rule for the function.

Input	1	2	4	7	9
Output	0	1	3	6	8

$y = x - 1$

Extra Example 5

At a community center, art lessons are offered at night. The fee is \$12 per lesson. You plan to attend up to 5 lessons. Write the amount you will spend as a function of the number of lessons you attend. Identify the independent and dependent variables. Then identify the domain and the range of the function. $A = 12n$; independent variable: n; dependent variable: A; domain: 0, 1, 2, 3, 4, 5; range: 0, 12, 24, 36, 48, 60

An **Animated Algebra** activity is available on-line for **Example 5**. This activity is also available on the **Power Presentations CD-ROM**.

Closing the Lesson

Have students summarize the major points of the lesson and answer the Essential Question: How do you represent functions as tables and as rules?

- For a function, no input value is paired with more than one output value.
- A function rule describes what must be done to the input to obtain the output.

To create a table for a function, use the domain of the function as the input values and apply the function rule to each input to find its corresponding output. To write a rule for a function, determine the pattern that links each dependent variable (output y) to its corresponding independent variable (input x).

4 PRACTICE AND APPLY

Assignment Guide

Answer Transparencies available for all exercises

Basic:
Day 1: pp. 38–40
Exs. 1–15
Day 2: pp. 38–40
Exs. 16–20, 23–27, 30–36

Average:
Day 1: pp. 38–40
Exs. 1, 2, 4, 5, 7–16
Day 2: pp. 38–40
Exs. 17–28, 30–36

Advanced:
Day 1: pp. 38–40
Exs. 1, 2, 5, 8, 11–13, 18, 19, 22*
Day 2: pp. 38–40
Exs. 23–36*

Block:
pp. 38–40
Exs. 1, 2, 4, 5, 7–16 (with 1.5)
pp. 38–40
Exs. 17–28, 30–36 (with 1.7)

Differentiated Instruction

See *Algebra 1 Best Practices Toolkit* for suggestions on addressing the needs of a diverse classroom.

Homework Check

For a quick check of student understanding of key concepts, go over the following exercises:

Basic: 3, 6, 15, 20, 23
Average: 4, 7, 16, 21, 24
Advanced: 5, 8, 18, 19, 25

Extra Practice

- Student Edition, p. 938
- Chapter 1 Resource Book: Practice levels A, B, C, pp. 62–64

Practice Worksheet

An easily-readable reduced practice page (with answers) for this lesson can be found on p. 1D.

1.6 EXERCISES

HOMEWORK KEY
○ = **WORKED-OUT SOLUTIONS** on p. WS2 for Exs. 7 and 23
★ = **STANDARDIZED TEST PRACTICE** Exs. 2, 11, 12, 13, 26, and 27
◆ = **MULTIPLE REPRESENTATIONS** Exs. 23 and 24

SKILL PRACTICE

A

1. **VOCABULARY** Copy and complete: A(n) _?_ is a number in the domain of a function. A(n) _?_ is a number in the range of a function. input; output

2. ★ **WRITING** In the equation $b = a - 2$, which variable is the independent variable and which is the dependent variable? *Explain.* a, b; the value of b depends on a.

EXAMPLES 1 and 2 on pp. 35–36 for Exs. 3–11

DOMAIN AND RANGE Identify the domain and range of the function.

3.

Input	Output
0	5
1	7
2	15
3	44

domain: 0, 1, 2, and 3, range: 5, 7, 15, and 44

4.

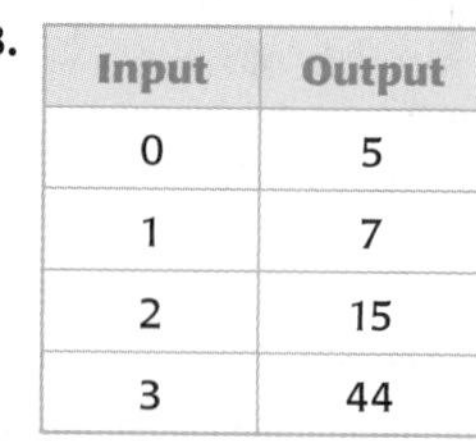

domain: 3, 5, 7, and 8, range: 2, 3, 5, and 7

5.

Input	Output
6	5
12	7
21	10
42	17

domain: 6, 12, 21, and 42, range: 5, 7, 10, and 17

IDENTIFYING FUNCTIONS Tell whether the pairing is a function.

6.

Input	Output
0	7.5
1	9.5
2	11.5
3	13.5

function

7.

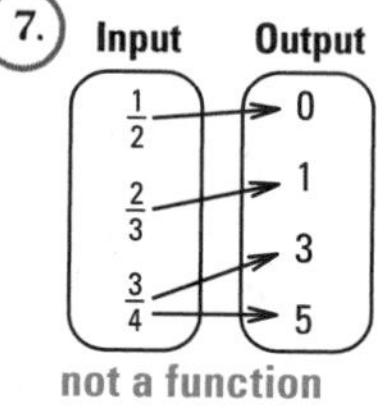

not a function

8.

Input	Output
7	13
11	8
21	13
35	20

function

ERROR ANALYSIS In Exercises 9 and 10, describe and correct the error related to the function represented by the table.

Input, x	1	2	3	4	5
Output, y	6	7	8	6	9

9, 10. See margin.

9. The pairing is not a function. One output is paired with two inputs. ✗

10. The pairing is a function. The range is 1, 2, 3, 4, and 5.

11. ★ **OPEN-ENDED** Draw a mapping diagram for a function with 6 inputs. Then make a table to represent the function. See margin.

EXAMPLES 3 and 4 on pp. 36–37 for Exs. 12–21

12. ★ **MULTIPLE CHOICE** The domain of the function $y = 5x - 1$ is 1, 3, 4, 5, and 6. Which number is in the range of the function? B

Ⓐ 0 Ⓑ 4 Ⓒ 9 Ⓓ 15

13. ★ **MULTIPLE CHOICE** Each output of a function is 0.5 less than the corresponding input. Which equation is a rule for the function? A

Ⓐ $y = x - 0.5$ Ⓑ $y = x + 0.5$ Ⓒ $y = 0.5 - x$ Ⓓ $y = 0.5x$

9. The pairing is a function. Each input is paired with only one output.

10. The numbers listed are the domain, not the range. The range of the function is 6, 7, 8, and 9.

11. *Sample:*

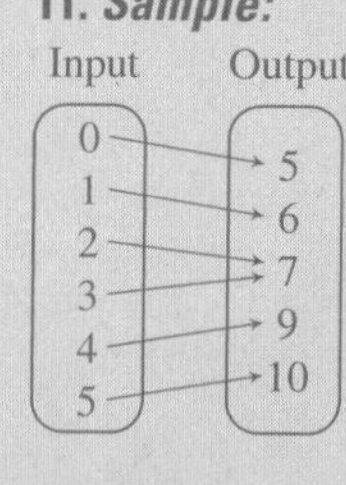

Input	Output
0	5
1	6
2	7
3	7
4	9
5	10

B **TABLES** **Make a table for the function. Identify the range of the function.**
14–19. See margin.

14. $y = x - 3$
Domain: 12, 15, 22, 30

15. $y = x + 3.5$
Domain: 4, 5, 7, 8, 12

16. $y = 3x + 4$
Domain: 0, 5, 7, 10

17. $y = \frac{1}{2}x + 3$
Domain: 4, 6, 9, 11

18. $y = \frac{2}{3}x + \frac{1}{3}$
Domain: 4, 6, 8, 12

19. $y = \frac{0.5x + 1}{2}$
Domain: 0, 2, 4, 6

FUNCTION RULES **Write a rule for the function.**

20.

Input, x	0	1	2	3
Output, y	2.2	3.2	4.2	5.2

$y = x + 2.2$

21.

Input, x	15	20	21	30	42
Output, y	7	12	13	22	34

$y = x - 8$

C **22. CHALLENGE** Fill in the table in such a way that when t is the independent variable, the pairing is a function, and when t is the dependent variable, the pairing is not a function.

Sample answer:

t	? 1	? 2	? 3	? 4
v	? 2	? 2	? 3	? 3

PROBLEM SOLVING

EXAMPLE 5 A on p. 37 for Exs. 23–26

23a. the number of quarters left; the number of quarters used

23. ◆ **MULTIPLE REPRESENTATIONS** You have 10 quarters that you can use for a parking meter.

a. **Describing in Words** Copy and complete: Each time you put 1 quarter in the meter, you have 1 less quarter, so _?_ is a function of _?_.

b. **Writing a Rule** Write a rule for the number y of quarters that you have left as a function of the number x of quarters you have used so far. Identify the domain of the function. $y = 10 - x$; domain: 0, 1, 2, 3, 4, 5, 6, 7, 8, 9, and 10

c. **Making a Table** Make a table and identify the range of the function. Range: 0, 1, 2, 3, 4, 5, 6, 7, 8, 9, and 10; see margin.

@HomeTutor for problem solving help at classzone.com

24. ◆ **MULTIPLE REPRESENTATIONS** At a yard sale, you find 5 paperback books by your favorite author. Each book is priced at $.75.

a. **Describing in Words** Copy and complete: For each book you buy, you spend $.75, so _?_ is a function of _?_. amount of money you spend; the number of books you buy

b. **Writing a Rule** Write a rule for the amount (in dollars) you spend as a function of the number of books you buy. Identify the domain of the function. $y = \$.75x$; domain: 0, 1, 2, 3, 4, and 5

c. **Making a Table** Make a table and identify the range of the function. Range: 0, 0.75, 1.5, 2.25, 3, and 3.75; see margin.

@HomeTutor for problem solving help at classzone.com

25. SAVINGS You have $100 saved and plan to save $20 each month. Write a rule for the amount saved (in dollars) as a function of the number of months from now. Identify the independent and dependent variables, the domain, and the range. How much will you have saved altogether 12 months from now? $y = 100 + 20m$; independent variable: m, the number of months; dependent variable: y, the amount of money saved; domain: $m > 0$, range: $y \geq 100$; $340

26. ★ **OPEN-ENDED** Write a function rule that models a real-world situation. Identify the independent variable and the dependent variable. *Sample answer:* $W = 8h$, where W is wages and h is hours worked; the independent variable is h, the dependent variable is W.

Vocabulary

Exercises 3–8 For students who confuse the connection between the terms *input* and *domain* and between the terms *output* and *range*, suggest they use the memory clue "*i* comes before *o* like *d* comes before *r*, so *input* goes with *domain* and *output* goes with *range*."

Avoiding Common Errors

Exercises 20–21 Some students may write the input as a function of the output. Remind them that the output is always a result of having done something with the input. Stress that they need to look at what must be done with the input value in order to obtain the corresponding output value.

Study Strategy

Exercise 25 To help students solve this problem, suggest they use Example 5 as a model. Point out that the problem states $100 is already saved, so students will need to show the addition of this amount in their rule.

14.

Input	12	15	22	30
Output	9	12	19	27

range: 9, 12, 19, and 27

15. See below.

16.

Input	0	5	7	10
Output	4	19	25	34

range: 4, 19, 25, and 34

17.

Input	4	6	9	11
Output	5	6	7.5	8.5

range: 5, 6, 7.5, and 8.5

18.

Input	4	6	8	12
Output	3	$4\frac{1}{3}$	$5\frac{2}{3}$	$8\frac{1}{3}$

range: 3, $4\frac{1}{3}$, $5\frac{2}{3}$, and $8\frac{1}{3}$

19.

Input	0	2	4	6
Output	$\frac{1}{2}$	1	$1\frac{1}{2}$	2

range: $\frac{1}{2}$, 1, $1\frac{1}{2}$, and 2

15.

Input	4	5	7	8	12
Output	7.5	8.5	10.5	11.5	15.5

range: 7.5, 8.5, 10.5, 11.5, and 15.5

23c.

Input	0	1	2	3	4	5	6	7	8	9	10
Output	10	9	8	7	6	5	4	3	2	1	0

24c.

Input	0	1	2	3	4	5
Output	0	0.75	1.5	2.25	3	3.75

5 ASSESS AND RETEACH

Daily Homework Quiz

Transparency Available

1. The domain of the function $y = \frac{2}{3}x + 1$ is 0, 3, 6, and 9. Make a table for the function. Identify the range of the function.

x	0	3	6	9
y	1	3	5	7

range: 1, 3, 5, 7

2. Write a rule for the function.

Input, x	2	3	4	5
Output, y	3	4.5	6	7.5

$y = 1.5x$

3. Jasmine sells bracelets. Her profit on each bracelet is $8. Write a rule that shows her total profit p as a function of the number of bracelets b she sells. Write the range of the function if the domain is 5, 10, 15, 20, and 25. $p = 8b$; range: 40, 80, 120, 160, 200

Available at **classzone.com**

Diagnosis/Remediation

- Practice A, B, C in Chapter 1 Resource Book, pp. 62–64
- Study Guide in Chapter 1 Resource Book, pp. 65–66
- Practice Workbook, pp. 11–12
- @HomeTutor

Challenge

Additional challenge is available in the Chapter 1 Resource Book, p. 69.

27a–b. See Additional Answers beginning on p. AA1.

27a, b. See margin.

B **27.** ★ **SHORT RESPONSE** Consider a pairing of the digits 2 through 9 on a telephone keypad with the associated letters.

a. Make a table showing the pairing with the digits as inputs and the letters as outputs. Is the pairing a function? *Explain.*

b. Make a table showing the pairing with the letters as inputs and the digits as outputs. Is the pairing a function? *Explain.*

28. **MULTI-STEP PROBLEM** The table shows the fuel efficiency of four compact cars from one manufacturer for model year 2004.

City fuel efficiency (mi/gal), c	24	26	27	28
Highway fuel efficiency (mi/gal), h	32	34	35	36

a. Write a Rule Use the table to write a rule for the cars' highway fuel efficiency as a function of their city fuel efficiency. $h = c + 8$

b. Predict Another of the manufacturer's compact cars has a city fuel efficiency of 30 miles per gallon. Predict the highway fuel efficiency. 38 mi/gal

c. Calculate A study found that if gas costs $2 per gallon, you can use the expression $\frac{11{,}550}{c} + \frac{9450}{h}$ to estimate a car's annual fuel cost (in dollars) for a typical driver. Evaluate the expression for the car in part (b). about $634

C **29.** **CHALLENGE** Each week you spend a total of 5 hours exercising. You swim part of the time and bike the rest.

300 calories per hour

440 calories per hour

a. Write a rule for the total number of calories you burn for the whole 5 hours as a function of the time you spend swimming. $c = 300s + 440(5 - s)$

b. One week you spend half the time swimming. How many calories do you burn during the whole 5 hours? 1850 cal

ILLINOIS MIXED REVIEW

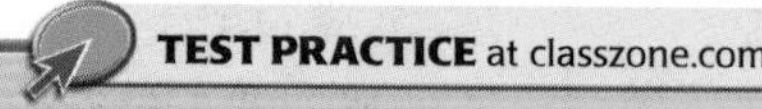

30. A train averages a speed of 75 miles per hour on a 300 mile trip. The train travels within a single time zone and leaves at 1 P.M. What time will the train arrive at its destination? D

(A) 3:00 P.M. (B) 3:30 P.M. (C) 4 P.M. (D) 5 P.M.

31. You pay a $5 processing fee to order concert tickets no matter how many tickets you order. Each ticket costs $18. Which equation best represents c, the total cost of ordering n tickets? A

(A) $c = 18n + 5$ (B) $18 = cn + 5$ (C) $c = 18(n + 5)$ (D) $18 = c(n + 5)$

@HomeTutor
classzone.com
Keystrokes

1.6 Make a Table

QUESTION **How can you use a graphing calculator to create a table for a function?**

You can use a graphing calculator to create a table for a function when you want to display many pairs of input values and output values or when you want to find the input value that corresponds to a given output value.

In the example below, you will make a table to compare temperatures in degrees Celsius and temperatures in degrees Fahrenheit for temperatures at or above the temperature at which water freezes, 32°F.

EXAMPLE **Use a graphing calculator to make a table**

The formula $C = \frac{5}{9}(F - 32)$ gives the temperature in degrees Celsius as a function of the temperature in degrees Fahrenheit. Make a table for the function.

STEP 1 ***Enter equation***
Rewrite the function using x for F and y for C. Press [Y=] and enter $\frac{5}{9}(x - 32)$.

```
Y1=(5/9)(X-32)
Y2=
Y3=
Y4=
Y5=
Y6=
Y7=
```

STEP 2 ***Set up table***
Go to the TABLE SETUP screen. Use a starting value (TblStart) of 32 and an increment (ΔTbl) of 1.

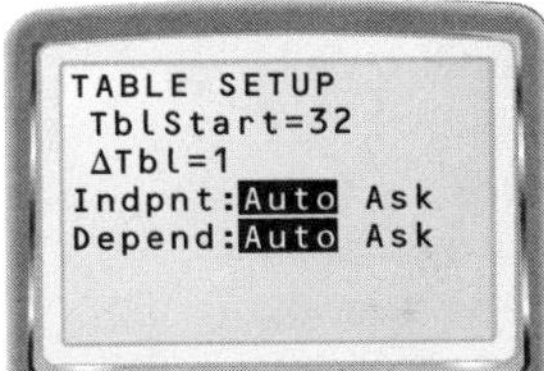

STEP 3 ***View table***
Display the table. Scroll down to see pairs of inputs and outputs.

X	Y1	Y2
32	0	
33	.55556	
34	1.1111	
35	1.6667	
36	2.2222	
37	2.7778	

PRACTICE

1. You see a sign that indicates that the outdoor temperature is 10°C. Find the temperature in degrees Fahrenheit. *Explain* how you found your answer. 50°F; scroll down until you see the output 10, look to see that the input is 50.
2. Water boils at 100°C. What is the temperature in degrees Fahrenheit? 212°F

Make a table for the function. Use the given starting value and increment. 3–6. See margin.

3. $y = \frac{3}{4}x + 5$
   TblStart = 0, ΔTbl = 1
4. $y = 4x + 2$
   TblStart = 0, ΔTbl = 0.5
5. $y = 7.5x - 0.5$
   TblStart = 1, ΔTbl = 1
6. $y = 0.5x + 6$
   TblStart = 3, ΔTbl = 3

1 PLAN AND PREPARE

Learn the Method

- Students will use a graphing calculator to make a table for a function.
- Students can use the skills learned in this activity to check their tables in Exercises 14–19 in Lesson 1.6.

Keystroke Help

Keystrokes for several models of calculators are available in blackline format in the *Chapter 1 Resource Book*.

2 TEACH

Tips for Success

When discussing Step 3, point out to students that the values for x and y are shown in the columns labeled X and Y_1, respectively. You may also wish to point out the unused column labeled Y_2. Remind students that the values in the X column are those for the variable F in the formula, and the values in the Y_1 column are those for the variable C.

Extra Example

Use your calculator to make a table for the function $y = 2x + 4$. Use a starting value of 4 and an increment of 0.25. Use your table to find the output when the input is 8.75. 21.5

3 ASSESS AND RETEACH

1. What are the key items you need to enter into the calculator to have it set up a table? the function, the starting value, and the increment
2. Explain how you would use the table in Step 3 to find the Celsius temperature that is equivalent to 98°F. Scroll down the table until you locate the value 98 in the X-column, and read the corresponding value in the Y_1-column.

3.

Input	0	1	2	3
Output	5	5.75	6.5	7.25

4.

Input	0	0.5	1	1.5
Output	2	4	6	8

5.

Input	1	2	3	4
Output	7	14.5	22	29.5

6.

Input	3	6	9	12
Output	7.5	9	10.5	12

1 PLAN AND PREPARE

Explore the Concept

- Students will collect data and make a scatter plot.
- This activity leads into the study of graphing data in Example 2 in Lesson 1.7.

Materials

Each group of students will need:

- tape measure
- graph paper

Recommended Time

Work activity: 15 min

Discuss results: 5 min

Grouping

Students can work in groups of 6–8. Students should take turns doing the measurements, recording the results, and plotting the points. All students should check the accuracy of the graph against the recorded results.

2 TEACH

Tips for Success

Exercise 3 hints at the vertical line test to determine if a relation is a function. If students are having trouble discovering this, you should lead them to seeing it. The vertical line test will be covered in the Extension on pages 49–50.

Key Discovery

You can plot points on a graph to show the relationship between two sets of data and to see if that relationship is a function.

3 ASSESS AND RETEACH

Do all scatter plots represent functions? Explain. No. Some scatter plots do not represent a function because there are some inputs that have more than one output associated with them.

1.7 Scatter Plots and Functions

MATERIALS • tape measure • graph paper

QUESTION **How can you tell whether a graph represents a function?**

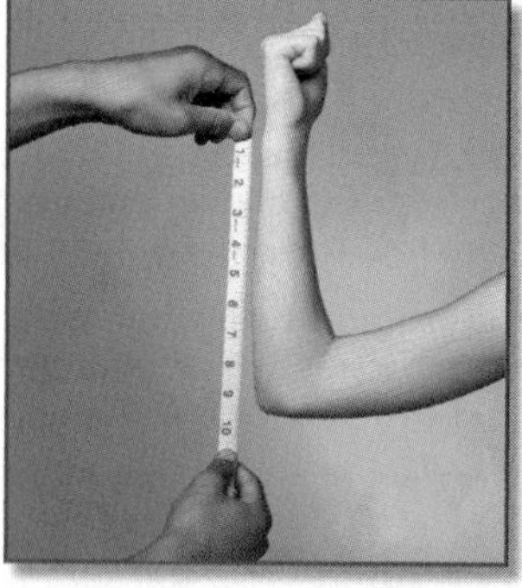

A *scatter plot* is a type of display for paired data. Each data pair is plotted as a point. In this activity, you will work in a group to make a scatter plot. You will measure the height of each student in your group and the length of his or her forearm. The length of the forearm is the distance from the elbow to the wrist.

EXPLORE **Collect data and make a scatter plot**

STEP 1 ***Collect data*** Measure the height of each student in your group and the length of his or her forearm. Record the results for each student in one row of a table like the one shown.

Height (inches)	Forearm length (inches)
63	10
?	?

STEP 2 ***Make a scatter plot*** Use graph paper to draw axes labeled as shown. Then plot the data pairs (*height*, *forearm length*). For example, plot the point (63, 10) for a student with a height of 63 inches and a forearm length of 10 inches.

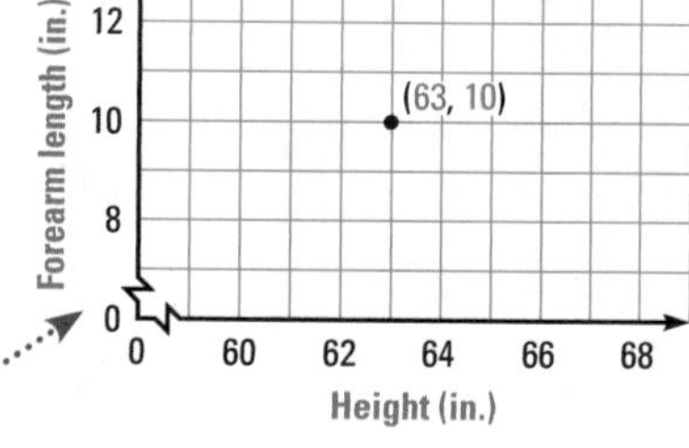

The symbol ⌇ on an axis represents a break in the axis.

DRAW CONCLUSIONS **Use your observations to complete these exercises**

1. Examine your scatter plot. What does it suggest about the relationship between a person's height and the person's forearm length?
   Sample answer: The greater the person's height, the greater the length of the forearm.
2. Compare your table with those of the other groups in your class. Determine which of the tables represent functions and which do not.
   Answers will vary. Tables that are functions should have only one forearm length for each height.
3. Is it possible to determine whether a table represents a function by looking at the corresponding scatter plot? *Explain.*
   Yes; if there is more than one y for an x it is not a function.

1.7 Represent Functions as Graphs

8.11.12	Create and connect representations that are tabular, graphic, numeric, and symbolic from a set of data.
Before	You represented functions as rules and tables.
Now	You will represent functions as graphs.
Why?	So you can describe sales trends, as in Example 4.

Key Vocabulary
- **function,** *p. 35*
- **domain,** *p. 35*
- **range,** *p. 35*

REVIEW THE COORDINATE PLANE
For help with the coordinate plane, see p. 921.

You can use a graph to represent a function. Given a table that represents a function, each corresponding pair of input and output values forms an ordered pair of numbers that can be plotted as a point. The x-coordinate is the input. The y-coordinate is the output.

Table

Input, x	Output, y
1	2
2	3
4	5

Ordered Pairs

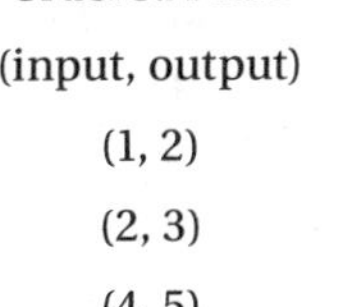

(input, output)
(1, 2)
(2, 3)
(4, 5)

Graph

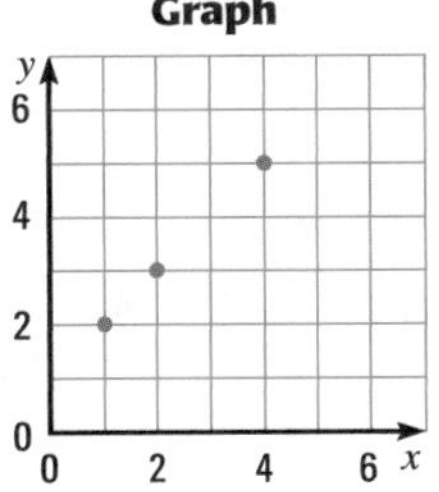

The horizontal axis of the graph is labeled with the input variable. The vertical axis is labeled with the output variable.

EXAMPLE 1 Graph a function

Graph the function $y = \frac{1}{2}x$ with domain 0, 2, 4, 6, and 8.

Solution

STEP 1 **Make** an input-output table.

x	0	2	4	6	8
y	0	1	2	3	4

STEP 2 **Plot** a point for each ordered pair (x, y).

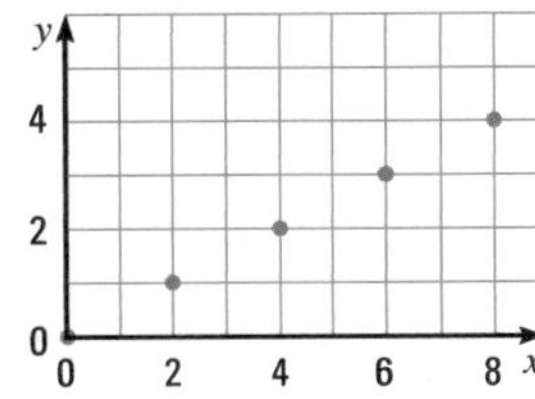

✓ GUIDED PRACTICE for Example 1

1. Graph the function $y = 2x - 1$ with domain 1, 2, 3, 4, and 5. See margin on p. 45.

1 PLAN AND PREPARE

Warm-Up Exercises

Transparency Available

1. Make a table for $y = 2x + 3$ with domain 0, 3, 6, and 9.

x	0	3	6	9
y	3	9	15	21

2. Write a rule for the function.

Input, x	0	2	4	9
Output, y	1	7	13	28

$y = 3x + 1$

Notetaking Guide

Transparency Available

Promotes interactive learning and notetaking skills, pp. 19–21.

Pacing

Basic: 1 day
Average: 1 day
Advanced: 1 day
Block: 0.5 block with 1.6
- See *Teaching Guide/Lesson Plan.*

2 FOCUS AND MOTIVATE

Essential Question

Big Idea 3, p. 1

How do you represent functions as graphs? Tell students they will learn how to answer this question by using the function's domain, range, and a table of values.

Resource Planning Guide

Chapter Resource Book
- Teaching Guide/Lesson Plan (pp. 70–71)
- Practice levels A, B, C (pp. 72–77)
- Study Guide (pp. 78–79)
- Catch-up for Absent Students (p. 80)
- Problem Solving Workshop (p. 81)
- Challenge (p. 82)

Workbooks
- Notetaking Guide (pp. 19–21)
- Practice Workbook (pp. 13–15)

Teaching Options
- **Power Presentations CD-ROM** provides dynamic electronic teaching resources for the classroom.
- **Activity Generator CD-ROM** provides editable activities for all ability levels.

Interactive Technology
- Easy Planner
- Power Presentations CD-ROM
- Activity Generator CD-ROM
- Animated Algebra
- Test Generator CD-ROM
- Online Quiz
- eWorkbook
- eEdition
- @HomeTutor

Resources for English Learners
- Quick Reference for English Learners
- Spanish Study Guide
- Multi-Language Visual Glossary
- Student Resources in Spanish

See also the *Algebra 1 Toolkit* for more strategies for meeting individual needs.

Motivating the Lesson

Tell students that graphs help to visualize the relationships between data values and that makes these relationships easier to recognize. Ask students to share instances where graphs have helped them to more easily visualize relationships.

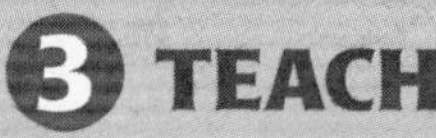

Extra Example 1

Graph the function $y = 2x - 3$ with domain 2, 3, 4, and 5.

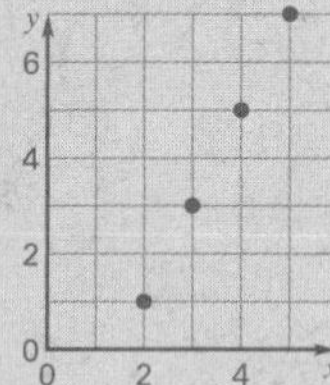

Extra Example 2

The table shows the profit p (in thousands of dollars) at a small toy store each year from 2000 to 2004 as a function of the time t in years since 2000. Graph the function.

t	0	1	2	3	4
p	19.5	20.3	22.7	21.1	21.8

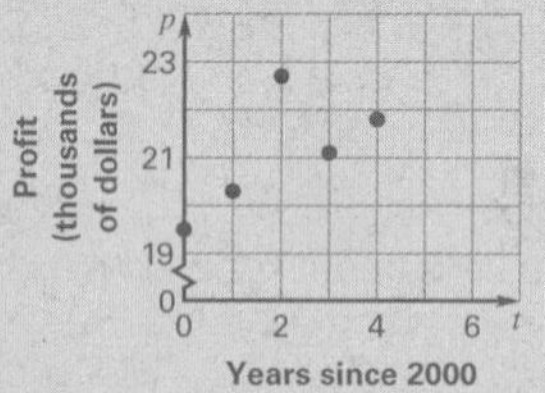

Extra Example 3

Write a rule for the function represented by the graph. Identify the domain and the range of the function.

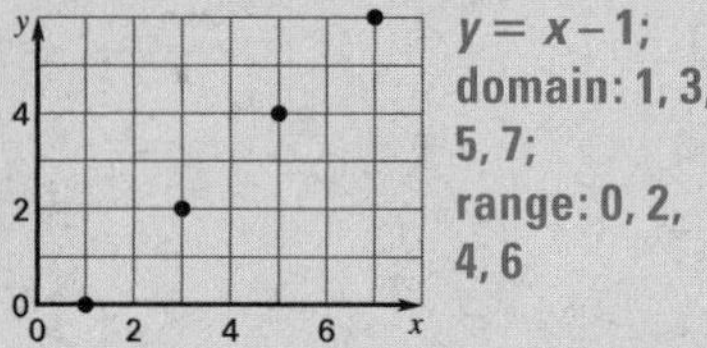

$y = x - 1$; domain: 1, 3, 5, 7; range: 0, 2, 4, 6

EXAMPLE 2 Graph a function

SAT SCORES The table shows the average score s on the mathematics section of the Scholastic Aptitude Test (SAT) in the United States from 1997 to 2003 as a function of the time t in years since 1997. In the table, 0 corresponds to the year 1997, 1 corresponds to 1998, and so on. Graph the function.

Years since 1997, t	0	1	2	3	4	5	6
Average score, s	511	512	511	514	514	516	519

Solution

READING

The symbol ⸗ on the vertical number line represents a break in the axis.

STEP 1 **Choose** a scale. The scale should allow you to plot all the points on a graph that is a reasonable size.

- The t-values range from 0 to 6, so label the t-axis from 0 to 6 in increments of 1 unit.
- The s-values range from 511 to 519, so label the s-axis from 510 to 520 in increments of 2 units.

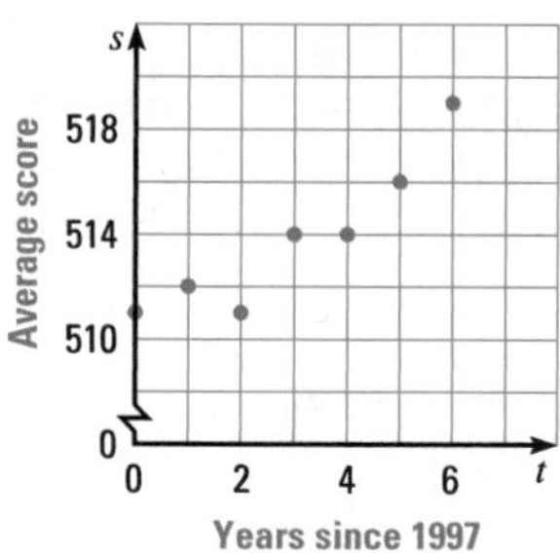

STEP 2 **Plot** the points.

✓ GUIDED PRACTICE for Example 2

2. **WHAT IF?** In Example 2, suppose that you use a scale on the s-axis from 0 to 520 in increments of 1 unit. *Describe* the appearance of the graph.
Sample answer: The graph would be very large with all the points near the top of the graph.

EXAMPLE 3 Write a function rule for a graph

Write a rule for the function represented by the graph. Identify the domain and the range of the function.

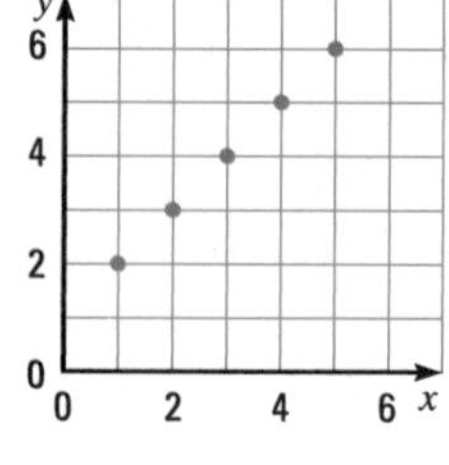

Solution

STEP 1 **Make** a table for the graph.

x	1	2	3	4	5
y	2	3	4	5	6

STEP 2 **Find** a relationship between the inputs and the outputs. Notice from the table that each output value is 1 more than the corresponding input value.

STEP 3 **Write** a function rule that describes the relationship: $y = x + 1$.

▶ A rule for the function is $y = x + 1$. The domain of the function is 1, 2, 3, 4, and 5. The range is 2, 3, 4, 5, and 6.

Differentiated Instruction

Inclusion Some students may find it counterintuitive to think of x-values increasing to the right and y-values increasing upward. Due to this, they may have difficulty constructing graphs on a coordinate plane. Have these students draw coordinate planes by first drawing the x- and y-axes with the arrows properly indicating the increasing direction of the x- and y-values.

See also the *Algebra 1 Toolkit* for more strategies.

GUIDED PRACTICE for Example 3

Write a rule for the function represented by the graph. Identify the domain and the range of the function.

3.

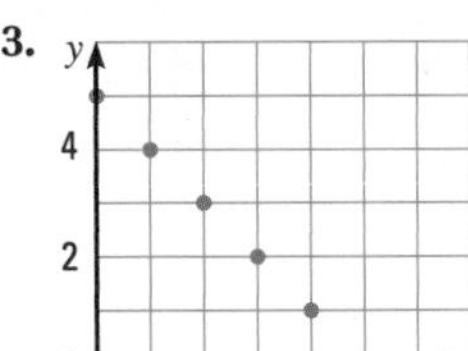

$y = 5 - x$; domain: 0, 1, 2, 3, and 4, range: 1, 2, 3, 4, and 5

4.

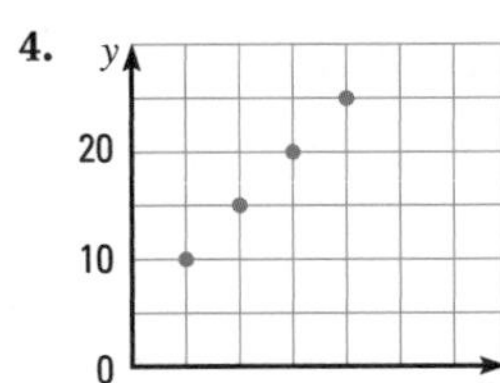

$y = 5x + 5$; domain: 1, 2, 3, and 4, range: 10, 15, 20, and 25

EXAMPLE 4 Analyze a graph

GUITAR SALES The graph shows guitar sales (in millions of dollars) for a chain of music stores for the period 1999–2005. Identify the independent variable and the dependent variable. Describe how sales changed over the period and how you would expect sales in 2006 to compare to sales in 2005.

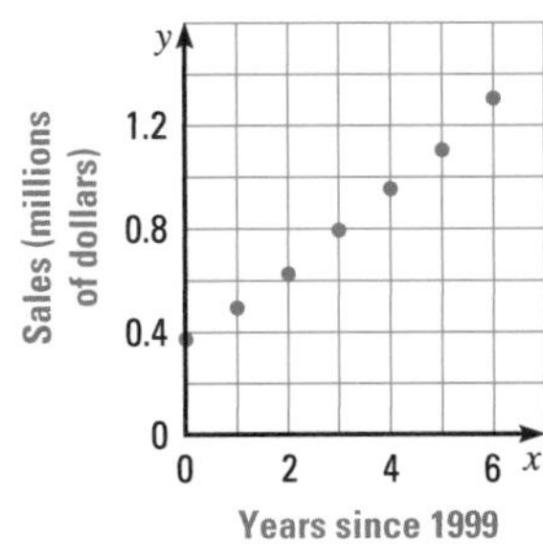

Solution

The independent variable is the number of years since 1999. The dependent variable is the sales (in millions of dollars). The graph shows that sales were increasing. If the trend continued, sales would be greater in 2006 than in 2005.

GUIDED PRACTICE for Example 4

5. **REASONING** Based on the graph in Example 4, is \$1.4 million a reasonable prediction of the chain's sales for 2006? *Explain.*
Yes; the graph seems to increase about \$0.2 million every two years.

CONCEPT SUMMARY *For Your Notebook*

Ways to Represent a Function

You can use a verbal rule, an equation, a table, or a graph to represent a function.

Verbal Rule

The output is 1 less than twice the input.

Equation

$y = 2x - 1$

Table

x	y
1	1
2	3
3	5
4	7

Graph

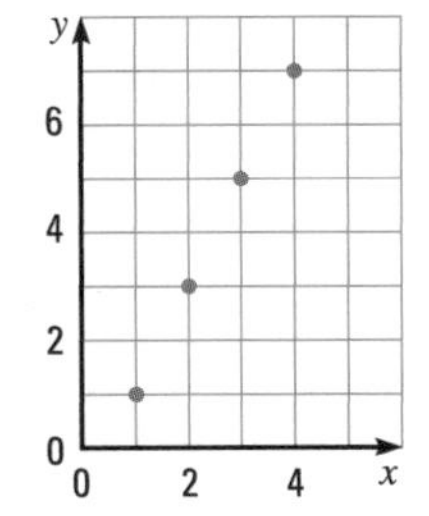

Extra Example 4

The graph shows the average number of video rentals per month at a video store for the years 2000–2006. Identify the independent variable and the dependent variable. Describe how the average number of rentals changed over the period and how you would expect the average number of rentals in 2006 to compare to the number in 2007.

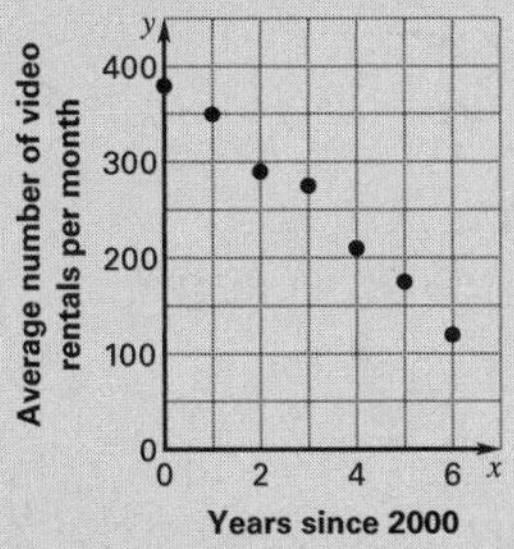

independent variable: years since 2000; dependent variable: average number of video rentals per month; The graph shows that the average number of video rentals per month was decreasing. If the trend continued, the average number of rentals in 2007 would be less than in 2006.

Closing the Lesson

Have students summarize the major points of the lesson and answer the Essential Question: How do you represent functions as graphs?

- You can use a graph to represent a function.
- An input-output table can be used to write a rule for a function whose graph is given.

You can graph a function by using its domain and function rule to create an input-output table, and then by graphing points for each ordered pair in the table.

p. 43

1.

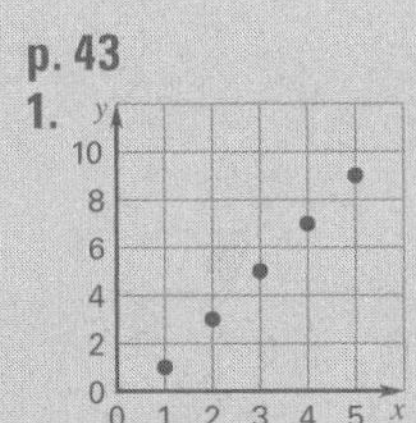

1.7 EXERCISES

HOMEWORK KEY
◯ = **WORKED-OUT SOLUTIONS** on p. WS2 for Exs. 3 and 17
★ = **STANDARDIZED TEST PRACTICE** Exs. 2, 13, 18, 19, and 20

4 PRACTICE AND APPLY

Assignment Guide

Answer Transparencies available for all exercises

Basic:
Day 1: pp. 46–48
Exs. 1–11, 15–19, 21–30

Average:
Day 1: pp. 46–48
Exs. 1, 2, 4–13, 15–19, 21–30

Advanced:
Day 1: pp. 46–48
Exs. 1, 2, 6–8, 11–20*, 23–30

Block:
pp. 46–48
Exs. 1, 2, 4–13, 15–19, 21–30 (with 1.6)

Differentiated Instruction

See *Algebra 1 Best Practices Toolkit* for suggestions on addressing the needs of a diverse classroom.

Homework Check

For a quick check of student understanding of key concepts, go over the following exercises:

Basic: 3, 6, 10, 15, 18
Average: 5, 11, 16, 18, 19
Advanced: 6, 12, 17, 18, 19

Extra Practice

- Student Edition, p. 938
- Chapter 1 Resource Book: Practice levels A, B, C, pp. 72–77

Practice Worksheet

An easily-readable reduced practice page (with answers) for this lesson can be found on p. 1D.

SKILL PRACTICE

A

1. **VOCABULARY** Copy and complete: Each point on the graph of a function corresponds to an ordered pair (x, y) where x is in the _?_ of the function and y is in the _?_ of the function. **domain; range**

2. ★ **WRITING** Given the graph of a function, describe how to write a rule for the function. **Find a relationship between the input values and the output values.**

EXAMPLE 1 on p. 43 for Exs. 3–9

GRAPHING FUNCTIONS **Graph the function.** **3–8. See margin.**

3. $y = x + 3$; domain: 0, 1, 2, 3, 4, and 5
4. $y = \frac{1}{2}x + 1$; domain: 0, 1, 2, 3, 4, and 5
5. $y = 2x + 2$; domain: 0, 2, 5, 7, and 10
6. $y = 3x - 1$; domain: 1, 2, 3, 4, and 5
7. $y = x + 5$; domain: 0, 2, 4, 6, 8, and 10
8. $y = 2.5x$; domain: 0, 1, 2, 3, and 4

9. **ERROR ANALYSIS** *Describe* and correct the error in graphing the function $y = x - 1$ with domain 1, 2, 3, 4, and 5.
The domain and range are graphed backwards; see margin.

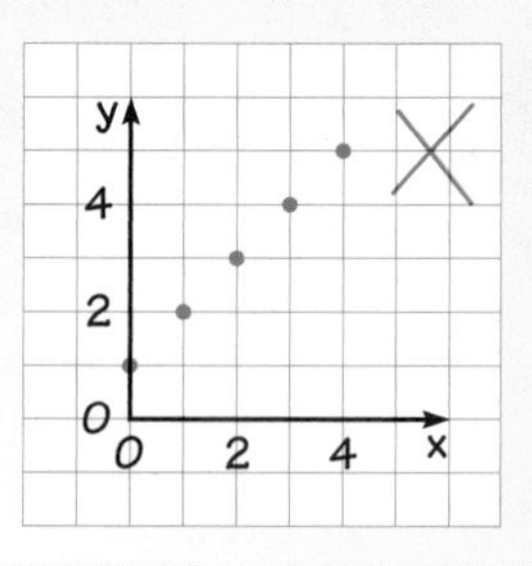

EXAMPLE 3 on p. 44 for Exs. 10–12

B

WRITING FUNCTION RULES **Write a rule for the function represented by the graph. Identify the domain and the range of the function.** **10–12. See margin.**

10.
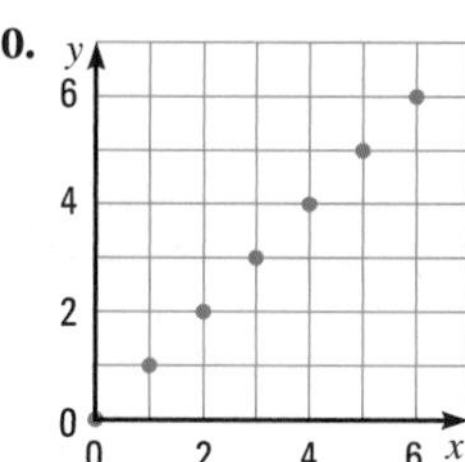

11.
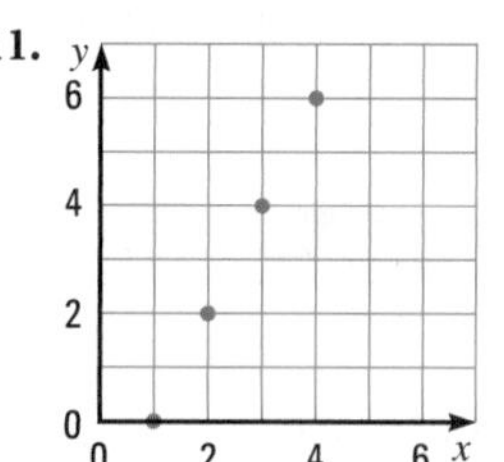

12.
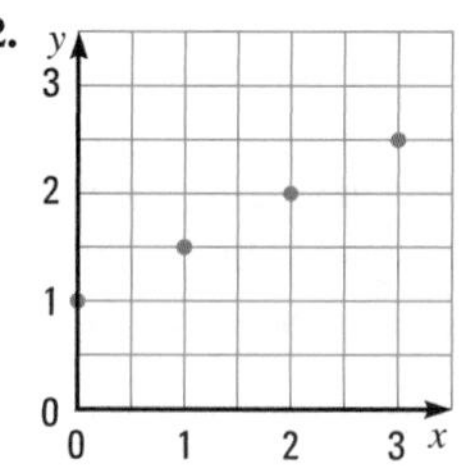

13. ★ **MULTIPLE CHOICE** The graph of which function is shown? **C**

Ⓐ $y = \frac{1}{2}x + \frac{1}{2}$
Ⓑ $y = x + \frac{1}{2}$
Ⓒ $y = \frac{3}{2}x + \frac{1}{2}$
Ⓓ $y = 2x + \frac{1}{2}$

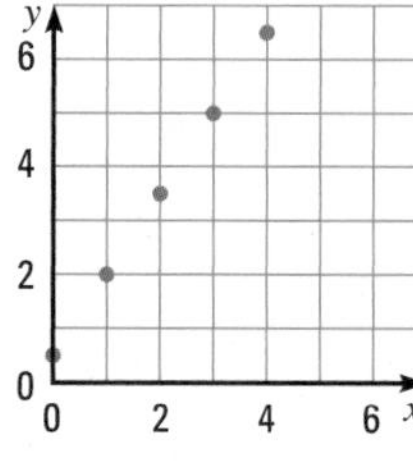

3–8. See Additional Answers beginning on p. AA1.

9.
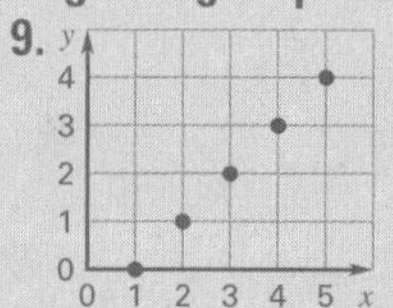

10. $y = x$; **domain: 0, 1, 2, 3, 4, 5, and 6, range: 0, 1, 2, 3, 4, 5, and 6**

11. $y = 2x - 2$; **domain: 1, 2, 3, and 4, range: 0, 2, 4, and 6**

12. $y = \frac{1}{2}x + 1$; **domain: 0, 1, 2, and 3, range: 1, $1\frac{1}{2}$, 2, $2\frac{1}{2}$**

15.
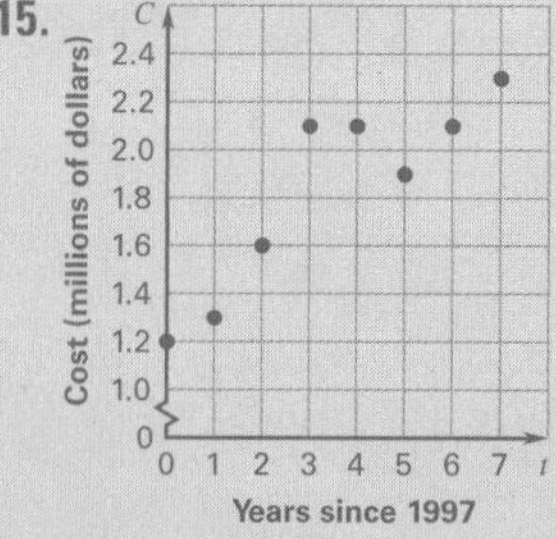

C 14. **CHALLENGE** The graph represents a function.

a. Write a rule for the function. $\frac{1}{2}x^2$

b. Find the value of y so that $(1.5, y)$ is on the graph of the function. 1.125

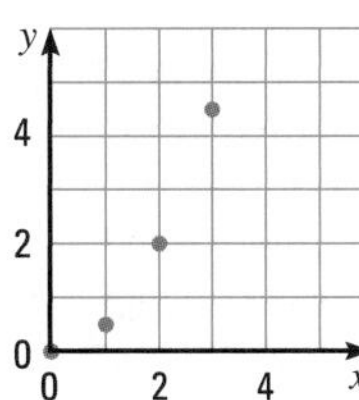

PROBLEM SOLVING

EXAMPLE 2 A on p. 44 for Exs. 15–17

15. **ADVERTISING** The table shows the cost C (in millions of dollars) of a 30 second Super Bowl ad on TV as a function of the time t (in years) since 1997. Graph the function. See margin.

Years since 1997, t	0	1	2	3	4	5	6	7
Cost (millions of dollars), C	1.2	1.3	1.6	2.1	2.1	1.9	2.1	2.3

@HomeTutor for problem solving help at classzone.com

16. **CONGRESS** The table shows the number r of U.S. representatives for Texas as a function of the time t (in years) since 1930. Graph the function. See margin.

Years since 1930, t	0	10	20	30	40	50	60	70
Number of representatives, r	21	21	22	23	24	27	30	32

@HomeTutor for problem solving help at classzone.com

17. **ELECTIONS** The table shows the number v of voters in U.S. presidential elections as a function of the time t (in years) since 1984. First copy and complete the table. Round to the nearest million. Then graph the function represented by the first and third columns. See margin for art.

Years since 1984	Voters	Voters (millions)
0	92,652,680	? 93
4	91,594,693	? 92
8	104,405,155	? 104
12	96,456,345	? 96
16	105,586,274	? 106

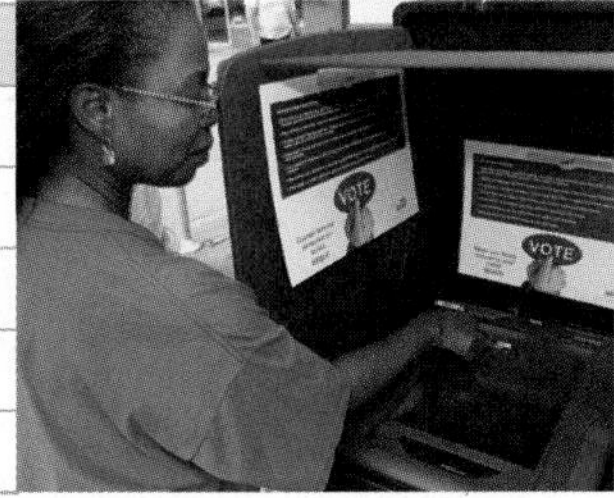

EXAMPLE 4 on p. 45 for Exs. 18–19

18. ★ **WRITING** The graph shows the number of hours of daylight in Houston, Texas, on the fifteenth day of the month, with 1 representing January, and so on. Identify the independent variable and the dependent variable. *Describe* how the number of hours of daylight changes over a year. Independent variable: the month, dependent variable: the hours of daylight; the number of daylight hours increases from January to May and then decreases through December.

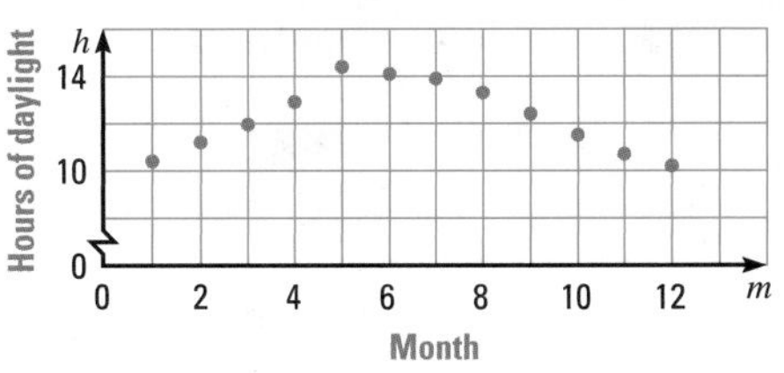

Differentiated Instruction

Advanced Ask students if it is possible to write a rule for the functions given in **Exercises 15 and 16**. Challenge them to explain why they can write rules for some functions and not for others. Suggest they graph a real-world situation in which they can write a rule for the function and then compare it to their graphs in Exercise 15 and 16. This will lead them into thinking about the differences between functions and prepare them for the concept of linear functions.

See also the *Algebra 1 Toolkit* for more strategies.

16.

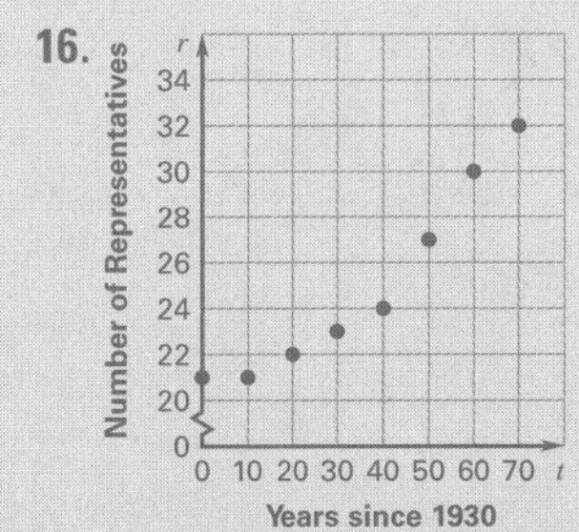

17.

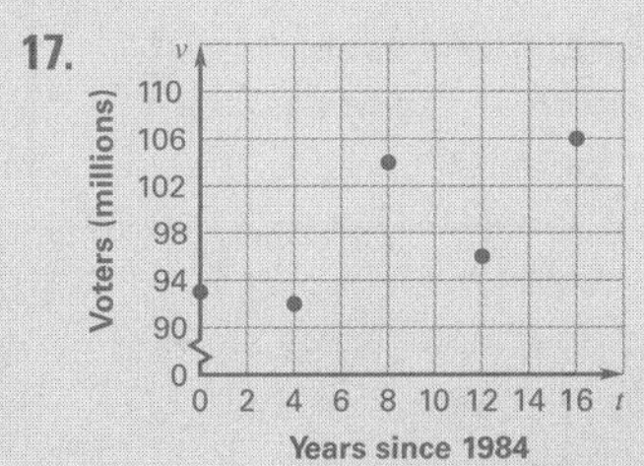

Avoiding Common Errors

Exercises 3–8 Students sometimes mistakenly reverse the x- and y-coordinates of a point when they plot it. Remind them that the domain values of a function are the x-coordinates of the points. Point out that they can quickly compare the given domain values to the labels of the vertical grid lines that have plotted points located on them.

Study Strategy

Exercises 10–12 Instruct students to use the solution steps shown in Example 3. Emphasize that a table will help them identify the relationship between the corresponding values of x and y.

Exercises 15–17 Suggest that students review Step 1 in Example 2 before graphing the functions. This will remind them to choose an appropriate scale and uniform increments for their graphs.

Mathematical Reasoning

Exercise 13 Lead students to see that the points are rising by $1\frac{1}{2}\left(\text{or } \frac{3}{2}\right)$ units on the y-axis for each increase of 1 unit on the x-axis. This suggests that answer C may be correct and should be checked first.

Exercise 15 Additional information about the Super Bowl, including a link to commercials, can be found at the official Super Bowl website www.superbowl.com.

Exercise 16 For information about the number of U.S. Representatives from other states, visit the official website for the U.S. House of Representatives at www.house.gov.

5 ASSESS AND RETEACH

Daily Homework Quiz

Transparency Available

1. Graph the function $y = \frac{1}{2}x + 2$ with domain 2, 4, 6, and 8.

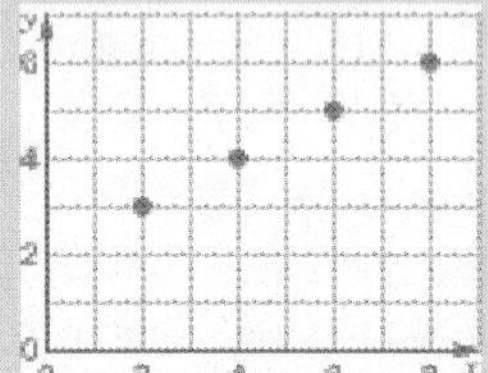

2. Write a rule for the function represented by the graph. Identify the domain and the range of the function.

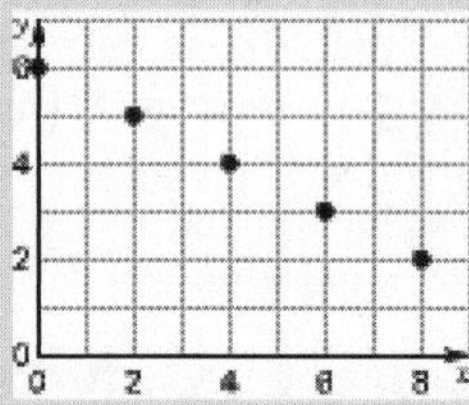

$y = -\frac{1}{2}x + 6$; domain: 0, 2, 4, 6, 8; range: 2, 3, 4, 5, 6

Available at **classzone.com**

Diagnosis/Remediation

- Practice A, B, C in Chapter 1 Resource Book, pp. 72–77
- Study Guide in Chapter 1 Resource Book, pp. 78–79
- Practice Workbook, pp. 13–15
- @HomeTutor

Challenge

Additional challenge is available in the Chapter 1 Resource Book, p. 82.

Quiz

An easily-readable reduced copy of the quiz (with answers) on Lessons 1.6–1.7 from the Assessment Book can be found on p. 1E.

20a, Quiz 1, 4, 5. See Additional Answers beginning on p. AA1.

B **19.** ★ **SHORT RESPONSE** A field biologist collected and measured alligator snapping turtle eggs. The graph shows the mass m (in grams) of an egg as a function of its length ℓ (in millimeters).

a. Describe As the lengths of the eggs increase, what happens to the masses of the eggs? increases

b. Estimate Is 27.5 g a reasonable estimate for the mass of an egg that is 38 mm long? *Explain.* Yes; 27.5 grams is between the mass of an egg that is just under 38 millimeters long and an egg that is just over 38 millimeters long.

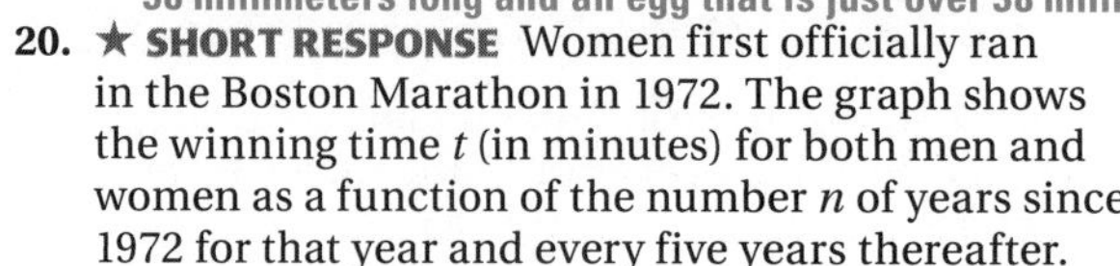

C **20.** ★ **SHORT RESPONSE** Women first officially ran in the Boston Marathon in 1972. The graph shows the winning time t (in minutes) for both men and women as a function of the number n of years since 1972 for that year and every five years thereafter.

a. CHALLENGE *Explain* how you can estimate the difference in the men's and women's winning time for any year shown. See margin.

b. CHALLENGE *Compare* any trends you see in the graphs. *Sample answer:* Between 1982 and 2002 the men's times are all within about 5 minutes of each other and the women's times are all within about 10 minutes of each other.

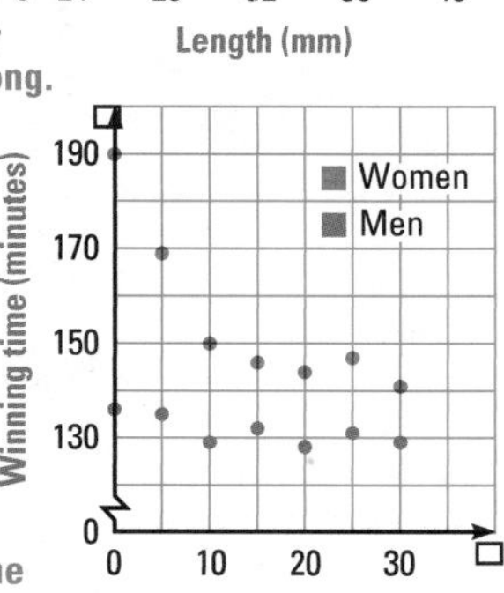

ILLINOIS MIXED REVIEW

TEST PRACTICE at classzone.com

21. A cylindrical can has a diameter of 2 inches and a height of 8 inches. What is the volume of the can? A

Ⓐ 8π in.^{3} Ⓑ 16π in.^{3} Ⓒ 32π in.^{3} Ⓓ 64π in.^{3}

22. Granite weighs about 1.5 ounces per cubic inch. Which expression gives the weight in ounces of a solid cube of granite that has an edge length of 10 inches? D

Ⓐ 15^3 Ⓑ $1.5^3 \cdot 10^3$ Ⓒ 150 Ⓓ $1.5 \cdot 10^3$

QUIZ *for Lessons 1.6–1.7*

1. The domain of the function $y = 12 - 2x$ is 0, 2, 3, 4, and 5. Make a table for the function, then identify the range of the function. *(p. 35)*
Range: 2, 4, 6, 8, and 12; see margin.

Tell whether the pairing is a function. *(p. 35)*

2.

x	5	6	7	11
y	1	2	3	7

function

3.

x	4	6	9	15
y	1	3	6	3

function

Graph the function. *(p. 43)* 4, 5. See margin.

4. $y = 2x - 5$; domain: 5, 6, 7, 8, and 9

5. $y = 7 - x$; domain: 1, 2, 3, 4, and 5

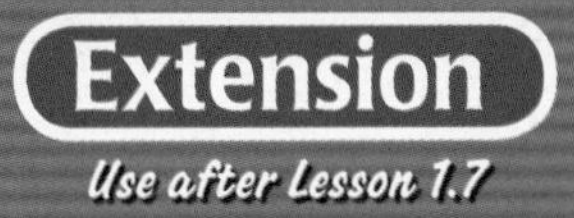

Determine Whether a Relation Is a Function

GOAL Determine whether a relation is a function when the relation is represented by a table or a graph.

Key Vocabulary
- **relation,** *p. 49*

A **relation** is any pairing of a set of inputs with a set of outputs. Every function is a relation, but not every relation is a function. A relation is a function if for every input there is exactly one output.

EXAMPLE 1 Determine whether a relation is a function

Determine whether the relation is a function.

a.

Input	4	4	5	6	7
Output	0	1	2	3	4

b.

Input	3	5	7	9
Output	1	2	3	2

Solution

a. The input 4 has two different outputs, 0 and 1. So, the relation is *not* a function.

b. Every input has exactly one output, so the relation is a function.

USING THE GRAPH OF A RELATION You can use the *vertical line test* to determine whether a relation represented by a graph is a function. When a relation is *not* a function, its graph contains at least two points with the same x-coordinate and different y-coordinates. Those points lie on a vertical line.

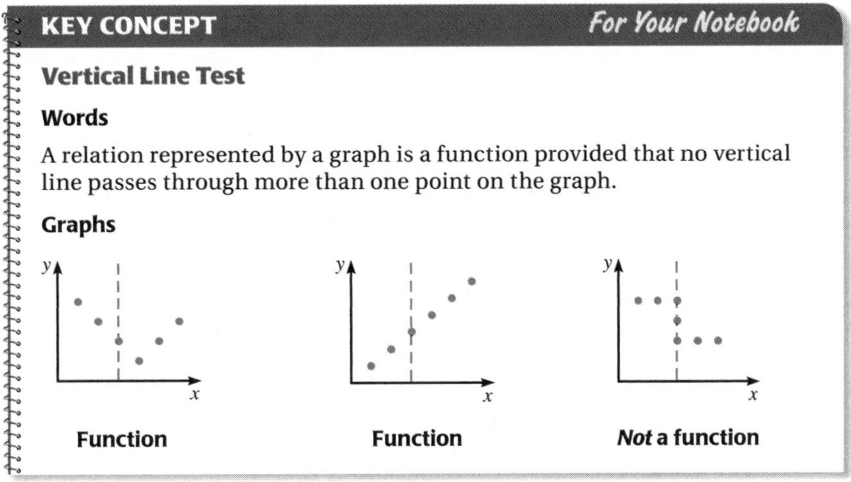

KEY CONCEPT
For Your Notebook
Vertical Line Test
Words
A relation represented by a graph is a function provided that no vertical line passes through more than one point on the graph.
Graphs
y
x
Function
Not a function

1 PLAN AND PREPARE

Warm-Up Exercises

1. Identify the domain and range.

Input	0	2	6	7	8
Output	1	4	5	9	11

domain: 0, 2, 6, 7, 8; range: 1, 4, 5, 9, 11

Tell whether the pairing is a function.

2. 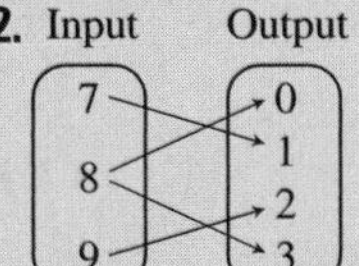

The pairing is *not* a function, because the input 8 is paired with both 0 and 3.

3. 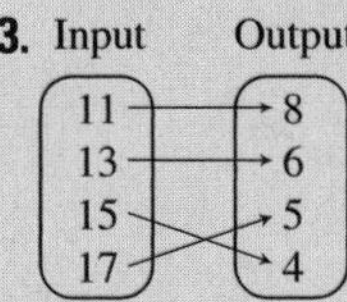

The pairing is a function, because each input is paired with exactly one output.

2 FOCUS AND MOTIVATE

Essential Question

Big Idea 3, p. 1

How do you determine whether a relation shown in a table or a graph is a function? **Tell students they will learn how to answer this question by examining input-output tables and by using the vertical line test on graphs.**

NCTM STANDARDS

Standard 2: Understand relations; Understand functions

3 TEACH

Extra Example 1

Determine whether the relation is a function. yes

Input	2	3	4	5	6
Output	9	4	1	0	1

Extra Example 2

Determine whether the graph represents a function. no

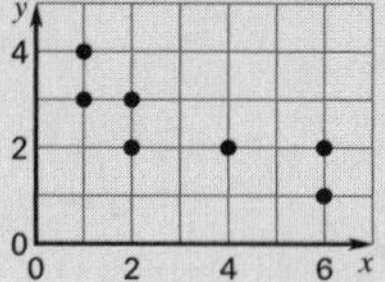

An **Animated Algebra** activity is available on-line for **Example 2**. This activity is also available on the **Power Presentations CD-ROM**.

Closing the Lesson

Have students summarize the major points of the lesson and answer the Essential Question: How do you determine whether a relation shown in a table or a graph is a function?

- A relation is a function if for every input there is exactly one output.
- A relation is a function if no vertical line passes through more than one point when the relation is graphed.

In a table, check that each input has exactly one output; in a graph, check that no vertical line passes through more than one point.

4 PRACTICE AND APPLY

Teaching Strategy

Exercises 8–9 Have students work in groups to create tables of realistic values and then have them graph them. Working with actual values may help students see the relationships more readily.

EXAMPLE 2 Use the vertical line test

Determine whether the graph represents a function.

a.

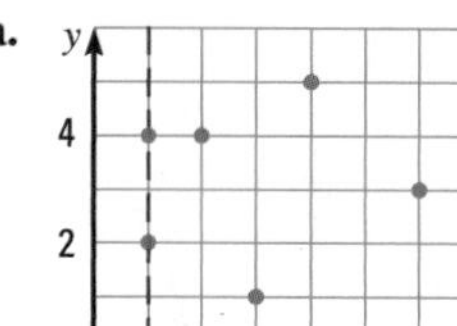

You can draw a vertical line through the points (1, 2) and (1, 4). The graph does *not* represent a function.

 at classzone.com

b.

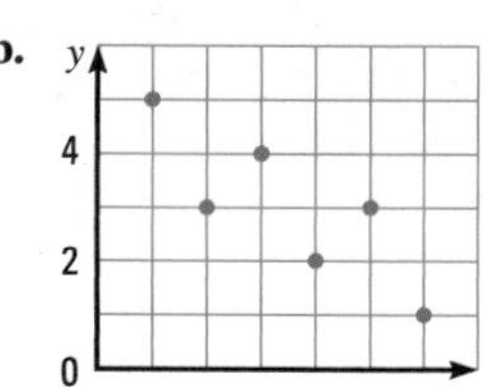

No vertical line can be drawn through more than one point. The graph represents a function.

PRACTICE

EXAMPLE 1 on p. 49 for Exs. 1–3

IDENTIFYING FUNCTIONS **Determine whether the relation is a function.**

1.

Input	Output
0	1
2	6
5	12
7	5
8	4

function

2.

Input	Output
3	7
4	8
4	9
5	10
6	11

not a function

3.

Input	Output
0.7	1.9
1.2	2.4
3.5	4.7
7.5	8.7
7.5	9.7

not a function

EXAMPLE 2 on p. 50 for Exs. 4–6

IDENTIFYING FUNCTIONS **Determine whether the graph represents a function.**

4.

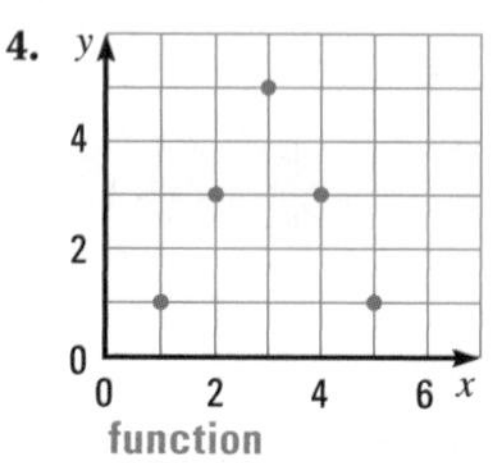

function

5.

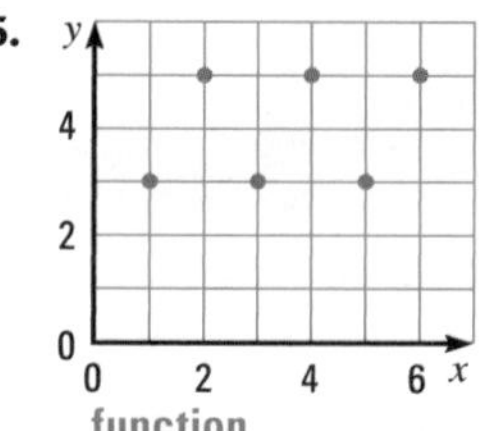

function

6.

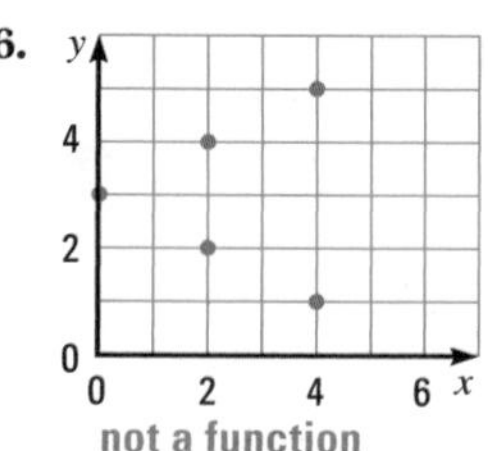

not a function

REASONING **Tell whether the pairing of x-values and y-values is necessarily a function. *Explain* your reasoning.** 7, 8. See margin.

7. A teacher makes a table that lists the number x of letters in the first name and the number y of letters in the last name of each student in the class.

8. Your doctor records your height x (in inches) and your weight y (in pounds) each time you have a medical exam.

9. You have a record of your age x (in years) and your height y (in inches) on each of your birthdays since you were born.
Function; for each of your birthdays, you have only one height.

7. Not a function. *Sample answer:* There could be many students whose first names have 4 letters, for instance, but their last names could all have a different number of letters.

8. Not a function. *Sample answer:* If your height stays the same, you could lose or gain weight, giving more than one output for an input.

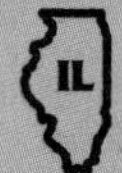

Illinois *Mixed Review*

TEST PRACTICE classzone.com

Lessons 1.5–1.7

1. **PAINTING** You are painting a room in a neighborhood recreation center. You need to cover a total area of 1080 square feet. The paint you choose is available only in 1 quart containers that each cover about 110 square feet. Each quart of paint costs $6. How much will it cost to give the entire area a single coat of paint?

   A. $54
   B. $58
   C. $60
   D. $66

2. **ROAD TRIP** Your family is taking a 250 mile road trip. The first 220 miles of the trip are on highways, where your average speed is 55 miles per hour. The rest of the trip is on local roads, where your average speed is 30 miles per hour. How much time does your family spend driving?

   F. 5 h
   G 5 h 30 min
   H. 6 h
   J. 6 h 30 min

3. **DANCE** You pay $50 to attend dance camp. You pay $5 for transportation each day. Which of the following expresses the total cost C (in dollars) as a function of the number of days d that you attend camp?

   A. $C = 50 + 5d$
   B. $C = 5 + 50d$
   C. $C = 55d$
   D. None of the above

4. **POSTERS** A store sells sets of 1, 2, 3, or 5 posters. For each set, the price (in dollars) is $2 more than twice the number of posters. Which of the following is a possible price for a set of posters?

   F. $7 **H.** $10
   G. $9 **J.** $12

5. **CAR WASH** Your class is planning a car wash. You need $75 worth of materials and plan to charge $5 per car. Which of the following is a verbal model for your class's profit?

   A. Cost of materials + Charge per car • Number of cars washed
   B. Cost of materials − Charge per car • Number of cars washed
   C. Charge per car • Number of cars washed − Cost of materials
   D. Charge per car + Number of cars washed − Cost of materials

6. **ROLLERBLADING** The graph shows the cost (in dollars) of renting rollerblades as a function of the number of hours they are rented. Which of the following is a rule for the function?

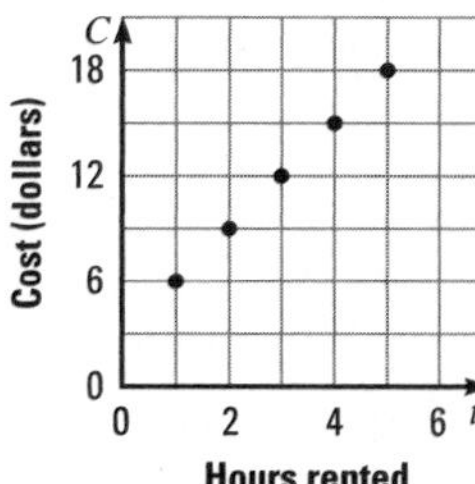

   F. $t = C - 5$ **H.** $C = 6t$
   G. $C = 3t + 6$ **J.** $C = 3t + 3$

7. **ROOM TEMPERATURE** You consider 68°F to be a comfortable room temperature. If the temperature in the room is 18°C, how many degrees Celsius should you raise the temperature so that it will be 68°F?

   A. 1.3 **C.** 3
   B. 2 **D.** 5.6

Illinois Mixed Review

1. C
2. F
3. A
4. J
5. C
6. J
7. B

Animated Algebra
classzone.com
Electronic Function Library

Additional Resources

The following resources are available to help review the materials in this chapter.

Chapter 1 Resource Book

- Chapter Review Games and Activities, p. 83
- Cumulative Practice, Ch. 1, pp. 86–87

Student Resources in Spanish

eWorkbook

@HomeTutor

Vocabulary Practice

Vocabulary practice is available at **classzone.com**

BIG IDEAS *For Your Notebook*

Big Idea 1

Writing and Evaluating Algebraic Expressions

The cost of admission for one student at a planetarium is \$6. You can use a verbal model to write an expression for the total cost of admission for any number of students.

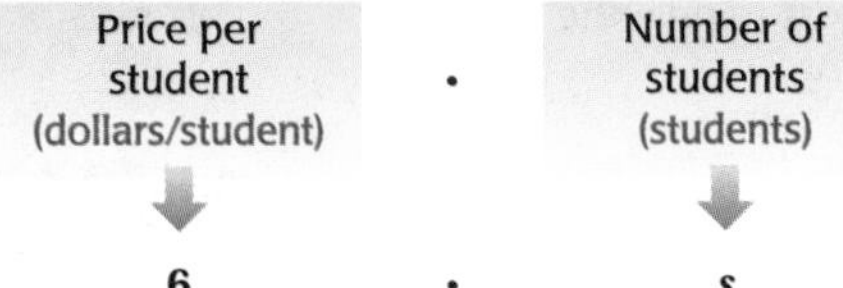

An expression is $6s$. Because $\frac{\text{dollars}}{\cancel{\text{student}}} \cdot \cancel{\text{students}} = \text{dollars}$, the expression produces an answer in dollars. The expression is reasonable.

Big Idea 2

Using Expressions to Write Equations and Inequalities

You can use symbols to write an equation or inequality that compares the expression $6s$ to another expression.

The total cost of admission to the planetarium for s students at a rate of \$6 per student is \$150.

$6s = 150$ **Equation**

The total cost of admission to the planetarium for s students at a rate of \$6 per student is no more than \$150.

$6s \leq 150$ **Inequality**

Big Idea 3

Representing Functions as Verbal Rules, Equations, Tables, and Graphs

You can use a verbal description, an equation, a table, or a graph to represent a function.

Words The total cost (in dollars) of admission to the planetarium is 6 times the number of students.

Equation

$C = 6s$

Table

Input, s	Input, C
0	0
1	6
2	12
3	18

Graph

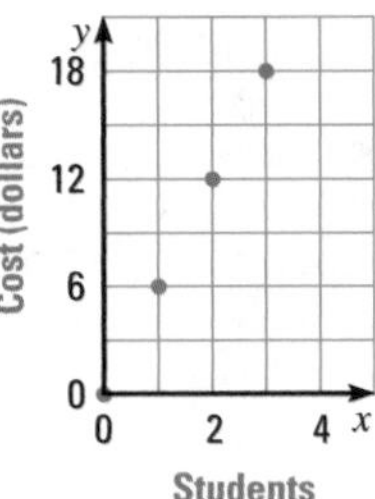

1 CHAPTER REVIEW

@HomeTutor
classzone.com
- Multi-Language Glossary
- Vocabulary practice

REVIEW KEY VOCABULARY

- variable, *p. 2*
- algebraic expression, *p. 2*
- evaluate an algebraic expression, *p. 2*
- power, exponent, base, *p. 3*
- order of operations, *p. 8*
- verbal model, *p. 16*
- rate, unit rate, *p. 17*
- equation, inequality, *p. 21*
- open sentence, *p. 21*
- solution of an equation or inequality, *p. 22*
- formula, *p. 30*
- function, *p. 35*
- input, output, *p. 35*
- domain, range, *p. 35*
- independent variable, *p. 36*
- dependent variable, *p. 36*

VOCABULARY EXERCISES

In Exercises 1–3, copy and complete the statement.

1. In the power 7^{12}, _?_ is the base and _?_ is the exponent.
2. A(n) _?_ is a statement that contains the symbol =.
3. A(n) _?_ is an expression that includes at least one variable.
4. **WRITING** *Describe* how you can tell by looking at the graph of a function which variable is the input variable and which is the output variable.

REVIEW EXAMPLES AND EXERCISES

Use the review examples and exercises below to check your understanding of the concepts you have learned in each lesson of Chapter 1.

1.1 Evaluate Expressions

pp. 2–7

EXAMPLE

Evaluate $6 - n$ when $n = 4$.

$6 - n = 6 - 4$ **Substitute 4 for *n*.**

$= 2$ **Simplify.**

EXERCISES

EXAMPLES 1, 4, and 5 on pp. 2–4 for Exs. 5–12

Evaluate the expression.

5. $3 + x$ when $x = 13$
6. $y - 2$ when $y = 18$
7. $\frac{20}{k}$ when $k = 2$
8. $40w$ when $w = 0.5$
9. z^2 when $z = 20$
10. w^3 when $w = 0.1$
11. **DVD STORAGE** A DVD storage sleeve has the shape of a square with an edge length of 5 inches. What is the area of the front of the sleeve?
12. **NOTEPAPER** You store square notepaper in a cube-shaped box with an inside edge length of 3 inches. What is the volume of the box?

Extra Example 1.1

Evaluate $\frac{36}{g}$ when $g = 4$. 9

1 CHAPTER REVIEW

Extra Example 1.2

Evaluate $32 - (4^2 + 8) \div 4$. 26

Extra Example 1.3

Write an expression for the height of a tree over time if the tree was 2.5 feet tall when planted and it grows at an average rate of 2 feet per year. $2t + 2.5$, where t represents the time in years

1.2 Apply Order of Operations

pp. 8–12

EXAMPLE

Evaluate $(5 + 3)^2 \div 2 \times 3$.

$(5 + 3)^2 \div 2 \times 3 = 8^2 \div 2 \times 3$ **Add within parentheses.**

$= 64 \div 2 \times 3$ **Evaluate power.**

$= 32 \times 3$ **Divide.**

$= 96$ **Multiply.**

EXERCISES

EXAMPLES 1, 2, and 3 on pp. 8–9 for Exs. 13–21

Evaluate the expression.

13. $12 - 6 \div 2$

14. $1 + 2 \cdot 9^2$

15. $3 + 2^3 - 6 \div 2$

16. $15 - (4 + 3^2)$

17. $\frac{20 - 12}{5^2 - 1}$

18. $50 - [7 + (3^2 \div 2)]$

Evaluate the expression when $x = 4$.

19. $15x - 8$

20. $3x^2 + 4$

21. $2(x - 1)^2$

1.3 Write Expressions

pp. 15–20

EXAMPLE

Write an expression for the entry fee in a jazz band competition if there is a base fee of $50 and a charge of $1 per member.

Write a verbal model. Then translate the verbal model into an algebraic expression. Let n represent the number of band members.

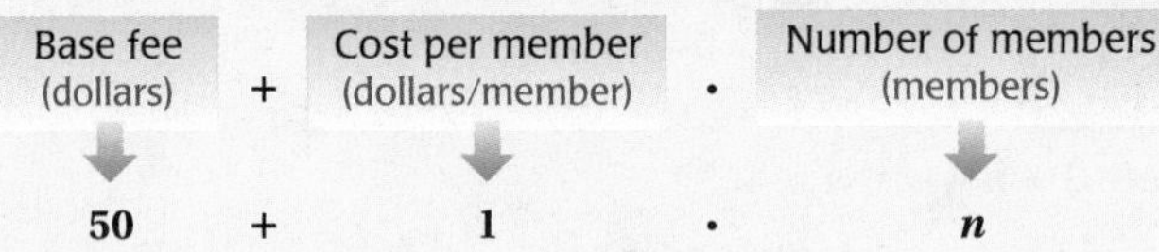

Base fee (dollars)
+
Cost per member (dollars/member)
•
Number of members (members)
50
+
1
•
n

▶ An expression for the entry fee (in dollars) is $50 + n$.

EXERCISES

EXAMPLES 1, 2, and 3 on pp. 15–16 for Exs. 22–27

Translate the verbal phrase into an expression.

22. The sum of a number k and 7

23. 5 less than a number z

24. The quotient of a number k and 12

25. 3 times the square of a number x

26. TOLL ROADS A toll road charges trucks a toll of $3 per axle. Write an expression for the total toll for a truck.

27. SCHOOL SUPPLIES You purchase some notebooks for $2.95 each and a package of pens for $2.19. Write an expression for the total amount (in dollars) that you spend.

@HomeTutor
classzone.com
Chapter Review Practice

1.4 Write Equations and Inequalities

pp. 21–26

EXAMPLE

Write an inequality for the sentence "The sum of 3 and twice a number k is no more than 15". Then check whether 4 is a solution of the inequality.

An inequality is $3 + 2k \leq 15$.

To check whether 4 is a solution of the inequality, substitute 4 for k.

$3 + 2(4) \overset{?}{\leq} 15$ **Substitute 4 for k.**

$11 \leq 15$ ✓ **The solution checks. So, 4 is a solution.**

EXERCISES

EXAMPLES 1 and 2 on pp. 21–22 for Exs. 28–32

Write an equation or an inequality.

28. The product of a number z and 12 is 60. $12z = 60$

29. The sum of 13 and a number t is at least 24. $13 + t \geq 24$

Check whether the given number is a solution of the equation or inequality.

30. $3x - 4 = 10$; 5
not a solution

31. $4y - 2 \geq 2$; 3
solution

32. $2d + 4 < 9d - 7$; 3
solution

1.5 Use a Problem Solving Plan

pp. 28–33

EXAMPLE

A rectangular banner is 12 feet long and has an area of 60 square feet. What is the perimeter of the banner?

STEP 1 **Read and Understand** You know the length of the rectangular banner and its area. You want to find the perimeter.

STEP 2 **Make a Plan** Use the area formula for a rectangle to find the width. Then use the perimeter formula for a rectangle.

STEP 3 **Solve the Problem** Substituting 12 for ℓ in the formula $A = \ell w$, $60 = 12w$. Because $12 \cdot 5 = 60$, $w = 5$. Then substituting 12 for ℓ and 5 for w in the formula $P = 2\ell + 2w$, $P = 2(12) + 2(5) = 34$ feet.

STEP 4 **Look Back** Use estimation. Since $\ell \approx 10$ and $A = 60$, $w \approx 6$. Then $P \approx 2(10) + 2(6) = 32$ feet, so your answer is reasonable.

EXERCISES

EXAMPLES 1, 2, and 3 on p. 28–30 for Exs. 33–34

33. **U.S. HISTORY** The flag that inspired the national anthem was a rectangle 30 feet wide and 42 feet long. Pieces of the flag have been lost. It is now 30 feet wide and 34 feet long. How many square feet have been lost? 240 ft^2

34. **PATTERNS** A grocery clerk stacks three rows of cans of fruit for a display. Each of the top two rows has 2 fewer cans than the row beneath it. There are 30 cans altogether. How many cans are there in each row? 8 cans, 10 cans, and 12 cans

Extra Example 1.4

Write an equation for the sentence "Nine more than the quantity 6 less than a number n is 18." Then check whether 10 is a solution of the equation. $9 + (n - 6) = 18$; 10 is not a solution since $9 + (10 - 6) = 13$ and $13 \neq 18$.

Extra Example 1.5

The floor of a rectangular building is 52 feet long and has a perimeter of 174 feet. What is the area of the floor? 1820 ft^2

1 CHAPTER REVIEW

Extra Example 1.6

The domain of the function $y = 4x + 1$ is 0, 2, 4, and 6. Make a table for the function, then identify the range of the function.

x	0	2	4	6
$y = 4x + 1$	1	9	17	25

range: 1, 9, 17, 25

Extra Example 1.7

Write a rule for the function represented by the graph. Identify the domain and the range of the function.

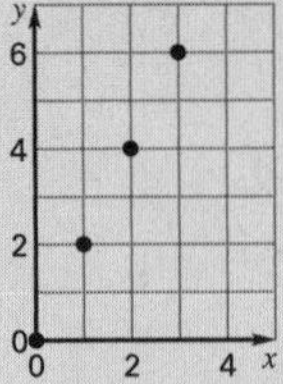

A rule for the function is $y = 2x$. The domain is 0, 1, 2, and 3. The range is 0, 2, 4, and 6.

35.

Input	10	12	15	20	21
Output	5	7	10	15	16

36.

Input	0	2	3	5	10
Output	1	7	10	16	31

39.

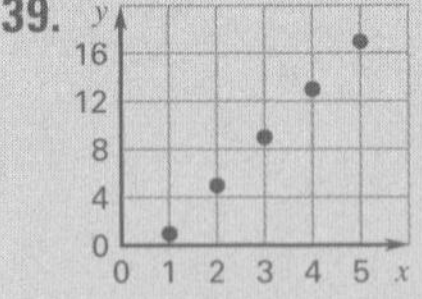

1.6 Represent Functions as Rules and Tables

pp. 35–40

EXAMPLE

The domain of the function $y = 3x - 5$ is 2, 3, 4, and 5. Make a table for the function, then identify the range of the function.

x	2	3	4	5
$y = 3x - 5$	$3(2) - 5 = 1$	$3(3) - 5 = 4$	$3(4) - 5 = 7$	$3(5) - 5 = 10$

The range of the function is 1, 4, 7, and 10.

EXERCISES

EXAMPLES 1, 3, and 4 on p. 35–37 for Exs. 35–38

Make a table for the function. Identify the range of the function.

35. $y = x - 5$
Domain: 10, 12, 15, 20, 21
Range: 5, 7, 10, 15, and 16; see margin.

36. $y = 3x + 1$
Domain: 0, 2, 3, 5, 10
Range: 1, 7, 10, 16, and 31; see margin.

Write a rule for the function.

37.

Input, x	0	2	4	5
Output, y	4	6	8	9

$y = x + 4$

38.

Input, x	0	3	4	6
Output, y	0	15	20	30

$y = 5x$

1.7 Represent Functions as Graphs

pp. 43–48

EXAMPLE

Write a rule for the function represented by the graph. Identify the domain and the range of the function.

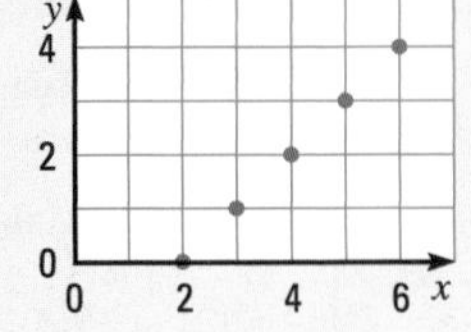

Make a table for the graph.

x	2	3	4	5	6
y	0	1	2	3	4

Each y-value is 2 less than the corresponding x-value. A rule for the function is $y = x - 2$. The domain is 2, 3, 4, 5, and 6. The range is 0, 1, 2, 3, and 4.

EXERCISES

EXAMPLES 1, 3, and 4 on pp. 43–45 for Exs. 39–40

39. Graph the function $y = 4x - 3$ with domain 1, 2, 3, 4, and 5. See margin.

40. Write a rule for the function represented by the graph. Identify the domain and the range of the function.
$\frac{1}{2}x + \frac{1}{2}$; domain: 1, 3, 5, and 7, range: 1, 2, 3, and 4

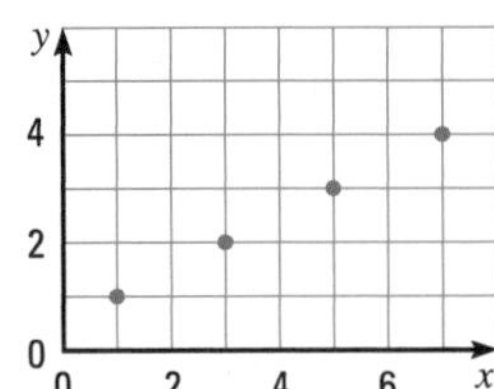

1 CHAPTER TEST

Evaluate the expression.

1. $7 + 3^2 \cdot 2$ 25
2. $(5^2 + 17) \div 7$ 6
3. $(24 - 11) - (3 + 2) \div 4$ 11.75
4. $\frac{x}{5}$ when $x = 30$ 6
5. n^3 when $n = 20$ 8000
6. $15 - t$ when $t = 11$ 4
7. $12 + 4x$ when $x = 1\frac{1}{2}$ 18
8. $3z^2 - 7$ when $z = 6$ 101
9. $2(4n + 5)$ when $n = 2$ 26

Write an expression, an equation, or an inequality.

10. The sum of 19 and the cube of a number x $19 + x^3$
11. The product of 3 and a number y is no more than 21. $3y \leq 21$
12. Twice the difference of a number z and 12 is equal to 10. $2(z - 12) = 10$

Check whether the given number is a solution of the equation or inequality.

13. $2 + 3x = 10$; 2 not a solution
14. $8 + 3b > 15$; 2 not a solution
15. $11y - 5 \leq 30$; 3 solution

16a. There is exactly one output for each input.

16b. domain: 1, 2, 3, 4, 5, and 6, range: 3, 4, 5, 6, 7, and 8

16. Refer to the graph.
    a. *Explain* why the graph represents a function.
    b. Identify the domain and the range.
    c. Write a rule for the function. $y = x + 2$

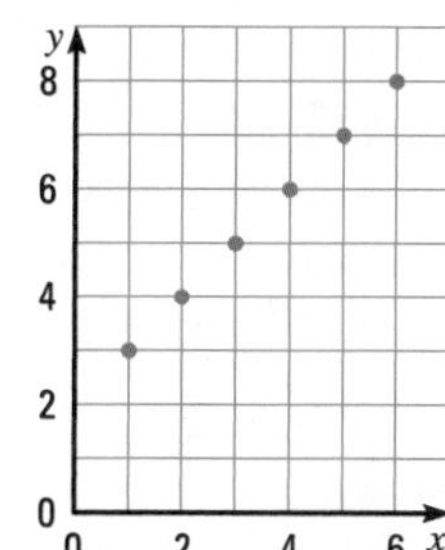

17. **FOOD PREPARATION** You buy tomatoes at \$1.29 per pound and peppers at \$3.99 per pound to make salsa. Write an expression for the total cost of the ingredients. Then find the total cost of 5 pounds of tomatoes and 2 pounds of peppers. $c = 1.29t + 3.99p$; \$14.43
18. **CAR EXPENSES** A family determined the average cost of maintaining and operating the family car to be about \$.30 per mile. On one trip, the family drove at an average rate of 50 miles per hour for a total of 6.5 hours. On a second trip, they drove at an average rate of 55 miles per hour for a total of 6 hours. Which trip cost more? How much more? the second trip; \$1.50
19. **SHOE SIZES** A man's size 6 shoe is the same size as a woman's size $7\frac{1}{2}$. The table shows other corresponding sizes of men's and women's shoes.

Men's size, x	6	$6\frac{1}{2}$	7	$7\frac{1}{2}$	8	$8\frac{1}{2}$	9
Women's size, y	$7\frac{1}{2}$	8	$8\frac{1}{2}$	9	$9\frac{1}{2}$	10	$10\frac{1}{2}$

    a. Using the data in the table, write a rule for women's shoe size as a function of men's shoe size. Identify the domain and the range.
    b. Graph the function. See margin.

19a. $y = x + 1\frac{1}{2}$; domain: 6, $6\frac{1}{2}$, 7, $7\frac{1}{2}$, 8, $8\frac{1}{2}$, and 9, range: $7\frac{1}{2}$, 8, $8\frac{1}{2}$, 9, $9\frac{1}{2}$, 10, and $10\frac{1}{2}$

Additional Resources

Assessment Book

- Chapter Test, Levels A, B, C, pp. 4–9
- Standardized Chapter Test, pp. 10–11
- SAT/ACT Chapter Test, pp. 12–13
- Alternative Assessment, pp. 14–15

Test Generator CD-ROM

Chapter Test

Easily-readable reduced copies (with answers) of Chapter Test B, the Standardized Chapter Test, and the Alternative Assessment from the Assessment Book can be found on pp. 1E–1F.

19b.

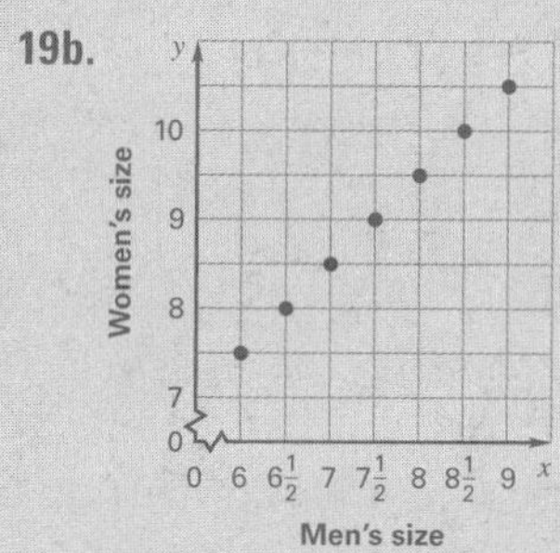

MULTIPLE CHOICE QUESTIONS

If you have difficulty solving a multiple choice problem directly, you may be able to use another approach to eliminate incorrect answer choices and obtain the correct answer.

PROBLEM 1

Mike and Aaron are inflating balloons for a graduation party. Mike can inflate 3 balloons per minute, and Aaron can inflate 2 balloons per minute. If Mike and Aaron start inflating balloons at the same time, how many minutes will it take them to inflate a total of 30 balloons?

A. 5 minutes

B. 6 minutes

C. 10 minutes

D. 150 minutes

METHOD 1

SOLVE DIRECTLY

STEP 1 **Write** equations.

Because Mike can inflate 3 balloons in 1 minute and Aaron can inflate 2 balloons in 1 minute, together they can inflate 5 balloons in 1 minute.

Let t equal the time (in minutes) that Mike and Aaron have been inflating balloons. Let b be the number of balloons inflated.

So the equation is $5t = b$.

STEP 2 **Solve** the equation.

We need to find the time when $b = 30$.

$5t = b$

$5t = 30$ Substitute $b = 30$.

$\frac{5t}{5} = \frac{30}{5}$ Divide by 5 on both sides.

$t = 6$ minutes
The correct answer is **B**.

METHOD 2

ELIMINATE CHOICES Another method is to consider the extremes to eliminate incorrect choices.

STEP 1 **Working** alone, Mike would take $\frac{30}{3}$ or 10 minutes to inflate 30 balloons. Working alone, Aaron would take $\frac{30}{2}$ or 15 minutes to inflate 30 balloons.

So together, their time must be less than 10 minutes. Since choices **C** and **D** are larger than 10 minutes, we can eliminate those choices.

STEP 2 **Calculate** the remaining answer choices.

Choice A:
Mike: 3 balloons × 5 minutes = 15 balloons
Aaron: 2 balloons × 5 minutes = 10 balloons

Total number = 25 balloons

Choice B:
Mike: 3 balloons × 6 minutes = 18 balloons
Aaron: 2 balloons × 6 minutes = 12 balloons

Total number = 30 balloons

So, the total number of balloons is 30 and the time is 6 minutes.

The correct answer is **B**.

PROBLEM SOLVING

Below are examples that test problem solving skills in multiple choice format. Try solving the problems before looking at the solutions. (Cover the solutions with a piece of paper.) Then check your solutions against the ones given.

1. The table shows the cost, in dollars, of renting a campsite for n days. What would you expect the cost of renting the campsite for 10 days to be?

Number of days	1	2	3	4	5
Cost (dollars)	25	40	55	70	85

A. $150

B. $160

C. $170

D. $250

Solution

The first day costs $25, and each additional day costs an additional $15. Use this pattern to write an expression.

The cost, in dollars, of renting the campsite for n days is given by the expression $25 + 15(n - 1)$. Evaluate the expression when $n = 10$.

$25 + 15(10 - 1) = 25 + 15(9) = 25 + 135 = 160$

When $n = 10$, the cost is $160, so the correct answer is **B.**

2. Jed has $2000 in a savings account and plans to save 20% of his salary each month. Erin has $1000 in her savings account and plans to save 25% of her salary each month. If you ignore interest, what information would allow you to determine whose account will have more money in it after 5 months?

F. Jed's salary

G. Jed's and Erin's salaries

H. The amount Jed deposits each month

J. The amount Erin deposits each month

Solution

Model the amount, in dollars, in each account after n months.

Jed: $2000 + 0.20 \cdot$ (Jed's salary) $\cdot\ n$

Erin: $1000 + 0.25 \cdot$ (Erin's salary) $\cdot\ n$

To evaluate the expressions and compare the values, you need to know both Jed's and Erin's salaries, so the correct answer is **G.**

3. The population of a town has doubled every 10 years for the last 30 years. The current population is 10,000. What was the population 30 years ago?

A. 1250

B. 1750

C. 2500

D. 5000

Solution

Consider that the population 10 years ago was half the current population. Make a table.

Years ago	0	10	20	30
Population	10,000	5000	2500	1250

The population 30 years ago was 1250, so the correct answer is **A.**

TEST PREPARATION

Illinois Test Practice

1. A
2. J
3. B
4. H
5. C
6. F
7. C
8. H
9. A
10. G
11. B
12. H
13. C
14. G
15. D
16. H
17. D
18. F

Illinois Test Practice

1. Which is a rule for the function given by the input-output table?

Input, x	8	10	12	14
Output, y	5	7	9	11

A. $y = x - 3$ **C.** $y = x + 3$

B. $y = x - 2$ **D.** $y = x - 2$

2. The number of adult tickets sold at a school talent show is 5 less than 3 times the number c of children's tickets sold. Which expression represents the number of adult tickets sold?

F. $3c + 5$ **H.** $5c + 3$

G. $5 - 3c$ **J.** $3c - 5$

3. The function $y = 2x + 4$ has a domain of 2, 3, 5, 7, and 8. Which number is *not* in the range of the function?

A. 8 **B.** 12 **C.** 18 **D.** 20

4. A train leaves at 10 A.M. and travels 500 miles to a destination in the same time zone. Which of the following pieces of information would allow you to estimate the time the train arrives at its destination?

F. The destination of the train.

G. The direction the train travels.

H. The average speed of the train.

J. The time zone in which the train travels.

5. Based on the pattern, how many squares would the diagram in Step 6 have?

Step number	Diagram	Number of squares
1		1
2		3
3		6

A. 15 **C.** 21

B. 18 **D.** 24

6. The domain of the function $y = 3x + 6$ is 0, 1, 2, and 3. What is the range of the function?

F. 6, 9, 12, and 15 **H.** 2, 3, 4, and 5

G. 0, 3, 6, and 9 **J.** 2, 5, 8, and 11

7. A shoe store is setting up a display of 100 pairs of shoes. Each shelf of the display can hold 13 pairs of shoes. What is the best method for determining the number of shelves that will be needed?

A. Find the remainder when 100 is divided by 13.

B. Round 13 to 10 and divide 100 by 10.

C. Divide 100 by 13 and round up.

D. Divide 100 by 13 and round down.

8. Maggie is twice as old as four more than Johnny's age. Which of the following equations could be used to find Maggie's age, M?

F. $M = 2J - 4$ **H.** $M = 2(J + 4)$

G. $M = 2J + 4$ **J.** $M = 2(J - 4)$

9. A hotel charges its guests \$0.50 to make a phone call plus \$0.10 a minute. Which equation best expresses the costs c, in dollars, of a call that lasts m minutes?

A. $c = 0.5 + 0.1m$ **C.** $c = 5 - m$

B. $c = 0.6m$ **D.** None of the above

10. Which of the following expressions could be used to represent the verbal phrase "the sum of the number m and 15?"

F. $m - 15$ **H.** $m \times 15$

G. $m + 15$ **J.** $m \div 15$

11. Which equation could be used to generate this table of values?

x	1	2	3	4
y	3	5	7	9

A. $y = x + 2$ **C.** $y = 3x$

B. $y = 2x + 1$ **D.** $y = 4x - 1$

12. The domain of the function $y = 5x + 5$ is 3, 4, 5, and 6. Which of the following is the range of the function?

F. 15, 20, 25 and 30

G. 20, 23, 26 and 29

H. 20, 25, 30 and 35

J. 25, 29, 33, and 37

13. A circular region is enclosed by 50 feet of rope. How can you best determine the diameter of the region?

A. Divide 50 by 2.

B. Find the square root of 50.

C. Divide 50 by π.

D. Divide 50 by 2π.

14. The distance around a figure is called the perimeter of the figure. Which of the expressions below could be used to find the perimeter of the figure shown?

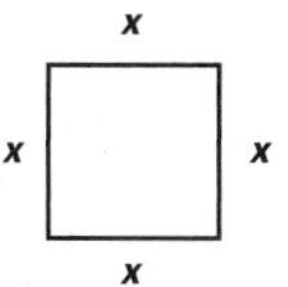

F. $x + 4$

G. $4x$

H. x^2

J. x^4

15. A room has the dimensions shown below. Part of the room is being carpeted. The remainder of the room is being laid with tile. The area to be tiled is $14x$ square feet. How can the area of the carpeted region be expressed in terms of x?

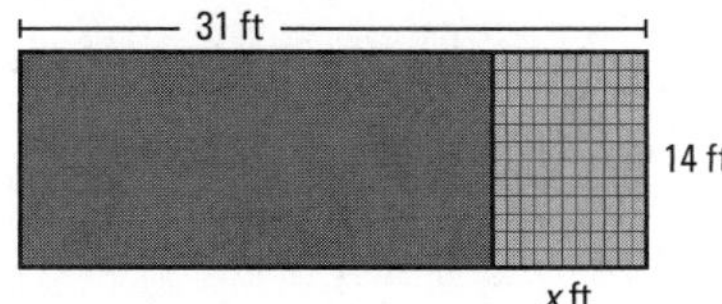

A. $31 - 14x$

B. $\frac{31(14)}{x}$

C. $\frac{(31 - x)}{14}$

D. $14(31 - x)$

16. The function $f(x) = \{(0, 4), (1, 3), (2, 2), (3, 1), (4,0)\}$ can be represented in several other ways. Which is *not* a correct representation of the function $f(x)$?

F. 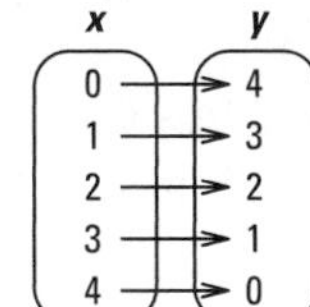

G. 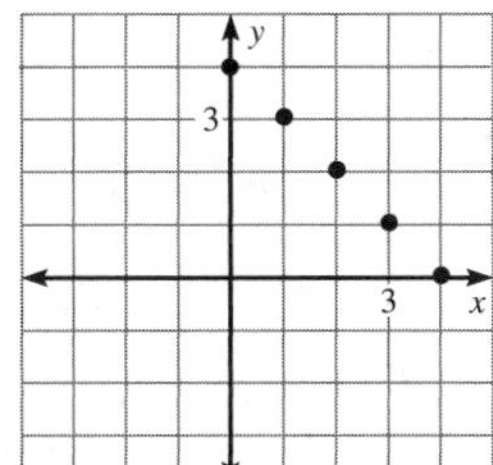

H. x is an number between 0 and 3, and y is 1 more than the opposite of x.

J. $y = -x + 4$, and the domain is $\{0, 1, 2, 3, 4\}$.

17. The length of a rectangular pool is four times the width of the pool. Which equation could be used to find the perimeter of the rectangular pool?

A. $P = w + 4$

B. $P = 5w$

C. $P = 4w$

D. $P = 10w$

18. A pool is a rectangular prism with a base of 90 square feet. If filled to the top, the pool can hold 495 cubic feet of water. However, the water level of the pool is currently x feet from the top. Which equation represents w, the number of cubic feet of water in the pool, as a function of x?

F. $w = 495 - 90x$

G. $w = 495x - 90$

H. $w = 495 + 90x$

J. $w = 495(90 + x)$

TEST PRACTICE

Illinois Resources Guide

Pacing and Assignment Guide

REGULAR SCHEDULE

Pre-AP For pacing and assignments for a Pre-AP course, see the *Algebra 1 Toolkit*.

Lesson	Les. Day	BASIC	AVERAGE	ADVANCED
2.1 6.11.01	Day 1	SRH p. 930 Exs. 1–4; pp. 67–70 Exs. 1, 3, 5–10, 14–19, 53, 54, 57, 67–75	pp. 67–70 Exs. 1, 3, 8–13, 17–22, 53, 54, 57–59, 67–75 odd	pp. 67–70 Exs. 1, 3, 10–13, 19–22, 53, 54, 57–60*, 68–74 even
	Day 2	pp. 67–70 Exs. 2, 4, 23–30, 35–44, 55, 56, 58, 61–66	pp. 67–70 Exs. 2, 4, 27–39 odd, 40–51, 55, 56, 61–66	pp. 67–70 Exs. 2, 4, 28–38 even, 39, 41–52*, 55, 56, 63, 65, 66
2.2 6.11.10	Day 1	SRH p. 914 Exs. 21–25; pp. 77–79 Exs. 1, 2, 3–23 odd, 24–31, 33–43 odd, 53–57, 60–66	pp. 77–79 Exs. 1, 2, 6–22 even, 24–31, 34–50 even, 53–59, 60–66 even	pp. 77–79 Exs. 1, 2, 8–22 even, 27–49 odd, 51–53*, 55–59*, 61–65 odd
2.3 6.11.10	Day 1	pp. 82–84 Exs. 1–16, 17–35 odd, 42–46, 49–55 odd	pp. 82–84 Exs. 1, 2, 6–14 even, 15, 16, 20–30 even, 32–46, 50–56 even	pp. 82–84 Exs. 1, 2, 10–14, 20–30 even, 32–41*, 43–48*, 52, 56
2.4 6.11.10	Day 1	pp. 91–93 Exs. 1–11, 19–41 odd, 43, 44, 50–54, 58–64 even	pp. 91–93 Exs. 1, 2, 10–42 even, 43–48, 50–55, 58–64 even	pp. 91–93 Exs. 1, 2, 12–42 even, 43–49*, 51–56*, 57–63 odd
2.5 6.11.05	Day 1	SRH p. 925 Exs. 1, 2, 4, 5, 12; pp. 99–101 Exs. 1–15, 21–24, 62–67	pp. 99–101 Exs. 1–4, 9–20, 23–27, 62–67	pp. 99–101 Exs. 1, 2, 11–20, 23–27, 65–67
	Day 2	pp. 99–101 Exs. 27–42, 50–53, 56–61	pp. 99–101 Exs. 32–48, 50–54, 56–61	pp. 99–101 Exs. 34–49*, 51–61*
2.6 6.11.10	Day 1	pp. 106–108 Exs. 1, 2, 3–23 odd, 24–28, 33–37, 42–45, 52–55, 59–63 odd	pp. 106–108 Exs. 1, 2, 7–10, 15–23 odd, 28–32, 37–49, 53, 60–64 even	pp. 106–108 Exs. 1, 2, 8–10, 19–23, 29–32, 38–41, 44–52*, 54–58*
2.7 6.11.01	Day 1	SRH p. 909 Exs. 11–17 odd; pp. 113–116 Exs. 1–10, 15–20, 23, 47–50, 56–63	pp. 113–116 Exs. 1, 2, 7–14, 17–23, 47–50, 56–63	pp. 113–116 Exs. 1, 2, 9–14, 19–23, 47–52, 56–62 even
	Day 2	pp. 113–116 Exs. 24–37, 51–53, 64–71	pp. 113–116 Exs. 24–32 even, 34–45, 51–54, 65–71 odd	pp. 113–116 Exs. 26–32 even, 36–46*, 53–55*, 64–70 even
Review	Day 1	pp. 121–124 Exs. 1–60	pp. 121–124 Exs. 1–60	pp. 121–124 Exs. 1–60
Assess	Day 1	Chapter 2 Test	Chapter 2 Test	Chapter 2 Test
Yearly Pacing		Chapter 2 Total – 12 days	Chapters 1–2 Total – 22 days	Remaining – 138 days

*Challenge Exercises EP = Extra Practice SRH = Skills Review Handbook

BLOCK SCHEDULE

DAY 1	DAY 2	DAY 3	DAY 4	DAY 5	DAY 6
2.1	**2.2**	**2.4**	**2.5 (CONT.)**	**2.7**	**REVIEW**
pp. 67–70 Exs. 1–4, 8–13, 17–22, 27–39 odd, 40–51, 53–59, 61–66, 67–75 odd	pp. 77–79 Exs. 1, 2, 6–22 even, 24–31, 34–50 even, 53–59, 60–66 even	pp. 91–93 Exs. 1, 2, 10–42 even, 43–48, 50–55, 58–64 even	pp. 99–101 Exs. 32–48, 50–54, 56–61	pp. 113–116 Exs. 1, 2, 7–14, 17–23, 24–32 even, 34–45, 47–54, 56–63, 65–71 odd	pp. 121–124 Exs. 1–60
	2.3	**2.5**	**2.6**		**ASSESS**
	pp. 82–84 Exs. 1, 2, 6–14 even, 15, 16, 20–30 even, 32–46, 50–56 even	pp. 99–101 Exs. 1–4, 9–20, 23–27, 62–67	pp. 106–108 Exs. 1, 2, 7–10, 15–23 odd, 28–32, 37–49, 60–64 even		Chapter 2 Test
Yearly Pacing	Chapter 2 Total – 6 days		Chapters 1–2 Total – 11 days	Remaining – 69 days	

Chapter Resource Guide

Chapter Resource Book

CHAPTER SUPPORT							
Parents as Partners (Chapter Overview with home involvement exercises and activity)						p. 1	
LESSON SUPPORT	**2.1**	**2.2**	**2.3**	**2.4**	**2.5**	**2.6**	**2.7**
Standard	**6.11.01**	**6.11.10**	**6.11.10**	**6.11.10**	**6.11.05**	**6.11.10**	**6.11.01**
Teaching Guide/Lesson Plan	p. 3	p. 13	p. 24	p. 37	p. 47	p. 58	p. 70
Activity Masters			p. 26				
Technology Activities & Keystrokes			p. 27			p. 60	
Activity Support Masters		p. 15			p. 49		
Practice (3 levels)	p. 5	p. 16	p. 28	p. 39	p. 50	p. 62	p. 72
Study Guide	p. 8	p. 19	p. 31	p. 42	p. 53	p. 65	p. 75
Catch-Up for Absent Students	p. 10	p. 21	p. 33	p. 44	p. 55	p. 67	p. 77
Problem Solving/Application	p. 11	p. 22	p. 34	p. 45	p. 56	p. 68	p. 78
Challenge Practice	p. 12	p. 23	p. 36	p. 46	p. 57	p. 69	p. 79
REVIEW							
Chapter Review Games and Activities		p. 80		Cumulative Practice		p. 83	
Project with Rubric		p. 81		Resource Book Answers		A1	

Transparencies	2.1	2.2	2.3	2.4	2.5	2.6	2.7
Warm-Up/Daily Homework Quiz	✔	✔	✔	✔	✔	✔	✔
Notetaking Guide	✔	✔	✔	✔	✔	✔	✔
Teacher Support	✔	✔					✔
Answer Transparencies	✔	✔	✔	✔	✔	✔	✔

ASSESSMENT BOOK

Quizzes	p. 16	SAT/ACT Chapter Test	p. 27
Chapter Tests (3 levels)	p. 19	Alternative Assessment with Rubric	p. 29
Standardized Chapter Test	p. 25		

TECHNOLOGY

- Easy Planner
- Test and Practice Generator
- Power Presentations
- @HomeTutor
- Activity Generator
- Animated Algebra
- Classzone.com
- eEdition Plus Online
- eWorkbook Plus Online
- ML Assessment System

ADDITIONAL RESOURCES

Illinois Additional Lessons

- Worked-Out Solution Key
- Notetaking Guide
- Practice Workbook
- Algebra 1 Toolkit
- Benchmark Tests
- Reteaching and Remediation
- Spanish Study Guide
- Spanish Assessment Book
- Spanish Resources in Spanish
- Multi-Language Visual Glossary

2 Lesson Practice Level B

LESSON 2.1 Practice B
For use with pages 64–70

4. whole number: none; integer: -3; rational number: $-1.9, \frac{3}{4}, 0.8, -3$; $-3, -1.9, \frac{3}{4}, 0.8$ 5. whole number: 0; integer: $0, -2$; rational number: $1.3, -2, \frac{1}{2}, 0$; $-2, 0, \frac{1}{2}, 1.3$

Graph the numbers on a number line. Then order the numbers from least to greatest.

1. $2, -3$, and 0 — $-3, 0, 2$
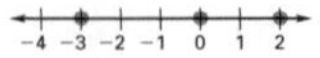
2. $-5, 7$, and -8 — $-8, -5, 7$
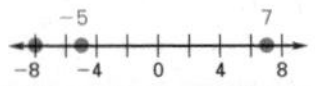
3. $-9, -12$, and 6 — $-12, -9, 6$
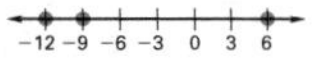

Tell whether each number in the list is a whole number, an integer, or a rational number. Then order the numbers from least to greatest.

4. $-1.9, \frac{3}{4}, 0.8, -3$
5. $1.3, -2, \frac{1}{2}, 0$
6. $2.5, -\frac{7}{8}, -0.5, \frac{1}{3}$

6. whole number: none; integer: none; rational number: $2.5, -\frac{7}{8}, -0.5, \frac{1}{3}$; $-\frac{7}{8}, -0.5, \frac{1}{3}, 2.5$

For the given value of *a*, find $-a$ and $|a|$.

7. $a = 10.2$ — $-10.2; 10.2$
8. $a = -14$ — $14; 14$
9. $a = \frac{1}{2}$ — $-\frac{1}{2}; \frac{1}{2}$

Identify the hypothesis and conclusion of the conditional statement. Tell whether the statement is *true* or *false*. If it is false, give a counterexample.

10. If a number is negative, then its opposite is positive.
11. If a number is even, then its opposite is a whole number.

10. hypothesis: a number is negative; conclusion: its opposite is positive; true
11. hypothesis: a number is even; conclusion: its opposite is a whole number; false; 2

Evaluate the expression when $x = -2.5$.

12. $-x$ — 2.5
13. $|x| + 3$ — 5.5
14. $|x| - 4$ — -1.5

15. **Fairbanks, Alaska** The table shows the monthly normal temperatures in Fairbanks, Alaska, during the winter months. Which monthly temperature is the lowest? Which months had temperatures below $-5°F$? January; December and January

Month	December	January	February	March
Temperature (°F)	−7°	−10°	−4°	11°

16. **Stock Market** The gains and losses of a stock for a week are shown in the table. Which day showed the greatest gain? Which day showed the greatest loss? Monday; Wednesday

Day	Monday	Tuesday	Wednesday	Thursday	Friday
Gain or loss	+0.02	−0.05	−0.12	−0.08	−0.01

17. **Class Enrollment** The table shows the growth in enrollment of the senior class at a high school between 1999 and 2004. Which year showed the greatest increase in class size? Which year showed the greatest decrease in class size? 2000; 2002

Year	1999	2000	2001	2002	2003	2004
Increase	15	22	−7	−12	10	18

LESSON 2.1

LESSON 2.2 Practice B
For use with pages 71–77

Use a number line to find the sum.

1. $-8 + 9$ — 1
2. $13 + (-4)$ — 9
3. $-5 + (-11)$ — -16
4. $-6 + (-7)$ — -13
5. $-15 + 6$ — -9
6. $-21 + 10$ — -11

Find the sum.

7. $-4.2 + 6.5$ — 2.3
8. $14.2 + (-9.1)$ — 5.1
9. $7.8 + (-3.9)$ — 3.9
10. $2\frac{2}{3} + \left(-1\frac{1}{3}\right)$ — $1\frac{1}{3}$
11. $-7\frac{1}{2} + 10\frac{3}{4}$ — $3\frac{1}{4}$
12. $8\frac{2}{3} + \left(-9\frac{1}{6}\right)$ — $-\frac{1}{2}$
13. $-10 + (-23) + 18$ — -15
14. $-1.25 + 2.5 + 3.5$ — 4.75
15. $-2.6 + 7.5 + 5.6$ — 10.5

Evaluate the expression for the given value of *x*.

16. $6 + x + (-11); x = 8$ — 3
17. $-14 + x + 14; x = 9$ — 9
18. $2.2 + x + (-3.4); x = -2.5$ — -3.7
19. $-4.3 + (-x) + 1.5; x = 3.1$ — -5.9
20. $-2.8 + (-x) + 8.1; x = -3.6$ — 8.9
21. $-6.8 + |x| + 2.6; x = -3.2$ — -1

Solve the equation.

22. $x + 15 + (-15) = 6$ — $x = 6$
23. $6 + x + (-3) = 0$ — $x = -3$
24. $x + (-2.5) + 6.8 = 0$ — $x = -4.3$

25. **Delivery Driver** A furniture delivery driver is given three deliveries for the morning. The first delivery is 7 miles west of the furniture store. The second delivery is 14 miles east of the first house, and the last delivery before lunch is 3 miles west of the second house. How far is the delivery driver from the store after the last delivery? 4 miles

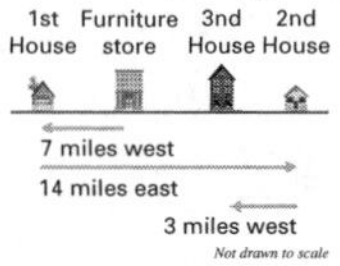

26. **Homework** Your history teacher gives you an extra credit question on each homework assignment. You've been keeping track of how many points you are above or below the number of regular points you can earn on each assignment. How many total points do you have if there are 125 regular homework points for the five assignments? 128 points

Assignment	1	2	3	4	5
Number of points above and below	−2	4	−1	5	−3

27. **Company Profits** The table shows the profits earned by a small company during the first six months of the year. Did the company make a positive profit for the first six months? If so, how much? yes; $500

Month	January	February	March	April	May	June
Profit	$1500	−$2000	$1000	$3000	−$2000	−$1000

LESSON 2.2

LESSON 2.3 Practice B
For use with pages 78–83

Find the difference.

1. $12 - (-7)$ — 19
2. $22 - (-28)$ — 50
3. $-6 - (-13)$ — 7
4. $-15 - (-9)$ — -6
5. $5.8 - (-7.9)$ — 13.7
6. $-4.1 - (-3.6)$ — -0.5
7. $-6.2 - (-3.6)$ — -2.6
8. $3.8 - (-5.9)$ — 9.7
9. $-2.6 - (-10.2)$ — 7.6
10. $\frac{1}{3} - \frac{4}{9}$ — $-\frac{1}{9}$
11. $\frac{1}{2} - \left(-\frac{7}{8}\right)$ — $1\frac{3}{8}$
12. $-\frac{2}{3} - \left(-\frac{3}{8}\right)$ — $-\frac{7}{24}$

Evaluate the expression when $x = -6.4$ and $y = 10.8$.

13. $y - x$ — 17.2
14. $x - (-y)$ — 4.4
15. $x - y$ — -17.2
16. $-y - x$ — -4.4
17. $x - y - 2.6$ — -19.8
18. $y - 5.4 - x$ — 11.8
19. $-7.3 - x + y$ — 9.9
20. $6.4 + y - x$ — 23.6
21. $10.8 - x - y$ — 6.4
22. $y - (-x) + 6.4$ — 10.8
23. $7.2 + y - x$ — 24.4
24. $4.25 - x - y$ — -0.15

Find the change in temperature or elevation.

25. From 15°C to −5°C — −20°C
26. From −250 meters to 175 meters — 425 m

27. **Planet Temperatures** The average temperature on the surface of Venus is 480°C and the average temperature on the surface of Mars is −65°C. How many degrees hotter is the temperature on Venus' surface than on Mars' surface? 545°C

28. **Manned Submersibles** Alvin, a manned submersible used in deep-sea exploration, has a maximum depth of −14,764 feet. Its first untethered dive was −35 feet. How many feet deeper is Alvin's maximum depth than the depth of its first dive? 14,729 ft

29. **Banana Prices** The table shows the weekly prices (in dollars) of a pound of bananas during a month at a local supermarket. Determine the change in the price per pound each week. Find the total of these changes to determine the total change in the price per pound over the 4 weeks.

Week	1	2	3	4
Price per pound (dollars)	0.49	0.49	0.39	0.49

Week 1 to Week 2: $0; Week 2 to Week 3: −$.10; Week 3 to Week 4: $.10; $0

30. **State Temperatures** The table shows the record high and low temperatures for several states. Find the difference between the record high and low temperatures for each state. Which state has the greatest temperature difference?

State	Alaska	North Dakota	Wyoming	Virginia	Nevada
High temperature (°F)	100°	121°	115°	110°	125°
Low temperature (°F)	−80°	−60°	−66°	−30°	−50°

Alaska: 180°; North Dakota: 181°; Wyoming: 181°; Virginia: 140°; Nevada: 175°; North Dakota and Wyoming

LESSON 2.3

LESSON 2.4 Practice B
For use with pages 86–91

LESSON 2.4

Find the product.

1. $10(-9)$ — -90
2. $-12(-3)$ — 36
3. $-11(7)$ — -77
4. $2.6(-8)$ — -20.8
5. $-3.2(15)$ — -48
6. $-9.5(5)$ — -47.5
7. $-\frac{1}{2}(28)$ — -14
8. $-\frac{2}{3}(-21)$ — 14
9. $\frac{4}{5}(-20)$ — -16
10. $-6(4)(-3.5)$ — 84
11. $-2.1(-10)(-5)$ — -105
12. $-6.5(21)(-6)$ — 819

Identify the property illustrated.

13. $5.6 \cdot (-3.2) = -3.2 \cdot 5.6$ — Commutative prop. of mult.
14. $0 \cdot 2.1 = 0$ — Multiplicative property of 0
15. $-1 \cdot (-1.5) = 1.5$ — Multiplicative property of −1

Find the product. Justify your steps. See below.

16. $-3(-5)(-4x)$
17. $-\frac{3}{4}(-20)(7y)$
18. $8x(4.2)(-5)$

Evaluate the expression when $x = -3$ and $y = 4.1$.

19. $x + 2y$ — 5.2
20. $y - 4x$ — 16.1
21. $5.2x - y$ — -19.7
22. $xy - 10.1$ — -22.4
23. $14.3 - xy$ — 26.6
24. $3x - |y|$ — -13.1

25. **Death Valley** The lowest point in North America is Death Valley, California. Its elevation is at −86 meters. What is this elevation in feet? *Hint:* Use the fact that 1 meter ≈ 3.281 feet. −282.166 m

26. **Lava Flow** A kind of lava, block lava, is moving away from the base of a volcano at a rate of 1.5 meters per day. If the lava continues to flow at this rate, how far away has the lava flowed from the base of the volcano in 30 days? 45 m

27. **Snow Melt** After a recent snowfall, the snow on the ground in a shaded area is melting at a rate of 0.01 inch per minute. Currently, there are 4 inches of snow on the ground. If the snow continues melting at this rate, how much snow will be on the ground in 6 hours? How much snow has melted? 0.4 in.; 3.6 in.

28. **City Population** In 1990, the population of Pittsburgh, Pennsylvania was 2468 thousand people. The table shows the average rate of change in the population for two periods of time. Find the total population in 2000 and 2002. 1990 to 2000: 2431 thousand people; 2000 to 2002: 2418 thousand people

Time period	Rate of change (thousand people/yr)
1990–2000	−3.7
2000–2002	−6.5

16. $-3(-5)(-4x)$
$= 15(-4x)$ — Product of −3 and −5 is 15.
$= [15(-4)]x$ — Assoc. prop. of mult.
$= -60x$ — Product of 15 and −4 is −60.

17. $-\frac{3}{4}(-20)(7y)$
$= 15(7y)$ — Product of $-\frac{3}{4}$ and −20 is 15.
$= (15 \cdot 7)y$ — Assoc. prop. of mult.
$= 105y$ — Product of 15 and 7 is 105.

18. $8x(4.2)(-5)$
$= 8x(-21)$ — Product of 4.2 and −5 is −21.
$= 8(-21)x$ — Comm. prop. of mult.
$= -168x$ — Product of 8 and −21 is −168.

LESSON 2.5

Practice B

For use with pages 94–100

Use the distributive property to write an equivalent expression.

1. $5(x + 11)$ $5x + 55$
2. $3(x - 12)$ $3x - 36$
3. $-4(x + 8)$ $-4x - 32$
4. $9(2x + 1)$ $18x + 9$
5. $(x - 7)(-10)$ $-10x + 70$
6. $(4x + 3)5$ $20x + 15$
7. $x(4x - 1)$ $4x^2 - x$
8. $2x(x - 1)$ $2x^2 - 2x$
9. $-x(5x + 2)$ $-5x^2 - 2x$

Identify the terms, like terms, coefficients, and constant terms of the expression.

10. $-8 + 2x + 5 + 11x$ **10.** Terms: $-8, 2x, 5, 11x$; Like terms: $2x$ and $11x$, -8 and 5; Coefficients: 2, 11; Constant terms: -8, 5
11. $4x^2 + 1 - 3x^2 + 5$ **11.** Terms: $4x^2, 1, -3x^2, 5$; Like terms: $4x^2$ and $-3x^2$, 1 and 5; Coefficients: 4, -3; Constant terms: 1, 5
12. $7y^2 - 6 + 3y^2 - 15$ See below.
13. $3xy + 5 - 2xy + 10$ See below.

Simplify the expression.

14. $6 + 10x + 3$ $10x + 9$
15. $2(3x + 1) + 4x$ $10x + 2$
16. $6(5 - x) + 12x$ $6x + 30$
17. $7(x - 1) - 5$ $7x - 12$
18. $8x + 3(2x - 1)$ $14x - 3$
19. $-2(x + 4) - 3$ $-2x - 11$
20. $11x - (x + 7)$ $10x - 7$
21. $9 - 2(x - 4)$ $-2x + 17$
22. $7x - 3(4 - 2x)$ $13x - 12$

23. **Curtains** You are making curtains by alternating strips of solid colored fabric and patterned fabric. The solid colored fabric costs \$.99 per strip and the patterned fabric costs \$1.25 per strip. You need 7 strips for one curtain. Write an equation that gives the total cost c as a function of the number n of solid colored strips used. Then find the total cost if you use 3 solid colored strips. $c = 0.99n + 1.25(7 - n)$; \$7.97

24. **Shoe Boxes** A department store is selling its plastic shoe boxes for \$1.50 off the regular price of a shoe box. You buy 4 shoe boxes. Write an equation that gives the total cost t as a function of the regular cost r of a shoe box. Then find the total cost if the boxes regularly cost \$3.59 each. $t = 4(r - 1.5)$; \$8.36

25. **Delivering Papers** You and your friend share a paper route. You can deliver 4 papers in one minute and your friend can deliver 3 papers in one minute. Seventy-five papers have to be delivered each day on the route. Let n be the number of papers you deliver.

    a. Use the verbal model to write an equation that you can use to find out how long it will take the both of you together to deliver the papers. $t = \frac{1}{4}n + \frac{1}{3}(75 - n)$

Total amount of time (min)	=	Your rate (min/paper)	•	Number of papers you deliver (papers)	+	Friend's rate (min/papers)	•	Number of papers friend delivers (papers)

    b. How long will it take the both of you to deliver the papers if you deliver 38 papers? 50 papers? about 21.8 min; about 20.8 min

12. Terms: $7y^2, -6, 3y^2, -15$; Like terms: $7y^2$ and $3y^2$, -6 and -15; Coefficients: 7, 3; Constant terms: -6, -15

13. Terms: $3xy, 5, -2xy, 10$; Like terms: $3xy$ and $-2xy$, 5 and 10; Coefficients: 3, -2; Constant terms: 5, 10

LESSON 2.5

LESSON 2.6

Practice B

For use with pages 101–106

Find the multiplicative inverse of the number.

1. -7 $-\frac{1}{7}$
2. $-\frac{1}{5}$ -5
3. $-\frac{7}{8}$ $-\frac{8}{7}$

Find the quotient.

4. $-32 \div (-2)$ 16
5. $-1 \div \left(-\frac{6}{5}\right)$ $\frac{5}{6}$
6. $14 \div \left(-\frac{2}{7}\right)$ -49
7. $17 \div \left(-2\frac{1}{8}\right)$ -8
8. $-\frac{3}{4} \div 4$ $-\frac{3}{16}$
9. $-\frac{1}{3} \div \frac{1}{5}$ $-1\frac{2}{3}$
10. $-\frac{1}{9} \div (-8)$ $\frac{1}{72}$
11. $-\frac{6}{11} \div (-3)$ $\frac{2}{11}$
12. $\frac{5}{8} \div \left(-2\frac{1}{2}\right)$ $-\frac{1}{4}$

Find the mean of the numbers.

13. $1, -3, -10$ -4
14. $-15, 4, -22$ -11
15. $-7.5, 3, -6.5$ $-3\frac{2}{3}$

Simplify the expression.

16. $\frac{-8x + 27}{9}$ $-\frac{8}{9}x + 3$
17. $\frac{15x - 5}{-5}$ $1 - 3x$
18. $\frac{12x - 20}{-4}$ $5 - 3x$

19. **Melting Point** The melting point of the element fluorine is $-219.62°C$. The melting point of the element bromine is $-7.2°C$. How many times lower is the melting point of fluorine than the melting point of bromine? Round your answer to the nearest tenth. about 30.5

20. **Website Traffic** During a 3-month period, the traffic to a website dropped by 126,000 visitors. Find the average rate of change in the traffic to the website (in visitors per month) over the 3-month period. $-42{,}000$ visitors/month

21. **Average Velocity** The velocity of an object indicates the object's speed and the direction in which the object is traveling. A negative velocity indicates that the object is moving downward or backward. A hawk is diving downward at a rate of 50 feet in 28 seconds. Find the hawk's average velocity (in feet per second). Round your answer to the nearest tenth. -1.8 ft/sec

22. **Health Club** The table below shows change in the number of memberships at a health club. What is the average change in the number of memberships (in members per month)? 5.6 memberships/month

Month	Nov.	Dec.	Jan.	Feb.	Mar.
Change in number of memberships	18	10	40	−25	−15

23. **Bank Account Activity** During a 14-day period, there is the following activity on your bank account. You deposit \$100, withdraw \$75, deposit \$85, and withdraw \$150. What is the rate of change (in dollars per day) in your bank account? Round your answer to the nearest cent. about $-\$2.86$/day

LESSON 2.6

LESSON 2.7

Practice B

For use with pages 107–114

Evaluate the expression.

1. $\pm\sqrt{81}$ ± 9
2. $\pm\sqrt{25}$ ± 5
3. $-\sqrt{400}$ -20
4. $\sqrt{625}$ 25
5. $\sqrt{4900}$ 70
6. $\pm\sqrt{169}$ ± 13

Approximate the square root to the nearest integer.

7. $-\sqrt{29}$ -5
8. $\sqrt{108}$ 10
9. $-\sqrt{53}$ -7
10. $\sqrt{138}$ 12
11. $-\sqrt{55}$ -7
12. $\sqrt{640}$ 25

Tell whether each number in the list is a real number, a rational number, an irrational number, an integer, or a whole number. Then order the numbers from least to greatest. See below.

13. $-\sqrt{16}, 3.2, -\frac{3}{2}, \sqrt{9}$
14. $\sqrt{5}, -6, 2.5, -\frac{24}{5}$

Evaluate the expression for the given value of x.

15. $14 + \sqrt{x}$ when $x = 16$ 18
16. $\sqrt{x} - 5.5$ when $x = 4$ -3.5
17. $-9 \cdot \sqrt{x}$ when $x = 25$ -45
18. $2\sqrt{x} - 1$ when $x = 100$ 19

19. **Park** A local park is in the shape of a square and covers an area of 3600 square feet. Find the side length of the park. 60 ft

20. **Wall Poster** You are considering buying a square wall poster that has an area of 6.25 square feet. Find the side length of the wall poster. 2.5 ft

21. **Road Sign** The U.S. Department of Transportation determines the sizes of the traffic control signs that you see along the roadways. The square Pennsylvania state route sign at the right has an area of 1296 square inches. Find the side length of the sign. 36 in.

22. **Flower Bed** You are building the square flower bed shown using railroad ties. You want to place another railroad tie on the diagonal to form two triangular beds. Find the length of the diagonal by using the expression $\sqrt{2s^2}$ where s is the side length of the flower bed. Round your answer to the nearest tenth. about 7.1 ft

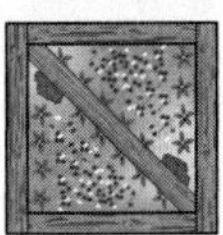

13. real number: $-\sqrt{16}, 3.2, -\frac{3}{2}, \sqrt{9}$; rational number: $-\sqrt{16}, 3.2, -\frac{3}{2}, \sqrt{9}$; irrational number: none; integer: $-\sqrt{16}, \sqrt{9}$; whole number: $\sqrt{9}$; $-\sqrt{16}, -\frac{3}{2}, \sqrt{9}, 3.2$

14. real number: $-6, -\frac{24}{5}, \sqrt{5}, 2.5$; rational number: $-6, -\frac{24}{5}, 2.5$; irrational number: $\sqrt{5}$; integer: -6; whole number: none; $-6, -\frac{24}{5}, \sqrt{5}, 2.5$

LESSON 2.7

CHAPTER 2 Quiz 1

For use after Lessons 2.1–2.3

Identify the property illustrated.

1. $x + (-7) = -7 + x$
2. $5 + (-5) = 0$
3. $(3 + 2) + 9 = 3 + (2 + 9)$
4. $0 + 12 = 12$

Find the sum or difference.

5. $2.7 + (-5.2)$
6. $18 - (-4)$
7. $-3 - (-5)$

Evaluate the expression when $x = 10$ and $y = -3$.

8. $-x + y + 4$
9. $y + |y| - 7$
10. $6 - x - y$

Answers

1. Commutative property of addition
2. Inverse property of addition
3. Associative property of addition
4. Identity property of addition
5. -2.5
6. 22
7. 2
8. -9
9. -7
10. -1

CHAPTER 2 Quiz 2

For use after Lessons 2.4–2.5

Identify the property illustrated.

1. $(-8 \cdot 2) \cdot 3 = -8 \cdot (2 \cdot 3)$
2. $5 \cdot (-1) = -5$
3. $3 \cdot (-6) = -6 \cdot 3$
4. $14 \cdot 0 = 0$

Find the product.

5. $3(-8)$
6. $-4(-5)$
7. $2(3)(-1)$
8. $(-6x) \cdot (-5)$
9. $-\frac{3}{4}x \cdot 28$
10. $1.8 \cdot x \cdot (-4.6)$

Use the distributive property to write an equivalent expression.

11. $-(3x + 1)$
12. $-9(y - 7)$
13. $(4x + 3)3$

Answers

1. Associative property of multiplication
2. Property of -1
3. Commutative property of multiplication
4. Property of zero
5. -24
6. 20
7. -6
8. $30x$
9. $-21x$
10. $-8.28x$
11. $-3x - 1$
12. $-9y + 63$
13. $12x + 9$

CHAPTER 2 Quiz 3

For use after Lessons 2.6–2.7

Find the multiplicative inverse of the number.

1. $-\frac{1}{3}$
2. 8

Find the quotient.

3. $-30 \div 3$
4. $-24 \div (-4)$
5. $-\frac{3}{4} \div 2$

Simplify the expression.

6. $\frac{35 - 14x}{7}$
7. $\frac{-16x + 8}{-4}$

Evaluate the expression.

8. $\sqrt{49}$
9. $\pm\sqrt{4}$
10. $-\sqrt{16}$

Answers

1. -3
2. $\frac{1}{8}$
3. -10
4. 6
5. $-\frac{3}{8}$
6. $5 - 2x$
7. $4x - 2$
8. 7
9. 2 and -2
10. -4

CHAPTER 2 Chapter Test B

For use after Chapter 2

Tell whether each number is a real number, a rational number, an irrational number, an integer, or a whole number.

1. -0.75
2. $\sqrt{12}$
3. 10

Tell whether the statement is *true* or *false*. If it is false, give a counterexample.

4. If a number is positive, then its opposite is negative.
5. If a number is an integer, then the number is an irrational number.

Order the numbers in the list from least to greatest.

6. $-\frac{1}{5}, -0.25, \frac{1}{3}, 1$
7. $-\frac{14}{3}, -4.6, -4.07, -4\frac{1}{3}$

Identify the property being illustrated.

8. $(x \cdot 0.5) \cdot 8 = x \cdot (0.5 \cdot 8)$
9. $x + (-y) = -y + x$
10. $2(5z - 9) = 10z - 18$
11. $3a + (-3a) = 0$

Find the sum or the difference.

12. $3 - (-12)$
13. $-22 + 16$
14. $-0.8 + (-8.9)$
15. $-16 - (-25.2)$
16. $\frac{1}{2} - \frac{7}{10}$
17. $7\frac{4}{5} + -2\frac{1}{4}$

In Exercises 18 and 19, use the table below.

Name	Double eagle	Eagle	Birdie	Par	Bogey	Double bogey
Score	-3	-2	-1	0	1	2

18. In golf, the best total score is the lowest score. In 4 holes, you score a birdie, a par, a double eagle, and a double bogey. Your friend scores an eagle, a double eagle, a bogey, and a par. Who has the better total score?
19. What is the difference between your friend's total score and your total score?

Answers

1. real number, rational number
2. real number, irrational number
3. real number, rational number, integer, whole number
4. true
5. false; 5
6. $-0.25, -\frac{1}{5}, \frac{1}{3}, 1$
7. $-\frac{14}{3}, -4.6, -4\frac{1}{3}, -4.07$
8. Assoc. prop. of mult.
9. Commutative property of addition
10. Distributive prop.
11. Inverse prop. of add.
12. 15
13. -6
14. -9.7
15. 9.2
16. $-\frac{1}{5}$
17. $5\frac{11}{20}$
18. your friend
19. -2

CHAPTER 2 Chapter Test B *continued*

For use after Chapter 2

Evaluate the expression when $x = -5.4$ and $y = 2.8$.

20. $y - x - 1.4$ **21.** $x + |y - 10|$

Find the product or the quotient.

22. $-6(-12)$ **23.** $45 \div (-3)$

24. $\frac{5}{9}\left(-\frac{3}{4}\right)$ **25.** $-7.2 \div 8$

26. $-4 \div \left(-\frac{2}{9}\right)$ **27.** $-\frac{2}{3}(18)\left(-\frac{1}{4}\right)$

28. A person buys items and sells them on a website. The table shows the profit earned for each item. Suppose that in one week the person sells 8 mantel clocks, 5 framed mirrors, and 3 candles. Find the average daily profit.

Item	Mantel clock	Framed mirror	Candle
Profit	\$4.13	−\$1.65	\$2.36

Simplify the expression.

29. $10x - (x + 3)$ **30.** $-2x(x - 6)$ **31.** $\frac{-6x + 15}{-10}$

32. Use the distributive property and mental math to find the total cost of 6 notebooks at \$3.95 each.

33. Find the perimeter and area of the rectangle with the given dimensions.

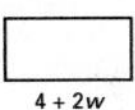

Approximate the square root to the nearest integer.

34. $\sqrt{35}$ **35.** $-\sqrt{150}$ **36.** $\sqrt{18}$

37. The area of a town's square is 14,400 square feet. Find the side length of the square.

Evaluate the expression for the given value of *x*.

38. $2 - \sqrt{x}$ when $x = 25$ **39.** $4\sqrt{x} + 9$ when $x = 1$

Answers

20. 6.8
21. 1.8
22. 72
23. -15
24. $-\frac{5}{12}$
25. -0.9
26. 18
27. 3
28. \$4.55
29. $9x - 3$
30. $-2x^2 + 12x$
31. $\frac{3}{5}x - \frac{3}{2}$
32. $6(4 - 0.05) = \$23.70$
33. $P = 20 + 4w$; $A = 24 + 12w$
34. 6
35. -12
36. 4
37. 120 ft
38. -3
39. 13

CHAPTER 2 Standardized Test

For use after Chapter 2

Multiple Choice

1. Which list of numbers is ordered from least to greatest? C

Ⓐ $-\frac{1}{2}, -1, \frac{3}{8}, 5$ Ⓑ $\frac{1}{2}, \frac{1}{3}, \frac{1}{4}, \frac{1}{5}$

Ⓒ $-\frac{1}{2}, 0.66, \frac{2}{3}, \frac{7}{8}$ Ⓓ $-0.16, -\frac{1}{6}, 0, 3$

2. Which number is an integer? A

Ⓐ $-\frac{32}{8}$ Ⓑ $\frac{1}{5}$

Ⓒ $|-3.8|$ Ⓓ $\left|\frac{24}{5}\right|$

3. What is the value of $5(-x)$ when $x = -\frac{1}{10}$? C

Ⓐ $-2\frac{1}{2}$ Ⓑ $\frac{4}{5}$

Ⓒ $\frac{1}{2}$ Ⓓ $4\frac{9}{10}$

4. Which number is a solution of $5 + |m| = 7.3$? B

Ⓐ -12.3 Ⓑ -2.3

Ⓒ 7.3 Ⓓ 12.3

5. What is the value of $-5.06 + -2.3$? B

Ⓐ -7.9 Ⓑ -7.36

Ⓒ 3.3 Ⓓ 3.76

6. What property is being illustrated in the equation $-12 + 12 = 0$? D

Ⓐ Associative Property

Ⓑ Commutative Property

Ⓒ Identity Property

Ⓓ Inverse Property

7. What is the solution of the equation $-9.7 + x - 5.4 = 12.1$? D

Ⓐ -3 Ⓑ 3 Ⓒ 16.5 Ⓓ 27.2

8. What is the value of $-\frac{5}{6} - \left(-\frac{2}{3}\right)$? C

Ⓐ $-1\frac{1}{2}$ Ⓑ $-\frac{7}{9}$

Ⓒ $-\frac{1}{6}$ Ⓓ $1\frac{1}{2}$

9. What is the change in temperature from −26°F to 78°F? D

Ⓐ −104°F Ⓑ −52°F

Ⓒ 52°F Ⓓ 104°F

10. What is the value of $|z - y| - x$ where $x = 25.3, y = -7.2, z = 15.8$? B

Ⓐ -16.7 Ⓑ -2.3

Ⓒ 2.3 Ⓓ 16.7

11. What property is being illustrated in the equation $-2 \cdot (5 \cdot 2) = (-2 \cdot 5) \cdot 2$? A

Ⓐ Associative Property

Ⓑ Commutative Property

Ⓒ Identity Property

Ⓓ Inverse Property

12. What is the product of $-\frac{1}{5}(-a)(-a)\left(\frac{5}{9}\right)$? A

Ⓐ $-\frac{1}{9} \cdot a^2$ Ⓑ $\frac{1}{9} \cdot a^2$

Ⓒ $-\frac{2}{9} \cdot a$ Ⓓ $\frac{2}{9} \cdot a$

13. What is the value of $|n| + m^2$ where $m = -2.4$ and $n = -3.8$? C

Ⓐ -1 Ⓑ 1.96

Ⓒ 9.56 Ⓓ 16.84

14. Which pair of terms are like terms? D

Ⓐ $2x, 2y$ Ⓑ $3x, 2x^2$

Ⓒ $-4, -4y$ Ⓓ $x^3, 5x^3$

CHAPTER 2 Standardized Test *continued*

For use after Chapter 2

15. Simplify the expression $4(n - 3) - 2(-3 + n)$. A

Ⓐ $2n - 6$ Ⓑ $2n + 6$

Ⓒ $4n - 18$ Ⓓ $6n - 2$

16. What is the perimeter of the rectangle? D

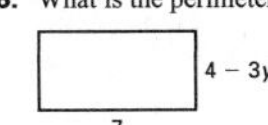

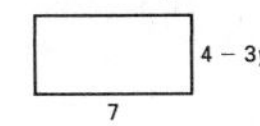

Ⓐ $-3y + 11$ Ⓑ $-21y + 28$

Ⓒ $-3y + 28$ Ⓓ $-6y + 22$

17. If $-\frac{4}{5}x = 1$, what is the value of x? B

Ⓐ $-1\frac{2}{5}$ Ⓑ $-1\frac{1}{4}$

Ⓒ $\frac{4}{5}$ Ⓓ $-1\frac{1}{5}$

18. Simplify the expression $\frac{27 - 6y}{-3}$. C

Ⓐ $-6y - 9$ Ⓑ $2y + 27$

Ⓒ $2y - 9$ Ⓓ $-7y$

19. Which number is between −20 and −15? C

Ⓐ $-\sqrt{1089}$ Ⓑ $-\sqrt{441}$

Ⓒ $-\sqrt{289}$ Ⓓ $-\sqrt{196}$

20. Which expression is a perfect square if $x = 81$? A

Ⓐ $2 \cdot \sqrt{x} + 31$ Ⓑ $\sqrt{x} + 3 \cdot 3$

Ⓒ $9 - 5\sqrt{x}$ Ⓓ $2 + 6\sqrt{x}$

21. Which number is irrational? D

Ⓐ $-\frac{5}{3}$ Ⓑ -2.4

Ⓒ $\sqrt{16}$ Ⓓ $\sqrt{18}$

Gridded Answer

22. What is the value of $\frac{5(2x - 6)}{x}$ when $x = -2$? 25

Short Response 23. a. $C = \$.15t + \$.10m$

23. Suppose you have a pre-paid cell phone where you pay a certain amount up front and the amount used is deducted. You pay \$.15 per minute and \$.10 per text message.

a. Write an equation for the total cost C where t represents each minute used and m represents each text message sent.

b. You have pre-paid \$20 on your phone. If you have used 104 minutes and have sent 7 text messages, what is your remaining balance? *Explain.* \$3.70

Extended Response

24. A gardener has a square garden with an area of 5476 square feet.

a. How many feet of fencing would the gardener need to fence around his garden? 296 ft

b. Fencing is sold in 50 feet rolls. Partial rolls cannot be purchased. How many rolls of fencing must the gardener purchase? *Explain.* 6 rolls

c. How many feet of fencing will the gardener have leftover? Explain. 4 ft

d. Each roll of fencing costs \$45.65 plus 6% tax. How much will the gardener pay for the fencing? Round to the nearest cent. *Explain.* \$290.33

CHAPTER 2 Alternative Assessment and Math Journal

For use after Chapter 2

Journal

1. Describe the relationship between integers and rational numbers. Explain the difference between rational numbers and irrational numbers, and provide an example of each type of number.

Multi-Step Problem

2. To discourage random guessing on a multiple-choice exam, a professor assigns 7 points for a correct answer, −3 points for an incorrect answer, and −1 point for leaving the question blank.

a. What is the score for a student who had 19 correct answers, 4 incorrect answers, and 2 questions left blank?

b. What is the maximum number of points available on the exam from part (a)?

c. The following calculation was used to compute Pete's score on the exam: $17(7) + 2(-1) + 6(-3)$. Determine the score for this student and describe Pete's performance on the exam.

d. Katie took the exam and had 19 correct answers, 3 incorrect answers, and left 3 questions blank. Katie calculated her score on the exam as shown.

$19(7) + 3(-3) + 3(-1) = 19(7) + 3(-3 - 1)$

Verify that both sides of this equation result in the same score and name the property that guarantees the equality.

e. Jason answered 20 questions correctly and 5 questions incorrectly. What fraction of the total points did Jason earn? Write your answer in simplest form.

f. Erin answered 18 questions correctly, 1 incorrectly, and left 6 blank. Stephen answered 19 questions correctly, 5 incorrectly, and left 1 blank. Who had the higher score on the exam?

g. If a student answers every question on the exam, the following expression can be used to calculate the number of points earned, where x represents the number of questions answered correctly.

$7x + (25 - x)(-3)$

Explain why this expression can be used to calculate the total number of points earned. Then simplify the expression.

h. Evaluate your expression from part (g) to determine the points earned by a student who answered all of the questions and had 16 correct answers.

1. Complete answers should include: an explanation that a rational number is a ratio of two integers; an explanation that irrational numbers cannot be expressed as a ratio of two integers, or a discussion of the differences between the decimal representations of rational numbers and irrational numbers; an example of a rational number and an example of an irrational number.

2. a. 199 points **b.** 175 points **c.** 99 points; 17 correct answers, 6 incorrect answers, 2 left blank **d.** 121 points; distributive property **e.** $\frac{5}{7}$ **f.** Neither; both scored 177 points. **g.** Explanations may vary; $10x - 75$ **h.** 85 points

PLAN AND PREPARE

Main Ideas

In Chapter 2, students will learn about the real number system. They will classify real numbers, compare and order integers and rational numbers, perform basic operations, find square roots, apply properties to evaluate and simplify expressions, and use the Distributive Property to write equivalent expressions. Students will use conditional statements and logical reasoning to reason with real numbers.

Prerequisite Skills

- Comparing and ordering numbers
- Evaluating expressions
- Applying order of operations

Additional resources for reviewing prerequisite skills are:

- Skills Review Handbook, pp. 909–937
- @HomeTutor

2 Properties of Real Numbers

Before

In previous courses and in Chapter 1, you learned the following skills, which you'll use in Chapter 2: comparing and ordering numbers, evaluating expressions, and applying the order of operations.

Prerequisite Skills

VOCABULARY CHECK

In Exercises 1 and 2, copy and complete the statement.

1. The **least common denominator** of the fractions $\frac{3}{8}$ and $\frac{5}{12}$ is _?_. 24
2. The **variable** in the expression $5x - 3$ is _?_. x
3. According to the **order of operations**, what is the first step in simplifying the expression $(3 + 4)^2 - 8$? Add 3 + 4.

SKILLS CHECK

Copy and complete the statement using <, >, or =. *(Review p. 909 for 2.1, 2.7.)*

4. 26.70 _?_ 29.69 < **5.** 15.09 _?_ 15.1 < **6.** 0.333 _?_ 0.34 < **7.** 2.5 _?_ 2.500 =

Evaluate the expression when $x = 5$. *(Review p. 2 for 2.2–2.4, 2.6.)*

8. $52 - x$ 47 **9.** $1.7x$ 8.5 **10.** $x + 39$ 44 **11.** $\frac{125}{x}$ 25

Evaluate the expression. *(Review p. 8 for 2.5.)*

12. $5m - 9$ when $m = 6$ 21 **13.** $16 - r - 3$ when $r = 10$ 3

@HomeTutor Prerequisite skills practice at classzone.com

Chapter Planning Guide

Chapter 2 Resource Book
- Teaching Guide/Lesson Plan (pp. 3, 13, 24, 37, 47, 58, 70)
- Project with Rubric (p. 81)

Assessment and Intervention
- Assessment Book (pp. 16–30)
- Benchmark Tests
- Reteaching and Remediation Book

Interactive Technology
- Easy Planner
- Power Presentations CD-ROM
- Activity Generator CD-ROM
- Animated Algebra
- Test Generator CD-ROM
- Online Quizzes
- eWorkbook
- eEdition
- @HomeTutor

Resources for English Learners
- Quick Reference for English Learners
- Spanish Study Guide
- Multi-Language Visual Glossary
- Student Resources in Spanish

Now

In Chapter 2, you will apply the big ideas listed below and reviewed in the Chapter Summary on page 120. You will also use the key vocabulary listed below.

Big Ideas

1. **Performing operations with real numbers**
2. **Applying properties of real numbers**
3. **Classifying and reasoning with real numbers**

KEY VOCABULARY

- whole numbers, integers, *p. 64*
- rational number, *p. 64*
- opposites, absolute value, *p. 66*
- conditional statement, *p. 66*
- additive identity, *p. 76*
- additive inverse, *p. 76*
- multiplicative identity, *p. 89*
- equivalent expressions, *p. 96*
- distributive property, *p. 96*
- term, coefficient, constant term, like terms, *p. 97*
- multiplicative inverse, *p. 103*
- square root, radicand, *p. 110*
- perfect square, *p. 111*
- irrational number, *p. 111*
- real numbers, *p. 112*

Why?

You can use multiple representations to solve a problem about a real-world situation. For example, you can write an equation and make a table to find a skydiver's altitude over time.

Animated Algebra

The animation illustrated below for Exercise 54 on page 93 helps you answer this question: How does the time spent in free fall after a skydiver reaches terminal velocity affect the altitude of the skydiver?

A skydiver in freefall wants to open the parachute at an altitude of 2500 feet.

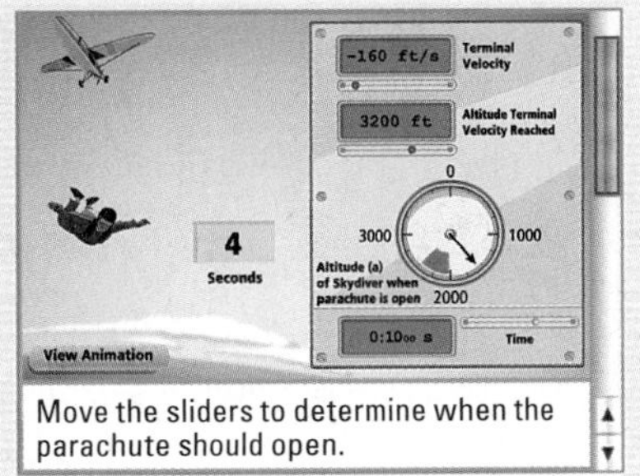

Move the sliders to determine when the parachute should open.

Animated Algebra at classzone.com

Other animations for Chapter 2: pages 73, 80, 90, and 98

Algebra 1 Toolkit

- Reading Strategies for Chapter 2, pp. 11–12
- Differentiated Instruction Notes, pp. 45–48
- English Learners Notes, pp. 99–100
- Inclusion Notes, pp. 131–132
- Teaching Strategies with Sample Worksheets, pp. 155–178
- Using Technology in the Classroom, pp. 179–184
- Tips for New Teachers, pp. 187–188
- Math Background Notes, pp. 213–214
- Pre-AP Strategies and Copymasters, pp. 280–281, 313–328
- Teacher Survival Activities, pp. 557–558, 583–584
- Bulletin Board Idea, p. 608
- Teacher Tool Transparencies, following p. 620

1 PLAN AND PREPARE

Warm-Up Exercises

Transparency Available

Complete the statement using <, >, or =.

1. 1.3 _?_ 1.03 > **2.** $\frac{5}{8}$ _?_ $\frac{6}{9}$ <

3. Order from least to greatest: $\frac{1}{2}$, 0.04, $\frac{3}{7}$, 0.45 0.04, $\frac{3}{7}$, 0.45, $\frac{1}{2}$

4. A hobby store has balsa wood strips in three thicknesses (in inches): $\frac{3}{16}$, $\frac{5}{32}$, and $\frac{1}{8}$. Which strip is the thickest? $\frac{3}{16}$-inch strip

Notetaking Guide

Transparency Available

Promotes interactive learning and notetaking skills, pp. 23–26.

Pacing

Basic: 2 days

Average: 2 days

Advanced: 2 days

Block: 1 block

- See *Teaching Guide/Lesson Plan.*

2 FOCUS AND MOTIVATE

Essential Question

Big Idea 3, p. 63

How do you compare positive and negative numbers? Tell students they will learn how to answer this question by graphing integers.

2.1 Use Integers and Rational Numbers

6.11.01 Recognize, represent, order, compare real numbers, and locate real numbers on a number line (e.g., ?, ? 2, ? 5, $\frac{2}{3}$, −1.6).

Before You performed operations with whole numbers.

Now You will graph and compare positive and negative numbers.

Why? So you can compare temperatures, as in Ex. 58.

Key Vocabulary
- whole numbers
- integers
- rational number
- opposites
- absolute value
- conditional statement

Whole numbers are the numbers 0, 1, 2, 3, . . . and **integers** are the numbers . . . , −3, −2, −1, 0, 1, 2, 3, ... (The dots indicate that the numbers continue without end in both directions.) **Positive integers** are integers that are greater than 0. **Negative integers** are integers that are less than 0. The integer 0 is neither negative nor positive.

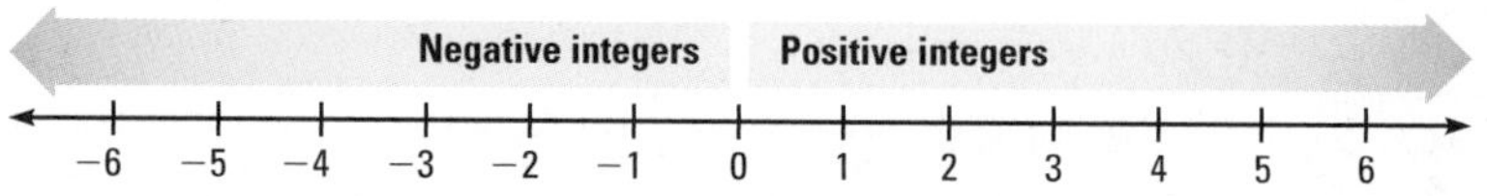

Zero is neither negative nor positive.

EXAMPLE 1 Graph and compare integers

Graph −3 and −4 on a number line. Then tell which number is greater.

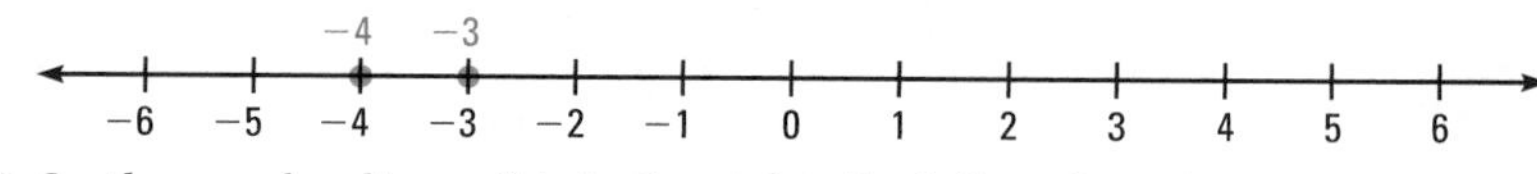

▶ On the number line, −3 is to the right of −4. So, −3 > −4.

RATIONAL NUMBERS The integers belong to the set of *rational numbers.* A **rational number** is a number $\frac{a}{b}$ where a and b are integers and $b \neq 0$. For example, $-\frac{1}{2}$ is a rational number because it can be written as $\frac{-1}{2}$ or $\frac{1}{-2}$. The rational numbers belong to the set of numbers called the *real numbers.*

READING Although you can write a negative fraction in different ways, you usually write it with the negative sign in front of the fraction.

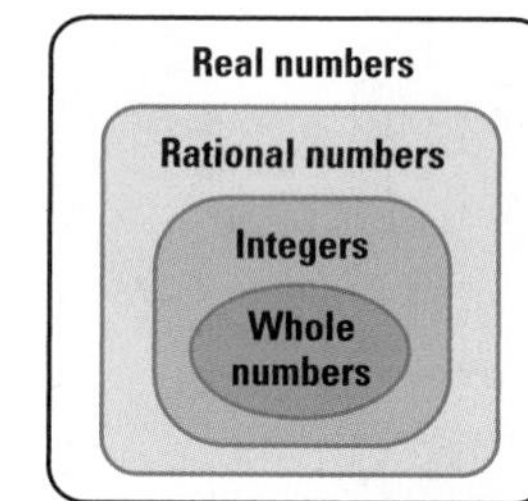

✓ GUIDED PRACTICE for Example 1

1–3. Check students' graphs.

Graph the numbers on a number line. Then tell which number is greater.

1. 4 and 0 4 **2.** 2 and −5 2 **3.** −1 and −6 −1

Resource Planning Guide

Chapter Resource Book
- Teaching Guide/Lesson Plan (pp. 3–4)
- Practice levels A, B, C (pp. 5–7)
- Study Guide (pp. 8–9)
- Catch-up for Absent Students (p. 10)
- Application (p. 11)
- Challenge (p. 12)

Workbooks
- Notetaking Guide (pp. 23–26)
- Practice Workbook (pp. 16–17)

Teaching Options
- **Power Presentations CD-ROM** provides dynamic electronic teaching resources for the classroom.
- **Activity Generator CD-ROM** provides editable activities for all ability levels.

Interactive Technology
- Easy Planner
- Power Presentations CD-ROM
- Activity Generator CD-ROM
- Animated Algebra
- Test Generator CD-ROM
- Online Quiz
- eWorkbook
- eEdition
- @HomeTutor

Resources for English Learners
- Quick Reference for English Learners
- Spanish Study Guide
- Multi-Language Visual Glossary
- Student Resources in Spanish

See also the *Algebra 1 Toolkit* for more strategies for meeting individual needs.

DECIMALS In decimal form, a rational number either terminates or repeats. For example, $\frac{3}{4} = 0.75$ is a *terminating decimal*, and $\frac{1}{3} = 0.333...$ is a *repeating decimal.*

REVIEW FRACTIONS For help with writing fractions as decimals, see p. 916.

EXAMPLE 2 Classify numbers

Tell whether each of the following numbers is a whole number, an integer, or a rational number: 5, 0.6, $-2\frac{2}{3}$, and −24.

Number	Whole number?	Integer?	Rational number?
5	Yes	Yes	Yes
0.6	No	No	Yes
$-2\frac{2}{3}$	No	No	Yes
−24	No	Yes	Yes

JUSTIFY AN ANSWER The number 0.6 is a rational number because it can be written as a quotient of two integers: $\frac{3}{5}$.

EXAMPLE 3 Order rational numbers

ASTRONOMY A star's color index is a measure of the temperature of the star. The greater the color index, the cooler the star. Order the stars in the table from hottest to coolest.

Star	Rigel	Arneb	Denebola	Shaula
Color index	−0.03	0.21	0.09	−0.22

Solution

Begin by graphing the numbers on a number line.

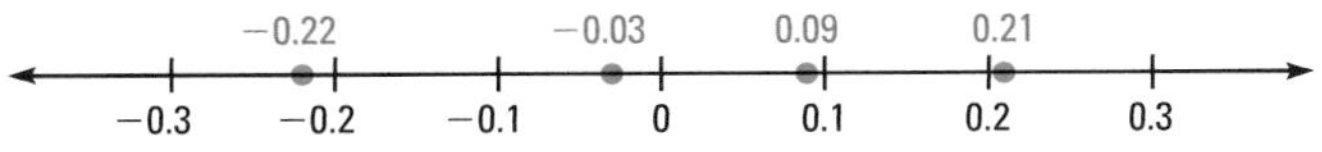

Read the numbers from left to right: −0.22, −0.03, 0.09, 0.21.

▶ From hottest to coolest, the stars are Shaula, Rigel, Denebola, and Arneb.

✓ GUIDED PRACTICE for Examples 2 and 3

Tell whether each number in the list is a whole number, an integer, or a rational number. Then order the numbers from least to greatest.

4–7. See margin.

4. 3, −1.2, −2, 0

5. 4.5, $-\frac{3}{4}$, −2.1, 0.5

6. 3.6, −1.5, −0.31, −2.8

7. $\frac{1}{6}$, 1.75, $-\frac{2}{3}$, 0

4. 3: whole number, integer, rational number, −1.2: rational number, −2: integer, rational number, 0: whole number, integer, rational number; −2, −1.2, 0, 3

5. 4.5: rational number, $-\frac{3}{4}$: rational number, −2.1: rational number, 0.5: rational number; −2.1, $-\frac{3}{4}$, 0.5, 4.5

6. 3.6: rational number, −1.5: rational number, −0.31: rational number, −2.8: rational number; −2.8, −1.5, −0.31, 3.6

7. $\frac{1}{6}$: rational number, 1.75: rational number, $-\frac{2}{3}$: rational number, 0: whole number, integer, rational number; $-\frac{2}{3}$, 0, $\frac{1}{6}$, 1.75

Motivating the Lesson

Ask students to give examples of situations where they might use negative numbers. Tell them by learning to compare positive and negative numbers they can determine who has a lower golf score.

3 TEACH

Extra Example 1

Graph 0 and −2 on a number line. Then tell which number is greater.

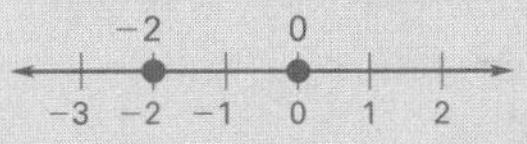

0 > −2

Extra Example 2

Tell whether each of the following numbers is a whole number, an integer, or a rational number: −19, 7, 0.3, and $-1\frac{1}{5}$. **−19: integer, rational number; 7: whole number, integer, rational number; 0.3: rational number; $-1\frac{1}{5}$: rational number**

Key Question to Ask for Example 2

- Why are all the numbers rational numbers? **They can all be written in the form $\frac{a}{b}$. $5 = \frac{5}{1}$; $0.6 = \frac{3}{5}$; $-2\frac{2}{3} = \frac{-8}{3}$; $-24 = \frac{-24}{1}$**

Extra Example 3

The apparent magnitude of a star is its brightness as observed from Earth. The greater the magnitude, the dimmer the star. Order the stars from brightest to dimmest.

Star	Magnitude
Arcturus	−0.06
Sirius	−1.47
Vega	0.03

Sirius, Arcturus, Vega

Differentiated Instruction

Below Level Students performing below level may not realize that all the numbers in **Guided Practice Exercises 4–7** are rational numbers. To help them see this fact, have these students write each of the numbers as a quotient of two integers. You may wish to do this as an activity in which below level students are paired with advanced students. If so, advanced students can give help where needed.

See also the *Algebra 1 Toolkit* for more strategies.

Extra Example 4

For the given value of a, find $-a$.

a. $a = \frac{3}{8}$ $-\frac{3}{8}$

b. $a = -0.65$ 0.65

Avoiding Common Errors

Tell students to get into the habit of reading $-a$ as "the opposite of a" to avoid mistaking $-a$ as a negative number when it may be positive. Have them practice reading Examples 4a and 4b aloud.

Extra Example 5

For the given value of a, find $|a|$.

a. $a = -16.2$ 16.2

b. $a = \frac{2}{3}$ $\frac{2}{3}$

Key Question to Ask for Example 5

- What do you know about the absolute values of a number and its opposite? Explain. The absolute values are the same. Both a number and its opposite are the same distance from 0 on a number line, and absolute value is defined as the distance from a number to 0 on a number line.

OPPOSITES Two numbers that are the same distance from 0 on a number line but are on opposite sides of 0 are called **opposites**. For example, 4 and -4 are opposites because they are both 4 units from 0 but are on opposite sides of 0. The opposite of 0 is 0. You read the expression $-a$ as "the opposite of a."

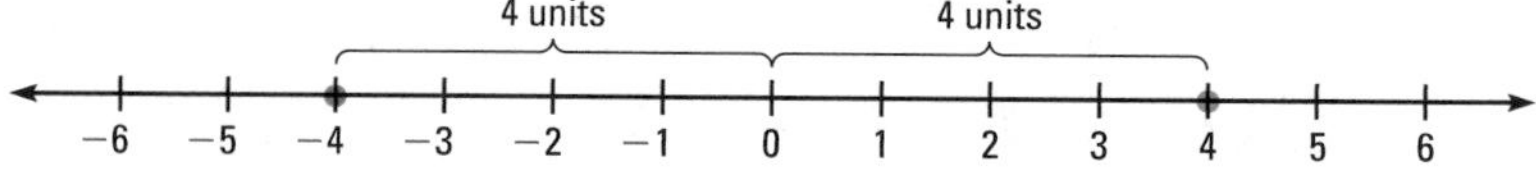

EXAMPLE 4 Find opposites of numbers

READING
Do not assume that $-a$ is a negative number. Notice that for $a = -2.5$, $-a = 2.5$.

a. If $a = -2.5$, then $-a = -(-2.5) = 2.5$.

b. If $a = \frac{3}{4}$, then $-a = -\frac{3}{4}$.

ABSOLUTE VALUE The **absolute value** of a number a is the distance between a and 0 on a number line. The symbol $|a|$ represents the absolute value of a.

KEY CONCEPT *For Your Notebook*

Absolute Value of a Number

Words If a is positive, then $\|a\| = a$.	**Example** $\|2\| = 2$
Words If a is 0, then $\|a\| = 0$.	**Example** $\|0\| = 0$
Words If a is negative, then $\|a\| = -a$.	**Example** $\|-2\| = -(-2) = 2$

EXAMPLE 5 Find absolute values of numbers

AVOID ERRORS
The absolute value of a number is never negative. If a number a is negative, then its absolute value, $-a$, is positive.

a. If $a = -\frac{2}{3}$, then $|a| = \left|-\frac{2}{3}\right| = -\left(-\frac{2}{3}\right) = \frac{2}{3}$.

b. If $a = 3.2$, then $|a| = |3.2| = 3.2$.

CONDITIONAL STATEMENTS A **conditional statement** has a hypothesis and a conclusion. An **if-then statement** is a form of a conditional statement. The *if* part contains the hypothesis. The *then* part contains the conclusion.

conditional statement

If a is a positive number, then $|a| = a$.

hypothesis **conclusion**

In mathematics, if-then statements are either true or false. An if-then statement is true if the conclusion is always true when the hypothesis is satisfied. An if-then statement is false if for just one example, called a **counterexample**, the conclusion is false when the hypothesis is satisfied.

Differentiated Instruction

Visual Learners Some students may not remember the distinction between whole numbers and integers. Whole numbers are integers greater than or equal to 0, and "0 ≥" looks like the letters "OL" in "WHOLE."

See also the *Algebra 1 Toolkit* for more strategies.

EXAMPLE 6 Analyze a conditional statement

Identify the hypothesis and the conclusion of the statement "If a number is a rational number, then the number is an integer." Tell whether the statement is *true* or *false*. If it is false, give a counterexample.

Solution

Hypothesis: a number is a rational number

Conclusion: the number is an integer

The statement is false. The number 0.5 is a counterexample, because 0.5 is a rational number but not an integer.

GUIDED PRACTICE for Examples 4, 5, and 6

For the given value of *a*, find $-a$ and $|a|$.

8. $a = 5.3$ −5.3, 5.3
9. $a = -7$ 7, 7
10. $a = -\frac{4}{9}$ $\frac{4}{9}, \frac{4}{9}$

Identify the hypothesis and the conclusion of the statement. Tell whether the statement is *true* or *false*. If it is false, give a counterexample.

11. If a number is a rational number, then the number is positive.

11. Hypothesis: a number is a rational number, conclusion: the number is positive; false. *Sample answer:* −1 is rational, but not positive.

12. If the absolute value of a number is positive, then the number is positive.
Hypothesis: the absolute value of a number is positive, conclusion: the number is positive; false. *Sample answer:* The absolute value of −2 is 2, but −2 is negative.

2.1 EXERCISES

HOMEWORK KEY
○ = **WORKED-OUT SOLUTIONS** on p. WS3 for Exs. 7, 29, and 53
★ = **STANDARDIZED TEST PRACTICE** Exs. 3, 4, 39, 50, 56, and 59

SKILL PRACTICE

A

1. **VOCABULARY** Copy and complete: A number is a(n) _?_ if it can be written in the form $\frac{a}{b}$ where a and b are integers and $b \neq 0$. rational number

2. **VOCABULARY** What is the opposite of −2? 2

3. ★ **WRITING** *Describe* the difference between whole numbers and positive integers. Zero is in the set of whole numbers, but not in the set of positive integers.

4. ★ **WRITING** For a negative number x, is the absolute value of x a *positive number* or a *negative number*? *Explain.* Positive number; the absolute value of a negative number is always positive.

EXAMPLE 1 on p. 64 for Exs. 5–13

GRAPHING AND COMPARING INTEGERS **Graph the numbers on a number line. Then tell which number is greater.** 5–13. Check students' graphs.

5. 0 and 7 7
6. 0 and −4 0
7. −5 and −6 −5
8. −2 and −3 −2
9. 5 and −2 5
10. −12 and 8 8
11. −1 and −5 −1
12. 3 and −13 3
13. −20 and −2 −2

Extra Example 6

Identify the hypothesis and conclusion of the statement "If a number is an integer, then the number is either positive or negative." Then tell whether the statement is *true* or *false*. If it is false, give a counterexample. Hypothesis: a number is an integer; Conclusion: the number is positive or negative; false: 0 is an integer and it is neither positive nor negative.

Key Question to Ask for Example 6

- If you switch the hypothesis and conclusion so that the statement reads "If a number is an integer, then it is a rational number," is the statement true or false? Why? True; an integer can be written as the quotient of two integers.

Closing the Lesson

Have students summarize the major points of the lesson and answer the Essential Question: How do you compare positive and negative numbers?

- A rational number can be written as the quotient of two integers.
- The absolute value of a number is the distance between the number and 0 on a number line. Opposites are the same distance from 0, but on opposite sides.
- Conditional statements contain a hypothesis and a conclusion, and can be either true or false.

Graph numbers on a number line so you can compare them and order them from least to greatest.

4 PRACTICE AND APPLY

Assignment Guide

Answer Transparencies available for all exercises

Basic:
Day 1: SRH p. 930 Exs. 1–4
pp. 67–70
Exs. 1, 3, 5–10, 14–19, 53, 54, 57, 67–75
Day 2: pp. 67–70
Exs. 2, 4, 23–30, 35–44, 55, 56, 58, 61–66

Average:
Day 1: pp. 67–70
Exs. 1, 3, 8–13, 17–22, 53, 54, 57–59, 67–75 odd
Day 2: pp. 67–70
Exs. 2, 4, 27–39 odd, 40–51, 55, 56, 61–66

Advanced:
Day 1: pp. 67–70
Exs. 1, 3, 10–13, 19–22, 53, 54, 57–60*, 68–74 even
Day 2: pp. 67–70
Exs. 2, 4, 28–38 even, 39, 41–52*, 55, 56, 63, 65, 66

Block:
pp. 67–70
Exs. 1–4, 8–13, 17–22, 27–39 odd, 40–51, 53–59, 61–66, 67–75 odd

Differentiated Instruction

See *Algebra 1 Best Practices Toolkit* for suggestions on addressing the needs of a diverse classroom.

Homework Check

For a quick check of student understanding of key concepts, go over the following exercises:

Basic: 16, 25, 35, 53, 55

Average: 18, 31, 37, 53, 56

Advanced: 20, 32, 38, 56, 57

Extra Practice

- Student Edition, p. 939
- Chapter 2 Resource Book: Practice levels A, B, C, pp. 5–7

Practice Worksheet

An easily-readable reduced practice page (with answers) for this lesson can be found on p. 62C.

EXAMPLES 2 and 3 on p. 65 for Exs. 14–22

CLASSIFYING AND ORDERING NUMBERS **Tell whether each number in the list is a whole number, an integer, or a rational number. Then order the numbers from least to greatest.** 14–22. See margin.

14. 3, −5, −2.4, 1 **15.** 1.6, 1, −4, 0 **16.** 0.25, −0.5, 0.2, −2

17. $-\frac{2}{3}, -0.6, -1, \frac{1}{3}$ **18.** $-0.01, 0.1, 0, -\frac{1}{10}$ **19.** $16, -1.66, \frac{5}{3}, -1.6$

20. $-2.7, \frac{1}{2}, 0.3, -7$ **21.** $-4.99, 5, \frac{16}{3}, -5.1$ **22.** $-\frac{3}{5}, -0.4, -1, -0.5$

EXAMPLES 4 and 5 on p. 66 for Exs. 23–34

FINDING OPPOSITES AND ABSOLUTE VALUES **For the given value of *a*, find $-a$ and $|a|$.**

23. $a = 6$ −6, 6 **24.** $a = -3$ 3, 3 **25.** $a = -18$ 18, 18 **26.** $a = 0$ 0, 0

27. $a = 13.4$ −13.4, 13.4 **28.** $a = 2.7$ −2.7, 2.7 **(29.)** $a = -6.1$ 6.1, 6.1 **30.** $a = -7.9$ 7.9, 7.9

31. $a = -1\frac{1}{9}$ $1\frac{1}{9}, 1\frac{1}{9}$ **32.** $a = -\frac{5}{6}$ $\frac{5}{6}, \frac{5}{6}$ **33.** $a = \frac{3}{4}$ $-\frac{3}{4}, \frac{3}{4}$ **34.** $a = 1\frac{1}{3}$ $-1\frac{1}{3}, 1\frac{1}{3}$

EXAMPLE 6 on p. 67 for Exs. 35–38

ANALYZING CONDITIONAL STATEMENTS **Identify the hypothesis and the conclusion of the conditional statement. Tell whether the statement is *true* or *false*. If it is false, give a counterexample.**

35. If a number is a positive integer, then the number is a whole number. Hypothesis: a number is a positive integer, conclusion: the number is a whole number; true.

36. If a number is negative, then its absolute value is negative.

37. If a number is positive, then its opposite is positive.

38. If a number is an integer, then the number is a rational number. Hypothesis: a number is an integer, conclusion: the number is a rational number; true.

39. ★ **MULTIPLE CHOICE** Which number is a whole number? A

Ⓐ $\left|-\frac{18}{9}\right|$ Ⓑ $-\frac{4}{3}$ Ⓒ 1.6 Ⓓ −(−7.963)

36. Hypothesis: a number is negative, conclusion: its absolute value is negative; false. *Sample answer:* |−3| is 3, a positive integer.

37. Hypothesis: a number is positive, conclusion: its opposite is positive; false. *Sample answer:* The opposite of 2 is −2, a negative number.

B

ERROR ANALYSIS ***Describe*** **and correct the error in the statement.** 40, 41. See margin.

40.

The numbers −(−2), −4, −|8|, and −0.3 are negative numbers.

41.

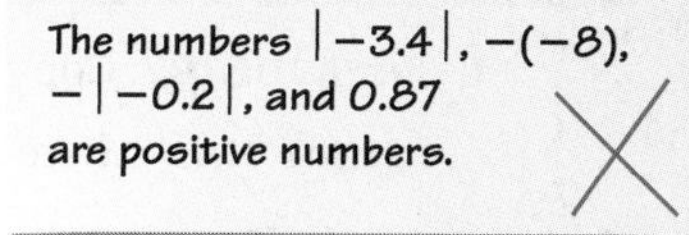

The numbers |−3.4|, −(−8), −|−0.2|, and 0.87 are positive numbers.

40. −(−2) is not negative. *Sample answer:* In the number −(−2), replace the parentheses with absolute value bars.

41. −|−0.2| is a negative number. *Sample answer:* In the number −|−0.2|, remove both negative signs.

EVALUATING EXPRESSIONS **Evaluate the expression when $x = -0.75$.**

42. $-x$ 0.75 **43.** $|x| + 0.25$ 1 **44.** $|x| - 0.75$ 0 **45.** $1 + |-x|$ 1.75

46. $2 \cdot (-x)$ 1.5 **47.** $(-x) \cdot 3$ 2.25 **48.** $|x| + |x|$ 1.5 **49.** $-x + |x|$ 1.5

50. ★ **MULTIPLE CHOICE** Which number is a solution of $|x| + 1 = 1.3$? B

Ⓐ −2.3 Ⓑ −0.3 Ⓒ 1.3 Ⓓ 2.3

C

51. **CHALLENGE** What can you conclude about the opposite of the opposite of a number? *Explain* your reasoning. It is the original number. *Sample answer:* The opposite of *a* is −*a* and the opposite of −*a* is *a*, which is the original number.

52. **CHALLENGE** For what values of *a* is the opposite of *a* greater than *a*? less than *a*? equal to *a*? See margin.

○ = WORKED-OUT SOLUTIONS on p. WS1 ★ = STANDARDIZED TEST PRACTICE

14. 3: whole number, integer, rational number, −5: integer, rational number, −2.4: rational number, 1: whole number, integer, rational number; −5, −2.4, 1, 3

15. 1.6: rational number, 1: whole number, integer, rational number, −4: integer, rational number, 0: whole number, integer, rational number; −4, 0, 1, 1.6

16. 0.25: rational number, −0.5: rational number, 0.2: rational number, −2: integer, rational number; −2, −0.5, 0.2, 0.25

PROBLEM SOLVING

EXAMPLE 3 A on p. 65 for Exs. 53, 57

53. Fondo, Frink, Alamorio, Calexico, Date City

53. GEOGRAPHY The map shows various locations in Imperial County, California, and their elevations above or below sea level. Order the locations from lowest elevation to highest elevation.

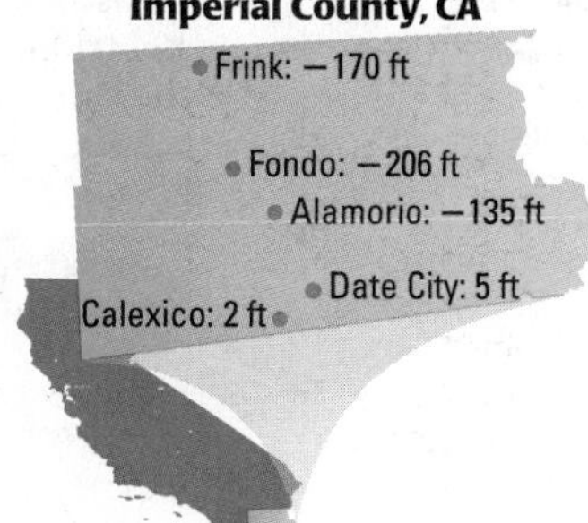

@HomeTutor for problem solving help at classzone.com

54. SPORTS In golf, the goal is to have the least score among all the players. Which golf score, −8 or −12, is the better score? −12

@HomeTutor for problem solving help at classzone.com

EXAMPLE 5 on p. 66 for Exs. 55–56

55. MUSIC A guitar tuner is a device that tunes a guitar string to its exact pitch. Some tuners use the measure *cents* to indicate how far above or below the exact pitch, marked as 0 cents, the string tone is. Suppose that one string tone measures −3.4 cents, and a second string tone measures −3.8 cents. Which string tone is closer to the exact pitch? *Explain.* −3.4; the absolute value of −3.4 is less than the absolute value of −3.8, so it is closer to 0, the exact pitch.

56. ★ MULTIPLE CHOICE The change in value of a share of a stock was −\$.45 on Monday, −\$1.32 on Tuesday, \$.27 on Wednesday, and \$1.03 on Thursday. On which day was the absolute value of the change the greatest? B

(A) Monday (B) Tuesday (C) Wednesday (D) Thursday

57. MULTI-STEP PROBLEM An equalizer on a stereo system is used to increase or decrease the intensity of sounds at different frequencies. The intensity is measured in decibels (dB), and the frequencies are measured in hertz (Hz). The table shows the intensity at different frequencies on a stereo system.

Frequency (Hz)	32	64	125	250	500	1000	2000	4000	8000
Intensity (dB)	8.8	7.1	5.8	1.5	−2.8	−1.5	2.7	2.8	2.9

a. Which frequency has the least sound intensity? 500 Hz

b. *Describe* the change in sound intensity as the frequency increases from 32 hertz to 8000 hertz. The intensity decreases until 1000 Hz and then increases.

B

58. WEATHER A wind chill index describes how much colder it feels outside when wind speed is considered with air temperature. The table shows the wind chill temperatures for given pairs of air temperature and wind speed.

Wind Chill Temperatures (°F)					
Wind speed (mi/h)	Air temperature (°F)				
	20	10	0	−10	−20
0	20	10	0	−10	−20
10	9	−4	−16	−28	−41
20	4	−9	−22	−35	−48
30	1	−12	−26	−39	−53

58a. −10°F with a wind speed of 10 miles per hour

a. **Compare** Which feels colder, an air temperature of 0°F with a wind speed of 30 miles per hour, or an air temperature of −10°F with a wind speed of 10 miles per hour?

b. **Analyze** How does the wind chill temperature change under constant wind speed and decreasing air temperature? under constant air temperature and increasing wind speed? decreases; decreases

17. $-\frac{2}{3}$: rational number, −0.6: rational number, −1: integer, rational number, $\frac{1}{3}$: rational number; −1, $-\frac{2}{3}$, −0.6, $\frac{1}{3}$

18. −0.01: rational number, 0.1: rational number, 0: whole number, integer, rational number, $-\frac{1}{10}$: rational number; $-\frac{1}{10}$, −0.01, 0, 0.1

19. 16: whole number, integer, rational number, −1.66: rational number, $\frac{5}{3}$: rational number, −1.6: rational number; −1.66, −1.6, $\frac{5}{3}$, 16

Study Strategy

Exercises 23–34 Remind students that $-a$ is read "the opposite of *a*." Give an example such as, "if *a* is −1, then the opposite of *a* is the opposite of −1."

Avoiding Common Errors

Exercises 42–49 Some students may read $-x$ as −0.75 rather than −(−0.75). Suggest that students use parenthesis around *x* to avoid this error.

Exercises 53–55 You may want to mention that students can avoid errors by graphing the numbers in these problems on a number line.

Reading Strategy

Exercise 56 Tell students to look for key words when they are reading a problem. Point out that this exercise asks for the day on which the *absolute value* of the change was the greatest.

Vocabulary

Exercise 58b Some students may need help with the word "constant." Tell these students that constant means that something does not change. Direct their attention to the chart so they can see that constant wind speed and decreasing air temperature are read in rows across the chart and constant air temperature and increasing wind speed are read in columns down the chart.

20. −2.7: rational number, $\frac{1}{2}$: rational number, 0.3: rational number, −7: integer, rational number; −7, −2.7, 0.3, $\frac{1}{2}$

21. −4.99: rational number, 5: whole number, integer, rational number, $\frac{16}{3}$: rational number, −5.1: rational number; −5.1, −4.99, 5, $\frac{16}{3}$

22. $-\frac{3}{5}$: rational number, −0.4: rational number, −1: integer, rational number, −0.5: rational number; −1, $-\frac{3}{5}$, −0.5, −0.4

52. See Additional Answers beginning on p. AA1.

5 ASSESS AND RETEACH

Daily Homework Quiz

Transparency Available

1. Graph −3 and −5 on a number line. Then tell which number is greater. **−3 > −5**

−5 −4 −3 −2 −1 0 1

2. Tell whether each number is a whole number, an integer, or a rational number: −2.24, 6, $3\frac{1}{4}$, −16. **−2.24: rational number; 6: whole number, integer, rational number; $3\frac{1}{4}$: rational number; −16: integer, rational number**

3. The table shows the boiling-point temperatures of some elements. Order the elements from lowest boiling-point temperature to highest.

Element	Temperature
Hydrogen	−2593°C
Mercury	357°C
Nitrogen	−196°C
Oxygen	−183°C

Hydrogen, Nitrogen, Oxygen, Mercury

Available at **classzone.com**

Diagnosis/Remediation

- Practice A, B, C in Chapter 2 Resource Book, pp. 5–7
- Study Guide in Chapter 2 Resource Book, pp. 8–9
- Practice Workbook, pp. 16–17
- @HomeTutor

Challenge

Additional challenge is available in the Chapter 2 Resource Book, p. 12.

59b. Rigel's apparent magnitude is greater than the Sun's apparent magnitude, so it is dimmer than the Sun; Rigel's absolute magnitude is less than the Sun's absolute magnitude, so it is brighter than the Sun.

59c. No. *Sample answer*: The apparent magnitude of Arcturus is less than the apparent magnitude of Achernar, but the absolute magnitude of Arcturus is greater than the absolute magnitude of Achernar.

59. ★ **EXTENDED RESPONSE** A star's apparent magnitude measures how bright the star appears to a person on Earth. A star's absolute magnitude measures its brightness if it were a distance of 33 light-years, or about 194 trillion miles, from Earth. The greater the magnitude, the dimmer the star.

Star	Arcturus	Achernar	Canopus	Capella	Sirius	Sun
Apparent magnitude	−0.04	0.46	−0.72	0.08	−1.46	−26.72
Absolute magnitude	0.2	−1.3	−2.5	0.4	1.4	4.8

Orion Constellation

a. **Order** Order the stars in the table from brightest to dimmest when viewed from Earth. Then order the stars from brightest to dimmest if they were 33 light-years from Earth.

b. **Compare** The star Rigel has an apparent magnitude of 0.12 and an absolute magnitude of −8.1. *Compare* its brightness with the Sun's brightness using both apparent magnitude and absolute magnitude.

c. **Analyze** Can you use the apparent magnitudes of two stars to predict which star is brighter in terms of absolute magnitude? *Explain* your answer using a comparison of the apparent and absolute magnitudes of two stars in the table.

59a. Sun, Sirius, Canopus, Arcturus, Capella, Achernar; Canopus, Achernar, Arcturus, Capella, Sirius, Sun

60. C **CHALLENGE** In an academic contest, the point values of the questions are given by the expression $50x$ where $x = 1, 2, 3,$ and 4. You earn $50x$ points for a correct answer to a question and $-(50x)$ points for an incorrect answer. Order from least to greatest all the possible points you can earn when answering a question. **−200, −150, −100, −50, 50, 100, 150, 200**

ILLINOIS MIXED REVIEW

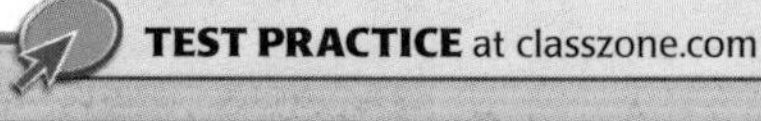

61. The graph of which function is shown? **D**

Ⓐ $y = 30x$

Ⓑ $y = 30 - x$

Ⓒ $y = 30 - (x + 5)$

Ⓓ $y = 30 - 5x$

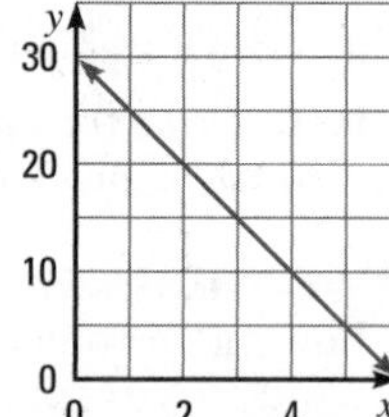

62. You are going to paint your room and need to determine the area of its walls and ceiling. The room is a rectangular prism with dimensions 10 feet by 10 feet by 8 feet. One of the walls contains a rectangular door that is 3 feet by 6 feet and two square windows each with a side length of 2 feet. What is the area you need to paint, not including the door and the two windows? **A**

Ⓐ 394 ft^2 Ⓑ 454 ft^2 Ⓒ 500 ft^2 Ⓓ 800 ft^2

Apply Sets to Numbers and Functions

GOAL Apply set theory to numbers and functions.

Key Vocabulary
- set
- element
- empty set
- universal set
- union
- intersection

A **set** is a collection of distinct objects. Each object in a set is called an **element** or *member* of the set. You can use *set notation* to write a set by enclosing the elements of the set in braces. For example, if A is the set of whole numbers less than 6, then $A = \{0, 1, 2, 3, 4, 5\}$.

Two special sets are the *empty set* and the *universal set*. The set with no elements is called the **empty set** and is written as $\emptyset$. The set of all elements under consideration is called the **universal set** and is written as U.

KEY CONCEPT *For Your Notebook*

Union and Intersection of Two Sets

The **union** of two sets A and B is the set of all elements in *either* A or B and is written as $A \cup B$.

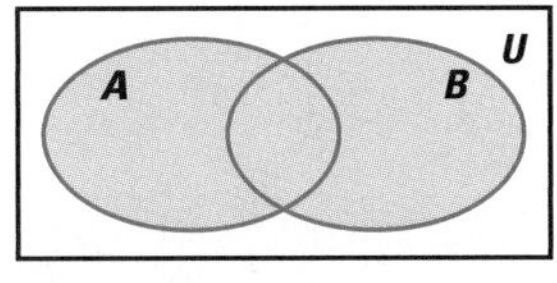

$A \cup B$

The **intersection** of two sets A and B is the set of all elements in *both* A and B and is written as $A \cap B$.

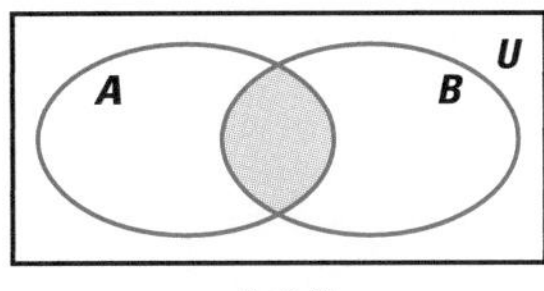

$A \cap B$

EXAMPLE 1 Find the union and intersection of two sets

Let U be the set of integers from 1 to 9. Let $A = \{2, 4, 6, 8\}$ and $B = \{2, 3, 5, 7\}$. Find (a) $A \cup B$ and (b) $A \cap B$.

Solution

a. The union of A and B consists of the elements that are in either set.

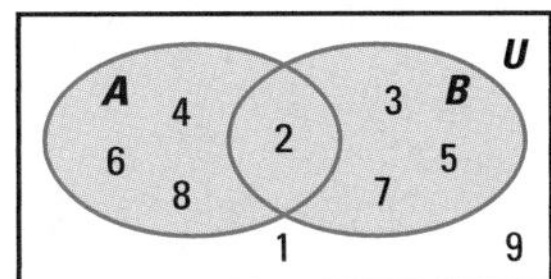

▶ $A \cup B = \{2, 3, 4, 5, 6, 7, 8\}$

b. The intersection of A and B consists of the elements that are in both sets.

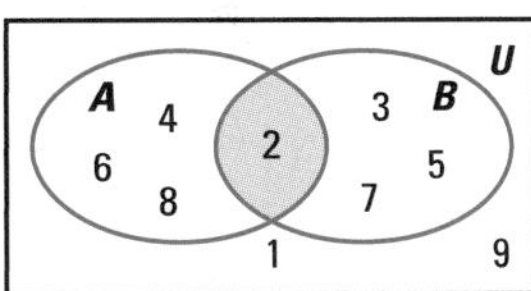

▶ $A \cap B = \{2\}$

1 PLAN AND PREPARE

Warm-Up Exercises

Find the range of the given function with the given domain.

1. $y = 2x$; Domain: 3, 5, 7 6, 10, 14
2. $y = x + 5$; Domain: 2, 5, 8 7, 10, 13
3. $y = x - 2$; Domain: 2, 4, 6 0, 2, 4

2 FOCUS AND MOTIVATE

Essential Question

Big Idea 3, p. 63

How do you apply sets to numbers and functions? Tell students they will learn how to answer this question by finding the union and intersection of two sets of numbers and by using set notation to write a function and its range.

3 TEACH

Extra Example 1

Let U be the set of rational numbers from -3 to 6.5. Let $A = \{-3, 1, 5\frac{1}{4}, 6.2\}$ and $B = \{-2, 1.5, 4, 6\}$. Find (a) $A \cup B$ and (b) $A \cap B$.

a. $A \cup B = \{-3, -2, 1, 1.5, 4, 5\frac{1}{4}, 6, 6.2\}$

b. $A \cap B = \emptyset$

NCTM STANDARDS

Standard 2: Understand functions; Use models to understand relationships

Extra Example 2

Consider the function $y = x - 4$ with domain $D = \{6, 7, 8, 9\}$. Write the range and function using set notation. The range is $R = \{2, 3, 4, 5\}$. The function is $f = \{(6, 2), (7, 3), (8, 4), (9, 5)\}$.

Key Question to Ask for Example 2

- How are the ordered pairs in f related to D and R? The elements if D are the first coordinates and the elements of R are the second coordinates of the ordered pairs.

Closing the Lesson

Have students summarize the major points of the lesson and answer the Essential Question: How do you apply sets to numbers and functions?

- Enclose the elements of a set in braces when using set notation.
- A function can be written as a set of ordered pairs.

The union of two sets of numbers is the set of all of the elements in either set. The intersection is the set of all of the numbers common to both sets. Write a function as a set of ordered pairs.

4 PRACTICE AND APPLY

Avoiding Common Errors

Exercises 1–10 Some students may confuse the symbols for union and intersection. Tell them to remember that union starts with the letter U and the symbol for union looks like the letter U.

FUNCTIONS AND SETS You can write the domain and range of a function as sets of input values and output values and the function as a set of ordered pairs, as illustrated for the mapping diagram below.

Function

Domain	Input	Output	Range
$D = \{1, 2, 3, 5\}$	1 →	2	$R = \{2, 3, 4\}$
	2 →	3	
	3 →	3	
	5 →	4	

$f = \{(1, 2), (2, 3), (3, 3), (5, 4)\}$

EXAMPLE 2 Write a function and its range as sets

Consider the function $y = x + 2$ with domain $D = \{0, 1, 2, 3\}$. Write the range and function using set notation.

Solution

x	0	1	2	3
y	$0 + 2 = 2$	$1 + 2 = 3$	$2 + 2 = 4$	$3 + 2 = 5$

▶ The range is $R = \{2, 3, 4, 5\}$.
The function is $f = \{(0, 2), (1, 3), (2, 4), (3, 5)\}$.

PRACTICE

EXAMPLE 1 on p. 71 for Exs. 1–4

Let U be the set of whole numbers from 0 to 10. Find $A \cup B$ and $A \cap B$ for the specified sets A and B.

1. $A = \{1, 3, 5, 7, 9\}$ and $B = \{3, 6, 9\}$ $\{1, 3, 5, 6, 7, 9\}, \{3, 9\}$
2. $A = \{1, 2, 3, 4, 5, 6\}$ and $B = \{4, 5, 6, 7, 8\}$ $\{1, 2, 3, 4, 5, 6, 7, 8\}, \{4, 5, 6\}$
3. $A = \{0, 2, 4, 6, 8, 10\}$ and $B = \{1, 3, 5, 7, 9\}$ $\{0, 1, 2, 3, 4, 5, 6, 7, 8, 9, 10\}, \emptyset$
4. $A = \{0, 5, 10\}$ and $B = \{1, 4, 7, 10\}$ $\{0, 1, 4, 5, 7, 10\}, \{10\}$

EXAMPLE 2 on p. 72 for Exs. 5–8

In Exercises 5–8, consider the specified function and domain. Write the range and function using set notation.

5. $y = 2x$ with domain $D = \{1, 2, 3, 4, 5\}$ $R = \{2, 4, 6, 8, 10\}$, $f = \{(1, 2), (2, 4), (3, 6), (4, 8), (5, 10)\}$
6. $y = x - 1$ with domain $D = \{2, 4, 6, 8, 10\}$ $R = \{1, 3, 5, 7, 9\}$, $f = \{(2, 1), (4, 3), (6, 5), (8, 7), (10, 9)\}$
7. $y = x + 3$ with domain $D = \{1, 5, 9, 13, 17\}$
8. $y = 3x + 2$ with domain $D = \{1, 2, 3, 4, 5\}$ $R = \{5, 8, 11, 14, 17\}$, $f = \{(1, 5), (2, 8), (3, 11), (4, 14), (5, 17)\}$
9. Let A be the set of positive integers, and let B be the set of negative integers and 0. Find $A \cup B$ and $A \cap B$. the set of integers, $\emptyset$
10. Let A be the set of integers, and let B be the set of rational numbers. Find $A \cup B$ and $A \cap B$. the set of rational numbers, the set of integers

7. $R = \{4, 8, 12, 16, 20\}$, $f = \{(1, 4), (5, 8), (9, 12), (13, 16), (17, 20)\}$

Investigating Algebra ACTIVITY Use before Lesson 2.2

Animated Algebra classzone.com

2.2 Addition of Integers

MATERIALS • algebra tiles

QUESTION How can you use algebra tiles to find the sum of two integers?

You can use algebra tiles to model addition of integers. Each + represents 1, and each − represents −1. Pairing a + with a − results in a sum of 0.

EXPLORE Find the sum of two integers

Find the sum −7 + 4.

STEP 1 Model −7 and 4 using algebra tiles.

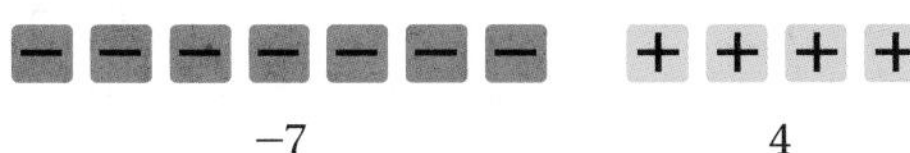

STEP 2 Group pairs of positive and negative tiles. Count the remaining tiles.

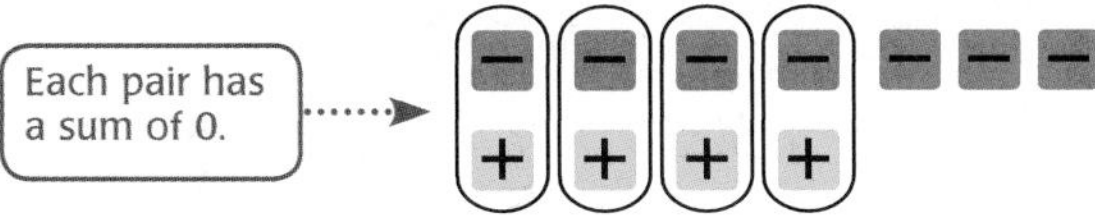

STEP 3 Copy and complete the statement: −7 + 4 = __?__. −3

DRAW CONCLUSIONS Use your observations to complete these exercises

Use algebra tiles to find the sum.

1. 3 + 8 11 **2.** 5 + (−1) 4 **3.** −9 + 6 −3 **4.** −2 + (−3) −5

5. −4 + 4 0 **6.** −7 + 5 −2 **7.** 5 + (−7) −2 **8.** −6 + 0 −6

REASONING In Exercises 9–13, answer the question and give an example from Exercises 1–8 to support your answer.

9. Is the sum of two positive integers *positive* or *negative?* positive, Ex. 1

10. Is the sum of two negative integers *positive* or *negative?* negative, Ex. 4

11. Is the sum of a positive integer and a negative integer *always* positive? no, Ex. 6

12. What is the sum of an integer and its opposite? 0, Ex. 5

13. What is the sum of an integer and 0? the integer, Ex. 8

14. In Exercises 6 and 7, the two integers being added are the same, but the order is reversed. What does this suggest about the sums $a + b$ and $b + a$ where a and b are integers? It does not affect the answer.

1 PLAN AND PREPARE

Explore the Concept

- Students will model integer addition with algebra tiles.
- This activity leads into the study of adding integers in Example 1 in Lesson 2.2.

Materials

Each student will need:

- algebra tiles
- Activity Support Master (*Chapter 2 Resource Book*, p. 15)

Recommended Time

Work activity: 10 min

Discuss results: 5 min

Grouping

Students should work individually.

2 TEACH

Tips for Success

Tell students that since the sum of a negative tile and a positive tile is zero, each such pair of tiles has no effect on the actual sum. Explain that this is why they need to pair one positive tile with one negative tile, and that they need to continue doing this until there are no pairs left.

Key Discovery

Students should see that the sum of an integer and its opposite is 0, the sum of two integers with the same sign has that same sign, and the sum of two integers with different signs has the sign of the integer modeled by the greater number of tiles.

3 ASSESS AND RETEACH

1. How many zero pairs can you make if you want to find the sum of 2 + (−5)? 2

2. Can you make zero pairs if you want to find the sum of −2 + (−3)? Explain. **No, only one negative and one positive tile form a zero pair.**

1 PLAN AND PREPARE

Warm-Up Exercises

Transparency Available

1. $0.43 + 1.27 = \underline{?}$ 1.7
2. $4\frac{5}{6} + 2\frac{2}{3} = \underline{?}$ $7\frac{1}{2}$
3. Ned wants to ship 3 books in a box with a weight limit of 25 pounds. The books weigh 8.4 pounds, 7.9 pounds, and 9.2 pounds. Can he ship them in the box? Explain. **No; the total weight of the books is 25.5 pounds and $25.5 > 25$.**

Notetaking Guide

Transparency Available

Promotes interactive learning and notetaking skills, pp. 27–29.

Pacing

Basic: 1 day
Average: 1 day
Advanced: 1 day
Block: 0.5 block with 2.3
• See *Teaching Guide/Lesson Plan.*

2 FOCUS AND MOTIVATE

Essential Question

Big Idea 1, p. 63

How do you add positive and negative numbers? **Tell students they will learn how to answer this question by using a number line, rules of addition, and properties of addition of real numbers.**

2.2 Add Real Numbers

6.11.10 Perform numerical computations with real numbers.

Before	You added positive numbers.
Now	You will add positive and negative numbers.
Why?	So you can calculate a sports score, as in Ex. 57.

Key Vocabulary
- **additive identity**
- **additive inverse**

One way to add two real numbers is to use a number line. Start at the first number. Use the sign of the second number to decide whether to move left or right. Then use the absolute value of the second number to decide how many units to move. The number where you stop is the sum of the two numbers.

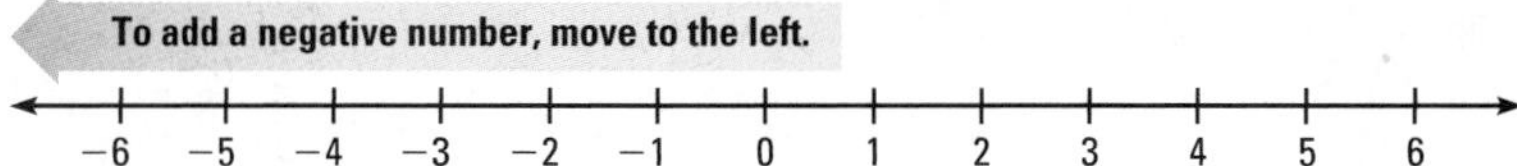

EXAMPLE 1 Add two integers using a number line

Use a number line to find the sum.

a. $-3 + 6$

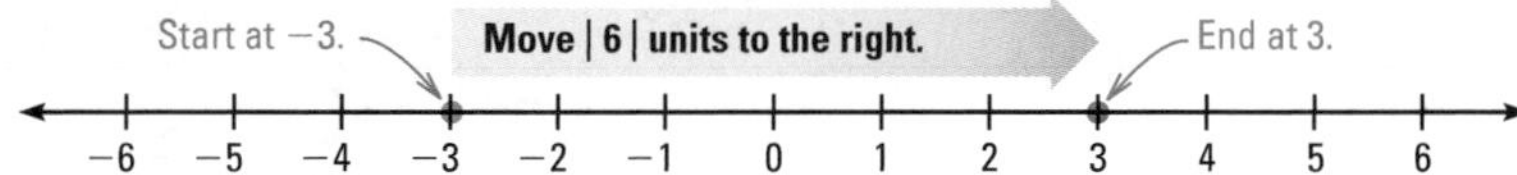

▶ The final position is 3. So, $-3 + 6 = 3$.

b. $-4 + (-5)$

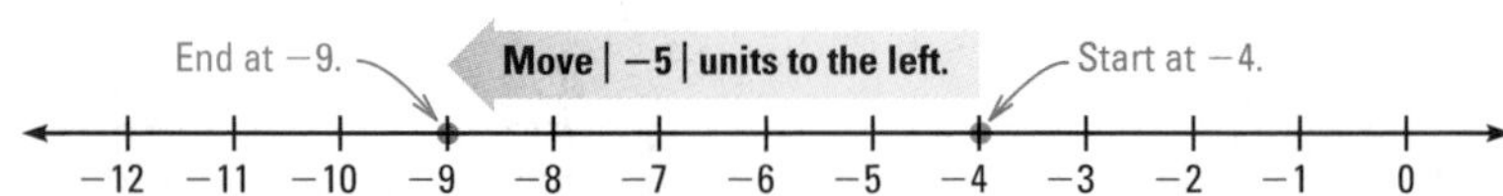

▶ The final position is −9. So, $-4 + (-5) = -9$.

✓ GUIDED PRACTICE for Example 1

Use a number line to find the sum.

1. $7 + (-2)$ **5** **2.** $8 + (-11)$ **−3** **3.** $-8 + 4$ **−4** **4.** $-1 + (-4)$ **−5**

Resource Planning Guide

Chapter Resource Book
- Teaching Guide/Lesson Plan (pp. 13–14)
- Practice levels A, B, C (pp. 16–18)
- Study Guide (pp. 19–20)
- Catch-up for Absent Students (p. 21)
- Application (p. 22)
- Challenge (p. 23)

Workbooks
- Notetaking Guide (pp. 27–29)
- Practice Workbook (pp. 18–19)

Teaching Options
- **Power Presentations CD-ROM** provides dynamic electronic teaching resources for the classroom.
- **Activity Generator CD-ROM** provides editable activities for all ability levels.

Interactive Technology
- Easy Planner
- Power Presentations CD-ROM
- Activity Generator CD-ROM
- Animated Algebra
- Test Generator CD-ROM
- Online Quiz
- eWorkbook
- eEdition
- @HomeTutor

Resources for English Learners
- Quick Reference for English Learners
- Spanish Study Guide
- Multi-Language Visual Glossary
- Student Resources in Spanish

See also the *Algebra 1 Toolkit* for more strategies for meeting individual needs.

KEY CONCEPT *For Your Notebook*

Rules of Addition

Words To add two numbers with the *same* sign, add their absolute values. The sum has the same sign as the numbers added.

Examples $8 + 7 = 15$ $-6 + (-10) = -16$

Words To add two numbers with *different* signs, subtract the lesser absolute value from the greater absolute value. The sum has the same sign as the number with the greater absolute value.

Examples $-12 + 7 = -5$ $18 + (-4) = 14$

EXAMPLE 2 Add real numbers

Find the sum.

a. $-5.3 + (-4.9) = -(|-5.3| + |-4.9|)$ **Rule of same signs**

$= -(5.3 + 4.9)$ **Take absolute values.**

$= -10.2$ **Add.**

b. $19.3 + (-12.2) = |19.3| - |-12.2|$ **Rule of different signs**

$= 19.3 - 12.2$ **Take absolute values.**

$= 7.1$ **Subtract.**

PROPERTIES OF ADDITION Notice that both $3 + (-2)$ and $-2 + 3$ have the same sum, 1. So, $3 + (-2) = -2 + 3$. This is an example of the *commutative property of addition.* The properties of addition are listed below.

KEY CONCEPT *For Your Notebook*

Properties of Addition

COMMUTATIVE PROPERTY The order in which you add two numbers does not change the sum.

Algebra $a + b = b + a$ **Example** $3 + (-2) = -2 + 3$

ASSOCIATIVE PROPERTY The way you group three numbers in a sum does not change the sum.

Algebra $(a + b) + c = a + (b + c)$ **Example** $(-3 + 2) + 1 = -3 + (2 + 1)$

IDENTITY PROPERTY The sum of a number and 0 is the number.

Algebra $a + 0 = 0 + a = a$ **Example** $-5 + 0 = -5$

INVERSE PROPERTY The sum of a number and its opposite is 0.

Algebra $a + (-a) = -a + a = 0$ **Example** $-6 + 6 = 0$

Motivating the Lesson

Have students imagine that they need to balance a checkbook, track a club's finances, or monitor a fund-raiser. Explain that learning how to add positive and negative numbers in this lesson will help them oversee activities that have money coming in and money going out.

3 TEACH

Extra Example 1

Use a number line to find the sum.

a. $-4 + 2$ -2

b. $3 + (-4)$ -1

Key Questions to Ask for Example 1

- In Example 1a, why do you start at -3? **-3 is the first number in the sum $-3 + 6$.**
- How do you know whether to move left or right? **Move right when the sign of the second number is positive and left when the sign is negative.**

Extra Example 2

Find the sum.

a. $-8.4 + (-0.7)$ -9.1

b. $-12.6 + 7.3$ -5.3

Key Question to Ask for Example 2

- In Example 2b, will $-12.2 + 19.3$ have the same answer as $19.3 + (-12.2)$? Why? **Yes, to add two numbers with different signs, you subtract the lesser absolute value from the greater absolute value, so for both, you will subtract 12.2 from 19.3.**

Extra Example 3

Identify the property being illustrated.

a. $-11.9 + 11.9 = 0$ Inverse property of addition

b. $-8 + (-x) = -x + (-8)$ Commutative property of addition

c. $-2 + 0 = 2$ Identity property of addition

Extra Example 4

The table shows how much weight two dieters lost or gained per month. Which dieter had the greater weight loss at the end of three months? dieter A

Month	Dieter A	Dieter B
1	−3.3	−7.8
2	−5.1	+1.2
3	+0.5	−0.8

Closing the Lesson

Have students summarize the major points of the lesson and answer the Essential Question: How do you add positive and negative numbers?

- Use the rules for like signs and different signs to add real numbers.
- Use the properties of addition to make adding easier, such as using the associative property to associate numbers that are easy to add.

Using the rules of addition, add the absolute value of two numbers with the same sign and use the sign of the numbers for the sum. If two numbers have different signs, subtract the lesser absolute value from the greater absolute value and use the sign of the greater absolute value for the sum.

The identity property states that the sum of a number a and 0 is a. The number 0 is the **additive identity**. The inverse property states that the sum of a number a and its opposite is 0. The opposite of a is its **additive inverse**.

EXAMPLE 3 Identify properties of addition

	Statement	Property illustrated
a.	$(x + 9) + 2 = x + (9 + 2)$	Associative property of addition
b.	$8.3 + (-8.3) = 0$	Inverse property of addition
c.	$-y + 0.7 = 0.7 + (-y)$	Commutative property of addition

EXAMPLE 4 Solve a multi-step problem

BUSINESS The table shows the annual profits of two piano manufacturers. Which manufacturer had the greater total profit for the three years?

Year	Profit (millions) for manufacturer A	Profit (millions) for manufacturer B
1	−$5.8	−$6.5
2	$8.7	$7.9
3	$6.8	$8.2

Solution

STEP 1 **Calculate** the total profit for each manufacturer.

ANOTHER WAY
You can also find the sums by adding from left to right, as shown for manufacturer A: $-5.8 + 8.7 + 6.8 = 2.9 + 6.8 = 9.7$.

Manufacturer A:

$$\begin{aligned}\text{Total profit} &= -5.8 + 8.7 + 6.8\\ &= -5.8 + (8.7 + 6.8)\\ &= -5.8 + 15.5\\ &= 9.7\end{aligned}$$

Manufacturer B:

$$\begin{aligned}\text{Total profit} &= -6.5 + 7.9 + 8.2\\ &= -6.5 + (7.9 + 8.2)\\ &= -6.5 + 16.1\\ &= 9.6\end{aligned}$$

STEP 2 **Compare** the total profits: $9.7 > 9.6$.

▶ Manufacturer A had the greater total profit.

✓ GUIDED PRACTICE for Examples 2, 3, and 4

Find the sum.

5. $-0.6 + (-6.7)$ -7.3 **6.** $10.1 + (-16.2)$ -6.1 **7.** $-13.1 + 8.7$ -4.4

Identify the property being illustrated.

8. $7 + (-7) = 0$ Inverse property of addition

9. $-12 + 0 = -12$ Identity property of addition

10. $4 + 8 = 8 + 4$ Commutative property of addition

11. **WHAT IF?** In Example 4, suppose that the profits for year 4 are −$1.7 million for manufacturer A and −$2.1 million for manufacturer B. Which manufacturer has the greater total profit for the four years? manufacturer A

2.2 EXERCISES

HOMEWORK KEY

○ = **WORKED-OUT SOLUTIONS** on p. WS3 for Exs. 13, 35, and 55

★ = **STANDARDIZED TEST PRACTICE** Exs. 2, 50, 56, 57, and 58

SKILL PRACTICE

1. VOCABULARY What number is called the additive identity? 0

2. ★ WRITING Without actually adding, how can you tell if the sum of two numbers will be zero? If they are opposites, their sum will be zero.

EXAMPLE 1 on p. 74 for Exs. 3–11

USING A NUMBER LINE **Use a number line to find the sum.**

3. $-11 + 3$ -8 **4.** $-1 + 6$ 5 **5.** $13 + (-7)$ 6

6. $5 + (-10)$ -5 **7.** $-9 + (-4)$ -13 **8.** $-8 + (-2)$ -10

9. $-14 + 8$ -6 **10.** $6 + (-12)$ -6 **11.** $-11 + (-9)$ -20

EXAMPLE 2 on p. 75 for Exs. 12–25

FINDING SUMS **Find the sum.**

12. $-2.4 + 3.9$ 1.5 **(13.)** $-8.7 + 4.2$ -4.5 **14.** $4.3 + (-10.2)$ -5.9

15. $9.1 + (-2.5)$ 6.6 **16.** $-6.5 + (-7.1)$ -13.6 **17.** $-11.4 + (-3.8)$ -15.2

18. $4\frac{1}{5} + \left(-9\frac{1}{2}\right)$ $-5\frac{3}{10}$ **19.** $8\frac{2}{3} + \left(-1\frac{3}{5}\right)$ $7\frac{1}{15}$ **20.** $-12\frac{3}{4} + 6\frac{9}{10}$ $-5\frac{17}{20}$

21. $-\frac{4}{9} + 1\frac{4}{5}$ $1\frac{16}{45}$ **22.** $-3\frac{3}{7} + \left(-14\frac{3}{4}\right)$ $-18\frac{5}{28}$ **23.** $-7\frac{1}{12} + \left(-13\frac{7}{8}\right)$ $-20\frac{23}{24}$

ERROR ANALYSIS ***Describe*** **and correct the error in finding the sum.**

24. $-13 + (-15) = 28$ ✗

The answer should be negative, $-13 + (-15) = -28$.

25. $17 + (-31) = -48$ ✗

The numbers have different signs, so their absolute values should have been subtracted, $17 + (-31) = -14$.

EXAMPLE 3 on p. 76 for Exs. 26–31

IDENTIFYING PROPERTIES **Identify the property being illustrated.**

26. $-3 + 3 = 0$ Inverse property of addition

27. $(-6 + 1) + 7 = -6 + (1 + 7)$ Associate property of addition

28. $9 + (-1) = -1 + 9$ Commutative property of addition

29. $-8 + 0 = -8$ Identity property of addition

30. $(x + 2) + 3 = x + (2 + 3)$ Associative property of addition

31. $y + (-4) = -4 + y$ Commutative property of addition

EXAMPLE 4 on p. 76 for Exs. 32–37

FINDING SUMS **Find the sum.**

32. $-13 + 5 + (-7)$ -15 **33.** $-18 + (-12) + (-19)$ -49

34. $0.47 + (-1.8) + (-3.8)$ -5.13 **(35.)** $-2.6 + (-3.4) + 7.6$ 1.6

36. $-3\frac{1}{2} + \left(-7\frac{2}{5}\right) + \left(-9\frac{3}{10}\right)$ $-20\frac{1}{5}$ **37.** $8\frac{2}{3} + \left(-6\frac{3}{5}\right) + 3\frac{1}{4}$ $5\frac{19}{60}$

B

EVALUATING EXPRESSIONS **Evaluate the expression for the given value of x.**

38. $3 + x + (-7); x = 6$ 2 **39.** $x + (-5) + 5; x = -3$ -3

40. $9.6 + (-x) + 2.3; x = -8.5$ 20.4 **41.** $-1.7 + (-5.4) + (-x); x = 2.4$ -9.5

42. $1\frac{1}{4} + |x| + \left(-3\frac{1}{2}\right); x = -8\frac{2}{5}$ $6\frac{3}{20}$ **43.** $|x| + \left(-3\frac{1}{4}\right) + \left(7\frac{3}{10}\right); x = -3\frac{1}{3}$ $7\frac{23}{60}$

4 PRACTICE AND APPLY

Assignment Guide

Answer Transparencies available for all exercises

Basic:
Day 1: SRH p. 914 Exs. 21–25
pp. 77–79
Exs. 1, 2, 3–23 odd, 24–31, 33–43 odd, 53–57, 60–66

Average:
Day 1: pp. 77–79
Exs. 1, 2, 6–22 even, 24–31, 34–50 even, 53–59, 60–66 even

Advanced:
Day 1: pp. 77–79
Exs. 1, 2, 8–22 even, 27–49 odd, 51–53*, 55–59*, 61–65 odd

Block:
pp. 77–79
Exs. 1, 2, 6–22 even, 24–31, 34–50 even, 53–59, 60–66 even (with 2.3)

Differentiated Instruction

See *Algebra 1 Best Practices Toolkit* for suggestions on addressing the needs of a diverse classroom.

Homework Check

For a quick check of student understanding of key concepts, go over the following exercises:

Basic: 7, 15, 28, 37, 54

Average: 8, 18, 30, 36, 54

Advanced: 10, 31, 37, 55, 57

Extra Practice

- Student Edition, p. 939
- Chapter 2 Resource Book: Practice levels A, B, C, pp. 16–18

Practice Worksheet

An easily-readable reduced practice page (with answers) for this lesson can be found on p. 62C.

Differentiated Instruction

Kinesthetic Learners While working on **Exercises 3–11**, some students may need to trace their fingertip along a number line in order to complete the exercises. Have them begin at the starting number, and trace to the right to add a positive number or to the left to add a negative number.

See also the *Algebra 1 Toolkit* for more strategies.

Teaching Strategy

Exercises 3–11 Some students may prefer using algebra tiles or the rules of addition to find the sums. Have these students find the sums using a number line and then check their answers using algebra tiles or the rules of addition.

Exercise 50 Tell students it may be easier to determine the answer if they first substitute real numbers for *a* and *b*.

Avoiding Common Errors

Exercises 12–23 Watch for students who add the greater absolute value to the lesser absolute value when adding numbers of different signs. Remind them that when the numbers have different signs, they need to subtract the lesser absolute value from the greater absolute value. This means if the lesser absolute value is the first number, it will become the second number when they subtract, such that $2.5 + (-8.2)$ becomes $8.2 - 2.5$ when they take the absolute values and subtract.

Mathematical Reasoning

Exercise 56 Suggest that students first look for ways to eliminate answers before adding the numbers. Point out that the answers for A and B overlap for the years 2000 and 2001. To determine which three-year period had the greater profit, all they need to do is compare profits for 1999 and 2002. They can do the same for answers C and D. After they eliminate two of the answers, they can add and then compare the profits for the remaining three-year periods.

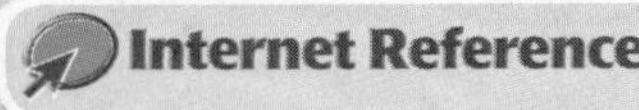

Exercise 58 For more information about atoms, visit the Jefferson Lab website at http://education.jlab.org/atomtour/index.html

51. 0; $|2x|$. *Sample answer:* If $x = 2$, then $|2| + (-2) = 2 + (-2) = 0$. If $x = -2$, then $|-2| + (-(-2)) = |-2| + |-2| = 4$.

FINDING SOLUTIONS **Solve the equation using mental math.**

44. $x + (-9) + 9 = 8$ 8
45. $(-8) + x + (-2) = -10$ 0
46. $x + (-2.8) + 9.2 = 0$ −6.4
47. $-8.7 + x + 1.3 = 0$ 7.4

TRANSLATING PHRASES **In Exercises 48 and 49, translate the verbal phrase into an addition expression. Then find the sum.**

48. The sum of the absolute value of −4 and the additive identity $|-4| + 0$; 4
49. The sum of the opposite of −18 and its additive inverse $-(-18) + (-18)$; 0

51. 0; $|2x|$. *Sample answer:* If $x = 2$, then $|2| + (-2) = 2 + (-2) = 0$. If $x = -2$, then $|-2| + (-(-2)) = |-2| + |-2| = 4$.

50. ★ **MULTIPLE CHOICE** If $a + b$ is negative, which statement must be true? D

Ⓐ $a < 0, b < 0$ Ⓑ $a < 0$ Ⓒ $a < 0, b > 0$ Ⓓ $a < -b$

51. C **CHALLENGE** Consider the expression $|x| + (-x)$. Write a simplified expression for the sum if x is positive. Then write a simplified expression for the sum if x is negative. Give examples to support your answers. See margin.

52. **CHALLENGE** Evaluate $-50 + (-49) + (-48) + \cdots + 48 + 49 + 50$. *Explain* how you can use the properties of addition to obtain the sum.
0; use the commutative property of addition to add each negative number and its opposite. By the additive inverse property, it will equal 0.

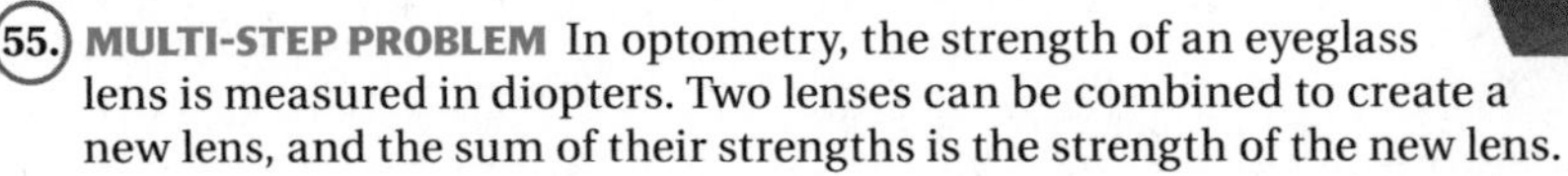

EXAMPLE 1 A on p. 74 for Ex. 53

53. **WEATHER** The temperature in your city at 6 A.M. was −8°F and increased by 15°F by noon. What was the temperature at noon? 7°F

@HomeTutor for problem solving help at classzone.com

EXAMPLE 2 on p. 75 for Exs. 54–55

54. **PARKING GARAGES** The bottom level of a parking garage has an elevation of −45 feet. The top level of the garage is 100 feet higher. What is the elevation of the top level? 55 ft

@HomeTutor for problem solving help at classzone.com

55. **MULTI-STEP PROBLEM** In optometry, the strength of an eyeglass lens is measured in diopters. Two lenses can be combined to create a new lens, and the sum of their strengths is the strength of the new lens.

a. A lens of −4.75 diopters is combined with a lens of 6.25 diopters to form a new lens. What is the strength of the new lens? 1.5 diopters

b. A lens of −2.5 diopters is combined with a lens of −1.25 diopters to form a new lens. What is the strength of the new lens? −3.75 diopters

c. The greater the absolute value of the strength of a lens, the stronger the lens. Which new lens is stronger, the one in part (a) or in part (b)? part (b)

EXAMPLE 4 on p. 76 for Exs. 56–57

56. ★ **MULTIPLE CHOICE** The table shows the profits for a company from 1999 to 2004. Which three-year period had the greatest total profit? C

Year	1999	2000	2001	2002	2003	2004
Profit (millions of dollars)	−13.76	54.91	38.54	−21.33	123.90	−14.82

Ⓐ 1999–2001 Ⓑ 2000–2002 Ⓒ 2001–2003 Ⓓ 2002–2004

○ = WORKED-OUT SOLUTIONS on p. WS1 ★ = STANDARDIZED TEST PRACTICE

B 57. ★ **SHORT RESPONSE** In golf, your score on a hole is the number of strokes above or below an expected number of strokes needed to hit a ball into the hole. As shown in the table, each score has a name. When you compare two scores, the lesser score is the better score.

Name	Double eagle	Eagle	Birdie	Par	Bogey	Double bogey
Score	−3	−2	−1	0	1	2

a. **Compare** For three holes, you score an eagle, a double bogey, and a birdie. Your friend scores a double eagle, a bogey, and a par. Who has the better total score? your friend

b. **Explain** Your friend scores a double eagle and an eagle for the next two holes. Is it possible for you to have a better score on all five holes after your next two holes? *Explain* your reasoning.
No, if you score 2 double eagles, you will have the same score.

58. ★ **EXTENDED RESPONSE** Atoms consist of protons, electrons, and neutrons. A group of x protons has a charge of x. A group of x electrons has a charge of $-x$. Neutrons have a charge of 0.

58c. 5 electrons should be added. *Sample answer*: $5 + x = 0$. For the expression to equal 0, add the additive inverse of 5, which is -5.

a. **Calculate** The total charge of an atom is the sum of the charges of its protons and electrons. Find the total charge of an atom that has 13 protons, 10 electrons, and 14 neutrons. 3

b. **Interpret** An atom is an ion only when it has a positive or a negative total charge. Is the atom in part (a) an ion? yes

c. **Explain** In an atom, only the number of electrons can change. Suppose an atom has a total charge of 5. For the atom not to be an ion, how should the number of electrons change? Your answer should include an algebraic equation that models the situation and an explanation of how you solved the equation.

C 59. **CHALLENGE** You sold three items in an Internet auction. The table shows the profit earned for each item. You now plan to sell a floor lamp. What is the least profit that you can earn on the lamp and have a positive total profit for the four items? *Explain* your answer. $12.40; the sum of the profit is −$12.39; to get a positive profit, you need to earn at least $12.40.

Item	Profit (dollars)
Mantel clock	4.13
Framed mirror	−10.65
Metal lunch box	−5.87

ILLINOIS MIXED REVIEW

TEST PRACTICE at classzone.com

60. A rectangular prism has dimensions ℓ, w, and h. Another rectangular prism has twice the volume of the first prism. Which of the following could be the dimensions of the second prism? D

Ⓐ ℓ, w, h Ⓑ $\ell, 2w, 2h$ Ⓒ $2\ell, 2w, 2h$ Ⓓ $\ell, \frac{w}{2}, 4h$

61. Which of the following values of x and y give the greatest value of z if $z = x^2 - 2y + 106$? C

Ⓐ $x = -5, y = 11$ Ⓒ $x = 3, y = -2$

Ⓑ $x = 2, y = 0$ Ⓓ $x = 5, y = 8$

5 ASSESS AND RETEACH

Daily Homework Quiz

Transparency Available

Find the sum.

1. $7.6 + (-9)$ −1.4

2. $-23.7 + 28.2 + 8.3$ 12.8

3. What property is illustrated by $(-y + 3) + 6 = -y + (3 + 6)$? Associative property of addition

4. The table shows the account ledgers for the Science Club and the Astronomy Club. Which club has the greater assets at the end of 3 weeks?

Week	Science Club	Astronomy Club
1	−$44.50	$106.00
2	$150.55	−$48.50
3	−$15.50	$35.00

The Astronomy Club has greater assets since $92.50 > $90.55.

Online Quiz

Available at **classzone.com**

Diagnosis/Remediation

- Practice A, B, C in Chapter 2 Resource Book, pp. 16–18
- Study Guide in Chapter 2 Resource Book, pp. 19–20
- Practice Workbook, pp. 18–19
- @HomeTutor

Challenge

Additional challenge is available in the Chapter 2 Resource Book, p. 23.

2.3 Subtract Real Numbers

6.11.10 Perform numerical computations with real numbers.

Before You added real numbers.

Now You will subtract real numbers.

Why? So you can find a change in temperature, as in Ex. 43.

1 PLAN AND PREPARE

Warm-Up Exercises

Transparency Available

Find the sum.

1. $-14 + 5$ -9
2. $6.4 + (-3.5)$ 2.9

Evaluate the expression when $x = 6$.

3. $x - 4.8$ 1.2
4. $6.3 - x$ 0.3
5. The temperature was $-3°F$ in the morning and then rose $2°F$ by noon. What was the temperature at noon? $-1°F$

Notetaking Guide

Transparency Available

Promotes interactive learning and notetaking skills, pp. 30–31.

Pacing

Basic: 1 day

Average: 1 day

Advanced: 1 day

Block: 0.5 block with 2.2

• See *Teaching Guide/Lesson Plan.*

2 FOCUS AND MOTIVATE

Essential Question

Big Idea 1, p. 63

How do you subtract real numbers? Tell students they will learn how to answer this question by using a subtraction rule that relates subtraction to addition.

Key Vocabulary
• **opposites,** *p. 66*

Because the expressions $12 - 3$ and $12 + (-3)$ have the same value, 9, you can conclude that $12 - 3 = 12 + (-3)$. Subtracting 3 from 12 is equivalent to adding the opposite of 3 to 12. This example illustrates the *subtraction rule.*

KEY CONCEPT *For Your Notebook*

Subtraction Rule

Words To subtract b from a, add the opposite of b to a.

Algebra $a - b = a + (-b)$ **Example** $14 - 8 = 14 + (-8)$

EXAMPLE 1 Subtract real numbers

Find the difference.

a. $-12 - 19 = -12 + (-19)$
$= -31$

b. $18 - (-7) = 18 + 7$
$= 25$

 at classzone.com

✓ GUIDED PRACTICE for Example 1

Find the difference.

1. $-2 - 7$ -9 **2.** $11.7 - (-5)$ 16.7 **3.** $\frac{1}{3} - \frac{1}{2}$ $-\frac{1}{6}$

EXAMPLE 2 Evaluate a variable expression

Evaluate the expression $y - x + 6.8$ when $x = -2$ and $y = 7.2$.

$y - x + 6.8 = 7.2 - (-2) + 6.8$ **Substitute −2 for *x* and 7.2 for *y*.**

$= 7.2 + 2 + 6.8$ **Add the opposite of −2.**

$= 16$ **Add.**

Resource Planning Guide

Chapter Resource Book
• Teaching Guide/Lesson Plan (pp. 24–25)
• Activity Master (p. 26)
• Practice levels A, B, C (pp. 28–30)
• Study Guide (pp. 31–32)
• Catch-up for Absent Students (p. 33)
• Problem Solving Workshop (p. 34)
• Challenge (p. 36)

Workbooks
• Notetaking Guide (pp. 30–31)
• Practice Workbook (pp. 20–21)

Teaching Options
• **Power Presentations CD-ROM** provides dynamic electronic teaching resources for the classroom.
• **Activity Generator CD-ROM** provides editable activities for all ability levels.

Interactive Technology
• Easy Planner
• Power Presentations CD-ROM
• Activity Generator CD-ROM
• Animated Algebra
• Test Generator CD-ROM
• Online Quiz
• eWorkbook
• eEdition
• @HomeTutor

Resources for English Learners
• Quick Reference for English Learners
• Spanish Study Guide
• Multi-Language Visual Glossary
• Student Resources in Spanish

See also the *Algebra 1 Toolkit* for more strategies for meeting individual needs.

EVALUATING CHANGE You can use subtraction to find the change in a quantity, such as elevation or temperature. The change in a quantity is the difference of the new amount and the original amount. If the new amount is greater than the original amount, the change is positive. If the new amount is less than the original amount, the change is negative.

EXAMPLE 3 Evaluate change

TEMPERATURES One of the most extreme temperature changes in United States history occurred in Fairfield, Montana, on December 24, 1924. At noon, the temperature was 63°F. By midnight, the temperature fell to −21°F. What was the change in temperature?

Solution

The change C in temperature is the difference of the temperature m at midnight and the temperature n at noon.

STEP 1 **Write** a verbal model. Then write an equation.

Change in temperature	=	Temperature at midnight	−	Temperature at noon
C	=	m	−	n

AVOID ERRORS
When a quantity decreases, the change is negative. So, the change found in Example 3 should be a negative number.

STEP 2 **Find** the change in temperature.

$C = m - n$ **Write equation.**

$= -21 - 63$ **Substitute values.**

$= -21 + (-63)$ **Add the opposite of 63.**

$= -84$ **Add −21 and −63.**

▸ The change in temperature was −84°F.

USING A CALCULATOR To enter a negative number on a calculator, use the (−) key. To enter a subtraction sign, use the − key. You can use a calculator to check your answer in Example 3 using the following keystrokes.

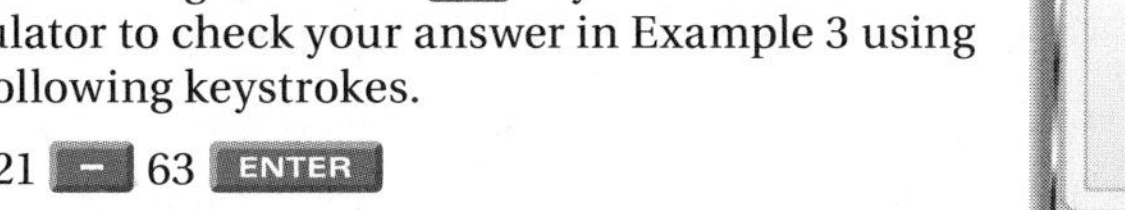

(−) 21 − 63 ENTER

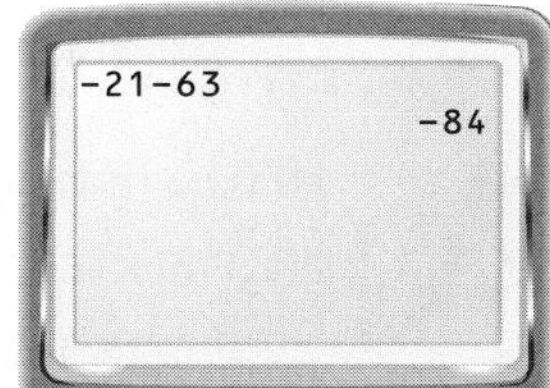

GUIDED PRACTICE for Examples 2 and 3

Evaluate the expression when $x = -3$ and $y = 5.2$.

4. $x - y + 8$ **−0.2**

5. $y - (x - 2)$ **10.2**

6. $(y - 4) - x$ **4.2**

7. **CAR VALUES** A new car is valued at \$15,000. One year later, the car is valued at \$12,300. What is the change in the value of the car? **−\$2700**

Motivating the Lesson

Tell students that learning to subtract real numbers allows them to evaluate changes in quantities, such as the change in value of a \$1500 computer that is valued at \$975 after two years.

3 TEACH

Extra Example 1

Find the difference.

a. −18 − 3 **−21** **b.** −9 − (−12) **3**

An **Animated Algebra** activity is available on-line for **Example 1**. This activity is also available on the **Power Presentations CD-ROM**.

Extra Example 2

Evaluate the expression $x - y + 2.3$ when $x = 8.8$ and $y = -1.4$. **12.5**

Extra Example 3

The temperature one morning was 14°C. By midday, the temperature was −3°C. What was the change in temperature? **−17°C**

Closing the Lesson

Have students summarize the major points of the lesson and answer the Essential Question: How do you subtract real numbers?

- **Subtracting b from a is the same as adding the opposite of b to a, so $a - b = a + (-b)$.**
- **The change in a quantity is the difference of the new amount and the original amount. If the quantity increases, the change is positive and if it decreases, the change is negative.**

To subtract two numbers, add the opposite of the second number to the first number.

Differentiated Instruction

Visual Learners On a calculator, some students may confuse the subtraction key with the negation key. Show them that the four operation keys (+, −, ×, ÷) are always together in a group. The negation key is not only set apart from the other keys, but it is often a different color.

See also the *Algebra 1 Toolkit* for more strategies.

4 PRACTICE AND APPLY

Assignment Guide

Answer Transparencies available for all exercises

Basic:
Day 1: pp. 82–84
Exs. 1–16, 17–35 odd, 42–46, 49–55 odd

Average:
Day 1: pp. 82–84
Exs. 1, 2, 6–14 even, 15, 16, 20–30 even, 32–46, 50–56 even

Advanced:
Day 1: pp. 82–84
Exs. 1, 2, 10–14, 20–30 even, 32–41*, 43–48*, 52, 56

Block:
pp. 82–84
Exs. 1, 2, 6–14 even, 15, 16, 20–30 even, 32–46, 50–56 even (with 2.2)

Differentiated Instruction

See *Algebra 1 Best Practices Toolkit* for suggestions on addressing the needs of a diverse classroom.

Homework Check

For a quick check of student understanding of key concepts, go over the following exercises:

Basic: 7, 19, 23, 27, 42
Average: 10, 22, 28, 32, 42
Advanced: 13, 24, 30, 35, 43

Extra Practice

- Student Edition, p. 939
- Chapter 2 Resource Book: Practice levels A, B, C, pp. 28–30

Practice Worksheet

An easily-readable reduced practice page (with answers) for this lesson can be found on p. 62C.

2.3 EXERCISES

HOMEWORK KEY
○ = WORKED-OUT SOLUTIONS on p. WS4 for Exs. 3, 21, and 43
★ = STANDARDIZED TEST PRACTICE Exs. 2, 38, 39, 40, and 46
◆ = MULTIPLE REPRESENTATIONS Ex. 45

SKILL PRACTICE

A

1. **VOCABULARY** Use the subtraction rule to rewrite the expression $-3 - 6$ as an addition expression. $-3 + (-6)$

2. ★ **WRITING** Without actually subtracting, how can you tell whether a change in a quantity will be negative? If the second number is greater than the first number.

EXAMPLE 1 on p. 80 for Exs. 3–14

FINDING DIFFERENCES **Find the difference.**

3. $13 - (-5)$ 18
4. $16 - 32$ -16
5. $-11 - (-3)$ -8
6. $-15 - 29$ -44
7. $-35.9 - (-50)$ 14.1
8. $14.7 - (-2.3)$ 17
9. $-3.6 - 22.2$ -25.8
10. $-18.2 - (-15.4)$ -2.8
11. $\frac{1}{2} - \frac{5}{6}$ $-\frac{1}{3}$
12. $-\frac{5}{3} - \frac{8}{3}$ $-4\frac{1}{3}$
13. $\frac{1}{2} - \left(-\frac{1}{4}\right)$ $\frac{3}{4}$
14. $-\frac{7}{10} - \left(-\frac{2}{5}\right)$ $-\frac{3}{10}$

EXAMPLE 2 on p. 80 for Exs. 15–25

ERROR ANALYSIS ***Describe*** **and correct the error in evaluating the expression when $x = 3$ and $y = -8$.**

15.
$$x - y + 2 = 3 - 8 + 2$$
$$= 3 + (-8) + 2$$
$$= -5 + 2$$
$$= -3$$

16.
$$x - (-4 + y) = 3 - [-4 + (-8)]$$
$$= 3 - (-12)$$
$$= 3 - 12$$
$$= -9$$

15. 8 was substituted for y instead of -8; $3 - (-8) + 2 = 3 + 8 + 2 = 13$.

16. The opposite of -12 was not added in step 3; $3 - [-4 + (-8)] = 3 - (-12) = 3 + 12 = 15$.

EVALUATING EXPRESSIONS **Evaluate the expression when $x = 7.1$ and $y = -2.5$.**

17. $x - (-y)$ 4.6
18. $y - x - 12$ -21.6
19. $x - (-6) + y$ 10.6
20. $x - (y - 13)$ 22.6
21. $-y - (1.9 - x)$ 7.7
22. $-y - x$ -4.6
23. $x - y - 2$ 7.6
24. $5.3 - (y - x)$ 14.9
25. $x + y - 2.8$ 1.8

EXAMPLE 3 on p. 81 for Exs. 26–31

EVALUATING CHANGE **Find the change in temperature or elevation.**

26. From −5°C to −13°C −8°C
27. From −45°F to 62°F 107°F
28. From −300 feet to −100 feet 200 ft
29. From 1200 meters to −80 meters −1280 m
30. From 4.8°F to −12.6°F −17.4°F
31. From −90.7 miles to 36.4 miles 127.1 mi

B

EVALUATING EXPRESSIONS **Evaluate the expression when $x = 3.6$, $y = 6.6$, and $z = -11$.**

32. $(x - y) - |z|$ -14
33. $(x - |-y|) - z$ 8
34. $x - |y - z|$ -14
35. $(-x - y) - z - 5$ -4.2
36. $x + y - z + 12.9$ 34.1
37. $-z + y - x - (-2.4)$ 16.4

38. ★ **MULTIPLE CHOICE** If the value of the expression $a - b$ is negative, which statement must be true? C

(A) $a > b$ (B) $a = 0$ (C) $a < b$ (D) $b = 0$

39. *Sample answer:* You are overdrawn on your checking account by \$23. You write two more checks for \$14 and \$8. What is your balance?; −\$45

39. ★ **OPEN-ENDED** Write a real-world problem that can be modeled by the expression $-23 - 14 - 8$. Then solve the problem.

40. ★ **WRITING** Tell whether the associative property and the commutative property hold for subtraction. Give examples to support your answers. No. *Sample answer*: $(2 - 3) - 4 \neq 2 - (3 - 4)$, $2 - 5 \neq 5 - 2$

C 41. **CHALLENGE** Let a and b be negative numbers. Tell whether the value of the expression is positive or negative. *Explain* your reasoning. See margin.

a. $|a + b|$ **b.** $-a - b$ **c.** $-|a| - |b|$ **d.** $a + b$

PROBLEM SOLVING

EXAMPLE 3 A on p. 81 for Exs. 42–43

42. **VOLCANOES** Mahukona is a Hawaiian volcano whose summit has an elevation of −3600 feet. The summit once had an elevation of 800 feet. What was the change in elevation of the volcano's summit? −4400 ft

@HomeTutor for problem solving help at classzone.com

43. **CAVES** The temperature inside Mammoth Cave in Kentucky is about 12.2°C year round. If the temperature outside the cave is −2.4°C, what is the change in temperature from outside to inside the cave? 14.6°C

@HomeTutor for problem solving help at classzone.com

44. **FOOTBALL** In four plays a football team gains 3 yards, loses 7 yards, loses 2 yards, and gains 15 yards. How many yards did the team gain after four plays? 9 yd

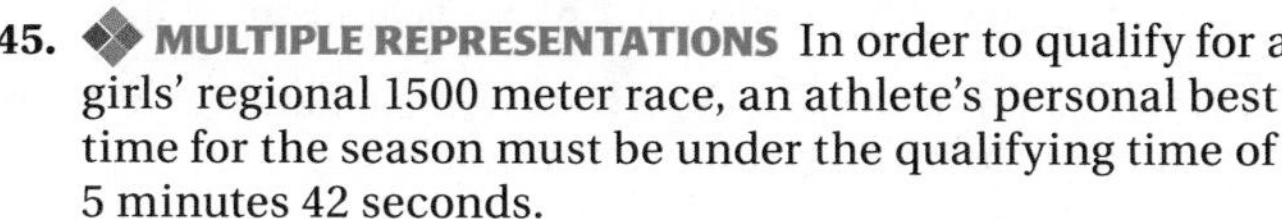

45a. $d = t - 342$

45b.

t	d
341.7	−0.3
343.8	1.8
340.9	−1.1
342.7	0.7

341.7 and 340.9; you can tell if $t - 342$ is negative.

45. ◆ **MULTIPLE REPRESENTATIONS** In order to qualify for a girls' regional 1500 meter race, an athlete's personal best time for the season must be under the qualifying time of 5 minutes 42 seconds.

a. Writing an Equation Write an equation that expresses d as the difference of the athlete's personal best time t (in seconds) and the qualifying time (in seconds).

b. Making a Table Make a table that gives the values of d for $t = 341.7$, 343.8, 340.9, and 342.7. Which values of t in the table are under the qualifying time? How can you tell from the differences?

B 46. ★ **SHORT RESPONSE** A trade surplus or deficit is the difference of the value of all exports and the value of all imports. A positive difference is a surplus, and a negative difference is a deficit. The table shows the values of the United States' imports and exports for the period 2000–2003.

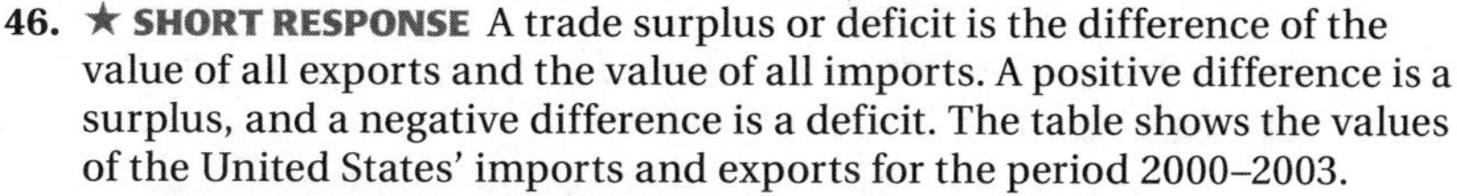

Year	2000	2001	2002	2003
Value of exports (trillions of dollars)	1.071	1.007	0.976	1.021
Value of imports (trillions of dollars)	1.449	1.369	1.398	1.517

a. Calculate Find the trade surplus or deficit for each year. −\$.378 trillion; −\$.362 trillion; −\$.422 trillion; −\$.496 trillion

b. Describe *Describe* any trends in the surplus or deficit over the years. *Sample answer:* There is a deficit each year and it has increased each year.

Avoiding Common Errors

Exercises 26–31 Remind students that a change is positive if the new amount is greater than the original and negative if the new amount is less than the original. Point out that the new amount could be greater than the original amount and still be a negative number.

Graphing Calculator

Exercises 26–31, 46 Students can use their calculators to check their answers for exercises 26–31 and to calculate trade surpluses and deficits for exercise 46. Tell them to use the instructions for the calculator in Example 3. Note that they do not need to use negative numbers for exercise 46.

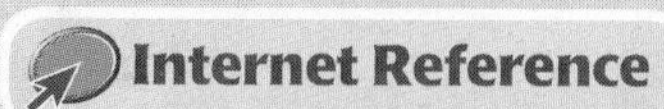

Internet Reference

Exercise 42 Additional information about volcanoes can be found at http://www.geology.sdsu.edu/how_volcanoes_work

Study Strategy

Exercises 42–43 Instruct students to write out detailed solutions for these exercises using Example 3 as a model. This will help them determine the original quantity and the new quantity and avoid confusing the two.

Reading Strategy

Exercise 45 Point out to students that part a on writing an equation states that the best time and the qualifying time are in seconds.

Exercise 47 Encourage students to read the introduction on snowboards and study the diagram before answering part a.

41a. Positive; the absolute value of a negative number is positive.

41b. Positive; if $-a - b$ is written as a sum, $-a + (-b)$, then the opposite of a negative number is positive. The sum of two positive numbers is positive.

41c. Negative; if $-|a| - |b|$ is written as a sum, $-|a| + (-|b|)$, the opposite of the absolute value of a number is negative. The sum of two negative numbers is negative.

41d. Negative; the sum of two negative numbers is negative.

5 ASSESS AND RETEACH

Daily Homework Quiz

 **Transparency Available**

Find the difference.

1. 37.5 − (−4.6) 42.1
2. −12 − (−8.5) −3.5

Evaluate the expression when $x = -2.5$ and $y = 6.2$.

3. $y - x + 2$ 10.7
4. $x - 4.7 - (-y)$ −1
5. On a hike through Benedict Canyon, Emma started at an elevation of 128 feet and then descended to −375 feet. What was Emma's change in elevation? −503 ft

Online Quiz

Available at **classzone.com**

Diagnosis/Remediation

- Practice A, B, C in Chapter 2 Resource Book, pp. 28–30
- Study Guide in Chapter 2 Resource Book, pp. 31–32
- Practice Workbook, pp. 20–21
- @HomeTutor

Challenge

Additional challenge is available in the Chapter 2 Resource Book, p. 36.

Quiz

An easily-readable reduced copy of the quiz (with answers) on Lessons 2.1–2.3 from the Assessment Book can be found on p. 62E.

47. SNOWBOARDS Snowboarders can rotate the shoe bindings on their snowboards. The binding setup shown below is written +24°/−18°. This means that the front angle is 24° counterclockwise from vertical, and the rear angle is 18° clockwise from vertical.

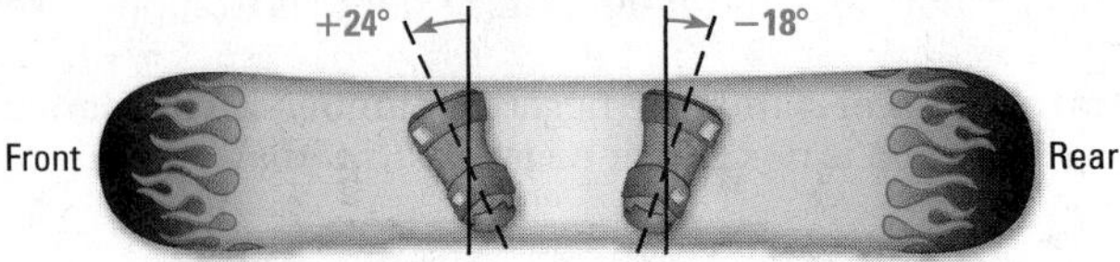

a. An instructor suggests a binding setup of +30°/+15° for beginners. Your setup is initially +24°/−4°. Find the changes in angle measures needed to match the instructor's suggestion. 6°; 19°

b. A mirror setup is a setup of $+n°/-n°$ where n is between 0 and 90. Your setup is initially +13°/−6°. You change the front angle measure by −3°. Find the change in the rear angle measure needed for a mirror setup. −4°

C **48. CHALLENGE** Greenwich Mean Time (GMT) is the time at the Royal Observatory in Greenwich, England. A location that is $+n$ hours from GMT is n hours ahead of GMT, and a location that is $-n$ hours from GMT is n hours behind GMT. Costa Rica is −6 hours from GMT, and India is +5.5 hours from GMT. If it is 7:45 A.M. in India, what time is it in Costa Rica? 8:15 P.M.

ILLINOIS MIXED REVIEW

TEST PRACTICE at classzone.com

49. The domain of the function $y = 3x - 1$ is 2, 5, and 10. What is the range of the function? D

Ⓐ 4, 14, and 29 Ⓑ 5, 11, and 14 Ⓒ 5, 11, and 29 Ⓓ 5, 14, and 29

50. How many times greater is the area of a circle with a diameter of $4x$ units than the area of a circle with a diameter of x units? D

Ⓐ 2 Ⓑ 4 Ⓒ 8 Ⓓ 16

QUIZ for Lessons 2.1–2.3

1. Tell whether each of the following numbers is a whole number, an integer, or a rational number: $-\frac{5}{6}$, −8.2, 0, −9. Then order the numbers from least to greatest. *(p. 64)* $-\frac{5}{6}$: rational number, −8.2: rational number, 0: whole number, integer, rational number, −9: integer, rational number; −9, −8.2, $-\frac{5}{6}$, 0

Find the sum or difference.

2. $5 + (-36)$ *(p. 74)* −31 **3.** $-8.2 + (-2.3)$ *(p. 74)* −10.5 **4.** $3\frac{1}{2} + (-2)$ *(p. 74)* $1\frac{1}{2}$

5. $-18 - (-9)$ *(p. 80)* −9 **6.** $-11.2 - 21.7$ *(p. 80)* −32.9 **7.** $4\frac{1}{2} - \left(-\frac{1}{5}\right)$ *(p. 80)* $4\frac{7}{10}$

Evaluate the expression when $x = 2.5$ and $y = -3.4$. *(p. 80)*

8. $x + y - 9$ −9.9 **9.** $x - (y - 5.1)$ 11 **10.** $12.1 - (y - x)$ 18

EXTRA PRACTICE for Lesson 2.3, p. 939

 **ONLINE QUIZ** at classzone.com

@HomeTutor
classzone.com
Keystrokes

2.3 Subtract Real Numbers

QUESTION How can you use a spreadsheet to subtract the same number from various numbers?

	A	B
1		
2		

In a spreadsheet, the columns are identified by letters, and the rows are identified by numbers. Each cell has a name that is made up of a letter and a number. For example, B2 is the cell in column B and row 2. A cell can contain a label, a number, or a formula.

EXAMPLE Find the difference of two numbers

A manufacturing company is making foam hand grips for bicycles and jump ropes. The ideal length of a hand grip is 5 inches. In a batch of ten hand grips, the actual lengths (in inches) are 4.878, 4.902, 5.115, 5.13, 4.877, 4.874, 4.799, 4.819, 4.879, and 5.124. Create a spreadsheet to find the difference of the actual length and the ideal length for each hand grip.

Solution

STEP 1 *Enter data*
Enter the labels in the first row of the spreadsheet. Then enter the grip numbers and grip lengths in successive rows.

	A	B	C
1	Grip	Length (inches)	Difference
2	1	4.878	
3	2	4.902	

STEP 2 *Calculate differences*
For each hand grip, enter the formula for the difference of the actual and ideal lengths in the appropriate cell in column C. See margin.

	A	B	C
1	Grip	Length (inches)	Difference
2	1	4.878	=B2−5
3	2	4.902	=B3−5

After you enter a formula, the cell should display the difference of the length of the grip and the ideal length. For example, C2 should display −0.122, and C3 should display −0.098.

DRAW CONCLUSIONS

1. The manufacturer will consider a hand grip acceptable if the absolute value of the difference of the actual length and the ideal length is at most 0.125 inch. How many hand grips from the batch are acceptable? **6 hand grips**
2. What are the least and greatest possible lengths that a hand grip can have and still be acceptable? *Explain* your reasoning. **4.875 in., 5.125 in.; adding and subtracting 0.125 from 5 will give the greatest and least acceptable lengths of a hand grip.**
3. For which of the ten hand grips is the length closest to the ideal length? How can you tell from the differences in column C? **4.902; the difference in the lengths has the smallest absolute value.**
4. In another batch of ten hand grips, the actual lengths (in inches) are 4.871, 5.019, 5.112, 4.987, 5.067, 4.899, 4.859, 5.132, 5.126, and 5.093. Create a spreadsheet to find the difference of the actual length and the ideal length for each hand grip. See margin.

1 PLAN AND PREPARE

Learn the Method

- Students will use a spreadsheet to subtract real numbers.
- After the activity, students can use a spreadsheet to check their table calculations in Exercise 46, Lesson 2.3.

2 TEACH

Alternative Strategy

Show students that they do not need to enter the formula in each cell in Step 2. Demonstrate that they can enter the formula for cell C2, click on the cell, move the cursor to the bottom right corner of the cell until the plus icon appears, click on the icon, and then move the cursor to the bottom of row 11. Students can check that the correct formula is entered by clicking on a cell. The formula will appear in the *fx* box at the top of the page. Warn that this works only if they have already entered all of the grip lengths in column B.

Extra Example

A manufacturing plant fills boxes with dog biscuits. The ideal weight per box is 12 ounces. In a batch of ten boxes, the actual weights (in ounces) are 11.025, 11.280, 11.275, 12.024, 11.685, 12.3, 11.45, 12.54, 11.955, and 12.2. Create a spreadsheet to find the difference of the actual weight and the ideal weight for each box of dog biscuits. **Enter box numbers in column A, actual weights in column B, and the formulas =B2–12, =B3–12, and so on in column C.**

3 ASSESS AND RETEACH

Suppose you made a spreadsheet to find the differences of the ideal and actual lengths of the grips. What would be the formula? Would the results be the same? **=5−B2, =5−B3, =5−B4, . . . ; yes**

Step 2, 4. See Additional Answers beginning on p. AA1.

Illinois Mixed Review

1. A
2. F
3. D
4. J
5. A
6. J
7. B

Illinois Mixed Review

Lessons 2.1–2.3

1. **ELEVATION** The table shows the recorded elevation of a diver as a function of time.

Time, t (minutes)	Elevation, e (meters)
0	0
2	−16
4	−32
7	−56
10	−80

Which equation represents the diver's elevation e (in meters) as a function of time t (in minutes)?

A. $e = -8t$

B. $e = \frac{8}{t}$

C. $e = 8t^2$

D. $e = 8t$

2. **TEMPERATURES** The record low temperatures (in degrees Fahrenheit) for Alaska, Arkansas, Hawaii, and California are −80°F, −29°F, 12°F, and −45°F, respectively. Which state recorded the lowest temperature?

F. Alaska

G. Arkansas

H. California

J. Hawaii

3. **DRY ICE** Dry ice changes directly from a solid to a gas when its temperature is about −79°C. Dry ice exists as a gas, liquid, and solid at the same time when it is at a certain pressure and its temperature increases by 22.4°C. What is the temperature (in degrees Celsius) at which this occurs?

A. −101.4°C

B. −57.6°C

C. −57.4°C

D. −56.6°C

4. **BUSINESS** In May, a store had an income of $22,556 and expenses of $17,491. In June, the store had an income of $19,418 and expenses of $24,950. What was the change in profit from May to June?

F. $467 **H.** −$467

G. $10,597 **J.** −$10,597

5. **MONEY** Your bank charges a $35 fee when the balance in your checking account is negative. You have a balance of $150 in your account. Suppose you withdraw $165 from the account. What will the balance be after the fee is charged?

A. −$50 **C.** −$20

B. −$40 **D.** $10

6. **MIGRATION** Net migration flow is the difference of the number of people migrating to a place and the number of people migrating out of a place. The table shows the number of people who migrated into and out of a certain city during the period 2002–2005. Which year had the greatest net migration flow?

Year	Number migrating into city	Number migrating out of city
2002	3179	3623
2003	3053	3632
2004	3180	3695
2005	3174	3396

F. 2002 **H.** 2004

G. 2003 **J.** 2005

7. **STOCK** An investor pays $8.64 per share of a stock. Over the next three days, the change in value of a share of the stock is −$.56, then −$1.02, and then $.94. What is the value (in dollars) of one share of the stock at the end of the three days?

A. $6.12 **C.** $9.12

B. $8.00 **D.** $9.38

Investigating Algebra ACTIVITY *Use before Lesson 2.4*

2.4 Multiplication by −1

MATERIALS • paper and pencil

QUESTION **What is the product of any integer *a* and −1?**

You can rewrite a multiplication expression as repeated addition. For example, $3 \cdot 8$ can be rewritten as $8 + 8 + 8$. Because the sum is 24, you can conclude that $3 \cdot 8 = 24$.

EXPLORE **Find the product of an integer and −1**

STEP 1 Copy and complete the table.

Multiplication Expression	Addition Expression	Sum
$5 \cdot (-1)$	$-1 + (-1) + (-1) + (-1) + (-1)$	−5
$4 \cdot (-1)$	?	?
$3 \cdot (-1)$	?	?
$2 \cdot (-1)$	?	?

$-1 + (-1) + (-1) + (-1)$; −4
$-1 + (-1) + (-1)$; −3
$-1 + (-1)$; −2

STEP 2 Copy and complete the multiplication equations below.

$5 \cdot (-1) = \underline{?}$ −5
$4 \cdot (-1) = \underline{?}$ −4
$3 \cdot (-1) = \underline{?}$ −3
$2 \cdot (-1) = \underline{?}$ −2

Complete using the table from Step 1.

$1 \cdot (-1) = \underline{?}$ −1
$0 \cdot (-1) = \underline{?}$ 0
$-1 \cdot (-1) = \underline{?}$ 1
$-2 \cdot (-1) = \underline{?}$ 2
$-3 \cdot (-1) = \underline{?}$ 3

Complete by extending the pattern in the first four products.

DRAW CONCLUSIONS **Use your observations to complete these exercises**

1. Copy and complete: For any integer *a*, $a \cdot (-1) = \underline{?}$. $-a$

Find the product.

2. $12 \cdot (-1)$ −12
3. $10 \cdot (-1)$ −10
4. $-23 \cdot (-1)$ 23
5. $-47 \cdot (-1)$ 47
6. $-18 \cdot (-1)$ 18
7. $15 \cdot (-1)$ −15

1 PLAN AND PREPARE

Explore the Concept

- Students will multiply an integer by −1.
- This activity leads into the study of properties of multiplication in Example 2 in Lesson 2.4.

Recommended Time

Work activity: 10 min
Discuss results: 5 min

Grouping

Students can work individually or in pairs. If students work in pairs, one student can copy and complete the table in Step 1 and the other student can copy and complete the multiplication equations in Step 2. Each student can check the work of the other.

2 TEACH

Key Questions

- What can you conclude from the table in Step 1? The product of a positive integer and −1 is the opposite of the integer.
- What is the pattern in Step 2? At each step, add 1 to the product from the step before.

Key Discovery

The product of an integer and −1 is the opposite of the integer.

3 ASSESS AND RETEACH

1. What is the sign of $a \cdot (-1)$ if *a* is a negative integer? positive
2. What is the sign of $a \cdot (-1)$ if *a* is a positive integer? negative

2.4 Multiply Real Numbers

 **6.11.10** Perform numerical computations with real numbers.

Before You added and subtracted real numbers.

Now You will multiply real numbers.

Why So you can calculate an elevation, as in Example 4.

Key Vocabulary
- **multiplicative identity**

In the activity on page 87, you saw that $a \cdot (-1) = -a$ for any integer a. This rule not only lets you write the product of a and -1 as $-a$, but it also lets you write $-a$ as $(-1)a$ and $a(-1)$. Using this rule, you can multiply any two real numbers. Here are two examples:

$$-2(3) = -1(2)(3) = -1(6) = -6 \qquad (-2)(-3) = -2(3)(-1) = -6(-1) = 6$$

KEY CONCEPT *For Your Notebook*

The Sign of a Product

Words The product of two real numbers with the *same* sign is positive.

Examples $3(4) = 12$ $\quad -6(-3) = 18$

Words The product of two real numbers with *different* signs is negative.

Examples $2(-5) = -10$ $\quad -7(2) = -14$

EXAMPLE 1 Multiply real numbers

Find the product.

a. $-3(6) = -18$ — Different signs; product is negative.

b. $2(-5)(-4) = (-10)(-4)$ — Multiply 2 and -5.

$= 40$ — Same signs; product is positive.

c. $-\frac{1}{2}(-4)(-3) = 2(-3)$ — Multiply $-\frac{1}{2}$ and -4.

$= -6$ — Different signs; product is negative.

MULTIPLY NEGATIVES
- A product is negative if it has an *odd* number of negative numbers.
- A product is positive if it has an *even* number of negative numbers.

 **GUIDED PRACTICE** for Example 1

Find the product.

1. $-2(-7)$ **14** **2.** $-0.5(-4)(-9)$ **−18** **3.** $\frac{4}{3}(-3)(7)$ **−28**

1 PLAN AND PREPARE

Warm-Up Exercises

Transparency Available

1. $-17.3 + 6.2 = \underline{?}$ **−11.1**
2. $26.9 - (-5.8) = \underline{?}$ **32.7**

Identify the property illustrated.

3. $(12 + 14) + 82 = 12 + (14 + 82)$ **Associative property of addition**
4. $-3 + 0 = -3$ **Identity property of addition**
5. A company had a profit of −\$8.6 million in 2005 and \$1.4 million in 2006. What is the change in profit? **\$10 million**

Notetaking Guide

Transparency Available

Promotes interactive learning and notetaking skills, pp. 32–35.

Pacing

Basic: 1 day
Average: 1 day
Advanced: 1 day
Block: 0.5 block with 2.5
- See *Teaching Guide/Lesson Plan*.

2 FOCUS AND MOTIVATE

Essential Question

Big Idea 1, p. 63

How do you multiply real numbers? **Tell students they will learn how to answer this question by using sign rules and properties of multiplication.**

Resource Planning Guide

Chapter Resource Book
- Teaching Guide/Lesson Plan (pp. 37–38)
- Practice levels A, B, C (pp. 39–41)
- Study Guide (pp. 42–43)
- Catch-up for Absent Students (p. 44)
- Problem Solving Workshop (p. 45)
- Challenge (p. 46)

Workbooks
- Notetaking Guide (pp. 32–35)
- Practice Workbook (pp. 22–23)

Teaching Options
- **Power Presentations CD-ROM** provides dynamic electronic teaching resources for the classroom.
- **Activity Generator CD-ROM** provides editable activities for all ability levels.

Interactive Technology
- Easy Planner
- Power Presentations CD-ROM
- Activity Generator CD-ROM
- Animated Algebra
- Test Generator CD-ROM
- Online Quiz
- eWorkbook
- eEdition
- @HomeTutor

Resources for English Learners
- Quick Reference for English Learners
- Spanish Study Guide
- Multi-Language Visual Glossary
- Student Resources in Spanish

See also the *Algebra 1 Toolkit* for more strategies for meeting individual needs.

PROPERTIES OF MULTIPLICATION Notice that both $4(-5)$ and $-5(4)$ have a product of -20, so $4(-5) = -5(4)$. This equation is an example of the *commutative property of multiplication*. Properties of multiplication are listed below.

KEY CONCEPT *For Your Notebook*

Properties of Multiplication

COMMUTATIVE PROPERTY The order in which you multiply two numbers does not change the product.

Algebra $a \cdot b = b \cdot a$ **Example** $4 \cdot (-5) = -5 \cdot 4$

ASSOCIATIVE PROPERTY The way you group three numbers in a product does not change the product.

Algebra $(a \cdot b) \cdot c = a \cdot (b \cdot c)$ **Example** $(-2 \cdot 7) \cdot 4 = -2 \cdot (7 \cdot 4)$

IDENTITY PROPERTY The product of a number and 1 is that number.

Algebra $a \cdot 1 = 1 \cdot a = a$ **Example** $(-5) \cdot 1 = -5$

PROPERTY OF ZERO The product of a number and 0 is 0.

Algebra $a \cdot 0 = 0 \cdot a = 0$ **Example** $-3 \cdot 0 = 0$

PROPERTY OF –1 The product of a number and -1 is the opposite of the number.

Algebra $a \cdot (-1) = -1 \cdot a = -a$ **Example** $-2 \cdot (-1) = 2$

The identity property states that the product of a number a and 1 is a. The number 1 is called the **multiplicative identity**.

EXAMPLE 2 Identify properties of multiplication

	Statement	Property illustrated
a.	$(x \cdot 7) \cdot 0.5 = x \cdot (7 \cdot 0.5)$	Associative property of multiplication
b.	$8 \cdot 0 = 0$	Multiplicative property of zero
c.	$-6 \cdot y = y \cdot (-6)$	Commutative property of multiplication
d.	$9 \cdot (-1) = -9$	Multiplicative property of -1
e.	$1 \cdot v = v$	Identity property of multiplication

GUIDED PRACTICE for Example 2

Identify the property illustrated.

4. $-1 \cdot 8 = -8$
Multiplicative property of -1

5. $12 \cdot x = x \cdot 12$
Commutative property of multiplication

6. $(y \cdot 4) \cdot 9 = y \cdot (4 \cdot 9)$
Associative property of multiplication

7. $0 \cdot (-41) = 0$
Multiplicative property of zero

8. $-5 \cdot (-6) = -6 \cdot (-5)$
Commutative property of multiplication

9. $-13 \cdot (-1) = 13$
Multiplicative property of -1

Motivating the Lesson

By learning to multiply real numbers, students can calculate the increase (or decrease) in a savings account if a fixed amount is added (or taken out) each week.

3 TEACH

Extra Example 1

Find the product.

a. $-8(-6)$ 48

b. $-2(3.5)(-4)$ 28

c. $\frac{1}{4}(-12)(3)$ -9

Key Question to Ask for Example 1

- How can you tell whether a product is positive or negative without multiplying? If the number of negative factors is even, the product is positive. If the number of negative factors is odd, the product is negative.

Extra Example 2

Identify the property illustrated.

a. $-7 \cdot 0 = 0$ Multiplicative property of zero

b. $b \cdot 1 = b$ Identity property of multiplication

c. $-1 \cdot (-13) = 13$ Multiplicative property of -1

d. $-a \cdot b = b \cdot (-a)$ Commutative property of multiplication

e. $(-2.5 \cdot y) \cdot (-4) = -2.5 \cdot (y \cdot (-4))$ Associative property of multiplication

Key Question to Ask for Example 2

- What is the difference between parts d and e? In part d, the product of -1 and a number is the opposite of the number, while in part e, the product of 1 and the number is the number.

Differentiated Instruction

Below Level To help students learn the properties of multiplication, have them write two of their own examples for each of the properties in the key concept box. Then have them use **Example 2** as a model to write statements that illustrate the properties. Ask them to exchange their statements with other students to see if they can identify the illustrated property. This will also help students justify their steps in **Example 3** and **Exercises 28–36**.

See also the *Algebra 1 Toolkit* for more strategies.

Extra Example 3

Find the product $-2 \cdot (c \cdot (-0.5))$. Justify your steps.

$-2 \cdot (c \cdot (-0.5)) = (c \cdot (-0.5)) \cdot (-2)$
$= c(-0.5 \cdot (-2))$
$= c \cdot 1$
$= c$

Justifications: Commutative property, Associative property, the product of -0.5 and -2 is 1, and the Identity property.

An **Animated Algebra** activity is available on-line for **Example 3**. This activity is also available on the **Power Presentations CD-ROM**.

Extra Example 4

From 1900 to 1940, a 250-foot wide beach on the Atlantic coast was eroding at a rate of about -0.02 feet per year. From 1940 to 2000, it was eroding at a rate of about -0.12 feet per year. Approximate the width of the beach in 2000.
about 242 ft

Closing the Lesson

Have students summarize the major points of the lesson and answer the Essential Question: How do you multiply real numbers?

- **The signs of the factors determine the sign of a product.**
- **The properties of multiplication hold for all real numbers.**

When multiplying real numbers, you use the properties of multiplication listed on page 89. The sign of the product of two numbers is positive if they have the same sign and negative if they have different signs.

10. $\frac{3}{2}y$; $\left(\frac{3}{10} \cdot 5\right)y$, **associative property of multiplication;** $\frac{3}{2} \cdot y$, **product of** $\frac{3}{10}$ **and 5 is** $\frac{3}{2}$; $\frac{3}{2}y$, **multiply.**

11. $0.8x$; $0.8(-1)(-x)$, **commutative property of multiplication;** $-0.8(-x)$, **multiplicative property of -1;** $0.8x$, **multiply**

12. $-3y$; $(-y)(3)$, **product of -0.5 and -6 is 3;** $-3y$, **commutative property of multiplication.**

EXAMPLE 3 Use properties of multiplication

JUSTIFY STEPS
To justify a step, you name the property used. Sometimes a step is a calculation, as when you multiply 0.25 and -4 in Example 3.

Find the product $(-4x) \cdot 0.25$. Justify your steps.

$(-4x) \cdot 0.25 = 0.25 \cdot (-4x)$	**Commutative property of multiplication**
$= [0.25 \cdot (-4)]x$	**Associative property of multiplication**
$= -1 \cdot x$	**Product of 0.25 and -4 is -1.**
$= -x$	**Multiplicative property of -1**

Animated Algebra at classzone.com

EXAMPLE 4 Solve a multi-step problem

READING
The average rate of change in elevation is the total change in elevation divided by the number of years that have passed.

LAKES In 1900 the elevation of Mono Lake in California was about 6416 feet. From 1900 to 1950, the average rate of change in elevation was about -0.12 foot per year. From 1950 to 2000, the average rate of change was about -0.526 foot per year. Approximate the elevation in 2000.

Solution

STEP 1 **Write** a verbal model.

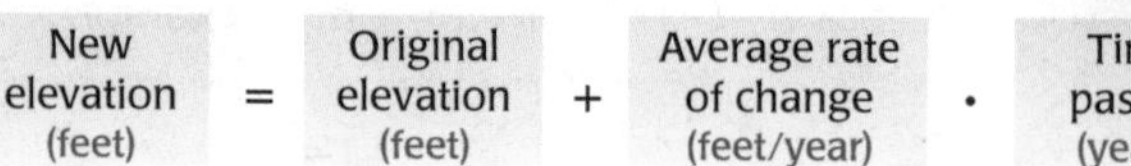

STEP 2 **Calculate** the elevation in 1950. Use the elevation in 1900 as the original elevation. The time span is $1950 - 1900 = 50$ years.

New elevation $= 6416 + (-0.12)(50)$	**Substitute values.**
$= 6416 + (-6)$	**Multiply -0.12 and 50.**
$= 6410$	**Add 6416 and -6.**

STEP 3 **Calculate** the elevation in 2000. Use the elevation in 1950 as the original elevation. The time span is $2000 - 1950 = 50$ years.

New elevation $= 6410 + (-0.526)(50)$	**Substitute values.**
$= 6410 + (-26.3)$	**Multiply -0.526 and 50.**
$= 6383.7$	**Add 6410 and -26.3.**

▸ The elevation in 2000 was about 6383.7 feet above sea level.

GUIDED PRACTICE for Examples 3 and 4

Find the product. *Justify* your steps. **10–12. See margin.**

10. $\frac{3}{10}(5y)$ **11.** $0.8(-x)(-1)$ **12.** $(-y)(-0.5)(-6)$

13. Using the data in Example 4, approximate the elevation of Mono Lake in 1925 and in 1965. **about 6413 ft; about 6402.11 ft**

Differentiated Instruction

Advanced When discussing **Example 4**, have advanced students use the average rate of change from 1950 to 2000 to predict when the elevation of Lake Mono will be about 6300 feet. Suggest they use a spreadsheet to make their prediction. They can write a formula for the spreadsheet using the information in the example. Some students may be interested in learning about the environmental effects of the change in elevation. They can share their research with the class.

See also the *Algebra 1 Toolkit* for more strategies.

2.4 EXERCISES

HOMEWORK KEY

 = **WORKED-OUT SOLUTIONS** on p. WS4 for Exs. 11, 31, and 51

★ = **STANDARDIZED TEST PRACTICE** Exs. 2, 48, 52, 53, and 55

◆ = **MULTIPLE REPRESENTATIONS** Ex. 54

SKILL PRACTICE

A

1. **VOCABULARY** What number is called the multiplicative identity? 1

2. ★ **WRITING** *Describe* the difference between the identity property of multiplication and the multiplicative property of −1. See margin.

EXAMPLE 1 on p. 88 for Exs. 3–18

FINDING PRODUCTS Find the product.

3. $-4(7)$ −28
4. $11(-2)$ −22
5. $-9(-10)$ 90
6. $-8(-11)$ 88
7. $5(-7.2)$ −36
8. $(-2.5)(-1.3)$ 3.25
9. $-42\left(-\frac{1}{6}\right)$ 7
10. $-\frac{1}{2}(-32)$ 16
11. $-1.9(3.3)(7)$ −43.89
12. $0.5(-20)(-3)$ 30
13. $-\frac{5}{6}(-12)(-4)$ −40
14. $-\frac{3}{4}(2)(-6)$ 9
15. $-8(-4)(-2.5)$ −80
16. $-1.6(-2)(-10)$ −32
17. $18\left(-\frac{2}{3}\right)\left(-\frac{1}{5}\right)$ $2\frac{2}{5}$
18. $-\frac{3}{4}\left(-\frac{1}{3}\right)\left(-\frac{8}{9}\right)$ $-\frac{2}{9}$

EXAMPLE 2 on p. 89 for Exs. 19–27

IDENTIFYING PROPERTIES Identify the property illustrated. 19–27. See margin.

19. $-\frac{2}{5} \cdot 0 = 0$
20. $0.3 \cdot (-3) = -3 \cdot 0.3$
21. $-143 \cdot 1 = -143$
22. $-1 \cdot (-6) = 6$
23. $(-2 \cdot 5) \cdot 4 = -2 \cdot (5 \cdot 4)$
24. $0 \cdot (-76.3) = 0$
25. $1 \cdot (ab) = ab$
26. $(3x)y = 3(xy)$
27. $s \cdot (-1) = -s$

EXAMPLE 3 on p. 90 for Exs. 28–36

USING PROPERTIES Find the product. *Justify* your steps. 28–36. See margin.

28. $y(-2)(-8)$
29. $-18(-x)$
30. $\frac{3}{5}(-5q)$
31. $-2(-6)(-7z)$
32. $-5(-4)(-2.1)(-z)$
33. $-\frac{1}{5}(-10)(4)(-5c)$
34. $-5t(-t)$
35. $-6r(-2.8r)$
36. $\frac{1}{3}\left(-\frac{9}{10}\right)(-m)(-m)$

B

EVALUATING EXPRESSIONS Evaluate the expression when $x = -2$ and $y = 3.6$.

37. $2x + y$ −0.4
38. $-x - 3y$ −8.8
39. $xy - 5.4$ −12.6
40. $|y| - 4x$ 11.6
41. $1.5x - |-y|$ −6.6
42. $x^2 - y^2$ −8.96

ERROR ANALYSIS *Describe* and correct the error in finding the product.

43.
$$-1(7)(-3)(-2x) = 7(-3)(-2x)$$
$$= -21(-2x)$$
$$= [-21 \cdot (-2)]x$$
$$= 42x$$

44.
$$(-5z)(-8)(z) = (-8)(-5z)(z)$$
$$= (-8)(-5)(z)(z)$$
$$= -40(z \cdot z)$$
$$= -40z^2$$

43. $-1(7) = -7$, not 7; $-1(7)(-3)(-2x) = -7(-3)(-2x) = 21(-2x) = [21 \cdot (-2)]x = -42x$

44. $(-8)(-5) = 40$, not −40; $(-8)(-5)(z)(z) = 40(z \cdot z) = 40z^2$

4 PRACTICE AND APPLY

Assignment Guide

Answer Transparencies available for all exercises

Basic:
Day 1: pp. 91–93
Exs. 1–11, 19–41 odd, 43, 44, 50–54, 58–64 even

Average:
Day 1: pp. 91–93
Exs. 1, 2, 10–42 even, 43–48, 50–55, 58–64 even

Advanced:
Day 1: pp. 91–93
Exs. 1, 2, 12–42 even, 43–49*, 51–56*, 57–63 odd

Block:
pp. 91–93
Exs. 1, 2, 10–42 even, 43–48, 50–55, 58–64 even (with 2.5)

Differentiated Instruction

See *Algebra 1 Best Practices Toolkit* for suggestions on addressing the needs of a diverse classroom.

Homework Check

For a quick check of student understanding of key concepts, go over the following exercises:

Basic: 7, 21, 29, 37, 50
Average: 12, 22, 32, 38, 51
Advanced: 16, 26, 34, 40, 52

Extra Practice

- Student Edition, p. 939
- Chapter 2 Resource Book: Practice levels A, B, C, pp. 39–41

Practice Worksheet

An easily-readable reduced practice page (with answers) for this lesson can be found on p. 62C.

2. *Sample answer:* The identity property of multiplication states that the product of a number and 1 is the number. The multiplicative property of −1 states that the product of a number and −1 is the *opposite* of the number.

19. Multiplicative property of zero
20. Commutative property of multiplication
21. Identity property of multiplication
22. Multiplicative property of −1
23. Associative property of multiplication
24. Multiplicative property of zero
25. Identity property of multiplication
26. Associative property of multiplication
27. Multiplicative property of −1
28–36. See Additional Answers beginning on p. AA1.

Mathematical Reasoning

Exercise 48 Suggest that students use numbers to help them determine which statement must be true. Ask "If *a* is –1, what must be the signs of *b* and *c* for the product of *abc* to be positive?" Lead students to see that one of the factors must be positive and one must be negative. They can then test their reasoning against each of the statements.

Graphing Calculator

Exercise 52 Students may want to use their calculators to find the volume of the glaciers. Remind them to use the negative key to enter the rates of change.

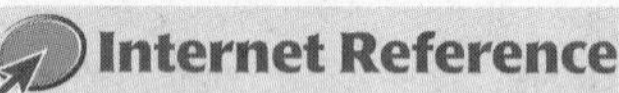

Internet Reference

Exercise 52 Additional information about Mount Rainier can be found on the National Park Service website at http://www.nps.gov/mora.

Avoiding Common Errors

Exercise 53 Some students may use –2 as the rate of change. Point out that the rate of change is in millimeters and the maximum clearance between the water and the Rialto Bridge is in meters. Students need to change millimeters to meters.

Study Strategy

Exercises 54–55 Suggest that students create spreadsheets for both of these exercises. They can use the equations from part a of the exercises to write a formula for the spreadsheet. This will enable them to find their answers quickly, particularly for parts b and c in Exercise 55.

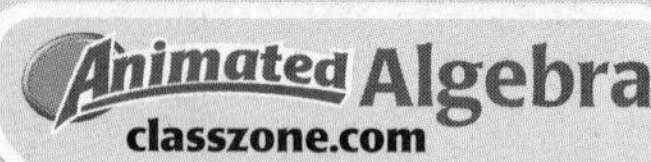

Animated Algebra
classzone.com

An **Animated Algebra** activity is available on-line for **Exercise 54**. This activity is also available on the **Power Presentations CD-ROM**.

REASONING In Exercises 45–47, tell whether the statement is *true* or *false*. If it is false, give a counterexample.

45. If x is negative, then x^2 is positive. true

46. If the product of three numbers is positive, then all three numbers are positive. False. *Sample answer:* $(-1)(-2)(3) = 6$

47. If the product of four numbers is 0, then at least one of the numbers is 0. true

48. ★ **MULTIPLE CHOICE** Let a be a negative number. If the product abc is positive, which statement must be true? B

Ⓐ $bc > 0$ Ⓑ $bc < 0$ Ⓒ $ac > 0$ Ⓓ $ab < 0$

C **49.** **CHALLENGE** The product of n factors is negative. What is the greatest possible number of negative factors if n is even? if n is odd? Give several examples to support your answers. $n - 1$; n. *Sample answer*: If you have 4 factors, $(-1)(-2)(-3)(4)$, the most that can be negative is 3, or $4 - 1$, for the product to be negative. If you have 5 factors, $(-1)(-2)(-3)(-4)(-5)$, all of them can be negative for the product to be negative.

PROBLEM SOLVING

EXAMPLE 4 A on p. 90 for Exs. 50–53

50. **DEAD SEA** In 1940 the surface area of the Dead Sea was about 980 square kilometers. From 1940 to 2001, the average rate of change in surface area was about -5.7 square kilometers per year. Find the surface area of the Dead Sea in 2001. about 632.3 km^2

@HomeTutor for problem solving help at classzone.com

51. **STOCKS** An investor purchases 50 shares of a stock at \$3.50 per share. The next day, the change in value of a share of the stock is $-\$.25$. What is the total value of the shares the next day? \$162.50

@HomeTutor for problem solving help at classzone.com

52b. about -0.47658 km^3; find the total change in the volume of the glaciers between 1913 and 1994, then multiply the change by $\frac{1}{3}$.

52. ★ **SHORT RESPONSE** In 1913 the total volume of the glaciers on Mount Rainier was 5.62 cubic kilometers. The table shows the average rate of change in the volume for two periods of time.

Time period	Rate of change (km^3/yr)
1913–1971	−0.02241
1971–1994	−0.00565

a. Find the total volume of the glaciers in 1971 and in 1994. 4.32022 km^3; 4.19027 km^3

b. About one third of the change in volume during the period 1913–1994 took place in the northeastern glaciers. Find the change in the volume of the northeastern glaciers. *Explain* your steps.

53. ★ **MULTIPLE CHOICE** The Rialto Bridge in Venice, Italy, is a footbridge built in the late 16th century. The maximum clearance between the water and the bridge is about 7.32 meters. Because of a rising sea level and a gradual sinking of the city, the clearance changes at an average rate of about -2 millimeters per year. Approximate the clearance after 15 years. C

Ⓐ 5.32 meters Ⓑ 7.02 meters

Ⓒ 7.29 meters Ⓓ 7.318 meters

○ = WORKED-OUT SOLUTIONS on p. WS1 ★ = STANDARDIZED TEST PRACTICE ◆ = MULTIPLE REPRESENTATIONS

B 54. ◆ **MULTIPLE REPRESENTATIONS** A skydiver in free fall will eventually reach a constant velocity, called terminal velocity. A skydiver reaches a terminal velocity of −160 feet per second at an altitude of 3200 feet.

4400 feet: Plane flies at this altitude.
3200 feet: Skydiver reaches terminal velocity.
2500 feet: Parachute opens.

a. **Writing an Equation** Write an equation for the altitude a (in feet) of the skydiver as a function of the time t (in seconds) after reaching terminal velocity. **$a = 3200 + (-160t)$**

b. **Making a Table** Make a table of values for $t = 1, 2, 3, 4,$ and 5 seconds. The skydiver wants to open the parachute after reaching an altitude of about 2500 feet. After how many seconds should the skydiver open the parachute? **See margin.**

at classzone.com

55. ★ **EXTENDED RESPONSE** The table shows the fuel capacities of two ferries in Puget Sound, Washington, and the average rates of change in tank fuel when the ferries are burning fuel.

Ferry	Fuel capacity (gal)	Rate of change (gal/h)
Rhododendron	11,250	−30
Spokane	135,000	−240

a. **Model** For each ferry, write an equation that gives the amount of tank fuel f (in gallons) as a function of the time t (in hours) that fuel is burned. **$f = 11{,}250 + (-30t)$, $f = 135{,}000 + (-240t)$**

b. **Calculate** Both ferries start with a full tank. How many gallons of fuel will each ferry have left after 3 hours? **11,160 gal, 134,280 gal**

c. **Explain** If both ferries continue to burn fuel without refueling, which ferry will run out of fuel first? How many gallons will the other ferry have at that time? Your answer should include the following: **See margin.**

- the number of hours that each ferry will take to burn all of its fuel
- an explanation of how you used the equations in part (a)

C 56. **CHALLENGE** Due to soil erosion, the surface area of Dongting Lake in China is decreasing. Its surface area was about 2626.5 square kilometers in 1995. From 1950 to 1995, the average rate of change in surface area was about −38.3 square kilometers per year. From 1825 to 1950, the average rate of change was about −13.2 square kilometers per year. Approximate the surface area in 1825. **6000 km²**

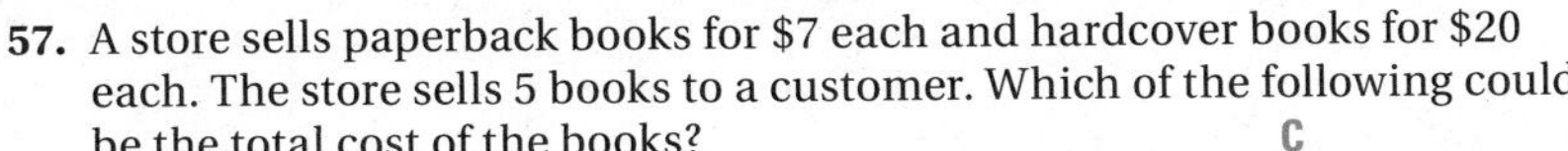

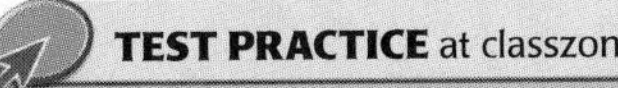
TEST PRACTICE at classzone.com

57. A store sells paperback books for \$7 each and hardcover books for \$20 each. The store sells 5 books to a customer. Which of the following could be the total cost of the books? **C**

Ⓐ \$40 Ⓑ \$44 Ⓒ \$74 Ⓓ \$80

58. The test scores for a class were 57, 62, 77, 80, 81, 81, and 90. Which measure of data is greatest for the class? **C**

Ⓐ Mean Ⓑ Median Ⓒ Mode Ⓓ Range

54b.

t	$3200 + (-160t)$
1	3040
2	2880
3	2720
4	2560
5	2400

4 sec

5 ASSESS AND RETEACH

Daily Homework Quiz

Transparency Available

Find the product.

1. −6.5(4)(−2) **52**
2. 7.4(−1.2)(3) **−26.64**

Identify the property illustrated.

3. $r \cdot 0 = 0$ **Multiplicative property of zero**
4. $-y \cdot (-1) = y$ **Multiplicative property of −1**
5. Since Javier began setting his thermostat lower, his energy bills have been declining at a rate of −0.88 dollar per year. If his average bill was \$130 in 1990, estimate his average bill in 2005. **\$116.80**

Available at **classzone.com**

Diagnosis/Remediation

- Practice A, B, C in Chapter 2 Resource Book, pp. 39–41
- Study Guide in Chapter 2 Resource Book, pp. 42–43
- Practice Workbook, pp. 22–23
- @HomeTutor

Challenge

Additional challenge is available in the Chapter 2 Resource Book, p. 46.

55c. Rhododendron; 45,000 gal; the Rhododendron takes 375 hours to burn all of its fuel; the Spokane takes 562.5 hours to burn all of its fuel; to find the number of hours the Rhododendron will take to burn all its fuel, use the equations in part (a) and find the additive inverse of 11,250, then divide it by −30; to find the number of hours the Spokane will take to burn all its fuel, use the equations in part (a) and find the additive inverse of 135,000, then divide it by −240.

1 PLAN AND PREPARE

Warm-Up Exercises

Perform the indicated operation.

1. $12.1 + (-15.2)$ -3.1
2. $-6 - (-9.8)$ 3.8
3. $-15(-2.4)$ 36
4. $4.8 \cdot (-5.5)(3)$ -79.2

2 FOCUS AND MOTIVATE

Essential Question

Big Idea 1, p. 63

How do you perform operations on matrices? Tell students they will learn how to answer this question by adding and subtracting two matrices and by performing scalar multiplication.

3 TEACH

Extra Example 1

Perform the indicated operation, if possible.

a. $\begin{bmatrix} 10 & -4 & -2 \\ 4 & -6 & 5 \end{bmatrix} - \begin{bmatrix} 11 & -1 & 3 \\ -4 & 0 & -8 \end{bmatrix}$ $\begin{bmatrix} -1 & -3 & -5 \\ 8 & -6 & 13 \end{bmatrix}$

b. $\begin{bmatrix} -5 & 14 & 0 \\ 6 & -7 & -4 \end{bmatrix} + \begin{bmatrix} -5 & -11 & -3 \\ -3 & -1 & 4 \end{bmatrix}$ $\begin{bmatrix} -10 & 3 & -3 \\ 3 & -8 & 0 \end{bmatrix}$

NCTM STANDARDS

Standard 2: Understand patterns

Standard 9: Use connections among mathematical ideas

Use after Lesson 2.4

Perform Matrix Addition, Subtraction, Scalar Multiplication

GOAL Perform operations on matrices.

Key Vocabulary
- **matrix**
- **dimensions of a matrix**
- **element**
- **scalar multiplication**
- **scalar**

A **matrix** is a rectangular arrangement of numbers in rows and columns. If a matrix has m rows and n columns, the **dimensions of the matrix** are written as $m \times n$. For example, matrix A below has two rows and three columns. The dimensions of matrix A are 2×3 (read "2 by 3"). Each number in a matrix is called an **element**, or *entry*. In matrix A, the element in the first row and second column is 4.

$$A = \begin{bmatrix} 0 & 4 & -1 \\ -3 & 2 & 5 \end{bmatrix} \text{ 2 rows}$$

3 columns

MATRIX ADDITION AND SUBTRACTION To add or subtract matrices (the plural of *matrix*), you add or subtract corresponding elements. You can add or subtract matrices only if they have the same dimensions.

EXAMPLE 1 Add or subtract two matrices

Perform the indicated operation, if possible.

a. $\begin{bmatrix} 0 & 4 & -1 \\ -3 & 2 & 5 \end{bmatrix} + \begin{bmatrix} 2 & 1 & 3 \\ -2 & -6 & 4 \end{bmatrix} = \begin{bmatrix} 0+2 & 4+1 & -1+3 \\ -3+(-2) & 2+(-6) & 5+4 \end{bmatrix}$

$= \begin{bmatrix} 2 & 5 & 2 \\ -5 & -4 & 9 \end{bmatrix}$

b. $\begin{bmatrix} -10 & 2 \\ -4 & 7 \\ 7 & -13 \end{bmatrix} - \begin{bmatrix} 9 & -2 \\ 4 & 8 \\ -5 & -11 \end{bmatrix} = \begin{bmatrix} -10-9 & 2-(-2) \\ -4-4 & 7-8 \\ 7-(-5) & -13-(-11) \end{bmatrix}$

$= \begin{bmatrix} -10+(-9) & 2+2 \\ -4+(-4) & 7+(-8) \\ 7+5 & -13+11 \end{bmatrix}$

$= \begin{bmatrix} -19 & 4 \\ -8 & -1 \\ 12 & -2 \end{bmatrix}$

c. You can't perform the subtraction $\begin{bmatrix} 6 & -4 & -8 \end{bmatrix} - \begin{bmatrix} 1 \\ 12 \\ -6 \end{bmatrix}$ because the first matrix is a 1×3 matrix and the second matrix is a 3×1 matrix.

SCALAR MULTIPLICATION In **scalar multiplication**, every element in a matrix is multiplied by a real number called a **scalar**.

EXAMPLE 2 Perform scalar multiplication

Perform the indicated operation.

a. $6\begin{bmatrix}-7 & -\frac{1}{3}\\ \frac{1}{2} & 11\end{bmatrix} = \begin{bmatrix}6(-7) & 6\left(-\frac{1}{3}\right)\\ 6\left(\frac{1}{2}\right) & 6(11)\end{bmatrix} = \begin{bmatrix}-42 & -2\\ 3 & 66\end{bmatrix}$

b. $-2\begin{bmatrix}0.5\\ -3.2\\ 8.1\end{bmatrix} = \begin{bmatrix}-2(0.5)\\ -2(-3.2)\\ -2(8.1)\end{bmatrix} = \begin{bmatrix}-1\\ 6.4\\ -16.2\end{bmatrix}$

PRACTICE

EXAMPLES 1 and 2 on pp. 94–95 for Exs. 1–10

Perform the indicated operation, if possible.

1. $\begin{bmatrix}7 & 6\\ 3 & 2\end{bmatrix} + \begin{bmatrix}9 & -2\\ 5 & 10\end{bmatrix}$ $\begin{bmatrix}16 & 4\\ 8 & 12\end{bmatrix}$

2. $\begin{bmatrix}-8\\ -4\\ 1\end{bmatrix} + \begin{bmatrix}11\\ -9\\ -6\end{bmatrix}$ $\begin{bmatrix}3\\ -13\\ -5\end{bmatrix}$

3. $\begin{bmatrix}-8 & -1 & -9\\ -4 & -3 & 2\end{bmatrix} - \begin{bmatrix}7 & 3 & 0\\ -2 & -5 & 7\end{bmatrix}$ See margin.

4. $\begin{bmatrix}11 & -12\\ 15 & -22\end{bmatrix} - \begin{bmatrix}7\\ 8\end{bmatrix}$ Cannot be performed.

5. $\begin{bmatrix}-9.1 & 5.4 & 3.7\end{bmatrix} + \begin{bmatrix}1.3 & -6.7\end{bmatrix}$ Cannot be performed.

6. $\begin{bmatrix}\frac{3}{4} & -2\\ 6 & -3\end{bmatrix} - \begin{bmatrix}8 & -2\\ 6 & -\frac{5}{6}\end{bmatrix}$ $\begin{bmatrix}-7\frac{1}{4} & 0\\ 0 & -2\frac{1}{6}\end{bmatrix}$

7. $7\begin{bmatrix}-4 & -7\\ \frac{1}{2} & \frac{4}{9}\end{bmatrix}$ $\begin{bmatrix}-28 & -49\\ 3\frac{1}{2} & 3\frac{1}{9}\end{bmatrix}$

8. $2\begin{bmatrix}1.5 & -6\\ -4.5 & 0\end{bmatrix}$ $\begin{bmatrix}3 & -12\\ -9 & 0\end{bmatrix}$

9. $-6\begin{bmatrix}12\\ -3.4\\ -0.7\end{bmatrix}$ $\begin{bmatrix}-72\\ 20.4\\ 4.2\end{bmatrix}$

10. $-\frac{1}{2}\begin{bmatrix}18 & -26 & \frac{7}{4}\\ -\frac{2}{3} & 20 & -2\end{bmatrix}$ $\begin{bmatrix}-9 & 13 & -\frac{7}{8}\\ \frac{1}{3} & -10 & 1\end{bmatrix}$

11. NUTRITION The matrix shows the amounts (in milligrams) of calcium and potassium in one ounce of different types of milk. Write a matrix for the amounts of calcium and potassium in 8 ounces of each type of milk.

	Calcium (mg)	Potassium (mg)	Calcium (mg)	Potassium (mg)
Lowfat milk	32.940	36.295	263.52	290.36
Reduced fat milk	33.855	42.700	270.84	341.6
Whole milk	30.805	40.565	246.44	324.52

CHALLENGE Perform the indicated operations.

12. $9\left(\begin{bmatrix}1 & -12 & 8\\ -7 & 10 & -4\end{bmatrix} + \begin{bmatrix}3 & -3 & -7\\ -5 & -21 & -12\end{bmatrix}\right)$ See margin.

13. $\begin{bmatrix}-6 & -8\\ 8 & 14\end{bmatrix} - 7\begin{bmatrix}5 & 13\\ -10 & -11\end{bmatrix}$ $\begin{bmatrix}-41 & -99\\ 78 & 91\end{bmatrix}$

Extra Example 2

Perform the indicated operation.

a. $4\begin{bmatrix}-8 & 0.5\\ \frac{1}{4} & -\frac{1}{2}\end{bmatrix}$ $\begin{bmatrix}-32 & 2\\ 1 & -2\end{bmatrix}$

b. $-2\begin{bmatrix}-1.6\\ 2.4\\ -5.5\end{bmatrix}$ $\begin{bmatrix}3.2\\ -4.8\\ 11\end{bmatrix}$

Closing the Lesson

Have students summarize the major points of the lesson and answer the Essential Question: How do you perform operations on matrices?

- Matrices must have the same dimensions to add or subtract.
- To perform scalar multiplication, multiply each element in the matrix by the scalar.

To add or subtract matrices with the same dimensions, add or subtract corresponding elements. For scalar multiplication, multiply all elements in the matrix by the scalar.

4 PRACTICE AND APPLY

Avoiding Common Errors

Exercises 1–10 Instruct students to write out the solutions, using Examples 1 and 2 as models. This will help them avoid adding, subtracting, or multiplying the wrong elements. It will also help them tell when two matrices do not have the same dimensions.

Reading Strategy

Exercise 11 For students who are having trouble solving this problem, ask whether it would make sense to add 8 ounces to find the number of milligrams of calcium and potassium, to subtract 8 ounces, or to multiply by 8 ounces.

3. $\begin{bmatrix}-15 & -4 & -9\\ -2 & 2 & -5\end{bmatrix}$

12. $\begin{bmatrix}36 & -135 & 9\\ -108 & -99 & -144\end{bmatrix}$

1 PLAN AND PREPARE

Warm-Up Exercises

Transparency Available

1. $-15 + (-19) + 16 = \underline{?}$ -18
2. $6(-x)(-4) = \underline{?}$ $24x$
3. $-9(-2)(-4b) = \underline{?}$ $-72b$
4. Kristin paid $1.90 per black-and-white photo b and $6.80 per color photo c to have some photos restored. What was the total amount A that she paid if she had 8 black-and-white and 12 color photos restored? **$96.80**

Notetaking Guide

Transparency Available

Promotes interactive learning and notetaking skills, pp. 36–38.

Pacing

Basic: 2 days
Average: 2 days
Advanced: 2 days
Block: 0.5 block with 2.4
0.5 block with 2.6

- See *Teaching Guide/Lesson Plan.*

2 FOCUS AND MOTIVATE

Essential Question

Big Idea 2, p. 63

How do you use the distributive property to simplify expressions?

Tell students they will learn how to answer this question by rewriting expressions.

2.5 Apply the Distributive Property

6.11.05 Simplify or test expressions by applying field properties. . . order properties. . . and properties of equality for the set of real numbers.

Before You used properties to add and multiply real numbers.
Now You will apply the distributive property.
Why? So you can find calories burned, as in Example 5.

Key Vocabulary
- equivalent expressions
- distributive property
- term
- coefficient
- constant term
- like terms

The models below show two methods for finding the area of a rectangle that has a length of $(x + 2)$ units and a width of 3 units.

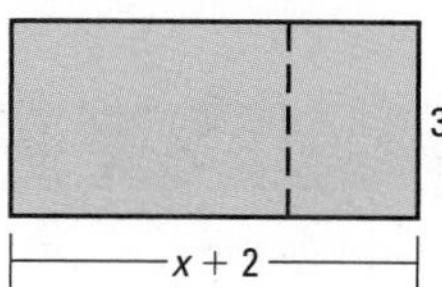

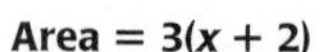

Area = 3(x + 2)

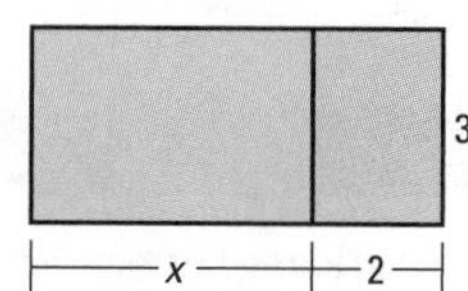

Area = 3(x) + 3(2)

The expressions $3(x + 2)$ and $3(x) + 3(2)$ are equivalent because they represent the same area. Two expressions that have the same value for all values of the variable are called **equivalent expressions**. The equation $3(x + 2) = 3(x) + 3(2)$ illustrates the **distributive property**, which can be used to find the product of a number and a sum or difference.

KEY CONCEPT *For Your Notebook*

The Distributive Property

Let a, b, and c be real numbers.

Words	Algebra	Examples
The product of a and $(b + c)$:	$a(b + c) = ab + ac$	$3(4 + 2) = 3(4) + 3(2)$
	$(b + c)a = ba + ca$	$(3 + 5)2 = 3(2) + 5(2)$
The product of a and $(b - c)$:	$a(b - c) = ab - ac$	$5(6 - 4) = 5(6) - 5(4)$
	$(b - c)a = ba - ca$	$(8 - 6)4 = 8(4) - 6(4)$

EXAMPLE 1 Apply the distributive property

AVOID ERRORS
Be sure to distribute the factor outside of the parentheses to *all* of the numbers inside the parentheses, not just to the first number.

Use the distributive property to write an equivalent expression.

a. $4(y + 3) = 4y + 12$

b. $(y + 7)y = y^2 + 7y$

c. $n(n - 9) = n^2 - 9n$

d. $(2 - n)8 = 16 - 8n$

Resource Planning Guide

Chapter Resource Book
- Teaching Guide/Lesson Plan (pp. 47–48)
- Activity Master (p. 49)
- Practice levels A, B, C (pp. 50–52)
- Study Guide (pp. 53–54)
- Catch-up for Absent Students (p. 55)
- Problem Solving Workshop (p. 56)
- Challenge (p. 57)

Workbooks
- Notetaking Guide (pp. 36–38)
- Practice Workbook (pp. 24–25)

Teaching Options
- **Power Presentations CD-ROM** provides dynamic electronic teaching resources for the classroom.
- **Activity Generator CD-ROM** provides editable activities for all ability levels.

Interactive Technology
- Easy Planner
- Power Presentations CD-ROM
- Activity Generator CD-ROM
- Animated Algebra
- Test Generator CD-ROM
- Online Quiz
- eWorkbook
- eEdition
- @HomeTutor

Resources for English Learners
- Quick Reference for English Learners
- Spanish Study Guide
- Multi-Language Visual Glossary
- Student Resources in Spanish

See also the *Algebra 1 Toolkit* for more strategies for meeting individual needs.

EXAMPLE 2 Distribute a negative number

Use the distributive property to write an equivalent expression.

a. $-2(x+7) = -2(x) + (-2)(7)$ — **Distribute −2.**
$= -2x - 14$ — **Simplify.**

b. $(5-y)(-3y) = 5(-3y) - y(-3y)$ — **Distribute −3y.**
$= -15y + 3y^2$ — **Simplify.**

c. $-(2x-11) = (-1)(2x-11)$ — **Multiplicative property of −1**
$= (-1)(2x) - (-1)(11)$ — **Distribute −1.**
$= -2x + 11$ — **Simplify.**

TERMS AND COEFFICIENTS The parts of an expression that are added together are called **terms**. The number part of a term with a variable part is called the **coefficient** of the term.

READING
Note that $-x$ has a coefficient of −1 even though the 1 isn't written. Similarly, x has a coefficient of 1.

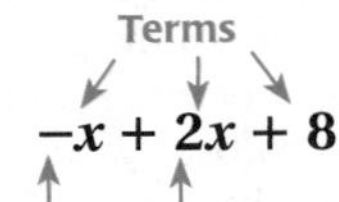

A **constant term** has a number part but no variable part, such as 8 in the expression above. **Like terms** are terms that have the same variable parts, such as $-x$ and $2x$ in the expression above. Constant terms are also like terms.

EXAMPLE 3 Identify parts of an expression

Identify the terms, like terms, coefficients, and constant terms of the expression $3x - 4 - 6x + 2$.

Solution

Write the expression as a sum: $3x + (-4) + (-6x) + 2$

Terms: $3x, -4, -6x, 2$ | **Like terms:** $3x$ and $-6x$; -4 and 2

Coefficients: $3, -6$ | **Constant terms:** $-4, 2$

GUIDED PRACTICE for Examples 1, 2, and 3

Use the distributive property to write an equivalent expression.

1. $2(x+3)$ $2x+6$
2. $-(4-y)$ $-4+y$
3. $(m-5)(-3m)$ $-3m^2+15m$
4. $(2n+6)\left(\frac{1}{2}\right)$ $n+3$
5. Identify the terms, like terms, coefficients, and constant terms of the expression $-7y + 8 - 6y - 13$.
terms: $-7y, 8, -6y, -13$; like terms: $-7y$ and $-6y$, 8 and −13; coefficients: −7, −6; constant terms: 8, −13

COMBINING LIKE TERMS The distributive property allows you to combine like terms that have variable parts. For example, $5x + 6x = (5+6)x = 11x$. A quick way to combine like terms with variable parts is to mentally add the coefficients and use the common variable part. An expression is *simplified* if it has no grouping symbols and if all of the like terms have been combined.

Differentiated Instruction

Kinesthetic Learners When students apply the distributive property, some of them may find it helpful to draw arrows as shown in **Example 1**. Furthermore, students may find it helpful to place one fingertip on the page and trace the arrows.

See also the *Algebra 1 Toolkit* for more strategies.

Motivating the Lesson

Knowing how to use the distributive property can make calculations easier. For example, suppose the coach of the swim team buys 12 T-shirts for \$11.96 each. By learning how to use the distributive property, you will be able to use mental math to find that the T-shirts cost \$143.52.

3 TEACH

Extra Example 1

Use the distributive property to write an equivalent expression.

a. $3(x+6)$ $3x+18$
b. $(n+5)n$ n^2+5n
c. $y(y-12)$ y^2-12y
d. $(8-x)9$ $72-9x$

Reading Strategy

When discussing Example 1, have students read "Avoid Errors." Point out that the arrows in each part of the example show where to distribute the factor that is outside the parentheses.

Extra Example 2

Use the distributive property to write an equivalent expression.

a. $(y-2)(-4)$ $-4y+8$
b. $-5x(4-x)$ $-20x+5x^2$
c. $-(3y-9)$ $-3y+9$

Key Question to Ask for Example 2

- When you distribute −1, what happens to the signs in the parentheses? They change to their opposites.

Extra Example 3

Identify the terms, like terms, coefficients, and constant terms of the expression $-2x - 8 + 6x + 5$. Terms: $-2x, -8, 6x, 5$; Like terms: $-2x$ and $6x$, −8 and 5; Coefficients: −2, 6; Constant terms: −8, 5

Extra Example 4

Which expression is equivalent to $6(x + 3) - 2(8 + x)$? A

Ⓐ $4x + 2$ Ⓑ $4x + 34$

Ⓒ $8x + 2$ Ⓓ $8x + 34$

Extra Example 5

Ms. Jenkins rented a rototiller from a garden shop. The rental charge is \$28 per day for the first two days and then \$15 per day for each additional day. If Ms. Jenkins kept the rototiller for 13 days, what was the total rental charge? \$221

Key Question to Ask for Example 5

- Why is the swimming time represented by $50 - r$? The swimming time is the time left from the total time after running. Since the total time is 50 minutes and the running time is r minutes, the swimming time must be $(50 - r)$ minutes.

An **Animated Algebra** activity is available on-line for **Example 5**. This activity is also available on the **Power Presentations CD-ROM**.

Closing the Lesson

Have students summarize the major points of the lesson and answer the Essential Question: How do you use the distributive property to simplify expressions?

- Distribute the outside factor in expressions to all of the terms inside the parentheses.
- Expressions are sums of variables and constant terms.

Use the distributive property to write equivalent expressions without parentheses. Then combine like terms to simplify expressions.

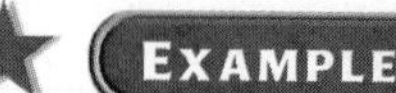

★ EXAMPLE 4 Standardized Test Practice

Simplify the expression $4(n + 9) - 3(2 + n)$.

Ⓐ $5n + 30$ Ⓑ $n + 30$ Ⓒ $5n + 3$ Ⓓ $n + 3$

ANOTHER WAY
In Example 4, you can rewrite the expression $4(n + 9) - 3(2 + n)$ as $4(n + 9) + (-3)(2 + n)$ and then distribute -3 to the terms in $2 + n$.

$4(n + 9) - 3(2 + n) = 4n + 36 - 6 - 3n$ **Distributive property**

$= n + 30$ **Combine like terms.**

▶ The correct answer is B. Ⓐ Ⓑ Ⓒ Ⓓ

EXAMPLE 5 Solve a multi-step problem

EXERCISING Your daily workout plan involves a total of 50 minutes of running and swimming. You burn 15 calories per minute when running and 9 calories per minute when swimming. Let r be the number of minutes that you run. Find the number of calories you burn in your 50 minute workout if you run for 20 minutes.

ANOTHER WAY
For an alternative method for solving the problem in Example 5, turn to page 102 for the **Problem Solving Workshop**.

Solution

The workout lasts 50 minutes, and your running time is r minutes. So, your swimming time is $(50 - r)$ minutes.

STEP 1 **Write** a verbal model. Then write an equation.

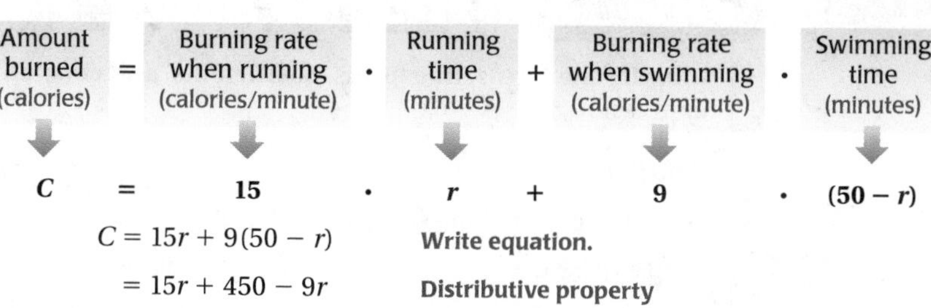

$C = 15r + 9(50 - r)$ **Write equation.**

$= 15r + 450 - 9r$ **Distributive property**

$= 6r + 450$ **Combine like terms.**

STEP 2 **Find** the value of C when $r = 20$.

$C = 6r + 450$ **Write equation.**

$= 6(20) + 450 = 570$ **Substitute 20 for r. Then simplify.**

▶ You burn 570 calories in your 50 minute workout if you run for 20 minutes.

Animated Algebra at classzone.com

GUIDED PRACTICE for Examples 4 and 5

6. Simplify the expression $5(6 + n) - 2(n - 2)$. $34 + 3n$

7. **WHAT IF?** In Example 5, suppose your workout lasts 45 minutes. How many calories do you burn if you run for 20 minutes? 30 minutes? 525 calories; 585 calories

21. terms: $-7, 13x, 2x, 8$; like terms: -7 and 8, $13x$ and $2x$; coefficients: 13, 2; constant terms: $-7, 8$

22. terms: $9, 7y, -2, -5y$; like terms: 9 and -2, $7y$ and $-5y$; coefficients: $7, -5$; constant terms: $9, -2$

2.5 EXERCISES

HOMEWORK KEY
○ = WORKED-OUT SOLUTIONS on p. WS4 for Exs. 9, 23, and 51
★ = STANDARDIZED TEST PRACTICE Exs. 2, 27, 52, and 54

SKILL PRACTICE

1. **VOCABULARY** What are the coefficients of the expression $4x + 8 - 9x + 2$? $4, -9$

2. ★ **WRITING** Are the expressions $2(x + 1)$ and $2x + 1$ equivalent? *Explain.*
No; the 2 was not distributed to the 1, $2(x + 1) = 2x + 2$.

ERROR ANALYSIS *Describe* **and correct the error in simplifying the expression.**

3. The negative was not distributed to the -8; $5y - (2y - 8) = 5y - 2y + 8 = 3y + 8$.

3. $5y - (2y - 8) = 5y - 2y - 8$
$= 3y - 8$ ✗

4. $8 + 2(4 + 3x) = 8 + 8 + 6x$
$= 22x$ ✗

4. Unlike terms cannot be combined; $8 + 2(4 + 3x) = 8 + 8 + 6x = 16 + 6x$.

EXAMPLES 1 and 2 on pp. 96–97 for Exs. 5–20

USING THE DISTRIBUTIVE PROPERTY **Use the distributive property to write an equivalent expression.**

5. $4(x + 3)$ $4x + 12$
6. $8(y + 2)$ $8y + 16$
7. $(m + 5)5$ $5m + 25$
8. $(n + 6)3$ $3n + 18$
9. $(p - 3)(-8)$ $-8p + 24$
10. $-4(q - 4)$ $-4q + 16$
11. $2(2r - 3)$ $4r - 6$
12. $(s - 9)9$ $9s - 81$
13. $6v(v + 1)$ $6v^2 + 6v$
14. $-w(2w + 7)$ $-2w^2 - 7w$
15. $-2x(3 - x)$ $2x^2 - 6x$
16. $3y(y - 6)$ $3y^2 - 18y$
17. $\frac{1}{2}\left(\frac{1}{2}m - 4\right)$ $\frac{1}{4}m - 2$
18. $-\frac{3}{4}(p - 1)$ $-\frac{3}{4}p + \frac{3}{4}$
19. $\frac{2}{3}(6n - 9)$ $4n - 6$
20. $\frac{5}{6}r(r - 1)$ $\frac{5}{6}r^2 - \frac{5}{6}r$

EXAMPLE 3 on p. 97 for Exs. 21–26

IDENTIFYING PARTS OF AN EXPRESSION **Identify the terms, like terms, coefficients, and constant terms of the expression.** 21–26. See margin.

21. $-7 + 13x + 2x + 8$
22. $9 + 7y - 2 - 5y$
23. $7x^2 - 10 - 2x^2 + 5$
24. $-3y^2 + 3y^2 - 7 + 9$
25. $2 + 3xy - 4xy + 6$
26. $6xy - 11xy + 2xy - 4xy + 7xy$

27. ★ **MULTIPLE CHOICE** Which two terms are like terms? B

Ⓐ $-2, -5x$ Ⓑ $4x, -x$ Ⓒ $-2, -2y$ Ⓓ $5x, -3y$

EXAMPLE 4 on p. 98 for Exs. 28–39

SIMPLIFYING EXPRESSIONS **Simplify the expression.**

28. $7x + (-11x)$ $-4x$
29. $6y - y$ $5y$
30. $5 + 2n + 2$ $2n + 7$
31. $(4a - 1)2 + a$ $9a - 2$
32. $3(2 - c) - c$ $6 - 4c$
33. $6r + 2(r + 4)$ $8r + 8$
34. $15t - (t - 4)$ $14t + 4$
35. $3(m + 5) - 10$ $3m + 5$
36. $-6(v + 1) + v$ $-5v - 6$
37. $7(w - 5) + 3w$ $10w - 35$
38. $6(5 - z) + 2z$ $30 - 4z$
39. $(s - 3)(-2) + 17s$ $15s + 6$

GEOMETRY **Find the perimeter and area of the rectangle.**

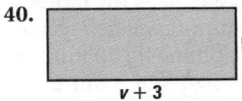

40. 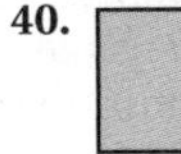
Rectangle: 5 by $v + 3$
$2v + 16$; $5v + 15$

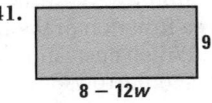

41. 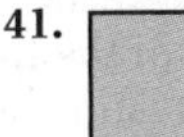
Rectangle: 9 by $8 - 12w$
$34 - 24w$; $72 - 108w$

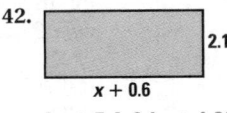

42. Rectangle: 2.1 by $x + 0.6$
$2x + 5.4$; $2.1x + 1.26$

4 PRACTICE AND APPLY

Assignment Guide

Answer Transparencies available for all exercises

Basic:
Day 1: SRH p. 925 Exs. 1, 2, 4, 5, 12
pp. 99–101
Exs. 1–15, 21–24, 62–67
Day 2: pp. 99–101
Exs. 27–42, 50–53, 56–61

Average:
Day 1: pp. 99–101
Exs. 1–4, 9–20, 23–27, 62–67
Day 2: pp. 99–101
Exs. 32–48, 50–54, 56–61

Advanced:
Day 1: pp. 99–101
Exs. 1, 2, 11–20, 23–27, 65–67
Day 2: pp. 99–101
Exs. 34–49*, 51–61*

Block:
pp. 99–101
Exs. 1–4, 9–20, 23–27, 62–67 (with 2.4)
pp. 99–101
Exs. 32–48, 50–54, 56–61 (with 2.6)

Differentiated Instruction

See *Algebra 1 Best Practices Toolkit* for suggestions on addressing the needs of a diverse classroom.

Homework Check

For a quick check of student understanding of key concepts, go over the following exercises:
Basic: 6, 10, 22, 31, 50
Average: 11, 15, 24, 35, 51
Advanced: 16, 18, 25, 37, 52

Extra Practice

- Student Edition, p. 939
- Chapter 2 Resource Book: Practice levels A, B, C, pp. 50–52

Practice Worksheet

An easily-readable reduced practice page (with answers) for this lesson can be found on p. 62D.

23. terms: $7x^2$, -10, $-2x^2$, 5; like terms: $7x^2$ and $-2x^2$, -10 and 5; coefficients: 7, -2; constant terms: -10, 5

24. terms: $-3y^2$, $3y^2$, -7, 9; like terms: $-3y^2$ and $3y^2$, -7 and 9; coefficients: -3, 3; constant terms: -7, 9

25. terms: 2, $3xy$, $-4xy$, 6; like terms: 2 and 6, $3xy$ and $-4xy$; coefficients: 3, -4; constant terms: 2, 6

26. terms: $6xy$, $-11xy$, $2xy$, $-4xy$, $7xy$; like terms: $6xy$, $-11xy$, $2xy$, $-4xy$, and $7xy$; coefficients: 6, -11, 2, -4, 7; constant terms: none

Avoiding Common Errors

Exercises 28–39 Some students may forget that x and $-x$ have a coefficient of 1 and -1, respectively. Encourage them to write x as "$1x$" and $-x$ as "$-1x$" so they do not overlook these variables when they combine like terms.

Study Strategy

Exercises 43–46 Suggest that students use the Example at the top of the page to write out the exercises in the same way. Tell them that once they become familiar with the method, they may no longer need to write out the steps.

Exercise 50 For more information about archery in the United States, visit http://www.usarchery.org

Teaching Strategy

Exercises 50, 54 You may want to refer students to Example 5 before they begin solving these problems. Step 1 is particularly useful and may help them write a verbal model and an equation. Note for students that in Exercise 54, parts a and b correspond to Steps 1 and 2 in Example 5.

Reading Strategy

Exercise 51 Some students may write the equation incorrectly. Tell them that the problem states the coupon for \$2 off is for *each* movie rental.

Mathematical Reasoning

Exercise 54 Encourage students to create a spreadsheet for part c. They can adapt the equation in part a for the formula and then generate a table of values.

USING MENTAL MATH **In Exercises 43–46, use the example below to find the total cost.**

EXAMPLE **Use the distributive property and mental math**

Use the distributive property and mental math to find the total cost of 5 picture frames at \$1.99 each.

Total cost $= 5(1.99)$	**Write expression for total cost.**
$= 5(2 - 0.01)$	**Rewrite 1.99 as 2 – 0.01.**
$= 5(2) - 5(0.01)$	**Distributive property**
$= 10 - 0.05$	**Multiply using mental math.**
$= 9.95$	**Subtract. The total cost is \$9.95.**

43. 3 CDs at \$12.99 each **\$38.97**

44. 5 magazines at \$3.99 each **\$19.95**

45. 6 pairs of socks at \$1.98 per pair **\$11.88**

46. 25 baseballs at \$2.98 each **\$74.50**

TRANSLATING PHRASES **In Exercises 47 and 48, translate the verbal phrase into an expression. Then simplify the expression.**

47. Twice the sum of 6 and x, increased by 5 less than x
$2(6 + x) + (x - 5)$; $3x + 7$

48. Three times the difference of x and 2, decreased by the sum of x and 10
$3(x - 2) - (x + 10)$; $2x - 16$

C **49. CHALLENGE** How can you use $a(b + c) = ab + ac$ to show that $(b + c)a = ba + ca$ is also true? *Justify* your steps.
$(b + c)a = a(b + c)$, Commutative property of multiplication; $= ab + ac$, Given statement; $= ba + ca$, Commutative property of multiplication

PROBLEM SOLVING

EXAMPLE 5 A on p. 98 for Exs. 50–52

50. SPORTS An archer shoots 6 arrows at a target. Some arrows hit the 9 point ring, and the rest hit the 10 point bull's-eye. Write an equation that gives the score s as a function of the number a of arrows that hit the 9 point ring. Then find the score if 2 arrows hit the 9 point ring. $s = -a + 60$; 58

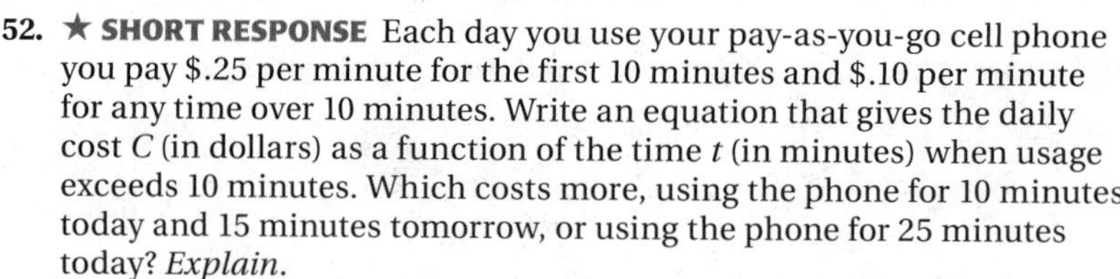

@HomeTutor for problem solving help at classzone.com

51. MOVIES You have a coupon for \$2 off the regular cost per movie rental. You rent 3 movies, and the regular cost of each rental is the same. Write an equation that gives the total cost C (in dollars) as a function of the regular cost r (in dollars) of a rental. Then find the total cost if a rental regularly costs \$3.99. $C = 3r - 6$; \$5.97

@HomeTutor for problem solving help at classzone.com

52. ★ **SHORT RESPONSE** Each day you use your pay-as-you-go cell phone you pay \$.25 per minute for the first 10 minutes and \$.10 per minute for any time over 10 minutes. Write an equation that gives the daily cost C (in dollars) as a function of the time t (in minutes) when usage exceeds 10 minutes. Which costs more, using the phone for 10 minutes today and 15 minutes tomorrow, or using the phone for 25 minutes today? *Explain.*

52. $C = 2.5 + 0.1(m - 10)$; 10 minutes today and 15 minutes tomorrow; the cost of using the phone 10 minutes today and 15 minutes tomorrow is $2.5 + 2.5 + 0.1(5) =$ \$5.50; the cost of using the phone for 25 minutes today is $2.5 + 0.1(15) =$ \$4.

○ = **WORKED-OUT SOLUTIONS on p. WS1** ★ = **STANDARDIZED TEST PRACTICE**

B **53. DIVING** In a diving competition, a diver's score is the product of the difficulty level d of a dive and the sum of the scores x, y, and z of 3 judges. Write a simplified expression that represents the diver's score. $s = d(x + y + z)$

54. ★ **EXTENDED RESPONSE** During the summer you give one hour saxophone lessons to 20 students each week. Use the information in the advertisement.

a. **Model** Write an equation that gives your weekly earnings y (in dollars) as a function of the number x of beginning students that you teach. $y = -15x + 700$

b. **Calculate** Find your weekly earnings if 15 of your 20 students are beginners. $475

c. **Explain** Suppose that you plan to teach for 10 weeks and want to earn $4000 for the summer. How many advanced students should you teach? Your answer should include the following:

- a table of values generated by the equation in part (a)
- an explanation of your method for answering the question See margin.

C **55. CHALLENGE** A drama club plans to sell 100 tickets to a school musical. An adult ticket costs $6, and a student ticket costs $4. Students who attend the school get a $1 discount. The club expects two thirds of the student tickets to be discounted. Write an equation that gives the total revenue r (in dollars) as a function of the number a of adult tickets sold. $r = \frac{8}{3}a + \frac{1000}{3}$

ILLINOIS MIXED REVIEW

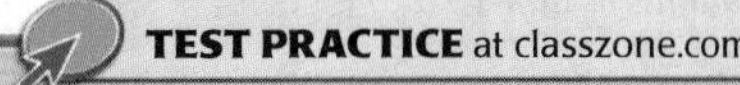
TEST PRACTICE at classzone.com

56. You have $75 and start a new job from which you are able to save $35 each week. How much will you have altogether after 5 weeks at your new job? C

Ⓐ $110 Ⓑ $175 Ⓒ $250 Ⓓ $550

57. What is the volume of a solid metal sphere with a diameter of 4 centimeters? B

Ⓐ $16\pi \text{ cm}^3$ Ⓑ $\frac{32\pi}{3} \text{ cm}^3$ Ⓒ $32\pi \text{ cm}^3$ Ⓓ $\frac{64\pi}{3} \text{ cm}^3$

QUIZ for Lessons 2.4–2.5

Find the product. *(p. 88)*

1. $-5 \cdot (-5)$ 25
2. $18 \cdot \left(-\frac{7}{6}\right)$ −21
3. $8 \cdot \frac{4}{5} \cdot (-10)$ −64
4. $9 \cdot (-7) \cdot (-1.2)$ 75.6
5. $(-3x) \cdot (-4)$ $12x$
6. $-\frac{2}{3}x \cdot 15$ $-10x$
7. $x \cdot 1.5 \cdot (-6.4)$ $-9.6x$
8. $(-2)(13x)$ $-26x$

Use the distributive property to write an equivalent expression. *(p. 96)*

9. $7(x + 14)$ $7x + 98$
10. $-4(5x + 9)$ $-20x - 36$
11. $-5(2x - 6)$ $-10x + 30$
12. $(3 - x)6$ $18 - 6x$

EXTRA PRACTICE for Lesson 2.5, p. 939  **ONLINE QUIZ** at classzone.com

5 ASSESS AND RETEACH

Daily Homework Quiz

 **Transparency Available**

Use the distributive property to write an equivalent expression.

1. $6(2 - x)$ $12 - 6x$
2. $-x(3x + 2)$ $-3x^2 - 2x$

Simplify the expression.

3. $4x - 5 + 3 - x$ $3x - 2$
4. $(3x - 2)4 + x$ $13x - 8$
5. You burn 18 calories per minute on an elliptical trainer and 7 calories per minute weight training. Suppose you work out at these two activities for 45 minutes. How many calories do you burn if you lift weights for 30 minutes? 480 calories

Online Quiz

Available at **classzone.com**

Diagnosis/Remediation

- Practice A, B, C in Chapter 2 Resource Book, pp. 50–52
- Study Guide in Chapter 2 Resource Book, pp. 53–54
- Practice Workbook, pp. 24–25
- @HomeTutor

Challenge

Additional challenge is available in the Chapter 2 Resource Book, p. 57.

Quiz

An easily-readable reduced copy of the quiz (with answers) on Lessons 2.4–2.5 from the Assessment Book can be found on p. 62E.

54c. You do not need to teach any advanced students.

Number of beginner students	Weekly pay (dollars)
15	475
16	460
17	445
18	430
19	415
20	400

You need to earn $4000 ÷ 10 = $400 a week. A table of values shows how much you can earn based on the number of beginner students you teach.

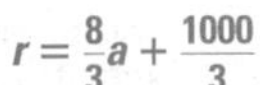

Alternative Strategy

Example 5 on page 98 can be solved by breaking the problem into parts. This method allows students to see the components of the problem and will help them better understand the algebraic solution given in Lesson 2.5.

Avoiding Common Errors

Students may confuse the time spent running with the time swimming or the number of calories burned per minute running with the number of calories burned per minute swimming. Have them check that their calculations match the numbers in the problem.

Teaching Strategy

Students may want to use this strategy for Exercises 50–55 in Lesson 2.5.

1. \$330; method 1: write an equation for c, the total cost as a function of n, the number of nights you spend at a campground; $c = 15n + 60(10 - n)$ or $c = -45n + 600$. Substitute 6 for n, giving you $c = \$330$; method 2: break the problem into parts. Find the cost of staying at the campground for 6 nights: \$15 per night • 6 nights = \$90. Find the number of nights spent at the motel: $10 - 6 =$ 4 nights. Find the cost of staying at the motel for 4 nights: \$60 per night • 4 nights = \$240. Add the cost of the campground to the cost of the motel: \$90 + \$240 = \$330.

2. \$450; method 1: write an equation for c, the total cost, as a function of n, the number of nights you spend at a campground; $c = 15n + 60(12 - n)$ or $c = -45n + 720$. Substitute 6 for n, giving you $c = \$450$; method 2: break the problem into parts. Find the cost of staying at the campground for 6 nights: \$15 per night • 6 nights = \$90. Find the number of nights spent at the motel: $12 - 6 =$ 6 nights. Find the cost of staying at the motel for 6 nights: \$60 per night • 6 nights = \$360. Add the cost of the campground to the cost of the motel: \$90 + \$360 = \$450.

PROBLEM SOLVING WORKSHOP LESSON 2.5 — *Using* ALTERNATIVE METHODS

Another Way to Solve Example 5, page 98

MULTIPLE REPRESENTATIONS In Example 5 on page 98, you saw how to solve a problem about exercising using a verbal model and an equation. You can also solve the problem by breaking it into parts.

PROBLEM

EXERCISING Your daily workout plan involves a total of 50 minutes of running and swimming. You burn 15 calories per minute when running and 9 calories per minute when swimming. Find the number of calories you burn in your 50 minute workout if you run for 20 minutes.

METHOD

Breaking into Parts You can solve the problem by breaking it into parts.

STEP 1 **Find** the number of calories you burn when running.

15 calories per minute • 20 minutes = 300 calories

Your running time is 20 minutes, so your swimming time is 50 − 20 = 30 minutes.

STEP 2 **Find** the calories you burn when swimming.

9 calories per minute • 30 minutes = 270 calories

STEP 3 **Add** the calories you burn when doing each activity. You burn a total of 570 calories.

300 calories + 270 calories = 570 calories

PRACTICE

1–4. See margin.

1. **VACATIONING** Your family is taking a vacation for 10 nights. You will spend some nights at a campground and the rest of the nights at a motel. A campground stay costs \$15 per night, and a motel stay costs \$60 per night. Find the total cost of lodging if you stay at a campground for 6 nights. Solve this problem using two different methods.

2. **WHAT IF?** In Exercise 1, suppose the vacation lasts 12 days. Find the total cost of lodging if you stay at the campground for 6 nights. Solve this problem using two different methods.

3. **FLORIST** During the summer, you work 35 hours per week at a florist shop. You get paid \$8 per hour for working at the register and \$9.50 per hour for making deliveries. Find the total amount you earn this week if you spend 5 hours making deliveries. Solve this problem using two different methods.

4. **ERROR ANALYSIS** *Describe* and correct the error in solving Exercise 3.

\$8 per hour • 5 hours = \$40
\$9.50 per hour • 30 hours = \$285
\$40 + \$285 = \$325

3. See Additional Answers beginning on p. AA1.

4. You earn \$9.50 per hour making deliveries, not working at the register; \$9.50 per hour • 5 hours = \$47.50; \$8 per hour • 30 hours = \$240; \$47.50 + \$240 = \$287.50.

2.6 Divide Real Numbers

 **6.11.10** Perform numerical computations with real numbers.

Before You multiplied real numbers.

Now You will divide real numbers.

Why? So you can calculate volleyball statistics, as in Ex. 57.

Key Vocabulary
- **multiplicative inverse**
- **reciprocal,** *p. 915*
- **mean,** *p. 918*

Reciprocals like $\frac{2}{3}$ and $\frac{3}{2}$ have the property that their product is 1:

$$\frac{2}{3} \cdot \frac{3}{2} = 1$$

The reciprocal of a nonzero number a, written $\frac{1}{a}$, is called the **multiplicative inverse** of a. Zero does not have a multiplicative inverse because there is no number a such that $0 \cdot a = 1$.

KEY CONCEPT *For Your Notebook*

Inverse Property of Multiplication

Words The product of a nonzero number and its multiplicative inverse is 1.

Algebra $a \cdot \frac{1}{a} = \frac{1}{a} \cdot a = 1, a \neq 0$ **Example** $8 \cdot \frac{1}{8} = 1$

EXAMPLE 1 **Find multiplicative inverses of numbers**

a. The multiplicative inverse of $-\frac{1}{5}$ is -5 because $-\frac{1}{5} \cdot (-5) = 1$.

b. The multiplicative inverse of $-\frac{6}{7}$ is $-\frac{7}{6}$ because $-\frac{6}{7} \cdot \left(-\frac{7}{6}\right) = 1$.

WRITE INVERSES
You can find the inverse of $-\frac{6}{7}$ as follows:

$$\frac{1}{-\frac{6}{7}} \cdot 1 = \frac{1}{-\frac{6}{7}} \cdot \frac{7}{7}$$
$$= -\frac{7}{6}$$

DIVISION Because the expressions $4 \div \frac{2}{3}$ and $4 \cdot \frac{3}{2}$ have the same value, 6, you can conclude that $4 \div \frac{2}{3} = 4 \cdot \frac{3}{2}$. This example illustrates the *division rule.*

KEY CONCEPT *For Your Notebook*

Division Rule

Words To divide a number a by a nonzero number b, multiply a by the multiplicative inverse of b.

Algebra $a \div b = a \cdot \frac{1}{b}, b \neq 0$ **Example** $5 \div 2 = 5 \cdot \frac{1}{2}$

1 PLAN AND PREPARE

Warm-Up Exercises

Transparency Available

Find the quotient.

1. $84 \div 14$ 6
2. $1.2 \div 5$ 0.24
3. $\frac{2}{3} \div 3$ $\frac{2}{9}$
4. $\frac{5}{8} \div \frac{1}{5}$ $3\frac{1}{8}$
5. The points Jeri scored in her last five basketball games were 28, 34, 19, 26, and 38. How many points did she average per game? 29 points

Notetaking Guide

Transparency Available

Promotes interactive learning and notetaking skills, pp. 39–41.

Pacing

Basic: 1 day
Average: 1 day
Advanced: 1 day
Block: 0.5 block with 2.5
- See *Teaching Guide/Lesson Plan.*

2 FOCUS AND MOTIVATE

Essential Question

Big Idea 1, p. 63

How do you divide real numbers? **Tell students they will learn how to answer this question by using the division rule and sign rules for products and quotients.**

Resource Planning Guide

Chapter Resource Book
- Teaching Guide/Lesson Plan (pp. 58–59)
- Activity Master (p. 60)
- Practice levels A, B, C (pp. 62–64)
- Study Guide (pp. 65–66)
- Catch-up for Absent Students (p. 67)
- Application (p. 68)
- Challenge (p. 69)

Workbooks
- Notetaking Guide (pp. 39–41)
- Practice Workbook (pp. 26–27)

Teaching Options
- **Power Presentations CD-ROM** provides dynamic electronic teaching resources for the classroom.
- **Activity Generator CD-ROM** provides editable activities for all ability levels.

Interactive Technology
- Easy Planner
- Power Presentations CD-ROM
- Activity Generator CD-ROM
- Animated Algebra
- Test Generator CD-ROM
- Online Quiz
- eWorkbook
- eEdition
- @HomeTutor

Resources for English Learners
- Quick Reference for English Learners
- Spanish Study Guide
- Multi-Language Visual Glossary
- Student Resources in Spanish

See also the *Algebra 1 Toolkit* for more strategies for meeting individual needs.

Motivating the Lesson

A top golfer has scores of −4, −3, −6 and −3 in four rounds of golf on a new course. In this lesson, you will learn how to find the average score on this course.

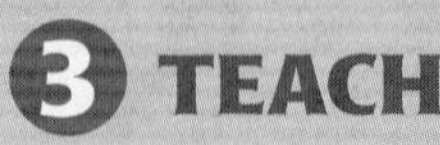

3 TEACH

Extra Example 1

Find the multiplicative inverse of the number.

a. $-\frac{1}{7}$ -7 b. $-\frac{5}{3}$ $-\frac{3}{5}$

Key Question to Ask for Example 1

- What is the multiplicative inverse of $\frac{a}{b}$, where $a \neq 0$ and $b \neq 0$? $\frac{b}{a}$

Extra Example 2

Find the quotient

a. $18 \div (-3)$ -6 b. $-16 \div \left(-\frac{8}{3}\right)$ 6

Extra Example 3

Andy recorded the low temperature each night at his home during January. Over five consecutive nights, he recorded the temperatures −2°C, −10°C, 6°C, −1°C, and 2°C. What was the mean low temperature at his home for these nights? −1°C

Key Question to Ask for Example 3

- Why do you divide by 5 in Example 3? because there are 5 values in the data set, one for each day

Vocabulary

In Example 3, remind students that the mean is sometimes referred to as the "average" of a set of data.

SIGN OF A QUOTIENT Because division can be expressed as multiplication, the sign rules for division are the same as the sign rules for multiplication.

AVOID ERRORS
You cannot divide a real number by 0, because 0 does not have a multiplicative inverse.

KEY CONCEPT *For Your Notebook*

The Sign of a Quotient

- The quotient of two real numbers with the *same* sign is positive.
- The quotient of two real numbers with *different* signs is negative.
- The quotient of 0 and any nonzero real number is 0.

EXAMPLE 2 Divide real numbers

Find the quotient.

a. $-16 \div 4 = -16 \cdot \frac{1}{4}$
$= -4$

b. $-20 \div \left(-\frac{5}{3}\right) = -20 \cdot \left(-\frac{3}{5}\right)$
$= 12$

GUIDED PRACTICE for Examples 1 and 2

Find the multiplicative inverse of the number.

1. -27 $-\frac{1}{27}$
2. -8 $-\frac{1}{8}$
3. $-\frac{4}{7}$ $-\frac{7}{4}$
4. $-\frac{1}{3}$ -3

Find the quotient.

5. $-64 \div (-4)$ 16
6. $-\frac{3}{8} \div \left(\frac{3}{10}\right)$ $-1\frac{1}{4}$
7. $18 \div \left(-\frac{2}{9}\right)$ -81
8. $-\frac{2}{5} \div 18$ $-\frac{1}{45}$

EXAMPLE 3 Find the mean

TEMPERATURES The table gives the daily minimum temperatures (in degrees Fahrenheit) in Barrow, Alaska, for the first 5 days of February 2004. Find the mean daily minimum temperature.

Day in February	1	2	3	4	5
Minimum temperature (°F)	−21	−29	−39	−39	−22

Point Barrow Observatory

Solution

To find the mean daily minimum temperature, find the sum of the minimum temperatures for the 5 days and then divide the sum by 5.

REVIEW MEAN
For help with finding a mean, see p. 918.

$$\text{Mean} = \frac{-21 + (-29) + (-39) + (-39) + (-22)}{5}$$

$$= -\frac{150}{5} = -30$$

▶ The mean daily minimum temperature was −30°F.

Differentiated Instruction

Inclusion Some students may find it easier to divide real numbers by first determining the sign of the final answer and then proceeding with the division of the numbers without regard to the sign. Give grouped examples like the following: $-4 \div 2 = -(4 \div 2) = -2$, $4 \div (-2) = -(4 \div 2) = -2$, $-4 \div (-2) = +(4 \div 2) = 2$. In these examples, once the sign was determined, the problem was reduced to dividing 4 by 2.

See also the *Algebra 1 Toolkit* for more strategies.

EXAMPLE 4 Simplify an expression

Simplify the expression $\frac{36x - 24}{6}$.

ANOTHER WAY
You can simplify the expression by first rewriting it as a difference of two fractions: $\frac{36x - 24}{6} = \frac{36x}{6} - \frac{24}{6} = 6x - 4$.

$\frac{36x - 24}{6} = (36x - 24) \div 6$ **Rewrite fraction as division.**

$= (36x - 24) \cdot \frac{1}{6}$ **Division rule**

$= 36x \cdot \frac{1}{6} - 24 \cdot \frac{1}{6}$ **Distributive property**

$= 6x - 4$ **Simplify.**

✓ GUIDED PRACTICE for Examples 3 and 4

9. Find the mean of the numbers −3, 4, 2.8, and −1.5. 0.575

10. **TEMPERATURES** Find the mean daily maximum temperature (in degrees Fahrenheit) in Barrow, Alaska, for the first 5 days of February 2004. −16.8°F

Day in February	1	2	3	4	5
Maximum temperature (°F)	−3	−20	−21	−22	−18

Simplify the expression.

11. $\frac{2x - 8}{-4}$ $-\frac{1}{2}x + 2$
12. $\frac{-6y + 18}{3}$ $-2y + 6$
13. $\frac{-10z - 20}{-5}$ $2z + 4$

OPERATIONS ON REAL NUMBERS In this chapter, you saw how to find the sum, difference, product, and quotient of two real numbers *a* and *b*. You can use the values of *a* and *b* to determine whether the result is positive, negative, or 0.

CONCEPT SUMMARY *For Your Notebook*

Rules for Addition, Subtraction, Multiplication, and Division

Let *a* and *b* be real numbers.

Expression	$a + b$	$a - b$	$a \cdot b$	$a \div b$
Positive if...	the number with the greater absolute value is positive.	$a > b$.	*a* and *b* have the same sign ($a \neq 0, b \neq 0$).	*a* and *b* have the same sign ($a \neq 0, b \neq 0$).
Negative if...	the number with the greater absolute value is negative.	$a < b$.	*a* and *b* have different signs ($a \neq 0, b \neq 0$).	*a* and *b* have different signs ($a \neq 0, b \neq 0$).
Zero if...	*a* and *b* are additive inverses.	$a = b$.	$a = 0$ or $b = 0$.	$a = 0$ and $b \neq 0$.

Extra Example 4
Simplify the expression $\frac{40x + 32}{8}$.
$5x + 4$

Reading Strategy
Be certain that students read and understand the Another Way note next to Example 4. This note presents another approach to simplifying expressions that some students may find preferable to use.

Closing the Lesson
Have students summarize the major points of the lesson and answer the Essential Question: How do you divide real numbers?

- To divide a number *a* by a nonzero number *b*, find the product $a \cdot \frac{1}{b}$.
- The sign rules for division are the same as for multiplication.
- The product of a nonzero number and its multiplicative inverse is 1.

To divide two real numbers, multiply the first number by the multiplicative inverse of the second number.

2.6 EXERCISES

HOMEWORK KEY
○ = WORKED-OUT SOLUTIONS on p. WS4 for Exs. 13, 35, and 53
★ = STANDARDIZED TEST PRACTICE Exs. 2, 23, 48, 49, 55, 56, and 57

4 PRACTICE AND APPLY

Assignment Guide

Answer Transparencies available for all exercises

Basic:
Day 1: pp. 106–108
Exs. 1, 2, 3–23 odd, 24–28, 33–37, 42–45, 52–55, 59–63 odd

Average:
Day 1: pp. 106–108
Exs. 1, 2, 7–10, 15–23 odd, 28–32, 37–49, 53, 60–64 even

Advanced:
Day 1: pp. 106–108
Exs. 1, 2, 8–10, 19–23, 29–32, 38–41, 44–52*, 54–58*

Block:
pp. 106–108
Exs. 1, 2, 7–10, 15–23 odd, 28–32, 37–49, 60–64 even (with 2.5)

Differentiated Instruction

See *Algebra 1 Best Practices Toolkit* for suggestions on addressing the needs of a diverse classroom.

Homework Check

For a quick check of student understanding of key concepts, go over the following exercises:
Basic: 5, 15, 25, 34, 52
Average: 8, 17, 30, 38, 53
Advanced: 9, 20, 31, 40, 54

Extra Practice

- Student Edition, p. 939
- Chapter 2 Resource Book: Practice levels A, B, C, pp. 62–64

Practice Worksheet

An easily-readable reduced practice page (with answers) for this lesson can be found on p. 62D.

SKILL PRACTICE

A

1. **VOCABULARY** Copy and complete: The product of a nonzero number and its __?__ is 1. multiplicative inverse

2. ★ **WRITING** How can you tell whether the mean of n numbers is negative without actually dividing the sum of the numbers by n? *Explain.*
If their sum is negative, the mean will be negative.

EXAMPLE 1 on p. 103 for Exs. 3–10, 23

FINDING INVERSES Find the multiplicative inverse of the number.

3. -18 $-\frac{1}{18}$
4. -9 $-\frac{1}{9}$
5. -1 -1
6. $-\frac{1}{2}$ -2
7. $-\frac{3}{4}$ $-1\frac{1}{3}$
8. $-\frac{5}{9}$ $-1\frac{4}{5}$
9. $-4\frac{1}{3}$ $-\frac{3}{13}$
10. $-2\frac{2}{5}$ $-\frac{5}{12}$

EXAMPLE 2 on p. 104 for Exs. 11–22

FINDING QUOTIENTS Find the quotient.

11. $-21 \div 3$ -7
12. $-18 \div (-6)$ 3
13. $-1 \div \left(-\frac{7}{2}\right)$ $\frac{2}{7}$
14. $15 \div \left(-\frac{3}{4}\right)$ -20
15. $13 \div \left(-4\frac{1}{3}\right)$ -3
16. $-\frac{2}{3} \div 2$ $-\frac{1}{3}$
17. $-\frac{1}{2} \div \frac{1}{5}$ $-2\frac{1}{2}$
18. $-\frac{1}{5} \div (-6)$ $\frac{1}{30}$
19. $-\frac{4}{7} \div (-2)$ $\frac{2}{7}$
20. $-1 \div \left(-\frac{6}{5}\right)$ $\frac{5}{6}$
21. $8 \div \left(-\frac{4}{11}\right)$ -22
22. $-\frac{1}{3} \div \frac{5}{3}$ $-\frac{1}{5}$

23. ★ **MULTIPLE CHOICE** If $-\frac{5}{7}x = 1$, what is the value of x? A

Ⓐ $-1\frac{2}{5}$ Ⓑ $\frac{5}{7}$ Ⓒ 1 Ⓓ $\frac{12}{5}$

EXAMPLE 3 on p. 104 for Exs. 24–32

FINDING MEANS Find the mean of the numbers.

24. $-10, -8, 3$ -5
25. $12, -8, -9$ $-1\frac{2}{3}$
26. $18, -9, 0, -5$ 1
27. $-2, 9, -3, 5$ $2\frac{1}{4}$
28. $-1, -4, -5, 10$ 0
29. $7, -4, 1, -9, -6$ $-2\frac{1}{5}$
30. $-5.3, -2, 1.3$ -2
31. $0.25, -4, -0.75, -1, 6$ 0.1
32. $-0.6, 0.18, -2, 5, -0.5$ 0.416

EXAMPLE 4 on p. 105 for Exs. 33–43

SIMPLIFYING EXPRESSIONS Simplify the expression.

33. $\frac{6x-14}{2}$ $3x-7$
34. $\frac{12y-8}{-4}$ $-3y+2$
35. $\frac{9z-6}{-3}$ $-3z+2$
36. $\frac{-6p+15}{6}$ $-p+2\frac{1}{2}$
37. $\frac{5-25q}{10}$ $\frac{1}{2}-\frac{5}{2}q$
38. $\frac{-18-21r}{-12}$ $\frac{3}{2}+\frac{7}{4}r$
39. $\frac{-24a-10}{-8}$ $3a+1\frac{1}{4}$
40. $\frac{-20b+12}{-5}$ $4b-2\frac{2}{5}$
41. $\frac{36-27c}{9}$ $4-3c$

ERROR ANALYSIS *Describe* and correct the error in simplifying the expression. 42, 43. See margin.

42.
$$\frac{12-18x}{6} = (12-18x)\cdot\left(-\frac{1}{6}\right) = 12\left(-\frac{1}{6}\right) - 18x\left(-\frac{1}{6}\right) = -2+3x$$

43.
$$\frac{-15x-10}{-5} = (-15x-10)\cdot\left(-\frac{1}{5}\right) = -15x\left(-\frac{1}{5}\right) - 10\left(-\frac{1}{5}\right) = 3x-2$$

42. The multiplicative inverse of 6 is $\frac{1}{6}$, not $-\frac{1}{6}$. $\frac{12-18x}{6} = (12-18x)\cdot\left(\frac{1}{6}\right) = 12\left(\frac{1}{6}\right) - 18x\left(\frac{1}{6}\right) = 2-3x.$

43. -2 was added instead of subtracted; $\frac{-15x-10}{-5} = (-15x-10)\cdot\left(-\frac{1}{5}\right) = -15x\left(-\frac{1}{5}\right) - 10\left(-\frac{1}{5}\right) = 3x+2.$

B **EVALUATING EXPRESSIONS** **Evaluate the expression.**

44. $\frac{2y - x}{x}$ when $x = 1$ and $y = -4$ **−9**

45. $\frac{4x}{3y + x}$ when $x = 6$ and $y = -8$ **$-1\frac{1}{3}$**

46. $\frac{-9x}{y^2 - 1}$ when $x = -3$ and $y = -2$ **9**

47. $\frac{y - x}{xy}$ when $x = -6$ and $y = -2$ **$\frac{1}{3}$**

48. No; no. *Sample answer:* $4 \div 2 = 2$ but $2 \div 4 = \frac{1}{2}$, $(20 \div 4) \div 2 = 2\frac{1}{2}$ but $20 \div (4 \div 2) = 10$.

48. ★ **WRITING** Tell whether division is commutative and associative. Give examples to support your answer.

49. ★ **MULTIPLE CHOICE** Let *a* and *b* be positive numbers, and let *c* and *d* be negative numbers. Which quotient has a value that is always negative? **C**

Ⓐ $\frac{a}{b} \div \frac{c}{d}$ Ⓑ $\frac{a}{c} \div \frac{b}{d}$ Ⓒ $\frac{c^2}{a} \div \frac{b}{d}$ Ⓓ $\frac{a}{cd} \div b$

C **50.** **CHALLENGE** Find the mean of the integers from −410 to 400. *Explain* how you got your answer. **See margin.**

51. **CHALLENGE** What is the mean of a number and three times its opposite? *Explain* your reasoning. **The opposite of the number; if you add *x* and 3 times $-x$, you get $-2x$; $-2x \div 2 = -x$.**

PROBLEM SOLVING

EXAMPLE 2 on p. 104 for Ex. 52

A **52.** **SPORTS** Free diving means diving without the aid of breathing equipment. Suppose that an athlete free dives to an elevation of −42 meters in 60 seconds. Find the average rate of change in the diver's elevation. **$-\frac{7}{10}$ m/sec**

@HomeTutor for problem solving help at classzone.com

EXAMPLE 3 on p. 104 for Exs. 53–54

53. **WEATHER** The daily mean temperature is the mean of the high and low temperatures for a given day. The high temperature for Boston, Massachusetts, on January 10, 2004, was −10.6°C. The low temperature was −18.9°C. Find the daily mean temperature for that day. **−14.75°C**

@HomeTutor for problem solving help at classzone.com

54. **MULTI-STEP PROBLEM** The table shows the changes in the values of one share of stock A and one share of stock B over 5 days.

Day of week	Monday	Tuesday	Wednesday	Thursday	Friday
Change in share value for stock A (dollars)	−0.45	−0.32	0.66	−1.12	1.53
Change in share value for stock B (dollars)	−0.37	0.14	0.59	−0.53	1.02

a. Find the average daily change in share value for each stock. **\$.06; \$.17**

b. Which stock performed better over the 5 days? How much more money did the better performing stock earn, on average, per day? **stock B; \$.11**

c. Can you conclude that the stock that performed better over all 5 days also performed better over the first 4 days of the week? *Explain* your reasoning.

54c. Yes. *Sample answer:* Over the first four days, stock A's average change in value was −0.3075 whereas stock B's was −0.0425.

Study Strategy

Exercises 33–41 In preparation for these exercises, students may want to review Example 4. Note that some students may find it easier to use the alternative method for simplifying expressions that is mentioned in "Another Way."

Avoiding Common Errors

Exercises 44–47 Students often substitute incorrectly when replacement values involve a negative sign. Encourage them to use parentheses to insert the values. This will help them avoid computational errors.

Reading Strategy

Exercise 56 Urge students to read all parts of the question carefully before completing part b. Note that the original prediction was off by 3.5 meters, which changes the rate of change for the whole period.

50. −5. ***Sample answer:*** **Using additive inverses you can determine that the sum of the integers −400 to 400 is 0. The sum of the integers from −410 to −401 is −4055. Divide this sum by the number of integers from −410 to 400, which is 811; −4055 ÷ 811 = −5.**

5 ASSESS AND RETEACH

Daily Homework Quiz

Transparency Available

Find the quotient.

1. $-14 \div 2\frac{1}{2}$ $-5\frac{3}{5}$
2. $-\frac{3}{4} \div (-4)$ $\frac{3}{16}$

Simplify the expression.

3. $\frac{9x - 15}{-3}$ $-3x + 5$
4. $\frac{-8x + 12}{5}$ $-1.6x + 2.4$
5. Ethan's team scored the following numbers of points in six rounds of a statewide History Quiz Contest: 86, −14, 58, −26, 74, and 20. What was the team's mean score? 33

Online Quiz

Available at **classzone.com**

Diagnosis/Remediation

- Practice A, B, C in Chapter 2 Resource Book, pp. 62–64
- Study Guide in Chapter 2 Resource Book, pp. 65–66
- Practice Workbook, pp. 26–27
- @HomeTutor

Challenge

Additional challenge is available in the Chapter 2 Resource Book, p. 69.

57c. If the player had the same number of aces as service errors, then $a = e$, so $f = \frac{a - a}{s} = 0$; if all the serves were aces, a would be equal to s and e would be 0, so $f = \frac{s - 0}{s} = \frac{s}{s} = 1$; if all the serves were errors, then $e = s$ and $a = 0$, so $f = \frac{0 - s}{s} = \frac{-s}{s} = -1$.

B

55. ★ **MULTIPLE CHOICE** In a trivia competition, your team earned 60, −100, 300, 120, and −80 points on 5 questions. The sixth question has a value of 300 points. By how many points will your team's mean score per question change if you answer the sixth question correctly? A

Ⓐ 40 points Ⓑ 50 points Ⓒ 60 points Ⓓ 100 points

56. ★ **SHORT RESPONSE** The South Aral Sea in Russia was about 57 meters above sea level in 1965. Scientists once predicted that the elevation would be about 34 meters above sea level in 2002.

a. Estimate the average rate of change in elevation for the period 1965–2002 using the scientists' prediction. Round to the nearest hundredth of a meter per year. −0.62 meter per year

b. More recent research suggests that the elevation decreased to about 30.5 meters above sea level in 2002. Use this information to predict the elevation in 2010. *Explain* the steps of your solution. About 24.74 m. *Sample answer:* Find the average rate of change based on the actual elevation in 2002, −0.72; use the equation 30.5 + (−0.72)(8) to predict the elevation on 2010.

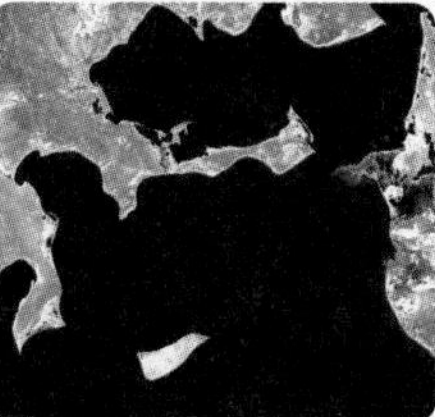
South Aral Sea, 1973

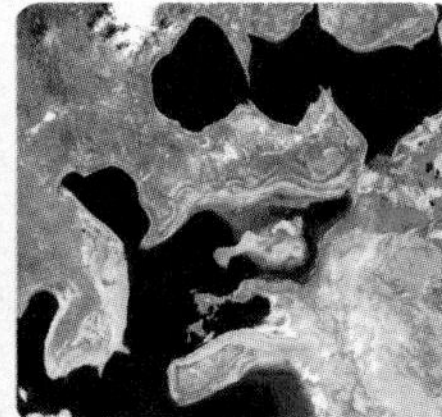
South Aral Sea, 2000

57. ★ **EXTENDED RESPONSE** In volleyball, an ace is a serve that the opponent doesn't hit. Ace efficiency is a measure of a player's ability to hit aces while minimizing service errors. The ace efficiency f is given by the formula $f = \frac{a - e}{s}$ where a is the number of aces, e is the number of service errors, and s is the total number of serves.

a. Calculate Find the ace efficiency for a player who has 108 aces and 125 service errors in 500 serves. −0.034

b. Compare If the player makes 30 more aces and 20 more service errors in the next 100 serves, will the ace efficiency improve? *Explain.* Yes; it will improve to −0.012.

c. Justify Under what conditions would a player's ace efficiency be 0? 1? −1? *Justify* your answers algebraically. See margin.

C

58. **CHALLENGE** The average daily balance of a checking account is the sum of the daily balances in a given period divided by the number of days in the period. Suppose that a period has 30 days. Find the average daily balance of an account that has a balance of $110 for 18 days, −$300 for 10 days, and $100 for the rest of the period. −$27.33

ILLINOIS MIXED REVIEW

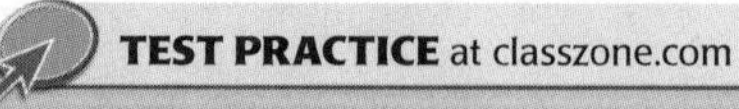

59. Which equation could be used to generate this table of values? C

x	5	10	15	20
y	0	10	20	30

Ⓐ $y = x - 5$ Ⓑ $y = 2x - 5$ Ⓒ $y = 2x - 10$ Ⓓ $y = 4x - 20$

60. A taxi driver charges $3.50 to drive 2 miles, $5.00 to drive 3 miles, and $6.50 to drive 4 miles. How much would you expect the taxi driver to charge to drive 6 miles? A

Ⓐ $9.50 Ⓑ $9.75 Ⓒ $10.00 Ⓓ $10.50

2.7 Writing Statements in If-Then Form

MATERIALS • paper and pencil

QUESTION How can you write an *all* or *none* statement in if-then form?

EXPLORE Tell whether certain statements are true about a group

STEP 1 ***Answer questions*** Copy the questions below and write your answers beside them.

1. Do you play an instrument?
2. Do you participate in a school sport?
3. Are you taking an art class?
4. Do you walk to school?

STEP 2 ***Write if-then statements*** Each of the *all* or *none* statements below can be written in if-then form. Copy each statement and complete its equivalent if-then form. The first one is done for you as an example.

1. All of the students in our group play an instrument.
   If a student is in our group, then the student plays an instrument.
2. None of the students in our group participates in a school sport.
   If ? , then ? . a student is in our group; the student doesn't participate in a school sport
3. None of the students in our group is taking an art class.
   If ? , then ? . a student is in our group; the student is not taking an art class
4. All of the students in our group walk to school.
   If ? , then ? . if a student is in our group; the student walks to school

STEP 3 ***Analyze statements*** Form a group with 2 or 3 classmates. Tell whether each if-then statement in Step 2 is *true* or *false* for your group. If the statement is false, give a counterexample.

DRAW CONCLUSIONS Use your observations to complete these exercises

1. *Describe* the similarity and difference in the if-then forms of the following statements: Both statements begin with "If a student is in our group" but the conclusion of the statement containing the word "all" is positive and the conclusion of the statement containing the word "none" is negative.

   All of the students in our group listen to rock music.

   None of the students in our group listens to rock music.

Rewrite the given conditional statement in if-then form. Then tell whether the statement is *true* or *false*. If it is false, give a counterexample.

2. All of the positive numbers are integers. If a number is positive, then it is an integer; false. *Sample answer*: $\frac{2}{3}$ is a positive number, but it is not an integer.
3. All of the rational numbers can be written as fractions. If a number is rational, then it can be written as a fraction; true.
4. None of the negative numbers is a whole number. If a number is negative, then it is not a whole number; true.
5. None of the rational numbers has an opposite equal to itself. If a number is rational, then it does not have an opposite equal to itself; false; 0 is a rational number and its opposite is 0.

1 PLAN AND PREPARE

Explore the Concept

- Students will write statements in if-then form.
- This activity leads into the study of rewriting conditional statements in Example 5 in Lesson 2.7.

Recommended Time

Work activity: 10 min
Discuss results:5 min

Grouping

Students should work in groups of 3–4. All students should answer the questions in Step 1. In Step 2, all students should write the if-then statements and then check that all the statements are written correctly. Students should complete Step 3 as a group.

2 TEACH

Tips for Success

In Step 2, point out that the "if" part of the if-then statement is the same for all of the statements and the "then" part of the if-then statement begins with "then the student."

Key Discovery

Generalizations that are true for all members of a set or for no members of a set can be written in if-then form.

3 ASSESS AND RETEACH

How many counterexamples does it take to prove that an if-then statement is false? one

1 PLAN AND PREPARE

Warm-Up Exercises

Transparency Available

Find the square of the number.

1. 14 196 **2.** 16 256

Complete the statements using <, >, or =.

3. $-2.5 \ \underline{?} \ -\frac{19}{8}$ < **4.** $\frac{5}{6} \ \underline{?} \ \frac{21}{25}$ <

5. A square room has a side length of 25 feet. What is its area? 625 ft^2

Notetaking Guide

Transparency Available

Promotes interactive learning and notetaking skills, pp. 42–44.

Pacing

Basic: 2 days

Average: 2 days

Advanced: 2 days

Block: 1 block

- See *Teaching Guide/Lesson Plan.*

2 FOCUS AND MOTIVATE

Essential Question

Big Idea 3, p. 63

How do you evaluate a square root and compare real numbers? **Tell students they will learn how to answer this question by finding and approximating square roots and graphing numbers on a number line.**

2.7 Find Square Roots and Compare Real Numbers

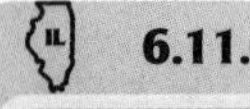
6.11.01 Recognize, represent, order, compare real numbers, and locate real numbers on a number line (e.g., ?, ? 2, ? 5, $\frac{2}{3}$, −1.6).

Before You found squares of numbers and compared rational numbers.

Now You will find square roots and compare real numbers.

Why? So you can find side lengths of geometric shapes, as in Ex. 54.

Key Vocabulary
- **square root**
- **radicand**
- **perfect square**
- **irrational number**
- **real numbers**

Recall that the square of 4 is $4^2 = 16$ and the square of -4 is $(-4)^2 = 16$. The numbers 4 and -4 are called the *square roots* of 16. In this lesson, you will find the square roots of nonnegative numbers.

KEY CONCEPT *For Your Notebook*

Square Root of a Number

Words If $b^2 = a$, then b is a **square root** of a.

Example $3^2 = 9$ and $(-3)^2 = 9$, so 3 and -3 are square roots of 9.

All positive real numbers have two square roots, a positive square root (or *principal* square root) and a negative square root. A square root is written with the radical symbol $\sqrt{\ }$. The number or expression inside a radical symbol is the **radicand.**

radical symbol ⟶ $\sqrt{a}$ ⟵ radicand

Zero has only one square root, 0. Negative real numbers do not have real square roots because the square of every real number is either positive or 0.

EXAMPLE 1 **Find square roots**

Evaluate the expression.

a. $\pm\sqrt{36} = \pm 6$ **The positive and negative square roots of 36 are 6 and −6.**

b. $\sqrt{49} = 7$ **The positive square root of 49 is 7.**

c. $-\sqrt{4} = -2$ **The negative square root of 4 is −2.**

READING
The symbol ± is read as "plus or minus" and refers to both the positive square root and the negative square root.

GUIDED PRACTICE for Example 1

Evaluate the expression.

1. $-\sqrt{9}$ **2.** $\sqrt{25}$ **3.** $\pm\sqrt{64}$ **4.** $-\sqrt{81}$

Resource Planning Guide

Chapter Resource Book
- Teaching Guide/Lesson Plan (pp. 70–71)
- Practice levels A, B, C (pp. 72–74)
- Study Guide (pp. 75–76)
- Catch-up for Absent Students (p. 77)
- Problem Solving Workshop (p. 78)
- Challenge (p. 79)

Workbooks
- Notetaking Guide (pp. 42–44)
- Practice Workbook (pp. 28–29)

Teaching Options
- **Power Presentations CD-ROM** provides dynamic electronic teaching resources for the classroom.
- **Activity Generator CD-ROM** provides editable activities for all ability levels.

Interactive Technology
- Easy Planner
- Power Presentations CD-ROM
- Activity Generator CD-ROM
- Animated Algebra
- Test Generator CD-ROM
- Online Quiz
- eWorkbook
- eEdition
- @HomeTutor

Resources for English Learners
- Quick Reference for English Learners
- Spanish Study Guide
- Multi-Language Visual Glossary
- Student Resources in Spanish

See also the *Algebra 1 Toolkit* for more strategies for meeting individual needs.

PERFECT SQUARES The square of an integer is called a **perfect square**. As shown in Example 1, the square root of a perfect square is an integer. As you will see in Example 2, you need to approximate a square root if the radicand is a whole number that is *not* a perfect square.

EXAMPLE 2 Approximate a square root

FURNITURE The top of a folding table is a square whose area is 945 square inches. Approximate the side length of the tabletop to the nearest inch.

Solution

You need to find the side length s of the tabletop such that $s^2 = 945$. This means that s is the positive square root of 945. You can use a table to determine whether 945 is a perfect square.

Number	28	29	30	31	32
Square of number	784	841	900	961	1024

As shown in the table, 945 is *not* a perfect square. The greatest perfect square less than 945 is 900. The least perfect square greater than 945 is 961.

$900 < 945 < 961$ **Write a compound inequality that compares 945 with both 900 and 961.**

$\sqrt{900} < \sqrt{945} < \sqrt{961}$ **Take positive square root of each number.**

$30 < \sqrt{945} < 31$ **Find square root of each perfect square.**

Because 945 is closer to 961 than to 900, $\sqrt{945}$ is closer to 31 than to 30.

▶ The side length of the tabletop is about 31 inches.

USING A CALCULATOR In Example 2, you can use a calculator to obtain a better approximation of the side length of the tabletop.

  945) ENTER

The side length is about 30.74 inches, which is closer to 31 than to 30.

GUIDED PRACTICE for Example 2

Approximate the square root to the nearest integer.

5. $\sqrt{32}$ 6 **6.** $\sqrt{103}$ 10 **7.** $-\sqrt{48}$ −7 **8.** $-\sqrt{350}$ −19

IRRATIONAL NUMBERS The square root of a whole number that is not a perfect square is an example of an *irrational number*. An **irrational number**, such as $\sqrt{945} = 30.74085...$, is a number that cannot be written as a quotient of two integers. The decimal form of an irrational number neither terminates nor repeats.

Motivating the Lesson

A square garden has an area of 225 square feet. You want to know how much fencing you should buy to go around the garden without measuring. By knowing how to find square roots, you can find the side length and then determine how much fencing you should buy.

3 TEACH

Extra Example 1

Evaluate the expression.

a. $\pm\sqrt{100}$ ±10

b. $\sqrt{121}$ 11

c. $-\sqrt{400}$ −20

Key Questions to Ask for Example 1

- How is Example 1a different from Examples 1b and 1c? The symbol ± in Example 1a means that the expression represents *both* the positive and negative square roots. In Examples 1b and 1c, only a *single* square root is indicated.
- In Example 1c, how is $-\sqrt{4}$ different from $\sqrt{-4}$? $-\sqrt{4}$ means the negative square root of 4; $\sqrt{-4}$ means the square root of −4, which is not a real number.

Extra Example 2

The top of a square box has an area of 320 square inches. Approximate the side length of the box top to the nearest inch. 18 in.

Teaching Strategy

When discussing Example 2, suggest that students make a list of the squares of numbers to 50 to use as a reference in approximating square roots.

Differentiated Instruction

Visual Learners Mathematicians chose the symbol √ for a square root because it is a distorted letter *r*, which is the first letter of the word "root." Be sure that students do not confuse it with the symbol ⟌ used in long division.

See also the *Algebra 1 Toolkit* for more strategies.

Extra Example 3

Tell whether each of the following numbers is a real number, a rational number, an irrational number, an integer, or a whole number: $-\sqrt{25}$, $\sqrt{361}$, $\sqrt{30}$. **$-\sqrt{25}$: real number, rational number, integer; $\sqrt{361}$: real number, rational number, integer, whole number; $\sqrt{30}$: real number, irrational number**

Extra Example 4

Order the numbers from least to greatest: $-\sqrt{10}$, $\frac{19}{5}$, -3, $\sqrt{12}$, $\sqrt{16}$. **$-\sqrt{10}$, -3, $\sqrt{12}$, $\frac{19}{5}$, $\sqrt{16}$**

Teaching Strategy

In Example 4, remind students to use a calculator, as shown on page 111, to approximate square roots that are irrational numbers.

9. $-\frac{9}{2}$: real number, rational number, 5.2: real number, rational number, 0: real number, rational number, integer, whole number, $\sqrt{7}$: real number, irrational number, 4.1: real number, rational number, $-\sqrt{20}$: real number, irrational number; $-\frac{9}{2}$, $-\sqrt{20}$, 0, $\sqrt{7}$, 4.1, 5.2

REAL NUMBERS The set of **real numbers** is the set of all rational and irrational numbers, as illustrated in the Venn diagram below. Every point on the real number line represents a real number.

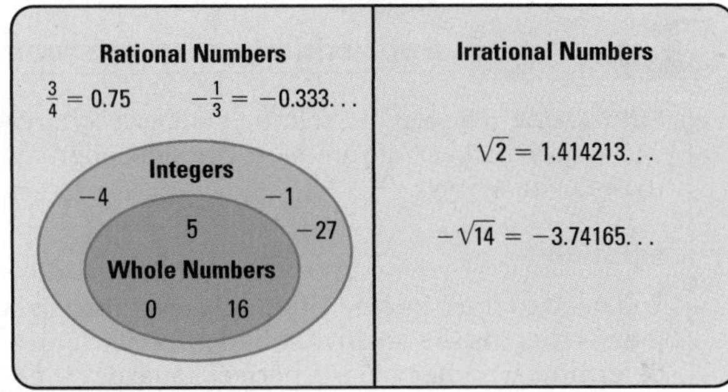

EXAMPLE 3 Classify numbers

Tell whether each of the following numbers is a real number, a rational number, an irrational number, an integer, or a whole number: $\sqrt{24}$, $\sqrt{100}$, $-\sqrt{81}$.

Number	Real number?	Rational number?	Irrational number?	Integer?	Whole number?
$\sqrt{24}$	Yes	No	Yes	No	No
$\sqrt{100}$	Yes	Yes	No	Yes	Yes
$-\sqrt{81}$	Yes	Yes	No	Yes	No

EXAMPLE 4 Graph and order real numbers

Order the numbers from least to greatest: $\frac{4}{3}$, $-\sqrt{5}$, $\sqrt{13}$, -2.5, $\sqrt{9}$.

Solution

Begin by graphing the numbers on a number line.

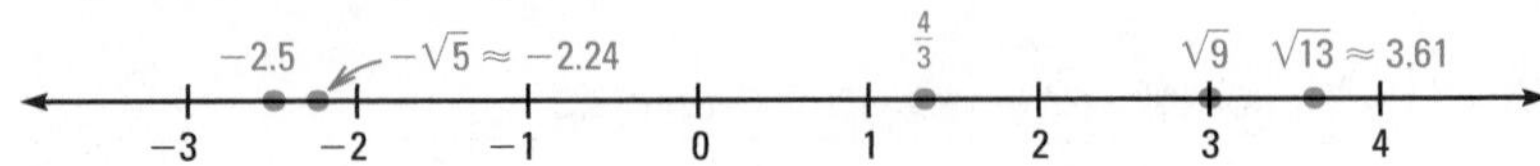

▶ Read the numbers from left to right: -2.5, $-\sqrt{5}$, $\frac{4}{3}$, $\sqrt{9}$, $\sqrt{13}$.

✓ **GUIDED PRACTICE** for Examples 3 and 4

9. Tell whether each of the following numbers is a real number, a rational number, an irrational number, an integer, or a whole number: $-\frac{9}{2}$, 5.2, 0, $\sqrt{7}$, 4.1, $-\sqrt{20}$. Then order the numbers from least to greatest. **See margin.**

CONDITIONAL STATEMENTS In the activity on page 109, you saw that a conditional statement not in if-then form can be written in that form.

EXAMPLE 5 Rewrite a conditional statement in if-then form

Rewrite the given conditional statement in if-then form. Then tell whether the statement is *true* or *false*. If it is false, give a counterexample.

Solution

a. Given: No fractions are irrational numbers.

If-then form: If a number is a fraction, then it is not an irrational number.

The statement is true.

b. Given: All real numbers are rational numbers.

If-then form: If a number is a real number, then it is a rational number.

The statement is false. For example, $\sqrt{2}$ is a real number but *not* a rational number.

✓ GUIDED PRACTICE for Example 5

Rewrite the conditional statement in if-then form. Then tell whether the statement is *true* or *false*. If it is false, give a counterexample.

10. All square roots of perfect squares are rational numbers.
If a number is the square root of a perfect square, then it is a rational number; true.
11. All repeating decimals are irrational numbers.
12. No integers are irrational numbers.
If a number is an integer, then it is not an irrational number; true.

11. If a number is a repeating decimal, then it is an irrational number; false. *Sample answer:* 0.333... is a repeating decimal and can be written as $\frac{1}{3}$, so it is a rational number.

2.7 EXERCISES

HOMEWORK KEY
○ = **WORKED-OUT SOLUTIONS** on p. WS5 for Exs. 9, 19, and 49
★ = **STANDARDIZED TEST PRACTICE** Exs. 2, 23, 42, 43, 44, 50, and 53
◆ = **MULTIPLE REPRESENTATIONS** Ex. 54

SKILL PRACTICE

1. **VOCABULARY** Copy and complete: The set of all rational and irrational numbers is called the set of __?__. real numbers

2. ★ **WRITING** Without calculating, how can you tell whether the square root of a whole number is rational or irrational?
If it is not a perfect square, the square root is irrational.

EXAMPLE 1 on p. 110 for Exs. 3–14

EVALUATING SQUARE ROOTS **Evaluate the expression.**

3. $\sqrt{4}$ 2	4. $-\sqrt{49}$ −7	5. $-\sqrt{9}$ −3	6. $\pm\sqrt{1}$ ±1
7. $\sqrt{196}$ 14	8. $\pm\sqrt{121}$ ±11	(9.) $\pm\sqrt{2500}$ ±50	10. $-\sqrt{256}$ −16
11. $-\sqrt{225}$ −15	12. $\sqrt{361}$ 19	13. $\pm\sqrt{169}$ ±13	14. $-\sqrt{1600}$ −40

Extra Example 5

Rewrite the given conditional statement in if-then form. Then tell whether the statement is true or false. If it is false, give a counterexample.

a. Given: No square roots are rational numbers. **If a number is a square root, then it is not a rational number. False; $\sqrt{16}$ is a rational number.**

b. Given: All integers are rational numbers. **If a number is an integer, then it is a rational number. True.**

Closing the Lesson

Have students summarize the major points of the lesson and answer the Essential Question: How do you evaluate a square root and compare real numbers?

- **All positive numbers have a positive and a negative square root.**
- **Square roots of positive integers or rational numbers that are not perfect squares are irrational numbers that can be approximated by nonrepeating decimals.**

To evaluate the square root of *a*, you need to find the number *b* such that $b^2 = a$. To compare real numbers, you can graph the numbers on a number line, using approximations for any square roots that are irrational numbers.

4 PRACTICE AND APPLY

Assignment Guide

Answer Transparencies available for all exercises

Basic:
Day 1: SRH p. 909 Exs. 11–17 odd
pp. 113–116
Exs. 1–10, 15–20, 23, 47–50, 56–63
Day 2: pp. 113–116
Exs. 24–37, 51–53, 64–71

Average:
Day 1: pp. 113–116
Exs. 1, 2, 7–14, 17–23, 47–50, 56–63
Day 2: pp. 113–116
Exs. 24–32 even, 34–45, 51–54, 65–71 odd

Advanced:
Day 1: pp. 113–116
Exs. 1, 2, 9–14, 19–23, 47–52, 56–62 even
Day 2: pp. 113–116
Exs. 26–32 even, 36–46*, 53–55*, 64–70 even

Block:
pp. 113–116
Exs. 1, 2, 7–14, 17–23, 24–32 even, 34–45, 47–54, 56–63, 65–71 odd

Differentiated Instruction

See *Algebra 1 Best Practices Toolkit* for suggestions on addressing the needs of a diverse classroom.

Homework Check

For a quick check of student understanding of key concepts, go over the following exercises:

Basic: 4, 16, 25, 30, 47
Average: 10, 20, 26, 30, 48
Advanced: 11, 21, 28, 32, 50

Extra Practice

- Student Edition, p. 939
- Chapter 2 Resource Book: Practice levels A, B, C, pp. 72–74

Practice Worksheet

An easily-readable reduced practice page (with answers) for this lesson can be found on p. 62D.

EXAMPLE 2 on p. 111 for Exs. 15–22

APPROXIMATING SQUARE ROOTS Approximate the square root to the nearest integer.

15. $\sqrt{10}$ 3
16. $-\sqrt{18}$ −4
17. $-\sqrt{3}$ −2
18. $\sqrt{150}$ 12
19. $-\sqrt{86}$ −9
20. $\sqrt{40}$ 6
21. $\sqrt{200}$ 14
22. $-\sqrt{65}$ −8

23. ★ **MULTIPLE CHOICE** Which number is between −30 and −25? B

Ⓐ $-\sqrt{1610}$ Ⓑ $-\sqrt{680}$ Ⓒ $-\sqrt{410}$ Ⓓ $-\sqrt{27}$

EXAMPLES 3 and 4 on p. 112 for Exs. 24–29

CLASSIFYING AND ORDERING REAL NUMBERS Tell whether each number in the list is a real number, a rational number, an irrational number, an integer, or a whole number. Then order the numbers from least to greatest.

24. $\sqrt{49}$, 8, $-\sqrt{4}$, −3 24–29. See margin.
25. $-\sqrt{12}$, −3.7, $\sqrt{9}$, 2.9
26. −11.5, $-\sqrt{121}$, −10, $\frac{25}{2}$, $\sqrt{144}$
27. $\sqrt{8}$, $-\frac{2}{5}$, −1, 0.6, $\sqrt{6}$
28. $-\frac{8}{3}$, $-\sqrt{5}$, 2.6, −1.5, $\sqrt{5}$
29. −8.3, $-\sqrt{80}$, $-\frac{17}{2}$, −8.25, $-\sqrt{100}$

EXAMPLE 5 on p. 113 for Exs. 30–33

ANALYZING CONDITIONAL STATEMENTS Rewrite the conditional statement in if-then form. Then tell whether the statement is *true* or *false*. If it is false, give a counterexample. 30–33. See margin.

30. All whole numbers are real numbers.
31. All real numbers are irrational numbers.
32. No perfect squares are whole numbers.
33. No irrational numbers are whole numbers.

B **EVALUATING EXPRESSIONS Evaluate the expression for the given value of *x*.**

34. $3 + \sqrt{x}$ when $x = 9$ 6
35. $11 - \sqrt{x}$ when $x = 81$ 2
36. $4 \cdot \sqrt{x}$ when $x = 49$ 28
37. $-7 \cdot \sqrt{x}$ when $x = 36$ −42
38. $-3 \cdot \sqrt{x} - 7$ when $x = 121$ −40
39. $6 \cdot \sqrt{x} + 3$ when $x = 100$ 63
40. $\frac{\sqrt{x}}{x}$ when $x = 4$ $\frac{1}{2}$
41. $\frac{\sqrt{x}}{5} - 17$ when $x = 25$ −16

42. ★ **OPEN-ENDED** Without using a calculator, find three rational numbers between $-\sqrt{26}$ and $-\sqrt{15}$. *Explain* how you found the numbers.

42. *Sample answer*: −5, −4.5, −4; $-\sqrt{26}$ is a little less than −5 and $-\sqrt{15}$ is a little more than −4, therefore −4, −4.5, and −5 are between $-\sqrt{26}$ and $-\sqrt{15}$.

43. ★ **MULTIPLE CHOICE** If $x = 36$, the value of which expression is a perfect square? B

Ⓐ $\sqrt{x} + 17$ Ⓑ $87 - \sqrt{x}$ Ⓒ $5 \cdot \sqrt{x}$ Ⓓ $8 \cdot \sqrt{x} + 2$

44. ★ **WRITING** Simplify $(\sqrt{x})^2$ for $x \geq 0$ using the definition of square root. Then verify your answer using several values of *x* that are perfect squares. See margin.

C 45. **CHALLENGE** Find the first five perfect squares *x* such that $2 \cdot \sqrt{x}$ is also a perfect square. *Describe* your method. 4, 64, 324, 1024, 2500; take $\frac{1}{2}$ of an even perfect square, and then square it.

46. **CHALLENGE** Let *n* be any whole number from 1 to 1000. For how many values of *n* is $\sqrt{n}$ a rational number? *Explain* your reasoning. 31; the square root of 1000 is between 31 and 32, so there are 31 perfect squares less than 1000.

◯ = WORKED-OUT SOLUTIONS on p. WS1 ★ = STANDARDIZED TEST PRACTICE

24–29. See Additional Answers beginning on p. AA1.

30. If a number is a whole number, then it is a real number; true.

31. If a number is a real number, then it is an irrational number; false. *Sample answer:* 3 is a real number and a rational number.

32. If a number is a perfect square, then it is not a whole number; false. *Sample answer:* 9 is a perfect square and a whole number.

33. If a number is an irrational number, then it is not a whole number; true.

PROBLEM SOLVING

EXAMPLE 1 on p. 110 for Exs. 47, 49

A

47. ART The area of a square painting is 3600 square inches. Find the side length of the painting. **60 in.**

@HomeTutor for problem solving help at classzone.com

EXAMPLE 2 on p. 111 for Exs. 48, 50

48. SOCCER Some soccer drills are practiced in a square section of a field. If the section of a field for a soccer drill is 1620 square yards, find the side length of the section. Round your answer to the nearest yard. **40 yd**

@HomeTutor for problem solving help at classzone.com

49. MAZES The table shows the locations and areas of various life-size square mazes. Find the side lengths of the mazes. Then tell whether the side lengths are *rational* or *irrational* numbers.
35 ft; 24 ft; 48 ft; 30 ft; they are all rational numbers.

Location of maze	Area (ft^2)
Dallas, Texas	1225
San Francisco, California	576
Corona, New York	2304
Waterville, Maine	900

Maze at Corona, New York

50. ★ SHORT RESPONSE You plan to use a square section of a park for a small outdoor concert. The section should have an area of 1450 square feet. You have 150 feet of rope to use to surround the section. Do you have enough rope? *Explain* your reasoning. **No; each side is a little more than 38 feet. 38 feet times 4 is 152 feet, which is more than 150 feet.**

51. MATH HISTORY To calculate the value of the irrational number π, the Greek mathematician Archimedes first estimated the square root of a certain integer x. He found that $\sqrt{x}$ was between $\frac{265}{153}$ and $\frac{1351}{780}$. Find the value of x. *Explain* how you got your answer.

51. 3; square each fraction, $\left(\frac{265}{153}\right)^2 < 3$, $\left(\frac{1351}{780}\right)^2 > 3$ so the value of x is 3.

B

52. MULTI-STEP PROBLEM The Kelvin temperature scale was invented by Lord Kelvin in the 19th century and is often used for scientific measurements. To convert a temperature from degrees Celsius (°C) to kelvin (K), you add 273 to the temperature in degrees Celsius.

a. Convert 17°C to kelvin. **290 K**

b. The speed s (in meters per second) of sound in air is given by the formula $s = 20.1 \cdot \sqrt{K}$ where K is the temperature in kelvin. Find the speed of sound in air at 17°C. Round your answer to the nearest meter per second. **342 m/sec**

53. ★ SHORT RESPONSE A homeowner is building a square patio and will cover the patio with square tiles. Each tile has an area of 256 square inches and costs $3.45. The homeowner has $500 to spend on tiles.

a. Calculate How many tiles can the homeowner buy? **144 tiles**

b. Explain Find the side length (in feet) of the largest patio that the homeowner can build. *Explain* how you got your answer. **See margin.**

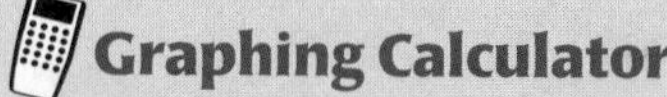

Graphing Calculator

Exercises 15–23 It may be helpful for students to use calculators to approximate the square roots. Tell them to use the instructions on how to approximate square roots on page 111.

Teaching Strategy

Exercise 42 For students who have difficulty with this exercise, suggest they first identify the opposites of the perfect squares closest to 26 and 15.

Study Strategy

Exercise 48 Students may be tempted to use their calculators to solve this problem. Encourage them to use their calculators to check their answers, but use the solution model for Example 2 to solve the problem. Explain that by using the model, they will develop a better understanding of square roots. By learning to approximate the square root of a number, they will develop estimation skills that can help them judge whether they entered numbers in their calculators incorrectly.

Avoiding Common Errors

Exercise 52 Some students overlook the different parts of a problem and then make errors because they lack information necessary to solve the problem. Some students may use 17°C for K in part b of this exercise. Remind students to read all parts of a problem before proceeding.

53b. 16 ft. *Sample answer:* If the homeowner can buy 144 tiles that are each 256 square inches, then the total area is (144 tiles) • (256 square inches per tile) = 36,864 square inches. Divide 36,864 square inches by 144 square inches to find the number of square feet, 256 square feet. If the area of the square is 256 square feet, take the square root of 256 to find the side length, 16 feet.

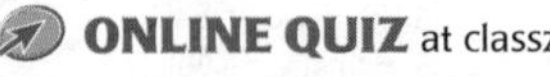

5 ASSESS AND RETEACH

Daily Homework Quiz

Transparency Available

Evaluate the expression.

1. $\pm\sqrt{289}$ ±17
2. $-\sqrt{36}$ −6

Approximate the square root to the nearest integer.

3. $-\sqrt{21}$ −5
4. $\sqrt{620}$ 25
5. A square courtyard has an area of 272 square feet. What is the side length of the courtyard to the nearest foot? 16 ft

Online Quiz

Available at **classzone.com**

Diagnosis/Remediation

- Practice A, B, C in Chapter 2 Resource Book, pp. 72–74
- Study Guide in Chapter 2 Resource Book, pp. 75–76
- Practice Workbook, pp. 28–29
- @HomeTutor

Challenge

Additional challenge is available in the Chapter 2 Resource Book, p. 79.

Quiz

An easily-readable reduced copy of the quiz (with answers) on Lessons 2.6–2.7 from the Assessment Book can be found on p. 62E.

54a. See Additional Answers beginning on p. AA1.

Quiz

6. −3: real number, rational number, integer, $-\sqrt{5}$: real number, irrational number, −3.7: real number, rational number, $\sqrt{3}$: real number, rational number; −3.7, −3, $-\sqrt{5}$, $\sqrt{3}$

54. **MULTIPLE REPRESENTATIONS** The diagram shows the approximate areas (in square meters) of the square bases for the pyramids of Giza.

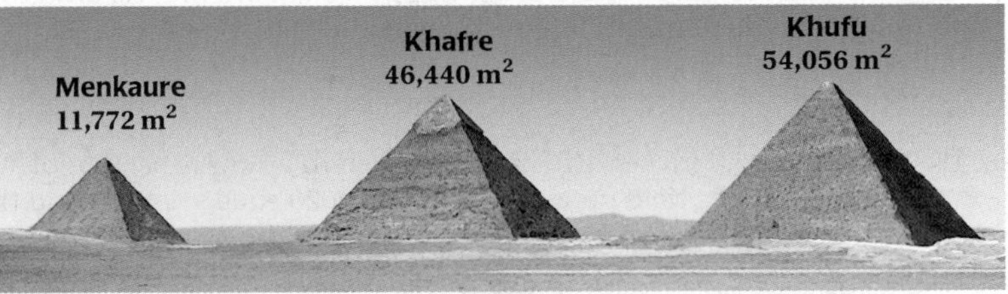

a. **Making a Table** Make a table that gives the following quotients (rounded to the nearest tenth) for each of the 3 pairs of pyramids:
- (area of larger base) ÷ (area of smaller base)
- (side length of larger base) ÷ (side length of smaller base)

For each pair of pyramids, how are the two quotients related?

b. **Writing an Equation** Write an equation that gives the quotient q of the side lengths as a function of the quotient r of the areas.

55. **CHALLENGE** Write an equation that gives the edge length ℓ of a cube as a function of the surface area A of the cube.

ILLINOIS MIXED REVIEW

TEST PRACTICE at classzone.com

56. The graph of a function contains the point (4, 6). Which of the following could NOT be a rule for the function?

Ⓐ $y = x + 2$ Ⓑ $y = \frac{2x}{3}$ Ⓒ $y = 3x - 6$ Ⓓ $y = 4x - 10$

57. A cup in the shape of a cylinder has a height of 6 centimeters, and its base has a radius of 3 centimeters. How much water will fill the cup?

Ⓐ 12π cm³ Ⓑ 18π cm³ Ⓒ 36π cm³ Ⓓ 54π cm³

QUIZ for Lessons 2.6–2.7

Find the quotient. *(p. 103)*

1. $-20 \div (-5)$
2. $-12 \div \frac{2}{3}$
3. $\frac{4}{5} \div \left(-\frac{3}{10}\right)$
4. $-18.2 \div (-3)$
5. Simplify the expression $\frac{15x - 6}{3}$. *(p. 103)*
6. Tell whether each of the following numbers is a real number, a rational number, an irrational number, an integer, or a whole number: −3, $-\sqrt{5}$, −3.7, $\sqrt{3}$. Then order the numbers from least to greatest. *(p. 110)*
7. Rewrite the following conditional statement in if-then form: "No irrational numbers are negative numbers." Tell whether the statement is *true* or *false*. If it is false, give a counterexample. *(p. 110)*

Use Logical Reasoning

Use after Lesson 2.7

GOAL Use inductive and deductive reasoning.

Key Vocabulary
- **inductive reasoning**
- **conjecture**
- **deductive reasoning**

When you make a conclusion based on several examples, you are using **inductive reasoning**. A conclusion reached using inductive reasoning is an example of a *conjecture*. A **conjecture** is a statement that is believed to be true but not yet shown to be true.

EXAMPLE 1 Use inductive reasoning

Your friend asks you to perform the following number trick: *Choose any number. Then double the number. Then add 8. Then multiply by 3. Then divide by 6. Then subtract 4.* Perform the number trick for three different numbers. Then make a conjecture based on the results.

Solution

Step 1: Choose any number.	Choose 5.	Choose 14.	Choose −6.
Step 2: Double the number.	10	28	−12
Step 3: Add 8.	18	36	−4
Step 4: Multiply by 3.	54	108	−12
Step 5: Divide by 6.	9	18	−2
Step 6: Subtract 4.	5	14	−6

Conjecture: The result in Step 6 is the same as the number in Step 1.

EXAMPLE 2 Show that a conjecture is true

Show that the conjecture made in Example 1 is true for all numbers x.

Solution

Step 1: Choose any number.	Choose x.
Step 2: Double the number.	$2x$
Step 3: Add 8.	$2x + 8$
Step 4: Multiply by 3.	$3(2x + 8) = 6x + 24$
Step 5: Divide by 6.	$\frac{6x + 24}{6} = x + 4$
Step 6: Subtract 4.	$(x + 4) - 4 = x$

The result in Step 6 is the same as the number chosen in Step 1. So, the conjecture made in Example 1 is true for all numbers x.

1 PLAN AND PREPARE

Warm-Up Exercises

Tell whether each statement is *true* or *false*. If it is false, give a counterexample.

1. If a number is negative, then it is a rational number. False; $-\sqrt{20}$ is a negative number and it is not rational.
2. If a number is an integer, then it is not a whole number. False; 7 is an integer and also a whole number.

2 FOCUS AND MOTIVATE

Essential Question

Big Idea 3, p. 63

How do you use reasoning with real numbers? Tell students they will learn how to answer this question by analyzing and proving conjectures.

3 TEACH

Extra Example 1

Choose any number. Then double it. Then subtract 4. Then multiply by 5. Then divide by 10. Then add 2. Perform the number trick for three different numbers. Then make a conjecture based on the results. Conjecture: The result in Step 6 is the same as the number in Step 1.

NCTM STANDARDS

Standard 7: Make mathematical conjectures; Investigate mathematical conjectures

Extra Example 2

Show that the conjecture in Example 1 is true for all numbers x.

Step 1: Choose x.

Step 2: $2x$

Step 3: $2x - 4$

Step 4: $5(2x - 4) = 10x - 20$

Step 5: $\frac{10x - 20}{10} = x - 2$

Step 6: $(x - 2) + 2 = x$

Extra Example 3

Show that $\frac{5(2x - 4)}{10} + 2 = x$. Justify each step.

$$\frac{5(2x - 4)}{10} + 2 = \frac{10x - 20}{10} + 2$$
$$= (x - 2) + 2$$
$$= (x + (-2)) + 2$$
$$= x + (-2 + 2)$$
$$= x + 0$$
$$= x$$

Justifications:

Step 1: Distributive property

Step 2: Divide $10x - 20$ by 10.

Step 3: Subtraction rule

Step 4: Associative property of addition

Step 5: Inverse property of addition

Step 6: Identity property of addition

Closing the Lesson

Have students summarize the major points of the lesson and answer the Essential Question: How do you use reasoning with real numbers?

- Inductive reasoning uses examples to draw conclusions.
- Deductive reasoning uses true statements, whether assumed true or shown to be true, to draw conclusions.
- A conjecture is a conclusion based on inductive reasoning.

You can use inductive and deductive methods to analyze statements about real numbers and determine if they are true or false.

DEDUCTIVE REASONING In Example 2, you simplified the expression at each step. Had you not done this, you would have obtained the expression $\frac{3(2x + 8)}{6} - 4$. You can still show that $\frac{3(2x + 8)}{6} - 4 = x$ by applying *deductive reasoning*. When you make a conclusion based on statements that are assumed or shown to be true, you are using **deductive reasoning**.

EXAMPLE 3 Use deductive reasoning

Show that $\frac{3(2x + 8)}{6} - 4 = x$. Justify each step.

Solution

Step	Justification
$\frac{3(2x + 8)}{6} - 4 = \frac{6x + 24}{6} - 4$	Distributive property
$= (x + 4) - 4$	Divide $(6x + 24)$ by 6.
$= (x + 4) + (-4)$	Subtraction rule
$= x + [4 + (-4)]$	Associative property of addition
$= x + 0$	Inverse property of addition
$= x$	Identity property of addition

PRACTICE

EXAMPLES 1, 2, and 3 on pp. 117–118 for Exs. 1–3

In Exercises 1 and 2, perform the given number trick for three numbers. Make a conjecture based on the results. Then show that your conjecture is true for all numbers. 1, 2. See margin.

1. Choose any number. Then subtract 5. Then multiply by 6. Then divide by 3. Then add 10.

2. Choose any number. Then double it. Then add 12. Then multiply by 4. Then divide by 8. Then subtract the number you chose.

3. The steps below show that $\frac{4(3x + 5) - 20}{12} = x$. *Justify* each step.

Step	Justification
$\frac{4(3x + 5) - 20}{12} = \frac{(12x + 20) - 20}{12}$	? Distributive property
$= \frac{(12x + 20) + (-20)}{12}$	? Subtraction rule
$= \frac{12x + [20 + (-20)]}{12}$	? Associative property of addition
$= \frac{12x + 0}{12}$	? Inverse property of addition
$= \frac{12x}{12}$	? Identity property of addition
$= x$	? Divide

4 PRACTICE AND APPLY

Avoiding Common Errors

Exercises 1–2 Students sometimes skip steps and then cannot prove their conclusions. Tell students to follow the step-by-step solutions offered in the three examples.

1. *Sample answer:* $3 - 5 = -2$, $-2(6) = -12$, $-12 \div 3 = -4$, $-4 + 10 = 6$; $-2 - 5 = -7$, $-7(6) = -42$, $-42 \div 3 = -14$, $-14 + 10 = -4$; $10 - 5 = 5$, $5(6) = 30$, $30 \div 3 = 10$, $10 + 10 = 20$; double the number; $\frac{(x - 5)6}{3} + 10 = (x - 5)2 + 10 = 2x - 10 + 10 = 2x$

2. *Sample answer:* $4(2) = 8$, $8 + 12 = 20$, $20(4) = 80$, $80 \div 8 = 10$, $10 - 4 = 6$; $(-5)(2) = 10$, $-10 + 12 = 2$, $2(4) = 8$, $8 \div 8 = 1$, $1 - (-5) = 6$; $10(2) = 20$, $20 + 12 = 32$, $32(4) = 128$, $128 \div 8 = 16$, $16 - 10 = 6$; the answer will be 6; $\frac{(2x + 12)4}{8} - x = \frac{8x + 48}{8} - x = x + 6 - x = 6$.

TEST PRACTICE
classzone.com

Lessons 2.4–2.7

1. **FARMING** A farmer is planting corn and soybeans in the rectangular field shown. The farmer spends \$.09 per square yard to plant corn and \$.07 per square yard to plant soybeans. How much money will the farmer spend on planting if the soybean section has a length of 300 yards?

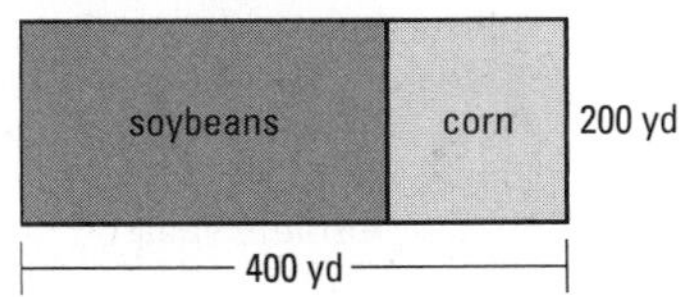

A. \$6000 **C.** \$10,400
B. \$6800 **D.** \$11,000

2. **PENTATHLON** The modern pentathlon consists of 5 events, including a distance run. For the men's run, each athlete starts with 1000 points and earns 2 points for every 0.5 second under a finishing time of 10 minutes and −2 points for every 0.5 second over a finishing time of 10 minutes. If an athlete finishes the run in 10 minutes 34 seconds, how many points does he earn?

F. 864 points
G. 932 points
H. 1068 points
J. 1136 points

3. **BASEBALL** The table shows the average cost of three items at a baseball stadium in 2002 and 2004. What is the change in the average amount spent from 2002 to 2004 if 2 of each item are bought?

Item	Cost in 2002	Cost in 2004
Ticket	\$20.44	\$17.90
Soda	\$2.75	\$2.00
Hot dog	\$2.75	\$2.75

A. −\$3.29 **C.** −\$6.58
B. −\$5.08 **D.** −\$7.88

4. **STORAGE BINS** Your friend is comparing two 6-sided cubic storage bins. The yellow bin has a surface area of 96 square feet and costs \$23.04. The blue bin has a surface area of 73.5 square feet and costs \$17.15. Which bin costs less per cubic foot and by approximately how much less than the other bin?

F. The yellow bin, by \$.04/ft^3
G. The yellow bin, by \$.01/ft^3
H. The blue bin, by \$.04/ft^3
J. The blue bin, by \$.01/ft^3

5. **TROPOSPHERE** The troposphere is the lowest layer of Earth's atmosphere. The temperature at Earth's surface is approximately 15°C and changes by about −0.0065°C for every meter of increase in elevation. What is the approximate temperature of the troposphere at 10,000 meters above the surface?

A. −65°C **C.** −6.5°C
B. −50°C **D.** 8.5°C

6. **AQUARIUM** A designer is creating an aquarium in the shape of a rectangular prism with a square base. The aquarium will have a height of 35 centimeters and a volume of 17,500 cubic centimeters. Which of the following is the best approximation of the side length of the base?

F. 20 cm **H.** 23 cm
G. 22 cm **J.** 25 cm

7. **RUGS** The table shows the areas of two square rugs. How many inches longer is the side length of the sorrel rug than the side length of the shaw rug?

Type of rug	Area (in.^{2})
Sorrel rug	8281
Shaw rug	7744

A. −537 inches **C.** 3 inches
B. −3 inches **D.** 537 inches

Illinois Mixed Review

1. A
2. F
3. C
4. F
5. B
6. G
7. C

Additional Resources

The following resources are available to help review the materials in this chapter.

Chapter 2 Resource Book

- Chapter Review Games and Activities, p. 80
- Cumulative Practice, Chs. 1–2, pp. 83–84

Student Resources in Spanish

eWorkbook

@HomeTutor

Vocabulary Practice

Vocabulary practice is available at **classzone.com**

2 CHAPTER SUMMARY

BIG IDEAS *For Your Notebook*

Big Idea 1

Performing Operations with Real Numbers

To add or multiply two real numbers *a* and *b*, you can use the following rules:

Expression	Rule when *a* and *b* have the same sign	Rule when *a* and *b* have different signs
$a + b$	Add $\lvert a \rvert$ and $\lvert b \rvert$. The sum has the same sign as *a* and *b*.	Subtract the lesser absolute value from the greater absolute value. The sum has the same sign as the number with the greater absolute value.
ab	The product is positive.	The product is negative.

You can use these rules to subtract or divide numbers, but first you rewrite the difference or quotient using the subtraction rule or the division rule.

Big Idea 2

Applying Properties of Real Numbers

You can apply the properties of real numbers to evaluate and simplify expressions. Many of the properties of addition and multiplication are similar.

Property	Addition	Multiplication
Commutative property	$a + b = b + a$	$ab = ba$
Associative property	$(a + b) + c = a + (b + c)$	$(ab)c = a(bc)$
Identity property	$a + 0 = 0 + a = a$	$a \cdot 1 = 1 \cdot a = a$
Inverse property	$a + (-a) = -a + a = 0$	$a \cdot \frac{1}{a} = \frac{1}{a} \cdot a = 1, a \neq 0$
Distributive property	$a(b + c) = ab + ac$ (and three variations)	

Big Idea 3

Classifying and Reasoning with Real Numbers

Being able to classify numbers can help you tell whether a conditional statement about real numbers is true or false. For example, the following statement is false: "All real numbers are integers." A counterexample is 3.5.

Numbers	Description
Whole numbers	The numbers 0, 1, 2, 3, 4, . . .
Integers	The numbers . . . , −3, −2, −1, 0, 1, 2, 3, . . .
Rational numbers	Numbers of the form $\frac{a}{b}$ where *a* and *b* are integers and $b \neq 0$
Irrational numbers	Numbers that cannot be written as a quotient of two integers
Real numbers	All rational and irrational numbers

2 CHAPTER REVIEW

@HomeTutor
classzone.com
• Multi-Language Glossary
• Vocabulary practice

REVIEW KEY VOCABULARY

- whole numbers, integers, positive integer, negative integer, *p. 64*
- rational number, *p. 64*
- opposites, absolute value, *p. 66*
- conditional statement, *p. 66*
- if-then statement, *p. 66*
- counterexample, *p. 66*
- additive identity, *p. 76*
- additive inverse, *p. 76*
- multiplicative identity, *p. 89*
- equivalent expressions, *p. 96*
- distributive property, *p. 96*
- term, coefficient, constant term, like terms, *p. 97*
- multiplicative inverse, *p. 103*
- square root, radicand, *p. 110*
- perfect square, *p. 111*
- irrational number, *p. 111*
- real numbers, *p. 112*

VOCABULARY EXERCISES

Identify the terms, coefficients, constant terms, and like terms of the expression. 1, 2. See margin.

1. $-3x - 5 - 7x - 9$ **2.** $-10c - 6 + c$

Tell whether the number is a real number, a rational number, an irrational number, an integer, or a whole number.

3. 0.3 real number, rational number

4. $-\sqrt{8}$ real number, irrational number

5. -15 real number, rational number, integer

6. $\sqrt{49}$ real number, rational number, integer, whole number

REVIEW EXAMPLES AND EXERCISES

Use the review examples and exercises below to check your understanding of the concepts you have learned in each lesson of Chapter 2.

2.1 Use Integers and Rational Numbers pp. 64–67

EXAMPLE

Order the following numbers from least to greatest: $\frac{1}{5}$, −0.10, 0.25, $-\frac{1}{6}$.

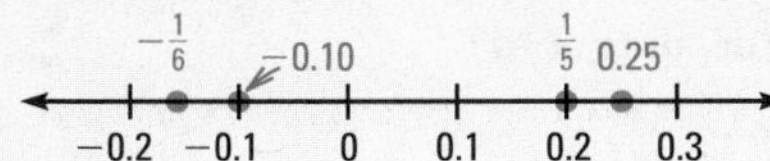

From least to greatest, the numbers are $-\frac{1}{6}$, −0.10, $\frac{1}{5}$, and 0.25.

EXERCISES

EXAMPLES 3, 4, and 5 on pp. 65–66 for Exs. 7–12

Order the numbers in the list from least to greatest.

7. $-5.2, -\frac{3}{8}, -6, 0.3, -\frac{1}{4}$ $-6, -5.2, -\frac{3}{8}, -\frac{1}{4}, 0.3$

8. $2.1, 0, -\frac{13}{10}, -1.38, \frac{3}{5}$ $-1.38, -\frac{13}{10}, 0, \frac{3}{5}, 2.1$

For the given value of *a*, find $-a$ and $|a|$.

9. $a = -0.2$ 0.2, 0.2

10. $a = 3$ −3, 3

11. $a = \frac{7}{8}$ $-\frac{7}{8}, \frac{7}{8}$

12. $a = -\frac{6}{11}$ $\frac{6}{11}, \frac{6}{11}$

Extra Example 2.1

Order the following numbers from least to greatest: −1.3, 0.15, $-\frac{1}{3}$, $\frac{1}{8}$, −0.2. −1.3, $-\frac{1}{3}$, −0.2, $\frac{1}{8}$, 0.15

1. terms: $-3x$, −5, $-7x$, −9; coefficients: −3, −7; constant terms: −5, −9; like terms: $-3x$ and $-7x$, −5 and −9

2. terms: $-10c$, −6, c; coefficients: −10, 1; constant terms: −6; like terms: $-10c$ and c

Extra Example 2.2

Find the sum.

a. $-12.8 + 6$ -6.8

b. $\frac{5}{8} + \left(-\frac{3}{4}\right)$ $-\frac{1}{8}$

Extra Example 2.3

Find the difference.

a. $-14 - 8$ -22

b. $6.3 - (-2.9)$ 9.2

2 CHAPTER REVIEW

2.2 Add Real Numbers

pp. 74–76

EXAMPLE

Find the sum.

a. $-3.6 + (-5.5) = -(|-3.6| + |-5.5|)$ **Rule of same signs**

$= -(3.6 + 5.5)$ **Take absolute values.**

$= -9.1$ **Add.**

b. $16.1 + (-9.3) = |16.1| - |-9.3|$ **Rule of different signs**

$= 16.1 - 9.3$ **Take absolute values.**

$= 6.8$ **Subtract.**

EXERCISES

EXAMPLES 1, 2, and 4 on pp. 74–76 for Exs. 13–19

Find the sum.

13. $-2 + 5$ 3 **14.** $-6 + (-4)$ -10 **15.** $6.2 + (-9.7)$ -3.5

16. $-4.61 + (-0.79)$ -5.4 **17.** $-\frac{4}{7} + \left(-\frac{9}{14}\right)$ $-1\frac{3}{14}$ **18.** $-\frac{4}{5} + \frac{11}{12}$ $\frac{7}{60}$

19. BUSINESS A company has a profit of \$2.07 million in its first year, −\$1.54 million in its second year, and −\$.76 million in its third year. Find the company's total profit for the three years. −\$.23 million

2.3 Subtract Real Numbers

pp. 80–81

EXAMPLE

Find the difference.

a. $12 - 19 = 12 + (-19)$ **Add the opposite of 19.**

$= -7$ **Simplify.**

b. $8.2 - (-1.6) = 8.2 + 1.6$ **Add the opposite of −1.6.**

$= 9.8$ **Simplify.**

EXERCISES

EXAMPLES 1 and 2 on p. 80 for Exs. 20–28

Find the difference.

20. $-8 - 3$ -11 **21.** $1 - 11$ -10 **22.** $7.7 - 16.3$ -8.6

23. $-20.3 - (-14.2)$ -6.1 **24.** $\frac{7}{3} - \frac{11}{3}$ $-1\frac{1}{3}$ **25.** $-\frac{4}{9} - \frac{5}{12}$ $-\frac{31}{36}$

Evaluate the expression when $x = 2$ and $y = -3$.

26. $(x - 7) + y$ -8 **27.** $\frac{3}{2} - x - y$ $2\frac{1}{2}$ **28.** $y - (2.4 - x)$ -3.4

2.4 Multiply Real Numbers

pp. 88–90

EXAMPLE

Find the product.

a. $-4(12) = -48$ — **Different signs; product is negative.**

b. $\frac{1}{2}(-6)(-3) = -3(-3)$ — **Multiply $\frac{1}{2}$ and -6.**

$= 9$ — **Same signs; product is positive.**

EXERCISES

EXAMPLES 1, 3, and 4 on pp. 88–90 for Exs. 29–35

Find the product.

29. $15(-4)$ -60 **30.** $-7.5(-8)$ 60 **31.** $-\frac{2}{5}(-5)(-9)$ -18

Find the product. *Justify* your steps. 32–34. See margin.

32. $-4(-y)(-7)$ **33.** $-\frac{1}{3}x \cdot (-18)$ **34.** $2.5(-4z)(-2)$

35. SWIMMING POOLS The water level of a swimming pool is 3.3 feet and changes at an average rate of -0.14 feet per day due to water evaporation. What will the water level of the pool be after 4 days? 2.74 ft

2.5 Apply the Distributive Property

pp. 96–98

EXAMPLE

Use the distributive property to write an equivalent expression.

a. $5(x + 3) = 5(x) + 5(3)$ — **Distribute 5.**

$= 5x + 15$ — **Simplify.**

b. $(7 - y)(-2y) = 7(-2y) - y(-2y)$ — **Distribute $-2y$.**

$= -14y + 2y^2$ — **Simplify.**

EXERCISES

EXAMPLES 1, 2, 4, and 5 on pp. 96–98 for Exs. 36–42

Use the distributive property to write an equivalent expression.

36. $8(5 - x)$ $40 - 8x$ **37.** $-3(y + 9)$ $-3y - 27$ **38.** $(z - 4)(-z)$ $-z^2 + 4z$

Simplify the expression.

39. $3(x - 2) + 14$ $3x + 8$ **40.** $9.1 - 4(m + 3.2)$ $-3.7 - 4m$ **41.** $5n + \frac{1}{2}(8n - 7)$ $9n - 3\frac{1}{2}$

42. PARTY COSTS You are buying 10 pizzas for a party. Cheese pizzas cost $11 each, and single topping pizzas cost $13 each. Write an equation that gives the total cost C (in dollars) as a function of the number p of cheese pizzas that you buy. Then find the total cost if you buy 4 cheese pizzas. $C = -2p + 130$; $122

Extra Example 2.4

Find the product.

a. $-8(-2.5)$ 20

b. $-\frac{1}{3}(9)(2)$ -6

Extra Example 2.5

Use the distributive property to write an equivalent expression.

a. $-6(y - 2)$ $-6y + 12$

b. $(5 - x)(-x)$ $-5x + x^2$

32. $-28y$; $-4(-y)(-7) = -4(-7)(-y)$, commutative property of multiplication; $28(-y)$, product of -4 and -7; $-28y$, multiply

33. $6x$; $-\frac{1}{3}x \cdot (-18) = -\frac{1}{3}(-18)(x)$, commutative property of multiplication; $6(x)$, product of $-\frac{1}{3}$ and -18; $6x$, multiply

34. $20z$; $2.5(-4z)(-2) = 2.5(-2)(-4z)$, commutative property of multiplication, $-5(-4z)$, product of 2.5 and -2; $[(-5)(-4)]z$, associative property of multiplication, $20z$, multiply

Extra Example 2.6

Find the quotient.

a. $-112 \div (-8)$ 14

b. $\frac{12}{21} \div \left(-\frac{6}{7}\right)$ $-\frac{2}{3}$

Extra Example 2.7

Order the following numbers from least to greatest: $\sqrt{12}$, 3.8, $-\sqrt{64}$, -8.2, 3. $-8.2, -\sqrt{64}, 3, \sqrt{12}, 3.8$

2.6 Divide Real Numbers

pp. 103–105

EXAMPLE

Find the quotient.

a. $196 \div (-7) = 196 \cdot \left(-\frac{1}{7}\right)$

$= -28$

b. $-\frac{14}{15} \div \left(-\frac{7}{3}\right) = -\frac{14}{15} \cdot \left(-\frac{3}{7}\right)$

$= \frac{2}{5}$

EXERCISES

EXAMPLES 2, 3, and 4 on pp. 104–105 for Exs. 43–49

Find the quotient.

43. $56 \div (-4)$ -14

44. $-6 \div \frac{3}{13}$ -26

45. $-\frac{4}{9} \div \left(-\frac{2}{3}\right)$ $\frac{2}{3}$

46. SCIENCE A scientist studies the diving abilities of three seals and records the elevations they reach before swimming back up to the surface. Find the mean of the following elevations (in meters) recorded: −380, −307, −354. −347 m

Simplify the expression.

47. $\frac{24x - 40}{8}$ $3x - 5$

48. $\frac{-36m + 18}{6}$ $-6m + 3$

49. $\frac{-18n - 9}{-9}$ $2n + 1$

2.7 Find Square Roots and Compare Real Numbers

pp. 110–113

EXAMPLE

Order the following numbers from least to greatest: $\sqrt{25}$, $-\sqrt{18}$, −4, 3.2.

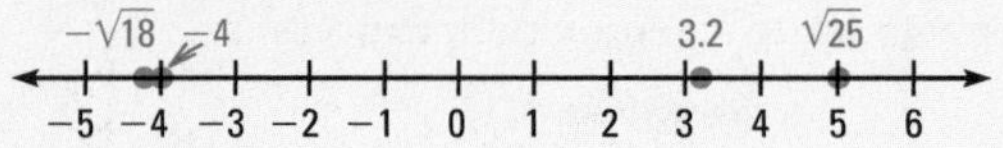

From least to greatest, the numbers are $-\sqrt{18}$, −4, 3.2, and $\sqrt{25}$.

EXERCISES

EXAMPLES 1, 2, 4, and 5 on pp. 110–113 for Exs. 50–60

Evaluate the expression.

50. $\sqrt{121}$ 11

51. $-\sqrt{36}$ -6

52. $\pm\sqrt{81}$ ± 9

53. $\pm\sqrt{225}$ ± 15

Approximate the square root to the nearest integer.

54. $\sqrt{97}$ 10

55. $-\sqrt{48}$ -7

56. $-\sqrt{142}$ -12

57. $\sqrt{300}$ 17

Order the numbers in the list from least to greatest.

58. $-\sqrt{49}$, −6.8, 2, $\sqrt{3}$, 1.58
$-\sqrt{49}$, −6.8, 1.58, $\sqrt{3}$, 2

59. 1.25, $\sqrt{11}$, −0.3, 0, $-\sqrt{4}$
$-\sqrt{4}$, −0.3, 0, 1.25, $\sqrt{11}$

60. Rewrite the following conditional statement in if-then form: "All real numbers are irrational numbers." Tell whether the statement is *true* or *false*. If it is false, give a counterexample. If a number is a real number, then it is irrational; false. *Sample answer:* 5 is a real number and it is rational.

2 CHAPTER TEST

Tell whether the number is a real number, a rational number, an irrational number, an integer, or a whole number.

1. $-\frac{1}{4}$ real number, rational number
2. $\sqrt{90}$ real number, irrational number
3. $-\sqrt{144}$ real number, rational number, integer
4. 8.95 real number, rational number

Order the numbers in the list from least to greatest.

5. $-\frac{5}{3}, -2, 3, \frac{1}{2}, -1.07$ $-2, -\frac{5}{3}, -1.07, \frac{1}{2}, 3$
6. $\sqrt{15}, -4.3, 4.2, 0, -\sqrt{25}$ $-\sqrt{25}, -4.3, 0, \sqrt{15}, 4.2$

Find the sum, difference, product, or quotient.

7. $-5 + 2$ -3
8. $1.3 + (-10.4)$ -9.1
9. $-\frac{1}{3} + \frac{1}{6}$ $-\frac{1}{6}$
10. $-\frac{2}{7} - \frac{5}{14}$ $-\frac{9}{14}$
11. $-41 - 32$ -73
12. $7.2 - (-11.6)$ 18.8
13. $-11(-7)$ 77
14. $-4.5(20)(2)$ -180
15. $-\frac{1}{5}(-20)(-5)$ -20
16. $-36 \div (-6)$ 6
17. $-\frac{3}{5} \div 12$ $-\frac{1}{20}$
18. $5 \div \left(-\frac{10}{11}\right)$ $-5\frac{1}{2}$

Evaluate the expression when $x = -6$ and $y = -10$.

19. $-x$ 6
20. $|y|$ 10
21. $8 - (x - y)$ 4
22. $-4x + y$ 14

Simplify the expression.

23. $-9(y - 7)$ $-9y + 63$
24. $8(x - 4) - 10x$ $-2x - 32$
25. $\frac{-7w - 21}{7}$ $-w - 3$
26. $\frac{-16v + 8}{-4}$ $4v - 2$

In Exercises 27 and 28, rewrite the conditional statement in if-then form. Then tell whether the statement is *true* or *false*. If it is false, give a counterexample.

27. No rational numbers are integers. If a number is rational, then it is not an integer; false. *Sample answer:* -2 is a rational number and an integer.
28. All irrational numbers are real numbers. If a number is irrational, then it is a real number; true.
29. **MUSIC** The revenue from sales of digital pianos in the United States was \$152.4 million in 2001 and \$149.0 million in 2002. Find the change in revenue from 2001 to 2002. $-\$3.4$ million
30. **ELEVATORS** An elevator moves at a rate of -5.8 feet per second from a height of 300 feet above the ground. It takes 3 seconds for the elevator to make its first stop. How many feet above the ground is the elevator now? 282.6 ft
31. **SUMMER JOBS** You plan to work a total of 25 hours per week at two summer jobs. You will earn \$8.75 per hour working at a cafe and \$10.50 per hour working at an auto shop. Write an equation that gives your weekly pay p (in dollars) as a function of the time t (in hours) spent working at the cafe. Then find your weekly pay if you work 10 hours at the cafe. $p = -1.75t + 262.5$; \$245
32. **TEMPERATURES** The low temperatures for Montreal, Quebec, in Canada on February 12 for each year during the period 2000–2004 are −6.7°F, −4.2°F, 4.1°F, −3.6°F, and 0.3°F. Find the mean of the temperatures. −2.02°F

Additional Resources

Assessment Book

- Chapter Test, Levels A, B, C, pp. 19–24
- Standardized Chapter Test, pp. 25–26
- SAT/ACT Chapter Test, pp. 27–28
- Alternative Assessment, pp. 29–30

Test Generator CD-ROM

Chapter Test

Easily-readable reduced copies (with answers) of Chapter Test B, the Standardized Chapter Test, and the Alternative Assessment from the Assessment Book can be found on pp. 62E–62F.

REVIEWING PROBLEM SOLVING

Many math problems require the ability to decide what action needs to be taken, recognize appropriate answers, and explain conclusions using mathematical language. Some problems may ask you to:

- identify the calculation that solves the problem
- determine the next step in the solution process
- justify your answer using mathematical properties
- select an answer that is reasonable given the constraints of the problem

EXAMPLE

The *Alvin* is an HOV (human-operated vehicle) used to explore the ocean. A new HOV is being built that will carry explorers deeper and faster. The table shows the capabilities of the two vehicles.

Vehicle	Lowest elevation (m)	Velocity (m/sec)
Alvin	−4500	−30
New HOV	−6500	−44

If both vehicles begin diving from the surface of the ocean at the same time and dive for 90 seconds, what is the difference in elevation between the two vehicles?

A. −6660 meters **B.** −3690 meters **C.** −2700 meters **D.** −1260 meters

STEP 1 **Write** a verbal model that you can use to find the elevation of each of the vehicles.

Number of seconds × Velocity of vehicle = Elevation of vehicle

STEP 2 **Calculate** the elevation for each of the vehicles.

Alvin: 90 seconds × (–30 m/sec) = e

−2700 m = e

New HOV: 90 seconds × (–44 m/sec) = e

−3960 m = e

STEP 3 **Calculate** the difference in the elevation of the vehicles.

$-3960 - (-2700) = -3960 + 2760 = -1260$ meters

The new HOV will be at an elevation of −1260 meters greater than Alvin.

PROBLEM SOLVING

Below are examples that test problem solving skills in multiple choice format. Try solving the problems before looking at the solutions. (Cover the solutions with a piece of paper.) Then check your solutions against the ones given.

1. Which description does *not* apply to $-\sqrt{9}$?

A. Real number

B. Whole number

C. Integer

D. Rational number

Solution

Start by solving for the square root of 9. The square root of nine is 3. There is a negative in front of the square root, so the answer is −3. Of the choices given, whole numbers do not include negative numbers.

The correct answer is **B**.

2. If the variables x and y represent integers and $xy = 24$, then which of the following could *not* be true?

F. $x = 6$

G. $x < y - 10$

H. $y < 0$

J. $x = y$

Solution

There is no integer which when multiplied by itself equals 24. So, x cannot equal y.

The correct answer is **J**.

3. A square parcel of land has an area of a square feet. Which expression gives the perimeter of the land?

A. $\frac{a}{4}$

B. $\sqrt{a}$

C. $4 \cdot \sqrt{a}$

D. None of the above

Solution

The perimeter of the square parcel of land is 4 times its side length. Each side of the square has a length of $\sqrt{a}$, so the perimeter is $4 \cdot \sqrt{a}$.

The correct answer is **C**.

4. Which of the following expressions is equivalent to the expression $-p(4p - 4)$?

F. $4p^2 - 4p$

G. $4p^2 + 4p$

H. $-4p^2 + 4p$

J. $-4p^2 - 4p$.

Solution

Use the distributive property to write the equivalent expression. The product of $-p$ and $4p$ is $-4p^2$. The product of $-p$ and -4 is $4p$. The sum of these two terms is $-4p^2 + 4p$.

The correct answer is **H**.

TEST PREPARATION

Illinois Test Practice

1. C
2. H
3. B
4. G
5. D
6. G
7. A
8. G
9. A
10. J
11. B
12. G
13. D
14. H
15. B
16. G
17. C
18. J

Illinois Test Practice

1. What is the value of the expression $-2.6x + |-6.1| - y$ when $x = 2.1$ and $y = 2$?

   A. -13.56

   B. -9.56

   C. -1.36

   D. 9.56

2. You have a plane ticket for a flight that departs at 1:30 P.M. You must get to the airport 1 hour before departure, and it takes 45 minutes to reach the airport from your house. Which of the following is the most reasonable time to leave your house?

   F. 9:00 A.M.

   G. 10:30 A.M.

   H. 11:15 A.M.

   J. 12:00 P.M.

3. Marcus wants to buy a stereo that costs \$85. He will work 5 hours as a server to cover the cost of the stereo. If he makes \$25 an hour when tips are added to his wages, how much money will he have left after he buys the stereo?

   A. \$15

   B. \$40

   C. \$125

   D. \$210

4. Simplify the algebraic expression $5(x + 1) - 2(4x - 2)$.

   F. $-3x + 1$

   G. $-3x + 9$

   H. $x + 1$

   J. $3x + 9$

5. A submarine is at an elevation of -632 feet and ascends at a rate of 10 feet per second. Which expression can be used to determine the elevation of the submarine after t seconds?

   A. $-10t - 632$

   B. $-10t + 632$

   C. $10t + 632$

   D. $10t - 632$

6. What is the sum of $-26 + 6 + (-8)$?

   F. -40 **H.** -24

   G. -28 **J.** -12

7. Which of the following numbers is between $\frac{5}{8}$ and $\frac{2}{3}$ when graphed on a number line?

   A. 0.6289

   B. $\sqrt{1.3}$

   C. $\frac{7}{10}$

   D. None of the above

8. An ice cream store sells ice cream in two sizes of cups. The large size costs \$3.75, and the small size costs \$2.50. Each size comes with one free topping, and every additional topping costs \$0.75. Two friends visit the ice cream store. One friend orders a large cup with 1 topping, and the other friend orders a small cup with 3 toppings. How much is the bill for the two friends?

   F. \$7.50 **H.** \$8.50

   G. \$7.75 **J.** \$8.75

9. Which expression shows $\frac{-40x + 64}{4}$ simplified?

   A. $-10x + 16$

   B. $-10x - 16$

   C. $10x + 16$

   D. $10x - 16$

10. Simplify the expression $5 - 2(1 - 3x)$.

F. $3 - 6x$

G. $3 - 3x$

H. $3 + 3x$

J. $3 + 6x$

11. It costs $6 for each hour you use the canoe. If you have $25, for how many hours can you rent the canoe?

A. 3 h

B. 4 h

C. 5 h

D. 6 h

12. Brent wants to write an expression that will always produce an odd integer. Which of the following will always produce an odd integer for any given integer, n?

F. $-n + 5$

G. $2n - 1$

H. $3n - 1$

J. n^2

13. Your friend believes that $y^2 + x^2$ is positive. Which pair of values for x and y could you use to disprove your friend's theory?

A. $x = -3$ and $y = 1$

B. $x = -1$ and $y = 2$

C. $x = -2$ and $y = 0$

D. $x = 0$ and $y = 0$

14. Which list of numbers is in order from least to greatest?

F. $5, -3.9, -3, \frac{1}{5}$

G. $-3, -3.9, \frac{1}{5}, 5$

H. $-3.9, -3, \frac{1}{5}, 5$

J. $5, \frac{1}{5}, -3, -3.9$

15. A certain stock is worth $7.59 when it is first purchased on a Monday. On Tuesday, the stock change is –$0.68. On Wednesday, the change was $0.80, and on Thursday, the change was –$1.03. How much was the value of the stock as of Thursday?

A. $5.08

B. $6.68

C. $8.04

D. $8.50

16. Simplify the expression $3(xy - 2x) - y(x + 2)$.

F. $2xy - 6x - 2$

G. $2xy - 6x - 2y$

H. $2xy - 8x$

J. $4xy - 6x - 2y$

17. A solid steel beam in the shape of a rectangular prism has a length of 2 feet, a width of $\sqrt{16}$ inches, and a height of $\frac{1}{2}$ inch. Find the volume of the beam. Use the formula $V = lwh$, where V is the volume, l is the length, w is the width, and h is the height.

A. 4 in.^{3}

B. 24 in.^{3}

C. 48 in.^{3}

D. 220 in.^{3}

18. Sam claims that $x^2 \geq x$ for all values of x. Which value of x proves Sam wrong?

F. -2

G. -1

H. 0

J. $\frac{1}{2}$

TEST PRACTICE

Illinois Resources Guide

Pacing and Assignment Guide

REGULAR SCHEDULE

Pre-AP For pacing and assignments for a Pre-AP course, see the *Algebra 1 Toolkit*.

Lesson	Les. Day	BASIC	AVERAGE	ADVANCED
3.1 8.11.16	Day 1	SRH p. 915 Exs. 16–20; pp. 137–140 Exs. 1, 2, 3–13 odd, 15, 16, 17–27 odd, 29–42, 53–59, 64–75	pp. 137–140 Exs. 1, 2, 8–14 even, 15, 16, 20–28 even, 29, 30, 32–50 even, 54–61, 64–75 even	pp. 137–140 Exs. 1, 2, 11–16, 20–26 even, 34–48 even, 49–52*, 56–63*, 69–75 odd
3.2 8.11.16	Day 1	SRH p. 938 Exs. 21–24; pp. 144–146 Exs. 1, 2, 3–21 odd, 22–29, 37–41, 46–60	pp. 144–146 Exs. 1, 2, 6–20 even, 21–26, 30–36, 38–44, 46–60	pp. 144–146 Exs. 1, 2, 8–14 even, 19–21, 24–26, 32–36*, 39–45*, 49–51, 54–60 even
3.3 8.11.16	Day 1	pp. 150–153 Exs. 1–18, 27, 28, 44–47	pp. 150–153 Exs. 1, 2, 4–10 even, 12–18, 27–32, 35, 45, 46	pp. 150–153 Exs. 1, 9–11, 15–18, 29–32, 35, 37*, 45, 46
	Day 2	pp. 150–153 Exs. 19–26, 29, 30, 38–41, 48–56	pp. 150–153 Exs. 19–26, 33, 34, 36, 38–42, 49–55 odd	pp. 150–153 Exs. 22–24, 33, 34, 36, 38–43*, 54–56
3.4 8.11.16	Day 1	EP p. 939 Exs. 38–41; pp. 157–159 Exs. 1, 2, 3–13 odd, 15–37, 49–52, 56–64 even	pp. 157–159 Exs. 1, 2, 7–13 odd, 15–29, 31–43 odd, 44–47, 49–53, 56–64 odd	pp. 157–159 Exs. 1, 7, 8, 12–26, 29, 38–48*, 50–55*, 58–64 even
3.5 6.11.17	Day 1	SRH p. 912 Exs. 6–10; pp. 165–167 Exs. 1–6, 7–17 odd, 19–26, 45–52, 56–66	pp. 165–167 Exs. 1, 2, 5, 6, 10–18 even, 19–22, 23–43 odd, 47–54, 56–66 even	pp. 165–167 Exs. 1, 2, 15–20, 27–30, 32–42 even, 43–55*, 57–65 odd
3.6 6.11.17	Day 1	pp. 171–173 Exs. 1–18, 19–25 odd, 33–39 odd, 40, 44–54 even	pp. 171–173 Exs. 1, 2, 4–14 even, 15–18, 19–29 odd, 31–42, 44–54 even	pp. 171–173 Exs. 1, 2, 11–16, 24–30 even, 31–34*, 37–43*, 46, 47, 53–55
3.7 6.11.18	Day 1	SRH p. 917 Exs. 11–17 odd; pp. 179–181 Exs. 1–14, 22, 23, 47–52	pp. 179–181 Exs. 1, 2, 3–13 odd, 22, 23, 26–29, 47–52	pp. 179–181 Exs. 1, 6–8, 12–14, 22, 23, 26–29
	Day 2	pp. 179–181 Exs. 15–21, 24, 25, 33–37, 41–46	pp. 179–181 Exs. 16, 19–21, 24, 25, 30, 31, 35–39, 41–46	pp. 179–181 Exs. 17–19, 24, 25, 30–32*, 35–40*, 42, 46
3.8 7.11.03	Day 1	pp. 187–189 Exs. 1–10, 11–19 odd, 20–25, 32–35, 38–45	pp. 187–189 Exs. 1, 2, 4, 6, 8–10, 12–18 even, 20–30, 32–36, 38–45	pp. 187–189 Exs. 1, 7, 8, 16–31*, 34–37*, 38–44 even
Review	Day 1	pp. 192–196 Exs. 1–61	pp. 192–196 Exs. 1–61	pp. 192–196 Exs. 1–61
Assess	Day 1	Chapter 3 Test	Chapter 3 Test	Chapter 3 Test
Yearly Pacing		Chapter 3 Total – 12 days	Chapters 1–3 Total – 34 days	Remaining – 126 days

*Challenge Exercises EP = Extra Practice SRH = Skills Review Handbook

BLOCK SCHEDULE

DAY 1	DAY 2	DAY 3	DAY 4	DAY 5	DAY 6
3.1	**3.3**	**3.4**	**3.6**	**3.7 (CONT.)**	**REVIEW**
pp. 137–140 Exs. 1, 2, 8–14 even, 15, 16, 20–28 even, 29, 30, 32–50 even, 54–61, 64–75 even	pp. 150–153 Exs. 1, 2, 4–10 even, 12–36, 38–42, 45, 46, 49–55 odd	pp. 157–159 Exs. 1, 2, 7–13 odd, 15–29, 31–43 odd, 44–47, 49–53, 56–64 odd	pp. 171–173 Exs. 1, 2, 4–14 even, 15–18, 19–29 odd, 31–42, 44–54 even	pp. 179–181 Exs. 16, 19–21, 24, 25, 30, 31, 35–39, 41–46	pp. 192–196 Exs. 1–61
3.2		**3.5**	**3.7**	**3.8**	**ASSESS**
pp. 144–146 Exs. 1, 2, 6–20 even, 21–26, 30–36, 38–44, 46–60		pp. 165–167 Exs. 1, 2, 5, 6, 10–18 even, 19–22, 23–43 odd, 47–54, 56–66 even	pp. 179–181 Exs. 1, 2, 3–13 odd, 22, 23, 26–29, 47–52	pp. 187–189 Exs. 1, 2, 4, 6, 8–10, 12–18 even, 20–30, 32–36, 38–45	Chapter 3 Test
Yearly Pacing	Chapter 3 Total – 6 days		Chapters 1–3 Total – 17 days		Remaining – 63 days

Chapter Resource Guide 3

Chapter Resource Book

CHAPTER SUPPORT								
Parents as Partners (Chapter Overview with home involvement exercises and activity)							p. 1	
LESSON SUPPORT / **Standard**	**3.1** 8.11.16	**3.2** 8.11.16	**3.3** 8.11.16	**3.4** 8.11.16	**3.5** 6.11.17	**3.6** 6.11.17	**3.7** 6.11.18	**3.8** 7.11.03
Teaching Guide/Lesson Plan	p. 3	p. 14	p. 25	p. 37	p. 50	p. 60	p. 70	p. 80
Activity Masters		p. 16		p. 39				
Technology Activities & Keystrokes			p. 27	p. 40				
Activity Support Masters	p. 5							
Practice (3 levels)	p. 6	p. 17	p. 29	p. 41	p. 52	p. 62	p. 72	p. 82
Study Guide	p. 9	p. 20	p. 32	p. 44	p. 55	p. 65	p. 75	p. 85
Catch-Up for Absent Students	p. 11	p. 22	p. 34	p. 46	p. 57	p. 67	p. 77	p. 87
Problem Solving/Application	p. 12	p. 23	p. 35	p. 47	p. 58	p. 68	p. 78	p. 88
Challenge Practice	p. 13	p. 24	p. 36	p. 49	p. 59	p. 69	p. 79	p. 89

REVIEW			
Chapter Review Games and Activities	p. 90	Cumulative Practice	p. 93
Project with Rubric	p. 91	Resource Book Answers	A1

Transparencies	*3.1*	*3.2*	*3.3*	*3.4*	*3.5*	*3.6*	*3.7*	*3.8*
Warm-Up/Daily Homework Quiz	✔	✔	✔	✔	✔	✔	✔	✔
Notetaking Guide	✔	✔	✔	✔	✔	✔	✔	✔
Teacher Support	✔							
Answer Transparencies	✔	✔	✔	✔	✔	✔	✔	✔

ASSESSMENT BOOK

Quizzes	p. 31	SAT/ACT Chapter Test	p. 42
Chapter Tests (3 levels)	p. 34	Alternative Assessment with Rubric	p. 44
Standardized Chapter Test	p. 40		

TECHNOLOGY

- Easy Planner
- Test and Practice Generator
- Power Presentations
- @HomeTutor
- Activity Generator
- Animated Algebra
- Classzone.com
- eEdition Plus Online
- eWorkbook Plus Online
- ML Assessment System

ADDITIONAL RESOURCES

Illinois Additional Lessons

- Worked-Out Solution Key
- Notetaking Guide
- Practice Workbook
- Algebra 1 Toolkit
- Benchmark Tests
- Reteaching and Remediation
- Spanish Study Guide
- Spanish Assessment Book
- Spanish Resources in Spanish
- Multi-Language Visual Glossary

3 Lesson Practice Level B

LESSON 3.1 Practice B
For use with pages 134–140

Solve the equation.

1. $x + 16 = 25$ $x = 9$
2. $n - 9 = 17$ $n = 26$
3. $-30 = w + 8$ $w = -38$
4. $y + 5 = -13$ $y = -18$
5. $a - 17 = -10$ $a = 7$
6. $41 = 52 + m$ $m = -11$
7. $c - 2.4 = 1.8$ $c = 4.2$
8. $z + 4.1 = 9.6$ $z = 5.5$
9. $-3.2 = 4.5 + p$ $p = -7.7$
10. $9x = 54$ $x = 6$
11. $-5b = 55$ $b = -11$
12. $-42 = 3m$ $m = -14$
13. $-52 = -4y$ $y = 13$
14. $\frac{1}{3}n = 36$ $n = 108$
15. $-\frac{3}{4}a = 12$ $a = -16$
16. $0.5y = 17$ $y = 34$
17. $-1.4a = 2.8$ $a = -2$
18. $-6.5 = -1.3m$ $m = 5$

The rectangle or triangle has area *A*. Write and solve an equation to find the value of *x*.

19. $A = 70 \text{ in.}^2$ $10x = 70; x = 7$ in.
20. $A = 30 \text{ in.}^2$ $\frac{1}{2}(12x) = 30; x = 5$ in.

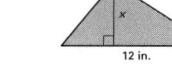

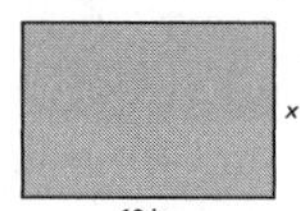

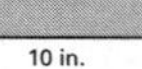

x

12 in.

21. **Caves** Cumberland Caverns in Tennessee is 44.4 kilometers long. This cave is 10.9 kilometers longer than Carlsbad Caverns in New Mexico. How long is Carlsbad Caverns? 33.5 km

22. **Bocce** Bocce is a lawn bowling game that originated in Italy. The bocce court below has an area of 1032 square feet. The width of the court is 12 feet. What is the length of the court? 86 ft

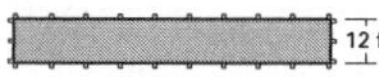

23. **Olympics** In the 2002 Winter Olympics, Cartriona LeMay Doan won the 500-meter race. Her winning time was 74.75 seconds. Find her average speed to the nearest tenth of a meter per second. 6.7 m/sec

24. **Part-Time Job** You work at a grocery store part-time. You estimate that you spend $\frac{3}{5}$ of your time stocking shelves. You work 20 hours each week. How many hours of your work week do you spend stocking shelves? 12 h

LESSON 3.1

LESSON 3.2 Practice B
For use with pages 141–146

Solve the equation.

1. $3n + 14 = 35$ $n = 7$
2. $7y - 10 = 11$ $y = 3$
3. $14 = 9 - x$ $x = -5$
4. $9c - 5 = 13$ $c = 2$
5. $4.6 = 4m - 3.4$ $m = 2$
6. $1.2 = 2.4 - 3b$ $b = 0.4$
7. $\frac{p}{6} + 9 = 14$ $p = 30$
8. $\frac{w}{7} - 2 = 9$ $w = 77$
9. $\frac{z}{3} - 8 = -4$ $z = 12$

Write an equation for the function described. Then find the input.

10. The output of a function is 5 more than 2 times the input. Find the input when the output is 17. $y = 2x + 5; 6$
11. The output of a function is 10 more than 4 times the input. Find the input when the output is -26. $y = 4x + 10; -9$
12. The output of a function is 14 less than 6 times the input. Find the input when the output is 22. $y = 6x - 14; 6$

Solve the equation.

13. $9a + 4a = 26$ $a = 2$
14. $14y - 6y = 48$ $y = 6$
15. $38 = 26x - 7x$ $x = 2$
16. $16x - 3x = -52$ $x = -4$
17. $-9 = 11m - 8m$ $m = -3$
18. $4.5z - 2.5z = 24$ $z = 12$

19. **Yoga Class** A fitness center offers yoga classes for $10 per class and sells yoga mats for $19.95. A person paid a total of $139.95 to the fitness center for yoga classes and a mat. Find the number of yoga classes the person took. 12 classes

20. **Library Books** Your school has a $1200 grant to buy books and magazine subscriptions for the school library. The average cost of a magazine subscription is $30. Your school decides to spend $870 on books and the remaining amount on magazine subscriptions. How many magazine subscriptions can the school buy? 11 subscriptions

21. **Walking** You have already walked 5 miles of an 18-mile trail. If you walk the rest of the trail at a pace of 1 mile in 17 minutes, how many hours will it take you to finish the trail? Use the following verbal model to answer the question. Round your answer to the nearest tenth. about 3.7 h

Walking rate (mi/min)	·	Number of minutes (min)	+	Number of miles already walked (mi)	=	Total number of miles walked (mi)

22. **Swimming Pool** The capacity of a small children's swimming pool is 106 gallons of water. There are currently 15 gallons of water in the pool. You are filling the pool with water at a rate of 2 gallons per minute.
    a. Write an equation that gives the amount *y* (in gallons) of water in the pool as a function of the number *x* of minutes from now. $y = 15 + 2x$
    b. After how many minutes will the pool be full? 45.5 min

LESSON 3.2

LESSON 3.3 Practice B
For use with pages 148–153

Solve the equation.

1. $16x - 15 - 9x = 13$ $x = 4$
2. $15m + 4 - 9m = -32$ $m = -6$
3. $3b - 9 - 8b = 11$ $b = -4$
4. $-31 = 8 - 6p - 7p$ $p = 3$
5. $9 + 4(x + 1) = 25$ $x = 3$
6. $7(d - 5) + 12 = 5$ $d = 4$
7. $10a + 5(a - 3) = 15$ $a = 2$
8. $19a - 3(a - 6) = 66$ $a = 3$
9. $\frac{1}{4}(x - 8) = 7$ $x = 36$
10. $\frac{1}{3}(d + 9) = -12$ $d = -45$
11. $\frac{3}{4}(n + 3) = 9$ $n = 9$
12. $-\frac{5}{2}(w - 1) = 15$ $w = -5$
13. $6.4 + 2.1(z - 2) = 8.5$ $z = 3$
14. $4.5 - 1.5(6m + 2) = 6$ $m = -0.5$
15. $15 = 4.3n - 2.1(n - 4)$ $n = 3$

Find the value of *x* for the triangle or rectangle.

16. Perimeter = 23 feet $x = 5$
17. Perimeter = 24 meters $x = 3$

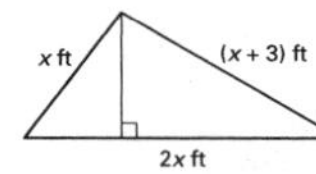

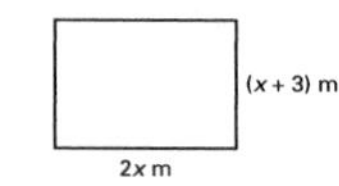

18. **Wrapping a Package** It takes 70 inches of ribbon to make a bow and wrap the ribbon around a box. The bow takes 32 inches of ribbon. The width of the box is 14 inches. What is the height of the box? 5 in.

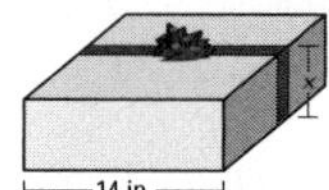

19. **Vacation** You are driving to a vacation spot that is 1500 miles away. Including rest stops, it takes you 42 hours to get to the vacation spot. You estimate that you drove at an average speed of 50 miles per hour. How many hours were you *not* driving? 12 h

20. **Moving** You helped a friend move a short distance recently. The friend rented a truck for $15 an hour and rented a dolly for $5. Your friend paid a total of $80 for the rental. How long did your friend rent the truck for? 5 h

21. **Painting** You and your friend are painting the walls in your apartment. You estimate that there is 1000 square feet of space to be painted. You paint at a rate of 4 square feet per minute and your friend paints at a rate of 3 square feet per minute. Your friend shows up to help you paint 45 minutes after you have already started painting.
    a. Write an equation that gives the total number of square feet *y* as a function of the number of minutes *x* it takes to paint all of the walls. $y = 4(x + 45) + 3x$
    b. How long will it take you and your friend to finish painting? Round your answer to the nearest minute. about 117 min

LESSON 3.3

LESSON 3.4 Practice B
For use with pages 154–159

1. $5x + 11 = 4x + 18$
   $x + 11 = 18$ Subtract $4x$ from each side.
   $x = 7$ Subtract 11 from each side.

Solve the equation and describe each step you use.

1. $5x + 11 = 4x + 18$
2. $11p - 4 = 6p + 1$ See below.
3. $-6 = 2(w + 5)$ See below.

Solve the equation, if possible.

4. $15x - 8 = 14x + 13$ $x = 21$
5. $9n - 7 = 5n + 5$ $n = 3$
6. $4z - 15 = 4z + 11$ no solution
7. $-7a + 9 = 3a + 49$ $a = -4$
8. $4(w + 3) = w - 15$ $w = -9$
9. $8(y - 5) = 6y - 18$ $y = 11$
10. $14m - 10 = 3(4 + m)$ $m = 2$
11. $7 + x = \frac{1}{2}(4x - 2)$ $x = 8$
12. $8b + 11 - 3b = 2b + 2$ $b = -3$
13. $10d - 6 = 4d - 15 - 3d$ $d = -1$
14. $16p - 4 = 4(2p - 3)$ $p = -1$
15. $0.25(8z - 4) = z + 8 - 2z$ $z = 3$

Write an expression for the perimeter of the square.

16. $16x - 16$ 17. $32x + 16$ 18. $18x - 30$

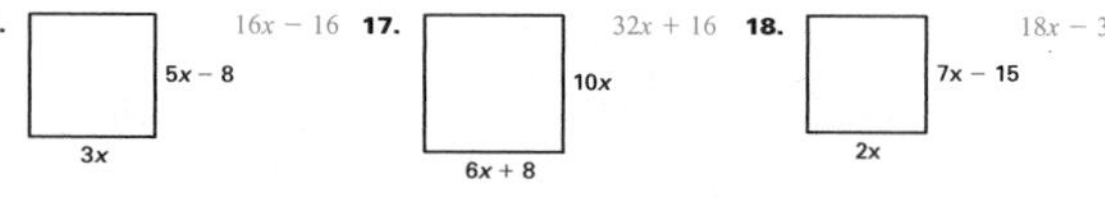

19. **Saving and Spending** Currently, you have $80 and your sister has $145. You decide to save $6 of your allowance each week, while your sister decides to spend her whole allowance plus $7 each week. How long will it be before you have as much money as your sister? 5 weeks

20. **Botanical Gardens** The membership fee for joining a gardening association is $24 per year. A local botanical garden charges members of the gardening association $3 for admission to the garden. Nonmembers of the association are charged $6. After how many visits to the garden is the total cost for members, including the membership fee, the same as the total cost for nonmembers? 8 visits

21. **College Enrollment** Information about students' choices of majors at a small college is shown in the table. In how many years will there be 2 times as many students majoring in engineering than in business? In how many years will there be 2 times as many students majoring in engineering than in biology? 3 years; 7.6 years

Major	Number of students enrolled in major	Average rate of change
Engineering	120	22 more students each year
Business	105	4 fewer students each year
Biology	98	6 more students each year

2. $11p - 4 = 6p + 1$
   $5p - 4 = 1$ Subtract $6p$ from each side.
   $5p = 5$ Add 4 to each side.
   $p = 1$ Divide each side by 5.

3. $-6 = 2(w + 5)$
   $-6 = 2w + 10$ Distribute 2 to $(w + 5)$.
   $-16 = 2w$ Subtract 10 from each side.
   $-8 = w$ Divide each side by 2.

LESSON 3.4

LESSON 3.5 Practice B

For use with pages 162–167

Tell whether the ratio is in simplest form. If not, write it in simplest form.

1. 16 to 34 no; 8 to 17 **2.** 17 : 65 yes **3.** $\frac{33}{108}$ no; $\frac{11}{36}$

Solve the proportion.

4. $\frac{1}{2}=\frac{p}{14}$ $p = 7$ **5.** $\frac{2}{3}=\frac{x}{21}$ $x = 14$ **6.** $\frac{14}{8}=\frac{y}{20}$ $y = 35$

7. $\frac{y}{6}=\frac{15}{9}$ $y = 10$ **8.** $\frac{10}{15}=\frac{m}{39}$ $m = 26$ **9.** $\frac{b}{8}=\frac{50}{20}$ $b = 20$

10. $\frac{8}{2.5}=\frac{d}{0.5}$ $d = 1.6$ **11.** $\frac{1.4}{1.6}=\frac{z}{10}$ $z = 8.75$ **12.** $\frac{n}{4}=\frac{0.3}{1.5}$ $n = 0.8$

Write the sentence as a proportion. Then solve the proportion.

13. 5 is to 12 as x is to 48. $\frac{5}{12}=\frac{x}{48}$; $x = 20$ **14.** w is to 9 as 7 is to 36. $\frac{w}{9}=\frac{7}{36}$; $w=\frac{7}{4}$

15. d is to 4 as 32 is to 56. $\frac{d}{4}=\frac{32}{56}$; $d=\frac{16}{7}$ **16.** 22 is to 50 as x is to 500. $\frac{22}{50}=\frac{x}{500}$; $x = 220$

17. 10 is to 45 as b is to 225. $\frac{10}{45}=\frac{b}{225}$; $b = 50$ **18.** n is to 18 as 64 is to 72. $\frac{n}{18}=\frac{64}{72}$; $n = 16$

19. Books Over the summer, you read 20 books. Eight of these books were biographies.

a. Find the ratio of biographies to the total number of books. $\frac{2}{5}$

b. Find the ratio of non-biographies to biographies. $\frac{3}{2}$

c. Find the ratio of non-biographies to the total number of books. $\frac{3}{5}$

20. Fitness Center The table shows the number of people attending classes at a fitness center during a recent evening.

Class	Aerobics	Spinning	Yoga
Number of people	32	28	16

a. Find the ratio of the number of people taking yoga to the number of people taking spinning class. $\frac{4}{7}$

b. Find the ratio of the number of people taking aerobics to the total number of people taking classes. $\frac{8}{19}$

21. Mailroom You work in the local mailroom at a college. One of your duties is to sort local mail from all of the other mail. You can sort 8 pieces of mail in 10 seconds. How many pieces of mail should you be able to sort in 45 minutes? 2160 pieces of mail

22. Music A music downloading website reports that nearly 5 out of every 7 songs downloaded are classified as pop music. According to this information, predict how many of the next 500 songs downloaded will be pop songs. Round your answer to the nearest whole number. about 357 songs

LESSON 3.5

LESSON 3.6 Practice B

For use with pages 168–173

Name the cross products of the proportion.

1. $\frac{n}{11}=\frac{40}{55}$ $55n$ and $11(40)$ **2.** $\frac{4}{9}=\frac{1}{x}$ $4x$ and $9(1)$ **3.** $\frac{1.8}{1.9}=\frac{b}{3.8}$ $1.8(3.8)$ and $1.9b$

4. $\frac{a+6}{21}=\frac{4}{7}$ $7(a+6)$ and $21(4)$ **5.** $\frac{5x}{x+1}=\frac{30}{9}$ $9(5x)$ and $30(x+1)$ **6.** $\frac{2.2}{3.3}=\frac{a-2}{a-1}$ $2.2(a-1)$ and $3.3(a-2)$

Solve the proportion.

7. $\frac{3}{5}=\frac{21}{m}$ $m = 35$ **8.** $\frac{12}{7}=\frac{60}{d}$ $d = 35$ **9.** $\frac{24}{x}=\frac{48}{60}$ $x = 30$

10. $\frac{5}{7}=\frac{3w}{21}$ $w = 5$ **11.** $\frac{2w}{16}=\frac{30}{80}$ $w = 3$ **12.** $\frac{2z}{24}=\frac{6}{8}$ $z = 9$

13. $\frac{8}{9}=\frac{30+a}{45}$ $a = 10$ **14.** $\frac{9-y}{44}=\frac{5}{22}$ $y = -1$ **15.** $\frac{26}{15}=\frac{104}{70-w}$ $w = 10$

16. $\frac{35}{16}=\frac{c-8}{2}$ $c = 12.375$ **17.** $\frac{1}{9}=\frac{a}{a+24}$ $a = 3$ **18.** $\frac{2}{n}=\frac{14}{n+30}$ $n = 5$

A map has a scale of 1 in. : 38 ft. Use the given map distance to find the actual distance.

19. 5.5 in. 209 ft **20.** 2.25 in. 85.5 ft **21.** 1.75 in. 66.5 ft

22. Concrete You are making up your own mix of concrete to patch a set of stairs. In order to have the proper mix, you need to mix 1 part of Portland cement with 2 parts of sand and 3 parts of gravel.

a. How many total parts are in one batch of concrete? 6

b. You make a mix with 4 parts of sand. How many total parts of cement, sand, and gravel are in your mix? 12 parts

23. Architectural Firm An architectural firm makes a model of a science center they are building. The ratio of the model to the actual size is 1 in. : 85 ft. Estimate the height of the building if the model is 1.5 inches tall. 127.5 ft

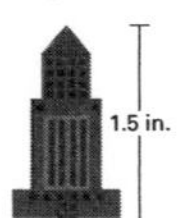

24. Tall Buildings You made a model of the Space Needle in Seattle, Washington, for a report on architecture in the United States. You used a scale of 1 in. : 50 ft. Your model is 12.1 inches tall. Estimate the actual height of the Space Needle. 605 ft

LESSON 3.6

LESSON 3.7 Practice B

For use with pages 176–181

Use a proportion to answer the question.

1. What percent of 125 is 25? 20% **2.** What percent of 70 is 14? 20%

3. What number is 15% of 80? 12 **4.** What number is 65% of 180? 117

5. 3 is 2% of what number? 150 **6.** 384 is 64% of what number? 600

Use the percent equation to answer the question.

7. What percent of 64 is 16? 25% **8.** What percent of 160 is 128? 80%

9. What number is 12% of 225? 27 **10.** What number is 85% of 360? 306

11. 4.8 is 8% of what number? 60 **12.** 25.8 is 86% of what number? 30

Find the percent. Round your answer to the nearest whole percent when necessary.

13. \$6 tip for a \$40 dinner 15% **14.** \$8.10 tax on an item priced at \$135 6%

15. 46 musicians out of 230 people 20% **16.** 18 action movies out of 45 movies 40%

17. Antarctica Antarctica comprises about 10.5% of the total land area on Earth. Antarctica has a surface area of about 5,400,000 square miles. What is the total land area on Earth? 51,428,571.43 mi^2

18. Part-Time Job So far this week, you have worked 10 hours at your part-time job. This is 80% of the number of hours you work each week. How many hours do you work each week? 12.5 h

19. Class Times The circle graph shows the results of a survey in which 500 college students were asked which time they preferred to start classes for the day.

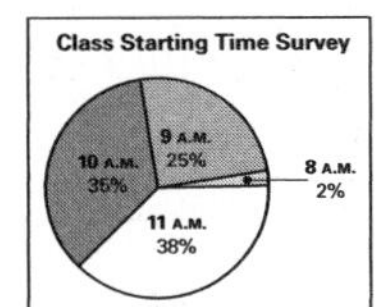

a. How many students who participated in the survey want to start classes at 8 A.M.? 10 students

b. How many students who participated in the survey want to start classes at 9 A.M.? 125 students

c. How many students who participated in the survey want to start classes at either 10 or 11 A.M.? 365 students

20. Boots Last year you bought a pair of designer boots on sale for \$84. Your friend bought the same boots this year for \$120. Which statements are correct? a and c

a. You paid 30% less than your friend paid.

b. Your friend paid 50% more than you did.

c. You paid 70% of what your friend paid.

LESSON 3.7

LESSON 3.8 Practice B

For use with pages 184–189

Write the equation in function form.

1. $4x + y = -10$ $y = -4x - 10$ **2.** $6 - y = 17x$ $y = 6 - 17x$ **3.** $y - 3x - 11 = 0$ $y = 3x + 11$

4. $2x + 2y = 8$ $y = 4 - x$ **5.** $6x - 3y = 12$ $y = 2x - 4$ **6.** $16 - 8y = 4x$ $y = 2 - \frac{1}{2}x$

7. $5x - 7y = 14$ $y = \frac{5}{7}x - 2$ **8.** $9y - 4x - 9 = 0$ $y = \frac{4}{9}x + 1$ **9.** $15 + 3y = -24x$ $y = -8x - 5$

10. $4 + 6y = 12x - 2$ $y = 2x - 1$ **11.** $4 - 10y = 22 - 6x$ $y = \frac{3}{5}x - \frac{9}{5}$ **12.** $8x - 2y - 5 = 11$ $y = 4x - 8$

Solve the literal equation.

13. Solve $R = R_1 + R_2$ for R_2. $R_2 = R - R_1$ **14.** Solve $I = Prt$ for r. $r = \frac{I}{Pt}$

15. Solve $C = \frac{Q}{V}$ for V. $V = \frac{Q}{C}$ **16.** Solve $y = mx + b$ for m. $m = \frac{y-b}{x}$

Solve the formula for the indicated variable.

17. Area of a trapezoid: $A = \frac{h}{2}(a + b)$. Solve for h. $h = \frac{2A}{a+b}$

18. Area of a rhombus: $A = \frac{1}{2}d_1d_2$. Solve for d_1. $d_1 = \frac{2A}{d_2}$

19. Guitar Practice You practice playing your guitar every day. You spend 15 minutes practicing chords and the rest of the time practicing a new song. So the total number of minutes y you practice for the week is given by $y = 7(15 + x)$, where x is the number of minutes you spend on practicing a new song.

a. Solve the equation for x. $x = \frac{y}{7} - 15$

b. How many minutes did you spend on a new song if you practiced 210 minutes last week? 245 minutes? 315 minutes? 15 min; 20 min; 30 min

20. Discounts Solve for r in the formula $S = L - rL$ where S is the sale price, L is the list price, and r is the discount rate. $r = \frac{L-S}{L}$

a. An item with a list price of \$128 goes on sale for \$51.20. Find the discount rate. 60%

b. An item with a list price of \$56.80 goes on sale for \$36.92. Find the discount rate. 35%

21. Cookbook You bought a cookbook while on a recent trip overseas. All of the oven temperatures are in degrees Celsius and the only formula you can remember for temperature is how to convert Fahrenheit to Celsius: $C = \frac{5}{9}(F - 32)$.

a. Solve the equation for F. $F = \frac{9}{5}C + 32$

b. A recipe tells you to bake a pie in the oven at 149°C. What is this temperature in degrees Fahrenheit? Round your answer to the nearest whole degree. about 300°F

LESSON 3.8

3 Assessment

CHAPTER 3 Quiz 1

For use after Lessons 3.1–3.3

Solve the equation. Check your solution.

1. $-112 = 7n$
2. $\frac{2}{3}t = 18$
3. $\frac{f}{-3} = -30$
4. $-28 = 10w - 3w$
5. $\frac{d}{5} + 1 = 7$
6. $\frac{9}{4}y - 2 = 25$
7. $24 = 13z - 4z + 6$
8. $7(h + 3) + 4 = -3$
9. $\frac{2}{3}(4x - 7) = -2$
10. A contractor purchases ceramic tile to remodel a kitchen floor. Each tile costs \$4, and the adhesive and grouting material costs \$17.82. If the contractor is charged a total of \$545.82, how many ceramic tiles did the contractor purchase?

Answers

1. $n = -16$
2. $t = 27$
3. $f = 90$
4. $w = -4$
5. $d = 30$
6. $y = 12$
7. $z = 2$
8. $h = -4$
9. $x = 1$
10. 132 tiles

CHAPTER 3 Quiz 2

For use after Lessons 3.4–3.6

Solve the equation, if possible.

1. $6 - 11x = 7x - 12$
2. $2y + 5 = 3(4y - 5)$
3. $12(x + 3) = 24 + 12x$

Solve the proportion. Check your solution.

4. $\frac{t}{65} = \frac{5}{13}$
5. $\frac{1.9}{2.1} = \frac{b}{8.4}$
6. $\frac{j + 4}{6} = \frac{18}{12}$
7. $\frac{m + 18}{m} = \frac{5}{2}$
8. $\frac{d + 4}{2d + 2} = \frac{3}{4}$
9. $\frac{f - 9}{-3} = \frac{11 - f}{5}$
10. At a pet show, the ratio of dogs to cats is 4 : 3. If the number of cats is 45, find the number of dogs at the show.

Answers

1. $x = 1$
2. $y = 2$
3. no solution
4. $t = 25$
5. $b = 7.6$
6. $j = 5$
7. $m = 12$
8. $d = 5$
9. $f = 6$
10. 60 dogs

CHAPTER 3 Quiz 3

For use after Lessons 3.7–3.8

Use the percent equation to answer the question.

1. 9 is 36 percent of what number?
2. What percent of 125 is 65?
3. What number is 15% of 120?
4. What percent of 110 is 8.8?
5. 62.4 is 48% of what number?
6. What number is 118% of 80?

Write the equation in function form.

7. $4 = 8x + 5y$
8. $2y - 10x = 16$
9. $10 + 7x = 19 - 3y$
10. The formula for simple interest is $I = Prt$ where P is the principal, r is the interest rate, and t is time. Solve the formula for r.

Answers

1. 25
2. 52%
3. 18
4. 8%
5. 130
6. 94.4
7. $y = -\frac{8}{5}x + \frac{4}{5}$
8. $y = 5x + 8$
9. $y = -\frac{7}{3}x + 3$
10. $r = \frac{I}{Pt}$

CHAPTER 3 Chapter Test B

For use after Chapter 3

Solve the equation, if posssible.

1. $-7 = -2 + x$
2. $b - \frac{2}{5} = \frac{3}{5}$
3. $-\frac{2}{3}d = 8$
4. $17 = 14 + 6y$
5. $2t - 5t = 9$
6. $13 - 9w = -14$
7. $7m - 4 - 2m = 6$
8. $\frac{3}{4}(c + 4) = 3$
9. $5(3 - 2y) + 4y = 3$
10. $4x - 1 = 2(2x + 3)$
11. $7a - 3.9a = 6.2$
12. $9 - 5z = 12 - (6z + 7)$
13. A new plasma-screen television costs \$5250. A family makes a down payment of \$552 and pays off the balance in 24 equal monthly payments. Write and solve an equation to find the monthly payment.
14. On a class trip, there were 45 more girls than boys. The total number of students on the trip was 211. Write and solve an equation to find the number of girls and the number of boys on the class trip.

Solve the proportion.

15. $\frac{4}{5} = \frac{12}{y}$
16. $\frac{1.1}{1.2} = \frac{w}{3.6}$
17. $\frac{16}{9} = \frac{-4t}{27}$
18. $\frac{8}{m + 3} = \frac{4}{m}$
19. $\frac{6}{x + 4} = \frac{12}{5x - 13}$
20. $\frac{5}{3z - 4} = \frac{-3}{1 - 2z}$
21. On Monday, biologists tagged 150 sunfish from a lake. On Friday, the biologists counted 12 tagged fish out of a sample of 400 sunfish from the same lake. Estimate the total number of sunfish in the lake.

Answers

1. $x = -5$
2. $b = 1$
3. $d = -12$
4. $y = \frac{1}{2}$
5. $t = -3$
6. $w = 3$
7. $m = 2$
8. $c = 0$
9. $y = 2$
10. no solution
11. $a = 2$
12. $z = -4$
13. $24x + 552 = 5250$; \$195.75
14. $x + x + 45 = 211$; 128 girls; 83 boys
15. $y = 15$
16. $w = 3.3$
17. $t = -12$
18. $m = 3$
19. $x = 7$
20. $z = -7$
21. 5000 sunfish

CHAPTER 3

Chapter Test B *continued*

For use after Chapter 3

22. A recipe for oatmeal raisin cookies calls for $1\frac{2}{3}$ cups of flour to make 4 dozen cookies. How many cups of flour are needed to make 6 dozen cookies?

Solve the percent problem.

23. 3 is 1.5% of what number?

24. 9 is what percent of 6?

25. What is 26.5% of 46?

26. 70 is 200% of what number?

27. In a renovation project, a football stadium increased its 60,000-seat capacity by 15%. How many seats will be available when the project is completed?

Write the equation in function form.

28. $5x - y = 7$

29. $10x + 3y + 2 = 9x + 8$

In Exercises 30–32, use the following information. Anthropologists can estimate the height of a woman by measuring the length of her radius bone (from the wrist to the elbow). The length of the radius bone b is given by $b = 0.26h - 18.85$ where h is the height (in centimeters) of the woman.

30. Solve the equation for h.

31. If the length of a woman's radius bone is 25 centimeters, estimate the height of the woman. Round your answer to the nearest centimeter.

32. If 1 in. = 2.54 cm, convert the woman's height to inches. Round your answer to the nearest inch.

Answers

22. $2\frac{1}{2}$ cups of flour

23. 200

24. 150%

25. 12.19

26. 35

27. 69,000 seats

28. $y = 5x - 7$

29. $y = -\frac{1}{3}x + 2$

30. $h = \frac{b + 18.85}{0.26}$

31. about 169 cm

32. about 67 in.

CHAPTER 3

Standardized Test

For use after Chapter 3

Multiple Choice

1. What is the solution of the equation $-25 = x - 12$? B

Ⓐ −37 Ⓑ −13 Ⓒ 13 Ⓓ 37

2. What is the solution of the equation $\frac{m}{3.6} = -1.2$? A

Ⓐ −4.32 Ⓑ −3 Ⓒ 2.4 Ⓓ 4.8

3. What is the solution of the equation $15 = \frac{3}{5}n$? D

Ⓐ 5 Ⓑ 9 Ⓒ $15\frac{3}{5}$ Ⓓ 25

4. What is the solution of the equation $\frac{2}{3}c + 6 = -12$? A

Ⓐ −27 Ⓑ −18 Ⓒ −9 Ⓓ 3

5. What is the first step in solving the equation $5 + \frac{12}{x} = -1$? C

Ⓐ Add 1 to each side.
Ⓑ Divide each side by 12.
Ⓒ Subtract 5 from each side.
Ⓓ Add 5 to each side.

6. Examine the problem below. Which line contains an error? A

$6x - 2(x - 5) = 22$	Line 1
$6x - 2x - 10 = 22$	Line 2
$4x - 10 = 22$	Line 3
$4x = 32$	Line 4
$x = 8$	Line 5

Ⓐ Line 2 Ⓑ Line 3 Ⓒ Line 4 Ⓓ Line 5

7. What is the solution of the equation $8x - 4(5 - x) = -44$? B

Ⓐ −6 Ⓑ −2 Ⓒ 5 Ⓓ 8

8. The perimeter of the triangle is 37 centimeters. What is the value of x? B

3x cm
2x + 1 cm
2(x + 4) cm

Ⓐ $2\frac{1}{4}$ Ⓑ 4 Ⓒ $4\frac{3}{7}$ Ⓓ 25

9. What is the solution of the equation $4t - 3(t - 2) = t + 6$? D

Ⓐ −16 Ⓑ −9 Ⓒ −7 Ⓓ 0

10. What equation does *not* have a solution? D

Ⓐ $3y - 2 = \frac{y}{2}$
Ⓑ $5(x - 3) = 2x + 7$
Ⓒ $4m - 15 = m - 15$
Ⓓ $3(6 - n) = -3(n - 8)$

11. What is the value of r in the proportion $\frac{2}{5} = \frac{18}{r}$? C

Ⓐ 10 Ⓑ 40 Ⓒ 45 Ⓓ 90

12. What is the value of p in the proportion $\frac{2}{3} = \frac{p}{35}$? A

Ⓐ $23\frac{1}{3}$ Ⓑ $52\frac{1}{2}$ Ⓒ 70 Ⓓ 105

CHAPTER 3

Standardized Test *continued*

For use after Chapter 3

13. Which proportion represents the statement 5 is to 4 as x is to 24? B

Ⓐ $\frac{5}{x} = \frac{24}{4}$ Ⓑ $\frac{5}{4} = \frac{x}{24}$ Ⓒ $\frac{5}{24} = \frac{4}{x}$ Ⓓ $\frac{4}{5} = \frac{x}{24}$

14. Which ratio represents the number of dogs to birds? C

Dogs	Cats	Birds
243	372	195

Ⓐ $\frac{81}{124}$ Ⓑ $\frac{65}{81}$ Ⓒ $\frac{81}{65}$ Ⓓ $\frac{124}{65}$

15. What is the value of y in the proportion $\frac{6}{y - 5} = \frac{18}{y + 1}$? C

Ⓐ $\frac{1}{2}$ Ⓑ 5 Ⓒ 8 Ⓓ 23

16. What number is 65% of 92? B

Ⓐ 5.98 Ⓑ 59.8 Ⓒ 598 Ⓓ 5980

17. What percent of 150 is 30? C

Ⓐ 2% Ⓑ 5% Ⓒ 20% Ⓓ 500%

18. Which equation is *not* equivalent to the formula $C = \frac{5}{9}(F - 32)$? A

Ⓐ $C - \frac{5}{9}F = -32$ Ⓑ $C = \frac{5}{9}F - \frac{160}{9}$ Ⓒ $\frac{9}{5}C = F - 32$ Ⓓ $C + 17\frac{7}{9} = \frac{5}{9}F$

Gridded Answer

19. What is the solution of the equation $15t - 3(t - 7) = 57$? 3

Short Response

20. You are shopping for a new jacket and find that your favorite store has jackets 35% off.

a. Write an equation representing the cost C before taxes where P represents the original price.

b. If the sale price of the jacket you want is \$55.25, what was the original price? *Explain.* \$85

20. a. $C = 0.75P$ or $C = P - 0.35P$

Extended Response

21. The formula for simple interest is $I = Prt$ where I is the interest, P is the principal, r is the interest rate, and t is time in years.

a. Calculate the amount of interest you would pay if you borrowed \$15,000 at a rate of 7.25% for 5 years. \$5437.50

b. Calculate the *total* amount of interest you would pay on a \$25,000 loan at a rate of 5.25% for 5 years. *Explain.*

c. Rewrite the formula for simple interest so that you can easily calculate the principal given the interest, rate, and time. $P = \frac{I}{rt}$

d. If the simple interest on a loan at a rate of 6.5% for 4 years is \$3250, what was the principal? \$12,500

21. b. \$31,562.50; The simple interest calculates to be \$6562.50. This amount must be added to the original \$25,000 borrowed for a total of \$31,562.50.

CHAPTER 3

Alternative Assessment and Math Journal

For use after Chapter 3

Journal

1. Explain the difference between a ratio and a proportion. Write an example of each, and explain how to solve a proportion.

Multi-Step Problem

2. A car rental agency charges \$25 per day to rent an economy class car, and also charges \$.08 per mile for each mile that the car is driven.

a. Write an equation that gives the cost C of a 3 day car rental as a function of the number of miles m that the car is driven.

b. Juanita needs to rent a car for a 3 day period. If she has \$150 budgeted to pay for the rental car, how many miles can she drive the car and not go over her budget? Write your answer in whole numbers of miles.

c. If Juanita changes her plans so that her rental is for 2 days, how many more miles can she drive the rental car and still stay within her \$150 budget? Write your answer in whole numbers of miles.

d. Write an equation that gives the cost C of a car rental for which 1000 miles were driven as a function of the number of days d that the car is rented.

e. Stephen needs to rent a car and knows that he will need to drive a total of 1000 miles. If Stephen has \$250 to spend on the rental car, how many days is he able to rent the car? Write your answer in whole numbers of days.

f. If Stephen decides to reduce the number of miles he drives to 800, how many more days is he able to rent the car? Write your answer in whole numbers of days.

1. Complete answers should include: an explanation that a ratio is a relationship between two quantities; an explanation that a proportion is created by equating two ratios; one example of a ratio and one example of a proportion; a written explanation describing how to solve a proportion.

2. a. $C = 75 + 0.08m$ **b.** 937 miles **c.** 313 more miles **d.** $C = 25d + 80$ **e.** 6 days **f.** 1 more day

PLAN AND PREPARE

Main Ideas

In Chapter 3, students use properties of equality to solve one-step, two-step, and multi-step equations in one variable. They also use properties of equality and the distributive property to solve equations with variables on both sides. Students write ratios and proportions, solve proportions using cross products, and solve percent problems, such as finding the percent of a number, a base, and part of a base. Finally, students rewrite equations in function form and solve formulas and literal equations for a given variable.

Prerequisite Skills

- Simplifying expressions
- Writing percents as decimals
- Using formulas

Additional resources for reviewing prerequisite skills are:

- Skills Review Handbook, pp. 909–937
- @HomeTutor

3 Solving Linear Equations

Before

In previous courses and chapters, you learned the following skills, which you'll use in Chapter 3: simplifying expressions, writing percents as decimals, and using formulas.

Prerequisite Skills

VOCABULARY CHECK

Copy and complete the statement.

1. In the expression $3x + 7 + 7x$, __?__ and __?__ are like terms. $3x, 7x$
2. The reciprocal of $\frac{5}{8}$ is __?__. $\frac{8}{5}$

SKILLS CHECK

Simplify the expression. *(Review p. 96 for 3.2–3.6.)*

3. $5x - (6 - x)$ $6x - 6$
4. $3(x - 9) - 16$ $3x - 43$
5. $23 + 4(x + 2)$ $4x + 31$
6. $x(7 + x) + 9x^2$ $10x^2 + 7x$

Write the percent as a decimal. *(Review p. 916 for 3.7.)*

7. 54% 0.54
8. 99% 0.99
9. 12.5% 0.125
10. 150% 1.5

Find the perimeter of the rectangle. *(Review p. 924 for 3.8.)*

11. 12. 13.

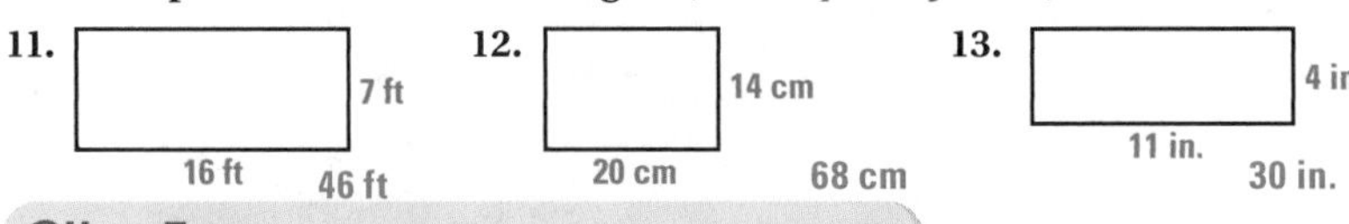

@HomeTutor Prerequisite skills practice at classzone.com

Chapter Planning Guide

Chapter 3 Resource Book
- Teaching Guide/Lesson Plan (pp. 3, 14, 25, 37, 50, 60, 70, 80)
- Project with Rubric (p. 91)

Assessment and Intervention
- Assessment Book (pp. 31–45)
- Benchmark Tests
- Reteaching and Remediation Book

Interactive Technology
- Easy Planner
- Power Presentations CD-ROM
- Activity Generator CD-ROM
- Animated Algebra
- Test Generator CD-ROM
- Online Quizzes
- eWorkbook
- eEdition
- @HomeTutor

Resources for English Learners
- Quick Reference for English Learners
- Spanish Study Guide
- Multi-Language Visual Glossary
- Student Resources in Spanish

Now

In Chapter 3, you will apply the big ideas listed below and reviewed in the Chapter Summary on page 191. You will also use the key vocabulary listed below.

Big Ideas

1. **Solving equations in one variable**
2. **Solving proportion and percent problems**
3. **Rewriting equations in two or more variables**

KEY VOCABULARY

- inverse operations, *p. 134*
- equivalent equations, *p. 134*
- identity, *p. 156*
- ratio, *p. 162*
- proportion, *p. 163*
- cross product, *p. 168*
- scale drawing, *p. 170*
- scale model, *p. 170*
- scale, *p. 170*
- literal equation, *p. 184*

Why?

Knowing how to solve a linear equation can help you solve problems involving distance, rate, and time. For example, you can solve an equation to find the time it takes a jellyfish to travel a given distance at a given rate.

Animated Algebra

The animation illustrated below for Exercise 59 on page 139 helps you answer this question: How long does it take the jellyfish to travel 26 feet?

You have to find the time it takes for the jellyfish to travel 26 feet.

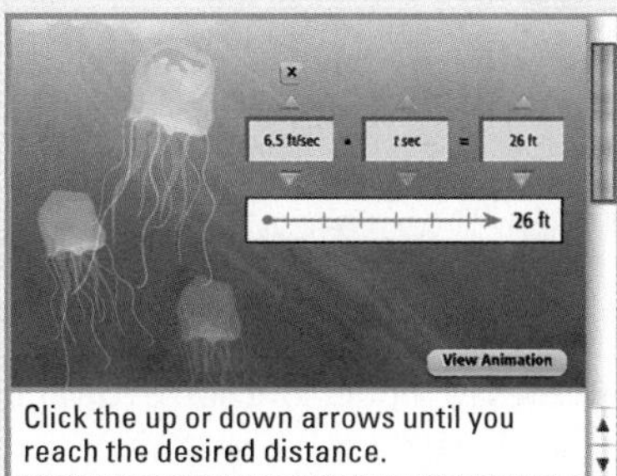

Click the up or down arrows until you reach the desired distance.

Animated Algebra at classzone.com

Other animations for Chapter 3: pages 133, 154, 176, 185, and 187

Algebra 1 Toolkit

- Reading Strategies for Chapter 3, pp. 13–14
- Differentiated Instruction Notes, pp. 49–52
- English Learners Notes, pp. 101–102
- Inclusion Notes, pp. 133–134
- Teaching Strategies with Sample Worksheets, pp. 155–178
- Using Technology in the Classroom, pp. 179–184
- Tips for New Teachers, pp. 189–190
- Math Background Notes, pp. 215–216
- Pre-AP Strategies and Copymasters, pp. 282–283, 329–344
- Teacher Survival Activities, pp. 559–560, 585–586
- Bulletin Board Idea, p. 609
- Teacher Tool Transparencies, following p. 620

1 PLAN AND PREPARE

Explore the Concept

- Students will use algebra tiles to model and solve one-step equations.
- This activity leads into the study of solving equations in Example 1 in Lesson 3.1.

Materials

Each student will need:

- algebra tiles
- Activity Support Master (*Chapter 3 Resource Book*, p. 5)

Recommended Time

Work activity: 10 min

Discuss results: 5 min

Grouping

Students should work individually.

2 TEACH

Tips for Success

In Explore 1, some students may think they should remove one 1-tile from each side of the equation since $1 + 1 = 2$. Point out that since there are two 1-tiles on the left side of the equation, they need to remove two 1-tiles to isolate the x-tile.

Key Questions

- In Explore 1, why do you remove the same number of 1-tiles from each side of the equation? **to keep the equation balanced**
- In Explore 2, why do you divide the 1-tiles into equal groups according to the number of x-tiles? **Since you want to isolate the x-tile, you need to find how many 1-tiles correspond to each x-tile.**

3.1 Modeling One-Step Equations

MATERIALS • algebra tiles

QUESTION **How can you use algebra tiles to solve one-step equations?**

You can model one-step equations using algebra tiles.

1-tile	**x-tile**
A 1-tile represents the number 1.	An x-tile represents the variable x.

EXPLORE 1 **Solve an equation using subtraction**

Solve $x + 2 = 5$.

STEP 1 Model $x + 2 = 5$ using algebra tiles.

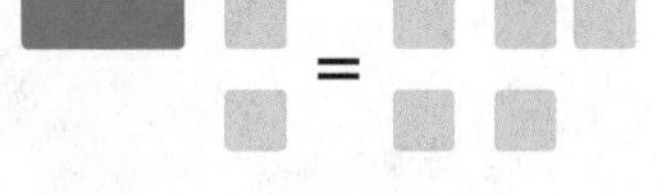

STEP 2 To find the value of x, isolate the x-tile on one side of the equation. You can do this by removing two 1-tiles from each side.

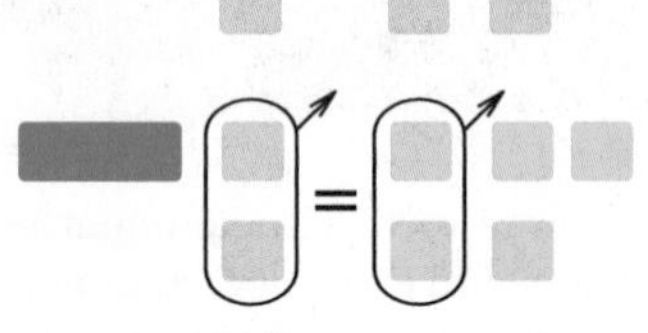

STEP 3 The x-tile is equal to three 1-tiles. So, the solution of $x + 2 = 5$ is 3.

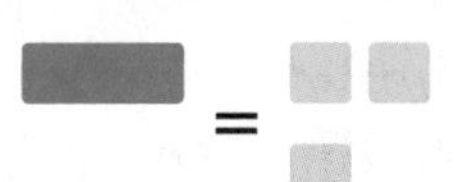

PRACTICE

Write the equation modeled by the algebra tiles.

1. 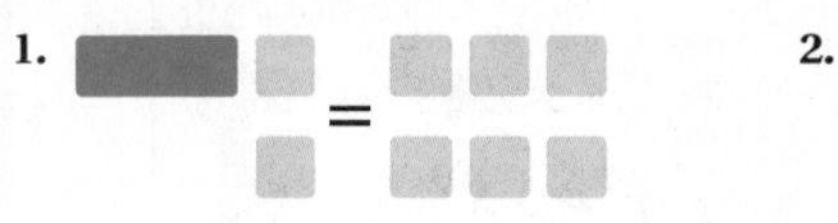

$x + 2 = 6$

2. 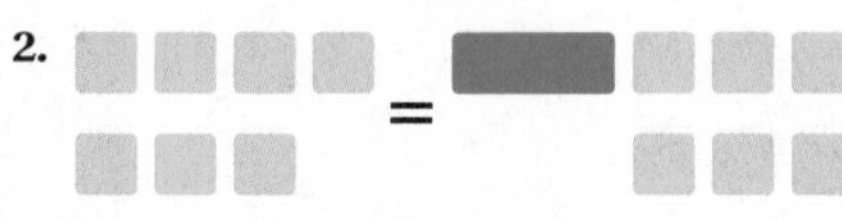

$7 = x + 6$

Use algebra tiles to model and solve the equation.

3. $x + 3 = 9$ **6**
4. $x + 2 = 7$ **5**
5. $x + 8 = 8$ **0**
6. $x + 3 = 7$ **4**
7. $x + 2 = 12$ **10**
8. $x + 7 = 12$ **5**
9. $15 = x + 5$ **10**
10. $13 = x + 10$ **3**

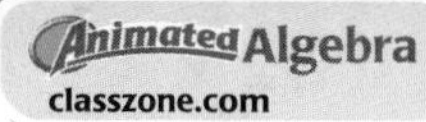

EXPLORE 2 Solve an equation using division

Solve $2x = 12$.

STEP 1 Model $2x = 12$ using algebra tiles.

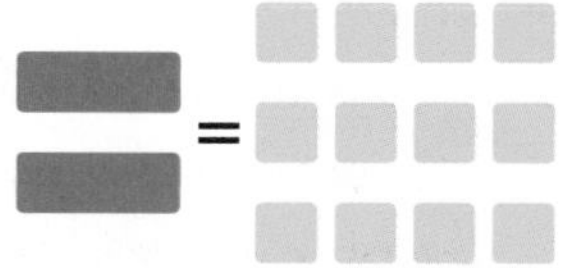

STEP 2 There are two x-tiles, so divide the x-tiles and 1-tiles into two equal groups.

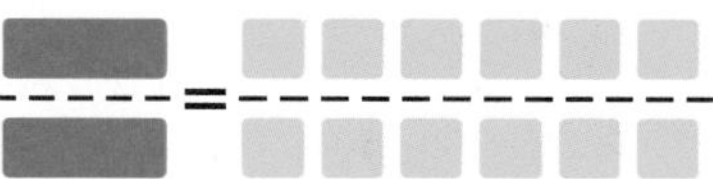

STEP 3 An x-tile is equal to six 1-tiles. So, the solution of $2x = 12$ is 6.

PRACTICE

Write the equation modeled by the algebra tiles.

11.

$4x = 4$

12.

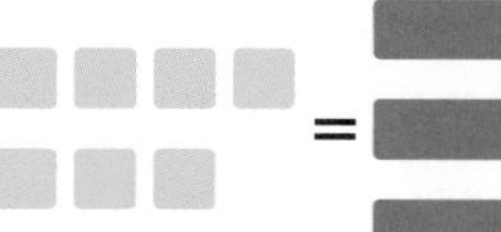

$7 = 3x$

Use algebra tiles to model and solve the equation.

13. $2x = 10$ 5 **14.** $3x = 12$ 4 **15.** $3x = 18$ 6 **16.** $4x = 16$ 4

17. $6 = 2x$ 3 **18.** $12 = 4x$ 3 **19.** $20 = 5x$ 4 **20.** $21 = 7x$ 3

DRAW CONCLUSIONS Use your observations to complete these exercises

21. An equation and explanation that correspond to each step in Explore 1 are shown below. Copy and complete the equations and explanations.

$x + 2 = 5$	**Original equation**
$x + 2 - \underline{?}^{2} = 5 - \underline{?}^{2}$	**Subtract $\underline{?}^{2}$ from each side.**
$x = \underline{?}^{3}$	**Simplify. Solution is $\underline{?}^{3}$.**

22. Write an equation that corresponds to the algebra tile equation in each step of Explore 2. Based on your results, describe an algebraic method that you can use to solve $12x = 180$. Then use your method to find the solution. $2x = 12, \frac{2x}{2} = \frac{12}{2}, x = 6$; divide each side by 12; 15.

Animated Algebra
classzone.com

An **Animated Algebra** activity is available on-line. This activity is also available on the **Power Presentations CD-ROM**.

Key Discovery

Subtract to isolate the variable in a one-step addition equation and divide to isolate the variable in a one-step multiplication equation.

3 ASSESS AND RETEACH

1. If you were modeling the solution of $x + 7 = 12$, how many 1-tiles would you remove from each side of the equation? 7
2. How many equal groups do you form when using algebra tiles to model and solve the equation $4x = 12$? Explain. Form 4 equal groups since there are 4 x-tiles.

1 PLAN AND PREPARE

Warm-Up Exercises

Transparency Available

Solve using mental math.

1. $x + 2 = 17$ 15 2. $\frac{x}{6} = 4$ 24
3. $x - 7 = 3$ 10 4. $9x = 54$ 6
5. Katrina divided her photos into three albums. Each album contains 26 photos. How many photos did Katrina have to begin with? 78 photos

Notetaking Guide

Transparency Available

Promotes interactive learning and notetaking skills, pp. 47–51.

Pacing

Basic: 1 day
Average: 1 day
Advanced: 1 day
Block: 0.5 block with 3.2
- See *Teaching Guide/Lesson Plan.*

2 FOCUS AND MOTIVATE

Essential Question

Big Idea 1, p. 131

How do you solve one-step equations using subtraction, addition, division, and multiplication? Tell students they will learn how to answer this question by using properties of equality and reciprocals to solve equations.

3.1 Solve One-Step Equations

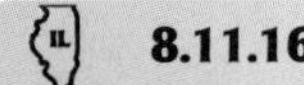

8.11.16 Solve linear equations and inequalities, including selecting and evaluating formulas.

Before You solved equations using mental math.
Now You will solve one-step equations using algebra.
Why? So you can determine a weight limit, as in Ex. 56.

Key Vocabulary
- **inverse operations**
- **equivalent equations**
- **reciprocal,** *p. 915*

Inverse operations are two operations that undo each other, such as addition and subtraction. When you perform the same inverse operation on each side of an equation, you produce an *equivalent equation*. **Equivalent equations** are equations that have the same solution(s).

KEY CONCEPT — *For Your Notebook*

Addition Property of Equality

Words Adding the same number to each side of an equation produces an equivalent equation.

Algebra If $x - a = b$, then $x - a + a = b + a$, or $x = b + a$.

Subtraction Property of Equality

Words Subtracting the same number from each side of an equation produces an equivalent equation.

Algebra If $x + a = b$, then $x + a - a = b - a$, or $x = b - a$.

EXAMPLE 1 Solve an equation using subtraction

Solve $x + 7 = 4$.

$x + 7 = 4$ — Write original equation.

$x + 7 - 7 = 4 - 7$ — Use subtraction property of equality: Subtract 7 from each side.

$x = -3$ — Simplify.

▸ The solution is -3.

AVOID ERRORS
To obtain an equivalent equation, be sure to subtract the same number from each side.

CHECK Substitute -3 for x in the original equation.

$x + 7 = 4$ — Write original equation.

$-3 + 7 \stackrel{?}{=} 4$ — Substitute -3 for x.

$4 = 4$ ✓ — Simplify. Solution checks.

Resource Planning Guide

Chapter Resource Book
- Teaching Guide/Lesson Plan (pp. 3–4)
- Practice levels A, B, C (pp. 6–8)
- Study Guide (pp. 9–10)
- Catch-up for Absent Students (p. 11)
- Application (p. 12)
- Challenge (p. 13)

Workbooks
- Notetaking Guide (pp. 47–51)
- Practice Workbook (pp. 30–31)

Teaching Options
- **Power Presentations CD-ROM** provides dynamic electronic teaching resources for the classroom.
- **Activity Generator CD-ROM** provides editable activities for all ability levels.

Interactive Technology
- Easy Planner
- Power Presentations CD-ROM
- Activity Generator CD-ROM
- Animated Algebra
- Test Generator CD-ROM
- Online Quiz
- eWorkbook
- eEdition
- @HomeTutor

Resources for English Learners
- Quick Reference for English Learners
- Spanish Study Guide
- Multi-Language Visual Glossary
- Student Resources in Spanish

See also the *Algebra 1 Toolkit* for more strategies for meeting individual needs.

EXAMPLE 2 Solve an equation using addition

USE HORIZONTAL FORMAT

In Example 2, both horizontal and vertical formats are used. In the rest of the book, equations will be solved using the horizontal format.

Solve $x - 12 = 3$.

Horizontal format		Vertical format
$x - 12 = 3$	Write original equation.	$x - 12 = 3$
$x - 12 + 12 = 3 + 12$	Add 12 to each side.	$+12 \quad +12$
$x = 15$	Simplify.	$x = 15$

MULTIPLICATION AND DIVISION EQUATIONS Multiplication and division are inverse operations. So, the multiplication property of equality can be used to solve equations involving division, and the division property of equality can be used to solve equations involving multiplication.

KEY CONCEPT *For Your Notebook*

Multiplication Property of Equality

Words Multiplying each side of an equation by the same nonzero number produces an equivalent equation.

Algebra If $\frac{x}{a} = b$ and $a \neq 0$, then $a \cdot \frac{x}{a} = a \cdot b$, or $x = ab$.

Division Property of Equality

Words Dividing each side of an equation by the same nonzero number produces an equivalent equation.

Algebra If $ax = b$ and $a \neq 0$, then $\frac{ax}{a} = \frac{b}{a}$, or $x = \frac{b}{a}$.

EXAMPLE 3 Solve an equation using division

Solve $-6x = 48$.

$-6x = 48$ Write original equation.

$\frac{-6x}{-6} = \frac{48}{-6}$ Divide each side by -6.

$x = -8$ Simplify.

GUIDED PRACTICE for Examples 1, 2, and 3

Solve the equation. Check your solution.

1. $y + 7 = 10$ 3
2. $x - 5 = 3$ 8
3. $q - 11 = -5$ 6
4. $6 = t - 2$ 8
5. $4x = 48$ 12
6. $-65 = -5y$ 13
7. $6w = -54$ -9
8. $24 = -8n$ -3

Motivating the Lesson

In 1979, Susan Montgomery set a world's record for blowing the biggest gum bubble—48.2 centimeters in diameter. She broke that record in 1994 by blowing a bubble with a 58.4-centimeter diameter. By knowing how to solve equations, you can compare and determine world records in feats such as Susan's or in sports and other activities.

3 TEACH

Extra Example 1

Solve $x + 9 = 3$. -6

Extra Example 2

Solve $x - 2 = 11$. 13

Key Questions to Ask for Example 2

- How are Examples 1 and 2 alike and how are they different? Both use inverse operations of addition and subtraction. In Example 1 you subtract to obtain an equivalent equation, while in Example 2 you add.
- Why do you perform the same operation on both sides of the equation? Explain. You need to produce an equation equivalent to the original equation so they have the same solution.

Extra Example 3

Solve $-4x = -28$. 7

Key Questions to Ask for Example 3

- Which property of equality do you use to solve the equation? Why? You use the division property of equality to undo multiplication of -6 times x.
- Why do you divide by -6? You want x to have a coefficient of 1.

Differentiated Instruction

Visual Learners The variable in an equation can be any letter, not just x. Instead of a letter, it may be easier for some students to use a box or a blank to be filled in with a number. After completing a few problems in this way, they can use a variable.

See also the *Algebra 1 Toolkit* for more strategies.

Extra Example 4

Solve $\frac{x}{3} = 7$. 21

Key Question to Ask for Example 4

- Could you solve the equation by multiplying by 5? Explain. No. If you multiply each side of the equation by 5, the new coefficient of x will be $\frac{5}{4}$. To isolate the variable, you have to multiply $\frac{x}{4}$ by 4.

Extra Example 5

Solve $\frac{3}{5}x = -9$. -15

Avoiding Common Errors

Students may overlook the negative sign when working with reciprocals. In Guided Practice for Examples 4 and 5, suggest they do an additional check by determining the sign of the solution before solving the problem.

Mathematical Reasoning

To help students understand the algebraic concepts in the Key Concept boxes on pages 134 and 135, provide a concrete demonstration by using numbers for the variables. On the board, you can show an algebraic and number version of the properties side-by-side or one underneath the other. By seeing how the concepts work with numbers, students will be able to make the connection to algebraic thinking. In discussing the multiplication and division properties of equality, show that a cannot equal 0 by giving the example that you can divide 8 into 2 groups but you cannot divide 8 into 0 groups.

EXAMPLE 4 Solve an equation using multiplication

Solve $\frac{x}{4} = 5$.

Solution

$\frac{x}{4} = 5$ Write original equation.

$4 \cdot \frac{x}{4} = 4 \cdot 5$ Multiply each side by 4.

$x = 20$ Simplify.

✓ GUIDED PRACTICE for Example 4

Solve the equation. Check your solution.

9. $\frac{t}{-3} = 9$ -27 **10.** $6 = \frac{c}{7}$ 42 **11.** $13 = \frac{z}{-2}$ -26 **12.** $\frac{a}{5} = -11$ -55

USING RECIPROCALS Recall that the product of a number and its reciprocal is 1. You can isolate a variable with a fractional coefficient by multiplying each side of the equation by the reciprocal of the fraction.

EXAMPLE 5 Solve an equation by multiplying by a reciprocal

Solve $-\frac{2}{7}x = 4$.

REVIEW RECIPROCALS
For help with finding reciprocals, see p. 915.

Solution

The coefficient of x is $-\frac{2}{7}$. The reciprocal of $-\frac{2}{7}$ is $-\frac{7}{2}$.

$-\frac{2}{7}x = 4$ Write original equation.

$-\frac{7}{2}\left(-\frac{2}{7}x\right) = -\frac{7}{2}(4)$ Multiply each side by the reciprocal, $-\frac{7}{2}$.

$x = -14$ Simplify.

▶ The solution is -14. Check by substituting -14 for x in the original equation.

CHECK $-\frac{2}{7}x = 4$ Write original equation.

$-\frac{2}{7}(-14) \stackrel{?}{=} 4$ Substitute -14 for x.

$4 = 4$ ✓ Simplify. Solution checks.

✓ GUIDED PRACTICE for Example 5

Solve the equation. Check your solution.

13. $\frac{5}{6}w = 10$ 12 **14.** $\frac{2}{3}p = 14$ 21 **15.** $9 = -\frac{3}{4}m$ -12 **16.** $-8 = -\frac{4}{5}v$ 10

Differentiated Instruction

Below Level Some students may find it difficult working with reciprocals in **Example 5**. Have these students use the stepped-out solution in Example 5 as a model to solve each of the exercises in the **Guided Practice**. In the second step of the solution, it may be useful to write 4 as $\frac{4}{1}$ to more easily discern that $-\frac{7}{2}(4)$ is -14. The same holds true for substituting -14 for x in checking the solution.

Advanced You may want to ask advanced students how they would solve **Example 5** if they did not use the reciprocal of $-\frac{2}{7}$. Have them write a stepped-out solution and justify each step. Ask them to share their solutions and explain the advantages and disadvantages of using the reciprocal.

See also the *Algebra 1 Toolkit* for more strategies.

EXAMPLE 6 Write and solve an equation

OLYMPICS In the 2004 Olympics, Shawn Crawford won the 200 meter dash. His winning time was 19.79 seconds. Find his average speed to the nearest tenth of a meter per second.

Solution

Let r represent Crawford's speed in meters per second. Write a verbal model. Then write and solve an equation.

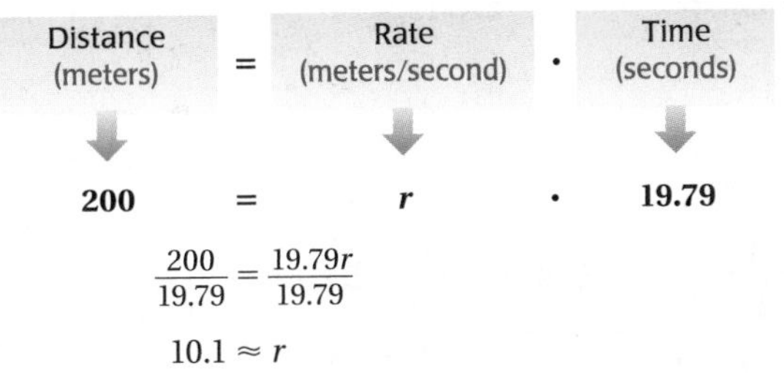

$$\frac{200}{19.79} = \frac{19.79r}{19.79}$$

$$10.1 \approx r$$

▶ Crawford's average speed was about 10.1 meters per second.

✓ **GUIDED PRACTICE** for Example 6

17. **WHAT IF?** In Example 6, suppose Shawn Crawford ran 100 meters at the same average speed he ran the 200 meters. How long would it take him to run 100 meters? Round your answer to the nearest tenth of a second. 9.9 sec

3.1 EXERCISES

HOMEWORK KEY
- ○ = **WORKED-OUT SOLUTIONS** on p. WS5 for Exs. 13 and 55
- ★ = **STANDARDIZED TEST PRACTICE** Exs. 2, 15, 16, 57, 58, and 61
-  = **MULTIPLE REPRESENTATIONS** Ex. 59

SKILL PRACTICE

A

1. **VOCABULARY** Copy and complete: Two operations that undo each other are called __?__. inverse operations

2. ★ **WRITING** Which property of equality would you use to solve the equation $14x = 35$? *Explain.* Division property of equality; to solve $14x = 35$, you need to divide each side by 14.

EXAMPLES 1 and 2 on pp. 134–135 for Exs. 3–14

SOLVING ADDITION AND SUBTRACTION EQUATIONS **Solve the equation. Check your solution.**

3. $x + 5 = 8$ 3
4. $m + 9 = 2$ −7
5. $11 = f + 6$ 5
6. $13 = 7 + z$ 6
7. $6 = 9 + h$ −3
8. $-3 = 5 + a$ −8
9. $y - 4 = 3$ 7
10. $t - 5 = 7$ 12
11. $14 = k - 3$ 17
12. $6 = w - 7$ 13
13. (circled) $-2 = n - 6$ 4
14. $-11 = b - 9$ −2

Extra Example 6

In the 2004 Summer Olympics, Inge de Bruijn won the women's 50-meter freestyle. Her winning time was 24.58 seconds. Find her average swimming speed to the nearest hundredth of a meter per second. about 2.03 m/sec

Key Question to Ask for Example 6

- If you knew Crawford's average speed and wanted to find how long it took him to run 200 meters, would you use a different property of equality to solve the equation? Explain. No, you would still use the division property of equality, and divide each side by the rate.

Reading Strategy

In Guided Practice for Example 6, tell students to make sure they understand the question. Point out that they will use the solution to Example 6 to determine the answer to Exercise 17, which uses Crawford's average rate of speed.

Closing the Lesson

Have students summarize the major points of the lesson and answer the Essential Question: How do you solve one-step equations using subtraction, addition, division, and multiplication?

- Use inverse operations and properties of equality to produce equivalent equations and isolate variables.
- Use reciprocals to isolate a variable with a fractional coefficient.

Solve one-step equations by using inverse operations to isolate the variable, for example, use addition to undo subtraction. If a coefficient is a fraction, multiply by its reciprocal to produce a coefficient of 1. Always perform the same operation on each side of the equation.

4 PRACTICE AND APPLY

Assignment Guide

Answer Transparencies available for all exercises

Basic:
Day 1: SRH p. 915 Exs. 16–20
pp. 137–140
Exs. 1, 2, 3–13 odd, 15, 16, 17–27 odd, 29–42, 53–59, 64–75

Average:
Day 1: pp. 137–140
Exs. 1, 2, 8–14 even, 15, 16, 20–28 even, 29, 30, 32–50 even, 54–61, 64–75 even

Advanced:
Day 1: pp. 137–140
Exs. 1, 2, 11–16, 20–26 even, 34–48 even, 49–52*, 56–63*, 69–75 odd

Block:
pp. 137–140
Exs. 1, 2, 8–14 even, 15, 16, 20–28 even, 29, 30, 32–50 even, 54–61, 64–75 even (with 3.2)

Differentiated Instruction

See *Algebra 1 Best Practices Toolkit* for suggestions on addressing the needs of a diverse classroom.

Homework Check

For a quick check of student understanding of key concepts, go over the following exercises:

Basic: 5, 19, 25, 40, 53
Average: 10, 20, 26, 44, 55
Advanced: 13, 22, 26, 46, 56

Extra Practice

- Student Edition, p. 940
- Chapter 3 Resource Book: Practice levels A, B, C, pp. 6–8

Practice Worksheet

An easily-readable reduced practice page (with answers) for this lesson can be found on p. 130C.

EXAMPLES 1 and 2 on pp. 134–135 for Exs. 15, 16

15. ★ **MULTIPLE CHOICE** What is the solution of $-8 = d - 13$? C

Ⓐ -21 Ⓑ -5 Ⓒ 5 Ⓓ 21

16. ★ **MULTIPLE CHOICE** What is the solution of $22 + v = -65$? A

Ⓐ -87 Ⓑ -43 Ⓒ 43 Ⓓ 87

EXAMPLES 3 and 4 on pp. 135–136 for Exs. 17–30

SOLVING MULTIPLICATION AND DIVISION EQUATIONS Solve the equation. Check your solution.

17. $5g = 20$ 4 **18.** $-4q = 52$ −13 **19.** $48 = 8c$ 6

20. $-108 = 9j$ −12 **21.** $15 = -h$ −15 **22.** $187 = -17r$ −11

23. $\frac{y}{3} = 5$ 15 **24.** $\frac{m}{2} = 14$ 28 **25.** $8 = \frac{x}{6}$ 48

26. $7 = \frac{t}{-7}$ −49 **27.** $-11 = \frac{z}{-2}$ 22 **28.** $-3 = \frac{d}{14}$ −42

ERROR ANALYSIS *Describe* and correct the error in solving the equation.

29.

$x + 3.8 = 2.3$
$x + 3.8 - 3.8 = 2.3 + 3.8$
$x = 6.1$

30.

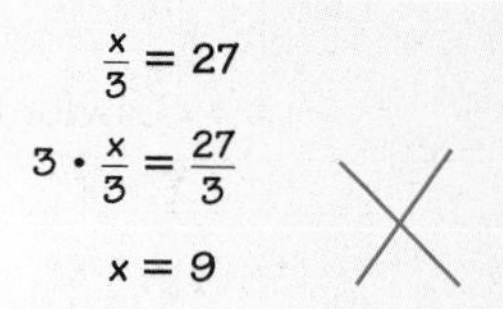
$\frac{x}{3} = 27$
$3 \cdot \frac{x}{3} = \frac{27}{3}$
$x = 9$

29. 3.8 should have been subtracted from both sides; $x + 3.8 - 3.8 = 2.3 - 3.8$, $x = -1.5$.

30. Both sides should have been multiplied by 3; $3 \cdot \frac{x}{3} = 27 \cdot 3$, $x = 81$.

B **SOLVING EQUATIONS** Solve the equation. Check your solution.

31. $b - 0.4 = 3.1$ 3.5 **32.** $-3.2 + z = -7.4$ −4.2 **33.** $-5.7 = w - 4.6$ −1.1

34. $-6.1 = p + 2.2$ −8.3 **35.** $8.2 = -4g$ −2.05 **36.** $-3.3a = 19.8$ −6

37. $\frac{3}{4} = \frac{1}{8} + v$ $\frac{5}{8}$ **38.** $\frac{n}{4.6} = -2.5$ −11.5 **39.** $-0.12 = \frac{y}{-0.5}$ 0.06

EXAMPLE 5 on p. 136 for Exs. 40–48

40. $\frac{1}{2}m = 21$ 42 **41.** $\frac{1}{3}c = 32$ 96 **42.** $-7 = \frac{1}{5}x$ −35

43. $\frac{3}{2}k = 18$ 12 **44.** $-21 = -\frac{3}{5}t$ 35 **45.** $-\frac{2}{7}v = 16$ −56

46. $\frac{8}{5}x = \frac{4}{15}$ $\frac{1}{6}$ **47.** $\frac{1}{3}y = \frac{1}{5}$ $\frac{3}{5}$ **48.** $-\frac{4}{3} = \frac{2}{3}z$ −2

C **GEOMETRY** The rectangle or triangle has area A. Write and solve an equation to find the value of x.

49. $A = 54 \text{ in.}^2$ $54 = 12x$; 4.5 in.

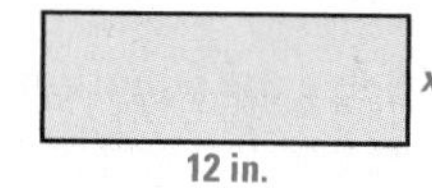

50. $A = 72 \text{ cm}^2$ $72 = \frac{1}{2}(16)x$; 9 cm

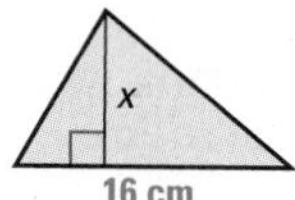

CHALLENGE Find the value of b using the given information.

51. $4a = 6$ and $b = a - 2$ −0.5 **52.** $a - 6.7 = 3.1$ and $b = 5a$ 49

○ = WORKED-OUT SOLUTIONS on p. WS1 ★ = STANDARDIZED TEST PRACTICE  = MULTIPLE REPRESENTATIONS

PROBLEM SOLVING

EXAMPLE 6 A on p. 137 for Exs. 53–57

53. THE DEAD SEA For the period 1999–2004, the maximum depth of the Dead Sea decreased by 9.9 feet. The maximum depth in 2004 was 1036.7 feet. What was the maximum depth in 1999? **1046.6 ft**

@HomeTutor for problem solving help at classzone.com

54. CRAFTS You purchase a cane of polymer clay to make pendants for necklaces. The cane is 50 millimeters long. How thick should you make each pendant so that you will have 20 pendants of uniform thickness? **2.5 mm**

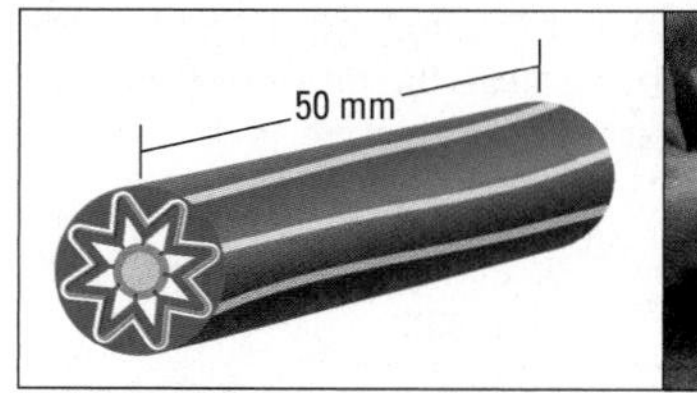

@HomeTutor for problem solving help at classzone.com

55. TRAMPOLINES A rectangular trampoline has an area of 187 square feet. The length of the trampoline is 17 feet. What is its width? **11 ft**

56. WHEELCHAIRS The van used to transport patients to and from a rehabilitation facility is equipped with a wheelchair lift. The maximum lifting capacity for the lift is 300 pounds. The wheelchairs used by the facility weigh 55 pounds each. What is the maximum weight of a wheelchair occupant who can use the lift? **245 lb**

57. ★ SHORT RESPONSE In Everglades National Park in Florida, there are 200 species of birds that migrate. This accounts for $\frac{4}{7}$ of all the species of birds sighted in the park.

a. Write an equation to find the number of species of birds that have been sighted in Everglades National Park. $\frac{4}{7}x = 200$

b. There are 600 species of plants in Everglades National Park. Are there more species of birds or of plants in the park? *Explain.* **Plants; if you solve the equation in part (a) you find that there are 350 species of birds.**

B

58. ★ OPEN-ENDED *Describe* a real-world situation that can be modeled by the equation $15x = 135$. Solve the equation and explain what the solution means in this situation.

58. *Sample answer:* Each member of the drama club needs to sell tickets to the upcoming play. If there are 15 members and you want to sell 135 tickets, how many tickets should each member sell? $x = 9$; each member should sell 9 tickets.

59. ◆ MULTIPLE REPRESENTATIONS A box jellyfish can travel at a rate of 6.5 feet per second.

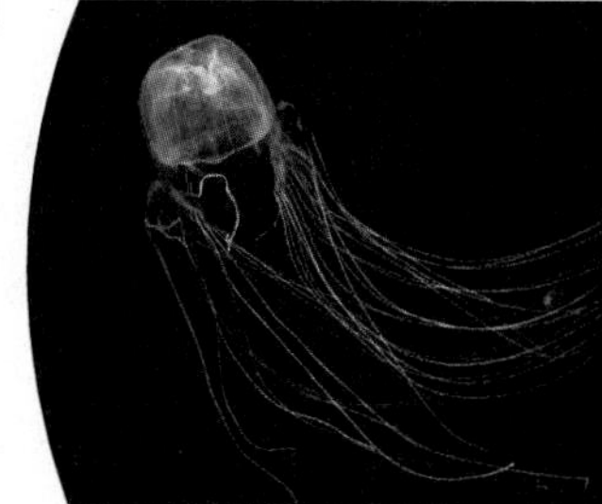

a. **Making a Table** Make a table that shows the distance d the jellyfish can travel after 1, 2, 3, 4, and 5 seconds. **See margin.**

b. **Drawing a Graph** Graph the ordered pairs from the table in a coordinate plane. How long does it take the jellyfish to travel 26 feet? **See margin for art.;4 sec.**

c. **Writing an Equation** Write and solve an equation to find the time it takes the jellyfish to travel 26 feet. $26 = 6.5t$; **4 sec**

Animated Algebra at classzone.com

Reading Strategy

Exercises 3–48 Some students may be confused when the variable is on the right side of the equation. Explain that the solution is the same whether the variable is on the right or the left side. If students find it distracting, they can rewrite the equation so that the variable is on the left side.

Exercises 47–48 Tell students to make sure they multiply by the reciprocal of the coefficient.

Avoiding Common Errors

Exercises 31–34 Remind students to align decimals when they add or subtract. They may want to use a vertical model for these exercises.

Study Strategy

Exercises 53–57 Encourage students to write a verbal model for each of these exercises using the model in Example 6 as a guide. This will help them organize all of the information in the problems so they write appropriate equations to solve the problems.

Internet Reference

Exercise 53 To learn more about the Dead Sea, visit i-cias.com/e.o/dead_sea.htm.

Exercise 57 More information about Everglades National Park can be found on the National Park Service's website www.nps.gov/ever.

An **Animated Algebra** activity is available on-line for **Exercise 59.** This activity is also available on the **Power Presentations CD-ROM**.

59a.

t	D
1	6.5
2	13
3	19.5
4	26
5	32.5

59b.

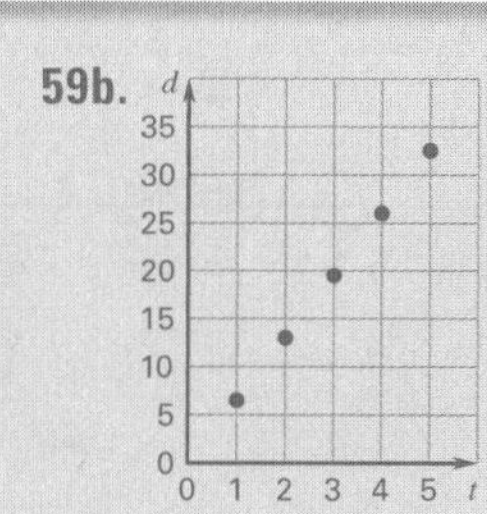

5 ASSESS AND RETEACH

Daily Homework Quiz

 **Transparency Available**

Solve the equation. Check your solution.

1. $-6 + a = -2$ **4**
2. $8 = m - 7$ **15**
3. $9k = -72$ **−8**
4. $12 = \frac{x}{-5}$ **−60**
5. Earth orbits the Sun at an average speed of 29.79 kilometers per second. Find how long it takes, to the nearest hundredth of a second, for Earth to travel 500 kilometers. **16.78 sec**

Online Quiz

Available at **classzone.com**

Diagnosis/Remediation

- Practice A, B, C in Chapter 3 Resource Book, pp. 6–8
- Study Guide in Chapter 3 Resource Book, pp. 9–10
- Practice Workbook, pp. 30–31
- @HomeTutor

Challenge

Additional challenge is available in the Chapter 3 Resource Book, p. 13.

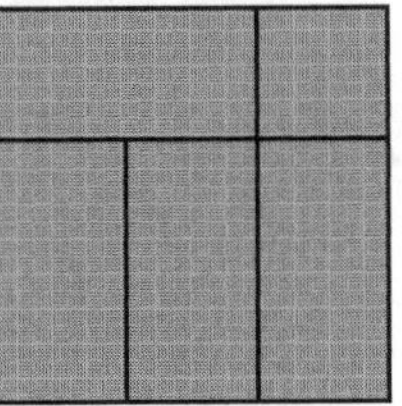

60. **MULTI-STEP PROBLEM** Tatami mats are a floor covering used in Japan. Tatami mats are equal in size, unless they are cut in half. The floor shown has an area of 81 square feet and is covered with 4.5 tatami mats.

    a. What is the area of one tatami mat? **18 ft²**

    b. What is the length of one tatami mat if it has a width of 3 feet? **6 ft**

61. ★ **EXTENDED RESPONSE** In baseball, a player's batting average is calculated by dividing the number of hits by the number of at bats.

    a. **Calculate** Use the information in the table to find the number of hits Bill Mueller had in the 2003 Major League Baseball regular season. Round your answer to the nearest whole number. **171 hits**

Player	Team	Batting average	At bats
Bill Mueller	Boston Red Sox	0.326	524

    b. **Calculate** The number of hits Bill Mueller had was 44 less than the number of hits Vernon Wells of the Toronto Blue Jays had in the 2003 regular season. How many hits did Vernon Wells have? **215 hits**

    c. **Compare** In the 2003 regular season, Mueller had a higher batting average than Wells. Did Wells have fewer at bats than Mueller? *Explain* your reasoning. **No; if Mueller had fewer hits than Wells but had a higher batting average, he must have had fewer at bats than Wells.**

C 62. **AMERICAN FLAGS** An American flag has a length that is 1.9 times its width. What is the area of a flag that has a length of 9.5 feet? **47.5 ft²**

63. **CHALLENGE** At a farm where you can pick your own strawberries, the cost of picked strawberries is calculated using only the weight of the strawberries. The total weight of a container full of strawberries is 2.1 pounds. The cost of the strawberries is \$4.68. The weight of the container is 0.3 pound. What is the cost per pound for strawberries? **\$2.60**

ILLINOIS MIXED REVIEW

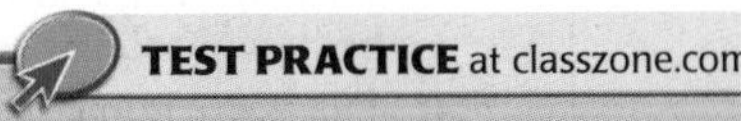

TEST PRACTICE at classzone.com

64. Which function includes the data set {(2, −1), (4, 5), (8, 17)}? **C**

    (A) $y = x - 3$ (B) $y = 2x - 3$ (C) $y = 3x - 7$ (D) $y = 5x - 15$

65. Simplify the expression $4(2x + 4) - 6(x + 1)$. **C**

    (A) $2x + 10$ (B) $2x + 15$ (C) $2x + 17$ (D) $2x + 22$

66. The drawing shows a 3-dimensional solid. Which best represents the shape of the solid when viewed from the top? **D**

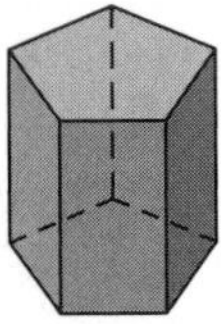

    (A) Square (B) Heptagon (C) Octagon (D) Pentagon

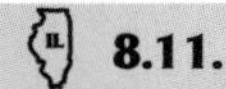

3.2 Solve Two-Step Equations

8.11.16 Solve linear equations and inequalities, including selecting and evaluating formulas.

Before You solved one-step equations.

Now You will solve two-step equations.

Why? So you can find a scuba diver's depth, as in Example 4.

Key Vocabulary
- **like terms,** *p. 97*
- **input,** *p. 35*
- **output,** *p. 35*

The equation $\frac{x}{2} + 5 = 11$ involves two operations performed on x: division by 2 and addition by 5. You typically solve such an equation by applying the inverse operations in the reverse order of the order of operations. This is shown in the table below.

Operations performed on x	Operations to isolate x
1. Divide by 2. 2. Add 5.	1. Subtract 5. 2. Multiply by 2.

EXAMPLE 1 Solve a two-step equation

Solve $\frac{x}{2} + 5 = 11$.

$\frac{x}{2} + 5 = 11$ Write original equation.

$\frac{x}{2} + 5 - 5 = 11 - 5$ Subtract 5 from each side.

$\frac{x}{2} = 6$ Simplify.

$2 \cdot \frac{x}{2} = 2 \cdot 6$ Multiply each side by 2.

$x = 12$ Simplify.

▶ The solution is 12. Check by substituting 12 for x in the original equation.

CHECK $\frac{x}{2} + 5 = 11$ Write original equation.

$\frac{12}{2} + 5 \stackrel{?}{=} 11$ Substitute 12 for x.

$11 = 11$ ✓ Simplify. Solution checks.

GUIDED PRACTICE for Example 1

Solve the equation. Check your solution.

1. $5x + 9 = 24$ 3
2. $4y - 4 = 16$ 5
3. $-1 = \frac{z}{3} - 7$ 18

1 PLAN AND PREPARE

Warm-Up Exercises

Transparency Available

Solve the equation.

1. $3x = -18$ -6
2. $b + 21 = 11$ -10
3. Simplify the expression $3(x + 2) - 4x + 1$. $-x + 7$
4. There are three times as many goats as sheep in a petting zoo. Find the number of sheep if the total number of goats and sheep is 28. 7 sheep

Notetaking Guide

Transparency Available

Promotes interactive learning and notetaking skills, pp. 52–54.

Pacing

Basic: 1 day
Average: 1 day
Advanced: 1 day
Block: 0.5 block with 3.1
- See *Teaching Guide/Lesson Plan*.

2 FOCUS AND MOTIVATE

Essential Question

Big Idea 1, p. 131

How do you solve two-step equations? Tell students they will learn how to answer this question by solving equations with more than one operation or with like terms.

Resource Planning Guide

Chapter Resource Book
- Teaching Guide/Lesson Plan (pp. 14–15)
- Activity Master (p. 16)
- Practice levels A, B, C (pp. 17–19)
- Study Guide (pp. 20–21)
- Catch-up for Absent Students (p. 22)
- Application (p. 23)
- Challenge (p. 24)

Workbooks
- Notetaking Guide (pp. 52–54)
- Practice Workbook (pp. 32–33)

Teaching Options
- **Power Presentations CD-ROM** provides dynamic electronic teaching resources for the classroom.
- **Activity Generator CD-ROM** provides editable activities for all ability levels.

Interactive Technology
- Easy Planner
- Power Presentations CD-ROM
- Activity Generator CD-ROM
- Animated Algebra
- Test Generator CD-ROM
- Online Quiz
- eWorkbook
- eEdition
- @HomeTutor

Resources for English Learners
- Quick Reference for English Learners
- Spanish Study Guide
- Multi-Language Visual Glossary
- Student Resources in Spanish

See also the *Algebra 1 Toolkit* for more strategies for meeting individual needs.

Motivating the Lesson

Ask students if they have shipped a package at a shipping outlet or bought items online. Tell them that outlets or online stores often charge handling fees, such as $.37 per ounce, on top of the cost of the items or the cost of shipping the package. Invite students to share some of their experiences. Tell them that these are examples of two-step equations that they will be solving in Lesson 3.2.

3 TEACH

Extra Example 1

Solve $\frac{x}{4} - 3 = 2$. 20

Key Questions to Ask for Example 1

- Could you multiply 2 by first? If so, what else would change? Yes, you could multiply by 2 first to get $x + 10 = 22$. Then you would subtract 10 from each side.
- Why is it simpler to subtract and then multiply? There are fewer steps. If you multiply first, you have to multiply all of the terms of the equation by 2, which adds a step.

Extra Example 2

Solve $5b - 7b = 4$. -2

Key Question to Ask for Example 2

- How do you use the distributive property to combine like terms? Add the coefficients mentally, and then write the common variable.

Extra Example 3

The output of a function is 7 more than 2 times the input. Write an equation for the function and then find the input when the output is 15. $y = 2x + 7$; 4

REVIEW LIKE TERMS
For help with combining like terms, see p. 97.

EXAMPLE 2 Solve a two-step equation by combining like terms

Solve $7x - 4x = 21$.

$7x - 4x = 21$	Write original equation.
$3x = 21$	Combine like terms.
$\frac{3x}{3} = \frac{21}{3}$	Divide each side by 3.
$x = 7$	Simplify.

EXAMPLE 3 Find an input of a function

The output of a function is 3 less than 5 times the input. Find the input when the output is 17.

Solution

STEP 1 **Write** an equation for the function. Let x be the input and y be the output.

$y = 5x - 3$	y is 3 less than 5 times x.

STEP 2 **Solve** the equation for x when $y = 17$.

$y = 5x - 3$	Write original function.
$17 = 5x - 3$	Substitute 17 for y.
$17 + 3 = 5x - 3 + 3$	Add 3 to each side.
$20 = 5x$	Simplify.
$\frac{20}{5} = \frac{5x}{5}$	Divide each side by 5.
$4 = x$	Simplify.

▶ An input of 4 produces an output of 17.

CHECK

$y = 5x - 3$	Write original function.
$17 \stackrel{?}{=} 5(4) - 3$	Substitute 17 for y and 4 for x.
$17 \stackrel{?}{=} 20 - 3$	Multiply 5 and 4.
$17 = 17$ ✓	Simplify. Solution checks.

✓ GUIDED PRACTICE for Examples 2 and 3

Solve the equation. Check your solution.

4. $4w + 2w = 24$ 4
5. $8t - 3t = 35$ 7
6. $-16 = 5d - 9d$ 4
7. The output of a function is 5 more than -2 times the input. Find the input when the output is 11. -3
8. The output of a function is 4 less than 4 times the input. Find the input when the output is 3. $1\frac{3}{4}$

EXAMPLE 4 Solve a multi-step problem

SCUBA DIVING As a scuba diver descends into deeper water, the pressure of the water on the diver's body steadily increases.

The pressure at the surface of the water is 2117 pounds per square foot (lb/ft^2). The pressure increases at a rate of 64 pounds per square foot for each foot the diver descends. Find the depth at which a diver experiences a pressure of 8517 pounds per square foot.

ANOTHER WAY
For an alternative method for solving Example 4, turn to page 147 for the **Problem Solving Workshop**.

Solution

STEP 1 **Write** a verbal model. Then write an equation.

Pressure at given depth (lb/ft^2)	=	Pressure at surface (lb/ft^2)	+	Rate of change of pressure (lb/ft^2 per foot of depth)	·	Diver's depth (ft)
P	=	2117	+	64	·	d

STEP 2 **Find** the depth at which the pressure is 8517 pounds per square foot.

$P = 2117 + 64d$ — **Write equation.**

$8517 = 2117 + 64d$ — **Substitute 8517 for *P*.**

$8517 - 2117 = 2117 - 2117 + 64d$ — **Subtract 2117 from each side.**

$6400 = 64d$ — **Simplify.**

$\frac{6400}{64} = \frac{64d}{64}$ — **Divide each side by 64.**

$100 = d$ — **Simplify.**

▶ A diver experiences a pressure of 8517 pounds per square foot at a depth of 100 feet.

CHECK

$P = 2117 + 64d$ — **Write original equation.**

$8517 \stackrel{?}{=} 2117 + 64(100)$ — **Substitute 8517 for *P* and 100 for *d*.**

$8517 \stackrel{?}{=} 2117 + 6400$ — **Multiply 64 and 100.**

$8517 = 8517$ ✓ — **Simplify. Solution checks.**

✓ **GUIDED PRACTICE** for Example 4

9. **WHAT IF?** In Example 4, suppose the diver experiences a pressure of 5317 pounds per square foot. Find the diver's depth. **50 ft**

10. **JOBS** Kim has a job where she makes $8 per hour plus tips. Yesterday, Kim made $53 dollars, $13 of which was from tips. How many hours did she work? **5 h**

Extra Example 4

To rent a booth at the county fairgrounds costs $42 per day plus a one-time equipment fee of $85. Find the number of days Mr. Batzle rented a booth if he paid a total of $337. **6 days**

Key Questions to Ask for Example 4

- How is Example 4 like the output and input of the function in Example 3? **The output is *P*, the pressure at a given depth, and the input is *d*, the diver's depth.**
- Which are the dependent and independent variables? ***P* is the dependent variable and *d* is the independent variable.**
- Why do you subtract and then divide to solve the equation? **This is using inverse operations in the reverse order of the operations performed on *d*. Since you multiplied *d* by 64 and then added 2117, you subtract 2117 and then divide by 64 to apply inverse operations in the reverse order.**

Closing the Lesson

Have students summarize the major points of the lesson and answer the Essential Question: How do you solve two-step equations?

- **To solve equations efficiently, apply inverse operations in the reverse order of the operations performed on the variable.**
- **Combine like terms before solving equations.**

First look for like terms and combine them when solving two-step equations. For equations with two operations, look at the original equation and apply the inverse operations in the reverse order.

Differentiated Instruction

Inclusion Students need to organize their solution steps. It may be helpful to refer to a mnemonic device such as "My Dear Aunt Sally" to remember the order of operations Multiplication, Division, Addition, and Subtraction. For the method of solving linear equations, the mnemonic is reversed; to isolate the variable, first do Subtraction or Addition, then do Division or Multiplication.

See also the *Algebra 1 Toolkit* for more strategies.

4 PRACTICE AND APPLY

Assignment Guide

Answer Transparencies available for all exercises

Basic:
Day 1: SRH p. 938 Exs. 21–24
pp. 144–146
Exs. 1, 2, 3–21 odd, 22–29, 37–41, 46–60

Average:
Day 1: pp. 144–146
Exs. 1, 2, 6–20 even, 21–26, 30–36, 38–44, 46–60

Advanced:
Day 1: pp. 144–146
Exs. 1, 2, 8–14 even, 19–21, 24–26, 32–36*, 39–45*, 49–51, 54–60 even

Block:
pp. 144–146
Exs. 1, 2, 6–20 even, 21–26, 30–36, 38–44, 46–60 (with 3.1)

Differentiated Instruction

See *Algebra 1 Best Practices Toolkit* for suggestions on addressing the needs of a diverse classroom.

Homework Check

For a quick check of student understanding of key concepts, go over the following exercises:

Basic: 7, 13, 17, 24, 37

Average: 8, 14, 18, 25, 38

Advanced: 10, 14, 20, 26, 39

Extra Practice

- Student Edition, p. 940
- Chapter 3 Resource Book: Practice levels A, B, C, pp. 17–19

Practice Worksheet

An easily-readable reduced practice page (with answers) for this lesson can be found on p. 130C.

3.2 EXERCISES

HOMEWORK KEY

○ = **WORKED-OUT SOLUTIONS** on p. WS5 for Exs. 13, 19, and 39

★ = **STANDARDIZED TEST PRACTICE** Exs. 2, 21, 40, 41, and 44

◆ = **MULTIPLE REPRESENTATIONS** Ex. 43

SKILL PRACTICE

A

1. **VOCABULARY** Copy and complete: To solve the equation $2x + 3x = 20$, you would begin by combining $2x$ and $3x$ because they are _?_. like terms

2. ★ **WRITING** *Describe* the steps you would use to solve the equation $4x + 7 = 15$. First, subtract 7 from each side to get $4x = 8$, then divide each side by 4 to get $x = 2$.

EXAMPLE 1 on p. 141 for Exs. 3–14

SOLVING TWO-STEP EQUATIONS **Solve the equation. Check your solution.**

3. $3x + 7 = 19$ 4
4. $5h + 4 = 19$ 3
5. $7d - 1 = 13$ 2
6. $2g - 13 = 3$ 8
7. $10 = 7 - m$ -3
8. $11 = 12 - q$ 1
9. $\frac{a}{3} + 4 = 6$ 6
10. $17 = \frac{w}{5} + 13$ 20
11. $\frac{b}{2} - 9 = 11$ 40
12. $-6 = \frac{z}{4} - 3$ -12
13. $7 = \frac{5}{6}c - 8$ 18
14. $10 = \frac{2}{7}n + 4$ 21

EXAMPLE 2 on p. 142 for Exs. 15–23

COMBINING LIKE TERMS **Solve the equation. Check your solution.**

15. $8y + 3y = 44$ 4
16. $2p + 7p = 54$ 6
17. $11x - 9x = 18$ 9
18. $36 = 9x - 3x$ 6
19. $-32 = -5k + 13k$ -4
20. $6 = -7f + 4f$ -2

21. ★ **MULTIPLE CHOICE** What is the first step you can take to solve the equation $6 + \frac{x}{3} = -2$? D

Ⓐ Subtract 2 from each side.
Ⓑ Add 6 to each side.
Ⓒ Divide each side by 3.
Ⓓ Subtract 6 from each side.

ERROR ANALYSIS ***Describe*** **and correct the error in solving the equation.**

22.
$7 - 3x = 12$
$4x = 12$
$x = 3$

Unlike terms were combined; $-3x = 5$, $x = -\frac{5}{3}$.

23.
$-2x + x = 10$
$\frac{-2x + x}{-2} = \frac{10}{-2}$
$x = -5$

See margin.

EXAMPLE 3 on p. 142 for Exs. 24–26

FINDING AN INPUT OF A FUNCTION **Write an equation for the function described. Then find the input.**

24. The output of a function is 7 more than 3 times the input. Find the input when the output is -8. $y = 3x + 7$; -5

25. The output of a function is 4 more than 2 times the input. Find the input when the output is -10. $y = 2x + 4$; -7

26. The output of a function is 9 less than 10 times the input. Find the input when the output is 11. $y = 10x - 9$; 2

23. The division of $-2x + x$ by -2 is done incorrectly. *Sample answer:* If like terms are combined as the first step, the second line would be $-x = 10$ and the final result would be $x = -10$.

B **SOLVING EQUATIONS** **Solve the equation. Check your solution.**

27. $5.6 = 1.1p + 1.2$ 4
28. $7.2y + 4.7 = 62.3$ 8
29. $1.2j - 4.3 = 1.7$ 5
30. $16 - 2.4d = -8$ 10
31. $14.4m - 5.1 = 2.1$ 0.5
32. $-5.3 = 2.2v - 8.6$ 1.5
33. $\frac{c}{5.3} + 8.3 = 11.3$ 15.9
34. $3.2 + \frac{x}{2.5} = 4.6$ 3.5
35. $-1.2 = \frac{z}{4.6} - 2.7$ 6.9

C 36. **CHALLENGE** Solve the equations $3x + 2 = 5$, $3x + 2 = 8$, and $3x + 2 = 11$. Predict the solution of the equation $3x + 2 = 14$. *Explain.* 1, 2, 3; 4; the output of each equation is increased by 3 because x is multiplied by 3, each solution increases by 1.

PROBLEM SOLVING

EXAMPLE 4 on p. 143 for Exs. 37–40

A 37. **DANCE CLASSES** A dance academy charges $24 per class and a one-time registration fee of $15. A student paid a total of $687 to the academy. Find the number of classes the student took. 28 classes

@HomeTutor for problem solving help at classzone.com

38. **CAR REPAIR** Tyler paid $124 to get his car repaired. The total cost for the repairs was the sum of the amount paid for parts and the amount paid for labor. Tyler was charged $76 for parts and $32 per hour for labor. Find the amount of time it took to repair his car. 1.5 h

@HomeTutor for problem solving help at classzone.com

39. **ADVERTISING** A science museum wants to promote an upcoming exhibit by advertising on city buses for one month. The costs of the two types of advertisements being considered are shown. The museum has budgeted $6000 for the advertisements. The museum decides to have 1 full bus wrap advertisement. How many half-side advertisements can the museum have? 5 half-side advertisements

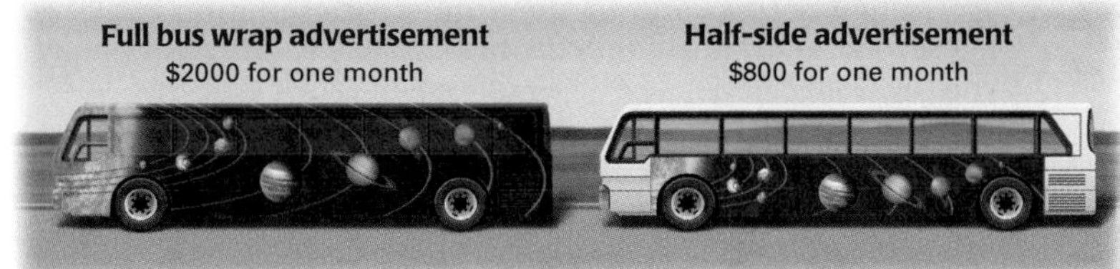

40. ★ **MULTIPLE CHOICE** A skateboarding park charges $7 per session to skate and $4 per session to rent safety equipment. Jared rents safety equipment every time he skates. During one year, he spends $99 for skating charges and equipment rentals. Which equation can be used to find x, the number of sessions Jared attended? B

Ⓐ $99 = 7x$ Ⓑ $99 = 7x + 4x$ Ⓒ $99 = 7x + 4$ Ⓓ $99 = 4x + 7$

B 41. ★ **SHORT RESPONSE** A guitar store offers a finance plan where you give a $50 down payment on a guitar and pay the remaining balance in 6 equal monthly payments. You have $50 and you can afford to pay up to $90 per month for a guitar. Can you afford a guitar that costs $542? *Explain.*

41. Yes; the equation $\$542 = \$50 + 6x$ gives the monthly cost of a guitar that costs $542. Solving the equation gives $x = \$82$ per month, so you can afford the guitar.

Avoiding Common Errors

Exercises 3–14 Students often use the wrong operation when solving an equation. Suggest they work with a partner prior to solving the equations to go over the operations they should use in each of the exercises. Refer them to the box in the explanation before Example 1. Have them go through each of the exercises using the box as a model to determine which operations they should use and in which order.

Reading Strategy

Exercises 13–14 Caution students to read these exercises carefully. Note that the coefficients are slightly different than those in Exercises 9–12.

Teaching Strategy

Exercises 24–26 It may be useful to review Example 3 and functions in general before students work on these exercises. Remind students that functions typically give the output y in terms of the input x.

Exercise 36 For students who request help on this exercise, tell them to look for a pattern in the equations and for a pattern in the value of x. They may want to line up the equations, one underneath the other, to visualize the pattern. Tell them to use the patterns to explain their prediction.

Exercises 37–40 Suggest that students first determine the variable in the problem. This will help them determine the coefficient of the variable and the constant.

5 ASSESS AND RETEACH

Daily Homework Quiz

Transparency Available

Solve the equation.

1. $\frac{a}{4} + 6 = -14$ -80
2. $6r - 12 = 6$ 3
3. $-36 = 7y + 2y$ -4
4. The output of a function is 9 less than 3 times the input. Write an equation for the function and then find the input when the output is -6. $y = 3x - 9$; 1
5. A bank charges $5.00 per month plus $.30 per check for a standard checking account. Find the number of checks Justine wrote if she paid $8.30 in fees last month. 11 checks

Available at **classzone.com**

Diagnosis/Remediation

- Practice A, B, C in Chapter 3 Resource Book, pp. 17–19
- Study Guide in Chapter 3 Resource Book, pp. 20–21
- Practice Workbook, pp. 32–33
- @HomeTutor

Challenge

Additional challenge is available in the Chapter 3 Resource Book, p. 24.

43b. See Additional Answers beginning on p. AA1.

43c.

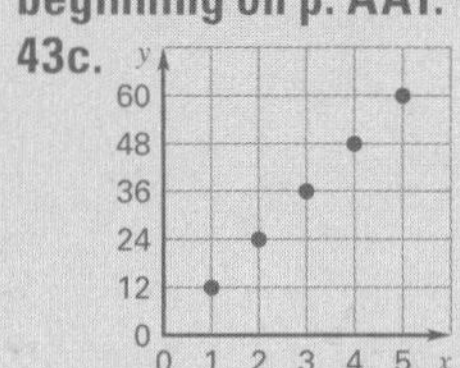

42. Sample answer: Estimate the number of days to be about 1200; $3{,}000{,}000 + 1600(1200) = 3{,}000{,}000 + 1{,}920{,}000 = 4{,}920{,}000$ so the solution makes sense.

42. **MULTI-STEP PROBLEM** The capacity of a landfill is 4,756,505 tons. The landfill currently holds 2,896,112 tons. A cell is added to the landfill every day, and each cell averages 1600 tons.
    a. Write an equation that gives the amount y (in tons) in the landfill as a function of the number x of days from now. $y = 2{,}896{,}112 + 1600x$
    b. After how many days will the landfill reach capacity? Round your answer to the nearest day. 1163 days
    c. Use estimation to check your answer to part (b).

Trash is compacted into a pocket called a cell.
Cells are separated by layers of soil.

43. **MULTIPLE REPRESENTATIONS** Two computer technicians are upgrading the software on the 54 computers in a school. On average, Marissa upgrades 5 computers in 1 hour and Ryan upgrades 7 computers in 1 hour.
    a. **Writing an Equation** Write an equation that gives the total number y of computers upgraded as a function of the number x of hours worked. $y = 12x$
    b. **Making a Table** Make a table that shows the number of computers upgraded by each technician and the total number of computers upgraded after 1, 2, 3, 4, and 5 hours. See margin.
    c. **Drawing a Graph** Graph the ordered pairs that represent the total number y of computers upgraded after x hours. Use the graph to estimate the number of hours it took to upgrade all of the computers. See margin for art; about 4.5 h.

44. ★ **SHORT RESPONSE** At a restaurant, customers can dine inside the restaurant or pick up food at the take-out window. On an average day, 400 customers are served inside the restaurant, and 120 customers pick up food at the take-out window. After how many days will the restaurant have served 2600 customers? *Explain.* 5 days; the restaurant serves $400 + 120 = 520$ customers each day, use the equation $2600 = 520x$ to find $x = 5$.

C 45. **CHALLENGE** During a 1 mile race, one runner is running at a rate of 14.6 feet per second, and another runner is running at a rate of 11.3 feet per second. One lap around the track is 660 feet. After how many seconds will the faster runner be exactly one lap ahead of the other runner? 200 sec

ILLINOIS MIXED REVIEW

TEST PRACTICE at classzone.com

46. Which equation best describes the graph shown? B

    (A) $y = x - 4$
    (B) $y = 24 - 4x$
    (C) $y = 24x - 4$
    (D) $y = -4(x + 24)$

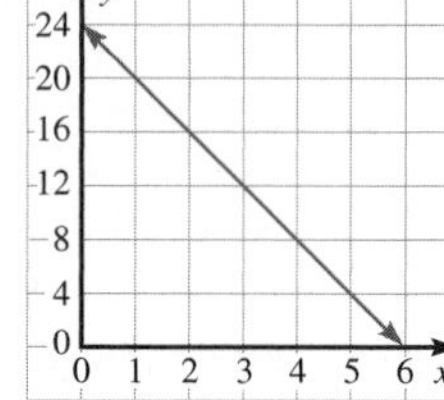

47. If a is positive, b is negative, and $c = 0$, which of the following expressions is positive? C

    (A) $a(b + c)$ (B) $c(a + b)$ (C) $b(b - a + c)$ (D) $c(a - b + ab)$

PROBLEM SOLVING WORKSHOP LESSON 3.2

Using ALTERNATIVE METHODS

Another Way to Solve Example 4, page 143

MULTIPLE REPRESENTATIONS In Example 4 on page 143, you saw how to solve a problem about scuba diving by using an equation. You can also solve the problem using a table.

PROBLEM

SCUBA DIVING As a scuba diver descends into deeper water, the pressure of the water on the diver's body steadily increases. The pressure at the surface of the water is 2117 pounds per square foot (lb/ft^2). The pressure increases at a rate of 64 pounds per square foot for each foot the diver descends. Find the depth at which a diver experiences a pressure of 8517 pounds per square foot.

METHOD

Making a Table An alternative approach is to make a table.

STEP 1 **Make** a table that shows the pressure as the depth increases. Because you are looking for a fairly high pressure, use larger increments in depth, such as 20 feet.

Every 1 ft of depth increases the pressure by 64 lb/ft^2.

Every 20 ft of depth increases the pressure by 64(20) = 1280 lb/ft^2.

Depth (ft)	Pressure (lb/ft^2)
0	2117
1	2181
2	2245
20	3397
40	4677
60	5957
80	7237
100	8517

STEP 2 **Look** for the depth at which the pressure reaches 8517 pounds per square foot. This happens at a depth of 100 feet.

PRACTICE

1. **BASKETBALL** A sports club offers an organized basketball league. A team pays $600 to join the league. In addition to paying their share of the $600, team members who are not members of the sports club must pay a $25 fee to play. A team pays a total of $775. How many team members who are not club members are on the team? Solve this problem using two different methods. See margin.

2. **WHAT IF?** In Exercise 1, suppose you are on a team, but not a club member. The $600 cost is divided equally among the team members. How many players must there be on your team for you to pay $100 to play? Make a table to find the answer. 8 players; see margin for table.

3. **FURNITURE** You have $370 to spend on a dining table and chairs. A table costs $220, and each chair costs $35. How many chairs can you buy in addition to the table? Solve this problem using two different methods. See margin.

Alternative Strategy

Example 4 on page 143 can be solved using a table. This method allows the student to grasp and solve a complex problem in which the numbers are large and the measurements are most likely unfamiliar. The table can also be used to help the student understand the algebraic solution given in Lesson 3.2.

Mathematical Reasoning

Multiple Representations Using a table to solve a problem is a useful strategy when students have a difficult time writing an equation. It is particularly helpful in Example 4 because students may feel overwhelmed by the numbers or the concepts and may be discouraged in finding a solution. By using the table alongside the algebraic solution, students are more likely to see the relationships in the equation between pressure at the surface, the rate of change, and the diver's depth. Once they see these interconnections, it could help them write an equation to model the problem. Have students discuss advantages and disadvantages of using tables to solve problems. One advantage is they can see how the pressure changes at different depths and thereby get a sense for a reasonable solution to the problem. Some disadvantages include more possibilities for making errors in calculations and missing the actual depth because they are using an increment that misses the target pressure.

1. See Additional Answers beginning on p. AA1.

2.

Team members	Your cost (dollars)
1	625
2	325
3	225
4	175
5	145
6	125
7	110.71
8	100

3. See Additional Answers beginning on p. AA1.

1 PLAN AND PREPARE

Warm-Up Exercises

Transparency Available

1. Simplify the expression $9x + 2(x - 1) + 7$. $11x + 5$

Solve the equation.

2. $5g - 7 = 58$ 13
3. $\frac{2}{3}x = 18$ 27
4. A surf shop charges $85 for surfing lessons and $35 per hour to rent a surfboard. Anna paid $225. Find the number of hours she spent surfing. 4 h

Notetaking Guide

Transparency Available

Promotes interactive learning and notetaking skills, pp. 55–56.

Pacing

Basic: 2 days
Average: 2 days
Advanced: 2 days
Block: 1 block
- See *Teaching Guide/Lesson Plan.*

2 FOCUS AND MOTIVATE

Essential Question

Big Idea 1, p. 131

How do you solve multi-step equations? Tell students they will learn how to answer this question by combining like terms, using the distributive property, and multiplying by a reciprocal.

3.3 Solve Multi-Step Equations

8.11.16 Solve linear equations and inequalities, including selecting and evaluating formulas.

Before You solved one-step and two-step equations.
Now You will solve multi-step equations.
Why? So you can solve a problem about lifeguarding, as in Ex. 40.

Key Vocabulary
- **like terms,** *p. 97*
- **distributive property,** *p. 96*
- **reciprocal,** *p. 915*

Solving a linear equation may take more than two steps. Start by simplifying one or both sides of the equation, if possible. Then use inverse operations to isolate the variable.

EXAMPLE 1 Solve an equation by combining like terms

Solve $8x - 3x - 10 = 20$.

$8x - 3x - 10 = 20$	Write original equation.
$5x - 10 = 20$	Combine like terms.
$5x - 10 + 10 = 20 + 10$	Add 10 to each side.
$5x = 30$	Simplify.
$\frac{5x}{5} = \frac{30}{5}$	Divide each side by 5.
$x = 6$	Simplify.

EXAMPLE 2 Solve an equation using the distributive property

Solve $7x + 2(x + 6) = 39$.

Solution

When solving an equation, you may feel comfortable doing some steps mentally. Method 2 shows a solution where some steps are done mentally.

REVIEW PROPERTIES
For help with using the distributive property, see p. 96.

METHOD 1 Show All Steps

$$7x + 2(x + 6) = 39$$
$$7x + 2x + 12 = 39$$
$$9x + 12 = 39$$
$$9x + 12 - 12 = 39 - 12$$
$$9x = 27$$
$$\frac{9x}{9} = \frac{27}{9}$$
$$x = 3$$

METHOD 2 Do Some Steps Mentally

$$7x + 2(x + 6) = 39$$
$$7x + 2x + 12 = 39$$
$$9x + 12 = 39$$
$$9x = 27$$
$$x = 3$$

Resource Planning Guide

Chapter Resource Book
- Teaching Guide/Lesson Plan (pp. 25–26)
- Activity Master (p. 27)
- Practice levels A, B, C (pp. 29–31)
- Study Guide (pp. 32–33)
- Catch-up for Absent Students (p. 34)
- Problem Solving Workshop (p. 35)
- Challenge (p. 36)

Workbooks
- Notetaking Guide (pp. 55–56)
- Practice Workbook (pp. 34–35)

Teaching Options
- **Power Presentations CD-ROM** provides dynamic electronic teaching resources for the classroom.
- **Activity Generator CD-ROM** provides editable activities for all ability levels.

Interactive Technology
- Easy Planner
- Power Presentations CD-ROM
- Activity Generator CD-ROM
- Animated Algebra
- Test Generator CD-ROM
- Online Quiz
- eWorkbook
- eEdition
- @HomeTutor

Resources for English Learners
- Quick Reference for English Learners
- Spanish Study Guide
- Multi-Language Visual Glossary
- Student Resources in Spanish

See also the *Algebra 1 Toolkit* for more strategies for meeting individual needs.

EXAMPLE 3 Standardized Test Practice

Which equation represents Step 2 in the solution process?

Step 1 $5x - 4(x - 3) = 17$

Step 2 ☐

Step 3 $x + 12 = 17$

Step 4 $x = 5$

ELIMINATE CHOICES
You can eliminate choices B and C because −4 has not been distributed to *both* terms in the parentheses.

Ⓐ $5x - 4x - 12 = 17$ Ⓑ $5x - 4x - 3 = 17$

Ⓒ $5x - 4x + 3 = 17$ Ⓓ $5x - 4x + 12 = 17$

Solution

In Step 2, the distributive property is used to simplify the left side of the equation. Because $-4(x - 3) = -4x + 12$, Step 2 should be $5x - 4x + 12 = 17$.

▶ The correct answer is D. Ⓐ Ⓑ Ⓒ Ⓓ

GUIDED PRACTICE for Examples 1, 2, and 3

Solve the equation. Check your solution.

1. $9d - 2d + 4 = 32$ 4 **2.** $2w + 3(w + 4) = 27$ 3 **3.** $6x - 2(x - 5) = 46$ 9

USING RECIPROCALS Although you can use the distributive property to solve an equation such as $\frac{3}{2}(3x + 5) = -24$, it is easier to multiply each side of the equation by the reciprocal of the fraction.

EXAMPLE 4 Multiply by a reciprocal to solve an equation

Solve $\frac{3}{2}(3x + 5) = -24$.

$\frac{3}{2}(3x + 5) = -24$ **Write original equation.**

$\frac{2}{3} \cdot \frac{3}{2}(3x + 5) = \frac{2}{3}(-24)$ **Multiply each side by $\frac{2}{3}$, the reciprocal of $\frac{3}{2}$.**

$3x + 5 = -16$ **Simplify.**

$3x = -21$ **Subtract 5 from each side.**

$x = -7$ **Divide each side by 3.**

GUIDED PRACTICE for Example 4

Solve the equation. Check your solution.

4. $\frac{3}{4}(z - 6) = 12$ 22 **5.** $\frac{2}{5}(3r + 4) = 10$ 7 **6.** $-\frac{4}{5}(4a - 1) = 28$ −8.5

Motivating the Lesson

Inform students that real-world problems often involve many parts. For example, you might want to know how long it takes to ride one section of a bike trail if you ride the whole trail in 55 minutes, pedaling at 14 miles per hour for part of the trail and 8 miles per hour for the rest. Tell students that this lesson offers several methods to solve problems such as this and others with many steps.

3 TEACH

Extra Example 1

Solve $9x + x - 7 = 13$. 2

Extra Example 2

Solve $4x - 7(x - 2) = 26$. −4

Key Question to Ask for Example 2

- Suppose you use Method 2 to solve Example 1. Which steps might you do mentally? Add 10 to each side; divide each side by 5.

Extra Example 3

Which equation represents Step 2 in the solution process? C

Step 1 $-3x + 4(x - 2) = 15$

Step 2 ☐

Step 3 $x - 8 = 15$

Step 4 $x = 23$

Ⓐ $-3x + 4x - 2 = 15$

Ⓑ $-3x + 4x + 2 = 15$

Ⓒ $-3x + 4x - 8 = 15$

Ⓓ $-3x + 4x + 8 = 15$

Extra Example 4

Solve $\frac{3}{5}(2x - 4) = 18$. 17

Extra Example 5

Edmund and Roberto took a 7-day (168 hours), 90-mile canoe trip down the Allagash River. If they paddled at an average rate of 2.5 miles per hour, how many hours did they spend *not* paddling? Write and solve an equation to find the answer. $90 = 2.5(168 - x)$; 132 h

Key Question to Ask for Example 5

- The Another Way sentence beside Example 5 suggests dividing by 25 as an alternative first step when solving the equation. When would it *not* be advantageous to divide by 25 as the first step? if the distance traveled was not a multiple of 25

Teaching Strategy

Ask a student to write the steps to solve Example 5 using the method presented on p. 147. Then have students discuss which method they prefer and why.

Closing the Lesson

Have students summarize the major points of the lesson and answer the Essential Question: How do you solve multi-step equations?

- To solve multi-step equations, first simplify one or both sides and then use inverse operations.
- If a fraction is being multiplied by a quantity, use reciprocals to simplify instead of the distributive property.

To solve a multi-step equation, first simplify and combine like terms. After simplifying, use inverse operations to isolate the variable.

EXAMPLE 5 Write and solve an equation

BIRD MIGRATION A flock of cranes migrates from Canada to Texas. The cranes take 14 days (336 hours) to travel 2500 miles. The cranes fly at an average speed of 25 miles per hour. How many hours of the migration are the cranes *not* flying?

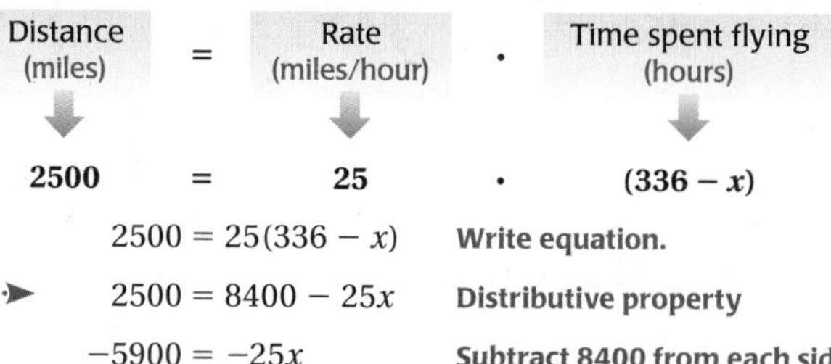

Solution

Let x be the amount of time the cranes are not flying. Then $336 - x$ is the amount of time the cranes are flying.

Distance (miles)	=	Rate (miles/hour)	•	Time spent flying (hours)
2500	=	**25**	•	**$(336 - x)$**

ANOTHER WAY
You can also begin solving the equation by dividing each side of the equation by 25.

$2500 = 25(336 - x)$	**Write equation.**
$2500 = 8400 - 25x$	**Distributive property**
$-5900 = -25x$	**Subtract 8400 from each side.**
$236 = x$	**Divide each side by −25.**

▶ The cranes were not flying for 236 hours of the migration.

✓ **GUIDED PRACTICE** for Example 5

7. **WHAT IF?** Suppose the cranes take 12 days (288 hours) to travel the 2500 miles. How many hours of this migration are the cranes *not* flying? 188 h

3.3 EXERCISES

HOMEWORK KEY
○ = **WORKED-OUT SOLUTIONS** on p. WS6 for Exs. 17 and 39
★ = **STANDARDIZED TEST PRACTICE** Exs. 2, 18, 35, 36, and 41
◆ = **MULTIPLE REPRESENTATIONS** Ex. 42

SKILL PRACTICE

A

1. **VOCABULARY** What is the reciprocal of the fraction in the equation $\frac{3}{5}(2x + 8) = 18$? $\frac{5}{3}$

2. ★ **WRITING** *Describe* the steps you would use to solve the equation $3(4y - 7) = 6$. Use the distributive property to get $12y - 21 = 6$, then add 21 to each side to get $12y = 27$, divide each side by 12 to get $y = 2.25$.

EXAMPLE 1 on p. 148 for Exs. 3–11

COMBINING LIKE TERMS **Solve the equation. Check your solution.**

3. $p + 2p - 3 = 6$ 3
4. $12v + 14 + 10v = 80$ 3
5. $11w - 9 - 7w = 15$ 6
6. $5a + 3 - 3a = -7$ −5
7. $6c - 8 - 2c = -16$ −2
8. $9 = 7z - 13z - 21$ −5
9. $-2 = 3y - 18 - 5y$ −8
10. $23 = -4m + 2 + m$ −7
11. $35 = -5 + 2x - 7x$ −8

EXAMPLES 2 and 3 on pp. 148–149 for Exs. 12–18, 25

USING THE DISTRIBUTIVE PROPERTY Solve the equation. Check your solution.

12. $3 + 4(z + 5) = 31$ 2
13. $14 + 2(4g - 3) = 40$ 4
14. $5m + 2(m + 1) = 23$ 3
15. $5h + 2(11 - h) = -5$ −9
16. $27 = 3c - 3(6 - 2c)$ 5
17. $-3 = 12y - 5(2y - 7)$ −19

18. ★ **MULTIPLE CHOICE** What is the solution of $7v - (6 - 2v) = 12$? C

(A) −3.6 (B) −2 (C) 2 (D) 3.6

EXAMPLE 4 on p. 149 for Exs. 19–24, 26

MULTIPLYING BY A RECIPROCAL Solve the equation. Check your solution.

19. $\frac{1}{3}(d + 3) = 5$ 12
20. $\frac{3}{2}(x - 5) = -6$ 1
21. $\frac{4}{3}(7 - n) = 12$ −2
22. $4 = \frac{2}{9}(4y - 2)$ 5
23. $-32 = \frac{8}{7}(3w - 1)$ −9
24. $-14 = \frac{2}{5}(9 - 2b)$ 22

ERROR ANALYSIS *Describe* and correct the error in solving the equation.

25.

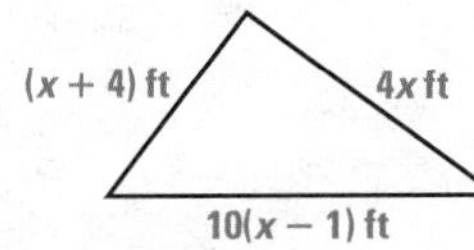

$5x - 3(x - 6) = 2$
$5x - 3x - 18 = 2$
$2x - 18 = 2$
$2x = 20$
$x = 10$

25. −3 times −6 is 18, not −18; $5x - 3x + 18 = 2$, $2x + 18 = 2$, $2x = -16$, $x = -8$.

26.

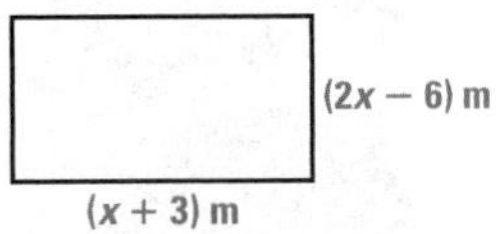

$\frac{1}{2}(2x - 10) = 4$
$2x - 10 = 2$
$2x = 12$
$x = 6$

Multiply each side by 2, not $\frac{1}{2}$; $2x - 10 = 8$, $2x = 18$, $x = 9$.

B

SOLVING EQUATIONS Solve the equation. Check your solution.

27. $8.9 + 1.2(3a - 1) = 14.9$ 2
28. $-11.2 + 4(2.1 + q) = -0.8$ 0.5
29. $1.3t + 3(t + 8.2) = 37.5$ 3
30. $1.6 = 7.6 - 5(k + 1.1)$ 0.1
31. $0.5 = 4.1x - 2(1.3x - 4)$ −5
32. $8.7 = 3.5m - 2.5(5.4 - 6m)$ 1.2

GEOMETRY Find the value of x for the triangle or rectangle.

33. Perimeter = 24 feet 2

$(x + 4)$ ft, $4x$ ft, $10(x - 1)$ ft

34. Perimeter = 26 meters $5\frac{1}{3}$

$(2x - 6)$ m, $(x + 3)$ m

35. ★ **WRITING** The length of a rectangle is 3.5 inches more than its width. The perimeter of the rectangle is 31 inches. Find the length and the width of the rectangle. *Explain* your reasoning. 9.5 in., 6 in.; if you use the perimeter formula $P = 2\ell + 2w$ and substitute $3.5 + w$ for ℓ, the solution is $w = 6$.

36. ★ **SHORT RESPONSE** Solve each equation by first dividing each side of the equation by the number outside the parentheses. When would you recommend using this method to solve an equation? *Explain.*

a. $9(x - 4) = 72$ 12
b. $8(x + 5) = 60$ 2.5

36. You should divide each side of the equation by the number outside the parentheses when the number is a factor of the number on the other side of the equals sign or it is a fraction.

C

37. **CHALLENGE** An even integer can be represented by the expression $2n$. Find three consecutive even integers that have a sum of 54. 16, 18, 20

4 PRACTICE AND APPLY

Assignment Guide

Answer Transparencies available for all exercises

Basic:
Day 1: pp. 150–153
Exs. 1–18, 27, 28, 44–47
Day 2: pp. 150–153
Exs. 19–26, 29, 30, 38–41, 48–56

Average:
Day 1: pp. 150–153
Exs. 1, 2, 4–10 even, 12–18, 27–32, 35, 45, 46
Day 2: pp. 150–153
Exs. 19–26, 33, 34, 36, 38–42, 49–55 odd

Advanced:
Day 1: pp. 150–153
Exs. 1, 9–11, 15–18, 29–32, 35, 37*, 45, 46
Day 2: pp. 150–153
Exs. 22–24, 33, 34, 36, 38–43*, 54–56

Block:
pp. 150–153
Exs. 1, 2, 4–10 even, 12–36, 38–42, 45, 46, 49–55 odd

Differentiated Instruction

See *Algebra 1 Best Practices Toolkit* for suggestions on addressing the needs of a diverse classroom.

Homework Check

For a quick check of student understanding of key concepts, go over the following exercises:

Basic: 4, 13, 18, 20, 38
Average: 8, 14, 18, 22, 39
Advanced: 11, 16, 18, 23, 40

Extra Practice

- Student Edition, p. 940
- Chapter 3 Resource Book: Practice levels A, B, C, pp. 29–31

Practice Worksheet

An easily-readable reduced practice page (with answers) for this lesson can be found on p. 130C.

Differentiated Instruction

English Learners While discussing **Exercise 37**, point out that the word "consecutive" comes from a Latin word meaning "to follow." Students may be more familiar with the related word "sequence," which is an ordered list. Show them examples of a list of consecutive integers, a list of consecutive even integers, and a list of consecutive odd integers.

See also the *Algebra 1 Toolkit* for more strategies.

Avoiding Common Errors

Exercises 3–11 Some students may overlook variables such as *p* in Exercise 3 when combining terms. Students should realize that these variables have a coefficient of 1.

Teaching Strategy

Exercise 18 For students who cannot solve this equation, suggest they rewrite it as an addition equation so that the equation reads $7v + (-1)(6 - 2v) = 12$.

Reading Strategy

Exercises 33–34 Point out to students that the known measurement for these exercises is perimeter, not area. Also, in Exercise 34 some students may think "m" is a variable. Note that *x* is the variable and the letter "m" stands for meters.

Study Strategy

Exercise 38 Some students may be confused by all the different dollar amounts. Suggest they look for like terms that can be combined to use the same variable.

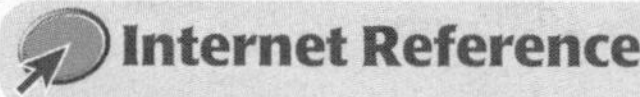

Exercise 41 For more information about the Colorado Midland Railway and the Busk-Ivanhoe Tunnel, visit www.daeunert.de/html/colorado_midland.html.

PROBLEM SOLVING

EXAMPLE 5 on p. 150 for Exs. 38–40

A

38. BASKETBALL A ticket agency sells tickets to a professional basketball game. The agency charges $32.50 for each ticket, a convenience charge of $3.30 for each ticket, and a processing fee of $5.90 for the entire order. The total charge for an order is $220.70. How many tickets were purchased? **6 tickets**

@HomeTutor for problem solving help at classzone.com

(39.) HANGING POSTERS You want to hang 3 equally-sized travel posters on the wall in your room so that the posters on the ends are each 3 feet from the end of the wall. You want the spacing between posters to be equal. How much space should you leave between the posters? **0.75 ft**

13.5 ft

@HomeTutor for problem solving help at classzone.com

40. LIFEGUARD TRAINING To qualify for a lifeguard training course, you have to swim continuously for 500 yards using either the front crawl or the breaststroke. You swim the front crawl at a rate of 45 yards per minute and the breaststroke at a rate of 35 yards per minute. You take 12 minutes to swim 500 yards. How much time did you spend swimming the front crawl? Use the verbal model below. **8 min**

Distance = Rate for front crawl · Time for front crawl + Rate for breaststroke (Total time − Time for front crawl)

B

41. ★ EXTENDED RESPONSE The Busk-Ivanhoe Tunnel on the Colorado Midland Railway was built in the 1890s with separate work crews starting on opposite ends at different times. The crew working from Ivanhoe started 0.75 month later than the crew working from Busk.

Cutaway of Busk-Ivanhoe Tunnel

a. Starting at the time construction began on the Busk end, find the time it took to complete a total of 8473 feet of the tunnel. Round your answer to the nearest month. **34 mo**

b. After 8473 feet were completed, the work crews merged under the same supervision. The combined crew took 3 months to complete the remaining 921 feet of the tunnel. Find the rate at which the remainder of the tunnel was completed. **307 ft per mo**

c. Was the tunnel being completed more rapidly before or after the work crews merged? *Explain* your reasoning.

41c. After the work crews merged; before the work crews merged they were working at a rate of 117 + 137 = 254 feet per month, and after merging at a rate of 307 feet per month.

○ = WORKED-OUT SOLUTIONS on p. WS1 ★ = STANDARDIZED TEST PRACTICE ◆ = MULTIPLE REPRESENTATIONS

42. MULTIPLE REPRESENTATIONS A roofing contractor gives estimates for shingling a roof in cost per square, where a square is a 10 foot by 10 foot section of roof. The contractor estimates \$27.50 per square for materials, \$17 per square for labor, \$30 per square for overhead and profit, and a total of \$750 for miscellaneous expenses.

a. **Writing an Equation** Write an equation that gives the estimate y (in dollars) as a function of the number x of squares of a roof. The contractor gives an estimate of \$2314.50. About how many squares does the roof have? $y = 74.5x + 750$; 21 squares

b. **Making a Table** Make a table that shows the estimates for shingling a roof that has 5, 10, 15, 20, or 25 squares. Use your table to check your answer to part (a). See margin.

C 43. CHALLENGE A person has quarters and dimes that total \$2.80. The number of dimes is 7 more than the number of quarters. How many of each coin does the person have? 6 quarters and 13 dimes

ILLINOIS MIXED REVIEW

TEST PRACTICE at classzone.com

44. A fire truck must travel 7 miles to reach a fire outside of town. If the truck travels 35 miles per hour, how long will it take the truck to reach the fire? B

Ⓐ 5 min Ⓑ 12 min Ⓒ 15 min Ⓓ 20 min

45. The trees in a grove have heights of 3.5 meters,4.2 meters, 5.2 meters, 6 meters, and 5.2 meters. A new tree that has a height of 8.2 meters is planted in the grove. Which measure of data would change the most as a result of planting the new tree?

Ⓐ Mean Ⓒ Mode A

Ⓑ Median Ⓓ Not here

QUIZ for Lessons 3.1–3.3

Solve the equation. Check your solution.

1. $x + 9 = 7$ (p. 134) -2
2. $y - 5 = -11$ (p. 134) -6
3. $-7b = -56$ (p. 134) 8
4. $\frac{z}{4} = 6$ (p. 134) 24
5. $-\frac{4}{3}t = -12$ (p. 134) 9
6. $9w - 4 = 14$ (p. 141) 2
7. $23 = 1 - d$ (p. 141) -22
8. $66 = 4m + 7m$ (p. 141) 6
9. $-104 = -5p - 3p$ (p. 141) 13
10. $2v + 5v - 8 = 13$ (p. 148) 3
11. $2a - 6(a - 4) = -4$ (p. 148) 7
12. $\frac{6}{5}(5 - 4g) = -18$ (p. 148) 5
13. **INTERNET SHOPPING** Dan purchases DVDs from a website. Each DVD costs \$11, and the shipping and handling fees are \$6.95. Dan is charged a total of \$50.95. How many DVDs did he purchase? (p. 141) 4 DVDs

5 ASSESS AND RETEACH

Daily Homework Quiz

Transparency Available

Solve the equation.

1. $8g - 2 + g = 16$ 2
2. $3b + 2(b - 4) = 47$ 11
3. $-6 + 4(2c + 1) = -34$ -4
4. $\frac{2}{3}(x - 6) = 12$ 24
5. Joe drove 405 miles in 7 hours. He drove at a rate of 55 miles per hour during the first part of the trip and 60 miles per hour during the second part. How many hours did he drive at a rate of 55 miles per hour? 3 h

Online Quiz

Available at **classzone.com**

Diagnosis/Remediation

- Practice A, B, C in Chapter 3 Resource Book, pp. 29–31
- Study Guide in Chapter 3 Resource Book, pp. 32–33
- Practice Workbook, pp. 34–35
- @HomeTutor

Challenge

Additional challenge is available in the Chapter 3 Resource Book, p. 36.

Quiz

An easily-readable reduced copy of the quiz (with answers) on Lessons 3.1–3.3 from the Assessment Book can be found on p. 130E.

42b.

Squares	Cost (dollars)
5	1122.50
10	1495
15	1867.50
20	2240
25	2612.50

1 PLAN AND PREPARE

Warm-Up Exercises

Transparency Available

Solve the equation.

1. $2m - 6 + 4m = 12$ 3
2. $6a - 5(a - 1) = 11$ 6
3. A charter bus company charges \$11.25 per ticket plus a handling charge of \$.50 per ticket, and a \$15 fee for booking the bus. If a group pays \$297 to charter a bus, how many tickets did they buy? 24 tickets

Notetaking Guide

Transparency Available

Promotes interactive learning and notetaking skills, pp. 57–59.

Pacing

Basic: 1 day

Average: 1 day

Advanced: 1 day

Block: 0.5 block with 3.5

- See *Teaching Guide/Lesson Plan.*

2 FOCUS AND MOTIVATE

Essential Question

Big Idea 1, p. 131

How do you solve equations with variables on both sides? **Tell students they will learn how to answer this question by collecting variable terms on one side and constants on the other.**

3.4 Solve Equations with Variables on Both Sides

 **8.11.16** Solve linear equations and inequalities, including selecting and evaluating formulas.

Before You solved equations with variables on one side.

Now You will solve equations with variables on both sides.

Why? So you can find the cost of a gym membership, as in Ex. 52.

Key Vocabulary
- **identity**

Some equations have variables on both sides. To solve such equations, you can collect the variable terms on one side of the equation and the constant terms on the other side of the equation.

EXAMPLE 1 Solve an equation with variables on both sides

Solve $7 - 8x = 4x - 17$.

$7 - 8x = 4x - 17$	Write original equation.
$7 - 8x + 8x = 4x - 17 + 8x$	Add $8x$ to each side.
$7 = 12x - 17$	Simplify each side.
$24 = 12x$	Add 17 to each side.
$2 = x$	Divide each side by 12.

ANOTHER WAY
You could also begin solving the equation by subtracting $4x$ from each side to obtain $7 - 12x = -17$. When you solve this equation for x, you get the same solution, 2.

▶ The solution is 2. Check by substituting 2 for x in the original equation.

CHECK	$7 - 8x = 4x - 17$	Write original equation.
	$7 - 8(2) \stackrel{?}{=} 4(2) - 17$	Substitute 2 for x.
	$-9 \stackrel{?}{=} 4(2) - 17$	Simplify left side.
	$-9 = -9$ ✓	Simplify right side. Solution checks.

 Animated Algebra at classzone.com

EXAMPLE 2 Solve an equation with grouping symbols

Solve $9x - 5 = \frac{1}{4}(16x + 60)$.

$9x - 5 = \frac{1}{4}(16x + 60)$	Write original equation.
$9x - 5 = 4x + 15$	Distributive property
$5x - 5 = 15$	Subtract $4x$ from each side.
$5x = 20$	Add 5 to each side.
$x = 4$	Divide each side by 5.

Resource Planning Guide

Chapter Resource Book
- Teaching Guide/Lesson Plan (pp. 37–38)
- Activity Master (p. 39)
- Practice levels A, B, C (pp. 41–43)
- Study Guide (pp. 44–45)
- Catch-up for Absent Students (p. 46)
- Problem Solving Workshop (p. 47)
- Challenge (p. 48)

Workbooks
- Notetaking Guide (pp. 57–59)
- Practice Workbook (pp. 36–37)

Teaching Options
- **Power Presentations CD-ROM** provides dynamic electronic teaching resources for the classroom.
- **Activity Generator CD-ROM** provides editable activities for all ability levels.

Interactive Technology
- Easy Planner
- Power Presentations CD-ROM
- Activity Generator CD-ROM
- Animated Algebra
- Test Generator CD-ROM
- Online Quiz
- eWorkbook
- eEdition
- @HomeTutor

Resources for English Learners
- Quick Reference for English Learners
- Spanish Study Guide
- Multi-Language Visual Glossary
- Student Resources in Spanish

See also the *Algebra 1 Toolkit* for more strategies for meeting individual needs.

 **GUIDED PRACTICE** for Examples 1 and 2

Solve the equation. Check your solution.

1. $24 - 3m = 5m$ 3
2. $20 + c = 4c - 7$ 9
3. $9 - 3k = 17 - 2k$ −8
4. $5z - 2 = 2(3z - 4)$ 6
5. $3 - 4a = 5(a - 3)$ 2
6. $8y - 6 = \frac{2}{3}(6y + 15)$ 4

EXAMPLE 3 Solve a real-world problem

CAR SALES A car dealership sold 78 new cars and 67 used cars this year. The number of new cars sold by the dealership has been increasing by 6 cars each year. The number of used cars sold by the dealership has been decreasing by 4 cars each year. If these trends continue, in how many years will the number of new cars sold be twice the number of used cars sold?

Solution

Let x represent the number of years from now. So, $6x$ represents the increase in the number of new cars sold over x years and $-4x$ represents the decrease in the number of used cars sold over x years. Write a verbal model.

New cars sold this year	+	Increase in new cars sold over x years	= 2 (	Used cars sold this year	+	Decrease in used cars sold over x years	)
78	+	$\mathbf{6x}$	= 2 (	**67**	+	$(-4x)$	)

$78 + 6x = 2(67 - 4x)$ **Write equation.**

$78 + 6x = 134 - 8x$ **Distributive property**

$78 + 14x = 134$ **Add 8x to each side.**

$14x = 56$ **Subtract 78 from each side.**

$x = 4$ **Divide each side by 14.**

▶ The number of new cars sold will be twice the number of used cars sold in 4 years.

CHECK You can use a table to check your answer.

Year	0	1	2	3	4
Used cars sold	67	63	59	55	51
New cars sold	78	84	90	96	102

The number of new cars sold is twice the number of used cars sold in 4 years.

 **GUIDED PRACTICE** for Example 3

7. **WHAT IF?** In Example 3, suppose the car dealership sold 50 new cars this year instead of 78. In how many years will the number of new cars sold be twice the number of used cars sold? 6 yr

Motivating the Lesson

Learning how to write and solve equations with variables on both sides allows you to determine when two quantities equal each other. Suppose you offer a dog grooming service to earn money during the summer. One plan could be to charge customers a flat fee of \$150 for two months of service, plus \$5 per comb out and shampoo. Another plan could be to charge \$10 per comb out and \$5 per shampoo. By setting these options equal to each other, you can find when the earnings from the two plans would be the same. This can help you decide which plan to use.

3 TEACH

Extra Example 1

Solve $13 + 5x = 2x - 8$. −7

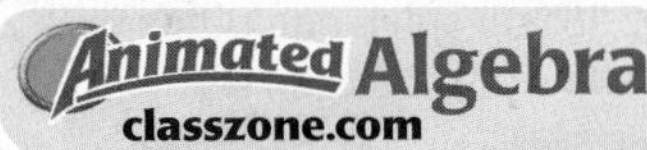

An **Animated Algebra** activity is available on-line for **Example 1**. This activity is also available on the **Power Presentations CD-ROM**.

Extra Example 2

Solve $4x - 5 = \frac{1}{5}(5x + 20)$. 3

Key Question to Ask for Example 2

- Another way is suggested for solving the equation in Example 1. What is another way to solve the equation in Example 2? **You could start by mutiplying each side by 4 to get $36x - 20 = 16x + 60$. Then $20x = 80$ and $x = 4$.**

Extra Example 3

A music website sold 94 single songs and 67 albums today. The number of single downloads has been increasing by 22 each day. The number of album downloads has been decreasing by 5 each day. If these trends continue, in how many days will the number of single downloads be ten times the number of album downloads? Write and solve an equation to find the number of days. $94 + 22x = 10(67 - 5x)$; 8

Extra Example 4

Solve the equation, if possible.

a. $5x - 6 = 5(x - 1)$ The equation has no solution.

b. $4(3x + 2) = 2(6x + 4)$ The equation is an identity.

Closing the Lesson

Have students summarize the major points of the lesson and answer the Essential Question: How do you solve equations with variables on both sides?

- To solve equations with variables on both sides, collect the variable terms on one side and the constant terms on the other.
- Some equations, called identities, are true for all values of the variable. Other equations have no solutions.

To solve equations with variables on both sides, first simplify the expressions on each side of the equation by using the distributive property to remove grouping symbols and then combining like terms. Next, use properties of equality to collect variable terms on one side of the equation and constants on the other. Then solve the equation by isolating the variable.

NUMBER OF SOLUTIONS Equations do not always have one solution. An equation that is true for all values of the variable is an **identity**. So, the solution of an identity is all real numbers. Some equations have no solution.

EXAMPLE 4 Identify the number of solutions of an equation

Solve the equation, if possible.

a. $3x = 3(x + 4)$ **b.** $2x + 10 = 2(x + 5)$

Solution

a. $3x = 3(x + 4)$ Original equation

$3x = 3x + 12$ Distributive property

The equation $3x = 3x + 12$ is not true because the number $3x$ cannot be equal to 12 more than itself. So, the equation has no solution. This can be demonstrated by continuing to solve the equation.

$3x - 3x = 3x + 12 - 3x$ Subtract $3x$ from each side.

$0 = 12$ ✗ Simplify.

▸ The statement $0 = 12$ is not true, so the equation has no solution.

b. $2x + 10 = 2(x + 5)$ Original equation

$2x + 10 = 2x + 10$ Distributive property

▸ Notice that the statement $2x + 10 = 2x + 10$ is true for all values of x. So, the equation is an identity, and the solution is all real numbers.

GUIDED PRACTICE for Example 4

Solve the equation, if possible.

8. $9z + 12 = 9(z + 3)$ no solution

9. $7w + 1 = 8w + 1$ 0

10. $3(2a + 2) = 2(3a + 3)$ identity

SOLVING LINEAR EQUATIONS You have learned several ways to transform an equation to an equivalent equation. These methods are combined in the steps listed below.

CONCEPT SUMMARY *For Your Notebook*

Steps for Solving Linear Equations

STEP 1 **Use** the distributive property to remove any grouping symbols.

STEP 2 **Simplify** the expression on each side of the equation.

STEP 3 **Use** properties of equality to collect the variable terms on one side of the equation and the constant terms on the other side of the equation.

STEP 4 **Use** properties of equality to solve for the variable.

STEP 5 **Check** your solution in the original equation.

Differentiated Instruction

Below Level As you discuss **Example 4**, it may be difficult for students to understand the concept of no solution or a solution that is true for all values of the variable. Have these students substitute 5 to 10 different values for x in the equations in parts a and b. After they have done this, ask them to describe why the equation in part a has no solution and why any value satisfies the equation in part b. Check their understanding by asking them to explain the solutions to **Guided Practice Exercises 8 and 10**.

Advanced For some students, the equations in **Example 4** and the **Guided Practice** may seem obvious. Challenge these students to create complicated equations with no solution, one solution, or infinitely many solutions. Ask them to create five of each and then exchange them with other students to solve. Remind them to mix the equations.

See also the *Algebra 1 Toolkit* for more strategies.

3.4 EXERCISES

HOMEWORK KEY
○ = **WORKED-OUT SOLUTIONS** on p. WS6 for Exs. 13 and 51
★ = **STANDARDIZED TEST PRACTICE** Exs. 2, 15, 16, 17, 29, and 53
◆ = **MULTIPLE REPRESENTATIONS** Ex. 52

SKILL PRACTICE

A

1. **VOCABULARY** Copy and complete: An equation that is true for all values of the variable is called a(n) _?_. identity

2. ★ **WRITING** *Explain* why the equation $4x + 3 = 4x + 1$ has no solution.
A number plus 3 can't be equal to itself plus 1. If you solve the equation, you get $0 = 2$.

EXAMPLES 1 and 2 on p. 154 for Exs. 3–17

SOLVING EQUATIONS **Solve the equation. Check your solution.**

3. $8t + 5 = 6t + 1$ −2
4. $k + 1 = 3k - 1$ 1
5. $8c + 5 = 4c - 11$ −4
6. $8 + 4m = 9m - 7$ 3
7. $10b + 18 = 8b + 4$ −7
8. $19 - 13p = -17p - 5$ −6
9. $9a = 6(a + 4)$ 8
10. $5h - 7 = 2(h + 1)$ 3
11. $3(d + 12) = 8 - 4d$ −4
12. $7(r + 7) = 5r + 59$ 5
13. $40 + 14j = 2(-4j - 13)$ −3
14. $5(n + 2) = \frac{3}{5}(5 + 10n)$ 7

15. ★ **MULTIPLE CHOICE** What is the solution of the equation $8x + 2x = 15x - 10$? C

Ⓐ −2 Ⓑ 0.4 Ⓒ 2 Ⓓ 5

16. ★ **MULTIPLE CHOICE** What is the solution of the equation $4y + y + 1 = 7(y - 1)$? D

Ⓐ −4 Ⓑ −3 Ⓒ 3 Ⓓ 4

17. ★ **WRITING** *Describe* the steps you would use to solve the equation $3(2z - 5) = 2z + 13$.

17. *Sample answer:* Distribute the 3 to get $6z - 15 = 2z + 13$, then subtract $2z$ from each side to get $4z - 15 = 13$, next add 15 to each side to get $4z = 28$, finally divide each side by 4 to get $z = 7$.

EXAMPLE 4 on p. 156 for Exs. 18–28

SOLVING EQUATIONS **Solve the equation, if possible.**

18. $w + 3 = w + 6$ no solution
19. $16d = 22 + 5d$ 2
20. $8z = 4(2z + 1)$ no solution
21. $12 + 5v = 2v - 9$ −7
22. $22x + 70 = 17x - 95$ −33
23. $2 - 15n = 5(-3n + 2)$ no solution
24. $12y + 6 = 6(2y + 1)$ identity
25. $5(1 + 4m) = 2(3 + 10m)$ no solution
26. $2(3g + 2) = \frac{1}{2}(12g + 8)$ identity

ERROR ANALYSIS ***Describe*** **and correct the error in solving the equation.**

27.
$3(x + 5) = 3x + 15$
$3x + 5 = 3x + 15$
$5 = 15$
The equation has no solution.

28.
$6(2y + 6) = 4(9 + 3y)$
$12y + 36 = 36 + 12y$
$12y = 12y$
$0 = 0$
The solution is $y = 0$.

27. The 3 was not distributed to both terms; $3x + 15 = 3x + 15$, $15 = 15$, so the equation is an identity.

28. When the equation is $0 = 0$, it means that it is true for all values of y, not just 0; the solution is an identity.

B

29. ★ **OPEN-ENDED** Give an example of an equation that has no solution. *Explain* why your equation does not have a solution.
Sample answer: $5x + 4 = 5x$; the number $5x$ cannot be equal to 4 more than itself.

4 PRACTICE AND APPLY

Assignment Guide

Answer Transparencies available for all exercises

Basic:
Day 1: EP p. 939 Exs. 38–41
pp. 157–159
Exs. 1, 2, 3–13 odd, 15–37, 49–52, 56–64 even

Average:
Day 1: pp. 157–159
Exs. 1, 2, 7–13 odd, 15–29, 31–43 odd, 44–47, 49–53, 56–64 odd

Advanced:
Day 1: pp. 157–159
Exs. 1, 7, 8, 12–17, 18–26, 29, 38–48*, 50–55*, 58–64 even

Block:
pp. 157–159
Exs. 1, 2, 7–13 odd, 15–29, 31–43 odd, 44–47, 49–53, 56–64 odd (with 3.5)

Differentiated Instruction

See *Algebra 1 Best Practices Toolkit* for suggestions on addressing the needs of a diverse classroom.

Homework Check

For a quick check of student understanding of key concepts, go over the following exercises:

Basic: 5, 11, 19, 31, 49
Average: 7, 13, 22, 37, 50
Advanced: 8, 14, 24, 39, 51

Extra Practice

- Student Edition, p. 940
- Chapter 3 Resource Book: Practice levels A, B, C, pp. 41–43

Practice Worksheet

An easily-readable reduced practice page (with answers) for this lesson can be found on p. 130C.

Avoiding Common Errors

Exercises 9–14 Students sometimes fail to distribute a factor to both terms in parentheses. Suggest that students confirm they distributed a factor to both terms if their solutions do not check.

Reading Strategy

Exercises 18–20, 30–43 Advise students that they may be able to solve some of these equations even though they are based on Example 4, which shows an equation with no solution and an equation that is an identity. Direct their attention to the instruction line, which indicates that an equation may or may not have a solution.

Teaching Strategy

Exercises 47–48 Before students try to solve these problems, you may want to review the meaning of an identity.

Study Strategy

Exercises 49–51 Suggest that students make a table to check their answers. This will also give them an opportunity to compare algebraic and tabular solutions to problems and gain facility in using each.

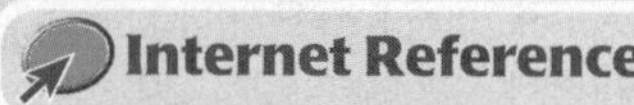

Exercise 53 More information about flyball can be found at the website www.flyballdogs.com/FAQ.html#flyball_is

SOLVING EQUATIONS **Solve the equation, if possible.**

30. $8w - 8 - 6w = 4w - 7$ $-\frac{1}{2}$

31. $3x - 4 = 2x + 8 - 5x$ 2

32. $-15c + 7c + 1 = 3 - 8c$ no solution

33. $\frac{3}{2} + \frac{3}{4}a = \frac{1}{4}a - \frac{1}{2}$ -4

34. $\frac{5}{8}m - \frac{3}{8} = \frac{1}{2}m + \frac{7}{8}$ 10

35. $n - 10 = \frac{5}{6}n - 7 - \frac{1}{3}n$ 6

36. $3.7b + 7 = 8.1b - 19.4$ 6

37. $6.2h + 5 - 1.4h = 4.8h + 5$ identity

38. $0.7z + 1.9 + 0.1z = 5.5 - 0.4z$ 3

39. $5.4t + 14.6 - 10.1t = 12.8 - 3.5t - 0.6$ 2

40. $\frac{1}{8}(5y + 64) = \frac{1}{4}(20 + 2y)$ -24

41. $14 - \frac{1}{5}(j - 10) = \frac{2}{5}(25 + j)$ 10

42. $5(1.2k + 6) = 7.1k + 34.4$ -4

43. $-0.25(4v - 8) = 0.5(4 - 2v)$ identity

GEOMETRY **Find the perimeter of the square.**

44. **45.**

44. $28x - 20$ **45.** $16x + 12$

46.

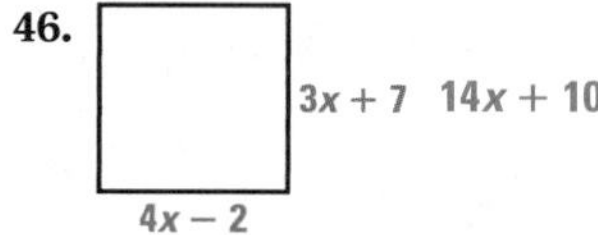

$14x + 10$

C **CHALLENGE** **Find the value(s) of a for which the equation is an identity.**

47. $a(2x + 3) = 9x + 12 - x$ 4

48. $10x - 35 + 3ax = 5ax - 7a$ 5

PROBLEM SOLVING

EXAMPLE 3 A on p. 155 for Exs. 49–51

49. CAMPING The membership fee for joining a camping association is \$45. A local campground charges members of the camping association \$35 per night for a campsite and nonmembers \$40 per night for a campsite. After how many nights of camping is the total cost for members, including the membership fee, the same as the total cost for nonmembers? 9 nights

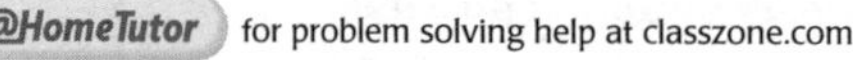

50. HIGH-SPEED INTERNET Dan and Sydney are getting high-speed Internet access at the same time. Dan's provider charges \$60 for installation and \$42.95 per month. Sydney's provider has free installation and charges \$57.95 per month. After how many months will Dan and Sydney have paid the same amount for high-speed Internet service? 4 mo

@HomeTutor for problem solving help at classzone.com

(51.) LANGUAGES Information about students who take Spanish and students who take French at a high school is shown in the table. If the trends continue, in how many years will there be 3 times as many students taking Spanish as French? about 4 yr

Language	Students enrolled this year	Average rate of change
Spanish	555	33 more students each year
French	230	2 fewer students each year

○ = WORKED-OUT SOLUTIONS on p. WS1 ★ = STANDARDIZED TEST PRACTICE

 = MULTIPLE REPRESENTATIONS

Differentiated Instruction

English Learners When solving **Exercises 49–55**, students will need to select their own variables. Students almost always create variables by using the first letter that a quantity represents (h for height, A for area, and so on). English learners may be more comfortable choosing variables from words in their native language. Explain that this still leads to a correct mathematical result, because the choice of variable is arbitrary. See also the *Algebra 1 Toolkit* for more strategies.

B 52. **MULTIPLE REPRESENTATIONS** For \$360, a rock-climbing gym offers a yearly membership where members can climb as many days as they want and pay \$4 per day for equipment rental. Nonmembers pay \$10 per day to use the gym and \$6 per day for equipment rental.

a. **Writing an Equation** Write an equation to find the number of visits after which the total cost for a member and the total cost for a nonmember are the same. Then solve the equation. $360 + 4x = 16x$; 30 visits

b. **Making a Table** Make a table for the costs of members and nonmembers after 5, 10, 15, 20, 25, 30, and 35 visits. Use the table to check your answer to part (a). See margin.

53. ★ **EXTENDED RESPONSE** Flyball is a relay race for dogs. In each of the four legs of the relay, a dog jumps over hurdles, retrieves a ball from a flybox, and runs back over the hurdles. The last leg of a relay is shown below. The collie starts the course 0.3 second before the sheepdog.

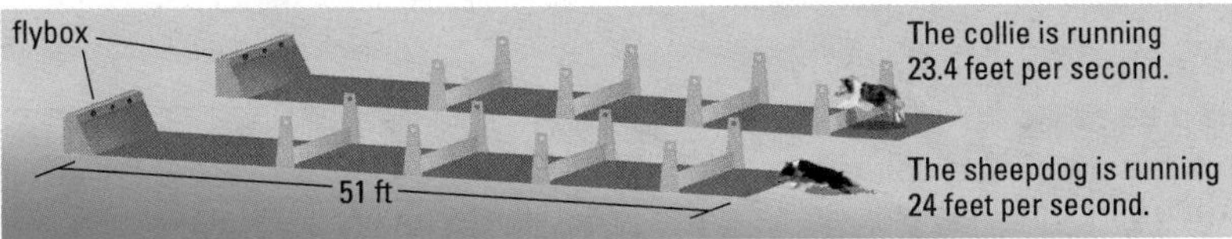
flybox
51 ft
The collie is running 23.4 feet per second.
The sheepdog is running 24 feet per second.

53c. No; it would take 12 seconds for the sheepdog to catch up to the collie and it only takes 4.4 seconds for the collie to complete the last leg.

a. Let t represent the time (in seconds) it takes the collie to run the last leg. Write and solve an equation to find the number of seconds after which the sheepdog would catch up with the collie. $23.4t = 24(t - 0.3)$; 12 sec

b. How long does it take the collie to run the last leg? about 4.4 sec

c. Use your answers from parts (a) and (b) to determine whether the sheepdog catches up and passes the collie during the last leg of the relay. *Explain* your reasoning.

C **CHALLENGE Find the length and the width of the rectangle described.**

54. The length is 12 units more than the width. The perimeter is 7 times the width. 20, 8

55. The length is 4 units less than 3 times the width. The perimeter is 22 units more than twice the width. 11, 5

IL

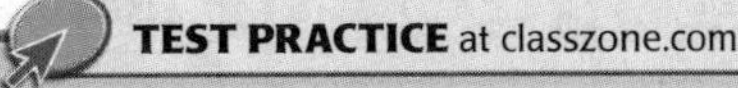

TEST PRACTICE at classzone.com

ILLINOIS MIXED REVIEW

56. If $(x, 12)$ is a solution to the equation $3x + 2y = 18$, what is the value of x?

(A) −6 (B) −3 (C) −2 (D) 3 C

57. A rectangular bulletin board is going to be covered by fourteen 10 inch by 10 inch pieces of paper. The bulletin board will be covered completely, and the pieces of paper will not overlap. Which of the following could be the dimensions of the bulletin board?

(A) 20 in. by 70 in. (C) 50 in. by 90 in. A

(B) 30 in. by 40 in. (D) 60 in. by 40 in.

5 ASSESS AND RETEACH

Daily Homework Quiz

Transparency Available

Solve the equation, if possible.

1. $3(3x + 6) = 9(x + 2)$ The equation is an identity.
2. $7(h - 4) = 2h + 17$ 9
3. $8 - 2w = 6w - 8$ 2
4. $4g + 3 = 2(2g + 3)$ The equation has no solution.
5. Bryson is looking for a repair service for general household maintenance. One service charges \$75 to join the service and \$30 per hour. Another service charges \$45 per hour. After how many hours of service is the total cost for the two services the same? 5 h

Online Quiz

Available at **classzone.com**

Diagnosis/Remediation

- Practice A, B, C in Chapter 3 Resource Book, pp. 41–43
- Study Guide in Chapter 3 Resource Book, pp. 44–45
- Practice Workbook, pp. 36–37
- @HomeTutor

Challenge

Additional challenge is available in the Chapter 3 Resource Book, p. 48.

52b. See Additional Answers beginning on p. AA1.

1 PLAN AND PREPARE

Learn the Method

- Students will use a spreadsheet to solve equations with variables on both sides.
- After the activity, students can use a spreadsheet to check their solutions in Exercises 3–16 and 49–53 in Lesson 3.4.

2 TEACH

Tips for Success

Make sure students enter an asterisk to indicate multiplication in columns b and c in Step 1. Point out that in Exercise 1 they need to place an asterisk in the spreadsheet between 15 and x for the left side of the equation and between 6 and x for the right side of the equation. It may be helpful for students to go through each of the exercises and mark where they need to place asterisks.

As students are working, point out that they do not need to simplify the sides of the equations to use a spreadsheet.

Extra Example

Solve $-9(x + 4) + 56 = -3x - 4$. 4

3 ASSESS AND RETEACH

Use a spreadsheet to solve the equation.

1. $7x + 12 = 6(x + 3)$ 6
2. $-4 + 3x = -3 + 2x$ 1

4a–b. See Additional Answers beginning on p. AA1.

Spreadsheet ACTIVITY Use after Lesson 3.4

@HomeTutor classzone.com Keystrokes

3.4 Solve Equations Using Tables

QUESTION How can you use a spreadsheet to solve an equation with variables on both sides?

You can use a spreadsheet to solve an equation with variables on both sides by evaluating the left side of the equation and the right side of the equation using the same value of the variable. If the left side and right side are equal, then the value of the variable is a solution.

EXAMPLE Solve an equation using a spreadsheet

Solve $19(x - 1) - 72 = 6x$.

***STEP 1* Enter data and formulas**

Label columns for possible solutions, left side, and right side in row 1. Enter the integers from 0 through 10 as possible solutions in column A. Then enter the formulas for the left side and the right side of the equation in columns B and C.

	A	B	C
1	Possible solutions	Left side	Right side
2	0	=19*(A2−1)−72	=6*A2
3	1	=19*(A3−1)−72	=6*A3
...	...	...	...
12	10	=19*(A12−1)−72	=6*A12

***STEP 2* Compare columns**

Compare the values of the left side and the values of the right side. The left side and right side values are equal when $x = 7$. So, the solution is 7.

	A	B	C
1	Possible solutions	Left side	Right side
...	...	...	...
8	6	23	36
9	7	42	42
10	8	61	48

DRAW CONCLUSIONS Use your observations to complete these exercises

In Exercises 1–3, use a spreadsheet to solve the equation.

1. $15x + 6 = 6x + 24$ 2
2. $8x - 17 = 5x + 70$ 29
3. $18 - 2(x + 3) = x$ 4
4. Not all equations have integer solutions. Consider the equation $4.9 + 4.8(7 - x) = 6.2x$.
   a. Follow Step 1 above using $4.9 + 4.8(7 - x) = 6.2x$. See answer to part (b).
   b. Add a fourth column that shows the difference of the value of the left side and the value of the right side. Find consecutive possible solutions between which the differences of the values of the left side and right side change sign. See margin for spreadsheet; 3 and 4.
   c. Repeat Step 1. This time use the lesser of the two possible solutions from part (b) as the first possible solution, and increase each possible solution by 0.1. Can you identify a solution now? If so, what is it? yes; 3.5

Illinois Mixed Review

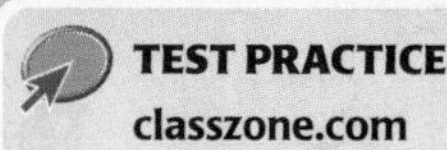

Lessons 3.1–3.4

1. **VOLCANOS** The eruption of Mount St. Helens in 1980 decreased its elevation by 1313 feet. The current elevation is 8364 feet. What was the volcano's elevation before the eruption?

   A. 7051 ft

   B. 8233 ft

   C. 8495 ft

   D. 9677 ft

2. **SKIING** A ski resort offers a super-saver pass for \$90 that allows you to buy lift tickets at half price. If you buy the pass, the cost (in dollars) of buying t tickets is $90 + 22.5t$. Otherwise the cost is $45t$ dollars. How many lift tickets would a skier have to buy for the two costs to be equal?

   F. 2 tickets

   G. 4 tickets

   H. 6 tickets

   J. 8 tickets

3. **CONCERTS** Eight friends buy tickets to a concert. Three of the tickets cost \$24 each, and the remaining tickets cost \$28 each. What is the mean cost?

   A. \$25.50

   B. \$26.00

   C. \$26.50

   D. \$27.00

4. **BOWLING** A bowling alley charges \$1.50 to rent bowling shoes and \$3.75 for each game. Matt and Veronica have a total of \$25 to spend at the bowling alley. Matt brings his own shoes, but Veronica rents hers. They each bowl 2 games. How much money do they have left?

   F. \$7.00

   G. \$8.50

   H. \$9.50

   J. \$16.50

5. **ORIGAMI** You are folding origami cranes to be used as wedding decorations. If you fold cranes for 1 hour without a break, you can make 40 cranes. During a 3 hour period, you made 100 cranes. How much time did you spend taking a break?

   A. 20 min

   B. 25 min

   C. 30 min

   D. 40 min

6. **LOANS** You borrow \$432 from your friend. You set up a payment plan in which you initially pay your friend \$60 and then pay back the rest in equal weekly payments for the next 12 weeks. If you assume no interest, how much are your weekly payments to your friend?

   F. \$31 **H.** \$124

   G. \$36 **J.** \$144

7. **CATS** Last year you adopted a cat from a local shelter for a \$60 donation. Over the past year, you spent \$300 on vet visits, and the rest of the cat's expenses came from food and litter. If there are no other costs and you spent a total of \$600, what were your mean monthly expenses on food and litter for the first year?

   A. \$20 **C.** \$240

   B. \$30 **D.** \$360

8. **GEOMETRY** The triangle below has a perimeter of 82 inches. What is the value of x?

   F. 4 **H.** 42

   G. 9 **J.** 84

Illinois Mixed Review

1. D
2. G
3. C
4. G
5. C
6. F
7. A
8. F

1 PLAN AND PREPARE

Warm-Up Exercises

Solve the equation.

1. $\frac{5}{6}x = 25$ 30
2. $\frac{2}{3}(6x + 3) = 14$ 3
3. $\frac{g}{5} - 7 = 12$ 95
4. You buy three identical polyester film balloons and a birthday card. The card costs $3.95. Find the cost of each balloon if your total bill before tax was $33.80. $9.95

Notetaking Guide

Transparency Available

Promotes interactive learning and notetaking skills, pp. 60–62.

Pacing

Basic: 1 day
Average: 1 day
Advanced: 1 day
Block: 0.5 block with 3.4
- See *Teaching Guide/Lesson Plan.*

2 FOCUS AND MOTIVATE

Essential Question

Big Idea 2, p. 131

How do you find ratios and write and solve proportions? Tell students they will learn how to answer this question by comparing quantities in the real world and by learning to recognize and set up proportions.

3.5 Write Ratios and Proportions

 **6.11.17** Set up, evaluate, or solve number sentences or word problems involving ratios and proportions with rational numbers . . .

Before You solved equations involving division.
Now You will find ratios and write and solve proportions.
Why? So you can find a ratio involving a contest, as in Ex. 46.

Key Vocabulary
- **ratio**
- **proportion**
- **simplest form,** *p. 912*

Throughout this book you have been using rates, such as 50 miles per hour. A rate is a special type of *ratio*.

KEY CONCEPT *For Your Notebook*

Ratios

A **ratio** uses division to compare two quantities. You can write the ratio of two quantities *a* and *b*, where *b* is not equal to 0, in three ways.

a to b $\qquad a:b \qquad \frac{a}{b}$

Each ratio is read "the ratio of *a* to *b*." Ratios should be written in simplest form.

EXAMPLE 1 Write a ratio

VOLLEYBALL A volleyball team plays 14 home matches and 10 away matches.

a. Find the ratio of home matches to away matches.

b. Find the ratio of home matches to all matches.

Solution

a. $\frac{\text{home matches}}{\text{away matches}} = \frac{14}{10} = \frac{7}{5}$

b. $\frac{\text{home matches}}{\text{all matches}} = \frac{14}{14 + 10} = \frac{14}{24} = \frac{7}{12}$

 **GUIDED PRACTICE** for Example 1

Derek and his brother decide to combine their CD collections. Derek has 44 CDs, and his brother has 52 CDs. Find the specified ratio.

1. The number of Derek's CDs to the number of his brother's CDs $\frac{11}{13}$
2. The number of Derek's CDs to the number of CDs in the entire collection $\frac{11}{24}$

Resource Planning Guide

Chapter Resource Book
- Teaching Guide/Lesson Plan (pp. 50–51)
- Practice levels A, B, C (pp. 52–54)
- Study Guide (pp. 55–56)
- Catch-up for Absent Students (p. 57)
- Problem Solving Workshop (p. 58)
- Challenge (p. 59)

Workbooks
- Notetaking Guide (pp. 60–62)
- Practice Workbook (pp. 38–39)

Teaching Options
- **Power Presentations CD-ROM** provides dynamic electronic teaching resources for the classroom.
- **Activity Generator CD-ROM** provides editable activities for all ability levels.

Interactive Technology
- Easy Planner
- Power Presentations CD-ROM
- Activity Generator CD-ROM
- Animated Algebra
- Test Generator CD-ROM
- Online Quiz
- eWorkbook
- eEdition
- @HomeTutor

Resources for English Learners
- Quick Reference for English Learners
- Spanish Study Guide
- Multi-Language Visual Glossary
- Student Resources in Spanish

See also the *Algebra 1 Toolkit* for more strategies for meeting individual needs.

PROPORTIONS A **proportion** is an equation that states that two ratios are equivalent. The general form of a proportion is given below.

READING
This proportion is read "*a* is to *b* as *c* is to *d*."

$$\frac{a}{b} = \frac{c}{d} \text{ where } b \neq 0, d \neq 0$$

If one of the numbers in a proportion is unknown, you can solve the proportion to find the unknown number. To solve a proportion with a variable in the numerator, you can use the same methods you used to solve equations.

EXAMPLE 2 Solve a proportion

Solve the proportion $\frac{11}{6} = \frac{x}{30}$.

$\frac{11}{6} = \frac{x}{30}$	Write original proportion.
$30 \cdot \frac{11}{6} = 30 \cdot \frac{x}{30}$	Multiply each side by 30.
$\frac{330}{6} = x$	Simplify.
$55 = x$	Divide.

GUIDED PRACTICE for Example 2

Solve the proportion. Check your solution.

3. $\frac{w}{35} = \frac{4}{7}$ 20
4. $\frac{9}{2} = \frac{m}{12}$ 54
5. $\frac{z}{54} = \frac{5}{9}$ 30

SETTING UP A PROPORTION There are different ways to set up a proportion. Consider the following problem.

A recipe for tomato salsa calls for 30 tomatoes to make 12 pints of salsa. How many tomatoes are needed to make 4 pints of salsa?

The tables below show two ways of arranging the information from the problem. In each table, x represents the number of tomatoes needed to make 4 pints of salsa. The proportions follow from the tables.

AVOID ERRORS
You cannot write a proportion that compares pints to tomatoes and tomatoes to pints.

$$\frac{\text{pints}}{\text{tomatoes}} \neq \frac{\text{tomatoes}}{\text{pints}}$$

	Tomatoes	Pints
Smaller recipe	x	4
Normal recipe	30	12

Proportion: $\frac{x}{30} = \frac{4}{12}$

	Smaller recipe	Normal recipe
Tomatoes	x	30
Pints	4	12

Proportion: $\frac{x}{4} = \frac{30}{12}$

Motivating the Lesson

Tell students that ratios and proportions are used to solve a wide range of problems in which the relationship between quantities is important. For example, you can use ratios to compare the number of math books to English books in the library, the number of boys to girls in drama classes, and the number of airplanes to cars at an airfield. Proportions can be used to find distance, time, speed, and cost, among other things.

3 TEACH

Extra Example 1

At a carwash fund raiser, 18 ninth grade students and 14 tenth grade students worked the first shift.

a. Find the ratio of ninth grade students to tenth grade students. $\frac{9}{7}$

b. Find the ratio of ninth grade students to all students. $\frac{9}{16}$

Key Question to Ask for Example 1

- Is the ratio of away matches to home matches the same as the ratio of home matches to away matches? Explain. **No, the ratio of away matches to home matches is 10 to 14 or 5 to 7, while the ratio of home matches to away matches is 7 to 5.**

Extra Example 2

Solve the proportion $\frac{12}{h} = \frac{3}{17}$. 68

Key Question to Ask for Example 2

- Why do you multiply by 30 and not by the reciprocal of $\frac{11}{6}$? **Multiplying by 30 isolates the variable.**

Differentiated Instruction

English Learners The similarities of the words *ratio* and *rational* may confuse some students. Explain that a rational number is the ratio of two integers. For instance, they can write the ratio 7 to 12 as 7 : 12 or as the rational number $\frac{7}{12}$. However, a ratio does not necessarily involve rational numbers. For example, the ratio of the area of a circle with radius r to a square with side length r is $\pi : 1$.

See also the *Algebra 1 Toolkit* for more strategies.

Extra Example 3

A backpacker in the Sierras hikes 5.5 miles in 2 hours. If the hiking rate remains the same, how far will the backpacker hike in 7 hours? Write and solve a proportion to find the answer. $\frac{5.5}{2} = \frac{x}{7}$; 19.25 mi

Key Questions to Ask for Example 3

- What is another way to set up the proportion? Explain. $\frac{5}{x} = \frac{150}{1029}$; it compares 5 seconds to 150 feet and the unknown number of seconds to 1029 feet.
- What is an incorrect way to set up the proportion? Explain. $\frac{5}{x} = \frac{1029}{150}$; it compares 5 seconds to 1029 feet and the unknown number of seconds to 150 feet.

Closing the Lesson

Have students summarize the major points of the lesson and answer the Essential Question: How do you find ratios and write and solve proportions?

- Ratios compare two quantities.
- A proportion states that two ratios are equivalent. When writing a proportion, put like quantities in the same location in each ratio, such as $\frac{\text{nuts}}{\text{ounces}} = \frac{\text{nuts}}{\text{ounces}}$.

A ratio is an expression that relates one quantity to another by division, while a proportion is an equation of two ratios. Solve proportions with unknown numbers in the same way as you solve equations, by isolating the variable.

EXAMPLE 3 Solve a multi-step problem

ELEVATORS The elevator that takes passengers from the lobby of the John Hancock Center in Chicago to the observation level travels 150 feet in 5 seconds. The observation level is located on the 94th floor, at 1029 feet above the ground. Find the time it takes the elevator to travel from the lobby to the observation level.

Solution

STEP 1 **Write** a proportion involving two ratios that compare the amount of time the elevator has ascended with the distance traveled.

$$\frac{5}{150} = \frac{x}{1029} \quad \begin{matrix}\leftarrow \text{seconds} \\ \leftarrow \text{feet}\end{matrix}$$

STEP 2 **Solve** the proportion.

$$\frac{5}{150} = \frac{x}{1029} \qquad \text{Write proportion.}$$

$$1029 \cdot \frac{5}{150} = 1029 \cdot \frac{x}{1029} \qquad \text{Multiply each side by 1029.}$$

$$\frac{5145}{150} = x \qquad \text{Simplify.}$$

$$34.3 = x \qquad \text{Use a calculator.}$$

▶ The elevator travels from the lobby to the observation level in 34.3 seconds.

CHECK You can use a table to check the reasonableness of your answer.

GENERATE TABLE As the amount of time increases by 5 seconds, the distance traveled increases by 150 feet.

Time (sec)	5	10	15	20	25	30	35
Distance traveled (ft)	150	300	450	600	750	900	1050

The solution, 34.3 seconds, is slightly less than 35 seconds, and 1029 feet is slightly less than 1050 feet. So, the solution is reasonable.

GUIDED PRACTICE for Example 3

6. **WHAT IF?** In Example 3, suppose the elevator travels 125 feet in 5 seconds. Find the time it will take for the elevator to travel from the lobby to the observation level. 41.16 sec

7. **ASTRONOMY** When two full moons appear in the same month, the second full moon is called a blue moon. On average, 2 blue moons occur every 5 years. Find the number of blue moons that are likely to occur in the next 25 years. 10 blue moons

3.5 EXERCISES

HOMEWORK KEY
○ = WORKED-OUT SOLUTIONS on p. WS6 for Exs. 17 and 49
★ = STANDARDIZED TEST PRACTICE Exs. 2, 19, 20, 43, and 54
◆ = MULTIPLE REPRESENTATIONS Ex. 52

SKILL PRACTICE

A

1. **VOCABULARY** Copy and complete: A proportion is an equation that states that two __?__ are equivalent. ratios

2. ★ **WRITING** Write a ratio of two quantities in three different ways. *Sample answer:* $\frac{2}{5}$, 2:5, 2 to 5

SIMPLIFYING RATIOS Tell whether the ratio is in simplest form. If not, write it in simplest form.

3. 14 to 18 no; 7 to 9
4. 5 : 13 yes
5. $\frac{24}{25}$ yes
6. 28 to 32 no; 7 to 8

EXAMPLE 2 on p. 163 for Exs. 7–22

SOLVING PROPORTIONS Solve the proportion. Check your solution.

7. $\frac{2}{5}=\frac{x}{3}$ $\frac{6}{5}$
8. $\frac{4}{1}=\frac{z}{16}$ 64
9. $\frac{c}{8}=\frac{11}{4}$ 22
10. $\frac{36}{12}=\frac{x}{2}$ 6
11. $\frac{16}{7}=\frac{m}{21}$ 48
12. $\frac{k}{9}=\frac{10}{18}$ 5
13. $\frac{5}{8}=\frac{t}{24}$ 15
14. $\frac{d}{5}=\frac{80}{100}$ 4
15. $\frac{v}{20}=\frac{8}{4}$ 40
16. $\frac{r}{60}=\frac{40}{50}$ 48
17. $\frac{16}{48}=\frac{n}{36}$ 12
18. $\frac{49}{98}=\frac{s}{112}$ 56

19. ★ **MULTIPLE CHOICE** What is the value of x in the proportion $\frac{8}{5}=\frac{x}{20}$? C

Ⓐ 2 Ⓑ 23 Ⓒ 32 Ⓓ 40

20. ★ **MULTIPLE CHOICE** What is the value of z in the proportion $\frac{z}{15}=\frac{28}{35}$? B

Ⓐ 8 Ⓑ 12 Ⓒ 18.75 Ⓓ 425

ERROR ANALYSIS *Describe* and correct the error in solving the proportion. 21, 22. See margin.

21.
$$\frac{3}{4}=\frac{x}{6}$$
$$\frac{1}{6}\cdot\frac{3}{4}=\frac{1}{6}\cdot\frac{x}{6}$$
$$\frac{1}{8}=x$$
✗

22.
$$\frac{m}{10}=\frac{50}{20}$$
$$10\cdot\frac{m}{10}=20\cdot\frac{50}{20}$$
$$m=50$$
✗

B

WRITING AND SOLVING PROPORTIONS Write the sentence as a proportion. Then solve the proportion.

23. 3 is to 8 as x is to 32. $\frac{3}{8}=\frac{x}{32}$; 12
24. 5 is to 7 as a is to 49. $\frac{5}{7}=\frac{a}{49}$; 35
25. x is to 4 as 8 is to 16.
26. y is to 20 as 9 is to 5.
27. b is to 10 as 7 is to 2. $\frac{b}{10}=\frac{7}{2}$; 35
28. 4 is to 12 as n is to 3. $\frac{4}{12}=\frac{n}{3}$; 1
29. 12 is to 18 as d is to 27.
30. t is to 21 as 40 is to 28.

25. $\frac{x}{4}=\frac{8}{16}$; 2
26. $\frac{y}{20}=\frac{9}{5}$; 36
29. $\frac{12}{18}=\frac{d}{27}$; 18
30. $\frac{t}{21}=\frac{40}{28}$; 30

4 PRACTICE AND APPLY

Assignment Guide

Answer Transparencies available for all exercises

Basic:
Day 1: SRH p. 912 Exs. 6–10
pp. 165–167
Exs. 1–6, 7–17 odd, 19–26, 45–52, 56–66

Average:
Day 1: pp. 165–167
Exs. 1, 2, 5, 6, 10–18 even, 19–22, 23–43 odd, 47–54, 56–66 even

Advanced:
Day 1: pp. 165–167
Exs. 1, 2, 15–20, 27–30, 32–42 even, 43–55*, 57–65 odd

Block:
pp. 165–167
Exs. 1, 2, 5, 6, 10–18 even, 19–22, 23–43 odd, 47–54, 56–66 even (with 3.4)

Differentiated Instruction

See *Algebra 1 Best Practices Toolkit* for suggestions on addressing the needs of a diverse classroom.

Homework Check

For a quick check of student understanding of key concepts, go over the following exercises:

Basic: 11, 13, 45, 47, 50
Average: 12, 16, 47, 48, 51
Advanced: 15, 20, 47, 48, 52

Extra Practice

- Student Edition, p. 940
- Chapter 3 Resource Book: Practice levels A, B, C, pp. 52–54

Practice Worksheet

An easily-readable reduced practice page (with answers) for this lesson can be found on p. 130D.

21. Multiply each side by 6, not $\frac{1}{6}$; $6\cdot\frac{3}{4}=6\cdot\frac{x}{6}$, $4\frac{1}{2}=x$.
22. Multiply each side by 10, not one side by 10 and the other side by 20; $10\cdot\frac{m}{10}=10\cdot\frac{50}{20}$, $m=25$.

Study Strategy

Exercises 7–18 Remind students that they solve proportions in the same way they solve equations, by isolating the variable. Also note that the variable can be on either side of the equation.

Exercises 34–42 Even though these proportions are more complex than those in the previous exercises, students should stay focused on isolating the variable.

Reading Strategy

Exercises 23–30 Before beginning these exercises, you may want to refer students to the reading note on page 163. Students can use this model to help them write the sentences as proportions.

Avoiding Common Errors

Exercises 45–49 Students often compare the wrong quantities when they write ratios. Point out that they should compare quantities in the same order as the words. For example, if they want to find the ratio between medium pizzas and small pizzas, the number for medium pizzas is first in the ratio and the number for small pizzas is second.

Exercises 50–52 Caution students to be sure to set up each proportion correctly. Suggest they reread the section on setting up proportions on page 163. They can then look over their proportions to make sure they are writing like quantities in the same location in each ratio.

SOLVING PROPORTIONS **Solve the proportion. Check your solution.**

31. $\frac{b}{0.5} = \frac{9}{2.5}$ 1.8

32. $\frac{1.1}{1.2} = \frac{n}{3.6}$ 3.3

33. $\frac{2.1}{7.7} = \frac{v}{8.8}$ 2.4

34. $\frac{36}{54} = \frac{2x}{6}$ 2

35. $\frac{3a}{4} = \frac{36}{12}$ 4

36. $\frac{10h}{108} = \frac{5}{9}$ 6

37. $\frac{6r}{10} = \frac{36}{15}$ 4

38. $\frac{12}{42} = \frac{4w}{56}$ 4

39. $\frac{m+3}{8} = \frac{40}{64}$ 2

40. $\frac{5}{13} = \frac{k-4}{39}$ 19

41. $\frac{7}{112} = \frac{c-3}{8}$ 3.5

42. $\frac{6+n}{60} = \frac{15}{90}$ 4

43. ★ **SHORT RESPONSE** Is it possible to write a proportion using the numbers 3, 4, 6, and 8? *Explain* your reasoning. Yes. *Sample answer:* $\frac{3}{6} = \frac{4}{8}$

C 44. **CHALLENGE** If $\frac{a}{b} = \frac{c}{d}$ for nonzero numbers a, b, c, and d, is it also true that $\frac{a}{c} = \frac{b}{d}$? *Explain.* Yes; multiply each side by b to get the equation $a = \frac{cb}{d}$, then divide each side by c to get $\frac{a}{c} = \frac{b}{d}$.

PROBLEM SOLVING

EXAMPLE 1 A on p. 162 for Exs. 45–49

45. **GOVERNMENT** There are 435 representatives in the U.S. House of Representatives. Of the 435 representatives, 6 are from Kentucky. Find the ratio of the number of representatives from Kentucky to the total number of representatives. $\frac{2}{145}$

@HomeTutor for problem solving help at classzone.com

46. **CONTEST** Of the 30 champions of the National Spelling Bee from 1974 to 2003, 16 are boys. Find the ratio of the number of champions who are girls to the number who are boys. $\frac{7}{8}$

@HomeTutor for problem solving help at classzone.com

PIZZA SALES **The table shows the number of pizzas sold at a pizzeria during a week. Use the information to find the specified ratio.**

47. Small pizzas to large pizzas $\frac{2}{5}$

48. Medium pizzas to large pizzas $\frac{3}{5}$

(49.) Large pizzas to all pizzas $\frac{1}{2}$

Size	Small	Medium	Large
Pizzas	96	144	240

EXAMPLE 3 on p. 164 for Exs. 50–52

50. **READING** A student can read 7 pages of a book in 10 minutes. How many pages of the book can the student read in 30 minutes? 21 pages

51. **SOCCER** In the first 4 games of the season, a soccer team scored a total of 10 goals. If this trend continues, how many goals will the team score in the 18 remaining games of the season? 45 goals

B 52. ◆ **MULTIPLE REPRESENTATIONS** A movie is filmed so that the ratio of the length to the width of the image on the screen is 1.85 : 1.

a. **Writing a Proportion** Write and solve a proportion to find the length of the image on the screen when the width of the image is 38 feet. *Sample answer:* $\frac{1.85}{1} = \frac{x}{38}$, 70.3 ft

b. **Making a Table** Make a table that shows the length of an image when the width of the image is 20, 25, 30, 35, and 40 feet. Use your table to check the reasonableness of your answer to part (a). See margin.

○ = WORKED-OUT SOLUTIONS on p. WS1 ★ = STANDARDIZED TEST PRACTICE ◆ = MULTIPLE REPRESENTATIONS

52b.

Width (ft)	Length (ft)
20	37
25	46.25
30	55.5
35	64.75
40	74

53. **MULTI-STEP PROBLEM** One day, the ratio of skiers to snowboarders on the mountain at a ski resort was 13 : 10. The resort sold a total of 253 lift tickets during the day.

a. Find the ratio of snowboarders on the mountain to all of the skiers and snowboarders on the mountain. $\frac{10}{23}$

b. Use the ratio from part (a) to find the number of lift tickets sold to snowboarders during the day. **110 lift tickets**

c. During the same day, the ratio of snowboarders who rented snowboards to snowboarders that have their own snowboards is 4 : 7. Find the number of snowboarders who rented a snowboard. **40 snowboarders**

54. ★ **EXTENDED RESPONSE** You and a friend are waiting in separate lines to purchase concert tickets.

a. **Interpret** Every 10 minutes, the cashier at the head of your line helps 3 people. There are 11 people in line in front of you. Write a proportion that can be used to determine how long you will have to wait to purchase tickets. *Sample answer:* $\frac{10}{3} = \frac{x}{11}$

b. **Interpret** Every 5 minutes, the cashier at the head of your friend's line helps 2 people. There are 14 people in line in front of your friend. Write a proportion that can be used to determine how long your friend will have to wait to purchase tickets. *Sample answer:* $\frac{5}{2} = \frac{x}{14}$

c. **Compare** Will you or your friend be able to purchase concert tickets first? *Explain.* **Your friend; you will wait in line for $36\frac{2}{3}$ minutes and your friend will wait only 35 minutes.**

C 55. **CHALLENGE** A car traveling 50 miles per hour goes 15 miles farther in the same amount of time as a car traveling 30 miles per hour. Find the distance that each car travels. **37.5 mi, 22.5 mi**

ILLINOIS MIXED REVIEW

TEST PRACTICE at classzone.com

56. If $2x + 3 = y$, which of the following is an equivalent equation?

Ⓐ $x + 7 = y + 4$

Ⓑ $2x - 3 = y - 3$

Ⓒ $3x + 3 = y + x$

Ⓓ $4x + 3 = 2y$

C

57. Which problem is best represented by the number sentence $x + 2(x - 3) = 42$?

Ⓐ Chris spent x dollars on lunch and $3 less than twice that much on dinner. He spent $42 altogether. How much did he spend on lunch?

Ⓑ Sonia earned x dollars one day at work. She used that money to buy 2 shirts that cost $(x - 3)$ dollars each. At the end of the day she had $42 left from her earnings. How much money did Sonia earn?

Ⓒ Anil has 2 jobs. One week, he worked 3 hours at one job and x hours at the other. He worked 42 hours that week. How many hours did he work at his other job?

Ⓓ Hernane bought a DVD and 2 CDs. The DVD cost x dollars, and each CD cost 3 dollars less than the DVD. Hernane spent $42. How much did the DVD cost?

D

5 ASSESS AND RETEACH

Daily Homework Quiz

Transparency Available

1. A chocolate chip cookie recipe calls for $2\frac{1}{4}$ cups of flour and $\frac{3}{4}$ cup of brown sugar. Find the ratio of brown sugar to flour. $\frac{1}{3}$

Solve the proportion.

2. $\frac{a}{7} = \frac{9}{21}$ 3

3. $\frac{32}{28} = \frac{m}{14}$ 16

4. A printer can print 12 color pages in 3 minutes. How many color pages can the printer print in 9 minutes? Write and solve a proportion to find the answer. $\frac{12}{3} = \frac{x}{9}$; **36 color pages**

Online Quiz

Available at **classzone.com**

Diagnosis/Remediation

- Practice A, B, C in Chapter 3 Resource Book, pp. 52–54
- Study Guide in Chapter 3 Resource Book, pp. 55–56
- Practice Workbook, pp. 38–39
- @HomeTutor

Challenge

Additional challenge is available in the Chapter 3 Resource Book, p. 59.

3.6 Solve Proportions Using Cross Products

6.11.17 Set up, evaluate, or solve number sentences or word problems involving ratios and proportions with rational numbers . . .

Before You solved proportions using the multiplication property of equality.

Now You will solve proportions using cross products.

Why? So you can find the height of a scale model, as in Ex. 39.

1 PLAN AND PREPARE

Warm-Up Exercises

Transparency Available

Solve the proportion.

1. $\frac{t}{32} = \frac{7}{16}$ 14
2. $\frac{18}{24} = \frac{b}{12}$ 9
3. $\frac{21}{n} = \frac{28}{32}$ 24
4. $\frac{4}{12} = \frac{11}{p}$ 33
5. It takes 30 tomatillos to make 8 ounces of enchilada sauce. How many tomatillos does it take to make 12 ounces of enchilada sauce? 45 tomatillos

Notetaking Guide

Transparency Available

Promotes interactive learning and notetaking skills, pp. 63–65.

Pacing

Basic: 1 day
Average: 1 day
Advanced: 1 day
Block: 0.5 block with 3.7
- See *Teaching Guide/Lesson Plan.*

2 FOCUS AND MOTIVATE

Essential Question

Big Idea 2, p. 131

How do you solve proportions using cross products? **Tell students they will learn how to answer this question by using the cross products property.**

Key Vocabulary
- **cross product**
- **scale drawing**
- **scale model**
- **scale**

In a proportion, a **cross product** is the product of the numerator of one ratio and the denominator of the other ratio. The following property involving cross products can be used to solve proportions.

KEY CONCEPT *For Your Notebook*

Cross Products Property

Words The cross products of a proportion are equal.

Example $\frac{3}{4} = \frac{6}{8}$ $4 \cdot 6 = 24$, $3 \cdot 8 = 24$

Algebra If $\frac{a}{b} = \frac{c}{d}$ where $b \neq 0$ and $d \neq 0$, then $ad = bc$.

The proportion $\frac{3}{4} = \frac{6}{8}$ can be written as $3:4 = 6:8$. In this form, 4 and 6 are called the *means* of the proportion, and 3 and 8 are called the *extremes* of the proportion. This is why the cross products property is also called the *means-extremes property.*

EXAMPLE 1 Use the cross products property

Solve the proportion $\frac{8}{x} = \frac{6}{15}$.

$\frac{8}{x} = \frac{6}{15}$	Write original proportion.
$8 \cdot 15 = x \cdot 6$	Cross products property
$120 = 6x$	Simplify.
$20 = x$	Divide each side by 6.

▶ The solution is 20. Check by substituting 20 for x in the original proportion.

CHECK $\frac{8}{20} \stackrel{?}{=} \frac{6}{15}$	Substitute 20 for x.
$8 \cdot 15 \stackrel{?}{=} 20 \cdot 6$	Cross products property
$120 = 120$ ✓	Simplify. Solution checks.

Resource Planning Guide

Chapter Resource Book
- Teaching Guide/Lesson Plan (pp. 60–61)
- Practice levels A, B, C (pp. 62–64)
- Study Guide (pp. 65–66)
- Catch-up for Absent Students (p. 67)
- Application (p. 68)
- Challenge (p. 69)

Workbooks
- Notetaking Guide (pp. 63–65)
- Practice Workbook (pp. 40–41)

Teaching Options
- **Power Presentations CD-ROM** provides dynamic electronic teaching resources for the classroom.
- **Activity Generator CD-ROM** provides editable activities for all ability levels.

Interactive Technology
- Easy Planner
- Power Presentations CD-ROM
- Activity Generator CD-ROM
- Animated Algebra
- Test Generator CD-ROM
- Online Quiz
- eWorkbook
- eEdition
- @HomeTutor

Resources for English Learners
- Quick Reference for English Learners
- Spanish Study Guide
- Multi-Language Visual Glossary
- Student Resources in Spanish

See also the *Algebra 1 Toolkit* for more strategies for meeting individual needs.

EXAMPLE 2 Standardized Test Practice

What is the value of x in the proportion $\frac{4}{x} = \frac{8}{x-3}$?

Ⓐ −6 Ⓑ −3 Ⓒ 3 Ⓓ 6

Solution

ANOTHER WAY
Because 8 is twice 4, you can reason that $x - 3$ must be twice x:
$x - 3 = 2x$
$-3 = x$

$\frac{4}{x} = \frac{8}{x-3}$ Write original proportion.

$4(x - 3) = x \cdot 8$ Cross products property

$4x - 12 = 8x$ Simplify.

$-12 = 4x$ Subtract $4x$ from each side.

$-3 = x$ Divide each side by 4.

▸ The value of x is −3. The correct answer is B. Ⓐ Ⓑ Ⓒ Ⓓ

EXAMPLE 3 Write and solve a proportion

SEALS Each day, the seals at an aquarium are each fed 8 pounds of food for every 100 pounds of their body weight. A seal at the aquarium weighs 280 pounds. How much food should the seal be fed per day?

Solution

STEP 1 **Write** a proportion involving two ratios that compare the amount of food with the weight of the seal.

$\frac{8}{100} = \frac{x}{280}$ ← amount of food / ← weight of seal

STEP 2 **Solve** the proportion.

ANOTHER WAY
You can also solve the proportion by multiplying each side of the equation by 280.

$\frac{8}{100} = \frac{x}{280}$ Write proportion.

$8 \cdot 280 = 100 \cdot x$ Cross products property

$2240 = 100x$ Simplify.

$22.4 = x$ Divide each side by 100.

▸ A 280 pound seal should be fed 22.4 pounds of food per day.

GUIDED PRACTICE for Examples 1, 2, and 3

Solve the proportion. Check your solution.

1. $\frac{4}{a} = \frac{24}{30}$ 5
2. $\frac{3}{x} = \frac{2}{x-6}$ 18
3. $\frac{m}{5} = \frac{m-6}{4}$ 30
4. **WHAT IF?** In Example 3, suppose the seal weighs 260 pounds. How much food should the seal be fed per day? 20.8 lb

Motivating the Lesson

Tell students that using cross products to solve proportions is useful in estimating actual distances on maps. Ask students to recount various times they have used the scale on a map to find the distance between two points. After a brief discussion, tell them they will learn how to use cross products to find map distances.

3 TEACH

Extra Example 1

Solve the proportion $\frac{4}{x} = \frac{12}{24}$. 8

Key Questions to Ask for Example 1

- What are the means of the proportion? x and 6
- What are the extremes of the proportion? 8 and 15

Extra Example 2

What is the value of x in the proportion $\frac{3}{x} = \frac{9}{x-4}$? C

Ⓐ 4 Ⓑ 2
Ⓒ −2 Ⓓ −4

Extra Example 3

Georgia is making her own potting soil. For every 4 buckets of peat moss, she mixes in 3 buckets of perlite. Suppose she uses 10 buckets of peat moss. How many buckets of perlite should she use? Write and solve a proportion to find the answer. $\frac{4}{3} = \frac{10}{x}$; she should use 7.5 buckets of perlite.

Differentiated Instruction

Visual Learners To solve problems like the one in **Example 3**, students may want to organize the information in a table first.

	100-lb seal	280-lb seal
Amount of food (lb)	8	?
Weight of seal (lb)	100	280

Then the students can set up ratios vertically, $\frac{8}{100}$ and $\frac{x}{280}$, or horizontally, $\frac{8}{x}$ and $\frac{100}{280}$, to write a proportion.

See also the *Algebra 1 Toolkit* for more strategies.

Extra Example 4

On a map, the distance between Red River Gorge and Pine Bluff is 3.8 centimeters. If the map scale is 1 cm = 25 km, estimate the actual distance between Red River Gorge and Pine Bluff. about 95 km

Key Question to Ask for Example 4

- If the distance between Columbus and Cincinnati is about 170 kilometers, could you use the proportion in Example 4 to find the distance between the two cities on the map? Explain. Yes, you could use the proportion $\frac{1}{85} = \frac{x}{170}$ to find the distance on the map.

Vocabulary

You may want to discuss the many meanings of the word "scale." You could have students look up *scale* in the dictionary and then have the class discuss the meanings. Finish by focusing on the meaning of scale in Example 4 as a ratio of map distance to actual distance.

Closing the Lesson

Have students summarize the major points of the lesson and answer the Essential Question: How do you solve proportions using cross products?

- Cross products of a proportion are equal.
- The scale of a scale drawing or model relates the drawing's or model's dimensions to the actual dimensions.

To use cross products, multiply the numerator of each ratio by the denominator of the other ratio, and write an equal sign between the two products. Then solve for the variable.

SCALE DRAWINGS AND SCALE MODELS The floor plan below is an example of a *scale drawing.* A **scale drawing** is a two-dimensional drawing of an object in which the dimensions of the drawing are in proportion to the dimensions of the object. A **scale model** is a three-dimensional model of an object in which the dimensions of the model are in proportion to the dimensions of the object.

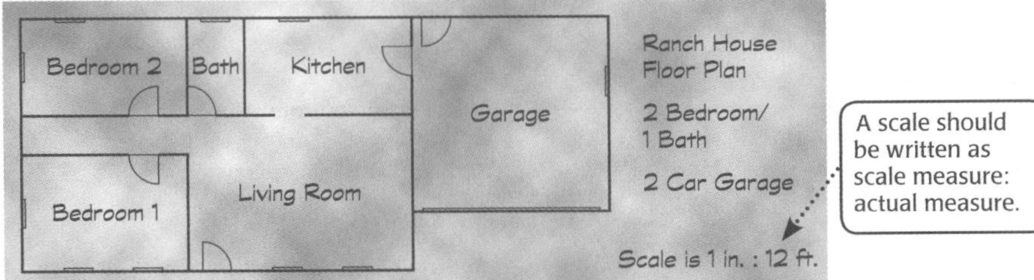

The **scale** of a scale drawing or scale model relates the drawing's or model's dimensions and the actual dimensions. For example, the scale 1 in. : 12 ft on the floor plan means that 1 inch in the floor plan represents an actual distance of 12 feet.

EXAMPLE 4 Use the scale on a map

MAPS Use a metric ruler and the map of Ohio to estimate the distance between Cleveland and Cincinnati.

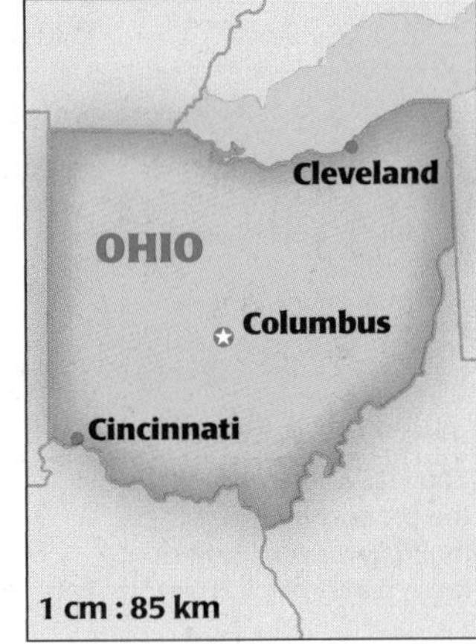

Solution

From the map's scale, 1 centimeter represents 85 kilometers. On the map, the distance between Cleveland and Cincinnati is about 4.2 centimeters.

Write and solve a proportion to find the distance d between the cities.

$$\frac{1}{85} = \frac{4.2}{d} \quad \begin{array}{l}\leftarrow \text{centimeters} \\ \leftarrow \text{kilometers}\end{array}$$

$1 \cdot d = 85 \cdot 4.2$ Cross products property

$d = 357$ Simplify.

▶ The actual distance between Cleveland and Cincinnati is about 357 kilometers.

GUIDED PRACTICE for Example 4

5. Use a metric ruler and the map in Example 4 to estimate the distance (in kilometers) between Columbus and Cleveland. about 212.5 km

6. **MODEL SHIPS** The ship model kits sold at a hobby store have a scale of 1 ft : 600 ft. A completed model of the *Queen Elizabeth II* is 1.6 feet long. Estimate the actual length of the *Queen Elizabeth II.* about 960 ft

3.6 EXERCISES

HOMEWORK KEY
- ○ = **WORKED-OUT SOLUTIONS** on p. WS7 for Exs. 13 and 39
- ★ = **STANDARDIZED TEST PRACTICE** Exs. 2, 15, 16, 41, and 42
- ◆ = **MULTIPLE REPRESENTATIONS** Ex. 40

SKILL PRACTICE

A

1. **VOCABULARY** Copy and complete: In a proportion, a(n) __?__ is the product of the numerator of one ratio and the denominator of the other ratio. cross product

2. ★ **WRITING** A scale drawing has a scale of 1 cm : 3 m. *Explain* how the scale can be used to find the actual distance between objects in the drawing. Measure the distance in centimeters, in the drawing and then substitute the value in the proportion, $\frac{1}{3} = \frac{\text{distance in drawing}}{\text{actual distance}}$.

EXAMPLES 1 and 2 on pp. 168–169 for Exs. 3–18

SOLVING PROPORTIONS Solve the proportion. Check your solution.

3. $\frac{2}{3} = \frac{4}{x}$ 6
4. $\frac{3}{y} = \frac{15}{35}$ 7
5. $\frac{13}{6} = \frac{52}{z}$ 24
6. $\frac{10}{45} = \frac{v}{27}$ 6
7. $\frac{5m}{6} = \frac{10}{12}$ 1
8. $\frac{3k}{27} = \frac{2}{3}$ 6
9. $\frac{-49}{7} = \frac{a+7}{6}$ −49
10. $\frac{6}{t+4} = \frac{42}{77}$ 7
11. $\frac{8}{12} = \frac{r}{r+1}$ 2
12. $\frac{n}{n-12} = \frac{9}{5}$ 27
13. ○ $\frac{11}{w} = \frac{33}{w+24}$ 12
14. $\frac{18}{d+13} = \frac{6}{d-13}$ 26

15. ★ **MULTIPLE CHOICE** What is the value of h in the proportion $\frac{15}{-2h} = \frac{5}{12}$? B

(A) −36 (B) −18 (C) 18 (D) 36

16. ★ **MULTIPLE CHOICE** What is the value of s in the proportion $\frac{7}{s-14} = \frac{21}{s+18}$? D

(A) −48 (B) −16 (C) 3 (D) 30

ERROR ANALYSIS *Describe* and correct the error in solving the proportion.

17.
$\frac{4}{3} = \frac{16}{x}$
$4 \cdot 16 = 4 \cdot x$
$64 = 4x$
$16 = x$

Use the cross products property to multiply 4 by x and 16 by 3; $4 \cdot x = 3 \cdot 16$, $4x = 48$, $x = 12$.

18.
$\frac{18}{14} = \frac{b+2}{b}$
$18b = 14b + 2$
$4b = 2$
$b = 0.5$

Distribute the 14 to both b and 2; $18b = 14b + 28$, $4b = 28$, $b = 7$.

B

SOLVING PROPORTIONS Solve the proportion. Check your solution.

19. $\frac{7}{3} = \frac{2x+5}{x}$ 15
20. $\frac{a}{9a-2} = \frac{1}{8}$ 2
21. $\frac{24}{5z+4} = \frac{4}{z-1}$ 10
22. $\frac{c-8}{-2} = \frac{11-4c}{11}$ 22
23. $\frac{k-8}{7+k} = \frac{-1}{5}$ 5.5
24. $\frac{2}{-3} = \frac{4v+4}{2v+14}$ −2.5
25. $\frac{m+1}{4} = \frac{3m+6}{7}$ −3.4
26. $\frac{6}{4+2w} = \frac{-2}{w-10}$ 5.2
27. $\frac{n+0.3}{n-3.2} = \frac{9}{2}$ 4.2
28. $\frac{-3}{11} = \frac{5-h}{h+1.4}$ 7.4
29. $\frac{4}{b-3.9} = \frac{2}{b+1}$ −5.9
30. $\frac{16.5+3t}{3} = \frac{0.9-t}{-5}$ −7.1

4 PRACTICE AND APPLY

Assignment Guide

Answer Transparencies available for all exercises

Basic:
Day 1: pp. 171–173
Exs. 1–18, 19–25 odd, 33–39 odd, 40, 44–54 even

Average:
Day 1: pp. 171–173
Exs. 1, 2, 4–14 even, 15–18, 19–29 odd, 31–42, 44–54 even

Advanced:
Day 1: pp. 171–173
Exs. 1, 2, 11–16, 24–30 even, 31–34*, 37–43*, 46, 47, 53–55

Block:
pp. 171–173
Exs. 1, 2, 4–14 even, 15–18, 19–29 odd, 31–42, 44–54 even (with 3.7)

Differentiated Instruction

See *Algebra 1 Best Practices Toolkit* for suggestions on addressing the needs of a diverse classroom.

Homework Check

For a quick check of student understanding of key concepts, go over the following exercises:

Basic: 7, 13, 15, 33, 35
Average: 10, 15, 23, 34, 37
Advanced: 12, 16, 30, 34, 39

Extra Practice

- Student Edition, p. 940
- Chapter 3 Resource Book: Practice levels A, B, C, pp. 62–64

Practice Worksheet

An easily-readable reduced practice page (with answers) for this lesson can be found on p. 130D.

Avoiding Common Errors

Exercises 3–30 Students sometimes multiply numerator by numerator and denominator by denominator when solving a proportion. Remind them that they find the cross products by multiplying the numerator of each ratio by the denominator of the other.

Study Strategy

Exercises 3–30 Tell students they can solve the proportions using the method with which they are most comfortable. Suggest they try a different method if they become stuck on a problem.

Teaching Strategy

Exercise 40 You may want to point out that the table in part (b) can be used to check the reasonableness of the answer in part (a) given that the diameter of the shell is between 4 and 5 inches.

Reading Strategy

Exercise 41 Urge students to read this problem carefully and to note that there are two steps to solving this problem. They need to determine the length of the field before they can set up a proportion.

31. REASONING The statements below justify the cross products property. Copy and complete the justification.

$\frac{a}{b} = \frac{c}{d}$	Given
$bd \cdot \frac{a}{b} = bd \cdot \frac{c}{d}$	**a.** ___?___ Multiplication property of equality
$\frac{bd \cdot a}{b} = \frac{bd \cdot c}{d}$	**b.** ___?___ Multiply
$ad = cb$	**c.** ___?___ Simplify

C **32. CHALLENGE** In the proportion $\frac{5}{h} = \frac{k}{14}$, what happens to the value of h as the value of k increases? *Explain.* Decreases; as k gets larger, the value of $\frac{k}{14}$ increases, so for the value of $\frac{5}{h}$ to increase, h must decrease.

PROBLEM SOLVING

EXAMPLE 3 on p. 169 for Exs. 33–34

A **33. RECIPES** A recipe that yields 12 buttermilk biscuits calls for 2 cups of flour. How much flour is needed to make 30 biscuits? 5 c

@HomeTutor for problem solving help at classzone.com

34. DIGITAL PHOTOGRAPHS It took 7.2 minutes to upload 8 digital photographs from your computer to a website. At this rate, how long will it take to upload 20 photographs? 18 min

@HomeTutor for problem solving help at classzone.com

EXAMPLE 4 on p. 170 for Exs. 35–39

MAPS A map has a scale of 1 cm : 15 km. Use the given map distance to find the actual distance.

35. 6 cm 90 km **36.** 3.2 cm 48 km **37.** 0.5 cm 7.5 km **38.** 4.7 cm 70.5 km

39. SCALE MODEL An exhibit at Tobu World Square in Japan includes a scale model of the Empire State Building. The model was built using a scale of 1 m : 25 m. The height of the actual Empire State Building is 443.2 meters. What is the height of the model? 17.728 m

B **40.**  **MULTIPLE REPRESENTATIONS** The diameter of the burst of a firework is proportional to the diameter of the shell of the firework.

a. Writing a Proportion Use the information in the diagram to find the burst diameter for a 4.75 inch shell. 213.75 ft

b. Making a Table Make a table of burst diameters for 2, 3, 4, 5, and 6 inch shells. Use the table to check your answer to part (a). See margin.

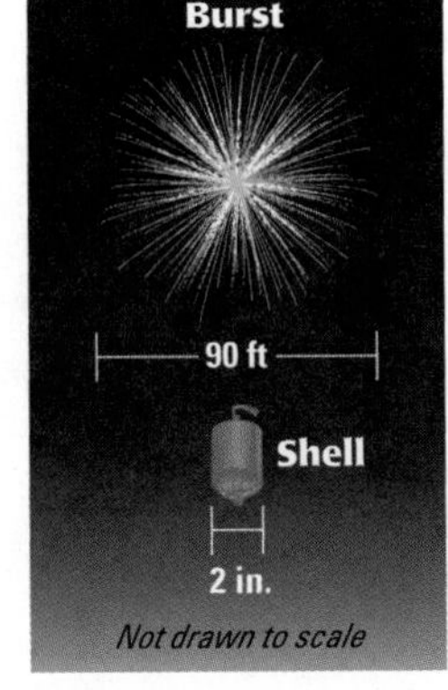

41. ★ SHORT RESPONSE The ratio of the length of a soccer field to the width of the field is 3 : 2. A scale drawing of a soccer field has a scale of 1 in. : 20 yd. The length of the field in the drawing is 6 inches. What is the actual width of the field? *Explain* your reasoning. 80 yd; find the actual length of the field by using the ratio 1 in. : 20 yd, then use that number to find the width of the soccer field by using the ratio 3 : 2.

◯ = WORKED-OUT SOLUTIONS on p. WS1 ★ = STANDARDIZED TEST PRACTICE ◆ = MULTIPLE REPRESENTATIONS

40b.

Shell diameter (ft)	Burst diameter (ft)
2	90
3	135
4	180
5	225
6	270

42c. Nearly equal. *Sample answer:* The ratio of moles of hydrogen to moles of carbon is about 1.33 to 1, the ratio of moles of hydrogen to moles of oxygen is about 1.32 to 1. The two ratios are nearly the same.

42. ★ **EXTENDED RESPONSE** A mole is a unit of measurement used in chemistry. The masses of one mole of three elements are in the table.

Element	Mass of 1 mole
Hydrogen	1.008 grams
Carbon	12.011 grams
Oxygen	15.999 grams

a. A 100 gram sample of ascorbic acid contains 4.58 grams of hydrogen. To the nearest tenth, find the number of moles of hydrogen. 4.5 moles

b. A 100 gram sample of ascorbic acid contains 54.5 grams of oxygen. To the nearest tenth, find the number of moles of oxygen in the sample. 3.4 moles

c. The ratio of moles of hydrogen to moles of carbon in ascorbic acid is 4:3. How does this ratio compare with the ratio of moles of hydrogen to moles of oxygen in ascorbic acid? *Explain.*

C **43.** **CHALLENGE** At a typical National Football League game, the ratio of females to males in attendance is 2 : 3. Estimate the number of male and female spectators at a game that has 75,000 spectators. 45,000 males, 30,000 females

ILLINOIS MIXED REVIEW

TEST PRACTICE at classzone.com

44. The function $y = 3x + 6$ has a domain of 2, 3, 5, and 8. What is the function's range?

Ⓐ 6, 9, 12, and 15

Ⓑ 12, 15, 18, and 21

Ⓒ 12, 15, 21, and 30 C

Ⓓ $-\frac{4}{3}, -1, -\frac{1}{3}$, and $\frac{2}{3}$

45. You pour 50 cubic centimeters of water into a cylindrical cup that has a height of 8 centimeters. The water fills half of the cup. Which is the best estimate of the radius of the cup?

Ⓐ 1 cm Ⓑ 2 cm Ⓒ 4 cm Ⓓ 5 cm B

QUIZ *for Lessons 3.4–3.6*

Solve the equation, if possible. *(p. 154)*

1. $y - 2 = y + 2$ no solution
2. $2x - 14 = -3x + 6$ 4
3. $10z - 4 = 2(5z - 2)$ identity
4. $6m + 5 - 3m = 7(m - 1)$ 3
5. $2(7 - g) = 9g + 14 - 11g$ identity
6. $13k + 3(k + 11) = 8k - 7$ −5
7. $\frac{1}{4}(8j - 3) = 2j - 3$ no solution
8. $8 - 4w = \frac{1}{3}(6w - 12)$ 2
9. $\frac{2}{5}(10t - 50) = 4(9 - 6t)$ 2

Solve the proportion. Check your solution. *(pp. 162, 168)*

10. $\frac{24}{20} = \frac{x}{5}$ 6
11. $\frac{6}{-7} = \frac{3z}{42}$ −12
12. $\frac{14}{12} = \frac{w + 11}{18}$ 10
13. $\frac{18}{5a} = \frac{3}{-5}$ −6
14. $\frac{10}{17} = \frac{k}{2k - 3}$ 10
15. $\frac{h - 1}{3} = \frac{2h + 1}{9}$ 4

16. **GEOMETRY** The ratio of the length to the width of a rectangle is 5 : 4. The length of the rectangle is 60 inches. What is the width? *(p. 168)* 48 in.

5 ASSESS AND RETEACH

Daily Homework Quiz

Transparency Available

Solve the proportion.

1. $\frac{10}{35} = \frac{y}{42}$ 12
2. $\frac{13}{h} = \frac{26}{16}$ 8
3. $\frac{5r}{6} = \frac{15}{2}$ 9
4. $\frac{9}{d + 3} = \frac{6}{17}$ 22.5
5. A figurine of a ballerina is based on a scale of 0.5 in. : 4 in. If the real ballerina used as a model for the figurine is 68 inches tall, what is the height of the figurine? 8.5 in.

Online Quiz

Available at **classzone.com**

Diagnosis/Remediation

- Practice A, B, C in Chapter 3 Resource Book, pp. 62–64
- Study Guide in Chapter 3 Resource Book, pp. 65–66
- Practice Workbook, pp. 40–41
- @HomeTutor

Challenge

Additional challenge is available in the Chapter 3 Resource Book, p. 69.

Quiz

An easily-readable reduced copy of the quiz (with answers) on Lessons 3.4–3.6 from the Assessment Book can be found on p. 130E.

1 PLAN AND PREPARE

Warm-Up Exercises

Solve the proportions.

1. $\frac{8}{k} = \frac{15}{6}$ 3.2
2. $\frac{46}{25} = \frac{h}{35}$ 64.4
3. $\frac{m}{2.5} = \frac{12}{6}$ 5
4. $\frac{0.5}{13} = \frac{6.5}{x}$ 169
5. The scale on a map is given as 1.5 cm : 8 km. The distance on the map between two cities is 2.25 centimeters. What is the actual distance between the cities? 12 km

2 FOCUS AND MOTIVATE

Essential Question

Big Idea 2, p. 131

How do you use similar figures to solve problems? Tell students they will learn how to answer this question by using similar figures to find unknown lengths of geometric figures and other objects that are difficult to measure.

3 TEACH

Extra Example 1

Given $\triangle EFG \sim \triangle QRS$, find GE. 12 m

S 24 m Q; 10 m; R; F 5 m E x G

NCTM STANDARDS

Standard 2: Analyze situations using algebraic symbols

Standard 9: Grasp how mathematical ideas interconnect

Extension

Use after Lesson 3.6

Apply Proportions to Similar Figures

GOAL Use similar figures to solve problems.

Key Vocabulary
- **congruent figures**
- **similar figures**
- **corresponding parts**

NAME SIMILAR FIGURES

When naming similar figures, list the letters of the corresponding vertices (corner points) in the same order.

Two figures are **congruent figures** if they have the same shape and size. The symbol $\cong$ indicates congruence. Of the triangles shown, $\triangle ABC \cong \triangle DEF$.

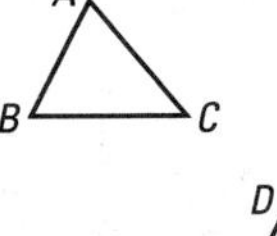

Two figures are **similar figures** if they have the same shape but not necessarily the same size. The symbol $\sim$ indicates that two figures are similar. All the triangles shown are similar; in particular, $\triangle ABC \sim \triangle JKL$.

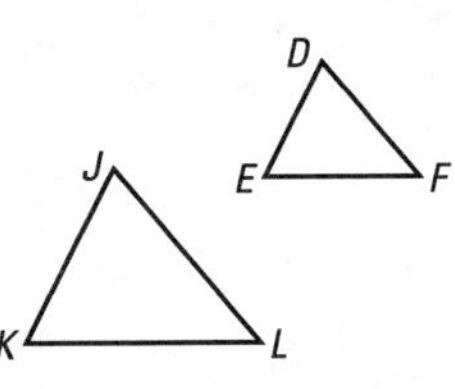

The sides or angles that have the same relative position within two figures are called **corresponding parts**.

NAME LENGTHS OF SIDES

AB represents the length of the side whose endpoints are *A* and *B*.

KEY CONCEPT — For Your Notebook

Properties of Similar Figures

In the diagram, $\triangle ABC \sim \triangle DEF$.

1. Corresponding angles of similar figures are congruent.
   $\angle A \cong \angle D, \angle B \cong \angle E, \angle C \cong \angle F$
2. The ratios of the lengths of corresponding sides of similar figures are equal.
   $\frac{AB}{DE} = \frac{BC}{EF} = \frac{AC}{DF} = \frac{1}{2}$

A 4 5 C 3 B

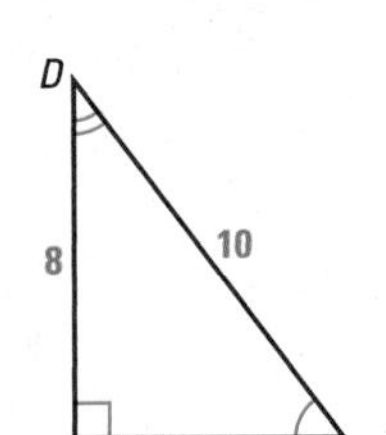

EXAMPLE 1 Find an unknown side length

Given $\triangle JKL \sim \triangle QRS$, find QR.

Solution

Use the ratios of the lengths of corresponding sides to write a proportion.

J 18 cm K; 8 cm; L

$\frac{JK}{QR} = \frac{KL}{RS}$	**Write proportion involving *QR*.**
$\frac{18}{x} = \frac{8}{12}$	**Substitute.**
$216 = 8x$	**Cross products property**
$27 = x$	**Divide each side by 8.**

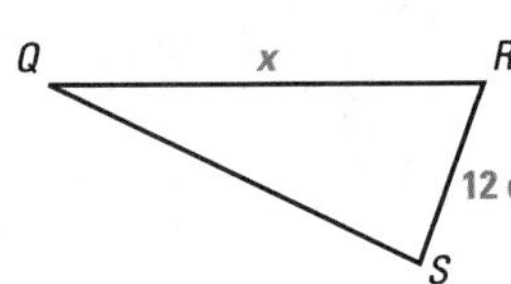

▶ QR is 27 centimeters.

INDIRECT MEASUREMENT You can use similar figures to find lengths that are difficult to measure directly.

EXAMPLE 2 Use similar figures to measure indirectly

CAPE HATTERAS LIGHTHOUSE A man stands next to the Cape Hatteras Lighthouse in North Carolina. The lighthouse and the man are perpendicular to the ground. The sun's rays strike the lighthouse and the man at the same angle, forming two similar triangles. Use indirect measurement to approximate the height of the lighthouse.

Not drawn to scale

Solution

Write and solve a proportion to find the height h (in feet) of the lighthouse.

ANOTHER WAY
You can also use the proportion below to find the height of the lighthouse.
$\frac{5.8}{2.5} = \frac{h}{83.2}$

height → $\frac{5.8}{h} = \frac{2.5}{83.2}$ ← **length of shadow**
height → ← **length of shadow**

$2.5h = 5.8 \cdot 83.2$ **Cross products property**

$2.5h = 482.56$ **Multiply.**

$h = 193.024$ **Divide each side by 2.5.**

▶ The height of the lighthouse is about 193 feet.

PRACTICE

EXAMPLE 1 on p. 174 for Exs. 1–4

1. Given $\triangle JKL \sim \triangle MNP$, find JL. 24 in.

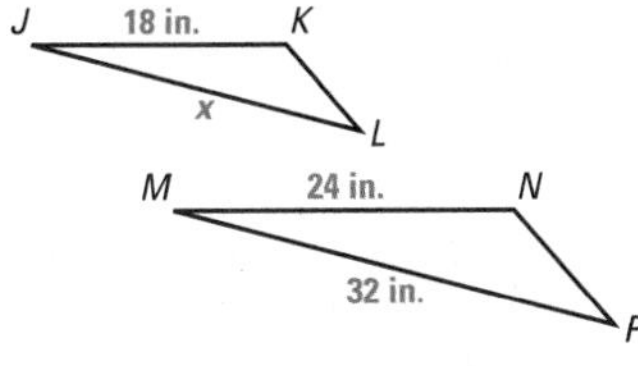

2. Given $\triangle EFG \sim \triangle UVW$, find UV. 10 cm

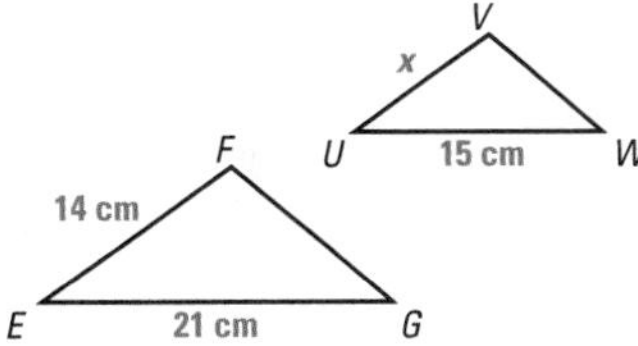

3. Given $ABCD \sim FGHJ$, find AD. 16 m

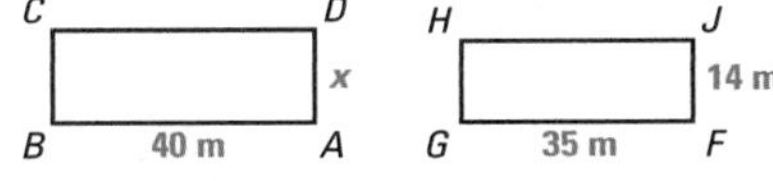

4. Given $JKLM \sim QRST$, find QT. 40 ft

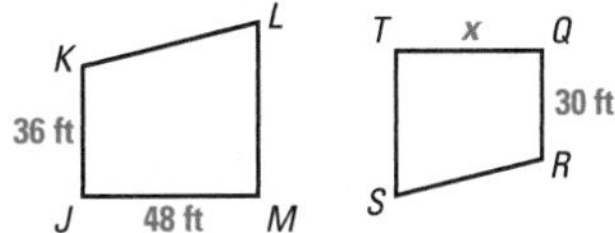

EXAMPLE 2 on p. 175 for Ex. 5

5. **FLAGPOLES** A 5 foot tall student stands near a flagpole. The flagpole and the student are perpendicular to the ground. The sun's rays strike the flagpole and the student at the same angle, forming two similar triangles. The flagpole casts a 15 foot shadow, and the student casts a 2 foot shadow. Use indirect measurement to find the height of the flagpole. 37.5 ft

Key Questions to Ask for Example 1

- How do you know that $\overline{JK}$ corresponds to $\overline{QR}$? The vertices appear in corresponding locations in the statement $\triangle JKL \sim \triangle QRS$.
- Can you find JL? Explain. No, you do not know the corresponding length QS in $\triangle QRS$.

Extra Example 2

A woman 5.5 feet tall stands next to a lamp post. The woman and the lamp post are perpendicular to the ground. The Sun's rays strike the lamp post and the woman at the same angle, forming two similar triangles. The woman casts a 2.2-foot shadow, and the lamppost casts a 6.4-foot shadow. Use indirect measurement to find the height of the lamp post. 16 ft

Closing the Lesson

Have students summarize the major points of the lesson and answer the Essential Question: How do you use similar figures to solve problems?

- In similar triangles, the ratios of the lengths of corresponding sides are equal.
- You can use similar figures to find unknown lengths.

If two figures are similar, you can use the ratios of corresponding side lengths to determine missing side lengths or to measure objects that are difficult to measure.

4 PRACTICE AND APPLY

Avoiding Common Errors

Exercises 1–4 Some students may try to determine corresponding sides in similar figures visually. Explain that this is difficult to do and often leads to inaccurate results. Remind them that the statement of similarity indicates how the vertices correspond. When they are setting up proportions, they should use the similarity statement to determine the corresponding sides.

1 PLAN AND PREPARE

Warm-Up Exercises

Transparency Available

Write the percent as a decimal.

1. 27% 0.27
2. 54.5% 0.545

Solve the proportion.

3. $\frac{6}{25} = \frac{12}{n}$ 50
4. $\frac{y}{18} = \frac{5}{8}$ 11.25
5. A tennis ball machine throws 2 balls every 3 seconds. How many balls will the machine throw in 18 seconds? 12 balls

Notetaking Guide

Transparency Available

Promotes interactive learning and notetaking skills, pp. 66–69.

Pacing

Basic: 2 days

Average: 2 days

Advanced: 2 days

Block: 0.5 block with 3.6
0.5 block with 3.8

- See *Teaching Guide/Lesson Plan.*

2 FOCUS AND MOTIVATE

Essential Question

Big Idea 2, p. 131

How do you solve percent problems? Tell students they will learn how to answer this question by using proportions and the percent equation to find a percent or a part of a base.

3.7 Solve Percent Problems

 **6.11.18** Set up, evaluate, or solve common problems involving percent . . .

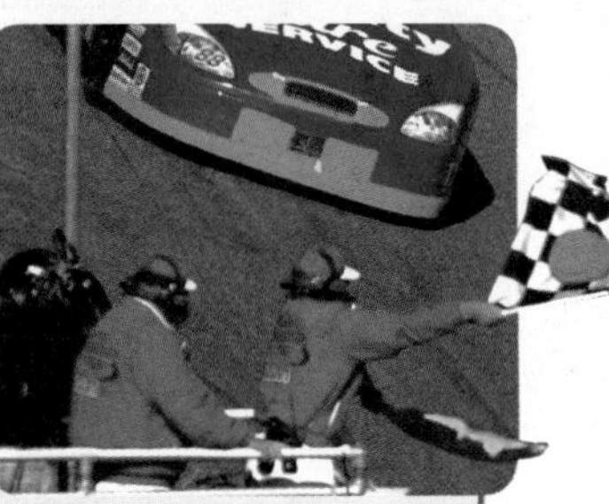

Before You solved proportions.

Now You will solve percent problems.

Why? So you can solve a problem about racing, as in Ex. 34.

Key Vocabulary
- **percent,** *p. 916*
- **proportion,** *p. 163*

Recall that *percent* means "divided by 100." For example $27\% = \frac{27}{100}$. By writing a percent as a fraction, you can use a proportion to solve a percent problem.

KEY CONCEPT *For Your Notebook*

Solving Percent Problems Using Proportions

You can represent "a is p percent of b" using the proportion

$$\frac{a}{b} = \frac{p}{100}$$

where a is a part of the base b and $\frac{p}{100}$, or $p\%$, is the percent.

EXAMPLE 1 Find a percent using a proportion

What percent of 25 is 17?

Solution

Write a proportion where 25 is the base and 17 is a part of the base.

$\frac{a}{b} = \frac{p}{100}$ **Write proportion.**

$\frac{17}{25} = \frac{p}{100}$ **Substitute 17 for *a* and 25 for *b*.**

$1700 = 25p$ **Cross products property**

$68 = p$ **Divide each side by 25.**

▶ 17 is 68% of 25.

AVOID ERRORS
You can also solve for p by multiplying each side of the equation by 100.

 Animated Algebra at classzone.com

✓ **GUIDED PRACTICE** for Example 1

Use a proportion to answer the question.

1. What percent of 20 is 15? 75%
2. What number is 30% of 90? 27

Resource Planning Guide

Chapter Resource Book
- Teaching Guide/Lesson Plan (pp. 70–71)
- Practice levels A, B, C (pp. 72–74)
- Study Guide (pp. 75–76)
- Catch-up for Absent Students (p. 77)
- Application (p. 78)
- Challenge (p. 79)

Workbooks
- Notetaking Guide (pp. 66–69)
- Practice Workbook (pp. 42–43)

Teaching Options
- **Power Presentations CD-ROM** provides dynamic electronic teaching resources for the classroom.
- **Activity Generator CD-ROM** provides editable activities for all ability levels.

Interactive Technology
- Easy Planner
- Power Presentations CD-ROM
- Activity Generator CD-ROM
- Animated Algebra
- Test Generator CD-ROM
- Online Quiz
- eWorkbook
- eEdition
- @HomeTutor

Resources for English Learners
- Quick Reference for English Learners
- Spanish Study Guide
- Multi-Language Visual Glossary
- Student Resources in Spanish

See also the *Algebra 1 Toolkit* for more strategies for meeting individual needs.

THE PERCENT EQUATION In Example 1, the proportion $\frac{a}{b} = \frac{p}{100}$ is used to find a percent. When you write $\frac{p}{100}$ as $p\%$ and solve for a, you get the equation $a = p\% \cdot b$.

KEY CONCEPT *For Your Notebook*

The Percent Equation

You can represent "a is p percent of b" using the equation

$$a = p\% \cdot b$$

where a is a part of the base b and $p\%$ is the percent.

EXAMPLE 2 Find a percent using the percent equation

What percent of 136 is 51?

DETERMINE THE BASE
When a problem talks about the percent *of* a number, the number is the base *b*, which is multiplied by the percent.

$a = p\% \cdot b$	**Write percent equation.**
$51 = p\% \cdot 136$	**Substitute 51 for *a* and 136 for *b*.**
$0.375 = p\%$	**Divide each side by 136.**
$37.5\% = p\%$	**Write decimal as percent.**

▶ 51 is 37.5% of 136.

CHECK Substitute 0.375 for $p\%$ in the original equation.

$51 = p\% \cdot 136$	**Write original equation.**
$51 \stackrel{?}{=} 0.375 \cdot 136$	**Substitute 0.375 for *p*%.**
$51 = 51$ ✓	**Multiply. Solution checks.**

EXAMPLE 3 Find a part of a base using the percent equation

What number is 15% of 88?

$a = p\% \cdot b$	**Write percent equation.**
$= 15\% \cdot 88$	**Substitute 15 for *p* and 88 for *b*.**
$= 0.15 \cdot 88$	**Write percent as decimal.**
$= 13.2$	**Multiply.**

▶ 13.2 is 15% of 88.

GUIDED PRACTICE for Examples 2 and 3

Use the percent equation to answer the question.

3. What percent of 56 is 49? 87.5%
4. What percent of 55 is 11? 20%
5. What number is 45% of 92? 41.4
6. What number is 140% of 50? 70

Motivating the Lesson

Ask students to give examples of surveys they have participated in or surveys they have taken. After discussing real-world surveys, point out that a common theme of all of these surveys is determining some kind of percent. For example, what percent of respondents prefer to travel by bicycle? Ask students to give other examples of survey percents. Close the discussion by telling students that this lesson will prepare them for solving problems that involve percents.

3 TEACH

Extra Example 1

What percent of 60 is 9? 15%

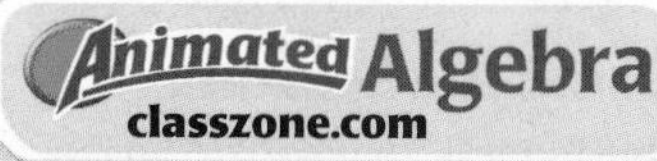

An **Animated Algebra** activity is available on-line for **Example 1**. This activity is also available on the **Power Presentations CD-ROM**.

Extra Example 2

What percent of 20 is 13? 65%

Key Questions to Ask for Example 2

- What is another way to write $p\%$? $\frac{p}{100}$, as in Example 1
- How would you write Example 2 as a proportion? $\frac{51}{136} = \frac{p}{100}$
- How do you know that 136 is the base, rather than 51? 136 follows the words "percent of".

Extra Example 3

What number is 12% of 85? 10.2

Extra Example 4

75 is 62.5% of what number? 120

Differentiated Instruction

Visual Learners Remind students that "percent" means hundredths by writing familiar words like "centimeter" $\left(\frac{1}{100}\text{ of a meter}\right)$ and "centipede" (hundred legs). Circle the word stem "centi-" to emphasize hundred (the "cent" in percent). Also note the resemblance of the percent sign (%) to one of the symbols for division (÷) to remind students that percent means to divide, not multiply, by 100.

See also the *Algebra 1 Toolkit* for more strategies.

Key Question to Ask for Example 4

- How can you represent this problem as a proportion? $\frac{20}{b} = \frac{12.5}{100}$

Extra Example 5

A survey asked 180 students how much they would tip for a $28 meal. Find the percent of students who would tip the given amount.

Amount of tip	Students
$2.00	16
$2.80	28
$3.00	45
$4.20	36
$5.00	47
$5.60	8

a. $4.20 20%

b. $5.60 about 4%

Closing the Lesson

Have students summarize the major points of the lesson and answer the Essential Question: How do you solve percent problems?

- Use "*a* is *p* percent of *b*" to represent percent problems, where *a* is part of a base, *b* is the base, and $\frac{p}{100}$ or $p\%$ is the percent.
- For proportions, use $\frac{a}{b} = \frac{p}{100}$.
- For equations, use $a = p\% \cdot b$.

Solve percent problems using the percent equation or a proportion. Of the three quantities—the percent, the base, and the part of the base—two will be known and one is unknown. The value that follows "percent of," in words or symbols, is the base.

EXAMPLE 4 Find a base using the percent equation

CHECK REASONABLENESS

Use 10%, or $\frac{1}{10}$, to check your answer:

$160 \cdot \frac{1}{10} = 16$

Because 16 is slightly less than 20, the solution is reasonable.

20 is 12.5% of what number?

$a = p\% \cdot b$ **Write percent equation.**

$20 = 12.5\% \cdot b$ **Substitute 20 for *a* and 12.5 for *p*.**

$20 = 0.125 \cdot b$ **Write percent as decimal.**

$160 = b$ **Divide each side by 0.125.**

▶ 20 is 12.5% of 160.

EXAMPLE 5 Solve a real-world percent problem

SURVEY A survey asked 220 students to name their favorite pasta dish. Find the percent of students who chose the given pasta dish.

a. macaroni and cheese

b. lasagna

Type of Pasta	Students
Spaghetti	83
Lasagna	40
Macaroni and cheese	33
Fettucine alfredo	22
Baked ziti	16
Pasta primavera	15
Other	11

Solution

a. The survey results show that 33 of the 220 students chose macaroni and cheese.

$a = p\% \cdot b$ **Write percent equation.**

$33 = p\% \cdot 220$ **Substitute 33 for *a* and 220 for *b*.**

$0.15 = p\%$ **Divide each side by 220.**

$15\% = p\%$ **Write decimal as percent.**

▶ 15% of the students chose macaroni and cheese as their favorite dish.

b. The survey results show that 40 of the 220 students chose lasagna.

$a = p\% \cdot b$ **Write percent equation.**

$40 = p\% \cdot 220$ **Substitute 40 for *a* and 220 for *b*.**

$0.18 \approx p\%$ **Divide each side by 220.**

$18\% \approx p\%$ **Write decimal as percent.**

▶ About 18% of the students chose lasagna as their favorite dish.

✓ GUIDED PRACTICE for Examples 4 and 5

In Exercises 7 and 8, use the percent equation to answer the question.

7. 65 is 62.5% of what number? 104

8. 50 is 125% of what number? 40

9. In Example 5, what percent of students chose fettucine alfredo? 10%

CONCEPT SUMMARY — *For Your Notebook*

Types of Percent Problems

Percent problem	Example	Equation
Find a percent.	What percent of 136 is 51?	$51 = p\% \cdot 136$
Find part of a base.	What number is 15% of 88?	$a = 15\% \cdot 88$
Find a base.	20 is 12.5% of what number?	$20 = 12.5\% \cdot b$

3.7 EXERCISES

HOMEWORK KEY
○ = **WORKED-OUT SOLUTIONS** on p. WS7 for Exs. 13 and 35
★ = **STANDARDIZED TEST PRACTICE** Exs. 2, 19, 30, 31, 38, and 39

SKILL PRACTICE

A

1. **VOCABULARY** Identify the percent, the base, and the part of the base in the following statement: 54 is 15% of 360. percent: 15, base: 360, part: 54

2. ★ **WRITING** Rewrite the statement "28 is 35% of 80" in the form $\frac{a}{b} = \frac{p}{100}$. *Explain* how you identified the values of a, b, and p. $\frac{28}{80} = \frac{35}{100}$; the statement identifies 28 as part of 80 so 28 is the part, a, and 80 is the base, b; 35 is p because it is a percent.

EXAMPLE 1 on p. 176 for Exs. 3–8

USING PROPORTIONS Use a proportion to answer the question.

3. What percent of 75 is 27? 36%
4. What percent of 120 is 66? 55%
5. What number is 35% of 80? 28
6. What number is 60% of 85? 51
7. 81 is 54% of what number? 150
8. 42 is 200% of what number? 21

EXAMPLES 2, 3, and 4 on pp. 177–178 for Exs. 9–21

USING THE PERCENT EQUATION Use the percent equation to answer the question.

9. What percent of 80 is 56? 70%
10. What percent of 225 is 99? 44%
11. What percent of 153 is 9.18? 6%
12. What number is 18% of 150? 27
13. What number is 115% of 60? 69
14. What number is 82% of 215? 176.3
15. 7 is 28% of what number? 25
16. 189 is 90% of what number? 210
17. 41.8 is 44% of what number? 95
18. 71.5 is 52% of what number? 137.5

19. ★ **MULTIPLE CHOICE** What number is 87.5% of 512? B

Ⓐ 5.85 Ⓑ 448 Ⓒ 585 Ⓓ 4480

ERROR ANALYSIS *Describe* and correct the error in answering the question.

20. What percent of 95 is 19? $p\%$ should be multiplied by 95; $19 = p\% \cdot 95$, $p\% = 20\%$.

$95 = p\% \cdot 19$
$5 = p\%$
$500\% = p\%$

21. 153 is 76.5% of what number? 76.5% needs to be changed to 0.765; $153 = 0.765 \cdot b$, $b = 200$.

$153 = 76.5\% \cdot b$
$153 = 76.5 \cdot b$
$2 = b$

4 PRACTICE AND APPLY

Assignment Guide

Answer Transparencies available for all exercises

Basic:
Day 1: SRH p. 917 Exs. 11–17 odd
pp. 179–181
Exs. 1–14, 22, 23, 47–52
Day 2: pp. 179–181
Exs. 15–21, 24, 25, 33–37, 41–46

Average:
Day 1: pp. 179–181
Exs. 1, 2, 3–13 odd, 22, 23, 26–29, 47–52
Day 2: pp. 179–181
Exs. 16, 19–21, 24, 25, 30, 31, 35–39, 41–46

Advanced:
Day 1: pp. 179–181
Exs. 1, 6–8, 12–14, 22, 23, 26–29
Day 2: pp. 179–181
Exs. 17–19, 24, 25, 30–32*, 35–40*, 42, 46

Block:
pp. 179–181
Exs. 1, 2, 3–13 odd, 22, 23, 26–29, 47–52 (with 3.6)
pp. 179–181
Exs. 16, 19–21, 24, 25, 30, 31, 35–39, 41–46 (with 3.8)

Differentiated Instruction

See *Algebra 1 Best Practices Toolkit* for suggestions on addressing the needs of a diverse classroom.

Homework Check

For a quick check of student understanding of key concepts, go over the following exercises:
Basic: 5, 10, 13, 16, 33
Average: 7, 11, 13, 16, 36
Advanced: 8, 12, 14, 18, 35

Extra Practice

- Student Edition, p. 940
- Chapter 3 Resource Book: Practice levels A, B, C, pp. 72–74

Practice Worksheet

An easily-readable reduced practice page (with answers) for this lesson can be found on p. 130D.

Avoiding Common Errors

Exercises 3–18 To avoid confusing the base and part of a base, suggest that students reread the note "determine the base" for Example 2 on page 177 on how to determine a base. Students can write this information on a 3 × 5 card to use until they become proficient in distinguishing between a base and a part of a base.

Exercise 35 Caution students that errors can occur when many categories and percents are used in a problem. Urge them to double check that they used the correct category and the correct percent when solving parts (a) and (b).

Exercise 36 You may want to suggest that students identify the base and the part of a base for years 2001 and 2002.

Teaching Strategy

Exercises 8, 13 Both of these exercises require using percents greater than 1. You may want to review how to write such percents before students begin these exercises. Point out that in Exercise 8, the base will be less than 42 since 42 is 200% of a number, and that in Exercise 13, a part of the base will be greater than 60 since it is 115% of 60. In Exercise 8, some students may recognize that 200% of a number is twice the number, and use the fact that 42 is twice 21.

Study Strategy

Exercise 19 Point out that students can eliminate two choices because the exercise asks for a part of the base, which in this exercise must be less than the base 512.

Reading Strategy

Exercises 22–25 For students who ask for help on these problems, point out that the direction line gives them the value for n, and they need to substitute for n before solving the percent problem.

B **SOLVING PERCENT PROBLEMS** **Answer the question when $n = 25$.**

22. What percent of 140 is $(n + 94)$? 85%
23. What percent of $(4n)$ is 96? 96%
24. What number is 52% of $(2n + 15)$? 33.8
25. 25.5 is $(n - 8)$% of what number? 150

SOLVING PERCENT PROBLEMS **Find the percent. Round your answer to the nearest whole percent, if necessary.**

26. \$3.00 tip for a \$18.70 taxi fare 16%
27. \$1.44 tax on an item priced at \$24.00 6%
28. 90 rock CDs out of 125 CDs 72%
29. 241 freshmen out of 804 students 30%

30. ★ **WRITING** Would you use a proportion or the percent equation to solve the following problem: What number is 25% of 600? *Explain.* *Sample answer:* Percent equation; you just need to multiply the percent by the base to find the part.

31. ★ **SHORT RESPONSE** The side length of a square is 40% of the side length of another square. Is the area of the smaller square 40% of the area of the larger square? *Explain.* No. *Sample answer:* The area of the smaller square would be 16% of the area of the larger square because the percent needs to be squared.

C 32. **CHALLENGE** Let y be 10% of a number. What is 50% of the number? Write your answer in terms of y. $5y$

Problem Solving

EXAMPLE 5 A on p. 178 for Exs. 33–36

33. **SCHOOL TRANSPORTATION** In a school transportation survey of 225 students, 18 of the students surveyed said that they walk to school. What percent of the students surveyed walk to school? 8%

@HomeTutor for problem solving help at classzone.com

34. **DAYTONA 500** After completing 10 laps in the Daytona 500, a driver has completed 5% of the race. How many laps does the race have? 200 laps

@HomeTutor for problem solving help at classzone.com

REVIEW CIRCLE GRAPHS
For help with using a circle graph, see p. 935.

35. **MUSIC** The circle graph shows the results of a radio survey in which 250 listeners were asked to rate a song.
    a. How many of the listeners who participated in the survey are "tired of" the song? 90 listeners
    b. How many of the listeners who participated in the survey "love" the song? 35 listeners

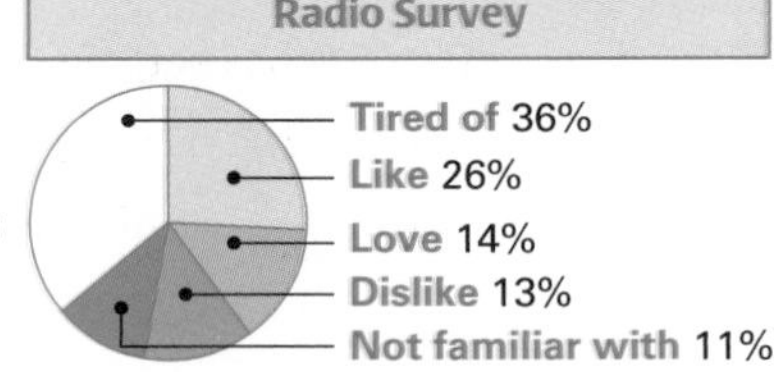

36. **HIKING** The table gives data about the number of people who started hiking the Appalachian Trail in Georgia and the number of those people who completed the trail in Maine. Copy and complete the table.

Year	Hikers who started	Hikers who completed	Percent completion
2001	2380	? 395	16.6%
2002	? 1880	376	20%
2003	1750	352	? 20%

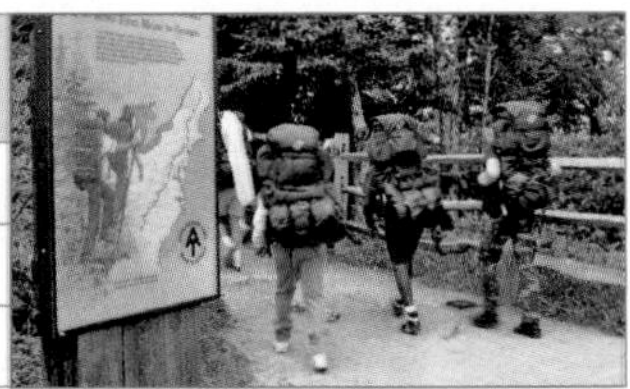

○ = WORKED-OUT SOLUTIONS on p. WS1 ★ = STANDARDIZED TEST PRACTICE

B **37. ART** The Louvre Museum, which is an art museum in France, has virtual tours of its exhibits on its website. The website can be viewed in four different languages. The table shows the number of hits received by each version of the website during one day. Find the percent of hits for each version of the website. **59.3%; 16.5%; 13.2%; 11%**

Version	English	French	Spanish	Japanese
Number of hits	4860	1350	1080	900

38. ★ OPEN-ENDED Write a real-world percent problem that can be solved using the proportion $\frac{x}{75} = \frac{15}{100}$. Then find the value of x and explain what the solution means in this situation. ***Sample answer:*** **You want to leave a 15% tip at a restaurant. If the bill came to $75, what tip should you leave? $x = 11.25$; you should leave $11.25 for a tip.**

39. ★ EXTENDED RESPONSE Two different stores are selling a bicycle that you want to buy.

a. **Solve** At one store, the bicycle is on sale for 20% off the original price of $240. How much money will you save by purchasing the bicycle on sale at this store? **$48**

b. **Solve** At the other store, the bicycle is on sale for 25% off the original price of $265. How much money will you save by purchasing the bicycle on sale at this store? **$66.25**

c. **Compare** Which bicycle should you buy? *Explain.* **The bicycle in part (a); it will cost $192, the bicycle in part (b) will cost $198.75.**

C **40. CHALLENGE** Julia deposits 20% of her paycheck in her savings account. Then she deposits 60% of the remaining money in her checking account. She deposits $108.24 in her checking account. How much money did she deposit in her savings account? **$45.10**

ILLINOIS MIXED REVIEW

TEST PRACTICE at classzone.com

41. A clothing designer uses $5 worth of fabric for each shirt she makes, and she sells each shirt for $15. She also spends $50 on supplies needed to make the shirts. Which of the following equations can be solved to determine how many shirts she needs to make to earn a profit of $100?

Ⓐ $100 = 5x + 15x - 50$

Ⓑ $100 = 5x + 15x + 50$

Ⓒ $100 = 15x - 5x - 50$ **C**

Ⓓ $100 = 5x - 15x - 50$

42. The polygon shown was made by connecting eight 1 centimeter sticks with four 4 centimeter sticks. All of the sticks meet at right angles. Find the area of the polygon.

Ⓐ 16 cm^2

Ⓑ 24 cm^2

Ⓒ 32 cm^2

Ⓓ 36 cm^2

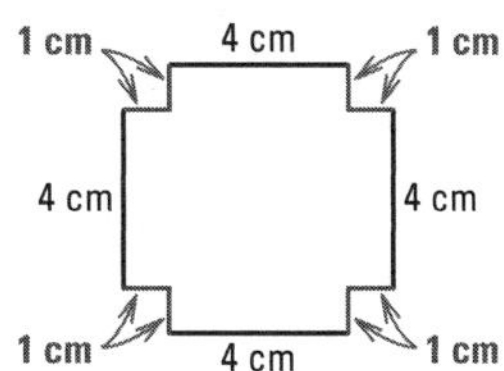

C

5 ASSESS AND RETEACH

Daily Homework Quiz

Transparency Available

Solve the percent problem.

1. What percent of 50 is 1? **2%**
2. What percent of 128 is 48? **37.5%**
3. What number is 16% of 45? **7.2**
4. 12 is 12.5% of what number? **96**
5. Leonard has read 1001 pages out of 1456 of Tolstoy's *War and Peace*. What percent of the novel has he read? **68.75%**

Online Quiz

Available at **classzone.com**

Diagnosis/Remediation

- Practice A, B, C in Chapter 3 Resource Book, pp. 72–74
- Study Guide in Chapter 3 Resource Book, pp. 75–76
- Practice Workbook, pp. 42–43
- @HomeTutor

Challenge

Additional challenge is available in the Chapter 3 Resource Book, p. 79.

1 PLAN AND PREPARE

Warm-Up Exercises

1. What percent of 75 is 18? 24%
2. What number is 45% of 180? 81
3. 28 is 16% percent of what number? 175
4. A particular Goliath Frog has a body that is 12 inches long. With its legs extended, it is 30 inches long. What percent of the frog's total length is its body? 40%

2 FOCUS AND MOTIVATE

Essential Question

Big Idea 2, p. 131

How do you solve percent of change problems? Tell students they will learn how to answer this question by finding the percent by which an amount increases or decreases from an original amount, and by finding a new amount when given an original amount and a percent of change.

3 TEACH

Extra Example 1

Identify the percent of change as an *increase* or *decrease*. Then find the percent of change.

a. Original: 90
New: 126 increase; 40%

b. Original: 160
New: 72 decrease; 55%

NCTM STANDARDS

Standard 1: Understand numbers; Compute fluently

Extension *Use after Lesson 3.7*

Find Percent of Change

GOAL Solve percent of change problems.

Key Vocabulary
- **percent of change**
- **percent of increase**
- **percent of decrease**

A **percent of change** indicates how much a quantity increases or decreases with respect to the original amount. If the new amount is greater than the original amount, the percent of change is called a **percent of increase**. If the new amount is less than the original amount, the percent of change is called a **percent of decrease**.

KEY CONCEPT *For Your Notebook*

Percent of Change

The percent of change is the ratio of the amount of increase or decrease to the original amount.

$$\text{Percent of change, } p\% = \frac{\text{Amount of increase or decrease}}{\text{Original amount}}$$

The amount of increase is the new amount minus the original amount. The amount of decrease is the original amount minus the new amount.

EXAMPLE 1 Find a percent of change

Identify the percent of change as an *increase* or *decrease*. Then find the percent of change.

a. Original: 140
New: 189

b. Original: 70
New: 59.5

Solution

a. Because the new amount is greater than the original amount, the percent of change is an increase.

$$p\% = \frac{\text{Amount of increase}}{\text{Original amount}}$$
$$= \frac{189 - 140}{140}$$
$$= \frac{49}{140}$$
$$= 0.35$$
$$= 35\%$$

▶ The percent of increase is 35%.

b. Because the new amount is less than the original amount, the percent of change is a decrease.

$$p\% = \frac{\text{Amount of decrease}}{\text{Original amount}}$$
$$= \frac{70 - 59.5}{70}$$
$$= \frac{10.5}{70}$$
$$= 0.15$$
$$= 15\%$$

▶ The percent of decrease is 15%.

CHECK REASONABLENESS
Because 50 is one third (about 33%) of 150, it is reasonable that 49 is 35% of 140.

FINDING A NEW AMOUNT If you know the original amount and the percent of change, you can find the new amount.

- For a $p\%$ increase, multiply the original amount by $(100\% + p\%)$.
- For a $p\%$ decrease, multiply the original amount by $(100\% - p\%)$.

EXAMPLE 2 Find a new amount

SHOPPING Find the sale price of the pair of jeans described in the table.

Original price	$48.00
Discount	40%
Sale price	?

Solution

ANOTHER WAY
You can also find the sale price by first finding the change in price:
$0.4 \cdot 48 = 19.2$.
Then subtract the change in price from the original price:
$\$48.00 - \$19.20 = \$28.80$.

The sale price is a decrease from the original price, so multiply the original price by $(100\% - p\%)$.

Sale price = Original price $\cdot (100\% - p\%)$

$= 48 \cdot (100\% - 40\%)$ **Substitute.**

$= 48 \cdot 0.6$ **Subtract percents. Then write as a decimal.**

$= 28.8$ **Multiply.**

▶ The sale price of the pair of jeans is $28.80.

PRACTICE

EXAMPLE 1 on p. 182 for Exs. 1–6

Identify the percent of change as an *increase* or *decrease*. Then find the percent of change.

1. Original: 16 increase; 25%
   New: 20
2. Original: 35 increase; 40%
   New: 49
3. Original: 80 decrease; 45%
   New: 44
4. Original: 120 decrease; 35%
   New: 78
5. Original: 360 decrease; 33%
   New: 241.2
6. Original: 170 increase; 67%
   New: 283.9

EXAMPLE 2 on p. 183 for Exs. 7–14

Find the new amount.

7. Increase 14 by 45%. 20.3
8. Increase 78 by 80%. 140.4
9. Decrease 44 by 20%. 35.2
10. Decrease 108 by 90%. 10.8
11. **SUBWAY** The price for a token to ride a city's subway system is changing from $1.25 to $1.50. Find the percent of change. 20% increase
12. **DVDS** The average price of a new DVD in 1998 was $24. In 2003, the average price was $21.12. Find the percent of change. 12% decrease
13. **POPULATION** In Arizona, the population increased by 48.6% from 1990 to 2002. Use the information in the table to find the population density in Arizona in 2002. 48.0 people per square mile
14. **DEPRECIATION** A new car is valued at $14,500. In one year, the car's value will depreciate, or decrease, by 15%. Find the value of the car after one year. $12,325

Year	Population density
1990	32.3 people per square mile
2002	?

Key Question to Ask for Example 1

- How can you check that the answers are correct? Multiply the original amount by the percent. Then add or subtract that amount to or from the original to obtain the new amount.

Extra Example 2

An adventure company discounted an Australian tour by 30%. The original price for the tour was $3500. Find the sale price. $2450

Closing the Lesson

Have students summarize the major points of the lesson and answer the Essential Question: How do you solve percent of change problems?

- Solve percent of change problems by dividing the amount of increase or decrease by the original amount.
- To find a new amount, multiply the original amount by $100\% + p\%$ for an increase or by $100\% - p\%$ for a decrease.

To find percent of change, first find the amount of change by subtracting the lesser number from the greater number and then dividing that difference by the original amount. To find new amounts, add or subtract the percent of change to or from 100% and then multiply that percent by the original number.

4 PRACTICE AND APPLY

Avoiding Common Errors

Exercises 1–6 Watch for students who divide the original amount by the new amount for a decrease and the new amount by the original amount for an increase. Remind students that they have to divide the *amount* of increase or decrease by the original amount.

1 PLAN AND PREPARE

Warm-Up Exercises

Transparency Available

1. Write an equation for "3 more than twice a is 24." $2a + 3 = 24$
2. A square has a side length of 8 feet. Find the area of the square using the formula $A = s^2$. 64 ft^2
3. A rectangular serving tray is 26 inches long and 18 inches wide. What is the tray's serving area? 468 in.^2

Notetaking Guide

Transparency Available

Promotes interactive learning and notetaking skills, pp. 70–71.

Pacing

Basic: 1 day

Average: 1 day

Advanced: 1 day

Block: 0.5 block with 3.7

- See *Teaching Guide/Lesson Plan.*

2 FOCUS AND MOTIVATE

Essential Question

Big Idea 3, p. 131

How do you rewrite equations? Tell students they will learn how to answer this question by rewriting equations and formulas with two or more variables so that any given variable is a function of the other variables.

3.8 Rewrite Equations and Formulas

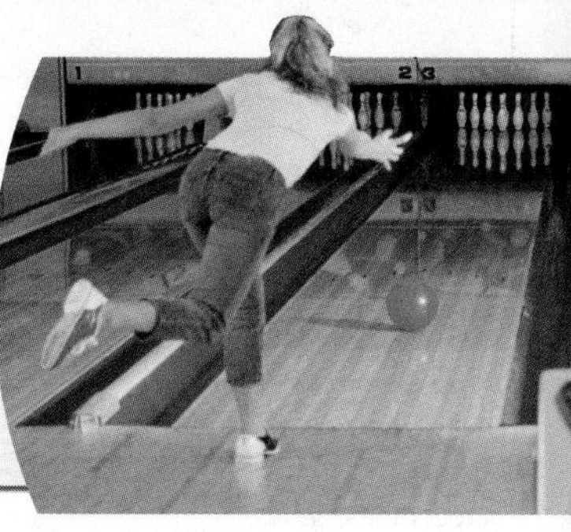

 **7.11.03** Determine and calculate . . . measures of common geometric figures or combinations of common geometric figures.

Before You wrote functions and used formulas.

Now You will rewrite equations and formulas.

Why? So you can solve a problem about bowling, as in Ex. 33.

Key Vocabulary
- **literal equation**
- **formula,** *p. 30*

The equations $2x + 5 = 11$ and $6x + 3 = 15$ have the general form $ax + b = c$. The equation $ax + b = c$ is called a **literal equation** because the coefficients and constants have been replaced by letters. When you solve a literal equation, you can use the result to solve any equation that has the same form as the literal equation.

EXAMPLE 1 Solve a literal equation

Solve $ax + b = c$ for x. Then use the solution to solve $2x + 5 = 11$.

Solution

STEP 1 **Solve** $ax + b = c$ for x.

$ax + b = c$ **Write original equation.**

$ax = c - b$ **Subtract b from each side.**

$x = \frac{c - b}{a}$ **Assume $a \neq 0$. Divide each side by a.**

STEP 2 **Use** the solution to solve $2x + 5 = 11$.

$x = \frac{c - b}{a}$ **Solution of literal equation**

$= \frac{11 - 5}{2}$ **Substitute 2 for a, 5 for b, and 11 for c.**

$= 3$ **Simplify.**

▶ The solution of $2x + 5 = 11$ is 3.

VARIABLES IN DENOMINATORS In Example 1, you must assume that $a \neq 0$ in order to divide by a. In general, if you have to divide by a variable when solving a literal equation, you should assume that the variable does not equal 0.

GUIDED PRACTICE for Example 1

Solve the literal equation for x. Then use the solution to solve the specific equation.

1. $a - bx = c$; $12 - 5x = -3$ $x = \frac{a - c}{b}$; 3
2. $ax = bx + c$; $11x = 6x + 20$ $x = \frac{c}{a - b}$; 4

Resource Planning Guide

Chapter Resource Book
- Teaching Guide/Lesson Plan (pp. 80–81)
- Practice levels A, B, C (pp. 82–84)
- Study Guide (pp. 85–86)
- Catch-up for Absent Students (p. 87)
- Problem Solving Workshop (p. 88)
- Challenge (p. 89)

Workbooks
- Notetaking Guide (pp. 70–71)
- Practice Workbook (pp. 44–45)

Teaching Options
- **Power Presentations CD-ROM** provides dynamic electronic teaching resources for the classroom.
- **Activity Generator CD-ROM** provides editable activities for all ability levels.

Interactive Technology
- Easy Planner
- Power Presentations CD-ROM
- Activity Generator CD-ROM
- Animated Algebra
- Test Generator CD-ROM
- Online Quiz
- eWorkbook
- eEdition
- @HomeTutor

Resources for English Learners
- Quick Reference for English Learners
- Spanish Study Guide
- Multi-Language Visual Glossary
- Student Resources in Spanish

See also the *Algebra 1 Toolkit* for more strategies for meeting individual needs.

TWO OR MORE VARIABLES An equation in two variables, such as $3x + 2y = 8$, or a formula in two or more variables, such as $A = \frac{1}{2}bh$, can be rewritten so that one variable is a function of the other variable(s).

EXAMPLE 2 Rewrite an equation

Write $3x + 2y = 8$ so that y is a function of x.

$3x + 2y = 8$	Write original equation.
$2y = 8 - 3x$	Subtract $3x$ from each side.
$y = 4 - \frac{3}{2}x$	Divide each side by 2.

EXAMPLE 3 Solve and use a geometric formula

The area A of a triangle is given by the formula $A = \frac{1}{2}bh$ where b is the base and h is the height.

a. Solve the formula for the height h.

b. Use the rewritten formula to find the height of the triangle shown, which has an area of 64.4 square meters.

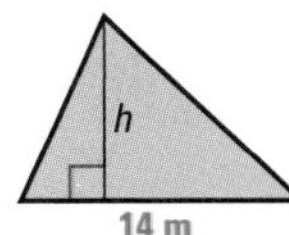

Solution

a.

$A = \frac{1}{2}bh$	Write original formula.
$2A = bh$	Multiply each side by 2.
$\frac{2A}{b} = h$	Divide each side by b.

b. Substitute 64.4 for A and 14 for b in the rewritten formula.

$h = \frac{2A}{b}$	Write rewritten formula.
$= \frac{2(64.4)}{14}$	Substitute 64.4 for A and 14 for b.
$= 9.2$	Simplify.

▶ The height of the triangle is 9.2 meters.

 at classzone.com

USE UNIT ANALYSIS
When area is measured in square meters and the base is measured in meters, dividing twice the area by the base gives a result measured in meters.

✓ GUIDED PRACTICE for Examples 2 and 3

3. Write $5x + 4y = 20$ so that y is a function of x. $y = 5 - \frac{5}{4}x$

4. The perimeter P of a rectangle is given by the formula $P = 2\ell + 2w$ where ℓ is the length and w is the width.

   a. Solve the formula for the width w.

   b. Use the rewritten formula to find the width of the rectangle shown. 2.4 ft

4a. $w = \frac{P - 2\ell}{2}$ or $w = \frac{P}{2} - \ell$

Motivating the Lesson

Tell students that in this lesson they will learn how to rewrite formulas to isolate different variables. Explain that often it is easier to solve a problem if they isolate a variable before they substitute numbers for the other variables. As an example, suppose they want to find how long it will take to drive to the beach. Instead of substituting values for the formula $d = rt$ and then isolating the variable t, they can isolate t as $t = \frac{d}{r}$ and then substitute values for d and r.

3 TEACH

Extra Example 1

Solve $p + qx = r$ for x. Then use the solution to solve $3 + 5x = -7$. $x = \frac{r - p}{q}$; -2

Key Question to Ask for Example 1

- How would you solve $2x + 5 = 11$ directly? Subtract 5 from both sides and then divide by 2.

Extra Example 2

Write $-2x + 3y = 6$ so that y is a function of x. $y = \frac{2}{3}x + 2$

Extra Example 3

The area for a rectangle is given by the formula $A = \ell w$, where ℓ is the length and w is the width.

a. Solve the formula for the length ℓ. $\ell = \frac{A}{w}$

b. Use the rewritten formula to find the length of this rectangle.

$A = 351\ \text{cm}^2$	13 cm

27 cm

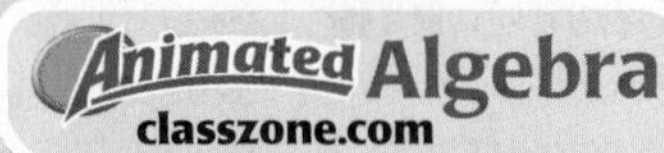

An **Animated Algebra** activity is available on-line for **Example 3**. This activity is also available on the **Power Presentations CD-ROM**.

Extra Example 4

Irina deposited $650 in a savings account. After two years her account balance was $682.50. Find the rate of interest for the two years. Use the formula $A = P(1 + rt)$, where A is the account balance, P is principal, r is rate, and t is time. Rewrite the formula to isolate r and then solve. $r = \frac{A - P}{Pt}$; $r = 0.025$ or 2.5%

Key Question to Ask for Example 4

- Do you have to rewrite the formula to find the low temperatures in degrees Fahrenheit? Explain. **No, you can use the given formula but the calculations are easier if you solve the given formula for F before you substitute 14°C or 10°C.**

Closing the Lesson

Have students summarize the major points of the lesson and answer the Essential Question: How do you rewrite equations?

- **In a literal equation, coefficients and constants have been replaced by letters. You can solve a literal equation for any variable.**
- **Use inverse operations when solving a formula or equation for a given variable.**

To rewrite an equation so that y is a function of x, rewrite the equation so that y is isolated on one side of the equation. For all literal equations, solve for the given variable by using properties of equality and inverse operations.

EXAMPLE 4 Solve a multi-step problem

TEMPERATURE You are visiting Toronto, Canada, over the weekend. A website gives the forecast shown. Find the low temperatures for Saturday and Sunday in degrees Fahrenheit. Use the formula $C = \frac{5}{9}(F - 32)$ where C is the temperature in degrees Celsius and F is the temperature in degrees Fahrenheit.

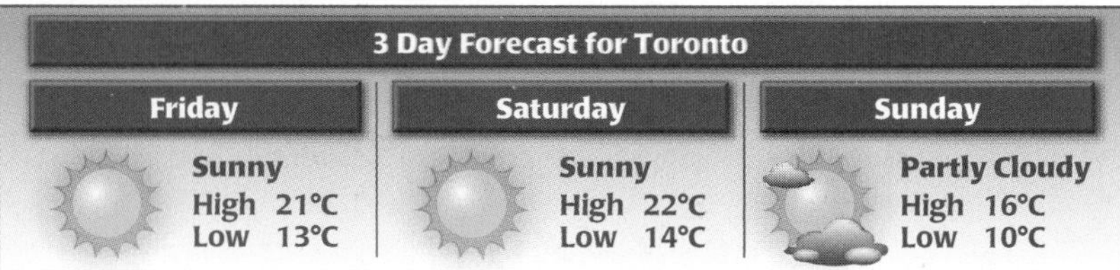

3 Day Forecast for Toronto
Friday
Sunny
High 21°C
Low 13°C
Saturday
Sunny
High 22°C
Low 14°C
Sunday
Partly Cloudy
High 16°C
Low 10°C

REWRITE FORMULAS
When using a formula for multiple calculations, you may find it easier to rewrite the formula first.

Solution

STEP 1 **Rewrite** the formula. In the problem, degrees Celsius are given and degrees Fahrenheit need to be calculated. The calculations will be easier if the formula is written so that F is a function of C.

$C = \frac{5}{9}(F - 32)$	**Write original formula.**
$\frac{9}{5} \cdot C = \frac{9}{5} \cdot \frac{5}{9}(F - 32)$	**Multiply each side by $\frac{9}{5}$, the reciprocal of $\frac{5}{9}$.**
$\frac{9}{5}C = F - 32$	**Simplify.**
$\frac{9}{5}C + 32 = F$	**Add 32 to each side.**

▶ The rewritten formula is $F = \frac{9}{5}C + 32$.

STEP 2 **Find** the low temperatures for Saturday and Sunday in degrees Fahrenheit.

Saturday (low of 14°C)	Sunday (low of 10°C)
$F = \frac{9}{5}C + 32$	$F = \frac{9}{5}C + 32$
$= \frac{9}{5}(14) + 32$	$= \frac{9}{5}(10) + 32$
$= 25.2 + 32$	$= 18 + 32$
$= 57.2$	$= 50$
▶ The low for Saturday is 57.2°F.	▶ The low for Sunday is 50°F.

✓ GUIDED PRACTICE for Example 4

5. Use the information in Example 4 to find the high temperatures for Saturday and Sunday in degrees Fahrenheit. **71.6°F, 60.8°F**

3.8 EXERCISES

HOMEWORK KEY

○ = **WORKED-OUT SOLUTIONS** on p. WS7 for Exs. 17 and 33

★ = **STANDARDIZED TEST PRACTICE** Exs. 2, 23, 29, 35, and 36

◆ = **MULTIPLE REPRESENTATIONS** Ex. 34

SKILL PRACTICE

1. **VOCABULARY** Copy and complete: When you write the equation $3x + 2 = 8$ as $ax + b = c$, the equation $ax + b = c$ is called a(n) __?__ because the coefficients and constants have been replaced by letters. literal equation

2. ★ **WRITING** *Describe* the steps you would take to solve $I = prt$ for t. Divide each side by pr to get $\frac{I}{pr} = t$.

EXAMPLE 1 on p. 184 for Exs. 3–10

LITERAL EQUATIONS **Solve the literal equation for x. Then use the solution to solve the specific equation.**

3. $ax = bx - c$; $8x = 3x - 10$ $x = \frac{c}{b-a}$; -2
4. $a(x + b) = c$; $2(x + 1) = 9$ $x = \frac{c}{a} - b$; 3.5
5. $c = \frac{x+a}{b}$; $2 = \frac{x+5}{7}$ $x = bc - a$; 9
6. $\frac{x}{a} = \frac{b}{c}$; $\frac{x}{8} = \frac{4.5}{12}$ $x = \frac{ab}{c}$; 3
7. $\frac{x}{a} + b = c$; $\frac{x}{4} + 6 = 13$ $x = a(c - b)$; 28
8. $ax + b = cx - d$; $2x + 9 = 7x - 1$ $x = \frac{b+d}{c-a}$; 2

ERROR ANALYSIS ***Describe*** **and correct the error in solving the equation for x.**

9. $ax + b = 0$
$ax = b$
$x = \frac{b}{a}$ ✗

9. b should have been subtracted from both sides, not added; $ax = -b$, $x = \frac{-b}{a}$.

10. $c = ax - bx$
$c = (a - b)x$
$c(a - b) = x$ ✗

10. Both sides should have been divided by $(a - b)$, not multiplied; $x = \frac{c}{a-b}$.

EXAMPLE 2 on p. 185 for Exs. 11–19

REWRITING EQUATIONS **Write the equation so that y is a function of x.**

11. $2x + y = 7$ $y = 7 - 2x$
12. $5x + 4y = 10$ $y = \frac{5}{2} - \frac{5}{4}x$
13. $12 = 9x + 3y$ $4 - 3x = y$
14. $18x - 2y = 26$ $y = -13 + 9x$
15. $14 = 7y - 6x$ $2 + \frac{6}{7}x = y$
16. $8x - 8y = 5$ $y = x - \frac{5}{8}$
17. $30 = 9x - 5y$ $\frac{9}{5}x - 6 = y$
18. $3 + 6x = 11 - 4y$ $2 - \frac{3}{2}x = y$
19. $2 + 6y = 3x + 4$ $y = \frac{1}{2}x + \frac{1}{3}$

EXAMPLE 3 on p. 185 for Exs. 20–23

REWRITING FORMULAS **Solve the formula for the indicated variable.**

20. Volume of a rectangular prism: $V = \ell wh$. Solve for w. $w = \frac{V}{\ell h}$
21. Surface area of a prism: $S = 2B + Ph$. Solve for h. $h = \frac{S - 2B}{P}$
22. Length of movie projected at 24 frames per second: $\ell = 24f$. Solve for f. $f = \frac{\ell}{24}$

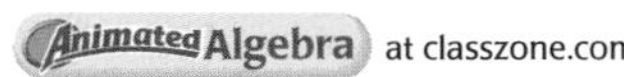
at classzone.com

23. ★ **MULTIPLE CHOICE** The formula for the area of a trapezoid is $A = \frac{1}{2}(b_1 + b_2)h$. Which equation is *not* equivalent to the formula? C

Ⓐ $h = \frac{2A}{b_1 + b_2}$ Ⓑ $b_1 = \frac{2A}{h} - b_2$ Ⓒ $b_2 = \frac{2A}{b_1} - h$ Ⓓ $b_2 = \frac{2A}{h} - b_1$

REWRITING EQUATIONS **Write the equation so that y is a function of x.**

24. $4.2x - 2y = 16.8$ $y = 2.1x - 8.4$
25. $9 - 0.5y = 2.5x$ $y = 18 - 5x$
26. $8x - 5x + 21 = 36 - 6y$ $y = -\frac{1}{2}x + \frac{5}{2}$

4 PRACTICE AND APPLY

Assignment Guide

Answer Transparencies available for all exercises

Basic:
Day 1: pp. 187–189
Exs. 1–10, 11–19 odd, 20–25, 32–35, 38–45

Average:
Day 1: pp. 187–189
Exs. 1, 2, 4, 6, 8–10, 12–18 even, 20–30, 32–36, 38–45

Advanced:
Day 1: pp. 187–189
Exs. 1, 7, 8, 16–31*, 34–37*, 38–44 even

Block:
pp. 187–189
Exs. 1, 2, 4, 6, 8–10, 12–18 even, 20–30, 32–36, 38–45 (with 3.7)

Differentiated Instruction

See *Algebra 1 Best Practices Toolkit* for suggestions on addressing the needs of a diverse classroom.

Homework Check

For a quick check of student understanding of key concepts, go over the following exercises:

Basic: 3, 6, 13, 20, 32
Average: 6, 16, 21, 24, 33
Advanced: 8, 18, 22, 26, 34

Extra Practice

- Student Edition, p. 940
- Chapter 3 Resource Book: Practice levels A, B, C, pp. 82–84

Practice Worksheet

An easily-readable reduced practice page (with answers) for this lesson can be found on p. 130D.

Differentiated Instruction

Auditory Learners While working on **Exercises 20–23**, students may benefit from reading the formulas aloud, including their meaning, in order to solve for a given variable. For example, in **Exercise 21**, students could read "Surface area is equal to twice the base area plus the product of the perimeter and the height" instead of just reading the formula as "S equals $2B$ plus Ph."

See also the *Algebra 1 Toolkit* for more strategies.

Avoiding Common Errors

Exercises 3–8, 11–19, 27–28 Caution students to check that they used inverse operations when solving for a given variable. One way to check is to list the operations used in the original equation and then to check that the operations in the new equation are inverses of the operations in that list.

An **Animated Algebra** activity is available on-line for **Exercise 22**. This activity is also available on the **Power Presentations CD-ROM**.

Vocabulary

Exercise 32 "Penny size" is an interesting term and it may lead to confusion between the length of a nail in inches *n* and the penny size *d*. Have a student look up the meaning of *penny size* and then discuss its meaning with the class.

34b.

r	x
50	173
51	169.86
52	166.72
53	163.58

34c.

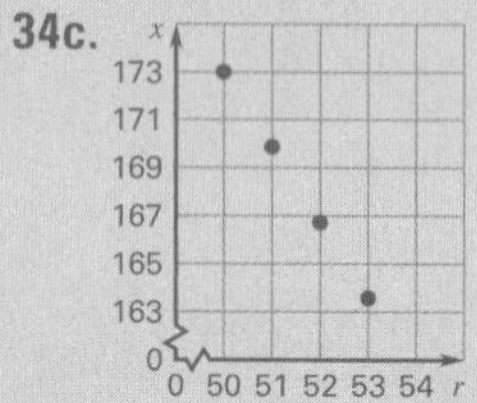

GEOMETRY Solve the formula for the indicated variable. Then evaluate the rewritten formula for the given values. (Use 3.14 for π.)

27. Surface area of a cone: $S = \pi r\ell + \pi r^2$. Solve for ℓ. Find ℓ when $S = 283 \text{ cm}^2$ and $r = 5$ cm. $\ell = \frac{S}{\pi r} - r$; 13.03 cm

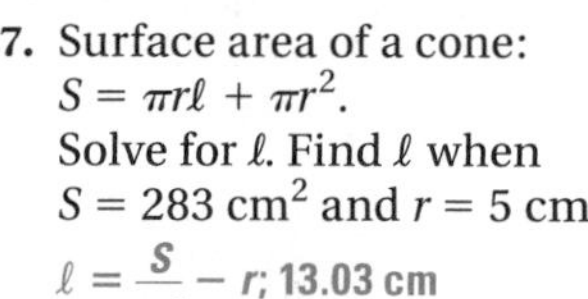

28. Area of a circular ring: $A = 4\pi pw$. Solve for p. Find p when $A = 905 \text{ ft}^2$ and $w = 9$ ft. $p = \frac{A}{4\pi w}$; 8.01 ft

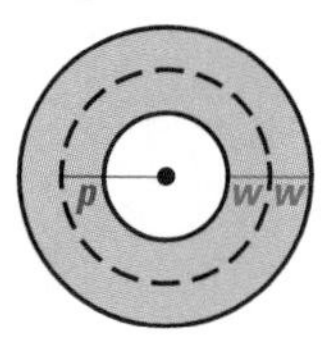

29. ★ **OPEN-ENDED** *Describe* a real-world situation where you would want to solve the distance traveled formula $d = rt$ for t. *Sample answer:* You want to find how long it will take to drive 150 miles if you drive at an average rate of 55 miles per hour.

C **CHALLENGE Solve the literal equation for *a*.**

30. $x = \frac{a + b + c}{ab}$ $\quad a = \frac{b + c}{bx - 1}$

31. $y = x\left(\frac{ab}{a - b}\right)$ $\quad a = \frac{by}{y - bx}$

PROBLEM SOLVING

EXAMPLE 4 A on p. 186 for Exs. 32–34

32. CARPENTRY The penny size d of a nail is given by $d = 4n - 2$ where n is the length (in inches) of the nail.

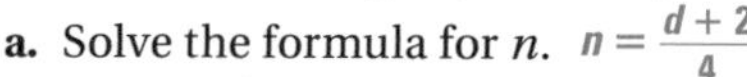

a. Solve the formula for n. $n = \frac{d + 2}{4}$

b. Use the new formula to find the lengths of nails with the following penny sizes: 5, 12, 16, and 20. 1.75 in., 3.5 in., 4.5 in., 5.5 in.

@HomeTutor for problem solving help at classzone.com

33. BOWLING To participate in a bowling league, you pay a \$25 sign-up fee and \$12 for each league night that you bowl. So, the total cost C (in dollars) is given by the equation $C = 12x + 25$ where x is the number of league nights you bowled.

a. Solve the equation for x. $x = \frac{C - 25}{12}$

b. How many league nights have you bowled if you spent a total of \$145? \$181? \$205? 10 league nights; 13 league nights; 15 league nights

@HomeTutor for problem solving help at classzone.com

34. ◆ **MULTIPLE REPRESENTATIONS** An athletic facility is building an indoor track like the one shown. The perimeter P (in feet) of the track is given by $P = 2\pi r + 2x$.

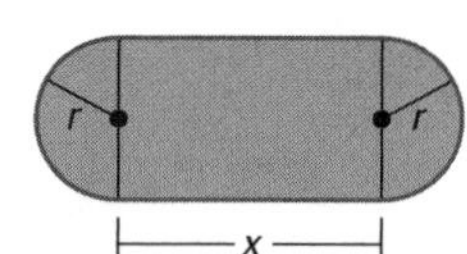

a. **Writing an Equation** Solve the formula for x. $x = \frac{P - 2\pi r}{2}$

b. **Making a Table** The perimeter of the track will be 660 feet. Use the rewritten formula to make a table that shows values of x to the nearest foot when r is 50 feet, 51 feet, 52 feet, and 53 feet. (Use 3.14 for π.) See margin.

c. **Drawing a Graph** Plot the ordered pairs from your table. Look for a pattern in the points. Use the pattern to find x when r is 54 feet. See margin for art; 160.44 ft.

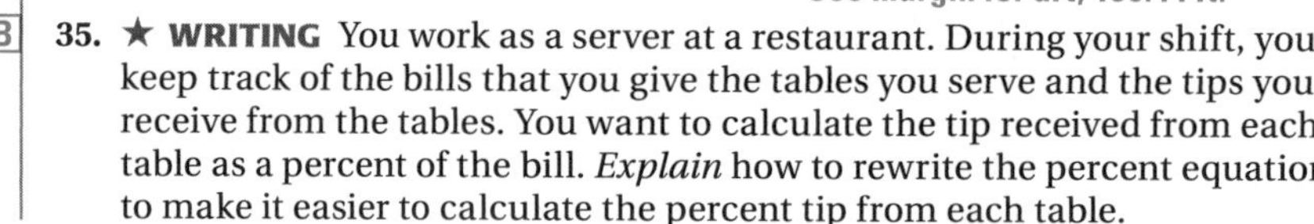

B **35.** ★ **WRITING** You work as a server at a restaurant. During your shift, you keep track of the bills that you give the tables you serve and the tips you receive from the tables. You want to calculate the tip received from each table as a percent of the bill. *Explain* how to rewrite the percent equation to make it easier to calculate the percent tip from each table. Divide each side by the total bill, b, to get $\frac{a}{b} = p\%$.

○ = WORKED-OUT SOLUTIONS on p. WS1 ★ = STANDARDIZED TEST PRACTICE

◆ = MULTIPLE REPRESENTATIONS

36b. 1.1 ft; 1.3 ft; 1.4 ft

36. ★ **EXTENDED RESPONSE** One type of stone formation found in Carlsbad Caverns in New Mexico is called a column. This cylindrical stone formation is connected to the ceiling and the floor of a cave.

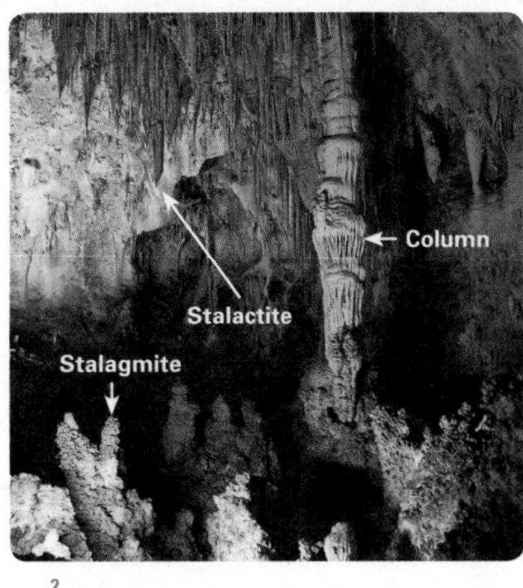

a. Rewrite the formula for the circumference of a circle, $C = 2\pi r$, so that you can easily calculate the radius of a column given its circumference. $r = \frac{C}{2\pi}$

b. What is the radius, to the nearest tenth of a foot, of a column that has a circumference of 7 feet? 8 feet? 9 feet? (Use 3.14 for π.)

c. *Explain* how you can find the *area* of a cross section of a column if you know its circumference. Solve for r using $\frac{C}{2\pi} = r$, then substitute r into the equation $A = \pi r^2$.

C **37. CHALLENGE** The distance d (in miles) traveled by a car is given by $d = 55t$ where t is the time (in hours) the car has traveled. The distance d (in miles) traveled is also given by $d = 20g$ where g is the number of gallons of gasoline used by the car. Write an equation that expresses g as a function of t. $g = \frac{11t}{4}$

ILLINOIS MIXED REVIEW

TEST PRACTICE at classzone.com

38. Which function includes the points (5, 11) and (9, 13)? D

Ⓐ $f(x) = 5x - 14$ Ⓑ $f(x) = 2x + 1$ Ⓒ $f(x) = 3x - 4$ Ⓓ $f(x) = 0.5(x + 17)$

39. Jed earns $12,500, and he puts $2000 into a savings fund. What percent of his earnings does he put into the fund? A

Ⓐ 16% Ⓑ 18% Ⓒ 22% Ⓓ 25%

QUIZ *for Lessons 3.7–3.8*

Use the percent equation to answer the question. *(p. 176)*

1. What percent of 150 is 72? 48%
2. What percent of 310 is 93? 30%
3. 31 is 5% of what number? 620
4. What number is 46% of 55? 25.3

Write the equation so that y is a function of x. *(p. 184)*

5. $5x - 3y = 9$ $y = \frac{5}{3}x - 3$
6. $3x + 2y + 5x = 12$ $y = 6 - 4x$
7. $4(2x - y) = 6$ $y = 2x - \frac{3}{2}$
8. **GEOMETRY** The volume V of a cylinder is given by the formula $V = \pi r^2 h$ where r is the radius of the cylinder and h is the height of the cylinder. Solve the formula for h. *(p. 184)* $h = \frac{V}{\pi r^2}$

5 ASSESS AND RETEACH

Daily Homework Quiz

Transparency Available

1. Write the equation $15 = 5y - 4x$ so that y is a function of x. $y = \frac{4}{5}x + 3$
2. Solve $C = 2\pi r$ for r. $r = \frac{C}{2\pi}$
3. Solve $V = \frac{1}{3}Bh$ for B. $B = \frac{3V}{h}$
4. On a round-trip bicycle trip from Santa Barbara to Canada, Phil rode 2850 miles in 63 days. Find his average miles per day for the trip. Use the formula $d = rt$ where d is distance, r is rate, and t is time. Solve for r to find the rate in miles per day to the nearest mile. about 45 miles per day

Online Quiz

Available at **classzone.com**

Diagnosis/Remediation

- Practice A, B, C in Chapter 3 Resource Book, pp. 82–84
- Study Guide in Chapter 3 Resource Book, pp. 85–86
- Practice Workbook, pp. 44–45
- @HomeTutor

Challenge

Additional challenge is available in the Chapter 3 Resource Book, p. 89.

Quiz

An easily-readable reduced copy of the quiz (with answers) on Lessons 3.7–3.8 from the Assessment Book can be found on p. 130E.

Illinois Mixed Review

1. C
2. G
3. C
4. G
5. B
6. G
7. D
8. H

190

Illinois Mixed Review

Lessons 3.5–3.8

1. **FLOOR PLANS** The dimensions of a rectangular room on a floor plan are 6 inches by 8 inches. Which of the following could be the actual dimensions of the room?

   A. 4 ft by 6 ft **C.** 9 ft by 12 ft
   B. 8 ft by 12 ft **D.** 12 ft by 18 ft

2. **DRAMA CLUB** The ratio of male students to female students in the drama club at a high school is 3 : 5. If there are 40 students in the club, how many are male?

   F. 12 **G.** 15 **H.** 24 **J.** 28

3. **SPORTS** The table shows the results of a survey in which students in a school were asked to name their favorite sport to watch on TV. If there are 1209 students in the school, predict how many students would name baseball as their favorite sport to watch on TV.

Sport	Students
Baseball	7
Basketball	6
Football	10
Other	8

   A. 226 students
   B. 234 students
   C. 273 students
   D. 353 students

4. **SCIENCE** In biology, the surface area-to-volume quotient Q of a single spherical cell is given by the formula $Q = \frac{3}{r}$ where r is the radius of the cell. Suppose a biologist needs to calculate the diameter d of a cell based on the value of Q. Given that $d = 2r$, which formula could the biologist use to find d?

   F. $d = \frac{6}{r}$ **H.** $d = 2Q$
   G. $d = 2\left(\frac{3}{Q}\right)$ **J.** $d = \frac{3}{2r}$

5. **GEOMETRY** The area A of a rhombus is given by the formula $A = \frac{1}{2}d_1d_2$ where d_1 and d_2 are the lengths of the diagonals. Suppose you need to find the value of d_1 for different values of d_2 and A. Which of the following equations could you use?

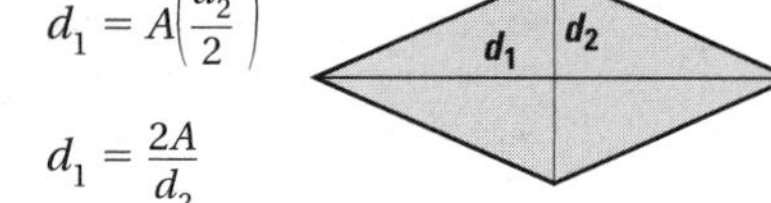

   A. $d_1 = A\left(\frac{d_2}{2}\right)$
   B. $d_1 = \frac{2A}{d_2}$
   C. $d_1 = \frac{A}{2d_2}$
   D. $2A = d_1d_2$

6. **REAL ESTATE** When a real estate agent sells a house, the agent receives 6% of the sale price as a commission. A house is sold for $208,000. How much commission does the agent receive?

   F. $1,248
   G. $12,480
   H. $124,800
   J. None of the above

7. **TRAVEL** During a recent trip, your car used 7 gallons of gasoline to travel 154 miles. If gasoline costs $2 per gallon, how much should you budget for gasoline for a 770 mile car trip?

   A. $35
   B. $45
   C. $53
   D. $70

8. **BASKETBALL** A basketball player made 60% of her free throw attempts last season. If she made 84 free throws, how many free throws did she attempt?

   F. 2
   G. 50
   H. 140
   J. 5040

3 CHAPTER SUMMARY

BIG IDEAS *For Your Notebook*

Big Idea 1

Solving Equations in One Variable

You can solve equations in one variable by adding, subtracting, multiplying by, or dividing by the same number on each side.

Property	Words	Algebra
Addition Property of Equality	Add the same number to each side.	If $x - a = b$, then $x - a + a = b + a$, or $x = b + a$.
Subtraction Property of Equality	Subtract the same number from each side.	If $x + a = b$, then $x + a - a = b - a$, or $x = b - a$.
Multiplication Property of Equality	Multiply each side by the same nonzero number.	If $\frac{x}{a} = b$ and $a \neq 0$, then $a \cdot \frac{x}{a} = a \cdot b$, or $x = ab$.
Division Property of Equality	Divide each side by the same nonzero number.	If $ax = b$ and $a \neq 0$, then $\frac{ax}{a} = \frac{b}{a}$, or $x = \frac{b}{a}$.

Big Idea 2

Solving Proportion and Percent Problems

When solving a proportion, you can take the cross products, then use properties of equality.

$\frac{x-3}{40} = \frac{4}{5}$	**Original proportion**
$5(x - 3) = 40 \cdot 4$	**Cross products property**
$5x - 15 = 160$	**Simplify.**
$5x = 175$	**Addition property of equality: Add 15 to each side.**
$x = 35$	**Division property of equality: Divide each side by 5.**

Rewriting Equations in Two or More Variables

If you have an equation in two or more variables, you can solve for one variable in terms of the others using properties of equality. For example, the formula for the perimeter P of a rectangle can be solved for the length ℓ.

$P = 2\ell + 2w$ (rectangle with width w and length ℓ)

$P = 2\ell + 2w$	**Original formula**
$P - 2w = 2\ell$	**Subtraction property of equality: Subtract $2w$ from each side.**
$\frac{P - 2w}{2} = \ell$	**Division property of equality: Divide each side by 2.**

Additional Resources

The following resources are available to help review the materials in this chapter.

Chapter 3 Resource Book

- Chapter Review Games and Activities, p. 90
- Cumulative Practice, Ch. 1–3, pp. 93–94

Student Resources in Spanish

eWorkbook

@HomeTutor

Vocabulary Practice

Vocabulary practice is available at **classzone.com**

Extra Example 3.1

Solve $6x = -96$. -16

3 CHAPTER REVIEW

@HomeTutor
classzone.com
- Multi-Language Glossary
- Vocabulary practice

REVIEW KEY VOCABULARY

- inverse operations, *p. 134*
- equivalent equations, *p. 134*
- identity, *p. 156*
- ratio, *p. 162*
- proportion, *p. 163*
- cross product, *p. 168*
- scale drawing, *p. 170*
- scale model, *p. 170*
- scale, *p. 170*
- literal equation, *p. 184*

VOCABULARY EXERCISES

1. Copy and complete: A(n) _?_ is a two-dimensional drawing of an object in which the dimensions of the drawing are in proportion to the dimensions of the object. scale drawing
2. Copy and complete: When you perform the same inverse operation on each side of an equation, you produce a(n) _?_ equation. equivalent
3. *Explain* why the equation $2x + 8x = 3x + 7x$ is an identity. If you collect like terms you get $10x = 10x$, so any value of x will make it true.
4. Copy and complete: In the proportion $\frac{7}{8} = \frac{28}{32}$, $7 \cdot 32$ and $8 \cdot 28$ are _?_. cross products
5. *Describe* the steps you would take to write the equation $6x - 2y = 16$ in function form. Subtract $6x$ from each side, then divide each side by -2.

REVIEW EXAMPLES AND EXERCISES

Use the review examples and exercises below to check your understanding of the concepts you have learned in each lesson of Chapter 3.

3.1 Solve One-Step Equations

pp. 134–140

EXAMPLE

Solve $\frac{x}{5} = 14$.

$\frac{x}{5} = 14$	Write original equation.
$5 \cdot \frac{x}{5} = 5 \cdot 14$	Multiply each side by 5.
$x = 70$	Simplify.

EXERCISES

EXAMPLES 1, 2, 3, 4 and 5 on pp. 134–136 for Exs. 6–12

Solve the equation. Check your solution.

6. $x - 4 = 3$ 7
7. $-8 + a = 5$ 13
8. $4m = -84$ -21
9. $-5z = 75$ -15
10. $11 = \frac{r}{6}$ 66
11. $-27 = \frac{3}{4}w$ -36
12. **PARKS** A rectangular city park has an area of 211,200 square feet. If the length of the park is 660 feet, what is the width of the park? 320 ft

@HomeTutor
classzone.com
Chapter Review Practice

3.2 Solve Two-Step Equations

pp. 141–146

EXAMPLE

Solve $4x - 9 = 3$.

$4x - 9 = 3$	Write original equation.
$4x - 9 + 9 = 3 + 9$	Add 9 to each side.
$4x = 12$	Simplify.
$\frac{4x}{4} = \frac{12}{4}$	Divide each side by 4.
$x = 3$	Simplify.

EXERCISES

EXAMPLES 1 and 2 on pp. 141–142 for Exs. 13–18

Solve the equation. Check your solution.

13. $9b + 5 = 23$ 2

14. $11 = 5y - 4$ 3

15. $\frac{n}{3} - 4 = 2$ 18

16. $\frac{3}{2}v + 2 = 20$ 12

17. $3t + 9t = 60$ 5

18. $-110 = -4c - 6c$ 11

3.3 Solve Multi-Step Equations

pp. 148–153

EXAMPLE

Solve $5x - 2(4x + 3) = 9$.

$5x - 2(4x + 3) = 9$	Write original equation.
$5x - 8x - 6 = 9$	Distributive property
$-3x - 6 = 9$	Combine like terms.
$-3x = 15$	Add 6 to each side.
$x = -5$	Divide each side by -3.

EXERCISES

EXAMPLES 1, 2, 3 and 4 on pp. 148–149 for Exs. 19–28

Solve the equation. Check your solution.

19. $3w + 4w - 2 = 12$ 2

20. $z + 5 - 4z = 8$ -1

21. $c + 2c - 5 - 5c = 7$ -6

22. $4y - (y - 4) = -20$ -8

23. $8a - 3(2a + 5) = 13$ 14

24. $16h - 4(5h - 7) = 4$ 6

25. $\frac{3}{2}(b + 1) = 3$ 1

26. $\frac{4}{3}(2x - 1) = -12$ -4

27. $\frac{6}{5}(8k + 2) = -36$ -4

28. **FOOTBALL** You purchase 5 tickets to a football game from an Internet ticket agency. In addition to the cost per ticket, the agency charges a convenience charge of \$2.50 per ticket. You choose to pay for rush delivery, which costs \$15. The total cost of your order is \$352.50. What is the price per ticket not including the convenience charge? \$65

Extra Example 3.2

Solve $\frac{a}{3} - 8 = 4$. 36

Extra Example 3.3

Solve $4b + 3(b - 2) = 15$. 3

3 CHAPTER REVIEW

Extra Example 3.4

Solve the equation, if possible.

a. $6(w - 4) = -2(12 - 3w)$ The equation is an identity.

b. $4a + 3 = 4(a + 3)$ The equation has no solution.

Extra Example 3.5

You know you can buy 6 tickets to the county fair for $18. How many tickets can you buy for $51? 17 tickets

3.4 Solve Equations with Variables on Both Sides

pp. 154–159

EXAMPLE

Solve the equation, if possible.

a. $-2(x - 5) = 7 - 2x$ **Original equation**

$-2x + 10 = 7 - 2x$ **Distributive property**

$-2x + 3 = -2x$ **Subtract 7 from each side.**

▶ The equation $-2x + 3 = -2x$ is not true because the number $-2x$ cannot be equal to 3 more than itself. So, the equation has no solution.

b. $5(3 - 2x) = -(10x - 15)$ **Original equation**

$15 - 10x = -10x + 15$ **Distributive property**

$15 - 10x = 15 - 10x$ **Rearrange terms.**

▶ The statement $15 - 10x = 15 - 10x$ is true for all values of x. So, the equation is an identity.

EXERCISES

EXAMPLES 1, 2, and 4 on pp. 154–156 for Exs. 29–37

Solve the equation, if possible.

29. $-3z - 1 = 8 - 3z$ no solution

30. $16 - 2m = 5m + 9$ 1

31 $2.9w + 5 = 4.7w - 7.6$ 7

32. $2y + 11.4 = 2.6 - 0.2y$ -4

33. $4(x - 3) = -2(6 - 2x)$ identity

34. $6(2a + 10) = 5(a + 5)$ -5

35. $\frac{1}{12}(48 + 24b) = 2(17 - 4b)$ 3

36. $1.5(n + 20) = 0.5(3n + 60)$ identity

37. **GEOMETRY** Refer to the square shown.

a. Find the value of x. 4

b. Find the perimeter of the square. 116

$6x + 5$

$8x - 3$

3.5 Write Ratios and Proportions

pp. 162–167

EXAMPLE

You know that 5 pizzas will feed 20 people. How many pizzas do you need to order to feed 88 people?

$\frac{5}{20} = \frac{x}{88}$ ← number of pizzas / ← number of people

$88 \cdot \frac{5}{20} = 88 \cdot \frac{x}{88}$ **Multiply each side by 88.**

$22 = x$ **Simplify.**

▶ You need to order 22 pizzas.

@HomeTutor
classzone.com
Chapter Review Practice

EXERCISES

EXAMPLES 2 and 3 on pp. 163–164 for Exs. 38–44

Solve the proportion. Check your solution.

38. $\frac{56}{16} = \frac{x}{2}$ 7

39. $\frac{y}{9} = \frac{25}{15}$ 15

40. $\frac{2}{7} = \frac{m}{91}$ 26

41. $\frac{5z}{3} = \frac{105}{6}$ 10.5

42. $\frac{9}{4} = \frac{3a}{20}$ 15

43. $\frac{c+2}{45} = \frac{8}{5}$ 70

44. PAINTING The label on a can of paint states that one gallon of the paint will cover 560 square feet. How many gallons of that paint are needed to cover 1400 square feet? 2.5 gal

3.6 Solve Proportions Using Cross Products

pp. 168–173

EXAMPLE

Solve the proportion $\frac{3}{10} = \frac{12}{x}$.

$\frac{3}{10} = \frac{12}{x}$	Write original proportion.
$3 \cdot x = 10 \cdot 12$	Cross products property
$3x = 120$	Simplify.
$x = 40$	Divide each side by 3.

EXAMPLE

A map has a scale of 1 cm : 15 km. The distance between two cities on the map is 7.2 centimeters. Estimate the actual distance between the cites.

$\frac{1}{15} = \frac{7.2}{d}$ ← centimeters / ← kilometers

$1 \cdot d = 15 \cdot 7.2$	Cross products property
$d = 108$	Simplify.

▶ The distance between the two cities is about 108 kilometers.

EXERCISES

EXAMPLES 1, 3, and 4 on pp. 168–170 for Exs. 45–52

Solve the proportion. Check your solution.

45. $\frac{5}{7} = \frac{20}{r}$ 28

46. $\frac{6}{z} = \frac{12}{5}$ 2.5

47. $\frac{126}{56} = \frac{9}{4b}$ 1

48. $\frac{10}{3m} = \frac{-5}{6}$ −4

49. $\frac{n+8}{5n-2} = \frac{3}{8}$ 10

50. $\frac{5-c}{3} = \frac{2c+2}{-4}$ −13

51. TYPING RATES A student can type 65 words in 2 minutes. How many words can the student type in 20 minutes? 650 words

52. MAPS A map has a scale of 1 cm : 12 km. The distance between two cities on the map is 6.8 centimeters. Estimate the actual distance between the cities. about 81.6 km

Extra Examples 3.6

1. Solve the proportion $\frac{3}{5} = \frac{s}{4}$. 2.4

2. A map has a scale of 1 cm : 8 km. The distance between 2 cities on the map is 6.5 centimeters. Estimate the actual distance between the cities. The distance between the two cities is about 52 kilometers.

3 CHAPTER REVIEW

Extra Example 3.7
What percent of 45 is 18? 40%

Extra Example 3.8
Write $ax + by = c$ so that y is a function of x. $y = \frac{c - ax}{b}$ or $y = -\frac{a}{b}x + \frac{c}{b}$

3.7 Solve Percent Problems

pp. 176–181

EXAMPLE

42 is 40% of what number?

$a = p\% \cdot b$	**Write percent equation.**
$42 = 40\% \cdot b$	**Substitute 42 for a and 40 for p.**
$42 = 0.4 \cdot b$	**Write percent as decimal.**
$105 = b$	**Divide each side by 0.4.**

▶ 42 is 40% of 105.

EXERCISES

EXAMPLES 2, 3, 4, and 5 on pp. 177–179 for Exs. 53–57

Use the percent equation to answer the question.

53. What number is 30% of 55? 16.5

54. 117 is 78% of what number? 150

55. What percent of 56 is 21? 37.5%

56. What percent of 60 is 18? 30%

57. CONCERTS There were 7500 tickets sold for a concert, 20% of which were general admission tickets. How many general admission tickets were sold?
1500 general admission tickets

3.8 Rewrite Equations and Formulas

pp. 184–189

EXAMPLE

Write $5x + 4y - 7 = 5$ so that y is a function of x.

$5x + 4y - 7 = 5$	**Write original equation.**
$5x + 4y = 12$	**Add 7 to each side.**
$4y = 12 - 5x$	**Subtract $5x$ from each side.**
$y = 3 - \frac{5}{4}x$	**Divide each side by 4.**

EXERCISES

EXAMPLES 2 and 3 on p. 185 for Exs. 58–61

Write the equation so that y is a function of x.

58. $x + 7y = 0$ $y = \frac{-x}{7}$

59. $3x = 2y - 18$ $y = \frac{3}{2}x + 9$

60. $4y - x = 20 - y$ $y = \frac{1}{5}x + 4$

61. AQUARIUMS A pet store sells aquariums that are rectangular prisms. The volume V of an aquarium is given by the formula $V = \ell wh$ where ℓ is the length, w is the width, and h is the height.

a. Solve the formula for h. $h = \frac{V}{\ell w}$

b. Use the rewritten formula to find the height of the aquarium shown, which has a volume of 5850 cubic inches. 15 in.

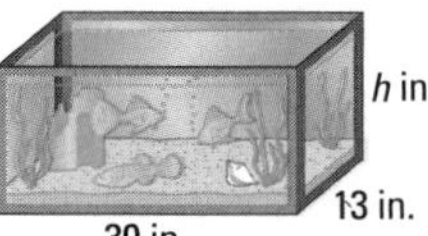

3 CHAPTER TEST

Solve the equation. Check your solution.

1. $5 + r = -19$ −24
2. $z - 8 = -12$ −4
3. $-11x = -77$ 7
4. $\frac{a}{9} = 6$ 54
5. $15q - 17 = 13$ 2
6. $3y + 2 = 26$ 8
7. $\frac{b}{4} + 5 = 14$ 36
8. $\frac{m}{10} - 6 = 20$ 260
9. $6j + 5j = 33$ 3
10. $4k - 9k = 10$ −2
11. $14c - 8c + 7 = 37$ 5
12. $4w - 21 + 5w = 51$ 8
13. $-19.4 - 15d + 22d = 4.4$ 3.4
14. $-12h + 39 = -4h - 17$ 7
15. $-5.7v - 44.2 = -8.3v$ 17
16. $-6.5t + 15 = -9.7t + 43.8$ 9
17. $3(3n + 4) = 54 + 6n$ 14
18. $\frac{1}{3}(24p - 66) = 3p + 43$ 13

Solve the proportion. Check your solution.

19. $\frac{3}{4} = \frac{z}{16}$ 12
20. $\frac{72}{45} = \frac{8}{w}$ 5
21. $\frac{k}{9} = \frac{63}{81}$ 7
22. $\frac{-5n}{4} = \frac{15}{2}$ −6
23. $\frac{34}{6} = \frac{2x + 1}{3}$ 8
24. $\frac{-4a - 1}{-10a} = \frac{3}{8}$ −4

Use the percent equation to answer the question.

25. What percent of 84 is 21? 25%
26. What percent of 124 is 93? 75%
27. What number is 15% of 64? 9.6
28. What number is 44% of 24.5? 10.78
29. 90 is what percent of 250? 36%
30. 79.8 is what percent of 95? 84%

Write the equation so that *y* is a function of *x*.

31. $8x + y = 14$ $y = 14 - 8x$
32. $-9x + 3y = 18$ $y = 3x + 6$
33. $4x = -2y + 26$ $13 - 2x = y$

34. **MOVIES** The ticket prices at a movie theater are shown in the table. A family purchases tickets for 2 adults and 3 children, and the family purchases 3 boxes of popcorn of the same size. The family spent a total of \$40.25. How much did each box of popcorn cost? \$2.25

Ticket	Price
Adults	\$8.50
Children	\$5.50

35. **ICE SKATING** To become a member of an ice skating rink, you have to pay a \$30 membership fee. The cost of admission to the rink is \$5 for members and \$7 for nonmembers. After how many visits to the rink is the total cost for members, including the membership fee, the same as the total cost for nonmembers? 15 visits

36. **SCALE DRAWING** You are making a scale drawing of your classroom using the scale 1 inch : 3 feet. The floor of your classroom is a rectangle with a length of 21 feet and a width of 18 feet. What should the length and width of the floor in your drawing be? 7 in., 6 in.

37. **SURVEYS** A survey asks high school seniors whether they would be willing to pay \$5 for their yearbook. Out of the 225 seniors surveyed, 198 said "yes." What percent of the seniors said "yes"? 88%

Additional Resources

Assessment Book

- Chapter Test, Levels A, B, C, pp. 34–39
- Standardized Chapter Test, pp. 40–41
- SAT/ACT Chapter Test, pp. 42–43
- Alternative Assessment, pp. 44–45

Test Generator CD-ROM

Chapter Test

Easily-readable reduced copies (with answers) of Chapter Test B, the Standardized Chapter Test, and the Alternative Assessment from the Assessment Book can be found on pp. 130E–130F.

Illinois Test Preparation

MULTIPLE CHOICE QUESTIONS

If you have difficulty solving a multiple choice problem directly, you may be able to use another approach to eliminate incorrect answer choices and obtain the correct answer.

PROBLEM 1

Sid's car gets 34 miles per gallon when driven on the highway and 26 miles per gallon when driven in the city. If Sid drove 414 miles on 13 gallons of gas, how many highway miles and how many city miles did Sid drive?

A. 91 highway miles, 323 city miles

B. 182 highway miles, 232 city miles

C. 232 highway miles, 182 city miles

D. 323 highway miles, 91 city miles

METHOD 1

SOLVE DIRECTLY Write and solve an equation for the situation.

STEP 1 **Write** an equation. Let x represent the amount of gas (in gallons) used for highway driving. Then $13 - x$ represents the amount of gas used for city driving.

$$414 = 34x + 26(13 - x)$$

STEP 2 **Solve** the equation.

$$414 = 34x + 338 - 26x$$

$$414 = 8x + 338$$

$$76 = 8x$$

$$9.5 = x$$

STEP 3 **Calculate** the number of highway miles driven.

$$34(9.5) = 323$$

STEP 4 **Calculate** the number of city miles driven.

$$26(13 - 9.5) = 91$$

Sid drove 323 highway miles and 91 city miles.

The correct answer is **D**.

METHOD 2

ELIMINATE CHOICES Another method is to consider the extremes to eliminate incorrect answer choices.

STEP 1 **Consider** driving all highway miles and all city miles.

All highway: $13 \text{ gal} \cdot \frac{34 \text{ mi}}{1 \text{ gal}} = 442 \text{ mi}$

All city: $13 \text{ gal} \cdot \frac{26 \text{ mi}}{1 \text{ gal}} = 338 \text{ mi}$

Because 414 is closer to 442 than to 338, you know that more highway miles were driven than city miles. So, you can eliminate choices A and B.

STEP 2 **Calculate** the gallons of gas that would be used for the remaining choices.

Choice C: $232 \text{ mi} \cdot \frac{1 \text{ gal}}{34 \text{ mi}} \approx 6.8 \text{ gal}$

$182 \text{ mi} \cdot \frac{1 \text{ gal}}{26 \text{ mi}} = 7 \text{ gal}$

Choice D: $323 \text{ mi} \cdot \frac{1 \text{ gal}}{34 \text{ mi}} = 9.5 \text{ gal}$

$91 \text{ mi} \cdot \frac{1 \text{ gal}}{26 \text{ mi}} = 3.5 \text{ gal}$

In choice D, the total number of gallons of gas is 13.

The correct answer is **D**.

PROBLEM 2

What is the value of x in the proportion $\frac{3}{2x-10} = \frac{12}{x+9}$?

F. 4 **G.** 6 **H.** 7 **J.** 8

METHOD 1

SOLVE DIRECTLY Find the value of x by using the cross products property to solve the proportion.

$$\frac{3}{2x-10} = \frac{12}{x+9}$$

$$3(x+9) = (2x-10) \cdot 12$$

$$3x + 27 = 24x - 120$$

$$147 = 21x$$

$$7 = x$$

The correct answer is **H**.

METHOD 2

ELIMINATE CHOICES Substitute each answer choice for x in the proportion and simplify.

Choice F: $\frac{3}{2(4)-10} \stackrel{?}{=} \frac{12}{4+9}$

$\frac{3}{-2} = \frac{12}{13}$ ✗

Choice G: $\frac{3}{2(6)-10} \stackrel{?}{=} \frac{12}{6+9}$

$\frac{3}{2} = \frac{4}{5}$ ✗

Choice H: $\frac{3}{2(7)-10} \stackrel{?}{=} \frac{12}{7+9}$

$\frac{3}{4} = \frac{3}{4}$ ✓

The correct answer is **H**.

PRACTICE

Explain why you can eliminate the highlighted answer choice.

1. What is the solution of the equation $5(x + 13) = 8(4 + x)$?

   A. −11 **B.** −4 **C.** ~~0~~ **D.** 11

2. 45 is 80% of what number?

   F. ~~36~~ **G.** 56.25 **H.** 60 **J.** 64.5

3. A grocery store sells apples by the pound. A 3 pound bag of apples costs $2.99. About how much does a 5 pound bag of apples cost?

   A. $3.24 **B.** $3.45 **C.** $4.98 **D.** ~~$5.98~~

4. The surface area S of a cylinder is given by the formula $S = 2\pi rh + 2\pi r^2$ where r is the radius and h is the height of the cylinder. Which of the given formulas is *not* equivalent to the original formula?

   F. $S = 2\pi r(h + r)$ **H.** ~~$h = \frac{S - 2\pi r^2}{2\pi r}$~~

   G. $h = 2\pi rS + 2\pi r^2$ **J.** $h = \frac{S}{2\pi r} - r$

TEST PREPARATION

Illinois Test Preparation

1. Substituting 0 for x into the equation gives $65 = 32$, which is not true.
2. 36 is less than 45, because 45 is only 80% of the number. The number must be greater than 45.
3. $5.98 is two times $2.99. Because 5 pounds is less than two times 3 pounds, the cost of the 5 pound bag should be less than two times the cost of the 3 pound bag.
4. Subtract $2\pi r^2$ from both sides of $S = 2\pi rh + 2\pi r^2$, and then divide both sides by $2\pi r$. The result is the formula given in answer H.

Illinois Test Practice

1. A
2. J
3. B
4. G
5. C
6. G
7. A
8. H
9. B
10. J
11. B
12. F
13. D
14. F
15. A
16. H
17. D
18. G
19. D
20. G

Illinois Test Practice

1. How many solutions does the equation $3(x - 3) = 3x - 6$ have?

   A. None **B.** 1 **C.** 2 **D.** Infinitely many

2. A karate studio offers a 6 week session for \$175. How much would you expect to pay for a 9 week session?

   F. \$117 **G.** \$200 **H.** \$229 **J.** \$262.50

3. Andrew decides to get cable TV for \$43 per month. Doug buys a satellite dish for \$104 and pays \$30 per month for satellite TV. After how many months will Andrew and Doug have paid the same amount for their TV services?

   A. 7 **B.** 8 **C.** 9 **D.** 10

4. The rates for using a swimming facility are given below. After how many visits will a family of 4 save money by having a membership rather than paying for all 4 family members for each visit?

Admission Prices	
One-day visit	\$3 per person
Family membership (unlimited visits)	\$150

   F. 12 **G.** 13 **H.** 38 **J.** 50

5. The record for the longest distance and longest time ever flown by a model airplane was set in 2003 by Maynard Hill. The airplane flew 1888 miles from Canada to Ireland in 38 hours and 53 minutes. What was the plane's average speed?

   A. About 36 mi/h
   B. About 45 mi/h
   C. About 49 mi/h
   D. About 71,744 mi/h

6. The perimeter of the triangle shown is 16.5 inches. What is the length of the shortest side?

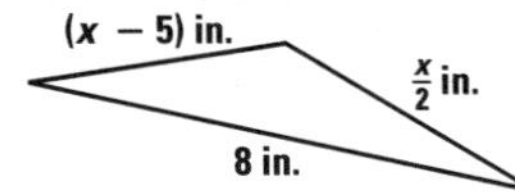

   F. 3.5 in. **G.** 4 in. **H.** 4.5 in. **J.** 9 in.

7. Jeanie completed a 27 mile duathlon (a race that is a combination of running and biking) in exactly 2 hours. She ran an average speed of 8.5 miles per hour and biked an average speed of 16 miles per hour. For how long did Jeanie bike during the race?

   A. 1 hour 20 minutes
   B. 1 hour 15 minutes
   C. 45 minutes
   D. 40 minutes

8. A model of the Gateway Arch in St. Louis, Missouri, was built using a scale of 1 ft : 500 ft. The model is 1.26 feet tall. What is the actual height of the Gateway Arch?

   F. 75.6 ft
   G. 396.8 ft
   H. 630 ft
   J. 7560 ft

9. A mountain biking park has a total of 48 trails, 37.5% of which are beginner trails. The rest are divided evenly between intermediate and expert trails. How many of each kind of trail is there?

   A. 12 beginner, 18 intermediate, 18 expert
   B. 18 beginner, 15 intermediate, 15 expert
   C. 18 beginner, 12 intermediate, 18 expert
   D. 30 beginner, 9 intermediate, 9 expert

10. What percent of 256 is 140.8?

   F. 45% **G.** 50% **H.** 52.5% **J.** 55%

11. A group of 5 salespeople earns 25% of all the money they bring in to their business. The salespeople then split the money, with each salesperson receiving one-fifth of the earnings. If the group brought in $8120 one day, how much did each salesperson earn?

A. $244

B. $406

C. $1624

D. $2030

12. Solve the literal equation $b(x - 3) = a$ for x.

F. $x = \frac{a}{b} + 3$

G. $x = \frac{a}{b} - 3$

H. $x = \frac{a}{b - 3}$

J. $x = ab - 3a$

13. Which of the following expressions does NOT equal 1.5?

A. $\frac{30}{20}$ **C.** 15% of 10

B. 5% of 30 **D.** $\frac{250}{150}$

14. What is the solution to the equation $2x - 4 = 4(x - 1)$?

F. $x = 0$

G. $x = 2$

H. No solution

J. Infinitely many solutions

15. A baseball team plays 15 home games and 9 away games. What is the ratio of away games to home games?

A. 3 : 5 **C.** 3 : 8

B. 5 : 3 **D.** 5 : 8

16. The length and width of a rectangle are tripled. What is the ratio of the rectangle's original area to its new area?

F. 1 : 3 **H.** 1 : 9

G. 1 : 6 **J.** 1 : 27

17. If ΔDEF is similar to ΔJKL, what is the length x?

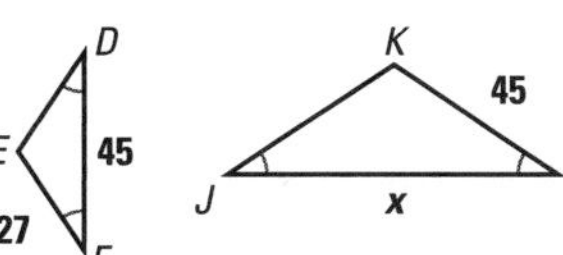

A. 27 **C.** 60

B. 45 **D.** 75

18. A parking meter accepts nickels, dimes, and quarters. You can buy 15 minutes of time on the meter for $0.25. How long can you park if you put $2.10 into the meter?

F. 1 h 50 min

G. 2 h 6 min

H. 2 h 10 min

J. 2 h 24 min

19. Payton went to the movies with her friends and purchased six tickets for a total of $45. The equation $6x = 45$ can be solved to find the cost of each ticket. Which of these methods should be used to solve for x?

A. Multiply both sides of the equation by $\frac{1}{45}$.

B. Multiply both sides of the equation by 6.

C. Divide both sides of the equation by 45.

D. Divide both sides of the equation by 6.

20. Simple interest I on an investment of P dollars at an annual interest rate r for t years is given by $I = Prt$. Samantha invests $2100 for 5 years in a simple interest bearing account and earns $178.50 in interest. Which of these formulas should she use to find the interest rate?

F. $\frac{I}{P} + t = r$

G. $\frac{I}{Pt} = r$

H. $\frac{I}{t} \cdot P = r$

J. $I \cdot P \cdot t = r$

TEST PRACTICE

Additional Resources

The following resources are available to help review the materials in Chapters 1–3.

Chapter Resource Books

- Chapter 1 CRB, Cumulative Review, pp. 86–87
- Chapter 2 CRB, Cumulative Review, pp. 83–84
- Chapter 3 CRB, Cumulative Review, pp. 93–94

3 CUMULATIVE REVIEW Chapters 1–3

Evaluate the expression. *(p. 8)*

1. $3 \cdot 4^2 - 21$ 27
2. $4 + 4^2 \div 8$ 6
3. $77 \div (11 - 4)$ 11
4. $\frac{1}{2}(8 \cdot 6) - 4^2$ 8
5. $3[50 - (13 - 7)^2]$ 42
6. $\frac{3}{4}[(6 + 4)^2 - 40]$ 45

Check whether the given number is a solution of the equation or inequality. *(p. 21)*

7. $7t - 11 = 52; 9$ solution
8. $3b - 2 = 2b + 3; 4$ not a solution
9. $8z - 11 > 21; 4$ not a solution
10. $5a + 3 \le 13; 2$ solution
11. $5 - y \ge 5; 3$ not a solution
12. $8x - 15 < 8; 7$ not a solution

Find the sum or difference.

13. $-2\frac{1}{6} + \left(-4\frac{2}{3}\right)$ *(p. 74)* $-6\frac{5}{6}$
14. $2.5 - (-2.05)$ *(p. 80)* 4.55
15. $-24.6 - (-5.5)$ *(p. 80)* −19.1

Find the product or quotient.

16. $\frac{5}{2}(-8)(-5)$ *(p. 88)* 100
17. $9 \div \left(-\frac{3}{7}\right)$ *(p. 103)* −21
18. $-\frac{7}{8} \div \frac{1}{2}$ *(p. 103)* $-1\frac{3}{4}$

Evaluate the expression for the given value of the variable(s).

19. $\frac{32}{w} - 2$ when $w = 4$ *(p. 8)* 6
20. $7 + 3m^2 - 8m$ when $m = 5$ *(p. 8)* 42
21. $\frac{5y}{32 - y^3}$ when $y = 3$ *(p. 8)* 3
22. $5.15 + (-h) + 6.6$ when $h = 4.3$ *(p. 74)* 7.45
23. $17.4 - |-p|$ when $p = 3.5$ *(p. 80)* 13.9
24. $k^2 - 12.2k$ when $k = -1.6$ *(p. 88)* 22.08
25. $8.3x - (-y)$ when $x = 6$ and $y = 9$ *(p. 88)* 58.8
26. $\frac{y}{5x - y}$ when $x = 2$ and $y = 4$ *(p. 103)* $\frac{2}{3}$

Solve the equation. Check your solution.

27. $m + 16 = 5$ *(p. 134)* −11
28. $-4 = \frac{w}{7}$ *(p. 134)* −28
29. $5 + 3x = 23$ *(p. 141)* 6
30. $\frac{a}{3} - 4 = 29$ *(p. 141)* 99
31. $-4 = -2b - 18 + 5b$ *(p. 148)* $4\frac{2}{3}$
32. $\frac{3}{8}(16n + 48) = 72$ *(p. 148)* 9
33. $-8z + 18 = 2(2z - 9)$ *(p. 154)* 3
34. $(15c + 30) = \frac{1}{3}(102 - 12c)$ *(p. 154)* $\frac{4}{19}$

Solve the proportion. *(p. 168)*

35. $\frac{6}{d} = \frac{12}{17}$ 8.5
36. $\frac{4}{7} = \frac{20}{m}$ 35
37. $\frac{1}{9} = \frac{5}{3x}$ 15
38. $\frac{3}{6h} = \frac{12}{72}$ 3
39. $\frac{2}{11} = \frac{4}{t - 1}$ 23
40. $\frac{12}{a + 1} = \frac{132}{35}$ $2\frac{2}{11}$
41. $\frac{w + 2}{8} = \frac{w}{3}$ 1.2
42. $\frac{4}{9} = \frac{z}{z + 10}$ 8

44. 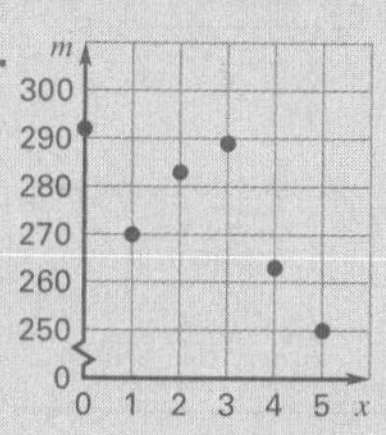

43. GARDENS You want to put edging around a rectangular flower garden that is 15 feet long and 12 feet wide. The edging comes in 3 foot pieces, as shown. How many pieces of edging do you need to buy? *(p. 28)* 18 pieces

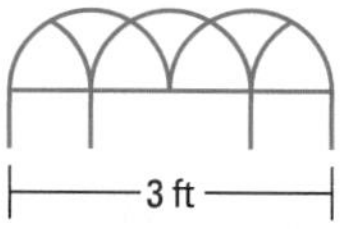

44. MUSIC The table shows the amount of time m (in hours per person per year) that adults listened to recorded music as a function of the time t (in years) since 1996. Graph the function. *(p. 43)* See margin.

Years since 1996, t	0	1	2	3	4	5
Hours listening to music, m	292	270	283	289	263	250

45. STOCKS The daily change in the price of a share of stock is the difference of the price of a share when trading closes and the price of a share when trading opened earlier that day. The table shows the prices of a share of stock during a 5 day period. Find the change in price for each day. *(p. 80)* −\$.34; −\$.45; −\$.25; \$1.02; \$.08

Day	1	2	3	4	5
Opening price (dollars)	39.16	38.82	38.37	38.12	39.14
Closing price (dollars)	38.82	38.37	38.12	39.14	39.22

46. CRAFTS You want to make a square mirror by applying silver leaf to a piece of glass. You have enough silver leaf to cover 854 square inches. Determine the side length of the square piece of glass you need to have cut for this project. Round your answer to the nearest inch. *(p. 110)* 29 in.

47. BANQUETS The senior class at your high school has its prom at a banquet facility. The banquet facility charges \$15.95 per person for a dinner buffet and \$400 to rent the banquet hall for an evening. The class paid the banquet facility a total of \$2633 for the dinner buffet and use of the banquet hall. How many people attended the prom? *(p. 141)* 140 people

48. TELEVISIONS The ratio of the length to the width of two different television screens is shown. The width of each screen is 16.2 inches. Find the length of each screen. *(p. 162)* 21.6 in., 28.8 in.

Standard

Wide screen

49. BASKETBALL The circle graph shows the positions of the 20 players on a basketball team. *(p. 176)*

a. How many players on the team play center? 2 players

b. How many players on the team play guard? 7 players

c. How many players on the team play forward? 11 players

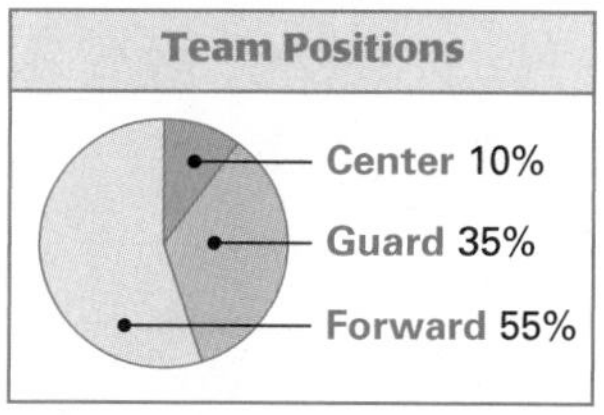

Illinois Resources Guide

Pacing and Assignment Guide

REGULAR SCHEDULE

Pre-AP For pacing and assignments for a Pre-AP course, see the *Algebra 1 Toolkit*.

Lesson	Les. Day	BASIC	AVERAGE	ADVANCED
4.1 9.11.11	Day 1	SRH p. 921 Exs. 7–21 odd; pp. 209–212 Exs. 1, 2, 3–11 odd, 13–17, 22–30, 36–39, 42–54 even	pp. 209–212 Exs. 1, 2, 7–13 odd, 16–22 even, 23, 24–32 even, 33–40, 43–53 odd	pp. 209–212 Exs. 1, 2, 10–13, 19–23, 26–28, 31–35*, 38–41*, 43–53 odd
4.2 8.11.11	Day 1	EP p. 938 Exs. 33–36; pp. 219–221 Exs. 1–10, 11–21 odd, 23–25, 42–47	pp. 219–221 Exs. 1–10, 16–25, 42–47	pp. 219–221 Exs. 1, 2, 5–10, 17–25, 34*, 42–47
	Day 2	pp. 219–221 Exs. 26–29, 35–39, 48–55	pp. 219–221 Exs. 26–32 even, 33, 35–40, 48–55	pp. 219–221 Exs. 29–33, 36–41*, 48–55
4.3 8.11.11	Day 1	EP p. 940 Exs. 1–7 odd; pp. 229–232 Exs. 1–10, 16–21, 28–33, 37, 44–47, 51–56	pp. 229–232 Exs. 1–3, 10–15, 22–27, 29, 30, 34–41, 44–49, 51–55 odd	pp. 229–232 Exs. 1, 2, 12–15, 24–27, 29, 30, 35–37, 39–43*, 46–50*, 52–56 even
4.4 8.11.09	Day 1	SRH p. 934 Exs. 6–14; pp. 239–242 Exs. 1–18, 42–56 even	pp. 239–242 Exs. 1–7, 11–18, 24–28, 43–55 odd	pp. 239–242 Exs. 1, 2, 12–18, 24–32, 43–55 odd
	Day 2	pp. 239–242 Exs. 19–27, 36–39, 57–62	pp. 239–242 Exs. 19–23, 31–33, 36–40, 57–62	pp. 239–242 Exs. 19–23, 35–41*, 57–62
4.5 8.11.11	Day 1	pp. 247–250 Exs. 1–13, 17–24, 30–33, 40–43, 46–56 even	pp. 247–250 Exs. 1–5, 9, 10, 13–20, 25–31, 32–38 even, 40–44, 46–56 even	pp. 247–250 Exs. 1, 2, 6–10, 14–19, 27–39*, 41–45*, 47–57 odd
4.6 6.11.19	Day 1	pp. 256–259 Exs. 1, 2, 3–9 odd, 10–22 even, 23–28, 40–45, 48–62 even	pp. 256–259 Exs. 1, 2, 6–10, 18–28, 29–35 odd, 40–46, 53–56, 60–62	pp. 256–259 Exs. 1, 2, 7–9, 19–22, 24–28, 33–39*, 41–47*, 54–56, 60–62
4.7 8.11.11	Day 1	pp. 265–268 Exs. 1, 3–11 odd, 12–18, 39–41, 46–54	pp. 265–268 Exs. 1, 7–13, 16–22, 39–41, 46–54	pp. 265–268 Exs. 1, 7–11, 13, 17–22, 37–41*, 46–54 even
	Day 2	pp. 265–268 Exs. 2, 19–29, 42, 55–60	pp. 265–268 Exs. 2, 27–37, 42–44, 55–60	pp. 265–268 Exs. 2, 28–36, 42–45*, 55–60
Review	Day 1	pp. 271–274 Exs. 1–34	pp. 271–274 Exs. 1–34	pp. 271–274 Exs. 1–34
Assess	Day 1	Chapter 4 Test	Chapter 4 Test	Chapter 4 Test
Yearly Pacing		Chapter 4 Total – 12 days	Chapters 1–4 Total – 46 days	Remaining – 114 days

*Challenge Exercises EP = Extra Practice SRH = Skills Review Handbook

BLOCK SCHEDULE

DAY 1	DAY 2	DAY 3	DAY 4	DAY 5	DAY 6
4.1	**4.2 (CONT.)**	**4.4**	**4.5**	**4.7**	**REVIEW**
pp. 209–212 Exs. 1, 2, 7–13 odd, 16–22 even, 23, 24–32 even, 33–40, 43–53 odd	pp. 219–221 Exs. 26–32 even, 33, 35–40, 48–55	pp. 239–242 Exs. 1–7, 11–28, 31–33, 36–40, 43–55 odd, 57–62	pp. 247–250 Exs. 1–5, 9, 10, 13–20, 25–31, 32–38 even, 40–44, 46–56 even	pp. 265–268 Exs. 1, 2, 7–13, 16–22, 27–37, 39–44, 46–60	pp. 271–274 Exs. 1–34
4.2	**4.3**		**4.6**		**ASSESS**
pp. 219–221 Exs. 1–10, 16–25, 42–47	pp. 229–232 Exs. 1–3, 10–15, 22–27, 29, 30, 34–41, 44–49, 51–55 odd		pp. 256–259 Exs. 1, 2, 6–10, 18–28, 29–35 odd, 40–46, 53–56, 60–62		Chapter 4 Test
Yearly Pacing	Chapter 4 Total – 6 days	Chapters 1–4 Total – 23 days	Remaining – 57 days		

Chapter Resource Guide

Chapter Resource Book							
CHAPTER SUPPORT							
Parents as Partners (Chapter Overview with home involvement exercises and activity)						p. 1	
LESSON SUPPORT **Standard**	4.1 **9.11.11**	4.2 **8.11.11**	4.3 **8.11.11**	4.4 **8.11.09**	4.5 **8.11.11**	4.6 **6.11.19**	4.7 **8.11.11**
Teaching Guide/Lesson Plan	p. 3	p. 16	p. 31	p. 45	p. 58	p. 75	p. 88
Activity Masters		p. 18					p. 90
Technology Activities & Keystrokes		p. 19			p. 60		
Activity Support Masters					p. 62		
Practice (3 levels)	p. 5	p. 20	p. 33	p. 47	p. 64	p. 77	p. 91
Study Guide	p. 11	p. 26	p. 39	p. 53	p. 70	p. 83	p. 97
Catch-Up for Absent Students	p. 13	p. 28	p. 41	p. 55	p. 72	p. 85	p. 99
Problem Solving/Application	p. 14	p. 29	p. 42	p. 56	p. 73	p. 86	p. 100
Challenge Practice	p. 15	p. 30	p. 44	p. 57	p. 74	p. 87	p. 101
REVIEW							
Chapter Review Games and Activities		p. 102		Cumulative Practice		p. 105	
Project with Rubric		p. 103		Resource Book Answers		A1	

Transparencies	4.1	4.2	4.3	4.4	4.5	4.6	4.7
Warm-Up/Daily Homework Quiz	✔	✔	✔	✔	✔	✔	✔
Notetaking Guide	✔	✔	✔	✔	✔	✔	✔
Teacher Support	✔	✔	✔	✔	✔	✔	✔
Answer Transparencies	✔	✔	✔	✔	✔	✔	✔

ASSESSMENT BOOK

Quizzes	p. 46	SAT/ACT Chapter Test	p. 57
Chapter Tests (3 levels)	p. 49	Alternative Assessment with Rubric	p. 59
Standardized Chapter Test	p. 55		

TECHNOLOGY

- Easy Planner
- Test and Practice Generator
- Power Presentations
- @HomeTutor
- Activity Generator
- Animated Algebra
- Classzone.com
- eEdition Plus Online
- eWorkbook Plus Online
- ML Assessment System

ADDITIONAL RESOURCES

Illinois Additional Lessons

- Additional Lesson G Vertex-Edge Graphs, Circuits, Networks, and Routing
- Additional lesson H Introduction to Vectors
- Worked-Out Solution Key
- Notetaking Guide
- Practice Workbook
- Algebra 1 Toolkit
- Benchmark Tests
- Reteaching and Remediation
- Spanish Study Guide
- Spanish Assessment Book
- Spanish Resources in Spanish
- Multi-Language Visual Glossary

LESSON 4.1 Practice B
For use with pages 206–212

Give the coordinates of the points labeled *A*, *B*, *C*, and *D*.

1. 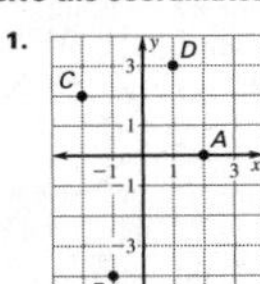

$A(2, 0), B(-1, -4), C(-2, 2), D(1, 3)$

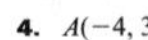

2. 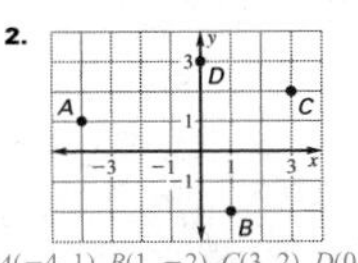

$A(-4, 1), B(1, -2), C(3, 2), D(0, 3)$

3. 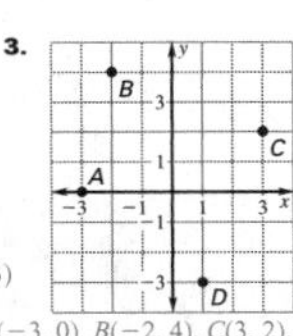

$A(-3, 0), B(-2, 4), C(3, 2), D(1, -3)$

Plot the point in a coordinate plane. *Describe* the location of the point.

4. $A(-4, 3)$

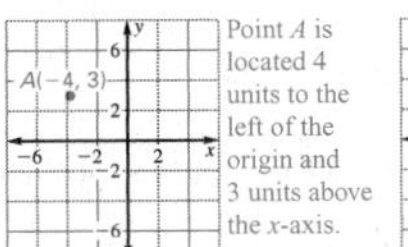

Point A is located 4 units to the left of the origin and 3 units above the x-axis.

5. $P(5, -6)$

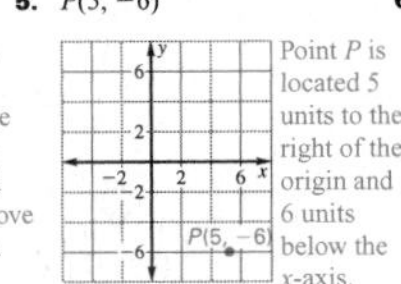

Point P is located 5 units to the right of the origin and 6 units below the x-axis.

6. $Q(0, 7)$

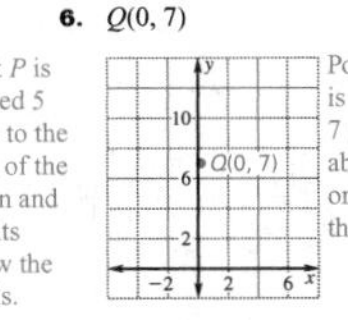

Point Q is located 7 units above the origin on the y-axis.

7. $B(-7, -5)$

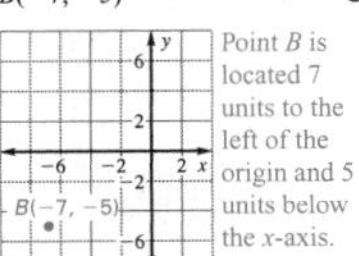

Point B is located 7 units to the left of the origin and 5 units below the x-axis.

8. $W(-5, 0)$

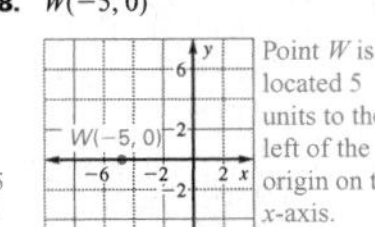

Point W is located 5 units to the left of the origin on the x-axis.

9. $V(-3, -3)$

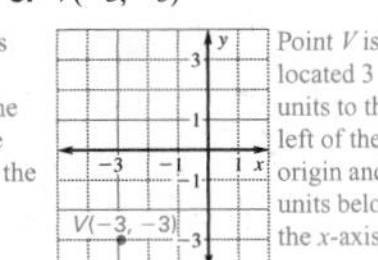

Point V is located 3 units to the left of the origin and 3 units below the x-axis.

Graph the function with the given domain. Then identify the range of the function.

10. $y = x + 4$; domain: $-2, -1, 0, 1, 2$

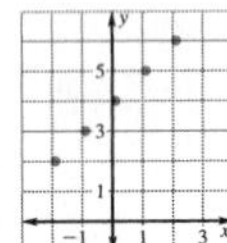

Range: 2, 3, 4, 5, 6

11. $y = 2x - 5$; domain: $-2, -1, 0, 1, 2$

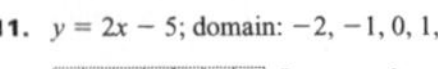

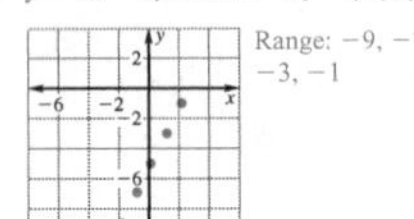

Range: $-9, -7, -5, -3, -1$

LESSON 4.1

LESSON 4.1 Practice B *continued*
For use with pages 206–212

12. $y = 3x - 1$; domain: $-2, -1, 0, 1, 2$

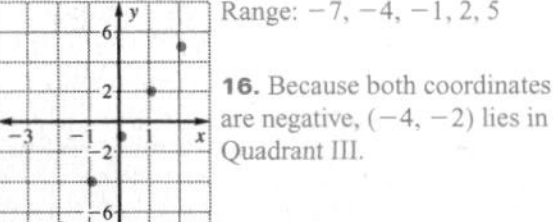

Range: $-7, -4, -1, 2, 5$

16. Because both coordinates are negative, $(-4, -2)$ lies in Quadrant III.

13. $y = 6x - 2$; domain: $-2, -1, 0, 1, 2$

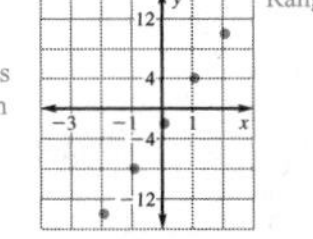

Range: $-14, -8, -2, 4, 10$

14. $y = 4x + 3$; domain: $-2, -1, 0, 1, 2$

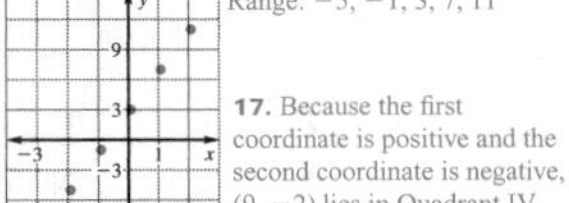

Range: $-5, -1, 3, 7, 11$

17. Because the first coordinate is positive and the second coordinate is negative, $(9, -2)$ lies in Quadrant IV.

15. $y = \frac{1}{2}x + 1$; domain: $-4, -2, 0, 2, 4$

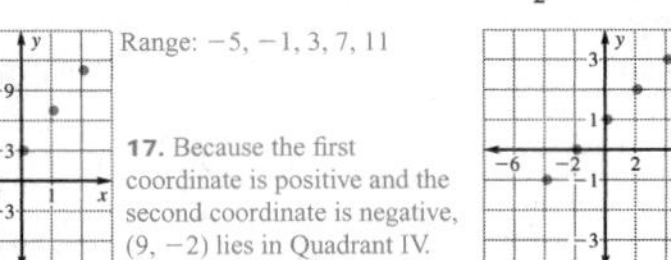

Range: $-1, 0, 1, 2, 3$

18. Because the first coordinate is negative and the second coordinate is positive, $(-1, 8)$ lies in Quadrant II.

Without plotting the point, tell whether it is in Quadrant I, Quadrant II, Quadrant III, or Quadrant IV. *Explain* your reasoning. See above.

16. $(-4, -2)$ **17.** $(9, -2)$ **18.** $(-1, 8)$

19. Jupiter's Moons The table shows some of the moons of Jupiter, their mean distances from Jupiter (in thousand kilometers), and their orbital periods (in Earth days). Graph the data from the table. Does the graph represent a function? Why or why not?

Moon	Io	Thebe	Ganymede	Callisto	Europa
Mean distance (thousand kilometers)	422	222	1070	1883	671
Orbital period (Earth days)	1.8	0.7	7.2	16.7	3.6

The graph represents a function because each input has exactly one output.

20. Cell Phone Use The table shows the number of cellular telephone subscribers in the United States since 1998.

Years since 1998	0	1	2	3	4
Subscribers (millions)	69	86	109	128	141

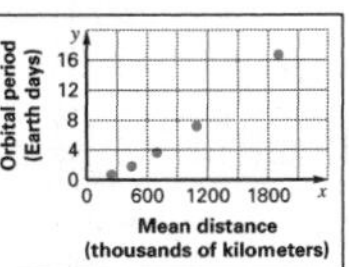

a. Graph the data from the table. Does the graph represent a function? Why or why not?

The graph represents a function because each input has exactly one output.

b. *Describe* any trend in the change in the number of subscribers.

The number of subscribers keeps increasing as time goes on.

LESSON 4.1

LESSON 4.2 Practice B
For use with pages 215–221

Decide which of the two points lies on the graph of the line.

1. $2x + y = 10$ b
a. $(4, 3)$ **b.** $(-4, 18)$

2. $x - 3y = 12$ b
a. $(9, 1)$ **b.** $(6, -2)$

3. $2y - x = 9$ b
a. $(5, 1)$ **b.** $(1, 5)$

Solve the equation for *y*.

4. $-6x + y = 11$ $y = 6x + 11$

5. $8x + 2y = 10$ $y = -4x + 5$

6. $6x - 3y = -9$ $y = 2x + 3$

7. $-4x + 2y = 16$ $y = 2x + 8$

8. $10x - 5y = 25$ $y = 2x - 5$

9. $3x + 2y = -8$ $y = -\frac{3}{2}x - 4$

Graph the equation.

10. $y + x = 14$

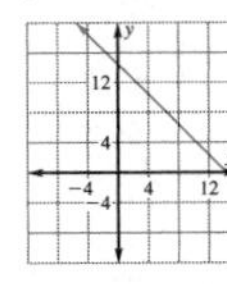

11. $y - 5x = 2$

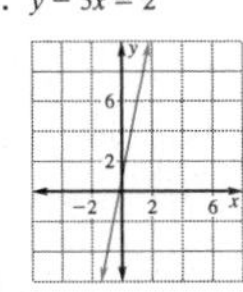

12. $2y - 4x = 10$

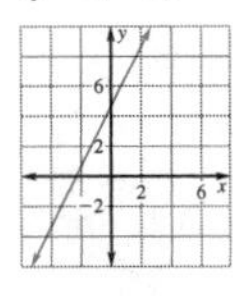

13. $x = -6$

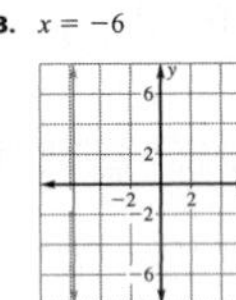

14. $y = 4$

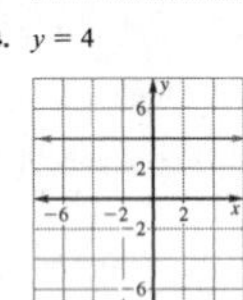

15. $3x - 2y = 0$

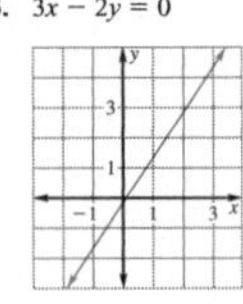

Graph the function with the given domain. Then identify the range of the function.

16. $y = 2x - 2$; domain: $x \geq 0$

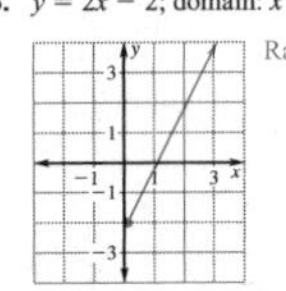

Range: $y \geq -2$

17. $y = -3x + 1$; domain: $x \leq 0$

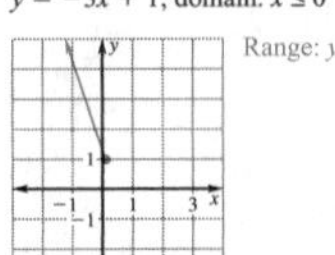

Range: $y \geq 1$

LESSON 4.2

LESSON 4.2 Practice B *continued*
For use with pages 215–221

18. $y = 3$; domain: $x \leq 2$

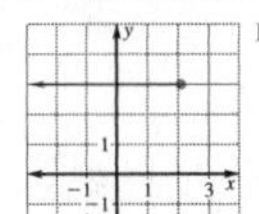

Range: $y = 3$

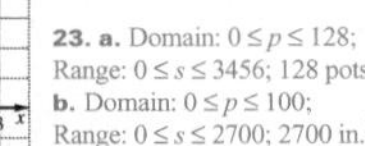

23. a. Domain: $0 \leq p \leq 128$; Range: $0 \leq s \leq 3456$; 128 pots
b. Domain: $0 \leq p \leq 100$; Range: $0 \leq s \leq 2700$; 2700 in.^{3}

19. $y = -1$; domain: $x \geq -1$

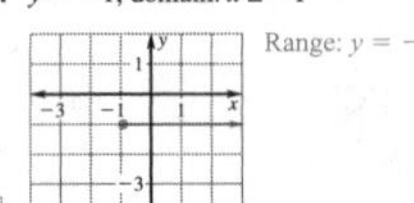

Range: $y = -1$

Identify the range of the function with the given domain.

20. $x + 3y = -8$; domain $x > 0$ $y < -\frac{8}{3}$

21. $6x - 3y = 9$; domain: $x < 1$ $y < -1$

22. Bicycle Rental A bicycle rental shop rents bicycles for \$8 per hour. The total cost c (in dollars) for renting a bicycle h hours is given by the function $c = 8h$. Once you get to the rental shop, you figure you can rent a bicycle for at most 5 hours. Graph the function and identify its domain and range. What is the most that you will pay for renting the bicycle? Domain: $0 \leq h \leq 5$; Range: $0 \leq c \leq 40$; \$40

24. Domain: $m \geq 0$; Range: $C \geq 700$; Rent for one year: Domain: $0 \leq m \leq 12$; Range: $0 \leq C \leq 6700$; The original graph was a ray. By restricting the domain, the graph becomes a line segment.

23. Plant Nursery A gardener at a nursery is filling pots with soil to prepare to transplant seedlings into these larger pots. Each new pot needs about 27 cubic inches of soil. The amount of soil s (in cubic inches) it takes to fill p pots is given by the function $s = 27p$. See above.

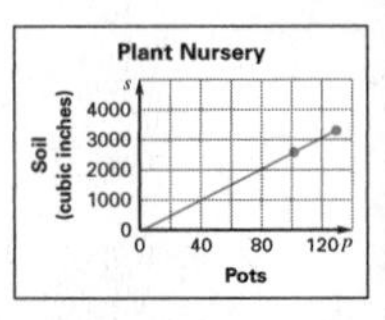

a. The gardener is filling the pots from a bag of soil that contains 3456 cubic inches of soil. Graph the function and identify its domain and range. How many pots can be filled from the bag?

b. Suppose the gardener needs to fill 100 pots. Graph the function on the same coordinate plane in part (a) and identify its domain and range. How much soil (in cubic inches) will the gardener need?

24. Apartment Lease Whenever you sign a lease for an apartment, you typically have to pay a security deposit in case you have caused any wear or tear on the apartment that has to be repaired before it can be re-leased. If no repairs need to be made, you get your entire deposit back. One apartment building has apartments that rent for \$500 a month and a security deposit of \$700. The total cost C (in dollars it costs to rent the apartment for m months is given by the function $C = 500m + 700$. Graph the function and identify its domain and range. Identify the domain and range if a renter only leases an apartment for one year and then moves out and doesn't get the security deposit back. How does this change the appearance of the graph? *Explain*. See above.

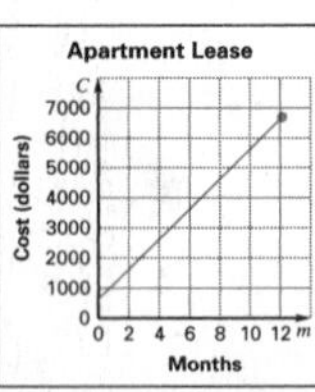

LESSON 4.2

Practice B

For use with pages 225–232

Find the *x*-intercept and the *y*-intercept of the graph of the equation.

1. $x + y = 1$ $x = 1; y = 1$
2. $x - y = -5$ $x = -5; y = 5$
3. $6x - 3y = -3$ $x = -\frac{1}{2}; y = 1$
4. $5x + 10y = 30$ $x = 6; y = 3$
5. $9y - 5x = 20$ $x = -4; y = \frac{20}{9}$
6. $8x - 2y = 16$ $x = 2; y = -8$
7. $7x + 8y = 18$ $x = \frac{18}{7}; y = \frac{9}{4}$
8. $2y - 12x = -6$ $x = \frac{1}{2}; y = -3$
9. $2x - 0.5y = 8$ $x = 4; y = -16$

Draw the line that has the given intercepts.

10. *x*-intercept: 5, *y*-intercept: 4

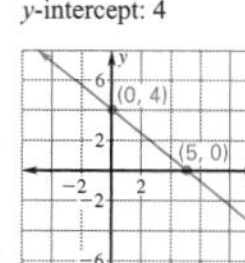

11. *x*-intercept: −1, *y*-intercept: 6

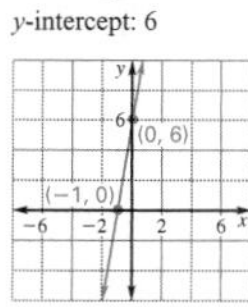

12. *x*-intercept: 2, *y*-intercept: −3

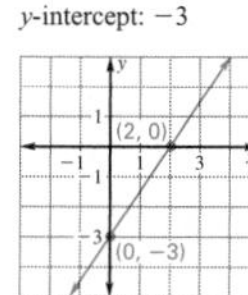

Graph the equation. Label the points where the line crosses the axes.

13. $y = -x - 4$

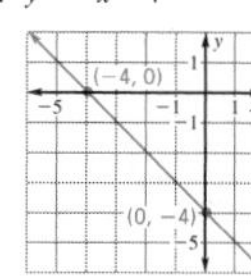

14. $y = 6 + 3x$

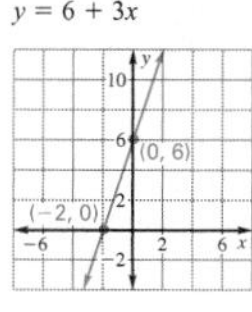

15. $y = 8x - 7$

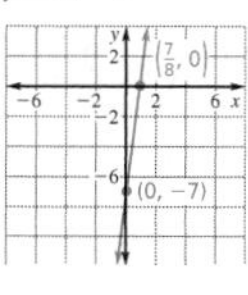

16. $y = 1 - 3x$

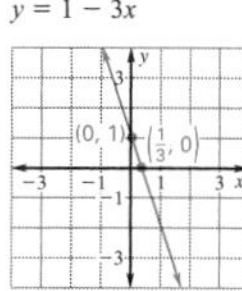

17. $7x - 7y = 42$

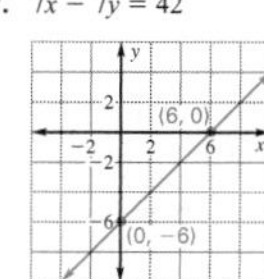

18. $3y + 2x = -5$

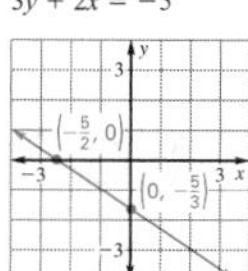

LESSON 4.3 Practice B *continued*

For use with pages 225–232

19. $4x - 9y = 16$

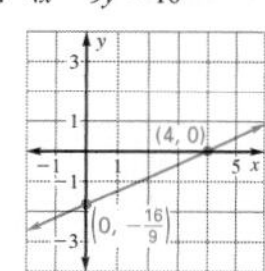

20. $y = 0.5x - 2$

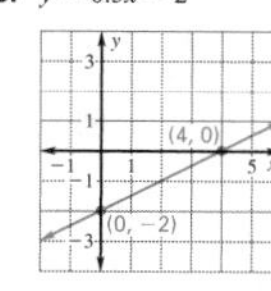

21. $y = 3x + 0.2$

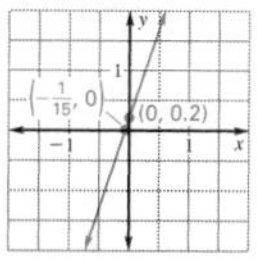

Match the equation with its intercepts.

22. $7y = 28 - 4x$ C
23. $7x = 4y + 28$ A
24. $4y = 7x + 28$ B

A. *x*-intercept: 4, *y*-intercept: −7

B. *x*-intercept: −4, *y*-intercept: 7

C. *x*-intercept: 7, *y*-intercept: 4

25. **Rabbit Hutch** The cage that you keep your rabbit in has a perimeter of 118 inches. Let *x* be the cage's width (in inches) and let *y* be its length (in inches).
   a. Write an equation for the perimeter. $2x + 2y = 118$
   b. Find the intercepts of the graph of the equation you wrote. Then graph the equation. $x = 59; y = 59$

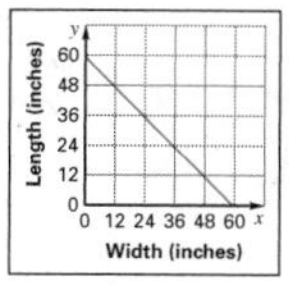

27. b. *x*-intercept: number of calories burnt when the man only bikes; *y*-intercept: number of calories burnt when the man only skates.

26. **Home and Garden Show** Admission to a home and garden show costs \$7 per person during the week and \$9 per person on the weekend. During one week of the show, a total of \$142,506 was paid in admissions. This situation can be represented by the equation $7x + 9y = 142{,}506$ where *x* is the number of tickets sold during the week and *y* is the number of tickets sold on the weekend.

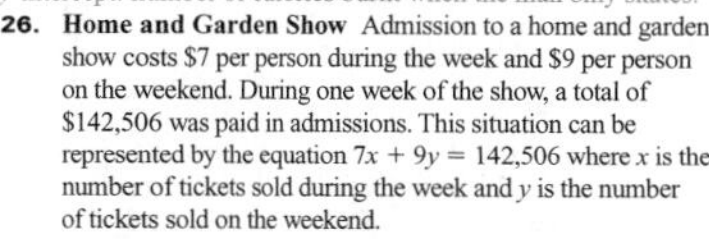

   a. Find the intercepts of the graph of the equation. Graph the equation. $x = 20{,}358; y = 15{,}834$
   b. Give three possibilities for the number of each kind of ticket that could have been sold for the week. Answers will vary.

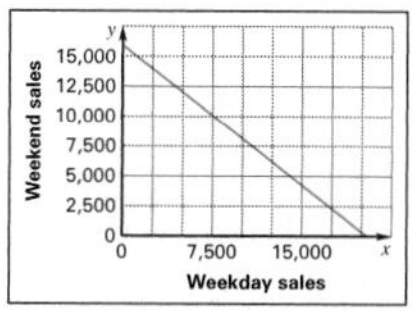

27. **Burning Calories** A man burns 10 calories per minute mountain biking and 7.5 calories per minute in-line skating. His goal is to burn approximately 420 calories daily. This situation can be represented by the equation $10x + 7.5y = 420$ where *x* is the number of minutes spent mountain biking and *y* is the number of minutes spent in-line skating.

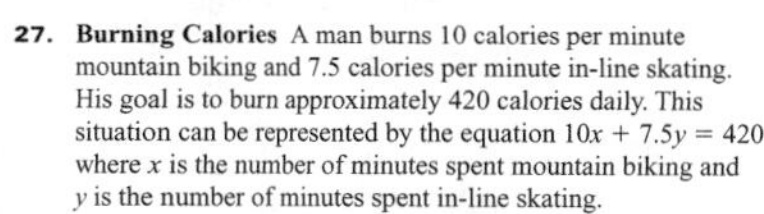

   a. Find the intercepts of the graph of the equation. Graph the equation. $x = 42; y = 56$
   b. What do the intercepts mean in this situation? See above.
   c. What are three possible numbers of minutes of biking and skating the man could do to reach his goal? Answers will vary.

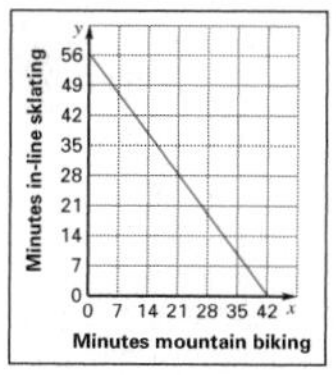

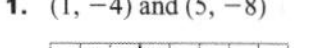

Practice B

For use with pages 235–242

Plot the points and draw a line through them. Without calculating, tell whether the slope of the line is *positive, negative, zero,* or *undefined.*

1. (1, −4) and (5, −8) negative

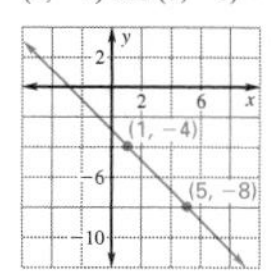

2. (−3, 6) and (−3, 0) undefined

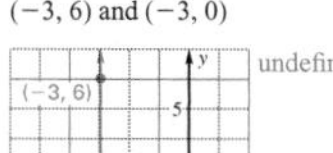

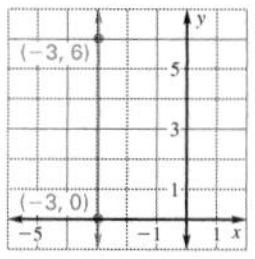

3. (−3, 3) and (7, −1) negative

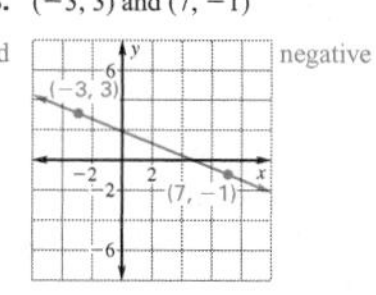

4. (0, −2) and (9, −5) negative

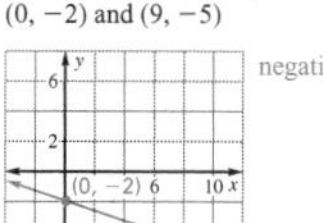

5. (7, 1) and (−2, 1) zero

6. (−3, −1) and (6, −2) negative

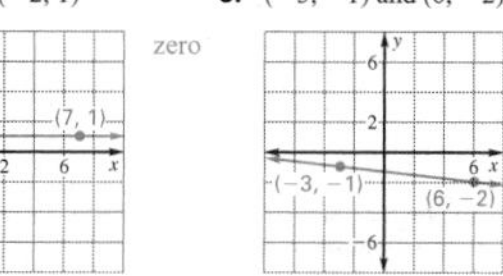

7. (−4, −5) and (−3, −2) positive

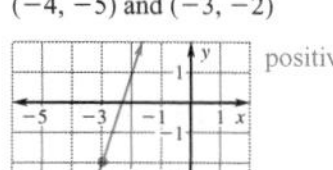

8. (−7, 1) and (−7, −8) undefined

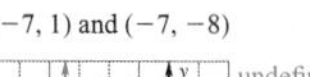

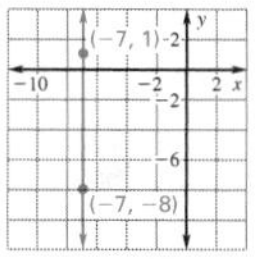

9. (2, −10) and (12, 10) positive

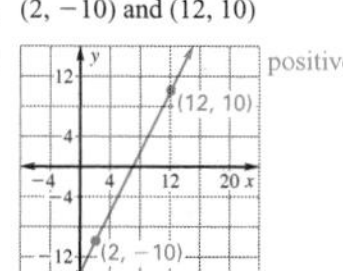

Find the slope of the line that passes through the points.

10. $\frac{2}{3}$

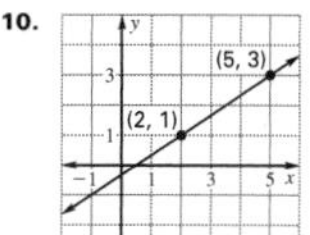

11. $-\frac{4}{5}$

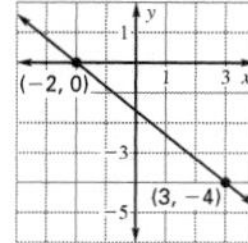

12. 0

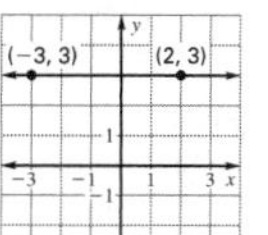

LESSON 4.4 Practice B *continued*

For use with pages 235–242

13. $-\frac{3}{5}$

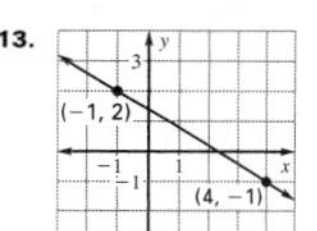

14. $\frac{3}{5}$

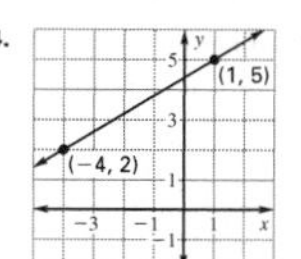

15. undefined

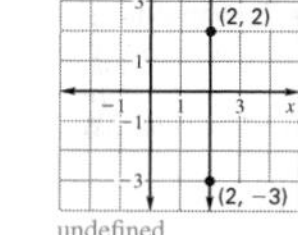

Find the slope of the line that passes through the points.

16. (1, 2) and (7, 7) $\frac{5}{6}$
17. (3, 4) and (−5, 0) $\frac{1}{2}$
18. (5, −2) and (5, 8) undefined
19. (3, 1) and (−5, 3) $-\frac{1}{4}$
20. (−7, 1) and (1, 5) $\frac{1}{2}$
21. (2, −5) and (5, −2) 1
22. (3, 0) and (8, 0) 0
23. (−6, −6) and (−2, −2) 1
24. (−5, −4) and (1, −2) $\frac{1}{3}$

Find the value of *x* or *y* so that the line passing through the two points has the given slope.

25. $(-3, y), (-9, -2); m = 1$ 4
26. $(-1, 4), (x, 3); m = \frac{1}{5}$ −6
27. $(8, 1), (1, y); m = -1$ 8
28. $(x, -7), (1, 2); m = 3$ −2
29. $(9, y), (3, 2); m = \frac{2}{3}$ 6
30. $(7, 5), (x, 2); m = \frac{3}{4}$ 3

31. **Trolley Bus** The table shows the number of trolley buses in operation in the United States during certain years.

Year	1980	1985	1990	1995	2000
Number of buses	823	676	832	885	951

   a. *Describe* the rates of change in the number of buses during the time period. See below.
   b. Determine the time intervals during which the number of trolley buses showed the greatest and least rates of change. Greatest: From 1985 to 1990; Least: From 1990 to 1995

32. **Postage Rate** The graph shows the cost (in dollars) (in dollars) to mail a letter that weighs one ounce during certain years.

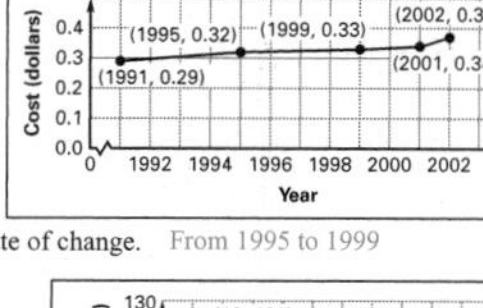

   a. Determine the time interval during which the cost to mail a one-ounce letter showed the greatest rate of change. From 2001 to 2002
   b. Determine the time interval during which the cost to mail a one-ounce letter showed the least rate of change. From 1995 to 1999

33. **Heart Rate** The graph shows the heart rate of a person during 30 minutes of exercise. Give a verbal description of the workout. The person's heartrate increased for 0 to 12 minutes, then it slowly decreased until the end of the workout.

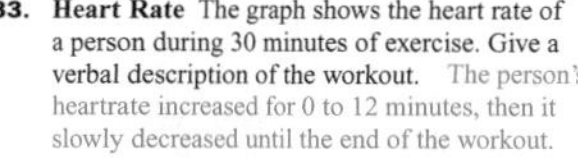

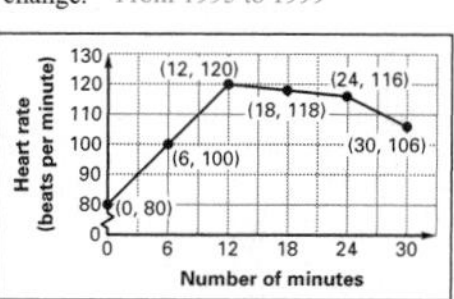

31. a. From 1980 to 1985: −29.4 buses per year; From 1985 to 1990: 31.2 buses per year; From 1990 to 1995: 10.6 buses per year; From 1995 to 2000: 13.2 buses per year; From 1980 to 1985, the number of buses decreased, but then the number of buses increased after that.

LESSON 4.5 Practice B
For use with pages 244–250

Identify the slope and y-intercept of the line with the given equation. See below.

1. $y = 5x - 4$
2. $y = 10 - 4x$
3. $9x + y = 8$
4. $12x + 3y = 9$
5. $6x - 2y = 2$
6. $2x + 5y = 10$
7. $9x - 3y = -1$
8. $4y + 6x = 2$
9. $8y - 2x = 5$
10. $5x + 5y = 3$
11. $-4y = 16$
12. $6x = 12$

Match the equation with its graph.

13. $3x + 4y = 12$ C
14. $3x + 4y = -12$ B
15. $3x - 4y = 12$ A

A. 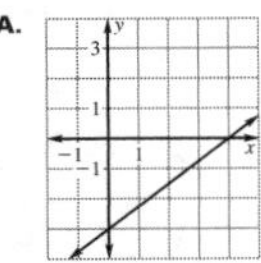

B. 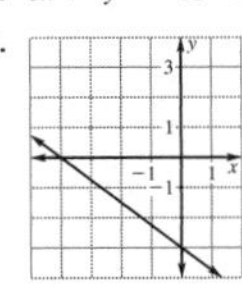

C. 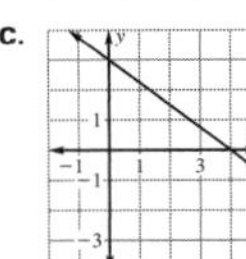

Graph the equation.

16. $y = -7x + 2$

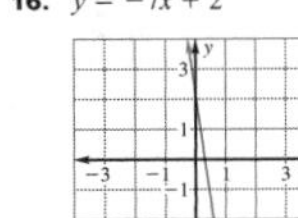

17. $y = 5x + 4$

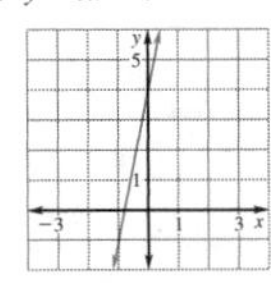

18. $y = -x + 9$

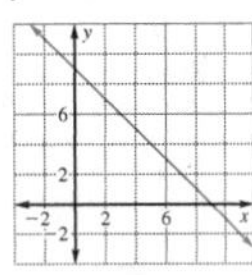

19. $y = \frac{1}{5}x$

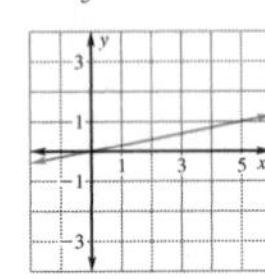

20. $y = -\frac{2}{3}x + 1$

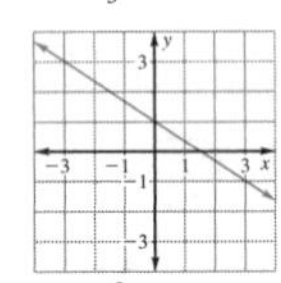

21. $y = \frac{4}{3}x - 5$

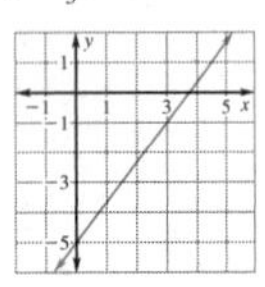

1. Slope: 5; y-intercept: −4
2. Slope: −4; y-intercept: 10
3. Slope: −9; y-intercept: 8
4. Slope: −4; y-intercept: 3
5. Slope: 3; y-intercept: −1
6. Slope: $-\frac{2}{5}$; y-intercept: 2
7. Slope: 3, y-intercept: $\frac{1}{3}$
8. Slope: $-\frac{3}{2}$; y-intercept: $\frac{1}{2}$
9. Slope: $\frac{1}{4}$; y-intercept: $\frac{5}{8}$
10. Slope: −1; y-intercept: $\frac{3}{5}$
11. Slope: 0; y-intercept: −4
12. Slope: undefined; y-intercept: none

LESSON 4.5 Practice B *continued*
For use with pages 244–250

Determine which lines are parallel.

22. 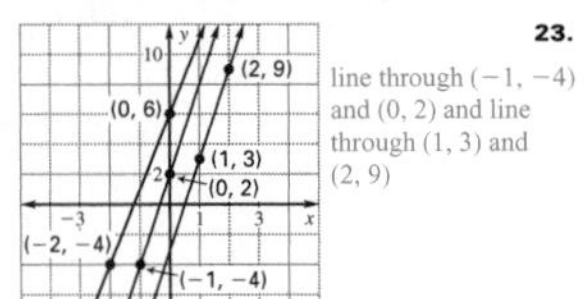
line through (−1, −4) and (0, 2) and line through (1, 3) and (2, 9)

23. 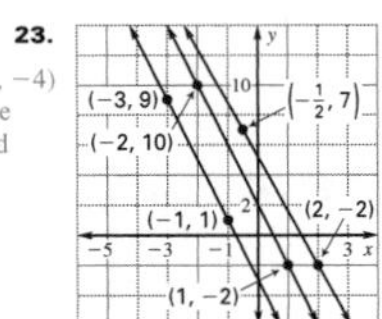
line through (−3, 9) and (−1, 1) and line through (−2, 10) and (1, −2)

Tell whether the graphs of the two equations are parallel lines.

24. $y = 8x - 3, 8x + y = 3$ no
25. $2x + y = 5, -6 + 2x = y$ no
26. $2x + y = 5, y = 0.5x - 3$ no
27. $y = -0.6x + 2, 5y + 3x = 8$ yes
28. $8x + 3y = 9, 3y - 4 = 8x$ yes
29. $10x + 2y = 7, 5x - y = 6$ no

30. **Squirrels** A family of squirrels takes up residence in the roof of your house. You call a company to get rid of the squirrels. The company traps the squirrels and then releases them in a wooded area. The company charges \$30 to drop off the traps and then charges \$15 for each squirrel it traps. The total cost C (in dollars) is given by the equation $C = 30 + 15s$ where s is the number of squirrels that are taken away.

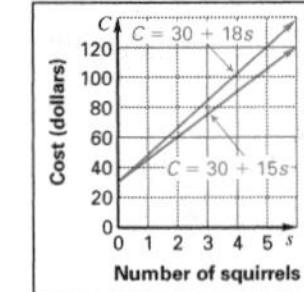

a. Graph the equation.
b. Suppose the company raises its fee to \$18 to take away each squirrel so that the total cost for s squirrels is given by the equation $C = 30 + 18s$. Graph the equation in the same coordinate plane as the equation in part (a).
c. How much more does it cost for the company to trap 4 squirrels after the fee is raised? \$12

31. **Water Usage** A new toilet model has two different flush settings in order to conserve water. One setting uses 1.6 gallons of water per flush and the other setting uses 0.8 gallon of water per flush. The total amount w (in gallons) of water used in the first setting is given by the equation $w = 1.6f$ where f is the number of times the toilet is flushed. The total amount of water used in the second setting is given by the equation $w = 0.8f$.

a. Graph both equations in the same coordinate plane. What do the slopes and the w-intercepts mean in this situation?
b. How much more water is used by the first setting if the toilet is flushed 10 times? 8 gal

31. a. The slopes indicate the number of gallons of water used per flush. The w-intercepts show how much water is used when the toilet is not flushed at all.

LESSON 4.6 Practice B
For use with pages 253–259

Tell whether the equation represents direct variation. If so, identify the constant of variation.

1. $y = 8x$ yes; 8
2. $y = 2x + 1$ no
3. $3x + y = 6$ no

Graph the direct variation equation.

4. $y = 9x$

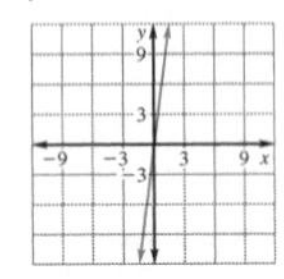

5. $y = -7x$

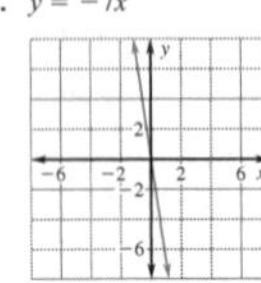

6. $3y = 4x$

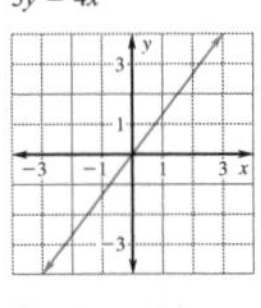

7. $4y = -12x$

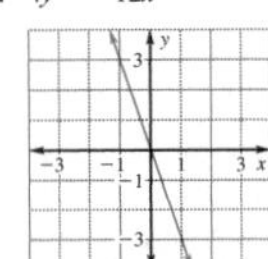

8. $8y = x$

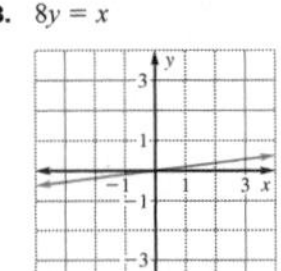

9. $8y = 6x$

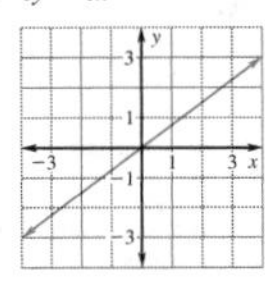

The graph of a direct variation equation is shown. Write the direct variation equation. Then find the value of y when x = 10.

10. 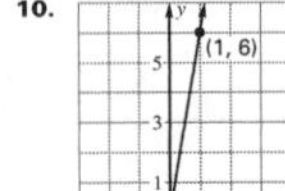
$y = 6x$; 60

11. 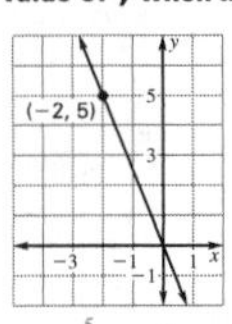
$y = -\frac{5}{2}x$; −25

12. 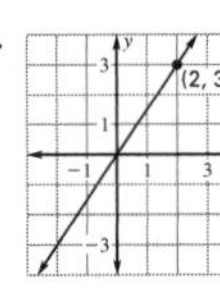
$y = \frac{3}{2}x$; 15

13. 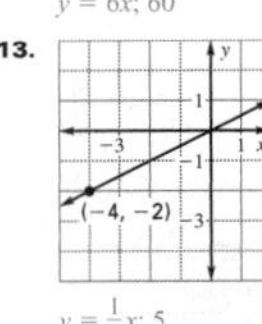
$y = \frac{1}{2}x$; 5

14. 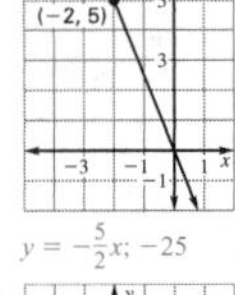
$y = \frac{2}{3}x$; $\frac{20}{3}$

15. 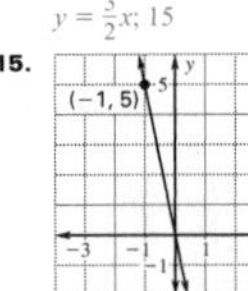
$y = -5x$; −50

LESSON 4.6 Practice B *continued*
For use with pages 253–259

16. 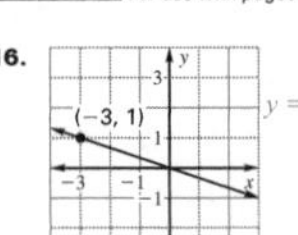
$y = -\frac{1}{3}x$; $-\frac{10}{3}$

17. 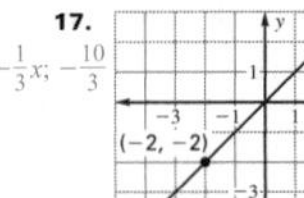
$y = x$; 10

18. 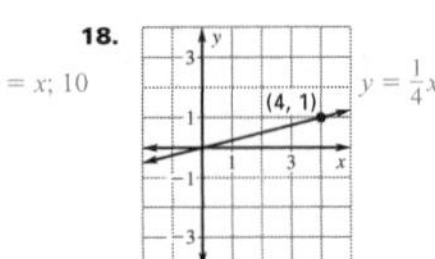
$y = \frac{1}{4}x$; $\frac{5}{2}$

Tell whether the table represents direct variation. If so, write the direct variation equation.

19.

x	0.5	3	−2	1	−8
y	9	54	−36	18	−144

yes; $y = 18x$

20.

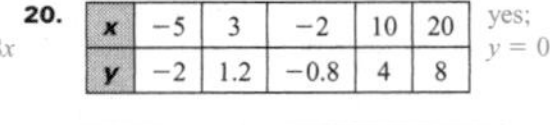

x	−5	3	−2	10	20
y	−2	1.2	−0.8	4	8

yes; $y = 0.4x$

21.

x	8	2	−4	−0.5	14
y	7	28	7	−112	4

no

22.

x	−0.2	−2	1	12	18
y	30	3	−6	−0.5	3

no

Given that y varies directly with x, use the specified values to write a direct variation equation that relates x and y.

23. $x = 24, y = 3$ $y = \frac{1}{8}x$
24. $x = -16, y = -4$ $y = \frac{1}{4}x$
25. $x = 28, y = -4$ $y = -\frac{1}{7}x$
26. $x = 5, y = -30$ $y = -6x$
27. $x = \frac{1}{6}, y = 1$ $y = 6x$
28. $x = 8, y = -3$ $y = -\frac{3}{8}x$
29. $x = 6, y = 102$ $y = 17x$
30. $x = -8, y = 64$ $y = -8x$
31. $x = 15, y = 9$ $y = \frac{3}{5}x$

32. **Hooke's Law** The force F required to stretch a spring varies directly with the amount the spring is stretched s. Eight pounds is needed to stretch a spring 8 inches.
a. Write a direct variation equation that relates F and s. $F = s$
b. How much force is required to stretch a spring 25 inches? 25 lb

33. **Basement Waterproofing** One way to keep moisture out of your basement is to paint the walls with a waterproof paint. The number g (of gallons) of paint you need varies directly with the area A of the basement. One gallon of paint covers 100 square feet.
a. Write a direct variation equation that relates g and A. $g = 0.01A$
b. How many gallons do you need to cover 530 square feet? 5.3 gal
c. How many square feet does 8.5 gallons of paint cover? 850 ft²

34. **Downloading Files** The table shows the amount of time t (in seconds) it takes to download a file of size s (in kilobytes).

Time, t (sec)	File size, s (kb)
15	420
30	840
45	1260

a. *Explain* why s varies directly with t.
b. Write a direct variation equation that relates s and t. $s = 28t$
c. How long will it take to download an 800-kilobyte file? Round your answer to the nearest second. about 29 sec

34. a. Because the ratios for each data pair is 28, s varies directly with t.

LESSON 4.7

Practice B

For use with pages 262–268

Evaluate the function when $x = -3$, 0, and 2.

1. $f(x) = 15x + 4$ −41; 4; 34
2. $g(x) = -9x + 1$ 28; 1; −17
3. $p(x) = -7x - 5$ 16; −5; −19
4. $h(x) = 3.25x$ −9.75; 0; 6.5
5. $m(x) = -4.4x$ 13.2; 0; −8.8
6. $f(x) = 6.1x - 3.3$ −21.6; −3.3; 8.9
7. $s(x) = \frac{4}{5}x - 2$ $-\frac{22}{5}$; −2; $-\frac{2}{5}$
8. $d(x) = -\frac{5}{3}x + 4$ 9; 4; $\frac{2}{3}$
9. $h(x) = \frac{3}{8}x - 6$ $-\frac{57}{8}$; −6; $-\frac{21}{4}$
10. $f(x) = -2.5x + 7$ 14.5; 7; 2
11. $h(x) = 4.2x - 3$ −15.6; −3; 5.4
12. $g(x) = 6.1x - 2.2$ −20.5; −2.2; 10

Find the value of x so that the function has the given value.

13. $f(x) = 4x - 2$; 18   5
14. $n(x) = 7x + 4$; 39   5
15. $q(x) = 6 - 5x$; 21   −3
16. $g(x) = -3x + 8$; 14   −2
17. $h(x) = 9x - 13$; 23   4
18. $m(x) = 12x - 30$; 30   5
19. $s(x) = -4x - 9$; 3   −3
20. $m(x) = 8.5x - 3$; 82   10
21. $p(x) = -2.4x + 6$; 18   −5
21. $d(x) = 3.3x - 1.1$; 31.9   10

Graph the function. *Compare* your graph to the graph of $f(x) = x$.

23. $h(x) = x - 4$

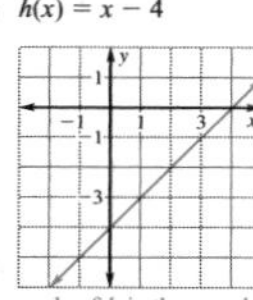

The graph of h is the graph of f shifted down 4 units.

24. $g(x) = x + 7$

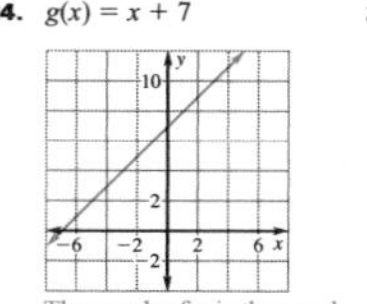

The graph of g is the graph of f shifted up 7 units.

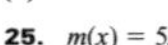

25. $m(x) = 5x$

The graph of m is a dilation of the graph of f using a scale factor of 5.

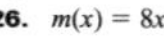

26. $m(x) = 8x$

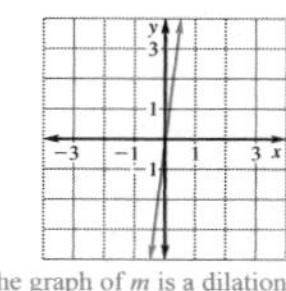

The graph of m is a dilation of the graph of f using a scale factor of 8.

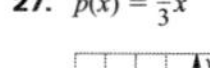

27. $p(x) = \frac{1}{3}x$

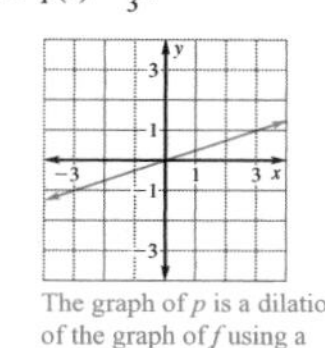

The graph of p is a dilation of the graph of f using a scale factor of $\frac{1}{3}$.

28. $n(x) = -2x$

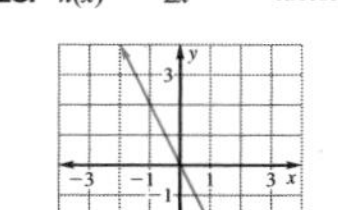

The graph of n is a dilation of the graph of f using a scale factor of 2 and a reflection in the x-axis.

LESSON 4.7

LESSON 4.7

Practice B *continued*

For use with pages 262–268

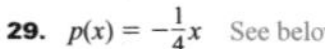

29. $p(x) = -\frac{1}{4}x$ See below.

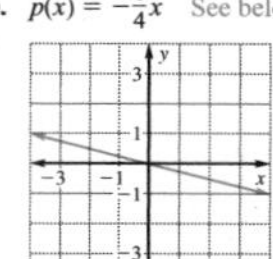

30. $d(x) = x - 1.5$ See below.

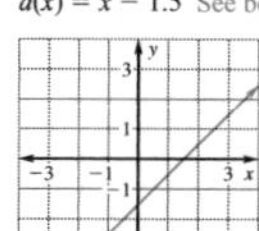

31. $g(x) = x + 4.5$ See below.

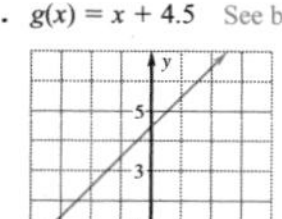

Match the function with the description of its graph in relation to the graph of $f(x) = x$.

32. $g(x) = 4x$ C
33. $g(x) = x + 4$ A
34. $g(x) = x - 4$ B

A. graph of f shifted up 4 units
B. graph of f shifted down 4 units
C. graph of f dilated by factor of 4

35. **Video Games** The number of hours people in the United States spend playing video games each year from 1998 to 2001 can be modeled by the function $f(x) = 11.9x + 46.4$ where x is the number of years since 1998. a. Domain: $0 \le x \le 3$ Range: $46.4 \le f(x) \le 82.1$
   a. Graph the function and identify its domain and range.
   b. Find the value of $f(x)$ when $x = 2$. *Explain* what the solution means in this situation. b. $f(2) = 70.2$; In 2000, people spent 70.2 hours each year playing video games.
   c. Find the value of x so that $f(x) = 60$. *Explain* what the solution means in this situation. See below.

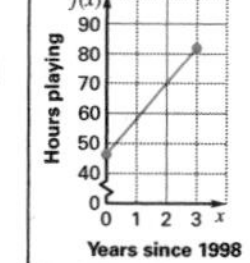

36. **Pool Membership** A pool membership during the summer costs \$7 per week. The total cost of a membership is given by $f(x) = 7x$. The pool also rents out lockers for \$2 per week. The total cost of a membership and a rental is given by $g(x) = 9x$.
   a. Graph both functions. How is the graph of f related to the graph of g? See below.
   b. What is the difference between a 12-week membership if you get a locker and if you don't? *Explain* how you got your answer. \$24; Because the difference is \$2 per week, multiply 2 by 12.

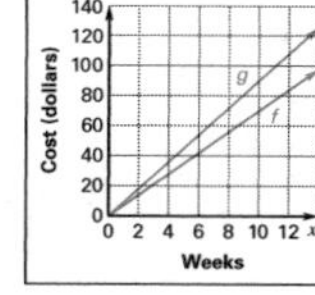

29. The graph of p is a dilation of the graph of f using a scale factor of $\frac{1}{4}$ and the reflection of f in the x-axis.

30. The graph of d is the graph of f shifted down 1.5 units.

31. The graph of s is the graph of f shifted up 4.5 units.

35. c. $f(1.1) \approx 60$; Near the beginning of 1999, people spent 60 hours each year playing video games.

36. a. The graphs have the same y-intercept but the slope of g is steeper than the slope of f.

LESSON 4.7

CHAPTER 4 Quiz 1
For use after Lessons 4.1–4.3

Plot the point in a coordinate plane. Describe the location of the point.

1. (1, −4)
2. (−3, −2)

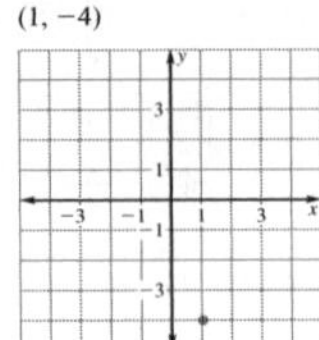

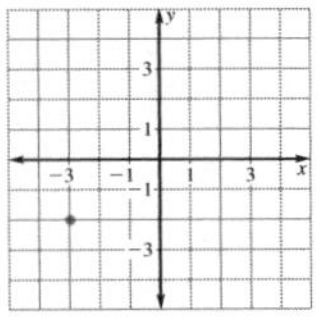

Graph the equation.

3. $x = 3$
4. $y = -3$

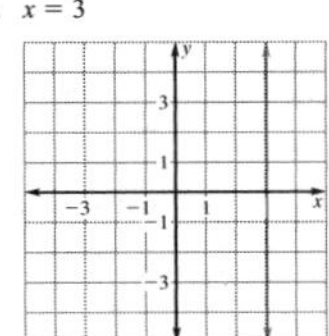

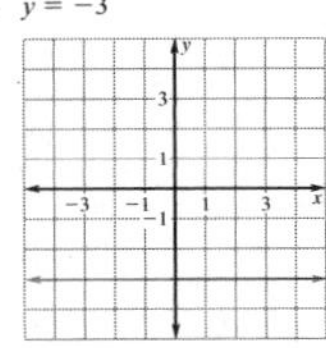

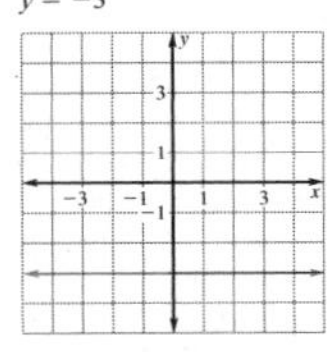

5. $y - 3x = 1$

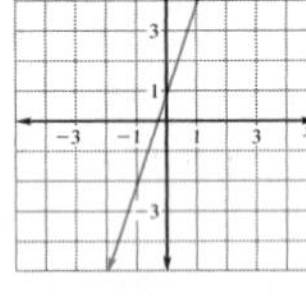

Find the *x*-intercept and the *y*-intercept of the graph of the equation.

6. $y = 7x - 3$
7. $-4y + x = 8$
8. $2x - 5y = 20$

9. Your school is selling tickets for a student concert. The total ticket sales can be modeled by the equation $90 = 6a + 3s$ where *a* is the number of adult tickets sold and *s* is the number of student tickets sold. Find the intercepts of the graph of the equation.

Answers

1. See left. Quadrant IV
2. See left. Quadrant III
3. See left.
4. See left.
5. See left.
6. *x*-intercept: $\left(\frac{3}{7}, 0\right)$; *y*-intercept: $(0, -3)$
7. *x*-intercept: $(8, 0)$; *y*-intercept: $(0, -2)$
8. *x*-intercept: $(10, 0)$; *y*-intercept: $(0, -4)$
9. *a*-intercept: $(15, 0)$; *s*-intercept: $(0, 30)$

CHAPTER 4 Quiz 2
For use after Lessons 4.4–4.5

Find the slope of the line that passes through the points.

1. (−4, 3) and (7, 5)
2. (1, 2) and (−2, 2)
3. (4, −1) and (4, 3)

Identify the slope and the *y*-intercept of the line with the given equation.

4. $y = 7x + 2$
5. $10x - 5y = 30$
6. $3x - 8y = -24$

Graph the equation.

7. $y = -\frac{7}{2}x - 1$
8. $-4x + 6y = 12$

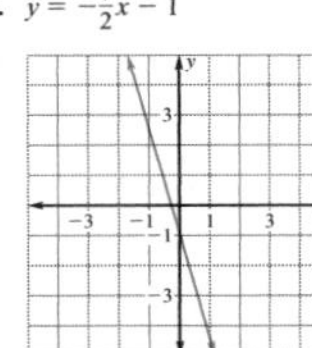

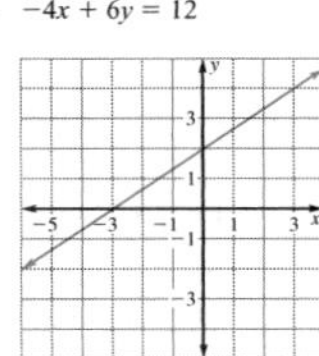

9. $9x + 2y = -7$

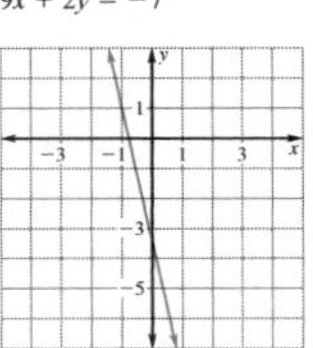

10. A campsite charges $12 per day for the site rental and $8 for parking. The total campsite charge *C* (in dollars) is given by $C = 12d + 8$ where *d* is the number of days that the site is rented. Graph the equation.

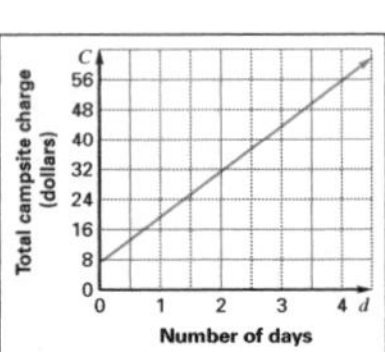

Answers

1. $\frac{2}{11}$
2. 0
3. undefined
4. 7; (0, 2)
5. 2; (0, −6)
6. $\frac{3}{8}$; (0, 3)
7. See left.
8. See left.
9. See left.
10. See left.

CHAPTER 4 Quiz 3
For use after Lessons 4.6–4.7

Given that *y* varies directly with *x*, use the specified values to write a direct variation equation that relates *x* and *y*.

1. $x = 4, y = 12$
2. $x = 6, y = 8$
3. $x = 3, y = -6$

Evaluate the function.

4. $f(x) = 7x + 2$ when $x = 5$
5. $h(x) = 0.3x + 9.7$ when $x = 15$
6. $p(x) = \frac{2}{5}x + \frac{1}{2}$ when $x = 3$

Graph the function. Compare the graph to the graph of $f(x) = x$.

7. $p(x) = x + 4$
8. $g(x) = 3x$

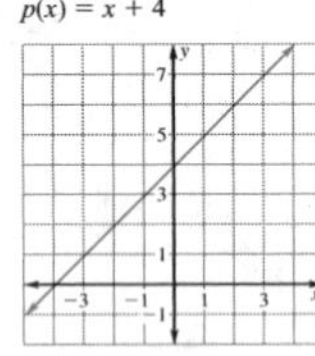

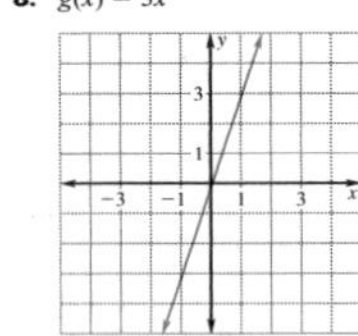

9. $h(x) = \frac{1}{2}x$

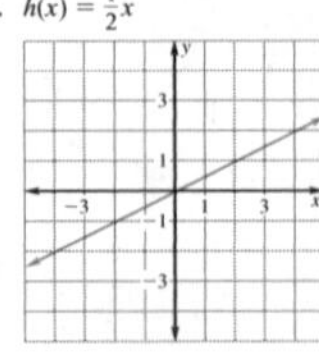

10. The area *A* of a square varies directly as the square of the side *s*. Write a direct variation equation that relates *s* and *A*.

Answers

1. $y = 3x$
2. $y = \frac{4}{3}x$
3. $y = -2x$
4. 37
5. 14.2
6. $\frac{17}{10}$
7. See left. Have the same slope; lines are parallel; the *y*-intercept of the graph of *p* is 4 more than the *y*-intercept of the graph of *f*.
8. See left. Slope of the graph of *g* > the slope of the graph of *f*; graph of *g* rises faster from left to right; the *y*-intercept for both graphs is 0; both lines pass through the origin.
9. See left. Slope of the graph of *h* < the slope of the graph of *f*; graph of *h* rises more slowly from left to right; the *y*-intercept for both graphs is 0; both lines pass through the origin.
10. $A = ks^2$

CHAPTER 4 Chapter Test
For use after Chapter 4

Plot the point in the coordinate plane. Describe the location of the point.

1. $A(-1, 3)$
2. $B(4, 0)$
3. $C(2, -2)$
4. $D(-1, -1)$

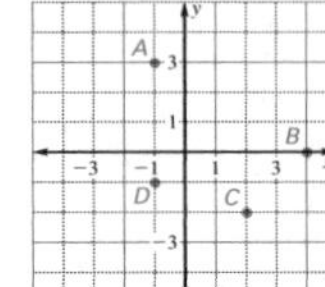

Graph the equation.

5. $3x - y = 5$
6. $3y - 2x = -3$
7. $y = -3$

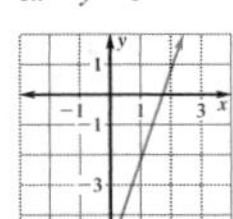

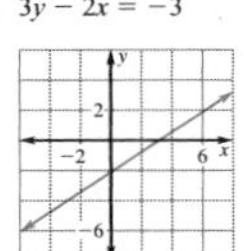

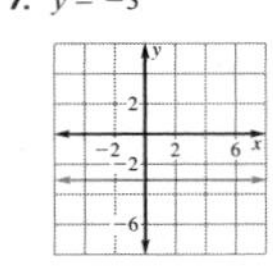

Find the *x*-intercept and the *y*-intercept of the graph of the equation.

8. $6x - 4y = 12$
9. $-2x + 5y = -10$
10. $y = \frac{1}{2}x - 2$

In Exercises 11–16, use the following information.

The graph shows the distance of a car traveling along a straight road for 8 hours. A positive velocity is motion to the right, and a negative velocity is motion to the left.

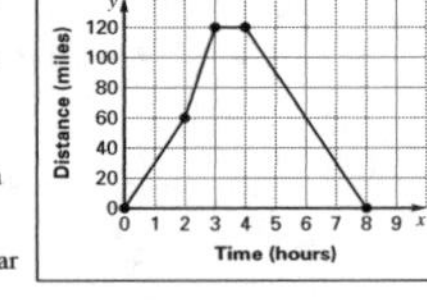

11. Determine the rates of change in distance with respect to time.
12. Between what two times is the car not moving?
13. Between what two times is the car traveling to the right?
14. Between what two times is the car traveling to the left.
15. Between what two times is the car traveling the fastest?
16. What does the *x*-intercept represent in this situation?

Answers

1. See left. Quadrant II
2. See left. *x*-axis
3. See left. Quadrant IV
4. See left. Quadrant III
5. See left.
6. See left.
7. See left.
8. *x*-intercept = 2, *y*-intercept = −3
9. *x*-intercept = 5, *y*-intercept = −2
10. *x*-intercept = 4, *y*-intercept = −2
11. 30 mi/h, 60 mi/h, 0 mi/h, −30 mi/h
12. hours 3 and 4
13. first 3 hours
14. hours 4 and 8
15. hours 2 and 3
16. After 8 hours, the car returns to its starting position.

CHAPTER 4 **Chapter Test B** *continued*
For use after Chapter 4

Identify the slope and *y*-intercept of the line with the given equation.

17. $y = 8x - 3$ **18.** $2x + 9y = 9$ **19.** $-3x - 4y = -16$

Determine whether the equation represents direct variation. If so, identify the constant of variation.

20. $y = -x$ **21.** $4x - 3y = 0$ **22.** $2x + y = 4$

Complete the table for the function.

23. $f(x) = 6 + x$

x	−1	−4	0
f(*x*)	5	2	6

24. $f(x) = -\frac{7}{2}x$

x	0	2	−4
f(*x*)	0	−7	14

In Exercises 25–27, use the following information.

An advertising company charges $150,000 each time a 30-second commercial is aired. The cost (in thousands of dollars) to produce the commercial and air it *x* times is given by the function $C(x) = 150x + 300$.

25. Graph the function.

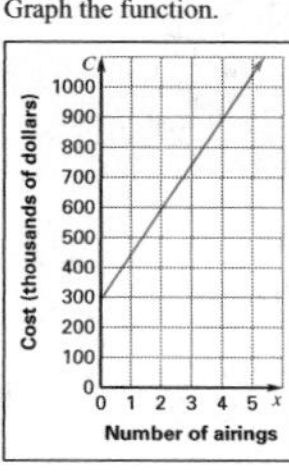

26. Identify the domain and the range of the function.

27. How many times could the station air the commercial if it wants to spend $900,000?

Answers

17. $m = 8, b = -3$
18. $m = -\frac{2}{9}, b = 1$
19. $m = -\frac{3}{4}, b = 4$
20. yes; $a = -1$
21. yes; $a = \frac{4}{3}$
22. no
23. See left.
24. See left.
25. See left.
26. domain: $x \geq 0$; range: $C \geq 300$
27. 4 times

CHAPTER 4 **Standardized Test**
For use after Chapter 4

Multiple Choice

1. A point is located 5 units to the right of the origin and 4 units down. What are the coordinates of the point? D

Ⓐ (5, 4) Ⓑ (−4, 5) Ⓒ (4, 5) Ⓓ (5, −4)

2. In which quadrant is the point (−2, 3) located? B

Ⓐ Quadrant I Ⓑ Quadrant II Ⓒ Quadrant III Ⓓ Quadrant IV

3. Which ordered pair is a solution of $5x + 4y = 18$? A

Ⓐ (−2, 7) Ⓑ (8, 2) Ⓒ (−3, 6) Ⓓ (2, 4)

4. Which statement is true for the function whose graph is shown? B

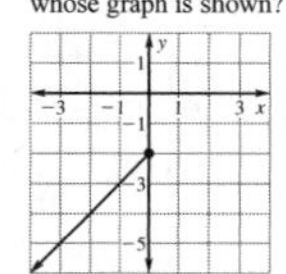

Ⓐ The domain is unrestricted.
Ⓑ The domain is $x \leq 0$.
Ⓒ The range is unrestricted.
Ⓓ The range is $y \leq 0$.

5. What is the *x*-intercept of the equation $3x - 2y = -12$? C

Ⓐ (0, 6) Ⓑ (0, −4) Ⓒ (−4, 0) Ⓓ (6, 0)

6. The slope of the line that passes through the points (−2, 4) and (−3, 7) is __?__. A

Ⓐ negative Ⓑ positive Ⓒ undefined Ⓓ zero

7. What is the slope of the line that passes through the points (5, −3) and (−7, 5)? B

Ⓐ $-\frac{1}{6}$ Ⓑ $-\frac{2}{3}$ Ⓒ −1 Ⓓ $-\frac{3}{2}$

8. What is the value of *y* for the line that has a slope of $-\frac{3}{2}$ and passes through the points (3, 5) and (7, *y*)? C

Ⓐ −11 Ⓑ −10 Ⓒ −1 Ⓓ 20

9. What is the slope of the line $y = \frac{1}{2}x + 2$? C

Ⓐ −2 Ⓑ $-\frac{1}{2}$ Ⓒ $\frac{1}{2}$ Ⓓ 2

10. What is the *y*-intercept of the line $5x - 4y = -12$? D

Ⓐ −3 Ⓑ $-\frac{5}{4}$ Ⓒ $\frac{5}{4}$ Ⓓ 3

11. Which line is parallel to the line $y = 4x - 2$? B

Ⓐ $12x - 4y = 8$ Ⓑ $4y - 16x = 10$ Ⓒ $5y - 25x = -10$ Ⓓ $-x + 4y = -8$

12. What is the value of *m* if Lines 1 and 2 are parallel? A

Line 1: (−2, −5) and (0, 0)
Line 2: (*m*, 12) and (−3, 2)

Ⓐ 1 Ⓑ 5 Ⓒ 7 Ⓓ 22

13. Which equation represents direct variation? A

Ⓐ $-2x = 3y$ Ⓑ $5y - x = 4$ Ⓒ $12x - 3 = 4y$ Ⓓ $5x - 2y + 3 = 0$

14. What is the constant of variation in the equation $5x - 3y = 0$? B

Ⓐ −3 Ⓑ $-\frac{5}{3}$ Ⓒ $-\frac{3}{5}$ Ⓓ 5

CHAPTER 4 **Standardized Test** *continued*
For use after Chapter 4

15. The graph of which function is shown? A

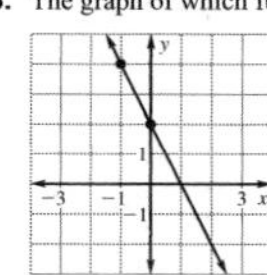

Ⓐ $f(x) = -2x + 2$ Ⓑ $f(x) = 2x + 2$ Ⓒ $f(x) = -2x - 2$ Ⓓ $f(x) = 2x - 2$

16. Examine the problem below. Which line contains an error? B

$g(x) = -\frac{2}{3}x - \frac{5}{6}$

$g(36) = -\frac{2}{3}(36) - \frac{5}{6}$ Line 1

$g(36) = -24 - \frac{5}{6}$ Line 2

$g(36) = -\frac{152}{6} - \frac{5}{6}$ Line 3

$g(36) = \frac{157}{6}$ Line 4

$g(36) = 26\frac{1}{6}$ Line 5

Ⓐ Line 2 Ⓑ Line 3 Ⓒ Line 4 Ⓓ Line 5

Gridded Answer

17. What is the value of $f(-3)$ if $f(x) = -4.2x + 6$?

18.6

18. a.

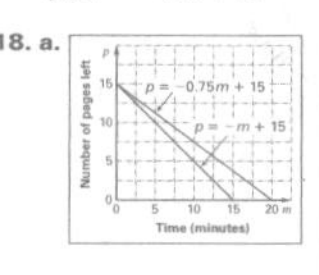

Short Response

18. You and a classmate are reading a short story that is 15 pages long. You read at a rate of 1 page per minute. Your classmate reads at a rate of 0.75 page per minute. The models below give the number of *p* pages you and your classmate have left to read after reading for *m* minutes.

You: $p = -m + 15$

Classmate: $p = -0.75m + 15$

a. Graph both equations on the same coordinate plane. See below.

b. How many more minutes would it take your classmate to read the short story than you? *Explain* how you used the graph to determine this information. 5 min

Extended Response

19. The table shows the difference *d* (in cents) of this year's average monthly gas price and the previous year's average monthly gas price. For example, in month 1, $d = -2$. So, the average gas price was 2 cents below the previous year's gas price.

Month *M*	1	2	3	4	5	6
Difference *d* (in cents)	−2	5	10	5	0	9

a. *Explain* how you know the table represents a function.

b. Graph the function and identify its domain and range.

c. What does a point in Quadrant IV mean in terms of this situation?

19. a. This table represents a function because for every month *M* there is exactly one difference *d*.
b.

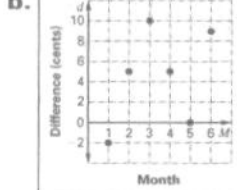

Domain = 1, 2, 3, 4, 5, and 6; Range = −2, 0, 5, 9, and 10 **c.** A point in Quadrant IV represents a decrease in the price of gas as compared to the average price that same month in the previous year.

CHAPTER 4 **Alternative Assessment and Math Journal**
For use after Chapter 4

Journal **1.** List the three different methods that can be used to graph a linear equation. Then briefly describe how to graph $2x + y = 3$ using each method.

Multi-Step Problem **2.** You are planning an ornamental garden that has a total area of 200 square feet. There are two sizes of ornamental plants you have chosen for your garden. Each small plant requires 2.5 square feet of space and each large plant requires 8 square feet of space. This situation can be modeled by the equation $2.5x + 8y = 200$ where *x* is the number of small plants and *y* is the number of large plants to be placed in the garden.

a. Find the intercepts of the graph of the equation.
b. Graph the equation.
c. What do the intercepts mean in this situation?
d. What are three possible numbers of small plants and large plants that you can plant in the garden?
e. What is the slope of this line?
f. Write the equation in slope-intercept form.
g. You decide to enlarge the space for the garden to a total of 240 square feet which means the new model will be $2.5x + 8y = 240$. Graph this equation on the same coordinate plane you used in part (b).
h. As you compare the two graphs, did increasing the size of the garden change the slope or *y*-intercept? Describe any changes that occurred.

1. Complete answers should include: a list of the three methods that can be used to graph a linear equation: make a table, use intercepts, and use the slope and *y*-intercept; an explanation of how to graph $2x + y = 3$ using each method. **2. a.** *x*-intercept: 80; *y*-intercept: 25 **b.**

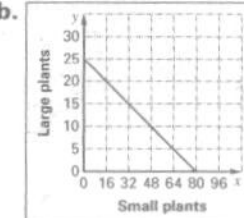

c. The *x*-intercept represents the number of small plants that can be placed in the garden if no large plants are used. The *y*-intercept represents the number of large plants that can be placed in the garden if no small plants are used. **d.** *Sample answer:* 16 small and 20 large; 32 small and 15 large; 48 small and 10 large **e.** $-\frac{5}{16}$ **f.** $y = -\frac{5}{16}x + 25$

g.

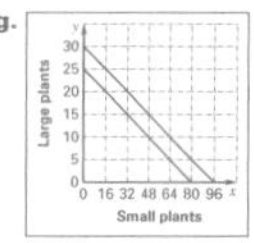

h. The slope remained the same, but the *y*-intercept increased by 5 units.

PLAN AND PREPARE

Main Ideas

In Chapter 4, students learn how to plot points in a coordinate plane and use tables, x- and y-intercepts, and the slope and y-intercept to graph linear equations and functions. They interpret slope as a rate of change in real-world situations and explore how changing the slope and y-intercept changes the graph. They use slope to identify parallel lines. They write and graph direct variation equations and use them to solve real-world problems. They learn how to use function notation and they compare families of graphs.

Prerequisite Skills

- Plotting ordered pairs
- Making a table of values for a function
- Graphing functions
- Writing equations in function form

Additional resources for reviewing prerequisite skills are:

- Skills Review Handbook, pp. 909–937
- @HomeTutor

4 Graphing Linear Equations and Functions

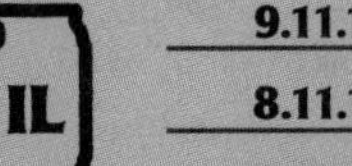

Before

In previous chapters, you learned the following skills, which you'll use in Chapter 4: graphing functions and writing equations and functions.

Prerequisite Skills

VOCABULARY CHECK

Copy and complete the statement.

1. The set of inputs of a function is called the _?_ of the function. The set of outputs of a function is called the _?_ of the function. **domain; range**
2. A(n) _?_ uses division to compare two quantities. **ratio**

SKILLS CHECK

Graph the function. *(Review p. 43 for 4.1–4.7.)* **3–8. See margin.**

3. $y = x + 6$; domain: 0, 2, 4, 6, and 8
4. $y = 2x + 1$; domain: 0, 1, 2, 3, and 4
5. $y = \frac{2}{3}x$; domain: 0, 3, 6, 9, and 12
6. $y = x - \frac{1}{2}$; domain: 1, 2, 3, 4, and 5
7. $y = x - 4$; 5, 6, 7, and 9
8. $y = \frac{1}{2}x + 1$; 2, 4, 6, and 8

Write the equation so that *y* is a function of *x*. *(Review p. 184 for 4.5.)*

9. $6x + 4y = 16$ $y = -\frac{3}{2}x + 4$
10. $x + 2y = 5$ $y = -\frac{1}{2}x + \frac{5}{2}$
11. $-12x + 6y = -12$ $y = 2x - 2$

@HomeTutor Prerequisite skills practice at classzone.com

Chapter Planning Guide

Chapter 4 Resource Book
- Teaching Guide/Lesson Plan (pp. 3, 16, 31, 45, 58, 75, 88)
- Project with Rubric (p. 103)

Assessment and Intervention
- Assessment Book (pp. 46–60)
- Benchmark Tests
- Reteaching and Remediation Book

Interactive Technology
- Easy Planner
- Power Presentations CD-ROM
- Activity Generator CD-ROM
- Animated Algebra
- Test Generator CD-ROM
- Online Quizzes
- eWorkbook
- eEdition
- @HomeTutor

Resources for English Learners
- Quick Reference for English Learners
- Spanish Study Guide
- Multi-Language Visual Glossary
- Student Resources in Spanish

Now

In Chapter 4, you will apply the big ideas listed below and reviewed in the Chapter Summary on page 270. You will also use the key vocabulary listed below.

Big Ideas

1. **Graphing linear equations and functions using a variety of methods**
2. **Recognizing how changes in linear equations and functions affect their graphs**
3. **Using graphs of linear equations and functions to solve real-world problems**

KEY VOCABULARY

- quadrant, *p. 206*
- standard form of a linear equation, *p. 216*
- linear function, *p. 217*
- *x*-intercept, *p. 225*
- *y*-intercept, *p. 225*
- slope, *p. 235*
- rate of change, *p. 237*
- slope-intercept form, *p. 244*
- parallel, *p. 246*
- direct variation, *p. 253*
- constant of variation, *p. 253*
- function notation, *p. 262*
- family of functions, *p. 263*
- parent linear function, *p. 263*

Why?

You can graph linear functions to solve problems involving distance. For example, you can graph a linear function to find the time it takes and in-line skater to travel a particular distance at a particular speed.

Animated Algebra

The animation illustrated below for Exercise 41 on page 267 helps you answer this question: How can you graph a function that models the distance an in-line skater travels over time?

Start
You want to graph a function that gives the distance traveled by an in-line skater.

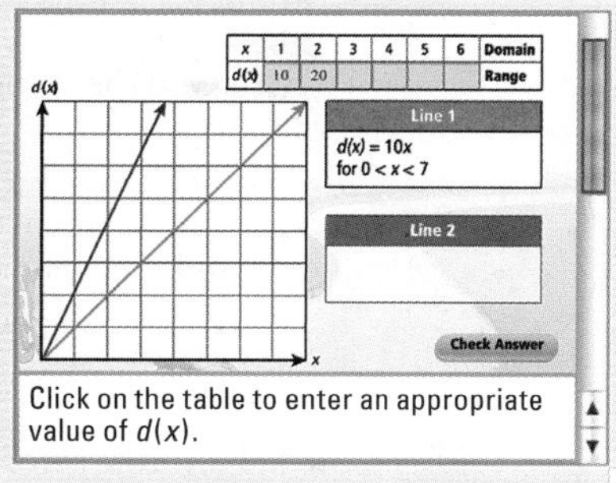

Animated Algebra at classzone.com

Other animations for Chapter 4: pages 207, 216, 226, 238, 245, and 254

Algebra 1 Toolkit

- Reading Strategies for Chapter 4, pp. 15–16
- Differentiated Instruction Notes, pp. 53–56
- English Learners Notes, pp. 103–104
- Inclusion Notes, pp. 135–136
- Teaching Strategies with Sample Worksheets, pp. 155–178
- Using Technology in the Classroom, pp. 179–184
- Tips for New Teachers, pp. 191–192
- Math Background Notes, pp. 217–218
- Pre-AP Strategies and Copymasters, pp. 284–285, 345–359
- Teacher Survival Activities, pp. 561–562, 587–588
- Bulletin Board Idea, p. 610
- Teacher Tool Transparencies, following p. 620

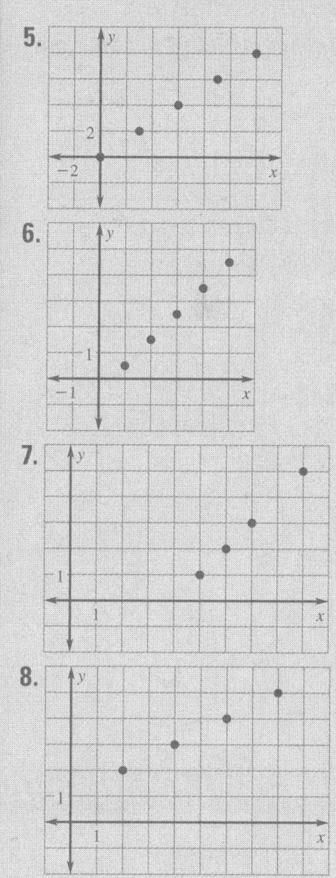

3.

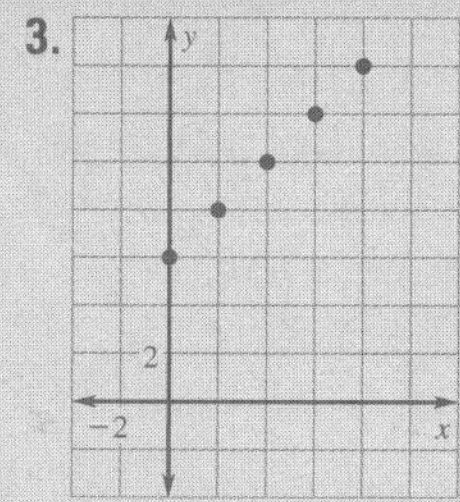

4.

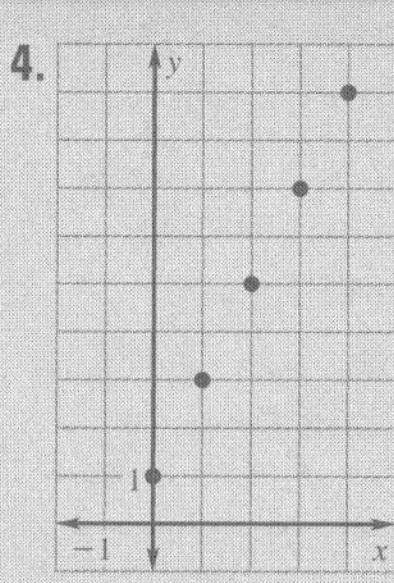

1 PLAN AND PREPARE

Warm-Up Exercises

Transparency Available

Plot the numbers on a number line.

1. −4, −2, 1, 3

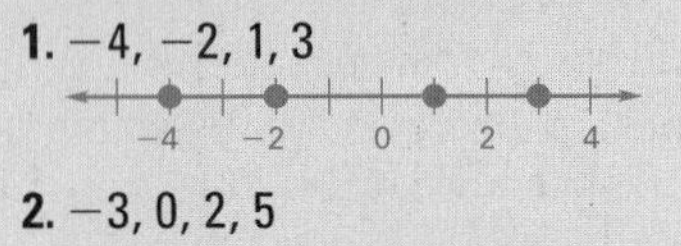

2. −3, 0, 2, 5

3. 0.4, 0.9, 1.3, 1.6

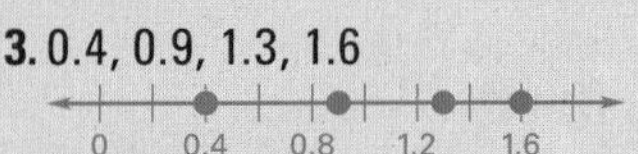

Notetaking Guide

Transparency Available

Promotes interactive learning and notetaking skills, pp. 73–75.

Pacing

Basic: 1 day
Average: 1 day
Advanced: 1 day
Block: 0.5 block with 4.2

- See *Teaching Guide/Lesson Plan.*

2 FOCUS AND MOTIVATE

Essential Question

Big Idea 1, p. 205

How do you plot points in a coordinate plane? **Tell students they will learn how to answer this question by locating points and graphing functions in all four quadrants of a coordinate plane.**

4.1 Plot Points in a Coordinate Plane

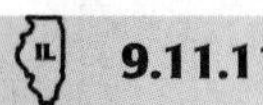
9.11.11 Graph, locate, and identify points on a coordinate system.

Before You graphed numbers on a number line.

Now You will identify and plot points in a coordinate plane.

Why? So you can interpret photos of Earth taken from space, as in Ex. 36.

Key Vocabulary
- **quadrants**
- **coordinate plane,** *p. 921*
- **ordered pair,** *p. 921*

In Chapter 1, you used a coordinate plane to graph ordered pairs whose coordinates were nonnegative. If you extend the x-axis and y-axis to include negative values, you divide the coordinate plane into four regions called **quadrants**, labeled I, II, III, and IV as shown.

Points in Quadrant I have two positive coordinates. Points in the other three quadrants have at least one negative coordinate.

READING
The x-coordinate of a point is sometimes called the *abscissa*. The y-coordinate of a point is sometimes called the *ordinate*.

For example, point P is in Quadrant IV and has an x-coordinate of 3 and a y-coordinate of −2. A point on an axis, such as point Q, is not considered to be in any of the four quadrants.

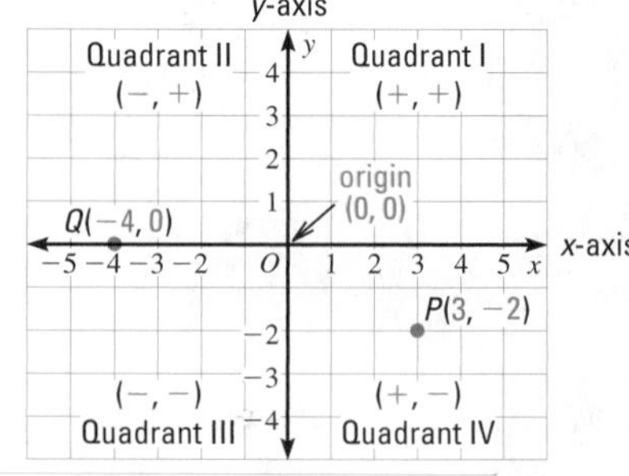

EXAMPLE 1 Name points in a coordinate plane

Give the coordinates of the point.

a. A **b.** B

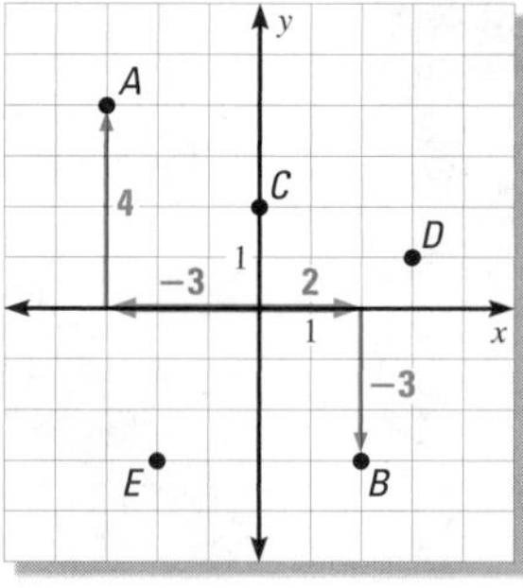

Solution

a. Point A is 3 units to the left of the origin and 4 units up. So, the x-coordinate is −3, and the y-coordinate is 4. The coordinates are (−3, 4).

b. Point B is 2 units to the right of the origin and 3 units down. So, the x-coordinate is 2, and the y-coordinate is −3. The coordinates are (2, −3).

✓ GUIDED PRACTICE for Example 1

1. Use the coordinate plane in Example 1 to give the coordinates of points C, D, and E. **C(0,2), D(3, 1), E(−2, −3)**
2. What is the y-coordinate of any point on the x-axis? **0**

Resource Planning Guide

Chapter Resource Book
- Teaching Guide/Lesson Plan (pp. 3–4)
- Practice levels A, B, C (pp. 5–10)
- Study Guide (pp. 11–12)
- Catch-up for Absent Students (p. 13)
- Application (p. 14)
- Challenge (p. 15)

Workbooks
- Notetaking Guide (pp. 73–75)
- Practice Workbook (pp. 46–48)

Teaching Options
- **Power Presentations CD-ROM** provides dynamic electronic teaching resources for the classroom.
- **Activity Generator CD-ROM** provides editable activities for all ability levels.

Interactive Technology
- Easy Planner
- Power Presentations CD-ROM
- Activity Generator CD-ROM
- Animated Algebra
- Test Generator CD-ROM
- Online Quiz
- eWorkbook
- eEdition
- @HomeTutor

Resources for English Learners
- Quick Reference for English Learners
- Spanish Study Guide
- Multi-Language Visual Glossary
- Student Resources in Spanish

See also the *Algebra 1 Toolkit* for more strategies for meeting individual needs.

EXAMPLE 2 Plot points in a coordinate plane

Plot the point in a coordinate plane. Describe the location of the point.

a. $A(-4, 4)$ **b.** $B(3, -2)$ **c.** $C(0, -4)$

Solution

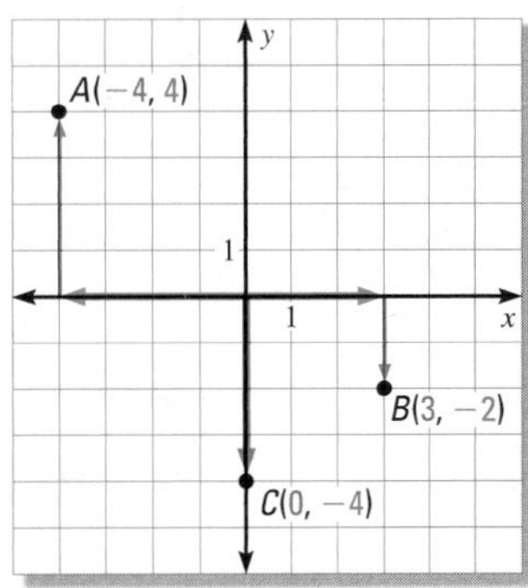

a. Begin at the origin. First move 4 units to the left, then 4 units up. Point A is in Quadrant II.

b. Begin at the origin. First move 3 units to the right, then 2 units down. Point B is in Quadrant IV.

c. Begin at the origin and move 4 units down. Point C is on the y-axis.

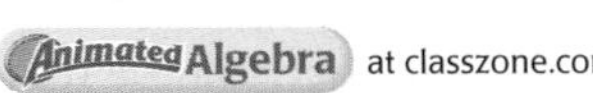

at classzone.com

EXAMPLE 3 Graph a function

Graph the function $y = 2x - 1$ with domain $-2, -1, 0, 1,$ and 2. Then identify the range of the function.

Solution

STEP 1 **Make** a table by substituting the domain values into the function.

x	$y = 2x - 1$
−2	$y = 2(-2) - 1 = -5$
−1	$y = 2(-1) - 1 = -3$
0	$y = 2(0) - 1 = -1$
1	$y = 2(1) - 1 = 1$
2	$y = 2(2) - 1 = 3$

STEP 2 **List** the ordered pairs: $(-2, -5)$, $(-1, -3)$, $(0, -1)$, $(1, 1)$, $(2, 3)$. Then graph the function.

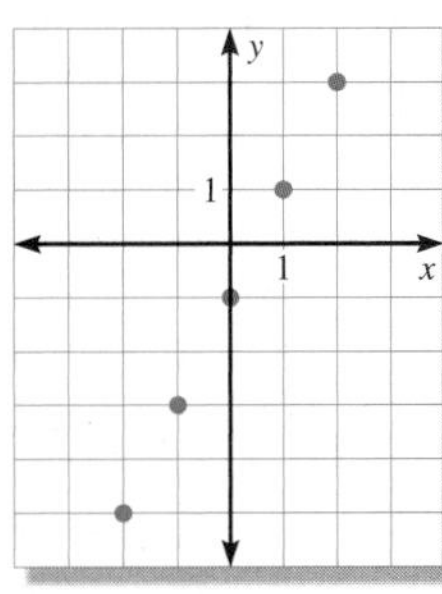

STEP 3 **Identify** the range. The range consists of the y-values from the table: $-5, -3, -1, 1,$ and 3.

ANALYZE A FUNCTION
The function in Example 3 is called a *discrete* function. To learn about discrete functions, see p. 223.

✓ GUIDED PRACTICE for Examples 2 and 3

Plot the point in a coordinate plane. *Describe* the location of the point.

3–6. See margin for art.

3. $A(2, 5)$ Quadrant I **4.** $B(-1, 0)$ x-axis **5.** $C(-2, -1)$ Quadrant III **6.** $D(-5, 3)$ Quadrant II

7. Graph the function $y = -\frac{1}{3}x + 2$ with domain $-6, -3, 0, 3,$ and 6. Then identify the range of the function. See margin for art; range: 0, 1, 2, 3, and 4.

Motivating the Lesson

You can use graphs in a coordinate plane to analyze trends that include negative quantities. For example, a member of the school golf team could plot her score above or below par for each round she plays, with round 0 being the first day of competition and rounds −1, −2, −3, . . . being earlier practice rounds

3 TEACH

Extra Example 1

Give the coordinates of the point.

a. A (−2, 1) **b.** B (4, −2)

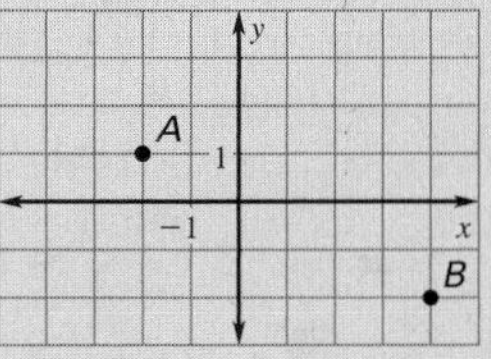

Extra Example 2

Plot the point in a coordinate plane. Describe the location of the point.

a. $A(-3, 0)$ **b.** $B(1, -4)$ **c.** $C(-4, -3)$

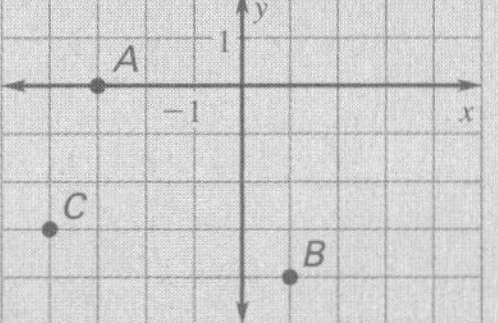

a. Point A is on the x-axis.
b. Point B is in Quadrant IV.
c. Point C is in Quadrant III.

An **Animated Algebra** activity is available on-line for **Example 2**. This activity is also available on the **Power Presentations CD-ROM**.

3–7. See Additional Answers beginning on p. AA1.

Differentiated Instruction

Below Level Students who confuse x- and y-coordinates and quadrants may want to create a note card with a model of a coordinate plane and instructions on how to plot points. Suggest they show the four quadrants, the origin, and the signs of the x- and y-coordinates in each quadrant. Instructions should indicate that they start at the origin, move right for positive x-coordinates and left for negative, and then up for positive y-coordinates and down for negative.

See also the *Algebra 1 Toolkit* for more strategies.

Extra Example 3

Graph the function $y = -\frac{1}{2}x + 1$ with domain −4, −2, 0, 2, and 4. Then identify the range.

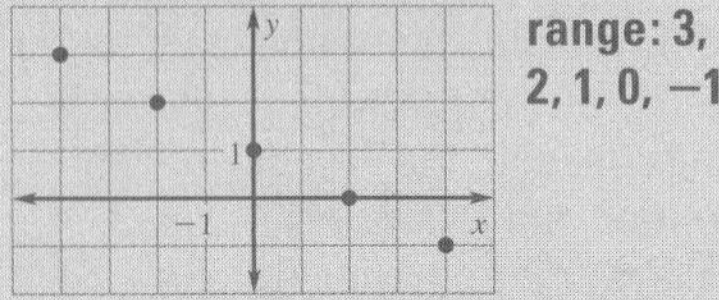

range: 3, 2, 1, 0, −1

Extra Example 4

The table shows attendance at a school carnival before and after the school added game booths in 2002.

Years, x, before or since 2002	−2	−1	0	1
Attendance, y (hundreds)	2.6	2.2	3.1	3.5

a. Explain how you know the table represents a function. **Each input has only one output.**

b. Graph the function.

c. Describe any trends. **Before 2002, attendance was below 300 and decreasing. After 2002, it increased to over 300 and it continued to climb in 2003.**

Closing the Lesson

Have students summarize the major points of the lesson and answer the Essential Question: How do you plot points in a coordinate plane?

- **A coordinate plane consists of four regions called quadrants.**
- **You plot points in a coordinate plane by moving left or right from the origin and then up or down from the x-axis.**

Begin at the origin and move to the right if the x-coordinate is positive and left if negative. Then move up if the y-coordinate is positive and down if negative.

 **EXAMPLE 4** **Graph a function represented by a table**

VOTING In 1920 the ratification of the 19th amendment to the United States Constitution gave women the right to vote. The table shows the number (to the nearest million) of votes cast in presidential elections both before and since women were able to vote.

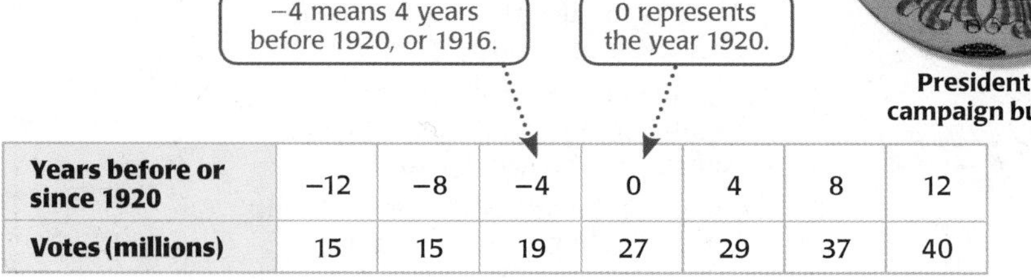

Presidential campaign button

Years before or since 1920	−12	−8	−4	0	4	8	12
Votes (millions)	15	15	19	27	29	37	40

a. Explain how you know that the table represents a function.

b. Graph the function represented by the table.

c. Describe any trend in the number of votes cast.

Solution

a. The table represents a function because each input has exactly one output.

b. To graph the function, let x be the number of years before or since 1920. Let y be the number of votes cast (in millions).

The graph of the function is shown.

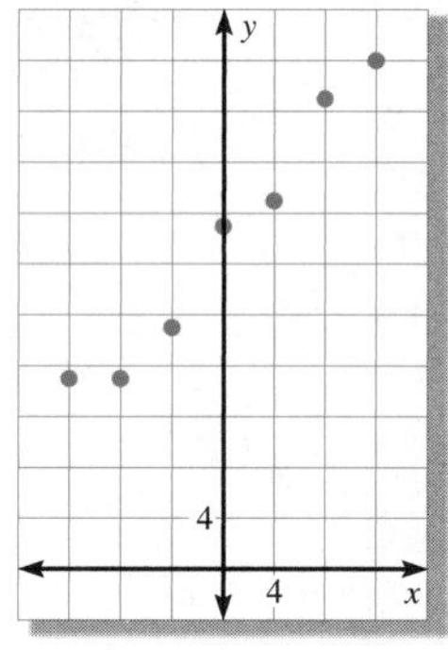

c. In the three election years before 1920, the number of votes cast was less than 20 million. In 1920, the number of votes cast was greater than 20 million. The number of votes cast continued to increase in the three election years since 1920.

✓ **GUIDED PRACTICE** for Example 4

8. VOTING The presidential election in 1972 was the first election in which 18-year-olds were allowed to vote. The table shows the number (to the nearest million) of votes cast in presidential elections both before and since 1972.

Years before or since 1972	−12	−8	−4	0	4	8	12
Votes (millions)	69	71	73	78	82	87	93

a. *Explain* how you know the graph represents a function.

b. Graph the function represented by the table. **See margin.**

c. *Describe* any trend in the number of votes cast. ***Sample answer:*** **Before 1972 the number of voters increased by 2 million every 4 years. In 1972 the number increased by 5 million and continued to increase by more than 2 million every 4 years since 1972.**

8a. The table represents a function because each input has exactly one output.

8b.

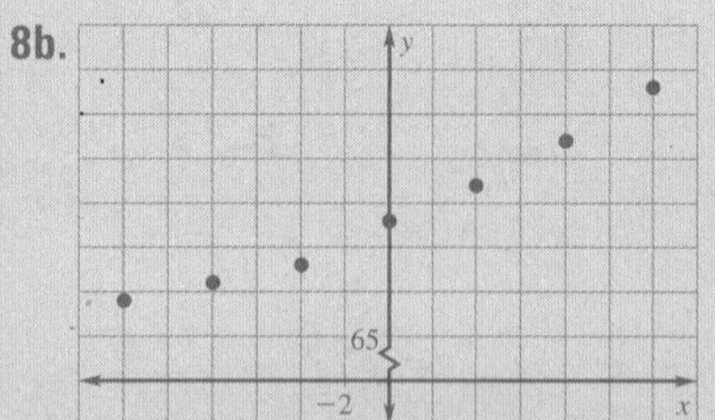

Differentiated Instruction

Inclusion If you use the words *abscissa* and *ordinate*, students sometimes cannot remember which coordinate is the ordinate and which is the abscissa. One way to avoid confusion is to point out that the words in the ordered pair (abscissa, ordinate) and the letters in the ordered pair (x, y) are both in alphabetical order.

See also the *Algebra 1 Toolkit* for more strategies.

4.1 EXERCISES

HOMEWORK KEY

○ = **WORKED-OUT SOLUTIONS** on p. WS7 for Exs. 15, 25, and 37

★ = **STANDARDIZED TEST PRACTICE** Exs. 2, 13, 23, 33, and 41

◆ = **MULTIPLE REPRESENTATIONS** Ex. 40

SKILL PRACTICE

A

1. **VOCABULARY** What is the x-coordinate of the point $(5, -3)$? What is the y-coordinate? 5; −3

2. ★ **WRITING** One of the coordinates of a point is negative while the other is positive. Can you determine the quadrant in which the point lies? *Explain.* No; the point could lie in either Quadrant II or Quadrant IV.

EXAMPLE 1 on p. 206 for Exs. 3–13

NAMING POINTS **Give the coordinates of the point.**

3. A (3, −2)
4. B (0, −1)
5. C (4, 4)
6. D (−4, 3)
7. E (4, −1)
8. F (3, 0)
9. G (−5, 4)
10. H(−3, −2)
11. J (−4, −1)
12. K (−1, 2)

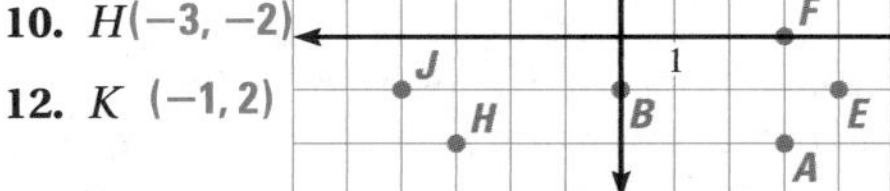

13. ★ **MULTIPLE CHOICE** A point is located 3 units to the left of the origin and 6 units up. What are the coordinates of the point? B

Ⓐ (3, 6) Ⓑ (−3, 6) Ⓒ (6, 3) Ⓓ (6, −3)

EXAMPLE 2 on p. 207 for Exs. 14–22

PLOTTING POINTS **Plot the point in a coordinate plane. *Describe* the location of the point.** 14–21. See margin for art.

14. $P(5, 5)$ Quadrant I
15. $Q(-1, 5)$ Quadrant II
16. $R(-3, 0)$ x-axis
17. $S(0, 0)$ origin
18. $T(-3, -4)$ Quadrant III
19. $U(0, 6)$ y-axis
20. $V(1.5, 4)$ Quadrant I
21. $W(3, -2.5)$ Quadrant IV

22. **ERROR ANALYSIS** *Describe* and correct the error in describing the location of the point $W(6, -6)$. The description of the location is backwards, the point is 6 units to the right of the origin and 6 units down.

> Point $W(6, -6)$ is 6 units to the left of the origin and 6 units up. ✗

EXAMPLE 3 on p. 207 for Exs. 23–27

23. ★ **MULTIPLE CHOICE** Which number is in the range of the function whose graph is shown? B

Ⓐ −2 Ⓑ −1
Ⓒ 0 Ⓓ 2

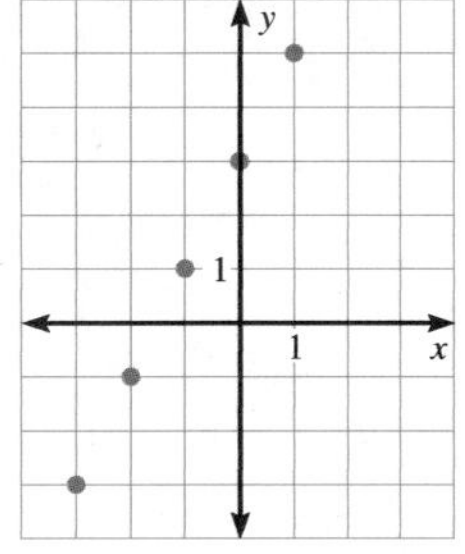

4 PRACTICE AND APPLY

Assignment Guide

Answer Transparencies available for all exercises

Basic:
Day 1: SRH p. 921 Exs. 7–21 odd
pp. 209–212
Exs. 1, 2, 3–11 odd, 13–17, 22–30, 36–39, 42–54 even

Average:
Day 1: pp. 209–212
Exs. 1, 2, 7–13 odd, 16–22 even, 23, 24–32 even, 33–40, 43–53 odd

Advanced:
Day 1: pp. 209–212
Exs. 1, 2, 10–13, 19–23, 26–28, 31–35*, 38–41*, 43–53 odd

Block:
pp. 209–212
Exs. 1, 2, 7–13 odd, 16–22 even, 23, 24–32 even, 33–40, 43–53 odd (with 4.2)

Differentiated Instruction

See *Algebra 1 Best Practices Toolkit* for suggestions on addressing the needs of a diverse classroom.

Homework Check

For a quick check of student understanding of key concepts, go over the following exercises:

Basic: 7, 16, 24, 36, 37
Average: 9, 18, 26, 36, 38
Advanced: 12, 20, 27, 38, 39

Extra Practice

- Student Edition, p. 941
- Chapter 4 Resource Book: Practice levels A, B, C, pp. 5–10

Practice Worksheet

An easily-readable reduced practice page (with answers) for this lesson can be found on p. 204C.

14–21. U(0, 6), P(5, 5), Q(−1, 5), V(1.5, 4), R(−3, 0), S(0, 0), W(3, −2.5), T(−3, −4)

Avoiding Common Errors

Exercises 3–21 Since students may switch x- and y-coordinates, you may want to remind them that the x-coordinate is the first number in an ordered pair and the y-coordinate the second.

Study Strategy

Exercise 23 Remind students that the range represents the y-values of the function. Have them rephrase the question as "Which y-value below is shown on the graph?"

Teaching Strategy

Exercise 35 Encourage students to create and use a visual model, such as the model of the coordinate plane shown in the introduction on page 206, to help determine the quadrant of each of the points.

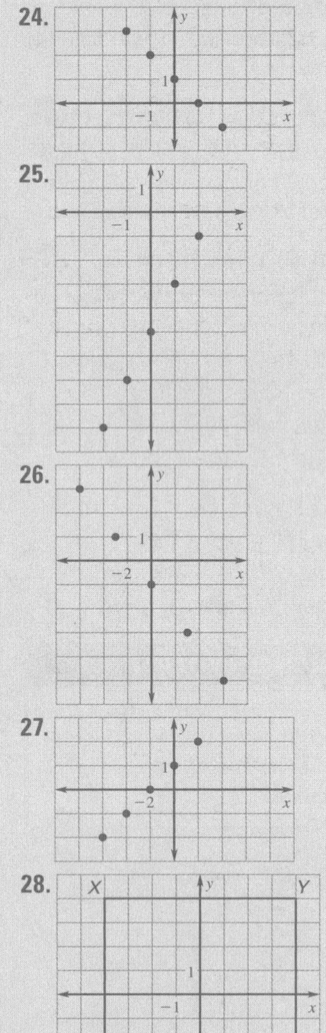

GRAPHING FUNCTIONS **Graph the function with the given domain. Then identify the range of the function.** 24–27. See margin for art.

24. $y = -x + 1$; domain: −2, −1, 0, 1, 2
−1, 0, 1, 2, 3

(25.) $y = 2x - 5$; domain: −2, −1, 0, 1, 2
−9, −7, −5, −3, −1

26. $y = -\frac{2}{3}x - 1$; domain: −6, −3, 0, 3, 6
−5, −3, −1, 1, 3

27. $y = \frac{1}{2}x + 1$; domain: −6, −4, −2, 0, 2
−2, −1, 0, 1, 2

B 28. **GEOMETRY** Plot the points $W(-4, -2)$, $X(-4, 4)$, $Y(4, 4)$, and $Z(4, -2)$ in a coordinate plane. Connect the points in order. Connect point Z to point W. Identify the resulting figure. Find its perimeter and area.
See margin for art; rectangle; perimeter: 28 units, area: 48 square units.

REASONING **Without plotting the point, tell whether it is in Quadrant I, II, III, or IV. *Explain* your reasoning.** 29–32. See margin.

29. (4, −11)
30. (40, −40)
31. (−18, 15)
32. (−32, −22)

33. ★ **WRITING** *Explain* how can you tell by looking at the coordinates of a point whether the point is on the x-axis or on the y-axis.

33. If the x-coordinate is 0, then the point is on the y-axis. If the y-coordinate is 0, then the point is on the x-axis.

C 34. **REASONING** Plot the point $J(-4, 3)$ in a coordinate plane. Plot three additional points in the same coordinate plane so that each of the four points lies in a different quadrant and the figure formed by connecting the points is a square. *Explain* how you located the points. See margin.

35. **CHALLENGE** Suppose the point (a, b) lies in Quadrant IV. *Describe* the location of the following points: (b, a), $(2a, -2b)$, and $(-b, -a)$. *Explain* your reasoning. See margin.

PROBLEM SOLVING

A 36. **ASTRONAUT PHOTOGRAPHY** Astronauts use a coordinate system to describe the locations of objects they photograph from space. The x-axis is the equator, 0° latitude. The y-axis is the prime meridian, 0° longitude. The names and coordinates of some lakes photographed from space are given. Use the map to determine on which continent each lake is located.

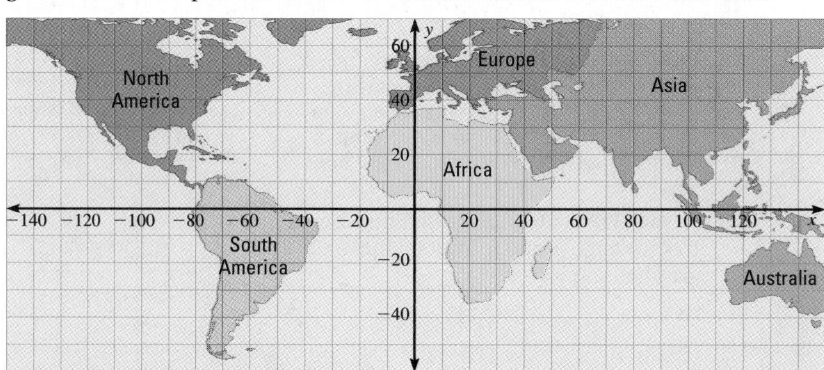

a. Lake Kulundinskoye: (80, 53) Asia
b. Lake Champlain: (−73, 45) North America
c. Lake Van: (43, 39) Asia
d. Lake Viedma: (−73, −50) South America
e. Lake Saint Clair: (−83, 43) North America
f. Starnberger Lake: (12, 48) Europe

@HomeTutor for problem solving help at classzone.com

○ = WORKED-OUT SOLUTIONS on p. WS1 ★ = STANDARDIZED TEST PRACTICE ◆ = MULTIPLE REPRESENTATIONS

29–32. See Additional Answers beginning on p. AA1.

34. *Sample answer:*

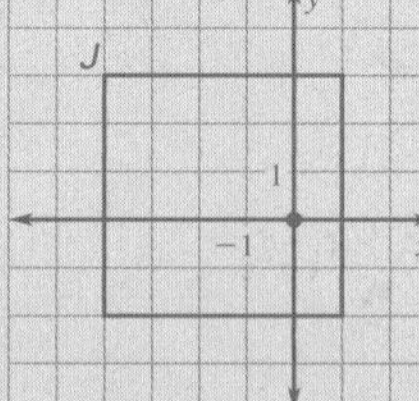

Decide on a side length of a square that is greater than 4, like 5, so the other points will be in different quadrants. Add 5 to the x-coordinate of J, −4, to find the point (1, 3) in Quadrant I. Then subtract 5 from the y-coordinate of J to find the point (−4, −2) in Quadrant 3. Then add 5 to the x-coordinate of (−4, −2) and subtract 5 from the y-coordinate of (1, 3) to find the point (1, −2) in Quadrant IV.

EXAMPLE 4 on p. 208 for Exs. 37–39

37. There is exactly one low temperature for each day in February; see margin for art.

37. RECORD TEMPERATURES The table shows the record low temperatures (in degrees Fahrenheit) for Odessa, Texas, for each day in the first week of February. *Explain* how you know the table represents a function. Graph the data from the table.

Day in February	1	2	3	4	5	6	7
Record low (degrees Fahrenheit)	−8	−11	10	8	10	9	11

@HomeTutor for problem solving help at classzone.com

38. STOCK VALUE The table shows the change in value (in dollars) of a stock over five days.

Day	1	2	3	4	5
Change in value (dollars)	−0.30	0.10	0.15	0.35	0.11

a. *Explain* how you know the table represents a function. Graph the data from the table. There is exactly one change in value for each day; see margin for art.

b. *Describe* any trend in the change in value of the stock.
Sample answer: The change in value increases until day 4, and then decreases.

B **39. MULTI-STEP PROBLEM** The difference between what the federal government collects and what it spends during a fiscal year is called the federal surplus or deficit. The table shows the federal surplus or deficit (in billions of dollars) in the 1990s. (A negative number represents a deficit.)

Years since 1990	0	1	2	3	4	5	6	7	8	9
Surplus or deficit (billions)	−221	−269	−290	−255	−203	−164	−108	−22	69	126

a. Graph the function represented by the table. See margin.

b. What conclusions can you make from the graph?
Sample answer: From 1992 to 1999 the federal deficit was decreasing.

40. MULTIPLE REPRESENTATIONS Low-density lipoproteins (LDL) transport cholesterol in the bloodstream throughout the body. A high LDL number is associated with an increased risk of cardiovascular disease. A patient's LDL number in 1999 was 189 milligrams per deciliter (mg/dL). To lower that number, the patient went on a diet. The annual LDL numbers for the patient in years after 1999 are 169, 154, 145, 139, and 136.

Years since 1999	1	2	? 3	? 4	? 5
Changes in LDL (mg/dL)	−20	−15	? −9	? −6	? −3

a. **Making a Table** Use the given information to copy and complete the table that shows the change in the patient's LDL number since 1999.

b. **Drawing a Graph** Graph the ordered pairs from the table. See margin.

c. **Describing in Words** Based on the graph, what can you conclude about the diet's effectiveness in lowering the patient's LDL number?
Sample answer: The diet is lowering the patient's LDL number.

35. For (b, a): Quadrant II; since (a, b) is in Quadrant IV, a must be positive and b must be negative, so the coordinates of (b, a) must be negative and positive. For $(2a, -2b)$: Quadrant I; since (a, b) is in Quadrant IV, a must be positive and b must be negative, so the coordinates of $(2a, -2b)$ must both be positive. For $(-b, -a)$: Quadrant IV; since (a, b) is in Quadrant IV, a must be positive and b must be negative, so the coordinates of $(-b, -a)$ must be positive and negative.

Vocabulary

Exercise 39 Students may be confused by the term "fiscal year." Tell them that a fiscal year refers to an accounting period of 12 months or 365 days, but the period may or may not correspond to the calendar year. The federal fiscal year runs from October through September.

Mathematical Reasoning

Exercises 39, 40 You may want to point out that both tables show years since a certain date, but the table in Exercise 39 begins with year 0, whereas the table in Exercise 40 begins with year 1. Lead students to see why the table in Exercise 40 must begin with year 1 and not year 0.

Internet Reference

Exercise 40 For more information about low-density lipoproteins, visit my.webmd.com/hw/cholesterol_management/hw207814.asp

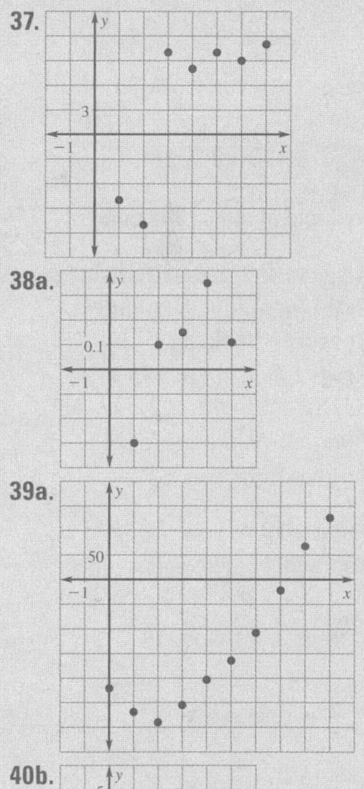

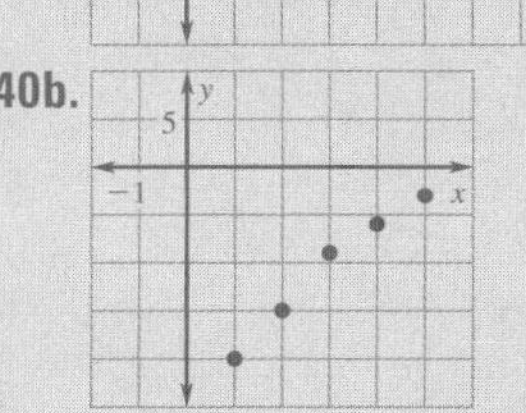

5 ASSESS AND RETEACH

Daily Homework Quiz

Transparency Available

Give the coordinates of the points.

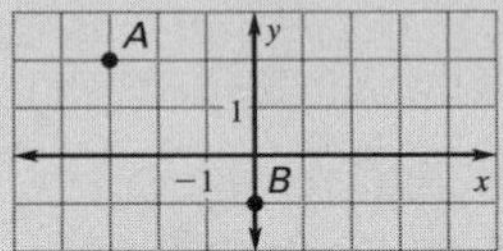

1. A (−3, 2) **2.** B (0, −1)

Plot the points in a coordinate plane.

3. $A(-2, -4)$ **4.** $B(3, 0)$

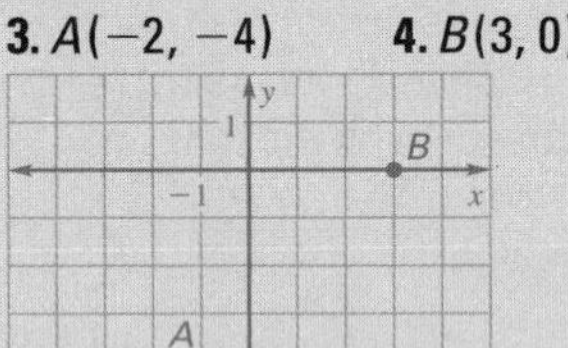

5. Graph $y = \frac{1}{2}x - 1$ with domain −4, −2, 0, 2, 4. Then identify the range. −4, −3, −2, −1, 0

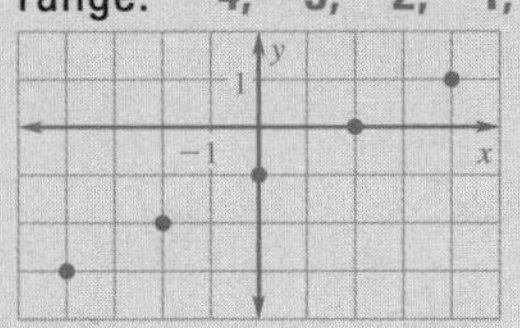

Online Quiz

Available at **classzone.com**

Diagnosis/Remediation

- Practice A, B, C in Chapter 4 Resource Book, pp. 5–10
- Study Guide in Chapter 4 Resource Book, pp. 11–12
- Practice Workbook, pp. 46–48
- @HomeTutor

Challenge

Additional challenge is available in the Chapter 4 Resource Book, p. 15.

41b.

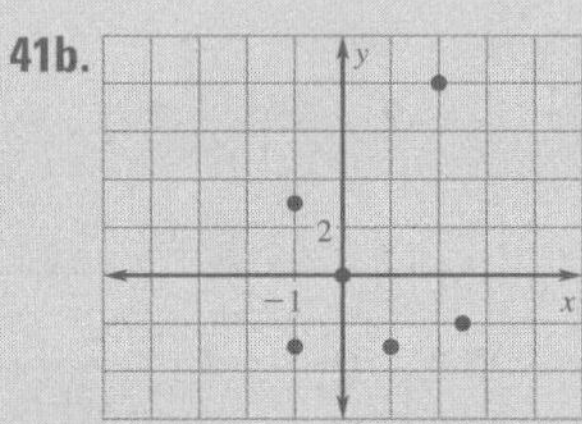

C **41.** ★ **EXTENDED RESPONSE** In a scientific study, researchers asked men to report their heights and weights. Then the researchers measured the actual heights and weights of the men. The data for six men are shown in the table. One row of the table represents the data for one man.

Height (inches)			Weight (pounds)		
Reported	**Measured**	**Difference**	**Reported**	**Measured**	**Difference**
70	68	70 − 68 = 2	154	146	154 − 146 = 8
70	67.5	? 2.5	141	143	? −2
78.5	77.5	? 1	165	168	? −3
68	69	? −1	146	143	? 3
71	72	? −1	220	223	? −3
70	70	? 0	176	176	? 0

a. Calculate Copy and complete the table.

b. Graph For each participant, write an ordered pair (x, y) where x is the difference of the reported and measured heights and y is the difference of the reported and measured weights. Then plot the ordered pairs in a coordinate plane. (2, 8), (2.5, −2), (1, −3), (−1, 3), (−1, −3), (0, 0); see margin for art.

c. CHALLENGE What does the origin represent in this situation?

41c. *Sample answer:* A person who reported the same information that was measured.

d. CHALLENGE Which quadrant has the greatest number of points? *Explain* what it means for a point to be in that quadrant.
Quadrant IV; the person reported a greater height than was measured and a lesser weight than was measured.

ILLINOIS MIXED REVIEW

TEST PRACTICE at classzone.com

42. The volume V of a cylinder is given by the formula $V = \pi r^2 h$. Solve the formula for h.

Ⓐ $h = V - \pi r^2$ Ⓑ $h = \frac{V}{\pi r^2}$ B

Ⓒ $h = \frac{V}{\pi r}$ Ⓓ $h = -\frac{V}{\pi r^2}$

43. If $\triangle ABC$ is similar to $\triangle DEF$, what is the length x?

Ⓐ 77

Ⓑ 84 D

Ⓒ 90

Ⓓ 99

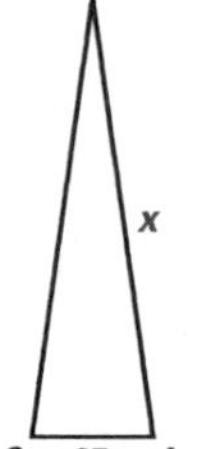

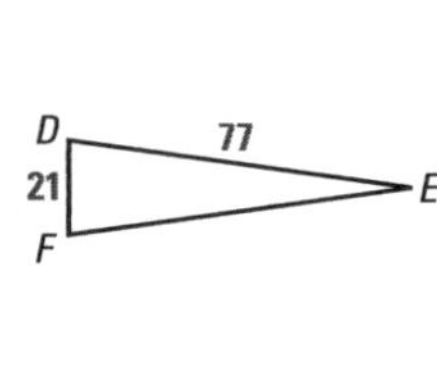

Perform Transformations

GOAL Perform and describe transformations in a coordinate plane.

Key Vocabulary
- **transformation**
- **translation**
- **vertical stretch or shrink**
- **reflection**

For a given set of points, a **transformation** produces an image by applying a rule to the coordinates of the points. Some types of transformations are *translations, vertical stretches, vertical shrinks,* and *reflections.*

A **translation** moves every point in a figure the same distance in the same direction either horizontally, vertically, or both. You can describe translations algebraically.

Horizontal translation: $(x, y) \to (x + h, y)$ **Vertical translation:** $(x, y) \to (x, y + k)$

EXAMPLE 1 Perform a translation

The transformation $(x, y) \to (x, y + 3)$ moves $\triangle ABC$ up 3 units.

Original		Image
$A(3, 0)$	$\to$	$A'(3, 3)$
$B(4, 2)$	$\to$	$B'(4, 5)$
$C(5, 0)$	$\to$	$C'(5, 3)$

The result of the transformation is $\triangle A'B'C'$.

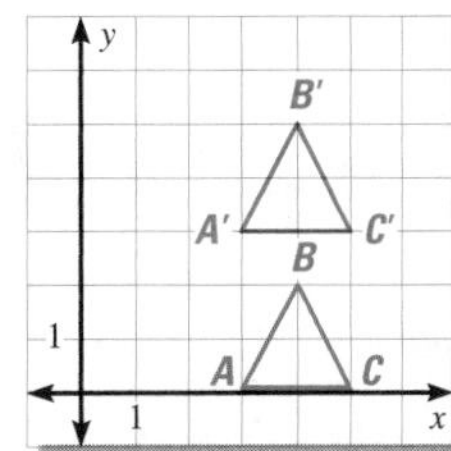

READ TRANSFORMATIONS
If a transformation is performed on a point A, the new location of point A is indicated by A' (read "A prime").

A **vertical stretch or shrink** moves every point in a figure away from the x-axis (a vertical stretch) or toward the x-axis (a vertical shrink), while points on the x-axis remain fixed. A **reflection** flips a figure in a line. You can describe vertical stretches and shrinks with or without reflection in the x-axis algebraically.

Vertical stretch:
$(x, y) \to (x, ay)$ where $a > 1$

Vertical shrink:
$(x, y) \to (x, ay)$ where $0 < a < 1$

Vertical stretch with reflection in the x-axis:
$(x, y) \to (x, ay)$ where $a < -1$

Vertical shrink with reflection in the x-axis:
$(x, y) \to (x, ay)$ where $-1 < a < 0$

EXAMPLE 2 Perform a vertical stretch with reflection

The transformation $(x, y) \to (x, -2y)$ vertically stretches $\triangle ABC$ and reflects it in the x-axis.

Original		Image
$A(3, 0)$	$\to$	$A'(3, 0)$
$B(4, 2)$	$\to$	$B'(4, -4)$
$C(5, 0)$	$\to$	$C'(5, 0)$

The result of the transformation is $\triangle A'B'C'$.

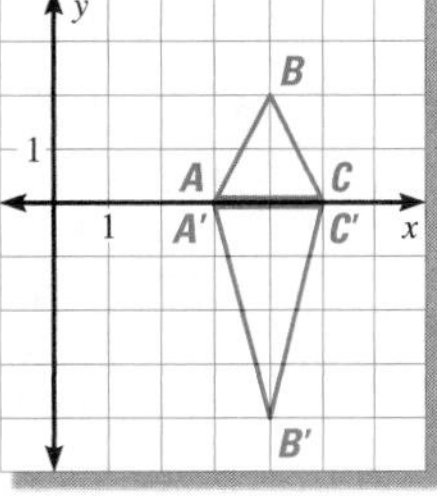

1 PLAN AND PREPARE

Warm-Up Exercises

Plot the points in a coordinate plane.

1. $A(-2, 1)$ **2.** $B(-1, -3)$
3. $C(4, -2)$ **4.** $D(1, 0)$

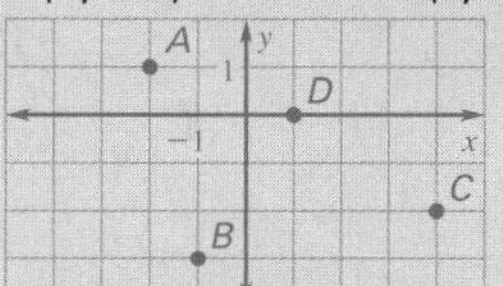

2 FOCUS AND MOTIVATE

Essential Question

Big Idea 2, p. 205

How do you transform figures in the coordinate plane? **Tell students they will learn how to answer this question by describing and performing translations, dilations, and reflections on figures in the coordinate plane.**

3 TEACH

Extra Example 1

Describe the transformation of $\triangle ABC$ to $\triangle A'B'C'$. **The transformation is $(x, y) \to (x - 4, y)$. $\triangle ABC$ is moved left 4 units.**

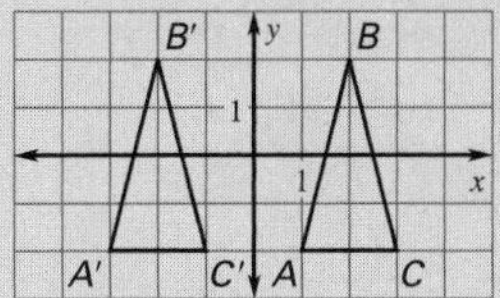

NCTM STANDARDS

Standard 3: Apply transformations to math situations

Standard 10: Use representations to communicate mathematical ideas

Extra Example 2

Describe the transformation of $\triangle ABC$ to $\triangle A'B'C'$. The transformation is $(x, y) \rightarrow \left(x, -\frac{1}{2}y\right)$. $\triangle A'B'C'$ shows a vertical shrink and reflection in the x-axis of $\triangle ABC$.

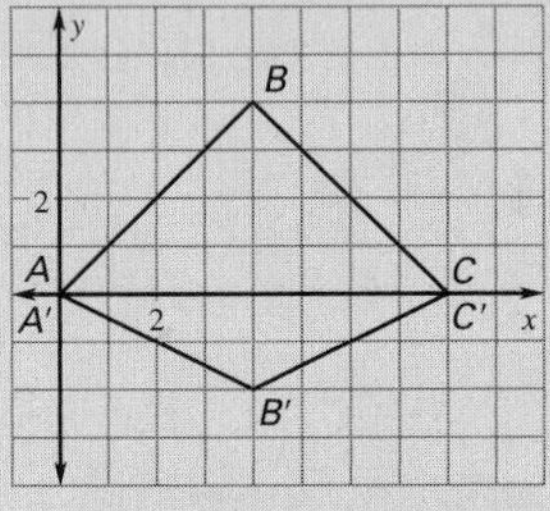

Closing the Lesson

Have students summarize the major points of the lesson and answer the Essential Question: How do you transform figures in the coordinate plane?

- A translation moves a figure horizontally or vertically.
- If a figure has one side along the x-axis, a vertical stretch or shrink moves a figure away from or towards the x-axis.
- A reflection flips a figure in a line.

Translate figures horizontally or vertically by adding to or subtracting from each x- or y-coordinate, respectively. Multiply the y-coordinates by positive numbers for stretches and shrinks and by negative numbers for reflections.

4 PRACTICE AND APPLY

Study Strategy

Exercises 9–11 Encourage students to check the indicated transformations against the descriptions of vertical stretches and shrinks and reflections on page 213. This allows them to anticipate the resulting transformation and to check that their calculations are correct.

CONCEPT SUMMARY — *For Your Notebook*

Identifying Transformations

Translation

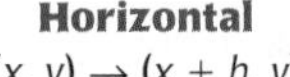

Horizontal
$(x, y) \rightarrow (x + h, y)$

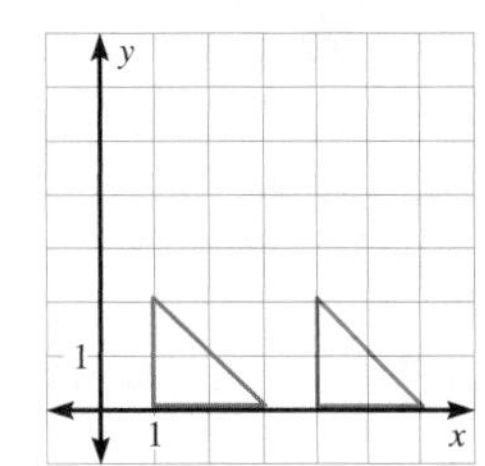

Vertical
$(x, y) \rightarrow (x, y + k)$

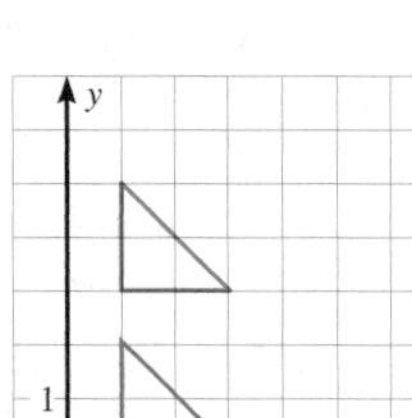

Vertical stretch or shrink

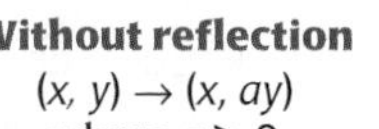

Without reflection
$(x, y) \rightarrow (x, ay)$
where $a > 0$

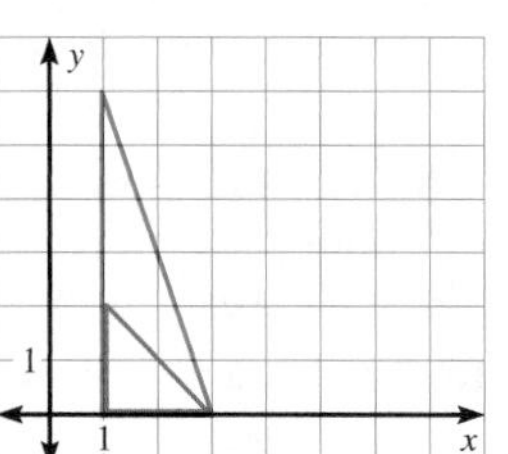

With reflection
$(x, y) \rightarrow (x, ay)$
where $a < 0$

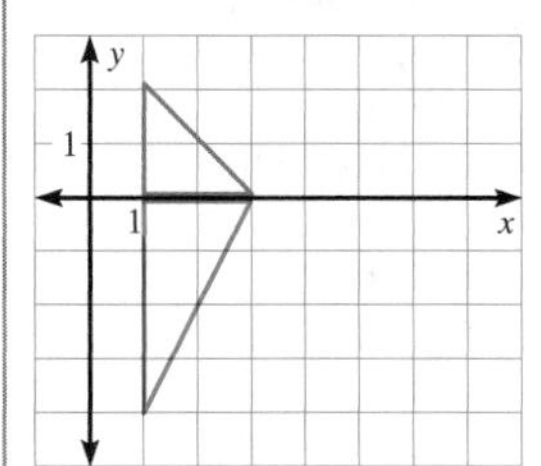

PRACTICE

1. **VOCABULARY** Does a translation or a vertical stretch always produce a figure that is the same size and shape as the original figure? *Explain.* See margin.

2. ★ **WRITING** *Describe* the vertical shrink $(x, y) \rightarrow (x, \frac{1}{2}y)$ in words. Multiply each y-coordinate by $\frac{1}{2}$.

EXAMPLES 1 and 2 on p. 213 for Exs. 3–14

1. Translation; a translation moves every point the same distance in the same direction so it will have the same shape and size as the original figure.

DESCRIBING TRANSFORMATIONS **Use words to describe the transformation of the blue figure to the red figure.**

3. Subtract 4 from each y-coordinate.

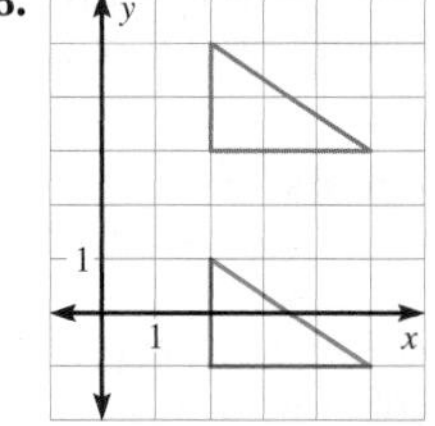

4. Multiply each y-coordinate by $-\frac{1}{2}$.

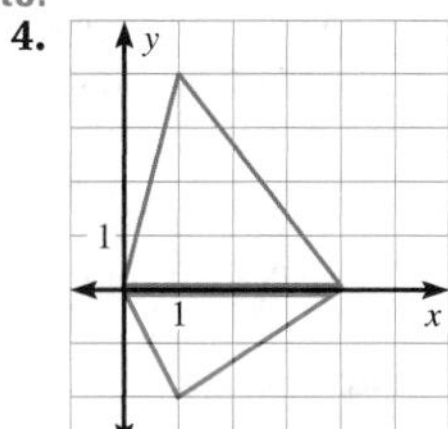

5. Add 2 to each y-coordinate.

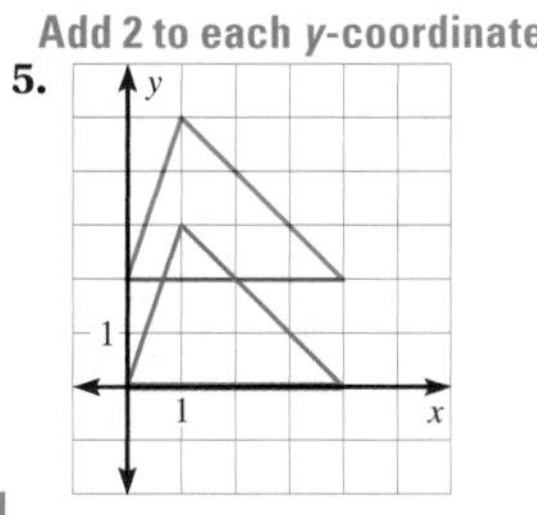

PERFORMING TRANSFORMATIONS **Square $ABCD$ has vertices at (0, 0), (0, 2), (2, 2), and (2, 0). Perform the indicated transformation. Then give the coordinates of figure $A'B'C'D'$.**

6. $(x, y) \rightarrow (x, y - 5)$
(0, −5), (0, −3), (2, −3), (2, −5)

7. $(x, y) \rightarrow (x, y + 1)$
(0, 1), (0, 3), (2, 3), (2, 1)

8. $(x, y) \rightarrow (x, y - 7)$
(0, −7), (0, −5), (2, −5), (2, −7)

9. $(x, y) \rightarrow (x, -y)$
(0, 0), (0, −2), (2, −2), (2, 0)

10. $(x, y) \rightarrow (x, 4y)$
(0, 0), (0, 8), (2, 8), (2, 0)

11. $(x, y) \rightarrow (x, -\frac{1}{2}y)$
(0, 0), (0, −1), (2, −1), (2, 0)

12. $(x, y) \rightarrow (x + 2, y + 3)$
(2, 3), (2, 5), (4, 5), (4, 3)

13. $(x, y) \rightarrow (x - 1, y + 4)$
(−1, 4), (−1, 6), (1, 6), (1, 4)

14. $(x, y) \rightarrow (x + 3, y)$
(3, 0), (3, 2), (5, 2), (5, 0)

15. ★ **WRITING** A square has vertices at (0, 0), (0, 3), (3, 3), and (3, 0). Tell how you could use a transformation to move the square so that it has new vertices at (0, 0), (0, −3), (3, −3), and (3, 0). Use the transformation $(x, y) \rightarrow (x, -y)$.

4.2 Graph Linear Equations

 **8.11.11** Analyze functions by investigating domain, range, rates of change, intercepts, and zeros.

Before You plotted points in a coordinate plane.

Now You will graph linear equations in a coordinate plane.

Why? So you can find how meteorologists collect data, as in Ex. 40.

Key Vocabulary
- **standard form of a linear equation**
- **linear function**

An example of an equation in two variables is $2x + 5y = 8$. A **solution of an equation in two variables**, x and y, is an ordered pair (x, y) that produces a true statement when the values of x and y are substituted into the equation.

EXAMPLE 1 Standardized Test Practice

Which ordered pair is a solution of $3x - y = 7$?

Ⓐ (3, 4) Ⓑ (1, −4) Ⓒ (5, −3) Ⓓ (−1, −2)

Solution

Check whether each ordered pair is a solution of the equation.

Test (3, 4):	$3x - y = 7$	**Write original equation.**
	$3(3) - 4 \stackrel{?}{=} 7$	**Substitute 3 for x and 4 for y.**
	$5 = 7$ ✗	**Simplify.**
Test (1, −4):	$3x - y = 7$	**Write original equation.**
	$3(1) - (-4) \stackrel{?}{=} 7$	**Substitute 1 for x and −4 for y.**
	$7 = 7$ ✓	**Simplify.**

So, (3, 4) is *not* a solution, but (1, −4) is a solution of $3x - y = 7$.

▶ The correct answer is B. Ⓐ Ⓑ Ⓒ Ⓓ

GUIDED PRACTICE for Example 1

1. Tell whether $\left(4, -\frac{1}{2}\right)$ is a solution of $x + 2y = 5$. not a solution

GRAPHS The **graph of an equation in two variables** is the set of points in a coordinate plane that represent all solutions of the equation. If the variables in an equation represent real numbers, one way to graph the equation is to make a table of values, plot enough points to recognize a pattern, and then connect the points. When making a table of values, choose convenient values of x that include negative values, zero, and positive values.

1 PLAN AND PREPARE

Warm-Up Exercises

Transparency Available

1. Graph $y = -x - 2$ with domain −2, −1, 0, 1, and 2.

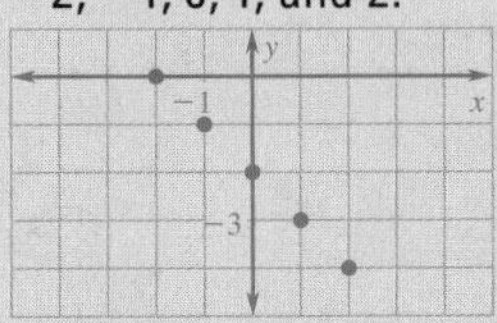

Rewrite the equation so y is a function of x.

2. $3x + 4y = 16$ $y = -\frac{3}{4}x + 4$

3. $-6x - 2y = -12$ $y = -3x + 6$

Notetaking Guide

Transparency Available

Promotes interactive learning and notetaking skills, pp. 76–79.

Pacing

Basic: 2 days

Average: 2 days

Advanced: 2 days

Block: 0.5 block with 4.1
0.5 block with 4.3

- See *Teaching Guide/Lesson Plan*.

2 FOCUS AND MOTIVATE

Essential Question

Big Idea 1, p. 205

How do you graph linear equations? Tell students they will learn how to answer this question by using tables to graph linear equations.

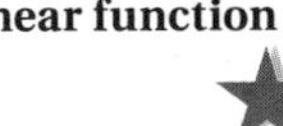

Resource Planning Guide

Chapter Resource Book
- Teaching Guide/Lesson Plan (pp. 16–17)
- Activity Master (p. 18)
- Practice levels A, B, C (pp. 20–25)
- Study Guide (pp. 26–27)
- Catch-up for Absent Students (p. 28)
- Problem Solving Workshop (p. 29)
- Challenge (p. 30)

Workbooks
- Notetaking Guide (pp. 76–79)
- Practice Workbook (pp. 49–51)

Teaching Options
- **Power Presentations CD-ROM** provides dynamic electronic teaching resources for the classroom.
- **Activity Generator CD-ROM** provides editable activities for all ability levels.

Interactive Technology
- Easy Planner
- Power Presentations CD-ROM
- Activity Generator CD-ROM
- Animated Algebra
- Test Generator CD-ROM
- Online Quiz
- eWorkbook
- eEdition
- @HomeTutor

Resources for English Learners
- Quick Reference for English Learners
- Spanish Study Guide
- Multi-Language Visual Glossary
- Student Resources in Spanish

See also the *Algebra 1 Toolkit* for more strategies for meeting individual needs.

Motivating the Lesson

You can use graphs of linear equations to determine information about real-world situations. For example, if you paid \$25 to join a skating rink and then \$15 per lesson, you could use a graph of the situation to find the cost after a specific number of lessons.

3 TEACH

Extra Example 1

Which ordered pair is a solution of $-x + 2y = 8$? D

Ⓐ (2, 3) Ⓑ (−2, 5)
Ⓒ (−1, 4) Ⓓ (−2, 3)

Key Questions to Ask for Example 1

- Are there other solutions of the equation? Explain. Yes. Any ordered pair that produces a true statement is a solution.
- What are some other solutions? (3, 2), (2, −1), (0, −7)

Extra Example 2

Graph the equation $2x + y = 2$.

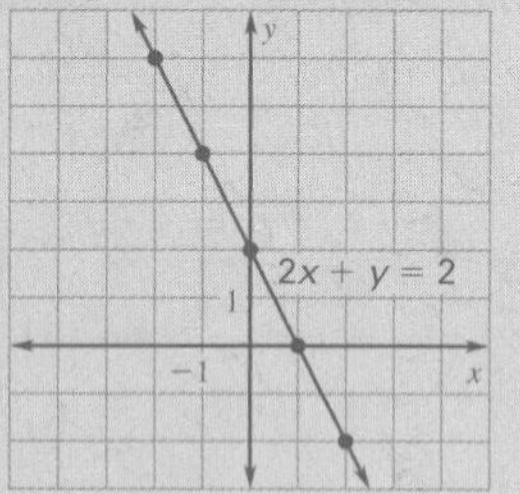

Key Question to Ask for Example 2

- How many points on the line represent solutions of the equation? Explain. Every point on the line is a solution of the equation, so there are an infinite number of solutions.

EXAMPLE 2 Graph an equation

Graph the equation $-2x + y = -3$.

Solution

STEP 1 **Solve** the equation for y.

$$-2x + y = -3$$

$$y = 2x - 3$$

STEP 2 **Make** a table by choosing a few values for x and finding the values of y.

x	−2	−1	0	1	2
y	−7	−5	−3	−1	1

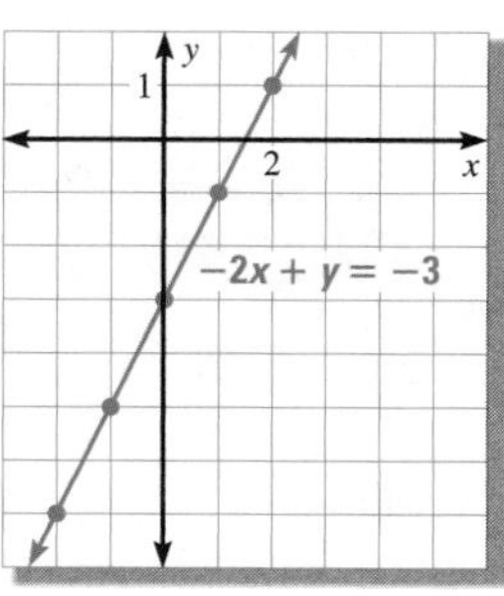

STEP 3 **Plot** the points. Notice that the points appear to lie on a line.

STEP 4 **Connect** the points by drawing a line through them. Use arrows to indicate that the graph goes on without end.

DRAW A GRAPH
If you continued to find solutions of the equation and plotted them, the line would fill in.

LINEAR EQUATIONS A **linear equation** is an equation whose graph is a line, such as the equation in Example 2. The **standard form** of a linear equation is

$$Ax + By = C$$

where A, B, and C are real numbers and A and B are not both zero.

Consider what happens when $A = 0$ or when $B = 0$. When $A = 0$, the equation becomes $By = C$, or $y = \frac{C}{B}$. Because $\frac{C}{B}$ is a constant, you can write $y = b$. Similarly, when $B = 0$, the equation becomes $Ax = C$, or $x = \frac{C}{A}$, and you can write $x = a$.

EXAMPLE 3 Graph $y = b$ and $x = a$

Graph (a) $y = 2$ and (b) $x = -1$.

Solution

a. For every value of x, the value of y is 2. The graph of the equation $y = 2$ is a horizontal line 2 units above the x-axis.

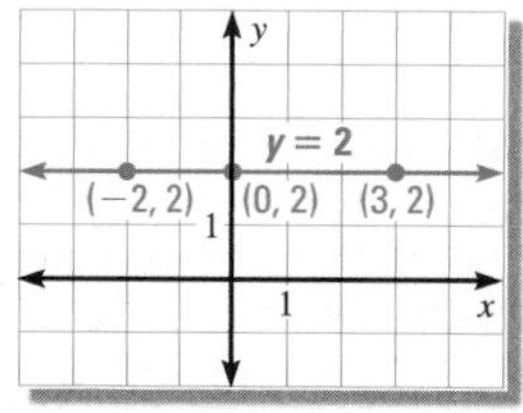

b. For every value of y, the value of x is −1. The graph of the equation $x = -1$ is a vertical line 1 unit to the left of the y-axis.

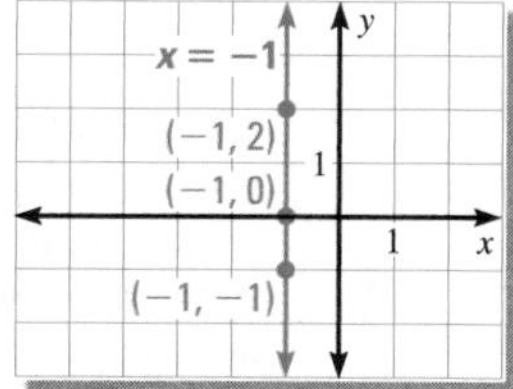

FIND A SOLUTION
The equations $y = 2$ and $0x + 1y = 2$ are equivalent. For any value of x, the ordered pair $(x, 2)$ is a solution of $y = 2$.

Animated Algebra at classzone.com

Differentiated Instruction

English Learners In Example 2, caution students that the figure is called a "graph of a line," and should not be confused with a *line graph* (p. 934). A line graph is a graph that uses line segments to connect data points. A graph of a line is a graph of a linear equation.

See also the *Algebra 1 Toolkit* for more strategies.

KEY CONCEPT *For Your Notebook*

Equations of Horizontal and Vertical Lines

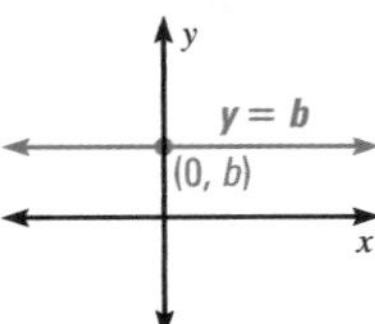

The graph of $y = b$ is a horizontal line. The line passes through the point $(0, b)$.

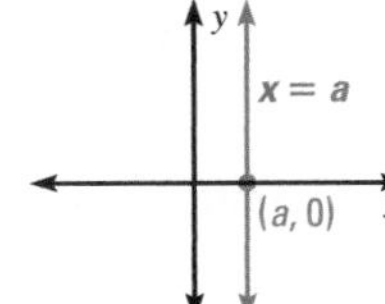

The graph of $x = a$ is a vertical line. The line passes through the point $(a, 0)$.

GUIDED PRACTICE for Examples 2 and 3

Graph the equation. 2–4. See margin.

2. $y + 3x = -2$
3. $y = 2.5$
4. $x = -4$

LINEAR FUNCTIONS In Example 3, $y = 2$ is a function, while $x = -1$ is not a function. The equation $Ax + By = C$ represents a **linear function** provided $B \neq 0$ (that is, provided the graph of the equation is not a vertical line). If the domain of a linear function is not specified, it is understood to be all real numbers. The domain can be restricted, as shown in Example 4.

EXAMPLE 4 Graph a linear function

Graph the function $y = -\frac{1}{2}x + 4$ with domain $x \geq 0$. Then identify the range of the function.

Solution

STEP 1 **Make** a table.

x	0	2	4	6	8
y	4	3	2	1	0

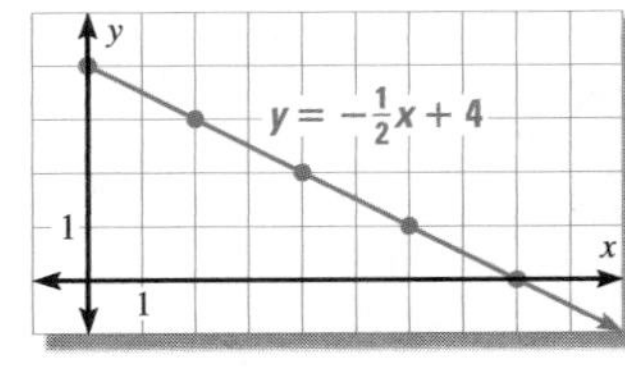

STEP 2 **Plot** the points.

STEP 3 **Connect** the points with a ray because the domain is restricted.

STEP 4 **Identify** the range. From the graph, you can see that all points have a y-coordinate of 4 or less, so the range of the function is $y \leq 4$.

ANALYZE A FUNCTION
The function in Example 4 is called a *continuous* function. To learn about continuous functions, see p. 223.

GUIDED PRACTICE for Example 4

5. Graph the function $y = -3x + 1$ with domain $x \leq 0$. Then identify the range of the function. See margin for art; $y \geq 1$.

Extra Example 3

Graph (a) $y = -3$ and (b) $x = 2$.

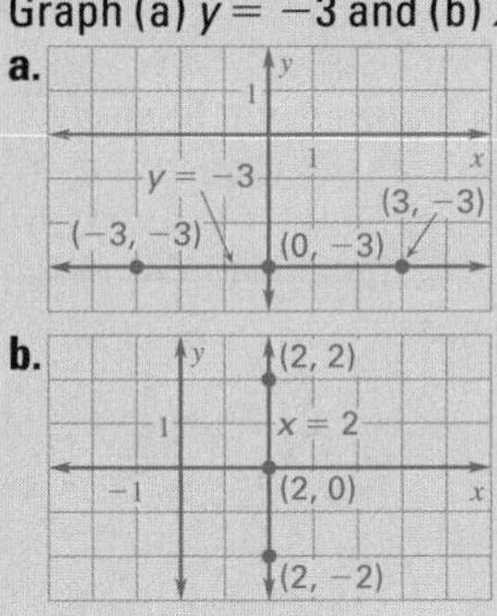

Key Question to Ask for Example 3

- Why is the graph of $y = b$ a horizontal line for any value of b? All the y-coordinates are the same, so a line connecting points on the graph is horizontal.

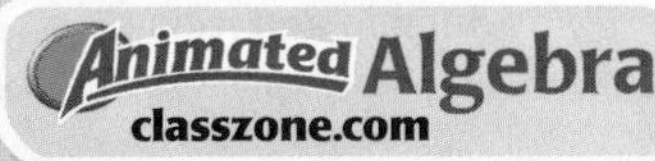

An **Animated Algebra** activity is available on-line for **Example 3**. This activity is also available on the **Power Presentations CD-ROM**.

Extra Example 4

Graph the function $y = \frac{1}{2}x - 1$ with domain $x \leq 0$. Then identify the range of the function. range: $y \leq -1$

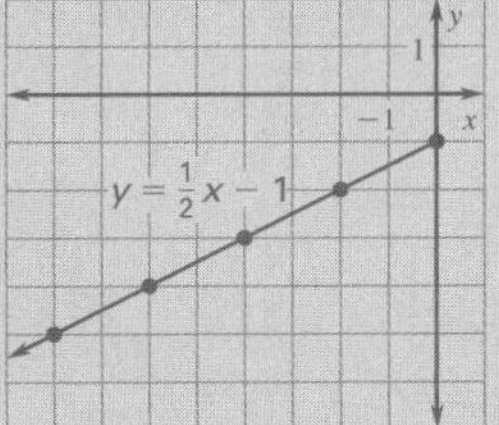

Key Questions to Ask for Example 4

- Why do the x-values in the table begin with 0? It is the least value in the domain $x \geq 0$.
- Does the range include negative numbers? Explain. Yes; when $x > 8$, the values of y are negative.

Differentiated Instruction

Kinesthetic Learners Some students may find it confusing that the y-axis is vertical line, but the graph of $y = b$ is a horizontal line, and that x-axis is horizontal line, but the graph of $x = a$ is a vertical line. Have students graph the equations $x = 0$ and $y = 0$ to identify them with the y- and x-axes, respectively, using an uncooked piece of spaghetti. Then have them graph $x = a$ and $y = b$ by sliding the spaghetti horizontally or vertically from the proper axis.

See also the *Algebra 1 Toolkit* for more strategies.

2–4. See Additional Answers beginning on p. AA1.

5.

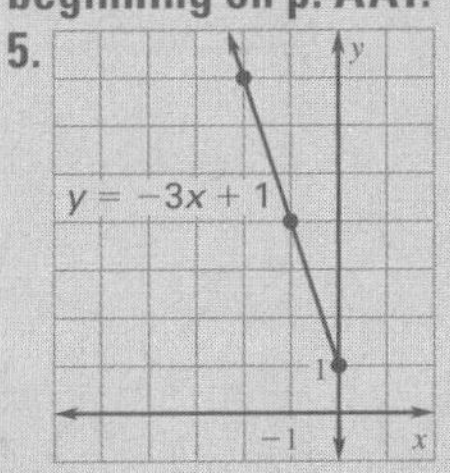

Extra Example 5

The number of pages a student types is given by $p = 4t$ where t is the time (in hours) spent typing. The student plans to type for at most 2.5 hours. Graph the function and identify its domain and range. **domain: $0 \le t \le 2.5$; range: $0 \le p \le 10$**

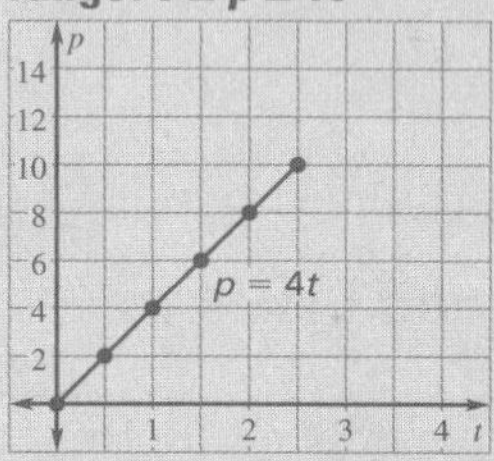

Extra Example 6

Suppose the student in Extra Example 5 plans to type at most 14 pages. Graph the function and identify its domain and range. **domain: $0 \le t \le 3.5$; range: $0 \le p \le 14$**

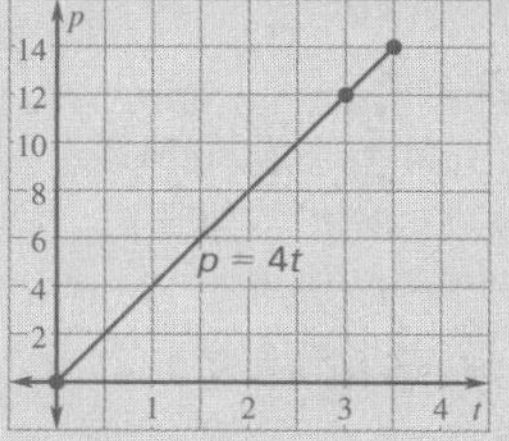

Closing the Lesson

Have students summarize the major points of the lesson and answer the Essential Question: How do you graph linear equations?

- **All points on the graph of a linear equation are solutions of the equation.**
- **Use a line to connect points when the domain is unrestricted, a ray when it is restricted, and a segment when both domain and range are restricted.**

Make a table of appropriate x-values, determine corresponding y-values, plot the points from the table, and connect the points with a line.

EXAMPLE 5 Solve a multi-step problem

RUNNING The distance d (in miles) that a runner travels is given by the function $d = 6t$ where t is the time (in hours) spent running. The runner plans to go for a 1.5 hour run. Graph the function and identify its domain and range.

Solution

STEP 1 **Identify** whether the problem specifies the domain or the range. You know the amount of time the runner plans to spend running. Because time is the independent variable, the domain is specified in this problem. The domain of the function is $0 \le t \le 1.5$.

STEP 2 **Graph** the function. Make a table of values. Then plot and connect the points.

t (hours)	0	0.5	1	1.5
d (miles)	0	3	6	9

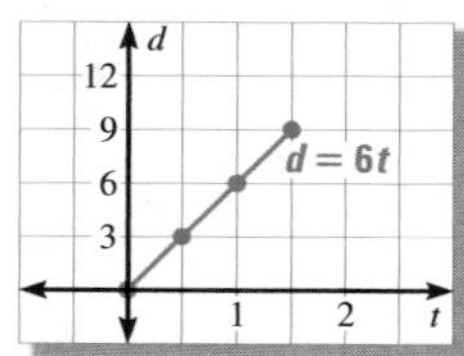

STEP 3 **Identify** the unspecified domain or range. From the table or graph, you can see that the range of the function is $0 \le d \le 9$.

ANALYZE GRAPHS
In Example 2, the domain is unrestricted, and the graph is a *line*. In Example 4, the domain is restricted to $x \ge 0$, and the graph is a *ray*. Here, the domain is restricted to $0 \le t \le 1.5$, and the graph is a *line segment*.

EXAMPLE 6 Solve a related problem

WHAT IF? Suppose the runner in Example 5 instead plans to run 12 miles. Graph the function and identify its domain and range.

Solution

STEP 1 **Identify** whether the problem specifies the domain or the range. You are given the distance that the runner plans to travel. Because distance is the dependent variable, the range is specified in this problem. The range of the function is $0 \le d \le 12$.

STEP 2 **Graph** the function. To make a table, you can substitute d-values (be sure to include 0 and 12) into the function $d = 6t$ and solve for t.

t (hours)	0	1	2
d (miles)	0	6	12

STEP 3 **Identify** the unspecified domain or range. From the table or graph, you can see that the domain of the function is $0 \le t \le 2$.

SOLVE FOR t
To find the time it takes the runner to run 12 miles, solve the equation $6t = 12$ to get $t = 2$.

✓ GUIDED PRACTICE for Examples 5 and 6

6. **GAS COSTS** For gas that costs \$2 per gallon, the equation $C = 2g$ gives the cost C (in dollars) of pumping g gallons of gas. You plan to pump \$10 worth of gas. Graph the function and identify its domain and range.
See margin for art; domain: $0 \le g \le 5$, range: $0 \le C \le 10$.

6. 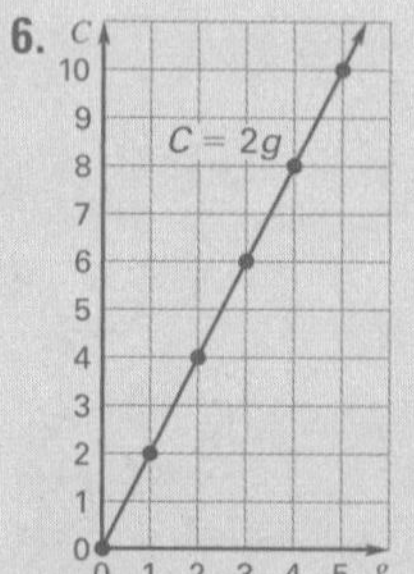

4.2 EXERCISES

HOMEWORK KEY
○ = WORKED-OUT SOLUTIONS on p. WS8 for Exs. 3, 11, and 37
★ = STANDARDIZED TEST PRACTICE Exs. 2, 10, 32, 33, 39, and 41
◆ = MULTIPLE REPRESENTATIONS Ex. 40

SKILL PRACTICE

A

1. **VOCABULARY** The equation $Ax + By = C$ represents a(n) _?_ provided $B \neq 0$. linear function

2. ★ **WRITING** Is the equation $y = 6x + 4$ in standard form? *Explain.*
No, to be in standard form it should be in the form $Ax + By = C$, so it should be $-6x + y = 4$.

EXAMPLE 1 on p. 215 for Exs. 3–10

CHECKING SOLUTIONS **Tell whether the ordered pair is a solution of the equation.**

3. $2y + x = 4$; $(-2, 3)$ solution
4. $3x - 2y = -5$; $(-1, 1)$ solution
5. $x = 9$; $(9, 6)$ solution
6. $y = -7$; $(-7, 0)$ not a solution
7. $-7x - 4y = 1$; $(-3, -5)$ not a solution
8. $-5y - 6x = 0$; $(-6, 5)$ not a solution

9. **ERROR ANALYSIS** *Describe* and correct the error in determining whether (8, 11) is a solution of $y - x = -3$.
The 8 should be substituted for x and 11 for y, $11 - 8 \neq -3$, so (8, 11) is not a solution.

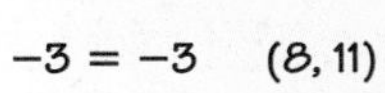

$y - x = -3$
$8 - 11 = -3$
$-3 = -3$ (8, 11) is a solution.

10. ★ **MULTIPLE CHOICE** Which ordered pair is a solution of $6x + 3y = 18$? B

Ⓐ $(-2, -10)$ Ⓑ $(-2, 10)$ Ⓒ $(2, 10)$ Ⓓ $(10, -2)$

EXAMPLES 2 and 3 on p. 216 for Exs. 11–25

GRAPHING EQUATIONS **Graph the equation.** 11–22. See margin.

11. $y + x = 2$
12. $y - 2x = 5$
13. $y - 3x = 0$
14. $y + 4x = 1$
15. $2y - 6x = 10$
16. $3y + 4x = 12$
17. $x - 2y = 3$
18. $3x + 2y = 8$
19. $x = 0$
20. $y = 0$
21. $y = -4$
22. $x = 2$

MATCHING EQUATIONS WITH GRAPHS **Match the equation with its graph.**

23. $y - x = 0$ C
24. $x = -2$ A
25. $y = -1$ B

A.
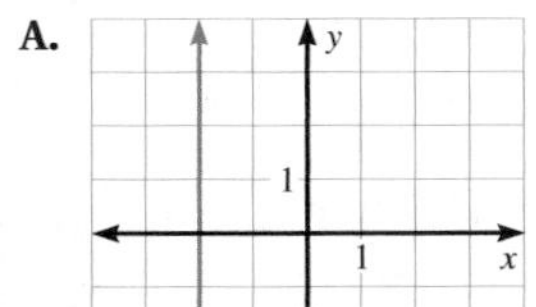

B.

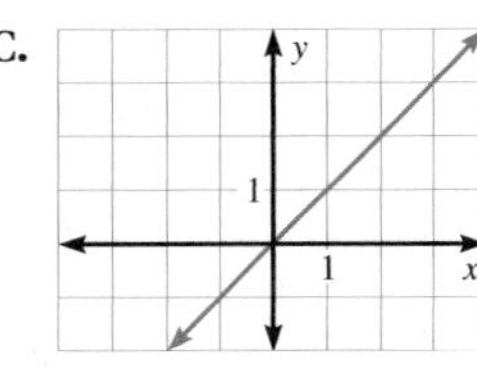

C.

EXAMPLE 4 on p. 217 for Exs. 26–31

B

GRAPHING FUNCTIONS **Graph the function with the given domain. Then identify the range of the function.** 26–31. See margin for art.

26. $y = 3x - 2$; domain: $x \geq 0$ $y \geq -2$
27. $y = -5x + 3$; domain: $x \leq 0$ $y \geq 3$
28. $y = 4$; domain: $x \leq 5$ $y = 4$
29. $y = -6$; domain: $x \geq 5$ $y = -6$
30. $y = 2x + 3$; domain: $-4 \leq x \leq 0$ $-5 \leq y \leq 3$
31. $y = -x - 1$; domain: $-1 \leq x \leq 3$ $-4 \leq y \leq 0$

32. ★ **OPEN-ENDED** Graph $x - y = 3$ and $2x - 2y = 6$. *Explain* why the equations look different but have the same graph. Find another equation that looks different from the two given equations but has the same graph.
See margin for art; the equations are the same, each term in the first equation was multiplied by 2 to get the second equation. *Sample answer:* $3x - 3y = 9$

11–22, 26–31. See Additional Answers beginning on p. AA1.

32.

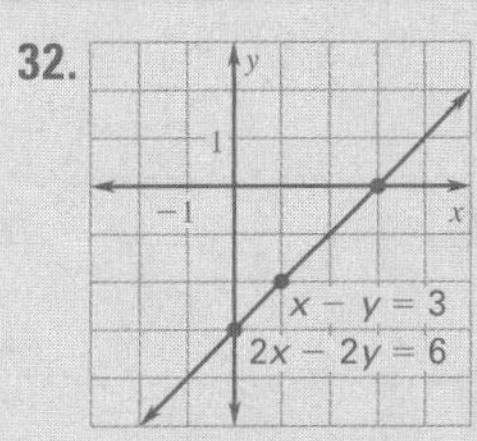

4 PRACTICE AND APPLY

Assignment Guide

Answer Transparencies available for all exercises

Basic:
Day 1: EP p. 938 Exs. 33–36
pp. 219–221
Exs. 1–10, 11–21 odd, 23–25, 42–47
Day 2: pp. 219–221
Exs. 26–29, 35–39, 48–55

Average:
Day 1: pp. 219–221
Exs. 1–10, 16–25, 42–47
Day 2: pp. 219–221
Exs. 26–32 even, 33, 35–40, 48–55

Advanced:
Day 1: pp. 219–221
Exs. 1, 2, 5–10, 17–25, 34*, 42–47
Day 2: pp. 219–221
Exs. 29–33, 36–41*, 48–55

Block:
pp. 219–221
Exs. 1–10, 16–25, 42–47 (with 4.1)
pp. 219–221
Exs. 26–32 even, 33, 35–40, 48–55 (with 4.3)

Differentiated Instruction

See *Algebra 1 Best Practices Toolkit* for suggestions on addressing the needs of a diverse classroom.

Homework Check

For a quick check of student understanding of key concepts, go over the following exercises:
Basic: 4, 13, 21, 26, 35
Average: 6, 17, 22, 28, 36
Advanced: 7, 18, 30, 37, 38

Extra Practice

- Student Edition, p. 941
- Chapter 4 Resource Book: Practice levels A, B, C, pp. 20–25

Practice Worksheet

An easily-readable reduced practice page (with answers) for this lesson can be found on p. 204C.

C 33. ★ **MULTIPLE CHOICE** Which statement is true for the function whose graph is shown? D

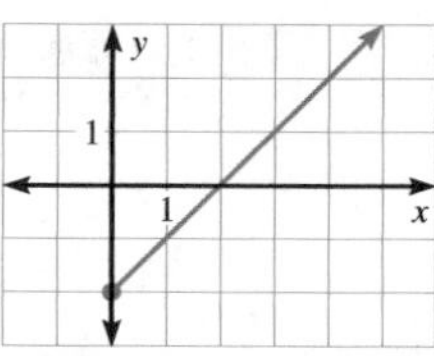

Ⓐ The domain is unrestricted.

Ⓑ The domain is $x \le -2$.

Ⓒ The range is $y \le -2$.

Ⓓ The range is $y \ge -2$.

34. **CHALLENGE** If $(3, n)$ is a solution of $Ax + 3y = 6$ and $(n, 5)$ is a solution of $5x + y = 20$, what is the value of A? -1

Avoiding Common Errors

Exercises 19–22 Since the *y*-axis is vertical and the *x*-axis is horizontal, some students may confuse axes with the graphs of equations. Watch for students who graph Exercises 19 and 22 as horizontal lines and 20 and 21 as vertical lines. Suggest they write ordered pairs for the equations before they begin to graph them. This should help students distinguish axes and graphs of equations.

Vocabulary

Exercise 33 Remind students that "unrestricted domain" means that the domain includes all the real numbers. A graph with an unrestricted domain therefore has an arrow on each end to show that the graph includes all the real numbers.

Mathematical Reasoning

Exercises 35, 36 Tell students that it makes sense to determine the domain or the range of the function before graphing it because that will help them decide what numbers to use in making a table of values. Ask students if values less than 0 make sense in these situations and how that affects the values they will use in their tables. Point out that upper limits on the domain or range also affect the values students use in their tables.

Exercise 40 To find more information about the weather balloons used by the National Weather Service, visit www.srh.noaa.gov/elp/kids/balloon.shtml

PROBLEM SOLVING

EXAMPLES 5 and 6 on p. 218 for Exs. 35–39

A 35. **BAKING** The weight w (in pounds) of a loaf of bread that a recipe yields is given by the function $w = \frac{1}{2}f$ where f is the number of cups of flour used. You have 4 cups of flour. Graph the function and identify its domain and range. What is the weight of the largest loaf of bread you can make?

@HomeTutor for problem solving help at classzone.com

See margin for art; domain: $0 \le f \le 4$, range: $0 \le w \le 2$; 2 lb.

36. **TRAVEL** After visiting relatives who live 200 miles away, your family drives home at an average speed of 50 miles per hour. Your distance d (in miles) from home is given by $d = 200 - 50t$ where t is the time (in hours) spent driving. Graph the function and identify its domain and range. What is your distance from home after driving for 1.5 hours?

@HomeTutor for problem solving help at classzone.com

See margin for art; domain: $0 \le t \le 4$, range: $0 \le d \le 200$; 125 mi.

(37.) **EARTH SCIENCE** The temperature T (in degrees Celsius) of Earth's crust can be modeled by the function $T = 20 + 25d$ where d is the distance (in kilometers) from the surface.

a. A scientist studies organisms in the first 4 kilometers of Earth's crust. Graph the function and identify its domain and range. What is the temperature at the deepest part of the section of crust? See margin for art; domain: $0 \le d \le 4$, range: $20 \le T \le 120$; 120°C.

b. Suppose the scientist studies organisms in a section of the crust where the temperature is between 20°C and 95°C. Graph the function and identify its domain and range. How many kilometers deep is the section of crust? See margin for art; domain: $0 \le d \le 3$, range: $20 \le T \le 95$; 3 km.

B 38. **MULTI-STEP PROBLEM** A fashion designer orders fabric that costs \$30 per yard. The designer wants the fabric to be dyed, which costs \$100. The total cost C (in dollars) of the fabric is given by the function

$$C = 30f + 100$$

where f is the number of yards of fabric.

a. The designer orders 3 yards of fabric. How much does the fabric cost? *Explain.* \$190; substitute 3 in for f and solve.

b. Suppose the designer can spend \$500 on fabric. How many yards of fabric can the designer buy? *Explain.*

38b. $13\frac{1}{3}$ yd; substitute 500 in for C and solve for f.

○ = WORKED-OUT SOLUTIONS on p. WS1 ★ = STANDARDIZED TEST PRACTICE ◆ = MULTIPLE REPRESENTATIONS

35.

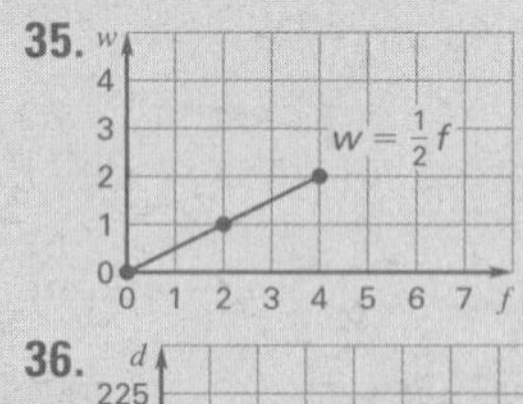

36.

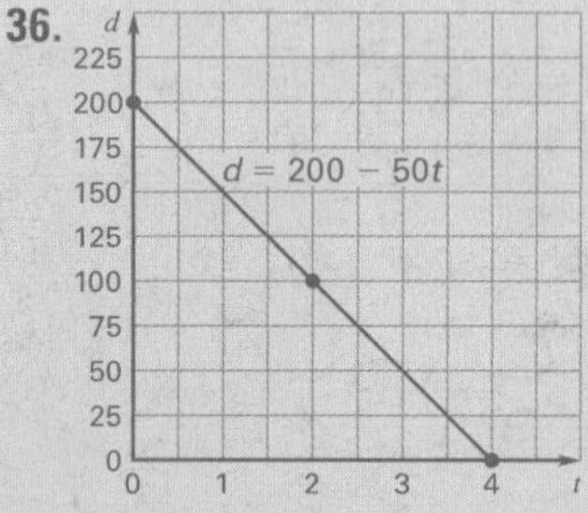

37a.

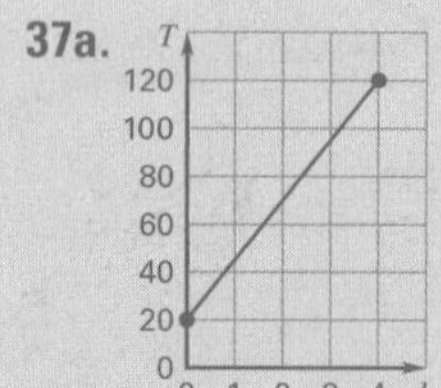

37b.

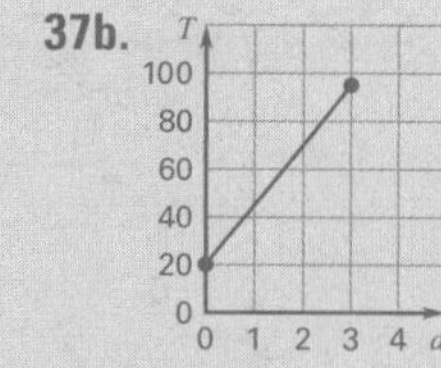

39a. See margin for art; domain: $t \geq 0$, range: $r \geq 0$.

39b. Domain: $0 \leq t \leq 4$, range: $0 \leq r \leq 480$; the graph was a ray, but is now a segment.

39. ★ **SHORT RESPONSE** An emergency cell phone charger requires you to turn a small crank in order to create the energy needed to recharge the phone's battery. If you turn the crank 120 times per minute, the total number r of revolutions that you turn the crank is given by

$$r = 120t$$

where t is the time (in minutes) spent turning the crank.

a. Graph the function and identify its domain and range.

b. Identify the domain and range if you stop turning the crank after 4 minutes. *Explain* how this affects the appearance of the graph.

40. ◆ **MULTIPLE REPRESENTATIONS** The National Weather Service releases weather balloons twice daily at over 90 locations in the United States in order to collect data for meteorologists. The height h (in feet) of a balloon is a function of the time t (in seconds) after the balloon is released, as shown.

a. **Making a Table** Make a table showing the height of a balloon after t seconds for $t = 0$ through $t = 10$. See margin.

b. **Drawing a Graph** A balloon bursts after a flight of about 7200 seconds. Graph the function and identify the domain and range.
See margin for art; domain: $0 \leq t \leq 7200$, range: $5 \leq h \leq 100,805$.

C **41.** ★ **EXTENDED RESPONSE** Students can pay for lunch at a school in one of two ways. Students can either make a payment of \$30 per month or they can buy lunch daily for \$2.50 per lunch.

a. **Graph** Graph the function $y = 30$ to represent the monthly payment plan. Using the same coordinate plane, graph the function $y = 2.5x$ to represent the daily payment plan. See margin.

b. **CHALLENGE** What are the coordinates of the point that is a solution of both functions? What does that point mean in this situation?

41b. (12, 30); at 12 days the cost is the same for both payment plans.

c. **CHALLENGE** A student eats an average of 15 school lunches per month. How should the student pay, daily or monthly? *Explain*.
Monthly; if he pays daily it will cost \$37.50, if he pays monthly it will cost only \$30.

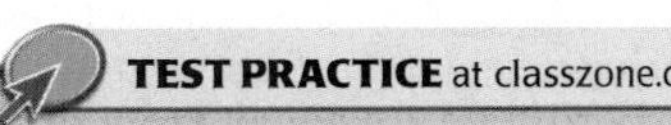

ILLINOIS MIXED REVIEW

42. A plumber charges \$64 per hour to do repair work and an additional \$92 for replacement parts. If the bill totals \$284, how many hours did the plumber work? D

Ⓐ 1.5 h Ⓑ 2 h Ⓒ 2.5 h Ⓓ 3 h

43. A specific shade of orange paint requires 3 parts red paint for every 4 parts yellow paint. A painter is mixing that shade of orange and uses 6 ounces of red paint and 2 tubes of yellow paint. How many ounces of paint are in one tube of yellow paint? B

Ⓐ $\frac{8}{3}$ oz Ⓑ 4 oz Ⓒ 6 oz Ⓓ 8 oz

5 ASSESS AND RETEACH

Daily Homework Quiz

Transparency Available

1. Graph $y + 2x = 4$.

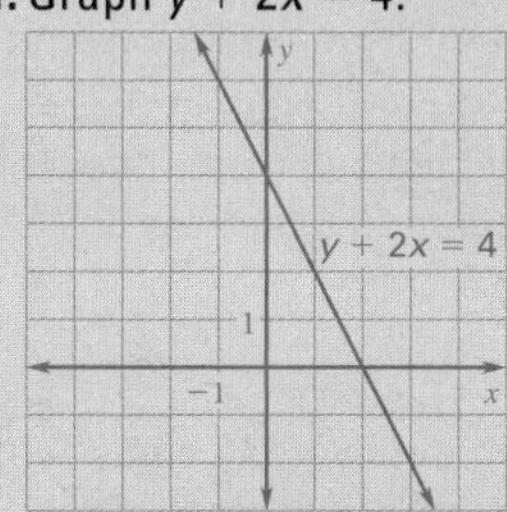

2. The distance in miles an elephant walks in t hours is given by $d = 5t$. The elephant walks for 2.5 hours. Graph the function and identify its domain and range. domain: $0 \leq t \leq 2.5$; range: $0 \leq d \leq 12.5$

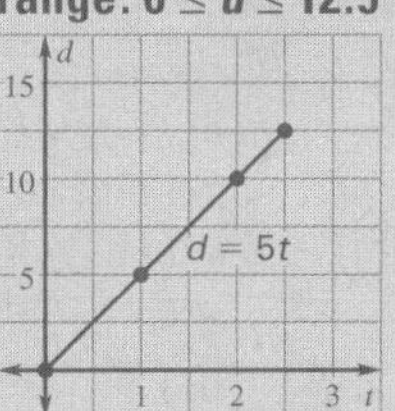

Available at **classzone.com**

Diagnosis/Remediation

- Practice A, B, C in Chapter 4 Resource Book, pp. 20–25
- Study Guide in Chapter 4 Resource Book, pp. 26–27
- Practice Workbook, pp. 49–51
- @HomeTutor

Challenge

Additional challenge is available in the Chapter 4 Resource Book, p. 30.

39a.

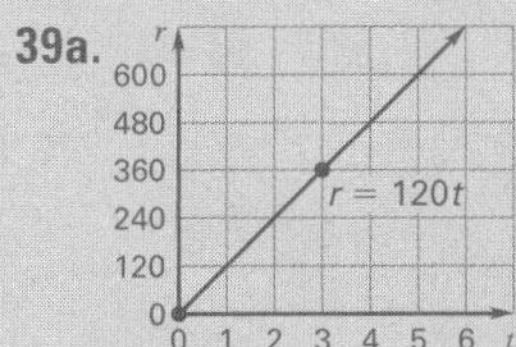

40a, 40b, 41a. See Additional Answers beginning on p. AA1.

1 PLAN AND PREPARE

Learn the Method

- Students will graph an equation on a graphing calculator and use the equation to solve a problem.
- After the activity, students can use a graphing calculator to check their solutions in Exercises 35–40 in Lesson 4.2.

Keystroke Help

Keystrokes for several models of calculators are available in blackline format in the *Chapter 4 Resource Book*.

2 TEACH

Tips for Success

As students are working on Step 2, mention that they can change existing minimums and maximums of a window by entering new data or by using the zoom feature on their calculators.

Extra Example

The total cost C to buy a water cooler and bottles of water can be modeled by $C = 115 + 5.65b$ where b is the number of bottles. Graph the equation. Estimate the total cost when the number of bottles is 18. about $217

3 ASSESS AND RETEACH

The fee f to use a photo lab can be modeled by $f = 12 + 4.25v$ where v is the number of visits.

1. Find the fee after 15 visits. $75.75
2. Find the number of visits if the fee is $63. 12 visits

Graphing Calculator ACTIVITY Use after Lesson 4.2

@HomeTutor classzone.com Keystrokes

4.2 Graphing Linear Equations

QUESTION How do you graph an equation on a graphing calculator?

EXAMPLE Use a graph to solve a problem

The formula to convert temperature from degrees Fahrenheit to degrees Celsius is $C = \frac{5}{9}(F - 32)$. Graph the equation. At what temperature are degrees Fahrenheit and degrees Celsius equal?

***STEP 1* Rewrite and enter equation**

Rewrite the equation using x for F and y for C. Enter the equation into the Y= screen. Put parentheses around the fraction $\frac{5}{9}$.

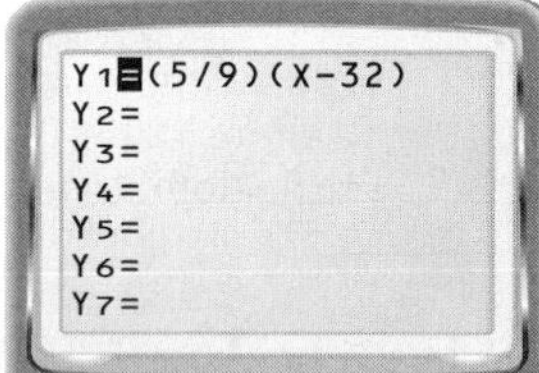

***STEP 2* Set window**

The screen is a "window" that lets you look at part of a coordinate plane. Press WINDOW to set the borders of the graph. A friendly window for this equation is $-94 \le x \le 94$ and $-100 \le y \le 100$.

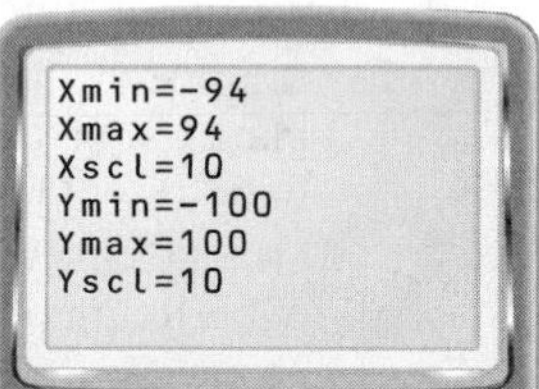

***STEP 3* Graph and trace equation**

Press TRACE and use the left and right arrows to move the cursor along the graph until the x-coordinate and y-coordinate are equal. From the graph, you can see that degrees Fahrenheit and degrees Celsius are equal at -40.

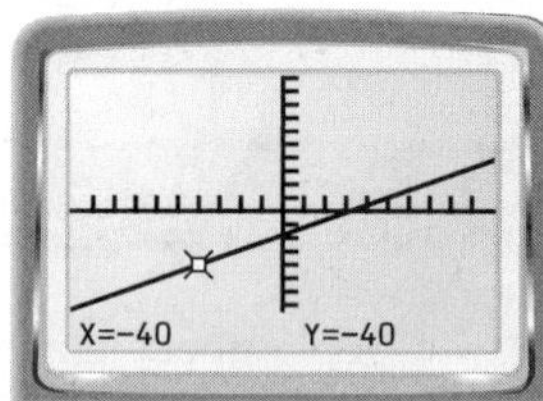

PRACTICE

Graph the equation. Find the unknown value in the ordered pair.

1. $y = 8 - x$; (2.4, ?) 5.6
2. $y = 2x + 3$; (?, 0.8) −1.1
3. $y = -4.5x + 1$; (1.4, ?) −5.3
4. **SPEED OF SOUND** The speed s (in meters per second) of sound in air can be modeled by $s = 331.1 + 0.61T$ where T is the air temperature in degrees Celsius. Graph the equation. Estimate the speed of sound when the temperature is 20°C. 343.3 m/sec

Use after Lesson 4.2

Identify Discrete and Continuous Functions

GOAL Graph and classify discrete and continuous functions.

Key Vocabulary
- **discrete function**
- **continuous function**

The graph of a function can consist of individual points, as in the graph in Example 3 on page 207. The graph of a function can also be a line or a part of a line with no breaks, as in the graph in Example 4 on page 217.

KEY CONCEPT *For Your Notebook*

Identifying Discrete and Continuous Functions

A **discrete function** has a graph that consists of isolated points.

A **continuous function** has a graph that is unbroken.

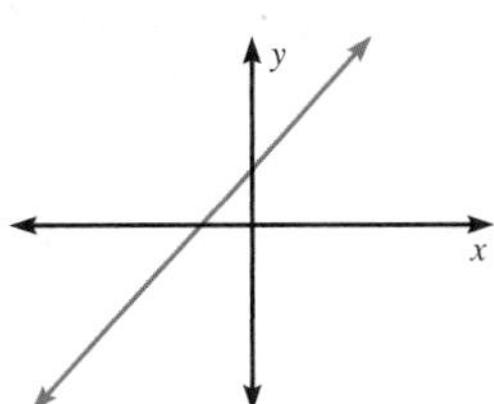

EXAMPLE 1 Graph and classify a function

Graph the function $y = 2x - 1$ with the given domain. Classify the function as discrete or continuous.

a. Domain: $x = 0, 1, 2, 3$

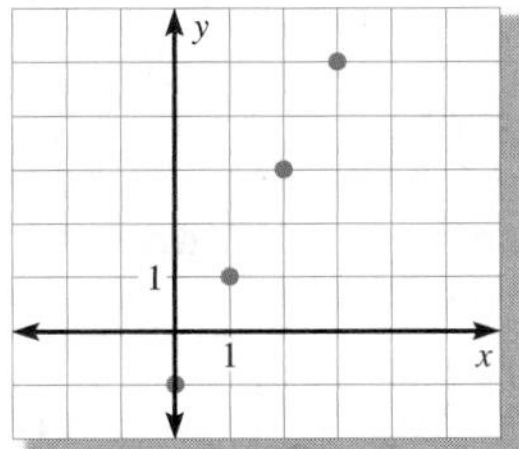

The graph consists of individual points, so the function is discrete.

b. Domain: $x \geq 0$

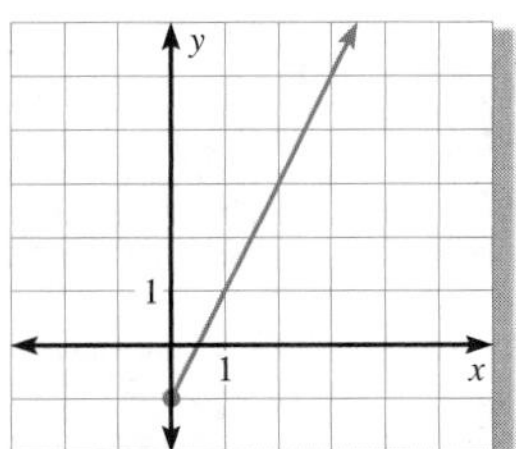

The graph is unbroken, so the function is continuous.

GRAPHS As a general rule, you can tell that a function is continuous if you do not have to lift your pencil from the paper to draw its graph, as in part (b) of Example 1.

1 PLAN AND PREPARE

Warm-Up Exercises

1. What is the range of $y = -x + 3$ with domain 0, 1, 2, and 4.
3, 2, 1, −1

2. Graph $y = \frac{1}{3}x + 1$.

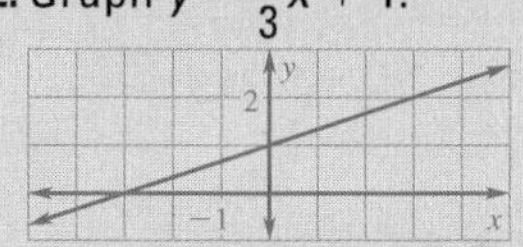

2 FOCUS AND MOTIVATE

Essential Question

Big Idea 1, p. 205

How do you tell if a function is discrete or continuous? Tell students they will learn how to answer this question by graphing functions with individual points and lines or parts of lines.

3 TEACH

Extra Example 1

Graph the function $y = \frac{1}{2}x + 1$ with the domain $x \geq 0$. Classify the function as discrete or continuous.

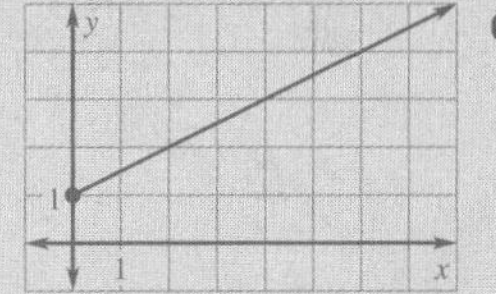

continuous

NCTM STANDARDS

Standard 2: Understand functions

Standard 10: Use representations to communicate mathematical ideas

Extra Example 2

Tell whether the function represented by the table is discrete or continuous. Explain. If continuous, graph the function and find the value of y when $x = 2.5$.

Hours hiked, x	1	2	3
Distance (mi), y	2.5	5	7.5

Since it makes sense to talk about the number of miles hiked after any amount of time, the table represents a continuous function. The distance hiked after 2.5 hours is about 6.25 miles.

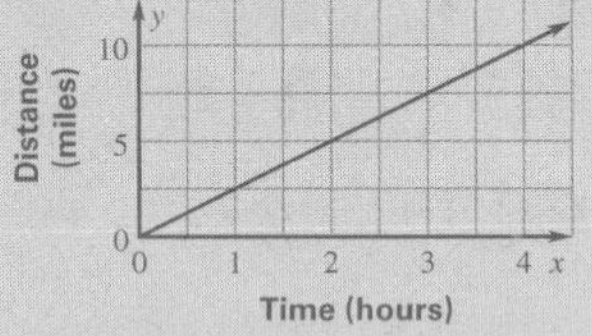

Closing the Lesson

Have students summarize the major points of the lesson and answer the Essential Question: How do you identify discrete and continuous functions?

- **A discrete function has a graph consisting of isolated points.**
- **A continuous function has a graph with no breaks in it.**

Given a situation or domain, determine whether you should represent the function with individual points or an unbroken line or part of a line.

4 PRACTICE AND APPLY

Study Strategy

Exercises 7–9 Instruct students to think in terms of what makes sense, as in Example 2, when considering whether the functions are discrete or continuous.

1–6. See Additional Answers beginning on p. AA1.

EXAMPLE 2 Classify and graph a real-world function

Tell whether the function represented by the table is discrete or continuous. Explain. If continuous, graph the function and find the value of y when $x = 1.5$.

Duration of storm (hours), x	1	2	3
Amount of rain (inches), y	0.5	1	1.5

Solution

Although the table shows the amount of rain that has fallen after whole numbers of hours only, it makes sense to talk about the amount of rain after any amount of time during the storm. So, the table represents a continuous function.

The graph of the function is shown. To find the value of y when $x = 1.5$, start at 1.5 on the x-axis, move up to the graph, and move over to the y-axis. The y-value is about 0.75. So, about 0.75 inch of rain has fallen after 1.5 hours.

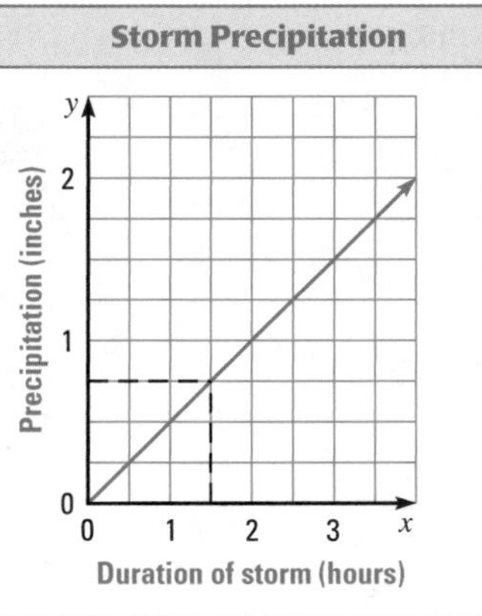

PRACTICE

EXAMPLE 1 on p. 223 for Exs. 1–6

Graph the function with the given domain. Classify the function as discrete or continuous. **1–6. See margin for art.**

1. $y = -2x + 3$; domain: $-2, -1, 0, 1, 2$ **discrete**
2. $y = x$; domain: all real numbers **continuous**
3. $y = -\frac{1}{3}x + 1$; domain: $-12, -6, 0, 6, 12$ **discrete**
4. $y = 0.5x$; domain: $-2, -1, 0, 1, 2$ **discrete**
5. $y = 3x - 4$; domain: $x \le 0$ **continuous**
6. $y = \frac{2}{3}x + \frac{1}{3}$; domain: $x \ge -2$ **continuous**

EXAMPLE 2 on p. 224 for Exs. 7–9

Tell whether the function represented by the table is discrete or continuous. *Explain.* If continuous, graph the function and find the value of y when $x = 3.5$. Round your answer to the nearest hundredth.

7.

Number of DVD rentals, x	1	2	3	4
Cost of rentals (dollars), y	4.50	9.00	13.50	18.00

Discrete; you can only rent a whole number of DVDs.

8.

Hours since 12 P.M., x	2	4	6	8
Distance driven (miles), y	100	200	300	400

8. Continuous; it makes sense to talk about the distance driven for any amount of time during the drive; 175.

9.

Volume of water (cubic inches), x	3	6	9	12
Approximate weight of water (pounds), y	0.1	0.2	0.3	0.4

Continuous; it makes sense to talk about the weight of water for any volume of water; about 0.12.

8. 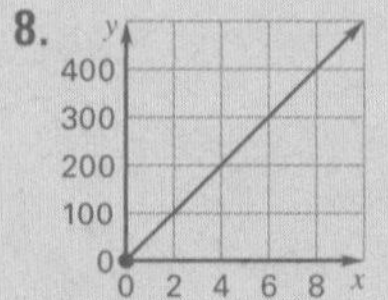

9. 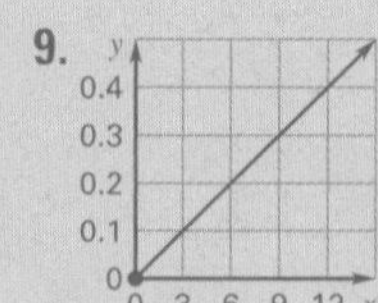

4.3 Graph Using Intercepts

8.11.11 Analyze functions by investigating domain, range, rates of change, intercepts, and zeros.

Before You graphed a linear equation using a table of values.

Now You will graph a linear equation using intercepts.

Why So you can find a submersible's location, as in Example 5.

Key Vocabulary
- ***x*-intercept**
- ***y*-intercept**

You can use the fact that two points determine a line to graph a linear equation. Two convenient points are the points where the graph crosses the axes.

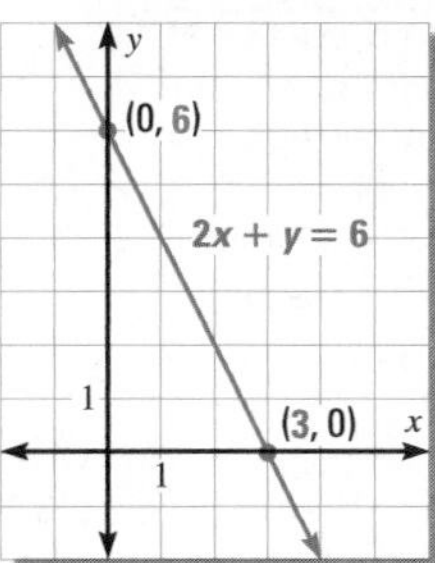

An ***x*-intercept** of a graph is the *x*-coordinate of a point where the graph crosses the *x*-axis. A ***y*-intercept** of a graph is the *y*-coordinate of a point where the graph crosses the *y*-axis.

To find the *x*-intercept of the graph of a linear equation, find the value of x when $y = 0$. To find the *y*-intercept of the graph, find the value of y when $x = 0$.

EXAMPLE 1 Find the intercepts of the graph of an equation

Find the *x*-intercept and the *y*-intercept of the graph of $2x + 7y = 28$.

Solution

To find the *x*-intercept, substitute 0 for y and solve for x.

$2x + 7y = 28$ Write original equation.

$2x + 7(0) = 28$ Substitute 0 for *y*.

$x = \frac{28}{2} = 14$ Solve for *x*.

To find the *y*-intercept, substitute 0 for x and solve for y.

$2x + 7y = 28$ Write original equation.

$2(0) + 7y = 28$ Substitute 0 for *x*.

$y = \frac{28}{7} = 4$ Solve for *y*.

▶ The *x*-intercept is 14. The *y*-intercept is 4.

GUIDED PRACTICE for Example 1

Find the *x*-intercept and the *y*-intercept of the graph of the equation.

1. $3x + 2y = 6$ 2, 3
2. $4x - 2y = 10$ 2.5, −5
3. $-3x + 5y = -15$ 5, −3

1 PLAN AND PREPARE

Warm-Up Exercises

Transparency Available

Evaluate the expression when $x = -3$.

1. $3x + 4$ −5
2. $-2x + 6$ 12
3. $4x - 3$ −15
4. The amount a that a taxi service charges is given by $a = 1.5m$ where m is the number of miles. Find a when m is 7. $10.50

Notetaking Guide

Transparency Available

Promotes interactive learning and notetaking skills, pp. 80–82.

Pacing

Basic: 1 day
Average: 1 day
Advanced: 1 day
Block: 0.5 block with 4.2
- See *Teaching Guide/Lesson Plan*.

2 FOCUS AND MOTIVATE

Essential Question

Big Idea 1, p. 205

How do you use intercepts to graph equations? Tell students they will learn how to answer this question by finding and using the *x*- and *y*-intercepts of the graph of an equation.

Resource Planning Guide

Chapter Resource Book
- Teaching Guide/Lesson Plan (pp. 31–32)
- Practice levels A, B, C (pp. 33–38)
- Study Guide (pp. 39–40)
- Catch-up for Absent Students (p. 41)
- Problem Solving Workshop (p. 42)
- Challenge (p. 44)

Workbooks
- Notetaking Guide (pp. 80–82)
- Practice Workbook (pp. 52–54)

Teaching Options
- **Power Presentations CD-ROM** provides dynamic electronic teaching resources for the classroom.
- **Activity Generator CD-ROM** provides editable activities for all ability levels.

Interactive Technology
- Easy Planner
- Power Presentations CD-ROM
- Activity Generator CD-ROM
- Animated Algebra
- Test Generator CD-ROM
- Online Quiz
- eWorkbook
- eEdition
- @HomeTutor

Resources for English Learners
- Quick Reference for English Learners
- Spanish Study Guide
- Multi-Language Visual Glossary
- Student Resources in Spanish

See also the *Algebra 1 Toolkit* for more strategies for meeting individual needs.

Motivating the Lesson

You know that your school sells T-shirts and sweatshirts with the school name on them. T-shirts cost \$9 and sweatshirts cost \$12. You have \$144. By writing an equation and finding the intercepts of the graph of the equation, you can find the possible numbers of T-shirts and sweatshirts you can buy.

3 TEACH

Extra Example 1

Find the x-intercept and the y-intercept of the graph of $3x - 4y = 12$. **x-intercept: 4, y-intercept: -3**

Key Question to Ask for Example 1

- What coordinates are associated with the x-intercept and the y-intercept? **(14, 0), (0, 4)**

Extra Example 2

Graph the equation $4x + 8y = 24$.

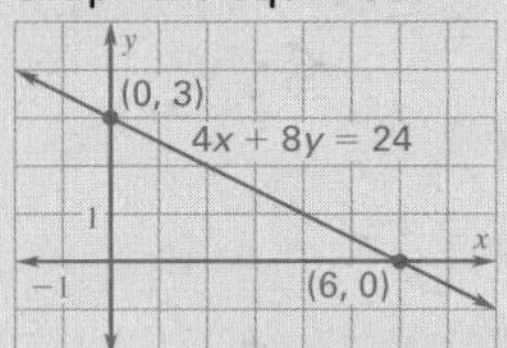

Key Question to Ask for Example 2

- Why is using intercepts an efficient way to graph an equation? **Since $x = 0$ and $y = 0$, it is easier to find the intercepts than other points on the line.**

An **Animated Algebra** activity is available on-line for **Example 2**. This activity is also available on the **Power Presentations CD-ROM**.

EXAMPLE 2 Use intercepts to graph an equation

Graph the equation $x + 2y = 4$.

Solution

STEP 1 **Find** the intercepts.

$x + 2y = 4$	$x + 2y = 4$
$x + 2(0) = 4$	$0 + 2y = 4$
$x = 4 \leftarrow$ **x-intercept**	$y = 2 \leftarrow$ **y-intercept**

STEP 2 **Plot** points. The x-intercept is 4, so plot the point (4, 0). The y-intercept is 2, so plot the point (0, 2). Draw a line through the points.

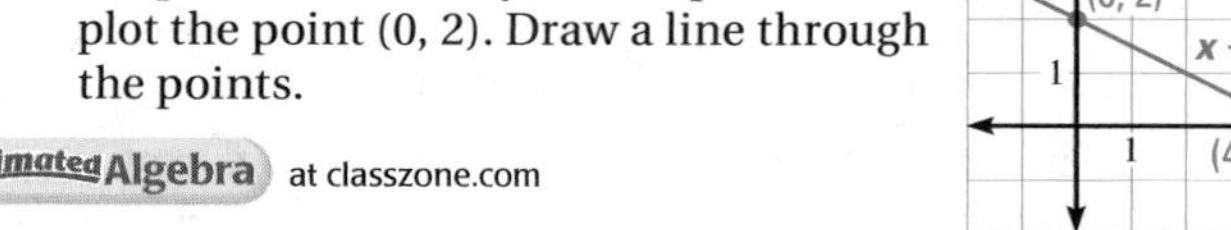

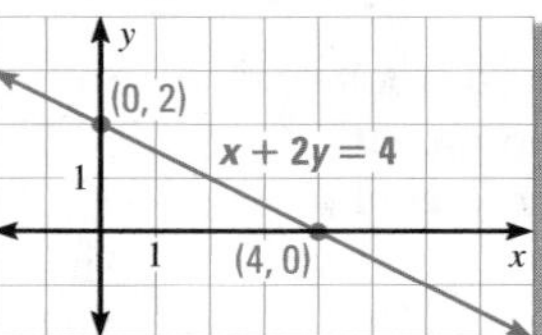

CHECK A GRAPH
Be sure to check the graph by finding a third solution of the equation and checking to see that the corresponding point is on the graph.

EXAMPLE 3 Use a graph to find intercepts

The graph crosses the x-axis at (2, 0). The x-intercept is 2. The graph crosses the y-axis at $(0, -1)$. The y-intercept is -1.

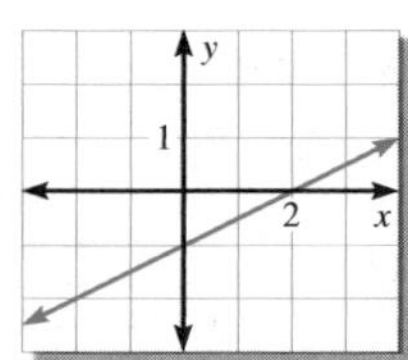

✓ GUIDED PRACTICE for Examples 2 and 3

4. Graph $6x + 7y = 42$. Label the points where the line crosses the axes. **See margin.**

5. Identify the x-intercept and the y-intercept of the graph shown at the right. **-4, 2**

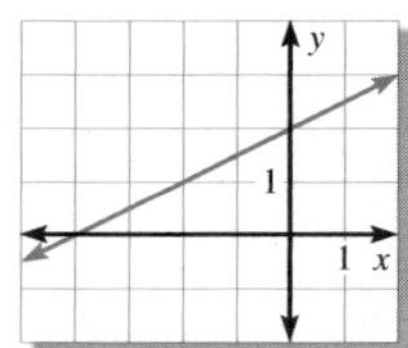

KEY CONCEPT *For Your Notebook*

Relating Intercepts, Points, and Graphs

Intercepts	Points
The x intercept of a graph is a.	The graph crosses the x-axis at $(a, 0)$.
The y-intercept of a graph is b.	The graph crosses the y-axis at $(0, b)$.

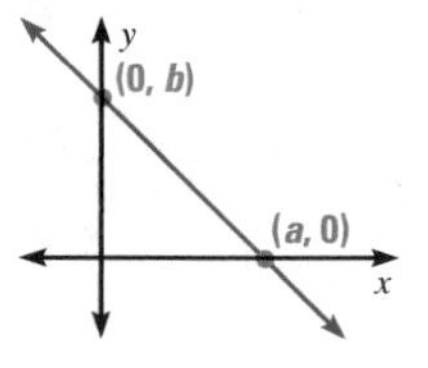

Differentiated Instruction

Visual Learners To help students remember how to find the intercepts in problems similar to Example 2, have them make the following table.

x-intercept	$x = 0$
y-intercept	$y = 0$

Have them connect the entries in this table with an "X," pairing "x-intercept" with "$y = 0$" and pairing "y-intercept" with "$x = 0$." See also the *Algebra 1 Toolkit* for more strategies.

EXAMPLE 4 Solve a multi-step problem

EVENT PLANNING You are helping to plan an awards banquet for your school, and you need to rent tables to seat 180 people. Tables come in two sizes. Small tables seat 4 people, and large tables seat 6 people. This situation can be modeled by the equation

$$4x + 6y = 180$$

where x is the number of small tables and y is the number of large tables.

- Find the intercepts of the graph of the equation.
- Graph the equation.
- Give four possibilities for the number of each size table you could rent.

Solution

STEP 1 **Find** the intercepts.

$4x + 6y = 180$	$4x + 6y = 180$
$4x + 6(0) = 180$	$4(0) + 6y = 180$
$x = 45 \leftarrow$ **x-intercept**	$y = 30 \leftarrow$ **y-intercept**

STEP 2 **Graph** the equation.

The x-intercept is 45, so plot the point (45, 0). The y-intercept is 30, so plot the point (0, 30).

Since x and y both represent numbers of tables, neither x nor y can be negative. So, instead of drawing a line, draw the part of the line that is in Quadrant I.

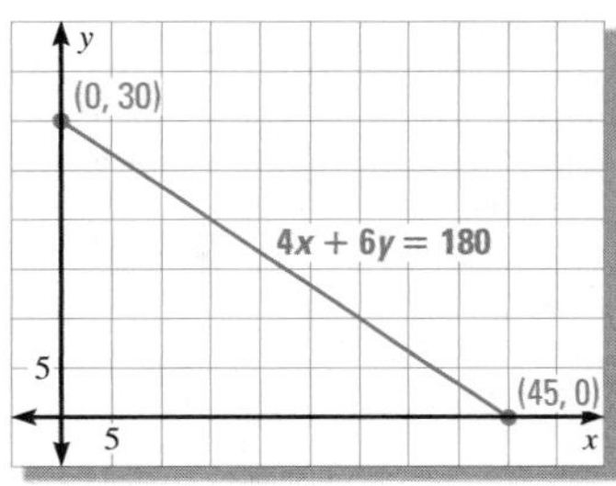

DRAW A GRAPH
Although x and y represent whole numbers, it is convenient to draw an unbroken line segment that includes points whose coordinates are not whole numbers.

STEP 3 **Find** the number of tables. For this problem, only whole-number values of x and y make sense. You can see that the line passes through the points (0, 30), (15, 20), (30, 10), and (45, 0).

So, four possible combinations of tables that will seat 180 people are: 0 small and 30 large, 15 small and 20 large, 30 small and 10 large, and 45 small and 0 large.

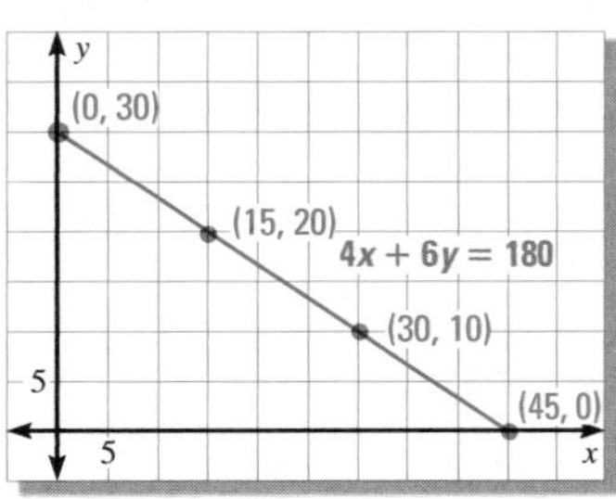

FIND SOLUTIONS
Other points, such as (12, 22), are also on the graph but are not as obvious as the points shown here because their coordinates are not multiples of 5.

GUIDED PRACTICE for Example 4

6. **WHAT IF?** In Example 4, suppose the small tables cost \$9 to rent and the large tables cost \$14. Of the four possible combinations of tables given in the example, which rental is the least expensive? *Explain.* **45 small tables and no large tables; if you rent 45 small tables it costs \$405, all other combinations are more expensive.**

4. 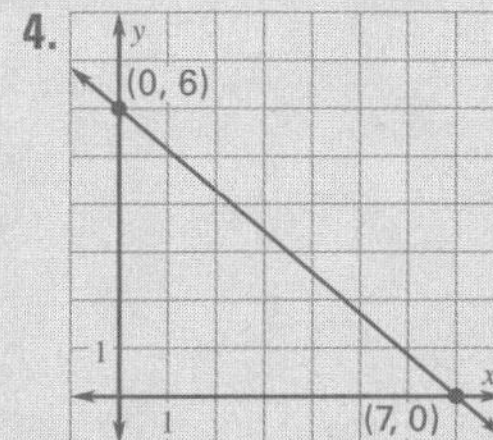

Extra Example 3

Identify the x-intercept and y-intercept of the graph.

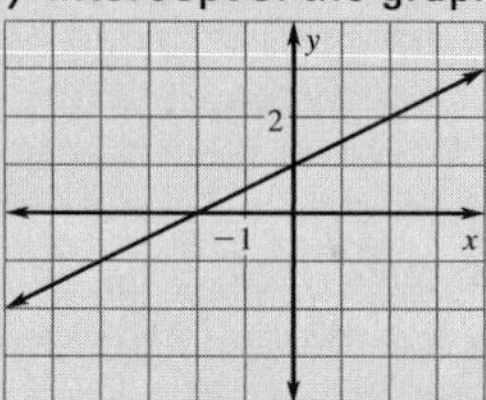

x-intercept: −2, y-intercept: 1

Extra Example 4

You make and sell decorative bows. You sell small bows for \$3 and large bows for \$5. You want to earn \$60 per week. This situation can be modeled by $3x + 5y = 60$ where x is the number of small bows and y is the number of large bows.

- Find the intercepts of the graph.
- Graph the equation.
- Give three possibilities for the number of each type of bow you can sell to earn \$60.

x-intercept: 20, y-intercept: 12

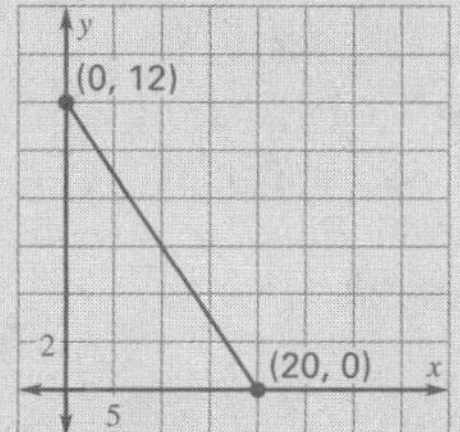

Possible combinations: 0 small and 12 large, 10 small and 6 large, 20 small and 0 large

Key Questions to Ask for Example 4

- How can you check the graph of the equation? Explain. **Test another point on the graph, such as (15, 20). If you substitute the values in the equation and they check, the graph is correct.**
- The point (10.5, 23) is a solution of the equation. Is it a solution of the problem? Explain. **No; you cannot rent 10.5 small tables.**

Teaching Strategy

In Step 2 of Example 5 on page 228, remind students that the scales on the x- and y-axes do not have to be the same and that it would be better in some situations to have two different scales.

Extra Example 5

You borrow \$1800 from your parents. To repay your debt, you give them \$150 per month. Your debt d (in dollars) is given by the function $d = 150t - 1800$ where t represents time (in months).

- Find the intercepts of the graph of the function and state what they represent. **t-intercept: 12, d-intercept: −1800; The t-intercept represents the number of months it takes to reduce the debt to 0 dollars. The d-intercept represents the amount of your debt at the time you begin to repay it.**
- Graph the function and identify its domain and range. **domain: $0 \le t \le 12$; range: $-1800 \le d \le 0$**

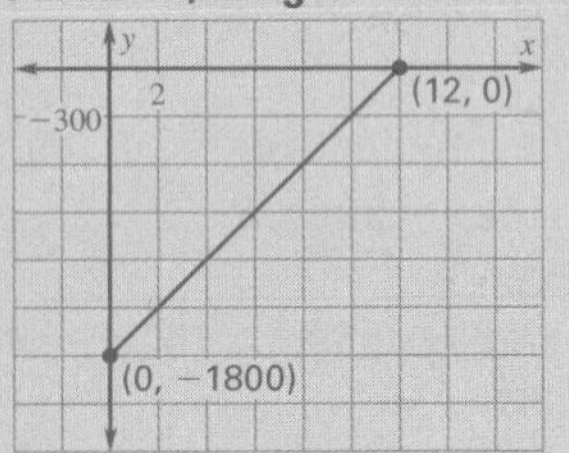

Closing the Lesson

Have students summarize the major points of the lesson and answer the Essential Question: How do you use intercepts to graph equations?

- **The x-intercept is the x-coordinate of the point where the graph crosses the x-axis.**
- **The y-intercept is the y-coordinate of the point where the graph crosses the y-axis.**

Find the x- and y-intercepts by substituting 0 for y in the equation and solving for x and then 0 for x and solving for y. Plot the points that correspond to the intercepts and then connect the points by drawing a line or part of a line through them.

EXAMPLE 5 Use a linear model

SUBMERSIBLES A submersible designed to explore the ocean floor is at an elevation of −13,000 feet (13,000 feet below sea level). The submersible ascends to the surface at an average rate of 650 feet per minute. The elevation e (in feet) of the submersible is given by the function

$$e = 650t - 13{,}000$$

where t is the time (in minutes) since the submersible began to ascend.

- Find the intercepts of the graph of the function and state what the intercepts represent.
- Graph the function and identify its domain and range.

NAME INTERCEPTS
Because t is the independent variable, the horizontal axis is the t-axis, and you refer to the "t-intercept" of the graph of the function. Similarly, the vertical axis is the e-axis, and you refer to the "e-intercept."

Solution

STEP 1 **Find** the intercepts.

$0 = 650t - 13{,}000$	$e = 650(0) - 13{,}000$
$13{,}000 = 650t$	$e = -13{,}000 \leftarrow$ **e-intercept**
$20 = t \leftarrow$ **t-intercept**	

The t-intercept represents the number of minutes the submersible takes to reach an elevation of 0 feet (sea level). The e-intercept represents the elevation of the submersible after 0 minutes (the time the ascent begins).

STEP 2 **Graph** the function using the intercepts.

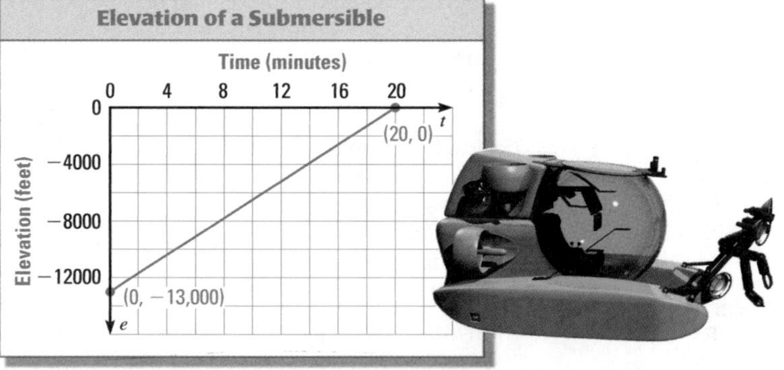

The submersible starts at an elevation of −13,000 feet and ascends to an elevation of 0 feet. So, the range of the function is $-13{,}000 \le e \le 0$. From the graph, you can see that the domain of the function is $0 \le t \le 20$.

✓ GUIDED PRACTICE for Example 5

7. **WHAT IF?** In Example 5, suppose the elevation of a second submersible is given by $e = 500t - 10{,}000$. Graph the function and identify its domain and range. **See margin for art; domain: $0 \le t \le 20$, range: $-10{,}000 \le e \le 0$.**

7.

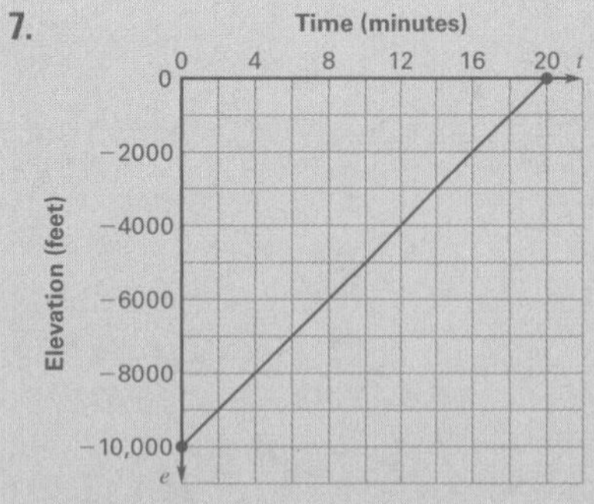

4.3 EXERCISES

HOMEWORK KEY
○ = WORKED-OUT SOLUTIONS on p. WS8 for Exs. 21 and 47
★ = STANDARDIZED TEST PRACTICE Exs. 2, 37, 41, 49, and 50
◆ = MULTIPLE REPRESENTATIONS Ex. 44

SKILL PRACTICE

A

1. **VOCABULARY** Copy and complete: The _?_ of the graph of an equation is the value of x when y is zero. x-intercept

2. ★ **WRITING** What are the x-intercept and the y-intercept of the line passing through the points (0, 3) and (−4, 0)? *Explain.*

2. −4, 3; the x-intercept is when y is 0, so the point (−4, 0) gives the x-intercept. The y-intercept is when x is 0, so the point (0, 3) gives the y-intercept.

3. **ERROR ANALYSIS** *Describe* and correct the error in finding the intercepts of the line shown. The intercepts are switched around; the x-intercept is −2, and the y-intercept is 1.

The x-intercept is 1, and the y-intercept is −2.

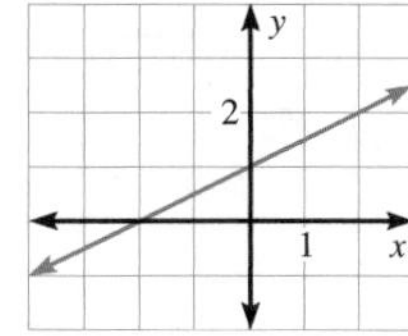

EXAMPLE 1 on p. 225 for Exs. 4–15

FINDING INTERCEPTS **Find the x-intercept and the y-intercept of the graph of the equation.**

4. $5x - y = 35$ 7, −35
5. $3x - 3y = 9$ 3, −3
6. $-3x + 9y = -18$ 6, −2
7. $4x + y = 4$ 1, 4
8. $2x + y = 10$ 5, 10
9. $2x - 8y = 24$ 12, −3
10. $3x + 0.5y = 6$ 2, 12
11. $0.2x + 3.2y = 12.8$ 64, 4
12. $y = 2x + 24$ −12, 24
13. $y = -14x + 7$ $\frac{1}{2}$, 7
14. $y = -4.8x + 1.2$ 0.25, 1.2
15. $y = \frac{3}{5}x - 12$ 20, −12

EXAMPLE 2 on p. 226 for Exs. 16–27

GRAPHING LINES **Graph the equation. Label the points where the line crosses the axes.** 16–27. See margin.

16. $y = x + 3$
17. $y = x - 2$
18. $y = 4x - 8$
19. $y = 5 + 10x$
20. $y = -2 + 8x$
21. $y = -4x + 3$
22. $3x + y = 15$
23. $x - 4y = 18$
24. $8x - 5y = 80$
25. $-2x + 5y = 15$
26. $0.5x + 3y = 9$
27. $y = \frac{1}{2}x + \frac{1}{4}$

EXAMPLE 3 on p. 226 for Exs. 28–30

USING GRAPHS TO FIND INTERCEPTS **Identify the x-intercept and the y-intercept of the graph.**

28. 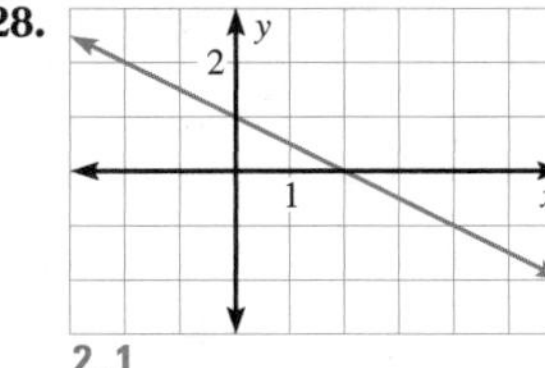

2, 1

29. 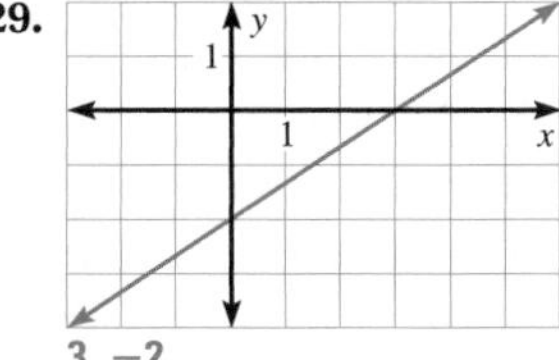

3, −2

30. 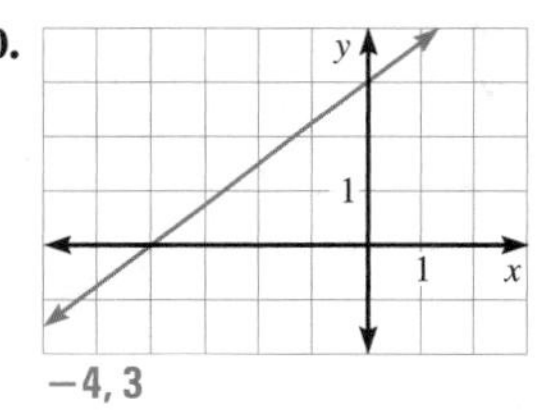

−4, 3

4 PRACTICE AND APPLY

Assignment Guide

Answer Transparencies available for all exercises

Basic:
Day 1: EP p. 940 Exs. 1–7 odd
pp. 229–232
Exs. 1–10, 16–21, 28–33, 37, 44–47, 51–56

Average:
Day 1: pp. 229–232
Exs. 1–3, 10–15, 22–27, 29, 30, 34–41, 44–49, 51–55 odd

Advanced:
Day 1: pp. 229–232
Exs. 1, 2, 12–15, 24–27, 29, 30, 35–37, 39–43*, 46–50*, 52–56 even

Block:
pp. 229–232
Exs. 1–3, 10–15, 22–27, 29, 30, 34–41, 44–49, 51–55 odd (with 4.2)

Differentiated Instruction

See *Algebra 1 Best Practices Toolkit* for suggestions on addressing the needs of a diverse classroom.

Homework Check

For a quick check of student understanding of key concepts, go over the following exercises:
Basic: 6, 17, 28, 44, 45
Average: 11, 24, 29, 46, 48
Advanced: 13, 26, 30, 48, 49

Extra Practice

- Student Edition, p. 941
- Chapter 4 Resource Book: Practice levels A, B, C, pp. 33–38

Practice Worksheet

An easily-readable reduced practice page (with answers) for this lesson can be found on p. 204D.

16–27. See Additional Answers beginning on p. AA1.

Avoiding Common Errors

Exercises 4–15 You may want to remind students before they begin these exercises that an intercept is either the x-coordinate or the y-coordinate of an ordered pair and therefore written as a number, not as an ordered pair.

Teaching Strategy

Exercises 31–36 Before students begin these exercises, suggest they write the ordered pairs that correspond to the intercepts.

31.

32.

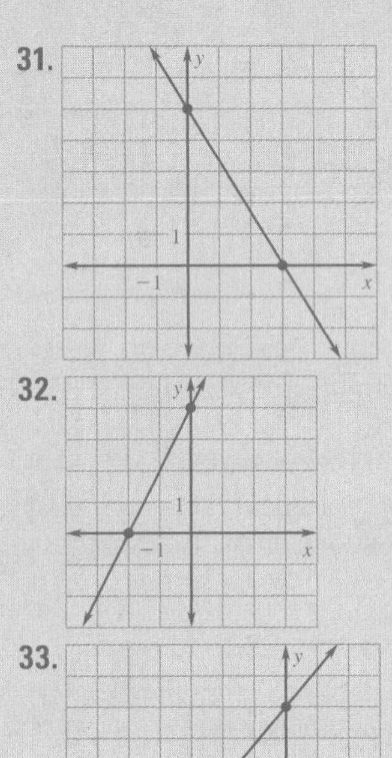

33.

34.

35.

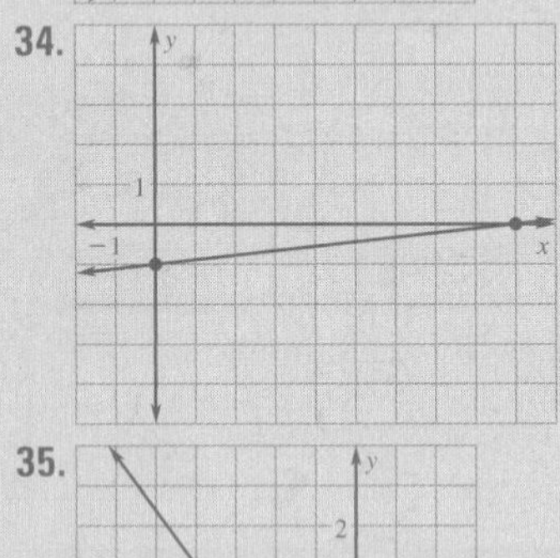

B **USING INTERCEPTS** **Draw the line that has the given intercepts.** 31–36. See margin.

31. x-intercept: 3
    y-intercept: 5
32. x-intercept: -2
    y-intercept: 4
33. x-intercept: -5
    y-intercept: 6
34. x-intercept: 9
    y-intercept: -1
35. x-intercept: -8
    y-intercept: -11
36. x-intercept: -2
    y-intercept: -6

37. ★ **MULTIPLE CHOICE** The x-intercept of the graph of $Ax + 5y = 20$ is 2. What is the value of A? D

    Ⓐ 2 Ⓑ 5 Ⓒ 7.5 Ⓓ 10

MATCHING EQUATIONS WITH GRAPHS **Match the equation with its graph.**

38. $2x - 6y = 6$ C
39. $2x - 6y = -6$ B
40. $2x - 6y = 12$ A

A.

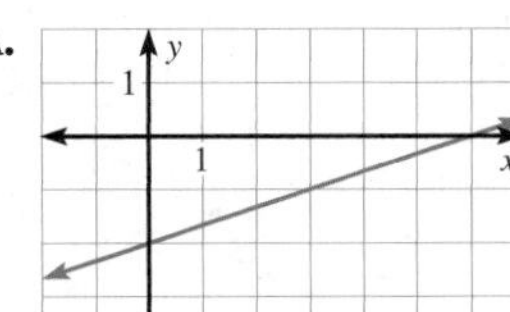

B.

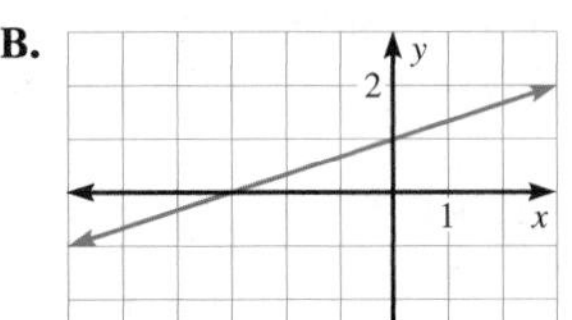

C.

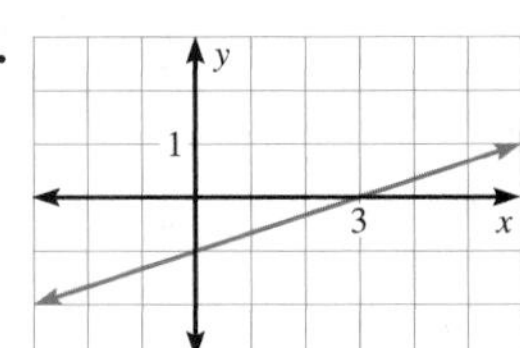

C 41. ★ **WRITING** Is it possible for a line *not* to have an x-intercept? Is it possible for a line *not* to have a y-intercept? *Explain.* Yes; yes; a horizontal line does not have an x-intercept if $y \neq 0$, a vertical line does not have a y-intercept if $x \neq 0$.

42. **REASONING** Consider the equation $3x + 5y = k$. What values could k have so that the x-intercept and the y-intercept of the equation's graph would both be integers? *Explain.* *Sample answer:* 15 and 30; k can be any multiple of both 3 and 5.

43. **CHALLENGE** If $a \neq 0$, find the intercepts of the graph of $y = ax + b$ in terms of a and b. $x = -\frac{b}{a}, y = b$

PROBLEM SOLVING

EXAMPLES A 4 and 5 on pp. 227–228 for Exs. 44–47

44. ◆ **MULTIPLE REPRESENTATIONS** The perimeter of a rectangular park is 72 feet. Let x be the park's width (in feet) and let y be its length (in feet).

    a. **Writing an Equation** Write an equation for the perimeter. $2x + 2y = 72$

    b. **Drawing a Graph** Find the intercepts of the graph of the equation you wrote. Then graph the equation. 36, 36; see margin for art.

    @HomeTutor for problem solving help at classzone.com

45. **RECYCLING** In one state, small bottles have a refund value of \$.04 each, and large bottles have a refund value of \$.08 each. Your friend returns both small and large bottles and receives \$.56. This situation is given by $4x + 8y = 56$ where x is the number of small bottles and y is the number of large bottles. $x = 14, y = 7$; see margin for art.

    a. Find the intercepts of the graph of the equation. Graph the equation.

    b. Give three possibilities for the number of each size bottle your friend could have returned. *Sample answer:* 2 and 6, 4 and 5, 6 and 4

    @HomeTutor for problem solving help at classzone.com

○ = WORKED-OUT SOLUTIONS on p. WS1 ★ = STANDARDIZED TEST PRACTICE

= MULTIPLE REPRESENTATIONS

36.

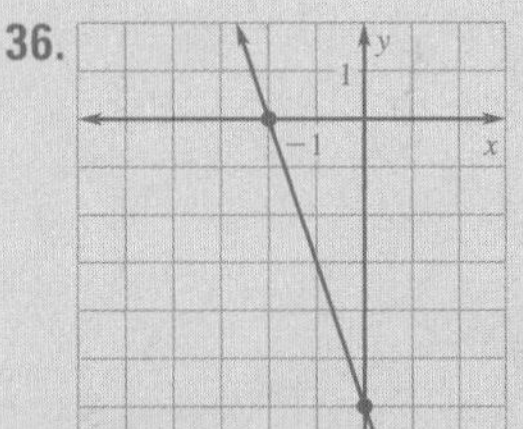

44b.

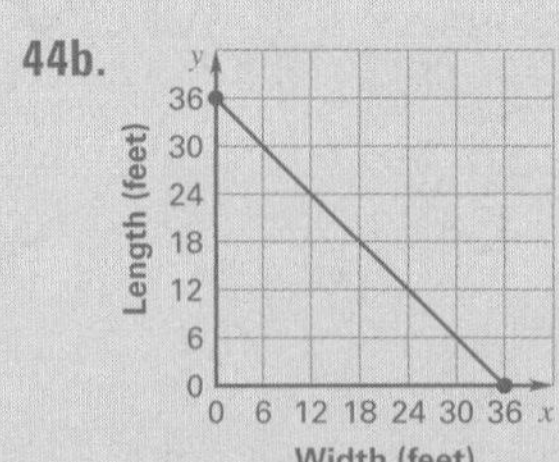

45a.

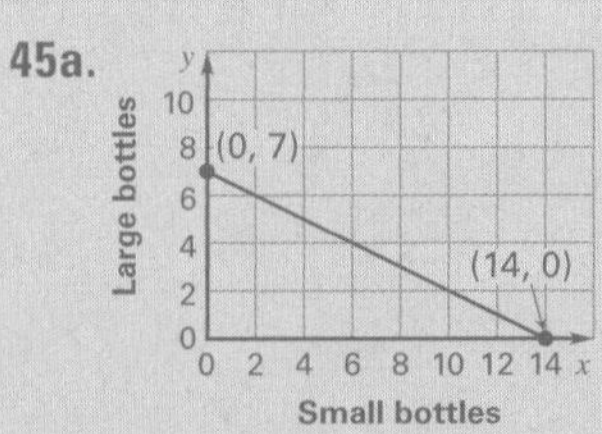

46b. The x-intercept means 64 field goals were scored and no free throws were scored. The y-intercept means that no field goals were scored and 128 free throws were scored.

46c. *Sample answer:* 40 field goals and 48 free throws, 50 field goals and 28 free throws, 60 field goals and 8 free throws

47a. v-intercept: 120, f-intercept: 180; the v-intercept means there are no flowers planted, the f-intercept means there are no vegetables planted.

47b. See margin for art; domain: $0 \le v \le 120$, range: $0 \le f \le 180$.

46. MULTI-STEP PROBLEM Before 1979, there was no 3-point shot in professional basketball; players could score only 2-point field goals and 1-point free throws. In a game before 1979, a team scored a total of 128 points. This situation is given by the equation $2x + y = 128$ where x is the possible number of field goals and y is the possible number of free throws.

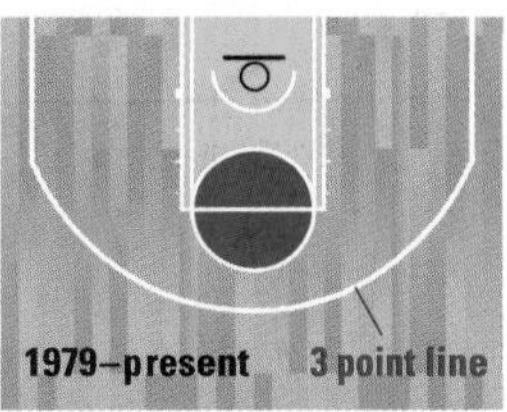

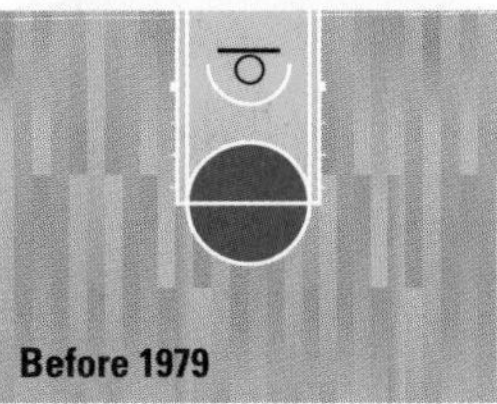

a. Find the intercepts of the graph of the equation. Graph the equation. $x = 64$, $y = 128$; see margin for art.

b. What do the intercepts mean in this situation?

c. What are three possible numbers of field goals and free throws the team could have scored?

d. If the team made 24 free throws, how many field goals were made? 52 field goals

47. COMMUNITY GARDENS A family has a plot in a community garden. The family is going to plant vegetables, flowers, or both. The diagram shows the area used by one vegetable plant and the area of the entire plot. The area f (in square feet) of the plot left for flowers is given by $f = 180 - 1.5v$ where v is the number of vegetable plants the family plants.

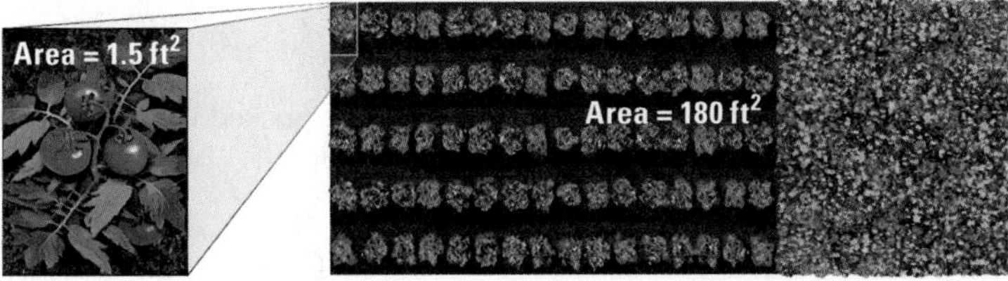

a. Find the intercepts of the graph of the function and state what the intercepts represent.

b. Graph the function and identify its domain and range.

c. The family decides to plant 80 vegetable plants. How many square feet are left to plant flowers? 60 ft²

B

48. CAR SHARING A member of a car-sharing program can use a car for \$6 per hour and \$.50 per mile. The member uses the car for one day and is charged \$44. This situation is given by

$$6t + 0.5d = 44$$

where t is the time (in hours) the car is used and d is the distance (in miles) the car is driven. Give three examples of the number of hours the member could have used the car and the number of miles the member could have driven the car. *Sample answer:* 1 h and 76 mi, 2 h and 64 mi, 3 h and 52 mi

49. ★ SHORT RESPONSE A humidifier is a device used to put moisture into the air by turning water to vapor. A humidifier has a tank that can hold 1.5 gallons of water. The humidifier can disperse the water at a rate of 0.12 gallon per hour. The amount of water w (in gallons) left in the humidifier after t hours of use is given by the function

$$w = 1.5 - 0.12t.$$

After how many hours of use will you have to refill the humidifier? *Explain* how you found your answer. 12.5 h. *Sample answer:* Since the tank will be empty when it needs to be refilled, replace w in the function with 0 and then solve the resulting equation for t.

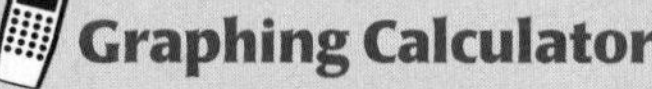

Graphing Calculator

Exercises 44–49 Students can use their graphing calculators to check their graphs. They can enter the equation using the **y=** key, set parameters for the window using the Window key, and then graph using the Graph key. They can use the Table key to check x-intercepts, y-intercepts, and possible solutions for each of the exercises.

46a.

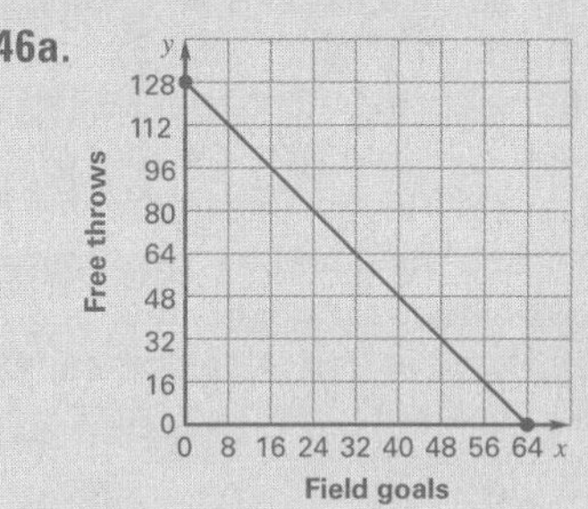

47b.

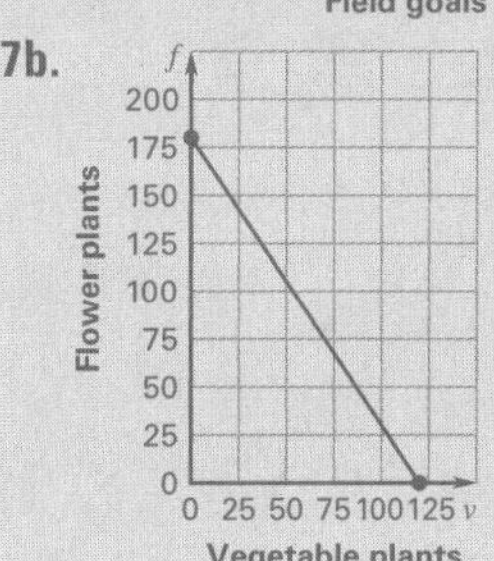

5 ASSESS AND RETEACH

Daily Homework Quiz

Transparency Available

1. Find the x-intercept and the y-intercept of the graph of $3x - y = 3$. x-int: 1, y-int: -3
2. A recycling company pays $1 per used ink jet cartridge and $2 per used laser cartridge. The company paid a customer $14. This situation is given by $x + 2y = 14$ where x is the number of ink jet cartridges and y the number of laser cartridges. Use intercepts to graph the equation. Give four possibilities for the number of each type of cartridge that could have been recycled. (0, 7), (6, 4), (10, 2), (14, 0)

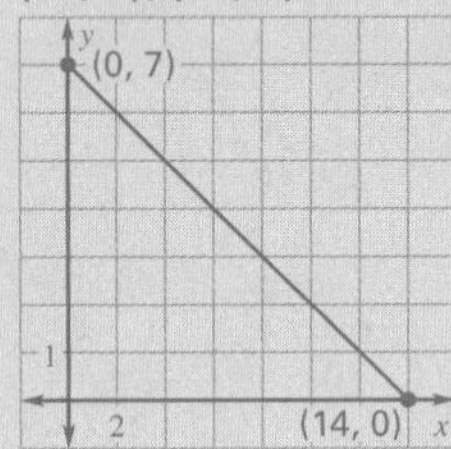

Available at **classzone.com**

Diagnosis/Remediation

- Practice A, B, C in Chapter 4 Resource Book, pp. 33–38
- Study Guide in Chapter 4 Resource Book, pp. 39–40
- Practice Workbook, pp. 52–54
- @HomeTutor

Challenge

Additional challenge is available in the Chapter 4 Resource Book, p. 44.

Quiz

An easily-readable reduced copy of the quiz (with answers) on Lessons 4.1–4.3 from the Assessment Book can be found on p. 204G.

50b, Quiz 1–6, 13. See Additional Answers beginning on p. AA1.

50. ★ **EXTENDED RESPONSE** You borrow $180 from a friend who doesn't charge you interest. You work out a payment schedule in which you will make weekly payments to your friend. The balance B (in dollars) of the loan is given by the function $B = 180 - pn$ where p is the weekly payment and n is the number of weeks you make payments.

    a. **Interpret** Without finding the intercepts, state what they represent.

    50a. The B-intercept is the balance of the loan after 0 weeks, the n-intercept is the amount of time it takes to pay off the loan.

    b. **Graph** Graph the function if you make weekly payments of $20. See margin.

    c. **Identify** Find the domain and range of the function in part (b). How long will it take to pay back your friend? domain: $0 \le n \le 9$, range: $0 \le B \le 180$; 9 wk

    d. **CHALLENGE** Suppose you make payments of $20 for three weeks. Then you make payments of $15 until you have paid your friend back. How does this affect the graph? How many payments do you make? The graph is two line segments; 11 payments.

ILLINOIS MIXED REVIEW

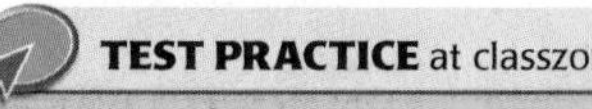

51. A hotel room costs $85 per night for 2 people, plus $10 per night for every additional person who stays in the room. If a family of 4 stays at the hotel for 3 nights, how much does the stay cost? B

    (A) $275 (B) $315 (C) $345 (D) $375

52. A solid sphere with a diameter of x units is packed within a cube-shaped crate. The inside of the crate has an edge length of x units. How much unused space does the crate have? B

    (A) $x^3 - \frac{4\pi x^3}{3}$ (B) $x^3 - \frac{\pi x^3}{6}$ (C) $x^3 - \frac{\pi x^3}{8}$ (D) $x^3 - \pi x^2$

QUIZ for Lessons 4.1–4.3

Plot the point in a coordinate plane. *Describe* the location of the point. *(p. 206)* 1–3. See margin for art.

1. $(-7, 2)$ Quadrant II
2. $(0, -5)$ y-axis
3. $(2, -6)$ Quadrant IV

Graph the equation. *(p. 215)* 4–6. See margin.

4. $-4x - 2y = 12$
5. $y = -5$
6. $x = 6$

Find the x-intercept and the y-intercept of the graph of the equation. *(p. 225)*

7. $y = x + 7$ $-7, 7$
8. $y = x - 3$ $3, -3$
9. $y = -5x + 2$ $\frac{2}{5}, 2$
10. $x + 3y = 15$ $15, 5$
11. $3x - 6y = 36$ $12, -6$
12. $-2x - 5y = 22$ $-11, -4\frac{2}{5}$
13. **SWIMMING POOLS** A public swimming pool that holds 45,000 gallons of water is going to be drained for maintenance at a rate of 100 gallons per minute. The amount of water w (in gallons) in the pool after t minutes is given by the function $w = 45{,}000 - 100t$. Graph the function. Identify its domain and range. How much water is in the pool after 60 minutes? How many minutes will it take to empty the pool? *(p. 225)* See margin for art; domain: $0 \le t \le 450$, range: $0 \le w \le 45{,}000$; 39,000 gal; 450 min.

 Illinois *Mixed Review*

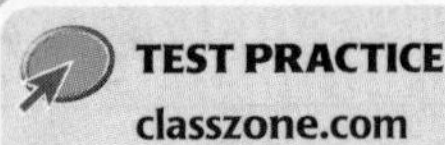

Lessons 4.1–4.3

1. **TEMPERATURE** The table shows the low temperature (in degrees Celsius) each day for a particular weekend. Let Friday be day 1, Saturday be day 2, and Sunday be day 3.

Day	1	2	3
Temperature (C)	5	−1	−2

If you plotted the data pair for Saturday, in which quadrant would the point lie?

A. Quadrant I **C.** Quadrant III

B. Quadrant II **D.** Quadrant IV

2. **BOOKS** The total cost C (in dollars) of books at a bookstore is given by the function $C = 8x$ where x is the number of books you buy. If you have $50, what is the greatest number of books you can buy?

F. 2 books **H.** 6 books

G. 3 books **J.** 7 books

3. **THEATER** Which statement is true for the graph shown?

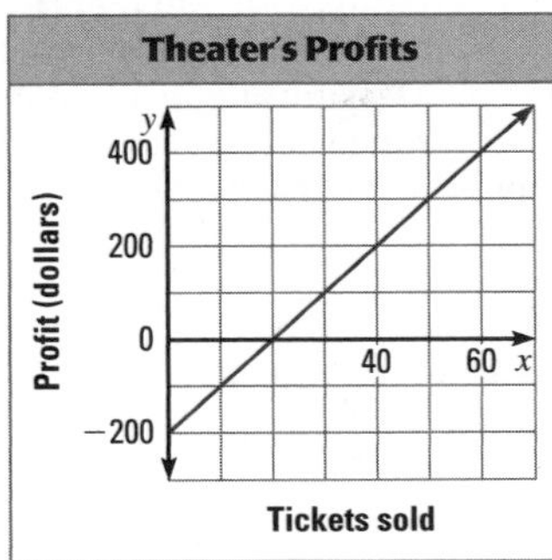

A. The theater needs to sell 20 tickets in order to earn a profit of $200.

B. The theater will earn a negative profit if it sells fewer than 20 tickets.

C. The theater will earn a profit of $100 if it sells 10 tickets.

D. The theater will earn a profit of $400 if it sells 40 tickets.

4. **CARNIVAL** A carnival charges $20 for an all-day pass and $10 for an evening pass. One day the carnival collects $1000 in pass sales. This situation is modeled by the equation $1000 = 20x + 10y$ where x is the number of all-day passes sold and y is the number of evening passes sold. Which ordered pair is a solution of the equation?

F. (20, 10) **H.** (40, 20)

G. (25, 25) **J.** (50, 10)

5. **CDS** You are selling your old CDs to a store so you can buy new ones. You can sell each old CD for $3, and each new one costs $13. You want to make a profit of $5 so you can buy lunch. This situation is modeled by the equation $3x - 13y = 5$ where x is the number of CDs you sell and y is the number of CDs you buy. If you buy 1 CD, how many CDs should you sell?

A. 1 CD **B.** 3 CDs **C.** 6 CDs **D.** 54 CDs

6. **CLOTHES** The graph shows the possible combinations of T-shirts and tank tops you can buy with the amount of money you have. If you buy only T-shirts, what is the greatest number you can buy?

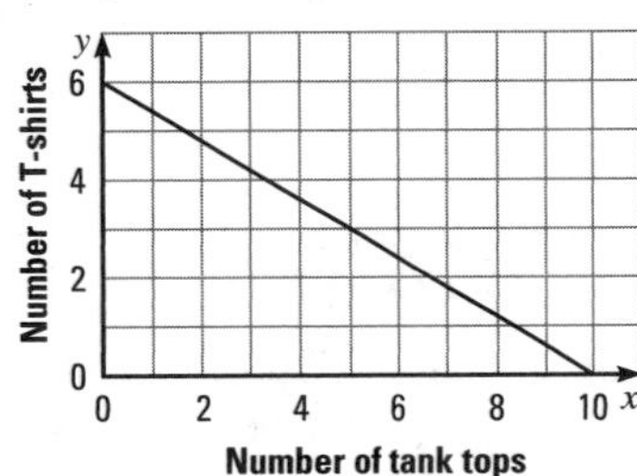

F. 2 T-shirts **H.** 6 T-shirts

G. 4 T-shirts **J.** 10 T-shirts

Illinois Mixed Review

1. D
2. H
3. B
4. H
5. C
6. H

1 PLAN AND PREPARE

Explore the Concept

- Students will measure the slope of a ramp.
- This activity leads into the study of finding slope in Example 1 in Lesson 4.4.

Materials

Each student or group of students will need:

- several books
- two rulers

Recommended Time

Work activity: 10 min

Discuss results: 5 min

Grouping

Students can work individually or in groups of three. If students work in groups, one student can make a ramp with books and ruler, one can measure the rise and run of the ramp, and the other can record measurements and calculate and record the slope.

2 TEACH

Tips for Success

Use whole numbers for the run to make calculations easier. Do not let the ruler slip when measuring the rise and run.

Key Discovery

Slope is dependent on the ratio of rise to run.

3 ASSESS AND RETEACH

How does the slope of a ramp change if the rise of the ramp decreases and the run increases? The slope decreases.

4.4 Slopes of Lines

MATERIALS • several books • two rulers

QUESTION How can you use algebra to describe the slope of a ramp?

You can use the ratio of the vertical rise to the horizontal run to describe the *slope* of a ramp.

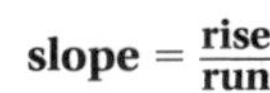

$$\text{slope} = \frac{\text{rise}}{\text{run}}$$

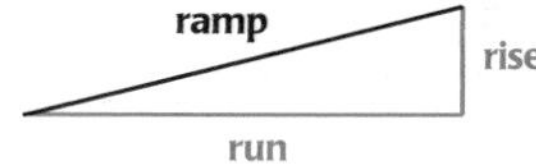

EXPLORE Calculate the slopes of ramps

STEP 1

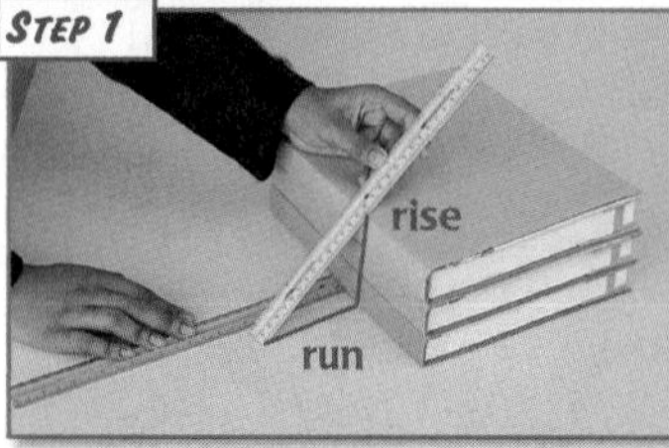

Make a ramp Make a stack of three books. Use a ruler as a ramp. Measure the rise and run of the ramp, and record them in a table. Calculate and record the slope of the ramp in your table.

STEP 2

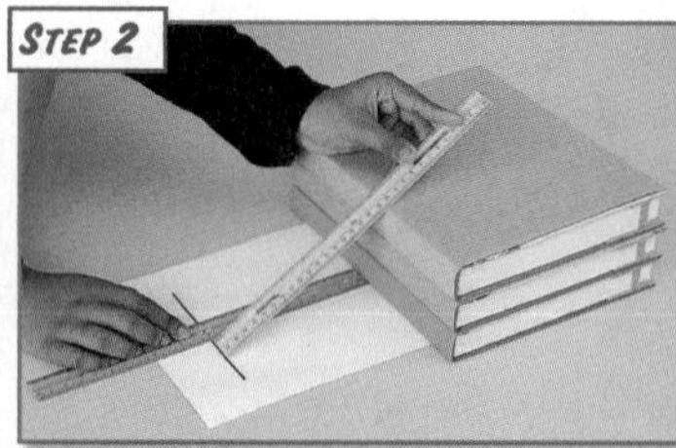

Change the run Without changing the rise, make three ramps with different runs by moving the lower end of the ruler. Measure and record the rise and run of each ramp. Calculate and record each slope.

STEP 3

Change the rise Without changing the run, make three ramps with different rises by adding or removing books. Measure and record the rise and run of each ramp. Calculate and record each slope.

DRAW CONCLUSIONS Use your observations to complete these exercises

Describe **how the slope of the ramp changes given the following conditions. Give three examples that support your answer.**

1. The run of the ramp increases, and the rise stays the same. The slope gets smaller. *Sample answer:* $\frac{1}{4}, \frac{1}{5}, \frac{1}{6}$
2. The rise of the ramp increases, and the run stays the same. The slope gets larger. *Sample answer:* $\frac{1}{5}, \frac{2}{5}, \frac{3}{5}$

In Exercises 3–5, describe the relationship between the rise and the run of the ramp.

3. A ramp with a slope of 1 The rise and the run are the same.
4. A ramp with a slope greater than 1 The rise is greater than the run.
5. A ramp with a slope less than 1 The rise is less than the run.
6. Ramp A has a rise of 6 feet and a run of 2 feet. Ramp B has a rise of 10 feet and a run of 4 feet. Which ramp is steeper? How do you know? Ramp A; the slope of ramp A is 3 while the slope of ramp B is $\frac{5}{2}$ or 2.5, and $3 > 2.5$.

4.4 Find Slope and Rate of Change

8.11.09 Identify slope from an equation, table of values, or graph.

Before	You graphed linear equations.
Now	You will find the slope of a line and interpret slope as a rate of change.
Why?	So you can find the slope of a boat ramp, as in Ex. 23.

Key Vocabulary
- **slope**
- **rate of change**

The **slope** of a nonvertical line is the ratio of the vertical change (the *rise*) to the horizontal change (the *run*) between any two points on the line. The slope of a line is represented by the letter m.

READING
Read x_1 as "x sub one." Think "x-coordinate of the first point."
Read y_1 as "y sub one." Think "y-coordinate of the first point."

KEY CONCEPT *For Your Notebook*

Finding the Slope of a Line

Words

The slope m of the nonvertical line passing through the two points (x_1, y_1) and (x_2, y_2) is the ratio of the rise (change in y) to the run (change in x).

$$\text{slope} = \frac{\text{rise}}{\text{run}} = \frac{\text{change in } y}{\text{change in } x}$$

Symbols

$$m = \frac{y_2 - y_1}{x_2 - x_1}$$

Graph

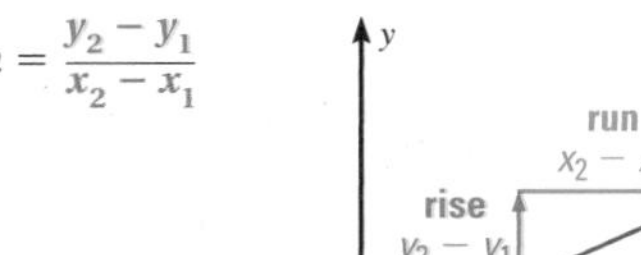

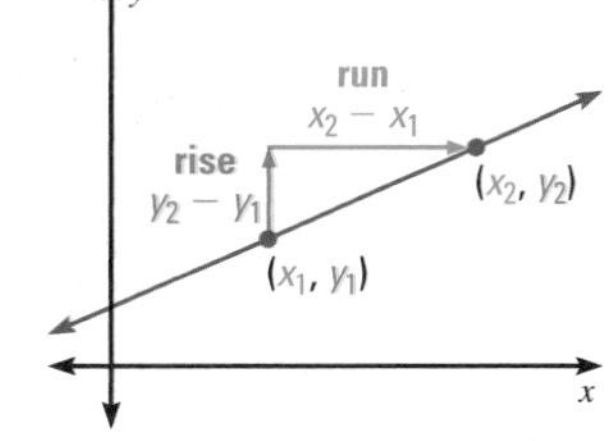

EXAMPLE 1 Find a positive slope

Find the slope of the line shown.

Let $(x_1, y_1) = (-4, 2)$ and $(x_2, y_2) = (2, 6)$.

$m = \frac{y_2 - y_1}{x_2 - x_1}$ **Write formula for slope.**

$= \frac{6 - 2}{2 - (-4)}$ **Substitute.**

$= \frac{4}{6} = \frac{2}{3}$ **Simplify.**

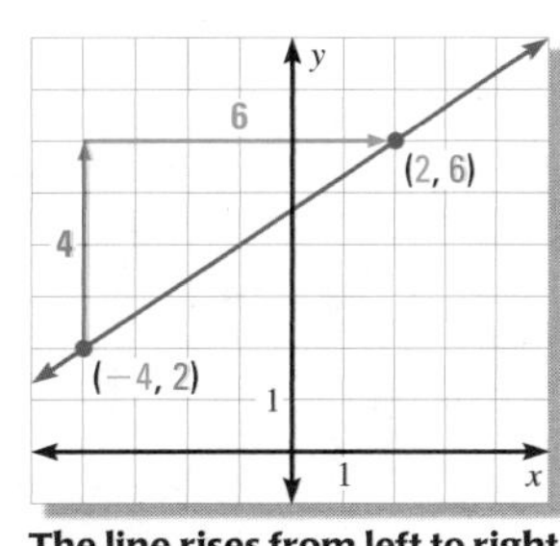

The line rises from left to right. The slope is positive.

AVOID ERRORS
Be sure to keep the x- and y-coordinates in the same order in both the numerator and denominator when calculating slope.

✓ **GUIDED PRACTICE** for Example 1

Find the slope of the line that passes through the points.

1. (5, 2) and (4, −1) 3
2. (−2, 3) and (4, 6) $\frac{1}{2}$
3. $\left(\frac{9}{2}, 5\right)$ and $\left(\frac{1}{2}, -3\right)$ 2

1 PLAN AND PREPARE

Warm-Up Exercises

Transparency Available

Evaluate and simplify the ratios when $x = 2$ and $y = -2$.

1. $\frac{y + 3}{x - 5}$ $-\frac{1}{3}$
2. $\frac{1 - y}{x - 6}$ $-\frac{3}{4}$
3. A cross-country skier traveled 14 miles in 3.5 hours. Use the formula $d = rt$ where d is distance, r is rate, and t is time, to find the average rate of speed. 4 mi/h

Notetaking Guide

Transparency Available

Promotes interactive learning and notetaking skills, pp. 83–86.

Pacing

Basic: 2 days
Average: 2 days
Advanced: 2 days
Block: 1 block
- See *Teaching Guide/Lesson Plan.*

2 FOCUS AND MOTIVATE

Essential Question

Big Idea 3, p. 205

How do you find the slope of a line and interpret slope as a rate of change? **Tell students they will learn how to answer this question by using the slope formula to find slope and to describe changes in a real-world situation.**

Resource Planning Guide

Chapter Resource Book
- Teaching Guide/Lesson Plan (pp. 45–46)
- Practice levels A, B, C (pp. 47–52)
- Study Guide (pp. 53–54)
- Catch-up for Absent Students (p. 55)
- Application (p. 56)
- Challenge (p. 57)

Workbooks
- Notetaking Guide (pp. 83–86)
- Practice Workbook (pp. 55–57)

Teaching Options
- **Power Presentations CD-ROM** provides dynamic electronic teaching resources for the classroom.
- **Activity Generator CD-ROM** provides editable activities for all ability levels.

Interactive Technology
- Easy Planner
- Power Presentations CD-ROM
- Activity Generator CD-ROM
- Animated Algebra
- Test Generator CD-ROM
- Online Quiz
- eWorkbook
- eEdition
- @HomeTutor

Resources for English Learners
- Quick Reference for English Learners
- Spanish Study Guide
- Multi-Language Visual Glossary
- Student Resources in Spanish

See also the *Algebra 1 Toolkit* for more strategies for meeting individual needs.

Motivating the Lesson

By learning how to use the slope formula, you can discover rates of change in real-world situations. For example, you are training for a marathon. After one hour, you have run 7 miles and after four hours, you have run 22 miles. By using the slope formula, you can find your average rate of change in distance with respect to time.

3 TEACH

Extra Example 1

Find the slope of the line shown. $\frac{3}{4}$

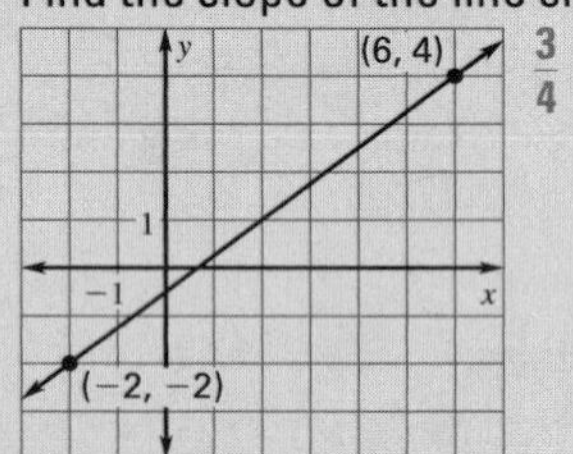

Extra Example 2

Find the slope of the line shown. $-\frac{1}{5}$

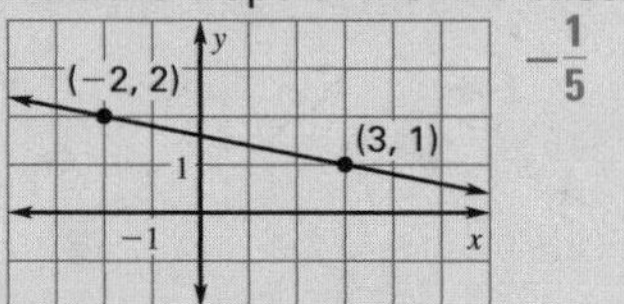

Key Question to Ask for Example 2

- If you let (6, −1) be (x_1, y_1) and (3, 5) be (x_2, y_2), will it change the slope? Explain. No, the slope will be −2 regardless of the order of the points.

Avoiding Common Errors

Example 2 Stress that the coordinates of the point chosen as (x_1, y_1) must be subtracted from the coordinates of (x_2, y_2) in the correct order in the numerator and the denominator.

FIND SLOPE

In Example 2, if you used two other points on the line, such as (4, 3) and (5, 1), in the slope formula, the slope would still be −2.

EXAMPLE 2 Find a negative slope

Find the slope of the line shown.

Let $(x_1, y_1) = (3, 5)$ and $(x_2, y_2) = (6, -1)$.

$m = \frac{y_2 - y_1}{x_2 - x_1}$ **Write formula for slope.**

$= \frac{-1 - 5}{6 - 3}$ **Substitute.**

$= \frac{-6}{3} = -2$ **Simplify.**

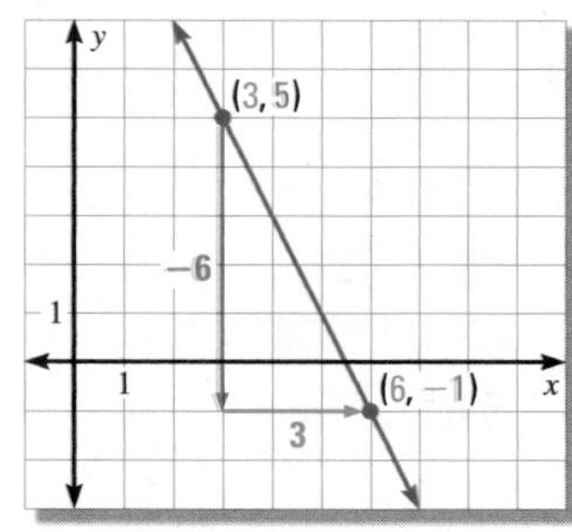

The line falls from left to right. The slope is negative.

EXAMPLE 3 Find the slope of a horizontal line

Find the slope of the line shown.

Let $(x_1, y_1) = (-2, 4)$ and $(x_2, y_2) = (4, 4)$.

$m = \frac{y_2 - y_1}{x_2 - x_1}$ **Write formula for slope.**

$= \frac{4 - 4}{4 - (-2)}$ **Substitute.**

$= \frac{0}{6} = 0$ **Simplify.**

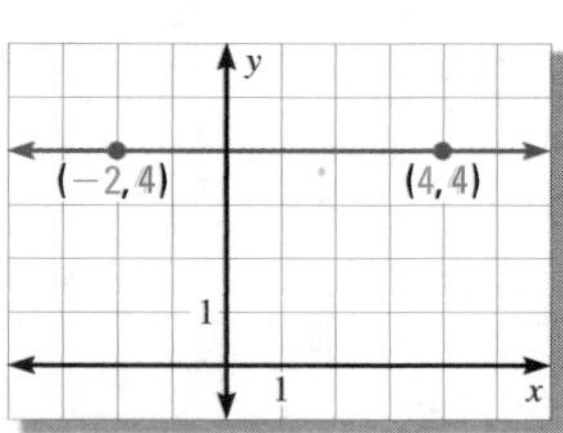

The line is horizontal. The slope is zero.

EXAMPLE 4 Find the slope of a vertical line

Find the slope of the line shown.

Let $(x_1, y_1) = (3, 5)$ and $(x_2, y_2) = (3, 1)$.

$m = \frac{y_2 - y_1}{x_2 - x_1}$ **Write formula for slope.**

$= \frac{1 - 5}{3 - 3}$ **Substitute.**

$= \frac{-4}{0}$ (crossed out) **Division by zero is undefined.**

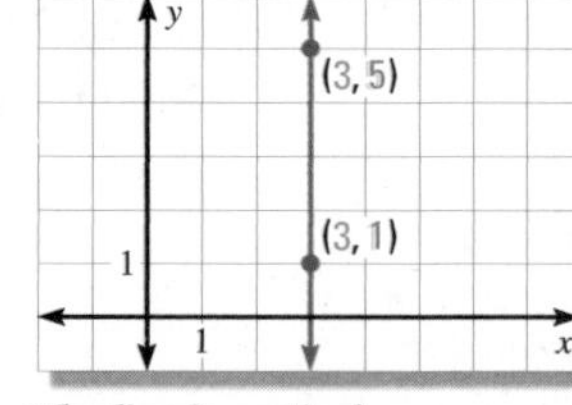

The line is vertical. The slope is undefined.

▶ Because division by zero is undefined, the slope of a vertical line is undefined.

✓ GUIDED PRACTICE for Examples 2, 3, and 4

Find the slope of the line that passes through the points.

4. (5, 2) and (5, −2) undefined
5. (0, 4) and (−3, 4) 0
6. (0, 6) and (5, −4) −2

Differentiated Instruction

English Learners Some students may need to be reminded that the small numbers in the formula $m = \frac{y_2 - y_1}{x_2 - x_1}$ are *not* exponents; they are called *subscripts* because they rest below the base line of the text. Tell students to remember that a submarine goes below the surface of the ocean. Remind students to read x_1 as "*x* sub one."

See also the *Algebra 1 Toolkit* for more strategies.

CONCEPT SUMMARY *For Your Notebook*

Classification of Lines by Slope

A line with positive slope ($m > 0$) *rises* from left to right.

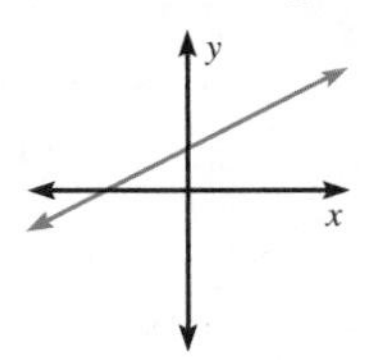

A line with negative slope ($m < 0$) *falls* from left to right.

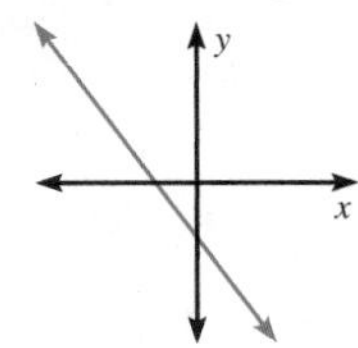

A line with zero slope ($m = 0$) is *horizontal*.

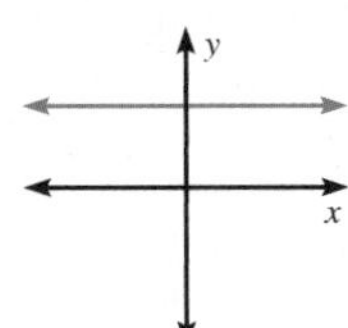

A line with undefined slope is *vertical*.

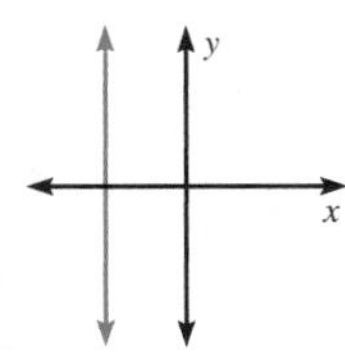

RATE OF CHANGE A **rate of change** compares a change in one quantity to a change in another quantity. For example, if you are paid $60 for working 5 hours, then your hourly wage is $12 per hour, a rate of change that describes how your pay increases with respect to time spent working.

EXAMPLE 5 Find a rate of change

INTERNET CAFE The table shows the cost of using a computer at an Internet cafe for a given amount of time. Find the rate of change in cost with respect to time.

Time (hours)	2	4	6
Cost (dollars)	7	14	21

Solution

ANALYZE UNITS
Because the cost is in dollars and time is in hours, the rate of change in cost with respect to time is expressed in dollars per hour.

$$\textbf{Rate of change} = \frac{\text{change in cost}}{\text{change in time}}$$

$$= \frac{14 - 7}{4 - 2} = \frac{7}{2} = 3.5$$

▶ The rate of change in cost is $3.50 per hour.

✓ GUIDED PRACTICE for Example 5

7. **EXERCISE** The table shows the distance a person walks for exercise. Find the rate of change in distance with respect to time.
0.05 mi/min

Time (minutes)	Distance (miles)
30	1.5
60	3
90	4.5

Differentiated Instruction

Below Level After discussing **Example 5**, have students determine the rate of change using two sets of quantities different from the set used in the example. Ask what would be the rise and run if they graphed the data. Then ask them to describe the slope of the line in terms of the rise and run.

Advanced Have students explore rates of change that are averages as well as constants. In **Example 5**, ask students to consider that the cost for 6 hours at the café is $18 rather than $21. Have them describe how this affects the rate of change by comparing rates at 2 hours and 4 hours, 2 hours and 6 hours, and 4 hours and 6 hours.

See also the *Algebra 1 Toolkit* for more strategies.

Extra Example 3

Find the slope of the line shown. 0

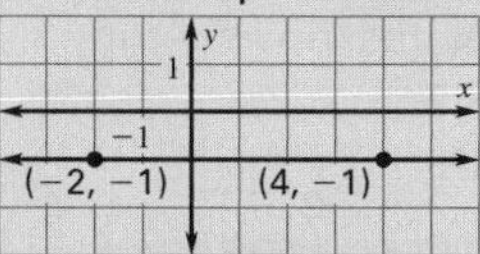

Key Question to Ask for Example 3

- What can you conclude about a line if the slope of the line is zero? The y-coordinates of the points on the line are the same and the line is horizontal.

Extra Example 4

Find the slope of the line shown. undefined

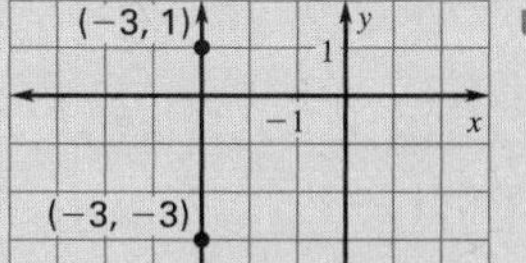

Key Question to Ask for Example 4

- What can you conclude about the slope of a line if two points on the line have the same x-coordinates? The slope is undefined and the line is vertical.

Extra Example 5

The table shows the cost to paint a house for a given number of hours. Find the rate of change in cost with respect to time. $22.50 per hour

Time (hours)	4	6	8
Cost ($)	90	135	180

Extra Example 6

The graph shows the number of computer games sold day 1, day 4, day 7, and day 9 of a sale. Describe the rates of change in sales with respect to time.

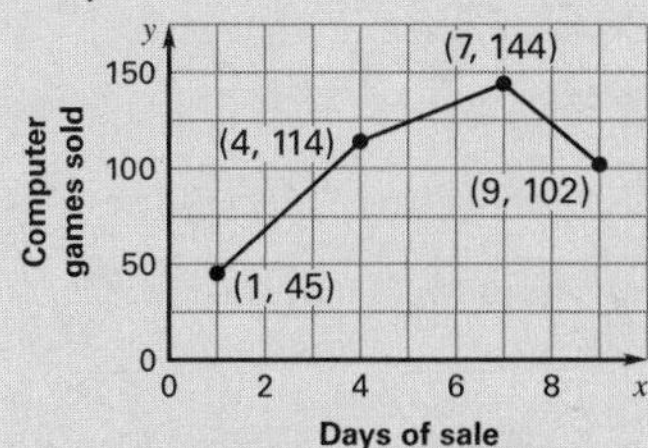

Sales increased at a fast rate, then at a slower rate, and finally decreased at a moderate rate.

Extra Example 7

The graph shows a ferry's trip across a lake. Describe the trip in words.

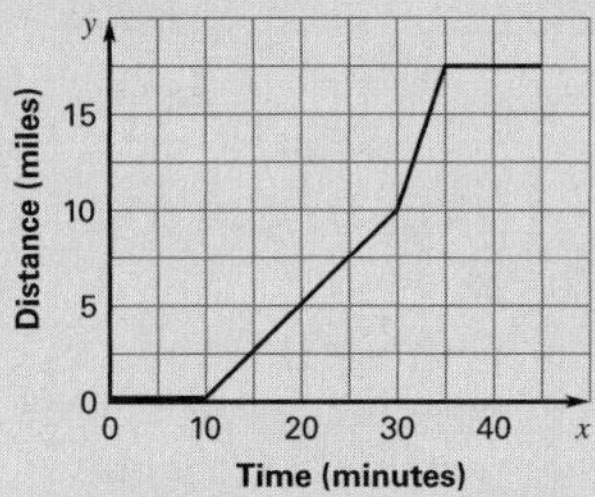

The slope is 0 at first, so the ferry must be loading. The ferry begins moving at a steady speed, picks up speed, and then unloads when the slope is 0 again.

An **Animated Algebra** activity is available on-line for **Example 7**. This activity is also available on the **Power Presentations CD-ROM**.

Closing the Lesson

Have students summarize the major points of the lesson and answer the Essential Question: How do you find the slope of a line and interpret slope as a rate of change?

- **The slope of a line is the ratio of the change in y (rise) to the change in x (the run). The slope is positive if the line slants upward and negative if the line slants downward.**
- **For real-world data, interpret slope as a rate of change.**

Use two points on a graph and the slope formula to find the slope of a line. In graphs of real-world data, use slope to describe the rate of change in the data.

9.

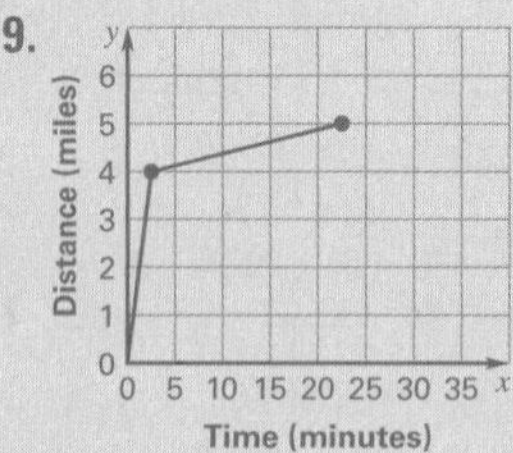

SLOPE AND RATE OF CHANGE You can interpret the slope of a line as a rate of change. When given graphs of real-world data, you can compare rates of change by comparing slopes of lines.

EXAMPLE 6 Use a graph to find and compare rates of change

COMMUNITY THEATER A community theater performed a play each Saturday evening for 10 consecutive weeks. The graph shows the attendance for the performances in weeks 1, 4, 6, and 10. Describe the rates of change in attendance with respect to time.

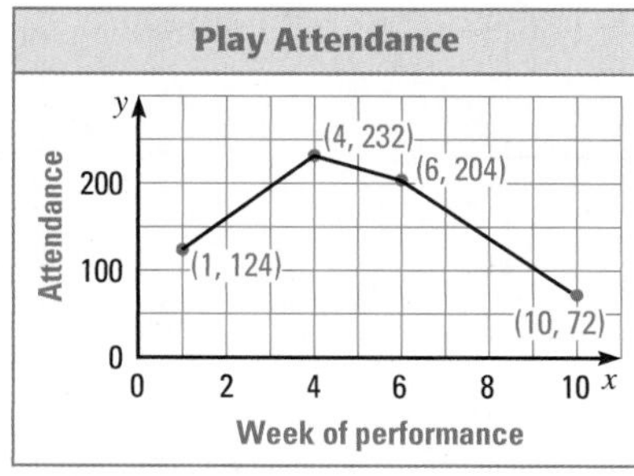

Solution

Find the rates of change using the slope formula.

INTERPRET RATE OF CHANGE
A negative rate of change indicates a decrease.

Weeks 1–4: $\frac{232 - 124}{4 - 1} = \frac{108}{3} = 36$ people per week

Weeks 4–6: $\frac{204 - 232}{6 - 4} = \frac{-28}{2} = -14$ people per week

Weeks 6–10: $\frac{72 - 204}{10 - 6} = \frac{-132}{4} = -33$ people per week

▶ Attendance increased during the early weeks of performing the play. Then attendance decreased, slowly at first, then more rapidly.

EXAMPLE 7 Interpret a graph

COMMUTING TO SCHOOL A student commutes from home to school by walking and by riding a bus. Describe the student's commute in words.

Solution

The first segment of the graph is not very steep, so the student is not traveling very far with respect to time. The student must be walking. The second segment has a zero slope, so the student must not be moving. He or she is waiting for the bus. The last segment is steep, so the student is traveling far with respect to time. The student must be riding the bus.

Animated Algebra at classzone.com

✓ GUIDED PRACTICE for Examples 6 and 7

8. **WHAT IF?** How would the answer to Example 6 change if you knew that attendance was 70 people in week 12? ***Sample answer:*** **The attendance did not decrease as rapidly between weeks 10 and 12.**
9. **WHAT IF?** Using the graph in Example 7, draw a graph that represents the student's commute from school to home. **See margin.**

4.4 EXERCISES

HOMEWORK KEY
○ = WORKED-OUT SOLUTIONS on p. WS9 for Exs. 11 and 37
★ = STANDARDIZED TEST PRACTICE Exs. 2, 17, 18, 34, and 40

SKILL PRACTICE

A

1. **VOCABULARY** Copy and complete: The _?_ of a nonvertical line is the ratio of the vertical change to the horizontal change between any two points on the line. slope

2. ★ **WRITING** Without calculating the slope, how can you tell that the slope of the line that passes through the points (−5, −3) and (2, 4) is positive?
The line between the two points rises from left to right.

3. **ERROR ANALYSIS** *Describe* and correct the error in calculating the slope of the line passing through the points (5, 3) and (2, 6). The denominator should be 2 − 5, not 5 − 2; $m = \frac{6-3}{2-5} = \frac{3}{-3} = -1$.

$m = \frac{6-3}{5-2} = \frac{3}{3} = 1$ ✗

EXAMPLES 1,2,3, and 4 on pp. 235–236 for Exs. 4–18

FINDING SLOPE Tell whether the slope of the line is *positive, negative, zero,* or *undefined*. Then find the slope if it exists.

4. 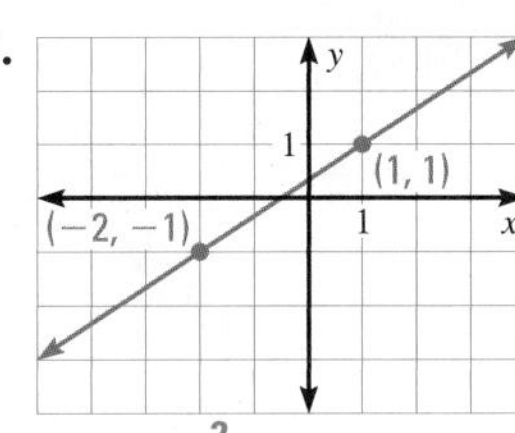

positive; $\frac{2}{3}$

5. 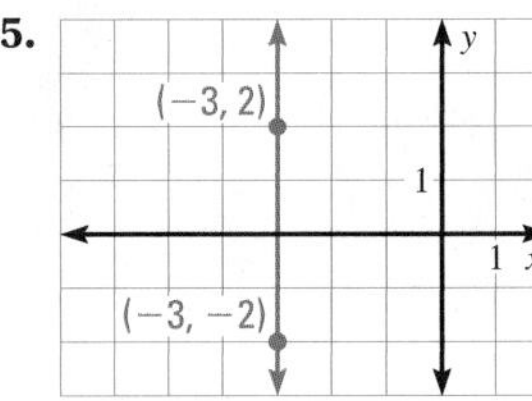

undefined

6. 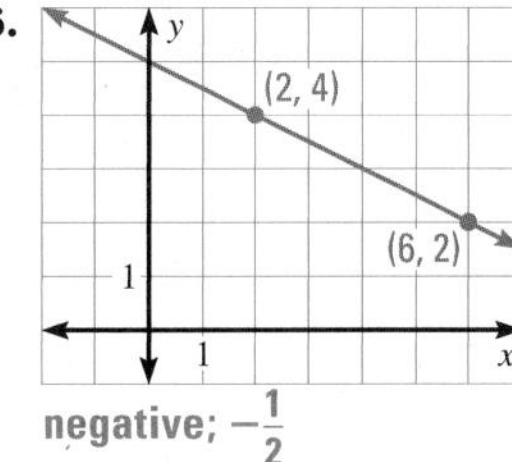

negative; $-\frac{1}{2}$

7. **ERROR ANALYSIS** *Describe* and correct the error in calculating the slope of the line shown.

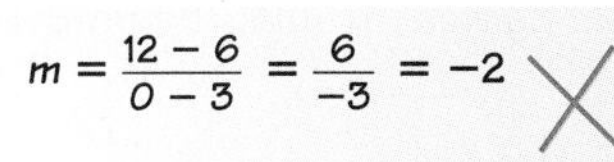
$m = \frac{12-6}{0-3} = \frac{6}{-3} = -2$ ✗

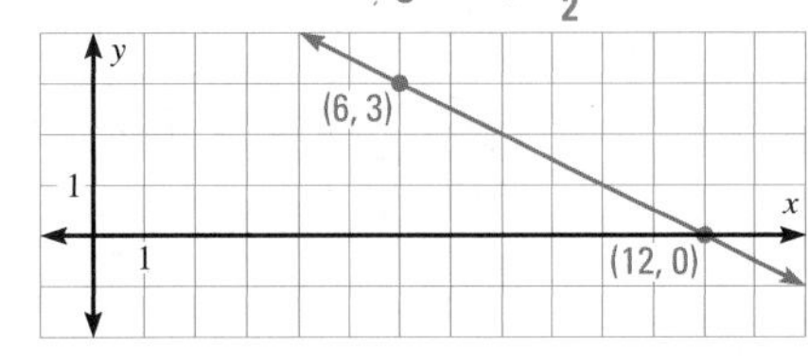

The slope was calculated using $\frac{\text{run}}{\text{rise}}$, not $\frac{\text{rise}}{\text{run}}$; $m = \frac{0-3}{12-6} = \frac{-3}{6} = -\frac{1}{2}$.

FINDING SLOPE Find the slope of the line that passes through the points.

8. (−2, −1) and (4, 5) 1
9. (−3, −2) and (−3, 6) undefined
10. (5, −3) and (−5, −3) 0
11. (1, 3) and (3, −2) $-\frac{5}{2}$
12. (−3, 4) and (4, 1) $-\frac{3}{7}$
13. (1, −3) and (7, 3) 1
14. (0, 0) and (0, −6) undefined
15. (−9, 1) and (1, 1) 0
16. (−10, −2) and (−8, 8) 5

17. ★ **MULTIPLE CHOICE** The slope of the line that passes through the points (−2, −3) and (8, −3) is _?_. C

Ⓐ positive Ⓑ negative Ⓒ zero Ⓓ undefined

18. ★ **MULTIPLE CHOICE** What is the slope of the line that passes through the points (7, −9) and (−13, −6)? A

Ⓐ $-\frac{3}{20}$ Ⓑ $\frac{3}{20}$ Ⓒ $\frac{3}{4}$ Ⓓ $\frac{5}{2}$

4 PRACTICE AND APPLY

Assignment Guide

Answer Transparencies available for all exercises

Basic:
Day 1: SRH p. 934 Exs. 6–14
pp. 239–242
Exs. 1–18, 42–56 even
Day 2: pp. 239–242
Exs. 19–27, 36–39, 57–62

Average:
Day 1: pp. 239–242
Exs. 1–7, 11–18, 24–28, 43–55 odd
Day 2: pp. 239–242
Exs. 19–23, 31–33, 36–40, 57–62

Advanced:
Day 1: pp. 239–242
Exs. 1, 2, 12–18, 24–32, 43–55 odd
Day 2: pp. 239–242
Exs. 19–23, 35–41*, 57–62

Block:
pp. 239–242
Exs. 1–7, 11–28, 31–33, 36–40, 43–55 odd, 57–62

Differentiated Instruction

See *Algebra 1 Best Practices Toolkit* for suggestions on addressing the needs of a diverse classroom.

Homework Check

For a quick check of student understanding of key concepts, go over the following exercises:

Basic: 4, 9, 19, 36, 38
Average: 11, 14, 20, 36, 39
Advanced: 12, 15, 20, 37, 39

Extra Practice

- Student Edition, p. 941
- Chapter 4 Resource Book: Practice levels A, B, C, pp. 47–52

Practice Worksheet

An easily-readable reduced practice page (with answers) for this lesson can be found on p. 204D.

Avoiding Common Errors

Exercises 3, 8–16 Students often switch the order of the x- and y-coordinates when finding slope. Caution students to double-check their calculations to make sure the coordinates are in the right order.

Vocabulary

Exercise 17 To help students understand the difference between 0 slope and undefined slope, point out that 0 slope implies identical y-coordinates, while undefined slope implies identical x-coordinates.

Teaching Strategy

Exercises 24–32 You may want to point out to students that the example for these exercises skips the step of adding 6 to each side and then dividing by 3. Also, encourage students to check their answers by substituting their solutions in the slope formula.

EXAMPLE 5 on p. 237 for Exs. 19–20

19. MOVIE RENTALS The table shows the number of days you keep a rented movie before returning it and the total cost of renting the movie. Find the rate of change in cost with respect to time and interpret its meaning.

Time (days)	4	5	6	7
Total cost (dollars)	6.00	8.25	10.50	12.75

$2.25 per day, it costs $2.25 per day to rent a movie.

20. AMUSEMENT PARK The table shows the amount of time spent at an amusement park and the admission fee the park charges. Find the rate of change in the fee with respect to time spent at the park and interpret its meaning.

Time (hours)	4	5	6
Admission fee (dollars)	34.99	34.99	34.99

0, it does not matter how long a person stays at the park, the admission is the same.

FINDING SLOPE Find the slope of the object. Round to the nearest tenth.

21. Skateboard ramp 0.3 **22.** Pet ramp 0.4 **23.** Boat ramp 0.1

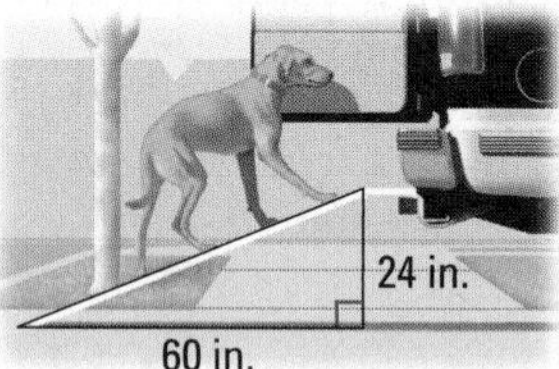

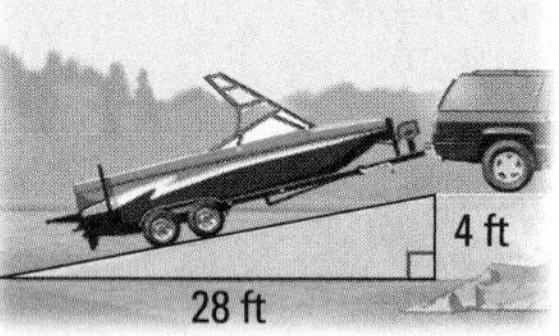

B **In Exercises 24–32, use the example below to find the value of x or y so that the line passing through the given points has the given slope.**

EXAMPLE Find a coordinate given the slope of a line

Find the value of x so that the line that passes through the points (2, 3) and $(x, 9)$ has a slope of $\frac{3}{2}$.

Solution

Let $(x_1, y_1) = (2, 3)$ and $(x_2, y_2) = (x, 9)$.

$m = \frac{y_2 - y_1}{x_2 - x_1}$ **Write formula for slope.**

$\frac{3}{2} = \frac{9 - 3}{x - 2}$ **Substitute values.**

$3(x - 2) = 2(9 - 3)$ **Cross products property**

$3x - 6 = 12$ **Simplify.**

$x = 6$ **Solve for x.**

24. $(x, 4), (6, -1); m = \frac{5}{6}$ 12 **25.** $(0, y), (-2, 1); m = -8$ −15 **26.** $(8, 1), (x, 7); m = -\frac{1}{2}$ −4

27. $(5, 4), (-5, y); m = \frac{3}{5}$ −2 **28.** $(-9, y), (0, -3); m = -\frac{7}{9}$ 4 **29.** $(x, 9), (-1, 19); m = 5$ −3

30. $(9, 3), (-6, 7y); m = 3$ −6 **31.** $(-3, y + 1), (0, 4); m = 6$ −15 **32.** $\left(\frac{x}{2}, 7\right), (-10, 15); m = 4$ −24

○ = WORKED-OUT SOLUTIONS on p. WS1 ★ = STANDARDIZED TEST PRACTICE

C 33. **REASONING** The point (−1, 8) is on a line that has a slope of −3. Is the point (4, −7) on the same line? *Explain* your reasoning.
Yes; the slope of the line containing both points is −3.

34. ★ **WRITING** Is a line with undefined slope the graph of a function? *Explain*.
No; a line with an undefined slope is a vertical line, which is not the graph of a function.

35. **CHALLENGE** Given two points (x_1, y_1) and (x_2, y_2) such that $x_1 \neq x_2$, show that $\frac{y_2 - y_1}{x_2 - x_1} = \frac{y_1 - y_2}{x_1 - x_2}$. What does this result tell you about calculating the slope of a line? See margin.

PROBLEM SOLVING

EXAMPLE 6 A on p. 238 for Exs. 36–37

36. **OCEANOGRAPHY** Ocean water levels are measured hourly at a monitoring station. The table shows the water level (in meters) on one particular morning. *Describe* the rates of change in water levels throughout the morning. *Sample answer:* The water level decreases until 8 A.M. and then it increases until 12 P.M.

Hours since 12:00 A.M.	1	3	8	10	12
Water level (meters)	2	1.4	0.5	1	1.8

@HomeTutor for problem solving help at classzone.com

37. **MULTI-STEP PROBLEM** Firing a piece of pottery in a kiln takes place at different temperatures for different amounts of time. The graph shows the temperatures in a kiln while firing a piece of pottery (after the kiln is preheated to 250°F).

a. Determine the time interval during which the temperature in the kiln showed the greatest rate of change. 0 h to 1.5 h

b. Determine the time interval during which the temperature in the kiln showed the least rate of change. 4.65 h to 8.95 h

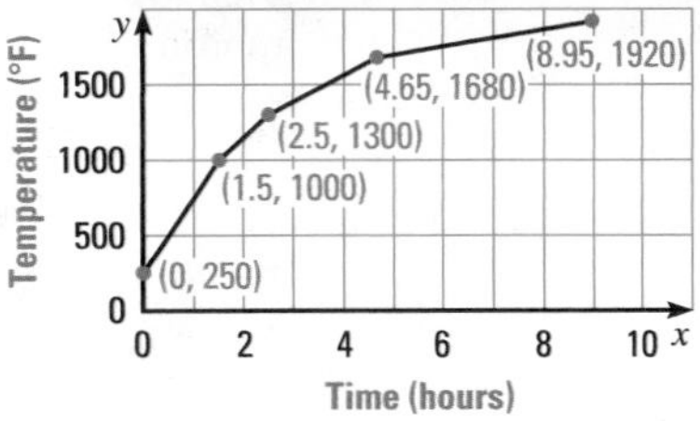

@HomeTutor for problem solving help at classzone.com

EXAMPLE 7 on p. 238 for Exs. 38–39

38. **FLYING** The graph shows the altitude of a plane during 4 hours of a flight. Give a verbal description of the flight. See margin.

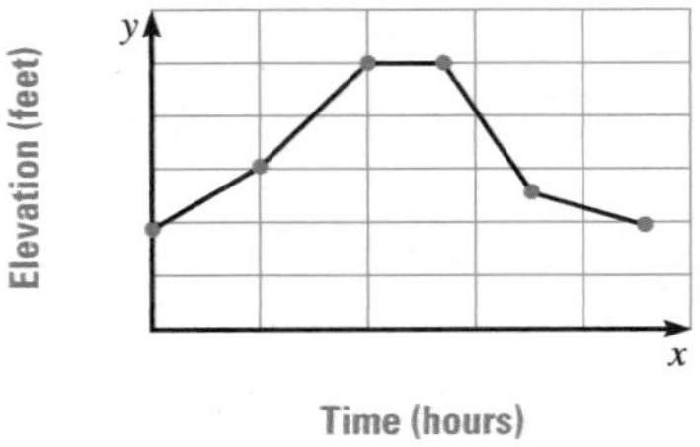

39. **HIKING** The graph shows the elevation of a hiker walking on a mountain trail. Give a verbal description of the hike. See margin.

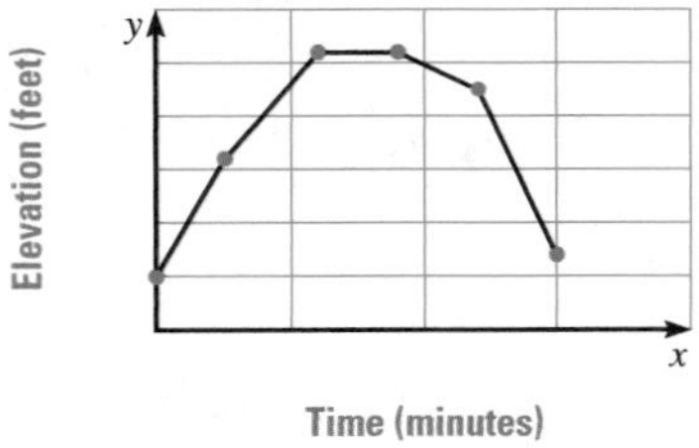

Study Strategy

Exercise 36 Tell students they can set up this problem using the solution in Example 6 as a model. Point out that instead of 3 intervals of time over weeks, there will be 4 intervals of time over hours for Exercise 36. Note that the independent variable is time and the dependent variable is water level. Ask students how this affects the use of the slope formula.

Exercises 38, 39 Suggest that students use Example 7 as a model for their descriptions. Note that the example describes the slope in each segment of the graph independently.

Internet Reference

Exercise 36 Additional information about oceanography can be found at the Office of Naval Research website at www.onr.navy.mil/focus/ocean

35. Multiply $\frac{y_2 - y_1}{x_2 - x_1}$ by $\frac{-1}{-1}$ to get $\frac{-y_2 + y_1}{-x_2 + x_1}$, which, by the commutative property of addition, is equal to $\frac{y_1 - y_2}{x_1 - x_2}$; it does not matter which point you choose to be (x_2, y_2) and which point is (x_1, y_1).

38. *Sample answer:* The altitude of the plane increases during the first 2 hours of the flight, then stays the same for about 45 minutes, and then decreases during the last hour and 45 minutes.

39. *Sample answer:* The elevation of the hiker increases for about 60 minutes, then stays the same for about 30 minutes, then decreases for the last 60 minutes.

5 ASSESS AND RETEACH

Daily Homework Quiz

Transparency Available

Find the slope of the line that passes through the points.

1. (12, −1) and (−3, −1) 0
2. (−2, 6) and (4, −3) $-\frac{3}{2}$
3. The graph shows the ticket sales for a school dance on day 1, day 3, day 6, and day 9 of ticket sales. Describe the rates of change in ticket sales with respect to time.

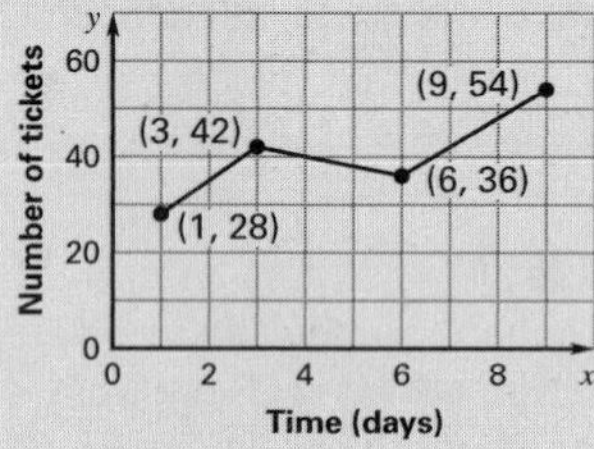

Ticket sales grew moderately, declined slightly, and then had another moderate rate of increase.

Online Quiz

Available at **classzone.com**

Diagnosis/Remediation

- Practice A, B, C in Chapter 4 Resource Book, pp. 47–52
- Study Guide in Chapter 4 Resource Book, pp. 53–54
- Practice Workbook, pp. 55–57
- @HomeTutor

Challenge

Additional challenge is available in the Chapter 4 Resource Book, p. 57.

41a–c. See Additional Answers beginning on p. AA1.

40a. 1996 to 1998; about −1500 students per year

40b. 1998 to 2000; about 1500 students per year

40c. It increased. *Sample answer:* Although the number of engineering majors decreased, the decrease was more than offset by the increase in the number of biological science majors and liberal arts majors.

B

40. ★ **EXTENDED RESPONSE** The graph shows the number (in thousands) of undergraduate students who majored in biological science, engineering, or liberal arts in the United States from 1990 to 2000.

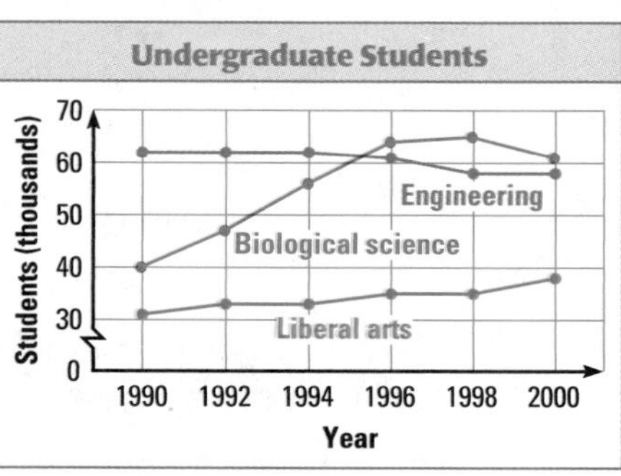

   a. During which two-year period did the number of engineering students decrease the most? Estimate the rate of change for this time period.
   b. During which two-year period did the number of liberal arts students increase the most? Estimate the rate of change for this time period.
   c. How did the total number of students majoring in biological science, engineering, and liberal arts change in the 10 year period? *Explain* your thinking.

C

41. **CHALLENGE** Imagine the containers below being filled with water at a constant rate. Sketch a graph that shows the water level for each container during the time it takes to fill the container with water. See margin.

a. 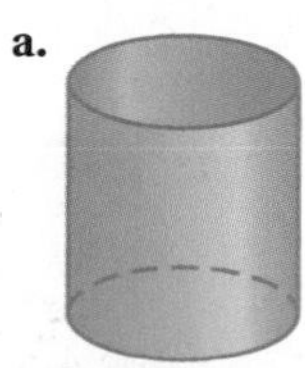

b. 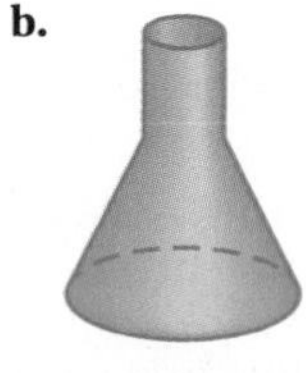

c. 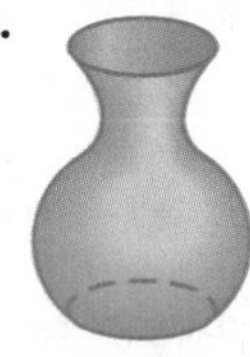

ILLINOIS MIXED REVIEW

TEST PRACTICE at classzone.com

42. What are the x- and y-intercepts of the function graphed at the right?

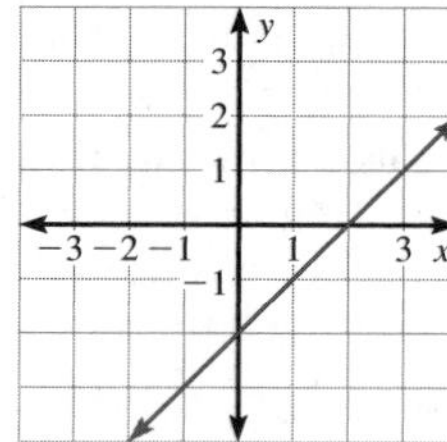

   (A) (0, 2) and (0, −2)
   (B) (2, 0) and (−2, 0)
   (C) (0, 2) and (−2, 0)
   (D) (2, 0) and (0, −2)

D

43. Which is always a correct conclusion about the quantities in the function $y = -x + 3$?

   (A) The variable x is always 3 more than y.
   (B) When the value of y is negative, the value of x is also negative.
   (C) When the value of x is negative, the value of y is positive.
   (D) As the value of x increases, the value of y also increases.

C

4.5 Slope and y-Intercept

QUESTION How can you use the equation of a line to find its slope and y-intercept?

EXPLORE Find the slopes and the y-intercepts of lines

STEP 1 *Find y when x = 0*

Copy the table below. Let $x_1 = 0$ and find y_1 for each equation. Use your answers to complete the second and fifth columns in the table.

STEP 2 *Find y when x = 2*

Let $x_2 = 2$ and find y_2 for each equation. Use your answers to complete the third column in the table.

STEP 3 *Compute the slope*

Use the slope formula and the ordered pairs you found in the second and third columns to complete the fourth column.

Line	$(0, y_1)$	$(2, y_2)$	Slope	y-intercept
$y = 4x + 3$	(0, 3)	(2, 11)	$\frac{11-3}{2-0} = 4$	3
$y = -2x + 3$	(0, ?) 3	(2, ?) −1	? −2	? 3
$y = \frac{1}{2}x + 4$	(0, ?) 4	(2, ?) 5	? $\frac{1}{2}$	? 4
$y = -4x - 3$	(0, ?) −3	(2, ?) −11	? −4	? −3
$y = -\frac{1}{4}x - 3$	(0, ?) −3	(2, ?) $-3\frac{1}{2}$	? $-\frac{1}{4}$	? −3

DRAW CONCLUSIONS Use your observations to complete these exercises

1. *Compare* the slope of each line with the equation of the line. What do you notice? It is the same as the coefficient of x in each equation.
2. *Compare* the y-intercept of each line with the equation of the line. What do you notice? It is the same as the constant in each equation.

Predict the slope and the y-intercept of the line with the given equation. Then check your predictions by finding the slope and y-intercept as you did in the table above.

3. $y = -5x + 1$ −5, 1
4. $y = \frac{3}{4}x + 2$ $\frac{3}{4}$, 2
5. $y = -\frac{3}{2}x - 1$ $-\frac{3}{2}$, −1

6. **REASONING** Use the procedure you followed to complete the table above to show that the y-intercept of the graph of $y = mx + b$ is b and the slope of the graph is m. If you substitute 0 for x you get $y = b$, giving the point $(0, b)$. This shows the y-intercept is b. Substitute 2 in for x giving the point $(2, 2m + b)$. Use the points $(0, b)$ and $(2, 2m + b)$ to find the slope. $\frac{(2m + b) - b}{2 - 0} = m$.

1 PLAN AND PREPARE

Explore the Concept

- Students will use the equation of a line to find the slope and y-intercept of the line.
- This activity leads into the study of finding the slope and y-intercept of a line in Example 1 in Lesson 4.5.

Materials

Each student will need:

- Activity Support Master (*Chapter 4 Resource Book*, p. 62)

Recommended Time

Work activity: 10 min
Discuss results: 5 min

Grouping

Students should work individually.

2 TEACH

Key Question

- What is the relationship between columns 2 and 5? Column 2 gives the coordinates of the y-intercept in column 5.

Key Discovery

The slope of a line written in the form $y = mx + b$ is m, the coefficient of x, and the y-intercept is the constant b.

3 ASSESS AND RETEACH

Predict the slope and y-intercept of the graph of $y = x$. Explain. Since the coefficient of x is 1, the slope is 1. Since the equation is equivalent to $y = x + 0$, the constant is 0, and the y-intercept is 0.

1 PLAN AND PREPARE

Warm-Up Exercises

Transparency Available

1. Rewrite $5x + y = 8$ so y is a function of x. $y = -5x + 8$
2. Find the slope of the line that passes through $(-5, 6)$ and $(0, 8)$. $\frac{2}{5}$
3. Find the intercepts of the graph of the function $a = 20t - 600$. a-intercept: -600, t-intercept: 30

Notetaking Guide

Transparency Available

Promotes interactive learning and notetaking skills, pp. 87–90.

Pacing

Basic: 1 day
Average: 1 day
Advanced: 1 day
Block: 0.5 block with 4.6
• See *Teaching Guide/Lesson Plan.*

2 FOCUS AND MOTIVATE

Essential Question

Big Idea 1, p. 205

How do you graph linear equations given in slope-intercept form? Tell students they will learn how to answer this question by using the y-intercept and the slope to determine two points on the graph.

4.5 Graph Using Slope-Intercept Form

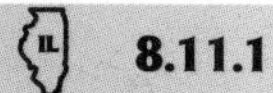

8.11.11 Analyze functions by investigating domain, range, rates of change, intercepts, and zeros.

Before You found slopes and graphed equations using intercepts.
Now You will graph linear equations using slope-intercept form.
Why? So you can model a worker's earnings, as in Ex. 43.

Key Vocabulary
• slope-intercept form
• parallel

In the activity on page 243, you saw how the slope and y-intercept of the graph of a linear equation in the form $y = mx + b$ are related to the equation.

KEY CONCEPT *For Your Notebook*

Finding the Slope and y-Intercept of a Line

Words	Symbols	Graph
A linear equation of the form $y = mx + b$ is written in **slope-intercept form** where m is the slope and b is the y-intercept of the equation's graph.	$y = mx + b$ (slope: m; y-intercept: b) → $y = \frac{1}{3}x + 1$	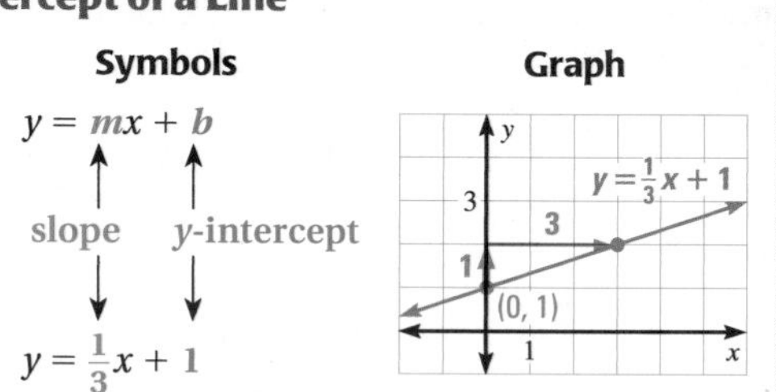

EXAMPLE 1 Identify slope and y-intercept

Identify the slope and y-intercept of the line with the given equation.

a. $y = 3x + 4$ **b.** $3x + y = 2$

Solution

a. The equation is in the form $y = mx + b$. So, the slope of the line is 3, and the y-intercept is 4.

b. Rewrite the equation in slope-intercept form by solving for y.

$3x + y = 2$ **Write original equation.**

$y = -3x + 2$ **Subtract $3x$ from each side.**

▸ The line has a slope of -3 and a y-intercept of 2.

REWRITE EQUATIONS
When you rewrite a linear equation in slope-intercept form, you are expressing y as a function of x.

GUIDED PRACTICE for Example 1

Identify the slope and y-intercept of the line with the given equation.

1. $y = 5x - 3$ $5, -3$ **2.** $3x - 3y = 12$ $1, -4$ **3.** $x + 4y = 6$ $-\frac{1}{4}, 1\frac{1}{2}$

Resource Planning Guide

Chapter Resource Book
• Teaching Guide/Lesson Plan (pp. 58–59)
• Activity Master (p. 60)
• Practice levels A, B, C (pp. 64–69)
• Study Guide (pp. 70–71)
• Catch-up for Absent Students (p. 72)
• Problem Solving Workshop (p. 73)
• Challenge (p. 74)

Workbooks
• Notetaking Guide (pp. 87–90)
• Practice Workbook (pp. 58–60)

Teaching Options
• **Power Presentations CD-ROM** provides dynamic electronic teaching resources for the classroom.
• **Activity Generator CD-ROM** provides editable activities for all ability levels.

Interactive Technology
• Easy Planner
• Power Presentations CD-ROM
• Activity Generator CD-ROM
• Animated Algebra
• Test Generator CD-ROM
• Online Quiz
• eWorkbook
• eEdition
• @HomeTutor

Resources for English Learners
• Quick Reference for English Learners
• Spanish Study Guide
• Multi-Language Visual Glossary
• Student Resources in Spanish

See also the *Algebra 1 Toolkit* for more strategies for meeting individual needs.

EXAMPLE 2 Graph an equation using slope-intercept form

Graph the equation $2x + y = 3$.

Solution

STEP 1 **Rewrite** the equation in slope-intercept form.

$y = -2x + 3$

STEP 2 **Identify** the slope and the y-intercept.

$m = -2$ and $b = 3$

STEP 3 **Plot** the point that corresponds to the y-intercept, $(0, 3)$.

STEP 4 **Use** the slope to locate a second point on the line. Draw a line through the two points.

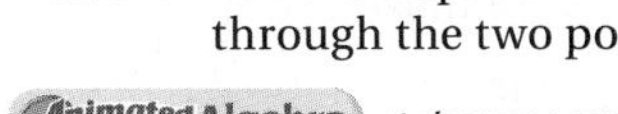

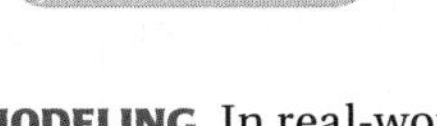

Animated Algebra at classzone.com

CHECK REASONABLENESS

To check the line drawn in Example 2, substitute the coordinates of the second point into the original equation. You should get a true statement.

MODELING In real-world problems that can be modeled by linear equations, the y-intercept is often an initial value, and the slope is a rate of change.

EXAMPLE 3 Change slopes of lines

ESCALATORS To get from one floor to another at a library, you can take either the stairs or the escalator. You can climb stairs at a rate of 1.75 feet per second, and the escalator rises at a rate of 2 feet per second. You have to travel a vertical distance of 28 feet. The equations model the vertical distance d (in feet) you have left to travel after t seconds.

Stairs: $d = -1.75t + 28$ **Escalator:** $d = -2t + 28$

a. Graph the equations in the same coordinate plane.

b. How much time do you save by taking the escalator?

Solution

a. Draw the graph of $d = -1.75t + 28$ using the fact that the d-intercept is 28 and the slope is -1.75. Similarly, draw the graph of $d = -2t + 28$. The graphs make sense only in the first quadrant.

b. The equation $d = -1.75t + 28$ has a t-intercept of 16. The equation $d = -2t + 28$ has a t-intercept of 14. So, you save $16 - 14 = 2$ seconds by taking the escalator.

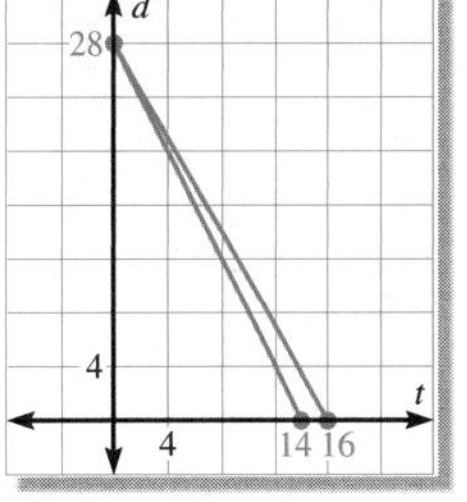

✓ GUIDED PRACTICE for Examples 2 and 3

4. Graph the equation $y = -2x + 5$. See margin.

5. WHAT IF? In Example 3, suppose a person can climb stairs at a rate of 1.4 feet per second. How much time does taking the escalator save? 6 sec

Motivating the Lesson

Which is cheaper, paying a certain fee to join an art museum and then paying \$5 for each special exhibit, or not joining and paying \$10 for each special exhibit? This lesson will help you decide.

3 TEACH

Extra Example 1

Identify the slope and y-intercept of the line $x + 3y = 9$. slope: $-\frac{1}{3}$, y-intercept: 3

Extra Example 2

Graph $x + 2y = 4$.

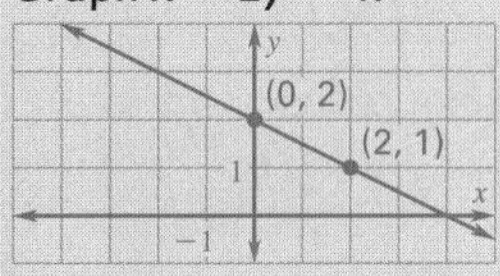

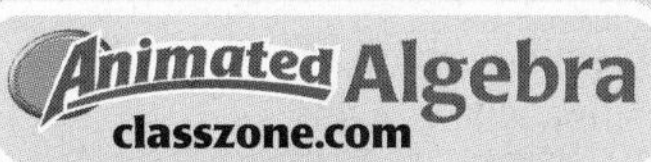

An **Animated Algebra** activity is available on-line for **Example 2.** This activity is also available on the **Power Presentations CD-ROM**.

Extra Example 3

You can use a laser or inkjet printer to print an 18-page report. The laser printer prints 6 pages/min and the inkjet printer prints 4.5 pages/min. The models give the number of pages p left to print after t minutes.

laser: $p = -6t + 18$

inkjet: $p = -4.5t + 18$

a. Graph both models in the same coordinate plane.

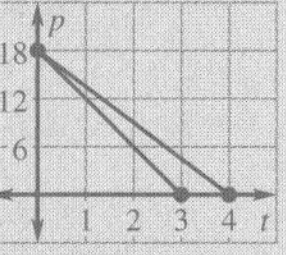

b. How many minutes do you save by using the laser printer? 1 min

4. See Additional Answers beginning on p. AA1.

Differentiated Instruction

Visual Learners Show students that if they let $x = 0$ in the slope-intercept form, $y = mx + b$, to find the y-intercept as they did in Section 4.3, they immediately find that the y-intercept is $y = b$.

See also the *Algebra 1 Toolkit* for more strategies.

Extra Example 4

A violin teacher charges a one-time sheet-music fee of $20 for adults and no fee for children. The charge per hour is $20 for both children and adults. The cost C for children for n lessons is given by $C = 20n$ and for adults by $C = 20n + 20$.

a. Graph both equations in the same coordinate plane.

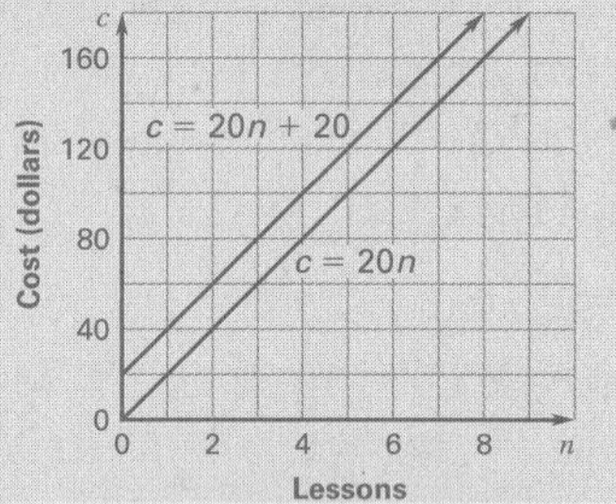

b. Based on the graphs, what is the difference in the costs? **$20, no matter how many lessons**

Extra Example 5

Determine which of the lines are parallel. **lines *a* and *b***

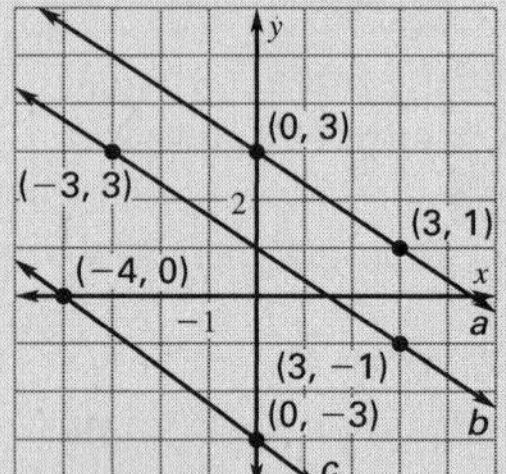

Closing the Lesson

Have students summarize the major points of the lesson and answer the Essential Question: How do you graph linear equations given in slope-intercept form?

- **The slope-intercept form of a linear equation is $y = mx + b$.**
- **In the slope-intercept form of the equation, m is slope and b is the y-intercept.**

Write the equation in slope-intercept form. Then plot the point that corresponds to the y-intercept, and use the slope to locate a second point.

EXAMPLE 4 Change intercepts of lines

TELEVISION A company produced two 30 second commercials, one for $300,000 and the second for $400,000. Each airing of either commercial on a particular station costs $150,000. The cost C (in thousands of dollars) to produce the first commercial and air it n times is given by $C = 150n + 300$. The cost to produce the second and air it n times is given by $C = 150n + 400$.

a. Graph both equations in the same coordinate plane.

b. Based on the graphs, what is the difference of the costs to produce each commercial and air it 2 times? 4 times? What do you notice about the differences of the costs?

Solution

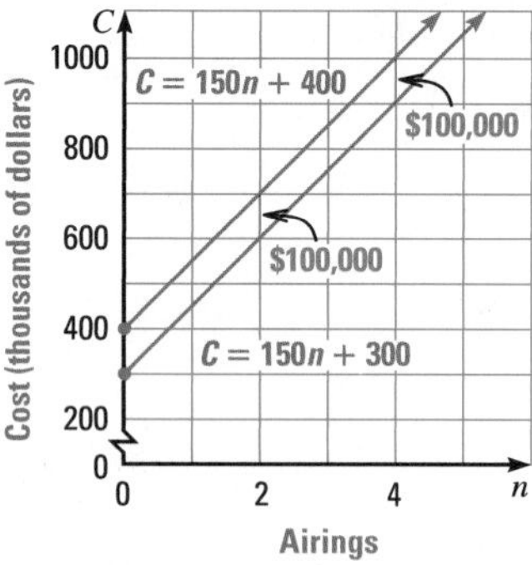

a. The graphs of the equations are shown.

b. You can see that the vertical distance between the lines is $100,000 when $n = 2$ and $n = 4$.

The difference of the costs is $100,000 no matter how many times the commercials are aired.

PARALLEL LINES Two lines in the same plane are **parallel** if they do not intersect. Because slope gives the rate at which a line rises or falls, two nonvertical lines with the same slope are parallel.

EXAMPLE 5 Identify parallel lines

Determine which of the lines are parallel.

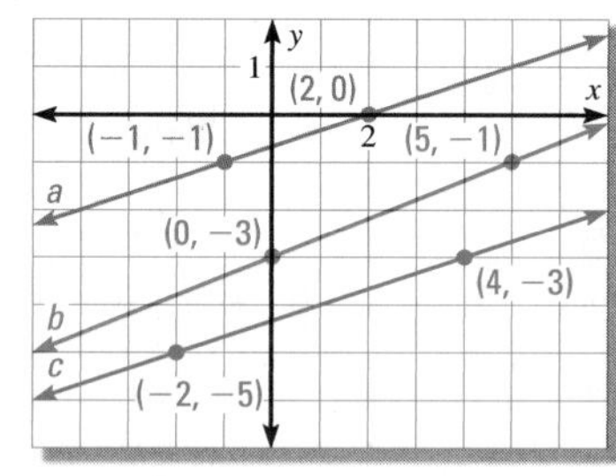

Find the slope of each line.

Line *a*: $m = \frac{-1 - 0}{-1 - 2} = \frac{-1}{-3} = \frac{1}{3}$

Line *b*: $m = \frac{-3 - (-1)}{0 - 5} = \frac{-2}{-5} = \frac{2}{5}$

Line *c*: $m = \frac{-5 - (-3)}{-2 - 4} = \frac{-2}{-6} = \frac{1}{3}$

▶ Line a and line c have the same slope, so they are parallel.

✓ GUIDED PRACTICE for Examples 4 and 5

6. **WHAT IF?** In Example 4, suppose that the cost of producing and airing a third commercial is given by $C = 150n + 200$. Graph the equation. Find the difference of the costs of the second commercial and the third. **See margin for art; $200,000.**
7. Determine which lines are parallel: line a through $(-1, 2)$ and $(3, 4)$; line b through $(3, 4)$ and $(5, 8)$; line c through $(-9, -2)$ and $(-1, 2)$. **a and c**

6.
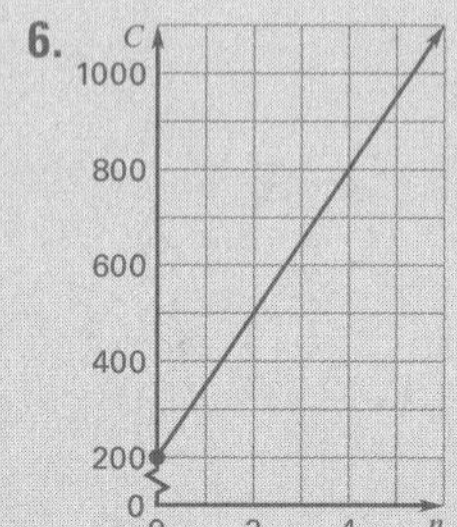

4.5 EXERCISES

HOMEWORK KEY
○ = **WORKED-OUT SOLUTIONS** on p. WS9 for Exs. 11, 21, and 41
★ = **STANDARDIZED TEST PRACTICE** Exs. 2, 9, 10, 36, 42, and 44

SKILL PRACTICE

A

1. **VOCABULARY** Copy and complete: Two lines in the same plane are _?_ if they do not intersect. parallel

2. ★ **WRITING** What is the slope-intercept form of a linear equation? *Explain* why this form is called slope-intercept form. $y = mx + b$; because m is the slope and b is the y-intercept.

EXAMPLE 1 on p. 244 for Exs. 3–16

SLOPE AND y-INTERCEPT Identify the slope and y-intercept of the line with the given equation.

3. $y = 2x + 1$ 2, 1
4. $y = -x$ −1, 0
5. $y = 6 - 3x$ −3, 6
6. $y = -7 + 5x$ 5, −7
7. $y = \frac{2}{3}x - 1$ $\frac{2}{3}$, −1
8. $y = -\frac{1}{4}x + 8$ $-\frac{1}{4}$, 8

9. ★ **MULTIPLE CHOICE** What is the slope of the line with the equation $y = -18x - 9$? A

Ⓐ −18 Ⓑ −9 Ⓒ 9 Ⓓ 18

10. ★ **MULTIPLE CHOICE** What is the y-intercept of the line with the equation $x - 3y = -12$? C

Ⓐ −12 Ⓑ −4 Ⓒ 4 Ⓓ 12

REWRITING EQUATIONS Rewrite the equation in slope-intercept form. Then identify the slope and the y-intercept of the line.

11. $4x + y = 1$ $y = -4x + 1$; −4, 1
12. $x - y = 6$ $y = x - 6$; 1, −6
13. $6x - 3y = -9$ $y = 2x + 3$; 2, 3
14. $-12x - 4y = 2$ $y = -3x - \frac{1}{2}$; −3, $-\frac{1}{2}$
15. $2x + 5y = -10$ $y = -\frac{2}{5}x - 2$; $-\frac{2}{5}$, −2
16. $-x - 10y = 20$ $y = -\frac{1}{10}x - 2$; $-\frac{1}{10}$, −2

EXAMPLE 2 on p. 245 for Exs. 17–29

MATCHING EQUATIONS WITH GRAPHS Match the equation with its graph.

17. $2x + 3y = 6$ B
18. $2x + 3y = -6$ A
19. $2x - 3y = 6$ C

A. 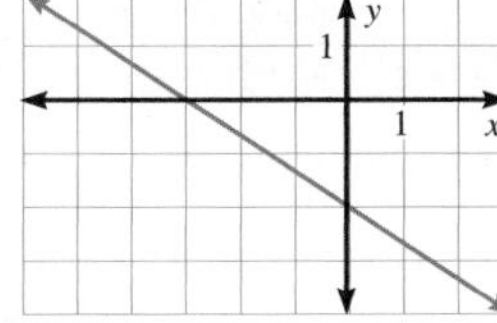

B. 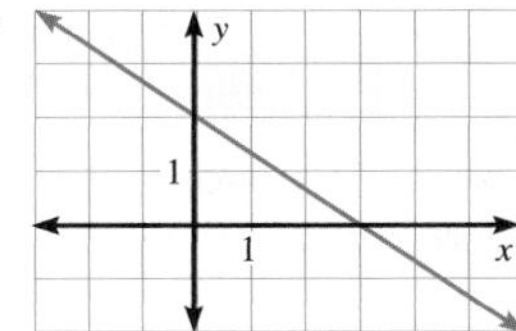

C. 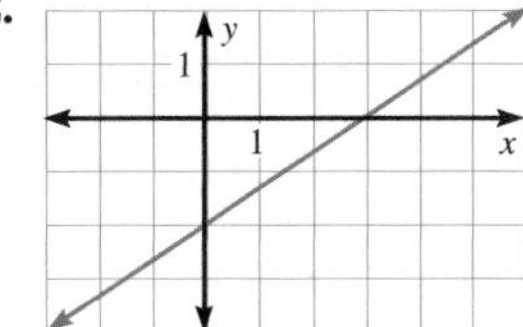

20. **ERROR ANALYSIS** *Describe* and correct the error in graphing the equation $y = 4x - 1$. The y-intercept is −1, not 1; see margin for art.

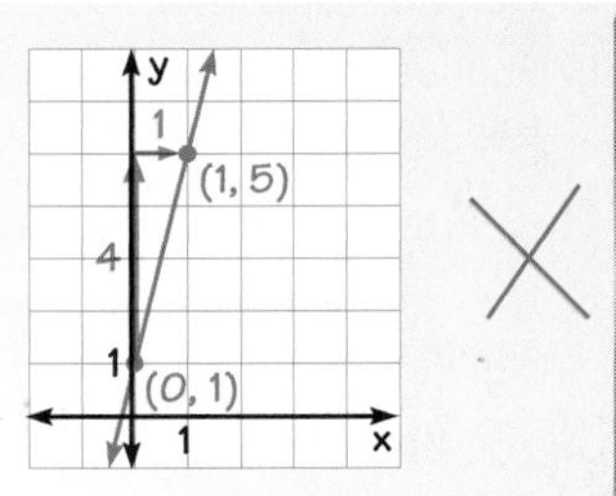

4 PRACTICE AND APPLY

Assignment Guide

Answer Transparencies available for all exercises

Basic:
Day 1: pp. 247–250
Exs. 1–13, 17–24, 30–33, 40–43, 46–56 even

Average:
Day 1: pp. 247–250
Exs. 1–5, 9, 10, 13–20, 25–31, 32–38 even, 40–44, 46–56 even

Advanced:
Day 1: pp. 247–250
Exs. 1, 2, 6–10, 14–19, 27–39*, 41–45*, 47–57 odd

Block:
pp. 247–250
Exs. 1–5, 9, 10, 13–20, 25–31, 32–38 even, 40–44, 46–56 even (with 4.6)

Differentiated Instruction

See *Algebra 1 Best Practices Toolkit* for suggestions on addressing the needs of a diverse classroom.

Homework Check

For a quick check of student understanding of key concepts, go over the following exercises:

Basic: 12, 22, 30, 40, 42
Average: 15, 26, 32, 41, 43
Advanced: 16, 29, 34, 41, 44

Extra Practice

- Student Edition, p. 941
- Chapter 4 Resource Book: Practice levels A, B, C, pp. 64–69

Practice Worksheet

An easily-readable reduced practice page (with answers) for this lesson can be found on p. 204E.

20. 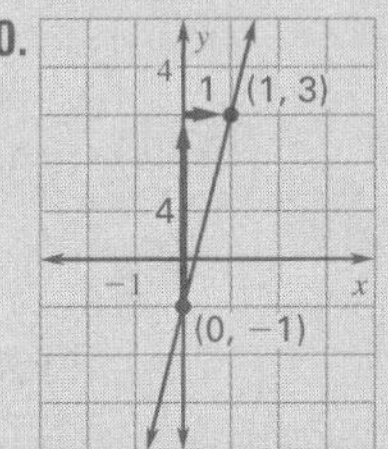

Avoiding Common Errors

Exercises 17–19 Caution students that the equation needs to be in slope-intercept form so they can visually match the equation with the graph.

Exercises 27–29, 32–35 Some students may think that the coefficient of x is the slope of the line of the equation regardless of the form of the equation. Remind them that the equation must be in the form $y = mx + b$.

Study Strategy

Exercises 37, 38 Students may want to review the slope formula before beginning these exercises. Remind them to pay attention to negative and positive numbers, especially when they replace k with a number.

21. 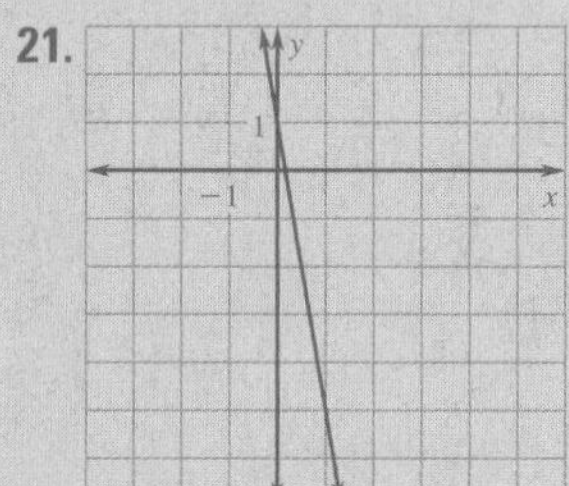

22. 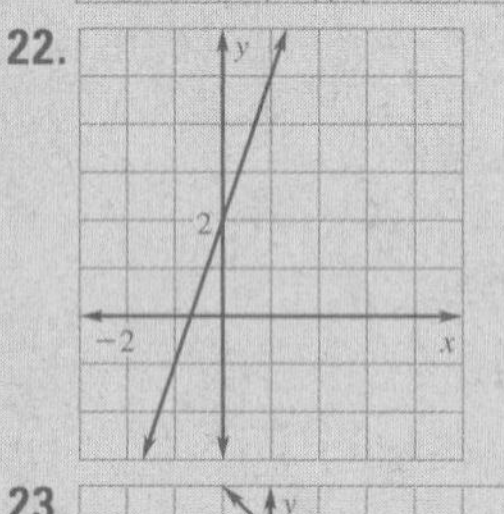

23. 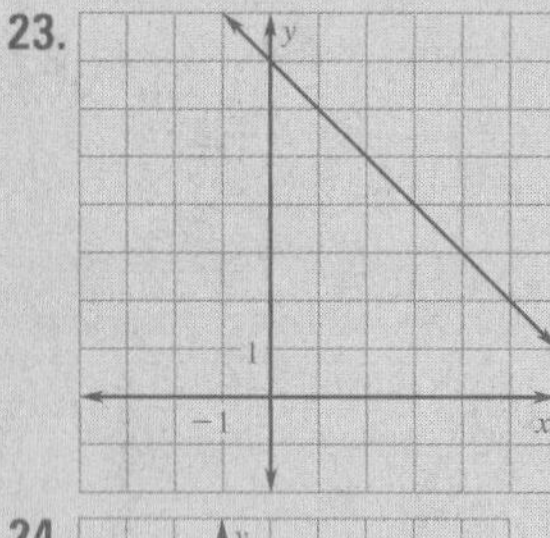

24. 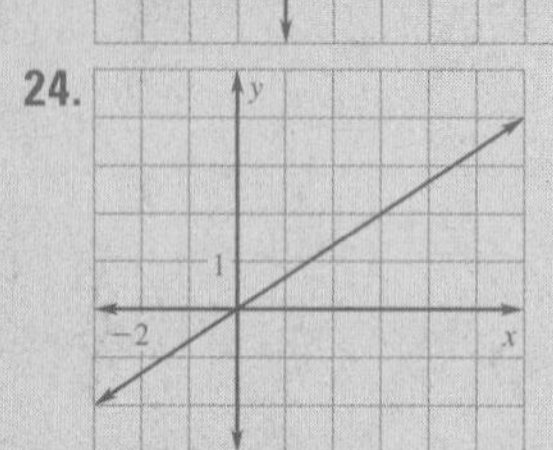

GRAPHING EQUATIONS Graph the equation. 21–29. See margin.

21. $y = -6x + 1$
22. $y = 3x + 2$
23. $y = -x + 7$
24. $y = \frac{2}{3}x$
25. $y = \frac{1}{4}x - 5$
26. $y = -\frac{5}{2}x + 2$
27. $7x - 2y = -11$
28. $-8x - 2y = 32$
29. $-x - 0.5y = 2.5$

EXAMPLE 5 on p. 246 for Exs. 30–35

PARALLEL LINES Determine which lines are parallel.

30. 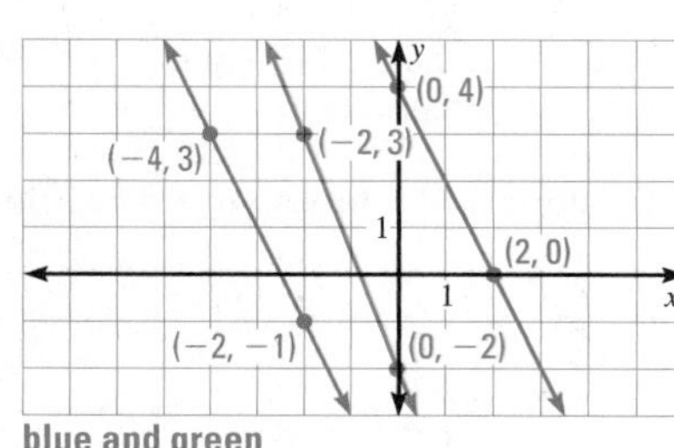

blue and green

31. 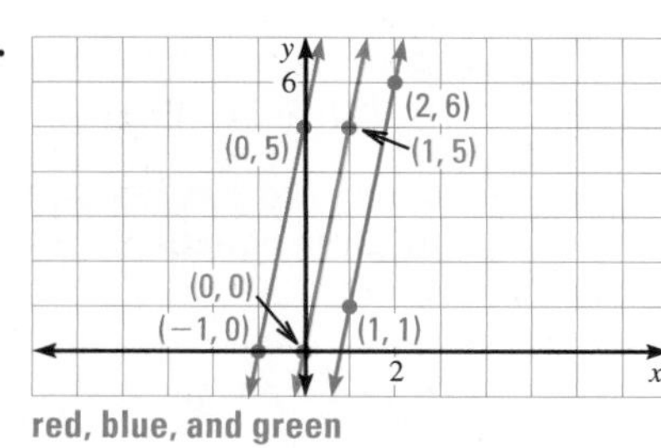

red, blue, and green

B **PARALLEL LINES Tell whether the graphs of the two equations are parallel lines. *Explain* your reasoning.**

32. $y = 5x - 7$, $5x + y = 7$ Not parallel; the slopes are 5 and −5.
33. $y = 3x + 2$, $-7 + 3x = y$ Parallel; the slopes are both 3.
34. $y = -0.5x$, $x + 2y = 18$ Parallel; the slopes are both −0.5.
35. $4x + y = 3$, $x + 4y = 3$ Not parallel; the slopes are −4 and $-\frac{1}{4}$.

36. ★ **OPEN-ENDED** Write the equation of a line that is parallel to $6x + y = 24$. *Explain* your reasoning. *Sample answer:* $y = -6x + 5$; the equation has the same slope as $6x + y = 24$, but a different y-intercept.

REASONING Find the value of *k* so that the lines through the given points are parallel.

37. Line 1: (−4, −2) and (0, 0)
Line 2: (2, 7) and (k, 5) −2

38. Line 1: (−1, 9) and (−6, −6)
Line 2: (−7, k) and (0, −2) −23

C 39. **CHALLENGE** Find the slope and y-intercept of the graph of the equation $Ax + By = C$ where $B \neq 0$. Use your results to find the slope and y-intercept of the graph of $3x + 2y = 18$. $m = -\frac{A}{B}$, y-intercept $= \frac{C}{B}$; $-\frac{3}{2}$, 9

PROBLEM SOLVING

EXAMPLES 3 and 4 on pp. 245–246 for Exs. 40–44

A 40. **HOCKEY** Your family spends \$60 on tickets to a hockey game and \$4 per hour for parking. The total cost C (in dollars) is given by $C = 60 + 4t$ where t is the time (in hours) your family's car is parked.

a. Graph the equation. a–b. See margin.

b. Suppose the parking fee is raised to \$5.50 per hour so that the total cost of tickets and parking for t hours is $C = 60 + 5.5t$. Graph the equation in the same coordinate plane as the equation in part (a).

c. How much more does it cost to go to a game for 4 hours after the parking fee is raised? \$6

@HomeTutor for problem solving help at classzone.com

○ = WORKED-OUT SOLUTIONS on p. WS1 ★ = STANDARDIZED TEST PRACTICE

25. 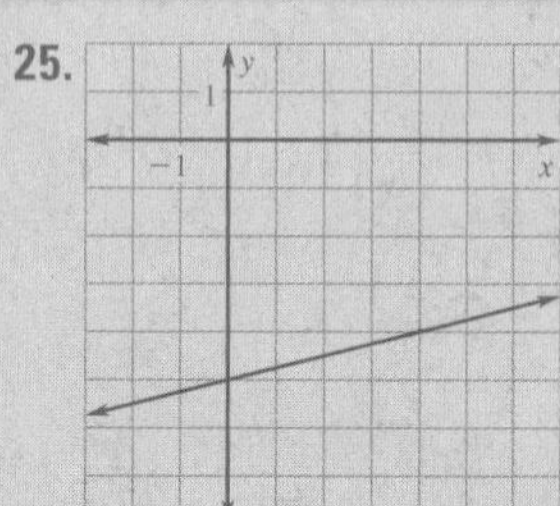

26. 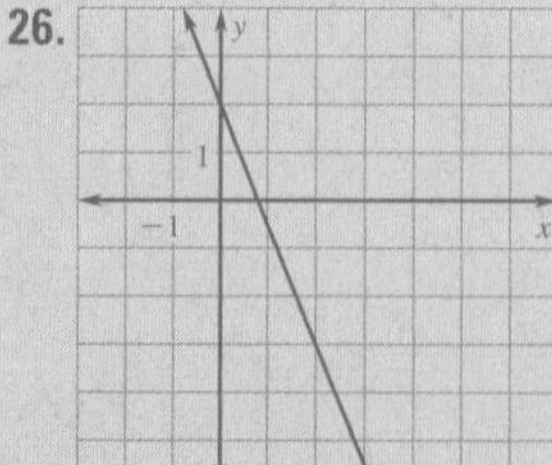

27. 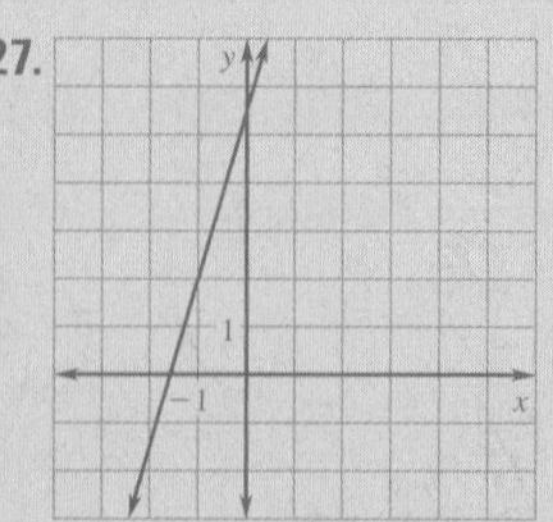

41. **SPEED LIMITS** In 1995 Pennsylvania changed its maximum speed limit on rural interstate highways, as shown below. The diagram also shows the distance d (in miles) a person could travel driving at the maximum speed limit for t hours both before and after 1995.

a. Graph both equations in the same coordinate plane. See margin.

b. Use the graphs to find the difference of the distances a person could drive in 3 hours before and after the speed limit was changed. 30 mi

@HomeTutor for problem solving help at classzone.com

42. ★ **SHORT RESPONSE** A service station charges $40 per hour for labor plus the cost of parts to repair a car. Parts can either be ordered from the car dealership for $250 or from a warehouse for $200. The equations below give the total repair cost C (in dollars) for a repair that takes t hours using parts from the dealership or from the warehouse.

Dealership: $C = 40t + 250$ **Warehouse:** $C = 40t + 200$

a. Graph both equations in the same coordinate plane. See margin.

b. Use the graphs to find the difference of the costs if the repair takes 3 hours. What if the repair takes 4 hours? What do you notice about the differences of the costs? *Explain.* $50; $50; the difference is $50 no matter how many hours it takes to repair a car because the slopes are the same.

B 43. **FACTORY SHIFTS** Welders at a factory can work one of two shifts. Welders on the first shift earn $12 per hour while workers on the second shift earn $14 per hour. The total amount a (in dollars) a first-shift worker earns is given by $a = 12t$ where t is the time (in hours) worked. The total amount a second-shift worker earns is given by $a = 14t$.

a. Graph both equations in the same coordinate plane. What do the slopes and the a-intercepts of the graphs mean in this situation?

b. How much more money does a welder earn for a 40 hour week if he or she works the second shift rather than the first shift? $80

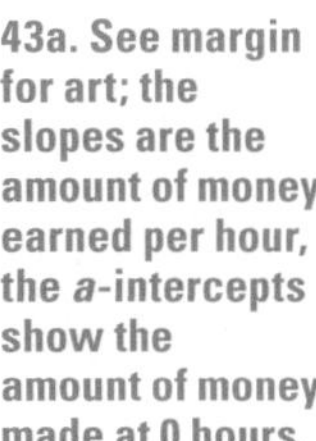

43a. See margin for art; the slopes are the amount of money earned per hour, the a-intercepts show the amount of money made at 0 hours.

44. ★ **EXTENDED RESPONSE** An artist is renting a booth at an art show. A small booth costs $350 to rent. The artist plans to sell framed pictures for $50 each. The profit P (in dollars) the artist makes after selling p pictures is given by $P = 50p - 350$.

a. Graph the equation. a–b. See margin for art.

b. If the artist decides to rent a larger booth for $500, the profit is given by $P = 50p - 500$. Graph this equation on the same coordinate plane you used in part (a).

c. The artist can display 80 pictures in the small booth and 120 in the larger booth. If the artist is able to sell all of the pictures, which booth should the artist rent? *Explain.* Larger booth; if the artist rents the larger booth and sells all the paintings, the artist will make $5500, if the artist rents the smaller booth and sells all the paintings, the artist will make only $3650.

Internet Reference

Exercise 41 To find a map showing the maximum speed limit on interstate highways for the entire United States, visit www.fhwa.dot.gov/policy/ohpi/speeds.htm

41a.

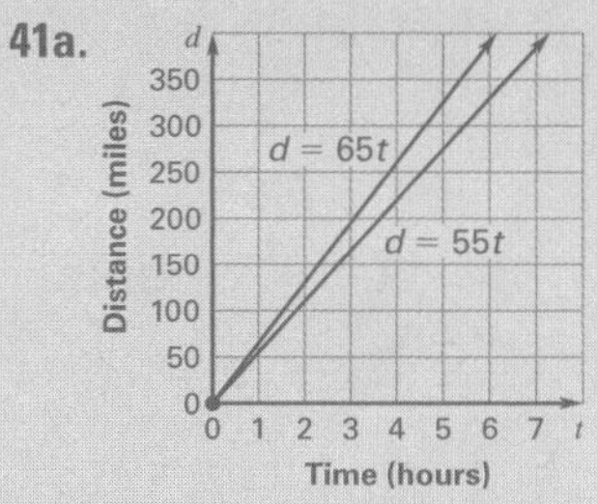

42a.

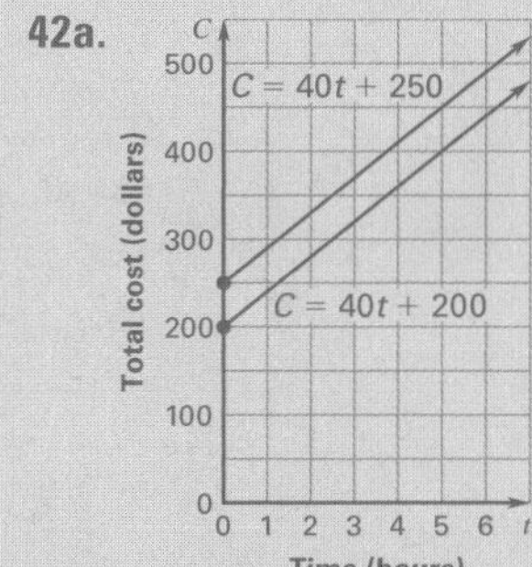

43a.

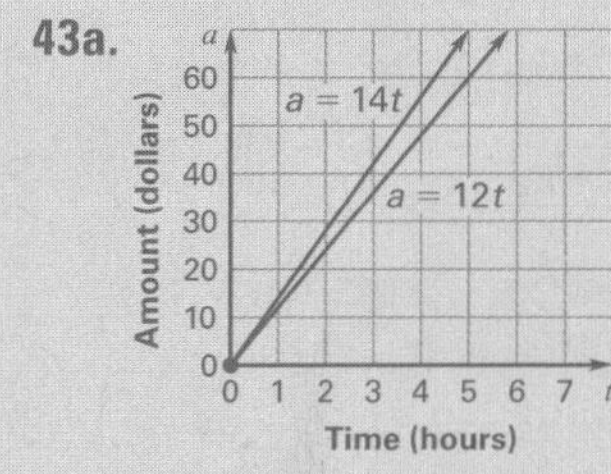

44a–b.

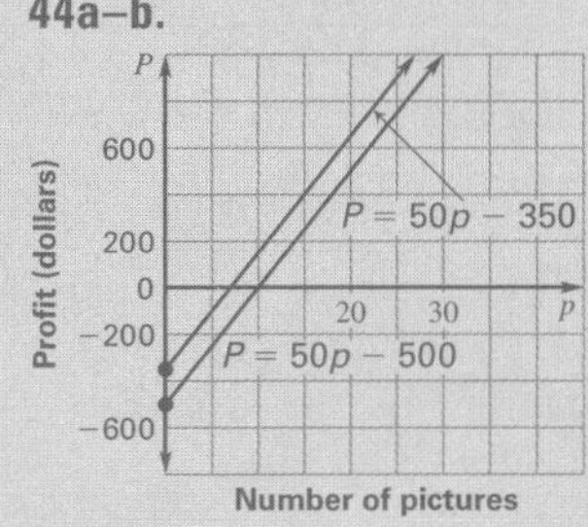

28.

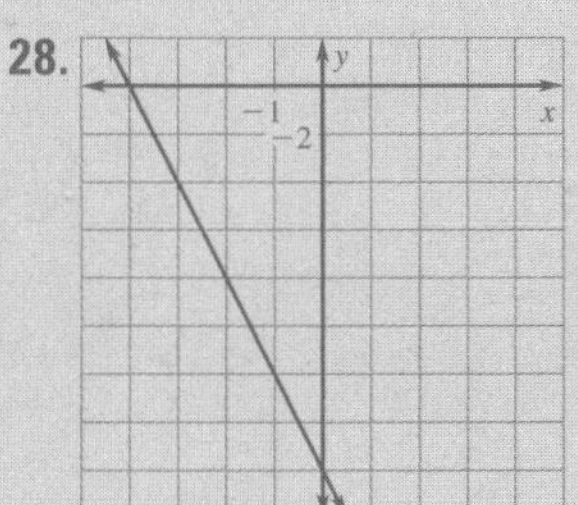

29.

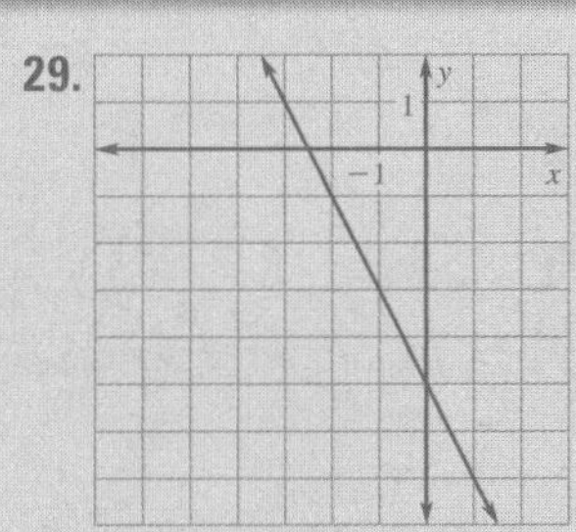

40a–b.

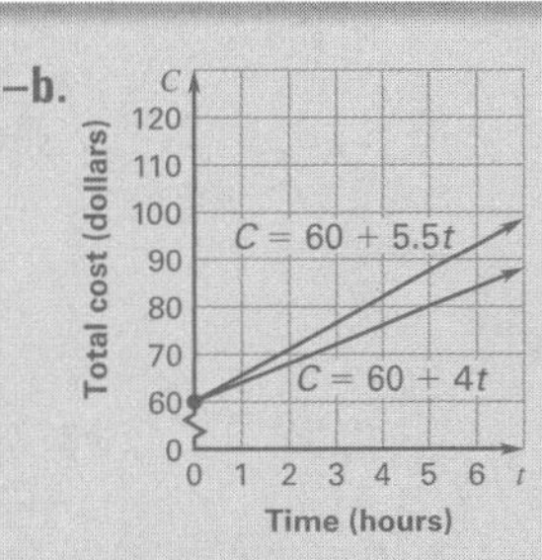

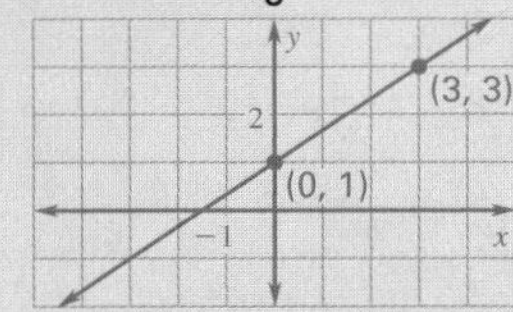

5 ASSESS AND RETEACH

Daily Homework Quiz

Transparency Available

1. Identify the slope and y-intercept of the line $2x + 4y = -16$. slope: $-\frac{1}{2}$, y-intercept: -4
2. Graph $y = \frac{2}{3}x + 1$.

3. Determine which of the lines are parallel. lines a and c

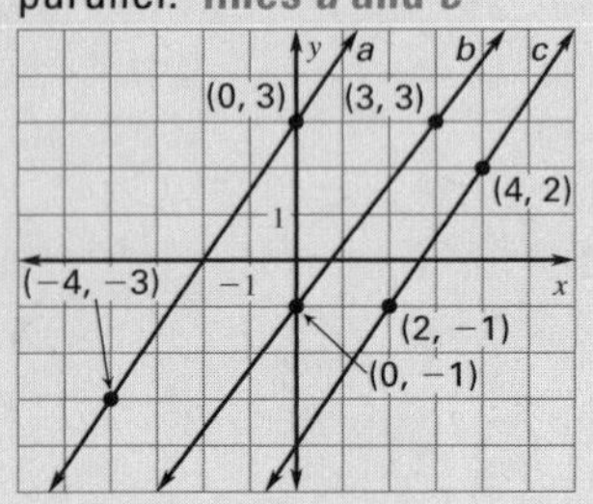

Online Quiz

Available at **classzone.com**

Diagnosis/Remediation

- Practice A, B, C in Chapter 4 Resource Book, pp. 64–69
- Study Guide in Chapter 4 Resource Book, pp. 70–71
- Practice Workbook, pp. 58–60
- @HomeTutor

Challenge

Additional challenge is available in the Chapter 4 Resource Book, p. 74.

Quiz

An easily-readable reduced copy of the quiz (with answers) on Lessons 4.4–4.5 from the Assessment Book can be found on p. 204G.

45a, Quiz 7–9, 10a. See Additional Answers beginning on p. AA1.

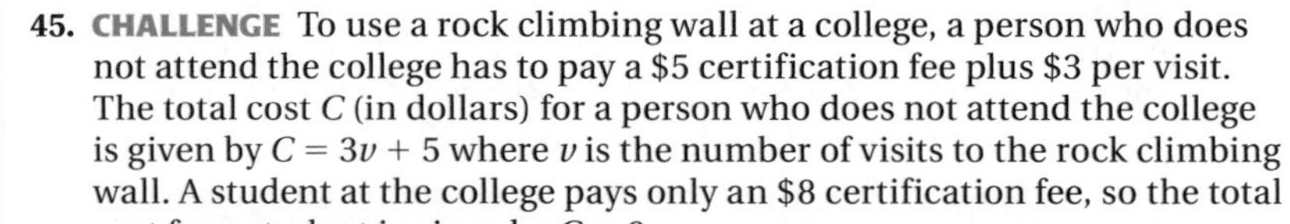

C **45. CHALLENGE** To use a rock climbing wall at a college, a person who does not attend the college has to pay a \$5 certification fee plus \$3 per visit. The total cost C (in dollars) for a person who does not attend the college is given by $C = 3v + 5$ where v is the number of visits to the rock climbing wall. A student at the college pays only an \$8 certification fee, so the total cost for a student is given by $C = 8$.

a. Graph both equations in the same coordinate plane. At what point do the lines intersect? What does the point of intersection represent? See margin for art; (1, 8); the point represents when the costs are equal.

b. When will a nonstudent pay more than a student? When will a student pay more than a nonstudent? *Explain.* A nonstudent pays more than a student after the first visit; a student pays more than a nonstudent when getting certified.

ILLINOIS MIXED REVIEW

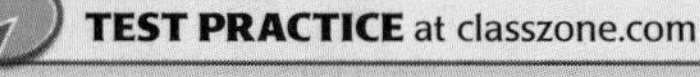

TEST PRACTICE at classzone.com

46. Which of the following equations is equivalent to $y = 3x + 9$? B

(A) $-3y = x - 9$ (B) $\frac{y}{3} = x + 3$ (C) $y = 2x + 6$ (D) $y = 5x + 15$

47. Triangle ABC is translated so that A is mapped to A'. Which coordinate pair represents B'? B

(A) $(-3, -1)$ (B) $(-1, 0)$

(C) $(0, 0)$ (D) $(0, -1)$

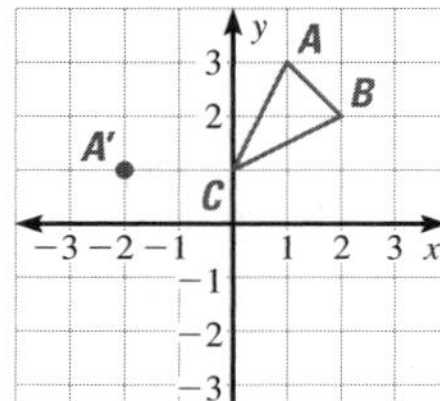

QUIZ for Lessons 4.4–4.5

Find the slope of the line that passes through the points. *(p. 235)*

1. $(3, -11)$ and $(0, 4)$ -5
2. $(2, 1)$ and $(8, 4)$ $\frac{1}{2}$
3. $(-4, -1)$ and $(-1, -1)$ 0

Identify the slope and y-intercept of the line with the given equation. *(p. 244)*

4. $y = -x + 9$ $-1, 9$
5. $2x + 9y = -18$ $-\frac{2}{9}, -2$
6. $-x + 6y = 21$ $\frac{1}{6}, 3\frac{1}{2}$

Graph the equation. *(p. 244)* 7–9. See margin.

7. $y = -2x + 11$
8. $y = \frac{5}{3}x - 8$
9. $-3x - 4y = -12$

10. RED OAKS Red oak trees grow at a rate of about 2 feet per year. You buy and plant two red oak trees, one that is 6 feet tall and one that is 8 feet tall. The height h (in feet) of the shorter tree can be modeled by $h = 2t + 6$ where t is the time (in years) since you planted the tree. The height of the taller tree can be modeled by $h = 2t + 8$. *(p. 244)*

a. Graph both equations in the same coordinate plane. See margin.

b. Use the graphs to find the difference of the heights of the trees 5 years after you plant them. What is the difference after 10 years? What do you notice about the difference of the heights of the two trees? 2 ft; 2 ft; it is always 2 feet.

Solve Linear Equations by Graphing

GOAL Use graphs to solve linear equations.

In Chapter 3, you learned how to solve linear equations in one variable algebraically. You can also solve linear equations graphically.

KEY CONCEPT *For Your Notebook*

Steps for Solving Linear Equations Graphically

Use the following steps to solve a linear equation in one variable graphically.

STEP 1 **Write** the equation in the form $ax + b = 0$.

STEP 2 **Write** the related function $y = ax + b$.

STEP 3 **Graph** the equation $y = ax + b$.

The solution of $ax + b = 0$ is the x-intercept of the graph of $y = ax + b$.

EXAMPLE 1 Solve an equation graphically

Solve $\frac{5}{2}x + 2 = 3x$ graphically. Check your solution algebraically.

Solution

STEP 1 **Write** the equation in the form $ax + b = 0$.

$\frac{5}{2}x + 2 = 3x$ **Write original equation.**

$-\frac{1}{2}x + 2 = 0$ **Subtract 3x from each side.**

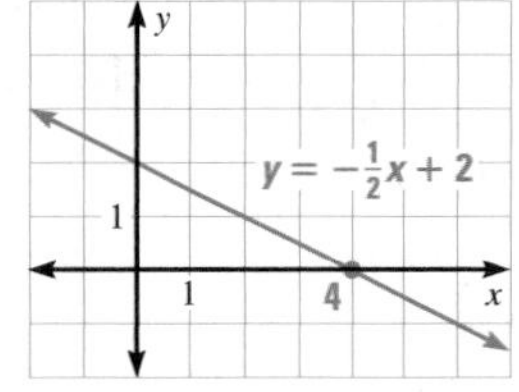

STEP 2 **Write** the related function $y = -\frac{1}{2}x + 2$.

STEP 3 **Graph** the equation $y = -\frac{1}{2}x + 2$. The x-intercept is 4.

▶ The solution of $\frac{5}{2}x + 2 = 3x$ is 4.

CHECK Use substitution.

$\frac{5}{2}x + 2 = 3x$ **Write original equation.**

$\frac{5}{2}(4) + 2 \stackrel{?}{=} 3(4)$ **Substitute 4 for x.**

$10 + 2 = 12$ **Simplify.**

$12 = 12$ ✓ **Solution checks.**

1 PLAN AND PREPARE

Warm-Up Exercises

Solve the equation.

1. $-3n + 13 = 7$ 2
2. $\frac{3}{4}x + 2 = -10$ −16
3. $-6 + 4d = 2d + 2$ 4
4. You buy a petrified rock and 6 postcards on a trip to the Petrified Forest. The petrified rock costs \$6.75. Find the cost of each postcard if your total cost is \$14.25 before tax and all the postcards cost the same. \$1.25

2 FOCUS AND MOTIVATE

Essential Question

Big Idea 1, p. 205

How do you use graphs to solve linear equations in one variable? Tell students they will learn how to answer this question by writing equations and their related functions to find the *x*-intercept of a graph.

3 TEACH

Extra Example 1

Solve $\frac{4}{3}x + 5 = 1$ graphically. −3

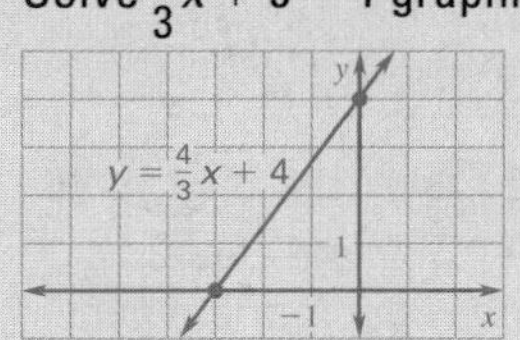

NCTM STANDARDS

Standard 2: Use models to understand relationships

Standard 10: Use representations to communicate mathematical ideas

Extra Example 2

The number s (in thousands) of subscribers to a local magazine can be modeled by the function $s = 3.128t + 12.58$ where t is the number of years since 1990. Use a graphing calculator to approximate the year when the number of subscribers will be 80 thousand.

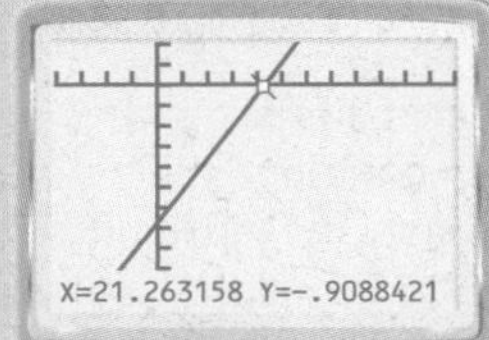

about 21 years after 1990, or 2011

Closing the Lesson

Have students summarize the major points of the lesson and answer the Essential Question: How do you use graphs to solve linear equations in one variable?

- To solve a linear equation in one variable by graphing, first find a related function.
- The x-intercept of the graph of the related function is the solution of the original equation.

Rewrite the given equation so it is equal to zero. Then write and graph the related function. The x-intercept of the graph is the solution of the equation.

4 PRACTICE AND APPLY

Avoiding Common Errors

Exercises 7–9 Remind students to substitute the appropriate numbers for s, b, and m in the equations and then write each equation in $ax + b = 0$ form.

EXAMPLE 2 Approximate a real-world solution

POPULATION The United States population P (in millions) can be modeled by the function $P = 2.683t + 213.1$ where t is the number of years since 1975. In approximately what year will the population be 350 million?

Solution

Substitute 350 for P in the linear model. You can answer the question by solving the resulting linear equation $350 = 2.683t + 213.1$.

STEP 1 **Write** the equation in the form $ax + b = 0$.

$350 = 2.683t + 213.1$ — **Write equation.**

$0 = 2.683t - 136.9$ — **Subtract 350 from each side.**

$0 = 2.683x - 136.9$ — **Substitute x for t.**

STEP 2 **Write** the related function: $y = 2.683x - 136.9$.

STEP 3 **Graph** the related function on a graphing calculator. Use the *trace* feature to approximate the x-intercept. You will know that you've crossed the x-axis when the y-values change from negative to positive. The x-intercept is about 51.

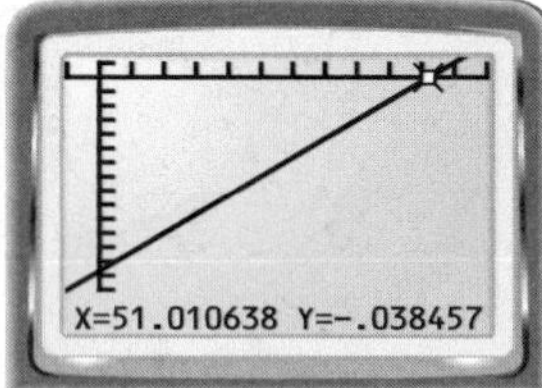

▶ Because x is the number of years since 1975, you can estimate that the population will be 350 million about 51 years after 1975, or in 2026.

SET THE WINDOW
Use the following viewing window for Example 2.
Xmin=−5
Xmax=60
Xscl=5
Ymin=−150
Ymax=10
Yscl=10

PRACTICE

EXAMPLE 1 on p. 251 for Exs. 1–6

Solve the equation graphically. Then check your solution algebraically.

1. $6x + 5 = -7$ −2
2. $-7x + 18 = -3$ 3
3. $2x - 4 = 3x$ −4
4. $\frac{1}{2}x - 3 = 2x$ −2
5. $-4 + 9x = -3x + 2$ $\frac{1}{2}$
6. $10x - 18x = 4x - 6$ $\frac{1}{2}$

EXAMPLE 2 on p. 252 for Exs. 7–9

7. **CABLE TELEVISION** The number s (in millions) of cable television subscribers can be modeled by the function $s = 1.79t + 51.1$ where t is the number of years since 1990. Use a graphing calculator to approximate the year when the number of subscribers was 70 million. 2000

8. **EDUCATION** The number b (in thousands) of bachelor's degrees in Spanish earned in the U.S. can be modeled by the function $b = 0.281t + 4.26$ where t is the number of years since 1990. Use a graphing calculator to approximate the year when the number of degrees will be 9000. 2006

9. **TRAVEL** The number of miles m (in billions) traveled by vehicles in New York can be modeled by $m = 2.56t + 113$ where t is the number of years since 1994. Use a graphing calculator to approximate the year in which the number of vehicle miles of travel in New York was 130 billion. 2000

4.6 Model Direct Variation

6.11.19 Set up, evaluate, or solve problems stated in terms of direct and inverse variation of simple quantities.

Before You wrote and graphed linear equations.

Now You will write and graph direct variation equations.

Why? So you can model distance traveled, as in Ex. 40.

Key Vocabulary
- **direct variation**
- **constant of variation**

Two variables x and y show **direct variation** provided $y = ax$ and $a \neq 0$. The nonzero number a is called the **constant of variation**, and y is said to *vary directly* with x.

The equation $y = 5x$ is an example of direct variation, and the constant of variation is 5. The equation $y = x + 5$ is *not* an example of direct variation.

EXAMPLE 1 Identify direct variation equations

Tell whether the equation represents direct variation. If so, identify the constant of variation.

a. $2x - 3y = 0$

b. $-x + y = 4$

Solution

To tell whether an equation represents direct variation, try to rewrite the equation in the form $y = ax$.

a. $2x - 3y = 0$ Write original equation.

$-3y = -2x$ Subtract $2x$ from each side.

$y = \frac{2}{3}x$ Simplify.

▶ Because the equation $2x - 3y = 0$ can be rewritten in the form $y = ax$, it represents direct variation. The constant of variation is $\frac{2}{3}$.

b. $-x + y = 4$ Write original equation.

$y = x + 4$ Add x to each side.

▶ Because the equation $-x + y = 4$ cannot be rewritten in the form $y = ax$, it does not represent direct variation.

GUIDED PRACTICE for Example 1

Tell whether the equation represents direct variation. If so, identify the constant of variation.

1. $-x + y = 1$ not direct variation

2. $2x + y = 0$ direct variation; -2

3. $4x - 5y = 0$ direct variation; $\frac{4}{5}$

1 PLAN AND PREPARE

Warm-Up Exercises

Transparency Available

Rewrite the equation so y is a function of x.

1. $4x - 2y = -8$ $y = 2x + 4$

2. $-9x + 3y = 21$ $y = 3x + 7$

3. You are traveling by bus. After 4.5 hours, the bus has traveled 234 miles. Use the formula $d = rt$ where d is distance, r is rate, and t is time to find the average rate of speed of the bus. 52 mi/h

Notetaking Guide

Transparency Available

Promotes interactive learning and notetaking skills, pp. 91–93.

Pacing

Basic: 1 day

Average: 1 day

Advanced: 1 day

Block: 0.5 block with 4.5

- See *Teaching Guide/Lesson Plan.*

2 FOCUS AND MOTIVATE

Essential Question

Big Idea 3, p. 205

How do you write and graph direct variation equations? Tell students they will learn how to answer this question by recognizing situations that represent direct variation and identifying the constant of variation.

Resource Planning Guide

Chapter Resource Book
- Teaching Guide/Lesson Plan (pp. 75–76)
- Practice levels A, B, C (pp. 77–82)
- Study Guide (pp. 83–84)
- Catch-up for Absent Students (p. 85)
- Application (p. 86)
- Challenge (p. 87)

Workbooks
- Notetaking Guide (pp. 91–93)
- Practice Workbook (pp. 61–63)

Teaching Options
- **Power Presentations CD-ROM** provides dynamic electronic teaching resources for the classroom.
- **Activity Generator CD-ROM** provides editable activities for all ability levels.

Interactive Technology
- Easy Planner
- Power Presentations CD-ROM
- Activity Generator CD-ROM
- Animated Algebra
- Test Generator CD-ROM
- Online Quiz
- eWorkbook
- eEdition
- @HomeTutor

Resources for English Learners
- Quick Reference for English Learners
- Spanish Study Guide
- Multi-Language Visual Glossary
- Student Resources in Spanish

See also the *Algebra 1 Toolkit* for more strategies for meeting individual needs.

Motivating the Lesson

Suppose an object that weighs 150 pounds on Earth would weigh 165 pounds on Neptune and that the weight of an object on Neptune varies directly with the weight of an object on Earth. You can use this information to determine an equation that relates the two weights. Then you can determine your weight, and the weight of your friends on Neptune.

3 TEACH

Extra Example 1

Tell whether the equation represents direct variation. If so, identify the constant of variation.

a. $4x + 5y = 0$ yes, $-\frac{4}{5}$

b. $2x - y = 3$ no

Extra Example 2

Graph the direct variation equation.

a. $y = \frac{2}{5}x$

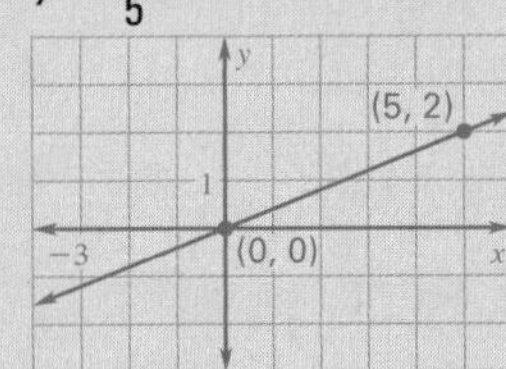

b. $y = -\frac{1}{2}x$

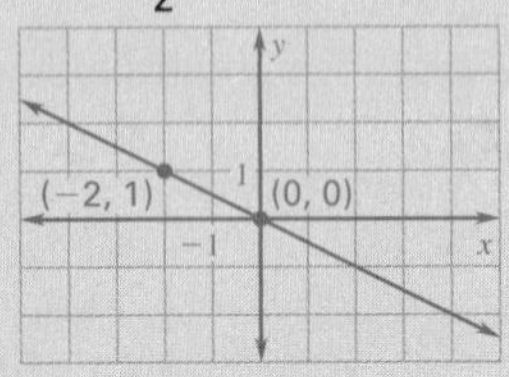

An **Animated Algebra** activity is available on-line for **Example 2**. This activity is also available on the **Power Presentations CD-ROM**.

DIRECT VARIATION GRAPHS Notice that a direct variation equation, $y = ax$, is a linear equation in slope-intercept form, $y = mx + b$, with $m = a$ and $b = 0$. The graph of a direct variation equation is a line with a slope of a and a y-intercept of 0. So, the line passes through the origin.

EXAMPLE 2 Graph direct variation equations

Graph the direct variation equation.

a. $y = \frac{2}{3}x$

b. $y = -3x$

Solution

a. Plot a point at the origin. The slope is equal to the constant of variation, or $\frac{2}{3}$. Find and plot a second point, then draw a line through the points.

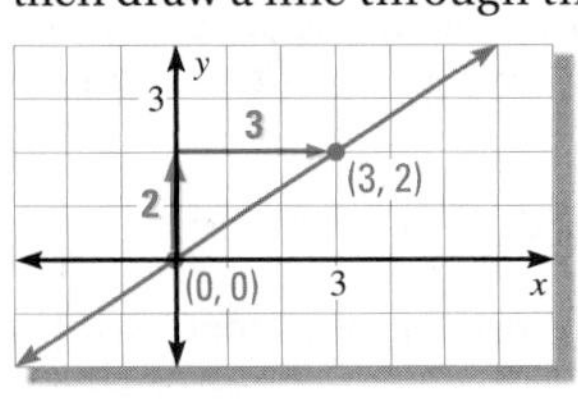

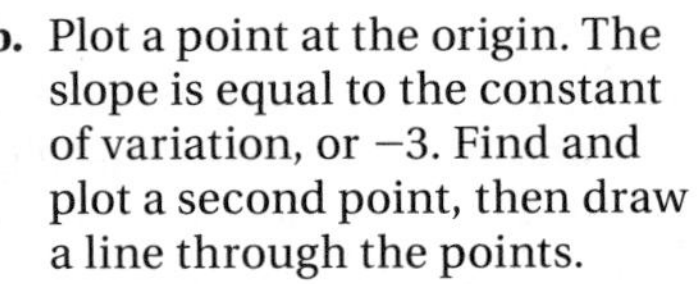

b. Plot a point at the origin. The slope is equal to the constant of variation, or −3. Find and plot a second point, then draw a line through the points.

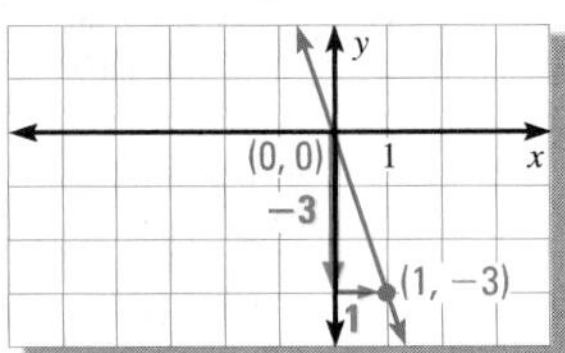

DRAW A GRAPH
If the constant of variation is positive, the graph of $y = ax$ passes through Quadrants I and III. If the constant of variation is negative, the graph of $y = ax$ passes through Quadrants II and IV.

Animated Algebra at classzone.com

EXAMPLE 3 Write and use a direct variation equation

The graph of a direct variation equation is shown.

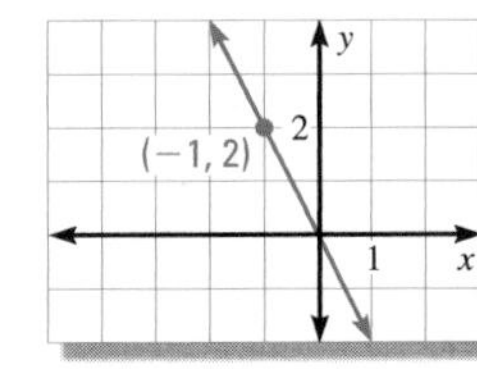

a. Write the direct variation equation.

b. Find the value of y when $x = 30$.

Solution

a. Because y varies directly with x, the equation has the form $y = ax$. Use the fact that $y = 2$ when $x = -1$ to find a.

$y = ax$	**Write direct variation equation.**
$2 = a(-1)$	**Substitute.**
$-2 = a$	**Solve for a.**

▶ A direct variation equation that relates x and y is $y = -2x$.

b. When $x = 30$, $y = -2(30) = -60$.

✓ **GUIDED PRACTICE** for Examples 2 and 3

4. Graph the direct variation equation $y = 2x$. See margin.

5. The graph of a direct variation equation passes through the point (4, 6). Write the direct variation equation and find the value of y when $x = 24$.
$y = \frac{3}{2}x$, 36

KEY CONCEPT *For Your Notebook*

Properties of Graphs of Direct Variation Equations

- The graph of a direct variation equation is a line through the origin.
- The slope of the graph of $y = ax$ is a.

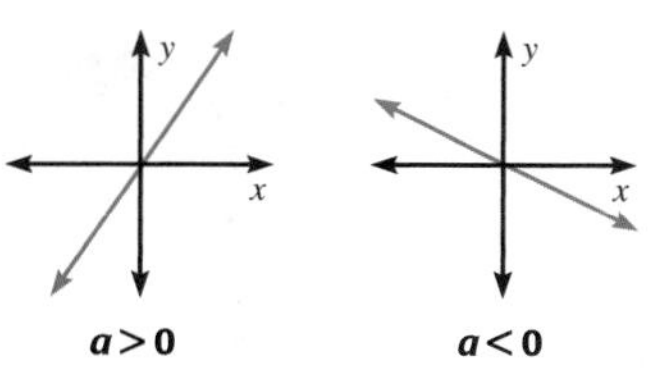

EXAMPLE 4 Solve a multi-step problem

ANOTHER WAY For alternative methods for solving Example 4, turn to page 260 for the **Problem Solving Workshop**.

SALTWATER AQUARIUM The number s of tablespoons of sea salt needed in a saltwater fish tank varies directly with the number w of gallons of water in the tank. A pet shop owner recommends adding 100 tablespoons of sea salt to a 20 gallon tank.

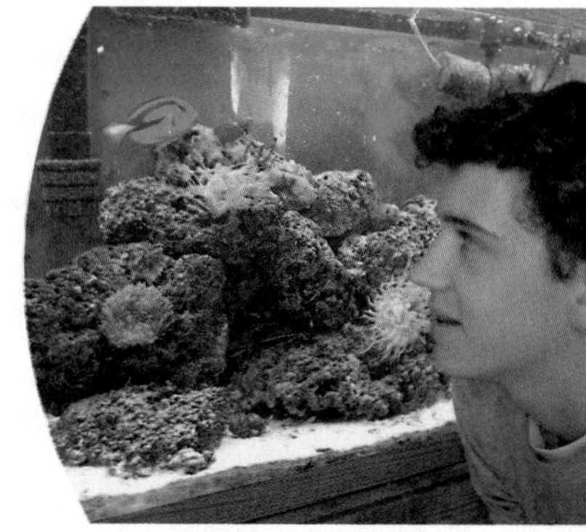

- Write a direct variation equation that relates w and s.
- How many tablespoons of salt should be added to a 30 gallon saltwater fish tank?

Solution

STEP 1 **Write** a direct variation equation. Because s varies directly with w, you can use the equation $s = aw$. Also use the fact that $s = 100$ when $w = 20$.

$s = aw$	**Write direct variation equation.**
$100 = a(20)$	**Substitute.**
$5 = a$	**Solve for *a*.**

RECOGNIZE RATE OF CHANGE The value of a in Example 4 is a rate of change: 5 tablespoons of sea salt per gallon of water.

▶ A direct variation equation that relates w and s is $s = 5w$.

STEP 2 **Find** the number of tablespoons of salt that should be added to a 30 gallon saltwater fish tank. Use your direct variation equation from Step 1.

$s = 5w$	**Write direct variation equation.**
$s = 5(30)$	**Substitute 30 for *w*.**
$s = 150$	**Simplify.**

▶ You should add 150 tablespoons of salt to a 30 gallon fish tank.

✓ GUIDED PRACTICE for Example 4

6. **WHAT IF?** In Example 4, suppose the fish tank is a 25 gallon tank. How many tablespoons of salt should be added to the tank? 125 tbsp

4.

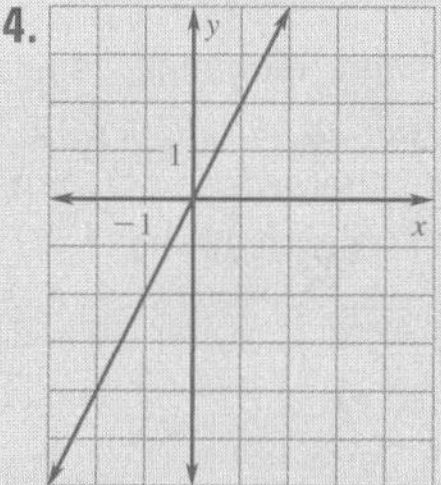

Key Questions to Ask for Example 2

- Can the y-intercept for the graph of a direct variation equation be a number other than zero? Explain. **No; a direct variation equation is of the form $y = ax + 0$, so the line must pass through the origin.**
- What is the relationship of slope to the constant of variation? **They are the same.**

Extra Example 3

The graph of a direct variation equation is shown.

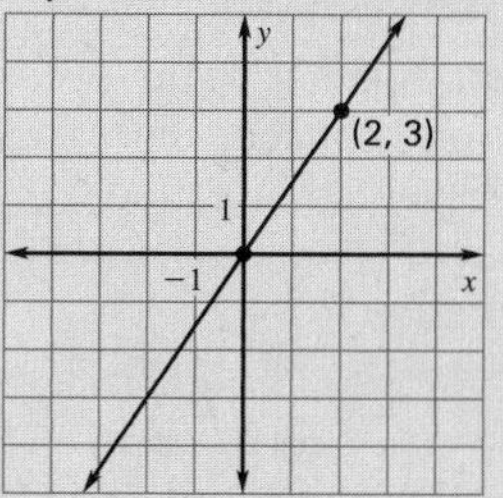

a. Write the direct variation equation. $y = \frac{3}{2}x$

b. Find the value of y when $x = 14$. 21

Key Questions to Ask for Example 3

- What do you need from a graph to write a direct variation equation? **the coordinates of one point on the graph, other than the origin**
- What can you tell about the constant of variation from looking at the graph? Explain. **The constant of variation must be negative, because the graph slants downward from left to right.**

Extra Example 4

An object that weighs 100 pounds on Earth would weigh just 6 pounds on Pluto. Assume that weight P on Pluto varies directly with weight E on Earth.

- Write a direct variation equation that relates P and E. $P = 0.06E$
- What would a boulder weighing 750 pounds on Earth weigh on Pluto? 45 lb

Extra Example 5

The table shows the cost of buying used DVDs at a music store.

Number of DVDs, d	Cost, c
3	$25.77
6	$51.54
9	$77.31

a. Explain why C varies directly with d. **All of the data pairs have the same ratio, 8.59.**

b. Write a direct variation equation that relates d and C. $C = 8.59d$

Closing the Lesson

Have students summarize the major points of the lesson and answer the Essential Question: How do you write and graph direct variation equations?

- **A direct variation equation is of the form $y = ax$, with a not equal to 0.**
- **The graph of a direct variation equation is a line through the origin with slope a.**

Use facts in a real-world situation or the coordinates of a point for the values of x and y in the direct variation equation $y = ax$. Then solve for the constant of variation. To graph a direct variation equation, plot a point at the origin and then use the constant of variation, which is the slope, to plot a second point.

RATIOS The direct variation equation $y = ax$ can be rewritten as $\frac{y}{x} = a$ for $x \neq 0$. So, in a direct variation, the ratio of y to x is constant for all nonzero data pairs (x, y).

EXAMPLE 5 Use a direct variation model

ONLINE MUSIC The table shows the cost C of downloading s songs at an Internet music site.

Number of songs, s	Cost, C (dollars)
3	2.97
5	4.95
7	6.93

a. Explain why C varies directly with s.

b. Write a direct variation equation that relates s and C.

CHECK RATIOS
For real-world data, the ratios may not be exactly equal. You may still be able to use a direct variation model when the ratios are approximately equal.

Solution

a. To explain why C varies directly with s, compare the ratios $\frac{C}{s}$ for all data pairs (s, C): $\frac{2.97}{3} = \frac{4.95}{5} = \frac{6.93}{7} = 0.99$.

Because the ratios all equal 0.99, C varies directly with s.

b. A direct variation equation is $C = 0.99s$.

✓ **GUIDED PRACTICE** for Example 5

7. WHAT IF? In Example 5, suppose the website charges a total of $1.99 for the first 5 songs you download and $.99 for each song after the first 5. Is it reasonable to use a direct variation model for this situation? *Explain.* **No; the equation that models this situation does not have the form $y = ax$.**

4.6 EXERCISES

HOMEWORK KEY
○ = **WORKED-OUT SOLUTIONS** on p. WS9 for Exs. 7, 21, and 43
★ = **STANDARDIZED TEST PRACTICE** Exs. 2, 9, 28, 38, 43, 44, and 46
◆ = **MULTIPLE REPRESENTATIONS** Ex. 45

SKILL PRACTICE

A

1. VOCABULARY Copy and complete: Two variables x and y show ___?___ provided $y = ax$ and $a \neq 0$. **direct variation**

2. ★ WRITING A line has a slope of −3 and a y-intercept of 4. Is the equation of the line a direct variation equation? *Explain.* **No; a direct variation equation has a y-intercept of 0.**

EXAMPLE 1 on p. 253 for Exs. 3–10

IDENTIFYING DIRECT VARIATION EQUATIONS **Tell whether the equation represents direct variation. If so, identify the constant of variation.**

3. $y = x$ **direct variation; 1**

4. $y = 5x - 1$ **not direct variation**

5. $2x + y = 3$ **not direct variation**

6. $x - 3y = 0$ **direct variation; $\frac{1}{3}$**

7. $8x + 2y = 0$ **direct variation; −4**

8. $2.4x + 6 = 1.2y$ **not direct variation**

Differentiated Instruction

English Learners The word *variation* means "a change," so students may be confused by the term *constant of variation* for a in the direct variation equation $y = ax$. Stress that a does not vary, but rather stays constant, in a given direct variation equation.

See also the *Algebra 1 Toolkit* for more strategies.

9. ★ **MULTIPLE CHOICE** Which equation is a direct variation equation? C

Ⓐ $y = 7 - 3x$ Ⓑ $3x - 7y = 1$ Ⓒ $3x - 7y = 0$ Ⓓ $3y = 7x - 1$

10. **ERROR ANALYSIS** *Describe* and correct the error in identifying the constant of variation for the direct variation equation $-5x + 3y = 0$. The coefficient of y should be 1, not 3; $y = \frac{5}{3}x$, the constant of variation is $\frac{5}{3}$.

$-5x + 3y = 0$
$3y = 5x$
The constant of variation is 5.

EXAMPLE 2 on p. 254 for Exs. 11–22

GRAPHING EQUATIONS **Graph the direct variation equation.** 11–22. See margin.

11. $y = x$ 12. $y = 3x$ 13. $y = -4x$ 14. $y = 5x$

15. $y = \frac{4}{3}x$ 16. $y = \frac{1}{2}x$ 17. $y = -\frac{1}{3}x$ 18. $y = -\frac{3}{2}x$

19. $12y = -24x$ 20. $10y = 25x$ 21. $4x + y = 0$ 22. $y - 1.25x = 0$

EXAMPLE 3 on p. 254 for Exs. 23–25

WRITING EQUATIONS **The graph of a direct variation equation is shown. Write the direct variation equation. Then find the value of y when $x = 8$.**

23.

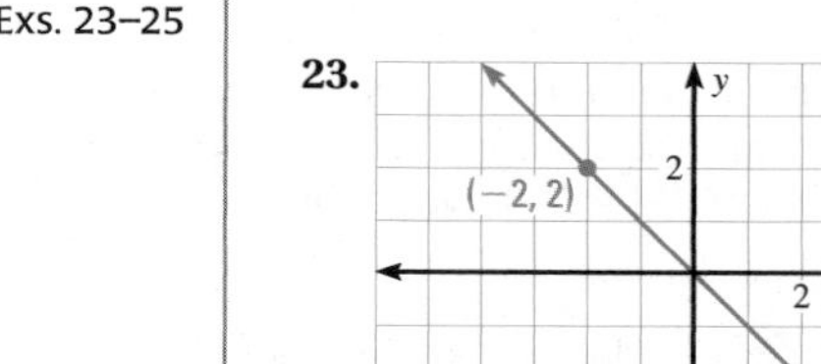

$y = -x$; -8

24.

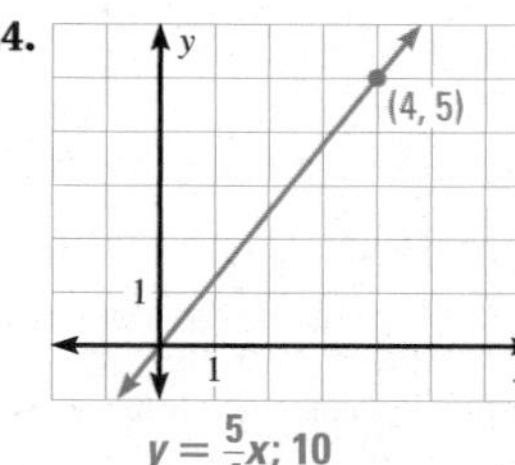

$y = \frac{5}{4}x$; 10

25.

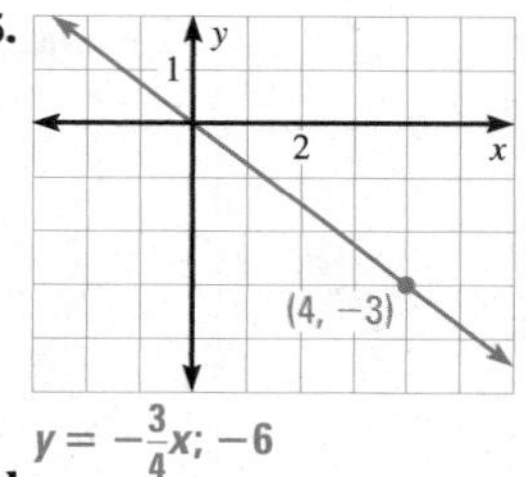

$y = -\frac{3}{4}x$; -6

B **IDENTIFYING DIRECT VARIATION EQUATIONS** **Tell whether the table represents direct variation. If so, write the direct variation equation.**

26.

x	1	2	3	4	6
y	5	10	15	20	30

direct variation; $y = 5x$

27.

x	−3	−1	1	3	5
y	−2	0	2	4	6

not a direct variation

28. ★ **WRITING** A student says that a direct variation equation can be used to model the data in the table. *Explain* why the student is mistaken.

x	2	4	8	16
y	1	2	4	6

Sample answer: Each of the ratios $\frac{y}{x}$ should be equal, $\frac{4}{8} \neq \frac{6}{16}$, so y does not vary directly with x.

WRITING EQUATIONS **Given that y varies directly with x, use the specified values to write a direct variation equation that relates x and y.**

29. $x = 3, y = 9$ $y = 3x$ 30. $x = 2, y = 26$ $y = 13x$ 31. $x = 14, y = 7$ $y = \frac{1}{2}x$

32. $x = 15, y = -5$ $y = -\frac{1}{3}x$ 33. $x = -2, y = -2$ $y = x$ 34. $x = -18, y = -4$ $y = \frac{2}{9}x$

35. $x = \frac{1}{4}, y = 1$ $y = 4x$ 36. $x = -6, y = 15$ $y = -\frac{5}{2}x$ 37. $x = -5.2, y = 1.4$ $y = -\frac{7}{26}x$

C 38. ★ **WRITING** If y varies directly with x, does x vary directly with y? If so, what is the relationship between the constants of variation? *Explain.*

38. Yes; the constants of variation are reciprocals of each other; if $y = a_1x$, then $a_1 = \frac{y}{x}$ and if $x = a_2y$, then $a_2 = \frac{x}{y}$, which shows the constants of variation, a_1 and a_2 are reciprocals of each other.

39. **CHALLENGE** The slope of a line is $-\frac{1}{3}$, and the point $(-6, 2)$ lies on the line. Use the formula for the slope of a line to determine if the equation of the line is a direct variation equation. direct variation

4 PRACTICE AND APPLY

Assignment Guide

Answer Transparencies available for all exercises

Basic:
Day 1: pp. 256–259
Exs. 1, 2, 3–9 odd, 10–22 even, 23–28, 40–45, 48–62 even

Average:
Day 1: pp. 256–259
Exs. 1, 2, 6–10, 18–28, 29–35 odd, 40–46, 53–56, 60–62

Advanced:
Day 1: pp. 256–259
Exs. 1, 2, 7–9, 19–22, 24–28, 33–39*, 41–47*, 54–56, 60–62

Block:
pp. 256–259
Exs. 1, 2, 6–10, 18–28, 29–35 odd, 40–46, 53–56, 60–62 (with 4.5)

Differentiated Instruction

See *Algebra 1 Best Practices Toolkit* for suggestions on addressing the needs of a diverse classroom.

Homework Check

For a quick check of student understanding of key concepts, go over the following exercises:

Basic: 5, 14, 23, 40, 43
Average: 7, 19, 24, 41, 43
Advanced: 8, 20, 25, 42, 44

Extra Practice

- Student Edition, p. 941
- Chapter 4 Resource Book: Practice levels A, B, C, pp. 77–82

Practice Worksheet

An easily-readable reduced practice page (with answers) for this lesson can be found on p. 204E.

11–22. See Additional Answers beginning on p. AA1.

Avoiding Common Errors

Exercises 19–22 Some students may forget to rewrite the equations in the form $y = ax$. Remind them to do this before graphing.

Exercises 23–25 Caution students to substitute the coordinates correctly in the direct variation equation.

Exercises 26–28 Some students may notice that the increments in the table are not equal and assume that the ratios are not the same for all the data pairs. Tell students they need to test all the data pairs to see if the ratios are equal.

Exercise 46 More statistical information for NCAA women's basketball can be found at www.ncaasports.com/basketball/womens/stats

PROBLEM SOLVING

EXAMPLE 4 on p. 255 for Exs. 40–42

40. BICYCLES The distance d (in meters) you travel on a bicycle varies directly with the number r of revolutions that the rear tire completes. You travel about 2 meters on a mountain bike for every revolution of the tire.

a. Write a direct variation equation that relates r and d. $d = 2r$

b. How many meters do you travel in 1500 tire revolutions? 3000 m

@HomeTutor for problem solving help at classzone.com

41. VACATION TIME At one company, the amount of vacation v (in hours) an employee earns varies directly with the amount of time t (in weeks) he or she works. An employee who works 2 weeks earns 3 hours of vacation.

a. Write a direct variation equation that relates t and v. $v = \frac{3}{2}t$

b. How many hours of vacation time does an employee earn in 8 weeks? 12 h

@HomeTutor for problem solving help at classzone.com

42. LANDSCAPING Landscapers plan to spread a layer of stone on a path. The number s of bags of stone needed depends on the depth d (in inches) of the layer. They need 10 bags to spread a layer of stone that is 2 inches deep. Write a direct variation equation that relates d and s. Then find the number of bags needed to spread a layer that is 3 inches deep. $s = 5d$; 15 bags

EXAMPLE 5 on p. 256 for Exs. 43–44

43a. Compare the ratios, $\frac{f}{w}$, for all data pairs (w, f). Since the ratios all equal 0.25, f varies directly with w.

44a. Compare the ratios, $\frac{p}{\ell}$, for all data pairs (ℓ, p). Since the ratios all equal 1.25, p varies directly with ℓ.

43. ★ **SHORT RESPONSE** At a recycling center, computers and computer accessories can be recycled for a fee f based on weight w, as shown in the table.

Weight, w (pounds)	Fee, f (dollars)
10	2.50
15	3.75
30	7.50

a. *Explain* why f varies directly with w.

b. Write a direct variation equation that relates w and f. Find the total recycling fee for a computer that weighs 18 pounds and a printer that weighs 10 pounds. $f = 0.25w$; \$7

44. ★ **SHORT RESPONSE** You can buy gold chain by the inch. The table shows the price of gold chain for various lengths.

Length, ℓ (inches)	7	9	16	18
Price, p (dollars)	8.75	11.25	20.00	22.50

a. *Explain* why p varies directly with ℓ.

b. Write a direct variation equation that relates ℓ and p. If you have \$30, what is the longest chain that you can buy? $p = 1.25\ell$; 24 in.

○ = WORKED-OUT SOLUTIONS on p. WS1 ★ = STANDARDIZED TEST PRACTICE  = MULTIPLE REPRESENTATIONS

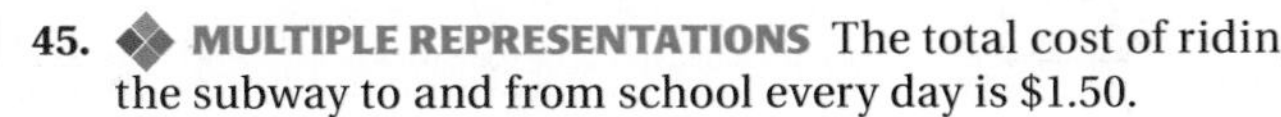

B 45. **MULTIPLE REPRESENTATIONS** The total cost of riding the subway to and from school every day is \$1.50.

a. **Making a Table** Make a table that shows the number d of school days and the total cost C (in dollars) for trips to and from school for some values of d. Assume you travel to school once each school day and home from school once each school day. See margin.

b. **Drawing a Graph** Graph the ordered pairs from the table and draw a ray through them. See margin.

c. **Writing an Equation** Write an equation of the graph from part (b). Is it a direct variation equation? *Explain.* If there are 22 school days in one month, what will it cost to ride the subway to and from school for that month? $C = 1.5d$; yes; it's in the form $y = ax$; \$33.

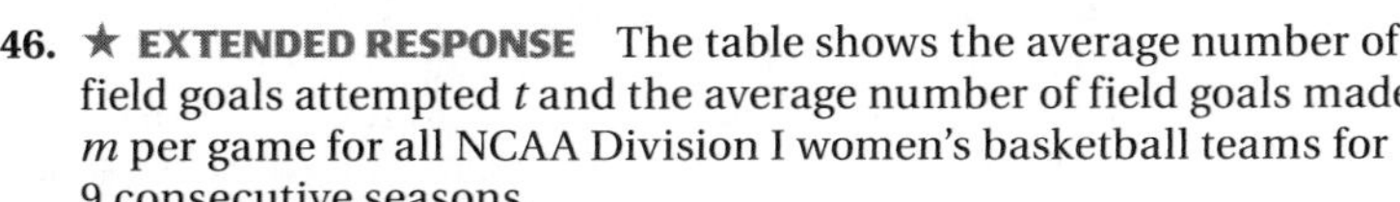

46. ★ **EXTENDED RESPONSE** The table shows the average number of field goals attempted t and the average number of field goals made m per game for all NCAA Division I women's basketball teams for 9 consecutive seasons.

Attempted field goals, t	61.8	61.9	61.8	60.8	59.5	59.0	58.9	59.2	58.4
Field goals made, m	25.7	25.6	25.6	25.2	24.5	24.6	24.5	24.3	24.0

a. **Write** Why is it reasonable to use a direct variation model for this situation? Write a direct variation equation that relates t and m. Find the constant of variation to the nearest tenth. All of the ratios, $\frac{m}{t}$, are approximately equal to 0.4; $m = 0.4t$; 0.4.

b. **Estimate** The highest average number of attempted field goals in one season was 66.2. Estimate the number of field goals made that season. about 26 field goals

c. **Explain** If the average number of field goals made was increasing rather than decreasing and the number of attempted field goals continued to decrease, would the data show direct variation? *Explain.* No; the ratios, $\frac{m}{t}$, for each season would not be equal to each other.

C 47. **CHALLENGE** In Exercise 40, you found an equation showing that the distance traveled on a bike varies directly with the number of revolutions that the rear tire completes. The number r of tire revolutions varies directly with the number p of pedal revolutions. In a particular gear, you travel about 1.3 meters for every 5 revolutions of the pedals. Show that distance traveled varies directly with pedal revolutions.

47. Because $d = 2r$ and r varies directly with p, you can write the equation $r = ap$. When $d = 1.3$ centimeters, $r = 0.65$. Substitute 0.65 for r when $p = 5$ to get $0.65 = 5a$. Solve to find $a = 0.13$. If you substitute ap for r into the equation $d = 2r$, you get $d = 2(0.13)p$, giving the direct variation equation $d = 0.26p$.

ILLINOIS MIXED REVIEW

TEST PRACTICE at classzone.com

48. The graph represents an employee's earnings as a function of the number of hours the employee works. How much money does the employee earn in 2 hours?

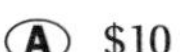

Ⓐ \$10 Ⓑ \$15 Ⓒ \$30 Ⓓ \$40

C

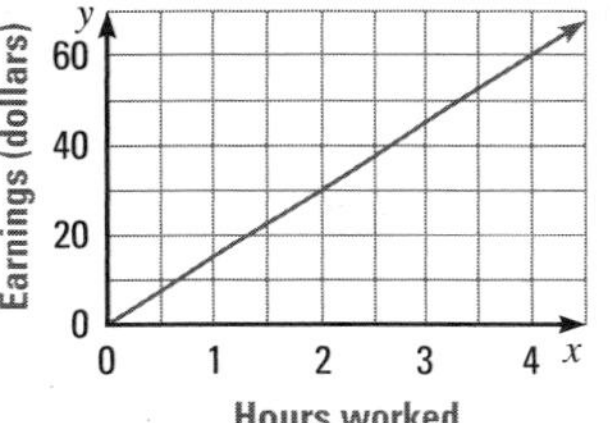

5 ASSESS AND RETEACH

Daily Homework Quiz

Transparency Available

Tell whether the equation represents direct variation. If so, identify the constant of variation.

1. $5x - 6y = 2$ no
2. $x + y = 0$ yes, −1
3. The number p of parts a machine produces varies directly with the time t (in minutes) the machine is in operation. The machine produces 84 parts in 14 minutes. Write a direct variation equation that relates t and p. How many parts does the machine produce in 25 minutes? $p = 6t$; 150 parts

Online Quiz

Available at **classzone.com**

Diagnosis/Remediation

- Practice A, B, C in Chapter 4 Resource Book, pp. 77–82
- Study Guide in Chapter 4 Resource Book, pp. 83–84
- Practice Workbook, pp. 61–63
- @HomeTutor

Challenge

Additional challenge is available in the Chapter 4 Resource Book, p. 87.

45a. *Sample answer:*

d	C (dollars)
1	1.5
2	3
3	4.5

45b.

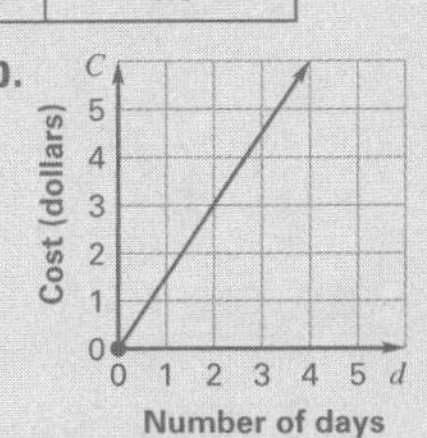

Alternative Strategy

Example 4 on page 255 can be solved by using a graph or by writing and solving a proportion. The method of using a graph allows students to visualize the solution. The method of using a proportion is useful when students cannot remember the direct variation equation. Both methods can help students understand the algebraic solution given in Lesson 4.6.

Reading Strategy

In Method 1, point out to students that the x-coordinates and x-values are color-coded blue and the y-coordinates and y-values are color-coded red for all three steps.

PROBLEM SOLVING WORKSHOP
LESSON 4.6

Using ALTERNATIVE METHODS

Another Way to Solve Example 4, page 255

MULTIPLE REPRESENTATIONS In Example 4 on page 255, you saw how to solve the problem about how much salt to add to a saltwater fish tank by writing and using a direct variation equation. You can also solve the problem using a graph or a proportion.

PROBLEM

SALTWATER AQUARIUM The number s of tablespoons of sea salt needed in a saltwater fish tank varies directly with the number w of gallons of water in the tank. A pet shop owner recommends adding 100 tablespoons of sea salt to a 20 gallon tank. How many tablespoons of salt should be added to a 30 gallon saltwater fish tank?

METHOD 1

Using a Graph An alternative approach is to use a graph.

STEP 1 **Read** the problem. It tells you an amount of salt for a certain size fish tank. You can also assume that if a fishtank has no water, then no salt needs to be added. Write ordered pairs for this information.

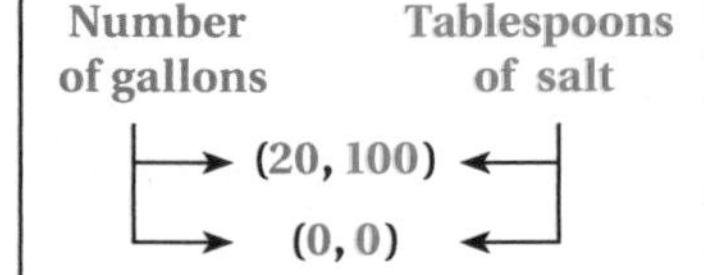

STEP 2 **Graph** the ordered pairs. Draw a line through the points.

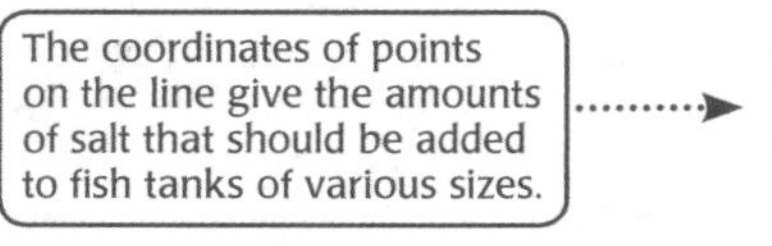

The coordinates of points on the line give the amounts of salt that should be added to fish tanks of various sizes.

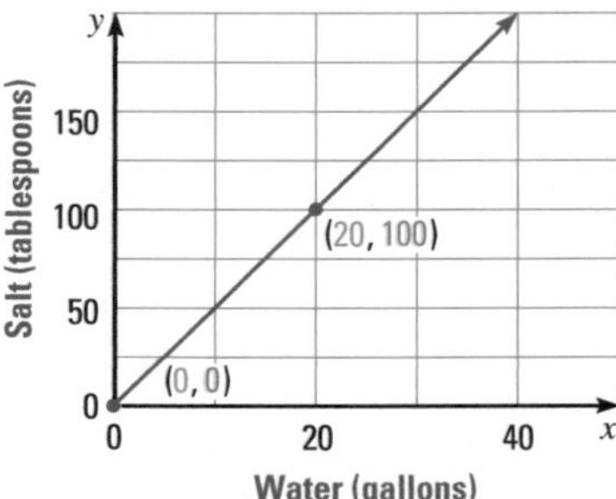

STEP 3 **Find** the point on the graph that has an x-coordinate of 30. The y-coordinate of this point is 150, so 150 tablespoons of salt should be added to a 30 gallon tank.

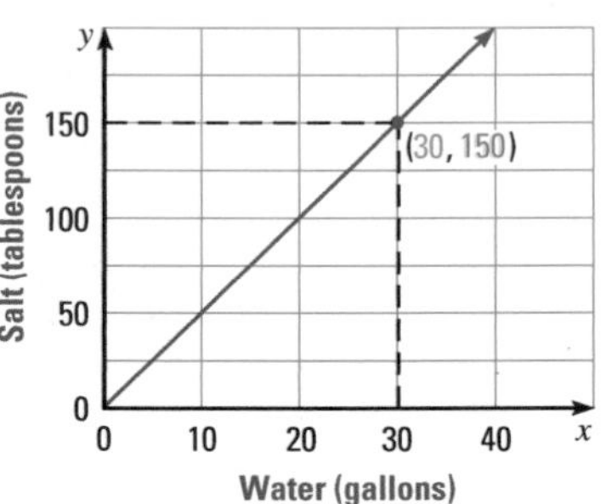

METHOD 2 **Writing a Proportion** Another alternative approach is to write and solve a proportion.

STEP 1 **Write** a proportion involving two ratios that each compare the amount of water (in gallons) to the amount of salt (in tablespoons).

$$\frac{20}{100} = \frac{30}{s}$$ ← amount of water (gallons) / ← amount of salt (tablespoons)

STEP 2 **Solve** the proportion.

$\frac{20}{100} = \frac{30}{s}$ — **Write proportion.**

$20s = 100 \cdot 30$ — **Cross products property**

$20s = 3000$ — **Simplify.**

$s = 150$ — **Divide each side by 20.**

▶ You should add 150 tablespoons of salt to a 30 gallon tank.

CHECK Check your answer by writing each ratio in simplest form.

$$\frac{20}{100} = \frac{1}{5} \text{ and } \frac{30}{150} = \frac{1}{5}$$

Because each ratio simplifies to $\frac{1}{5}$, the answer is correct.

PRACTICE

1. **WHAT IF?** Suppose the fish tank in the problem above is a 22 gallon tank. How many tablespoons of salt should be added to the tank? *Describe* which method you used to solve this problem. See margin.

2. **ADVERTISING** A local newspaper charges by the word for printing classified ads. A 14 word ad costs \$5.88. How much would a 21 word ad cost? Solve this problem using two different methods. See margin.

3. **REASONING** In Exercise 2, how can you quickly determine the cost of a 7 word ad? *Explain* how you could use the cost of a 7 word ad to solve the problem. See margin.

4. **NUTRITION** A company sells fruit smoothies in two sizes of bottles: 6 fluid ounces and 10 fluid ounces. You know that a 6 ounce bottle contains 96 milligrams of sodium. How many milligrams of sodium does a 10 ounce bottle contain? 160 mg

5. **ERROR ANALYSIS** A student solved the problem in Exercise 4 as shown. *Describe* and correct the error made.

> Let x = the number of milligrams of sodium in a 10 ounce bottle.
>
> $\frac{6}{x} = \frac{10}{96}$
>
> $576 = 10x$
>
> $57.6 = x$ ✗

The proportion should be $\frac{6}{96} = \frac{10}{x}$; $\frac{6}{96} = \frac{10}{x}$, $960 = 6x$, $x = 160$.

6. **SLEEPING** You find an online calculator that calculates the number of calories you burn while sleeping. The results for various sleeping times are shown. About how many more calories would you burn by sleeping for 9.5 hours than for 8 hours? Choose any method for solving the problem. 90 calories

Hours of sleep	6.5	7	8.5	9
Calories burned	390	420	510	540

Avoiding Common Errors

In Method 2, point out to students that units of water are compared to units of salt. Caution students to check that their proportions in the Practice exercises are set up correctly. When using a graph to solve a Practice exercise, tell students to make sure they do not switch *x*- and *y*-coordinates. Suggest they use the algebraic or proportion method to check the reasonableness of their answer.

Teaching Strategy

You may want to discuss the relationship of dependent and independent variables before students solve Exercise 6.

1. 110 tbsp. *Sample answer:* Use the proportion $\frac{20}{100} = \frac{22}{x}$.

2. \$8.82; Method 1: Use a graph. Graph the points (0, 0) and (14, 5.88) and draw a line through the points. Find the point on the graph that has an *x*-coordinate of 21. The *y*-coordinate is about 8.82, so it costs \$8.82 for 21 words.

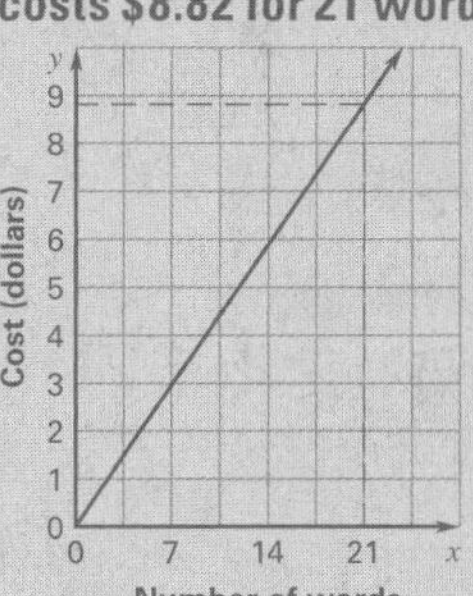

Method 2: Write a proportion. $\frac{14}{5.88} = \frac{21}{x}$, solve the proportion to find $x = 8.82$, so it costs \$8.82 for 21 words.

3. Because 7 is half of 14, you can take half of 5.88 to find 7 words cost \$2.94. Because 21 is 3 times 7, multiply \$2.94 by 3 to get \$8.82.

1 PLAN AND PREPARE

Warm-Up Exercises

Transparency Available

Tell whether the ordered pair is a solution of the equation.

1. $2x + 3y = 2$; $(3, -2)$ no
2. $-x - 4y = -3$; $(-5, 2)$ yes
3. The weight of a person on Mars is given by the function $y = 0.371x$ where x is the weight of a person on Earth. A person weighs 130 pounds on Earth. Find the weight of the person on Mars. 48.23 lb

Notetaking Guide

Transparency Available

Promotes interactive learning and notetaking skills, pp. 94–97.

Pacing

Basic: 2 days
Average: 2 days
Advanced: 2 days
Block: 1 block

- See *Teaching Guide/Lesson Plan.*

2 FOCUS AND MOTIVATE

Essential Question

Big Idea 3, p. 205

What is function notation? Tell students they will learn how to answer this question by finding values of a function for given x-values, by finding x-values for given function values, and by graphing.

4.7 Graph Linear Functions

 **8.11.11** Analyze functions by investigating domain, range, rates of change, intercepts, and zeros.

Before You graphed linear equations and functions.
Now You will use function notation.
Why? So you can model an animal population, as in Example 3.

Key Vocabulary
- **function notation**
- **family of functions**
- **parent linear function**

You have seen linear functions written in the form $y = mx + b$. By naming a function f, you can write it using **function notation**.

$$f(x) = mx + b \quad \text{Function notation}$$

The symbol $f(x)$ is another name for y and is read as "the value of f at x," or simply as "f of x." It does *not* means f times x. You can use letters other than f, such as g or h, to name functions.

EXAMPLE 1 Standardized Test Practice

What is the value of the function $f(x) = 3x - 15$ when $x = -3$?

Ⓐ -24 Ⓑ -6 Ⓒ -2 Ⓓ 8

Solution

$f(x) = 3x - 15$ Write original function.

$f(-3) = 3(-3) - 15$ Substitute -3 for x.

$= -24$ Simplify.

▶ The correct answer is A.  Ⓑ Ⓒ Ⓓ

✓ GUIDED PRACTICE for Example 1

1. Evaluate the function $h(x) = -7x$ when $x = 7$. -49

EXAMPLE 2 Find an x-value

For the function $f(x) = 2x - 10$, find the value of x so that $f(x) = 6$.

$f(x) = 2x - 10$ Write original function.

$6 = 2x - 10$ Substitute 6 for $f(x)$.

$8 = x$ Solve for x.

▶ When $x = 8$, $f(x) = 6$.

Resource Planning Guide

Chapter Resource Book
- Teaching Guide/Lesson Plan (pp. 88–89)
- Activity Master (p. 90)
- Practice levels A, B, C (pp. 91–96)
- Study Guide (pp. 97–98)
- Catch-up for Absent Students (p. 99)
- Problem Solving Workshop (p. 100)
- Challenge (p. 101)

Workbooks
- Notetaking Guide (pp. 94–97)
- Practice Workbook (pp. 64–66)

Teaching Options
- **Power Presentations CD-ROM** provides dynamic electronic teaching resources for the classroom.
- **Activity Generator CD-ROM** provides editable activities for all ability levels.

Interactive Technology
- Easy Planner
- Power Presentations CD-ROM
- Activity Generator CD-ROM
- Animated Algebra
- Test Generator CD-ROM
- Online Quiz
- eWorkbook
- eEdition
- @HomeTutor

Resources for English Learners
- Quick Reference for English Learners
- Spanish Study Guide
- Multi-Language Visual Glossary
- Student Resources in Spanish

See also the *Algebra 1 Toolkit* for more strategies for meeting individual needs.

DOMAIN AND RANGE The domain of a function consists of the values of x for which the function is defined. The range consists of the values of $f(x)$ where x is in the domain of f. The graph of a function f is the set of all points $(x, f(x))$.

EXAMPLE 3 Graph a function

INTERPRET MODELS
The rate of change in the wolf population actually varied over time. The model simplifies the situation by assuming a steady rate of change.

GRAY WOLF The gray wolf population in central Idaho was monitored over several years for a project aimed at boosting the number of wolves. The number of wolves can be modeled by the function $f(x) = 37x + 7$ where x is the number of years since 1995. Graph the function and identify its domain and range.

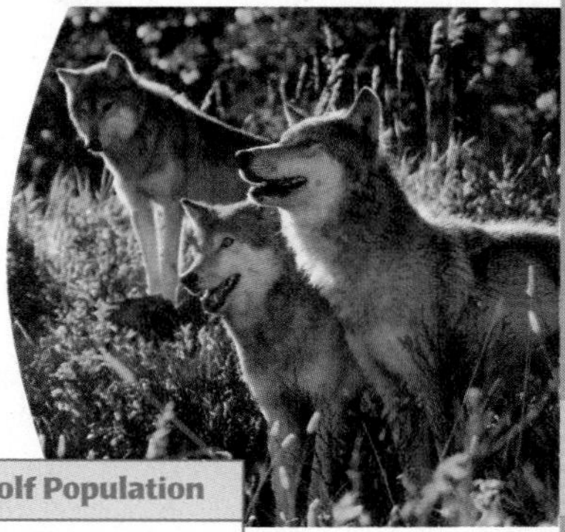

Solution

To graph the function, make a table.

x	$f(x)$
0	$37(0) + 7 = 7$
1	$37(1) + 7 = 44$
2	$37(2) + 7 = 81$

Gray Wolf Population

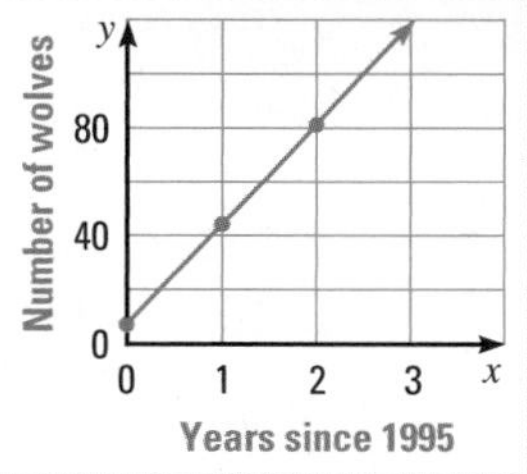

The domain of the function is $x \geq 0$. From the graph or table, you can see that the range of the function is $f(x) \geq 7$.

GUIDED PRACTICE for Examples 2 and 3

2. **WOLF POPULATION** Use the model from Example 3 to find the value of x so that $f(x) = 155$. *Explain* what the solution means in this situation.
4; in 1999, 4 years after 1995, the wolf population will be 155.

FAMILIES OF FUNCTIONS A **family of functions** is a group of functions with similar characteristics. For example, functions that have the form $f(x) = mx + b$ constitute the family of *linear* functions.

KEY CONCEPT *For Your Notebook*

Parent Function for Linear Functions

The most basic linear function in the family of all linear functions, called the **parent linear function**, is:

$$f(x) = x$$

The graph of the parent linear function is shown.

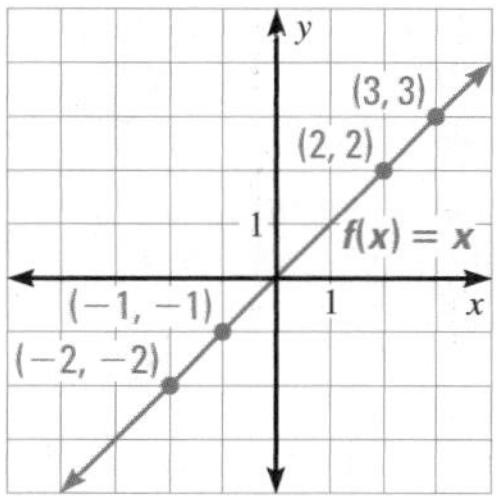

Motivating the Lesson

You are comparing the costs of two veterinarians for the care of your horses. One veterinarian charges \$50 per house call plus \$25 per hour. Another charges \$25 per house call plus \$45 per hour. By learning how to use function notation, you can compare the two rates by graphing both functions on the same coordinate plane.

3 TEACH

Extra Example 1

What is the value of the function $f(x) = 2x + 12$ when $x = -8$? **B**

Ⓐ -12 Ⓑ -4
Ⓒ 4 Ⓓ 28

Extra Example 2

For the function $f(x) = -2x + 4$, find the value of x so that $f(x) = 16$.
-6

Key Question to Ask for Example 2

- How is Example 2 different from Example 1? **In Example 1, x is replaced with a number to find $f(x)$; and in Example 2, $f(x)$ is replaced with a number to find x.**

Extra Example 3

A bowling alley charges \$5 to rent shoes and \$4 per game. The cost after playing x games is given by $f(x) = 4x + 5$. Graph the function and identify its domain and range.

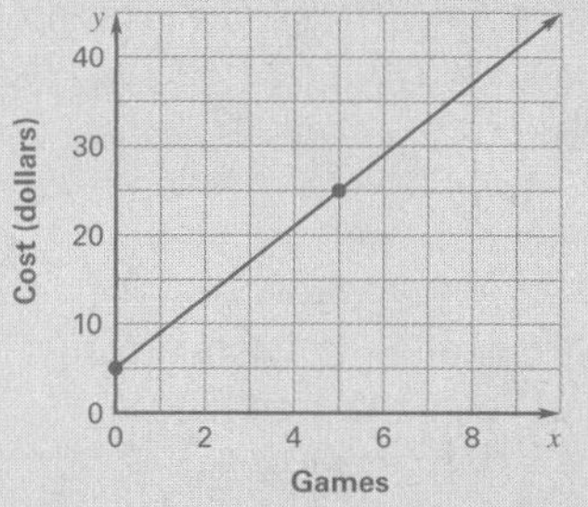

domain: $x \geq 0$; range: $f(x) \geq 5$

Differentiated Instruction

Kinesthetic Learners Explain that $y = x$ is called the *parent function* because any linear function can be obtained by changing the slope from 1 and moving the y-intercept from 0. Changing m and b in the linear function $f(x) = mx + b$ generates the family of linear functions. Draw a line on a transparency and place it on a grid to show the graph of $y = x$. Then show how this can be used to create any line on the coordinate plane by moving the transparency.

See also the *Algebra 1 Toolkit* for more strategies.

Extra Example 4

Graph the function. Compare the graph with the graph of $f(x) = x$.

a. $g(x) = -2x$

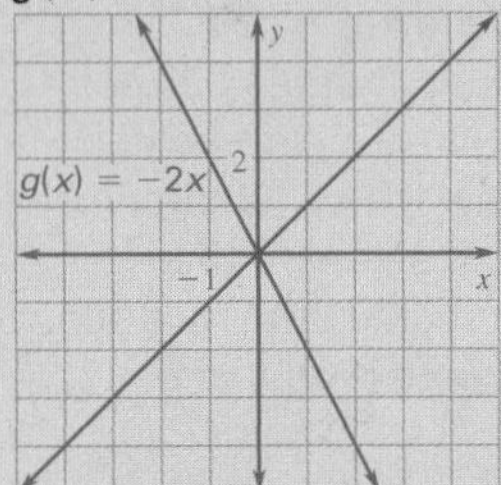

The graph of f has a positive slope, whereas the graph of g has a negative slope. The y-intercept for both graphs is 0, so both lines of pass through the origin.

b. $h(x) = \frac{1}{2}x$

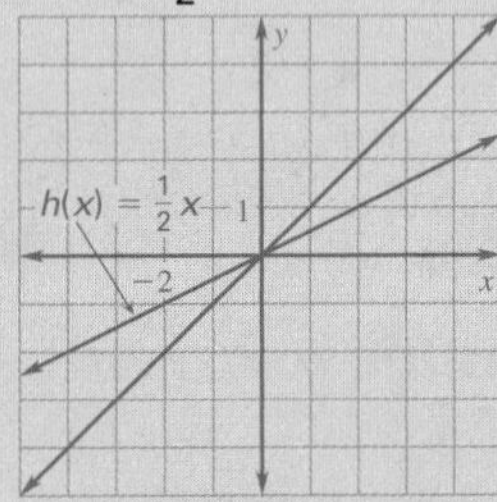

Because the slope of the graph of h is less than the slope of the graph of f, the graph of h is less steep than the graph of f. The lines of both graphs pass through the origin, since they have the same y-intercept of 0.

Key Questions to Ask for Example 4

- How can you describe the graphs of g and h in parts a and b in terms of changes in m and b from the graph of $f(x) = mx + b$? *For g, m remains the same, while b changes. For h, m changes and b remains the same.*
- What is another graph that would be parallel to the graph of f in part a? *Sample answer:* $k(x) = x - 3$

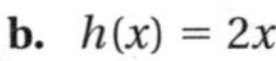

EXAMPLE 4 Compare graphs with the graph $f(x) = x$

Graph the function. Compare the graph with the graph of $f(x) = x$.

a. $g(x) = x + 3$ **b.** $h(x) = 2x$

Solution

a.

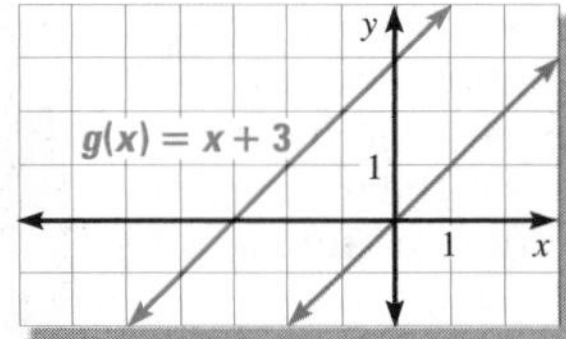

Because the graphs of g and f have the same slope, $m = 1$, the lines are parallel. Also, the y-intercept of the graph of g is 3 more than the y-intercept of the graph of f.

b.

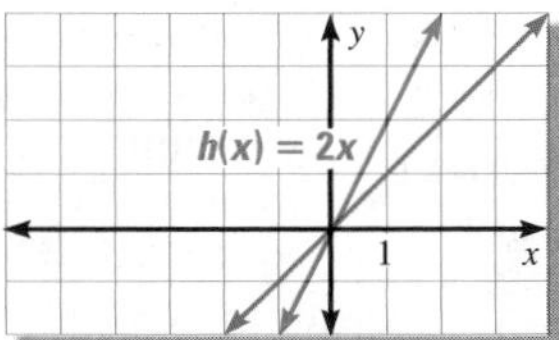

Because the slope of the graph of h is greater than the slope of the graph of f, the graph of h rises faster from left to right. The y-intercept for both graphs is 0, so both lines pass through the origin.

✓ **GUIDED PRACTICE** for Example 4

3. Graph $h(x) = -3x$. Compare the graph with the graph of $f(x) = x$.
See margin for art; since the slope of the graph of h is negative the graph of h falls from left to right. The y-intercept for both graphs is 0, so both lines pass through the origin.

CONCEPT SUMMARY *For Your Notebook*

Comparing Graphs of Linear Functions with the Graph of $f(x) = x$

Changing m or b in the general linear function $g(x) = mx + b$ creates families of linear functions whose graphs are related to the graph of $f(x) = x$.

$g(x) = x + b$

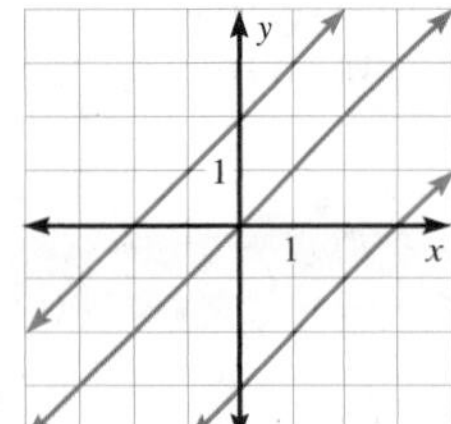

- The graphs have the same slope, but different y-intercepts.
- Graphs of this family are vertical translations of the graph of $f(x) = x$.

$g(x) = mx$ where $m > 0$

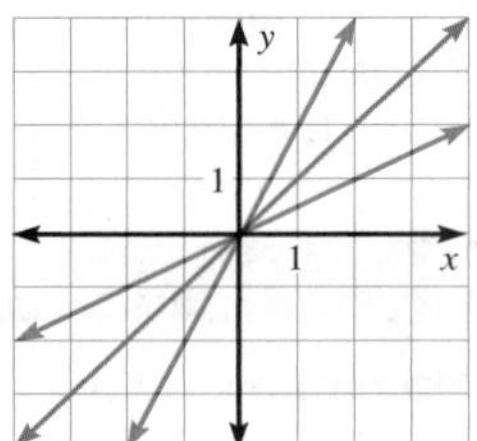

- The graphs have different (positive) slopes, but the same y-intercept.
- Graphs of this family are vertical stretches or shrinks of the graph of $f(x) = x$.

$g(x) = mx$ where $m < 0$

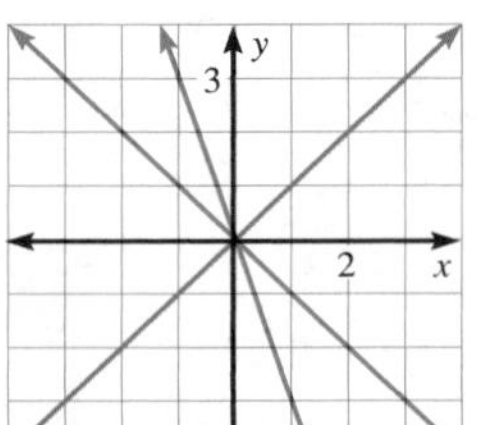

- The graphs have different (negative) slopes, but the same y-intercept.
- Graphs of this family are vertical stretches or shrinks with reflections in the x-axis of the graph of $f(x) = x$.

3.

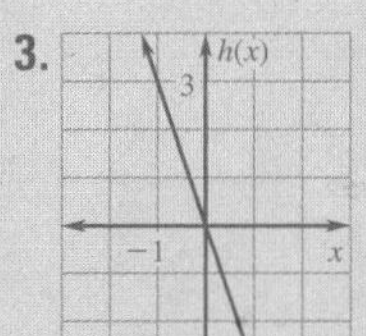

EXAMPLE 5 Graph real-world functions

CABLE A cable company charges new customers $40 for installation and $60 per month for its service. The cost to the customer is given by the function $f(x) = 60x + 40$ where x is the number of months of service. To attract new customers, the cable company reduces the installation fee to $5. A function for the cost with the reduced installation fee is $g(x) = 60x + 5$. Graph both functions. How is the graph of g related to the graph of f?

Solution

The graphs of both functions are shown. Both functions have a slope of 60, so they are parallel. The y-intercept of the graph of g is 35 less than the graph of f. So, the graph of g is a vertical translation of the graph of f.

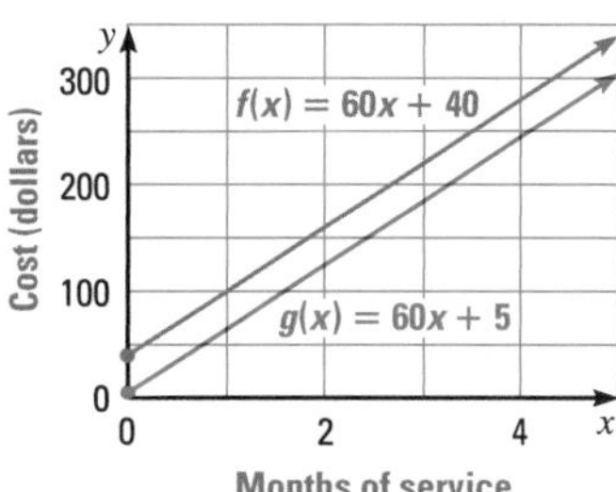

REVIEW TRANSFORMATIONS
For help with transformations, see pp. 922–923.

GUIDED PRACTICE for Example 5

4. **WHAT IF?** In Example 5, suppose the monthly fee is $70 so that the cost to the customer is given by $h(x) = 70x + 40$. Graph f and h in the same coordinate plane. How is the graph of h related to the graph of f? See margin for art; since the slope of the graph of h is greater than the slope of the graph of f, the graph of h rises faster from left to right. The y-intercept for both graphs is 40, so both lines pass through (0, 40).

4.7 EXERCISES

HOMEWORK KEY
○ = WORKED-OUT SOLUTIONS on p. WS10 for Exs. 3, 17, and 39
★ = STANDARDIZED TEST PRACTICE Exs. 2, 13, 22, 35, 36, 44, and 45

SKILL PRACTICE

A

1. **VOCABULARY** When you write the function $y = 3x + 12$ as $f(x) = 3x + 12$, you are using _?_. function notation

2. ★ **WRITING** Would the functions $f(x) = -9x + 12$, $g(x) = -9x - 2$, and $h(x) = -9x$ be considered a family of functions? *Explain.* Yes; they are all linear functions.

EXAMPLE 1 on p. 262 for Exs. 3–13

EVALUATING FUNCTIONS Evaluate the function when $x = -2, 0,$ and 3.

3. $f(x) = 12x + 1$ −23, 1, 37
4. $g(x) = -3x + 5$ 11, 5, −4
5. $p(x) = -8x - 2$ 14, −2, −26
6. $h(x) = 2.25x$ −4.5, 0, 6.75
7. $m(x) = -6.5x$ 13, 0, −19.5
8. $f(x) = -0.75x - 1$ 0.5, −1, −3.25
9. $s(x) = \frac{2}{5}x + 3$ $2\frac{1}{5}, 3, 4\frac{1}{5}$
10. $d(x) = -\frac{3}{2}x + 5$ $8, 5, \frac{1}{2}$
11. $h(x) = \frac{3}{4}x - 6$ $-7\frac{1}{2}, -6, -3\frac{3}{4}$

12. **ERROR ANALYSIS** *Describe* and correct the error in evaluating the function $g(x) = -5x + 3$ when $x = -3$. $g(-3)$ does not mean multiply −3 and g, it means to find the value of the function when $g = -3$, $g(-3) = 18$.

$g(-3) = -5(-3) + 3$
$-3g = 18$
$g = -6$

Extra Example 5

A state park charges $5 per car as an entrance fee. The amount collected is given by the function $f(x) = 5x$. The park recently restructured its fees and now charges $10 per car. The function for the new fee is $g(x) = 10x$. Graph both functions. How is the graph of g related to the graph of f?

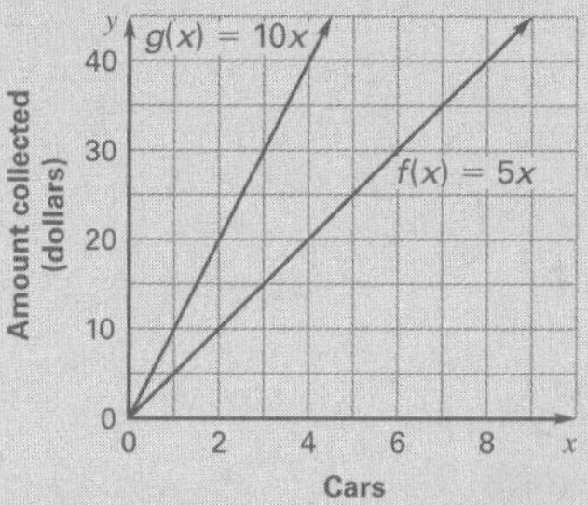

Both functions have the same y-intercept of 0. They have different slopes. The slope of the graph of g is steeper than the graph of f, so the graph of g is a vertical stretch of the graph of f.

Closing the Lesson

Have students summarize the major points of the lesson and answer the Essential Question: What is function notation?

- $f(x)$ means "the value of f at x" and is function notation for y.
- Graphs of linear functions can be analyzed and categorized in terms of their relation to the graph of $f(x) = x$.

Function notation is the use of $f(x)$ to replace y in functions. $f(x)$ represents the range of the function f for all values of x in its domain, so $f(3)$ represents the value of the function when $x = 3$. You can use g, h, and other letters to name functions.

4.
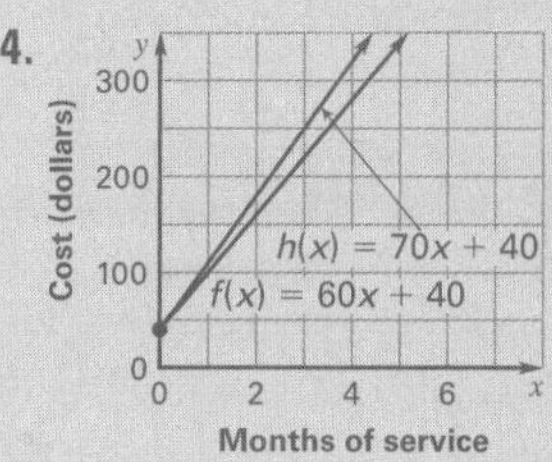

4 PRACTICE AND APPLY

Assignment Guide

Answer Transparencies available for all exercises

Basic:
Day 1: pp. 265–268
Exs. 1, 3–11 odd, 12–18, 39–41, 46–54
Day 2: pp. 265–268
Exs. 2, 19–29, 42, 55–60

Average:
Day 1: pp. 265–268
Exs. 1, 7–13, 16–22, 39–41, 46–54
Day 2: pp. 265–268
Exs. 2, 27–37, 42–44, 55–60

Advanced:
Day 1: pp. 265–268
Exs. 1, 7–11, 13, 17–22, 37–41*, 46–54 even
Day 2: pp. 265–268
Exs. 2, 28–36, 42–45*, 55–60

Block:
pp. 265–268
Exs. 1, 2, 7–13, 16–22, 27–37, 39–44, 46–60

Differentiated Instruction

See *Algebra 1 Best Practices Toolkit* for suggestions on addressing the needs of a diverse classroom.

Homework Check

For a quick check of student understanding of key concepts, go over the following exercises:

Basic: 5, 16, 24, 39, 42
Average: 8, 18, 28, 40, 42
Advanced: 9, 20, 31, 41, 43

Extra Practice

- Student Edition, p. 941
- Chapter 4 Resource Book: Practice levels A, B, C, pp. 91–96

Practice Worksheet

An easily-readable reduced practice page (with answers) for this lesson can be found on p. 204F.

23–34, 36a–c. See Additional Answers beginning on p. AA1.

---

13. ★ **MULTIPLE CHOICE** Given $f(x) = -6.8x + 5$, what is the value of $f(-2)$? D

(A) −18.6 (B) −8.6 (C) 8.6 (D) 18.6

EXAMPLE 2 on p. 262 for Exs. 14–22

FINDING X-VALUES Find the value of x so that the function has the given value.

14. $f(x) = 6x + 9; 3$ −1
15. $g(x) = -x + 5; 2$ 3
16. $h(x) = -7x + 12; -9$ 3
(17.) $j(x) = 4x + 11; -13$ −6
18. $m(x) = 9x - 5; -2$ $\frac{1}{3}$
19. $n(x) = -2x - 21; -6$ −7.5
20. $p(x) = -12x - 36; -3$ −2.75
21. $q(x) = 8x - 32; -4$ 3.5

22. ★ **MULTIPLE CHOICE** What value of x makes $f(x) = 5$ if $f(x) = -2x + 25$? C

(A) −15 (B) −10 (C) 10 (D) 15

EXAMPLE 4 on p. 264 for Exs. 23–34

B **TRANSFORMATIONS OF LINEAR FUNCTIONS Graph the function. Compare the graph with the graph of $f(x) = x$.** 23–34. See margin.

23. $g(x) = x + 5$
24. $h(x) = 6 + x$
25. $q(x) = x - 1$
26. $m(x) = x - 6$
27. $d(x) = x + 7$
28. $t(x) = x - 3$
29. $r(x) = 4x$
30. $w(x) = 5x$
31. $h(x) = -3x$
32. $k(x) = -6x$
33. $g(x) = \frac{1}{3}x$
34. $m(x) = -\frac{7}{2}x$

35. ★ **MULTIPLE CHOICE** The graph of which function is shown? B

(A) $f(x) = 3x + 8$
(B) $f(x) = 3x - 8$
(C) $f(x) = 8x + 3$
(D) $f(x) = 8x - 3$

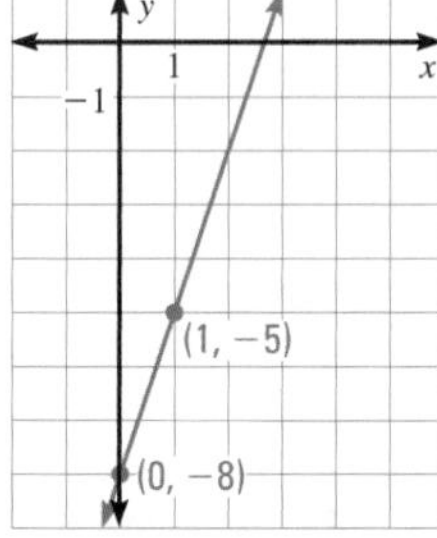

36. ★ **OPEN-ENDED** In this exercise you will compare the graphs of linear functions when their slopes and y-intercepts are changed.

a. Choose a linear function of the form $f(x) = mx + b$ where $m \neq 0$. Then graph the function. *Sample answer:* $f(x) = 2x + 3$; see margin for art.

b. Using the same m and b values as in part (a), graph the function $g(x) = 2mx + b$. How are the slope and y-intercept of the graph of g related to the slope and y-intercept of the graph of f? See margin.

c. Using the same m and b values as in part (a), graph the function $h(x) = mx + (b - 3)$. How are the slope and y-intercept of the graph of h related to the slope and y-intercept of the graph of f? See margin.

C **37.** **REASONING** How is the graph of $g(x) = 1$ related to the graph of $h(x) = -1$? Since the graphs of g and h have the same slope, $m = 0$, the lines are parallel. The y-intercept of the graph of h is 2 less than the y-intercept of the graph of g.

38. **CHALLENGE** Suppose that $f(x) = 4x + 7$ and $g(x) = 2x$. What is a rule for $g(f(x))$? What is a rule for $f(g(x))$? $8x + 14$; $8x + 7$

○ = WORKED-OUT SOLUTIONS on p. WS1 ★ = STANDARDIZED TEST PRACTICE

PROBLEM SOLVING

EXAMPLE 3 A on p. 263 for Exs. 39–41

39. **MOVIE TICKETS** The average price of a movie ticket in the United States from 1980 to 2000 can be modeled by the function $f(x) = 0.10x + 2.75$ where x is the number of years since 1980.

a. Graph the function and identify its domain and range.

b. Find the value of x so that $f(x) = 4.55$. *Explain* what the solution means in this situation.

@HomeTutor for problem solving help at classzone.com

39a. See margin for art; domain: $0 \le x \le 20$, range: $2.75 \le f(x) \le 4.75$.

39b. 18; in 1998, 18 years after 1980, the price of a movie ticket was \$4.55.

40. **DVD PLAYERS** The number (in thousands) of DVD players sold in the United States from 1998 to 2003 can be modeled by $f(x) = 4250x + 330$ where x is the number of years since 1998.

a. Graph the function and identify its domain and range.

b. Find the value of x so that $f(x) = 13{,}080$. *Explain* what the solution means in this situation.

@HomeTutor for problem solving help at classzone.com

40a. See margin for art; domain: $0 \le x \le 5$, range: $330 \le f(x) \le 21{,}580$

3; in 2001, 3 years after 1998, the number of DVD players sold was 13,080,000.

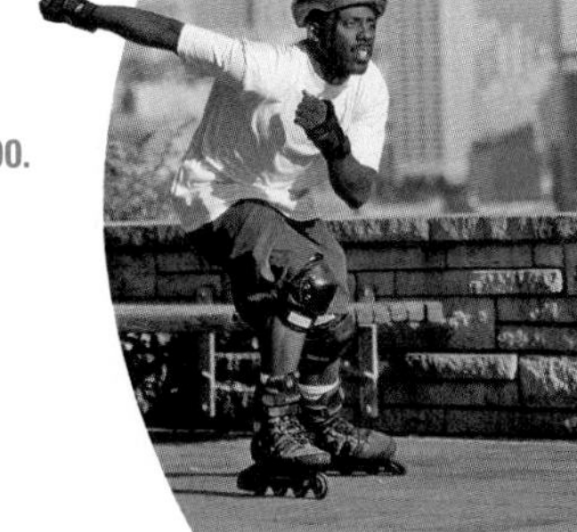

41. **IN-LINE SKATING** An in-line skater's average speed is 10 miles per hour. The distance traveled after skating for x hours is given by the function $d(x) = 10x$. Graph the function and identify its domain and range. How long did it take the skater to travel 15 miles? *Explain.*

Animated Algebra at classzone.com

41. See margin for art; domain: $x \ge 0$, range: $d(x) \ge 0$; 1.5 h; substitute 15 for $d(x)$ to get the equation $15 = 10x$, solve for x.

EXAMPLE 5 B on p. 265 for Exs. 42–43

42. **HOME SECURITY** A home security company charges new customers \$155 for the installation of security equipment and a monthly fee of \$40. To attract more customers, the company reduces its installation fee to \$75. The functions below give the total cost for x months of service:

Regular fee: $f(x) = 40x + 155$ **Reduced fee:** $g(x) = 40x + 75$

Graph both functions. How is the graph of g related to the graph of f? See margin.

43. **THEATERS** A ticket for a play at a theater costs \$16. The revenue (in dollars) generated from the sale of x tickets is given by $s(x) = 16x$. The theater managers raise the cost of tickets to \$20. The revenue generated from the sale of x tickets at that price is given by $r(x) = 20x$. Graph both functions. How is the graph of r related to the graph of s? See margin.

C **44.** ★ **EXTENDED RESPONSE** The cost of supplies, such as mustard and napkins, a pretzel vendor needs for one day is \$75. Each pretzel costs the vendor \$.50 to make. The total daily cost to the vendor is given by $C(x) = 0.5x + 75$ where x is the number of pretzels the vendor makes.

a. **Graph** Graph the cost function. See margin.

b. **Graph** The vendor sells each pretzel for \$3. The revenue is given by $R(x) = 3x$ where x is the number of pretzels sold. Graph the function. See margin.

c. **Explain** The vendor's profit is the difference of the revenue and the cost. *Explain* how you could use the graphs to find the vendor's profit for any given number of pretzels made and sold.
Sample answer: Find the values of y on each graph for any value of x. Subtract $C(x)$ from $R(x)$ to find the vendor's profit.

Teaching Strategy

Exercises 3–11 To remind students that $f(x)$ does not mean f times x, you may wish to have them write the function name with x replaced by −2, 0, and 3. For example, students would write $f(-2) = -23$, $f(0) = 1$, and $f(3) = 37$ when answering Exercise 3.

Exercises 23–34 You may want to review the concept box on page 264 before the students begin these exercises. Ask students to give examples of vertical stretches and shrinks with and without reflections.

Reading Strategy

Exercises 14–21 Tell students to read the instruction line for the exercises carefully. They may want to review Examples 1 and 2 so they are clear on the difference between finding an x-value and finding the value of a function for a given x-value.

An **Animated Algebra** activity is available on-line for **Exercise 41**. This activity is also available on the **Power Presentations CD-ROM**.

42, 43. See Additional Answers beginning on p. AA1.

44a.
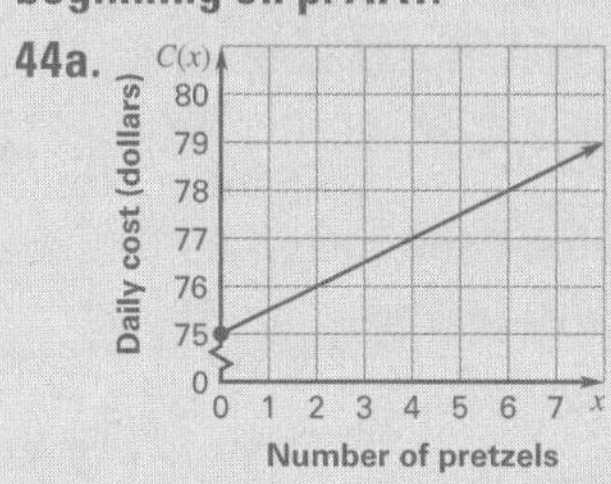

44b.
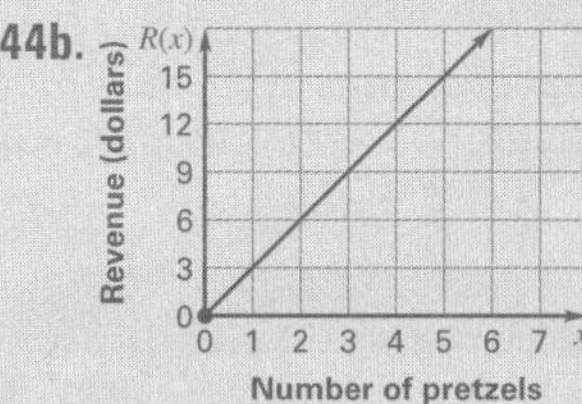

39a.
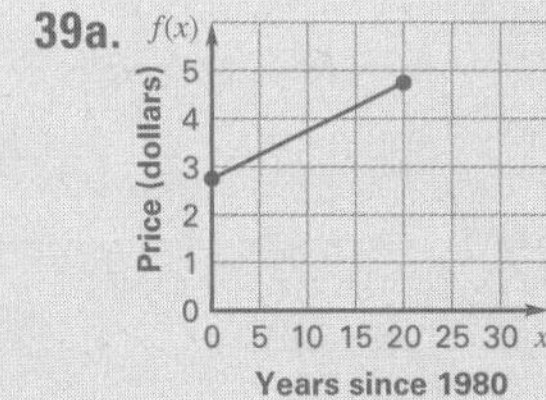

40a.
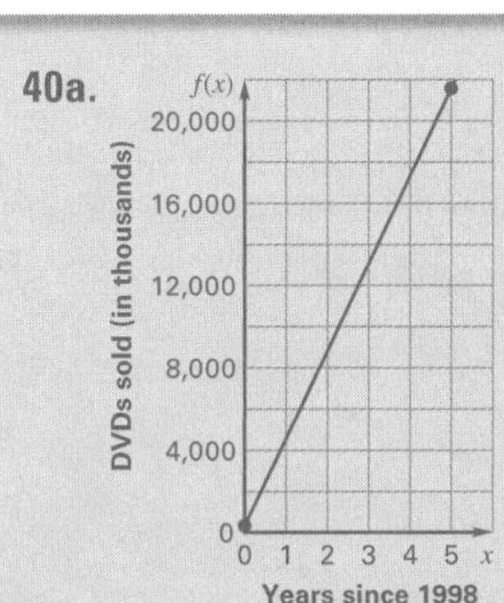

41.
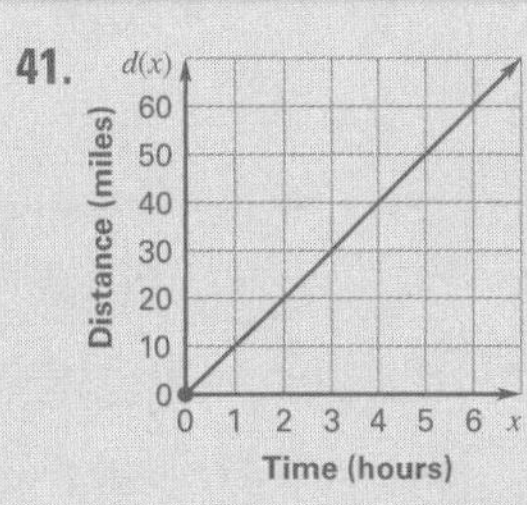

5 ASSESS AND RETEACH

Daily Homework Quiz

Transparency Available

1. Evaluate $f(x) = 8x - 4$ when $x = -3, 0$, and 2. $-28, -4, 12$
2. Find the value of x so $g(x) = -2x + 1$ has the value -3. 2
3. A stable charges \$25 for feed and \$50 per day to stable horses. The cost is given by $f(x) = 50x + 25$. Recently, the stable raised its fee for food to \$50. The new fee is given by $g(x) = 50x + 50$. Graph the functions and then compare the two graphs.

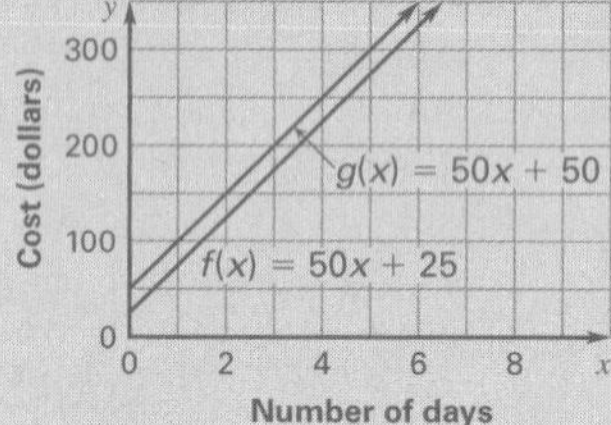

The graphs have the same slope. The y-intercept of g is 25 units greater than that of f, so g is a vertical translation.

Available at **classzone.com**

Diagnosis/Remediation

- Practice A, B, C in Chapter 4 Resource Book, pp. 91–96
- Study Guide in Chapter 4 Resource Book, pp. 97–98
- Practice Workbook, pp. 64–66
- @HomeTutor

Challenge

Additional challenge is available in the Chapter 4 Resource Book, p. 101.

Quiz

An easily-readable reduced copy of the quiz (with answers) on Lessons 4.6–4.7 from the Assessment Book can be found on p. 204G.

45b, Quiz 8, 9. See Additional Answers beginning on p. AA1.

45. ★ **EXTENDED RESPONSE** The number of hours of daylight in Austin, Texas, during the month of March can be modeled by the function $\ell(x) = 0.03x + 11.5$ where x is the day of the month.
    a. **Graph** Graph the function and identify its domain and range. See graph in part (b); domain: $1 \le x \le 31$, range: $11.53 \le \ell(x) \le 12.43$
    b. **Graph** The number of hours of darkness can be modeled by the function $d(x) = 24 - \ell(x)$. Graph the function on the same coordinate plane as you used in part (a). Identify its domain and range. See margin for art; domain: $11.53 \le \ell(x) \le 12.43$, range: $11.57 \le d(x) \le 12.47$
    c. **CHALLENGE** *Explain* how you could have obtained the graph of d from the graph of ℓ using translations and reflections. The graph of d is a reflection of the line ℓ.
    d. **CHALLENGE** What does the point where the graphs intersect mean in terms of the number of hours of daylight and darkness? The number of hours of daylight equals the number of hours of darkness.

ILLINOIS MIXED REVIEW

TEST PRACTICE at classzone.com

46. Simplify the expression $8(x + 3) - 4x - (x + 1)$. C

    Ⓐ $3x + 2$ Ⓑ $3x + 4$ Ⓒ $3x + 23$ Ⓓ $3x + 25$

47. A poll predicts that candidate A will receive 48% of the total votes in an election. If 60,000 people vote in the election, how many votes does the poll predict candidate A will receive? B

    Ⓐ 28,200 Ⓑ 28,800 Ⓒ 31,200 Ⓓ 32,800

QUIZ *for Lessons 4.6–4.7*

Given that y varies directly with x, use the specified values to write a direct variation equation that relates x and y. *(p. 253)*

1. $x = 5, y = 10$ $y = 2x$
2. $x = 4, y = 6$ $y = \frac{3}{2}x$
3. $x = 2, y = -16$ $y = -8x$

Evaluate the function. *(p. 262)*

4. $g(x) = 6x - 5$ when $x = 4$ 19
5. $h(x) = 14x + 7$ when $x = 2$ 35
6. $j(x) = 0.2x + 12.2$ when $x = 244$ 61
7. $k(x) = \frac{5}{6}x + \frac{1}{3}$ when $x = 4$ $3\frac{2}{3}$

Graph the function. Compare the graph to the graph of $f(x) = x$. *(p. 262)* 8–9. See margin.

8. $g(x) = -4x$
9. $h(x) = x - 2$

10. **HOURLY WAGE** The table shows the number of hours that you worked for each of three weeks and the amount that you were paid. What is your hourly wage? *(p. 253)* \$7/h

Hours	12	16	14
Pay (dollars)	84	112	98

EXTRA PRACTICE for Lesson 4.7, p. 941 **ONLINE QUIZ** at classzone.com

Illinois Mixed Review

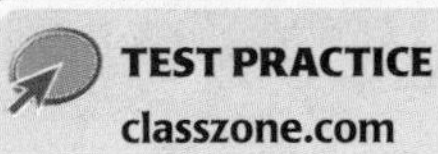

TEST PRACTICE
classzone.com

Lessons 4.4–4.7

1. **DRINK MIX** The amount d (in tablespoons) of drink mix needed to make a drink varies directly with the amount w (in fluid ounces) of water used. A package of the mix recommends using 3 tablespoons of drink mix and 12 fluid ounces of water. Which of the following equations can be used to relate w and d?

   A. $w = 4d$

   B. $w = \frac{1}{4}d$

   C. $d = 4w$

   D. $d = 36w$

2. **NOVEL** You have to read 15 pages of a novel for homework. The number of pages, $p(x)$, that you have left to read after reading for x minutes is given by $p(x) = -x + 15$. What is $p(7)$?

   F. 7 **H.** 15

   G. 8 **J.** 22

3. **CELL PHONE** Your family bought a cell phone for \$50 and pays \$30 per month for service. If x is the number of months you use the phone, your total cost C is given by the equation $C = 30x + 50$. The cost of a friend's cell phone service is given by the equation $C = 30x + 30$. How does your friend's plan differ from yours?

   A. The monthly charge is \$20 less.

   B. The cost of the phone is \$20 less.

   C. The cost of the phone is \$30 more.

   D. It has an additional \$30 activation fee.

4. **FREE THROWS** On average, a basketball player makes 16 free throws for every 20 attempts. Suppose you write a direct variation model that relates the number of free throws made, m, to the number of free throws attempted, a. What is the constant of variation?

   F. 0.8 **H.** 16

   G. 1.25 **J.** 20

5. **SUNSPOTS** A central observatory averages and then reports the number of sunspots recorded by various observatories. The table shows the average number of sunspots reported by the central observatory every two years from 1995 to 2001. Which of the following time periods has the greatest rate of change in the average number of sunspots with respect to time?

Year	Average number of sunspots
1995	17.5
1997	21.0
1999	93.2
2001	110.9

   A. 1995 to 1997

   B. 1995 to 1999

   C. 1997 to 1999

   D. 1999 to 2001

6. **GYM FEES** To become a member at a gym, you have to pay a sign-up fee of \$75 and a monthly fee of \$40. To increase its profit, the gym increases the sign-up fee to \$125. The function f gives the total cost with the regular sign-up fee. The function g gives the total cost with the increased sign-up fee. The graphs of f and g are shown. The graph of g is a vertical translation of the graph of f by how many units?

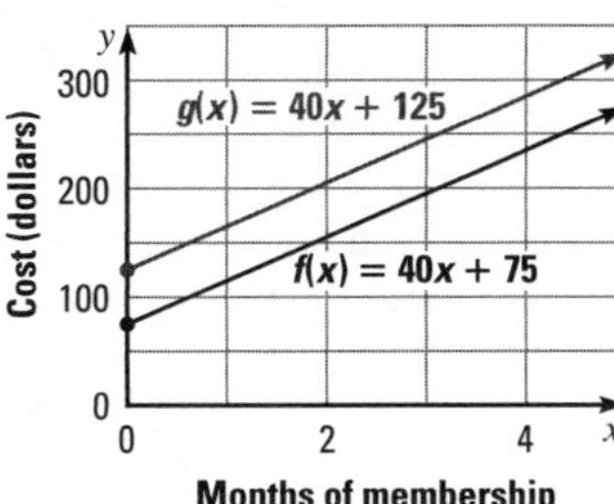

   F. 40 **H.** 75

   G. 50 **J.** 125

Illinois Mixed Review

1. A
2. G
3. B
4. F
5. C
6. G

4 CHAPTER SUMMARY

Animated Algebra
classzone.com
Electronic Function Library

Additional Resources

The following resources are available to help review the materials in this chapter.

Chapter 4 Resource Book

- Chapter Review Games and Activities, p. 103
- Cumulative Practice, Chs. 1–4, pp. 105–106

Student Resources in Spanish

eWorkbook

@HomeTutor

Vocabulary Practice

Vocabulary practice is available at **classzone.com**

BIG IDEAS *For Your Notebook*

Big Idea 1

Graphing Linear Equations and Functions Using a Variety of Methods

You can graph a linear equation or function by making a table, using intercepts, or using the slope and y-intercept.

A taxi company charges a $2 fee to pick up a customer plus $1 per mile to drive to the customer's destination. The total cost C (in dollars) that a customer pays to travel d miles is given by $C = d + 2$. Graph this function.

Method: Make a table.

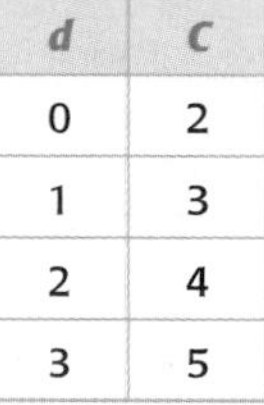

d	C
0	2
1	3
2	4
3	5

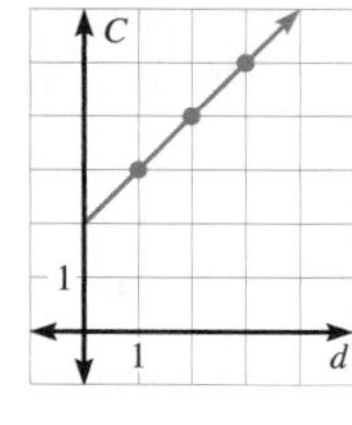

Method: Use slope and C-intercept.

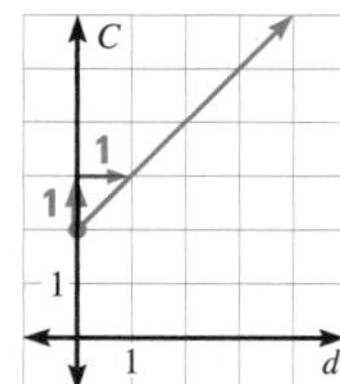

Big Idea 2

Recognizing How Changes in Linear Equations and Functions Affect Their Graphs

When you change the value of m or b in the equation $y = mx + b$, you produce an equation whose graph is related to the graph of the original equation.

Suppose the taxi company raises its rate to $1.50 per mile. The total amount that a customer pays is given by $C = 1.5d + 2$. Graph the function.

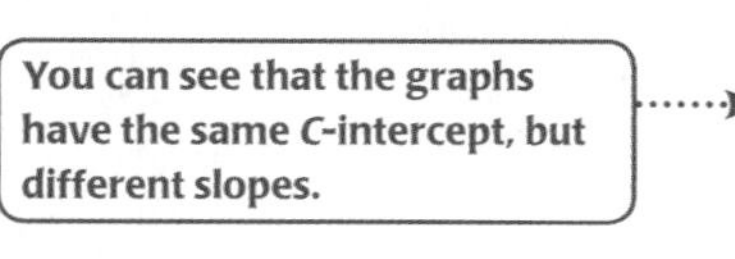

You can see that the graphs have the same C-intercept, but different slopes.

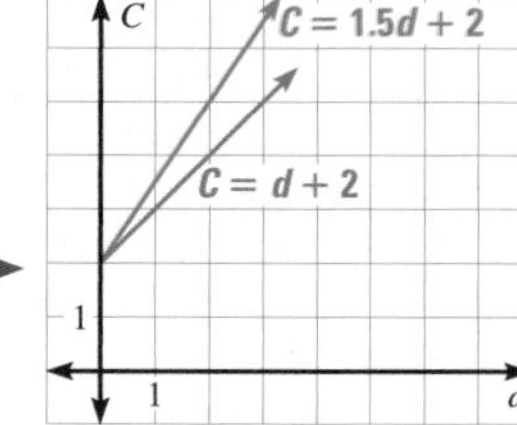

Big Idea 3

Using Graphs of Linear Equations and Functions to Solve Real-world Problems

You can use the graphs of $C = d + 2$ and $C = 1.5d + 2$ to find out how much more a customer pays to travel 4 miles at the new rate than at the old rate.

A customer pays $2 more to travel 4 miles at the new rate.

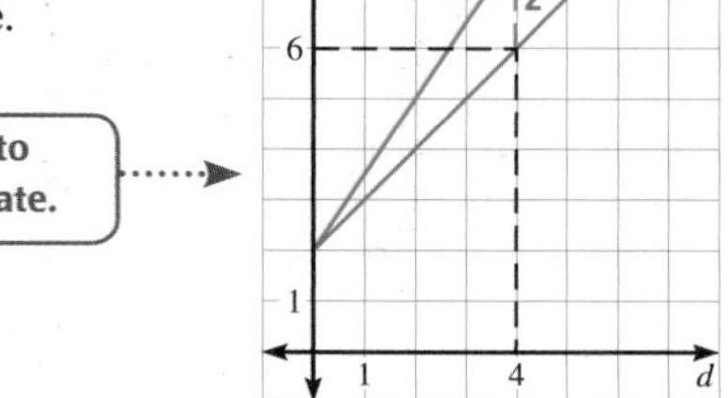

CHAPTER REVIEW

@HomeTutor
classzone.com
- Multi-Language Glossary
- Vocabulary practice

REVIEW KEY VOCABULARY

- quadrant, *p. 206*
- solution of an equation in two variables, *p. 215*
- graph of an equation in two variables, *p. 215*
- linear equation, *p. 216*
- standard form of a linear equation, *p. 216*
- linear function, *p. 217*
- *x*-intercept, *p. 225*
- *y*-intercept, *p. 225*
- slope, *p. 235*
- rate of change, *p. 237*
- slope-intercept form, *p. 244*
- parallel, *p. 246*
- direct variation, *p. 253*
- constant of variation, *p. 253*
- function notation, *p. 262*
- family of functions, *p. 263*
- parent linear function, *p. 263*

VOCABULARY EXERCISES

1. Copy and complete: The __?__ of a nonvertical line is the ratio of vertical change to horizontal change. **slope**

2. Copy and complete: When you write $y = 2x + 3$ as $f(x) = 2x + 3$, you use __?__. **function notation**

3. **WRITING** *Describe* three different methods you could use to graph the equation $5x + 3y = 12$. ***Sample answer:* Make a table, use intercepts, and use the slope and *y*-intercept.**

4. Tell whether the equation is written in slope-intercept form. If the equation is not in slope-intercept form, write it in slope-intercept form.

   a. $3x + y = 6$ **not slope-intercept form; $y = -3x + 6$**
   b. $y = 5x + 2$ **slope-intercept form**
   c. $x = 4y - 1$ **not slope-intercept form; $y = \frac{1}{4}x + \frac{1}{4}$**
   d. $y = -x + 6$ **slope-intercept form**

REVIEW EXAMPLES AND EXERCISES

Use the review examples and exercises below to check your understanding of the concepts you have learned in each lesson of Chapter 4.

4.1 Plot Points in a Coordinate Plane

pp. 206–212

EXAMPLE

Plot the points $A(-2, 3)$ and $B(0, -2)$ in a coordinate plane. Describe the location of the points.

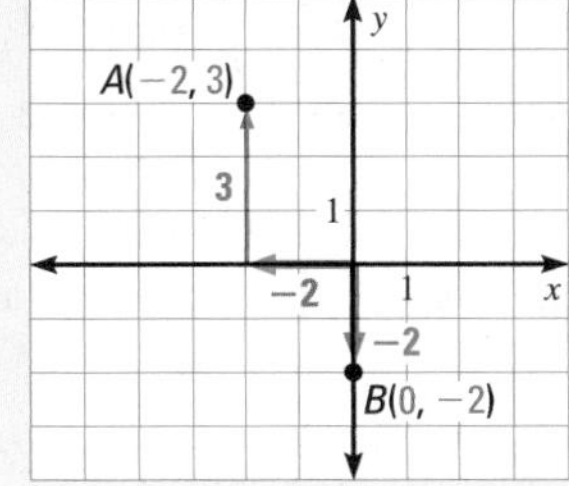

Point $A(-2, 3)$: Begin at the origin and move 2 units to the left, then 3 units up. Point A is in Quadrant II.

Point $B(0, -2)$: Begin at the origin and move 2 units down. Point B is on the y-axis.

EXERCISES

EXAMPLE 2 on p. 207 for Exs. 5–7

Plot the point in a coordinate plane. *Describe* the location of the point. **5–7. See margin for art.**

5. $A(3, 4)$ **Quadrant I**
6. $B(-5, 0)$ ***x*-axis**
7. $C(-7, -2)$ **Quadrant III**

Extra Example 4.1

Plot the points $A(0, 3)$ and $B(-2, -1)$ in a coordinate plane. Describe the location of the points.

Point $A(0, 3)$: Begin at the origin and move 3 units up. Point A is on the y-axis.

Point B: Begin at the origin and move to the left 2 points, then 1 unit down. Point B is in Quadrant III.

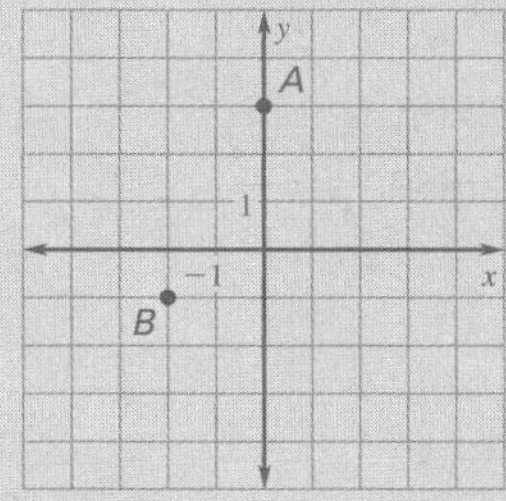

5–7.

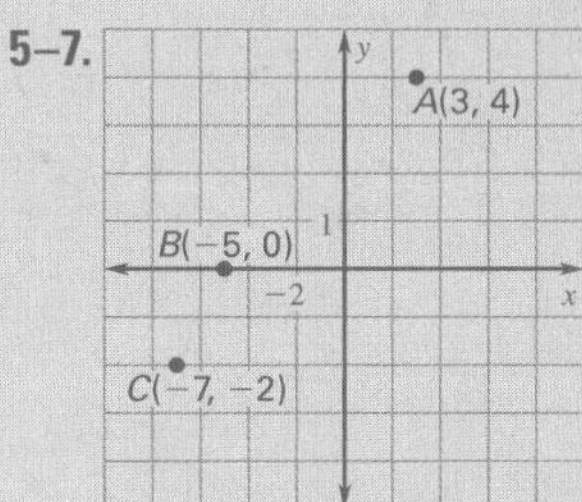

4 CHAPTER REVIEW

Extra Example 4.2

Graph the equation $y + 2x = -3$.

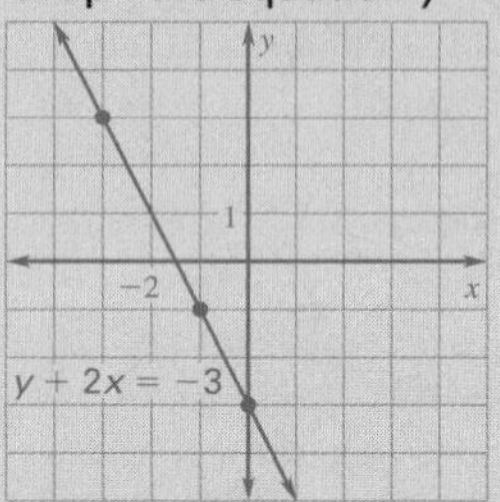

Extra Example 4.3

Graph the equation $-2x + 4y = 12$ using intercepts.

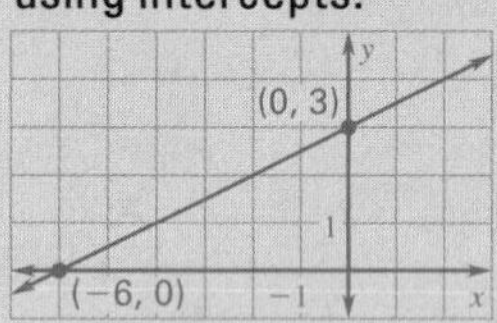

8\.

9\.

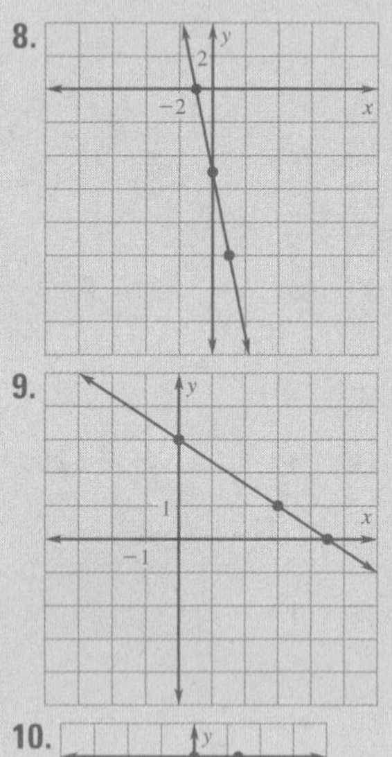

10\.

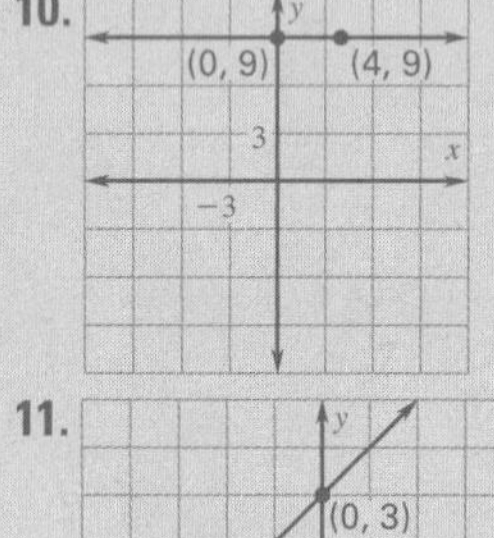

11\.

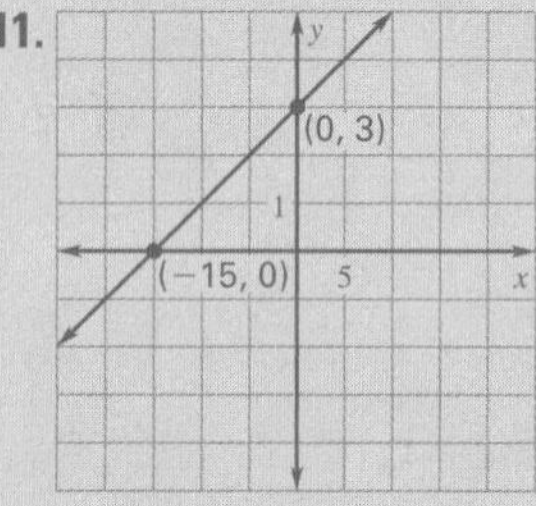

4.2 Graph Linear Equations

pp. 215–221

EXAMPLE

Graph the equation $y + 3x = 1$.

STEP 1 **Solve** the equation for y.

$$y + 3x = 1$$

$$y = -3x + 1$$

STEP 2 **Make** a table by choosing a few values for x and finding the values for y.

x	−1	0	1
y	4	1	−2

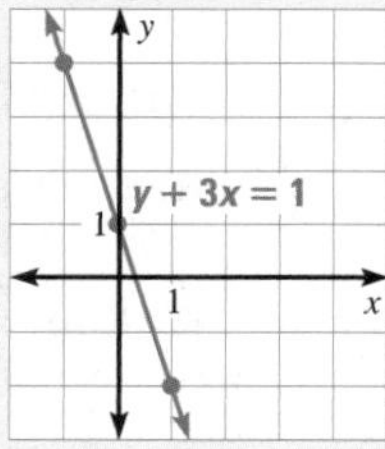

STEP 3 **Plot** the points.

STEP 4 **Connect** the points by drawing a line through them.

EXERCISES

EXAMPLE 2 on p. 216 for Exs. 8–10

Graph the equation. 8–10. See margin.

8. $y + 5x = -5$ **9.** $2x + 3y = 9$ **10.** $2y - 14 = 4$

4.3 Graph Using Intercepts

pp. 225–232

EXAMPLE

Graph the equation $-0.5x + 2y = 4$.

STEP 1 **Find** the intercepts.

$-0.5x + 2y = 4$	$-0.5x + 2y = 4$
$-0.5x + 2(0) = 4$	$-0.5(0) + 2y = 4$
$x = -8 \leftarrow$ ***x*-intercept**	$y = 2 \leftarrow$ ***y*-intercept**

STEP 2 **Plot** the points that correspond to the intercepts: $(-8, 0)$ and $(0, 2)$.

STEP 3 **Connect** the points by drawing a line through them.

EXERCISES

EXAMPLES 2 and 4 on pp. 226–227 for Exs. 11–14

Graph the equation. 11–13. See margin.

11. $-x + 5y = 15$ **12.** $4x + 4y = -16$ **13.** $2x - 6y = 18$

14. CRAFT FAIR You sell necklaces for \$10 and bracelets for \$5 at a craft fair. You want to earn \$50. This situation is modeled by the equation $10n + 5b = 50$ where n is the number of necklaces you sell and b is the number of bracelets you sell. Find the intercepts of the graph of the equation. Then graph the equation. Give three possibilities for the number of bracelets and necklaces that you could sell. *n*-intercept: 5, *b*-intercept: 10; see margin for art. *Sample answer:* 1 necklace and 8 bracelets, 2 necklaces and 6 bracelets, 3 necklaces and 4 bracelets

12\.

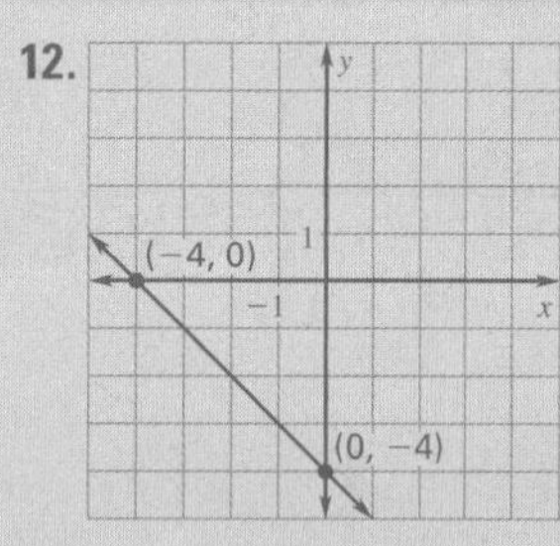

13\.

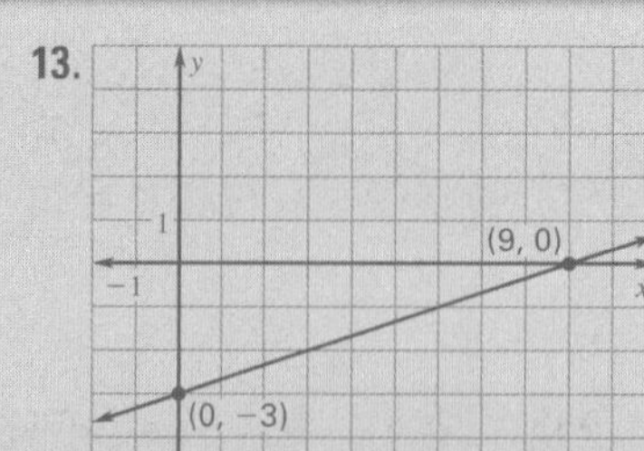

14\.

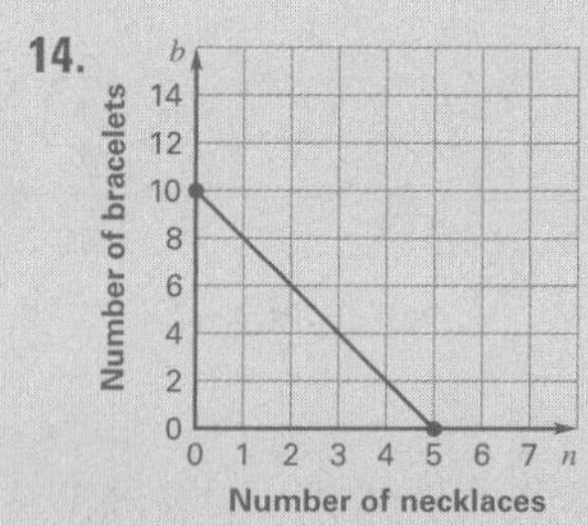

@HomeTutor
classzone.com
Chapter Review Practice

4.4 Find Slope and Rate of Change

pp. 235–242

EXAMPLE

Find the slope of the line shown.

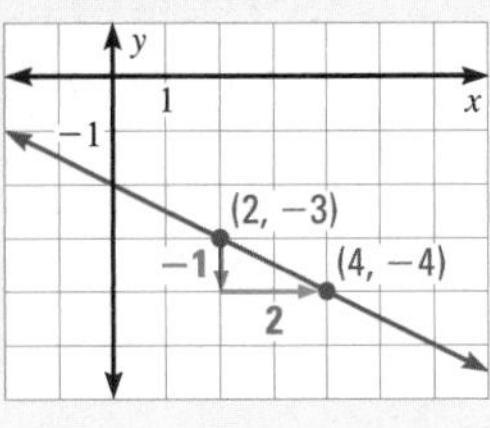

Let $(x_1, y_1) = (2, -3)$ and $(x_2, y_2) = (4, -4)$.

$m = \frac{y_2 - y_1}{x_2 - x_1}$ **Write formula for slope.**

$= \frac{-4 - (-3)}{4 - 2}$ **Substitute values.**

$= -\frac{1}{2}$ **Simplify.**

EXAMPLES 1,2,3, and 4 on pp. 235–236 for Exs. 15–17

EXERCISES

Find the slope of the line that passes through the points.

15. (−1, 11) and (2, 10) $-\frac{1}{3}$ **16.** (−2, 0) and (4, 9) $\frac{3}{2}$ **17.** (−5, 4) and (1, −8) −2

4.5 Graph Using Slope-Intercept Form

pp. 244–250

EXAMPLE

Graph the equation $2x + y = -1$.

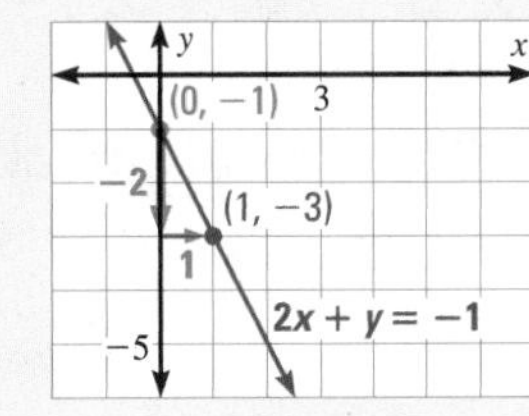

STEP 1 **Rewrite** the equation in slope-intercept form.

$2x + y = -1 \rightarrow y = -2x - 1$

STEP 2 **Identify** the slope and the y-intercept.

$m = -2$ and $b = -1$

STEP 3 **Plot** the point that corresponds to the y-intercept, (0, −1).

STEP 4 **Use** the slope to locate a second point on the line. Draw a line through the two points.

EXAMPLES 2 and 3 on p. 245 for Exs. 18–21

EXERCISES

Graph the equation. 18–20. See margin.

18. $4x - y = 3$ **19.** $3x - 6y = 9$ **20.** $-3x + 4y - 12 = 0$

21. RUNNING One athlete can run a 60 meter race at an average rate of 7 meters per second. A second athlete can run the race at an average rate of 6 meters per second. The distance d (in meters) the athletes have left to run after t seconds is given by the following equations:

Athlete 1: $d = -7t + 60$ **Athlete 2:** $d = -6t + 60$

Graph both models in the same coordinate plane. About how many seconds faster does the first athlete finish the race than the second athlete?

See margin for art; about 1.4 sec.

Extra Example 4.4

Find the slope of the line shown. $\frac{3}{2}$

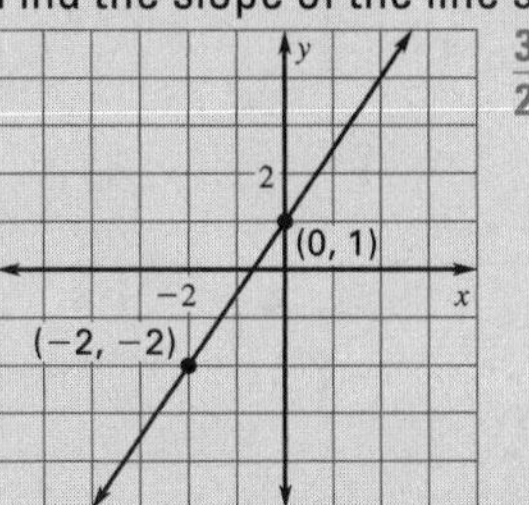

Extra Example 4.5

Graph the equation $3x + y = 2$ using slope-intercept form.

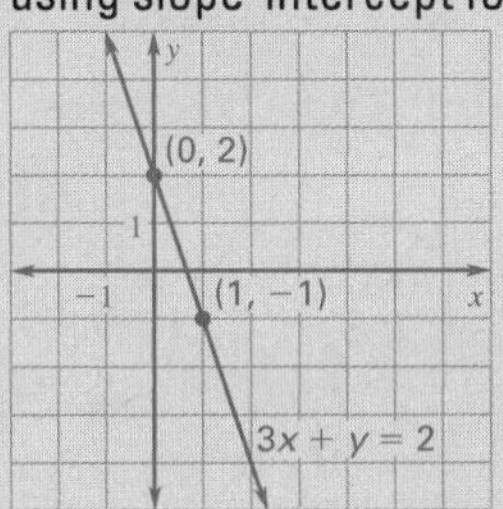

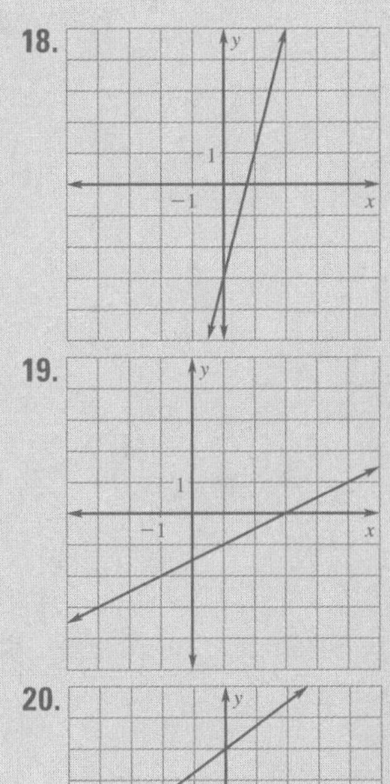

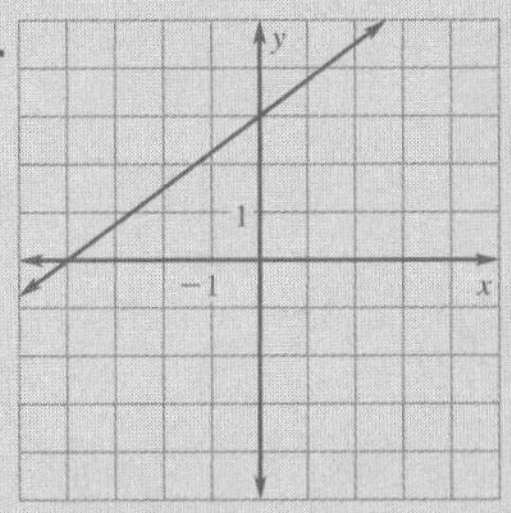

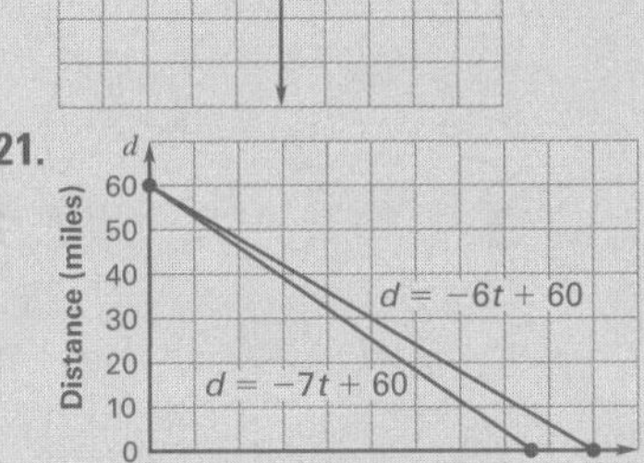

Extra Example 4.6

Graph the direct variation equation $y = \frac{1}{4}x$.

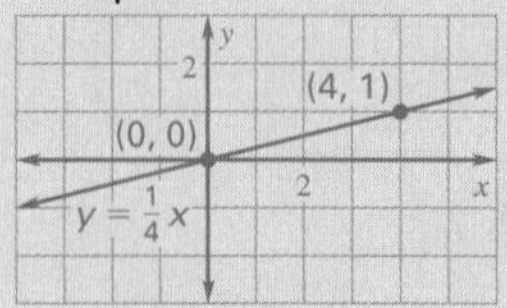

Extra Example 4.7

Evaluate the function $f(x) = 3x + 5$ when $x = -2$. -1

25.

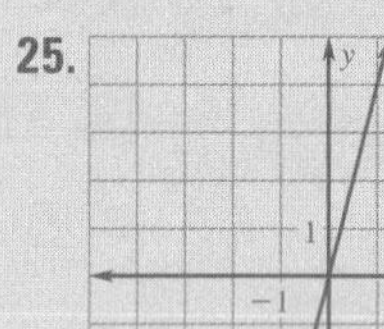

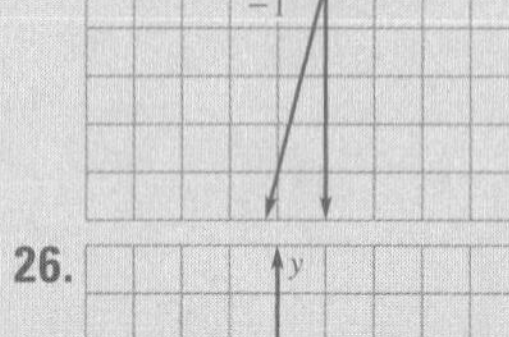

26.

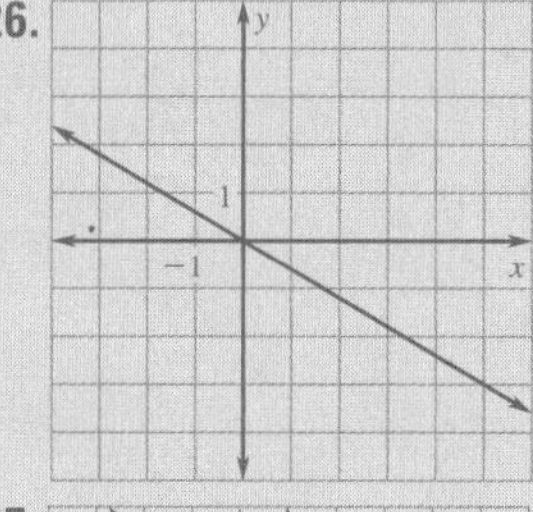

27.

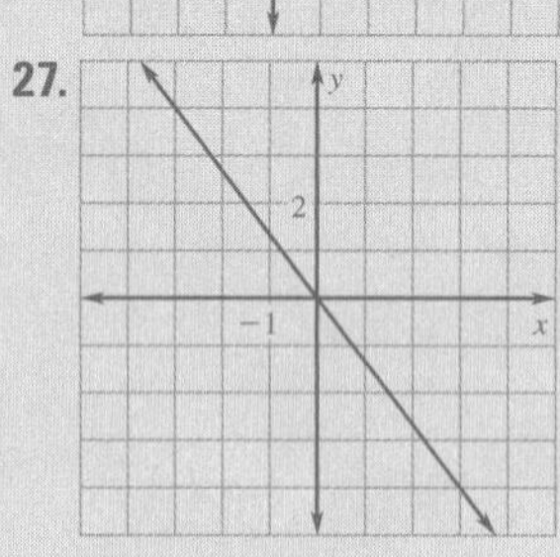

31–33. See Additional Answers beginning on p. AA1.

34.

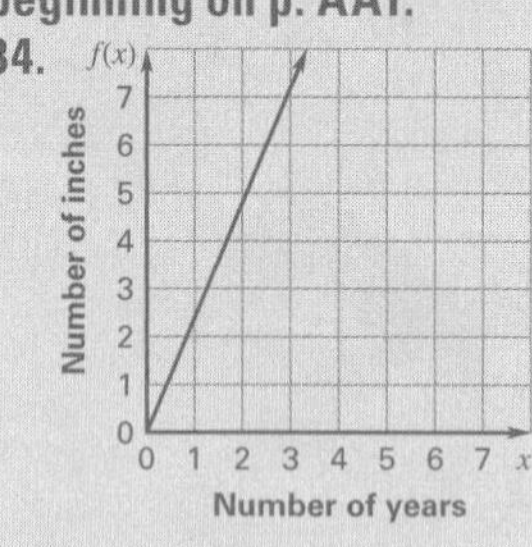

4 CHAPTER REVIEW

4.6 Model Direct Variation *pp. 253–259*

EXAMPLE

Graph the direct variation equation $y = -\frac{2}{3}x$.

Plot a point at the origin. The slope is equal to the constant of variation, $-\frac{2}{3}$. Find and plot a second point, then draw a line through the points.

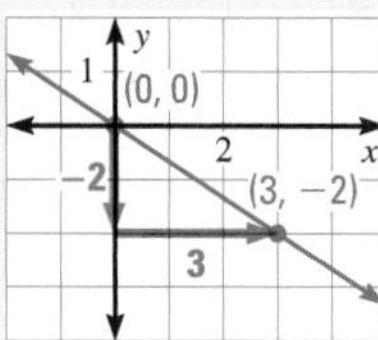

EXERCISES

EXAMPLES 1, 2, and 4 on pp. 253–255 for Exs. 22–28

Tell whether the equation represents direct variation. If so, identify the constant of variation.

22. $x - y = 3$ not direct variation

23. $x + 2y = 0$ direct variation; $-\frac{1}{2}$

24. $8x - 2y = 0$ direct variation; 4

Graph the direct variation equation. 25–27. See margin.

25. $y = 4x$

26. $-5y = 3x$

27. $4x + 3y = 0$

28. SNOWSTORMS The amount s (in inches) of snow that fell during a snowstorm varied directly with the duration d (in hours) of the storm. In the first 2 hours of the storm 5 inches of snow fell. Write a direct variation equation that relates d and s. How many inches of snow fell in 6 hours? $s = \frac{5}{2}d$; 15 in.

4.7 Graph Linear Functions *pp. 262–268*

EXAMPLE

Evaluate the function $f(x) = -6x + 5$ when $x = 3$.

$f(x) = -6x + 5$ **Write function.**

$f(3) = -6(3) + 5$ **Substitute 3 for x.**

$= -13$ **Simplify.**

EXERCISES

EXAMPLES 1 and 3 on pp. 262–263 for Exs. 29–34

Evaluate the function.

29. $g(x) = 2x - 3$ when $x = 7$ 11

30. $h(x) = -\frac{1}{2}x - 7$ when $x = -6$ -4

Graph the function. Compare the graph with the graph of $f(x) = x$. 31–33. See margin.

31. $j(x) = x - 6$

32. $k(x) = -2.5x$

33. $t(x) = 2x + 1$

34. MOUNT EVEREST Mount Everest is rising at a rate of 2.4 inches per year. The number of inches that Mount Everest rises in x years is given by the function $f(x) = 2.4x$. Graph the function and identify its domain and range. Find the value of x so that $f(x) = 250$. *Explain* what the solution means in this situation. See margin for art; domain: $x \ge 0$, range: $f(x) \ge 0$; about 104; Mount Everest will have grown 250 inches in 104 years.

4 CHAPTER TEST

Plot the point in a coordinate plane. *Describe* the location of the point. 1–3. See margin for art.

1. $A(7, 1)$ Quadrant I
2. $B(-4, 0)$ x-axis
3. $C(3, -9)$ Quadrant IV

Draw the line that has the given intercepts. 4–6. See margin.

4. x-intercept: 2
   y-intercept: -6
5. x-intercept: -1
   y-intercept: 8
6. x-intercept: -3
   y-intercept: -5

Find the slope of the line that passes through the points.

7. (2, 1) and (8, 4) $\frac{1}{2}$
8. $(-2, 7)$ and $(0, -1)$ -4
9. (3, 5) and (3, 14) undefined

Identify the slope and y-intercept of the line with the given equation.

10. $y = -\frac{3}{2}x - 10$ $-\frac{3}{2}, -10$
11. $7x + 2y = -28$ $-\frac{7}{2}, -14$
12. $3x - 8y = 48$ $\frac{3}{8}, -6$

Tell whether the equation represents direct variation. If so, identify the constant of variation.

13. $x + 4y = 4$ not direct variation
14. $-\frac{1}{3}x - y = 0$ direct variation; $-\frac{1}{3}$
15. $3x - 3y = 0$ direct variation; 1

Graph the equation. 16–18. See margin.

16. $x = 3$
17. $y + x = 6$
18. $2x + 8y = -32$

Evaluate the function for the given value.

19. $f(x) = -4x$ when $x = 2.5$ -10
20. $g(x) = \frac{5}{2}x - 6$ when $x = -2$ -11

21. **BUSINESS** To start a dog washing business, you invest \$300 in supplies. You charge \$10 per hour for your services. Your profit P (in dollars) for working t hours is given by $P = 10t - 300$. Graph the equation. You will break even when your profit is \$0. Use the graph to find the number of hours you must work in order to break even. See margin for art; 30 h.

22. **PEDIATRICS** The dose d (in milligrams) of a particular medicine that a pediatrician prescribes for a patient varies directly with the patient's mass m (in kilograms). The pediatrician recommends a dose of 150 mg of medicine for a patient whose mass is 30 kg.
    a. Write a direct variation equation that relates m and d. $d = 5m$
    b. What would the dose of medicine be for a patient whose mass is 50 kg? 250 mg

23. **SCISSOR LIFT** The scissor lift is a device that can lower and raise a platform. The maximum and minimum heights of the platform of a particular scissor lift are shown. The scissor lift can raise the platform at a rate of 3.5 inches per second. The height of the platform after t seconds is given by $h(t) = 3.5t + 48$. Graph the function and identify its domain and range. See margin for art; domain: $0 \le t \le 58.3$, range: $48 \le h(t) \le 252$.

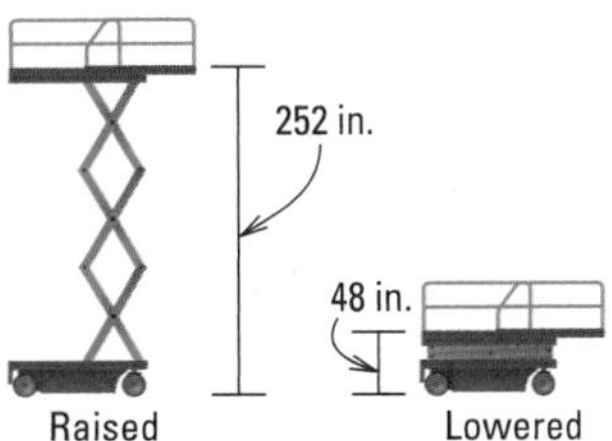

Additional Resources

Assessment Book

- Chapter Test, Levels A, B, C, pp. 49–54
- Standardized Chapter Test, pp. 55–56
- SAT/ACT Chapter Test, pp. 57–58
- Alternative Assessment, pp. 59–60

Test Generator CD-ROM

Chapter Test

Easily-readable reduced copies (with answers) of Chapter Test B, the Standardized Chapter Test, and the Alternative Assessment from the Assessment Book can be found on pp. 204G–204H.

5., 6.

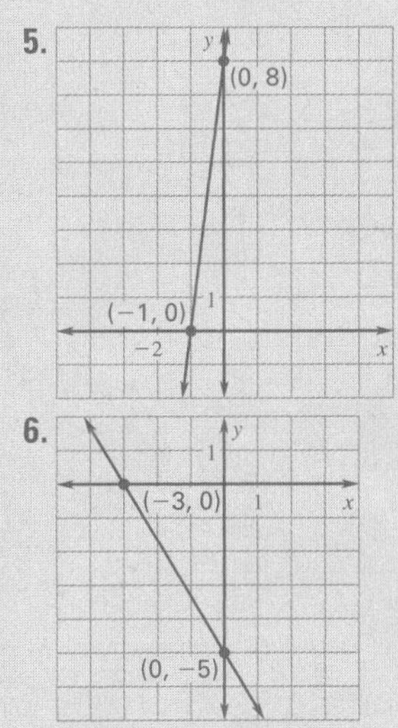

16–18. See Additional Answers beginning on p. AA1.

21.

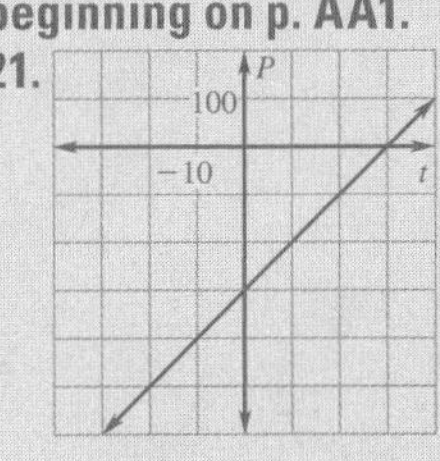

23.

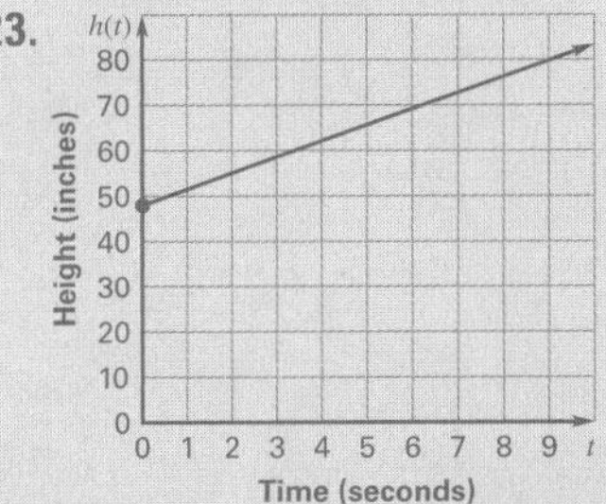

1–3.

A(7, 1)
B(−4, 0)
C(3, −9)

4.

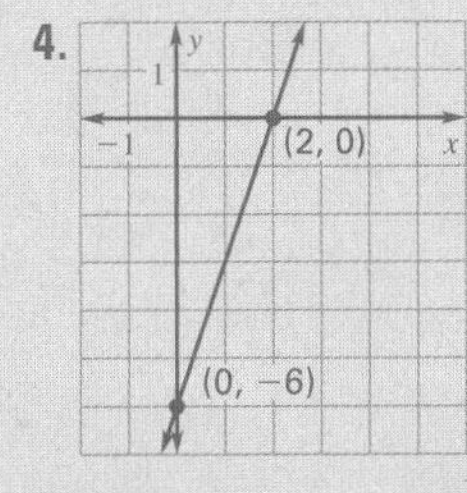

MULTIPLE CHOICE QUESTIONS

Some of the information you need to solve a multiple choice question may appear in a table, a diagram, or a graph.

PROBLEM 1

A recipe from a box of pancake mix is shown. The number p of pancakes you can make varies directly with the number m of cups of mix you use. A full box of pancake mix contains 9 cups of mix. How many pancakes can you make when you use the full box?

A. 63 **C.** 126

B. 65 **D.** 131

2 cups pancake mix
1 cup milk
2 eggs
Combine ingredients. Pour batter on hot greased griddle. Flip when edges are dry. Makes 14 pancakes.

Plan

INTERPRET THE INFORMATION Use the number of pancakes and the number of cups of mix given in the recipe to write a direct variation equation. Then use the equation to find the number of pancakes that you can make when you use 9 cups of mix.

Solution

STEP 1 Use the values given in the recipe to find a direct variation equation.

Because the number p of pancakes you can make varies directly with the number m of cups of mix you use, you can write the equation $p = am$. From the recipe, you know that $p = 14$ when $m = 2$.

$p = am$ **Write direct variation equation.**

$14 = a(2)$ **Substitute.**

$7 = a$ **Solve for a.**

So, a direct variation equation that relates p and m is $p = 7m$.

STEP 2 Substitute 9 for m in the direct variation equation and solve for p.

Use the direct variation equation to find the number of pancakes you can make when you use a full box of mix.

$p = 7m$ **Write direct variation equation.**

$p = 7(9)$ **Substitute 9 for m.**

$p = 63$ **Simplify.**

You can make 63 pancakes when you use a full box of mix.

The correct answer is **A**.

Illinois Test Preparation

1. B
2. H

PROBLEM 2

At a yard sale, Jack made $54 selling cassettes for $1 each and CDs for $3 each. This situation is modeled by the equation $x + 3y = 54$ where x is the number of cassettes and y is the number of CDs that Jack sold. The graph of the equation is shown. Which is a possible combination of cassettes and CDs that Jack sold?

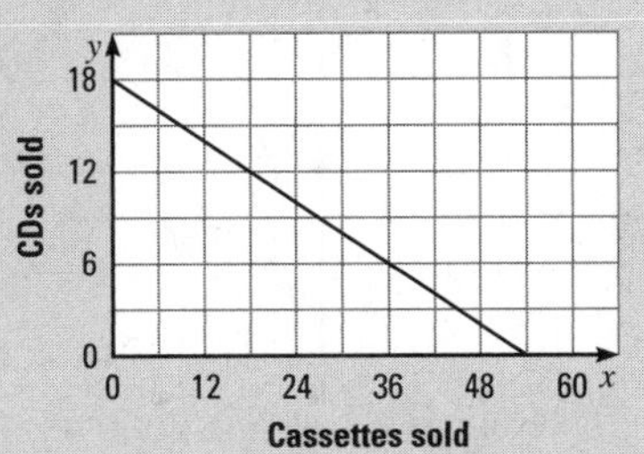

F. 12 cassettes, 4 CDs

G. 4 cassettes, 12 CDs

H. 18 cassettes, 12 CDs

J. 28.5 cassettes, 8.5 CDs

Plan

INTERPRET THE INFORMATION Each point on the line represents a solution of the equation. Identify the answer choice that describes a point on the graph shown and that makes sense in the context of the problem.

Solution

STEP 1 Write an ordered pair for each answer choice.

The answer choices correspond to the following ordered pairs.

F. (12, 4) **G.** (4, 12) **H.** (18, 12) **J.** (28.5, 8.5)

STEP 2 Eliminate points not on the line and points that don't make sense. Check ordered pairs not eliminated to find the solution.

You can eliminate answer choices F and G because the points do not lie on the graph shown. You can also eliminate answer choice J because only whole number solutions make sense in this situation. Check that (18, 12) is a solution of the equation.

$x + 3y = 54$ **Write original equation.**

$\mathbf{18} + 3(\mathbf{12}) = 54$ **Substitute.**

$54 = 54 \checkmark$ **Solution checks.**

The correct answer is **H**.

PRACTICE

1. In Problem 2, what is the greatest number of CDs Jack could have sold?

   A. 3 **B.** 18 **C.** 36 **D.** 54

2. The table shows the total cost for a certain number of people to ice skate at a particular rink. What is the cost per person?

   F. $.20 **H.** $5

   G. $1 **J.** $10

Number of people	Cost (dollars)
2	10
4	20
6	30

TEST PREPARATION

Illinois Test Practice

1. B
2. J
3. D
4. H
5. D
6. F
7. C
8. G
9. C
10. F
11. C
12. H
13. A
14. J
15. D
16. F

Illinois Test Practice

In Exercises 1 and 2, use the graph below.

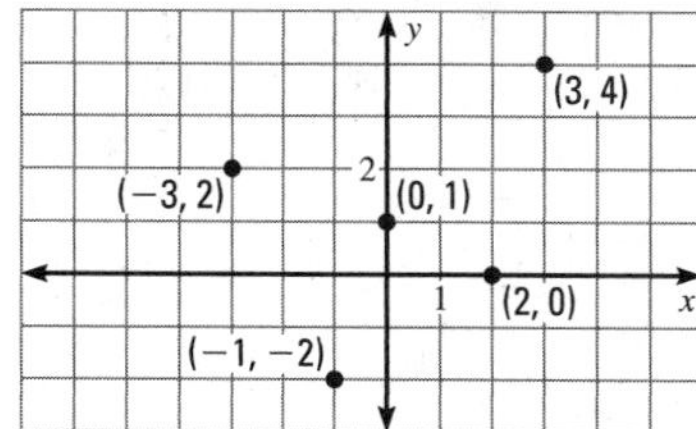

1. The graph represents a function. Which number is in the domain of the function?

   A. 22 **C.** 1

   B. −1 **D.** 4

2. The graph would no longer represent a function if which point were included?

   F. (−4, −2) **H.** (1, 3)

   G. (−2, 0) **J.** (3, −1)

In Exercises 3 and 4, use the graph below, which shows a traveler's movements through an airport to a terminal. The traveler has to walk and take a shuttle bus to get to the terminal.

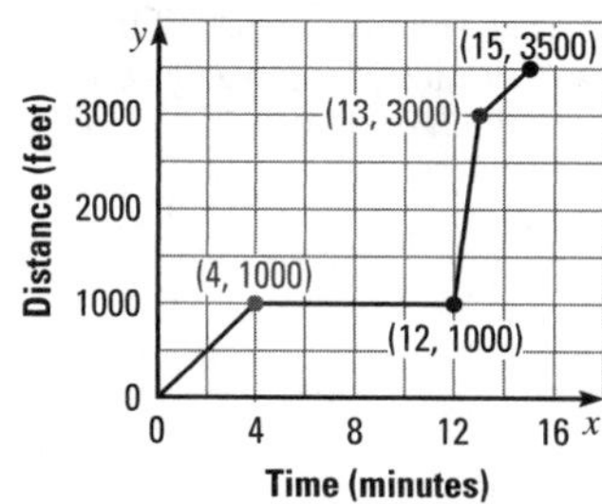

3. For how many minutes does the traveler wait for the shuttle bus?

   A. 1 min **C.** 4 min

   B. 2 min **D.** 8 min

4. For about what distance does the traveler ride on the shuttle bus?

   F. 100 ft **H.** 2000 ft

   G. 1000 ft **J.** 3000 ft

In Exercises 5–7, use the following information.

At a yoga studio, new members pay a sign-up fee of \$50 plus a monthly fee of \$25. The total cost C (in dollars) of a new membership is given by $C = 25m + 50$ where m is the number of months of membership. The owner of the studio is considering changing the cost of a new membership. A graph of four different options for changing the cost is shown.

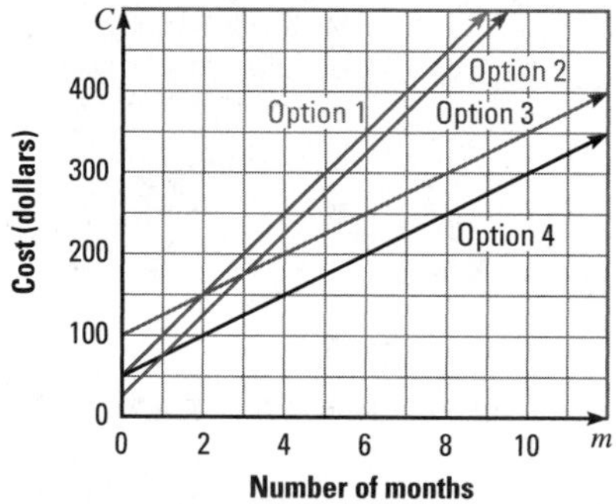

5. For which option are the sign-up fee and monthly fee kept the same?

   A. Option 1 **C.** Option 3

   B. Option 2 **D.** Option 4

6. For which option is the sign-up fee kept the same and the monthly fee raised?

   F. Option 1 **H.** Option 3

   G. Option 2 **J.** Option 4

7. For which option is the monthly fee kept the same and the sign-up fee raised?

   A. Option 1 **C.** Option 3

   B. Option 2 **D.** Option 4

8. The table shows the cost of a therapeutic massage for a given amount of time. What is the cost per minute?

Time (minutes)	30	45	60
Cost (dollars)	42.00	63.00	84.00

   F. \$.71 **H.** \$2.80

   G. \$1.40 **J.** \$14.00

9. Which point on the coordinate plane below satisfies the conditions $x > 0.8$ and $y < 1.5$?

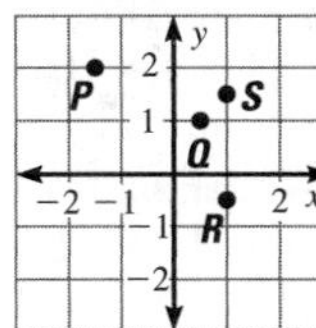

A. Point P **C.** Point R

B. Point Q **D.** Point S

10. Which function includes the data set {(1, 5), (2, 3), (5, −3)}?

F. $y = -2x + 7$ **H.** $y = 5x - 4$

G. $y = \frac{x}{2} + 7$ **J.** $y = 5x - 7$

11. What is the value of the function $g(x) = 4x - 9$ when $x = 5$?

A. −10 **C.** 11

B. 0 **D.** 36

12. If $(x, 3)$ is a solution to the equation $5x - 2y = 44$, what is the value of x?

F. 6 **H.** 10

G. 9 **J.** 12

13. Triangle XYZ has coordinates $X(-2, -0.5)$, $Y(1, 1)$, and $Z(-1, -1.5)$. What will be the new coordinates of point X if the triangle is translated 2 units to the right and 3 units up?

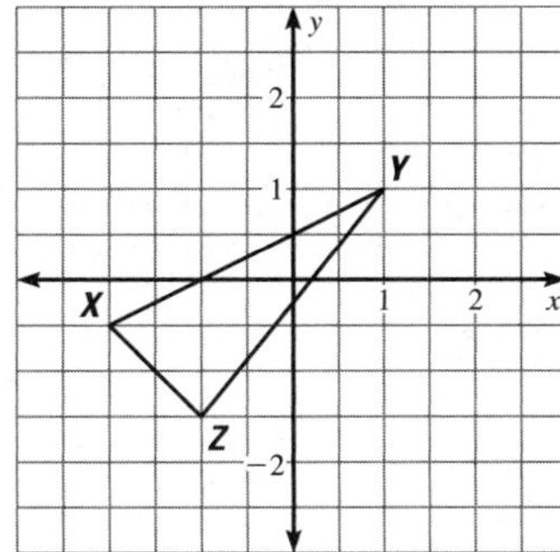

A. (0, 2.5) **C.** (1, −2.5)

B. (0, 3.5) **D.** (−0.5, 1)

14. What is the y-intercept of the graph of the equation $4x + 8y = 16$?

F. −2 **H.** $\frac{1}{2}$

G. $-\frac{1}{2}$ **J.** 2

15. The graph below was drawn by a business. Which of the following is *not* true for the graph below?

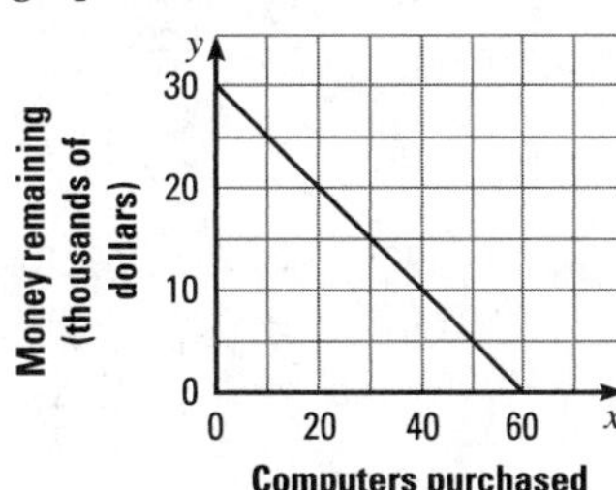

A. The business will have $30,000 if it purchases no computers.

B. The business can purchase 10 computers for about $5000.

C. If the business purchases 30 computers, it will have $15,000 remaining.

D. The business will have $5 remaining if it purchases 50 computers.

16. In the distance formula $d = rt$, r represents the rate of change, or slope. Which ray on the graph best represents a slope of 65 miles per hour?

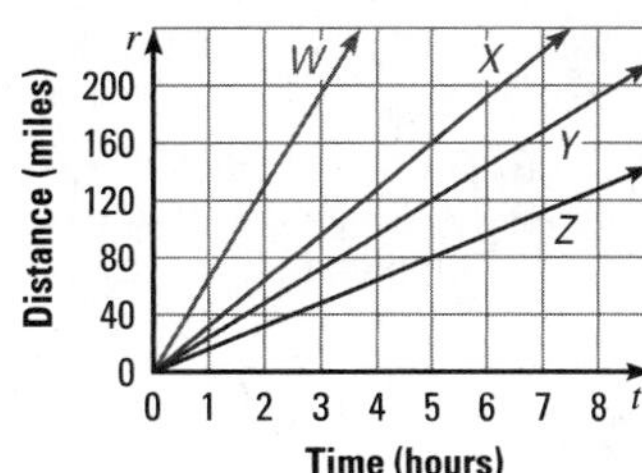

F. W **G.** X **H.** Y **J.** Z

TEST PRACTICE

Illinois Resources Guide

Pacing and Assignment Guide

REGULAR SCHEDULE

Pre-AP For pacing and assignments for a Pre-AP course, see the *Algebra 1 Toolkit*.

Lesson	Les. Day	BASIC	AVERAGE	ADVANCED
5.1 8.11.07	Day 1	EP p. 941 Exs. 33–36; pp. 286–289 Exs. 1–5, 9–12, 16–20, 24–26, 30–32, 39, 40, 45–49, 53–63 odd	pp. 286–289 Exs. 1, 2, 6–9, 13–17, 21–24, 26, 28, 33–35, 39–43, 46–51, 56, 57, 62, 63	pp. 286–289 Exs. 1, 7–9, 13–15, 21–23, 27–29, 36–44*, 47–52*, 58, 64
5.2 8.11.07	Day 1	EP p. 941 Exs. 27–32; pp. 296–299 Exs. 1–5, 11–13, 17–19, 23–26, 55–58	pp. 296–299 Exs. 1, 2, 6–8, 14–16, 20–22, 25–29, 55–58	pp. 296–299 Exs. 1, 7, 8, 15, 16, 21, 22, 27–37, 57, 58
	Day 2	pp. 296–299 Exs. 9, 10, 29–35, 47–52, 59–64	pp. 296–299 Exs. 9, 10, 31–43 odd, 48–53, 59–64	pp. 296–299 Exs. 10, 38–46*, 49–54*, 63, 64
5.3 8.11.07	Day 1	EP p. 939 Exs. 42–45; pp. 305–308 Exs. 1–8, 12–17, 45–53	pp. 305–308 Exs. 1, 2, 6–13, 17–19, 45–53	pp. 305–308 Exs. 1, 2, 7–12, 17–19, 35*, 36*, 45–53 odd
	Day 2	pp. 305–308 Exs. 20–32, 37–42, 54–57	pp. 305–308 Exs. 20–28 even, 29–34, 37–43, 54–57	pp. 305–308 Exs. 24–28, 30–34, 37–44*, 55, 57
5.4 8.11.07	Day 1	EP p. 941 Exs. 37–40; pp. 314–316 Exs. 1–8, 11–19, 47–49	pp. 314–316 Exs. 1–4, 8–10, 14–22, 47–49	pp. 314–316 Exs. 1–4, 8–10, 16–22, 37*, 47–49
	Day 2	pp. 314–316 Exs. 23–32, 38–41, 45, 46	pp. 314–316 Exs. 23–29 odd, 30–36, 38–43, 45, 46	pp. 314–316 Exs. 26–28, 30–36, 41–46*
5.5 8.11.11	Day 1	pp. 322–324 Exs. 1–8, 12–22, 27, 28, 32–35, 38–42	pp. 322–324 Exs. 1, 2, 7–17, 23–30, 32–37, 39, 41, 42	pp. 322–324 Exs. 1, 2, 8–11, 13–17, 24–37*, 40–42
5.6 8.11.07	Day 1	EP p. 941 Exs. 1–7 odd; pp. 328–331 Exs. 1–12, 16–18, 22–28	pp. 328–331 Exs. 1, 2, 4–14, 16–20, 22–28	pp. 328–331 Exs. 1, 2, 4–8, 11–28*
5.7 8.11.07	Day 1	pp. 338–341 Exs. 1–15, 18–21, 24–32	pp. 338–341 Exs. 1–6, 9–16, 18–22, 24–32	pp. 338–341 Exs. 1–6, 10–14, 16–32*
Review	Day 1	pp. 345–348 Exs. 1–22	pp. 345–348 Exs. 1–22	pp. 345–348 Exs. 1–22
Assess	Day 1	Chapter 5 Test	Chapter 5 Test	Chapter 5 Test
Yearly Pacing		Chapter 5 Total – 12 days	Chapters 1–5 Total – 58 days	Remaining – 102 days

*Challenge Exercises EP = Extra Practice SRH = Skills Review Handbook

BLOCK SCHEDULE

DAY 1	DAY 2	DAY 3	DAY 4	DAY 5	DAY 6
5.1	**5.2 (CONT.)**	**5.3 (CONT.)**	**5.4 (CONT.)**	**5.6**	**REVIEW**
pp. 286–289 Exs. 1, 2, 6–9, 13–17, 21–24, 26, 28, 33–35, 39–43, 46–51, 56, 57, 62, 63	pp. 296–299 Exs. 9, 10, 31–43 odd, 48–53, 59–64	pp. 305–308 Exs. 20–28 even, 29–34, 37–43, 54–57	pp. 314–316 Exs. 23–29 odd, 30–36, 38–43, 45, 46	pp. 328–331 Exs. 1, 2, 4–14, 16–20, 22–28	pp. 345–348 Exs. 1–22
5.2	**5.3**	**5.4**	**5.5**	**5.7**	**ASSESS**
pp. 296–299 Exs. 1, 2, 6–8, 14–16, 20–22, 25–29, 55–58	pp. 305–308 Exs. 1, 2, 6–13, 17–19, 45–53	pp. 314–316 Exs. 1–4, 8–10, 14–22, 47–49	pp. 322–324 Exs. 1, 2, 7–17, 23–30, 32–37, 39, 41, 42	pp. 338–341 Exs. 1–6, 9–16, 18–22, 24–32	Chapter 5 Test
Yearly Pacing	Chapter 5 Total – 6 days	Chapters 1–5 Total – 29 days	Remaining – 51 days		

Chapter Resource Guide 5

Chapter Resource Book							
CHAPTER SUPPORT							
Parents as Partners (Chapter Overview with home involvement exercises and activity)						p. 1	
LESSON SUPPORT Standard	**5.1 8.11.07**	**5.2 8.11.07**	**5.3 8.11.07**	**5.4 8.11.07**	**5.5 8.11.11**	**5.6 8.11.07**	**5.7 8.11.07**
Teaching Guide/Lesson Plan	p. 3	p. 14	p. 24	p. 38	p. 50	p. 60	p. 74
Activity Masters			p. 26	p. 40			
Technology Activities & Keystrokes	p. 5					p. 62	p. 76
Activity Support Masters							
Practice (3 levels)	p. 6	p. 16	p. 27	p. 41	p. 52	p. 63	p. 78
Study Guide	p. 9	p. 19	p. 33	p. 44	p. 55	p. 69	p. 84
Catch-Up for Absent Students	p. 11	p. 21	p. 35	p. 46	p. 57	p. 71	p. 86
Problem Solving/Application	p. 12	p. 22	p. 36	p. 47	p. 58	p. 72	p. 87
Challenge Practice	p. 13	p. 23	p. 37	p. 49	p. 59	p. 73	p. 88
REVIEW							
Chapter Review Games and Activities		p. 89		Cumulative Practice		p. 92	
Project with Rubric		p. 90		Resource Book Answers		A1	

Transparencies	5.1	5.2	5.3	5.4	5.5	5.6	5.7
Warm-Up/Daily Homework Quiz	✔	✔	✔	✔	✔	✔	✔
Notetaking Guide	✔	✔	✔	✔	✔	✔	✔
Teacher Support	✔		✔	✔		✔	
Answer Transparencies	✔	✔	✔	✔	✔	✔	✔

ASSESSMENT BOOK

Quizzes	p. 61	SAT/ACT Chapter Test	p. 71
Chapter Tests (3 levels)	p. 63	Alternative Assessment with Rubric	p. 73
Standardized Chapter Test	p. 69		

TECHNOLOGY

- Easy Planner
- Test and Practice Generator
- Power Presentations
- @HomeTutor
- Activity Generator
- Animated Algebra
- Classzone.com
- eEdition Plus Online
- eWorkbook Plus Online
- ML Assessment System

ADDITIONAL RESOURCES

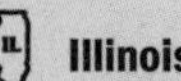
Illinois Additional Lessons

- Additional Lesson J Introduction to Vectors
- Worked-Out Solution Key
- Notetaking Guide
- Practice Workbook
- Algebra 1 Toolkit
- Benchmark Tests
- Reteaching and Remediation
- Spanish Study Guide
- Spanish Assessment Book
- Spanish Resources in Spanish
- Multi-Language Visual Glossary

5 Lesson Practice Level B

LESSON 5.1 Practice B
For use with pages 283–289

Write an equation of the line with the given slope and y-intercept.

1. slope: 7; y-intercept: 4 $y = 7x + 4$
2. slope: −3; y-intercept: 5 $y = -3x + 5$
3. slope: 1; y-intercept: −6 $y = x - 6$

Write an equation of the line shown.

4.
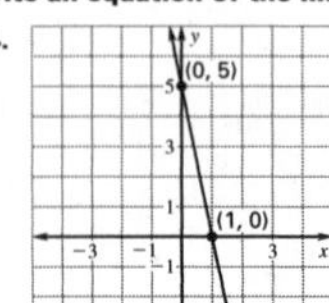

$y = -5x + 5$

5.
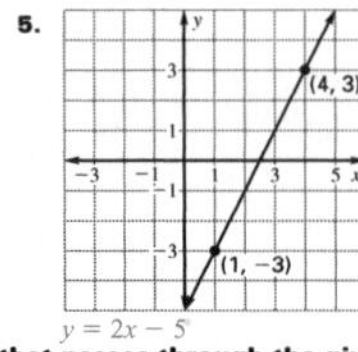

$y = 2x - 5$

6.
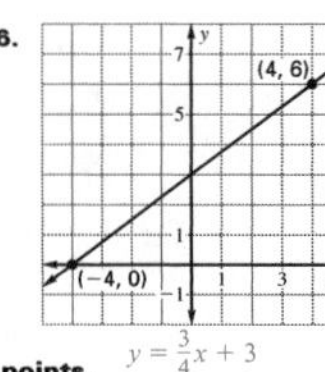

$y = \frac{3}{4}x + 3$

Write an equation of the line that passes through the given points.

7. (−1, 0), (0, −2) $y = -2x - 2$
8. (0, 4), (6, 13) $y = \frac{3}{2}x + 4$
9. (4, 5), (8, 2) $y = -\frac{3}{4}x + 8$
10. (−1, −9), (6, 5) $y = 2x - 7$
11. (2, −13), (−3, 12) $y = -5x - 3$
12. (−4, −21), (1, −1) $y = 4x - 5$

Write an equation for the linear function f with the given values.

13. $f(0) = -1, f(3) = -10$ $f(x) = -3x - 1$
14. $f(-4) = 5, f(2) = 2$ $f(x) = -\frac{1}{2}x + 3$
15. $f(-4) = -2, f(2) = 7$ $f(x) = \frac{3}{2}x + 4$

16. Landscape Supply A landscape supply business charges $30 to deliver mulch. The mulch costs $23 per cubic yard.

a. Write an equation that gives the total cost (in dollars) of having mulch delivered to a site as a function of the number of cubic yards ordered. $y = 23x + 30$

b. *Identify* the dependent and independent variables in this situation. b. independent: x, number of cubic yards ordered; dependent: y, total cost

c. Find the cost of having 8 cubic yards of mulch delivered to a site. $214

17. Cable Television A cable company charges $44 per month for basic service. Each premium channel costs an additional $16 per month.

a. Write an equation that gives the total cost (in dollars) of cable each month as a function of the number of premium channels. $y = 16x + 44$

b. *Identify* the dependent and independent variables in this situation. b. independent: x, number of premium channels; dependent: y, total cost

c. *Explain* how you can use the equation from part (a) to approximate how many premium channels you can have for $80 a month. Substitute 80 for y in the equation and solve for x.

18. Laser Printer A laser printer has a "sleep" mode that is an energy-saving feature. When a job is sent to the printer, it takes 45 seconds for the printer to warm up and then the printer prints pages at a rate of 6 pages per minute.

a. Write the time it takes the printer to warm up in minutes. 0.75 min

b. Write an equation that gives the total amount of time (in minutes) it takes the printer to warm up and print a job as a function of the number of pages in the job. $y = \frac{1}{6}x + 0.75$

c. Find out how long it takes the printer to print a 50-page job if it must first warm up. about 9 min

LESSON 5.2 Practice B
For use with pages 292–299

Write an equation of the line that passes through the given point and has slope m.

1. (−1, 6); $m = 5$ $y = 5x + 11$
2. (10, 3); $m = -2$ $y = -2x + 23$
3. (2, −3); $m = 7$ $y = 7x - 17$
4. (−4, −9); $m = 2$ $y = 2x - 1$
5. (5, −4); $m = \frac{1}{3}$ $y = \frac{1}{3}x - \frac{17}{3}$
6. (−8, 1); $m = -\frac{3}{4}$ $y = -\frac{3}{4}x - 5$

Write an equation of the line shown.

7.
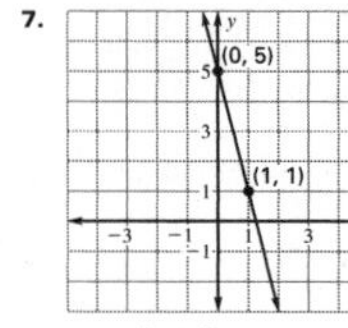

$y = -4x + 5$

8.
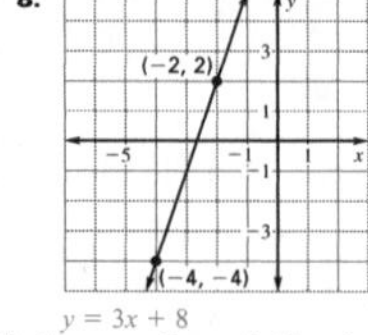

$y = 3x + 8$

9.
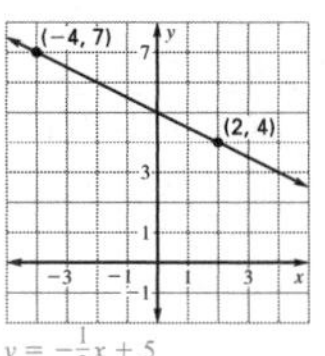

$y = -\frac{1}{2}x + 5$

Write an equation of the line that passes through the given points.

10. (−10, 7), (5, −3) $y = -\frac{2}{3}x + \frac{1}{3}$
11. (−5, −3), (12, 17.4) $y = 1.2x + 3$
12. (−8, 84), (5, −46) $y = -10x + 4$

Write an equation for the linear function f with the given values.

13. $f(4) = -8, f(-3) = 1$ $f(x) = \frac{9}{7}x - \frac{20}{7}$
14. $f(6) = -4, f(9) = -9$ $f(x) = -\frac{5}{3}x + 6$
15. $f(-1) = -6, f(4) = -14$ $f(x) = -\frac{8}{5}x - \frac{38}{5}$

16. Oil Changes You are scheduled to start your job at an oil change shop 2 hours after the shop opens. Two hours after you start, a total of 11 cars have had their oil changed since the shop opened. Three hours later, a total of 14 cars have had their oil changed. At what rate are cars getting their oil changed since you started working? How many cars had their oil changed before you started work? 1 car per hour; 9 cars

17. Motor Vehicle Licenses The amount of revenue brought in by states from motor vehicle licenses increased at a relatively constant rate of 499.79 million dollars per year from 1990 to 2000. In 2000, the states brought in 15,099 million dollars in revenue from motor vehicle licenses.

a. What was the approximate revenue (in million dollars) from licenses in 1990? 10,101.1 million dollars

b. Write an equation that gives the revenue (in million dollars) as a function of the number of years since 1990. $y = 499.79x + 10{,}101.1$

c. Find the revenue from licenses in 1999. 14,599.21 million dollars

18. Imports The number of metric tons of fruits, nuts, and vegetables imported into the United States increased at a relatively constant rate of 437.5 thousand metric tons per year from 1990 to 2002. In 2002, about 9900.5 thousand metric tons of fruits, nuts, and vegetables were imported. Write an equation that gives the number of thousand metric tons imported as a function of the number of years since 1990. Find the year in which the number of metric tons reached 8000 thousand metric tons.
$y = 437.5x + 4650.5$; between 1997 and 1998

LESSON 5.3 Practice B
For use with pages 302–308

Write an equation in point-slope form of the line that passes through the given point and has the given slope m.

1. (1, 9); $m = -3$ $y - 9 = -3(x - 1)$
2. (4, −10); $m = 2$ $y + 10 = 2(x - 4)$
3. (−5, 6); $m = 4$ $y - 6 = 4(x + 5)$
4. (−2, −8); $m = 3$ $y + 8 = 3(x + 2)$
5. (−4, −7); $m = -\frac{1}{2}$ $y + 7 = -\frac{1}{2}(x + 4)$
6. (−9, 2); $m = -5$ $y - 2 = -5(x + 9)$
7. (6, −4); $m = \frac{2}{3}$ $y + 4 = \frac{2}{3}(x - 6)$
8. (0, 15); $m = \frac{4}{5}$ $y - 15 = \frac{4}{5}x$
9. (−8, 0); $m = 2$ $y = 2(x + 8)$

Graph the equation.

10. $y - 6 = 3(x - 4)$

11. $y + 1 = 2(x - 5)$
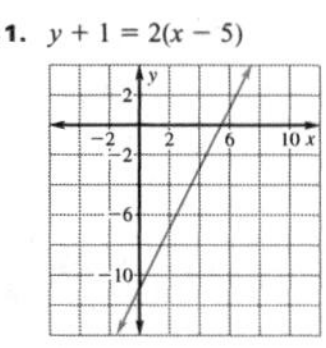

12. $y - 2 = -4(x + 3)$
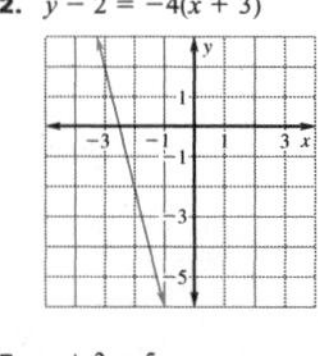

13. $y + 2 = -(x - 1)$
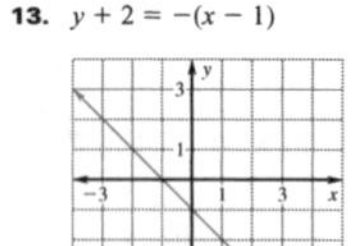
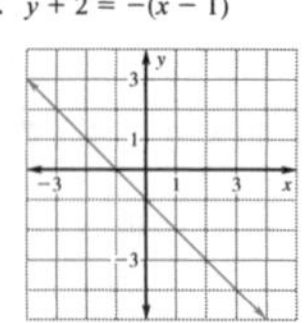

14. $y = \frac{1}{2}(x - 5)$
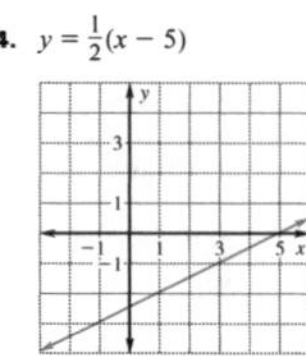

15. $y + 3 = 5x$
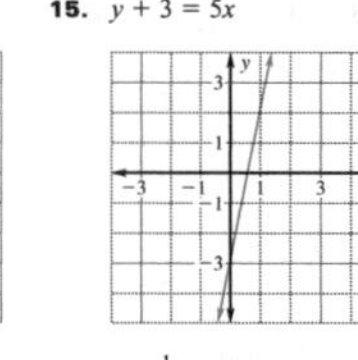

16. $y + 1 = \frac{2}{3}(x + 1)$
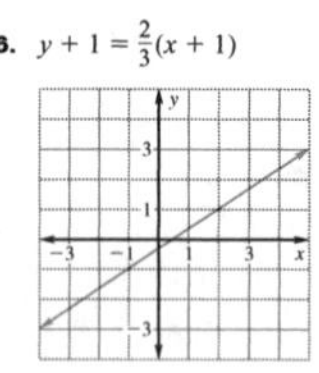

17. $y - 2 = -\frac{1}{2}(x - 3)$
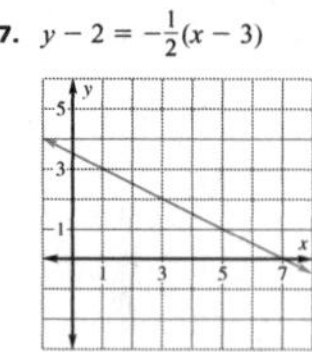

18. $y + \frac{1}{2} = 2(x - 1)$
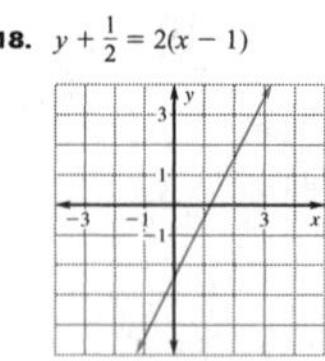

LESSON 5.3 Practice B *continued*
For use with pages 302–308

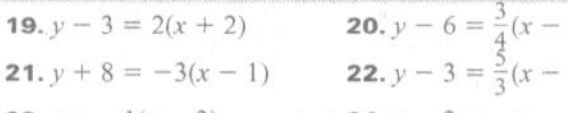
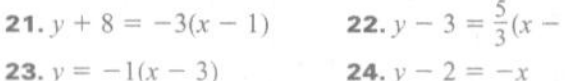
19. $y - 3 = 2(x + 2)$
20. $y - 6 = \frac{3}{4}(x - 4)$
21. $y + 8 = -3(x - 1)$
22. $y - 3 = \frac{5}{3}(x - 1)$
23. $y = -1(x - 3)$
24. $y - 2 = -x$

Write an equation of the line shown.

19. **20.** **21.**
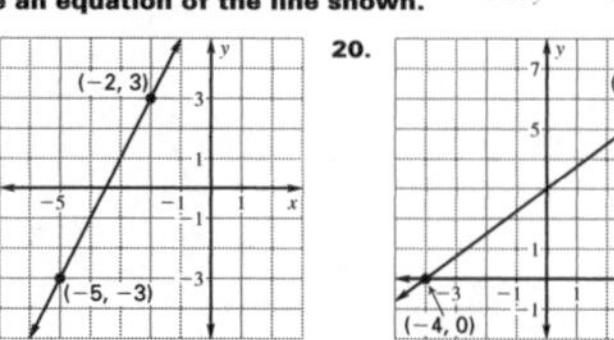
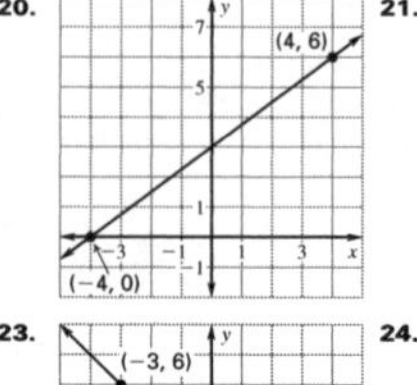

22. **23.** **24.**
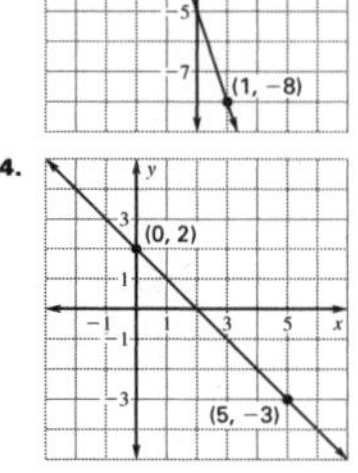

Write an equation of the line that passes through the given points.

25. (9, 4), (17, 6) $y - 4 = \frac{1}{4}(x - 9)$
26. (−3, 10), (4, 2) $y - 2 = -\frac{8}{7}(x - 4)$
27. (3, −8), (7, −2) $y + 8 = \frac{3}{2}(x - 3)$
28. (−4, −4), (2, 5) $y + 4 = \frac{3}{2}(x + 4)$

29. Bryce Canyon National Park From 1990 to 2000, the number of thousand visits by people to Bryce Canyon National Park increased by about 23.9 thousand visits per year. In 2000, there were about 1102.4 thousand visits to the park.

a. Write an equation that gives the number of thousand visits as a function of the number of years since 1990. $y - 1102.4 = 23.9(x - 10)$

b. How many visits were made to the park in 1995? 982.9 thousand visits

30. Airmail Letter Rates The table shows the cost of mailing different weights of airmail letters to Canada.

Weight (oz)	2	3	4	8
Cost (dollars)	0.85	1.10	1.35	2.35

a. *Explain* why the situation can be modeled using a linear equation. The slope between each pair of points is the same.

b. Write an equation that gives the cost (in dollars) as a function of the weight of an airmail letter (in ounces). $y - 0.85 = 0.25(x - 2)$

c. How much does it cost to mail a 5-ounce airmail letter to Canada? $1.60

31. New Mexico The population density of New Mexico increased at a relatively constant rate from 1980 to 1999. In 1985, the population density was about 11.62 people per square mile. In 1999, the population density was about 14.28 people per square mile. Write an equation that gives the population density (in people per square mile) as a function of the number of years since 1980. What was the population density in 1990?
$y - 11.62 = 0.19(x - 5)$; 12.57 people per square mile

LESSON 5.4

Practice B
For use with pages 311–316

Write two equations in standard form that are equivalent to the given equation. 1–6. Answers will vary.

1. $6x + 24y = 18$
2. $8x - 14y = 2$
3. $6x + y = 1$
4. $-4x - 2y = 16$
5. $2x + 3y = 11$
6. $-9x + 4y = 5$

Write an equation in standard form of the line that passes through the given point and has the given slope *m*.

7. $(4, 3), m = 7$ $7x - y = 25$
8. $(5, -1), m = 2$ $2x - y = 11$
9. $(-2, 6), m = 1$ $x - y = -8$
10. $(-7, 8), m = -3$ $3x + y = -13$
11. $(9, -10), m = -4$ $4x + y = 26$
12. $(-15, -4), m = \frac{1}{2}$ $x - 2y = -7$

Write an equation in standard form of the line that passes through the given points.

13. $(2, 6), (3, 8)$ $2x - y = -2$
14. $(-1, 2), (5, 4)$ $x - 3y = -7$
15. $(7, -3), (4, 1)$ $4x + 3y = 19$
16. $(3, -8), (5, -9)$ $x + 2y = -13$
17. $(-5, 6), (2, -3)$ $9x + 7y = -3$
18. $(-3, -1), (6, -8)$ $7x + 9y = -30$

Write equations of the horizontal and the vertical lines that pass through the given point.

19. $(8, 3)$ $x = 8, y = 3$
20. $(-2, 6)$ $x = -2, y = 6$
21. $(5, -5)$ $x = 5, y = -5$

22. **Text Messaging** Your cell phone plan charges you \$.02 to send a text message and \$.07 to receive a text message. You plan to spend no more than \$5 a month on text messaging.
    a. Write an equation in standard form that models the possible combinations of sent text messages and received text messages. $0.02x + 0.07y = 5$
    b. Graph the equation from part (a). *Explain* what the intercepts of the graph mean in this situation. b. x-intercept: the number of messages you can send when no messages are received; y-intercept: the number of messages you can receive when no messages are sent
    c. List three other possible combinations of the number of messages you can send and receive. Answers will vary.

23. **Potting Soil Mix** You are making 24 pounds of your own potting soil mix of sphagnum peat moss and coarse sand. You buy the peat moss in bags that weigh approximately 2 pounds.
    a. Last time you made potting soil, you used 9 bags of sphagnum peat moss and 4 bags of coarse sand. Use this information to find the number of pounds in a bag of coarse sand. 1.5 lb
    b. Write an equation in standard form that models the possible combinations of bags of sphagnum peat moss and coarse sand you can use. $2x + 1.5y = 24$
    c. List three possible combinations of whole bags of sphagnum peat moss and coarse sand you can use to make the potting soil. Answers will vary.

LESSON 5.5

Practice B
For use with pages 319–324

Write an equation of the line that passes through the given point and is parallel to the given line. See below.

1. $(4, 7), y = 5x - 3$
2. $(3, -2), y = \frac{2}{3}x + 1$
3. $(-6, 1), 4x + y = 7$
4. $(-5, -5), 6x - y = 1$
5. $(0, -8), 8x + 4y = 5$
6. $(-9, 11), 5x - 10y = 3$

Write an equation of the line that passes through the given point and is perpendicular to the given line. See below.

7. $(1, -1), y = 3x + 2$
8. $(5, 0), y = \frac{2}{3}x - 4$
9. $(3, -7), y = -\frac{1}{5}x + 1$
10. $(-9, 2), 10x - 5y = 6$
11. $(10, -11), -2x + 5y = 1$
12. $(-4, -8), 8x + 3y = 7$

Determine which of the following lines, if any, are parallel or perpendicular.

13. Line *a*: $y = 8x - 5$, Line *b*: $y = \frac{1}{8}x + 1$, Line *c*: $8x + y = 2$
14. Line *a*: $y = -2x + 5$, Line *b*: $2y - x = 3$, Line *c*: $2x + y = 1$
15. Line *a*: $6x + 2y = 5$, Line *b*: $y = \frac{1}{3}x - 4$, Line *c*: $y = -3x + 5$

13. Lines *b* and *c* are perpendicular. 14. Lines *a* and *b* and lines *b* and *c* are perpendicular. Lines *a* and *c* are parallel. 15. Lines *a* and *b* and lines *b* and *c* are perpendicular. Lines *a* and *c* are parallel.

16. **Kite Design** You are beginning to model a kite design on the coordinate plane, as shown.

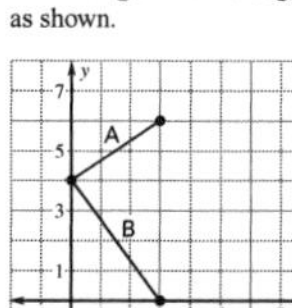

1. $y - 7 = 5(x - 4)$ 2. $y + 2 = \frac{2}{3}(x - 3)$ 3. $y - 1 = -4(x + 6)$ 4. $y + 5 = 6(x + 5)$ 5. $y + 8 = -2x$ 6. $y - 11 = \frac{1}{2}(x + 9)$ 7. $y + 1 = -\frac{1}{3}(x - 1)$ 8. $y = -\frac{3}{2}(x - 5)$ 9. $y + 7 = 5(x - 3)$ 10. $y - 2 = -\frac{1}{2}(x + 9)$ 11. $y + 11 = -\frac{5}{2}(x - 10)$ 12. $y + 8 = \frac{3}{8}(x + 4)$ 17. a. you: $y = \frac{1}{2}x$; your friend: $y = \frac{1}{2}x + 5$

a. Write an equation that models part A of the kite. $y = \frac{2}{3}x + 4$
b. Write an equation that models part B of the kite. $y = -\frac{4}{3}x + 4$
c. Do the kite parts form a right angle? *Justify* your answer. No. The lines for part A and part B are not perpendicular.

17. **Lunch Duty** Everyone at summer camp takes turns being on lunch duty. You and your friend are in charge of making turkey sandwiches. You both can make 1 sandwich in 2 minutes. Your friend arrives 10 minutes earlier and starts making sandwiches.
    a. Write equations that model the number of sandwiches made as a function of the number of minutes it takes you and your friend to each make sandwiches.
    b. How many sandwiches will each of you make in 20 minutes? you: 10 sandwiches; your friend: 15 sandwiches
    c. How are the graphs of the equations from part (a) related? *Justify* your answer. The graphs are parallel; they have the same slope but different y-intercepts.

LESSON 5.6

Practice B
For use with pages 325–331

Tell whether *x* and *y* show a *positive correlation*, a *negative correlation*, or *relatively no correlation*.

1. 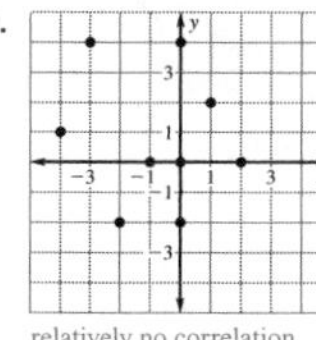
relatively no correlation

2. 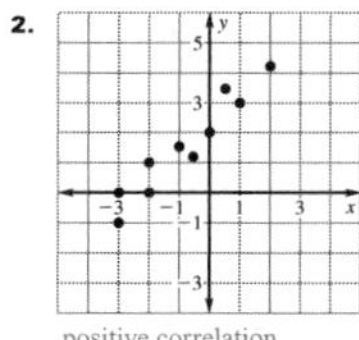
positive correlation

3. 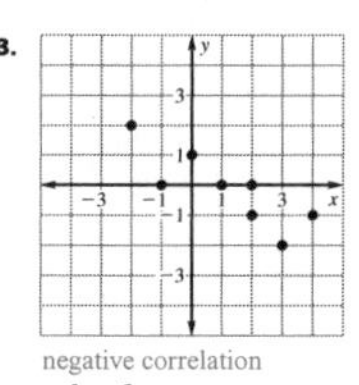
negative correlation

Make a scatter plot of the data. Draw a line of fit. Write an equation for the line.

4.

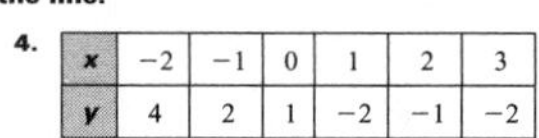
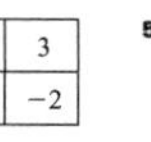

x	−2	−1	0	1	2	3
y	4	2	1	−2	−1	−2

Answers will vary.

5.

x	0	0	0.5	1.5	2	2.5
y	−4	−3	−1.5	1	3	4

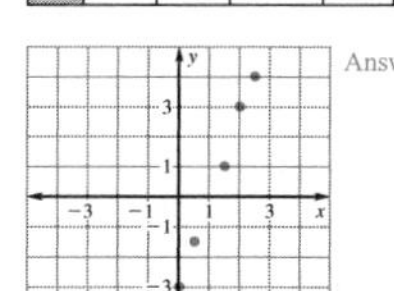
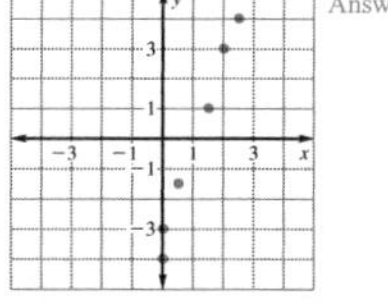
Answers will vary.

6.

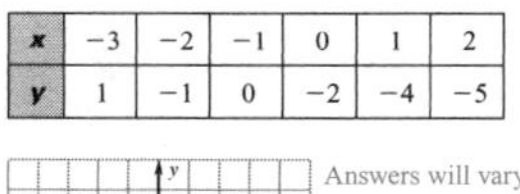

x	−3	−2	−1	0	1	2
y	1	−1	0	−2	−4	−5

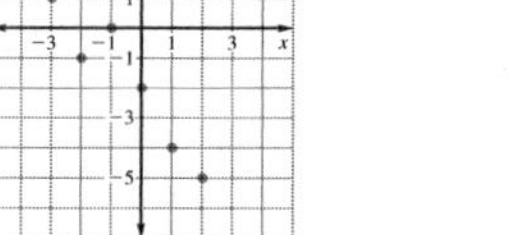
Answers will vary.

7.

x	0	4	3	2	1	0
y	−3	−2	0	−1	1	1

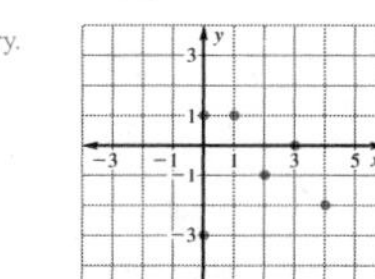
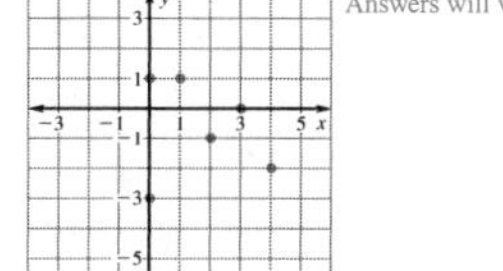
Answers will vary.

LESSON 5.6

Practice B *continued*
For use with pages 325–331

Make a scatter plot of the data. *Describe* the correlation of the data. If possible, fit a line to the data and write an equation of the line.

8.

x	−2	−2	−1	0	1	1	2
y	−4	−3	−2	−1	0	2	1

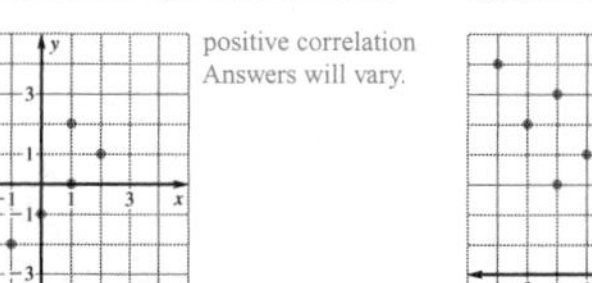
positive correlation
Answers will vary.

9.

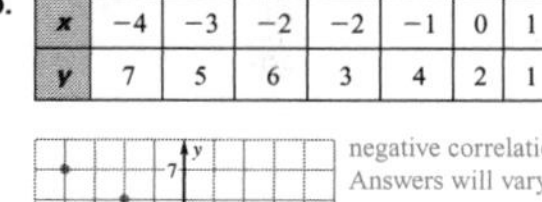

x	−4	−3	−2	−2	−1	0	1
y	7	5	6	3	4	2	1

negative correlation
Answers will vary.

10. **Thermostat** The table shows the thermostat setting (in units called gas marks) on a British gas oven and the corresponding temperature in degrees Celsius.

Setting (gas mark)	2	3	4	5	6	7	8
Temperature (°C)	150	160	180	190	200	220	230

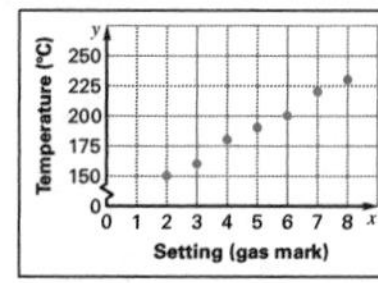

a. Make a scatter plot of the data where *x* represents the thermostat setting (in gas marks) and *y* represents the temperature (in degrees Celsius).
b. *Describe* the correlation of the data. positive correlation
c. An oven set to gas mark 10 heats to a temperature of 260°C. Does this fit the trend shown by your scatter plot? *Explain* your reasoning. Yes; tshe temperature increases as the setting increases.

11. **Fruits** The table shows the amount of energy (in kilocalories) and amount of carbohydrates (in grams) in a 100-gram serving of different fruits.

Fruit	Apple	Banana	Blueberries	Kiwi	Pear	Strawberries	Mango
Energy (kcal)	59	92	56	61	59	30	65
Carbohydrates (g)	15.25	23.43	14.13	14.88	15.11	7.02	17

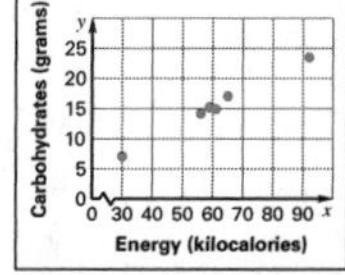

a. Make a scatter plot of the data where *x* represents the energy (in kilocalories) and *y* represents the carbohydrates (in grams).
b. *Describe* the correlation of the data. positive correlation
c. A 100-gram serving of an avocado contains 161 kilocalories of energy and 7.39 grams of carbohydrates. Does an avocado fit the trend shown by your scatter plot? *Explain* your reasoning. No; the number of carbohydrates appears to increase as the number of kilocalories increases.

LESSON 5.7 **Practice B**
For use with pages 335–341

Make a scatter plot of the data. Find the equation of the best-fitting line. Approximate the value of y for $x = 3$.

1.
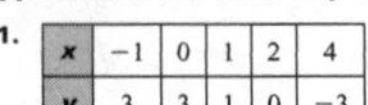

x	−1	0	1	2	4
y	3	3	1	0	−3

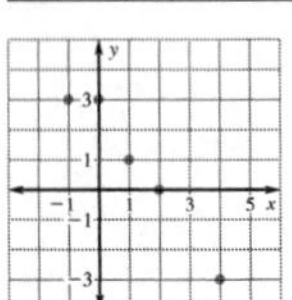
Answers will vary.

2.

x	−1	0	1	2	4
y	−1	1	2	1	5

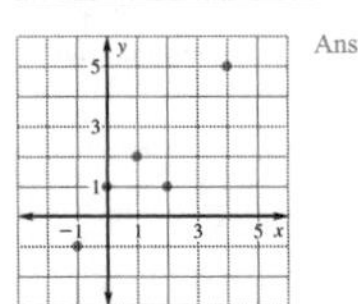
Answers will vary.

Make a scatter plot of the data. Find the equation of the best-fitting line. Approximate the value of y for $x = 5$.

3.
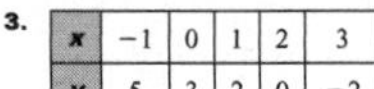

x	−1	0	1	2	3
y	5	3	2	0	−2

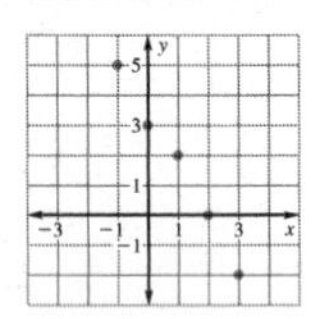
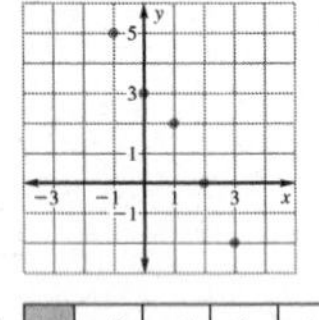
Answers will vary.

4.

x	−5	−3	−1	1	2
y	−4	−2	−1	1	0

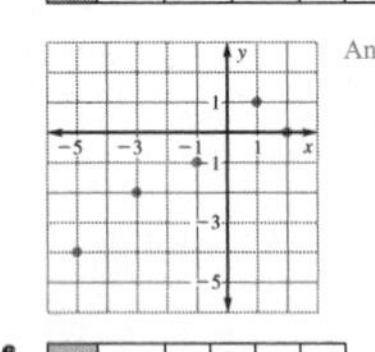
Answers will vary.

5.
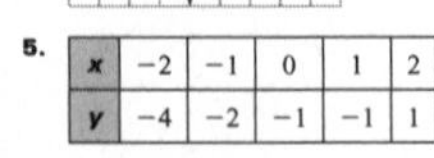

x	−2	−1	0	1	2
y	−4	−2	−1	−1	1

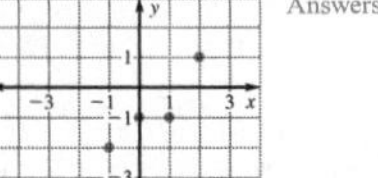
Answers will vary.

6.
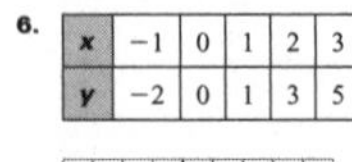

x	−1	0	1	2	3
y	−2	0	1	3	5

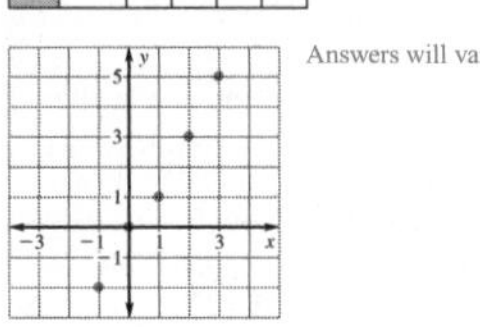
Answers will vary.

LESSON 5.7

LESSON 5.7 **Practice B** *continued*
For use with pages 335–341

Find the zero of the function.

7. $f(x) = 16x - 4$ 0.25
8. $f(x) = 2 - 4x$ 0.5
9. $f(x) = 0.5x + 5$ −10
10. $f(x) = -0.1x - 3$ −30
11. $f(x) = \frac{3}{4}x - 3$ 4
12. $f(x) = -\frac{2}{5}x + 4$ 10
13. $f(x) = 0.25x + 0.5$ −2
14. $f(x) = 9 - 0.7x$ $\frac{90}{7}$
15. $f(x) = 1.2x + 10$ $-\frac{25}{3}$
16. $f(x) = \frac{1}{2}x - 6$ 12
17. $f(x) = -\frac{2}{5}x - 4$ −10
18. $f(x) = -0.8x + 15$ 18.75
19. $f(x) = 1.25x - 5$ 4
20. $f(x) = 6 - 0.2x$ 30
21. $f(x) = 2.5x - 3$ 1.2

22. **Profit** The table shows the monthly profit of a small company.

Month	January	February	March	April	May
Profit (dollars)	1200	1250	1400	1380	1450

a. Make a scatter plot of the data. Let x represent the number of months since January and let y represent the profit.
b. Find an equation that models the profit (in dollars) as a function of the number of months since January. Answers will vary.
c. Approximate the profit in August. Answers will vary.

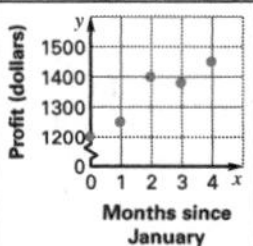

23. **Escape Velocity** The table shows several planet diameters and escape velocities. The escape velocity is the velocity at which an object has to travel in order to escape the effect of a planet's gravity.

Planet	Mercury	Uranus	Earth	Mars	Venus
Diameter (km)	4879	51,118	12,756	6794	12,104
Escape velocity (km/sec)	4.3	21.3	11.186	5.03	10.36

a. Make a scatter plot of the data. Let x represent the diameter of the planet and let y represent the escape velocity.
b. Find an equation that models the escape velocity (in kilometers per second) as a function of the diameter (in kilometers). Answers will vary.
c. Approximate the escape velocity of Neptune, which has a diameter of 49,528 kilometers. Answers will vary.

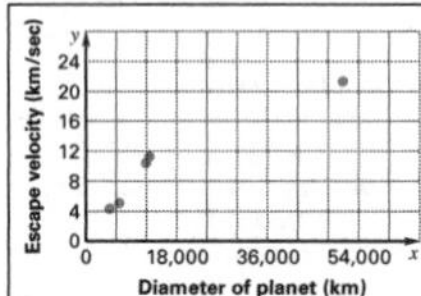

5 Assessment

CHAPTER 5 Quiz 1
For use after Lessons 5.1–5.4

Write an equation in slope-intercept form of the line that passes through the given point and has the given slope m.

1. $(2, 3); m = 2$
2. $(5, -4); m = -1$
3. $(6, 2); m = -\frac{1}{2}$
4. $(-3, -1); m = \frac{4}{5}$

Write an equation in point-slope form of the line that passes through the given points.

5. $(2, -2), (5, 7)$
6. $(6, 4), (2, 1)$

Write an equation in standard form of the line that passes through the given points.

7. $(0, 3), (2, -3)$
8. $(1, -1), (4, 2)$
9. A racquetball club charges \$10 for a one-month trial membership. After the trial month, the regular membership fee is \$12 per month. Write an equation that gives the total cost of a membership C as a function of the length of membership m (in months).
10. Use your equation from Exercise 9 to find the total cost of membership after 8 months.

Answers

1. $y = 2x - 1$
2. $y = -x + 1$
3. $y = -\frac{1}{2}x + 5$
4. $y = \frac{4}{5}x + \frac{7}{5}$
5. $y + 2 = 3(x - 2)$ or $y - 7 = 3(x - 5)$
6. $y - 4 = \frac{3}{4}(x - 6)$ or $y - 1 = \frac{3}{4}(x - 2)$
7. $3x + y = 3$
8. $x - y = 2$
9. $C = 12(m - 1) + 10$
10. \$94

CHAPTER 5 Quiz 2
For use after Lessons 5.5–5.7

Write an equation of the line that passes through the given point and is parallel to the given line.

1. $(1, -2), -5x + y = 9$
2. $(-3, -4), 2y = 4 + 3x$

Write an equation of the line that passes through the given point and is perpendicular to the given line.

3. $(5, -8), y = \frac{5}{2}x + 4$
4. $(2, -3), 6y = -2x + 1$

Determine which of the following lines, if any, are parallel or perpendicular.

5. Line a: $3y + x = 6$, Line b: $y = 3x + 2$, Line c: $3x + y = 0$
6. Line a: $y = -\frac{4}{5}x - 2$, Line b: $y = -\frac{5}{4}x + 7$, Line c: $5y = -4x + 5$

Tell whether x and y show a *positive correlation*, a *negative correlation*, or *relatively no correlation*.

7.

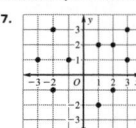

8.

Find the zero of the function.

9. $f(x) = -13x + 52$
10. $f(x) = \frac{1}{6}x - 3$

Answers

1. $y = 5x - 7$
2. $y = \frac{3}{2}x + \frac{1}{2}$
3. $y = -\frac{2}{5}x - 6$
4. $y = 3x - 9$
5. Lines a and b are perpendicular.
6. Lines a and c are parallel.
7. relatively no correlation
8. negative correlation
9. 4
10. 18

CHAPTER 5 Chapter Test B
For use after Chapter 5

Write an equation in slope-intercept form of the line shown.

1. 2.

In Exercises 3 and 4, use the following information.

A delivery service charges a base price for an overnight delivery of a package plus an extra charge for each pound the package weighs. A customer is billed \$22.85 for shipping a 3-pound package and \$40 for shipping a 10-pound package.

3. Write an equation that gives the total cost of shipping a package as a function of the weight of the package.
4. Find the cost of shipping a 15-pound package.

Find the missing coefficient in the equation of the line that passes through the given point.

5. $Ax + y = 3; (2, -5)$
6. $3x + By = -1; (2, 7)$

Graph the equation.

7. $y - 2 = \frac{2}{3}(x - 4)$
8. $y + 4 = -3(x + 2)$

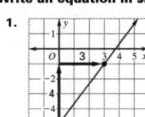

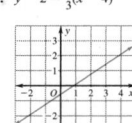

In Exercises 9 and 10, use the table.

x	2	4	6	9	11
y	−3	5	13	25	33

9. Explain why the data can be modeled by a linear equation.
10. Write an equation in point-slope form that relates y to x.

Answers

1. $y = \frac{4}{3}x - 5$
2. $y = -x - 1$
3. $y = 2.45x + 15.50$
4. \$52.25
5. $A = 4$
6. $B = -1$
7. See left.
8. See left.
9. The y-values increase at a constant rate of 4 for each x-value.
10. *Sample answer:* $y + 3 = 4(x - 2)$

CHAPTER 5 Chapter Test B *continued*
For use after Chapter 5

Write an equation in standard form of the line that passes through the given point and has the given slope m or that passes through the given points.

11. $(-4, 3), m = \frac{1}{2}$
12. $(2, -3), m = -4$
13. $(-2, -1), (2, -6)$
14. $(-2, 5), (3, 5)$

In Exercises 15 and 16, use the following information.

A piggy bank contains only nickels and quarters. The total value in the bank is \$3.80.

15. Write an equation in standard form that models the possible combinations of nickels and quarters in the piggy bank.
16. List two of these possible combinations.
17. Write an equation of the line that passes through the point $(-4, -1)$ and is (a) parallel to and (b) perpendicular to the line $2x + 7y = 14$.

In Exercises 18–22, use the table.

Fat (g)	31	39	19	34	43	39	35
Calories	580	680	410	590	660	640	570

18. Make a scatter plot of the data.

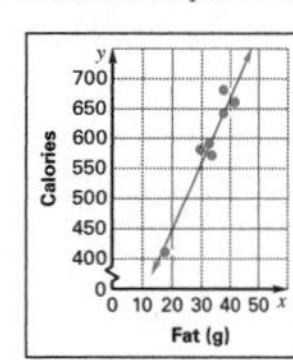
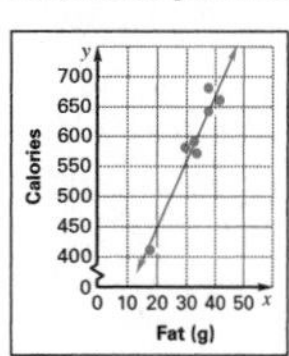

19. Describe the correlation.
20. Use technology to find the equation of the best-fitting line for the data.
21. Graph the best-fitting line for the data on the scatter plot.
22. Predict the number of calories in a hamburger that contains 34 grams of fat.

Answers

11. $y = \frac{1}{2}x + 5$
12. $4x + y = 5$
13. $5x + 4y = -14$
14. $y = 5$
15. $0.05n + 0.25q = 3.80$
16. *Sample answers:* 26 nickels and 10 quarters; 1 nickel and 15 quarters
17. Parallel: $y = -\frac{2}{7}x - \frac{15}{7}$; Perpendicular: $y = \frac{7}{2}x + 13$
18. See left.
19. The scatter plot shows a positive correlation. As the grams of fat increase, the number of calories tends to increase.
20. $y = 11x + 211$
21. See left.
22. 585 calories

CHAPTER 5 Standardized Test
For use after Chapter 5

Multiple Choice

1. Which equation is an equation of the line with a slope of -2 and a y-intercept of 4? D

Ⓐ $y = 4x - 2$ Ⓑ $y = -2x - 4$

Ⓒ $y = 2x - 4$ Ⓓ $y = -2x + 4$

2. Which equation represents the line shown? A

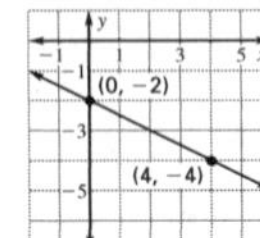

Ⓐ $y = -\frac{1}{2}x - 2$ Ⓑ $y = -2x - 2$

Ⓒ $y = \frac{1}{2}x - 2$ Ⓓ $y = -\frac{1}{2}x + 4$

3. Which function has the values $f(-3) = -11$ and $f(2) = -1$? D

Ⓐ $f(x) = x - 8$ Ⓑ $f(x) = -2x + 3$

Ⓒ $f(x) = \frac{1}{3}x - 10$ Ⓓ $f(x) = 2x - 5$

4. What is the equation of the line that passes through the points $(1, 8)$ and $(-2, -7)$? B

Ⓐ $y = -x + 9$ Ⓑ $y = 5x + 3$

Ⓒ $y = 2x - 3$ Ⓓ $y = \frac{1}{5}x - 5$

5. Which equation is an equation of the line that passes through the point $(2, -1)$ and has a slope of -1? A

Ⓐ $y + 1 = -(x - 2)$

Ⓑ $y - 1 = -(x - 2)$

Ⓒ $y - 1 = -(x + 2)$

Ⓓ $y + 1 = -(x + 2)$

6. Which equation is the point-slope equation of the line that passes through the points $(-2, -1)$ and $(7, -4)$? C

Ⓐ $y + 1 = -3(x + 2)$

Ⓑ $y - 1 = -\frac{1}{3}(x - 2)$

Ⓒ $y + 4 = -\frac{1}{3}(x - 7)$

Ⓓ $y + 4 = \frac{1}{3}(x - 7)$

7. What is the equation of the vertical line that passes through the point $(6, -2)$? C

Ⓐ $y = -2$ Ⓑ $y = 6$

Ⓒ $x = 6$ Ⓓ $x = -2$

8. Which equation is the standard form equation of the line that passes through the point $(-2, 0)$ and has a slope of 4? D

Ⓐ $-4x + y = 2$ Ⓑ $4x - y = 8$

Ⓒ $4x + y = -8$ Ⓓ $-4x + y = 8$

9. The graph of the equation $Ax + 3y = -3$ is a line that passes through $(2, -5)$. What is the value of A? B

Ⓐ 5 Ⓑ 6

Ⓒ 7 Ⓓ 8

10. Which of the following statements is true of the given lines? C

Line a: $2x + y = -4$

Line b: $x + 2y = -10$

Line c: $-2x + 4y = -12$

Ⓐ Lines a and b are parallel.

Ⓑ Lines b and c are parallel.

Ⓒ Lines a and c are perpendicular.

Ⓓ Lines b and c are perpendicular.

CHAPTER 5 Standardized Test *continued*
For use after Chapter 5

11. Which equation represents the line that passes through $(1, 1)$ and is parallel to the line passing through $(2, 3)$ and $(1, 5)$? D

Ⓐ $y = \frac{1}{2}x + 1$ Ⓑ $y = \frac{1}{2}x + 3$

Ⓒ $y = -2x + 1$ Ⓓ $y = -2x + 3$

12. Which equation best models the data in the scatter plot? A

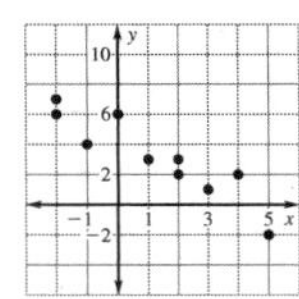

Ⓐ $y = -x + 4$ Ⓑ $y = x + 5$

Ⓒ $y = -5x + 2$ Ⓓ $y = 3x - 2$

13. Given the function $y = -5.2x + 28$, for what value of x does $y = -206$? C

Ⓐ -45 Ⓑ 0

Ⓒ 45 Ⓓ 54

Gridded Answer

14. What is the zero of the function $f(x) = 4x - 5$?

5 / 4

Short Response

15. You pay an activation fee and a monthly fee for cellular phone service. The table shows the total cost of cellular service over different numbers of months.

Months of Service	2	4	6	8	10
Total Cost (dollars)	137	209	281	353	425

a. *Explain* why the situation can be modeled by a linear equation. See below.

b. What is the activation fee? \$65

c. What is the monthly service fee? \$36

Extended Response

16. If you sign up for a gym membership during the month of May, you are charged a joining fee of \$78. Otherwise, you are charged a joining fee of \$155. The monthly membership cost is \$33.32.

a. Write an equation that gives the total cost (in dollars) of membership as a function of the number of months of membership if you join in May.

b. Write an equation that gives the total cost (in dollars) of membership as a function of the number of months of membership if you join in a month other than May. $C = 155 + 33.32m$

c. How are the graphs of these functions related? *Explain.*

d. After 6 months, what is the difference in total cost for a person who paid \$78 to join and a person who paid \$155 to join? After 12 months? *Explain.*

15. a. The situation can be modeled by a linear equation because the monthly fee is constant.
16. a. $C = 78 + 33.32m$ **c.** The graphs are parallel. The slopes of both lines are equal.
d. Regardless of the number of months, the difference will always be \$77. They both pay the same amount each month. The only difference was in their joining fee.

CHAPTER 5

Alternative Assessment and Math Journal

For use after Chapter 5

Journal

1. Explain the process that is used to fit a line to data.

Multi-Step Problem

2. A car wash charges a flat rate for the first 8 minutes of washing time and also charges a certain amount for each additional minute of washing time. Gina took 12 minutes to wash her car and it cost her a total of $5.00. Kris took 17 minutes to wash his truck at a total cost of $6.25.

   a. Write an equation that models the total cost of a car wash as a function of the number of minutes spent washing a vehicle.

   b. How much is the flat rate for the first 8 minutes?

   c. How much is charged for each additional minute of washing time?

   d. It took Jermaine 15 minutes to wash his car. How much did he spend?

   e. Darci has $10 to spend at the car wash. What is the maximum number of minutes she can take to wash her vehicle?

   f. What is the slope of a line parallel to the line in part (a)?

   g. What is the slope of a line perpendicular to the line in part (a)?

1. Complete answers should include mention of: making a scatter plot of the data; deciding if the data can be modeled by a line; sketching a line that follows the trend in the data; determining two points on the line drawn in order to determine the equation of the line.

2. a. $C = 0.25x + 2$ **b.** $4.00 **c.** $.25 **d.** $5.75 **e.** 32 minutes **f.** 0.25 **g.** -4

CHAPTER 5

Alternative Assessment Rubric *continued*

For use after Chapter 5

Journal Solution

1. Complete answers should include mention of:
   - making a scatter plot of the data.
   - deciding if the data can be modeled by a line.
   - sketching a line that follows the trend in the data.
   - determining two points on the line drawn in order to determine the equation of the line.

Multi-Step Problem Solution

2. **a.** $C = 0.25x + 2$
   b. $4.00
   c. $.25
   d. $5.75
   e. 32 minutes
   f. 0.25
   g. -4

Multi-Step Problem Rubric

4 The student answers all parts of the problem correctly and completely. The student shows all work. The student's work is neat.

3 The student answers all parts of the problem. The student's work may contain one or two errors in the calculations or equation. The student shows most work. The student's work is neat.

2 The student answers all parts of the problem, but there are more than two errors in the calculations or equation. The student shows some work. The student's work is sloppy.

1 The student does not complete all parts of the problem. The student's work has several errors in the calculations and equation. The student's work is sloppy, or no work is shown.

PLAN AND PREPARE

Main Ideas

In Chapter 5, students write equations of lines in slope-intercept form given three situations: the slope and y-intercept; the slope and a point; or two points. Also, they write and graph equations using the slope and a point, using a graph of the line, or using real-world data. They write equations of lines in standard form, and use their equations to solve real-world problems. They write and find equations of lines parallel or perpendicular to a given line. They make scatter plots of data and use a line of fit to model and interpret the data. They perform linear regression to find the best-fitting line for data, and make predictions using the graph and the equation.

Prerequisite Skills

- Evaluating functions
- Finding the slope of lines
- Finding the y-intercept of lines

Additional resources for reviewing prerequisite skills are:

- Skills Review Handbook, pp. 909–937
- @HomeTutor

5 Writing Linear Equations

Before

In previous chapters, you learned the following skills, which you'll use in Chapter 5: evaluating functions and finding the slopes and y-intercepts of lines.

Prerequisite Skills

VOCABULARY CHECK

Copy and complete the statement.

1. In the equation $y = mx + b$, the value of m is the _?_ of the graph of the equation. slope
2. In the equation $y = mx + b$, the value of b is the _?_ of the graph of the equation. y-intercept
3. Two lines are _?_ if their slopes are equal. parallel

SKILLS CHECK

Find the slope of the line that passes through the points.
(Review p. 235 for 5.1–5.6.)

4. $(4, 5), (2, 3)$ 1
5. $(0, -6), (8, 0)$ $\frac{3}{4}$
6. $(0, 0), (-1, 2)$ -2

Identify the slope and the y-intercept of the line with the equation.
(Review p. 244 for 5.1–5.6.)

7. $y = x + 1$ 1, 1
8. $y = \frac{3}{4}x - 6$ $\frac{3}{4}, -6$
9. $y = -\frac{2}{5}x - 2$ $-\frac{2}{5}, -2$

Evaluate the function when $x = -2, 0,$ and 4. *(Review p. 262 for 5.7.)*

10. $f(x) = x - 10$ $-12, -10, -6$
11. $f(x) = 2x + 4$ $0, 4, 12$
12. $f(x) = -5x - 7$ $3, -7, -27$

@HomeTutor Prerequisite skills practice at classzone.com

280

Chapter Planning Guide

Chapter 5 Resource Book
- Teaching Guide/Lesson Plan (pp. 3, 14, 24, 38, 50, 60, 74)
- Project with Rubric (p. 90)

Assessment and Intervention
- Assessment Book (pp. 61–74)
- Benchmark Tests
- Reteaching and Remediation Book

Interactive Technology
- Easy Planner
- Power Presentations CD-ROM
- Activity Generator CD-ROM
- Animated Algebra
- Test Generator CD-ROM
- Online Quizzes
- eWorkbook
- eEdition
- @HomeTutor

Resources for English Learners
- Quick Reference for English Learners
- Spanish Study Guide
- Multi-Language Visual Glossary
- Student Resources in Spanish

Now

In Chapter 5, you will apply the big ideas listed below and reviewed in the Chapter Summary on page 344. You will also use the key vocabulary listed below.

Big Ideas

1. **Writing linear equations in a variety of forms**
2. **Using linear models to solve problems**
3. **Modeling data with a line of fit**

KEY VOCABULARY

- point-slope form, *p. 302*
- converse, *p. 319*
- perpendicular, *p. 320*
- scatter plot, *p. 325*
- correlation, *p. 325*
- line of fit, *p. 326*
- best-fitting line, *p. 335*
- linear regression, *p. 335*
- interpolation, *p. 335*
- extrapolation, *p. 336*
- zero of a function, *p. 337*

Why?

You can use linear equations to solve problems involving a constant rate of change. For example, you can write an equation that models how traffic delays affected excess fuel consumption over time.

Animated Algebra

The animation illustrated below for Exercise 40 on p. 307 helps you to answer the question: In what year was a certain amount of excess fuel consumed?

Find the year in which the given amount of excess fuel was consumed.

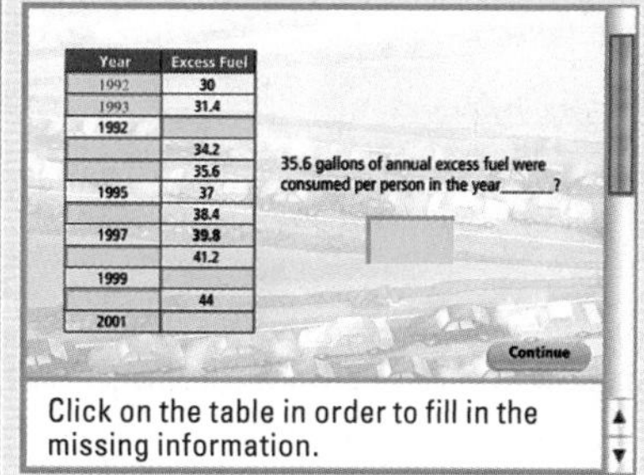

Click on the table in order to fill in the missing information.

Animated Algebra at classzone.com

Other animations for Chapter 5: pages 283, 303, 307, 311, 322, 327, and 335

Algebra 1 Toolkit

- Reading Strategies for Chapter 5, pp. 17–18
- Differentiated Instruction Notes, pp. 57–60
- English Learners Notes, pp. 105–106
- Inclusion Notes, pp. 137–138
- Teaching Strategies with Sample Worksheets, pp. 155–178
- Using Technology in the Classroom, pp. 179–184
- Tips for New Teachers, pp. 193–194
- Math Background Notes, pp. 219–220
- Pre-AP Strategies and Copymasters, pp. 286–287, 360–366
- Teacher Survival Activities, pp. 563–564, 589–590
- Bulletin Board Idea, p. 611
- Teacher Tool Transparencies, following p. 620

1 PLAN AND PREPARE

Explore the Concept

- Students model a linear relationship using the perimeter formula.
- This activity leads into the study of writing linear equations in slope-intercept form in Example 5 in Lesson 5.1.

Materials

Each student or pair of students will need:

- 8.5 by 11-inch sheet of paper
- inch ruler

Recommended Time

Work activity: 10 min

Discuss results: 5 min

Grouping

Students can work individually or in pairs. If students work in pairs, one can measure and fold the paper and the other can find the paper's perimeter and record the data.

2 TEACH

Key Questions

- What are the independent and dependent variables? **Width of fold; perimeter**
- What is the starting value of the perimeter? **39 in.**
- What happens to the perimeter as the width of the fold increases by one inch? **It decreases by 2 inches.**

Key Discovery

Use a constant rate of change and a starting value to describe a linear relationship.

3 ASSESS AND RETEACH

How do you find the perimeter if the fold is 8 inches? **Multiply 8 by −2 and add 39 to get 23 inches.**

5.1 Modeling Linear Relationships

MATERIALS • 8.5 inch by 11 inch piece of paper • inch ruler

QUESTION How can you model a linear relationship?

You know that the perimeter of a rectangle is given by the formula $P = 2\ell + 2w$. In this activity, you will find a linear relationship using that formula.

EXPLORE Find perimeters of rectangles

Width of fold (inches)	Perimeter of rectangle (inches)
0	39
1	?
2	?
3	?
4	?

STEP 1 ***Find perimeter***
Find the perimeter of a piece of paper that is 8.5 inches wide and 11 inches long. Record the result in a table like the one shown.

STEP 2 ***Change paper size***
Measure 1 inch from a short edge of the paper. Fold over 1 inch of the paper. You now have a rectangle with the same width and a different length than the original piece of paper. Find the perimeter of this new rectangle and record it in your table.

STEP 3 ***Find additional perimeters***
Unfold the paper and repeat Step 2, this time folding the paper 2 inches from a short edge. Find the perimeter of this rectangle and record the result in your table. Repeat with a fold of 3 inches and a fold of 4 inches.

DRAW CONCLUSIONS Use your observations to complete these exercises

1. What were the length and the width of the piece of paper before it was folded? By how much did these dimensions change with each fold? **11 in., 8.5 in.; length: reduced by 1 in., width: did not change**
2. What was the perimeter of the piece of paper before it was folded? By how much did the perimeter change with each fold? **39 in.; reduced by 2 in.**
3. Use the values from your table to predict the perimeter of the piece of paper after a fold of 5 inches. *Explain* your reasoning. **29 in.; with each 1 inch fold, the perimeter is reduced by 2 inches.**
4. Write a rule you could use to find the perimeter of the piece of paper after a fold of n inches. Use the data in the table to show that this rule gives accurate results. **$39 - 2n$; $39 - (2)(1) = 37$; $39 - (2)(2) = 35$; $39 - (2)(3) = 33$; $39 - (2)(4) = 31$**

5.1 Write Linear Equations in Slope-Intercept Form

 **8.11.07** Identify an equation of a line or an equation of a line of best fit from given information . . .

Before You graphed equations of lines.
Now You will write equations of lines.
Why? So you can model distances in sports, as in Ex. 52.

Key Vocabulary
- *y*-intercept, *p. 225*
- slope, *p. 235*
- slope-intercept form, *p. 244*

Recall that the graph of an equation in slope-intercept form, $y = mx + b$, is a line with a slope of m and a y-intercept of b. You can use this form to write an equation of a line if you know its slope and y-intercept.

EXAMPLE 1 Use slope and *y*-intercept to write an equation

Write an equation of the line with a slope of −2 and a *y*-intercept of 5.

$y = mx + b$ Write slope-intercept form.

$y = -2x + 5$ Substitute −2 for *m* and 5 for *b*.

EXAMPLE 2 Standardized Test Practice

ELIMINATE CHOICES
In Example 2, you can eliminate choices C and D because the *y*-intercepts of the graphs of these equations are not 3.

Which equation represents the line shown?

(A) $y = -\frac{2}{5}x + 3$ (B) $y = -\frac{5}{2}x + 3$

(C) $y = -\frac{2}{5}x + 1$ (D) $y = 3x + \frac{2}{5}$

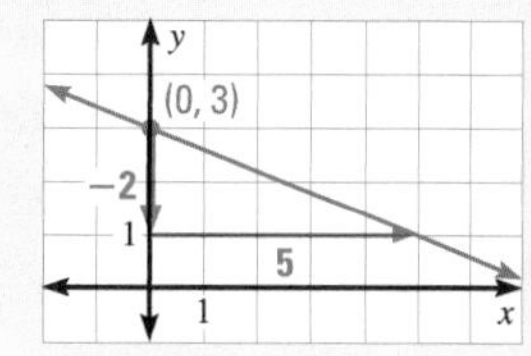

The slope of the line is $\frac{\text{rise}}{\text{run}} = \frac{-2}{5} = -\frac{2}{5}$.

The line crosses the y-axis at (0, 3). So, the y-intercept is 3.

$y = mx + b$ Write slope-intercept form.

$y = -\frac{2}{5}x + 3$ Substitute $-\frac{2}{5}$ for *m* and 3 for *b*.

▶ The correct answer is A. (A) (B) (C) (D)

 Animated Algebra at classzone.com

GUIDED PRACTICE for Examples 1 and 2

Write an equation of the line with the given slope and *y*-intercept.

1. Slope is 8; *y*-intercept is −7. $y = 8x - 7$

2. Slope is $\frac{3}{4}$; *y*-intercept is −3. $y = \frac{3}{4}x - 3$

1 PLAN AND PREPARE

Warm-Up Exercises
Transparency Available

Find the slope of the line that passes through the points.

1. (2, −1), (4, 0) $\frac{1}{2}$
2. (−1, −3), (1, 5) 4
3. A landscape architect charges $75 for a consulting fee and $30 per hour. Write an equation that shows the cost *C* as a function of time *t* (in hours). $C = 30t + 75$

Notetaking Guide
Transparency Available

Promotes interactive learning and notetaking skills, pp. 100–102.

Pacing
Basic: 1 day
Average: 1 day
Advanced: 1 day
Block: 0.5 block with 5.2
- See *Teaching Guide/Lesson Plan.*

2 FOCUS AND MOTIVATE

Essential Question
Big Idea 1, p. 281

How do you write an equation of a line in slope-intercept form? Tell students they will learn how to answer this question by using the slope and *y*-intercept or two points to write an equation of the line.

Resource Planning Guide

Chapter Resource Book
- Teaching Guide/Lesson Plan (pp. 3–4)
- Activity Master (p. 5)
- Practice levels A, B, C (pp. 6–8)
- Study Guide (pp. 9–10)
- Catch-up for Absent Students (p. 11)
- Application (p. 12)
- Challenge (p. 13)

Workbooks
- Notetaking Guide (pp. 100–102)
- Practice Workbook (pp. 67–68)

Teaching Options
- **Power Presentations CD-ROM** provides dynamic electronic teaching resources for the classroom.
- **Activity Generator CD-ROM** provides editable activities for all ability levels.

Interactive Technology
- Easy Planner
- Power Presentations CD-ROM
- Activity Generator CD-ROM
- Animated Algebra
- Test Generator CD-ROM
- Online Quiz
- eWorkbook
- eEdition
- @HomeTutor

Resources for English Learners
- Quick Reference for English Learners
- Spanish Study Guide
- Multi-Language Visual Glossary
- Student Resources in Spanish

See also the *Algebra 1 Toolkit* for more strategies for meeting individual needs.

Motivating the Lesson

Your family has a monthly long distance telephone plan that charges \$3.99 plus \$.05 per minute. If you know how to write an equation that models the plan, and you know the number of minutes you talked on the phone, you can find what you owe on the monthly bill.

3 TEACH

Extra Example 1

Write an equation of the line with a slope of 4 and a y-intercept of -3.
$y = 4x - 3$

Extra Example 2

Which equation represents the line shown? **B**

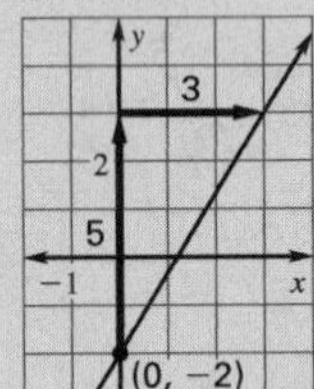

Ⓐ $y = \frac{3}{5}x - 2$

Ⓑ $y = \frac{5}{3}x - 2$

Ⓒ $y = -2x + \frac{3}{5}$

Ⓓ $-2x + \frac{5}{3}$

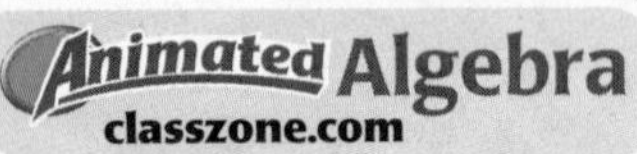

An **Animated Algebra** activity is available on-line for **Example 2**. This activity is also available on the **Power Presentations CD-ROM**.

Extra Example 3

Write an equation of the line shown.

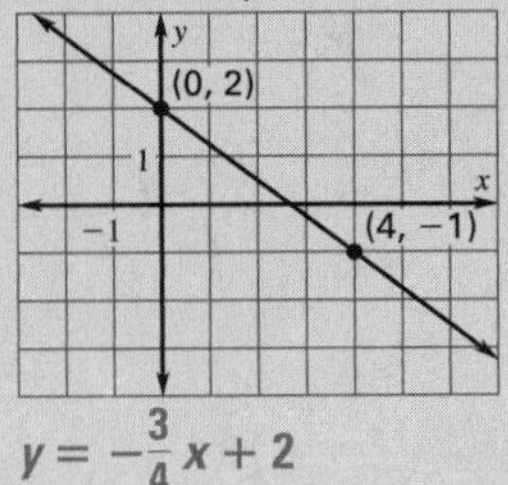

$y = -\frac{3}{4}x + 2$

USING TWO POINTS If you know the point where a line crosses the y-axis and any other point on the line, you can write an equation of the line.

EXAMPLE 3 Write an equation of a line given two points

Write an equation of the line shown.

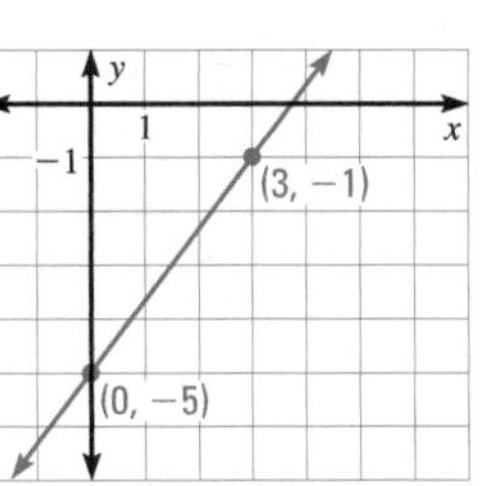

Solution

STEP 1 **Calculate** the slope.

$$m = \frac{y_2 - y_1}{x_2 - x_1} = \frac{-1 - (-5)}{3 - 0} = \frac{4}{3}$$

STEP 2 **Write** an equation of the line. The line crosses the y-axis at $(0, -5)$. So, the y-intercept is -5.

$y = mx + b$ **Write slope-intercept form.**

$y = \frac{4}{3}x - 5$ **Substitute $\frac{4}{3}$ for m and -5 for b.**

WRITING FUNCTIONS Recall that the graphs of linear functions are lines. You can use slope-intercept form to write a linear function.

EXAMPLE 4 Write a linear function

REVIEW FUNCTIONS
For help with using function notation, see p. 262.

Write an equation for the linear function f with the values $f(0) = 5$ and $f(4) = 17$.

Solution

STEP 1 **Write** $f(0) = 5$ as $(0, 5)$ and $f(4) = 17$ as $(4, 17)$.

STEP 2 **Calculate** the slope of the line that passes through $(0, 5)$ and $(4, 17)$.

$$m = \frac{y_2 - y_1}{x_2 - x_1} = \frac{17 - 5}{4 - 0} = \frac{12}{4} = 3$$

STEP 3 **Write** an equation of the line. The line crosses the y-axis at $(0, 5)$. So, the y-intercept is 5.

$y = mx + b$ **Write slope-intercept form.**

$y = 3x + 5$ **Substitute 3 for m and 5 for b.**

▶ The function is $f(x) = 3x + 5$.

✓ GUIDED PRACTICE for Examples 3 and 4

3. Write an equation of the line shown. $y = -\frac{1}{2}x + 1$

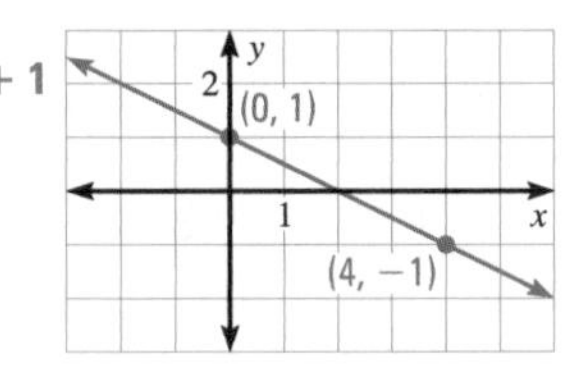

Write an equation for the linear function f with the given values.

4. $f(0) = -2, f(8) = 4$ $y = \frac{3}{4}x - 2$

5. $f(-3) = 6, f(0) = 5$ $y = -\frac{1}{3}x + 5$

READING
The value b is a starting value in a real-world situation modeled by $y = mx + b$, because when $x = 0$, the value of y is b.

MODELING REAL-WORLD SITUATIONS When a quantity y changes at a constant rate with respect to a quantity x, you can use the equation $y = mx + b$ to model the relationship. The value of m is the constant rate of change, and the value of b is an initial, or starting, value for y.

EXAMPLE 5 Solve a multi-step problem

RECORDING STUDIO A recording studio charges musicians an initial fee of \$50 to record an album. Studio time costs an additional \$35 per hour.

a. Write an equation that gives the total cost of an album as a function of studio time (in hours).

b. Find the total cost of recording an album that takes 10 hours of studio time.

Solution

a. The cost changes at a constant rate, so you can write an equation in slope-intercept form to model the total cost.

STEP 1 **Identify** the rate of change and the starting value.

Rate of change, m: cost per hour
Starting value, b: initial fee

STEP 2 **Write** a verbal model. Then write the equation.

Total cost (dollars)	=	Cost per hour (dollars per hour)	•	Studio time (hours)	+	Initial fee (dollars)
C	=	35	•	t	+	50

CHECK Use unit analysis to check the equation.

$$\text{dollars} = \frac{\text{dollars}}{\cancel{\text{hour}}} \cdot \cancel{\text{hours}} + \text{dollars} \checkmark$$

▶ The total cost C is given by the function $C = 35t + 50$ where t is the studio time (in hours).

b. Evaluate the function for $t = 10$.

$C = 35(10) + 50 = 400$ **Substitute 10 for t and simplify.**

▶ The total cost for 10 hours of studio time is \$400.

✓ GUIDED PRACTICE for Example 5

6. **WHAT IF?** In Example 5, suppose the recording studio raises its initial fee to \$75 and charges \$40 per hour for studio time.

a. Write an equation that gives the total cost of an album as a function of studio time (in hours). $C = 40t + 75$

b. Find the total cost of recording an album that takes 10 hours of studio time. \$475

Extra Example 4

Write an equation for the linear function f with the values $f(0) = 3$ and $f(-4) = 11$. $f(x) = -2x + 3$

Key Question to Ask for Example 4

- How does $f(4) = 17$ correspond to the ordered pair (x, y)? Writing the function as $f(x) = y$ and comparing that to $f(4) = 17$, the value of x is 4 and the value of y is 17.

Extra Example 5

A dance academy charges \$20 to use the facility and \$25 per hour of instruction.

a. Write an equation that gives the total cost to learn dance at the academy as a function of hours of instruction. The total cost C is given by $C = 25t + 20$, where t is time in hours.

b. Find the total cost of 2 hours of dance instruction. \$70

Closing the Lesson

Have students summarize the major points of the lesson and answer the Essential Question: How do you write an equation of a line in slope-intercept form?

- An equation in slope-intercept form, $y = mx + b$, has slope m and y-intercept b.
- Given two points on a graph, one of which gives the y-intercept, you can find the slope m and the y-intercept b and substitute those values into $y = mx + b$.
- You can write a function in slope-intercept form given values of $f(0)$, x, and $f(x)$.

To write an equation in slope-intercept form, substitute the slope for m and the y-intercept for b in the equation $y = mx + b$. In real-world situations, use the constant rate of change for m and the starting value for b.

Differentiated Instruction

Inclusion Students may have difficulty working with equations when the variables are not x and y. To graph the equation in **Example 5**, have students write the following two equations.

$C = 35t + 50$

$y = 35x + 50$

Because t matches up with x and C matches up with y, it is easy to explain why t is plotted on the x-axis and C is plotted on the y-axis. See also the *Algebra 1 Toolkit* for more strategies.

4 PRACTICE AND APPLY

Assignment Guide

Answer Transparencies available for all exercises

Basic:
Day 1: EP p. 941 Exs. 33–36
pp. 286–289
Exs. 1–5, 9–12, 16–20, 24–26, 30–32, 39, 40, 45–49, 53–63 odd

Average:
Day 1: pp. 286–289
Exs. 1, 2, 6–9, 13–17, 21–24, 26, 28, 33–35, 39–43, 46–51, 56, 57, 62, 63

Advanced:
Day 1: pp. 286–289
Exs. 1, 7–9, 13–15, 21–23, 27–29, 36–44*, 47–52*, 58, 64

Block:
pp. 286–289
Exs. 1, 2, 6–9, 13–17, 21–24, 26, 28, 33–35, 39–43, 46–51, 56, 57, 62, 63 (with 5.2)

Differentiated Instruction

See *Algebra 1 Best Practices Toolkit* for suggestions on addressing the needs of a diverse classroom.

Homework Check

For a quick check of student understanding of key concepts, go over the following exercises:

Basic: 4, 10, 20, 32, 45
Average: 6, 13, 26, 34, 46
Advanced: 8, 14, 28, 38, 48

Extra Practice

- Student Edition, p. 942
- Chapter 5 Resource Book: Practice levels A, B, C, pp. 6–8

Practice Worksheet

An easily-readable reduced practice page (with answers) for this lesson can be found on p. 280C.

5.1 EXERCISES

HOMEWORK KEY
○ = **WORKED-OUT SOLUTIONS** on p. WS10 for Exs. 11, 19, and 47
★ = **STANDARDIZED TEST PRACTICE** Exs. 2, 9, 40, 43, 48, and 50
◆ = **MULTIPLE REPRESENTATIONS** Ex. 49

SKILL PRACTICE

A

1. **VOCABULARY** Copy and complete: The ratio of the rise to the run between any two points on a nonvertical line is called the _?_. slope

2. ★ **WRITING** *Explain* how you can use slope-intercept form to write an equation of a line given its slope and y-intercept. You can substitute the slope for m and the y-intercept for b to get the equation of the line.

EXAMPLE 1 on p. 283 for Exs. 3–9, 16

WRITING EQUATIONS Write an equation of the line with the given slope and y-intercept.

3. slope: 2, y-intercept: 9 — $y = 2x + 9$
4. slope: 1, y-intercept: 5 — $y = x + 5$
5. slope: −3, y-intercept: 0 — $y = -3x$
6. slope: −7, y-intercept: 1 — $y = -7x + 1$
7. slope: $\frac{2}{3}$, y-intercept: −9 — $y = \frac{2}{3}x - 9$
8. slope: $\frac{3}{4}$, y-intercept: −6 — $y = \frac{3}{4}x - 6$

9. ★ **MULTIPLE CHOICE** Which equation represents the line with a slope of −1 and a y-intercept of 2? A

Ⓐ $y = -x + 2$ Ⓑ $y = 2x - 1$ Ⓒ $y = x - 2$ Ⓓ $y = 2x + 1$

EXAMPLE 2 on p. 283 for Exs. 10–15

WRITING EQUATIONS Write an equation of the line shown.

10. 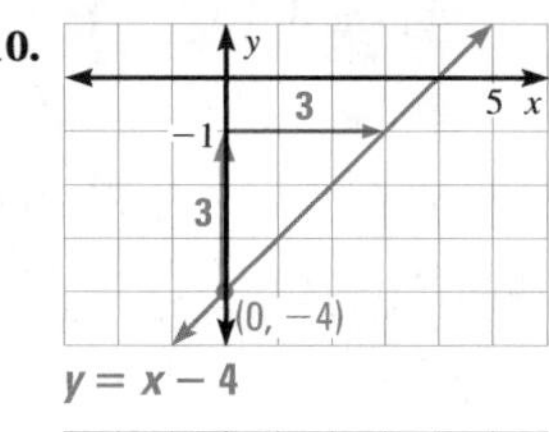

$y = x - 4$

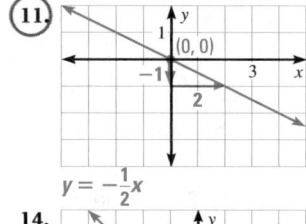

11. $y = -\frac{1}{2}x$

12. 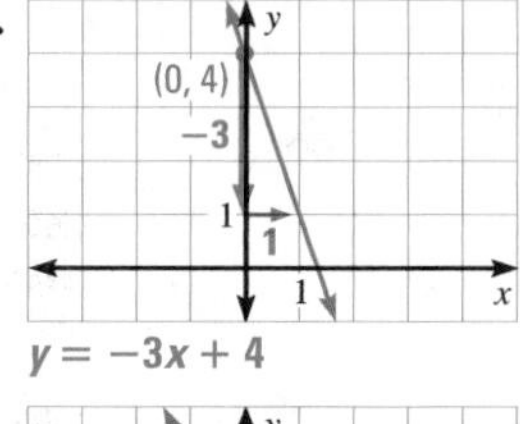

$y = -3x + 4$

13. 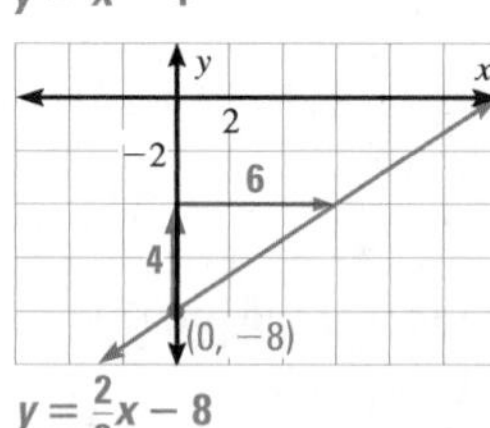

$y = \frac{2}{3}x - 8$

14. 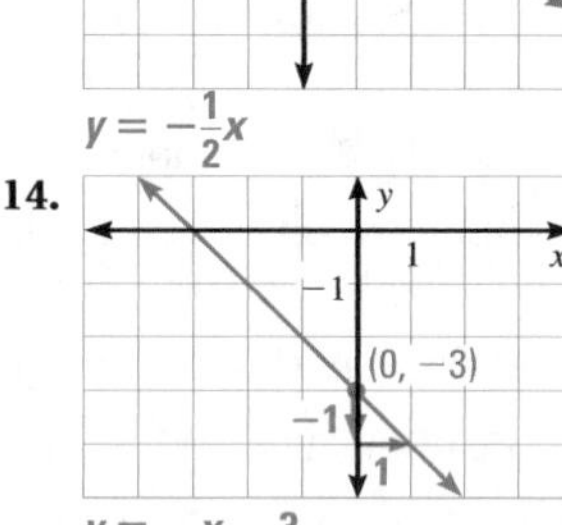

$y = -x - 3$

15. 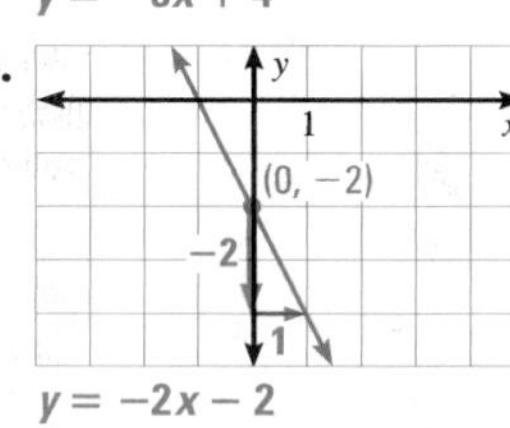

$y = -2x - 2$

16. **ERROR ANALYSIS** *Describe* and correct the error in writing an equation of the line with a slope of 2 and a y-intercept of 7.

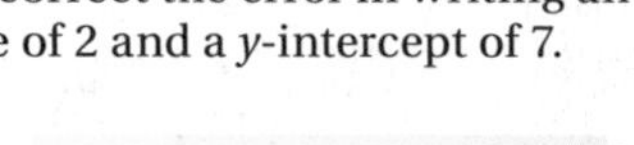

16. The given slope and y-intercept were interchanged in the slope-intercept form of the equation; $y = 2x + 7$.

EXAMPLE 3 on p. 284 for Exs. 17–29

17. **ERROR ANALYSIS** *Describe* and correct the error in writing an equation of the line shown.

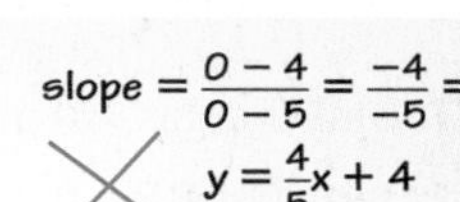

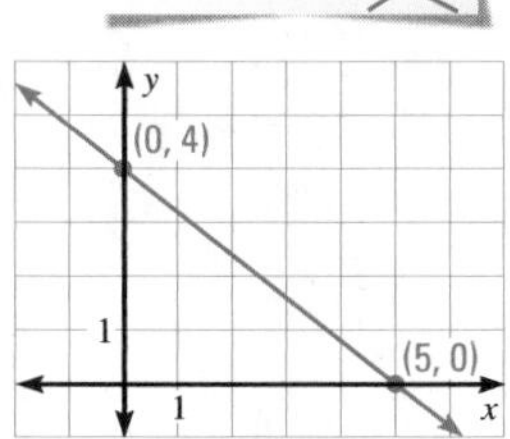

The slope should be $\frac{0-4}{5-0}$, $y = -\frac{4}{5}x + 4$.

USING A GRAPH **Write an equation of the line shown.**

18.

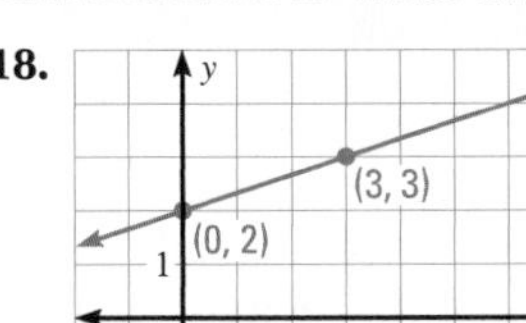

$y = \frac{1}{3}x + 2$

19.

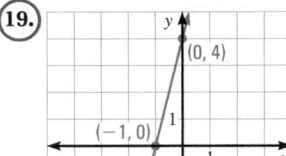

$y = 4x + 4$

20.

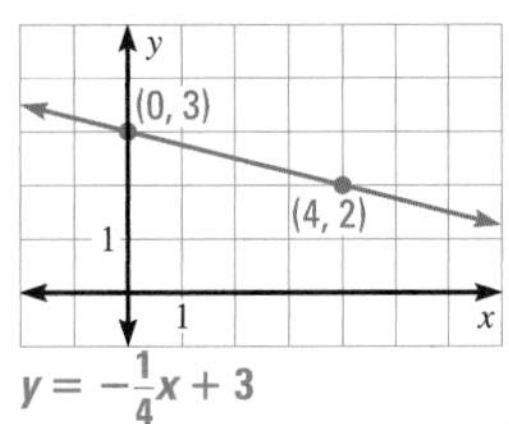

$y = -\frac{1}{4}x + 3$

21.

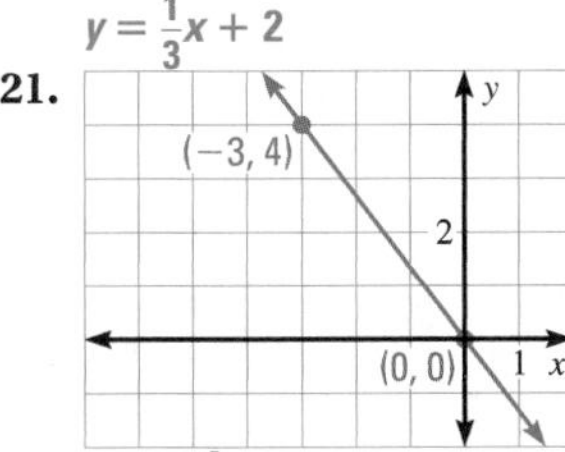

$y = -\frac{4}{3}x$

22.

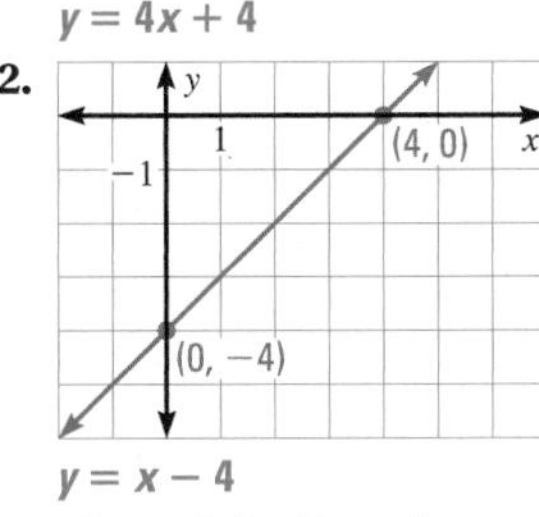

$y = x - 4$

23.

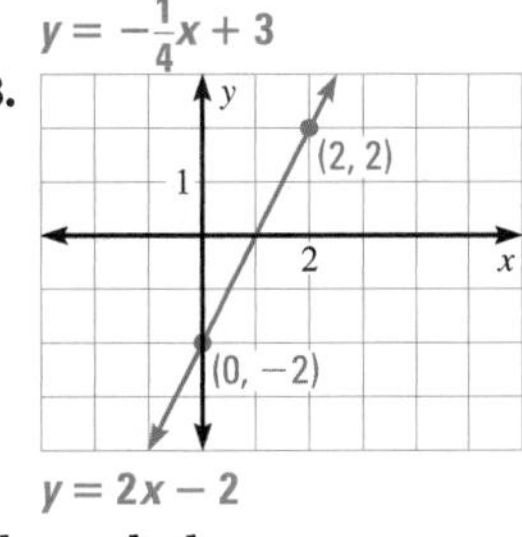

$y = 2x - 2$

USING TWO POINTS **Write an equation of the line that passes through the given points.**

24. $(-3, 1), (0, -8)$ $y = -3x - 8$

25. $(2, -7), (0, -5)$ $y = -x - 5$

26. $(2, -4), (0, -4)$ $y = -4$

27. $(0, 4), (8, 3.5)$ $y = -0.0625x + 4$

28. $(0, 5), (1.5, 1)$ $y = -\frac{8}{3}x + 5$

29. $(-6, 0), (0, -24)$ $y = -4x - 24$

EXAMPLE 4 on p. 284 for Exs. 30–38

WRITING FUNCTIONS **Write an equation for the linear function *f* with the given values.**

30. $f(0) = 2, f(2) = 4$ $y = x + 2$

31. $f(0) = 7, f(3) = 1$ $y = -2x + 7$

32. $f(0) = -2, f(4) = -3$ $y = -\frac{1}{4}x - 2$

33. $f(0) = -1, f(5) = -5$ $y = -\frac{4}{5}x - 1$

34. $f(-2) = 6, f(0) = -4$ $y = -5x - 4$

35. $f(-6) = -1, f(0) = 3$ $y = \frac{2}{3}x + 3$

36. $f(4) = 13, f(0) = 21$ $y = -2x + 21$

37. $f(0) = 9, f(3) = 0$ $y = -3x + 9$

38. $f(0.2) = 1, f(0) = 0.6$ $y = 2x + 0.6$

B **39.** **VISUAL THINKING** Write an equation of the line with a slope that is half the slope of the line shown and a *y*-intercept that is 2 less than the *y*-intercept of the line shown. $y = x - 3$

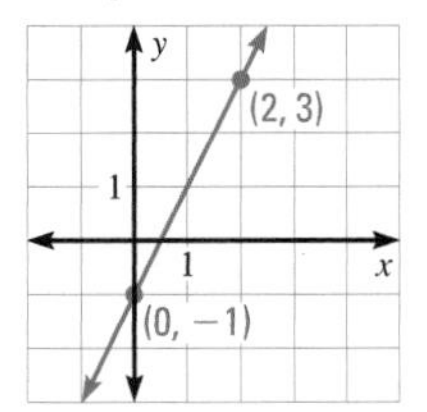

40. ★ **OPEN-ENDED** *Describe* a real-world situation that can be modeled by the function $y = 4x + 9$.

40. *Sample answer:* A health club offers an aerobics membership that charges \$9 plus \$4 per class.

USING A DIAGRAM OR TABLE **Write an equation that represents the linear function shown in the mapping diagram or table.**

41. $y = -2x + 1$

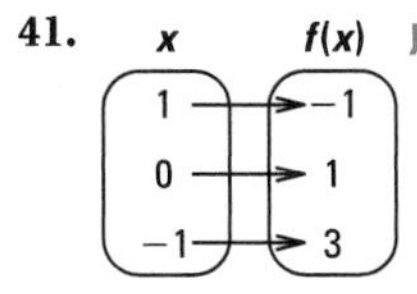

42. $y = \frac{1}{2}x$

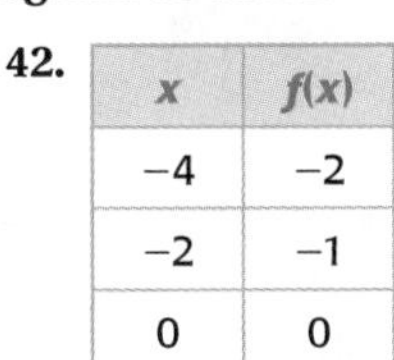

x	$f(x)$
−4	−2
−2	−1
0	0

43. ★ **WRITING** A line passes through the points (3, 5) and (3, −7). Is it possible to write an equation of the line in slope-intercept form? *Justify* your answer. **No; the slope of the line is undefined, the equation is $x = 3$, which is not in slope-intercept form.**

C **44.** **CHALLENGE** Show that the equation of the line that passes through the points $(0, b)$ and $(1, b + m)$ is $y = mx + b$. *Explain* how you can be sure that the point $(-1, b - m)$ also lies on the line. See margin.

Avoiding Common Errors

Exercises 3–9 Students sometimes interchange the slope and the *y*-intercept when replacing *m* and *b* in the slope-intercept form of an equation of the line. Suggest that students double-check that *m* is the slope and *b* is the *y*-intercept in their equations.

Teaching Strategy

Exercises 10–15 Prior to these exercises, you may want to review how to use the ratio of rise to run to determine slope. In discussing the ratio, you might want to point out that a ratio of 4 to 4, for example, is 1, whereas a ratio of 4 to 1 is 4.

Study Strategy

Exercises 18–23 Tell students they can use the ratio of rise to run to check their slope calculations.

Reading Strategy

Exercises 30–38 Remind students that $f(x)$ is read "the value of *f* at *x*." When *x* in the parentheses is replaced by a number such as 3, it can be read "the value of *f* when *x* is 3."

44. Find the slope by substituting the values: $\frac{b + m - b}{1 - 0} = m$. The *y*-intercept is when $x = 0$, so the *y*-intercept is *b*. If you substitute $(-1, b - m)$ into the equation $y = mx + b$, you get $b - m = -m + b$ which is a true statement.

Reading Strategy

Exercise 49 Remind students to read instructions carefully. Point out in part a that *x* is the number of years since 1970. Tell them that this affects whether they use 0 or 1 to designate 1970 and, in turn, affects the numbers they use to designate subsequent years.

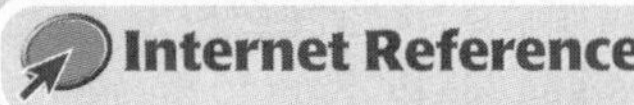

Exercise 49 For more information about Mt. Kilimanjaro and its glaciers, visit nationalgeographic.com and do a search for "Mt. Kilimanjaro AND glaciers."

Mathematical Reasoning

Exercises 50–51 You may want to discuss with students how an equation of the form $y = mx + b$ can model these situations. Ask them to identify the independent and dependent variables, the values for *m*, and the values for *b*. The starting values of *b* may give students problems in both of these exercises. Point out that, depending on the context, a starting value may require calculation.

49a.

x (years since 1970)	y (km²)
0	5.2
10	4.1
20	3.0
30	1.9

49b.

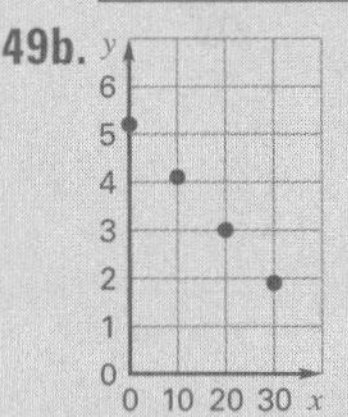

PROBLEM SOLVING

EXAMPLE 5 A on p. 285 for Exs. 45–49

45. WEB SERVER The initial fee to have a website set up using a server is \$48. It costs \$44 per month to maintain the website.

a. Write an equation that gives the total cost of setting up and maintaining a website as a function of the number of months it is maintained. $C = 44m + 48$

b. Find the total cost of setting up and maintaining the website for 6 months. \$312

@HomeTutor for problem solving help at classzone.com

46. PHOTOGRAPHS A camera shop charges \$3.99 for an enlargement of a photograph. Enlargements can be delivered for a charge of \$1.49 per order. Write an equation that gives the total cost of an order with delivery as a function of the number of enlargements. Find the total cost of ordering 8 photograph enlargements with delivery. $C = 3.99e + 1.49$; \$33.41

@HomeTutor for problem solving help at classzone.com

47. AQUARIUM Your family spends \$30 for tickets to an aquarium and \$3 per hour for parking. Write an equation that gives the total cost of your family's visit to the aquarium as a function of the number of hours that you are there. Find the total cost of 4 hours at the aquarium. $C = 3h + 30$; \$42

48. ★ SHORT RESPONSE Scientists found that the number of ant species in Clark Canyon, Nevada, increases at a rate of 0.0037 species per meter of elevation. There are approximately 3 ant species at sea level.

a. Write an equation that gives the number of ant species as a function of the elevation (in meters). $a = 0.0037e + 3$

b. Identify the dependent and independent variables in this situation. dependent variable: *a*, independent variable: *e*

c. *Explain* how you can use the equation from part (a) to approximate the number of ant species at an elevation of 2 meters. Substitute 2 for *e* to get approximately 3.

B **49. ◆ MULTIPLE REPRESENTATIONS** The timeline shows the approximate total area of glaciers on Mount Kilimanjaro from 1970 to 2000.

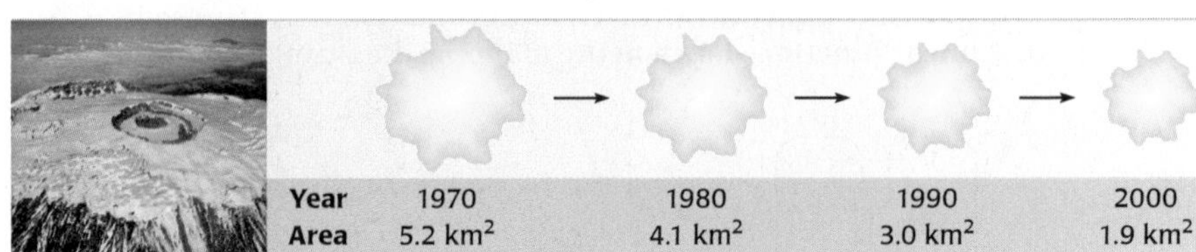

Year	1970	1980	1990	2000
Area	5.2 km²	4.1 km²	3.0 km²	1.9 km²

a. **Making a Table** Make a table that shows the number of years *x* since 1970 and the area of the glaciers *y* (in square kilometers). See margin.

b. **Drawing a Graph** Graph the data in the table. *Explain* how you know the area of glaciers changed at a constant rate. See margin for art; the area of the glaciers changed −1.1 square kilometers between every 10 year interval.

c. **Writing an Equation** Write an equation that models the area of glaciers as a function of the number of years since 1970. By how much did the area of the glaciers decrease each year from 1970 to 2000? $y = -0.11x + 5.2$; -0.11 km²

○ = WORKED-OUT SOLUTIONS on p. WS1 ★ = STANDARDIZED TEST PRACTICE ◆ = MULTIPLE REPRESENTATIONS

50. ★ **EXTENDED RESPONSE** The Harris Dam in Maine releases water into the Kennebec River. From 10:00 A.M. to 1:00 P.M. during each day of whitewater rafting season, water is released at a greater rate than usual.

Time interval	Release rate (gallons per hour)
12:00 A.M. to 10:00 A.M.	8.1 million
10:00 A.M. to 1:00 P.M.	130 million

a. On a day during rafting season, how much water is released by 10:00 A.M.? 81 million gal

b. Write an equation that gives, for a day during rafting season, the total amount of water (in gallons) released as a function of the number of hours since 10:00 A.M. $y = 130{,}000{,}000h$

c. What is the domain of the function from part (b)? *Explain.*
$0 \le h \le 3$; water is only released for 3 hours after 10:00 A.M.

51. FIREFIGHTING The diagram shows the time a firefighting aircraft takes to scoop water from a lake, fly to a fire, and drop the water on the fire.

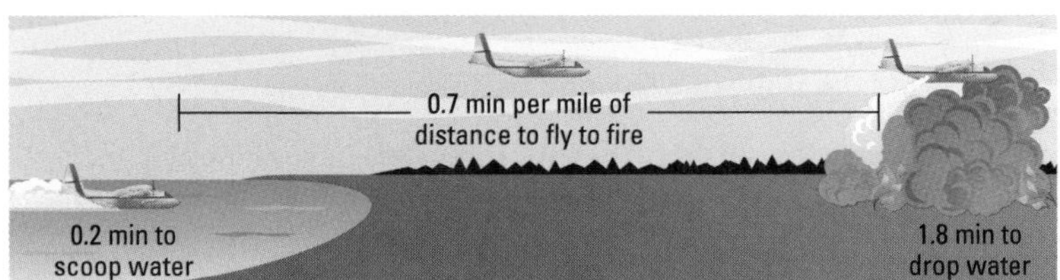

a. Model Write an equation that gives the total time (in minutes) that the aircraft takes to scoop, fly, and drop as a function of the distance (in miles) flown from the lake to the fire. $t = 0.7d + 2$

b. Predict Find the time the aircraft takes to scoop, fly, and drop if it travels 20 miles from the lake to the fire. 16 min

C **52. CHALLENGE** The elevation at which a baseball game is played affects the distance a ball travels when hit. For every increase of 1000 feet in elevation, the ball travels about 7 feet farther. Suppose a baseball travels 400 feet when hit in a ball park at sea level.

a. Model Write an equation that gives the distance (in feet) the baseball travels as a function of the elevation of the ball park in which it is hit. $d = \frac{7}{1000}e + 400$

b. Justify *Justify* the equation from part (a) using unit analysis. $d \text{ ft} = \frac{7}{1000} \cdot e \text{ ft} + 400 \text{ ft}$

c. Predict If the ball were hit in exactly the same way at a park with an elevation of 3500 feet, how far would it travel? 424.5 ft

ILLINOIS MIXED REVIEW

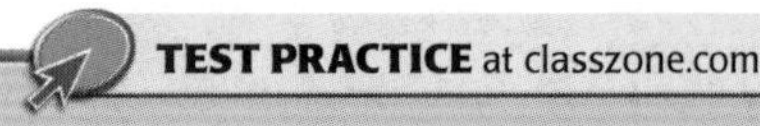

TEST PRACTICE at classzone.com

53. Which function includes the data set {(−4, 6), (−2, 2) (0, −2)}? B

Ⓐ $y = -2x$ Ⓑ $y = -2x - 2$ Ⓒ $y = -\frac{x}{2}$ Ⓓ $y = 2x - 2$

54. If the length of a rectangle doubles and its width triples, by what factor does the rectangle's area increase? C

Ⓐ 2.5 Ⓑ 5 Ⓒ 6 Ⓓ 8

5 ASSESS AND RETEACH

Daily Homework Quiz

Transparency Available

1. Write an equation of the line with a slope of −4 and a y-intercept of 1. $y = -4x + 1$

Write an equation of the line that passes through the given points.

2. (−9, 1), (0, −8) $y = -x - 8$

3. (−4, −6), (0, 6) $y = 3x + 6$

4. Write an equation for the linear function f with $f(0) = -4$ and $f(-1) = -9$. $y = 5x - 4$

5. An electronics game store sells used games for $12.99 with a $20 membership fee. Write an equation that gives the total cost to become a member and buy games as a function of the number of games that are purchased. Then find the cost for 6 games. $C = 12.99g + 20$ where C is total cost and g is the number of games; $97.94

Online Quiz

Available at **classzone.com**

Diagnosis/Remediation

- Practice A, B, C in Chapter 5 Resource Book, pp. 6–8
- Study Guide in Chapter 5 Resource Book, pp. 9–10
- Practice Workbook, pp. 67–68
- @HomeTutor

Challenge

Additional challenge is available in the Chapter 5 Resource Book, p. 13.

1 PLAN AND PREPARE

Learn the Method

- Students will find the slope and the y-intercept of a line using a graphing calculator and then write an equation of the line.
- After the activity, students can use a graphing calculator to check their solutions in Exercises 24–38 in Lesson 5.1.

Keystroke Help

Keystrokes for several models of calculators are available in blackline format in the *Chapter 5 Resource Book*.

2 TEACH

Tips for Success

In Example 1, remind students that a line with a positive slope rises from left to right and a line with a negative slope falls from left to right.

Extra Example 1

In the same viewing window, display the four lines that have slopes of −2, −1, 1, and 2 and a y-intercept of −3. Then use the graphs to determine which line passes through the point (1, −4). Write an equation of the line.

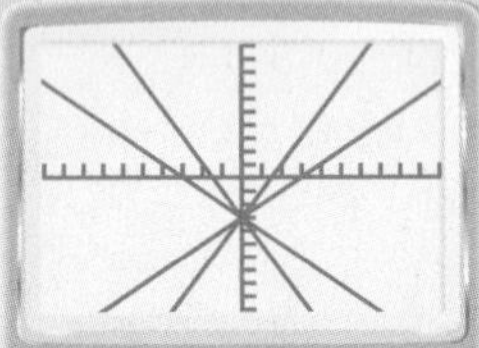

The line that passes through the point (1, −4) is the line with a slope of −1. An equation of the line is $y = -x - 3$.

5.1 Investigate Families of Lines

QUESTION How can you use a graphing calculator to find equations of lines using slopes and y-intercepts?

Recall from Chapter 4 that you can create families of lines by varying the value of either m or b in $y = mx + b$. The constants m and b are called *parameters*. Given the value of one parameter, you can determine the value of the other parameter if you also have information that uniquely identifies one member of the family of lines.

EXAMPLE 1 Find the slope of a line and write an equation

In the same viewing window, display the four lines that have slopes of −1, −0.5, 0.5, and 1 and a y-intercept of 2. Then use the graphs to determine which line passes through the point (12, 8). Write an equation of the line.

STEP 1 ***Enter equations***

Press Y= and enter the four equations. Because the lines all have the same y-intercept, they constitute a family of lines and can be entered as shown.

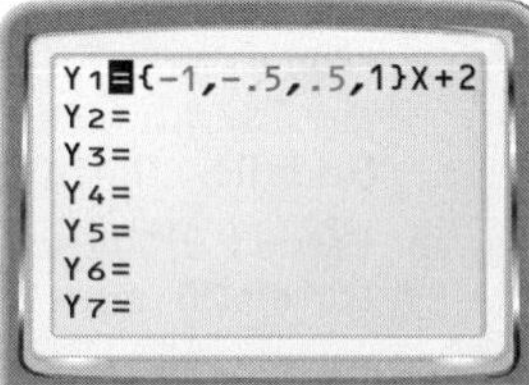

STEP 2 ***Display graphs***

Graph the equations in an appropriate viewing window. Press TRACE and use the left and right arrow keys to move along one of the lines until $x = 12$. Use the up and down arrow keys to see which line passes through (12, 8).

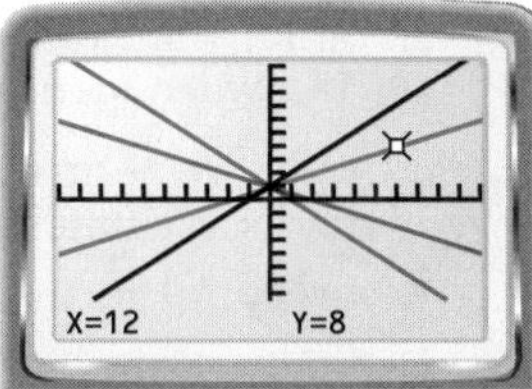

STEP 3 ***Find the line***

The line that passes through (12, 8) is the line with a slope of 0.5. So, an equation of the line is $y = 0.5x + 2$.

PRACTICE

Display the lines that have the same y-intercept but different slopes, as given, in the same viewing window. Determine which line passes through the given point. Write an equation of the line.

1. Slopes: −3, −2, 2, 3; y-intercept: 5; point: (−3, 11) $y = -2x + 5$
2. Slopes: 4, −2.5, 2.5, 4; y-intercept: −1; point: (4, −11) $y = -2.5x - 1$
3. Slopes: −2, −1, 1, 2; y-intercept: 1.5; point: (1, 3.5) $y = 2x + 1.5$

@HomeTutor
classzone.com
Keystrokes

EXAMPLE 2 Find the y-intercept of a line and write an equation

In the same viewing window, display the five lines that have a slope of 0.5 and y-intercepts of −2, −1, 0, 1, and 2. Then use the graphs to determine which line passes through the point (−2, −2). Write an equation of the line.

STEP 1 ***Enter equations***

Press Y= and enter the five equations. Because the lines all have the same slope, they constitute a family of lines and can be entered as shown below.

```
Y1=.5X+{-2,-1,0,1,2}
Y2=
Y3=
Y4=
Y5=
Y6=
Y7=
```

STEP 2 ***Display graphs***

Graph the equations in an appropriate viewing window. Press TRACE and use the left and right arrow keys to move along one of the lines until $x = -2$. Use the up and down arrow keys to see which line passes through (−2, −2).

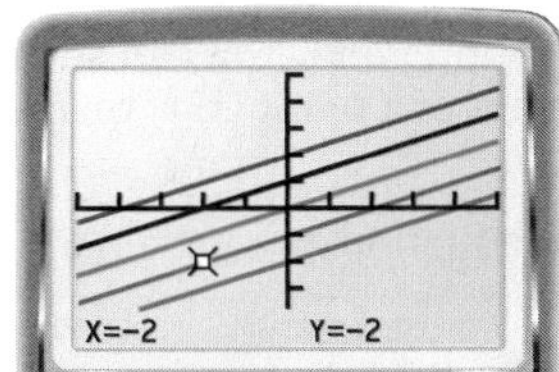

STEP 3 ***Find the line***

The line that passes through (−2, −2) is the line with a y-intercept of −1. So, an equation of the line is $y = 0.5x - 1$.

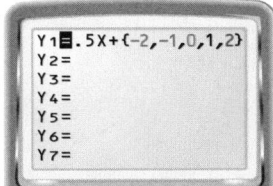

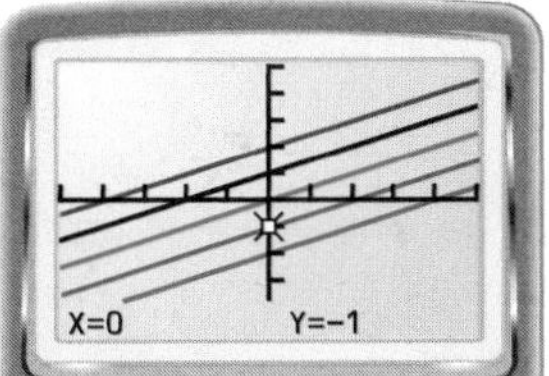

PRACTICE

Display the lines that have the same slope but different y-intercepts, as given, in the same viewing window. Determine which line passes through the given point. Write an equation of the line.

4. Slope: −3; y-intercepts: −2, −1, 0, 1, 2; point: (4, −13) $y = -3x - 1$
5. Slope: 1.5; y-intercepts: −2, −1, 0, 1, 2; point: (−2, −1) $y = 1.5x + 2$
6. Slope: −0.5; y-intercepts: −3, −1.5, 0, 1.5, 3; point: (−4, 3.5) $y = -0.5x + 1.5$
7. Slope: 4; y-intercepts: −3, −1, 0, 1, 3; point: (2, 5) $y = 4x - 3$
8. Slope: 2; y-intercepts: −6, −3, 0, 3, 6; point: (−2, −7) $y = 2x - 3$

DRAW CONCLUSIONS

9. Of all the lines having equations of the form $y = 0.5x + b$, which one passes through the point (2, 2)? *Explain* how you found your answer. $y = 0.5x + 1$; substitute 2 for x, 2 for y, and solve for b.
10. *Describe* a process you could use to find an equation of a line that has a slope of −0.25 and passes through the point (8, −2). *Sample answer:* Substitute −0.25 for m, 8 for x, and −2 for y and solve for b.

Extra Example 2

In the same viewing window, display the five lines that have a slope of −2 and y-intercepts of −4, −2, 0, 2, and 4. Then use the graphs to determine which line passes through the point (−1, 2). Write an equation of the line.

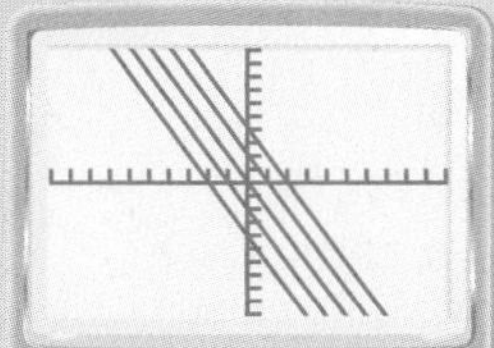

The line that passes through the point (−1, 2) is the line with a y-intercept of 0. An equation of the line is $y = -2x$.

3 ASSESS AND RETEACH

1. Describe a process you could use to find an equation of a line that has a y-intercept of 1 and passes through the point (2, 4). In the same viewing window, display graphs through (0, 1) with several slopes, such as 0.5, 1, 1.5, and 2. Then use trace to find the line that passes through (2, 4).
2. Of all the lines having equations of the form $y = mx - 2$, which one passes through the point (3, 4)? Explain how you found your answer. An equation of the line is $y = 2x - 2$. I first tried $y = x - 2$. That line passes through (3, 1), so in order to pass through (3, 4) I needed a greater slope. I graphed equations of lines through (0, −2) with slopes of 1.5, 2, and 2.5. I used trace to find that a line with a slope of 2 passes through (3, 4).

1 PLAN AND PREPARE

Warm-Up Exercises

Transparency Available

Find the slope of the line that passes through the points.

1. (0, −2), (1, 3) 5
2. (3, 2), (5, −2) −2
3. Bill borrowed \$75 from his parents. He is paying back \$5 per week. Write an equation that models this situation. $y = -5x + 75$

Notetaking Guide

Transparency Available

Promotes interactive learning and notetaking skills, pp. 103–105.

Pacing

Basic: 2 days
Average: 2 days
Advanced: 2 days
Block: 0.5 block with 5.1
0.5 block with 5.3

• See *Teaching Guide/Lesson Plan.*

2 FOCUS AND MOTIVATE

Essential Question

Big Idea 2, p. 281

How do you find the equation of a line given two points? Tell students they will learn how to answer this question by using the slope formula and finding the *y*-intercept.

5.2 Use Linear Equations in Slope-Intercept Form

8.11.07 Identify an equation of a line or an equation of a line of best fit from given information . . .

Before You wrote an equation of a line using its slope and *y*-intercept.
Now You will write an equation of a line using points on the line.
Why So you can write a model for total cost, as in Example 5.

Key Vocabulary
• ***y*-intercept,** *p. 225*
• **slope,** *p. 235*
• **slope-intercept form,** *p. 244*

KEY CONCEPT *For Your Notebook*

Writing an Equation of a Line in Slope-Intercept Form

STEP 1 **Identify** the slope m. You can use the slope formula to calculate the slope if you know two points on the line.

STEP 2 **Find** the y-intercept. You can substitute the slope and the coordinates of a point (x, y) on the line in $y = mx + b$. Then solve for b.

STEP 3 **Write** an equation using $y = mx + b$.

EXAMPLE 1 Write an equation given the slope and a point

Write an equation of the line that passes through the point (−1, 3) and has a slope of −4.

Solution

STEP 1 **Identify** the slope. The slope is −4.

STEP 2 **Find** the y-intercept. Substitute the slope and the coordinates of the given point in $y = mx + b$. Solve for b.

$y = mx + b$ Write slope-intercept form.

$3 = -4(-1) + b$ Substitute −4 for m, −1 for x, and 3 for y.

$-1 = b$ Solve for b.

AVOID ERRORS
When you substitute, be careful not to mix up the *x*- and *y*-values.

STEP 3 **Write** an equation of the line.

$y = mx + b$ Write slope-intercept form.

$y = -4x - 1$ Substitute −4 for m and −1 for b.

✓ **GUIDED PRACTICE** for Example 1

1. Write an equation of the line that passes through the point (6, 3) and has a slope of 2. $y = 2x - 9$

Resource Planning Guide

Chapter Resource Book
• Teaching Guide/Lesson Plan (pp. 14–15)
• Practice levels A, B, C (pp. 16–18)
• Study Guide (pp. 19–20)
• Catch-up for Absent Students (p. 21)
• Application (p. 22)
• Challenge (p. 23)

Workbooks
• Notetaking Guide (pp. 103–105)
• Practice Workbook (pp. 69–70)

Teaching Options
• **Power Presentations CD-ROM** provides dynamic electronic teaching resources for the classroom.
• **Activity Generator CD-ROM** provides editable activities for all ability levels.

Interactive Technology
• Easy Planner
• Power Presentations CD-ROM
• Activity Generator CD-ROM
• Animated Algebra
• Test Generator CD-ROM
• Online Quiz
• eWorkbook
• eEdition
• @HomeTutor

Resources for English Learners
• Quick Reference for English Learners
• Spanish Study Guide
• Multi-Language Visual Glossary
• Student Resources in Spanish

See also the *Algebra 1 Toolkit* for more strategies for meeting individual needs.

EXAMPLE 2 Write an equation given two points

Write an equation of the line that passes through (−2, 5) and (2, −1).

Solution

STEP 1 **Calculate** the slope.

$$m = \frac{y_2 - y_1}{x_2 - x_1} = \frac{-1 - 5}{2 - (-2)} = \frac{-6}{4} = -\frac{3}{2}$$

ANOTHER WAY
You can also find the y-intercept using the coordinates of the other given point, (2, −1):
$y = mx + b$
$-1 = -\frac{3}{2}(2) + b$
$2 = b$

STEP 2 **Find** the y-intercept. Use the slope and the point (−2, 5).

$y = mx + b$	**Write slope-intercept form.**
$5 = -\frac{3}{2}(-2) + b$	**Substitute $-\frac{3}{2}$ for m, −2 for x, and 5 for y.**
$2 = b$	**Solve for b.**

STEP 3 **Write** an equation of the line.

$y = mx + b$	**Write slope-intercept form.**
$y = -\frac{3}{2}x + 2$	**Substitute $-\frac{3}{2}$ for m and 2 for b.**

EXAMPLE 3 Standardized Test Practice

Which function has the values $f(4) = 9$ and $f(-4) = -7$?

Ⓐ $f(x) = 2x + 10$ Ⓑ $f(x) = 2x + 1$

Ⓒ $f(x) = 2x - 13$ Ⓓ $f(x) = 2x - 14$

ELIMINATE CHOICES
You can also evaluate each function when $x = 4$ and $x = -4$. Eliminate any choices for which $f(4) \neq 9$ or $f(-4) \neq -7$.

STEP 1 **Calculate** the slope. Write $f(4) = 9$ as (4, 9) and $f(-4) = -7$ as (−4, −7).

$$m = \frac{y_2 - y_1}{x_2 - x_1} = \frac{-7 - 9}{-4 - 4} = \frac{-16}{-8} = 2$$

STEP 2 **Find** the y-intercept. Use the slope and the point (4, 9).

$y = mx + b$	**Write slope-intercept form.**
$9 = 2(4) + b$	**Substitute 2 for m, 4 for x, and 9 for y.**
$1 = b$	**Solve for b.**

STEP 3 **Write** an equation for the function. Use function notation.

$f(x) = 2x + 1$	**Substitute 2 for m and 1 for b.**

▶ The answer is B. Ⓐ Ⓑ Ⓒ Ⓓ

✓ GUIDED PRACTICE for Examples 2 and 3

2. Write an equation of the line that passes through (1, −2) and (−5, 4). $y = -x - 1$
3. Write an equation for the linear function with the values $f(-2) = 10$ and $f(4) = -2$. $y = -2x + 6$

Motivating the Lesson

Knowing how to write a linear equation that represents a real-world situation will help you determine information about the situation. For example, if you know that one person paid $135 for a ski club membership and 5 ski lessons and another person paid $183 for membership and 9 lessons, you could determine the membership fee and the cost per ski lesson.

3 TEACH

Extra Example 1

Write an equation of the line that passes through the point (6, 3) and has a slope of −2. $y = -2x + 15$

Extra Example 2

Write an equation of the line that passes through (3, 0) and (2, −4). $y = 4x - 12$

Key Questions to Ask for Example 2

- How is Example 2 different from Example 1? **In Example 1 you are given the slope and in Example 2 you have to use the two points to calculate the slope.**
- What values do you need from the graph of a line to write an equation of the line in slope-intercept form? **You need the coordinates of two points to calculate the slope and to determine the y-intercept.**

Extra Example 3

Which function has the values $f(2) = 8$ and $f(-2) = -4$? A

Ⓐ $f(x) = 3x + 2$
Ⓑ $f(x) = 3x + 14$
Ⓒ $f(x) = 3x - 10$
Ⓓ $f(x) = 3x - 12$

Extra Example 4

A carnival charges \$2.50 per ride after an entrance fee. You paid a total of \$22.50 after 6 rides. Write an equation that gives the total cost as a function of the number of rides. Find the total cost for 15 rides.
$C = 2.5n + 7.5$, where C is the total cost and n is the number of rides. The total cost for 15 rides is \$45.

Key Questions to Ask for Example 4

- In a graph of the situation, which values would you graph on the x-and y-axes? **Graph the independent variable, t, time in months, on the x-axis, and the dependent variable, C, total cost, on the y-axis.**
- What would be the coordinates of the y-intercept in a graph of the equation? **(0, 30)**
- Which are two other points that the graph of the equation would pass through? **(1, 63), (9, 327)**
- What do the points (x, y) on the graph represent? **The points represent the total cost y after x months.**

CONCEPT SUMMARY *For Your Notebook*

How to Write Equations in Slope-Intercept Form

Given slope m and y-intercept b

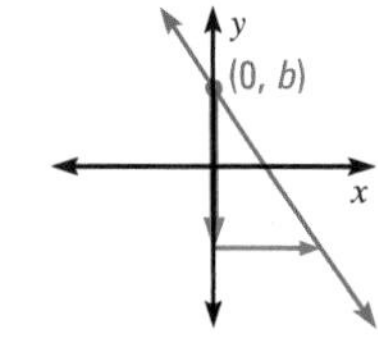

Substitute m and b in the equation $y = mx + b$.

Given slope m and one point

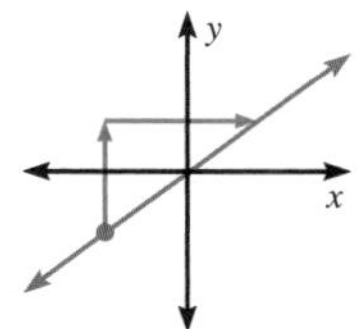

Substitute m and the coordinates of the point in $y = mx + b$. Solve for b. Write the equation.

Given two points

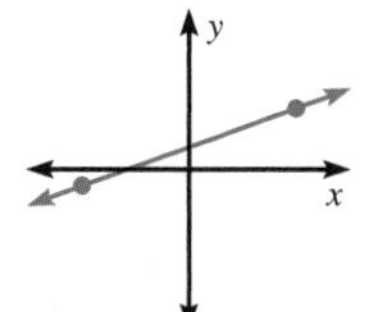

Use the points to find the slope m. Then follow the same steps described at the left.

MODELING REAL-WORLD SITUATIONS You can model a real-world situation that involves a constant rate of change with an equation in slope-intercept form.

EXAMPLE 4 Solve a multi-step problem

GYM MEMBERSHIP Your gym membership costs \$33 per month after an initial membership fee. You paid a total of \$228 after 6 months. Write an equation that gives the total cost as a function of the length of your gym membership (in months). Find the total cost after 9 months.

Solution

STEP 1 **Identify** the rate of change and starting value.

Rate of change, m: monthly cost, \$33 per month
Starting value, b: initial membership fee

STEP 2 **Write** a verbal model. Then write an equation.

Total cost	=	Monthly cost	·	Number of months	+	Membership fee
C	=	33	·	t	+	b

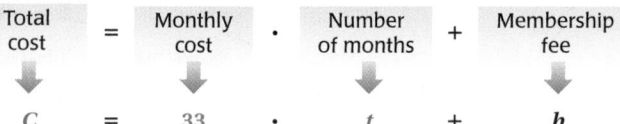

STEP 3 **Find** the starting value. Membership for 6 months costs \$228, so you can substitute 6 for t and 228 for C in the equation $C = 33t + b$.

$228 = 33(6) + b$ **Substitute 6 for t and 228 for C.**

$30 = b$ **Solve for b.**

STEP 4 **Write** an equation. Use the function from Step 2.

$C = 33t + 30$ **Substitute 30 for b.**

STEP 5 **Evaluate** the function when $t = 9$.

$C = 33(9) + 30 = 327$ **Substitute 9 for t. Simplify.**

▶ Your total cost after 9 months is \$327.

Differentiated Instruction

English Learners The letter t is used for the number of months in **Example 4** because it is a time (and this word begins with the letter t). Tell students that t is commonly used as a variable for most measures of time (seconds, minutes, hours, days, and so on) in algebraic expressions and equations.

See also the *Algebra 1 Toolkit* for more strategies.

EXAMPLE 5 Solve a multi-step problem

BMX RACING In Bicycle Moto Cross (BMX) racing, racers purchase a one year membership to a track. They also pay an entry fee for each race at that track. One racer paid a total of \$125 after 5 races. A second racer paid a total of \$170 after 8 races. How much does the track membership cost? What is the entry fee per race?

ANOTHER WAY
For alternative methods for solving the problem in Example 5, turn to page 300 for the **Problem Solving Workshop**.

Solution

STEP 1 **Identify** the rate of change and starting value.

Rate of change, *m*: entry fee per race
Starting value, *b*: track membership cost

STEP 2 **Write** a verbal model. Then write an equation.

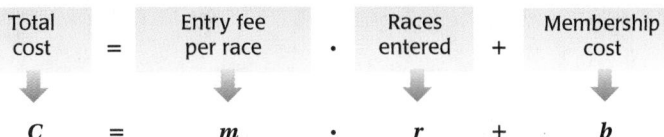

Total cost	=	Entry fee per race	·	Races entered	+	Membership cost
C	=	m	·	r	+	b

STEP 3 **Calculate** the rate of change. This is the entry fee per race. Use the slope formula. Racer 1 is represented by (5, 125). Racer 2 is represented by (8, 170).

$$m = \frac{y_2 - y_1}{x_2 - x_1} = \frac{170 - 125}{8 - 5} = \frac{45}{3} = 15$$

STEP 4 **Find** the track membership cost b. Use the data pair (5, 125) for racer 1 and the entry fee per race from Step 3.

$C = mr + b$ **Write the equation from Step 2.**

$125 = 15(5) + b$ **Substitute 15 for *m*, 5 for *r*, and 125 for *C*.**

$50 = b$ **Solve for *b*.**

▶ The track membership cost is \$50. The entry fee per race is \$15.

✓ GUIDED PRACTICE for Examples 4 and 5

4. **GYM MEMBERSHIP** A gym charges \$35 per month after an initial membership fee. A member has paid a total of \$250 after 6 months. Write an equation that gives the total cost of a gym membership as a function of the length of membership (in months). Find the total cost of membership after 10 months. $C = 35m + 40$; \$390

5. **BMX RACING** A BMX race track charges a membership fee and an entry fee per race. One racer paid a total of \$76 after 3 races. Another racer paid a total of \$124 after 7 races.
   a. How much does the track membership cost? \$40
   b. What is the entry fee per race? \$12
   c. Write an equation that gives the total cost as a function of the number of races entered. $C = 12r + 40$

Extra Example 5

For science class, you need to know the Celsius equivalent of a room temperature of 70°F. To estimate the Celsius equivalent, you use the facts that 32°F is equivalent to 0°C and that 212°F is equivalent to 100°C. Estimate the Celsius equivalent of 70°F. about 21°C

Key Questions to Ask for Example 5

- What are the variable quantities? Which variable is dependent on the other? **The variable quantities are the number of races and the amount paid. The amount paid depends on the number of races.**
- How are the values of m and b related to the racing problem? **The slope *m* is the entry fee per race. The *y*-intercept *b* is the cost of track membership.**

Closing the Lesson

Have students summarize the major points of the lesson and answer the Essential Question: How do you find the equation of a line given two points?

- **You can write an equation of a line given the slope and a point on the line or given two points on the line.**

Use the slope formula to find the slope. Use the slope and the slope-intercept form to find the *y*-intercept. Substitute the slope and *y*-intercept in the slope-intercept form.

Differentiated Instruction

Below Level A graph may help students better understand the relationships in **Example 5**. Have students graph $y = 15x + 50$. Ask how much it would cost if a racer participated in 0 races and what this cost represents. Have students determine the cost to participate in 1, 2, and 3 races. Ask them to find the differences between the costs of consecutive races. Then ask what this difference represents.

Advanced Have students graph the equation $y = 15x + 50$ from **Example 5** and the equation $y = 12x + 40$ they found in **Guided Practice Exercise 5c** on the same coordinate plane. Then ask them to evaluate the savings for various numbers of races under the fees from **Exercise 5** as opposed to the fee from **Example 5**.

See also the *Algebra 1 Toolkit* for more strategies.

4 PRACTICE AND APPLY

Assignment Guide

Answer Transparencies available for all exercises

Basic:
Day 1: EP p. 941 Exs. 27–32
pp. 296–299
Exs. 1–5, 11–13, 17–19, 23–26, 55–58
Day 2: pp. 296–299
Exs. 9, 10, 29–35, 47–52, 59–64

Average:
Day 1: pp. 296–299
Exs. 1, 2, 6–8, 14–16, 20–22, 25–29, 55–58
Day 2: pp. 296–299
Exs. 9, 10, 31–43 odd, 48–53, 59–64

Advanced:
Day 1: pp. 296–299
Exs. 1, 7, 8, 15, 16, 21, 22, 27–37, 57, 58
Day 2: pp. 296–299
Exs. 10, 38–46*, 49–54*, 63, 64

Block:
pp. 296–299
Exs. 1, 2, 6–8, 14–16, 20–22, 25–29, 55–58 (with 5.1)
pp. 296–299
Exs. 9, 10, 31–43 odd, 48–53, 59–64 (with 5.3)

Differentiated Instruction

See *Algebra 1 Best Practices Toolkit* for suggestions on addressing the needs of a diverse classroom.

Homework Check

For a quick check of student understanding of key concepts, go over the following exercises:

Basic: 4, 12, 25, 47, 48
Average: 7, 20, 31, 48, 49
Advanced: 8, 22, 32, 49, 50

Extra Practice

- Student Edition, p. 942
- Chapter 5 Resource Book: Practice levels A, B, C, pp. 16–18

Practice Worksheet

An easily-readable reduced practice page (with answers) for this lesson can be found on p. 280C.

5.2 EXERCISES

HOMEWORK KEY
○ = **WORKED-OUT SOLUTIONS** on p. WS11 for Exs. 5, 11, and 49
★ = **STANDARDIZED TEST PRACTICE** Exs. 2, 29, 34–37, 41, and 49
◆ = **MULTIPLE REPRESENTATIONS** Ex. 53

SKILL PRACTICE

A

1. **VOCABULARY** What is the y-coordinate of a point where a graph crosses the y-axis called? *y-intercept*

2. ★ **WRITING** If the equation $y = mx + b$ is used to model a quantity y as a function of the quantity x, why is b considered to be the starting value? *It is the point where x is 0.*

EXAMPLE 1 on p. 292 for Exs. 3–9

WRITING EQUATIONS **Write an equation of the line that passes through the given point and has the given slope m.**

3. $(1, 1)$; $m = 3$ $\quad y = 3x - 2$
4. $(5, 1)$; $m = 2$ $\quad y = 2x - 9$
5. $(-4, 7)$; $m = -5$ $\quad y = -5x - 13$
6. $(5, -5)$; $m = -2$ $\quad y = -2x + 5$
7. $(8, -4)$; $m = -\frac{3}{4}$ $\quad y = -\frac{3}{4}x + 2$
8. $(-3, -11)$; $m = \frac{1}{2}$ $\quad y = \frac{1}{2}x - \frac{19}{2}$

9. **ERROR ANALYSIS** *Describe* and correct the error in finding the y-intercept of the line that passes through the point $(6, -3)$ and has a slope of -2.
−3 was substituted for x instead of y and 6 was substituted for y instead of x, $-3 = -2(6) + b$, $-3 = -12 + b$, $9 = b$.

$y = mx + b$
$6 = -2(-3) + b$
$6 = 6 + b$
$0 = b$
✗

EXAMPLE 4 on p. 294 for Ex. 10

10. **ERROR ANALYSIS** An Internet service provider charges $18 per month plus an initial set-up fee. One customer paid a total of $81 after 2 months of service. *Describe* and correct the error in finding the set-up fee.
18 should have been substituted for m, not b, $81 = (18)2 + b$, $81 = 36 + b$, $b = \$45$.

$C = mt + b$
$81 = m(2) + 18$
$63 = m(2)$
$31.50 = m$
✗

EXAMPLE 2 on p. 293 for Exs. 11–22

USING TWO POINTS **Write an equation of the line that passes through the given points.**

11. $(1, 4), (2, 7)$ $\quad y = 3x + 1$
12. $(3, 2), (4, 9)$ $\quad y = 7x - 19$
13. $(10, -5), (-5, 1)$ $\quad y = -\frac{2}{5}x - 1$
14. $(-2, 8), (-6, 0)$ $\quad y = 2x + 12$
15. $\left(\frac{9}{2}, 1\right), \left(-\frac{7}{2}, 7\right)$ $\quad y = -\frac{3}{4}x + \frac{35}{8}$
16. $\left(-5, \frac{3}{4}\right), \left(-2, -\frac{3}{4}\right)$ $\quad y = -\frac{1}{2}x - \frac{7}{4}$

USING A GRAPH **Write an equation of the line shown.**

17. $y = 4x - 15$
18. $y = \frac{2}{5}x + \frac{4}{5}$
19. $y = -\frac{1}{2}x + \frac{1}{2}$
20. $y = -\frac{7}{6}x + \frac{11}{6}$
21. $y = \frac{1}{3}x - \frac{4}{3}$
22. $y = -3x - 7$

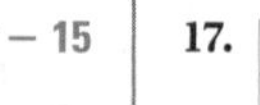

17.
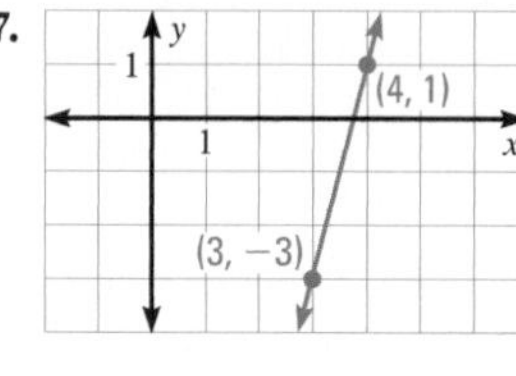

18.
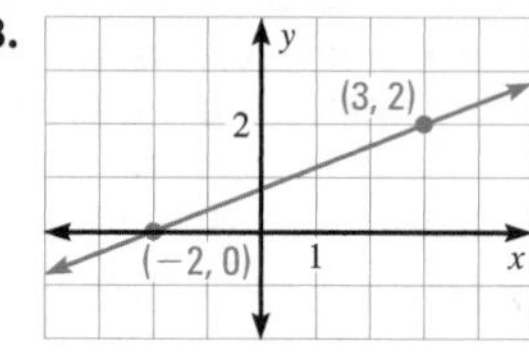

19.
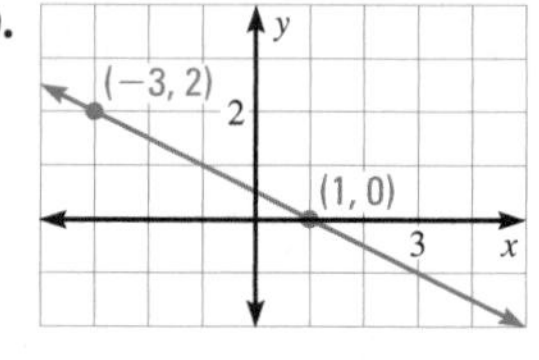

20.
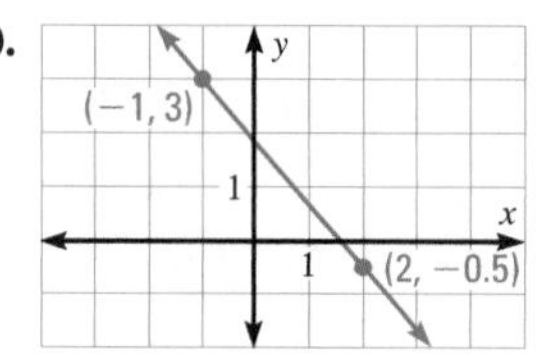

21.
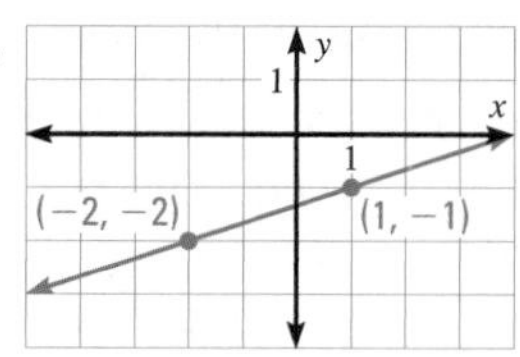

22.
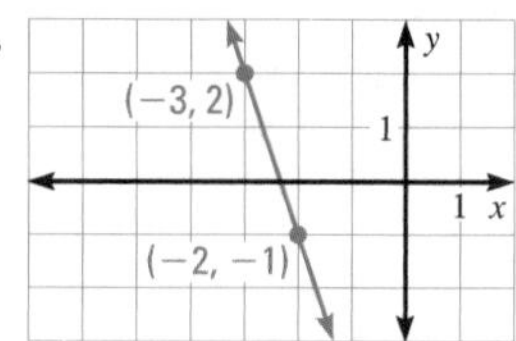

EXAMPLE 3 on p. 293 for Exs. 23–33

WRITING LINEAR FUNCTIONS Write an equation for a linear function f that has the given values.

23. $f(-2) = 15, f(1) = 9$ $y = -2x + 11$

24. $f(-2) = -2, f(4) = -8$ $y = -x - 4$

25. $f(2) = 7, f(4) = 6$ $y = -\frac{1}{2}x + 8$

26. $f(-4) = -8, f(-8) = -11$ $y = \frac{3}{4}x - 5$

27. $f(3) = 1, f(6) = 4$ $y = x - 2$

28. $f(-5) = 9, f(11) = -39$ $y = -3x - 6$

29. ★ **MULTIPLE CHOICE** Which function has the values $f(4) = -15$ and $f(7) = 57$? D

Ⓐ $f(x) = 14x - 71$ Ⓑ $f(x) = 24x - 1361$

Ⓒ $f(x) = 24x + 360$ Ⓓ $f(x) = 24x - 111$

B **USING A TABLE OR DIAGRAM Write an equation that represents the linear function shown in the table or mapping diagram.**

30.

x	$f(x)$
−4	6
4	4
8	3
12	2

$y = -\frac{1}{4}x + 5$

31.

x	$f(x)$
−3	8
3	4
6	2
9	0

$y = -\frac{2}{3}x + 6$

32.

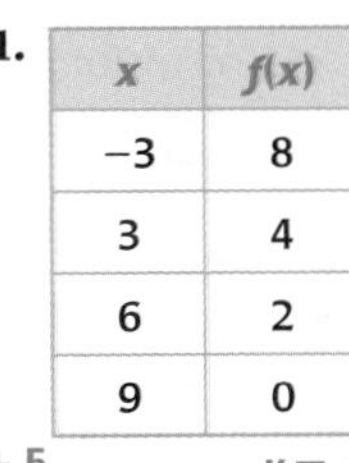

$y = -\frac{1}{2}x + 3$

33.

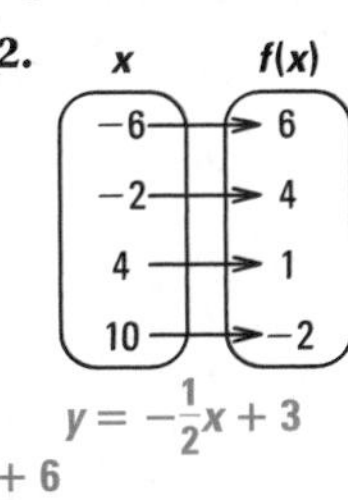

$y = 6x - 4$

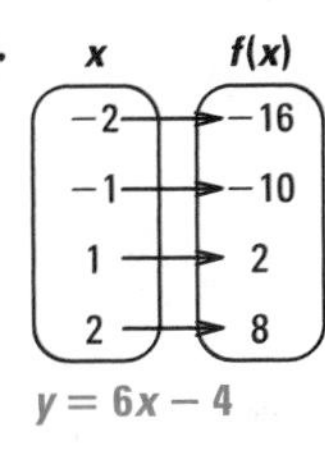

★ **SHORT RESPONSE Tell whether the given information is enough to write an equation of a line. *Justify* your answer.** 34–37. See margin.

34. Two points on the line

35. The slope and a point on the line

36. The slope of the line

37. Both intercepts of the line

USING A GRAPH In Exercises 38–41, use the graph at the right.

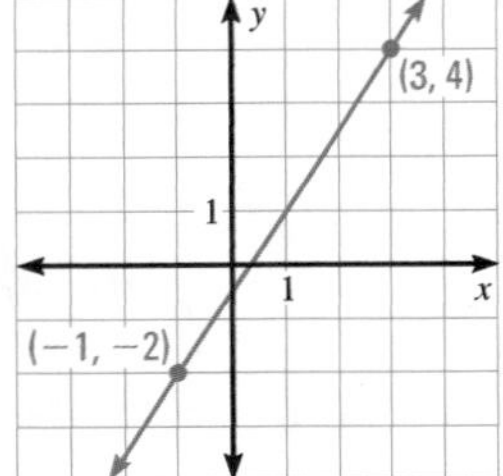

38. Write an equation of the line shown. $y = \frac{3}{2}x - \frac{1}{2}$

39. Write an equation of a line that has the same y-intercept as the line shown but has a slope that is 3 times the slope of the line shown. $y = \frac{9}{2}x - \frac{1}{2}$

40. Write an equation of a line that has the same slope as the line shown but has a y-intercept that is 6 more than the y-intercept of the line shown. $y = \frac{3}{2}x + \frac{11}{2}$

41. ★ **WRITING** Which of the lines from Exercises 38–40 intersect? Which of the lines never intersect? *Justify* your answers.

41. The lines $y = \frac{3}{2}x - \frac{1}{2}$ and $y = \frac{9}{2}x - \frac{1}{2}$ and the lines $y = \frac{9}{2}x - \frac{1}{2}$ and $y = \frac{3}{2}x + \frac{11}{2}$ intersect because they have different slopes; the lines $y = \frac{3}{2}x - \frac{1}{2}$ and $y = \frac{3}{2}x + \frac{11}{2}$ will not intersect, they have the same slope, so they are parallel.

C **REASONING Decide whether the three points lie on the same line. *Explain* how you know. If the points do lie on the same line, write an equation of the line that passes through all three points.** 42–45. See margin.

42. (−4, −2), (2, 2.5), (8, 7)

43. (2, 2), (−4, 5), (6, 1)

44. (−10, 4), (−3, 2.8), (−17, 6.8)

45. (−5.5, 3), (−7.5, 4), (−4, 5)

46. **CHALLENGE** A line passes through the points (−2, 3), (2, 5), and (6, k). Find the value of k. *Explain* your steps.
7; find the equation of the line through (−2, 3) and (2, 5) to be $y = \frac{1}{2}x + 4$, then substitute 6 for x to find k.

Avoiding Common Errors

Exercises 11–22 Students often make errors in computing slope. Remind them that it is helpful to write out the slope formula and then substitute the numbers before simplifying.

Exercises 18, 19 In these exercises, some students may use the x-intercept as the y-intercept. Remind those students that they are being given $(a, 0)$, not $(0, b)$.

Graphing Calculator

Exercises 11–22 Students can check their answers to these exercises by using the *calculate* feature. Students should enter their equation into the calculator, select *value* from the calculate menu, enter the x-values from the exercise, and use the calculator's y-values to check their answers.

42. The three points lie on the same line. If you find the equation of the line between two of the points and then check to see that the third point is a solution, you can see that all three points are on the line $y = \frac{3}{4}x + 1$.

43. The three points do not lie on the same line. If you find the equation of the line between two of the points and then check to see that the third point is a solution, you can see they do not lie on the same line.

44. The three points do not lie on the same line. If you find the equation of the line between two of the points and then check to see that the third point is a solution, you can see they do not lie on the same line.

45. The three points do not lie on the same line. If you find the equation of the line between two of the points and then check to see that the third point is a solution, you can see they do not lie on the same line.

34. Yes; you can find the slope and then substitute m and the coordinates of the point in $y = mx + b$, solve for b, and write the equation.

35. Yes; you can substitute m and the coordinates of the point in $y = mx + b$, solve for b, and write the equation.

36. No; many lines have the same slope but different y-intercepts.

37. Yes; you can find the slope of the line, then substitute the y-intercept for b, and write the equation.

Teaching Strategy

Exercises 47–48 To help students begin these exercises, you may wish to stress that they follow each of the four steps given in Example 5 on page 295. For Exercise 48, point out that part a corresponds to Step 3 and part b corresponds to Step 4. Emphasize that they should perform Steps 1 and 2 before proceeding to Steps 3 and 4.

Exercises 50–52 Similarly, stress that students may want to follow the five steps in Example 4 on page 294 for these exercises. You may want to point out that part a corresponds to Step 3, part b to Step 4, and part c to Step 5. Again, students can use the information given in the problems to perform Step 1 and Step 2.

53b.

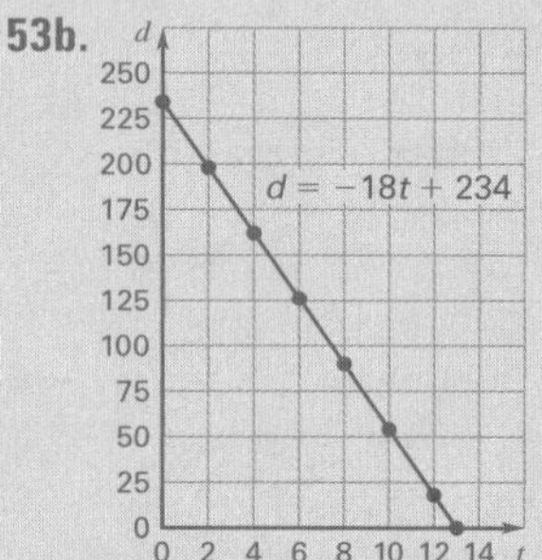

The slope is the rate that the hurricane is traveling, the y-intercept represents the distance from the town at 12 P.M.

53c. 1 A.M.; find the t-intercept to find the value of t when the distance to the town is 0; substitute 0 for d and solve for t; $t = 13$, so you need to add 13 hours to 12 P.M. to get 1 A.M.

54b. The rate of change, 10 meters per second, represents the skaters' top racing speed; the initial value, 60, represents the distance the skater traveled from a standstill to where he reached his top racing speed; d meters $= \left(10 \frac{\text{meters}}{\text{second}}\right)(x \text{ seconds}) +$ 60 meters.

PROBLEM SOLVING

EXAMPLES 4 and 5 on pp. 294–295 for Exs. 47–50 [A]

47. **BIOLOGY** Four years after a hedge maple tree was planted, its height was 9 feet. Eight years after it was planted, the hedge maple tree's height was 12 feet. What is the growth rate of the hedge maple? What was its height when it was planted? $\frac{3}{4}$ ft/yr; 6 ft

@HomeTutor for problem solving help at classzone.com

48. **TECHNOLOGY** You have a subscription to an online magazine that allows you to view 25 articles from the magazine's archives. You are charged an additional fee for each article after the first 25 articles viewed. After viewing 28 archived articles, you paid a total of \$34.80. After viewing 30 archived articles, you paid a total of \$40.70.

a. What is the cost per archived article after the first 25 articles viewed? \$2.95

b. What is cost of the magazine subscription? \$25.95

@HomeTutor for problem solving help at classzone.com

49. 115 min or 1 h 55 min; substitute 30 for m, 2 for x and 85 for y into the equation $y = mx + b$ to find $b = 25$. Then substitute 3 for x into the equation $y = 30x + 25$ to solve for y.

(49.) ★ **SHORT RESPONSE** You are cooking a roast beef until it is well-done. You must allow 30 minutes of cooking time for every pound of beef, plus some extra time. The last time you cooked a 2 pound roast, it was well-done after 1 hour and 25 minutes. How much time will it take to cook a 3 pound roast? *Explain* how you found your answer. See margin.

HINT In part (b), let t represent the number of years since 1981.

50. **TELEPHONE SERVICE** The annual household cost of telephone service in the United States increased at a relatively constant rate of \$27.80 per year from 1981 to 2001. In 2001 the annual household cost of telephone service was \$914.

a. What was the annual household cost of telephone service in 1981? \$358

b. Write an equation that gives the annual household cost of telephone service as a function of the number of years since 1981. $y = 27.8x + 358$

c. Find the household cost of telephone service in 2000. \$886.20

51. **NEWSPAPERS** Use the information in the article about the circulation of Sunday newspapers.

a. About how many Sunday newspapers were in circulation in 1970? about 584 newspapers

b. Write an equation that gives the number of Sunday newspapers in circulation as a function of the number of years since 1970. $y = 11.8x + 584$

c. About how many Sunday newspapers were in circulation in 2000? about 938 newspapers

> Sunday Edition C9
>
> **SUNDAY PAPERS INCREASE**
>
> **From 1970 to 2000,** the number of Sunday newspapers in circulation increased at a relatively constant rate of 11.8 newspapers per year. In 1997 there were 903 Sunday newspapers in circulation.

[B]

52. **AIRPORTS** From 1990 to 2001, the number of airports in the United States increased at a relatively constant rate of 175 airports per year. There were 19,306 airports in the United States in 2001.

a. How many U.S. airports were there in 1990? 17,381 airports

b. Write an equation that gives the number of U.S. airports as a function of the number of years since 1990. $y = 175x + 17,381$

c. Find the year in which the number of U.S. airports reached 19,200. 2000

○ = WORKED-OUT SOLUTIONS on p. WS1 ★ = STANDARDIZED TEST PRACTICE  = MULTIPLE REPRESENTATIONS

53. **MULTIPLE REPRESENTATIONS** A hurricane is traveling at a constant speed on a straight path toward a coastal town, as shown below.

Hurricane position at 1:00 P.M.

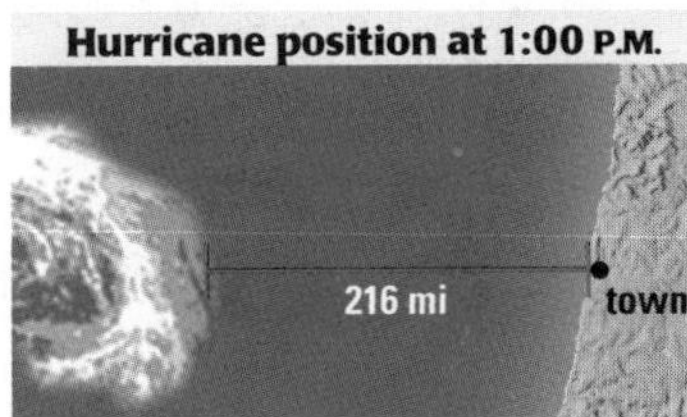

Hurricane position at 5:00 P.M.

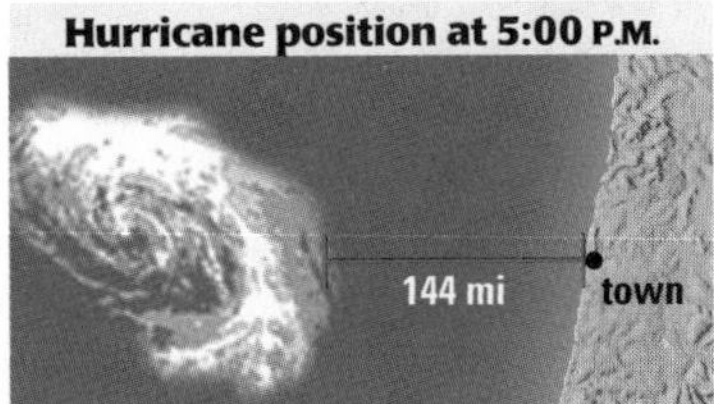

a. **Writing an Equation** Write an equation that gives the distance (in miles) of the hurricane from the town as a function of the number of hours since 12:00 P.M. $d = -18t + 234$

b. **Drawing a Graph** Graph the equation from part (a). *Explain* what the slope and the *y*-intercept of the graph mean in this situation. b–c. See margin.

c. **Describing in Words** Predict the time at which the hurricane will reach the town. Your answer should include the following information:

- an explanation of how you used your equation
- a description of the steps you followed to obtain your prediction

C 54. **CHALLENGE** An in-line skater practices at a race track. In two trials, the skater travels the same distance going from a standstill to his top racing speed. He then travels at his top racing speed for different distances.

Trial number	Time at top racing speed (seconds)	Total distance traveled (meters)
1	24	300
2	29	350

a. **Model** Write an equation that gives the total distance traveled (in meters) as a function of the time (in seconds) at top racing speed. $d = 10t + 60$

b. **Justify** What do the rate of change and initial value in your equation represent? *Explain* your answer using unit analysis. See margin.

c. **Predict** One lap around the race track is 200 meters. The skater starts at a standstill and completes 3 laps. Predict the number of seconds the skater travels at his top racing speed. *Explain* your method. 54 sec; the total distance is the length of the race track times 3 laps, 600 meters. If you substitute 600 for d, $t = 54$.

ILLINOIS MIXED REVIEW

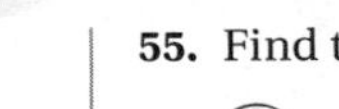

TEST PRACTICE at classzone.com

55. Find the slope of the line $-4x - y = -1$. A

Ⓐ -4 Ⓑ $\frac{1}{4}$ Ⓒ 1 Ⓓ 4

56. Which of the following is the best estimate for the length of the piece of wire shown? B

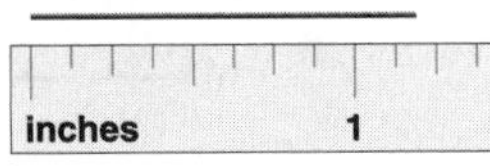

Ⓐ $1\frac{1}{8}$ in. Ⓑ $1\frac{3}{16}$ in. Ⓒ $1\frac{1}{4}$ in. Ⓓ $1\frac{1}{2}$ in.

5 ASSESS AND RETEACH

Daily Homework Quiz

Transparency Available

Write an equation of the line that passes through the given point with the given slope.

1. (4, −1), $m = -1$ $y = -x + 3$
2. (2, 0), $m = 4$ $y = 4x - 8$

Write an equation of the line that passes through the given points.

3. (2, 3), (4, 7) $y = 2x - 1$
4. (−5, 7), (2, −7) $y = -2x - 3$
5. A camp charges a registration fee and a daily amount. If the total bill for one camper was $338 for 12 days and the total bill for another camper was $506 for 19 days, how much will the bill be for a camper who enrolls for 30 days? $770

Available at **classzone.com**

Diagnosis/Remediation

- Practice A, B, C in Chapter 5 Resource Book, pp. 16–18
- Study Guide in Chapter 5 Resource Book, pp. 19–20
- Practice Workbook, pp. 69–70
- @HomeTutor

Challenge

Additional challenge is available in the Chapter 5 Resource Book, p. 23.

Using ALTERNATIVE METHODS

Another Way to Solve Example 5, page 295

MULTIPLE REPRESENTATIONS In Example 5 on page 295, you saw how to solve a problem about BMX racing using an equation. You can also solve this problem using a graph or a table.

PROBLEM

BMX RACING In Bicycle Moto Cross (BMX) racing, racers purchase a one year membership to a track. They also pay an entry fee for each race at that track. One racer paid a total of $125 after 5 races. A second racer paid a total of $170 after 8 races. How much does the track membership cost? What is the entry fee per race?

METHOD 1

Using a Graph One alternative approach is to use a graph.

STEP 1 **Read** the problem. It tells you the number of races and amount paid for each racer. Write this information as ordered pairs.

Racer 1: (5, 125)
Racer 2: (8, 170)

STEP 2 **Graph** the ordered pairs. Draw a line through the points.

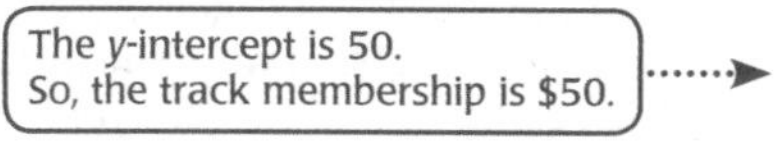

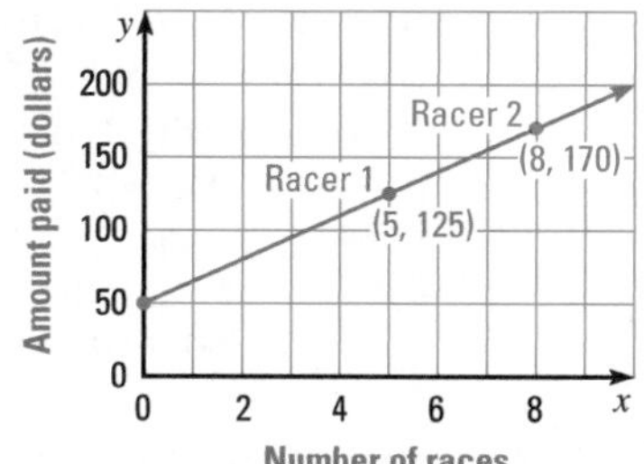

STEP 3 **Find** the slope of the line. This is the entry fee per race.

$$\text{Fee} = \frac{45 \text{ dollars}}{3 \text{ races}} = \$15 \text{ per race}$$

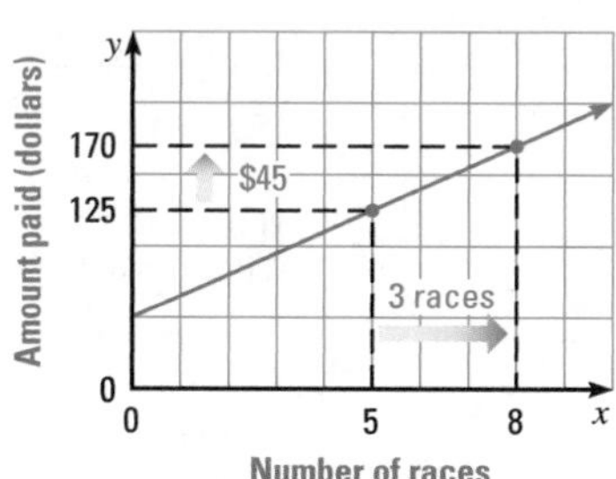

Alternative Strategy

Students can solve Example 5 on page 295 by using a graph or a table. A graph can help students visualize the racing problem, while a table can help students see the linear pattern. Both methods help students to understand the algebraic solution to the problem.

Mathematical Reasoning

Multiple Representations You may want to discuss the advantages of finding an algebraic solution of the racing problem, and using a graph or table to check the reasonableness of the solution. For example, an algebraic solution allows the student to calculate the total cost for any input value, whereas the graph and the table are limited by scale and by size. The graph readily shows the slope of the line and the table lends itself to calculating the y-intercept, both of which confirm the algebraic solution of the problem.

1. $5; $19; Method 1: Use a graph.

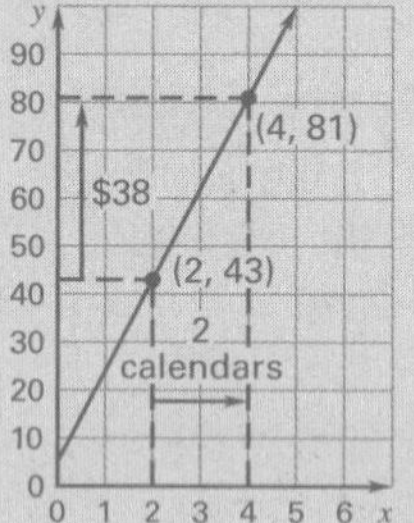

Graph the ordered pairs, (2, 43) and (4, 81), draw a line through the points and find the y-intercept, or the delivery fee, to be $5. Then find the slope of the line, or the cost per calendar, to be $\frac{38}{2} = \$19$; Method 2: Use a table to calculate the cost of the calendars.

Number of calendars	Cost (dollars)
2	43
3	?
4	81

The number of calendars increased by 2 and the cost increased by $38, so the cost per calendar is $38 ÷ 2 = $19. The delivery fee is the cost when the number of calendars is 0. Use the cost per calendar and work backwards to fill in the table. $43 − $19 = $24; $24 − $19 = $5.

Number of calendars	Cost (dollars)
0	5
1	24
2	43

The delivery fee is $5.

2. $119.18; Method 1: Use a graph.

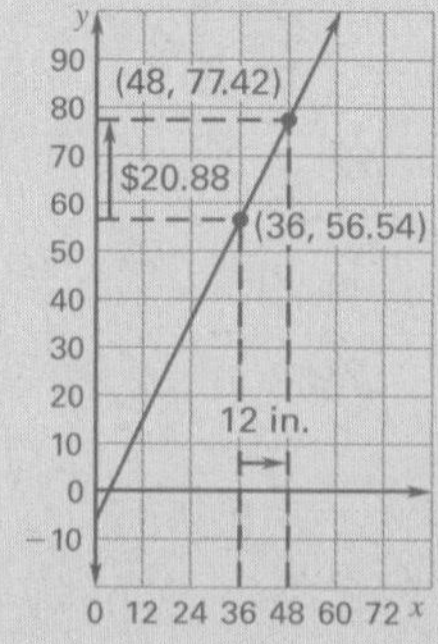

METHOD 2 **Using a Table** Another approach is to use a table showing the amount paid for various numbers of races.

STEP 1 **Calculate** the race entry fee.

Number of races	Amount paid
5	$125
6	?
7	?
8	$170

(+ 3 in number of races; + $45 in amount paid)

The number of races increased by 3, and the amount paid increased by $45, so the race entry fee is $\$45 \div 3 = \$15$.

STEP 2 **Find** the membership cost.

Number of races	Amount paid
0	$50
1	$65
2	$80
3	$95
4	$110
5	$125

(– $15 between each pair of rows)

The membership cost is the cost with no races. Use the race entry fee and work backwards to fill in the table. The membership cost is $50.

PRACTICE

1. **CALENDARS** A company makes calendars from personal photos. You pay a delivery fee for each order plus a cost per calendar. The cost of 2 calendars plus delivery is $43. The cost of 4 calendars plus delivery is $81. What is the delivery fee? What is the cost per calendar? Solve this problem using two different methods. See margin.

2. **BOOKSHELVES** A furniture maker offers bookshelves that have the same width and depth but that differ in height and price, as shown in the table. Find the cost of a bookshelf that is 72 inches high. Solve this problem using two different methods. See margin.

Height (inches)	Price (dollars)
36	56.54
48	77.42
60	98.30

3. **WHAT IF?** In Exercise 2, suppose the price of the 60 inch bookshelf was $99.30. Can you still solve the problem? *Explain.* See margin.

4. **CONCERT TICKETS** All tickets for a concert are the same price. The ticket agency adds a fixed fee to every order. A person who orders 5 tickets pays $93. A person who orders 3 tickets pays $57. How much will 4 tickets cost? Solve this problem using two different methods. See margin.

5. **ERROR ANALYSIS** A student solved the problem in Exercise 4 as shown below. *Describe* and correct the error.

Let p = price paid for 4 tickets

$$\frac{57}{3} = \frac{p}{4}$$

$$228 = 3p$$

$$76 = p$$

The student assumes that there is no fixed fee by using a proportion; $93 - 57 = 36$, $36 \div 2 = 18$, $57 + 18 = 75$.

Avoiding Common Errors

While discussing Method 2, remind students that in Step 1 they need to calculate the increase in both columns to determine the slope.

Study Strategy

Exercises 1–5 Point out to students that if they use a graph, they may not be able to determine an exact y-intercept if the x-coordinates of the ordered pairs fall between the numbers on the scale. Note that Method 1, Step 2 finds the y-intercept by drawing a line through two points. If they plot the points slightly higher or lower on the graph, the line will not pass through (0, 50). Suggest they verify the y-intercept using the slope ratio.

3. No; if the cost of the 60 inch bookshelf changes, the cost no longer increases at a constant rate.

4. $75; Method 1: Use a graph.

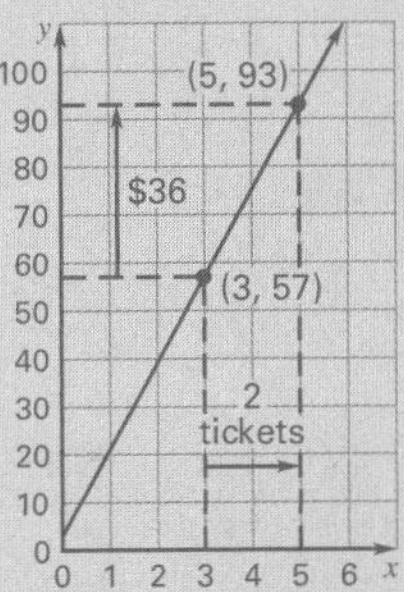

Graph the ordered pairs, (5, 93) and (3, 57), draw a line through the points, and find the y-intercept to be 3, so the fixed fee on every order is $3. Then find the slope of the line to be $\frac{36}{2} = \$18$ per ticket. Write the equation $y = 18x + 3$ and substitute 4 for x to find the total cost of 4 tickets to be $75; Method 2: Use a table to calculate the cost per ticket.

Number of tickets	Total cost (dollars)
3	57
4	?
5	93

The number of tickets increased by 2 and the total cost of tickets increased by $36, so the cost per ticket is $\$36 \div 2 = \$18$; $\$57 + \$18 = \$75$; $\$39 - \$18 = \$21$; $\$21 - \$18 = \$3$; the total cost of 4 tickets is $75.

(Exercise 2 continued)
Graph the ordered pairs, (36, 56.54) and (48, 77.42), draw a line through the points and find the y-intercept to be -6.1. Then find the slope of the line to be $\frac{20.88}{12} = \$1.74$. Write the equation $y = 1.74x - 6.1$ and substitute 72 for x to find the cost to be $119.18; Method 2: Use a table to calculate the cost of the bookshelf.

Height (inches)	Cost (dollars)
36	56.54
48	77.42
60	98.30

The height increased by 12 and the cost increased by $20.88, so the cost per inch is $\$20.88 \div 12 = \$1.74$; $98.30 + 20.88 = 119.18$.

The cost of a bookshelf that is 72 inches is $119.18.

5.3 Write Linear Equations in Point-Slope Form

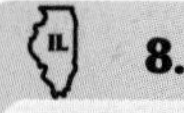

8.11.07 Identify an equation of a line or an equation of a line of best fit from given information . . .

Before You wrote linear equations in slope-intercept form.

Now You will write linear equations in point-slope form.

Why? So you can model sports statistics, as in Ex. 43.

Key Vocabulary
- **point-slope form**

Consider the line that passes through the point (2, 3) with a slope of $\frac{1}{2}$.

Let (x, y) where $x \neq 2$ be another point on the line. You can write an equation relating x and y using the slope formula, with $(x_1, y_1) = (2, 3)$ and $(x_2, y_2) = (x, y)$.

$$m = \frac{y_2 - y_1}{x_2 - x_1}$$ **Write slope formula.**

$$\frac{1}{2} = \frac{y - 3}{x - 2}$$ **Substitute $\frac{1}{2}$ for m, 3 for y_1, and 2 for x_1.**

$$\frac{1}{2}(x - 2) = y - 3$$ **Multiply each side by $(x - 2)$.**

USE POINT-SLOPE FORM
When an equation is in point-slope form, you can read the x- and y-coordinates of a point on the line and the slope of the line.

The equation in *point-slope form* is $y - 3 = \frac{1}{2}(x - 2)$.

KEY CONCEPT *For Your Notebook*

Point-Slope Form

The **point-slope form** of the equation of the nonvertical line through a given point (x_1, y_1) with a slope of m is $y - y_1 = m(x - x_1)$.

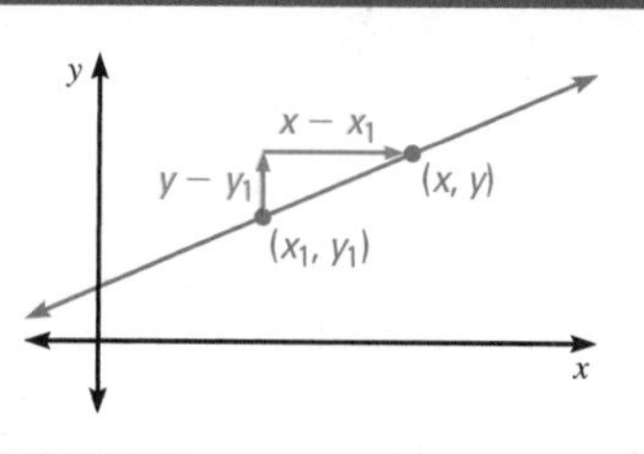

EXAMPLE 1 **Write an equation in point-slope form**

Write an equation in point-slope form of the line that passes through the point (4, −3) and has a slope of 2.

$y - y_1 = m(x - x_1)$ **Write point-slope form.**

$y + 3 = 2(x - 4)$ **Substitute 2 for m, 4 for x_1, and −3 for y_1.**

GUIDED PRACTICE for Example 1

1. Write an equation in point-slope form of the line that passes through the point (−1, 4) and has a slope of −2. $y - 4 = -2(x + 1)$

1 PLAN AND PREPARE

Warm-Up Exercises

Transparency Available

Write an equation of the line.

1. passes through (3, 4), $m = 3$ $y = 3x - 5$
2. passes through (−2, 2) and (1, 8) $y = 2x + 6$
3. A carnival charges an entrance fee and a ticket fee. One person paid $27.50 and bought 5 tickets. Another paid $45.00 and bought 12 tickets. How much will 22 tickets cost? $70

Notetaking Guide

Transparency Available

Promotes interactive learning and notetaking skills, pp. 106–108.

Pacing

Basic: 2 days
Average: 2 days
Advanced: 2 days
Block: 0.5 block with 5.2
0.5 block with 5.4

- See *Teaching Guide/Lesson Plan.*

2 FOCUS AND MOTIVATE

Essential Question

Big Idea 1, p. 281

How do you write linear equations in point-slope form? **Tell students they will learn how to answer this question by using two points, or the slope and one point.**

Resource Planning Guide

Chapter Resource Book
- Teaching Guide/Lesson Plan (pp. 24–25)
- Activity Master (p. 26)
- Practice levels A, B, C (pp. 27–32)
- Study Guide (pp. 33–34)
- Catch-up for Absent Students (p. 35)
- Problem Solving Workshop (p. 36)
- Challenge (p. 38)

Workbooks
- Notetaking Guide (pp. 106–108)
- Practice Workbook (pp. 71–73)

Teaching Options
- **Power Presentations CD-ROM** provides dynamic electronic teaching resources for the classroom.
- **Activity Generator CD-ROM** provides editable activities for all ability levels.

Interactive Technology
- Easy Planner
- Power Presentations CD-ROM
- Activity Generator CD-ROM
- Animated Algebra
- Test Generator CD-ROM
- Online Quiz
- eWorkbook
- eEdition
- @HomeTutor

Resources for English Learners
- Quick Reference for English Learners
- Spanish Study Guide
- Multi-Language Visual Glossary
- Student Resources in Spanish

See also the *Algebra 1 Toolkit* for more strategies for meeting individual needs.

EXAMPLE 2 Graph an equation in point-slope form

Graph the equation $y + 2 = \frac{2}{3}(x - 3)$.

Solution

Because the equation is in point-slope form, you know that the line has a slope of $\frac{2}{3}$ and passes through the point (3, −2).

Plot the point (3, −2). Find a second point on the line using the slope. Draw a line through both points.

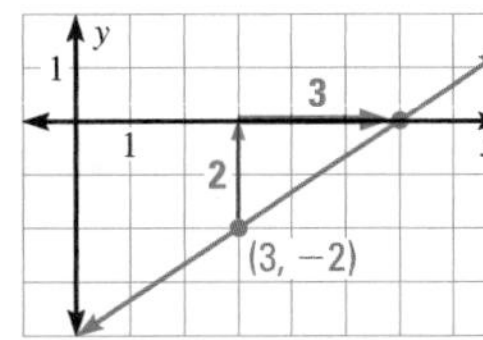

GUIDED PRACTICE for Example 2

2. Graph the equation $y - 1 = -(x - 2)$. See margin.

EXAMPLE 3 Use point-slope form to write an equation

Write an equation in point-slope form of the line shown.

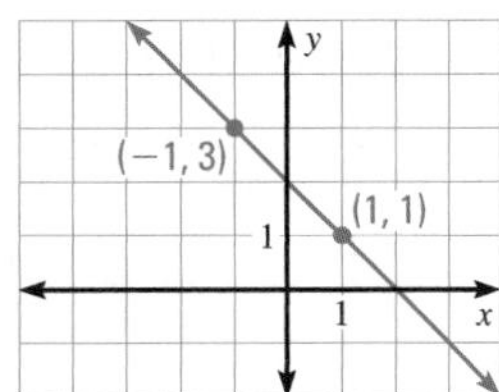

Solution

STEP 1 **Find** the slope of the line.

$$m = \frac{y_2 - y_1}{x_2 - x_1} = \frac{3 - 1}{-1 - 1} = \frac{2}{-2} = -1$$

STEP 2 **Write** the equation in point-slope form. You can use either given point.

Method 1 Use (−1, 3).

$y - y_1 = m(x - x_1)$

$y - 3 = -(x + 1)$

Method 2 Use (1, 1).

$y - y_1 = m(x - x_1)$

$y - 1 = -(x - 1)$

CHECK Check that the equations are equivalent by writing them in slope-intercept form.

$y - 3 = -x - 1$

$y = -x + 2$

$y - 1 = -x + 1$

$y = -x + 2$

 activity at classzone.com

GUIDED PRACTICE for Example 3

3. Write an equation in point-slope form of the line that passes through the points (2, 3) and (4, 4). $y - 3 = \frac{1}{2}(x - 2)$ or $y - 4 = \frac{1}{2}(x - 4)$

Motivating the Lesson

You need to print and bind a report for a project. You have a price list showing a printing company charges \$10.50 for 10 pages, \$11.75 for 15 pages, \$14.25 for 25 pages, and \$18 for 40 pages. You can use this list to determine if the company charges a constant rate to print each page. If so, you can determine the cost to print and bind your report.

3 TEACH

Extra Example 1

Write an equation in point-slope form of the line that passes through the point (−3, 1) and has a slope of 3. $y - 1 = 3(x + 3)$

Extra Example 2

Graph $y - 2 = \frac{1}{2}(x + 2)$.

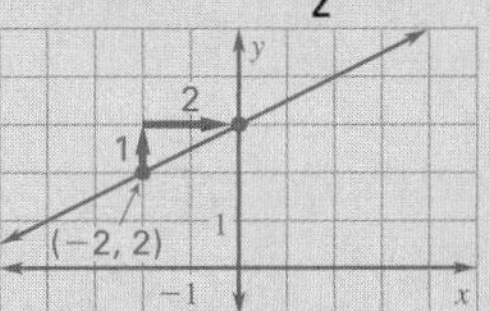

Extra Example 3

Write an equation in point-slope form of the line shown.

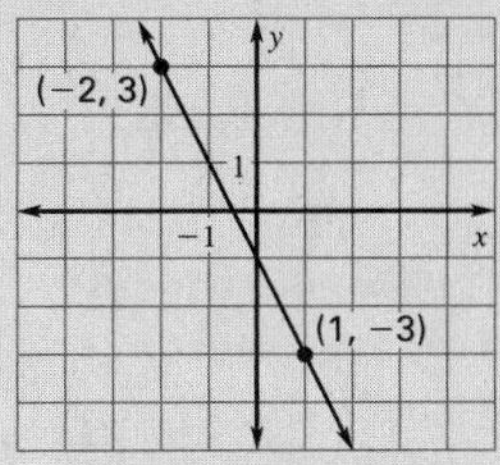

$y - 3 = -2(x + 2)$ or $y + 3 = -2(x - 1)$

2. See Additional Answers beginning on p. AA1.

Differentiated Instruction

Auditory Learners To write the equation of a line in point-slope form, students need to know the slope and a point on the line. Students can state the point-slope form as follows. "For a given *point*, *y* minus the *y*-coordinate equals the *slope* times the quantity *x* minus the *x*-coordinate."

See also the *Algebra 1 Toolkit* for more strategies.

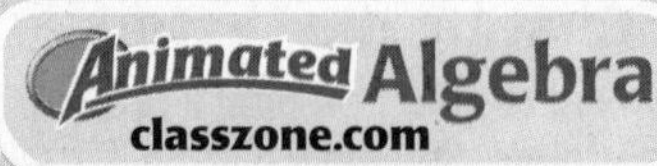

An **Animated Algebra** activity is available on-line for **Example 3**. This activity is also available on the **Power Presentations CD-ROM**.

Extra Example 4

A radio station charges $650 for the first minute of ad time and then $340 for each additional minute. Write an equation that gives the total cost (in dollars) to run an ad as a function of the number of minutes the ad runs. Find the cost of 7 minutes of ad time. **$C = 340t + 310$, where C is total cost (in dollars) and t is time (in minutes). The cost to run the ad for 7 minutes is $2690.**

Extra Example 5

The table shows the cost of renting a canoe for different times (in hours). Can the situation be modeled by a linear equation? *Explain.* If possible, write an equation that gives the cost as a function of time (in hours).

Time (hours)	Cost (dollars)
2	22
4	32
6	42
8	52
10	62

Because the cost increases at a constant rate of $5 per hour, the situation can be modeled by a linear equation. An equation that models the situation is $C = 5t + 12$, where C is the total cost (in dollars) and t is time (in hours).

Key Questions to Ask for Example 5

- When the equation is written in slope-intercept form, what does the y-intercept represent? **a one-time cost of $50**
- If you use the data pair (12, 650), how does it affect the point-slope form and slope-intercept form of the equation? **The point-slope form changes to $C - 650 = 50(p - 12)$, but the slope-intercept form remains the same.**

EXAMPLE 4 Solve a multi-step problem

STICKERS You are designing a sticker to advertise your band. A company charges $225 for the first 1000 stickers and $80 for each additional 1000 stickers. Write an equation that gives the total cost (in dollars) of stickers as a function of the number (in thousands) of stickers ordered. Find the cost of 9000 stickers.

Solution

STEP 1 **Identify** the rate of change and a data pair. Let C be the cost (in dollars) and s be the number of stickers (in thousands).

Rate of change, m: $80 per 1 thousand stickers
Data pair (s_1, C_1): (1 thousand stickers, $225)

STEP 2 **Write** an equation using point-slope form. Rewrite the equation in slope-intercept form so that cost is a function of the number of stickers.

$C - C_1 = m(s - s_1)$ **Write point-slope form.**

$C - 225 = 80(s - 1)$ **Substitute 80 for m, 1 for s_1, and 225 for C_1.**

$C = 80s + 145$ **Solve for C.**

STEP 3 **Find** the cost of 9000 stickers.

$C = 80(9) + 145 = 865$ **Substitute 9 for s. Simplify.**

▶ The cost of 9000 stickers is $865.

AVOID ERRORS
Remember that s is given in thousands. To find the cost of 9000 stickers, substitute 9 for s.

EXAMPLE 5 Write a real-world linear model from a table

WORKING RANCH The table shows the cost of visiting a working ranch for one day and night for different numbers of people. Can the situation be modeled by a linear equation? *Explain.* If possible, write an equation that gives the cost as a function of the number of people in the group.

Number of people	4	6	8	10	12
Cost (dollars)	250	350	450	550	650

Solution

STEP 1 **Find** the rate of change for consecutive data pairs in the table.

$$\frac{350 - 250}{6 - 4} = 50, \quad \frac{450 - 350}{8 - 6} = 50, \quad \frac{550 - 450}{10 - 8} = 50, \quad \frac{650 - 550}{12 - 10} = 50$$

Because the cost increases at a constant rate of $50 per person, the situation can be modeled by a linear equation.

STEP 2 **Use** point-slope form to write the equation. Let C be the cost (in dollars) and p be the number of people. Use the data pair (4, 250).

$C - C_1 = m(p - p_1)$ **Write point-slope form.**

$C - 250 = 50(p - 4)$ **Substitute 50 for m, 4 for p_1, and 250 for C_1.**

$C = 50p + 50$ **Solve for C.**

✓ **GUIDED PRACTICE** for Examples 4 and 5

4. **WHAT IF?** In Example 4, suppose a second company charges $250 for the first 1000 stickers. The cost of each additional 1000 stickers is $60.

   a. Write an equation that gives the total cost (in dollars) of the stickers as a function of the number (in thousands) of stickers ordered. $C = 60s + 190$

   b. Which company would charge you less for 9000 stickers? second company

5. **MAILING COSTS** The table shows the cost (in dollars) of sending a single piece of first class mail for different weights. Can the situation be modeled by a linear equation? *Explain.* If possible, write an equation that gives the cost of sending a piece of mail as a function of its weight (in ounces).

Weight (ounces)	1	4	5	10	12
Cost (dollars)	0.37	1.06	1.29	2.44	2.90

Yes; because the cost increases at a constant rate of $.23 per ounce, the situation can be modeled by a linear equation; $C = 0.23w + 0.14$.

5.3 EXERCISES

HOMEWORK KEY

○ = **WORKED-OUT SOLUTIONS** on p. WS11 for Exs. 3 and 39

★ = **STANDARDIZED TEST PRACTICE** Exs. 2, 12, 30–34, 38, and 41

SKILL PRACTICE

1. **VOCABULARY** Identify the slope of the line given by the equation $y - 5 = -2(x + 5)$. Then identify one point on the line. -2; $(-5, 5)$

2. ★ **WRITING** *Describe* the steps you would take to write an equation in point-slope form of the line that passes through the points (3, −2) and (4, 5). Find the slope and substitute it for m in the equation $y - y_1 = m(x - x_1)$. Then pick one of the points and substitute the coordinates in for y_1 and x_1.

EXAMPLE 1 on p. 302 for Exs. 3–13

WRITING EQUATIONS Write an equation in point-slope form of the line that passes through the given point and has the given slope *m*.

3. (2, 1), $m = 2$ $y - 1 = 2(x - 2)$
4. (3, 5), $m = -1$ $y - 5 = -(x - 3)$
5. (7, −1), $m = -6$ $y + 1 = -6(x - 7)$
6. (5, −1), $m = -2$ $y + 1 = -2(x - 5)$
7. (−8, 2), $m = 5$ $y - 2 = 5(x + 8)$
8. (−6, 6), $m = \frac{3}{2}$ $y - 6 = \frac{3}{2}(x + 6)$
9. (−11, −3), $m = -9$ $y + 3 = -9(x + 11)$
10. (−3, −9), $m = \frac{7}{3}$ $y + 9 = \frac{7}{3}(x + 3)$
11. (5, −12), $m = -\frac{2}{5}$ $y + 12 = -\frac{2}{5}(x - 5)$

12. ★ **MULTIPLE CHOICE** Which equation represents the line that passes through the point (−6, 2) and has a slope of −1? C

    Ⓐ $y + 2 = -(x + 6)$ Ⓑ $y + 2 = -(x - 6)$

    Ⓒ $y - 2 = -(x + 6)$ Ⓓ $y + 1 = -2(x + 6)$

13. **ERROR ANALYSIS** *Describe* and correct the error in writing an equation of the line that passes through the point (1, −5) and has a slope of −2.

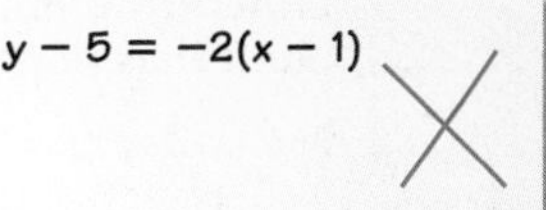

The form is $y - y_1$, so the left side should be $y - (-5)$ or $y + 5$; $y + 5 = -2(x - 1)$.

Mathematical Reasoning

You may want to discuss the relationship between the point-slope form and the slope-intercept form of an equation. Tell students that data as ordered pairs fit well with the point-slope form. The ordered pairs allow them to determine quickly whether there is a constant rate of change, and the pairing allows them to plug the data directly into the point-slope form. Point out that to make calculations and graphing easier, they can rewrite the equation in slope-intercept form. Stress that they can use the form that works best in a situation, and then move from one form to the other as needed to help solve the problem.

Closing the Lesson

Have students summarize the major points of the lesson and answer the Essential Question: How do you write linear equations in point-slope form?

- The point-slope form of an equation is $y - y_1 = m(x - x_1)$.
- The point-slope form uses the *x*-and *y*-coordinates of a point and the slope.

If you are given two points, use the slope formula to find the slope. Substitute the slope and the coordinates of a given point into the point-slope form.

EXAMPLE 2 on p. 303 for Exs. 14–19

GRAPHING EQUATIONS Graph the equation. 14–19. See margin.

14. $y - 5 = 3(x - 1)$ **15.** $y + 3 = -2(x - 2)$ **16.** $y - 1 = 3(x + 6)$

17. $y + 8 = -(x + 4)$ **18.** $y - 1 = \frac{3}{4}(x + 1)$ **19.** $y + 4 = -\frac{5}{2}(x - 3)$

EXAMPLE 3 on p. 303 for Exs. 20–30

USING A GRAPH Write an equation in point-slope form of the line shown.

20.

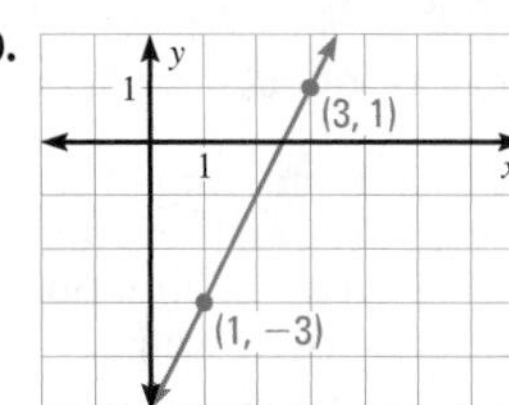

$y - 1 = 2(x - 3)$ or $y + 3 = 2(x - 1)$

21.

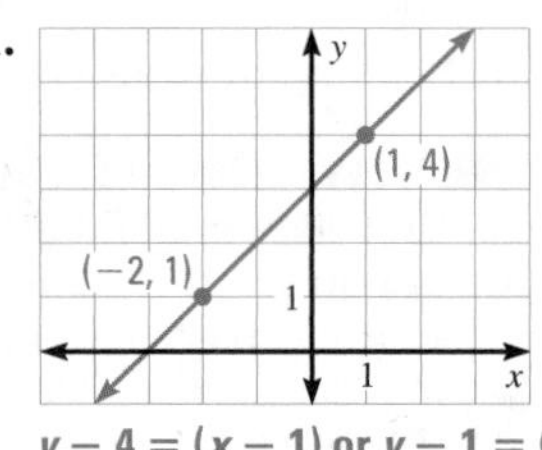

$y - 4 = (x - 1)$ or $y - 1 = (x + 2)$

22.

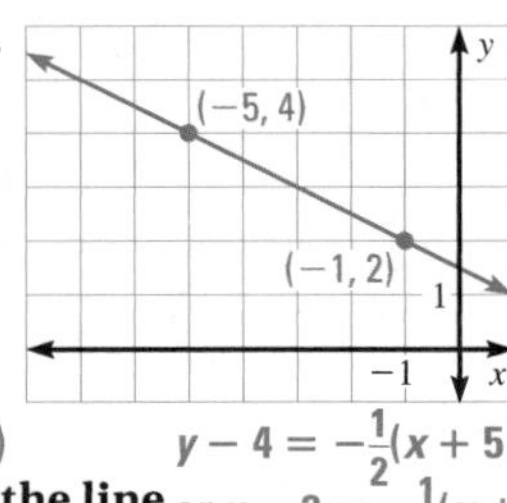

$y - 4 = -\frac{1}{2}(x + 5)$ or $y - 2 = -\frac{1}{2}(x + 1)$

WRITING EQUATIONS Write an equation in point-slope form of the line that passes through the given points. 23–28. See margin.

23. (7, 2), (2, 12) **24.** (6, −2), (12, 1) **25.** (−4, −1), (6, −7)

26. (4, 5), (−4, −5) **27.** (−3, −20), (4, 36) **28.** (−5, −19), (5, 13)

29. ERROR ANALYSIS *Describe* and correct the error in writing an equation of the line shown.

$m = \frac{4 - 2}{4 - 1} = \frac{2}{3}$ $y - 2 = \frac{2}{3}(x - 4)$

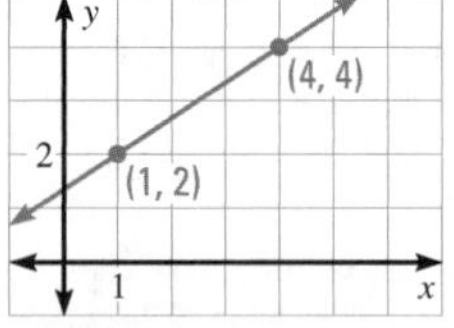

29. A point was not substituted into the equation, the y-coordinates of the two points were substituted; $y - 2 = \frac{2}{3}(x - 1)$.

30. ★ MULTIPLE CHOICE The graph of which equation is shown? B

Ⓐ $y + 4 = -3(x + 2)$ Ⓑ $y - 4 = -3(x - 2)$

Ⓒ $y - 4 = -3(x + 2)$ Ⓓ $y + 4 = -3(x - 2)$

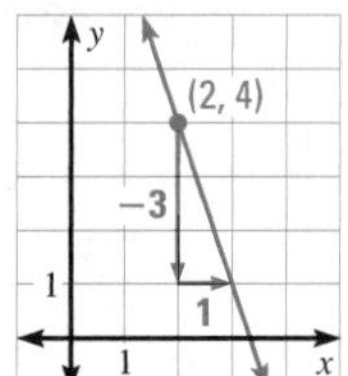

B **★ SHORT RESPONSE Tell whether the data in the table can be modeled by a linear equation. *Explain.* If possible, write an equation in point-slope form that relates y and x.** 31–34. See margin.

31.

x	2	4	6	8	10
y	−1	5	15	29	47

32.

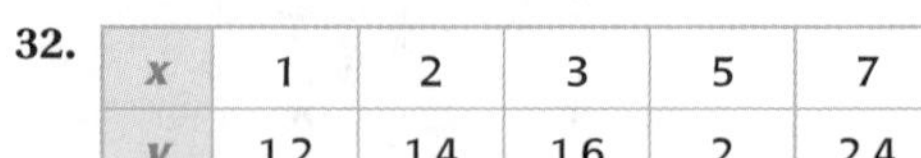

x	1	2	3	5	7
y	1.2	1.4	1.6	2	2.4

33.

x	1	2	3	4	5
y	2	−3	4	−5	6

34.

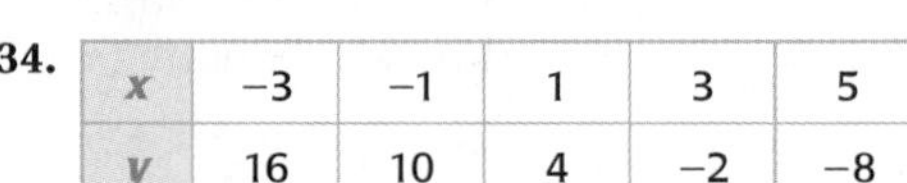

x	−3	−1	1	3	5
y	16	10	4	−2	−8

C **CHALLENGE Find the value of k so that the line passing through the given points has slope m. Write an equation of the line in point-slope form.**

35. $(k, 4k), (k + 2, 3k), m = -1$
2; $y - 8 = -(x - 2)$ or $y - 6 = -(x - 4)$

36. $(-k + 1, 3), (3, k + 3), m = 3$
−3; $y - 3 = 3(x - 4)$ or $y = 3(x - 3)$

○ = WORKED-OUT SOLUTIONS on p. WS1 ★ = STANDARDIZED TEST PRACTICE

4 PRACTICE AND APPLY

Assignment Guide

Answer Transparencies available for all exercises

Basic:
Day 1: EP p. 939 Exs. 42–45
pp. 305–308
Exs. 1–8, 12–17, 45–53
Day 2: pp. 305–308
Exs. 20–32, 37–42, 54–57

Average:
Day 1: pp. 305–308
Exs. 1, 2, 6–13, 17–19, 45–53
Day 2: pp. 305–308
Exs. 20–28 even, 29–34, 37–43, 54–57

Advanced:
Day 1: pp. 305–308
Exs. 1, 2, 7–12, 17–19, 35*, 36*, 45–53 odd
Day 2: pp. 305–308
Exs. 24–28, 30–34, 37–44*, 55, 57

Block:
pp. 305–308
Exs. 1, 2, 6–13, 17–19, 45–53 (with 5.2)
pp. 305–308
Exs. 20–28 even, 29–34, 37–43, 54–57 (with 5.4)

Differentiated Instruction

See *Algebra 1 Best Practices Toolkit* for suggestions on addressing the needs of a diverse classroom.

Homework Check

For a quick check of student understanding of key concepts, go over the following exercises:

Basic: 4, 16, 22, 37, 38
Average: 8, 17, 24, 38, 39
Advanced: 10, 18, 27, 38, 40

Extra Practice

- Student Edition, p. 942
- Chapter 5 Resource Book: Practice levels A, B, C, pp. 27–32

Practice Worksheet

An easily-readable reduced practice page (with answers) for this lesson can be found on p. 280C.

14.

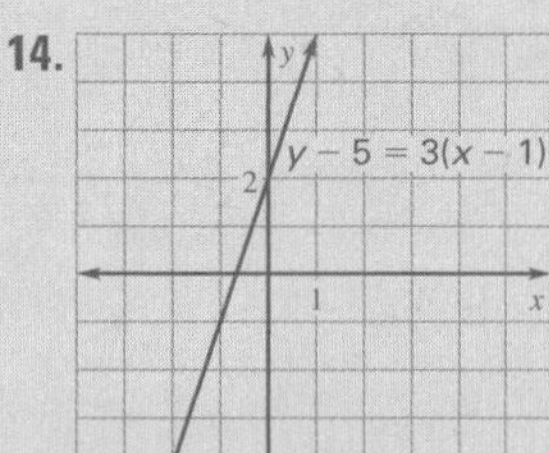

15.

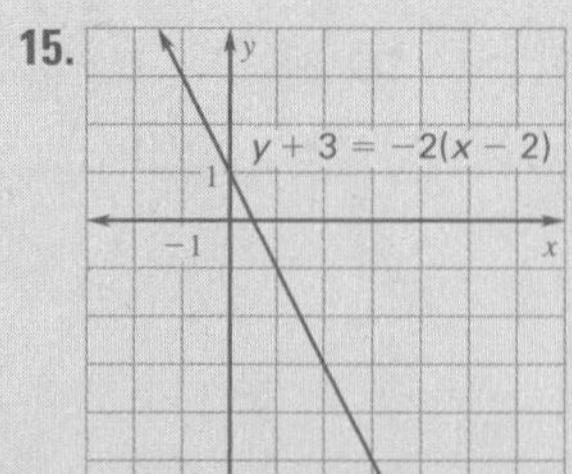

16.

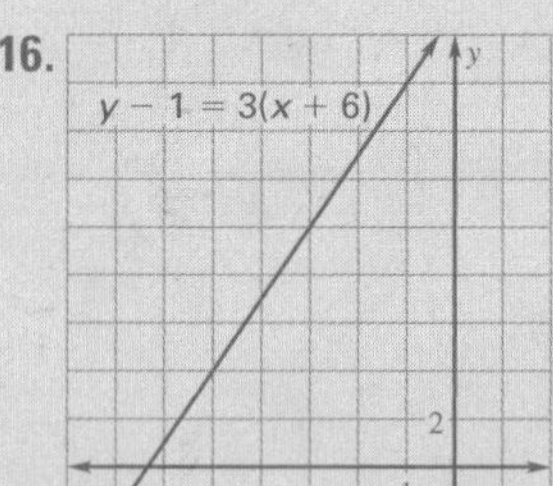

PROBLEM SOLVING

EXAMPLE 4 A on p. 304 for Exs. 37, 39, 40

37. TELEVISION In order to use an excerpt from a movie in a new television show, the television producer must pay the director of the movie \$790 for the first 2 minutes of the excerpt and \$130 per minute after that.

a. Write an equation that gives the total cost (in dollars) of using the excerpt as a function of the length (in minutes) of the excerpt. $y = 130x + 530$

b. Find the total cost of using an excerpt that is 8 minutes long. \$1570

@HomeTutor for problem solving help at classzone.com

EXAMPLE 5 on p. 304 for Exs. 38, 41

38. Since the cost increases at a constant rate of \$1714 per month, the situation can be modeled by a linear equation; \$5950; \$1714.

38. ★ SHORT RESPONSE A school district pays an installation fee and a monthly fee for Internet service. The table shows the total cost of Internet service for the school district over different numbers of months. *Explain* why the situation can be modeled by a linear equation. What is the installation fee? What is the monthly service fee?

Months of service	2	4	6	8	10	12
Total cost (dollars)	9,378	12,806	16,234	19,662	23,090	26,518

@HomeTutor for problem solving help at classzone.com

39. COMPANY SALES During the period 1994–2004, the annual sales of a small company increased by \$10,000 per year. In 1997 the annual sales were \$97,000. Write an equation that gives the annual sales as a function of the number of years since 1994. Find the sales in 2000. $y = 10000x + 67000$; \$127,000

Animated Algebra at classzone.com

40. TRAFFIC DELAYS From 1990 to 2001 in Boston, Massachusetts, the annual excess fuel (in gallons per person) consumed due to traffic delays increased by about 1.4 gallons per person each year. In 1995 each person consumed about 37 gallons of excess fuel.

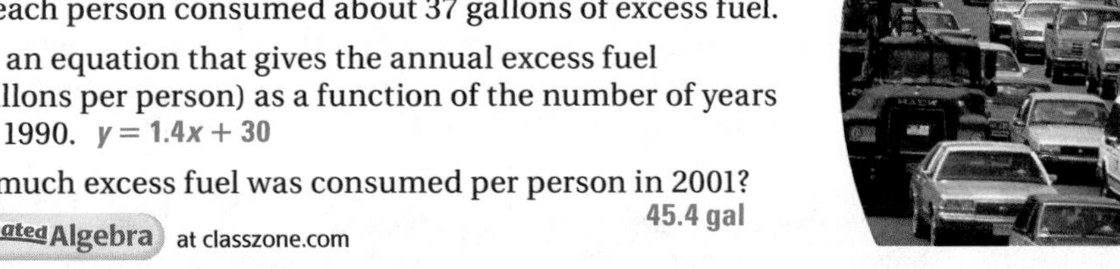

a. Write an equation that gives the annual excess fuel (in gallons per person) as a function of the number of years since 1990. $y = 1.4x + 30$

b. How much excess fuel was consumed per person in 2001? 45.4 gal

Animated Algebra at classzone.com

41a. Since the cost increases at a constant rate of \$.49 per print, the situation can be modeled by a linear equation.

41. ★ EXTENDED RESPONSE The table shows the cost of ordering sets of prints of digital photos from an online service. The cost per print is the same for the first 30 prints. There is also a shipping charge.

Number of prints	1	2	5	8
Total cost (dollars)	1.98	2.47	3.94	5.41

a. *Explain* why the situation can be modeled by a linear equation.

b. Write an equation in point-slope form that relates the total cost (in dollars) of a set of prints to the number of prints ordered. *Sample answer:* $y - 1.98 = 0.49(x - 1)$

c. Find the shipping charge for up to 10 prints. \$1.49

d. The cost of 15 prints is \$9.14. The shipping charge increases after the first 10 prints. Find the shipping charge for 15 prints. \$1.79

Avoiding Common Errors

Exercises 3–11, 23–28 Watch for students who fail to write both the subtraction symbol and negative symbol when they substitute negative values in the point-slope form.

Exercises 31, 32, 38, 41 Caution students that intervals for the data pairs are not always equal. To avoid errors, suggest they model Step 1 in Example 5 on page 304.

Study Strategy

Exercises 23–28 Suggest that students follow Example 3 on page 303 and use both points to write equations in point-slope form. They can then check that the equations are equivalent by writing them in slope-intercept form.

An **Animated Algebra** activity is available on-line for **Exercise 40.** This activity is also available on the **Power Presentations CD-ROM**.

23. $y - 2 = -2(x - 7)$ or $y - 12 = -2(x - 2)$

24. $y + 2 = \frac{1}{2}(x - 6)$ or $y - 1 = \frac{1}{2}(x - 12)$

25. $y + 1 = -\frac{3}{5}(x + 4)$ or $y + 7 = -\frac{3}{5}(x - 6)$

26. $y - 5 = \frac{5}{4}(x - 4)$ or $y + 5 = \frac{5}{4}(x + 4)$

27. $y + 20 = 8(x + 3)$ or $y - 36 = 8(x - 4)$

28. $y + 19 = \frac{16}{5}(x + 5)$ or $y - 13 = \frac{16}{5}(x - 5)$

31–34. See Additional Answers beginning on p. AA1.

17.

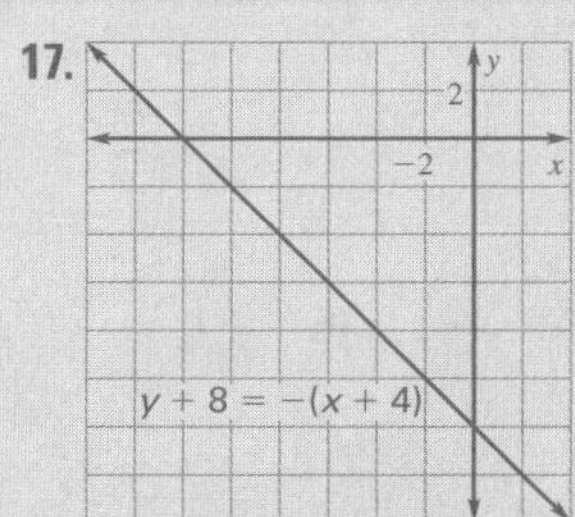

18.

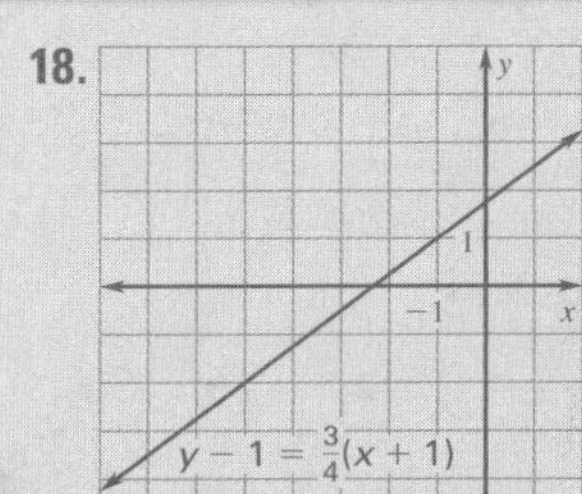

19.

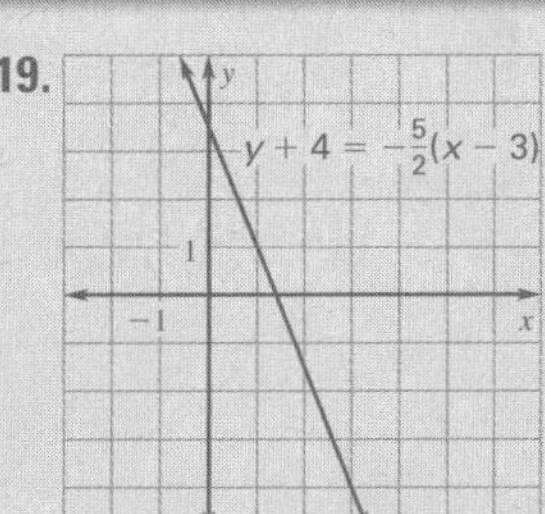

5 ASSESS AND RETEACH

Daily Homework Quiz

Transparency Available

1. Write an equation in point-slope form of the line that passes through (6, −4) and has slope 2. $y + 4 = 2(x - 6)$
2. Write an equation in point-slope form of the line that passes through (−1, −6) and (3, 10). $y + 6 = 4(x + 1)$ or $y - 10 = 4(x - 3)$
3. A travel company offers guided rafting trips for $875 for the first three days and $235 for each additional day. Write an equation that gives the total cost (in dollars) of a rafting trip as a function of the length of the trip. Find the cost for a 7-day trip. $C = 235t + 170$, where C is total cost and t is time (in days); $1815

Online Quiz

Available at **classzone.com**

Diagnosis/Remediation

- Practice A, B, C in Chapter 5 Resource Book, pp. 27–32
- Study Guide in Chapter 5 Resource Book, pp. 33–34
- Practice Workbook, pp. 71–73
- @HomeTutor

Challenge

Additional challenge is available in the Chapter 5 Resource Book, p. 37.

B

42. **AQUACULTURE** Aquaculture is the farming of fish and other aquatic animals. World aquaculture increased at a relatively constant rate from 1991 to 2002. In 1994 world aquaculture was about 20.8 million metric tons. In 2000 world aquaculture was about 35.5 million metric tons.

    a. Write an equation that gives world aquaculture (in millions of metric tons) as a function of the number of years since 1991. $y = 2.45x + 13.45$

    b. In 2001 China was responsible for 70.2% of world aquaculture. Approximate China's aquaculture in 2001. about 26.64 million metric tons

43. **MARATHON** The diagram shows a marathon runner's speed at several outdoor temperatures.

    a. Write an equation in point-slope form that relates running speed (in feet per second) to temperature (in degrees Fahrenheit). $y - 17.6 = -0.06(x - 60)$

    b. Estimate the runner's speed when the temperature is 80°F. 16.4 ft/sec

C

44. **CHALLENGE** The number of cans recycled per pound of aluminum recycled in the U.S. increased at a relatively constant rate from 1972 to 2002. In 1977 about 23.5 cans per pound of aluminum were recycled. In 2000, about 33.1 cans per pound of aluminum were recycled.

    a. Write an equation that gives the number of cans recycled per pound of aluminum recycled as a function of the number of years since 1972. $y = 0.417391x + 21.413$

    b. In 2002, there were 53.8 billion aluminum cans collected for recycling. Approximately how many pounds of aluminum were collected? *Explain* how you found your answer.

44b. 1.59 billion lb; find the number of cans recycled per pound of aluminum in 2002 by substituting 30 for x to get about 33.9 cans per pound. Divide 53.8 billion aluminum cans by 33.9 cans per pound to find the number of pounds of aluminum.

ILLINOIS MIXED REVIEW

TEST PRACTICE at classzone.com

45. You want to write an expression that will always produce an odd number. Which of the following will always produce an odd number for any integer, n? B

    Ⓐ $3n$ Ⓑ $2n + 1$ Ⓒ $5n - 1$ Ⓓ $5n + 1$

46. A 60 inch piece of wire was cut into equal segments, and the segments were then soldered together to form a cube. What is the volume of the cube? B

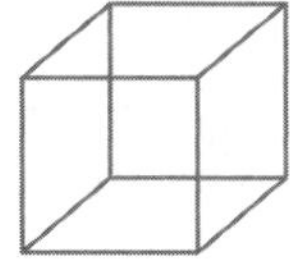

    Ⓐ 100 in.^{3} Ⓑ 125 in.^{3}
    Ⓒ 1000 in.^{3} Ⓓ 1728 in.^{3}

Extension
Use after Lesson 5.3

Relate Arithmetic Sequences to Linear Functions

GOAL Identify, graph, and write the general form of arithmetic sequences.

Key Vocabulary
- sequence
- arithmetic sequence
- common difference

A **sequence** is an ordered list of numbers. The numbers in a sequence are called *terms*. In an **arithmetic sequence**, the difference between consecutive terms is constant. The constant difference is called the **common difference**.

An arithmetic sequence has the form $a_1, a_1 + d, a_1 + 2d, \ldots$ where a_1 is the first term and d is the common difference. For instance, if $a_1 = 2$ and $d = 6$, then the sequence $2, 2 + 6, 2 + 2(6), \ldots$ or $2, 8, 14, \ldots$ is arithmetic.

EXAMPLE 1 Identify an arithmetic sequence

Tell whether the sequence is arithmetic. If it is, find the next two terms.

a. $-4, 1, 6, 11, 16, \ldots$ **b.** $3, 5, 9, 15, 23, \ldots$

Solution

a. The first term is $a_1 = -4$. Find the differences of consecutive terms.

$a_2 - a_1 = 1 - (-4) = 5$ $a_3 - a_2 = 6 - 1 = 5$

$a_4 - a_3 = 11 - 6 = 5$ $a_5 - a_4 = 16 - 11 = 5$

▶ Because the terms have a common difference ($d = 5$), the sequence is arithmetic. The next two terms are $a_6 = 21$ and $a_7 = 26$.

b. The first term is $a_1 = 3$. Find the differences of consecutive terms.

$a_2 - a_1 = 5 - 3 = 2$ $a_3 - a_2 = 9 - 5 = 4$

$a_4 - a_3 = 15 - 9 = 6$ $a_5 - a_4 = 23 - 15 = 8$

▶ There is no common difference, so the sequence is not arithmetic.

GRAPHING A SEQUENCE To graph a sequence, let a term's position number in the sequence be the x-value. The term is the corresponding y-value.

EXAMPLE 2 Graph a sequence

Graph the sequence $-4, 1, 6, 11, 16, \ldots$.

Make a table pairing each term with its position number.

Position, x	1	2	3	4	5
Term, y	−4	1	6	11	16

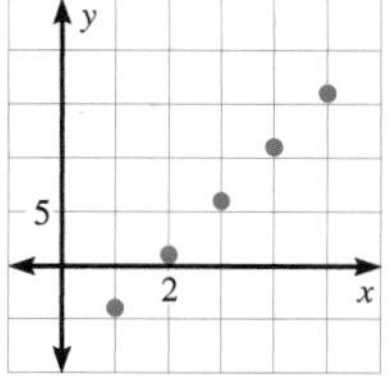

Plot the pairs in the table as points in a coordinate plane.

1 PLAN AND PREPARE

Warm-Up Exercises

Find the next two numbers in the pattern.

1. 6, 13, 20, 27, 34, . . . 41, 48

2. 2, 3, 5, 8, 12, . . . 17, 23

3. 54, 43, 32, 21, . . . 10, −1

4. −5, −2, 1, 4, 7, . . . 10, 13

2 FOCUS AND MOTIVATE

Essential Question

Big Idea 2, p. 281

How do you use a linear model to identify, graph, and write the general form of arithmetic sequences? Tell students they will learn how to answer this question by using the difference between terms in a sequence to extend the sequence or to find the *n*th term.

3 TEACH

Extra Example 1

Tell whether the sequence is arithmetic. If it is, find the next two terms.

a. 3, 4, 7, 12, 19, . . . no

b. 13, 9, 5, 1, −3, . . . yes; −7, −11

NCTM STANDARDS

Standard 9: Understand how mathematical ideas build on one another

Standard 10: Use representations to communicate mathematical ideas

Extra Example 2

Graph the sequence 13, 9, 5, 1, −3, ...

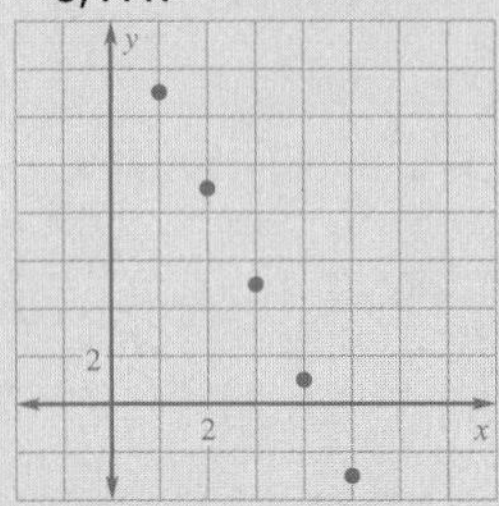

Extra Example 3

Write a rule for the nth term of the sequence 13, 9, 5, 1, −3, ... Find a_{100}. $a_n = 13 + (n - 1)(-4)$; −383

Closing the Lesson

Have students summarize the major points of the lesson and answer the Essential Question: How do you use a linear model to identify, graph, and write the general form of arithmetic sequences?

- A sequence is arithmetic if consecutive terms have a common difference.
- The rule for an arithmetic sequence is $a_n = a_1 + (n - 1)d$ where a_n is the nth term, a_1 is the first term, and d is the common difference.

Use the common difference between consecutive terms to find the next term. Pair a term with its position in the sequence to graph the sequence. Substitute the first term, the value of n, and the common difference into the arithmetic sequence rule to find the nth term.

4 PRACTICE AND APPLY

Avoiding Common Errors

Exercises 1–3 Some students may use a positive number as a common difference when it should be a negative number. Tell students that the common difference between consecutive terms can be a positive or a negative number. Remind them to subtract each term from the one right after it to find the common difference.

FUNCTIONS Notice that the points plotted in Example 2 appear to lie on a line. In fact, an arithmetic sequence is a linear function. You can think of the common difference d as the slope and $(1, a_1)$ as a point on the graph of the function. An equation in point-slope form for the function is $a_n - a_1 = d(n - 1)$. This equation can be rewritten as $a_n = a_1 + (n - 1)d$.

KEY CONCEPT *For Your Notebook*

Rule for an Arithmetic Sequence

The nth term of an arithmetic sequence with first term a_1 and common difference d is given by $a_n = a_1 + (n - 1)d$.

EXAMPLE 3 Write a rule for the nth term of a sequence

Write a rule for the nth term of the sequence −4, 1, 6, 11, 16, ... Find a_{100}.

Solution

The first term of the sequence is $a_1 = -4$, and the common difference is $d = 5$.

$a_n = a_1 + (n - 1)d$ — Write general rule for an arithmetic sequence.

$a_n = -4 + (n - 1)5$ — Substitute −4 for a_1 and 5 for d.

Find a_{100} by substituting 100 for n.

$a_n = -4 + (n - 1)5$ — Write the rule for the sequence.

$a_{100} = -4 + (100 - 1)5$ — Substitute 100 for n.

$a_{100} = 491$ — Evaluate.

PRACTICE

EXAMPLE 1 on p. 309 for Exs. 1–3

Tell whether the sequence is arithmetic. If it is, find the next two terms. If it is not, explain why not.

1. 17, 14, 11, 8, 5, . . . yes; 2, −1
2. 1, 4, 16, 64, 256, . . . No; there is no common difference.
3. −8, −15, −22, −29, −36, . . . yes; −43, −50

EXAMPLE 2 on p. 309 for Exs. 4–9

Graph the sequence. 4–9. See margin.

4. 1, 4, 7, 11, 14, . . .
5. 4, −3, −10, −17, −24, . . .
6. 5, −1, −7, −13, −19, . . .
7. 2, $3\frac{1}{2}$, 5, $6\frac{1}{2}$, 8, . . .
8. 0, 2, 4, 6, 8, . . .
9. −3, −4, −5, −6, −7, . . .

EXAMPLE 3 on p. 310 for Exs. 10–15

Write a rule for the nth term of the sequence. Find a_{100}. 10–15. See margin.

10. −12, −5, 2, 9, 16, . . .
11. 51, 72, 93, 114, 135, . . .
12. 0.25, −0.75, −1.75, −2.75, . . .
13. $\frac{1}{4}, \frac{3}{8}, \frac{1}{2}, \frac{5}{8}, \frac{3}{4}, \ldots$
14. 0, −5, −10, −15, −20, . . .
15. 1, $1\frac{1}{3}$, $1\frac{2}{3}$, 2, $2\frac{1}{3}$, . . .
16. **REASONING** For an arithmetic sequence with a first term of a_1 and a common difference of d, show that $a_{n+1} - a_n = d$. A term after the first term is the sum of the previous term and the common difference, so $a_{n+1} = a_n + d$, subtract a_n from both sides, $a_{n+1} - a_n = d$.

4–9. See Additional Answers beginning on p. AA1.

10. $a_n = -12 + (n - 1)7$; 681
11. $a_n = 51 + (n - 1)21$; 2130
12. $a_n = 0.25 + (n - 1)(-1)$; −98.75
13. $a_n = \frac{1}{4} + (n - 1)\frac{1}{8}$; $12\frac{5}{8}$
14. $a_n = (n - 1)(-5)$; −495
15. $a_n = 1 + (n - 1)\frac{1}{3}$; 34

5.4 Write Linear Equations in Standard Form

 **8.11.07** Analyze functions by investigating domain, range, rates of change, intercepts, and zeros.

Before You wrote equations in point-slope form.

Now You will write equations in standard form.

Why? So you can find possible combinations of objects, as in Ex. 41.

Key Vocabulary
- **standard form,** *p. 215*

Recall that the linear equation $Ax + By = C$ is in standard form, where A, B, and C are real numbers and A and B are not both zero. All linear equations can be written in standard form.

EXAMPLE 1 Write equivalent equations in standard form

Write two equations in standard form that are equivalent to $2x - 6y = 4$.

Solution

To write one equivalent equation, multiply each side by 2.

$$4x - 12y = 8$$

To write another equivalent equation, multiply each side by 0.5.

$$x - 3y = 2$$

EXAMPLE 2 Write an equation from a graph

Write an equation in standard form of the line shown.

Solution

STEP 1 **Calculate** the slope.

$$m = \frac{1 - (-2)}{1 - 2} = \frac{3}{-1} = -3$$

STEP 2 **Write** an equation in point-slope form. Use (1, 1).

$y - y_1 = m(x - x_1)$ **Write point-slope form.**

$y - 1 = -3(x - 1)$ **Substitute 1 for y_1, −3 for m, and 1 for x_1.**

STEP 3 **Rewrite** the equation in standard form.

$3x + y = 4$ **Simplify. Collect variable terms on one side, constants on the other.**

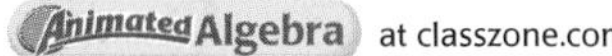 at classzone.com

✓ GUIDED PRACTICE for Examples 1 and 2

1. Write two equations in standard form that are equivalent to $x - y = 3$. *Sample answer:* $2x - 2y = 6$, $3x - 3y = 9$
2. Write an equation in standard form of the line through (3, −1) and (2, −3). $-2x + y = -7$

1 PLAN AND PREPARE

Warm-Up Exercises

Transparency Available

Write an equation in point-slope form of the line that passes through the given points.

1. (1, 4), (6, −1) $y - 4 = -(x - 1)$ or $y + 1 = -(x - 6)$
2. (−1, −2), (2, 7) $y + 2 = 3(x + 1)$ or $y - 7 = 3(x - 2)$
3. A store rents 3 DVDs for \$5, plus \$3 for each additional DVD. Find the cost of renting 20 DVDs. \$56

Notetaking Guide

Transparency Available

Promotes interactive learning and notetaking skills, pp. 109–112.

Pacing

Basic: 2 days
Average: 2 days
Advanced: 2 days
Block: 0.5 block with 5.3
0.5 block with 5.5
- See *Teaching Guide/Lesson Plan.*

2 FOCUS AND MOTIVATE

Essential Question

Big Idea 1, p. 281

How do you write an equation in standard form? **Tell students they will learn how to answer this question by rewriting equations.**

Resource Planning Guide

Chapter Resource Book
- Teaching Guide/Lesson Plan (pp. 38–39)
- Activity Master (p. 40)
- Practice levels A, B, C (pp. 41–43)
- Study Guide (pp. 44–45)
- Catch-up for Absent Students (p. 46)
- Problem Solving Workshop (p. 47)
- Challenge (p. 49)

Workbooks
- Notetaking Guide (pp. 109–112)
- Practice Workbook (pp. 74–75)

Teaching Options
- **Power Presentations CD-ROM** provides dynamic electronic teaching resources for the classroom.
- **Activity Generator CD-ROM** provides editable activities for all ability levels.

Interactive Technology
- Easy Planner
- Power Presentations CD-ROM
- Activity Generator CD-ROM
- Animated Algebra
- Test Generator CD-ROM
- Online Quiz
- eWorkbook
- eEdition
- @HomeTutor

Resources for English Learners
- Quick Reference for English Learners
- Spanish Study Guide
- Multi-Language Visual Glossary
- Student Resources in Spanish

See also the *Algebra 1 Toolkit* for more strategies for meeting individual needs.

Motivating the Lesson

You want to earn \$1000 teaching children how to swim. You earn \$10 per hour for individual instruction and \$25 per hour for instructing groups. By knowing how to write equations in standard form, you can determine the possible combinations of hours of individual and group instruction that will result in \$1000 in earnings.

3 TEACH

Extra Example 1

Write two equations in standard form that are equivalent to $x + 4y = 3$. $-2x - 8y = -6$; $3x + 12y = 9$

Extra Example 2

Write an equation in standard form of the line shown. $2x + y = 6$

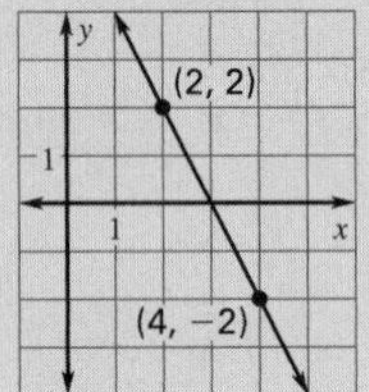

An **Animated Algebra** activity is available on-line for **Example 2**. This activity is also available on the **Power Presentations CD-ROM**.

Extra Example 3

Write an equation of the line.

a. Line a $x = -3$

b. Line b $y = 2$

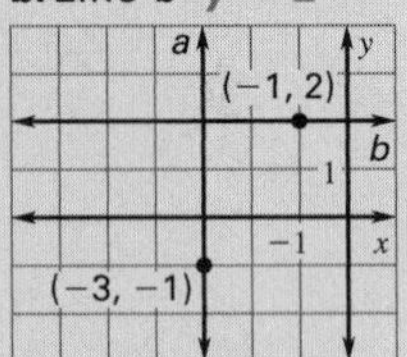

HORIZONTAL AND VERTICAL LINES Recall that equations of horizontal lines have the form $y = a$. Equations of vertical lines have the form $x = b$. You cannot write an equation for a vertical line in slope-intercept form or point-slope form, because a vertical line has no slope. However, you can write an equation for a vertical line in standard form.

EXAMPLE 3 Write an equation of a line

Write an equation of the specified line.

a. Blue line **b.** Red line

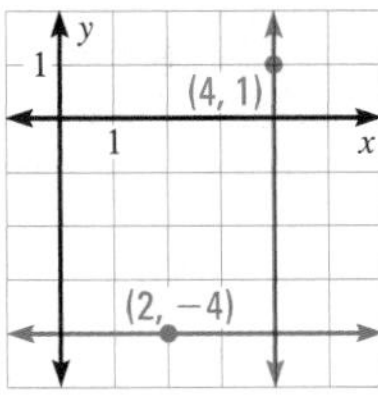

Solution

ANOTHER WAY Using the slope-intercept form to find an equation of the horizontal line gives you $y = 0x - 4$, or $y = -4$.

a. The y-coordinate of the given point on the blue line is -4. This means that all points on the line have a y-coordinate of -4. An equation of the line is $y = -4$.

b. The x-coordinate of the given point on the red line is 4. This means that all points on the line have an x-coordinate of 4. An equation of the line is $x = 4$.

EXAMPLE 4 Complete an equation in standard form

Find the missing coefficient in the equation of the line shown. Write the completed equation.

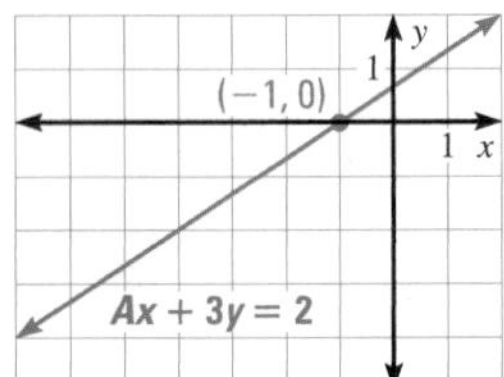

Solution

STEP 1 **Find** the value of A. Substitute the coordinates of the given point for x and y in the equation. Solve for A.

$Ax + 3y = 2$	Write equation.
$A(-1) + 3(0) = 2$	Substitute −1 for x and 0 for y.
$-A = 2$	Simplify.
$A = -2$	Divide by −1.

STEP 2 **Complete** the equation.

$-2x + 3y = 2$ Substitute −2 for A.

✓ GUIDED PRACTICE for Examples 3 and 4

Write equations of the horizontal and vertical lines that pass through the given point.

3. $(-8, -9)$ $y = -9, x = -8$

4. $(13, -5)$ $y = -5, x = 13$

Find the missing coefficient in the equation of the line that passes through the given point. Write the completed equation.

5. $-4x + By = 7, (-1, 1)$ $3; -4x + 3y = 7$

6. $Ax + y = -3, (2, 11)$ $-7; -7x + y = -3$

Differentiated Instruction

Visual Learners For the equations of vertical lines ($x = a$) and horizontal lines ($y = b$), remind students that the constants a and b are not the same as the A and B in the equation for the standard form of a line. Constants a and b correspond to C in the standard form of a line.

See also the *Algebra 1 Toolkit* for more strategies.

EXAMPLE 5 Solve a multi-step problem

LIBRARY Your class is taking a trip to the public library. You can travel in small and large vans. A small van holds 8 people and a large van holds 12 people. Your class could fill 15 small vans and 2 large vans.

a. **Write** an equation in standard form that models the possible combinations of small vans and large vans that your class could fill.

b. **Graph** the equation from part (a).

c. **List** several possible combinations.

Solution

a. Write a verbal model. Then write an equation.

Capacity of small van	·	Number of small vans	+	Capacity of large van	·	Number of large vans	=	People on trip
8	·	s	+	12	·	ℓ	=	p

Because your class could fill 15 small vans and 2 large vans, use (15, 2) as the s- and ℓ-values to substitute in the equation $8s + 12\ell = p$ to find the value of p.

$8(15) + 12(2) = p$ **Substitute 15 for s and 2 for ℓ.**

$144 = p$ **Simplify.**

Substitute 144 for p in the equation $8s + 12\ell = p$.

▶ The equation $8s + 12\ell = 144$ models the possible combinations.

b. Find the intercepts of the graph.

Substitute 0 for s.	Substitute 0 for ℓ.
$8(0) + 12\ell = 144$	$8s + 12(0) = 144$
$\ell = 12$	$s = 18$

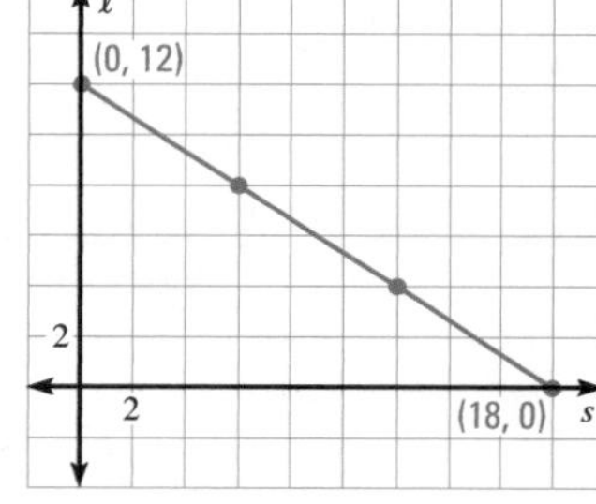

Plot the points (0, 12) and (18, 0). Connect them with a line segment. For this problem only nonnegative whole-number values of s and ℓ make sense.

c. The graph passes through (0, 12), (6, 8),(12, 4), and (18, 0). So, four possible combinations are 0 small and 12 large, 6 small and 8 large, 12 small and 4 large, 18 small and 0 large.

LISTING COMBINATIONS
Other combinations of small and large vans are possible. Another way to find possible combinations is by substituting values for s or ℓ in the equation.

GUIDED PRACTICE for Example 5

7. **WHAT IF?** In Example 5, suppose that 8 students decide not to go on the class trip. Write an equation that models the possible combinations of small and large vans that your class could fill. List several possible combinations. $8s + 12l = 136$. *Sample answer:* 17 small, 0 large; 14 small, 2 large; 11 small, 4 large; 8 small, 6 large; 5 small, 8 large; 2 small, 10 large

Extra Example 4

Find the missing coefficient in the equation of the line shown. Write the completed equation.

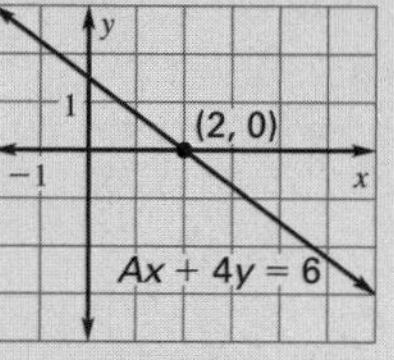

$3x + 4y = 6$

Extra Example 5

T-shirts at a flea market cost $4.50 each and shorts cost $6 each. You have enough money to buy exactly 12 T-shirts and 9 pairs of shorts.

a. Write an equation in standard form that models the possible combinations of T-shirts and shorts you can buy. $4.5t + 6s = 108$

b. Graph the equation.

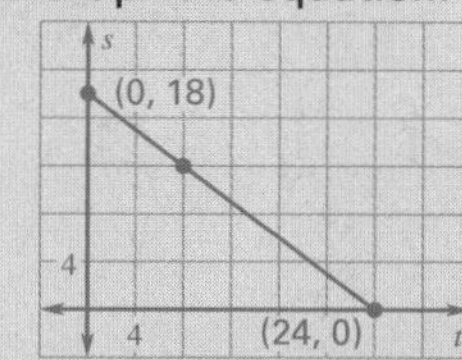

c. List several possible combinations. 0 T-shirts and 18 shorts; 8 T-shirts and 12 shorts; 24 T-shirts and 0 shorts

Closing the Lesson

Have students summarize the major points of the lesson and answer the Essential Question: How do you write an equation in standard form?

- $Ax + By = C$ is the standard form of an equation where A, B, and C are real numbers, and A and B are not both 0.

Use the slope formula to find the slope. Write the equation in point-slope form. Collect variable terms on one side of the equation and constants on the other to rewrite the equation in standard form.

Differentiated Instruction

Below Level Have students find two other combinations in **Example 5** part (c) using the suggestion in the side note to substitute values for s or ℓ in the equation. After the students find the combinations (3, 10) and (9, 6), ask them to describe the combinations in terms of small and large vans and coordinates on a graph. Ask them to compare the methods of using an equation and a graph to obtain possible combinations, leading them to discuss the advantages and disadvantages of both methods.

See also the *Algebra 1 Toolkit* for more strategies.

4 PRACTICE AND APPLY

Assignment Guide

Answer Transparencies available for all exercises

Basic:
Day 1: EP p. 941 Exs. 37–40
pp. 314–316
Exs. 1–8, 11–19, 47–49
Day 2: pp. 314–316
Exs. 23–32, 38–41, 45, 46

Average:
Day 1: pp. 314–316
Exs. 1–4, 8–10, 14–22, 47–49
Day 2: pp. 314–316
Exs. 23–29 odd, 30–36, 38–43, 45, 46

Advanced:
Day 1: pp. 314–316
Exs. 1–4, 8–10, 16–22, 37*, 47–49
Day 2: pp. 314–316
Exs. 26–28, 30–36, 41–46*

Block:
pp. 314–316
Exs. 1–4, 8–10, 14–22, 47–49 (with 5.3)
pp. 314–316
Exs. 23–29 odd, 30–36, 38–43, 45, 46 (with 5.5)

Differentiated Instruction

See *Algebra 1 Best Practices Toolkit* for suggestions on addressing the needs of a diverse classroom.

Homework Check

For a quick check of student understanding of key concepts, go over the following exercises:

Basic: 6, 12, 24, 29, 38
Average: 9, 16, 27, 32, 39
Advanced: 10, 20, 27, 34, 38

Extra Practice

- Student Edition, p. 942
- Chapter 5 Resource Book: Practice levels A, B, C, pp. 41–43

Practice Worksheet

An easily-readable reduced practice page (with answers) for this lesson can be found on p. 280D.

5.4 EXERCISES

HOMEWORK KEY
○ = WORKED-OUT SOLUTIONS on p. WS11 for Exs. 17 and 39
★ = STANDARDIZED TEST PRACTICE Exs. 4, 30, 40, and 42
◆ = MULTIPLE REPRESENTATIONS Ex. 41

SKILL PRACTICE

A

VOCABULARY **Identify the form of the equation.**

1. $2x + 8y = -3$ standard form
2. $y = -5x + 8$ slope-intercept form
3. $y + 4 = 2(x - 6)$ point-slope form

4. ★ **WRITING** *Explain* how to write an equation of a line in standard form when two points on the line are given. Find the slope of the line then substitute the slope and one of the points into the point-slope form. Collect variables on one side and constants on the other side.

EXAMPLE 1 on p. 311 for Exs. 5–10

EQUIVALENT EQUATIONS **Write two equations in standard form that are equivalent to the given equation.** 5–10. See margin.

5. $x + y = -10$
6. $5x + 10y = 15$
7. $-x + 2y = 9$
8. $-9x - 12y = 6$
9. $9x - 3y = -12$
10. $-2x + 4y = -5$

EXAMPLE 2 on p. 311 for Exs. 11–22

17. $\frac{2}{3}x + y = -\frac{4}{3}$
19. $-\frac{4}{3}x + y = -1$
21. $-\frac{1}{2}x + y = 1$

WRITING EQUATIONS **Write an equation in standard form of the line that passes through the given point and has the given slope m or that passes through the two given points.**

11. $(-3, 2), m = 1$ $-x + y = 5$
12. $(4, -1), m = 3$ $-3x + y = -13$
13. $(0, 5), m = -2$ $2x + y = 5$
14. $(-8, 0), m = -4$ $4x + y = -32$
15. $(-4, -4), m = -\frac{3}{2}$ $\frac{3}{2}x + y = -10$
16. $(-6, -10), m = \frac{1}{6}$ $-\frac{1}{6}x + y = -9$
17. $(-8, 4), (4, -4)$
18. $(-5, 2), (-4, 3)$ $-x + y = 7$
19. $(0, -1), (-6, -9)$
20. $(3, 9), (1, 1)$ $-4x + y = -3$
21. $(10, 6), (-12, -5)$
22. $(-6, -2), (-1, -2)$ $y = -2$

EXAMPLE 3 on p. 312 for Exs. 23–28

HORIZONTAL AND VERTICAL LINES **Write equations of the horizontal and vertical lines that pass through the given point.**

23. $(3, 2)$ $y = 2, x = 3$
24. $(-5, -3)$ $y = -3, x = -5$
25. $(-1, 3)$ $y = 3, x = -1$
26. $(5, 3)$ $y = 3, x = 5$
27. $(-1, 4)$ $y = 4, x = -1$
28. $(-6, -2)$ $y = -2, x = -6$

EXAMPLE 4 on p. 312 for Exs. 29–36

B

29. (1, −4) was substituted incorrectly, 1 should be substituted for x and −4 substituted for y, $A(1) - 3(-4) = 5$, $A + 12 = 5$, $A = -7$.

32. $\frac{1}{2}$; $\frac{1}{2}x - 4y = -1$

29. **ERROR ANALYSIS** *Describe* and correct the error in finding the value of A for the equation $Ax - 3y = 5$, if the graph of the equation passes through the point $(1, -4)$.

$$A(-4) - 3(1) = 5$$
$$A = -2$$

30. ★ **MULTIPLE CHOICE** The graph of the equation $Ax + 2y = -2$ is a line that passes through $(2, -2)$. What is the value of A? B

(A) −1 (B) 1 (C) 2 (D) 3

COMPLETING EQUATIONS **Find the missing coefficient in the equation of the line that passes through the given point. Write the completed equation.**

31. $Ax + 3y = 5, (2, -1)$ 4; $4x + 3y = 5$
32. $Ax - 4y = -1, (6, 1)$
33. $-x + By = 10, (-2, -2)$ −4; $-x - 4y = 10$
34. $8x + By = 4, (-5, 4)$ 11; $8x + 11y = 4$
35. $Ax - 3y = -5, (1, 0)$ −5; $-5x - 3y = -5$
36. $2x + By = -4, (-3, 7)$ $\frac{2}{7}$; $2x + \frac{2}{7}y = -4$

C

37. **CHALLENGE** Write an equation in standard form of the line that passes through $(0, a)$ and $(b, 0)$ where $a \neq 0$ and $b \neq 0$. $\frac{a}{b}x + y = a$

5–10. Sample answers are given.
5. $2x + 2y = -20$, $3x + 3y = -30$
6. $x + 2y = 3$, $10x + 20y = 30$
7. $x - 2y = -9$, $-2x + 4y = 18$
8. $-3x - 4y = 2$, $-6x - 8y = 4$
9. $3x - y = -4$, $6x - 2y = -8$
10. $2x - 4y = 5$, $-4x + 8y = -10$

PROBLEM SOLVING

EXAMPLE 5 [A] on p. 313 for Exs. 38–41

38. GARDENING The diagram shows the prices of two types of ground cover plants. Write an equation in standard form that models the possible combinations of vinca and phlox plants a gardener can buy for $300. List three of these possible combinations. $2.5p + 1.2v = 300$; *Sample answer:* 120 phlox plants and 0 vinca plants, 0 phlox plants and 250 vinca plants, 60 phlox plants and 125 vinca plants

@HomeTutor for problem solving help at classzone.com

39. NUTRITION A snack mix requires a total of 120 ounces of some corn cereal and some wheat cereal. Corn cereal comes in 12 ounce boxes.

a. The last time you made this mix, you used 5 boxes of corn cereal and 4 boxes of wheat cereal. How many ounces are in a box of wheat cereal? 15 oz

b. Write an equation in standard form that models the possible combinations of boxes of wheat and corn cereal you can use. $12c + 15w = 120$

c. List all possible combinations of whole boxes of wheat and corn cereal you can use to make the snack mix. 10 corn, 0 wheat; 5 corn, 4 wheat; 0 corn, 8 wheat

@HomeTutor for problem solving help at classzone.com

40. $20n + 5t = 100$; see margin for art. The n-intercept, 5, is the number of nights of boarding the dog at the kennel without any treats. The t-intercept, 20, is the number of treats that can be bought without boarding the dog for any nights.

40. ★ SHORT RESPONSE A dog kennel charges $20 per night to board your dog. You can also have a doggie treat delivered to your dog for $5. Write an equation that models the possible combinations of nights at the kennel and doggie treats that you can buy for $100. Graph the equation. *Explain* what the intercepts of the graph mean in this situation.

[B]

41. ◆ MULTIPLE REPRESENTATIONS As the student council treasurer, you prepare the budget for your class rafting trip. Each large raft costs $100 to rent, and each small raft costs $40 to rent. You have $1600 to spend.

a. **Writing an Equation** Write an equation in standard form that models the possible combinations of small rafts and large rafts that you can rent. $100\ell + 40s = 1600$

b. **Drawing a Graph** Graph the equation from part (a). See margin.

c. **Making a Table** Make a table that shows several combinations of small and large rafts that you can rent. See margin.

42. ★ SHORT RESPONSE One bus ride costs $.75. One subway ride costs $1.00. A monthly pass can be used for unlimited subway and bus rides and costs the same as 36 subway rides plus 36 bus rides.

a. Write an equation in standard form that models the possible combinations of bus and subway rides with the same value as the pass. $0.75b + s = 63$

b. You ride the bus 60 times in one month. How many times must you ride the subway in order for the cost of the rides to equal the value of the pass? *Explain* your answer. 18 subway rides; if you ride the bus 60 times, it costs $(0.75)\$60 = \$45$ without the pass. The pass costs $63, you need to spend $18 on subway rides, $\$18 \div 1 = \$18$.

Avoiding Common Errors

Exercises 5–10 Watch for students who overlook one of the terms of the equation or one of the sides of the equation when multiplying to write an equivalent equation. Remind these students that they must use every term of the equation as a factor to obtain an equivalent equation.

Teaching Strategy

Exercise 42 You may want to use this exercise to illustrate why it makes sense in some problems to substitute values in an equation to find possible combinations. Point out the side note to Example 5 which mentions the method of substitution as another way to find possible combinations. Point out that either method works well for Example 5. Then draw students' attention to Exercise 42. After they write the equation in part (a), ask them to find the intercepts of the equation. Discuss how the points (0, 63) and (84, 0) would make this a difficult problem to graph. Suggest that students pay attention to practical matters such as very large numbers when solving problems of this type.

41c.

Large rafts	Small rafts
16	0
14	5
12	10
10	15
8	20
6	25
4	30
2	35
0	40

40.

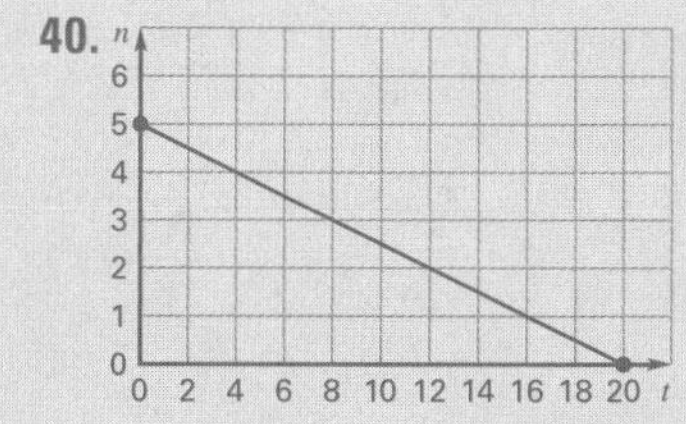

41b.

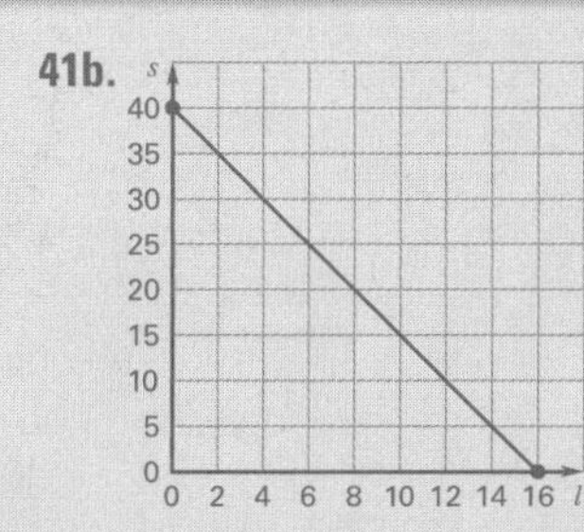

5 ASSESS AND RETEACH

Daily Homework Quiz

Transparency Available

Write an equation in standard form of the line that passes through the given point and has the given slope m or that passes through the two given points.

1. $(1, -6)$, $m = -2$ $2x + y = -4$
2. $(-4, -3)$, $(2, 9)$ $-2x + y = 5$
3. You have \$96 to spend on campground activities. You can rent a paddleboat for \$8 per hour and a kayak for \$6 per hour. Write an equation in standard form that models the possible hourly combinations of activities you can afford. List three possible combinations. $8p + 6c = 96$; 16 h kayak and 0 h paddleboat; 12 h paddleboat and 0 h kayak; 6 h paddleboat and 8 h kayak

Available at **classzone.com**

Diagnosis/Remediation

- Practice A, B, C in Chapter 5 Resource Book, pp. 41–43
- Study Guide in Chapter 5 Resource Book, pp. 44–45
- Practice Workbook, pp. 74–75
- @HomeTutor

Challenge

Additional challenge is available in the Chapter 5 Resource Book, p. 49.

Quiz

An easily-readable reduced copy of the quiz (with answers) on Lessons 5.1–5.4 from the Assessment Book can be found on p. 280F.

43, Quiz 7–9. See Additional Answers beginning on p. AA1.

43. **GEOMETRY** Write an equation in standard form that models the possible lengths and widths (in feet) of a rectangle having the same perimeter as a rectangle that is 10 feet wide and 20 feet long. Make a table that shows five possible lengths and widths of the rectangle. $2\ell + 2w = 60$; see margin for table.

C 44. **CHALLENGE** You are working in a chemistry lab. You have 1000 milliliters of pure acid. A dilution of acid is created by adding pure acid to water. A 40% dilution contains 40% acid and 60% water. You have been asked to make a 40% dilution and a 60% dilution of pure acid.

a. Write an equation in standard form that models the possible quantities of each dilution you can prepare using all 1000 milliliters of pure acid. $0.4x + 0.6y = 1000$

b. You prepare 700 milliliters of the 40% dilution. How much of the 60% dilution can you prepare? 1200 mL

c. How much water do you need to prepare 700 milliliters of the 40% dilution? 420 mL

ILLINOIS MIXED REVIEW

TEST PRACTICE at classzone.com

45. The dollar amount that a catering company charges for a party is $19x + 100$ where x is the number of guests. If the catering budget for a certain party is \$600, how many guests can attend? B

Ⓐ 21 Ⓑ 26 Ⓒ 31 Ⓓ 36

46. The amount of liquid that can fill a jar represents the jar's ____. C

Ⓐ area Ⓑ surface area Ⓒ volume Ⓓ circumference

QUIZ *for Lessons 5.1–5.4*

Write an equation in slope-intercept form of the line that passes through the given point and has the given slope m.

1. $(2, 5)$, $m = 3$ *(p. 292)* $y = 3x - 1$
2. $(-1, 4)$, $m = -2$ *(p. 292)* $y = -2x + 2$
3. $(0, -7)$, $m = 5$ *(p. 283)* $y = 5x - 7$

Write an equation in slope-intercept form of the line that passes through the given points.

4. $(0, 2)$, $(9, 5)$ *(p. 283)* $y = \frac{1}{3}x + 2$
5. $(5, 7)$, $(19, 14)$ *(p. 292)* $y = \frac{1}{2}x + \frac{9}{2}$
6. $(4, 24)$, $(-11, 19)$ *(p. 292)* $y = \frac{1}{3}x + \frac{68}{3}$

Write an equation in (a) point-slope form and (b) standard form of the line that passes through the given points. *(pp. 302, 311)* 7–9. See margin.

7. $(-5, 2)$, $(-4, 3)$
8. $(0, -1)$, $(-6, -9)$
9. $(3, 9)$, $(1, 1)$

10. **DVDS** The table shows the price per DVD for different quantities of DVDs. Write an equation that models the price per DVD as a function of the number of DVDs purchased. *(p. 302)* $y = -2x + 22$

Number of DVDs purchased	1	2	3	4	5	6
Price per DVD (dollars)	20	18	16	14	12	10

EXTRA PRACTICE for Lesson 5.4, p. 942

ONLINE QUIZ at classzone.com

Illinois *Mixed Review*

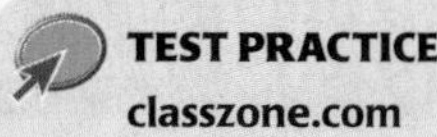

TEST PRACTICE
classzone.com

Lessons 5.1–5.4

1. **HIKING** You hike 5 miles before noon, at which time you take a break to eat lunch. After lunch, you hike at an average rate of 3.5 miles per hour. If you use an equation in slope-intercept form to represent the total number of miles hiked as a function of time, what does the slope represent?

 A. Miles hiked before your break
 B. Miles hiked per hour before your break
 C. Total number of miles hiked
 D. Miles hiked per hour after your break

2. **PHOTOCOPIES** You have \$10 on a copy card. The copy store charges \$0.10 for each black and white copy, and \$1 for each color copy. Which of the following equations models the different combinations of the number b of black and white copies you can make and the number c of color copies you can make?

 F. $b + 10c = 10$ **H.** $c - 10b = 0$
 G. $c + 10b = 100$ **J.** $b + 10c = 100$

3. **TREE GROWTH** A tree is 76 inches tall and is expected to grow 2 inches per year. If the height of the tree is graphed as a function of the number of years from now, what does the graph's y-intercept represent?

 A. The tree's growth rate
 B. The tree's height now
 C. The tree's age now
 D. The tree's height x years from now

4. **SWIMMING POOL** You use a garden hose to fill an empty swimming pool at a constant rate. After 5 minutes, there are 15 gallons of water in the pool. After 30 minutes, there are 90 gallons of water in the pool. Which of the following equations gives the volume V (in gallons) of water as a function of the time t (in minutes) since you began filling the pool?

 F. $V = 2t + 3$ **H.** $V = 3t$
 G. $V = 15t$ **J.** $V = 5t - 30$

5. **BIKE PATH** Your city is paving a bike path that is 14 miles long. The same length of path is paved each day. After 4 days of paving, there are 8 miles of path left to be paved. Which equation gives y, the number of miles of bike path left to be paved, as a function of x, the number of days since paving began?

 A. $y = -\frac{3}{2}x + 14$
 B. $y = 14x - \frac{3}{2}$
 C. $y = -\frac{2}{3}x + 14$
 D. $y = 14x - \frac{2}{3}$

6. **CATERING** The table shows the cost of a catered lunch buffet for different numbers of people. Which of the following is an equation that relates the total cost C (in dollars) of a catered lunch buffet to the number of people p?

Number of people	12	18	24	30
Cost (dollars)	192	288	384	480

 F. $C - 192 = 12(p - 12)$
 G. $C - 192 = 16(p - 12)$
 H. $C - 30 = 12(p - 480)$
 J. $C - 2 = 16(p - 192)$

7. **MOVING VANS** The cost of renting a moving van includes a rental fee and a charge per mile. A 26 mile trip costs \$62.50, and a 38 mile trip costs \$65.50. What is the cost (in dollars) for a 54 mile trip?

 A. \$56.00
 B. \$56.25
 C. \$69.50
 D. \$96.50

Illinois Mixed Review

1. D
2. J
3. B
4. H
5. A
6. G
7. C

Investigating Algebra ACTIVITY *Use before Lesson 5.5*

1 PLAN AND PREPARE

Explore the Concept

- Students will explore whether converses of conditional statements are true.
- This activity leads into the study of parallel lines and perpendicular lines in Lesson 5.5.

Materials

Each student will need 10 index cards.

Recommended Time

Work activity: 10 min

Discuss results: 5 min

Grouping

Students should work individually.

2 TEACH

Alternative Strategy

When you begin this activity, have one student select two cards, and then write the conditional statement on the board. If the statement is false, have the student write a counterexample. Ask a second student to write the converse of the conditional statement on the board. Ask the class whether the converse is true or false.

Key Discovery

The converse of a conditional statement may be true or false.

3 ASSESS AND RETEACH

If a conditional statement is false, is the converse always false? Always true? Justify your answer. The converse of a false statement may be true or false. Examples: The statement "if it swims, it is a duck" is false, while its converse "if it is a duck, it swims" is true. The statement "If it is a tree, it has wings" is false, and its converse "if it has wings, it is a tree" also is false.

5.5 If–Then Statements and Their Converses

MATERIALS • index cards

QUESTION **Is the converse of a conditional statement true?**

In Lesson 2.1, you learned that an if-then statement is a form of a conditional statement where the *if* part contains the hypothesis and the *then* part contains the conclusion. The *converse* of an if-then statement interchanges the hypothesis and conclusion of the original statement.

EXPLORE **Write the converse**

STEP 1 ***Make cards***
Write each phrase below on a separate index card.

it swims	it is a tree	it flies	it needs water	it has wings
it is a duck	it grows	it is a bird	it is an airplane	it is a frog

STEP 2 ***Write the conditional statement***
Place the cards face down. Select a card at random to be the hypothesis. Select another card at random to be the conclusion. Write the statement and determine whether it is true or false. If it is false, give a counterexample.

Hypothesis: it is a duck   Conclusion: it has wings

Statement: If it is a duck, then it has wings.

The statement is true. All ducks have wings.

STEP 3 ***Write the converse***
Switch the order of the cards to create the converse statement. Determine whether the converse is true or false. If it is false, give a counterexample.

Hypothesis: it has wings   Conclusion: it is a duck

Statement: If it has wings, then it is a duck.

The statement is false. Airplanes have wings, but they are not ducks.

STEP 4 ***Repeat***
Repeat Steps 2 and 3 ten times. Keep a record of your conditional statements and their converses.

DRAW CONCLUSIONS **Use your observations to complete these exercises**

1. **REASONING** If a conditional statement is true, can you be sure that its converse is true? *Justify* your answer. See margin.
2. **REASONING** If the converse of a statement is true, can you be sure that the original statement is true? *Justify* your answer. No. *Sample answer:* If you picked *it needs water* and *it is a tree*, the converse would be *If it is a tree, then it needs water*, which is true. The original statement is *If it needs water, then it is a tree*, which is not true, a duck needs water, but it is not a tree.

1. No. *Sample answer:* If you picked *it is a bird* and *it flies*, the statement would be *If it is a bird, then it flies*, which is true. The converse statement is *If it flies, then it is a bird*, which is not true; an airplane flies, but it is not a bird.

5.5 Write Equations of Parallel and Perpendicular Lines

 **8.11.11** Analyze functions by investigating domain, range, rates of change, intercepts, and zeros.

Before You used slope to determine whether lines are parallel.

Now You will write equations of parallel and perpendicular lines.

Why? So you can analyze growth rates, as in Ex. 33.

Key Vocabulary
- **converse**
- **perpendicular lines**
- **conditional statement,** *p. 66*

The **converse** of a conditional statement interchanges the hypothesis and conclusion. The converse of a true statement is not necessarily true.

In Chapter 4, you learned that the statement "If two nonvertical lines have the same slope, then they are parallel" is true. Its converse is also true.

KEY CONCEPT *For Your Notebook*

Parallel Lines

- If two nonvertical lines in the same plane have the same slope, then they are parallel.
- If two nonvertical lines in the same plane are parallel, then they have the same slope.

EXAMPLE 1 Write an equation of a parallel line

Write an equation of the line that passes through $(-3, -5)$ and is parallel to the line $y = 3x - 1$.

Solution

STEP 1 **Identify** the slope. The graph of the given equation has a slope of 3. So, the parallel line through $(-3, -5)$ has a slope of 3.

STEP 2 **Find** the y-intercept. Use the slope and the given point.

$y = mx + b$ — **Write slope-intercept form.**

$-5 = 3(-3) + b$ — **Substitute 3 for m, -3 for x, and -5 for y.**

$4 = b$ — **Solve for b.**

STEP 3 **Write** an equation. Use $y = mx + b$.

$y = 3x + 4$ — **Substitute 3 for m and 4 for b.**

CHECK REASONABLENESS
You can check that your answer is reasonable by graphing both lines.

✓ **GUIDED PRACTICE** for Example 1

1. Write an equation of the line that passes through $(-2, 11)$ and is parallel to the line $y = -x + 5$. $y = -x + 9$

1 PLAN AND PREPARE

Warm-Up Exercises

Transparency Available

Are the lines parallel? Explain.

1. $y - 2 = 2x$, $2x + y = 7$ **No; one slope is 2 and the other is -2.**
2. $-x = y + 4$, $3x + 3y = 5$ **Yes; both slopes are -1.**
3. You play tennis at two clubs. The total cost C (in dollars) to play for time t (in hours) and rent equipment is given by $C = 15t + 23$ at one club and $C = 15t + 17$ at the other. What is the difference in total cost after 4 hours of play? **$6**

Notetaking Guide

Transparency Available

Promotes interactive learning and notetaking skills, pp. 113–116.

Pacing

Basic: 1 day
Average: 1 day
Advanced: 1 day
Block: 0.5 block with 5.4
- See *Teaching Guide/Lesson Plan.*

2 FOCUS AND MOTIVATE

Essential Question

Big Idea 1, p. 281

How do you write equations of parallel and perpendicular lines? **Tell students they will learn how to answer this question by comparing slopes.**

Resource Planning Guide

Chapter Resource Book
- Teaching Guide/Lesson Plan (pp. 50–51)
- Practice levels A, B, C (pp. 52–54)
- Study Guide (pp. 55–56)
- Catch-up for Absent Students (p. 57)
- Problem Solving Workshop (p. 58)
- Challenge (p. 59)

Workbooks
- Notetaking Guide (pp. 113–116)
- Practice Workbook (pp. 76–77)

Teaching Options
- **Power Presentations CD-ROM** provides dynamic electronic teaching resources for the classroom.
- **Activity Generator CD-ROM** provides editable activities for all ability levels.

Interactive Technology
- Easy Planner
- Power Presentations CD-ROM
- Activity Generator CD-ROM
- Animated Algebra
- Test Generator CD-ROM
- Online Quiz
- eWorkbook
- eEdition
- @HomeTutor

Resources for English Learners
- Quick Reference for English Learners
- Spanish Study Guide
- Multi-Language Visual Glossary
- Student Resources in Spanish

See also the *Algebra 1 Toolkit* for more strategies for meeting individual needs.

Motivating the Lesson

Your dad is planning to plant two red oak trees in your backyard. He wants to know how tall they will be in six years. One tree is 56 inches high and the other is 63 inches high. Red oaks grow at an average rate of 24 inches per year. By writing two equations that model the growth of the trees, you can predict the height of each tree in six years.

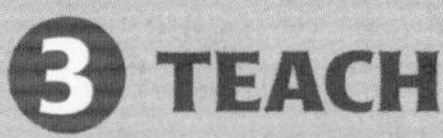

Extra Example 1

Write an equation of the line that passes through $(-3, 3)$ and is parallel to the line $y = -2x + 1$.
$y = -2x - 3$

Key Questions to Ask for Example 1

- How are the parallel lines different? They have different y-intercepts.
- If two lines have different y-intercepts, are they parallel? Explain. No. The line $y = x + 3$ and the line $y = 2x + 1$ have different y-intercepts, but they are not parallel since they have different slopes.

Extra Example 2

Determine which lines, if any, are parallel or perpendicular.
Line a: $-x + 3y = 1$
Line b: $y = -3x + 1$
Line c: $2x - 6y = 4$
Lines a and c have slopes of $\frac{1}{3}$, so they are parallel. Line b has a slope of -3, the negative reciprocal of $\frac{1}{3}$, so it is perpendicular to lines a and c.

PERPENDICULAR LINES Two lines in the same plane are **perpendicular** if they intersect to form a right angle. Horizontal and vertical lines are perpendicular to each other.

Compare the slopes of the perpendicular lines shown below.

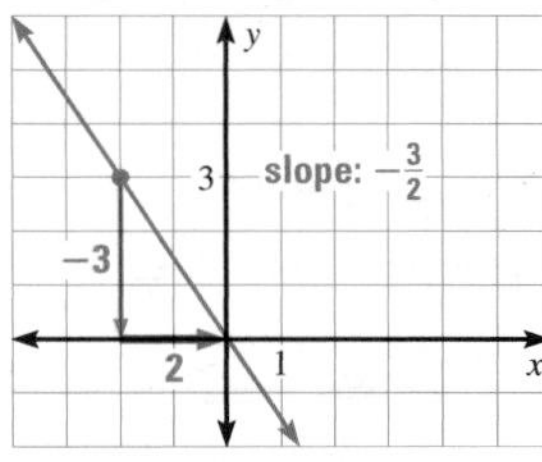

Rotate the line 90° in a clockwise direction about the origin to find a perpendicular line.

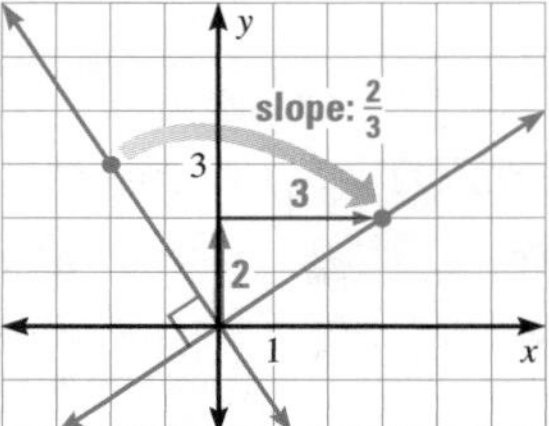

USE FRACTIONS
The product of a nonzero number m and its negative reciprocal is -1:
$m\left(-\frac{1}{m}\right) = -1.$

KEY CONCEPT *For Your Notebook*

Perpendicular Lines

- If two nonvertical lines in the same plane have slopes that are negative reciprocals, then the lines are perpendicular.
- If two nonvertical lines in the same plane are perpendicular, then their slopes are negative reciprocals.

EXAMPLE 2 Determine whether lines are parallel or perpendicular

Determine which lines, if any, are parallel or perpendicular.

Line *a*: $y = 5x - 3$ **Line *b*:** $x + 5y = 2$ **Line *c*:** $-10y - 2x = 0$

Solution

Find the slopes of the lines.

Line *a*: The equation is in slope-intercept form. The slope is 5.

Write the equations for lines b and c in slope-intercept form.

Line *b*: $x + 5y = 2$
$5y = -x + 2$
$y = -\frac{1}{5}x + \frac{2}{5}$

Line *c*: $-10y - 2x = 0$
$-10y = 2x$
$y = -\frac{1}{5}x$

▶ Lines b and c have slopes of $-\frac{1}{5}$, so they are parallel. Line a has a slope of 5, the negative reciprocal of $-\frac{1}{5}$, so it is perpendicular to lines b and c.

✓ **GUIDED PRACTICE** for Example 2

2. Determine which lines, if any, are parallel or perpendicular.
Line *a*: $2x + 6y = -3$ **Line *b*:** $y = 3x - 8$ **Line *c*:** $-1.5y + 4.5x = 6$
parallel: b and c; perpendicular: a and b, a and c

Differentiated Instruction

English Learners Some students may have trouble with the converse. The statements about parallel and perpendicular lines give examples with converses that are true. Give examples to illustrate that the converse of a logical statement is not always true. For example, "If a figure is a square, then it has four sides" is a true statement. The converse, "If a figure has four sides, then it is a square" is false (for example, the figure could be a rectangle).
See also the *Algebra 1 Toolkit* for more strategies.

EXAMPLE 3 Determine whether lines are perpendicular

STATE FLAG The Arizona state flag is shown in a coordinate plane. Lines a and b appear to be perpendicular. Are they?

Line a: $12y = -7x + 42$

Line b: $11y = 16x - 52$

Solution

Find the slopes of the lines. Write the equations in slope-intercept form.

Line a: $12y = -7x + 42$	**Line b:** $11y = 16x - 52$
$y = -\frac{7}{12}x + \frac{42}{12}$	$y = \frac{16}{11}x - \frac{52}{11}$

▶ The slope of line a is $-\frac{7}{12}$. The slope of line b is $\frac{16}{11}$. The two slopes are not negative reciprocals, so lines a and b are not perpendicular.

Extra Example 3

The path of a golf ball bouncing off a curved wall on a miniature golf course is shown in a coordinate plane. Lines a and b of the path appear to be perpendicular. Are they?

Line a: $3y = 2x - 1$

Line b: $2y = -3x + 21$

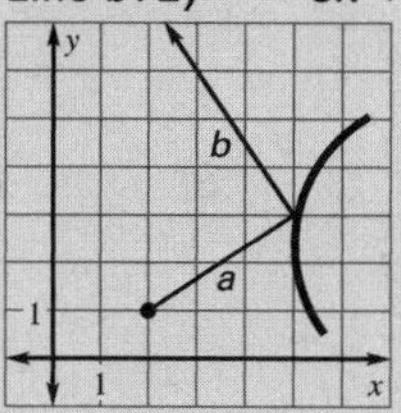

The slope of line a is $\frac{2}{3}$. The slope of line b is $-\frac{3}{2}$. The two slopes are negative reciprocals, so the lines are perpendicular.

EXAMPLE 4 Write an equation of a perpendicular line

Write an equation of the line that passes through (4, −5) and is perpendicular to the line $y = 2x + 3$.

Solution

STEP 1 **Identify** the slope. The graph of the given equation has a slope of 2. Because the slopes of perpendicular lines are negative reciprocals, the slope of the perpendicular line through (4, −5) is $-\frac{1}{2}$.

STEP 2 **Find** the y-intercept. Use the slope and the given point.

$y = mx + b$	Write slope-intercept form.
$-5 = -\frac{1}{2}(4) + b$	Substitute $-\frac{1}{2}$ for m, 4 for x, and −5 for y.
$-3 = b$	Solve for b.

STEP 3 **Write** an equation.

$y = mx + b$	Write slope-intercept form.
$y = -\frac{1}{2}x - 3$	Substitute $-\frac{1}{2}$ for m and −3 for b.

Extra Example 4

Write an equation of the line that passes through (4, −2) and is perpendicular to the line $y = 4x + 2$. $y = -\frac{1}{4}x - 1$

Closing the Lesson

Have students summarize the major points of the lesson and answer the Essential Question: How do you write equations of parallel and perpendicular lines?

- Two nonvertical lines have the same slope if and only if they are parallel.
- The slopes of two nonvertical lines are negative reciprocals if and only if the lines are perpendicular.

Identify the slope of the line. Use the same slope and a different y-intercept to write an equation of a parallel line. Use the negative reciprocal of the slope to write an equation of a perpendicular line.

✓ GUIDED PRACTICE for Examples 3 and 4

3. Is line a perpendicular to line b? *Justify* your answer using slopes.

   Line a: $2y + x = -12$ **Line b**: $2y = 3x - 8$

   3. No; the slope of line a is $-\frac{1}{2}$, the slope of line b is $\frac{3}{2}$. The slopes are not negative reciprocals so the lines are not perpendicular.

4. Write an equation of the line that passes through (4, 3) and is perpendicular to the line $y = 4x - 7$. $y = -\frac{1}{4}x + 4$

4 PRACTICE AND APPLY

Assignment Guide

Answer Transparencies available for all exercises

Basic:
Day 1: pp. 322–324
Exs. 1–8, 12–22, 27, 28, 32–35, 38–42

Average:
Day 1: pp. 322–324
Exs. 1, 2, 7–17, 23–30, 32–37, 39, 41, 42

Advanced:
Day 1: pp. 322–324
Exs. 1, 2, 8–11, 13–17, 24–37*, 40–42

Block:
pp. 322–324
Exs. 1, 2, 7–17, 23–30, 32–37, 39, 41, 42 (with 5.4)

Differentiated Instruction

See *Algebra 1 Best Practices Toolkit* for suggestions on addressing the needs of a diverse classroom.

Homework Check

For a quick check of student understanding of key concepts, go over the following exercises:

Basic: 6, 12, 16, 20, 32
Average: 8, 14, 24, 32, 34
Advanced: 10, 15, 26, 32, 34

Extra Practice

- Student Edition, p. 942
- Chapter 5 Resource Book: Practice levels A, B, C, pp. 52–54

Practice Worksheet

An easily-readable reduced practice page (with answers) for this lesson can be found on p. 280D.

5.5 EXERCISES

HOMEWORK KEY ○ = **WORKED-OUT SOLUTIONS** on p. WS12 for Exs. 19 and 33
★ = **STANDARDIZED TEST PRACTICE** Exs. 2, 16, 17, 28, 30, 34, and 36

SKILL PRACTICE

A

1. **VOCABULARY** Copy and complete: Two lines in a plane are _?_ if they intersect to form a right angle. perpendicular

2. ★ **WRITING** *Explain* how you can tell whether two lines are perpendicular, given the equations of the lines. Identify the slopes of the lines. If the slopes are negative reciprocals, then the lines are perpendicular.

EXAMPLE 1 on p. 319 for Exs. 3–11

PARALLEL LINES **Write an equation of the line that passes through the given point and is parallel to the given line.**

3. $(-1, 3)$, $y = 2x + 2$ $y = 2x + 5$
4. $(6, 8)$, $y = -\frac{5}{2}x + 10$ $y = -\frac{5}{2}x + 23$
5. $(5, -1)$, $y = -\frac{3}{5}x - 3$ $y = -\frac{3}{5}x + 2$
6. $(-1, 2)$, $y = 5x + 4$ $y = 5x + 7$
7. $(1, 7)$, $-6x + y = -1$ $y = 6x + 1$
8. $(18, 2)$, $3y = x - 12$ $y = \frac{1}{3}x - 4$
9. $(-2, 5)$, $2y = 4x - 6$ $y = 2x + 9$
10. $(9, 4)$, $y - x = 3$ $y = x - 5$
11. $(-10, 0)$, $-y + 3x = 16$ $y = 3x + 30$

EXAMPLE 2 on p. 320 for Exs. 12–16

PARALLEL OR PERPENDICULAR **Determine which lines, if any, are parallel or perpendicular.**

12. Line a: $y = 4x - 2$, Line b: $y = -\frac{1}{4}x$, Line c: $y = -4x + 1$
parallel: none; perpendicular: a and b
13. Line a: $y = \frac{3}{5}x + 1$, Line b: $5y = 3x - 2$, Line c: $10x - 6y = -4$
parallel: a and b; perpendicular: none
14. Line a: $y = 3x + 6$, Line b: $3x + y = 6$, Line c: $3y = 2x + 18$
parallel: none; perpendicular: none
15. Line a: $4x - 3y = 2$, Line b: $3x + 4y = -1$, Line c: $4y - 3x = 20$
parallel: none; perpendicular: a and b

16. ★ **MULTIPLE CHOICE** Which statement is true of the given lines? D

Line a: $-2x + y = 4$ Line b: $2x + 5y = 2$ Line c: $x + 2y = 4$

(A) Lines a and b are parallel. (B) Lines a and c are parallel.
(C) Lines a and b are perpendicular. (D) Lines a and c are perpendicular.

17. ★ **SHORT RESPONSE** Determine which of the lines shown, if any, are parallel or perpendicular. *Justify* your answer using slopes.

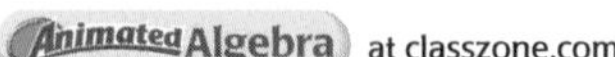 at classzone.com

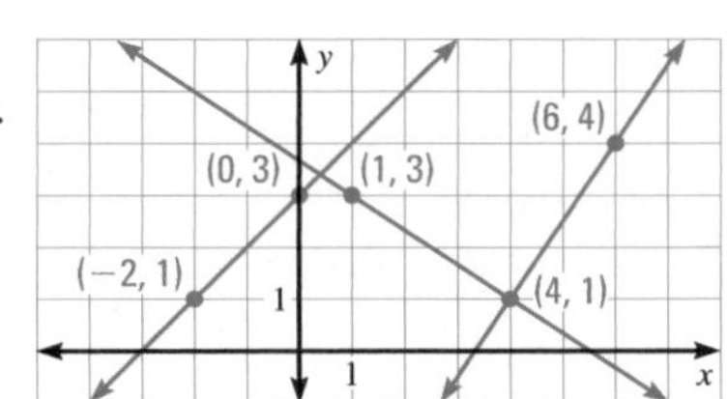

17. The line through points (6, 4) and (4, 1) is perpendicular to the line through points (1, 3) and (4, 1); the slope of the line through the points (6, 4) and (4, 1) is $\frac{3}{2}$, the slope of the line through the points (1, 3) and (4, 1) is $-\frac{2}{3}$. The slopes are negative reciprocals, so the lines are perpendicular.

EXAMPLE 4 on p. 321 for Exs. 18–27

PERPENDICULAR LINES **Write an equation of the line that passes through the given point and is perpendicular to the given line.**

18. $(3, -3)$, $y = x + 5$ $y = -x$
19. $(-9, 2)$, $y = 3x - 12$ $y = -\frac{1}{3}x - 1$
20. $(5, 1)$, $y = 5x - 2$ $y = -\frac{1}{5}x + 2$
21. $(7, 10)$, $y = 0.5x - 9$ $y = -2x + 24$
22. $(-2, -4)$, $y = -\frac{2}{7}x + 1$ $y = \frac{7}{2}x + 3$
23. $(-4, -1)$, $y = \frac{4}{3}x + 6$ $y = -\frac{3}{4}x - 4$
24. $(3, 3)$, $2y = 3x - 6$ $y = -\frac{2}{3}x + 5$
25. $(-5, 2)$, $y + 3 = 2x$ $y = -\frac{1}{2}x - \frac{1}{2}$
26. $(8, -1)$, $4y + 2x = 12$ $y = 2x - 17$

27. **ERROR ANALYSIS** *Describe* and correct the error in finding the y-intercept of the line that passes through (2, 1) and is perpendicular to the line $y = -\frac{1}{2}x + 3$.

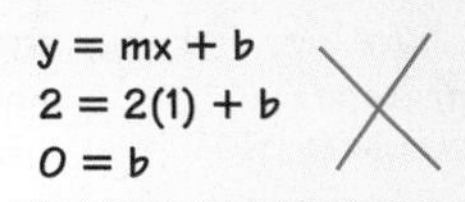

(2, 1) was substituted incorrectly, 2 should be substituted for x, and 1 should be substituted for y; $1 = 2(2) + b$, $1 = 4 + b$, $-3 = b$.

B 28. ★ **MULTIPLE CHOICE** Which equation represents the line that passes through (0, 0) and is parallel to the line passing through (2, 3) and (6, 1)? B

Ⓐ $y = \frac{1}{2}x$ Ⓑ $y = -\frac{1}{2}x$ Ⓒ $y = -2x$ Ⓓ $y = 2x$

29. **REASONING** Is the line through (4, 3) and (3, −1) perpendicular to the line through (−3, 3) and (1, 2)? *Justify* your answer using slopes. See margin.

30. *Sample answer:* $y = 2x + 1$ and $y = 2x + 3$; $y = -\frac{1}{2}x + 2$

C 30. ★ **OPEN-ENDED** Write equations of two lines that are parallel. Then write an equation of a line that is perpendicular to those lines.

31. **CHALLENGE** Write a formula for the slope of a line that is perpendicular to the line through the points (x_1, y_1) and (x_2, y_2). $m = \frac{x_1 - x_2}{y_1 - y_2}$

PROBLEM SOLVING

EXAMPLES 3 and 4 on p. 321 for Exs. 32, 34

A 32. **HOCKEY** A hockey puck leaves the blade of a hockey stick, bounces off a wall, and travels in a new direction, as shown.

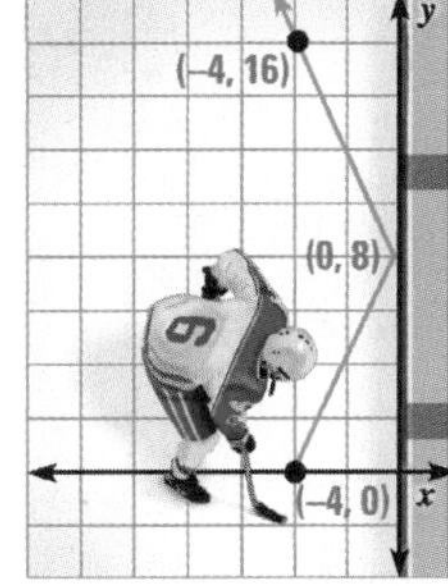

a. Write an equation that models the path of the puck from the blade of the hockey stick to the wall. $y = 2x + 8$

b. Write an equation that models the path of the puck after it bounces off the wall. $y = -2x + 8$

c. Does the path of the puck form a right angle? *Justify* your answer.

32c. No; the slopes −2 and 2 are not negative reciprocals.

@HomeTutor for problem solving help at classzone.com

33. **BIOLOGY** While nursing, blue whale calves can gain weight at a rate of 200 pounds per day. Two particular calves weigh 6000 pounds and 6250 pounds at birth.

a. Write equations that model the weight of each calf as a function of the number of days since birth. $w_1 = 200d + 6000$; $w_2 = 200d + 6250$

b. How much is each calf expected to weigh 30 days after birth? 12,000 lb; 12,250 lb

c. How are the graphs of the equations from part (a) related? *Justify* your answer.

33c. The graphs of the lines are parallel because they have the same slope, 200. The w-intercept of the second line is 250 more than the w-intercept of the first line.

@HomeTutor for problem solving help at classzone.com

34. ★ **SHORT RESPONSE** The map shows several streets in a city. Determine which of the streets, if any, are parallel or perpendicular. *Justify* your answer using slopes. See margin.

Park: $3y - 2x = 12$ Main: $y = -6x + 44$

2nd St.: $3y = 2x - 13$ Sea: $2y = -3x + 37$

29. Yes; the slope of the line through (4, 3) and (3, −1) is 4 and the slope of the line through (−3, 3) and (1, 2) is $-\frac{1}{4}$. The slopes are negative reciprocals, so the lines are perpendicular.

Graphing Calculator

Exercises 3–11, 18–26 Students can use their graphing calculators to check that their equations are reasonable. Have them enter both equations on the same viewing screen and then use trace to verify that each equation passes through the point.

Avoiding Common Errors

Exercises 7–11, 13–15, 24, 26 Some students may use the coefficient of x as the slope before rewriting the equation in slope-intercept form. Remind these students that the equation must be in slope-intercept form in order to read the value of m.

An **Animated Algebra** activity is available on-line for **Exercise 17**. This activity is also available on the **Power Presentations CD-ROM**.

Study Strategy

Exercises 18–26 Remind students that the product of negative reciprocals is −1. They can use this information to check whether or not two numbers are negative reciprocals.

Exercise 33 More information about blue whales can be found at the American Cetacean Society website, www.acsonline.org/factpack/bluewhl.htm

34. Parallel: 2nd Street and Park Street; the slope of both streets is $\frac{2}{3}$. Since they have the same slope, the streets are parallel. Perpendicular: 2nd Street and Sea Street, Park Street and Sea Street; the slope of Sea Street is $-\frac{3}{2}$, which is the negative reciprocal of $\frac{2}{3}$, the slope of 2nd Street and Park Street. Since the slopes are negative reciprocals, the streets are perpendicular.

5 ASSESS AND RETEACH

Daily Homework Quiz

Transparency Available

1. Write an equation of the line that passes through the point $(-1, 4)$ and is parallel to the line $y = 5x - 2$. $y = 5x + 9$
2. Write an equation of the line that passes through the point $(-1, -1)$ and is perpendicular to the line $y = -\frac{1}{4}x + 2$.
   $y = 4x + 3$
3. Paths a, b, and c are shown in the coordinate grid. Determine which paths, if any, are parallel or perpendicular. Justify your answer using slopes.

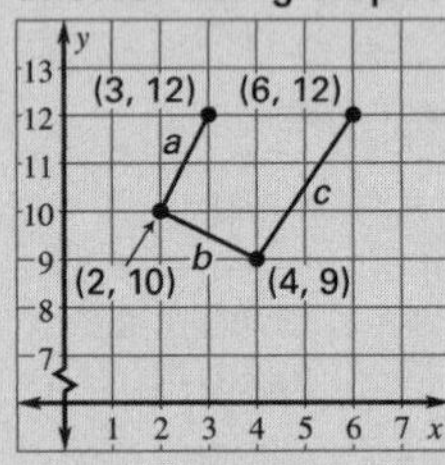

Paths a and b are perpendicular because their slopes, 2 and $-\frac{1}{2}$, are negative reciprocals. No paths are parallel.

Available at **classzone.com**

Diagnosis/Remediation

- Practice A, B, C in Chapter 5 Resource Book, pp. 52–54
- Study Guide in Chapter 5 Resource Book, pp. 55–56
- Practice Workbook, pp. 76–77
- @HomeTutor

Challenge

Additional challenge is available in the Chapter 5 Resource Book, p. 59.

35. Different registration fees; because the lines are parallel, the rate of change, the monthly fee, for each must be equal. Therefore, the students paid different registration fees.

36c. The graphs of the lines are parallel; they have the same slope, 38.75. The C-intercept of the second graph is 100 more than the C-intercept of the first graph.

37b. The graphs of the lines are parallel; they have the same slope, -2.5. The y–intercept of the second line is 20 less than the y-intercept of the first line.

B

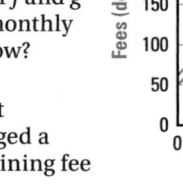

35. SOFTBALL A softball training academy charges students a monthly fee plus an initial registration fee. The total amounts paid by two students are given by the functions $f(x)$ and $g(x)$ where x is the numbers of months the students have been members of the academy. The graphs of f and g are parallel lines. Did the students pay different monthly fees or different registration fees? How do you know?

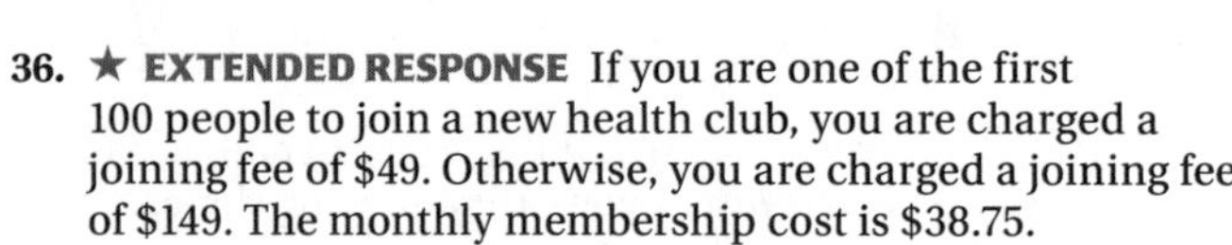

36. ★ EXTENDED RESPONSE If you are one of the first 100 people to join a new health club, you are charged a joining fee of \$49. Otherwise, you are charged a joining fee of \$149. The monthly membership cost is \$38.75.

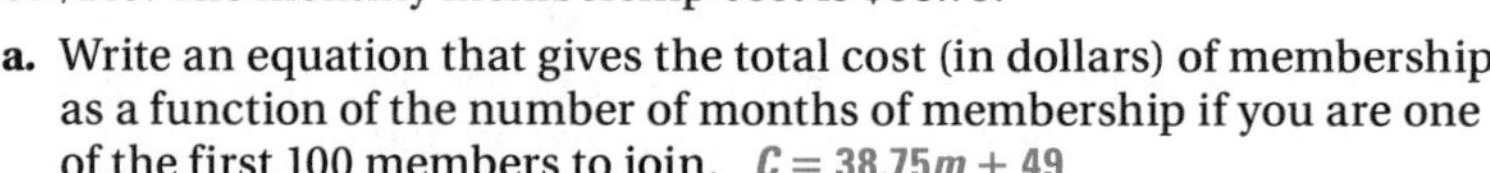

a. Write an equation that gives the total cost (in dollars) of membership as a function of the number of months of membership if you are one of the first 100 members to join. $C = 38.75m + 49$

b. Write an equation that gives the total cost (in dollars) of membership as a function of the number of months of membership if you are *not* one of the first 100 members to join. $C = 38.75m + 149$

c. How are the graphs of these functions related? How do you know?

d. After 6 months, what is the difference in total cost for a person who paid \$149 to join and a person who paid \$49 to join? after 12 months? \$100; \$100

C

37. CHALLENGE You and your friend have gift cards to a shopping mall. Your card has a value of \$50, and your friend's card has a value of \$30. If neither of you uses the cards, the value begins to decrease at a rate of \$2.50 per month after 6 months.

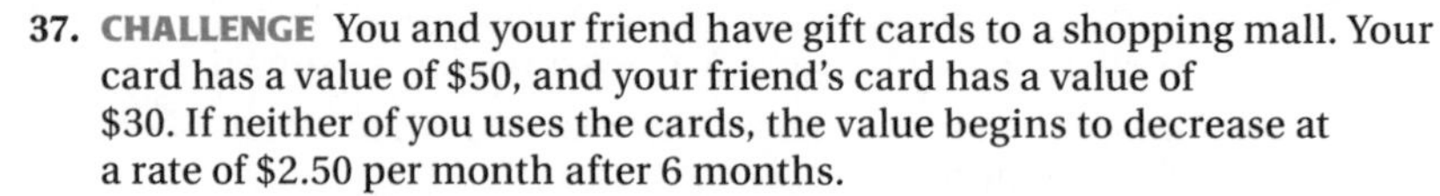

a. Write two equations, one that gives the value of your card and another that gives the value of your friend's card as functions of the number of months after 6 months of nonuse. $y = -2.5x + 50$; $y = -2.5x + 30$

b. How are the graphs of these functions related? How do you know?

c. What are the x-intercepts of the graphs of the functions, and what do they mean in this situation? 20; 12; the x-intercepts show the number of months of nonuse it would take for the value of the gift card to be \$0.

ILLINOIS MIXED REVIEW

38. You plan to travel on a train to visit your cousins. A train leaves 10 minutes past every hour and takes 1 hour and 20 minutes to reach your cousins' town. It is 9:45 A.M. now, and it will take you 25 minutes to pack and 30 minutes to get to the train station. What time will you reach your cousins' town? D

Ⓐ 11:30 A.M. Ⓑ 12 P.M. Ⓒ 12:20 P.M. Ⓓ 12:30 P.M.

39. If $(x, 9)$ is a solution to the equation $3x - 4y = 9$, what is the value of x?

Ⓐ -15 Ⓑ -9 Ⓒ 15 Ⓓ 45 C

5.6 Fit a Line to Data

8.11.07 Identify an equation of a line or an equation of a line of best fit from given information . . .

Before You modeled situations involving a constant rate of change.

Now You will make scatter plots and write equations to model data.

Why? So you can model scientific data, as in Ex. 19.

Key Vocabulary
- scatter plot
- correlation
- line of fit

A **scatter plot** is a graph used to determine whether there is a relationship between paired data. Scatter plots can show trends in the data.

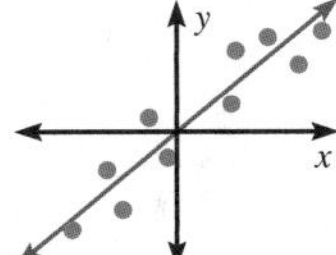

If y tends to increase as x increases, the paired data are said to have a **positive correlation**.

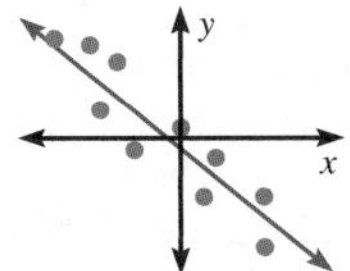

If y tends to decrease as x increases, the paired data are said to have a **negative correlation**.

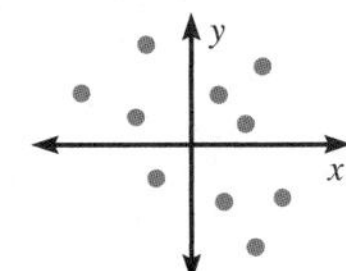

If x and y have no apparent relationship, the paired data are said to have **relatively no correlation**.

EXAMPLE 1 Describe the correlation of data

Describe **the correlation of the data graphed in the scatter plot.**

a.

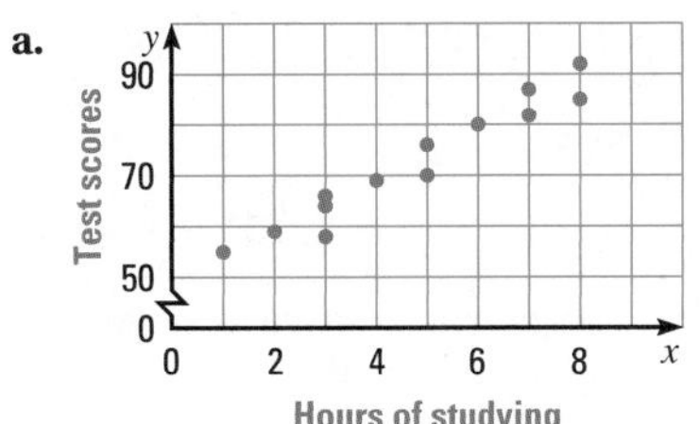

b.

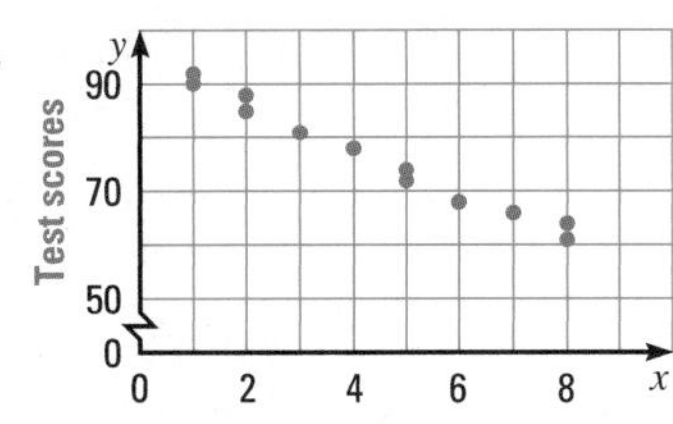

a. The scatter plot shows a positive correlation between hours of studying and test scores. This means that as the hours of studying increased, the test scores tended to increase.

b. The scatter plot shows a negative correlation between hours of television watched and test scores. This means that as the hours of television watched increased, the test scores tended to decrease.

✓ **GUIDED PRACTICE** for Example 1

1. Using the scatter plots in Example 1, predict a reasonable test score for 4.5 hours of studying and 4.5 hours of television watched. *Sample answer: 72, 77*

1 PLAN AND PREPARE

Warm-Up Exercises

Transparency Available

Find the slope of the line that passes through the points.

1. $(-4, 1)$ and $(6, -4)$ $-\frac{1}{2}$
2. $(2, -3)$ and $(-1, 6)$ -3
3. Your commission c varies directly with the number s of pairs you sell. You made \$180 when you sold 15 pairs of shoes. Write a direct variation equation that relates c to s. $c = 12s$

Notetaking Guide

Transparency Available

Promotes interactive learning and notetaking skills, pp. 117–120.

Pacing

Basic: 1 day
Average: 1 day
Advanced: 1 day
Block: 0.5 block with 5.7
- See *Teaching Guide/Lesson Plan.*

2 FOCUS AND MOTIVATE

Essential Question

Big Idea 3, p. 281

How do you make scatter plots and write equations to model data? **Tell students they will learn how to answer this question by graphing data pairs and by finding a line of fit for the data pairs.**

Resource Planning Guide

Chapter Resource Book
- Teaching Guide/Lesson Plan (pp. 60–61)
- Activity Master (p. 62)
- Practice levels A, B, C (pp. 63–68)
- Study Guide (pp. 69–70)
- Catch-up for Absent Students (p. 71)
- Application (p. 72)
- Challenge (p. 73)

Workbooks
- Notetaking Guide (pp. 117–120)
- Practice Workbook (pp. 78–80)

Teaching Options
- **Power Presentations CD-ROM** provides dynamic electronic teaching resources for the classroom.
- **Activity Generator CD-ROM** provides editable activities for all ability levels.

Interactive Technology
- Easy Planner
- Power Presentations CD-ROM
- Activity Generator CD-ROM
- Animated Algebra
- Test Generator CD-ROM
- Online Quiz
- eWorkbook
- eEdition
- @HomeTutor

Resources for English Learners
- Quick Reference for English Learners
- Spanish Study Guide
- Multi-Language Visual Glossary
- Student Resources in Spanish

See also the *Algebra 1 Toolkit* for more strategies for meeting individual needs.

Motivating the Lesson

For a science project, you are exploring the relationship between the densities of substances and their melting points. By knowing how to make a scatter plot, you can graph the paired data on a coordinate grid and then determine whether there is a positive relationship, a negative relationship, or relatively no relationship between the densities and the melting points of the substances.

3 TEACH

Extra Example 1

Describe the correlation of the data graphed in the scatter plot.

a.

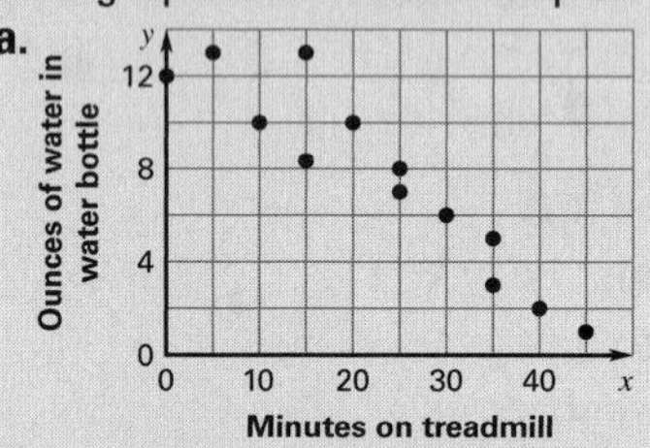

The scatter plot shows a negative correlation between minutes on a treadmill and ounces of water in a water bottle. This means that as the minutes on the treadmill increased, the ounces of water in the water bottle tended to decrease.

b.

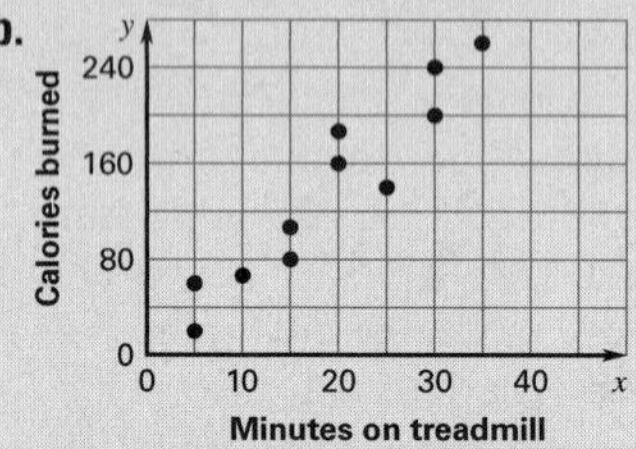

The scatter plot shows a positive correlation between minutes on a treadmill and calories burned. This means that as the minutes on the treadmill increased, the number of calories burned tended to increase.

EXAMPLE 2 Make a scatter plot

SWIMMING SPEEDS The table shows the lengths (in centimeters) and swimming speeds (in centimeters per second) of six fish.

Fish	Pike	Red gurnard	Black bass	Gurnard	Norway haddock
Length (cm)	37.8	19.2	21.3	26.2	26.8
Speed (cm/sec)	148	47	88	131	98

a. Make a scatter plot of the data.

b. *Describe* the correlation of the data.

Solution

a. Treat the data as ordered pairs. Let x represent the fish length (in centimeters), and let y represent the speed (in centimeters per second). Plot the ordered pairs as points in a coordinate plane.

b. The scatter plot shows a positive correlation, which means that longer fish tend to swim faster.

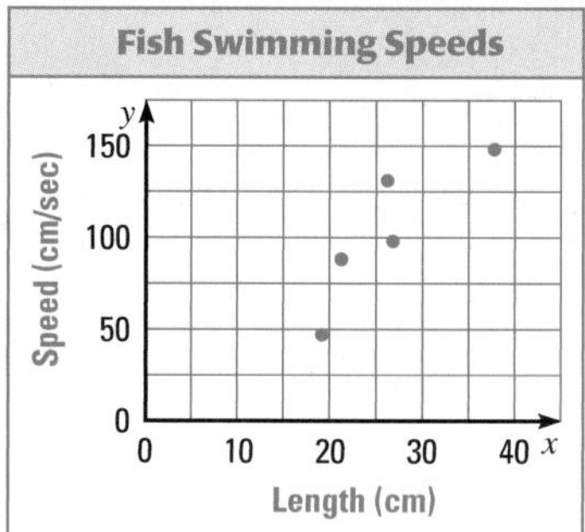

✓ GUIDED PRACTICE for Example 2

2. Make a scatter plot of the data in the table. *Describe* the correlation of the data.

x	1	1	2	3	3	4	5	5	6
y	2	3	4	4	5	5	5	7	8

See margin for art; the scatter plot shows a positive correlation.

MODELING DATA When data show a positive or negative correlation, you can model the trend in the data using a **line of fit**.

KEY CONCEPT — *For Your Notebook*

Using a Line of Fit to Model Data

STEP 1 **Make** a scatter plot of the data.

STEP 2 **Decide** whether the data can be modeled by a line.

STEP 3 **Draw** a line that appears to fit the data closely. There should be approximately as many points above the line as below it.

STEP 4 **Write** an equation using two points on the line. The points do not have to represent actual data pairs, but they must lie on the line of fit.

Differentiated Instruction

Visual Learners After introducing the line of fit, have students go back and draw lines of fit for **Example 1**. Students should observe that a line drawn through positively correlated data has a positive slope and that a line drawn through negatively correlated data has a negative slope. For some students, it may be easier to draw the line of fit before determining the type of correlation. Point out that if a line of fit is not possible, there is no correlation.

See also the *Algebra 1 Toolkit* for more strategies.

EXAMPLE 3 Write an equation to model data

BIRD POPULATIONS The table shows the number of active red-cockaded woodpecker clusters in a part of the De Soto National Forest in Mississippi. Write an equation that models the number of active clusters as a function of the number of years since 1990.

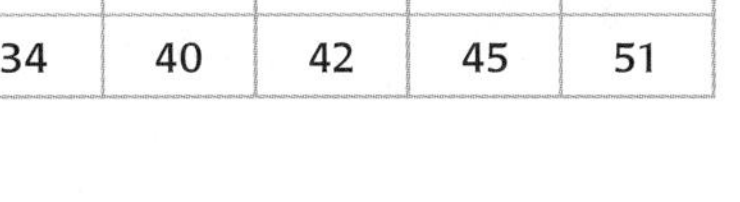

Year	1992	1993	1994	1995	1996	1997	1998	1999	2000
Active clusters	22	24	27	27	34	40	42	45	51

Solution

STEP 1 **Make** a scatter plot of the data. Let x represent the number of years since 1990. Let y represent the number of active clusters.

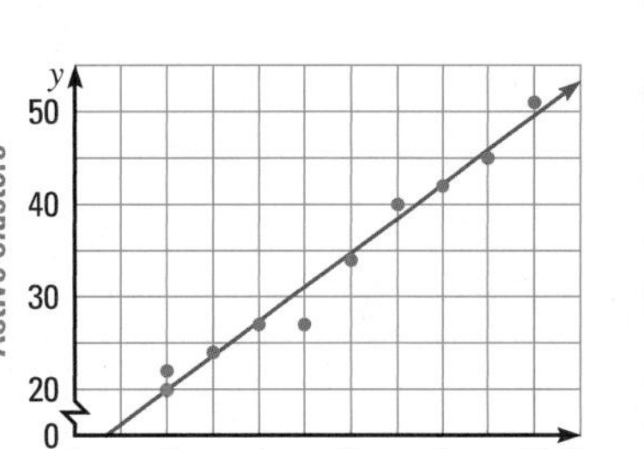

STEP 2 **Decide** whether the data can be modeled by a line. Because the scatter plot shows a positive correlation, you can fit a line to the data.

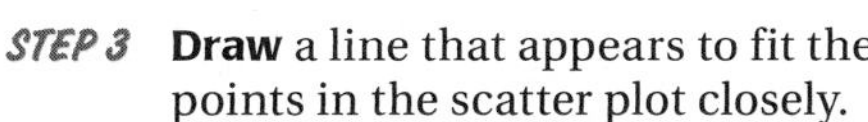

STEP 3 **Draw** a line that appears to fit the points in the scatter plot closely.

STEP 4 **Write** an equation using two points on the line. Use (2, 20) and (8, 42).

Find the slope of the line.

$$m = \frac{y_2 - y_1}{x_2 - x_1} = \frac{42 - 20}{8 - 2} = \frac{22}{6} = \frac{11}{3}$$

Find the y-intercept of the line. Use the point (2, 20).

$y = mx + b$ **Write slope-intercept form.**

$20 = \frac{11}{3}(2) + b$ **Substitute $\frac{11}{3}$ for m, 2 for x, and 20 for y.**

$\frac{38}{3} = b$ **Solve for b.**

An equation of the line of fit is $y = \frac{11}{3}x + \frac{38}{3}$.

▶ The number y of active woodpecker clusters can be modeled by the function $y = \frac{11}{3}x + \frac{38}{3}$ where x is the number of years since 1990.

Animated Algebra at classzone.com

GUIDED PRACTICE for Example 3

3. Use the data in the table to write an equation that models y as a function of x.

x	1	2	3	4	5	6	8
y	3	5	8	9	11	12	14

Sample answer: $y = 1.6x + 2.3$

2.

Extra Example 2

The table shows the carbohydrates (in grams) and the fiber (in grams) in six types of fruit.

Fruit	Fiber	Carb.
Apple	5	22
Banana	4	29
Blackberries	8	18
Figs	2	12
Guava	5	11
Peach	2	11

a. Make a scatter plot of the data.

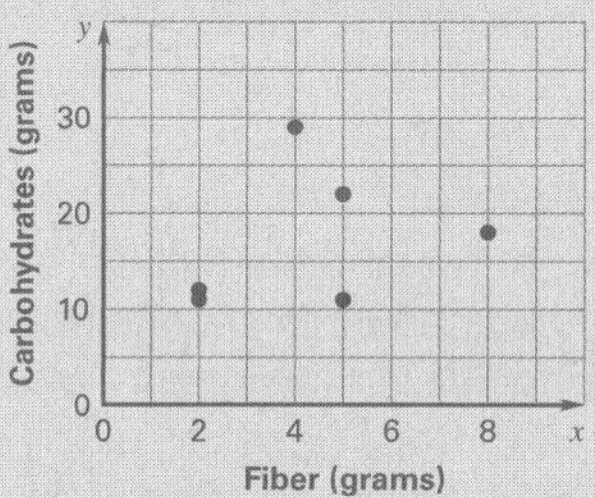

b. Describe the correlation of the data. **The scatter plot shows relatively no correlation, which means there is no general relationship between fiber and carbohydrates in fruit.**

Extra Example 3

The table shows the number of injured birds a person rehabilitated at a veterinary service. Write an equation that models the number of rehabilitated birds as a function of the number of years years since 1995.

Year	Birds
1997	8
1998	11
1999	12
2000	12
2001	15
2002	19
2003	21

The number of rehabilitated birds can be modeled by the function $y = 2.07x + 3.64$ where x is the number of years since 1995.

An **Animated Algebra** activity is available on-line for **Example 3**. This activity is also available on the **Power Presentations CD-ROM**.

Extra Example 4

Refer to the model on the number of birds in Extra Example 3.

a. Describe the domain and range of the function. The domain is the period 1997 to 2003. Since x is the number of years after 1995, the domain is $2 \le x \le 8$. The range is the number of birds given by the model, so the range is about $8 \le y \le 20$.

b. At what rate did the number of rehabilitated birds change from 1997 to 2003? The number of rehabilitated birds increased at a rate of 2 birds per year.

Closing the Lesson

Have students summarize the major points of the lesson and answer the Essential Question: How do you make scatter plots and write equations to model data?

- A scatter plot shows whether there is a positive, negative, or no correlation in the data.
- A line of fit can model data. The points you use to find the equation must be on the line, but they do not have to be actual data values.

Plot paired data in a coordinate plane. For a positive or negative correlation, draw a line of fit, with about the same number of points above and below the line. Use two points on the line to find the slope and then use the slope and a point to find the y-intercept. Write an equation of the line.

2. When data has a positive correlation, the dependent variable tends to increase as the independent variable increases. When data has a negative correlation, the dependent variable tends to decrease as the independent variable increases. When data has relatively no correlation there is no apparent relationship between the independent variable and the dependent variable.

EXAMPLE 4 Interpret a model

Refer to the model for the number of woodpecker clusters in Example 3.

a. *Describe* the domain and range of the function.

b. At about what rate did the number of active woodpecker clusters change during the period 1992–2000?

Solution

a. The domain of the function is the the period from 1992 to 2000, or $2 \le x \le 10$. The range is the the number of active clusters given by the function for $2 \le x \le 10$, or $20 \le y \le 49.3$.

b. The number of active woodpecker clusters increased at a rate of $\frac{11}{3}$ or about 3.7 woodpecker clusters per year.

GUIDED PRACTICE for Example 4

4. In Guided Practice Exercise 2, at about what rate does y change with respect to x? about 1.6

5.6 EXERCISES

HOMEWORK KEY

 = **WORKED-OUT SOLUTIONS** on p. WS12 for Exs. 7 and 17

★ = **STANDARDIZED TEST PRACTICE** Exs. 2, 8, 11, 12, and 16

SKILL PRACTICE

A

1. **VOCABULARY** Copy and complete: When data have a positive correlation, the dependent variable tends to _?_ as the independent variable increases. increase

2. ★ **WRITING** *Describe* how paired data with a positive correlation, a negative correlation, and relatively no correlation differ. See margin.

EXAMPLE 1 on p. 325 for Exs. 3–5, 10, 11

DESCRIBING CORRELATIONS **Tell whether x and y show a *positive correlation*, a *negative correlation*, or *relatively no correlation*.**

3. 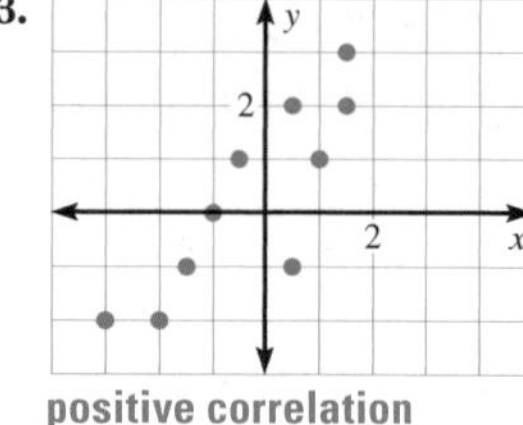

positive correlation

4. 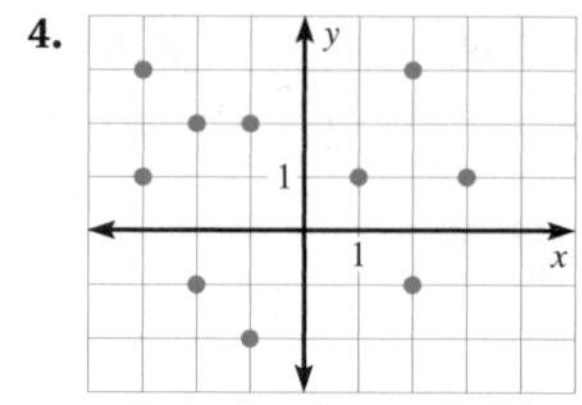

relatively no correlation

5. 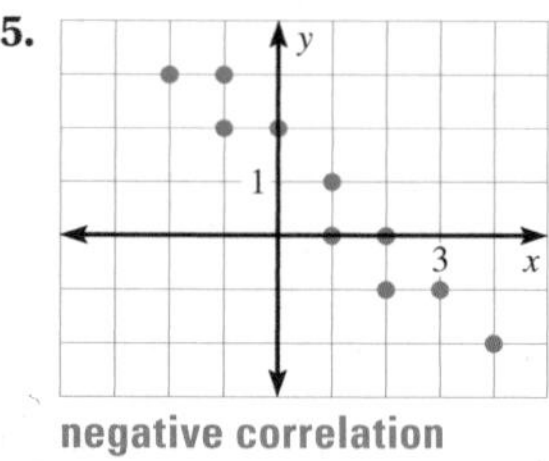

negative correlation

EXAMPLES 2 and 3 on pp. 326–327 for Exs. 6–9

FITTING LINES TO DATA **Make a scatter plot of the data in the table. Draw a line of fit. Write an equation of the line.** 6–7. See margin for art.

6.

x	1	1	3	4	5	6	9
y	10	12	33	46	59	70	102

Sample answer: $y = 11.5x - 0.28$

7.

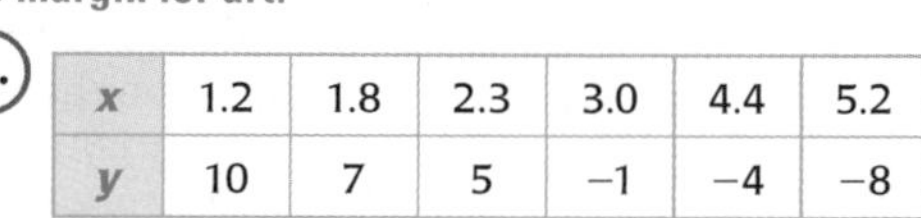

x	1.2	1.8	2.3	3.0	4.4	5.2
y	10	7	5	−1	−4	−8

Sample answer: $y = -4.4x + 14.88$

6. 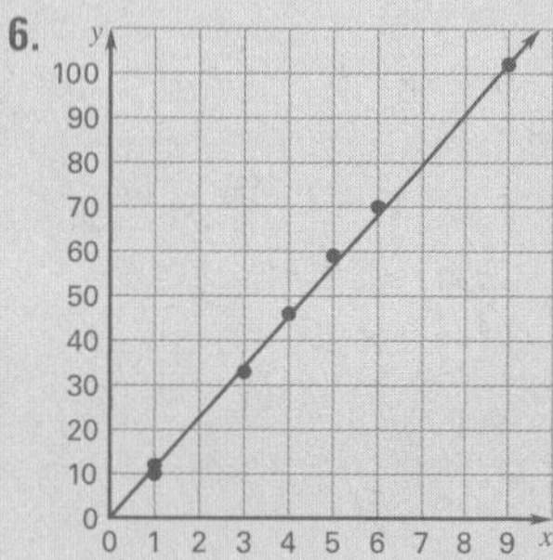

7. 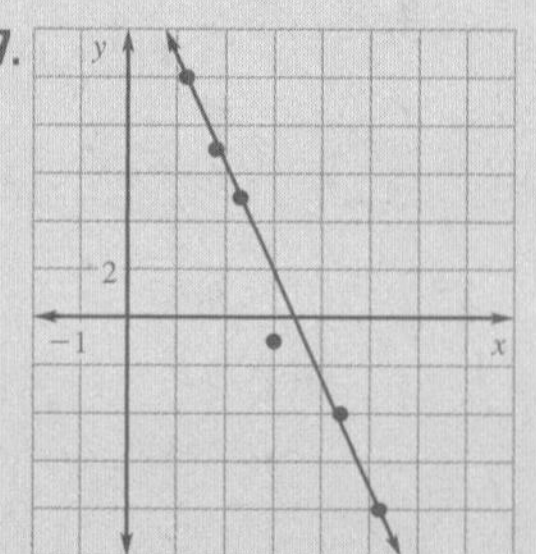

8. ★ **MULTIPLE CHOICE** Which equation best models the data in the scatter plot? C

Ⓐ $y = -x - 6$ Ⓑ $y = x - 6$

Ⓒ $y = -x + 8$ Ⓓ $y = x + 8$

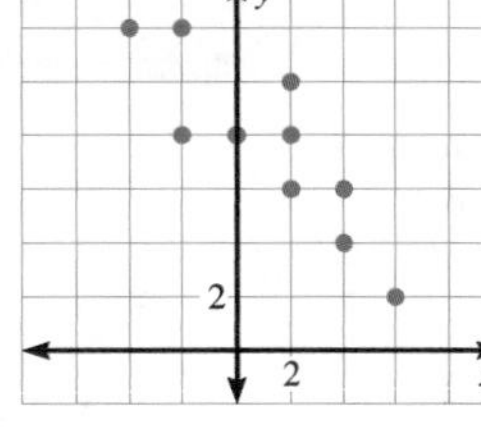

9. **ERROR ANALYSIS** *Describe* and correct the error in fitting the line to the data in the scatter plot.

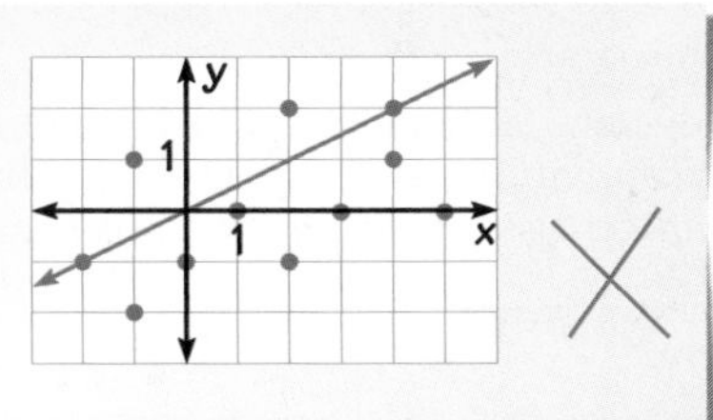

10. **ERROR ANALYSIS** *Describe* and correct the error in describing the correlation of the data in the scatter plot.

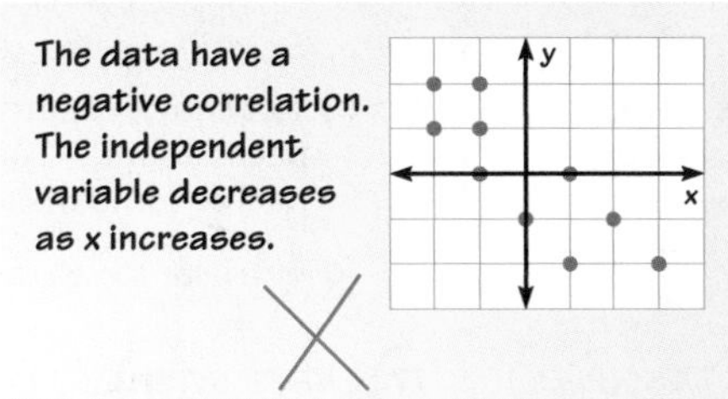

11. ★ **OPEN-ENDED** Give an example of a data set that shows a negative correlation. *Sample answer:* The amount of time driving a car and the amount of gas left in the gas tank.

B

12. ★ **SHORT RESPONSE** Make a scatter plot of the data. *Describe* the correlation of the data. Is it possible to fit a line to the data? If so, write an equation of the line. If not, explain why.

x	−12	−7	−4	−3	−1	2	5	6	7	9	15
y	150	50	15	10	1	5	22	37	52	90	226

MODELING DATA Make a scatter plot of the data. *Describe* the correlation of the data. If possible, fit a line to the data and write an equation of the line.

13–14. See margin for art.

13.

x	10	12	15	20	30	45	60	99
y	−2	4	9	16	32	55	87	128

positive correlation; *Sample answer:* $y = 1.49x - 13$

14.

x	−5	−3	−3	0	1	2	5	6
y	−4	12	10	−6	8	0	3	−9

relatively no correlation

C

15. **CHALLENGE** Which line shown is a better line of fit for the scatter plot? *Explain* your reasoning.
Line b; line a has too many points below the line, but line b has about half the points above the line and about half the points below the line.

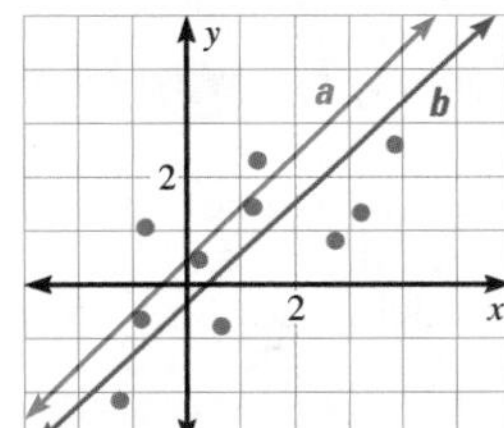

9. The line does not have approximately half the data above it and half below it; see margin for art.

10. The independent variable is x, not y; the dependent variable decreases as x increases.

12. See margin for art; relatively no correlation; no; because there is relatively no correlation in the data you cannot write an equation.

4 PRACTICE AND APPLY

Assignment Guide

Answer Transparencies available for all exercises

Basic:
Day 1: EP p. 941 Exs. 1–7 odd
pp. 328–331
Exs. 1–12, 16–18, 22–28

Average:
Day 1: pp. 328–331
Exs. 1, 2, 4–14, 16–20, 22–28

Advanced:
Day 1: pp. 328–331
Exs. 1, 2, 4–8, 11–28*

Block:
pp. 328–331
Exs. 1, 2, 4–14, 16–20, 22–28 (with 5.7)

Differentiated Instruction

See *Algebra 1 Best Practices Toolkit* for suggestions on addressing the needs of a diverse classroom.

Homework Check

For a quick check of student understanding of key concepts, go over the following exercises:

Basic: 3, 6, 16, 17, 18

Average: 4, 7, 16, 17, 18

Advanced: 5, 7, 16, 17, 18

Extra Practice

- Student Edition, p. 942
- Chapter 5 Resource Book: Practice levels A, B, C, pp. 63–68

Practice Worksheet

An easily-readable reduced practice page (with answers) for this lesson can be found on p. 280D.

9.
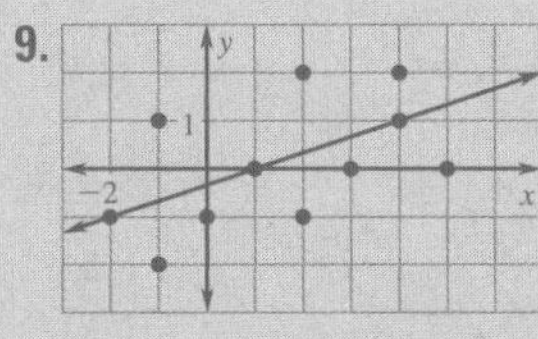

12.
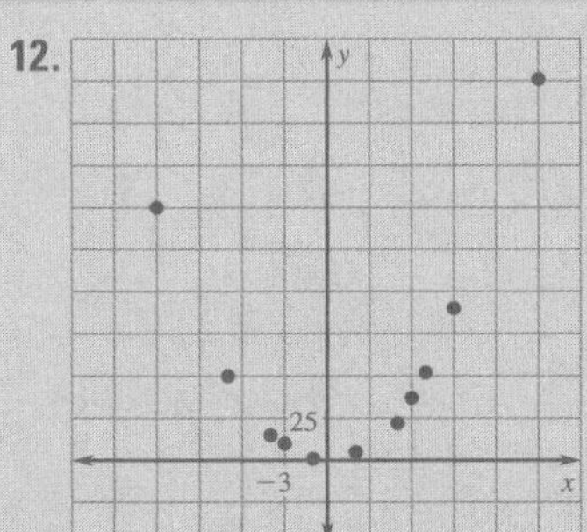

13.
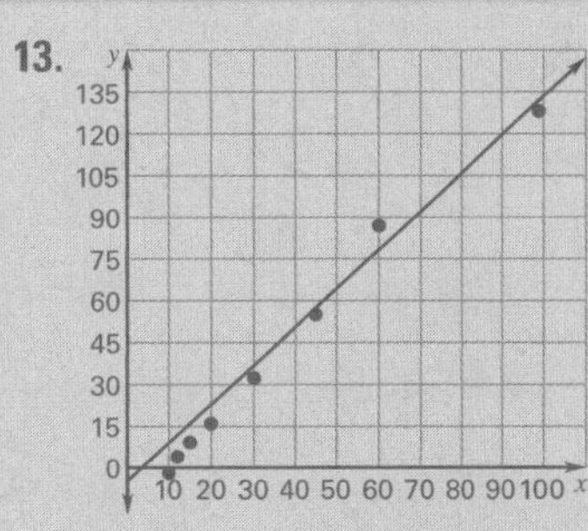
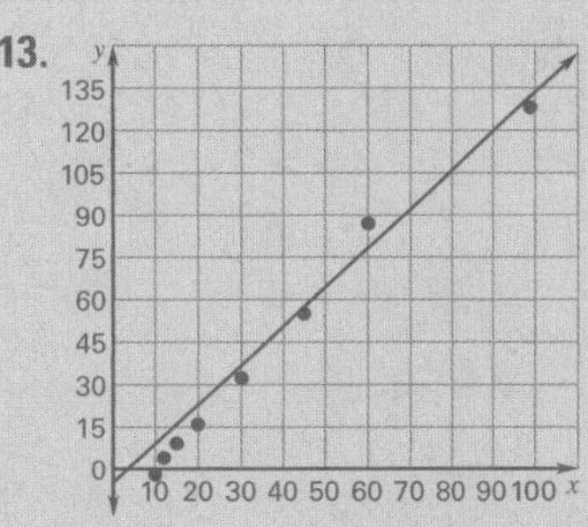

14.

Teaching Strategy

Exercise 8 You may want to point out to students that they can immediately eliminate the two choices with positive slope based on the correlation shown on the scatter plot.

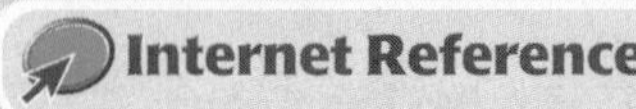

Exercise 17 Additional information about the layers of Earth's atmosphere can be found at liftoff. msfc.nasa.gov/academy/space/ atmosphere.html

Avoiding Common Errors

Exercises 17–21 Some students may draw a line through two of the points rather than a line of fit that models the data. Remind them that approximately the same number of points should lie above the line as below it, but that none of the points in the data set actually have to lie on the line.

Exercises 19–21 Some students may attempt to write an equation that models the data without making a scatter plot first. Remind these students that there is not a constant rate of change in the data, and that because of this, they need to plot the data so they can draw a line of fit.

16a.

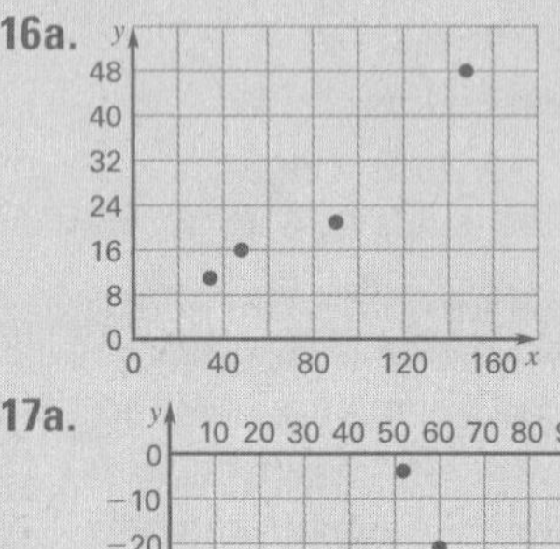

17a.

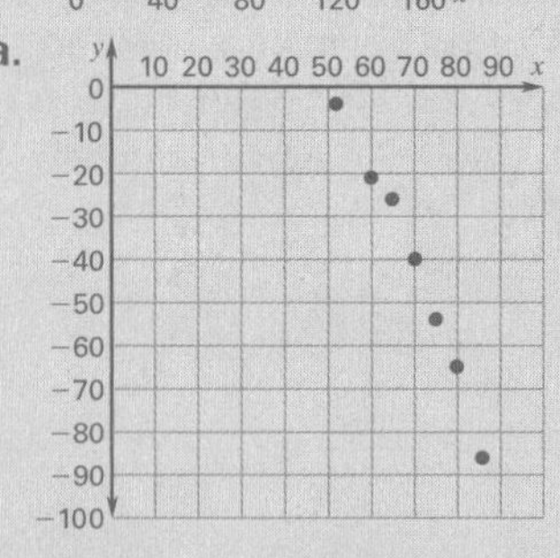

PROBLEM SOLVING

EXAMPLE 2 on p. 326 for Exs. 16

A

16. ★ **SHORT RESPONSE** The table shows the approximate home range size of big cats (members of the *Panthera* genus) in their natural habitat and the percent of time that the cats spend pacing in captivity.

Big cat (*Panthera* genus)	Lion	Jaguar	Leopard	Tiger
Home range size (km^2)	148	90	34	48
Pacing (percent of time)	48	21	11	16

a. Make a scatter plot of the data. See margin.

b. *Describe* the correlation of the data.

16b. Positive correlation; the larger the home range size the larger the percent of pacing time.

c. The snow leopard's home range size is about 39 square kilometers. It paces about 7% of its time in captivity. Does the snow leopard fit the pacing trend of cats in the *Panthera* genus? *Explain* your reasoning. No; it is below the expected percent of time spent pacing.

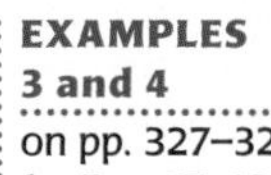

for problem solving help at classzone.com

EXAMPLES 3 and 4 on pp. 327–328 for Exs. 17–18

17. **EARTH SCIENCE** The mesosphere is a layer of atmosphere that lies from about 50 kilometers above Earth's surface to about 90 kilometers above Earth's surface. The diagram shows the temperature at certain altitudes in the mesosphere.

100 km, 86 km, 52 km, 0 km

Mesosphere

Altitude (km)	Temperature (°C)
86	−86
80	−65
75	−54
70	−40
65	−26
60	−21
52	−4

a. Make a scatter plot of the data. See margin.

b. Write an equation that models the temperature (in degrees Celsius) as a function of the altitude (in kilometers) above 50 kilometers.

17b. *Sample answer:* $y = -2.2x + 111$

c. At about what rate does the temperature change with increasing altitude in the mesosphere? *Sample answer:* −2.2 degrees per kilometer

@HomeTutor for problem solving help at classzone.com

B

18. **ALLIGATORS** The table shows the weights of two alligators at various times during a feeding trial. Make two scatter plots, one for each alligator, where x is the number of weeks and y is the weight of the alligator. Draw lines of fit for both scatter plots. *Compare* the approximate growth rates.

18. See margin for art; the growth rate of alligator 2 is slightly greater than the growth rate of alligator 1.

Weeks	0	9	18	27	34	43	49
Alligator 1 weight (pounds)	6	8.6	10	13.6	15	17.2	19.8
Alligator 2 weight (pounds)	6	9.2	12.8	13.6	20.2	21.4	24.3

19. **GEOLOGY** The table shows the duration of several eruptions of the geyser Old Faithful and the interval between eruptions. Write an equation that models the interval as a function of an eruption's duration.

19. *Sample answer*: $y = 12.6x + 32$

Duration (minutes)	1.5	2.0	2.5	3.0	3.5	4.0	4.5	5.0
Interval (minutes)	50	57	65	71	76	82	89	95

○ = WORKED-OUT SOLUTIONS on p. WS1

★ = STANDARDIZED TEST PRACTICE

18.

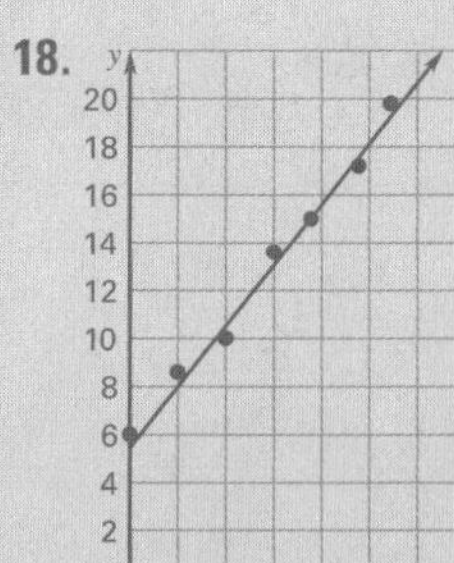

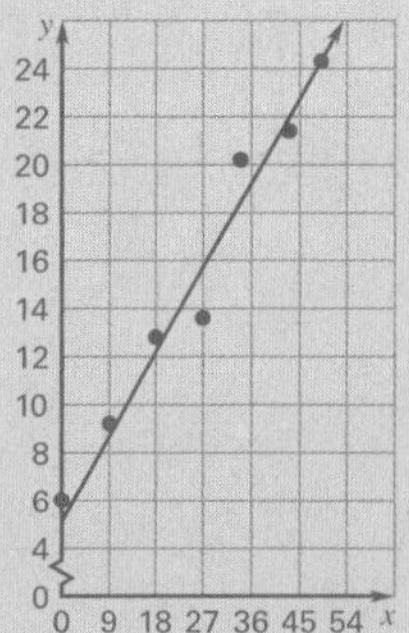

20. **DAYLIGHT** The table shows the number of hours and minutes of daylight in Baltimore, Maryland, for ten days in January.

Day in January	5	6	7	8	9	10	11	12	13	14
Daylight (hours and minutes)	9:30	9:31	9:32	9:34	9:35	9:36	9:37	9:38	9:40	9:41

a. Write an equation that models the hours of daylight (in minutes in excess of 9 hours) as a function of the number of days since January 5. *Sample answer:* $y = 1.2x + 30$

b. At what rate do the hours of daylight change over time in early January? *Sample answer:* 1.2 min per day

c. Do you expect the trend described by the equation to continue indefinitely? *Explain.* No; it will continue through June and then start decreasing.

21c. *Sample answer:* $m = 13.884y + 39.808$; the function models the amount of money, m, spent on the Internet as a function of the number of years, y, since 1999.

21d. Yes, if you substitute the number of years since 1999 for y, you get about the amount of money, m, given in the data.

21. **CHALLENGE** The table shows the estimated amount of time and the estimated amount of money the average person in the U.S. spent on the Internet each year from 1999 to 2005.

Year	1999	2000	2001	2002	2003	2004	2005
Internet time (hours)	88	107	136	154	169	182	193
Internet spending (dollars)	40.55	49.64	68.70	84.73	97.76	110.46	122.67

a. Write an equation that models the amount of time h (in hours) spent on the Internet as a function of the number of years y since 1999. *Sample answer:* $h = 17.8y + 93.6$

b. Write an equation that models the amount of money m spent on the Internet as a function of the time h (in hours) spent on the Internet. *Sample answer:* $m = 0.78h - 33.2$

c. Substitute the expression that is equal to h from part (a) in the function from part (b). What does the new function tell you? See margin.

d. Does the function from part (c) agree with the data given? *Explain.*

ILLINOIS MIXED REVIEW

TEST PRACTICE at classzone.com

22. You are making a rectangular quilt with dimensions 48 inches by 60 inches. The fabric you are using costs $1.50 per square foot. How much will the fabric for the quilt cost? C

Ⓐ $20 Ⓑ $25 Ⓒ $30 Ⓓ $32

23. Find the slope of the line shown.

Ⓐ −2 Ⓑ −1
Ⓒ −0.5 Ⓓ 2 C

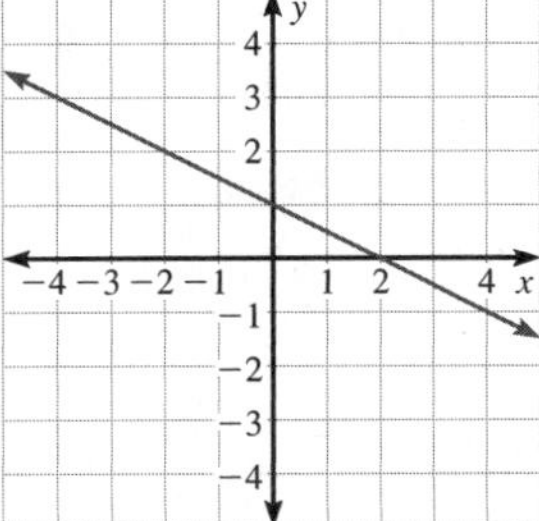

5 ASSESS AND RETEACH

Daily Homework Quiz

Transparency Available

Tell whether x and y show a *positive correlation*, a *negative correlation*, or *relatively no correlation*.

1.

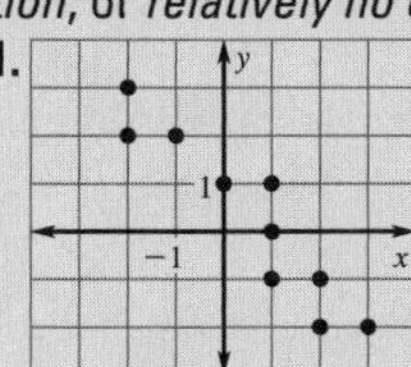

negative correlation

2. The table shows the body length and wingspan (both in inches) of seven birds. Write an equation that models the wingspan as a function of body length.

Bird	Body Length	Wing-span
Cuckoo	12	18
Falcon	16	41
Harrier	18	43
Hawk	19	51
Osprey	23	63
Sandpiper	9	22
Warbler	5	7

$y = 3.1x - 10.3$, where x is body length and y is wingspan

Online Quiz

Available at **classzone.com**

Diagnosis/Remediation

- Practice A, B, C in Chapter 5 Resource Book, pp. 63–68
- Study Guide in Chapter 5 Resource Book, pp. 69–70
- Practice Workbook, pp. 78–80
- @HomeTutor

Challenge

Additional challenge is available in the Chapter 5 Resource Book, p. 73.

1 PLAN AND PREPARE

Learn the Method

- Students will use a graphing calculator to create a scatter plot and perform linear regression on a data set.
- After the activity, students can use a graphing calculator to check their solutions in Exercises 17–21 in Lesson 5.6.

Keystroke Help

Keystrokes for several models of calculators are available in blackline format in the *Chapter 5 Resource Book*.

2 TEACH

Extra Example 1

The table shows the number of endangered plants in the U.S. from 1997 to 2002. Make a scatter plot of the data. *Describe* the correlation of the data.

Year	Endangered Plants
1997	553
1998	567
1999	581
2000	592
2001	595
2002	599

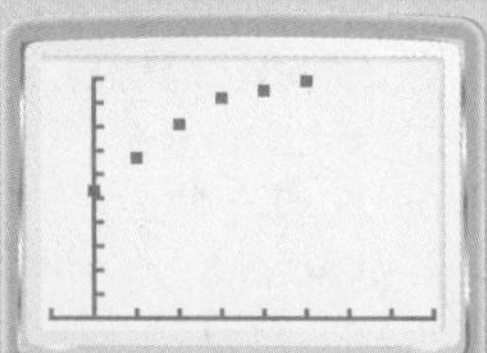

The data have a positive correlation. This means that with each passing year, the number of endangered plants tended to increase.

5.6 Perform Linear Regression

QUESTION How can you model data with the best-fitting line?

The line that most closely follows a trend in data is the *best-fitting line.* The process of finding the best-fitting line to model a set of data is called *linear regression.* This process can be tedious to perform by hand, but you can use a graphing calculator to make a scatter plot and perform linear regression on a data set.

EXAMPLE 1 Create a scatter plot

The table shows the total sales from women's clothing stores in the United States from 1997 to 2002. Make a scatter plot of the data. *Describe* the correlation of the data.

Year	1997	1998	1999	2000	2001	2002
Sales (billions of dollars)	27.9	28.7	30.2	32.5	33.1	34.3

STEP 1 *Enter data*

Press STAT and select Edit. Enter years since 1997 (0, 1, 2, 3, 4, 5) into List 1 (L_1). These will be the x-values. Enter sales (in billions of dollars) into List 2 (L_2). These will be the y-values.

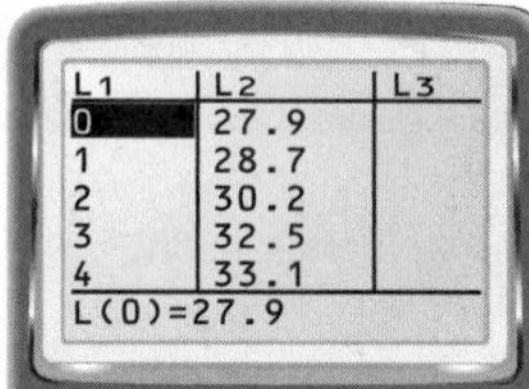

STEP 2 *Choose plot settings*

Press 2nd Y= and select Plot1. Turn Plot1 On. Select scatter plot as the type of display. Enter L_1 for the Xlist and L_2 for the Ylist.

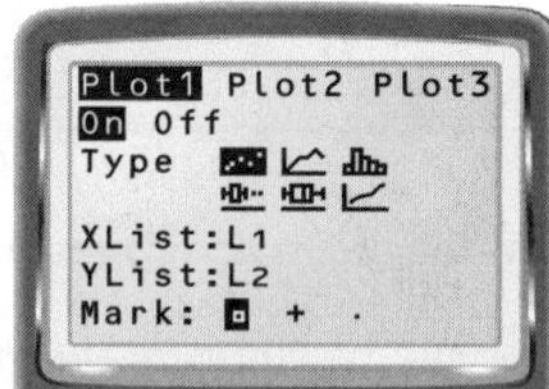

STEP 3 *Make a scatter plot*

Press ZOOM 9 to display the scatter plot so that the points for all data pairs are visible.

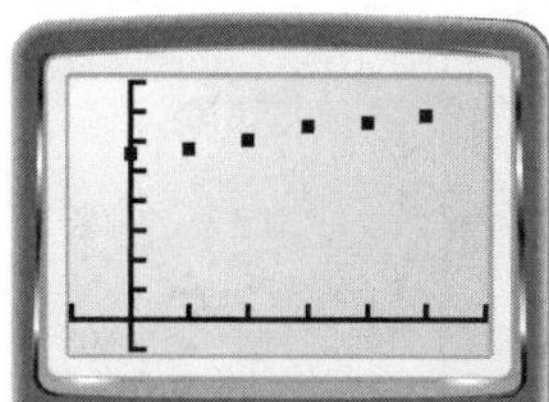

STEP 4 *Describe the correlation*

Describe the correlation of the data in the scatter plot.

The data have a positive correlation. This means that with each passing year, the sales of women's clothing tended to increase.

@HomeTutor classzone.com Keystrokes

MODELING DATA The *correlation coefficient* r for a set of paired data measures how well the best-fitting line fits the data. You can use a graphing calculator to find a value for r.

For r close to 1, the data have a strong positive correlation. For r close to -1, the data have a strong negative correlation. For r close to 0, the data have relatively no correlation.

EXAMPLE 2 Find the best-fitting line

Find an equation of the best-fitting line for the scatter plot from Example 1. Determine the correlation coefficient of the data. Graph the best-fitting line.

STEP 1 Perform regression

Press STAT. From the CALC menu, choose LinReg(ax+b). The a- and b-values given are for an equation of the form $y = ax + b$. Rounding these values gives the equation $y = 1.36x + 27.7$. Because r is close to 1, the data have a strong positive correlation.

STEP 2 Draw the best-fitting line

Press Y= and enter $1.36x + 27.7$ for y_1. Press GRAPH.

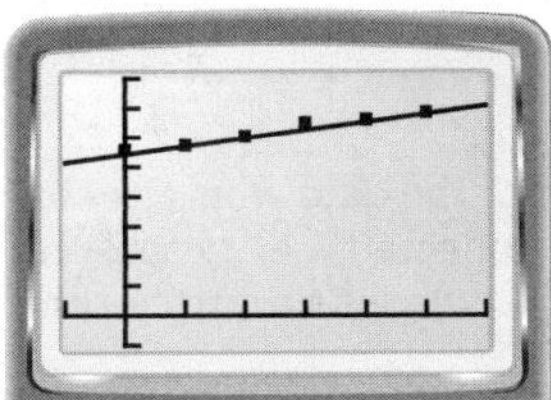

PRACTICE

In Exercises 1–5, refer to the table, which shows the total sales from men's clothing stores in the United States from 1997 to 2002.

Year	1997	1998	1999	2000	2001	2002
Sales (billions of dollars)	10.1	10.6	10.5	10.8	10.3	9.9

1. Make a scatter plot of the data. *Describe* the correlation. **See art in Exercise 3; negative correlation.**
2. Find the equation of the best-fitting line for the data. **$S = -0.046y + 10.5$**
3. Draw the best-fitting line for the data. **See margin.**

DRAW CONCLUSIONS

4. What does the value of r for the equation in Exercise 2 tell you about the correlation of the data? **The data have relatively no correlation.**
5. **PREDICT** How could you use the best-fitting line to predict future sales of men's clothing? *Explain* your answer. ***Sample answer:* You cannot use the best-fitting line to predict future sales because the data do not show a strong correlation.**

Extra Example 2

Find an equation of the best-fitting line for the scatter plot from Extra Example 1. Determine the correlation coefficient of the data. Graph the best-fitting line. **Rounding the values from the graphing calculator, the equation of the best-fitting line is $y = 9.29x + 558$. The correlation coefficient is 0.965. Since r is close to 1, the data have a strong positive correlation.**

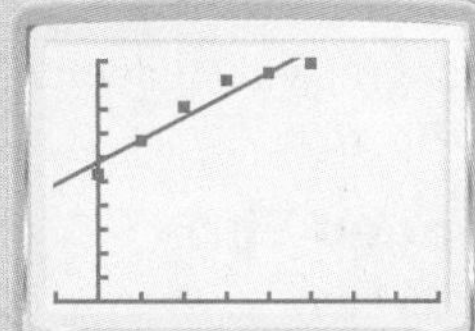

3 ASSESS AND RETEACH

A friend performs linear regression on a data set and tells you that the correlation coefficient is 0.213.

1. What does the value of r tell you about the data set? **Since the value of r is positive but close to zero, there is almost no correlation in the data even though the y values tend to increase as the x values increase.**
2. How reliable is the best-fitting line for predicting future trends in the data? **Since the correlation is low, the best-fitting line would not be accurate in predicting future trends.**

3.

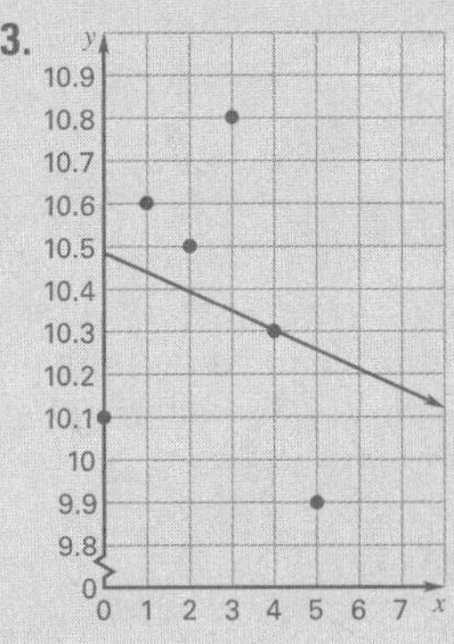

1 PLAN AND PREPARE

Explore the Concept

- Students will make a prediction using a line of fit.
- This activity leads into the study of using the equation of a best-fitting line to make a prediction in Example 1 in Lesson 5.7.

Materials

Each student or group of students will need a metric ruler.

Recommended Time

Work activity: 15 min

Discuss results: 5 min

Grouping

Students can work individually or in groups of four. If students work in groups, they can divide the tasks into collecting (and drawing) the rectangles, measuring the rectangles and recording data, and plotting the data and drawing a line of fit. Two students can share the last task.

2 TEACH

Tips for Success

Remind students to use care in plotting the points on the scatter plot and in drawing the line of fit.

Key Discovery

The closer a line of fit models the data, the better the prediction.

3 ASSESS AND RETEACH

How accurate is your model in predicting the long side of a rectangle if the short side is 2 centimeters? Explain. **Students should give reasons why their model is or is not accurate.**

5.7 Collecting and Organizing Data

MATERIALS • metric ruler

QUESTION How can you make a prediction using a line of fit?

EXPLORE Make a prediction using a line of fit

A student in your class draws a rectangle with a short side that is 4 centimeters in length. Predict the length of the long side of the rectangle.

STEP 1 ***Collect data***

Ask each of 10 people to draw a rectangle. Do not let anyone drawing a rectangle see a rectangle drawn by someone else.

cm 1 2 3

STEP 2 ***Organize data***

Measure the lengths (in centimeters) of the short and long sides of the rectangles you collected. Create a table like the one shown.

Short side (cm)	2.7	2.7	1.8	2.6	1.4	1.5	1.2	0.8	3.8
Long side (cm)	4.4	6.5	3.4	6	3.4	3	2.8	1.6	6.5

STEP 3 ***Graph data***

Make a scatter plot of the data where each point represents a rectangle that you collected. Let x represent the length of the short side of the rectangle, and let y represent the length of the long side.

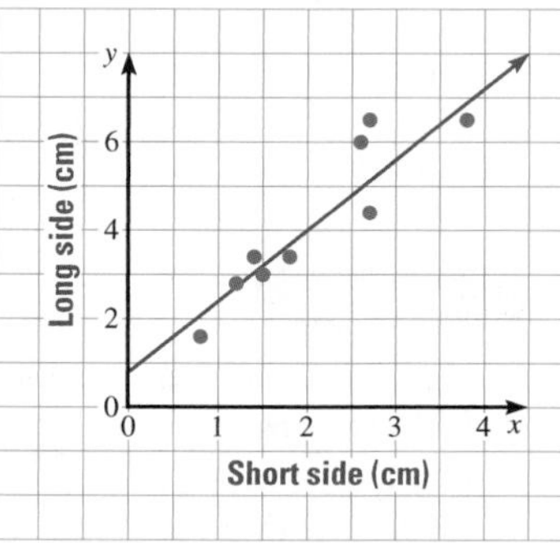

STEP 4 ***Model data***

Draw a line of fit.

STEP 5 ***Predict***

Use the line of fit to find the length of the long side that corresponds to a short side with a length of 4 centimeters. In this case, the long side length predicted by the line of fit has a length of about 7 centimeters.

DRAW CONCLUSIONS Use your observations to complete these exercises

1–3. Answers may vary.

1. **COMPARE** What is the slope of your line of fit? How does this slope compare with the slope of the line shown above?
2. **PREDICT** Suppose a student in your class draws a rectangle that has a long side with a length of 5 centimeters. Predict the length of the shorter side. *Explain* how you made your prediction.
3. **EXTEND** The *golden ratio* appears frequently in architectural structures, paintings, sculptures, and even in nature. This ratio of the long side of a rectangle to its short side is approximately 1.618. How does this ratio compare with the slopes of the lines you compared in Exercise 1?

5.7 Predict with Linear Models

8.11.07 Identify an equation of a line or an equation of a line of best fit from given information . . .

Before You made scatter plots and wrote equations of lines of fit.

Now You will make predictions using best-fitting lines.

Why? So you can model trends, as in Ex. 21.

Key Vocabulary
- **best-fitting line**
- **linear regression**
- **interpolation**
- **extrapolation**
- **zero of a function**

The line that most closely follows a trend in data is called the **best-fitting line**. The process of finding the best-fitting line to model a set of data is called **linear regression**. You can perform linear regression using technology. Using a line or its equation to approximate a value between two known values is called **linear interpolation**.

EXAMPLE 1 Interpolate using an equation

CD SINGLES The table shows the total number of CD singles shipped (in millions) by manufacturers for several years during the period 1993–1997.

Year	1993	1995	1996	1997
CD singles shipped (millions)	7.8	22	43	67

REVIEW REGRESSION
For help with performing a linear regression to find the best-fitting line, see p. 332.

a. Make a scatter plot of the data.

b. Find an equation that models the number of CD singles shipped (in millions) as a function of the number of years since 1993.

c. Approximate the number of CD singles shipped in 1994.

Solution

a. Enter the data into lists on a graphing calculator. Make a scatter plot, letting the number of years since 1993 be the x-values (0, 2, 3, 4) and the number of CD singles shipped be the y-values.

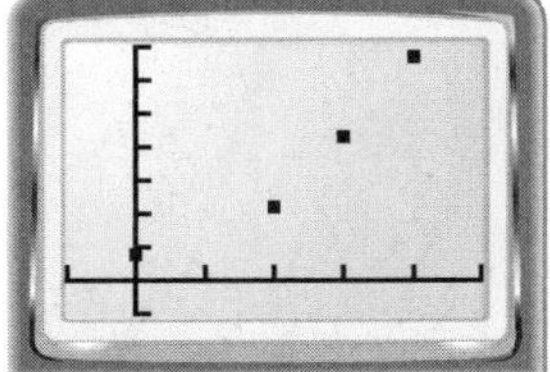

b. Perform linear regression using the paired data. The equation of the best-fitting line is approximately $y = 14x + 2.4$.

ANOTHER WAY
You can also estimate the number of CDs shipped in 1994 by evaluating $y = 14x + 2.4$ when $x = 1$.

c. Graph the best-fitting line. Use the *trace* feature and the arrow keys to find the value of the equation when $x = 1$.

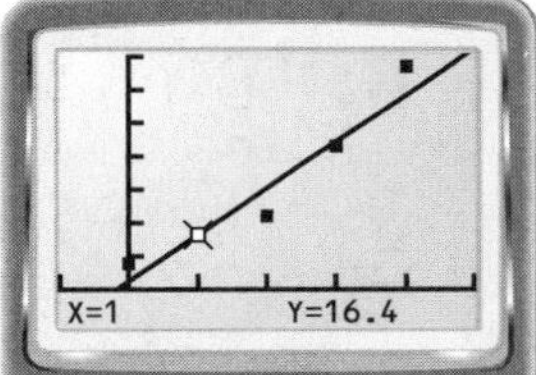

▶ About 16 million CD singles were shipped in 1994.

Animated Algebra at classzone.com

1 PLAN AND PREPARE

Warm-Up Exercises
Transparency Available

1. Evaluate $f(x) = 2.5x + 8$ when x is 3 or 5. **15.5; 20.5**
2. The table shows the profits of a company. Write an equation modeling the profit y as a function of the number of years x since 1998. $y = 2.8x + 16.4$

Year	'98	'99	'00	'01	'02
Profit (millions)	15	21	22	25	27

Notetaking Guide
Transparency Available

Promotes interactive learning and notetaking skills, pp. 121–124.

Pacing
Basic: 1 day
Average: 1 day
Advanced: 1 day
Block: 0.5 block with 5.6
- See *Teaching Guide/Lesson Plan.*

2 FOCUS AND MOTIVATE

Essential Question
Big Idea 3, p. 281
How can you use a best-fitting line to make predictions about data? **Tell students they will learn how to answer this question by performing a linear regression.**

Resource Planning Guide

Chapter Resource Book
- Teaching Guide/Lesson Plan (pp. 74–75)
- Activity Master (p. 76)
- Practice levels A, B, C (pp. 78–83)
- Study Guide (pp. 84–85)
- Catch-up for Absent Students (p. 86)
- Problem Solving Workshop (p. 87)
- Challenge (p. 88)

Workbooks
- Notetaking Guide (pp. 121–124)
- Practice Workbook (pp. 81–83)

Teaching Options
- **Power Presentations CD-ROM** provides dynamic electronic teaching resources for the classroom.
- **Activity Generator CD-ROM** provides editable activities for all ability levels.

Interactive Technology
- Easy Planner
- Power Presentations CD-ROM
- Activity Generator CD-ROM
- Animated Algebra
- Test Generator CD-ROM
- Online Quiz
- eWorkbook
- eEdition
- @HomeTutor

Resources for English Learners
- Quick Reference for English Learners
- Spanish Study Guide
- Multi-Language Visual Glossary
- Student Resources in Spanish

See also the *Algebra 1 Toolkit* for more strategies for meeting individual needs.

EXTRAPOLATION Using a line or its equation to approximate a value outside the range of known values is called **linear extrapolation**.

EXAMPLE 2 Extrapolate using an equation

CD SINGLES Look back at Example 1.

a. Use the equation from Example 1 to approximate the number of CD singles shipped in 1998 and in 2000.

b. In 1998 there were actually 56 million CD singles shipped. In 2000 there were actually 34 million CD singles shipped. *Describe* the accuracy of the extrapolations made in part (a).

Solution

a. Evaluate the equation of the best-fitting line from Example 1 for $x = 5$ and $x = 7$.

Y1(5)
72.4
Y1(7)
100.4

The model predicts about 72 million CD singles shipped in 1998 and about 100 million CD singles shipped in 2000.

b. The differences between the predicted number of CD singles shipped and the actual number of CD singles shipped in 1998 and 2000 are 16 million CDs and 66 million CDs, respectively. The difference in the actual and predicted numbers increased from 1998 to 2000. So, the equation of the best-fitting line gives a less accurate prediction for the year that is farther from the given years.

ACCURACY As Example 2 illustrates, the farther removed an x-value is from the known x-values, the less confidence you can have in the accuracy of the predicted y-value. This is true in general but not in every case.

GUIDED PRACTICE for Examples 1 and 2

1. **HOUSE SIZE** The table shows the median floor area of new single-family houses in the United States during the period 1995–1999.

Year	1995	1996	1997	1998	1999
Median floor area (square feet)	1920	1950	1975	2000	2028

a. Find an equation that models the floor area (in square feet) of a new single-family house as a function of the number of years since 1995. $y = 26.6x + 1921.4$

b. Predict the median floor area of a new single-family house in 2000 and in 2001. about 2054.4 ft^2, about 2081 ft^2

c. Which of the predictions from part (b) would you expect to be more accurate? *Explain* your reasoning. The prediction for 2000 because the farther removed an x-value is from the known x-values, the less confidence you can have in the accuracy of the predicted y-value.

Motivating the Lesson

You have data that gives the yearly sea turtle strandings off North Carolina from 1993 to 2004, with the exception of 1995 and 1998. By using a best-fitting line, you can predict the number of strandings that occurred in 1995 and 1998. You can also predict the number of strandings that are likely in future years.

3 TEACH

Extra Example 1

The table shows the number of hikers who have completed the Appalachian Trail from 1996 to 2000.

Year	Hikers completing trail
1996	405
1998	403
1999	552
2000	623

a. Make a scatter plot of the data.

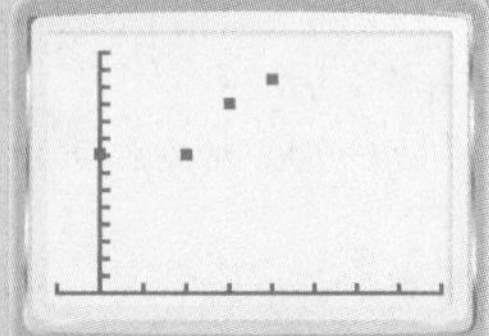

b. Find an equation that models the number of hikers completing the trail as a function of the number of years since 1996. *Sample answer:* $y = 56x + 369$

c. Approximate the number of hikers who completed the entire trail in 1997. about 425 hikers

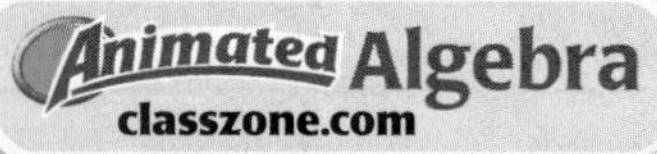

An **Animated Algebra** activity is available on-line for **Example 1**. This activity is also available on the **Power Presentations CD-ROM**.

Differentiated Instruction

Auditory Learners Point out that linear *in*terpolation predicts a point *in*side the range of the data points. Linear *ex*trapolation predicts a point *ex*terior to, or outside of, the range of the data points.

See also the *Algebra 1 Toolkit* for more strategies.

EXAMPLE 3 Predict using an equation

SOFTBALL The table shows the number of participants in U.S. youth softball during the period 1997–2001. Predict the year in which the number of youth softball participants reaches 1.2 million.

Year	1997	1998	1999	2000	2001
Participants (millions)	1.44	1.4	1.411	1.37	1.355

Solution

STEP 1 Perform linear regression. Let x represent the number of years since 1997, and let y represent the number of youth softball participants (in millions). The equation for the best-fitting line is approximately $y = -0.02x + 1.435$.

STEP 2 Graph the equation of the best-fitting line. Trace the line until the cursor reaches $y = 1.2$. The corresponding x-value is shown at the bottom of the calculator screen.

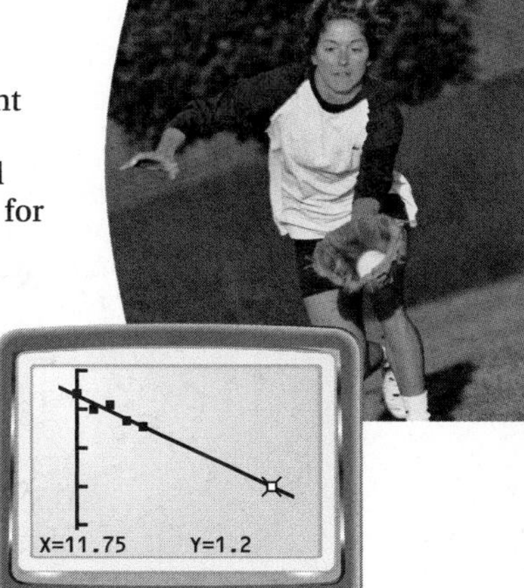

▶ There will be 1.2 million participants about 12 years after 1997, or in 2009.

ANOTHER WAY

You can also predict the year by substituting 1.2 for y in the equation and solving for x:

$y = 0.02x + 1.435$

$1.2 = -0.02x + 1.435$

$x = 11.75$

✓ **GUIDED PRACTICE** for Example 3

2. **SOFTBALL** In Example 3, in what year will there be 1.25 million youth softball participants in the U.S? 2006

ZERO OF A FUNCTION A **zero of a function** $y = f(x)$ is an x-value for which $f(x) = 0$ (or $y = 0$). Because $y = 0$ along the x-axis of the coordinate plane, a zero of a function is an x-intercept of the function's graph.

KEY CONCEPT *For Your Notebook*

Relating Solutions of Equations, x-Intercepts of Graphs, and Zeros of Functions

In Chapter 3 you learned to solve an equation like $2x - 4 = 0$:

$$2x - 4 = 0$$
$$2x = 4$$
$$x = 2$$

The solution of $2x - 4 = 0$ is 2.

In Chapter 4 you found the x-intercept of the graph of a function like $y = 2x - 4$:

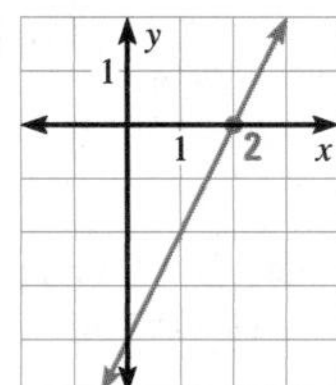

Now you are finding the zero of a function like $f(x) = 2x - 4$:

$$f(x) = 0$$
$$2x - 4 = 0$$
$$x = 2$$

The zero of $f(x) = 2x - 4$ is 2.

Extra Example 2

Look back at Extra Example 1.

a. Use the equation from Extra Example 1 to approximate the number of hikers who completed the entire trail in 2001 and 2003. about 649 hikers in 2001 and about 761 hikers in 2003

b. In 2001, 610 hikers actually completed the entire trail. In 2003, 555 hikers completed the entire trail. Describe the accuracy of the extrapolation made in part (a). The differences between the predicted number of hikers and the actual number in 2001 and 2003 are 39 and 206, respectively. The actual and the predicted numbers are close for 2001, but very different for 2003. So, the equation of the best-fitting line gives a less accurate prediction for the year that is farther from the given years.

Extra Example 3

The Federal Communications Commission issues licenses for amateur radio stations. The table shows the number of new general class licenses the FCC issued during the period September, 2004, to January, 2005. Predict the month and year in which the number of new general class amateur radio licenses issued reaches 50.

Month/Year	New Licenses
September, 2004	203
October, 2004	185
November, 2004	144
December, 2004	135
January, 2005	138

about 8 months after September, 2004, or about May, 2005

Extra Example 4

Look back at Extra Example 3. Find the zero of the function. *Explain* what the zero means in this situation. **The zero of the function is about 11. The function has a negative slope, which means that the number of new issues of amateur radio licenses in the general class is decreasing. According to the model, there will be no new general licenses issued about 11 months after September, 2004, which will be August, 2005.**

Closing the Lesson

Have students summarize the major points of the lesson and answer the Essential Question: How can you use a best-fitting line to make predictions about data?

- **You can approximate an unknown data value by using the equation of the best-fitting line found by linear regression.**
- **The zero of a function is the x value of the point where the line crosses the x-axis.**

Make a scatter plot of the data and then perform a linear regression to find the equation of the best-fitting line. Use the trace feature of the graphing calculator to trace the line of the equation or evaluate the equation of the best-fitting line to find the predicted values. Substitute 0 for y in the equation to find the zero of the function.

2. Extrapolation is finding an approximate value outside the range of known values. Interpolation is finding an approximate value within the range of known values.

3.

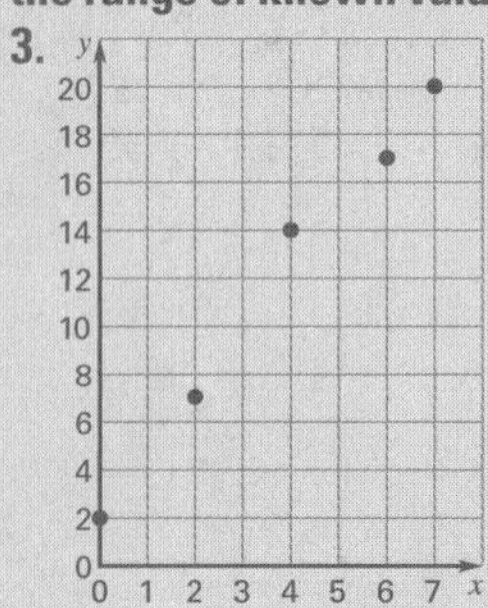

EXAMPLE 4 Find the zero of a function

SOFTBALL Look back at Example 3. Find the zero of the function. *Explain* what the zero means in this situation.

Solution

Substitute 0 for y in the equation of the best-fitting line and solve for x.

$y = -0.02x + 1.435$	**Write the equation.**
$0 = -0.02x + 1.435$	**Substitute 0 for y.**
$x \approx 72$	**Solve for x.**

▶ The zero of the function is about 72. The function has a negative slope, which means that the number of youth softball participants is decreasing. According to the model, there will be no youth softball participants 72 years after 1997, or in 2069.

GUIDED PRACTICE for Example 4

3. **JET BOATS** The number y (in thousands) of jet boats purchased in the U.S. can be modeled by the function $y = -1.23x + 14$ where x is the number of years since 1995. Find the zero of the function. *Explain* what the zero means in this situation. **11.4; the function has a negative slope, which means that the number of jet boats purchased in the U.S. is decreasing. According to the model, there will be no jet boats purchased 11.4 years after 1995, or in 2006.**

5.7 EXERCISES

HOMEWORK KEY

○ = **WORKED-OUT SOLUTIONS** on p. WS13 for Exs. 3 and 19

★ = **STANDARDIZED TEST PRACTICE** Exs. 2, 14, 16, and 21

◆ = **MULTIPLE REPRESENTATIONS** Exs. 22

SKILL PRACTICE

A

1. **VOCABULARY** Copy and complete: Using a linear function to approximate a value within a range of known data values is called _?_. **linear interpolation**

2. ★ **WRITING** *Explain* how extrapolation differs from interpolation. **See margin.**

EXAMPLE 1 on p. 335 for Exs. 3–4

LINEAR INTERPOLATION **Make a scatter plot of the data. Find the equation of the best-fitting line. Approximate the value of y for $x = 5$.** **3–4. See margin for art.**

3.

x	0	2	4	6	7
y	2	7	14	17	20

$y = 2.6x + 2.3$; 15.3

4.

x	2	4	6	8	10
y	6.2	22.5	40.2	55.4	72.1

$y = 8.2x - 10.1$; 30.9

EXAMPLE 2 on p. 336 for Exs. 5–6

LINEAR EXTRAPOLATION **Make a scatter plot of the data. Find the equation of the best-fitting line. Approximate the value of y for $x = 10$.** **5–6. See margin for art.**

5.

x	0	1	2	3	4
y	20	32	39	53	63

$y = 10.7x + 20$; 127

6.

x	1	3	5	7	9
y	0.4	1.4	1.9	2.3	3.2

$y = 0.33x + 0.22$; 3.52

4.

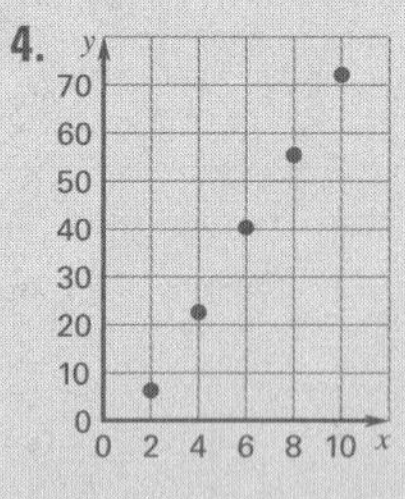

5.

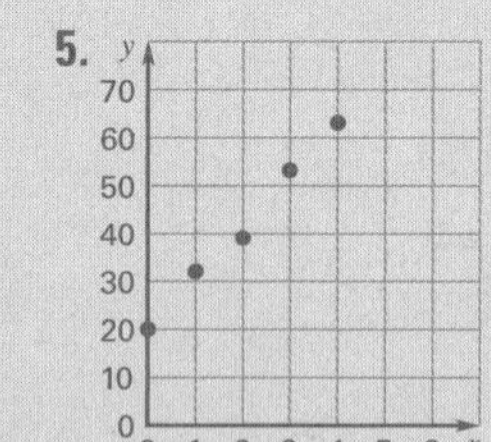

6.

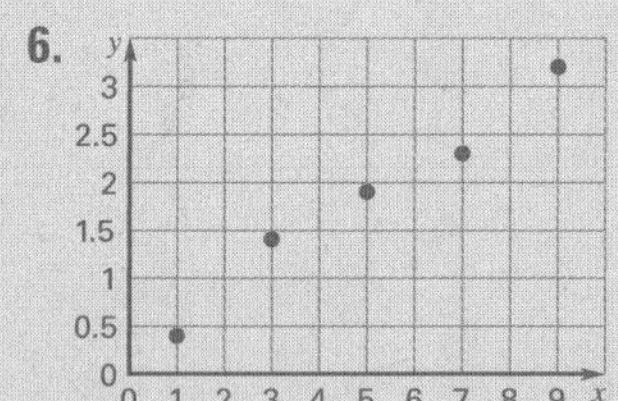

EXAMPLE 4
on p. 338
for Exs. 7–13

ZERO OF A FUNCTION **Find the zero of the function.**

7. $f(x) = 7.5x - 20$ $2\frac{2}{3}$
8. $f(x) = -x + 7$ 7
9. $f(x) = \frac{1}{8}x + 2$ −16
10. $f(x) = 17x - 68$ 4
11. $f(x) = -0.5x + 0.75$ 1.5
12. $f(x) = 5x - 7$ 1.4

13. **ERROR ANALYSIS** *Describe* and correct the error made in finding the zero of the function $y = 2.3x - 2$. To find the zero of a function, substitute 0 for y, not x; $0 = 2.3x - 2$, $2 = 2.3x$, $x = \frac{20}{23}$.

$y = 2.3(0) - 2$
$y = -2$

14. ★ **MULTIPLE CHOICE** Given the function $y = 12.6x + 3$, for what x-value does $y = 66$? B

Ⓐ 0.2 Ⓑ 5 Ⓒ 5.5 Ⓓ 78.6

B 15. **ERROR ANALYSIS** *Describe* and correct the error in finding an equation of the best-fitting line using a graphing calculator.

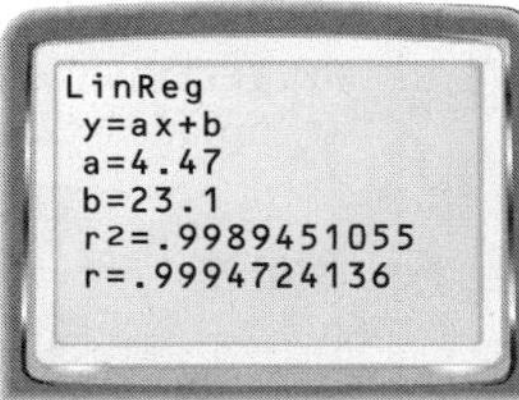

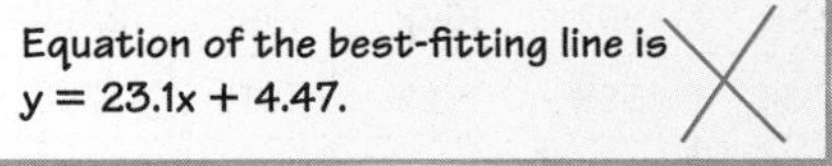

a and *b* were not substituted correctly; $y = 4.47x + 23.1$.

16. ★ **OPEN-ENDED** Give an example of a real-life situation in which you can use linear interpolation to find the zero of a function. *Explain* what the zero means in this situation. *Sample answer:* Temperature on a mountain depends on the elevation. The zero indicates the elevation at which the temperature is 0°F.

C 17. **CHALLENGE** A quantity increases rapidly for 10 years. During the next 10 years, the quantity decreases rapidly.
   a. Can you fit a line to the data? *Explain.* No; the data would first have a positive slope and then a negative slope.
   b. How could you model the data using more than one line? *Explain* the steps you could take. You could fit a line to the data for the first 10 years and then fit another line to the data for the following 10 years.

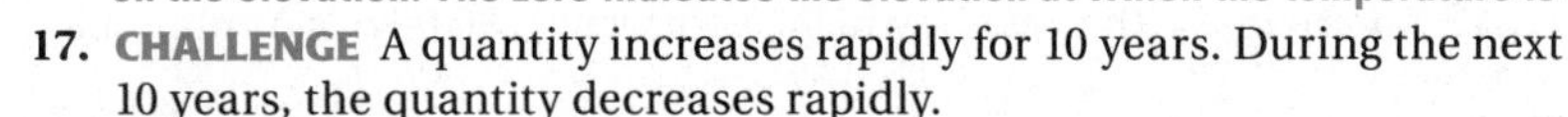

PROBLEM SOLVING

EXAMPLE 1
on p. 335
for Ex. 18

A 18. **SAILBOATS** Your school's sailing club wants to buy a sailboat. The table shows the lengths and costs of sailboats.

Length (feet)	11	12	14	14	16	22	23
Cost (dollars)	600	500	1900	1700	3500	6500	6000

   a. Make a scatter plot of the data. Let x represent the length of the sailboat. Let y represent the cost of the sailboat. See margin.
   b. Find an equation that models the cost (in dollars) of a sailboat as a function of its length (in feet). $y = 513x - 5258$
   c. Approximate the cost of a sailboat that is 20 feet long. \$5002

for problem solving help at classzone.com

4 PRACTICE AND APPLY

Assignment Guide

Answer Transparencies available for all exercises

Basic:
Day 1: pp. 338–341
Exs. 1–15, 18–21, 24–32

Average:
Day 1: pp. 338–341
Exs. 1–6, 9–16, 18–22, 24–32

Advanced:
Day 1: pp. 338–341
Exs. 1–6, 10–14, 16–32*

Block:
pp. 338–341
Exs. 1–6, 9–16, 18–22, 24–32 (with 5.6)

Differentiated Instruction

See *Algebra 1 Best Practices Toolkit* for suggestions on addressing the needs of a diverse classroom.

Homework Check

For a quick check of student understanding of key concepts, go over the following exercises:

Basic: 3, 5, 8, 20, 21
Average: 4, 5, 10, 20, 21
Advanced: 6, 12, 18, 20, 22

Extra Practice

- Student Edition, p. 942
- Chapter 5 Resource Book: Practice levels A, B, C, pp. 78–83

Practice Worksheet

An easily-readable reduced practice page (with answers) for this lesson can be found on p. 280C.

18a.

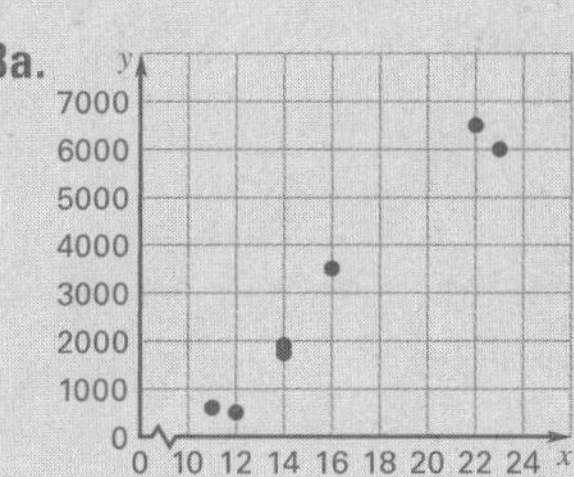

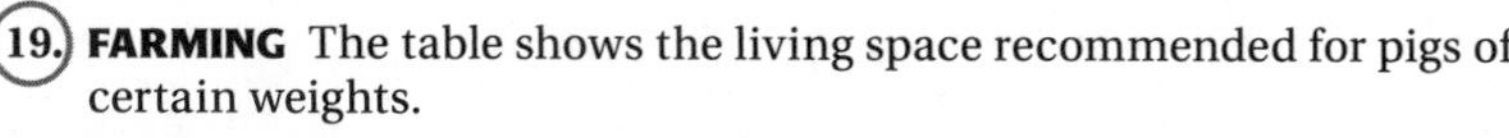

Graphing Calculator

Exercises 3–6, 18–23 If students cannot view the entire scatter plot in the viewing window, remind them that they can press Zoom 9 to display the scatter plot properly. They also can press window to set the bounds of the x-and y-axes and the scale on the axes.

Avoiding Common Errors

Exercises 7–12 Some students, in following Example 4 on page 338, may substitute 0 for x instead of 0 for $f(x)$. Remind these students that $f(x)$ replaces y, so they need to substitute 0 for $f(x)$.

Teaching Strategy

Exercise 22 Prior to students working on this exercise, you may want to discuss the meaning of the zero of a function in real-world situations. Review the meaning when data show a negative correlation. Then ask what occurs on the graph when data show a positive correlation.

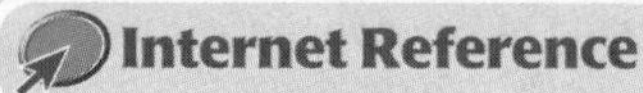

Exercise 23 For more information about ducks, visit www.npwrc.usgs.gov/resource/tools/duckdist/duckdist.htm

19a.

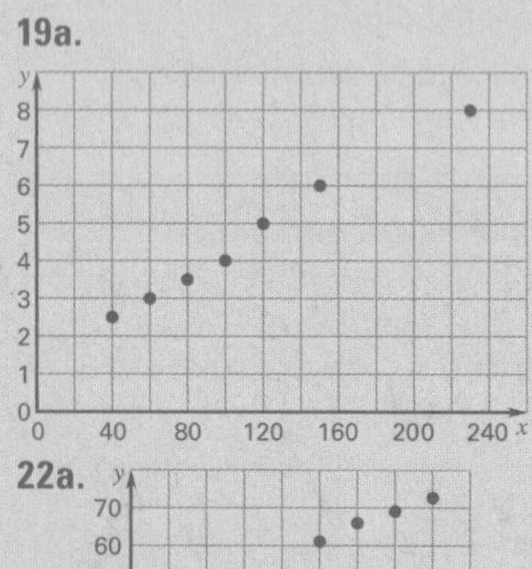

22a.

EXAMPLE 2 on p. 336 for Ex. 19

19. FARMING The table shows the living space recommended for pigs of certain weights.

Weight (pounds)	40	60	80	100	120	150	230
Area (square feet)	2.5	3	3.5	4	5	6	8

a. Make a scatter plot of the data. See margin.

b. Write an equation that models the recommended living space (in square feet) as a function of a pig's weight (in pounds). $y = 0.03x + 1.23$

c. About how much living space is recommended for a pig weighing 250 pounds? about 8.73 ft^2

@HomeTutor for problem solving help at classzone.com

EXAMPLE 3 B on p. 338 for Ex. 20

20. TELEVISION STATIONS The table shows the number of UHF and VHF broadcast television stations each year from 1996 to 2002.

Year	1996	1997	1998	1999	2000	2001	2002
Television stations	1551	1563	1583	1616	1730	1686	1714

a. Find an equation that models the number of broadcast television stations as a function of the number of years since 1996. $y = 31.5x + 1540$

b. At approximately what rate did the number of television stations change from 1996 to 2002? 31.5 stations per year

c. Approximate the year in which there were 1790 television stations. 2004

EXAMPLE 4 on p. 338 for Exs. 21–22

21b. about 17.9; 17.9 years from 1985, or 2002, the number of people living in high noise areas will be 0; no.

21. ★ SHORT RESPONSE The table shows the number of people who lived in high noise areas near U.S. airports for several years during the period 1985–2000.

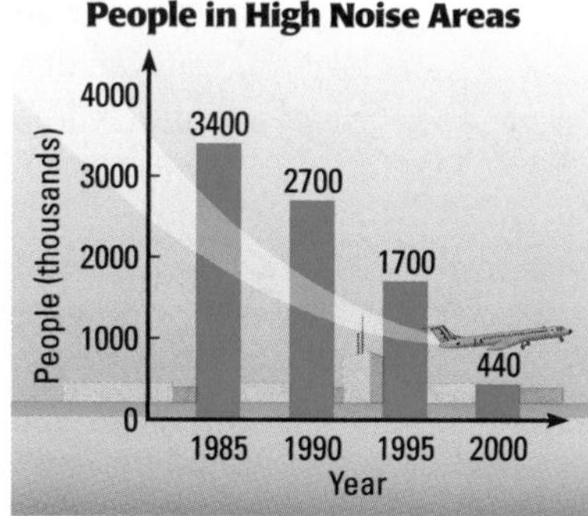

a. Find an equation that models the number of people (in thousands) living in high noise areas as a function of the number of years since 1985. $y = -197.6x + 3542$

b. Find the zero of the function from part (a). *Explain* what the zero means in this situation. Is this reasonable?

22. ◆ MULTIPLE REPRESENTATIONS The table shows the number of U.S. households with personal computers (PCs) from 1994 to 2002.

Year	1994	1995	1996	1997	1998	1999	2000	2001	2002
Households with PCs (millions)	32.0	33.6	38.8	44.0	51.2	61.1	66.0	69.1	72.7

a. Drawing a Graph Make a scatter plot of the data in the table. See margin.

b. Writing an Equation Find an equation that models the number of households with personal computers (in millions) as a function of the number of years since 1994. $y = 5.7x + 29.3$

c. Describing in Words Find the zero of the function from part (b). *Explain* what the zero means in this situation. About -5.14; about 5.14 years before 1994, or 1988, the number of households with PCs was 0.

○ = WORKED-OUT SOLUTIONS on p. WS1 ★ = STANDARDIZED TEST PRACTICE ◆ = MULTIPLE REPRESENTATIONS

23a.

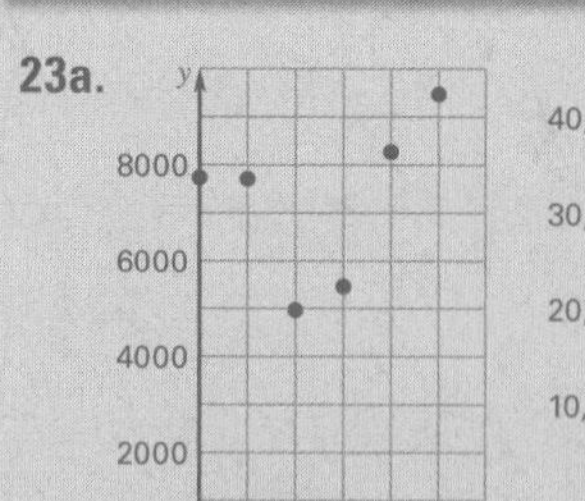

There is relatively no correlation in either scatter plot.

C **23. CHALLENGE** The table shows the estimated populations of mallard ducks and all ducks in North America for several years during the period 1975–2000.

Year	1975	1980	1985	1990	1995	2000
Mallards (thousands)	7727	7707	4961	5452	8269	9470
All ducks (thousands)	37,790	36,220	25,640	25,080	35,870	41,840

a. Make two scatter plots where x is the number of years since 1975 and y is the number of mallards (in thousands) for one scatter plot, while y is the number of ducks (in thousands) for the other scatter plot. *Describe* the correlation of the data in each scatter plot. See margin.

b. Can you use the mallard duck population to predict the total duck population? *Explain.* No; because you cannot find a line of best fit for either correlation, you cannot use the mallard duck population to predict the total duck population.

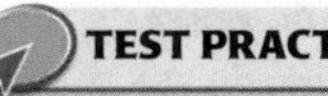

TEST PRACTICE at classzone.com

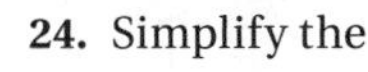

ILLINOIS MIXED REVIEW

24. Simplify the expression $3(-x + 1) - 2(2 + x)$. B

Ⓐ $-5x - 5$ Ⓑ $-5x - 1$ Ⓒ $-x + 7$ Ⓓ $x + 1$

25. A watch loses 2 minutes every 12 hours. After how many days will the watch have lost an hour? A

Ⓐ 15 Ⓑ 30 Ⓒ 60 Ⓓ 90

QUIZ *for Lessons 5.5–5.7*

1. PARALLEL LINES Write an equation of the line that passes through $(-6, 8)$ and is parallel to the line $y = 3x - 15$. *(p. 319)* $y = 3x + 26$

PERPENDICULAR LINES Write an equation of the line that passes through the given point and is perpendicular to the given line. *(p. 319)*

2. $(5, 5), y = -x + 2$ $y = x$ **3.** $(10, -3), y = 2x + 24$ $y = -\frac{1}{2}x + 2$ **4.** $(2, 3), x + 2y = -7$ $y = 2x - 1$

5. CASSETTE TAPES The table shows the number of audio cassette tapes shipped for several years during the period 1994–2002. *(pp. 325, 335)*

Year	1994	1996	1998	2000	2002
Tapes shipped (millions)	345	225	159	76	31

a. Write an equation that models the number of tapes shipped (in millions) as a function of the number of years since 1994. $y = -38.85x + 322.6$

b. At about what rate did the number of tapes shipped change over time?

5b. about −38.85 million tapes per year

c. Approximate the year in which 125 million tapes were shipped. 1999

d. Find the zero of the function from part (a). *Explain* what the zero means in this situation.
About 8.3; 8.3 years after 1994, or 2002, there will be no tapes shipped.

5 ASSESS AND RETEACH

Daily Homework Quiz

Transparency Available

1. Find the zero of the function $f(x) = 2.5x - 6$. 2.4

2. The table shows the number of video rentals at a store from 1998 to 2002. Find an equation that models the number of video rentals as a function of the number of years since 1998. Predict the number of rentals in 1999 and 2003.

Year	Video Rentals (thousands)
1998	2.3
2000	2.0
2001	1.85
2002	1.45

$y = -0.2x + 2.35$, where x is the number of years after 1998. The model predicts about 2150 video rentals in 1999 and 1350 video rentals in 2003.

Online Quiz

Available at **classzone.com**

Diagnosis/Remediation

- Practice A, B, C in Chapter 5 Resource Book, pp. 78–83
- Study Guide in Chapter 5 Resource Book, pp. 84–85
- Practice Workbook, pp. 81–83
- @HomeTutor

Challenge

Additional challenge is available in the Chapter 5 Resource Book, p. 88.

Quiz

An easily-readable reduced copy of the quiz (with answers) on Lessons 5.5–5.7 from the Assessment Book can be found on p. 280F.

1 PLAN AND PREPARE

Learn the Method

- Students will find data on the Internet and use the data to make a prediction about the total U.S. voting-age population in 2010.
- After the activity, students can use the techniques they learned to find data for a real-life situation in Exercise 16 in Lesson 5.7, and then find the zero of the function.

2 TEACH

Tips for Success

Urge students to pay attention to the year of the data as there may be gaps in the years. Remind them that they need to enter the correct year to plot accurate data for the scatter plots.

Extra Example 1

Find data on U.S. postal rates for the first ounce of a letter since 1995. Use an equation that models the data to predict the cost of postage for the first ounce of a letter in 2010. You can find postal rates in the most recent "Transportation" document. **Using the data (1995, 32), (1999, 33), (2001, 34), (2002, 37), an equation is $y = 0.591x + 28.5$, where x is the number of years after 1990. The model predicts that in 2010 the first ounce of postage on a letter will be about 40 cents.**

3 ASSESS AND RETEACH

Looking at the online *Statistical Abstract*, name three different types of data that you can use to explore real-life situations.
Sample answer: **Total energy consumption from 1996 to 2002; the number of oil spills from 1–100 gallons from 1998 to 2001; attendance at major league baseball games from 1985 to 2003.**

@HomeTutor classzone.com Keystrokes

5.7 Model Data from the Internet

QUESTION **How can you find reliable data on the Internet and use it to predict the total U.S voting-age population in 2010?**

EXAMPLE 1 **Collect and analyze data**

Find data for the total U.S. voting-age population over several years. Use an equation that models the data to predict the total U.S. voting-age population in 2010.

STEP 1 ***Find a data source***

Reliable data about the U.S. population can be found in the online *Statistical Abstract*. Go to the address shown below. Click on a link to the most recent version of the *Statistical Abstract*.

Address http://www.census.gov

Voting-Age Population

Year	Total (mil.)
1980	157.1
1988	178.1
1990	182.1
1994	190.3
1996	193.7
1998	198.2

STEP 2 ***Find an appropriate data set***

Choose the most recent "Elections" document. In this document, find the table of data entitled "Voting-Age Population."

STEP 3 ***Find a model***

Use a graphing calculator to make a scatter plot. Let x represent the number of years since 1980. Let y represent the total U.S. voting-age population (in millions). Find an equation that models the total U.S. voting-age population (in millions) as a function of the number of years since 1980.

▶ $y = 2.23x + 159$

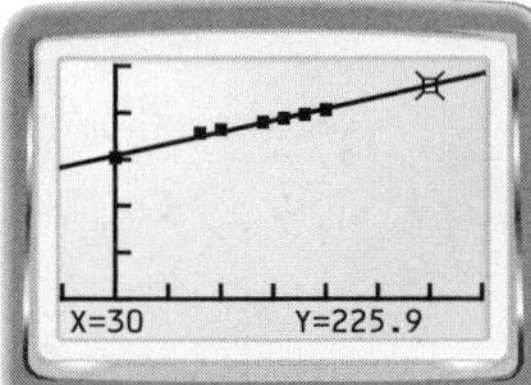

STEP 4 ***Predict***

Use the model to predict the total voting-age population in 2010. You can either evaluate the equation for $x = 30$ or trace the graph of the equation, as shown.

▶ The total U.S. voting-age population will be about 225.9 million in 2010.

DRAW CONCLUSIONS **1–3. Answers may vary.**

1. In the online *Statistical Abstract*, find data for the total value of agricultural imports over several years beginning with 1990.
2. Make a scatter plot of the data you found in Exercise 1. Find an equation that models the total value of agricultural imports (in millions of dollars) as a function of the number of years since 1990.
3. Predict the year in which the total value of agricultural imports will be \$45,000 million. *Describe* the method you used.

Illinois *Mixed Review*

TEST PRACTICE classzone.com

Lessons 5.5–5.7

1. **SCHOOLS** The table shows the value of primary and secondary schools built in the U.S. each year from 1996 to 2000. Which equation best models the data?

Years since 1996, t	0	1	2	3	4
Value v (millions of dollars)	1560	2032	2174	2420	2948

A. $v = 1594t + 316$

B. $v = 316t + 1594$

C. $v = 338t + 1560$

D. $v = 347t + 1560$

2. **BUTTER** The scatter plot shows the annual average price of 1 pound of butter from 1994 to 2001. If the trend in price continues, which is the best estimate for the price of 1 pound of butter in 2008?

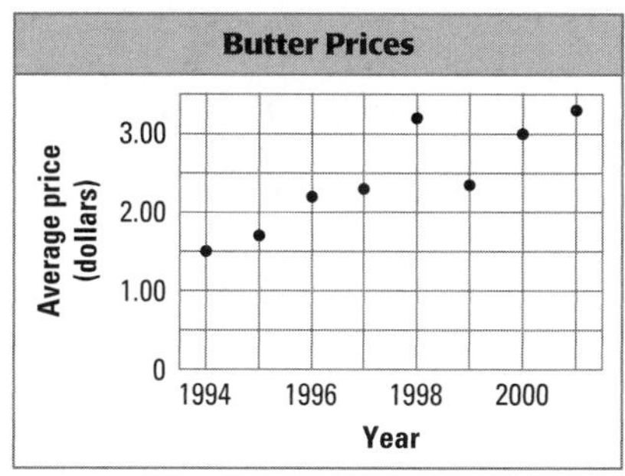

F. \$2.75 **H.** \$4.25

G. \$3.50 **J.** \$5.00

3. **MAPS** A map of a city shows streets as lines on a coordinate grid. State Street has a slope of $-\frac{1}{2}$. Park Street runs perpendicular to State Street. What is the slope of Park Street on the map?

A. -2 **C.** $\frac{1}{2}$

B. $-\frac{1}{2}$ **D.** 2

4. **HORSES** Gail collected data on the heights and corresponding lengths of a random sample of horses. If she plots the data on a scatter plot, what relationship will she most likely see between height and length?

F. Negative correlation

G. Positive correlation

H. Relatively no correlation

J. None of the above

5. **ADVERTISING** The table shows the number of advertisers that used network television for various years during the period 1975–2000.

Year	Advertisers using network TV
1975	513
1980	558
1985	606
1990	630
1995	750

If the trend in the number of advertisers using network television continued, approximately how many advertisers would have used television in 1997?

A. 744 **C.** 788

B. 778 **D.** 800

6. **BOARD SEATS** The percent of seats that were held by women on the board of directors of Fortune 500 companies from 1995 to 2001 can be modeled by the equation $y = 0.47x + 9.6$ where y is the percent of seats held by women and x is the number of years since 1995. In what year would you expect the percent of seats held by women to reach 15%?

F. 1996 **H.** 2020

G. 2006 **J.** 2047

Illinois Mixed Review

1. B
2. J
3. D
4. G
5. B
6. G

5 CHAPTER SUMMARY

Additional Resources

The following resources are available to help review the materials in this chapter.

Chapter 5 Resource Book

- Chapter Review Games and Activities, p. 89
- Cumulative Practice, Chs. 1–5, pp. 92–93

Student Resources in Spanish

eWorkbook

@HomeTutor

Vocabulary Practice

Vocabulary practice is available at **classzone.com**

BIG IDEAS *For Your Notebook*

Big Idea 1

Writing Linear Equations in a Variety of Forms

Using given information about a line, you can write an equation of the line in three different forms.

Form	Equation	Important information
Slope-intercept form	$y = mx + b$	• The slope of the line is m. • The y-intercept of the line is b.
Point-slope form	$y - y_1 = m(x - x_1)$	• The slope of the line is m. • The line passes through (x_1, y_1).
Standard form	$Ax + By = C$	• A, B, and C are real numbers. • A and B are not both zero.

Big Idea 2

Using Linear Models to Solve Problems

You can write a linear equation that models a situation involving a constant rate of change. Analyzing given information helps you choose a linear model.

Choosing a Linear Model	
If this is what you know . . .	**. . . then use this equation form**
constant rate of change and initial value	slope-intercept form
constant rate of change and one data pair	slope-intercept form or point-slope form
two data pairs and the fact that the rate of change is constant	slope-intercept form or point-slope form
the sum of two variable quantities is constant	standard form

Big Idea 3

Modeling Data with a Line of Fit

You can use a line of fit to model data that have a positive or negative correlation. The line or an equation of the line can be used to make predictions.

Step 1 Make a scatter plot of the data.

Step 2 Decide whether the data can be modeled by a line.

Step 3 Draw a line that appears to follow the trend in data closely.

Step 4 Write an equation using two points on the line.

Step 5 Interpolate (between known values) or extrapolate (beyond known values) using the line or its equation.

5 CHAPTER REVIEW

@HomeTutor
classzone.com
- Multi-Language Glossary
- Vocabulary practice

REVIEW KEY VOCABULARY

- point-slope form, *p. 302*
- converse, *p. 319*
- perpendicular, *p. 320*
- scatter plot, *p. 325*
- positive correlation, negative correlation, relatively no correlation, *p. 325*
- line of fit, *p. 326*
- best-fitting line, *p. 335*
- linear regression, *p. 335*
- interpolation, *p. 335*
- extrapolation, *p. 336*
- zero of a function, *p. 337*

VOCABULARY EXERCISES

1. Copy and complete: If a best-fitting line falls from left to right, then the data have a(n) _?_ correlation. **negative**

2. Copy and complete: Using a linear function to approximate a value beyond a range of known values is called _?_. **extrapolation**

3. **WRITING** What is the zero of a function, and how does it relate to the function's graph? *Explain.* **The zero of a function is the x-value of the function when $y = 0$; it is the x-intercept of the graph.**

REVIEW EXAMPLES AND EXERCISES

Use the review examples and exercises below to check your understanding of the concepts you have learned in each lesson of Chapter 5.

5.1 Write Linear Equations in Slope-Intercept Form *pp. 283–289*

EXAMPLE

Write an equation of the line shown.

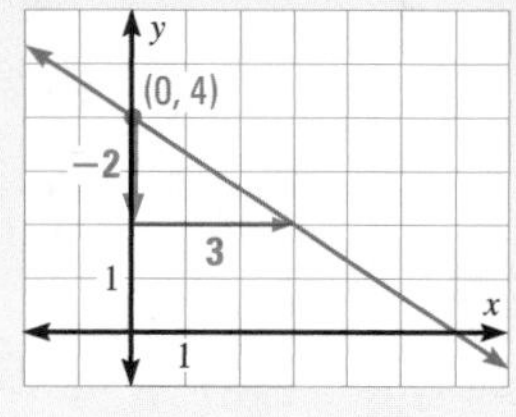

$y = mx + b$ **Write slope-intercept form.**

$y = -\frac{2}{3}x + 4$ **Substitute $-\frac{2}{3}$ for m and 4 for b.**

EXERCISES

EXAMPLES 1 and 5 on pp. 283, 285 for Exs. 4–7

Write an equation in slope-intercept form of the line with the given slope and y-intercept.

4. slope: 3
   y-intercept: −10
   $y = 3x - 10$

5. slope: $\frac{4}{9}$
   y-intercept: 5 $y = \frac{4}{9}x + 5$

6. slope: $-\frac{2}{11}$
   y-intercept: 7
   $y = -\frac{2}{11}x + 7$

7. **GIFT CARD** You have a \$25 gift card for a bagel shop. A bagel costs \$1.25. Write an equation that gives the amount (in dollars) that remains on the card as a function of the total number of bagels you have purchased so far. How much money is on the card after you buy 2 bagels? $y = -1.25x + 25$; \$22.50

Extra Example 5.1

Write an equation of the line shown.

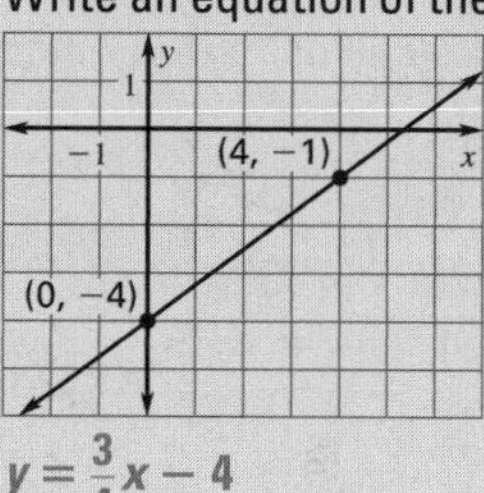

$y = \frac{3}{4}x - 4$

5 CHAPTER REVIEW

Extra Example 5.2

Write an equation of the line that passes through the point (6, 4) and has a slope of 3. $y = 3x - 14$

Extra Example 5.3

Write an equation in point-slope form of the line shown.

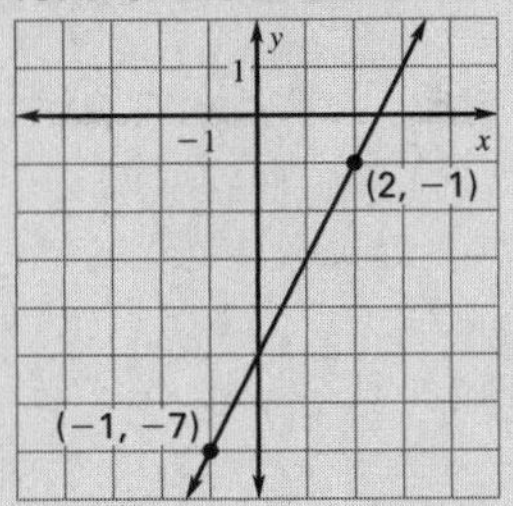

$y + 7 = 2(x + 1)$ or $y + 1 = 2(x - 2)$

11. $y - 7 = -6(x - 4)$ or $y - 1 = -6(x - 5)$

12. $y + 2 = -\frac{1}{3}(x - 9)$ or $y - 2 = -\frac{1}{3}(x + 3)$

13. $y + 2 = -\frac{6}{11}(x + 3)$ or $y + 8 = -\frac{6}{11}(x - 8)$

5.2 Use Linear Equations in Slope-Intercept Form

pp. 292–299

EXAMPLE

Write an equation of the line that passes through the point (−2, −6) and has a slope of 2.

STEP 1 **Find** the *y*-intercept.

$y = mx + b$ — **Write slope-intercept form.**

$-6 = 2(-2) + b$ — **Substitute 2 for *m*, −2 for *x*, and −6 for *y*.**

$-2 = b$ — **Solve for *b*.**

STEP 2 **Write** an equation of the line.

$y = mx + b$ — **Write slope intercept form.**

$y = 2x - 2$ — **Substitute 2 for *m* and −2 for *b*.**

EXERCISES

EXAMPLE 1 on p. 292 for Exs. 8–10

Write an equation in slope-intercept form of the line that passes through the given point and has the given slope *m*.

8. (−3, −1); $m = 4$ $y = 4x + 11$

9. (−2, 1); $m = 1$ $y = x + 3$

10. (8, −4); $m = -3$ $y = -3x + 20$

5.3 Write Linear Equations in Point-Slope Form

pp. 302–308

EXAMPLE

Write an equation in point-slope form of the line shown.

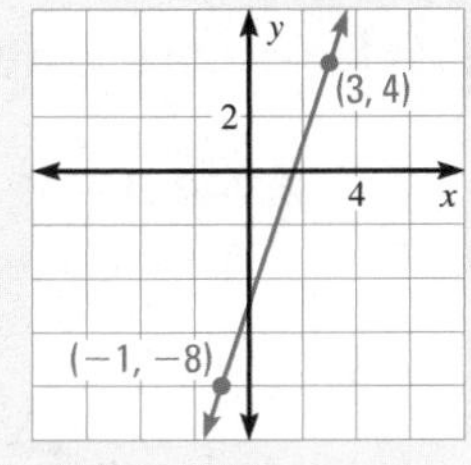

STEP 1 **Find** the slope of the line.

$$m = \frac{y_2 - y_1}{x_2 - x_1} = \frac{-8 - 4}{-1 - 3} = \frac{-12}{-4} = 3$$

STEP 2 **Write** an equation. Use (3, 4).

$y - y_1 = m(x - x_1)$ — **Write point-slope form.**

$y - 4 = 3(x - 3)$ — **Substitute 3 for *m*, 3 for x_1, and 4 for y_1.**

EXERCISES

EXAMPLES 3 and 5 on pp. 303, 304 for Exs. 11–14

Write an equation in point-slope form of the line that passes through the given points. 11–13. See margin.

11. (4, 7), (5, 1)

12. (9, −2), (−3, 2)

13. (8, −8), (−3, −2)

14. BUS TRIP A bus leaves at 10 A.M. to take students on a field trip to a historic site. At 10:25 A.M., the bus is 100 miles from the site. At 11:15 A.M., the bus is 65 miles from the site. The bus travels at a constant speed. Write an equation in point-slope form that relates the distance (in miles) from the site and the time (in minutes) after 10:00 A.M. How far is the bus from the site at 11:30 A.M.? $y - 100 = -\frac{7}{10}(x - 25)$ or $y - 65 = -\frac{7}{10}(x - 75)$; 54.5 mi

@HomeTutor
classzone.com
Chapter Review Practice

5.4 Write Linear Equations in Standard Form

pp. 311–316

EXAMPLE

Write an equation in standard form of the line shown.

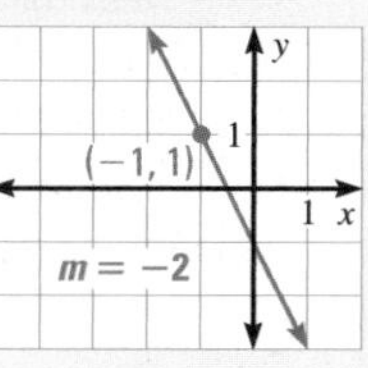

$y - y_1 = m(x - x_1)$	**Write point-slope form.**
$y - 1 = -2(x - (-1))$	**Substitute 1 for y_1, −2 for m, and −1 for x_1.**
$y - 1 = -2x - 2$	**Distributive property**
$2x + y = -1$	**Collect variable terms on one side, constants on the other.**

EXERCISES

EXAMPLES 2 and 5 on pp. 311, 313 for Exs. 15–17

Write an equation in standard form of the line that has the given characteristics.

15. Slope: −4; passes through (−2, 7) $4x + y = -1$
16. Passes through (−1, −5) and (3, 7) $-3x + y = -2$
17. **COSTUMES** You are buying ribbon to make costumes for a school play. Organza ribbon costs \$.07 per yard. Satin ribbon costs \$.04 per yard. Write an equation to model the possible combinations of yards of organza ribbon and yards of satin ribbon you can buy for \$5. List several possible combinations. $0.07r + 0.04s = 5$. *Sample answer:* 4 organza, 118 satin; 8 organza, 111 satin; 12 organza, 104 satin

5.5 Write Equations of Parallel and Perpendicular Lines

pp. 319–324

EXAMPLE

Write an equation of the line that passes through (−4, −2) and is perpendicular to the line $y = 4x - 7$.

The slope of the line $y = 4x - 7$ is 4. The slope of the perpendicular line through (−4, −2) is $-\frac{1}{4}$. Find the y-intercept of the perpendicular line.

$y = mx + b$	**Write slope-intercept form.**
$-2 = -\frac{1}{4}(-4) + b$	**Substitute $-\frac{1}{4}$ for m, −4 for x, and −2 for y.**
$-3 = b$	**Solve for b.**

An equation of the perpendicular line through (−4, −2) is $y = -\frac{1}{4}x - 3$.

EXERCISES

EXAMPLES 1 and 4 on pp. 319, 321 for Exs. 18–20

Write an equation of the line that passes through the given point and is (a) parallel to the given line and (b) perpendicular to the given line.

18. (0, 2), $y = -4x + 6$
    a. $y = -4x + 2$
    b. $y = \frac{1}{4}x + 2$
19. (2, −3), $y = -2x - 3$
    a. $y = -2x + 1$
    b. $y = \frac{1}{2}x - 4$
20. (6, 0), $y = \frac{3}{4}x - \frac{1}{4}$
    a. $y = \frac{3}{4}x - 4\frac{1}{2}$; b. $y = -\frac{4}{3}x + 8$

Extra Example 5.4

Write an equation in standard form of the line shown. $3x + y = 4$

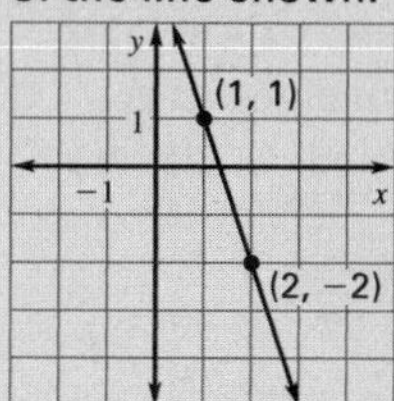

Extra Example 5.5

Write an equation of the line that passes through (−2, −2) and is parallel to the line $y = \frac{3}{2}x - 5$. $y = \frac{3}{2}x + 1$

5 CHAPTER REVIEW

Extra Example 5.6

The table shows the number of students who joined the astronomy club at a school from 1996 to 2003. Make a scatter plot of the data. *Describe* the correlation of the data.

Year	Students in the Astronomy Club
1996	8
1999	15
2000	18
2001	22
2003	24

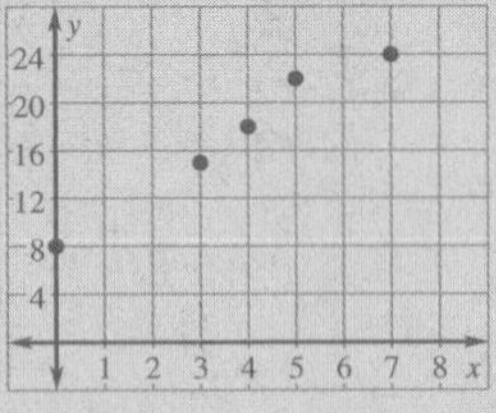

The scatter plot shows a positive correlation, which means that the number of students who joined the astronomy club tended to increase with each passing year.

Extra Example 5.7

Use the scatter plot from Extra Example 5.6 to estimate the number of students who joined the club in 1998. About 13 students joined the astronomy club in 1998.

21.

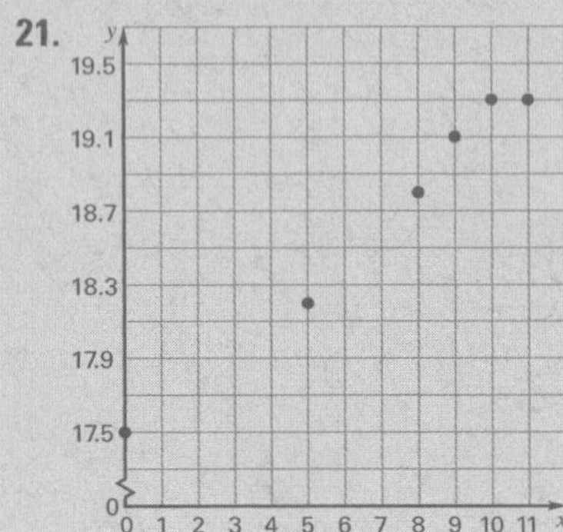

5.6 Fit a Line to Data

pp. 325–331

EXAMPLE

The table shows the time needed to roast turkeys of different weights. Make a scatter plot of the data. *Describe* the correlation of the data.

Weight (pounds)	6	8	12	14	18	20	24
Roast time (hours)	2.75	3.00	3.50	4.00	4.25	4.75	5.25

Treat the data as ordered pairs. Let x represent the turkey weight (in pounds), and let y represent the time (in hours) it takes to roast the turkey. Plot the ordered pairs as points in a coordinate plane.

The scatter plot shows a positive correlation, which means that heavier turkeys tend to require more time to roast.

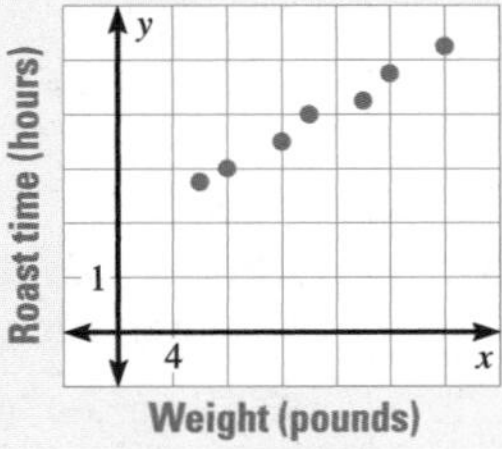

EXERCISES

EXAMPLE 2 on p. 326 for Ex. 21

21. **AIRPORTS** The table shows the number of airports in the Unites States for several years during the period 1990–2001. Make a scatter plot of the data. *Describe* the correlation of the data. See margin for art; positive correlation.

Years	1990	1995	1998	1999	2000	2001
Airports (thousands)	17.5	18.2	18.8	19.1	19.3	19.3

5.7 Predict with Linear Models

pp. 335–341

EXAMPLE

Use the scatter plot from the example for Lesson 5.6 above to estimate the time (in hours) it takes to roast a 10 pound turkey.

Draw a line that appears to fit the points in the scatter plot closely. There should be approximately as many points above the line as below it.

Find the point on the line whose x-coordinate is 10. At that point, you can see that the y-coordinate is about 3.25.

▸ It takes about 3.25 hours to roast a 10 pound turkey.

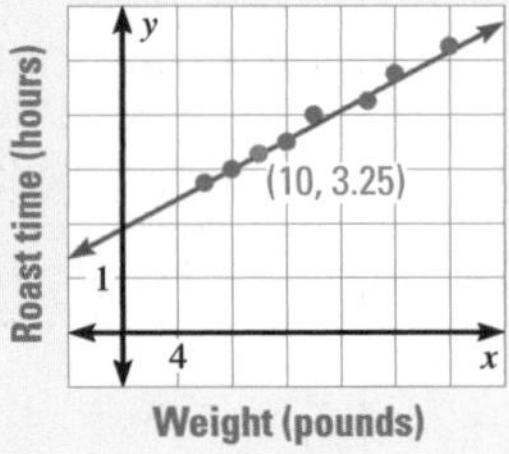

EXERCISES

EXAMPLE 2 on p. 336 for Ex. 22

22. **COOKING TIMES** Use the graph in the Example above to estimate the time (in hours) it takes to roast a turkey that weighs 30 pounds. *Explain* how you found your answer. About 5.75 h. *Sample answer:* Use the points (10, 3.25) and (8, 3) to find the slope of the line to be 0.125. Looking at the graph, you can see that the y-intercept is 2, so the equation of the line is $y = 0.125x + 2$. Substitute 30 for x to find $y = 5.75$.

5 CHAPTER TEST

Write an equation in slope-intercept form of the line with the given slope and y-intercept.

1. slope: 5; y-intercept: −7 $y = 5x - 7$

2. slope: $\frac{2}{5}$; y-intercept: −2 $y = \frac{2}{5}x - 2$

3. slope: $-\frac{4}{3}$; y-intercept: 1 $y = -\frac{4}{3}x + 1$

Write an equation in slope-intercept form of the line that passes through the given point and has the given slope m.

4. $(-2, -8)$; $m = 3$ $y = 3x - 2$

5. $(1, 1)$; $m = -4$ $y = -4x + 5$

6. $(-1, 3)$; $m = -6$ $y = -6x - 3$

Write an equation in point-slope form of the line that passes through the given points. 7–9. See margin.

7. (4, 5), (2, 9)

8. (−2, 2), (8, −3)

9. (3, 4), (1, −6)

Write an equation in standard form of the line with the given characteristics.

10. Slope: 10; passes through (6, 2) $-10x + y = -58$

11. Passes through (−3, 2) and (6, −1) $\frac{1}{3}x + y = 1$

Write an equation of the line that passes through the given point and is (a) parallel to the given line and (b) perpendicular to the given line. 12–14. See margin.

12. $(2, 0)$, $y = -5x + 3$

13. $(-1, 4)$, $y = -x - 4$

14. $(4, -9)$, $y = \frac{1}{4}x + 2$

Make a scatter plot of the data. Draw a line of fit. Write an equation of the line. 15, 16. See margin.

15.

x	0	1	2	3	4
y	15	35	53	74	94

16.

x	0	2	4	8	10
y	−2	6	15	38	50

17. FIELD TRIP Your science class is taking a field trip to an observatory. The cost of a presentation and a tour of the telescope is \$60 for the group plus an additional \$3 per person. Write an equation that gives the total cost C as a function of the number of people p in the group. $C = 3p + 60$

18. GOLF FACILITIES The table shows the number of golf facilities in the United States during the period 1997–2001.

Year	Golf facilities (thousands)
1997	14.6
1998	14.9
1999	15.2
2000	15.5
2001	15.7

a. Make a scatter plot of the data where x is the number of years since 1997 and y is the number of golf facilities (in thousands). See margin.

b. Write an equation that models the number of golf facilities (in thousands) as a function of the number of years since 1997. *Sample answer:* $y = 0.28x + 14.6$

c. At about what rate did the number of golf facilities change during the period 1997–2001? *Sample answer:* About 280 golf facilities per year

d. Use the equation from part (b) to predict the number of golf facilities in 2004. *Sample answer:* About 16,560 golf facilities

e. Predict the year in which the number of golf facilities reached 16,000. *Explain* how you found your answer. *Sample answer:* 2002; substitute 16 for y in the equation $y = 0.28x + 14.6$ and solve for x.

7. $y - 5 = -2(x - 4)$ or $y - 9 = -2(x - 2)$

8. $y - 2 = -\frac{1}{2}(x + 2)$ or $y + 3 = -\frac{1}{2}(x - 8)$

9. $y - 4 = 5(x - 3)$ or $y + 6 = 5(x - 1)$

12a. $y = -5x + 10$

12b. $y = \frac{2}{5}x - \frac{2}{5}$

13a. $y = -x + 3$

13b. $y = x + 5$

14a. $y = \frac{1}{4}x - 10$

14b. $y = -4x + 7$

Additional Resources

Assessment Book

- Chapter Test, Levels A, B, C, pp. 63–68
- Standardized Chapter Test, pp. 69–70
- SAT/ACT Chapter Test, pp. 71–72
- Alternative Assessment, pp. 73–74

Test Generator CD-ROM

Chapter Test

Easily-readable reduced copies (with answers) of Chapter Test B, the Standardized Chapter Test, and the Alternative Assessment from the Assessment Book can be found on pp. 280F–280H.

15.

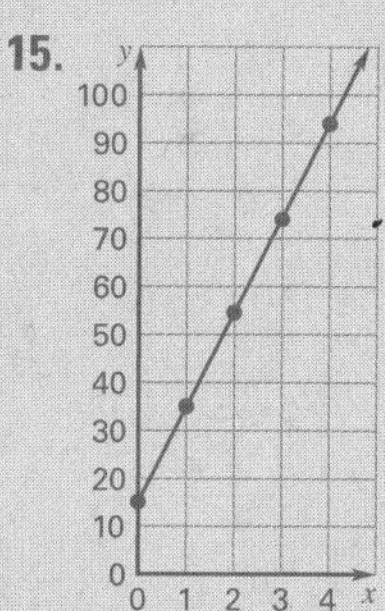

Sample answer: $y = 19.7x + 14.8$

16.

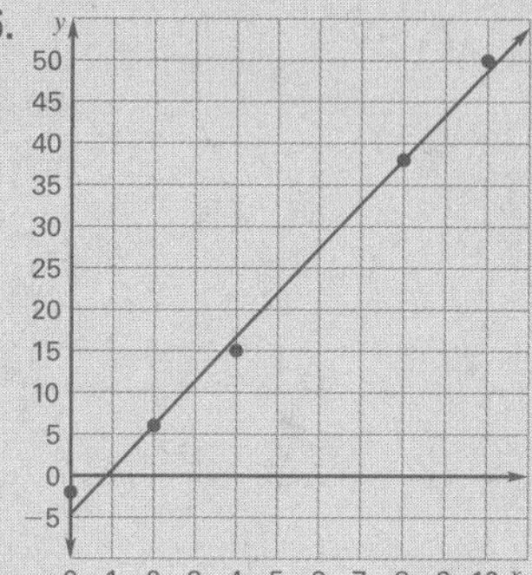

Sample answer: $y = 5.3x - 3.9$

18a.

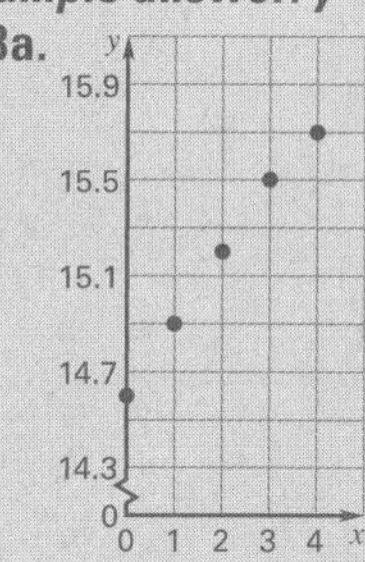

MULTIPLE CHOICE QUESTIONS

Some of the information you need to solve a multiple choice question may appear in a table, a diagram, or a graph.

PROBLEM 1

What is the equation of the line shown?

A. $y = -\frac{1}{2}x + 5$

B. $y = \frac{1}{2}x + 5$

C. $y = 2x + 5$

D. $y = -2x + 5$

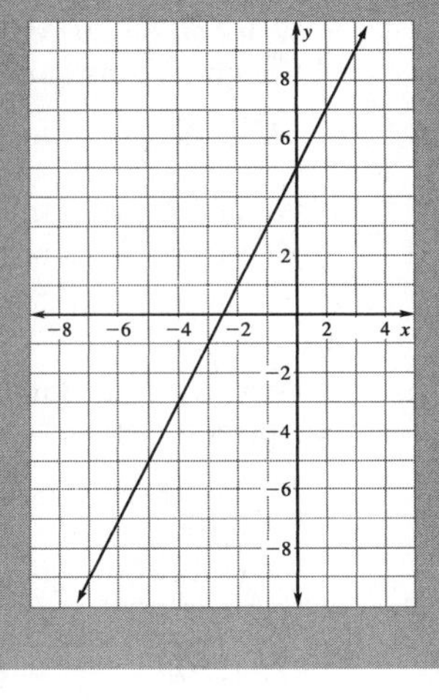

Plan

INTERPRET THE GRAPH Find the slope m by counting the "rise" (change in y) and the "run" (change in x) from one point to another on the line. Then find the y-intercept. Write the equation in slope-intercept form.

Solution

STEP 1 Find the slope by dividing the rise by the run.

Mark 2 points on the graph so that you can count the "rise" and the "run". Choose (1, 7) and (2, 9).

From (1, 7) to (2, 9), $m = \frac{\text{rise}}{\text{run}} = \frac{\text{up } 2}{\text{right } 1} = \frac{+2}{+1} = 2$.

Find the y-intercept, b, by identifying where the line crosses the y-axis.

STEP 2 Find the y-intercept.

This line crosses the y-axis at (0, 5), so $b = 5$.

Write the equation by substituting the slope and y-intercept into $y = mx + b$.

STEP 3 Write the equation.

The equation of the line is $y = 2x + 5$.

The correct answer is **C**.

Problem 2

Suzy's weekly earnings are summarized in the table shown. Which linear equation best describes her weekly earnings as a function of the units sold?

Units Sold	5	7	9	11
Weekly Earnings ($)	550	640	730	820

F. $y = 90x + 100$ **H.** $y = 45x - 325$

G. $y = 45x + 325$ **J.** $y = -45x + 775$

Plan

INTERPRET THE INFORMATION Use the information in the table to write ordered pairs. Then find the slope and *y*-intercept. Write the equation.

Solution

STEP 1 Use 2 ordered pairs to find the slope.

With the points (5, 550) and (7, 640), $m = \frac{640 - 550}{7 - 5} = \frac{90}{2} = 45$.

Find the *y*-intercept *b*, using the point (5, 550) and the slope, 45.

STEP 2 Use one of the points and the slope to find the *y*-intercept

$y = mx + b$

$550 = 45(5) + b$

$325 = b$

The slope is 45 and the y-intercept is 325.

STEP 3 Write the equation.

The equation is $y = 45x + 325$.

The correct answer is **G**.

PRACTICE

1. Which equation best represents the relation between *y* as a function of *x*?

x	−4	−2	0	2	4
y	1	2	3	4	5

A. $y = \frac{1}{2}x + 3$ **C.** $y = 2x + 3$

B. $y = -\frac{1}{2}x + 3$ **D.** $y = -2x + 3$

2. What is the equation of the line shown?

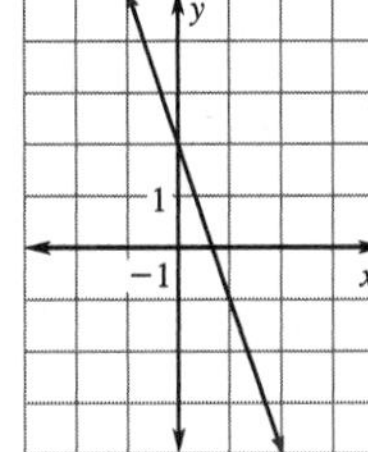

F. $y = 3x + 2$ **H.** $y = -3x + 2$

G. $y = \frac{1}{3}x + 2$ **J.** $y = -\frac{1}{3}x + 2$

TEST PREPARATION

Illinois Test Practice

1. A
2. H

Illinois Test Practice

1. D
2. H
3. A
4. G
5. C
6. G
7. B
8. F
9. C
10. F
11. B
12. G
13. C
14. H
15. B

Illinois Test Practice

1. Which equation represents the line that passes through (0, 8) and (2, 0)?

A. $y = 4x + 2$

B. $y = -4x + 2$

C. $y = 4x + 8$

D. $y = -4x + 8$

2. Which equation represents the line with a slope of 5 and a y-intercept of 2?

F. $y = 2x + 5$

G. $y = 2x - 5$

H. $y = 5x + 2$

J. $y = 5x - 2$

3. Which function has the values $f(1) = 8$ and $f(7) = -10$?

A. $f(x) = -3x + 11$

B. $f(x) = -2x + 10$

C. $f(x) = -3x + 25$

D. $f(x) = 3x - 24$

4. Which equation best represents the line shown?

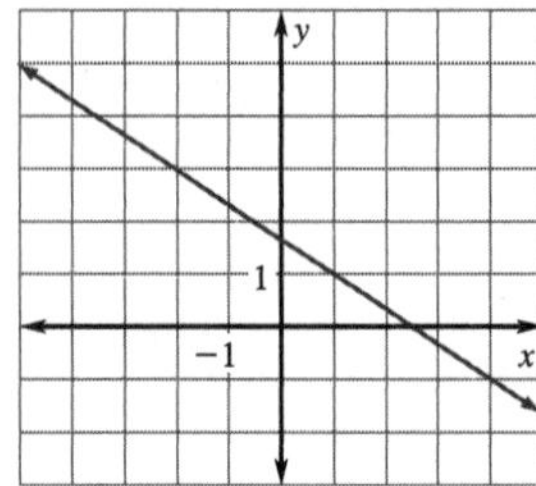

F. $y - 1 = \frac{2}{3}(x - 1)$

G. $y - 1 = -\frac{2}{3}(x - 1)$

H. $y + 1 = \frac{3}{2}(x + 1)$

J. $y + 1 = -\frac{3}{2}(x + 1)$

5. The cost of a taxi ride is the initial charge plus a charge per mile. The graph shows the cost of a taxi ride for a given taxi company.

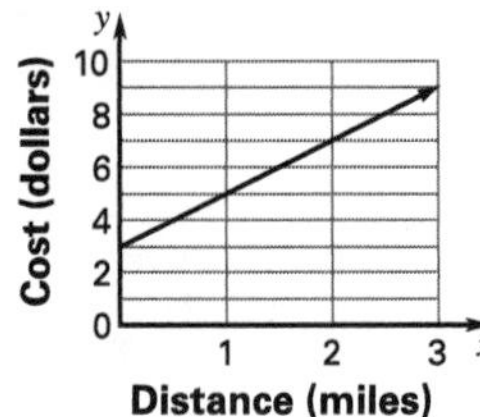

Suppose the company changes the cost so that the initial charge is \$1.75 and the charge per mile is \$3. How would the graph of the new cost of a taxi ride compare with the graph of the original cost?

A. The y-intercept is greater.

B. The y-intercept is the same.

C. The slope is greater.

D. The slope is the same.

6. A hiker begins hiking a mountain at a height of 3075 feet above sea level. If the hiker's altitude increases at a constant rate of 3 feet per minute, which equation could be used to determine h, the hiker's height in feet above sea level after t minutes?

F. $h = 3 + 3075t$ **H.** $h = 3(t + 3075)$

G. $h = 3075 + 3t$ **J.** $h = (3075 + 3)t$

7. Using the line shown, find the equation of a second line by multiplying the slope by 2 and adding 3 to the y-intercept.

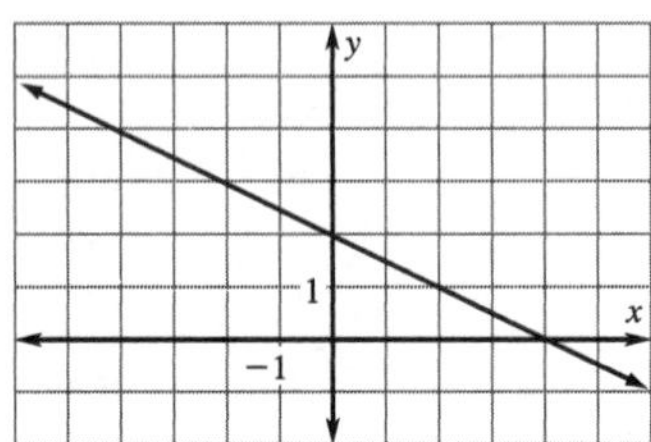

A. $y = -4x + 5$ **C.** $y = x + 5$

B. $y = -x + 5$ **D.** $y = \frac{5}{2}x + 5$

8. Which equation represents a vertical line that passes through the point (–3, 5)?

F. $x = -3$ H. $y = -3$

G. $x = 5$ J. $y = 5$

9. Which equation represents the line that passes through (1, –4) and has slope 2?

A. $y - 4 = 2(x + 1)$

B. $y - 1 = 2(x - 4)$

C. $y + 4 = 2(x - 1)$

D. $y + 1 = -4(x + 2)$

10. According to data from 1992 to 1995, a model for the United States consumer price index n is $n = 4t + 140.35$ where t is the number of years since 1992. On the basis of this model, in what year will the United States have a consumer price index of 180.4?

F. 2002 H. 2027

G. 2005 J. 2035

11. What is an equation of a line that best fits this scatter plot?

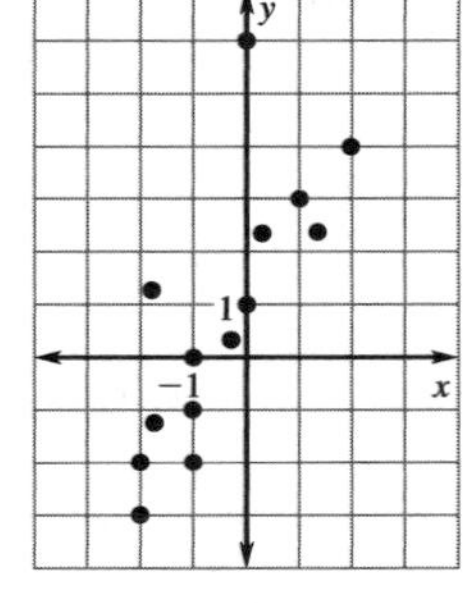

A. $y = 2x$

B. $y = 2x + 1$

C. $y = 4x + 1$

D. $y = -2x - 1$

12. This chart shows the cost of a movie ticket at the Midtown Theatre from 1960 to 1980. Using a linear model, what is the best prediction for the cost of a movie ticket in the year 1990?

Year	1960	1965	1970	1975	1980
Cost	$.90	$1.25	$1.60	$2.00	$2.70

F. $3.00 H. $4.00

G. $3.50 J. $5.00

13. Preet studied the effect of cold temperatures on seed germination. Here is the data she collected.

Days	*% of Seeds to Germinate*
10	13
15	20
20	31
25	42
30	52
35	60
40	73

She graphed the data. Which of these equations would represent the line of best fit?

A. $y = 2$ C. $y = 2x - 8$

B. $y = 2x - 10$ D. $y = 2x - 3$

14. Which equation represents a line parallel to $y = 3x + 2$?

F. $y = \frac{1}{3}x + 2$ H. $y = 3x - 2$

G. $y = -3x + 2$ J. $y = -\frac{1}{3}x - 2$

15. The graph shows the correlation between the heights of 10 women and their shoe sizes.

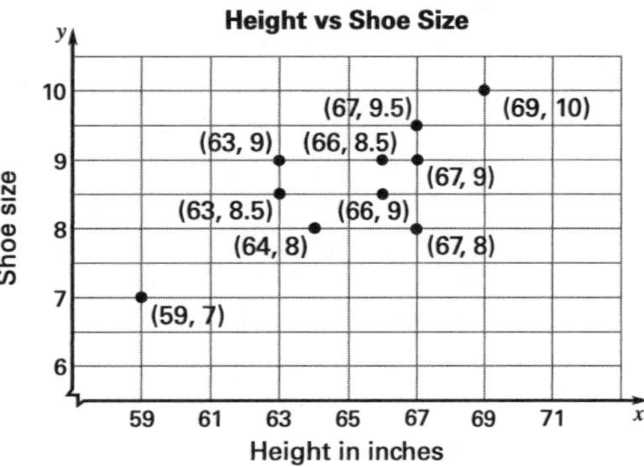

What would be the best terminology to use to describe the correlation?

A. Relatively no correlation

B. Positive correlation

C. Negative correlation

D. Weak correlation

TEST PRACTICE

Illinois Resources Guide

Pacing and Assignment Guide

REGULAR SCHEDULE

Pre-AP For pacing and assignments for a Pre-AP course, see the *Algebra 1 Toolkit*.

Lesson	Les. Day	BASIC	AVERAGE	ADVANCED
6.1	Day 1	EP p. 939 Exs.12–19; pp. 359–361 Exs. 1–17, 22–25, 31–36, 40–50 even	pp. 359–361 Exs. 1–9, 14–28, 31–38, 41, 44, 47, 50	pp. 359–361 Exs. 1, 2, 4, 5, 8, 9, 14–21, 24–39*, 42, 45, 48, 51
6.2	Day 1	pp. 366–368 Exs. 1–18, 27–31, 36–40, 43–53 odd	pp. 366–368 Exs. 1, 2, 15–34, 36–41, 44–52 even	pp. 366–368 Exs. 1, 2, 17–27, 30–42*, 44–52 even
6.3	Day 1	EP p. 940 Exs. 9–14; pp. 372–374 Exs. 1–10, 17–24, 29, 30, 37–41, 44–56 even	pp. 372–374 Exs. 1, 2, 4–14 even, 15, 16, 21–27 odd, 29–34, 37–42, 44, 45–55 odd	pp. 372–374 Exs. 1, 2, 4–8 even, 13, 14, 22–28 even, 29–36*, 38–43*, 44–56 even
6.4 **6.11.08**	Day 1	pp. 384–387 Exs. 1–8, 23–27, 47–50, 55	pp. 384–387 Exs. 1–8, 23–31, 48, 55	pp. 384–387 Exs. 1, 2, 5–8, 23–32, 50, 55
	Day 2	pp. 384–387 Exs. 9–22, 37–43, 51–54	pp. 384–387 Exs. 12–22, 32, 33, 39–45, 51–54	pp. 384–387 Exs. 13–20, 33–36*, 40–46*, 52, 54
6.5 **8.11.19**	Day 1	EP p. 940 Exs. 12–20; pp. 393–395 Exs. 1–22, 51–53	pp. 393–395 Exs. 1, 2, 6–17, 37–40, 51–53	pp. 393–395 Exs. 1, 2, 6–8, 12–20, 37–41*, 54–59
	Day 2	pp. 393–395 Exs. 23–37, 42–47, 54–59	pp. 393–395 Exs. 21–36, 42–49, 54–59	pp. 393–395 Exs. 24–36, 43–50*, 54–58 even
6.6 **8.11.19**	Day 1	SRH p. 918 Exs. 1–5; pp. 401–403 Exs. 1, 2, 3–21 odd, 22–28, 35–38, 42–52 even	pp. 401–403 Exs. 1, 2, 6–20 even, 21–24, 25–31 odd, 35–40, 45–50	pp. 401–403 Exs. 1, 6–20 even, 21, 22, 26–32 even, 33*, 34*, 36–41*, 44, 47, 52
6.7	Day 1	EP p. 941 Exs. 41–44; pp. 409–412 Exs. 1–11, 15–25, 62–70 even	pp. 409–412 Exs. 1, 2, 8–16, 20–28, 44–46, 63–69 odd	pp. 409–412 Exs. 1, 10–16, 21–28, 44–46, 51*, 52*, 63–69 odd
	Day 2	pp. 409–412 Exs. 29–41, 53–58, 71–76	pp. 409–412 Exs. 29–43, 47–50, 54–59, 71–75 odd	pp. 409–412 Exs. 29–43, 47–50, 55–61*, 73, 76
Review	Day 1	pp. 415–418 Exs. 1–44	pp. 415–418 Exs. 1–44	pp. 415–418 Exs. 1–44
Assess	Day 1	Chapter 6 Test	Chapter 6 Test	Chapter 6 Test
Yearly Pacing		Chapter 6 Total – 12 days	Chapters 1–6 Total – 70 days	Remaining – 90 days

*Challenge Exercises EP = Extra Practice SRH = Skills Review Handbook

BLOCK SCHEDULE

DAY 1	DAY 2	DAY 3	DAY 4	DAY 5	DAY 6
6.1	**6.3**	**6.4 (CONT.)**	**6.5 (CONT.)**	**6.7**	**REVIEW**
pp. 359–361 Exs. 1–9, 14–28, 31–38, 41, 44, 47, 50	pp. 372–374 Exs. 1, 2, 4–14 even, 15, 16, 21–27 odd, 29–34, 37–42, 44, 45–55 odd	pp. 384–387 Exs. 12–22, 32, 33, 39–45, 51–54	pp. 393–395 Exs. 21–36, 42–49, 54–59	pp. 409–412 Exs. 1, 2, 8–16, 20–50, 54–59, 63–75 odd	pp. 415–418 Exs. 1–44
6.2	**6.4**	**6.5**	**6.6**		**ASSESS**
pp. 366–368 Exs. 1, 2, 15–34, 36–41, 44–52 even	pp. 384–387 Exs. 1–8, 23–31, 48, 55	pp. 393–395 Exs. 1, 2, 6–17, 37–40, 51–53	pp. 401–403 Exs. 1, 2, 6–20 even, 21–24, 25–31 odd, 35–40, 45–50		Chapter 6 Test
Yearly Pacing	Chapter 6 Total – 6 days	Chapters 1–6 Total – 35 days	Remaining – 45 days		

Chapter Resource Guide

RESOURCE MANAGER

Chapter Resource Book

CHAPTER SUPPORT							
Parents as Partners (Chapter Overview with home involvement exercises and activity)						p. 1	
LESSON SUPPORT **Standard**	6.1	6.2	6.3	6.4 6.11.08	6.5 8.11.19	6.6 8.11.19	6.7
Teaching Guide/Lesson Plan	p. 3	p. 17	p. 30	p. 43	p. 58	p. 68	p. 82
Activity Masters	p. 5					p. 70	
Technology Activities & Keystrokes				p. 45			p. 84
Activity Support Masters							p. 86
Practice (3 levels)	p. 6	p. 19	p. 32	p. 46	p. 60	p. 71	p. 87
Study Guide	p. 12	p. 25	p. 38	p. 52	p. 63	p. 77	p. 93
Catch-Up for Absent Students	p. 14	p. 27	p. 40	p. 54	p. 65	p. 79	p. 95
Problem Solving/Application	p. 15	p. 28	p. 41	p. 55	p. 66	p. 80	p. 96
Challenge Practice	p. 16	p. 29	p. 42	p. 57	p. 67	p. 81	p. 97

REVIEW			
Chapter Review Games and Activities	p. 98	Cumulative Practice	p. 101
Project with Rubric	p. 99	Resource Book Answers	A1

Transparencies	6.1	6.2	6.3	6.4	6.5	6.6	6.7
Warm-Up/Daily Homework Quiz	✔	✔	✔	✔	✔	✔	✔
Notetaking Guide	✔	✔	✔	✔	✔	✔	✔
Teacher Support	✔	✔	✔	✔		✔	✔
Answer Transparencies	✔	✔	✔	✔	✔	✔	✔

ASSESSMENT BOOK

Quizzes	p. 75	SAT/ACT Chapter Test	p. 86
Chapter Tests (3 levels)	p. 78	Alternative Assessment with Rubric	p. 88
Standardized Chapter Test	p. 84		

TECHNOLOGY

- Easy Planner
- Test and Practice Generator
- Power Presentations
- @HomeTutor
- Activity Generator
- Animated Algebra
- Classzone.com
- eEdition Plus Online
- eWorkbook Plus Online
- ML Assessment System

ADDITIONAL RESOURCES

Illinois Additional Lessons

- Worked-Out Solution Key
- Notetaking Guide
- Practice Workbook
- Algebra 1 Toolkit
- Benchmark Tests
- Reteaching and Remediation
- Spanish Study Guide
- Spanish Assessment Book
- Spanish Resources in Spanish
- Multi-Language Visual Glossary

LESSON 6.1

Practice B

For use with pages 356–361

Write an inequality that is represented by the graph.

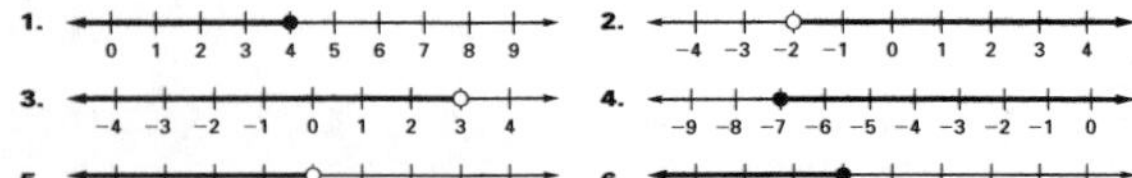

1. $x \le 4$ 2. $x > -2$ 3. $x < 3$ 4. $x \ge -7$ 5. $x < 0$ 6. $x \le -1$

Solve the inequality. Graph your solution.

7. $x + 7 > 1$ $x > -6$

8. $n - 3 \le 9$ $n \le 12$

9. $10 \ge a + 7$ $a \le 3$

10. $m - 3 < -2$ $m < 1$

11. $p - 5 > -5$ $p > 0$

12. $x + 3 \le -4.5$ $x \le -7.5$

13. $b + 9.5 \le -6.4$ $b \le -15.9$

14. $y + 2.5 < 7.3$ $y < 4.8$

15. $z - 10.2 > 18.3$ $z > 28.5$

16. $d - 8 > 2.2$ $d > 10.2$

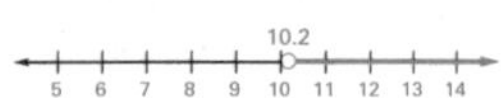

Write the verbal sentence as an inequality. Then solve the inequality and graph your solution.

17. The sum of 15 and n is less than 8. $15 + n < 8$; $n < -7$

LESSON 6.1

Practice B *continued*

For use with pages 356–361

18. The difference of m and 3 is greater than or equal to 10. $m - 3 \ge 10$; $m \ge 13$

19. Twenty-four is less than or equal to the sum of 35 and x. $24 \le 35 + x$; $x \ge -11$

20. Eighty-five is greater than the difference of x and 63. $85 < x - 63$; $x > 148$

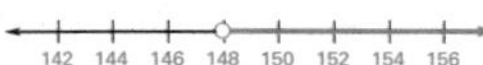

21. **Summer Reading** During the summer you want to read at least 32 books. You have read 21 books so far this summer. What are the possible numbers of books you can read to pass your goal? 11 books or more

22. **Baseball Hats** You are a big baseball fan. You have a goal of attending a baseball game in every major league stadium in the country. Every time you go to a different stadium, you buy a baseball hat. You keep your hats in a display case that holds 25 hats. You have 8 baseball hats so far. What are the possible numbers of hats you can collect without needing another display case? 17 hats or less

23. **Gift Card** You received a $25 gift card to a sporting goods store for your birthday. You are looking at skateboards and want to spend no more than $85 of your own money.
    a. Write and solve an inequality to find the prices p in dollars of skateboards you can buy. $p - 25 \le 85$; $p \le 110$
    b. What is the most expensive skateboard you can buy? A $110 skateboard

24. **Video Games** You and your friend are having a video game competition. The person with the highest score after two games wins. The table shows your friend's first and second scores and your first score.

Game	Friend's score	Your score
1	6532	5034
2	4887	?

a. Write and solve an inequality to find the scores s that you can earn in your second game in order to beat your friend. $6532 + 4887 < 5034 + s$; $s > 6385$

b. Will you win if you earn 6392 points? 6385 points? 6377 points? *Justify* your answers. Yes, because $6392 > 6385$. No, because $6385 \not> 6385$; No, because $6377 \not> 6385$.

LESSON 6.2

Practice B

For use with pages 363–368

Match the verbal sentence with the inequality. Then solve the inequality.

1. The product of 3 and x is less than or equal to 18. C; $x \le 6$ **A.** $\frac{x}{18} \ge 3$
2. The product of 18 and x is greater than or equal to 3. B; $x \ge \frac{1}{6}$ **B.** $18x \ge 3$
3. The quotient of x and 18 is greater than or equal to 3. A; $x \ge 54$ **C.** $3x \le 18$

Solve the inequality. Graph your solution.

4. $3y \ge 4$ $y \ge \frac{4}{3}$

5. $\frac{x}{2} < 6$ $x < 12$

6. $\frac{m}{5} > -5$ $m > -25$

7. $\frac{c}{-10} \le -2$ $c \ge 20$

8. $8n > -1$ $n > -\frac{1}{8}$

9. $42 < 6z$ $z > 7$

10. $-5p \le 2$ $p \ge -\frac{2}{5}$

11. $\frac{w}{-4} < 8$ $w > -32$

12. $-7a \ge -3$ $a \le \frac{3}{7}$

13. $52 \le -13x$ $x \le -4$

14. $0.25x > 18$ $x > 72$

15. $-2d < 3$ $d > -\frac{3}{2}$

LESSON 6.2

Practice B *continued*

For use with pages 363–368

Write the verbal sentence as an inequality. Then solve the inequality and graph your solution.

16. The product of 12 and y is greater than or equal to 60. $12y \ge 60$; $y \ge 5$

17. The product of 7 and b is less than -35. $7b < -35$; $b < -5$

18. The quotient of m and 2 is greater than 23. $\frac{m}{2} > 23$; $m > 46$

19. The quotient of p and 4.5 is less than or equal to 10. $\frac{p}{4.5} \le 10$; $p \le 45$

20. **Flower Beds** You are in charge of buying the flowers for the flower beds around your school. You cannot spend over $80 on flowers. The flowers cost $10.99 for a flat of flowers. What are the possible numbers of flats of flowers you can buy? 7 flats or less

21. **Pavilion Rental** You and three of your friends decide to rent a pavilion at a local park for an end-of-the-school-year party. The group budget is $80. The group decides to split the cost equally.
    a. What are the possible amounts of money that each of you can spend? $20 or less
    b. If two more of your friends decide to pitch in for the party, what are the possible amounts of money that each of you can spend if you all split the cost equally? about $13.33 or less

22. **Waiting Tables** Restaurants typically pay wait staff an hourly wage that is lower than minimum wage. The wait staff is expected to make up the difference in tips. The minimum wage is $5.15 per hour and a restaurant pays the wait staff $4 per hour.
    a. If a waitress works an 8-hour shift, write and solve an inequality that gives the total tips t in dollars that the waitress must earn in an 8-hour shift in order to meet or exceed the minimum wage. $\frac{t}{8} \ge 1.15$; $t \ge 9.2$
    b. If the waitress makes $10.40 in tips during an 8-hour shift, will she meet or exceed the minimum wage? By how much? yes; by $1.20
    c. If the waitress makes $9.20 in tips during an 8-hour shift, will she meet or exceed the minimum wage? By how much? yes; by $0

LESSON 6.3

Practice B

For use with pages 369–374

Solve the inequality. Graph your solution.

1. $4x - 7 \geq 1$ $x \geq 2$

2. $7p + 3 < -11$ $p < -2$

3. $8 - 2n \geq 26$ $n \leq -9$

4. $3(a - 4) \leq 33$ $a \leq 15$

5. $6(y + 1) > 6$ $y > 0$

6. $-2(c - 1) < -22$ $c > 12$

7. $8m - 7 < 4m + 5$ $m < 3$

8. $10 - 11d > -5d - 4$ $d < \frac{7}{3}$

9. $9z \leq -7z + 14$ $z \leq \frac{7}{8}$

10. $6w + 3 < 2w + 15$ $w < 3$

Solve the inequality, if possible.

11. $6y - 9 \leq 4y + 2y - 16$ no solution

12. $7p - 11p + 3 \geq 3 - 4p$ all real numbers

13. $4(c - 5) < 2(c - 10)$ $c < 0$

14. $5(a - 3) \leq 5a - 6$ all real numbers

15. $6(x - 8) > 6x - 48$ no solution

16. $2(3d - 4) < 4 + 6d - 15$ no solution

17. $4m + 14 - 2m \leq 2(m + 7)$ all real numbers

18. $-2(n - 3) \geq 1 - 2n + 5$ all real numbers

19. $4(3 - 2x) > 2(6 - 4x)$ no solution

20. $2(5 - a) > 4a + 13 - 6a$ no solution

21. $-4n + 11 < -4(n + 6)$ no solution

22. $3(5 - 6x) \leq 2(11 - 9x)$ all real numbers

23. $2m + 10 - 7m \leq 5(4 - m)$ all real numbers

24. $6(1-2n) \leq 5 - 12n$ no solution

LESSON 6.3

Practice B *continued*

For use with pages 369–374

Translate the verbal phrase into an inequality. Then solve the inequality and graph your solution.

25. Six more than 5 times a number x is greater than or equal to 31. $6 + 5x \geq 31; x \geq 5$

26. Twice the sum of 4 and x is less than -16. $2(4 + x) < -16; x < -12$

27. The difference of $10x$ and $3x$ is less than or equal to the sum of $4x$ and 21. $10x - 3x \leq 4x + 21; x \leq 7$

28. The sum of $2x$ and $4x$ is greater than or equal to the sum of $3x$ and 36. $2x + 4x \geq 3x + 36; x \geq 9$

29. The difference of $2x$ and 15 is less than or equal to the sum of $4x$ and 17. $2x - 15 \leq 4x + 17; x \geq -16$

30. Weaving A weaver spends $420 on supplies to make wall hangings and plans to sell the wall hangings for $80 each.

a. Write an inequality that gives the possible numbers w of wall hangings the weaver needs to sell in order for the profit to be positive. $80w - 420 > 0$

b. What are the possible numbers of wall hangings the weaver needs to sell in order for the profit to be positive? 6 wall hangings or more

31. School Spirit Your club is in charge of making pins that students can buy to show their school spirit for the upcoming football game. You have made 225 pins so far, and you only have 2 hours left to make the rest of the pins. You need to make at least 400 pins.

a. Write an inequality that gives the possible numbers p of pins you have to make per minute in order to exceed your goal. $225 + 120p \geq 400$

b. What are the possible numbers of pins you have to make per minute in order to exceed your goal? 2 pins or more

32. Aquarium You are getting a larger aquarium for your neon tetra fish and you also want to add more neon tetras to the larger aquarium. The general rule is that each fish needs 2 gallons of water. You currently have 6 neon tetras. If you buy a 20-gallon aquarium, what are the possible numbers of fish you can put in your aquarium? *Explain* how you got your answer. 4 fish or less; First find the number of gallons needed by the 6 fish by finding the product of 6 and 2, which is 12. Then subtract this amount from 20 to get 8, the number of gallons left for new fish. Then solve the inequality $2f \leq 8$, where f is the number of new fish.

LESSON 6.4

Practice B

For use with pages 380–387

Translate the verbal phrase into an inequality. Then graph the inequality.

1. All real numbers that are less than or equal to -3 *and* greater than or equal to -8 $-8 \leq x \leq -3$

2. All real numbers that are greater than 5 *or* less than or equal to -1 $x \leq -1$ *or* $x > 5$

3. All real numbers that are greater than or equal to -2.5 *and* less than 3.5 $-2.5 \leq x < 3.5$

Solve the inequality. Graph your solution.

4. $-3 < x + 1 \leq 5$ $-4 < x \leq 4$

5. $-7 < x - 8 < 2$ $1 < x < 10$

6. $-5 < -5x \leq 20$ $-4 \leq x < 1$

7. $0 \leq 2(x - 3) < 8$ $3 \leq x < 7$

8. $3x + 2 < 8$ *or* $-x + 3 < -2$ $x < 2$ *or* $x > 5$

9. $2(x + 4) < 6$ *or* $-x - 3 \leq -7$ $x < -1$ *or* $x \geq 4$

10. $5x < -30$ *or* $x + 10 > 7$ $x < -6$ *or* $x > -3$

11. $3x + 5 \leq 1$ *or* $8 - x < 5$ $x \leq -\frac{4}{3}$ *or* $x > 3$

LESSON 6.4

Practice B *continued*

For use with pages 380–387

Write the verbal sentence as an inequality. Then solve the inequality and graph your solution.

12. Three times x is less than -6 *and* greater than -21. $-21 < 3x < -6; -7 < x < -2$

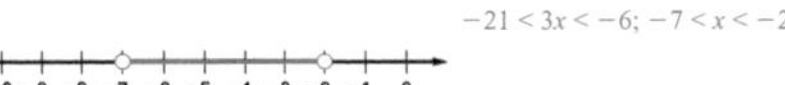

13. One less than x is less than -1 *or* 3 more than x is greater than or equal to 7. $x - 1 < -1$ *or* $3 + x \geq 7; x < 0$ *or* $x \geq 4$

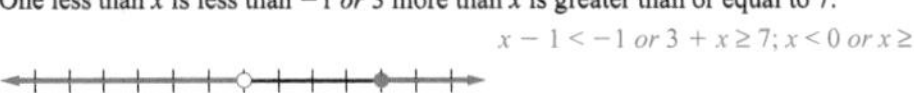

14. The difference of $2x$ and 5 is greater than -3 *and* less than or equal to 11. $-3 < 2x - 5 \leq 11; 1 < x \leq 8$

15. The sum of $3x$ and 1 is greater than -5 *and* less than or equal to 10. $-5 < 3x + 1 \leq 10; -2 < x \leq 3$

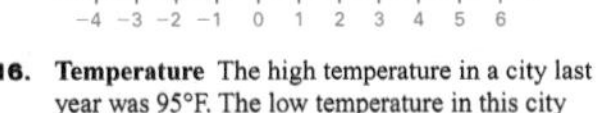

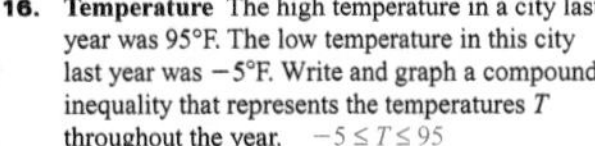

16. Temperature The high temperature in a city last year was 95°F. The low temperature in this city last year was -5°F. Write and graph a compound inequality that represents the temperatures T throughout the year. $-5 \leq T \leq 95$

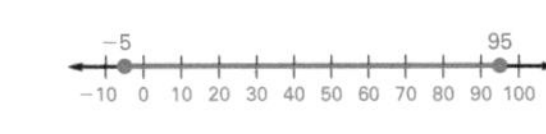

17. Pollen Count Weather forecasts will often give reports on the pollen count. For people suffering from allergies, the pollen count indicates the severity of their symptoms. If a pollen count is high, the severity of the symptoms are increased. The table shows ranges for high, medium, and low pollen counts. Write an inequality to find the range at which the pollen count is not medium. $x \leq 4$ *or* $x > 8$

Pollen Count	High	Medium	Low
Range	Greater than 8	Greater than 4 and less than or equal to 8	Less than or equal to 4

18. Distances You live 5 miles from work and the gym you go to is 3 miles from work.

a. Find the minimum distance d between your home and the gym. 2 mi

b. Find the maximum distance d between your home and the gym. 8 mi

c. Write an inequality that describes the possible distances d between your home and the gym. $2 \leq d \leq 8$

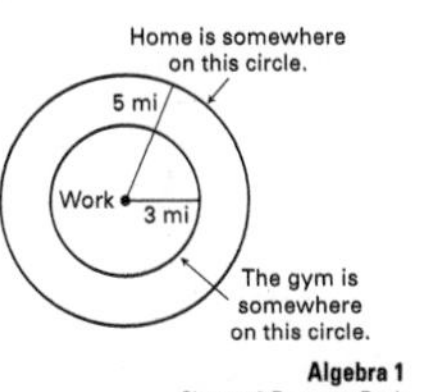

LESSON 6.5 Practice B
For use with pages 390–397

13. $x = -6, 0$ 14. $x = 4, 12$ 15. $x = -\frac{7}{2}, -\frac{5}{2}$
16. no solution 17. $x = -\frac{3}{2}, 0$ 18. $x = -\frac{9}{2}, -\frac{1}{2}$
19. no solution 20. $x = \frac{5}{2}, \frac{17}{6}$ 21. no solution

Solve the equation.

1. $|x| = 9$ $x = -9, 9$
2. $|x| = 2.25$ $x = -2.25, 2.25$
3. $|x| = \frac{3}{2}$ $x = -\frac{3}{2}, \frac{3}{2}$
4. $|x - 6| = 14$ $x = -8, 20$
5. $|x + 1| = 8$ $x = -9, 7$
6. $|2x - 3| = 15$ $x = -6, 9$
7. $|4x + 1| = 15$ $x = -4, \frac{7}{2}$
8. $|7x + 2| = 23$ $x = -\frac{25}{7}, 3$
9. $|5 - 2x| = 9$ $x = -2, 7$
10. $3|2x - 2| = 18$ $x = -2, 4$
11. $4|5x - 1| = 36$ $x = -\frac{8}{5}, 2$
12. $2|6x + 5| - 1 = 25$ $x = -3, \frac{4}{3}$

Solve the equation, if possible. See above.

13. $|x + 3| - 4 = -1$
14. $|x - 8| - 9 = -5$
15. $|x + 3| + 2.5 = 3$
16. $-6|10 - 2x| = 24$
17. $-3|4x + 3| = -9$
18. $-4|5 + 2x| = -16$
19. $-\frac{1}{3}|1 - 8x| = 2$
20. $|3x - 8| + 0.25 = 0.75$
21. $|6x + 5| - 1.3 = -1.9$

Find the values of *x* that satisfy the definition of absolute value for the given value and the given absolute deviation.

22. Given value: 3; absolute deviation: 5
23. Given value: 1; absolute deviation: 7
24. Given value: −4; absolute deviation: 2
25. Given value: −2.5; absolute deviation: 8

22. $x = -2, 8$ 23. $x = -6, 8$ 24. $x = -6, -2$ 25. $x = -10.5, 5.5$

26. **Food Scale** Bakers will typically weigh out flour for recipes rather than use a measuring cup because weighing is a more accurate measure. A baker is using a scale that has an absolute error of 0.05 gram.
    a. Find the minimum and maximum possible weights if the scale is used to measure out 225 grams of flour. 224.95 g; 225.05 g
    b. Find the minimum and maximum possible weights if the scale is used to measure out 300 grams of flour. 299.95 g; 300.05 g
    c. Find the minimum and maximum possible weights if the scale is used to measure out 420 grams of flour. 419.95 g; 420.05 g

27. **Toothpaste Prices** The average price of the brand of toothpaste that you buy is $2.49 for an 8.2-ounce tube. Depending on where you shop, the prices vary by as much as $.15.
    a. Write an absolute value equation that represents the minimum and maximum prices of the toothpaste. $|x - 2.49| = 0.15$
    b. Find the minimum and maximum prices of the toothpaste. $2.34; $2.64
    c. You have a coupon for $.50 off two tubes of toothpaste. If you go to the store that has the minimum price for the toothpaste, how much will you pay for two tubes? $4.18

LESSON 6.5

LESSON 6.6 Practice B
For use with pages 398–403

Solve the inequality. Graph your solution.

1. $|x| \geq 5$ $x \leq -5$ *or* $x \geq 5$

2. $|x| < 6.5$ $-6.5 < x < 6.5$

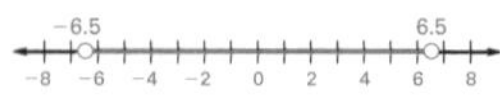

3. $|x| \geq \frac{3}{2}$ $x \leq -\frac{3}{2}$ *or* $x \geq \frac{3}{2}$
4. $|x - 6| \leq 1$ $5 \leq x \leq 7$
5. $|x + 7| > 11$ $x < -18$ *or* $x > 4$
6. $|10 - x| < 2$ $8 < x < 12$
7. $|-x - 5| < 1$ $-6 < x < -4$
8. $|2x + 1| \geq 5$ $x \leq -3$ *or* $x \geq 2$
9. $|3x - 2| \leq 7$ $-\frac{5}{3} \leq x \leq 3$
10. $|8 - 3x| \geq 7$ $x \leq \frac{1}{3}$ *or* $x \geq 5$
11. $\left|\frac{1}{2}x - 4\right| > 20$ $x < -32$ *or* $x > 48$
12. $\left|1 - \frac{4}{3}x\right| < 5$ $-3 < x < 4.5$

Write the verbal sentence as an inequality. Then solve the inequality and graph your solution.

13. The distance between x and 8 is less than 14. $|x - 8| < 14; -6 < x < 22$

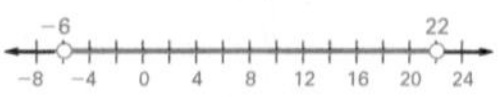

LESSON 6.6

LESSON 6.6 Practice B *continued*
For use with pages 398–403

14. The distance between x and -5 is greater than or equal to 12. $|x + 5| \geq 12; x \leq -17$ *or* $x \geq 7$

15. The distance between 9 and x is less than or equal to 8. $|9 - x| \leq 8; 1 \leq x \leq 17$

16. The distance between 10 and $2x$ is greater than 34. $|10 - 2x| > 34; x < -12$ *or* $x > 22$

Tell whether the statement is *true* or *false*. If it is false, give a counterexample.

17. If a is a solution of $|x + 4| < 7$, then a is also a solution of $x + 4 < 7$. true
18. If a is a solution of $|x - 6| \geq 4$, then a is also a solution of $x - 6 \leq -4$. true

19. **DVDs** The average price of a standard DVD is $15.99 with a standard deviation of $4. Write an absolute value inequality that describes this range in prices. $|x - 15.99| = 4$

20. **Body Temperature** A canine's body temperature is considered to be normal if it is 101°F with an absolute deviation of 1.5°F. $|x - 101| = 1.5$
    a. Write an absolute value inequality that represents the normal temperature range.
    b. Solve the inequality. What is the normal temperature range? Between 99.5°F and 102.5°F

21. **Baseball** A baseball should weigh 5.12 ounces with an absolute deviation of 0.035 ounce. The circumference of a baseball should be 9.05 inches with an absolute deviation of 0.05 inch.
    a. Write absolute value inequalities that represent the ranges for the weight and circumference of a baseball. weight: $|x - 5.12| = 0.035$; circumference: $|x - 9.05| = 0.05$
    b. Is a ball that weighs 5.16 ounces and has a circumference of 9 inches within the ranges that it should be? *Explain* why or why not. No, because the ball weighs too much.
    c. What are the maximum and minimum circumferences of a baseball? 9.1 in.; 9 in.
    d. What are the maximum and minimum weights of a baseball? 5.155 oz; 5.085 oz

LESSON 6.6

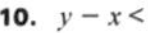

LESSON 6.7

Practice B

For use with pages 405–412

Tell whether the ordered pair is a solution of the inequality.

1. $x + y > -9$; $(0, 0)$ yes
2. $x - y \geq 8$; $(14, 9)$ no
3. $2x - y > 4$; $(-6, -15)$ no
4. $2x + y > -5$; $(-5, 12)$ yes
5. $5x + 2y \leq 8$; $(-3, 6)$ yes
6. $4x - 3y \geq -5$; $(6, 8)$ yes
7. $0.5x + 2.5y \geq 2$; $(0, 0)$ no
8. $1.2x - 3.1y < 4$; $(3, -1)$ no
9. $0.2y - 0.5x > -1$; $(-4, -8)$ yes

Graph the inequality.

10. $y - x < 6$

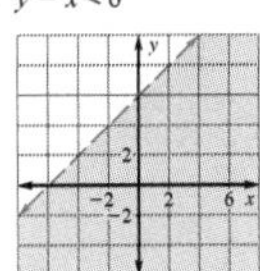

11. $x - y > -4$

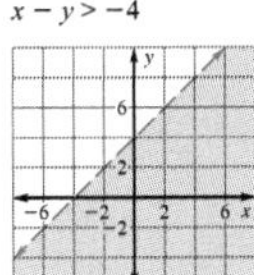

12. $2y - x < 2$

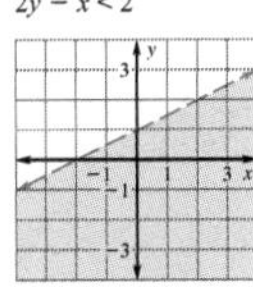

13. $4y \leq 6x - 2$

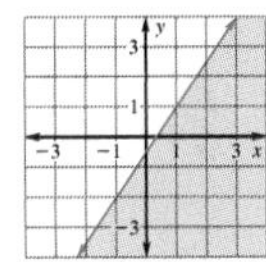

14. $5y \leq 10x + 15$

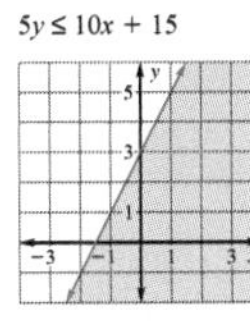

15. $6y + 3 \geq -18x$

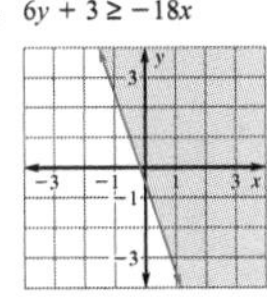

16. $2(y + 3) < 4x$

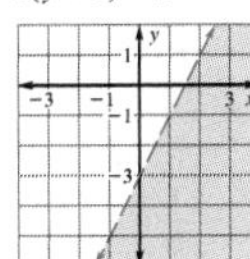

17. $2y - 3x \geq -8$

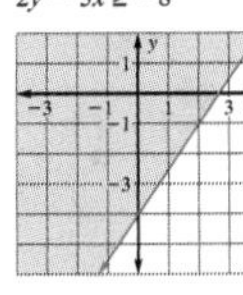

18. $2(x - y) < -5$

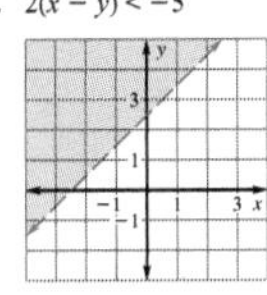

19. $y > 7$

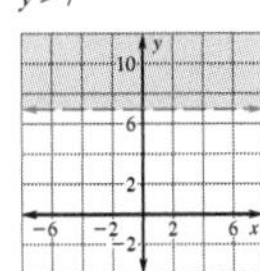

20. $x \leq -5$

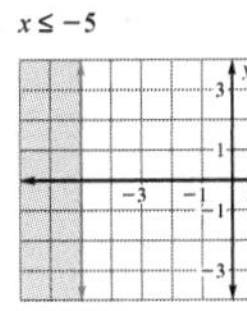

21. $y < -4$

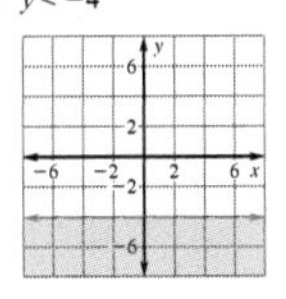

LESSON 6.7

LESSON 6.7

Practice B *continued*

For use with pages 405–412

Write an inequality of the graph shown.

22.

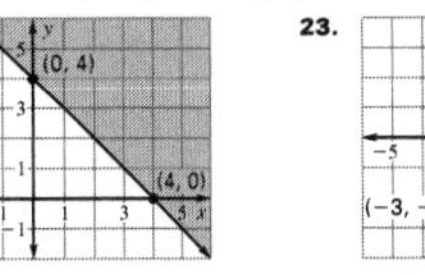

$y \geq -x + 4$

23.

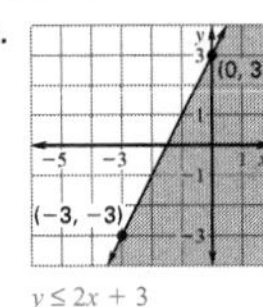

$y \leq 2x + 3$

24.

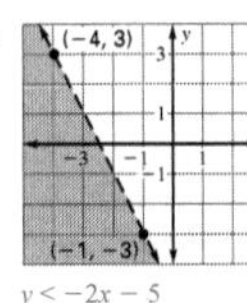

$y < -2x - 5$

25. **Clothes** You are going clothes shopping and can spend at most \$130 on clothes. It costs \$30 for a pair of pants and \$22 for a shirt. Let x represent the number of pants you can buy. Let y represent the number of shirts you can buy.

 a. Write and graph an inequality that describes the different number of shirts and pants you can buy. $30x + 22y \leq 130$

 b. Give three possible combinations of pants and shirts that you can buy. Answers will vary.

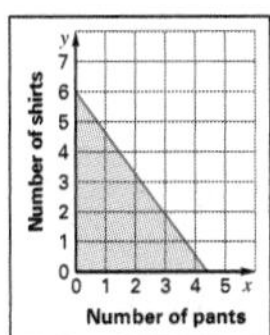

26. **Window** The area of the window shown is less than 42 square feet. Let x and y represent the heights of the triangular and rectangular portions of the window, respectively.

 a. Write and graph an inequality that describes the different dimensions of the window. $4y + 2x < 42$

 b. Could the height of the triangular portion be 2 feet and the height of the rectangular portion be 8 feet? yes

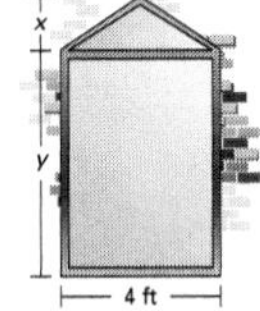

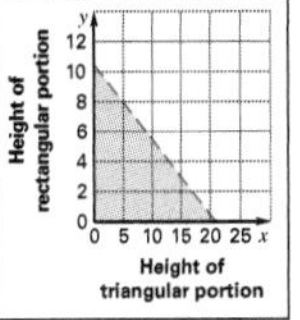

LESSON 6.7

CHAPTER 6 Quiz 1

For use after Lessons 6.1–6.2

Solve the inequality. Graph your solution.

1. $y - 9 < -4$
2. $4 + m \geq 1$
3. $k + 12 \leq 3$
4. $-1 > p - 8$
5. $-15 \leq 3d$
6. $-2t > -16$
7. $\frac{b}{3} < 2$
8. $48 \geq -4n$
9. $\frac{h}{-5} > 7$
10. You are buying pizzas for a neighborhood party. Each pizza costs \$9. If you have \$72, what are the possible numbers of pizzas that you can buy?

Answers

1. $y < 5$ See left.
2. $m \geq -3$ See left.
3. $k \leq -9$ See left.
4. $p < 7$ See left.
5. $d \geq -5$ See left.
6. $t < 8$ See left.
7. $b < 6$ See left.
8. $n \geq -12$ See left.
9. $h < -35$ See left.
10. $p \leq 8$ pizzas

CHAPTER 6 Quiz 2

For use after Lessons 6.3–6.4

Solve the inequality, if possible.

1. $5x + 7 \geq 2$
2. $8x - 9 < -2x + 11$
3. $4(3x - 2) > 12(x + 1)$
4. $-3(x - 2) \leq -3x + 7$
5. $x + 3 \leq -2$ *or* $10x - 3 > x + 15$
6. $\frac{1}{2}(x + 10) > -(x + 1)$

Answers

1. $x \geq -1$
2. $x < 2$
3. no solution
4. all real numbers
5. $x \leq -5$ *or* $x > 2$
6. $x > -4$

CHAPTER 6 Quiz 3

For use after Lessons 6.5–6.7

Solve the equation.

1. $|x| = 0.3$
2. $|x + 4| = 2$
3. $2|5x - 1| = 8$

Solve the inequality. Graph your solution.

4. $|x| \geq 5$
5. $|3x - 2| < 2$
6. $2|x + 3| - 1 \leq 3$

Graph the inequality.

7. $y > 3x - 2$

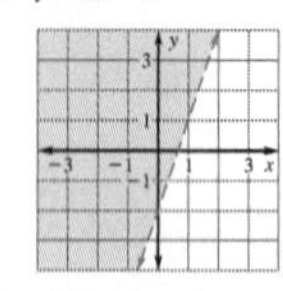

8. $4x + y \leq 0$
9. $x \geq 3$

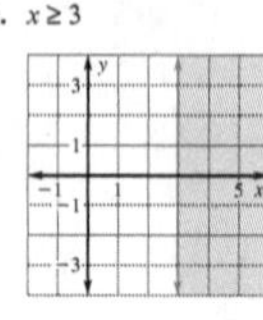

Answers

1. 0.3 and -0.3
2. -2 and -6
3. 1 and $-\frac{3}{5}$
4. $x \leq -5$ *or* $x \geq 5$ See left.
5. $0 < x < \frac{4}{3}$ See left.
6. $-5 \leq x \leq -1$ See left.
7. See left.
8. See left.
9. See left.

CHAPTER 6 Chapter Test B

For use after Chapter 6

Solve the inequality. Graph your solution.

1. $x + 8 > -10$
2. $\frac{y}{-4} < -3$
3. $7 - 5d < -3$
4. $4a - 8 < 2a$

In Exercises 5 and 6, use the following information.

To be eligible for the playoffs, a baseball team cannot lose more than 40% of its remaining games. The team has 18 games remaining in the regular season.

5. Write and solve an inequality to find the number of games g that the team could lose and still be eligible for the playoffs.
6. If the baseball team loses 8 of its remaining games, will the team advance to the playoffs? Explain your answer.

Solve the inequality, if possible.

7. $2(3x - 1) > 6(x + 1)$
8. $3(2p - 5) \geq 8p - 5$
9. $5(2s + 7) - 4 > 10s - 7$

Translate the verbal statement into an inequality. Then solve the inequality.

10. Five-eighths of a number x is greater than or equal to -10.
11. The difference of 9 and $3x$ is less than or equal to -6.

In Exercises 12 and 13, use the following information.

The photography club at your school decides to publish a calendar to raise money. The initial cost for equipment and software is \$600. In addition to the initial cost, each calendar costs \$2.50 to produce. The club plans to sell the calendars for \$8 each.

12. Write and solve an inequality to find the number n of calendars that the photography club must sell in order to raise at least \$1200.
13. Will the club reach their fundraising goal if they sell 110 calendars? Explain your answer.

Answers

1. $x > -18$ See left.
2. $y > 12$ See left.
3. $d > 2$ See left.
4. $a < 4$ See left.
5. $\frac{g}{18} \leq 0.40$; $g \leq 7.2$
6. No, the team can lose at most 7 games.
7. no solution
8. $p \leq -5$
9. all real numbers
10. $\frac{5}{8}x \geq -10$; $x \geq -16$
11. $9 - 3x \leq -6$; $x \geq 5$
12. $8n - 2.50n - 600 \geq 1200$; $n \geq \frac{3600}{11}$
13. No, they must sell at least 328 calendars.

CHAPTER 6

Chapter Test B

For use after Chapter 6

Solve the compound inequality. Graph your solution.

14. $5 - x > 2$ *or* $5 \le x - 7$

15. $-10 \le 2(x - 1) < 14$

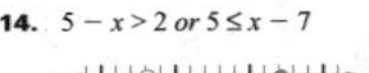

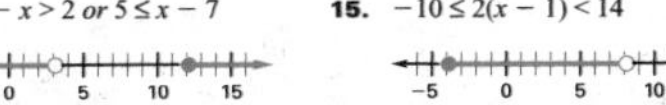

16. The water pressure p (in pounds per square inch) exerted on an object in the ocean can be given by the function $p = 15 + \frac{6}{11}d$ where d is the depth (in feet) below the surface of the water. What are the possible water pressures of an object when the depth ranges from 102 feet to 468 feet?

Solve the equation or inequality, if possible.

17. $|3x - 1| = 2$

18. $2|x| - 7 = 3$

19. $2|x + 8| + 6 = 0$

20. $|x - 2| + 6 > 9$

21. $-2|4 - x| \le -4$

22. $|2x - 8| < 0$

Graph the inequality.

23. $y > -3x - 2$

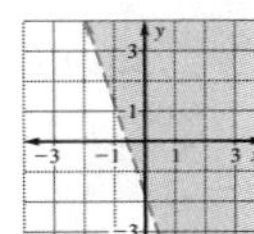

24. $x - 3y < 6$

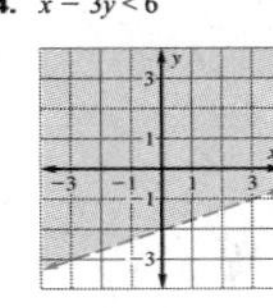

In Exercises 25 and 26, use the following information.

A concert promoter needs to take in at least \$380,000 from ticket sales. The promoter charges \$30 for floor seats and \$20 for bleacher seats.

25. Write and graph an inequality that describes his goal in terms of selling bleacher seat tickets and selling floor seat tickets.

26. Identify and interpret one of the solutions.

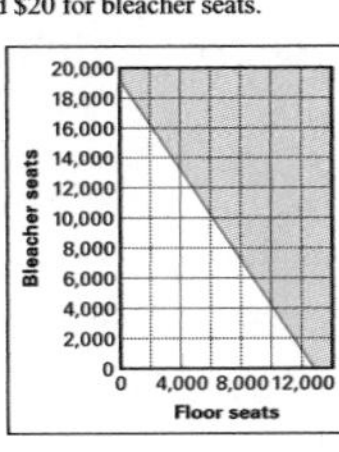

Answers

14. $x < 3$ *or* $x > 12$; See left.

15. $-4 \le x < 8$; See left.

16. The depths are between 159.5 ft and 830.5 ft.

17. $x = -\frac{1}{3}; x = 1$

18. $x = \pm 5$

19. no solution

20. $x > 5$ or $x < -1$

21. $6 \ge x \ge 2$

22. no solution

23. See left.

24. See left.

25. $30x + 20y \ge 380{,}000$; See left.

26. *Sample answer:* (10,000, 12,000); He could sell 10,000 tickets for bleacher seats and 12,000 tickets for floor seats.

CHAPTER 6

Standardized Test

For use after Chapter 6

Multiple Choice

1. Which inequality is represented by the graph? D

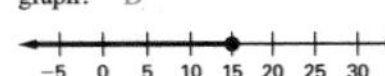

Ⓐ $x + 9 > 24$ Ⓑ $x + 7 \ge 22$
Ⓒ $x - 5 < 10$ Ⓓ $x - 7 \le 8$

2. Which inequality is equivalent to $3.4 \ge p - 2.3$? B

Ⓐ $1.1 \ge p$ Ⓑ $p \le 5.7$
Ⓒ $p \ge 1.1$ Ⓓ $5.7 \le p$

3. Which inequality represents the sentence "The difference of r and 12 is less than or equal to 22."? A

Ⓐ $r - 12 \le 22$ Ⓑ $r - 12 > 22$
Ⓒ $r - 12 \ge 22$ Ⓓ $r - 12 < 22$

4. You need to buy 5 notebooks but only have \$6 to spend. Which inequality can you use to find the possible number of notebooks that you can afford if n represents the price of one notebook? B

Ⓐ $5n < 6$ Ⓑ $5n \le 6$
Ⓒ $\frac{5}{n} < 6$ Ⓓ $\frac{5}{n} \le 6$

5. Which inequality is equivalent to $\frac{m}{-8} > 7$? D

Ⓐ $m > 56$ Ⓑ $m < 56$
Ⓒ $m > -56$ Ⓓ $m < -56$

6. Which inequality represents the sentence "The product of w and 12 is greater than 54."? C

Ⓐ $\frac{w}{12} > 54$ Ⓑ $\frac{w}{12} < 54$
Ⓒ $12w > 54$ Ⓓ $12w < 54$

7. What is the first step in solving the inequality $5x - 12 < 18$? B

Ⓐ Subtract 12 from each side of the inequality.
Ⓑ Add 12 to each side of the inequality.
Ⓒ Multiply each side of the inequality by 5.
Ⓓ Divide each side of the inequality by 5.

8. Which inequality is equivalent to $\frac{1}{2}f + 5 < 21$? D

Ⓐ $f < 16$ Ⓑ $f < 13$
Ⓒ $f < 8$ Ⓓ $f < 32$

9. Which inequality is equivalent to $5(r - 2) \le -10r + 5$? A

Ⓐ $r \le 1$ Ⓑ $r \ge 1$
Ⓒ $r \le \frac{7}{15}$ Ⓓ $r \ge \frac{7}{15}$

10. For which values of m and n are all the solutions of $mx - n > 0$ negative? C

Ⓐ $m > 0, n > 0$ Ⓑ $m < 0, n < 0$
Ⓒ $m > 0, n < 0$ Ⓓ $m > 0, n = 0$

11. Which inequality is equivalent to $4 \le \frac{2}{3}(9x + 15) < 34$? B

Ⓐ $-\frac{11}{6} \le x < \frac{19}{6}$ Ⓑ $-1 \le x < 4$
Ⓒ $\frac{14}{6} \le x < \frac{44}{6}$ Ⓓ $-36 \le x < 144$

12. Which inequality represents the verbal phrase "All real numbers that are greater than or equal to $-5\frac{1}{3}$ *and* less than $25\frac{2}{3}$"? A

Ⓐ $-5\frac{1}{3} \le x < 25\frac{2}{3}$ Ⓑ $-5\frac{1}{3} \ge x < 25\frac{2}{3}$
Ⓒ $-5\frac{1}{3} \ge x > 25\frac{2}{3}$ Ⓓ $-5\frac{1}{3} \le x > 25\frac{2}{3}$

CHAPTER 6

Standardized Test *continued*

For use after Chapter 6

13. Which of the following are the solutions to the equation $3|x - 8| = 132$? D

Ⓐ $x = 44$ and $x = -44$
Ⓑ $x = 36$ and $x = -36$
Ⓒ $x = 52$ and $x = -52$
Ⓓ $x = 52$ and $x = -36$

14. A toolmaker is making a part that must have a diameter of 2.5 centimeters with an absolute error of 0.0025 centimeter. What is the minimum possible diameter that this part can have? B

Ⓐ 0.00625 cm Ⓑ 2.4975 cm
Ⓒ 2.5025 cm Ⓓ 1000 cm

15. Which inequality is equivalent to $x < -6$ *or* $x > 11$? C

Ⓐ $|x - 7| < -13$ Ⓑ $5|x - 5| > 50$
Ⓒ $4|5 - 2x| > 68$ Ⓓ $2|2 - 4x| > 86$

16. The graph of which inequality is shown? D

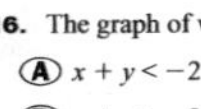

Ⓐ $x + y < -2$
Ⓑ $x + y > -2$
Ⓒ $x + y \le -2$
Ⓓ $x + y \ge -2$

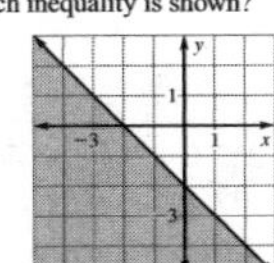

Gridded Answer

17. You will be giving a presentation in your Algebra I class. Your teacher gives you a time limit of 12 minutes with an absolute deviation of 1.5 minutes. What is the minimum possible duration (in minutes) of your presentation?

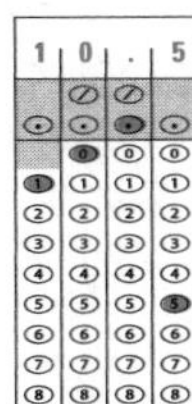

18\. a. $\frac{98 + 85 + 72 + 78 + x}{5} \ge 85$; $x \ge 92$
b. No, it is not possible to earn an average of 92. A score of 100 on the last test would still only give you an average of 86.6.

Short Response

18. You earned the following scores on four English tests: 98, 85, 72, and 78. You want to have an average of at least 85 after you take the fifth test.

a. Write and solve an inequality to find the possible scores that you can earn on your fifth test in order to meet your goal. See above.

b. The greatest score you can earn on a test is 100. Is it possible for you to have an average score of 92 after the fifth test? *Explain* your reasoning. See above.

Extended Response

19. The math club at your school is selling chances to win a computer in order to help raise funds for a local tournament. Each ticket is \$2. The club has 1000 tickets to sell and must sell at least 750 to raise enough money. The table shows the number of tickets sold so far by each member.

Member	1	2	3	4	5
Tickets Sold	98	68	112	75	112

a. Find the possible numbers a of additional tickets that the club can sell in order to meet its goal. $a \ge 285$

b. If the club raises more than \$1500, any additional amount will be used to purchase calculators. Find the possible total numbers t of tickets that the club can sell in order to purchase at least \$100 worth of calculators. $t \ge 800$

c. Write an inequality that describes the possible amounts c that the club can use toward the purchase of calculators. *Explain* your answer.

$c \le \$500$ or $\$0 \le c \le \$500$; Selling 750 tickets would raise \$1500 for the club. Anything over that amount is used to purchase calculators. After selling 750 tickets, there are 250 tickets remaining, which would total \$500. So, the maximum amount that can be used towards calculators is \$500 and the minimum amount is \$0.

CHAPTER 6

Alternative Assessment and Math Journal

For use after Chapter 6

Journal

1. Explain how to solve the absolute value inequality $|ax + b| > 9$ and give a rough sketch of the graph of the resulting solution.

Multi-Step Problem

2. The Math Club has \$1500 to spend on a party. The club decides to use a portion of the money to reserve a banquet room and purchase door prizes. The banquet room costs \$125 to reserve and the door prizes each cost \$8.50.

a. Write and solve an inequality representing the number of door prizes p that can be purchased if the club decides to use no more than \$250 to reserve the banquet room and purchase the door prizes.

b. Graph the solution in part (a). What is the maximum number of door prizes that can be purchased?

c. The club decides to purchase the maximum number of door prizes. Determine the maximum amount that remains in the \$1500 budget after purchasing door prizes and reserving the banquet room.

d. The remaining money in the budget will be used to pay for the food for the banquet. Vegetarian, beef, and chicken entrée options are available at prices of \$7, \$11, and \$9, respectively. Write an inequality representing the purchase of x beef, y chicken, and 8 vegetarian entrees that stays within the budget.

e. Graph the inequality in part (d).

f. Give 3 possible combinations of numbers of beef and chicken entrees.

g. For each answer given in part (f), determine the amount of money in the budget that was not spent.

1\. Complete answers should include: a discussion of the equivalent compound inequality $ax + b > 9$ or $ax + b < -9$; a discussion of how to solve each part of this compound inequality; a rough sketch of a solution consisting of two rays having open circles that point in opposite directions.

2\. a. $125 + 8.5p \le 250$; $p \le 14$ b.  (number line 0 2 6 4 8 10 12 14); 14 door prizes

c. \$1256 d. $11x + 9y + 56 \le 1256$

e.

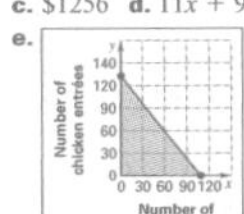

f. *Sample answer:* 100 beef and 10 chicken; 50 beef and 70 chicken; 25 beef and 100 chicken g. For sample answer in part (f): \$10, \$20, and \$25, respectively.

PLAN AND PREPARE

Main Ideas

In Chapter 6, students write, solve, and graph one-step and multi-step inequalities using addition, subtraction, multiplication, and division. They learn to reverse an inequality sign when multiplying or dividing by a negative number. Students solve and graph compound inequalities using *and* and *or*. They solve absolute value equations using *or* and they solve and graph absolute value inequalities using *and* and *or*. Finally, students graph linear inequalities in two variables.

Prerequisite Skills

- Solving equations
- Graphing equations
- Writing equations

Additional resources for reviewing prerequisite skills are:

- Skills Review Handbook, pp. 909–937
- @HomeTutor

2. No; because the solution of $7x - 4 = 10$ is $x = 2$, the two equations do not have the same solution.

16.

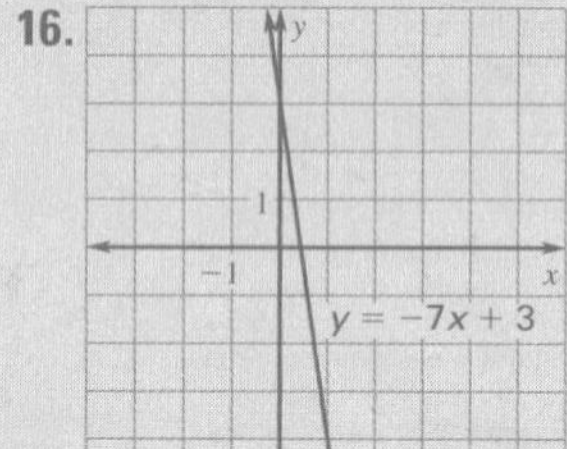

6 Solving and Graphing Linear Inequalities

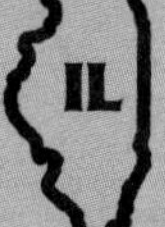

Before

In previous chapters, you learned the following skills, which you'll use in Chapter 6: solving equations, graphing equations, and writing equations.

Prerequisite Skills

VOCABULARY CHECK

1. Identify one **ordered pair** that is a solution of $8x - 5y = -2$. *Sample answer:* (1, 2)
2. Are $7x - 4 = 10$ and $x = 3$ **equivalent equations**? *Explain.* See margin.
3. The **absolute value** of a number a is the distance between a and _?_ on a number line. 0

SKILLS CHECK

Check whether the given number is a solution of the equation or inequality. *(Review p. 21 for 6.1–6.6.)*

4. $x - 2 = 3; 5$ solution **5.** $s + 3 = 12; 9$ solution **6.** $6y > 20; 3$ not a solution **7.** $\frac{p-3}{5} \le 4; 23$ solution

Solve the equation. Check your solution. *(Review pp. 134, 141, 148 for 6.1–6.6.)*

8. $m + 8 = -20$ -28 **9.** $-7x = 35$ -5 **10.** $-9r - 4 = 25$ $-\frac{29}{9}$ **11.** $4t - 7t = 9$ -3

For the given value of a, find $-a$ and $|a|$. *(Review p. 64 for 6.5–6.6.)*

12. $a = -3$ 3, 3 **13.** $a = -5.6$ 5.6, 5.6 **14.** $a = 14$ −14, 14 **15.** $a = 0$ 0, 0

Graph the equation. *(Review p. 215 for 6.7.)* 16–19. See margin for art.

16. $y = -7x + 3$ **17.** $6x + 3y = -5$ **18.** $x = -8$ **19.** $y = 4$

@HomeTutor Prerequisite skills practice at classzone.com

Chapter Planning Guide

Chapter 6 Resource Book
- Teaching Guide/Lesson Plan (pp. 3, 17, 30, 43, 58, 68, 82)
- Project with Rubric (p. 99)

Assessment and Intervention
- Assessment Book (pp. 75–89)
- Benchmark Tests
- Reteaching and Remediation Book

Interactive Technology
- Easy Planner
- Power Presentations CD-ROM
- Activity Generator CD-ROM
- Animated Algebra
- Test Generator CD-ROM
- Online Quizzes
- eWorkbook
- eEdition
- @HomeTutor

Resources for English Learners
- Quick Reference for English Learners
- Spanish Study Guide
- Multi-Language Visual Glossary
- Student Resources in Spanish

Now

In Chapter 6, you will apply the big ideas listed below and reviewed in the Chapter Summary on page 414. You will also use the key vocabulary listed below.

Big Ideas

1. **Applying properties of inequality**
2. **Using statements with *and* or *or***
3. **Graphing inequalities**

KEY VOCABULARY

- graph of an inequality, *p. 356*
- equivalent inequalities, *p. 357*
- compound inequality, *p. 380*
- absolute value equation, *p. 390*
- absolute deviation, *p. 392*
- linear inequality in two variables, *p. 405*
- graph of an inequality in two variables, *p. 405*

Why?

You can use inequalities to solve problems in sound amplification. For example, you can solve an inequality to determine whether an amplifier provides enough amplification for a given number of people in an audience.

Animated Algebra

The animation illustrated below for Exercise 45 on page 387 helps you answer this question: Is a 2900 watt amplifier adequate for an audience of 350 people?

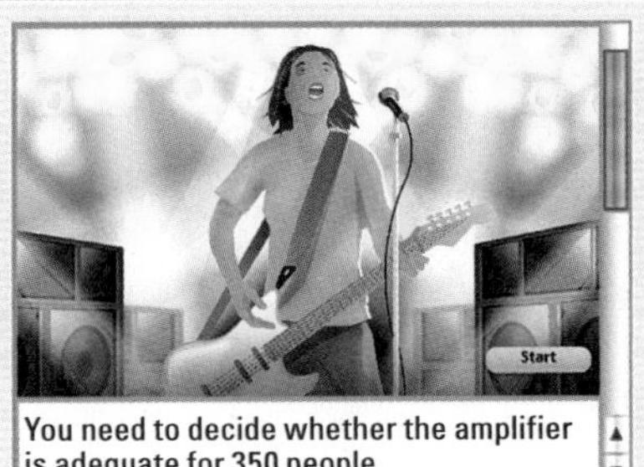

Start
You need to decide whether the amplifier is adequate for 350 people.

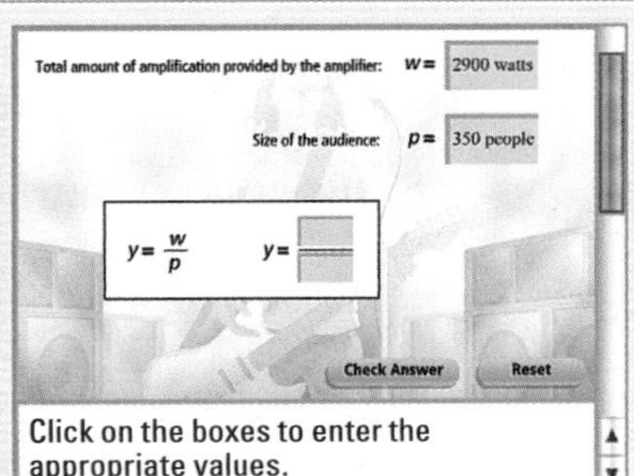

Animated Algebra at classzone.com

Other animations for Chapter 6: pages 358, 364, 382, 390, 391, 399, and 407

355

Algebra 1 Toolkit

- Reading Strategies for Chapter 6, pp. 19–20
- Differentiated Instruction Notes, pp. 65–68
- English Learners Notes, pp. 107–108
- Inclusion Notes, pp. 139–140
- Teaching Strategies with Sample Worksheets, pp. 155–178
- Using Technology in the Classroom, pp. 179–184
- Tips for New Teachers, pp. 195–196
- Math Background Notes, pp. 221–222
- Pre-AP Strategies and Copymasters, pp. 288–289, 367–383
- Teacher Survival Activities, pp. 565–566, 591–592
- Bulletin Board Idea, p. 612
- Teacher Tool Transparencies, following p. 620

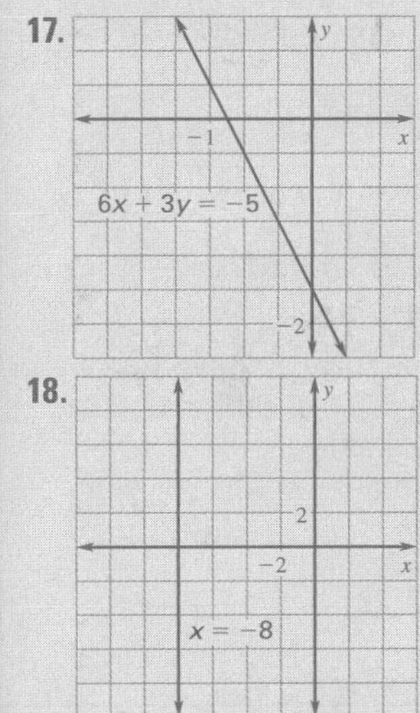

19.

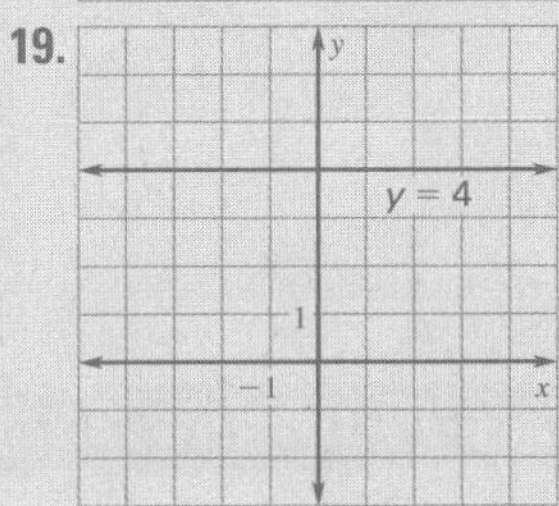

1 PLAN AND PREPARE

Warm-Up Exercises

Transparency Available

1. Is -9 a solution of $a + 7 = -2$? yes
2. Solve the equation $h + 12 = -8$. -20
3. Write an inequality that describes the number of CDs you can buy for \$12 each if you have no more than \$60 to spend. Can you buy 6 CDs? $12x \leq 60$; no

Notetaking Guide

Transparency Available

Promotes interactive learning and notetaking skills, pp. 127–129.

Pacing

Basic: 1 day

Average: 1 day

Advanced: 1 day

Block: 0.5 block with 6.2

- See *Teaching Guide/Lesson Plan.*

2 FOCUS AND MOTIVATE

Essential Question

Big Idea 1, p. 355

How do you solve and graph inequalities using addition and subtraction? Tell students they will learn how to answer this question by using addition and subtraction properties of inequality.

6.1 Solve Inequalities Using Addition and Subtraction

Before You solved equations using addition and subtraction.

Now You will solve inequalities using addition and subtraction.

Why So you can describe desert temperatures, as in Example 1.

Key Vocabulary
- graph of an inequality
- equivalent inequalities
- inequality, *p. 21*
- solution of an inequality, *p. 22*

On a number line, the **graph of an inequality** in one variable is the set of points that represent all solutions of the inequality. To graph an inequality in one variable, use an open circle for $<$ or $>$ and a closed circle for $\leq$ or $\geq$. The graphs of $x < 3$ and $x \geq -1$ are shown below.

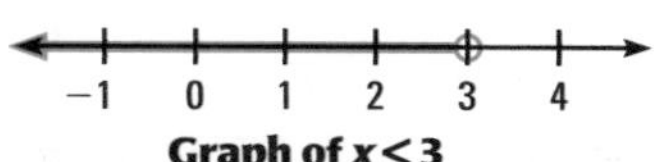

Graph of $x < 3$

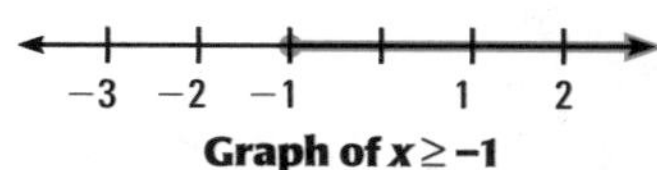

Graph of $x \geq -1$

EXAMPLE 1 Write and graph an inequality

DEATH VALLEY The highest temperature recorded in the United States was 134°F at Death Valley, California, in 1913. Use only this fact to write and graph an inequality that describes the temperatures in the United States.

Solution

Let T represent a temperature (in degrees Fahrenheit) in the United States. The value of T must be less than or equal to 134. So, an inequality is $T \leq 134$.

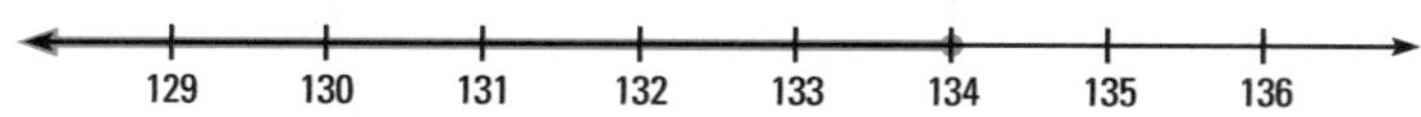

EXAMPLE 2 Write inequalities from graphs

Write an inequality represented by the graph.

a. 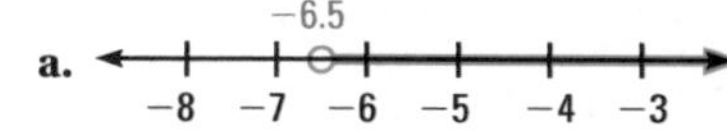

b. 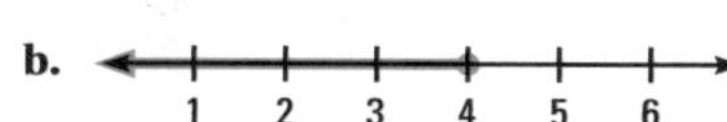

Solution

a. The open circle means that -6.5 is not a solution of the inequality. Because the arrow points to the right, all numbers greater than -6.5 are solutions.

▸ An inequality represented by the graph is $x > -6.5$.

b. The closed circle means that 4 is a solution of the inequality. Because the arrow points to the left, all numbers less than 4 are solutions.

▸ An inequality represented by the graph is $x \leq 4$.

Resource Planning Guide

Chapter Resource Book
- Teaching Guide/Lesson Plan (pp. 3–4)
- Activity Master (p. 5)
- Practice levels A, B, C (pp. 6–11)
- Study Guide (pp. 12–13)
- Catch-up for Absent Students (p. 14)
- Application (p. 15)
- Challenge (p. 16)

Workbooks
- Notetaking Guide (pp. 127–129)
- Practice Workbook (pp. 84–86)

Teaching Options
- **Power Presentations CD-ROM** provides dynamic electronic teaching resources for the classroom.
- **Activity Generator CD-ROM** provides editable activities for all ability levels.

Interactive Technology
- Easy Planner
- Power Presentations CD-ROM
- Activity Generator CD-ROM
- Animated Algebra
- Test Generator CD-ROM
- Online Quiz
- eWorkbook
- eEdition
- @HomeTutor

Resources for English Learners
- Quick Reference for English Learners
- Spanish Study Guide
- Multi-Language Visual Glossary
- Student Resources in Spanish

See also the *Algebra 1 Toolkit* for more strategies for meeting individual needs.

✓ GUIDED PRACTICE for Examples 1 and 2

1. **ANTARCTICA** The lowest temperature recorded in Antarctica was −129°F at the Russian Vostok station in 1983. Use only this fact to write and graph an inequality that describes the temperatures in Antarctica. $x \ge -129$; see margin for art.

Write an inequality represented by the graph.

2. 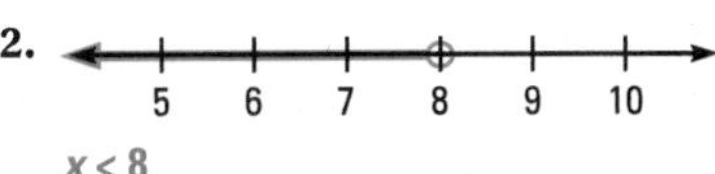
$x < 8$

3. 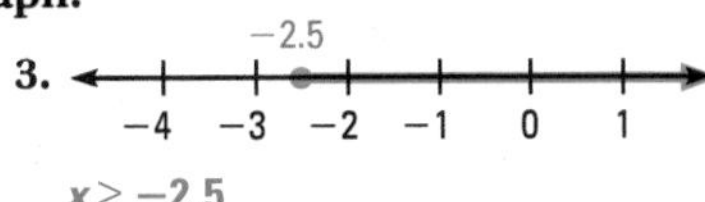
$x \ge -2.5$

EQUIVALENT INEQUALITIES Just as you used properties of equality to produce equivalent equations, you can use properties of inequality to produce *equivalent inequalities*. **Equivalent inequalities** are inequalities that have the same solutions.

KEY CONCEPT *For Your Notebook*

Addition Property of Inequality

Words Adding the same number to each side of an inequality produces an equivalent inequality.

Algebra If $a > b$, then $a + c > b + c$. If $a \ge b$, then $a + c \ge b + c$.

If $a < b$, then $a + c < b + c$. If $a \le b$, then $a + c \le b + c$.

EXAMPLE 3 Solve an inequality using addition

Solve $x - 5 > -3.5$. Graph your solution.

$x - 5 > -3.5$	Write original inequality.
$x - 5 + 5 > -3.5 + 5$	Add 5 to each side.
$x > 1.5$	Simplify.

▶ The solutions are all real numbers greater than 1.5. Check by substituting a number greater than 1.5 for x in the original inequality.

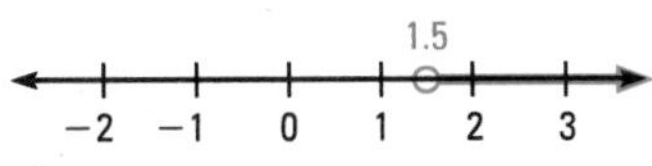

CHECK $x - 5 > -3.5$	Write original inequality.
$6 - 5 \overset{?}{>} -3.5$	Substitute 6 for x.
$1 > -3.5$ ✓	Solution checks.

✓ GUIDED PRACTICE for Example 3

Solve the inequality. Graph your solution. 4–6. See margin for art.

4. $x - 9 \le 3$ $x \le 12$
5. $p - 9.2 < -5$ $p < 4.2$
6. $-1 \ge m - \frac{1}{2}$ $m \le -\frac{1}{2}$

Motivating the Lesson

You know that you can send no more than 50 text messages on your monthly cell phone plan without incurring additional charges. You sent 18 messages yesterday and 9 today. By knowing how to write and solve inequalities, you can find the maximum number of text messages you can send this month without additional charges.

3 TEACH

Extra Example 1

The lowest elevation recorded in the United States is −282 feet at Death Valley, California. Use this fact to write and graph an inequality that describes the elevations in the United States. $E \ge -282$, where E is elevation in feet

Extra Example 2

Write an inequality represented by the graph. $x \le -1.5$

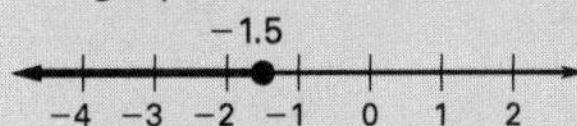

Key Question to Ask for Example 2

- How are the graphs in parts a and b different? In part a, the graph points to the right and does not include the endpoint. In part b, the graph points to the left and does include the endpoint.

Extra Example 3

Solve $m - 3.8 < -1$. Graph your solution. all real numbers less than 2.8

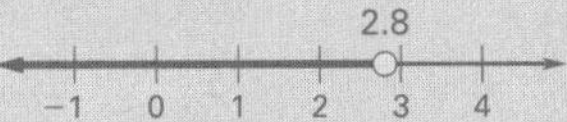

1, 4–6. See Additional Answers beginning on p. AA1.

Extra Example 4

Solve $b + 7 > 3$. Graph your solution. all real numbers greater than −4

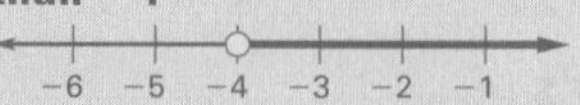

An **Animated Algebra** activity is available on-line for **Example 4**. This activity is also available on the **Power Presentations CD-ROM**.

Extra Example 5

You are shopping for bicycles. The type you want costs at least \$185. You have saved \$97. Find the possible amounts of money you need to save to buy the bicycle you want. \$88 or more

Closing the Lesson

Have students summarize the major points of the lesson and answer the Essential Question: How do you solve and graph inequalities using addition and subtraction?

- The addition property of inequality can be used to produce equivalent inequalities.
- On a number line, an open circle on the graph means the number is not a solution of the inequality, while a closed circle means it is a solution.

Solve the inequality by adding or subtracting the same number from each side of the inequality. To graph the inequality, use an open circle for < or > or use a closed circle for ≤ or ≥. Shade the numbers on the number line in the appropriate direction.

7.

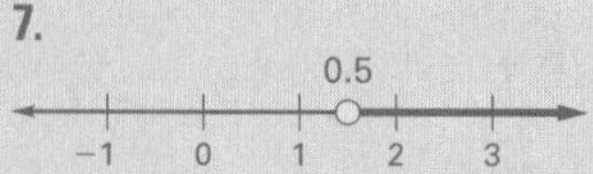

KEY CONCEPT *For Your Notebook*

Subtraction Property of Inequality

Words Subtracting the same number from each side of an inequality produces an equivalent inequality.

Algebra If $a > b$, then $a - c > b - c$. If $a \geq b$, then $a - c \geq b - c$.

If $a < b$, then $a - c < b - c$. If $a \leq b$, then $a - c \leq b - c$.

EXAMPLE 4 Solve an inequality using subtraction

Solve $9 \geq x + 7$. Graph your solution.

$9 \geq x + 7$	Write original inequality.
$9 - 7 \geq x + 7 - 7$	Subtract 7 from each side.
$2 \geq x$	Simplify.

▶ You can rewrite $2 \geq x$ as $x \leq 2$. The solutions are all real numbers less than or equal to 2.

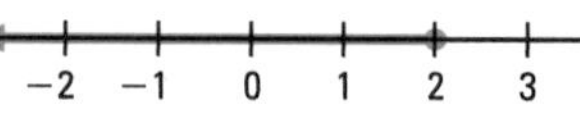

Animated Algebra at classzone.com

EXAMPLE 5 Solve a real-world problem

READING The phrase "no more than" indicates that you use the ≤ symbol.

LUGGAGE WEIGHTS You are checking a bag at an airport. Bags can weigh no more than 50 pounds. Your bag weighs 16.8 pounds. Find the possible weights w (in pounds) that you can add to the bag.

Solution

Write a verbal model. Then write and solve an inequality.

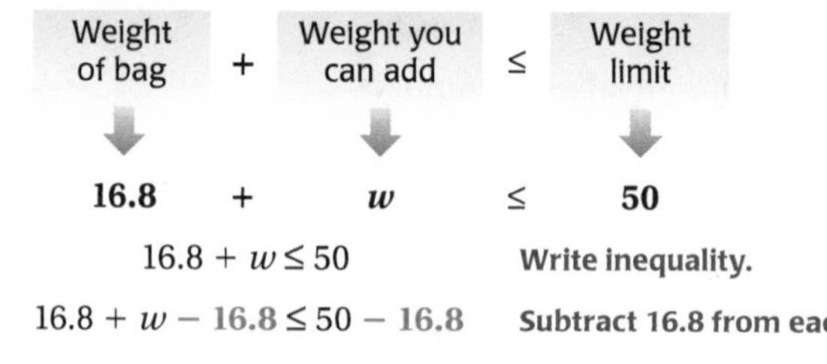

$16.8 + w \leq 50$	Write inequality.
$16.8 + w - 16.8 \leq 50 - 16.8$	Subtract 16.8 from each side.
$w \leq 33.2$	Simplify.

▶ You can add no more than 33.2 pounds.

GUIDED PRACTICE for Examples 4 and 5

7. Solve $y + 5.5 > 6$. Graph your solution. $y > 0.5$; see margin for art.

8. **WHAT IF?** In Example 5, suppose your bag weighs 29.1 pounds. Find the possible weights (in pounds) that you can add to the bag. $w \leq 20.9$ lb

6.1 EXERCISES

HOMEWORK KEY
- ○ = **WORKED-OUT SOLUTIONS** on p. WS13 for Exs. 7, 15, and 33
- ★ = **STANDARDIZED TEST PRACTICE** Exs. 2, 29, 34, 35, and 38
- ◆ = **MULTIPLE REPRESENTATIONS** Ex. 37

SKILL PRACTICE

A

1. **VOCABULARY** Copy and complete: To graph $x < -8$, you draw a(n) __?__ circle at -8, and you draw an arrow to the __?__. open, left of -8

2. ★ **WRITING** Are $x + 7 \geq 18$ and $x \geq 25$ equivalent inequalities? *Explain.*
No; because the solution of $x + 7 \geq 18$ is $x \geq 11$, the two inequalities do not have the same solution.

EXAMPLE 1 on p. 356 for Exs. 3–5

WRITING AND GRAPHING INEQUALITIES **Write and graph an inequality that describes the situation.** 3–5. See margin for art.

3. The speed limit on a highway is 60 miles per hour. $s \leq 60$
4. You must be at least 16 years old to go on a field trip. $a \geq 16$
5. A child must be taller than 48 inches to get on an amusement park ride. $h > 48$

EXAMPLE 2 on p. 356 for Exs. 6–9

WRITING INEQUALITIES **Write an inequality represented by the graph.**

6. 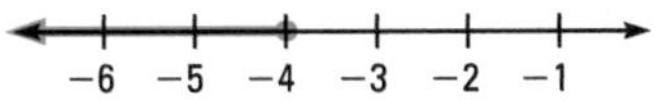

$x \leq -4$

7. 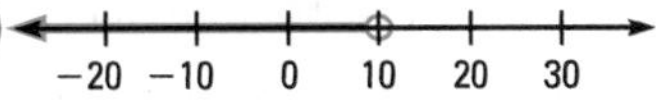

$x < 10$

8. 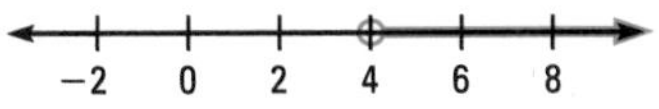

$x > 4$

9. 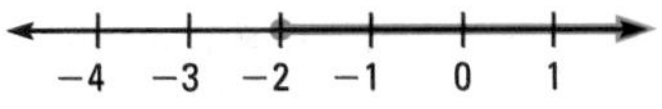

$x \geq -2$

EXAMPLES 3 and 4 on pp. 357–358 for Exs. 10–23

SOLVING INEQUALITIES **Solve the inequality. Graph your solution.** 10–21. See margin for art.

10. $x + 4 < 5$ $x < 1$
11. $-8 \leq 8 + y$ $y \geq -16$
12. $-1\frac{1}{4} \leq m + 3$ $m \geq -4\frac{1}{4}$
13. $n + 17 \leq 16\frac{4}{5}$ $n \leq -\frac{1}{5}$
14. $8.2 + v > -7.6$ $v > -15.8$
15. $w + 14.9 > -2.7$ $w > -17.6$
16. $r - 4 < -5$ $r < -1$
17. $1 \leq s - 8$ $s \geq 9$
18. $-1\frac{1}{3} \leq p - 8\frac{1}{3}$ $p \geq 7$
19. $q - 1\frac{1}{3} > -2\frac{1}{2}$ $q > -1\frac{1}{6}$
20. $2.1 \geq c - 6.7$ $c \leq 8.8$
21. $d - 1.92 > -8.76$ $d > -6.84$

ERROR ANALYSIS ***Describe*** **and correct the error in solving the inequality or in graphing the solution.** 22, 23. See margin for art.

22.
$x + 8 < -3$
$x + 8 - 8 < -3 + 8$
$x < 5$
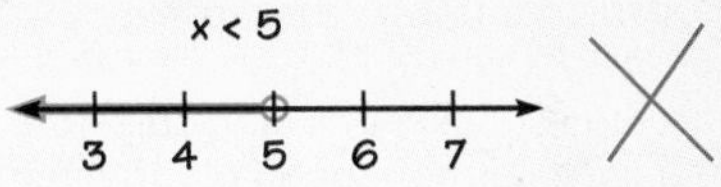

23.
$-17 \leq x - 14$
$-17 + 14 \leq x - 14 + 14$
$-3 \leq x$
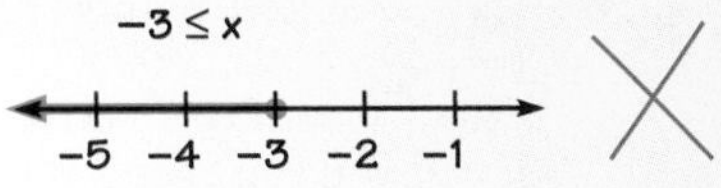

22. 8 must be subtracted from both sides of the equation, not subtracted from one and added to the other; $x + 8 - 8 < -3 - 8$, $x < -11$.

23. The number line should be shaded to the right of -3, not the left.

B

TRANSLATING SENTENCES **Write the verbal sentence as an inequality. Then solve the inequality and graph your solution.** 24–26. See margin for art.

24. The sum of 11 and m is greater than -23. $11 + m > -23$; $m > -34$
25. The difference of n and 15 is less than or equal to 37. $n - 15 \leq 37$; $n \leq 52$
26. The difference of c and 13 is less than -19. $c - 13 < -19$; $c < -6$

4 PRACTICE AND APPLY

Assignment Guide

Answer Transparencies available for all exercises

Basic:
Day 1: EP p. 939 Exs. 12–19
pp. 359–361
Exs. 1–17, 22–25, 31–36, 40–50 even

Average:
Day 1: pp. 359–361
Exs. 1–9, 14–28, 31–38, 41, 44, 47, 50

Advanced:
Day 1: pp. 359–361
Exs. 1, 2, 4, 5, 8, 9, 14–21, 24–39*, 42, 45, 48, 51

Block:
pp. 359–361
Exs. 1–9, 14–28, 31–38, 41, 44, 47, 50 (with 6.2)

Differentiated Instruction

See *Algebra 1 Best Practices Toolkit* for suggestions on addressing the needs of a diverse classroom.

Homework Check

For a quick check of student understanding of key concepts, go over the following exercises:

Basic: 3, 6, 12, 16, 31
Average: 4, 8, 14, 18, 32
Advanced: 5, 9, 15, 20, 33

Extra Practice

- Student Edition, p. 943
- Chapter 6 Resource Book: Practice levels A, B, C, pp. 6–11

Practice Worksheet

An easily-readable reduced practice page (with answers) for this lesson can be found on p. 354C.

Differentiated Instruction

Inclusion Some students may have difficulty remembering which inequality symbols to use for an open circle and which to use for a closed circle while doing **Exercises 6–9**. Stress that when the circle is open, the symbol (< or >) is an open triangle; when the circle is closed, the inequality sign (≤ or ≥) shows three lines that can be used to form a closed triangle.

See also the *Algebra 1 Toolkit* for more strategies.

3. 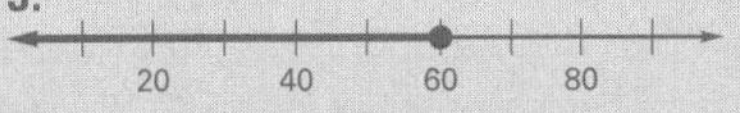

4. 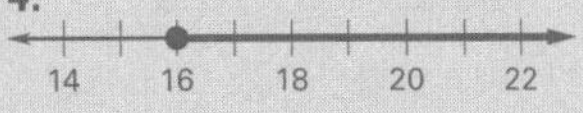

5. 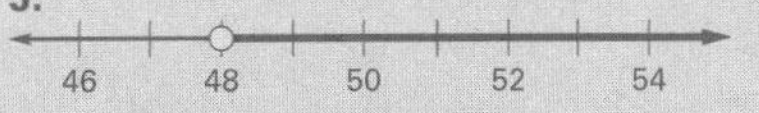

10–23. See Additional Answers beginning on p. AA1.

24. 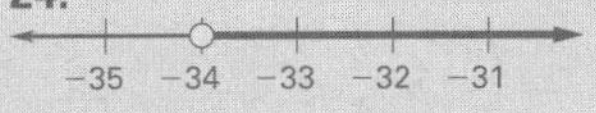

25. 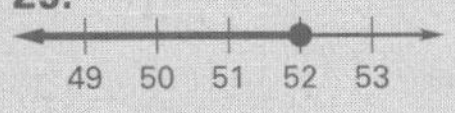

26. 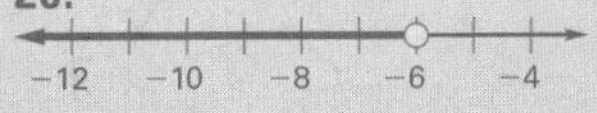

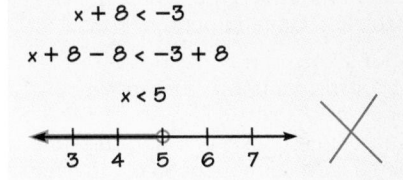

GEOMETRY Write and solve an inequality to find the possible values of x.

27. Perimeter < 51.3 inches $x < 21.6$

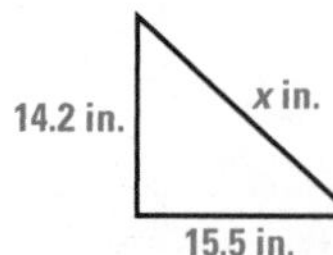

28. Perimeter ≤ 18.7 feet $x \le 3.3$

4.1 ft
4.9 ft
x ft
6.4 ft

29. ★ **WRITING** Is it possible to check all the numbers that are solutions of an inequality? Does checking one solution guarantee that you have solved an inequality correctly? *Explain* your answers. See margin.

C **30.** **CHALLENGE** Write and graph an inequality that represents the numbers that are *not* solutions of $x - 12 \ge 5.7$. $x < 17.7$; see margin for art.

PROBLEM SOLVING

EXAMPLE 5 A
on p. 358
for Exs. 31–35

31. **INTERNET** You earn points from buying items at an Internet shopping site. You would like to redeem 2350 points to get an item for free, but you want to be sure to have more than 6000 points left over. What are the possible numbers of points you can have before making a redemption?

@HomeTutor for problem solving help at classzone.com

more than 8350 points

32. **SPORTS RECORDS** In 1982 Wayne Gretsky set a new record for the greatest number of hockey goals in one season with 92 goals. Suppose that a hockey player has 59 goals so far in a season. What are the possible numbers of additional goals that the player can make in order to match or break Wayne Gretsky's record? at least 33 goals

@HomeTutor for problem solving help at classzone.com

(33.) **MULTI-STEP PROBLEM** In aerial ski competitions, athletes perform two acrobatic ski jumps, and the scores on both jumps are added together. The table shows your competitor's first and second scores and your first score.

Ski jump	Competitor's score	Your score
1	127.04	129.49
2	129.98	?

a. Write and solve an inequality to find the scores s that you can earn in your second jump in order to beat your competitor. $s > 127.53$

b. Will you beat your competitor if you earn 128.13 points? 126.78 points? 127.53 points? *Justify* your answers. Yes; no; no; $128.13 > 127.53$; $126.78 < 127.53$; when your score is 127.53, you and your competitor will tie.

34. ★ **MULTIPLE CHOICE** You want to buy a jacket at a clothing store, and you can spend at most \$30. You have a coupon for \$3 off any item at the store. Which inequality can you use to find the original prices p of jackets that you can buy? C

Ⓐ $3 + p \ge 30$ Ⓑ $30 + p \le 3$ Ⓒ $p - 3 \le 30$ Ⓓ $p - 30 \ge 3$

35. ★ **OPEN-ENDED** *Describe* a real-world situation that can be modeled by the inequality $x + 14 \ge 17$. *Explain* what the solution of the inequality means in this situation. See margin.

○ = WORKED-OUT SOLUTIONS on p. WS1 ★ = STANDARDIZED TEST PRACTICE ◆ = MULTIPLE REPRESENTATIONS

Avoiding Common Errors

Exercises 10–21 Some students may graph the solution of an inequality correctly, except their "open circle" may look like a closed circle or vice versa. Stress the importance of clearly showing open and closed circles.

Teaching Strategy

Exercises 11, 12, 17, 18, 20 Some students may want to rewrite an inequality such as $-16 \le y$ as $y \ge -16$, with the variable on the left side. Students should realize that is OK, as long as the inequality symbol describes the same relationship between the variable and the constant.

Exercise 32 You can find information about Wayne Gretzky's career and his hockey records at nhl.com/hockeyu/history/gretzky

Vocabulary

Exercises 32–38 These exercises use words such as "at most" and "no more than" and concepts such as "match a record" or "beat a record." Discuss the meanings of these words as they relate to inequality symbols, leading students to see the connections between "at most" and "no more than," and the differences between "match a record" and "beat a record."

29. No; no; there are an infinite number of solutions of an inequality, so it is not possible to check them all. One solution might check in the inequality while another does not. For example, if you incorrectly solve $x + 7 > 10$ as $x > 2$, the solution $x = 4$ checks in the original inequality.

30.

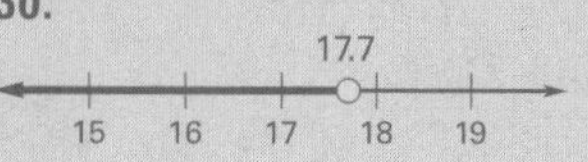

35. *Sample answer:* You want to improve on your personal best of 16 points scored in a basketball game. In the first three quarters of the game, you scored 14 points. Write and solve an inequality to find the possible numbers of points that you can score in the fourth quarter to give yourself a new personal best; $x \ge 3$, if you score at least 3 points in the fourth quarter, you will have a new personal best.

36. VEHICLE WEIGHTS According to a state law for vehicles traveling on state roads, the maximum total weight of the vehicle and its contents depends on the number of axles the vehicle has.

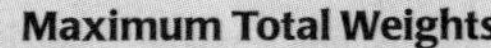

For each type of vehicle, write and solve an inequality to find the possible weights w (in pounds) of a vehicle when its contents weigh 14,200 pounds. Can a vehicle that has 2 axles and weighs 20,000 pounds hold 14,200 pounds of contents? *Explain.* See margin.

37. MULTIPLE REPRESENTATIONS Your friend is willing to spend no more than \$17,000 for a new car. The car dealership offers \$3000 cash back for the purchase of a new car.

a. **Making a Table** Make a table of values that gives the final price y of a car after the cash back offer is applied to the original price x. Use the following values for x: 19,459, 19,989, 20,549, 22,679, 23,999. See margin.

b. **Writing an Inequality** Write and solve an inequality to find the original prices of the cars that your friend will consider buying.
$x - 3000 \le 17{,}000$, $x \le 20{,}000$

38b. Yes; with a fastest time of 53.18 seconds and an average time of 53.92 seconds, his slowest time must be greater than 53.92 seconds. If his time is in between 53.92 seconds and his slowest time, the team will not meet its goal.

38. ★ SHORT RESPONSE A 4-member track team is trying to match or beat last year's winning time of 3 minutes 41.1 seconds for a 1600 meter relay race. The table shows the 400 meter times for the first three athletes.

Athlete	Time (sec)
1	53.34
2	56.38
3	57.46

a. **Calculate** What are the possible times that the last athlete can run 400 meters in order for the team to match or beat last year's time? at most 53.92 sec

b. **Decide** So far this season the last athlete's fastest 400 meter time is 53.18 seconds, and his average 400 meter time is 53.92 seconds. In this race the last athlete expects to run faster than his slowest time this season. Is it possible for the team to fail to meet its goal? *Explain.*

C **39. CHALLENGE** A public television station wants to raise at least \$72,000 in a pledge drive. The station raised an average of \$5953 per day for the first 3 days and an average of \$6153 per day for the next 3 days. What are the possible additional amounts that the station can raise to meet its goal? at least \$35,682

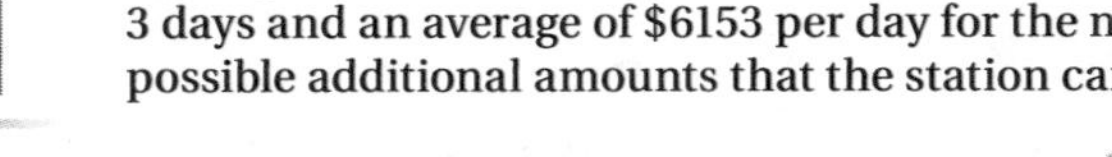

ILLINOIS MIXED REVIEW

TEST PRACTICE at classzone.com

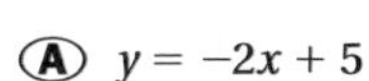

40. Which linear function includes the points (−2, 4), (0, 5), and (2, 6)? B

Ⓐ $y = -2x + 5$ Ⓑ $y = \frac{x}{2} + 5$ Ⓒ $y = -\frac{x}{2} + 5$ Ⓓ $y = 2x + 5$

41. The circumference of a circle is doubled. By how many times does the diameter increase? B

Ⓐ 1 Ⓑ 2 Ⓒ 3 Ⓓ 4

5 ASSESS AND RETEACH

Daily Homework Quiz

Transparency Available

Solve the inequality. Graph your solution.

1. $s + 0.5 \ge -1.5$ all real numbers greater than or equal to −2

2. $k - 6 < -5$ all real numbers less than 1

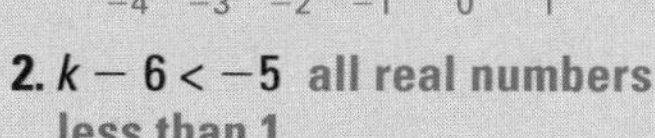

3. A theater can seat at most 625 people. The box office has sold tickets for 284 seats. Write and solve an inequality to find the possible numbers of remaining tickets t the box office can sell. $t + 284 \le 625$; $t \le 341$; no more than 341 tickets.

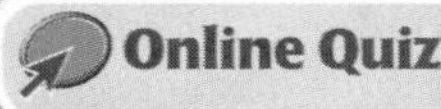

Available at **classzone.com**

Diagnosis/Remediation

- Practice A, B, C in Chapter 6 Resource Book, pp. 6–11
- Study Guide in Chapter 6 Resource Book, pp. 12–13
- Practice Workbook, pp. 84–86
- @HomeTutor

Challenge

Additional challenge is available in the Chapter 6 Resource Book, p. 16.

36, 37a. See Additional Answers beginning on p. AA1.

Investigating Algebra ACTIVITY Use before Lesson 6.2

6.2 Inequalities with Negative Coefficients

MATERIALS • index cards

QUESTION How do you solve an inequality with a negative coefficient?

EXPLORE Check solutions of inequalities

STEP 1 ***Write integers*** Write the integers from -5 to 5 on index cards. Place the cards face up as shown.

-5 -4 -3 -2 -1 0 1 2 3 4 5

STEP 2 ***Check solutions*** Determine whether each integer is a solution of $4x \geq 8$. If the integer is *not* a solution, turn over the card.

2 3 4 5

STEP 3 ***Check solutions*** Turn all the cards face up. Repeat Step 2 for $-4x \geq 8$.

-5 -4 -3 -2

DRAW CONCLUSIONS Use your observations to complete these exercises

1. State an operation that you can perform on both sides of $4x \geq 8$ to obtain the solutions found in Step 2. Then solve the inequality. **divide each side by 4; $x \geq 2$**
2. Copy and complete the steps below for solving $-4x \geq 8$.

$-4x \geq 8$	Write original inequality.
?	Add $4x$ to each side. **$0 \geq 8 + 4x$**
?	Subtract 8 from each side. **$-8 \geq 4x$**
?	Divide each side by 4. **$-2 \geq x$**
?	Rewrite inequality with x on the left side. **$x \leq -2$**

3. Does dividing both sides of $-4x \geq 8$ by -4 give the solution found in Exercise 2? If not, what else must you do to the inequality when you divide by -4? **No; reverse the direction of the inequality symbol.**
4. Do you need to change the direction of the inequality symbol when you divide each side of an inequality by a positive number? by a negative number? **no; yes**

Solve the inequality.

5. $20x \geq 5$ **$x \geq \frac{1}{4}$**
6. $-9x \leq 45$ **$x \geq -5$**
7. $-8x > 40$ **$x < -5$**
8. $7x < 21$ **$x < 3$**

1 PLAN AND PREPARE

Explore the Concept

- Students will solve an inequality with a negative coefficient.
- This activity leads into the study of solving inequalities in Examples 2 and 3 in Lesson 6.2.

Materials

Each student will need 11 index cards.

Recommended Time

Work activity: 10 min

Discuss results: 5 min

Grouping

Students should work individually.

2 TEACH

Key Question

In Step 3, why is the number -2 a solution of $-4x \geq 8$? **When $x = -2$ the value of $-4x$ is $(-4)(-2) = 8$, and the statement $8 \geq 8$ is true.**

Key Discovery

Change the direction of the inequality symbol when you multiply or divide both sides of the inequality by a negative number.

3 ASSESS AND RETEACH

Explain whether you need to change the direction of the inequality symbol to find the value of x for these inequalities: $3x > -27$, $-3x < 27$, and $-3x \geq -27$. **No for $3x > -27$ because the coefficient of the variable is positive; yes for $-3x < 27$ and for $-3x \geq -27$ because the value of each coefficient is negative.**

6.2 Solve Inequalities Using Multiplication and Division

Before You solved inequalities using addition and subtraction.
Now You will solve inequalities using multiplication and division.
Why? So you can find possible distances traveled, as in Ex. 40.

Key Vocabulary
- **inequality,** *p. 21*
- **equivalent inequalities,** *p. 357*

Solving an inequality using multiplication is similar to solving an equation using multiplication, but it is different in an important way.

KEY CONCEPT *For Your Notebook*

Multiplication Property of Inequality

Words Multiplying each side of an inequality by a *positive* number produces an equivalent inequality.

Multiplying each side of an inequality by a *negative* number and *reversing the direction of the inequality symbol* produces an equivalent inequality.

Algebra If $a < b$ and $c > 0$, then $ac < bc$. If $a < b$ and $c < 0$, then $ac > bc$.

If $a > b$ and $c > 0$, then $ac > bc$. If $a > b$ and $c < 0$, then $ac < bc$.

This property is also true for inequalities involving $\le$ and $\ge$.

EXAMPLE 1 **Solve an inequality using multiplication**

Solve $\frac{x}{4} < 5$. Graph your solution.

$\frac{x}{4} < 5$ **Write original inequality.**

$4 \cdot \frac{x}{4} < 4 \cdot 5$ **Multiply each side by 4.**

$x < 20$ **Simplify.**

▶ The solutions are all real numbers less than 20. Check by substituting a number less than 20 in the original inequality.

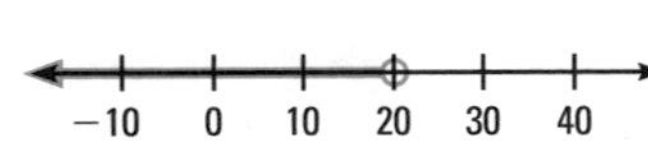

GUIDED PRACTICE for Example 1

Solve the inequality. Graph your solution. 1–3. See margin on p. 364 for art.

1. $\frac{x}{3} > 8$ $x > 24$
2. $\frac{m}{8} \le -2$ $m \le -16$
3. $\frac{y}{2.5} \ge -4$ $y \ge -10$

1 PLAN AND PREPARE

Warm-Up Exercises

Transparency Available

Check whether the given number is a solution of the inequality.

1. $\frac{x}{3} \le 7$; 20 yes
2. $4m > -23$; -6 no
3. How long will it take a diver to ascend 36 feet if the average rate of ascent is 30 feet per minute? 1.2 min or 1 min 12 sec

Notetaking Guide

Transparency Available

Promotes interactive learning and notetaking skills, pp. 130–133.

Pacing

Basic: 1 day
Average: 1 day
Advanced: 1 day
Block: 0.5 block with 6.1
- See *Teaching Guide/Lesson Plan.*

2 FOCUS AND MOTIVATE

Essential Question

Big Idea 1, p. 355

How do you solve inequalities using multiplication and division? Tell students they will learn how to answer this question by applying multiplication and division properties of inequality and by learning when to reverse the direction of the inequality symbol.

Resource Planning Guide

Chapter Resource Book
- Teaching Guide/Lesson Plan (pp. 17–18)
- Practice levels A, B, C (pp. 19–24)
- Study Guide (pp. 25–26)
- Catch-up for Absent Students (p. 27)
- Problem Solving Workshop (p. 28)
- Challenge (p. 29)

Workbooks
- Notetaking Guide (pp. 130–133)
- Practice Workbook (pp. 87–89)

Teaching Options
- **Power Presentations CD-ROM** provides dynamic electronic teaching resources for the classroom.
- **Activity Generator CD-ROM** provides editable activities for all ability levels.

Interactive Technology
- Easy Planner
- Power Presentations CD-ROM
- Activity Generator CD-ROM
- Animated Algebra
- Test Generator CD-ROM
- Online Quiz
- eWorkbook
- eEdition
- @HomeTutor

Resources for English Learners
- Quick Reference for English Learners
- Spanish Study Guide
- Multi-Language Visual Glossary
- Student Resources in Spanish

See also the *Algebra 1 Toolkit* for more strategies for meeting individual needs.

Motivating the Lesson

Can you think of a time while shopping when you had to decide how many CDs, or shirts, or video games you could possibly buy with the money you had? Answering such a question involves solving an inequality.

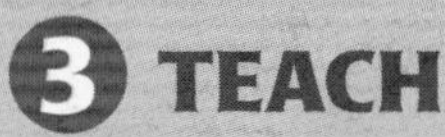

3 TEACH

Extra Example 1

Solve $\frac{y}{7} \geq -4$. Graph your solution. all real numbers greater than or equal to -28

Extra Example 2

Solve $\frac{x}{-3} > -2$. Graph your solution. all real numbers less than 6

Extra Example 3

Solve $-6x \leq 18$. $x \geq -3$

Key Question to Ask for Example 3

- If you graph $x < -8$, would you use an open or a closed circle? open

Animated Algebra classzone.com

An **Animated Algebra** activity is available on-line for **Example 3**. This activity is also available on the **Power Presentations CD-ROM**.

p. 363

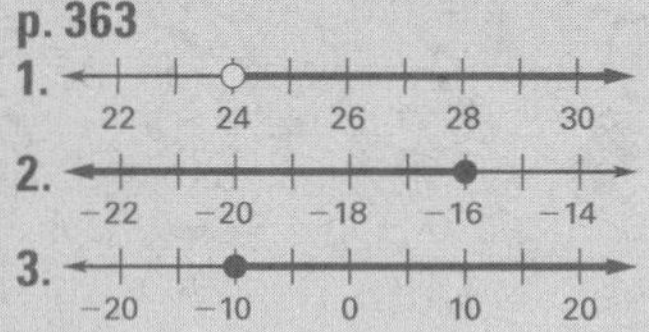

EXAMPLE 2 Solve an inequality using multiplication

Solve $\frac{x}{-6} < 7$. Graph your solution.

$\frac{x}{-6} < 7$	Write original inequality.
$-6 \cdot \frac{x}{-6} > -6 \cdot 7$	Multiply each side by -6. Reverse inequality symbol.
$x > -42$	Simplify.

AVOID ERRORS
Because you are multiplying by a negative number, be sure to reverse the inequality symbol.

▶ The solutions are all real numbers greater than -42. Check by substituting a number greater than -42 in the original inequality.

CHECK

$\frac{x}{-6} < 7$	Write original inequality.
$\frac{0}{-6} \stackrel{?}{<} 7$	Substitute 0 for x.
$0 < 7$ ✓	Solution checks.

USING DIVISION The rules for solving an inequality using division are similar to the rules for solving an inequality using multiplication.

KEY CONCEPT *For Your Notebook*

Division Property of Inequality

Words Dividing each side of an inequality by a *positive* number produces an equivalent inequality.

Dividing each side of an inequality by a *negative* number and *reversing the direction of the inequality symbol* produces an equivalent inequality.

Algebra If $a < b$ and $c > 0$, then $\frac{a}{c} < \frac{b}{c}$. If $a < b$ and $c < 0$, then $\frac{a}{c} > \frac{b}{c}$.

If $a > b$ and $c > 0$, then $\frac{a}{c} > \frac{b}{c}$. If $a > b$ and $c < 0$, then $\frac{a}{c} < \frac{b}{c}$.

This property is also true for inequalities involving $\leq$ and $\geq$.

EXAMPLE 3 Solve an inequality using division

Solve $-3x > 24$.

$-3x > 24$	Write original inequality.
$\frac{-3x}{-3} < \frac{24}{-3}$	Divide each side by -3. Reverse inequality symbol.
$x < -8$	Simplify.

Animated Algebra at classzone.com

Differentiated Instruction

Visual Learners The Division Property of Inequality is equivalent to the Multiplication Property of Inequality. Write both properties on the board. Then replace c with $\frac{1}{c}$ in the Multiplication Property of Inequality to show the equivalence. See also the *Algebra 1 Toolkit* for more strategies.

GUIDED PRACTICE for Examples 2 and 3

Solve the inequality. Graph your solution. 4–7. See margin for art.

4. $\frac{x}{-4} > 12$ $x < -48$

5. $\frac{m}{-7} < 1.6$ $m > -11.2$

6. $5v \geq 45$ $v \geq 9$

7. $-6n < 24$ $n > -4$

EXAMPLE 4 Standardized Test Practice

A student pilot plans to spend 80 hours on flight training to earn a private license. The student has saved $6000 for training. Which inequality can you use to find the possible hourly rates *r* that the student can afford to pay for training?

Ⓐ $80r \geq 6000$ Ⓑ $80r \leq 6000$ Ⓒ $6000r \geq 80$ Ⓓ $6000r \leq 80$

Solution

The total cost of training can be at most the amount of money that the student has saved. Write a verbal model for the situation. Then write an inequality.

ELIMINATE CHOICES
You need to multiply the hourly rate and the number of hours, which is 80, not 6000. So, you can eliminate choices C and D.

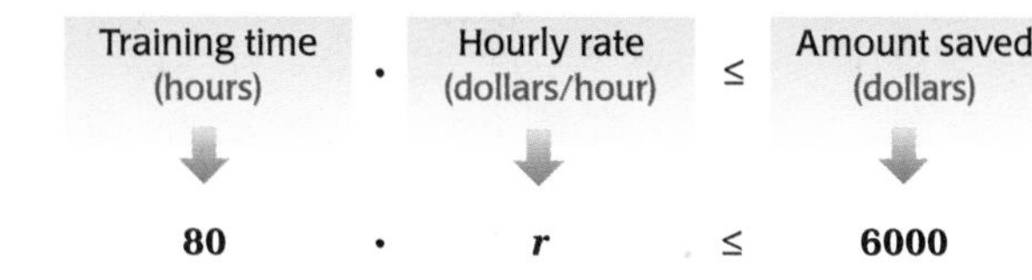

$$80 \cdot r \leq 6000$$

▶ The correct answer is B. Ⓐ Ⓑ Ⓒ Ⓓ

EXAMPLE 5 Solve a real-world problem

PILOTING In Example 4, what are the possible hourly rates that the student can afford to pay for training?

Solution

$80 \cdot r \leq 6000$ Write inequality.

$\frac{80r}{80} \leq \frac{6000}{80}$ Divide each side by 80.

$r \leq 75$ Simplify.

▶ The student can afford to pay at most $75 per hour for training.

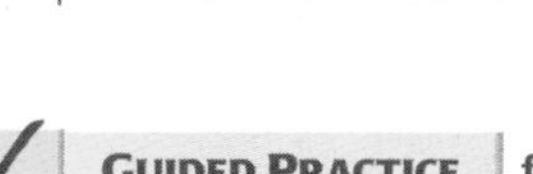

GUIDED PRACTICE for Examples 4 and 5

8. WHAT IF? In Example 5, suppose the student plans to spend 90 hours on flight training and has saved $6300. Write and solve an inequality to find the possible hourly rates that the student can afford to pay for training. $90r \leq 6300$, at most $70/h

Extra Example 4

A restaurant owner plans to place identical bouquets of flowers on 35 tables for opening night. The owner wants to spend no more than $400 for all the bouquets. Which inequality can you use to find the possible amounts of money *m* that the owner should budget for each bouquet of flowers? B

Ⓐ $400 \leq 35m$ Ⓑ $400 \geq 35m$
Ⓒ $400m \geq 35$ Ⓓ $400m \leq 35$

Extra Example 5

In Extra Example 4, what are the possible amounts of money the owner should budget for each bouquet of flowers? up to $11.42

Closing the Lesson

Have students summarize the major points of the lesson and answer the Essential Question: How do you solve inequalities using multiplication and division?

- The multiplication and division properties of inequality can be used to produce equivalent inequalities.
- Reverse the direction of the inequality symbol when multiplying or dividing by a negative number.

Multiply or divide each side of the inequality by the same number to isolate the variable and produce an equivalent inequality. Reverse the direction of the inequality symbol if you multiply or divide by a negative number.

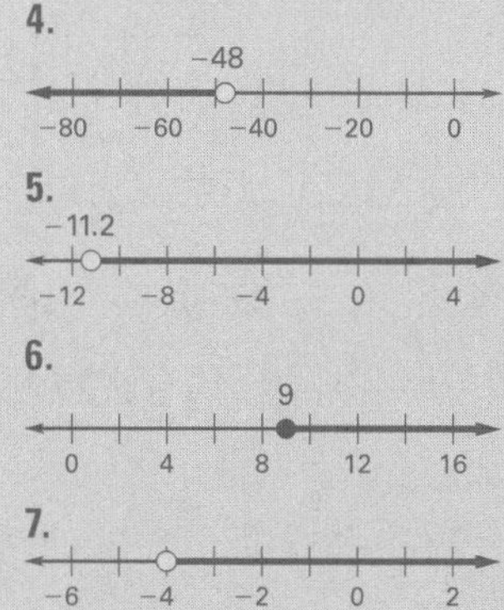

4 PRACTICE AND APPLY

Assignment Guide

Answer Transparencies available for all exercises

Basic:
Day 1: pp. 366–368
Exs. 1–18, 27–31, 36–40, 43–53 odd

Average:
Day 1: pp. 366–368
Exs. 1, 2, 15–34, 36–41, 44–52 even

Advanced:
Day 1: pp. 366–368
Exs. 1, 2, 17–27, 30–42*, 44–52 even

Block:
pp. 366–368
Exs. 1, 2, 15–34, 36–41, 44–52 even (with 6.1)

Differentiated Instruction

See *Algebra 1 Best Practices Toolkit* for suggestions on addressing the needs of a diverse classroom.

Homework Check

For a quick check of student understanding of key concepts, go over the following exercises:

Basic: 4, 6, 10, 36, 37

Average: 16, 18, 21, 37, 38

Advanced: 20, 24, 25, 38, 39

Extra Practice

- Student Edition, p. 943
- Chapter 6 Resource Book: Practice levels A, B, C, pp. 19–24

Practice Worksheet

An easily-readable reduced practice page (with answers) for this lesson can be found on p. 354C.

3–26. See Additional Answers beginning on p. AA1.

6.2 EXERCISES

HOMEWORK KEY
○ = WORKED-OUT SOLUTIONS on p. WS14 for Exs. 5, 9, and 39
★ = STANDARDIZED TEST PRACTICE Exs. 2, 27, 34, and 41
◆ = MULTIPLE REPRESENTATIONS Ex. 38

SKILL PRACTICE

A

1. **VOCABULARY** Which property are you using when you solve $5x \geq 30$ by dividing each side by 5? Division property of inequality

2. ★ **WRITING** Are $\frac{x}{-4} < -9$ and $x < 36$ equivalent inequalities? *Explain* your answer. No; when you multiply both sides of $\frac{x}{-4} < -9$ by -4 you must reverse the inequality symbol, producing the inequality $x > 36$.

EXAMPLES 1, 2, and 3 on pp. 363–364 for Exs. 3–29

SOLVING INEQUALITIES Solve the inequality. Graph your solution. 3–26. See margin for art.

3. $2p \geq 14$ $p \geq 7$
4. $\frac{x}{-3} < -10$ $x > 30$
5. $-6y < -36$ $y > 6$
6. $40 > \frac{w}{5}$ $w < 200$
7. $\frac{q}{4} < 7$ $q < 28$
8. $72 \leq 9r$ $r \geq 8$
9. $\frac{g}{6} > -20$ $g > -120$
10. $-11m \leq -22$ $m \geq 2$
11. $-90 \geq 4t$ $t \leq -22.5$
12. $\frac{n}{3} < -9$ $n < -27$
13. $60 \leq -12s$ $s \leq -5$
14. $\frac{v}{-4} \geq -8$ $v \leq 32$
15. $-8.4f > 2.1$ $f < -0.25$
16. $\frac{d}{-2} \leq 18.6$ $d \geq -37.2$
17. $9.6 < -16c$ $c < -0.6$
18. $0.07 \geq \frac{k}{7}$ $k \leq 0.49$
19. $-1.5 \geq 6z$ $z \leq -0.25$
20. $\frac{x}{-5} \leq -7.5$ $x \geq 37.5$
21. $1.02 < -3j$ $j < -0.34$
22. $\frac{y}{-4.5} \geq -10$ $y \leq 45$
23. $\frac{r}{-30} < 1.8$ $r > -54$
24. $1.9 \leq -5p$ $p \leq -0.38$
25. $\frac{m}{0.6} > -40$ $m > -24$
26. $-2t > -1.22$ $t < 0.61$

27. ★ **WRITING** How is solving $ax > b$ where $a > 0$ similar to solving $ax > b$ where $a < 0$? How is it different? In both cases, you divide both sides of the inequality by a; when $a > 0$, you do not reverse the inequality symbol, but when $a < 0$, you do.

ERROR ANALYSIS ***Describe*** **and correct the error in solving the inequality.**

28.

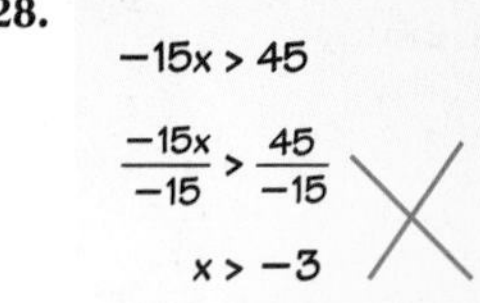

The inequality symbol was not reversed when dividing both sides by -15; $\frac{-15x}{-15} < \frac{45}{-15}$, $x < -3$.

29.

$\frac{x}{9} \leq -7$

$9 \cdot \frac{x}{9} \leq 9 \cdot (-7)$

$x \geq -63$

29. Both sides of the inequality were multiplied by a positive number, so the inequality symbol should not have been reversed; $x \leq -63$.

B

TRANSLATING SENTENCES In Exercises 30–33, write the verbal sentence as an inequality. Then solve the inequality and graph your solution. 30–33. See margin for art.

30. The product of 8 and x is greater than 50. $8x > 50$; $x > \frac{25}{4}$
31. The product of -15 and y is less than or equal to 90. $-15y \leq 90$; $y \geq -6$
32. The quotient of v and -9 is less than -18. $\frac{v}{-9} < -18$; $v > 162$
33. The quotient of w and 24 is greater than or equal to $-\frac{1}{6}$. $\frac{w}{24} \geq -\frac{1}{6}$; $w \geq -4$

34. ★ **OPEN-ENDED** Write an inequality in the form $ax < b$ such that the solutions are all real numbers greater than 4. *Sample answer:* $-3x < -12$

30. 31.

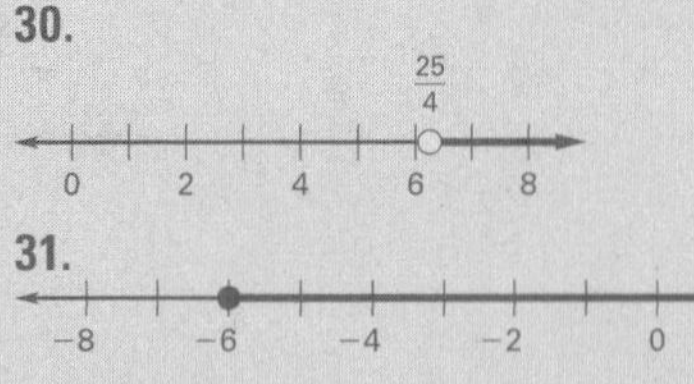

32. 33.

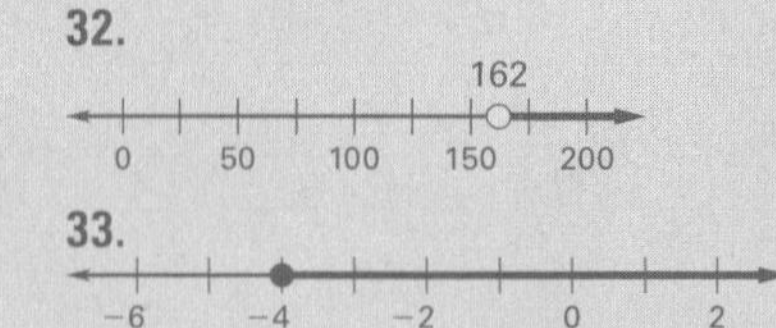

35. **CHALLENGE** For the given values of a and b, tell whether the solution of $ax > b$ consists of *positive numbers, negative numbers,* or *both. Explain.* See margin.

a. $a < 0, b > 0$ b. $a > 0, b > 0$ c. $a > 0, b < 0$ d. $a < 0, b < 0$

PROBLEM SOLVING

EXAMPLES 4 and 5 on p. 365 for Exs. 36–39

36. **MUSIC** You have \$90 to buy CDs for your friend's party. The CDs cost \$18 each. What are the possible numbers of CDs that you can buy? at most 5 CDs

@HomeTutor for problem solving help at classzone.com

37. **JOB SKILLS** You apply for a job that requires the ability to type 40 words per minute. You practice typing on a keyboard for 5 minutes. The average number of words you type per minute must at least meet the job requirement. What are the possible numbers of words that you can type in 5 minutes in order to meet or exceed the job requirement? at least 200 words

@HomeTutor for problem solving help at classzone.com

38. **MULTIPLE REPRESENTATIONS** You are stacking books on a shelf that has a height of 66 centimeters. Each book has a thickness of 4 centimeters.

a. **Using a Model** Use a concrete model to find the possible numbers of books that you can stack as follows: Cut strips of paper 4 centimeters wide to represent the books. Then place the strips one above the other until they form a column no taller than 66 centimeters. at most 16 books

b. **Writing an Inequality** Write and solve an inequality to find the possible numbers of books that you can stack. $4x \le 66$, $x \le 16.5$, at most 16 books

c. **Drawing a Graph** Write and graph an equation that gives the height y of stacked books as a function of the number x of books. Then graph $y = 66$ in the same coordinate plane. To find the possible numbers of books that you can stack, identify the integer x-coordinates of the points on the first graph that lie *on or below* the graph of $y = 66$. See margin.

d. **Choosing a Method** Suppose the shelf has a height of 100 centimeters. Which method would you use to find the possible numbers of books, *a concrete model, solving an inequality,* or *drawing a graph*? *Explain.* Answers may vary.

39. **MANUFACTURING** A manufacturer of architectural moldings recommends that the length of a piece be no more than 15 times its minimum width w (in inches) in order to prevent cracking. For the piece shown, what could the values of w be? at least 3.2

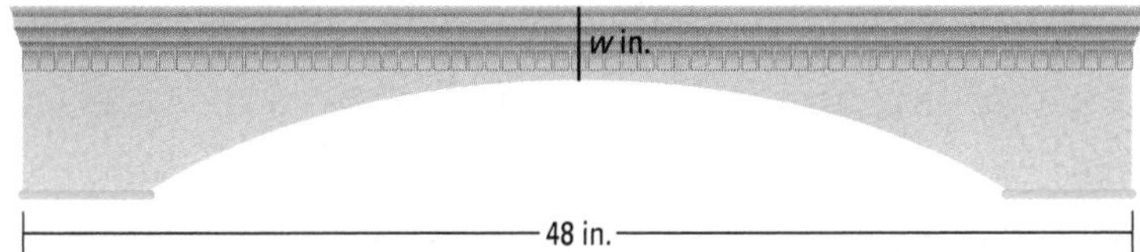

40. **RECREATION** A water-skiing instructor recommends that a boat pulling a beginning skier have a speed less than 18 miles per hour. Write and solve an inequality that you can use to find the possible distances d (in miles) that a beginner can travel in 45 minutes of practice time. $d < 18(0.75)$, $d < 13.5$, less than 13.5 mi

Avoiding Common Errors

Exercises 3–26 Watch for students who do not reverse the inequality symbol when multiplying by a negative number. Suggest that students write the phrase "reverse the symbol" as soon as they see that an exercise has a negative coefficient.

Reading Strategy

Exercise 34 Suggest to students that they read this exercise carefully. Urge them to pay attention to the inequality symbol and how it is connected to the solutions of the inequality.

Study Strategy

Exercise 35 Remind students that some challenge problems may be more manageable if they substitute numbers for the variables and use their observations to explain their reasoning. Tell them that sometimes they will need to substitute several numbers for the variables before they see a pattern.

35a. Negative; when you divide both sides of the inequality by the negative number a, the inequality symbol becomes < and $\frac{b}{a}$ is negative, because $(+) \div (-) = (-)$. Thus, the answer is in the form $x <$ (a negative number), so x itself must be negative.

35b. Positive; when you divide both sides of the inequality by the positive number a, the inequality symbol stays the same and $\frac{b}{a}$ is positive, because $(+) \div (+) = (+)$. Thus, the answer is in the form $x >$ (a positive number), so x itself must be positive.

35c. Both; when you divide both sides of the inequality by the positive number a, the inequality symbol stays the same and $\frac{b}{a}$ is negative, because $(-) \div (+) = (-)$. Thus, the answer is in the form $x >$ (a negative number), so x itself can be either positive or negative (or 0).

35d. Both; when you divide both sides of the inequality by the negative number a, the inequality symbol becomes < and $\frac{b}{a}$ is positive, because $(-) \div (-) = (+)$. Thus, the answer is in the form $x <$ (a positive number), so x itself can be either positive or negative (or 0).

38c. $y = 4x$;

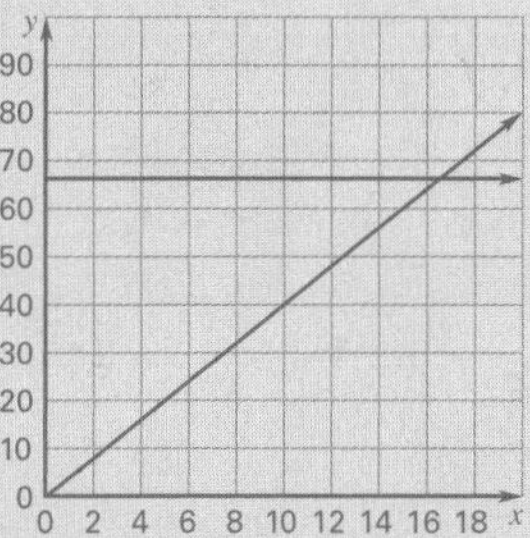

0, 1, 2, 3, 4, 5, 6, 7, 8, 9, 10, 11, 12, 13, 14, 15, 16

5 ASSESS AND RETEACH

Daily Homework Quiz

Transparency Available

Solve each inequality. Graph your solution.

1. $-72 < 8p$ $p > -9$

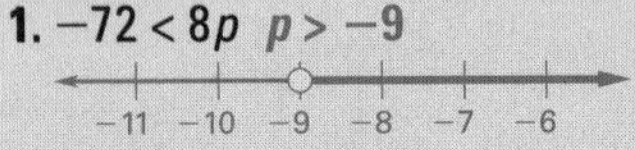

2. $\frac{w}{-6} \geq -5$ $w \leq 30$

0 10 20 30 40 50

3. A fitness walking group walks 4 days each week with a goal of at least 12 miles per week. Write and solve an inequality to find the average number of possible miles m the group should walk each day to meet its goal. $4m \geq 12$; an average of at least 3 miles per day

Available at **classzone.com**

Diagnosis/Remediation

- Practice A, B, C in Chapter 6 Resource Book, pp. 19–24
- Study Guide in Chapter 6 Resource Book, pp. 25–26
- Practice Workbook, pp. 87–89
- @HomeTutor

Challenge

Additional challenge is available in the Chapter 6 Resource Book, p. 29.

Quiz

An easily-readable reduced copy of the quiz (with answers) on Lessons 6.1–6.2 from the Assessment Book can be found on p. 345G.

41b, Quiz 1–9. See Additional Answers beginning on p. AA1.

41c. $h \leq 23$ horses; the area of the new corral is $(80 + 15)(82 + 15) = 9215$ square feet. Find the possible numbers, h, of horses the corral can hold by solving the inequality $9215 \geq 400h$; $h \leq 23.04$.

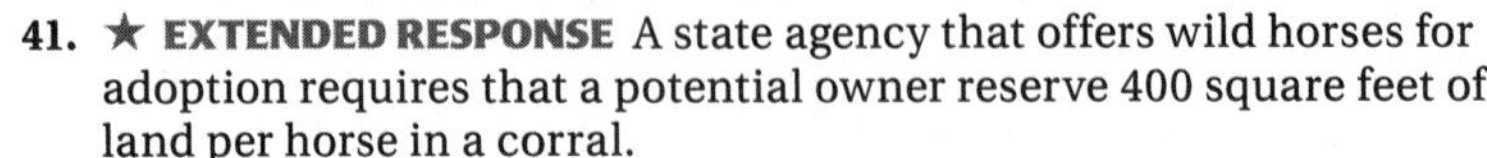

41. ★ **EXTENDED RESPONSE** A state agency that offers wild horses for adoption requires that a potential owner reserve 400 square feet of land per horse in a corral.

 a. **Solve** A farmer has a rectangular corral whose length is 80 feet and whose width is 82 feet. Write and solve an inequality to find the possible numbers h of horses that the corral can hold. $400h \leq 6560$, $h \leq 16.4$, no more than 16 horses

 b. **Explain** If the farmer increases the length and width of the corral by 20 feet each, will the corral be able to hold only 1 more horse? *Explain* your answer without calculating the new area of the corral. See margin.

 c. **Calculate** The farmer decides to increase the length and width of the corral by 15 feet each. Find the possible numbers of horses that the corral can hold. Your answer should include the following:

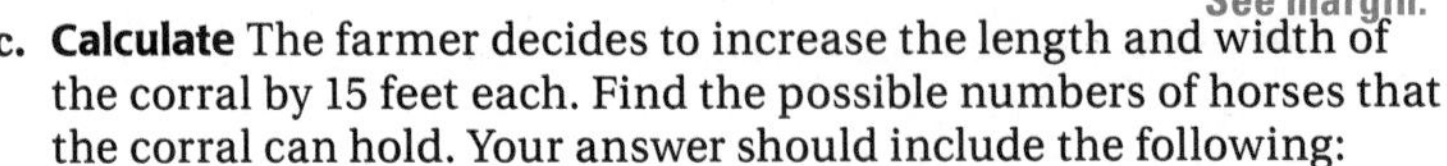

 - a calculation of the new area of the corral
 - a description of your steps for solving the problem

C 42. **CHALLENGE** An electronics store is selling a laptop computer for \$1050. You can spend no more than \$900 for the laptop, so you wait for it to go on sale. Also, you plan to use a store coupon for 5% off the sale price. For which decreases in price will you consider buying the laptop? decreases of at least \$102.63

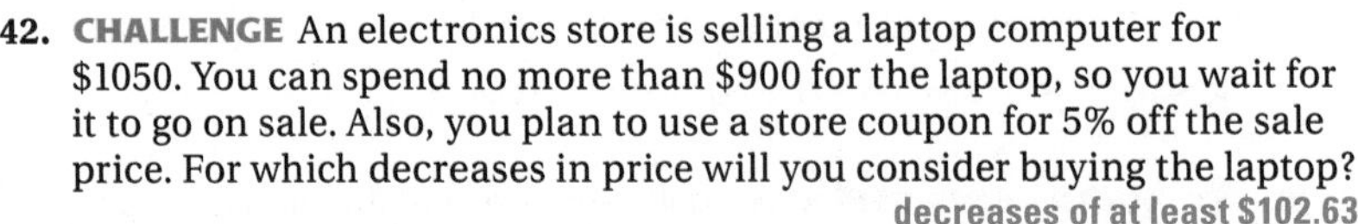

ILLINOIS MIXED REVIEW

TEST PRACTICE at classzone.com

43. The cost of parking in a parking garage is described by the function $c(x) = 2(x - 2) + 3$ in which $c(x)$ is the cost and x is the time in hours. If you need to spend less than \$10 for parking, what is the maximum whole number of hours you can park in the garage? C

 Ⓐ 2 h Ⓑ 3 h Ⓒ 5 h Ⓓ 6 h

44. A couple decided that they would put 12% of their combined annual income of \$89,500 into a retirement fund. Approximately how much will the couple put into the retirement fund? D

 Ⓐ \$110 Ⓑ \$1,074 Ⓒ \$7,458 Ⓓ \$10,740

QUIZ *for Lessons 6.1–6.2*

Solve the inequality. Graph your solution. 1–9. See margin for art.

1. $x + 8 \geq -5$ *(p. 356)* $x \geq -13$
2. $y + 6 < 14$ *(p. 356)* $y < 8$
3. $-8 \leq v - 5$ *(p. 356)* $v \geq -3$
4. $w - 11 > 2$ *(p. 356)* $w > 13$
5. $-40 < -5r$ *(p. 363)* $r < 8$
6. $-93 < 3s$ *(p. 363)* $s > -31$
7. $-2m \geq 26$ *(p. 363)* $m \leq -13$
8. $\frac{n}{-4} > -7$ *(p. 363)* $n < 28$
9. $\frac{c}{6} \leq -8$ *(p. 363)* $c \leq -48$
10. **FOOD PREPARATION** You need to make at least 150 sandwiches for a charity event. You can make 3 sandwiches per minute. How long will it take you to make the number of sandwiches you need? *(p. 363)* at least 50 min

6.3 Solve Multi-Step Inequalities

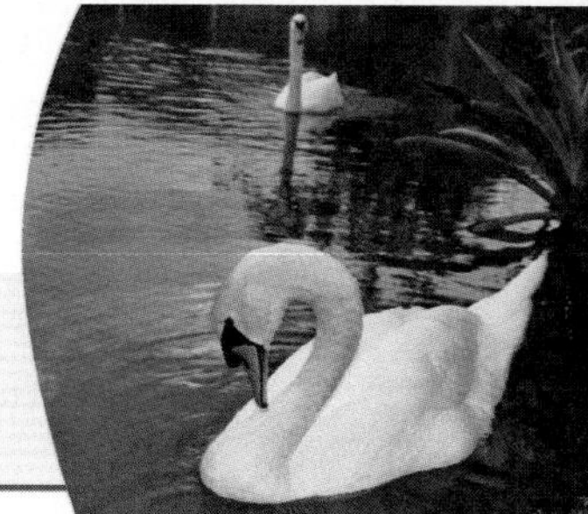

Before You solved one-step inequalities.
Now You will solve multi-step inequalities.
Why? So you can compare animal habitats, as in Ex. 39.

Key Vocabulary
- **inequality,** *p. 21*

The steps for solving two-step and multi-step equations can be applied to linear inequalities. For inequalities, be sure to reverse the inequality symbol when multiplying or dividing by a negative number.

EXAMPLE 1 Solve a two-step inequality

Solve $3x - 7 < 8$. Graph your solution.

$3x - 7 < 8$	Write original inequality.
$3x < 15$	Add 7 to each side.
$x < 5$	Divide each side by 3.

▶ The solutions are all real numbers less than 5. Check by substituting a number less than 5 in the original inequality.

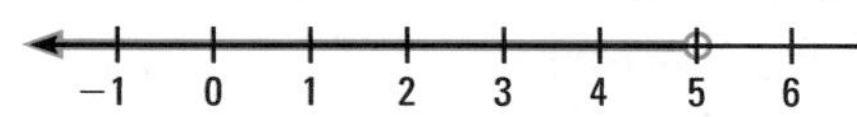

CHECK

$3x - 7 < 8$	Write original inequality.
$3(0) - 7 \overset{?}{<} 8$	Substitute 0 for *x*.
$-7 < 8$ ✓	Solution checks.

EXAMPLE 2 Solve a multi-step inequality

Solve $-0.6(x - 5) \le 15$.

$-0.6(x - 5) \le 15$	Write original inequality.
$-0.6x + 3 \le 15$	Distributive property
$-0.6x \le 12$	Subtract 3 from each side.
$x \ge -20$	Divide each side by -0.6. Reverse inequality symbol.

GUIDED PRACTICE for Examples 1 and 2

Solve the inequality. Graph your solution. 1–3. See margin on p. 371 for art.

1. $2x - 5 \le 23$ $x \le 14$
2. $-6y + 5 \le -16$ $y \ge 3.5$
3. $-\frac{1}{4}(p - 12) > -2$ $p < 20$

1 PLAN AND PREPARE

Warm-Up Exercises

Transparency Available

1. Is 4 a solution of the inequality $2a - 1.5 \ge 6$? yes
2. Solve the equation $\frac{f}{4} + 8 = 7$. -4
3. All hats sell for the same price at a swap meet. You buy one pair of sunglasses for \$7 and 2 hats. You spend \$26.50. How much did each hat cost? \$9.75

Notetaking Guide

Transparency Available

Promotes interactive learning and notetaking skills, pp. 134–136.

Pacing

Basic: 1 day
Average: 1 day
Advanced: 1 day
Block: 0.5 block with 6.4
- See *Teaching Guide/Lesson Plan.*

2 FOCUS AND MOTIVATE

Essential Question

Big Idea 1, p. 355

How do you solve multi-step inequalities? Tell students they will learn how to answer this question by using the distributive property and the properties of inequality.

Resource Planning Guide

Chapter Resource Book
- Teaching Guide/Lesson Plan (pp. 30–31)
- Practice levels A, B, C (pp. 32–37)
- Study Guide (pp. 38–39)
- Catch-up for Absent Students (p. 40)
- Application (p. 41)
- Challenge (p. 42)

Workbooks
- Notetaking Guide (pp. 134–136)
- Practice Workbook (pp. 90–92)

Teaching Options
- **Power Presentations CD-ROM** provides dynamic electronic teaching resources for the classroom.
- **Activity Generator CD-ROM** provides editable activities for all ability levels.

Interactive Technology
- Easy Planner
- Power Presentations CD-ROM
- Activity Generator CD-ROM
- Animated Algebra
- Test Generator CD-ROM
- Online Quiz
- eWorkbook
- eEdition
- @HomeTutor

Resources for English Learners
- Quick Reference for English Learners
- Spanish Study Guide
- Multi-Language Visual Glossary
- Student Resources in Spanish

See also the *Algebra 1 Toolkit* for more strategies for meeting individual needs.

EXAMPLE 3 Solve a multi-step inequality

ANOTHER WAY

You can also solve the inequality by subtracting 17 and $6x$ from each side, as follows:

$$6x - 7 > 2x + 17$$
$$6x - 24 > 2x$$
$$-24 > -4x$$
$$6 < x$$

The inequality $6 < x$ is equivalent to $x > 6$.

Solve $6x - 7 > 2x + 17$. Graph your solution.

$6x - 7 > 2x + 17$	**Write original inequality.**
$6x > 2x + 24$	**Add 7 to each side.**
$4x > 24$	**Subtract $2x$ from each side.**
$x > 6$	**Divide each side by 4.**

▶ The solutions are all real numbers greater than 6.

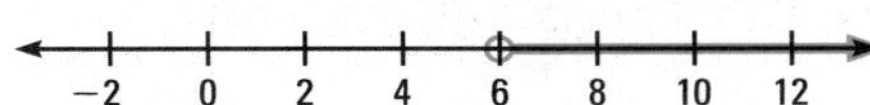

NUMBER OF SOLUTIONS If an inequality is equivalent to an inequality that is true, such as $-3 < 0$, then the solutions of the inequality are *all real numbers.* If an inequality is equivalent to an inequality that is false, such as $4 < -1$, then the inequality has *no solution.*

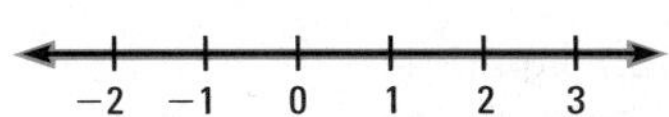

Graph of an inequality whose solutions are all real numbers

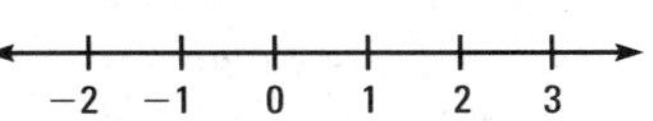

Graph of an inequality that has no solution

EXAMPLE 4 Identify the number of solutions of an inequality

Solve the inequality, if possible.

a. $14x + 5 < 7(2x - 3)$ **b.** $12x - 1 > 6(2x - 1)$

Solution

a. $14x + 5 < 7(2x - 3)$	**Write original inequality.**
$14x + 5 < 14x - 21$	**Distributive property**
$5 < -21$	**Subtract $14x$ from each side.**

▶ There are no solutions because $5 < -21$ is false.

b. $12x - 1 > 6(2x - 1)$	**Write original inequality.**
$12x - 1 > 12x - 6$	**Distributive property**
$-1 > -6$	**Subtract $12x$ from each side.**

▶ All real numbers are solutions because $-1 > -6$ is true.

GUIDED PRACTICE for Examples 3 and 4

Solve the inequality, if possible. Graph your solution. 4–6. See margin for art.

4. $5x - 12 \le 3x - 4$ $x \le 4$

5. $5(m + 5) < 5m + 17$ no solution

6. $1 - 8s \le -4(2s - 1)$ all real numbers

Motivating the Lesson

Ask students if the typical problems they solve in everyday life tend to be one-step or multi-step problems. Invite them to support their views by providing examples. After a short discussion, tell students that many people have trouble solving multi-step problems because they do not know where to begin. Tell them that by learning how to solve a multi-step problem, they will be able to break a problem into its parts, recognize key words, and choose from a variety of methods to solve the problem.

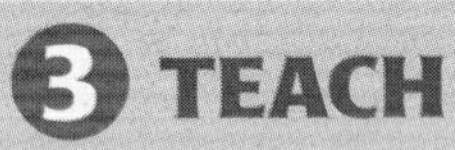

Extra Example 1

Solve $-7x + 2 < -5$. Graph your solution. all real numbers greater than 1

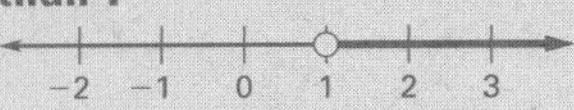

Extra Example 2

Solve $\frac{1}{3}(3x + 6) \ge -1$. $x \ge -3$

Key Question to Ask for Example 2

- Is -21 a solution of the inequality? Explain. No. The inequality is not true for $x = -21$ because $-21 < -20$ and the solutions are all real numbers greater than -20.

Extra Example 3

Solve $9x + 6 \le 6x + 21$. Graph your solution. all real numbers less than or equal to 5

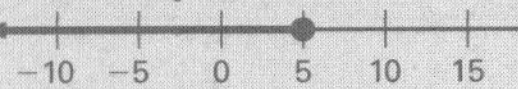

Differentiated Instruction

Auditory Learners While discussing **Example 3**, students follow the same steps for solving a multi-step inequality that they would use for solving a multi-step equation. Ask them if there are any differences between solving an inequality and the related equation. Stress that there is an additional step when solving an inequality; they must remember to reverse the symbol when multiplying or dividing by a negative number.

See also the *Algebra 1 Toolkit* for more strategies.

EXAMPLE 5 Solve a multi-step problem

CAR WASH Use the sign shown. A gas station charges $.10 less per gallon of gasoline if a customer also gets a car wash. What are the possible amounts (in gallons) of gasoline that you can buy if you also get a car wash and can spend at most $20?

ANOTHER WAY
For an alternative method for solving the problem in Example 5, turn to page 375 for the Problem Solving Workshop.

Solution

Because you are getting a car wash, you will pay $2.09 − $.10 = $1.99 per gallon of gasoline. Let g be the amount (in gallons) of gasoline that you buy.

STEP 1 **Write** a verbal model. Then write an inequality.

Price of gasoline (dollars/gallon)	·	Amount of gasoline (gallons)	+	Price of car wash (dollars)	≤	Maximum amount (dollars)
1.99	·	g	+	**8**	≤	**20**

STEP 2 **Solve** the inequality.

$1.99g + 8 \le 20$ — Write inequality.

$1.99g \le 12$ — Subtract 8 from each side.

$g \le 6.03015\ldots$ — Divide each side by 1.99.

▶ You can buy up to slightly more than 6 gallons of gasoline.

CHECK You can use a table to check the reasonableness of your answer.

The table shows that you will pay $19.94 for exactly 6 gallons of gasoline. Because $19.94 is less than $20, it is reasonable to conclude that you can buy slightly more than 6 gallons of gasoline.

Gasoline (gal)	Total amount spent (dollars)
0	8.00
1	9.99
2	11.98
3	13.97
4	15.96
5	17.95
6	19.94

✓ **GUIDED PRACTICE** for Example 5

7. **WHAT IF?** In Example 5, suppose that a car wash costs $9 and gasoline regularly costs $2.19 per gallon. What are the possible amounts (in gallons) of gasoline that you can buy? at most 5.26 gal

8. **CAMP COSTS** You are saving money for a summer camp that costs $1800. You have saved $500 so far, and you have 14 more weeks to save the total amount. What are the possible average amounts of money that you can save per week in order to have a total of at least $1800 saved? at least $92.86/wk

Extra Example 4

Solve the inequality, if possible.

a. $8x - 4 \ge 4(2x - 1)$ all real numbers because $-4 \ge -4$ is true

b. $-2x + 9 < -2(x - 3)$ no solutions because $9 < 6$ is false

Extra Example 5

You can work at most 24 hours per week as a nurse's aid. So far this week you have worked 7 hours. If the remaining shifts for the week are each 4 hours long, how many possible full shifts can you work? You can work up to 4 full shifts.

Closing the Lesson

Have students summarize the major points of the lesson and answer the Essential Question: How do you solve multi-step inequalities?

- You can solve multi-step inequalities by applying the same steps used for solving multi-step equations, with the additional step of reversing an inequality symbol if you multiply or divide by a negative number.

Use the distributive property and the properties of inequality to produce equivalent inequalities. Reverse the direction of the inequality symbol when dividing or multiplying by a negative number. If you reach an inequality that is false, there are no solutions; if you reach an inequality that is always true, then all real numbers are solutions.

pp. 369–370

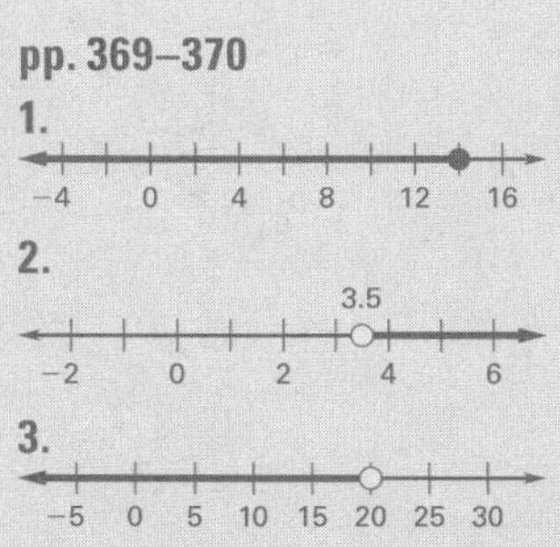

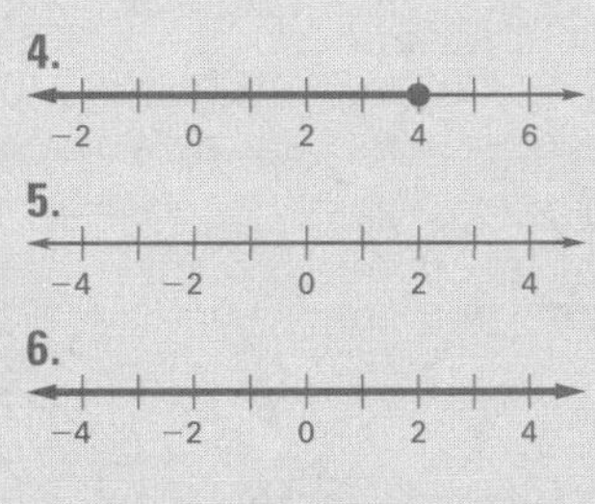

6.3 EXERCISES

HOMEWORK KEY
○ = WORKED-OUT SOLUTIONS on p. WS14 for Exs. 5, 19, and 39
★ = STANDARDIZED TEST PRACTICE Exs. 2, 33, 39, 40, and 42
◆ = MULTIPLE REPRESENTATIONS Ex. 41

4 PRACTICE AND APPLY

Assignment Guide

Answer Transparencies available for all exercises

Basic:
Day 1: EP p. 940 Exs. 9–14
pp. 372–374
Exs. 1–10, 17–24, 29, 30, 37–41, 44–56 even

Average:
Day 1: pp. 372–374
Exs. 1, 2, 4–14 even, 15, 16, 21–27 odd, 29–34, 37–42, 44, 45–55 odd

Advanced:
Day 1: pp. 372–374
Exs. 1, 2, 4–8 even, 13, 14, 22–28 even, 29–36*, 38–43*, 44–56 even

Block:
pp. 372–374
Exs. 1, 2, 4–14 even, 15, 16, 21–27 odd, 29–34, 37–42, 44, 45–55 odd (with 6.4)

Differentiated Instruction

See *Algebra 1 Best Practices Toolkit* for suggestions on addressing the needs of a diverse classroom.

Homework Check

For a quick check of student understanding of key concepts, go over the following exercises:

Basic: 3, 6, 9, 20, 37
Average: 4, 6, 12, 25, 38
Advanced: 4, 8, 13, 26, 39

Extra Practice

- Student Edition, p. 943
- Chapter 6 Resource Book: Practice levels A, B, C, pp. 32–37

Practice Worksheet

An easily-readable reduced practice page (with answers) for this lesson can be found on p. 354D.

2. An inequality has no solutions if it is equivalent to a false inequality such as $0 > 2$. All real numbers are solutions of the inequality if it is equivalent to a true inequality such as $0 < 2$.

SKILL PRACTICE

A

1. **VOCABULARY** Copy and complete: The inequalities $3x - 1 < 11$, $3x < 12$, and $x < 4$ are called __?__. equivalent inequalities

2. ★ **WRITING** How do you know whether an inequality has no solutions? How do you know whether the solutions are all real numbers? See margin.

EXAMPLES 1, 2, and 3 on pp. 369–370 for Exs. 3–16

SOLVING INEQUALITIES **Solve the inequality. Graph your solution.** 3–14. See margin for art.

3. $2x - 3 > 7$ $x > 5$
4. $5y + 9 \leq 4$ $y \leq -1$
5. $8v - 3 \geq -11$ $v \geq -1$
6. $3(w + 12) < 0$ $w < -12$
7. $7(r - 3) \geq -13$ $r \geq 1\frac{1}{7}$
8. $2(s + 4) \leq 16$ $s \leq 4$
9. $4 - 2m > 7 - 3m$ $m > 3$
10. $8n - 2 > 17n + 9$ $n < -1\frac{2}{9}$
11. $-10p > 6p - 8$ $p < \frac{1}{2}$
12. $4 - \frac{1}{2}q \leq 33 - q$ $q \leq 58$
13. $-\frac{2}{3}d - 2 < \frac{1}{3}d + 8$ $d > -10$
14. $8 - \frac{4}{5}f > -14 - 2f$ $f > -18\frac{1}{3}$

ERROR ANALYSIS ***Describe*** **and correct the error in solving the inequality.** 15, 16. See margin.

15.
$17 - 3x \geq 56$
$-3x \geq 39$
$x \geq -13$ ✗

16.
$-4(2x - 3) < 28$
$-8x - 12 < 28$
$-8x < 40$
$x > -5$ ✗

EXAMPLE 4 on p. 370 for Exs. 17–28

SOLVING INEQUALITIES **Solve the inequality, if possible.**

17. $3p - 5 > 2p + p - 7$ all real numbers
18. $5d - 8d - 4 \leq -4 + 3d$ $d \geq 0$
19. $3(s - 4) \geq 2(s - 6)$ $s \geq 0$
20. $2(t - 3) > 2t - 8$ all real numbers
21. $5(b + 9) \leq 5b + 45$ all real numbers
22. $2(4c - 7) \geq 8(c - 3)$ all real numbers
23. $6(x + 3) < 5x + 18 + x$ no solution
24. $4 + 9y - 3 \geq 3(3y + 2)$ no solution
25. $2.2h + 0.4 \leq 2(1.1h - 0.1)$ no solution
26. $9.5j - 6 + 5.5j \geq 3(5j - 2)$ all real numbers
27. $\frac{1}{5}(4m + 10) < \frac{4}{5}m + 2$ no solution
28. $\frac{3}{4}(8n - 4) < -3(1 - 2n)$ no solution

B

TRANSLATING PHRASES **Translate the verbal phrase into an inequality. Then solve the inequality and graph your solution.** 29–32. See margin for art.

29. Four more than the product of 3 and x is less than 40. $3x + 4 < 40$; $x < 12$
30. Twice the sum of x and 8 is greater than or equal to -36. $2(x + 8) \geq -36$; $x \geq -26$
31. The sum of $5x$ and $2x$ is greater than the difference of $9x$ and 4. $5x + 2x > 9x - 4$; $x < 2$
32. The product of 6 and the difference of $6x$ and 3 is less than or equal to the product of -2 and the sum of 4 and $8x$. $6(6x - 3) \leq -2(4 + 8x)$; $x \leq \frac{5}{26}$

33. ★ **MULTIPLE CHOICE** For which values of a and b are all the solutions of $ax + b > 0$ positive? C

Ⓐ $a > 0, b > 0$ Ⓑ $a < 0, b < 0$ Ⓒ $a > 0, b < 0$ Ⓓ $a < 0, b = 0$

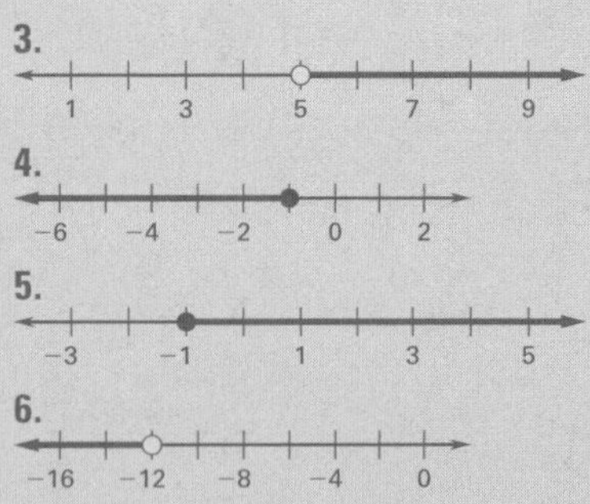

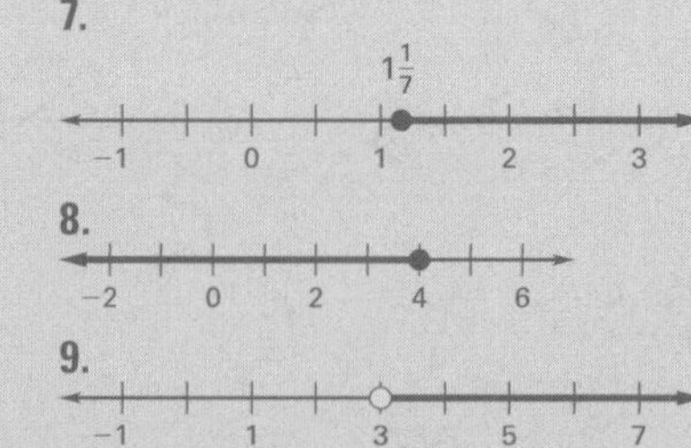

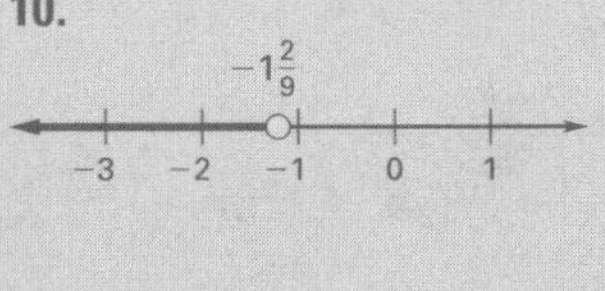

GEOMETRY Write and solve an inequality to find the possible values of x.

34. Area > 81 square feet $9(x+2) > 81;\ x > 7$

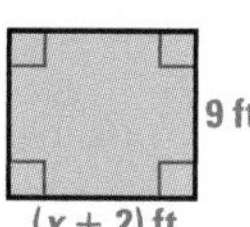

35. Area ≤ 44 square centimeters $\frac{1}{2} \cdot 8(x+1) \le 44;\ x \le 10$

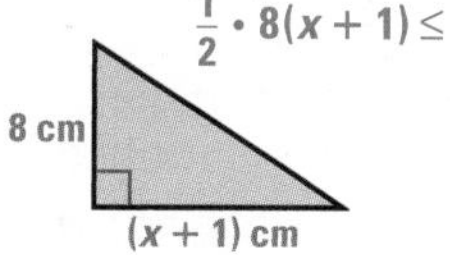

C 36. **CHALLENGE** For which value of a are all the solutions of $2(x-5) \ge 3x + a$ less than or equal to 5? -15

Problem Solving

EXAMPLE 5 A on p. 371 for Exs. 37–40

37. **CD BURNING** A blank CD can hold 70 minutes of music. So far you have burned 25 minutes of music onto the CD. You estimate that each song lasts 4 minutes. What are the possible numbers of additional songs that you can burn onto the CD? at most 11 songs

@HomeTutor for problem solving help at classzone.com

38. **BUSINESS** You spend \$46 on supplies to make wooden ornaments and plan to sell the ornaments for \$8.50 each. What are the possible numbers of ornaments that you can sell in order for your profit to be positive? at least 6 ornaments

@HomeTutor for problem solving help at classzone.com

39a. Up to 6 swans; the area of the habitat is (20 feet) (50 feet) = 1000 square feet. 500 square feet are needed for the first two swans and the remaining 1000 − 500 = 500 square feet can hold up to 500 ÷ 125 = 4 more swans; so, the maximum number of swans is 2 + 4 = 6 swans.

39. ★ **SHORT RESPONSE** A zookeeper is designing a rectangular habitat for swans, as shown. The zookeeper needs to reserve 500 square feet for the first 2 swans and 125 square feet for each additional swan.

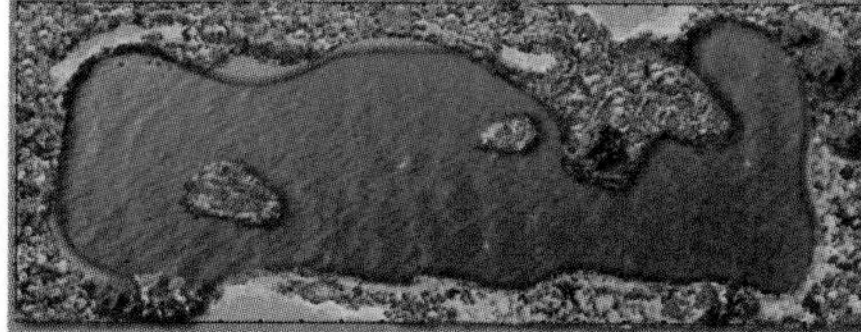

a. **Calculate** What are the possible numbers of swans that the habitat can hold? *Explain* how you got your answer. See margin.

b. **Compare** Suppose that the zookeeper increases both the length and width of the habitat by 20 feet. What are the possible numbers of additional swans that the habitat can hold? at most 14 more swans

40. ★ **MULTIPLE CHOICE** A gym is offering a trial membership for 3 months by discounting the regular monthly rate by \$50. You will consider joining the gym if the total cost of the trial membership is less than \$100. Which inequality can you use to find the possible regular monthly rates that you are willing to pay? C

(A) $3x - 50 < 100$ (B) $3x - 50 > 100$

(C) $3(x - 50) < 100$ (D) $3(x - 50) > 100$

Avoiding Common Errors

Exercises 3–14 Students should always check that their written solution for an inequality matches the graph of the solution. Specifically, they should check that their inequality uses an open circle for < or > and a closed circle for ≤ or ≥.

Exercises 17–28 When using the distributive property, students who use mental math sometimes fail to distribute the factor to all the numbers inside the parentheses. Encourage all students to get into the habit of checking for this error.

Reading Strategy

Exercises 37–43 As in the previous lessons, students should read the problems carefully in order to determine which inequality symbol to use. Remind them to look for key words and phrases, such as "no more than," "at most," and "at least."

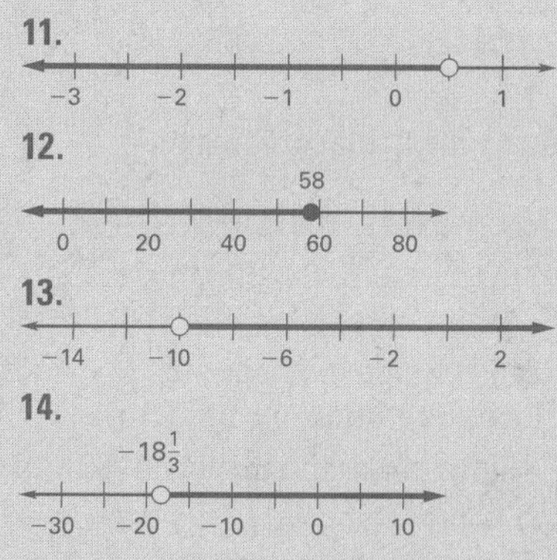

15. The inequality symbol was not reversed when dividing both sides by −3; $x \le -13$.

16. The distributive property was not used correctly, $-8x + 12 < 28$, $-8x < 16$, $x > -2$.

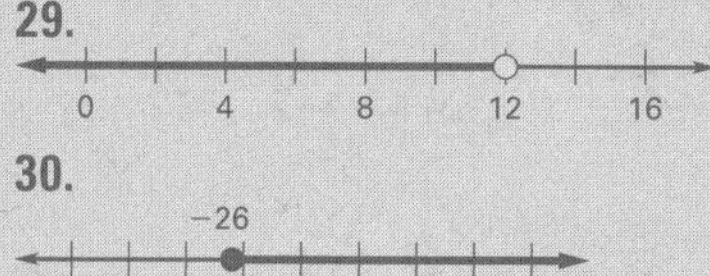

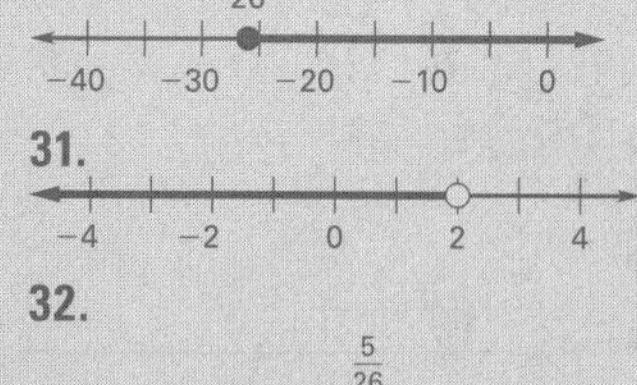

5 ASSESS AND RETEACH

Daily Homework Quiz

Transparency Available

1. Solve $3(x + 8) < 9$. Graph your solution. **all real numbers less than -5**

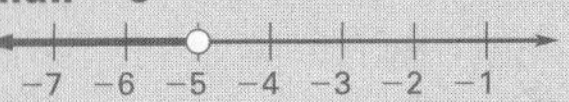

Solve the inequality, if possible.

3. $6k + 1 > 3(2k - 3)$ **all real numbers because $1 > -9$ is true**

4. $5(a - 2) < 5a - 14$ **no solutions because $-10 < -14$ is false**

5. A box of cat treats contains at least 50 treats. So far you have fed your cats 18 treats. If you want the box of treats to last 8 days, what are the possible average numbers of treats you can feed the cats per day? **an average of no more than 4 treats per day**

Available at **classzone.com**

Diagnosis/Remediation

- Practice A, B, C in Chapter 6 Resource Book, pp. 32–37
- Study Guide in Chapter 6 Resource Book, pp. 38–39
- Practice Workbook, pp. 90–92
- @HomeTutor

Challenge

Additional challenge is available in the Chapter 6 Resource Book, p. 42.

41a, 42c. See Additional Answers beginning on p. AA1.

B

41. **MULTIPLE REPRESENTATIONS** A baseball pitcher makes 53 pitches in the first four innings of a game and plans to pitch in the next 3 innings.

a. Making a Table Make a table that gives the total number t of pitches made if the pitcher makes an average of p pitches per inning in the next 3 innings. Use the following values for p: 15, 16, 17, 18, 19. **See margin.**

b. Writing an Inequality The baseball coach assigns a maximum of 105 pitches to the pitcher for the game. Write and solve an inequality to find the possible average numbers of pitches that the pitcher can make in each of the next three innings. **$53 + 3p \le 105$, $p \le 17\frac{1}{3}$, at most 17 pitches**

42a. 5%; the amount that was taxed was $300 − $175 = $125. To find the tax rate, solve the proportion $\frac{x}{100} = \frac{6.25}{125}$.

42. ★ **EXTENDED RESPONSE** A state imposes a sales tax on items of clothing that cost more than $175. The tax applies only to the difference of the price of the item and $175.

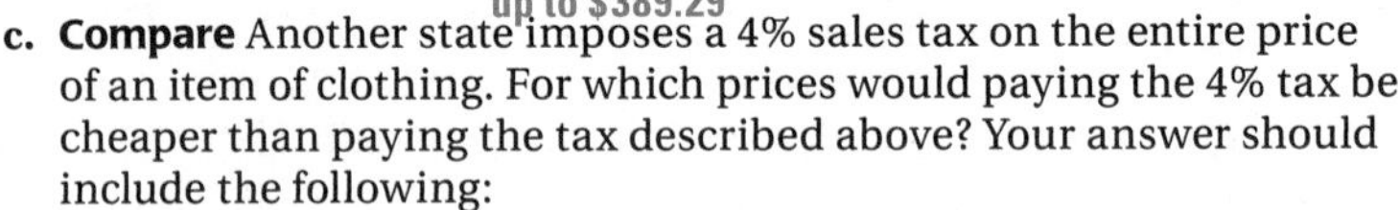

a. Calculate Use the receipt shown to find the tax rate (as a percent). *Explain* how you got your answer.

b. Apply A shopper has $400 to spend on a winter coat. Write and solve an inequality to find the prices p of coats that the shopper can afford. Assume that $p \ge 175$. **$p + 0.05(p - 175) \le 400$, $p \le 389.29$; up to $389.29**

c. Compare Another state imposes a 4% sales tax on the entire price of an item of clothing. For which prices would paying the 4% tax be cheaper than paying the tax described above? Your answer should include the following:

- writing and solving an inequality that describes the situation
- checking the reasonableness of your answer using one of the solutions of the inequality **See margin.**

C

43. **CHALLENGE** Your scores in four bowling league tournaments are 157, 161, 149, and 172. After the next game, you want your average score to be at least 167. What are the possible scores that you can earn in your next tournament in order to meet your goal? **at least 196**

ILLINOIS MIXED REVIEW

TEST PRACTICE at classzone.com

44. A math class consists of 6 freshmen and 25 sophomores. On a test, the freshmen had an average of x points. The sophomores had an average of y points. Which expression gives the average test score per student for the entire class? **C**

Ⓐ $\frac{6x + 25y}{x + y}$ Ⓑ $\frac{6x + 25y}{2}$ Ⓒ $\frac{6x + 25y}{31}$ Ⓓ $\frac{6x + 25y}{150}$

45. Last soccer season Jason made 72% of his attempted shots on goal. In the first game of this season, Jason attempted 8 shots on goal. About how many goals did Jason make if his success rate from last season continued? **C**

Ⓐ 3 Ⓑ 4 Ⓒ 6 Ⓓ 7

PROBLEM SOLVING WORKSHOP
LESSON 6.3

Using ALTERNATIVE METHODS

Another Way to Solve Example 5, page 371

MULTIPLE REPRESENTATIONS In Example 5 on page 371, you saw how to solve a problem about buying gasoline using an inequality. You can also solve the problem by working backward or by using a graph.

PROBLEM

CAR WASH Use the sign shown. A gas station charges \$.10 less per gallon of gasoline if a customer also gets a car wash. What are the possible amounts (in gallons) of gasoline that you can buy if you also get a car wash and can spend at most \$20?

METHOD 1

Work backward One alternative approach is to work backward.

STEP 1 **Read** the problem. It gives you the following information:

- amount you can spend: up to \$20
- price of a car wash: \$8
- regular price per gallon of gasoline: \$2.09
- discount per gallon of gasoline when you get a car wash: \$.10

Because you are getting a car wash, gasoline costs \$2.09 − \$.10, or \$1.99, per gallon.

STEP 2 **Work** backward.

- Start with the amount you have to spend: \$20.
- Subtract the cost of a car wash: \$20 − \$8 = \$12.
- Make a table of values showing the amount of money you have left after buying various amounts of gasoline.

Gasoline (gal)	Amount of money left
0	\$12.00
1	\$10.01
2	\$8.02
3	\$6.03
4	\$4.04
5	\$2.05
6	\$.06

(Each row: − \$1.99)

▸ You can buy up to slightly more than 6 gallons of gasoline.

Alternative Strategy

Example 5 on page 371 can be solved by working backward or by using a graph. Working backward is a good strategy because the problem provides a maximum amount and a constant amount, which gives the student an immediate starting point and a quick means to a solution. A graph is a good strategy because it gives an approximate answer, which is all that is needed for this problem.

Avoiding Common Errors

In Method 1, Step 2, you may want to point out a quick way to subtract \$1.99 is to subtract \$2 and add \$.01. This can help students avoid calculation errors and give faster results.

Reading Strategy

Tell students that italicized words usually emphasize important ideas. Draw their attention to the italicized words in Method 2, Step 4. Ask them to explain why they think these words are italicized. Emphasize that they should look for words such as "at most" or "at least" in the Practice exercises so they know whether the solutions are "on-or-below" or "on-or-above" the graph of the line.

1. At least 9 batches; Method 1: Work backward. Begin with 100 cookies and make a table of values showing the number of cookies you have left to make after each batch of 12 cookies.

Number of batches baked	Number of cookies to bake
0	100
1	88
2	76
3	64
4	52
5	40
6	28
7	16
8	4
9	less than 0

After 9 batches you will have at least 100 cookies. Method 2: Use a graph. Write and graph an equation that gives the total number y of cookies baked as a function of the number x of batches baked: $y = 12x$. Graph $y = 100$ on the same coordinate plane.

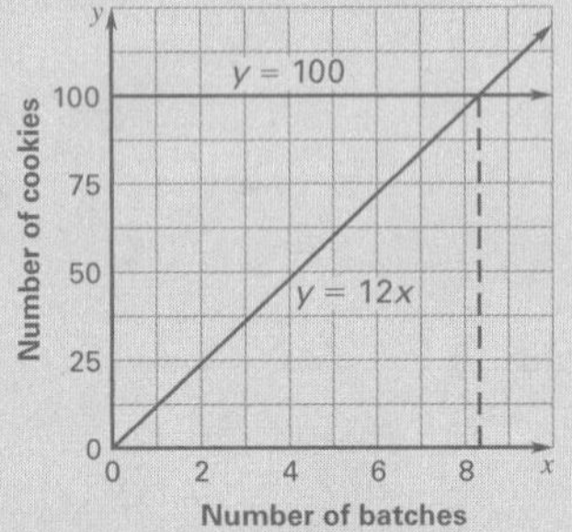

The graphs intersect between $x = 8$ and $x = 9$. Because you must bake at least 100 cookies, the solutions are the x-coordinates of the points on the graph of $y = 12x$ that lie on or above the graph of $y = 100$. Only integer values of x make sense in this situation, so you must bake at least 9 batches.

2, 4. See Additional Answers beginning on p. AA1.

METHOD 2 **Using a graph** Another alternative approach is to use a graph.

STEP 1 **Write** a verbal model. Then write an equation that gives the total amount of money y (in dollars) that you spend as a function of the amount x (in gallons) of gasoline that you buy.

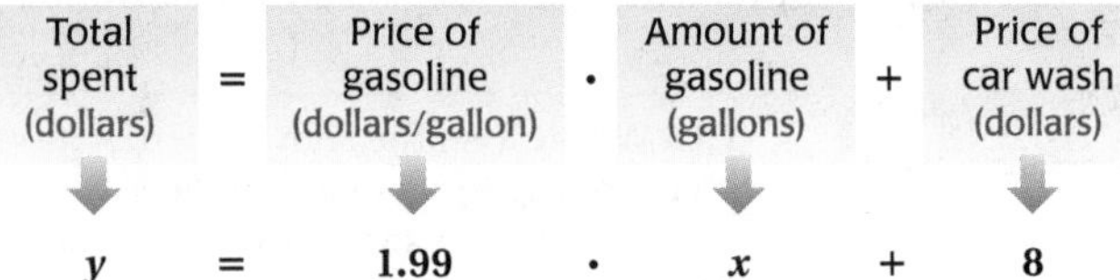

Total spent (dollars)
=
Price of gasoline (dollars/gallon)
·
Amount of gasoline (gallons)
+
Price of car wash (dollars)

$$y = 1.99 \cdot x + 8$$

STEP 2 **Graph** $y = 1.99x + 8$.

STEP 3 **Graph** $y = 20$ in the same coordinate plane. This equation gives the maximum amount of money that you can spend for gasoline and a car wash.

STEP 4 **Analyze** the graphs. The point of intersection shows that you can buy slightly more than 6 gallons of gasoline when you spend \$20. Because you can spend *at most* \$20, the solutions are the x-coordinates of the points on the graph of $y = 1.99x + 8$ that lie *on or below* the graph of $y = 20$.

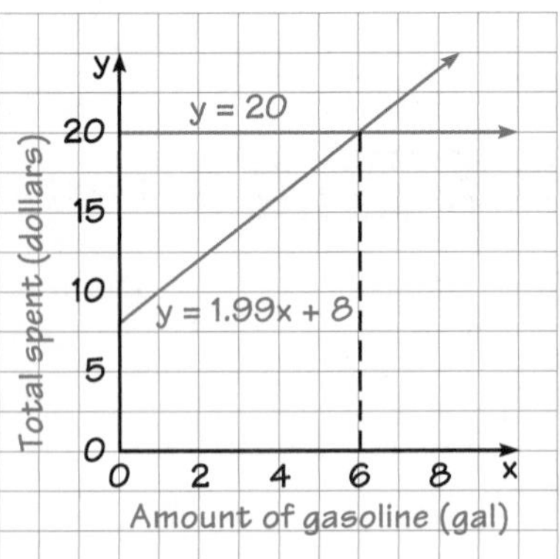

▶ You can buy up to slightly more than 6 gallons of gasoline.

PRACTICE

1. **BAKING** You need to bake at least 100 cookies for a bake sale. You can bake 12 cookies per batch of dough. What are the possible numbers of batches that will allow you to bake enough cookies? Solve this problem using two different methods. See margin.

2. **VIDEO GAMES** A video game console costs \$259, and games cost \$29 each. You saved \$400 to buy a console and games. What are the possible numbers of games that you can buy? Solve this problem using two different methods. See margin.

3. **WHAT IF?** In Exercise 2, suppose that you saved \$500 and decide to buy a video game console that costs \$299. What are the possible numbers of games that you can buy? **at most 6 games**

4. **MONEY** You need to have at least \$100 in your checking account to avoid a low balance fee. You have \$247 in your account, and you make withdrawals of \$20 per week. What are the possible numbers of weeks that you can withdraw money and avoid paying the fee? Solve this problem using two different methods. See margin.

5. **RUNNING TIMES** You are running a 10 mile race. You run the first 3 miles in 24.7 minutes. Your goal is to finish the race in less than 1 hour 20 minutes. What should your average running time (in minutes per mile) be for the remaining miles? **less than 7.9 min/mi**

Solve Linear Inequalities by Graphing

GOAL Use graphs to solve linear inequalities.

So far in Chapter 6 you have seen how to solve linear inequalities algebraically. You can also solve linear inequalities graphically.

KEY CONCEPT *For Your Notebook*

Solving Linear Inequalities Graphically

STEP 1 **Write** the inequality in one of the following forms: $ax + b < 0$, $ax + b \le 0$, $ax + b > 0$, or $ax + b \ge 0$.

STEP 2 **Write** the related equation $y = ax + b$.

STEP 3 **Graph** the equation $y = ax + b$.

- The solutions of $ax + b > 0$ are the x-coordinates of the points on the graph of $y = ax + b$ that lie above the x-axis.
- The solutions of $ax + b < 0$ are the x-coordinates of the points on the graph of $y = ax + b$ that lie below the x-axis.
- If the inequality symbol is $\le$ or $\ge$, then the x-intercept of the graph is also a solution.

EXAMPLE 1 Solve an inequality graphically

Solve $3x + 2 > 8$ graphically.

Solution

STEP 1 **Write** the inequality in the form $ax + b > 0$.

$3x + 2 > 8$ Write original inequality.

$3x - 6 > 0$ Subtract 8 from each side.

STEP 2 **Write** the related equation $y = 3x - 6$.

STEP 3 **Graph** the equation $y = 3x - 6$.

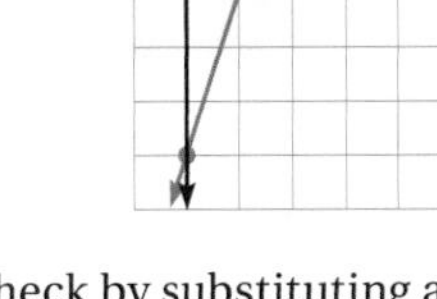

The inequality in Step 1 is in the form $ax + b > 0$, and the x-intercept of the graph in Step 3 is 2. So, $x > 2$.

▶ The solutions are all real numbers greater than 2. Check by substituting a number greater than 2 in the original inequality.

CHECK $3x + 2 > 8$ Write original inequality.

$3(4) + 2 \overset{?}{>} 8$ Substitute 4 for x.

$14 > 8$ ✓ Solution checks.

1 PLAN AND PREPARE

Warm-Up Exercises

1. Write $4x + 2 = 5$ in the form $ax + b = 0$. Then write the related function $y = ax + b$. $4x - 3 = 0$; $y = 4x - 3$
2. Solve $2x + 3 = x$ by graphing the related function $y = f(x)$. -3

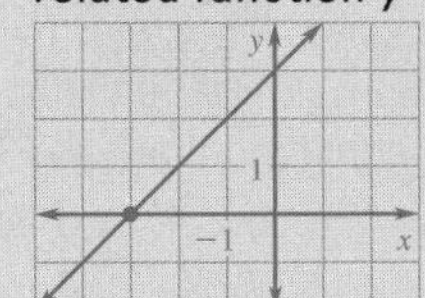

2 FOCUS AND MOTIVATE

Essential Question

Big Idea 3, p. 355

How do you use graphs to solve linear inequalities? **Tell students they will learn how to answer this question by graphing the related function and shading one of the half-planes.**

3 TEACH

Extra Example 1

Solve $2x - 1 < 5$ graphically.

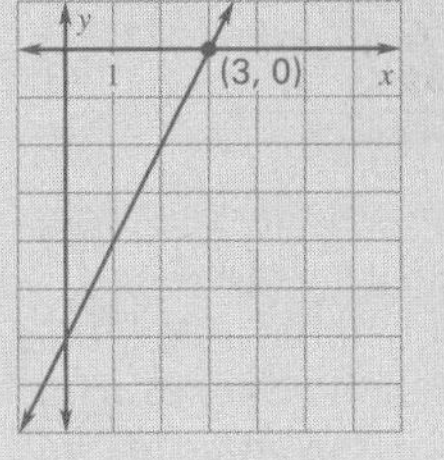

all real numbers less than 3

NCTM STANDARDS

Standard 2: Use models to understand relationships

Standard 6: Solve problems in math and other contexts

Extra Example 2

Your gym membership costs \$18.95 per month. Yoga classes cost \$3.25 each. You budget \$30 per month for gym costs. What are the possible numbers of yoga classes that you can afford each month? **no more than 3 yoga classes per month**

Closing the Lesson

Have students summarize the major points of the lesson and answer the Essential Question: How do you use graphs to solve linear inequalities?

- **You can solve a linear inequality graphically by writing and graphing the related function.**

Write the inequality in a form that sets it to zero. Then write the related function and graph the equation. The inequality symbol specifies whether or not the solutions contain the *x*-intercept and whether the solutions are to the right or to the left of the *x*-intercept.

Avoiding Common Errors

Exercises 1–3 Some students may find the *y*-intercept instead of the *x*-intercept for these exercises. Remind these students that they are solving for *x* and not for *y*.

Study Strategy

Exercise 4 Point out that the problem in the exercise is similar to Example 2. Suggest that students closely model their solutions on the patterns shown in the steps of Example 2.

EXAMPLE 2 Approximate a real-world solution

CELL PHONES Your cell phone plan costs \$49.99 per month for a given number of minutes. Each additional minute or part of a minute costs \$.40. You budgeted \$55 per month for phone costs. What are the possible additional minutes x that you can afford each month?

Solution

STEP 1 **Write** a verbal model. Then write an inequality.

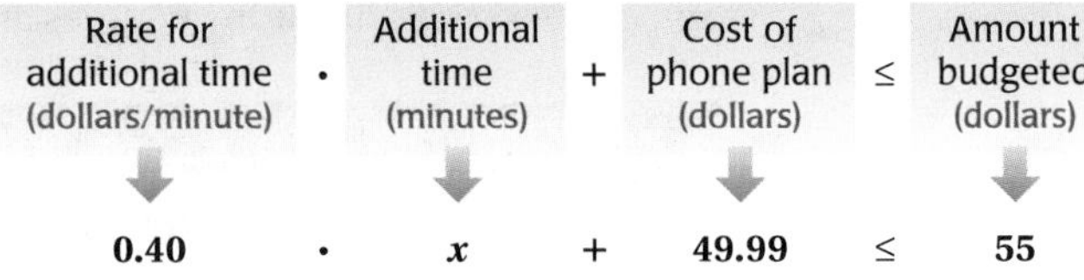

Rate for additional time (dollars/minute) · Additional time (minutes) + Cost of phone plan (dollars) ≤ Amount budgeted (dollars)
0.40 · x + 49.99 ≤ 55

Write the inequality in the form $ax + b \leq 0$.

$0.40x + 49.99 \leq 55$ **Write original inequality.**

$0.40x - 5.01 \leq 0$ **Subtract 55 from each side.**

STEP 2 **Write** the related equation $y = 0.40x - 5.01$.

STEP 3 **Graph** the equation $y = 0.40x - 5.01$ on a graphing calculator.

Use the *trace* feature of the graphing calculator to find the x-intercept of the graph.

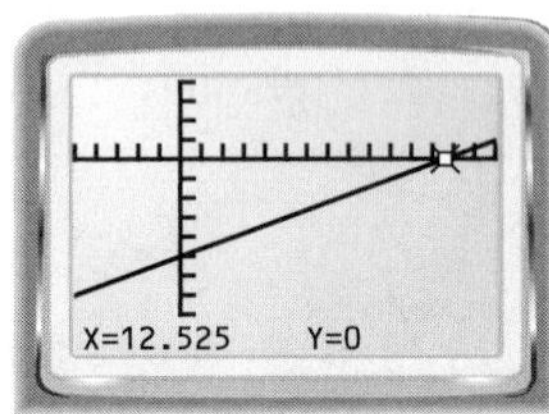

The inequality in Step 1 is in the form $ax + b \leq 0$, and the x-intercept is about 12.5. Because a part of a minute costs \$.40, round 12.5 down to 12 to be sure that you stay within your budget.

▶ You can afford up to 12 additional minutes.

PRACTICE

EXAMPLES 1 and 2 on pp. 377–378 for Exs. 1–4

Solve the inequality graphically.

1. $2x + 5 > 11$ **$x > 3$**
2. $\frac{1}{2}x + 6 \leq 13$ **$x \leq 14$**
3. $0.2x - 15.75 < 27$ **$x < 213.75$**
4. **CABLE COSTS** Your family has a cable television package that costs \$40.99 per month. Pay-per-view movies cost \$3.95 each. Your family budgets \$55 per month for cable television costs. What are the possible numbers of pay-per-view movies that your family can afford each month? **up to 3 movies**

6.4 Statements with *And* and *Or*

MATERIALS • paper and pencil

QUESTION **What is the difference between a statement with *and* and a statement with *or*?**

EXPLORE **Use a Venn diagram to answer questions about a group**

STEP 1 ***Answer questions*** Copy the questions below and write your answers beside them. Steps 1, 2. Answers may vary.

1. Are you taking an art class?
2. Are you taking a foreign language class?

STEP 2 ***Complete a Venn diagram*** Form a group with 3 or 4 classmates. Draw a Venn diagram, like the one shown below, where set *A* consists of students taking an art class, and set *B* consists of students taking a foreign language class. Then write the name of each student in the appropriate section of the diagram.

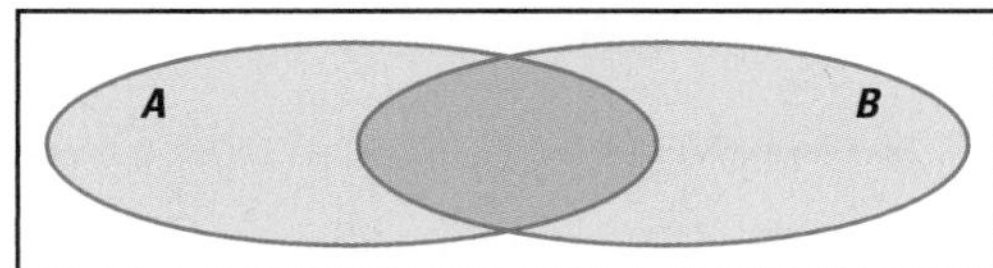

DRAW CONCLUSIONS **Use your observations to complete these exercises**

In Exercises 1–3, use your Venn diagram to list the students who belong in the given set. 1–6. Answers may vary.

1. Set *A*
2. Set *B*
3. Set *A and* set *B*
4. The students who belong in set *A or* set *B* are all of the students who belong only in set *A*, only in set *B*, or in set *A and* set *B*. List the students in your group who belong in set *A or* set *B*.
5. **OPEN-ENDED** Write a statement with *and* so that the statement is true for all students in your group.
6. **OPEN-ENDED** Write a statement with *or* so that the statement is true for all students in your group.

REASONING **Tell whether the statement is *true* or *false*.**

7. If a student belongs in set *A and* set *B*, then the student belongs in set *A or* set *B*. true
8. If a student belongs in set *A or* set *B*, then the student belongs in set *A and* set *B*. false

1 PLAN AND PREPARE

Explore the Concept

- Students will use a Venn diagram to explore the difference between statements with *and* and with *or*.
- This activity leads into the study of compound inequalities in Example 1 in Lesson 6.4.

Recommended Time

Work activity: 10 min
Discuss results: 5 min

Grouping

Students can work individually or in groups of 4. If students work in groups, two can ask questions and write answers and two can draw and label the Venn diagram.

2 TEACH

Tips for Success

If students are not taking art or foreign language, then suggest other classes such as science or English.

Key Discovery

Statements with *and* describe the intersection of two sets, while statements with *or* describe the union of two sets.

3 ASSESS AND RETEACH

Which usually contains more students, "Set *A and* Set *B*" or "Set *A or* Set *B*"? Explain. **"Set *A or* Set *B*" includes students in either set, so it usually contains more than "Set *A and* Set *B*," for which students must be in both sets.**

1 PLAN AND PREPARE

Warm-Up Exercises

Transparency Available

Solve the inequality.

1. $8 > x + 10$ **all real numbers less than −2**
2. $6 \le 2x - 4$ **all real numbers greater than or equal to 5**
3. You estimate you can read at least 8 history text pages per day. What are the possible numbers of days it will take you to read at most 118 pages? **at most 15 days**

Notetaking Guide

Transparency Available

Promotes interactive learning and notetaking skills, pp. 137–139.

Pacing

Basic: 2 days
Average: 2 days
Advanced: 2 days
Block: 0.5 block with 6.3
0.5 block with 6.5

• See *Teaching Guide/Lesson Plan.*

2 FOCUS AND MOTIVATE

Essential Question

Big Idea 2, p. 355

How do you solve compound inequalities? **Tell students they will learn how to answer this question by solving the two parts of the inequality separately.**

6.4 Solve Compound Inequalities

6.11.08 Determine the appropriate solution, including rounding, from a context (e.g., rounding up, down, to the nearest integer).

Before You solved one-step and multi-step inequalities.

Now You will solve compound inequalities.

Why? So you can describe possible heights, as in Example 2.

Key Vocabulary
• compound inequality

A **compound inequality** consists of two separate inequalities joined by *and* or *or.*

The graph of a compound inequality with *and* is the *intersection* of the graphs of the inequalities.

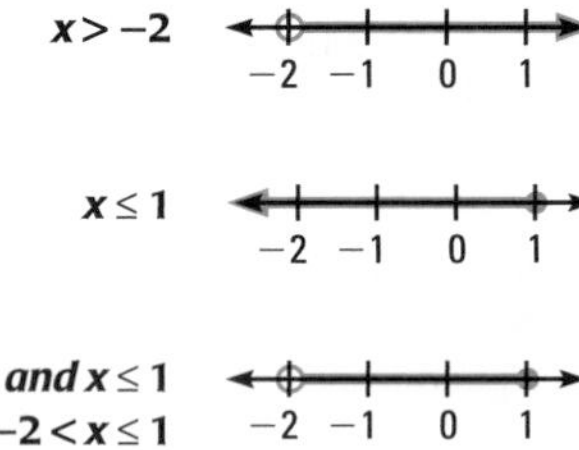

The graph of a compound inequality with *or* is the *union* of the graphs of the inequalities.

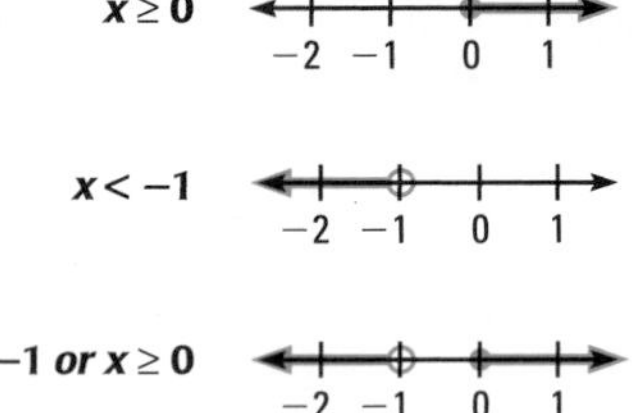

EXAMPLE 1 Write and graph compound inequalities

Translate the verbal phrase into an inequality. Then graph the inequality.

a. All real numbers that are greater than −2 *and* less than 3

Inequality: $-2 < x < 3$

Graph: −3 −2 −1 0 1 2 3 4 5

b. All real numbers that are less than 0 *or* greater than or equal to 2

Inequality: $x < 0$ *or* $x \ge 2$

Graph: −3 −2 −1 0 1 2 3 4 5

GUIDED PRACTICE for Example 1

Translate the verbal phrase into an inequality. Then graph the inequality. **1–2. See margin for art.**

1. All real numbers that are less than −1 *or* greater than or equal to 4 **$x < -1$ or $x \ge 4$**
2. All real numbers that are greater than or equal to −3 *and* less than 5 **$-3 \le x < 5$**

Resource Planning Guide

Chapter Resource Book
• Teaching Guide/Lesson Plan (pp. 43–44)
• Activity Master (p. 45)
• Practice levels A, B, C (pp. 46–51)
• Study Guide (pp. 52–53)
• Catch-up for Absent Students (p. 54)
• Problem Solving Workshop (p. 55)
• Challenge (p. 57)

Workbooks
• Notetaking Guide (pp. 137–139)
• Practice Workbook (pp. 93–95)

Teaching Options
• **Power Presentations CD-ROM** provides dynamic electronic teaching resources for the classroom.
• **Activity Generator CD-ROM** provides editable activities for all ability levels.

Interactive Technology
• Easy Planner
• Power Presentations CD-ROM
• Activity Generator CD-ROM
• Animated Algebra
• Test Generator CD-ROM
• Online Quiz
• eWorkbook
• eEdition
• @HomeTutor

Resources for English Learners
• Quick Reference for English Learners
• Spanish Study Guide
• Multi-Language Visual Glossary
• Student Resources in Spanish

See also the *Algebra 1 Toolkit* for more strategies for meeting individual needs.

EXAMPLE 2 Write and graph a real-world compound inequality

CAMERA CARS A crane sits on top of a camera car and faces toward the front. The crane's maximum height and minimum height above the ground are shown. Write and graph a compound inequality that describes the possible heights of the crane.

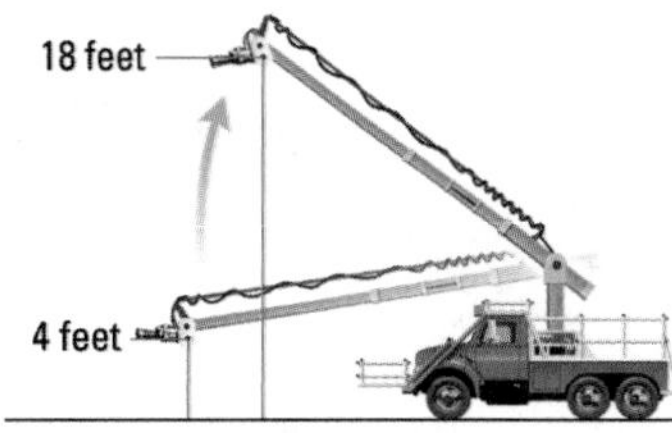

Solution

Let h represent the height (in feet) of the crane. All possible heights are greater than or equal to 4 feet *and* less than or equal to 18 feet. So, the inequality is $4 \le h \le 18$.

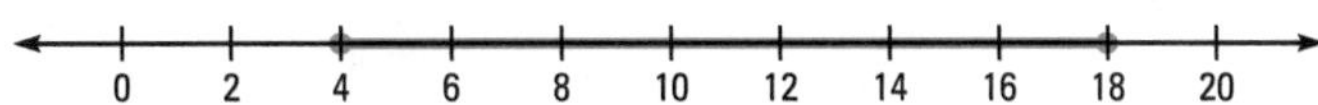

SOLVING COMPOUND INEQUALITIES A number is a solution of a compound inequality with *and* if the number is a solution of *both* inequalities. A number is a solution of a compound inequality with *or* if the number is a solution of *at least one* of the inequalities.

EXAMPLE 3 Solve a compound inequality with *and*

Solve $2 < x + 5 < 9$. Graph your solution.

Solution

Separate the compound inequality into two inequalities. Then solve each inequality separately.

$2 < x + 5$	*and*	$x + 5 < 9$	**Write two inequalities.**
$2 - 5 < x + 5 - 5$	*and*	$x + 5 - 5 < 9 - 5$	**Subtract 5 from each side.**
$-3 < x$	*and*	$x < 4$	**Simplify.**

The compound inequality can be written as $-3 < x < 4$.

▶ The solutions are all real numbers greater than -3 *and* less than 4.

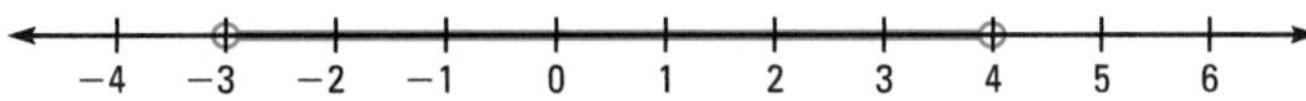

GUIDED PRACTICE for Examples 2 and 3

3. **INVESTING** An investor buys shares of a stock and will sell them if the change c in value from the purchase price of a share is less than $-\$3.00$ or greater than \$4.50. Write and graph a compound inequality that describes the changes in value for which the shares will be sold. $c < -3$ or $c > 4.5$; see margin for art.

Solve the inequality. Graph your solution. 4–6. See margin for art.

4. $-7 < x - 5 < 4$ $-2 < x < 9$
5. $10 \le 2y + 4 \le 24$ $3 \le y \le 10$
6. $-7 < -z - 1 < 3$ $-4 < z < 6$

Motivating the Lesson

Your veterinarian wants you to monitor your dog's weight if it dips 3 pounds below a minimum weight of 8 pounds or increases 5 pounds above a maximum weight of 12 pounds. Knowing how to solve compound inequalities will help you determine the possible weights you need to monitor.

3 TEACH

Extra Example 1

Translate the verbal phrase into an inequality. Then graph the inequality.

a. All real numbers that are greater than or equal to -4 *and* less than 4 $-4 \le x < 4$

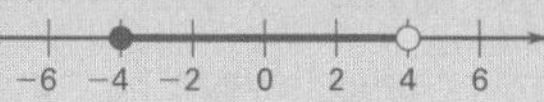

b. All real numbers that are less than -1 or greater than 2 $x < -1$ *or* $x > 2$

−3 −2 −1 0 1 2 3 4

Extra Example 2

At an auction, the lowest bid for an autographed trading card is \$20. The highest bid is \$54. Write and graph a compound inequality that describes the possible bids. All bids b are greater than or equal to \$20 *and* less than or equal to \$54; $20 \le b \le 54$.

Extra Example 3

Solve $-1 < x + 1 \le 7$. Graph your solution. all real numbers greater than -2 *and* less than or equal to 6

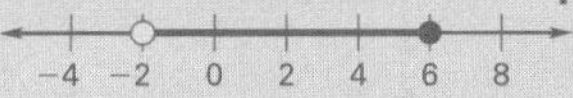

1–6. See Additional Answers beginning on p. AA1.

Extra Example 4

Solve $1 < -2x + 3 < 19$. Graph your solution. all real numbers greater than -8 *and* less than 1

Extra Example 5

Solve $3x - 2 \leq -11$ *or* $2x + 8 > 16$. Graph your solution. all real numbers less than or equal to -3 *or* greater than 4

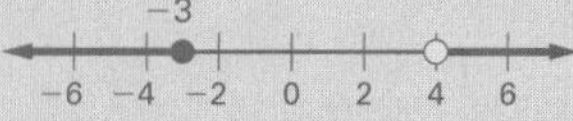

Key Questions to Ask for Example 5

- According to the graph, is 3 a solution of the compound inequality? Explain. No; the inequality $x < 3$ is not true when x is 3.
- Does a number have to be a solution of both inequalities to be a solution of the compound inequality? Explain. No; a number has to be a solution of at least one of the inequalities for an *or* compound inequality.

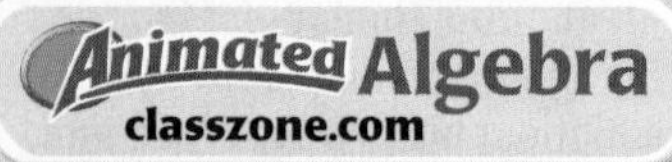

An **Animated Algebra** activity is available on-line for **Example 5**. This activity is also available on the **Power Presentations CD-ROM**.

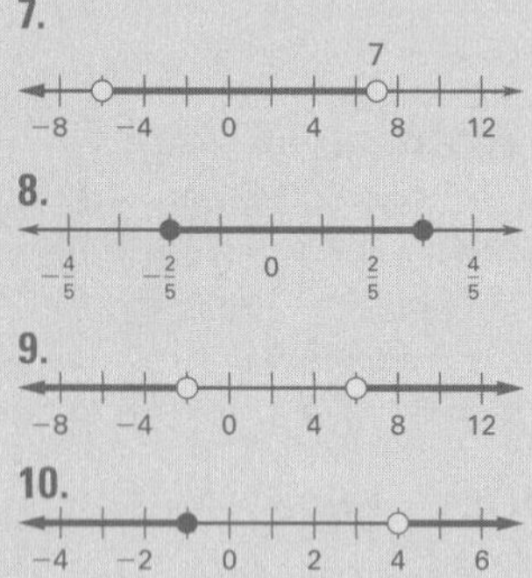

ANOTHER WAY In Example 3, you could solve $2 < x + 5 < 9$ by subtracting 5 from 2, $x + 5$, and 9 without first separating the compound inequality into two separate inequalities. To solve a compound inequality with *and*, you perform the same operation on each expression.

EXAMPLE 4 Solve a compound inequality with *and*

Solve $-5 \leq -x - 3 \leq 2$. Graph your solution.

$-5 \leq -x - 3 \leq 2$	Write original inequality.
$-5 + 3 \leq -x - 3 + 3 \leq 2 + 3$	Add 3 to each expression.
$-2 \leq -x \leq 5$	Simplify.
$-1(-2) \geq -1(-x) \geq -1(5)$	Multiply each expression by -1 and reverse *both* inequality symbols.
$2 \geq x \geq -5$	Simplify.
$-5 \leq x \leq 2$	Rewrite in the form $a \leq x \leq b$.

▶ The solutions are all real numbers greater than or equal to -5 *and* less than or equal to 2.

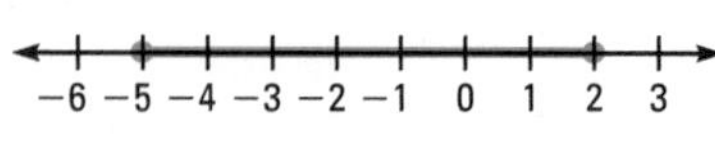

EXAMPLE 5 Solve a compound inequality with *or*

Solve $2x + 3 < 9$ *or* $3x - 6 > 12$. Graph your solution.

Solution

Solve the two inequalities separately.

$2x + 3 < 9$	*or*	$3x - 6 > 12$	Write original inequality.
$2x + 3 - 3 < 9 - 3$	*or*	$3x - 6 + 6 > 12 + 6$	Addition or subtraction property of inequality
$2x < 6$	*or*	$3x > 18$	Simplify.
$\frac{2x}{2} < \frac{6}{2}$	*or*	$\frac{3x}{3} > \frac{18}{3}$	Division property of inequality
$x < 3$	*or*	$x > 6$	Simplify.

▶ The solutions are all real numbers less than 3 *or* greater than 6.

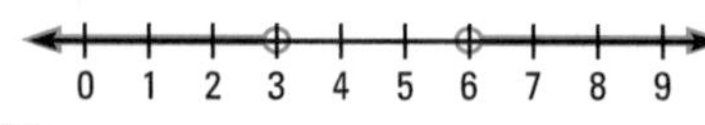

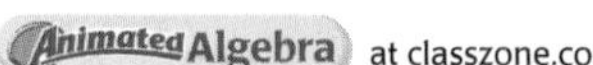

at classzone.com

✓ GUIDED PRACTICE for Examples 4 and 5

Solve the inequality. Graph your solution. 7–10. See margin for art.

7. $-14 < x - 8 < -1$ $\quad -6 < x < 7$
8. $-1 \leq -5t + 2 \leq 4$ $\quad -\frac{2}{5} \leq t \leq \frac{3}{5}$
9. $3h + 1 < -5$ *or* $2h - 5 > 7$ $\quad h < -2$ or $h > 6$
10. $4c + 1 \leq -3$ *or* $5c - 3 > 17$ $\quad c \leq -1$ or $c > 4$

Differentiated Instruction

Below Level Some students may have difficulty recognizing differences between compound inequalities with *and* and with *or*. Stress that compound inequalities with *and* have solutions that overlap. Have students graph $x \geq -5$ and $x \leq 2$ in **Example 4** on separate graphs. This may help them see that the solutions overlap. Point out that graphs of most compound inequalities with *or* have gaps, with arrows heading in opposite directions. See also the *Algebra 1 Toolkit* for more strategies.

EXAMPLE 6 Solve a multi-step problem

ASTRONOMY The Mars Exploration Rovers *Opportunity* and *Spirit* are robots that were sent to Mars in 2003 in order to gather geological data about the planet. The temperature at the landing sites of the robots can range from −100°C to 0°C.

- Write a compound inequality that describes the possible temperatures (in degrees Fahrenheit) at a landing site.
- Solve the inequality. Then graph your solution.
- Identify three possible temperatures (in degrees Fahrenheit) at a landing site.

Solution

Let F represent the temperature in degrees Fahrenheit, and let C represent the temperature in degrees Celsius. Use the formula $C = \frac{5}{9}(F - 32)$.

STEP 1 **Write** a compound inequality. Because the temperature at a landing site ranges from −100°C to 0°C, the lowest possible temperature is −100°C, and the highest possible temperature is 0°C.

$-100 \le C \le 0$ **Write inequality using *C*.**

$-100 \le \frac{5}{9}(F - 32) \le 0$ **Substitute $\frac{5}{9}(F - 32)$ for *C*.**

STEP 2 **Solve** the inequality. Then graph your solution.

$-100 \le \frac{5}{9}(F - 32) \le 0$ **Write inequality from Step 1.**

$-180 \le F - 32 \le 0$ **Multiply each expression by $\frac{9}{5}$.**

$-148 \le F \le 32$ **Add 32 to each expression.**

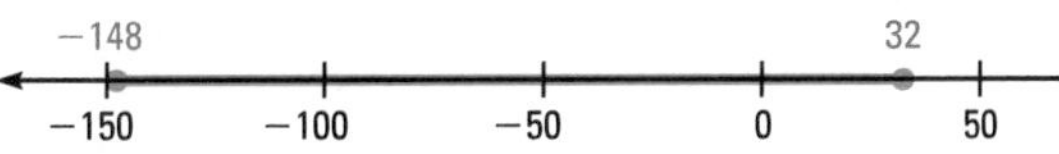

ANOTHER WAY
You can solve the compound inequality by multiplying through by 9:

$-100 \le \frac{5}{9}(F - 32) \le 0$

$-900 \le 5(F - 32) \le 0$

$-900 \le 5F - 160 \le 0$

$-740 \le 5F \le 160$

$-148 \le F \le 32$

STEP 3 **Identify** three possible temperatures.

The temperature at a landing site is greater than or equal to −148°F *and* less than or equal to 32°F. Three possible temperatures are −115°F, 15°F, and 32°F.

✓ GUIDED PRACTICE for Example 6

11. **MARS** Mars has a maximum temperature of 27°C at the equator and a minimum temperature of −133°C at the winter pole.
    - Write and solve a compound inequality that describes the possible temperatures (in degrees Fahrenheit) on Mars.
    - Graph your solution. Then identify three possible temperatures (in degrees Fahrenheit) on Mars.

    $-133 \le \frac{5}{9}(F - 32) \le 27$; $-207.4 \le F \le 80.6$; see margin for art.
    ***Sample answer:* −100°F, 0°F, 25°F**

Extra Example 6

The eggs of a Rocky Mountain Tailed frog can survive in streams where the temperature ranges from 5°C to 18°C. Write a compound inequality that describes the possible stream temperatures (in degrees Fahrenheit) for egg survival. Solve the inequality. Then graph your solution. Identify three possible stream temperatures (in degrees Fahrenheit) for egg survival.

$5 \le \frac{5}{9}(F - 32) \le 18$; $41 \le F \le 64.4$

41 64.4
35 40 45 50 55 60 65 70

examples: 45°F, 53°F, 61°F

Closing the Lesson

Have students summarize the major points of the lesson and answer the Essential Question: How do you solve and graph compound inequalities?

- **Compound inequalities are two inequalities joined by *and* or joined by *or*.**
- **The graph of a compound inequality with *and* is the intersection of the graphs of the inequalities. The graph of an inequality with *or* is the union of the graphs.**

Solve the two inequalities in the compound inequality separately. On the graph of a compound inequality with *and*, shade all the numbers that satisfy both inequalities together. On the graph of a compound inequality with *or*, shade the numbers that satisfy the separate inequalities.

11.

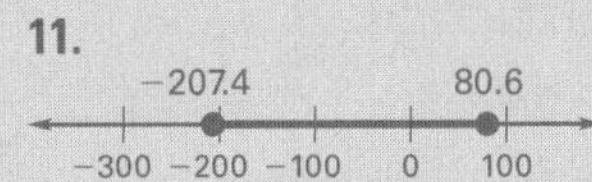

Differentiated Instruction

Advanced Have students search the Internet for astronomical or other scientific data that involve a range and a conversion, as in **Example 6**. Ask them to create a multi-step problem that uses a compound inequality with *and* or *or* and that involves a conversion. Encourage them to share their problems with the class.

See also the *Algebra 1 Toolkit* for more strategies.

6.4 EXERCISES

HOMEWORK KEY
○ = **WORKED-OUT SOLUTIONS** on p. WS14 for Exs. 7, 11, and 41
★ = **STANDARDIZED TEST PRACTICE** Exs. 2, 27, 39, and 45
◆ = **MULTIPLE REPRESENTATIONS** Ex. 43

SKILL PRACTICE

A

1. **VOCABULARY** Copy and complete: A(n) _?_ is an inequality that consists of two inequalities joined by *and* or *or*. compound inequality

2. ★ **WRITING** *Describe* the difference between the graphs of $-6 \le x \le -4$ and $x \le -6$ *or* $x \ge -4$. See margin.

EXAMPLE 1 on p. 380 for Exs. 3–6

TRANSLATING VERBAL PHRASES Translate the verbal phrase into an inequality. Then graph the inequality. 3–6. See margin for art.

3. All real numbers that are less than 6 *and* greater than 2 $2 < x < 6$
4. All real numbers that are less than or equal to -8 *or* greater than 12 $x \le -8$ or $x > 12$
5. All real numbers that are greater than or equal to -1.5 *and* less than 9.2 $-1.5 \le x < 9.2$
6. All real numbers that are greater than or equal to $-7\frac{1}{2}$ *or* less than or equal to -10 $x \le -10$ or $x \ge -7\frac{1}{2}$

EXAMPLE 2 on p. 381 for Exs. 7–8

WRITING AND GRAPHING INEQUALITIES Write and graph an inequality that describes the situation. 7, 8. See margin for art.

7. The minimum speed on a highway is 40 miles per hour, and the maximum speed is 60 miles per hour. $40 \le s \le 60$
8. The temperature inside a room is uncomfortable if the temperature is lower than 60°F or higher than 75°F. $t < 60$ or $t > 75$

EXAMPLES 3, 4, and 5 on pp. 381–382 for Exs. 9–22

SOLVING COMPOUND INEQUALITIES Solve the inequality. Graph your solution. 9–20. See margin for art.

9. $6 < x + 5 \le 11$ $1 < x \le 6$
10. $-7 > y - 8 \ge -12$ $-4 \le y < 1$
11. $-1 \le -4m \le 16$ $-4 \le m \le \frac{1}{4}$
12. $-6 < 3n + 9 < 21$ $-5 < n < 4$
13. $-15 \le 5(3p - 2) < 20$ $-\frac{1}{3} \le p < 2$
14. $7 > \frac{2}{3}(6q + 18) \ge -9$ $-5\frac{1}{4} \le q < -1\frac{1}{4}$
15. $2r + 3 < 7$ *or* $-r + 9 \le 2$ $r < 2$ or $r \ge 7$
16. $16 < -s - 6$ *or* $2s + 5 \ge 11$ $s < -22$ or $s \ge 3$
17. $v + 13 < 8$ *or* $-8v < -40$ $v < -5$ or $v > 5$
18. $-14 > w + 3$ *or* $5w - 13 > w + 7$ $w < -17$ or $w > 5$
19. $9g - 6 > 12g + 1$ *or* $4 > -\frac{2}{5}g + 8$ $g < -2\frac{1}{3}$ or $g > 10$
20. $-2h - 7 > h + 5$ *or* $\frac{1}{4}(h + 8) \ge 9$ $h < -4$ or $h \ge 28$

ERROR ANALYSIS *Describe* and correct the error in solving the inequality or in graphing the solution. 21, 22. See margin for art.

21.
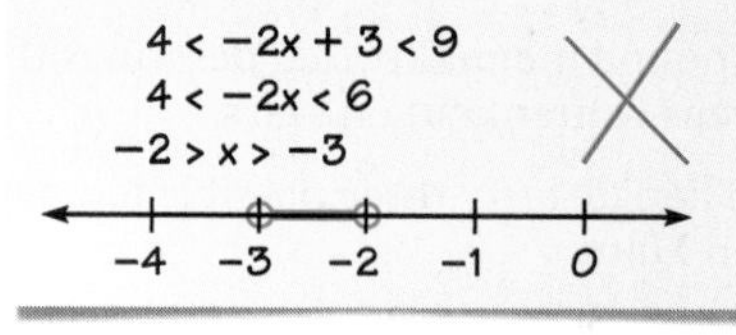

22.
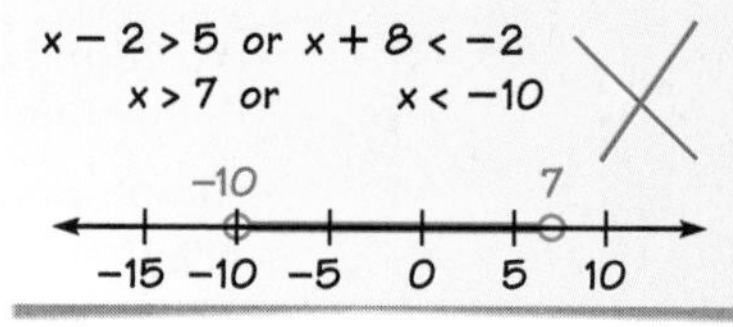

21. 3 was subtracted from only two of the three expressions of the inequality; $1 < -2x < 6$, $-\frac{1}{2} > x > -3$.

22. The graph should include the points of the number line to the left of −10 and to the right of 7, not the points between −10 and 7.

4 PRACTICE AND APPLY

Assignment Guide

Answer Transparencies available for all exercises

Basic:
Day 1: pp. 384–387
Exs. 1–8, 23–27, 47–50, 55
Day 2: pp. 384–387
Exs. 9–22, 37–43, 51–54

Average:
Day 1: pp. 384–387
Exs. 1–8, 23–31, 48, 55
Day 2: pp. 384–387
Exs. 12–22, 32, 33, 39–45, 51–54

Advanced:
Day 1: pp. 384–387
Exs. 1, 2, 5–8, 23–32, 50, 55
Day 2: pp. 384–387
Exs. 13–20, 33–36*, 40–46*, 52, 54

Block:
pp. 384–387
Exs. 1–8, 23–31, 48, 55 (with 6.3)
pp. 384–387
Exs. 12–22, 32, 33, 39–45, 51–54 (with 6.5)

Differentiated Instruction

See *Algebra 1 Best Practices Toolkit* for suggestions on addressing the needs of a diverse classroom.

Homework Check

For a quick check of student understanding of key concepts, go over the following exercises:
Basic: 3, 7, 10, 18, 41
Average: 4, 8, 13, 19, 42
Advanced: 6, 8, 14, 20, 43

Extra Practice

- Student Edition, p. 943
- Chapter 6 Resource Book: Practice levels A, B, C, pp. 46–51

Practice Worksheet

An easily-readable reduced practice page (with answers) for this lesson can be found on p. 354D.

2. The graph of $-6 \le x \le -4$ consists of -6, -4, and all the points on the number line between -6 and -4. The graph of $x \le -6$ *or* $x \ge -4$ consists of -6 and all the points on the number line to the left of -6, along with -4 and all the points on the number line to the right of -4.

3.
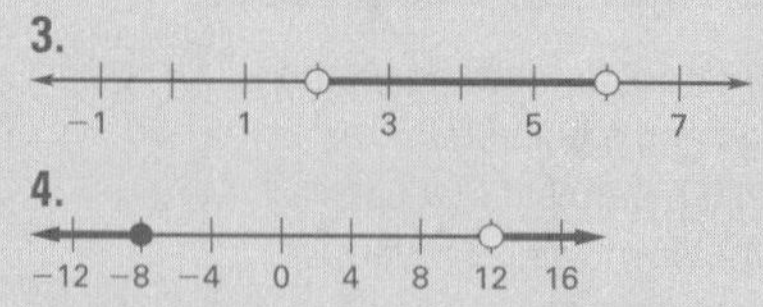

4.
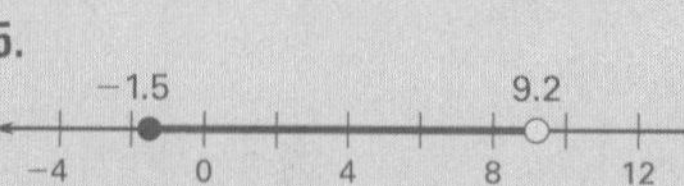

5.

6.
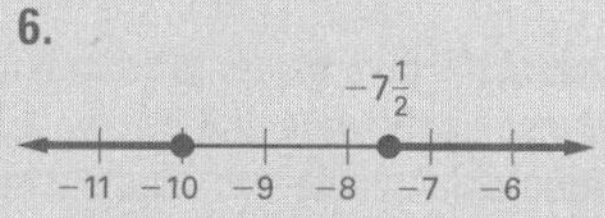

B **TRANSLATING SENTENCES** **Write the verbal sentence as an inequality. Then solve the inequality and graph your solution.** 23–26. See margin for art.

23. Five more than x is less than 8 *or* 3 less than x is greater than 5. $x + 5 < 8$ or $x - 3 > 5$; $x < 3$ or $x > 8$

24. Three less than x is greater than -4 *and* less than -1. $-4 < x - 3 < -1$; $-1 < x < 2$

25. Three times the difference of x and 4 is greater than or equal to -8 *and* less than or equal to 10. $-8 \le 3(x - 4) \le 10$; $1\frac{1}{3} \le x \le 7\frac{1}{3}$

26. The sum of $-2x$ and 8 is less than or equal to -5 *or* 6 is less than $-2x$. $-2x + 8 \le -5$ or $6 < -2x$; $x < -3$ or $x \ge 6\frac{1}{2}$

27. ★ **MULTIPLE CHOICE** Consider the compound inequality $a > 3x + 8$ *or* $a > -4x - 1$. For which value of a does the solution consist of numbers greater than -6 *and* less than 5? C

Ⓐ 16 Ⓑ 19 Ⓒ 23 Ⓓ 26

REASONING **In Exercises 28 and 29, tell whether the statement is *true* or *false*. If it is false, give a counterexample.**

28. If a is a solution of $x < 5$, then a is also a solution of $x < 5$ *and* $x \ge -4$. False. *Sample answer:* $a = -5$

29. If a is a solution of $x > 5$, then a is also a solution of $x > 5$ *or* $x \le -4$. true

30. Is the converse of the statement in Exercise 28 *true* or *false*? *Explain.*

30. True; any solution of $x < 5$ *and* $x \ge -4$ lies between -4 and 5 on the number line, so it is to the left of 5 and is therefore a solution of $x < 5$.

31. Is the converse of the statement in Exercise 29 *true* or *false*? *Explain.* False. *Sample answer:* $a = -4$ is a solution of $x > 5$ or $x \le -4$, but it is not a solution of $x > 5$.

32. **GEOMETRY** The sum of the lengths of any two sides of a triangle is greater than the length of the third side.

a. Write and solve three inequalities for the triangle shown. $x + 5 > 7$, $x > 2$; $5 + 7 > x$, $x < 12$; $x + 7 > 5$, $x > -2$

b. Use the inequalities that you wrote in part (a) to write one inequality that describes all the possible values of x. $2 < x < 12$

c. Give three possible lengths for the third side of the triangle. *Sample answer:* 3, 7, 10

C **CHALLENGE** **Solve the inequality, if possible. Graph your solution.** 33–36. See margin for art.

33. $-18 < x - 23$ *and* $x - 16 < -22$ no solution

34. $-3y + 7 \le 11$ *and* $y + 4 > 11$ $y > 7$

35. $2m - 1 \ge 5$ *or* $5m > -25$ $m > -5$

36. $n + 19 \ge 10$ *or* $-5n + 3 > 33$ all real numbers

PROBLEM SOLVING

EXAMPLE 2 **A** on p. 381 for Exs. 37, 39, 40

37. **SLITSNAILS** Slitsnails are large mollusks that live in deep waters. Slitsnails have been found at elevations from -2600 feet to -100 feet. Write and graph a compound inequality that represents the elevations at which slitsnails have been found.

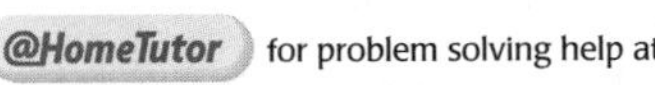
@HomeTutor for problem solving help at classzone.com

$-2600 \le e \le -100$; see margin for art.

EXAMPLE 6 on p. 383 for Exs. 38, 41–43

38. **ICEBERGS** The temperature inside an iceberg off the coast of Newfoundland, Canada, ranges from −20°C to −15°C. Write and graph a compound inequality that describes the possible temperatures (in degrees Fahrenheit) of the iceberg's interior. $-4 \le t \le 5$; see margin for art.

@HomeTutor for problem solving help at classzone.com

Avoiding Common Errors

Exercises 9–20 Some students who do not separate compound inequalities with *and* before solving them make calculation errors. Encourage students to break apart the compound inequality and solve the inequalities separately until they are familiar with the solution process.

Internet Reference

Exercise 38 Additional information about icebergs can be found at oceanworld.tamu.edu/students/iceberg/iceberg1.htm

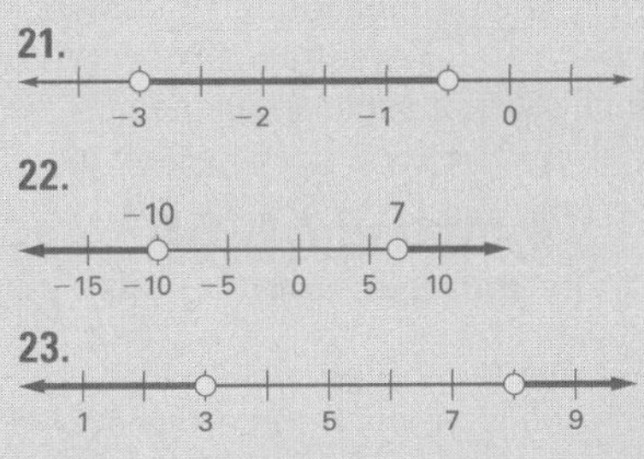
21. 22.

23.

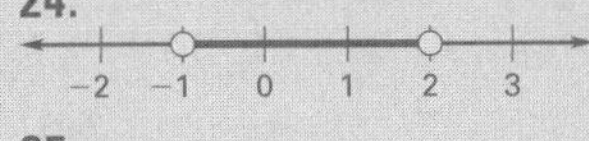
24.

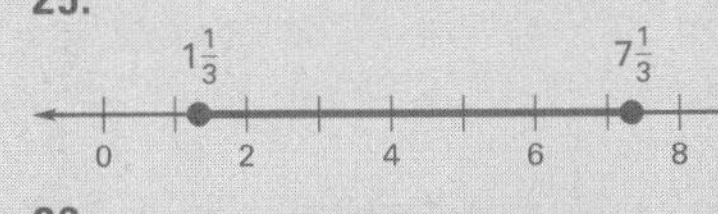
25.

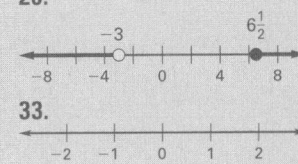

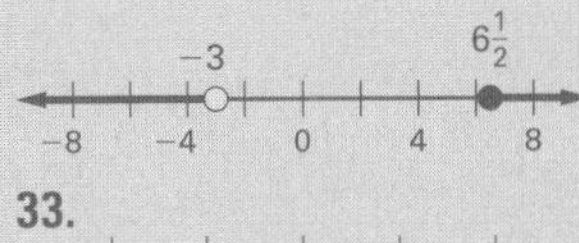
26. 33.

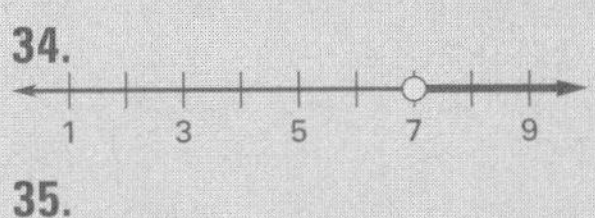
34.

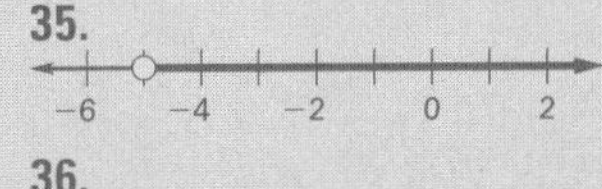
35. 36.

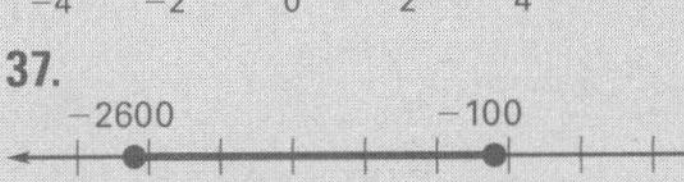
37.

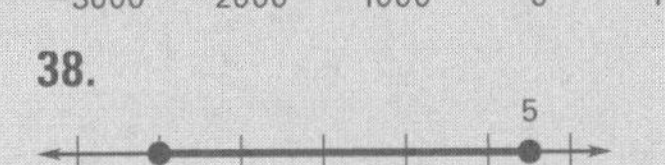
38.

Differentiated Instruction

English Learners Explain the use of the word *or* while discussing **Exercises 35 and 36**. "Left *or* right" means that you can take only one direction, but weather that is "sunny *or* cold" could mean both on a clear winter day. In English, there is no single word to explain if both choices are included. Other languages, including mathematics, are more precise: *or* means to include points from the first inequality, the second, and the intersection (if it exists).

See also the *Algebra 1 Toolkit* for more strategies.

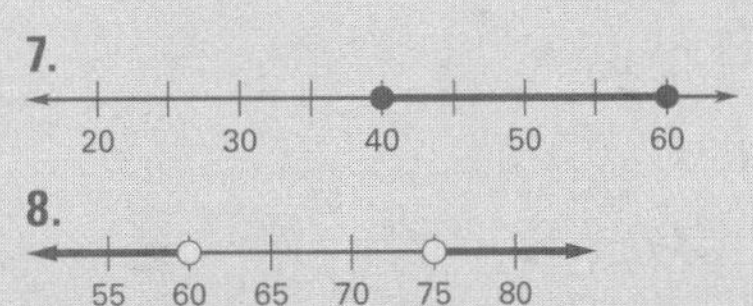
7. 8.

9–20. See Additional Answers beginning on p. AA1.

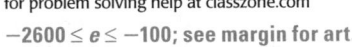

39. ★ **MULTIPLE CHOICE** The euro is the currency in several countries in Europe. In 2003, the dollar value of one euro ranged from \$1.0361 to \$1.2597. Which inequality represents the dollar values v that the euro was *not* worth during the year? B

Ⓐ $1.0361 < v < 1.2597$ Ⓑ $v < 1.0361$ *or* $v > 1.2597$

Ⓒ $1.0361 \le v \le 1.2597$ Ⓓ $v \le 1.0361$ *or* $v \ge 1.2597$

40. **CURRENCY** On October 25, 1865, the steamship *S.S. Republic* sank along with a cargo of gold and silver coins. The list gives the prices of several recovered gold coins. Use the least price and greatest price to write a compound inequality that describes the prices p of the coins. $5319 \le p \le 73{,}486$

Prices of Recovered Gold Coins

\$9,098	\$20,995	\$9,798	\$33,592	\$12,597
\$16,796	\$9,798	\$10,498	\$5,319	\$73,486
\$11,897	\$32,895	\$7,349	\$6,578	\$29,395

(41.) **ANIMALS** A deer can eat 2% to 4% of its body weight in food per day. The percent p of the deer's body weight eaten in food is given by the equation $p = \frac{f}{d}$ where f is the amount (in pounds) of food eaten and d is the weight (in pounds) of the deer. Find the possible amounts of food that a 160 pound deer can eat per day. $3.2 \text{ lb} \le f \le 6.4 \text{ lb}$

42. **SKIS** A ski shop sells recreational skis with lengths ranging from 150 centimeters to 220 centimeters. The shop recommends that recreational skis be 1.16 times the skier's height (in centimeters). For which heights of skiers does the shop *not* provide recreational skis? less than 129.31 cm or greater than 189.66 cm

B

43. ◆ **MULTIPLE REPRESENTATIONS** Water can exist as either a solid, a liquid, or a gas. The table shows the temperatures (in degrees Celsius) at which water can exist in each state.

State of water	Solid	Liquid	Gas
Temperatures (°C)	Less than 0	0 to 100	Greater than 100

a. **Writing an Inequality** Write and solve a compound inequality to find the temperatures (in degrees Fahrenheit) at which water is *not* a liquid. $\frac{5}{9}(F - 32) < 0$ or $\frac{5}{9}(F - 32) > 100$, $F < 32°F$ or $F > 212°F$

b. **Making a Table** Make a table that gives the temperature (in degrees Celsius) when the temperature (in degrees Fahrenheit) of water is 23°F, 86°F, 140°F, 194°F, and 239°F. For which temperatures in the table is water *not* a liquid? 23°F, 239°F; see margin for table.

44. **WEATHER** Wind chill temperature describes how much colder it feels when the speed of the wind is combined with air temperature. At a wind speed of 20 miles per hour, the wind chill temperature w (in degrees Fahrenheit) can be given by the model $w = -22 + 1.3a$ where a is the air temperature (in degrees Fahrenheit). What are the possible air temperatures if the wind chill temperature ranges from $-9°F$ to $-2.5°F$ at a wind speed of 20 miles per hour? from 10°F to 15°F

○ = WORKED-OUT SOLUTIONS on p. WS1 ★ = STANDARDIZED TEST PRACTICE ◆ = MULTIPLE REPRESENTATIONS

Study Strategy

Exercises 39–40, 43–45 Recommend to students that they think through whether a compound inequality describing a real-world situation uses *and* or *or*. They can look for clues in the problem, such as the word *range*, which indicates a continuum and an *and* compound inequality. Similarly, there may be clues in the problem that the solution set has two parts, which would indicate an *or* compound inequality. They can also ask themselves whether a compound inequality with *and* or with *or* makes the most sense in the situation. Encourage students to draw on their own experiences in determining what seems reasonable.

An **Animated Algebra** activity is available on-line for **Exercise 45**. This activity is also available on the **Power Presentations CD-ROM**.

43b.

°F	23	86	140	194	239
°C	−5	30	60	90	115

45c. 4800 watts; because each person requires at least 8 watts of amplification, and you want to be sure to provide enough amplification for 600 people, you need at least $8(600) = 4800$ watts of amplification.

Quiz

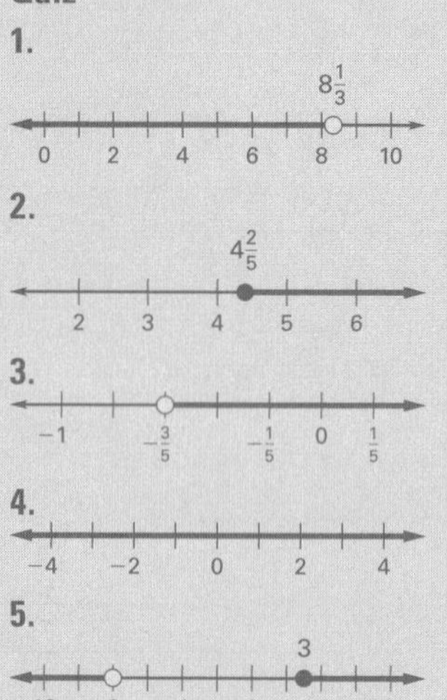

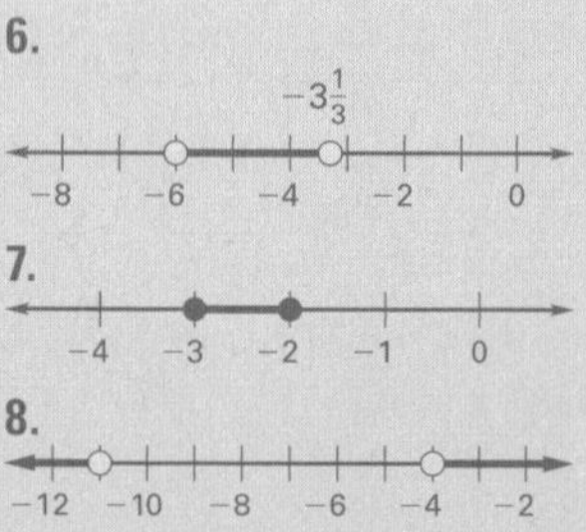

386

45a. $8 \le \frac{w}{300} \le 10$, $2400 \le w \le 3000$; 2400 watts to 3000 watts

45b. Yes; no; the amplification per person for 350 people is $\frac{2900}{350} \approx 8.3$ watts, which is between 8 watts and 10 watts, the amplification for 400 people is $\frac{2900}{400} = 7.25$ watts, which is not between 8 watts and 10 watts.

45. ★ **EXTENDED RESPONSE** Some musicians use audio amplifiers so that everyone in the audience can hear the performance. The amount y of amplification per person is given by the equation $y = \frac{w}{p}$ where w is the total amount (in watts) of amplification provided by the amplifier and p is the number of people in the audience.

a. **Solve** Each person requires 8 watts to 10 watts of amplification. Write and solve an inequality to find the possible total amounts of amplification that an amplifier would need to provide for 300 people.

b. **Decide** Will an amplifier that provides 2900 watts of amplification be strong enough for an audience of 350 people? 400 people? *Explain.*

c. **Justify** Your band usually performs before an audience of 500 to 600 people. What is the least amount of amplification that your amplifier should provide? *Justify* your answer. See margin.

Animated Algebra at classzone.com

46. **CHALLENGE** You and three friends are planning to eat at a restaurant, and all of you agree to divide the total cost of the meals and the 15% tip equally. Each person agrees to pay at least \$10 but no more than \$20. How much can you spend altogether on meals before the tip is applied? from \$34.78 up to \$69.57

ILLINOIS MIXED REVIEW

TEST PRACTICE at classzone.com

47. Which circle has a center located at coordinates $(-2, 2)$? C

Ⓐ 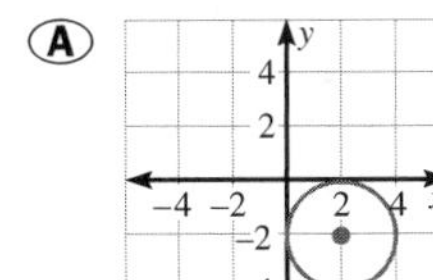

Ⓑ 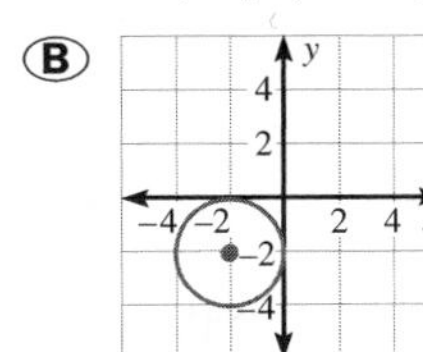

Ⓒ 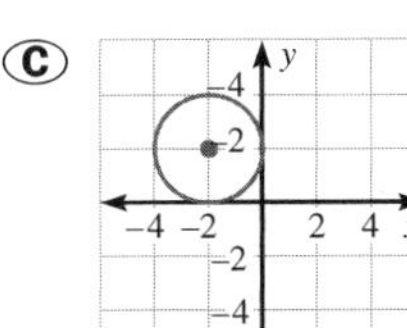

Ⓓ 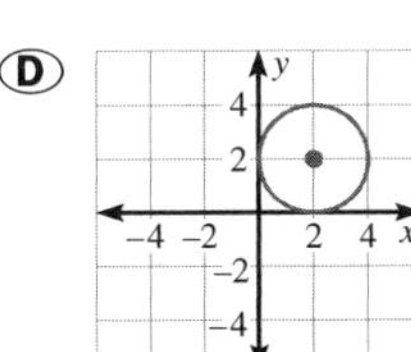

QUIZ for Lessons 6.3–6.4

Solve the inequality, if possible. Graph your solution. 1–8. See margin for art.

1. $-\frac{1}{5}(x - 5) > x - 9$ (p. 369) $x < 8\frac{1}{3}$
2. $\frac{1}{2}y - 8 \ge -2y + 3$ (p. 369) $y \ge 4\frac{2}{5}$
3. $-4r + 7 \le r + 10$ (p. 369) $r \ge -\frac{3}{5}$
4. $-2(s + 6) \le -2s + 8$ (p. 369) all real numbers
5. $a - 4 \ge -1$ *or* $3a < -24$ (p. 380) $a < -8$ or $a \ge 3$
6. $22 > -3c + 4 > 14$ (p. 380) $-6 < c < -3\frac{1}{3}$
7. $-27 \le 9m \le -18$ (p. 380) $-3 \le m \le -2$
8. $5n + 2 > -18$ *or* $-3(n + 4) > 21$ (p. 380) $n < -11$ or $n > -4$

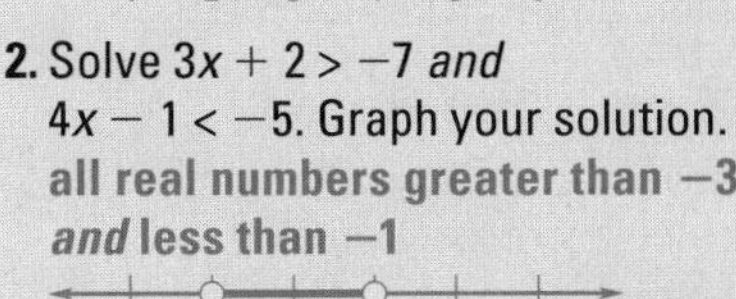

ASSESS AND RETEACH

Daily Homework Quiz

Transparency Available

1. Solve $x + 4 < 7$ *or* $2x - 5 > 3$. Graph your solution. all real numbers less than 3 *or* greater than 4

2. Solve $3x + 2 > -7$ *and* $4x - 1 < -5$. Graph your solution. all real numbers greater than -3 *and* less than -1

3. The smallest praying mantis is 0.4 inch in length. The largest is 6 inches. Write and graph a compound inequality that describes the possible lengths L of a praying mantis. $0.4 \le L \le 6$

Online Quiz

Available at **classzone.com**

Diagnosis/Remediation

- Practice A, B, C in Chapter 6 Resource Book, pp. 46–51
- Study Guide in Chapter 6 Resource Book, pp. 52–53
- Practice Workbook, pp. 93–95
- @HomeTutor

Challenge

Additional challenge is available in the Chapter 6 Resource Book, p. 57.

Quiz

An easily-readable reduced copy of the quiz (with answers) on Lessons 6.3–6.4 from the Assessment Book can be found on p. 354G.

1 PLAN AND PREPARE

Learn the Method

- Students will use a graphing calculator to solve compound inequalities.
- After the activity, students can use a graphing calculator to check their solutions in Exercises 9–20 and 33–36 in Lesson 6.4.

Keystroke Help

Keystrokes for several models of calculators are available in blackline format in the *Chapter 6 Resource Book*.

2 TEACH

Tips for Success

Stress to students that the graphing calculator does not draw open or closed circles so they need to pay attention to the inequality symbols in the compound inequality.

Extra Example

Solve $-28 < -4x < 4$ using a graphing calculator. all real numbers greater than -1 *and* less than 7

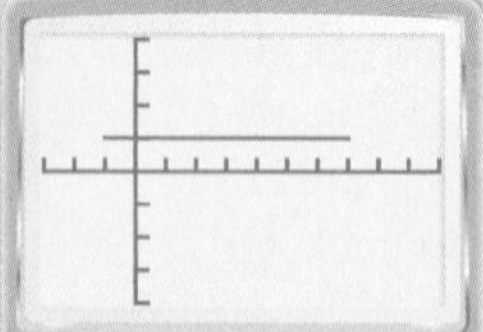

3 ASSESS AND RETEACH

Solve $-5x \le -30$ *or* $-2x > 8$ using a graphing calculator. What inequality symbols should you use in your solution? Explain. $\ge$ and $<$; you have to reverse both of the original inequality symbols because each solution involves dividing by a negative number.

@HomeTutor classzone.com Keystrokes

6.4 Solve Compound Inequalities

QUESTION How can you use a graphing calculator to display the solutions of a compound inequality?

EXAMPLE Display the solutions of a compound inequality on a graphing calculator

Display the solutions of $12 \le 3x \le 21$ on a graphing calculator.

STEP 1 Rewrite inequality

Rewrite $12 \le 3x \le 21$ as two separate inequalities joined by *and*.

$12 \le 3x \le 21$ Write original inequality.

$12 \le 3x$ *and* $3x \le 21$ Write as two inequalities joined by *and*.

STEP 2 Enter inequalities

Press Y= and enter the two inequalities, as shown. Inequality signs can be found in the TEST menu, and *and* and *or* can be found in the LOGIC menu.

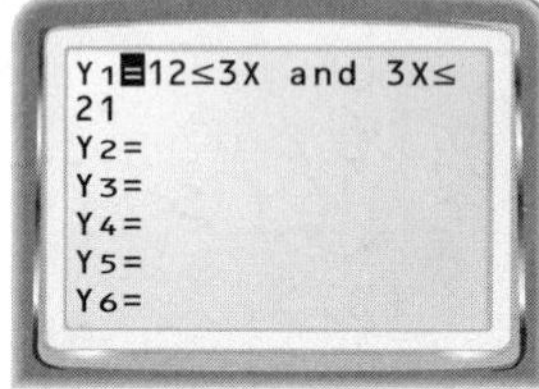

STEP 3 Display solutions

Press GRAPH to display the solutions of $12 \le 3x$ *and* $3x \le 21$. For each value of x that makes the inequality true, the calculator assigns a value of 1 to y and plots the point $(x, 1)$. For each value of x that makes the inequality false, the calculator assigns a value of 0 to y and plots the point $(x, 0)$.

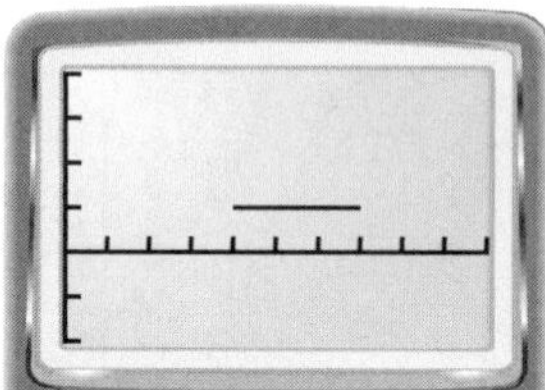

The screen in Step 3 shows the graph of $y = 1$ over the interval $4 \le x \le 7$. This suggests that the solutions are all real numbers greater than or equal to 4 *and* less than or equal to 7.

DRAW CONCLUSIONS

1. Display the solutions of $12 < 3x < 21$ on a graphing calculator. Then compare the graph of $12 < 3x < 21$ with the graph of $12 \le 3x \le 21$. $4 < x < 7$; the graphs are the same.
2. When displaying the solutions of an inequality on a graphing calculator, how do you know which inequality symbols you should use in your solution? Use the inequality symbols from the original inequality.

Display the solutions of the inequality on a graphing calculator.

3. $9 \le 3x \le 21$ $3 \le x \le 7$
4. $4 < 4x < 8$ $1 < x < 2$
5. $2 \le \frac{1}{4}x \le 12$ $8 \le x \le 48$
6. $-6x > 18$ *or* $9x > 45$ $x < -3$ or $x > 5$
7. $4x \le 18$ *or* $5x \ge 25$ $x \le 4\frac{1}{2}$ or $x \ge 5$
8. $8x \le 16$ *or* $3x \ge 30$ $x \le 2$ or $x \ge 10$

Illinois *Mixed Review*

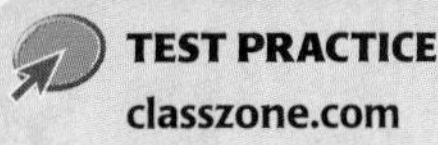

TEST PRACTICE
classzone.com

Lessons 6.1–6.4

1. **SPORTING GOODS** You have a $150 gift card to use at a sporting goods store. You buy 2 pairs of shoes for $65 each. You plan to spend the rest of the money on socks. Socks cost $4.75 per pair. Of all the possible numbers of pairs of socks that you can buy, which is the greatest number?

   A. 2 pairs
   B. 4 pairs
   C. 5 pairs
   D. 8 pairs

2. **SCIENCE TESTS** On the five science tests you have taken this semester, you received the following scores: 75, 82, 90, 84, and 71. You want an average score of at least 80 after you take the sixth test. Which inequality describes the possible scores s you can earn on your sixth test to meet your goal?

   F. $s > 76$ **H.** $s > 78$
   G. $s \geq 78$ **J.** $s \geq 80$

3. **NANOTUBE THERMOMETER** A nanotube thermometer is so tiny that it is invisible to the human eye. The thermometer can measure temperatures from 50°C to 500°C. Which temperature could the nanotube thermometer measure?

   A. 55°F **C.** 700°F
   B. 105°F **D.** 1450°F

4. **MODELING** Which situation can be modeled by the inequality $17x \leq 240$?

   F. A store sells 17 CDs for $240. Each CD costs x dollars.
   G. A customer has $240 and wants to buy at least 17 books. Each book costs x dollars.
   H. A business purchases 17 items for x dollars each. The business can spend no more than $240.
   J. You save x dollars every week in order to buy a bike that costs $240. After 17 weeks, you still cannot afford the bike.

5. **RAFTING TRIP** A rafting guide plans to take 6 children on a rafting trip. The raft can hold up to 550 pounds. The guide weighs 160 pounds and estimates that each child will bring 5 pounds of baggage. Which inequality describes the possible average weight w (in pounds) of the children?

   A. $w \leq 55$
   B. $w \leq 60$
   C. $w \leq 64.18$
   D. $w \leq 91.67$

6. **INCOME TAX** In 1862 the United States imposed a tax on annual income in order to pay for the expenses of the Civil War. The table shows the tax rates for different incomes. Which compound inequality describes the possible incomes of x dollars for which the tax was between $450 and $600?

Annual income	Tax rate
$600 to $10,000	3% of income
Greater than $10,000	3% of first $10,000 plus 5% of income over $10,000

   F. $3,000 \leq x \leq 6,000$
   G. $9,000 \leq x \leq 12,000$
   H. $13,000 \leq x \leq 16,000$
   J. $15,000 \leq x \leq 20,000$

7. **BAKE SALE** You need 34 eggs to make enough chiffon cakes for a bake sale. Your grocer sells cartons of eggs by the dozen. Of all the possible numbers of cartons that you can buy, what is the least number that you need?

   A. 1 carton
   B. 2 cartons
   C. 3 cartons
   D. 4 cartons

Illinois Mixed Review

1. B
2. G
3. C
4. H
5. B
6. H
7. C

1 PLAN AND PREPARE

Warm-Up Exercises

Transparency Available

1. For $a = -12$, find $-a$ and $|a|$. 12, 12
2. Evaluate $|x| - 2$ when $x = -3$. 1
3. The change in elevation as a diver explored a reef was −0.5 feet, 1.5 feet, −2.5 feet, and 2.25 feet. Which change in elevation had the greatest absolute value? −2.5 ft

Notetaking Guide

Transparency Available

Promotes interactive learning and notetaking skills, pp. 140–142.

Pacing

Basic: 2 days

Average: 2 days

Advanced: 2 days

Block: 0.5 block with 6.4
0.5 block with 6.6

- See *Teaching Guide/Lesson Plan.*

2 FOCUS AND MOTIVATE

Essential Question

Big Idea 2, p. 355

How do you solve absolute value equations? Tell students they will learn how to answer this question by rewriting absolute value equations as two equations and then solving the equations.

6.5 Solve Absolute Value Equations

8.11.19 Solve problems that include nonlinear functions, including selecting and evaluating formulas . . .

Before You solved linear equations.

Now You will solve absolute value equations.

Why? So you can analyze rules of a competition, as in Ex. 43.

Key Vocabulary
- **absolute value equation**
- **absolute deviation**
- **absolute value,** *p. 66*

The absolute value of a number a, written $|a|$, is the distance between a and 0 on a number line. An **absolute value equation**, such as $|x| = 4$, is an equation that contains an absolute value expression. The equation $|x| = 4$ means that the distance between x and 0 is 4. The solutions of the equation are 4 and −4, because they are the only numbers whose distance from 0 is 4.

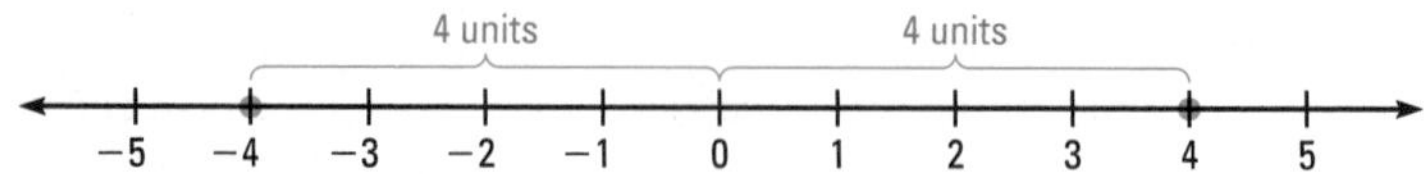

EXAMPLE 1 Solve an absolute value equation

Solve $|x| = 7$.

Solution

The distance between x and 0 is 7. So, $x = 7$ *or* $x = -7$.

▶ The solutions are 7 and −7.

at classzone.com

✓ GUIDED PRACTICE for Example 1

1. Solve (a) $|x| = 3$ and (b) $|x| = 15$.
   a. 3, −3
   b. 15, −15

SOLVING ABSOLUTE VALUE EQUATIONS In Example 1, notice that the expression inside the absolute value symbols equals 7 or the opposite of 7. This suggests the following rule for solving an absolute value equation.

KEY CONCEPT *For Your Notebook*

Solving an Absolute Value Equation

The equation $|ax + b| = c$ where $c \geq 0$ is equivalent to the statement $ax + b = c$ *or* $ax + b = -c$.

Resource Planning Guide

Chapter Resource Book
- Teaching Guide/Lesson Plan (pp. 58–59)
- Practice levels A, B, C (pp. 60–62)
- Study Guide (pp. 63–64)
- Catch-up for Absent Students (p. 65)
- Problem Solving Workshop (p. 66)
- Challenge (p. 67)

Workbooks
- Notetaking Guide (pp. 140–142)
- Practice Workbook (pp. 96–97)

Teaching Options
- **Power Presentations CD-ROM** provides dynamic electronic teaching resources for the classroom.
- **Activity Generator CD-ROM** provides editable activities for all ability levels.

Interactive Technology
- Easy Planner
- Power Presentations CD-ROM
- Activity Generator CD-ROM
- Animated Algebra
- Test Generator CD-ROM
- Online Quiz
- eWorkbook
- eEdition
- @HomeTutor

Resources for English Learners
- Quick Reference for English Learners
- Spanish Study Guide
- Multi-Language Visual Glossary
- Student Resources in Spanish

See also the *Algebra 1 Toolkit* for more strategies for meeting individual needs.

EXAMPLE 2 Solve an absolute value equation

Solve $|x - 3| = 8$.

Solution

Rewrite the absolute value equation as two equations. Then solve each equation separately.

AVOID ERRORS
You cannot solve the equation $|x - 3| = 8$ by adding 3 to each side because $|x - 3| + 3 \neq |x|$.

$|x - 3| = 8$	**Write original equation.**
$x - 3 = 8$ *or* $x - 3 = -8$	**Rewrite as two equations.**
$x = 11$ *or* $x = -5$	**Add 3 to each side.**

▶ The solutions are 11 and −5. Check your solutions.

CHECK			
	$|x - 3| = 8$	$|x - 3| = 8$	**Write original inequality.**
	$|11 - 3| \stackrel{?}{=} 8$	$|-5 - 3| \stackrel{?}{=} 8$	**Substitute for x.**
	$|8| \stackrel{?}{=} 8$	$|-8| \stackrel{?}{=} 8$	**Subtract.**
	$8 = 8$ ✓	$8 = 8$ ✓	**Simplify. The solution checks.**

REWRITING EQUATIONS To solve an absolute value equation, you may first need to rewrite the equation in the form $|ax + b| = c$.

EXAMPLE 3 Rewrite an absolute value equation

Solve $3|2x - 7| - 5 = 4$.

Solution

First, rewrite the equation in the form $|ax + b| = c$.

$3|2x - 7| - 5 = 4$	**Write original equation.**
$3|2x - 7| = 9$	**Add 5 to each side.**
$|2x - 7| = 3$	**Divide each side by 3.**

Next, solve the absolute value equation.

$|2x - 7| = 3$	**Write absolute value equation.**
$2x - 7 = 3$ *or* $2x - 7 = -3$	**Rewrite as two equations.**
$2x = 10$ *or* $2x = 4$	**Add 7 to each side.**
$x = 5$ *or* $x = 2$	**Divide each side by 2.**

▶ The solutions are 5 and 2.

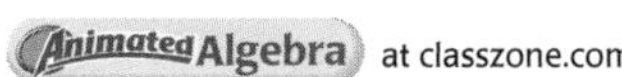 at classzone.com

 **GUIDED PRACTICE** for Examples 2 and 3

Solve the equation.

2. $|r - 7| = 9$ 16, −2 **3.** $2|s| + 4.1 = 18.9$ 7.4, −7.4 **4.** $4|t + 9| - 5 = 19$ −3, −15

Motivating the Lesson

Ask students what they think it means when a sports item such as a tennis racquet or a soccer ball is advertised as "official." Invite students to share any specialized knowledge they might have concerning specifications of sports equipment. Point out that some deviations from an official standard generally are permitted. Then tell students that knowing how to solve absolute value equations will help them determine whether a sports item is within the "official" range.

3 TEACH

Extra Example 1

Solve $|x| = 9$. 9, −9

An **Animated Algebra** activity is available on-line for **Examples 1 and 3**. These activities are also available on the **Power Presentations CD-ROM**.

Extra Example 2

Solve $|x + 4| = 3$. −1, −7

Key Questions to Ask for Example 2

- When can you perform operations on an absolute value expression? after you remove the absolute value symbols and rewrite the equation as two equations
- Why is the expression $x - 3$ inside the absolute value symbol equal to 8 or −8? because 8 and −8 are 8 units from 0 on a number line

Extra Example 3

Solve $3|4x + 2| - 7 = 11$. 1, −2

NO SOLUTIONS The absolute value of a number is never negative. So, when an absolute value expression equals a negative number, there are *no solutions.*

EXAMPLE 4 Decide if an equation has no solutions

Solve $|3x + 5| + 6 = -2$, if possible.

$|3x + 5| + 6 = -2$ **Write original equation.**

$|3x + 5| = -8$ **Subtract 6 from each side.**

▶ The absolute value of a number is never negative. So, there are no solutions.

ABSOLUTE DEVIATION The **absolute deviation** of a number x from a given value is the absolute value of the difference of x and the given value: absolute deviation $= |x - \text{given value}|$.

EXAMPLE 5 Use absolute deviation

BASKETBALLS Before the start of a professional basketball game, a basketball must be inflated to an air pressure of 8 pounds per square inch (psi) with an absolute error of 0.5 psi. (*Absolute error* is the absolute deviation of a measured value from an accepted value.) Find the minimum and maximum acceptable air pressures for the basketball.

Solution

Let p be the air pressure (in psi) of a basketball. Write a verbal model. Then write and solve an absolute value equation.

Absolute error	= |	Measured air pressure	−	Accepted air pressure	|
↓		↓		↓	
0.5	= |	***p***	−	**8**	|

$0.5 = |p - 8|$ **Write original equation.**

$0.5 = p - 8$ *or* $-0.5 = p - 8$ **Rewrite as two equations.**

$8.5 = p$ *or* $7.5 = p$ **Add 8 to each side.**

▶ The minimum and maximum acceptable pressures are 7.5 psi and 8.5 psi.

GUIDED PRACTICE for Examples 4 and 5

Solve the equation, if possible.

5. $2|m - 5| + 4 = 2$ no solution

6. $-3|n + 2| - 7 = -10$ −1, −3

7. The absolute deviation of x from 7.6 is 5.2. What are the values of x that satisfy this requirement? 12.8, 2.4

Extra Example 4

Solve $3|2x - 8| + 3 = 2$, if possible. In $|ax + b| = c$ form, the exercise is $|2x - 8| = -\frac{1}{3}$, but the absolute value of a number is never negative. So, there are no solutions.

Key Question to Ask for Example 4

- Why is the absolute value of a number never negative? Absolute value is the distance of a number from 0 on the number line. Distance cannot be negative, so absolute value is never negative.

Extra Example 5

A volleyball league is preparing a two minute radio ad to announce tryouts. The ad has an absolute deviation of 0.05 minute. Find the minimum and maximum acceptable times the radio ad can run. minimum: 1.95 min; maximum: 2.05 min

Closing the Lesson

Have students summarize the major points of the lesson and answer the Essential Question: How do you solve absolute value equations?

- You can rewrite an absolute value equation as two equations and then solve each equation separately to solve the absolute value equation.
- Some absolute value equations have no solution.

Rewrite an absolute value equation in the form $|ax + b| = c$, if necessary, and then rewrite it as two equations $ax + b = c$ and $ax + b = -c$. Solve each equation separately.

Differentiated Instruction

Kinesthetic Learners Students can use a compass to understand the absolute deviation. In **Example 5**, the pressure is centered around 8, so have students plot 8 on a number line with increments of 0.1. Have them set a compass so the radius is equal to 0.5 (the absolute deviation) and draw a circle with center at 8. The points of the circle on the number line give the maximum and minimum values with the desired absolute deviation.

See also the *Algebra 1 Toolkit* for more strategies.

6.5 EXERCISES

HOMEWORK KEY
○ = **WORKED-OUT SOLUTIONS** on p. WS14 for Exs. 11, 23, and 45
★ = **STANDARDIZED TEST PRACTICE** Exs. 2, 32, 44, 48, and 49

SKILL PRACTICE

A

1. **VOCABULARY** Copy and complete: The equation $|x - 7| = 0.15$ is an example of a(n) _?_. absolute value equation

2. ★ **WRITING** Given $|x - 9| = 5$, describe the relationship between x, 9, and 5 using absolute deviation. The absolute deviation of x from 9 is 5.

EXAMPLES 1, 2, and 3 on pp. 390–391 for Exs. 3–20

SOLVING EQUATIONS Solve the equation.

3. $|x| = 5$ 5, −5
4. $|y| = 36$ 36, −36
5. $|v| = 0.7$ 0.7, −0.7
6. $|w| = 9.2$ 9.2, −9.2
7. $|r| = \frac{1}{2}$ $\frac{1}{2}, -\frac{1}{2}$
8. $|s| = \frac{7}{4}$ $\frac{7}{4}, -\frac{7}{4}$
9. $|m + 3| = 7$ 4, −10
10. $|4n - 5| = 18$ $5\frac{3}{4}, -3\frac{1}{4}$
11. $|3p + 7| = 4$ $-1, -3\frac{2}{3}$
12. $|q + 8| = 2$ −6, −10
13. $|2d + 7| = 11$ 2, −9
14. $|f - 8| = 14$ 22, −6
15. $3|13 - 2t| = 15$ 4, 9
16. $4|b - 1| - 7 = 17$ 7, −5
17. $\frac{1}{3}|2c - 5| + 3 = 7$ $8\frac{1}{2}, -3\frac{1}{2}$
18. $\frac{7}{4}|3j + 5| + 1 = 15$ $1, -4\frac{1}{3}$
19. $4|2k + 3| - 2 = 6$ $-\frac{1}{2}, -2\frac{1}{2}$
20. $-3|5g + 1| - 6 = -9$ $0, -\frac{2}{5}$

ERROR ANALYSIS *Describe* and correct the error in solving the absolute value equation.

21.
$|x + 4| = 13$
$x + 4 = 13$
$x = 9$

21. The absolute value symbol was removed without writing the second equation, $x + 4 = -13$; $x = 9$ or $x = -17$.

22.
$|x - 6| = -2$
$x - 6 = -2$ or $x - 6 = 2$
$x = 4$ or $x = 8$

22. The absolute value of a number is never negative, so it is incorrect to rewrite this absolute value equation as two equations; there are no solutions.

EXAMPLE 4 on p. 392 for Exs. 23–31

SOLVING EQUATIONS Solve the equation, if possible.

23. $|x - 1| + 5 = 2$ no solution
24. $|y - 4| + 8 = 6$ no solution
25. $|m + 5| + 1.5 = 2$ −4.5, −5.5
26. $-4|8 - 5n| = 13$ no solution
27. $-3\left|1 - \frac{2}{3}v\right| = -9$ −3, 6
28. $-5\left|\frac{4}{5}w + 6\right| = -10$ −5, −10
29. $-10|14 - r| - 2 = -7$ $13\frac{1}{2}, 14\frac{1}{2}$
30. $-2\left|\frac{1}{3}s - 5\right| + 3 = 8$ no solution
31. $-9|4p + 2| - 8 = -35$ $\frac{1}{4}, -1\frac{1}{4}$

32. ★ **MULTIPLE CHOICE** Which number is a solution of $|4x - 1| + 2 = 1$? D

Ⓐ $-\frac{1}{2}$ Ⓑ 0 Ⓒ 1 Ⓓ There is no solution.

EXAMPLE 5 on p. 392 for Exs. 33–36

USING ABSOLUTE DEVIATION Find the values of x that satisfy the definition of absolute deviation for the given value and the given absolute deviation.

33. Given value: 5; absolute deviation: 8 13, −3
34. Given value: 20; absolute deviation: 5 25, 15
35. Given value: −9.1; absolute deviation: 1.6 −7.5, −10.7
36. Given value: −3.4; absolute deviation: 6.7 3.3, −10.1

4 PRACTICE AND APPLY

Assignment Guide

Answer Transparencies available for all exercises

Basic:
Day 1: EP p. 940 Exs. 12–20 pp. 393–395 Exs. 1–22, 51–53
Day 2: pp. 393–395 Exs. 23–37, 42–47, 54–59

Average:
Day 1: pp. 393–395 Exs. 1, 2, 6–17, 37–40, 51–53
Day 2: pp. 393–395 Exs. 21–36, 42–49, 54–59

Advanced:
Day 1: pp. 393–395 Exs. 1, 2, 6–8, 12–20, 37–41*, 54–59
Day 2: pp. 393–395 Exs. 24–36, 43–50*, 54–58 even

Block:
pp. 393–395 Exs. 1, 2, 6–17, 37–40, 51–53 (with 6.4)
pp. 393–395 Exs. 21–36, 42–49, 54–59 (with 6.6)

Differentiated Instruction

See *Algebra 1 Best Practices Toolkit* for suggestions on addressing the needs of a diverse classroom.

Homework Check

For a quick check of student understanding of key concepts, go over the following exercises:

Basic: 4, 10, 16, 24, 42
Average: 6, 12, 17, 26, 44
Advanced: 8, 14, 20, 30, 45

Extra Practice

- Student Edition, p. 943
- Chapter 6 Resource Book: Practice levels A, B, C, pp. 60–62

Practice Worksheet

An easily-readable reduced practice page (with answers) for this lesson can be found on p. 354E.

Differentiated Instruction

Below Level Some students may need help in determining whether they can solve **Exercises 23–31**. Demonstrate strategies they can use to determine whether the absolute value equation is equal to a negative number and, thus, has no solution. In **Exercise 24**, point out that the right side becomes $6 - 8$, and in **Exercise 26**, point out that the right side becomes $\frac{13}{-4}$. Have students use these strategies to identify all the exercises that have no solutions.

See also the *Algebra 1 Toolkit* for more strategies.

Avoiding Common Errors

Exercises 15–20 Watch for students who try to solve these equations without rewriting them in the form $|ax + b| = c$. Remind them that the absolute value expression must be equal to a nonnegative number before they can rewrite it as two equations.

Mathematical Reasoning

Exercise 37 Students should know that $|x| = b$ means x is b units from 0 on the number line. You may want to ask them to interpret $|x - 0| = b$ as a middle step in understanding that $|x - a| = b$ means x is b units from a.

B **37. SOLVING AN EQUATION** Interpreted geometrically, the equation $|x - a| = b$ means that the distance between x and a on a number line is b. Solve $|x - 3| = 7$ both geometrically and algebraically. *Compare* your solutions. The distance between x and 3 is 7, 10, −4; $x - 3 = 7$ or $x - 3 = -7$, 10, −4; the solutions are the same.

TRANSLATING SENTENCES In Exercises 38 and 39, write the verbal sentence as an absolute value equation. Then solve the equation.

38. Four more than the absolute deviation of x from 3 is 8. $|x - 3| + 4 = 8$; 7, −1

39. Five times the absolute deviation of $2x$ from −9 is 15. $5|2x + 9| = 15$; −3, −6

40. REASONING Is $a|x|$ equivalent to $|ax|$ when a is positive? when a is negative? when a is 0? Give examples to support your answers. See margin.

C **41. CHALLENGE** How many solutions does the equation $a|x + b| + c = d$ have if $a > 0$ and $c = d$? if $a < 0$ and $c > d$? one, two

PROBLEM SOLVING

EXAMPLE 5 on p. 392 for Exs. 42–46

A **42. GUARDRAILS** A safety regulation requires that the height of a guardrail be 42 inches with an absolute deviation of 3 inches. Find the minimum and maximum heights of a guardrail. 39 in., 45 in.

@HomeTutor for problem solving help at classzone.com

40. Yes; no; yes; when $a = 3$ and $x = -2$, $3|-2| = 3(2) = 6 = |-6| = |3(-2)|$; when $a = -3$ and $x = -2$, $-3|-2| = -3(2) = -6 \neq |6| = |-3(-2)|$; when $a = 0$ and $x = -2$, $0|-2| = 0 = |0| = |0(-2)|$.

43. CHEERLEADING A cheerleading team is preparing a dance program for a competition. The program must last 4 minutes with an absolute deviation of 5 seconds. Find the least and greatest possible times (in seconds) that the program can last. 235 sec, 245 sec

@HomeTutor for problem solving help at classzone.com

44. ★ MULTIPLE CHOICE The diameter of a billiard ball must be 2.25 inches with an absolute error of 0.005 inch. What is the maximum possible diameter that a billiard ball can have? C

Ⓐ 2.2 inches Ⓑ 2.245 inches Ⓒ 2.255 inches Ⓓ 2.3 inches

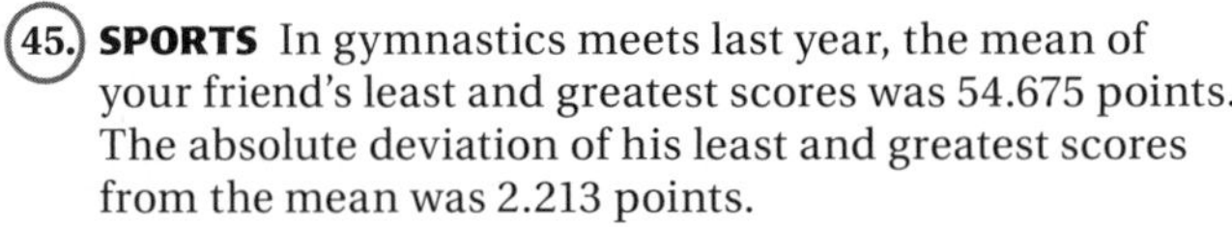

45. SPORTS In gymnastics meets last year, the mean of your friend's least and greatest scores was 54.675 points. The absolute deviation of his least and greatest scores from the mean was 2.213 points.

a. What were the least and greatest scores that he earned? 52.462 points, 56.888 points

b. This year the mean of his least and greatest scores is 56.738 points, and the absolute deviation of the least and greatest scores from the mean is 0.45 point. How many points more than last year's greatest score is this year's greatest score? 0.3 point

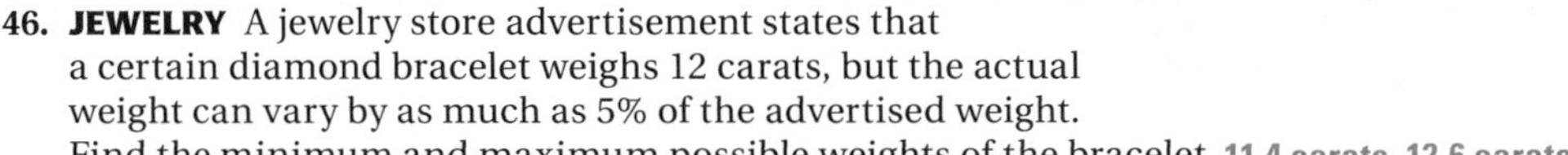

46. JEWELRY A jewelry store advertisement states that a certain diamond bracelet weighs 12 carats, but the actual weight can vary by as much as 5% of the advertised weight. Find the minimum and maximum possible weights of the bracelet. 11.4 carats, 12.6 carats

◯ = WORKED-OUT SOLUTIONS on p. WS1 ★ = STANDARDIZED TEST PRACTICE

394

B 47. **CONTESTS** You currently have 450 points in an academic contest. You choose the value p of the question you want to answer. The value p represents the absolute deviation of your new score s from 450.

a. Write an absolute value equation that gives p in terms of s. $p = |s - 450|$

b. If you choose a question worth 150 points, what are the possible new scores that you can have after answering the question? 300 points, 600 points

48. ★ **EXTENDED RESPONSE** The percent p of United States residents who were foreign born, or born outside of the United States, during the period 1910–2000 can be modeled by the equation $p = 0.165|t - 60| + 4.8$ where t is the number of years since 1910.

a. **Approximate** During the period 1910–2000, in approximately what year did foreign-born residents account for 13% of all residents? 1920

b. **Predict** If the model holds for years after 2000, predict the year in which foreign-born residents will again account for 13% of all residents. 2020

c. **Decide** According to the model, did foreign-born residents account for 4% of all residents at any time during the period 1910–2000? *Explain* your answer. No; if you substitute 4 for p in the model, the equation has no solution.

49b. Yes; make a table of values for (m, p) using integer values of m from 0 to 8. Look for the lowest value of p in the table.

49. ★ **SHORT RESPONSE** A stock's average price p (in dollars) during the period February 2005 to October 2005 can be modeled by the equation $p = 2.3|m - 7| + 9.57$ where m is the number of months since February 2005.

a. **Approximate** In approximately what month and year was the average price \$16.15? If the model holds for months after October 2005, predict the month and year in which the average price will again be \$16.15. June 2005; November 2005

b. **Justify** Is it possible to use the model to estimate the stock's lowest average price during this period? *Justify* your answer.

C 50. **CHALLENGE** In a recent Olympics, swimmers in a men's 200 meter butterfly event finished with times from 1 minute 54.04 seconds to 1 minute 57.48 seconds. Let t represent the slowest or fastest time (in seconds). Write an absolute value equation that describes the situation. $|t - 115.76| \leq 1.72$

ILLINOIS MIXED REVIEW

TEST PRACTICE at classzone.com

51. What are the x- and y-intercepts of the graph of the function $2x - 3y = 6$? D

Ⓐ (2, 0) and (0, −3)
Ⓑ (−2, 0) and (0, 3)
Ⓒ (−3, 0) and (0, −2)
Ⓓ (3, 0) and (0, −2)

52. A rectangular prism with a volume of 50 cm^3 has length ℓ, width w, and height h. A second rectangular prism has length 3ℓ, width $2w$, and height $\frac{h}{2}$. What is the volume of the second prism? B

Ⓐ 100 cm^3 Ⓑ 150 cm^3 Ⓒ 300 cm^3 Ⓓ 600 cm^3

5 ASSESS AND RETEACH

Daily Homework Quiz

Transparency Available

Solve the equation, if possible.

1. $|x - 4| = 13$ −9, 17
2. $|x + 2| + 7 = 3$ no solutions
3. $|2x - 6| + 4 = 20$ −5, 11
4. $-2|x - 5| + 7 = 12$ no solutions
5. A pattern for a 26-inch skirt allows for an absolute deviation of 1.5 inches. Find the minimum and maximum skirt lengths that can be made from the pattern. minimum: 24.5 in.; maximum: 27.5 in.

Online Quiz

Available at **classzone.com**

Diagnosis/Remediation

- Practice A, B, C in Chapter 6 Resource Book, pp. 60–62
- Study Guide in Chapter 6 Resource Book, pp. 63–64
- Practice Workbook, pp. 96–97
- @HomeTutor

Challenge

Additional challenge is available in the Chapter 6 Resource Book, p. 67.

Extension
Use after Lesson 6.5

Graph Absolute Value Functions

1 PLAN AND PREPARE

Warm-Up Exercises

Evaluate the expression when $x = -2$.

1. $|x - 3|$ 5
2. $-4|x|$ −8

2 FOCUS AND MOTIVATE

Essential Question

Big Idea 2, p. 355

How do you graph absolute value functions? Tell students they will learn how to answer this question by using a table to plot points.

3 TEACH

Extra Example 1

Graph each function. Compare the graph with the graph of $f(x) = |x|$.

a. $g(x) = |x + 1|$

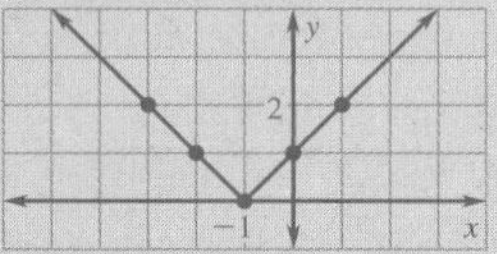

The graph is 1 unit to the left of the graph of $f(x) = |x|$.

b. $g(x) = |x| + 2$

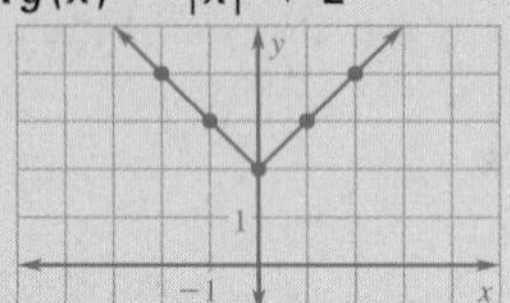

The graph is 2 units above the graph of $f(x) = |x|$.

NCTM STANDARDS

Standard 2: Understand functions

Standard 3: Apply transformations to math situations

GOAL Graph absolute value functions.

Key Vocabulary
- **absolute value,** *p. 66*

The function $f(x) = |x|$ is an example of an *absolute value function* and is the parent function for all absolute value functions. You can graph absolute value functions by using a table of values, as shown below for $f(x) = |x|$.

KEY CONCEPT *For Your Notebook*

Graph of Parent Function for Absolute Value Functions

x	$f(x) = \|x\|$
−2	$\|-2\| = 2$
−1	$\|-1\| = 1$
0	$\|0\| = 0$
1	$\|1\| = 1$
2	$\|2\| = 2$

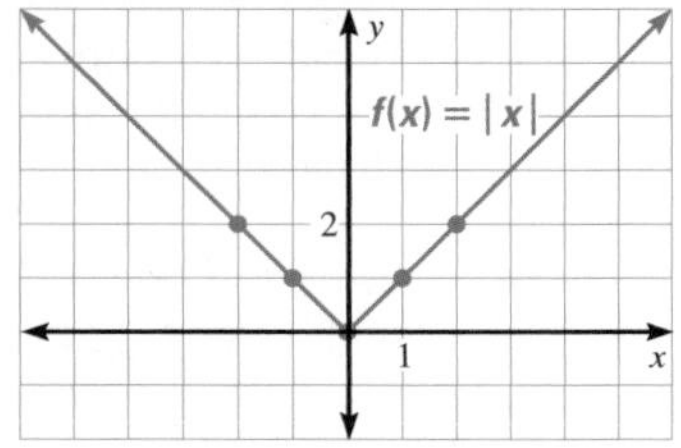

EXAMPLE 1 Graph $g(x) = |x - h|$ and $g(x) = |x| + k$

Graph each function. Compare the graph with the graph of $f(x) = |x|$.

a. $g(x) = |x - 2|$

STEP 1 **Make** a table of values.

x	0	1	2	3	4
$g(x)$	2	1	0	1	2

STEP 2 **Graph** the function.

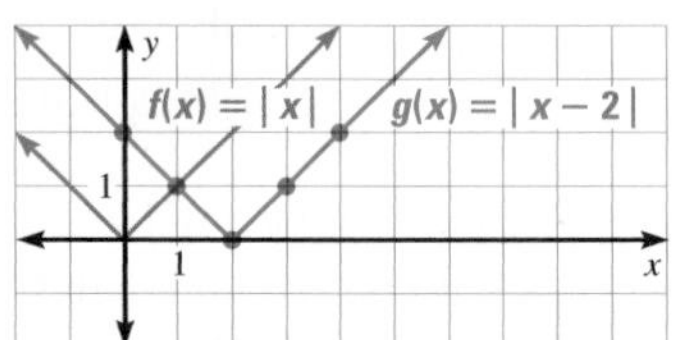

STEP 3 **Compare** the graphs of g and f. The graph of $g(x) = |x - 2|$ is 2 units to the right of the graph of $f(x) = |x|$.

b. $g(x) = |x| - 1$

STEP 1 **Make** a table of values.

x	−2	−1	0	1	2
$g(x)$	1	0	−1	0	1

STEP 2 **Graph** the function.

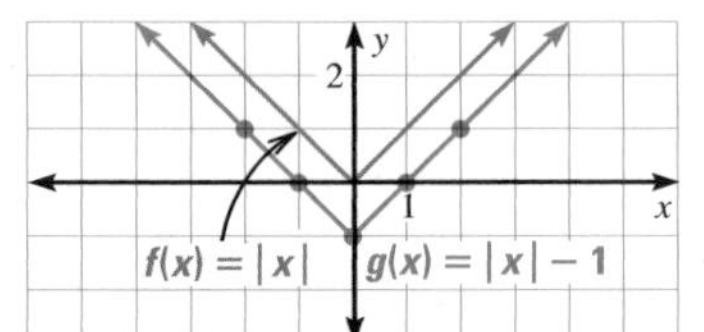

STEP 3 **Compare** the graphs of g and f. The graph of $g(x) = |x| - 1$ is 1 unit below the graph of $f(x) = |x|$.

APPLY TRANSFORMATIONS
The two graphs in Example 1 are translations of the graph of $f(x) = |x|$. The graph in part (a) is a horizontal translation. The graph in part (b) is a vertical translation.

EXAMPLE 2 Graph $g(x) = a|x|$

Graph each function. Compare the graph with the graph of $f(x) = |x|$.

a. $g(x) = 4|x|$

STEP 1 **Make** a table of values.

x	−2	−1	0	1	2
$g(x)$	8	4	0	4	8

STEP 2 **Graph** the function.

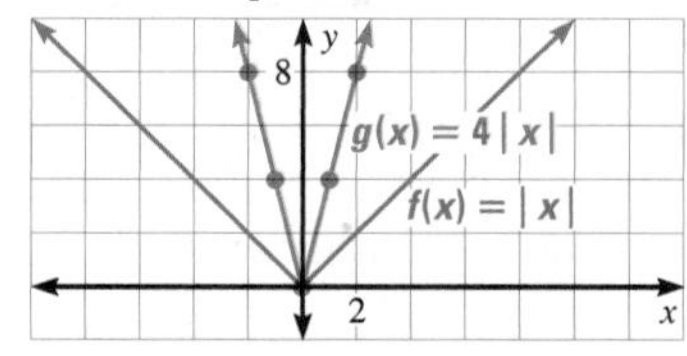

STEP 3 **Compare** the graphs of g and f. The graph of $g(x) = 4|x|$ opens up and is narrower than the graph of $f(x) = |x|$.

b. $g(x) = -0.5|x|$

STEP 1 **Make** a table of values.

x	−4	−2	0	2	4
$g(x)$	−2	−1	0	−1	−2

STEP 2 **Graph** the function.

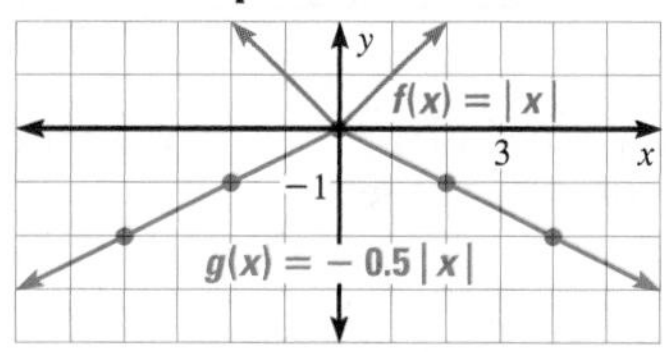

STEP 3 **Compare** the graphs of g and f. The graph of $g(x) = -0.5|x|$ opens down and is wider than the graph of $f(x) = |x|$.

APPLY TRANSFORMATIONS
The graph in part (a) of Example 2 is a vertical stretch of the graph of $f(x) = |x|$. The graph in part (b) is a vertical shrink with a reflection in the x-axis of the graph of $f(x) = |x|$.

KEY CONCEPT *For Your Notebook*

Comparing Graphs of Absolute Value Functions with the Graph of $f(x) = |x|$

$g(x) = |x - h|$

If $h > 0$, the graph of g is $|h|$ units to the right of the graph of $f(x) = |x|$.

If $h < 0$, the graph of g is $|h|$ units to the left of the graph of $f(x) = |x|$.

$g(x) = |x| + k$

If $k > 0$, the graph of g is $|k|$ units above the graph of $f(x) = |x|$.

If $k < 0$, the graph of g is $|k|$ units below the graph of $f(x) = |x|$.

$g(x) = a|x|$

If $|a| > 1$, the graph of g is narrower than the graph of $f(x) = |x|$. If $0 < |a| < 1$, the graph of g is wider.

If $a > 0$, the graph of g opens up. If $a < 0$, the graph opens down.

PRACTICE

EXAMPLES 1 and 2
on pp. 396–397 for Exs. 1–6

Graph the function. ***Compare*** **the graph with the graph of $f(x) = |x|$.** 1–6. See margin.

1. $g(x) = |x + 3|$
2. $g(x) = |x| + 5$
3. $g(x) = |x| - 7$
4. $g(x) = 2|x|$
5. $g(x) = 0.6|x|$
6. $g(x) = -3|x|$
7. Make a table of values for $g(x) = 2|x - 3| + 4$. Use the following values for x: 1, 2, 3, 4, 5. Then graph the function and compare the graph with the graph of $f(x) = |x|$. See margin.

Extra Example 2

Graph each function. Compare the graph with the graph of $f(x) = |x|$.

a. $g(x) = -2|x|$

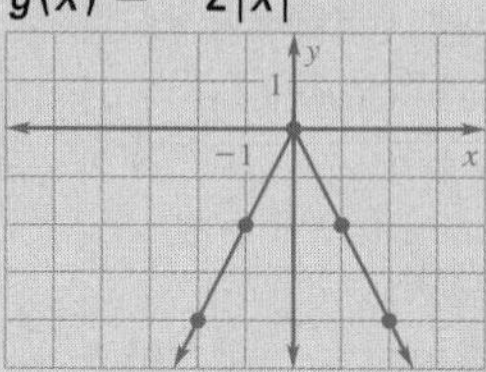

The graph opens down and is narrower than the graph of $f(x) = |x|$.

b. $g(x) = 0.5|x|$

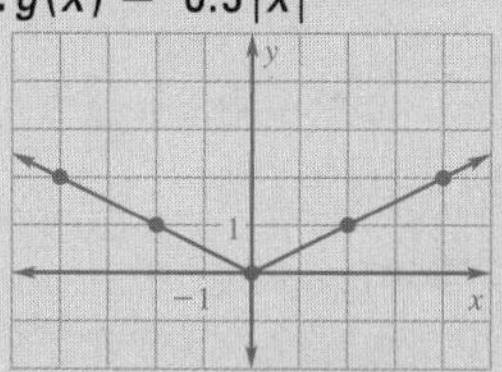

The graph is wider than the graph of $f(x) = |x|$.

Closing the Lesson

Have students summarize the major points of the lesson and answer the Essential Question: How do you graph absolute value functions?

- Absolute value functions are transformations of the parent function $f(x) = |x|$.

Make a table of values for the function. Plot points and connect them.

4 PRACTICE AND APPLY

Avoiding Common Errors

Exercises 1–7 Some students may make a table of values for one side of the function only. Have them start in the middle of the table with an x value that gives 0 for the expression inside the absolute value symbols. Then assign x values on each side of that first value.

1–6. See Additional Answers beginning on p. AA1.

7.

x	1	2	3	4	5
$g(x)$	8	6	4	6	8

See graph at right. The graph of g is the graph of f moved 3 units right and 4 units up, and made narrower.

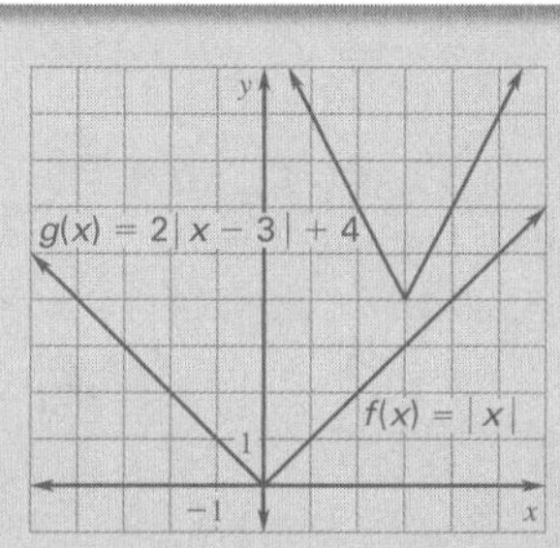

1 PLAN AND PREPARE

Warm-Up Exercises

Transparency Available

1. Solve $|x - 6| = 4$. **2, 10**
2. Solve $|x + 5| - 8 = 2$. **−15, 5**
3. A frame will hold photographs that are 5 inches by 8 inches with an absolute deviation of 0.25 inch for length and width. What are the minimum and maximum dimensions for photos? **min: 4.75 in. by 7.75 in.; max: 5.25 in. by 8.25 in.**

Notetaking Guide

Transparency Available

Promotes interactive learning and notetaking skills, pp. 143–145.

Pacing

Basic: 1 day
Average: 1 day
Advanced: 1 day
Block: 0.5 block with 6.5

- See *Teaching Guide/Lesson Plan*.

2 FOCUS AND MOTIVATE

Essential Question

Big Idea 1, p. 355

How do you solve absolute value inequalities? **Tell students they will learn how to answer this question by rewriting absolute value inequalities as compound inequalities and solving them.**

6.6 Solve Absolute Value Inequalities

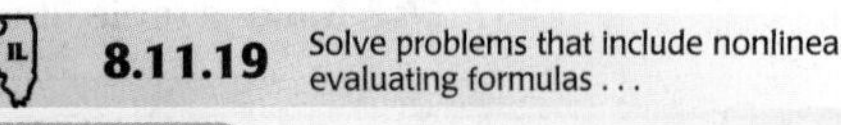

8.11.19 Solve problems that include nonlinear functions, including selecting and evaluating formulas . . .

Before You solved absolute value equations.

Now You will solve absolute value inequalities.

Why So you can analyze softball compression, as in Ex. 38.

Key Vocabulary
- **absolute value,** *p. 66*
- **equivalent inequalities,** *p. 357*
- **compound inequality,** *p. 380*
- **absolute deviation,** *p. 392*
- **mean,** *p. 918*

Recall that $|x| = 3$ means that the distance between x and 0 is 3. The inequality $|x| < 3$ means that the distance between x and 0 is *less than* 3, and $|x| > 3$ means that the distance between x and 0 is *greater than* 3. The graphs of $|x| < 3$ and $|x| > 3$ are shown below.

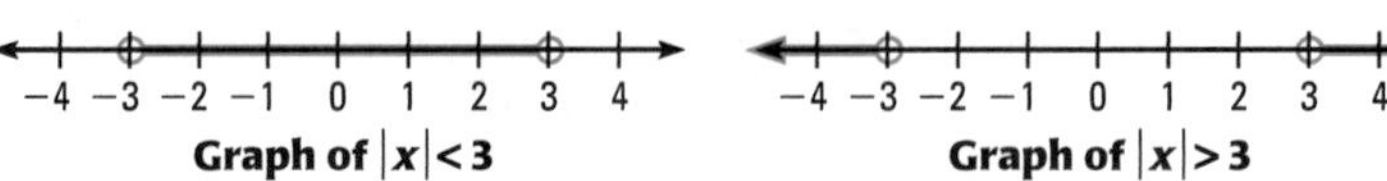

EXAMPLE 1 Solve absolute value inequalities

Solve the inequality. Graph your solution.

a. $|x| \geq 6$ **b.** $|x| \leq 0.5$

Solution

a. The distance between x and 0 is greater than or equal to 6. So, $x \leq -6$ *or* $x \geq 6$.

▶ The solutions are all real numbers less than or equal to −6 *or* greater than or equal to 6.

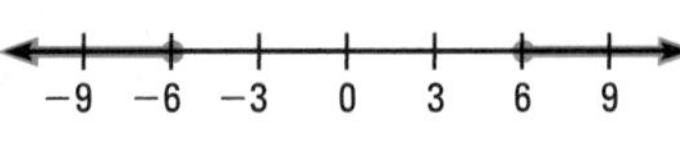

b. The distance between x and 0 is less than or equal to 0.5. So, $-0.5 \leq x \leq 0.5$.

▶ The solutions are all real numbers greater than or equal to −0.5 *and* less than or equal to 0.5.

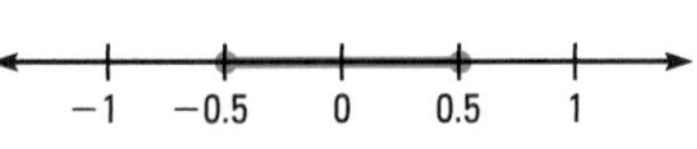

✓ GUIDED PRACTICE for Example 1

Solve the inequality. Graph your solution. **1–3. See margin for art.**

1. $|x| \leq 8$ **$-8 \leq x \leq 8$**
2. $|u| < 3.5$ **$-3.5 < u < 3.5$**
3. $|v| > \frac{2}{3}$ **$v < -\frac{2}{3}$ or $v > \frac{2}{3}$**

SOLVING ABSOLUTE VALUE INEQUALITIES In Example 1, the solutions of $|x| \geq 6$ and $|x| \leq 0.5$ suggest that you can rewrite an absolute value inequality as a compound inequality.

Resource Planning Guide

Chapter Resource Book
- Teaching Guide/Lesson Plan (pp. 68–69)
- Activity Master (p. 70)
- Practice levels A, B, C (pp. 71–76)
- Study Guide (pp. 77–78)
- Catch-up for Absent Students (p. 79)
- Application (p. 80)
- Challenge (p. 81)

Workbooks
- Notetaking Guide (pp. 143–145)
- Practice Workbook (pp. 98–100)

Teaching Options
- **Power Presentations CD-ROM** provides dynamic electronic teaching resources for the classroom.
- **Activity Generator CD-ROM** provides editable activities for all ability levels.

Interactive Technology
- Easy Planner
- Power Presentations CD-ROM
- Activity Generator CD-ROM
- Animated Algebra
- Test Generator CD-ROM
- Online Quiz
- eWorkbook
- eEdition
- @HomeTutor

Resources for English Learners
- Quick Reference for English Learners
- Spanish Study Guide
- Multi-Language Visual Glossary
- Student Resources in Spanish

See also the *Algebra 1 Toolkit* for more strategies for meeting individual needs.

READING
You can use the words *between* and *beyond* to describe absolute value inequalites. For example, $|x| < 2$ means that x is between -2 *and* 2; $|x| > 2$ means that x is beyond -2 *or* beyond 2.

KEY CONCEPT *For Your Notebook*

Solving Absolute Value Inequalities

- The inequality $|ax + b| < c$ where $c > 0$ is equivalent to the compound inequality $-c < ax + b < c$.
- The inequality $|ax + b| > c$ where $c > 0$ is equivalent to the compound inequality $ax + b < -c$ *or* $ax + b > c$.

In the inequalities above, $<$ can be replaced by $\le$ and $>$ can be replaced by $\ge$.

EXAMPLE 2 Solve an absolute value inequality

Solve $|x - 5| \ge 7$. Graph your solution.

$\lvert x - 5\rvert \ge 7$	Write original inequality.
$x - 5 \le -7$ *or* $x - 5 \ge 7$	Rewrite as compound inequality.
$x \le -2$ *or* $x \ge 12$	Add 5 to each side.

▶ The solutions are all real numbers less than or equal to -2 *or* greater than or equal to 12. Check several solutions in the original inequality.

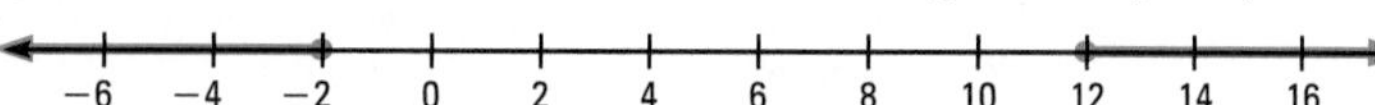

EXAMPLE 3 Solve an absolute value inequality

Solve $|-4x - 5| + 3 < 9$. Graph your solution.

$\lvert -4x - 5\rvert + 3 < 9$	Write original inequality.
$\lvert -4x - 5\rvert < 6$	Subtract 3 from each side.
$-6 < -4x - 5 < 6$	Rewrite as compound inequality.
$-1 < -4x < 11$	Add 5 to each expression.
$0.25 > x > -2.75$	Divide each expression by -4. Reverse inequality symbol.
$-2.75 < x < 0.25$	Rewrite in the form $a < x < b$.

▶ The solutions are all real numbers greater than -2.75 *and* less than 0.25.

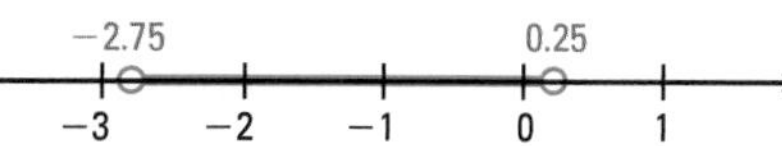

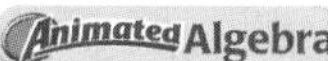

at classzone.com

GUIDED PRACTICE for Examples 2 and 3

Solve the inequality. Graph your solution. 4–6. See margin for art.

4. $|x + 3| > 8$
 $x < -11$ or $x > 5$
5. $|2w - 1| < 11$
 $-5 < w < 6$
6. $3|5m - 6| - 8 \le 13$
 $-0.2 \le m \le 2.6$

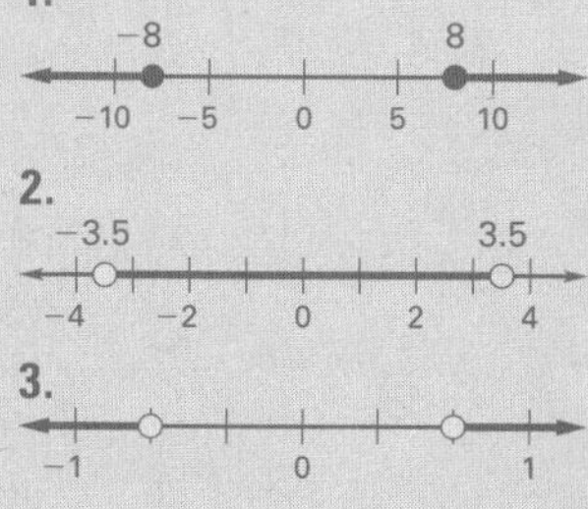

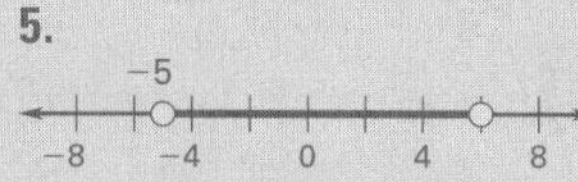

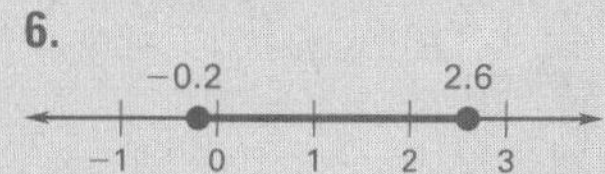

Motivating the Lesson

Knowing how to solve absolute value inequalities can help you analyze statistical data. For example, if you know that 582 people in a poll voted for a candidate and the poll has a 2% margin of error, you can determine the least and greatest number of people who voted for the candidate.

3 TEACH

Extra Example 1

Solve the inequality. Graph your solution.

a. $|x| > 2$ all real numbers less than -2 *or* greater than 2

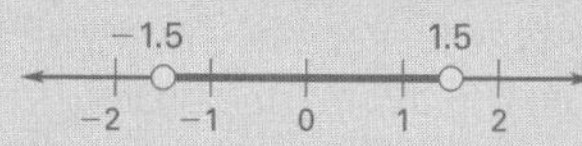

b. $|x| < 1.5$ all real numbers greater than -1.5 *and* less than 1.5

−1.5 1.5
−2 −1 0 1 2

Extra Example 2

Solve $|x + 2| > 1$. Graph your solution. all real numbers less than -3 *or* greater than -1

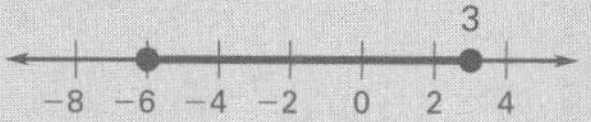

Extra Example 3

Solve $|2x + 3| - 4 \le 5$. Graph your solution. all real numbers greater than or equal to -6 *and* less than or equal to 3

Animated Algebra classzone.com

An **Animated Algebra** activity is available on-line for **Example 3**. This activity is also available on the **Power Presentations CD-ROM**.

Extra Example 4

You are on the planning committee for a school dance. Ticket sales for the last ten dances are 133, 178, 205, 220, 186, 142, 138, 204, 216, and 198.

- Find the mean number of tickets sold.
- The dance committee estimates they will sell the mean number of tickets with an absolute deviation of at most 40 tickets. How many of the ticket sales to the previous ten dances were within this range?

The mean number of tickets sold is 182. The range of sales within 40 tickets of the mean is 142 to 222 tickets. Eight previous ticket sales fell within this range: 178, 205, 220, 186, 142, 204, 216, and 198.

Closing the Lesson

Have students summarize the major points of the lesson and answer the Essential Question: How do you solve absolute value inequalities?

- **You can rewrite an absolute value inequality as a compound inequality. Inequalities using > or ≥ can be rewritten using *or*. Inequalities using < or ≤ can be rewritten using *and*.**

Rewrite the absolute value inequality so one side is $|ax + b|$. Then write the compound inequality as two inequalities joined by *or* for > and ≥, or by *and* for < and ≤, and solve the inequalities.

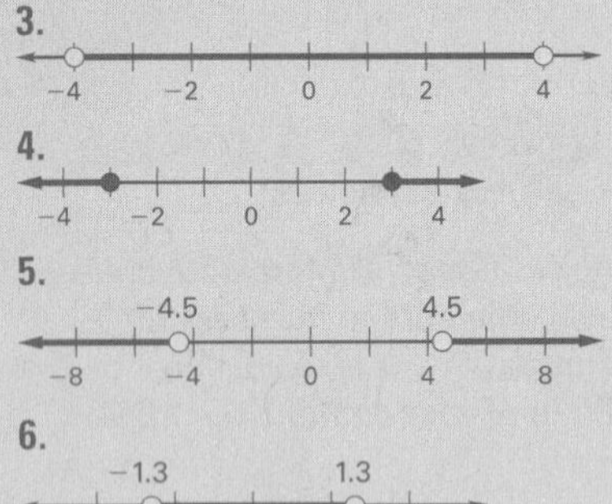

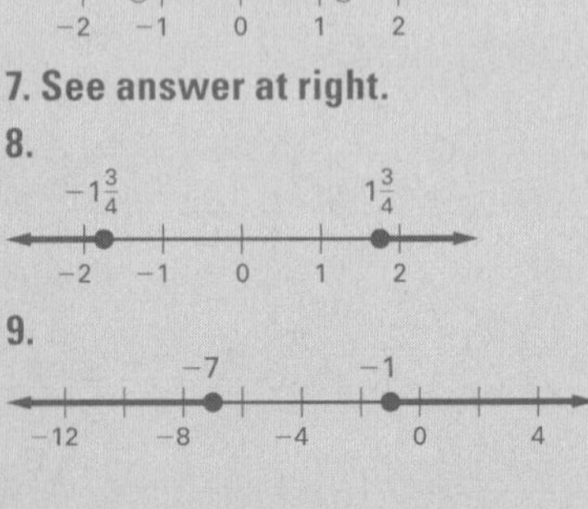

EXAMPLE 4 Solve a multi-step problem

COMPUTERS You are buying a new computer and find 10 models in a store advertisement. The prices are \$890, \$750, \$650, \$370, \$660, \$670, \$450, \$650, \$725, and \$825.

- Find the mean of the computer prices.
- You are willing to pay the mean price with an absolute deviation of at most \$100. How many of the computer prices meet your condition?

Solution

REVIEW MEAN
For help with finding a mean, see p. 918.

STEP 1 **Find** the mean by dividing the sum of the prices by 10.

$$\text{Mean} = \frac{890 + 750 + 650 + 370 + 660 + 670 + 450 + 650 + 725 + 825}{10}$$

$$= \frac{6640}{10} = 664$$

STEP 2 **Write** and solve an inequality. An absolute deviation of at most \$100 from the mean, \$664, is given by the inequality $|x - 664| \le 100$.

$\lvert x - 664 \rvert \le 100$	**Write absolute value inequality.**
$-100 \le x - 664 \le 100$	**Write as compound inequality.**
$564 \le x \le 764$	**Add 664 to each expression.**

▶ The prices you will consider must be at least \$564 and at most \$764. Six prices meet your condition: \$750, \$650, \$660, \$670, \$650, and \$725.

✓ GUIDED PRACTICE for Example 4

7. **WHAT IF?** In Example 4, suppose that you are willing to pay the mean price with an absolute deviation of at most \$75. How many of the computer prices meet this condition? **5 computer prices**

CONCEPT SUMMARY *For Your Notebook*

Solving Inequalities

One-Step and Multi-Step Inequalities

- Follow the steps for solving an equation, but reverse the inequality symbol when multiplying or dividing by a negative number.

Compound Inequalities

- If necessary, rewrite the inequality as two separate inequalities. Then solve each inequality separately. Include *and* or *or* in the solution.

Absolute Value Inequalities

- If necessary, isolate the absolute value expression on one side of the inequality. Rewrite the absolute value inequality as a compound inequality. Then solve the compound inequality.

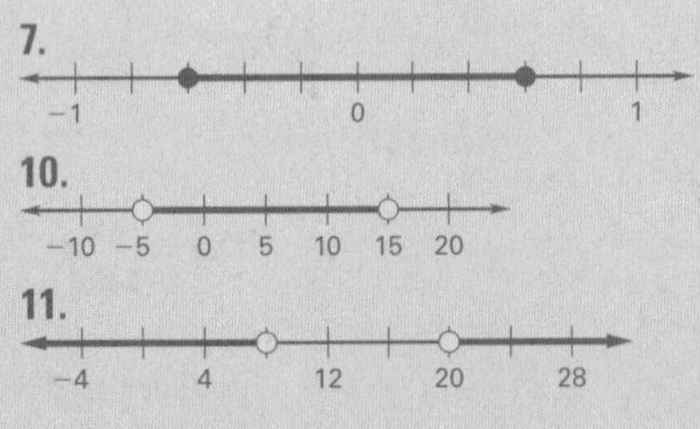

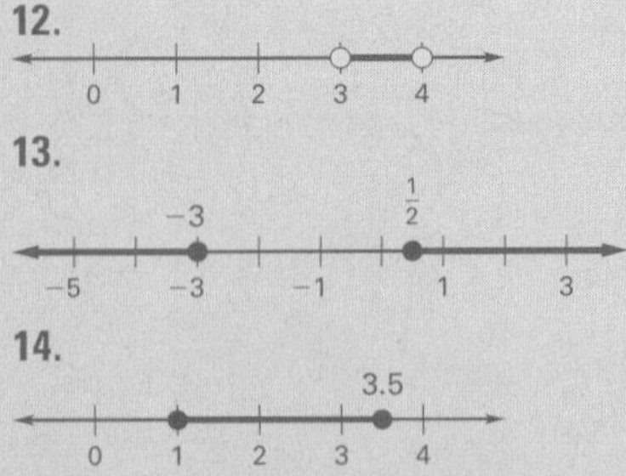

6.6 EXERCISES

HOMEWORK KEY

○ = **WORKED-OUT SOLUTIONS** on p. WS15 for Exs. 9, 15, and 37

★ = **STANDARDIZED TEST PRACTICE** Exs. 2, 21, 22, 37, and 40

◆ = **MULTIPLE REPRESENTATIONS** Ex. 38

SKILL PRACTICE

A

1. **VOCABULARY** Copy and complete: The inequalities $|x| > 8$ and $x > 8$ *or* $x < -8$ are ___?___. equivalent inequalities

2. ★ **WRITING** *Describe* the difference between solving $|x| \le 5$ and solving $|x| \ge 5$. Solving $|x| \le 5$ involves solving a compound inequality with *and*, while solving $|x| \ge 5$ involves solving a compound inequality with *or*.

EXAMPLES 1, 2, and 3 on pp. 398–399 for Exs. 3–24

SOLVING INEQUALITIES **Solve the inequality. Graph your solution.** 3–20. See margin for art.

3. $|x| < 4$ $-4 < x < 4$
4. $|y| \ge 3$ $y \le -3$ or $y \ge 3$
5. $|h| > 4.5$ $h < -4.5$ or $h > 4.5$
6. $|p| < 1.3$ $-1.3 < p < 1.3$
7. $|t| \le \frac{3}{5}$ $-\frac{3}{5} \le t \le \frac{3}{5}$
8. $|j| \ge 1\frac{3}{4}$ $j \le -1\frac{3}{4}$ or $j \ge 1\frac{3}{4}$
9. $|d + 4| \ge 3$ $d \le -7$ or $d \ge -1$
10. $|b - 5| < 10$ $-5 < b < 15$
11. $|14 - m| > 6$ $m < 8$ or $m > 20$
12. $|2s - 7| < 1$ $3 < s < 4$
13. $|4c + 5| \ge 7$ $c \le -3$ or $c \ge \frac{1}{2}$
14. $|9 - 4n| \le 5$ $1 \le n \le 3.5$
15. $5\left|\frac{1}{2}r + 3\right| > 5$ $r < -8$ or $r > -4$
16. $\left|\frac{4}{3}s - 7\right| - 8 > 3$ $s < -3$ or $s > 13\frac{1}{2}$
17. $-3\left|2 - \frac{5}{4}u\right| \le -18$ $u \le -3\frac{1}{5}$ or $u \ge 6\frac{2}{5}$
18. $2|3w + 8| - 13 < -5$ $-4 < w < -1\frac{1}{3}$
19. $2\left|\frac{1}{4}v - 5\right| - 4 > 3$ $v < 6$ or $v > 34$
20. $\frac{2}{7}|4f + 6| - 2 \ge 10$ $f \le -12$ or $f \ge 9$

21. ★ **MULTIPLE CHOICE** Which inequality is equivalent to $x < 1$ *or* $x > 5$? B

Ⓐ $|x + 8| - 2 > 10$ Ⓑ $3|6 - 2x| > 12$

Ⓒ $|5x + 9| < 10$ Ⓓ $|7 - 4x| - 9 < 8$

22. ★ **WRITING** How can you tell whether an absolute value inequality is equivalent to a compound inequality with *and* or to a compound inequality with *or*?

22. When the inequality has the absolute value expression isolated on the left side, the equivalent compound inequality will use *and* if the symbol is < *or* ≤, and it will use *or* if the symbol is > or ≥.

ERROR ANALYSIS ***Describe*** **and correct the error in solving the inequality.**

23.
$|x + 4| > 13$
$13 > x + 4 > -13$
$9 > x > -17$
✗

24.
$|x - 5| < 20$
$x - 5 < 20$
$x < 25$
✗

23. The compound inequality should use *or*: $x + 4 > 13$ *or* $x + 4 < -13$; $x > 9$ *or* $x < -17$.

24. Part of the compound inequality is missing; the compound inequality should be $-20 < x - 5 < 20$; $-15 < x < 25$.

B

TRANSLATING SENTENCES **Write the verbal sentence as an inequality. Then solve the inequality and graph your solution.** 25–28. See margin for art.

25. The absolute deviation of x from 6 is less than or equal to 4. $|x - 6| \le 4$; $2 \le x \le 10$
26. The absolute deviation of $2x$ from -7 is greater than or equal to 15. $|2x + 7| \ge 15$; $x \le -11$ *or* $x \ge 4$
27. Three more than the absolute deviation of $-4x$ from 7 is greater than 10. $|-4x - 7| + 3 > 10$; $x < -3.5$ *or* $x > 0$
28. Four times the absolute deviation of x from 9 is less than 8. $4|x - 9| < 8$; $7 < x < 11$

4 PRACTICE AND APPLY

Assignment Guide

Answer Transparencies available for all exercises

Basic:
Day 1: SRH p. 918 Exs. 1–5
pp. 401–403
Exs. 1, 2, 3–21 odd, 22–28, 35–38, 42–52 even

Average:
Day 1: pp. 401–403
Exs. 1, 2, 6–20 even, 21–24, 25–31 odd, 35–40, 45–50

Advanced:
Day 1: pp. 401–403
Exs. 1, 6–20 even, 21, 22, 26–32 even, 33*, 34*, 36–41*, 44, 47, 52

Block:
pp. 401–403
Exs. 1, 2, 6–20 even, 21–24, 25–31 odd, 35–40, 45–50 (with 6.5)

Differentiated Instruction

See *Algebra 1 Best Practices Toolkit* for suggestions on addressing the needs of a diverse classroom.

Homework Check

For a quick check of student understanding of key concepts, go over the following exercises:

Basic: 5, 11, 17, 25, 35
Average: 6, 10, 18, 25, 36
Advanced: 8, 12, 20, 28, 37

Extra Practice

- Student Edition, p. 943
- Chapter 6 Resource Book: Practice levels A, B, C, pp. 71–76

Practice Worksheet

An easily-readable reduced practice page (with answers) for this lesson can be found on p. 354E.

15.
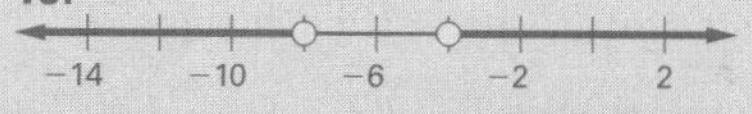

16.
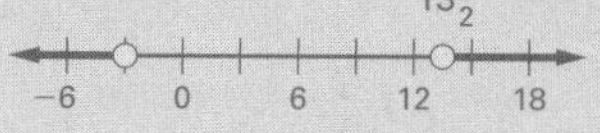

17.
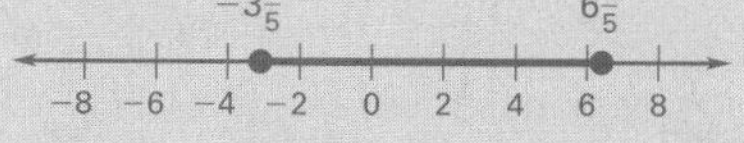

18.
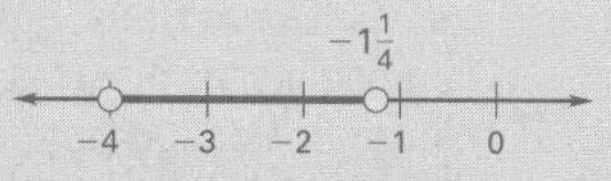

19.
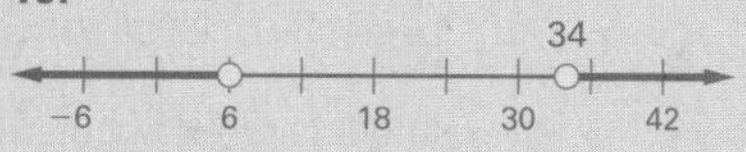

20.
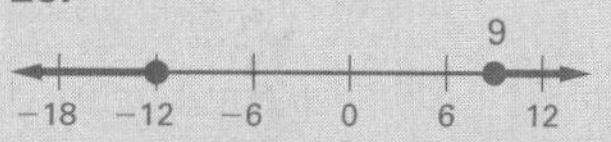

25.
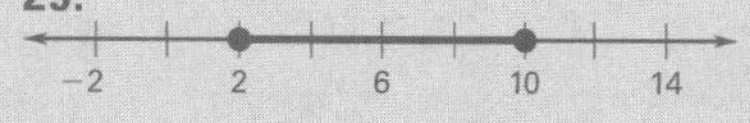

26.
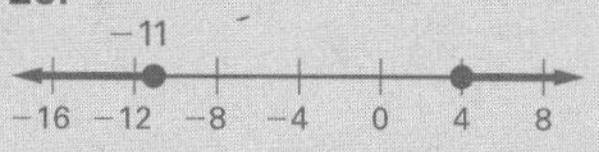

27.
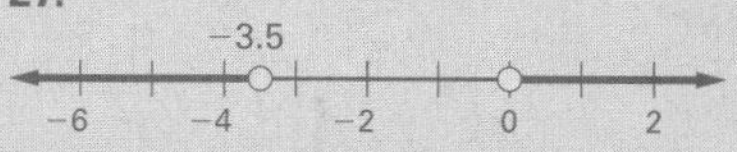

28.
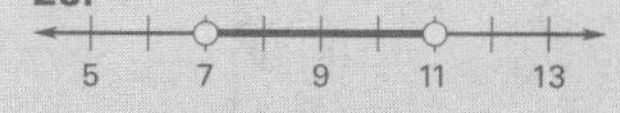

Avoiding Common Errors

Exercises 9–20 Some students may switch *and* and *or* when they rewrite absolute value inequalities. Remind students that $|ax + b| < c$ and $|ax + b| \le c$ are rewritten using *and* and that $|ax + b| > c$ and $|ax + b| \ge c$ are rewritten using *or*.

Mathematical Reasoning

Multiple Representations

Exercise 38 You may want to discuss the advantages of using tables to organize data. Stress that presenting numbers in tables allows students to find the data they need quickly. Suggest they create a table that has three columns with a title at the top of each, such as minimum, *p*, and maximum. They can also use the top of each column to indicate the calculation they need to perform.

Graphing Calculator

Exercise 39 Students can use a graphing calculator to calculate the mean. They should use the STAT option, then EDIT, and enter the data in the list. After they enter the data, they should go to STAT, then CALC, and then choose 1-VAR stats and the list number, such as L1. This will produce a screen that includes the mean.

Exercise 40 For more information about pronghorn antelope, visit www.nps.gov/wica/Pronghorn.htm

38a. See Additional Answers beginning on p. AA1.

REASONING **Tell whether the statement is *true* or *false*. If it is false, give a counterexample.**

29. If a is a solution of $|x + 3| \le 8$, then a is also a solution of $x + 3 \ge -8$. true

30. If a is a solution of $|x + 3| > 8$, then a is also a solution of $x + 3 > 8$. False. *Sample answer:* -20

31. If a is a solution of $|x + 3| \ge 8$, then a is also a solution of $x + 3 \le -8$. False. *Sample answer:* 20

32. If a is a solution of $x + 3 \le -8$, then a is also a solution of $|x + 3| \ge 8$. true

33. $6 < x < 7$; solve each absolute value inequality by rewriting it as a compound inequality. Graph the solutions and find the intersection of the graphs.

C **33. CHALLENGE** Solve $|x - 3| < 4$ *and* $|x + 2| > 8$. *Describe* your steps.

34. CHALLENGE If $|ax + b| < c$ where $c < 0$, what is the solution of the inequality? If $|ax + b| > c$ where $c < 0$, what is the solution of the inequality? *Explain* your answers.
No solution; all real numbers; because an absolute value cannot be negative, for any real number x, $|ax + b|$ is nonnegative, so if c is a negative number, $|ax + b| > c$ for any real number x.

PROBLEM SOLVING

EXAMPLE 4 on p. 400 for Exs. 35–38

A **35. ESSAY CONTEST** An essay contest requires that essay entries consist of 500 words with an absolute deviation of at most 30 words. What are the possible numbers of words that the essay can have? at least 470 words and at most 530 words

@HomeTutor for problem solving help at classzone.com

36. SWIMMING POOL The saturation index for a pool measures the balance between the acid level and the amount of minerals in pool water. Balanced water has an index value of 0. Water is highly corrosive or highly scale forming if the absolute deviation of the index value from 0 is greater than 0.5. Find the index values for which pool water is highly corrosive or highly scale forming. greater than 0.5 or less than -0.5

@HomeTutor for problem solving help at classzone.com

37. ★ **SHORT RESPONSE** You are preheating an oven to 350°F before you bake muffins. Several minutes later, the oven thermometer reads 346°F. The measured temperature has an absolute deviation of at most 2°F. Write and solve an inequality to find the possible temperatures in the oven. Should you continue to preheat the oven, or should you start baking the muffins? *Explain* your choice. $|t - 346| \le 2$, at least 344°F and at most 348°F; continue to preheat; the temperature is still below 350°F.

38. ◆ **MULTIPLE REPRESENTATIONS** Softball compression measures the hardness of a softball and affects the distance that the softball can travel upon contact with a bat. A softball organization requires that the compression of a softball be 350 pounds but allows an absolute deviation of at most 50 pounds.

a. **Making a Table** Make a table that shows the absolute deviation from the required compression when the measured compression of a softball is p pounds. Use the following values for p: 275, 325, 375, 425, 475. See margin.

b. **Writing an Inequality** Write and solve an inequality to find the softball compressions that the organization will allow. Which values of p in the table are solutions of the inequality?
$|p - 350| \le 50$, at least 300 lb and at most 400 lb; 325, 375

○ = WORKED-OUT SOLUTIONS on p. WS1 ★ = STANDARDIZED TEST PRACTICE ◆ = MULTIPLE REPRESENTATIONS

Differentiated Instruction

Visual Learners Students probably understand that acceleration means an increase in velocity, but may be confused by the mathematical notation. In **Exercise 39**, an acceleration of 10 m/sec^2 means a velocity of 10 meters per second in 1 second, a velocity of 20 meters per second in 2 seconds, and so on. Have students write acceleration as $10\frac{\text{m}}{\text{sec}}$ per sec or $10\frac{\frac{\text{m}}{\text{sec}}}{\text{sec}}$. Show that this is equal to $10\frac{\text{m}}{\text{sec}^2}$.
See also the *Algebra 1 Toolkit* for more strategies.

B 39. **MULTI-STEP PROBLEM** In a physics class, 7 groups of students experimentally determine the acceleration (in meters per second per second) of an object in free fall. The table below shows the value calculated by each group.

Group	1	2	3	4	5	6	7
Calculated value (m/sec^2)	10.50	9.52	9.73	9.86	9.78	10.90	9.86

a. **Calculate** Find the mean of the measured values given in the table. Round to the nearest hundredth. 10.02 m/sec^2

b. **Solve** When writing up their lab reports, the students wanted to state that the absolute deviation of each measured value x from the mean was at most d. What is the value of d in this situation? 0.88 m/sec^2

40b. $|p - 18{,}000| \le 3600$; at least 14,400 antelope and at most 21,600 antelope.

40. ★ **EXTENDED RESPONSE** *Relative absolute deviation* of a number from a given value is the absolute deviation expressed as a percent of the given value. A wildlife biologist estimates that the number of pronghorn antelope in Nevada is 18,000 with a relative absolute deviation of at most 20%.

a. **Calculate** Find the absolute deviation from the estimated population of pronghorn antelope by multiplying the estimated population by the relative absolute deviation. 3600 antelope

b. **Solve** Write and solve an inequality to find the possible numbers of pronghorn antelope in Nevada.

c. **Explain** If the relative absolute deviation were 25%, could you conclude that the actual population is necessarily greater than if the relative absolute deviation were 20%? *Explain* your reasoning. See margin.

C 41. **CHALLENGE** According to the rules for a women's figure skating event, a skater should finish a routine in an ideal time of 3 minutes 30 seconds. The skater receives a 0.1 point penalty if the absolute deviation of the finishing time from the ideal time is greater than 10 seconds *and* less than or equal to 20 seconds. Write and solve an inequality to find the finishing times for which the skater receives a 0.1 penalty point. at least 3 minutes 10 seconds and less than 3 minutes 20 seconds, more than 3 minutes 40 seconds and at most 3 minutes 50 seconds

ILLINOIS MIXED REVIEW

TEST PRACTICE at classzone.com

42. Which equation describes a function that has a y-intercept of 5 and a slope of $\frac{1}{3}$? A

Ⓐ $y = \frac{x}{3} + 5$ Ⓑ $y = \frac{x + 5}{3}$ Ⓒ $y = 5x + \frac{1}{3}$ Ⓓ $y = x + \frac{5}{3}$

43. Alyssia's age is 5 years less than half her mother's age. If Alyssia is 25 years old, which equation can be used to determine her mother's age? B

Ⓐ $2(x - 5) = 25$ Ⓑ $\frac{x}{2} - 5 = 25$ Ⓒ $2x - 5 = 25$ Ⓓ $\frac{x - 5}{2} = 25$

5 ASSESS AND RETEACH

Daily Homework Quiz

Transparency Available

Solve the inequality. Graph your solution.

1. $|x - 5| > 3$ all real numbers less than 2 *or* greater than 8

2. $|x + 3| + 6 \le 8$ all real numbers greater than or equal to -5 *and* less than or equal to -1

3. The clock in your car has an absolute deviation of at most 4 minutes after 6 months. After 6 months, the clock reads 7:38. Write and solve an inequality to find the possible times. $|x - 7{:}38| \le 4$; from 7:34 through 7:42

Online Quiz

Available at **classzone.com**

Diagnosis/Remediation

- Practice A, B, C in Chapter 6 Resource Book, pp. 71–76
- Study Guide in Chapter 6 Resource Book, pp. 77–78
- Practice Workbook, pp. 98–100
- @HomeTutor

Challenge

Additional challenge is available in the Chapter 6 Resource Book, p. 81.

40c. No; if the relative absolute deviation is 25%, then the actual population is between 13,500 and 22,500 antelope. For the 25% relative absolute deviation the actual population might be 14,000 antelope, which is less than any possible actual population for the 20% relative absolute deviation.

1 PLAN AND PREPARE

Explore the Concept

- Students will use inequalities to describe an overestimate and an underestimate.
- This activity leads into the study of linear inequalities in two variables in Example 2 in Lesson 6.7.

Materials

Each pair of students will need:

- set of tangram pieces
- 4 tangram puzzles
- stopwatch
- Activity Support Master (*Chapter 6 Resource Book*, p. 86)

Recommended Time

Work activity: 15 min

Discuss results: 5 min

Grouping

Students should work in pairs. Students can take turns conducting the experiment and recording and graphing the results.

2 TEACH

Tips for Success

Test the stopwatch before you begin the experiment.

Key Discovery

You can write inequalities that describe points that are either above or below the graph of a line.

3 ASSESS AND RETEACH

Does the inequality that represents an overestimate or underestimate include the points that lie on the line? Explain. **No; the points that are on the line are neither overestimates nor underestimates.**

6.7 Linear Inequalities in Two Variables

MATERIALS • set of tangram pieces • 4 tangram puzzles • stopwatch

QUESTION **How can you use inequalities to describe an overestimate or an underestimate?**

EXPLORE **Conduct an experiment**

To solve a tangram puzzle, you use seven pieces to create a figure. Each piece must lie flat and touch at least one other piece, and the pieces cannot overlap.

STEP 1 ***Predict a time***

Have your partner give you a tangram puzzle, such as the dog shown below. Predict how long it will take you to create the figure.

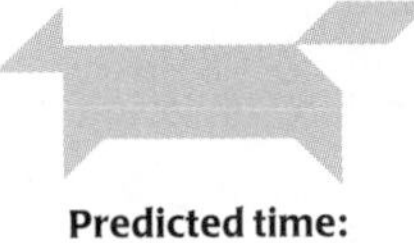

Predicted time: 50 seconds

STEP 2 ***Create figure***

Use the tangrams to create the figure. Your partner will use a stopwatch to record the actual time it takes you to finish.

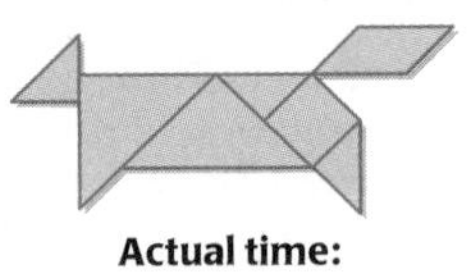

Actual time: 73 seconds

STEP 3 ***Record times***

Record the actual time x and the predicted time y in a table, as below. Repeat Steps 1–3 for three more puzzles. Then switch roles with your partner.

Figure	Actual time x (sec)	Predicted time y (sec)
1	73	50
2	67	67
3	70	88
4	90	74

STEP 4 ***Plot points***

Graph $y = x$ in Quadrant I. Then plot the points (x, y) from the table.

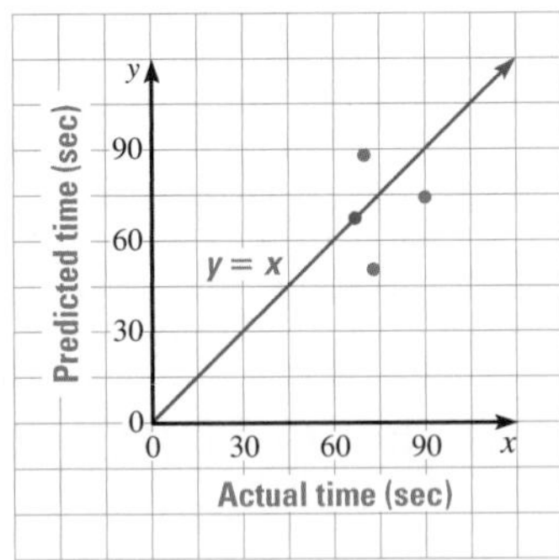

DRAW CONCLUSIONS **Use your observations to complete these exercises**

1. *Describe* the points that represent an *overestimate* of the actual finishing time. Then write an inequality that describes the location of the points in the coordinate plane. **points that lie above the line $y = x$; $y > x$**

2. *Describe* the points that represent an *underestimate* of the actual finishing time. Then write an inequality that describes the location of the points in the coordinate plane. **points that lie below the line $y = x$; $y < x$**

6.7 Graph Linear Inequalities in Two Variables

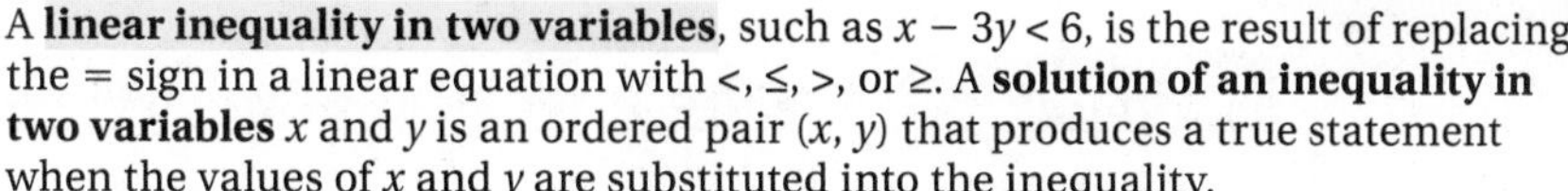

Before You graphed linear equations in two variables.
Now You will graph linear inequalities in two variables.
Why? So you can analyze a music competition, as in Ex. 56.

Key Vocabulary
- **linear inequality in two variables**
- **graph of an inequality in two variables**

A **linear inequality in two variables**, such as $x - 3y < 6$, is the result of replacing the = sign in a linear equation with <, ≤, >, or ≥. A **solution of an inequality in two variables** x and y is an ordered pair (x, y) that produces a true statement when the values of x and y are substituted into the inequality.

EXAMPLE 1 Standardized Test Practice

Which ordered pair is *not* a solution of $x - 3y \le 6$?

Ⓐ (0, 0) Ⓑ (6, −1) Ⓒ (10, 3) Ⓓ (−1, 2)

Solution

Check whether each ordered pair is a solution of the inequality.

Test (0, 0): $x - 3y \le 6$ Write inequality.

$0 - 3(0) \le 6$ Substitute 0 for x and 0 for y.

$0 \le 6$ ✓ Simplify.

Test (6, −1): $x - 3y \le 6$ Write inequality.

$6 - 3(-1) \le 6$ Substitute 6 for x and −1 for y.

$9 \le 6$ ✗ Simplify.

So, (0, 0) is a solution of $x - 3y \le 6$ but (6, −1) is *not* a solution.

▶ The correct answer is B. Ⓐ Ⓑ Ⓒ Ⓓ

✓ **GUIDED PRACTICE** for Example 1

Tell whether the ordered pair is a solution of $-x + 2y < 8$.

1. (0, 0) solution
2. (0, 4) not a solution
3. (3, 5) solution

GRAPH OF AN INEQUALITY In a coordinate plane, the **graph of an inequality in two variables** is the set of points that represent all solutions of the inequality. The *boundary line* of a linear inequality divides the coordinate plane into two **half-planes**. Only one half-plane contains the points that represent the solutions of the inequality.

1 PLAN AND PREPARE

Warm-Up Exercises

Transparency Available

Tell whether the ordered pair is a solution of the equation.

1. $x + 2y = 4$; (2, −1) no

2. $4x + 3y = 22$; (7, −2) yes

3. Graph the equation $y - 2x = 4$.

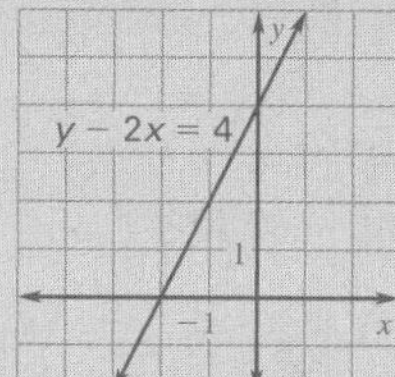

Notetaking Guide

Transparency Available

Promotes interactive learning and notetaking skills, pp. 146–148.

Pacing

Basic: 2 days
Average: 2 days
Advanced: 2 days
Block: 1 block
- See *Teaching Guide/Lesson Plan.*

2 FOCUS AND MOTIVATE

Essential Question

Big Idea 3, p. 355

How do you graph a linear inequality in two variables? Tell students they will learn how to answer this question by graphing a boundary line and shading one half-plane.

Resource Planning Guide

Chapter Resource Book
- Teaching Guide/Lesson Plan (pp. 82–83)
- Activity Master (p. 84)
- Practice levels A, B, C (pp. 87–92)
- Study Guide (pp. 93–94)
- Catch-up for Absent Students (p. 95)
- Problem Solving Workshop (p. 96)
- Challenge (p. 97)

Workbooks
- Notetaking Guide (pp. 146–148)
- Practice Workbook (pp. 101–103)

Teaching Options
- **Power Presentations CD-ROM** provides dynamic electronic teaching resources for the classroom.
- **Activity Generator CD-ROM** provides editable activities for all ability levels.

Interactive Technology
- Easy Planner
- Power Presentations CD-ROM
- Activity Generator CD-ROM
- Animated Algebra
- Test Generator CD-ROM
- Online Quiz
- eWorkbook
- eEdition
- @HomeTutor

Resources for English Learners
- Quick Reference for English Learners
- Spanish Study Guide
- Multi-Language Visual Glossary
- Student Resources in Spanish

See also the *Algebra 1 Toolkit* for more strategies for meeting individual needs.

Motivating the Lesson

Your two favorite rides at the State Fair are the Ferris wheel and the spinner. You need 4 tickets for the Ferris wheel and 6 tickets for the spinner. You have at least 42 tickets. If you know how to write and solve an inequality in two variables, you can determine the possible numbers of times you can go on each ride.

3 TEACH

Extra Example 1

Which point is *not* a solution of $x + 2y \geq 7$? **D**

Ⓐ $(-1, 4)$ Ⓑ $(2, 4)$

Ⓒ $(11, -2)$ Ⓓ $(8, -1)$

Extra Example 2

Graph the inequality $y \geq 3x + 1$.

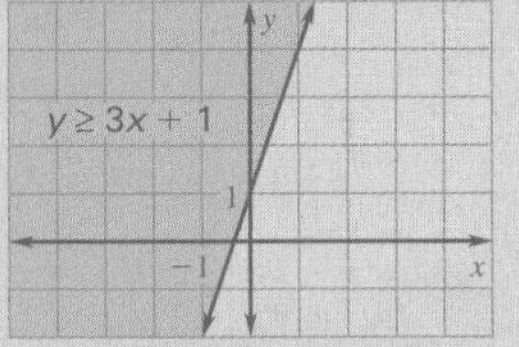

Key Questions to Ask for Example 2

- Why do you test a point that is not on the boundary line? **If the point is on the boundary line, you cannot tell which half-plane should be shaded.**
- What is a point on the graph that is *not* a solution of the inequality? **any point in the unshaded region**

Extra Example 3

Graph the inequality $x + 4y < -8$.

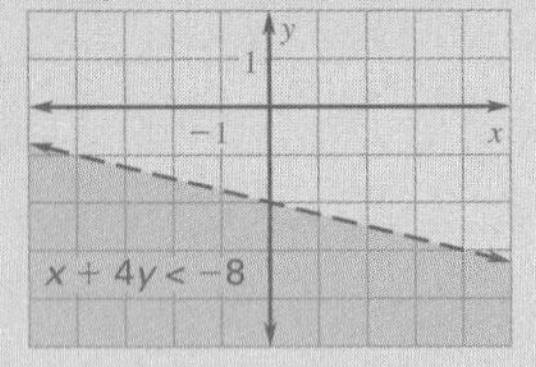

KEY CONCEPT *For Your Notebook*

Graphing a Linear Inequality in Two Variables

STEP 1 **Graph** the boundary line. Use a *dashed line* for < or >, and use a *solid line* for ≤ or ≥.

STEP 2 **Test** a point not on the boundary line by checking whether the ordered pair is a solution of the inequality.

STEP 3 **Shade** the half-plane containing the point if the ordered pair is a solution of the inequality. Shade the other half-plane if the ordered pair is *not* a solution.

EXAMPLE 2 Graph a linear inequality in two variables

Graph the inequality $y > 4x - 3$.

Solution

STEP 1 **Graph** the equation $y = 4x - 3$. The inequality is >, so use a dashed line.

STEP 2 **Test** $(0, 0)$ in $y > 4x - 3$.

$$0 \overset{?}{>} 4(0) - 3$$

$$0 > -3 \checkmark$$

STEP 3 **Shade** the half-plane that contains $(0, 0)$, because $(0, 0)$ is a solution of the inequality.

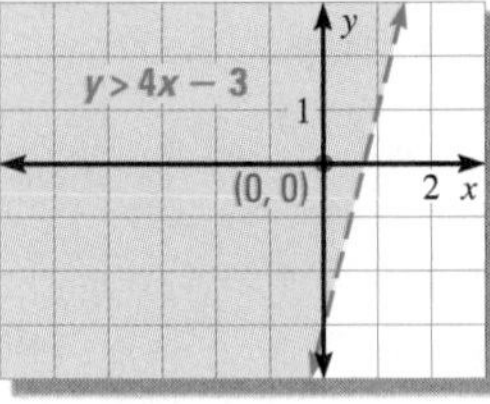

EXAMPLE 3 Graph a linear inequality in two variables

Graph the inequality $x + 2y \leq 0$.

Solution

STEP 1 **Graph** the equation $x + 2y = 0$. The inequality is ≤, so use a solid line.

STEP 2 **Test** $(1, 0)$ in $x + 2y \leq 0$.

$$1 + 2(0) \overset{?}{\leq} 0$$

$$1 \leq 0 \text{ ✗}$$

STEP 3 **Shade** the half-plane that does not contain $(1, 0)$, because $(1, 0)$ is *not* a solution of the inequality.

AVOID ERRORS
Be sure to test a point that is not on the boundary line. In Example 3, you can't test (0, 0) because it lies on the boundary line $x + 2y = 0$.

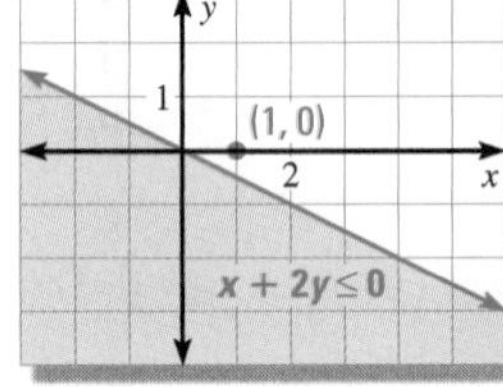

✓ **GUIDED PRACTICE** for Examples 2 and 3

4. Graph the inequality $x + 3y \geq -1$. **See margin.**

Differentiated Instruction

Inclusion Some students may have difficulty remembering which inequality symbol to use when the graph includes a solid line, and which to use when the graph includes a dashed line. Have students make the following connection: when the graph includes a solid line, the inequality symbol has a solid line under it (≤ or ≥), and when the graph includes a dashed line, the symbol does not (< or >).

See also the *Algebra 1 Toolkit* for more strategies.

LINEAR INEQUALITIES IN ONE VARIABLE The steps for graphing a linear inequality in two variables can be used to graph a linear inequality in one variable in a coordinate plane.

The boundary line for an inequality in one variable is either vertical or horizontal. When testing a point to determine which half-plane to shade, do the following:

- If an inequality has only the variable x, substitute the x-coordinate of the test point into the inequality.
- If an inequality has only the variable y, substitute the y-coordinate of the test point into the inequality.

EXAMPLE 4 Graph a linear inequality in one variable

Graph the inequality $y \geq -3$.

Solution

STEP 1 **Graph** the equation $y = -3$.
The inequality is $\geq$, so use a solid line.

STEP 2 **Test** (2, 0) in $y \geq -3$. You substitute only the y-coordinate, because the inequality does not have the variable x.

$$0 \geq -3 \checkmark$$

STEP 3 **Shade** the half-plane that contains (2, 0), because (2, 0) is a solution of the inequality.

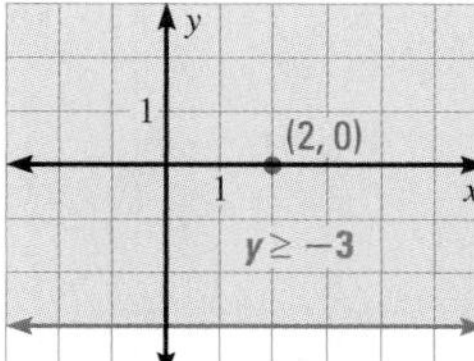

EXAMPLE 5 Graph a linear inequality in one variable

Graph the inequality $x < -1$.

Solution

STEP 1 **Graph** the equation $x = -1$.
The inequality is <, so use a dashed line.

STEP 2 **Test** (3, 0) in $x < -1$. You substitute only the x-coordinate, because the inequality does not have the variable y.

$$3 < -1 \ \text{✗}$$

STEP 3 **Shade** the half-plane that does *not* contain (3, 0), because (3, 0) is not a solution of the inequality.

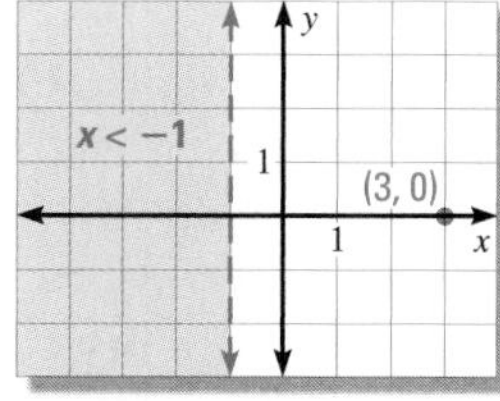

Animated Algebra at classzone.com

✓ GUIDED PRACTICE for Examples 4 and 5

Graph the inequality. 5–7. See margin.

5. $y > 1$ **6.** $y \leq 3$ **7.** $x < -2$

Extra Example 4

Graph the inequality $y < 1$.

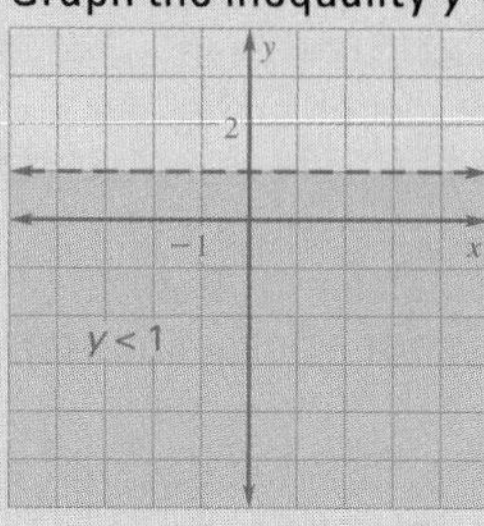

Key Questions to Ask for Example 4

- How is graphing a linear inequality in one variable different from graphing a linear inequality in two variables? **When you test a point for a linear inequality in one variable, you substitute only the variable that appears in the inequality. To test a point for a two-variable inequality, you substitute both coordinates.**
- Does it matter which point you test? **As with linear inequalities in two variables, you should not test a point on the boundary line.**

Extra Example 5

Graph the inequality $x \geq 2$.

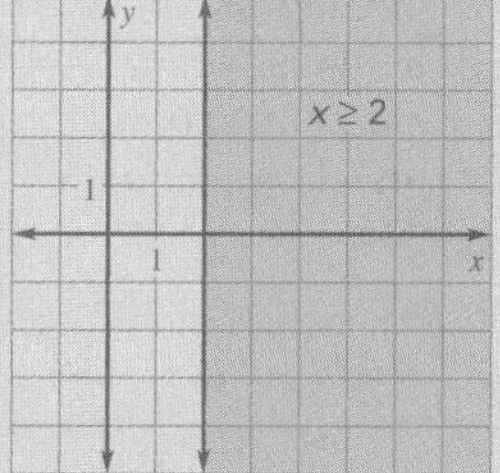

Key Question to Ask for Example 5

- Is the point $(-1, y)$ a solution of the inequality? Explain. **No; the inequality $x < -1$ is not true when x is -1.**

4.

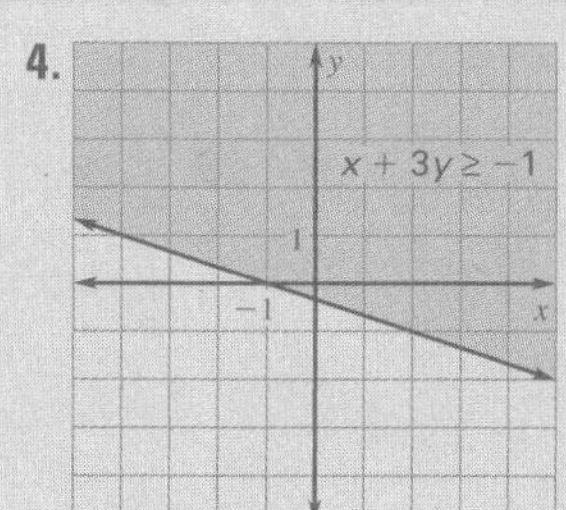

5.

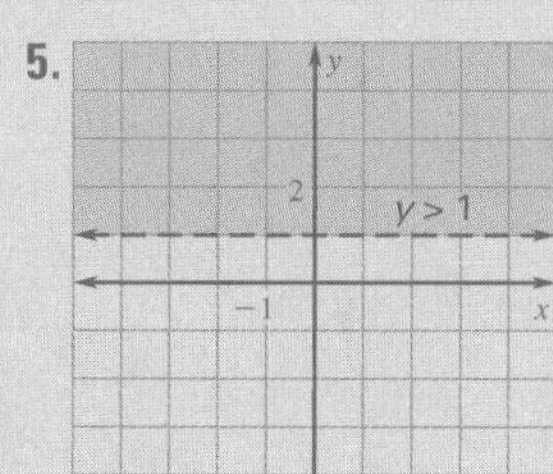

6.

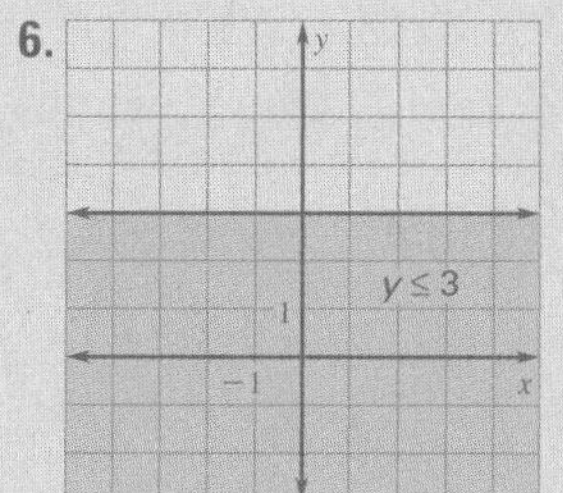

7.

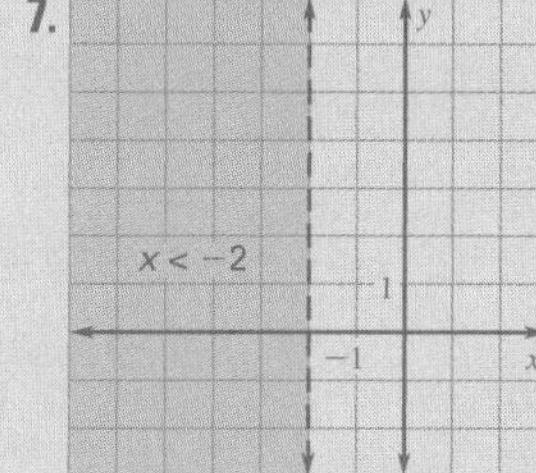

EXAMPLE 6 Solve a multi-step problem

JOB EARNINGS You have two summer jobs at a youth center. You earn \$8 per hour teaching basketball and \$10 per hour teaching swimming. Let x represent the amount of time (in hours) you teach basketball each week, and let y represent the amount of time (in hours) you teach swimming each week. Your goal is to earn at least \$200 per week.

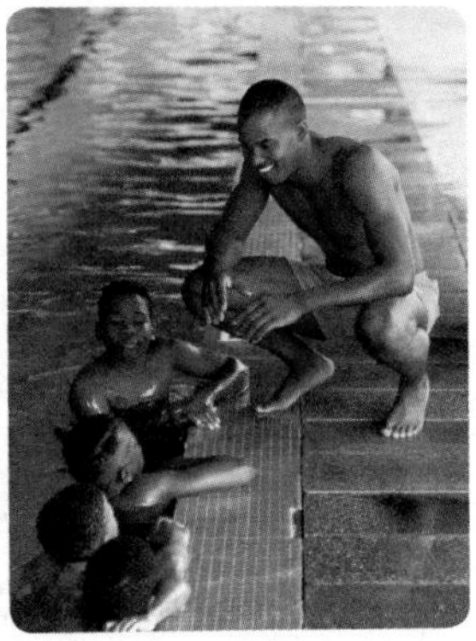

- Write an inequality that describes your goal in terms of x and y.
- Graph the inequality.
- Give three possible combinations of hours that will allow you to meet your goal.

Solution

STEP 1 **Write** a verbal model. Then write an inequality.

Basketball pay rate (dollars/hour)	•	Basketball time (hours)	+	Swimming pay rate (dollars/hour)	•	Swimming time (hours)	≥	Total earnings (dollars)
8	•	x	+	10	•	y	≥	200

STEP 2 **Graph** the inequality $8x + 10y \geq 200$.

First, graph the equation $8x + 10y = 200$ in Quadrant I. The inequality is ≥, so use a solid line.

Next, test (5, 5) in $8x + 10y \geq 200$:

$$8(5) + 10(5) \geq 200$$

$$90 \geq 200 \text{ ✗}$$

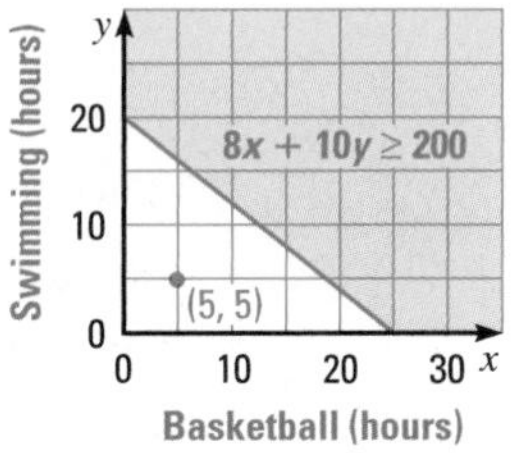

Finally, shade the part of Quadrant I that does not contain (5, 5), because (5, 5) is not a solution of the inequality.

AVOID ERRORS
The variables can't represent negative numbers. So, the graph of the inequality does not include points in Quadrants II, III, or IV.

STEP 3 **Choose** three points on the graph, such as (13, 12), (14, 10), and (16, 9). The table shows the total earnings for each combination of hours.

Basketball time (hours)	13	14	16
Swimming time (hours)	12	10	9
Total earnings (dollars)	224	212	218

✓ **GUIDED PRACTICE** for Example 6

8. **WHAT IF?** In Example 6, suppose that next summer you earn \$9 per hour teaching basketball and \$12.50 per hour teaching swimming. Write and graph an inequality that describes your goal. Then give three possible combinations of hours that will help you meet your goal.
$9x + 12.5y \geq 200$; see margin for art. *Sample answer:* (8, 12), (12, 10), (16, 6)

Extra Example 6

A party shop makes gift bags for birthday parties. They charge \$4 per glow stick placed in the bag and \$10 per T-shirt. Let x represent the number of glow sticks and y represent the number of T-shirts. The goal is to earn at least \$500 for the bags.

- Write an inequality that describes the goal in terms of x and y.
- Graph the inequality.
- Give three possible combinations of pairs of items that will allow the shop to meet its goal.

$4x + 10y \geq 500$

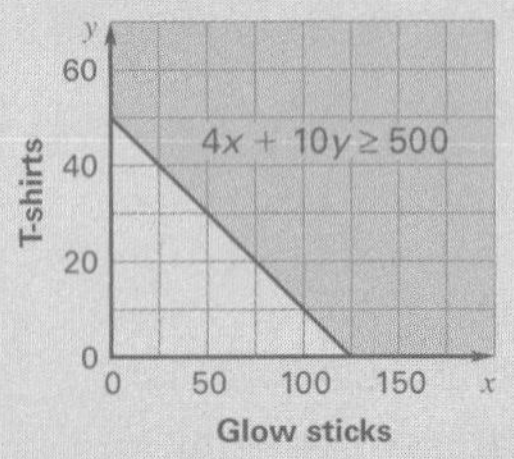

Possible pair combinations:
25 glow sticks, 52 T-shirts;
75 glow sticks, 30 T-shirts;
100 glow sticks, 12 T-shirts

Closing the Lesson

Have students summarize the major points of the lesson and answer the Essential Question: How do you graph linear inequalities in two variables?

- Graph the boundary line, using a solid or a dashed line.
- Use a test point and shade one of the two half-planes.

Graph the boundary line, using a dashed or solid line. Test a point not on the boundary line. If it is a solution, shade the half-plane that contains the test point. If it is not a solution, shade the half-plane that does not contain the test point.

8.

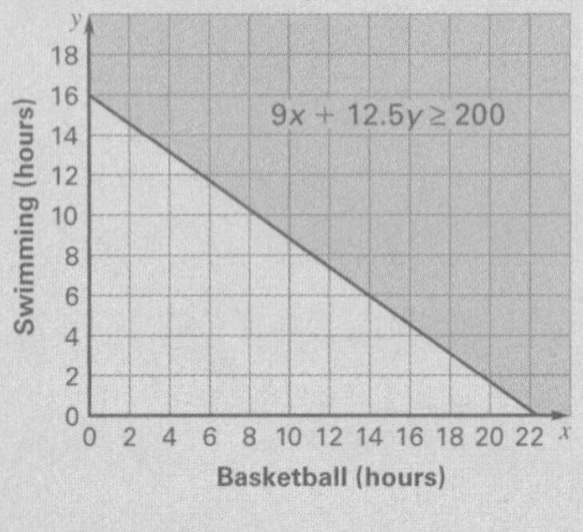

6.7 EXERCISES

HOMEWORK KEY

 = **WORKED-OUT SOLUTIONS** on p. WS15 for Exs. 5, 19, and 57

★ = **STANDARDIZED TEST PRACTICE** Exs. 2, 15, 16, 39, 56, 59, and 60

◆ = **MULTIPLE REPRESENTATIONS** Ex. 55

SKILL PRACTICE

A

1. **VOCABULARY** Copy and complete: The ordered pair $(2, -4)$ is a(n) __?__ of $3x - y > 7$. solution

2. ★ **WRITING** *Describe* the difference between graphing a linear inequality in two variables and graphing a linear equation in two variables. See margin.

EXAMPLE 1 on p. 405 for Exs. 3–15

CHECKING SOLUTIONS **Tell whether the ordered pair is a solution of the inequality.**

3. $x + y < -4$; $(0, 0)$ not a solution
4. $x - y \le 5$; $(8, 3)$ solution
5. $y - x > -2$; $(-1, -4)$ not a solution
6. $2x + 3y \ge 14$; $(5, 2)$ solution
7. $4x - 7y > 28$; $(-2, 4)$ not a solution
8. $-3y - 2x < 12$; $(5, -6)$ solution
9. $2.8x + 4.1y \le 1$; $(0, 0)$ solution
10. $0.5y - 0.5x > 3.5$; $(6, 2)$ not a solution
11. $x \ge -3$; $(-4, 0)$ not a solution
12. $y \le 8$; $(-9, -7)$ solution
13. $\frac{3}{4}x - \frac{1}{3}y < 6$; $(-8, 12)$ solution
14. $\frac{2}{5}x + y \ge 2$; $(1, 2)$ solution

15. ★ **MULTIPLE CHOICE** Which ordered pair is *not* a solution of $x + 5y < 15$? C

Ⓐ $(-1, -3)$ Ⓑ $(-1, 3)$ Ⓒ $(1, 3)$ Ⓓ $(3, 2)$

EXAMPLES 2, 3, 4, and 5 on pp. 406–407 for Exs. 16–38

16. ★ **MULTIPLE CHOICE** The graph of which inequality is shown? A

Ⓐ $x + y \le -1$ Ⓑ $x + y \ge -1$

Ⓒ $x - y \le -1$ Ⓓ $x - y \ge -1$

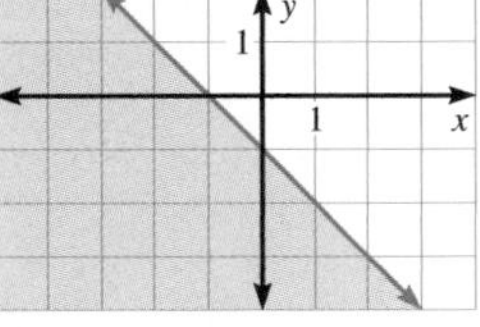

GRAPHING INEQUALITIES **Graph the inequality.** 17–36. See margin.

17. $y > x + 3$
18. $y \le x - 2$
19. $y < 3x + 5$
20. $y \ge -2x + 8$
21. $x + y < -8$
22. $x - y \le -11$
23. $x + 8y > 16$
24. $5x - y \ge 1$
25. $2(x + 2) > 7y$
26. $y - 4 < x - 6$
27. $-4y \le 16x$
28. $6(2x) \ge -24y$
29. $y < -3$
30. $x \ge 5$
31. $x > -2$
32. $y \le 4$
33. $3(x - 2) > y + 8$
34. $x - 4 \le -2(y + 6)$
35. $\frac{1}{2}(x + 2) + 3y < 8$
36. $2(x + 1) \ge \frac{1}{4}y - 1$

ERROR ANALYSIS *Describe* **and correct the error in graphing the inequality.**

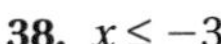

37, 38. See margin for art.

37. $2y - x \ge 2$

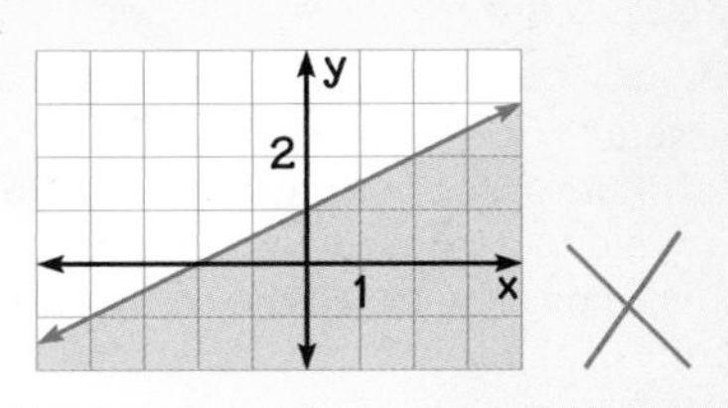

The wrong half-plane is shaded.

38. $x \le -3$

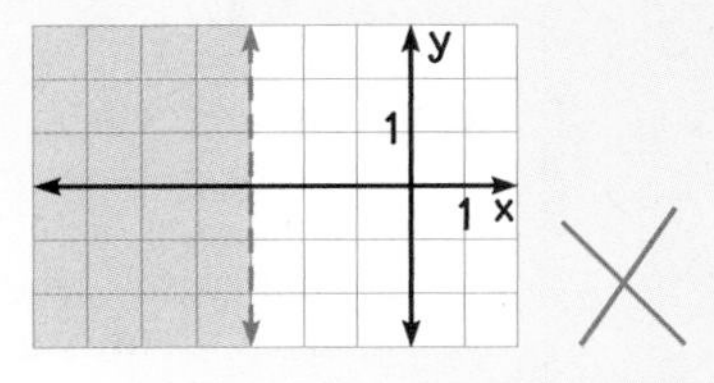

The boundary line should be solid.

2. Graphing a linear inequality in two variables involves graphing the boundary line (as either a solid or dashed line) and then shading the appropriate half-plane. Graphing a linear equation in two variables involves only the graphing of one (solid) line.

17–38. See Additional Answers beginning on p. AA1.

4 PRACTICE AND APPLY

Assignment Guide

Answer Transparencies available for all exercises

Basic:
Day 1: EP p. 941 Exs. 41–44
pp. 409–412
Exs. 1–11, 15–25, 62–70 even
Day 2: pp. 409–412
Exs. 29–41, 53–58, 71–76

Average:
Day 1: pp. 409–412
Exs. 1, 2, 8–16, 20–28, 44–46, 63–69 odd
Day 2: pp. 409–412
Exs. 29–43, 47–50, 54–59, 71–75 odd

Advanced:
Day 1: pp. 409–412
Exs. 1, 10–16, 21–28, 44–46, 51*, 52*, 63–69 odd
Day 2: pp. 409–412
Exs. 29–43, 47–50, 55–61*, 73, 76

Block:
pp. 409–412
Exs. 1, 2, 8–16, 20–50, 54–59, 63–75 odd

Differentiated Instruction

See *Algebra 1 Best Practices Toolkit* for suggestions on addressing the needs of a diverse classroom.

Homework Check

For a quick check of student understanding of key concepts, go over the following exercises:

Basic: 4, 18, 25, 30, 53
Average: 12, 20, 27, 31, 54
Advanced: 14, 22, 28, 32, 55

Extra Practice

- Student Edition, p. 943
- Chapter 6 Resource Book: Practice levels A, B, C, pp. 87–92

Practice Worksheet

An easily-readable reduced practice page (with answers) for this lesson can be found on p. 354F.

Avoiding Common Errors

Exercises 17–36 Some students may test a point on the boundary line. Remind students that a point on the boundary line cannot be used to determine which half-plane to shade.

Graphing Calculator

Exercises 17–36 Students may want to check the boundary lines using a graphing calculator. They should use the **y=** key, enter the equation, and then select GRAPH.

Teaching Strategy

Exercises 44–46 Before assigning these exercises, you may want to review how to write a linear equation given two points. Remind students to choose an inequality symbol by looking at whether the boundary line is solid or dashed and by observing which half-plane is shaded.

Internet Reference

Exercise 53 Information about the history of the sport of bobsledding can be found at the U.S. Bobsled and Skeleton Federation's website www.usbsf.com/bobhistory.htm

40.

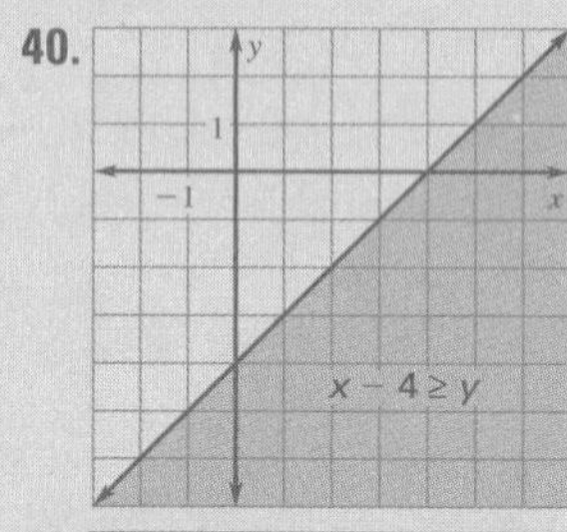

41.

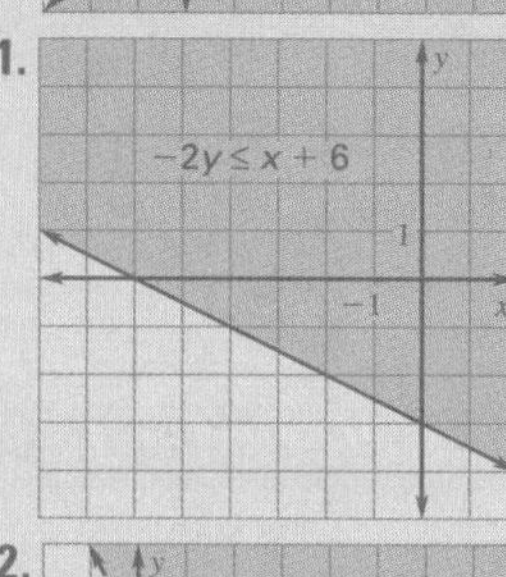

42.

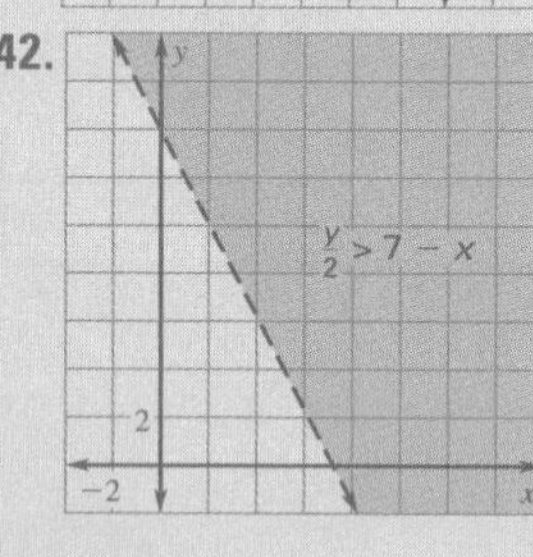

39. ★ **WRITING** Can you use (0, 0) as a test point when graphing $2x > -5y$? *Explain* your reasoning. No; (0, 0) is a point on the boundary line $2x = -5y$.

B **TRANSLATING SENTENCES** **Write the verbal sentence as an inequality. Then graph the inequality.** 40–43. See margin for art.

40. Four less than x is greater than or equal to y. $x - 4 \geq y$

41. The product of -2 and y is less than or equal to the sum of x and 6. $-2y \leq x + 6$

42. The quotient of y and 2 is greater than the difference of 7 and x. $\frac{y}{2} > 7 - x$

43. The sum of x and the product of 4 and y is less than -3. $x + 4y < -3$

USING A GRAPH **Write an inequality of the graph shown.**

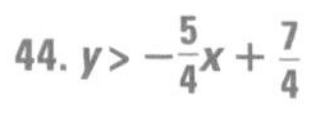

44. $y > -\frac{5}{4}x + \frac{7}{4}$

45. $y \leq \frac{5}{7}x - \frac{9}{7}$

46. $y > \frac{1}{2}x + 2$

44.

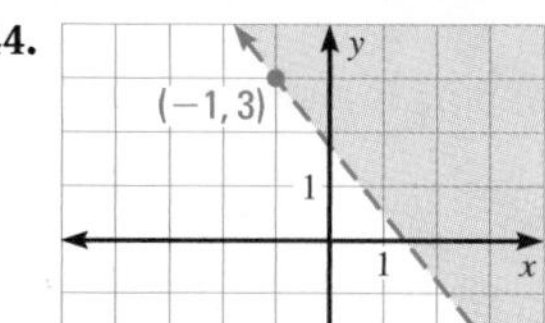

45.

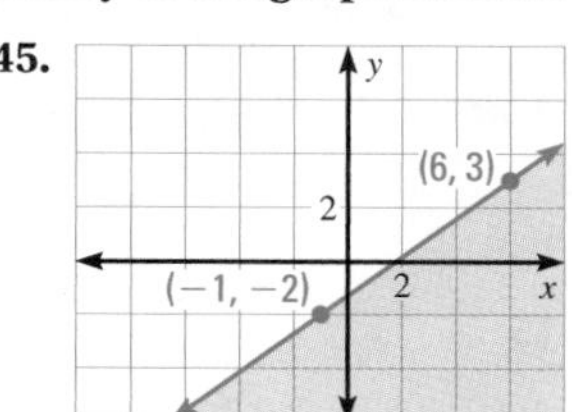

46.

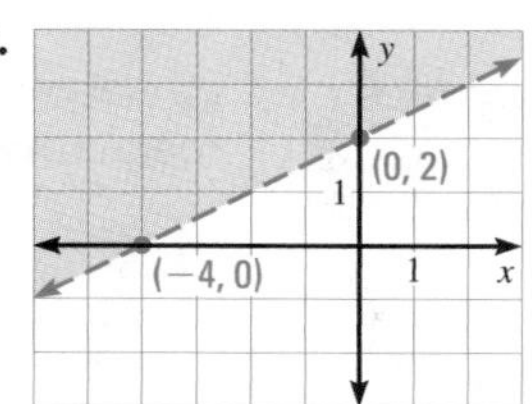

WRITING INEQUALITIES **Write an inequality whose graph contains only the points in the given quadrants.**

47. Quadrants I and II $y > 0$

48. Quadrants II and III $x < 0$

49. Quadrants III and IV $y < 0$

50. Quadrants I and IV $x > 0$

C **CHALLENGE** **In Exercises 51 and 52, write and graph an inequality whose graph is described by the given information.** 51, 52. See margin for art.

51. The points (2, 5) and (−3, −5) lie on the boundary line. The points (6, 5) and (−2, −3) are solutions of the inequality. $y \leq 2x + 1$

52. The points (−7, −16) and (1, 8) lie on the boundary line. The points (−7, 0) and (3, 14) are *not* solutions of the inequality. $y < 3x + 5$

PROBLEM SOLVING

EXAMPLE 6 **A** on p. 408 for Exs. 53–57

53. **BOBSLEDS** In a two-man bobsled competition, the sum of the weight x (in pounds) of the bobsled and the combined weight y (in pounds) of the athletes must not exceed 860 pounds. Write and graph an inequality that describes the possible weights of the bobsled and the athletes. Identify and interpret one of the solutions.

@HomeTutor for problem solving help at classzone.com

See margin.

54. **ELEVATORS** The number y of passengers riding an elevator can be no greater than the elevator's maximum weight capacity x (in pounds) divided by 150. Write and graph an inequality that relates the number of passengers to the maximum weight capacity. Identify and interpret one of the solutions. See margin.

@HomeTutor for problem solving help at classzone.com

○ = WORKED-OUT SOLUTIONS on p. WS1 ★ = STANDARDIZED TEST PRACTICE

= MULTIPLE REPRESENTATIONS

43.

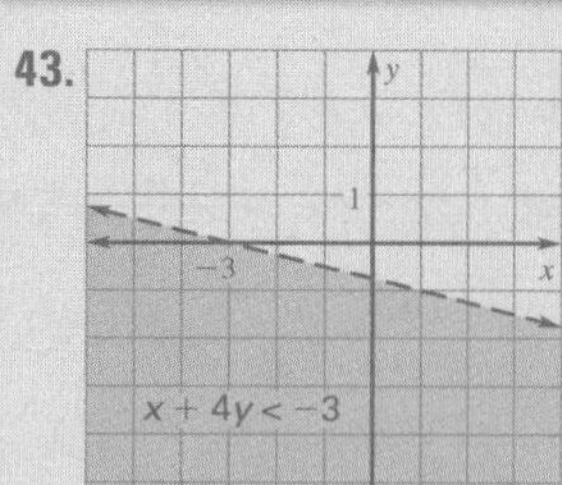

51.

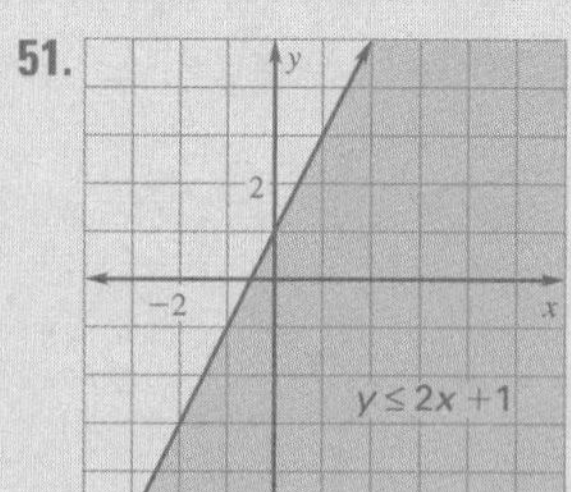

52.

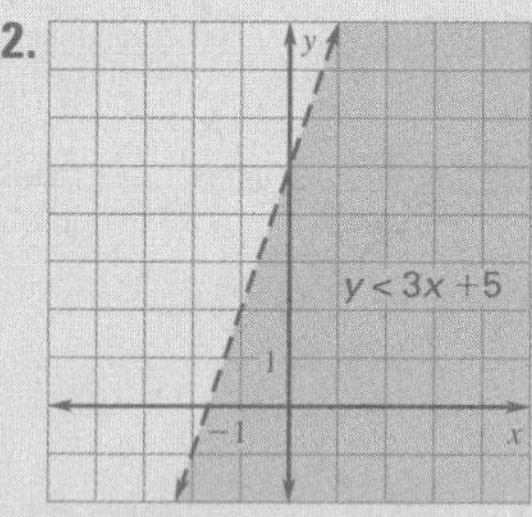

55. ◆ **MULTIPLE REPRESENTATIONS** You tutor Spanish for \$15 per hour and French for \$10 per hour. You want to earn at least \$100 per week.

a. **Writing an Inequality** Write an inequality that describes your goal in terms of hours spent tutoring Spanish and hours spent tutoring French. **$15x + 10y \geq 100$**

b. **Drawing a Graph** Graph the inequality. Then give three possible combinations of hours that meet your goal. **See margin.**

c. **Making a Table** Make a table that gives the amount of money that you will earn for each combination of hours given in part (b). **See margin.**

56. ★ **MULTIPLE CHOICE** To compete in a piano competition, you need to perform two musical pieces whose combined duration is no greater than 15 minutes. Which inequality describes the possible durations x and y (in minutes) of the pieces? **B**

Ⓐ $x + y < 15$ Ⓑ $x + y \leq 15$ Ⓒ $x + y > 15$ Ⓓ $x + y \geq 15$

(57.) **MULTI-STEP PROBLEM** You are making muffins and loaves of bread for a bake sale. You need $\frac{1}{6}$ batch of batter per muffin and $\frac{1}{2}$ batch of batter per loaf of bread. You have enough ingredients to make up to 12 batches of batter. **$\frac{1}{6}m + \frac{1}{2}\ell \leq 12$; See margin for art.**

a. Write and graph an inequality that describes the possible combinations of muffins m and loaves ℓ of bread that you can make.

b. You make 4 loaves of bread. What are the possible numbers of muffins that you can make? **$m \leq 60$**

B 58. **NUTRITION** A nutritionist recommends that the fat calories y consumed per day should be at most 30% of the total calories x consumed per day.

a. Write and graph an inequality that relates the number of fat calories consumed to the total calories consumed. **$y \leq 0.3x$; see margin for art.**

b. Use the nutrition labels below. You normally consume 2000 calories per day. So far today you have eaten 6 crackers and 1 container of yogurt. What are the possible additional fat calories that you can consume today? **$y \leq 500$**

59. ★ **SHORT RESPONSE** You need to bring a duffel and a bedroll for a trip in the mountains. The sum of the weight x (in pounds) of the duffel and the weight y (in pounds) of the bedroll cannot exceed 30 pounds.

a. **Graph and Apply** Write and graph a linear inequality that describes the possible weights of the duffel and bedroll. Then give three possible combinations of weights of the duffel and bedroll. **See margin.**

b. **Interpret** Are (0, 30) and (30, 0) solutions of the inequality in part (a)? Do these ordered pairs make sense for this situation? *Explain.*

Study Strategy

Exercise 55 Suggest that students review Example 6 before they begin this exercise. This will help them write a verbal model for the problem, graph the inequality, and create a table.

55b.

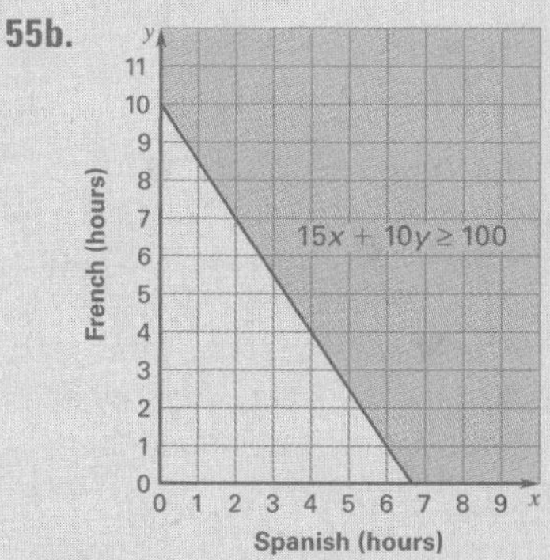

55c. ***Sample answer:***

Spanish time (hours)	4	5	6
French time (hours)	8	3	1
Total earnings (dollars)	140	105	100

57a.

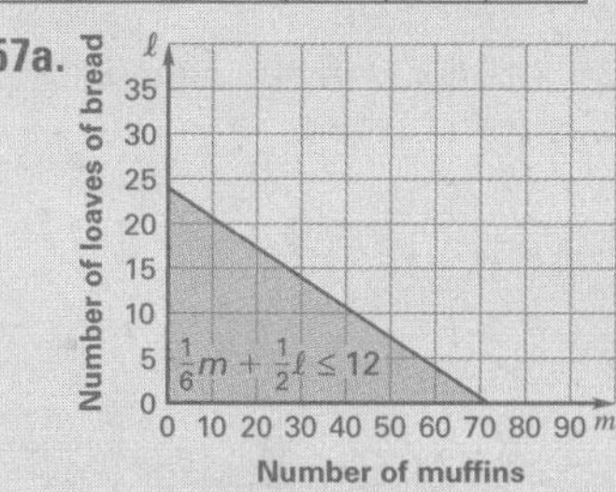

58a.

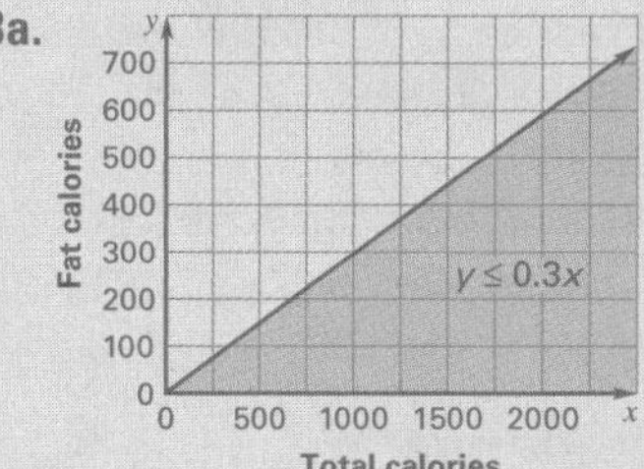

59a.

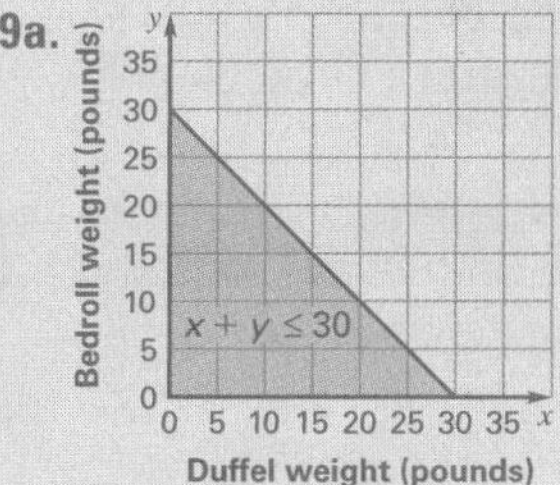

59a. $x + y \leq 30$, see margin for art. ***Sample answer:*** (20, 4), (25, 5), (26, 2)

59b. Yes; no; (0, 30) means that you do not take a duffel and have a 30 pound bedroll, while (30, 0) means you take a 30 pound duffel and do not take a bedroll. You need to bring both a duffel and a bedroll.

53, 54. See Additional Answers beginning on p. AA1.

5 ASSESS AND RETEACH

Daily Homework Quiz

Transparency Available

Tell whether the ordered pair is a solution of the inequality.

1. $x + 4y \geq 16$; (3, 3) no
2. $3x - 2y < 20$; (5, −2) yes
3. For a fundraiser, students offer a basic car wash for \$2 and a deluxe for \$5. They want to earn at least \$100 per day. Write an inequality that describes the goal. Graph the inequality. Identify and interpret one combination that meets the goal. $2x + 5y \geq 100$, where x represents basic washes and y represents deluxe washes

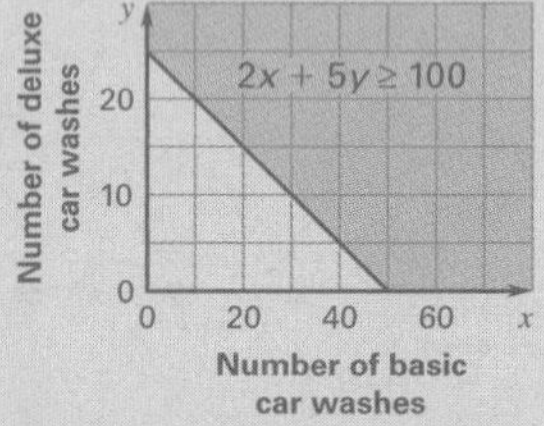

(40, 15); 40 basic washes and 15 deluxe washes

Available at **classzone.com**

Diagnosis/Remediation

- Practice A, B, C in Chapter 6 Resource Book, pp. 87–92
- Study Guide in Chapter 6 Resource Book, pp. 93–94
- Practice Workbook, pp. 101–103
- @HomeTutor

Challenge

Additional challenge is available in the Chapter 6 Resource Book, p. 97.

Quiz

An easily-readable reduced copy of the quiz (with answers) on Lessons 6.5–6.7 from the Assessment Book can be found on p. 354G.

60a, 60b, 61a, Quiz 4–9. See Additional Answers beginning on p. AA1.

60c. Less than or equal to 10 years; when x is less than 10 years, y will be greater than 100%. You cannot invest more than 100% of your money.

60. ★ **EXTENDED RESPONSE** A financial advisor suggests that if a person is an aggressive investor, the percent y of money that the person invests in stocks should be greater than the difference of 110 and the person's age x.
    a. **Graph** Write and graph a linear inequality that relates the percent of money invested in stocks to an aggressive investor's age. $y > 110 - x$; see margin for art.
    b. **Calculate** If an aggressive investor is 30 years old, what are the possible percents that the investor can invest in stocks? *Explain* your answer. See margin.
    c. **Justify** Are there any ages for which none of the solutions of the inequality makes sense for this situation? *Justify* your answer.

C 61. **CHALLENGE** The formula $m = dV$ gives the mass m of an object in terms of the object's density d and its volume V. Water has a density of 1 gram per cubic centimeter. An object immersed in water will sink if its density is greater than the density of water. An object will float in water if its density is less than the density of water.
    a. For an object that sinks, write and graph an inequality that relates its mass (in grams) to its volume (in cubic centimeters). For an object that floats, write and graph an inequality that relates its mass (in grams) to its volume (in cubic centimeters). See margin.
    b. A cylindrical can has a radius of 5 centimeters, a height of 10 centimeters, and a mass of 2119.5 grams. Will the can sink or float in water? *Explain* your answer.
    Sink; the volume of the cylindrical can is $\pi r^2 h = \pi(25)(10) \approx 785.40$ cubic centimeters. Since the mass, 2119.5 grams, is greater than the volume, 785.40 cubic centimeters, the can will sink.

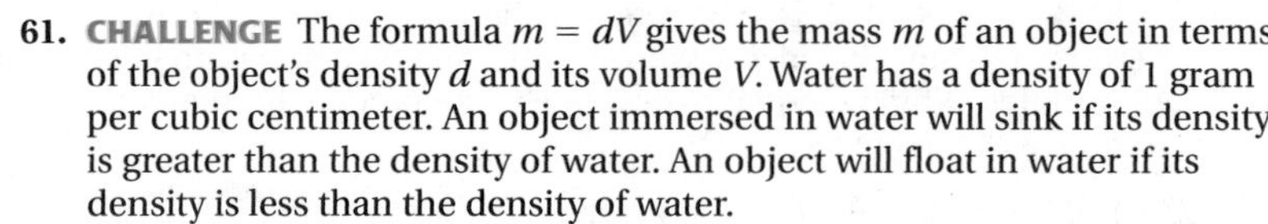

62. $\triangle FGH$ has vertices $F(-2, 3)$, $G(-1, 2)$, and $H(-2, -1.5)$. $\triangle FGH$ is dilated by a scale factor of 2 and has the origin as the center of dilation. What are the coordinates of H'? A

    Ⓐ (−4, −3) Ⓑ (−4, 6) Ⓒ (−1.5, −2) Ⓓ (0, 0.5)

63. What is the y-intercept of the function $f(x) = 4(x - 3)$? A

    Ⓐ −12 Ⓑ −3 Ⓒ 3 Ⓓ 4

QUIZ for Lessons 6.5–6.7

Solve the equation. *(p. 390)*

1. $|x| = 5$ 5, −5
2. $|c - 8| = 24$ 32, −16
3. $-2|r - 5| = -6$ 8, 2

Solve the inequality. Graph your solution. *(p. 398)* 4–6. See margin for art.

4. $|y| > 4$ $y < -4$ or $y > 4$
5. $|2t - 5| < 3$ $1 < t < 4$
6. $4|3s + 7| - 5 \geq 7$ $s \leq -3\frac{1}{3}$ or $s \geq -1\frac{1}{3}$

Graph the inequality. *(p. 405)* 7–9. See margin.

7. $x + y \geq 3$
8. $\frac{5}{7}x < 10$
9. $2y - x \leq 8$

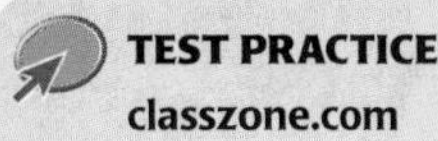

TEST PRACTICE classzone.com

Lessons 6.5–6.7

1. **FOOD PREPARATION** You and your friends have picked 360 apples at an orchard and plan to use them to create apple pies and applesauce. You use 7 apples to make an apple pie and 5 apples to fill a jar of applesauce. Which inequality can you use to find the possible numbers p of apple pies and jars s of applesauce that you and your friends can make?

   A. $5p + 7s < 360$ **C.** $7p + 5s \le 360$

   B. $7p - 5s \le 360$ **D.** $360 - 7p \le 5s$

2. **ELECTION POLL** A poll taken before an election predicts that candidate A will receive 47 percent of the vote with an absolute deviation of at most 4 percent. Which of the following equations can you use to find the minimum and maximum percent of the vote that candidate A is predicted to receive in the election?

   F. $|47 - 4| = x$ **H.** $|x - 4| = 47$

   G. $|47 - x| = 4$ **J.** $|47 + x| = 4$

3. **JOB TRAINING** You are scooping ice cream as part of your training to work at an ice cream shop. The weight of a scoop should be 4 ounces with an absolute deviation of at most 0.5 ounce. Your first 10 scoops have the following weights (in ounces): 3.8, 4.2, 3.9, 4.5, 3.7, 4.6, 4.1, 3.3, 4.3, and 4.2. What percent of your scoops meet the weight requirement?

   A. 60% **C.** 80%

   B. 70% **D.** 90%

4. **INVESTING** An investor purchases shares of a stock for \$30 each and will sell them if the absolute deviation of the selling price from the purchase price is at least \$15. Which inequality can you use to find the possible prices y (in dollars) at which the shares will be sold?

   F. $|y - 15| \ge 30$ **H.** $|y - 30| \le 15$

   G. $|y - 30| \ge 15$ **J.** $|y - 15| \le 30$

5. **RAFTING** A tour operator requires that river rafters wear protective suits if the following condition applies:

   Water temperature + Air temperature < 100°F

   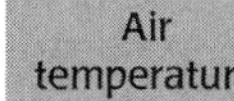

   Which graph represents the possible air temperatures x and water temperatures y for which a protective suit is required?

   A. 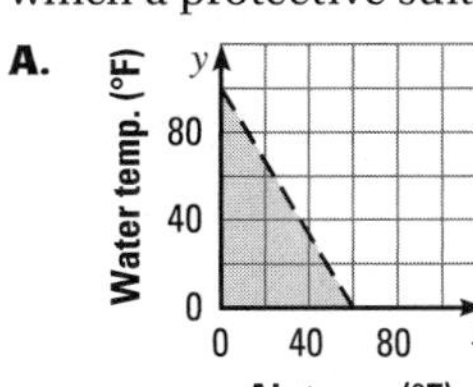

   B. 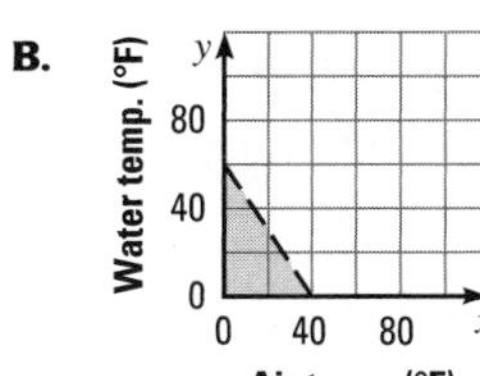

   C. 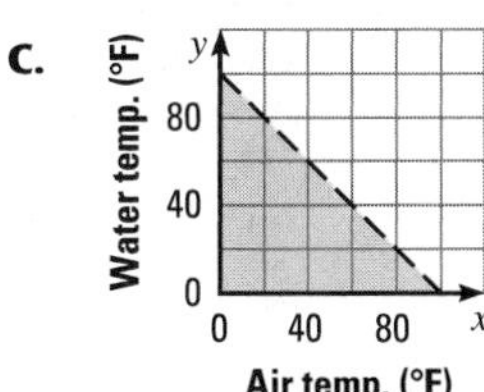

   D. 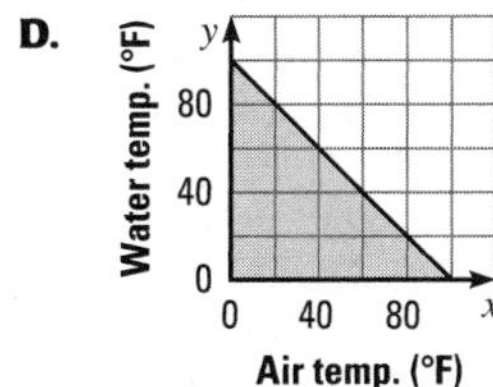

6. **PRESENTATION** You will be making a presentation for your history class. Your teacher gives you a time limit of 15 minutes with an absolute deviation of at most 1.5 minutes. What is the minimum duration (in minutes) for your presentation?

   F. 13.5 minutes **H.** 16.5 minutes

   G. 15 minutes **J.** 22.5 minutes

Illinois Mixed Review

1. C
2. G
3. C
4. G
5. C
6. F

6 CHAPTER SUMMARY

Additional Resources

The following resources are available to help review the materials in this chapter.

Chapter 6 Resource Book

- Chapter Review Games and Activities, p. 98
- Cumulative Practice, Chs. 1–6, pp. 101–102

Student Resources in Spanish

eWorkbook

@HomeTutor

Vocabulary Practice

Vocabulary practice is available at **classzone.com**

BIG IDEAS — For Your Notebook

Big Idea 1

Applying Properties of Inequality

You can apply the properties of inequality to solve inequalities. The properties listed below are also true for inequalities involving ≤ and ≥.

Property	If $a < b$, then ...	If $a > b$, then ...
Addition property of inequality	$a + c < b + c$.	$a + c > b + c$.
Subtraction property of inequality	$a - c < b - c$.	$a - c > b - c$.
Multiplication property of inequality	$ac < bc$ if $c > 0$. $ac > bc$ if $c < 0$.	$ac > bc$ if $c > 0$. $ac < bc$ if $c < 0$.
Division property of inequality	$\frac{a}{c} < \frac{b}{c}$ if $c > 0$. $\frac{a}{c} > \frac{b}{c}$ if $c < 0$.	$\frac{a}{c} > \frac{b}{c}$ if $c > 0$. $\frac{a}{c} < \frac{b}{c}$ if $c < 0$.

Big Idea 2

Using Statements with *And* or *Or*

An absolute value equation can be rewritten as two equations joined by *or.* An absolute value inequality can be rewritten as a compound inequality with *and* or *or.* In the statements below, < can be replaced by ≤, and > can be replaced by ≥.

Absolute value equation or inequality	Equivalent statement with *and* or *or*
$\|ax + b\| = c, c \ge 0$	$ax + b = c$ *or* $ax + b = -c$
$\|ax + b\| < c, c \ge 0$	$-c < ax + b < c$
$\|ax + b\| > c, c \ge 0$	$ax + b < -c$ *or* $ax + b > c$

Big Idea 3

Graphing Inequalities

You use a number line to graph an inequality in one variable. Similarly, you use a coordinate plane to graph a linear inequality in two variables (including cases where one of the variables has a coefficient of 0, such as $0x + y < 1$, or $y < 1$).

Graphing inequalities in one variable	Graphing linear inequalities in two variables
Graph simple inequalities: 1. Solve for the variable. 2. Draw an open circle for < or > and a closed circle for ≤ or ≥. Draw an arrow in the appropriate direction. Graph compound inequalities: 1. Solve the compound inequality. 2. Use the union of graphs of simple inequalities for *or.* Use the intersection for *and.*	1. Graph the boundary line. Use a solid line for ≤ or ≥ and a dashed line for < or >. 2. Test a point that does not lie on the boundary line. 3. Shade the half-plane containing the point if the ordered pair is a solution of the inequality. Shade the other half-plane if the ordered pair is *not* a solution.

CHAPTER REVIEW

@HomeTutor
classzone.com
• Multi-Language Glossary
• Vocabulary practice

REVIEW KEY VOCABULARY

- graph of an inequality, *p. 356*
- equivalent inequalities, *p. 357*
- compound inequality, *p. 380*
- absolute value equation, *p. 390*
- absolute deviation, *p. 392*
- linear inequality in two variables, *p. 405*
- solution of an inequality in two variables, *p. 405*
- graph of an inequality in two variables, half-plane, *p. 405*

VOCABULARY EXERCISES

1. Translate the verbal sentence into an absolute value equation: "The absolute deviation of x from 19 is 8." $|x - 19| = 8$
2. Identify three ordered pairs that are solutions of $2x - 3y \geq -10$. *Sample answer:* (1, 1), (−2, 1), (4, 2)
3. **WRITING** When you graph a linear inequality in two variables, how do you know whether the boundary line is a solid line or a dashed line? How do you know which half-plane to shade? The boundary line is solid if the inequality symbol is ≤ or ≥, the boundary line is dashed if the inequality symbol is < or >; choose a test point that is not on the boundary line. If the ordered pair is a solution to the inequality, shade the half-plane that contains the test point; if it not a solution, shade the other half-plane.

REVIEW EXAMPLES AND EXERCISES

Use the review examples and exercises below to check your understanding of the concepts you have learned in each lesson of Chapter 6.

6.1 Solve Inequalities Using Addition and Subtraction *pp. 356–361*

EXAMPLE

Solve $x - 2.1 \leq 1.4$. Graph your solution.

$x - 2.1 \leq 1.4$	**Write original inequality.**
$x - 2.1 + 2.1 \leq 1.4 + 2.1$	**Add 2.1 to each side.**
$x \leq 3.5$	**Simplify.**

▶ The solutions are all real numbers less than or equal to 3.5.

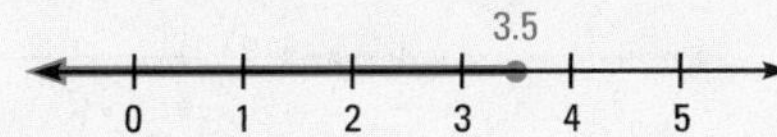

EXERCISES

EXAMPLES 1, 2, 3, and 4 on pp. 356–358 for Exs. 4–7

4. **GEOGRAPHY** The lowest elevation in Mexico is −10 meters at Laguna Salada. Write and graph an inequality that describes all elevations in Mexico that are greater than the lowest elevation. $x > -10$; see margin for art.

Solve the inequality. Graph your solution. 5–7. See margin for art.

5. $x + 5 > -13$ $x > -18$
6. $m - 9 \geq -4$ $m \geq 5$
7. $s + 3.7 < 1$ $s < -2.7$

Extra Example 6.1

Solve $x + 6 > 9$. Graph your solution. all real numbers greater than 3

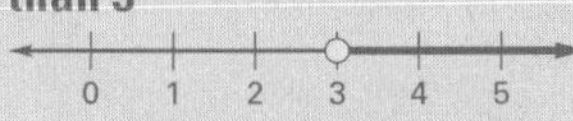

4.

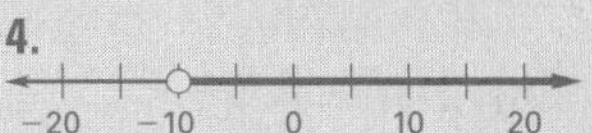

5.

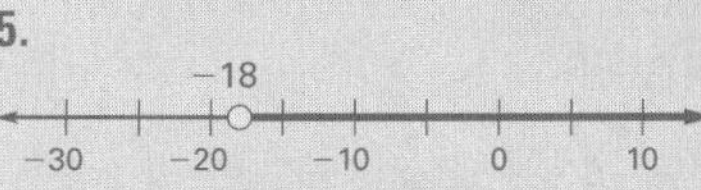

6.

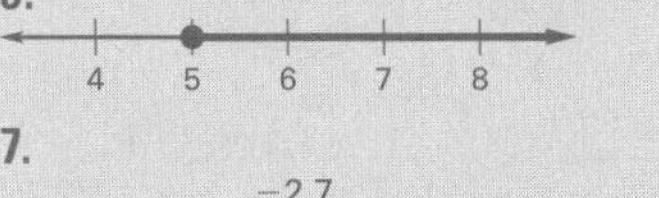

7.

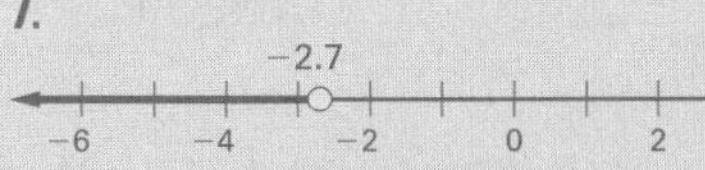

Extra Example 6.2

Solve $\frac{x}{-6} \geq 4$. Graph your solution. all real numbers less than or equal to -24

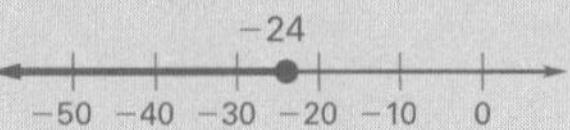

Extra Example 6.3

Solve $-3x - 2 < 10$. Graph your solution. all real numbers greater than -4

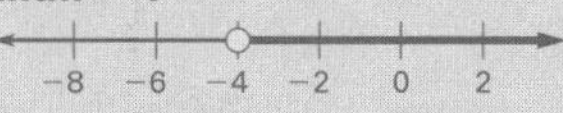

8.

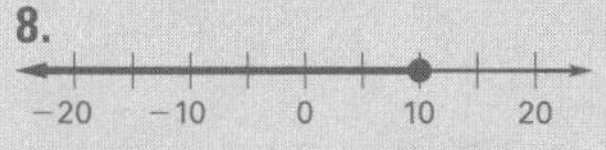

9.

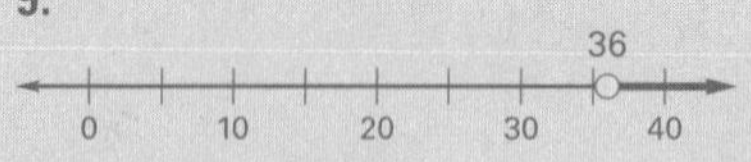

10.

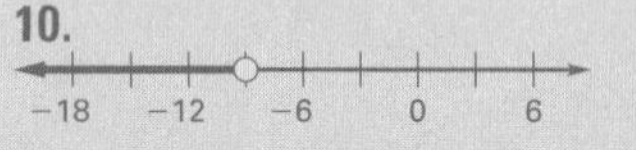

11.

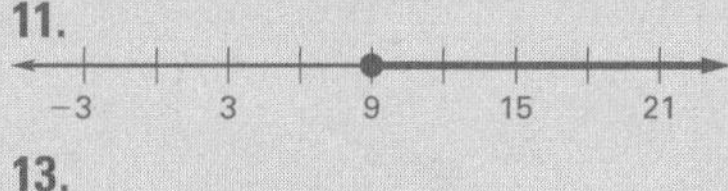

13.

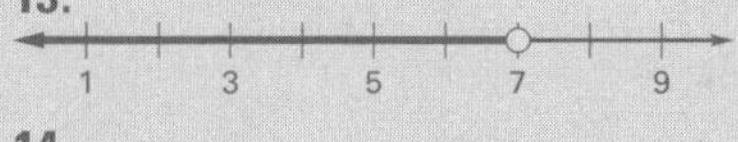

14.

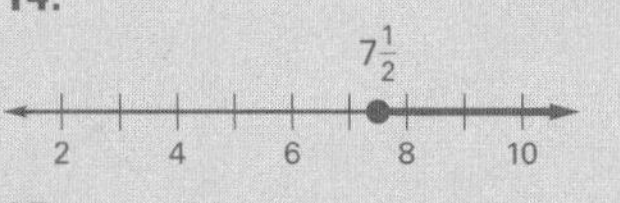

15.

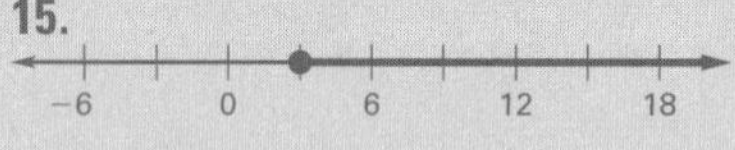

16.

17.

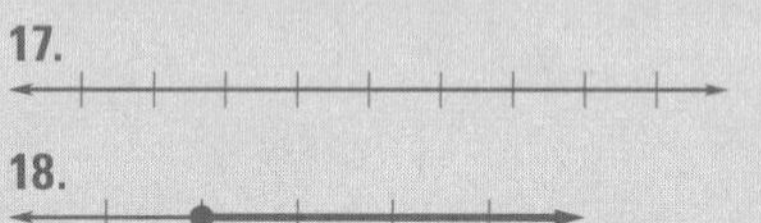

18.

−2 −1 0 1 2

6 CHAPTER REVIEW

6.2 Solve Inequalities Using Multiplication and Division *pp. 363–368*

EXAMPLE

Solve $\frac{x}{-4} < 9$. Graph your solution.

$\frac{x}{-4} < 9$	**Write original inequality.**
$-4 \cdot \frac{x}{-4} > -4 \cdot 9$	**Multiply each side by −4. Reverse inequality symbol.**
$x > -36$	**Simplify.**

▶ The solutions are all real numbers greater than -36.

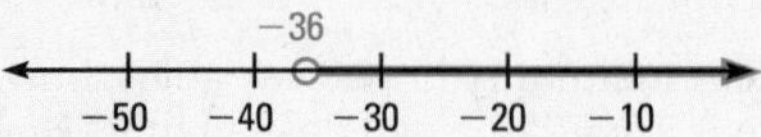

EXERCISES

EXAMPLES 1, 2, 3, 4, and 5 on pp. 363–365 for Exs. 8–12

Solve the inequality. Graph your solution. 8–11. See margin for art.

8. $\frac{p}{2} \leq 5$ $p \leq 10$ **9.** $\frac{n}{-4.5} < -8$ $n > 36$ **10.** $-3x > 27$ $x < -9$ **11.** $2y \geq 18$ $y \geq 9$

12. GYMNASTICS In men's gymnastics, an athlete competes in 6 events. Suppose that an athlete's average score per event is at most 9.7 points. Write and solve an inequality to find the possible total scores for the athlete. $\frac{x}{6} \leq 9.7$, at most 58.2 points

6.3 Solve Multi-Step Inequalities *pp. 369–374*

EXAMPLE

Solve $-4x + 7 \geq -13$. Graph your solution.

$-4x + 7 \geq -13$	**Write original inequality.**
$-4x \geq -20$	**Subtract 7 from each side.**
$x \leq 5$	**Divide each side by −4. Reverse inequality symbol.**

▶ The solutions are all real numbers less than or equal to 5.

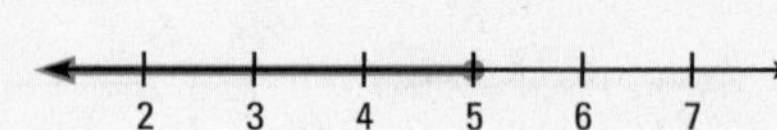

EXERCISES

EXAMPLES 1, 2, 3, and 4 on pp. 369–370 for Exs. 13–19

Solve the inequality, if possible. Graph your solution. 13–18. See margin for art.

13. $2g + 11 < 25$ $g < 7$ **14.** $\frac{2}{3}r - 4 \geq 1$ $r \geq 7\frac{1}{2}$ **15.** $1 - 3x \leq -14 + 2x$ $x \geq 3$

16. $3(q + 1) < 3q + 7$ all real numbers **17.** $8(t - 1) > -8 + 8t$ no solution **18.** $-3(2n - 1) \geq 1 - 8n$ $n \geq -1$

19. TICKET PURCHASES You can order discount movie tickets from a website for \$7 each. You must also pay a shipping fee of \$4. You want to spend no more than \$40 on movie tickets. Find the possible numbers of movie tickets that you can order. at most 5 tickets

@HomeTutor
classzone.com
Chapter Review Practice

6.4 Solve Compound Inequalities *pp. 380–387*

EXAMPLE

Solve $-1 < -2x + 7 < 9$. Graph your solution.

$-1 < -2x + 7 < 9$	**Write original inequality.**
$-8 < -2x < 2$	**Subtract 7 from each expression.**
$4 > x > -1$	**Divide each expression by −2. Reverse both inequality symbols.**
$-1 < x < 4$	**Rewrite in the form $a < x < b$.**

▶ The solutions are all real numbers greater than −1 *and* less than 4.

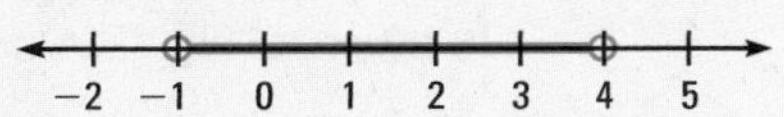

EXERCISES

EXAMPLES 3, 4, and 5 on pp. 381–382 for Exs. 20–23

Solve the inequality. Graph your solution. 20–23. See margin for art.

20. $-6 \le 2t - 5 \le -3$ $-\frac{1}{2} \le t \le 1$

21. $-3 < -3x + 8 < 11$ $-1 < x < 3\frac{2}{3}$

22. $9s - 6 < 12$ *or* $3s + 1 > 13$ $s < 2$ or $s > 4$

23. $-4w + 12 \ge 10$ *or* $5w - 14 > -4$ $w \le \frac{1}{2}$ or $w > 2$

6.5 Solve Absolute Value Equations *pp. 390–395*

EXAMPLE

Solve $4|5x - 3| + 6 = 30$.

First, rewrite the equation in the form $|ax + b| = c$.

$4|5x - 3| + 6 = 30$	**Write original equation.**
$4|5x - 3| = 24$	**Subtract 6 from each side.**
$|5x - 3| = 6$	**Divide each side by 4.**

Next, solve the absolute value equation.

$5x - 3 = 6$ *or* $5x - 3 = -6$	**Rewrite as two equations.**
$5x = 9$ *or* $5x = -3$	**Add 3 to each side.**
$x = 1.8$ *or* $x = -0.6$	**Divide each side by 5.**

▶ The solutions are −0.6 and 1.8.

EXERCISES

EXAMPLES 1, 2, 3, 4, and 5 on pp. 390–392 for Exs. 24–30

Solve the equation, if possible.

24. $|r| = 7$ 7, −7

25. $|a + 6| = 2$ −4, −8

26. $|2c + 5| = 21$ 8, −13

27. $2|x - 3| + 1 = 5$ 5, 1

28. $3|2q + 1| - 5 = 1$ 0.5, −1.5

29. $4|3p - 2| + 5 = 11$ $1\frac{1}{6}, \frac{1}{6}$

30. **BOWLING** In tenpin bowling, the height of each bowling pin must be 15 inches with an absolute deviation of 0.03125 inch. Find the minimum and maximum possible heights of a bowling pin. 14.96875 in., 15.03125 in.

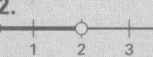

Extra Example 6.4

Solve $2x + 3 \le 5$ *or* $5x + 2 > 12$. Graph your solution. all real numbers less than or equal to 1 *or* greater than 2

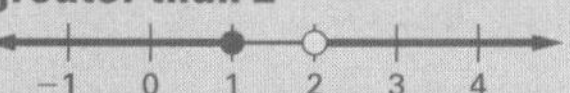

Extra Example 6.5

Solve $3|4x + 2| - 5 = 13$. 1, −2

20.

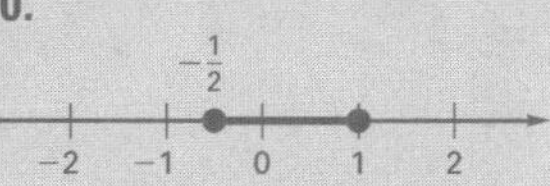

21.

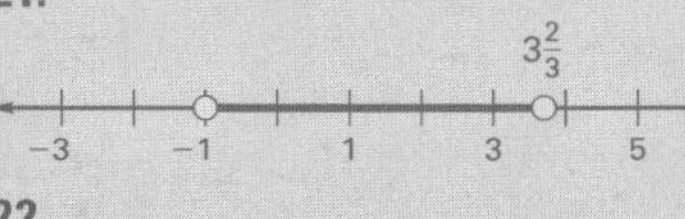

22.

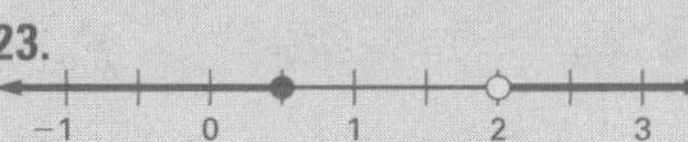

23.

−1 0 1 2 3

Extra Example 6.6

Solve $|-2x - 3| + 6 < 17$. Graph your solution. **all real numbers greater than -7 and less than 4**

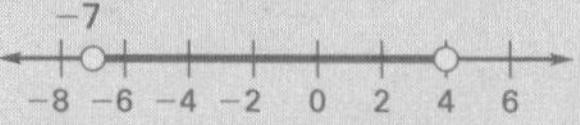

Extra Example 6.7

Graph the inequality $2x + y \geq 4$.

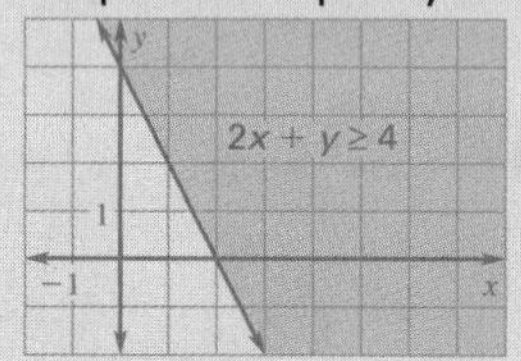

31.

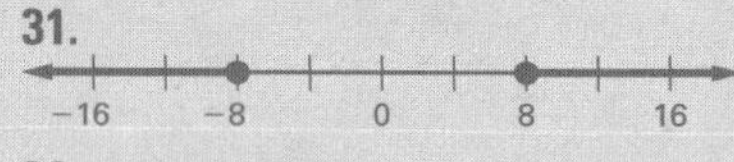

32.

$\frac{1}{6}$

−1 $-\frac{1}{2}$ 0 $\frac{1}{2}$ 1

33.

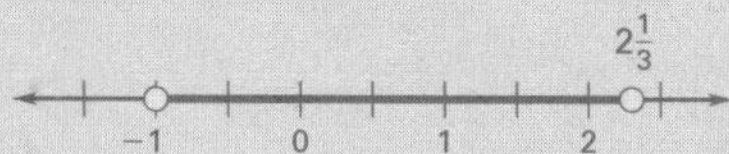

34.

$-2\frac{4}{9}$ $-\frac{8}{9}$

−4 −3 −2 −1 0

35.

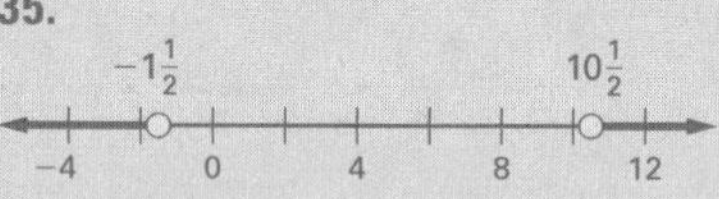

36.

−16 −12 −8 −4 0 4 8

41.

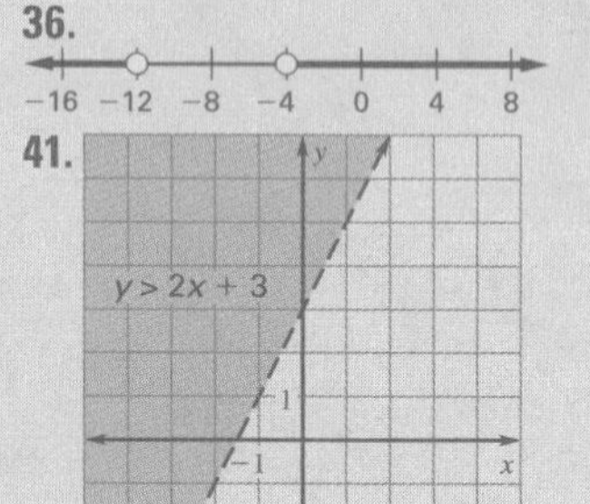

42.

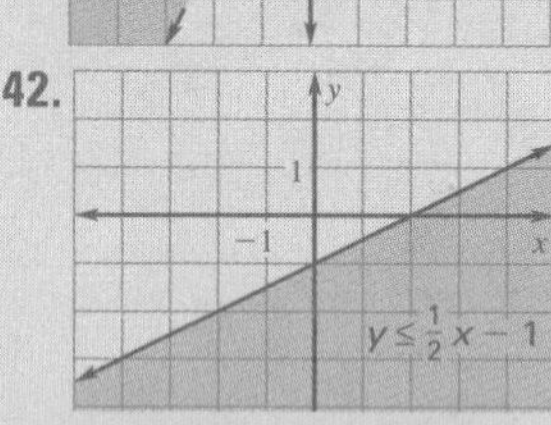

43.

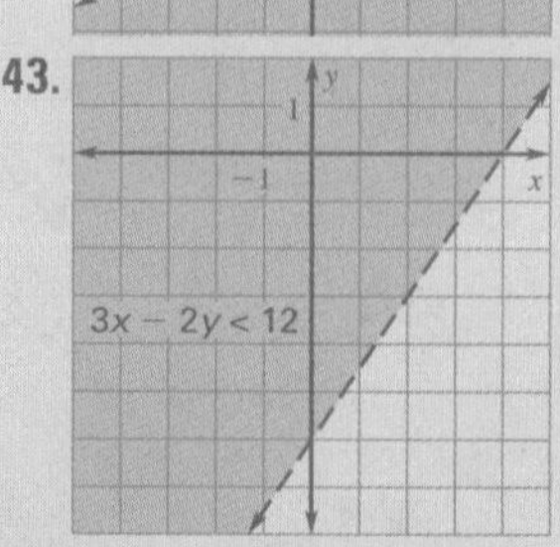

6 CHAPTER REVIEW

6.6 Solve Absolute Value Inequalities

pp. 398–403

EXAMPLE

Solve $3|2x + 11| + 2 \leq 17$. Graph your solution.

$3\|2x + 11\| + 2 \leq 17$	**Write original inequality.**
$3\|2x + 11\| \leq 15$	**Subtract 2 from each side.**
$\|2x + 11\| \leq 5$	**Divide each side by 3.**
$-5 \leq 2x + 11 \leq 5$	**Rewrite as compound inequality.**
$-16 \leq 2x \leq -6$	**Subtract 11 from each expression.**
$-8 \leq x \leq -3$	**Divide each expression by 2.**

▶ The solutions are all real numbers greater than or equal to -8 *and* less than or equal to -3.

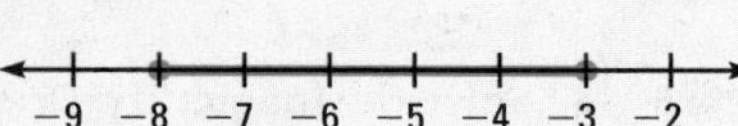

EXERCISES

EXAMPLES 1, 2, and 3 on pp. 398–399 for Exs. 31–36

Solve the inequality. Graph your solution. 31–36. See margin for art.

31. $|m| \geq 8$ $m \geq 8$ *or* $m \leq -8$
32. $|6k + 1| \geq 2$ $k \geq \frac{1}{6}$ *or* $k \leq -\frac{1}{2}$
33. $|3g - 2| < 5$ $-1 < g < 2\frac{1}{3}$

34. $6|3x + 5| \leq 14$ $-2\frac{4}{9} \leq x \leq -\frac{8}{9}$
35. $|2j - 9| - 2 > 10$ $j < -1\frac{1}{2}$ or $j > 10\frac{1}{2}$
36. $5|d + 8| - 7 > 13$ $d < -12$ or $d > -4$

6.7 Graph Linear Inequalities in Two Variables

pp. 405–412

EXAMPLE

Graph the inequality $y < 3x - 1$.

STEP 1 **Graph** the equation $y = 3x - 1$. The inequality is <, so use a dashed line.

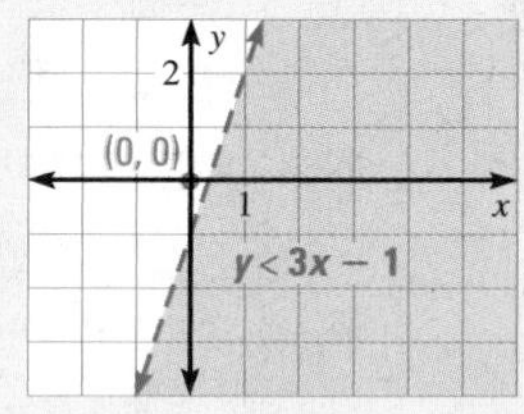

STEP 2 **Test** (0, 0) in $y < 3x - 1$.

$$0 \overset{?}{<} 3(0) - 1$$

$$0 < -1 \text{ ✗}$$

STEP 3 **Shade** the half-plane that does not contain (0, 0), because (0, 0) is *not* a solution of the inequality.

EXERCISES

EXAMPLES 1, 2, 3, 4, and 5 on pp. 405–407 for Exs. 37–44

Tell whether the ordered pair is a solution of $-3x + 2y \geq 16$.

37. (−2, 8) solution
38. (−1, −1) not a solution
39. (−2, 10) solution
40. (9, −5) not a solution

Graph the inequality. 41–44. See margin.

41. $y > 2x + 3$
42. $y \leq \frac{1}{2}x - 1$
43. $3x - 2y < 12$
44. $y \geq 3$

44.

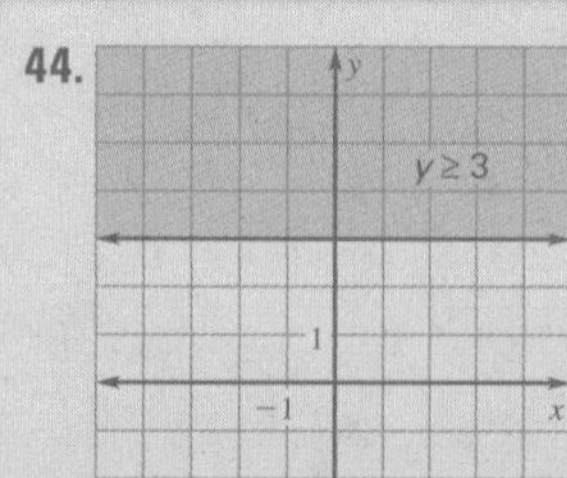

Chapter Test

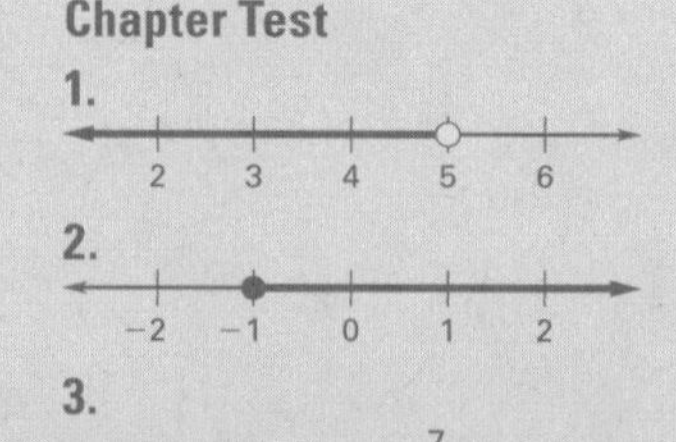

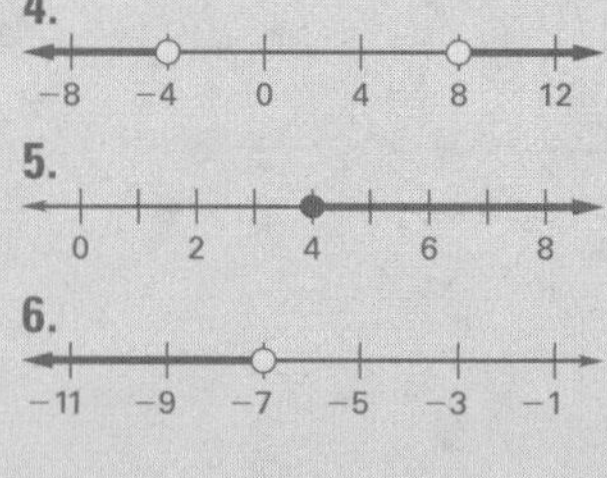

6 CHAPTER TEST

Translate the verbal phrase into an inequality. Then graph the inequality. **1–4. See margin for art.**

1. All real numbers that are less than 5 **$x < 5$**
2. All real numbers that are greater than or equal to -1 **$x \geq -1$**
3. All real numbers that are greater than -2 *and* less than or equal to 7 **$-2 < x \leq 7$**
4. All real numbers that are greater than 8 *or* less than -4 **$x > 8$ *or* $x < -4$**

Solve the inequality, if possible. Graph your solution. **5–22. See margin for art.**

5. $x - 9 \geq -5$ **$x \geq 4$**
6. $-2 > 5 + y$ **$y < -7$**
7. $-0.8 \leq z + 7.7$ **$z \geq -8.5$**
8. $5m \geq 35$ **$m \geq 7$**
9. $\frac{n}{6} < -1$ **$n < -6$**
10. $\frac{r}{-3} \leq 4$ **$r \geq -12$**
11. $-4s < 6s + 1$ **$s > -0.1$**
12. $4t - 7 \leq 13$ **$t \leq 5$**
13. $-8 > 5 - v$ **$v > 13$**
14. $3(5w + 4) < 12w - 11$ **$w < -7\frac{2}{3}$**
15. $4p - 3 > 2(2p + 1)$ **no solution**
16. $9q - 12 \geq 3(3q - 4)$ **all real numbers**
17. $-2 \leq 4 - 3a \leq 13$ **$-3 \leq a \leq 2$**
18. $-7 < 2c - 1 < 10\frac{1}{2}$ **$-3 < c < 5.75$**
19. $-5 \leq 2 - h$ *or* $6h + 5 \geq 71$ **$h \leq 7$ or $h \geq 11$**
20. $|2d + 8| > 3$ **$d < -5.5$ *or* $d > -2.5$**
21. $2|3f - 7| + 5 < 11$ **$1\frac{1}{3} < f < 3\frac{1}{3}$**
22. $|j - 7| - 1 \leq 3\frac{5}{6}$ **$2\frac{1}{6} \leq j \leq 11\frac{5}{6}$**

Solve the equation, if possible.

23. $-\frac{3}{4}|x - 3| = \frac{1}{4}$ **no solution**
24. $|3y + 1| - 6 = -2$ **$1, -1\frac{2}{3}$**
25. $4|2z + 5| + 9 = 5$ **no solution**

Check whether the ordered pair is a solution of the inequality.

26. $2x - y < 4$; $(2, -1)$ **not a solution**
27. $y + 3x \geq -5$; $(-3, -4)$ **not a solution**
28. $y \leq -3$; $(4, -7)$ **solution**

Graph the inequality. **29–31. See margin.**

29. $y < x + 4$
30. $y \geq 2x - 5$
31. $y \geq -6$

32. **BUSINESS** Your friend is starting a small business baking and decorating cakes and wants to make a profit of at least \$250 for the first month. The expenses for the first month are \$155. What are the possible revenues that your friend can earn in order to meet the profit goal? **at least \$405**

33. **BICYCLES** A manufacturer of bicycle parts requires that a bicycle chain have a width of 0.3 inch with an absolute error of at most 0.0003 inch. Find the possible widths of bicycle chains that the manufacturer will accept. **0.2997 in. up to 0.3003 in.**

34. **HORSES** You are planning to ride a horse to a campsite. The sum of your weight x (in pounds) and the combined weight y (in pounds) of your camping supplies can be at most 20% of the weight of the horse.
    a. Suppose that the horse weighs 1000 pounds. Write and graph an inequality that describes the possible combinations of your weight and the combined weight of the camping supplies. **$x + y \leq 200$; see margin for art.**
    b. Identify and interpret one of the solutions of the inequality in part (a). ***Sample answer:* (130, 60); if you weigh 130 pounds and the combined weight of your camping supplies is 60 pounds, the combined weight is 190, so you will be able to ride the horse to the campsite.**

Additional Resources

Assessment Book

- Chapter Test, Levels A, B, C, pp. 78–83
- Standardized Chapter Test, pp. 84–85
- SAT/ACT Chapter Test, pp. 86–87
- Alternative Assessment, pp. 88–89

Test Generator CD-ROM

Chapter Test

Easily-readable reduced copies (with answers) of Chapter Test B, the Standardized Chapter Test, and the Alternative Assessment from the Assessment Book can be found on pp. 354G–354H.

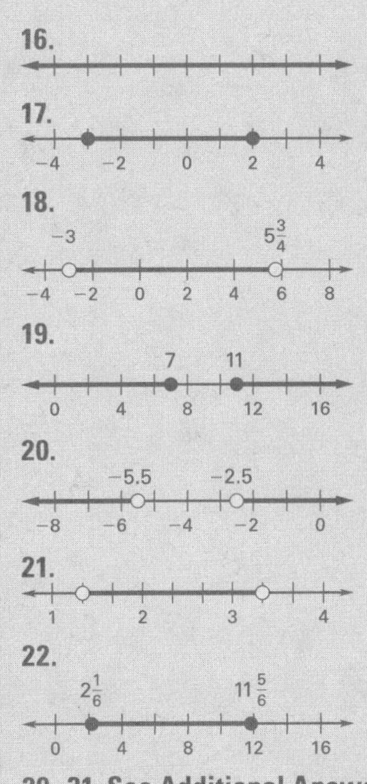

29–31. See Additional Answers beginning on p. AA1.

34a.

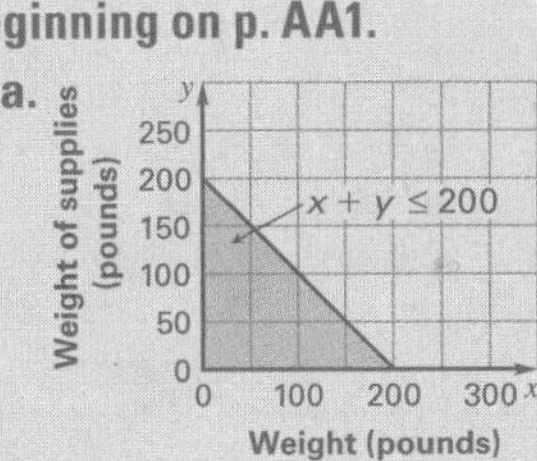

7. −8.5; −10 −8 −6 −4 −2

8. 1 3 5 7 9

9. −8 −6 −4 −2 0

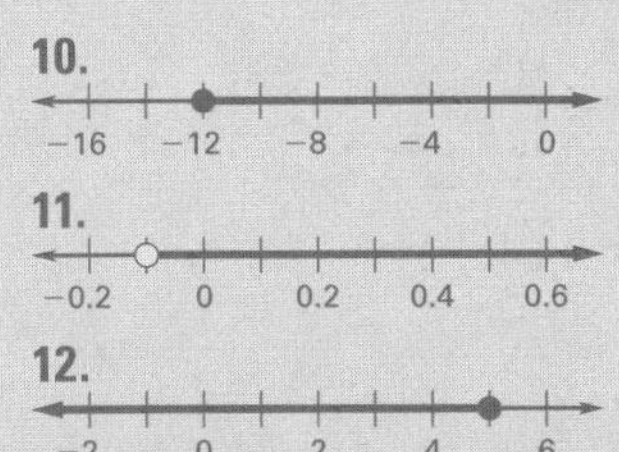

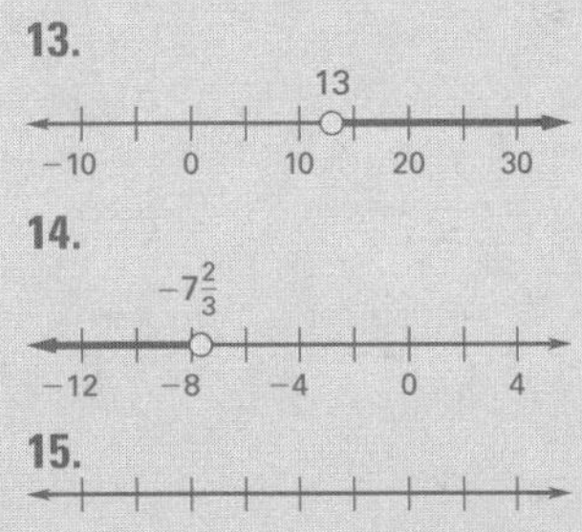

MULTIPLE CHOICE QUESTIONS

If you have difficulty solving a multiple choice problem directly, you may be able to use another approach to eliminate incorrect answer choices and obtain the correct answer.

PROBLEM 1

What are the solutions of $|-x + 1| - 5 = 8$?

A. -14 and 12 **C.** -4 and 14

B. -12 and 14 **D.** 12 and 14

Method 1

SOLVE DIRECTLY

STEP 1 **Write** the equation in the form $|ax + b| = c$.

$|-x + 1| - 5 = 8$

$|-x + 1| = 13$ Add 5 to each side.

STEP 2 **Solve** the absolute value equation.

Rewrite $|-x + 1| = 13$ as 2 equations.

$-x + 1 = 13$ or $-x + 1 = -13$

Solve $-x + 1 = 13$

$-x + 1 = 13$

$-x = 12$ Subtract 1 from each side.

$x = -12$ Divide both sides by -1.

Solve $-x + 1 = -13$

$-x + 1 = -14$

$-x = -14$ Subtract 1 from each side.

$x = 14$ Divide both sides by -1.

The solutions are -12 and 14.

The answer is **B**.

Method 2

ELIMINATE CHOICES Substitute the values given in each answer choice for x in the equation.

Choice A: -14 and 12

$|-(-14) + 1| - 5 \stackrel{?}{=} 8$ $|-(12) + 1| - 5 \stackrel{?}{=} 8$

$|-(-14) + 1| \stackrel{?}{=} 13$ $|-(12) + 1| \stackrel{?}{=} 13$

$|14 + 1| \stackrel{?}{=} 13$ $|-12 + 1| \stackrel{?}{=} 13$

$|15| \stackrel{?}{=} 13$ $|-11| \stackrel{?}{=} 13$

$15 = 13$ ✗ $11 = 13$ ✗

Because neither –14 or 12 checks, we can eliminate Choices **A** and **D**.

Let's check answer choice **B**.

Choice B: -12 and 14

$|-(-12) + 1| - 5 \stackrel{?}{=} 8$ $|-(14) + 1 - 5| \stackrel{?}{=} 8$

$|-(-12) + 1| \stackrel{?}{=} 13$ $|-(14) + 1| \stackrel{?}{=} 13$

$|12 + 1| \stackrel{?}{=} 13$ $|-14 + 1| \stackrel{?}{=} 13$

$|13| \stackrel{?}{=} 13$ $|-13| \stackrel{?}{=} 13$

$13 = 13$ ✓ $13 = 13$ ✓

Both -12 and 14 are solutions.

The answer is **B**.

Illinois Test Practice

1. B
2. F
3. D

PROBLEM 2

What is the solution to the compound inequality?

$$-5 < 4x - 17 \le -1$$

F. $3 < x \le 4$ **G.** $-3 \le x < 4$ **H.** $-3 < x \le 4$ **J.** $3 < x < 4$

METHOD 1

SOLVE DIRECTLY

STEP 1 **Write** the compound inequality as 2 inequalities.

$-5 < 4x - 17$ and $4x - 17 \le -1$

STEP 2 **Solve** the inequalities.

$-5 < 4x - 17$

$12 < 4x$ Add 17 to each side.

$3 < x$ Divide each side by 4.

$4x - 17 \le -1$

$4x \le 16$ Add 17 to each side.

$x \le 4$ Divide each side by 4.

The solution is $3 < x \le 4$.

The answer is **F**.

METHOD 2

ELIMINATE CHOICES Another method is to consider the extremes to eliminate incorrect choices.

STEP 1 It is not necessary to multiply or divide by a negative number when solving the inequality. Therefore, the inequality symbols will remain the same.

Eliminate Choices **G** and **J**.

STEP 2 The right sides of the compound inequalities in Choices **F** and **H** are the same. Solve the left side to determine the correct answer.

$-5 < 4x - 17$

$12 < 4x$ Add 17 to each side.

$3 < x$ Divide each side by 4.

The solution is $3 < x \le 4$.

The answer is **F**.

TEST PREPARATION

PRACTICE

1. Which describes the solution of the inequality $4x - 13 \ge 19$?

   A. $x \le 8$ **B.** $x \ge 8$ **C.** $x > 8$ **D.** $x \ge -8$

2. Which describes the solution to the compound inequality $13 \ge 5x - 7 > 3$?

   F. $4 \ge x > 2$ **G.** $4 \le x < 2$ **H.** $20 \ge x > 10$ **J.** $20 \le x < 10$

3. What are the solutions of $|-2x + 4| + 3 = 11$?

   A. -9 and 5 **B.** -6 and 2 **C.** -5 and 9 **D.** -2 and 6

Illinois Test Practice

1. C
2. H
3. B
4. G
5. B
6. G
7. D
8. H
9. C
10. F
11. B
12. G
13. D
14. H
15. C
16. J
17. D
18. H
19. D

Illinois Test Practice

1. In a piano competition, a pianist must perform a sonata that lasts no less than 8 minutes and no more than 10 minutes. Which inequality represents the durations d (in minutes) of sonatas that can be performed?

A. $8 < d < 10$

B. $d \leq 8$ or $d \geq 10$

C. $8 \leq d \leq 10$

D. $d < 8$ or $d > 10$

2. Which ordered pair is a solution of the inequality $4x - y \geq 3$?

F. (0, 0) **H.** (1, 1)

G. (−1, 2) **J.** (0, −2)

3. You are designing an obstacle course for a dog agility event. The course includes a tunnel that must have a height of 24 inches with an absolute deviation of 2 inches. Which equation can you use to find the minimum and maximum heights of the tunnel?

A. $|x + 24| = 2$

B. $|x - 24| = 2$

C. $|x + 2| = 24$

D. $|x - 2| = 24$

4. What is the solution of the inequality $4 + 2x < 10$?

F. $x < -3$ **H.** $x > -3$

G. $x < 3$ **J.** $x > 3$

5. The cost of renting a truck from a rental company is described by the equation $y = 28x + 15$ in which y is the cost and x is the time in days. If Jake has $90 to spend, what is the maximum number of days that he can rent a single truck if tax is not considered?

A. 1 **C.** 3

B. 2 **D.** 4

6. Which graph represents the solution of $|2x + 6| > 10$?

F.
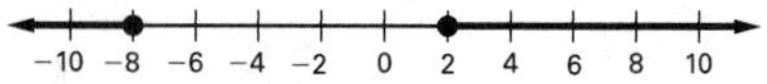

G.
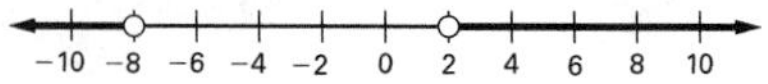

H.
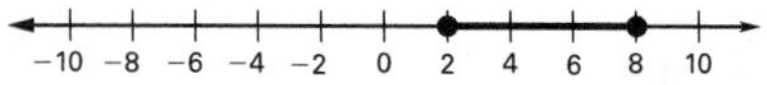

J.
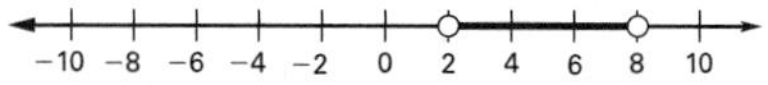

7. Which describes the solution of the inequality $3x - 11 \geq 7$?

A. $x \geq -6$

B. $x \leq 6$

C. $x > 6$

D. $x \geq 6$

8. Which inequality is equivalent to $4 - x < 4x + 9$?

F. $1 < x$

G. $1 > x$

H. $-1 < x$

J. $-1 > x$

9. What is the solution of the compound inequality?

$-2 \leq 3x - 5 \leq 7$

A. $-1 \leq x \leq 2$

B. $2 \leq x \leq 4$

C. $1 \leq x \leq 4$

D. $-1 \leq x \leq -4$

10. For which values of x is the inequality true?

$3(x + 2) \geq 4x - 3$

F. $x \leq 9$

G. $x < -9$

H. $x > -9$

J. $x \geq -9$

11. Which point is *not* a solution of $-3x + 4y \geq -(x + 8)$?

A. $(-2, -3)$ **C.** $(2, -1)$

B. $(-2, -7)$ **D.** $(-4, -4)$

12. The solution for which inequality is shown in the graph?

F. $x + 3y \geq 0$

G. $2x + 3y < 6$

H. $x - 3y < 5$

J. $2x - 3y \leq 6$

13. What are the solutions of the equation $|3x - 5| = 10$?

A. $-5, 5$ **C.** $-\frac{3}{5}, 5$

B. $-5, 2$ **D.** $-\frac{5}{3}, 5$

14. Brian and four friends each purchased a fishing license that cost \$25. Each plans to spend \$45 a day for food and lodging. Which inequality can be solved to find out how many days Brian can spend fishing with at most \$500? How many days can he fish?

F. $45x + 5(25) \leq 500$; 8 days

G. $45x + 5(25) \geq 500$; 9 days

H. $45x + 25 \leq 500$; 10 days

J. $45x + 25 \geq 500$; 11 days

15. Which inequality has the solution shown on the graph?

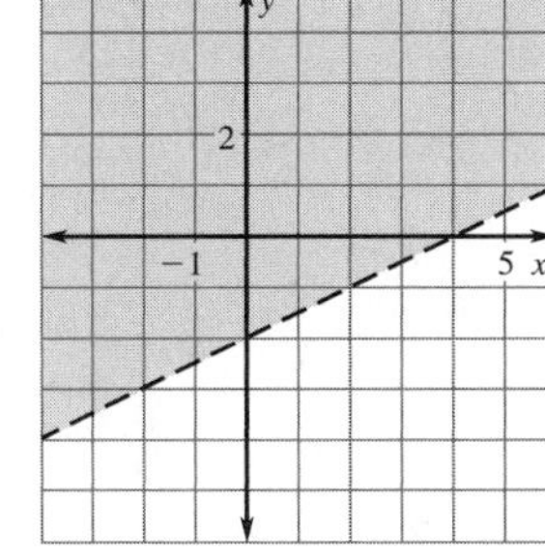

A. $y \leq 2x - 2$

B. $y \geq 2x - 2$

C. $y > \frac{1}{2}x - 2$

D. $y < \frac{1}{2}x - 2$

16. The sum of the lengths of any two sides of a triangle is greater than the length of the third side. Which compound inequality describes all the possible lengths of the side of the triangle labeled x?

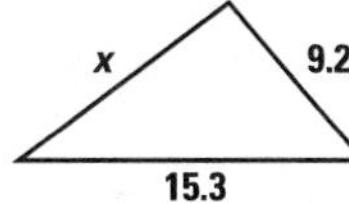

F. $6.1 > x > 24.5$ **H.** $6.1 \leq x \leq 24.5$

G. $6.1 \geq x \geq 24.5$ **J.** $6.1 < x < 24.5$

17. Which of the following compound inequalities describes the graph below?

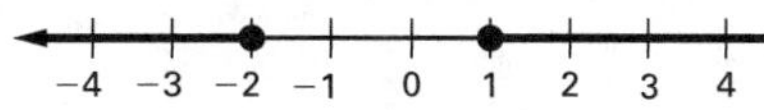

A. $-2 \geq x \geq 1$ **C.** $x \leq -2$ and $x \geq 1$

B. $-2 \leq x \leq 1$ **D.** $x \leq -2$ or $x \geq 1$

18. The rectangle below has an area greater than 42 square meters. Use an inquality to solve for x.?

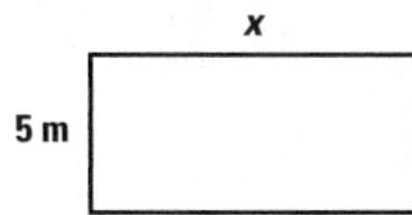

F. $x < 8.4$ m **H.** $x > 8.4$ m

G. $x \leq 8.4$ m **J.** $x \geq 8.4$ m

19. For what values of x is $|5x - 20| + 16 = 12$?

A. 0 **C.** $\frac{24}{5}$ and $\frac{16}{5}$

B. $\frac{16}{5}$ **D.** None of the above

TEST PRACTICE

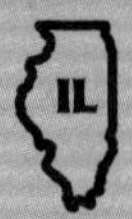

Illinois Resources Guide

Pacing and Assignment Guide

REGULAR SCHEDULE

Pre-AP For pacing and assignments for a Pre-AP course, see the *Algebra 1 Toolkit.*

Lesson	Les. Day	BASIC	AVERAGE	ADVANCED
7.1 8.11.17	Day 1	EP p. 941 Exs. 19–22; pp. 430–433 Exs. 1–17, 31–34, 38–42 even, 43–48	pp. 430–433 Exs. 1–11, 18–35, 37–41 odd, 43–48	pp. 430–433 Exs. 1, 4–7, 9, 10, 21–36*, 38–48 even
7.2 8.11.17	Day 1	EP p. 940 Exs. 21–26; pp. 439–441 Exs. 1–19	pp. 439–441 Exs. 1, 2, 4–18 even, 19–29 odd	pp. 439–441 Exs. 1, 6–8, 15–18, 20–28
	Day 2	pp. 439–441 Exs. 20–25, 31–35, 39–50	pp. 439–441 Exs. 31–37, 39–50	pp. 439–441 Exs. 29–38*, 42–44, 48–50
7.3 8.11.17	Day 1	pp. 447–450 Exs. 1, 2, 3–21 odd, 22–30, 39–43, 46–54 even	pp. 447–450 Exs. 1, 2, 6–8, 12–15, 19–24, 26–36 even, 39–44, 47–55 odd	pp. 447–450 Exs. 1, 2, 7, 8, 13–15, 19–22, 25–33 odd, 34–45*, 49, 52, 54
7.4 8.11.17	Day 1	SRH p. 911 Exs. 25, 26, 32, 36; pp. 454–457 Exs. 1, 2, 3–17 odd, 18–25, 37–41, 46–58 even	pp. 454–457 Exs. 1, 2, 6–8, 13–20, 21–33 odd, 34, 37–42, 45–57 odd	pp. 454–457 Exs. 1, 7, 8, 15–18, 21–36*, 39–44*, 47, 52, 58
7.5 8.11.17	Day 1	pp. 462–465 Exs. 1–20, 24, 25, 42–45	pp. 462–465 Exs. 1–14, 18–25, 42–45	pp. 462–465 Exs. 1–4, 11–13, 18–25, 44, 45
	Day 2	pp. 462–465 Exs. 26–30, 36–39, 46–60	pp. 462–465 Exs. 26–34, 36–40, 46–54 even, 56–61	pp. 462–465 Exs. 26–35*, 37–41*, 51, 52, 55, 59
7.6 8.11.17	Day 1	EP p. 943 Exs. 67–70, 72, 73; pp. 469–472 Exs. 1–8, 9–21 odd, 22–26, 36–39, 43–53 odd	pp. 469–472 Exs. 1–8, 15–23, 25–33 odd, 36–40, 42–52 even	pp. 469–472 Exs. 1, 2, 16–22, 24–41*, 47, 52
Review	Day 1	pp. 475–478 Exs. 1–31	pp. 475–478 Exs. 1–31	pp. 475–478 Exs. 1–31
Assess	Day 1	Chapter 7 Test	Chapter 7 Test	Chapter 7 Test

Yearly Pacing Chapter 7 Total – 10 days Chapters 1–7 Total – 80 days Remaining – 80 days

*Challenge Exercises EP = Extra Practice SRH = Skills Review Handbook

BLOCK SCHEDULE

DAY 1	DAY 2	DAY 3	DAY 4	DAY 5
7.1	**7.2 (CONT.)**	**7.4**	**7.5 (CONT.)**	**REVIEW**
pp. 430–433 Exs. 1–11, 18–35, 37–41 odd, 43–48	pp. 439–441 Exs. 31–37, 39–50	pp. 454–457 Exs. 1, 2, 6–8, 13–20, 21–33 odd, 34, 37–42, 45–57 odd	pp. 462–465 Exs. 26–34, 36–40, 46–54 even, 56–61	pp. 475–478 Exs. 1–31
7.2	**7.3**	**7.5**	**7.6**	**ASSESS**
pp. 439–441 Exs. 1, 2, 4–18 even, 19–29 odd	pp. 447–450 Exs. 1, 2, 6–8, 12–15, 19–24, 26–36 even, 39–44, 47–55 odd	pp. 462–465 Exs. 1–14, 18–25, 42–45	pp. 469–472 Exs. 1–8, 15–23, 25–33 odd, 36–40, 42–52 even	Chapter 7 Test

Yearly Pacing Chapter 7 Total – 5 days Chapters 1–7 Total – 40 days Remaining – 40 days

7 Chapter Resource Guide

Chapter Resource Book						
CHAPTER SUPPORT						
Parents as Partners (Chapter Overview with home involvement exercises and activity)					p. 1	
LESSON SUPPORT	**7.1**	**7.2**	**7.3**	**7.4**	**7.5**	**7.6**
Standard	**8.11.17**	**8.11.17**	**8.11.17**	**8.11.17**	**8.11.17**	**8.11.17**
Teaching Guide/Lesson Plan	p. 3	p. 17	p. 27	p. 38	p. 50	p. 64
Activity Masters				p. 40	p. 52	
Technology Activities & Keystrokes	p. 5					p. 66
Activity Support Masters			p. 29			
Practice (3 levels)	p. 6	p. 19	p. 30	p. 41	p. 53	p. 68
Study Guide	p. 12	p. 22	p. 33	p. 44	p. 59	p. 74
Catch-Up for Absent Students	p. 14	p. 24	p. 35	p. 46	p. 61	p. 76
Problem Solving/Application	p. 15	p. 25	p. 36	p. 47	p. 62	p. 77
Challenge Practice	p. 16	p. 26	p. 37	p. 49	p. 63	p. 78
REVIEW						
Chapter Review Games and Activities		p. 79	Cumulative Practice			p. 82
Project with Rubric		p. 80	Resource Book Answers			A1

Transparencies	*7.1*	*7.2*	*7.3*	*7.4*	*7.5*	*7.6*
Warm-Up/Daily Homework Quiz	✔	✔	✔	✔	✔	✔
Notetaking Guide	✔	✔	✔	✔	✔	✔
Teacher Support	✔				✔	✔
Answer Transparencies	✔	✔	✔	✔	✔	✔

ASSESSMENT BOOK

Quizzes	p. 90	SAT/ACT Chapter Test	p. 101
Chapter Tests (3 levels)	p. 93	Alternative Assessment with Rubric	p. 103
Standardized Chapter Test	p. 99	Cumulative Test	p. 105

TECHNOLOGY

- Easy Planner
- Test and Practice Generator
- Power Presentations
- @HomeTutor
- Activity Generator
- Animated Algebra
- Classzone.com
- eEdition Plus Online
- eWorkbook Plus Online
- ML Assessment System

ADDITIONAL RESOURCES

Illinois Additional Lessons

- Worked-Out Solution Key
- Notetaking Guide
- Practice Workbook
- Algebra 1 Toolkit
- Benchmark Tests
- Reteaching and Remediation
- Spanish Study Guide
- Spanish Assessment Book
- Spanish Resources in Spanish
- Multi-Language Visual Glossary

Lesson Practice Level B

LESSON 7.1

Practice B

For use with pages 427–433

Tell whether the ordered pair is a solution of the linear system.

1. (4, 1); no
$x + 2y = 6$
$3x + y = 11$

2. (−2, 1); yes
$5x - 2y = -12$
$x + 3y = 1$

3. (4, −3); yes
$-3x + 2y = -18$
$6x - y = 27$

4. (−4, −6); no
$3x - y = 6$
$-x + 2y = 8$

5. (−4, 3); no
$4x + 3y = -12$
$x + 2y = -6$

6. (−2, −5); yes
$-x + y = -3$
$-x + 3y = -13$

LESSON 7.1

Use the graph to solve the linear system. Check your solution.

7. $x - y = 8$ (3, −5)
$x + y = -2$

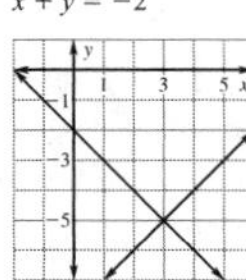

8. $5x - y = -9$ (−1, 4)
$y + 2x = 2$

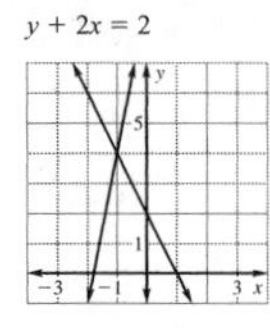

9. $2x + 3y = 2$ (−2, 2)
$-2x + y = 6$

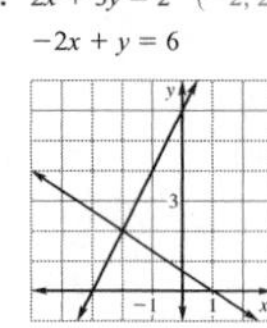

10. $3x - 2y = 16$ (4, −2)
$5x + y = 18$

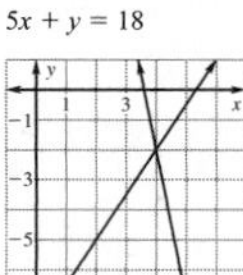

11. $2x - y = -13$ (−5, 3)
$y + 3x = -12$

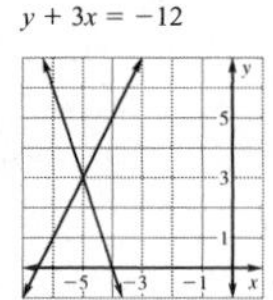

12. $6x + 2y = 8$ (0, 4)
$-3x + 4y = 16$

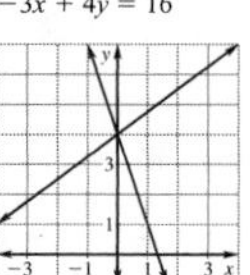

Solve the linear system by graphing. Check your solution.

13. $y = 3x$ (1, 3)
$y = 4x - 1$

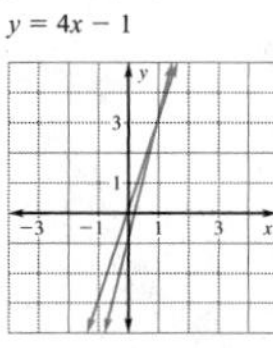

14. $2x + y = -4$ (−4, 4)
$x - y = -8$

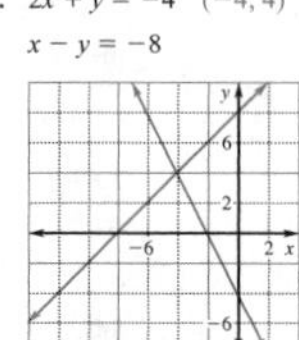

15. $-3x - y = -1$ (2, −5)
$2x + 4y = -16$

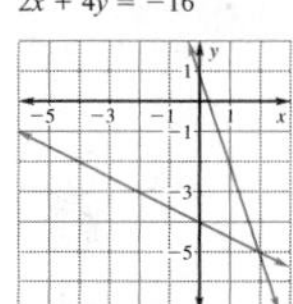

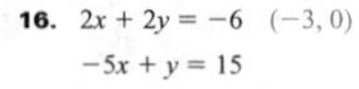

LESSON 7.1

Practice B

For use with pages 427–433

16. $2x + 2y = -6$ (−3, 0)
$-5x + y = 15$

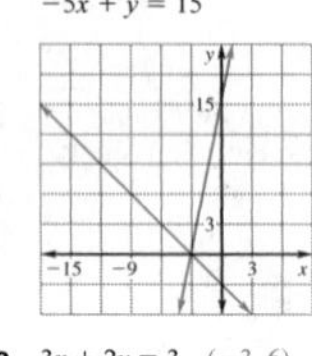

17. $-6x + y = 33$ (−5, 3)
$2x - 8y = -34$

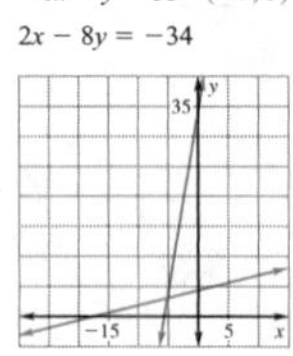

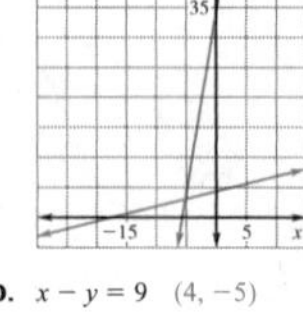

18. $-9x + 6y = -6$ (−2, −4)
$2x - 3y = 8$

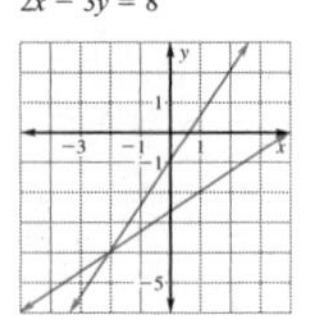

19. $3x + 2y = 3$ (−3, 6)
$5x + y = -9$

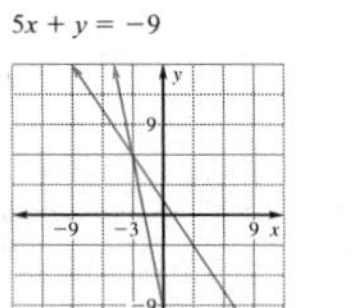

20. $x - y = 9$ (4, −5)
$3x + 2y = 2$

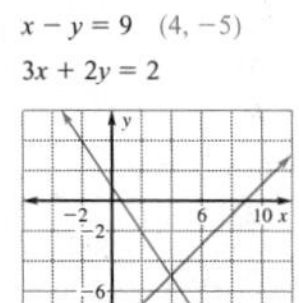

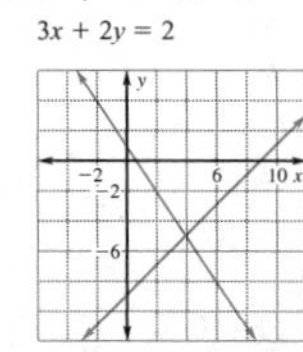

21. $6x + y = 19$ (2, 7)
$5x - 2y = -4$

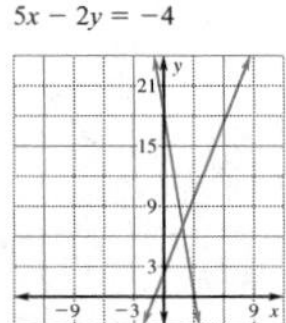

22. Hanging Flower Baskets You will be making hanging flower baskets. The plants you have picked out are blooming annuals and non-blooming annuals. The blooming annuals cost \$3.20 each and the non-blooming annuals cost \$1.50 each. You bought a total of 24 plants for \$49.60. Write a linear system of equations that you can use to find out how many of each type of plant you bought. Then graph the linear system and use the graph to find how many of each type of plant you bought.
8 blooming annuals and 16 non-blooming annuals

23. Baseball Outs In a game, 12 of a baseball team's 27 outs were fly balls. Twenty-five percent of the outs made by infielders and 100% of the outs made by outfielders were fly balls.

a. Write a linear system you can use to find the number of outs made by infielders and the number of outs made by outfielders. (*Hint:* Write one equation for the total number of outs and another equation for the number of fly ball outs.)

b. Graph your linear system. **a.** $x + y = 27$ and $0.25x + y = 12$

c. How many outs were made by infielders? How many outs were made by outfielders? infielders: 20 outs; outfielders: 7 outs

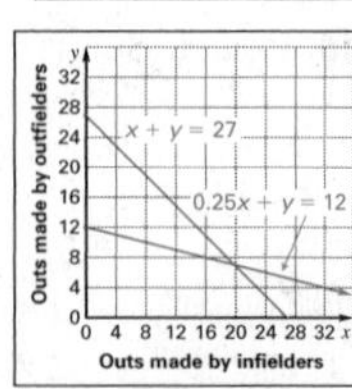

LESSON 7.2

Practice B

For use with pages 435–441

Solve for the indicated variable.

1. $8x + 4y = 12$; y $y = -2x + 3$ **2.** $3x - 4y = 12$; y $y = \frac{3}{4}x - 3$ **3.** $6x - 4y = 8$; x $x = \frac{2}{3}y + \frac{4}{3}$

Tell which equation you would use to isolate a variable. *Explain* your reasoning.

4. $x = 8y - 3$
$3x - 4y = 1$
Answers will vary.

5. $-4x + 5y = 11$
$y = 4x - 1$
Answers will vary.

6. $9 - 3x = y$
$3x - y = -2$
Answers will vary.

Solve the linear system by using substitution.

7. $x = 6 - 4y$ (2, 1)
$2x - 3y = 1$

8. $4x + 3y = 0$ (−3, 4)
$2x + y = -2$

9. $-x + 2y = -6$ (4, −1)
$8x + y = 31$

10. $6x - y = -35$ (−5, 5)
$5x - 2y = -35$

11. $-x + 3y = -9$ (3, −2)
$8x - 4y = 32$

12. $3x + 3y = -18$ (−4, −2)
$4x - y = -14$

13. $2x + 2y = 6$ (6, −3)
$-3x + 5y = -33$

14. $5x + 2y = 43$ (7, 4)
$-6x + 3y = -30$

15. $4x - 2y = -4$ (3, 8)
$7x - 5y = -19$

16. $3x + 2y = 5$ (1, 1)
$5x - 9y = -4$

17. $4x - 3y = 28$ (4, −4)
$2x + 3y = -4$

18. $8x + 8y = 24$ (1, 2)
$x + 5y = 11$

LESSON 7.2

19. Drum Sticks A drummer is stocking up on his drum sticks and brushes. The wood sticks that he buys are \$10.50 a pair and the brushes are \$24 a pair. He ends up spending \$90 on sticks and brushes and buys two times as many pairs of sticks as brushes. How many pairs of sticks and brushes did he buy? 4 pairs of sticks and 2 pairs of brushes

20. Mowing and Shoveling Last year you mowed grass and shoveled snow for 12 households. You earned \$225 for mowing a household's lawn for the entire year and you earned \$200 for shoveling a household's walk and driveway for an entire year. You earned a total of \$2600 last year.

a. Let x be the number of households you mowed for and let y be the number of households you shoveled for. Write an equation in x and y that shows the total number of households you worked for. Then write an equation in x and y that shows the total amount of money you earned. $x + y = 12$; $225x + 200y = 2600$

b. How many households did you mow the lawn for and how many households did you shovel the walk and driveway for? households mowed: 8 households; households shoveled: 4 households

21. Dimensions of a Metal Sheet A rectangular hole 3 centimeters wide and x centimeters long is cut in a rectangular sheet of metal that is 4 centimeters wide and y centimeters long. The length of the hole is 1 centimeter less than the length of the metal sheet. After the hole is cut, the area of the remaining metal sheet is 20 square centimeters. Find the length of the hole and the length of the metal sheet.
length of hole: 16 cm; length of sheet: 17 cm

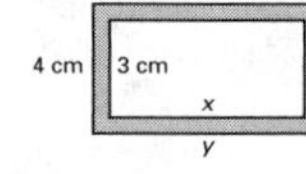

LESSON 7.3

Practice B

For use with pages 444–450

Rewrite the linear system so that the like terms are arranged in columns.

1. $8x - y = 19$ $8x - y = 19$ and $3x + y = 7$
   $y + 3x = 7$
2. $4x = y - 11$
   $6y + 4x = -3$
   $4x - y = -11$ and $4x + 6y = -3$
3. $9x - 2y = 5$
   $2y = -11x + 8$
   $9x - 2y = 5$ and $11x + 2y = 8$

Describe the first step you would use to solve the linear system.

4. $22x - y = -4$
   $y = 6x - 5$
   Arrange the terms.
5. $25 = x - 7y$
   $x + 12y = -8$
   Arrange the terms.
6. $3x + 7 = 2y$
   $-2y - 1 = 10x$
   Arrange the terms.
7. $x + 9y = 2$
   $14x - 9y = -4$
   Add the equations.
8. $4x + 3y = -6$
   $3y = -5x + 1$
   Arrange the terms.
9. $4x + y = -10$
   $x + y = -14$
   Subtract the equations.

Solve the linear system by using elimination.

10. $x + 5y = 28$ (3, 5)
    $-x - 2y = -13$
11. $7x - 4y = -30$ (−2, 4)
    $3x + 4y = 10$
12. $6x + y = 39$ (7, −3)
    $-2x + y = -17$
13. $3x = y - 20$ (−6, 2)
    $-7x - y = 40$
14. $2x - 6y = -10$ (10, 5)
    $4x = 10 + 6y$
15. $x - 3y = 6$ (−9, −5)
    $-2x = 3y + 33$
16. $-3x = y - 20$ (3, 11)
    $-y = -5x + 4$
17. $x - \frac{1}{2}y = \frac{11}{2}$ (10, 9)
    $-x + 4y = 26$
18. $-\frac{2}{3}x + 6y = 38$ (15, 8)
    $x - 6y = -33$
19. $\frac{3}{2}x + y = -\frac{5}{2}$ (−1, −1)
    $4x + y = -5$
20. $7x - \frac{1}{3}y = -29$ (−4, 3)
    $2x - \frac{1}{3}y = -9$
21. $\frac{1}{2}x - \frac{3}{2}y = -\frac{29}{2}$ $\left(8, \frac{37}{3}\right)$
    $-\frac{1}{2}x + 3y = 33$

22. **Fishing Barge** A fishing barge leaves from a dock and moves upstream (against the current) at a rate of 3.8 miles per hour until it reaches its destination. After the people on the barge are done fishing, the barge moves the same distance downstream (with the current) at a rate of 8 miles per hour until it returns to the dock. The speed of the current remains constant. Use the models below to write and solve a system of equations to find the average speed of the barge in still water and the speed of the current. Speed of barge in still water: 5.9 mi/h; Speed of current: 2.1 mi/h

    Upstream: Speed of barge in still water − Speed of current = Speed of barge
    Downstream: Speed of barge in still water + Speed of current = Speed of barge

23. **Floor Sander Rental** A rental company charges a flat fee of x dollars for a floor sander rental plus y dollars per hour of the rental. One customer rents a floor sander for 4 hours and pays $63. Another customer rents a floor sander for 6 hours and pays $87.
    a. Find the flat fee and the cost per hour for the rental. Flat fee: $15; Hourly fee: $12
    b. How much would it cost someone to rent a sander for 11 hours? $147

LESSON 7.3

LESSON 7.4

Practice B

For use with pages 451–457

1. *Sample answer:* Multiply the first equation by 2.
2. *Sample answer:* Multiply the second equation by −3.
3. *Sample answer:* Multiply the first equation by −3.

Describe the first step you would use to solve the linear system.

1. $3x - 4y = 7$
   $5x + 8y = 10$
2. $9x + 4y = 13$
   $3x + 5y = 9$
3. $5x + 7y = -3$
   $15x + 4y = -5$
4. $7x - 4y = 6$ See below.
   $3x - 2y = -15$
5. $7x + 9y = -6$ See below.
   $-5x + 14y = 11$
6. $9x - 5y = 14$ See below.
   $-6x + 8y = 13$

Solve the linear system by using elimination.

7. $x + 3y = 1$ (4, −1)
   $-5x + 4y = -24$
8. $-3x - y = -15$ (3, 6)
   $8x + 4y = 48$
9. $x + 7y = -37$ (−2, −5)
   $2x - 5y = 21$
10. $8x - 4y = -76$ (−6, 7)
    $5x + 2y = -16$
11. $-3x + 10y = 23$ (9, 5)
    $5x + 2y = 55$
12. $9x - 4y = 26$ (2, −2)
    $18x + 7y = 22$
13. $4x - 3y = 16$ (10, 8)
    $16x + 10y = 240$
14. $20x + 10y = 100$ (−1, 12)
    $-5x + 4y = 53$
15. $3x - 10y = -25$ (5, 4)
    $5x - 20y = -55$
16. $-3x - 4y = 27$ (−5, −3)
    $5x - 6y = -7$
17. $2x + 7y = 2$ (15, −4)
    $5x - 2y = 83$
18. $3x - 5y = -16$ (8, 8)
    $2x - 3y = -8$

19. **Hockey Game** Two families go to a hockey game. One family purchases two adult tickets and four youth tickets for $28. Another family purchases four adult tickets and five youth tickets for $45.50. Let x represent the cost in dollars of one adult ticket and let y represent the cost in dollars of one youth ticket.
    a. Write a linear system that represents this situation. $2x + 4y = 28$ and $4x + 5y = 45.5$
    b. Solve the linear system to find the cost of one adult and one youth ticket. Adult: $7; Youth: $3.50
    c. How much would it cost two adults and five youths to attend the game? $31.50

20. **Travel Agency** A travel agency offers two Chicago outings. Plan A includes hotel accommodations for three nights and two pairs of baseball tickets worth a total of $557. Plan B includes hotel accommodations for five nights and four pairs of baseball tickets worth a total of $974. Let x represent the cost in dollars of one night's hotel accommodations and let y represent the cost in dollars of one pair of baseball tickets.
    a. Write a linear system you could use to find the cost of one night's hotel accommodations and the cost of one pair of baseball tickets. $3x + 2y = 557$ and $5x + 4y = 974$
    b. Solve the linear system to find the cost of one night's hotel accommodations and the cost of one pair of baseball tickets. Hotel: $140/night; Tickets: $68.50/pair

21. **Highway Project** There are fifteen workers employed on a highway project, some at $180 per day and some at $155 per day. The daily payroll is $2400. Let x represent the number of $180 per day workers and let y represent the number of $155 per day workers. Write and solve a linear system to find the number of workers employed at each wage. $x + y = 15$ and $180x + 155y = 2400$; $180/day: 3 workers; $155/day: 12 workers

4. *Sample answer:* Multiply the second equation by −2.
5. *Sample answer:* Multiply the first equation by −5.
6. *Sample answer:* Multiply the first equation by 2.

LESSON 7.5

Practice B

For use with pages 459–465

Match the linear system with its graph. Then use the graph to tell whether the linear system has *one solution, no solution,* or *infinitely many solutions.*

1. $y + 3 = 4x$ C
   $3y = 12x - 9$
2. $2x + y = 1$ A
   $2x + y = 5$
3. $3x + y = 1$ B
   $-2x + y = -3$

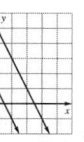

A. B. C.

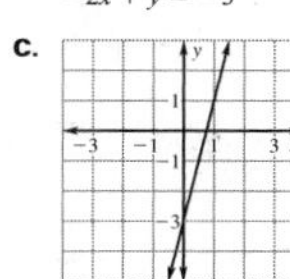

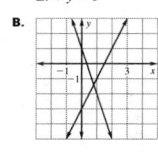

Graph the linear system. Then use the graph to tell whether the linear system has *one solution, no solution,* or *infinitely many solutions.*

4. $-6x + 2y = -2$
   $-3x + y = 2$ no solution
5. $2y - x = -4$
   $2x + y = 3$ one solution
6. $4x - y = 2$
   $-x + 3y = 9$ one solution

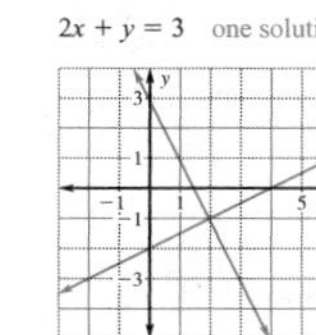

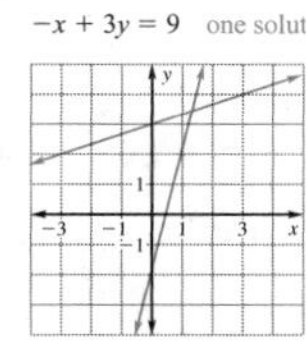

7. $x + 2y = 3$ one solution
   $-x + 2y = -2$
8. $3x + y = 4$ no solution
   $x + \frac{1}{3}y = 2$
9. $2x - y = 4$ infinitely many solutions
   $-2x + y = -4$

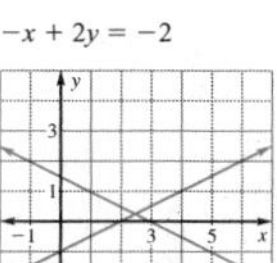

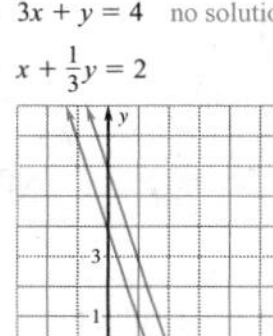

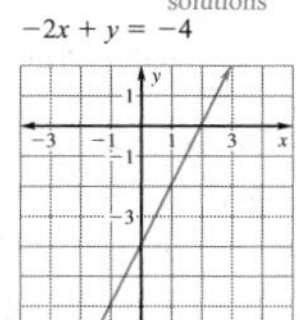

LESSON 7.5

LESSON 7.5

Practice B *continued*

For use with pages 459–465

Solve the linear system by using substitution or elimination.

10. $3x - 2y = 24$ (8, 0)
    $x + 2y = 8$
11. $3x + 2y = 4$ infinitely many solutions
    $-6x - 4y = -8$
12. $x + y = 50$ (20, 30)
    $-3x + 2y = 0$
13. $-x + 4y = -3$ (−1, −1)
    $-3x + 2y = 1$
14. $-x + 3y = 9$ (3, 4)
    $2x + y = 10$
15. $2x + y = 6$ no solution
    $2x + y = -7$

Without solving the linear system, tell whether the linear system has *one solution, no solution, or infinitely many solutions.*

16. $-6x + 6y = -4$ no solution
    $2x - 2y = 5$
17. $y + 2x = \frac{8}{3}$ no solution
    $2x + y = -10$
18. $4x + 3y = 9$ one solution
    $\frac{3}{4}x + y = 3$
19. $4x - 6y = -1$ one solution
    $-\frac{3}{2}x + y = \frac{1}{4}$
20. $-\frac{2}{3}x + y = 2$ one solution
    $-6x + 3y = 6$
21. $9x - 15y = 15$ one solution
    $x + \frac{3}{5}y = 1$
22. $-3x + 4y = 2$
    $2y = \frac{3}{2}x + 1$ infinitely many solutions
23. $3x + y = 4$ no solution
    $x + \frac{1}{3}y = 2$
24. $-4x + 3y = 2$ infinitely many solutions
    $4 - 6y = -8x$

25. **Golf Clubs** A sporting goods store stocks a "better" set of golf clubs in both left-handed and right-handed sets. The set of left-handed golf clubs sells for x dollars and the set of right-handed golf clubs sells for y dollars. In one month, the store sells 2 sets of left-handed golf clubs and 12 sets of right-handed golf clubs for a total of $1859.30. The next month, the store sells 2 sets of left-handed golf clubs and 22 sets of right-handed golf clubs for a total of $3158.80. Is there enough information to determine the cost of each kind of set? *Explain.* Yes; Answers will vary.

26. **Comedy Tickets** The table below shows the tickets sales at an all-ages comedy club on a Friday night and a Saturday night.

Day	Number of adult tickets	Number of student tickets	Total sales (dollars)
Friday	30	20	910
Saturday	45	30	1365

    a. Let x represent the cost (in dollars) of one adult ticket and let y represent the cost (in dollars) of one student ticket. Write a linear system that models the situation.
    b. Solve the linear system. infinitely many solutions
    c. Can you determine how much each kind of ticket costs? Why or why not? No, because one equation in the system is a multiple of the other, specific values for neither x nor y can be found.

26. a. $30x + 20y = 910$ and $45x + 30y = 1365$

7 Lesson Practice Level B

LESSON 7.6 **Practice B**
For use with pages 466–472

Tell whether the ordered pair is a solution of the system of inequalities.

1. (3, 0) yes **2.** (2, 2) yes **3.** $(-2, 2)$ no

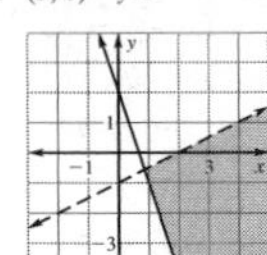
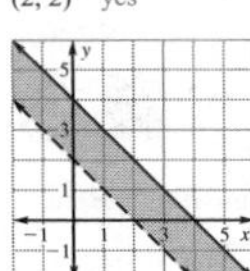
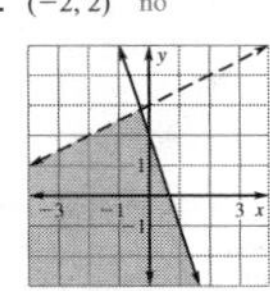

Match the system of inequalities with its graph.

4. $\frac{1}{2}x + y \geq 3$ B
$x > -1$

5. $y - \frac{1}{2}x \leq 3$ A
$x < -1$

6. $y \leq \frac{1}{2}x + 3$ C
$x > -1$

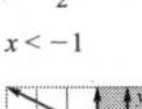
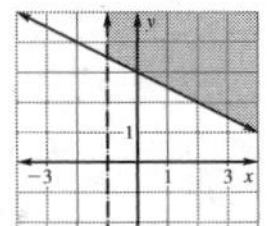

A. **B.** **C.**

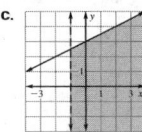

Graph the system of inequalities.

7. $x > -1$
$x < 1$

8. $y \geq 2$
$y < 3$

9. $x + y > 1$
$x \leq y$

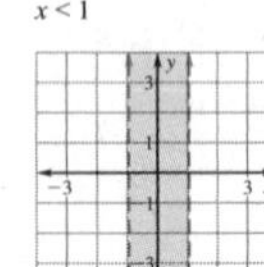
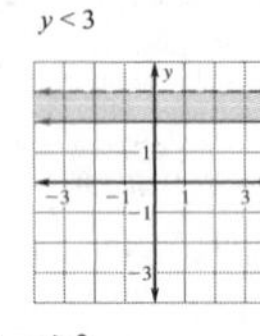
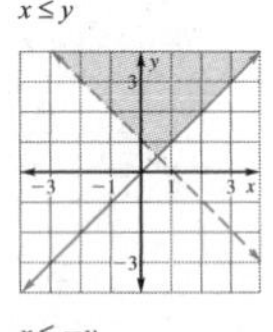

10. $x \geq y + 2$
$2x + y < 4$

11. $y \geq 2$
$x + y \leq -3$

12. $x \leq -y$
$2x - y < 4$

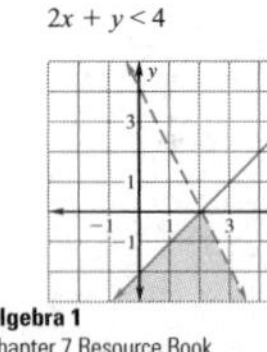
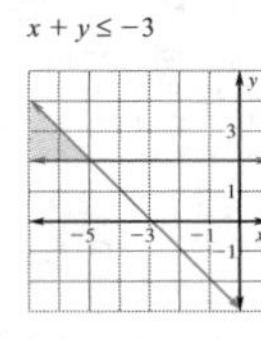
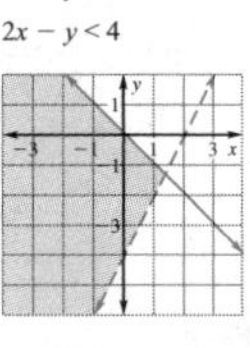

LESSON 7.6

LESSON 7.6 **Practice B** *continued*
For use with pages 466–472

13. $y \geq -4$ and $y < 1$
14. $x \geq -4$ and $y < -3$
15. $y \geq x + 1$ and $x \leq 0$
16. $y \leq 4 - x$ and $y > 2$
17. $y \leq x$ and $y \leq 1 - x$
18. $x \geq 0$, $y \geq 0$, and $y \leq x + 2$

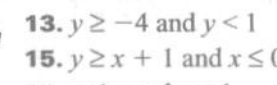
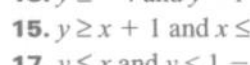

Write a system of inequalities for the shaded region.

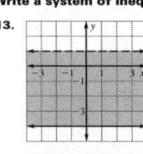

13. **14.** **15.**

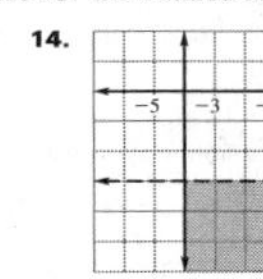
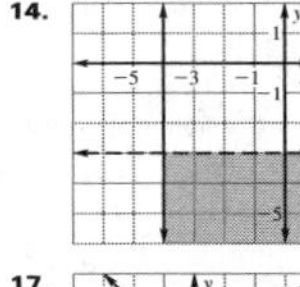
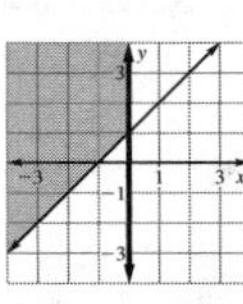

16. **17.** **18.**

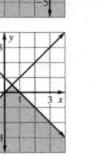

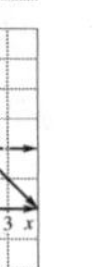
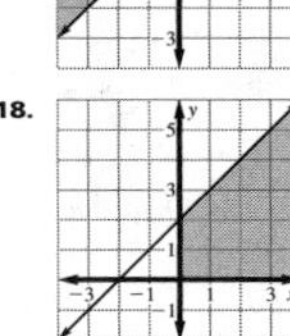

19. Cookout You are planning a cookout. You figure that you will need at least 5 packages of hot dogs and hamburgers. A package of hot dogs costs \$1.90 and a package of hamburgers costs \$5.20. You can spend a maximum of \$20 on the hot dogs and hamburgers.

a. Let x represent the number of packages of hot dogs and let y represent the number of packages of hamburgers. Write a system of linear inequalities for the number of packages of each that can be bought. $x + y \geq 5$ and $1.9x + 5.2y \leq 20$

b. Graph the system of inequalities.

c. Identify two possible combinations of packages of hot dogs and hamburgers you can buy. Answers will vary.

20. Chores You need at least 4 hours to do your chores, which is cleaning out the garage and weeding the flower beds around your house. It is 1:30 P.M. on Sunday and your friend wants you to go to the movies at 7:00 P.M.

a. How much time do you have between now and 7:00 P.M. to do your chores? 5.5 h

b. Let x represent the number of hours spent cleaning out the garage and let y represent the number of hours spent on weeding the flower beds. Write and graph a system of linear inequalities that shows the number of hours you can work on each chore if you go to the movies.

c. Identify two possible combinations of time you can spend on each chore. Answers will vary.

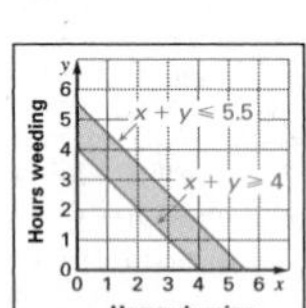

CHAPTER 7
Quiz 1
For use after Lessons 7.1–7.2

Solve the linear system by graphing. Check your solution.

1. $x - y = 1$
   $x + y = -5$

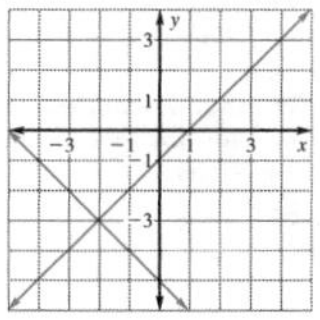

2. $x - 4y = 10$
   $2x + y = 2$

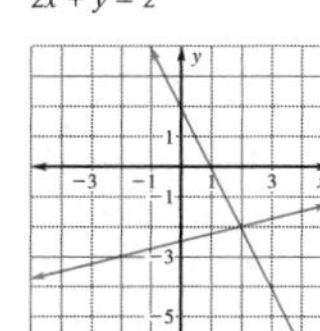

3. $-5x + y = 0$
   $x + y = 6$

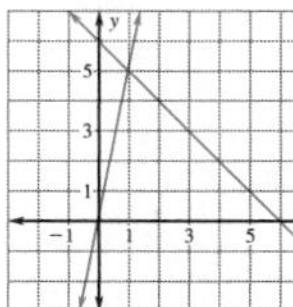

Solve the linear system using substitution.

4. $y = 6 - 2x$
   $7x - y = 3$
5. $x = y - 4$
   $3x + y = 12$
6. $y - 5 = x$
   $4x - y = 4$
7. $y - 2x = -6$
   $5x - y = 9$
8. $3y + x = 2$
   $y - x = -6$

Answers

1. (−2, −3) See left.
2. (2, −2) See left.
3. (1, 5) See left.
4. (1, 4)
5. (2, 6)
6. (3, 8)
7. (1, −4)
8. (5, −1)

CHAPTER 7
Quiz 2
For use after Lessons 7.3–7.4

Solve the linear system using elimination.

1. $5x + y = 4$
   $6x - y = 7$
2. $-3x + 4y = 2$
   $3x + y = 8$
3. $x + 3y = 14$
   $x + 2y = 10$
4. $5x + 3y = 1$
   $5x + y = -3$
5. $6x - y = 8$
   $7x - y = 9$
6. $x - 2y = 8$
   $4x + y = 5$
7. $7x + y = 11$
   $4x + 2y = 12$
8. $3x + y = 10$
   $5x - 2y = 13$

Answers

1. (1, −1)
2. (2, 2)
3. (2, 4)
4. (−1, 2)
5. (1, −2)
6. (2, −3)
7. (1, 4)
8. (3, 1)

CHAPTER 7
Quiz 3
For use after Lessons 7.5–7.6

Graph the linear system. Then use the graph to tell whether the linear system has *one solution, no solution,* or *infinitely many solutions.*

1. $3y - 7x = -4$
   $3y - 2x = 1$

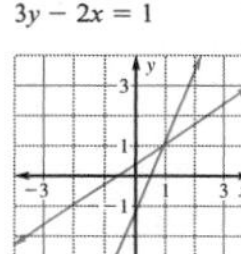

2. $-8x + 2y = -16$
   $4x - y = 10$

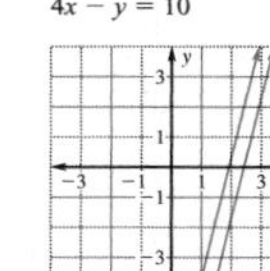

3. $3x + y = 2$
   $-9x - 3y = -6$

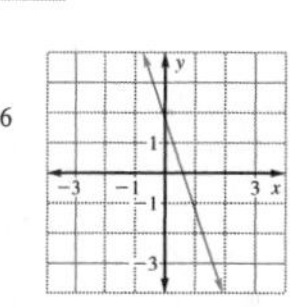

Graph the system of inequalities.

4. $x > 2$
   $y < 3$

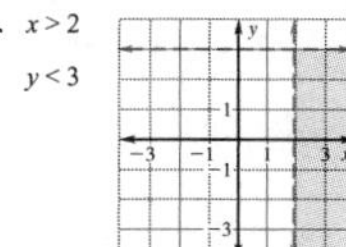

5. $y \le x + 2$
   $y \ge 1$

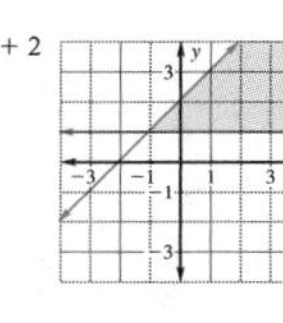

6. $x \ge 0$
   $y > 3x$

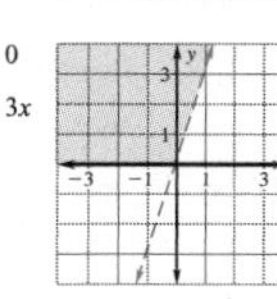

7. $y \le -x$
   $y > 1$
   $x < -1$

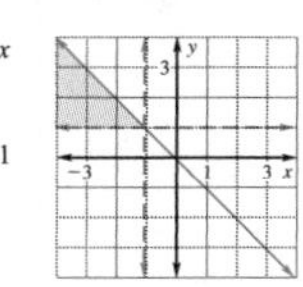

Answers

1. See left. one solution
2. See left. no solution
3. See left. infinitely many solutions
4. See left.
5. See left.
6. See left.
7. See left.

CHAPTER 7 Chapter Test B

For use after Chapter 7

Tell whether the ordered pair is a solution of the linear system.

1. (4, –1)
   $x + 2y = 2$
   $x - 2y = 6$
2. (8, 5)
   $5x - 4y = 20$
   $3y = 2x + 1$
3. (–3, 5)
   $9x + 7y = 8$
   $8x - 9y = -69$

In Exercises 4–6, use the following information.

Tickets for a school play cost $4 for adults and $2 for students. At the end of the play, the school sold a total of 105 tickets and collected $360.

4. Write a linear system. Let x be the number of adult tickets sold and let y be the number of student tickets sold.
5. Graph the linear system.

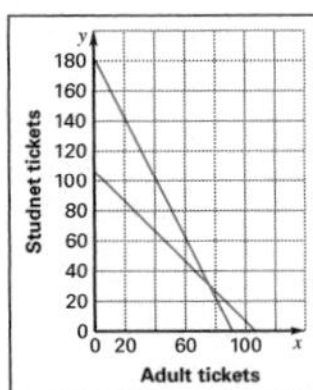

6. Find the number of adult tickets sold and the number of student tickets sold.

Solve the linear system using substitution.

7. $4x + 3y = -5$
   $x = y - 3$
8. $x + 3y = -28$
   $y = -5x$
9. $x + 4y = -1$
   $2x - 5y = 11$
10. $3x + y = -4$
    $2x + y = 0$
11. $3x - y = 13$
    $2x + 5y = 20$
12. $x - 4y = -3$
    $-3x + 5y = 2$
13. A hotel rents a double-occupancy room for $20 more than a single-occupancy room. One night, the hotel took in $3115 after renting 15 double-occupancy rooms and 26 single-occupancy rooms. Write and solve a linear system to find the cost of renting a double-occupancy room and the cost of renting a single-occupancy room.

Answers

1. yes
2. no
3. yes
4. $x + y = 105$, $4x + 2y = 360$
5. See left.
6. 75 adult tickets and 30 student tickets
7. $(-2, 1)$
8. $(2, -10)$
9. $(3, -1)$
10. $(-4, 8)$
11. $(5, 2)$
12. $(1, 1)$
13. $y = x + 20$, $26x + 15y = 3115$; $65 for a single-occupancy room and $95 for a double-occupancy room

CHAPTER 7 Chapter Test B *continued*

For use after Chapter 7

Solve the linear system using elimination.

14. $3x - y = 9$
    $2x + y = 1$
15. $5x + 7y = 10$
    $3x - 14y = 6$
16. $4x + 3y = 15$
    $2x - 5y = 1$
17. $2x + 3y = 1$
    $3x - 5y = -8$
18. $2x - 3y = -2$
    $-2y + 3x = 12$
19. $2x + 9y = 16$
    $5x = 1 - 3y$

Without solving the linear system, tell whether the linear system has *one solution, no solution,* or *infinitely many solutions.*

20. $y = 2 - 3x$
    $6x + 2y = 7$
21. $y = x + 2$
    $x + y = 6$
22. $2x - y = 1$
    $4x - 2y = 2$
23. On Monday, the office staff at your school paid $8.77 for 4 cups of coffee and 7 bagels. On Wednesday, they paid $15.80 for 8 cups of coffee and 14 bagels. Can you determine the cost of a bagel? Explain.

Graph the system of linear inequalities.

24. $y \geq x - 3$
    $y \leq -x + 2$

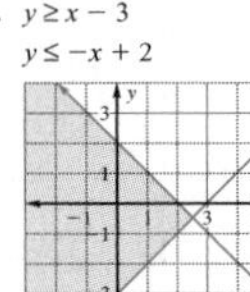

25. $x < 3$
    $y > 1$
    $y \geq -x$

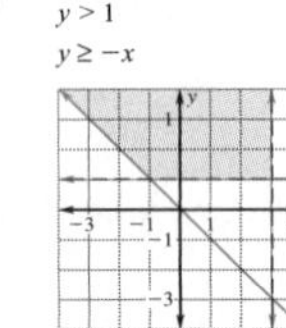

26. In an academic competition, scoring is based on a written examination and an oral presentation. The written examination score cannot exceed 65 points and the oral presentation cannot exceed 35 points. Write and graph a system of inequalities for the scores a school team can receive.

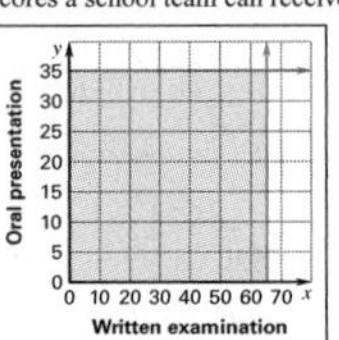

Answers

14. $(2, -3)$
15. $(2, 0)$
16. $(3, 1)$
17. $(-1, 1)$
18. $(8, 6)$
19. $(-1, 2)$
20. no solution
21. one solution
22. infinitely many solutions
23. There is no solution, so you cannot determine the cost of a bagel.
24. See left.
25. See left.
26. $x \geq 0, y \geq 0,$ $x \leq 65, y \leq 35$ See left.

CHAPTER 7 Standardized Test

For use after Chapter 7

Multiple Choice

1. Which ordered pair is a solution of the linear system $x + y = -3$ and $2x + -3y = -16$? D
   (A) $(-8, 5)$ (B) $(-2, 4)$
   (C) $(-2, -1)$ (D) $(-5, 2)$
2. Which ordered pair is a solution of the linear system $5x + 2y = 29$ and $8x - 8y = 80$? B
   (A) $(5, 2)$ (B) $(7, -3)$
   (C) $(10, 0)$ (D) $(1, 12)$
3. Which ordered pair is a solution of the linear system shown? A

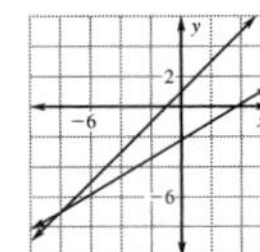

   (A) $(-8, -7)$ (B) $(7, 2)$
   (C) $(-7, -8)$ (D) $(2, 7)$
4. Which ordered pair is a solution of the linear system $y - x = 2$ and $5x + 4y = 30.5$? B
   (A) $(3, 5)$ (B) $(2.5, 4.5)$
   (C) $(5.2, 7.2)$ (D) $(2.1, 5)$
5. Which ordered pair is a solution of the linear system $6x - 3y = 2$ and $2x - 9y = -2$? D
   (A) $\left(1, \frac{4}{3}\right)$ (B) $(8, 2)$
   (C) $\left(\frac{10}{3}, 6\right)$ (D) $\left(\frac{1}{2}, \frac{1}{3}\right)$
6. Which step below contains an error in solving the linear system $2x + y = 10$ and $5y - 6x = 2$? B

   Step 1
   $2x + y = 10$
   $y = 10 - 2x$

   Step 2
   $5(10 - 2x) - 6x = 2$
   $50 - 10x - 6x = 2$
   $50 - 4x = 2$
   $48 = 4x$
   $12 = x$

   Step 3
   $2(12) + y = 10$
   $24 + y = 10$
   $y = -14$

   Step 4
   $(12, -14)$

   (A) Step 1 (B) Step 2
   (C) Step 3 (D) Step 4
7. Which ordered pair is a solution of the linear system $5x + 3y = 22$ and $4x - 3y = -4$? C
   (A) $(5, -1)$ (B) $(-1, 0)$
   (C) $(2, 4)$ (D) $(8, -6)$
8. Which of the linear systems has *exactly* one solution? A
   (A) $5x + 3y = -22$, $4x - 5y = 12$
   (B) $2x + 3y = 45$, $2y + \frac{4}{3}x = 30$
   (C) $2x - 3y = -15$, $\frac{2}{3}x - y = 3$
   (D) $x + y = 2$, $\frac{1}{2}x + \frac{1}{2}y = 1$
9. Which of the linear systems has no solution? C
   (A) $5x + 3y = -22$, $4x - 5y = 12$
   (B) $2x + 3y = 45$, $2y + \frac{4}{3}x = 30$
   (C) $2x - 3y = -15$, $\frac{2}{3}x - y = 3$
   (D) $x + y = 2$, $\frac{1}{2}x + \frac{1}{2}y = 1$

CHAPTER 7 Standardized Test *continued*

For use after Chapter 7

10. Which ordered pair is a solution of the system $x < 5$ and $x + 2y \geq 1$? D
    (A) $(4, -2)$ (B) $(8, 2)$
    (C) $(1, -1)$ (D) $(4, 5)$
11. The graph of which system of inequalities is shown? C

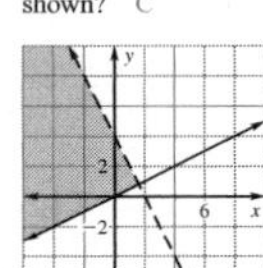

    (A) $y \leq \frac{1}{2}x$, $4x + 2y < 8$
    (B) $y \leq \frac{1}{2}x$, $4x + 2y > 8$
    (C) $y \geq \frac{1}{2}x$, $4x + 2y < 8$
    (D) $y \geq \frac{1}{2}x$, $4x + 2y > 8$

Gridded Answer

12. What is the x-coordinate of the solution of the system whose graph is shown?

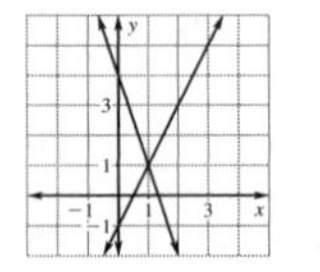

Answer grid: 1

Short Response

13. Use the linear system below.
    $3x + 8y = 32$
    $y = -\frac{3}{8}x + m$
    a. Find a value for m so that the linear system has infinitely many solutions. $m = 4$
    b. Is it possible to find a value for m so that the linear system has exactly one solution? *Explain.* See below.

Extended Response

14. The owner of a car wash combines x gallons of a 2% liquid soap and 98% water mix with y gallons of a 7% liquid soap and 93% water mix to make 500 gallons of a 5% liquid soap and 95% water mix. See below.
    a. Write a system of linear equations that represents the situation.
    b. How many fluid ounces of the 2% liquid soap and 98% water mix and the 7% liquid soap and 93% water mix did the car wash owner combine to make 500 gallons of the 5% liquid soap and 95% water mix?
    c. Suppose the car wash owner combines pure (100%) water and the 7% liquid soap and 93% water mix to make the 500 gallons of the 5% liquid soap and 95% water mix. Is more of the 7% liquid soap and 93% water mix used in this mix than in the original mix? *Explain.*

13. b. No; because the lines have the same slope, they are parallel. Therefore, there will never be exactly one solution.

14. a. $x + y = 500$ and $0.02x + 0.07y = 25$ **b.** The car wash owner would use 200 gallons of the 2% liquid soap and 98% water solution and 300 gallons of the 7% liquid soap and 93% water solution. **c.** The car wash owner would use more of the 7% liquid soap and 93% water mix than in the original mix because in the original mix the other solution contained soap. In the new mix, there is no soap being added to the 7% liquid soap and 93% water mix.

CHAPTER 7

Alternative Assessment and Math Journal

For use after Chapter 7

Journal **1.** There are three different categories for the number of solutions to a system of two linear equations. Name each category and describe the graph of the system for each case.

Multi-Step Problem **2.** Last week a football team ran a total of 108 offensive plays. There were twice as many running plays as passing plays.

a. Write a system of equations to represent this information given that x is the number of running plays and y is the number of passing plays.

b. Use the graphing method to solve the system in part (a).

c. Use the method of substitution to solve the system in part (a) and compare this answer to the one that resulted from your work in part (b). Are the solutions the same?

d. How many offensive plays were running plays last week?

e. The team sets some offensive goals for the next game. The first goal is to execute a total of at least 80 offensive plays, and the second goal is to gain at least 360 offensive yards. The team averages 3 yards on each running play and 7 yards on each passing play. The system of inequalities used to model this situation is

$$x + y \geq 80$$
$$3x + 7y \geq 360$$
$$x \geq 0$$
$$y \geq 0$$

Graph this system of inequalities.

f. Give 3 solutions to this system.

g. Suppose the team decided to also set a goal of having more running plays than passing plays. Write an inequality to represent this new goal.

h. Add the graph of the inequality for the new goal to the graph in part (e).

1. Complete answers should include: mention of all three categories for the number of solutions to a system of two linear equations (one solution, no solution, infinitely many solutions); a description of the graph of the system as intersecting, parallel, or coincidental lines.

2. a. $x + y = 108$

$x = 2y$

b. **c.** (72, 36) **d.** 72 running plays **e.**

f. *Sample answer:* (50, 30); (70, 25); (30, 50) **g.** $x > y$

h.

CHAPTER 7

Alternative Assessment Rubric *continued*

For use after Chapter 7

Journal Solution **1.** Complete answers should include:

- mention of all three categories for the number of solutions to a system of two linear equations (one solution, no solution, infinitely many solutions).
- a description of the graph of the system as intersecting, parallel, or coincidental lines.

Multi-Step Problem Solution **2. a.** $x + y = 108$

$x = 2y$

b.

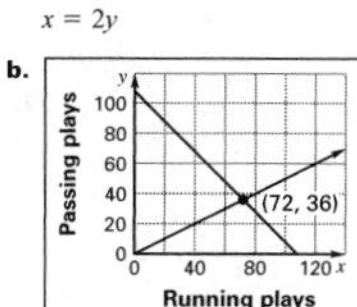

c. (72, 36) **d.** 72 running plays

e.

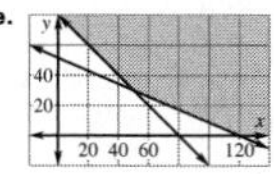

f. *Sample answer:* (50, 30); (70, 25); (30, 50)

g. $x > y$

h.

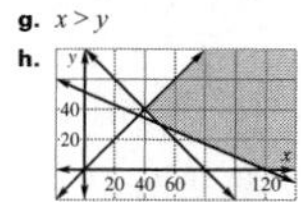

Multi-Step Problem Rubric

4 The student answers all parts of the problem correctly and completely. The student shows all work. The student's work is neat.

3 The student answers all parts of the problem. The student's work may contain one or two errors in the calculations, equations, or graphs. The student shows most work. The student's work is neat.

2 The student answers all parts of the problem, but there are more than two errors in the calculations, equations, or graphs. The student shows some work. The student's work is sloppy.

1 The student does not complete all parts of the problem. The student's work has several errors in the calculations, equations, and graphs. The student's work is sloppy, or no work is shown.

PLAN AND PREPARE

Main Ideas

In Chapter 7, students use graphing, substitution, and elimination to solve systems of linear equations. When solving by the elimination method, they either add or subtract, or they multiply first and then add or subtract. Students identify linear systems as having one solution, no solution, or infinitely many solutions. Students solve systems of linear inequalities.

Prerequisite Skills

- Graphing linear equations
- Solving equations
- Determining whether lines are parallel
- Graphing linear inequalities in two variables

Additional resources for reviewing prerequisite skills are:

- Skills Review Handbook, pp. 909–937
- @HomeTutor

3–6. See p. 425.

9. Not parallel; the slope of the graph of the first equation is 2, while the slope of the graph of the second equation is −2.

10. Parallel; the 2 lines have a slope of 5, but different y-intercepts.

11. Parallel; the 2 lines have a slope of 1, but different y-intercepts.

12. Not parallel; the slope of the graph of the first equation is 6, while the slope of the graph of the second equation is 4.

13–16. See p. 425.

7 Systems of Equations and Inequalities

Before

In previous chapters, you learned the following skills, which you'll use in Chapter 7: graphing linear equations, solving equations, determining whether lines are parallel, and graphing linear inequalities in two variables.

Prerequisite Skills

VOCABULARY CHECK

Copy and complete the statement.

1. The least common multiple of 10 and 15 is _?_. 30
2. Two lines in the same plane are _?_ if they do not intersect. parallel

SKILLS CHECK

Graph the equation. *(Review p. 225 for 7.1.)* 3–6. See margin.

3. $x - y = 4$ 4. $6x - y = -1$ 5. $4x + 5y = 20$ 6. $3x - 2y = -12$

Solve the equation. *(Review p. 148 for 7.2–7.4.)*

7. $5m + 4 - m = 20$ 4 8. $10(z + 5) + z = 6$ −4

Tell whether the graphs of the two equations are parallel lines. *Explain* your reasoning. *(Review p. 244 for 7.5.)* 9–12. See margin.

9. $y = 2x - 3, y + 2x = -3$ 10. $y - 5x = -1, y - 5x = 1$

11. $y = x + 10, x - y = -9$ 12. $6x - y = 4, 4x - y = 6$

Graph the inequality. *(Review p. 405 for 7.6.)* 13–16. See margin.

13. $y \le -2x + 1$ 14. $x - y < 5$ 15. $x \ge -4$ 16. $y > 3$

@HomeTutor Prerequisite skills practice at classzone.com

424

Chapter Planning Guide

Chapter 7 Resource Book
- Teaching Guide/Lesson Plan (pp. 3, 17, 27, 38, 50, 64)
- Project with Rubric (p. 80)

Assessment and Intervention
- Assessment Book (pp. 90–108)
- Benchmark Tests
- Reteaching and Remediation Book

Interactive Technology
- Easy Planner
- Power Presentations CD-ROM
- Activity Generator CD-ROM
- Animated Algebra
- Test Generator CD-ROM
- Online Quizzes
- eWorkbook
- eEdition
- @HomeTutor

Resources for English Learners
- Quick Reference for English Learners
- Spanish Study Guide
- Multi-Language Visual Glossary
- Student Resources in Spanish

Now

In Chapter 7, you will apply the big ideas listed below and reviewed in the Chapter Summary on page 474. You will also use the key vocabulary listed below.

Big Ideas

1. **Solving linear systems by graphing**
2. **Solving linear systems using algebra**
3. **Solving systems of linear inequalities**

KEY VOCABULARY

- system of linear equations, *p. 427*
- solution of a system of linear equations, *p. 427*
- consistent independent system, *p. 427*
- inconsistent system, *p. 459*
- consistent dependent system, *p. 459*
- system of linear inequalities, *p. 466*
- solution of a system of linear inequalities, *p. 466*
- graph of a system of linear inequalities, *p. 466*

Why?

You can use a system of linear equations to solve problems about traveling with and against a current. For example, you can write and solve a system of linear equations to find the average speed of a kayak in still water.

Animated Algebra

The animation illustrated below for Example 4 on page 446 helps you answer this question: What is the average speed of the kayak in still water?

Start
You have to find the speed of the kayak in still water.

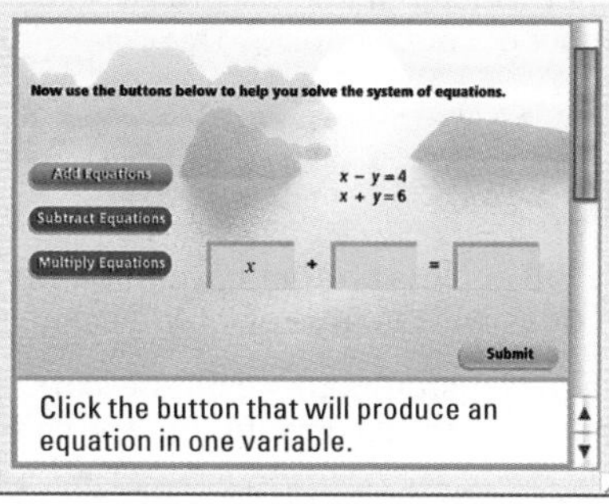

Animated Algebra at classzone.com

Other animations for Chapter 7: pages 428, 435, 441, 446, 452, 459, and 466

425

Algebra 1 Toolkit

- Reading Strategies for Chapter 7, pp. 21–22
- Differentiated Instruction Notes, pp. 65–68
- English Learners Notes, pp. 109–110
- Inclusion Notes, pp. 141–142
- Teaching Strategies with Sample Worksheets, pp. 155–178
- Using Technology in the Classroom, pp. 179–184
- Tips for New Teachers, pp. 197–198
- Math Background Notes, pp. 223–224
- Pre-AP Strategies and Copymasters, pp. 290–291, 384–399
- Teacher Survival Activities, pp. 567–568, 593–594
- Bulletin Board Idea, p. 613
- Teacher Tool Transparencies, following p. 620

6.
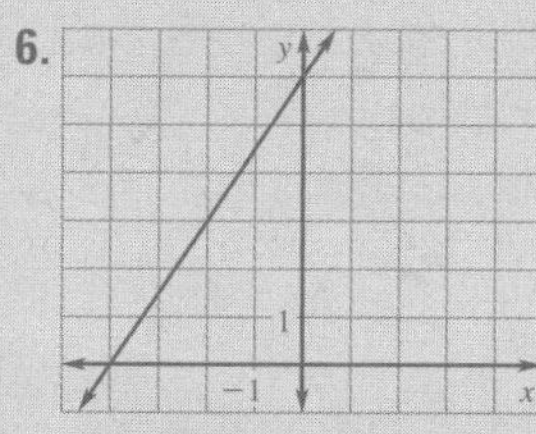

13.
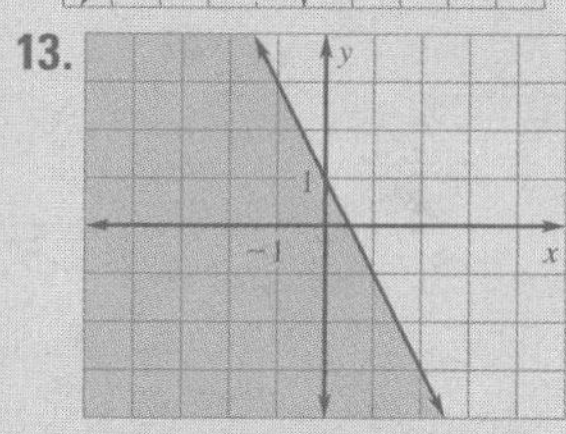

14.
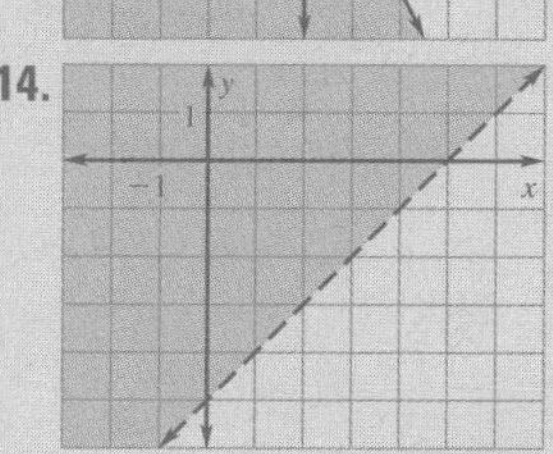

15.
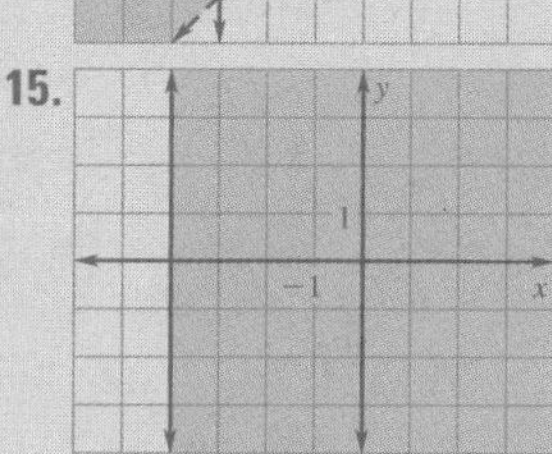

16.
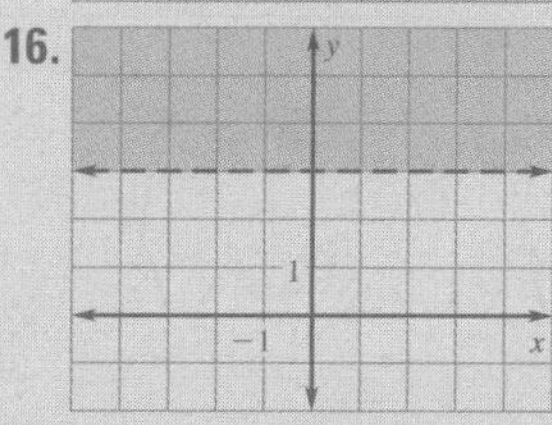

3.
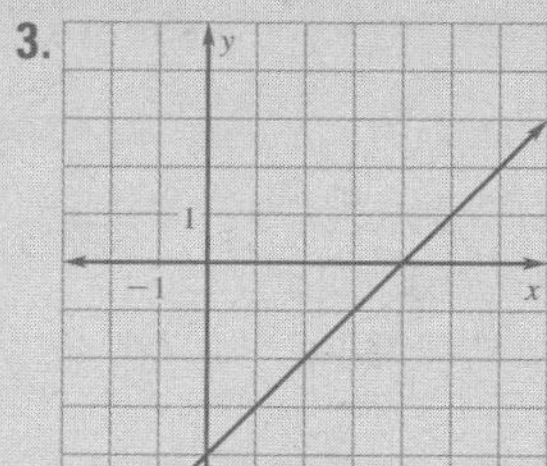

4.
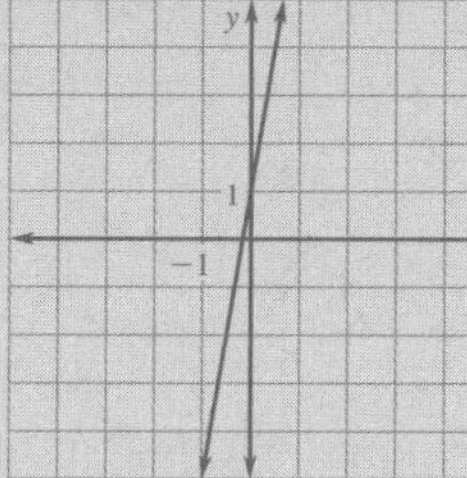

5.
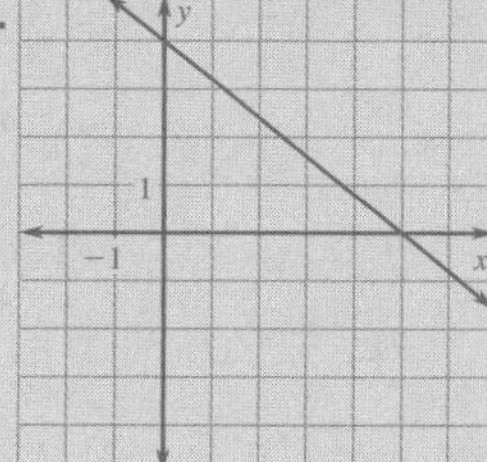

7.1 Solving Linear Systems Using Tables

MATERIALS • pencil and paper

QUESTION How can you use a table to solve a linear system?

A *system of linear equations*, or *linear system*, consists of two or more linear equations in the same variables. A *solution of a linear system* is an ordered pair that satisfies each equation in the system. You can use a table to find a solution to a linear system.

EXPLORE Solve a linear system

Bill and his brother collect comic books. Bill currently has 15 books and adds 2 books to his collection every month. His brother currently has 7 books and adds 4 books to his collection every month. Use the equations below to find the number x of months after which Bill and his brother will have the same number y of comic books in their collections.

$y = 2x + 15$ Number of comic books in Bill's collection

$y = 4x + 7$ Number of comic books in his brother's collection

STEP 1 *Make a table*
Copy and complete the table of values shown.

x	$y = 2x + 15$	$y = 4x + 7$
0	15	7
1	? 17	? 11
2	? 19	? 15
3	? 21	? 19
4	? 23	? 23
5	? 25	? 27

STEP 2 *Find a solution*
Find an x-value that gives the same y-value for both equations. 4

STEP 3 *Interpret the solution*
Use your answer to Step 2 to find the number of months after which Bill and his brother have the same number of comic books. 4 mo

DRAW CONCLUSIONS Use your observations to complete these exercises

1. When Bill and his brother have the same number of books in their collections, how many books will each of them have? 23 books
2. Graph the equations above on the same coordinate plane. What do you notice about the graphs and the solution you found above? See margin for art; the graphs intersect at (4, 23), which is a solution of both equations.

Use a table to solve the linear system.

3. $y = 2x + 3$
   $y = -3x + 18$
   (3, 9)
4. $y = -x + 1$
   $y = 2x - 5$
   (2, −1)
5. $y = -3x + 1$
   $y = 5x - 31$
   (4, −11)

2.
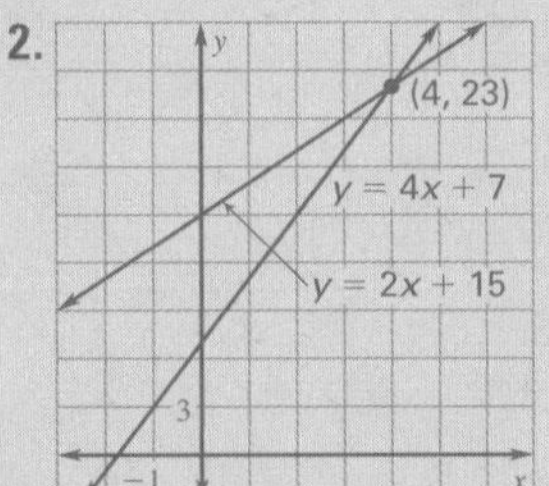

1 PLAN AND PREPARE

Explore the Concept

- Students will use a table to solve a linear system.
- This activity leads into the study of solving linear systems by graphing in Example 1 in Lesson 7.1.

Recommended Time

Work activity: 15 min
Discuss results: 5 min

Grouping

Students should work individually.

2 TEACH

Tips for Success

Students may want to write the two ordered pairs in a fourth column as a visual reminder that the x-value is the same for both y-value columns.

Key Discovery

A solution of a linear system is an ordered pair that must satisfy each equation in the system.

3 ASSESS AND RETEACH

1. If Bill adds 3 books to his collection each month instead of 2, when will he and his brother have the same number of books in their collections? after 8 mo
2. Use a table to solve this linear system. (−4, −16)
   $y = 5x + 4$
   $y = 2x - 8$

7.1 Solve Linear Systems by Graphing

8.11.17 Solve systems of equations and inequalities.

Before You graphed linear equations.

Now You will graph and solve systems of linear equations.

Why? So you can analyze craft fair sales, as in Ex. 33.

Key Vocabulary
- system of linear equations
- solution of a system of linear equations
- consistent independent system

A **system of linear equations,** or simply a *linear system*, consists of two or more linear equations in the same variables. An example is shown below.

$x + 2y = 7$ **Equation 1**

$3x - 2y = 5$ **Equation 2**

A **solution of a system of linear equations** in two variables is an ordered pair that satisfies each equation in the system.

One way to find the solution of a linear system is by graphing. If the lines intersect in a single point, then the coordinates of the point are the solution of the linear system. A solution found using graphical methods should be checked algebraically.

EXAMPLE 1 Check the intersection point

Use the graph to solve the system. Then check your solution algebraically.

$x + 2y = 7$ **Equation 1**

$3x - 2y = 5$ **Equation 2**

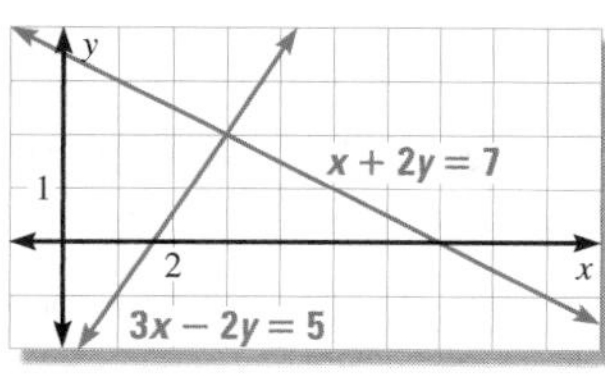

Solution

The lines appear to intersect at the point (3, 2).

CHECK Substitute 3 for x and 2 for y in each equation.

$x + 2y = 7$	$3x - 2y = 5$
$3 + 2(2) \stackrel{?}{=} 7$	$3(3) - 2(2) \stackrel{?}{=} 5$
$7 = 7$ ✓	$5 = 5$ ✓

▶ Because the ordered pair (3, 2) is a solution of each equation, it is a solution of the system.

TYPES OF LINEAR SYSTEMS In Example 1, the linear system has exactly one solution. A linear system that has exactly one solution is called a **consistent independent system** because the lines are distinct (are independent) and intersect (are consistent). You will solve consistent independent systems in Lessons 7.1–7.4. In Lesson 7.5 you will consider other types of systems.

1 PLAN AND PREPARE

Warm-Up Exercises

Transparency Available

1. Graph the equation $-2x + y = 1$.

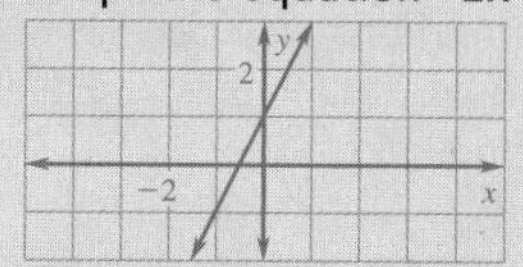

2. It takes 3 hours to mow a lawn and 2 hours to trim hedges. You spend 16 hours doing yard work. What are two possible numbers of lawns you mowed and hedges you trimmed? **2 lawns and 5 hedges, or 4 lawns and 2 hedges**

Notetaking Guide

Transparency Available

Promotes interactive learning and notetaking skills, pp. 150–152.

Pacing

Basic: 1 day
Average: 1 day
Advanced: 1 day
Block: 0.5 block with 7.2
- See *Teaching Guide/Lesson Plan*.

2 FOCUS AND MOTIVATE

Essential Question

Big Idea 1, p. 425

How do you solve systems of linear equations by graphing? **Tell students they will learn how to answer this question by graphing the equations in the same coordinate plane.**

Resource Planning Guide

Chapter Resource Book
- Teaching Guide/Lesson Plan (pp. 3–4)
- Activity Master (p. 5)
- Practice levels A, B, C (pp. 6–11)
- Study Guide (pp. 12–13)
- Catch-up for Absent Students (p. 14)
- Problem Solving Workshop (p. 15)
- Challenge (p. 16)

Workbooks
- Notetaking Guide (pp. 150–152)
- Practice Workbook (pp. 104–106)

Teaching Options
- **Power Presentations CD-ROM** provides dynamic electronic teaching resources for the classroom.
- **Activity Generator CD-ROM** provides editable activities for all ability levels.

Interactive Technology
- Easy Planner
- Power Presentations CD-ROM
- Activity Generator CD-ROM
- Animated Algebra
- Test Generator CD-ROM
- Online Quiz
- eWorkbook
- eEdition
- @HomeTutor

Resources for English Learners
- Quick Reference for English Learners
- Spanish Study Guide
- Multi-Language Visual Glossary
- Student Resources in Spanish

See also the *Algebra 1 Toolkit* for more strategies for meeting individual needs.

Motivating the Lesson

You raised \$260 for the swim team selling calendars and desk planners. You know you sold 22 items and that the calendars are \$15 each and the planners are \$8 each. By knowing how to solve a system of linear equations, you can determine how many calendars and desk planners you sold.

3 TEACH

Extra Example 1

Use the graph to solve the system. Then check your solution algebraically.

$2x + 5y = 7$

$-x + 2y = -8$ (6, −1)

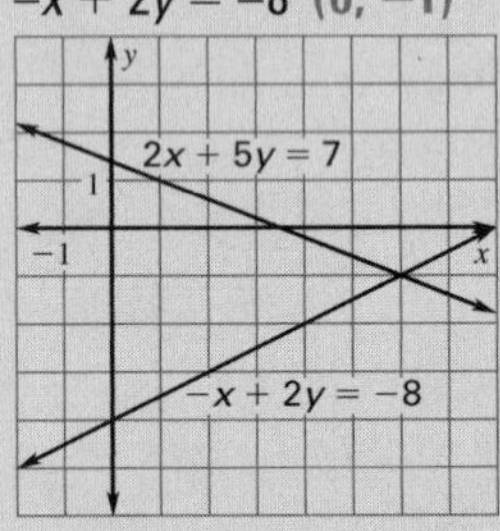

Key Question to Ask for Example 1

- Why is it a good idea to check a solution algebraically? An algebraic check confirms that you read the point of intersection correctly.

Extra Example 2

Solve the linear system by graphing.

$-x + y = 5$

$2x + y = 8$ (1, 6)

An **Animated Algebra** activity is available on-line for **Example 2**. This activity is also available on the **Power Presentations CD-ROM**.

KEY CONCEPT *For Your Notebook*

Solving a Linear System Using the Graph-and-Check Method

STEP 1 **Graph** both equations in the same coordinate plane. For ease of graphing, you may want to write each equation in slope-intercept form.

STEP 2 **Estimate** the coordinates of the point of intersection.

STEP 3 **Check** the coordinates algebraically by substituting into each equation of the original linear system.

EXAMPLE 2 Use the graph-and-check method

Solve the linear system: $-x + y = -7$ Equation 1

$x + 4y = -8$ Equation 2

Solution

STEP 1 **Graph** both equations.

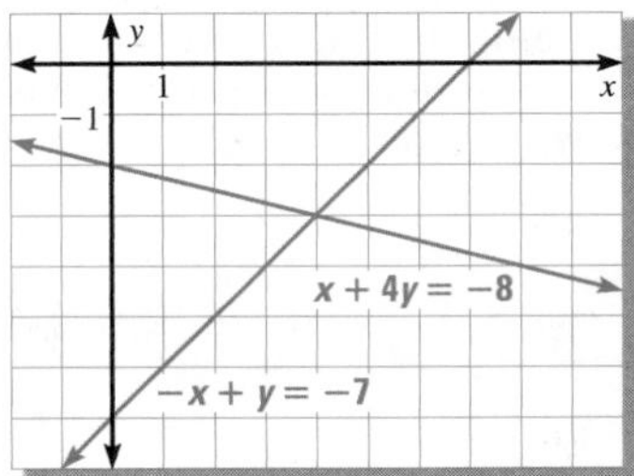

STEP 2 **Estimate** the point of intersection. The two lines appear to intersect at (4, −3).

STEP 3 **Check** whether (4, −3) is a solution by substituting 4 for x and −3 for y in each of the original equations.

Equation 1	Equation 2
$-x + y = -7$	$x + 4y = -8$
$-(4) + (-3) \stackrel{?}{=} -7$	$4 + 4(-3) \stackrel{?}{=} -8$
$-7 = -7$ ✓	$-8 = -8$ ✓

▶ Because (4, −3) is a solution of each equation, it is a solution of the linear system.

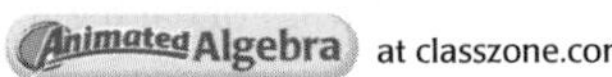 at classzone.com

 **GUIDED PRACTICE** for Examples 1 and 2

Solve the linear system by graphing. Check your solution.

1. $-5x + y = 0$ (1, 5)
   $5x + y = 10$
2. $-x + 2y = 3$ (1, 2)
   $2x + y = 4$
3. $x - y = 5$ (2, −3)
   $3x + y = 3$

Differentiated Instruction

Below Level Some students may need help graphing linear systems. In **Example 2** and **Guided Practice Exercises 1–3**, remind students that they can solve the equation for y to give the slope-intercept form of the equation. They can then plot the point for the y-intercept, use the slope to find another point, and then draw a line through the points. If they prefer, they can make a table of values for the equations, plot the points, and then draw a line through the points.

See also the *Algebra 1 Toolkit* for more strategies.

EXAMPLE 3 Standardized Test Practice

The parks and recreation department in your town offers a season pass for \$90.

- As a season pass holder, you pay \$4 per session to use the town's tennis courts.
- Without the season pass, you pay \$13 per session to use the tennis courts.

Which system of equations can be used to find the number x of sessions of tennis after which the total cost y with a season pass, including the cost of the pass, is the same as the total cost without a season pass?

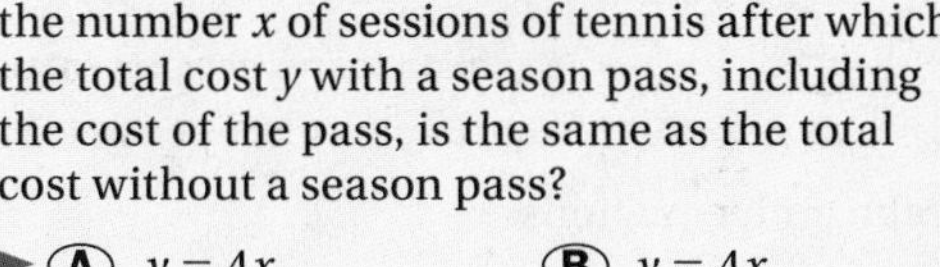

Ⓐ $y = 4x$, $y = 13x$ Ⓑ $y = 4x$, $y = 90 + 13x$

Ⓒ $y = 13x$, $y = 90 + 4x$ Ⓓ $y = 90 + 4x$, $y = 90 + 13x$

ELIMINATE CHOICES You can eliminate choice A because neither of the equations include the cost of a season pass.

Solution

Write a system of equations where y is the total cost (in dollars) for x sessions.

EQUATION 1

Total cost (dollars)	=	Cost per session (dollars/session)	·	Number of sessions (sessions)
y	=	13	·	x

EQUATION 2

Total cost (dollars)	=	Cost for season pass (dollars)	+	Cost per session (dollars/session)	·	Number of sessions (sessions)
y	=	90	+	4	·	x

▶ The correct answer is C. Ⓐ Ⓑ Ⓒ Ⓓ

✓ GUIDED PRACTICE for Example 3

4. Solve the linear system in Example 3 to find the number of sessions after which the total cost with a season pass, including the cost of the pass, is the same as the total cost without a season pass. **10 sessions**

5. **WHAT IF?** In Example 3, suppose a season pass costs \$135. After how many sessions is the total cost with a season pass, including the cost of the pass, the same as the total cost without a season pass? **15 sessions**

Extra Example 3

The cost to join an art museum is \$60. If you are a member, you can take lessons at the museum for \$2 each. If you are not a member, lessons cost \$6 each. Which system of equations can be used to find the number x of lessons after which the total cost y of lessons with a membership is the same as the total cost of lessons without a membership? **D**

Ⓐ $y = 2x$, $y = 6x$ Ⓑ $y = 60x + 2$, $y = 6x$

Ⓒ $y = 2x + 60$, $y = 6x + 60$ Ⓓ $y = 2x + 60$, $y = 6x$

Key Questions to Ask for Example 3

- Why is it possible to eliminate choice D? Explain. **Both equations include the cost of a season pass.**
- How would a graph of the system of equations in Example 3 be different from the graph of the system of equations in Example 2? **The graph in Example 3 would be restricted to Quadrant I, since the costs would be positive numbers only.**

Differentiated Instruction

English Learners Make mathematical language easier to understand by using more common terms. In **Example 2**, tell stuidents that the coordinates of the intersecting lines "agree" at one point. Mathematicians might say that the two lines are "consistent" at that point. In ordinary language, to be consistent means to be in agreement.

See also the *Algebra 1 Toolkit* for more strategies.

Extra Example 4

Your school is selling football tickets for a home game. The school sold 35 tickets for $86 on the first day of the sale. Student tickets cost $2 each and non-student tickets cost $3 each. Find the number of student tickets and the number of non-student tickets the gym sold. **19 student tickets and 16 non-student tickets**

Key Question to Ask for Example 4

- What does the ordered pair (20, 5) represent? **20 pairs of skates and 5 bicycles**

Closing the Lesson

Have students summarize the major points of the lesson and answer the Essential Question: How do you solve systems of linear equations by graphing?

- **You can find the solution of a linear system by graphing both equations in the same coordinate plane.**

Graph the equations in the linear system in the same coordinate plane. The point of intersection is the solution of the system. Check the solution by substituting the coordinates of the point into each equation of the original system.

EXAMPLE 4 Solve a multi-step problem

RENTAL BUSINESS A business rents in-line skates and bicycles. During one day, the business has a total of 25 rentals and collects $450 for the rentals. Find the number of pairs of skates rented and the number of bicycles rented.

Solution

STEP 1 **Write** a linear system. Let x be the number of pairs of skates rented, and let y be the number of bicycles rented.

$x + y = 25$ Equation for number of rentals

$15x + 30y = 450$ Equation for money collected from rentals

STEP 2 **Graph** both equations.

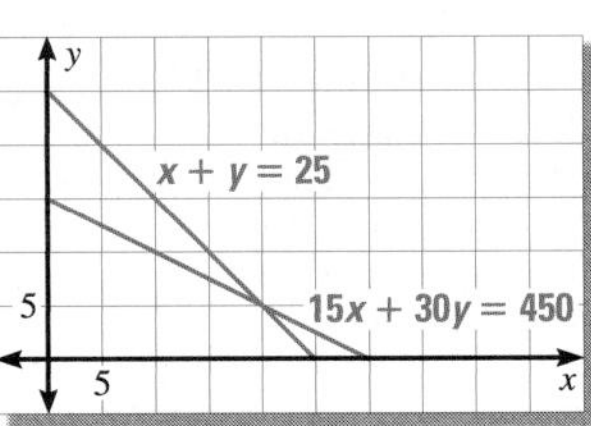

STEP 3 **Estimate** the point of intersection. The two lines appear to intersect at (20, 5).

STEP 4 **Check** whether (20, 5) is a solution.

$20 + 5 \stackrel{?}{=} 25$ | $15(20) + 30(5) \stackrel{?}{=} 450$

$25 = 25$ ✓ | $450 = 450$ ✓

▶ The business rented 20 pairs of skates and 5 bicycles.

✓ **GUIDED PRACTICE** for Example 4

6. **WHAT IF?** In Example 4, suppose the business has a total of 20 rentals and collects $420. Find the number of bicycles rented. **8 bicycles**

7.1 EXERCISES

HOMEWORK KEY
○ = **WORKED-OUT SOLUTIONS** on p. WS16 for Exs. 15 and 31
★ = **STANDARDIZED TEST PRACTICE** Exs. 2, 6, 7, 27, 28, 29, and 32
◆ = **MULTIPLE REPRESENTATIONS** Ex. 35

SKILL PRACTICE

A

1. **VOCABULARY** Copy and complete: A(n) __?__ of a system of linear equations in two variables is an ordered pair that satisfies each equation in the system. **solution**

2. ★ **WRITING** *Explain* how to use the graph-and-check method to solve a linear system of two equations in two variables. **See margin.**

CHECKING SOLUTIONS Tell whether the ordered pair is a solution of the linear system.

3. (−3, 1); **solution**
$x + y = -2$
$x + 5y = 2$

4. (5, 2); **not a solution**
$2x - 3y = 4$
$2x + 8y = 11$

5. (−2, 1); **not a solution**
$6x + 5y = -7$
$x - 2y = 0$

2. *Sample answer:* Graph both equations and then estimate the point at which the graphs intersect. Then check whether the point is a solution of each equation.

EXAMPLE 1
on p. 427
for Exs. 6–11

6. ★ **MULTIPLE CHOICE** Which ordered pair is a solution of the linear system $x + y = -2$ and $7x - 4y = 8$? B

Ⓐ $(-2, 0)$ Ⓑ $(0, -2)$ Ⓒ $(2, 0)$ Ⓓ $(0, 2)$

7. ★ **MULTIPLE CHOICE** Which ordered pair is a solution of the linear system $2x + 3y = 12$ and $10x + 3y = -12$? B

Ⓐ $(-3, 3)$ Ⓑ $(-3, 6)$ Ⓒ $(3, 3)$ Ⓓ $(3, 6)$

SOLVING SYSTEMS GRAPHICALLY Use the graph to solve the linear system. Check your solution.

8. $x - y = 4$ (1, −3)
$4x + y = 1$

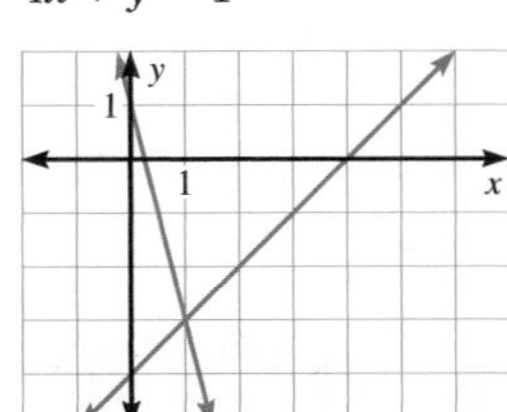

9. $-x + y = -2$ (4, 2)
$2x - y = 6$

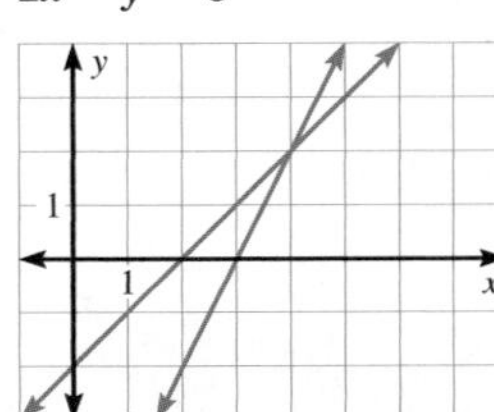

10. $x + y = 5$ (3, 2)
$-2x + y = -4$

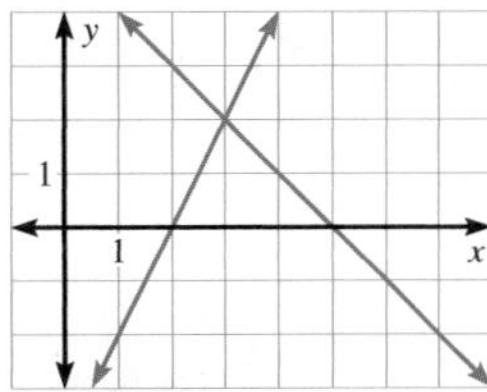

11. **ERROR ANALYSIS** *Describe* and correct the error in solving the linear system below.

$x - 3y = 6$ Equation 1
$2x - 3y = 3$ Equation 2

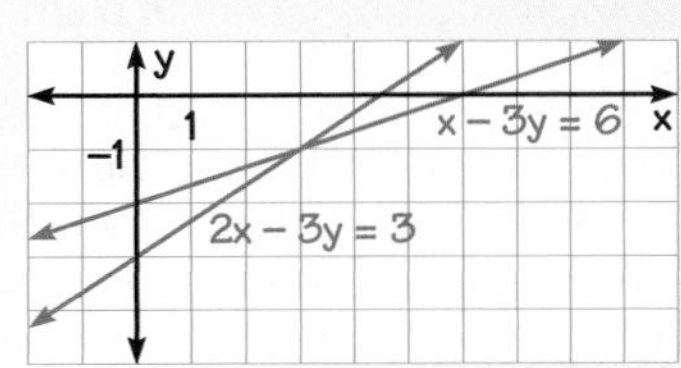

The solution (3, −1) does not satisfy Equation 2. The graph of Equation 2 is incorrect; if properly graphed, the lines would intersect at (−3, −3); see margin for art.

EXAMPLE 2 B
on p. 428
for Exs. 12–26

GRAPH-AND-CHECK METHOD Solve the linear system by graphing. Check your solution.

12. $y = -x + 3$ (1, 2)
$y = x + 1$

13. $y = -x + 4$ (4, 0)
$y = 2x - 8$

14. $y = 2x + 2$ (−2, −2)
$y = 4x + 6$

15. $x - y = 2$ (−3, −5)
$x + y = -8$

16. $x + 2y = 1$ (1.8, −0.4)
$-2x + y = -4$

17. $3x + y = 15$ (10, −15)
$y = -15$

18. $2x - 3y = -1$ (4, 3)
$5x + 2y = 26$

19. $6x + y = 37$ (7, −5)
$4x + 2y = 18$

20. $7x + 5y = -3$ (1, −2)
$-9x + y = -11$

21. $6x + 12y = -6$ (−5, 2)
$2x + 5y = 0$

22. $2x + y = 9$ (3, 3)
$2x + 3y = 15$

23. $-5x + 3y = 3$ (3, 6)
$4x + 3y = 30$

24. $\frac{3}{4}x + \frac{1}{4}y = \frac{13}{2}$ (8, 2)
$x - \frac{3}{4}y = \frac{13}{2}$

25. $\frac{1}{5}x - \frac{2}{5}y = -\frac{8}{5}$ (4, 6)
$-\frac{3}{4}x + y = 3$

26. $-1.6x - 3.2y = -24$ (5, 5)
$2.6x + 2.6y = 26$

27. ★ **OPEN-ENDED** Find values for m and b so that the system $y = \frac{3}{5}x - 1$ and $y = mx + b$ has (5, 2) as a solution. *Sample answer:* $m = 0$ and $b = 2$

28. ★ **WRITING** Solve the linear system shown by graphing. *Explain* why it is important to check your solution.

$y = 4x - 1.5$ Equation 1
$y = -2x + 1.5$ Equation 2

28. (0.5, 0.5). *Sample answer:* It is important to check the solution because the lines do not intersect at integer values.

4 PRACTICE AND APPLY

Assignment Guide

Answer Transparencies available for all exercises

Basic:
Day 1: EP p. 941 Exs. 19–22
pp. 430–433
Exs. 1–17, 31–34, 38–42 even, 43–48

Average:
Day 1: pp. 430–433
Exs. 1–11, 18–35, 37–41 odd, 43–48

Advanced:
Day 1: pp. 430–433
Exs. 1, 4–7, 9, 10, 21–36*, 38–48 even

Block:
pp. 430–433
Exs. 1–11, 18–35, 37–41 odd, 43–48 (with 7.2)

Differentiated Instruction

See *Algebra 1 Best Practices Toolkit* for suggestions on addressing the needs of a diverse classroom.

Homework Check

For a quick check of student understanding of key concepts, go over the following exercises:

Basic: 8, 14, 16, 31, 32
Average: 9, 20, 21, 32, 33
Advanced: 10, 22, 24, 32, 33

Extra Practice

- Student Edition, p. 944
- Chapter 7 Resource Book: Practice levels A, B, C, pp. 6–11

Practice Worksheet

An easily-readable reduced practice page (with answers) for this lesson can be found on p. 424C.

11.

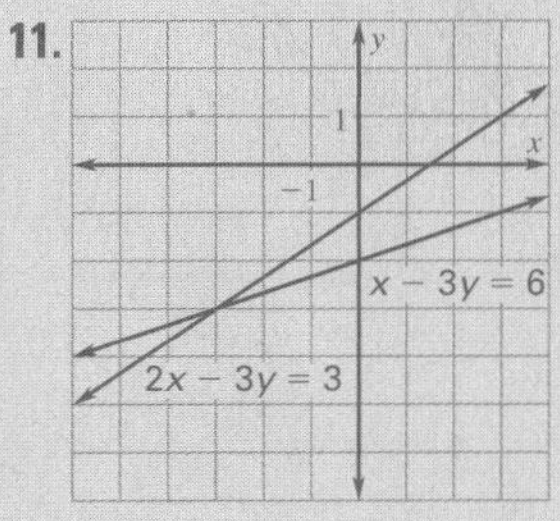

Avoiding Common Errors

Exercises 3–10 Some students may substitute the *x*- and *y*-coordinates of a solution into one equation of the linear system only. Remind these students that a solution of a linear system must satisfy both equations of the system.

Exercises 12–26 Some students may reverse the *x*- and *y*-coordinates in their solutions. Emphasize that checking their solutions will help correct such errors.

Reading Strategy

Exercises 15, 31 Remind students that there is a worked-out solution for exercises circled in red. Point out the Homework Key at the beginning of the exercises on page 430 and at the bottom of the page on page 432.

Teaching Strategy

Exercise 36 You may want to point out that 20% off of the purchase is the same as paying 80% of the purchase.

29d. *Sample answer:* Set each side of the equation equal to *y* to create a system of two equations. Then solve the system using the graph-and-check method. The *x*-coordinate of the system's solution is the solution of the orginal equation.

29. ★ **EXTENDED RESPONSE** Consider the equation $-\frac{1}{4}x + 6 = \frac{1}{2}x + 3$.
   a. Solve the equation using algebra. 4
   b. Solve the linear system below using a graph. (4, 5)

   $y = -\frac{1}{4}x + 6$ Equation 1

   $y = \frac{1}{2}x + 3$ Equation 2

   c. How is the linear system in part (b) related to the original equation? *Sample answer:* Each side of the equation is set equal to *y*.
   d. *Explain* how to use a graph to solve the equation $-\frac{2}{5}x + 5 = \frac{1}{5}x + 2$.

C 30. **CHALLENGE** The three lines given below form a triangle. Find the coordinates of the vertices of the triangle.

Line 1: $-3x + 2y = 1$ **Line 2:** $2x + y = 11$ **Line 3:** $x + 4y = 9$

(3, 5), (1, 2), and (5, 1)

PROBLEM SOLVING

EXAMPLES 3 and 4 on pp. 429–430 for Exs. 31–33

A 31. **TELEVISION** The graph shows a projection, from 1990 on, of the percent of eighth graders who watch 1 hour or less of television on a weekday and the percent of eighth graders who watch more than 1 hour of television on a weekday. Use the graph to predict the year when the percent of eighth graders who watch 1 hour or less will equal the percent who watch more than 1 hour. 2040

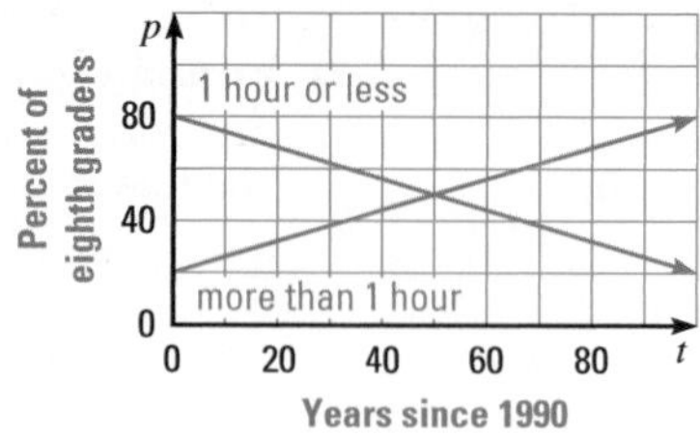

@HomeTutor for problem solving help at classzone.com

32. ★ **MULTIPLE CHOICE** A car dealership is offering interest-free car loans for one day only. During this day, a salesperson at the dealership sells two cars. One of his clients decides to pay off his \$17,424 car in 36 monthly payments of \$484. His other client decides to pay off his \$15,840 car in 48 monthly payments of \$330. Which system of equations can be used to determine the number *x* of months after which both clients will have the same loan balance *y*? B

   Ⓐ $y = -484x$, $y = -330x$
   Ⓑ $y = -484x + 17,424$, $y = -330x + 15,840$
   Ⓒ $y = -484x + 15,840$, $y = -330x + 17,424$
   Ⓓ $y = 484x + 17,424$, $y = 330x + 15,840$

@HomeTutor for problem solving help at classzone.com

33. **CRAFTS** Kirigami is the Japanese art of making paper designs by folding and cutting paper. A student sells small and large greeting cards decorated with kirigami at a craft fair. The small cards cost \$3 per card, and the large cards cost \$5 per card. The student collects \$95 for selling a total of 25 cards. How many of each type of card did the student sell?
   15 small cards and 10 large cards

○ = WORKED-OUT SOLUTIONS on p. WS1 ★ = STANDARDIZED TEST PRACTICE

35b.

Tickets	Cost for members	Cost for non-members
1	\$20	\$8
2	\$25	\$16
3	\$30	\$24
4	\$35	\$32
5	\$40	\$40
6	\$45	\$48

35c.

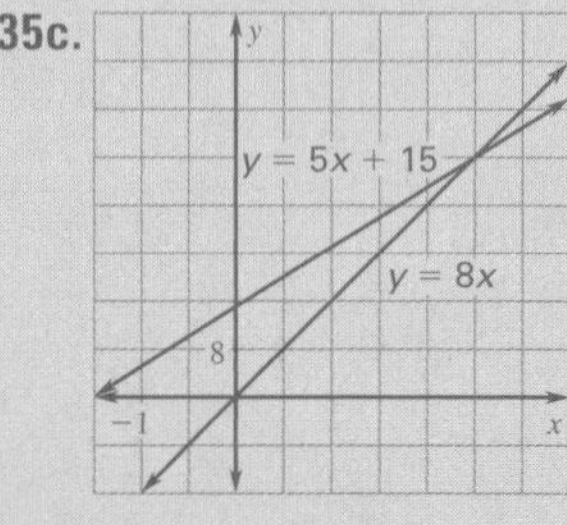

When you rent 6 or more movies. *Sample answer:* The graph for a non-member is below the graph for a member up through 4 movies. For 5 movies, the cost is the same. The graph for members is lower than the graph for non-members for 6 or more movies.

Differentiated Instruction

Advanced When discussing **Exercise 27**, ask students to describe values for *b* in the equation $y = mx + b$ when the value of *m* is negative and when the value of *m* is positive. Have them support their reasoning by graphing several equations in the system $y = \frac{3}{5}x - 1$ and $y = mx + b$ with a solution of (5, 2) and then describing the pattern of graphs in the system as they relate to the values of *m* and *b*.

See also the *Algebra 1 Toolkit* for more strategies.

B **34. FITNESS** You want to burn 225 calories while exercising at a gym. The number of calories that you burn per minute on different machines at the gym is shown below.

Stair machine	*Elliptical trainer*	*Stationary bike*
You burn 5 Cal/min.	You burn 8 Cal/min.	You burn 6 Cal/min.

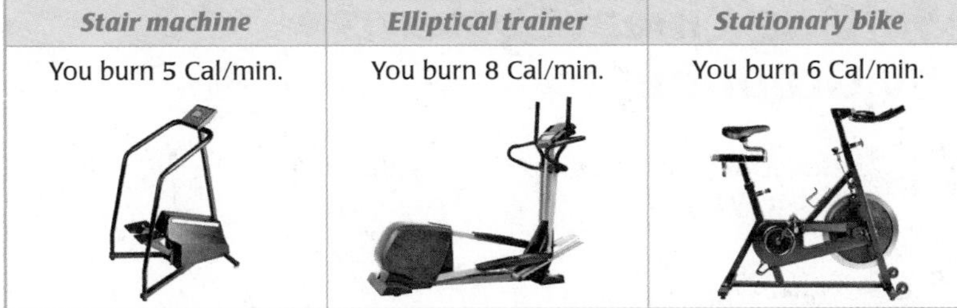

34a. 25 min on the stationary bike and 15 min on the stair machine

34b. 25 min on the ellipitical trainer and 5 min on the stair machine

a. Suppose you have 40 minutes to exercise at the gym and you want to use the stair machine and stationary bike. How many minutes should you spend on each machine so that you burn 225 calories?

b. Suppose you have 30 minutes to exercise at the gym and you want to use the stair machine and the elliptical trainer. How many minutes should you spend on each machine so that you burn 225 calories?

35. ◆ **MULTIPLE REPRESENTATIONS** It costs \$15 for a yearly membership to a movie club at a movie theater. A movie ticket costs \$5 for club members and \$8 for nonmembers.

a. **Writing a System of Equations** Write a system of equations that you can use to find the number x of movies viewed after which the total cost y for a club member, including the membership fee, is the same as the cost for a nonmember. $y = 5x + 15$, $y = 8x$

b. **Making a Table** Make a table of values that shows the total cost for a club member and a nonmember after paying to see 1, 2, 3, 4, 5, and 6 movies. See margin.

c. **Drawing a Graph** Use the table to graph the system of equations. Under what circumstances does it make sense to become a movie club member? *Explain* your answer by using the graph. See margin.

36. You should choose \$25 off if your purchase is less than \$125, and choose 20% off purchases greater than \$125. *Sample answer*: For values less than \$125, 20% off is less than \$25 off. For values greater than \$125, 20% off is greater than \$25 off.

C **36. CHALLENGE** With a minimum purchase of \$25, you can open a credit account with a clothing store. The store is offering either \$25 or 20% off of your purchase if you open a credit account. You decide to open a credit account. Should you choose \$25 or 20% off of your purchase? *Explain*.

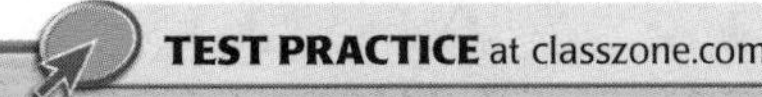

TEST PRACTICE at classzone.com

ILLINOIS MIXED REVIEW

37. A teacher collects data on the number of hours her students spent studying for a test and the scores they received on the test. If the teacher plots the data on a scatter plot, what relationship will the teacher most likely see between the number of hours spent studying and the students' test scores?

Ⓐ A positive correlation A Ⓑ A negative correlation

Ⓒ A constant correlation Ⓓ No correlation

5 ASSESS AND RETEACH

Daily Homework Quiz

Transparency Available

1. Use the graph to solve the linear system.
$3x - y = 5$
$-x + 3y = 1$ (2, 1)

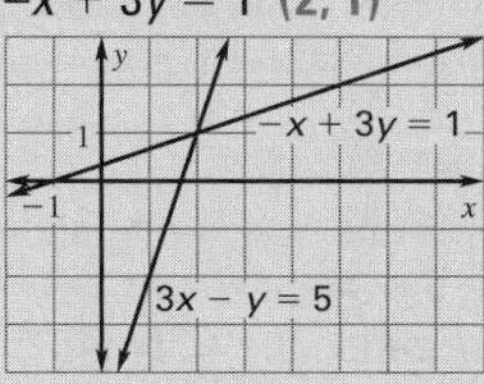

2. Solve the linear system by graphing.
$2x + y = -3$
$-6x + 3y = 3$ (−1, −1)

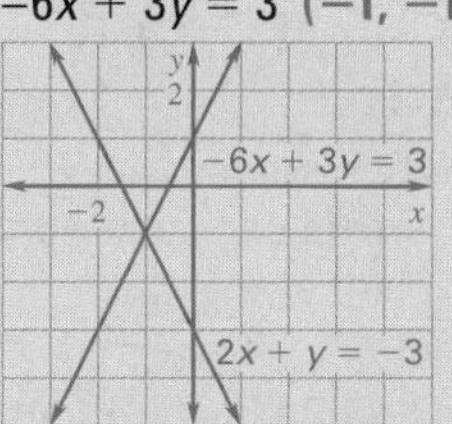

3. A pet store sells angel fish for \$6 each and clown loaches for \$4 each. If the pet store sold 8 fish for \$36, how many of each type of fish did it sell? 2 angel fish and 6 clown loaches

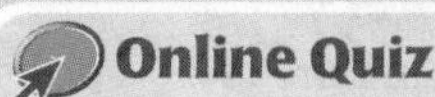

Online Quiz

Available at **classzone.com**

Diagnosis/Remediation

- Practice A, B, C in Chapter 7 Resource Book, pp. 6–11
- Study Guide in Chapter 7 Resource Book, pp. 12–13
- Practice Workbook, pp. 104–106
- @HomeTutor

Challenge

Additional challenge is available in the Chapter 7 Resource Book, p. 16.

1 PLAN AND PREPARE

Learn the Method

- Students will use a graphing calculator to solve a linear system.
- After the activity, students can use a graphing calculator to check their solutions in Exercises 3–7 and 12–26 in Lesson 7.1.

Keystroke Help

Keystrokes for several models of calculators are available in blackline format in the *Chapter 7 Resource Book*.

2 TEACH

Tips for Success

In Step 1, caution students to divide each term in each equation by the coefficient of y.

In Step 2, remind students to use parentheses around the fractions.

Extra Example

Solve the linear system using a graphing calculator.

$4x - 3y = 2$

$x + 5y = -6$ **about (−0.35, −1.13)**

Key Discovery

The intercept feature of a graphing calculator can be used to approximate a solution to a system of linear equations.

3 ASSESS AND RETEACH

Solve the linear system using a graphing calculator.

$-5x + y = -8$

$x - 4y = 9$ **about (1.21, −1.95)**

Graphing Calculator ACTIVITY *Use after Lesson 7.1*

@HomeTutor classzone.com Keystrokes

7.1 Solving Linear Systems by Graphing

QUESTION How can you use a graphing calculator to solve a linear system?

EXAMPLE Solve a linear system

Solve the linear system using a graphing calculator.

$5x + 2y = 6$ **Equation 1**

$x - 3y = -5$ **Equation 2**

STEP 1 ***Rewrite equations***

Solve each equation for y.

Equation 1	Equation 2
$5x + 2y = 6$	$x - 3y = -5$
$2y = -5x + 6$	$-3y = -x - 5$
$y = -\frac{5}{2}x + 3$	$y = \frac{1}{3}x + \frac{5}{3}$

STEP 2 ***Enter equations***

Press Y= and enter the equations.

```
Y1=-(5/2)X+3
Y2=(1/3)X+(5/3)
Y3=
Y4=
Y5=
Y6=
Y7=
```

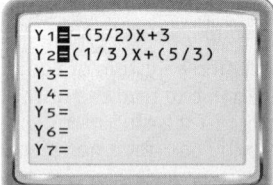

STEP 3 ***Display graph***

Graph the equations using a standard viewing window.

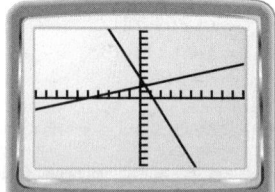

STEP 4 ***Find point of intersection***

Use the *intersect* feature to find the point where the graphs intersect.

X=.47058824 Y=1.8235294

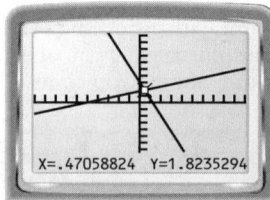

The solution is about (0.47, 1.8).

PRACTICE

Solve the linear system using a graphing calculator.

1. $y = x + 4$
$y = -3x - 2$
(−1.5, 2.5)

2. $5x + y = -4$
$x - y = -2$
(−1, 1)

3. $-0.45x - y = 1.35$
$-1.8x + y = -1.8$
(0.2, −1.44)

4. $-0.4x + 0.8y = -16$
$1.2x + 0.4y = 1$
(6.43, −16.79)

7.2 Solve Linear Systems by Substitution

8.11.17 Solve systems of equations and inequalities.

Before You solved systems of linear equations by graphing.

Now You will solve systems of linear equations by substitution.

Why? So you can find tubing costs, as in Ex. 32.

Key Vocabulary
- **system of linear equations,** *p. 427*

KEY CONCEPT *For Your Notebook*

Solving a Linear System Using the Substitution Method

STEP 1 **Solve** one of the equations for one of its variables. When possible, solve for a variable that has a coefficient of 1 or −1.

STEP 2 **Substitute** the expression from Step 1 into the other equation and solve for the other variable.

STEP 3 **Substitute** the value from Step 2 into the revised equation from Step 1 and solve.

EXAMPLE 1 Use the substitution method

Solve the linear system: $y = 3x + 2$ **Equation 1**
$x + 2y = 11$ **Equation 2**

Solution

STEP 1 **Solve** for y. Equation 1 is already solved for y.

STEP 2 **Substitute** $3x + 2$ for y in Equation 2 and solve for x.

$x + 2y = 11$ **Write Equation 2.**

$x + 2(3x + 2) = 11$ **Substitute 3x + 2 for y.**

$7x + 4 = 11$ **Simplify.**

$7x = 7$ **Subtract 4 from each side.**

$x = 1$ **Divide each side by 7.**

STEP 3 **Substitute** 1 for x in the original Equation 1 to find the value of y.

$y = 3x + 2 = 3(1) + 2 = 3 + 2 = 5$

▶ The solution is (1, 5).

CHECK Substitute 1 for x and 5 for y in each of the original equations.

$y = 3x + 2$	$x + 2y = 11$
$5 \stackrel{?}{=} 3(1) + 2$	$1 + 2(5) \stackrel{?}{=} 11$
$5 = 5$ ✓	$11 = 11$ ✓

Animated Algebra at classzone.com

1 PLAN AND PREPARE

Warm-Up Exercises

Transparency Available

Solve the equation.

1. $6a - 3 + 2a = 13$ 2
2. $4(n + 2) - n = 11$ 1
3. You burned 8 calories per minute on a treadmill and 10 calories per minute on an elliptical trainer for a total of 560 calories in 60 minutes. How many minutes did you spend on each machine? **treadmill: 20 min, elliptical trainer: 40 min**

Notetaking Guide

Transparency Available

Promotes interactive learning and notetaking skills, pp. 153–154.

Pacing

Basic: 2 days

Average: 2 days

Advanced: 2 days

Block: 0.5 block with 7.1
0.5 block with 7.3

• See *Teaching Guide/Lesson Plan.*

2 FOCUS AND MOTIVATE

Essential Question

Big Idea 2, p. 425

How do you solve systems of linear equations by substitution? **Tell students they will learn how to answer this question by substituting an expression for a variable in one equation into the other equation.**

Resource Planning Guide

Chapter Resource Book
- Teaching Guide/Lesson Plan (pp. 17–18)
- Practice levels A, B, C (pp. 19–21)
- Study Guide (pp. 22–23)
- Catch-up for Absent Students (p. 24)
- Application (p. 25)
- Challenge (p. 26)

Workbooks
- Notetaking Guide (pp. 153–154)
- Practice Workbook (pp. 107–108)

Teaching Options
- **Power Presentations CD-ROM** provides dynamic electronic teaching resources for the classroom.
- **Activity Generator CD-ROM** provides editable activities for all ability levels.

Interactive Technology
- Easy Planner
- Power Presentations CD-ROM
- Activity Generator CD-ROM
- Animated Algebra
- Test Generator CD-ROM
- Online Quiz
- eWorkbook
- eEdition
- @HomeTutor

Resources for English Learners
- Quick Reference for English Learners
- Spanish Study Guide
- Multi-Language Visual Glossary
- Student Resources in Spanish

See also the *Algebra 1 Toolkit* for more strategies for meeting individual needs.

Motivating the Lesson

In the previous lesson you solved systems of equations by graphing. But what if the point of intersection is not where two grid lines cross? You could approximate the coordinates of the point, but the substitution method provides a means for finding the exact coordinates.

3 TEACH

Extra Example 1

Solve the linear system:
$y = 2x - 3$
$x + 3y = 5$ (2, 1)

An **Animated Algebra** activity is available on-line for **Example 1**. This activity is also available on the **Power Presentations CD-ROM**.

Extra Example 2

Solve the linear system:
$-5x - y = 12$
$3x - 5y = 4$ (−2, −2)

Key Question to Ask for Example 2

- How is Example 2 different from Example 1? In Example 2, you first solve one equation in the system for *x* or *y*. In Example 1, an equation is already solved for *y*.

Avoiding Common Errors

When students solve an equation for *x*, as in Example 2, the first value they find is the *y*-value. Caution them that this number is the *second* coordinate of the ordered pair solution.

EXAMPLE 2 Use the substitution method

Solve the linear system: $x - 2y = -6$ **Equation 1**
$4x + 6y = 4$ **Equation 2**

CHOOSE AN EQUATION
Equation 1 was chosen in Step 1 because *x* has a coefficient of 1. So, only one step is needed to solve Equation 1 for *x*.

Solution

STEP 1 **Solve** Equation 1 for *x*.

$x - 2y = -6$ **Write original Equation 1.**

$x = 2y - 6$ **Revised Equation 1**

STEP 2 **Substitute** $2y - 6$ for *x* in Equation 2 and solve for *y*.

$4x + 6y = 4$ **Write Equation 2.**

$4(2y - 6) + 6y = 4$ **Substitute 2*y* − 6 for *x*.**

$8y - 24 + 6y = 4$ **Distributive property**

$14y - 24 = 4$ **Simplify.**

$14y = 28$ **Add 24 to each side.**

$y = 2$ **Divide each side by 14.**

STEP 3 **Substitute** 2 for *y* in the revised Equation 1 to find the value of *x*.

$x = 2y - 6$ **Revised Equation 1**

$x = 2(2) - 6$ **Substitute 2 for *y*.**

$x = -2$ **Simplify.**

▶ The solution is (−2, 2).

CHECK Substitute −2 for *x* and 2 for *y* in each of the original equations.

Equation 1	Equation 2
$x - 2y = -6$	$4x + 6y = 4$
$-2 - 2(2) \stackrel{?}{=} -6$	$4(-2) + 6(2) \stackrel{?}{=} 4$
$-6 = -6$ ✓	$4 = 4$ ✓

CHECK REASONABLENESS When solving a linear system using the substitution method, you can use a graph to check the reasonableness of your solution. For example, the graph at the right verifies that (−2, 2) is a solution of the linear system in Example 2.

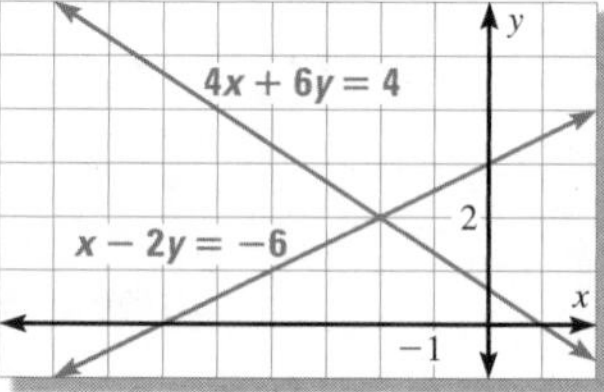

GUIDED PRACTICE for Examples 1 and 2

Solve the linear system using the substitution method.

1. $y = 2x + 5$ (1, 7)
$3x + y = 10$

2. $x - y = 3$ (0, −3)
$x + 2y = -6$

3. $3x + y = -7$ (−2, −1)
$-2x + 4y = 0$

Differentiated Instruction

Visual Learners The substitution method involves many steps when written out verbally. Some students may find it helpful to visualize getting one variable (*x* or *y*) by itself in one equation, and then substituting an expression for that variable into the other equation. Students should look at the equations and highlight any variable with a coefficient of 1 or −1. In **Example 2**, the variable *x* in the first equation would be highlighted.

See also the *Algebra 1 Toolkit* for more strategies.

EXAMPLE 3 Solve a multi-step problem

ANOTHER WAY
For an alternative method for solving the problem in Example 3, turn to page 442 for the **Problem Solving Workshop**.

WEBSITES Many businesses pay website hosting companies to store and maintain the computer files that make up their websites. Internet service providers also offer website hosting. The costs for website hosting offered by a website hosting company and an Internet service provider are shown in the table. Find the number of months after which the total cost for website hosting will be the same for both companies.

Company	Set-up fee (dollars)	Cost per month (dollars)
Internet service provider	10	21.95
Website hosting company	None	22.45

Solution

STEP 1 **Write** a system of equations. Let y be the total cost after x months.

Equation 1: Internet service provider

Total cost = Set-up fee + Cost per month · Number of months

$$y = 10 + 21.95 \cdot x$$

Equation 2: Website hosting company

Total cost = Cost per month · Number of months

$$y = 22.45 \cdot x$$

The system of equations is: $y = 10 + 21.95x$ **Equation 1**

$y = 22.45x$ **Equation 2**

STEP 2 **Substitute** $22.45x$ for y in Equation 1 and solve for x.

$y = 10 + 21.95x$ **Write Equation 1.**

$22.45x = 10 + 21.95x$ **Substitute 22.45x for y.**

$0.5x = 10$ **Subtract 21.95x from each side.**

$x = 20$ **Divide each side by 0.5.**

▶ The total cost will be the same for both companies after 20 months.

✓ GUIDED PRACTICE for Example 3

4. In Example 3, what is the total cost for website hosting for each company after 20 months? **$449**

5. **WHAT IF?** In Example 3, suppose the Internet service provider offers $5 off the set-up fee. After how many months will the total cost for website hosting be the same for both companies? **10 mo**

Extra Example 3

A food cooperative is a business that usually offers special prices on locally grown food and produce. Some cooperatives are clubs and others are retail stores. The weekly costs for seasonal produce offered by a club-based and a store-based food cooperative are shown in the table. Find the number of weeks at which the total cost of weekly produce will be the same.

Type of cooperative	Club fee (dollars)	Cost per week (dollars)
Club	$20	$15
Retail	None	$17.50

The total cost will be the same for both cooperatives at 8 weeks.

Key Question to Ask for Example 3

- Which company will have the greater total cost for 21 months? Explain. **The website hosting company, since its monthly cost is greater than the monthly cost for the Internet service provider.**

Avoiding Common Errors

In Step 2 of Example 3, some students may substitute 22.45 for y instead of $22.45x$. Remind these students that y is equivalent to $22.45 \cdot x$ in Equation 2.

Extra Example 4

A chemist needs 15 liters of a 60% alcohol solution. The chemist has a solution that is 50% alcohol. How many liters of the 50% alcohol solution and pure alcohol should the chemist mix together to make 15 liters of a 60% alcohol solution? **3 liters of pure alcohol and 12 liters of the 50% alcohol solution**

Key Question to Ask for Example 4

- In Step 2, why should you solve Equation 1 for x? **The variable x has a coefficient of 1 in Equation 2 and thus the step where you need to multiply by a coefficient is eliminated.**

Closing the Lesson

Have students summarize the major points of the lesson and answer the Essential Question: How do you solve systems of linear equations by substitution?

- **You can solve a linear system by substituting an expression for one variable in an equation into the other equation and then solving for the other variable.**

Solve one of the equations in the system for x or y. Substitute the expression for x or y into the other equation. Solve for the other variable. Substitute the value of this variable into the original equation in the first step. Solve for the other variable.

EXAMPLE 4 Solve a mixture problem

ANTIFREEZE For extremely cold temperatures, an automobile manufacturer recommends that a 70% antifreeze and 30% water mix be used in the cooling system of a car. How many quarts of pure (100%) antifreeze and a 50% antifreeze and 50% water mix should be combined to make 11 quarts of a 70% antifreeze and 30% water mix?

Solution

STEP 1 **Write** an equation for the total number of quarts and an equation for the number of quarts of antifreeze. Let x be the number of quarts of 100% antifreeze, and let y be the number of quarts of a 50% antifreeze and 50% water mix.

Equation 1: Total number of quarts

$x + y = 11$

Equation 2: Number of quarts of antifreeze

DRAW A DIAGRAM
Each bar shows the liquid in each mix. The green portion shows the percent of the mix that is antifreeze.

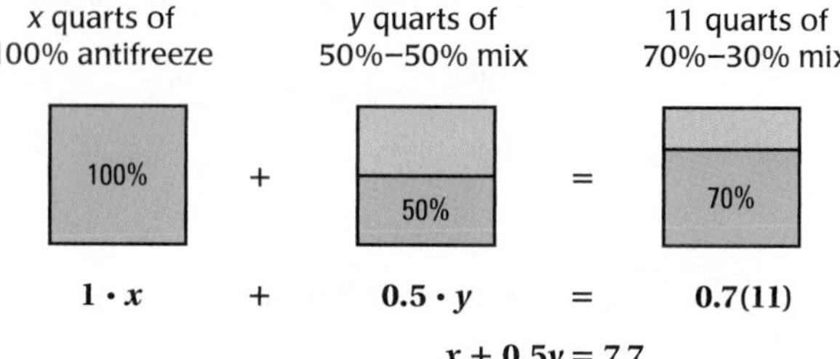

$$x + 0.5y = 7.7$$

The system of equations is: $x + y = 11$ Equation 1

$x + 0.5y = 7.7$ Equation 2

STEP 2 **Solve** Equation 1 for x.

$x + y = 11$ Write Equation 1.

$x = 11 - y$ Revised Equation 1

STEP 3 **Substitute** $11 - y$ for x in Equation 2 and solve for y.

$x + 0.5y = 7.7$ Write Equation 2.

$(11 - y) + 0.5y = 7.7$ Substitute $11 - y$ for x.

$y = 6.6$ Solve for y.

STEP 4 **Substitute** 6.6 for y in the revised Equation 1 to find the value of x.

$x = 11 - y = 11 - 6.6 = 4.4$

▶ Mix 4.4 quarts of 100% antifreeze and 6.6 quarts of a 50% antifreeze and 50% water mix to get 11 quarts of a 70% antifreeze and 30% water mix.

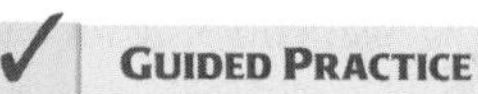

GUIDED PRACTICE for Example 4

6. **WHAT IF?** How many quarts of 100% antifreeze and a 50% antifreeze and 50% water mix should be combined to make 16 quarts of a 70% antifreeze and 30% water mix? **6.4 quarts of 100% antifreeze and 9.6 quarts of 50% antifreeze and 50% water mix**

Differentiated Instruction

Below Level Some students avoid mixture problems, such as the one in **Example 4**, because they look complicated. Tell students that following the steps in the example and using diagrams will help them learn how to break mixture problems into parts. Suggest that they solve the problem for 10 quarts of antifreeze instead of 11. This will make the computation more manageable. Break Step 3 into a stepped-out solution so students see how to get a positive value for y. Students can then solve **Guided Practice Exercise 6** for 16 quarts.

See also the *Algebra 1 Toolkit* for more strategies.

7.2 EXERCISES

HOMEWORK KEY
○ = **WORKED-OUT SOLUTIONS** on p. WS16 for Exs. 13 and 33
★ = **STANDARDIZED TEST PRACTICE** Exs. 2, 18, 29, 33, and 37

SKILL PRACTICE

A

1. **VOCABULARY** Give an example of a system of linear equations.
Sample answer: $y = x + 1$, $y = 2x + 1$

2. ★ **WRITING** If you are solving the linear system shown using the substitution method, which equation would you solve for which variable? *Explain.* *Sample answer:* Solve Equation 2 for y; the y term does not have a coefficient.

$2x - 3y = 24$ **Equation 1**
$2x + y = 8$ **Equation 2**

EXAMPLE 1 on p. 435 for Exs. 3–8

SOLVING LINEAR SYSTEMS **Solve the linear system using substitution.**

3. $x = 17 - 4y$, $y = x - 2$ (5, 3)
4. $y = 2x - 1$, $2x + y = 3$ (1, 1)
5. $x = y + 3$, $2x - y = 5$ (2, −1)
6. $4x - 7y = 10$, $y = x - 7$ (13, 6)
7. $x = 16 - 4y$, $3x + 4y = 8$ (−4, 5)
8. $-5x + 3y = 51$, $y = 10x - 8$ (3, 22)

EXAMPLE 2 on p. 436 for Exs. 9–19

9. $2x = 12$, $x - 5y = -29$ (6, 7)
10. $2x - y = 23$, $x - 9 = -1$ (8, −7)
11. $x + y = 0$, $x - 2y = 6$ (2, −2)
12. $2x + y = 9$, $4x - y = -15$ (−1, 11)
13. $5x + 2y = 9$, $x + y = -3$ (5, −8)
14. $5x + 4y = 32$, $9x - y = 33$ (4, 3)
15. $11x - 7y = -14$, $x - 2y = -4$ (0, 2)
16. $20x - 30y = -50$, $x + 2y = 1$ (−1, 1)
17. $6x + y = 4$, $x - 4y = 19$ (1.4, −4.4)

18. ★ **MULTIPLE CHOICE** Which ordered pair is a solution of the linear system $4x - y = 17$ and $-9x + 8y = 2$? A

Ⓐ (6, 7) Ⓑ (7, 6) Ⓒ (7, 11) Ⓓ (11, 7)

19. **ERROR ANALYSIS** *Describe* and correct the error in solving the linear system $4x + 2y = 6$ and $3x + y = 9$.

Step 1	Step 2	Step 3	The solution is (6, 1).
$3x + y = 9$	$4x + 2(9 - 3x) = 6$	$y = 9 - 3x$	
$y = 9 - 3x$	$4x + 18 - 6x = 6$	$6 = 9 - 3x$	
	$-2x = -12$	$-3 = -3x$	
	$x = 6$	$1 = x$	

Sample answer: In Step 3, 6 is substituted for y instead of x; $y = 9 - 3(6)$, $y = -9$, the solution is (6, −9).

B

SOLVING LINEAR SYSTEMS **Solve the linear system using substitution.**

20. $4.5x + 1.5y = 24$, $x - y = 4$ (5, 1)
21. $35x + y = 20$, $1.5x - 0.1y = 18$ (4, −120)
22. $3x - 2y = 8$, $0.5x + y = 17$ (10.5, 11.75)
23. $0.5x + 0.6y = 5.7$, $2x - y = -1$ (3, 7)
24. $x - 9 = 0.5y$, $2.2x - 3.1y = -0.2$ (14, 10)
25. $0.2x + y = -1.8$, $1.8y + 5.5x = 27.6$ (6, −3)
26. $\frac{1}{2}x + \frac{1}{4}y = 5$, $x - \frac{1}{2}y = 1$ $\left(5\frac{1}{2}, 9\right)$
27. $x + \frac{1}{3}y = -2$, $-8x - \frac{2}{3}y = 4$ (0, −6)
28. $\frac{3}{8}x + \frac{3}{4}y = 12$, $\frac{2}{3}x + \frac{1}{2}y = 13$ (12, 10)

4 PRACTICE AND APPLY

Assignment Guide

Answer Transparencies available for all exercises

Basic:
Day 1: EP p. 940 Exs. 21–26
pp. 439–441
Exs. 1–19
Day 2: pp. 439–441
Exs. 20–25, 31–35, 39–50

Average:
Day 1: pp. 439–441
Exs. 1, 2, 4–18 even, 19–29 odd
Day 2: pp. 439–441
Exs. 31–37, 39–50

Advanced:
Day 1: pp. 439–441
Exs. 1, 6–8, 15–18, 20–28
Day 2: pp. 439–441
Exs. 29–38*, 42–44, 48–50

Block:
pp. 439–441
Exs. 1, 2, 4–18 even, 19–29 odd (with 7.1)
pp. 439–441
Exs. 31–37, 39–50 (with 7.3)

Differentiated Instruction

See *Algebra 1 Best Practices Toolkit* for suggestions on addressing the needs of a diverse classroom.

Homework Check

For a quick check of student understanding of key concepts, go over the following exercises:
Basic: 4, 10, 14, 31, 35
Average: 6, 14, 21, 32, 35
Advanced: 8, 16, 24, 33, 35

Extra Practice

- Student Edition, p. 944
- Chapter 7 Resource Book: Practice levels A, B, C, pp. 19–21

Practice Worksheet

An easily-readable reduced practice page (with answers) for this lesson can be found on p. 424C.

29. ★ **WRITING** Suppose you solve a linear system using substitution. *Explain* how you can use a graph to check your solution. ***Sample answer:*** **The graphs of the equations should intersect at the solution you found using the substitution method.**

C 30. **CHALLENGE** Find values of a and b so that the linear system shown has a solution of $(-9, 4)$. $a = 4, b = 5$

$ax + by = -16$ **Equation 1**

$ax - by = -56$ **Equation 2**

PROBLEM SOLVING

EXAMPLE 3 on p. 437 for Exs. 31–33

A 31. **FUNDRAISING** During a football game, the parents of the football players sell pretzels and popcorn to raise money for new uniforms. They charge \$2.50 for a bag of popcorn and \$2 for a pretzel. The parents collect \$336 in sales during the game. They sell twice as many bags of popcorn as pretzels. How many bags of popcorn do they sell? How many pretzels do they sell? **96 bags of popcorn; 48 pretzels**

@HomeTutor for problem solving help at classzone.com

32. **TUBING COSTS** A group of friends takes a day-long tubing trip down a river. The company that offers the tubing trip charges \$15 to rent a tube for a person to use and \$7.50 to rent a "cooler" tube, which is used to carry food and water in a cooler. The friends spend \$360 to rent a total of 26 tubes. How many of each type of tube do they rent? **22 tubes for a person and 4 "cooler" tubes**

@HomeTutor for problem solving help at classzone.com

(33.) ★ **SHORT RESPONSE** In the mobile shown, objects are attached to each end of a dowel. For the dowel to balance, the following must be true:

$x \cdot$ (Weight hanging from point A) $= y \cdot$ (Weight hanging from point B)

The weight of the objects hanging from point A is 1.5 pounds, and the weight of the objects hanging from point B is 1.2 pounds. The length of the dowel is 9 inches. How far from point A should the string be placed? *Explain.*
4 in. *Sample answer:* (4, 5) is the solution to the appropriate linear system, so *x* should equal 4.

B 34. **MULTI-STEP PROBLEM** Two swimming teams are competing in a 400 meter medley relay. During the last leg of the race, the swimmer in lane 1 has a 1.2 second head start on the swimmer in lane 2, as shown.

a. Let t be the time since the swimmer in lane 2 started the last leg. After how many seconds into the leg will the swimmer in lane 2 catch up to the swimmer in lane 1? **21.6 sec**

b. Does the swimmer in lane 2 catch up to the swimmer in lane 1 before the race ends? *Explain.*

34b. Yes. *Sample answer:* After 21.6 seconds they have swam 41.04 meters, so the race is not over.

○ = WORKED-OUT SOLUTIONS on p. WS1 ★ = STANDARDIZED TEST PRACTICE

Graphing Calculator

Exercises 3–17, 20–28 Students may want to check their solutions by graphing the equations. They should enter the equations in the graphing calculator using y= key, set and then select Graph. They can use the Zoom feature if the standard window does not allow them to view the point of intersection of the graphs. The intersect feature will display the coordinates of the point of intersection.

Avoiding Common Errors

Exercises 35–36 A common error in mixture problems is failing to multiply the percentage of the mixture times the amount of the mixture when writing the equation that represents the contents of the mixture. Suggest that students review Step 1 in Example 4 before writing the equations for the linear system.

Exercise 37 For more information about gazelles, visit the website www.zoo.org/educate/fact_sheets/savana/g_gazelle/g_gazelle.htm

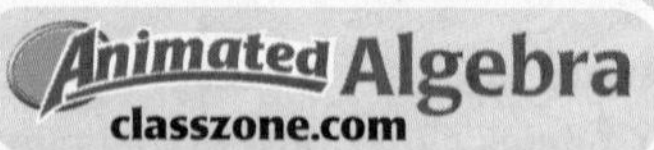

An **Animated Algebra** activity is available on-line for **Exercise 37**. This activity is also available on the **Power Presentations CD-ROM**.

EXAMPLE 4 on p. 438 for Ex. 35

35. **CHEMISTRY** In your chemistry lab, you have a bottle of 1% hydrochloric acid solution and a bottle of 5% hydrochloric acid solution. You need 100 milliliters of a 3% hydrochloric acid solution for an experiment. How many milliliters of each solution do you need to mix together?
50 milliliters of 1% hydrochloric acid solution and 50 milliliters of 5% hydrochloric acid solution

36. **MONEY** Laura has $4.50 in dimes and quarters. She has 3 more dimes than quarters. How many quarters does she have? **12 quarters**

37. ★ **SHORT RESPONSE** A gazelle can run 73 feet per second for several minutes. A cheetah can run 88 feet per second, but it can sustain this speed for only 20 seconds. A gazelle is 350 feet from a cheetah when both animals start running. Can the gazelle stay ahead of the cheetah? *Explain.* **Yes.** ***Sample answer:*** **The cheetah would have to run at 88 feet per second for 23.3 seconds to catch the gazelle.**

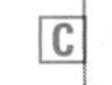
Animated Algebra at classzone.com

C 38. **CHALLENGE** A gardener needs 6 bushels of a potting medium of 40% peat moss and 60% vermiculite. He decides to add 100% vermiculite to his current potting medium that is 50% peat moss and 50% vermiculite. The gardener has 5 bushels of the 50% peat moss and 50% vermiculite mix. Does he have enough of the 50% peat moss and 50% vermiculite mix to make 6 bushels of the 40% peat moss and 60% vermiculite mix? *Explain.*
Yes. ***Sample answer:*** **The gardener needs 4.8 bushels of the 50% peat moss and 50% vermiculite mix, and the gardener had 5 bushels.**

ILLINOIS MIXED REVIEW

TEST PRACTICE at classzone.com

39. Jim wants to write an expression that will always produce a positive number. Which of the following expressions is positive for any real number, x? **D**

   (A) $2x - x$ (B) $x^2 - 0.01$ (C) $|x + 2| - 1$ (D) $x^2 + 2$

40. A box that is a rectangular prism has a volume of 150 cubic centimeters. Another box has twice the length, twice the width, and twice the height of the first box. What is the volume of the second box? **C**

   (A) 300 cm^3 (B) 450 cm^3 (C) 1200 cm^3 (D) 1500 cm^3

QUIZ for Lessons 7.1–7.2

Solve the linear system by graphing. Check your solution. *(p. 427)*

1. $x + y = -2$, $-x + y = 6$ **(−4, 2)**
2. $x - y = 0$, $5x + 2y = -7$ **(−1, −1)**
3. $x - 2y = 12$, $-3x + y = -1$ **(−2, −7)**

Solve the linear system using substitution. *(p. 435)*

4. $y = x - 4$, $-2x + y = 18$ **(−22, −26)**
5. $y = 4 - 3x$, $5x - y = 22$ **(3.25, −5.75)**
6. $x = y + 9$, $5x - 3y = 7$ **(−10, −19)**
7. $2y + x = -4$, $y - x = -5$ **(2, −3)**
8. $5x - 4y = 27$, $-2x + y = 3$ **(−13, −23)**
9. $3x - 5y = 13$, $x + 4y = 10$ **(6, 1)**

5 ASSESS AND RETEACH

Daily Homework Quiz

Transparency Available

Solve the linear system using substitution.

1. $-5x - y = 12$, $3x - 5y = 4$ **(−2, −2)**
2. $2x + 9y = -4$, $x - 2y = 11$ **(7, −2)**
3. You are making 6 quarts of fruit punch for a party. You want the punch to contain 80% fruit juice. You have bottles of 100% fruit juice and 20% fruit juice. How many quarts of 100% fruit juice and how many quarts of 20% fruit juice should you mix to make 6 quarts of 80% fruit juice? **4.5 quarts of 100% fruit juice and 1.5 quarts of 20% fruit juice**

Online Quiz

Available at **classzone.com**

Diagnosis/Remediation

- Practice A, B, C in Chapter 7 Resource Book, pp. 19–21
- Study Guide in Chapter 7 Resource Book, pp. 22–23
- Practice Workbook, pp. 107–108
- @HomeTutor

Challenge

Additional challenge is available in the Chapter 7 Resource Book, p. 26.

Quiz

An easily-readable reduced copy of the quiz (with answers) on Lessons 7.1–7.2 from the Assessment Book can be found on p. 424F.

Alternative Strategy

Example 3 on page 437 can be solved by making a table rather than by writing a system of equations. Making a table is a good alternative for students who have difficulties with algebraic representations. A table in this situation has the added benefit of showing a detailed analysis of the costs of both companies. This allows the student to reason about the benefits of choosing one company over another, which is often the goal in this type of exercise.

Avoiding Common Errors

Calculation errors are the biggest drawback in using this method. One way to avoid these errors is to make tables using a spreadsheet. After students enter the formulas in the appropriate cells, the spreadsheet will enter the correct calculations.

PROBLEM SOLVING WORKSHOP
LESSON 7.2

Using ALTERNATIVE METHODS

Another Way to Solve Example 3, page 437

MULTIPLE REPRESENTATIONS In Example 3 on page 437, you saw how to solve the problem about website hosting by solving a linear system algebraically. You can also solve the problem using a table.

PROBLEM

WEBSITES Many businesses pay website hosting companies to store and maintain the computer files that make up their websites. Internet service providers also offer website hosting. The costs for website hosting offered by a website hosting company and an Internet service provider are shown in the table. Find the number of months after which the total cost for website hosting will be the same for both companies.

Company	Set-up fee	Cost per month
Internet service provider	$10	$21.95
Website hosting company	None	$22.45

METHOD

Making a Table An alternative approach is to make a table.

STEP 1 **Make** a table for the total cost of website hosting for both companies.

Include the set-up fee in the cost for the first month.

STEP 2 **Look** for the month in which the total cost of the service from the Internet service provider and the website hosting company is the same. This happens after 20 months.

Months	Internet service provider	Website hosting company
1	$31.95	$22.45
2	$53.90	$44.90
3	$75.85	$67.35
⋮	⋮	⋮
19	$427.05	$426.55
20	$449.00	$449.00
21	$470.95	$471.45

PRACTICE

1. **TAXIS** A taxi company charges $2.80 for the first mile and $1.60 for each additional mile. Another taxi company charges $3.20 for the first mile and $1.50 for each additional mile. After how many miles will each taxi cost the same? Use a table to solve the problem. **5 mi**

2. **SCHOOL PLAY** An adult ticket to a school play costs $5 and a student ticket costs $3. A total of $460 was collected from the sale of 120 tickets. How many student tickets were purchased? Solve the problem using algebra. Then use a table to check your answer. **70 student tickets**

7.3 Linear Systems and Elimination

MATERIALS • algebra tiles

QUESTION How can you solve a linear system using algebra tiles?

You can use the following algebra tiles to model equations.

1-tiles **x-tiles** **y-tiles**

EXPLORE Solve a linear system using algebra tiles.

Solve the linear system: $3x - y = 5$ Equation 1
$x + y = 3$ Equation 2

STEP 1 Model equations
Model each equation using algebra tiles. Arrange the algebra tiles so that one equation is directly below the other equation.

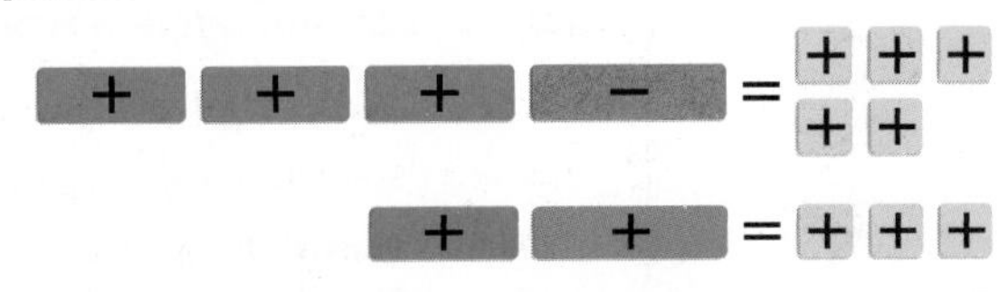

STEP 2 Add equations
Combine the two equations to form one equation. Notice that the new equation has one positive y-tile and one negative y-tile. The y-tiles can be removed because the pair of y-tiles has a value of 0.

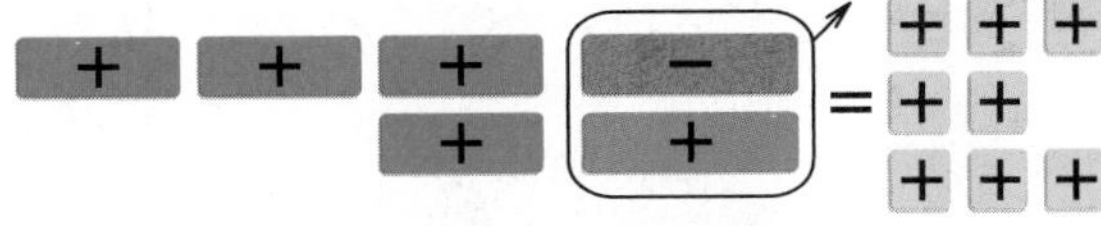

STEP 3 Solve for x
Divide the remaining tiles into four equal groups. Each x-tile is equal to two 1-tiles. So, $x = 2$.

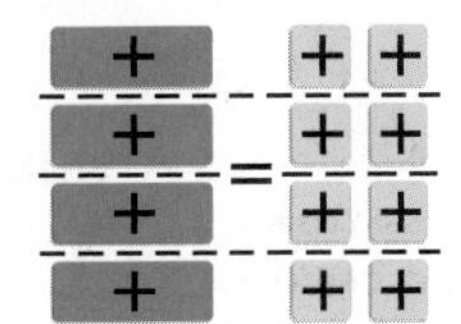

STEP 4 Solve for y
To find the value of y, use the model for Equation 2. Because $x = 2$, you can replace the x-tile with two 1-tiles. Solve the new equation for y. So $y = 1$, and the solution of the system is (2, 1).

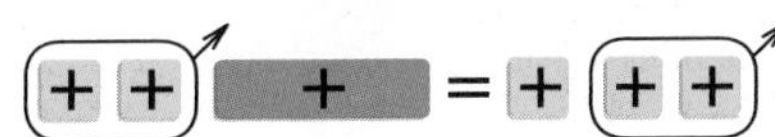

DRAW CONCLUSIONS Use your observations to complete these exercises

Use algebra tiles to model and solve the linear system.

1. $x + 3y = 8$
$4x - 3y = 2$
(2, 2)
2. $2x + y = 5$
$-2x + 3y = 7$
(1, 3)
3. $5x - 2y = -2$
$x + 2y = 14$
(2, 6)
4. $x + 2y = 3$
$-x + 3y = 2$
(1, 1)
5. **REASONING** Is it possible to solve the linear system $3x - 2y = 6$ and $2x + y = 11$ using the steps shown above? *Explain* your reasoning. See margin.

1 PLAN AND PREPARE

Explore the Concept
- Students will use algebra tiles to solve a linear system.
- This activity leads into the study of solving linear systems by adding, as in Example 1 in Lesson 7.3.

Materials
Each student will need:
- algebra tiles
- Activity Support Master (*Chapter 7 Resource Book*, p. 29)

Recommended Time
Work activity: 15 min
Discuss results: 5 min

Grouping
Students should work individually.

2 TEACH

Tips for Success
Make sure that the models of the equations are directly beneath each other.

Key Question
- In Step 4, why should you use the model for Equation 2? **Equation 2 is easier to solve for y because the coefficient of y is 1.**

Key Discovery
You can eliminate a variable if the coefficients are opposites.

3 ASSESS AND RETEACH

If you model the linear system $3x - 2y = 1$ and $-3x + y = 4$, which tiles can you remove when you combine the equations? **3 positive x-tiles and 3 negative x-tiles**

5. No. *Sample answer:* When you combine the two equations, the result still has 2 variables.

1 PLAN AND PREPARE

Warm-Up Exercises

Transparency Available

1. Solve the linear system using substitution.
   $2x + y = 12$
   $3x - 2y = 11$ **(5, 2)**
2. One auto repair shop charges \$30 for a diagnosis and \$25 per hour for labor. Another auto repair shop charges \$35 per hour for labor. For how many hours are the total charges for both of the shops the same? **3 h**

Notetaking Guide

Transparency Available

Promotes interactive learning and notetaking skills, pp. 155–157.

Pacing

Basic: 1 day
Average: 1 day
Advanced: 1 day
Block: 0.5 block with 7.2
• See *Teaching Guide/Lesson Plan.*

2 FOCUS AND MOTIVATE

Essential Question

Big Idea 2, p. 425

How do you solve linear systems by eliminating a variable? **Tell students they will learn how to answer this question by adding or subtracting equations to eliminate one of the variables.**

7.3 Solve Linear Systems by Adding or Subtracting

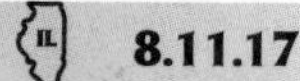

8.11.17 Solve systems of equations and inequalities.

Before You solved linear systems by graphing and using substitution.
Now You will solve linear systems using elimination.
Why? So you can solve a problem about arranging flowers, as in Ex. 42.

Key Vocabulary
• **system of linear equations,** *p. 427*

When solving a linear system, you can sometimes add or subtract the equations to obtain a new equation in one variable. This method is called *elimination.*

KEY CONCEPT *For Your Notebook*

Solving a Linear System Using the Elimination Method

STEP 1 **Add or subtract** the equations to eliminate one variable.

STEP 2 **Solve** the resulting equation for the other variable.

STEP 3 **Substitute** in either original equation to find the value of the eliminated variable.

EXAMPLE 1 Use addition to eliminate a variable

Solve the linear system: $2x + 3y = 11$ **Equation 1**
$-2x + 5y = 13$ **Equation 2**

Solution

ADD EQUATIONS When the coefficients of one variable are opposites, add the equations to eliminate the variable.

STEP 1 **Add** the equations to eliminate one variable.
$2x + 3y = 11$
$-2x + 5y = 13$
$8y = 24$

STEP 2 **Solve** for y.
$y = 3$

STEP 3 **Substitute** 3 for y in either equation and solve for x.

$2x + 3y = 11$ **Write Equation 1.**
$2x + 3(3) = 11$ **Substitute 3 for y.**
$x = 1$ **Solve for x.**

▶ The solution is (1, 3).

CHECK Substitute 1 for x and 3 for y in each of the original equations.

$2x + 3y = 11$	$-2x + 5y = 13$
$2(1) + 3(3) \stackrel{?}{=} 11$	$-2(1) + 5(3) \stackrel{?}{=} 13$
$11 = 11$ ✓	$13 = 13$ ✓

Resource Planning Guide

Chapter Resource Book
• Teaching Guide/Lesson Plan (pp. 27–28)
• Practice levels A, B, C (pp. 30–32)
• Study Guide (pp. 33–34)
• Catch-up for Absent Students (p. 35)
• Problem Solving Workshop (p. 36)
• Challenge (p. 37)

Workbooks
• Notetaking Guide (pp. 155–157)
• Practice Workbook (pp. 109–110)

Teaching Options
• **Power Presentations CD-ROM** provides dynamic electronic teaching resources for the classroom.
• **Activity Generator CD-ROM** provides editable activities for all ability levels.

Interactive Technology
• Easy Planner
• Power Presentations CD-ROM
• Activity Generator CD-ROM
• Animated Algebra
• Test Generator CD-ROM
• Online Quiz
• eWorkbook
• eEdition
• @HomeTutor

Resources for English Learners
• Quick Reference for English Learners
• Spanish Study Guide
• Multi-Language Visual Glossary
• Student Resources in Spanish

See also the *Algebra 1 Toolkit* for more strategies for meeting individual needs.

EXAMPLE 2 Use subtraction to eliminate a variable

Solve the linear system: $4x + 3y = 2$ **Equation 1**
$5x + 3y = -2$ **Equation 2**

SUBTRACT EQUATIONS
When the coefficients of one variable are the same, subtract the equations to eliminate the variable.

Solution

STEP 1 **Subtract** the equations to eliminate one variable.

$$\begin{array}{r} 4x + 3y = 2 \\ 5x + 3y = -2 \\ \hline -x \qquad = 4 \end{array}$$

STEP 2 **Solve** for x.

$$x = -4$$

STEP 3 **Substitute** -4 for x in either equation and solve for y.

$4x + 3y = 2$ **Write Equation 1.**

$4(-4) + 3y = 2$ **Substitute −4 for x.**

$y = 6$ **Solve for y.**

▶ The solution is $(-4, 6)$.

EXAMPLE 3 Arrange like terms

Solve the linear system: $8x - 4y = -4$ **Equation 1**
$4y = 3x + 14$ **Equation 2**

AVOID ERRORS
Make sure that the equal signs are in the same column, just as the like terms are.

Solution

STEP 1 **Rewrite** Equation 2 so that the like terms are arranged in columns.

$8x - 4y = -4$
$4y = 3x + 14$

$$\begin{array}{r} 8x - 4y = -4 \\ -3x + 4y = 14 \\ \hline 5x \qquad = 10 \end{array}$$

STEP 2 **Add** the equations.

STEP 3 **Solve** for x.

$$x = 2$$

STEP 4 **Substitute** 2 for x in either equation and solve for y.

$4y = 3x + 14$ **Write Equation 2.**

$4y = 3(2) + 14$ **Substitute 2 for x.**

$y = 5$ **Solve for y.**

▶ The solution is $(2, 5)$.

GUIDED PRACTICE for Examples 1, 2, and 3

Solve the linear system.

1. $4x - 3y = 5$ $(-1, -3)$
$-2x + 3y = -7$

2. $-5x - 6y = 8$ $(2, -3)$
$5x + 2y = 4$

3. $6x - 4y = 14$ $(5, 4)$
$-3x + 4y = 1$

4. $7x - 2y = 5$ $(1, 1)$
$7x - 3y = 4$

5. $3x + 4y = -6$ $(-2, 0)$
$2y = 3x + 6$

6. $2x + 5y = 12$ $(1, 2)$
$5y = 4x + 6$

Motivating the Lesson

You and a friend go to a county fair. Your friend pays an entrance fee and buys 8 tickets for rides, and the total cost is $16.50. You buy 6 tickets for rides and your total cost, with the entrance fee, is $14. By writing and solving a linear system, you can determine the entrance fee for the county fair and the cost per ticket for rides at the fair.

3 TEACH

Extra Example 1

Solve the linear system.
$3x + 4y = 8$
$-3x + 5y = 10$ $(0, 2)$

Extra Example 2

Solve the linear system.
$5x + 6y = 4$
$7x + 6y = 8$ $(2, -1)$

Avoiding Common Errors

When using subtraction to solve, as in Example 2, some students may add terms rather than subtract. One way to avoid this error is to use the definition of subtraction to rewrite Equation 2 with opposite signs and then add the equations.

Extra Example 3

Solve the linear system.
$9x - 3y = 18$
$3y = -7x + 30$ $(3, 3)$

Key Question to Ask for Example 3

- How do you know that you need to add the equations in Example 3? **Since the coefficients of y are opposites, you add to solve the system.**

Extra Example 4

A riverboat travels 28 miles upstream in 7 hours. It travels 28 miles downstream in 5 hours. The speed of the current remains the same during the travel upstream and downstream. Find the average speed of the riverboat in still water and the speed of the current. **speed in still water: 4.8 mi/h; speed of current: 0.8 mi/h**

Key Question to Ask for Example 4

- Why is the speed of the current added to the speed of the kayak going downstream? **When the kayak travels downstream, it is moving with the current, which causes its speed to increase.**

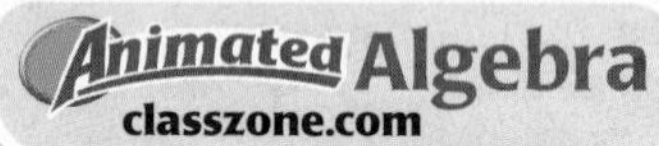

An **Animated Algebra** activity is available on-line for **Example 4**. This activity is also available on the **Power Presentations CD-ROM**.

Closing the Lesson

Have students summarize the major points of the lesson and answer the Essential Question: How do you solve linear systems by eliminating a variable?

- **If the coefficients of one variable are opposites, you add the equations to begin solving the system.**
- **If the coefficients of one variable are the same, you subtract the equations to begin solving the system.**

Add or subtract the equations to eliminate one of the variables. Solve the resulting equation for whichever variable remains, *x* or *y*. Substitute this value of *x* or *y* in either of the original equations to find the value of the eliminated variable.

EXAMPLE 4 Write and solve a linear system

KAYAKING During a kayaking trip, a kayaker travels 12 miles upstream (against the current) and 12 miles downstream (with the current), as shown. The speed of the current remained constant during the trip. Find the average speed of the kayak in still water and the speed of the current.

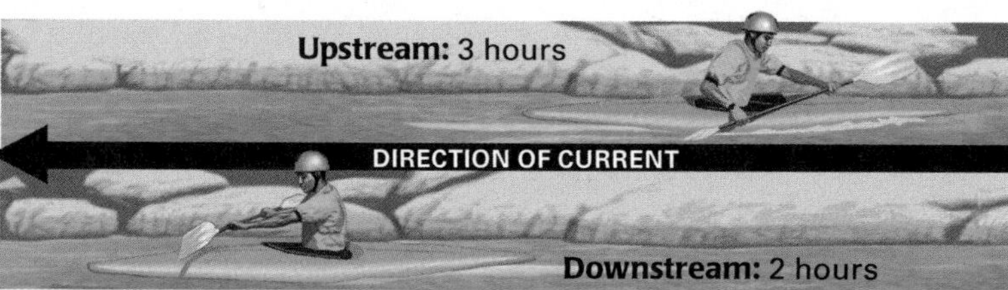

STEP 1 **Write** a system of equations. First find the speed of the kayak going upstream and the speed of the kayak going downstream.

Upstream: $d = rt$ | **Downstream:** $d = rt$

$12 = r \cdot 3$ | $12 = r \cdot 2$

$4 = r$ | $6 = r$

Use the speeds to write a linear system. Let x be the average speed of the kayak in still water, and let y be the speed of the current.

COMBINE SPEEDS
When you go upstream, the speed at which you can travel in still water is decreased by the speed of the current. The opposite is true when you go downstream.

Equation 1: Going upstream

Speed of kayak in still water	−	Speed of current	=	Speed of kayak going upstream
x	−	y	=	4

Equation 2: Going downstream

Speed of kayak in still water	+	Speed of current	=	Speed of kayak going downstream
x	+	y	=	6

STEP 2 **Solve** the system of equations.

$x - y = 4$ **Write Equation 1.**

$x + y = 6$ **Write Equation 2.**

$2x = 10$ **Add equations.**

$x = 5$ **Solve for *x*.**

Substitute 5 for x in Equation 2 and solve for y.

$5 + y = 6$ **Substitute 5 for *x* in Equation 2.**

$y = 1$ **Subtract 5 from each side.**

▶ The average speed of the kayak in still water is 5 miles per hour, and the speed of the current is 1 mile per hour.

Differentiated Instruction

English Learners When discussing **Example 4**, students may have difficulty with the meanings of "upstream" and "downstream". When you go up, you move against the force of gravity; so going upstream is going against the force of the river flow. Similarly, going down is moving with the force of gravity; so going downstream is going with the river flow.

See also the *Algebra 1 Toolkit* for more strategies.

 **GUIDED PRACTICE** for Example 4

7. **WHAT IF?** In Example 4, suppose it takes the kayaker 5 hours to travel 10 miles upstream and 2 hours to travel 10 miles downstream. The speed of the current remains constant during the trip. Find the average speed of the kayak in still water and the speed of the current.
average speed of the kayak: 3.5 mi/h, speed of the current: 1.5 mi/h

7.3 EXERCISES

HOMEWORK KEY
- ◯ = **WORKED-OUT SOLUTIONS** on p. WS16 for Exs. 17 and 41
- ★ = **STANDARDIZED TEST PRACTICE** Exs. 2, 15, 22, 36, and 44
- ◆ = **MULTIPLE REPRESENTATIONS** Ex. 42

SKILL PRACTICE

A

1. **VOCABULARY** Give an example of a linear system in two variables that can be solved by first adding the equations to eliminate one variable.
Sample answer: $x + y = 10$, $x - y = 5$

2. ★ **WRITING** *Explain* how to solve the linear system shown using the elimination method. $2x - y = 2$ Equation 1; $2x + 3y = 22$ Equation 2 *Sample answer:* Subtract Equation 2 from Equation 1 then solve the resulting equation for *y*. Then substitute the value of *y* and solve for *x*.

EXAMPLE 1 on p. 444 for Exs. 3–8

USING ADDITION **Solve the linear system using elimination.**

3. $x + 2y = 13$, $-x + y = 5$ (1, 6)
4. $9x + y = 2$, $-4x - y = -17$ (−3, 29)
5. $-3x - y = 8$, $7x + y = -12$ (−1, −5)
6. $3x - y = 30$, $-3x + 7y = 6$ (12, 6)
7. $-9x + 4y = -17$, $9x - 6y = 3$ (5, 7)
8. $-3x - 5y = -7$, $-4x + 5y = 14$ (−1, 2)

EXAMPLE 2 on p. 445 for Exs. 9–15

USING SUBTRACTION **Solve the linear system using elimination.**

9. $x + y = 1$, $-2x + y = 4$ (−1, 2)
10. $x - y = -4$, $x + 3y = 4$ (−2, 2)
11. $2x - y = 7$, $2x + 7y = 31$ (5, 3)
12. $6x + y = -10$, $5x + y = -10$ (0, −10)
13. $5x + 6y = 50$, $-x + 6y = 26$ (4, 5)
14. $4x - 9y = -21$, $4x + 3y = -9$ (−3, 1)

15. ★ **MULTIPLE CHOICE** Which ordered pair is a solution of the linear system $4x + 9y = -2$ and $11x + 9y = 26$? C

Ⓐ (−2, 4) Ⓑ (2, −4) Ⓒ (4, −2) Ⓓ (4, 2)

EXAMPLE 3 on p. 445 for Exs. 16–22

ARRANGING LIKE TERMS **Solve the linear system using elimination.**

16. $2x - y = 32$, $y - 5x = 13$ (−15, −62)
17. $-8y + 6x = 36$, $6x - y = 15$ (2, −3)
18. $2x - y = -11$, $y = -2x - 13$ (−6, −1)
19. $-x - y = 14$, $x = 5y - 38$ (−18, 4)
20. $11y - 3x = 18$, $-3x = -16y + 33$ (5, 3)
21. $-5x + y = -23$, $-y = 3x - 9$ (4, −3)

22. ★ **MULTIPLE CHOICE** Which ordered pair is a solution of the linear system $2x + y = 10$ and $3y = 2x + 6$? B

Ⓐ (−3, −4) Ⓑ (3, 4) Ⓒ (−4, 3) Ⓓ (4, 3)

4 PRACTICE AND APPLY

Assignment Guide

 **Answer Transparencies available for all exercises**

Basic:
Day 1: pp. 447–450
Exs. 1, 2, 3–21 odd, 22–30, 39–43, 46–54 even

Average:
Day 1: pp. 447–450
Exs. 1, 2, 6–8, 12–15, 19–24, 26–36 even, 39–44, 47–55 odd

Advanced:
Day 1: pp. 447–450
Exs. 1, 2, 7, 8, 13–15, 19–22, 25–33 odd, 34–45*, 49, 52, 54

Block:
pp. 447–450
Exs. 1, 2, 6–8, 12–15, 19–24, 26–36 even, 39–44, 47–55 odd (with 7.2)

Differentiated Instruction

See *Algebra 1 Best Practices Toolkit* for suggestions on addressing the needs of a diverse classroom.

Homework Check

For a quick check of student understanding of key concepts, go over the following exercises:
Basic: 5, 11, 17, 19, 39
Average: 6, 12, 19, 21, 40
Advanced: 8, 14, 20, 21, 41

Extra Practice

- Student Edition, p. 944
- Chapter 7 Resource Book: Practice levels A, B, C, pp. 30–32

Practice Worksheet

An easily-readable reduced practice page (with answers) for this lesson can be found on p. 424C.

Mathematical Reasoning

Exercise 15–22, 25–33 Remind students that after the like terms have been arranged in columns, they need to determine whether to add or subtract to solve the system. Refer them to the notes next to Examples 1 and 2 for guidance on whether to add or subtract.

Exercise 36 Point out to students that they should use the same reasoning for eliminating a variable in a system of three equations as they use in a system of two equations.

23. *Sample answer:* The two equations should be subtracted rather than added; $6x = 8$, $x = \frac{4}{3}$.

24. *Sample answer:* When $-3x$ is moved to the other side, it should become $3x$, the equations should then be subtracted; $3x - 2y = -3$, $3x + 5y = 60$, $-7y = -63$, $y = 9$.

ERROR ANALYSIS ***Describe*** **and correct the error in finding the value of one of the variables in the given linear system.**

23. $5x - 7y = 16$
$-x - 7y = 8$

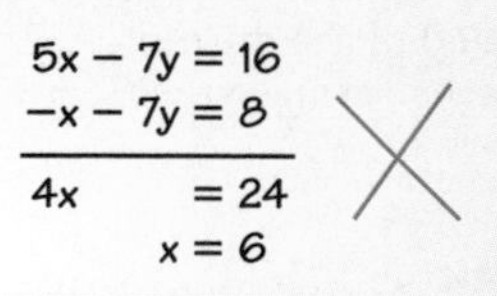

24. $3x - 2y = -3$
$5y = 60 - 3x$

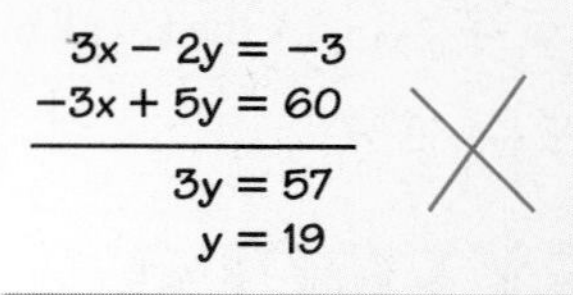

B **SOLVING LINEAR SYSTEMS** **Solve the linear system using elimination.**

25. $-x + \frac{1}{2}y = -19$ (26, 14)
$x - y = 12$

26. $\frac{1}{4}x - \frac{2}{3}y = 7$ (4, −9)
$\frac{1}{2}x + \frac{2}{3}y = -4$

27. $8x - \frac{1}{2}y = -38$ (−4, 12)
$\frac{1}{4}x - \frac{1}{2}y = -7$

28. $5.2x + 3.5y = 54$ (5, 8)
$-3.6x + 3.5y = 10$

29. $1.3x - 3y = -17.6$ (−2, 5)
$-1.3x + 4.5y = 25.1$

30. $-2.6x - 3.2y = 4.8$
$1.9x - 3.2y = -4.2$
(−2, 0.125)

31. $\frac{4}{5}x + \frac{2}{5}y = 14$ (5, 25)
$\frac{2}{5}y + \frac{1}{5}x = 11$

32. $2.7x + 1.5y = 36$ (10, 6)
$3.5y = 2.7x - 6$

33. $4 - 4.8x = 1.7y$ (−2, 8)
$12.8 + 1.7y = -13.2x$

34. WRITING AN EQUATION OF A LINE Use the following steps to write an equation of the line that passes through the points (1, 2) and (−4, 12).

a. Write a system of linear equations by substituting 1 for x and 2 for y in $y = mx + b$ and −4 for x and 12 for y in $y = mx + b$. $2 = m + b$, $12 = -4m + b$

b. Solve the system of linear equations from part (a). What is the slope of the line? What is the y-intercept? slope: −2; y-intercept: 4

c. Write an equation of the line that passes through (1, 2) and (−4, 12). $y = -2x + 4$

35. **GEOMETRY** The rectangle has a perimeter P of 14 feet, and twice its length ℓ is equal to 1 less than 4 times its width w. Write and solve a system of linear equations to find the length and the width of the rectangle. $\ell = 4.5$ ft, $w = 2.5$ ft

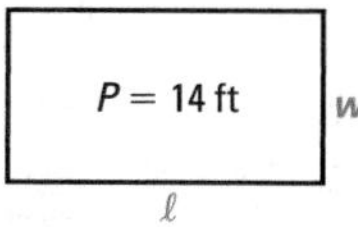

36. ★ **SHORT RESPONSE** Find the solution of the system of linear equations below. *Explain* your steps. (−1, 3). *Sample answer:* First solve the system that consists of Equations 1 and 2 using elimination. Then check the solution for all three equations.

$x + 3y = 8$ Equation 1
$x - 6y = -19$ Equation 2
$5x - 3y = -14$ Equation 3

C **37. CHALLENGE** For $a \neq 0$, what is the solution of the system $ax + 2y = 4$ and $ax - 3y = -6$? (0, 2)

38. CHALLENGE Solve for x, y, and z in the system of equations below. *Explain* your steps. (−5, 4, 2). *Sample answer:* Subtract Equation 2 from Equation 1 to solve for y. Then substitute y into Equation 3 to solve for x. Then substitute x and y into Equation 1 or Equation 2 to solve for z. Check solution in all three equations.

$x + 7y + 3z = 29$ Equation 1
$3z + x - 2y = -7$ Equation 2
$5y = 10 - 2x$ Equation 3

◯ = **WORKED-OUT SOLUTIONS on p. WS1** ★ = **STANDARDIZED TEST PRACTICE**

PROBLEM SOLVING

EXAMPLE 4 A on p. 446 for Exs. 39–41

39. ROWING During a practice, a 4 person crew team rows a rowing shell upstream (against the current) and then rows the same distance downstream (with the current). The shell moves upstream at a speed of 4.3 meters per second and downstream at a speed of 4.9 meters per second. The speed of the current remains constant. Use the models below to write and solve a system of equations to find the average speed of the shell in still water and the speed of the current.
speed in still water: 4.6 m/sec, speed of current: 0.3 m/sec

Upstream

Speed of shell in still water − Speed of current = Speed of shell

Downstream

Speed of shell in still water + Speed of current = Speed of shell

@HomeTutor for problem solving help at classzone.com

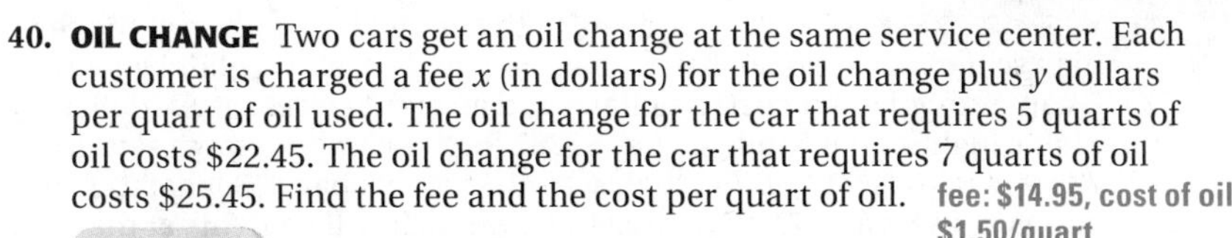

40. OIL CHANGE Two cars get an oil change at the same service center. Each customer is charged a fee x (in dollars) for the oil change plus y dollars per quart of oil used. The oil change for the car that requires 5 quarts of oil costs $22.45. The oil change for the car that requires 7 quarts of oil costs $25.45. Find the fee and the cost per quart of oil. **fee: $14.95, cost of oil: $1.50/quart**

@HomeTutor for problem solving help at classzone.com

41. PHONES Cellular phone ring tones can be monophonic or polyphonic. Monophonic ring tones play one tone at a time, and polyphonic ring tones play multiple tones at a time. The table shows the ring tones downloaded from a website by two customers. Use the information to find the cost of a monophonic ring tone and a polyphonic ring tone, assuming that all monophonic ring tones cost the same and all polyphonic ring tones cost the same. **monophonic ring tone: $1.95, polyphonic ring tone: $3.50**

Customer	Monophonic ring tones	Polyphonic ring tones	Total cost (dollars)
Julie	3	2	12.85
Tate	1	2	8.95

42. MULTIPLE REPRESENTATIONS For a floral arrangement class, Alicia has to create an arrangement of twigs and flowers that has a total of 9 objects. She has to pay for the twigs and flowers that she uses in her arrangement. Each twig costs $1, and each flower costs $3.

a. Writing a System Alicia spends $15 on the twigs and flowers. Write and solve a linear system to find the number of twigs and the number of flowers she used.

b. Making a Table Make a table showing the number of twigs in the arrangement and the total cost of the arrangement when the number of flowers purchased is 0, 1, 2, 3, 4, or 5. Use the table to check your answer to part (a). **See margin.**

42a. Let x represent the number of twigs and y represent the number of flowers; $x + 3y = 15$, $x + y = 9$, 6 twigs and 3 flowers.

Avoiding Common Errors

Exercise 40 When some students use Example 4 as a model for this exercise, they may believe that they should subtract the x- and y-values for the first equation and add the x- and y-values for the second equation. Remind these students that the context of the problem determines whether they add or subtract the x- and y-values in each equation.

Study Strategy

Exercise 43 Suggest that students use Example 4 as a model for solving this problem. Point out that wind speed is comparable to current speed and that flying into the wind is comparable to going upstream, while flying with the wind is comparable to going downstream.

42b.

Flowers	Twigs	Cost
0	9	$9
1	8	$11
2	7	$13
3	6	$15
4	5	$17
5	4	$19

5 ASSESS AND RETEACH

Daily Homework Quiz

 **Transparency Available**

Solve the linear system using elimination.

1. $-5x + y = 18$
   $3x - y = -10$ $(-4, -2)$
2. $4x + 2y = 14$
   $4x - 3y = -11$ $(1, 5)$
3. $2x - y = -14$
   $y = 3x + 6$ $(8, 30)$
4. $x + 4y = 15$
   $2y = x - 9$ $(11, 1)$
5. A business center charges a flat fee to send faxes plus a fee per page. You send one fax with 4 pages for \$5.36 and another fax with 7 pages for \$7.88. Find the flat fee and the cost per page to send a fax. flat fee: \$2, price per page: \$.84

Online Quiz

Available at **classzone.com**

Diagnosis/Remediation

- Practice A, B, C in Chapter 7 Resource Book, pp. 30–32
- Study Guide in Chapter 7 Resource Book, pp. 33–34
- Practice Workbook, pp. 109–110
- @HomeTutor

Challenge

Additional challenge is available in the Chapter 7 Resource Book, p. 37.

B **43. MULTI-STEP PROBLEM** On a typical day with light winds, the 1800 mile flight from Charlotte, North Carolina, to Phoenix, Arizona, takes longer than the return trip because the plane has to fly into the wind.

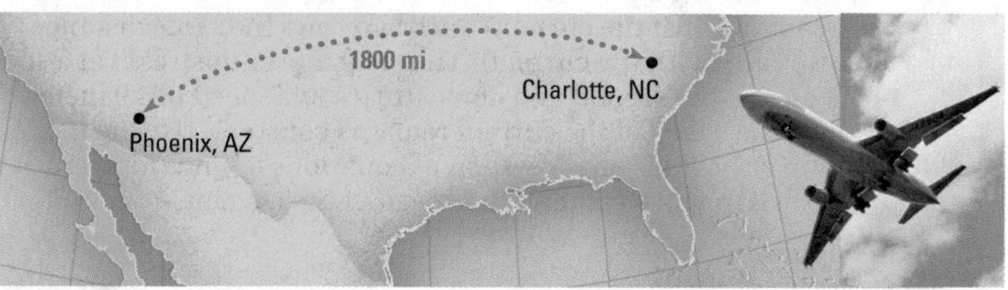

a. The flight from Charlotte to Phoenix is 4 hours 30 minutes long, and the flight from Phoenix to Charlotte is 4 hours long. Find the average speed (in miles per hour) of the airplane on the way to Phoenix and on the return trip to Charlotte. flight to Phoenix: 400 mi/h, flight to Charlotte: 450 mi/h

b. Let s be the speed (in miles per hour) of the plane with no wind, and let w be the speed (in miles per hour) of the wind. Use your answer to part (a) to write and solve a system of equations to find the speed of the plane with no wind and the speed of the wind.
$s + w = 450$, $s - w = 400$; plane: 425 mi/h, wind: 25 mi/h

44. ★ SHORT RESPONSE The students in the graduating classes at the three high schools in a school district have to pay for their caps and gowns. A cap-and-gown set costs x dollars, and an extra tassel costs y dollars. At one high school, students pay \$3262 for 215 cap-and-gown sets and 72 extra tassels. At another high school, students pay \$3346 for 221 cap-and-gown sets and 72 extra tassels. How much will students at the third high school pay for 218 cap-and-gown sets and 56 extra tassels? *Explain.*
\$3248. *Sample answer:* Each cap-and-gown costs \$14 and each extra tassel costs \$3.50.

C **45. CHALLENGE** A clothing manufacturer makes men's dress shirts. For the production process, an ideal sleeve length x (in centimeters) for each shirt size and an allowable deviation y (in centimeters) from the ideal length are established. The deviation is expressed as $\pm y$. For a specific shirt size, the minimum allowable sleeve length is 62.2 centimeters and the maximum allowable sleeve length is 64.8 centimeters. Find the ideal sleeve length and the allowable deviation.
ideal sleeve length: 63.5 cm, allowable deviation: 1.3 cm

ILLINOIS MIXED REVIEW

TEST PRACTICE at classzone.com

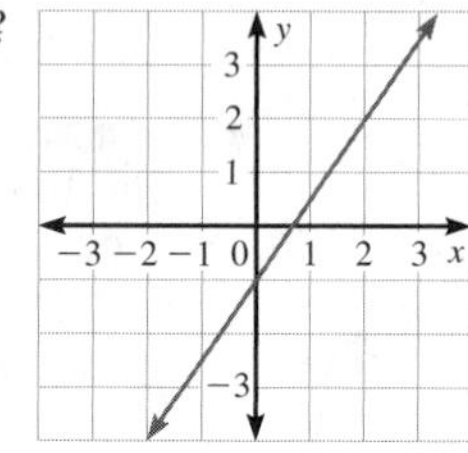

46. What is the slope of the linear function shown in the graph?

Ⓐ $\frac{1}{3}$ Ⓑ $\frac{2}{3}$ C

Ⓒ $\frac{3}{2}$ Ⓓ 3

47. Suppose the line shown is translated 2 units to the left and 1 unit down. Which point would lie on the translated line?

Ⓐ $(-2, -2)$ Ⓑ $(-1, 1)$ Ⓒ $(0, 2)$ Ⓓ $(2, 3)$

A

7.4 Solve Linear Systems by Multiplying First

8.11.17 Solve systems of equations and inequalities.

Before You solved linear systems by adding or subtracting.

Now You will solve linear systems by multiplying first.

Why So you can solve a problem about preparing food, as in Ex. 39.

Key Vocabulary
- **least common multiple,** *p. 910*

In a linear system like the one below, neither variable can be eliminated by adding or subtracting the equations. For systems like these, you can multiply one or both of the equations by a constant so that adding or subtracting the equations will eliminate one variable.

$5x + 2y = 16 \xrightarrow{\times 2} 10x + 4y = 32$

$3x - 4y = 20 \longrightarrow 3x - 4y = 20$

The new system is equivalent to the original system.

EXAMPLE 1 Multiply one equation, then add

Solve the linear system: $6x + 5y = 19$ **Equation 1**
$2x + 3y = 5$ **Equation 2**

Solution

STEP 1 **Multiply** Equation 2 by -3 so that the coefficients of x are opposites.

$6x + 5y = 19 \qquad\qquad 6x + 5y = 19$

$2x + 3y = 5 \xrightarrow{\times(-3)} -6x - 9y = -15$

STEP 2 **Add** the equations. $-4y = 4$

ANOTHER WAY You can also multiply Equation 2 by 3 and subtract the equations.

STEP 3 **Solve** for y. $y = -1$

STEP 4 **Substitute** -1 for y in either of the original equations and solve for x.

$2x + 3y = 5$ **Write Equation 2.**

$2x + 3(-1) = 5$ **Substitute −1 for y.**

$2x + (-3) = 5$ **Multiply.**

$2x = 8$ **Subtract −3 from each side.**

$x = 4$ **Divide each side by 2.**

▶ The solution is $(4, -1)$.

CHECK Substitute 4 for x and -1 for y in each of the original equations.

Equation 1	Equation 2
$6x + 5y = 19$	$2x + 3y = 5$
$6(4) + 5(-1) \stackrel{?}{=} 19$	$2(4) + 3(-1) \stackrel{?}{=} 5$
$19 = 19$ ✓	$5 = 5$ ✓

1 PLAN AND PREPARE

Warm-Up Exercises

Transparency Available

Solve the linear system.

1. $4x - 3y = 15$
$2x - 3y = 9$ **(3, −1)**

2. $-2x + y = -8$
$2x - 2y = 8$ **(4, 0)**

3. You row a canoe 10 miles upstream in 2.5 hours and 10 miles downstream in 2 hours. What is the average speed of the canoe in still water? **4.5 mi/h**

Notetaking Guide

Transparency Available

Promotes interactive learning and notetaking skills, pp. 158–159.

Pacing

Basic: 1 day
Average: 1 day
Advanced: 1 day
Block: 0.5 block with 7.5
- See *Teaching Guide/Lesson Plan.*

2 FOCUS AND MOTIVATE

Essential Question

Big Idea 2, p. 425

How do you solve linear systems by multiplying first? **Tell students they will learn how to answer this question by multiplying one or both equations by a constant and then adding or subtracting to eliminate a variable.**

Resource Planning Guide

Chapter Resource Book
- Teaching Guide/Lesson Plan (pp. 38–39)
- Activity Master (p. 40)
- Practice levels A, B, C (pp. 41–43)
- Study Guide (pp. 44–45)
- Catch-up for Absent Students (p. 46)
- Problem Solving Workshop (p. 47)
- Challenge (p. 49)

Workbooks
- Notetaking Guide (pp. 158–159)
- Practice Workbook (pp. 111–112)

Teaching Options
- **Power Presentations CD-ROM** provides dynamic electronic teaching resources for the classroom.
- **Activity Generator CD-ROM** provides editable activities for all ability levels.

Interactive Technology
- Easy Planner
- Power Presentations CD-ROM
- Activity Generator CD-ROM
- Animated Algebra
- Test Generator CD-ROM
- Online Quiz
- eWorkbook
- eEdition
- @HomeTutor

Resources for English Learners
- Quick Reference for English Learners
- Spanish Study Guide
- Multi-Language Visual Glossary
- Student Resources in Spanish

See also the *Algebra 1 Toolkit* for more strategies for meeting individual needs.

Motivating the Lesson

A concession stand offers two different soft drink specials. One special has 3 large drinks and 2 medium drinks for \$15. The other has 2 large drinks and 3 medium drinks for \$13.75. By knowing how to use multiplication with elimination to solve a linear system, you can determine the cost of each drink size.

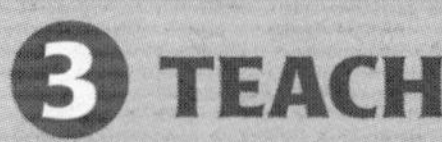

3 TEACH

Extra Example 1

Solve the linear system.
$2x + y = -9$
$4x + 11y = 9$ **(−6, 3)**

Key Question to Ask for Example 1

- Why do you eliminate x rather than y? **Since 6 is a multiple of 2, it is easier to eliminate x. To eliminate y, you would need to multiply by a fraction, either $\frac{5}{3}$ or $\frac{3}{5}$.**

Extra Example 2

Solve the linear system.
$2x - 3y = 6$
$4y = -7x - 8$ **(0, −2)**

Key Question to Ask for Example 2

- Is it possible to eliminate x by multiplying each equation by a constant? Explain. **You can eliminate x by multiplying Equation 1 by 3 and Equation 2 by 4.**

An **Animated Algebra** activity is available on-line for **Example 2**. This activity is also available on the **Power Presentations CD-ROM**.

MULTIPLYING BOTH EQUATIONS To eliminate one variable when adding or subtracting equations in a linear system, you may need to multiply both equations by constants. Use the least common multiple of the coefficients of one of the variables to determine the constants.

$2x - 9y = 1$ → × 4 → $8x - 36y = 4$

$7x - 12y = 23$ → × 3 → $21x - 36y = 69$

The least common multiple of −9 and −12 is −36.

EXAMPLE 2 Multiply both equations, then subtract

Solve the linear system: $4x + 5y = 35$ **Equation 1**
$2y = 3x - 9$ **Equation 2**

Solution

STEP 1 **Arrange** the equations so that like terms are in columns.

$4x + 5y = 35$ **Write Equation 1.**

$-3x + 2y = -9$ **Rewrite Equation 2.**

ANOTHER WAY
You can also multiply Equation 1 by 3 and Equation 2 by 4. Then add the revised equations to eliminate x.

STEP 2 **Multiply** Equation 1 by 2 and Equation 2 by 5 so that the coeffcient of y in each equation is the least common multiple of 5 and 2, or 10.

$4x + 5y = 35$ → × 2 → $8x + 10y = 70$

$-3x + 2y = -9$ → × 5 → $-15x + 10y = -45$

STEP 3 **Subtract** the equations. $23x = 115$

STEP 4 **Solve** for x. → $x = 5$

STEP 5 **Substitute** 5 for x in either of the original equations and solve for y.

$4x + 5y = 35$ **Write Equation 1.**

$4(5) + 5y = 35$ **Substitute 5 for x.**

$y = 3$ **Solve for y.**

▶ The solution is (5, 3).

CHECK Substitute 5 for x and 3 for y in each of the original equations.

Equation 1	Equation 2
$4x + 5y = 35$	$2y = 3x - 9$
$4(5) + 5(3) \stackrel{?}{=} 35$	$2(3) \stackrel{?}{=} 3(5) - 9$
$35 = 35$ ✓	$6 = 6$ ✓

Animated Algebra at classzone.com

GUIDED PRACTICE for Examples 1 and 2

Solve the linear system using elimination.

1. $6x - 2y = 1$ **(−0.5, −2)**
$-2x + 3y = -5$

2. $2x + 5y = 3$ **(9, −3)**
$3x + 10y = -3$

3. $3x - 7y = 5$ **(−10, −5)**
$9y = 5x + 5$

Differentiated Instruction

English Learners Caution students not to confuse the words "equal" and "equivalent". In **Example 2**, multiplying the first equation by 2 and the second equation by 5 produces "equivalent" equations, because the solution set is not changed. The sides of each equation are "equal".

See also the *Algebra 1 Toolkit* for more strategies.

EXAMPLE 3 Standardized Test Practice

Darlene is making a quilt that has alternating stripes of regular quilting fabric and sateen fabric. She spends $76 on a total of 16 yards of the two fabrics at a fabric store. Which system of equations can be used to find the amount x (in yards) of regular quilting fabric and the amount y (in yards) of sateen fabric she purchased?

Sateen fabric costs $6 per yard.
Quilting fabric costs $4 per yard.

ELIMINATE CHOICES
You can eliminate choice A because $x + y$ cannot equal both 16 and 76.

Ⓐ $x + y = 16$
$x + y = 76$

Ⓑ $x + y = 16$
$4x + 6y = 76$

Ⓒ $x + y = 76$
$4x + 6y = 16$

Ⓓ $x + y = 16$
$6x + 4y = 76$

Solution

Write a system of equations where x is the number of yards of regular quilting fabric purchased and y is the number of yards of sateen fabric purchased.

Equation 1: Amount of fabric

Amount of quilting fabric	+	Amount of sateen fabric	=	Total yards of fabric
x	+	y	=	16

Equation 2: Cost of fabric

Quilting fabric price (dollars/yd)	·	Amount of quilting fabric (yd)	+	Sateen fabric price (dollars/yd)	·	Amount of sateen fabric (yd)	=	Total cost (dollars)
4	·	x	+	6	·	y	=	76

The system of equations is: $x + y = 16$ **Equation 1**
$4x + 6y = 76$ **Equation 2**

▶ The correct answer is B. Ⓐ Ⓑ Ⓒ Ⓓ

GUIDED PRACTICE for Example 3

4. **SOCCER** A sports equipment store is having a sale on soccer balls. A soccer coach purchases 10 soccer balls and 2 soccer ball bags for $155. Another soccer coach purchases 12 soccer balls and 3 soccer ball bags for $189. Find the cost of a soccer ball and the cost of a soccer ball bag.
soccer ball: $14.50, soccer ball bag: $5

Extra Example 3

Mr. Alvarado bought a total of 20 pounds of grass seed at the nursery for $168. He paid $9 per pound for Kentucky bluegrass and $6 per pound for Tall Fescue. Which system of equations can be used to find the amount x (in pounds) of Kentucky bluegrass and the amount y (in pounds) of Tall Fescue Mr. Alvarado purchased? **D**

Ⓐ $x + y = 168$
$9x + 6y = 20$

Ⓑ $x + y = 20$
$6x + 9y = 168$

Ⓒ $x + y = 168$
$6x + 9y = 20$

Ⓓ $x + y = 20$
$9x + 6y = 168$

Mathematical Reasoning

You may want to point out that choice C does not make sense mathematically because one yard each of quilting fabric and sateen cannot cost $76 if one costs $4 per yard and one costs $6 per yard.

Closing the Lesson

Have students summarize the major points of the lesson and answer the Essential Question: How do you solve linear systems by multiplying first?

- **Multiply one or both equations of a linear system by a constant or constants and then add or subtract to eliminate a variable.**

Determine whether you need to multiply one equation or both equations by constants so you can eliminate one of the variables. After multiplying, use addition or subtraction to eliminate the variable. Solve the equation and then substitute in one of the original equations to find the value of the eliminated variable.

4 PRACTICE AND APPLY

Assignment Guide

Answer Transparencies available for all exercises

Basic:
Day 1: SRH p. 911 Exs. 25, 26, 32, 36
pp. 454–457
Exs. 1, 2, 3–17 odd, 18–25, 37–41, 46–58 even

Average:
Day 1: pp. 454–457
Exs. 1, 2, 6–8, 13–20, 21–33 odd, 34, 37–42, 45–57 odd

Advanced:
Day 1: pp. 454–457
Exs. 1, 7, 8, 15–18, 21–36*, 39–44*, 47, 52, 58

Block:
pp. 454–457
Exs. 1, 2, 6–8, 13–20, 21–33 odd, 34, 37–42, 45–57 odd (with 7.5)

Differentiated Instruction

See *Algebra 1 Best Practices Toolkit* for suggestions on addressing the needs of a diverse classroom.

Homework Check

For a quick check of student understanding of key concepts, go over the following exercises:

Basic: 5, 11, 13, 37, 38
Average: 7, 14, 21, 38, 39
Advanced: 8, 16, 28, 39, 40

Extra Practice

- Student Edition, p. 944
- Chapter 7 Resource Book: Practice levels A, B, C, pp. 41–43

Practice Worksheet

An easily-readable reduced practice page (with answers) for this lesson can be found on p. 424C.

CONCEPT SUMMARY *For Your Notebook*

Methods for Solving Linear Systems

Method	Example	When to Use
Table (p. 426)		When x-values are integers, so that equal values can be seen in the table
Graphing (p. 427)	$3x - 2y = 2$; $x + y = 4$	When you want to see the lines that the equations represent
Substitution (p. 435)	$y = 4 - 2x$ $4x + 2y = 8$	When one equation is already solved for x or y
Addition (p. 444)	$4x + 7y = 15$ $6x - 7y = 5$	When the coefficients of one variable are opposites
Subtraction (p. 445)	$3x + 5y = -13$ $3x + y = -5$	When the coefficients of one variable are the same
Multiplication (p. 451)	$9x + 2y = 38$ $3x - 5y = 7$	When no corresponding coefficients are the same or opposites

Table example:

x	$y = 2x$	$y = 3x - 1$
0	0	−1
1	2	2
2	4	5

7.4 EXERCISES

HOMEWORK KEY
○ = **WORKED-OUT SOLUTIONS** on p. WS17 for Exs. 15 and 39
★ = **STANDARDIZED TEST PRACTICE** Exs. 2, 18, 34, 41, and 42
◆ = **MULTIPLE REPRESENTATIONS** Ex. 40

SKILL PRACTICE

1. **VOCABULARY** What is the least common multiple of 12 and 18? 36

2. ★ **WRITING** *Explain* how to solve the linear system using the elimination method.
$2x - 3y = -4$ **Equation 1**
$7x + 9y = -5$ **Equation 2**
Sample answer: Multiply Equation 1 by 3 and add to Equation 2. Then solve for x and substitute to find y.

EXAMPLE 1 on p. 451 for Exs. 3–8

SOLVING LINEAR SYSTEMS **Solve the linear system using elimination.**

3. $x + y = 2$ (1, 1)
$2x + 7y = 9$

4. $3x - 2y = 3$ (5, 6)
$-x + y = 1$

5. $4x + 3y = 8$ (5, −4)
$x - 2y = 13$

6. $10x - 9y = 46$ (19, 16)
$-2x + 3y = 10$

7. $8x - 5y = 11$ (2, 1)
$4x - 3y = 5$

8. $11x - 20y = 28$ (8, 3)
$3x + 4y = 36$

EXAMPLE 2 on p. 452 for Exs. 9–20

19. *Sample answer:* The two equations should be subtracted rather than added; $-x = -9, x = 9$.

SOLVING LINEAR SYSTEMS Solve the linear system using elimination.

9. $4x - 3y = 8$ $(-7, -12)$
$5x - 2y = -11$

10. $-2x - 5y = 9$ $(-17, 5)$
$3x + 11y = 4$

11. $7x - 6y = -1$ $(5, 6)$
$5x - 4y = 1$

12. $7x + 3y = -12$ $(-6, 10)$
$2x + 5y = 38$

13. $9x - 8y = 4$ $(4, 4)$
$2x - 3y = -4$

14. $12x - 7y = -2$ $(1, 2)$
$-8x + 11y = 14$

15. $9x + 2y = 39$ $(5, -3)$
$6x + 13y = -9$

16. $-7x + 10y = 11$ $(7, 6)$
$-8x + 15y = 34$

17. $-14x + 15y = 15$ $\left(4\frac{2}{7}, 5\right)$
$21x - 20y = -10$

18. ★ **MULTIPLE CHOICE** Which ordered pair is a solution of the linear system $15x + 8y = 6$ and $25x + 12y = 14$? D

Ⓐ $(-3, -2)$ Ⓑ $(-3, 2)$ Ⓒ $(-2, -3)$ Ⓓ $(2, -3)$

ERROR ANALYSIS ***Describe*** **and correct the error when solving the linear system.** 19–20. See margin.

20. *Sample answer:* The right side of the equations were not multiplied; $27x + 24y = 33$, $28x + 24y = 36$, $-x = -3, x = 3$.

19.

$2x - 3y = -9 \xrightarrow{\times 2} 4x - 6y = -18$
$5x - 6y = -9 \qquad 5x - 6y = -9$
$9x = -27$
$x = -3$

20.

$9x + 8y = 11 \xrightarrow{\times 3} 27x + 24y = 11$
$7x + 6y = 9 \xrightarrow{\times 4} 28x + 24y = 9$
$-x = 2$
$x = -2$

B **SOLVING LINEAR SYSTEMS Solve the linear system using any algebraic method.**

21. $3x + 2y = 4$ $(2, -1)$
$2y = 8 - 5x$

22. $4x - 5y = 18$ $\left(3\frac{4}{11}, -\frac{10}{11}\right)$
$3x = y + 11$

23. $8x - 9y = -15$ $\left(-4\frac{5}{22}, -2\frac{1}{11}\right)$
$-4x = 19 + y$

24. $0.3x + 0.1y = -0.1$ $(-1, 2)$
$-x + y = 3$

25. $4.4x - 3.6y = 7.6$ $(5, 4)$
$x - y = 1$

26. $3x - 2y = -20$ $(-2, 7)$
$x + 1.2y = 6.4$

27. $0.2x - 1.5y = -1$ $(10, 2)$
$x - 4.5y = 1$

28. $1.5x - 3.5y = -5$ $(20, 10)$
$-1.2x + 2.5y = 1$

29. $4.9x + 2.4y = 7.4$ $(2, -1)$
$0.7x + 3.6y = -2.2$

30. $x + y = 0$ $(2, -2)$
$\frac{1}{2}x - \frac{1}{2}y = 2$

31. $3x + y = \frac{1}{3}$ $\left(\frac{1}{3}, -\frac{2}{3}\right)$
$2x - 3y = \frac{8}{3}$

32. $\frac{3}{5}x - \frac{3}{4}y = -3$ $(10, 12)$
$\frac{2}{5}x + \frac{1}{3}y = 8$

33. **GEOMETRY** A rectangle has a perimeter of 18 inches. A new rectangle is formed by doubling the width w and tripling the length ℓ, as shown. The new rectangle has a perimeter P of 46 inches.

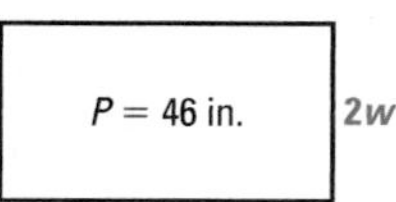

a. Write and solve a system of linear equations to find the length and width of the original rectangle.
$2\ell + 2w = 18$, $6\ell + 4w = 46$; length: 5 in., width: 4 in.

b. Find the length and width of the new rectangle.
length: 15 in., width: 8 in.

34. ★ **WRITING** For which values of a can you solve the linear system $ax + 3y = 2$ and $4x + 5y = 6$ without multiplying first? *Explain.*
4 and −4. *Sample answer:* For these values, you can add or subtract to eliminate the x term.

C **CHALLENGE Find the values of *a* and *b* so that the linear system has the given solution.**

$ax - by = 4$ Equation 1
$bx - ay = 10$ Equation 2

35. $(4, 2)$ $a = 3, b = 4$

36. $(2, 1)$ $a = 6, b = 8$

Avoiding Common Errors

Exercises 9–17, 21–32 Some students may fail to subtract the equations in a linear system when the coefficients of a variable are the same. Suggest that they give the equations a second look to make sure that the coefficients of the eliminated variable are opposites.

Graphing Calculator

Exercises 24–32 Students may want to graph these linear systems to check their solutions. They should enter the equations using [y=], and adjust the standard viewing window if necessary. The intersect feature will show the coordinates of the intersection point.

Mathematical Reasoning

Exercises 37–40 Before students begin these exercises, you may want to discuss how a system of linear equations represents a real-world situation. You could point out in Exercise 37 that one equation represents the total number of books and the other equation represents the cost of the books. In contrast, in Exercise 38, one equation represents the number of individual songs and albums and their cost for one person and the other equation represents the same information for a different person.

Internet Reference

Exercise 39 Information about the various apple varieties can be found at www.urbanext.uiuc.edu/apple.varieties.html

40b.

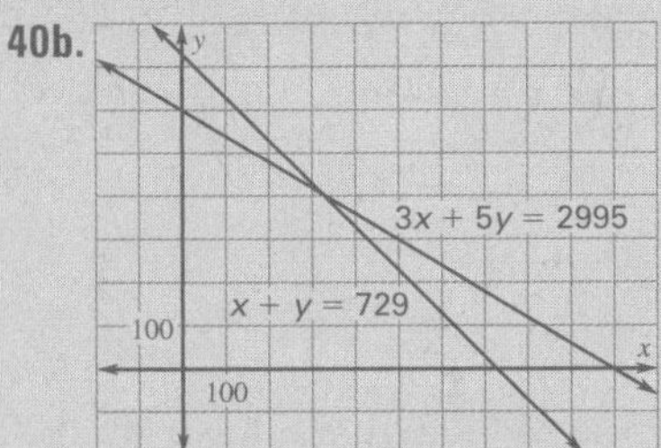

42. *Sample answer:* Two cars are traveling on the same route. One car leaves 30 minutes before the other car and travels at a rate of 40 miles per hour. If the other car travels 45 miles per hour, how many hours will it take for the second car to catch the first car? 4 h, the second car will have to travel 4 hours in order to catch the first car.

PROBLEM SOLVING

EXAMPLE 3 A on p. 453 for Exs. 37–39

37. BOOK SALE A library is having a book sale to raise money. Hardcover books cost \$4 each and paperback books cost \$2 each. A person spends \$26 for 8 books. How many hardcover books did she purchase? **5 hardcover books**

@HomeTutor for problem solving help at classzone.com

38. MUSIC A website allows users to download individual songs or an entire album. All individual songs cost the same to download, and all albums cost the same to download. Ryan pays \$14.94 to download 5 individual songs and 1 album. Seth pays \$22.95 to download 3 individual songs and 2 albums. How much does the website charge to download a song? an entire album? **\$.99; \$9.99**

@HomeTutor for problem solving help at classzone.com

(39.) FARM PRODUCTS The table shows the number of apples needed to make the apple pies and applesauce sold at a farm store. During a recent apple picking at the farm, 169 Granny Smith apples and 95 Golden Delicious apples were picked. How many apple pies and batches of applesauce can be made if every apple is used? **21 pies, 16 batches of applesauce**

Type of apple	Granny Smith	Golden Delicious
Needed for a pie	5	3
Needed for a batch of applesauce	4	2

B

40. ◆ MULTIPLE REPRESENTATIONS Tickets for admission to a high school football game cost \$3 for students and \$5 for adults. During one game, \$2995 was collected from the sale of 729 tickets.

a. **Writing a System** Write and solve a system of linear equations to find the number of tickets sold to students and the number of tickets sold to adults.

b. **Drawing a Graph** Graph the system of linear equations. Use the graph to determine whether your answer to part (a) is reasonable. **The answer is reasonable; see margin for art.**

40a. Let x represent the number of student tickets and y represent the number of adult tickets; $3x + 5y = 2995$, $x + y = 729$, 325 student tickets and 404 adult tickets.

41. ★ SHORT RESPONSE A dim sum restaurant offers two sizes of dishes: small and large. All small dishes cost the same and all large dishes cost the same. The bills show the cost of the food before the tip is included. What will 3 small and 2 large dishes cost before the tip is included? *Explain.*

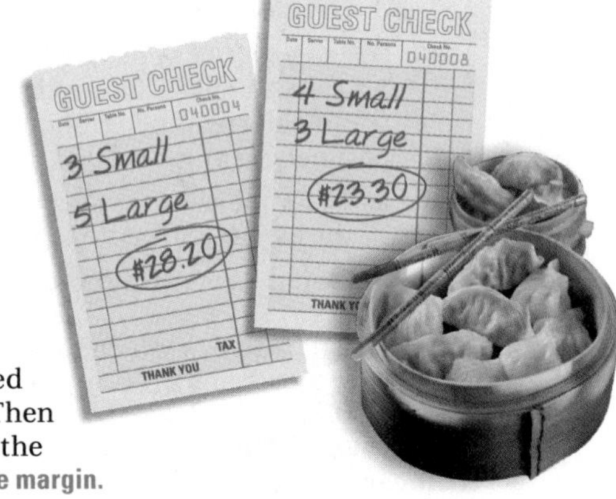

41. \$16.50; a small costs \$2.90, and a large costs \$3.90; $3(2.90) + 2(3.90) = 16.50$.

42. ★ OPEN-ENDED *Describe* a real-world problem that can be solved using a system of linear equations. Then solve the problem and explain what the solution means in this situation. **See margin.**

○ = WORKED-OUT SOLUTIONS on p. WS1 ★ = STANDARDIZED TEST PRACTICE ◆ = MULTIPLE REPRESENTATIONS

C **43. INVESTMENTS** Matt invested \$2000 in stocks and bonds. This year the bonds paid 8% interest, and the stocks paid 6% in dividends. Matt received a total of \$144 in interest and dividends. How much money did he invest in stocks? in bonds? **\$800; \$1200**

44. CHALLENGE You drive a car 45 miles at an average speed r (in miles per hour) to reach your destination. Due to traffic, your average speed on the return trip is $\frac{3}{4}r$. The round trip took a total of 1 hour 45 minutes. Find the average speed for each leg of your trip. **first leg: 60 mi/h, second leg: 45 mi/h**

ILLINOIS MIXED REVIEW

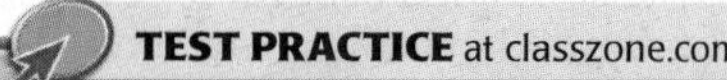

45. The net of a cube is shown. Use a ruler to measure the dimensions of the cube to the nearest half centimeter. Find the volume of the cube to the nearest cubic centimeter.

Ⓐ 6 cm^3 **B**

Ⓑ 8 cm^3

Ⓒ 16 cm^3

Ⓓ 38 cm^3

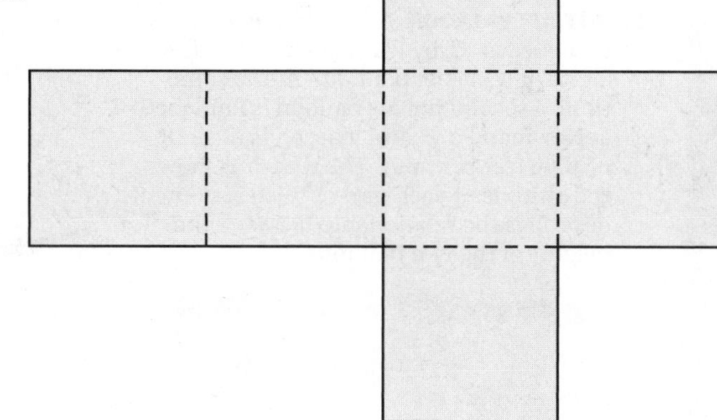

QUIZ *for Lessons 7.3–7.4*

Solve the linear system using elimination. *(pp. 444, 451)*

1. $x + y = 4$, $-3x + y = -8$ **(3, 1)**
2. $2x - y = 2$, $6x - y = -2$ **(−1, −4)**
3. $x + y = 5$, $-x + y = -3$ **(4, 1)**
4. $x + 3y = -10$, $-x + 5y = -30$ **(5, −5)**
5. $x + 3y = 10$, $3x - y = 13$ **(4.9, 1.7)**
6. $x + 7y = 10$, $x + 2y = -8$ **(−15.2, 3.6)**
7. $4x - y = -2$, $3x + 2y = 7$ $\left(\frac{3}{11}, 3\frac{1}{11}\right)$
8. $x + 3y = 1$, $5x + 6y = 14$ **(4, −1)**
9. $3x + y = 21$, $x + y = 1$ **(10, −9)**
10. $2x - 3y = -5$, $5x + 2y = 16$ **(2, 3)**
11. $7x + 2y = 13$, $4x + 3y = 13$ **(1, 3)**
12. $\frac{1}{3}x + 5y = -3$, $-\frac{2}{3}x + 6y = -10$ **(6, −1)**

5 ASSESS AND RETEACH

Daily Homework Quiz

Transparency Available

Solve the linear system using elimination.

1. $8x + 3y = 12$, $-2x + y = 4$ **(0, 4)**
2. $-3x + 2y = 7$, $5x - 4y = -15$ **(1, 5)**
3. $-7x - 3y = 11$, $4x - 2y = 16$ **(1, −6)**
4. A recreation center charges nonmembers \$3 to use the pool and \$5 to use the basketball courts. A person pays \$42 to use the recreation facilities 12 times. How many times did the person use the pool? **9 times**

Available at **classzone.com**

Diagnosis/Remediation

- Practice A, B, C in Chapter 7 Resource Book, pp. 41–43
- Study Guide in Chapter 7 Resource Book, pp. 44–45
- Practice Workbook, pp. 111–112
- @HomeTutor

Challenge

Additional challenge is available in the Chapter 7 Resource Book, p. 49.

Quiz

An easily-readable reduced copy of the quiz (with answers) on Lessons 7.3–7.4 from the Assessment Book can be found on p. 424F.

1. D
2. G
3. D
4. H
5. C

Illinois Mixed Review

Lessons 7.1–7.4

1. **LEMONADE** You have \$35 to spend on lemons and sugar to make lemonade for your lemonade stand. Lemons cost \$.40 each, and sugar costs \$1 per pound. You need to buy 1 pound of sugar for every 10 lemons you buy. What is the greatest number of lemons and pounds of sugar that you can buy for your lemonade stand?

   A. 3 lemons, 3 pounds of sugar

   B. 28 lemons, 7 pounds of sugar

   C. 50 lemons, 5 pounds of sugar

   D. 70 lemons, 7 pounds of sugar

2. **HOT AIR BALLOON** A hot air balloon is launched at Kirby Park, and it ascends at a rate of 7200 feet per hour. At the same time, a second hot air balloon is launched at Newman Park, and it ascends at a rate of 4000 feet per hour. The diagram shows the altitude of each park. Which statement describes the relationship between the heights of the two balloons?

   Kirby Park | Newman Park
   1705 ft | 3940 ft
   SEA LEVEL *Not drawn to scale*

   F. The balloon launched at Newman Park will always be higher.

   G. After one hour, the balloon launched at Kirby Park will be higher than the balloon launched at Newman Park.

   H. After 30 minutes, the balloon launched at Kirby Park will be higher than the balloon launched at Newman Park.

   J. The relationship cannot be determined.

3. **HELICOPTER** Flying into the wind, a helicopter takes 15 minutes to travel 15 kilometers. The return flight takes 12 minutes. If the wind speed and direction remain constant during the trip, which system of equations can be used to represent the situation?

   A. $15x = y$
   $12x = y - 3$

   B. $x + y = 15$
   $x - y = 12$

   C. $x + y = 60$
   $x - y = 75$

   D. $x + y = 75$
   $x - y = 60$

4. **CHEMISTRY** A chemist needs 500 milliliters of a solution that is 20% acid and 80% water. She combines x milliliters of a 10% acid and 90% water mix and y milliliters of a 30% acid and 70% water mix. Find the values of x and y.

   F. $x = 100$, $y = 400$ **H.** $x = 250$, $y = 250$

   G. $x = 225$, $y = 275$ **J.** $x = 350$, $y = 150$

5. **COMPUTERS** Two customers each buy a computer from a salesperson one day. Each customer arranges a payment plan. The graph shows the amount y (in dollars) paid for the computers after x months. After how many months will each customer have paid the same amount?

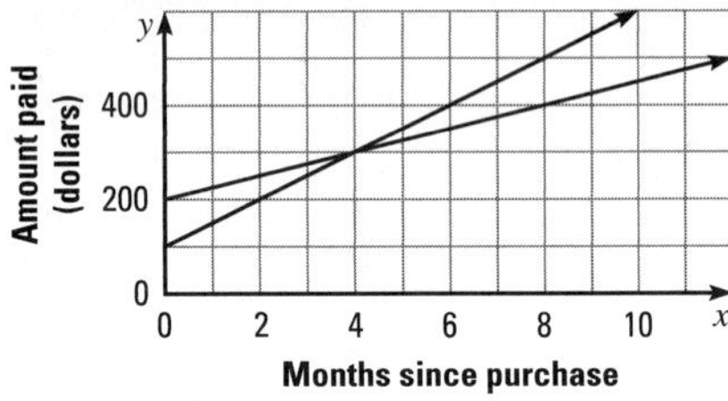

   A. 2 months **C.** 4 months

   B. 3 months **D.** 5 months

7.5 Solve Special Types of Linear Systems

 **8.11.17** Solve systems of equations and inequalities.

Before You found the solution of a linear system.

Now You will identify the number of solutions of a linear system.

Why? So you can compare distances traveled, as in Ex. 39.

Key Vocabulary
- **inconsistent system**
- **consistent dependent system**
- **system of linear equations,** *p. 427*
- **parallel,** *p. 244*

A linear system can have no solution or infinitely many solutions. A linear system has no solution when the graphs of the equations are parallel. A linear system with no solution is called an **inconsistent system**.

A linear system has infinitely many solutions when the graphs of the equations are the same line. A linear system with infinitely many solutions is called a **consistent dependent system**.

EXAMPLE 1 A linear system with no solution

Show that the linear system has no solution.

$3x + 2y = 10$ **Equation 1**
$3x + 2y = 2$ **Equation 2**

Solution

METHOD 1 Graphing

REVIEW GRAPHING
For help with graphing linear equations, see pp. 215, 225, and 244.

Graph the linear system.

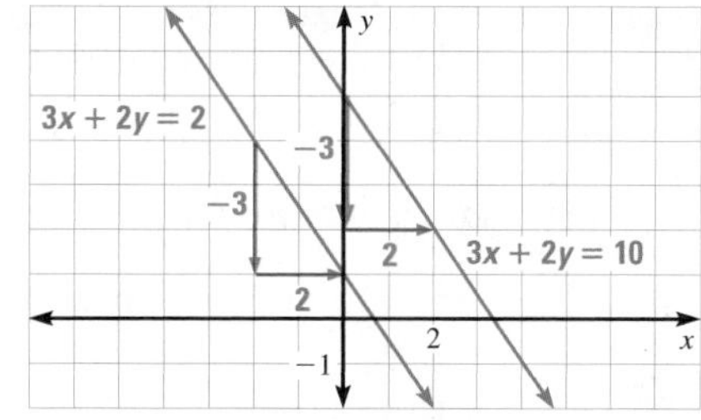

▶ The lines are parallel because they have the same slope but different y-intercepts. Parallel lines do not intersect, so the system has no solution.

METHOD 2 Elimination

Subtract the equations.

$$\begin{array}{r} 3x + 2y = 10 \\ \underline{3x + 2y = 2} \\ 0 = 8 \end{array}$$

← This is a false statement.

IDENTIFY TYPES OF SYSTEMS
The linear system in Example 1 is called an inconsistent system because the lines do not intersect (are not consistent).

▶ The variables are eliminated and you are left with a false statement regardless of the values of x and y. This tells you that the system has no solution.

 at classzone.com

1 PLAN AND PREPARE

Warm-Up Exercises

Transparency Available

1. Solve the linear system.
$2x + 3y = -9$
$x - 2y = 6$ (0, −3)
2. You buy 8 pencils for $8 at the bookstore. Standard pencils cost $.85 and specialty pencils cost $1.25. How many specialty pencils did you buy? 3 specialty pencils

Notetaking Guide

Transparency Available

Promotes interactive learning and notetaking skills, pp. 160–162.

Pacing

Basic: 2 days
Average: 2 days
Advanced: 2 days
Block: 0.5 block with 7.4
0.5 block with 7.6
- See *Teaching Guide/Lesson Plan.*

2 FOCUS AND MOTIVATE

Essential Question

Big Idea 1, p. 425

How can you identify the number of solutions of a linear system? Tell students they will learn how to answer this question by graphing and solving linear systems and by looking at the slopes and the y-intercepts of the equations.

Resource Planning Guide

Chapter Resource Book
- Teaching Guide/Lesson Plan (pp. 50–51)
- Activity Master (p. 52)
- Practice levels A, B, C (pp. 53–58)
- Study Guide (pp. 59–60)
- Catch-up for Absent Students (p. 61)
- Application (p. 62)
- Challenge (p. 63)

Workbooks
- Notetaking Guide (pp. 160–162)
- Practice Workbook (pp. 113–115)

Teaching Options
- **Power Presentations CD-ROM** provides dynamic electronic teaching resources for the classroom.
- **Activity Generator CD-ROM** provides editable activities for all ability levels.

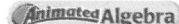

Interactive Technology
- Easy Planner
- Power Presentations CD-ROM
- Activity Generator CD-ROM
- Animated Algebra
- Test Generator CD-ROM
- Online Quiz
- eWorkbook
- eEdition
- @HomeTutor

Resources for English Learners
- Quick Reference for English Learners
- Spanish Study Guide
- Multi-Language Visual Glossary
- Student Resources in Spanish

See also the *Algebra 1 Toolkit* for more strategies for meeting individual needs.

Motivating the Lesson

A group of people bought 15 bus tickets and 12 transfers for \$63. Another group bought 5 bus tickets and 4 transfers for \$21. You want to know the cost of one bus ticket. By knowing how to identify whether a system has one solution, no solution, or infinitely many solutions, you will be able to determine if you have enough information to find the cost of one ticket.

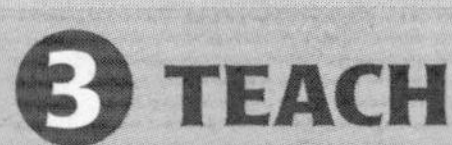

3 TEACH

Extra Example 1

Show that the linear system has no solution.

$2x - 3y = 6$

$2x - 3y = -4$

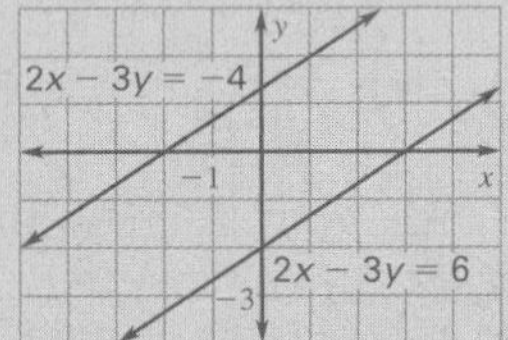

The lines are parallel, so the system has no solution.

An **Animated Algebra** activity is available on-line for **Example 1**. This activity is also available on the **Power Presentations CD-ROM**.

Extra Example 2

Show that the linear system has infinitely many solutions.

$4x - 2y = 8$

$y = 2x - 4$

Substitute $2x - 4$ for y in the first equation.

$4x - 2(2x - 4) = 8$

$4x - 4x + 8 = 8$

$8 = 8$

The statement is true; the system has infinitely many solutions.

EXAMPLE 2 A linear system with infinitely many solutions

Show that the linear system has infinitely many solutions.

$x - 2y = -4$ **Equation 1**

$y = \frac{1}{2}x + 2$ **Equation 2**

Solution

METHOD 1 Graphing

Graph the linear system.

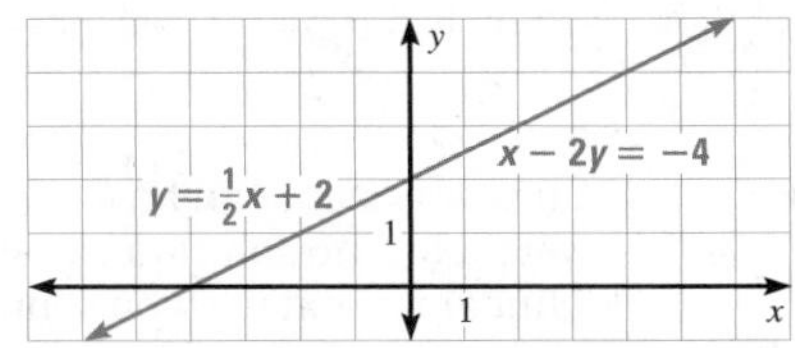

▶ The equations represent the same line, so any point on the line is a solution. So, the linear system has infinitely many solutions.

METHOD 2 Substitution

Substitute $\frac{1}{2}x + 2$ for y in Equation 1 and solve for x.

$x - 2y = -4$ **Write Equation 1.**

$x - 2\left(\frac{1}{2}x + 2\right) = -4$ **Substitute $\frac{1}{2}x + 2$ for y.**

$-4 = -4$ **Simplify.**

▶ The variables are eliminated and you are left with a statement that is true regardless of the values of x and y. This tells you that the system has infinitely many solutions.

IDENTIFY TYPES OF SYSTEMS

The linear system in Example 2 is called a consistent dependent system because the lines intersect (are consistent) and the equations are equivalent (are dependent).

GUIDED PRACTICE for Examples 1 and 2

Tell whether the linear system has *no solution* or *infinitely many solutions*. Explain.

1. $5x + 3y = 6$
$-5x - 3y = 3$

2. $y = 2x - 4$
$-6x + 3y = -12$

1. No solution. ***Sample answer:*** **When you solve the system you get $0 = 9$, which is a false statement.**

2. Infinitely many solutions. ***Sample answer:*** **When you solve the system you get $-12 = -12$, which is a true statement.**

IDENTIFYING THE NUMBER OF SOLUTIONS When the equations of a linear system are written in slope-intercept form, you can identify the number of solutions of the system by looking at the slopes and y-intercepts of the lines.

Number of solutions	Slopes and y-intercepts
One solution	Different slopes
No solution	Same slope Different y-intercepts
Infinitely many solutions	Same slope Same y-intercept

Differentiated Instruction

Inclusion Some students may need help understanding the concept of linear dependence. In **Example 2**, have students solve $x - 2y = 24$ for y. By doing so, students will get the second equation. This shows that the two equations are algebraically equivalent.

See also the *Algebra 1 Toolkit* for more strategies.

EXAMPLE 3 Identify the number of solutions

Without solving the linear system, tell whether the linear system has *one solution*, *no solution*, or *infinitely many solutions*.

a. $5x + y = -2$ Equation 1
$-10x - 2y = 4$ Equation 2

b. $6x + 2y = 3$ Equation 1
$6x + 2y = -5$ Equation 2

Solution

a. $y = -5x - 2$ Write Equation 1 in slope-intercept form.

$y = -5x - 2$ Write Equation 2 in slope-intercept form.

▸ Because the lines have the same slope and the same y-intercept, the system has infinitely many solutions.

b. $y = -3x + \frac{3}{2}$ Write Equation 1 in slope-intercept form.

$y = -3x - \frac{5}{2}$ Write Equation 2 in slope-intercept form.

▸ Because the lines have the same slope but different y-intercepts, the system has no solution.

EXAMPLE 4 Write and solve a system of linear equations

ART An artist wants to sell prints of her paintings. She orders a set of prints for each of two of her paintings. Each set contains regular prints and glossy prints, as shown in the table. Find the cost of one glossy print.

Regular	Glossy	Cost
45	30	$465
15	10	$155

Solution

STEP 1 **Write** a linear system. Let x be the cost (in dollars) of a regular print, and let y be the cost (in dollars) of a glossy print.

$45x + 30y = 465$ Cost of prints for one painting
$15x + 10y = 155$ Cost of prints for other painting

STEP 2 **Solve** the linear system using elimination.

$$\begin{aligned} 45x + 30y &= 465 & &\rightarrow & 45x + 30y &= 465 \\ 15x + 10y &= 155 & \times(-3) &\rightarrow & -45x - 30y &= -465 \\ & & & & 0 &= 0 \end{aligned}$$

▸ There are infinitely many solutions, so you cannot determine the cost of one glossy print. You need more information.

✓ GUIDED PRACTICE for Examples 3 and 4

3. Without solving the linear system, tell whether it has *one solution*, *no solution*, or *infinitely many solutions*. one solution

$x - 3y = -15$ Equation 1
$2x - 3y = -18$ Equation 2

4. WHAT IF? In Example 4, suppose a glossy print costs $3 more than a regular print. Find the cost of a glossy print. $8

Key Question to Ask for Example 2

- What happens if you multiply Equation 2 by 2? You get $2y = x + 4$, which is the same as Equation 1.

Extra Example 3

Without solving the linear system, tell whether the linear system has *one solution*, *no solution*, or *infinitely many solutions*.

a. $-3x + 5y = 6$
$6x - 10y = -12$ infinitely many solutions

b. $9x - 5y = 12$
$9x - 5y = 8$ no solution

Extra Example 4

A pizza parlor fills two pizza orders. Find the cost of one medium pizza.

Medium	Large	Cost
4	12	$168
8	24	$336

You cannot determine the cost of one medium pizza, since there are infinitely many solutions.

Closing the Lesson

Have students summarize the major points of the lesson and answer the Essential Question: How can you identify the number of solutions of a linear system?

- Linear systems can have one solution, no solution, or infinitely many solutions.

Systems with one solution have graphs with intersecting lines and equations with different slopes. Systems with no solution have graphs with parallel lines, equations with the same slope but different y-intercepts, and result in false statements when solved algebraically. Systems with infinitely many solutions have graphs with coinciding lines, identical equations, and result in true statements when solved algebraically.

4 PRACTICE AND APPLY

Assignment Guide

Answer Transparencies available for all exercises

Basic:
Day 1: pp. 462–465
Exs. 1–20, 24, 25, 42–45
Day 2: pp. 462–465
Exs. 26–30, 36–39, 46–60

Average:
Day 1: pp. 462–465
Exs. 1–14, 18–25, 42–45
Day 2: pp. 462–465
Exs. 26–34, 36–40, 46–54 even, 56–61

Advanced:
Day 1: pp. 462–465
Exs. 1–4, 11–13, 18–25, 44, 45
Day 2: pp. 462–465
Exs. 26–35*, 37–41*, 51, 52, 55, 59

Block:
pp. 462–465
Exs. 1–14, 18–25, 42–45 (with 7.4)
pp. 462–465
Exs. 26–34, 36–40, 46–54 even, 56–61 (with 7.6)

Differentiated Instruction

See *Algebra 1 Best Practices Toolkit* for suggestions on addressing the needs of a diverse classroom.

Homework Check

For a quick check of student understanding of key concepts, go over the following exercises:

Basic: 9, 20, 26, 36, 37
Average: 13, 18, 28, 36, 38
Advanced: 12, 21, 30, 37, 38

Extra Practice

- Student Edition, p. 944
- Chapter 7 Resource Book: Practice levels A, B, C, pp. 53–58

Practice Worksheet

An easily-readable reduced practice page (with answers) for this lesson can be found on p. 424C.

CONCEPT SUMMARY *For Your Notebook*

Number of Solutions of a Linear System

One solution	No solution	Infinitely many solutions
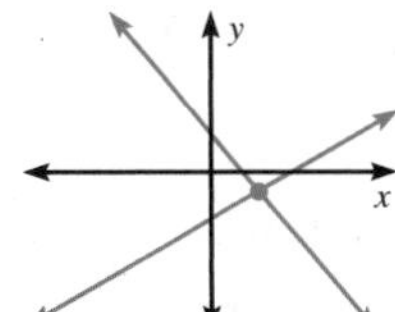	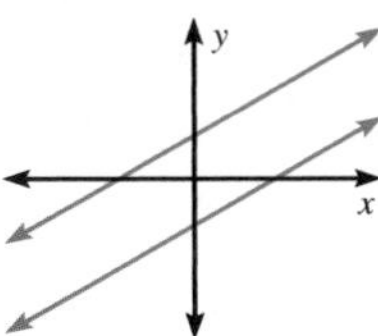	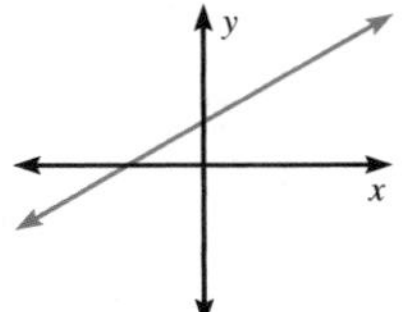
The lines intersect.	The lines are parallel.	The lines coincide.
The lines have different slopes.	The lines have the same slope and different y-intercepts.	The lines have the same slope and the same y-intercept.

7.5 EXERCISES

HOMEWORK KEY
○ = **WORKED-OUT SOLUTIONS** on p. WS17 for Exs. 11 and 37
★ = **STANDARDIZED TEST PRACTICE** Exs. 3, 4, 24, 25, 32, 33, and 40

SKILL PRACTICE

A

1. **VOCABULARY** Copy and complete: A linear system with no solution is called a(n) _?_ system. inconsistent

2. **VOCABULARY** Copy and complete: A linear system with infinitely many solutions is called a(n) _?_ system. consistent dependent

3. ★ **WRITING** *Describe* the graph of a linear system that has no solution. *Sample answer:* The lines have the same slope but different y-intercepts.

4. ★ **WRITING** *Describe* the graph of a linear system that has infinitely many solutions. *Sample answer:* The graph would show only one line.

INTERPRETING GRAPHS Match the linear system with its graph. Then use the graph to tell whether the linear system has *one solution*, *no solution*, or *infinitely many solutions*.

5. $x - 3y = -9$
$x - y = -1$
B; one solution

6. $x - y = -4$
$-3x + 3y = 2$
C; no solution

7. $x + 3y = -1$
$-2x - 6y = 2$
A; infinitely many solutions

A. 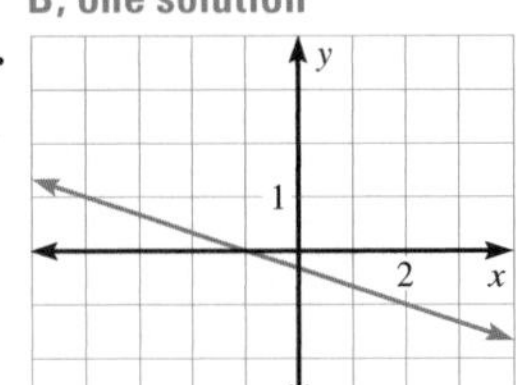

B. 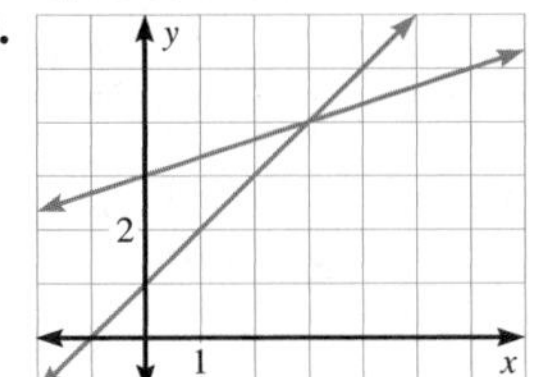

C. 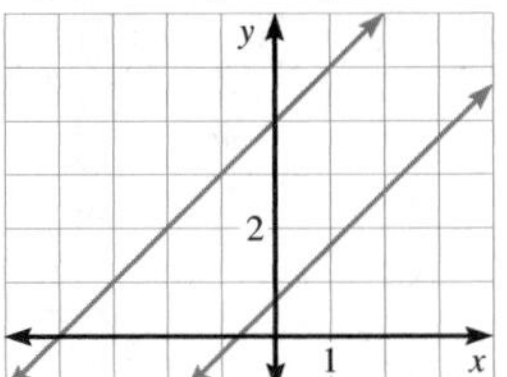

EXAMPLES 1 and 2 on pp. 459–460 for Exs. 8–25

INTERPRETING GRAPHS **Graph the linear system. Then use the graph to tell whether the linear system has *one solution, no solution,* or *infinitely many solutions.*** 8–13. See margin for graphs.

8. $x + y = -2$
$y = -x + 5$
no solution

9. $3x - 4y = 12$
$y = \frac{3}{4}x - 3$
infinitely many solutions

10. $3x - y = -9$
$3x + 5y = -15$
one solution

11. $-2x + 2y = -16$
$3x - 6y = 30$
one solution

12. $-9x + 6y = 18$
$6x - 4y = -12$
infinitely many solutions

13. $-3x + 4y = 12$
$-3x + 4y = 24$
no solution

14. *Sample answer:* The lines do not have the same slope, so they are not parallel and they do have a solution. If the graph were larger the lines would intersect at (4, 12); see margin for art.

14. ERROR ANALYSIS *Describe* and correct the error in solving the linear system below.

$6x + y = 36$
$5x - y = 8$

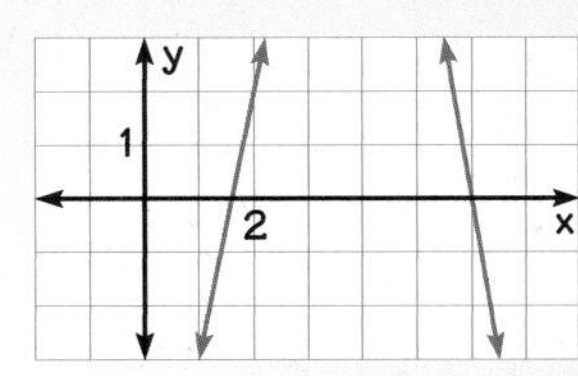

The lines do not intersect, so there is no solution.

SOLVING LINEAR SYSTEMS **Solve the linear system using substitution or elimination.**

15. $2x + 5y = 14$
$6x + 7y = 10$ (−3, 4)

16. $-16x + 2y = -2$
$y = 8x - 1$ infinitely many solutions

17. $3x - 2y = -5$
$4x + 5y = 47$ (3, 7)

18. $5x - 5y = -3$
$y = x + 0.6$ infinitely many solutions

19. $x - y = 0$
$5x - 2y = 6$ (2, 2)

20. $x - 2y = 7$
$-x + 2y = 7$ no solution

21. $-18x + 6y = 24$
$3x - y = -2$ no solution

22. $4y + 5x = 15$
$x = 8y + 3$ (3, 0)

23. $6x + 3y = 9$
$2x + 9y = 27$ (0, 3)

24. ★ MULTIPLE CHOICE Which of the linear systems has *exactly* one solution? C

Ⓐ $-x + y = 9$
$x - y = 9$

Ⓑ $-x + y = 9$
$x - y = -9$

Ⓒ $-x + y = 9$
$-x - y = 9$

Ⓓ $x - y = -9$
$-x + y = -9$

25. ★ MULTIPLE CHOICE Which of the linear systems has infinitely many solutions? D

Ⓐ $15x + 5y = 20$
$6x - 2y = 8$

Ⓑ $15x - 5y = 20$
$6x - 2y = -8$

Ⓒ $15x - 5y = -20$
$6x - 2y = 8$

Ⓓ $15x - 5y = 20$
$6x - 2y = 8$

EXAMPLE 3 on p. 461 for Exs. 26–31

B **IDENTIFYING THE NUMBER OF SOLUTIONS** **Without solving the linear system, tell whether the linear system has *one solution, no solution,* or *infinitely many solutions.***

26. $y = -6x - 2$
$12x + 2y = -6$
no solution

27. $y = 7x + 13$
$-21x + 3y = 39$
infinitely many solutions

28. $4x + 3y = 27$
$4x - 3y = -27$
one solution

29. $9x - 15y = 24$
$6x - 10y = 16$
infinitely many solutions

30. $0.3x + 0.4y = 2.4$
$0.5x - 0.6y = 0.2$
one solution

31. $0.9x - 2.1y = 12.3$
$1.5x - 3.5y = 20.5$
infinitely many solutions

Avoiding Common Errors

Exercises 15–23 Some students may erroneously correlate true statements with no solution and false statements with infinitely many solutions. Stress that a true statement means that all points on a line are solutions and a false statement means that none of the points on either line are solutions. To reinforce these concepts, suggest that students write the equations of these systems in slope-intercept form and then look at the slopes and y-intercepts to determine the number of solutions. This will also help them associate true statements with infinitely many solutions and false statements with no solution.

11.
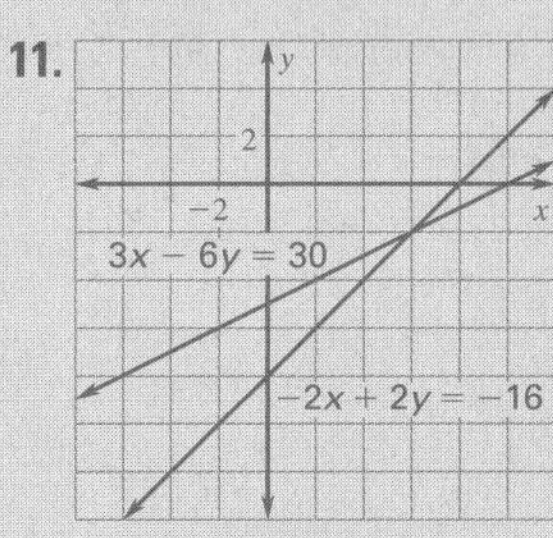

12.
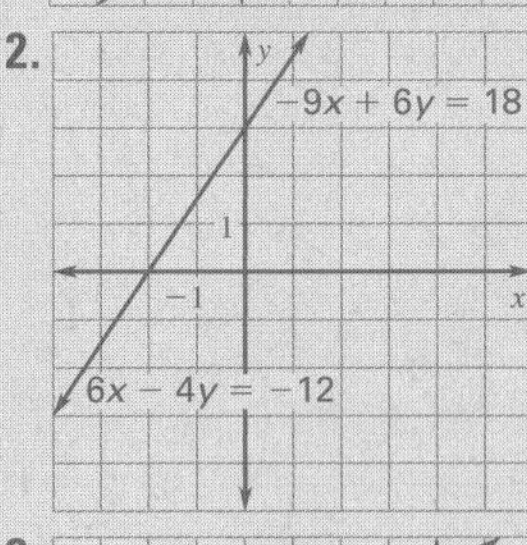

13.
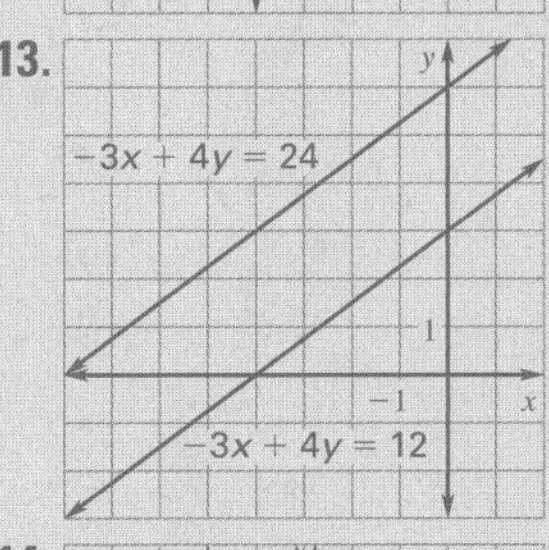

14.
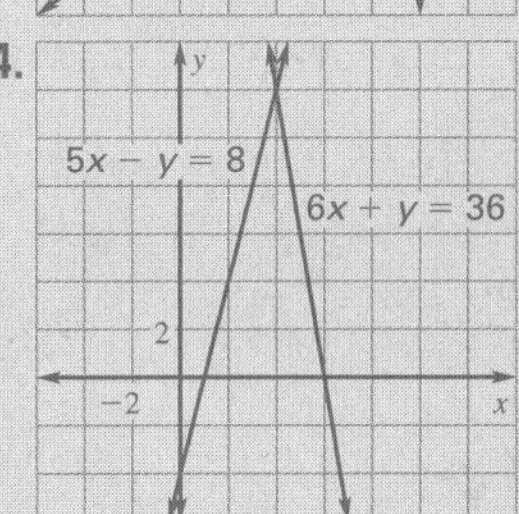

8.
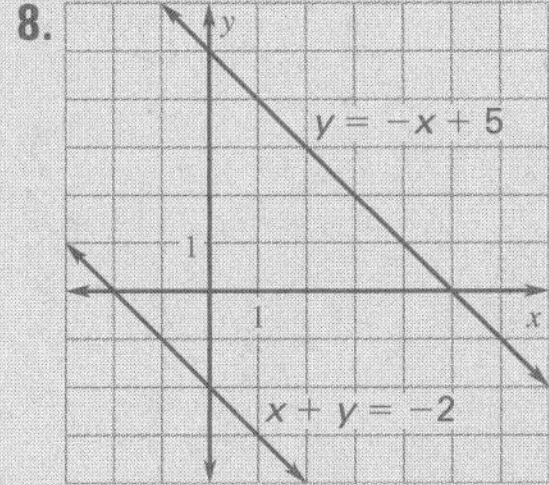

9.
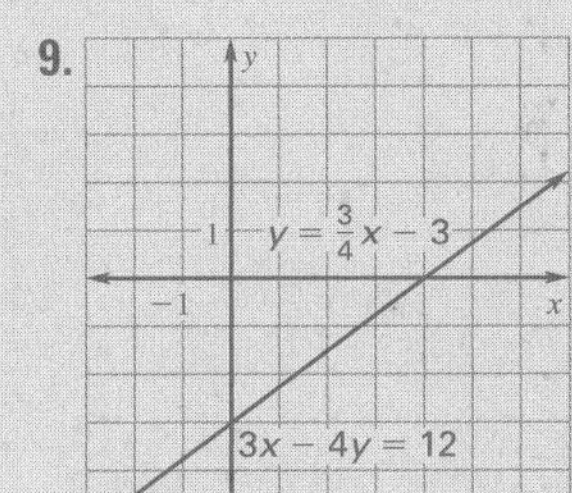

10.
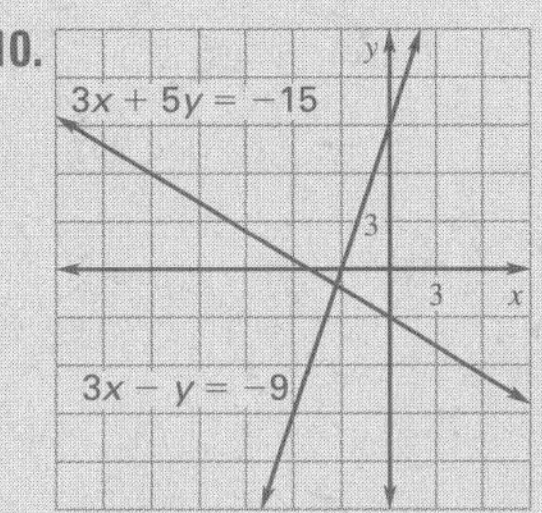

Teaching Strategy

Exercise 37 You may want to point out to students that after they write the equations for this system, they can write the equations in slope-intercept form and then look at the slopes and y-intercepts to determine whether there is enough information to find the cost of one ticket. Note that if the slopes are different, then there is enough information to find the cost of one ticket. If the slopes are the same, then there are either infinitely many solutions or no solution, and in either case, there is not enough information to find the cost of one ticket.

Avoiding Common Errors

Exercise 38 Some students may write the equations in the system, using the first row of the table for x and the second for y. Caution students to read the description in the problem to determine what x and y should represent.

32. ★ **OPEN-ENDED** Write a linear system so that it has infinitely many solutions, and one of the equations is $y = 3x + 2$. *Sample answer:* $y = 3x + 2, 2y = 6x + 4$

33. ★ **OPEN-ENDED** Write a linear system so that it has no solution and one of the equations is $7x - 8y = -9$.
Sample answer: $7x - 8y = -9, 7x - 8y = 4$

C

34. **REASONING** Give a counterexample for the following statement: If the graphs of the equations of a linear system have the same slope, then the linear system has no solution.
Sample answer: $y = 3x, 2y = 6x$

35. **CHALLENGE** Find values of p, q, and r that produce the solution(s).

$px + qy = r$ **Equation 1**

$2x - 3y = 5$ **Equation 2**

a. No solution *Sample answer:* $p = 2, q = -3, r = 0$

b. Infinitely many solutions
Sample answer: $p = 4, q = -6, r = 10$

c. One solution of (4, 1)
Sample answer: $p = 1, q = 1, r = 5$

Problem Solving

EXAMPLE 4 A
on p. 461
for Exs. 36–38

36. **RECREATION** One admission to a roller skating rink costs x dollars and renting a pair of skates costs y dollars. A group pays \$243 for admission for 36 people and 21 skate rentals. Another group pays \$81 for admission for 12 people and 7 skate rentals. Is there enough information to determine the cost of one admission to the roller skating rink? *Explain.*

@HomeTutor for problem solving help at classzone.com

No. *Sample answer:* There are infinitely many solutions to the resulting linear system.

37. **TRANSPORTATION** A passenger train travels from New York City to Washington, D.C., then back to New York City. The table shows the number of coach tickets and business class tickets purchased for each leg of the trip. Is there enough information to determine the cost of one coach ticket? *Explain.* Yes. *Sample answer:* There is one solution to the resulting linear system.

Destination	Coach tickets	Business class tickets	Money collected (dollars)
Washington, D.C.	150	80	22,860
New York City	170	100	27,280

@HomeTutor for problem solving help at classzone.com

38. **PHOTOGRAPHY** In addition to taking pictures on your digital camera, you can record 30 second movies. All pictures use the same amount of memory, and all 30 second movies use the same amount of memory. The number of pictures and 30 second movies on 2 memory cards is shown.

a. Is there enough information given to determine the amount of memory used by a 30 second movie? *Explain.*

b. Given that a 30 second movie uses 50 times the amount of memory that a digital picture uses, can you determine the amount of memory used by a 30 second movie? *Explain.*

Size of card (megabytes)	64	256
Pictures	450	1800
Movies	7	28

38a. No. *Sample answer:* There are infinitely many solutions to the resulting linear system.

38b. Yes. *Sample answer:* You can write a new equation and create a linear system that has only one solution.

○ = WORKED-OUT SOLUTIONS on p. WS1 ★ = STANDARDIZED TEST PRACTICE

B 39. **MULTI-STEP PROBLEM** Two people are training for a speed ice-climbing event. During a practice climb, one climber starts 15 seconds after the first climber. The rates that the climbers ascend are shown.

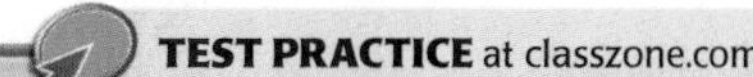

a. Let *d* be the distance (in feet) traveled by a climber *t* seconds after the first person starts climbing. Write a linear system that models the situation. $d = \frac{t}{3}, d = \frac{t}{3} - 5$

b. Graph the linear system from part (a). Does the second climber catch up to the first climber? *Explain.*

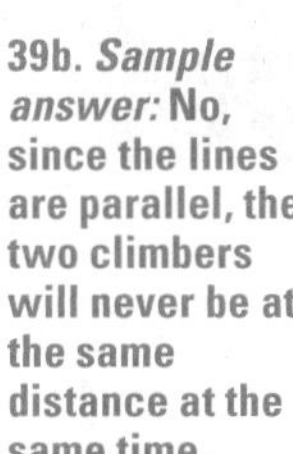
39b. *Sample answer:* No, since the lines are parallel, the two climbers will never be at the same distance at the same time.

40. ★ **EXTENDED RESPONSE** Two employees at a banquet facility are given the task of folding napkins. One person starts folding napkins at a rate of 5 napkins per minute. The second person starts 10 minutes after the first person and folds napkins at a rate of 4 napkins per minute.

a. **Model** Let *y* be the number of napkins folded *x* minutes after the first person starts folding. Write a linear system that models the situation. $y = 5x, y = 4(x - 10)$

b. **Solve** Solve the linear system. $(-40, -200)$

c. **Interpret** Does the solution of the linear system make sense in the context of the problem? *Explain.* No. *Sample answer: x* and *y* only make sense for positive values.

C 41. **CHALLENGE** An airplane has an average air speed of 160 miles per hour. The airplane takes 3 hours to travel with the wind from Salem to Lancaster. The airplane has to travel against the wind on the return trip. After 3 hours into the return trip, the airplane is 120 miles from Salem. Find the distance from Salem to Lancaster. If the problem cannot be solved with the information given, *explain* why. 540 mi

ILLINOIS MIXED REVIEW

TEST PRACTICE at classzone.com

42. A restaurant served 625 customers over a 2 week period. The store owner estimates that 150% as many customers were served in the first week as in the second week. Which system of equations can be used to determine *x*, the number of customers served in the first week, and *y*, the number of customers served in the second week? B

(A) $x = 625$, $y = 1.5x$
(B) $x + y = 625$, $x = 1.5y$
(C) $xy = 625$, $x = 1.5y$
(D) $x + 1.5y = 625$, $y = 1.5x$

43. $\triangle ABC$ is similar to $\triangle DEF$. Which scale factor was used to transform $\triangle ABC$ to $\triangle DEF$?

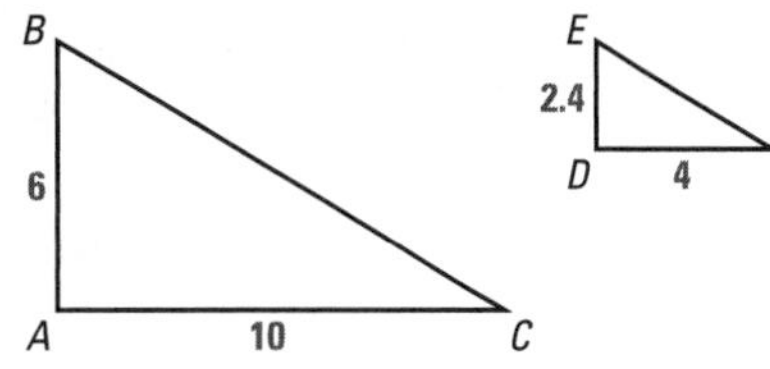

(A) $\frac{2}{5}$ (B) $\frac{3}{5}$ A

(C) $\frac{2}{3}$ (D) $\frac{5}{2}$

5 ASSESS AND RETEACH

Daily Homework Quiz

Transparency Available

Without solving the linear system, tell whether the linear system has *one solution, no solution,* or *infinitely many solutions.*

1. $4x + 2y = 12$
   $y = -2x + 8$ no solution
2. $-2x + 5y = 5$
   $y = \frac{2}{5}x + 1$ infinitely many solutions
3. A group of 12 students and 3 teachers pays $57 for admission to a primate research center. Another group of 14 students and 4 teachers pays $69. Find the cost of one student ticket. $3.50

Online Quiz

Available at **classzone.com**

Diagnosis/Remediation

- Practice A, B, C in Chapter 7 Resource Book, pp. 53–58
- Study Guide in Chapter 7 Resource Book, pp. 59–60
- Practice Workbook, pp. 113–115
- @HomeTutor

Challenge

Additional challenge is available in the Chapter 7 Resource Book, p. 63.

39b.

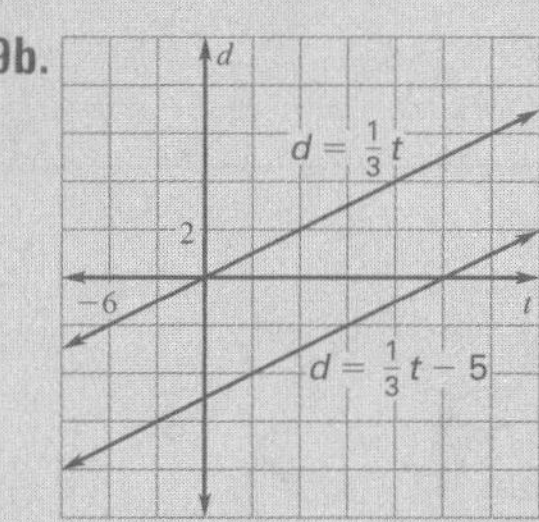

1 PLAN AND PREPARE

Warm-Up Exercises

Transparency Available

1. Graph $y < \frac{2}{3}x - 1$.

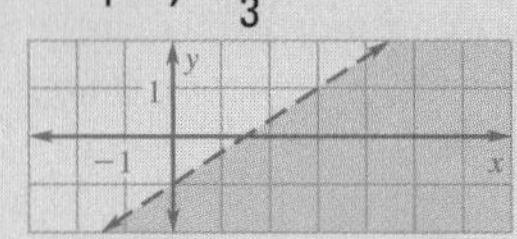

2. You are running one ad that costs \$6 per day and another that costs \$8 per day. You can spend no more than \$120. Name a possible combination of days that you can run the ads. ***Sample:* 16 days of the \$6 ad and 3 days of the \$8 ad**

Notetaking Guide

Transparency Available

Promotes interactive learning and notetaking skills, pp. 163–165.

Pacing

Basic: 1 day
Average: 1 day
Advanced: 1 day
Block: 0.5 block with 7.5
• See *Teaching Guide/Lesson Plan.*

2 FOCUS AND MOTIVATE

Essential Question

Big Idea 3, p. 425

How do you solve systems of linear inequalities in two variables? **Tell students they will learn how to answer this question by graphing in the same coordinate plane.**

7.6 Solve Systems of Linear Inequalities

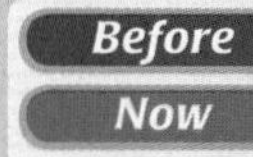

8.11.17 Solve systems of equations and inequalities.

Before You graphed linear inequalities in two variables.
Now You will solve systems of linear inequalities in two variables.
Why So you can find a marching band's competition score, as in Ex. 36.

Key Vocabulary
- system of linear inequalities
- solution of a system of linear inequalities
- graph of a system of linear inequalities

A **system of linear inequalities** in two variables, or simply a *system of inequalities*, consists of two or more linear inequalities in the same variables. An example is shown.

$$x - y > 7 \quad \text{Inequality 1}$$
$$2x + y < 8 \quad \text{Inequality 2}$$

A **solution of a system of linear inequalities** is an ordered pair that is a solution of each inequality in the system. For example, (6, −5) is a solution of the system above. The **graph of a system of linear inequalities** is the graph of all solutions of the system.

KEY CONCEPT *For Your Notebook*

Graphing a System of Linear Inequalities

STEP 1 **Graph** each inequality (as you learned to do in Lesson 6.7).

STEP 2 **Find** the intersection of the half-planes. The graph of the system is this intersection.

EXAMPLE 1 Graph a system of two linear inequalities

Graph the system of inequalities. $y > -x - 2$ Inequality 1
$y \le 3x + 6$ Inequality 2

Solution

REVIEW GRAPHING INEQUALITIES
For help with graphing a linear inequality in two variables, see p. 405.

Graph both inequalities in the same coordinate plane. The graph of the system is the intersection of the two half-planes, which is shown as the darker shade of blue.

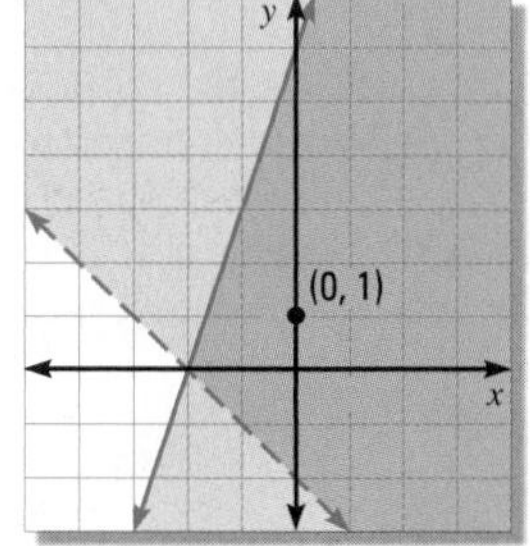

CHECK Choose a point in the dark blue region, such as (0, 1). To check this solution, substitute 0 for x and 1 for y into each inequality.

$1 \overset{?}{>} 0 - 2$	$1 \overset{?}{\le} 0 + 6$
$1 > -2$ ✓	$1 \le 6$ ✓

Animated Algebra at classzone.com

Resource Planning Guide

Chapter Resource Book
- Teaching Guide/Lesson Plan (pp. 64–65)
- Activity Master (p. 66)
- Practice levels A, B, C (pp. 68–73)
- Study Guide (pp. 74–75)
- Catch-up for Absent Students (p. 76)
- Problem Solving Workshop (p. 77)
- Challenge (p. 78)

Workbooks
- Notetaking Guide (pp. 163–165)
- Practice Workbook (pp. 116–118)

Teaching Options
- **Power Presentations CD-ROM** provides dynamic electronic teaching resources for the classroom.
- **Activity Generator CD-ROM** provides editable activities for all ability levels.

Interactive Technology
- Easy Planner
- Power Presentations CD-ROM
- Activity Generator CD-ROM
- Animated Algebra
- Test Generator CD-ROM
- Online Quiz
- eWorkbook
- eEdition
- @HomeTutor

Resources for English Learners
- Quick Reference for English Learners
- Spanish Study Guide
- Multi-Language Visual Glossary
- Student Resources in Spanish

See also the *Algebra 1 Toolkit* for more strategies for meeting individual needs.

THE SOLUTION REGION In Example 1, the half-plane for each inequality is shaded, and the solution region is the intersection of the half-planes. From this point on, only the solution region will be shaded.

EXAMPLE 2 Graph a system of three linear inequalities

Graph the system of inequalities.

$y \geq -1$ Inequality 1
$x > -2$ Inequality 2
$x + 2y \leq 4$ Inequality 3

Solution

Graph all three inequalities in the same coordinate plane. The graph of the system is the triangular region shown.

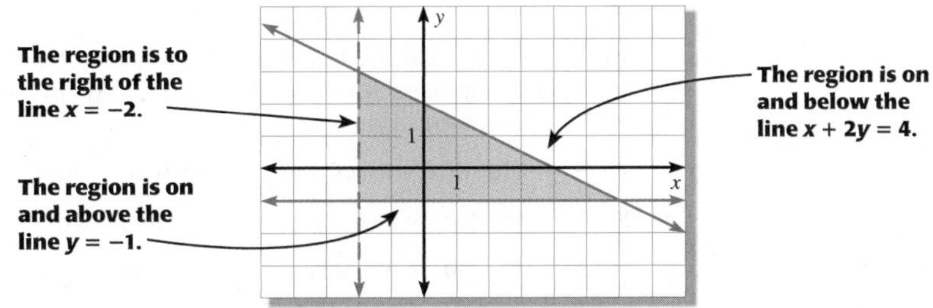

The region is to the right of the line x = −2.
The region is on and above the line y = −1.
The region is on and below the line x + 2y = 4.
y
x
1
1

GUIDED PRACTICE for Examples 1 and 2

Graph the system of linear inequalities. 1–3. See margin.

1. $y < x - 4$
   $y \geq -x + 3$
2. $y \geq -x + 2$
   $y < 4$
   $x < 3$
3. $y > -x$
   $y \geq x - 4$
   $y < 5$

EXAMPLE 3 Write a system of linear inequalities

Write a system of inequalities for the shaded region.

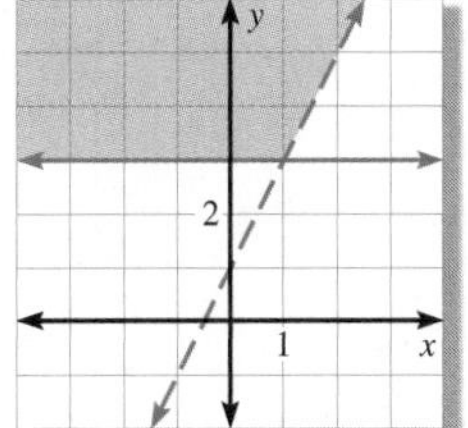

y
x
2
1

REVIEW EQUATIONS OF LINES
For help with writing an equation of a line, see pp. 283, 302, and 311.

Solution

INEQUALITY 1: One boundary line for the shaded region is $y = 3$. Because the shaded region is *above* the *solid* line, the inequality is $y \geq 3$.

INEQUALITY 2: Another boundary line for the shaded region has a slope of 2 and a y-intercept of 1. So, its equation is $y = 2x + 1$. Because the shaded region is *above* the *dashed* line, the inequality is $y > 2x + 1$.

▶ The system of inequalities for the shaded region is:

$y \geq 3$ Inequality 1
$y > 2x + 1$ Inequality 2

Differentiated Instruction

Auditory Learners Tell students that the method used in **Example 1** is sometimes called the "graph-and-check" method, because students *graph* the inequalities and then *check* points in each test region. Students should get in the habit of checking their graphs by verifying that points in their solution satisfy each inequality.

See also the *Algebra 1 Toolkit* for more strategies.

Motivating the Lesson

Your science teacher tells you that the written portion of lab reports can be no longer than 4 pages, the illustrated portions can be no longer than 8 pages, and the total number of pages can be no more than 12 pages. By knowing how to write and graph systems of linear inequalities, you can determine whether your lab report fits within the guidelines.

3 TEACH

Extra Example 1

Graph the system of inequalities.
$y < 3x$
$y \geq -2x + 1$

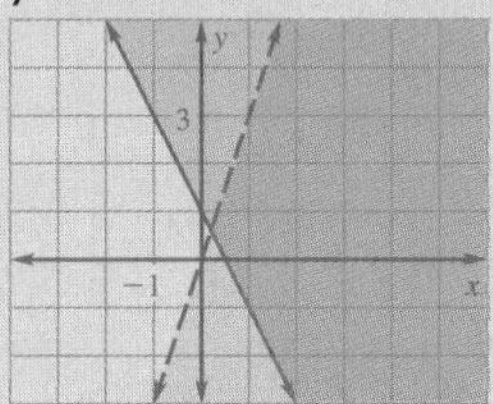

y
3
−1
x

Animated Algebra
classzone.com

An **Animated Algebra** activity is available on-line for **Example 1**. This activity is also available on the **Power Presentations CD-ROM**.

Extra Example 2

Graph the system of inequalities.
$y \geq 0$
$x > -3$
$2x + 3y \leq 6$

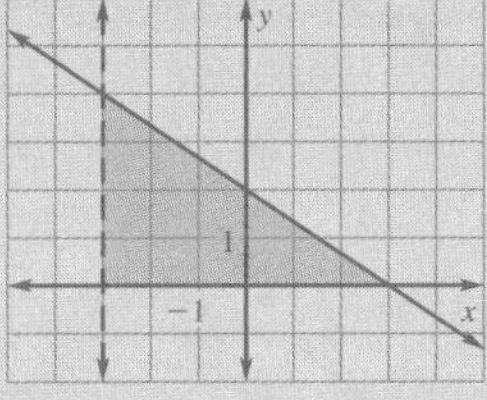

y
1
−1
x

1–3. See Additional Answers beginning on p. AA1.

Extra Example 3

Write a system of inequalities for the shaded region.

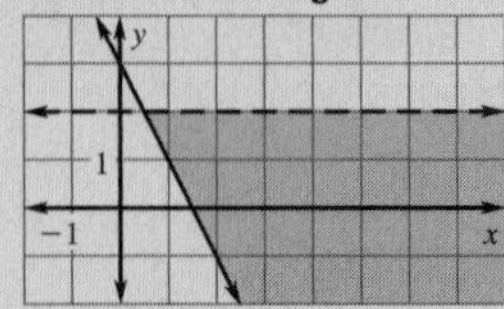

$y < 2$ and $y \geq -2x + 3$

Extra Example 4

A logo contest requires that the logo width be between 3 and 5 inches, the height no less than 2 inches, and the sum of the width and height no more than 9.

a. Write and graph a system of linear inequalities that describes the information given above. **inequalities: $x \geq 3$, $x \leq 5$, $x + y \leq 9$, $y \geq 2$**

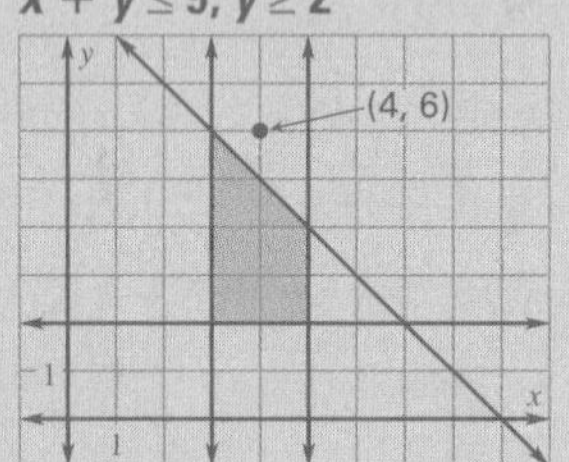

b. You enter a logo 4 inches wide and 6 inches high. Use the graph to determine if it meets contest requirements. **Because the point falls outside the solution region, the logo does not meet requirements.**

Closing the Lesson

Have students summarize the major points of the lesson and answer the Essential Question: How do you solve systems of linear inequalities in two variables?

- **You can use a graph of a system of inequalities to find all the solutions of the system.**

Graph each inequality in the same coordinate plane. The graph of the system is the intersection of all of the graphs.

6. 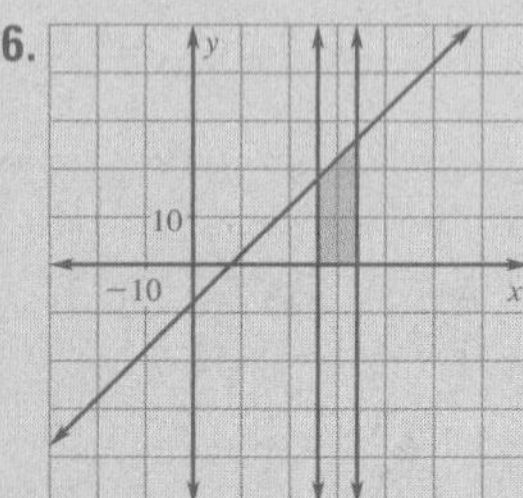

EXAMPLE 4 Write and solve a system of linear inequalities

BASEBALL The National Collegiate Athletic Association (NCAA) regulates the lengths of aluminum baseball bats used by college baseball teams. The NCAA states that the length (in inches) of the bat minus the weight (in ounces) of the bat cannot exceed 3. Bats can be purchased at lengths from 26 to 34 inches.

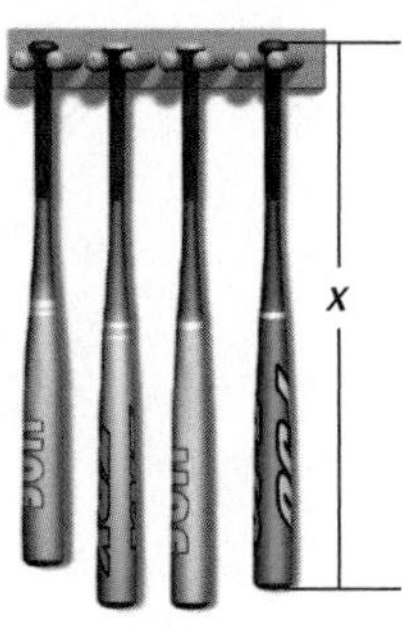

a. Write and graph a system of linear inequalities that describes the information given above.

b. A sporting goods store sells an aluminum bat that is 31 inches long and weighs 25 ounces. Use the graph to determine if this bat can be used by a player on an NCAA team.

Solution

a. Let x be the length (in inches) of the bat, and let y be the weight (in ounces) of the bat. From the given information, you can write the following inequalities:

$x - y \leq 3$	The difference of the bat's length and weight can be at most 3.
$x \geq 26$	The length of the bat must be at least 26 inches.
$x \leq 34$	The length of the bat can be at most 34 inches.
$y \geq 0$	The weight of the bat cannot be a negative number.

WRITING SYSTEMS OF INEQUALITIES
Consider the values of the variables when writing a system of inequalities. In many real-world problems, the values cannot be negative.

Graph each inequality in the system. Then identify the region that is common to all of the graphs of the inequalities. This region is shaded in the graph shown.

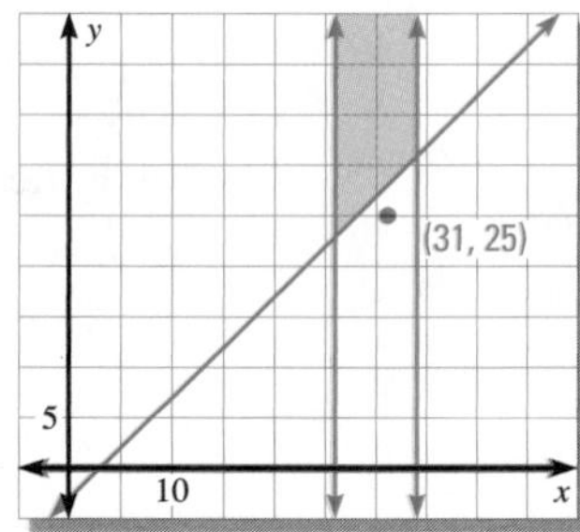

b. Graph the point that represents a bat that is 31 inches long and weighs 25 ounces.

▶ Because the point falls outside the solution region, the bat cannot be used by a player on an NCAA team.

✓ GUIDED PRACTICE for Examples 3 and 4

Write a system of inequalities that defines the shaded region.

4. 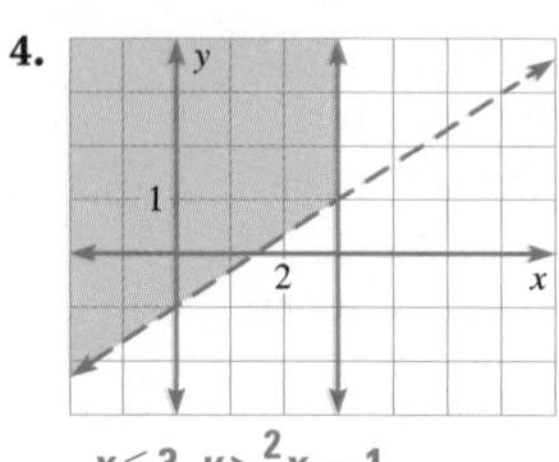

$x \leq 3$, $y > \frac{2}{3}x - 1$

5. 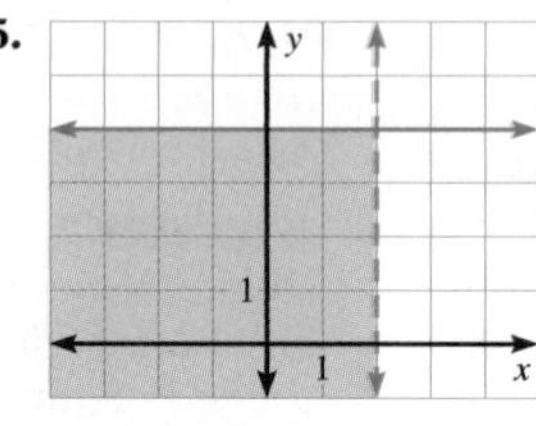

$y \leq 4$, $x < 2$

6. WHAT IF? In Example 4, suppose a Senior League (ages 10–14) player wants to buy the bat described in part (b). In Senior League, the length (in inches) of the bat minus the weight (in ounces) of the bat cannot exceed 8. Write and graph a system of inequalities to determine whether the described bat can be used by the Senior League player.
$x - y \leq 8$, $x \geq 26$, $x \leq 34$, $y \geq 0$, see margin for art; the bat can be used.

7.6 EXERCISES

HOMEWORK KEY
○ = **WORKED-OUT SOLUTIONS** on p. WS18 for Exs. 13 and 39
★ = **STANDARDIZED TEST PRACTICE** Exs. 2, 21, 22, 33, and 40

SKILL PRACTICE

A

1. **VOCABULARY** Copy and complete: A(n) _?_ of a system of linear inequalities is an ordered pair that is a solution of each inequality in the system. solution

2. ★ **WRITING** *Describe* the steps you would take to graph the system of inequalities shown.

$x - y < 7$ Inequality 1
$y \geq 3$ Inequality 2

2. *Sample answer:* Graph each inequality then shade the region that is the intersection of the solutions to each inequality. Then check the solution with a test point.

CHECKING A SOLUTION Tell whether the ordered pair is a solution of the system of inequalities.

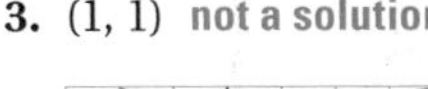

3. (1, 1) not a solution

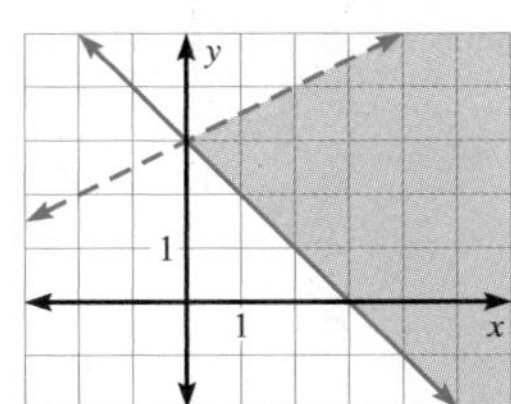

4. (0, 6) solution

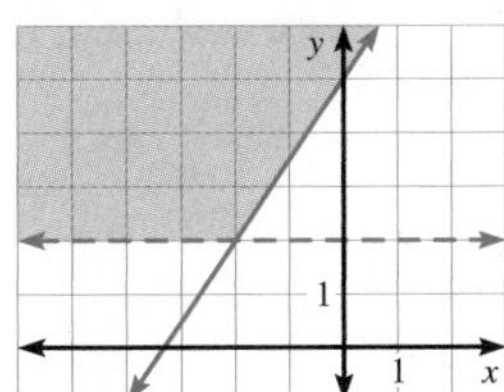

5. (3, −1) not a solution

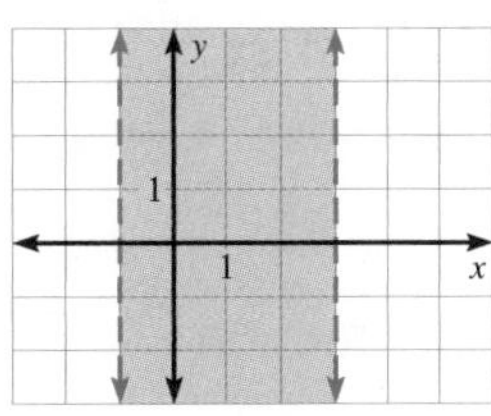

EXAMPLE 1 on p. 466 for Exs. 6–17

MATCHING SYSTEMS AND GRAPHS Match the system of inequalities with its graph.

6. $x - 4y > -8$
$x \geq 2$ C

7. $x - 4y \geq -8$
$x < 2$ A

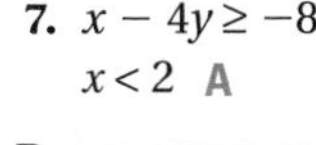

8. $x - 4y > -8$
$y \geq 2$ B

A.
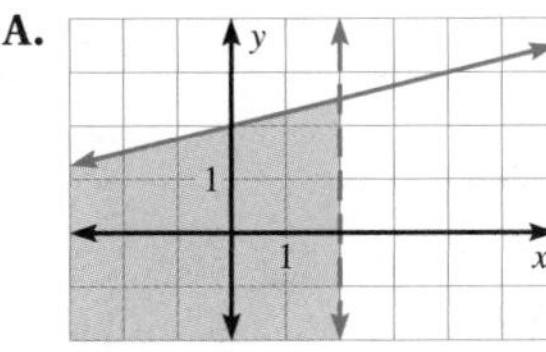

B.
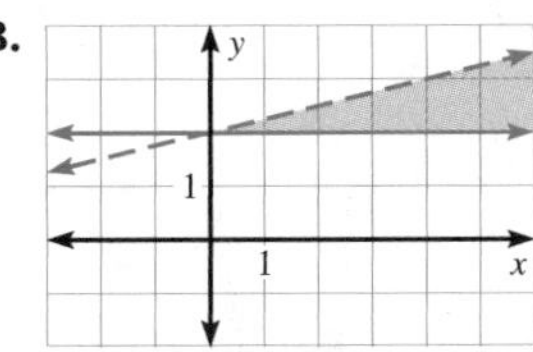

C.
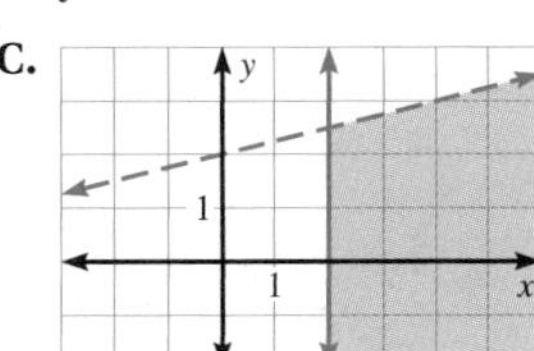

GRAPHING A SYSTEM Graph the system of inequalities. 9–20. See margin.

9. $x > -5$
$x < 2$

10. $y \leq 10$
$y \geq 6$

11. $x > 3$
$y > x$

12. $y < -2x + 3$
$y \geq 4$

13. $y \geq 0$
$y < 2.5x - 1$

14. $y \geq 2x + 1$
$y < -x + 4$

15. $x < 8$
$x - 4y \leq -8$

16. $y \geq -2$
$2x + 3y > -6$

17. $y - 2x < 7$
$y + 2x > -1$

EXAMPLE 2 on p. 467 for Exs. 18–21

18. $x < 4$
$y > 1$
$y \geq -x + 1$

19. $x \geq 0$
$y \geq 0$
$6x - y < 12$

20. $x + y \leq 10$
$x - y \geq 2$
$y \geq 2$

21. ★ **MULTIPLE CHOICE** Which ordered pair is a solution of the system $2x - y \leq 5$ and $x + 2y > 2$? D

Ⓐ (1, −1) Ⓑ (4, 1) Ⓒ (2, 0) Ⓓ (3, 2)

4 PRACTICE AND APPLY

Assignment Guide

Answer Transparencies available for all exercises

Basic:
Day 1: EP p. 943 Exs. 67–70, 72, 73
pp. 469–472
Exs. 1–8, 9–21 odd, 22–26, 36–39, 43–53 odd

Average:
Day 1: pp. 469–472
Exs. 1–8, 15–23, 25–33 odd, 36–40, 42–52 even

Advanced:
Day 1: pp. 469–472
Exs. 1, 2, 16–22, 24–41*, 47, 52

Block:
pp. 469–472
Exs. 1–8, 15–23, 25–33 odd, 36–40, 42–52 even (with 7.5)

Differentiated Instruction

See *Algebra 1 Best Practices Toolkit* for suggestions on addressing the needs of a diverse classroom.

Homework Check

For a quick check of student understanding of key concepts, go over the following exercises:

Basic: 11, 19, 21, 24, 36
Average: 16, 18, 22, 27, 37
Advanced: 16, 20, 22, 28, 38

Extra Practice

- Student Edition, p. 944
- Chapter 7 Resource Book: Practice levels A, B, C, pp. 68–73

Practice Worksheet

An easily-readable reduced practice page (with answers) for this lesson can be found on p. 424C.

9–20. See Additional Answers beginning on p. AA1.

Avoiding Common Errors

Exercise 5 Some students may think the ordered pair is a solution of the system of inequalities since it appears on the boundary. Remind these students that a dashed line is the graph of an inequality containing < or >, so an ordered pair on a dashed line cannot be a solution of the system. You may want to point out that an ordered pair on a solid line is a solution of the system of inequalities.

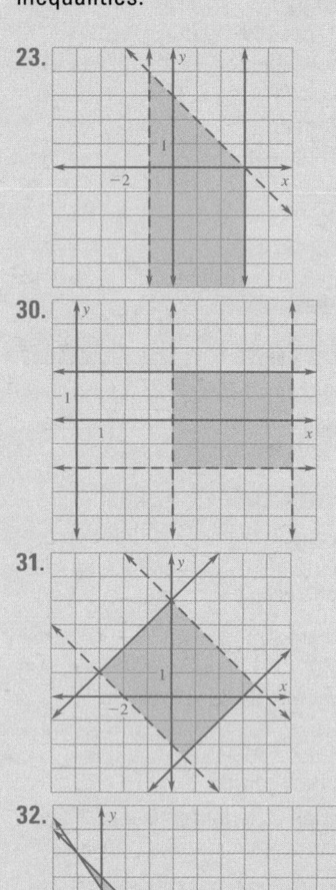

EXAMPLE 2 on p. 467 for Exs. 22–23

22. ★ **MULTIPLE CHOICE** The graph of which system of inequalities is shown? B

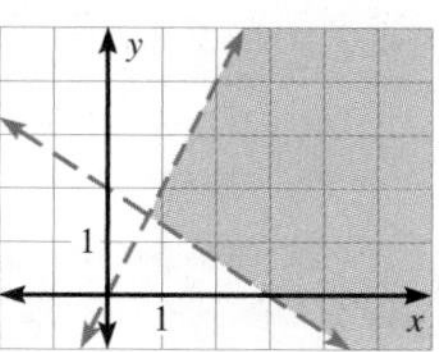

Ⓐ $y < 2x$, $2x + 3y < 6$

Ⓑ $y < 2x$, $2x + 3y > 6$

Ⓒ $y > 2x$, $2x + 3y < 6$

Ⓓ $y > 2x$, $2x + 3y > 6$

23. **ERROR ANALYSIS** *Describe* and correct the error in graphing this system of inequalities:

$x + y < 3$ **Inequality 1**
$x > -1$ **Inequality 2**
$x \leq 3$ **Inequality 3**

The graph is shaded to include $x + y > 3$, not $x + y < 3$; see margin for art.

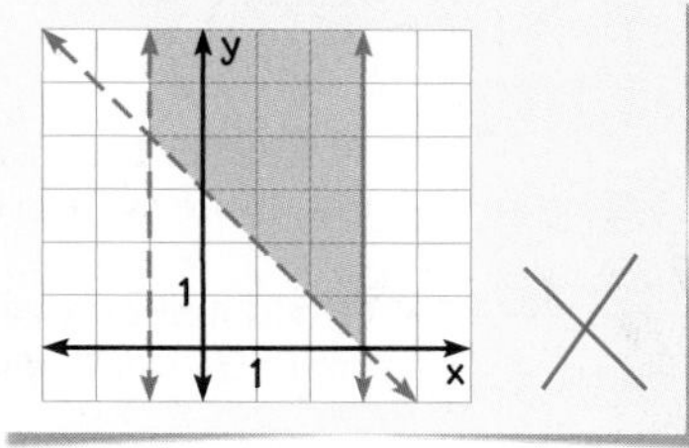

EXAMPLE 3 B on p. 467 for Exs. 24–29

WRITING A SYSTEM Write a system of inequalities for the shaded region.

24.

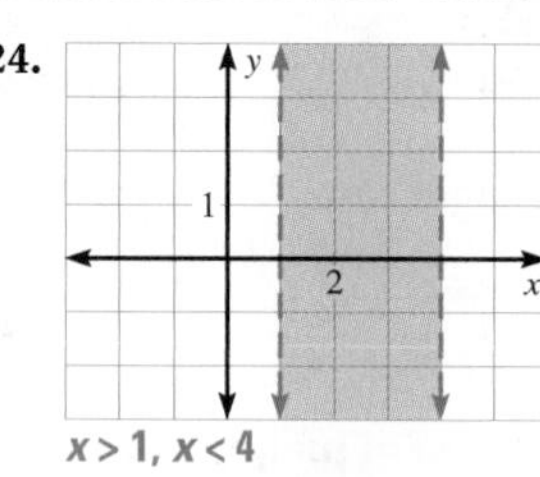

$x > 1, x < 4$

25.

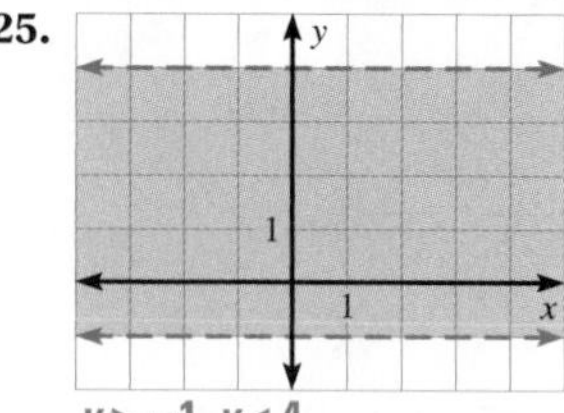

$y > -1, y < 4$

26.

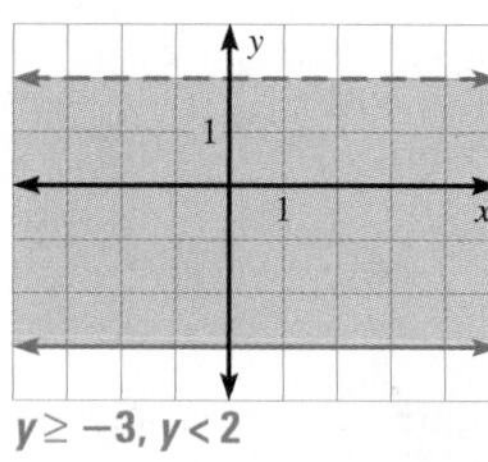

$y \geq -3, y < 2$

27.

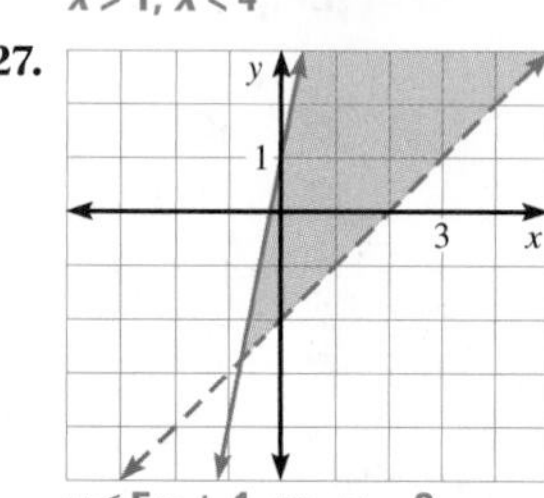

$y \leq 5x + 1, y > x - 2$

28.

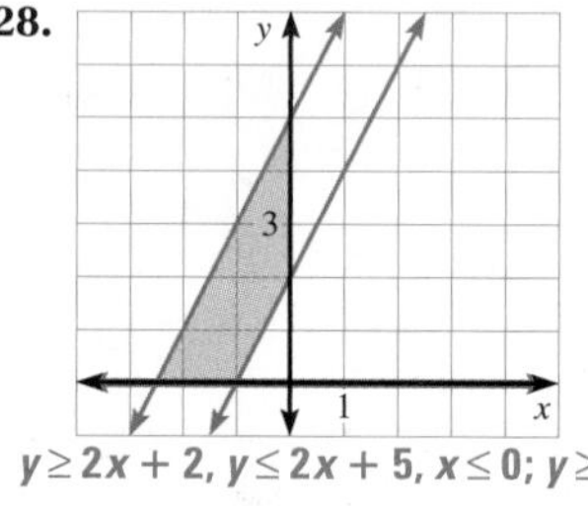

$y \geq 2x + 2, y \leq 2x + 5, x \leq 0; y \geq 0$

29.

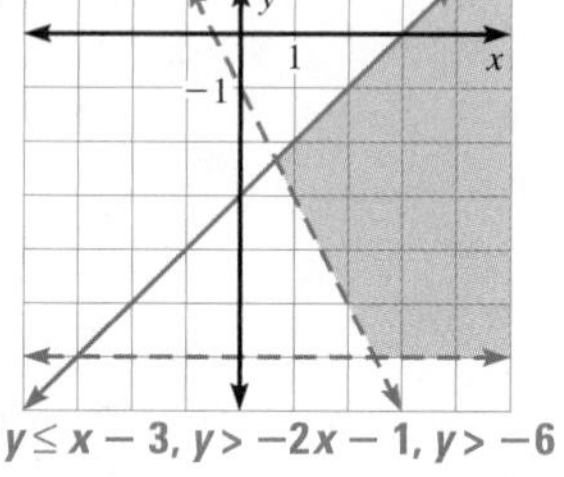

$y \leq x - 3, y > -2x - 1, y > -6$

GRAPHING A SYSTEM Graph the system of inequalities. 30–32. See margin.

30. $x > 4$, $x < 9$, $y \leq 2$, $y > -2$

31. $x + y < 4$, $x + y > -2$, $x - y \leq 3$, $x - y \geq -4$

32. $x \leq 10$, $3x + 2y \geq 9$, $x - 2y \leq 6$, $x + y \leq 5$

33. ★ **SHORT RESPONSE** Does the system of inequalities have any solutions? *Explain.* No; there are no possible values for *x* and *y* that satisfy both equations.

$x - y > 5$ **Inequality 1**
$x - y < 1$ **Inequality 2**

C **CHALLENGE** Write a system of inequalities for the shaded region described.

34. The shaded region is a rectangle with vertices at (2, 1), (2, 4), (6, 4), and (6, 1). $x \geq 2, x \leq 6, y \geq 1, y \leq 4$

35. The shaded region is a triangle with vertices at (−3, 0), (3, 2), and (0, −2). $y \leq \frac{1}{3}x + 1, y \geq -\frac{2}{3}x - 2, y \geq \frac{4}{3}x - 2$

○ = WORKED-OUT SOLUTIONS on p. WS1 ★ = STANDARDIZED TEST PRACTICE

PROBLEM SOLVING

EXAMPLE 4 A on p. 468 for Exs. 36–38

36. COMPETITION SCORES In a marching band competition, scoring is based on a musical evaluation and a visual evaluation. The musical evaluation score cannot exceed 60 points, the visual evaluation score cannot exceed 40 points. Write and graph a system of inequalities for the scores that a marching band can receive. **Let x represent the musical evaluation score and y represent the visual evaluation score. $x \le 60$, $y \le 40$, $x \ge 0$, $y \ge 0$, see margin for art.**

@HomeTutor for problem solving help at classzone.com

37. NUTRITION For a hiking trip, you are making a mix of x ounces of peanuts and y ounces of chocolate pieces. You want the mix to have less than 70 grams of fat and weigh less than 8 ounces. An ounce of peanuts has 14 grams of fat, and an ounce of chocolate pieces has 7 grams of fat. Write and graph a system of inequalities that models the situation. **$14x + 7y < 70$, $x + y < 8$, $x \ge 0$, $y \ge 0$, see margin for art.**

@HomeTutor for problem solving help at classzone.com

38. FISHING LIMITS You are fishing in a marina for surfperch and rockfish, which are two species of bottomfish. Gaming laws in the marina allow you to catch no more than 15 surfperch per day, no more than 10 rockfish per day, and no more than 15 total bottomfish per day.

a. Write and graph a system of inequalities that models the situation.

b. Use the graph to determine whether you can catch 11 surfperch and 9 rockfish in one day. **no**

39. HEALTH A person's maximum heart rate (in beats per minute) is given by $220 - x$ where x is the person's age in years ($20 \le x \le 65$). When exercising, a person should aim for a heart rate that is at least 70% of the maximum heart rate and at most 85% of the maximum heart rate.

a. Write and graph a system of inequalities that models the situation.

b. A 40-year-old person's heart rate varies from 104 to 120 beats per minute while exercising. Does his heart rate stay in the suggested target range for his age? *Explain.*

B **40. ★ SHORT RESPONSE** A photography shop has a self-service photo center that allows you to make prints of pictures. Each sheet of printed pictures costs $8. The number of pictures that fit on each sheet is shown.

a. You want at least 16 pictures of any size, and you are willing to spend up to $48. Write and graph a system of inequalities that models the situation.

b. Will you be able to purchase 12 pictures that are 3 inches by 5 inches and 6 pictures that are 4 inches by 6 inches? *Explain.*

Four 3 inch by 5 inch pictures fit on one sheet.

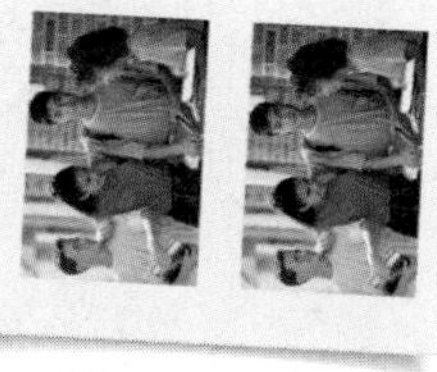

Two 4 inch by 6 inch pictures fit on one sheet.

38a. Let s represent the number of surfperch and r represent the number of rockfish. $s \le 15$, $s + r \le 15$, $r \le 10$, $s \ge 0$, $r \ge 0$, see margin for art.

39a. $20 \le x \le 65$, $y \ge 154 - 0.7x$, $y \le 187 - 0.85x$, see margin for art.

39b. No. *Sample answer:* The heart rate is below 70% of the maximum heart rate.

40a. $8x + 8y \le 48$, $4x + 2y \ge 16$, $x \ge 0$, $y \ge 0$, see margin for art.

40b. Yes. *Sample answer:* It would cost $48 and give you 18 pictures.

Vocabulary

Exercises 36, 38, 39 Encourage students to pay close attention to the phrases "cannot exceed," "no more than," "at least," and "at most." Point out that all of these phrases share a common meaning of "less than or equal to."

Study Strategy

Exercises 36–40 Remind students that real-world situations often do not include negative solutions. If the situation warrants a restriction to a certain quadrant, students should include that inequality when they write the system of inequalities.

Exercise 38 For more information about bottomfish and local fishing laws, visit Hawaii's Department of Aquatic Resources at www.state.hi.us/dlnr/dar/bottomfish/index.htm

Exercise 39 To learn more about maximum heart rates, visit the American Heart Association's website at www.americanheart.org and do a search for "target heart rates."

39a.

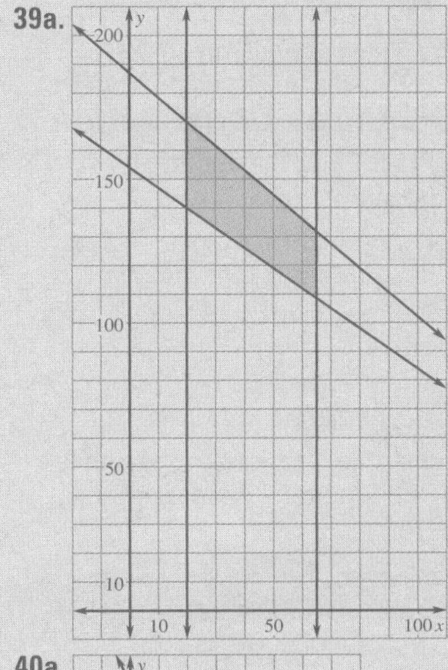

40a.

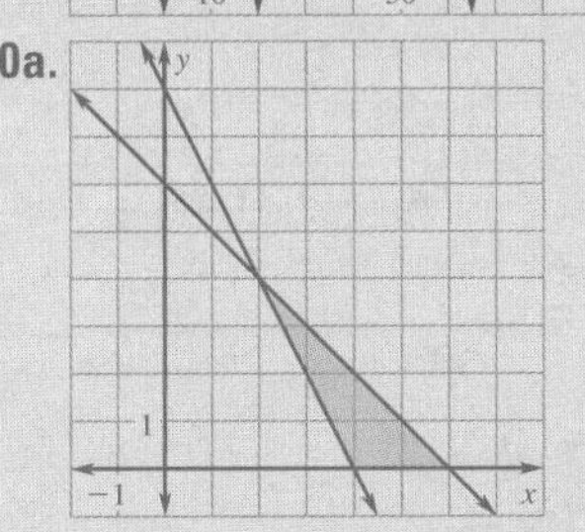

36.

y
10
−10
x

37.

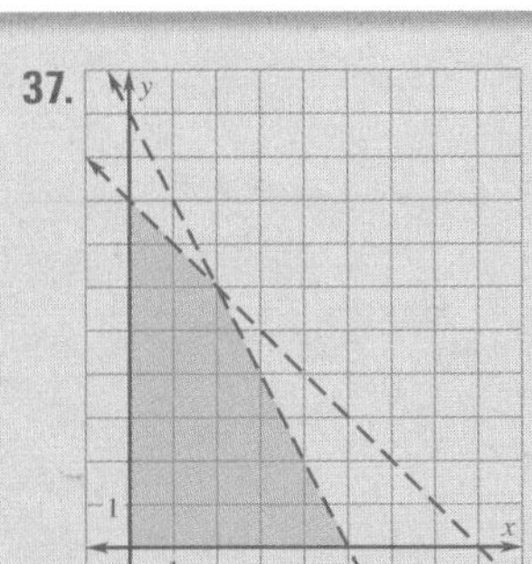

38.

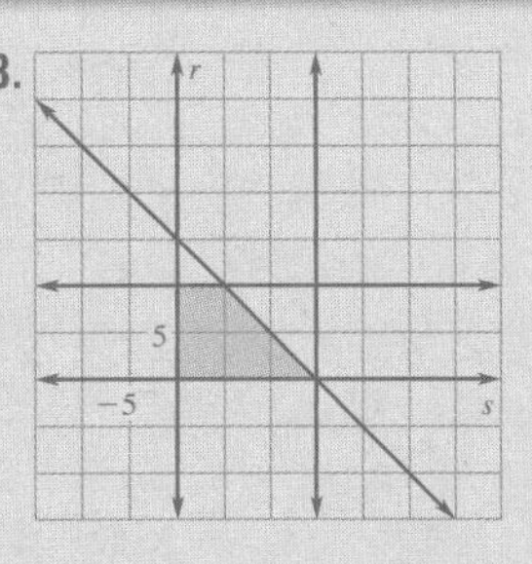

5 ASSESS AND RETEACH

Daily Homework Quiz

Transparency Available

1. Write a system of inequalities for the shaded region.

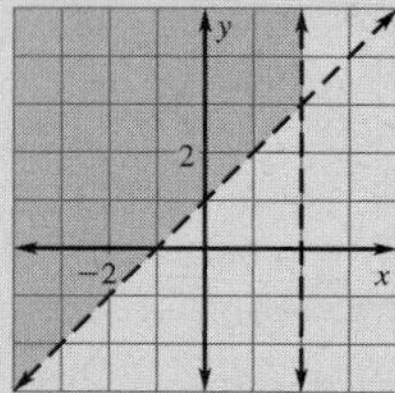

$x < 2$, $y > x + 1$

2. A bibliography can refer to at most 8 articles, at most 4 books, and at most 8 references in all. Write and graph a system of inequalities that models the situation. x = articles, y = books; $x \le 8$, $y \le 4$, $x + y \le 8$, $x \ge 0$, and $y \ge 0$

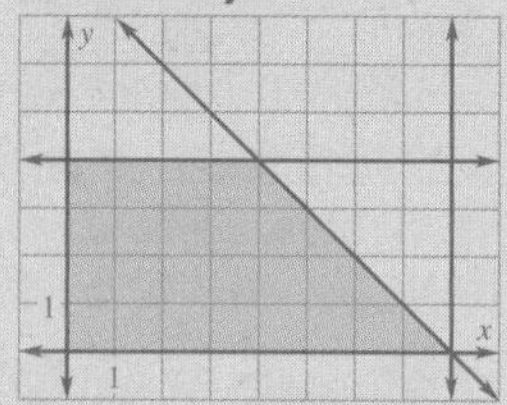

Online Quiz

Available at **classzone.com**

Diagnosis/Remediation

- Practice A, B, C in Chapter 7 Resource Book, pp. 68–73
- Study Guide in Chapter 7 Resource Book, pp. 74–75
- Practice Workbook, pp. 116–118
- @HomeTutor

Challenge

Additional challenge is available in the Chapter 7 Resource Book, p. 78.

Quiz

An easily-readable reduced copy of the quiz (with answers) on Lessons 7.5–7.6 from the Assessment Book can be found on p. 424F.

41a, Quiz 1–9. See Additional Answers beginning on p. AA1.

C **41. CHALLENGE** You make necklaces and keychains to sell at a craft fair. The table shows the time that it takes to make each necklace and keychain, the cost of materials for each necklace and keychain, and the time and money that you can devote to making necklaces and keychains.

	Necklace	Keychain	Available
Time to make (hours)	0.5	0.25	20
Cost to make (dollars)	2	3	120

41a. $0.5x + 0.25y \le 20$, $2x + 3y \le 120$, $y \ge 0$, $x \ge 0$, see margin for art.

a. Write and graph a system of inequalities for the number x of necklaces and the number y of keychains that you can make under the given constraints.

b. Find the vertices (corner points) of the graph. (0, 0), (40, 0), (0, 40), (30, 20)

c. You sell each necklace for \$10 and each keychain for \$8. The revenue R is given by the equation $R = 10x + 8y$. Find the revenue for each ordered pair in part (b). Which vertex results in the maximum revenue? (0, 0): \$0, (40, 0): \$400, (0, 40): \$320, (30, 20): \$460. The maximum revenue is at (30, 20), or 30 necklaces and 20 keychains.

ILLINOIS MIXED REVIEW

TEST PRACTICE at classzone.com

42. The cost of renting a condominium for a week at a resort is described by the function $f(n) = 800 + 75(n - 1)$, where $f(n)$ is the cost and n is the number of people staying in the condominium. If a maximum of 7 people can stay in the condominium, what is the most a group can pay for the condominium for one week? B

(A) \$1,150 (B) \$1,250 (C) \$1,325 (D) \$1,400

43. Susan believes that $(xy)^2 \ge xy$ for all values of x and y. Which pair of values for x and y could be used to disprove Susan's theory? D

(A) $x = -1, y = -1$ (B) $x = -1, y = 1$

(C) $x = 0, y = 1$ (D) $x = 1, y = \frac{1}{2}$

QUIZ *for Lessons 7.5–7.6*

Graph the linear system. Then use the graph to tell whether the linear system has *one solution, no solution,* or *infinitely many solutions.* *(p. 459)* 1–3. See margin for art.

1. $x - y = 1$, $x - y = 6$ no solution

2. $6x + 2y = 16$, $2x - y = 2$ one solution

3. $3x - 3y = -2$, $-6x + 6y = 4$ infinitely many solutions

Graph the system of linear inequalities. *(p. 466)* 4–9. See margin.

4. $x > -3$, $x < 7$

5. $y \le 2$, $y < 6x + 2$

6. $4x \ge y$, $-x + 4y < 4$

7. $x + y < 2$, $2x + y > -3$, $y \ge 0$

8. $y \ge 3x - 4$, $y \le x$, $y \ge -5x - 15$

9. $x > -5$, $x < 0$, $y \le 2x + 7$

Illinois *Mixed Review*

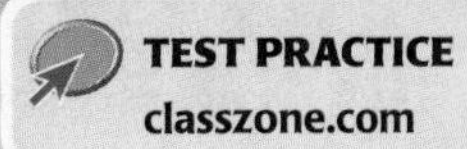

TEST PRACTICE
classzone.com

Lessons 7.5–7.6

1. **PAINT** You are painting a room and spend \$120 on 4 cans of yellow paint and 2 cans of white paint. You decide to paint another room using the same colors, and you spend \$60 for 2 cans of yellow paint and 1 can of white paint. How much does one can of each color of paint cost?

   A. yellow: \$10, white: \$30

   B. yellow: \$20, white: \$20

   C. yellow: \$30, white: \$10

   D. The cost cannot be determined.

2. **SUMMER JOBS** During the summer, you want to earn at least \$250 per week. You earn \$10 per hour working as a lifeguard, and you earn \$8 per hour working at a retail store. You can work at most 30 hours per week. Suppose you are scheduled to work at the retail store for 10 hours per week. Which inequality gives the range of hours x you must work as a lifeguard to meet your goal?

   F. $x \geq 20$ **H.** $15 \leq x \leq 20$

   G. $10 \leq x \leq 20$ **J.** $17 \leq x \leq 20$

3. **POPULATION** The table shows the current population and rate of growth for four towns. You want to use the data to predict when each pair of towns will have the same population. For which pair of towns will this *not* occur?

Town	Population (people)	Rate of growth (people per year)
Baker	12,000	1,800
Lincoln	18,000	1,400
Riverton	20,000	1,400
Thorton	24,000	1,200

   A. Baker and Thorton

   B. Baker and Riverton

   C. Lincoln and Riverton

   D. Lincoln and Thorton

4. **CONSTRUCTION** A minimum of 600 bricks and 12 bags of sand are needed for a construction job. Each brick weighs 2 pounds, and each bag of sand weighs 50 pounds. The maximum weight that a delivery truck can carry is 2000 pounds. Which amount of bricks and sand cannot be delivered by the truck in one load?

   F. 600 bricks, 15 bags of sand

   G. 650 bricks, 14 bags of sand

   H. 750 bricks, 10 bags of sand

   J. 700 bricks, 13 bags of sand

5. **MUSIC** During a sale at a music store, all CDs are priced the same and all music videos on DVD are priced the same. Tyler buys 4 CDs and 2 DVDs for \$78. The next day, while the sale is still in progress, Tyler goes back and buys 2 CDs and 1 DVD. What is the cost (in dollars) of his second purchase?

   A. \$26

   B. \$34

   C. \$39

   D. \$52

6. **GARDEN** What is the area (in square units) of the rectangular garden defined by the following system of inequalities?

   $x \geq -2$
   $x \leq 6$
   $y \geq -2$
   $y \leq 4$

   F. 8 square units

   G. 12 square units

   H. 24 square units

   J. 48 square units

Illinois Mixed Review

1. D
2. J
3. C
4. J
5. C
6. J

7 CHAPTER SUMMARY

Additional Resources

The following resources are available to help review the materials in this chapter.

Chapter 7 Resource Book

- Chapter Review Games and Activities, p. 79
- Cumulative Practice, Chs. 1–7, pp. 82–83

Student Resources in Spanish

eWorkbook

@HomeTutor

Vocabulary Practice

Vocabulary practice is available at **classzone.com**

BIG IDEAS — *For Your Notebook*

Big Idea 1

Solving Linear Systems by Graphing

The graph of a system of two linear equations tells you how many solutions the system has.

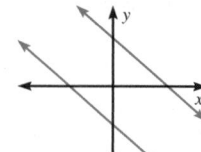

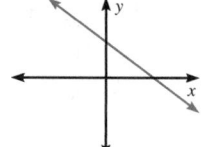

One solution	**No solution**	**Infinitely many solutions**
The lines intersect.	The lines are parallel.	The lines coincide.

Big Idea 2

Solving Linear Systems Using Algebra

You can use any of the following algebraic methods to solve a system of linear equations. Sometimes it is easier to use one method instead of another.

Method	Procedure	When to use
Substitution	Solve one equation for x or y. Substitute the expression for x or y into the other equation.	When one equation is already solved for x or y
Addition	Add the equations to eliminate x or y.	When the coefficients of one variable are opposites
Subtraction	Subtract the equations to eliminate x or y.	When the coefficients of one variable are the same
Multiplication	Multiply one or both equations by a constant so that adding or subtracting the equations will eliminate x or y.	When no corresponding coefficients are the same or opposites

Big Idea 3

Solving Systems of Linear Inequalities

The graph of a system of linear inequalities is the intersection of the half-planes of each inequality in the system. For example, the graph of the system of inequalities below is the shaded region.

$x \leq 6$	Inequality 1
$y < 2$	Inequality 2
$2x + 3y \geq 6$	Inequality 3

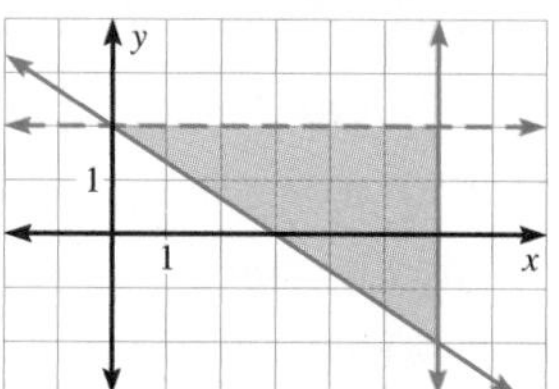

7 CHAPTER REVIEW

@HomeTutor
classzone.com
• Multi-Language Glossary
• Vocabulary practice

REVIEW KEY VOCABULARY

- system of linear equations, *p. 427*
- solution of a system of linear equations, *p. 427*
- consistent independent system, *p. 427*
- inconsistent system, *p. 459*
- consistent dependent system, *p. 459*
- system of linear inequalities, *p. 466*
- solution of a system of linear inequalities, *p. 466*
- graph of a system of linear inequalities, *p. 466*

VOCABULARY EXERCISES

1. Copy and complete: A(n) _?_ consists of two or more linear inequalities in the same variables. **system of linear inequalities**
2. Copy and complete: A(n) _?_ consists of two or more linear equations in the same variables. **system of linear equations**
3. *Describe* how you would graph a system of two linear inequalities. **See margin.**
4. Give an example of a consistent dependent system. *Explain* why the system is a consistent dependent system. ***Sample answer:*** **$y = 2x + 3$, $2y = 4x + 6$; the lines intersect (are consistent) and the equations are equivalent (are dependent).**

REVIEW EXAMPLES AND EXERCISES

Use the review examples and exercises below to check your understanding of the concepts you have learned in each lesson of Chapter 7.

7.1 Solve Linear Systems by Graphing

pp. 427–433

EXAMPLE

Solve the linear system by graphing. Check your solution.

$y = x - 2$ **Equation 1**
$y = -3x + 2$ **Equation 2**

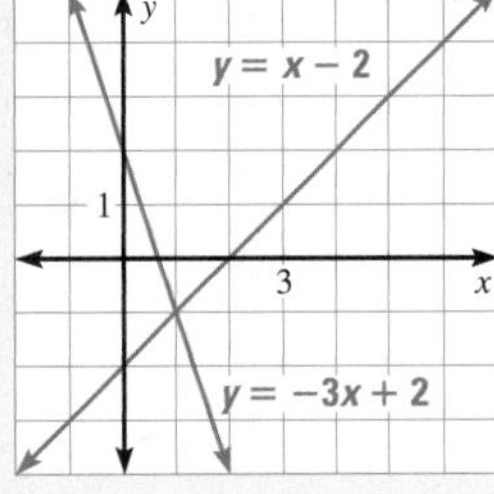

Graph both equations. The lines appear to intersect at (1, −1). Check the solution by substituting 1 for x and −1 for y in each equation.

$y = x - 2$	$y = -3x + 2$
$-1 \stackrel{?}{=} 1 - 2$	$-1 \stackrel{?}{=} -3(1) + 2$
$-1 = -1$ ✓	$-1 = -1$ ✓

EXERCISES

EXAMPLES 1 and 2 on pp. 427–428 for Exs. 5–7

Solve the linear system by graphing. Check your solution.

5. $y = -3x + 1$ **(2, −5)**
$y = x - 7$

6. $y = 3x + 4$ **(−1, 1)**
$y = -2x - 1$

7. $x + y = 3$ **(4, −1)**
$x - y = 5$

Extra Example 7.1

Solve the linear system by graphing. Check your solution.
$y = -x + 4$
$y = 2x - 5$ **(3, 1)**

3. ***Sample answer:*** **Graph each inequality then shade the region that is the intersection of the solutions to each inequality. Then check the solution with a test point.**

Extra Example 7.2

Solve the linear system using substitution.

$y + 2x = 13$
$-x + 4y = -2$ (6, 1)

Extra Example 7.3

Solve the linear system using elimination.

$-2x + 3y = 6$
$-2x + 5y = -6$ (−12, −6)

7 CHAPTER REVIEW

7.2 Solve Linear Systems by Substitution

pp. 435–441

EXAMPLE

Solve the linear system: $3x + y = -9$ **Equation 1**
$y = 5x + 7$ **Equation 2**

STEP 1 **Substitute** $5x + 7$ for y in Equation 1 and solve for x.

$3x + y = -9$ **Write Equation 1.**

$3x + 5x + 7 = -9$ **Substitute 5x + 7 for y.**

$x = -2$ **Solve for x.**

STEP 2 **Substitute** -2 for x in Equation 2 to find the value of y.

$$y = 5x + 7 = 5(-2) + 7 = -10 + 7 = -3$$

▸ The solution is (−2, −3). Check the solution by substituting −2 for x and −3 for y in each of the original equations.

EXERCISES

EXAMPLES 1, 2, and 3 on pp. 435–437 for Exs. 8–11

Solve the linear system using substitution.

8. $y = 2x - 7$ (3, −1)
$x + 2y = 1$

9. $x + 4y = 9$ (5, 1)
$x - y = 4$

10. $2x + y = -15$ (−3, −9)
$y - 5x = 6$

11. ART Kara spends \$16 on tubes of paint and disposable brushes for an art project. Each tube of paint costs \$3, and each disposable brush costs \$.50. Kara purchases twice as many brushes as tubes of paint. Find the number of brushes and the number of tubes of paint that she purchases. **4 tubes of paint, 8 brushes**

7.3 Solve Linear Systems by Adding or Subtracting

pp. 444–450

EXAMPLE

Solve the linear system: $5x - y = 8$ **Equation 1**
$-5x + 4y = -17$ **Equation 2**

STEP 1 **Add** the equations to eliminate one variable.

$$\begin{array}{r} 5x - y = 8 \\ -5x + 4y = -17 \\ \hline 3y = -9 \end{array}$$

STEP 2 **Solve** for y. $y = -3$

STEP 3 **Substitute** -3 for y in either equation and solve for x.

$5x - y = 8$ **Write Equation 1.**

$5x - (-3) = 8$ **Substitute −3 for y.**

$x = 1$ **Solve for x.**

▸ The solution is (1, −3). Check the solution by substituting 1 for x and −3 for y in each of the original equations.

@HomeTutor
classzone.com
Chapter Review Practice

EXERCISES

EXAMPLES 1, 2, and 3 on pp. 444–445 for Exs. 12–17

Solve the linear system using elimination.

12. $x + 2y = 13$ (3, 5)
$x - 2y = -7$

13. $4x - 5y = 14$ (1, −2)
$-4x + y = -6$

14. $x + 7y = 12$ (−2, 2)
$-2x + 7y = 18$

15. $9x - 2y = 34$ (6, 10)
$5x - 2y = 10$

16. $3x = y + 1$ (−8, −25)
$2x - y = 9$

17. $4y = 11 - 3x$ (−7, 8)
$3x + 2y = -5$

7.4 Solve Linear Systems by Multiplying First

pp. 451–457

EXAMPLE

Solve the linear system: $x - 2y = -7$ **Equation 1**
$3x - y = 4$ **Equation 2**

STEP 1 **Multiply** the first equation by −3.

$$\begin{array}{ll} x - 2y = -7 & \xrightarrow{\times(-3)} \quad -3x + 6y = 21 \\ 3x - y = 4 & \qquad\qquad\; 3x - y = 4 \end{array}$$

STEP 2 **Add** the equations. $5y = 25$

STEP 3 **Solve** for *y*. $y = 5$

STEP 4 **Substitute** 5 for *y* in either of the original equations and solve for *x*.

$x - 2y = -7$ **Write Equation 1.**

$x - 2(5) = -7$ **Substitute 5 for *y*.**

$x = 3$ **Solve for *x*.**

▶ The solution is (3, 5).

CHECK Substitute 3 for *x* and 5 for *y* in each of the original equations.

Equation 1	Equation 2
$x - 2y = -7$	$3x - y = 4$
$3 - 2(5) \stackrel{?}{=} -7$	$3(3) - 5 \stackrel{?}{=} 4$
$-7 = -7$ ✓	$4 = 4$ ✓

EXERCISES

EXAMPLES 1 and 2 on pp. 451–452 for Exs. 18–24

Solve the linear system using elimination.

18. $-x + y = -4$ (7, 3)
$2x - 3y = 5$

19. $x + 6y = 28$ (−2, 5)
$2x - 3y = -19$

20. $3x - 5y = -7$ (−9, −4)
$-4x + 7y = 8$

21. $8x - 7y = -3$ (4, 5)
$6x - 5y = -1$

22. $5x = 3y - 2$ (2, 4)
$3x + 2y = 14$

23. $11x = 2y - 1$ (1, 6)
$3y = 10 + 8x$

24. **CAR MAINTENANCE** You pay \$24.50 for 10 gallons of gasoline and 1 quart of oil at a gas station. Your friend pays \$22 for 8 gallons of the same gasoline and 2 quarts of the same oil. Find the cost of 1 quart of oil. \$2

Extra Example 7.4

Solve the linear system using elimination.
$3x - 2y = 5$
$2x - 3y = 5$ (1, −1)

Extra Example 7.5

Show that the linear system has infinitely many solutions.

$y = -2x - 4$
$6x + 3y = -12$

Substitute $-2x - 4$ for y in the equation $6x + 3y = -12$ and solve for x.

$$6x + 3y = -12$$
$$6x + 3(-2x - 4) = -12$$
$$6x - 6x - 12 = -12$$
$$-12 = -12$$

Since this is a true statement, the system has infinitely many solutions.

Extra Example 7.6

Graph the system of linear inequalities.

$y \geq x - 1$
$y < -2x$

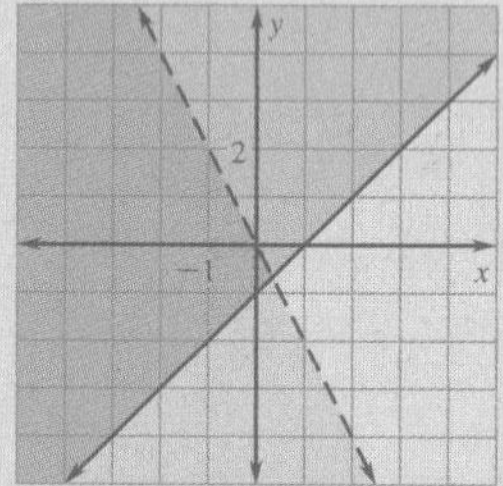

25. No solution. *Sample answer:* When the variables are eliminated, a false statement remains, which means there is no solution.

26. Infinitely many solutions. *Sample answer:* When the variables are eliminated, a true statement remains, which means there are infinitely many solutions.

27. One solution. *Sample answer:* The lines have different slopes, so there is only one solution.

28. 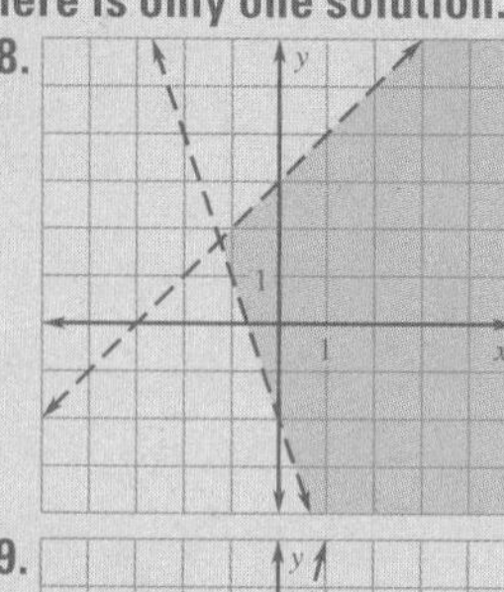

29. 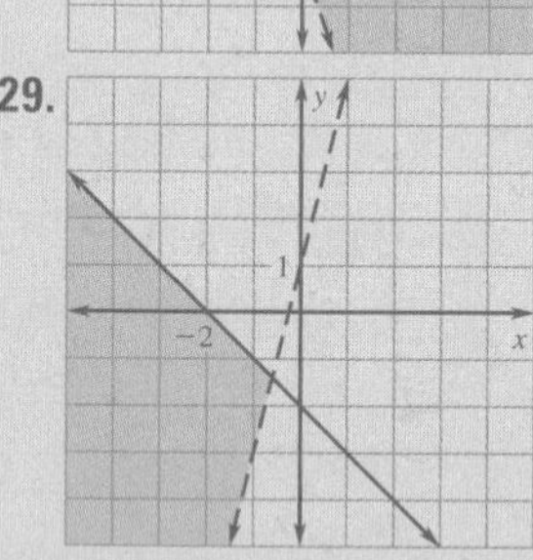

7 CHAPTER REVIEW

7.5 Solve Special Types of Linear Systems

pp. 459–465

EXAMPLE

Show that the linear system has no solution.

$-2x + y = -3$ **Equation 1**
$y = 2x + 1$ **Equation 2**

Graph the linear system.

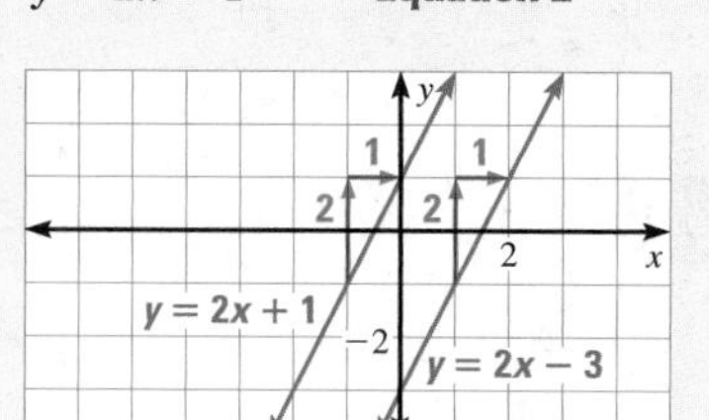

The lines are parallel because they have the same slope but different y-intercepts. Parallel lines do not intersect, so the system has no solution.

EXERCISES

EXAMPLES 1, 2, and 3 on pp. 459–461 for Exs. 25–27

Tell whether the linear system has *one solution, no solution,* or *infinitely many solutions. Explain.* 25–27. See margin.

25. $x = 2y - 3$
$1.5x - 3y = 0$

26. $-x + y = 8$
$x + 8 = y$

27. $4x = 2y + 6$
$4x + 2y = 10$

7.6 Solve Systems of Linear Inequalities

pp. 466–472

EXAMPLE

Graph the system of linear inequalities.

$y < -2x + 3$ **Inequality 1**
$y \geq x - 3$ **Inequality 2**

The graph of $y < -2x + 3$ is the half-plane *below* the *dashed* line $y = -2x + 3$.

The graph of $y \geq x - 3$ is the half-plane *on and above* the *solid* line $y = x - 3$.

The graph of the system is the intersection of the two half-planes shown as the darker shade of blue.

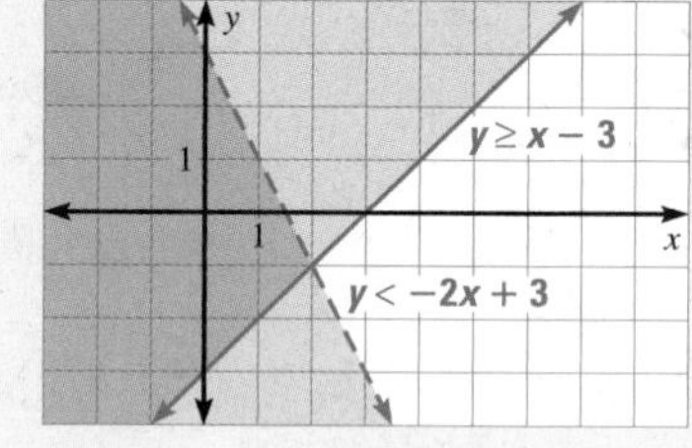

EXERCISES

EXAMPLES 1, 2, 3, and 4 on pp. 466–468 for Exs. 28–31

Graph the system of linear inequalities. 28–30. See margin.

28. $y < x + 3$
$y > -3x - 2$

29. $y \leq -x - 2$
$y > 4x + 1$

30. $y \geq 0$
$x \leq 2$
$y < x + 4$

31. MOVIE COSTS You receive a \$40 gift card to a movie theater. A ticket to a matinee movie costs \$5, and a ticket to an evening movie costs \$8. Write and graph a system of inequalities for the number of tickets you can purchase using the gift card. Let m represent the number of matinee movies and n represent the number of evening movies. $5m + 8n \leq 40$, $m \geq 0$, $n \geq 0$, see margin for art.

30. 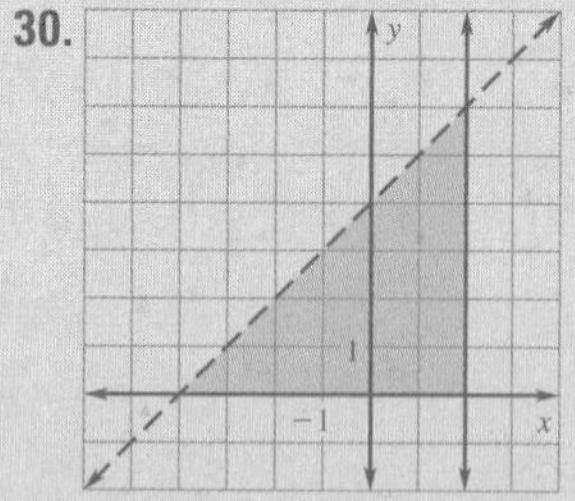

31. 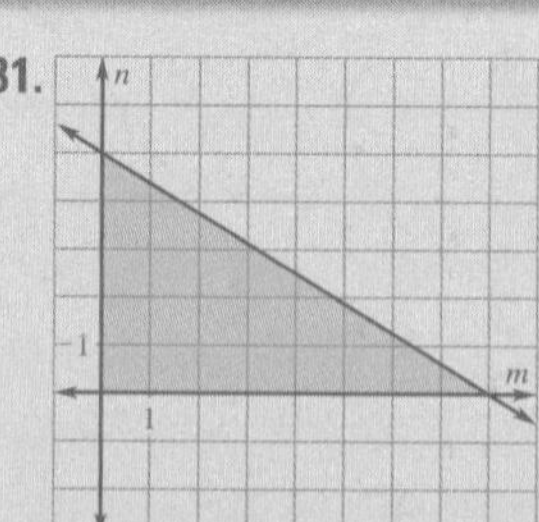

7 CHAPTER TEST

Solve the linear system by graphing. Check your solution.

1. $3x - y = -6$; $x + y = 2$ $(-1, 3)$

2. $-2x + y = 5$; $x + y = -1$ $(-2, 1)$

3. $y = 4x + 4$; $3x + 2y = 12$ $\left(\frac{4}{11}, 5\frac{5}{11}\right)$

4. $5x - 4y = 20$; $x + 2y = 4$ $(4, 0)$

5. $x + 3y = 9$; $2x - y = 4$ $(3, 2)$

6. $2x + 7y = 14$; $5x + 7y = -7$ $(-7, 4)$

Solve the linear system using substitution.

7. $y = 5x - 7$; $-4x + y = -1$ $(6, 23)$

8. $x = y - 11$; $x - 3y = 1$ $(-17, -6)$

9. $3x + y = -19$; $x - y = 7$ $(-3, -10)$

10. $15x + y = 70$; $3x - 2y = -8$ $(4, 10)$

11. $3y + x = 17$; $x + y = 8$ $(3.5, 4.5)$

12. $0.5x + y = 9$; $1.6x + 0.2y = 13$ $\left(7\frac{7}{15}, 5\frac{4}{15}\right)$

Solve the linear system using elimination.

13. $8x + 3y = -9$; $-8x + y = 29$ $(-3, 5)$

14. $x - 5y = -3$; $3x - 5y = 11$ $(7, 2)$

15. $4x + y = 17$; $7y = 4x - 9$ $(4, 1)$

16. $3x + 2y = -5$; $x - y = 10$ $(3, -7)$

17. $3y = x + 5$; $-3x + 8y = 8$ $(16, 7)$

18. $6x - 5y = 9$; $9x - 7y = 15$ $(4, 3)$

Tell whether the linear system has *one solution, no solution,* or *infinitely many solutions.*

19. $15x - 3y = 12$; $y = 5x - 4$ infinitely many solutions

20. $4x - y = -4$; $-8x + 2y = 2$ no solution

21. $-12x + 3y = 18$; $4x + y = -6$ one solution

22. $6x - 7y = 5$; $-12x + 14y = 10$ no solution

23. $3x - 4y = 24$; $3x + 4y = 24$ one solution

24. $10x - 2y = 14$; $15x - 3y = 21$ infinitely many solutions

Graph the system of linear inequalities. 25–27. See margin.

25. $y < 2x + 2$; $y \geq -x - 1$

26. $y \leq 3x - 2$; $y > x + 4$

27. $y \leq 3$; $x > -1$; $y > 3x - 3$

28. TRUCK RENTALS Carrie and Dave each rent the same size moving truck for one day. They pay a fee of x dollars for the truck and y dollars per mile they drive. Carrie drives 150 miles and pays \$215. Dave drives 120 miles and pays \$176. Find the amount of the fee and the cost per mile. fee: \$20, cost per mile: \$1.30

29. GEOMETRY The rectangle has a perimeter P of 58 inches. The length ℓ is one more than 3 times the width w. Write and solve a system of linear equations to find the length and width of the rectangle. $2\ell + 2w = 58$, $\ell = 3w + 1$, $\ell = 22$ in., $w = 7$ in.

$P = 58$ in. (width w, length ℓ)

30. COMMUNITY SERVICE A town committee has a budget of \$75 to spend on snacks for the volunteers participating in a clean-up day. The committee chairperson decides to purchase granola bars and at least 50 bottles of water. Granola bars cost \$.50 each, and bottles of water cost \$.75 each. Write and graph a system of linear inequalities for the number of bottles of water and the number of granola bars that can be purchased. See margin.

25.

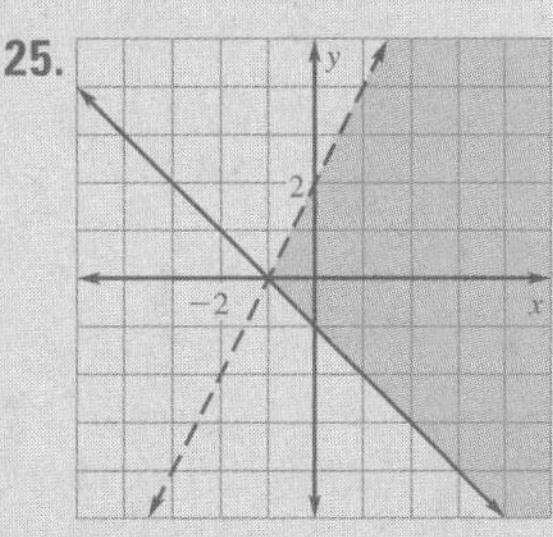

Additional Resources

Assessment Book

- Chapter Test, Levels A, B, C, pp. 93–98
- Standardized Chapter Test, pp. 99–100
- SAT/ACT Chapter Test, pp. 101–102
- Alternative Assessment, pp. 103–104

Test Generator CD-ROM

Chapter Test

Easily-readable reduced copies (with answers) of Chapter Test B, the Standardized Chapter Test, and the Alternative Assessment from the Assessment Book can be found on pp. 424G–424H.

26.

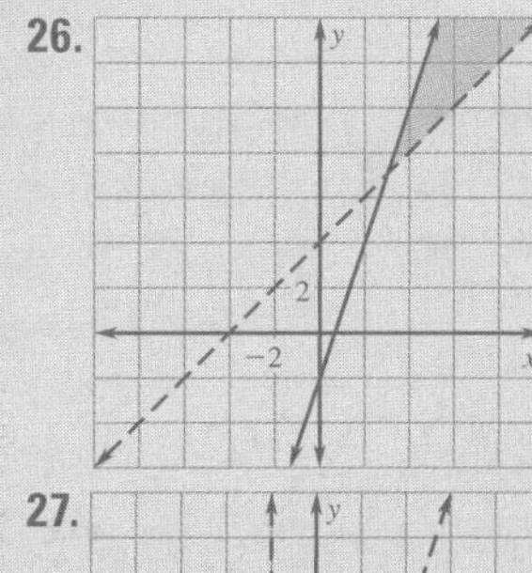

27.

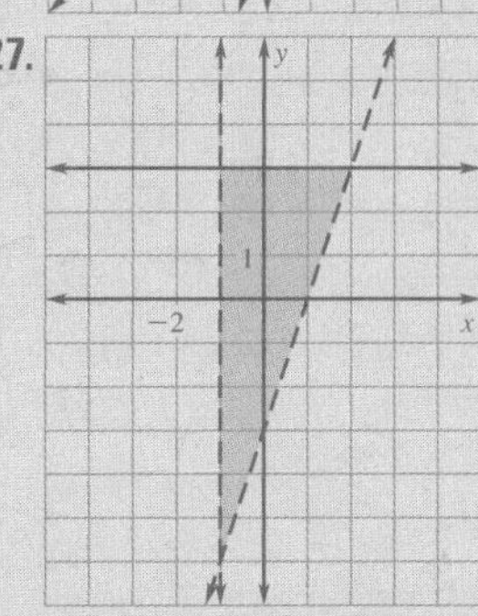

30. Let w represent the number of water bottles and g represent the number of granola bars; $w \geq 50$, $g \geq 0$, $0.5g + 0.75w \leq 75$.

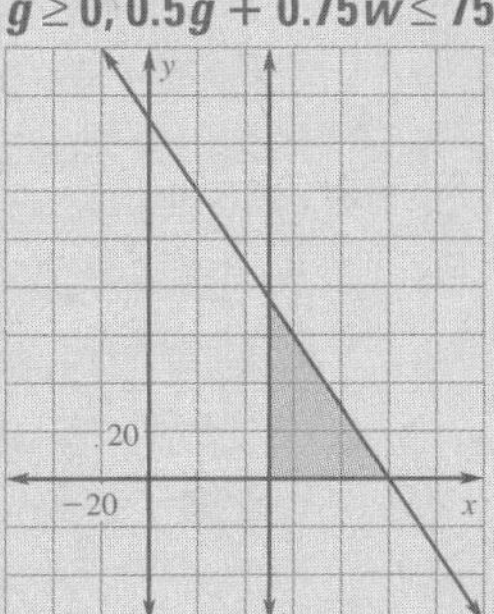

MULTIPLE CHOICE QUESTIONS

If you have difficulty solving a multiple choice problem directly, you may be able to use another approach to eliminate incorrect answer choices and obtain the correct answer.

PROBLEM 1

Which ordered pair is the solution of the linear system $y = \frac{1}{2}x$ and $2x + 3y = -7$?

A. (2, 1) **B.** (1, −3) **C.** (−2, −1) **D.** (4, 2)

Method 1

SOLVE DIRECTLY Use substitution to solve the linear system.

STEP 1 **Substitute** $\frac{1}{2}x$ for y in the equation $2x + 3y = -7$ and solve for x.

$$2x + 3y = -7$$

$$2x + 3\left(\frac{1}{2}x\right) = -7$$

$$2x + \frac{3}{2}x = -7$$

$$\frac{7}{2}x = -7$$

$$x = -2$$

STEP 2 **Substitute** −2 for x in $y = \frac{1}{2}x$ to find the value of y.

$$y = \frac{1}{2}x$$

$$= \frac{1}{2}(-2)$$

$$= -1$$

The solution of the system is (−2, −1).

The correct answer is **C**.

Method 2

ELIMINATE CHOICES Substitute the values given in each answer choice for x and y in both equations.

Choice A: (2, 1)
Substitute 2 for x and 1 for y.

$y = \frac{1}{2}x$ $\qquad$ $2x + 3y = -7$

$1 \stackrel{?}{=} \frac{1}{2}(2)$ $\qquad$ $2(2) + 3(1) \stackrel{?}{=} -7$

$1 = 1$ ✓ $\qquad$ $7 = -7$ ✗

Choice B: (1, −3)
Substitute 1 for x and −3 for y.

$y = \frac{1}{2}x$

$-3 \stackrel{?}{=} \frac{1}{2}(1)$

$-3 = \frac{1}{2}$ ✗

Choice C: (−2, −1)
Substitute −2 for x and −1 for y.

$y = \frac{1}{2}x$ $\qquad$ $2x + 3y = -7$

$-1 \stackrel{?}{=} \frac{1}{2}(-2)$ $\qquad$ $2(-2) + 3(-1) \stackrel{?}{=} -7$

$-1 = -1$ ✓ $\qquad$ $-7 = -7$ ✓

The correct answer is **C**.

PROBLEM 2

The sum of two numbers is −1, and the difference of the two numbers is 5. What are the numbers?

F. −5 and 4 **G.** 1 and 6 **H.** 2 and −3 **J.** −2 and 3

Method 1

SOLVE DIRECTLY Write and solve a system of equations for the numbers.

STEP 1 **Write** a system of equations. Let x and y be the numbers.

$x + y = -1$ **Equation 1**
$x - y = 5$ **Equation 2**

STEP 2 **Add** the equations to eliminate one variable. Then find the value of the other variable.

$$\begin{aligned} x + y &= -1 \\ x - y &= 5 \\ \hline 2x = 4, \text{ so } x &= 2 \end{aligned}$$

STEP 3 **Substitute** 2 for x in Equation 1 and solve for y.

$2 + y = -1$, so $y = -3$

The correct answer is **H.**

Method 2

ELIMINATE CHOICES Find the sum and difference of each pair of numbers. Because the difference is positive, be sure to subtract the lesser number from the greater number.

Choice F: −5 and 4

Sum: $-5 + 4 = -1$ ✓

Difference: $-5 - 4 = -9$ ✗

Choice G: 1 and 6

Sum: $1 + 6 = 7$ ✗

Choice H: 2 and −3

Sum: $2 + (-3) = -1$ ✓

Difference: $2 - (-3) = 5$ ✓

The correct answer is **H.**

PRACTICE

Explain why you can eliminate the highlighted answer choice.

1. The sum of two numbers is –27. One number is twice the other. What are the numbers?

   A. ✗ 9 and 18 **B.** −3 and 24 **C.** −18 and −9 **D.** −14 and −13

2. Which ordered pair is a solution of the linear system $5x + 2y = -11$ and $x = -\frac{1}{2}y - 4$?

   F. $\left(-\frac{7}{6}, -\frac{17}{3}\right)$ **G.** $\left(-\frac{23}{3}, \frac{1}{3}\right)$ **H.** $(-3, 2)$ **J.** ✗ $(-3, -13)$

3. Long-sleeve and short-sleeve T-shirts can be purchased at a concert. A long-sleeve T-shirt costs $25 and a short-sleeve T-shirt costs $15. During a concert, the T-shirt vendor collects $8415 from the sale of 441 T-shirts. How many short-sleeve T-shirts were sold?

   A. 100 **B.** ✗ 180 **C.** 261 **D.** 441

TEST PREPARATION

Illinois Test Practice

1. The sum of 9 and 18 is not negative.
2. $5(-3) + 3(-13)$ does not equal -11.
3. If 180 short-sleeve T-shirts are sold, then 261 long-sleeve T-shirts would be sold, and 261($25) + 180($15) does not equal $8415.

Illinois Test Practice

1. B
2. F
3. D
4. J
5. B
6. G
7. B
8. J
9. A
10. G
11. D
12. F
13. A
14. H
15. B
16. H
17. B
18. F

Illinois Test Practice

1. Which ordered pair is the solution of the linear system $y = \frac{1}{2}x + 1$ and $y = \frac{3}{2}x + 4$?

   A. $\left(3, \frac{5}{2}\right)$ **C.** $\left(\frac{3}{2}, \frac{7}{4}\right)$
   B. $\left(-3, -\frac{1}{2}\right)$ **D.** $(0, 1)$

2. How many solutions does the linear system $3x + 5y = 8$ and $3x + 5y = 1$ have?

   F. 0 **H.** 2
   G. 1 **J.** Infinitely many

3. The sum of two numbers is −3, and the difference of the two numbers is 11. What are the numbers?

   A. 4 and 7 **C.** 3 and 14
   B. −3 and 8 **D.** −7 and 4

4. Which ordered pair is the solution of the system of linear equations whose graph is shown?

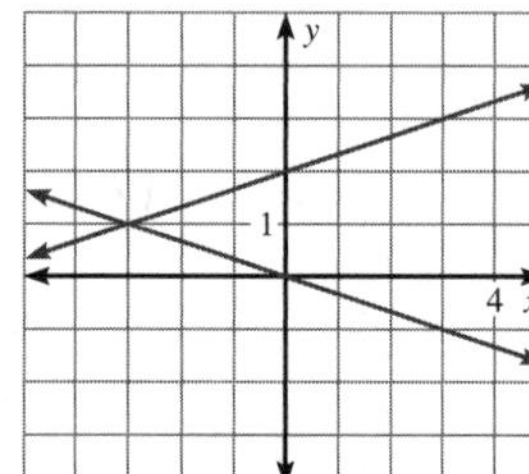

   F. $(3, -1)$ **H.** $(0, 2)$
   G. $(0, 0)$ **J.** $(-3, 1)$

5. Which ordered pair is the solution of the linear system $3x + y = -1$ and $y = -\frac{1}{2}x - \frac{7}{2}$?

   A. $\left(\frac{5}{2}, -\frac{17}{2}\right)$ **C.** $(-1, -3)$
   B. $(1, -4)$ **D.** $(0, -1)$

6. Which ordered pair is a solution of the system $x + 2y \leq -2$ and $y \leq -3x + 4$?

   F. $(0, 0)$ **H.** $(-2, 2)$
   G. $(2, -2)$ **J.** $(5, -4)$

7. How many solutions does the system of linear equations whose graph is shown have?

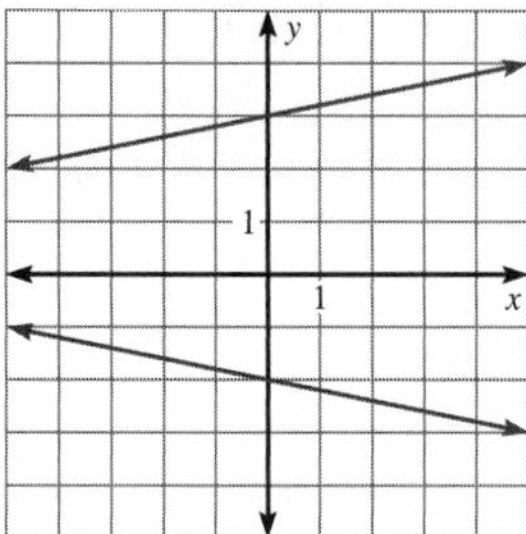

   A. 0 **C.** 2
   B. 1 **D.** Infinitely many

8. At a bakery, one customer pays \$5.67 for 3 bagels and 4 muffins. Another customer pays \$6.70 for 5 bagels and 3 muffins. Which system of equations can be used to determine the cost x (in dollars) of one bagel and the cost y (in dollars) of one muffin at the bakery?

   F. $x + y = 7$, $x + y = 8$ **H.** $3x + 4y = 6.7$, $5x + 3y = 5.67$
   G. $y = 3x + 5.67$, $y = 5x + 6.7$ **J.** $3x + 4y = 5.67$, $5x + 3y = 6.7$

9. The perimeter P (in feet) of each of the two rectangles below is given. What are the values of ℓ and w?

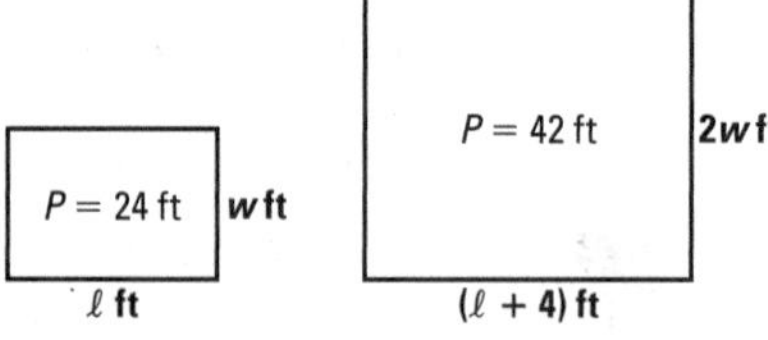

   A. $\ell = 7$ and $w = 5$
   B. $\ell = 8$ and $w = 4$
   C. $\ell = 11$ and $w = 10$
   D. $\ell = 12$ and $w = 9$

10. Which point represents the solution of the system of linear equations?

$3x - 2y = 8$
$x + 4y = -2$

F. (−2, −1) **H.** (−2, 1)

G. (2, −1 **J.** (2, 1)

11. What is the value of xy if $x + 5y = 26$ and $-x + y - 4$?

A. −5 **C.** 4

B. −4 **D.** 5

12. What is the value of $x - y$ if $5x - 3y = 3$ and $-x + 3y = 9$?

F. −1 **H.** 4

G. 3 **J.** 12

13. How many solutions does the linear system have?

$3x - 11y = 4$
$3x - 11y = 22$

A. None

B. Exactly one

C. Two

D. Infinitely many

14. Which system of linear equations has a solution represented by the ordered pair (−1, 2)?

F. $2x + y = 1$
$5x - y = 13$

H. $2x + y = 0$
$3x - y = -5$

G. $2x + y = 4$
$2x - y = 6$

J. $2x - y = 0$
$3x + y = -5$

15. Which point is a solution of the system of linear inequalities?

$y < -2x$
$y > 3x + 5$

A. (2, −1) **C.** (−1, 4)

B. (−4, 1) **D.** (1, −2)

16. Use the graph to determine which ordered pair is a solution of the linear system.

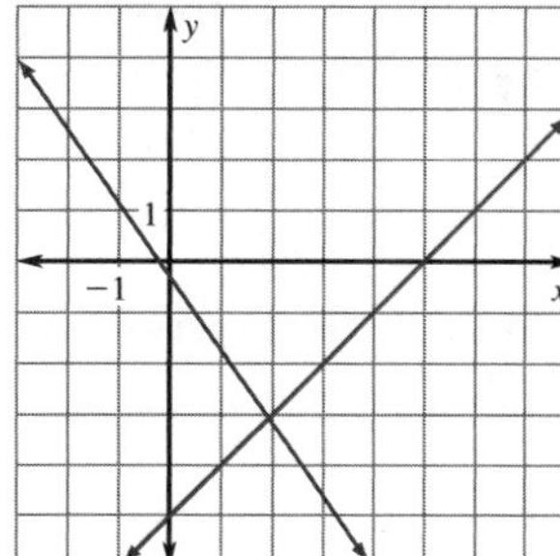

F. (−3, 2)

G. (−2, 3)

H. (2, −3)

J. (3, −2)

17. To solve the linear system below, which substitution of unknowns is proper?

$3x - 7y = 12$
$5x - y = -16$

A. Substitute $5x - 16$ for y in the first equation.

B. Substitute $5x + 16$ for y in the first equation.

C. Substitute $5x + 12$ for y in the first equation.

D. Substitute $7y - 4$ for x in the second equation.

18. One plane is traveling toward the airport following the line $3x - 2y = 1$. Another plane is traveling toward the airport following the line $-x + 4y = -27$. What are the coordinates of the airport?

F. (−5, −8)

G. (5, −8)

H. (−8, 5)

J. (5, 8)

TEST PRACTICE

Additional Resources

The following resources are available to help review the materials in Chapters 1–7.

Chapter Resource Books

- Chapter 4 CRB, Cumulative Review, pp. 105–106
- Chapter 5 CRB, Cumulative Review, pp. 92–93
- Chapter 6 CRB, Cumulative Review, pp. 101–102
- Chapter 7 CRB, Cumulative Review, pp. 82–83

Assessment Book

- Cumulative Test, Chapters 1–7, pp. 105–108

Evaluate the expression.

1. $2^5 \cdot 2 - 4 \div 2$ *(p. 8)* 62
2. $24 \div 6 + (9 - 6)$ *(p. 8)* 7
3. $5[(6 - 2)^2 - 5]$ *(p. 8)* 55
4. $\sqrt{144}$ *(p. 110)* 12
5. $-\sqrt{2500}$ *(p. 110)* -50
6. $\pm\sqrt{400}$ *(p. 110)* ± 20

Check whether the given number is a solution of the equation or inequality. *(p. 21)*

7. $7 + 3x = 16; 3$ solution
8. $21y + 1 = 1; 0$ solution
9. $20 - 12h = 12; 1$ not a solution
10. $g - 3 > 2; 5$ not a solution
11. $10 \geq 4 - x; 0$ solution
12. $30 - 4p \geq 5; 6$ solution

Simplify the expression.

13. $5(y - 1) + 4$ *(p. 96)* $5y - 1$
14. $12w + (w - 2)3$ *(p. 96)* $15w - 6$
15. $(g - 1)(-4) + 3g$ *(p. 96)* $-g + 4$
16. $\frac{10h - 25}{5}$ *(p. 103)* $2h - 5$
17. $\frac{21 - 4x}{-7}$ *(p. 103)* $-3 + \frac{4}{7}x$
18. $\frac{32 - 20m}{2}$ *(p. 103)* $16 - 10m$

Solve the equation.

19. $x - 8 = 21$ *(p. 134)* 29
20. $-1 = x + 3$ *(p. 134)* -4
21. $6x = -42$ *(p. 134)* -7
22. $\frac{x}{3} = 8$ *(p. 134)* 24
23. $5 - 2x = 11$ *(p. 141)* -3
24. $\frac{2}{3}x - 3 = 17$ *(p. 141)* 30
25. $3(x - 2) = -15$ *(p. 148)* -3
26. $3(5x - 7) = 5x - 1$ *(p. 154)* 2
27. $-7(2x - 10) = 4x - 10$ *(p. 154)* $4\frac{4}{9}$

Graph the equation. 28–33. See margin.

28. $x + 2y = -8$ *(p. 225)*
29. $-2x + 5y = -10$ *(p. 225)*
30. $3x - 4y = 12$ *(p. 225)*
31. $y = 3x - 7$ *(p. 244)*
32. $y = x + 6$ *(p. 244)*
33. $y = -\frac{1}{3}x$ *(p. 253)*

Write an equation of the line in slope-intercept form with the given slope and *y*-intercept. *(p. 283)*

34. slope: 5, *y*-intercept: -1 $y = 5x - 1$
35. slope: -1, *y*-intercept: 3 $y = -x + 3$
36. slope: -7, *y*-intercept: 0 $y = -7x$

Write an equation in point-slope form of the line that passes through the given points. *(p. 302)* 37–42. See margin.

37. $(1, -10), (-5, 2)$
38. $(4, 7), (-4, 3)$
39. $(-9, -2), (-6, 8)$
40. $(-1, 1), (1, -3)$
41. $(2, 4), (8, 2)$
42. $(-6, 1), (3, -5)$

Solve the inequality. Then graph your solution. 43–54. See margin for art.

43. $x - 9 < -13$ *(p. 356)* $x < -4$
44. $8 \leq x + 7$ *(p. 356)* $x \geq 1$
45. $8x \geq 56$ *(p. 363)* $x \geq 7$
46. $\frac{x}{-4} > 7$ *(p. 363)* $x < -28$
47. $1 - 2x < 11$ *(p. 369)* $x > -5$
48. $8 > -3x - 1$ *(p. 369)* $x > -3$
49. $4x - 10 \leq 7x + 8$ *(p. 369)* $x \geq -6$
50. $7x - 5 < 6x - 4$ *(p. 369)* $x < 1$
51. $-4 < 3x - 1 < 5$ *(p. 380)* $-1 < x < 2$
52. $3 \leq 9 - 2x \leq 15$ *(p. 380)* $-3 \leq x \leq 3$
53. $|3x| < 15$ *(p. 398)* $-5 < x < 5$
54. $|4x - 2| \geq 18$ *(p. 398)* $x \leq -4$ or $x \geq 5$

28.

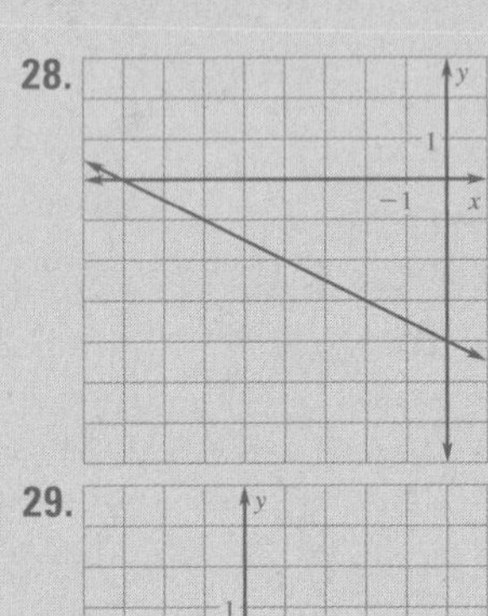

29.

30.

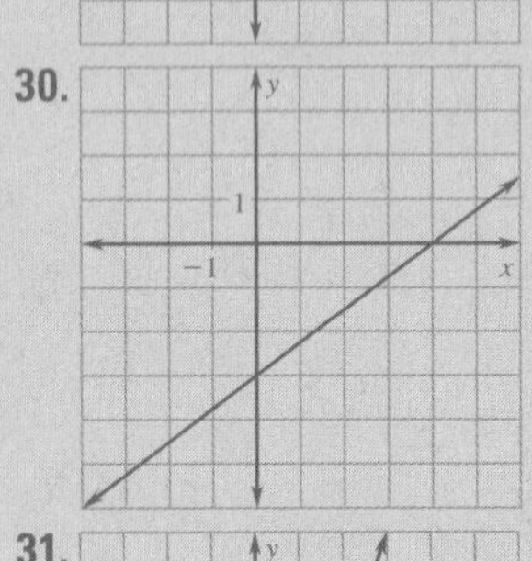

31.

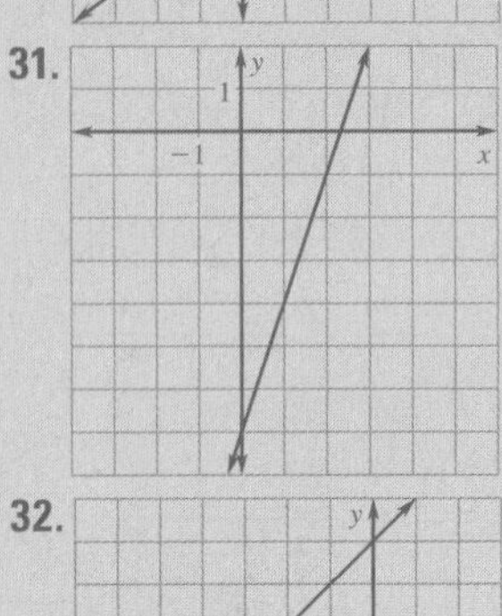

32.

33.

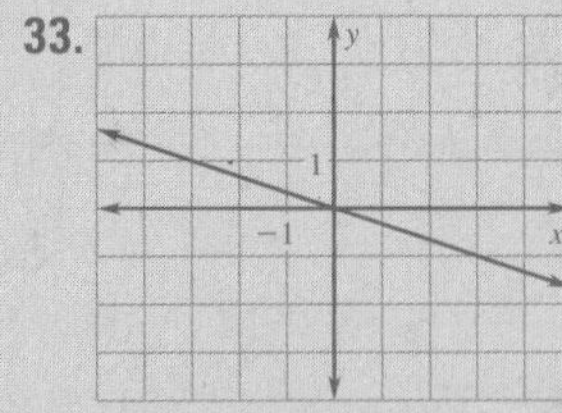

37. $y + 10 = -2(x - 1)$ or $y - 2 = -2(x + 5)$

38. $y - 7 = \frac{1}{2}(x - 4)$ or $y - 3 = \frac{1}{2}(x + 4)$

39. $y + 2 = \frac{10}{3}(x + 9)$ or $y - 8 = \frac{10}{3}(x + 6)$

40. $y - 1 = -2(x + 1)$ or $y + 3 = -2(x - 1)$

41. $y - 4 = -\frac{1}{3}(x - 2)$ or $y - 2 = -\frac{1}{3}(x - 8)$

42. $y - 1 = -\frac{2}{3}(x + 6)$ or $y + 5 = -\frac{2}{3}(x - 3)$

Solve the linear system using elimination. *(p. 451)*

55. $4x + y = 8$
$5x - 2y = -3$ (1, 4)

56. $3x - 5y = 5$
$x - 5y = -4$ (4.5, 1.7)

57. $12x + 7y = 3$
$8x + 5y = 1$ (2, −3)

58. **ART PROJECT** You are making a tile mosaic on the rectangular tabletop shown. A bag of porcelain tiles costs \$3.95 and covers 36 square inches. How much will it cost to buy enough tiles to cover the tabletop? *(p. 28)* \$79

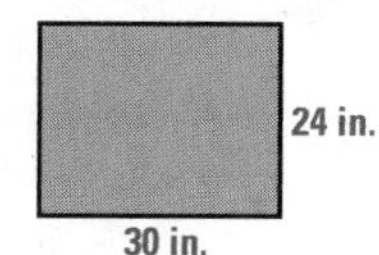

59. **FOOD** The table shows the changes in the price for a dozen grade A, large eggs over 4 years. Find the average yearly change to the nearest cent in the price for a dozen grade A, large eggs during the period 1999–2002. *(p. 103)* \$.02

Year	1999	2000	2001	2002
Change in price for a dozen grade A, large eggs (dollars)	−0.17	0.04	−0.03	0.25

60. **HONEY PRODUCTION** Honeybees visit about 2,000,000 flowers to make 16 ounces of honey. About how many flowers do honeybees visit to make 6 ounces of honey? *(p. 168)* 750,000 flowers

61. **MUSIC** The table shows the price p (in dollars) for various lengths of speaker cable. *(p. 253)*

Length, ℓ (feet)	3	5	12	15
Price, p (dollars)	7.50	12.50	30.00	37.50

a. *Explain* why p varies directly with ℓ. The ratio $\frac{p}{\ell}$ is always the same, so p varies directly with ℓ.

b. Write a direct variation equation that relates ℓ and p. $p = 2.5\ell$

62. **CURRENCY** The table shows the exchange rate between the currency of Bolivia (bolivianos) and U.S. dollars from 1998 to 2003. *(p. 335)*

Year	1998	1999	2000	2001	2002	2003
Bolivianos per U.S. dollar	5.51	5.81	6.18	6.61	7.17	7.66

a. Find an equation that models the bolivianos per U.S. dollar as a function of the number of years since 1998. See margin.

b. If the trend continues, predict the number of bolivianos per U.S. dollar in 2010. *Sample answer:* 10.63 bolivianos

63. **BATTERIES** A manufacturer of nickel-cadmium batteries recommends storing the batteries at temperatures ranging from −20°C to 45°C. Use an inequality to describe the temperatures (in degrees Fahrenheit) at which the batteries can be stored. *(p. 380)* $-4 < F < 113$

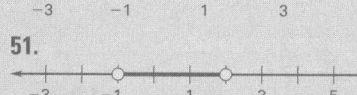

53.
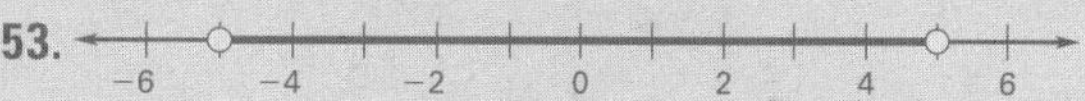

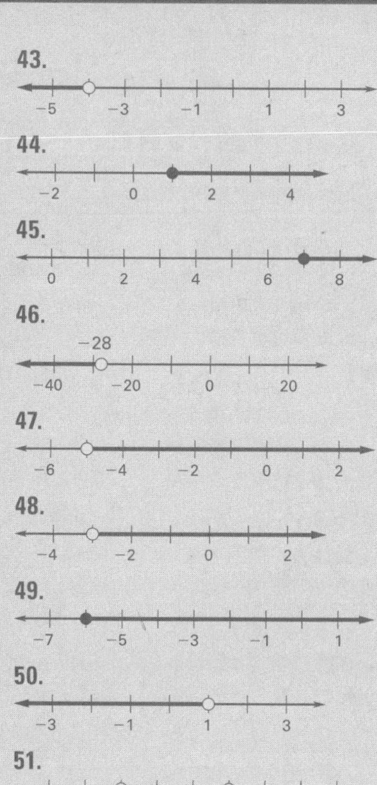

52.
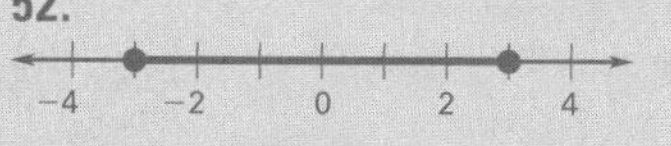

53. See below.

54.
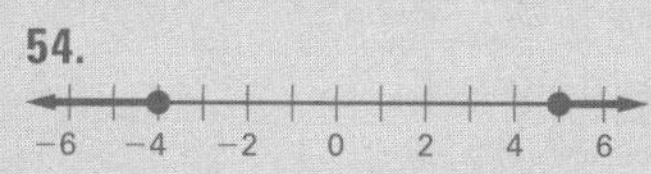

62a. *Sample answer:* Let x = number of years since 1998 and y = bolivianos per U.S. dollar; $y = 0.436x + 5.4$.

Illinois Resources Guide

Pacing and Assignment Guide

REGULAR SCHEDULE

Pre-AP For pacing and assignments for a Pre-AP course, see the *Algebra 1 Toolkit*.

Lesson	Les. Day	BASIC	AVERAGE	ADVANCED
8.1 6.11.07	Day 1	pp. 492–494 Exs. 1, 2, 3–15 odd, 19–39 odd, 40–42, 52–57, 60–74 even	pp. 492–494 Exs. 1, 2, 4–18 even, 29–49, 53–58, 61, 64, 67, 73	pp. 492–494 Exs. 1, 2, 8–18 even, 31–38, 40–51*, 54–59*, 62, 65, 68, 74
8.2 8.11.01	Day 1	pp. 498–501 Exs. 1–28	pp. 498–501 Exs. 1, 2, 7–28, 38–40	pp. 498–501 Exs. 1, 2, 9–19, 21–28, 38–40, 47, 48*
	Day 2	pp. 498–501 Exs. 29–39, 49–52, 55–66	pp. 498–501 Exs. 31–37, 41–46, 49–53, 55–66	pp. 498–501 Exs. 32–37, 41–46, 49–66*
8.3 8.11.01	Day 1	pp. 506–508 Exs. 1, 2, 3–35 odd, 50–55, 60–68 even	pp. 506–508 Exs. 1, 2, 9–14, 21–27, 28–44 even, 45, 51–57, 60–68 even	pp. 506–508 Exs. 1, 2, 11–14, 22–26, 29–43 odd, 44–49*, 52–58*, 59, 61, 68
8.4 6.11.02	Day 1	EP p. 939 Exs. 32–37; pp. 514–518 Exs. 1–28	pp. 514–518 Exs. 1, 2, 6–15, 19–28, 39–44	pp. 514–518 Exs. 1, 2, 8–15, 21–27, 39–47
	Day 2	pp. 514–518 Exs. 29–36, 39–41, 51–56, 61–74	pp. 514–518 Exs. 29–38, 45–49, 51–59, 62–74 even	pp. 514–518 Exs. 29–38, 48–60*, 64, 67, 68, 71
8.5 8.11.12	Day 1	SRH p. 923 Exs. 9–13; pp. 523–527 Exs. 1–21	pp. 523–527 Exs. 1–8, 11–21, 35, 60, 61	pp. 523–527 Exs. 1, 2, 4–8, 13–21, 35–37*, 60
	Day 2	pp. 523–527 Exs. 22–27, 38–43, 52–61	pp. 523–527 Exs. 22–34, 38–46, 52–58 even	pp. 523–527 Exs. 26–34, 39–51*, 54, 58
8.6 8.11.12	Day 1	pp. 535–538 Exs. 1–18, 63–66	pp. 535–538 Exs. 1–6, 10–18, 32–34, 63–66	pp. 535–538 Exs. 1, 4–6, 12–18, 32–37, 63–66
	Day 2	pp. 535–538 Exs. 19–35 odd, 36–40, 47–50, 54–62 even	pp. 535–538 Exs. 19, 20–30 even, 35–44, 47–52, 55, 58, 61	pp. 535–538 Exs. 19, 24–31, 38–53*, 56, 59, 62
Review	Day 1	pp. 543–546 Exs. 1–42	pp. 543–546 Exs. 1–42	pp. 543–546 Exs. 1–42
Assess	Day 1	Chapter 8 Test	Chapter 8 Test	Chapter 8 Test
Yearly Pacing		Chapter 8 Total – 12 days	Chapters 1–8 Total – 92 days	Remaining – 68 days

*Challenge Exercises EP = Extra Practice SRH = Skills Review Handbook

BLOCK SCHEDULE

*Challenge Exercises EP = Extra Practice SRH = Skills Review Handbook

DAY 1	DAY 2	DAY 3	DAY 4	DAY 5	DAY 6
8.1	**8.2 (CONT.)**	**8.4**	**8.5**	**8.6**	**REVIEW**
pp. 492–494 Exs. 1, 2, 4–18 even, 29–49, 53–58, 61, 64, 67, 73	pp. 498–501 Exs. 31–37, 41–46, 49–53, 55–66	pp. 514–518 Exs. 1, 2, 6–15, 19–49, 51–59, 62–74 even	pp. 523–527 Exs. 1–8, 11–35, 38–46, 52–58 even, 60, 61	pp. 535–538 Exs. 1–6, 10–19, 20–30 even, 32–44, 47–52, 55, 58, 61, 63–66	pp. 543–546 Exs. 1–42
8.2	**8.3**				**ASSESS**
pp. 498–501 Exs. 1, 2, 7–28, 38–40	pp. 506–508 Exs. 1, 2, 9–14, 21–27, 28–44 even, 45, 51–57, 60–68 even				Chapter 8 Test
Yearly Pacing	Chapter 8 Total – 6 days	Chapters 1–8 Total – 46 days	Remaining – 34 days		

Chapter Resource Guide

Chapter Resource Book

CHAPTER SUPPORT						
Parents as Partners (Chapter Overview with home involvement exercises and activity)					p. 1	
LESSON SUPPORT **Standard**	8.1 **6.11.07**	8.2 **8.11.01**	8.3 **8.11.01**	8.4 **6.11.02**	8.5 **8.11.12**	8.6 **8.11.12**
Teaching Guide/Lesson Plan	p. 3	p. 14	p. 25	p. 36	p. 47	p. 62
Activity Masters		p. 16			p. 49	
Technology Activities & Keystrokes				p. 38	p. 50	p. 64
Activity Support Masters	p. 5					
Practice (3 levels)	p. 6	p. 17	p. 27	p. 39	p. 51	p. 66
Study Guide	p. 9	p. 20	p. 30	p. 42	p. 57	p. 72
Catch-Up for Absent Students	p. 11	p. 22	p. 32	p. 44	p. 59	p. 74
Problem Solving/Application	p. 12	p. 23	p. 33	p. 45	p. 60	p. 75
Challenge Practice	p. 13	p. 24	p. 35	p. 46	p. 61	p. 76

REVIEW			
Chapter Review Games and Activities	p. 77	Cumulative Practice	p. 80
Project with Rubric	p. 78	Resource Book Answers	A1

Transparencies	*8.1*	*8.2*	*8.3*	*8.4*	*8.5*	*8.6*
Warm-Up/Daily Homework Quiz	✔	✔	✔	✔	✔	✔
Notetaking Guide	✔	✔	✔	✔	✔	✔
Teacher Support					✔	✔
Answer Transparencies	✔	✔	✔	✔	✔	✔

ASSESSMENT BOOK

Quizzes	p. 109	SAT/ACT Chapter Test	p. 120
Chapter Tests (3 levels)	p. 112	Alternative Assessment with Rubric	p. 122
Standardized Chapter Test	p. 118		

TECHNOLOGY

- Easy Planner
- Test and Practice Generator
- Power Presentations
- @HomeTutor
- Activity Generator
- Animated Algebra
- Classzone.com
- eEdition Plus Online
- eWorkbook Plus Online
- ML Assessment System

ADDITIONAL RESOURCES

Illinois Additional Lessons

- Worked-Out Solution Key
- Notetaking Guide
- Practice Workbook
- Algebra 1 Toolkit
- Benchmark Tests
- Reteaching and Remediation
- Spanish Study Guide
- Spanish Assessment Book
- Spanish Resources in Spanish
- Multi-Language Visual Glossary

8 Lesson Practice Level B

LESSON 8.1 Practice B

For use with pages 489–494

Simplify the expression. Write your answer using exponents.

1. $5^4 \cdot 5^8$ 5^{12}
2. $(-4)^7 \cdot (-4)^3$ $(-4)^{10}$
3. $(-10)^5 \cdot (-10)^2$ $(-10)^7$
4. $8^2 \cdot 8^4 \cdot 8$ 8^7
5. $2^5 \cdot 2 \cdot 2^4$ 2^{10}
6. $(3^5)^2$ 3^{10}
7. $(9^3)^7$ 9^{21}
8. $(15^2)^4$ 15^8
9. $[(-4)^5]^9$ $(-4)^{45}$
10. $(13 \cdot 19)^4$ $13^4 \cdot 19^4$
11. $(48 \cdot 27)^6$ $48^6 \cdot 27^6$
12. $(135 \cdot 8)^5$ $135^5 \cdot 8^5$

Simplify the expression.

13. $x^5 \cdot x^2$ x^7
14. $y^3 \cdot y \cdot y^4$ y^8
15. $a^{10} \cdot a^2 \cdot a^6$ a^{18}
16. $(z^5)^5$ z^{25}
17. $(b^7)^2$ b^{14}
18. $[(b+1)^2]^3$ $(b+1)^6$
19. $(-3x)^4$ $81x^4$
20. $-(3x)^4$ $-81x^4$
21. $(2ab)^5$ $32a^5b^5$
22. $(2x^3y)^6$ $64x^{18}y^6$
23. $(3m^7)^4 \cdot m^3$ $81m^{31}$
24. $4p^2 \cdot (3p^5)^2$ $36p^{12}$

Find the missing exponent.

25. $x^6 \cdot x^? = x^{12}$ 6
26. $(x^4)^? = x^{12}$ 3
27. $(3z^?)^3 = 27z^{18}$ 6

28. **Newspaper Circulation** In 1996, the newspaper circulation in the country of Algeria was approximately 10^3 times the newspaper circulation in the country of Mauritania. The newspaper circulation in Mauritania was 10^3. What was the newspaper circulation in Algeria? 10^6 newspapers

29. **Metric System** The metric system has names for very large weights.
   a. One gigaton is 10^2 times the weight of a hectaton. One hectaton is 10^2 ton. Write one gigaton in tons. 10^4 tons
   b. One teraton is 10^9 times the weight of a kiloton. One kiloton is 10^2 ton. Write one teraton in tons. 10^{11} tons
   c. One exaton is 10^6 times the weight of a teraton. Use your answer to part (b) to write one exaton in tons. 10^{17} tons

30. **Wall Mural** You are designing a wall mural that will be composed of squares of different sizes. One of the requirements of your design is that the side length of each square is itself a perfect square.
   a. If you represent the side length of a square as x^2, write an expression for the area of a mural square. x^4 square units
   b. Find the area of a mural square when $x = 5$. 625 square units
   c. Find the area of a mural square when $x = 10$. 10,000 square units

LESSON 8.1

LESSON 8.2 Practice B

For use with pages 495–501

Simplify the expression. Write your answer using exponents.

1. $\frac{6^{14}}{6^8}$ 6^6
2. $\frac{14^5}{14^4}$ 14^1
3. $\frac{(-5)^7}{(-5)^2}$ $(-5)^5$
4. $\frac{12^5 \cdot 12^3}{12^4}$ 12^4
5. $\frac{8^{17}}{8^3 \cdot 8^7}$ 8^7
6. $\left(\frac{3}{4}\right)^5$ $\frac{3^5}{4^5}$
7. $\left(-\frac{1}{5}\right)^6$ $\frac{(-1)^6}{5^6}$
8. $3^8 \cdot \frac{1}{3^1}$ 3^7
9. $\left(\frac{1}{4}\right)^5 \cdot 4^{13}$ 4^8

Simplify the expression.

10. $\frac{1}{y^9} \cdot y^{15}$ y^6
11. $z^{16} \cdot \frac{1}{z^7}$ z^9
12. $\left(\frac{a}{b}\right)^8$ $\frac{a^8}{b^8}$
13. $\left(-\frac{6}{z}\right)^3$ $-\frac{216}{z^3}$
14. $\left(\frac{a^3}{2b^5}\right)^4$ $\frac{a^{12}}{16b^{20}}$
15. $\left(\frac{3x^4}{y^6}\right)^5$ $\frac{243x^{20}}{y^{30}}$
16. $\left(\frac{m^4}{5n^9}\right)^3$ $\frac{m^{12}}{125n^{27}}$
17. $\left(\frac{3x^7}{2y^{12}}\right)^4$ $\frac{81x^{28}}{16y^{48}}$
18. $\left(\frac{2m^5}{3n^9}\right)^5$ $\frac{32m^{25}}{243n^{45}}$

19. **Area** The area of New Zealand is 104,454 square miles and the area of Saint Kitts and Nevis, islands in the Caribbean Sea, is 104 square miles. Use order of magnitude to estimate how many times greater New Zealand's area is than Saint Kitts and Nevis' area. 10^4

20. **Cell Phone Subscribers** The table below shows the approximate number of cell phone subscribers in selected countries in 2001.

Country	Algeria	Dominican Republic	Poland	Solomon Islands
Number of subscribers	10^5	10^6	10^7	10^3

   a. How many times greater is the number of cell phone subscribers in Poland than in the Solomon Islands? 10^4
   b. How many times greater is the number of cell phone subscribers in the Dominican Republic than in the Solomon Islands? 10^3

21. **Glass Vase** You are taking a glass-blowing class and have created a vase in the shape of a sphere. The vase will have a hole in the top so you can put flowers in it and it will sit on a stand. The radius of your vase is $\frac{21}{2}$ inches. Use the formula $V = \frac{4}{3}\pi r^3$ to write an expression for the volume of your vase. $\frac{3087\pi}{2}$ in.^{3}

LESSON 8.2

LESSON 8.3 Practice B

For use with pages 503–508

Evaluate the expression.

1. 3^{-5} $\frac{1}{243}$
2. 10^{-3} $\frac{1}{1000}$
3. $(-2)^{-6}$ $\frac{1}{64}$
4. 5^0 1
5. $(-6)^0$ 1
6. $\left(\frac{4}{3}\right)^0$ 1
7. $\left(\frac{5}{8}\right)^{-2}$ $\frac{64}{25}$
8. $\left(\frac{7}{4}\right)^3$ $\frac{343}{64}$
9. 0^{-5} undefined
10. $10^{-2} \cdot 10^{-3}$ $\frac{1}{100{,}000}$
11. $4^{-6} \cdot 4^3$ $\frac{1}{64}$
12. $\frac{1}{5^{-4}}$ 625

Simplify the expression. Write your answer using only positive exponents.

13. x^{-7} $\frac{1}{x^7}$
14. $6y^{-4}$ $\frac{6}{y^4}$
15. $(2b)^{-5}$ $\frac{1}{32b^5}$
16. $(-3m)^{-4}$ $\frac{1}{81m^4}$
17. a^2b^{-4} $\frac{a^2}{b^4}$
18. $3x^{-2}y^{-5}$ $\frac{3}{x^2y^5}$
19. $(4x^{-4}y^2)^{-3}$ $\frac{x^{12}}{64y^6}$
20. $(8mn^3)^0$ 1
21. $\frac{c^{-3}}{d^{-5}}$ $\frac{d^5}{c^3}$
22. $\frac{x^2}{y^{-4}}$ x^2y^4
23. $\frac{x^{-6}}{4y^5}$ $\frac{1}{4x^6y^5}$
24. $\frac{1}{3x^{-3}y^{-7}}$ $\frac{x^3y^7}{3}$

25. **Paper** A sheet of 67-pound paper has a thickness of 100^{-1} inch.
   a. Write and evaluate an expression for the total thickness of 5 sheets of 67-pound paper. $\frac{1}{20}$ in.
   b. Write and evaluate an expression for the total thickness of 2^3 sheets of 67-pound paper. $\frac{2}{25}$ in.

26. **Frogs** A frog egg currently has a radius of 5^{-1} centimeter. Write an expression using positive exponents for the volume of the frog egg. Use the formula for the volume of a sphere $V = \frac{4}{3}\pi r^3$. $\frac{4\pi}{375}$ cm^3

27. **Metric System** The metric system has names for very small lengths.
   a. One micrometer is 10^3 times the length of one nanometer. One nanometer is 10^{-9} meter. Write one micrometer in meters. 10^{-6} m
   b. One femtometer is 10^3 times the length of one attometer. One attometer is 10^{-18} meter. Write one femtometer in meters. 10^{-15} m
   c. One centimeter is 10^{10} times the length of one picometer. One picometer is 10^{-12} meter. Write one centimeter in meters. 10^{-2} m

LESSON 8.3

LESSON 8.4 Practice B

For use with pages 512–518

Write the number in scientific notation.

1. 10.4 1.04×10^1
2. 6751 6.751×10^3
3. 0.54 5.4×10^{-1}
4. 0.000103 1.03×10^{-4}
5. 415,620 4.1562×10^5
6. 0.08104 8.104×10^{-2}
7. 3,412,000 3.412×10^6
8. 525.5 5.255×10^2
9. 104.25 1.0425×10^2
10. 0.0000456 4.56×10^{-5}
11. 0.000000207 2.07×10^{-7}
12. 23,551 2.3551×10^4

Write the number in standard form.

13. 15.8×10^4 158,000
14. 3.21×10^8 321,000,000
15. 450.21×10^7 4,502,100,000
16. 8.1045×10^5 810,450
17. 17.22×10^6 17,220,000
18. 1.012×10^2 101.2
19. 8.12×10^{-4} 0.000812
20. 4.014×10^{-7} 0.0000004014
21. 8.1025×10^{-3} 0.0081025
22. 3.12056×10^{-9} 0.00000000312056
23. 1.211×10^{-2} 0.01211
24. 7.00135×10^{-5} 0.0000700135

Order the numbers from least to greatest.

25. 1.3759×10^4; 14,205; 9.287×10^3; 3.0214×10^4 9.287×10^3; 1.3759×10^4; 14,205; 3.0214×10^4
26. 0.16; 2.5×10^{-3}; 1.04×10^{-3}; 0.0985 1.04×10^{-3}; 2.5×10^{-3}; 0.0985; 0.16
27. 8.79×10^2; 1146; 1.0085×10^3; 1023 8.79×10^2; 1.0085×10^3; 1023; 1146
28. 1.2×10^{-5}; 0.001023; 1.045×10^{-3}; 0.01036 1.2×10^{-5}; 0.001023; 1.045×10^{-3}; 0.01036

Evaluate the expression. Write your answer in scientific notation.

29. $(6 \times 10^8)(5 \times 10^{-2})$ 3×10^7
30. $\frac{4.5 \times 10^{-5}}{9 \times 10^{-2}}$ 5×10^{-4}
31. $(2 \times 10^{-5})^5$ 3.2×10^{-24}

32. **Pixels** The images on a computer screen are made up of more than 5000 pixels, or dots, per square inch. How many pixels are on a computer screen that measures 108 square inches? Write your answer in scientific notation. 5.4×10^5 pixels

33. **Oregon** Oregon has an area of approximately 2.52×10^5 square kilometers. In 2000, the population of Oregon was approximately 3.42×10^6 people. How many people were there per square kilometer in Oregon in 2000? about 13.57 people/km^2

34. **Uranus' Moons** The table below shows the masses in kilograms of some of Uranus' moons.

Moon	Miranda	Titania	Ariel	Oberon	Umbriel
Mass (kg)	6.6×10^{19}	3.52×10^{21}	13.5×10^{20}	30.1×10^{20}	11.7×10^{20}

   a. Write the moons in order of largest mass to smallest mass. Titania, Oberon, Ariel, Umbriel, Miranda
   b. How many times larger is the moon of largest mass than the moon of smallest mass? about 53

LESSON 8.4

LESSON 8.5 Practice B
For use with pages 520–527

Write a rule for the function.

1.

x	-2	-1	0	1	2
y	$\frac{1}{121}$	$\frac{1}{11}$	1	11	121

$y = 11^x$

2.

x	-1	0	1	2	3
y	$\frac{1}{8}$	$\frac{1}{4}$	$\frac{1}{2}$	1	2

$y = 0.25(2)^x$

Graph the function and identify its domain and range.

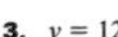

3. $y = 12^x$ **4.** $y = (1.75)^x$ **5.** $y = (3.1)^x$

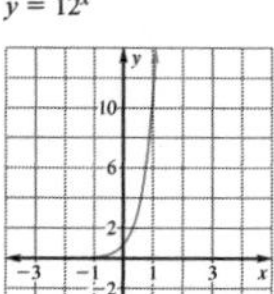
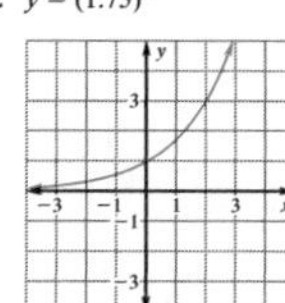
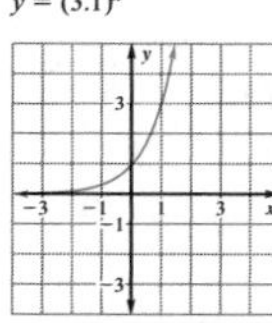

3. domain: all real numbers; range: all positive real numbers
4. domain: all real numbers; range: all positive real numbers
5. domain: all real numbers; range: all positive real numbers

6. $y = \left(\frac{9}{2}\right)^x$ See below. **7.** $y = -5^x$ See below. **8.** $y = -\left(\frac{3}{2}\right)^x$ See below.

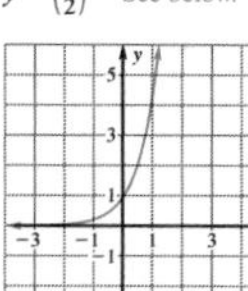
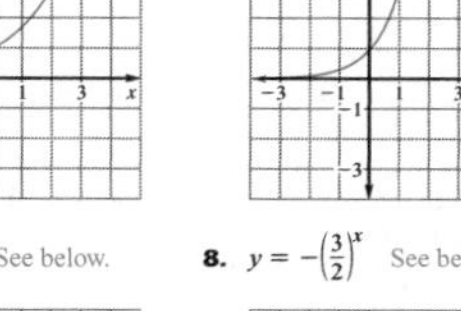
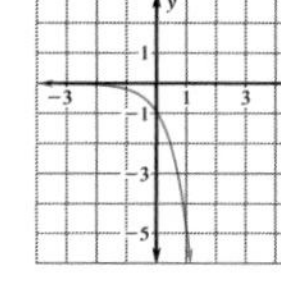
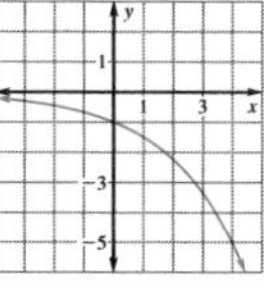

9. $y = 5 \cdot 2^x$ See below. **10.** $y = 2 \cdot \left(\frac{4}{3}\right)^x$ See below. **11.** $y = -3 \cdot 2^x$ See below.

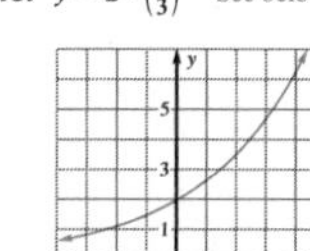
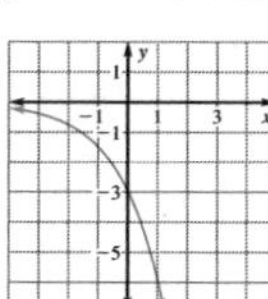

6. domain: all real numbers; range: all positive real numbers
7. domain: all real numbers; range: all negative real numbers
8. domain: all real numbers; range: all negative real numbers
9. domain: all real numbers; range: all positive real numbers
10. domain: all real numbers; range: all positive real numbers
11. domain: all real numbers; range: all negative real numbers

LESSON 8.5

LESSON 8.5 Practice B *continued*
For use with pages 520–527

Graph the function. Compare the graph with the graph of $y = 6^x$.

12. $y = 2 \cdot 6^x$ vertical stretch **13.** $y = -6^x$ reflection in x-axis **14.** $y = \frac{1}{2} \cdot 6^x$ vertical shrink

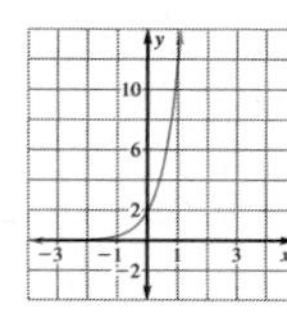
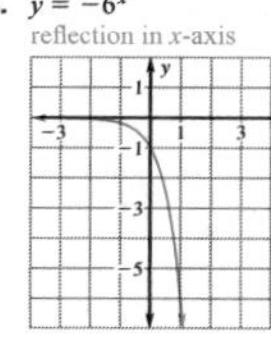
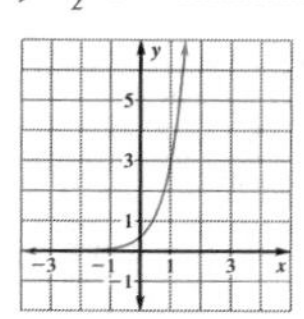

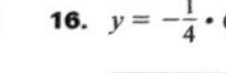

15. $y = -3 \cdot 6^x$ See below. **16.** $y = -\frac{1}{4} \cdot 6^x$ See below. **17.** $y = -\frac{3}{2} \cdot 6^x$ See below.

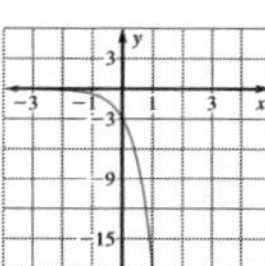
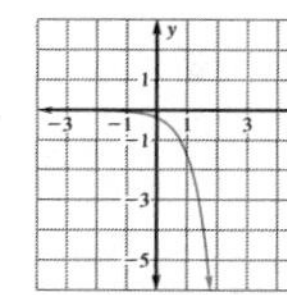

18. Investments You deposit \$500 in a savings account that earns 2.5% interest compounded yearly. Find the balance in the account after the given amounts of time.

a. 1 year \$512.50 **b.** 5 years \$565.70 **c.** 20 years \$819.31

19. College Tuition From 1995 to 2005, the tuition at a college increased by about 7% per year. Use the graph to write an exponential growth function that models the tuition over time. $y = 8000(1.07)^t$

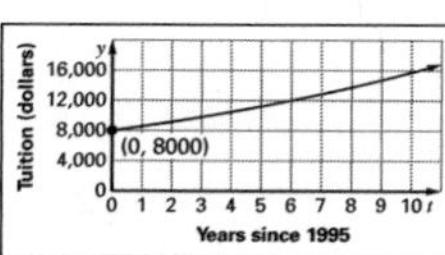

20. Profit A business had \$10,000 profit in 2000. Then the profit increased by 8% each year for the next 10 years.

a. Write a function that models the profit in dollars over time. $y = 10{,}000(1.08)^t$

b. Use the function to predict the profit in 2009. \$19,990.05

15. vertical stretch and reflection in x-axis
16. vertical shrink and reflection in x-axis
17. vertical stretch and reflection in x-axis

LESSON 8.5

LESSON 8.6 Practice B
For use with pages 531–538

Tell whether the table represents an exponential function. If so, write a rule for the function.

1.

x	-2	-1	0	1	2
y	25	5	1	$\frac{1}{5}$	$\frac{1}{25}$

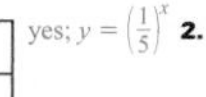

yes; $y = \left(\frac{1}{5}\right)^x$

2.

x	-1	0	1	2	3
y	1	4	7	10	13

no

Graph the function and identify its domain and range.

3. $y = \left(\frac{1}{12}\right)^x$ **4.** $y = \left(\frac{7}{8}\right)^x$ **5.** $y = \left(\frac{8}{9}\right)^x$

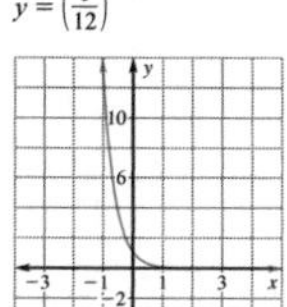
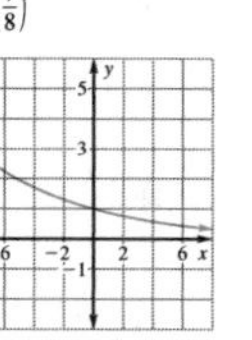
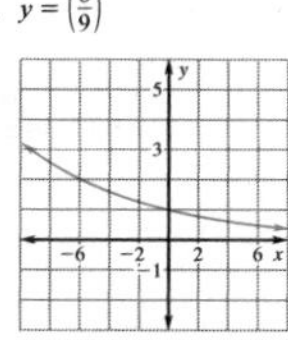

3. domain: all real numbers; range: all positive real numbers
4. domain: all real numbers; range: all positive real numbers
5. domain: all real numbers; range: all positive real numbers

6. $y = -\left(\frac{1}{8}\right)^x$ See below. **7.** $y = 2 \cdot \left(\frac{1}{5}\right)^x$ See below. **8.** $y = -2 \cdot \left(\frac{2}{3}\right)^x$ See below.

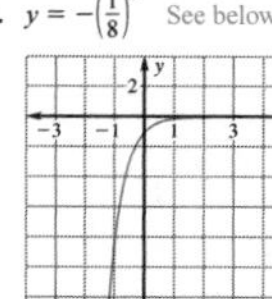
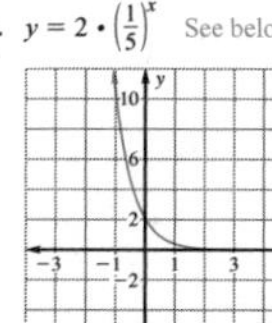
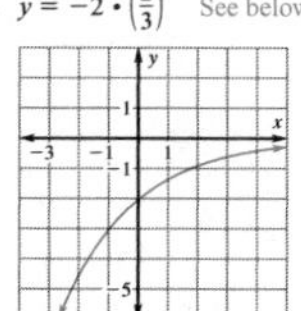

9. $y = 2 \cdot (0.25)^x$ See below. **10.** $y = -0.5 \cdot (0.3)^x$ See below. **11.** $y = -0.2 \cdot (0.2)^x$ See below.

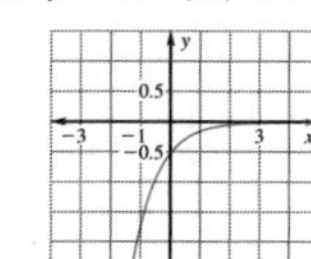
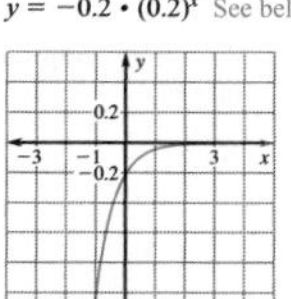

6. domain: all real numbers; range: all negative real numbers
7. domain: all real numbers; range: all positive real numbers
8. domain: all real numbers; range: all negative real numbers
9. domain: all real numbers; range: all positive real numbers
10. domain: all real numbers; range: all negative real numbers
11. domain: all real numbers; range: all negative real numbers

LESSON 8.6

LESSON 8.6 Practice B *continued*
For use with pages 531–538

Graph the function. Compare the graph with the graph of $y = \left(\frac{1}{8}\right)^x$.

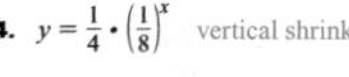

12. $y = 2 \cdot \left(\frac{1}{8}\right)^x$ vertical stretch **13.** $y = -\left(\frac{1}{8}\right)^x$ reflection in x-axis **14.** $y = \frac{1}{4} \cdot \left(\frac{1}{8}\right)^x$ vertical shrink

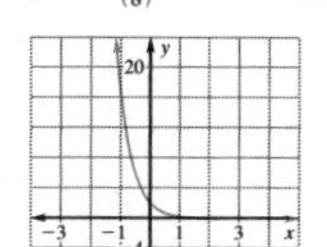
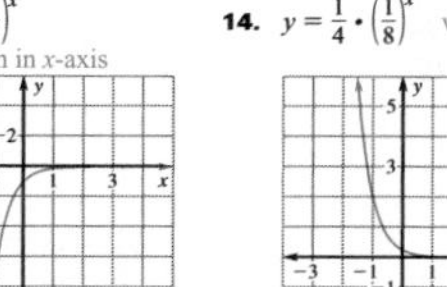
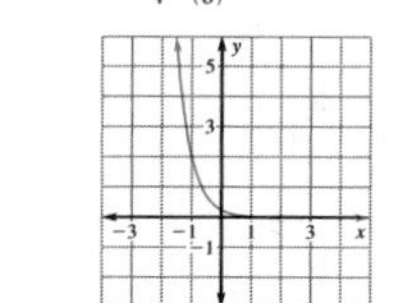

Tell whether the graph represents exponential growth or exponential decay. Then write a rule for the function.

15. **16.** **17.**

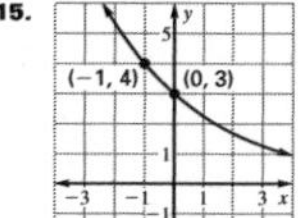

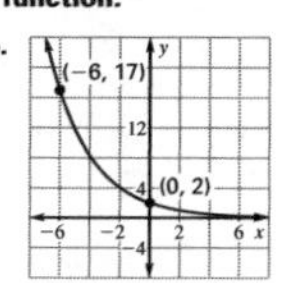

exponential decay; $y = 3(0.75)^x$ exponential decay; $y = 2(0.7)^x$ exponential growth; $y = 4(2)^x$

18. Computer Value You buy a computer for \$3000. It depreciates at the rate of 20% per year. Find the value of the computer for the given year.

a. 1 year \$2400 **b.** 3 years \$1536 **c.** 5 years \$983.04

19. Unemployment Rate In 2000, the unemployment rate of a city decreased by approximately 2.1% each month. In January, the unemployment rate was 7%.

a. Use the graph at the right to write a function that models the unemployment rate of the city over time.

b. What was the unemployment rate in December? about 5.4% **19. a.** $y = 7(0.979)^t$

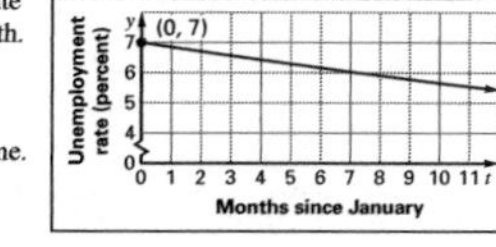

20. Indoor Water Park An indoor water park had a declining attendance from 2000 to 2005. The attendance in 2000 was 18,000. Each year for the next 5 years, the attendance decreased by 5.5%.

a. Write a function that models the attendance since 2000. $y = 18{,}000(0.945)^t$

b. What was the attendance in 2005? about 13,565 people

8 Assessment

CHAPTER 8 Quiz 1
For use after Lessons 8.1–8.2

Simplify the expression. Write your answer using exponents.

1. $8^2 \cdot 8^3$
2. $(-3)^4(-3)^2$
3. $(6^3)^5$
4. $[(-2)^2]^5$
5. $(16 \cdot 7)^4$
6. $4^3 \cdot 4 \cdot 4^5$
7. $\frac{9^{12}}{9^5}$
8. $\frac{2^7 \cdot 2^8}{2^3}$

Simplify the expression.

9. $x^3 \cdot x^7$
10. $-(x^7)^2$
11. $(x^2)^4(3x^5)$
12. $(3x^3)^2(2x)^3$
13. $\frac{1}{x^2} \cdot x^{17}$
14. $\left(-\frac{x^5}{2}\right)^4$

Answers

1. 8^5
2. $(-3)^6$
3. 6^{15}
4. $(-2)^{10}$
5. $16^4 \cdot 7^4$
6. 4^9
7. 9^7
8. 2^{12}
9. x^{10}
10. $-x^{14}$
11. $3x^{13}$
12. $72x^9$
13. x^{15}
14. $\frac{x^{20}}{16}$

CHAPTER 8 Quiz 2
For use after Lessons 8.3–8.4

Simplify the expression. Write your answer using only positive exponents.

1. $(8x)^3 \cdot 8^{-4}$
2. $2x^{-5} \cdot y^{-3}$
3. $(4x^4y^{-3})^{-2}$
4. $\frac{1}{(3x)^{-2}}$

Write the number in standard form.

5. 9.3×10^5
6. 7.04×10^4
7. 5.62×10^{-3}
8. 4.209×10^{-6}

9. The distance from Earth to the sun is approximately 93 million miles. Write this distance in scientific notation.

Answers

1. $\frac{x^3}{8}$
2. $\frac{2}{x^5y^3}$
3. $\frac{y^6}{16x^8}$
4. $9x^2$
5. 930,000
6. 70,400
7. 0.00562
8. 0.000004209
9. 9.3×10^7

CHAPTER 8 Quiz 3
For use after Lessons 8.5–8.6

Graph the function.

1. $y = 4$

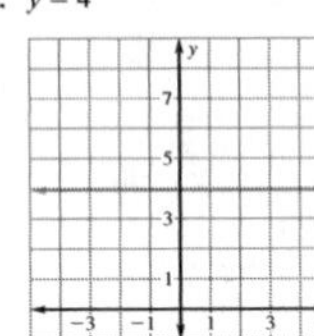

2. $y = \left(\frac{1}{4}\right)^x$

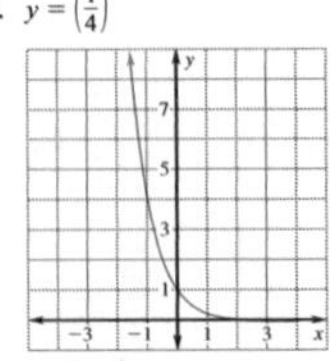

3. $y = 4 \cdot 2^x$

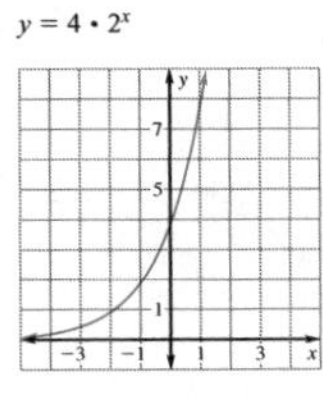

4. $y = \left(\frac{2}{3}\right)^x$

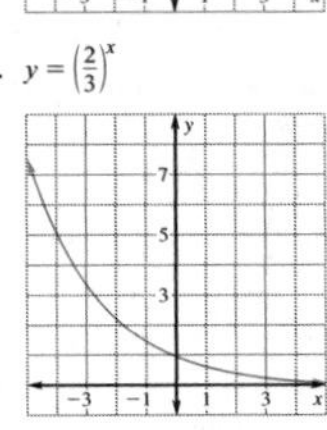

5. $y = 2 \cdot 4^x$

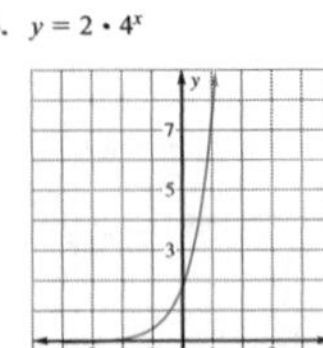

6. $y = 6^x$

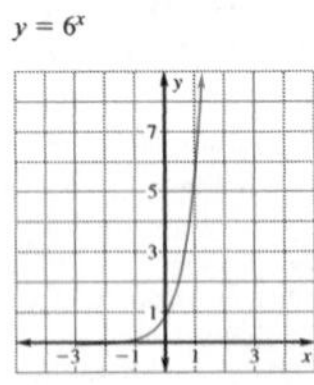

7. A family purchased a house for $80,000. Each year the value of the house increases by 5%. Write a function that models the value of the house over time. Then find the value of the house after 6 years. Round your answer to the nearest dollar.

Answers

1. See left.
2. See left.
3. See left.
4. See left.
5. See left.
6. See left.
7. $y = 80{,}000(1.05)^t$; $107,208

CHAPTER 8 Chapter Test
For use after Chapter 8

Simplify the expression. Write your answer using exponents.

1. $(-7)^9(-7)^2$
2. $(5^3)^8$
3. $\frac{12^2 \cdot 12^4}{12^3}$

In Exercises 4 and 5, use the table.

Unit	tera	giga	mega	kilo	hecto	deka
Meters	10^{12}	10^9	10^6	10^3	10^2	10^1

4. How many hectometers are there in 1 gigameter?
5. How many kilometers are there in 1 terameter?

Simplify the expression.

6. $x^4 \cdot x$
7. $(9pq)^2$
8. $(-5m^6)^2 \cdot m^3$
9. $\frac{1}{y} \cdot y^{11}$
10. $\left(-\frac{1}{t}\right)^5$
11. $\left(\frac{a^8}{2b}\right)^4$
12. Write and simplify an expression for the area of the triangle.

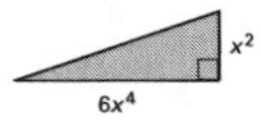

Simplify the expression. Write your answer using only positive exponents.

13. $2w^{-7}$
14. $(5g)^{-3}$
15. $\frac{1}{8c^{10}d^{-6}}$

Complete the statement using <, >, or =.

16. 9.27×10^{-4} ? 0.00927
17. 527,000,000 ? 5.27×10^8

Evaluate the expression. Write your answer in scientific notation.

18. $(4 \times 10^8)^3$
19. $(4 \times 10^{13})(5 \times 10^{-9})$
20. $\frac{9.3 \times 10^{12}}{3.1 \times 10^{-3}}$

Answers

1. $(-7)^{11}$
2. 5^{24}
3. 12^3
4. 10^7
5. 10^9
6. x^5
7. $81p^2q^2$
8. $25m^{15}$
9. y^{10}
10. $-\frac{1}{t^5}$
11. $\frac{a^{32}}{16b^4}$
12. $A = \frac{1}{2}x^2(6x^4) = 3x^6$ square units
13. $\frac{2}{w^7}$
14. $\frac{1}{125g^3}$
15. $\frac{d^6}{8c^{10}}$
16. <
17. =
18. 6.4×10^{25}
19. 2×10^5
20. 3×10^{15}

CHAPTER 8

Chapter Test B *continued*

For use after Chapter 8

21. In a recent year, 6.5×10^8 metric tons of wheat were produced in the world. One metric ton is equivalent to 1000 kilograms. A grain of wheat weighs about 0.000008 kilogram. Find the number of grains of wheat that were produced in the world.

Write a rule for the function.

22.

x	−2	−1	0	1	2
y	$\frac{1}{8}$	$\frac{1}{2}$	2	8	32

23.

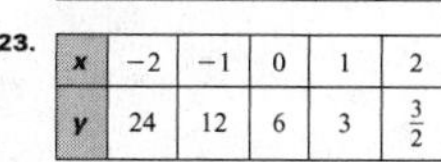

x	−2	−1	0	1	2
y	24	12	6	3	$\frac{3}{2}$

In Exercises 24–26, use the following information.

A house was bought 20 years ago for $160,000. Due to inflation, its value has increased about 5% each year.

24. Write a function that models the value of the home over time.

25. Identify the initial value, the growth factor, and the growth rate.

26. What is the home worth today?

27. Graph the function $y = -5\left(\frac{1}{3}\right)^x$ and compare it to the graph of $y = \left(\frac{1}{3}\right)^x$. Then identify its domain and range.

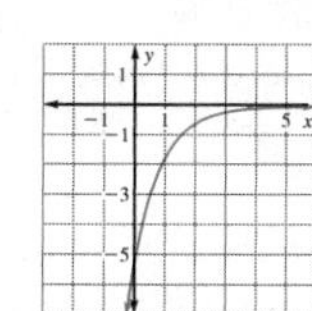

Tell whether the graph represents exponential growth or exponential decay. Then write a rule for the function.

28.

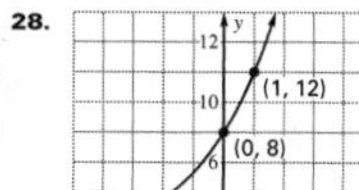

29.

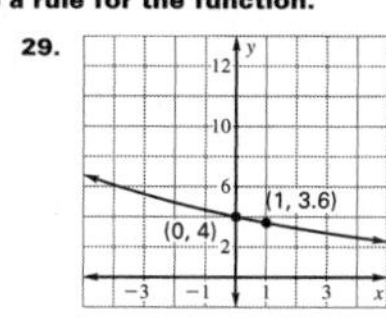

Answers

21. 8.125×10^{16}

22. $y = 2 \cdot 4^x$

23. $y = 6 \cdot \left(\frac{1}{2}\right)^x$

24. $y = 160{,}000(1.05)^t$

25. $160,000; 1.05; 0.05

26. $424,528

27. See left. The graph is a vertical stretch and reflection in the x-axis of the graph of $y = \left(\frac{1}{3}\right)^x$; The domain is all real numbers and the range is all negative real numbers.

28. exponential growth; $y = 8 \cdot (1.5)^x$

29. exponential decay; $y = 4 \cdot (0.9)^x$

CHAPTER 8

Standardized Test

For use after Chapter 8

Multiple Choice

1. Which expression is equivalent to $(-2)^8$? B

Ⓐ $(-2)^2(-2)^4$ Ⓑ $(-2)(-2)^7$
Ⓒ $[(-2)^4]^4$ Ⓓ $[(-2)^5]^3$

2. Which expression is equivalent to $16x^{15}$? A

Ⓐ $(4x^6)^2 \cdot x^3$ Ⓑ $2x^5 \cdot 8x^3$
Ⓒ $2x^5 \cdot (2x)^3$ Ⓓ $(2x^3)^5$

3. Which expression is equivalent to $(-2a)(-4a^2b^3c)^2(-5a^4b^3c^6)^2$? D

Ⓐ $-40a^{13}b^{12}c^{14}$ Ⓑ $800a^{11}b^{10}c^{11}$
Ⓒ $400a^{11}b^{10}c^{10}$ Ⓓ $-800a^{13}b^{12}c^{14}$

4. Which expression is equivalent to 14^6? B

Ⓐ $\frac{14^4}{14^2}$ Ⓑ $\frac{(14^5)^3}{14^9}$
Ⓒ $\frac{14^{12}}{14^2}$ Ⓓ $\left(\frac{14^{11}}{14^5}\right)^3$

5. Which expression is equivalent to $\left(\frac{4x^4}{2x^3}\right)^3$? C

Ⓐ $2x$ Ⓑ $8x$
Ⓒ $8x^3$ Ⓓ $16x^{21}$

6. Which value of x makes the equation $\frac{ax \cdot a^8}{a^3} = a^6$ true? B

Ⓐ $x = 0$ Ⓑ $x = 1$
Ⓒ $x = 2$ Ⓓ $x = 3$

7. Which expression simplifies to $3x^5$? A

Ⓐ $\frac{3}{x^{-5}}$ Ⓑ $3x^{-5}$
Ⓒ $\frac{1}{3x^{-5}}$ Ⓓ $\left(\frac{1}{3x}\right)^{-5}$

8. Which expression is equivalent to $(-5 \cdot 2^2 \cdot 2^0)^{-2}$? D

Ⓐ -80 Ⓑ -40
Ⓒ $-\frac{1}{40}$ Ⓓ $-\frac{1}{400}$

9. Which of the following equations is *not* true? C

Ⓐ $\frac{m^{-1}}{p^{-1}} = \frac{p}{m}$
Ⓑ $\frac{2}{(5p)^{-2}} = 50p^2$
Ⓒ $\left(\frac{p^2}{3p}\right)^{-1} = \frac{3p^2}{p}$
Ⓓ $m^{-1} + p^{-1} = \frac{1}{m} + \frac{1}{p}$

10. Which number represents 65,006,000 in scientific notation? B

Ⓐ 6.5006×10^{-7} Ⓑ 6.5006×10^7
Ⓒ 65.006×10^{-6} Ⓓ 65.006×10^6

11. Which number represents 0.00007605 in scientific notation? A

Ⓐ 7.605×10^{-5} Ⓑ 7.605×10^5
Ⓒ 0.7605×10^{-4} Ⓓ 0.7605×10^4

12. Which number represents 8.205×10^{-4} in standard form? B

Ⓐ 0.00008205 Ⓑ 0.0008205
Ⓒ 82,050 Ⓓ 82,050,000

13. Which number represents 5.4289×10^{-3} in standard form? B

Ⓐ 0.00054289 Ⓑ 0.0054289
Ⓒ 54,289 Ⓓ 5428.9

14. Which number is the value of $\frac{1.728 \times 10^6}{5.4 \times 10^8}$? C

Ⓐ 3.2×10^3 Ⓑ 0.32×10^{-1}
Ⓒ 3.2×10^{-3} Ⓓ 3.2×10^{-2}

CHAPTER 8

Standardized Test *continued*

For use after Chapter 8

15. Which expression is written in scientific notation and equivalent to $(7.2 \times 10^{-4})(2.3 \times 10^6)$? D

Ⓐ 16.56×10^2 Ⓑ 16.56×10^{-2}
Ⓒ 1.656×10 Ⓓ 1.656×10^3

16. Which rule applies to the table below? C

x	−2	−1	0	1	2
y	1	2	4	8	16

Ⓐ $y = 2 \cdot 4^x$ Ⓑ $y = 2 \cdot x^4$
Ⓒ $y = 4 \cdot 2^x$ Ⓓ $y = 4 \cdot x^2$

17. The graph of which function is shown? A

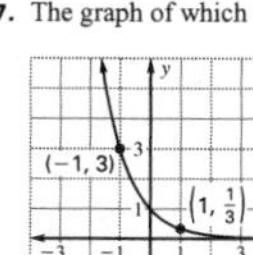

Ⓐ $y = \left(\frac{1}{3}\right)^x$ Ⓑ $y = 3^x$
Ⓒ $y = 2 \cdot \left(\frac{1}{3}\right)^x$ Ⓓ $y = 2 \cdot 3^x$

Gridded Answer

18. The distance from the Sun to Earth is 1.5×10^8 kilometers. Mercury is 5.8×10^7 kilometers from the Sun. What is the difference between these distances in millions of kilometers?

Short Response

19. The graph shows the value of a car over time. **a.** $y = 20{,}000 \cdot \left(\frac{37}{40}\right)^x$

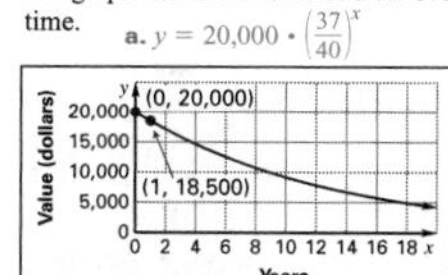

a. Write an equation for the function whose graph is shown. See above.

b. At what rate is the car losing value? *Explain.* The car is losing value at a rate of $\frac{37}{40}$ each year.

Extended Response

20. You are saving money to buy a car. You put $2500 in a savings account that pays 4% annual interest compounded yearly.

a. Write a function that models the amount of the money in the account over time. $A = 2500(1 + 0.04)^t$

b. Graph the function. See below.

c. Suppose you want to buy a car for $3,000. Will there be enough money in the account after 5 years? *Explain.* Yes. After 5 years there will be approximately $3041.63 in the account. This is about $41.63 more than what he needs to buy the car.

20. b.

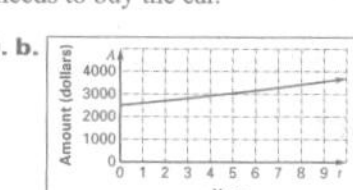

CHAPTER 8

Alternative Assessment and Math Journal

For use after Chapter 8

Journal

1. Describe the difference between numbers that have positive exponents versus negative exponents when written in scientific notation. Give an example of each type of number and include both the scientific notation and the standard form for each.

Multi-Step Problem

2. Let $L = 2^x$ be the function representing the number of layers of paper that has been folded in half x times.

a. Determine the value of L for $x = 0$. Explain the meaning of your answer.

b. Complete the table.

x	0	1	2	3	4
L	?	?	?	?	?

c. What pattern do you notice in the values in part (b)?

d. How many folds are needed to have 128 layers of paper?

e. Consider the function $T = (0.1)2^{x-4}$ where T is the thickness (in centimeters) of a piece of paper folded in half x times. Use properties of exponents to show that an equivalent function is $T = (0.00625)2^x$.

f. Graph the function $T = (0.00625)2^x$.

g. Does this graph represent exponential growth or exponential decay?

h. How thick is a piece of paper that has been folded 10 times?

1. Complete answers should include: an explanation that numbers larger than 10 will have positive exponents when written in scientific notation; an explanation that numbers between 0 and 1 will have negative exponents when written in scientific notation; an example of each case in both scientific notation and standard form.

2. **a.** $L = 1$; A paper folded 0 times will have 1 layer.

b.

x	0	1	2	3	4
L	1	2	4	8	16

c. Each additional fold results in twice as many layers. **d.** 7 folds

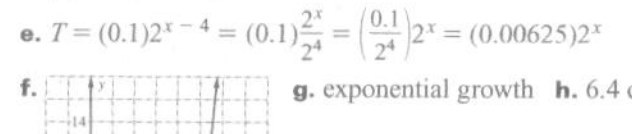

e. $T = (0.1)2^{x-4} = (0.1)\frac{2^x}{2^4} = \left(\frac{0.1}{2^4}\right)2^x = (0.00625)2^x$

f.

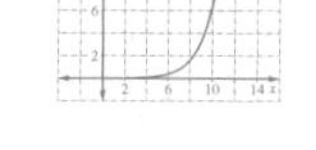

g. exponential growth **h.** 6.4 cm

PLAN AND PREPARE

Main Ideas

In Chapter 8, students learn and use properties of exponents involving products and quotients. They learn how to apply the product of powers property, the power of a power property, the power of a product property, the quotient of powers property, and the power of a quotient property. Students also use zero and negative exponents. Students learn how to read, write, and compute with numbers in scientific notation. Students also learn how to graph and write rules for exponential functions, including exponential growth and exponential decay functions.

Prerequisite Skills

- Evaluating expressions involving exponents
- Ordering numbers
- Writing percents as decimals
- Writing function rules

Additional resources for reviewing prerequisite skills are:

- Skills Review Handbook, pp. 909–937
- @HomeTutor

8 Exponents and Exponential Functions

Before

In previous chapters and courses, you learned the following skills, which you'll use in Chapter 8: evaluating expressions involving exponents, ordering numbers, writing percents as decimals, and writing function rules.

Prerequisite Skills

VOCABULARY CHECK

1. Identify the exponent and the base in the expression 13^8. exponent: 8, base: 13
2. Copy and complete: An expression that represents repeated multiplication of the same factor is called a(n) _?_. power

SKILLS CHECK

Evaluate the expression. *(Review p. 2 for 8.1–8.3.)*

3. x^2 when $x = 10$ 100
4. a^3 when $a = 3$ 27
5. r^2 when $r = \frac{5}{6}$ $\frac{25}{36}$
6. z^3 when $z = \frac{1}{2}$ $\frac{1}{8}$

Order the numbers from least to greatest. *(Review p. 909 for 8.4.)*

7. 6.12, 6.2, 6.01 6.01, 6.12, 6.2
8. 0.073, 0.101, 0.0098 0.0098, 0.073, 0.101

Write the percent as a decimal. *(Review p. 916 for 8.5 and 8.6.)*

9. 4% 0.04
10. 0.5% 0.005
11. 13.8% 0.138
12. 145% 1.45

13. Write a rule for the function. *(Review p. 35 for 8.5 and 8.6.)* $f(x) = x + 2$

Input	0	1	4	6	10
Output	2	3	6	8	12

@HomeTutor Prerequisite skills practice at classzone.com

486

Chapter Planning Guide

Chapter 8 Resource Book
- Teaching Guide/Lesson Plan (pp. 3, 14, 25, 36, 47, 62)
- Project with Rubric (p. 78)

Assessment and Intervention
- Assessment Book (pp. 109–123)
- Benchmark Tests
- Reteaching and Remediation Book

Interactive Technology
- Easy Planner
- Power Presentations CD-ROM
- Activity Generator CD-ROM
- Animated Algebra
- Test Generator CD-ROM
- Online Quizzes
- eWorkbook
- eEdition
- @HomeTutor

Resources for English Learners
- Quick Reference for English Learners
- Spanish Study Guide
- Multi-Language Visual Glossary
- Student Resources in Spanish

In Chapter 8, you will apply the big ideas listed below and reviewed in the Chapter Summary on page 542. You will also use the key vocabulary listed below.

Big Ideas

1. **Applying properties of exponents to simplify expressions**
2. **Working with numbers in scientific notation**
3. **Writing and graphing exponential functions**

KEY VOCABULARY

- order of magnitude, *p. 491*
- scientific notation, *p. 512*
- exponential function, *p. 520*
- exponential growth, *p. 522*
- compound interest, *p. 523*
- exponential decay, *p. 533*

You can use exponents to explore exponential growth and decay. For example, you can write an exponential function to find the value of a collector car over time.

Animated Algebra

The animation illustrated below for Example 4 on page 522 helps you answer this question: If you know the growth rate of the value of a collector car over time, can you predict what the car will sell for at an auction?

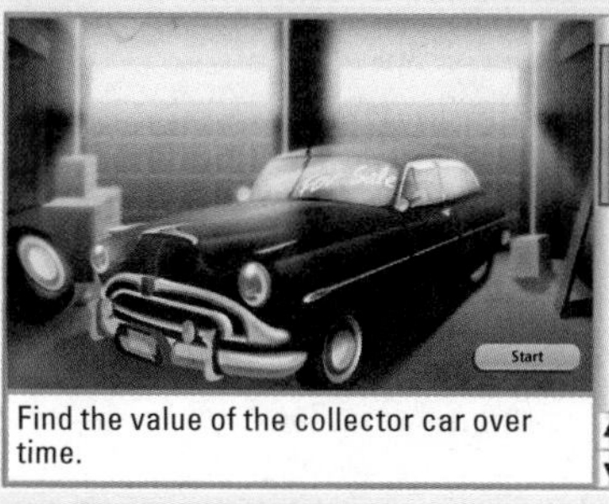

Find the value of the collector car over time.

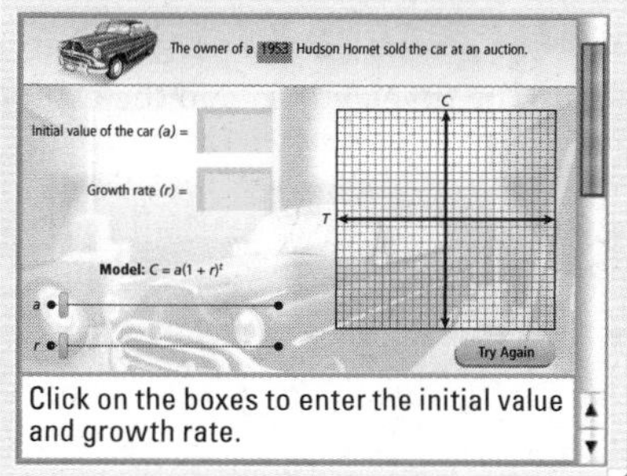

Click on the boxes to enter the initial value and growth rate.

Animated Algebra at classzone.com

Other animations for Chapter 8: pages 491, 505, 512, 534, and 536

Algebra 1 Toolkit

- Reading Strategies for Chapter 8, pp. 23–24
- Differentiated Instruction Notes, pp. 69–72
- English Learners Notes, pp. 111–112
- Inclusion Notes, pp. 143–144
- Teaching Strategies with Sample Worksheets, pp. 155–178
- Using Technology in the Classroom, pp. 179–184
- Tips for New Teachers, pp. 199–200
- Math Background Notes, pp. 225–226
- Pre-AP Strategies and Copymasters, pp. 292–293, 400–419
- Teacher Survival Activities, pp. 569–570, 595–596
- Bulletin Board Idea, p. 614
- Teacher Tool Transparencies, following p. 620

Investigating Algebra ACTIVITY *Use before Lesson 8.1*

1 PLAN AND PREPARE

Explore the Concept

- Students will find products of powers and powers of powers.
- This activity leads into the study of using the product of powers property in Example 1 and the power of a power property in Example 2 in Lesson 8.1.

Materials

Each student will need:

- Activity Support Master (*Chapter 8 Resource Book*, p. 5)

Recommended Time

Work activity: 10 min

Discuss results: 5 min

Grouping

Students should work individually.

2 TEACH

Tips for Success

In Explore 2, help students understand how a power of a power is different from a product of powers. For example, contrast the expression $(5^3)^2$, which means $5^3 \cdot 5^3$, with the expression $5^3 \cdot 5^2$.

Key Discovery

When you find a product of powers for powers that have the same base, you add the exponents. When you find a power of a power, you multiply the exponents.

3 ASSESS AND RETEACH

Does $(2x)^3 = 2x^3$? *Explain* your reasoning. No. The expression $(2x)^3$ means $2x \cdot 2x \cdot 2x$, or $8x^3$.

Explore 2: Step 1. $[(-6) \cdot (-6)] \cdot [(-6) \cdot (-6)] \cdot [(-6) \cdot (-6)] \cdot [(-6) \cdot (-6)]$

8.1 Products and Powers

MATERIALS • paper and pencil

QUESTION How can you find a product of powers and a power of a power?

EXPLORE 1 Find products of powers

STEP 1 ***Copy and complete*** Copy and complete the table.

Expression	Expression as repeated multiplication	Number of factors	Simplified expression
$7^4 \cdot 7^5$	$(7 \cdot 7 \cdot 7 \cdot 7) \cdot (7 \cdot 7 \cdot 7 \cdot 7 \cdot 7)$	9	7^9
$(-4)^2 \cdot (-4)^3$	$[(-4) \cdot (-4)] \cdot [(-4) \cdot (-4) \cdot (-4)]$	? 5	? $(-4)^5$
$x^1 \cdot x^5$	? $(x) \cdot (x \cdot x \cdot x \cdot x \cdot x)$	? 6	? x^6

STEP 2 ***Analyze results*** Find a pattern that relates the exponents of the factors in the first column and the exponent of the expression in the last column. See margin.

EXPLORE 2 Find powers of powers

STEP 1 ***Copy and complete*** Copy and complete the table.

Expression	Expanded expression	Expression as repeated multiplication	Number of factors	Simplified expression
$(5^3)^2$	$(5^3) \cdot (5^3)$	$(5 \cdot 5 \cdot 5) \cdot (5 \cdot 5 \cdot 5)$	6	5^6
$[(-6)^2]^4$	$[(-6)^2] \cdot [(-6)^2] \cdot [(-6)^2] \cdot [(-6)^2]$	? See margin.	? 8	? $(-6)^8$
$(a^3)^3$	? $(a^3) \cdot (a^3) \cdot (a^3)$	? $(a \cdot a \cdot a) \cdot (a \cdot a \cdot a) \cdot (a \cdot a \cdot a)$	? 9	? a^9

STEP 2 ***Analyze results*** Find a pattern that relates the exponents of the expression in the first column and the exponent of the expression in the last column. *Sample answer:* The exponent of the simplified expression is equal to the product of the exponents in the first column.

DRAW CONCLUSIONS Use your observations to complete these exercises

Simplify the expression. Write your answer using exponents.

1. $5^2 \cdot 5^3$ 5^5
2. $(-6)^1 \cdot (-6)^4$ $(-6)^5$
3. $m^6 \cdot m^4$ m^{10}
4. $(10^3)^3$ 10^9
5. $[(-2)^3]^4$ $(-2)^{12}$
6. $(c^2)^6$ c^{12}

In Exercises 7 and 8, copy and complete the statement.

7. If a is a real number and m and n are positive integers, then $a^m \cdot a^n =$ __?__. a^{m+n}
8. If a is a real number and m and n are positive integers, then $(a^m)^n =$ __?__. a^{mn}

8.1 Apply Exponent Properties Involving Products

6.11.07 Determine the effects of operations on the magnitudes of quantities (e.g., multiplication, division, powers, roots).

Before You evaluated exponential expressions.
Now You will use properties of exponents involving products.
Why? So you can evaluate agricultural data, as in Example 5.

Key Vocabulary
- **order of magnitude**
- **power,** *p. 3*
- **exponent,** *p. 3*
- **base,** *p. 3*

Notice what happens when you multiply two powers that have the same base.

$$a^2 \cdot a^3 = \underbrace{(a \cdot a)}_{\text{2 factors}} \cdot \underbrace{(a \cdot a \cdot a)}_{\text{3 factors}} = a^5 = a^{2+3}$$

(5 factors)

The example above suggests the following property of exponents, known as the product of powers property.

KEY CONCEPT *For Your Notebook*

Product of Powers Property

Let a be a real number, and let m and n be positive integers.

Words To multiply powers having the same base, add the exponents.

Algebra $a^m \cdot a^n = a^{m+n}$ **Example** $5^6 \cdot 5^3 = 5^{6+3} = 5^9$

EXAMPLE 1 Use the product of powers property

SIMPLIFY EXPRESSIONS
When simplifying powers with numerical bases only, write your answers using exponents, as in parts (a), (b), and (c).

a. $7^3 \cdot 7^5 = 7^{3+5} = 7^8$

b. $9 \cdot 9^8 \cdot 9^2 = 9^1 \cdot 9^8 \cdot 9^2$
$= 9^{1+8+2}$
$= 9^{11}$

c. $(-5)(-5)^6 = (-5)^1 \cdot (-5)^6$
$= (-5)^{1+6}$
$= (-5)^7$

d. $x^4 \cdot x^3 = x^{4+3} = x^7$

✓ **GUIDED PRACTICE** for Example 1

Simplify the expression.

1. $3^2 \cdot 3^7$ 3^9 **2.** $5 \cdot 5^9$ 5^{10} **3.** $(-7)^2(-7)$ $(-7)^3$ **4.** $x^2 \cdot x^6 \cdot x$ x^9

1 PLAN AND PREPARE

Warm-Up Exercises
Transparency Available

Evaluate the expression.

1. x^4 when $x = 3$ 81
2. a^2 when $a = -6$ 36
3. m^3 when $m = -5$ −125
4. A food storage container is in the shape of a cube. What is the volume of the container if one side is 4 inches long? Use $V = s^3$. 64 in.^{3}

Notetaking Guide
Transparency Available

Promotes interactive learning and notetaking skills, pp. 167–169.

Pacing
Basic: 1 day
Average: 1 day
Advanced: 1 day
Block: 0.5 block with 8.2
- See *Teaching Guide/Lesson Plan.*

2 FOCUS AND MOTIVATE

Essential Question
Big Idea 1, p. 487

How do you use properties of exponents involving products?
Tell students they will learn how to answer this question by applying properties of exponents to simplify expressions.

Resource Planning Guide

Chapter Resource Book
- Teaching Guide/Lesson Plan (pp. 3–4)
- Practice levels A, B, C (pp. 6–8)
- Study Guide (pp. 9–10)
- Catch-up for Absent Students (p. 11)
- Application (p. 12)
- Challenge (p. 13)

Workbooks
- Notetaking Guide (pp. 167–169)
- Practice Workbook (pp. 119–120)

Teaching Options
- **Power Presentations CD-ROM** provides dynamic electronic teaching resources for the classroom.
- **Activity Generator CD-ROM** provides editable activities for all ability levels.

Interactive Technology
- Easy Planner
- Power Presentations CD-ROM
- Activity Generator CD-ROM
- Animated Algebra
- Test Generator CD-ROM
- Online Quiz
- eWorkbook
- eEdition
- @HomeTutor

Resources for English Learners
- Quick Reference for English Learners
- Spanish Study Guide
- Multi-Language Visual Glossary
- Student Resources in Spanish

See also the *Algebra 1 Toolkit* for more strategies for meeting individual needs.

Motivating the Lesson

By knowing how to use properties of exponents and order of magnitude, you will be able to estimate data using powers of ten. For example, you can estimate and compare the amount of energy released by earthquakes, the brightness and luminosity of stars, and numerous other real-world data.

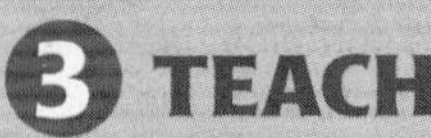

3 TEACH

Extra Example 1

Use the product of powers property.

a. $4^7 \cdot 4^6$ 4^{13}

b. $8^5 \cdot 8 \cdot 8^2$ 8^8

c. $(-3)^3 \cdot (-3)$ $(-3)^4$

d. $b \cdot b^3 \cdot b^5 \cdot b^2$ b^{11}

Avoiding Common Errors

In parts b and c of Example 1, students often forget that factors like 9 and -5 have an exponent of 1 that must be included in the sum. Suggest that they rewrite the products as shown in the Example to avoid this error.

Extra Example 2

Use the power of a power property.

a. $(7^4)^5$ 7^{20}

b. $[(-3)^4]^2$ $(-3)^8$

c. $(y^3)^3$ y^9

d. $[(n+8)^2]^9$ $(n+8)^{18}$

Key Question to Ask for Example 2

- In part d, why is it not possible to write $(y+2)^{12}$ as $y^{12} + 2^{12}$? **Because $y + 2$ is a quantity, you must add the value of y to 2 before you can raise the base to the power of 12.**

POWER OF A POWER Notice what happens when you raise a power to a power.

$$(a^2)^3 = a^2 \cdot a^2 \cdot a^2 = (a \cdot a) \cdot (a \cdot a) \cdot (a \cdot a) = a^6 = a^{2 \cdot 3}$$

The example above suggests the following property of exponents, known as the power of a power property.

KEY CONCEPT *For Your Notebook*

Power of a Power Property

Let a be a real number, and let m and n be positive integers.

Words To find a power of a power, multiply exponents.

Algebra $(a^m)^n = a^{mn}$

Example $(3^4)^2 = 3^{4 \cdot 2} = 3^8$

EXAMPLE 2 Use the power of a power property

AVOID ERRORS
In part (d), notice that you can write $[(y+2)^6]^2$ as $(y+2)^{12}$, but you cannot write $(y+2)^{12}$ as $y^{12} + 2^{12}$.

a. $(2^5)^3 = 2^{5 \cdot 3}$
$= 2^{15}$

b. $[(-6)^2]^5 = (-6)^{2 \cdot 5}$
$= (-6)^{10}$

c. $(x^2)^4 = x^{2 \cdot 4}$
$= x^8$

d. $[(y+2)^6]^2 = (y+2)^{6 \cdot 2}$
$= (y+2)^{12}$

✓ **GUIDED PRACTICE** for Example 2

Simplify the expression.

5. $(4^2)^7$ 4^{14} **6.** $[(-2)^4]^5$ $(-2)^{20}$ **7.** $(n^3)^6$ n^{18} **8.** $[(m+1)^5]^4$ $(m+1)^{20}$

POWER OF A PRODUCT Notice what happens when you raise a product to a power.

$$(ab)^3 = (ab) \cdot (ab) \cdot (ab) = (a \cdot a \cdot a) \cdot (b \cdot b \cdot b) = a^3b^3$$

The example above suggests the following property of exponents, known as the power of a product property.

KEY CONCEPT *For Your Notebook*

Power of a Product Property

Let a and b be real numbers, and let m be a positive integer.

Words To find a power of a product, find the power of each factor and multiply.

Algebra $(ab)^m = a^m b^m$

Example $(23 \cdot 17)^5 = 23^5 \cdot 17^5$

Differentiated Instruction

Inclusion Students may have difficulty interpreting the symbols used in mathematics (such as exponents), and in memorizing complex rules. At first, it may be more instructive to allow them to write out terms like a^3 as *aaa*, rather than memorize rules like the power of a power property. Later, they should have no need of this particular technique.

See also the *Algebra 1 Toolkit* for more strategies.

SIMPLIFY EXPRESSIONS
When simplifying powers with numerical *and* variable bases, be sure to evaluate the numerical power, as in parts (b), (c), and (d).

EXAMPLE 3 Use the power of a product property

a. $(24 \cdot 13)^8 = 24^8 \cdot 13^8$

b. $(9xy)^2 = (9 \cdot x \cdot y)^2 = 9^2 \cdot x^2 \cdot y^2 = 81x^2y^2$

c. $(-4z)^2 = (-4 \cdot z)^2 = (-4)^2 \cdot z^2 = 16z^2$

d. $-(4z)^2 = -(4 \cdot z)^2 = -(4^2 \cdot z^2) = -16z^2$

EXAMPLE 4 Use all three properties

Simplify $(2x^3)^2 \cdot x^4$.

$(2x^3)^2 \cdot x^4 = 2^2 \cdot (x^3)^2 \cdot x^4$ Power of a product property

$= 4 \cdot x^6 \cdot x^4$ Power of a power property

$= 4x^{10}$ Product of powers property

Animated Algebra at classzone.com

ORDER OF MAGNITUDE The **order of magnitude** of a quantity can be defined as the power of 10 nearest the quantity. Order of magnitude can be used to estimate or perform rough calculations. For instance, there are about 91,000 species of insects in the United States. The power of 10 closest to 91,000 is 10^5, or 100,000. So, there are about 10^5 species of insects in the United States.

EXAMPLE 5 Solve a real-world problem

BEES In 2003 the U.S. Department of Agriculture (USDA) collected data on about 10^3 honeybee colonies. There are about 10^4 bees in an average colony during honey production season. About how many bees were in the USDA study?

Solution

To find the total number of bees, find the product of the number of colonies, 10^3, and the number of bees per colony, 10^4.

$10^3 \cdot 10^4 = 10^{3+4} = 10^7$

▶ The USDA studied about 10^7, or 10,000,000, bees.

✓ **GUIDED PRACTICE** for Examples 3, 4, and 5

Simplify the expression.

9. $42^2 \cdot 12^2$

11. $6561m^{12}n^4$

9. $(42 \cdot 12)^2$ **10.** $(-3n)^2$ $9n^2$ **11.** $(9m^3n)^4$ **12.** $5 \cdot (5x^2)^4$ $3125x^8$

13. WHAT IF? In Example 5, 10^2 honeybee colonies in the study were located in Idaho. About how many bees were studied in Idaho? about 1,000,000 bees

Extra Example 3

Use the power of a product property.

a. $(34 \cdot 9)^6$ $34^6 \cdot 9^6$

b. $(4mn)^3$ $64m^3n^3$

c. $(-2g)^4$ $16g^4$

d. $-(5x)^2$ $-25x^2$

Key Question to Ask for Example 3

- Why is the simplified expression in part (c) positive and in part (d) negative? In part (c), −4 is squared, so it simplifies to 16. In part (d), the negative sign represents −1 and since it is outside the parentheses, it is not squared and −1 • 16 = −16.

Extra Example 4

Simplify $(3d^5)^3 \cdot d$. $27d^{16}$

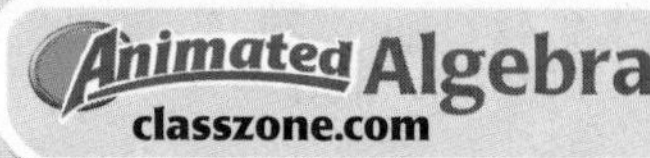

An **Animated Algebra** activity is available on-line for **Example 4**. This activity is also available on the **Power Presentations CD-ROM**.

Extra Example 5

A box of staples contains 10^4 staples. How many staples do 10^2 boxes contain? 1,000,000 staples

Closing the Lesson

Have students summarize the major points of the lesson and answer the Essential Question: How do you use properties of exponents involving products?

- Add exponents when using the product of a powers property.
- Multiply exponents when using the power of a power or the power of a product property.

When simplifying expressions, add exponents when multiplying powers and multiply exponents when raising a power to a power or raising a product to a power.

8.1 EXERCISES

HOMEWORK KEY
○ = **WORKED-OUT SOLUTIONS** on p. WS18 for Exs. 31 and 55
★ = **STANDARDIZED TEST PRACTICE** Exs. 2, 40, 41, 50, and 58
◆ = **MULTIPLE REPRESENTATIONS** Ex. 55

4 PRACTICE AND APPLY

Assignment Guide

Answer Transparencies available for all exercises

Basic:
Day 1: pp. 492–494
Exs. 1, 2, 3–15 odd, 19–39 odd, 40–42, 52–57, 60–74 even

Average:
Day 1: pp. 492–494
Exs. 1, 2, 4–18 even, 29–49, 53–58, 61, 64, 67, 73

Advanced:
Day 1: pp. 492–494
Exs. 1, 2, 8–18 even, 31–38, 40–51*, 54–59*, 62, 65, 68, 74

Block:
pp. 492–494
Exs. 1, 2, 4–18 even, 29–49, 53–58, 61, 64, 67, 73 (with 8.2)

Differentiated Instruction

See *Algebra 1 Best Practices Toolkit* for suggestions on addressing the needs of a diverse classroom.

Homework Check

For a quick check of student understanding of key concepts, go over the following exercises:

Basic: 7, 11, 15, 27, 52
Average: 8, 12, 16, 33, 53
Advanced: 10, 14, 18, 36, 54

Extra Practice

- Student Edition, p. 945
- Chapter 8 Resource Book: Practice levels A, B, C, pp. 6–8

Practice Worksheet

An easily-readable reduced practice page (with answers) for this lesson can be found on p. 486C.

SKILL PRACTICE

A

1. **VOCABULARY** Copy and complete: The _?_ of the quantity 93,534,004 people is the power of 10 nearest the quantity, or 10^8 people. order of magnitude

2. ★ **WRITING** *Explain* when and how to use the product of powers property. When powers have the same base, their product is the base raised to the sum of the exponents.

EXAMPLES 1,2,3, and 4 on pp. 489–491 for Exs. 3–41

SIMPLIFYING EXPRESSIONS **Simplify the expression. Write your answer using exponents.**

3. $4^2 \cdot 4^6$ 4^8
4. $8^5 \cdot 8^2$ 8^7
5. $3^3 \cdot 3$ 3^4
6. $9 \cdot 9^5$ 9^6
7. $(-7)^4(-7)^5$ $(-7)^9$
8. $(-6)^6(-6)$ $(-6)^7$
9. $2^4 \cdot 2^9 \cdot 2$ 2^{14}
10. $(-3)^2(-3)^{11}(-3)$ $(-3)^{14}$
11. $(3^5)^2$ 3^{10}
12. $(7^4)^3$ 7^{12}
13. $[(-5)^3]^4$ $(-5)^{12}$
14. $[(-8)^9]^2$ $(-8)^{18}$
15. $(15 \cdot 29)^3$ $15^3 \cdot 29^3$
16. $(17 \cdot 16)^4$ $17^4 \cdot 16^4$
17. $(132 \cdot 9)^6$ $132^6 \cdot 9^6$
18. $((-14) \cdot 22)^5$ $(-14)^5 \cdot 22^5$

SIMPLIFYING EXPRESSIONS **Simplify the expression.**

19. $x^4 \cdot x^2$ x^6
20. $y^9 \cdot y$ y^{10}
21. $z^2 \cdot z \cdot z^3$ z^6
22. $a^4 \cdot a^3 \cdot a^{10}$ a^{17}
23. $(x^5)^2$ x^{10}
24. $(y^4)^6$ y^{24}
25. $[(b-2)^2]^6$ $(b-2)^{12}$
26. $[(d+9)^7]^3$ $(d+9)^{21}$
27. $(-5x)^2$ $25x^2$
28. $-(5x)^2$ $-25x^2$
29. $(7xy)^2$ $49x^2y^2$
30. $(5pq)^3$ $125p^3q^3$
31. $(-10x^6)^2 \cdot x^2$ $100x^{14}$
32. $(-8m^4)^2 \cdot m^3$ $64m^{11}$
33. $6d^2 \cdot (2d^5)^4$ $96d^{22}$
34. $(-20x^3)^2(-x^7)$ $-400x^{13}$
35. $-(2p^4)^3(-1.5p^7)$ $12p^{19}$
36. $\left(\frac{1}{2}y^5\right)^3(2y^2)^4$ $2y^{23}$
37. $(3x^5)^3(2x^7)^2$ $108x^{29}$
38. $(-10n)^2(-4n^3)^3$ $-6400n^{11}$

39. **ERROR ANALYSIS** *Describe* and correct the error in simplifying $c \cdot c^4 \cdot c^5$. *Sample answer*: The exponents should be added, not multiplied; $c^1 \cdot c^4 \cdot c^5 = c^{1+4+5} = c^{10}$.

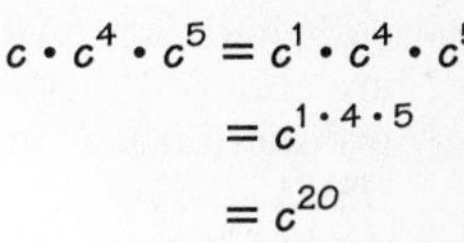

$c \cdot c^4 \cdot c^5 = c^1 \cdot c^4 \cdot c^5$
$= c^{1 \cdot 4 \cdot 5}$
$= c^{20}$

B

40. ★ **MULTIPLE CHOICE** Which expression is equivalent to $(-9)^6$? B

Ⓐ $(-9)^2(-9)^3$ Ⓑ $(-9)(-9)^5$ Ⓒ $[(-9)^4]^2$ Ⓓ $[(-9)^3]^3$

41. ★ **MULTIPLE CHOICE** Which expression is equivalent to $36x^{12}$? D

Ⓐ $(6x^3)^4$ Ⓑ $12x^4 \cdot 3x^3$ Ⓒ $3x^3 \cdot (4x^3)^3$ Ⓓ $(6x^5)^2 \cdot x^2$

SIMPLIFYING EXPRESSIONS **Find the missing exponent.**

42. $x^4 \cdot x^? = x^5$ 1
43. $(y^8)^? = y^{16}$ 2
44. $(2z^?)^3 = 8z^{15}$ 5
45. $(3a^3)^? \cdot 2a^3 = 18a^9$ 2

46. **POPULATION** The population of New York City in 2000 was 8,008,278. What was the order of magnitude of the population of New York City? 10^7 people

SIMPLIFYING EXPRESSIONS **Simplify the expression.**

47. $(-3x^2y)^3(11x^3y^5)^2$ $-3267x^{12}y^{13}$
48. $-(-xy^2z^3)^5(x^4yz)^2$ $x^{13}y^{12}z^{17}$
49. $(-2s)(-5r^3st)^3(-2r^4st^7)^2$ $1000r^{17}s^6t^{17}$

C 50. ★ **OPEN-ENDED** Write three expressions involving products of powers, powers of powers, or powers of products that are equivalent to $12x^8$.
Sample answer: $3x^2 \cdot 4x^6$, $12(x^4)^2$, $3(2x^4)^2$

51. **CHALLENGE** Show that when a and b are real numbers and n is a positive integer, $(ab)^n = a^n b^n$. See margin.

PROBLEM SOLVING

EXAMPLE 5 A on p. 491 for Exs. 52–56

52. **ICE CREAM COMPOSITION** There are about 954,930 air bubbles in 1 cubic centimeter of ice cream. There are about 946 cubic centimeters in 1 quart. Use order of magnitude to find the approximate number of air bubbles in 1 quart of ice cream. 10^9 air bubbles

@HomeTutor for problem solving help at classzone.com

53. **ASTRONOMY** The order of magnitude of the radius of our solar system is 10^{13} meters. The order of magnitude of the radius of the visible universe is 10^{13} times as great. Find the approximate radius of the visible universe. 10^{26} m

@HomeTutor for problem solving help at classzone.com

54. **COASTAL LANDSLIDE** There are about 1 billion grains of sand in 1 cubic foot of sand. In 1995 a stretch of beach at Sleeping Bear Dunes National Lakeshore in Michigan slid into Lake Michigan. Scientists believe that around 35 million cubic feet of sand fell into the lake. Use order of magnitude to find about how many grains of sand slid into the lake. 10^{16} grains of sand

55. ◆ **MULTIPLE REPRESENTATIONS** There are about 10^{23} atoms of gold in 1 ounce of gold.

a. **Making a Table** Copy and complete the table by finding the number of atoms of gold for the given amounts of gold (in ounces).

Gold (ounces)	10	100	1000	10,000	100,000
Number of atoms	?	?	?	?	?

10^{24} 10^{25} 10^{26} 10^{27} 10^{28}

b. **Writing an Expression** A particular mine in California extracted about 96,000 ounces of gold in 1 year. Use order of magnitude to write an expression you can use to find the approximate number of atoms of gold extracted in the mine that year. Simplify the expression. Verify your answer using the table. $10^5 \cdot 10^{23}$; 10^{28} atoms

56. **MULTI-STEP PROBLEM** A microscope has two lenses, the objective lens and the eyepiece, that work together to magnify an object. The total magnification of the microscope is the product of the magnification of the objective lens and the magnification of the eyepiece.

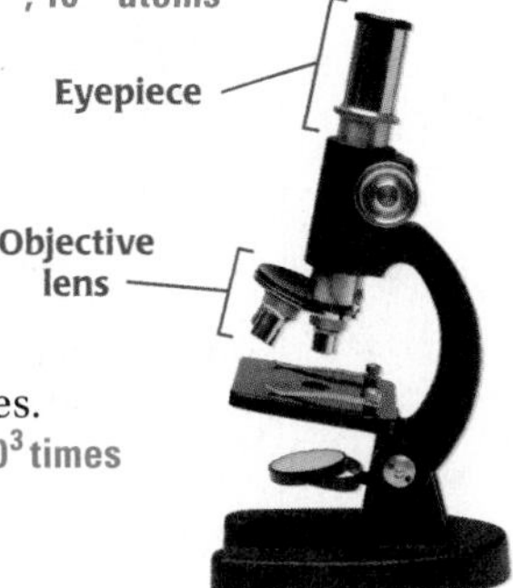

a. Your microscope's objective lens magnifies an object 10^2 times, and the eyepiece magnifies an object 10 times. What is the total magnification of your microscope? 10^3 times

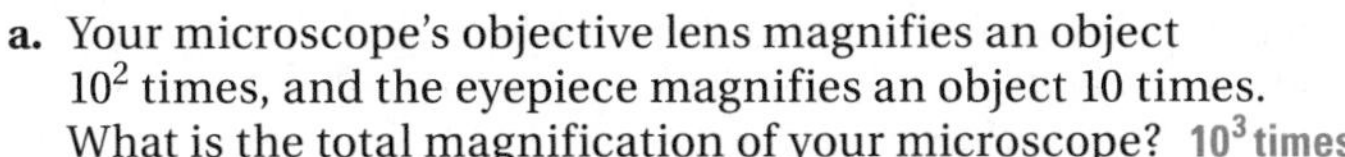

b. You magnify an object that is 10^2 nanometers long. How long is the magnified image? 10^5 nanometers

Vocabulary

Exercise 2 Encourage students to write out explanations and give specific examples for all three properties covered in this lesson.

Avoiding Common Errors

Exercises 3–38 Watch for students who fail to account for numerical or variable bases that have an exponent of 1. Remind these students that a base without an exponent is raised to the power of 1 and that they need to add 1 or multiply by 1 when simplifying expressions. Also, some students may overlook the numerical factor when simplifying powers with numerical and variable bases. Remind these students to evaluate the numerical power first.

Study Strategy

Exercise 54 You may want to suggest that students write the standard form of 1 billion and 35 million before they determine the order of magnitude. Students may want to review order of magnitude and estimation on page 491 before they begin this exercise.

51. *Sample answer:* $(ab)^n = (ab) \cdot (ab) \cdot \ldots \cdot (ab)$ so that there are n total terms (ab). By the commutative property, the n a's can be grouped as a repeated multiplication equal to a^n and the n b's can be grouped as a repeated multiplication equal to b^n. $(ab)^n$ is equal to the product of these two groups, or $a^n \cdot b^n$.

5 ASSESS AND RETEACH

Daily Homework Quiz

Transparency Available

Simplify the expression. Write your answer using exponents.

1. $14^5 \cdot 14^2$ 14^7
2. $[(-8)^4]^3$ $(-8)^{12}$

Simplify the expression.

3. $[(m-3)^6]^4$ $(m-3)^{24}$
4. $-(2s)^3$ $-8s^3$
5. A website had about 102 hits after a week. After a year, it had about 103 times the number of hits of the first week. About how many hits did it have at the end of the year? **about 10,000 hits**

Online Quiz

Available at **classzone.com**

Diagnosis/Remediation

- Practice A, B, C in Chapter 8 Resource Book, pp. 6–8
- Study Guide in Chapter 8 Resource Book, pp. 9–10
- Practice Workbook, pp. 119–120
- @HomeTutor

Challenge

Additional challenge is available in the Chapter 8 Resource Book, p. 13.

B **57. VOLUME OF THE SUN** The radius of the sun is about 695,000,000 meters. The formula for the volume of a sphere, such as the sun, is $V = \frac{4}{3}\pi r^3$. Because the order of magnitude of $\frac{4}{3}\pi$ is 1, it does not contribute to the formula in a significant way. So, you can find the order of magnitude of the volume of the sun by cubing its radius. Find the order of magnitude of the volume of the sun. 10^{27}

58. ★ **EXTENDED RESPONSE** Rock salt can be mined from large deposits of salt called salt domes. A particular salt dome is roughly cylindrical in shape. The order of magnitude of the radius of the salt dome is 10^3 feet. The order of magnitude of the height of the salt dome is about 10 times that of its radius. The formula for the volume of a cylinder is $V = \pi r^2 h$.

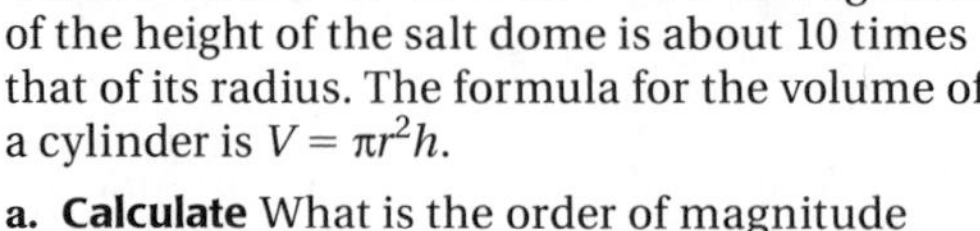

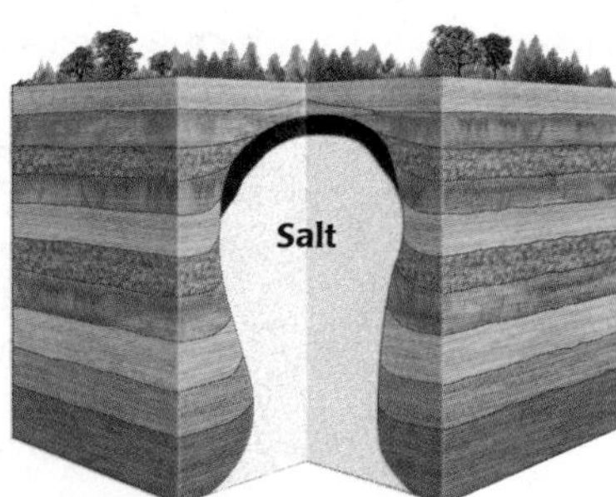

a. **Calculate** What is the order of magnitude of the height of the salt dome? 10^4

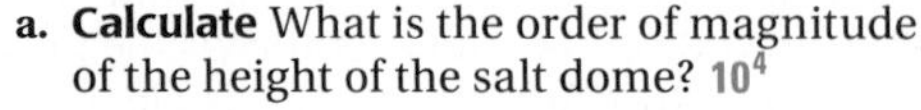

b. **Calculate** What is the order of magnitude of the volume of the salt dome? 10^{10}

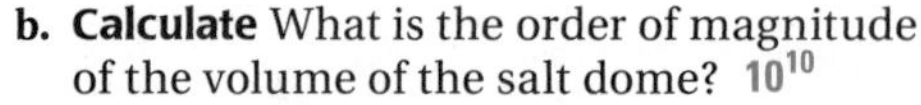

c. **Explain** The order of magnitude of the radius of a salt dome can be 10 times the radius of the salt dome described in this exercise. What effect does multiplying the order of magnitude of the radius of the salt dome by 10 have on the volume of the salt dome? *Explain.*

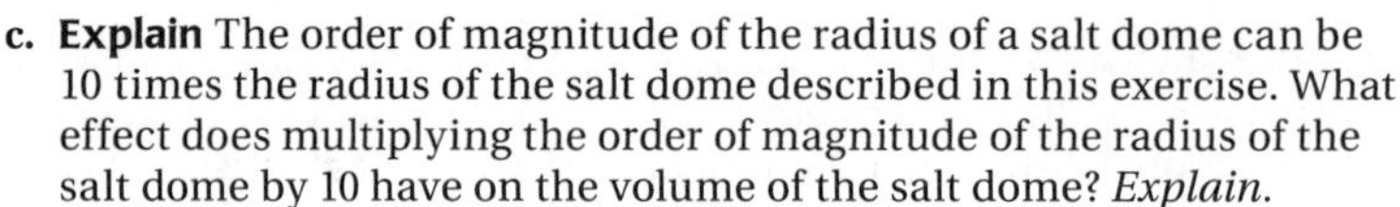

58c. Multiplies the volume by a factor of 10^2. *Sample answer:* Since the radius is squared in the formula for volume, multiplying the radius by 10 would multiply the volume by a factor of $10 \cdot 10$, or 10^2.

C **59. CHALLENGE** Your school is conducting a poll that has two parts, one part that has 13 questions and a second part that has 10 questions. Students can answer the questions in either part with "agree" or "disagree." What power of 2 represents the number of ways there are to answer the questions in the first part of the poll? What power of 2 represents the number of ways there are to answer the questions in the second part of the poll? What power of 2 represents the number of ways there are to answer all of the questions on the poll? 2^{13} ways; 2^{10} ways; 2^{23} ways

ILLINOIS MIXED REVIEW

TEST PRACTICE at classzone.com

60. Which is always a correct conclusion about the quantities in the function $y = 3x$? C

Ⓐ The variable y is always greater than x.

Ⓑ When the value of x is negative, the value of y is positive.

Ⓒ As the value of x decreases, the value of y decreases.

Ⓓ The variable x is 3 times the value of y.

61. A photograph of a surfer on a surfboard is enlarged by a scale factor of 8 to make a poster. If the surfboard in the photograph is 1.5 inches long, how long is the surfboard in the poster? B

Ⓐ 8 in. Ⓑ 12 in. Ⓒ 18 in. Ⓓ 96 in.

EXTRA PRACTICE for Lesson 8.1, p. 945

ONLINE QUIZ at classzone.com

8.2 Apply Exponent Properties Involving Quotients

 **8.11.01** Simplify or identify equivalent algebraic expressions (e.g., exponential, rational, logarithmic, factored, polynomial).

Before You used properties of exponents involving products.

Now You will use properties of exponents involving quotients.

Why? So you can compare magnitudes of earthquakes, as in Ex. 53.

Key Vocabulary
- **power,** *p. 3*
- **exponent,** *p. 3*
- **base,** *p. 3*

Notice what happens when you divide powers with the same base.

$$\frac{a^5}{a^3} = \frac{a \cdot a \cdot \cancel{a} \cdot \cancel{a} \cdot \cancel{a}}{\cancel{a} \cdot \cancel{a} \cdot \cancel{a}} = a \cdot a = a^2 = a^{5-3}$$

The example above suggests the following property of exponents, known as the quotient of powers property.

KEY CONCEPT *For Your Notebook*

Quotient of Powers Property

Let a be a nonzero real number, and let m and n be positive integers such that $m > n$.

Words To divide powers having the same base, subtract exponents.

Algebra $\frac{a^m}{a^n} = a^{m-n}, a \neq 0$ **Example** $\frac{4^7}{4^2} = 4^{7-2} = 4^5$

EXAMPLE 1 Use the quotient of powers property

SIMPLIFY EXPRESSIONS
When simplifying powers with numerical bases only, write your answers using exponents, as in parts (a), (b), and (c).

a. $\frac{8^{10}}{8^4} = 8^{10-4}$
$= 8^6$

b. $\frac{(-3)^9}{(-3)^3} = (-3)^{9-3}$
$= (-3)^6$

c. $\frac{5^4 \cdot 5^8}{5^7} = \frac{5^{12}}{5^7}$
$= 5^{12-7}$
$= 5^5$

d. $\frac{1}{x^4} \cdot x^6 = \frac{x^6}{x^4}$
$= x^{6-4}$
$= x^2$

 **GUIDED PRACTICE** for Example 1

Simplify the expression.

1. $\frac{6^{11}}{6^5}$ 6^6
2. $\frac{(-4)^9}{(-4)^2}$ $(-4)^7$
3. $\frac{9^4 \cdot 9^3}{9^2}$ 9^5
4. $\frac{1}{y^5} \cdot y^8$ y^3

1 PLAN AND PREPARE

Warm-Up Exercises
Transparency Available

1. Evaluate q^3 when $q = \frac{1}{4}$. $\frac{1}{64}$

2. Evaluate c^2 when $c = \frac{3}{5}$. $\frac{9}{25}$

3. A magazine had a circulation of 9364 in 2001. The circulation was about 125 times greater in 2006. Use order of magnitude to estimate the circulation in 2006. about 10^6 or 1,000,000

Notetaking Guide
Transparency Available
Promotes interactive learning and notetaking skills, pp. 170–172.

Pacing
Basic: 2 days
Average: 2 days
Advanced: 2 days
Block: 0.5 block with 8.1
0.5 block with 8.3
- See *Teaching Guide/Lesson Plan.*

2 FOCUS AND MOTIVATE

Essential Question
Big Idea 1, p. 487
How do you use properties of exponents involving quotients?
Tell students they will learn how to answer this question by simplifying expressions that involve division of powers.

Resource Planning Guide

Chapter Resource Book
- Teaching Guide/Lesson Plan (pp. 14–15)
- Activity Master (p. 16)
- Practice levels A, B, C (pp. 17–19)
- Study Guide (pp. 20–21)
- Catch-up for Absent Students (p. 22)
- Application (p. 23)
- Challenge (p. 24)

Workbooks
- Notetaking Guide (pp. 170–172)
- Practice Workbook (pp. 121–122)

Teaching Options
- **Power Presentations CD-ROM** provides dynamic electronic teaching resources for the classroom.
- **Activity Generator CD-ROM** provides editable activities for all ability levels.

Interactive Technology
- Easy Planner
- Power Presentations CD-ROM
- Activity Generator CD-ROM
- Animated Algebra
- Test Generator CD-ROM
- Online Quiz
- eWorkbook
- eEdition
- @HomeTutor

Resources for English Learners
- Quick Reference for English Learners
- Spanish Study Guide
- Multi-Language Visual Glossary
- Student Resources in Spanish

See also the *Algebra 1 Toolkit* for more strategies for meeting individual needs.

Motivating the Lesson

You are preparing a report that compares the radius of Earth at an order of magnitude of 10^7 meters to the radius of the Milky Way galaxy at an order of magnitude of 10^{21} meters. By knowing how to apply properties of exponents that involve quotients, you will be able to approximate how many times as great the radius of the Milky Way galaxy is as the radius of Earth.

Extra Example 1

Use the quotient of powers property.

a. $\frac{9^{12}}{9^5}$ 9^7

b. $\frac{(-2)^4}{(-2)^3}$ -2

c. $\frac{6^3 \cdot 6^4}{6^2}$ 6^5

d. $\frac{1}{r^5} \cdot r^8$ r^3

Key Question to Ask for Example 1

- How is dividing powers different from multiplying powers? You subtract exponents when you divide powers and add exponents when you multiply powers.

Extra Example 2

Use the power of a quotient property.

a. $\left(\frac{c}{d}\right)^6$ $\frac{c^6}{d^6}$

b. $\left(\frac{-2}{y}\right)^4$ $\frac{16}{y^4}$

POWER OF A QUOTIENT Notice what happens when you raise a quotient to a power.

$$\left(\frac{a}{b}\right)^4 = \frac{a}{b} \cdot \frac{a}{b} \cdot \frac{a}{b} \cdot \frac{a}{b} = \frac{a \cdot a \cdot a \cdot a}{b \cdot b \cdot b \cdot b} = \frac{a^4}{b^4}$$

The example above suggests the following property of exponents, known as the power of a quotient property.

KEY CONCEPT *For Your Notebook*

Power of a Quotient Property

Let a and b be real numbers with $b \neq 0$, and let m be a positive integer.

Words To find a power of a quotient, find the power of the numerator and the power of the denominator and divide.

Algebra $\left(\frac{a}{b}\right)^m = \frac{a^m}{b^m}$, $b \neq 0$

Example $\left(\frac{3}{2}\right)^7 = \frac{3^7}{2^7}$

EXAMPLE 2 Use the power of a quotient property

SIMPLIFY EXPRESSIONS
When simplifying powers with numerical *and* variable bases, evaluate the numerical power, as in part (b).

a. $\left(\frac{x}{y}\right)^3 = \frac{x^3}{y^3}$

b. $\left(-\frac{7}{x}\right)^2 = \left(\frac{-7}{x}\right)^2 = \frac{(-7)^2}{x^2} = \frac{49}{x^2}$

EXAMPLE 3 Use properties of exponents

a. $\left(\frac{4x^2}{5y}\right)^3 = \frac{(4x^2)^3}{(5y)^3}$ Power of a quotient property

$= \frac{4^3 \cdot (x^2)^3}{5^3y^3}$ Power of a product property

$= \frac{64x^6}{125y^3}$ Power of a power property

b. $\left(\frac{a^2}{b}\right)^5 \cdot \frac{1}{2a^2} = \frac{(a^2)^5}{b^5} \cdot \frac{1}{2a^2}$ Power of a quotient property

$= \frac{a^{10}}{b^5} \cdot \frac{1}{2a^2}$ Power of a power property

$= \frac{a^{10}}{2a^2b^5}$ Multiply fractions.

$= \frac{a^8}{2b^5}$ Quotient of powers property

Differentiated Instruction

Inclusion For smaller exponents, explicitly writing out the factors of each power works for division as well as multiplication. As practice, students can attempt a similar problem with very large exponents. This will allow them to see why the quotient of powers property works, without having to memorize its verbal form.

See also the *Algebra 1 Toolkit* for more strategies.

 **GUIDED PRACTICE** for Examples 2 and 3

Simplify the expression.

5. $\left(\frac{a}{b}\right)^2$ $\frac{a^2}{b^2}$

6. $\left(-\frac{5}{y}\right)^3$ $-\frac{125}{y^3}$

7. $\left(\frac{x^2}{4y}\right)^2$ $\frac{x^4}{16y^2}$

8. $\left(\frac{2s}{3t}\right)^3 \cdot \left(\frac{t^5}{16}\right)$ $\frac{s^3t^2}{54}$

EXAMPLE 4 Solve a multi-step problem

FRACTAL TREE To construct what is known as a *fractal tree*, begin with a single segment (the trunk) that is 1 unit long, as in Step 0. Add three shorter segments that are $\frac{1}{2}$ unit long to form the first set of branches, as in Step 1. Then continue adding sets of successively shorter branches so that each new set of branches is half the length of the previous set, as in Steps 2 and 3.

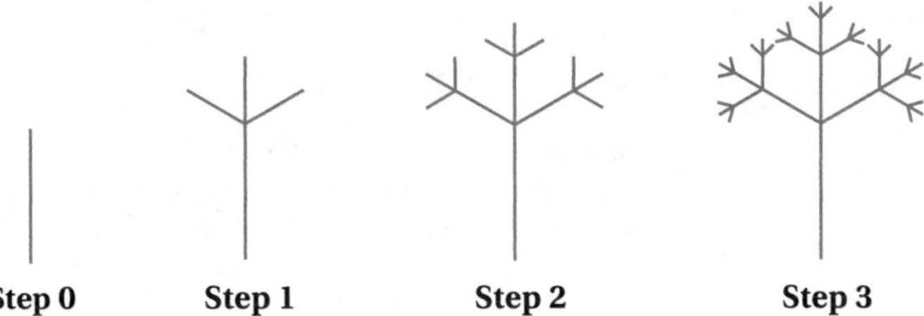

a. Make a table showing the number of new branches at each step for Steps 1–4. Write the number of new branches as a power of 3.

b. How many times greater is the number of new branches added at Step 5 than the number of new branches added at Step 2?

Solution

a.

Step	Number of new branches
1	$3 = 3^1$
2	$9 = 3^2$
3	$27 = 3^3$
4	$81 = 3^4$

b. The number of new branches added at Step 5 is 3^5. The number of new branches added at Step 2 is 3^2. So, the number of new branches added at Step 5 is $\frac{3^5}{3^2} = 3^3 = 27$ times the number of new branches added at Step 2.

 **GUIDED PRACTICE** for Example 4

9. **FRACTAL TREE** In Example 4, add a column to the table for the length of the new branches at each step. Write the lengths of the new branches as powers of $\frac{1}{2}$. What is the length of a new branch added at Step 9? See margin.

Extra Example 3

Use properties of exponents.

a. $\left(\frac{3a^4}{5b}\right)^3$ $\frac{27a^{12}}{125b^3}$

b. $\left(\frac{x^3}{y}\right)^7 \cdot \frac{1}{3x^8}$ $\frac{x^{13}}{3y^7}$

Extra Example 4

Construct a fractal tree that begins with a V-shaped segment, with each side of the V-shape 1 unit long. Then add a V-shaped segment on each end with each side $\frac{1}{2}$ unit long. Continue adding sets of successively shorter branches so that each new set of branches is half the length of the previous set.

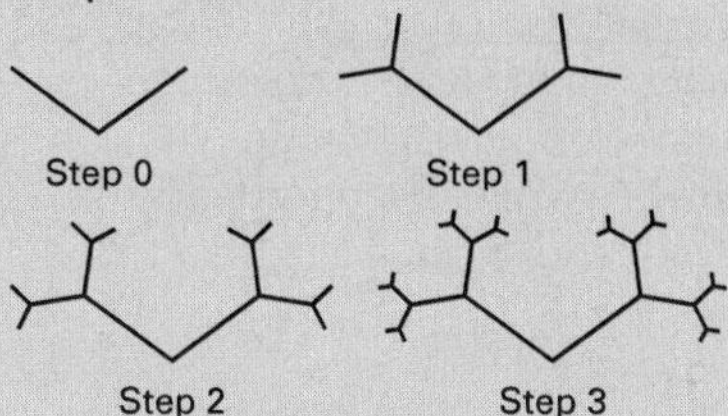

a. Make a table showing the number of new branches at each step for Steps 1–3. Write the number of new branches as a power of 2.

Step	New branches
1	$4 = 2^2$
2	$8 = 2^3$
3	$16 = 2^4$

b. How many times as great is the number of new branches at Step 6 as the number of new branches at Step 2? 16

Key Question to Ask for Example 4

- Why do you write the number of new branches as a power of 3? Since you add 3 segments to each set of successive branches, the steps are 3, then 3 × 3, then 3 × 3 × 3, and so on.

9.

Step	Number of new branches	Length of new branches
1	$3 = 3^1$	$\frac{1}{2} = \left(\frac{1}{2}\right)^1$
2	$9 = 3^2$	$\frac{1}{4} = \left(\frac{1}{2}\right)^2$
3	$27 = 3^3$	$\frac{1}{8} = \left(\frac{1}{2}\right)^3$
4	$81 = 3^4$	$\frac{1}{16} = \left(\frac{1}{2}\right)^4$

$\left(\frac{1}{2}\right)^9 = \frac{1}{512}$ unit

Extra Example 5

The order of magnitude of the luminosity of the Milky Way galaxy is 10^{36} watts. The order of magnitude of the luminosity of a gamma ray burster is 10^{45} watts. How many times as luminous is a gamma ray burster as the Milky Way galaxy? **about 10^9 times as luminous**

Key Question to Ask for Example 5

- How do you know that you need to divide to find the solution to this problem? **The problem asks for a ratio and you divide to find ratios.**

Closing the Lesson

Have students summarize the major points of the lesson and answer the Essential Question: How do you use properties of exponents involving quotients?

- **Subtract exponents to divide powers.**
- **To find the power of a quotient, find the powers of the numerator and the powers of denominator before dividing.**

To simplify an expression involving quotients, subtract the exponent of the denominator from the exponent of the numerator. To raise a quotient to a power, find the power of the numerator and the power of the denominator and divide.

EXAMPLE 5 Solve a real-world problem

ASTRONOMY The luminosity (in watts) of a star is the total amount of energy emitted from the star per unit of time. The order of magnitude of the luminosity of the sun is 10^{26} watts. The star Canopus is one of the brightest stars in the sky. The order of magnitude of the luminosity of Canopus is 10^{30} watts. How many times more luminous is Canopus than the sun?

Canopus

Solution

$$\frac{\text{Luminosity of Canopus (watts)}}{\text{Luminosity of the sun (watts)}} = \frac{10^{30}}{10^{26}} = 10^{30-26} = 10^4$$

▶ Canopus is about 10^4 times as luminous as the sun.

✓ GUIDED PRACTICE for Example 5

10. **WHAT IF?** Sirius is considered the brightest star in the sky. Sirius is less luminous than Canopus, but Sirius appears to be brighter because it is much closer to Earth. The order of magnitude of the luminosity of Sirius is 10^{28} watts. How many times more luminous is Canopus than Sirius? **10^2**

8.2 EXERCISES

HOMEWORK KEY

○ = **WORKED-OUT SOLUTIONS** on p. WS18 for Exs. 33 and 51

★ = **STANDARDIZED TEST PRACTICE** Exs. 2, 19, 37, 46, and 54

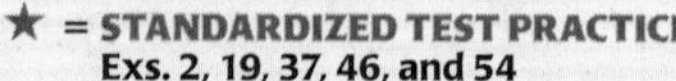

◆ = **MULTIPLE REPRESENTATIONS** Ex. 49

SKILL PRACTICE

A

1. **VOCABULARY** Copy and complete: In the power 4^3, 4 is the _?_ and 3 is the _?_. **base, exponent**

2. ★ **WRITING** *Explain* when and how to use the quotient of powers property. **When powers have the same base, their quotient is the base raised to the difference of the exponents.**

EXAMPLES 1 and 2 on pp. 495–496 for Exs. 3–20

SIMPLIFYING EXPRESSIONS **Simplify the expression. Write your answer using exponents.**

3. $\frac{5^6}{5^2}$ **5^4**
4. $\frac{2^{11}}{2^6}$ **2^5**
5. $\frac{3^9}{3^5}$ **3^4**
6. $\frac{(-6)^8}{(-6)^5}$ **$(-6)^3$**
7. $\frac{(-4)^7}{(-4)^4}$ **$(-4)^3$**
8. $\frac{(-12)^9}{(-12)^3}$ **$(-12)^6$**
9. $\frac{10^5 \cdot 10^5}{10^4}$ **10^6**
10. $\frac{6^7 \cdot 6^4}{6^6}$ **6^5**
11. $\left(\frac{1}{3}\right)^5$ **$\frac{1}{3^5}$**
12. $\left(\frac{3}{2}\right)^4$ **$\frac{3^4}{2^4}$**
13. $\left(-\frac{5}{4}\right)^4$ **$\frac{5^4}{4^4}$**
14. $\left(-\frac{2}{5}\right)^5$ **$-\frac{2^5}{5^5}$**
15. $7^9 \cdot \frac{1}{7^2}$ **7^7**
16. $\frac{1}{9^5} \cdot 9^{11}$ **9^6**
17. $\left(\frac{1}{3}\right)^4 \cdot 3^{12}$ **3^8**
18. $4^9 \cdot \left(-\frac{1}{4}\right)^5$ **-4^4**

Differentiated Instruction

Advanced In **Example 5**, some students may see that if Canopus is 10,000 times as bright as the sun, then the sun is $\frac{1}{10{,}000}$ as bright as Canopus. Challenge students to use this observation to write a ratio of the luminosity of the sun to the luminosity of Canopus using exponents. Ask them to explain their reasoning by describing the relationship between the two ratios. This prepares students for the definition of negative exponents in Lesson 8.3.

See also the *Algebra 1 Toolkit* for more strategies.

19. ★ **MULTIPLE CHOICE** Which expression is equivalent to 16^6? C

Ⓐ $\frac{16^4}{16^2}$ Ⓑ $\frac{16^{12}}{16^2}$ Ⓒ $\left(\frac{16^6}{16^3}\right)^2$ Ⓓ $\left(\frac{16^9}{16^6}\right)^3$

20. **ERROR ANALYSIS** *Describe* and correct the error in simplifying $\frac{9^5 \cdot 9^3}{9^4}$. See margin.

$$\frac{9^5 \cdot 9^3}{9^4} = \frac{9^8}{9^4} = 9^{12} \quad ✗$$

EXAMPLES 1, 2, and 3 on pp. 495–496 for Exs. 21–37

SIMPLIFYING EXPRESSIONS **Simplify the expression.**

21. $\frac{1}{y^8} \cdot y^{15}$ y^7 22. $z^8 \cdot \frac{1}{z^7}$ z 23. $\left(\frac{a}{y}\right)^9$ $\frac{a^9}{y^9}$ 24. $\left(\frac{j}{k}\right)^{11}$ $\frac{j^{11}}{k^{11}}$

25. $\left(\frac{p}{q}\right)^4$ $\frac{p^4}{q^4}$ 26. $\left(-\frac{1}{x}\right)^5$ $-\frac{1}{x^5}$ 27. $\left(-\frac{4}{x}\right)^3$ $-\frac{64}{x^3}$ 28. $\left(-\frac{a}{b}\right)^4$ $\frac{a^4}{b^4}$

29. $\left(\frac{4c}{d^2}\right)^3$ $\frac{64c^3}{d^6}$ 30. $\left(\frac{a^7}{2b}\right)^5$ $\frac{a^{35}}{32b^5}$ 31. $\left(\frac{x^2}{3y^3}\right)^2$ $\frac{x^4}{9y^6}$ 32. $\left(\frac{3x^5}{7y^2}\right)^3$ $\frac{27x^{15}}{343y^6}$

(33.) $\left(\frac{3x^3}{2y}\right)^2 \cdot \frac{1}{x^2}$ $\frac{9x^4}{4y^2}$ 34. $\left(\frac{2x^3}{y}\right)^3 \cdot \frac{1}{6x^3}$ $\frac{4x^6}{3y^3}$ 35. $\frac{3}{8m^5} \cdot \left(\frac{m^4}{n^2}\right)^3$ $\frac{3m^7}{8n^6}$ 36. $\left(-\frac{5}{x}\right)^2 \cdot \left(\frac{2x^4}{y^3}\right)^2$ $\frac{100x^6}{y^6}$

B 37. ★ **MULTIPLE CHOICE** Which expression is equivalent to $\left(\frac{7x^3}{2y^4}\right)^2$? D

Ⓐ $\frac{7x^5}{2y^6}$ Ⓑ $\frac{7x^6}{2y^8}$ Ⓒ $\frac{49x^5}{4y^6}$ Ⓓ $\frac{49x^6}{4y^8}$

SIMPLIFYING EXPRESSIONS **Find the missing exponent.**

38. $\frac{(-8)^7}{(-8)^?} = (-8)^3$ 4 39. $\frac{7^? \cdot 7^2}{7^4} = 7^6$ 8 40. $\frac{1}{p^5} \cdot p^? = p^9$ 14 41. $\left(\frac{2c^3}{d^2}\right)^? = \frac{16c^{12}}{d^8}$ 4

SIMPLIFYING EXPRESSIONS **Simplify the expression.**

42. $\left(\frac{2f^2g^3}{3fg}\right)^4$ $\frac{16f^4g^8}{81}$ 43. $\frac{2s^3t^3}{st^2} \cdot \frac{(3st)^3}{s^2t}$ $54s^3t^3$ 44. $\left(\frac{2m^5n}{4m^2}\right)^2 \cdot \left(\frac{mn^4}{5n}\right)^2$ $\frac{m^8n^8}{100}$ 45. $\left(\frac{3x^3y}{x^2}\right)^3 \cdot \left(\frac{y^2x^4}{5y}\right)^2$ $\frac{27x^{11}y^5}{25}$

46. ★ **OPEN-ENDED** Write three expressions involving quotients that are equivalent to 14^7. *Sample answer:* $\frac{14^8}{14}, \frac{14^{10}}{14^3}, \frac{14^{14}}{14^7}$

C 47. **REASONING** Name the definition or property that justifies each step to show that $\frac{a^m}{a^n} = \frac{1}{a^{n-m}}$ for $m < n$.

Let $m < n$. Given

$\frac{a^m}{a^n} = \frac{a^m}{a^n}\left(\frac{\frac{1}{a^m}}{\frac{1}{a^m}}\right)$? Identity property of multiplication

$= \frac{1}{\frac{a^n}{a^m}}$? Multiply fractions.

$= \frac{1}{a^{n-m}}$? Quotient of powers property

48. **CHALLENGE** Find the values of x and y if you know that $\frac{b^x}{b^y} = b^9$ and $\frac{b^x \cdot b^2}{b^{3y}} = b^{13}$. *Explain* how you found your answer.

48. $x = 8$, $y = -1$. *Sample answer:* Using the quotient of a power property, write two equations for x and y: $x - y = 9$, and $x + 2 - 3y = 13$. Solve the equations.

20. *Sample answer:* When using the quotient of powers property, the base is raised to the difference of the exponents, not the sum; $\frac{9^8}{9^4} = 9^{(8-4)} = 9^4$.

4 PRACTICE AND APPLY

Assignment Guide

Answer Transparencies available for all exercises

Basic:
Day 1: pp. 498–501
Exs. 1–28
Day 2: pp. 498–501
Exs. 29–39, 49–52, 55–66

Average:
Day 1: pp. 498–501
Exs. 1, 2, 7–28, 38–40
Day 2: pp. 498–501
Exs. 31–37, 41–46, 49–53, 55–66

Advanced:
Day 1: pp. 498–501
Exs. 1, 2, 9–19, 21–28, 38–40, 47, 48*
Day 2: pp. 498–501
Exs. 32–37, 41–46, 49–66*

Block:
pp. 498–501
Exs. 1, 2, 7–28, 38–40 (with 8.1)
pp. 498–501
Exs. 31–37, 41–46, 49–53, 55–66 (with 8.3)

Differentiated Instruction

See *Algebra 1 Best Practices Toolkit* for suggestions on addressing the needs of a diverse classroom.

Homework Check

For a quick check of student understanding of key concepts, go over the following exercises:

Basic: 6, 23, 30, 49, 50
Average: 12, 24, 32, 49, 51
Advanced: 16, 27, 34, 50, 51

Extra Practice

- Student Edition, p. 945
- Chapter 8 Resource Book: Practice levels A, B, C, pp. 17–19

Practice Worksheet

An easily-readable reduced practice page (with answers) for this lesson can be found on p. 486C.

Avoiding Common Errors

Exercises 3–18, 21–36 Watch for students who add exponents when finding a quotient. Remind these students that you subtract exponents when dividing and add exponents when multiplying.

Study Strategy

Exercises 19, 37 Suggest that students look for ways to eliminate answers. In Exercise 19, point out that they can eliminate two choices quickly by subtracting exponents. In Exercise 37, suggest that students evaluate the numerical bases to eliminate two choices.

Mathematical Reasoning

Exercises 38–40 For students who have difficulty solving these exercises, suggest that they expand numbers and variables into their basic factors and then work backward from what they know. For example, in Exercise 38, tell them that they know there are 7 factors of (-8) in the numerator. They also know that the number of factors in the numerator and denominator cancel so that 3 factors of (-8) remain. So the question they need to ask is how many factors of (-8) are in the denominator so that only 3 factors of (-8) remain in the numerator after canceling.

Exercise 53 More information about earthquakes can be found at pubs.usgs.gov/gip/earthq1

PROBLEM SOLVING

EXAMPLES A **4 and 5** on pp. 497–498 for Exs. 49–51

49. ◆ **MULTIPLE REPRESENTATIONS** Draw a square with side lengths that are 1 unit long. Divide it into four new squares with side lengths that are one half the side length of the original square, as shown in Step 1. Keep dividing the squares into new squares, as shown in Steps 2 and 3.

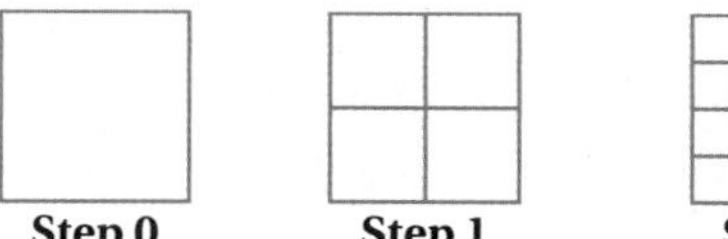

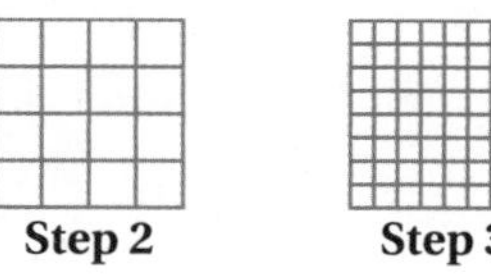

a. Making a Table Make a table showing the number of new squares and the side length of a new square at each step for Steps 1–4. Write the number of new squares as a power of 4. Write the side length of a new square as a power of $\frac{1}{2}$. See margin.

b. Writing an Expression Write and simplify an expression to find by how many times the number of new squares increased from Step 2 to Step 4. $\frac{4^4}{4^2}$; 16 times

@HomeTutor for problem solving help at classzone.com

50. GROSS DOMESTIC PRODUCT In 2003 the gross domestic product (GDP) for the United States was about 11 trillion dollars, and the order of magnitude of the population of the U.S. was 10^8. Use order of magnitude to find the approximate per capita (per person) GDP. about 10^5 dollars

@HomeTutor for problem solving help at classzone.com

(51.) SPACE TRAVEL Alpha Centauri is the closest star system to Earth. Alpha Centauri is about 10^{13} kilometers away from Earth. A spacecraft leaves Earth and travels at an average speed of 10^4 meters per second. About how many years would it take the spacecraft to reach Alpha Centauri? about 31,710 yr

B

52. ASTRONOMY The brightness of one star relative to another star can be measured by comparing the magnitudes of the stars. For every increase in magnitude of 1, the relative brightness is diminished by a factor of 2.512. For instance, a star of magnitude 8 is 2.512 times less bright than a star of magnitude 7.

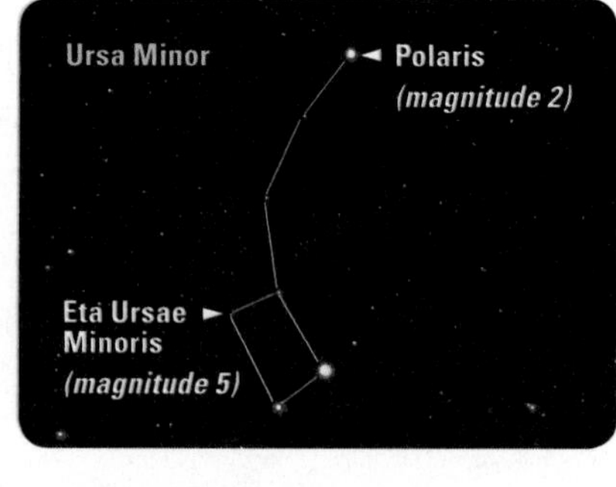

The constellation Ursa Minor (the Little Dipper) is shown. How many times less bright is Eta Ursae Minoris than Polaris? 2.512^3 times

53. EARTHQUAKES The energy released by one earthquake relative to another earthquake can be measured by comparing the magnitudes (as determined by the Richter scale) of the earthquakes. For every increase of 1 in magnitude, the energy released is multiplied by a factor of about 31. How many times greater is the energy released by an earthquake of magnitude 7 than the energy released by an earthquake of magnitude 4? 31^3 times greater

○ = WORKED-OUT SOLUTIONS on p. WS1 ★ = STANDARDIZED TEST PRACTICE ◆ = MULTIPLE REPRESENTATIONS

49a.

Step	Number of new squares	Side length of new square
1	$4 = 4^1$	$\frac{1}{2} = \left(\frac{1}{2}\right)^1$
2	$16 = 4^2$	$\frac{1}{4} = \left(\frac{1}{2}\right)^2$
3	$64 = 4^3$	$\frac{1}{8} = \left(\frac{1}{2}\right)^3$
4	$256 = 4^4$	$\frac{1}{16} = \left(\frac{1}{2}\right)^4$

C 54. ★ **EXTENDED RESPONSE** A byte is a unit used to measure computer memory. Other units are based on the number of bytes they represent. The table shows the number of bytes in certain units. For example, from the table you can calculate that 1 terabyte is equivalent to 2^{10} gigabytes.

Unit	Number of bytes
Kilobyte	2^{10}
Megabyte	2^{20}
Gigabyte	2^{30}
Terabyte	2^{40}
Petabyte	2^{50}

a. **Calculate** How many kilobytes are there in 1 terabyte? 2^{30} kilobytes

b. **Calculate** How many megabytes are there in 1 petabyte? 2^{30} megabytes

c. **CHALLENGE** Another unit used to measure computer memory is a bit. There are 8 bits in a byte. *Explain* how you can convert the number of bytes per unit given in the table to the number of bits per unit. Multiply the number of bytes in each unit by 8, or 2^3.

ILLINOIS MIXED REVIEW

TEST PRACTICE at classzone.com

55. For a car traveling at a speed of 45 miles per hour, the relationship between the distance traveled, d, and the time traveled, t, is described by the function $d = 45t$. Which statement is true? B

(A) The time traveled depends on the distance traveled.

(B) The distance traveled depends on the time traveled.

(C) The speed of the car depends on the distance traveled.

(D) The speed of the car depends on the time traveled.

QUIZ for Lessons 8.1–8.2

Simplify the expression. Write your answer using exponents.

1. $3^2 \cdot 3^6$ *(p. 489)* 3^8
2. $(5^4)^3$ *(p. 489)* 5^{12}
3. $(32 \cdot 14)^7$ *(p. 489)* $32^7 \cdot 14^7$
4. $7^2 \cdot 7^6 \cdot 7$ *(p. 489)* 7^9
5. $(-4)(-4)^9$ *(p. 489)* $(-4)^{10}$
6. $\frac{7^{12}}{7^4}$ *(p. 495)* 7^8
7. $\frac{(-9)^9}{(-9)^7}$ *(p. 495)* $(-9)^2$
8. $\frac{3^7 \cdot 3^4}{3^6}$ *(p. 495)* 3^5
9. $\left(\frac{5}{4}\right)^4$ *(p. 495)* $\frac{5^4}{4^4}$

Simplify the expression.

10. $x^2 \cdot x^5$ *(p. 489)* x^7
11. $(3x^3)^2$ *(p. 489)* $9x^6$
12. $-(7x)^2$ *(p. 489)* $-49x^2$
13. $(6x^5)^3 \cdot x$ *(p. 489)* $216x^{16}$
14. $(2x^5)^3(7x^7)^2$ *(p. 489)* $392x^{29}$
15. $\frac{1}{x^9} \cdot x^{21}$ *(p. 495)* x^{12}
16. $\left(-\frac{4}{x}\right)^3$ *(p. 495)* $-\frac{64}{x^3}$
17. $\left(\frac{w}{v}\right)^6$ *(p. 495)* $\frac{w^6}{v^6}$
18. $\left(\frac{x^3}{4}\right)^2$ *(p. 495)* $\frac{x^6}{16}$

19. **AGRICULTURE** In 2004 the order of magnitude of the number of pounds of oranges produced in the United States was 10^{10}. The order of magnitude of the number of acres used for growing oranges was 10^6. About how many pounds of oranges per acre were produced in in the United States in 2004? *(p. 495)* about 10^4 pounds

EXTRA PRACTICE for Lesson 8.2, p. 945  **ONLINE QUIZ** at classzone.com

5 ASSESS AND RETEACH

Daily Homework Quiz

Transparency Available

1. Simplify $\frac{6^3 \cdot 6^5}{6^4}$ 6^4
2. Simplify $10^7 \cdot \left(\frac{-1}{10}\right)^4$ 10^3
3. Simplify $\left(\frac{s^8}{3r}\right)^3$ $\frac{s^{24}}{27r^3}$
4. The order of magnitude of the power output of a nuclear-powered aircraft carrier is about 10^6 watts. The order of magnitude of peak power at Hoover Dam is about 10^9 watts. How many times as great is the power output of Hoover Dam as the power output of a nuclear-powered aircraft carrier? 10^3

Available at **classzone.com**

Diagnosis/Remediation

- Practice A, B, C in Chapter 8 Resource Book, pp. 17–19
- Study Guide in Chapter 8 Resource Book, pp. 20–21
- Practice Workbook, pp. 121–122
- @HomeTutor

Challenge

Additional challenge is available in the Chapter 8 Resource Book, p. 24.

Quiz

An easily-readable reduced copy of the quiz (with answers) on Lessons 8.1–8.2 from the Assessment Book can be found on p. 486E.

1 PLAN AND PREPARE

Explore the Concept

- Students will simplify expressions with zero or negative exponents.
- This activity leads into the study of using the definitions of zero and negative exponents in Example 1 in Lesson 8.3.

Recommended Time

Work activity: 10 min

Discuss results: 5 min

Grouping

Students should work individually.

2 TEACH

Tips for Success

When students read the table from the bottom up in Step 1, make sure that they look for the pattern in the second column. Point out that the value of 2^n is multiplied by 2, the base of 2^n, and not by the value of the exponent in column 1.

Key Discovery

A number to the zero power is 1. A power with a negative exponent can be written with a positive exponent by taking the reciprocal of the base.

3 ASSESS AND RETEACH

1. What is the value of $(-2xy)^0$? 1
2. How do you write a^{-n} using a positive exponent if a is a nonzero number and n is a positive integer? $\frac{1}{a^n}$

8.3 Zero and Negative Exponents

MATERIALS • paper and pencil

QUESTION How can you simplify expressions with zero or negative exponents?

EXPLORE Evaluate powers with zero and negative exponents

STEP 1 ***Find a pattern***

Copy and complete the tables for the powers of 2 and 3.

Exponent, n	Value of 2^n
4	16
3	? 8
2	? 4
1	? 2

Exponent, n	Value of 3^n
4	81
3	? 27
2	? 9
1	? 3

As you read the tables from the *bottom up*, you see that each time the exponent is increased by 1, the value of the power is multiplied by the base. What can you say about the exponents and the values of the powers as you read the table from the *top down*?

STEP 2 ***Extend the pattern***

Copy and complete the tables using the pattern you observed in Step 1.

Exponent, n	Power, 2^n
3	8
2	? 4
1	? 2
0	? 1
−1	? $\frac{1}{2}$
−2	? $\frac{1}{4}$

Exponent, n	Power, 3^n
3	27
2	? 9
1	? 3
0	? 1
−1	? $\frac{1}{3}$
−2	? $\frac{1}{9}$

DRAW CONCLUSIONS Use your observations to complete these exercises

1. Find 2^n and 3^n for $n = -3, -4$, and -5. $2^{-3} = \frac{1}{8}, 3^{-3} = \frac{1}{27}; 2^{-4} = \frac{1}{16}, 3^{-4} = \frac{1}{81}; 2^{-5} = \frac{1}{32}, 3^{-5} = \frac{1}{243}$
2. What appears to be the value of a^0 for any nonzero number a? 1
3. Write each power in the tables above as a power with a positive exponent. For example, you can write 3^{-1} as $\frac{1}{3^1}$. See margin.

3.

Power, 2^n	Exponent
8	2^3
4	2^2
2	2^1
1	2^0
$\frac{1}{2}$	$\frac{1}{2^1}$
$\frac{1}{4}$	$\frac{1}{2^2}$

Power, 3^n	Exponent
27	3^3
9	3^2
3	3^1
1	3^0
$\frac{1}{3}$	$\frac{1}{3^1}$
$\frac{1}{9}$	$\frac{1}{3^2}$

8.3 Define and Use Zero and Negative Exponents

8.11.01 Simplify or identify equivalent algebraic expressions (e.g., exponential, rational, logarithmic, factored, polynomial).

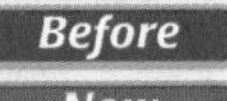

Before You used properties of exponents to simplify expressions.

Now You will use zero and negative exponents.

Why? So you can compare masses, as in Ex. 52.

Key Vocabulary
- **reciprocal,** *p. 915*

In the activity, you saw what happens when you raise a number to a zero or negative exponent. The activity suggests the following definitions.

KEY CONCEPT *For Your Notebook*

Definition of Zero and Negative Exponents

Words	Algebra	Example
a to the zero power is 1.	$a^0 = 1, a \neq 0$	$5^0 = 1$
a^{-n} is the reciprocal of a^n.	$a^{-n} = \frac{1}{a^n}, a \neq 0$	$2^{-1} = \frac{1}{2}$
a^n is the reciprocal of a^{-n}.	$a^n = \frac{1}{a^{-n}}, a \neq 0$	$2 = \frac{1}{2^{-1}}$

EXAMPLE 1 Use definition of zero and negative exponents

SIMPLIFY EXPRESSIONS
In this lesson, when simplifying powers with numerical bases, evaluate the numerical power.

a. $3^{-2} = \frac{1}{3^2}$ — Definition of negative exponents

$= \frac{1}{9}$ — Evaluate exponent.

b. $(-7)^0 = 1$ — Definition of zero exponent

c. $\left(\frac{1}{5}\right)^{-2} = \frac{1}{\left(\frac{1}{5}\right)^2}$ — Definition of negative exponents

$= \frac{1}{\frac{1}{25}}$ — Evaluate exponent.

$= 25$ — Simplify by multiplying numerator and denominator by 25.

d. $0^{-5} = \frac{1}{0^5}$ (Undefined) — a^{-n} is defined only for a *nonzero* number a.

GUIDED PRACTICE for Example 1

Evaluate the expression.

1. $\left(\frac{2}{3}\right)^0$ 1 **2.** $(-8)^{-2}$ $\frac{1}{64}$ **3.** $\frac{1}{2^{-3}}$ 8 **4.** $(-1)^0$ 1

1 PLAN AND PREPARE

Warm-Up Exercises

Transparency Available

1. Simplify $(-3x)^2$. $9x^2$

2. Simplify $\left(\frac{a^3}{2b}\right)^5$. $\frac{a^{15}}{32b^5}$

3. The order of magnitude of Earth's mass is about 10^{27} grams. The order of magnitude of the sun's mass is about 10^{33} grams. About how many times as great is the sun's mass as Earth's mass? about 10^6

Notetaking Guide

Transparency Available

Promotes interactive learning and notetaking skills, pp. 173–175.

Pacing

Basic: 1 day
Average: 1 day
Advanced: 1 day
Block: 0.5 block with 8.2
- See *Teaching Guide/Lesson Plan.*

2 FOCUS AND MOTIVATE

Essential Question

Big Idea 1, p. 487

How do you use zero and negative exponents? Tell students they will learn how to answer this question by using properties of exponents to simplify and evaluate expressions.

Resource Planning Guide

Chapter Resource Book
- Teaching Guide/Lesson Plan (pp. 25–26)
- Practice levels A, B, C (pp. 27–29)
- Study Guide (pp. 30–31)
- Catch-up for Absent Students (p. 32)
- Problem Solving Workshop (p. 33)
- Challenge (p. 35)

Workbooks
- Notetaking Guide (pp. 173–175)
- Practice Workbook (pp. 123–124)

Teaching Options
- **Power Presentations CD-ROM** provides dynamic electronic teaching resources for the classroom.
- **Activity Generator CD-ROM** provides editable activities for all ability levels.

Interactive Technology
- Easy Planner
- Power Presentations CD-ROM
- Activity Generator CD-ROM
- Animated Algebra
- Test Generator CD-ROM
- Online Quiz
- eWorkbook
- eEdition
- @HomeTutor

Resources for English Learners
- Quick Reference for English Learners
- Spanish Study Guide
- Multi-Language Visual Glossary
- Student Resources in Spanish

See also the *Algebra 1 Toolkit* for more strategies for meeting individual needs.

Motivating the Lesson

The mass of an amoeba is about 10^{-5} grams. The mass of a raindrop is about 1,000 times as great as the mass of an amoeba. By knowing how to evaluate numbers with negative exponents, you can determine the approximate mass of a raindrop.

Extra Example 1

Use the definition of zero and negative exponents.

a. 6^{-2} $\frac{1}{36}$

b. x^0 1

c. $\left(\frac{2}{3}\right)^{-2}$ $\frac{9}{4}$

d. 0^{-7} undefined

Key Questions to Ask for Example 1

- Why is the expression in part d undefined? Division by zero is not defined.
- If the base of a power is positive and the exponent is negative, is the power always positive? Explain. Yes; the reciprocal of a positive number is positive, and the power of a positive number is positive.

Extra Example 2

Evaluate exponential expressions.

a. $(-2)^5 \cdot (-2)^{-5}$ 1

b. $(3^3)^{-2}$ $\frac{1}{729}$

c. $\frac{1}{8^{-2}}$ 64

d. $\frac{7^3}{7^5}$ $\frac{1}{49}$

Key Question to Ask for Example 2

- In part (c), why is $\frac{1}{3^{-4}}$ equal to 3^4? 3^4 is the reciprocal of 3^{-4}.

PROPERTIES OF EXPONENTS The properties of exponents you learned in Lessons 8.1 and 8.2 can be used with negative or zero exponents.

KEY CONCEPT *For Your Notebook*

Properties of Exponents

Let a and b be real numbers, and let m and n be integers.

$a^m \cdot a^n = a^{m+n}$	Product of powers property
$(a^m)^n = a^{mn}$	Power of a power property
$(ab)^m = a^m b^m$	Power of a product property
$\frac{a^m}{a^n} = a^{m-n}, a \neq 0$	Quotient of powers property
$\left(\frac{a}{b}\right)^m = \frac{a^m}{b^m}, b \neq 0$	Power of a quotient property

EXAMPLE 2 Evaluate exponential expressions

a. $6^{-4} \cdot 6^4 = 6^{-4+4}$	Product of powers property
$= 6^0$	Add exponents.
$= 1$	Definition of zero exponent
b. $(4^{-2})^2 = 4^{-2 \cdot 2}$	Power of a power property
$= 4^{-4}$	Multiply exponents.
$= \frac{1}{4^4}$	Definition of negative exponents
$= \frac{1}{256}$	Evaluate power.
c. $\frac{1}{3^{-4}} = 3^4$	Definition of negative exponents
$= 81$	Evaluate power.
d. $\frac{5^{-1}}{5^2} = 5^{-1-2}$	Quotient of powers property
$= 5^{-3}$	Subtract exponents.
$= \frac{1}{5^3}$	Definition of negative exponents
$= \frac{1}{125}$	Evaluate power.

GUIDED PRACTICE for Example 2

Evaluate the expression.

5. $\frac{1}{4^{-3}}$ 64 **6.** $(5^{-3})^{-1}$ 125 **7.** $(-3)^5 \cdot (-3)^{-5}$ 1 **8.** $\frac{6^{-2}}{6^2}$ $\frac{1}{1296}$

Differentiated Instruction

Visual Learners Some of these examples give students a way to visualize zero and negative exponents. In **Example 2a**, 6^0 is simplified from $6^{-4} \cdot 6^4$, which by the quotient of powers property is $\frac{6^4}{6^4}$, or 1. In **Example 2b**, 4^{-4} is 4^{0-4}, which by the quotient of powers property is $\frac{4^0}{4^4}$, or $\frac{1}{256}$.

See also the *Algebra 1 Toolkit* for more strategies.

EXAMPLE 3 Use properties of exponents

Simplify the expression. Write your answer using only positive exponents.

a. $(2xy^{-5})^3 = 2^3 \cdot x^3 \cdot (y^{-5})^3$ — **Power of a product property**

$= 8 \cdot x^3 \cdot y^{-15}$ — **Power of a power property**

$= \frac{8x^3}{y^{15}}$ — **Definition of negative exponents**

b. $\frac{(2x)^{-2}y^5}{-4x^2y^2} = \frac{y^5}{(2x)^2(-4x^2y^2)}$ — **Definition of negative exponents**

$= \frac{y^5}{(4x^2)(-4x^2y^2)}$ — **Power of a product property**

$= \frac{y^5}{-16x^4y^2}$ — **Product of powers property**

$= -\frac{y^3}{16x^4}$ — **Quotient of powers property**

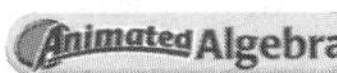 at classzone.com

EXAMPLE 4 Standardized Test Practice

The order of magnitude of the mass of a polyphemus moth larva when it hatches is 10^{-3} gram. During the first 56 days of its life, the moth larva can eat about 10^5 times its own mass in food. About how many grams of food can the moth larva eat during its first 56 days?

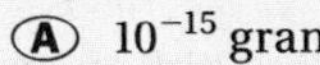

Ⓐ 10^{-15} gram Ⓑ 0.00000001 gram

Ⓒ 100 grams Ⓓ 10,000,000 grams

Not to scale

Solution

To find the amount of food the moth larva can eat in the first 56 days of its life, multiply its original mass, 10^{-3}, by 10^5.

$10^5 \cdot 10^{-3} = 10^{5+(-3)} = 10^2 = 100$

The moth larva can eat about 100 grams of food in the first 56 days of its life.

▶ The correct answer is C. Ⓐ Ⓑ Ⓒ Ⓓ

GUIDED PRACTICE for Examples 3 and 4

9. Simplify the expression $\frac{3xy^{-3}}{9x^3y}$. Write your answer using only positive exponents. $\frac{1}{3x^2y^4}$

10. **SCIENCE** The order of magnitude of the mass of a proton is 10^4 times greater than the order of magnitude of the mass of an electron, which is 10^{-27} gram. Find the order of magnitude of the mass of a proton. 10^{-23} g

Extra Example 3

Simplify the expression. Write your answer using only positive exponents.

a. $(3x^{-2}y^2)^3$ $\frac{27y^6}{x^6}$

b. $\frac{4x^{-2}y^4}{8xy^6}$ $\frac{1}{2x^3y^2}$

Key Question to Ask for Example 3

- In part a, why is the variable y in the denominator after simplifying the expression? **It has a negative exponent.**

An **Animated Algebra** activity is available on-line for **Example 3**. This activity is also available on the **Power Presentations CD-ROM**.

Extra Example 4

The order of magnitude of the radius of an atom is about 10^5 times as great as the order of magnitude of the radius of a proton, which is about 10^{-15} meters. What is the order of magnitude of the radius of an atom? **about 10^{-10} m**

Closing the Lesson

Have students summarize the major points of the lesson and answer the Essential Question: How do you use zero and negative exponents?

- **A nonzero number raised to the zero power is always 1.**
- **A power with a negative exponent is the reciprocal of the power with a positive exponent.**

To evaluate an expression, write powers with negative exponents as their reciprocals and powers with a zero exponent as 1. Use the properties of exponents to multiply and divide powers and to raise a power or a quotient to a power.

4 PRACTICE AND APPLY

Assignment Guide

Answer Transparencies available for all exercises

Basic:
Day 1: pp. 506–508
Exs. 1, 2, 3–35 odd, 50–55, 60–68 even

Average:
Day 1: pp. 506–508
Exs. 1, 2, 9–14, 21–27, 28–44 even, 45, 51–57, 60–68 even

Advanced:
Day 1: pp. 506–508
Exs. 1, 2, 11–14, 22–26, 29–43 odd, 44–49*, 52–58*, 59, 61, 68

Block:
pp. 506–508
Exs. 1, 2, 9–14, 21–27, 28–44 even, 45, 51–57, 60–68 even (with 8.2)

Differentiated Instruction

See *Algebra 1 Best Practices Toolkit* for suggestions on addressing the needs of a diverse classroom.

Homework Check

For a quick check of student understanding of key concepts, go over the following exercises:
Basic: 5, 19, 25, 29, 51
Average: 10, 22, 26, 34, 52
Advanced: 12, 24, 33, 43, 53

Extra Practice

- Student Edition, p. 945
- Chapter 8 Resource Book: Practice levels A, B, C, pp. 27–29

Practice Worksheet

An easily-readable reduced practice page (with answers) for this lesson can be found on p. 486C.

8.3 EXERCISES

HOMEWORK KEY
○ = **WORKED-OUT SOLUTIONS** on p. WS19 for Exs. 11 and 53
★ = **STANDARDIZED TEST PRACTICE** Exs. 2, 44, 45, 54, and 57
◆ = **MULTIPLE REPRESENTATIONS** Ex. 55

SKILL PRACTICE

A

1. **VOCABULARY** Which definitions or properties would you use to simplify the expression $3^5 \cdot 3^{-5}$? *Explain.* Product of powers property and definition of zero exponent; the expression simplifies using the product of powers property to 3^0, which by definition equals 1.
2. ★ **WRITING** *Explain* why the expression 0^{-4} is undefined.
Sample answer: The definition of negative exponents is defined only for nonzero bases.

EXAMPLE 1 on p. 503 for Exs. 3–14

EVALUATING EXPRESSIONS Evaluate the expression.

3. 4^{-3} $\frac{1}{64}$
4. 7^{-3} $\frac{1}{343}$
5. $(-3)^{-1}$ $-\frac{1}{3}$
6. $(-2)^{-6}$ $\frac{1}{64}$
7. 2^0 1
8. $(-4)^0$ 1
9. $\left(\frac{3}{4}\right)^0$ 1
10. $\left(\frac{-9}{16}\right)^0$ 1
11. $\left(\frac{2}{7}\right)^{-2}$ $\frac{49}{4}$
12. $\left(\frac{4}{3}\right)^{-3}$ $\frac{27}{64}$
13. 0^{-3} undefined
14. 0^{-2} undefined

EXAMPLE 2 on p. 504 for Exs. 15–27

15. $2^{-2} \cdot 2^{-3}$ $\frac{1}{32}$
16. $7^{-6} \cdot 7^4$ $\frac{1}{49}$
17. $(2^{-1})^5$ $\frac{1}{32}$
18. $(3^{-2})^2$ $\frac{1}{81}$
19. $\frac{1}{3^{-3}}$ 27
20. $\frac{1}{6^{-2}}$ 36
21. $\frac{3^{-3}}{3^2}$ $\frac{1}{243}$
22. $\frac{6^{-3}}{6^{-5}}$ 36
23. $4\left(\frac{3}{2}\right)^{-1}$ $\frac{8}{3}$
24. $16\left(\frac{2^{-3}}{2^2}\right)$ $\frac{1}{2}$
25. $6^0 \cdot \left(\frac{1}{4^{-2}}\right)$ 16
26. $3^{-2} \cdot \left(\frac{5}{7^0}\right)$ $\frac{5}{9}$

27. **ERROR ANALYSIS** *Describe* and correct the error in evaluating the expression $-6 \cdot 3^0$.
3^0 is not equivalent to 0, but to 1; $-6 \cdot 3^0 = -6 \cdot 1 = -6$.

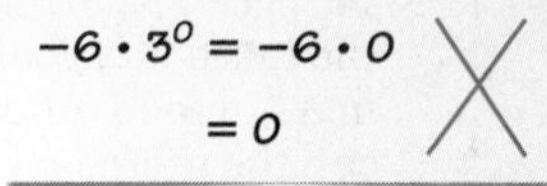

EXAMPLE 3 on p. 505 for Exs. 28–43

B

SIMPLIFYING EXPRESSIONS Simplify the expression. Write your answer using only positive exponents.

28. x^{-4} $\frac{1}{x^4}$
29. $2y^{-3}$ $\frac{2}{y^3}$
30. $(4g)^{-3}$ $\frac{1}{64g^3}$
31. $(-11h)^{-2}$ $\frac{1}{121h^2}$
32. x^2y^{-3} $\frac{x^2}{y^3}$
33. $5m^{-3}n^{-4}$ $\frac{5}{m^3n^4}$
34. $(6x^{-2}y^3)^{-3}$ $\frac{x^6}{216y^9}$
35. $(-15fg^2)^0$ 1
36. $\frac{r^{-2}}{s^{-4}}$ $\frac{s^4}{r^2}$
37. $\frac{x^{-5}}{y^2}$ $\frac{1}{x^5y^2}$
38. $\frac{1}{8x^{-2}y^{-6}}$ $\frac{x^2y^6}{8}$
39. $\frac{1}{15x^{10}y^{-8}}$ $\frac{y^8}{15x^{10}}$
40. $\frac{1}{(-2z)^{-2}}$ $4z^2$
41. $\frac{9}{(3d)^{-3}}$ $243d^3$
42. $\frac{(3x)^{-3}y^4}{-x^2y^{-6}}$ $-\frac{y^{10}}{27x^5}$
43. $\frac{12x^8y^{-7}}{(4x^{-2}y^{-6})^2}$ $\frac{3x^{12}y^5}{4}$

44. ★ **MULTIPLE CHOICE** Which expression simplifies to $2x^4$? D
Ⓐ $2x^{-4}$ Ⓑ $\frac{32}{(2x)^{-4}}$ Ⓒ $\frac{1}{2x^{-4}}$ Ⓓ $\frac{8}{4x^{-4}}$

45. ★ **MULTIPLE CHOICE** Which expression is equivalent to $(-4 \cdot 2^0 \cdot 3)^{-2}$? D
Ⓐ -12 Ⓑ $-\frac{1}{144}$ Ⓒ 0 Ⓓ $\frac{1}{144}$

46. Not true. *Sample answer:* $\frac{2^{-3}}{2^{-4}} = 2$

48. Not true. *Sample answer:* $2^{-1} + 2^{-1} = 1$

C **CHALLENGE In Exercises 46–48, tell whether the statement is true for all nonzero values of *a* and *b*. If it is not true, give a counterexample.**

46. $\frac{a^{-3}}{a^{-4}} = \frac{1}{a}$ **47.** $\frac{a^{-1}}{b^{-1}} = \frac{b}{a}$ true **48.** $a^{-1} + b^{-1} = \frac{1}{a+b}$

49. REASONING For $n > 0$, what happens to the value of a^{-n} as n increases? *Sample answer:* It approaches 0.

PROBLEM SOLVING

EXAMPLE 4 A on p. 505 for Exs. 50–54

50. MASS The mass of a grain of salt is about 10^{-4} gram. About how many grains of salt are in a box containing 100 grams of salt? about 10^6 grains of salt

@HomeTutor for problem solving help at classzone.com

51. MASS The mass of a grain of a certain type of rice is about 10^{-2} gram. About how many grains of rice are in a box containing 10^3 grams of rice? about 10^5 grains of rice

@HomeTutor for problem solving help at classzone.com

52. BOTANY The average mass of the fruit of the wolffia angusta plant is about 10^{-4} gram. The largest pumpkin ever recorded had a mass of about 10^4 kilograms. About how many times greater is the mass of the largest pumpkin than the mass of the fruit of the wolffia angusta plant? about 10^{11} times greater

53. MEDICINE A doctor collected about 10^{-2} liter of blood from a patient to run some tests. The doctor determined that a drop of the patient's blood, or about 10^{-6} liter, contained about 10^7 red blood cells. How many red blood cells did the entire sample contain? about 10^{11} red blood cells

54. ★ SHORT RESPONSE One of the smallest plant seeds comes from an orchid, and one of the largest plant seeds comes from a giant fan palm. A seed from an orchid has a mass of 10^{-9} gram and is 10^{13} times less massive than a seed from a giant fan palm. A student says that the seed from the giant fan palm has a mass of about 1 kilogram. Is the student correct? *Explain.* No. *Sample answer:* The giant fan palm has a mass of about 10^4 grams or 10,000 grams, which equals 10 kilograms.

Orchid

Giant fan palm

B **55. ◆ MULTIPLE REPRESENTATIONS** Consider folding a piece of paper in half a number of times.

a. **Making a Table** Each time the paper is folded, record the number of folds and the fraction of the original area in a table like the one shown.

Number of folds	0	1	2	3
Fraction of original area	? 1	? $\frac{1}{2}$	? $\frac{1}{4}$	? $\frac{1}{8}$

b. **Writing an Expression** Write an exponential expression for the fraction of the original area of the paper using a base of $\frac{1}{2}$. $\left(\frac{1}{2}\right)^x$ where x is the number of folds

Avoiding Common Errors

Exercises 3–26, 28–43 Students often evaluate an expression with an exponent of zero as equal to 0. Remind these students that any nonzero expression with an exponent of 0 is equal to 1.

Exercises 28–43 Caution students to distinguish between a negative number or variable in the base of an expression and a negative exponent. Remind them that they take the reciprocal when the exponent in a power is negative, not when the base is negative.

Study Strategy

Exercises 28–43 Tell students that a variety of strategies and steps can be used to solve these problems and that the best strategy overall is to take their time in simplifying the expressions. Urge them to pay attention to the sign of the exponent, to expressions in parentheses, and to whether an exponent applies to a number or variable. Remind them that they can always expand factors if necessary.

Mathematical Reasoning

Exercises 50, 51 You may want to point out to students that they can determine a reasonable answer to these exercises by asking how many grains of salt are in 1 gram of salt and how many grains of rice are in 1 gram of rice. Suggest that they first write the mass of the grains of salt and rice using positive exponents, then determine how many grains are in a gram, and finally multiply by the number of respective grams in the boxes of salt and rice.

5 ASSESS AND RETEACH

Daily Homework Quiz

Transparency Available

1. Evaluate $\left(\frac{5}{2}\right)^{-3}$. $\frac{8}{125}$
2. Evaluate $4^{-7} \cdot 4^3$. $\frac{1}{256}$
3. Simplify $6a^{-4}b^0$. $\frac{6}{a^4}$
4. Simplify $\frac{8x^3y^{-4}}{12x^2y^{-3}}$. $\frac{2x}{3y}$
5. A human cell uses on average about 10^{-12} watts of power. The laser in a CD-R drive uses about 10^9 times as many watts. About how many watts of power does the laser in a CD-R drive use? about 10^{-3}

Online Quiz

Available at **classzone.com**

Diagnosis/Remediation

- Practice A, B, C in Chapter 8 Resource Book, pp. 27–29
- Study Guide in Chapter 8 Resource Book, pp. 30–31
- Practice Workbook, pp. 123–124
- @HomeTutor

Challenge

Additional challenge is available in the Chapter 8 Resource Book, p. 35.

56. **SCIENCE** Diffusion is the movement of molecules from one location to another. The time t (in seconds) it takes molecules to diffuse a distance of x centimeters is given by $t = \frac{x^2}{2D}$ where D is the diffusion coefficient.
    a. You can examine a cross section of a drop of ink in water to see how the ink diffuses. The diffusion coefficient for the molecules in the drop of ink is about 10^{-5} square centimeter per second. How long will it take the ink to diffuse 1 micrometer (10^{-4} centimeter)? 0.0005 sec
    b. Check your answer to part (a) using unit analysis. $\frac{(\text{cm})^2}{\frac{\text{cm}^2}{\text{sec}}} = \text{cm}^2 \cdot \frac{\text{sec}}{\text{cm}^2} = \text{sec}$

57. ★ **EXTENDED RESPONSE** The intensity of sound I (in watts per square meter) can be modeled by $I = 0.08Pd^{-2}$ where P is the power (in watts) of the sound's source and d is the distance (in meters) that you are from the source of the sound.

Not to scale

    a. What is the power (in watts) of the siren of the firetruck shown in the diagram? 112.5 watts
    b. Using the power of the siren you found in part (a), simplify the formula for the intensity of sound from the siren. $I = 9d^{-2}$
    c. *Explain* what happens to the intensity of the siren when you double your distance from it. The intensity is divided by 4.

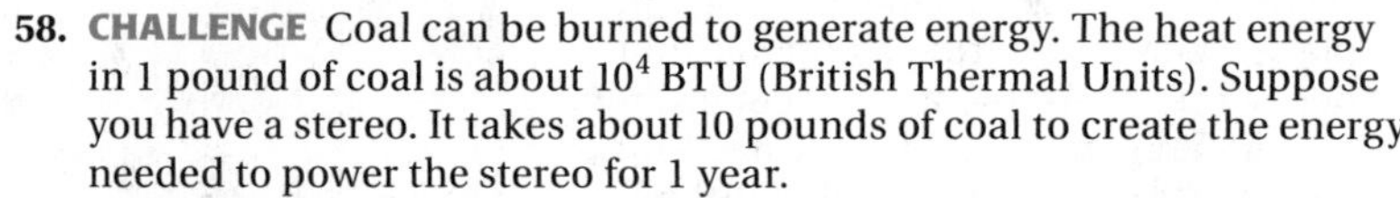

C 58. **CHALLENGE** Coal can be burned to generate energy. The heat energy in 1 pound of coal is about 10^4 BTU (British Thermal Units). Suppose you have a stereo. It takes about 10 pounds of coal to create the energy needed to power the stereo for 1 year.
    a. About how many BTUs does your stereo use in 1 year? 10^5 BTUs
    b. Suppose the power plant that delivers energy to your home produces 10^{-1} pound of sulfur dioxide for each 10^6 BTU of energy that it creates. How much sulfur dioxide is added to the air by generating the energy needed to power your stereo for 1 year? 0.01 lb

ILLINOIS MIXED REVIEW

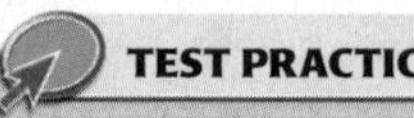

TEST PRACTICE at classzone.com

59. Which expression describes the area in square units of a rectangle that has a width of $3x^3y^2$ and a length of $2x^4y^3$? B

    Ⓐ $6xy$　Ⓑ $6x^7y^5$　Ⓒ $6x^7y^6$　Ⓓ $6x^{12}y^6$

60. The edge length of one cube is 3 times the edge length of another cube. How many times greater is the volume of the first cube than the volume of the second cube? C

    Ⓐ 3　Ⓑ 9　Ⓒ 27　Ⓓ 81

Use after Lesson 8.3

Define and Use Fractional Exponents

GOAL Use fractional exponents.

Key Vocabulary
- cube root

In Lesson 2.7, you learned to write the square root of a number using a radical sign. You can also write a square root of a number using exponents.

For any $a \ge 0$, suppose you want to write $\sqrt{a}$ as a^k. Recall that a number b (in this case, a^k) is a square root of a number a provided $b^2 = a$. Use this definition to find a value for k as follows.

$b^2 = a$ **Definition of square root**

$(a^k)^2 = a$ **Substitute a^k for b.**

$a^{2k} = a^1$ **Product of powers property**

Because the bases are the same in the equation $a^{2k} = a^1$, the exponents must be equal:

$2k = 1$ **Set exponents equal.**

$k = \frac{1}{2}$ **Solve for k.**

So, for a nonnegative number a, $\sqrt{a} = a^{1/2}$.

You can work with exponents of $\frac{1}{2}$ and multiples of $\frac{1}{2}$ just as you work with integer exponents.

EXAMPLE 1 Evaluate expressions involving square roots

a. $16^{1/2} = \sqrt{16}$
$= 4$

b. $25^{-1/2} = \frac{1}{25^{1/2}}$
$= \frac{1}{\sqrt{25}}$
$= \frac{1}{5}$

c. $9^{5/2} = 9^{(1/2) \cdot 5}$
$= (9^{1/2})^5$
$= (\sqrt{9})^5$
$= 3^5$
$= 243$

d. $4^{-3/2} = 4^{(1/2) \cdot (-3)}$
$= (4^{1/2})^{-3}$
$= (\sqrt{4})^{-3}$
$= 2^{-3}$
$= \frac{1}{2^3}$
$= \frac{1}{8}$

FRACTIONAL EXPONENTS You can work with other fractional exponents just as you did with $\frac{1}{2}$.

1 PLAN AND PREPARE

Warm-Up Exercises

Evaluate the expression.

1. $\sqrt{49}$ 7
2. $\sqrt{121}$ 11
3. 2^{-5} $\frac{1}{32}$
4. 13^2 169

2 FOCUS AND MOTIVATE

Essential Question

Big Idea 1, p. 487

How do you evaluate expressions with fractional exponents? Tell students they will learn how to answer this question by writing expressions as square roots and cube roots and evaluating them using the properties of exponents.

3 TEACH

Extra Example 1

Evaluate the expression.

a. $49^{1/2}$ 7
b. $36^{-1/2}$ $\frac{1}{6}$
c. $25^{3/2}$ 125
d. $4^{-7/2}$ $\frac{1}{128}$

Key Questions to Ask for Example 1

- Which part of the fractional exponent is the same for all parts of the example? denominator
- Which part of the exponent determines the power to which the base is raised? numerator

NCTM STANDARDS

Standard 1: Understand meanings of operations

Standard 9: Understand how mathematical ideas build on one another

Extra Example 2

Evaluate the expression.

a. $216^{1/3}$ 6 b. $64^{-1/3}$ $\frac{1}{4}$

c. $27^{2/3}$ 9 d. $8^{-5/3}$ $\frac{1}{32}$

Key Questions to Ask for Example 2

- How is Example 2 different from Example 1? The denominators are 3 instead of 2 in Example 2.
- What does the denominator 3 tell you? take the cube root

Extra Example 3

Use properties of exponents.

a. $8^{1/2} \cdot 8^{-5/2}$ $\frac{1}{64}$

b. $\frac{(3^{5/3} \cdot 3^0)}{3^{2/3}}$ 3

Closing the Lesson

Have students summarize the major points of the lesson and answer the Essential Question: How do you evaluate expressions with fractional exponents?

- The square root of a can be written as $a^{1/2}$, and the cube root of a can be written as $a^{1/3}$.

If an exponent in an expression is $\frac{1}{2}$, take the square root of the base. If an exponent is $\frac{1}{3}$, take the cube root of the base. If the exponent is negative, take the reciprocal. If the exponent is a multiple of $\frac{1}{2}$ or $\frac{1}{3}$, use $\frac{1}{2}$ for the square root, $\frac{1}{3}$ for the cube root, and the other factor as the power. All the properties of integral exponents apply to fractional exponents.

4 PRACTICE AND APPLY

Avoiding Common Errors

Exercises 1–12 Watch for students who multiply the exponent by the base. Remind students that the denominator of the exponent tells them what root to take and the numerator what power to use.

CUBE ROOTS If $b^3 = a$, then b is the **cube root** of a. For example, $2^3 = 8$, so 2 is the cube root of 8. The cube root of a can be written as $\sqrt[3]{a}$ or $a^{1/3}$.

EXAMPLE 2 Evaluate expressions involving cube roots

a. $27^{1/3} = \sqrt[3]{27} = \sqrt[3]{3^3} = 3$

b. $8^{-1/3} = \frac{1}{8^{1/3}} = \frac{1}{\sqrt[3]{8}} = \frac{1}{2}$

c. $64^{4/3} = 64^{(1/3) \cdot 4} = (64^{1/3})^4 = (\sqrt[3]{64})^4 = 4^4 = 256$

d. $125^{-2/3} = 125^{(1/3) \cdot (-2)} = (125^{1/3})^{-2} = (\sqrt[3]{125})^{-2} = 5^{-2} = \frac{1}{5^2} = \frac{1}{25}$

PROPERTIES OF EXPONENTS The properties of exponents for integer exponents also apply to fractional exponents.

EXAMPLE 3 Use properties of exponents

a. $12^{-1/2} \cdot 12^{5/2} = 12^{(-1/2) + (5/2)} = 12^{4/2} = 12^2 = 144$

b. $\frac{6^{4/3} \cdot 6}{6^{1/3}} = \frac{6^{(4/3)+1}}{6^{1/3}} = \frac{6^{7/3}}{6^{1/3}} = 6^{(7/3) - (1/3)} = 6^2 = 36$

PRACTICE

EXAMPLES 1, 2, and 3 on pp. 509–510 for Exs. 1–12

Evaluate the expression.

1. $100^{3/2}$ 1000
2. $121^{-1/2}$ $\frac{1}{11}$
3. $81^{-3/2}$ $\frac{1}{729}$
4. $216^{2/3}$ 36
5. $27^{-1/3}$ $\frac{1}{3}$
6. $343^{-2/3}$ $\frac{1}{49}$
7. $9^{7/2} \cdot 9^{-3/2}$ 81
8. $\left(\frac{1}{16}\right)^{1/2}\left(\frac{1}{16}\right)^{-1/2}$ 1
9. $36^{5/2} \cdot \frac{36^{-1/2}}{(36^{-1})^{-7/2}}$ $\frac{1}{216}$
10. $(27^{-1/3})^3$ $\frac{1}{27}$
11. $(-64)^{-5/3}(-64)^{4/3}$ $-\frac{1}{4}$
12. $(-8)^{1/3}(-8)^{-2/3}(-8)^{1/3}$ 1
13. **REASONING** Show that the cube root of a can be written as $a^{1/3}$ using an argument similar to the one given for square roots on the previous page. See margin.

13. *Sample answer:* $b^3 = a$, substitute a^k for b to create $(a^k)^3 = a$. $a^{3k} = a^1$ by the power of a power property. Solving for k, $3k = 1$ so $k = \frac{1}{3}$.

Illinois *Mixed Review*

Lessons 8.1–8.3

1. **TIME** The table shows units of measurement of time and the durations of the units in seconds.

Name of unit	Duration (seconds)
Gigasecond	10^9
Megasecond	10^6
Millisecond	10^{-3}
Nanosecond	10^{-9}

Which is the greatest number?

A. The number of nanoseconds in 1 millisecond
B. The number of nanoseconds in 1 megasecond
C. The number of megaseconds in 1 gigasecond
D. The number of milliseconds in 1 gigasecond

2. **SOUND** The least intense sound that is audible to the human ear has an intensity of about 10^{-12} watt per square meter. The intensity of sound from a jet engine at a distance of 30 meters is about 10^{15} times greater than the least intense sound. How intense is the sound (in watts per square meter) 30 meters from the jet engine?

F. $\left(\frac{1}{10}\right)^3$ **H.** 1000
G. 100 **J.** 10,000

3. **OIL** For an experiment, a scientist dropped a spoonful, or about 10^{-1} cubic inch, of biodegradable olive oil into a pond to see how the oil would spread out over the surface of the pond. She found that the oil spread until it covered an area of about 10^5 square inches. About how deep was the layer of oil that spread across the pond?

A. 10^{-6} in. **C.** 10^4 in.
B. 10^{-4} in. **D.** 10^6 in.

4. **SUPPLIES** A store sells cubical containers that can be used to store office supplies.

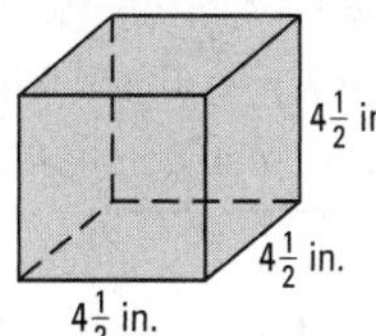

Write the edge length as an improper fraction and substitute the length into the formula for the volume of a cube. Which is the volume (in cubic inches) of the cube?

F. $\frac{9^3}{2^3}$ **H.** $\frac{9^3}{2}$
G. $43 + \left(\frac{1}{2}\right)^3$ **J.** None of the above

5. **RAINDROPS** Clouds contain millions of tiny spherical water droplets. The radius of a droplet is around 10^{-4} centimeter. By combining their volumes, the droplets form a raindrop. The radius of a spherical raindrop is 10^{-2} centimeter. How many droplets combine to form 1 raindrop?

A. 10^{-2} **C.** 10^{12}
B. 10^2 **D.** 10^{56}

6. **COMPUTERS** In 2004, the fastest computers could record about 10^{10} bits per second. (A bit is the smallest unit of memory storage for computers.) At the time, scientists believed that the speed limit at which computers could record was about 10^{12} bits per second. How many times more bits per second was the speed limit than the fastest computers?

F. 2 **H.** 10^2
G. 10 **J.** 10^{22}

Illinois Mixed Review

1. B
2. H
3. A
4. F
5. B
6. H

8.4 Use Scientific Notation

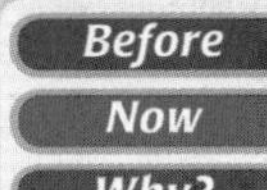

6.11.02 Represent numbers in equivalent forms (e.g., . . . scientific notation).

Before You used properties of exponents.

Now You will read and write numbers in scientific notation.

Why? So you can compare lengths of insects, as in Ex. 51.

Key Vocabulary
- **scientific notation**

Numbers such as 1,000,000, 153,000, and 0.0009 are written in *standard form.* Another way to write a number is to use *scientific notation.*

KEY CONCEPT *For Your Notebook*

Scientific Notation

A number is written in **scientific notation** when it is of the form $c \times 10^n$ where $1 \le c < 10$ and n is an integer.

Number	Standard form	Scientific notation
Two million	2,000,000	2×10^6
Five thousandths	0.005	5×10^{-3}

EXAMPLE 1 Write numbers in scientific notation

a. $42{,}590{,}000 = 4.259 \times 10^7$ — **Move decimal point 7 places to the left. Exponent is 7.**

b. $0.0000574 = 5.74 \times 10^{-5}$ — **Move decimal point 5 places to the right. Exponent is −5.**

EXAMPLE 2 Write numbers in standard form

READING
A positive number in scientific notation is greater than 1 if the exponent is positive. A positive number in scientific notation is between 0 and 1 if the exponent is negative.

a. $2.0075 \times 10^6 = 2{,}007{,}500$ — **Exponent is 6. Move decimal point 6 places to the right.**

b. $1.685 \times 10^{-4} = 0.0001685$ — **Exponent is −4. Move decimal point 4 places to the left.**

 Animated Algebra at classzone.com

✓ **GUIDED PRACTICE** for Examples 1 and 2

1. Write the number 539,000 in scientific notation. Then write the number 4.5×10^{-4} in standard form. 5.39×10^5; 0.00045

1 PLAN AND PREPARE

Warm-Up Exercises

Transparency Available

1. Order the numbers 0.014, 0.1, 0.01 from least to greatest. 0.01, 0.014, 0.1
2. Find the ratio of the mass of the Milky Way galaxy, which is about 10^{44} grams, to the mass of the universe, which is about 10^{55} grams. about $\frac{1}{10^{11}}$

Notetaking Guide

Transparency Available

Promotes interactive learning and notetaking skills, pp. 176–178.

Pacing

Basic: 2 days
Average: 2 days
Advanced: 2 days
Block: 1 block
- See *Teaching Guide/Lesson Plan.*

2 FOCUS AND MOTIVATE

Essential Question

Big Idea 2, p. 487

How do you write a number in scientific notation? Tell students they will learn how to answer this question by rewriting a number as the product of a number from 1 up to 10 and a power of 10.

Resource Planning Guide

Chapter Resource Book
- Teaching Guide/Lesson Plan (pp. 36–37)
- Activity Master (p. 38)
- Practice levels A, B, C (pp. 39–41)
- Study Guide (pp. 42–43)
- Catch-up for Absent Students (p. 44)
- Application (p. 45)
- Challenge (p. 46)

Workbooks
- Notetaking Guide (pp. 176–178)
- Practice Workbook (pp. 125–126)

Teaching Options
- **Power Presentations CD-ROM** provides dynamic electronic teaching resources for the classroom.
- **Activity Generator CD-ROM** provides editable activities for all ability levels.

Interactive Technology
- Easy Planner
- Power Presentations CD-ROM
- Activity Generator CD-ROM
- Animated Algebra
- Test Generator CD-ROM
- Online Quiz
- eWorkbook
- eEdition
- @HomeTutor

Resources for English Learners
- Quick Reference for English Learners
- Spanish Study Guide
- Multi-Language Visual Glossary
- Student Resources in Spanish

See also the *Algebra 1 Toolkit* for more strategies for meeting individual needs.

EXAMPLE 3 Order numbers in scientific notation

Order 103,400,000, 7.8×10^8, and 80,760,000 from least to greatest.

Solution

STEP 1 **Write** each number in scientific notation, if necessary.
$103,400,000 = 1.034 \times 10^8$ $80,760,000 = 8.076 \times 10^7$

STEP 2 **Order** the numbers. First order the numbers with different powers of 10. Then order the numbers with the same power of 10.

Because $10^7 < 10^8$, you know that 8.076×10^7 is less than both 1.034×10^8 and 7.8×10^8. Because $1.034 < 7.8$, you know that 1.034×10^8 is less than 7.8×10^8.

So, $8.076 \times 10^7 < 1.034 \times 10^8 < 7.8 \times 10^8$.

STEP 3 **Write** the original numbers in order from least to greatest.
80,760,000; 103,400,000; 7.8×10^8

EXAMPLE 4 Compute with numbers in scientific notation

Evaluate the expression. Write your answer in scientific notation.

a. $(8.5 \times 10^2)(1.7 \times 10^6)$

$= (8.5 \cdot 1.7) \times (10^2 \cdot 10^6)$	Commutative property and associative property
$= 14.45 \times 10^8$	Product of powers property
$= (1.445 \times 10^1) \times 10^8$	Write 14.45 in scientific notation.
$= 1.445 \times (10^1 \times 10^8)$	Associative property
$= 1.445 \times 10^9$	Product of powers property

AVOID ERRORS
Notice that 14.45×10^8 is *not* written in scientific notation because $14.45 > 10$.

b.

$(1.5 \times 10^{-3})^2 = 1.5^2 \times (10^{-3})^2$	Power of a product property
$= 2.25 \times 10^{-6}$	Power of a power property

REVIEW FRACTIONS
For help with fractions, see p. 915.

c.

$\frac{1.2 \times 10^4}{1.6 \times 10^{-3}} = \frac{1.2}{1.6} \times \frac{10^4}{10^{-3}}$	Product rule for fractions
$= 0.75 \times 10^7$	Quotient of powers property
$= (7.5 \times 10^{-1}) \times 10^7$	Write 0.75 in scientific notation.
$= 7.5 \times (10^{-1} \times 10^7)$	Associative property
$= 7.5 \times 10^6$	Product of powers property

GUIDED PRACTICE for Examples 3 and 4

2. Order 2.7×10^5, 3.401×10^4, and 27,500 from least to greatest. 27,500; 3.401×10^4; 2.7×10^5

Evaluate the expression. Write your answer in scientific notation.

3. $(1.3 \times 10^{-5})^2$ 1.69×10^{-10}
4. $\frac{4.5 \times 10^5}{1.5 \times 10^{-2}}$ 3×10^7
5. $(1.1 \times 10^7)(4.2 \times 10^2)$ 4.62×10^9

Motivating the Lesson

Knowing how to write numbers in scientific notation allows you to better manage extremely large or small numbers with lots of zeros. For example, the number of electrons that pass through a 1-amp circuit every second is 625 followed by 16 zeros. It is easier to write the number in scientific notation in order to determine how many electrons pass through the circuit in 60 seconds.

3 TEACH

Extra Example 1

Write in scientific notation.

a. 267,500,000 2.675×10^8
b. 0.000486 4.86×10^{-4}

Key Question to Ask for Example 1

- How do you know if the exponent of 10 is positive or negative? If the original number is greater than 1, the exponent is positive. If the original number is between 0 and 1, the exponent is negative.

Extra Example 2

Write in standard form.

a. 7.0234×10^5 702,340
b. 3.096×10^{-6} 0.000003096

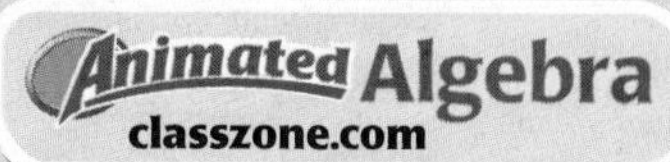

An **Animated Algebra** activity is available on-line for **Example 2**. This activity is also available on the **Power Presentations CD-ROM**.

Extra Example 3

Order 93,000,000, 9.2×10^6, and 9,028,000 from least to greatest. 9,028,000, 9.2×10^6, 93,000,000

Extra Example 4

Evaluate the expression. Write your answer in scientific notation.

a. $(5.7 \times 10^3)(2.6 \times 10^4)$ 1.482×10^8

b. $(2.4 \times 10^{-4})^2$ 5.76×10^{-8}

c. $\frac{2.4 \times 10^5}{2.5 \times 10^{-4}}$ 9.6×10^8

Extra Example 5

The radius of a red blood cell is about 4.5×10^{-6} meter. The radius of *Mycoplasma* bacteria is about 1.25×10^{-8} meter.

a. Find the ratio of the radius of a red blood cell to the radius of *Mycoplasma* bacteria. What does the ratio tell you? **360; the radius of the red blood cell is about 360 times that of the *Mycoplasma* bacteria.**

b. Find the ratio of the volumes of the red blood cell and the *Mycoplasma* bacteria. What does the ratio tell you? **46,656,000; the volume of the red blood cell is about 46,656,000 times that of the *Mycoplasma* bacteria.**

Closing the Lesson

Have students summarize the major points of the lesson and answer the Essential Question: How do you write numbers in scientific notation?

- **A number written in scientific notation is in the form $c \times 10^n$, where $1 \le c < 10$ and n is an integer.**

Write a positive number as the product of a decimal from 1 up to 10 and a power of 10. If the original number is greater than 1, the power of 10 has a positive exponent. If the number is between 0 and 1, the exponent is negative.

EXAMPLE 5 Solve a multi-step problem

BLOOD VESSELS Blood flow is partially controlled by the cross-sectional area of the blood vessel through which the blood is traveling. Three types of blood vessels are venules, capillaries, and arterioles.

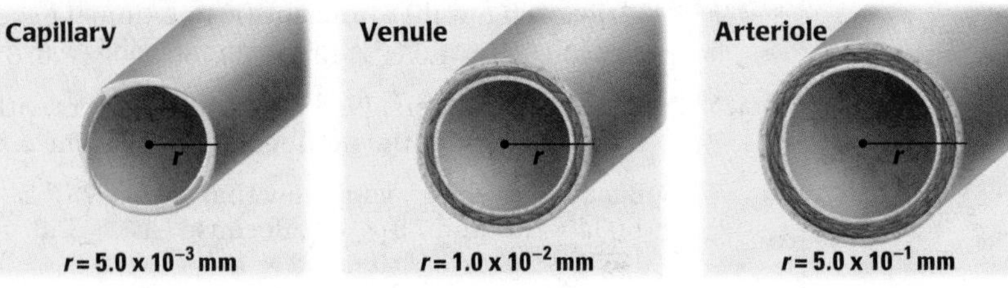

a. Let r_1 be the radius of a venule, and let r_2 be the radius of a capillary. Find the ratio of r_1 to r_2. What does the ratio tell you?

b. Let A_1 be the cross-sectional area of a venule, and let A_2 be the cross-sectional area of a capillary. Find the ratio of A_1 to A_2. What does the ratio tell you?

c. What is the relationship between the ratio of the radii of the blood vessels and the ratio of their cross-sectional areas?

Solution

a. From the diagram, you can see that the radius of the venule r_1 is 1.0×10^{-2} millimeter and the radius of the capillary r_2 is 5.0×10^{-3} millimeter.

$$\frac{r_1}{r_2} = \frac{1.0 \times 10^{-2}}{5.0 \times 10^{-3}} = \frac{1.0}{5.0} \times \frac{10^{-2}}{10^{-3}} = 0.2 \times 10^1 = 2$$

The ratio tells you that the radius of the venule is twice the radius of the capillary.

ANOTHER WAY You can also find the ratio of the cross-sectional areas by finding the areas using the values for r_1 and r_2, setting up a ratio, and then simplifying.

b. To find the cross-sectional areas, use the formula for the area of a circle.

$$\frac{A_1}{A_2} = \frac{\pi r_1^2}{\pi r_2^2}$$ **Write ratio.**

$$= \frac{r_1^2}{r_2^2}$$ **Divide numerator and denominator by π.**

$$= \left(\frac{r_1}{r_2}\right)^2$$ **Power of a quotient property**

$$= 2^2 = 4$$ **Substitute and simplify.**

The ratio tells you that the cross-sectional area of the venule is four times the cross-sectional area of the capillary.

c. The ratio of the cross-sectional areas of the blood vessels is the square of the ratio of the radii of the blood vessels.

GUIDED PRACTICE for Example 5

6. **WHAT IF?** *Compare* the radius and cross-sectional area of an arteriole with the radius and cross-sectional area of a capillary.

6. The radius of an arteriole is 10^2 times greater than the radius of a capillary. The cross-sectional area of an arteriole is 10^4 times greater than the cross-sectional area of a capillary.

Differentiated Instruction

Below Level Some students may need extra practice writing numbers in scientific and standard notation. Have students search the Internet for very large and very small numbers. For example, they can search for astronomical data for large numbers and cellular biology data for small numbers. Suggest that they exchange numbers with partners for more practice.

See also the *Algebra 1 Toolkit* for more strategies.

8.4 EXERCISES

HOMEWORK KEY

◯ = **WORKED-OUT SOLUTIONS** on p. WS19 for Exs. 3, 17, and 53

★ = **STANDARDIZED TEST PRACTICE** Exs. 2, 15, 48, 49, 54, and 59

◆ = **MULTIPLE REPRESENTATIONS** Ex. 58

SKILL PRACTICE

A

1. **VOCABULARY** Is 0.5×10^6 written in scientific notation? *Explain* why or why not. No; 0.5 is not a number greater than or equal to 1.0 and less than 10.

2. ★ **WRITING** Is 7.89×10^6 between 0 and 1 or greater than 1? *Explain* how you know. Greater than 1; the exponent is positive.

EXAMPLE 1 on p. 512 for Exs. 3–15

WRITING IN SCIENTIFIC NOTATION **Write the number in scientific notation.**

3. 8.5 8.5×10^0
4. 0.72 7.2×10^{-1}
5. 82.4 8.24×10^1
6. 0.005 5×10^{-3}
7. 72,000,000 7.2×10^7
8. 0.00406 4.06×10^{-3}
9. 1,065,250 1.06525×10^6
10. 0.000045 4.5×10^{-5}
11. 1,060,000,000 1.06×10^9
12. 0.00000526 5.26×10^{-6}
13. 900,000,000,000,000 9×10^{14}
14. 0.00000007008 7.008×10^{-8}

15. ★ **MULTIPLE CHOICE** Which number represents 54,004,000,000 written in scientific notation? C

    Ⓐ 54004×10^6 Ⓑ 54.004×10^9

    Ⓒ 5.4004×10^{10} Ⓓ 0.54004×10^{11}

EXAMPLE 2 on p. 512 for Exs. 16–28

WRITING IN STANDARD FORM **Write the number in standard form.**

16. 2.6×10^3 2600
17. 7.5×10^7 75,000,000
18. 1.11×10^2 111
19. 3.03×10^4 30,300
20. 4.709×10^6 4,709,000
21. 1.544×10^{10} 15,440,000,000
22. 6.1×10^{-3} 0.0061
23. 4.4×10^{-10} 0.00000000044
24. 2.23×10^{-6} 0.00000223
25. 8.52×10^{-8} 0.0000000852
26. 6.4111×10^{-10} 0.00000000064111
27. 1.2034×10^{-6} 0.0000012034

28. **ERROR ANALYSIS** *Describe* and correct the error in writing 1.24×10^{-3} in standard form. The decimal point should be moved to the left, not the right; $1.24 \times 10^{-3} = 0.00124$.

    $1.24 \times 10^{-3} = 1240$ ✗

EXAMPLE 3 on p. 513 for Exs. 29–32

B

ORDERING NUMBERS **Order the numbers from least to greatest.**

29. 45,000; 6.7×10^3; 12,439; 2×10^4 6.7×10^3; 12,439; 2×10^4; 45,000
30. 65,000,000; 6.2×10^6; 3.557×10^7; 55,004,000; 6.07×10^6
31. 0.0005; 9.8×10^{-6}; 5×10^{-3}; 0.00008; 0.04065; 8.2×10^{-3}
32. 0.0000395; 0.00010068; 2.4×10^{-5}; 5.08×10^{-6}; 0.000005 0.000005; 5.08×10^{-6}; 2.4×10^{-5}; 0.0000395; 0.00010068

30. 6.07×10^6; 6.2×10^6; 3.557×10^7; 55,004,000; 65,000,000

31. 9.8×10^{-6}; 0.00008; 0.0005; 5×10^{-3}; 8.2×10^{-3}; 0.04065

COMPARING NUMBERS **Copy and complete the statement using <, >, or =.**

33. 5.6×10^3 _?_ 56,000 <
34. 404,000.1 _?_ 4.04001×10^5 <
35. 9.86×10^{-3} _?_ 0.00986 =
36. 0.003309 _?_ 3.309×10^{-3} =
37. 2.203×10^{-4} _?_ 0.0000203 >
38. 604,589,000 _?_ 6.04589×10^7 >

4 PRACTICE AND APPLY

Assignment Guide

Answer Transparencies available for all exercises

Basic:
Day 1: EP p. 939 Exs. 32–37
pp. 514–518
Exs. 1–28
Day 2: pp. 514–518
Exs. 29–36, 39–41, 51–56, 61–74

Average:
Day 1: pp. 514–518
Exs. 1, 2, 6–15, 19–28, 39–44
Day 2: pp. 514–518
Exs. 29–38, 45–49, 51–59, 62–74 even

Advanced:
Day 1: pp. 514–518
Exs. 1, 2, 8–15, 21–27, 39–47
Day 2: pp. 514–518
Exs. 29–38, 48–60*, 64, 67, 68, 71

Block:
pp. 514–518
Exs. 1, 2, 6–15, 19–49, 51–59, 62–74 even

Differentiated Instruction

See *Algebra 1 Best Practices Toolkit* for suggestions on addressing the needs of a diverse classroom.

Homework Check

For a quick check of student understanding of key concepts, go over the following exercises:

Basic: 8, 20, 29, 53, 54

Average: 10, 24, 42, 51, 55

Advanced: 12, 26, 45, 52, 55

Extra Practice

- Student Edition, p. 945
- Chapter 8 Resource Book: Practice levels A, B, C, pp. 39–41

Practice Worksheet

An easily-readable reduced practice page (with answers) for this lesson can be found on p. 486C.

Differentiated Instruction

Kinesthetic Learners In mathematics, a left-shift is associated with negative numbers, and a right-shift is associated with positive numbers. Another way to complete **Exercises 3–14** is as follows. To write 93,000,000 in scientific notation, place the decimal point to the right of 9 and count 7 places right to the last 0 to get 9.3×10^7. Similarly, place the decimal point to the right of 1 in 0.0017 and count 3 places to the left to the last 0 to get 1.7×10^{-3}. See also the *Algebra 1 Toolkit* for more strategies.

Avoiding Common Errors

Exercises 3–15 Some students may write scientific notation with two or more digits to the left of the decimal point. Remind them that the decimal must be less than 10 but greater than or equal to 1. Suggest that students check their answers by expanding the scientific notation to make sure they have written the numbers correctly.

Exercises 16–28 Caution students that they need to move the decimal to the right for numbers with positive exponents and to the left for numbers with negative exponents when writing numbers in standard form.

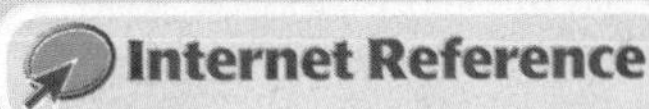

Exercise 52 For more information about the *Voyager 1* and *Voyager 2* spacecrafts, visit NASA's website voyager.jpl.nasa.gov

Reading Strategy

Exercise 53 Encourage students to read the problem carefully for clues on what operation they should use to solve the problem. Draw their attention to the phrase "per acre."

EXAMPLE 4 on p. 513 for Exs. 39–48

EVALUATING EXPRESSIONS **Evaluate the expression. Write your answer in scientific notation.**

39. $(4.4 \times 10^3)(1.5 \times 10^{-7})$ 6.6×10^{-4}

40. $(7.3 \times 10^{-5})(5.8 \times 10^2)$ 4.234×10^{-2}

41. $(8.1 \times 10^{-4})(9 \times 10^{-6})$ 7.29×10^{-9}

42. $\frac{6 \times 10^{-3}}{8 \times 10^{-6}}$ 7.5×10^2

43. $\frac{5.4 \times 10^{-5}}{1.8 \times 10^{-2}}$ 3×10^{-3}

44. $\frac{4.1 \times 10^4}{8.2 \times 10^8}$ 5×10^{-5}

45. $(5 \times 10^{-8})^3$ 1.25×10^{-22}

46. $(7 \times 10^{-5})^4$ 2.401×10^{-17}

47. $(1.4 \times 10^3)^2$ 1.96×10^6

48. ★ **MULTIPLE CHOICE** Which number is the value of $\frac{1.235 \times 10^4}{9.5 \times 10^7}$? B

Ⓐ 0.13×10^{-4} Ⓑ 1.3×10^{-4} Ⓒ 1.3×10^{-3} Ⓓ 0.13×10^3

49. ★ **OPEN-ENDED** Write two numbers in scientific notation whose product is 2.8×10^4. Write two numbers in scientific notation whose quotient is 2.8×10^4. *Sample answer:* 2.8×10^1 and 1×10^3; 11.2×10^5 and 4.0×10^1

C 50. **CHALLENGE** Add the numbers 3.6×10^5 and 6.7×10^4 *without* writing the numbers in standard form. Write your answer in scientific notation. *Describe* the steps you take. 4.27×10^5. *Sample answer:* Rewrite 6.7×10^4 as 0.67×10^5, then add $3.6 + 0.67 = 4.27$. Since the answer is between 1 and 10, the exponent does not change, so the answer is 4.27×10^5.

PROBLEM SOLVING

EXAMPLE 3 A on p. 513 for Exs. 51–52

51a. 1.4×10^{-4}; 2.5×10^{-1}; 1.67×10^2; 555

51. **INSECT LENGTHS** The lengths of several insects are shown in the table.

a. List the lengths of the insects in order from least to greatest.

b. Which insects are longer than the fringed ant beetle? the elephant beetle and the walking stick

Insect	Length (millimeters)
Fringed ant beetle	2.5×10^{-1}
Walking stick	555
Parasitic wasp	1.4×10^{-4}
Elephant beetle	1.67×10^2

@HomeTutor for problem solving help at classzone.com

54. 14; the flow rate of the Amazon River is about 14 times faster than the flow rate of the Mississippi River.

52. **ASTRONOMY** The spacecrafts *Voyager 1* and *Voyager 2* were launched in 1977 to gather data about our solar system. As of March 12, 2004, *Voyager 1* had traveled a total distance of about 9,643,000,000 miles, and *Voyager 2* had traveled a total distance of about 9.065×10^9 miles. Which spacecraft had traveled the greater distance at that time? *Voyager 1*

@HomeTutor for problem solving help at classzone.com

EXAMPLE 4 on p. 513 for Ex. 53

53. **AGRICULTURE** In 2002, about 9.7×10^8 pounds of cotton were produced in California. The cotton was planted on 6.9×10^5 acres of land. What was the average number of pounds of cotton produced per acre? Round your answer to the nearest whole number. 1406 pounds per acre

EXAMPLE 5 on p. 514 for Exs. 54–55

54. ★ **SHORT RESPONSE** The average flow rate of the Amazon River is about 7.6×10^6 cubic feet per second. The average flow rate of the Mississippi River is about 5.53×10^5 cubic feet per second. Find the ratio of the flow rate of the Amazon to the flow rate of the Mississippi. Round to the nearest whole number. What does the ratio tell you?

◯ = WORKED-OUT SOLUTIONS on p. WS1 ★ = STANDARDIZED TEST PRACTICE ◆ = MULTIPLE REPRESENTATIONS

55a. About 3.67; the radius of Earth is about 3.67 times greater than the radius of the moon.

55b. About 49.30; the volume of Earth is about 49.30 times greater than the volume of the moon.

55. ASTRONOMY The radius of Earth and the radius of the moon are shown.

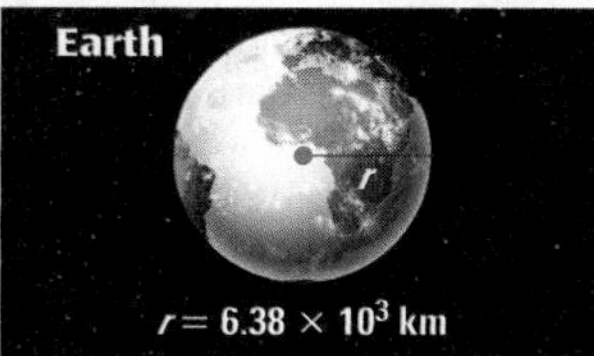

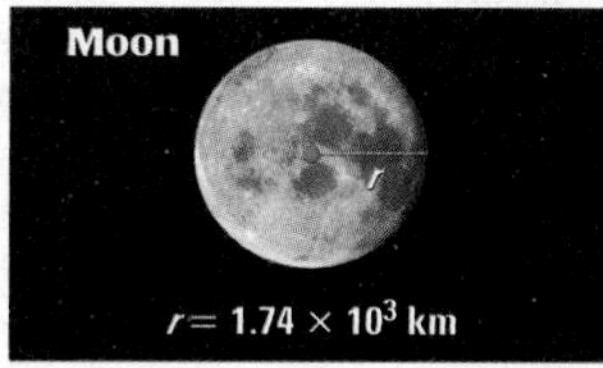

a. Find the ratio of the radius of Earth to the radius of the moon. Round to the nearest hundredth. What does the ratio tell you?

b. Assume Earth and the moon are spheres. Find the ratio of the volume of Earth to the volume of the moon. Round to the nearest hundredth. What does the ratio tell you?

c. What is the relationship between the ratios of the radii and the ratios of the volumes? The ratio of the volumes is the cube of the ratio of the radii.

B **56. MULTI-STEP PROBLEM** In 1954, 50 swarms of locusts were observed in Kenya. The largest swarm covered an area of 200 square kilometers. The average number of locusts in a swarm is about 5×10^7 locusts per square kilometer.

a. About how many locusts were in Kenya's largest swarm? Write your answer in scientific notation. about 1×10^{10} locusts

b. The average mass of a desert locust is 2 grams. What was the total mass (in kilograms) of Kenya's largest swarm? Write your answer in scientific notation. 2×10^7 kg

57. DIGITAL PHOTOGRAPHY When a picture is taken with a digital camera, the resulting image is made up of square pixels (the smallest unit that can be displayed on a monitor). For one image, the side length of a pixel is 4×10^{-3} inch. A print of the image measures 1×10^3 pixels by 1.5×10^3 pixels. What are the dimensions of the print in inches? 4 in. by 6 in.

58. MULTIPLE REPRESENTATIONS The speed of light is 1.863×10^5 miles per second.

a. **Writing an Expression** Assume 1 year is 365 days. Write an expression to convert the speed of light from miles per second to miles per year. See margin.

b. **Making a Table** Make a table that shows the distance light travels in 1, 10, 100, 1000, 10,000, and 100,000 years. Our galaxy has a diameter of about 5.875×10^{17} miles. Based on the table, about how long would it take for light to travel across our galaxy? See margin.

59b. about 2.58×10^6 L, about 2.58×10^7 L, about 2.06×10^8 L

C **59. ★ EXTENDED RESPONSE** When a person is at rest, approximately 7×10^{-2} liter of blood flows through the heart with each heartbeat. The human heart beats about 70 times per minute.

a. **Calculate** About how many liters of blood flow through the heart each minute when a person is at rest? 4.9 L

b. **Estimate** There are approximately 5.265×10^5 minutes in a year. Use your answer from part (a) to estimate the number of liters of blood that flow through the human heart in 1 year, in 10 years, and in 80 years. Write your answers in scientific notation.

c. **Explain** Are your answers to part (b) underestimates or overestimates? *Explain.*

59c. Underestimates. *Sample answer:* They are calculated when a person is at rest. When a person is not resting, the rate will go up.

Study Strategy

Exercise 55 Haves students use Example 5 as a model for this exercise. Caution them that part b asks them to find the ratio for volumes, whereas Example 5 has them compare areas.

Exercise 60 Additional information about solar flares can be found at NASA's website hesperia.gsfc.nasa.gov/sftheory

58a. $\frac{1.863 \times 10^5 \text{ mi}}{1 \text{ sec}} \cdot \frac{60 \text{ sec}}{1 \text{ min}} \cdot \frac{60 \text{ min}}{1 \text{ h}} \cdot \frac{24 \text{ h}}{1 \text{ day}} \cdot \frac{365 \text{ days}}{1 \text{ yr}} \approx 5.875 \times 10^{12}$ mi/yr

58b.

Years	1	10	100	1000	10,000	100,000
Miles traveled	5.875×10^{12}	5.875×10^{13}	5.875×10^{14}	5.875×10^{15}	5.875×10^{16}	5.875×10^{17}

100,000 yr

5 ASSESS AND RETEACH

Daily Homework Quiz

Transparency Available

Write the number in scientific notation.

1. 100,500 1.005×10^5
2. 0.0203 2.03×10^{-2}
3. Write 3.06×10^7 in standard form. 30,600,000
4. The diameter of Mercury is about 4.9×10^3 kilometers. The diameter of Venus is about 1.2×10^4 kilometers. Find the ratio of the diameter of Venus to that of Mercury. Round to the nearest hundredth. about 2.5

Available at **classzone.com**

Diagnosis/Remediation

- Practice A, B, C in Chapter 8 Resource Book, pp. 39–41
- Study Guide in Chapter 8 Resource Book, pp. 42–43
- Practice Workbook, pp. 125–126
- @HomeTutor

Challenge

Additional challenge is available in the Chapter 8 Resource Book, p. 46.

Quiz

An easily-readable reduced copy of the quiz (with answers) on Lessons 8.3–8.4 from the Assessment Book can be found on p. 486E.

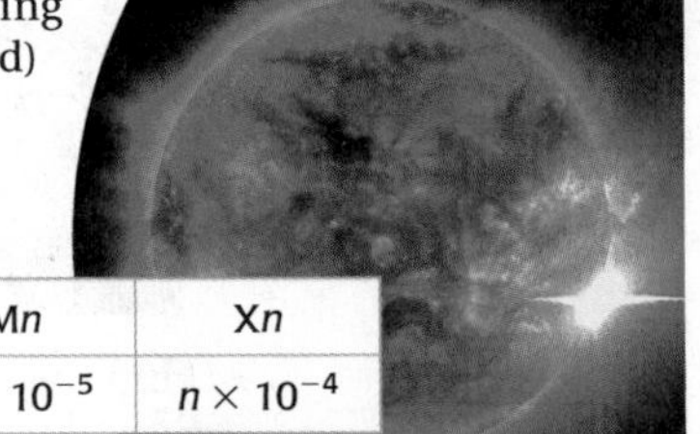

60. **CHALLENGE** A solar flare is a sudden eruption of energy in the sun's atmosphere. Solar flares are classified according to their peak X-ray intensity (in watts per meter squared) and are denoted with a capital letter and a number, as shown in the table. For example, a C4 flare has a peak intensity of 4×10^{-6} watt per square meter.

Class	Bn	Cn	Mn	Xn
Peak intensity (w/m^2)	$n \times 10^{-7}$	$n \times 10^{-6}$	$n \times 10^{-5}$	$n \times 10^{-4}$

a. In November 2003, a massive X45 solar flare was observed. In April 2004, a C9 flare was observed. How many times greater was the intensity of the X45 flare than that of the C9 flare? 500 times greater

b. A solar flare may be accompanied by a coronal mass ejection (CME), a bubble of mass ejected from the sun. A CME related to the X45 flare was estimated to be traveling at 8.2 million kilometers per hour. At that rate, how long would it take the CME to travel from the sun to Earth, a distance of about 1.5×10^{11} meters? about 18 h

ILLINOIS MIXED REVIEW

TEST PRACTICE at classzone.com

61. The Ambriz family paid \$120 per ticket for 5 concert tickets and \$6 per hour for parking. The car was parked for 4 hours. How much did they spend on the concert and parking? C

Ⓐ \$144 Ⓑ \$606 Ⓒ \$624 Ⓓ \$630

62. If $y = x^2$, which of the following is equivalent to x^8? C

Ⓐ y^2 Ⓑ y^3 Ⓒ y^4 Ⓓ y^6

QUIZ for Lessons 8.3–8.4

Simplify the expression. Write your answer using only positive exponents. *(p. 503)*

1. $(-4x)^4 \cdot (-4)^{-6}$ $\frac{x^4}{16}$
2. $(-3x^7y^{-2})^{-3}$ $-\frac{y^6}{27x^{21}}$
3. $\frac{1}{(5z)^{-3}}$ $125z^3$
4. $\frac{(6x)^{-2}y^5}{-x^3y^{-7}}$ $-\frac{y^{12}}{36x^5}$

Write the number in standard form. *(p. 512)*

5. 6.02×10^6 6,020,000
6. 5.41×10^{11} 541,000,000,000
7. 8.007×10^{-5} 0.00008007
8. 9.253×10^{-7} 0.0000009253

9. **DINOSAURS** The estimated masses of several dinosaurs are shown in the table. *(p. 512)*

a. List the masses of the dinosaurs in order from least to greatest.

b. Which dinosaurs are more massive than Brachiosaurus? Ultrasaurus

9a. 1.06×10^4; 29,900; 77,100; 1.36×10^5

Dinosaur	Mass (kilograms)
Brachiosaurus	77,100
Diplodocus	1.06×10^4
Apatosaurus	29,900
Ultrasaurus	1.36×10^5

EXTRA PRACTICE for Lesson 8.4, p. 945

ONLINE QUIZ at classzone.com

Graphing Calculator ACTIVITY *Use after Lesson 8.4*

@HomeTutor classzone.com Keystrokes

8.4 Use Scientific Notation

QUESTION How can you use a graphing calculator to solve problems that involve numbers in scientific notation?

EXAMPLE Use numbers in scientific notation

Gold is one of many trace elements dissolved in seawater. There is about 1.1×10^{-8} gram of gold per kilogram of seawater. The mass of the oceans is about 1.4×10^{21} kilograms. About how much gold is present in the oceans?

STEP 1 ***Write a verbal model***

Amount of gold present in oceans (grams)	=	Amount of gold in 1 kilogram of seawater (gram/kilogram)	•	Amount of seawater in oceans (kilograms)

STEP 2 ***Find product*** The product is $(1.1 \times 10^{-8}) \cdot (1.4 \times 10^{21})$.

(1.1 × 10 ^ (−) 8) (1.4 × 10 ^ 21) ENTER

STEP 3 ***Read result***

The calculator indicates that a number is in scientific notation by using "E." You can read the calculator's result 1.54E13 as 1.54×10^{13}.

There are about 1.54×10^{13} grams of gold present in the oceans.

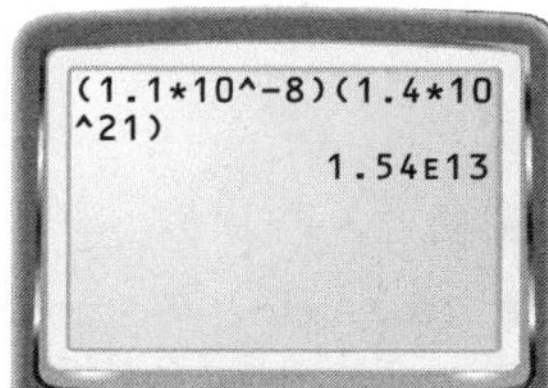

PRACTICE

Evaluate the expression. Write the result in scientific notation.

1. $(1.5 \times 10^4)(1.8 \times 10^9)$ **2.7×10^{13}**
2. $(2.6 \times 10^{-14})(1.4 \times 10^{20})$ **3.64×10^6**
3. $(7.0 \times 10^{25}) \div (2.8 \times 10^6)$ **2.5×10^{19}**
4. $(4.5 \times 10^{15}) \div (9.0 \times 10^{-2})$ **5.0×10^{16}**
5. **GASOLINE** A scientist estimates that it takes about 4.45×10^7 grams of carbon from ancient plant matter to produce 1 gallon of gasoline. In 2002 motor vehicles in the U.S. used about 1.37×10^{11} gallons of gasoline.
   a. If all of the gasoline used in 2002 by motor vehicles in the U.S. came from carbon from ancient plant matter, how many grams of carbon were used to produce the gasoline? **about 6.10×10^{18} g**
   b. There are about 5.0×10^{22} atoms of carbon in 1 gram of carbon. How many atoms of carbon were used? **about 3.05×10^{41} atoms**

1 PLAN AND PREPARE

Learn the Method

- Students will use a graphing calculator to solve a problem involving scientific notation.
- After the activity, students can use a graphing calculator to check their solutions in Exercises 39–48 in Lesson 8.4.

Keystroke Help

Keystrokes for several models of calculators are available in blackline format in the *Chapter 8 Resource Book.*

2 TEACH

Tips for Success

Make sure that students place parentheses around the numbers in scientific notation.

Extra Example

In 2003, about 1.35×10^6 acres of beans were harvested in the United States. The yield per acre was about 1.67×10^3 pounds of beans. About how many pounds of beans were produced in the United States in 2003? **about 2.25×10^9 lb**

3 ASSESS AND RETEACH

Evaluate the expression. Write the result in scientific notation.

1. $(3.6 \times 10^{-16})(1.8 \times 10^5)$ **6.48×10^{-11}**
2. $(2.4 \times 10^{12}) \div (1.5 \times 10^{-3})$ **1.6×10^{15}**

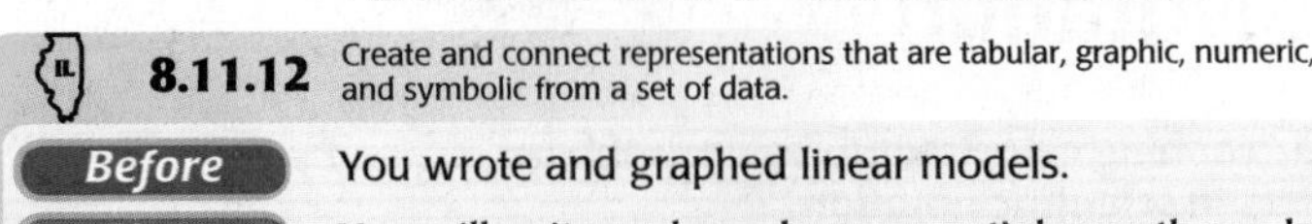

8.5 Write and Graph Exponential Growth Functions

8.11.12 Create and connect representations that are tabular, graphic, numeric, and symbolic from a set of data.

Before You wrote and graphed linear models.

Now You will write and graph exponential growth models.

Why? So you can find the value of a collector car, as in Example 4.

1 PLAN AND PREPARE

Warm-Up Exercises

Transparency Available

Write the percent as a decimal.

1. 2% 0.02
2. 5.5% 0.055
3. The table shows the cost of tickets for a matinee. Write a rule for the function. $c = 2t$

Tickets, t	2	4	6	8
Cost, c	4	8	12	16

Notetaking Guide

Transparency Available

Promotes interactive learning and notetaking skills, pp. 179–182.

Pacing

Basic: 2 days
Average: 2 days
Advanced: 2 days
Block: 1 block
- See *Teaching Guide/Lesson Plan.*

2 FOCUS AND MOTIVATE

Essential Question

Big Idea 3, p. 487

How do you write and graph equations for exponential growth functions? Tell students they will learn how to answer this question by using models to write functions and tables to graph functions.

Key Vocabulary
- exponential function
- exponential growth
- compound interest

An **exponential function** is a function of the form $y = ab^x$ where $a \neq 0$, $b > 0$, and $b \neq 1$. Exponential functions are *nonlinear* functions. Observe how an exponential function compares with a linear function.

Linear function: $y = 3x + 2$

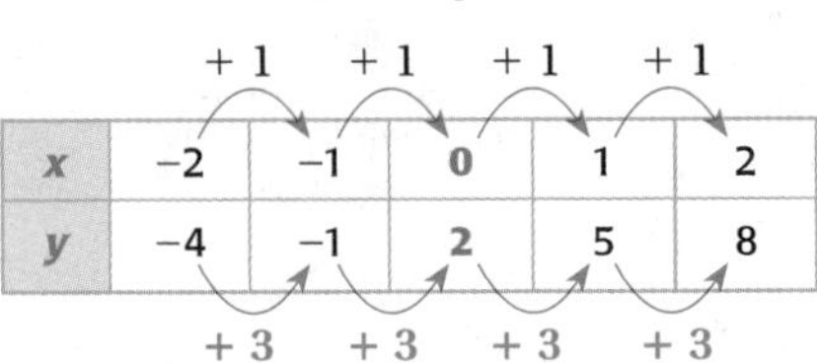

x	−2	−1	0	1	2
y	−4	−1	2	5	8

Exponential function: $y = 2 \cdot 3^x$

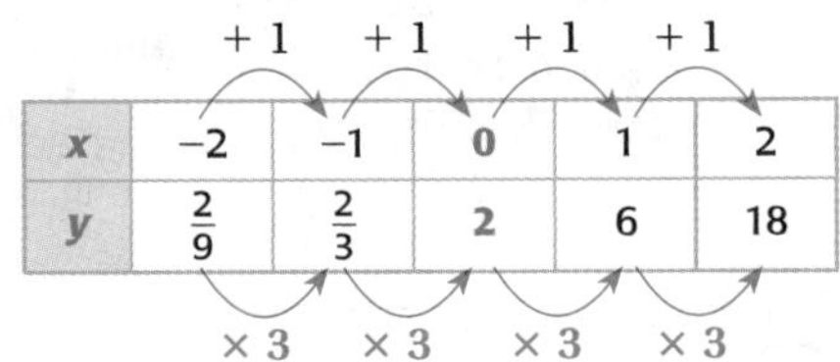

x	−2	−1	0	1	2
y	$\frac{2}{9}$	$\frac{2}{3}$	2	6	18

EXAMPLE 1 Write a function rule

Write a rule for the function.

x	−2	−1	0	1	2
y	2	4	8	16	32

Solution

STEP 1 **Tell** whether the function is exponential.

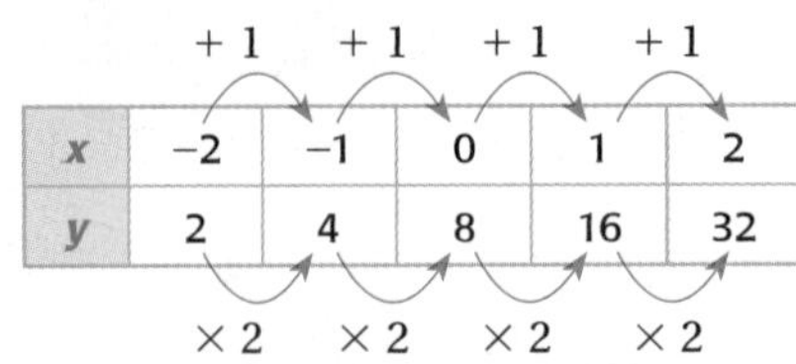

x	−2	−1	0	1	2
y	2	4	8	16	32

Here, the y-values are multiplied by 2 for each increase of 1 in x, so the table represents an exponential function of the form $y = ab^x$ where $b = 2$.

STEP 2 **Find** the value of a by finding the value of y when $x = 0$. When $x = 0$, $y = ab^0 = a \cdot 1 = a$. The value of y when $x = 0$ is 8, so $a = 8$.

STEP 3 **Write** the function rule. A rule for the function is $y = 8 \cdot 2^x$.

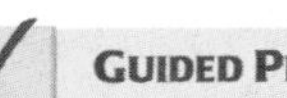

GUIDED PRACTICE for Example 1

1. Write a rule for the function. $y = 27 \cdot 3^x$

x	−2	−1	0	1	2
y	3	9	27	81	243

Resource Planning Guide

Chapter Resource Book
- Teaching Guide/Lesson Plan (pp. 47–48)
- Activity Master (p. 49)
- Practice levels A, B, C (pp. 51–56)
- Study Guide (pp. 57–58)
- Catch-up for Absent Students (p. 59)
- Problem Solving Workshop (p. 60)
- Challenge (p. 61)

Workbooks
- Notetaking Guide (pp. 179–182)
- Practice Workbook (pp. 127–129)

Teaching Options
- **Power Presentations CD-ROM** provides dynamic electronic teaching resources for the classroom.
- **Activity Generator CD-ROM** provides editable activities for all ability levels.

Interactive Technology
- Easy Planner
- Power Presentations CD-ROM
- Activity Generator CD-ROM
- Animated Algebra
- Test Generator CD-ROM
- Online Quiz
- eWorkbook
- eEdition
- @HomeTutor

Resources for English Learners
- Quick Reference for English Learners
- Spanish Study Guide
- Multi-Language Visual Glossary
- Student Resources in Spanish

See also the *Algebra 1 Toolkit* for more strategies for meeting individual needs.

EXAMPLE 2 Graph an exponential function

Graph the function $y = 2^x$. Identify its domain and range.

Solution

READ A GRAPH
Notice that the graph has a y-intercept of 1 and that it gets closer to the negative x-axis as the x-values decrease.

STEP 1 **Make** a table by choosing a few values for x and finding the values of y. The domain is all real numbers.

x	-2	-1	0	1	2
y	$\frac{1}{4}$	$\frac{1}{2}$	1	2	4

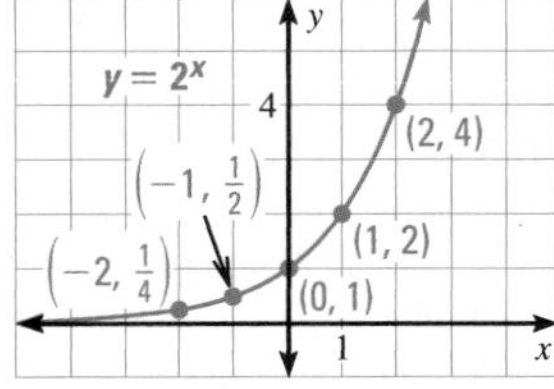

STEP 2 **Plot** the points.

STEP 3 **Draw** a smooth curve through the points. From either the table or the graph, you can see that the range is all positive real numbers.

EXAMPLE 3 Compare graphs of exponential functions

Graph the functions $y = 3 \cdot 2^x$ and $y = -3 \cdot 2^x$. Compare each graph with the graph of $y = 2^x$.

Solution

To graph each function, make a table of values, plot the points, and draw a smooth curve through the points.

x	$y = 2^x$	$y = 3 \cdot 2^x$	$y = -3 \cdot 2^x$
-2	$\frac{1}{4}$	$\frac{3}{4}$	$-\frac{3}{4}$
-1	$\frac{1}{2}$	$\frac{3}{2}$	$-\frac{3}{2}$
0	1	3	-3
1	2	6	-6
2	4	12	-12

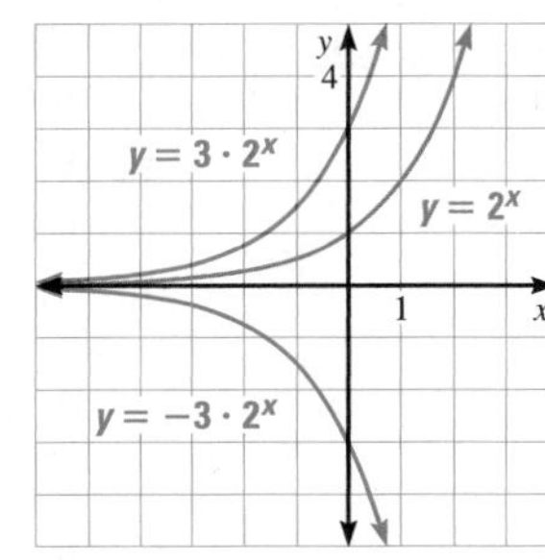

Because the y-values for $y = 3 \cdot 2^x$ are 3 times the corresponding y-values for $y = 2^x$, the graph of $y = 3 \cdot 2^x$ is a vertical stretch of the graph of $y = 2^x$.

Because the y-values for $y = -3 \cdot 2^x$ are -3 times the corresponding y-values for $y = 2^x$, the graph of $y = -3 \cdot 2^x$ is a vertical stretch with a reflection in the x-axis of the graph of $y = 2^x$.

GUIDED PRACTICE for Examples 2 and 3

2–4. See margin for art.

2. Graph $y = 5^x$ and identify its domain and range.
   domain: all real numbers, range: all positive real numbers
3. Graph $y = \frac{1}{3} \cdot 2^x$. Compare the graph with the graph of $y = 2^x$.
   The graph is a vertical shrink of the graph of $y = 2^x$.
4. Graph $y = -\frac{1}{3} \cdot 2^x$. Compare the graph with the graph of $y = 2^x$.
   The graph is a vertical shrink with a reflection in the x–axis of the graph of $y = 2^x$.

Motivating the Lesson

You are studying population growth in your city. You know the current population is 128,256 and the annual rate of growth averages 3%. By knowing how to write and evaluate an exponential growth model, you can estimate the population in 2012.

3 TEACH

Extra Example 1

Write a rule for the function.

x	-2	-1	0	1	2
y	1	4	16	64	256

$y = 16 \cdot 4^x$

Extra Example 2

Graph the function $y = 3^x$. Identify its domain and range. Domain: all real numbers; Range: all positive real numbers

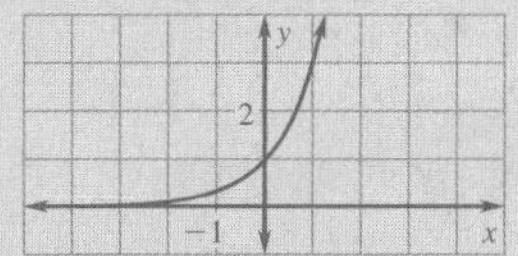

Extra Example 3

Graph $y = \frac{1}{2} \cdot 2^x$ and $y = -\frac{1}{2} \cdot 2^x$.

Compare each graph with the graph of $y = 2^x$.

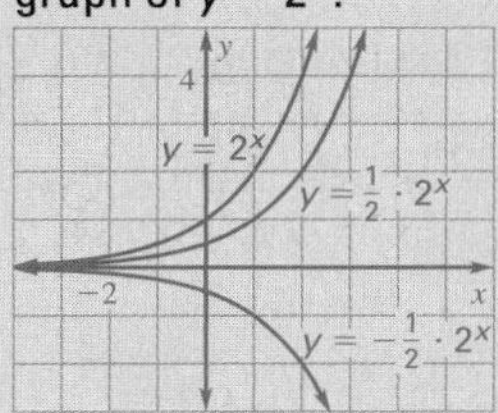

The graph of $y = \frac{1}{2} \cdot 2^x$ is a vertical shrink of the graph of $y = 2^x$. The graph of $y = -\frac{1}{2} \cdot 2^x$ is a vertical shrink and reflection in the x-axis of the graph of $y = 2^x$.

2–4. See Additional Answers beginning on p. AA1.

Differentiated Instruction

Inclusion Students with fine-motor problems may find it difficult to graph exponential functions and thus get frustrated. Have these students understand the general shape of an exponential function and have them graph on a coordinate plane without grid lines. Also show how a spreadsheet program or graphing calculator can be used to generate a graph.

See also the *Algebra 1 Toolkit* for more strategies.

Extra Example 4

The owner of an original copy of a 1938 comic book sold it at an auction in 2005. The owner bought the comic book for \$55 in 1980. The value of the comic book increased at a rate of 2.8% per year.

a. Write a function that models the value of the comic book over time. $C = 55(1.028)^t$

b. What was the approximate value of the comic book at the time of the auction in 2005? Round your answer to the nearest dollar. about \$110

Key Questions to Ask for Example 4

- How is an exponential growth model different from a linear model? The increase in an exponential model is the same percent every year, while the increase in a linear model is the same amount every year.
- What types of quantities can be represented by an exponential growth model? quantities that increase by the same percent in equal periods of time

An **Animated Algebra** activity is available on-line for **Example 4**. This activity is also available on the **Power Presentations CD-ROM**.

EXPONENTIAL GROWTH When $a > 0$ and $b > 1$, the function $y = ab^x$ represents **exponential growth**. When a quantity grows exponentially, it increases by the same percent over equal time periods. To find the amount to which the quantity grows after t time periods, use the following model.

REWRITE EQUATIONS
Notice that you can rewrite $y = ab^x$ as $y = a(1 + r)^t$ by replacing b with $1 + r$ and x with t (for time).

KEY CONCEPT — *For Your Notebook*

Exponential Growth Model

$$y = a(1 + r)^t$$

a is the **initial amount**.

r is the **growth rate**.

$1 + r$ is the **growth factor**.

t is the **time period**.

Notice the relationship between the growth rate r and the growth factor $1 + r$. If the initial amount of a quantity is a units and the quantity is growing at a rate of r, then after one time period the new amount is:

$$\text{Initial amount} + \text{amount of increase} = a + r \cdot a = a(1 + r)$$

EXAMPLE 4 Solve a multi-step problem

ANOTHER WAY
For alternative methods for solving Example 4, turn to page 528 for the **Problem Solving Workshop**.

COLLECTOR CAR The owner of a 1953 Hudson Hornet convertible sold the car at an auction. The owner bought it in 1984 when its value was \$11,000. The value of the car increased at a rate of 6.9% per year.

a. Write a function that models the value of the car over time.

b. The auction took place in 2004. What was the approximate value of the car at the time of the auction? Round your answer to the nearest dollar.

Solution

a. Let C be the value of the car (in dollars), and let t be the time (in years) since 1984. The initial value a is \$11,000, and the growth rate r is 0.069.

$C = a(1 + r)^t$	**Write exponential growth model.**
$= 11{,}000(1 + 0.069)^t$	**Substitute 11,000 for *a* and 0.069 for *r*.**
$= 11{,}000(1.069)^t$	**Simplify.**

AVOID ERRORS
The growth rate in this example is 6.9%, or 0.069. So, the growth factor is 1 + 0.069, or 1.069, not 0.069.

b. To find the value of the car in 2004, 20 years after 1984, substitute 20 for t.

$C = 11{,}000(1.069)^{20}$	**Substitute 20 for *t*.**
$\approx 41{,}778$	**Use a calculator.**

▶ In 2004 the value of the car was about \$41,778.

Animated Algebra at classzone.com

COMPOUND INTEREST **Compound interest** is interest earned on both an initial investment and on previously earned interest. Compounding of interest can be modeled by exponential growth where a is the initial investment, r is the annual interest rate, and t is the number of years the money is invested.

EXAMPLE 5 Standardized Test Practice

You put \$250 in a savings account that earns 4% annual interest compounded yearly. You do not make any deposits or withdrawals. How much will your investment be worth in 5 years?

Ⓐ \$300 Ⓑ \$304.16 Ⓒ \$1344.56 Ⓓ \$781,250

ESTIMATE
You can use the simple interest formula, $I = prt$, to estimate the amount of interest earned: $(250)(0.04)(5) = 50$. Compounding interest will result in slightly more than \$50.

Solution

$y = a(1 + r)^t$ Write exponential growth model.

$= 250(1 + 0.04)^5$ Substitute 250 for a, 0.04 for r, and 5 for t.

$= 250(1.04)^5$ Simplify.

≈ 304.16 Use a calculator.

You will have \$304.16 in 5 years.

▶ The correct answer is B. Ⓐ Ⓑ Ⓒ Ⓓ

GUIDED PRACTICE for Examples 4 and 5

5. **WHAT IF?** In Example 4, suppose the owner of the car sold it in 1994. Find the value of the car to the nearest dollar. \$21,437

6. **WHAT IF?** In Example 5, suppose the annual interest rate is 3.5%. How much will your investment be worth in 5 years? \$296.92

8.5 EXERCISES

HOMEWORK KEY
○ = **WORKED-OUT SOLUTIONS** on p. WS19 for Exs. 13 and 41
★ = **STANDARDIZED TEST PRACTICE** Exs. 3, 8, 34, 35, 42, 43, 46, and 50
◆ = **MULTIPLE REPRESENTATIONS** Ex. 41

SKILL PRACTICE

A

1. **VOCABULARY** In the exponential growth model $y = a(1 + r)^t$, the quantity $1 + r$ is called the _?_. growth factor

2. **VOCABULARY** For what values of b does the exponential function $y = ab^x$ (where $a > 0$) represent exponential growth? $b > 1$

3. ★ **WRITING** How does the graph of $y = 2 \cdot 5^x$ compare with the graph of $y = 5^x$? *Explain.* The graph would be a vertical stretch. *Sample answer:* Since the y-values of $y = 2 \cdot 5^x$ are double those of $y = 5^x$.

Extra Example 5

You put \$125 in a savings account that earns 2% interest compounded yearly. You do not make any deposits or withdrawals. How much will your investment be worth in 5 years? B

Ⓐ \$130 Ⓑ \$138.01
Ⓒ \$311.04 Ⓓ \$4000

Key Question to Ask for Example 5

- Why is an estimate using the simple interest formula useful? **Since it shows that simple interest is \$50 and compound interest would be slightly more than \$50, you can eliminate all answer choices except B.**

Closing the Lesson

Have students summarize the major points of the lesson and answer the Essential Question: How do you write and graph equations for exponential growth functions?

- **An exponential function has the form $y = ab^x$, where $a \neq 0$, $b > 0$, and $b \neq 1$.**
- **The exponential growth model is $y = a(1 + r)^t$, where a is the initial amount, r is the growth rate, and t is the time period.**

Use the exponential growth model to write an equation. Substitute the initial amount for a, the rate for r, written as a decimal, and the time period for t. When graphing an exponential function, make a table of negative and positive values, determine the y-intercept, plot the points on a coordinate plane, and connect them with a smooth curve.

Differentiated Instruction

Advanced Suggest that students research several banks, either locally or online, for interest rates on savings accounts, money market accounts, and CDs. Have them develop exponential growth models for each type of account at each bank on an initial deposit of \$500 after 2 years. Ask students to make a chart comparing the rates and potential earnings for the different types of accounts and the different banks.

See also the *Algebra 1 Toolkit* for more strategies.

4 PRACTICE AND APPLY

Assignment Guide

Answer Transparencies available for all exercises

Basic:
Day 1: SRH p. 923 Exs. 9–13
pp. 523–527
Exs. 1–21
Day 2: pp. 523–527
Exs. 22–27, 38–43, 52–61

Average:
Day 1: pp. 523–527
Exs. 1–8, 11–21, 35, 60, 61
Day 2: pp. 523–527
Exs. 22–34, 38–46, 52–58 even

Advanced:
Day 1: pp. 523–527
Exs. 1, 2, 4–8, 13–21, 35–37*, 60
Day 2: pp. 523–527
Exs. 26–34, 39–51*, 54, 58

Block:
pp. 523–527
Exs. 1–8, 11–35, 38–46,
52–58 even, 60, 61

Differentiated Instruction

See *Algebra 1 Best Practices Toolkit* for suggestions on addressing the needs of a diverse classroom.

Homework Check

For a quick check of student understanding of key concepts, go over the following exercises:

Basic: 4, 12, 24, 38, 39
Average: 5, 16, 28, 38, 40
Advanced: 6, 20, 32, 39, 41

Extra Practice

- Student Edition, p. 945
- Chapter 8 Resource Book: Practice levels A, B, C, pp. 51–56

Practice Worksheet

An easily-readable reduced practice page (with answers) for this lesson can be found on p. 486C.

EXAMPLE 1 on p. 520 for Exs. 4–8

4. $y = 4 \cdot 2^x$
5. $y = 125 \cdot 5^x$
6. $y = \frac{1}{2} \cdot 2^x$
7. $y = \frac{1}{9} \cdot 3^x$

WRITING FUNCTIONS **Write a rule for the function.**

4.

x	−2	−1	0	1	2
y	1	2	4	8	16

5.

x	−2	−1	0	1	2
y	5	25	125	625	3125

6.

x	−2	−1	0	1	2
y	$\frac{1}{8}$	$\frac{1}{4}$	$\frac{1}{2}$	1	2

7.

x	−2	−1	0	1	2
y	$\frac{1}{81}$	$\frac{1}{27}$	$\frac{1}{9}$	$\frac{1}{3}$	1

8. ★ **WRITING** Given a table of values, describe how can you tell if the table represents a linear function or an exponential function. See margin.

EXAMPLE 2 on p. 521 for Exs. 9–21

GRAPHING FUNCTIONS **Graph the function and identify its domain and range.** 9–20. See margin.

9. $y = 4^x$
10. $y = 7^x$
11. $y = 8^x$
12. $y = 9^x$
13. $y = (1.5)^x$
14. $y = (2.5)^x$
15. $y = (1.2)^x$
16. $y = (4.3)^x$
17. $y = \left(\frac{4}{3}\right)^x$
18. $y = \left(\frac{7}{2}\right)^x$
19. $y = \left(\frac{5}{3}\right)^x$
20. $y = \left(\frac{5}{4}\right)^x$

21. The percent increase was not written as a decimal; $0.27(1 + 0.02)^3 = 0.27(1.02)^3 \approx \$.29$.

21. **ERROR ANALYSIS** The price P (in dollars) of a pound of flour was \$.27 in 1999. The price has increased by about 2% each year. Let t be the number of years since 1999. *Describe* and correct the error in finding the price of a pound of flour in 2002.

$P = a(1 + r)^t$
$= 0.27(1 + 2)^3 = 0.27(3)^3 = 7.29$ ✗
In 2002 the price of a pound of flour was \$7.29.

EXAMPLE 3 [B] on p. 521 for Exs. 22–34

COMPARING GRAPHS OF FUNCTIONS **Graph the function. Compare the graph with the graph of $y = 3^x$.** 22–33. See margin.

22. $y = 2 \cdot 3^x$
23. $y = 4 \cdot 3^x$
24. $y = \frac{1}{4} \cdot 3^x$
25. $y = \frac{2}{3} \cdot 3^x$
26. $y = 0.5 \cdot 3^x$
27. $y = 2.5 \cdot 3^x$
28. $y = -2 \cdot 3^x$
29. $y = -4 \cdot 3^x$
30. $y = -\frac{1}{4} \cdot 3^x$
31. $y = -\frac{2}{3} \cdot 3^x$
32. $y = -0.5 \cdot 3^x$
33. $y = -2.5 \cdot 3^x$

34. ★ **MULTIPLE CHOICE** The graph of which function is shown? C

(A) $f(x) = 6^x$
(B) $f(x) = \left(\frac{1}{3}\right)^x$
(C) $f(x) = \frac{1}{3} \cdot 6^x$
(D) $f(x) = 6 \cdot \left(\frac{1}{3}\right)^x$

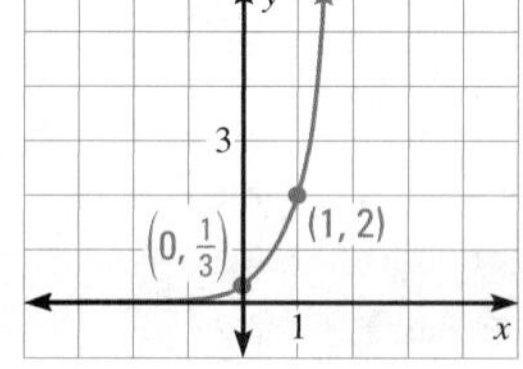

35. 200%. *Sample answer:* A growth rate of 200% would create a growth factor of 1 + 2 = 3, which would represent the tripling of the population every year.

[C] 35. ★ **WRITING** If a population triples each year, what is the population's growth rate (as a percent)? *Explain.*

36. **CHALLENGE** Write a linear function and an exponential function whose graphs pass through the points (0, 2) and (1, 6). *Sample answer:* $f(x) = 4x + 2$, $f(x) = 2 \cdot 3^x$

37. **CHALLENGE** Compare the graph of the function $f(x) = 2^{x+2}$ with the graph of the function $g(x) = 4 \cdot 2^x$. Use properties of exponents to explain your observations. *Sample answer:* The graphs are the same. Since by the product of a power property $2^{x+2} = 2^x \cdot 2^2$, and $2^x \cdot 2^2$ simplifies to $4 \cdot 2^x$, $2^{x+2} = 4 \cdot 2^x$.

○ = WORKED-OUT SOLUTIONS on p. WS1 ★ = STANDARDIZED TEST PRACTICE

= MULTIPLE REPRESENTATIONS

8. *Sample answer:* If the difference between successive terms is constant, the function is linear and if the ratio of successive terms is constant, the function is exponential.

9–20, 22–33. See Additional Answers beginning on p. AA1.

PROBLEM SOLVING

GRAPHING CALCULATOR **You may wish to use a graphing calculator to complete the following Problem Solving exercises.**

EXAMPLES A 4 and 5 on pp. 522–523 for Exs. 38–41

38. **INVESTMENTS** You deposit \$125 in a savings account that earns 5% annual interest compounded yearly. Find the balance in the account after the given amounts of time.

a. 1 year **\$131.25** **b.** 2 years **\$137.81** **c.** 5 years **\$159.54** **d.** 20 years **\$331.66**

@HomeTutor for problem solving help at classzone.com

39a. Let x represent the number of years since 2001 and $f(x)$ represent the number of computers (in hundreds of millions); $f(x) = 6 \cdot (1.1)^x$.

39. **MULTI-STEP PROBLEM** One computer industry expert reported that there were about 600 million computers in use worldwide in 2001 and that the number was increasing at an annual rate of about 10%.

a. Write a function that models the number of computers in use over time.

b. Use the function to predict the number of computers that will be in use worldwide in 2009. **about 1,286,153,286 computers**

@HomeTutor for problem solving help at classzone.com

40a. Let x represent the number of years since 1985 and $f(x)$ represent the number of grills shipped; $f(x) = 3{,}173{,}000 \cdot (1.07)^x$.

40. **MULTI-STEP PROBLEM** A research association reported that 3,173,000 gas grills were shipped by various manufacturers in the U.S. in 1985. Shipments increased by about 7% per year from 1985 to 2002.

a. Write a function that models the number of gas grills shipped over time.

b. About how many gas grills were shipped in 2002? **about 10,022,921 gas grills**

41. **MULTIPLE REPRESENTATIONS** A tree's cross-sectional area taken at a height of 4.5 feet from the ground is called its basal area and is measured in square inches. Tree growth can be measured by the growth of the tree's basal area. The initial basal area and annual growth rate for two particular trees are shown.

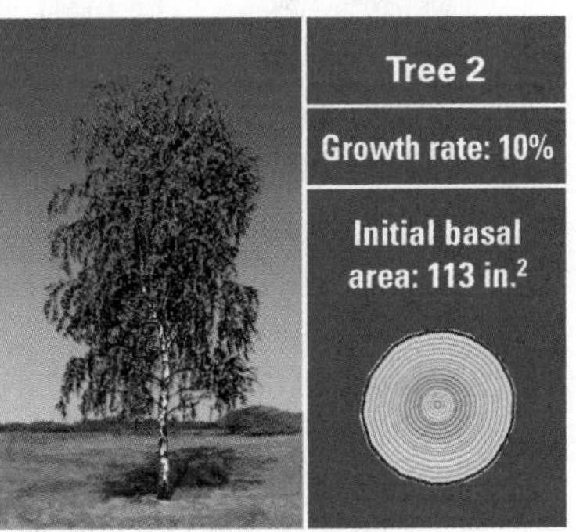

a. Writing a Model Write a function that models the basal area A of each tree over time. **tree 1: $A = 154 \cdot (1.06)^t$, tree 2: $A = 113 \cdot (1.1)^t$**

b. Graphing a Function Use a graphing calculator to graph the functions from part (a) in the same coordinate plane. In about how many years will the trees have the same basal area? **See margin for art; about 8.4 yr.**

Avoiding Common Errors

Exercises 4–6 Some students may fail to find the value of a. Remind students that an exponential function is in the form of $y = ab^x$ and that they can find the value of a by finding the value of y when $x = 0$.

Exercises 38–41 Watch for students who do not write percents as decimals before applying the exponential growth model.

Graphing Calculator

Exercises 9–20, 22–34 Students may want to check their graphs on a graphing calculator. They can enter the function in the Y = menu and then press Graph. They can press Table to check values. They can scroll up or down to see more values.

Reading Strategy

Exercises 38–41 Draw students' attention to the graphing calculator logo at the top of page 525. Point out that the logo appears whenever a graphing calculator is suggested for the exercises.

41b.

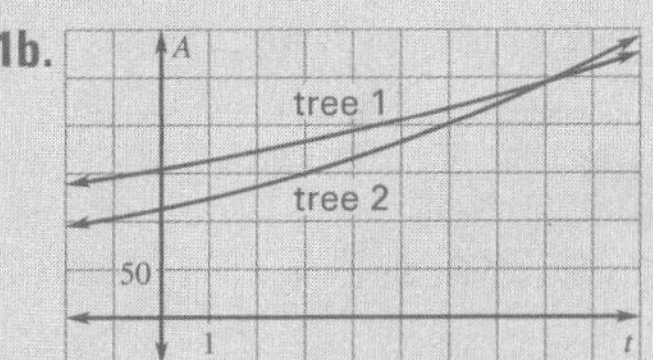

Avoiding Common Errors

Exercises 42–46 Some students may forget to add 1 to the rate of growth in the exponential growth model. Remind students that $1 + r$ is the growth factor in the model.

Study Strategy

Exercises 47–50 Encourage students to study the Example on page 527 in detail. You may wish to present this Example to students to be certain they understand what each variable in the formula represents.

44b.

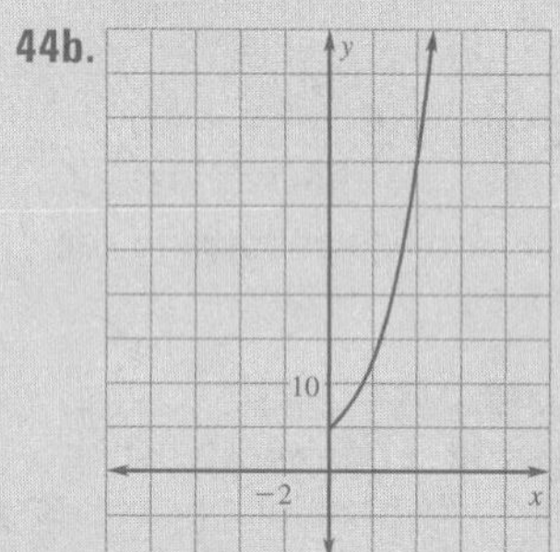

46c. *Sample answer:* The exponential model is more accurate from 1850–1890. The exponential model underestimates the actual totals by less than 2 million in 1850 and 1870, while the linear model overestimates by more than 5 million in each year.

42. Yes. *Sample answer:* The quotient of each pair of adjacent terms is the same, $\frac{7}{4}$.

44a. initial amount: 4.67 million, growth factor: 1.65, growth rate: 0.65

44b. See margin for art; domain: $0 \le x \le 10$, range: 4.67 million $\le y \le$ 698.5 million.

45. $y = 25.96(1.059)^x$; about 145 Hz

B

42. ★ **SHORT RESPONSE** A company sells advertising blimps. The table shows the costs of advertising blimps of different lengths. Does the table represent an exponential function? *Explain.*

Length, ℓ (feet)	10	15	20	25
Cost, c (dollars)	400.00	700.00	1225.00	2143.75

43. ★ **MULTIPLE CHOICE** A weblog, or blog, refers to a website that contains a personal journal. According to one analyst, over one 18 month period, the number of blogs in existence doubled about every 6 months. The analyst estimated that there were about 600,000 blogs at the beginning of the period. How many blogs were there at the end of the period? C

Ⓐ 660,000 Ⓑ 1,200,000 Ⓒ 4,800,000 Ⓓ 16,200,000

44. TELECOMMUNICATIONS For the period 1991–2001, the number y (in millions) of Internet users worldwide can be modeled by the function $y = 4.67(1.65)^x$ where x is the number of years since 1991.

a. Identify the initial amount, the growth factor, and the growth rate.

b. Graph the function. Identify its domain and range.

c. Use the graph to estimate the year in which the number of Internet users worldwide was about 21 million. 1994

45. GRAPHING CALCULATOR The frequency (in hertz) of a note played on a piano is a function of the position of the key that creates the note. The position of some piano keys and the frequencies of the notes created by the keys are shown below. Use the exponential regression feature on a graphing calculator to find an exponential model for the frequency of piano notes. What is the frequency of the note created by the 30th key?

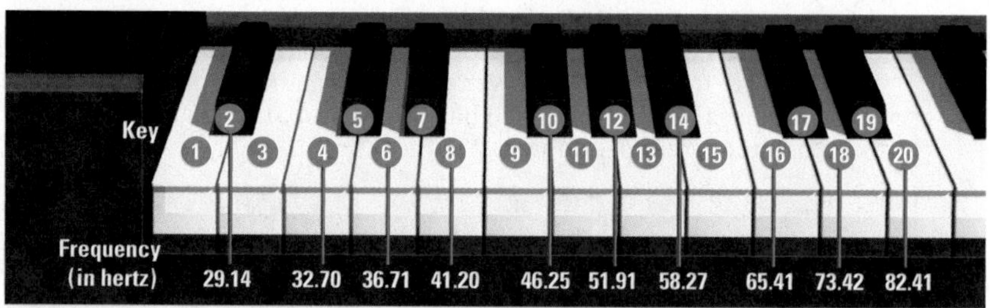

C

46. ★ **EXTENDED RESPONSE** In 1830, the population of the United States was 12,866,020. By 1890, the population was 62,947,714.

a. Model Assume the population growth from 1830 to 1890 was linear. Write a linear model for the U.S. population from 1830 to 1890. By about how much did the population grow per year from 1830 to 1890? $y = 834694.9x + 12,866,020$; 834694.9 people

b. Model Assume the population growth from 1830 to 1890 was exponential. Write an exponential model for the U.S. population from 1830 to 1890. By approximately what percent did the population grow per year from 1830 to 1890? $y = 12,866,020(1.0268)^x$; about 2.68%

c. Explain The U.S. population was 23,191,876 in 1850 and 38,558,371 in 1870. Which of the models in parts (a) and (b) is a better approximation of actual U.S. population for the time period 1850–1890? *Explain.* See margin.

★ = STANDARDIZED TEST PRACTICE

COMPOUND INTEREST **In Exercises 47–49, use the example below to find the balance of the account compounded with the given frequency.**

EXAMPLE **Use the general compound interest formula**

FINANCE You deposit \$1000 in an account that pays 3% annual interest. Find the balance after 8 years if the interest is compounded monthly.

Solution

The general formula for compound interest is $A = P\left(1 + \frac{r}{n}\right)^{nt}$. In this formula, P is the initial amount, called principal, in an account that pays interest at an annual rate r and that is compounded n times per year. The amount A (in dollars) is the amount in the account after t years.

Here, the interest is compounded monthly. So, $n = 12$.

$A = P\left(1 + \frac{r}{n}\right)^{nt}$ **Write compound interest formula.**

$= 1000\left(1 + \frac{0.03}{12}\right)^{12(8)}$ **Substitute 1000 for P, 0.03 for r, 12 for n, and 8 for t.**

$= 1000(1.0025)^{96}$ **Simplify.**

≈ 1270.868467 **Use a calculator.**

▶ The account balance after 8 years will be about \$1270.87.

47. Yearly **\$1266.77** **48.** Quarterly **\$1270.11** **49.** Daily ($n = 365$) **\$1271.24**

50. ★ **WRITING** Which compounding frequency yields the highest balance in the account in the example above: monthly, yearly, quarterly, or daily? *Explain* why this is so.

50. Daily; in an account compounded daily, each day you earn interest on both the principal and the interest that was accrued on the previous days.

51. **CHALLENGE** You invest \$500 in an account that earns interest compounded monthly. Use a table or graph to find the least annual interest rate (to the nearest tenth of a percent) that the account would have to earn if you want to have a balance of \$600 in 4 years. **4.6%**

ILLINOIS MIXED REVIEW

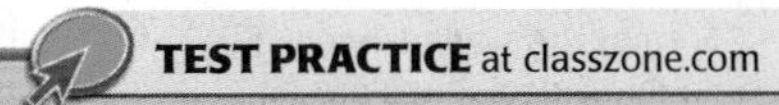

52. Which graph is the best representation of $y = x$? **C**

Ⓐ
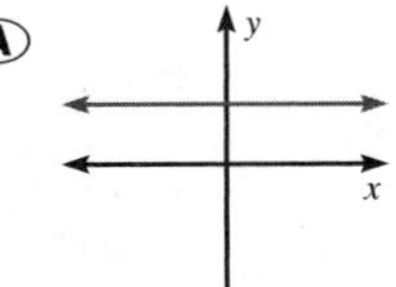

Ⓑ
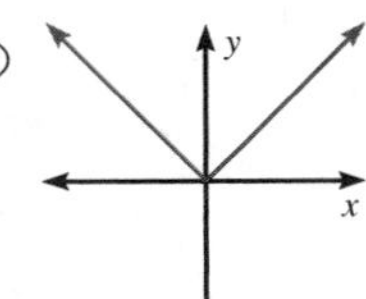

Ⓒ
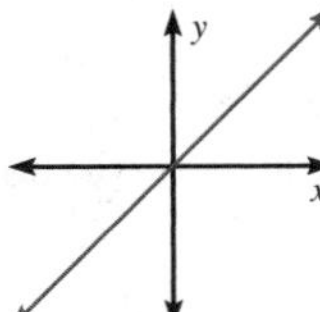

Ⓓ
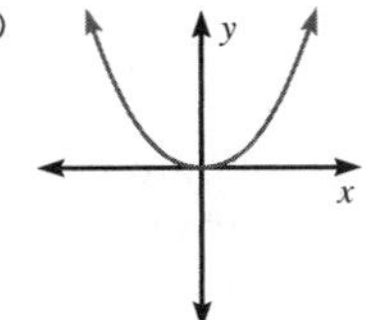

EXTRA PRACTICE for Lesson 8.5, p. 945 **ONLINE QUIZ** at classzone.com

5 ASSESS AND RETEACH

Daily Homework Quiz

Transparency Available

1. Graph $y = 1.4^x$.

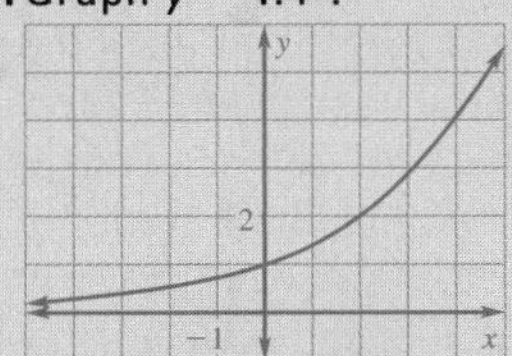

2. Your family bought a house for \$150,000 in 2000. The value of the house increases at an annual rate of 8%. What is the value of the house after 5 years? **about \$220,399**

Available at **classzone.com**

Diagnosis/Remediation

- Practice A, B, C in Chapter 8 Resource Book, pp. 51–56
- Study Guide in Chapter 8 Resource Book, pp. 57–58
- Practice Workbook, pp. 127–129
- @HomeTutor

Challenge

Additional challenge is available in the Chapter 8 Resource Book, p. 61.

Using ALTERNATIVE METHODS

Alternative Strategy

Example 4 on page 522 can be solved by using a spreadsheet. A spreadsheet has the advantage of showing the value of the car each year after1984. If the student wants to find the value for a different year or knows the value of the car but not the year, all the information can be readily found on the spreadsheet. Should the student want to find the value of the car in future years, using the *fill down* feature on the spreadsheet will quickly furnish the value.

Avoiding Common Errors

Watch for students who enter the formula incorrectly. Suggest that they double-check their formulas for accuracy.

Reading Strategy

Point out the note on formatting a spreadsheet. Tell students that the number of decimal places becomes unwieldy if they do not format the cells to round to 2 decimal places.

Another Way to Solve Example 4, page 522

MULTIPLE REPRESENTATIONS In Example 4 on page 522, you saw how to solve a problem about the value of a collector car over time by using an exponential model. You can also solve the problem by using a spreadsheet.

PROBLEM

COLLECTOR CAR The owner of a 1953 Hudson Hornet convertible sold the car at an auction. The owner bought it in 1984 when its value was \$11,000. The value of the car increased at a rate of 6.9% per year.

a. Write a function that models the value of the car over time.

b. The auction took place in 2004. What was the approximate value of the car at the time of the auction? Round your answer to the nearest dollar.

METHOD

Using a Spreadsheet An alternative approach is to use a spreadsheet.

a. The model for the value of the car over time is $C = 11{,}000(1.069)^t$, as shown in Example 4 on page 522.

b. You can find the value of the car in 2004 by creating a spreadsheet.

STEP 1 **Create** a table showing the years since 1984 and the value of the car. Enter the car's value in 1984. To find the value in any year after 1984, multiply the car's value in the preceding year by the growth factor, as shown in cell B3 below.

FORMAT A SPREADSHEET
Format the spreadsheet so that calculations are rounded to 2 decimal places.

	A	B
1	Years since 1984, *t*	Value, *C* (dollars)
2	0	11000
3	1	=B2*1.069

STEP 2 **Find** the value of the car in 2004 by using the *fill down* feature until you get to the desired cell.

	A	B
1	Years since 1984, *t*	Value, *C* (dollars)
2	0	11000
3	1	11759
...	...	...
21	19	39081.31
22	20	41777.92

▸ From the spreadsheet, you can see the value of the car was about \$41,778 in 2004.

PROBLEM **WHAT IF?** Suppose the owner decided to sell the car when it was worth about \$28,000. In what year did the owner sell the car?

METHOD **Using a Spreadsheet** To solve the equation algebraically, you need to substitute 28,000 for C and solve for t, but you have not yet learned how to solve this type of equation. An alternative to the algebraic approach is using a spreadsheet.

STEP 1 **Use** the same spreadsheet as on the previous page.

STEP 2 **Find** when the value of the car is about \$28,000.

	A	B
1	Years since 1984, t	Value, C (dollars)
2	0	11000
...	...	...
15	13	26188.03
16	14	27995.01

The value of the car is about \$28,000 when $t = 14$.

▸ The owner sold the car in 1998.

PRACTICE

1. **TRANSPORTATION** In 1997 the average intercity bus fare for a particular state was \$20. For the period 1997–2000, the bus fare increased at a rate of about 12% each year.
   a. Write a function that models the intercity bus fare for the period 1997–2000. See margin.
   b. Find the intercity bus fare in 1998. Use two different methods to solve the problem. \$22.40
   c. In what year was the intercity bus fare \$28.10? *Explain* how you found your answer. 2000. *Sample answer:* Make a table of values.

2. **ERROR ANALYSIS** *Describe* and correct the error in writing the function for part (a) of Exercise 1.

   Let b be the bus fare (in dollars) and t be the number of years since 1997.
   $b = 20(0.12)^t$ ✗

   The growth factor should be 1.12, not 0.12; $b = 20(1.12)^t$.

3. **TECHNOLOGY** A computer's Central Processing Unit (CPU) is made up of transistors. One manufacturer released a CPU in May 1997 that had 7.5 million transistors. The number of transistors in the CPUs sold by the company increased at a rate of 3.9% per month.
   a. Write a function that models the number T (in millions) of transistors in the company's CPUs t months after May 1997. $T = 7.5(1.039)^t$
   b. Use a spreadsheet to find the number of transistors in a CPU released by the company in November 2000. about 37.4 million

4. **HOUSING** The value of a home in 2002 was \$150,000. The value of the home increased at a rate of about 6.5% per year.
   a. Write a function that models the value of the home over time. See margin.
   b. Use a spreadsheet to find the year in which the value of the home was about \$200,000. 2007

Study Strategy

Suggest that students check their exponential growth models in the Practice problems against the model given at the top of page 522. If they are unsure on how to use the model, suggest that they review Example 4 on page 522.

1a. Let t represent the number of years since 1997 and F represent the bus fare. $F = 20(1.12)^t$

4a. Let V represent the home's value and t represent the number of years since 2002. $V = 150{,}000(1.065)^t$.

1 PLAN AND PREPARE

Explore the Concept

- Students will model a situation using an exponential function.
- This activity leads into the study of writing function rules in Example 1 in Lesson 8.6.

Materials

Each student or group of students will need:

- yarn
- scissors

Recommended Time

Work activity: 10 min

Discuss results: 5 min

Grouping

Students can work individually or in pairs. If students work in pairs, one student can fold and cut the yarn and the other student can record the data in the chart.

2 TEACH

Tips for Success

Make sure that students fold all the pieces of yarn in half at each stage and then cut all of the pieces.

Key Discovery

Some exponential functions model increases in value, while others model decreases.

3 ASSESS AND RETEACH

How does the function in Exercise 2 differ from the one in Exercise 1?. **The values in Exercise 2 are decreasing rather than increasing as in Exercise 1.**

1a. Yes. *Sample answer:* Each value is twice the value of the previous stage.

2a. Yes. *Sample answer:* Each value is half the value of the previous stage.

8.6 Exponential Models

MATERIALS • yarn • scissors

QUESTION **How can you model a situation using an exponential function?**

EXPLORE **Collect data so that you can write exponential models**

STEP 1 ***Fold and cut*** Take about 1 yard of yarn and consider it to be 1 unit long. Fold it in half and cut, as shown. You are left with two pieces of yarn, each half the length of the original piece of yarn.

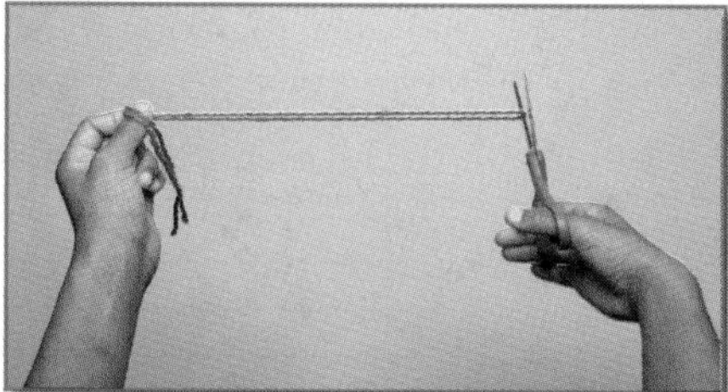

STEP 2 ***Copy and complete*** Copy the table. Notice that the row for stage 1 has the data from Step 1. For each successive stage, fold *all* the pieces of yarn in half and cut. Then record the number of new pieces and the length of each new piece until the table is complete.

Stage	Number of pieces	Length of each new piece
1	2	$\frac{1}{2}$
2	? **4**	? $\frac{1}{4}$
3	? **8**	? $\frac{1}{8}$
4	? **16**	? $\frac{1}{16}$
5	? **32**	? $\frac{1}{32}$

DRAW CONCLUSIONS **Use your observations to complete these exercises**

1. Use the data in the first and second columns of the table.
   a. Do the data represent an exponential function? *Explain* how you know. **See margin.**
   b. Write a function that models the number of pieces of yarn at stage x. **$y = 2^x$**
   c. Use the function to find the number of pieces of yarn at stage 10. **1024 pieces of yarn**
2. Use the data in the first and third columns of the table.
   a. Do the data represent an exponential function? *Explain* how you know. **See margin.**
   b. Write a function that models the length of each new piece of yarn at stage x. **$y = \left(\frac{1}{2}\right)^x$**
   c. Use the function to find the length of each new piece of yarn at stage 10. **$\frac{1}{1024}$ units**

8.6 Write and Graph Exponential Decay Functions

 **8.11.12** Create and connect representations that are tabular, graphic, numeric, and symbolic from a set of data.

Before You wrote and graphed exponential growth functions.

Now You will write and graph exponential decay functions.

Why? So you can use a graph to solve a sports problem, as in Ex. 50.

Key Vocabulary
- **exponential decay**

A table of values represents an exponential function $y = ab^x$ provided successive y-values are multiplied by b each time the x-values increase by 1.

EXAMPLE 1 Write a function rule

Tell whether the table represents an exponential function. If so, write a rule for the function.

a.

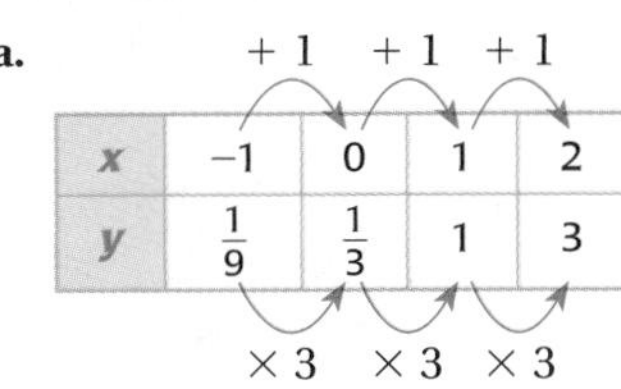

x	−1	0	1	2
y	$\frac{1}{9}$	$\frac{1}{3}$	1	3

The y-values are multiplied by 3 for each increase of 1 in x, so the table represents an exponential function of the form $y = ab^x$ with $b = 3$.

The value of y when $x = 0$ is $\frac{1}{3}$, so $a = \frac{1}{3}$.

The table represents the exponential function $y = \frac{1}{3} \cdot 3^x$.

b.

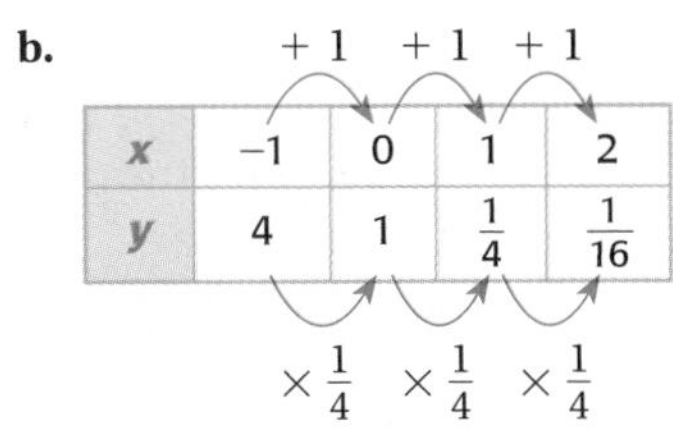

x	−1	0	1	2
y	4	1	$\frac{1}{4}$	$\frac{1}{16}$

The y-values are multiplied by $\frac{1}{4}$ for each increase of 1 in x, so the table represents an exponential function of the form $y = ab^x$ with $b = \frac{1}{4}$.

The value of y when $x = 0$ is 1, so $a = 1$.

The table represents the exponential function $y = \left(\frac{1}{4}\right)^x$.

✓ GUIDED PRACTICE for Example 1

1. Tell whether the table represents an exponential function. If so, write a rule for the function. yes; $y = \left(\frac{1}{5}\right)^x$

x	−1	0	1	2
y	5	1	$\frac{1}{5}$	$\frac{1}{25}$

1 PLAN AND PREPARE

Warm-Up Exercises

Transparency Available

1. Evaluate $\left(\frac{1}{2}\right)^3$. $\frac{1}{8}$
2. Evaluate $\left(\frac{1}{4}\right)^{-2}$. 16
3. The table shows how much money Tess owes after w weeks. Write a rule for the function.

Week, w	0	1	2	3
Owes, m	50	45	40	35

$m = 50 - 5w$

Notetaking Guide

Transparency Available

Promotes interactive learning and notetaking skills, pp. 183–186.

Pacing

Basic: 2 days
Average: 2 days
Advanced: 2 days
Block: 1 block
- See *Teaching Guide/Lesson Plan.*

2 FOCUS AND MOTIVATE

Essential Question

Big Idea 3, p. 487

How do you write and graph exponential decay functions?
Tell students they will learn how to answer this question by using tables, graphs, and exponential decay models.

Resource Planning Guide

Chapter Resource Book
- Teaching Guide/Lesson Plan (pp. 62–63)
- Activity Master (p. 64)
- Practice levels A, B, C (pp. 66–71)
- Study Guide (pp. 72–73)
- Catch-up for Absent Students (p. 74)
- Problem Solving Workshop (p. 75)
- Challenge (p. 76)

Workbooks
- Notetaking Guide (pp. 183–186)
- Practice Workbook (pp. 130–132)

Teaching Options
- **Power Presentations CD-ROM** provides dynamic electronic teaching resources for the classroom.
- **Activity Generator CD-ROM** provides editable activities for all ability levels.

Interactive Technology
- Easy Planner
- Power Presentations CD-ROM
- Activity Generator CD-ROM
- Animated Algebra
- Test Generator CD-ROM
- Online Quiz
- eWorkbook
- eEdition
- @HomeTutor

Resources for English Learners
- Quick Reference for English Learners
- Spanish Study Guide
- Multi-Language Visual Glossary
- Student Resources in Spanish

See also the *Algebra 1 Toolkit* for more strategies for meeting individual needs.

Motivating the Lesson

Your aunt bought a car two years ago for $12,000 and now she wants to sell it. She knows that the value of similar models has been decreasing at a rate of 17% per year. By knowing how to write and use an exponential decay model, she will be able to determine the value of the car at the time that she sells it.

3 TEACH

Extra Example 1

Tell whether the table represents an exponential function. If so, write a rule for the function.

x	−1	0	1	2
y	$\frac{1}{8}$	$\frac{1}{2}$	2	8

yes; $y = \frac{1}{2} \cdot 4^x$

Extra Example 2

Graph the function $y = \left(\frac{1}{3}\right)^x$ and identify its domain and range.

Domain: all real numbers; Range: all positive real numbers

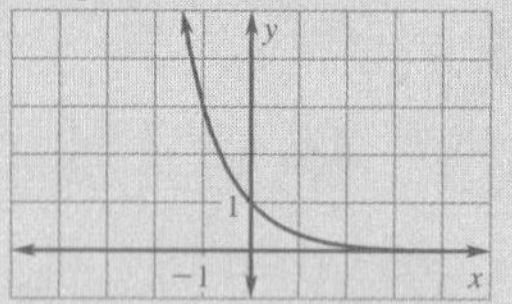

Key Question to Ask for Example 2

- How does the graph in Example 2 differ from a graph that represents exponential growth? **The graph in Example 2 falls from left to right and gets closer to the x-axis as x gets larger. A graph of exponential growth rises from left to right and gets closer to the x-axis as x gets smaller.**

2, 3. See Additional Answers beginning on p. AA1.

EXAMPLE 2 Graph an exponential function

Graph the function $y = \left(\frac{1}{2}\right)^x$ and identify its domain and range.

Solution

READ A GRAPH
Notice that the graph has a y-intercept of 1 and that it gets closer to the positive x-axis as the x-values increase.

STEP 1 **Make** a table of values. The domain is all real numbers.

x	−2	−1	0	1	2
y	4	2	1	$\frac{1}{2}$	$\frac{1}{4}$

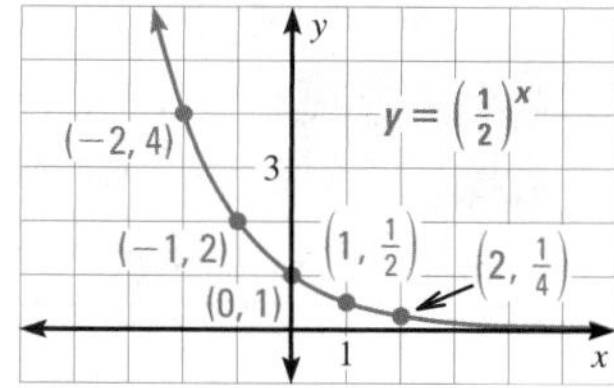

STEP 2 **Plot** the points.

STEP 3 **Draw** a smooth curve through the points. From either the table or the graph, you can see the range is all positive real numbers.

EXAMPLE 3 Compare graphs of exponential functions

Graph the functions $y = 3 \cdot \left(\frac{1}{2}\right)^x$ and $y = -\frac{1}{3} \cdot \left(\frac{1}{2}\right)^x$. Compare each graph with the graph of $y = \left(\frac{1}{2}\right)^x$.

Solution

x	$y = \left(\frac{1}{2}\right)^x$	$y = 3 \cdot \left(\frac{1}{2}\right)^x$	$y = -\frac{1}{3} \cdot \left(\frac{1}{2}\right)^x$
−2	4	12	$-\frac{4}{3}$
−1	2	6	$-\frac{2}{3}$
0	1	3	$-\frac{1}{3}$
1	$\frac{1}{2}$	$\frac{3}{2}$	$-\frac{1}{6}$
2	$\frac{1}{4}$	$\frac{3}{4}$	$-\frac{1}{12}$

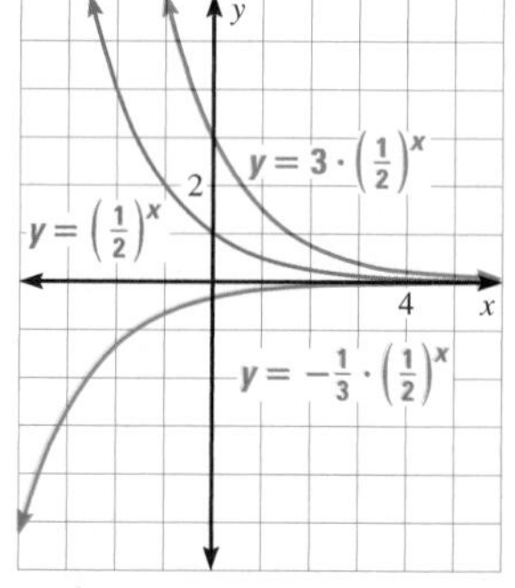

Because the y-values for $y = 3 \cdot \left(\frac{1}{2}\right)^x$ are 3 times the corresponding y-values for $y = \left(\frac{1}{2}\right)^x$, the graph of $y = 3 \cdot \left(\frac{1}{2}\right)^x$ is a vertical stretch of the graph of $y = \left(\frac{1}{2}\right)^x$.

Because the y-values for $y = -\frac{1}{3} \cdot \left(\frac{1}{2}\right)^x$ are $-\frac{1}{3}$ times the corresponding y-values for $y = \left(\frac{1}{2}\right)^x$, the graph of $y = -\frac{1}{3} \cdot \left(\frac{1}{2}\right)^x$ is a vertical shrink with reflection in the x-axis of the graph of $y = \left(\frac{1}{2}\right)^x$.

✓ GUIDED PRACTICE for Examples 2 and 3

2. Graph $y = (0.4)^x$ and identify its domain and range.
3. Graph $y = 5 \cdot (0.4)^x$. Compare the graph with the graph of $y = (0.4)^x$. **See margin for art; the graph is a vertical stretch of $y = (0.4)^x$.**

2. See margin for art; domain: all real numbers, range: all positive real numbers.

COMPARE GRAPHS When $a > 0$ and $0 < b < 1$, the function $y = ab^x$ represents **exponential decay**. The graph of an exponential decay function falls from left to right. In comparison, the graph of an exponential growth function $y = ab^x$ where $a > 0$ and $b > 1$ rises from the left.

EXAMPLE 4 Classify and write rules for functions

Tell whether the graph represents *exponential growth* or *exponential decay*. Then write a rule for the function.

a.

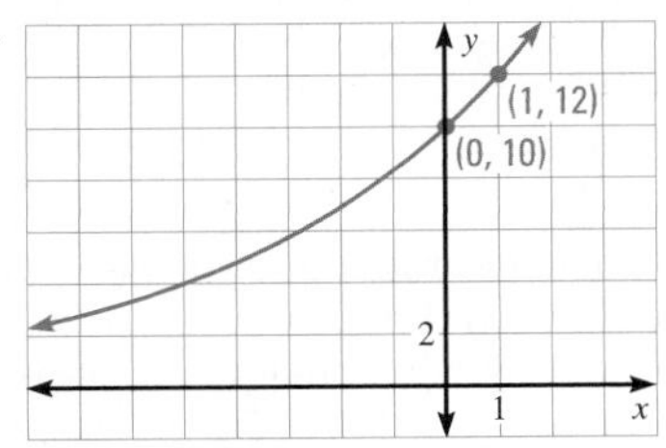

b.

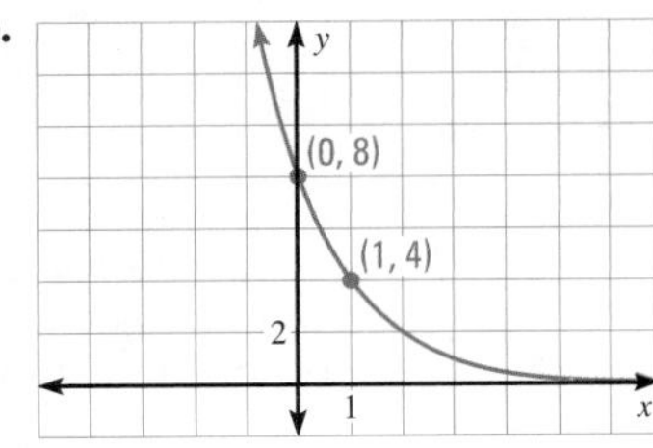

Solution

a. The graph represents exponential growth ($y = ab^x$ where $b > 1$). The y-intercept is 10, so $a = 10$. Find the value of b by using the point (1, 12) and $a = 10$.

$y = ab^x$ **Write function.**

$12 = 10 \cdot b^1$ **Substitute.**

$1.2 = b$ **Solve.**

A function rule is $y = 10(1.2)^x$.

b. The graph represents exponential decay ($y = ab^x$ where $0 < b < 1$). The y-intercept is 8, so $a = 8$. Find the value of b by using the point (1, 4) and $a = 8$.

$y = ab^x$ **Write function.**

$4 = 8 \cdot b^1$ **Substitute.**

$0.5 = b$ **Solve.**

A function rule is $y = 8(0.5)^x$.

ANALYZE GRAPHS
For the function $y = ab^x$, where $x = 0$, the value of y is $y = ax^0 = a$. This means that the graph of $y = ab^x$ has a y-intercept of a.

GUIDED PRACTICE for Example 4

4. The graph of an exponential function passes through the points (0, 10) and (1, 8). Graph the function. Tell whether the graph represents *exponential growth* or *exponential decay*. Write a rule for the function.
See margin for art; exponential decay; $y = 10 \cdot (0.8)^x$.

CONCEPT SUMMARY *For Your Notebook*

Exponential Growth and Decay

Exponential Growth

$y = ab^x$, $a > 0$ and $b > 1$

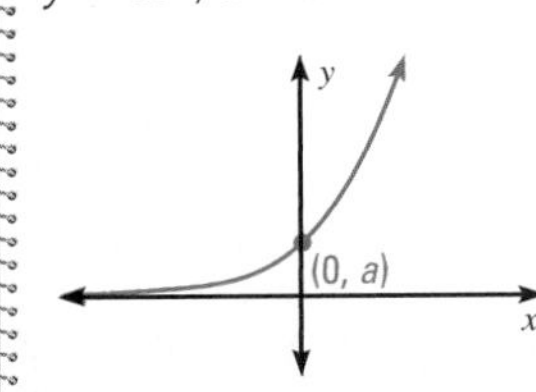

Exponential Decay

$y = ab^x$, $a > 0$ and $0 < b < 1$

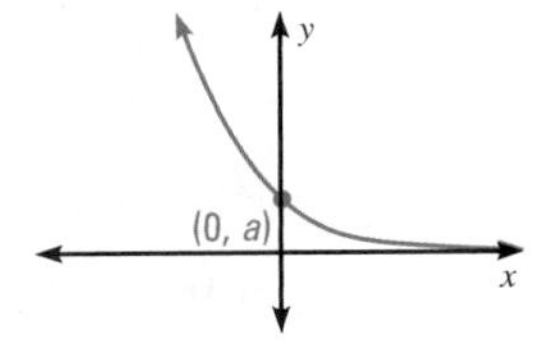

Differentiated Instruction

Visual Learners Have students include in their notebooks general sketches for the graphs of $y = ab^x$ for $a < 0$ and $b > 1$, and $y = ab^x$ for $a < 0$ and $0 < b < 1$. Students should note that even though the first graph is decreasing, it does not model exponential decay. Likewise, even though the second graph is increasing, it does not model exponential growth.

See also the *Algebra 1 Toolkit* for more strategies.

4.

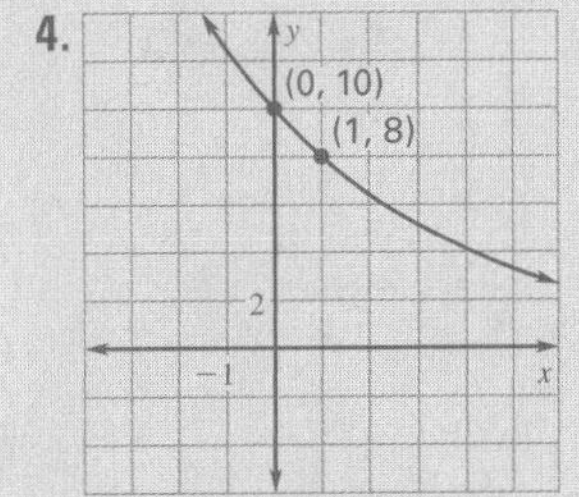

Extra Example 3

Graph the functions $y = 2 \cdot \left(\frac{1}{3}\right)^x$ and $y = -\frac{1}{2} \cdot \left(\frac{1}{3}\right)^x$. Compare each graph with the graph of $y = \left(\frac{1}{3}\right)^x$.

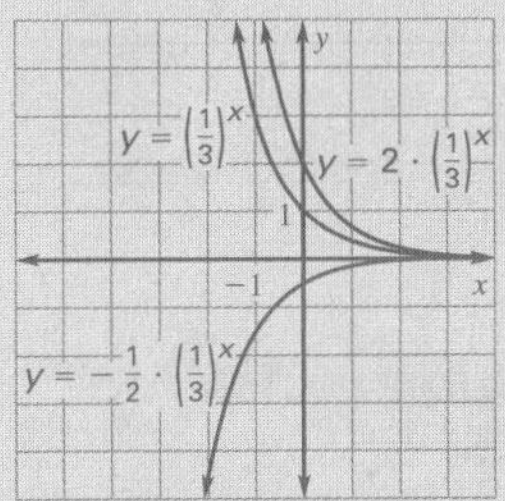

The graph of $y = 2 \cdot \left(\frac{1}{3}\right)^x$ is a vertical stretch of the graph of $y = \left(\frac{1}{3}\right)^x$. The graph of $y = -\frac{1}{2} \cdot \left(\frac{1}{3}\right)^x$ is a vertical shrink and reflection of the graph of $y = \left(\frac{1}{3}\right)^x$.

Key Question to Ask for Example 3

- Why is the graph of $y = 3 \cdot \left(\frac{1}{2}\right)^x$ a vertical stretch of the graph of $y = \left(\frac{1}{2}\right)^x$? **For given x-values, the y-values for $y = 3 \cdot \left(\frac{1}{2}\right)^x$ are 3 times as great as the y-values for $y = \left(\frac{1}{2}\right)^x$.**

Extra Example 4

Tell whether the graph represents exponential growth or exponential decay. Then write a rule for the function.

a.

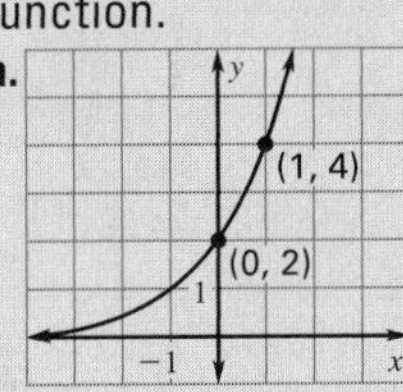

exponential growth; $y = 2(2)^x$

b.

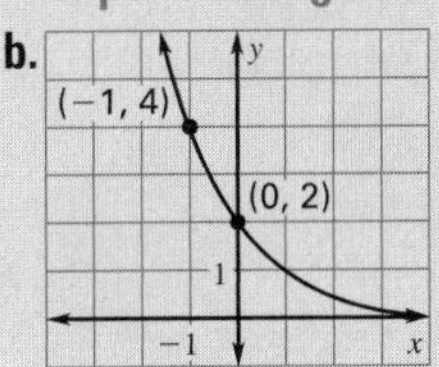

exponential decay; $y = 2(0.5)^x$

Extra Example 5

A farmer bought a tractor in 1999 for $30,000. The value of the tractor has been decreasing at a rate of 18% per year.

a. Write a function that models the value of the tractor over time. $V = 30{,}000(1 - 0.18)^t$

b. What was the approximate value of the tractor in 2005? about $9120

Key Question to Ask for Example 5

- Why do you subtract the decay rate from 1 in the exponential decay model? Because the acreage is decreasing, the decay factor is less than 1.

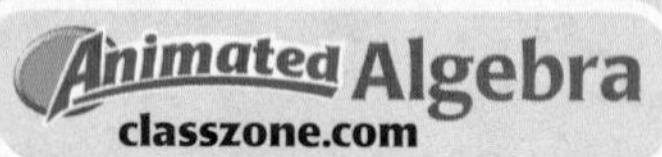

An **Animated Algebra** activity is available on-line for **Example 5**. This activity is also available on the **Power Presentations CD-ROM**.

Closing the Lesson

Have students summarize the major points of the lesson and answer the Essential Question: How do you write and graph exponential decay functions?

- The function $y = ab^x$ represents exponential decay when $a > 0$ and $0 < b < 1$.
- The exponential decay model is $y = a(1 - r)^t$, where a is the initial amount, $1 - r$ is the decay factor, and t is the time period.

To write a function rule, use the form $y = ab^x$. Substitute the y-intercept for a and then use another point from the table to solve the equation for b. To graph a function of the form $y = ab^x$, create a table of values, plot the points, and connect the points with a smooth curve.

EXPONENTIAL DECAY When a quantity decays exponentially, it decreases by the same percent over equal time periods. To find the amount of the quantity left after t time periods, use the following model.

REWRITE EQUATIONS
Notice that you can rewrite $y = ab^x$ as $y = a(1 - r)^t$ by replacing b with $1 - r$ and x with t (for time).

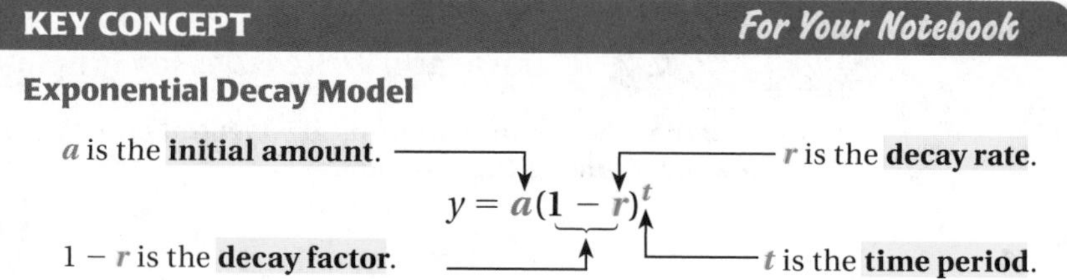

KEY CONCEPT *For Your Notebook*

Exponential Decay Model

a is the **initial amount**. r is the **decay rate**.

$$y = a(1 - r)^t$$

$1 - r$ is the **decay factor**. t is the **time period**.

The relationship between the decay rate r and the decay factor $1 - r$ is similar to the relationship between the growth rate and growth factor in an exponential growth model. You will explore this relationship in Exercise 45.

EXAMPLE 5 Solve a multi-step problem

FORESTRY The number of acres of Ponderosa pine forests decreased in the western United States from 1963 to 2002 by 0.5% annually. In 1963 there were about 41 million acres of Ponderosa pine forests.

a. Write a function that models the number of acres of Ponderosa pine forests in the western United States over time.

b. To the nearest tenth, about how many million acres of Ponderosa pine forests were there in 2002?

Solution

a. Let P be the number of acres (in millions), and let t be the time (in years) since 1963. The initial value is 41, and the decay rate is 0.005.

$P = a(1 - r)^t$ **Write exponential decay model.**

$= 41(1 - 0.005)^t$ **Substitute 41 for a and 0.005 for r.**

$= 41(0.995)^t$ **Simplify.**

AVOID ERRORS
The decay rate in this example is 0.5%, or 0.005. So, the decay factor is 1 − 0.005, or 0.995, not 0.005.

b. To find the number of acres in 2002, 39 years after 1963, substitute 39 for t.

$P = 41(0.995)^{39} \approx 33.7$ **Substitute 39 for t. Use a calculator.**

▶ There were about 33.7 million acres of Ponderosa pine forests in 2002.

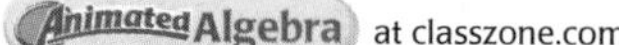

GUIDED PRACTICE for Example 5

5. WHAT IF? In Example 5, suppose the decay rate of the forests remains the same beyond 2002. About how many acres will be left in 2010? about 32.4 million

8.6 EXERCISES

HOMEWORK KEY
○ = **WORKED-OUT SOLUTIONS** on p. WS19 for Exs. 7 and 49
★ = **STANDARDIZED TEST PRACTICE** Exs. 2, 19, 36, 45, and 49
◆ = **MULTIPLE REPRESENTATIONS** Ex. 50

SKILL PRACTICE

A

1. **VOCABULARY** What is the decay factor in the exponential decay model $y = a(1 - r)^t$? $1 - r$

2. ★ **WRITING** *Explain* how you can tell if a graph represents *exponential growth* or *exponential decay.* See margin.

EXAMPLE 1 on p. 531 for Exs. 3–6

WRITING FUNCTIONS **Tell whether the table represents an exponential function. If so, write a rule for the function.**

3.

x	−1	0	1	2
y	2	8	32	128

exponential function; $y = 8 \cdot 4^x$

4.

x	−1	0	1	2
y	50	10	2	0.4

exponential function; $y = 10(0.2)^x$

5.

x	−1	0	1	2
y	6	2	$\frac{2}{3}$	$\frac{2}{9}$

exponential function; $y = 2\left(\frac{1}{3}\right)^x$

6.

x	−1	0	1	2
y	−11	−7	−3	1

not an exponential function

EXAMPLE 2 on p. 532 for Exs. 7–18

GRAPHING FUNCTIONS **Graph the function and identify its domain and range.** 7–18. See margin.

7. $y = \left(\frac{1}{5}\right)^x$ 8. $y = \left(\frac{1}{6}\right)^x$ 9. $y = \left(\frac{2}{3}\right)^x$ 10. $y = \left(\frac{3}{4}\right)^x$

11. $y = \left(\frac{4}{5}\right)^x$ 12. $y = \left(\frac{3}{5}\right)^x$ 13. $y = (0.3)^x$ 14. $y = (0.5)^x$

15. $y = (0.1)^x$ 16. $y = (0.9)^x$ 17. $y = (0.7)^x$ 18. $y = (0.25)^x$

EXAMPLE 3 on p. 532 for Exs. 19–31

19. ★ **MULTIPLE CHOICE** The graph of which function is shown? D

Ⓐ $y = (0.25)^x$ Ⓑ $y = (0.5)^x$

Ⓒ $y = 0.25 \cdot (0.5)^x$ Ⓓ $y = 4 \cdot (0.5)^x$

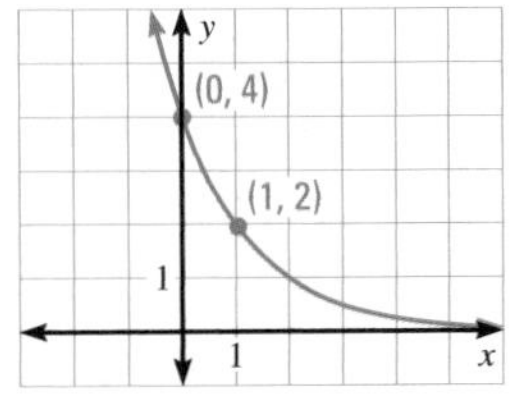

2. *Sample answer:* If the graph increases from left to right, then it represents growth; if it decreases from left to right, then it represents decay.

COMPARING FUNCTIONS **Graph the function. Compare the graph with the graph of $y = \left(\frac{1}{4}\right)^x$.** 20–31. See margin.

20. $y = 5 \cdot \left(\frac{1}{4}\right)^x$ 21. $y = 3 \cdot \left(\frac{1}{4}\right)^x$ 22. $y = \frac{1}{2} \cdot \left(\frac{1}{4}\right)^x$ 23. $y = \frac{1}{3} \cdot \left(\frac{1}{4}\right)^x$

24. $y = 0.2 \cdot \left(\frac{1}{4}\right)^x$ 25. $y = 1.5 \cdot \left(\frac{1}{4}\right)^x$ 26. $y = -5 \cdot \left(\frac{1}{4}\right)^x$ 27. $y = -3 \cdot \left(\frac{1}{4}\right)^x$

28. $y = -\frac{1}{2} \cdot \left(\frac{1}{4}\right)^x$ 29. $y = -\frac{1}{3} \cdot \left(\frac{1}{4}\right)^x$ 30. $y = -0.2 \cdot \left(\frac{1}{4}\right)^x$ 31. $y = -1.5 \cdot \left(\frac{1}{4}\right)^x$

4 PRACTICE AND APPLY

Assignment Guide

Answer Transparencies available for all exercises

Basic:
Day 1: pp. 535–538
Exs. 1–18, 63–66
Day 2: pp. 535–538
Exs. 19–35 odd, 36–40, 47–50, 54–62 even

Average:
Day 1: pp. 535–538
Exs. 1–6, 10–18, 32–34, 63–66
Day 2: pp. 535–538
Exs. 19, 20–30 even, 35–44, 47–52, 55, 58, 61

Advanced:
Day 1: pp. 535–538
Exs. 1, 4–6, 12–18, 32–37, 63–66
Day 2: pp. 535–538
Exs. 19, 24–31, 38–53*, 56, 59, 62

Block:
pp. 535–538
Exs. 1–6, 10–19, 20–30 even, 32–44, 47–52, 55, 58, 61, 63–66

Differentiated Instruction

See *Algebra 1 Best Practices Toolkit* for suggestions on addressing the needs of a diverse classroom.

Homework Check

For a quick check of student understanding of key concepts, go over the following exercises:

Basic: 4, 8, 21, 38, 47
Average: 5, 12, 24, 39, 48
Advanced: 6, 16, 28, 40, 49

Extra Practice

- Student Edition, p. 945
- Chapter 8 Resource Book: Practice levels A, B, C, pp. 66–71

Practice Worksheet

An easily-readable reduced practice page (with answers) for this lesson can be found on p. 486C.

7–18, 20–31. See Additional Answers beginning on p. AA1.

Avoiding Common Errors

Exercises 7–18 Some students' graphs may cross the x-axis. Remind these students that graphs of exponential functions get closer and closer to the x-axis, but do not cross it.

Exercises 20–31 Students may want to use their graphing calculators to compare the graphs. Remind them to use parentheses around the fractions and carets to indicate the exponent.

An **Animated Algebra** activity is available on-line for **Exercise 38**. This activity is also available on the **Power Presentations CD-ROM**.

35. initial amount: 90,000 people, decay factor: 0.975, decay rate: 2.5%; Let P represent the population and t represent the number of years. $P = 90{,}000(0.975)^t$

45. *Sample answer:* Since the quantity loses the same percent each time period, the amount y remaining after x time periods can be modeled using the exponential function $y = a(1 - r)^x$. After 1 time period, when x is 1, $y = a(1 - r)^1$, or $a(1 - r)$.

B **MATCHING** **Match the function with its graph.**

32. $y = (0.2)^x$ A

33. $y = 5(0.2)^x$ C

34. $y = \frac{1}{2}(0.2)^x$ B

A. 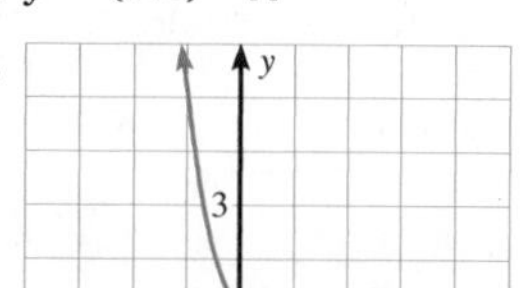

B. 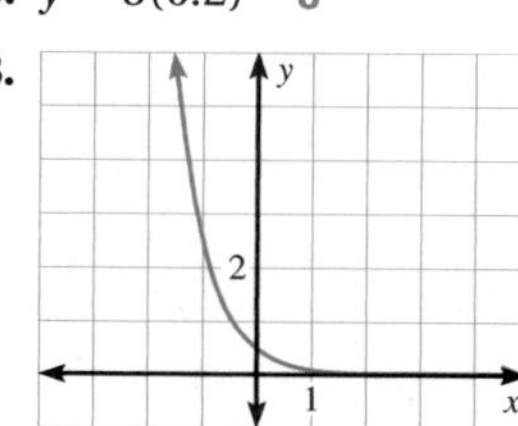

C. 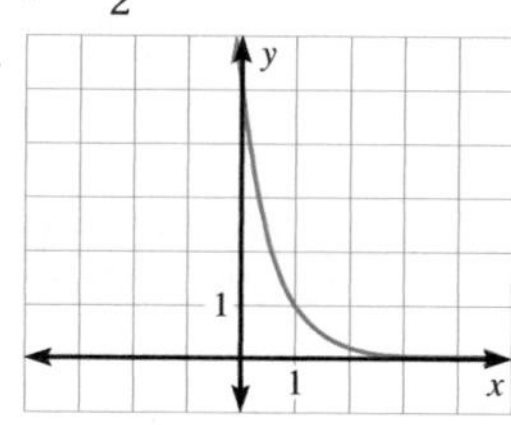

35. **POPULATION** A population of 90,000 decreases by 2.5% per year. Identify the initial amount, the decay factor, and the decay rate. Then write a function that models the population over time. See margin.

36. ★ **MULTIPLE CHOICE** What is the decay rate of the function $y = 4(0.97)^t$? D

(A) 4 (B) 0.97 (C) 0.3 (D) 0.03

37. The decay rate, r, is 0.14. So the decay factor $(1 - r)$ should be 0.86, not 0.14; $y = 25{,}000(0.86)^t$.

37. **ERROR ANALYSIS** In 2004 a person purchased a car for \$25,000. The value of the car decreased by 14% annually. *Describe* and correct the error in writing a function that models the value of the car since 2004.

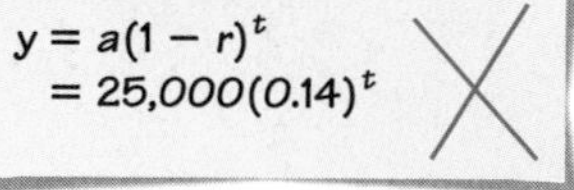

EXAMPLE 4 on p. 533 for Exs. 38–40

RECOGNIZING EXPONENTIAL MODELS **Tell whether the graph represents *exponential growth* or *exponential decay*. Then write a rule for the function.**

38. 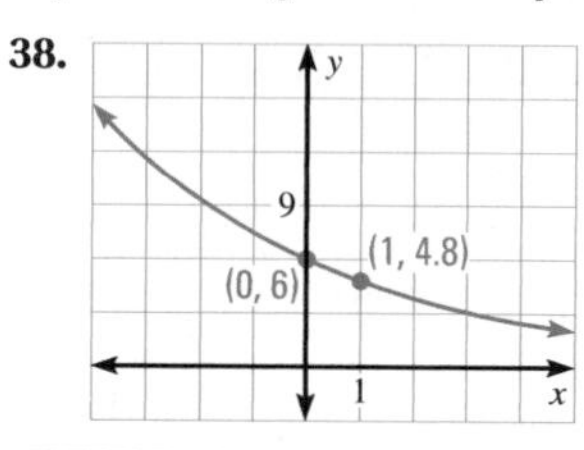

38. exponential decay; $y = 6 \cdot 0.8^x$

39. 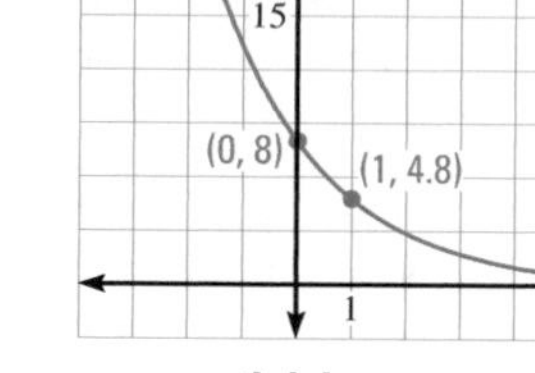

exponential decay; $y = 8 \cdot 0.6^x$

40. 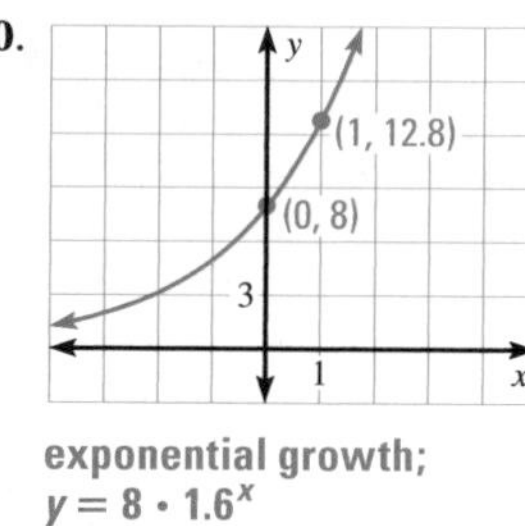

exponential growth; $y = 8 \cdot 1.6^x$

Animated Algebra at classzone.com

41. **REASONING** Without graphing, explain how the graphs of the given functions are related to the graph of $f(x) = (0.5)^x$.

a. $m(x) = \frac{1}{3} \cdot (0.5)^x$ The graph is a vertical shrink.

b. $n(x) = -4 \cdot (0.5)^x$

c. $p(x) = (0.5)^x + 1$

41b. The graph is a vertical stretch with a reflection in the x-axis.

41c. The graph is a vertical shift up 1 unit.

C **CHALLENGE** **Write an exponential function of the form $y = ab^x$ whose graph passes through the given points.**

42. $(0, 1), \left(2, \frac{1}{4}\right)$ $y = \left(\frac{1}{2}\right)^x$

43. $(1, 20), (2, 4)$ $y = 100 \cdot \left(\frac{1}{5}\right)^x$

44. $\left(1, \frac{3}{2}\right), \left(2, \frac{3}{4}\right)$ $y = 3 \cdot \left(\frac{1}{2}\right)^x$

45. ★ **WRITING** The initial amount of a quantity is a units and the quantity is decaying at a rate of r (a percent per time period). Show that the amount of the quantity after one time period is $a(1 - r)$. *Explain* how you found your answer. See margin.

46. *Sample answer:* The graphs are the same. By the product of powers property, $4^{x-2} = 4^x \cdot 4^{-2}$, or $\frac{1}{16} \cdot 4^x$.

46. **CHALLENGE** Compare the graph of the function $f(x) = 4^{x-2}$ with the graph of the function $g(x) = \frac{1}{16} \cdot 4^x$. Use properties of exponents to explain your observation.

○ = WORKED-OUT SOLUTIONS for on p. WS1 ★ = STANDARDIZED TEST PRACTICE

 = MULTIPLE REPRESENTATIONS

PROBLEM SOLVING

GRAPHING CALCULATOR You may wish to use a graphing calculator to complete the following Problem Solving exercises.

EXAMPLE 5 A on p. 534 for Exs. 47–50

47. CELL PHONES You purchase a cell phone for \$125. The value of the cell phone decreases by about 20% annually. Write a function that models the value of the cell phone over time. Then find the value of the cell phone after 3 years. Let V represent the value of the cell phone and t represent the number of years since purchase, $V = 125(0.8)^t$; \$64.

@HomeTutor for problem solving help at classzone.com

48a. initial amount: 141,200; decay factor: 0.89; decay rate: 11%

48b. Let B represent the number of bats and t represent the number of years since 1983, $B = 141{,}200(0.89)^t$; 13,729 bats.

48. ANIMAL POPULATION Scientists studied the population of a species of bat in some caves in Missouri from 1983 to 2003. In 1983, there were 141,200 bats living in the caves. That number decreased by about 11% annually until 2003.

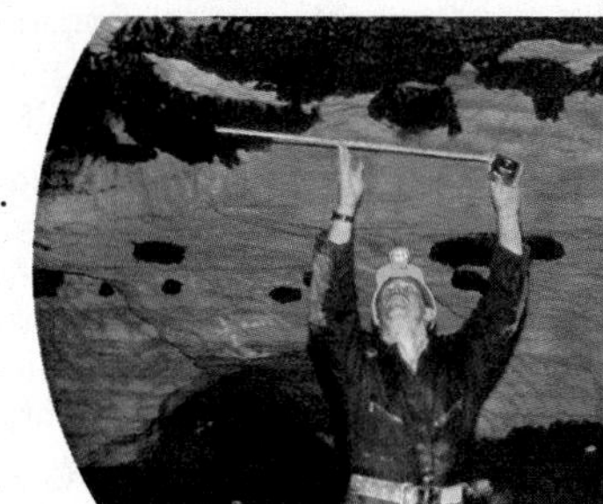

a. Identify the initial amount, the decay factor, and the decay rate.

b. Write a function that models the number of bats since 1983. Then find the number of bats in 2003.

@HomeTutor for problem solving help at classzone.com

49. ★ **SHORT RESPONSE** In 2003 a family bought a boat for \$4000. The boat depreciates (loses value) at a rate of 7% annually. In 2006 a person offers to buy the boat for \$3000. Should the family sell the boat? *Explain.* No. *Sample answer:* The boat's value is about \$3217.

50. MULTIPLE REPRESENTATIONS There are a total of 128 teams at the start of a citywide 3-on-3 basketball tournament. Half of the teams are eliminated after each round.

a. **Writing a Model** Write a function for the number of teams left after x rounds. $f(x) = 128(0.5)^x$

b. **Making a Table** Make a table for the function using $x = 0, 1, 2, \ldots, 7$. See margin.

c. **Drawing a Graph** Use the table in part (b) to graph the function. After which round are there 4 teams left in the tournament? See margin for art; round 5.

B **51. GUITARS** The frets on a guitar are the small metal bars that divide the fingerboard. The distance d (in inches) between the nut and the first fret or any two consecutive frets can be modeled by the function $d = 1.516(0.9439)^f$ where f is the number of the fret farthest from the nut.

51a. decay factor: 0.9439, decay rate: 5.61%

a. Identify the decay factor and the decay rate for the model.

b. What is the distance between the nut and the first fret? about 1.431 in.

c. The distance between the 12th and 13th frets is about half the distance between the nut and the first fret. Use this fact to find the distance between the 12th and 13th frets. Use the model to verify your answer. about 0.716 in.

Study Strategy

Exercise 48 Suggest that students use the exponential decay model on page 534 to check their solutions to parts (a) and (b).

Vocabulary

Exercise 49 You may want to ask a student to use a dictionary or thesaurus to define the word *depreciate*. Have the student look up the word *appreciate* as an antonym to depreciate. Then ask them to discuss the relationship of these terms to exponential functions.

Internet Reference

Exercise 53 More information about maximal oxygen consumption can be found at www.nismat.org/physcor/max_o2.html

50b.

Rounds completed	Teams remaining
0	128
1	64
2	32
3	16
4	8
5	4
6	2
7	1

50c.

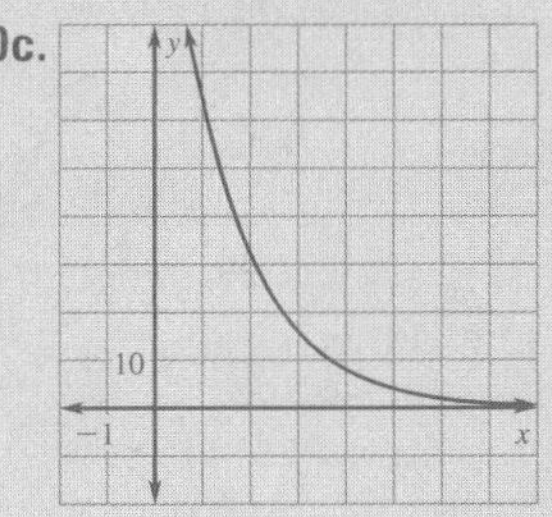

5 ASSESS AND RETEACH

Daily Homework Quiz

Transparency Available

1. Graph $y = \left(\frac{1}{3}\right)^x$.

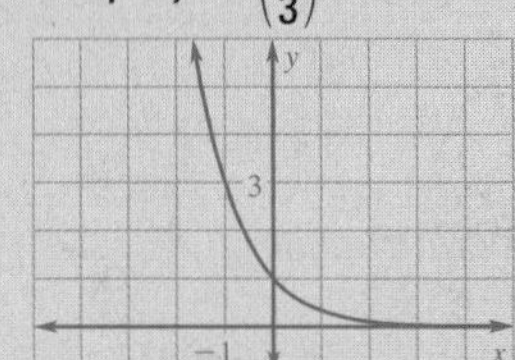

2. The population in a town has been declining at a rate of 2% per year since 2001. The population was 84,223 in 2001. What was the population in 2006? about 76,130

Available at **classzone.com**

Diagnosis/Remediation

- Practice A, B, C in Chapter 8 Resource Book, pp. 66–71
- Study Guide in Chapter 8 Resource Book, pp. 72–73
- Practice Workbook, pp. 130–132
- @HomeTutor

Challenge

Additional challenge is available in the Chapter 8 Resource Book, p. 76.

Quiz

An easily-readable reduced copy of the quiz (with answers) on Lessons 8.5–8.6 from the Assessment Book can be found on p. 486E.

53b.

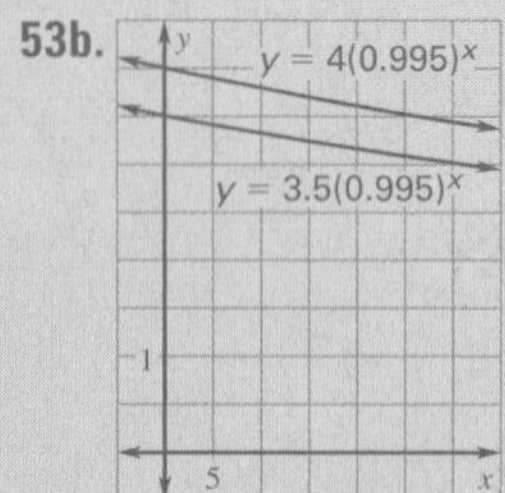

Quiz 1–6. See Additional Answers beginning on p. AA1.

52. CHALLENGE A college student finances a computer that costs \$1850. The financing plan states that as long as a minimum monthly payment of 2.25% of the remaining balance is made, the student does not have to pay interest for 24 months. The student makes only the minimum monthly payments until the last payment. What is the amount of the last payment if the student buys the computer without paying interest? Round your answer to the nearest cent. **\$1096.12**

C **53. MULTI-STEP PROBLEM** Maximal oxygen consumption is the maximum volume of oxygen (in liters per minute) that the body uses during exercise. Maximal oxygen consumption varies from person to person and decreases with age by about 0.5% per year after age 25 for active adults.

a. **Model** A 25-year-old female athlete has a maximal oxygen consumption of 4 liters per minute. Another 25-year-old female athlete has a maximal oxygen consumption of 3.5 liters per minute. Write a function for each athlete that models the maximal consumption each year after age 25. $y = 4(0.995)^x$, $y = 3.5(0.995)^x$

b. **Graph** Graph the models in the same coordinate plane. See margin.

c. **Estimate** About how old will the first athlete be when her maximal oxygen consumption is equal to what the second athlete's maximal oxygen consumption is at age 25? **about 52 yr**

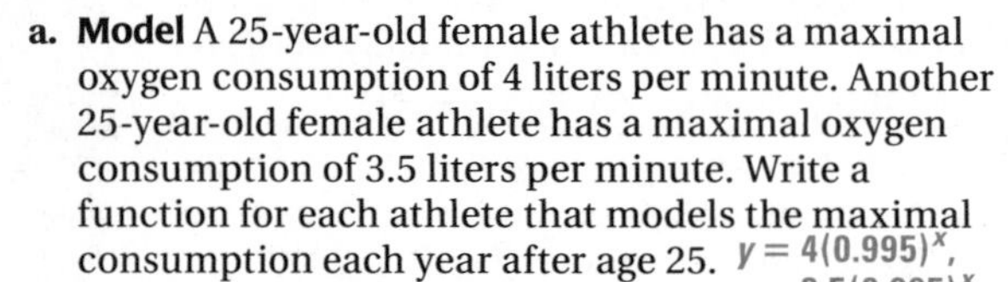

ILLINOIS MIXED REVIEW

TEST PRACTICE at classzone.com

54. On a certain day, a pound of apples costs $\frac{3}{4}$ the price of a pound of oranges. If you have enough money to buy 12 pounds of apples, how many pounds of oranges can you buy? **B**

Ⓐ 8 Ⓑ 9 Ⓒ 15 Ⓓ 16

55. A cylindrical container has a volume of 100 cubic centimeters. If the container is dilated by a scale factor of 3, what is the volume of the resulting container? **D**

Ⓐ 300 cm³ Ⓑ 900 cm³ Ⓒ 10,000 cm³ Ⓓ Not here

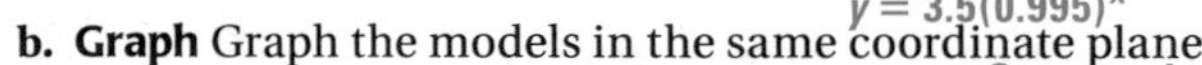

QUIZ for Lessons 8.5–8.6

Graph the function. 1–6. See margin.

1. $y = \left(\frac{5}{2}\right)^x$ *(p. 520)*
2. $y = 3 \cdot \left(\frac{1}{4}\right)^x$ *(p. 531)*
3. $y = \frac{1}{4} \cdot 3^x$ *(p. 520)*
4. $y = (0.1)^x$ *(p. 531)*
5. $y = 10 \cdot 5^x$ *(p. 520)*
6. $y = 7(0.4)^x$ *(p. 531)*

7. **COINS** You purchase a coin from a coin collector for \$25. Each year the value of the coin increases by 8%. Write a function that models the value of the coin over time. Then find the value of the coin after 10 years. Round to the nearest cent. *(p. 520)*

7. Let V represent the value of the coin and t represent the number of years since purchase, $V = 25(1.08)^t$; about \$53.97.

EXTRA PRACTICE for Lesson 8.6, p. 945

ONLINE QUIZ at classzone.com

Extension

Use after Lesson 8.6

Relate Geometric Sequences to Exponential Functions

GOAL Identify, graph, and write geometric sequences.

Key Vocabulary
- **geometric sequence**
- **common ratio**

In a **geometric sequence**, the ratio of any term to the previous term is constant. This constant ratio is called the **common ratio** and is denoted by r.

A geometric sequence with first term a_1 and common ratio r has the form a_1, $a_1r, a_1r^2, a_1r^3, \ldots$. For instance, if $a_1 = 5$ and $r = 2$, the sequence $5, 5 \cdot 2, 5 \cdot 2^2, 5 \cdot 2^3, \ldots$, or 5, 10, 20, 40, . . . , is geometric.

EXAMPLE 1 Identify a geometric sequence

Tell whether the sequence is *arithmetic* or *geometric*. Then write the next term of the sequence.

a. 3, 6, 9, 12, 15, . . . **b.** 128, 64, 32, 16, 8, . . .

Solution

a. The first term is $a_1 = 3$. Find the ratios of consecutive terms:

$$\frac{a_2}{a_1} = \frac{6}{3} = 2 \qquad \frac{a_3}{a_2} = \frac{9}{6} = 1\frac{1}{2} \qquad \frac{a_4}{a_3} = \frac{12}{9} = 1\frac{1}{3} \qquad \frac{a_5}{a_4} = \frac{15}{12} = 1\frac{1}{4}$$

Because the ratios are not constant, the sequence is not geometric. To see if the sequence is arithmetic, find the differences of consecutive terms.

REVIEW ARITHMETIC SEQUENCES
For help with identifying an arithmetic sequence and finding a common difference, see p. 309.

$$a_2 - a_1 = 6 - 3 = 3 \qquad a_3 - a_2 = 9 - 6 = 3$$

$$a_4 - a_3 = 12 - 9 = 3 \qquad a_5 - a_4 = 15 - 12 = 3$$

The common difference is 3, so the sequence is arithmetic. The next term of the sequence is $a_6 = a_5 + 3 = 18$.

b. The first term is $a_1 = 128$. Find the ratios of consecutive terms:

$$\frac{a_2}{a_1} = \frac{64}{128} = \frac{1}{2} \qquad \frac{a_3}{a_2} = \frac{32}{64} = \frac{1}{2} \qquad \frac{a_4}{a_3} = \frac{16}{32} = \frac{1}{2} \qquad \frac{a_5}{a_4} = \frac{8}{16} = \frac{1}{2}$$

Because the ratios are constant, the sequence is geometric. The common ratio is $\frac{1}{2}$. The next term of the sequence is $a_6 = a_5 \cdot \frac{1}{2} = 4$.

EXAMPLE 2 Graph a geometric sequence

ANALYZE A GRAPH
Notice that the graph in Example 2 appears to be exponential.

To graph the sequence from part (b) of Example 1, let each term's position number in the sequence be the x-value. The term is the corresponding y-value. Then make and plot the points.

Position, x	1	2	3	4	5
Term, y	128	64	32	16	8

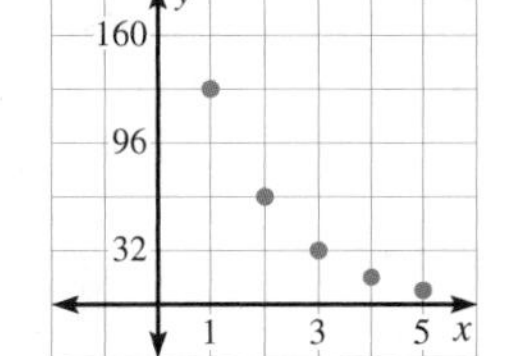

1 PLAN AND PREPARE

Warm-Up Exercises

1. Write the next term in the pattern 1, 2, 4, 7, 11, ... 16
2. Bill earns $16 in 2 hours, $32 in 4 hours, and $48 in 6 hours. What does he earn in 12 hours? $96

2 FOCUS AND MOTIVATE

Essential Question

Big Idea 3, p. 487

How do you identify and write geometric sequences? **Tell students they will learn how to answer this question by examining patterns and writing rules.**

3 TEACH

Extra Example 1

Tell whether the sequence is *arithmetic* or *geometric*. Then write the next term of the sequence.

a. 81, 77, 73, 69, 65, . . . **arithmetic; 61**

b. 3, 6, 12, 24, 48, . . . **geometric; 96**

Extra Example 2

Graph the geometric sequence from part b of Extra Example 1.

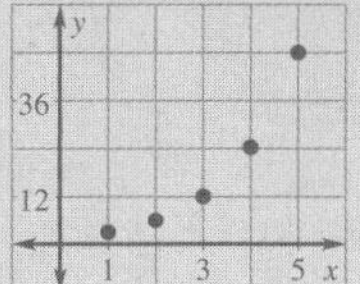

NCTM STANDARDS

Standard 2: Analyze situations using algebraic symbols

Standard 9: Grasp how mathematical ideas interconnect

Extra Example 3

Write a rule for the nth term of the geometric sequence in Extra Example 1. Then find a_{10}.
$a_n = 3 \cdot 2^{n-1}$; $a_{10} = 1536$

Key Question to Ask for Example 3

- Can you substitute any term in the sequence for a_1? Explain. **No; the correct terms would not be generated if a term other than a_1 were substituted.**

Closing the Lesson

Have students summarize the major points of the lesson and answer the Essential Question: How do you identify and write geometric sequences?

- **In a geometric sequence, the ratio of any term to the previous term is constant.**
- **To find the nth term of a geometric sequence, use the general rule $a_n = a_1 r^{n-1}$.**

To identify a geometric sequence, find the ratios of consecutive terms. If the ratios are constant, the sequence is geometric. Use the general rule for a geometric sequence to write a specific rule by substituting the first term in the sequence for a_1 and the ratio for r. Substitute the position in the sequence for n to find the nth term.

4 PRACTICE AND APPLY

Avoiding Common Errors

Exercises 1–6 Some students may only look for a common difference between terms of a sequence and fail to see that a sequence is geometric. Remind students to check the ratios of consecutive terms and then determine if the ratios are constant.

1–6. See Additional Answers beginning on p. AA1.

FUNCTIONS The table shows that a rule for finding the nth term of a geometric sequence is $a_n = a_1r^{n-1}$. Notice that the rule is an exponential function.

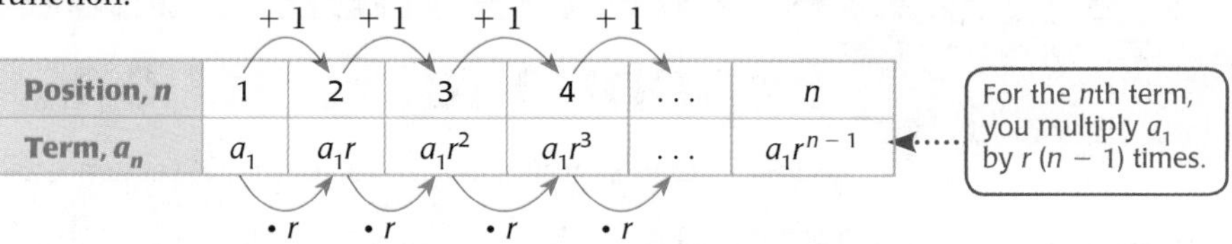

Position, n	1	2	3	4	...	n
Term, a_n	a_1	a_1r	a_1r^2	a_1r^3	...	a_1r^{n-1}

KEY CONCEPT — *For Your Notebook*

General Rule for a Geometric Sequence

The nth term of a geometric sequence with first term a_1 and common ratio r is given by: $a_n = a_1r^{n-1}$.

EXAMPLE 3 Write a rule for a geometric sequence

Write a rule for the nth term of the geometric sequence in Example 1. Then find a_{10}.

Solution

To write a rule for the nth term of the sequence, substitute the values for a_1 and r in the general rule $a_n = a_1r^{n-1}$. Because $a_1 = 128$ and $r = \frac{1}{2}$, $a_n = 128 \cdot \left(\frac{1}{2}\right)^{n-1}$. The 10th term of the sequence is $a_{10} = 128 \cdot \left(\frac{1}{2}\right)^{10-1} = \frac{1}{4}$.

PRACTICE

EXAMPLES 1, 2, and 3 on pp. 539–540 for Exs. 1–10

Tell whether the sequence is *arithmetic* or *geometric*. Then graph the sequence. **1–6. See margin for art.**

1. 3, 12, 48, 192, . . . **geometric**
2. 7, 16, 25, 34, . . . **arithmetic**
3. 34, 28, 22, 16, . . . **arithmetic**
4. 1024, 128, 16, 2, . . . **geometric**
5. 9, −18, 36, −72, . . . **geometric**
6. 29, 43, 57, 71, . . . **arithmetic**

Write a rule for the nth term of the geometric sequence. Then find a_7.

7. 1, −5, 25, −125, . . . **$a_n = (-5)^{n-1}$; 15,625**
8. 13, 26, 52, 104, . . . **$a_n = 13 \cdot 2^{n-1}$; 832**
9. 432, 72, 12, 2, . . . **$a_n = 432\left(\frac{1}{6}\right)^{n-1}$; $\frac{1}{108}$**
10. **E-MAIL** A chain e-mail instructs the recipient to forward the e-mail to four more people. The table shows the number of rounds of sending the e-mail and the number of new e-mails generated. Write a rule for the nth term of the sequence. Then graph the first six terms of the sequence. **$a_n = 4^{n-1}$; see margin for art.**

Number of rounds sending e-mail, n	1	2	3	4
Number of new e-mails generated, a_n	1	4	16	64

10.

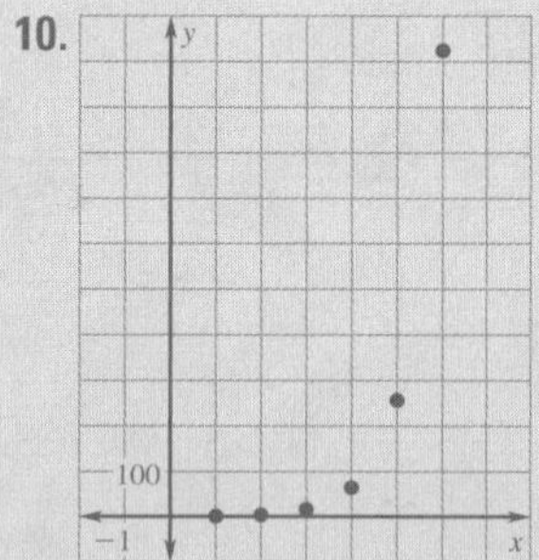

Illinois *Mixed Review*

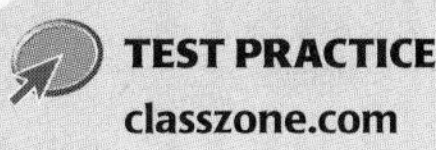

Lessons 8.4–8.6

1. **EARTH** The radius of Earth is about 6370 kilometers. The surface area S of a sphere with radius r is given by $S = 4\pi r^2$. If you assume that Earth is a perfect sphere, which of the following is the surface area of Earth?

 A. $5.10 \times 10^4\ \text{km}^2$

 B. $5.10 \times 10^5\ \text{km}^2$

 C. $5.10 \times 10^6\ \text{km}^2$

 D. $5.10 \times 10^8\ \text{km}^2$

2. **BUSINESS** The graph of the exponential growth function shows the value of a business over time.

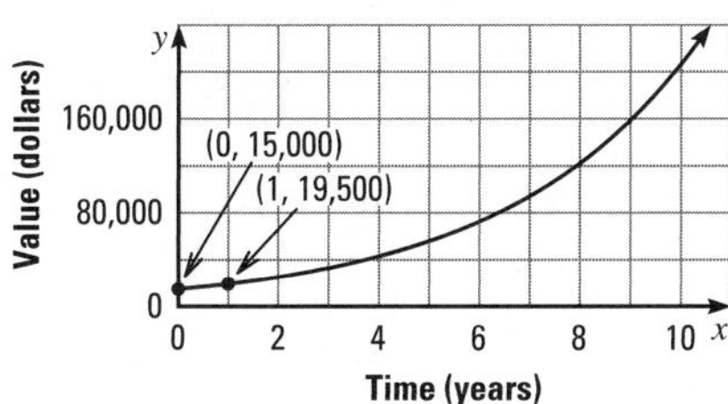

 Which of the following equations models the value v (in dollars) of the business over time t (in years)?

 F. $v = 15{,}000(1.30)^t$

 G. $v = 15{,}000(0.70)^t$

 H. $v = 15{,}000(0.50)^t$

 J. $v = 15{,}000(0.30)^t$

3. **CHEMISTRY** Avogadro's number is a number chemists use to describe quantities of atoms. Avogadro's number is defined as the number of atoms in exactly 12 grams of carbon, or 6.022×10^{23}. Divide 12 grams by Avogadro's number to find the mass (in grams) of a single carbon atom.

 A. 1.993×10^{-24}

 B. 5.018×10^{-24}

 C. 1.993×10^{-23}

 D. 5.018×10^{-22}

4. **TRUCK** The exponential decay graph shows the value of a truck over time.

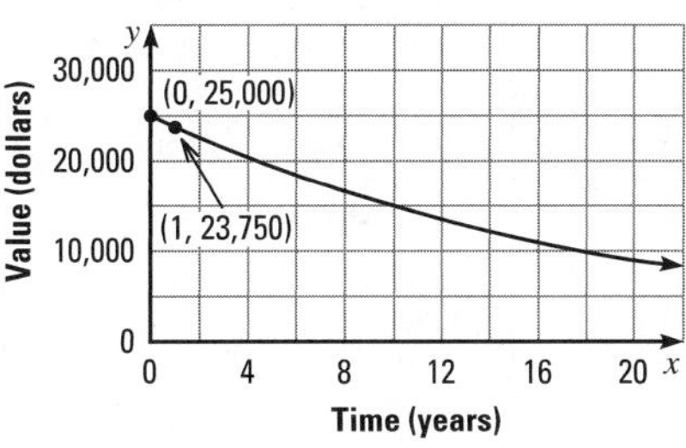

 How is the value changing?

 F. Decreasing by 5% each year

 G. Decreasing by \$1250 each year

 H. Decreasing by 95% each year

 J. Decreasing by \$2250 each year

5. **SAVINGS** An employee earns \$35,000 one year. She deposits 10% of the money into a savings account that earns 4% annual interest compounded yearly. After 2 years, how much more money does she have than if she had not put her money into the account?

 A. \$280   **C.** \$3780

 B. \$285.60   **D.** \$3785.60

6. **MEDICINE** The half-life of a medication is the time it takes for the medication to reduce to half of its original amount in a patient's bloodstream. A certain antibiotic has a half-life of about 8 hours. A patient is administered 500 milligrams of the antibiotic. How much of the dose will be in the patient's bloodstream after 24 hours?

 F. 0 mg   **H.** 75 mg

 G. 62.5 mg   **J.** 125 mg

7. **LAPTOP** A new laptop costs \$2000. The value of the laptop decreases over time. A model for the value v (in dollars) of the laptop after t years is given by $v = 2000(0.90)^t$. What is the decay rate (as an annual percent in decimal form) of the value of the laptop?

 A. 10%   **C.** 70%

 B. 50%   **D.** 90%

Illinois Mixed Review

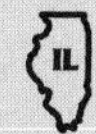

1. D
2. F
3. C
4. F
5. B
6. G
7. A

8 CHAPTER SUMMARY

Additional Resources

The following resources are available to help review the materials in this chapter.

Chapter 8 Resource Book

- Chapter Review Games and Activities, p. 77
- Cumulative Practice, Chs. 1–8, pp. 80–81

Student Resources in Spanish

eWorkbook

@HomeTutor

Vocabulary Practice

Vocabulary practice is available at **classzone.com**

BIG IDEAS

For Your Notebook

Big Idea 1

Applying Properties of Exponents to Simplify Expressions

You can use the properties of exponents to simplify expressions. For the properties listed below, a and b are real numbers, and m and n are integers.

Expression	Property
$a^m \cdot a^n = a^{m+n}$	**Product of powers property**
$(a^m)^n = a^{mn}$	**Power of a power property**
$(ab)^m = a^m b^m$	**Power of a product property**
$\frac{a^m}{a^n} = a^{m-n}, a \neq 0$	**Quotient of powers property**
$\left(\frac{a}{b}\right)^m = \frac{a^m}{b^m}, b \neq 0$	**Power of a quotient property**

Big Idea 2

Working with Numbers in Scientific Notation

You can write numbers in scientific notation.

Number	Standard form	Scientific notation
Four billion	4,000,000,000	4×10^9
Thirty-two thousandths	0.032	3.2×10^{-2}

You can also compute with numbers in scientific notation. For example:

$$(4 \times 10^9) \times (3.2 \times 10^{-2}) = 12.8 \times 10^7 = 1.28 \times 10^8, \text{ or } 128{,}000{,}000$$

Big Idea 3

Writing and Graphing Exponential Functions

You can write and graph exponential growth and decay functions. You can also model real-world situations involving exponential growth and exponential decay.

Exponential growth	Exponential decay
Function $y = ab^x, a > 0$ and $b > 1$	**Function** $y = ab^x, a > 0$ and $0 < b < 1$
Graph y, (0, a), x	**Graph** y, (0, a), x
Model $y = a(1 + r)^t$	**Model** $y = a(1 - r)^t$

8 CHAPTER REVIEW

@HomeTutor
classzone.com
• Multi-Language Glossary
• Vocabulary practice

REVIEW KEY VOCABULARY

- order of magnitude, *p. 491*
- zero exponent, *p. 503*
- negative exponent, *p. 503*
- scientific notation, *p. 512*
- exponential function, *p. 520*
- exponential growth, *p. 522*
- growth factor, growth rate, *p. 522*
- compound interest, *p. 523*
- exponential decay, *p. 533*
- decay factor, decay rate, *p. 534*

VOCABULARY EXERCISES

1. Copy and complete: The function $y = 1200(0.3)^t$ is an exponential _?_ function, and the base 0.3 is called the _?_. decay, decay factor

2. **WRITING** *Explain* how you can tell whether a table represents a linear function or an exponential function. See margin.

Tell whether the function represents exponential growth or exponential decay. *Explain.* 3–5. See margin.

3. $y = 3(0.85)^x$
4. $y = \frac{1}{2}(1.01)^x$
5. $y = 2(2.1)^x$

REVIEW EXAMPLES AND EXERCISES

Use the review examples and exercises below to check your understanding of the concepts you have learned in each lesson of Chapter 8.

8.1 Apply Exponent Properties Involving Products *pp. 489–494*

EXAMPLE

Simplify $(3y^3)^4 \cdot y^5$.

$(3y^3)^4 \cdot y^5 = 3^4 \cdot (y^3)^4 \cdot y^5$ **Power of a product property**

$= 81 \cdot y^{12} \cdot y^5$ **Power of a power property**

$= 81y^{17}$ **Product of powers property**

EXERCISES

EXAMPLES 1, 2, 3, 4, and 5 on pp. 489–491 for Exs. 6–15

Simplify the expression.

6. $4^4 \cdot 4^3$ 4^7
7. $(-3)^7(-3)$ $(-3)^8$
8. $z^3 \cdot z^5 \cdot z^5$ z^{13}
9. $(y^4)^5$ y^{20}
10. $[(-7)^4]^4$ $(-7)^{16}$
11. $[(b+2)^8]^3$ $(b+2)^{24}$
12. $(6^4 \cdot 31)^5$ $6^{20} \cdot 31^5$
13. $-(8xy)^2$ $-64x^2y^2$
14. $(2x^2)^4 \cdot x^5$ $16x^{13}$

15. **EARTH SCIENCE** The order of magnitude of the mass of Earth's atmosphere is 10^{18} kilograms. The order of magnitude of the mass of Earth's oceans is 10^3 times greater. What is the order of magnitude of the mass of Earth's oceans? 10^{21}

Extra Example 8.1
Simplify $[(d+4)^3]^2$. $(d+4)^6$

2. *Sample answer:* If the difference of each pair of successive terms is constant, the table represents a linear function. If the ratio of each pair of successive terms is constant, the table represents an exponential function.

3. Exponential decay; $b = 0.85$ which is between 0 and 1, therefore it is exponential decay.

4. Exponential growth; $b = 1.01$ which is greater than 1, therefore it is exponential growth.

5. Exponential growth; $b = 2.1$ which is greater than 1, therefore it is exponential growth.

8 CHAPTER REVIEW

Extra Example 8.2

Simplify $\left(\frac{2y^3}{z}\right)^5 \cdot \frac{1}{y^2}$. $\frac{32y^{13}}{z^5}$

Extra Example 8.3

Evaluate $(4x^{-4}y^0)^{-2}$. $\frac{x^8}{16}$

8.2 Apply Exponent Properties Involving Quotients

pp. 495–501

EXAMPLE

Simplify $\left(\frac{x^3}{y}\right)^4 \cdot \frac{2}{x^5}$.

$\left(\frac{x^3}{y}\right)^4 \cdot \frac{2}{x^5} = \frac{(x^3)^4}{y^4} \cdot \frac{2}{x^5}$ — Power of a quotient property

$= \frac{x^{12}}{y^4} \cdot \frac{2}{x^5}$ — Power of a power property

$= \frac{2x^{12}}{y^4x^5}$ — Multiply fractions.

$= \frac{2x^7}{y^4}$ — Quotient of powers property

EXERCISES

EXAMPLES 1, 2, and 3 on pp. 495–496 for Exs. 16–24

Simplify the expression.

16. $\frac{(-3)^7}{(-3)^3}$ $(-3)^4$

17. $\frac{5^2 \cdot 5^4}{5^3}$ 5^3

18. $\left(\frac{m}{n}\right)^3$ $\frac{m^3}{n^3}$

19. $\frac{17^{12}}{17^8}$ 17^4

20. $\left(-\frac{1}{x}\right)^4$ $\frac{1}{x^4}$

21. $\left(\frac{7x^5}{y^2}\right)^2$ $\frac{49x^{10}}{y^4}$

22. $\frac{1}{p^2} \cdot p^6$ p^4

23. $\frac{6}{7r^{10}} \cdot \left(\frac{r^5}{s}\right)^5$ $\frac{6r^{15}}{7s^5}$

24. PER CAPITA INCOME The order of magnitude of the population of Montana in 2003 was 10^6 people. The order of magnitude of the total personal income (in dollars) for Montana in 2003 was 10^{10}. What was the order of magnitude of the mean personal income in Montana in 2003? 10^4

8.3 Define and Use Zero and Negative Exponents

pp. 503–508

EXAMPLE

Evaluate $(2x^0y^{-5})^3$.

$(2x^0y^{-5})^3 = 2^3 \cdot x^0 \cdot y^{-15}$ — Power of a power property

$= 8 \cdot 1 \cdot y^{-15}$ — Definition of zero exponent

$= \frac{8}{y^{15}}$ — Definition of negative exponents

EXERCISES

EXAMPLES 1, 2, and 4 on pp. 503–505 for Exs. 25–29

Evaluate the expression.

25. 14^0 1

26. 3^{-4} $\frac{1}{81}$

27. $\left(\frac{2}{3}\right)^{-3}$ $\frac{27}{8}$

28. $7^{-5} \cdot 7^5$ 1

29. UNITS OF MEASURE Use the fact that 1 femtogram = 10^{-18} kilogram and 1 nanogram = 10^{-12} kilogram to complete the following statement: 1 nanogram = ? femtogram(s). 10^6

@HomeTutor
classzone.com
Chapter Review Practice

8.4 Use Scientific Notation *pp. 512–518*

EXAMPLE

Write the number in scientific notation.

a. $2097 = 2.097 \times 10^3$ — **Move decimal point left 3 places. Exponent is 3.**

b. $0.00032 = 3.2 \times 10^{-4}$ — **Move decimal point right 4 places. Exponent is −4.**

Write the number in standard form.

a. $4.3201 \times 10^2 = 432.01$ — **Exponent is 2. Move decimal point right 2 places.**

b. $2.068 \times 10^{-3} = 0.002068$ — **Exponent is −3. Move decimal point left 3 places.**

EXERCISES

EXAMPLES 1, 2, 4, and 5 on pp. 512–514 for Exs. 30–34

30. Write 78,120 in scientific notation. 7.812×10^4

31. Write 7.5×10^{-5} in standard form. 0.000075

Evaluate the expression. Write your answer in scientific notation.

32. $(6.3 \times 10^3)(1.9 \times 10^{-5})$ 1.197×10^{-1}

33. $\frac{6.5 \times 10^9}{1.6 \times 10^{-4}}$ 4.0625×10^{13}

34. MASS The mass m_1 of a gate of the Thames Barrier in London is about 1.5×10^6 kilograms. The mass m_2 of the Great Pyramid of Giza is about 6×10^9 kilograms. Find the ratio of m_1 to m_2. What does the ratio tell you?
2.5×10^{-4}; the mass of the gate is 0.00025 or $\frac{1}{4000}$ the mass of the pyramid.

8.5 Write and Graph Exponential Growth Functions *pp. 520–527*

EXAMPLE

Graph the function $y = 4^x$ and identify its domain and range.

STEP 1 **Make** a table. The domain is all real numbers.

x	−1	0	1	2
y	$\frac{1}{4}$	1	4	16

STEP 2 **Plot** the points.

STEP 3 **Draw** a smooth curve through the points.

STEP 4 **Identify** the range. As you can see from the graph, the range is all positive real numbers.

EXERCISES

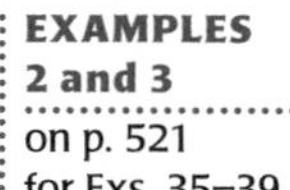
EXAMPLES 2 and 3 on p. 521 for Exs. 35–39

Graph the function and identify its domain and range. 35–38. See margin.

35. $y = 6^x$

36. $y = (1.1)^x$

37. $y = (3.5)^x$

38. $y = \left(\frac{5}{2}\right)^x$

39. Graph the function $y = -5 \cdot 2^x$. Compare the graph with the graph of $y = 2^x$. See margin.

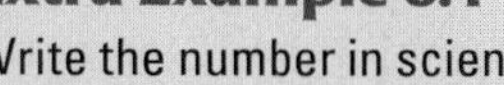
Extra Example 8.4

Write the number in scientific notation.

a. 463,250 4.6325×10^5

b. 0.3457 3.457×10^{-1}

Write the number in standard form.

a. 5.23×10^4 52,300

b. 9.021×10^{-6} 0.000009021

Extra Example 8.5

Graph the function $y = \left(\frac{5}{2}\right)^x$ and identify its domain and range.

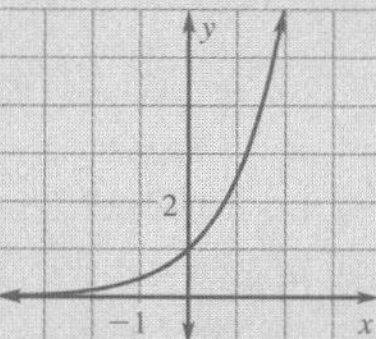

domain: all real numbers; range: all positive real numbers

38.

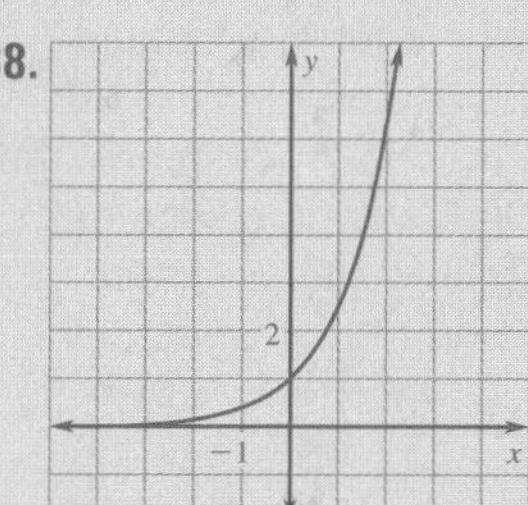

domain: all real numbers, range: all positive real numbers

39.

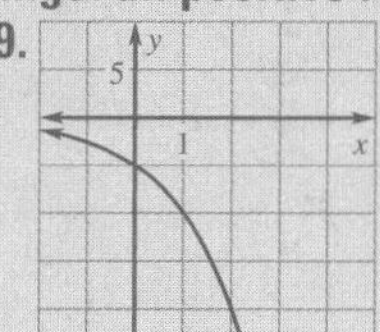

The graph is a vertical stretch with a reflection in the x-axis.

35.

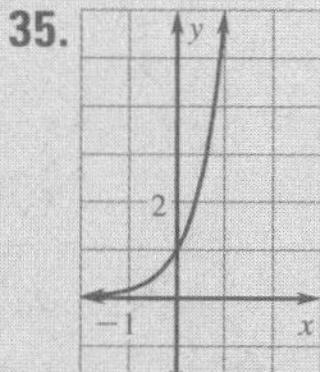
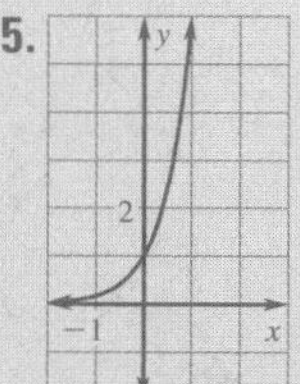

domain: all real numbers, range: all positive real numbers

36.

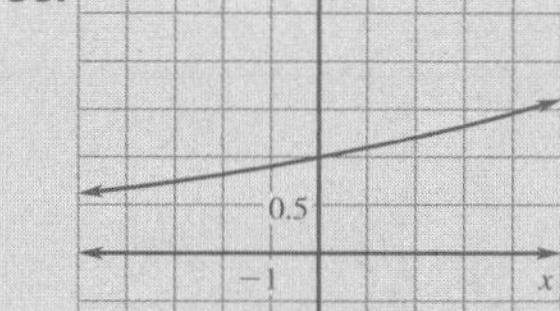

domain: all real numbers, range: all positive real numbers

37.

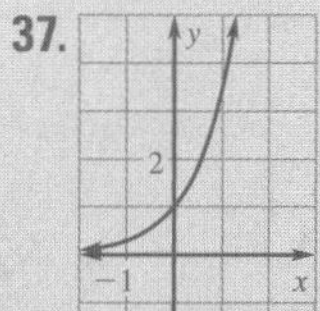

domain: all real numbers, range: all positive real numbers

8 CHAPTER REVIEW

Extra Examples 8.6

1. Tell whether the graph represents exponential growth or exponential decay. Then write a rule for the function.

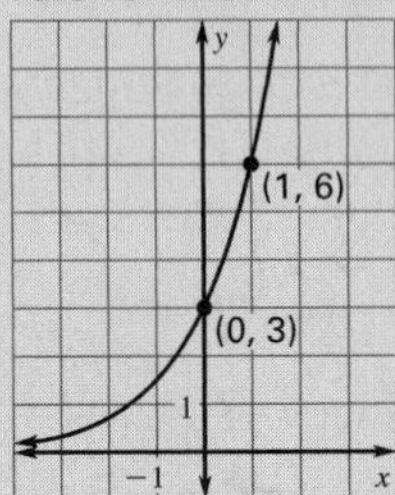

The graph represents exponential growth. A function rule is $y = 3(2)^x$.

2. A high school issued a report that enrollment in physical education classes at their school has been declining at a rate of 6% per year since 1984. For all grades at the high school, enrollment in physical education classes was 2864 in 1984. Write a function that models the enrollment over time. Find the approximate number of students enrolled in physical education in 2006. $y = 2864(1 - 0.06)^t$; There were about 734 students enrolled in physical education classes at the high school in 2006.

42. Let V represent the value of the car (in dollars) and x represent the number of years since the initial value. $V = 13{,}000(0.85)^x$; about \$6786.

8.6 Write and Graph Exponential Decay Functions

pp. 531–538

EXAMPLE 1

Tell whether the graph represents *exponential growth* or *exponential decay*. Then write a rule for the function.

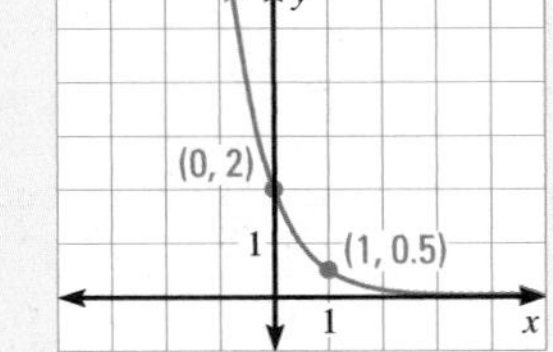

The graph represents exponential decay ($y = ab^x$ where $0 < b < 1$). The y-intercept is 2, so $a = 2$. Find the value of b by using the point (1, 0.5) and $a = 2$.

$y = ab^x$ **Write function.**

$0.5 = 2 \cdot b^1$ **Substitute.**

$0.25 = b$ **Solve for *b*.**

A function rule is $y = 2(0.25)^x$.

EXAMPLE 2

CAR VALUE A family purchases a car for \$11,000. The car depreciates (loses value) at a rate of about 16% annually. Write a function that models the value of the car over time. Find the approximate value of the car in 4 years.

Let V represent the value (in dollars) of the car, and let t represent the time (in years since the car was purchased). The initial value is 11,000, and the decay rate is 0.16.

$V = a(1 - r)^t$ **Write exponential decay model.**

$= 11{,}000(1 - 0.16)^t$ **Substitute 11,000 for *a* and 0.16 for *r*.**

$= 11{,}000(0.84)^t$ **Simplify.**

To find the approximate value of the car in 4 years, substitute 4 for t.

$V = 11{,}000(0.84)^t = 11{,}000(0.84)^4 \approx \$5477$

The approximate value of the car in 4 years is \$5477.

EXERCISES

EXAMPLES 4 and 5 on pp. 533–534 for Exs. 40–42

Tell whether the graph represents *exponential growth* or *exponential decay*. Then write a rule for the function.

40. 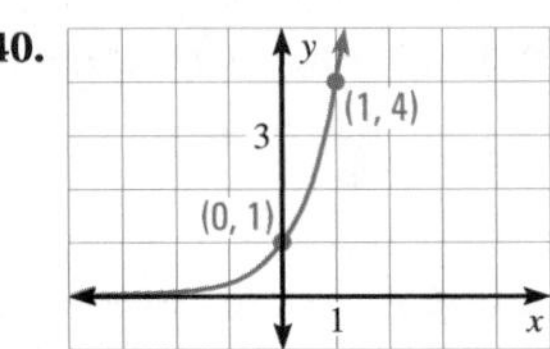

exponential growth; $y = 4^x$

41. 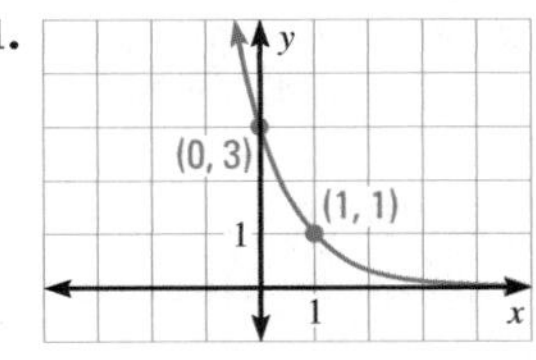

exponential decay; $y = 3 \cdot \left(\frac{1}{3}\right)^x$

42. **CAR VALUE** The value of a car is \$13,000. The car depreciates (loses value) at a rate of about 15% annually. Write an exponential decay model for the value of the car. Find the approximate value of the car in 4 years. See margin.

8 CHAPTER TEST

Simplify the expression. Write your answer using exponents.

1. $(62 \cdot 17)^4$ $62^4 \cdot 17^4$
2. $(-3)(-3)^6$ $(-3)^7$
3. $\frac{8^4 \cdot 8^5}{8^3}$ 8^6
4. $(8^4)^3$ 8^{12}
5. $\frac{2^{15}}{2^8}$ 2^7
6. $5^3 \cdot 5^0 \cdot 5^5$ 5^8
7. $[(-4)^3]^2$ $(-4)^6$
8. $\frac{(-5)^{10}}{(-5)^3}$ $(-5)^7$

Simplify the expression.

9. $t^2 \cdot t^6$ t^8
10. $\left(\frac{s}{t}\right)^6$ $\frac{s^6}{t^6}$
11. $\frac{1}{9^{-2}}$ 81
12. $-(6p)^2$ $-36p^2$
13. $(5xy)^2$ $25x^2y^2$
14. $\frac{1}{z^7} \cdot z^9$ z^2
15. $(x^5)^3$ x^{15}
16. $\left(-\frac{4}{c}\right)^2$ $\frac{16}{c^2}$

Simplify the expression. Write your answer using only positive exponents.

17. $\left(\frac{a^{-3}}{3b}\right)^4$ $\frac{1}{81a^{12}b^4}$
18. $\frac{3}{4d} \cdot \frac{(2d)^4}{c^3}$ $\frac{12d^3}{c^3}$
19. $y^0 \cdot (8x^6y^{-3})^{-2}$ $\frac{y^6}{64x^{12}}$
20. $(5r^5)^3 \cdot r^{-2}$ $125r^{13}$

Write the number in scientific notation.

21. 423.6 4.236×10^2
22. 7,194,548 7.194548×10^6
23. 500.32 5.0032×10^2
24. 71.23884 7.123884×10^1
25. 0.562 5.62×10^{-1}
26. 0.0348 3.48×10^{-2}
27. 0.000123 1.23×10^{-4}
28. 0.5603002 5.603002×10^{-1}

Write the number in standard form.

29. 4.02×10^5 402,000
30. 5.3121×10^4 53,121
31. 9.354×10^8 935,400,000
32. 1.307×10^{19} See margin.
33. 1.3×10^{-3} 0.0013
34. 3.32×10^{-4} 0.000332
35. 7.506×10^{-5} 0.00007506
36. 9.3119×10^{-7} 0.00000093119

37. Graph the function $y = 4^x$. Identify its domain and range. See margin.

38. Graph the function $y = \frac{1}{2} \cdot 4^x$. Compare the graph with the graph of $y = 4^x$. See margin.

39. **ANIMATION** About 1.2×10^7 bytes of data make up a single frame of an animated film. There are 24 frames in 1 second of a film. About how many bytes of data are there in 1 hour of an animated film? about 1.04×10^{12} bytes

40. **SALARY** A recent college graduate accepts a job at a law firm. The job has a salary of $32,000 per year. The law firm guarantees an annual pay increase of 3% of the employee's salary.
    a. Write a function that models the employee's salary over time. Assume that the employee receives only the guaranteed pay increase. See margin.
    b. Use the function to find the employee's salary after 5 years. $37,096.77

41. **SCIENCE** At sea level, Earth's atmosphere exerts a pressure of 1 atmosphere. Atmospheric pressure P (in atmospheres) decreases with altitude and can be modeled by $P = (0.99987)^a$ where a is the altitude (in meters).
    a. Identify the initial amount, decay factor, and decay rate. initial amount: 1, decay factor: 0.99987, decay rate: 0.013%
    b. Use a graphing calculator to graph the function. See margin.
    c. Estimate the altitude at which the atmospheric pressure is about half of what it is at sea level. about 5332 m

Additional Resources

Assessment Book

- Chapter Test, Levels A, B, C, pp. 112–117
- Standardized Chapter Test, pp. 118–119
- SAT/ACT Chapter Test, pp. 120–121
- Alternative Assessment, pp. 122–123

Test Generator CD-ROM

Chapter Test

Easily-readable reduced copies (with answers) of Chapter Test B, the Standardized Chapter Test, and the Alternative Assessment from the Assessment Book can be found on pp. 486E–486F.

37.

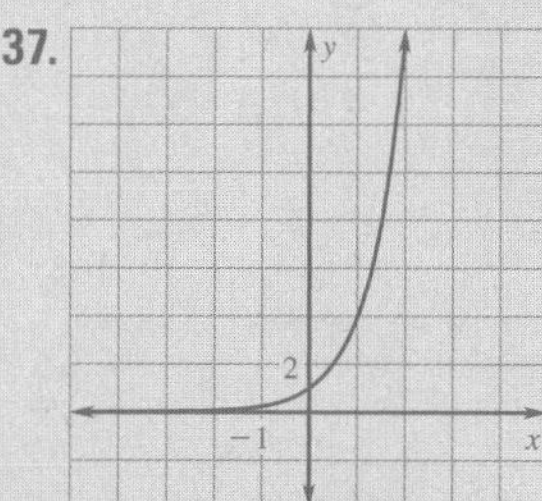

domain: all real numbers, range: all positive real numbers

25.

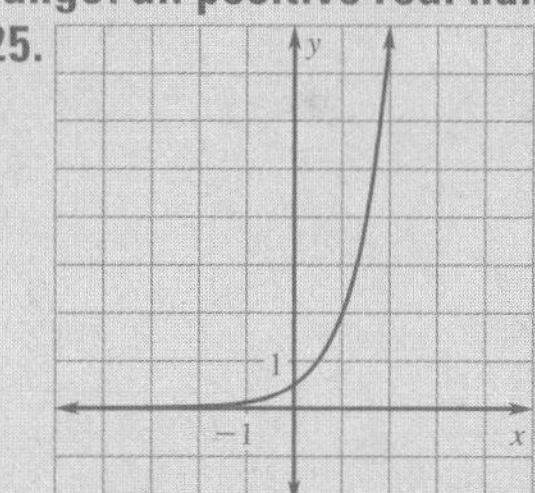

The graph is a vertical shrink of $y = 4^x$.

40a. Let y represent the yearly salary and x represent the number of years since accepting the job. $y = 32{,}000(1.03)^x$.

41b.

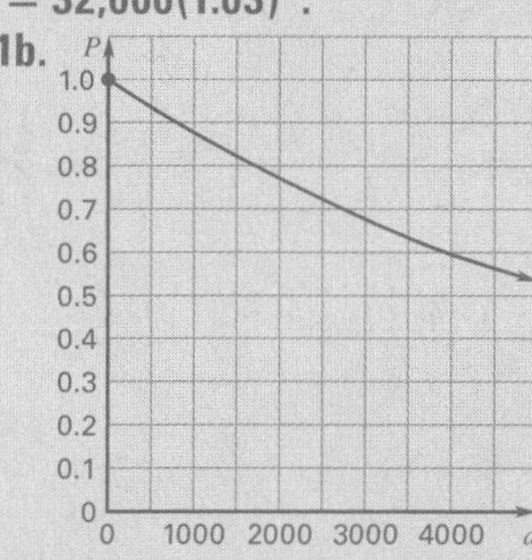

Illinois Test Preparation

MULTIPLE CHOICE QUESTIONS

Some of the information you need to solve a multiple choice question may appear in a table, a diagram, or a graph.

PROBLEM 1

A scientist monitors bacteria cell growth in an experiment. The scientist records the number of bacteria cells in a petri dish every 20 minutes, as shown in the table.

Number of 20 minute time periods, t	0	1	2	3	4
Number of bacteria cells, c	15	30	60	120	240

How many bacteria cells will there be after 3 hours?

A. 7.69×10^{10} **B.** 7680 **C.** 270 **D.** 120

Plan

INTERPRET THE TABLE Determine whether the table represents a linear or an exponential function. Use the information in the table to write a function. Then use the function to find the number of bacteria cells after 3 hours.

Solution

STEP 1 Determine whether the function is exponential.

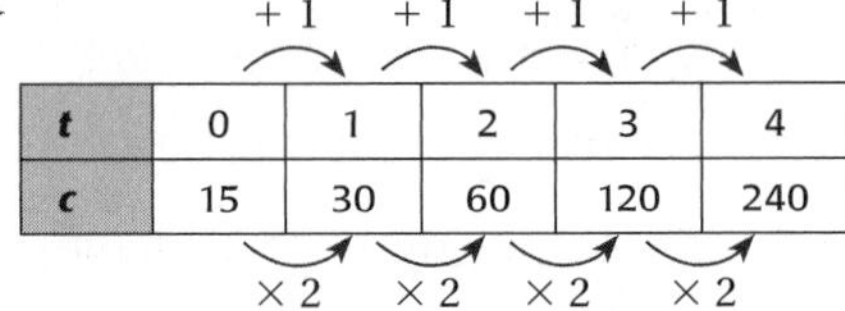

Because the c-values are multiplied by 2 for each increase of 1 in t, the table represents an exponential function of the form $c = ab^t$ where $b = 2$.

STEP 2 Write the function rule.

The value of c when $t = 0$ is 15, as shown in the table, so $a = 15$. Substitute the values of a and b in the function $c = ab^t$.

A function rule is $c = 15 \cdot 2^t$.

STEP 3 Find the number of cells after 3 hours.

There are 180 minutes in 3 hours. So there are nine 20 minute periods in 3 hours. Substitute 9 for t in the function rule you wrote in Step 2.

$c = 15 \cdot 2^t$

$= 15 \cdot 2^9$

$= 7680$

There are 7680 bacteria cells in the petri dish after 3 hours.

The correct answer is **B**.

PROBLEM 2

A fish tank is a rectangular prism and is partially filled with sand, as shown. The dimensions of the fish tank are given. The order of magnitude of the number of grains of sand in 1 cubic inch is 10^3. Find the order of magnitude of the total number of grains of sand in the fish tank.

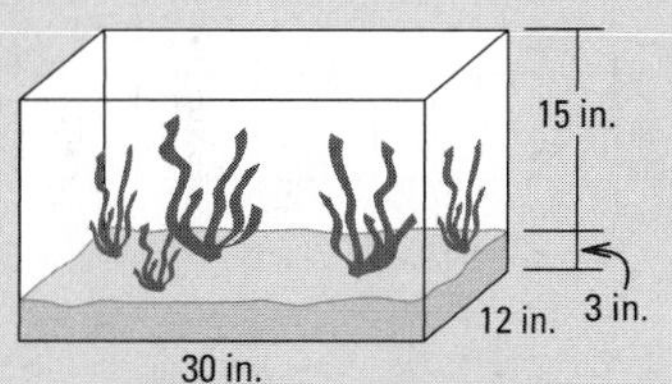

F. 10^2 grains **G.** 10^3 grains **H.** 10^5 grains **J.** 10^6 grains

Plan

INTERPRET THE DIAGRAM Use the information in the diagram to find the order of magnitude of the volume of sand in the fish tank. Multiply the volume by the order of magnitude of the number of grains of sand in 1 cubic inch.

Solution

STEP 1 Find the order of magnitude of the volume of sand in the fish tank.

Use the formula for the volume of a rectangular prism.

$V = lwh$ **Write formula for volume of rectangular prism.**

$= 30 \cdot 12 \cdot 3$ **Substitute given values.**

$= 1080$ **Multiply.**

The order of magnitude of the volume of sand is 10^3 cubic inches.

STEP 2 Find the order of magnitude of the number of grains of sand in the fish tank.

Multiply the order of magnitude of the volume of sand in the fish tank by the order of magnitude of the grains of sand in 1 cubic inch.

$10^3 \cdot 10^3 = 10^{3+3} = 10^6$

The order of magnitude of the total number of grains of sand in the fish tank is 10^6.

The correct answer is **J**.

PRACTICE

1. In Problem 2, consider the section of the fish tank occupied by water only. The order of magnitude of the weight of water per cubic inch is 10^{-2} pound. The tank is filled to the top. What is the order of magnitude of the weight of the water in the fish tank?

   A. 10^{-8} pound **B.** 10^{-6} pound **C.** 10^2 pounds **D.** 10^6 pounds

2. What is the volume of the cylinder shown?

   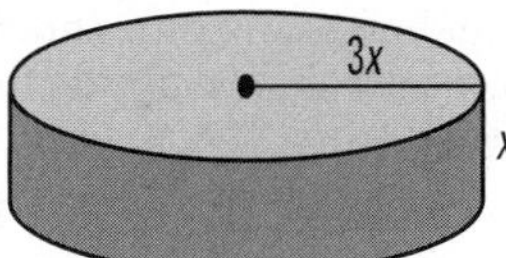

   F. $9\pi x^3$ **H.** $9\pi x^2$

   G. $3\pi x^3$ **J.** $3\pi x^2$

TEST PREPARATION

Illinois Test Preparation

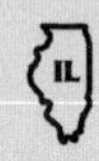

1. C
2. F

Illinois Test Practice

1. A
2. J
3. D
4. J
5. D
6. H
7. C
8. J
9. A
10. F
11. B
12. G
13. A
14. G
15. B
16. F
17. D
18. G
19. C
20. F

Illinois Test Practice

1. The table represents which function?

x	-2	-1	0	1	2
y	$\frac{1}{75}$	$\frac{1}{15}$	$\frac{1}{3}$	$\frac{5}{3}$	$\frac{25}{3}$

A. $y = \frac{1}{3} \cdot 5^x$ **C.** $y = 3 \cdot 5^x$

B. $y = -\frac{1}{3} \cdot 5^x$ **D.** $y = -3 \cdot 5^x$

2. What is the volume of the cube?

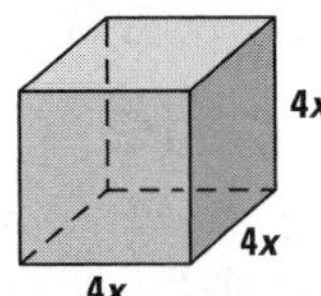

F. $4x^3$

G. $12x^3$

H. $16x^2$

J. $64x^3$

In Exercises 3 and 4, use the table below.

3. List the elements in order from least concentration to greatest concentration.

Element in Seawater	Concentration (parts per million)
Sulfur	904
Chloride	1.95×10^4
Magnesium	1.29×10^3
Sodium	10,770

A. Sulfur, sodium, magnesium, chloride

B. Chloride, sodium, magnesium, sulfur

C. Sulfur, chloride, magnesium, sodium

D. Sulfur, magnesium, sodium, chloride

4. About how many times greater is the concentration of chloride than the concentration of magnesium?

F. 0.066 **H.** 1.5

G. 0.66 **J.** 15

In Exercises 5–7, use the table below.

Unit	Number of meters
Kilometer	10^3
Centimeter	10^{-2}
Millimeter	10^{-3}
Nanometer	10^{-9}

5. How many millimeters are in 1 kilometer?

A. 1 **C.** 10^3

B. 10 **D.** 10^6

6. How many nanometers are in a centimeter?

F. 10^{-11} **H.** 10^7

G. 10^{-7} **J.** 10^{18}

7. A micrometer is 10^3 times greater than a nanometer. How many meters are in a micrometer?

A. 10^{-27} **C.** 10^{-6}

B. 10^{-12} **D.** 10^6

In Exercises 8 and 9, use the graph below.

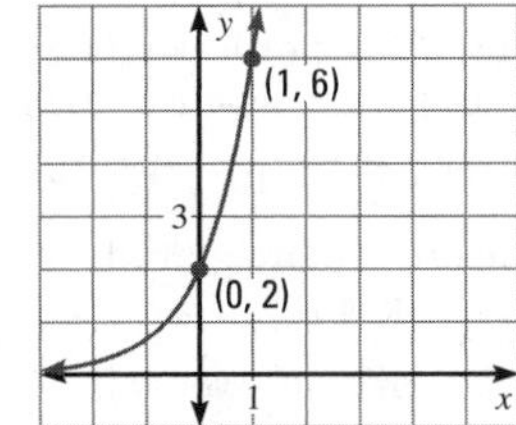

8. The graph of which exponential function is shown?

F. $y = 3^x$ **H.** $y = -2 \cdot 3^x$

G. $y = -3^x$ **J.** $y = 2 \cdot 3^x$

9. How does the graph compare with the graph of $y = 3^x$?

A. It is a vertical stretch.

B. It is a vertical shrink.

C. It is a reflection in the x-axis.

D. It is the same graph.

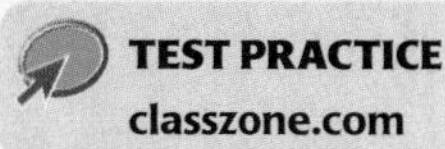

10. What is a simplified form of the expression $(-5)^4 \cdot (-5)^3 \cdot (-5)^3$?

F. $(-5)^{10}$ **H.** $(-125)^{10}$

G. $(-5)^{36}$ **J.** $(-125)^{36}$

11. What is the value of the expression $\left(-\frac{1}{2}xy\right)^{-1}$ when $x = 4$ and $y = -3$?

A. 0 **C.** $\frac{8}{3}$

B. $\frac{1}{6}$ **D.** 6

12. What is a simplified form of the expression $\frac{-2x^7y^4}{3x^3y^5} \cdot \frac{6x^3y^5}{xy^2}$?

F. $-2x^6y^3$ **H.** $-6x^{18}y^6$

G. $-4x^6y^2$ **J.** $4x^8y^6$

13. Which of the following numbers is *not* written in scientific notation?

A. 83.2×10^5 **C.** 4.52×10^{-2}

B. 7.28×10^{-7} **D.** 1.23×10^9

14. What is a simplified form of the expression $(-5dc)^0$?

F. 0 **H.** $-5cd$

G. 1 **J.** $5cd$

15. Which model best represents the growth curve shown to the right?

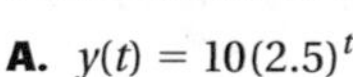

A. $y(t) = 10(2.5)^t$

B. $y(t) = 10(3.5)^t$

C. $y(t) = -10(3.5)^t$

D. $y(t) = 10(3.5)^{-t}$

16. The purchase value of a car is \$14,000. The value of the car will depreciate (lose value) at the rate of 14% per year. What will be the value of the car in 4 years?

F. \$7658.11 **H.** \$8904.75

G. \$7732.78 **J.** \$9540.61

17. Which models below are exponential decay models?

I. $y = (0.032)^x$
II. $y = (1.01)^{x+3}$
II. $y = (3022)^x$
IV. $y = (1 - 0.12)^x$

A. I and II **C.** II and III

B. III and IV **D.** I and IV

18. Todd can earn extra credit on his math test if he writes the correct expression in the blank space.

$5^2 \cdot 5^3 = 5^{2+3}$
$= \underline{\ ?\ }$

Which of these expressions should he write?

F. 5^6 **H.** 5^1

G. 5^5 **J.** 5^0

19. The mass of an object is given by $M = VD$, where V is the volume of the object and D is its density. The mass of Earth is 5.97×10^{24} kg. The density of Earth is 5.52×10^3 kg/m^3. What is the volume of Earth?

A. 32.95×10^{28} m^3 **C.** 1.08×10^{21} m^3

B. 32.95×10^{27} m^3 **D.** 1.08×10^8 m^3

20. A car is purchased for \$25,000. The value of the car depreciates at a rate of 12% per year. This change in value is shown in the graph.

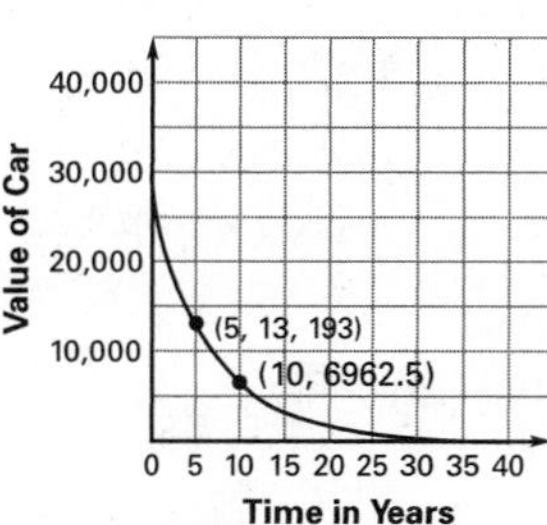

How would the graph change if the car **gained** value at a rate of 5% per year?

F. The graph would increase from left to right.

G. The graph would decrease from left to right at a quicker rate.

H. The graph would appear steeper.

J. The graph would appear less steep.

TEST PRACTICE

551

Illinois Resources Guide

Pacing and Assignment Guide

REGULAR SCHEDULE

Pre-AP For pacing and assignments for a Pre-AP course, see the *Algebra 1 Toolkit.*

Lesson	Les. Day	BASIC	AVERAGE	ADVANCED
9.1 8.11.01	Day 1	pp. 557–559 Exs. 1, 2, 3–7 odd, 9, 10, 11–25 odd, 27–31, 37–40, 43–53 odd	pp. 557–559 Exs. 1, 2, 6–10, 12–26 even, 27–34, 37–41, 44, 47, 50, 53	pp. 557–559 Exs. 1, 2, 7–10, 14–16, 18–26 even, 29–42*, 48, 51, 54
9.2 8.11.01	Day 1	pp. 565–568 Exs. 1, 2, 4–14 even, 15, 16, 17–39 odd, 49–52, 56–66 even	pp. 565–568 Exs. 1, 2, 3–43 odd, 45, 46, 49–53, 56, 59, 62, 65	pp. 565–568 Exs. 1, 2, 7, 8, 14, 21–26, 30–32, 33–41 odd, 43–54*, 60, 63, 66
9.3 8.11.01	Day 1	SRH p. 917 Exs. 1–9 odd; pp. 572–574 Exs. 1, 2, 4–8 even, 9–13, 17–22, 24–34 even, 40–43, 46–56 even	pp. 572–574 Exs. 1, 2, 4–22, 24–34 even, 35–37, 40–44, 48, 52, 54, 56	pp. 572–574 Exs. 1, 2, 6–8, 14–18, 19–33 odd, 35–45*, 53, 57
9.4 8.11.19	Day 1	SRH p. 911 Exs. 13–23 odd; pp. 578–580 Exs. 2, 3–15 odd, 16–26, 72–74	pp. 578–580 Exs. 2, 9–16, 18–26 even, 40–45, 72–74	pp. 578–580 Exs. 2, 10–15, 22–26, 40–45, 72–74
	Day 2	pp. 578–580 Exs. 1, 27–42, 51–56, 60–70 even	pp. 578–580 Exs. 1, 31–39, 46–49, 51–58, 61–71 odd	pp. 578–580 Exs. 1, 32–39, 46–50*, 52–59*, 60–70 even
9.5 8.11.01	Day 1	SRH p. 911 Exs. 1–11 odd; pp. 586–589 Exs. 1–19, 66–73	pp. 586–589 Exs. 1, 2, 3–17 odd, 18, 19, 47–55, 66–72 even	pp. 586–589 Exs. 1, 2, 12–17, 47–58*, 66–72 even
	Day 2	pp. 586–589 Exs. 20–28 even, 29, 30–43, 59–62, 74–80 even	pp. 586–589 Exs. 21–29 odd, 33–46, 59–64, 74, 78	pp. 586–589 Exs. 24–29, 34–46, 60–65*, 76, 80
9.6 8.11.01	Day 1	pp. 596–599 Exs. 1–22, 64–72 even	pp. 596–599 Exs. 1–3, 8–21, 52–55, 65–71 odd	pp. 596–599 Exs. 1–3, 12–21, 52–57*, 65–71 odd
	Day 2	pp. 596–599 Exs. 23–37 odd, 38–45, 58–62, 73–81 odd	pp. 596–599 Exs. 26–38 even, 39–51, 58–62, 74, 77, 80	pp. 596–599 Exs. 30–37, 40–51, 58–63*, 75, 78, 81
9.7 8.11.01	Day 1	pp. 603–605 Exs. 1, 2, 3–21 odd, 22–30, 46–50, 53–75 odd	pp. 603–605 Exs. 1, 2, 6–8, 12–24, 25–39 odd, 46–51, 54–76 even	pp. 603–605 Exs. 1, 2, 6–9, 12–20, 23, 24, 26–38 even, 40–52*, 61, 70, 76
9.8 8.11.01	Day 1	SRH p. 928 Exs. 1, 2, 4, 6, 10; pp. 610–613 Exs. 1–22, 87–89	pp. 610–613 Exs. 1–12, 14–22 even, 61–66, 87–89	pp. 610–613 Exs. 1, 6–12, 16–21, 61–67*, 87–89
	Day 2	pp. 610–613 Exs. 23–41 odd, 42–50, 68–72, 76–86 even	pp. 610–613 Exs. 32–60, 68–73, 76, 80, 84	pp. 610–613 Exs. 34–42, 48–60, 68–74*, 78, 82, 86
Review	Day 1	pp. 616–620 Exs. 1–66	pp. 616–620 Exs. 1–66	pp. 616–620 Exs. 1–66
Assess	Day 1	Chapter 9 Test	Chapter 9 Test	Chapter 9 Test
Yearly Pacing		Chapter 9 Total – 14 days	Chapters 1–9 Total – 106 days	Remaining – 54 days

*Challenge Exercises EP = Extra Practice SRH = Skills Review Handbook

BLOCK SCHEDULE

DAY 1	DAY 2	DAY 3	DAY 4	DAY 5	DAY 6	DAY 7
9.1	**9.3**	**9.4 (CONT.)**	**9.5 (CONT.)**	**9.6 (CONT.)**	**9.8**	**REVIEW**
pp. 557–559 Exs. 1, 2, 6–10, 12–26 even, 27–34, 37–41, 44, 47, 50, 53	pp. 572–574 Exs. 1, 2, 4–22, 24–34 even, 35–37, 40–44, 48, 52, 54, 56	pp. 578–580 Exs. 1, 31–39, 46–49, 51–58, 61–71 odd	pp. 586–589 Exs. 21–29 odd, 33–46, 59–64, 74, 78	pp. 596–599 Exs. 26–38 even, 39–51, 58–62, 74, 77, 80	pp. 610–613 Exs. 1–12, 14–22 even, 32–66, 68–73, 76, 80, 84, 87–89	pp. 616–620 Exs. 1–66
9.2	**9.4**	**9.5**	**9.6**	**9.7**		**ASSESS**
pp. 565–568 Exs. 1, 2, 3–43 odd, 45, 46, 49–53, 56, 59, 62, 65	pp. 578–580 Exs. 2, 9–16, 18–26 even, 40–45, 72–74	pp. 586–589 Exs. 1, 2, 3–17 odd, 18, 19, 47–55, 66–72 even	pp. 596–599 Exs. 1–3, 8–21, 52–55, 65–71 odd	pp. 603–605 Exs. 1, 2, 6–8, 12–24, 25–39 odd, 46–51, 54–76 even		Chapter 9 Test
Yearly Pacing	Chapter 9 Total – 7 days		Chapters 1–9 Total – 53 days		Remaining – 27 days	

Chapter Resource Guide

Chapter Resource Book								
CHAPTER SUPPORT								
Parents as Partners (Chapter Overview with home involvement exercises and activity)							p. 1	
LESSON SUPPORT **Standard**	**9.1** 8.11.01	**9.2** 8.11.01	**9.3** 8.11.01	**9.4** 8.11.19	**9.5** 8.11.01	**9.6** 8.11.01	**9.7** 8.11.01	**9.8** 8.11.01
Teaching Guide/Lesson Plan	p. 3	p. 15	p. 26	p. 36	p. 50	p. 61	p. 72	p. 82
Activity Masters	p. 5			p. 38				
Technology Activities & Keystrokes	p. 6			p. 39				
Activity Support Masters		p. 17			p. 52	p. 63		
Practice (3 levels)	p. 7	p. 18	p. 28	p. 41	p. 53	p. 64	p. 74	p. 84
Study Guide	p. 10	p. 21	p. 31	p. 44	p. 56	p. 67	p. 77	p. 87
Catch-Up for Absent Students	p. 12	p. 23	p. 33	p. 46	p. 58	p. 69	p. 79	p. 89
Problem Solving/Application	p. 13	p. 24	p. 34	p. 47	p. 59	p. 70	p. 80	p. 90
Challenge Practice	p. 14	p. 25	p. 35	p. 49	p. 60	p. 71	p. 81	p. 91
REVIEW								
Chapter Review Games and Activities		p. 92		Cumulative Practice			p. 95	
Project with Rubric		p. 93		Resource Book Answers			A1	

Transparencies	*9.1*	*9.2*	*9.3*	*9.4*	*9.5*	*9.6*	*9.7*	*9.8*
Warm-Up/Daily Homework Quiz	✔	✔	✔	✔	✔	✔	✔	✔
Notetaking Guide	✔	✔	✔	✔	✔	✔	✔	✔
Teacher Support		✔			✔	✔		
Answer Transparencies	✔	✔	✔	✔	✔	✔	✔	✔

ASSESSMENT BOOK

Quizzes	p. 124	SAT/ACT Chapter Test	p. 135
Chapter Tests (3 levels)	p. 127	Alternative Assessment with Rubric	p. 137
Standardized Chapter Test	p. 133		

TECHNOLOGY

- Easy Planner
- Test and Practice Generator
- Power Presentations
- @HomeTutor
- Activity Generator
- Animated Algebra
- Classzone.com
- eEdition Plus Online
- eWorkbook Plus Online
- ML Assessment System

ADDITIONAL RESOURCES

Illinois Additional Lessons

- Worked-Out Solution Key
- Notetaking Guide
- Practice Workbook
- Algebra 1 Toolkit
- Benchmark Tests
- Reteaching and Remediation
- Spanish Study Guide
- Spanish Assessment Book
- Spanish Resources in Spanish
- Multi-Language Visual Glossary

LESSON 9.1 Practice B
For use with pages 554–559

Write the polynomial so that the exponents decrease from left to right. Identify the degree and leading coefficient of the polynomial.

1. $4n^5$
2. $4x - 2x^2 + 3$
3. $6y^3 - 2y^2 + 4y^4 - 5$

1. $4n^5$; degree: 5; leading coefficient: 4
2. $-2x^2 + 4x + 3$; degree: 2; leading coefficient: -2
3. $4y^4 + 6y^3 - 2y^2 - 5$; degree: 4; leading coefficient: 4

Tell whether the expression is a polynomial. If it is a polynomial, find its degree and classify it by the number of its terms. Otherwise, tell why it is not a polynomial.

4. 10^x not a polynomial
5. $-6n^2 - n^3 + 4$ polynomial; degree: 3; trinomial
6. $w^{-3} + 5$ not a polynomial

Find the sum or difference.

7. $(3z^2 + z - 4) + (2z^2 + 2z - 3)$ $5z^2 + 3z - 7$
8. $(8c^2 - 4c + 1) + (-3c^2 + c + 5)$
9. $(2x^2 + 5x - 1) + (x^2 - 5x + 7)$ $3x^2 + 6$
10. $(10b^2 - 3b + 2) - (4b^2 + 5b + 1)$
11. $(-4m^2 + 3m - 1) - (m + 2)$
12. $(3m + 4) - (2m^2 - 6m + 5)$ $-2m^2 + 9m - 1$

8. $5c^2 - 3c + 6$ 10. $6b^2 - 8b + 1$ 11. $-4m^2 + 2m - 3$

Write a polynomial that represents the perimeter of the figure.

13.

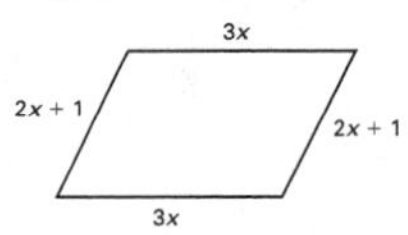

$10x + 2$

14.
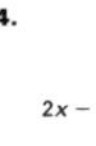
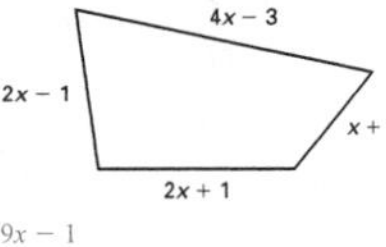

$9x - 1$

15. **Floor Plan** The first floor of a home has the floor plan shown. Find the area of the first floor.

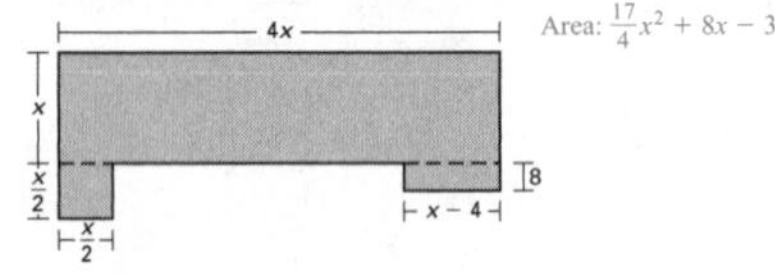

Area: $\frac{17}{4}x^2 + 8x - 32$

16. **Profit** For 1995 through 2005, the revenue R (in dollars) and the cost C (in dollars) of producing a product can be modeled by

$R = \frac{1}{4}t^2 + \frac{21}{4}t + 400$ and $C = \frac{1}{12}t^2 + \frac{13}{4}t + 200$

where t is the number of years since 1995. Write an equation for the profit earned from 1995 to 2005. (*Hint:* Profit = Revenue − Cost)

$P = \frac{1}{6}t^2 + 2t + 200$

LESSON 9.2 Practice B
For use with pages 562–568

Find the product.

1. $x^2(6x^2 - 3x - 1)$
2. $-5a^3(4a^4 - 3a + 1)$
3. $4d^2(-2d^3 + 5d^2 - 6d + 2)$
4. $(3x + 1)(2x - 5)$
5. $(2y + 3)(y - 5)$
6. $(6a - 3)(4a - 1)$
7. $(b - 8)(5b - 2)$
8. $(8m + 7)(2m + 3)$
9. $(-p + 2)(3p^2 + 1)$
10. $(2z - 7)(-z + 3)$
11. $(-3d + 10)(2d - 1)$
12. $(n + 1)(n^2 + 4n + 5)$
13. $(w - 3)(w^2 + 8w + 1)$
14. $(2s + 5)(s^2 + 3s - 1)$
15. $(x^2 - 4xy + y^2)(5xy)$

1. $6x^4 - 3x^3 - x^2$ 2. $-20a^7 + 15a^4 - 5a^3$ 3. $-8d^5 + 20d^4 - 24d^3 + 8d^2$ 4. $6x^2 - 13x - 5$ 5. $2y^2 - 7y - 15$ 6. $24a^2 - 18a + 3$ 7. $5b^2 - 42b + 16$ 8. $16m^2 + 38m + 21$ 9. $-3p^3 + 6p^2 - p + 2$ 10. $-2z^2 + 13z - 21$ 11. $-6d^2 + 23d - 10$ 12. $n^3 + 5n^2 + 9n + 5$ 13. $w^3 + 5w^2 - 23w - 3$ 14. $2s^3 + 11s^2 + 13s - 5$ 15. $5x^3y - 20x^2y^2 + 5xy^3$

Simplify the expression.

16. $a(3a + 1) + (a + 1)(a - 1)$ $4a^2 + a - 1$
17. $(x + 2)(x + 5) - x(4x - 1)$ $-3x^2 - 2x - 10$
18. $(m + 7)(m - 3) + (m - 4)(m + 5)$ $2m^2 + 5m - 41$

Write a polynomial for the area of the shaded region.

19.
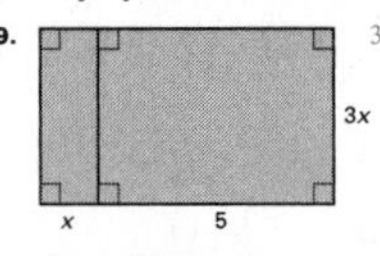

$3x^2 + 15x$

20.
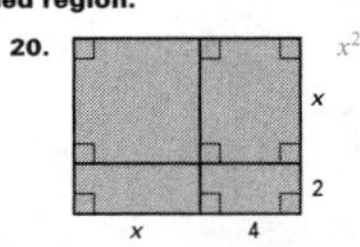

$x^2 + 6x + 8$

21. **Flower Bed** You are designing a rectangular flower bed that you will border using brick pavers. The width of the border around the bed will be the same on every side, as shown.

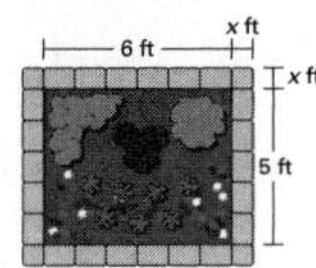

a. Write a polynomial that represents the total area of the flower bed and the border. $A = 4x^2 + 22x + 30$

b. Find the total area of the flower bed and border when the width of the border is 1.5 feet. 72 ft²

22. **School Enrollment** During the period 1995–2002, the number S of students (in thousands) enrolled in school in the U.S. and the percent P (in decimal form) of this amount that are between 7 and 13 years old can be modeled by

$S = 32.6t^3 - 376.45t^2 + 1624.2t + 66{,}939$

and

$P = 0.000005t^4 - 0.0003t^3 + 0.003t^2 - 0.007t + 0.4$

where t is the number of years since 1995.

a. Find the values of S and P for $t = 0$. What does the product $S \cdot P$ mean for $t = 0$ in the context of this problem? S: 66,939 students; P: 40%; $A \cdot P$ indicates the number of students that are between 7 and 13.

b. Write an equation that models the number of students (in thousands) that are between 7 and 13 years old as a function of the number of years since 1995.

c. How many students between 7 and 13 years old were enrolled in 1995? about 26,776

22. b. $A \cdot P = 0.000163t^7 - 0.01166225t^6 + 0.2188565t^5 - 1.510115t^4 + 0.46605t^3 + 38.8676t^2 + 181.107t + 26{,}775.6$

LESSON 9.3 Practice B
For use with pages 569–574

Find the product of the square of the binomial.

1. $(x - 9)^2$ $x^2 - 18x + 81$
2. $(m + 11)^2$ $m^2 + 22m + 121$
3. $(5s + 2)^2$ $25s^2 + 20s + 4$
4. $(3m + 7)^2$ $9m^2 + 42m + 49$
5. $(4p - 5)^2$ $16p^2 - 40p + 25$
6. $(7a - 6)^2$ $49a^2 - 84a + 36$
7. $(10z - 3)^2$ $100z^2 - 60z + 9$
8. $(2x + y)^2$ $4x^2 + 4xy + y^2$
9. $(3y - x)^2$ $9y^2 - 6xy + x^2$

Find the product of the sum and difference.

10. $(a - 9)(a + 9)$ $a^2 - 81$
11. $(z - 20)(z + 20)$ $z^2 - 400$
12. $(5r + 1)(5r - 1)$ $25r^2 - 1$
13. $(6m + 10)(6m - 10)$
14. $(7p - 2)(7p + 2)$ $49p^2 - 4$
15. $(9c - 1)(9c + 1)$ $81c^2 - 1$
16. $(4x + 3)(4x - 3)$ $16x^2 - 9$
17. $(4 - w)(4 + w)$ $-w^2 + 16$
18. $(5 - 2y)(5 + 2y)$ $-4y^2 + 25$

13. $36m^2 - 100$

Describe **how you can use mental math to find the product.**

19. $15 \cdot 25$ Find the product $(20 - 5)(20 + 5)$.
20. $43 \cdot 57$ Find the product $(50 - 7)(50 + 7)$.
21. 18^2 Find the product $(20 - 2)^2$.

Perform the indicated operation using the functions $f(x) = 4x + 0.5$ and $g(x) = 4x - 0.5$.

22. $f(x) \cdot g(x)$ $16x^2 - 0.25$
23. $(f(x))^2$ $16x^2 + 4x + 0.25$
24. $(g(x))^2$ $16x^2 - 4x + 0.25$

25. **Pea Plants** In pea plants, the gene S is for spherical seed shape, and the gene s is for wrinkled seed shape. Any gene combination with an S results in a spherical seed shape. Suppose two pea plants have the same gene combination Ss.

a. Make a Punnett square that shows the possible gene combinations of an offspring pea plant and the resulting seed shape. See below.

b. Write a polynomial that models the possible gene combinations of an offspring pea plant. $0.25S^2 + 0.5Ss + 0.25s^2$

c. What percent of the possible gene combinations of the offspring results in a wrinkled seed shape? 25%

26. **Basketball Statistics** You are on the basketball team and you want to figure out some statistics about foul shots. The area model shows the possible outcomes of two attempted foul shots.

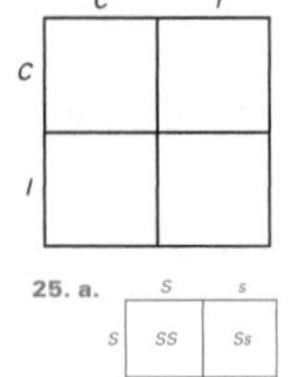

a. What percent of the two possible outcomes of two attempted foul shots results in you making at least one foul shot? *Explain* how you found your answer using the table. 75%; Three of the four squares in the area model represent at least one foul shot being made.

b. Show how you could use a polynomial to model the possible results of two attempted foul shots.
The chance of making a foul shot is 50% and the chance of not making a foul shot is 50%. So the polynomial $(0.5C + 0.5I)^2 = 0.25C^2 + 0.5CI + 0.25I^2$ represents this situation where C represents a foul shot made and I represents a foul shot missed.

25. a.

	S	s
S	SS	Ss
s	sS	ss

LESSON 9.4 Practice B
For use with pages 575–580

Solve the equation.

1. $(x + 14)(x - 3) = 0$ $-14, 3$
2. $(m - 12)(m + 5) = 0$ $-5, 12$
3. $(p + 15)(p + 24) = 0$ $-24, -15$
4. $(n - 8)(n - 9) = 0$ $8, 9$
5. $(d + 8)\left(d - \frac{1}{2}\right) = 0$ $-8, \frac{1}{2}$
6. $\left(c + \frac{3}{4}\right)(c - 6) = 0$ $-\frac{3}{4}, 6$
7. $(2z - 8)(z + 5) = 0$ $-5, 4$
8. $(y - 3)(5y + 10) = 0$ $-2, 3$
9. $(6b - 4)(b - 8) = 0$ $\frac{2}{3}, 8$
10. $(8x + 4)(6x - 3) = 0$ $-\frac{1}{2}, \frac{1}{2}$
11. $(3x + 9)(6x - 3) = 0$ $-3, \frac{1}{2}$
12. $(4x + 5)(4x - 5) = 0$ $-\frac{5}{4}, \frac{5}{4}$

Factor out the greatest common monomial factor.

13. $10x - 10y$ $10(x - y)$
14. $8x^2 + 20y$ $4(2x^2 + 5y)$
15. $18a^2 - 6b$ $6(3a^2 - b)$
16. $4x^2 - 4x$ $4x(x - 1)$
17. $r^2 + 2rs$ $r(r + 2s)$
18. $2m^2 + 6mn$ $2m(m + 3n)$
19. $5p^2q + 10q$ $5q(p^2 + 2)$
20. $9a^5 + a^3$ $a^3(9a^2 + 1)$
21. $6w^3 - 14w^2$ $2w^2(3w - 7)$

Solve the equation.

22. $m^2 - 10m = 0$ $0, 10$
23. $b^2 + 14b = 0$ $-14, 0$
24. $5w^2 - 5w = 0$ $0, 1$
25. $24k^2 + 24k = 0$ $-1, 0$
26. $8r^2 - 24r = 0$ $0, 3$
27. $9p^2 + 18p = 0$ $-2, 0$
28. $6n^2 - 15n = 0$ $0, \frac{5}{2}$
29. $-8y^2 - 10y = 0$ $-\frac{5}{4}, 0$
30. $-10b^2 + 25b = 0$ $0, \frac{5}{2}$
31. $8c^2 = 4c$ $0, \frac{1}{2}$
32. $30r^2 = -15r$ $-\frac{1}{2}, 0$
33. $-24y^2 = 9y$ $-\frac{3}{8}, 0$

34. **Diving Board** A diver jumps from a diving board that is 24 feet above the water. The height of the diver is given by $h = -16(t - 1.5)(t + 1)$ where the height h is measured in feet, and the time t is measured in seconds. When will the diver hit the water? Can you see a quick way to find the answer? *Explain.* 1.5 sec; Yes. From the equation, you can see that the factor $t - 1.5$ will be zero when $t = 1.5$.

35. **Dog** A dog leaps into the air to catch a frisbee with an initial velocity of 14 feet per second.

a. Write a model for the height of the dog above the ground. $h = -16t^2 + 14t$

b. After how many seconds does the dog land on the ground? $\frac{7}{8}$ sec

36. **Desktop Areas** You have two components to the desktop where you do your homework that fit together into an L shape. The two components have the same area.

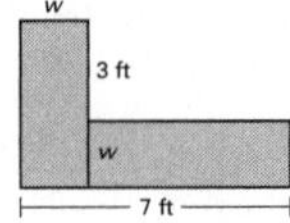

a. Write an equation that relates the areas of the desktop components. $w(w + 3) = w(7 - w)$

b. Find the value of w. 2 ft

c. What is the combined area of the desktop components? 20 ft²

LESSON 9.5 Practice B
For use with pages 583–589

Factor the trinomial.

1. $x^2 + 8x + 7$ $(x + 7)(x + 1)$
2. $b^2 - 7b + 10$ $(b - 5)(b - 2)$
3. $w^2 - 12w - 13$
4. $p^2 + 10p + 25$ $(p + 5)^2$
5. $m^2 - 10m + 24$
6. $y^2 - 5y - 24$ $(y - 8)(y + 3)$
7. $a^2 + 13a + 36$ $(a + 9)(a + 4)$
8. $n^2 + 2n - 48$ $(n - 6)(n + 8)$
9. $z^2 - 14z + 40$ $(z - 10)(z - 4)$

3. $(w - 13)(w + 1)$ 5. $(m - 6)(m - 4)$

Solve the equation.

10. $y^2 + 17y + 72 = 0$ $-9, -8$
11. $a^2 - 9a - 36 = 0$ $-3, 12$
12. $w^2 - 13w + 42 = 0$ $6, 7$
13. $m^2 - 5m - 14 = 0$ $-2, 7$
14. $x^2 + 11x + 24 = 0$
15. $n^2 - 12n + 27 = 0$ $3, 9$
16. $d^2 + 5d - 50 = 0$ $-10, 5$
17. $p^2 + 16p + 48 = 0$
18. $z^2 - z - 30 = 0$ $-5, 6$

14. $-8, -3$ 17. $-12, -4$

Find the zeros of the polynomial function.

19. $f(x) = x^2 - 5x - 36$
20. $g(x) = x^2 + 8x - 20$
21. $h(x) = x^2 - 11x + 24$ $3, 8$
22. $f(x) = x^2 + 11x + 28$
23. $g(x) = x^2 + 11x - 12$
24. $h(x) = x^2 + 3x - 18$ $-6, 3$

19. $-4, 9$ 20. $-10, 2$ 22. $-7, -4$ 23. $-12, 1$

Solve the equation.

25. $x(x + 17) = -60$ $-12, -5$
26. $p(p - 4) = 32$ $-4, 8$
27. $w(w + 8) = -15$ $-5, -3$
28. $n(n + 6) = 7$ $-7, 1$
29. $s^2 - 3(s + 2) = 4$ $-2, 5$
30. $d^2 + 18(d + 4) = -9$ -9

31. **Patio Area** A community center is building a patio area along two sides of its pool. The pool is rectangular with a width of 50 feet and a length of 100 feet. The patio area will have the same width on each side of the pool.

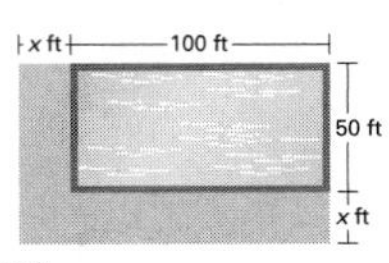

   a. Write a polynomial that represents the combined area of the pool and the patio area. $x^2 + 150x + 5000$
   b. The combined area of the pool and patio area should be 8400 square feet. How wide should the patio area be? 20 ft

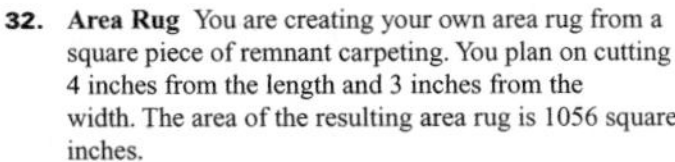

32. **Area Rug** You are creating your own area rug from a square piece of remnant carpeting. You plan on cutting 4 inches from the length and 3 inches from the width. The area of the resulting area rug is 1056 square inches.

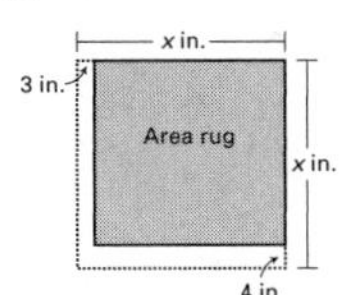

   a. Write a polynomial that represents the area of your area rug. $x^2 - 7x + 12$
   b. What is the perimeter of the original piece of remnant carpeting? 144 in.

LESSON 9.6 Practice B
For use with pages 593–599

1. $(-x + 4)(x + 7)$ 2. $(-p + 2)(p - 6)$ 3. $(-m - 8)(m + 5)$ 4. $(2y + 1)(y + 7)$ 5. $(3a - 1)(a - 4)$ 6. $(5d + 2)(d - 4)$ 7. $(3c + 2)(2c + 1)$ 8. $2(5n - 3)(n - 2)$ 9. $(2w + 3)(6w - 5)$ 10. $(b + 4)(-2b + 3)$ 11. $(r + 5)(-3r - 2)$ 12. $(s - 2)(-4s - 2)$

Factor the trinomial.

1. $-x^2 - 3x + 28$
2. $-p^2 + 8p - 12$
3. $-m^2 - 13m - 40$
4. $2y^2 + 15y + 7$
5. $3a^2 - 13a + 4$
6. $5d^2 - 18d - 8$
7. $6c^2 + 7c + 2$
8. $10n^2 - 26n + 12$
9. $12w^2 + 8w - 15$
10. $-2b^2 - 5b + 12$
11. $-3r^2 - 17r - 10$
12. $-4s^2 + 6s + 4$

Solve the equation. See below.

13. $-x^2 + x + 20 = 0$
14. $-m^2 - 10m - 16 = 0$
15. $-p^2 + 13p - 42 = 0$
16. $2c^2 - 11c + 5 = 0$
17. $2y^2 + y - 10 = 0$
18. $16r^2 + 18r + 5 = 0$
19. $3w^2 + 19w + 6 = 0$
20. $12n^2 - 11n + 2 = 0$
21. $15a^2 - 2a - 8 = 0$
22. $-2x^2 - 9x - 4 = 0$
23. $-3s^2 - s + 10 = 0$
24. $8d^2 - 6d - 5 = 0$

Find the zeros of the polynomial function. See below.

25. $f(x) = -x^2 + 6x + 27$
26. $f(x) = 6x^2 + 45x - 24$
27. $f(x) = -3x^2 - 14x + 24$
28. $f(x) = -2x^2 + 2x + 4$
29. $f(x) = 3x^2 - 17x + 20$
30. $f(x) = 8x^2 + 53x - 21$
31. $f(x) = 4x^2 + 29x + 30$
32. $f(x) = -2x^2 - 17x + 30$
33. $f(x) = 10x^2 + 5x - 5$

34. **Summer Business** Your weekly revenue R (in dollars) from your tie-dye T-shirt business can be modeled by
$R = -2t^2 + 87t + 90$
where t represents the number of weeks since the first week you started selling T-shirts. How much did you make your first week? \$90

35. **Cliff Diving** A cliff diver jumps from a ledge 96 feet above the ocean with an initial upward velocity of 16 feet per second. How long will it take until the diver enters the water? 3 sec

36. **Wall Mirror** You plan on making a wall hanging that contains two small mirrors as shown.

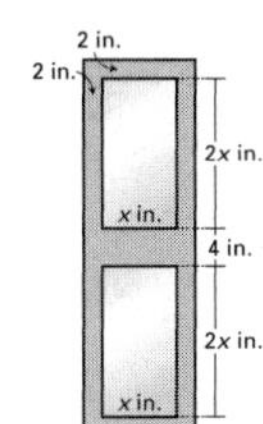

   a. Write a polynomial that represents the area of the wall hanging. $4x^2 + 24x + 32$
   b. The area of the wall hanging will be 480 square inches. Find the length and width of the mirrors you will use. 8 in. by 16 in.

13. $-4, 5$ 14. $-8, -2$ 15. $6, 7$ 16. $\frac{1}{2}, 5$ 17. $-\frac{5}{2}, 2$ 18. $-\frac{5}{8}, -\frac{1}{2}$ 19. $-6, -\frac{1}{3}$ 20. $\frac{1}{4}, \frac{2}{3}$ 21. $-\frac{2}{3}, \frac{4}{5}$ 22. $-4, -\frac{1}{2}$ 23. $-2, \frac{5}{3}$ 24. $-\frac{1}{2}, \frac{5}{4}$ 25. $-3, 9$ 26. $-8, \frac{1}{2}$ 27. $-6, \frac{4}{3}$ 28. $-1, 2$ 29. $\frac{5}{3}, 4$ 30. $-7, \frac{3}{8}$ 31. $-6, -\frac{5}{4}$ 32. $-10, \frac{3}{2}$ 33. $-1, \frac{1}{2}$

LESSON 9.7 Practice B
For use with pages 600–605

2. $(5p - 12)(5p + 12)$ 3. $(2b - 10)(2b + 10)$ 5. $-2(x - 4)(x + 4)$ 6. $-4(r - 5s)(r + 5s)$ 7. $(y + 12)^2$ 8. $(3c + 4)^2$

Factor the polynomial.

1. $x^2 - 36$ $(x - 6)(x + 6)$
2. $25p^2 - 144$
3. $4b^2 - 100$
4. $36m^2 - 81$ $(6m - 9)(6m + 9)$
5. $-2x^2 + 32$
6. $-4r^2 + 100s^2$
7. $y^2 + 24y + 144$
8. $9c^2 + 24c + 16$
9. $25w^2 - 20w + 4$ $(5w - 2)^2$
10. $16n^2 - 56n + 49$ $(4n - 7)^2$
11. $-18a^2 - 12a - 2$ $-2(3a + 1)^2$
12. $20z^2 - 140z + 245$ $5(2z - 7)^2$

Solve the equation.

13. $x^2 + 14x + 49 = 0$ -7
14. $8w^2 = 50$ $-\frac{5}{2}, \frac{5}{2}$
15. $64p^2 - 16p + 1 = 0$ $\frac{1}{8}$
16. $8a^2 - 72 = 0$ $-3, 3$
17. $3m^2 + 30m + 75 = 0$ -5
18. $-4y^2 + 32y - 64 = 0$ 4
19. $-5x^2 + 125 = 0$ $-5, 5$
20. $-7r^2 + 140r - 700 = 0$ 10
21. $24w^2 - 24w + 6 = 0$ $\frac{1}{2}$
22. $18n^2 + 60n + 50 = 0$ $-\frac{5}{3}$
23. $\frac{25}{2}x^2 + 15x + \frac{9}{2} = 0$ $-\frac{3}{5}$
24. $4x^2 = \frac{9}{16}$ $-\frac{3}{8}, \frac{3}{8}$

Find the value of *x* in the geometric shape.

25. Area $= 144\pi$ cm^2 8

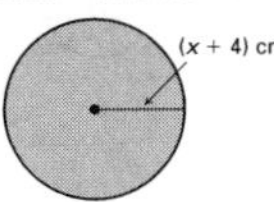

26. Area $= 225$ in.^{2} 3

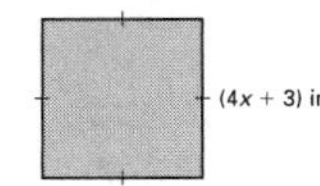

27. **Measuring Tape** A measuring tape drops from a roof that is 16 feet above the ground. After how many seconds does the measuring tape land on the ground? 1 sec

28. **Playground** A curved ladder that children can climb on can be modeled by the equation

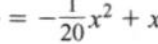

$y = -\frac{1}{20}x^2 + x$

where x and y are measured in feet.

   a. Make a table of values that shows the height of the ladder for $x = 0, 5, 10, 15,$ and 20 feet from the left end. 0; 3.75; 5; 3.75; 0
   b. For what additional values of x does the equation make sense? *Explain.*
   c. Plot the ordered pairs in the table from part (a) as points in the coordinate plane. Connect the points with a smooth curve.
   d. At approximately what distance from the left end does the ladder reach a height of 5 feet? Check your answer algebraically. 10 ft

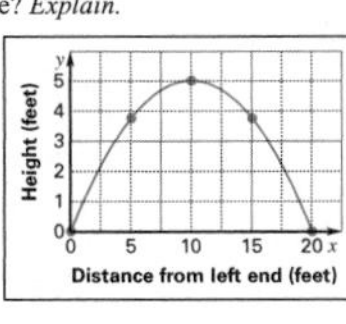

b. Any other values between 0 and 20 because the ladder is on the ground at $x = 0$ and meets the ground again at $x = 20$.

LESSON 9.8 Practice B
For use with pages 606–613

14. $4m(m - 2)(m + 2)$ 19. $5(m^2 + 4m + 8)$ 20. $6(x + 5)(x - 4)$ 21. $4z(z - 2)(z + 1)$ 22. $9(x^3 + 4x^2 + 4)$ 23. $(x^2 + 5)(x + 1)$ 24. $(d^2 + 5)(d + 4)$

Factor the expression.

1. $4x(x + 5) - 3(x + 5)$ $(4x - 3)(x + 5)$
2. $12(a - 3) - 2a(a - 3)$ $(12 - 2a)(a - 3)$
3. $w^2(w + 8) - 5(w + 8)$ $(w^2 - 5)(w + 8)$
4. $2b^2(b + 6) + 3(b + 6)$ $(2b^2 + 3)(b + 6)$
5. $y(15 + x) - (x + 15)$ $(y - 1)(x + 15)$
6. $3x(4 + y) - 6(4 + y)$ $(3x - 6)(y + 4)$

Factor the polynomial by grouping.

7. $x^3 + x^2 + 5x + 5$ $(x^2 + 5)(x + 1)$
8. $y^3 - 14y^2 + y - 14$ $(y^2 + 1)(y - 14)$
9. $m^3 - 6m^2 + 2m - 12$ $(m^2 + 2)(m - 6)$
10. $p^3 + 9p^2 + 4p + 36$ $(p^2 + 4)(p + 9)$
11. $t^3 + 12t^2 - 2t - 24$ $(t^2 - 2)(t + 12)$
12. $3n^3 - 3n^2 + n - 1$ $(3n^2 + 1)(n - 1)$

Factor the polynomial completely.

13. $7x^3 + 28x^2$ $7x^2(x + 4)$
14. $4m^3 - 16m$ See above.
15. $-16p^3 - 2p$ $-2p(8p^2 + 1)$
16. $48r^3 - 30r^2$ $6r^2(8r - 5)$
17. $15y - 60y^2$ $15y(1 - 4y)$
18. $18xy - 24x^2$ $6x(3y - 4x)$
19. $5m^2 + 20m + 40$ See above.
20. $6x^2 + 6x - 120$ See above.
21. $4z^3 - 4z^2 - 8z$ See above.
22. $9x^3 + 36x^2 + 36$ See above.
23. $x^3 + x^2 + 5x + 5$ See above.
24. $d^3 + 4d^2 + 5d + 20$ See above.

Solve the equation.

25. $3x^2 + 18x + 24 = 0$
26. $10x^2 = 250$ $-5, 5$
27. $4m^2 - 28m + 49 = 0$ $\frac{7}{2}$
28. $12x^2 + 18x + 6 = 0$
29. $18x^2 - 48x + 32 = 0$ $\frac{4}{3}$
30. $-18x^2 - 60x - 50 = 0$ $-\frac{5}{3}$

25. $-4, -2$ 28. $-\frac{1}{2}, -1$

31. **Countertop** A countertop will have a hole drilled in it to hold a cylindrical container that will function as a utensil holder. The area of the entire countertop is given by $5x^2 + 12x + 7$. The area of the hole is given by $x^2 + 2x + 1$. Write an expression for the area in factored form of the countertop that is left after the hole is drilled. $2(2x + 3)(x + 1)$

32. **Film Canister** A film canister in the shape of a cylinder has a height of 8 centimeters and a volume of 32π cubic centimeters.
   a. Write an equation for the volume of the film canister. $8\pi r^2 - 32\pi = 0$
   b. What is the radius of the film canister? 2 cm

33. **Badminton** You hit a badminton birdie upward with a racket from a height of 2 feet with an initial velocity of 8 feet per second.
   a. Write an equation that models this situation. $-16t^2 + 8t + 2$
   b. How high is the birdie at 0.1 second? 2.64 ft
   c. How high is the birdie at 0.25 second? 3 ft
   d. How long will it take the birdie to reach the ground? about 0.7 sec

9 Assessment

CHAPTER 9 Quiz 1

For use after Lessons 9.1–9.3

Find the sum, difference, or product.

1. $(-3x^2 - 8x + 5) + (x^2 - 6x + 2)$
2. $(q^3 - 7q^2 - 3q) - (q^3 + 10q^2 - 4)$
3. $-5k^2(k^4 - 3k^3)$
4. $(y + 2)(y^2 + y - 1)$
5. $(4z + 9)(z - 2)$
6. $(p - 7)(p + 1)$
7. $(8m + 3)^2$
8. $(5y - 6)^2$
9. A flower garden is 4 feet longer that its width w. Write a polynomial that represents the area of the garden.

Answers

1. $-2x^2 - 14x + 7$
2. $-17q^2 - 3q + 4$
3. $-5k^6 + 15k^4$
4. $y^3 + 3y^2 + y - 2$
5. $4z^2 + z - 18$
6. $p^2 - 6p - 7$
7. $64m^2 + 48m + 9$
8. $25y^2 - 60y + 36$
9. $w^2 + 4w$

CHAPTER 9 Quiz 2

For use after Lessons 9.4–9.6

Factor out the greatest common monomial factor.

1. $12x^2 + 3xy$
2. $21ab^2 + 35ab$
3. $9z^2 - 18z^3$
4. $4p - 8p^2$

Factor the trinomial.

5. $w^2 + 15w + 14$
6. $m^2 - 12m + 20$
7. $2k^2 + 5k - 3$
8. $3b^2 - 20b - 7$
9. $8y^2 + 26y + 15$
10. $-2d^2 - 7d - 5$

Solve the equation.

11. $(h + 6)(h - 4) = 0$
12. $21d^2 - 7d = 0$
13. $s^2 - 7s + 14 = 2$
14. $-5z^2 - 10z = 0$
15. $2g^2 - 14g = -20$
16. $-r^2 - 5r - 6 = 0$

Answers

1. $3x(4x + y)$
2. $7ab(3b + 5)$
3. $9z^2(1 - 2z)$
4. $4p(1 - 2p)$
5. $(w + 1)(w + 14)$
6. $(m - 10)(m - 2)$
7. $(2k - 1)(k + 3)$
8. $(3b + 1)(b - 7)$
9. $(2y + 5)(4y + 3)$
10. $-(2d + 5)(d + 1)$
11. $-6, 4$
12. $0, \frac{1}{3}$
13. $3, 4$
14. $-2, 0$
15. $2, 5$
16. $-3, -2$

CHAPTER 9 Quiz 3

For use after Lessons 9.7–9.8

Factor the polynomial.

1. $x^2 - 81$
2. $9z^2 - 121$
3. $100m^2 - 49n^2$
4. $h^2 + 14h + 49$
5. $64t^2 - 16t + 1$
6. $4a^2 + 4b^2$

Factor the polynomial completely.

7. $6x^2 - 6y^2$
8. $5m^2 - 20n^2$
9. $x^3 - 3x^2 - 10x$
10. $3z^2 + 30z + 75$
11. $2k^3 - 36k^2 + 162k$
12. $x^2 + 2x + xy + 2y$

Solve the equation.

13. $d^2 + 10d + 25 = 0$
14. $20 - 5s^2 = 0$
15. $y^3 - 49y = 0$
16. $6x^3 - 36x^2 + 30x = 0$
17. A box of crackers has a volume of 96 cubic inches. The box has a height of x inches, a width of $(x - 6)$ inches, and a length of $(x - 2)$ inches. Find the dimensions of the box.

Answers

1. $(x + 9)(x - 9)$
2. $(3z + 11)(3z - 11)$
3. $(10m + 7n) \cdot (10m - 7n)$
4. $(h + 7)^2$
5. $(8t - 1)^2$
6. $4(a^2 + b^2)$
7. $6(x + y)(x - y)$
8. $5(m + 2n)(m - 2n)$
9. $x(x - 5)(x + 2)$
10. $3(z + 5)^2$
11. $2k(k - 9)^2$
12. $(x + y)(x + 2)$
13. -5
14. $-2, 2$
15. $-7, 0, 7$
16. $0, 1, 5$
17. 6 in. long by 2 in. wide by 8 in. high

CHAPTER 9 Chapter Test B

For use after Chapter 9

Find the sum or difference.

1. $(4a^3 - 2a + 1) - (a^3 - 2a + 3)$
2. $(3x^3 + 4x + 14) + (-4x^2 + 21)$
3. $(3d - 5d^3 + 2d^2) - (8d^3 + 6d - 1)$
4. $(-3n + 7n) + (4n^3 - 2n^2 + 12)$

In Exercises 5 and 6, use the following information.

During the period 1985–2012, the projected enrollment B (in thousands of students) in public schools and the projected enrollment R (in thousands of students) in private schools can be modeled by

$$B = -18.53t^2 + 975.8t + 48{,}140 \quad \text{and} \quad R = 80.8t + 8049$$

where t is the number of years since 1985.

5. Write an equation that models the difference in the projected enrollments for public schools and private schools as a function of the number of years since 1985.
6. Find the difference in projected enrollments for public schools and private schools in 2005.

Find the product.

7. $-4c(-9c^2 + 5c + 8)$
8. $(y + 4)(5y - 3)$
9. $(s^2 + 6s - 5)(5s + 2)$
10. $(4p + 1)(4p - 1)$
11. $(w - 5)^2$
12. $(2b + 3)^2$

In Exercises 13 and 14, use the following information.

You are making an open box from a rectangular sheet of cardboard by cutting squares 2 inches in length from each corner and folding up the sides. The length of the sheet of cardboard is 8 inches more than the width.

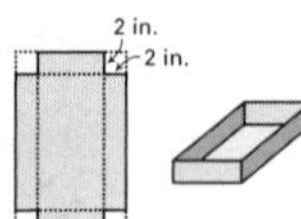

13. Write a polynomial that represents the total volume of the open box.
14. Find the volume of the open box when the width of the sheet of cardboard is 6 inches.

Answers

1. $3a^3 - 2$
2. $3x^3 - 4x^2 + 4x + 35$
3. $-13d^3 + 2d^2 - 3d + 1$
4. $4n^3 - 2n^2 + 4n + 12$
5. $D = -18.53t^2 - 895t + 40{,}091$
6. 14,779,000 students
7. $36c^3 - 20c^2 - 32c$
8. $5y^2 + 7y - 12$
9. $5s^3 + 32s^2 - 13s - 10$
10. $16p^2 - 1$
11. $w^2 - 10w + 25$
12. $4b^2 + 12b + 9$
13. $V = 2x(x + 8) = 2x^2 + 16x$
14. 168 in.^{3}

CHAPTER 9

Chapter Test B *continued*

For use after Chapter 9

Solve the equation.

15. $(h - 7)(2h + 1) = 0$

16. $4g^2 - 32g = 0$

17. $3m^2 = -6m$

In Exercises 18 and 19, use the following information.

The room and the hallway shown in the floor plan below have different dimensions but the same area.

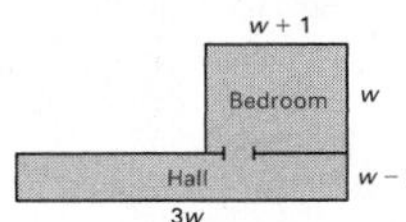

18. Write an equation that relates the areas of the rooms.

19. Find the value of w.

Factor the trinomial.

20. $n^2 - 14n - 72$ **21.** $-x^2 + 14x - 45$ **22.** $6k^2 - k - 12$

In Exercises 23 and 24, use the following information.

A juggler throws a ball from an initial height of 4 feet with an initial vertical velocity of 30 feet per second. The height h (in feet) of the ball can be modeled by $h = -16t^2 + vt + s$ where t is the time (in seconds) the ball has been in the air, v is the initial vertical velocity (in feet per second), and s is the initial height.

23. Write an equation that gives the height (in feet) of the ball as a function of the time (in seconds) since it left the juggler's hand.

24. If the juggler misses the ball, after how many seconds does it hit the ground?

Factor the polynomial completely.

25. $x^6 - x^3$ **26.** $5a(a - 3) - 7(a - 3)$

27. $9t^4 + 30t^3 + 25t^2$ **28.** $b^3 + 5b^2 - 3b - 15$

Solve the equation.

29. $x^2 + 8x + 15 = 0$ **30.** $7y - 2 = 5y^2$

31. $72 = 32q^2$ **32.** $u^3 + 6u^2 = 4u + 24$

Answers

15. $-\frac{1}{2}, 7$

16. $0, 8$

17. $-2, 0$

18. $3w(w - 2) = w(w + 1)$

19. $\frac{7}{2}$

20. $(n - 18)(n + 4)$

21. $-(x - 9)(x - 5)$

22. $(3k + 4)(2k - 3)$

23. $h = -16t^2 + 30t + 4$

24. 2 sec

25. $x^3(x + 1)(x - 1)$

26. $(a - 3)(5a - 7)$

27. $t^2(3t + 5)^2$

28. $(b - 5)(b^2 - 3)$

29. $-5, -3$

30. $1, \frac{2}{5}$

31. $\pm\frac{3}{2}$

32. $-6, \pm 2$

CHAPTER 9

Standardized Test

For use after Chapter 9

Multiple Choice

1. What is the degree of $-5a^2b + 4a^2 - 2b + 5$? C

Ⓐ −5 Ⓑ 2 Ⓒ 3 Ⓓ 4

2. Which expression is *not* a monomial? D

Ⓐ $-2n$ Ⓑ $\frac{m}{2}$ Ⓒ r^2 Ⓓ $3p^{-3}$

3. What is the sum of $6m^2 - 5m + 4$ and $7m^2 + 2m - 5$? B

Ⓐ $13m^2 - 7m - 9$

Ⓑ $13m^2 - 3m - 1$

Ⓒ $13m^2 + 3m - 1$

Ⓓ $13m^2 - 3m + 1$

4. What is $(12s^2 + 8s - 6) - (9s^2 - 2s + 5)$ in simplest form? B

Ⓐ $3s^2 + 6s - 1$ Ⓑ $3s^2 + 10s - 11$

Ⓒ $3s^2 + 10s + 11$ Ⓓ $3s^2 + 6s - 11$

5. What is the product of $x + 5$ and $3x - 2$? A

Ⓐ $3x^2 + 13x - 10$ Ⓑ $3x^2 - 10$

Ⓒ $3x^2 + 17x - 10$ Ⓓ $3x^2 - 13x - 10$

6. Which polynomial represents $f(x) \cdot g(x)$ if $f(x) = -4x^2$ and $g(x) = x^3 + 2x^2 - 5x + 3$? C

Ⓐ $-4x^5 + 8x^4 - 20x^3 - 12x^2$

Ⓑ $-4x^5 - 8x^3 - 20x^3 - 12x^2$

Ⓒ $-4x^5 - 8x^4 + 20x^3 - 12x^2$

Ⓓ $-4x^5 + 8x^4 + 20x^3 - 12x^2$

7. What is the simplest form of $(5x + 2)(5x - 2)$? A

Ⓐ $25x^2 - 4$ Ⓑ $10x^2$

Ⓒ $25x^2 + 10x - 4$ Ⓓ $25x^2 - 20x - 4$

8. What is the simplest form of $(2n + 3)^2$? D

Ⓐ $4n^2 + 12n + 6$ Ⓑ $4n^2 + 6n + 9$

Ⓒ $4n^2 + 9$ Ⓓ $4n^2 + 12n + 9$

9. Which of the following are the roots of the equation $(y - 3)(y + 2) = 0$? B

Ⓐ 2 and 3 Ⓑ −2 and 3

Ⓒ −3 and 2 Ⓓ −3 and −2

10. What is the greatest monomial factor of $32x^5 - 12x^2$? A

Ⓐ $4x^2$ Ⓑ $32x^5$

Ⓒ $12x^2$ Ⓓ $20x^3$

11. What are the roots of the equation $5x^2 = x$? C

Ⓐ −5 and 0 Ⓑ 0 and $-\frac{1}{5}$

Ⓒ 0 and $\frac{1}{5}$ Ⓓ 0 and 5

12. Which of the following is the correct factorization of $x^2 - 15x + 56$? A

Ⓐ $(x - 7)(x - 8)$

Ⓑ $(x + 7)(x - 8)$

Ⓒ $(x - 7)(x + 8)$

Ⓓ $(x + 7)(x + 8)$

13. What are the roots of the equation $x^2 + 30x = 1000$? D

Ⓐ 20 and 50 Ⓑ −50 and −20

Ⓒ −20 and 50 Ⓓ −50 and 20

14. Which of the following is the correct factorization of $6x^2 - 2x - 20$? B

Ⓐ $(3x - 5)(2x + 4)$

Ⓑ $(3x + 5)(2x - 4)$

Ⓒ $(6x - 10)(x + 2)$

Ⓓ $(6x + 2)(x - 10)$

CHAPTER 9

Standardized Test *continued*

For use after Chapter 9

15. Which of the following is the correct factorization of $-y^2 + y + 6$? C

Ⓐ $(-y + 3)(y - 2)$

Ⓑ $-(y + 6)(y + 1)$

Ⓒ $-(y + 2)(y - 3)$

Ⓓ $-(y + 2)(y + 3)$

16. What are the roots of the equation $1.5x^2 - 4.5x = -3$? C

Ⓐ −2 and −1 Ⓑ −1 and 1

Ⓒ 1 and 2 Ⓓ 2 and 3

17. Which of the following is the correct factorization of $-60m^2 + 15n^2$? D

Ⓐ $15(2m + n)^2$

Ⓑ $15(2m - n)(2m + n)$

Ⓒ $-15(2m - n)^2$

Ⓓ $-15(2m - n)(2m + n)$

18. Which of the following is the correct factorization of $3x^3 + 24x^2 - 27x$? A

Ⓐ $3x(x + 9)(x - 1)$

Ⓑ $3x(x - 9)(x + 1)$

Ⓒ $3x(x - 9)(x - 1)$

Ⓓ $3x(x + 9)(x + 1)$

19. What is the completely factored form of $4x^5 - 256x^3$? B

Ⓐ $4x^3(x - 8)^2$

Ⓑ $4x^3(x + 8)(x - 8)$

Ⓒ $4x^3(x^2 - 64)$

Ⓓ $4x^3(x + 8)^2$

22. a.

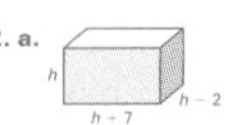

22. c. 222 cm²; If you set the polynomial in part (b) equal to 180 and solve for h, you will find that the height is 5 centimeters. From there, you find the area of each side and add to find the total surface area.

Gridded Answer

20. The square of the binomial $x - 4$ has the form $x^2 - ax + 16$. What is the value of a?

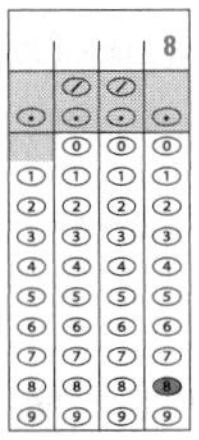

8

Short Response

21. You made a square card to send to a friend. The card did not fit in the envelope so you had to trim the card. You trimmed 4 inches from the length and 5 inches from the width. The area of the resulting card is 20 square inches.

a. What were the original dimensions of the card? 9 in. × 9 in.

b. What was the perimeter of the original card? 36 in.

c. What is the difference in the areas of the original and trimmed cards? 61 in.²

Extended Response

22. The length of a box is 2 centimeters less than its height. The width of the box is 7 centimeters more than its height.

a. Draw a diagram of the box and label its dimensions in terms of the height h. See left.

b. Write a polynomial that represents the volume of the box. $h^3 + 5h^2 - 14h$

c. If the box has a volume of 180 cubic centimeters, what is its surface area? *Explain.* See left.

CHAPTER 9

Alternative Assessment and Math Journal

For use after Chapter 9

Journal **1.** Explain the four steps that you should try when factoring a polynomial completely.

Multi-Step Problem **2.** The diagram below represents a picture frame that is being built.

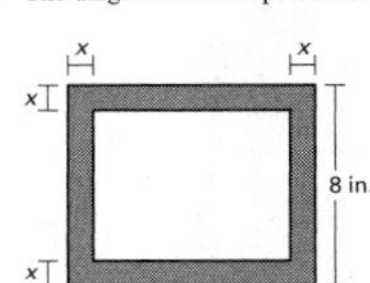

a. Write a polynomial expression to represent each dimension of the inner rectangle.

b. A gold ribbon is to be placed around the outside of each rectangle of the frame. Write a polynomial expression to represent the amount of ribbon needed.

c. How much gold ribbon is needed if the value of x is 1.5 inches?

d. Write a polynomial expression to represent the area of the interior portion of the picture frame.

e. What is the interior area of the picture frame if the value of x is 1.5 inches?

f. Write and solve a polynomial equation to determine the value of x that will make the interior area of the picture frame measure 63 square inches.

g. Write a polynomial expression to represent the area of the shaded portion of the frame.

h. Write and solve a polynomial equation to determine the value of x that will make the shaded area of the picture frame measure 38.75 square inches.

1. Complete answers should include: a brief description of the four steps of factoring a polynomial completely:

1. Factor out the greatest common monomial factor.
2. Look for a difference of two squares or a perfect square trinomial.
3. Factor a trinomial of the form $ax^2 + bx + c$ into a product of binomial factors.
4. Factor a polynomial with four terms by grouping; mention that some of the steps may not work for the polynomial that is being factored.

2. a. $10 - 2x$; $8 - 2x$ **b.** $72 - 8x$ **c.** 60 in. **d.** $4x^2 - 36x + 80$ **e.** 35 in.²

f. $\frac{1}{2}$ in. **g.** $-4x^2 + 36x$ **h.** 1.25 in.

PLAN AND PREPARE

Main Ideas

In Chapter 9 students identify, classify, add, subtract, and multiply polynomials. They use vertical and horizontal formats to find sums and differences. To find products, they use the distributive property, tables of products, and patterns (including the FOIL pattern, the square of a binomial pattern, and the sum and difference patterns). They write polynomials to describe and solve real-world problems and solve polynomial equations. Students factor polynomials and use factoring to solve equations, to find the zeros of functions, and to find the roots of equations. Finally, they factor polynomials completely using a variety of techniques.

Prerequisite Skills

- using the distributive property
- combining like terms
- using the properties of exponents

Additional resources for reviewing prerequisite skills are:

- Skills Review Handbook, pp. 909–937
- @HomeTutor

9 Polynomials and Factoring

Before

In previous chapters, you learned the following skills, which you'll use in Chapter 9: using the distributive property, combining like terms, and using the properties of exponents.

Prerequisite Skills

VOCABULARY CHECK

Copy and complete the statement.

1. Terms that have the same variable part are called __?__. like terms
2. For a function $f(x)$, a(n) _?_ is an x-value for which $f(x) = 0$. zero

SKILLS CHECK

Find the greatest common factor of the pair of numbers. *(Review p. 910 for 9.4.)*

3. 121, 77 11
4. 96, 32 32
5. 81, 42 3
6. 12, 56 4

Simplify the expression. *(Review p. 96 for 9.1–9.8.)*

7. $3x + (-6x)$ $-3x$
8. $5 + 4x + 2$ $4x + 7$
9. $4(2x - 1) + x$ $9x - 4$
10. $-(x + 4) - 6x$ $-7x - 4$

Simplify the expression. *(Review p. 489 for 9.2–9.8.)*

11. $(3xy)^3$ $27x^3y^3$
12. $xy^2 \cdot xy^3$ x^2y^5
13. $(x^5)^3$ x^{15}
14. $(-x)^3$ $-x^3$

@HomeTutor Prerequisite skills practice at classzone.com

552

Chapter Planning Guide

Chapter 9 Resource Book
- Teaching Guide/Lesson Plan (pp. 3, 15, 26, 36, 50, 61, 72, 82)
- Project with Rubric (p. 93)

Assessment and Intervention
- Assessment Book (pp. 124–138)
- Benchmark Tests
- Reteaching and Remediation Book

Interactive Technology
- Easy Planner
- Power Presentations CD-ROM
- Activity Generator CD-ROM
- Animated Algebra
- Test Generator CD-ROM
- Online Quizzes
- eWorkbook
- eEdition
- @HomeTutor

Resources for English Learners
- Quick Reference for English Learners
- Spanish Study Guide
- Multi-Language Visual Glossary
- Student Resources in Spanish

Now

In Chapter 9, you will apply the big ideas listed below and reviewed in the Chapter Summary on page 615. You will also use the key vocabulary listed below.

Big Ideas

1. **Adding, subtracting, and multiplying polynomials**
2. **Factoring polynomials**
3. **Writing and solving polynomial equations to solve problems**

KEY VOCABULARY

- monomial, *p. 554*
- degree, *p. 554*
- polynomial, *p. 554*
- leading coefficient, *p. 554*
- binomial, *p. 555*
- trinomial, *p. 555*
- roots, *p. 575*
- vertical motion model, *p. 577*
- perfect square trinomial, *p. 601*
- factor by grouping, *p. 606*
- factor completely, *p. 607*

Why?

You can use a polynomial function to model vertical motion. For example, you can use a polynomial function to model the height of a jumping animal as a function of time.

Animated Algebra

The animation illustrated below for Exercise 62 on page 598 helps you to answer this question: How does changing the initial vertical velocity of a serval, an African cat, affect its jumping height?

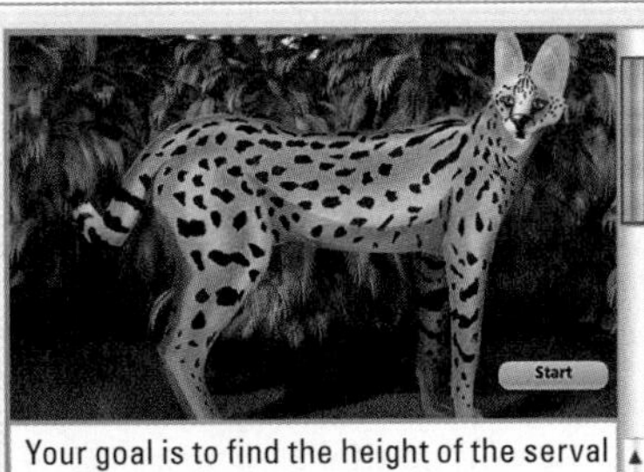

Your goal is to find the height of the serval at different times.

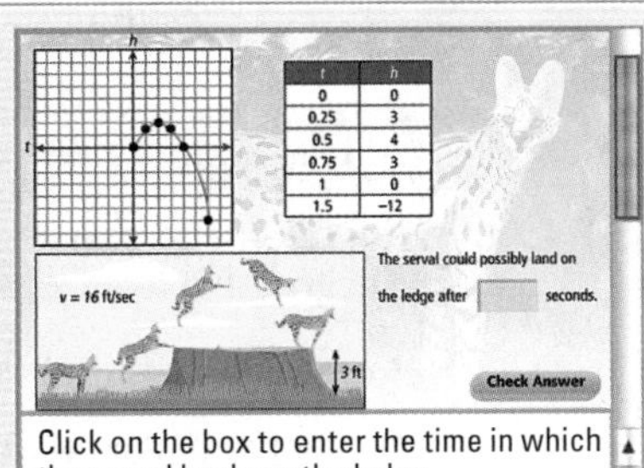

Click on the box to enter the time in which the serval lands on the ledge.

Animated Algebra at classzone.com

Other animations for Chapter 9: pages 555, 582, 592, and 601

553

Algebra 1 Toolkit

- Reading Strategies for Chapter 9, pp. 25–26
- Differentiated Instruction Notes, pp. 73–76
- English Learners Notes, pp. 113–114
- Inclusion Notes, pp. 145–146
- Teaching Strategies with Sample Worksheets, pp. 155–178
- Using Technology in the Classroom, pp. 179–184
- Tips for New Teachers, pp. 201–202
- Math Background Notes, pp. 227–228
- Pre-AP Strategies and Copymasters, pp. 294–295, 420–426
- Teacher Survival Activities, pp. 571–572, 597–598
- Bulletin Board Idea, p. 615
- Teacher Tool Transparencies, following p. 620

9.1 Add and Subtract Polynomials

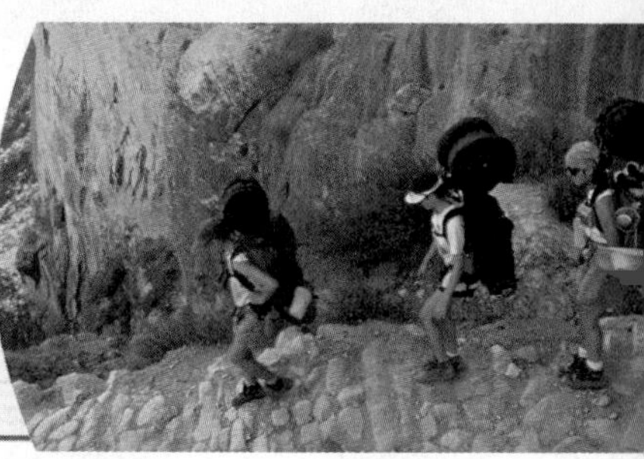

8.11.01 Simplify or identify equivalent algebraic expressions (e.g., exponential, rational, logarithmic, factored, polynomial).

Before You added and subtracted integers.

Now You will add and subtract polynomials.

Why? So you can model trends in recreation, as in Ex. 37.

Key Vocabulary
- **monomial**
- **degree**
- **polynomial**
- **leading coefficient**
- **binomial**
- **trinomial**

A **monomial** is a number, a variable, or the product of a number and one or more variables with whole number exponents. The **degree of a monomial** is the sum of the exponents of the variables in the monomial. The degree of a nonzero constant term is 0. The constant 0 does not have a degree.

Monomial	Degree
10	0
$3x$	1
$\frac{1}{2}ab^2$	$1 + 2 = 3$
$-1.8m^5$	5

Not a monomial	Reason
$5 + x$	A sum is not a monomial.
$\frac{2}{n}$	A monomial cannot have a variable in the denominator.
4^a	A monomial cannot have a variable exponent.
x^{-1}	The variable must have a whole number exponent.

A **polynomial** is a monomial or a sum of monomials, each called a *term* of the polynomial. The **degree of a polynomial** is the greatest degree of its terms.

When a polynomial is written so that the exponents of a variable decrease from left to right, the coefficient of the first term is called the **leading coefficient**.

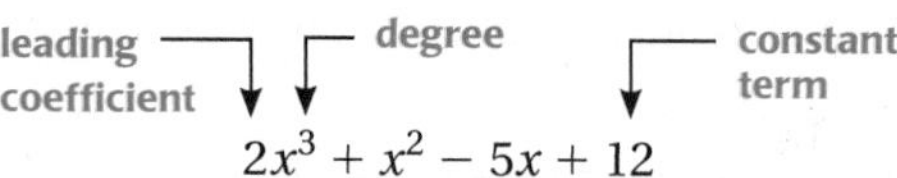

EXAMPLE 1 Rewrite a polynomial

Write $15x - x^3 + 3$ so that the exponents decrease from left to right. Identify the degree and leading coefficient of the polynomial.

Solution

Consider the degree of each of the polynomial's terms.

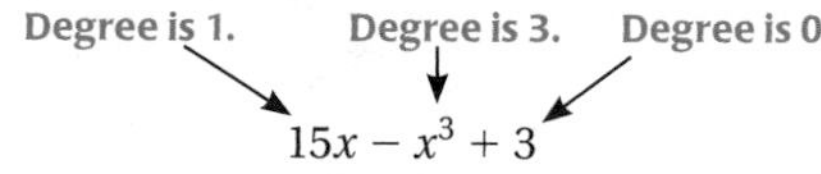

The polynomial can be written as $-x^3 + 15x + 3$. The greatest degree is 3, so the degree of the polynomial is 3, and the leading coefficient is -1.

1 PLAN AND PREPARE

Warm-Up Exercises

Transparency Available

Simplify the expression.

1. $5x + 4(2x + 7)$ $13x + 28$
2. $9x - 6(x + 2) + 3$ $3x - 9$
3. Imported square tiles used for a kitchen floor measure 18 centimeters on one side. What is the area of a floor composed of 50 tiles? Use $A = s^2$ for the area of a tile. 16,200 cm^2

Notetaking Guide

Transparency Available

Promotes interactive learning and notetaking skills, pp. 188–190.

Pacing

Basic: 1 day

Average: 1 day

Advanced: 1 day

Block: 0.5 block with 9.2

- See *Teaching Guide/Lesson Plan*.

2 FOCUS AND MOTIVATE

Essential Question

Big Idea 1, p. 553

How do you add and subtract polynomials? **Tell students they will learn how to answer this question by using vertical and horizontal formats to find sums and differences of polynomials.**

Resource Planning Guide

Chapter Resource Book
- Teaching Guide/Lesson Plan (pp. 3–4)
- Activity Master (p. 5)
- Practice levels A, B, C (pp. 7–9)
- Study Guide (pp. 10–11)
- Catch-up for Absent Students (p. 12)
- Problem Solving Workshop (p. 13)
- Challenge (p. 14)

Workbooks
- Notetaking Guide (pp. 188–190)
- Practice Workbook (pp. 133–134)

Teaching Options
- **Power Presentations CD-ROM** provides dynamic electronic teaching resources for the classroom.
- **Activity Generator CD-ROM** provides editable activities for all ability levels.

Interactive Technology
- Easy Planner
- Power Presentations CD-ROM
- Activity Generator CD-ROM
- Animated Algebra
- Test Generator CD-ROM
- Online Quiz
- eWorkbook
- eEdition
- @HomeTutor

Resources for English Learners
- Quick Reference for English Learners
- Spanish Study Guide
- Multi-Language Visual Glossary
- Student Resources in Spanish

See also the *Algebra 1 Toolkit* for more strategies for meeting individual needs.

BINOMIALS AND TRINOMIALS A polynomial with two terms is called a **binomial**. A polynomial with three terms is called a **trinomial**.

EXAMPLE 2 Identify and classify polynomials

Tell whether the expression is a polynomial. If it is a polynomial, find its degree and classify it by the number of its terms. Otherwise, tell why it is not a polynomial.

	Expression	Is it a polynomial?	Classify by degree and number of terms
a.	9	Yes	0 degree monomial
b.	$2x^2 + x - 5$	Yes	2nd degree trinomial
c.	$6n^4 - 8^n$	No; variable exponent	
d.	$n^{-2} - 3$	No; negative exponent	
e.	$7bc^3 + 4b^4c$	Yes	5th degree binomial

ADDING POLYNOMIALS To add polynomials, add like terms. You can use a vertical or a horizontal format.

EXAMPLE 3 Add polynomials

Find the sum.

a. $(2x^3 - 5x^2 + x) + (2x^2 + x^3 - 1)$ **b.** $(3x^2 + x - 6) + (x^2 + 4x + 10)$

Solution

ALIGN TERMS
If a particular power of the variable appears in one polynomial but not the other, leave a space in that column, or write the term with a coefficient of 0.

a. Vertical format: Align like terms in vertical columns.

$$\begin{array}{r} 2x^3 - 5x^2 + x \phantom{{}-1} \\ + \quad x^3 + 2x^2 \phantom{{}+x} - 1 \\ \hline 3x^3 - 3x^2 + x - 1 \end{array}$$

b. Horizontal format: Group like terms and simplify.

$$(3x^2 + x - 6) + (x^2 + 4x + 10) = (3x^2 + x^2) + (x + 4x) + (-6 + 10)$$
$$= 4x^2 + 5x + 4$$

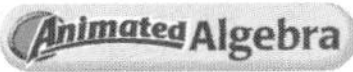 at classzone.com

✓ GUIDED PRACTICE for Examples 1, 2, and 3

1. Write $5y - 2y^2 + 9$ so that the exponents decrease from left to right. Identify the degree and leading coefficient of the polynomial. $-2y^2 + 5y + 9$; 2, −2
2. Tell whether $y^3 - 4y + 3$ is a polynomial. If it is a polynomial, find its degree and classify it by the number of its terms. Otherwise, tell why it is not a polynomial. polynomial; 3, trinomial
3. Find the sum $(5x^3 + 4x - 2x) + (4x^2 + 3x^3 - 6)$. $8x^3 + 4x^2 + 2x - 6$

Motivating the Lesson

Tell students that they can add or subtract polynomials to model a real-world situation. For example, if one polynomial models ticket sales for boys' sports and another models ticket sales for girls' sports, they can add the polynomials and evaluate the sum to find total ticket sales.

3 TEACH

Extra Example 1

Write $3b^3 - 4b^4 + b^2$ so that the exponents decrease from left to right. Identify the degree and leading coefficient of the polynomial. $-4b^4 + 3b^3 + b^2$; degree: 4; leading coefficient: −4

Extra Example 2

Tell whether the expression is a polynomial. If it is a polynomial, find its degree and classify it by the number of its terms. Otherwise, tell why it is not a polynomial.

a. $5xy^2$ yes, 3rd degree monomial
b. $3a^{-5}$ no, negative exponent
c. $x^4 + 3x^3 - x$ yes, 4th degree trinomial
d. $\frac{9}{m}$ no, variable in denominator
e. $6a^2c + 5ac^5$ yes, 6th degree binomial

Extra Example 3

Find the sum.

a. $(-2x^2 + 3x - x^3) + (3x^2 + x^3 - 12)$ $x^2 + 3x - 12$
b. $(4x^3 + 2x^2 - 4) + (x^3 - 3x^2 + x)$ $5x^3 - x^2 + x - 4$

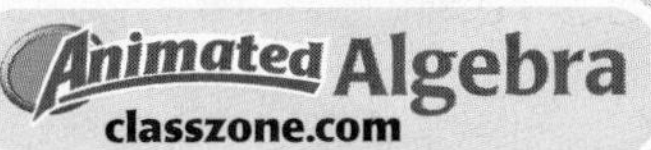

An **Animated Algebra** activity is available on-line for **Example 3**. This activity is also available on the **Power Presentations CD-ROM**.

Differentiated Instruction

Below Level To help students gain confidence in recognizing polynomials, have them work with partners to write examples of 1st degree through 6th degree monomials, binomials, and trinomials. Suggest that they create a table to organize their work. Encourage students to write some polynomials with more than one variable per term. Have partners exchange their polynomials so that other partners can check that the polynomials fit the descriptions.

See also the *Algebra 1 Toolkit* for more strategies.

Extra Example 4

Find the difference.

a. $(2c^2 - 8) - (3c^2 - 4c + 1)$
$-c^2 + 4c - 9$

b. $(5y^2 + 2y - 4) - (-y^2 + 4y - 3)$
$6y^2 - 2y - 1$

Key Question to Ask for Example 4

- How do you group terms in the horizontal format for part (a)? $(4n^2 - (-2n^2)) + (-2n) + (5 - (-4))$

Extra Example 5

During the period 1999–2005, the number of hours an individual person watched broadcast television B and cable and satellite television C can be modeled by
$B = 2.8t^2 - 35t + 879$ and
$C = -5t^2 + 80t + 712$
where t is the number of years since 1999. About how many hours did people watch television in 2002? about 1706 h

Closing the Lesson

Have students summarize the major points of the lesson and answer the Essential Question: How do you add and subtract polynomials?

- A polynomial is a monomial or the sum of monomials. The degree of a polynomial is the greatest degree of its terms.
- Use a vertical or horizontal format to add and subtract polynomials.

To use a vertical format, align like terms in columns. To use a horizontal format, group like terms and simplify. To add, add the terms. To subtract, add the opposite of each term of the subtracted polynomial.

SUBTRACTING POLYNOMIALS To subtract a polynomial, add its opposite. To find the opposite of a polynomial, multiply each of its terms by -1.

EXAMPLE 4 Subtract polynomials

Find the difference.

a. $(4n^2 + 5) - (-2n^2 + 2n - 4)$ **b.** $(4x^2 - 3x + 5) - (3x^2 - x - 8)$

Solution

AVOID ERRORS
Remember to multiply *each* term in the polynomial by -1 when you write the subtraction as addition.

a.

$$\begin{array}{r} (4n^2 \qquad + 5) \\ -(-2n^2 + 2n - 4) \\ \hline \end{array} \quad \longrightarrow \quad \begin{array}{r} 4n^2 \qquad + 5 \\ +\ 2n^2 - 2n + 4 \\ \hline 6n^2 - 2n + 9 \end{array}$$

b. $(4x^2 - 3x + 5) - (3x^2 - x - 8) = 4x^2 - 3x + 5 - 3x^2 + x + 8$
$= (4x^2 - 3x^2) + (-3x + x) + (5 + 8)$
$= x^2 - 2x + 13$

EXAMPLE 5 Solve a multi-step problem

BASEBALL ATTENDANCE Major League Baseball teams are divided into two leagues. During the period 1995–2001, the attendance N and A (in thousands) at National and American League baseball games, respectively, can be modeled by

$N = -488t^2 + 5430t + 24{,}700$ and

$A = -318t^2 + 3040t + 25{,}600$

where t is the number of years since 1995. About how many people attended Major League Baseball games in 2001?

Solution

STEP 1 **Add** the models for the attendance in each league to find a model for M, the total attendance (in thousands).

$M = (-488t^2 + 5430t + 24{,}700) + (-318t^2 + 3040t + 25{,}600)$
$= (-488t^2 - 318t^2) + (5430t + 3040t) + (24{,}700 + 25{,}600)$
$= -806t^2 + 8470t + 50{,}300$

AVOID ERRORS
Because a value of M represents *thousands* of people, $M \approx 72{,}100$ represents 72,100,000 people.

STEP 2 **Substitute** 6 for t in the model, because 2001 is 6 years after 1995.

$M = -806(6)^2 + 8470(6) + 50{,}300 \approx 72{,}100$

▸ About 72,100,000 people attended Major League Baseball games in 2001.

GUIDED PRACTICE for Examples 4 and 5

4. Find the difference $(4x^2 - 7x) - (5x^2 + 4x - 9)$. $-x^2 - 11x + 9$

5. **BASEBALL ATTENDANCE** Look back at Example 5. Find the difference in attendance at National and American League baseball games in 2001.

5. about 7,320,000 people

Differentiated Instruction

Advanced Have students use the online U.S. Statistical Abstract to research a favorite sport or activity. Have them create a problem similar to **Example 5** using data that appear nonlinear. If necessary, they can review the Activity on page 342 on using the Abstract. They can enter data on a graphing calculator and use the quadratic and cubic regression option to find a best-fit equation. Students can discuss which equations best fit the data and exchange and solve each other's problems.

See also the *Algebra 1 Toolkit* for more strategies.

9.1 EXERCISES

HOMEWORK KEY
◯ = **WORKED-OUT SOLUTIONS** on p. WS20 for Exs. 21 and 39
★ = **STANDARDIZED TEST PRACTICE** Exs. 2, 9, 10, 39, and 41

SKILL PRACTICE

1. **VOCABULARY** Copy and complete: A number, a variable, or the product of one or more variables is called a(n) __?__. monomial

2. ★ **WRITING** Is 6 a polynomial? *Explain* why or why not. Yes; a polynomial is a monomial or a sum of monomials. Since 6 is a monomial, it is also a polynomial.

EXAMPLE 1 on p. 554 for Exs. 3–9

REWRITING POLYNOMIALS **Write the polynomial so that the exponents decrease from left to right. Identify the degree and leading coefficient of the polynomial.**

3. $9m^5$ $9m^5$; 5, 9
4. $2 - 6y$ $-6y + 2$; 1, -6
5. $2x^2y^2 - 8xy$ $2x^2y^2 - 8xy$; 4, 2
6. $5n^3 + 2n - 7$ $5n^3 + 2n - 7$; 3, 5
7. $5z + 2z^3 - z^2 + 3z^4$ $3z^4 + 2z^3 - z^2 + 5z$; 4, 3
8. $-2h^2 + 2h^4 - h^6$ $-h^6 + 2h^4 - 2h^2$; 6, -1
9. ★ **MULTIPLE CHOICE** What is the degree of $-4x^3 + 6x^4 - 1$? C

   Ⓐ -4 Ⓑ 3 Ⓒ 4 Ⓓ 6

EXAMPLE 2 on p. 555 for Exs. 10–16

10. ★ **MULTIPLE CHOICE** Which expression is *not* a monomial? D

    Ⓐ $-5x^2$ Ⓑ $0.2y^4$ Ⓒ $3mn$ Ⓓ $3s^{-2}$

IDENTIFYING AND CLASSIFYING POLYNOMIALS **Tell whether the expression is a polynomial. If it is a polynomial, find its degree and classify it by the number of its terms. Otherwise, tell why it is not a polynomial.**

11. -4^x not a polynomial; variable exponent
12. $w^{-3} + 1$ not a polynomial; negative exponent
13. $3x - 5$ polynomial; 1, binomial
14. $\frac{4}{5}f^2 - \frac{1}{2}f + \frac{2}{3}$ polynomial; 2, trinomial
15. $6 - n^2 + 5n^3$ polynomial; 3, trinomial
16. $10y^4 - 3y^2 + 11$ polynomial; 4, trinomial

EXAMPLES 3 and 4 on pp. 555–556 for Exs. 17–28

ADDING AND SUBTRACTING POLYNOMIALS **Find the sum or difference.**

17. $(5a^2 - 3) + (8a^2 - 1)$ $13a^2 - 4$
18. $(h^2 + 4h - 4) + (5h^2 - 8h + 2)$ $6h^2 - 4h - 2$
19. $(4m^2 - m + 2) + (-3m^2 + 10m + 7)$ $m^2 + 9m + 9$
20. $(7k^2 + 2k - 6) + (3k^2 - 11k - 8)$ $10k^2 - 9k - 14$
21. $(6c^2 + 3c + 9) - (3c - 5)$ $6c^2 + 14$
22. $(3x^2 - 8) - (4x^3 + x^2 - 15x + 1)$ $-4x^3 + 2x^2 + 15x - 9$
23. $(-n^2 + 2n) - (2n^3 - n^2 + n + 12)$ $-2n^3 + n - 12$
24. $(9b^3 - 13b^2 + b) - (-13b^2 - 5b + 14)$ $9b^3 + 6b - 14$
25. $(4d - 6d^3 + 3d^2) - (9d^3 + 7d - 2)$ $-15d^3 + 3d^2 - 3d + 2$
26. $(9p^2 - 6p^3 + 3 - 11p) + (7p^3 - 3p^2 + 4)$ $p^3 + 6p^2 - 11p + 7$

ERROR ANALYSIS ***Describe*** **and correct the error in finding the sum or difference of the polynomials.**

27.
$$\begin{array}{r} x^3 - 4x^2 + 3 \\ +\ -3x^3 + 8x - 2 \\ \hline -2x^3 + 4x^2 + 1 \end{array}$$
✗

28.
$(6x^2 - 5x) - (2x^2 + 3x - 2)$
$= (6x^2 - 2x^2) + (-5x + 3x) - 2$
$= 4x^2 - 2x - 2$
✗

27. Two unlike terms, $-4x^2$ and $8x$, were combined; $-2x^3 - 4x^2 + 8x + 1$.

28. When the subtraction was rewritten as addition, the last two terms of the second polynomial were not multiplied by -1; $(6x^2 - 2x^2) + (-5x - 3x) + 2$, $4x^2 - 8x + 2$.

B

29. **POLYNOMIAL FUNCTIONS** Find the sum $f(x) + g(x)$ and the difference $f(x) - g(x)$ for the functions $f(x) = 3x^2 + x - 7$ and $g(x) = -x^2 + 5x - 2$. $2x^2 + 6x - 9$, $4x^2 - 4x - 5$

4 PRACTICE AND APPLY

Assignment Guide

Answer Transparencies available for all exercises

Basic:
Day 1: pp. 557–559
Exs. 1, 2, 3–7 odd, 9, 10, 11–25 odd, 27–31, 37–40, 43–53 odd

Average:
Day 1: pp. 557–559
Exs. 1, 2, 6–10, 12–26 even, 27–34, 37–41, 44, 47, 50, 53

Advanced:
Day 1: pp. 557–559
Exs. 1, 2, 7–10, 14–16, 18–26 even, 29–42*, 48, 51, 54

Block:
pp. 557–559
Exs. 1, 2, 6–10, 12–26 even, 27–34, 37–41, 44, 47, 50, 53 (with 9.2)

Differentiated Instruction

See *Algebra 1 Best Practices Toolkit* for suggestions on addressing the needs of a diverse classroom.

Homework Check

For a quick check of student understanding of key concepts, go over the following exercises:
Basic: 3, 13, 17, 23, 37
Average: 6, 14, 18, 24, 38
Advanced: 8, 16, 20, 24, 39

Extra Practice

- Student Edition, p. 946
- Chapter 9 Resource Book: Practice levels A, B, C, pp. 7–9

Practice Worksheet

An easily-readable reduced practice page (with answers) for this lesson can be found on p. 552C.

Differentiated Instruction

English Learners Prefixes such as *mono-*, *bi-*, *tri-*, and *poly-* occur often in English. For example, the word *monotonous* means "one tone" and the word *bisect* means "cut into two." For some English learners, these prefixes do not occur in their native language, so the meanings of the terms *monomial*, *binomial*, *trinomial*, and *polynomial* may not be familiar. Try using more common language such as saying "one term" instead of monomial in classifying various polynomials.

See also the *Algebra 1 Toolkit* for more strategies.

Mathematical Reasoning

Exercise 2 Some students may ask why a monomial such as 6 has degree 0. Remind them that a variable to the zero power, such as x^0, is equal to 1. So, $6 \cdot x^0 = 6 \cdot 1$ or 6. Since 6 can be written as $6x^0$, the degree of 6 or any constant term is 0. After discussing this concept, you may want to ask if it is possible to have a 0 degree binomial. Have students use examples such as $6x^0 + 5y^0 = 6 + 5 = 11$ to support their reasoning.

Vocabulary

Exercises 11–16 Some students may confuse monomials, binomials, and trinomials. Point out that the prefixes mono, bi, and tri, mean one, two, and three, respectively. Suggest that they pair each term with a more familiar term, such as monorail, bicycle, and tricycle, to help them distinguish between the three types of polynomials.

Avoiding Common Errors

Exercises 21–25, 34–35 Caution students to pay attention to signs when subtracting polynomials. To avoid errors, urge them to first multiply each term of the subtrahend by −1 and then add like terms.

Reading Strategy

Exercise 41 Point out to students that the key at the bottom of page 558 indicates that problem 41 is an example of an extended response question on a standardized test. Tell them that a good reading strategy for this type of question is to read all of the parts of the question to see if one part is dependent upon an answer to a previous part, as part (b) is on part (a).

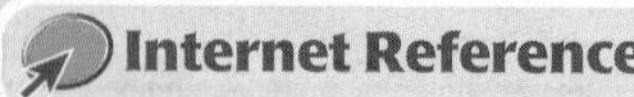

Internet Reference

Exercise 41 To find more information about Cy Young, go to www.baseballhalloffame.org and do a search for "Cy Young."

GEOMETRY **Write a polynomial that represents the perimeter of the figure.**

30. 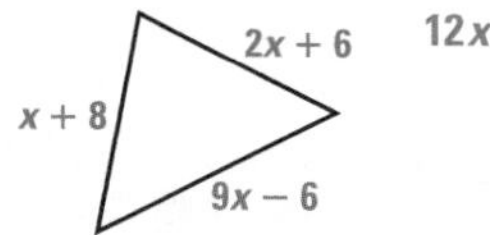

$12x + 8$

31. 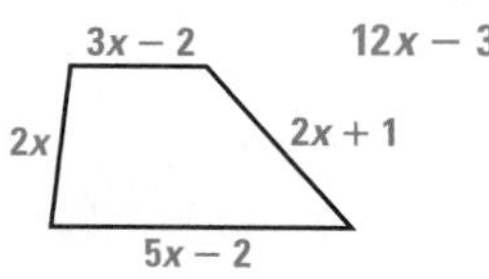

$12x - 3$

ADDING AND SUBTRACTING POLYNOMIALS **Find the sum or difference.**

32. $(3r^2s + 5rs + 3) + (-8rs^2 - 9rs - 12)$ $3r^2s - 8rs^2 - 4rs - 9$

33. $(x^2 + 11xy - 3y^2) + (-2x^2 - xy + 4y^2)$ $-x^2 + 10xy + y^2$

34. $(5mn + 3m - 9n) - (13mn + 2m)$ $-8mn + m - 9n$

35. $(8a^2b - 6a) - (2a^2b - 4b + 19)$ $6a^2b - 6a + 4b - 19$

C **36. CHALLENGE** Consider any integer x. The next consecutive integer can be represented by the binomial $(x + 1)$.

a. Write a polynomial for the sum of any two consecutive integers. $2x + 1$

b. *Explain* how you can be sure that the sum of two consecutive integers is always odd. Use the polynomial from part (a) in your explanation. The sum of any two consecutive integers can be written in the form $2x + 1$ where x is an integer. Since x is an integer, $2x$ is an integer with a factor of 2, so $2x$ must be even. Then $2x + 1$ must be odd.

PROBLEM SOLVING

EXAMPLE 5 A on p. 556 for Exs. 37–39

37. BACKPACKING AND CAMPING During the period 1992–2002, the participation B (in millions of people) in backpacking and the participation C (in millions of people) in camping can be modeled by

$$B = -0.0262t^3 + 0.376t^2 - 0.574t + 9.67 \text{ and}$$
$$C = -0.0182t^3 + 0.522t^2 - 2.59t + 47$$

about 39,800,000 people

where t is the number of years since 1992. About how many more people camped than backpacked in 2002?

@HomeTutor for problem solving help at classzone.com

38. CAR COSTS During the period 1990–2002, the average costs D (in dollars) for a new domestic car and the average costs I (in dollars) for a new imported car can be modeled by

$$D = 442.14t + 14{,}433 \quad \text{and} \quad I = -137.63t^2 + 2705.2t + 15{,}111$$

where t is the number of years since 1990. Find the difference in average costs (in dollars) for a new imported car and a new domestic car in 2002. $8016

@HomeTutor for problem solving help at classzone.com

39. ★ **SHORT RESPONSE** During the period 1998–2002, the number A (in millions) of books for adults and the number J (in millions) of books for juveniles sold can be modeled by

$$A = 9.5t^3 - 58t^2 + 66t + 500 \quad \text{and} \quad J = -15t^2 + 64t + 360$$

where t is the number of years since 1998.

a. Write an equation that gives the total number (in millions) of books for adults and for juveniles sold as a function of the number of years since 1998. $T = 9.5t^3 - 73t^2 + 130t + 860$

b. Were more books sold in 1998 or in 2002? *Explain* your answer.

39b. 1998; substitute $t = 0$ into the equation for T to find the number of books sold in 1998 to get 860 million books. Substitute 4 into the equation for T to find the number of books sold in 2002 to get 820 million books. More books were sold in 1998.

○ = WORKED-OUT SOLUTIONS on p. WS1 ★ = STANDARDIZED TEST PRACTICE

B 40. **SCHOOL ENROLLMENT** During the period 1985–2012, the projected enrollment B (in thousands of students) in public schools and the projected enrollment R (in thousands of students) in private schools can be modeled by

$$B = -18.53t^2 + 975.8t + 48{,}140 \quad \text{and} \quad R = 80.8t + 8049$$

where t is the number of years since 1985. Write an equation that models the total school enrollment (in thousands of students) as a function of the number of years since 1985. What percent of all students is expected to be enrolled in public schools in 2012? $T = -18.53t^2 + 1056.6t + 56{,}189$; about 86%

41c. about 61%; Cy Young's career lasted 1911 − 1890 = 21 years. To find the number of wins in his career, find the value of W when $t = 21$; about 525 wins. From part (b), we know that the total number of decisions in his career is about 855, so to find the percent of the decisions that were wins, find 525 ÷ 855 ≈ 0.614, or about 61%.

41. ★ **EXTENDED RESPONSE** The award for the best pitchers in baseball is named after the pitcher Cy Young. During the period 1890–1911, the total number of Cy Young's wins W and losses L can be modeled by

$$W = -0.44t^2 + 34t + 4.7 \quad \text{and} \quad L = 15t + 15$$

where t is the number of years since 1890.

a. A game credited to a pitcher as a win or a loss is called a decision. Write an equation that models the number of decisions for Cy Young as a function of the number of years since 1890. $D = -0.44t^2 + 49t + 19.7$

b. Cy Young's career in Major League Baseball lasted from 1890 to 1911. Approximately how many total decisions did Cy Young have during his career? about 855 decisions

c. About what percent of the decisions in Cy Young's career were wins? *Explain* how you found your answer.

Cy Young Award

C 42. **CHALLENGE** In 1970 the United States produced 63.5 quadrillion BTU (British Thermal Units) of energy and consumed 67.86 quadrillion BTU. From 1970 through 2001, the total U.S. energy production increased by about 0.2813 quadrillion BTU per year, and the total U.S. energy consumption increased by about 0.912 quadrillion BTU per year.

a. Write two equations that model the total U.S. energy production and consumption (in quadrillion BTU) as functions of the number of years since 1970. $P = 0.2813t + 63.5$, $C = 0.912t + 67.86$

b. How much more energy was consumed than produced in the U.S. in 1970 and in 2001? What was the change in the amount of energy consumed from 1970 to 2001? 4.36 quadrillion BTU, about 23.91 quadrillion BTU; 28.272 quadrillion BTU

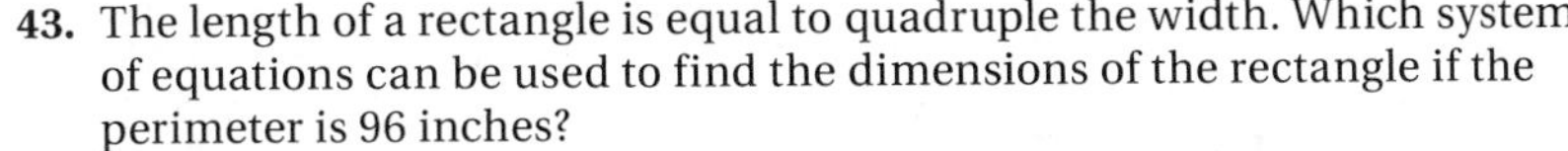

ILLINOIS MIXED REVIEW

TEST PRACTICE at classzone.com

43. The length of a rectangle is equal to quadruple the width. Which system of equations can be used to find the dimensions of the rectangle if the perimeter is 96 inches?

Ⓐ $\ell = w + 4$
$2(\ell + w) = 96$

Ⓑ $\ell = 4w$
$2\ell + 8w = 96$

C

Ⓒ $\ell = 4w$
$2(\ell + w) = 96$

Ⓓ $\ell = w + 4$
$2\ell + 8w = 96$

5 ASSESS AND RETEACH

Daily Homework Quiz

Transparency Available

If the expression is a polynomial, find its degree and classify it by the number of terms. Otherwise, tell why it is not a polynomial.

1. $m^3 + n^4m^2 + m^{-2}$ No; one exponent is not a whole number.
2. $-3b^3c^4 - 4b^2c + c^8$ 8th degree trinomial

Find the sum or difference.

3. $(3m^2 - 2m + 9) + (m^2 + 2m - 4)$ $4m^2 + 5$
4. $(-4a^2 + 3a - 1) - (a^2 + 2a - 6)$ $-5a^2 + a + 5$
5. The number of dog adoptions D and cat adoptions C can be modeled by $D = 1.35t^2 - 9.8t + 131$ and $C = 0.1t^2 - 3t + 79$ where t represents the years since 1998. About how many dogs and cats were adopted in 2004? about 185 dogs and cats

Available at **classzone.com**

Diagnosis/Remediation

- Practice A, B, C in Chapter 9 Resource Book, pp. 7–9
- Study Guide in Chapter 9 Resource Book, pp. 10–11
- Practice Workbook, pp. 133–134
- @HomeTutor

Challenge

Additional challenge is available in the Chapter 9 Resource Book, p. 14.

@HomeTutor
classzone.com
Keystrokes

1 PLAN AND PREPARE

Learn the Method

- Students will graph polynomial functions to check whether a sum or difference of polynomials is correct.
- After the activity, students can use a graphing calculator to check their solutions for Exercises 17–26 and 32–35 in Lesson 9.1.

Keystroke Help

Keystrokes for several models of calculators are available in blackline format in the *Chapter 9 Resource Book*.

2 TEACH

Tips for Success

Remind students to use the caret key to indicate powers. If students cannot see a graph in the viewing window, suggest that they use the zoom feature on their graphing calculator.

Extra Example

Tell whether the sum or difference is correct.

a. $(2x^2 + x + 2) + (3x^2 - x - 4) \stackrel{?}{=} 5x^2 + 2$ The thick curve deviates from the thin curve, so the sum is incorrect.

b. $(4x^3 + 2x^2 - 3) - (2x^3 + x^2 + 2) \stackrel{?}{=} 2x^3 + x^2 - 5$ The thick curve coincides with the thin curve, so the difference is correct.

3 ASSESS AND RETEACH

Is $(-x^3 + 2x^2 + 3x) - (2x^3 + x^2 - x) \stackrel{?}{=} -3x^3 + x^2 + 2x$ correct? Explain. The two curves do not coincide, so the difference is incorrect. The correct difference is $-3x^3 + x^2 + 4x$.

9.1 Graph Polynomial Functions

QUESTION How can you use a graph to check your work with polynomials?

EXAMPLE Check a sum or difference of polynomials

Tell whether the sum or difference is correct.

a. $(x^2 - 2x + 3) + (2x^2 + 4x - 5) \stackrel{?}{=} 3x^2 + 2x - 2$

b. $(x^3 + x + 1) - (5x^3 - 2x + 7) \stackrel{?}{=} -4x^3 - x - 6$

STEP 1 *Enter expressions*

Let y_1 equal the original expression.
Let y_2 equal the sum.

a.

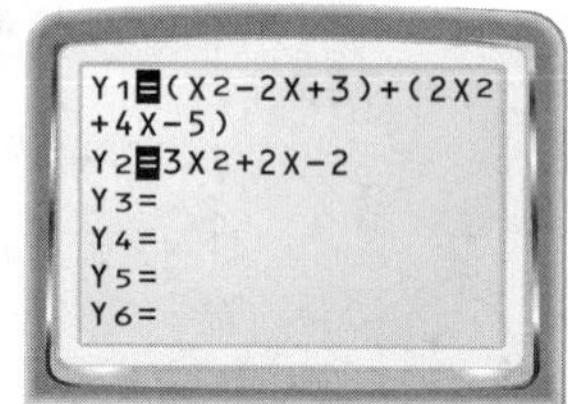

b.

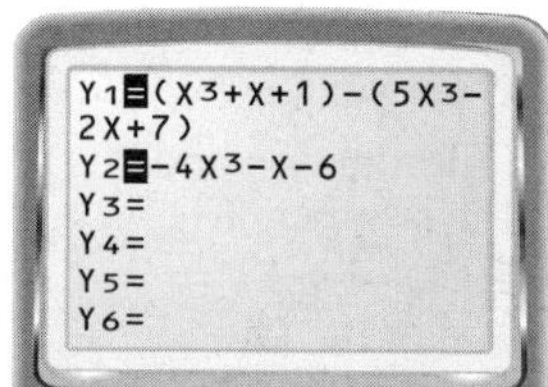

STEP 2 *Graph expressions*

For y_1, choose a normal graph style.
For y_2, choose a thicker graph style.

a.

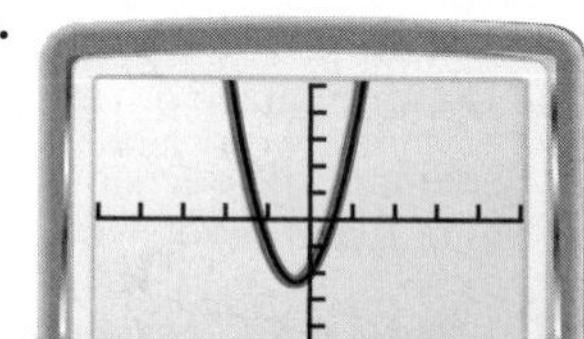

b.

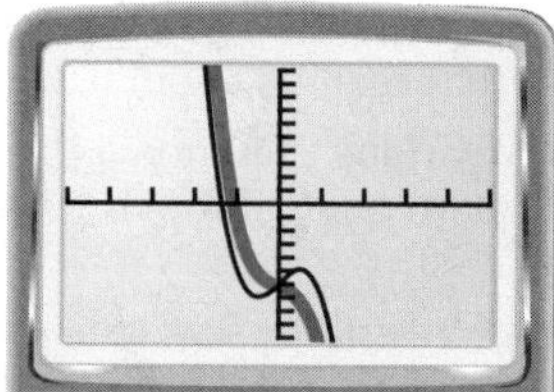

STEP 3 *Analyze graphs*

a. The thick curve coincides with the thin curve, so the sum is correct.

b. The thick curve deviates from the thin curve, so the difference is incorrect.

PRACTICE

Find the sum or difference. Use a graphing calculator to check your answer.

1. $(6x^2 + 4x - 1) + (x^2 - 2x + 2)$ $7x^2 + 2x + 1$

2. $(3x^2 - 2x + 1) - (4x^2 - 5x + 1)$ $-x^2 + 3x$

Tell whether the sum or difference is correct. Correct any incorrect answers.

3. $(3x^2 - 2x + 4) + (-x^2 + 3x + 2) \stackrel{?}{=} 2x^2 + x + 6$ correct

4. $(-4x^2 - 5x - 1) - (-5x^2 + 6x + 3) \stackrel{?}{=} -9x^2 + x + 2$ not correct; $x^2 - 11x - 4$

Investigating Algebra ACTIVITY *Use before Lesson 9.2*

9.2 Multiplication with Algebra Tiles

MATERIALS • algebra tiles

QUESTION How can you multiply binomials using algebra tiles?

You can use the following algebra tiles to model polynomials. Notice that the value of each tile is the same as its area.

1-tile

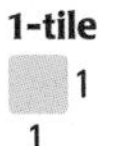

x-tile

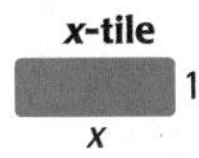

x^2-tile

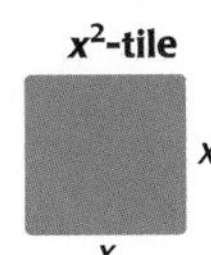

EXPLORE Multiply binomials

Find the product $(x + 3)(2x + 1)$.

STEP 1 ***Model the rectangle's dimensions***

Model each binomial with algebra tiles. Arrange the first binomial vertically and the second horizontally, as shown. These polynomials model the length and width of a rectangle.

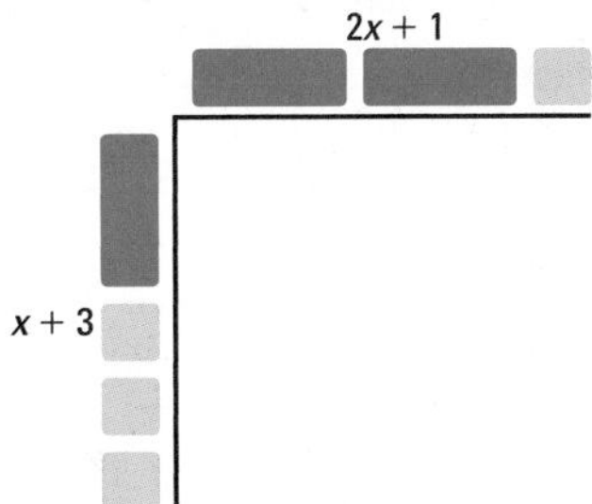

STEP 2 ***Fill in the area***

Fill in the rectangle with the appropriate algebra tiles.

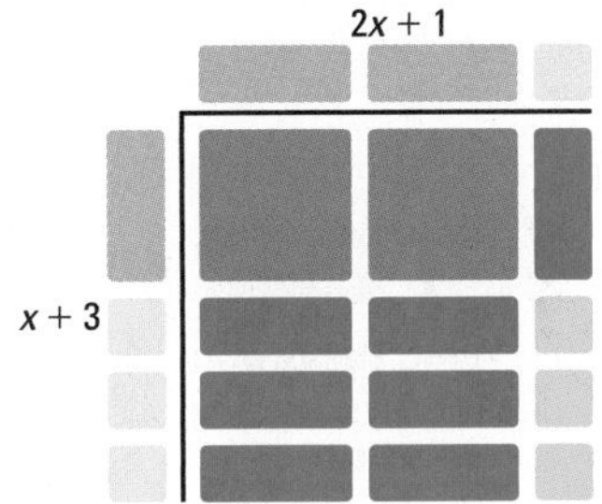

STEP 3 ***Find the product***

The rectangle you created represents the polynomial $2x^2 + 7x + 3$.
So, $(x + 3)(2x + 1) = 2x^2 + 7x + 3$.

DRAW CONCLUSIONS Use your observations to complete these exercises

Use algebra tiles to find the product. Include a drawing of your model. 1–6. See margin for art.

1. $(x + 1)(x + 3)$ $x^2 + 4x + 3$
2. $(x + 5)(x + 4)$ $x^2 + 9x + 20$
3. $(2x + 1)(x + 2)$ $2x^2 + 5x + 2$
4. $(3x + 2)(x + 1)$ $3x^2 + 5x + 2$
5. $(3x + 2)(2x + 1)$ $6x^2 + 7x + 2$
6. $(4x + 1)(2x + 3)$ $8x^2 + 14x + 3$
7. **REASONING** Find the product $x(2x + 1)$ and the product $3(2x + 1)$. What is the sum of these two products? What do your answers suggest you can do to find the product $(x + 3)(2x + 1)$? See margin.

1 PLAN AND PREPARE

Explore the Concept

- Students will use algebra tiles to multiply binomials.
- This activity leads into the study of multiplying polynomials using a table of products in Example 2 of Lesson 9.2.

Materials

Each student will need:

- algebra tiles
- Activity Support Master (*Chapter 9 Resource Book*, p. 17)

Recommended Time

Work activity: 10 min
Discuss results: 5 min

Grouping

Students should work individually.

2 TEACH

Key Question

- How do you know which are appropriate algebra tiles to fill in the rectangle? The length and width of each tile matches the tiles at the left of and above the rectangle.

Key Discovery

Multiplying binomials is based on the distributive property.

3 ASSESS AND RETEACH

If you use algebra tiles to multiply $(3x + 1)(3x + 4)$, how many x^2-tiles will you need to fill in the rectangle? Explain. 9, since you need to fill in 3 columns and 3 rows of tiles where both dimensions are determined by x-tiles.

1–6. See Additional Answers beginning on p. AA1.

7. $2x^2 + x$, $6x + 3$; $2x^2 + 7x + 3$; multiply $(2x + 1)$ by each term of $(x + 3)$ and then add the products.

1 PLAN AND PREPARE

Warm-Up Exercises

Transparency Available

1. Simplify $-2(9a - b)$. $-18a + 2b$
2. Simplify $r^2s \bullet rs^3$. r^3s^4
3. The number of hardback h and paperback p books (in hundreds) sold from 1999–2005 can be modeled by $h = 0.2t^2 - 1.7t + 14$ and $p = 0.17t^3 - 2.7t^2 + 11.7t + 27$ where t is the number of years since 1999. About how many books sold in 2003? 5200

Notetaking Guide

Transparency Available

Promotes interactive learning and notetaking skills, pp. 191–194.

Pacing

Basic: 1 day
Average: 1 day
Advanced: 1 day
Block: 0.5 block with 9.1
- See *Teaching Guide/Lesson Plan.*

2 FOCUS AND MOTIVATE

Essential Question

Big Idea 1, p. 553

How do you multiply polynomials? Tell students they will learn how to answer this question by using the distributive property to find the product of two polynomials.

9.2 Multiply Polynomials

8.11.01 Simplify or identify equivalent algebraic expressions (e.g., exponential, rational, logarithmic, factored, polynomial).

Before You added and subtracted polynomials.
Now You will multiply polynomials.
Why? So you can determine areas, as in Example 7.

Key Vocabulary
- **polynomial,** *p. 554*
- **binomial,** *p. 555*

The diagram shows that a rectangle with width x and length $2x + 3$ has an area of $2x^2 + 3x$. You can also find this product by using the distributive property.

$$x(2x + 3) = x(2x) + x(3) = 2x^2 + 3x$$

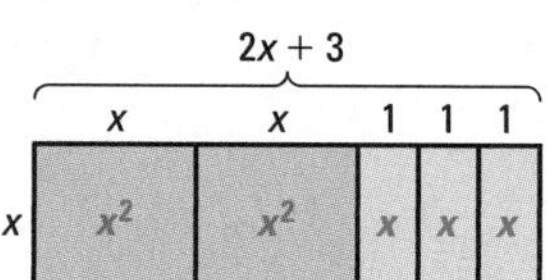

In this lesson, you will learn several methods for multiplying polynomials. Each method is based on the distributive property.

EXAMPLE 1 Multiply a monomial and a polynomial

REVIEW PROPERTIES OF EXPONENTS
For help with using the properties of exponents, see p. 489.

Find the product $2x^3(x^3 + 3x^2 - 2x + 5)$.

$2x^3(x^3 + 3x^2 - 2x + 5)$	Write product.
$= 2x^3(x^3) + 2x^3(3x^2) - 2x^3(2x) + 2x^3(5)$	Distributive property
$= 2x^6 + 6x^5 - 4x^4 + 10x^3$	Product of powers property

EXAMPLE 2 Multiply polynomials using a table

Find the product $(x - 4)(3x + 2)$.

Solution

STEP 1 **Write** subtraction as addition in each polynomial.

$$(x - 4)(3x + 2) = [x + (-4)](3x + 2)$$

STEP 2 **Make** a table of products.

	$3x$	2
x	$3x^2$	
-4		

→

	$3x$	2
x	$3x^2$	$2x$
-4	$-12x$	-8

▶ The product is $3x^2 + 2x - 12x - 8$, or $3x^2 - 10x - 8$.

GUIDED PRACTICE for Examples 1 and 2

Find the product.

1. $x(7x^2 + 4)$ $7x^3 + 4x$
2. $(a + 3)(2a + 1)$ $2a^2 + 7a + 3$
3. $(4n - 1)(n + 5)$ $4n^2 + 19n - 5$

Resource Planning Guide

Chapter Resource Book
- Teaching Guide/Lesson Plan (pp. 15–16)
- Practice levels A, B, C (pp. 18–20)
- Study Guide (pp. 21–22)
- Catch-up for Absent Students (p. 23)
- Application (p. 24)
- Challenge (p. 25)

Workbooks
- Notetaking Guide (pp. 191–194)
- Practice Workbook (pp. 135–136)

Teaching Options
- **Power Presentations CD-ROM** provides dynamic electronic teaching resources for the classroom.
- **Activity Generator CD-ROM** provides editable activities for all ability levels.

Interactive Technology
- Easy Planner
- Power Presentations CD-ROM
- Activity Generator CD-ROM
- Animated Algebra
- Test Generator CD-ROM
- Online Quiz
- eWorkbook
- eEdition
- @HomeTutor

Resources for English Learners
- Quick Reference for English Learners
- Spanish Study Guide
- Multi-Language Visual Glossary
- Student Resources in Spanish

See also the *Algebra 1 Toolkit* for more strategies for meeting individual needs.

EXAMPLE 3 Multiply polynomials vertically

Find the product $(b^2 + 6b - 7)(3b - 4)$.

Solution

AVOID ERRORS
Remember that the terms of $(3b - 4)$ are $3b$ and -4. They are *not* $3b$ and 4.

STEP 1 **Multiply** by -4.

$$\begin{array}{r} b^2 + 6b - 7 \\ \times \qquad\qquad 3b - 4 \\ \hline -4b^2 - 24b + 28 \end{array}$$

STEP 2 **Multiply** by $3b$.

$$\begin{array}{r} b^2 + 6b - 7 \\ \times \qquad\qquad 3b - 4 \\ \hline -4b^2 - 24b + 28 \\ 3b^3 + 18b^2 - 21b \qquad \end{array}$$

STEP 3 **Add** products.

$$\begin{array}{r} b^2 + 6b - 7 \\ \times \qquad\qquad 3b - 4 \\ \hline -4b^2 - 24b + 28 \\ 3b^3 + 18b^2 - 21b \qquad \\ \hline 3b^3 + 14b^2 - 45b + 28 \end{array}$$

EXAMPLE 4 Multiply polynomials horizontally

Find the product $(2x^2 + 5x - 1)(4x - 3)$.

$(2x^2 + 5x - 1)(4x - 3)$	Write product.
$= 2x^2(4x - 3) + 5x(4x - 3) - 1(4x - 3)$	Distributive property
$= 8x^3 - 6x^2 + 20x^2 - 15x - 4x + 3$	Distributive property
$= 8x^3 + 14x^2 - 19x + 3$	Combine like terms.

FOIL PATTERN The letters of the word FOIL can help you to remember how to use the distributive property to multiply binomials. The letters should remind you of the words **F**irst, **O**uter, **I**nner, and **L**ast.

First Outer Inner Last

$$(2x + 3)(4x + 1) = 8x^2 + 2x + 12x + 3$$

EXAMPLE 5 Multiply binomials using the FOIL pattern

Find the product $(3a + 4)(a - 2)$.

$(3a + 4)(a - 2)$	
$= (3a)(a) + (3a)(-2) + (4)(a) + (4)(-2)$	Write products of terms.
$= 3a^2 + (-6a) + 4a + (-8)$	Multiply.
$= 3a^2 - 2a - 8$	Combine like terms.

GUIDED PRACTICE for Examples 3, 4, and 5

Find the product.

4. $(x^2 + 2x + 1)(x + 2)$ $x^3 + 4x^2 + 5x + 2$

5. $(3y^2 - y + 5)(2y - 3)$ $6y^3 - 11y^2 + 13y - 15$

6. $(4b - 5)(b - 2)$ $4b^2 - 13b + 10$

Motivating the Lesson

You want to know how much wall space you need for a poster surrounded by different borders. If you know the length and width of the poster, you can write an expression that models the total area of the poster and its border. You can then evaluate the expression to determine how much wall space you need.

3 TEACH

Extra Example 1

Find the product $3x^2(2x^3 - x^2 + 4x - 3)$. $6x^5 - 3x^4 + 12x^3 - 9x^2$

Key Question to Ask for Example 1

- How do you multiply powers that have the same base? Write the base, add the exponents.

Extra Example 2

Find the product $(x + 4)(2x - 1)$. $2x^2 + 7x - 4$

Extra Example 3

Find the product $(a^2 + 3a - 4)(2a + 3)$. $2a^3 + 9a^2 + a - 12$

Extra Example 4

Find the product $(2x^2 - x - 2)(3x - 1)$. $6x^3 - 5x^2 - 5x + 2$

Extra Example 5

Find the product $(4a + 3)(a + 2)$. $4a^2 + 11a + 6$

Differentiated Instruction

Below Level Some students may find the FOIL pattern confusing. To help these students, you may want to use algebra tiles to show how the filled-in rectangle corresponds to each letter of the FOIL pattern. After they have a better understanding of the pattern, encourage them to use notecards to write out each step of the pattern. Suggest that they write an example at the top of the card, such as $(4x + 2)(3x - 1)$, and then First, Outer, Inner, and Last, each on one line of the card. They should show the step next to each word and explain the step in words.

See also the *Algebra 1 Toolkit* for more strategies.

EXAMPLE 6 Standardized Test Practice

The dimensions of a rectangle are $x + 3$ and $x + 2$. Which expression represents the area of the rectangle?

Ⓐ $x^2 + 6$ Ⓑ $x^2 + 5x + 6$ Ⓒ $x^2 + 6x + 6$ Ⓓ $x^2 + 6x$

ELIMINATE CHOICES
When you multiply $x + 3$ and $x + 2$, the product will have a constant term of $3 \cdot 2 = 6$. So, you can eliminate choice D.

Solution

Area = length • width	Formula for area of a rectangle
$= (x + 3)(x + 2)$	Substitute for length and width.
$= x^2 + 2x + 3x + 6$	Multiply binomials.
$= x^2 + 5x + 6$	Combine like terms.

▶ The correct answer is B. Ⓐ Ⓑ Ⓒ Ⓓ

CHECK You can use a graph to check your answer. Use a graphing calculator to display the graphs of $y_1 = (x + 3)(x + 2)$ and $y_2 = x^2 + 5x + 6$ in the same viewing window. Because the graphs coincide, you know that the product of $x + 3$ and $x + 2$ is $x^2 + 5x + 6$.

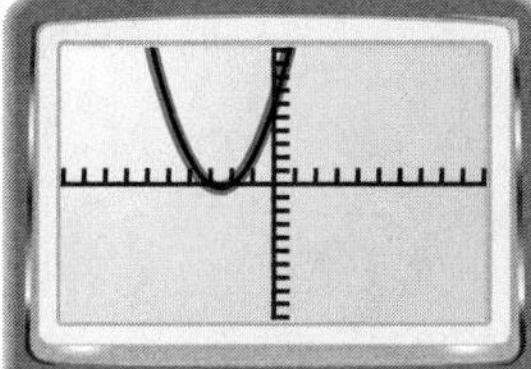

EXAMPLE 7 Solve a multi-step problem

SKATEBOARDING You are designing a rectangular skateboard park on a lot that is on the corner of a city block. The park will have a walkway along two sides. The dimensions of the lot and the walkway are shown in the diagram.

- Write a polynomial that represents the area of the skateboard park.
- What is the area of the park if the walkway is 3 feet wide?

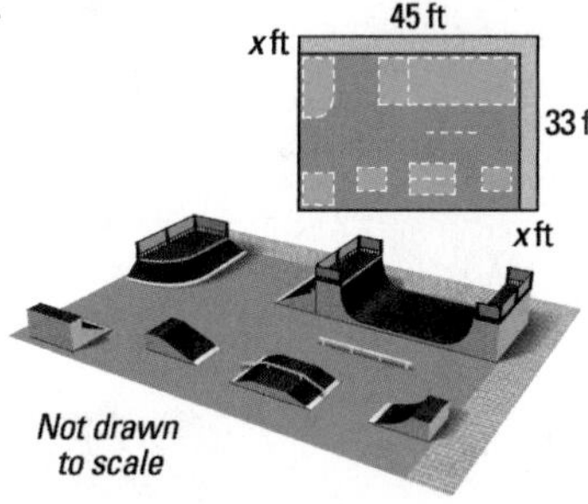

Solution

STEP 1 **Write** a polynomial using the formula for the area of a rectangle. The length is $45 - x$. The width is $33 - x$.

Area = length • width	Formula for area of a rectangle
$= (45 - x)(33 - x)$	Substitute for length and width.
$= 1485 - 45x - 33x + x^2$	Multiply binomials.
$= 1485 - 78x + x^2$	Combine like terms.

STEP 2 **Substitute** 3 for x and evaluate.

Area $= 1485 - 78(3) + (3)^2 = 1260$

▶ The area of the park is 1260 square feet.

Extra Example 6

A rectangle has dimensions $x + 3$ and $x + 5$. Which expression shows the area of the rectangle? C

Ⓐ $x^2 + 15$
Ⓑ $x^2 + 3x + 15$
Ⓒ $x^2 + 8x + 15$
Ⓓ $x^2 + 8x$

Extra Example 7

A rectangular trivet has a ceramic center and a wooden border. The dimensions of the center and border are shown in the diagram.

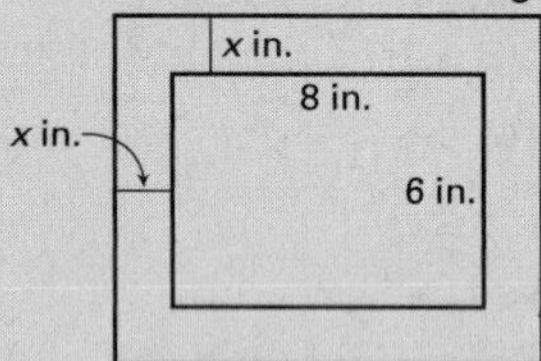

- Write a polynomial that represents the total area of the trivet. $48 + 28x + 4x^2$
- What is the total area of the trivet if the width of the border is 2 inches? 120 in.^{2}

Closing the Lesson

Have students summarize the major points of the lesson and answer the Essential Question: How do you multiply polynomials?

- Use the distributive property to multiply polynomials.
- Use the FOIL pattern to multiply binomials.

To use the distributive property, multiply each term of one polynomial by each term of the other, using properties of exponents if necessary. Then combine like terms. To use the FOIL pattern, multiply the two First terms of each binomial, the two Outer terms, the two Inner terms, the two Last terms, and then combine like terms.

 **GUIDED PRACTICE** for Examples 6 and 7

7. The dimensions of a rectangle are $x + 5$ and $x + 9$. Which expression represents the area of the rectangle? C

   (A) $x^2 + 45x$ (B) $x^2 + 45$

   (C) $x^2 + 14x + 45$ (D) $x^2 + 45x + 45$

8. **GARDEN DESIGN** You are planning to build a walkway that surrounds a rectangular garden, as shown. The width of the walkway around the garden is the same on every side.

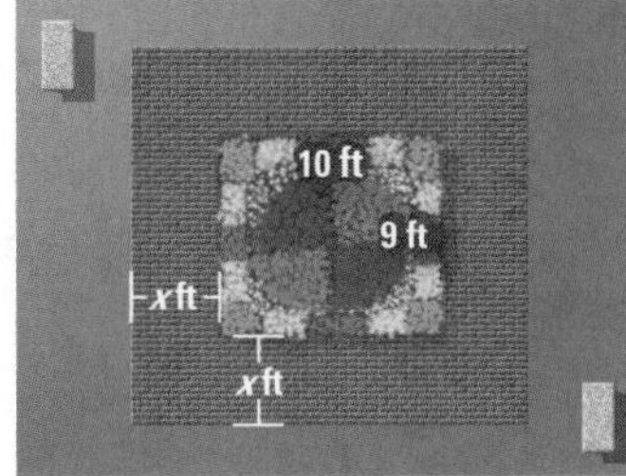

   a. Write a polynomial that represents the combined area of the garden and the walkway. $4x^2 + 38x + 90$

   b. Find the combined area when the width of the walkway is 4 feet. 306 ft^2

9.2 EXERCISES

HOMEWORK KEY
○ = WORKED-OUT SOLUTIONS on p. WS20 for Exs. 23 and 51
★ = STANDARDIZED TEST PRACTICE Exs. 2, 26, 44, 52, and 53

SKILL PRACTICE

1. **VOCABULARY** Copy and complete: The FOIL pattern can be used to multiply any two __?__. binomials

2. ★ **WRITING** *Explain* how the letters of the word FOIL can help you multiply polynomials. See margin.

EXAMPLE 1 on p. 562 for Exs. 3–8

MULTIPLYING POLYNOMIALS Find the product.

3. $x(2x^2 - 3x + 9)$ $2x^3 - 3x^2 + 9x$
4. $4y(-y^3 - 2y - 1)$ $-4y^4 - 8y^2 - 4y$
5. $z^2(4z^4 + z^3 - 11z^2 - 6)$ $4z^6 + z^5 - 11z^4 - 6z^2$
6. $3c^3(8c^4 - c^2 - 3c + 5)$ $24c^7 - 3c^5 - 9c^4 + 15c^3$
7. $-a^5(-9a^2 + 5a + 13)$ $9a^7 - 5a^6 - 13a^5$
8. $-5b^3(4b^5 - 2b^3 + b - 11)$ $-20b^8 + 10b^6 - 5b^4 + 55b^3$

EXAMPLE 2 on p. 562 for Exs. 9–15

USING TABLES Use a table to find the product.

9. $(x + 2)(x - 3)$ $x^2 - x - 6$
10. $(y - 5)(2y + 3)$ $2y^2 - 7y - 15$
11. $(4b - 3)(b - 7)$ $4b^2 - 31b + 21$
12. $(5s + 2)(s + 8)$ $5s^2 + 42s + 16$
13. $(3k - 1)(4k + 9)$ $12k^2 + 23k - 9$
14. $(8n - 5)(3n - 6)$ $24n^2 - 63n + 30$

EXAMPLES 3 and 4 on p. 563 for Exs. 16–26

ERROR ANALYSIS *Describe* and correct the error in finding the product of the polynomials.

15. $(x - 5)(3x + 1)$

	3x	1
x	$3x^2$	x
5	15x	5

$(x - 5)(3x + 1) = 3x^2 + 16x + 5$

15. The second term of the first binomial is −5, not 5, so the entries in the second row of the diagram should be $-15x$ and -5; $3x^2 - 14x - 5$.

16.
$$\begin{array}{r} 2x^2 - 3x - 4 \\ \times \qquad x + 7 \\ \hline 14x^2 - 21x - 28 \\ 2x^3 - 3x^2 - 4x \\ \hline 2x^3 + 11x^4 - 25x^2 - 28 \end{array}$$

When combining like terms, the exponents on the variables should stay the same, rather than being added together; $2x^3 + 11x^2 - 25x - 28$.

4 PRACTICE AND APPLY

Assignment Guide

Answer Transparencies available for all exercises

Basic:
Day 1: pp. 565–568
Exs. 1, 2, 4–14 even, 15, 16, 17–39 odd, 49–52, 56–66 even

Average:
Day 1: pp. 565–568
Exs. 1, 2, 3–43 odd, 45, 46, 49–53, 56, 59, 62, 65

Advanced:
Day 1: pp. 565–568
Exs. 1, 2, 7, 8, 14, 21–26, 30–32, 33–41 odd, 43–54*, 60, 63, 66

Block:
pp. 565–568
Exs. 1, 2, 3–43 odd, 45, 46, 49–53, 56, 59, 62, 65 (with 9.1)

Differentiated Instruction

See *Algebra 1 Best Practices Toolkit* for suggestions on addressing the needs of a diverse classroom.

Homework Check

For a quick check of student understanding of key concepts, go over the following exercises:

Basic: 6, 19, 27, 39, 49
Average: 11, 22, 29, 41, 50
Advanced: 14, 24, 31, 41, 50

Extra Practice

- Student Edition, p. 946
- Chapter 9 Resource Book: Practice levels A, B, C, pp. 18–20

Practice Worksheet

An easily-readable reduced practice page (with answers) for this lesson can be found on p. 552C.

2. The letters of the word FOIL remind you to find the sum of the products of these terms: First terms of each binomial, Outer terms of each binomial, Inner terms of each binomial, Last terms of each binomial.

Graphing Calculator

Exercises 9–14, 17–32 Encourage students to use a graphing calculator to check their answers. They should display two graphs in the same viewing window, using a thin line and a thick line. If the two graphs for an exercise do not coincide, students should review the method they used to find the product.

Avoiding Common Errors

Exercises 17–25 Caution students to align like terms in columns when they are using the vertical format. This will help them avoid errors such as combining unlike terms.

Study Strategy

Exercises 27–32 Refer students who are having trouble using FOIL to the diagram on page 563. Tell them to draw arrows as in the diagram to help them see and use the pattern. Reinforce the idea that the more they use the pattern, the more familiar it will become.

MULTIPLYING POLYNOMIALS **Use a vertical or a horizontal format to find the product.**

17. $(y + 6)(y - 5)$ $y^2 + y - 30$
18. $(5x - 8)(2x - 5)$ $10x^2 - 41x + 40$
19. $(7w + 5)(11w - 3)$ $77w^2 + 34w - 15$
20. $(b - 2)(b^2 - b + 1)$ $b^3 - 3b^2 + 3b - 2$
21. $(s + 4)(s^2 + 6s - 5)$ $s^3 + 10s^2 + 19s - 20$
22. $(-r + 7)(2r^2 - r - 9)$ $-2r^3 + 15r^2 + 2r - 63$
23. $(5x + 2)(-3x^2 + 4x - 1)$ $-15x^3 + 14x^2 + 3x - 2$
24. $(y^2 + 8y - 6)(4y - 3)$ $4y^3 + 29y^2 - 48y + 18$
25. $(6z^2 + z - 1)(9z - 5)$ $54z^3 - 21z^2 - 14z + 5$
26. ★ **MULTIPLE CHOICE** What is the product of $2x - 9$ and $4x + 1$? B

   (A) $8x^2 - 38x - 9$ (B) $8x^2 - 34x - 9$

   (C) $8x^2 + 34x - 9$ (D) $8x^2 + 38x - 9$

EXAMPLE 5 on p. 563 for Exs. 27–32

USING THE FOIL PATTERN **Use the FOIL pattern to find the product.**

27. $(2r - 1)(5r + 3)$ $10r^2 + r - 3$
28. $(7a - 2)(3a - 4)$ $21a^2 - 34a + 8$
29. $(4m + 9)(2m + 7)$ $8m^2 + 46m + 63$
30. $(8t + 11)(6t - 1)$ $48t^2 + 58t - 11$
31. $(4x - 5)(12x - 7)$ $48x^2 - 88x + 35$
32. $(8z + 3)(5z + 4)$ $40z^2 + 47z + 12$

B **SIMPLIFYING EXPRESSIONS** **Simplify the expression.**

33. $p(2p - 3) + (p - 3)(p + 3)$ $3p^2 - 3p - 9$
34. $x^2(7x + 5) - (2x + 6)(x - 1)$ $7x^3 + 3x^2 - 4x + 6$
35. $-3c^2(c + 11) - (4c - 5)(3c - 2)$ $-3c^3 - 45c^2 + 23c - 10$
36. $2w^3(2w^3 - 7w - 1) + w(5w^2 + 2w)$ $4w^6 - 14w^4 + 3w^3 + 2w^2$

EXAMPLES 6 and 7 on p. 564 for Exs. 37–42

GEOMETRY **Write a polynomial that represents the area of the shaded region.**

37. 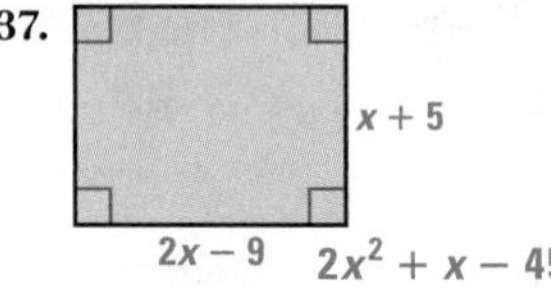

$2x^2 + x - 45$

38. 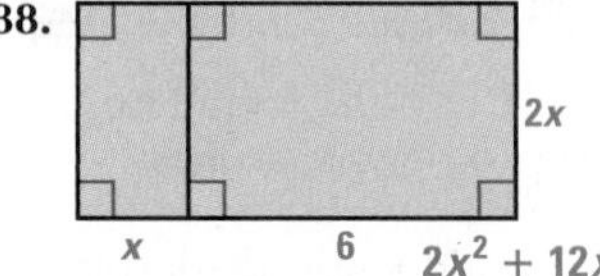

$2x^2 + 12x$

39. 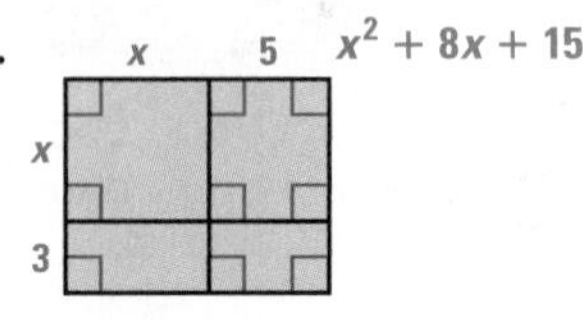

$x^2 + 8x + 15$

40. 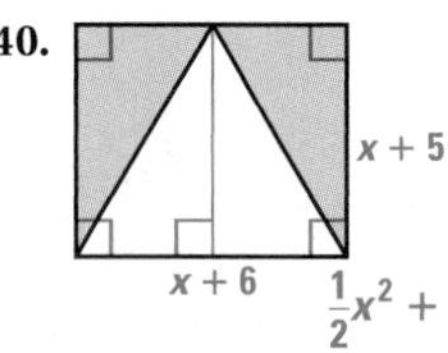

$\frac{1}{2}x^2 + \frac{11}{2}x + 15$

41. 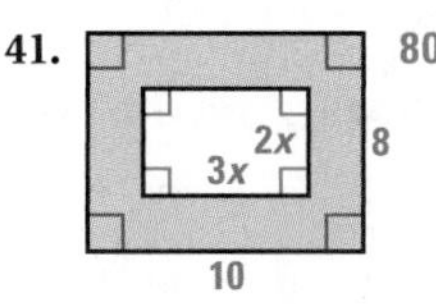

$80 - 6x^2$

42. 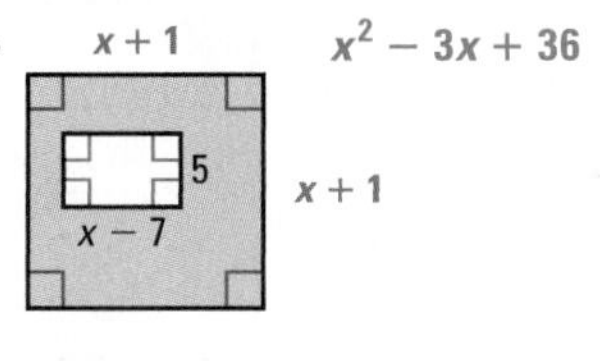

$x^2 - 3x + 36$

43. **POLYNOMIAL FUNCTIONS** Find the product $f(x) \cdot g(x)$ for the functions $f(x) = x - 11$ and $g(x) = 2x + 12$. $2x^2 - 10x - 132$

44. ★ **MULTIPLE CHOICE** Which polynomial represents $f(x) \cdot g(x)$ if $f(x) = -2x^2$ and $g(x) = x^3 - 5x^2 + 2x - 1$? C

   (A) $-2x^5 - 10x^4 + 4x^3 - 2x^2$ (B) $-2x^5 + 10x^4 - 4x^3 - 2x^2$

   (C) $-2x^5 + 10x^4 - 4x^3 + 2x^2$ (D) $2x^5 - 10x^4 + 4x^3 - 2x^2$

45. **REASONING** Find the product $(x^2 - 7x)(2x^2 + 3x + 1)$. Show that the product is correct by using a graphing calculator. *Explain* your reasoning.

45. $2x^4 - 11x^3 - 20x^2 - 7x$; graph $Y_1 = (x^2 - 7x)(2x^2 + 3x + 1)$ and $Y_2 = 2x^4 - 11x^3 - 20x^2 - 7x$ in the same viewing window. Because the graphs coincide, the expressions for Y_1 and Y_2 must be equivalent.

C **CHALLENGE** **Find the product.**

46. $(x - y)(3x + 4y)$ $3x^2 + xy - 4y^2$
47. $(x^2y + 9y)(2x + 3y)$ $2x^3y + 3x^2y^2 + 18xy + 27y^2$
48. $(x^2 - 5xy + y^2)(4xy)$ $4x^3y - 20x^2y^2 + 4xy^3$

◯ = WORKED-OUT SOLUTIONS p. WS1 ★ = STANDARDIZED TEST PRACTICE

PROBLEM SOLVING

EXAMPLE 7 A on p. 564 for Exs. 49–50

49. PICTURE FRAME You are designing a frame to surround a rectangular picture. The width of the frame around the picture is the same on every side, as shown.

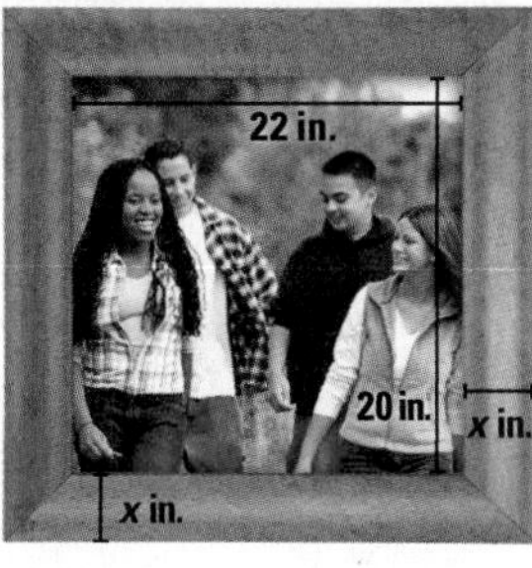

a. Write a polynomial that represents the total area of the picture and the frame. $4x^2 + 84x + 440$

b. Find the combined area of the picture and the frame when the width of the frame is 4 inches. 840 in.^2

@HomeTutor for problem solving help at classzone.com

50. SWIMMING POOL A rectangular swimming pool is bordered on one side by a deck. A contractor is hired to build a walkway along the remaining three sides of the pool. The width of the walkway is the same on every side, as shown.

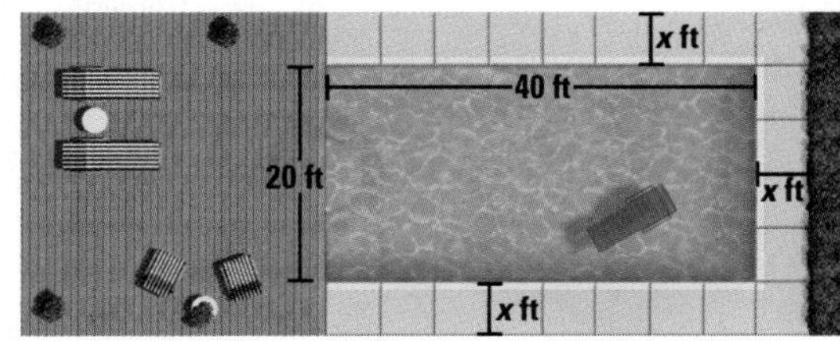

a. Write a polynomial that represents the total area of the pool and the walkway. $2x^2 + 100x + 800$

b. Find the combined area of the pool and the walkway when the width of the walkway is 5 feet. 1350 ft^2

@HomeTutor for problem solving help at classzone.com

51a. $12,300 million, 0.171; for $t = 0$, the amount of money (in millions of dollars) people between 15 and 19 years old spent on sound recordings in the U.S. in 1997.

(51.) SOUND RECORDINGS During the period 1997–2002, the amount of money R (in millions of dollars) spent on sound recordings in the U.S. and the percent P (in decimal form) of this amount spent by people who are between 15 and 19 years old can be modeled by

$$R = -336t^2 + 1730t + 12{,}300 \text{ and } P = 0.00351t^2 - 0.0249t + 0.171$$

where t is the number of years since 1997.

a. Find the values of R and P for $t = 0$. What does the product $R \cdot P$ mean for $t = 0$ in this situation?

b. Write an equation that models the amount spent on sound recordings by people who are between 15 and 19 years old as a function of the number of years since 1997. $R \cdot P \approx -1.18t^4 + 14.4t^3 - 57.4t^2 - 10.4t + 2100$

c. How much money did people between 15 and 19 years old spend on sound recordings in 2002? about $1680 million

52a. $H \cdot P \approx 2t^2 + 263t + 8366$; find the product $H \cdot P$, because the number of housing units times the percent of housing units that were vacant will give the number of vacant housing units.

52. ★ SHORT RESPONSE During the period 1980–2002, the number H (in thousands) of housing units in the U.S. and the percent P (in decimal form) of housing units that were vacant can be modeled by

$$H = 1570t + 89{,}000 \quad \text{and} \quad P = 0.0013t + 0.094$$

where t is the number of years since 1980.

a. Write an equation that models the number (in thousands) of vacant housing units as a function of the number of years since 1980. *Explain* how you found this equation.

b. How many housing units were vacant in 2002? about 15,120 housing units

Mathematical Reasoning

Exercise 49 You may want to discuss the usefulness of using a variable to represent the width of the frame. Lead students to see that the ease of manipulating a variable at the design stage allows them to consider the impact of various widths.

Reading Strategy

Exercises 51–52 You may want to point out that Exercise 51 has a worked-out solution and that Exercise 52 uses the same concepts. Exercise 52 is also an example of a short response question, so the worked-out solution for Exercise 51 can provide useful strategies for this type of test question. Suggest that students carefully read Exercise 51 so they understand the problem before they attempt a solution.

5 ASSESS AND RETEACH

Daily Homework Quiz

Transparency Available

Find the product.

1. $3x(x^3 - 3x^2 + 2x - 4)$ $3x^4 - 9x^3 + 6x^2 - 12x$
2. $(y - 4)(2y + 5)$ $2y^2 - 3y - 20$
3. $(4x + 3)(3x - 2)$ $12x^2 + x - 6$
4. $(b^2 - 2b - 1)(3b - 5)$ $3b^3 - 11b^2 + 7b + 5$
5. The dimensions of a rectangle are $x + 4$ and $3x - 1$. Write an expression to represent the area of the rectangle. $3x^2 + 11x - 4$

Available at **classzone.com**

Diagnosis/Remediation

- Practice A, B, C in Chapter 9 Resource Book, pp. 18–20
- Study Guide in Chapter 9 Resource Book, pp. 21–22
- Practice Workbook, pp. 135–136
- @HomeTutor

Challenge

Additional challenge is available in the Chapter 9 Resource Book, p. 25.

53a. *Sample answer:* $T = t + 90$; use the data points from 1995–1999: (5, 95), (6, 96), (7, 97), (8, 98), (9, 99). All these points lie on a line with slope $m = 1$; use any one of the points to find the y-intercept $b = 90$. The other data points, (0, 92), (10, 101), and (11, 102), lie close to the line $T = t + 90$.

B **53.** ★ **EXTENDED RESPONSE** The bar graph shows the number of households with a television for various years during the period 1990–2001.

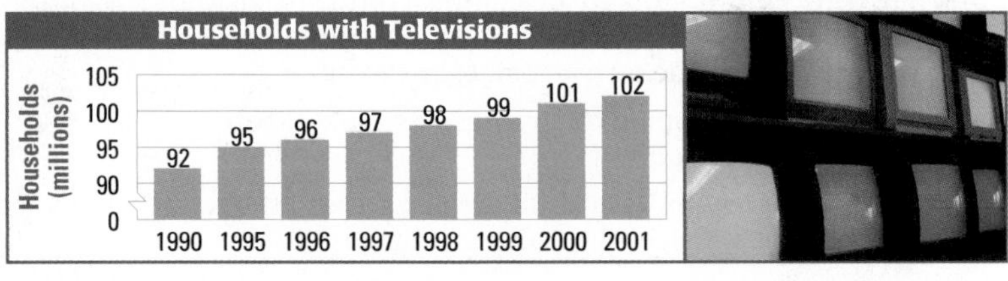

a. Find a linear equation that models the number of households T (in millions) with a television as a function of the number of years since 1990. *Explain* how you found your model.

b. During the period 1990–2001, the percent P (in decimal form) of television households that also have a VCR can be modeled by

$$P = -0.0015t^2 + 0.032t + 0.069$$

where t is the number of years since 1990. Write an equation that models the number of households V (in millions) with a VCR and a television as a function of the number of years since 1990. $V = -0.0015t^3 - 0.103t^2 + 2.949t + 6.21$

c. Use the equation from part (b) to predict the number of households that had a VCR and a television in 2002 and in 2005. about 24.2 million households, about 22.2 million households

C **54.** **CHALLENGE** For the period 1990–2001, the total United States energy consumption C (in quadrillion British Thermal Units, or BTU) and the percent P of the total energy that was consumed in the United States for industrial purposes can be modeled by

$$C = 1.5t + 84$$
$$P = -0.05t^2 + 0.25t + 38$$

where t is the number of years since 1990.

a. Find the percent of total energy that was consumed in the United States for industrial purposes in 2000. 35.5%

b. Write an equation that gives the total energy (in quadrillion BTU) consumed in the United States for industrial purposes as a function of the number of years since 1990. To write the equation, you may need to rewrite one of the given equations. $C \cdot 0.01P = -0.00075t^3 - 0.03825t^2 + 0.78t + 31.92$

ILLINOIS MIXED REVIEW

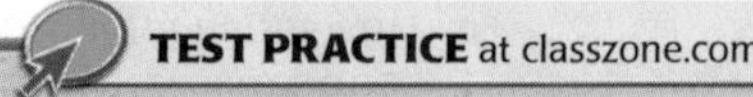

55. A class consists of 12 girls and 17 boys. Girls had an average of x points on a test, while boys had an average of y points. Which expression gives the average test score for the entire class? B

Ⓐ $\frac{x + y}{2}$ Ⓑ $\frac{12x + 17y}{29}$ Ⓒ $\frac{x + y}{29}$ Ⓓ $29\left(\frac{x}{12} + \frac{y}{17}\right)$

56. Mrs. Smith invested some money that will double in value every 14 years. If she invested \$4,000 on the first of the year 2005, how much will the investment be worth on the first of the year 2061? C

Ⓐ \$24,000 Ⓑ \$32,000 Ⓒ \$64,000 Ⓓ \$128,000

9.3 Find Special Products of Polynomials

8.11.01 Simplify or identify equivalent algebraic expressions (e.g., exponential, rational, logarithmic, factored, polynomial).

Before You multiplied polynomials.

Now You will use special product patterns to multiply polynomials.

Why? So you can make a scientific prediction, as in Example 4.

Key Vocabulary
- **binomial,** *p. 555*
- **trinomial,** *p. 555*

The diagram shows a square with a side length of $(a + b)$ units. You can see that the area of the square is

$$(a + b)^2 = a^2 + 2ab + b^2.$$

This is one version of a pattern called the square of a binomial. To find another version of this pattern, use algebra: replace b with $-b$.

	a	b
a	a^2	ab
b	ab	b^2

$(a + (-b))^2 = a^2 + 2a(-b) + (-b)^2$ — **Replace *b* with $-b$ in the pattern above.**

$(a - b)^2 = a^2 - 2ab + b^2$ — **Simplify.**

KEY CONCEPT *For Your Notebook*

Square of a Binomial Pattern

Algebra	Example
$(a + b)^2 = a^2 + 2ab + b^2$	$(x + 5)^2 = x^2 + 10x + 25$
$(a - b)^2 = a^2 - 2ab + b^2$	$(2x - 3)^2 = 4x^2 - 12x + 9$

EXAMPLE 1 Use the square of a binomial pattern

USE PATTERNS
When you use special product patterns, remember that *a* and *b* can be numbers, variables, or variable expressions.

Find the product.

a. $(3x + 4)^2 = (3x)^2 + 2(3x)(4) + 4^2$ — **Square of a binomial pattern**

$= 9x^2 + 24x + 16$ — **Simplify.**

b. $(5x - 2y)^2 = (5x)^2 - 2(5x)(2y) + (2y)^2$ — **Square of a binomial pattern**

$= 25x^2 - 20xy + 4y^2$ — **Simplify.**

✓ **GUIDED PRACTICE** for Example 1

Find the product.

1. $(x + 3)^2$ $x^2 + 6x + 9$

2. $(2x + 1)^2$ $4x^2 + 4x + 1$

3. $(4x - y)^2$ $16x^2 - 8xy + y^2$

4. $(3m + n)^2$ $9m^2 + 6mn + n^2$

1 PLAN AND PREPARE

Warm-Up Exercises
Transparency Available

Find the product.

1. $(x + 7)(x + 2)$ $x^2 + 9x + 14$

2. $(3x - 1)(3x + 2)$ $9x^2 + 3x - 2$

3. The dimensions of a rectangular playground can be represented by $3x + 8$ and $5x + 2$. Write a polynomial that represents the area of the playground. What is the area of the playground if x is 8 meters? $15x^2 + 46x + 16$; 1344 m^2

Notetaking Guide
Transparency Available

Promotes interactive learning and notetaking skills, pp. 195–198.

Pacing
Basic: 1 day
Average: 1 day
Advanced: 1 day
Block: 0.5 block with 9.4
- See *Teaching Guide/Lesson Plan.*

2 FOCUS AND MOTIVATE

Essential Question
Big Idea 1, p. 553

How do you use special product patterns to multiply binomials? Tell students they will learn how to answer this question by using patterns to write products of binomials.

Resource Planning Guide

Chapter Resource Book
- Teaching Guide/Lesson Plan (pp. 26–27)
- Practice levels A, B, C (pp. 28–30)
- Study Guide (pp. 31–32)
- Catch-up for Absent Students (p. 33)
- Application (p. 34)
- Challenge (p. 35)

Workbooks
- Notetaking Guide (pp. 195–198)
- Practice Workbook (pp. 137–138)

Teaching Options
- **Power Presentations CD-ROM** provides dynamic electronic teaching resources for the classroom.
- **Activity Generator CD-ROM** provides editable activities for all ability levels.

Interactive Technology
- Easy Planner
- Power Presentations CD-ROM
- Activity Generator CD-ROM
- Animated Algebra
- Test Generator CD-ROM
- Online Quiz
- eWorkbook
- eEdition
- @HomeTutor

Resources for English Learners
- Quick Reference for English Learners
- Spanish Study Guide
- Multi-Language Visual Glossary
- Student Resources in Spanish

See also the *Algebra 1 Toolkit* for more strategies for meeting individual needs.

Motivating the Lesson

If both parents have brown eyes, it is possible for one child to have brown eyes while another child has blue eyes. By using a special pattern to multiply binomials, you can calculate the likelihood of such an occurrence.

3 TEACH

Extra Example 1

Find the product.

a. $(2x + 5)^2$ $4x^2 + 20x + 25$

b. $(3x - y)^2$ $9x^2 - 6xy + y^2$

Key Question to Ask for Example 1

- How would the product $(3x - 4)^2$ be different from the product in part (a)? **The middle term would be negative rather than positive.**

Extra Example 2

Find the product.

a. $(r + 3)(r - 3)$ $r^2 - 9$

b. $(4x + y)(4x - y)$ $16x^2 - y^2$

Key Question to Ask for Example 2

- What happens to the middle terms when you find the product using the sum and difference pattern? **The sum of the two middle terms is zero.**

Extra Example 3

Use special products to find the product 18 • 22. **396**

SUM AND DIFFERENCE PATTERN To find the product $(x + 2)(x - 2)$, you can multiply the two binomials using the FOIL pattern.

$(x + 2)(x - 2) = x^2 - 2x + 2x - 4$ **Use FOIL pattern.**

$= x^2 - 4$ **Combine like terms.**

This suggests a pattern for the product of the sum and difference of two terms.

KEY CONCEPT *For Your Notebook*

Sum and Difference Pattern

Algebra	Example
$(a + b)(a - b) = a^2 - b^2$	$(x + 3)(x - 3) = x^2 - 9$

EXAMPLE 2 Use the sum and difference pattern

Find the product.

a. $(t + 5)(t - 5) = t^2 - 5^2$ **Sum and difference pattern**

$= t^2 - 25$ **Simplify.**

b. $(3x + y)(3x - y) = (3x)^2 - y^2$ **Sum and difference pattern**

$= 9x^2 - y^2$ **Simplify.**

✓ **GUIDED PRACTICE** for Example 2

Find the product.

5. $(x + 10)(x - 10)$ $x^2 - 100$

6. $(2x + 1)(2x - 1)$ $4x^2 - 1$

7. $(x + 3y)(x - 3y)$ $x^2 - 9y^2$

SPECIAL PRODUCTS AND MENTAL MATH The special product patterns can help you use mental math to find certain products of numbers.

EXAMPLE 3 Use special products and mental math

Use special products to find the product 26 • 34.

Solution

Notice that 26 is 4 less than 30 while 34 is 4 more than 30.

$26 \cdot 34 = (30 - 4)(30 + 4)$ **Write as product of difference and sum.**

$= 30^2 - 4^2$ **Sum and difference pattern**

$= 900 - 16$ **Evaluate powers.**

$= 884$ **Simplify.**

Differentiated Instruction

Visual Learners Students sometimes forget the coefficient of the linear term *ab* in the square of a binomial, or they misplace the minus sign. In addition to the colored tiles shown on page 569, another way to remember the formulas is to apply the FOIL method to the product of two binomials using mental math. See also the *Algebra 1 Toolkit* for more strategies.

EXAMPLE 4 Solve a multi-step problem

BORDER COLLIES The color of the dark patches of a border collie's coat is determined by a combination of two genes. An offspring inherits one patch color gene from each parent. Each parent has two color genes, and the offspring has an equal chance of inheriting either one.

The gene B is for black patches, and the gene r is for red patches. Any gene combination with a B results in black patches. Suppose each parent has the same gene combination Br. The Punnett square shows the possible gene combinations of the offspring and the resulting patch color.

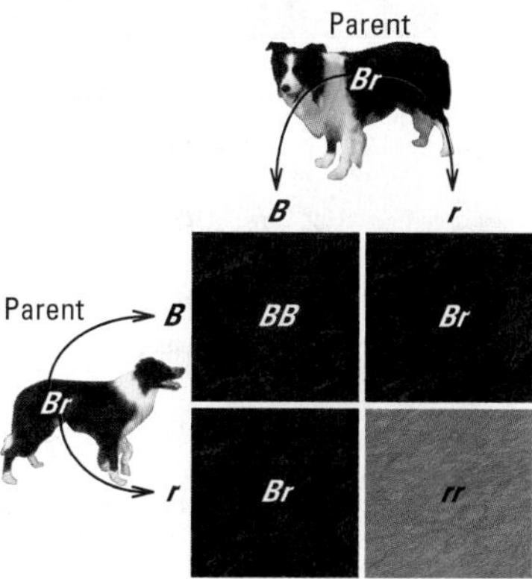

- What percent of the possible gene combinations of the offspring result in black patches?
- Show how you could use a polynomial to model the possible gene combinations of the offspring.

Solution

STEP 1 **Notice** that the Punnett square shows 4 possible gene combinations of the offspring. Of these combinations, 3 result in black patches.

▶ 75% of the possible gene combinations result in black patches.

STEP 2 **Model** the gene from each parent with $0.5B + 0.5r$. There is an equal chance that the collie inherits a black or red gene from each parent.

The possible genes of the offspring can be modeled by $(0.5B + 0.5r)^2$. Notice that this product also represents the area of the Punnett square.

Expand the product to find the possible patch colors of the offspring.

$$(0.5B + 0.5r)^2 = (0.5B)^2 + 2(0.5B)(0.5r) + (0.5r)^2$$

$$= 0.25B^2 + 0.5Br + 0.25r^2$$

Consider the coefficients in the polynomial.

$$0.25B^2 + 0.5Br + 0.25r^2$$

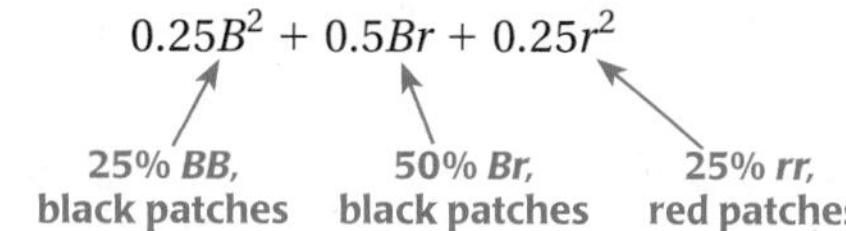

The coefficients show that 25% + 50% = 75% of the possible gene combinations will result in black patches.

✓ GUIDED PRACTICE for Examples 3 and 4

8. *Describe* how you can use special products to find 21^2.
Use the square of a binomial pattern to find the product $(20 + 1)^2$.
9. **BORDER COLLIES** Look back at Example 4. What percent of the possible gene combinations of the offspring result in red patches? 25%

Extra Example 4

In dogs, the gene E is for erect ears and the gene e is for droopy ears. Any gene combination with an E results in erect ears. The Punnett square shows the possible gene combinations of the offspring and the resulting type of ear.

	E	e
E	EE erect	Ee erect
e	Ee erect	ee droopy

- What percent of the possible gene combinations of the offspring result in droopy ears? 25%
- Show how you could use a polynomial to model the possible gene combinations of the offspring. **Use $(0.5E + 0.5e)^2$ to model the possible genes of the offspring. Expand the product to find the possible gene combinations: $0.25E^2 + 0.5Ee + 0.25e^2$. The coefficient of e^2 shows that 25% of the possible gene combinations will result in droopy ears.**

Closing the Lesson

Have students summarize the major points of the lesson and answer the Essential Question: How do you use special product patterns to multiply binomials?

- **The square of a binomial pattern is for $(a + b)^2$ or $(a - b)^2$.**
- **The sum and difference pattern is for $(a + b)(a - b)$.**

To find $(a + b)^2$ or $(a - b)^2$, square a, add (or subtract) twice the product ab, and add the square of c. The product $(a + b)(a - b)$ is $a^2 - b^2$.

4 PRACTICE AND APPLY

Assignment Guide

Answer Transparencies available for all exercises

Basic:
Day 1: SRH p. 917 Exs. 1–9 odd
pp. 572–574
Exs. 1, 2, 4–8 even, 9–13, 17–22, 24–34 even, 40–43, 46–56 even

Average:
Day 1: pp. 572–574
Exs. 1, 2, 4–22, 24–34 even, 35–37, 40–44, 48, 52, 54, 56

Advanced:
Day 1: pp. 572–574
Exs. 1, 2, 6–8, 14–18, 19–33 odd, 35–45*, 53, 57

Block:
pp. 572–574
Exs. 1, 2, 4–22, 24–34 even, 35–37, 40–44, 48, 52, 54, 56 (with 9.4)

Differentiated Instruction

See *Algebra 1 Best Practices Toolkit* for suggestions on addressing the needs of a diverse classroom.

Homework Check

For a quick check of student understanding of key concepts, go over the following exercises:

Basic: 4, 12, 19, 26, 40
Average: 6, 15, 20, 28, 41
Advanced: 8, 16, 21, 31, 42

Extra Practice

- Student Edition, p. 946
- Chapter 9 Resource Book: Practice levels A, B, C, pp. 28–30

Practice Worksheet

An easily-readable reduced practice page (with answers) for this lesson can be found on p. 552C.

9.3 EXERCISES

HOMEWORK KEY
○ = WORKED-OUT SOLUTIONS on p. WS21 for Exs. 11 and 41
★ = STANDARDIZED TEST PRACTICE Exs. 2, 17, 18, 42, and 44
◆ = MULTIPLE REPRESENTATIONS Ex. 41

SKILL PRACTICE

A

1. **VOCABULARY** Give an example of two binomials whose product you can find using the sum and difference pattern. *Sample answer:* $x - 5, x + 5$

2. ★ **WRITING** *Explain* how to use the square of a binomial pattern. See margin.

EXAMPLE 1 on p. 569 for Exs. 3–10, 18

SQUARE OF A BINOMIAL Find the product.

3. $(x + 8)^2$ $x^2 + 16x + 64$
4. $(a + 6)^2$ $a^2 + 12a + 36$
5. $(2y + 5)^2$ $4y^2 + 20y + 25$
6. $(t - 7)^2$ $t^2 - 14t + 49$
7. $(n - 11)^2$ $n^2 - 22n + 121$
8. $(6b - 1)^2$ $36b^2 - 12b + 1$

ERROR ANALYSIS *Describe* and correct the error in multiplying. 9, 10. See margin.

9. $(s - 3)^2 = s^2 + 9$ ✗

10. $(2d - 10)^2 = 4d^2 - 20d + 100$ 

EXAMPLE 2 on p. 570 for Exs. 11–17

SUM AND DIFFERENCE PATTERN Find the product.

11. $(t + 4)(t - 4)$ $t^2 - 16$
12. $(m - 6)(m + 6)$ $m^2 - 36$
13. $(2x + 1)(2x - 1)$ $4x^2 - 1$
14. $(3x - 1)(3x + 1)$ $9x^2 - 1$
15. $(7 + w)(7 - w)$ $49 - w^2$
16. $(3s - 8)(3s + 8)$ $9s^2 - 64$

9. The middle term of the product, $2s(-3)$, was left out; $s^2 - 6s + 9$.

17. ★ **MULTIPLE CHOICE** Find the product $(7x + 3)(7x - 3)$. B

Ⓐ $7x^2 - 9$ Ⓑ $49x^2 - 9$ Ⓒ $49x^2 - 21x - 9$ Ⓓ $49x^2 - 42x - 9$

18. ★ **MULTIPLE CHOICE** Find the product $(5n - 3)^2$. D

Ⓐ $5n^2 - 9$ Ⓑ $25n^2 - 9$ Ⓒ $25n^2 - 15n + 9$ Ⓓ $25n^2 - 30n + 9$

EXAMPLE 3 on p. 570 for Exs. 19–22

MENTAL MATH *Describe* how you can use mental math to find the product. 19–22. See margin.

19. $16 \cdot 24$
20. $28 \cdot 32$
21. 17^2
22. 44^2

10. The middle term of the products should be twice the product of the terms of the binomial; $4d^2 - 40d + 100$.

SPECIAL PRODUCT PATTERNS Find the product.

23. $(r + 9s)^2$ $r^2 + 18rs + 81s^2$
24. $(6x + 5)^2$ $36x^2 + 60x + 25$
25. $(3m + 11n)(3m - 11n)$ $9m^2 - 121n^2$
26. $(7a + 8b)(7a - 8b)$ $49a^2 - 64b^2$
27. $(3m - 7n)^2$ $9m^2 - 42mn + 49n^2$
28. $(13 - 2x)^2$ $169 - 52x + 4x^2$
29. $(3f - 9)(3f + 9)$ $9f^2 - 81$
30. $(9 - 4t)(9 + 4t)$ $81 - 16t^2$
31. $(3x + 8y)^2$ $9x^2 + 48xy + 64y^2$
32. $(-x - 2y)^2$ $x^2 + 4xy + 4y^2$
33. $(2a - 5b)(2a + 5b)$ $4a^2 - 25b^2$
34. $(6x + y)(6x - y)$ $36x^2 - y^2$

B

MULTIPLYING FUNCTIONS Perform the indicated operation using the functions $f(x) = 3x + 0.5$ and $g(x) = 3x - 0.5$.

35. $f(x) \cdot g(x)$ $9x^2 - 0.25$
36. $(f(x))^2$ $9x^2 + 3x + 0.25$
37. $(g(x))^2$ $9x^2 - 3x + 0.25$

C

38. **CHALLENGE** Write two binomials that have the product $x^2 - 121$. *Explain.* See margin.

39. **CHALLENGE** Write a pattern for the cube of a binomial $(a + b)^3$. $a^3 + 3a^2b + 3ab^2 + b^3$

2. See Additional Answers beginning on p. AA1.

19. Use the sum and difference pattern to find the product $(20 - 4)(20 + 4)$.

20. Use the sum and difference pattern to find the product $(30 - 2)(30 + 2)$.

21. Use the square of a binomial pattern to find the product $(20 - 3)^2$.

22. Use the square of a binomial pattern to find the product $(40 + 4)^2$.

38. $x - 11, x + 11$; since $x^2 - 121 = x^2 - 11^2$ is in the form $a^2 - b^2$, you can use the sum and difference pattern in reverse to find the binomials $a - b = x - 11$ and $a + b = x + 11$.

PROBLEM SOLVING

EXAMPLE 4 A on p. 571 for Exs. 40–42

40. **PEA PLANTS** In pea plants, the gene G is for green pods, and the gene y is for yellow pods. Any gene combination with a G results in a green pod. Suppose two pea plants have the same gene combination Gy. The Punnett square shows the possible gene combinations of an offspring pea plant and the resulting pod color.

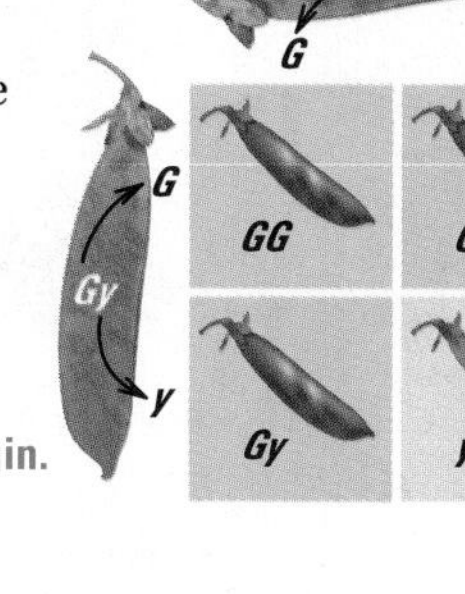

   a. What percent of possible gene combinations of the offspring plant result in a yellow pod? 25%

   b. Show how you could use a polynomial to model the possible gene combinations of the offspring. See margin.

   @HomeTutor for problem solving help at classzone.com

41. ◆ **MULTIPLE REPRESENTATIONS** In humans, the gene s is for straight thumbs, and the gene C is for curved thumbs. Any gene combination with a C results in a curved thumb. Suppose each parent has the same gene combination Cs.

   a. **Making a Diagram** Make a Punnett square that shows the possible gene combinations inherited by a child. See margin.

   b. **Writing a Model** Write a polynomial that models the possible gene combinations of the child. $0.25C^2 + 0.5Cs + 0.25s^2$

   c. **Interpreting a Model** What percent of the possible gene combinations of the child result in a curved thumb? 75%

   @HomeTutor for problem solving help at classzone.com

42. ★ **SHORT RESPONSE** In ball pythons, the gene N is for normal coloring, and the gene a is for no coloring, or albino. Any gene combination with an N results in normal coloring. Suppose one parent python has the gene combination Na and the other parent python has the gene combination aa. What percent of the possible gene combinations of the offspring result in an albino python? *Explain* how you found your answer. See margin.

B

43. **FOOTBALL STATISTICS** During the 2004 regular season, the San Diego Chargers' quarterback Drew Brees completed 65.5% of the passes he attempted. The area model shows the possible outcomes of two attempted passes. a, b. See margin.

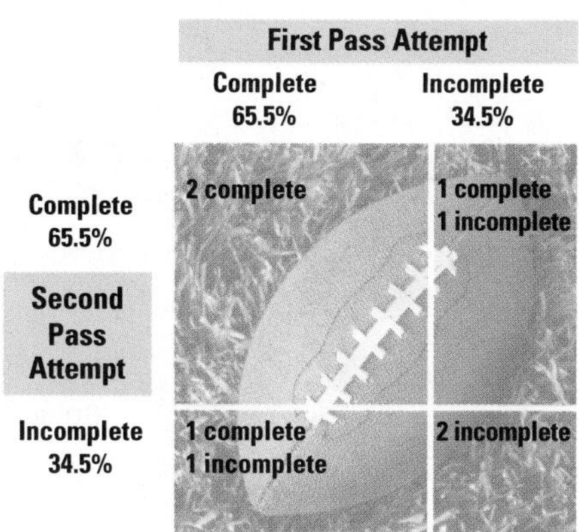

First Pass Attempt
Complete 65.5%
Incomplete 34.5%
Second Pass Attempt
Complete 65.5%
Incomplete 34.5%
2 complete
1 complete 1 incomplete
1 complete 1 incomplete
2 incomplete

   a. What percent of the possible outcomes of two attempted passes results in Drew Brees's throwing at least one complete pass? *Explain* how you found your answer using the area model.

   b. Show how you could use a polynomial to model the possible results of two attempted passes.

Avoiding Common Errors

Exercises 23–34 Students often use an incorrect pattern when finding products of binomials. Suggest that students go through all of the exercises before finding the products to determine which pattern they should use for each exercise. If the square of a binomial pattern is appropriate, encourage them to indicate whether the middle term is positive or negative.

Teaching Strategy

Exercise 42 It may be useful to have students make Punnet squares for several other possible combinations of genes, such as *NN* and *aa* or *NN* and *Na*, so they can see the range of possible combinations. They may find it interesting to compare the Punnett squares. Ask students to determine the percent of each of the possible gene combinations for each of the Punnett squares. You may want to challenge students to write offspring polynomials for each of the possible parent combinations.

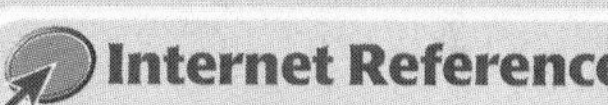

Exercises 40–42 To learn more about Mendel and his pea plant experiment, visit anthro.palomar.edu/mendel/mendel_1.htm

42. 50%; the gene from one parent is modeled by $0.5N + 0.5a$ and the gene from the other parent in modeled by $0.5a + 0.5a = a$, so the possible gene combinations of the offspring are modeled by $a(0.5N + 0.5a) = 0.5Na + 0.5a^2$. Because any gene combination with an N results in normal coloring, only the second term, $0.5a^2$, represents albino offspring. The coefficient of a^2, 0.5, shows that 50% of the offspring will be albino.

43a–b. See Additional Answers beginning on p. AA1.

40b. The gene from each parent is modeled by $0.5G + 0.5y$. The possible genes of the offspring are modeled by $(0.5G + 0.5y)^2 = 0.25G^2 + 0.5Gy + 0.25y^2$. Because any gene combination with a G results in a green pod, the coefficients of the first two terms show that 25% + 50% = 75% of the offspring will have green pods, and the coefficient of the last term shows that 25% of the offspring will have yellow pods.

41a.

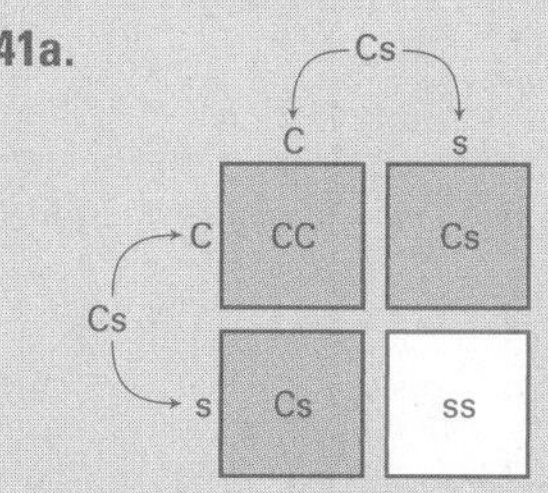

5 ASSESS AND RETEACH

Daily Homework Quiz

Transparency Available

Find the product.

1. $(y + 8)(y - 8)$ $y^2 - 64$
2. $(3m - 2n)^2$ $9m^2 - 12mn + 4n^2$
3. $(2m + 5)^2$ $4m^2 + 20m + 25$
4. In humans, the genes for being able to roll and not roll the tongue are R and r, respectively. Offspring with R can roll the tongue. If one parent is Rr and the other is rr, what percent of the offspring will not be able to roll the tongue? 50%

Available at **classzone.com**

Diagnosis/Remediation

- Practice A, B, C in Chapter 9 Resource Book, pp. 28–30
- Study Guide in Chapter 9 Resource Book, pp. 31–32
- Practice Workbook, pp. 137–138
- @HomeTutor

Challenge

Additional challenge is available in the Chapter 9 Resource Book, p. 35.

Quiz

An easily-readable reduced copy of the quiz (with answers) on Lessons 9.1–9.3 from the Assessment Book can be found on p. 552E.

44c. 30.25π, 4π; substitute the least width $w = 0.5$ millimeters into the polynomial from part (b) to find the greatest possible area: $\pi(0.5)^2 - 12\pi(0.5) + 36\pi = 0.25\pi - 6\pi + 36\pi = 30.25\pi$ square millimeters. Substitute the greatest width $w = 4$ millimeters into the polynomial from part (b) to find the least possible area: $\pi(4)^2 - 12\pi(4) + 36\pi = 16\pi - 48\pi + 36\pi = 4\pi$ square millimeters.

44. ★ **EXTENDED RESPONSE** The iris of an eye surrounds the pupil. It regulates the amount of light entering the eye by opening and closing the pupil. For parts (a)–(c) below, leave your answers in terms of π.

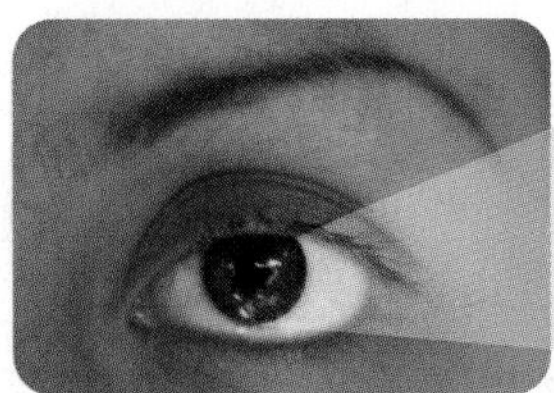

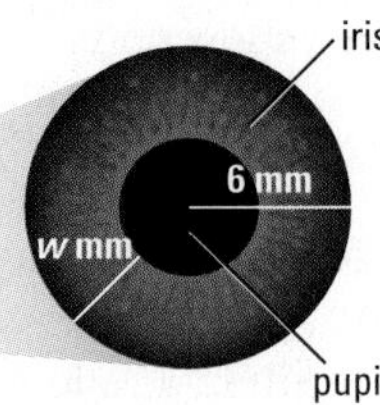

The iris of a human eye has a width w that varies from 0.5 millimeter to 4 millimeters.

a. Write a polynomial that represents the pupil's radius. $6 - w$

b. Write a polynomial that represents the pupil's area. $\pi w^2 - 12\pi w + 36\pi$

c. What is the least possible area and the greatest possible area of the pupil? *Explain* how you found your answers. See margin.

C **45.** **CHALLENGE** You use 100 feet of fencing to form a square with a side length of 25 feet. You want to change the dimensions of the enclosed region. For every 1 foot you increase the width, you must decrease the length by 1 foot. Write a polynomial that gives the area of the rectangle after you increase the width by x feet and decrease the length by x feet. *Explain* why *any* change in dimensions results in an area less than that of the original square. $625 - x^2$; the area of the original square is $25^2 = 625$ square feet, and the area of a square when the dimensions are changed is $(25 - x)(25 + x) = 625 - x^2$ square feet; since x^2 is always positive, the area of the new square will be less than 625 square feet.

ILLINOIS MIXED REVIEW

TEST PRACTICE at classzone.com

46. The table gives the cost for one person to stay at a campground for different lengths of time. Which equation best describes the relationship between the cost in dollars, c, and the number of days, t? B

Ⓐ $c = 15t$ Ⓑ $c = 15t + 25$

Ⓒ $c = 25t - 5$ Ⓓ $t = \frac{c}{15}$

Time (days)	Cost (dollars)
2	55
3	70
4	85

QUIZ for Lessons 9.1–9.3

Find the sum, difference, or product.

1. $(x^2 - 3x + 5) + (-2x^2 + 11x + 1)$ *(p. 554)* $-x^2 + 8x + 6$
2. $(8y^3 - 7y^2 + y) - (9y^2 - 5y + 7)$ *(p. 554)* $8y^3 - 16y^2 + 6y - 7$
3. $(2r + 11)(r - 6)$ *(p. 562)* $2r^2 - r - 66$
4. $(m + 3)(-2m^2 + 5m - 1)$ *(p. 562)* $-2m^3 - m^2 + 14m - 3$
5. $(2 + 8p)(2 - 10p)$ *(p. 562)* $4 - 4p - 80p^2$
6. $(15 - 2s)^2$ *(p. 569)* $225 - 60s + 4s^2$
7. $(5w + 9z)^2$ *(p. 569)* $25w^2 + 90wz + 81z^2$
8. $(5x - 4y)(5x + 4y)$ *(p. 569)* $25x^2 - 16y^2$
9. **AREA** The length of a rectangular rug is 2 times its width. The rug is centered in a rectangular room. Each edge is 3 feet from the nearest wall. Write a polynomial that represents the area of the room. *(p. 564)* $2w^2 + 18w + 36$

EXTRA PRACTICE for Lesson 9.3, p. 946

ONLINE QUIZ at classzone.com

9.4 Solve Polynomial Equations in Factored Form

8.11.19 Solve problems that include nonlinear functions, including selecting and evaluating formulas . . .

Before You solved linear equations.

Now You will solve polynomial equations.

Why So you can analyze vertical motion, as in Ex. 55.

Key Vocabulary
- **roots**
- **vertical motion model**

In Lesson 2.4, you learned the property of zero: For any real number a, $a \cdot 0 = 0$. This is equivalent to saying:

For real numbers a and b, if $a = 0$ or $b = 0$, then $ab = 0$.

The converse of this statement is also true (as shown in Exercise 49), and it is called the zero-product property.

KEY CONCEPT *For Your Notebook*

Zero-Product Property

Let a and b be real numbers. If $ab = 0$, then $a = 0$ or $b = 0$.

The zero-product property is used to solve an equation when one side is zero and the other side is a product of polynomial factors. The solutions of such an equation are also called **roots**.

EXAMPLE 1 Use the zero-product property

Solve $(x - 4)(x + 2) = 0$.

$(x - 4)(x + 2) = 0$ — Write original equation.

$x - 4 = 0$ *or* $x + 2 = 0$ — Zero-product property

$x = 4$ *or* $x = -2$ — Solve for x.

▶ The solutions of the equation are 4 and −2.

CHECK Substitute each solution into the original equation to check.

$(4 - 4)(4 + 2) \stackrel{?}{=} 0$ $\quad$ $(-2 - 4)(-2 + 2) \stackrel{?}{=} 0$

$0 \cdot 6 \stackrel{?}{=} 0$ $\quad$ $-6 \cdot 0 \stackrel{?}{=} 0$

$0 = 0$ ✓ $\quad$ $0 = 0$ ✓

GUIDED PRACTICE for Example 1

1. Solve the equation $(x - 5)(x - 1) = 0$. 5, 1

1 PLAN AND PREPARE

Warm-Up Exercises

Transparency Available

1. Find the GCF of 12 and 28. 4
2. Find the GCF of 18 and 42. 6
3. The number (in hundreds) of sunscreen and sun tanning products sold at a pharmacy from 1999–2005 can be modeled by $-0.8t^2 + 0.3x + 107$, where t is the number of years since 1999. About how many products were sold in 2002? about 10,070

Notetaking Guide

Transparency Available

Promotes interactive learning and notetaking skills, pp. 199–202.

Pacing

Basic: 2 days

Average: 2 days

Advanced: 2 days

Block: 0.5 block with 9.3
0.5 block with 9.5

- See *Teaching Guide/Lesson Plan.*

2 FOCUS AND MOTIVATE

Essential Question

Big Idea 3, p. 553

How do you solve polynomial equations in factored form? Tell students they will learn how to answer this question by using the zero-product property.

Resource Planning Guide

Chapter Resource Book
- Teaching Guide/Lesson Plan (pp. 36–37)
- Activity Master (p. 38)
- Practice levels A, B, C (pp. 41–43)
- Study Guide (pp. 44–45)
- Catch-up for Absent Students (p. 46)
- Problem Solving Workshop (p. 47)
- Challenge (p. 49)

Workbooks
- Notetaking Guide (pp. 199–202)
- Practice Workbook (pp. 139–140)

Teaching Options
- **Power Presentations CD-ROM** provides dynamic electronic teaching resources for the classroom.
- **Activity Generator CD-ROM** provides editable activities for all ability levels.

Interactive Technology
- Easy Planner
- Power Presentations CD-ROM
- Activity Generator CD-ROM
- Animated Algebra
- Test Generator CD-ROM
- Online Quiz
- eWorkbook
- eEdition
- @HomeTutor

Resources for English Learners
- Quick Reference for English Learners
- Spanish Study Guide
- Multi-Language Visual Glossary
- Student Resources in Spanish

See also the *Algebra 1 Toolkit* for more strategies for meeting individual needs.

Motivating the Lesson

Ask students to recount events in which they experienced or witnessed a person or animal jumping in an upward motion. After they share some of their experiences, tell them that this lesson offers a way to calculate how long the person or animal will be in the air.

3 TEACH

Extra Example 1

Solve $(x + 3)(x - 5) = 0$. $-3, 5$

Key Question to Ask for Example 1

- Why does this type of equation have two solutions? The left side of the equation is the product of two quantities. By the zero-product property, either of them could be zero. This allows for the equation to have two solutions.

Extra Example 2

Factor out the greatest common monomial factor.

a. $8x + 12y$ $4(2x + 3y)$

b. $14y^2 + 21y$ $7y(2y + 3)$

Key Question to Ask for Example 2

- In part (b), how do you know x^3 is a factor of x^3 and x^4?

$\frac{x^4}{x^3} = x^{4-3}$ or x and

$\frac{x^3}{x^3} = x^{3-3} = x^0$ or 1

Extra Example 3

Solve $3x^2 + 18x = 0$ $-6, 0$

Extra Example 4

Solve $4s^2 = 14s$. $0, \frac{7}{2}$

REVIEW GCF
For help with finding the GCF, see p. 910.

FACTORING To solve a polynomial equation using the zero-product property, you may need to *factor* the polynomial, or write it as a product of other polynomials. Look for the *greatest common factor* (GCF) of the polynomial's terms. This is a monomial with an integer coefficient that divides evenly into each term.

EXAMPLE 2 Find the greatest common monomial factor

Factor out the greatest common monomial factor.

a. $12x + 42y$ **b.** $4x^4 + 24x^3$

Solution

a. The GCF of 12 and 42 is 6. The variables x and y have no common factor. So, the greatest common monomial factor of the terms is 6.

▶ $12x + 42y = 6(2x + 7y)$

b. The GCF of 4 and 24 is 4. The GCF of x^4 and x^3 is x^3. So, the greatest common monomial factor of the terms is $4x^3$.

▶ $4x^4 + 24x^3 = 4x^3(x + 6)$

GUIDED PRACTICE for Example 2

2. Factor out the greatest common monomial factor from $14m + 35n$. $7(2m + 5n)$

EXAMPLE 3 Solve an equation by factoring

Solve $2x^2 + 8x = 0$.

$2x^2 + 8x = 0$	Write original equation.
$2x(x + 4) = 0$	Factor left side.
$2x = 0$ *or* $x + 4 = 0$	Zero-product property
$x = 0$ *or* $x = -4$	Solve for x.

▶ The solutions of the equation are 0 and -4.

EXAMPLE 4 Solve an equation by factoring

Solve $6n^2 = 15n$.

AVOID ERRORS
To use the zero-product property, you must write the equation so that one side is 0. For this reason, $15n$ must be subtracted from each side.

$6n^2 - 15n = 0$	Subtract $15n$ from each side.
$3n(2n - 5) = 0$	Factor left side.
$3n = 0$ *or* $2n - 5 = 0$	Zero-product property
$n = 0$ *or* $n = \frac{5}{2}$	Solve for n.

▶ The solutions of the equation are 0 and $\frac{5}{2}$.

✓ **GUIDED PRACTICE** for Examples 3 and 4

Solve the equation.

3. $a^2 + 5a = 0$ 0, −5 **4.** $3s^2 - 9s = 0$ 0, 3 **5.** $4x^2 = 2x$ $0, \frac{1}{2}$

VERTICAL MOTION A *projectile* is an object that is propelled into the air but has no power to keep itself in the air. A thrown ball is a projectile, but an airplane is not. The height of a projectile can be described by the **vertical motion model**.

UNDERSTAND THE MODEL
The vertical motion model takes into account the effect of gravity but ignores other, less significant, factors such as air resistance.

KEY CONCEPT *For Your Notebook*

Vertical Motion Model

The height h (in feet) of a projectile can be modeled by

$$h = -16t^2 + vt + s$$

where t is the time (in seconds) the object has been in the air, v is the initial vertical velocity (in feet per second), and s is the initial height (in feet).

EXAMPLE 5 Solve a multi-step problem

ARMADILLO A startled armadillo jumps straight into the air with an initial vertical velocity of 14 feet per second. After how many seconds does it land on the ground?

Solution

STEP 1 **Write** a model for the armadillo's height above the ground.

$h = -16t^2 + vt + s$	Vertical motion model
$h = -16t^2 + 14t + 0$	Substitute 14 for v and 0 for s.
$h = -16t^2 + 14t$	Simplify.

STEP 2 **Substitute** 0 for h. When the armadillo lands, its height above the ground is 0 feet. Solve for t.

$0 = -16t^2 + 14t$	Substitute 0 for h.
$0 = 2t(-8t + 7)$	Factor right side.
$2t = 0$ *or* $-8t + 7 = 0$	Zero-product property
$t = 0$ *or* $t = 0.875$	Solve for t.

AVOID ERRORS
The solution $t = 0$ means that before the armadillo jumps, its height above the ground is 0 feet.

▶ The armadillo lands on the ground 0.875 second after the armadillo jumps.

 **GUIDED PRACTICE** for Example 5

6. WHAT IF? In Example 5, suppose the initial vertical velocity is 12 feet per second. After how many seconds does the armadillo land on the ground? 0.75 sec

Extra Example 5

A dolphin jumped out of the water with an initial velocity of 32 feet per second. After how many seconds did the dolphin enter the water? 2 sec

Key Questions to Ask for Example 5

- Can you use the vertical motion model to calculate when a hot air balloon will return to the ground? Explain. No, a hot air balloon is not a projectile.
- What steps can you use to solve $-8t + 7 = 0$? Subtract 7 from both sides of the equation and then divide both sides of the equation by −8.

Closing the Lesson

Have students summarize the major points of the lesson and answer the Essential Question: How do you solve polynomial equations in factored form?

- The zero-product property can be used to solve a polynomial equation in factored form.
- If a polynomial expression can be factored, rewrite it in factored form before solving the equation.

If necessary, rewrite the equation so one side is 0 and factor out any monomial factor. Then use the zero-product property to set each factor equal to 0 and find the solutions.

9.4 EXERCISES

HOMEWORK KEY
- ○ = **WORKED-OUT SOLUTIONS** on p. WS21 for Exs. 3 and 55
- ★ = **STANDARDIZED TEST PRACTICE** Exs. 2, 15, 39, 53, and 56
- ◆ = **MULTIPLE REPRESENTATIONS** Ex. 58

SKILL PRACTICE

A

1. **VOCABULARY** What is the vertical motion model and what does each variable in the model represent? See margin.

2. ★ **WRITING** *Explain* how to use the zero-product property to find the solutions of the equation $3x(x - 7) = 0$. Set each of the two polynomial factors, $3x$ and $x - 7$, equal to zero and then solve each equation for x.

EXAMPLE 1 on p. 575 for Exs. 3–16

ZERO-PRODUCT PROPERTY Solve the equation.

3. $(x - 5)(x + 3) = 0$ $5, -3$
4. $(y + 9)(y - 1) = 0$ $-9, 1$
5. $(z - 13)(z - 14) = 0$ $13, 14$
6. $(c + 6)(c + 8) = 0$ $-6, -8$
7. $(d - 7)\left(d + \frac{4}{3}\right) = 0$ $7, -\frac{4}{3}$
8. $\left(g - \frac{1}{8}\right)(g + 18) = 0$ $\frac{1}{8}, -18$
9. $(m - 3)(4m + 12) = 0$ ± 3
10. $(2n - 14)(3n + 9) = 0$ $7, -3$
11. $(3n + 11)(n + 1) = 0$ $-\frac{11}{3}, -1$
12. $(3x + 1)(x + 6) = 0$ $-\frac{1}{3}, -6$
13. $(2y + 5)(7y - 5) = 0$ $-\frac{5}{2}, \frac{5}{7}$
14. $(8z - 6)(12z + 14) = 0$ $\frac{3}{4}, -\frac{7}{6}$

15. ★ **MULTIPLE CHOICE** What are the solutions of the equation $(y - 12)(y + 6) = 0$? C

    Ⓐ -12 and -6 Ⓑ -12 and 6 Ⓒ -6 and 12 Ⓓ 6 and 12

16. **ERROR ANALYSIS** *Describe* and correct the error in solving $(z - 15)(z + 21) = 0$. The step of setting each factor equal to zero was left out; $z - 15 = 0$ or $z + 21 = 0$, $z = 15$ or $z = -21$.

    $(z - 15)(z + 21) = 0$
    $z = -15$ or $z = 21$

EXAMPLE 2 on p. 576 for Exs. 17–26

26. A common monomial factor, $3x$, was factored out, but not the greatest common factor, which is $3x^3$; $3x^3(6x^5 - 3x - 2)$.

FACTORING EXPRESSIONS Factor out the greatest common monomial factor.

17. $2x + 2y$ $2(x + y)$
18. $6x^2 - 15y$ $3(2x^2 - 5y)$
19. $3s^4 + 16s$ $s(3s^3 + 16)$
20. $5d^6 + 2d^5$ $d^5(5d + 2)$
21. $7w^5 - 35w^2$ $7w^2(w^3 - 5)$
22. $9m^7 - 3m^2$ $3m^2(3m^5 - 1)$
23. $15n^3 + 25n$ $5n(3n^2 + 5)$
24. $12a^5 + 8a$ $4a(3a^4 + 2)$
25. $\frac{5}{2}x^6 - \frac{1}{2}x^4$ $\frac{1}{2}x^4(5x^2 - 1)$

26. **ERROR ANALYSIS** *Describe* and correct the error in factoring out the greatest common monomial factor of $18x^8 - 9x^4 - 6x^3$. See margin.

    $18x^8 - 9x^4 - 6x^3 = 3x(6x^7 - 3x^3 - 2x^2)$

EXAMPLES 3 and 4 on p. 576 for Exs. 27–39

SOLVING EQUATIONS Solve the equation.

27. $b^2 + 6b = 0$ $0, -6$
28. $5w^2 - 5w = 0$ $0, 1$
29. $-10n^2 + 35n = 0$ $0, \frac{7}{2}$
30. $2x^2 + 15x = 0$ $0, -\frac{15}{2}$
31. $18c^2 + 6c = 0$ $0, -\frac{1}{3}$
32. $-32y^2 - 24y = 0$ $0, -\frac{3}{4}$
33. $3k^2 = 6k$ $0, 2$
34. $6h^2 = 3h$ $0, \frac{1}{2}$
35. $4s^2 = 10s$ $0, \frac{5}{2}$
36. $-42z^2 = 14z$ $0, -\frac{1}{3}$
37. $28m^2 = -8m$ $0, -\frac{2}{7}$
38. $-12p^2 = -30p$ $0, \frac{5}{2}$

39. ★ **MULTIPLE CHOICE** What are the solutions of $4x^2 = x$? C

    Ⓐ -4 and 0 Ⓑ $-\frac{1}{4}$ and 0 Ⓒ 0 and $\frac{1}{4}$ Ⓓ 0 and 4

4 PRACTICE AND APPLY

Assignment Guide

Answer Transparencies available for all exercises

Basic:
Day 1: SRH p. 911 Exs. 13–23 odd
pp. 578–580
Exs. 2, 3–15 odd, 16–26, 72–74
Day 2: pp. 578–580
Exs. 1, 27–42, 51–56, 60–70 even

Average:
Day 1: pp. 578–580
Exs. 2, 9–16, 18–26 even, 40–45, 72–74
Day 2: pp. 578–580
Exs. 1, 31–39, 46–49, 51–58, 61–71 odd

Advanced:
Day 1: pp. 578–580
Exs. 2, 10–15, 22–26, 40–45, 72–74
Day 2: pp. 578–580
Exs. 1, 32–39, 46–50*, 52–59*, 60–70 even

Block:
pp. 578–580
Exs. 2, 9–16, 18–26 even, 40–45, 72–74 (with 9.3)
pp. 578–580
Exs. 1, 31–39, 46–49, 51–58, 61–71 odd (with 9.5)

Differentiated Instruction

See *Algebra 1 Best Practices Toolkit* for suggestions on addressing the needs of a diverse classroom.

Homework Check

For a quick check of student understanding of key concepts, go over the following exercises:

Basic: 5, 18, 28, 34, 51
Average: 10, 22, 31, 36, 52
Advanced: 12, 24, 32, 38, 53

Extra Practice

- Student Edition, p. 946
- Chapter 9 Resource Book: Practice levels A, B, C, pp. 41–43

Practice Worksheet

An easily-readable reduced practice page (with answers) for this lesson can be found on p. 552C.

1. The vertical motion model is the equation $h = -16t^2 + vt + s$, where h is the height (in feet) of a projectile after t seconds in the air, given an initial velocity of v feet per second and an initial height of s feet.

B **FACTORING EXPRESSIONS Factor out the greatest common monomial factor.**

40. $20x^2y^2 - 4xy$ $4xy(5xy - 1)$ **41.** $8a^2b - 6ab^2$ $2ab(4a - 3b)$ **42.** $18s^2t^5 - 2s^3t$ $2s^2t(9t^4 - s)$

43. $v^3 - 5v^2 + 9v$ $v(v^2 - 5v + 9)$ **44.** $-2g^4 + 14g^2 + 6g$ $-2g(g^3 - 7g - 3)$ **45.** $6q^5 - 21q^4 - 15q^2$ $3q^2(2q^3 - 7q^2 - 5)$

HINT For help with finding zeros of functions, see p. 335.

FINDING ZEROS OF FUNCTIONS Find the zeros of the function.

46. $f(x) = x^2 - 15x$ 0, 15 **47.** $f(x) = -2x^2 + x$ $0, \frac{1}{2}$ **48.** $f(x) = 3x^2 - 27x$ 0, 9

C **49. CHALLENGE** Consider the equation $ab = 0$. Assume that $a \neq 0$ and solve the equation for b. Then assume that $b \neq 0$ and solve the equation for a. What conclusion can you draw about the values of a and b? 0; 0; at least one of them must be 0.

50. CHALLENGE Consider the equation $z = x^2 - xy$. For what values of x and y does $z = 0$? for $x = 0$ and y any real number, or for all real numbers x and y where $x = y$

PROBLEM SOLVING

EXAMPLE 5 A on p. 577 for Exs. 51–53

51. MOTION A cat leaps from the ground into the air with an initial vertical velocity of 11 feet per second. After how many seconds does the cat land on the ground? about 0.69 sec

@HomeTutor for problem solving help at classzone.com

52. SPITTLEBUG A spittlebug jumps into the air with an initial vertical velocity of 10 feet per second.

a. Write an equation that gives the height of the spittlebug as a function of the time (in seconds) since it left the ground. $h = -16t^2 + 10t$

b. The spittlebug reaches its maximum height after 0.3125 second. How high can it jump?

52b. about 1.563 ft

 for problem solving help at classzone.com

53. ★ SHORT RESPONSE A penguin jumps out of the water while swimming. This action is called porpoising. The height h (in feet) of the porpoising penguin can be modeled by $h = -16t^2 + 4.5t$ where t is the time (in seconds) since the penguin jumped out of the water. Find the zeros of the function. *Explain* what the zeros mean in this situation. See margin.

VERTICAL MOTION In Exercises 54 and 55, use the information below.

The height h (in meters) of a projectile can be modeled by $h = -4.9t^2 + vt + s$ where t is the time (in seconds) the object has been in the air, v is the initial vertical velocity (in meters per second), and s is the initial height (in meters).

54. SOCCER A soccer ball is kicked upward from the ground with an initial vertical velocity of 3.6 meters per second. After how many seconds does it land? about 0.73 sec

55. RABBIT HIGH JUMP A rabbit in a high jump competition leaves the ground with an initial vertical velocity of 4.9 meters per second.

a. Write an equation that gives the height of the rabbit as a function of the time (in seconds) since it left the ground. $h = -4.9t^2 + 4.9t$

b. What is a reasonable domain for the function? *Explain* your answer. See margin.

Avoiding Common Errors

Exercises 3–14, 27–38 Urge students to pay attention to the sign of each solution. Remind them that they must use properties of equality to solve an equation.

Exercises 17–25 Watch for students who factor a common factor that is not the greatest common monomial factor. Suggest to all students that they check each non-monomial factor to see if the terms still have a common factor.

Graphing Calculator

Exercise 58 Students can check their graphs by graphing $y = -2x^2 + 8x$ on a graphing calculator using the y= key. They can use the trace feature to check the value of y for the given x-values.

53. 0, about 0.28; the zero $t = 0$ seconds means that the penguin begins at a height of 0 feet in the air as it leaves the water; the zero $t \approx 0.28$ second means that the penguin lands back in the water (at a height of 0 feet in the air) after about 0.28 second.

55b. $0 \le t \le 1$; a reasonable domain for the function will cover the time from when the rabbit leaves the ground until the rabbit lands back on the ground; these times t are the zeros of the function, 0 seconds and 1 second.

5 ASSESS AND RETEACH

Daily Homework Quiz

Transparency Available

Solve the equation.

1. $(y + 5)(y - 9) = 0$ $-5, 9$
2. $(2n + 3)(n - 4) = 0$ $-\frac{3}{2}, 4$
3. $6x^2 = 20x$ $0, \frac{10}{3}$
4. $12x^2 = 18x$ $0, \frac{3}{2}$
5. A dog jumps in the air with an initial velocity of 18 feet per second to catch a flying disc. How long does the dog remain in the air? 1.125 sec

Online Quiz

Available at **classzone.com**

Diagnosis/Remediation

- Practice A, B, C in Chapter 9 Resource Book, pp. 41–43
- Study Guide in Chapter 9 Resource Book, pp. 44–45
- Practice Workbook, pp. 139–140
- @HomeTutor

Challenge

Additional challenge is available in the Chapter 9 Resource Book, p. 49.

58a.

x (feet)	y (feet)
0	0
1	6
2	8
3	6
4	0

58b.

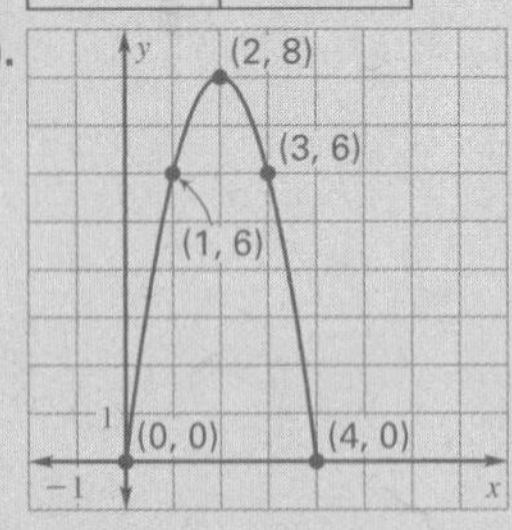

59a–b. See Additional Answers beginning on p. AA1.

B **56.** ★ **MULTIPLE CHOICE** Two rectangular rooms in a building's floor plan have different dimensions but the same area. The dimensions (in meters) are shown. What is the value of w? B

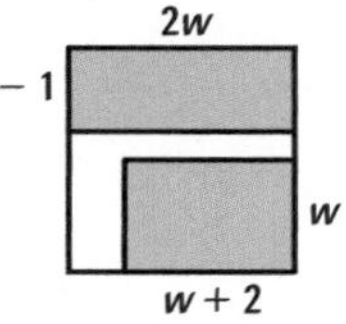

Ⓐ 3 m Ⓑ 4 m Ⓒ 6 m Ⓓ 8 m

57. TABLETOP AREAS A display in your school library sits on top of two rectangular tables arranged in an L shape, as shown. The tabletops have the same area.

a. Write an equation that relates the areas of the tabletops. $w(w + 2) = w(10 - w)$

b. Find the value of w. 4

c. What is the combined area of the tabletops? 48 ft²

58. ◆ **MULTIPLE REPRESENTATIONS** An arch frames the entrance to a garden. The shape of the arch is modeled by the graph of the equation $y = -2x^2 + 8x$ where x and y are measured in feet. On a coordinate plane, the ground is represented by the x-axis.

a. **Making a Table** Make a table of values that shows the height of the arch for $x = 0, 1, 2, 3,$ and 4 feet. See margin.

b. **Drawing a Graph** Plot the ordered pairs in the table as points in a coordinate plane. Connect the points with a smooth curve that represents the arch. See margin.

c. **Interpreting a Graph** How wide is the base of the arch? 4 ft

C **59. CHALLENGE** The shape of an arched doorway is modeled by the graph of the function $y = -0.5x(x - 8)$ where x and y are measured in feet. On a coordinate plane, the floor is represented by the x-axis. a, b. See margin.

a. How wide is the doorway at its base? *Justify* your answer using the zeros of the function.

b. The doorway's highest point occurs above the center of its base. How high is the highest point of the arched doorway? *Explain* how you found your answer.

ILLINOIS MIXED REVIEW

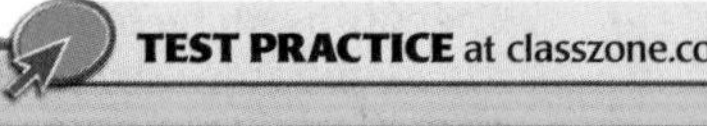

60. If $y = 3x^3$, which of the following is equivalent to x^9? C

Ⓐ y^3 Ⓑ $\frac{y^3}{3}$ Ⓒ $\frac{y^3}{27}$ Ⓓ $\frac{y^6}{3}$

61. Cam has two similar triangular pieces of paper, as shown. Using the dimensions given, find the approximate length of the side labeled x.

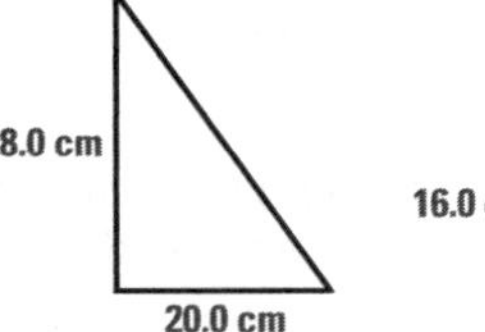

Ⓐ 8.0 cm Ⓑ 11.4 cm B

Ⓒ 13.2 cm Ⓓ 22.4 cm

Illinois Mixed Review

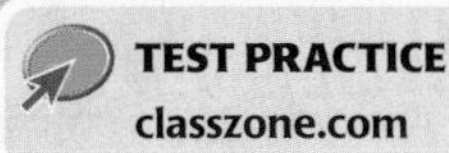

Lessons 9.1–9.4

1. **DOGS** A dog leaps from the ground into the air with an initial vertical velocity of 12 feet per second. After how many seconds does the dog land on the ground.

   A. 0.75 sec

   B. 1.3 sec

   C. 3 sec

   D. 4 sec

2. **SNOW SPORTS** During the period 1992–2000, the number C (in millions) of people participating in cross-country skiing and the number S (in millions) of people participating in snowboarding can be modeled by

   $C = 0.067t^3 - 0.107t^2 + 0.27t + 3.5$

   $S = 0.416t + 1.24$

   where t is the number of years since 1992. Which equation models the total number T (in millions) of people participating in cross-country skiing and snowboarding as a function of the number of years since 1992?

   F. $T = 0.067t^3 - 0.107t^2 + 0.686t + 4.74$

   G. $T = 0.067t^3 - 0.523t^2 + 0.27t + 4.74$

   H. $T = 0.483t^3 - 1.331t^2 + 0.27t + 3.5$

   J. $T = 0.483t^3 + 1.133t^2 + 0.27t + 3.5$

3. **HORSES** A horse with pinto coloring has white fur with patches of color. The gene P is for pinto coloring, and the gene s is for solid coloring. Any gene combination with a P results in pinto coloring.

   Suppose a male horse has the gene combination Ps and a female horse has the gene combination ss. What percent of the possible gene combinations of their offspring result in pinto coloring?

   A. 25%

   B. 50%

   C. 75%

   D. 100%

4. **BLANKET** You are making a blanket with a fringe border of equal width on each edge, as shown. Which polynomial represents the total area (in square inches) of the blanket with the fringe?

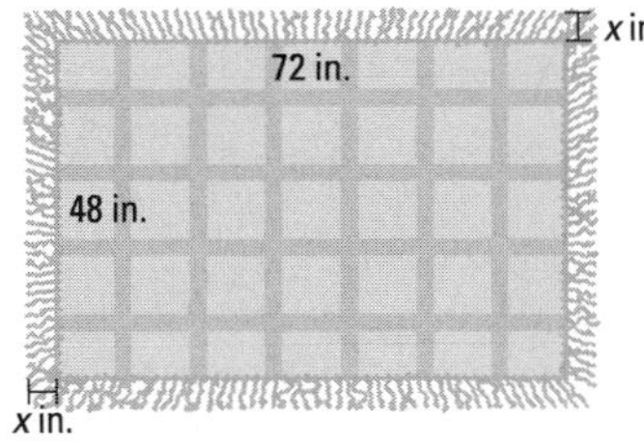

   F. $3456x^2$

   G. $3456 + 120x + x^2$

   H. $120x^2$

   J. $3456 + 240x + 4x^2$

5. **RUG** A circular rug has an interior circle and two rings around the circle, as shown. Which polynomial represents the total area of the rug?

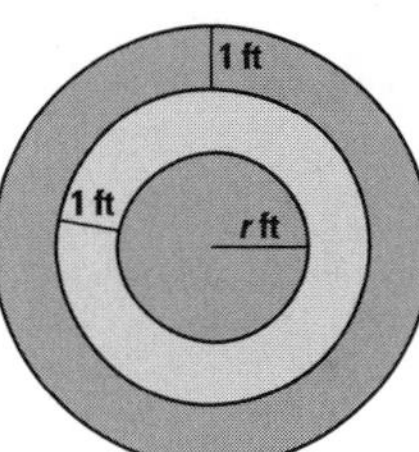

   A. $\pi r^2 + 2\pi$

   B. $\pi r^2 + 2\pi + \pi r$

   C. $\pi r^2 + 4\pi + 2r\pi$

   D. $\pi r^2 + 4\pi + 4\pi r$

6. **TOYS** During the period 1996–2000, the total value T (in millions of dollars) of toys imported to the United States can be modeled by

   $T = 82.9t^3 - 848t^2 + 3030t + 9610$

   where t is the number of years since 1996. What is the degree of the polynomial?

   F. 3 **H.** 6

   G. 5 **J.** 7

Illinois Mixed Review

1. A
2. F
3. B
4. J
5. D
6. F

Animated Algebra classzone.com

9.5 Factorization with Algebra Tiles

MATERIALS • algebra tiles

QUESTION **How can you factor a trinomial using algebra tiles?**

You have seen that algebra tiles can be used to model polynomials and to multiply binomials. Now, you will use algebra tiles to factor trinomials.

EXPLORE **Factor the trinomial $x^2 + 6x + 8$**

STEP 1 ***Make a rectangle***

Model the trinomial with algebra tiles. You will need one x^2-tile, six x-tiles, and eight 1-tiles. Arrange all of the tiles to form a rectangle. There can be no gaps or leftover tiles. The area of the rectangle represents the trinomial.

STEP 2 ***Find the side lengths***

The side lengths of the rectangle represent the polynomials $x + 2$ and $x + 4$. So, $x^2 + 6x + 8 = (x + 2)(x + 4)$.

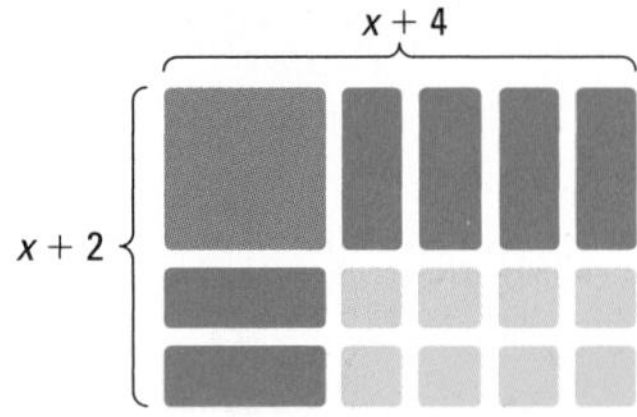

DRAW CONCLUSIONS **Use your observations to complete these exercises**

1. Use multiplication to show that $x + 4$ and $x + 2$ are factors of the polynomial $x^2 + 6x + 8$. $(x + 4)(x + 2) = x^2 + 2x + 4x + 8 = x^2 + 6x + 8$

Use algebra tiles to factor the trinomial. Include a drawing of your model. 2–7. See margin for art.

2. $x^2 + 6x + 5$ $(x + 5)(x + 1)$
3. $x^2 + 9x + 14$ $(x + 7)(x + 2)$
4. $x^2 + 5x + 6$ $(x + 3)(x + 2)$
5. $x^2 + 8x + 16$ $(x + 4)^2$
6. $x^2 + 5x + 4$ $(x + 4)(x + 1)$
7. $x^2 + 8x + 12$ $(x + 6)(x + 2)$
8. **REASONING** The factors of the trinomial $x^2 + 6x + 8$ have the form $x + p$ and $x + q$, as shown above. How are p and q related to 6 and 8? $p + q = 6$, $pq = 8$

2–7. See Additional Answers beginning on p. AA1.

1 PLAN AND PREPARE

Explore the Concept

- Students will factor a trinomial using algebra tiles.
- This activity leads into the study of factoring trinomials in Example 1 of Lesson 9.5.

Materials

Each student will need:

- algebra tiles
- Activity Support Master (*Chapter 9 Resource Book*, p. 52)

Recommended Time

Work activity: 10 min

Discuss results: 5 min

Grouping

Students should work individually.

2 TEACH

Tips for Success

If students cannot see that $x + 4$ and $x + 2$ are factors of the trinomial, have them arrange algebra tiles above and to the left of the rectangle to model the factors.

An **Animated Algebra** activity is available on-line. This activity is also available on the **Power Presentations CD-ROM**.

Key Discovery

If 1 is the coefficient of the x^2-term of a factorable trinomial, then the coefficient of the x-term is the sum of the constant terms of the factors.

3 ASSESS AND RETEACH

What factors should you use to factor $x^2 + 7x + 12$? Explain.
4 and 3, because $4 + 3 = 7$ and $4 \cdot 3 = 12$.

9.5 Factor $x^2 + bx + c$

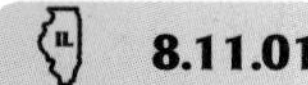

8.11.01 Simplify or identify equivalent algebraic expressions (e.g., exponential, rational, logarithmic, factored, polynomial).

Before You factored out the greatest common monomial factor.

Now You will factor trinomials of the form $x^2 + bx + c$.

Why So you can find the dimensions of figures, as in Ex. 61.

Key Vocabulary
- **zero of a function,** *p. 337*

From Lesson 9.2, you know that

$$(x + 3)(x + 4) = x^2 + (4 + 3)x + 4 \cdot 3 = x^2 + 7x + 12.$$

You will reverse this process to factor trinomials of the form $x^2 + bx + c$.

KEY CONCEPT *For Your Notebook*

Factoring $x^2 + bx + c$

Algebra $x^2 + bx + c = (x + p)(x + q)$ provided $p + q = b$ and $pq = c$.

Example $x^2 + 5x + 6 = (x + 3)(x + 2)$ because $3 + 2 = 5$ and $3 \cdot 2 = 6$.

EXAMPLE 1 Factor when b and c are positive

Factor $x^2 + 11x + 18$.

Solution

Find two positive factors of 18 whose sum is 11. Make an organized list.

Factors of 18	Sum of factors	
18, 1	$18 + 1 = 19$	✗
9, 2	$9 + 2 = 11$	← Correct sum
6, 3	$6 + 3 = 9$	✗

The factors 9 and 2 have a sum of 11, so they are the correct values of p and q.

▶ $x^2 + 11x + 18 = (x + 9)(x + 2)$

CHECK $(x + 9)(x + 2) = x^2 + 2x + 9x + 18$ **Multiply binomials.**

$= x^2 + 11x + 18$ ✓ **Simplify.**

GUIDED PRACTICE for Example 1

Factor the trinomial.

1. $x^2 + 3x + 2$ $(x + 2)(x + 1)$
2. $a^2 + 7a + 10$ $(a + 5)(a + 2)$
3. $t^2 + 9t + 14$ $(t + 7)(t + 2)$

1 PLAN AND PREPARE

Warm-Up Exercises

Transparency Available

Find the product.

1. $(x + 6)(x - 4)$ $x^2 + 2x - 24$
2. $(2y + 3)(y + 5)$ $2y^2 + 13y + 15$
3. The dimensions of a rectangular print can be represented by $x - 2$ and $2x + 1$. Write an expression that models the area of the print. What is its area if x is 4 inches? $2x^2 - 3x - 2$; 18 in.^{2}

Notetaking Guide

Transparency Available

Promotes interactive learning and notetaking skills, pp. 203–206.

Pacing

Basic: 2 days
Average: 2 days
Advanced: 2 days
Block: 0.5 block with 9.4
0.5 block with 9.6
- See *Teaching Guide/Lesson Plan.*

2 FOCUS AND MOTIVATE

Essential Question

Big Idea 2, p. 553

How do you factor trinomials of the form $x^2 + bx + c$? **Tell students they will learn how to answer this question by making lists of the possible factors.**

Resource Planning Guide

Chapter Resource Book
- Teaching Guide/Lesson Plan (pp. 50–51)
- Practice levels A, B, C (pp. 53–55)
- Study Guide (pp. 56–57)
- Catch-up for Absent Students (p. 58)
- Application (p. 59)
- Challenge (p. 60)

Workbooks
- Notetaking Guide (pp. 203–206)
- Practice Workbook (pp. 141–142)

Teaching Options
- **Power Presentations CD-ROM** provides dynamic electronic teaching resources for the classroom.
- **Activity Generator CD-ROM** provides editable activities for all ability levels.

Interactive Technology
- Easy Planner
- Power Presentations CD-ROM
- Activity Generator CD-ROM
- Animated Algebra
- Test Generator CD-ROM
- Online Quiz
- eWorkbook
- eEdition
- @HomeTutor

Resources for English Learners
- Quick Reference for English Learners
- Spanish Study Guide
- Multi-Language Visual Glossary
- Student Resources in Spanish

See also the *Algebra 1 Toolkit* for more strategies for meeting individual needs.

Motivating the Lesson

Ask students to give examples of situations in which they wanted to find one of the dimensions of an object. After students give some examples, tell them that this lesson teaches them how to find the length or the width of a rectangular figure if they know the other dimension and the area of the figure.

3 TEACH

Extra Example 1

Factor $x^2 + 8x + 12$. $(x + 6)(x + 2)$

Key Questions to Ask for Example 1

- In the Key Concept, what do b and c represent? **b represents the coefficient of the x-term and c represents the constant; in Example 1, b and c are 11 and 18, respectively.**
- What do p and q represent? **p and q represent the constant terms in the binomial factors of the trinomial; $p + q$ is equal to b and $p \cdot q$ is equal to c. In Example 1, p is 9 and q is 2.**

Extra Example 2

Factor $n^2 - 5n + 6$. $(n - 3)(n - 2)$

Key Question to Ask for Example 2

- Why must p and q both be negative when b is negative and c is positive? **Since $c = p \cdot q$, c is positive when p and q are either both positive or both negative. Since b is negative and c is positive, p and q must be negative.**

Extra Example 3

Factor $y^2 + 3y - 10$. $(y + 5)(y - 2)$

FACTORING When factoring a trinomial, first consider the signs of p and q.

$(x + p)(x + q)$	$x^2 + bx + c$	Signs of b and c
$(x + 2)(x + 3)$	$x^2 + 5x + 6$	b is positive; c is positive.
$(x + 2)(x + (-3))$	$x^2 - x - 6$	b is negative; c is negative.
$(x + (-2))(x + 3)$	$x^2 + x - 6$	b is positive; c is negative.
$(x + (-2))(x + (-3))$	$x^2 - 5x + 6$	b is negative; c is positive.

By observing the signs of b and c in the table, you can see that:

- b and c are positive when both p and q are positive.
- b is negative and c is positive when both p and q are negative.
- c is negative when p and q have different signs.

EXAMPLE 2 Factor when b is negative and c is positive

Factor $n^2 - 6n + 8$.

Because b is negative and c is positive, p and q must both be negative.

Factors of 8	Sum of factors	
−8, −1	$-8 + (-1) = -9$	✗
−4, −2	$-4 + (-2) = -6$	← Correct sum

▸ $n^2 - 6n + 8 = (n - 4)(n - 2)$

EXAMPLE 3 Factor when b is positive and c is negative

Factor $y^2 + 2y - 15$.

Because c is negative, p and q must have different signs.

Factors of −15	Sum of factors	
−15, 1	$-15 + 1 = -14$	✗
15, −1	$15 + (-1) = 14$	✗
−5, 3	$-5 + 3 = -2$	✗
5, −3	$5 + (-3) = 2$	← Correct sum

▸ $y^2 + 2y - 15 = (y + 5)(y - 3)$

GUIDED PRACTICE for Examples 2 and 3

Factor the trinomial.

4. $x^2 - 4x + 3$ $(x - 3)(x - 1)$
5. $t^2 - 8t + 12$ $(t - 6)(t - 2)$
6. $m^2 + m - 20$ $(m + 5)(m - 4)$
7. $w^2 + 6w - 16$ $(w + 8)(w - 2)$

Differentiated Instruction

Inclusion Some students may have difficulty using and organizing a table. Instead, they can begin by partially writing out the answer, and then fill in the blanks. When discussing **Example 2**, begin by writing $(n - \quad)(n - \quad)$, since p and q are both negative. Then, ask students to try various factors of 8, and add the Outer and Inner terms generated by the FOIL method. Point out that the product $(n - 4)(n - 2)$ is correct because the sum of the Outer and Inner terms is $-2n + (-4n) = -6n$.

See also the *Algebra 1 Toolkit* for more strategies.

EXAMPLE 4 Solve a polynomial equation

Solve the equation $x^2 + 3x = 18$.

$x^2 + 3x = 18$	Write original equation.
$x^2 + 3x - 18 = 0$	Subtract 18 from each side.
$(x + 6)(x - 3) = 0$	Factor left side.
$x + 6 = 0$ *or* $x - 3 = 0$	Zero-product property
$x = -6$ *or* $x = 3$	Solve for x.

▶ The solutions of the equation are −6 and 3.

GUIDED PRACTICE for Example 4

8. Solve the equation $s^2 - 2s = 24$. −4, 6

EXAMPLE 5 Solve a multi-step problem

ANOTHER WAY
For alternative methods for solving Example 5, turn to page 590 for the Problem Solving Workshop.

BANNER DIMENSIONS You are making banners to hang during school spirit week. Each banner requires 16.5 square feet of felt and will be cut as shown. Find the width of one banner.

Solution

STEP 1 **Draw** a diagram of two banners together.

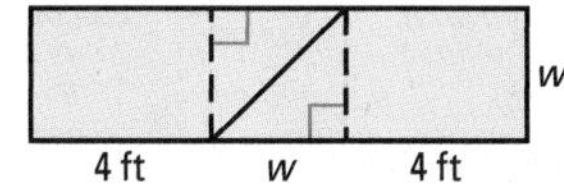

STEP 2 **Write** an equation using the fact that the area of 2 banners is $2(16.5) = 33$ square feet. Solve the equation for w.

$A = \ell \cdot w$	Formula for area of a rectangle
$33 = (4 + w + 4) \cdot w$	Substitute 33 for A and $(4 + w + 4)$ for ℓ.
$0 = w^2 + 8w - 33$	Simplify and subtract 33 from each side.
$0 = (w + 11)(w - 3)$	Factor right side.
$w + 11 = 0$ *or* $w - 3 = 0$	Zero-product property
$w = -11$ *or* $w = 3$	Solve for w.

▶ The banner cannot have a negative width, so the width is 3 feet.

GUIDED PRACTICE for Example 5

9. **WHAT IF?** In Example 5, suppose the area of a banner is to be 10 square feet. What is the width of one banner? 2 ft

Extra Example 4

Solve the equation $x^2 - 3x = 28$. −4, 7

Extra Example 5

You are designing a flag for the school football team with the dimensions shown in the diagram. The shaded region will show the team name. The flag requires 117 square inches of fabric. Find the width w of the flag. 9 in.

Key Question to Ask for Example 5

- In Step 2, why do you subtract 33 from both sides of the equation? One side of the equation must be 0 to use the zero-product property.

Closing the Lesson

Have students summarize the major points of the lesson and answer the Essential Question: How do you factor trinomials of the form $x^2 + bx + c$?

- To factor $x^2 + bx + c$, find factors of the form $(x + p)(x + q)$ where $p + q = b$ and $pq = c$.

Find factors of c whose sum $p + q$ is b. When b and c are positive, p and q are positive. When b is negative and c is positive, p and q are negative. When c is negative, p and q have different signs.

Differentiated Instruction

Advanced Some students may be interested in learning about Descartes' Rule of Signs. Tell them they can use this rule to determine the maximum number of positive and negative real roots of a polynomial. Suggest that students research the rule and then test it on polynomials in the lesson or on ones they create for their classmates.

See also the *Algebra 1 Toolkit* for more strategies.

9.5 EXERCISES

HOMEWORK KEY
○ = WORKED-OUT SOLUTIONS on p. WS21 for Exs. 7 and 61
★ = STANDARDIZED TEST PRACTICE Exs. 2, 29, 42, 61, 62, and 63
◆ = MULTIPLE REPRESENTATIONS Ex. 64

SKILL PRACTICE

A

1. **VOCABULARY** Copy and complete: The _?_ of $t^2 + 3t + 2$ are $t + 2$ and $t + 1$. factors

2. ★ **WRITING** If $x^2 - 8x + 12 = (x + p)(x + q)$, what are the signs of p and q? *Justify* your answer. See margin.

EXAMPLES 1, 2, and 3 on pp. 583–584 for Exs. 3–19

FACTORING TRINOMIALS Factor the trinomial.

3. $x^2 + 4x + 3$ $(x + 3)(x + 1)$
4. $a^2 + 6a + 8$ $(a + 4)(a + 2)$
5. $b^2 - 17b + 72$ $(b - 9)(b - 8)$
6. $s^2 - 10s + 16$ $(s - 8)(s - 2)$
7. $z^2 + 8z - 48$ $(z + 12)(z - 4)$
8. $w^2 + 18w + 56$ $(w + 14)(w + 4)$
9. $y^2 - 7y - 18$ $(y - 9)(y + 2)$
10. $n^2 - 9n + 14$ $(n - 7)(n - 2)$
11. $x^2 + 3x - 70$ $(x + 10)(x - 7)$
12. $f^2 + 4f - 32$ $(f + 8)(f - 4)$
13. $m^2 - 7m - 120$ $(m - 15)(m + 8)$
14. $d^2 - 20d + 99$ $(d - 11)(d - 9)$
15. $p^2 + 20p + 64$ $(p + 16)(p + 4)$
16. $x^2 + 6x - 72$ $(x + 12)(x - 6)$
17. $c^2 + 15c + 44$ $(c + 11)(c + 4)$

ERROR ANALYSIS *Describe* and correct the error in factoring the trinomial.

18. $s^2 - 17s - 60 = (s - 5)(s - 12)$

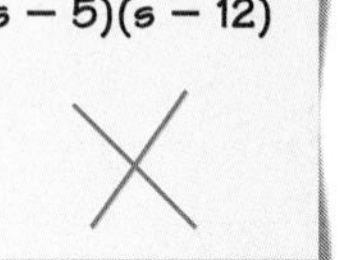

18. In order to have a product of −60, p and q cannot both be negative; $(s - 20)(s + 3)$.

19. $m^2 - 10m + 24 = (m - 12)(m + 2)$

In order to have a product of +24, p and q must have the same sign; $(m - 6)(m - 4)$.

EXAMPLE 4 on p. 585 for Exs. 20–29

SOLVING EQUATIONS Solve the equation.

20. $x^2 - 10x + 21 = 0$ 7, 3
21. $n^2 - 7n - 30 = 0$ 10, −3
22. $w^2 - 15w + 44 = 0$ 11, 4
23. $a^2 + 5a = 50$ −10, 5
24. $r^2 + 2r = 24$ −6, 4
25. $t^2 + 9t = -20$ −5, −4
26. $y^2 - 2y - 8 = 7$ 5, −3
27. $m^2 + 22 = -23m$ −22, −1
28. $b^2 + 5 = 8b - 10$ 5, 3

29. ★ **MULTIPLE CHOICE** What are the solutions of the equation $x^2 - 8x = 240$? C

Ⓐ −20 and −12　Ⓑ −20 and 12　Ⓒ 20 and −12　Ⓓ 12 and 20

B

FINDING ZEROS OF FUNCTIONS Find the zeros of the polynomial function.

30. $f(x) = x^2 + 11x + 18$ −9, −2
31. $g(x) = x^2 + 5x + 6$ −3, −2
32. $h(x) = x^2 - 18x + 32$ 16, 2
33. $f(x) = x^2 - 14x + 45$ 9, 5
34. $h(x) = x^2 - 5x - 24$ 8, −3
35. $g(x) = x^2 - 14x - 51$ 17, −3
36. $g(x) = x^2 + 10x - 39$ −13, 3
37. $f(x) = -x^2 + 16x - 28$ 14, 2
38. $f(x) = -x^2 + 24x + 180$ 30, −6

SOLVING EQUATIONS Solve the equation.

39. $s(s + 1) = 72$ −9, 8
40. $x^2 - 10(x - 1) = -11$ 7, 3
41. $q(q + 19) = -34$ −17, −2

2. p and q are both negative; $pq = 12$, so the product pq is positive, which means p and q are either both positive or both negative. Also, $p + q = -8$. In order for p and q to have the same sign and have a negative sum, both p and q must be negative.

4 PRACTICE AND APPLY

Assignment Guide

Answer Transparencies available for all exercises

Basic:
Day 1: SRH p. 911 Exs. 1–11 odd pp. 586–589 Exs. 1–19, 66–73
Day 2: pp. 586–589 Exs. 20–28 even, 29, 30–43, 59–62, 74–80 even

Average:
Day 1: pp. 586–589 Exs. 1, 2, 3–17 odd, 18, 19, 47–55, 66–72 even
Day 2: pp. 586–589 Exs. 21–29 odd, 33–46, 59–64, 74, 78

Advanced:
Day 1: pp. 586–589 Exs. 1, 2, 12–17, 47–58*, 66–72 even
Day 2: pp. 586–589 Exs. 24–29, 34–46, 60–65*, 76, 80

Block:
pp. 586–589 Exs. 1, 2, 3–17 odd, 18, 19, 47–55, 66–72 even (with 9.4)
pp. 586–589 Exs. 21–29 odd, 33–46, 59–64, 74, 78 (with 9.6)

Differentiated Instruction

See *Algebra 1 Best Practices Toolkit* for suggestions on addressing the needs of a diverse classroom.

Homework Check

For a quick check of student understanding of key concepts, go over the following exercises:
Basic: 4, 10, 13, 22, 59
Average: 5, 11, 15, 25, 60
Advanced: 13, 14, 17, 27, 61

Extra Practice

- Student Edition, p. 946
- Chapter 9 Resource Book: Practice levels A, B, C, pp. 53–55

Practice Worksheet

An easily-readable reduced practice page (with answers) for this lesson can be found on p. 552C.

42. ★ **SHORT RESPONSE** Write an equation of the form $x^2 + bx + c = 0$ that has the solutions -4 and 6. *Explain* how you found your answer. See margin.

GEOMETRY Find the dimensions of the rectangle or triangle that has the given area.

43. Area: 100 square inches **20 in., 5 in.**

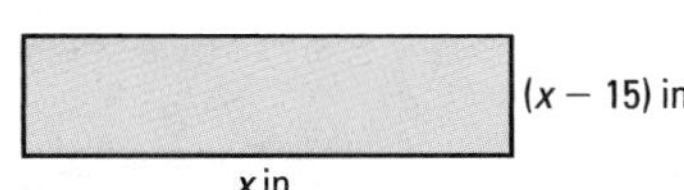

44. Area: 34 square meters **17 m, 2 m**

(x − 4) m
(x + 11) m

45. Area: 78 square yards **26 yd, 6 yd**

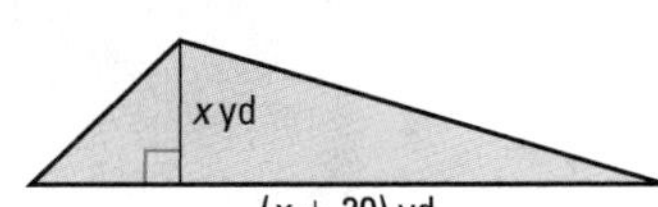

46. Area: 119 square feet **17 ft, 14 ft**

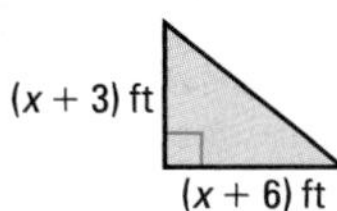

FACTORING TRINOMIALS In Exercises 47–55, use the example below to factor the trinomial.

EXAMPLE Factor a trinomial in two variables

Factor $x^2 + 9xy + 14y^2$.

Solution

To factor the trinomial, you must find factors of the form $x + py$ and $x + qy$.

First, consider the signs of the factors needed. In this example, b is 9, and c is 14. Because both b and c are positive, you must find two positive factors of 14 that have a sum of 9.

Factors of 14	Sum of factors	
14, 1	14 + 1 = 15	✗
7, 2	7 + 2 = 9	← Correct sum

The factors 7 and 2 have a sum of 9, so 7 and 2 are the correct values of p and q.

▶ $x^2 + 9xy + 14y^2 = (x + 7y)(x + 2y)$

47. $x^2 - 4xy + 4y^2$ $(x - 2y)^2$

48. $y^2 - 6yz + 5z^2$ $(y - 5z)(y - z)$

49. $c^2 + 13cd + 36d^2$ $(c + 9d)(c + 4d)$

50. $r^2 + 15rs + 50s^2$ $(r + 10s)(r + 5s)$

51. $a^2 + 2ab - 15b^2$ $(a + 5b)(a - 3b)$

52. $x^2 + 8xy - 65y^2$ $(x + 13y)(x - 5y)$

53. $m^2 - mn - 42n^2$ $(m - 7n)(m + 6n)$

54. $u^2 - 3uv - 108v^2$ $(u - 12v)(u + 9v)$

55. $g^2 + 4gh - 60h^2$ $(g + 10h)(g - 6h)$

C **CHALLENGE Find all integer values of b for which the trinomial has factors of the form $x + p$ and $x + q$ where p and q are integers.**

56. $x^2 + bx + 15$ $\pm 8, \pm 16$

57. $x^2 - bx + 21$ $\pm 10, \pm 22$

58. $x^2 + bx - 42$ $\pm 1, \pm 11, \pm 19, \pm 41$

Avoiding Common Errors

Exercises 3–17 Warn students that it is easy to use the wrong signs when factoring trinomials. After they complete the exercises, suggest that they use FOIL to check the binomial factors against the original trinomials.

Study Strategy

Exercises 20–28 Remind students that they may need to combine like terms or write the equation so that one side is equal to 0.

Teaching Strategy

Exercises 47–55 For each exercise, students can begin by identifying the variable parts of the two factors and confirming that those variables will give the variable part of the middle term of the original trinomial.

42. $x^2 - 2x - 24$; any root $x = r$ of $x^2 + bx + c = 0$ comes from setting the factor $x - r$ equal to zero after $x^2 + bx + c$ is written in factored form; so, the roots -4 and 6 come from the factors $x - (-4)$, or $x + 4$, and $x - 6$. The product of these factors is $(x + 4)(x - 6) = x^2 - 6x + 4x - 24 = x^2 - 2x - 24$.

Teaching Strategy

Exercise 59 If students do not see how to start a solution, tell them that they can use Step 2 in Example 5 as a model for finding the dimensions of the white part of the card.

61. 40 in.; the side lengths of the trimmed photo can be represented by $x - 5$ and $x - 6$; the area of the trimmed photo is 20 square inches, so to find the side length x of the original square photo, solve the equation $(x - 5)(x - 6) = 20$. The equation has two solutions, 10 and 1, but when $x = 1$ inch, both $x - 5$ and $x - 6$ are negative, which does not make sense in this situation. So, $x = 10$ inches, and the perimeter of the original square photo was $4(10) = 40$ inches.

PROBLEM SOLVING

EXAMPLE 5 A
on p. 585
for Exs. 59–61

62c. 625 feet does not make sense as a path width in this problem situation because it is wider than the length of either path. In the diagram w is also the side length of the overlapping square. If $w = 625$ feet, the square is larger than either part of the path. Only the solution $w = 5$ feet makes sense as a path width.

59. **CARD DESIGN** You are designing a gift card that has a border along one side, as shown. The area of the white part of the card is 30 square centimeters. What is the area of the border? 10 cm^2

s cm; $(s + 1)$ cm; 2 cm

@HomeTutor for problem solving help at classzone.com

60. **CONSTRUCTION** A contractor is building a porch along two sides of a house. The house is rectangular with a width of 32 feet and a length of 50 feet. The porch will have the same width on each side of the house.

50 ft; x ft; 32 ft; x ft

a. Write a polynomial that represents the combined area of the first floor of the house and the porch. $x^2 + 82x + 1600$

b. The owners want the combined area of the first floor and the porch to be 2320 square feet. How wide should the contractor build the porch? 8 ft

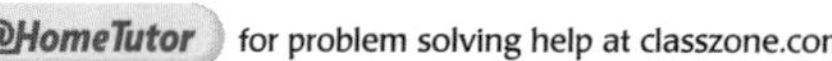
@HomeTutor for problem solving help at classzone.com

61. ★ **SHORT RESPONSE** You trimmed a large square picture so that you could fit it into a frame. You trimmed 6 inches from the length and 5 inches from the width. The area of the resulting picture is 20 square inches. What was the perimeter of the original large square picture? *Explain* how you found your answer. See margin.

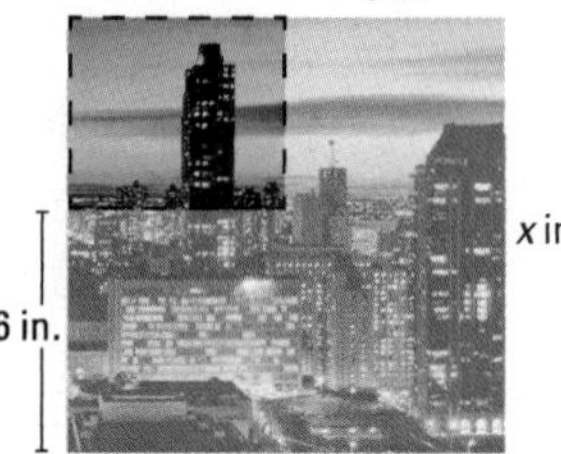

B

62. ★ **EXTENDED RESPONSE** A town has a rectangular park. The parks department is planning to install two brick paths that will intersect at right angles. One path will be 130 feet long, and the other path will be 500 feet long. The paths will have the same width.

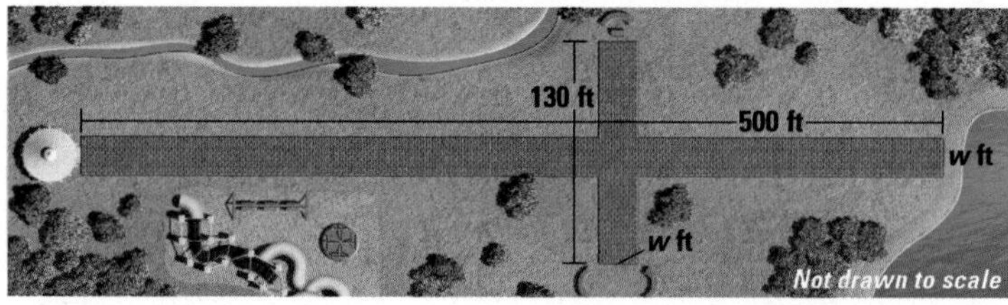

HINT
Add the path areas, but subtract the overlap, so that it is not counted twice.

a. Write a polynomial that represents the combined area of the two paths. $630w - w^2$

b. The parks department can afford brick for 3125 square feet of path. Write and solve an equation to find the width of the paths. $630w - w^2 = 3125$; 625, 5; 5 ft

c. In part (b) you used one solution of the equation to find your answer. *Explain* how you chose which solution to use. See margin.

○ = WORKED-OUT SOLUTIONS on p. WS1 ★ = STANDARDIZED TEST PRACTICE  = MULTIPLE REPRESENTATIONS

64a.

x (feet)	y (feet)
2	17
4	21
6	17
8	0

64b.

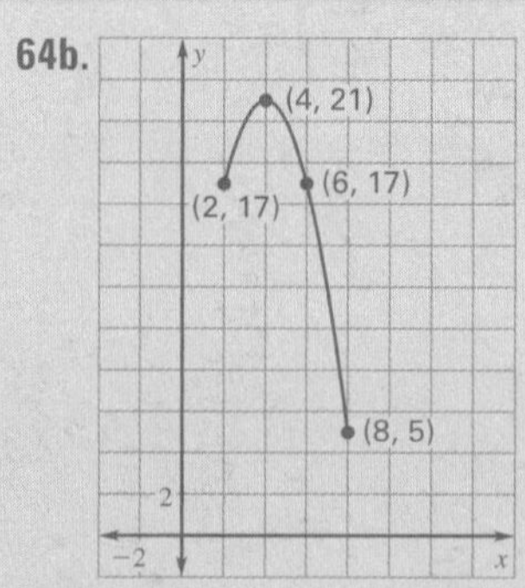

63. ★ **MULTIPLE CHOICE** A square quilt has a border that is 1 foot wide on each side. The quilt has an area of 25 square feet. What is the side length of the quilt without the border? B

Ⓐ 2 feet Ⓑ 3 feet Ⓒ 4 feet Ⓓ 5 feet

64. **MULTIPLE REPRESENTATIONS** You toss a set of keys to a friend who is standing at a window 20 feet above the ground in a building that is 5 feet away from where you are standing. The path of the keys can be modeled by the graph of the equation $y = -x^2 + 8x + 5$ where x and y are measured in feet. On a coordinate plane, the ground is represented by the x-axis, and you are standing at the origin. a–d. See margin.

a. **Making a Table** Make a table of values that shows the height of the keys for $x = 2, 4, 6$, and 8 feet.

b. **Drawing a Graph** Plot the ordered pairs in the table as points in a coordinate plane. Connect the points with a smooth curve.

c. **Interpreting a Graph** Based on your graph, do you expect the keys to reach your friend? *Explain* your answer.

d. **Using an Equation** Find the value of x when $y = 20$. (You may need to factor out a -1 in order to factor the trinomial.) What do you notice? *Explain* how the x-value justifies your answer from part (c).

C 65. **CHALLENGE** A rectangular stage is positioned in the center of a rectangular room, as shown. The area of the stage is 120 square feet.

a. Use the dimensions given in the diagram to find the length and width of the stage. 10 ft, 12 ft

b. The combined area of the stage and the surrounding floor is 360 square feet. Find the length and width of the room. 20 ft, 18 ft

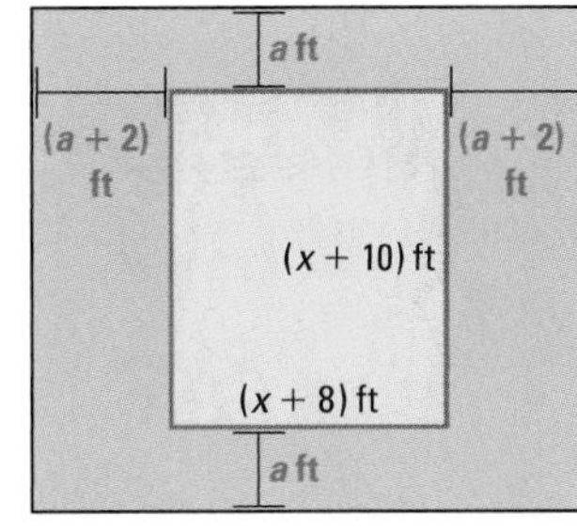

ILLINOIS MIXED REVIEW

TEST PRACTICE at classzone.com

66. What are the x- and y-intercepts of the function graphed?

Ⓐ (1, 0) and (0, 2) B

Ⓑ (2, 0) and (0, 4)

Ⓒ (2, 0) and (0, 1)

Ⓓ (4, 0) and (0, 2)

67. Which of the following would be least helpful in determining the amount of time it would take you to walk around a city block? B

Ⓐ Your walking speed Ⓑ The block's area

Ⓒ The block's perimeter Ⓓ The block's dimensions

5 ASSESS AND RETEACH

Daily Homework Quiz

Transparency Available

Factor the trinomial.

1. $x^2 - 6x - 16$ $(x + 2)(x - 8)$
2. $y^2 + 11y + 24$ $(y + 3)(y + 8)$
3. $x^2 + x - 12$ $(x + 4)(x - 3)$
4. Solve $a^2 - a = 20$. $-4, 5$
5. Each wooden slat on a set of blinds has width w and length $w + 17$. The area of one slat is 38 square inches. What are the dimensions of a slat? 2 in. by 19 in.

Online Quiz

Available at **classzone.com**

Diagnosis/Remediation

- Practice A, B, C in Chapter 9 Resource Book, pp. 53–55
- Study Guide in Chapter 9 Resource Book, pp. 56–57
- Practice Workbook, pp. 141–142
- @HomeTutor

Challenge

Additional challenge is available in the Chapter 9 Resource Book, p. 60.

64c. Yes. *Sample answer:* From the graph it appears that the keys reach a height of 21 feet when they are still 1 foot from the edge of the building (when $x = 4$ feet); when the keys are at the edge of the building ($x = 5$ feet), they have started to fall back down and appear to be at a height of about 20 feet, the height of the window.

64d. 3, 5; there are two points at which the keys reach a height of 20 feet; because you are standing 5 feet from the building, the x-value of 5 feet means that when the keys reach the edge of the building they are at a height of 20 feet.

PROBLEM SOLVING WORKSHOP
LESSON 9.5

Using ALTERNATIVE METHODS

Another Way to Solve Example 5, page 585

MULTIPLE REPRESENTATIONS In Example 5 on page 585, you saw how to solve the problem about a school banner by solving an equation. You can also solve the problem using a table or a graph.

PROBLEM

BANNER DIMENSIONS You are making banners to hang during school spirit week. Each banner requires 16.5 square feet of felt and will be cut as shown. Find the width of one banner.

METHOD 1

Using a Table Consider the separate geometric figures that form one banner and find their areas in terms of w. Then find the total area of the banner for different values of w until you find a value that gives a total area of 16.5 square feet. Use a table to organize your work.

STEP 1 **Write** equations for the area of the pieces and the total area.

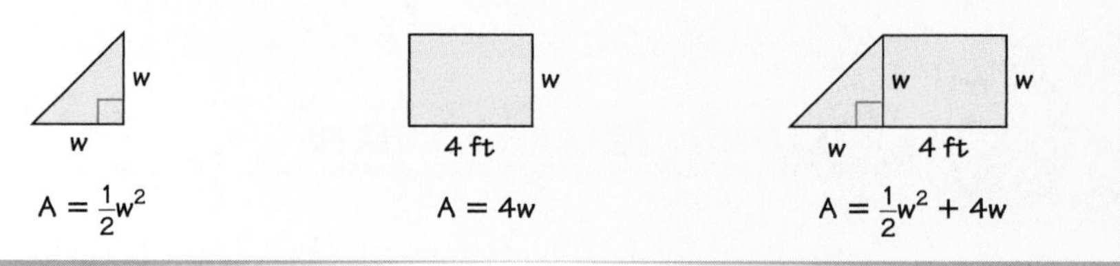

STEP 2 **Organize** your work in a table.

w	Triangle's area $\left(\frac{1}{2}w^2\right)$	Rectangle's area $(4w)$	Total area $\left(\frac{1}{2}w^2 + 4w\right)$	
1	0.5	4	4.5	← $4.5 < 16.5$, so try a greater value of w.
2	2	8	10	← $10 < 16.5$, so try a greater value of w.
3	4.5	12	16.5	← Correct area

▶ The width of the banner is 3 feet.

Alternative Strategy

Example 5 on page 585 can be solved using a table or a graph. Both methods work well for students who prefer to use one of the figures to determine the width of the banner rather than combining the two complex figures. Though both alternative methods require a few more steps to determine an area formula for the figure, many students find it easier to break a figure into its component parts, determine an appropriate formula for each, and then combine the formulas. The table method aids students by using the familiar guess and check strategy in an organized way. The graphing method aids students who prefer visual solutions to problems.

Avoiding Common Errors

Because both the base and height of the triangle are w, some students may write the formula for the area of a triangle as $A = \frac{1}{2}w$. Remind these students to substitute into the area formula $A = \frac{1}{2}bh$ to get $A = \frac{1}{2} \cdot w \cdot w$ or $A = \frac{1}{2}w^2$.

1. 2 ft; Method 1: Use a table. Write the area of the countertop as the sum of the areas of the two triangles and the rectangle: $A = \left(\frac{1}{2}w^2\right) + 4w = w^2 + 4w$. Make a table showing the total area A for various values of w and look for the value of w that gives a total area of 12 square feet.

w	Total area ($A = w^2 + 4w$)
1	5
2	12

The total area is 12 square feet when $w = 2$ feet. Method 2: Use a graph. Write the area of the countertop as the sum of the areas of the two triangles and the rectangle: $A = \left(\frac{1}{2}w^2\right) + 4w = w^2 + 4w$. Graph the equations $A = w^2 + 4w$ and $A = 12$ on the same coordinate plane. To use a graphing calculator, enter the equations as $y = x^2 + 4x$ and $y = 12$ in the same viewing window. To find the w-value for which $A = 12$ square feet, use the calculator's *intersect* feature to find that the graphs intersect at (2, 12).

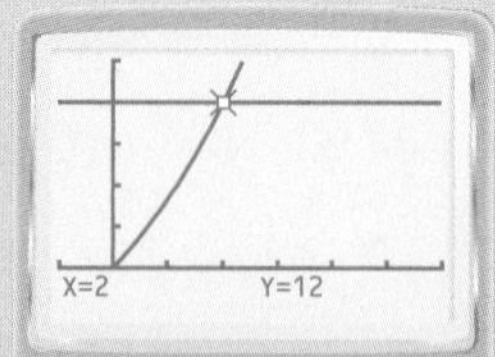

The total area is 12 square feet when the width is 2 feet.

2. The signs are reversed in the factorization of $w^2 + 4w - 12$; $(w + 2)(w - 6)$ gives a middle term of $-4w$ instead of $+4w$. The correct factorization is $(w - 2)(w + 6)$, which leads to solutions of 2 and -6. The width cannot be negative, so the width is 2 feet.

METHOD 2 **Using a Graph** Another approach is to use a graph.

STEP 1 **Write** an equation for the area of the banner. The area of the banner can be thought of as the area of a triangle plus the area of a rectangle.

Area of banner = Area of triangle + Area of rectangle

$$A = \frac{1}{2}w^2 + 4w$$

STEP 2 **Graph** the equation for the area of the banner using a graphing calculator. Graph $y_1 = 0.5x^2 + 4x$. Because you are looking for the value of x that gives an area of 16.5 square feet, you should display the graph of $y_2 = 16.5$ in the same viewing window.

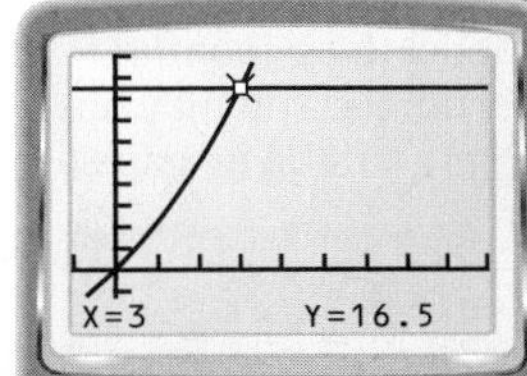

STEP 3 **Find** the intersection of the graphs by using the *intersect* feature on your calculator. The graphs intersect at (3, 16.5).

▶ The width of the banner is 3 feet.

PRACTICE

1–4. See margin.

1. **COUNTER DESIGN** A contractor is building a counter in a kitchen using the diagram shown. The countertop will have an area of 12 square feet. How wide should it be? Solve this problem using two different methods.

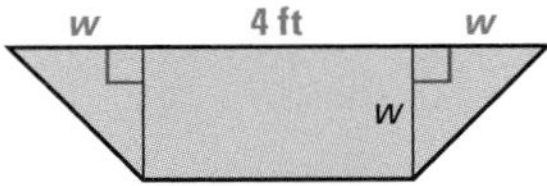

2. **ERROR ANALYSIS** *Describe* and correct the error in using an equation to solve the problem in Exercise 1.

$12 = 4w + \frac{1}{2}w^2 + \frac{1}{2}w^2$

$0 = w^2 + 4w - 12$

$0 = (w + 2)(w - 6)$

$w + 2 = 0$ or $w - 6 = 0$

$w = -2$ or $w = 6$

The width is 6 feet.

3. **FOUNTAIN DESIGN** A square fountain in a city plaza is surrounded by brick patios as shown. The combined area of the fountain and brick patios is 205 square feet. What is the side length of the fountain? Solve this problem using two different methods.

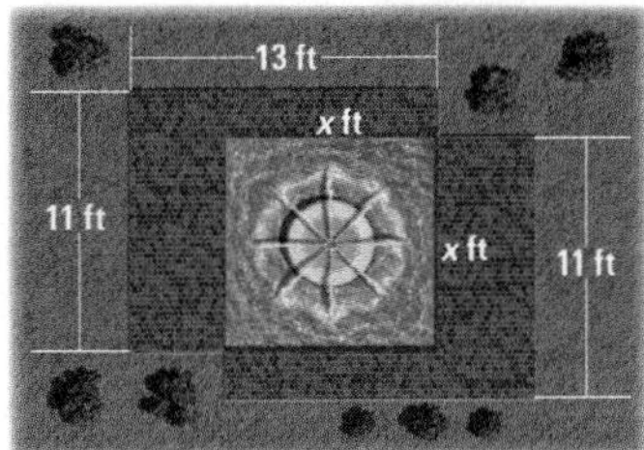

4. **WHAT IF?** You want to make a larger banner using the same pattern shown in the problem on page 585. The new banner will have an area of 24 square feet. Find the width of the new banner. *Describe* the method you used to find your answer.

3. 9 ft; Method 1: Use a table. To write a polynomial that represents the combined area of the fountain and the brick patios, find the sum of the areas of the rectangles and subtract the area of the fountain (so that the fountain's area is not counted twice): $A = 2(13)(11) - x^2$, or $A = 286 - x^2$. Make a table showing the combined area A for various values of x and look for the value of x that gives a combined area of 205 square feet.

x	Combined area ($A = 286 - x^2$)
5	261
6	250
7	237
8	222
9	205

(Exercise 3 continued)

The combined area is 205 square feet when $x = 9$ feet. Method 2: Use a graph. Write the combined area of the fountain and the brick patios as the sum of the areas of the rectangles minus the area of the fountain (so that the fountain's area is not counted twice): $A = 2(13)(11) - x^2$, or $A = 286 - x^2$. Graph the equations $A = 286 - x^2$ and $A = 205$ on the same coordinate plane. To use a graphing calculator, enter the equations as $y = 286 - x^2$ and $y = 205$ in the same viewing window. To find the x-value for which $A = 205$ square feet, use the calculator's *intersect* feature to find that the graphs intersect at (9, 205).

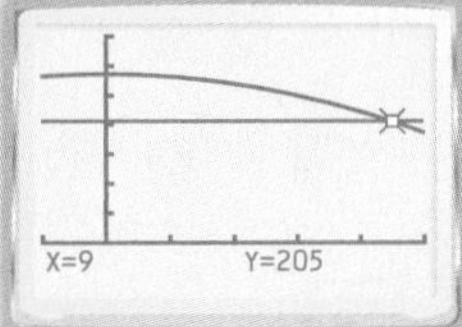

The combined area is 205 square feet when the side length of the fountain is 9 feet.

4. 4 ft. *Sample answer:* Use a graph. Write the area of the banner as the sum of the area of the triangle and the rectangle: $A = \frac{1}{2}w^2 + 4w$. Graph the equations $A = \frac{1}{2}w^2 + 4w$ and $A = 24$ on the same coordinate plane. To use a graphing calculator, enter the equations as $y = 0.5x^2 + 4x$ and $y = 24$ in the same viewing window. To find the w-value for which $A = 24$ square feet, use the calculator's *intersect* feature to find the x-value of the intersection point of the graphs.

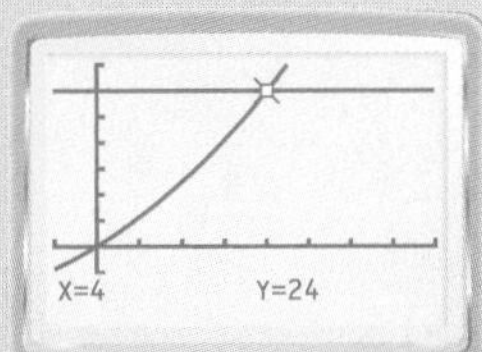

9.6 More Factorization with Algebra Tiles

MATERIALS • algebra tiles

QUESTION How can you factor a trinomial using algebra tiles?

EXPLORE Factor the trinomial $2x^2 + 7x + 3$

STEP 1 ***Make a rectangle***

Model the trinomial with algebra tiles. Arrange all of the tiles to form a rectangle. You may have to try a few arrangements to make the rectangle. There can be no gaps or leftover tiles.

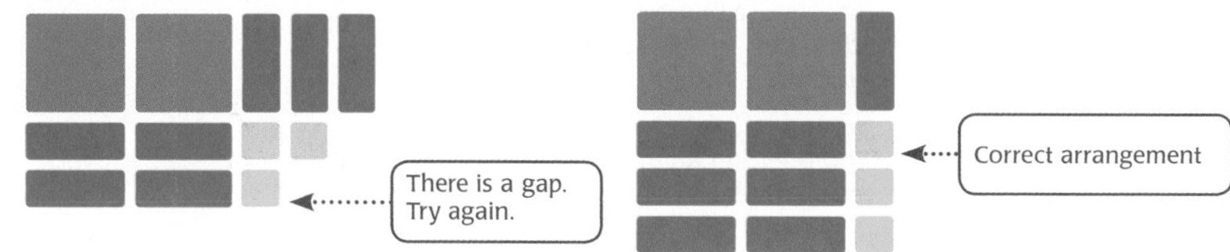

STEP 2 ***Find the side lengths***

The side lengths of the rectangle represent the polynomials $x + 3$ and $2x + 1$. So $2x^2 + 7x + 3 = (x + 3)(2x + 1)$.

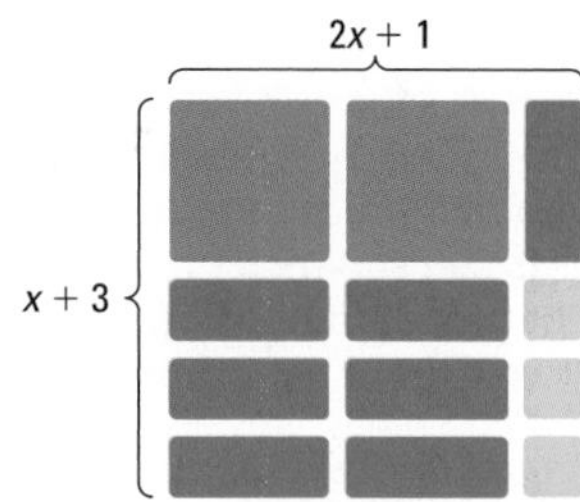

DRAW CONCLUSIONS Use your observations to complete these exercises

1. Use multiplication to show that $x + 3$ and $2x + 1$ are factors of the polynomial $2x^2 + 7x + 3$. $(x + 3)(2x + 1) = 2x^2 + x + 6x + 3 = 2x^2 + 7x + 3$

Use algebra tiles to factor the trinomial. Include a drawing of your model. 2–7. See margin for art.

2. $2x^2 + 5x + 3$ $(x + 1)(2x + 3)$
3. $3x^2 + 5x + 2$ $(x + 1)(3x + 2)$
4. $4x^2 + 9x + 2$ $(x + 2)(4x + 1)$
5. $3x^2 + 13x + 4$ $(x + 4)(3x + 1)$
6. $4x^2 + 11x + 6$ $(x + 2)(4x + 3)$
7. $4x^2 + 8x + 3$ $(2x + 1)(2x + 3)$
8. **REASONING** Factor the trinomial $2x^2 + 11x + 5$ into two binomials. How is the leading coefficient of the trinomial related to the leading coefficients of its binomial factors? $(x + 5)(2x + 1)$; the leading coefficient of the trinomial is the product of the leading coefficients of its binomial factors.

2–7. See Additional Answers beginning on p. AA1.

1 PLAN AND PREPARE

Explore the Concept

- Students will use algebra tiles to factor a trinomial.
- This activity leads into the study of factoring a trinomial in Example 1 of Lesson 9.6.

Materials

Each student will need:

- algebra tiles
- Activity Support Master (*Chapter 9 Resource Book*, p. 63)

Recommended Time

Work activity: 10 min

Discuss results: 5 min

Grouping

Students should work individually.

2 TEACH

Tips for Success

Tell students to begin forming the rectangle by placing all the x^2-tiles at the upper left corner of the rectangle.

An **Animated Algebra** activity is available on-line. This activity is also available on the **Power Presentations CD-ROM**.

Key Discovery

The leading coefficient of the original trinomial is the product of the leading coefficients of the factors.

3 ASSESS AND RETEACH

Without factoring $4x^2 - 4x - 3$, what are the possible leading coefficients of the factors? Explain. 4 and 1, 2 and 2; their product must be 4, the coefficient of the x^2-term.

9.6 Factor $ax^2 + bx + c$

8.11.01 Simplify or identify equivalent algebraic expressions (e.g., exponential, rational, logarithmic, factored, polynomial).

Before You factored trinomials of the form $x^2 + bx + c$.

Now You will factor trinomials of the form $ax^2 + bx + c$.

Why? So you can find the dimensions of a building, as in Ex. 61.

Key Vocabulary
- **trinomial,** *p. 555*

When factoring a trinomial of the form $ax^2 + bx + c$, first consider the signs of b and c, as in Lesson 9.5. This approach works when a is positive.

REVIEW FACTORING
For help with determining the signs of the factors of a trinomial, see p. 584.

EXAMPLE 1 Factor when b is negative and c is positive

Factor $2x^2 - 7x + 3$.

Solution

Because b is negative and c is positive, both factors of c must be negative. Make a table to organize your work.

You must consider the order of the factors of 3, because the x-terms of the possible factorizations are different.

Factors of 2	Factors of 3	Possible factorization	Middle term when multiplied	
1, 2	−1, −3	$(x-1)(2x-3)$	$-3x - 2x = -5x$	✗
1, 2	−3, −1	$(x-3)(2x-1)$	$-x - 6x = -7x$	← Correct

▸ $2x^2 - 7x + 3 = (x-3)(2x-1)$

EXAMPLE 2 Factor when b is positive and c is negative

Factor $3n^2 + 14n - 5$.

Solution

Because b is positive and c is negative, the factors of c have different signs.

Factors of 3	Factors of −5	Possible factorization	Middle term when multiplied	
1, 3	1, −5	$(n+1)(3n-5)$	$-5n + 3n = -2n$	✗
1, 3	−1, 5	$(n-1)(3n+5)$	$5n - 3n = 2n$	✗
1, 3	5, −1	$(n+5)(3n-1)$	$-n + 15n = 14n$	← Correct
1, 3	−5, 1	$(n-5)(3n+1)$	$n - 15n = -14n$	✗

▸ $3n^2 + 14n - 5 = (n+5)(3n-1)$

1 PLAN AND PREPARE

Warm-Up Exercises

Transparency Available

Find the product.

1. $(3c + 3)(2c - 3)$ $6c^2 - 3c - 9$

2. $(2y + 3)(2y + 1)$ $4y^2 + 8y + 3$

3. A cat leaps into the air with an initial velocity of 12 feet per second to catch a speck of dust, and then falls back to the floor. How long does the cat remain in the air? 0.75 sec

Notetaking Guide

Transparency Available

Promotes interactive learning and notetaking skills, pp. 207–209.

Pacing

Basic: 2 days
Average: 2 days
Advanced: 2 days
Block: 0.5 block with 9.5
0.5 block with 9.7

- See *Teaching Guide/Lesson Plan.*

2 FOCUS AND MOTIVATE

Essential Question

Big Idea 2, p. 553

How do you factor trinomials of the form $ax^2 + bx + c$? **Tell students they will learn how to answer this question by factoring polynomials with positive and negative leading coefficients other than 1 or −1.**

Resource Planning Guide

Chapter Resource Book
- Teaching Guide/Lesson Plan (pp. 61–62)
- Practice levels A, B, C (pp. 64–66)
- Study Guide (pp. 67–68)
- Catch-up for Absent Students (p. 69)
- Problem Solving Workshop (p. 70)
- Challenge (p. 71)

Workbooks
- Notetaking Guide (pp. 207–209)
- Practice Workbook (pp. 143–144)

Teaching Options
- **Power Presentations CD-ROM** provides dynamic electronic teaching resources for the classroom.
- **Activity Generator CD-ROM** provides editable activities for all ability levels.

Interactive Technology
- Easy Planner
- Power Presentations CD-ROM
- Activity Generator CD-ROM
- Animated Algebra
- Test Generator CD-ROM
- Online Quiz
- eWorkbook
- eEdition
- @HomeTutor

Resources for English Learners
- Quick Reference for English Learners
- Spanish Study Guide
- Multi-Language Visual Glossary
- Student Resources in Spanish

See also the *Algebra 1 Toolkit* for more strategies for meeting individual needs.

Motivating the Lesson

Engage students in a discussion about football, baseball, or soccer. Remark that when a ball is kicked, thrown, or hit in the air, sometimes the ball's starting position is some distance above the ground. Tell students that if they know the initial velocity of the ball and the height at which it was kicked or thrown, they can calculate when it will hit the ground.

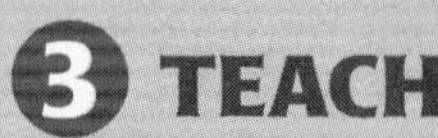

3 TEACH

Extra Example 1

Factor $2x^2 - 13x + 6$.
$(x - 6)(2x - 1)$

Key Question to Ask for Example 1

- Which terms of the binomial factors do you multiply to find the middle term? the two outer terms, the two inner terms

Extra Example 2

Factor $4n^2 + 11n - 3$.
$(n + 3)(4n - 1)$

Extra Example 3

Factor $-3x^2 - 13x - 4$.
$-(3x + 1)(x + 4)$

Key Question to Ask for Example 3

- What are the possible first terms for the binomial factors? What are the possible second terms? 4 and −1, −4 and 1, 2 and −2; 1 and 7; −1 and −7

✓ GUIDED PRACTICE for Examples 1 and 2

Factor the trinomial.

1. $3t^2 + 8t + 4$ $(t + 2)(3t + 2)$
2. $4s^2 - 9s + 5$ $(s - 1)(4s - 5)$
3. $2h^2 + 13h - 7$ $(h + 7)(2h - 1)$

FACTORING WHEN *a* IS NEGATIVE To factor a trinomial of the form $ax^2 + bx + c$ when a is negative, first factor −1 from each term of the trinomial. Then factor the resulting trinomial as in the previous examples.

EXAMPLE 3 Factor when *a* is negative

Factor $-4x^2 + 12x + 7$.

Solution

STEP 1 **Factor** −1 from each term of the trinomial.

$$-4x^2 + 12x + 7 = -(4x^2 - 12x - 7)$$

STEP 2 **Factor** the trinomial $4x^2 - 12x - 7$. Because b and c are both negative, the factors of c must have different signs. As in the previous examples, use a table to organize information about the factors of a and c.

Factors of 4	Factors of −7	Possible factorization	Middle term when multiplied	
1, 4	1, −7	$(x + 1)(4x - 7)$	$-7x + 4x = -3x$	✗
1, 4	7, −1	$(x + 7)(4x - 1)$	$-x + 28x = 27x$	✗
1, 4	−1, 7	$(x - 1)(4x + 7)$	$7x - 4x = 3x$	✗
1, 4	−7, 1	$(x - 7)(4x + 1)$	$x - 28x = -27x$	✗
2, 2	1, −7	$(2x + 1)(2x - 7)$	$-14x + 2x = -12x$	← Correct
2, 2	−1, 7	$(2x - 1)(2x + 7)$	$14x - 2x = 12x$	✗

AVOID ERRORS Remember to include the −1 that you factored out in Step 1.

▶ $-4x^2 + 12x + 7 = -(2x + 1)(2x - 7)$

CHECK You can check your factorization using a graphing calculator. Graph $y_1 = -4x^2 + 12x + 7$ and $y_2 = -(2x + 1)(2x - 7)$. Because the graphs coincide, you know that your factorization is correct.

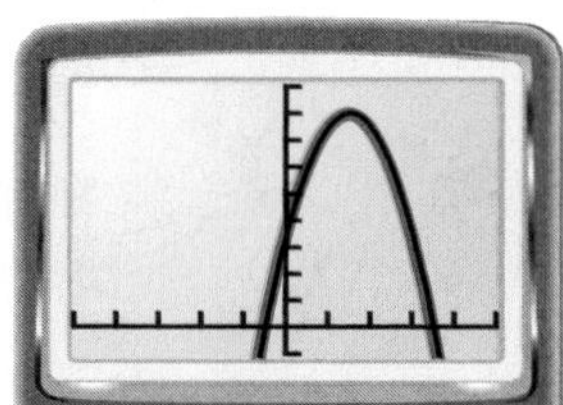

✓ GUIDED PRACTICE for Example 3

Factor the trinomial.

4. $-2y^2 - 5y - 3$ $-(y + 1)(2y + 3)$
5. $-5m^2 + 6m - 1$ $-(m - 1)(5m - 1)$
6. $-3x^2 - x + 2$ $-(x + 1)(3x - 2)$

Differentiated Instruction

Inclusion Organizing a table may be difficult for some students. When discussing **Example 3**, consider adding an additional column for the factors of a and c. Start the table as follows.

Factors of 4		Factors of −7		Possible factorization	Middle term when multiplied
1	4	1	−7	$(x + 1)(4x - 7)$	$-7x + 4x = -3x$

See also the *Algebra 1 Toolkit* for more strategies.

FINDING A COMMON FACTOR In Lesson 9.4, you learned to factor out the greatest common monomial factor from the terms of a polynomial. Sometimes you may need to do this before finding two binomial factors of a trinomial.

EXAMPLE 4 Write and solve a polynomial equation

DISCUS An athlete throws a discus from an initial height of 6 feet and with an initial vertical velocity of 46 feet per second.

a. Write an equation that gives the height (in feet) of the discus as a function of the time (in seconds) since it left the athlete's hand.

b. After how many seconds does the discus hit the ground?

Solution

USE VERTICAL MOTION MODEL
For help with using the vertical motion model, see p. 577.

a. Use the vertical motion model to write an equation for the height h (in feet) of the discus. In this case, $v = 46$ and $s = 6$.

$h = -16t^2 + vt + s$ Vertical motion model

$h = -16t^2 + 46t + 6$ Substitute 46 for v and 6 for s.

b. To find the number of seconds that pass before the discus lands, find the value of t for which the height of the discus is 0. Substitute 0 for h and solve the equation for t.

$0 = -16t^2 + 46t + 6$ Substitute 0 for h.

$0 = -2(8t^2 - 23t - 3)$ Factor out -2.

$0 = -2(8t + 1)(t - 3)$ Factor the trinomial. Find factors of 8 and -3 that produce a middle term with a coefficient of -23.

$8t + 1 = 0$ *or* $t - 3 = 0$ Zero-product property

$t = -\frac{1}{8}$ *or* $t = 3$ Solve for t.

The solutions of the equation are $-\frac{1}{8}$ and 3. A negative solution does not make sense in this situation, so disregard $-\frac{1}{8}$.

▶ The discus hits the ground after 3 seconds.

✓ **GUIDED PRACTICE** for Example 4

7. **WHAT IF?** In Example 4, suppose another athlete throws the discus with an initial vertical velocity of 38 feet per second and releases it from a height of 5 feet. After how many seconds does the discus hit the ground? 2.5 sec

8. **SHOT PUT** In a shot put event, an athlete throws the shot put from an initial height of 6 feet and with an initial vertical velocity of 29 feet per second. After how many seconds does the shot put hit the ground? 2 sec

Extra Example 4

A soccer goalie throws a ball into the air at an initial height of 8 feet and an initial vertical velocity of 28 feet per second.

a. Write an equation that gives the height (in feet) of the soccer ball as a function of the time (in seconds) since it left the goalie's hand. $h = -16t^2 + 28t + 8$

b. After how many seconds does it hit the ground? 2 sec

Key Questions to Ask for Example 4

- Why do you substitute 0 for h in the vertical motion model? $h = 0$ means that the discus is at 0 height or ground level. You use 0 because you want to find the number of seconds it takes the discus to reach the ground.
- How could you use the model if you want to know how long it takes the discus to reach a height of 6 feet on the way down? Substitute 6 for h, get 0 on one side of the equation, and solve.
- Can you use the model if the vertical motion is given in miles per hour or meters per second? Explain. No, for this model the motion must be measured in feet per second. You can convert miles per hour to feet per second and then use the model. A different model is used for metric units.

Extra Example 5

A rectangle's length is 5 feet more than 4 times its width. The area is 6 square feet. What is the width? B

Ⓐ $\frac{1}{2}$ ft Ⓑ $\frac{3}{4}$ ft

Ⓒ 2 ft Ⓓ $\frac{4}{3}$ ft

Key Question to Ask for Example 5

- Is there a way to eliminate any of the answer choices? Since the length of the rectangle is greater than 13 meters and the area is 10 square meters, the width has to be less than 1 meter. You can eliminate all answer choices except A.

Closing the Lesson

Have students summarize the major points of the lesson and answer the Essential Question: How do you factor trinomials of the form $ax^2 + bx + c$?

- You can use the factors of a and c to determine possible terms of the factors.
- If the leading coefficient is negative, first factor out -1 from each term of the trinomial.

The leading coefficient of the trinomial should be positive before you factor. If it is negative, factor out -1 from each term of the trinomial. Then use the signs of b and c to determine the signs of the second terms. After you determine possible factors of a and c, find out which of the possible factors gives the middle term of the original trinomial.

2. Enter the polynomial as Y_1 and enter the polynomial in factored form as Y_2. Graph Y_1 and Y_2 in the same viewing window. If the graphs coincide then the factorization is correct.

3. To factor the polynomial that has a leading coefficient of 1, $x^2 - x - 2$, you only need to find factors of the constant term, -2, that add to the coefficient of the middle term, -1. To factor the polynomial that has a leading coefficient that is not 1, $6x^2 - x - 2$, you must also take into account how the factors of the leading coefficient, 6, affect the coefficient of the middle term.

EXAMPLE 5 Standardized Test Practice

A rectangle's length is 13 meters more than 3 times its width. The area is 10 square meters. What is the width?

Ⓐ $\frac{2}{3}$ m Ⓑ 3 m Ⓒ 5 m Ⓓ 10 m

$w(3w + 13) = 10$	Write an equation to model area.
$3w^2 + 13w - 10 = 0$	Simplify and subtract 10 from each side.
$(w + 5)(3w - 2) = 0$	Factor left side.
$w + 5 = 0$ *or* $3w - 2 = 0$	Zero-product property
$w = -5$ *or* $w = \frac{2}{3}$	Solve for w.

Reject the negative width.

▸ The correct answer is A. Ⓐ Ⓑ Ⓒ Ⓓ

✓ GUIDED PRACTICE for Example 5

9. A rectangle's length is 1 inch more than twice its width. The area is 6 square inches. What is the width? B

Ⓐ $\frac{1}{2}$ in. Ⓑ $\frac{3}{2}$ in. Ⓒ 2 in. Ⓓ $\frac{5}{2}$ in.

9.6 EXERCISES

HOMEWORK KEY

○ = **WORKED-OUT SOLUTIONS** on p. WS22 for Exs. 5, 25, and 61

★ = **STANDARDIZED TEST PRACTICE** Exs. 2, 3, 22, 41, 51, and 60

◆ = **MULTIPLE REPRESENTATIONS** Ex. 62

SKILL PRACTICE

1. **VOCABULARY** What is another word for the solutions of $x^2 + 2x + 1 = 0$? roots

2. ★ **WRITING** *Explain* how you can use a graph to check a factorization. See margin.

3. ★ **WRITING** *Compare* factoring $6x^2 - x - 2$ with factoring $x^2 - x - 2$. See margin.

EXAMPLES 1, 2, and 3 on pp. 593–594 for Exs. 4–22

FACTORING TRINOMIALS Factor the trinomial.

4. $-x^2 + x + 20$ $-(x - 5)(x + 4)$
5. $-y^2 + 2y + 8$ $-(y - 4)(y + 2)$
6. $-a^2 + 12a - 27$ $-(a - 3)(a - 9)$
7. $5w^2 - 6w + 1$ $(5w - 1)(w - 1)$
8. $-3p^2 - 10p - 3$ $-(3p + 1)(p + 3)$
9. $6s^2 - s - 5$ $(6s + 5)(s - 1)$
10. $2t^2 + 5t - 63$ $(2t - 9)(t + 7)$
11. $2c^2 - 7c + 3$ $(2c - 1)(c - 3)$
12. $3n^2 - 17n + 10$ $(3n - 2)(n - 5)$
13. $-2h^2 + 5h + 3$ $-(2h + 1)(h - 3)$
14. $-6k^2 - 13k - 6$ $-(2k + 3)(3k + 2)$
15. $10x^2 - 3x - 27$ $(2x + 3)(5x - 9)$
16. $4m^2 + 9m + 5$ $(4m + 5)(m + 1)$
17. $3z^2 + z - 14$ $(3z + 7)(z - 2)$
18. $4a^2 + 9a - 9$ $(4a - 3)(a + 3)$
19. $4n^2 + 16n + 15$ $(2n + 3)(2n + 5)$
20. $-5b^2 + 7b - 2$ $-(5b - 2)(b - 1)$
21. $6y^2 - 5y - 4$ $(3y - 4)(2y + 1)$

38. In order to solve an equation by factoring and using the zero-product property, the equation must first be put in the form $ax^2 + bx + c = 0$. The left side of the equation should not be factored until 4 is subtracted from each side, making the right side of the equation zero; $5x^2 + x - 4 = 0$, $(5x - 4)(x + 1) = 0$, $5x - 4 = 0$ or $x + 1 = 0$, $x = \frac{4}{5}$ or $x = -1$; $\frac{4}{5}$, -1.

22. ★ **MULTIPLE CHOICE** What is the correct factorization of $8x^2 - 10x + 3$? **B**

Ⓐ $(2x - 3)(4x - 1)$ Ⓑ $(2x - 1)(4x - 3)$

Ⓒ $(4x + 1)(2x - 3)$ Ⓓ $(8x - 3)(x - 1)$

EXAMPLES 4 and 5 on pp. 595–596 for Exs. 23–39

SOLVING EQUATIONS **Solve the equation.**

23. $2x^2 - 3x - 35 = 0$ $-\frac{7}{2}, 5$
24. $3w^2 + 22w + 7 = 0$ $-\frac{1}{3}, -7$
25. $4s^2 + 11s - 3 = 0$ $\frac{1}{4}, -3$
26. $7a^2 + 2a = 5$ $\frac{5}{7}, -1$
27. $8t^2 - 2t = 3$ $\frac{3}{4}, -\frac{1}{2}$
28. $6m^2 - 5m = 14$ $-\frac{7}{6}, 2$
29. $b(20b - 3) - 2 = 0$ $-\frac{1}{4}, \frac{2}{5}$
30. $4(3y^2 - 7y + 4) = 1$ $\frac{5}{6}, \frac{3}{2}$
31. $p(3p + 14) = 5$ $\frac{1}{3}, -5$
32. $4n^2 - 2n - 90 = 0$ $-\frac{9}{2}, 5$
33. $10c^2 - 14c + 4 = 0$ $\frac{2}{5}, 1$
34. $-16k^2 + 8k + 24 = 0$ $\frac{3}{2}, -1$
35. $6r^2 - 15r = 99$ $\frac{11}{2}, -3$
36. $56z^2 + 2 = 22z$ $\frac{1}{7}, \frac{1}{4}$
37. $30x^2 + 25x = 20$ $-\frac{4}{3}, \frac{1}{2}$

ERROR ANALYSIS ***Describe*** **and correct the error in solving the equation.**

38.
$5x^2 + x = 4$
$x(5x + 1) = 4$
$x = 4$ or $5x + 1 = 4$
$x = 4$ or $x = \frac{3}{5}$

See margin.

39.
$12x^2 + 5x - 2 = 0$
$(3x - 1)(4x + 2) = 0$
$3x - 1 = 0$ or $4x + 2 = 0$
$x = \frac{1}{3}$ or $x = -\frac{1}{2}$

39. The factorization of the polynomial should be $(3x + 2)(4x - 1)$ instead of $(3x - 1)(4x + 2)$; $-\frac{2}{3}, \frac{1}{4}$.

40. **GEOMETRY** The length of a rectangle is 7 inches more than 5 times its width. The area of the rectangle is 6 square inches. What is the width? $\frac{3}{5}$ in.

41. ★ **SHORT RESPONSE** The length of a rectangle is 1 inch more than 4 times its width. The area of the rectangle is 3 square inches. What is the perimeter of the rectangle? *Explain* how you found your answer. See margin.

B **FINDING ZEROS OF FUNCTIONS** **Find the zeros of the polynomial function.**

42. $g(x) = 2x^2 + x - 1$ $\frac{1}{2}, -1$
43. $f(x) = -x^2 + 12x - 35$ $5, 7$
44. $h(x) = -3x^2 + 2x + 5$ $\frac{5}{3}, -1$
45. $f(x) = 3x^2 + x - 14$ $-\frac{7}{3}, 2$
46. $g(x) = 8x^2 - 6x - 14$ $\frac{7}{4}, -1$
47. $f(x) = 12x^2 - 24x - 63$ $\frac{7}{2}, -\frac{3}{2}$

SOLVING EQUATIONS **Multiply each side of the equation by an appropriate power of 10 to obtain integer coefficients. Then solve the equation.**

48. $0.3x^2 - 0.7x - 4.0 = 0$ $-\frac{8}{3}, 5$
49. $0.8x^2 - 1.8x - 0.5 = 0$ $-\frac{1}{4}, \frac{5}{2}$
50. $0.4x^2 - 0.4x = 9.9$ $-\frac{9}{2}, \frac{11}{2}$

51. ★ **MULTIPLE CHOICE** What are the solutions of the equation $0.4x^2 - 1.1x = 2$? **C**

Ⓐ −12.5 AND 40 Ⓑ −4 AND 1.25 Ⓒ −1.25 AND 4 Ⓓ −0.125 AND 0.4

WRITING EQUATIONS **Write a polynomial equation that has the given solutions. The equation must have integer coefficients.** ***Explain*** **your reasoning.** 52–54. See margin.

52. −3 and 2
53. $-\frac{1}{2}$ and 5
54. $-\frac{3}{4}$ and $-\frac{1}{3}$

C **CHALLENGE** **Factor the trinomial.**

55. $2x^2 - 11xy + 5y^2$ $(2x - y)(x - 5y)$
56. $3x^2 + 2xy - 8y^2$ $(3x - 4y)(x + 2y)$
57. $6x^3 - 10x^2y - 56xy^2$ $2x(3x + 7y)(x - 4y)$

4 PRACTICE AND APPLY

Assignment Guide

Answer Transparencies available for all exercises

Basic:
Day 1: pp. 596–599
Exs. 1–22, 64–72 even
Day 2: pp. 596–599
Exs. 23–37 odd, 38–45, 58–62, 73–81 odd

Average:
Day 1: pp. 596–599
Exs. 1–3, 8–21, 52–55, 65–71 odd
Day 2: pp. 596–599
Exs. 26–38 even, 39–51, 58–62, 74, 77, 80

Advanced:
Day 1: pp. 596–599
Exs. 1–3, 12–21, 52–57*, 65–71 odd
Day 2: pp. 596–599
Exs. 30–37, 40–51, 58–63*, 75, 78, 81

Block:
pp. 596–599
Exs. 1–3, 8–21, 52–55, 65–71 odd (with 9.5)
pp. 596–599
Exs. 26–38 even, 39–51, 58–62, 74, 77, 80 (with 9.7)

Differentiated Instruction

See *Algebra 1 Best Practices Toolkit* for suggestions on addressing the needs of a diverse classroom.

Homework Check

For a quick check of student understanding of key concepts, go over the following exercises:

Basic: 7, 10, 13, 27, 59
Average: 12, 14, 18, 30, 60
Advanced: 17, 20, 21, 58, 61

Extra Practice

- Student Edition, p. 946
- Chapter 9 Resource Book: Practice levels A, B, C, pp. 64–66

Practice Worksheet

An easily-readable reduced practice page (with answers) for this lesson can be found on p. 552C.

41. $9\frac{1}{2}$ in.; to find the width, solve the equation $w(4w + 1) = 3$ to get $w = \frac{3}{4}$ or $w = -1$. The width cannot be negative, so the width is $\frac{3}{4}$ inch. Then the length is $4\left(\frac{3}{4}\right) + 1 = 4$ inches, and the perimeter is $2\left(\frac{3}{4}\right) + 2(4) = 9\frac{1}{2}$ inches.

52–54. See Additional Answers beginning on p. AA1.

Avoiding Common Errors

Exercises 4–21 Remind students to factor out −1 before they factor trinomials with a negative leading coefficient. Remind them to include it after they have factored the trinomial.

Graphing Calculator

Exercises 4–21 Have students use a graphing calculator to check their factorizations. They can graph the trinomial and the factorization in the same viewing window using a thin line and a thick line. If the graphs do not coincide, they can try different factors.

Vocabulary

Exercise 58 Some students may not know what "center of gravity" means. Explain that *center of gravity* generally means the point on which a person or object will balance.

An **Animated Algebra** activity is available on-line for **Exercise 62**. This activity is also available on the **Power Presentations CD-ROM**.

Exercise 62 For more information about serval cats, visit the African Wildlife Foundation's website www.awf.org/wildlives/185

60. 2 sec; the ball's height (in feet) is modeled by the equation $h = -16t^2 + 31t + 6$, where t is the time (in seconds) since you threw it. To find when the height is 4 feet, substitute 4 for h. Solve the equation $4 = -16t^2 + 31t + 6$, or $16t^2 - 31t - 2 = 0$. The roots of this equation are $-\frac{1}{16}$ and 2. The time t cannot be negative, so disregard the root $-\frac{1}{16}$; the ball reaches a height of 4 feet after 2 seconds.

PROBLEM SOLVING

EXAMPLE 4 A
on p. 595
for Exs. 58, 60

58. DIVING A diver dives from a cliff when her center of gravity is 46 feet above the surface of the water. Her initial vertical velocity leaving the cliff is 9 feet per second. After how many seconds does her center of gravity enter the water? **2 sec**

@HomeTutor for problem solving help at classzone.com

EXAMPLE 5
on p. 596
for Exs. 59, 61

59. SCRAPBOOK DESIGN You plan to make a scrapbook. On the cover, you want to show three pictures with space between them, as shown. Each of the pictures is twice as long as it is wide.

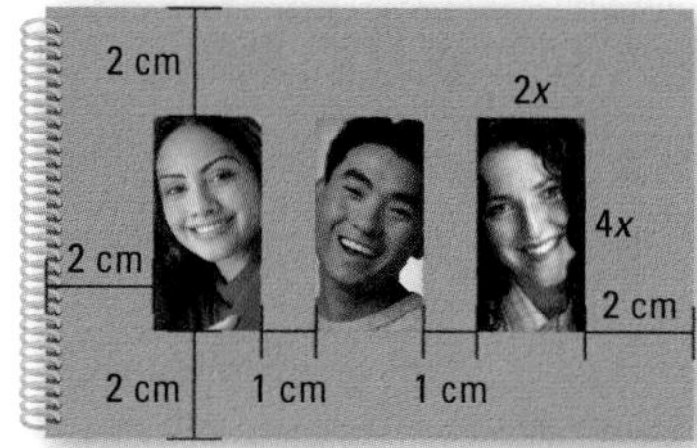

a. Write a polynomial that represents the area of the scrapbook cover. $24x^2 + 48x + 24$

b. The area of the cover will be 96 square centimeters. Find the length and width of the pictures you will use. **4 cm, 2 cm**

@HomeTutor for problem solving help at classzone.com

60. ★ SHORT RESPONSE You throw a ball into the air with an initial vertical velocity of 31 feet per second. The ball leaves your hand when it is 6 feet above the ground. You catch the ball when it reaches a height of 4 feet. After how many seconds do you catch the ball? *Explain* how you can use the solutions of an equation to find your answer. **See margin.**

(61.) PARTHENON The Parthenon in Athens, Greece, is an ancient structure that has a rectangular base. The length of the Parthenon's base is 8 meters more than twice its width. The area of the base is about 2170 square meters. Find the length and width of the Parthenon's base. **70 m, 31 m**

B **62. ◆ MULTIPLE REPRESENTATIONS** An African cat called a serval leaps from the ground in an attempt to catch a bird. The serval's initial vertical velocity is 24 feet per second.

a. **Writing an Equation** Write an equation that gives the serval's height (in feet) as a function of the time (in seconds) since it left the ground. $h = -16t^2 + 24t$

b. **Making a Table** Use the equation from part (a) to make a table that shows the height of the serval for $t = 0, 0.3, 0.6, 0.9, 1.2$, and 1.5 seconds. **See margin.**

c. **Drawing a Graph** Plot the ordered pairs in the table as points in a coordinate plane. Connect the points with a smooth curve. After how many seconds does the serval reach a height of 9 feet? *Justify* your answer using the equation from part (a).

Animated Algebra at classzone.com

See margin for art; 0.75 sec; substitute $h = 9$ feet into the equation $h = -16t^2 + 24t$ and solve for t, $t = 0.75$ second.

○ = WORKED-OUT SOLUTIONS on p. WS1 ★ = STANDARDIZED TEST PRACTICE  = MULTIPLE REPRESENTATIONS

62b.

x (feet)	y (feet)
0	0
0.3	5.76
0.6	8.64
0.9	8.64
1.2	5.76
1.5	0

62c.

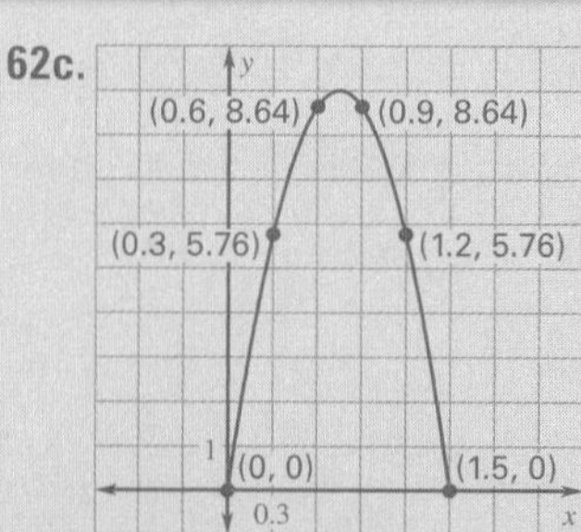

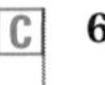 63. **CHALLENGE** A bush cricket jumps from the ground into the air with an initial vertical velocity of 4 feet per second.

a. Write an equation that gives the cricket's height (in feet) as a function of the time (in seconds) since it left the ground. $h = -16t^2 + 4t$

b. After how many seconds is the cricket 3 inches off the ground? 0.125 sec

c. Does the cricket jump higher than 3 inches? *Explain* your reasoning using your answer from part (b). See margin.

ILLINOIS MIXED REVIEW

 **TEST PRACTICE** at classzone.com

64. The net of a cube is shown. Use a ruler to measure the dimensions of the cube to the nearest tenth of a centimeter. Which best represents the surface area of this cube to the nearest square centimeter?

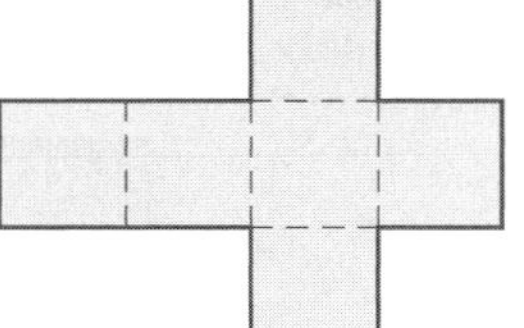

Ⓐ 1 cm² Ⓑ 3 cm²

Ⓒ 4 cm² D Ⓓ 6 cm²

QUIZ *for Lessons 9.4–9.6*

Factor out the greatest common monomial factor. *(p. 575)*

1. $16a^2 - 40b$ $8(2a^2 - 5b)$
2. $9xy^2 + 6x^2y$ $3xy(3y + 2x)$
3. $4n^4 - 22n^3 - 8n^2$ $2n^2(2n^2 - 11n - 4)$
4. $3x^2 + 6xy - 3y^2$ $3(x^2 + 2xy - y^2)$
5. $12abc^2 - 6a^2c$ $6ac(2bc - a)$
6. $-36s^3 + 18s^2 - 54s$ $-18s(2s^2 - s + 3)$

Factor the trinomial.

7. $r^2 + 15r + 56$ *(p. 583)* $(r + 7)(r + 8)$
8. $s^2 - 6s + 5$ *(p. 583)* $(s - 5)(s - 1)$
9. $w^2 + 6w - 40$ *(p. 583)* $(w + 10)(w - 4)$
10. $-a^2 + 9a + 22$ *(p. 593)* $-(a - 11)(a + 2)$
11. $2x^2 - 9x + 4$ *(p. 593)* $(2x - 1)(x - 4)$
12. $5m^2 + m - 6$ *(p. 593)* $(5m + 6)(m - 1)$
13. $6h^2 - 19h + 3$ *(p. 593)* $(6h - 1)(h - 3)$
14. $-7y^2 - 23y - 6$ *(p. 593)* $-(7y + 2)(y + 3)$
15. $18c^2 + 12c - 6$ *(p. 593)* $6(3c - 1)(c + 1)$

Solve the equation.

16. $(4p - 7)(p + 5) = 0$ *(p. 575)*
17. $-8u^2 + 28u = 0$ *(p. 575)* $0, \frac{7}{2}$
18. $51x^2 = -17x$ *(p. 575)* $0, -\frac{1}{3}$
19. $b^2 - 11b = -24$ *(p. 583)* 3, 8
20. $m^2 + 12m = -35$ *(p. 583)* −7, −5
21. $q^2 + 19 = -20q$ *(p. 583)* −19, −1
22. $3t^2 - 11t + 10 = 0$ *(p. 593)* $\frac{5}{3}, 2$
23. $4y^2 + 31y = 8$ *(p. 593)* $\frac{1}{4}, -8$
24. $14s^2 + 12s = 2$ *(p. 593)* $\frac{1}{7}, -1$

16. $\frac{7}{4}, -5$

25. **BASEBALL** A baseball player hits a baseball into the air with an initial vertical velocity of 72 feet per second. The player hits the ball from a height of 3 feet. *(p. 593)*

a. Write an equation that gives the baseball's height as a function of the time (in seconds) after it is hit. $h = -16t^2 + 72t + 3$

b. After how many seconds is the baseball 84 feet above the ground? 2.25 sec

5 ASSESS AND RETEACH

Daily Homework Quiz

Transparency Available

Factor the trinomial.

1. $-x^2 + x + 30$ $-(x + 5)(x - 6)$
2. $5b^2 + 3b - 14$ $(b + 2)(5b - 7)$
3. $6y^2 - 13y - 5$ $(3y + 1)(2y - 5)$
4. Solve $2x^2 + 7x = -3$. $-\frac{1}{2}, -3$
5. A baseball is hit into the air at an initial height of 4 feet and an initial velocity of 30 feet per second. For how many seconds is it in the air? 2 sec

Online Quiz

Available at **classzone.com**

Diagnosis/Remediation

- Practice A, B, C in Chapter 9 Resource Book, pp. 64–66
- Study Guide in Chapter 9 Resource Book, pp. 67–68
- Practice Workbook, pp. 143–144
- @HomeTutor

Challenge

Additional challenge is available in the Chapter 9 Resource Book, p. 71.

Quiz

An easily-readable reduced copy of the quiz (with answers) on Lessons 9.4–9.6 from the Assessment Book can be found on p. 552E.

63c. No; $t = 0.125$ is the only solution of the equation $\frac{1}{4} = -16t^2 + 4t$, so the cricket is 3 inches off the ground only once. This happens only at the highest point of the cricket's jump; all other heights are reached twice, once on the way up and once on the way down.

1 PLAN AND PREPARE

Warm-Up Exercises

Transparency Available

Find the product.

1. $(m + 2)(m - 2)$ $m^2 - 4$
2. $(2y - 3)^2$ $4y^2 - 12y + 9$
3. $(s + 2t)(s - 2t)$ $s^2 - 4t^2$
4. A football is thrown in the air at an initial height of 5 feet and an initial velocity of 16 feet per second. After how many seconds does it hit the ground? 1.25 sec

Notetaking Guide

Transparency Available

Promotes interactive learning and notetaking skills, pp. 210–213.

Pacing

Basic: 1 day
Average: 1 day
Advanced: 1 day
Block: 0.5 block with 9.6

- See *Teaching Guide/Lesson Plan*.

2 FOCUS AND MOTIVATE

Essential Question

Big Idea 2, p. 553

How do you factor special products? Tell students they will learn how to answer this question by using the difference of two squares pattern and the perfect square trinomial patterns.

9.7 Factor Special Products

 **8.11.01** Simplify or identify equivalent algebraic expressions (e.g., exponential, rational, logarithmic, factored, polynomial).

Before You factored polynomials of the form $ax^2 + bx + c$.

Now You will factor special products.

Why? So you can use a scientific model, as in Ex. 48.

Key Vocabulary
- **perfect square trinomial**

You can use the special product patterns you studied in Lesson 9.3 to factor polynomials, such as the difference of two squares.

KEY CONCEPT *For Your Notebook*

Difference of Two Squares Pattern

Algebra	**Example**
$a^2 - b^2 = (a + b)(a - b)$	$4x^2 - 9 = (2x)^2 - 3^2 = (2x + 3)(2x - 3)$

EXAMPLE 1 Factor the difference of two squares

Factor the polynomial.

a. $y^2 - 16 = y^2 - 4^2$ — Write as $a^2 - b^2$.
$= (y + 4)(y - 4)$ — Difference of two squares pattern

b. $25m^2 - 36 = (5m)^2 - 6^2$ — Write as $a^2 - b^2$.
$= (5m + 6)(5m - 6)$ — Difference of two squares pattern

c. $x^2 - 49y^2 = x^2 - (7y)^2$ — Write as $a^2 - b^2$.
$= (x + 7y)(x - 7y)$ — Difference of two squares pattern

EXAMPLE 2 Factor the difference of two squares

Factor the polynomial $8 - 18n^2$.

$8 - 18n^2 = 2(4 - 9n^2)$ — Factor out common factor.
$= 2[2^2 - (3n)^2]$ — Write $4 - 9n^2$ as $a^2 - b^2$.
$= 2(2 + 3n)(2 - 3n)$ — Difference of two squares pattern

 **GUIDED PRACTICE** for Examples 1 and 2

1. Factor the polynomial $4y^2 - 64$. $(2y + 8)(2y - 8)$

Resource Planning Guide

Chapter Resource Book
- Teaching Guide/Lesson Plan (pp. 72–73)
- Practice levels A, B, C (pp. 74–76)
- Study Guide (pp. 77–78)
- Catch-up for Absent Students (p. 79)
- Application (p. 80)
- Challenge (p. 81)

Workbooks
- Notetaking Guide (pp. 210–213)
- Practice Workbook (pp. 145–146)

Teaching Options
- **Power Presentations CD-ROM** provides dynamic electronic teaching resources for the classroom.
- **Activity Generator CD-ROM** provides editable activities for all ability levels.

Interactive Technology
- Easy Planner
- Power Presentations CD-ROM
- Activity Generator CD-ROM
- Animated Algebra
- Test Generator CD-ROM
- Online Quiz
- eWorkbook
- eEdition
- @HomeTutor

Resources for English Learners
- Quick Reference for English Learners
- Spanish Study Guide
- Multi-Language Visual Glossary
- Student Resources in Spanish

See also the *Algebra 1 Toolkit* for more strategies for meeting individual needs.

PERFECT SQUARE TRINOMIALS The pattern for finding the square of a binomial gives you the pattern for factoring trinomials of the form $a^2 + 2ab + b^2$ and $a^2 - 2ab + b^2$. These are called **perfect square trinomials**.

KEY CONCEPT *For Your Notebook*

Perfect Square Trinomial Pattern

Algebra	Example
$a^2 + 2ab + b^2 = (a + b)^2$	$x^2 + 6x + 9 = x^2 + 2(x \cdot 3) + 3^2 = (x + 3)^2$
$a^2 - 2ab + b^2 = (a - b)^2$	$x^2 - 10x + 25 = x^2 - 2(x \cdot 5) + 5^2 = (x - 5)^2$

EXAMPLE 3 Factor perfect square trinomials

Factor the polynomial.

a. $n^2 - 12n + 36 = n^2 - 2(n \cdot 6) + 6^2$ — Write as $a^2 - 2ab + b^2$.

$= (n - 6)^2$ — Perfect square trinomial pattern

b. $9x^2 - 12x + 4 = (3x)^2 - 2(3x \cdot 2) + 2^2$ — Write as $a^2 - 2ab + b^2$.

$= (3x - 2)^2$ — Perfect square trinomial pattern

c. $4s^2 + 4st + t^2 = (2s)^2 + 2(2s \cdot t) + t^2$ — Write as $a^2 + 2ab + b^2$.

$= (2s + t)^2$ — Perfect square trinomial pattern

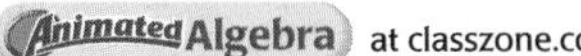
at classzone.com

EXAMPLE 4 Factor a perfect square trinomial

Factor the polynomial $-3y^2 + 36y - 108$.

$-3y^2 + 36y - 108 = -3(y^2 - 12y + 36)$ — Factor out -3.

$= -3[y^2 - 2(y \cdot 6) + 6^2]$ — Write $y^2 - 12y + 36$ as $a^2 - 2ab + b^2$.

$= -3(y - 6)^2$ — Perfect square trinomial pattern

CHECK Check your factorization using a graphing calculator. Graph $y_1 = -3x^2 + 36x - 108$ and $y_2 = -3(x - 6)^2$. Because the graphs coincide, you know that your factorization is correct.

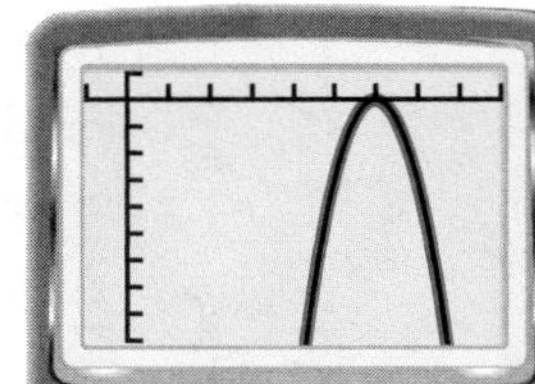

✓ **GUIDED PRACTICE** for Examples 3 and 4

Factor the polynomial.

2. $h^2 + 4h + 4$ $(h + 2)^2$ **3.** $2y^2 - 20y + 50$ $2(y - 5)^2$ **4.** $3x^2 + 6xy + 3y^2$ $3(x + y)^2$

Motivating the Lesson

Ask students to discuss how long it takes objects to fall from different heights. Tell them that if they know the height from which an object is dropped, they can calculate the time it takes the object to reach the ground.

3 TEACH

Extra Example 1

Factor the polynomial.

a. $y^2 - 9$ $(y + 3)(y - 3)$

b. $64c^2 - 16$ $(8c + 4)(8c - 4)$

c. $x^2 - 81y^2$ $(x + 9y)(x - 9y)$

Extra Example 2

Factor the polynomial $12 - 48m^2$. $12(1 + 2m)(1 - 2m)$

Extra Example 3

Factor the polynomial.

a. $a^2 + 6a + 9$ $(a + 3)^2$

b. $4n^2 + 20n + 25$ $(2n + 5)^2$

c. $9c^2 - 6cd + d^2$ $(3c - d)^2$

Animated Algebra classzone.com

An **Animated Algebra** activity is available on-line for **Example 3**. This activity is also available on the **Power Presentations CD-ROM**.

Extra Example 4

Factor the polynomial $-2x^2 - 16x - 32$. $-2(x + 4)^2$

Key Question to Ask for Example 4

- How can you check the factorization other than by graphing? Use FOIL and then multiply each term by -3.

Differentiated Instruction

Inclusion The number of formulas in this section may overwhelm students. Instead of asking students to memorize the formulas, have them apply the FOIL method to the products $(a + b)(a + b)$, $(a + b)(a - b)$, and $(a - b)(a - b)$ to learn the patterns of the special products.

See also the *Algebra 1 Toolkit* for more strategies.

Extra Example 5

Solve the equation $x^2 - 5x + \frac{25}{4} = 0$. $\frac{5}{2}$

Key Question to Ask for Example 5

- Why does the equation have only one solution? The factored form is $(3x + 1)^2 = 0$ or $(3x + 1)(3x + 1) = 0$. Since the two factors are the same, the equation has only one solution.

Extra Example 6

A rock is dropped from a riverbank that is 4 feet above the surface of the river. After how many seconds does the rock hit the surface of the water? 0.5 sec

Key Question to Ask for Example 6

- How is the vertical motion model in Example 6 different from the model for an object launched from ground level? For the vertical motion model in Example 6, the initial vertical velocity is 0.

Closing the Lesson

Have students summarize the major points of the lesson and answer the Essential Question: How do you factor special products?

- You can use patterns to factor the difference of two squares, $a^2 - b^2$, and perfect square trinomials, $a^2 + 2ab + b^2$ and $a^2 - 2ab + b^2$.

Use the pattern $a^2 - b^2 = (a + b)(a - b)$ to factor a polynomial that is the difference of two squares. Use the patterns $a^2 + 2ab + b^2 = (a + b)^2$ and $a^2 - 2ab + b^2 = (a - b)^2$ to factor perfect square trinomials.

EXAMPLE 5 Solve a polynomial equation

Solve the equation $x^2 + \frac{2}{3}x + \frac{1}{9} = 0$.

$x^2 + \frac{2}{3}x + \frac{1}{9} = 0$	Write original equation.
$9x^2 + 6x + 1 = 0$	Multiply each side by 9.
$(3x)^2 + 2(3x \cdot 1) + (1)^2 = 0$	Write left side as $a^2 + 2ab + b^2$.
$(3x + 1)^2 = 0$	Perfect square trinomial pattern
$3x + 1 = 0$	Zero-product property
$x = -\frac{1}{3}$	Solve for x.

FIND SOLUTIONS This equation has two identical solutions, because it has two identical factors.

▶ The solution of the equation is $-\frac{1}{3}$.

EXAMPLE 6 Solve a vertical motion problem

FALLING OBJECT A window washer drops a wet sponge from a height of 64 feet. After how many seconds does the sponge land on the ground?

Solution

Use the vertical motion model to write an equation for the height h (in feet) of the sponge as a function of the time t (in seconds) after it is dropped.

The sponge was dropped, so it has no initial vertical velocity. Find the value of t for which the height is 0.

$h = -16t^2 + vt + s$	Vertical motion model
$0 = -16t^2 + (0)t + 64$	Substitute 0 for h, 0 for v, and 64 for s.
$0 = -16(t^2 - 4)$	Factor out -16.
$0 = -16(t - 2)(t + 2)$	Difference of two squares pattern
$t - 2 = 0$ *or* $t + 2 = 0$	Zero-product property
$t = 2$ *or* $t = -2$	Solve for t.

Disregard the negative solution of the equation.

▶ The sponge lands on the ground 2 seconds after it is dropped.

GUIDED PRACTICE for Examples 5 and 6

Solve the equation.

5. $a^2 + 6a + 9 = 0$ -3 **6.** $w^2 - 14w + 49 = 0$ 7 **7.** $n^2 - 81 = 0$ ± 9

8. WHAT IF? In Example 6, suppose the sponge is dropped from a height of 16 feet. After how many seconds does it land on the ground? 1 sec

9.7 EXERCISES

HOMEWORK KEY ○ = **WORKED-OUT SOLUTIONS** on p. WS22 for Exs. 11 and 49
★ = **STANDARDIZED TEST PRACTICE** Exs. 2, 23, 24, 49, and 50

SKILL PRACTICE

A

1. **VOCABULARY** Copy and complete: The polynomial $9n^2 + 6n + 1$ is called a(n) __?__ trinomial. perfect square

2. ★ **WRITING** *Explain* how to factor the difference of two squares. Write the binomial in the form $a^2 - b^2$ and then factor it as $(a + b)(a - b)$, the sum and difference of a and b.

EXAMPLES 1 and 2 on p. 600 for Exs. 3–8

DIFFERENCE OF TWO SQUARES **Factor the polynomial.**

3. $x^2 - 25$ $(x + 5)(x - 5)$
4. $n^2 - 64$ $(n + 8)(n - 8)$
5. $81c^2 - 4$ $(9c + 2)(9c - 2)$
6. $49 - 121p^2$ $(7 + 11p)(7 - 11p)$
7. $-3m^2 + 48n^2$ $-3(m + 4n)(m - 4n)$
8. $225x^2 - 144y^2$ $9(5x + 4y)(5x - 4y)$

EXAMPLES 3 and 4 on p. 601 for Exs. 9–14

PERFECT SQUARE TRINOMIALS **Factor the polynomial.**

9. $x^2 - 4x + 4$ $(x - 2)^2$
10. $y^2 - 10y + 25$ $(y - 5)^2$
11. $49a^2 + 14a + 1$ $(7a + 1)^2$
12. $9t^2 - 12t + 4$ $(3t - 2)^2$
13. $m^2 + m + \frac{1}{4}$ $\left(m + \frac{1}{2}\right)^2$
14. $2x^2 + 12xy + 18y^2$ $2(x + 3y)^2$

EXAMPLES 1, 2, 3, and 4 on pp. 600–601 for Exs. 15–24

FACTORING POLYNOMIALS **Factor the polynomial.**

15. $4c^2 - 400$ $4(c + 10)(c - 10)$
16. $4f^2 - 36f + 81$ $(2f - 9)^2$
17. $-9r^2 + 4s^2$ $(2s + 3r)(2s - 3r)$
18. $z^2 + 12z + 36$ $(z + 6)^2$
19. $72 - 32y^2$ $8(3 + 2y)(3 - 2y)$
20. $45r^2 - 120rs + 80s^2$ $5(3r - 4s)^2$

ERROR ANALYSIS *Describe* and correct the error in factoring. 21, 22. See margin.

21.
$$36x^2 - 81 = 9(4x^2 - 9)$$
$$= 9((2x)^2 - 3^2)$$
$$= 9(2x - 3)^2$$

22.
$$y^2 - 6y + 9 = y^2 - 2(y \cdot 3) + 3^2$$
$$= (y - 3)(y + 3)$$

23. ★ **MULTIPLE CHOICE** Which is the correct factorization of $-45x^2 + 20y^2$? C

Ⓐ $-5(3x + 2y)^2$ Ⓑ $5(3x - 2y)^2$
Ⓒ $-5(3x + 2y)(3x - 2y)$ Ⓓ $5(3x + 2y)(3x - 2y)$

24. ★ **MULTIPLE CHOICE** Which is the correct factorization of $16m^2 - 8mn + n^2$? A

Ⓐ $(4m - n)^2$ Ⓑ $(4m + n)^2$
Ⓒ $(8m - n)^2$ Ⓓ $(4m - n)(4m + n)$

EXAMPLE 5 on p. 602 for Exs. 25–39

B

SOLVING EQUATIONS **Solve the equation.**

25. $x^2 + 8x + 16 = 0$ -4
26. $16a^2 - 8a + 1 = 0$ $\frac{1}{4}$
27. $4w^2 - 36 = 0$ ± 3
28. $32 - 18m^2 = 0$ $\pm\frac{4}{3}$
29. $27c^2 + 108c + 108 = 0$ -2
30. $-2h^2 - 28h - 98 = 0$ -7
31. $6p^2 = 864$ ± 12
32. $-3t^2 = -108$ ± 6
33. $8k^2 = 98$ $\pm\frac{7}{2}$
34. $-\frac{4}{3}x + \frac{4}{9} = -x^2$ $\frac{2}{3}$
35. $y^2 - \frac{5}{3}y = -\frac{25}{36}$ $\frac{5}{6}$
36. $\frac{2}{9} = 8n^2$ $\pm\frac{1}{6}$
37. $-9c^2 = -16$ $\pm\frac{4}{3}$
38. $-20s - 3 = 25s^2 + 1$ $-\frac{2}{5}$
39. $y^4 - 2y^3 + y^2 = 0$ 0, 1

21. $(2x)^2 - 3^2$ is in the form $a^2 - b^2$, so it must be factored using the difference of two squares pattern, not the perfect square trinomial pattern; $9(2x + 3)(2x - 3)$.

22. $y^2 - 2(y \cdot 3) + 3^2$ is in the form $a^2 - 2ab + b^2$, so it must be factored using the perfect square trinomial pattern, not the difference of two squares pattern; $(y - 3)^2$.

4 PRACTICE AND APPLY

Assignment Guide

Answer Transparencies available for all exercises

Basic:
Day 1: pp. 603–605
Exs. 1, 2, 3–21 odd, 22–30, 46–50, 53–75 odd

Average:
Day 1: pp. 603–605
Exs. 1, 2, 6–8, 12–24, 25–39 odd, 46–51, 54–76 even

Advanced:
Day 1: pp. 603–605
Exs. 1, 2, 6–9, 12–20, 23, 24, 26–38 even, 40–52*, 61, 70, 76

Block:
pp. 603–605
Exs. 1, 2, 6–8, 12–24, 25–39 odd, 46–51, 54–76 even (with 9.6)

Differentiated Instruction

See *Algebra 1 Best Practices Toolkit* for suggestions on addressing the needs of a diverse classroom.

Homework Check

For a quick check of student understanding of key concepts, go over the following exercises:

Basic: 5, 9, 17, 26, 46
Average: 6, 12, 19, 29, 47
Advanced: 8, 14, 20, 38, 48

Extra Practice

- Student Edition, p. 946
- Chapter 9 Resource Book: Practice levels A, B, C, pp. 74–76

Practice Worksheet

An easily-readable reduced practice page (with answers) for this lesson can be found on p. 552C.

Avoiding Common Errors

Exercises 15–20 Some students confuse the patterns associated with $a^2 - b^2$ and $(a - b)^2$. Remind students to watch for this error. Sometimes it helps students to say the pattern aloud, listening for the difference between "the difference of two squares" and "the square of a difference."

Study Strategy

Exercises 23–24 Recommend that students eliminate answer choices before factoring the polynomials. Tell them that using elimination not only helps them in choosing the correct answer choice, but also helps them become better at recognizing patterns.

Teaching Strategy

Exercise 49 It may help some students to graph the equation so they can better explain the number of times the ball reaches a height of 54 feet. You may also want to ask students the number of times the ball reaches a height of 53 feet.

49. Once; the ball's height (in feet) is modeled by the equation $h = -16t^2 + 56t + 5$, where t is the time (in seconds) since it was thrown. To find when the height is 54 feet, substitute 54 for h and solve the equation $54 = -16t^2 + 56t + 5$, or $16t^2 - 56t + 49 = 0$. Because the left side of the equation factors as a perfect square trinomial, $(4t - 7)^2$, the equation has only one solution, $\frac{7}{4}$ or 1.75; so, the ball reaches a height of 54 feet only once, 1.75 seconds after being thrown.

50a.

x (feet)	y (feet)
0	0
2	5
5	8.75
8	8
11	2.75

C **CHALLENGE** **Determine the value(s) of k for which the expression is a perfect square trinomial.**

40. $x^2 + kx + 36$ ± 12

41. $4x^2 + kx + 9$ ± 12

42. $16x^2 + kx + 4$ ± 16

43. $25x^2 + 10x + k$ 1

44. $49x^2 - 84x + k$ 36

45. $4x^2 - 48x + k$ 144

PROBLEM SOLVING

EXAMPLE 6 on p. 602 for Exs. 46–48

A **46. FALLING BRUSH** While standing on a ladder, you drop a paintbrush from a height of 25 feet. After how many seconds does the paintbrush land on the ground? 1.25 sec

@HomeTutor for problem solving help at classzone.com

47. FALLING OBJECT A hickory nut falls from a branch that is 100 feet above the ground. After how many seconds does the hickory nut land on the ground? 2.5 sec

@HomeTutor for problem solving help at classzone.com

48. GRASSHOPPER A grasshopper jumps straight up from the ground with an initial vertical velocity of 8 feet per second.

a. Write an equation that gives the height (in feet) of the grasshopper as a function of the time (in seconds) since it leaves the ground. $h = -16t^2 + 8t$

b. After how many seconds is the grasshopper 1 foot off the ground? 0.25 sec

49. ★ **SHORT RESPONSE** A ball is thrown up into the air from a height of 5 feet with an initial vertical velocity of 56 feet per second. How many times does the ball reach a height of 54 feet? *Explain* your answer. See margin.

B **50.** ★ **EXTENDED RESPONSE** An arch of balloons decorates the stage at a high school graduation. The balloons are tied to a frame. The shape of the frame can be modeled by the graph of the equation $y = -\frac{1}{4}x^2 + 3x$ where x and y are measured in feet.

a. Make a table of values that shows the height of the balloon arch for $x = 0, 2, 5, 8$, and 11 feet. See margin.

b. For what additional values of x does the equation make sense? *Explain.* See margin.

c. At approximately what distance from the left end does the arch reach a height of 9 feet? Check your answer algebraically. 6 ft

○ = WORKED-OUT SOLUTIONS on p. WS1 ★ = STANDARDIZED TEST PRACTICE

50b. $0 \le x \le 12$; the table in part (a) shows the heights of the arch for various values of x from 0 to 11; to find the greatest x-value for which the equation gives a height that makes sense, find the other value of x for which the height is 0. Solve the equation $0 = -\frac{1}{4}x^2 + 3x$; the roots are 0 and 12, so the equation makes sense for $0 \le x \le 12$.

51. **FRAMING** A square mirror is framed with stained glass as shown. Each corner of the frame began as a square with a side length of d inches before it was cut to fit the mirror. The mirror has a side length of 3 inches. The area of the stained glass frame is 91 square inches.

a. Write a polynomial that represents the area of the stained glass frame. $4d^2 - 9$

b. What is the side length of the frame? 10 in.

C 52. **CHALLENGE** You have 120 folding chairs to set up in a park for an outdoor play. You want each row to have an odd number of chairs. You also want each row after the first to have 2 more chairs than the row in front of it. The first row will have 15 chairs.

a. Copy and complete the table below.

n	nth odd integer	Sum of first n odd integers	Sum as a power
1	1	1	1^2
2	3	$1 + 3 = 4$	2^2
3	5	$1 + 3 + 5 = 9$	? 3^2
4	7	? $1 + 3 + 5 + 7 = 16$	? 4^2
5	9	? $1 + 3 + 5 + 7 + 9 = 25$	? 5^2

b. *Describe* the relationship between n and the sum of the first n odd integers. Then find the sum of the first 10 odd integers. The sum of the first n odd integers is n^2; 100.

c. *Explain* how to find the sum of the odd integers from 11 to 21. See margin.

d. How many rows of chairs will you need for the outdoor play? *Explain* your thinking. See margin.

ILLINOIS MIXED REVIEW

TEST PRACTICE at classzone.com

53. $\triangle ABC \sim \triangle DEF$. What scale factor was used to transform $\triangle ABC$ to $\triangle DEF$? B

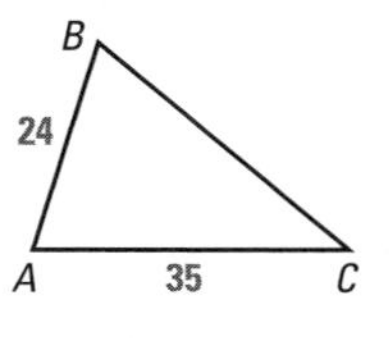

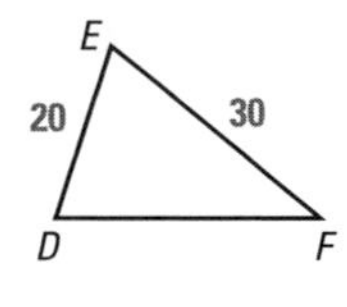

Ⓐ $\frac{4}{5}$ Ⓑ $\frac{5}{6}$ Ⓒ $\frac{6}{5}$ Ⓓ $\frac{7}{4}$

54. A teacher gives a test to 24 students. The teacher wants to use the test scores to divide the students into two groups of approximately equal size. Which measure of the test scores would be most useful to the teacher? B

Ⓐ Mean Ⓑ Median Ⓒ Mode Ⓓ Range

5 ASSESS AND RETEACH

Daily Homework Quiz

Transparency Available

Factor the polynomial.

1. $4m^2 - n^2$ $(2m - n)(2m + n)$

2. $x^2 + 6x + 9$ $(x + 3)^2$

3. $4y^2 - 16y + 16$ $(2y - 4)^2$

4. Solve the equation $x^2 + x + \frac{1}{4} = 0$. $-\frac{1}{2}$

5. An apple falls from a branch 9 feet above the ground. After how many seconds does the apple hit the ground? 0.75 sec

Online Quiz

Available at **classzone.com**

Diagnosis/Remediation

- Practice A, B, C in Chapter 9 Resource Book, pp. 74–76
- Study Guide in Chapter 9 Resource Book, pp. 77–78
- Practice Workbook, pp. 145–146
- @HomeTutor

Challenge

Additional challenge is available in the Chapter 9 Resource Book, p. 81.

52c. The nth odd integer is in the form $2n - 1$, so 11 is the sixth odd integer and 21 is the eleventh odd integer. To find the sum of the odd integers from 11 to 21, find the sum of the first 11 odd integers ($11^2 = 121$) and subtract the sum of the first 5 odd integers ($5^2 = 25$) to get $121 - 25 = 96$.

52d. See Additional Answers beginning on p. AA1.

1 PLAN AND PREPARE

Warm-Up Exercises

Transparency Available

1. Solve $2x^2 + 11x = 21$. $\frac{3}{2}, -7$
2. Factor $4x^2 + 10x + 4$. $2(x + 2)(2x + 1)$
3. A replacement piece of sod for a lawn has an area of 112 square inches. The width is w and the length is $2w - 2$. What are the dimensions of the sod? width: 8 in., length: 14 in.

Notetaking Guide

Transparency Available

Promotes interactive learning and notetaking skills, pp. 214–218.

Pacing

Basic: 2 days
Average: 2 days
Advanced: 2 days
Block: 1 block
• See *Teaching Guide/Lesson Plan.*

2 FOCUS AND MOTIVATE

Essential Question

Big Idea 3, p. 553

How do you factor polynomials completely? Tell students they will learn how to answer this question by grouping terms and factoring out binomials.

9.8 Factor Polynomials Completely

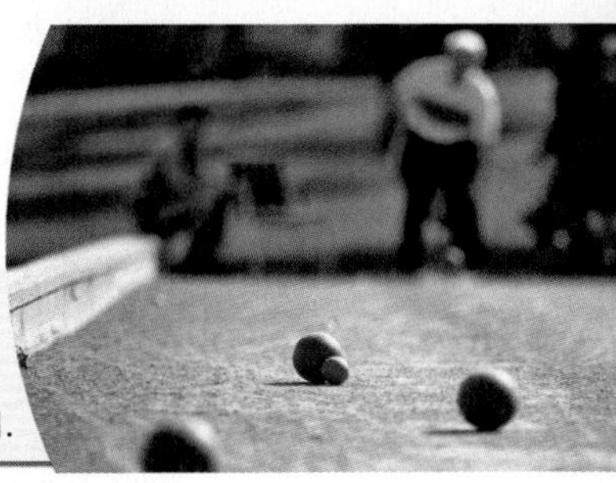

8.11.01 Simplify or identify equivalent algebraic expressions (e.g., exponential, rational, logarithmic, factored, polynomial).

Before You factored polynomials.
Now You will factor polynomials completely.
Why? So you can model the height of a projectile, as in Ex. 71.

Key Vocabulary
• factor by grouping
• factor completely

You have used the distributive property to factor a greatest common monomial from a polynomial. Sometimes, you can factor out a common binomial.

EXAMPLE 1 Factor out a common binomial

Factor the expression.

a. $2x(x + 4) - 3(x + 4)$ **b.** $3y^2(y - 2) + 5(2 - y)$

Solution

a. $2x(x + 4) - 3(x + 4) = (x + 4)(2x - 3)$

b. The binomials $y - 2$ and $2 - y$ are opposites. Factor -1 from $2 - y$ to obtain a common binomial factor.

$3y^2(y - 2) + 5(2 - y) = 3y^2(y - 2) - 5(y - 2)$ Factor -1 from $(2 - y)$.
$= (y - 2)(3y^2 - 5)$ Distributive property

GROUPING You may be able to use the distributive property to factor polynomials with four terms. Factor a common monomial from pairs of terms, then look for a common binomial factor. This is called **factor by grouping**.

EXAMPLE 2 Factor by grouping

Factor the polynomial.

a. $x^3 + 3x^2 + 5x + 15$ **b.** $y^2 + y + yx + x$

Solution

a. $x^3 + 3x^2 + 5x + 15 = (x^3 + 3x^2) + (5x + 15)$ Group terms.
$= x^2(x + 3) + 5(x + 3)$ Factor each group.
$= (x + 3)(x^2 + 5)$ Distributive property

b. $y^2 + y + yx + x = (y^2 + y) + (yx + x)$ Group terms.
$= y(y + 1) + x(y + 1)$ Factor each group.
$= (y + 1)(y + x)$ Distributive property

CHECK WORK
Remember that you can check a factorization by multiplying the factors.

Resource Planning Guide

Chapter Resource Book
• Teaching Guide/Lesson Plan (pp. 82–83)
• Practice levels A, B, C (pp. 84–86)
• Study Guide (pp. 87–88)
• Catch-up for Absent Students (p. 89)
• Problem Solving Workshop (p. 90)
• Challenge (p. 91)

Workbooks
• Notetaking Guide (pp. 214–218)
• Practice Workbook (pp. 147–148)

Teaching Options
• **Power Presentations CD-ROM** provides dynamic electronic teaching resources for the classroom.
• **Activity Generator CD-ROM** provides editable activities for all ability levels.

Interactive Technology
• Easy Planner
• Power Presentations CD-ROM
• Activity Generator CD-ROM
• Animated Algebra
• Test Generator CD-ROM
• Online Quiz
• eWorkbook
• eEdition
• @HomeTutor

Resources for English Learners
• Quick Reference for English Learners
• Spanish Study Guide
• Multi-Language Visual Glossary
• Student Resources in Spanish

See also the *Algebra 1 Toolkit* for more strategies for meeting individual needs.

EXAMPLE 3 Factor by grouping

Factor $x^3 - 6 + 2x - 3x^2$.

Solution

The terms x^3 and -6 have no common factor. Use the commutative property to rearrange the terms so that you can group terms with a common factor.

$x^3 - 6 + 2x - 3x^2 = x^3 - 3x^2 + 2x - 6$	**Rearrange terms.**
$= (x^3 - 3x^2) + (2x - 6)$	**Group terms.**
$= x^2(x - 3) + 2(x - 3)$	**Factor each group.**
$= (x - 3)(x^2 + 2)$	**Distributive property**

CHECK Check your factorization using a graphing calculator. Graph $y_1 = x^3 - 6 + 2x - 3x^2$ and $y_2 = (x - 3)(x^2 + 2)$. Because the graphs coincide, you know that your factorization is correct.

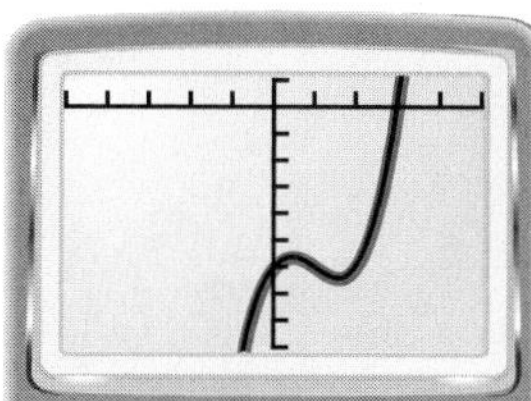

✓ GUIDED PRACTICE for Examples 1, 2, and 3

Factor the expression.

1. $x(x - 2) + (x - 2)$ $(x - 2)(x + 1)$
2. $a^3 + 3a^2 + a + 3$ $(a + 3)(a^2 + 1)$
3. $y^2 + 2x + yx + 2y$ $(y + 2)(y + x)$

READING If a polynomial has two or more terms and is unfactorable, it is called a *prime polynomial.*

FACTORING COMPLETELY You have seen that the polynomial $x^2 - 1$ can be factored as $(x + 1)(x - 1)$. This polynomial is factorable. Notice that the polynomial $x^2 + 1$ cannot be written as the product of polynomials with integer coefficients. This polynomial is unfactorable. A factorable polynomial with integer coefficients is **factored completely** if it is written as a product of unfactorable polynomials with integer coefficients.

CONCEPT SUMMARY *For Your Notebook*

Guidelines for Factoring Polynomials Completely

To factor a polynomial completely, you should try each of these steps.

1. Factor out the greatest common monomial factor. *(Lesson 9.4)*	$3x^2 + 6x = 3x(x + 2)$
2. Look for a difference of two squares or a perfect square trinomial. *(Lesson 9.7)*	$x^2 + 4x + 4 = (x + 2)^2$
3. Factor a trinomial of the form $ax^2 + bx + c$ into a product of binomial factors. *(Lessons 9.5 and 9.6)*	$3x^2 - 5x - 2 = (3x + 1)(x - 2)$
4. Factor a polynomial with four terms by grouping. *(Lesson 9.8)*	$x^3 + x - 4x^2 - 4 = (x^2 + 1)(x - 4)$

Differentiated Instruction

Visual Learners Some students may see that the grouping method is not unique. Show the following for **Example 3**.

$$x^3 - 6 + 2x - 3x^2 = x^3 + 2x - 6 - 3x^2$$
$$= (x^3 + 2x) - (6 + 3x^2)$$
$$= x(x^2 + 2) - 3(2 + x^2)$$
$$= x(x^2 + 2) - 3(x^2 + 2)$$
$$= (x - 3)(x^2 + 2)$$

See also the *Algebra 1 Toolkit* for more strategies.

Motivating the Lesson

Food packagers often know what the volume of a package must be and have to decide what the package's dimensions can be. If they know how the dimensions are related, they can use factoring to find the dimensions.

3 TEACH

Extra Example 1

Factor the expression.

a. $4x(x - 3) + 5(x - 3)$ $(x - 3)(4x + 5)$

b. $2y^2(y - 5) - 3(5 - y)$ $(y - 5)(2y^2 + 3)$

Key Questions to Ask for Example 1

- In part (b), why is one of the factors $3y^2 - 5$ instead of $3y^2 + 5$? **When you factor out −1 to obtain the common binomial factor $y - 2$, you are left with the factor $-1 \cdot 5$, or -5.**
- In part (b), if the binomials were $(y + 2)(2 + y)$, how would you obtain a common binomial? **Use the commutative property to change $2 + y$ to $y + 2$.**

Extra Example 2

Factor the polynomial.

a. $x^3 + 2x^2 + 8x + 16$ $(x + 2)(x^2 + 8)$

b. $r^2 + 4r + rs + 4s$ $(r + 4)(r + s)$

Extra Example 3

Factor $x^3 - 10 - 5x + 2x^2$.

$(x + 2)(x^2 - 5)$

Extra Example 4

Factor the polynomial completely.

a. $x^2 - 4x - 3$ cannot be factored

b. $3x^3 - 21x^2 - 54x$
$3x(x + 2)(x - 9)$

c. $8d^3 + 24d$ $8d(d^2 + 3)$

Key Question to Ask for Example 4

- How do you determine if a polynomial is not factorable? If the terms have no common factors, if it does not follow one of the factor patterns, and if none of the possible factors gives the middle term of the original trinomial, then it is not factorable.

Extra Example 5

Solve $2x^3 - 18x^2 = -36x$. 0, 3, 6

Key Question to Ask for Example 5

- Could the equation have more than 3 solutions? Explain. No; a 3rd degree equation can have at most 3 factors and thus at most 3 solutions.

EXAMPLE 4 Factor completely

Factor the polynomial completely.

a. $n^2 + 2n - 1$ **b.** $4x^3 - 44x^2 + 96x$ **c.** $50h^4 - 2h^2$

Solution

a. The terms of the polynomial have no common monomial factor. Also, there are no factors of -1 that have a sum of 2. This polynomial cannot be factored.

b. $4x^3 - 44x^2 + 96x = 4x(x^2 - 11x + 24)$ **Factor out 4x.**

$= 4x(x - 3)(x - 8)$ **Find two negative factors of 24 that have a sum of −11.**

c. $50h^4 - 2h^2 = 2h^2(25h^2 - 1)$ **Factor out $2h^2$.**

$= 2h^2(5h - 1)(5h + 1)$ **Difference of two squares pattern**

✓ **GUIDED PRACTICE** for Example 4

Factor the polynomial completely.

4. $3x^3 - 12x$ $3x(x - 2)(x + 2)$ **5.** $2y^3 - 12y^2 + 18y$ $2y(y - 3)^2$ **6.** $m^3 - 2m^2 - 8m$ $m(m - 4)(m + 2)$

EXAMPLE 5 Solve a polynomial equation

Solve $3x^3 + 18x^2 = -24x$.

$3x^3 + 18x^2 = -24x$ **Write original equation.**

$3x^3 + 18x^2 + 24x = 0$ **Add 24x to each side.**

$3x(x^2 + 6x + 8) = 0$ **Factor out 3x.**

$3x(x + 2)(x + 4) = 0$ **Factor trinomial.**

$3x = 0$ *or* $x + 2 = 0$ *or* $x + 4 = 0$ **Zero-product property**

$x = 0$ $x = -2$ $x = -4$ **Solve for x.**

▶ The solutions of the equation are 0, −2, and −4.

CHECK Check each solution by substituting it for x in the equation. One check is shown here.

$3(-2)^3 + 18(-2)^2 \stackrel{?}{=} -24(-2)$

$-24 + 72 \stackrel{?}{=} 48$

$48 = 48$ ✓

GUIDED PRACTICE for Example 5

Solve the equation.

7. $w^3 - 8w^2 + 16w = 0$ 0, 4 **8.** $x^3 - 25x = 0$ 0, ±5 **9.** $c^3 - 7c^2 + 12c = 0$ 0, 3, 4

EXAMPLE 6 Solve a multi-step problem

TERRARIUM A terrarium in the shape of a rectangular prism has a volume of 4608 cubic inches. Its length is more than 10 inches. The dimensions of the terrarium are shown. Find the length, width, and height of the terrarium.

Solution

STEP 1 **Write** a verbal model. Then write an equation.

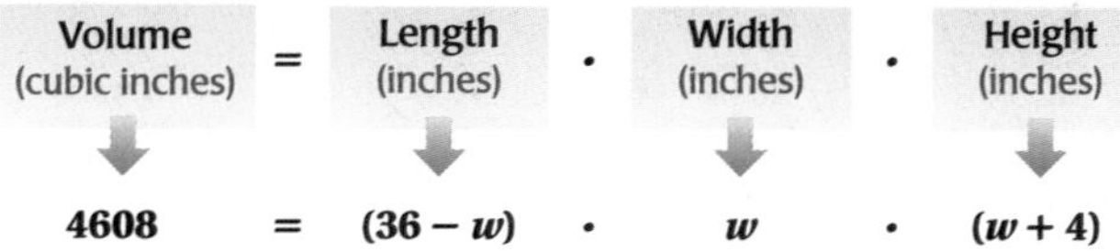

Volume (cubic inches) = Length (inches) · Width (inches) · Height (inches)

$$4608 = (36 - w) \cdot w \cdot (w + 4)$$

STEP 2 **Solve** the equation for w.

$4608 = (36 - w)(w)(w + 4)$ — Write equation.

$0 = 32w^2 + 144w - w^3 - 4608$ — Multiply. Subtract 4608 from each side.

$0 = (-w^3 + 32w^2) + (144w - 4608)$ — Group terms.

$0 = -w^2(w - 32) + 144(w - 32)$ — Factor each group.

$0 = (w - 32)(-w^2 + 144)$ — Distributive property

$0 = -1(w - 32)(w^2 - 144)$ — Factor -1 from $-w^2 + 144$.

$0 = -1(w - 32)(w - 12)(w + 12)$ — Difference of two squares pattern

$w - 32 = 0$ *or* $w - 12 = 0$ *or* $w + 12 = 0$ — Zero-product property

$w = 32 \quad w = 12 \quad w = -12$ — Solve for w.

STEP 3 **Choose** the solution of the equation that is the correct value of w. Disregard $w = -12$, because the width cannot be negative.

You know that the length is more than 10 inches. Test the solutions 12 and 32 in the expression for the length.

Length $= 36 - 12 = 24$ ✓ *or* Length $= 36 - 32 = 4$ ✗

The solution 12 gives a length of 24 inches, so 12 is the correct value of w.

STEP 4 **Find** the height.

Height $= w + 4 = 12 + 4 = 16$

▶ The width is 12 inches, the length is 24 inches, and the height is 16 inches.

✓ **GUIDED PRACTICE** for Example 6

10. 3 ft long by 2 ft wide by 12 ft high

10. **DIMENSIONS OF A BOX** A box in the shape of a rectangular prism has a volume of 72 cubic feet. The box has a length of x feet, a width of $(x - 1)$ feet, and a height of $(x + 9)$ feet. Find the dimensions of the box.

Extra Example 6

A kitchen drawer has a volume of 768 cubic inches. The dimensions of the drawer are shown. Find the length, width, and height of the drawer. width: 12 in., length: 16 in., height: 4 in.

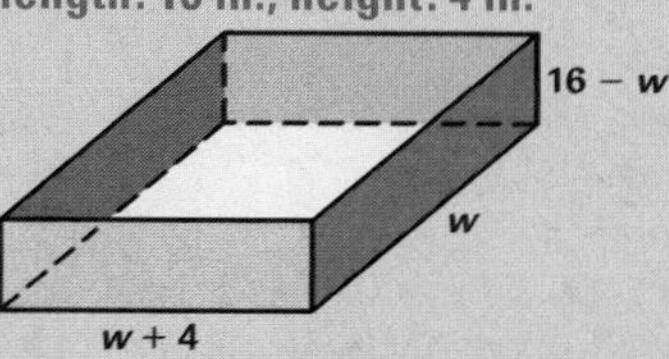

Key Question to Ask for Example 6

- How do you get $32w^2 + 144w - w^3 - 4608$ in Step 2? Multiply $(36 - w)$, w, and $(w + 4)$, and subtract 4608.

Closing the Lesson

Have students summarize the major points of the lesson and answer the Essential Question: How do you factor polynomials completely?

- Factor a polynomial completely by writing it as a monomial or the product of a monomial and one or more prime polynomials.
- A polynomial is unfactorable if you cannot write it as the product of polynomials of lesser degrees.

Before trying to factor a polynomial, look for a greatest common monomial and common binomials and factor them out. If a trinomial is in the form of $ax^2 + bx + c$, look for binomial factors. If a polynomial has four terms, factor by grouping the terms. Look for a difference of two squares pattern or a perfect square trinomial pattern.

4 PRACTICE AND APPLY

Assignment Guide

Answer Transparencies available for all exercises

Basic:
Day 1: SRH p. 928 Exs. 1, 2, 4, 6, 10
pp. 610–613
Exs. 1–22, 87–89
Day 2: pp. 610–613
Exs. 23–41 odd, 42–50, 68–72, 76–86 even

Average:
Day 1: pp. 610–613
Exs. 1–12, 14–22 even, 61–66, 87–89
Day 2: pp. 610–613
Exs. 32–60, 68–73, 76, 80, 84

Advanced:
Day 1: pp. 610–613
Exs. 1, 6–12, 16–21, 61–67*, 87–89
Day 2: pp. 610–613
Exs. 34–42, 48–60, 68–74*, 78, 82, 86

Block:
pp. 610–613
Exs. 1–12, 14–22 even, 32–66, 68–73, 76, 80, 84, 87–89

Differentiated Instruction

See *Algebra 1 Best Practices Toolkit* for suggestions on addressing the needs of a diverse classroom.

Homework Check

For a quick check of student understanding of key concepts, go over the following exercises:

Basic: 6, 15, 29, 44, 68
Average: 8, 18, 34, 50, 69
Advanced: 10, 20, 37, 53, 70

Extra Practice

- Student Edition, p. 946
- Chapter 9 Resource Book: Practice levels A, B, C, pp. 84–86

Practice Worksheet

An easily-readable reduced practice page (with answers) for this lesson can be found on p. 552C.

9.8 EXERCISES

HOMEWORK KEY
○ = WORKED-OUT SOLUTIONS on p. WS23 for Exs. 13, 23, and 71
★ = STANDARDIZED TEST PRACTICE Exs. 2, 12, 41, 55, 71, and 73

SKILL PRACTICE

A

1. **VOCABULARY** What does it mean for a polynomial to be factored completely? The polynomial is written as a monomial or as a product of a monomial and one or more prime polynomials.

2. ★ **WRITING** *Explain* how you know if a polynomial is unfactorable. See margin.

EXAMPLE 1 on p. 606 for Exs. 3–12

BINOMIAL FACTORS **Factor the expression.**

3. $x(x-8)+(x-8)$ $(x-8)(x+1)$
4. $5y(y+3)-2(y+3)$ $(y+3)(5y-2)$
5. $6z(z-4)-7(z-4)$ $(z-4)(6z-7)$
6. $10(a-6)-3a(a-6)$ $(a-6)(10-3a)$
7. $b^2(b+5)-3(b+5)$ $(b+5)(b^2-3)$
8. $7c^2(c+9)+2(c+9)$ $(c+9)(7c^2+2)$
9. $x(13+x)-(x+13)$ $(x+13)(x-1)$
10. $y^2(y-4)+5(4-y)$ $(y-4)(y^2-5)$
11. $12(z-1)-5z^2(1-z)$ $(z-1)(12+5z^2)$

12. ★ **MULTIPLE CHOICE** Which is the correct factorization of $x^2(x-8)+5(8-x)$? C

Ⓐ $(x^2+5)(x-8)$ Ⓑ $(x^2+5)(8-x)$
Ⓒ $(x^2-5)(x-8)$ Ⓓ $(x^2-5)(8-x)$

EXAMPLES 2 and 3 on pp. 606–607 for Exs. 13–22

FACTORING BY GROUPING **Factor the polynomial.** 13–21. See margin.

13. x^3+x^2+2x+2
14. y^3-9y^2+y-9
15. $z^3-4z^2+3z-12$
16. $c^3+7c^2+5c+35$
17. $a^3+13a^2-5a-65$
18. $2s^3-3s^2+18s-27$
19. $5n^3-4n^2+25n-20$
20. $x^2+8x-xy-8y$
21. $y^2+y+5xy+5x$

22. **ERROR ANALYSIS** *Describe* and correct the error in factoring. See margin.

$$a^3+8a^2-6a-48=a^2(a+8)+6(a+8)$$
$$=(a+8)(a^2+6)$$

EXAMPLE 4 on p. 608 for Exs. 23–42

FACTORING COMPLETELY **Factor the polynomial completely.**

23. x^4-x^2 $x^2(x-1)(x+1)$
24. $36a^4-4a^2$ $4a^2(3a-1)(3a+1)$
25. $3n^5-48n^3$ $3n^3(n-4)(n+4)$
26. $4y^6-16y^4$ $4y^4(y-2)(y+2)$
27. $75c^9-3c^7$ $3c^7(5c-1)(5c+1)$
28. $72p-2p^3$ $2p(6-p)(6+p)$
29. $32s^4-8s^2$ $8s^2(2s-1)(2s+1)$
30. $80z^8-45z^6$ $5z^6(4z-3)(4z+3)$
31. $m^2-5m-35$ cannot be factored
32. $6g^3-24g^2+24g$ $6g(g-2)^2$
33. $3w^4+24w^3+48w^2$ $3w^2(w+4)^2$
34. $3r^5+3r^4-90r^3$ $3r^3(r+6)(r-5)$
35. $b^3-5b^2-4b+20$ $(b-5)(b-2)(b+2)$
36. $h^3+4h^2-25h-100$ $(h+4)(h-5)(h+5)$
37. $9t^3+18t-t^2-2$ $(9t-1)(t^2+2)$
38. $2x^5y-162x^3y$ $2x^3y(x-9)(x+9)$
39. $7a^3b^3-63ab^3$ $7ab^3(a-3)(a+3)$
40. $-4s^3t^3+24s^2t^2-36st$ $-4st(st-3)^2$

41. ★ **MULTIPLE CHOICE** What is the completely factored form of $3x^6-75x^4$? D

Ⓐ $3x^4(x^2-25)$ Ⓑ $3x^4(x-5)^2$ Ⓒ $3x^4(x+5)^2$ Ⓓ $3x^4(x-5)(x+5)$

B

42. **ERROR ANALYSIS** *Describe* and correct the error in factoring the polynomial completely.

$$x^3-6x^2-9x+54=x^2(x-6)-9(x-6)$$
$$=(x-6)(x^2-9)$$

42. The factorization is correct, but the polynomial has not been factored completely. The binomial factor (x^2-9) can be factored using the difference of two squares pattern; $(x-6)(x-3)(x+3)$.

2. A polynomial with integer coefficients is not factorable if it cannot be written as the product of polynomials of lesser degree using only integer coefficients and constants, and if the only common factors of its terms are 1 and −1.
13. $(x+1)(x^2+2)$
14. $(y-9)(y^2+1)$
15. $(z-4)(z^2+3)$
16. $(c+7)(c^2+5)$
17. $(a+13)(a^2-5)$
18. $(2s-3)(s^2+9)$
19. $(5n-4)(n^2+5)$
20. $(x+8)(x-y)$
21. $(y+1)(y+5x)$
22. −6, not +6, was the common monomial factored out of the third and fourth terms of the polynomial, so the sign between the two groups of factors should be − not +; $(a+8)(a^2-6)$.

EXAMPLE 5 on p. 608 for Exs. 43–54

45. $\frac{7}{4}, \pm 2$

SOLVING EQUATIONS **Solve the equation.**

43. $x^3 + x^2 - 4x - 4 = 0$ $-1, \pm 2$

44. $a^3 - 11a^2 - 9a + 99 = 0$ $11, \pm 3$

45. $4y^3 - 7y^2 - 16y + 28 = 0$

46. $5n^3 - 30n^2 + 40n = 0$ $0, 2, 4$

47. $3b^3 + 24b^2 + 45b = 0$ $0, -5, -3$

48. $2t^5 + 2t^4 - 144t^3 = 0$ $0, -9, 8$

49. $z^3 - 81z = 0$ $0, \pm 9$

50. $c^4 - 100c^2 = 0$ $0, \pm 10$

51. $12s - 3s^3 = 0$ $0, \pm 2$

52. $2x^3 - 10x^2 + 40 = 8x$ $5, \pm 2$

53. $3p + 1 = p^2 + 3p^3$ $-\frac{1}{3}, \pm 1$

54. $m^3 - 3m^2 = 4m - 12$ $3, \pm 2$

55. ★ **WRITING** Is it possible to find three solutions of the equation $x^3 + 2x^2 + 3x + 6 = 0$? *Explain* why or why not. See margin.

GEOMETRY **Find the length, width, and height of the rectangular prism with the given volume.**

56. Volume = 12 cubic inches 6 in., 1 in., 2 in.

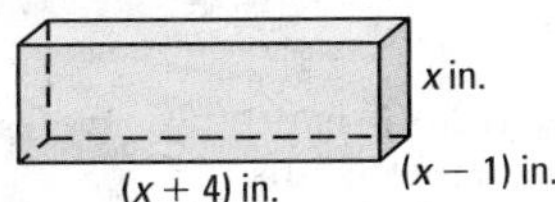

57. Volume = 96 cubic feet 12 ft, 4 ft, 2 ft

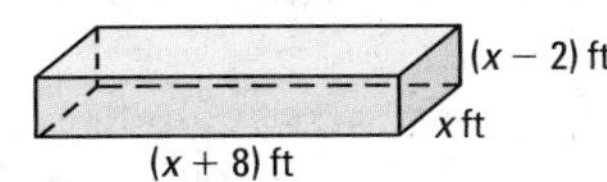

FACTORING COMPLETELY **Factor the polynomial completely.**

58. $x^3 + 2x^2y - x - 2y$ $(x + 2y)(x - 1)(x + 1)$

59. $8b^3 - 4b^2a - 18b + 9a$ $(2b - a)(2b - 3)(2b + 3)$

60. $4s^2 - s + 12st - 3t$ $(4s - 1)(s + 3t)$

FACTOR BY GROUPING **In Exercises 61–66, use the example below to factor the trinomial by grouping.**

EXAMPLE **Factor a trinomial by grouping**

Factor $8x^2 + 10x - 3$ by grouping.

Solution

Notice that the polynomial is in the form $ax^2 + bx + c$.

STEP 1 **Write** the product ac as the product of two factors that have a sum of b. In this case, the product ac is $8(-3) = -24$. Find two factors of -24 that have a sum of 10.

$-24 = 12 \cdot (-2)$ and $12 + (-2) = 10$

STEP 2 **Rewrite** the middle term as two terms with coefficients 12 and -2.

$8x^2 + 10x - 3 = 8x^2 + 12x - 2x - 3$

STEP 3 **Factor** by grouping.

$8x^2 + 12x - 2x - 3 = (8x^2 + 12x) + (-2x - 3)$ **Group terms.**

$= 4x(2x + 3) - (2x + 3)$ **Factor each group.**

$= (2x + 3)(4x - 1)$ **Distributive property**

61. $6x^2 + 5x - 4$ $(3x + 4)(2x - 1)$

62. $10s^2 + 19s + 6$ $(2s + 3)(5s + 2)$

63. $12n^2 - 13n + 3$ $(4n - 3)(3n - 1)$

64. $16a^2 + 14a + 3$ $(8a + 3)(2a + 1)$

65. $21w^2 + 8w - 4$ $(3w + 2)(7w - 2)$

66. $15y^2 - 31y + 10$ $(3y - 5)(5y - 2)$

C **67.** **CHALLENGE** Use factoring by grouping to show that a trinomial of the form $a^2 + 2ab + b^2$ can be factored as $(a + b)^2$. *Justify* your steps. See margin.

Avoiding Common Errors

Exercises 10–11 Watch for students who identify and rewrite opposite binomial factors but who do not multiply the rest of the term by -1.

Exercises 43–54 Remind students that 3rd degree or higher degree polynomials may have 3 or more roots. Encourage students to examine their solutions to make sure they have not missed one of the solutions.

Study Strategy

Exercises 23–40 Students may find it easier to factor completely if they follow a systematic plan for factoring. Suggest that they develop a set of steps in which they look for common monomial factors, grouping, and so on. Suggest that they write the steps on notecards for reference.

55. No; when the polynomial is factored completely, the equation becomes $(x + 2)(x^2 + 3) = 0$. When the factor $x^2 + 3$ is set equal to zero, the resulting equation, $x^2 + 3 = 0$, or $x^2 = -3$, has no real number solutions because x^2 cannot be negative.

67. First, rewrite the middle term as $ab + ab$ and group the terms: $a^2 + 2ab + b^2 = (a^2 + ab) + (ab + b^2)$. Factor each group and then use the distributive property to factor out the common binomial: $(a^2 + ab) + (ab + b^2) = a(a + b) + b(a + b) = (a + b)(a + b) = (a + b)^2$.

Study Strategy

Exercises 69–70 You may want to point out that in Exercise 69, part (a) corresponds to Step 1 in Example 6 and that part (b) corresponds to Steps 2–4. Suggest that students write a stepped-out solution to Exercise 70 using Example 6 as a model.

Exercise 71 Additional information about the game of bocce can be found on the Bocce Standards Association's website at www.boccestandardsassociation.org

72b. 3 ft; to find how far the robot has traveled horizontally when it lands back on the ground, find the non-zero x-value that makes the height y equal to zero. Solve $0 = -10x^2 + 30x$; the roots are $x = 0$ feet (which is the starting point of the jump) and $x = 3$ feet (which is the ending point of the jump).

PROBLEM SOLVING

EXAMPLE 6 on p. 609 for Exs. 68–70

68. CYLINDRICAL VASE A vase in the shape of a cylinder has a height of 6 inches and a volume of 24π cubic inches. What is the radius of the vase? 2 in.

@HomeTutor for problem solving help at classzone.com

69b. 4 in. long by 4 in. wide by 8 in. high

69. CARPENTRY You are building a birdhouse that will have a volume of 128 cubic inches. The birdhouse will have the dimensions shown.

(w + 4) in.
w in.
4 in.

a. Write a polynomial that represents the volume of the birdhouse. $4w^2 + 16w$

b. What are the dimensions of the birdhouse?

@HomeTutor for problem solving help at classzone.com

70. BAG SIZE A gift bag is shaped like a rectangular prism and has a volume of 1152 cubic inches. The dimensions of the gift bag are shown. The height is greater than the width. What are the dimensions of the gift bag? 16 in. long by 6 in. wide by 12 in. high

71b. The zero $t \approx -0.2$ has no meaning because t, which represents time in seconds, cannot be negative in this situation. The zero $t = 1$ means that the ball hits the ground 1 second after you throw it.

71. ★ **SHORT RESPONSE** A pallino is the small target ball that is tossed in the air at the beginning of a game of bocce. The height h (in meters) of the pallino after you throw it can be modeled by $h = -4.9t^2 + 3.9t + 1$ where t is the time (in seconds) since you released it.

a. Find the zeros of the function. 1, about −0.2

b. Do the zeros of the function have any meaning in this situation? *Explain* your reasoning.

72. JUMPING ROBOT The path of a jumping robot can be modeled by the graph of the equation $y = -10x^2 + 30x$ where x and y are both measured in feet. On a coordinate plane, the ground is represented by the x-axis, and the robot's starting position is the origin.

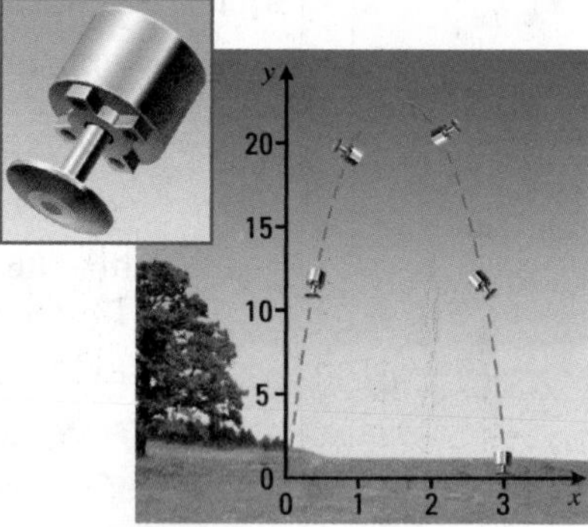

a. The robot's maximum height is 22.5 feet. What is the robot's horizontal distance from its starting point when its height is 22.5 feet? 1.5 ft

b. How far has the robot traveled horizontally when it lands on the ground? *Explain* your answer. See margin.

73. ★ **EXTENDED RESPONSE** The width of a box is 4 inches more than the height h. The length is the difference of 9 inches and the height.

a. Write a polynomial that represents the volume of the box. $-h^3 + 5h^2 + 36h$

b. The volume of the box is 180 cubic inches. What are all the possible dimensions of the box? 4 in. long by 9 in. wide by 5 in. high, 3 in. long by 10 in. wide by 6 in. high

c. Which dimensions result in a box with the smallest possible surface area? *Explain* your reasoning. 4 in. long by 9 in. wide by 5 in. high; the 4-inch long box has a surface area of 202 square inches and the 3-inch long box has a surface area of 216 square inches.

○ = WORKED-OUT SOLUTIONS on p. WS1 ★ = STANDARDIZED TEST PRACTICE

74. **CHALLENGE** A plastic cube is used to display an autographed baseball. The cube has an outer surface area of 54 square inches.

a. What is the length of an outer edge of the cube? 3 in.

b. What is the greatest volume the cube can possibly have? *Explain* why the actual volume inside of the cube may be less than the greatest possible volume. 27 in.^{3}; the thickness of the plastic used to make the sides of the box will make the edge length of the interior of the cube be less than 3 inches, so the volume of the interior will be less than 27 cubic inches.

ILLINOIS MIXED REVIEW

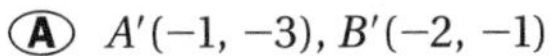

TEST PRACTICE at classzone.com

75. Which equation describes a line that has a y-intercept of -4 and a slope of 2? C

(A) $y = -4x + 2$ (B) $y = 2(x - 4)$ (C) $y = 2x - 4$ (D) $y = -4(x + 2)$

76. $\overline{AB}$ is shown in the coordinate plane. Find the coordinates of the endpoints of the image of $\overline{AB}$ reflected across the y-axis. D

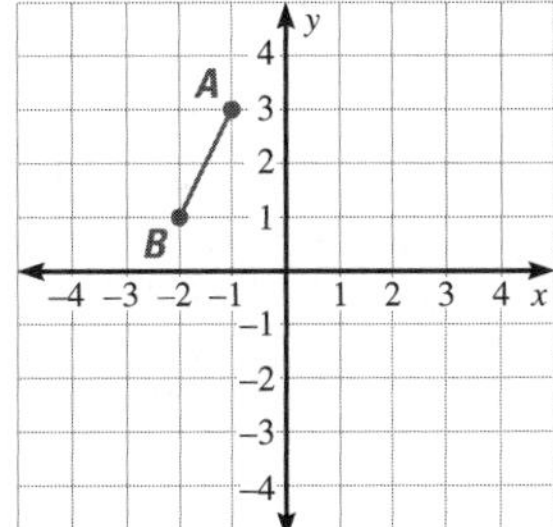

(A) $A'(-1, -3), B'(-2, -1)$

(B) $A'(-1, 3), B'(-2, 1)$

(C) $A'(1, -3), B'(2, -1)$

(D) $A'(1, 3), B'(2, 1)$

QUIZ for Lessons 9.7–9.8

Factor the polynomial. *(p. 600)*

1. $x^2 - 400$ $(x - 20)(x + 20)$
2. $18 - 32z^2$ $2(3 - 4z)(3 + 4z)$
3. $169x^2 - 25y^2$ $(13x - 5y)(13x + 5y)$
4. $n^2 - 6n + 9$ $(n - 3)^2$
5. $100a^2 + 20a + 1$ $(10a + 1)^2$
6. $8r^2 - 40rs + 50s^2$ $2(2r - 5s)^2$

Factor the polynomial completely. *(p. 606)*

7. $3x^5 - 75x^3$ $3x^3(x - 5)(x + 5)$
8. $72s^4 - 8s^2$ $8s^2(3s - 1)(3s + 1)$
9. $3x^4y - 300x^2y$ $3x^2y(x - 10)(x + 10)$
10. $a^3 - 4a^2 - 21a$ $a(a - 7)(a + 3)$
11. $2h^4 + 28h^3 + 98h^2$ $2h^2(h + 7)^2$
12. $z^3 - 4z^2 - 16z + 64$ $(z + 4)(z - 4)^2$

Solve the equation.

13. $x^2 + 10x + 25 = 0$ *(p. 600)* -5
14. $48 - 27m^2 = 0$ *(p. 600)* $\pm\frac{4}{3}$
15. $w^3 - w^2 - 4w + 4 = 0$ *(p. 606)* 1, ± 2
16. $4x^3 - 28x^2 + 40x = 0$ *(p. 606)* 0, 2, 5
17. $3x^5 - 6x^4 - 45x^3 = 0$ *(p. 606)* 0, -3, 5
18. $x^3 - 121x = 0$ *(p. 606)* 0, ± 11

19. **VOLUME** The cylinder shown has a volume of 72π cubic inches. *(p. 600)*

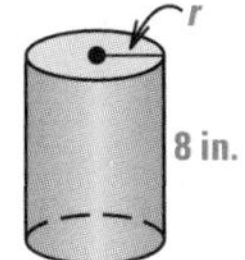

a. Write a polynomial that represents the volume of the cylinder. Leave your answer in terms of π. $8\pi r^2$

b. Find the radius of the cylinder. 3 in.

EXTRA PRACTICE for Lesson 9.8, p. 946

 **ONLINE QUIZ** at classzone.com

5 ASSESS AND RETEACH

Daily Homework Quiz

Transparency Available

Factor the polynomial completely.

1. $40b^5 - 5b^3$ $5b^3(8b^2 - 1)$
2. $x^3 + 6x^2 - 7x$ $x(x - 1)(x + 7)$
3. $y^3 + 6y^2 - y - 6$ $(y + 6)(y^2 - 1)$
4. Solve $2x^3 + 18x^2 = -40x$. $-5, -4, 0$
5. A sewing kit has a volume of 72 cubic inches. Its dimensions are w, $w + 1$, and $9 - w$ units. Find the dimensions of the kit. 8 in. by 9 in. by 1 in.

Online Quiz

Available at **classzone.com**

Diagnosis/Remediation

- Practice A, B, C in Chapter 9 Resource Book, pp. 84–86
- Study Guide in Chapter 9 Resource Book, pp. 87–88
- Practice Workbook, pp. 147–148
- @HomeTutor

Challenge

Additional challenge is available in the Chapter 9 Resource Book, p. 91.

Quiz

An easily-readable reduced copy of the quiz (with answers) on Lessons 9.7–9.8 from the Assessment Book can be found on p. 552E.

Illinois Mixed Review

1. C
2. F
3. B
4. F
5. B
6. H
7. B
8. H

Illinois Mixed Review

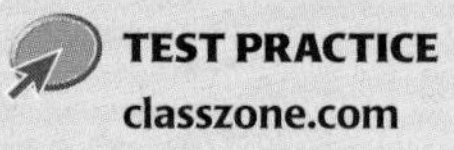

Lessons 9.5–9.8

1. **CLAY DIMENSIONS** A block of clay has the dimensions shown. The clay has a volume of 180 cubic inches. Find the length, width, and height of the block.

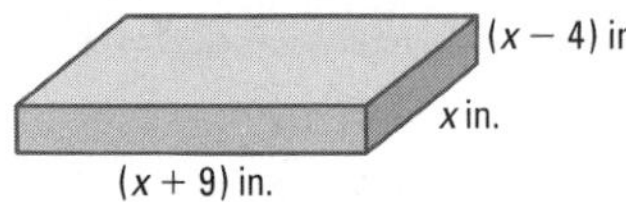

A. 10 in., 6 in., 3 in.

B. 12 in., 3 in., 5 in.

C. 15 in., 6 in., 2 in.

D. 16 in., 5 in., 2 in.

2. **BASEBALL** You hit a baseball straight up into the air. The baseball is hit with an initial vertical velocity of 88 feet per second when it is 3 feet off the ground. After how many seconds does the ball first reach a height of 99 feet?

F. 1.5 sec **H.** 4 sec

G. 3 sec **J.** 7 sec

3. **TILES** Each rectangular tile in a box of floor tiles has a width of x inches and is 2 inches longer than it is wide. Four of the tiles cover an area of 77 square inches. What are the dimensions of a tile?

A. 2 in. by 4 in. **C.** 4 in. by 6 in.

B. 3.5 in. by 5.5 in. **D.** 5.5 in. by 7.5 in.

4. **GARDENING** A square house has a lawn on two sides. Together, the house and lawn form a square with the dimensions shown. The lawn is being reseeded. The gardener determined that the lawn has an area of 900 square feet. Find the width of the lawn.

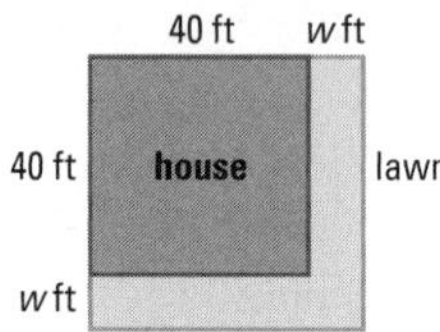

F. 10 ft **H.** 25 ft

G. 15 ft **J.** 90 ft

5. **TENNIS** A tennis player hits a ball with an initial vertical velocity of 63 feet per second from an initial height of 4 feet. After how many seconds does the tennis ball hit the ground?

A. 1 sec

B. 4 sec

C. 6 sec

D. 7 sec

6. **GAME BOARD** You are making a square game board. You cut the game board from a square piece of wood, as shown. The area of the game board is 100 square inches. What is the area of the original piece of wood?

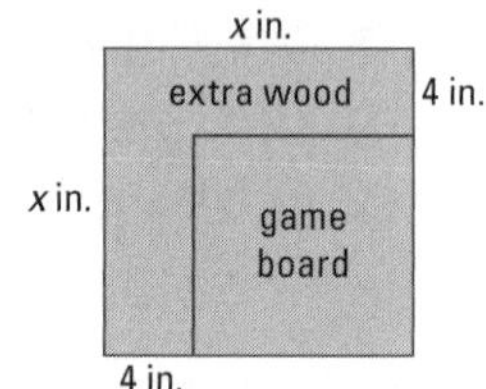

F. 116 in.^{2} **H.** 196 in.^{2}

G. 164 in.^{2} **J.** 224 in.^{2}

7. **BOX** A box is a rectangular prism having the dimensions shown.

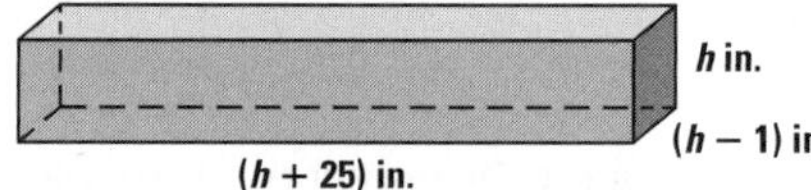

The box has a volume of 600 cubic inches. What is the area of the top of the box?

A. 20 in.^{2} **C.** 150 in.^{2}

B. 120 in.^{2} **D.** 240 in.^{2}

8. **DIMENSIONS** The floor of a rectangular room has an area of 204 square feet. The room is 5 feet longer than it is wide. What is the length (in feet) of the room?

F. 5 ft **H.** 17 ft

G. 12 ft **J.** 18 ft

9 CHAPTER SUMMARY

BIG IDEAS — For Your Notebook

Big Idea 1

Adding, Subtracting, and Multiplying Polynomials

You can perform operations with polynomials using the steps below.

Operation	Steps
Add	Group like terms and add.
Subtract	First, rewrite subtraction as addition. Second, group like terms and add.
Multiply	First, multiply terms using the distributive property. Second, combine like terms.

Big Idea 2

Factoring Polynomials

When factoring a polynomial, you should use the following checklist so that you can be sure you have factored the polynomial completely.

STEP 1 **Factor** out the greatest common monomial factor.

STEP 2 **Look** for special products to factor.

STEP 3 **Factor** a trinomial into a pair of binomials, if possible.

STEP 4 **Factor** a polynomial with four terms by grouping, if possible.

Big Idea 3

Writing and Solving Polynomial Equations to Solve Problems

You can write polynomials that model real-world situations in order to solve problems. For example, you can use the vertical motion model.

Height (in feet) of a projectile: $h = -16t^2 + vt + s$ where t is the time (in seconds) the object has been in the air, v is the initial vertical velocity (in feet per second), and s is the initial height (in feet).

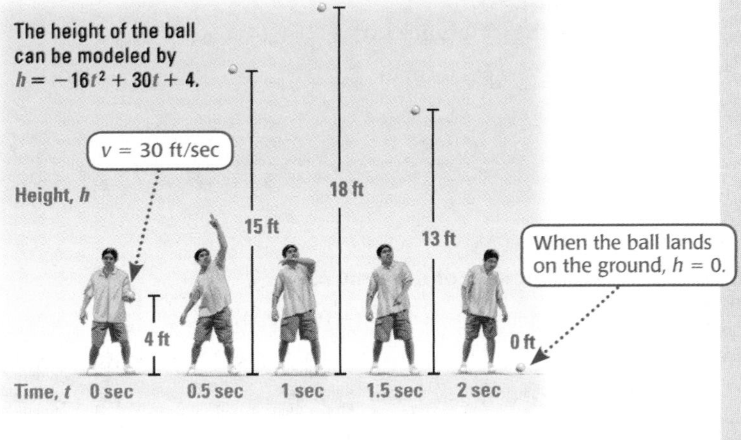

Additional Resources

The following resources are available to help review the materials in this chapter.

Chapter 9 Resource Book
- Chapter Review Games and Activities, p. 92
- Cumulative Practice, Chs. 1–9, pp. 95–96

Student Resources in Spanish

eWorkbook

@HomeTutor

Vocabulary Practice

Vocabulary practice is available at **classzone.com**

Extra Example 9.1

Find the sum
$(3x^3 - x^2 + 6) + (-x^3 + 3x^2 + x)$.
$2x^3 + 2x^2 + x + 6$

3. A factorable polynomial with integer coefficients is factored completely if it is written as a product of unfactorable polynomials with integer coefficients. *Sample answer:* $3x(x - 4)(2x + 1)$

9 CHAPTER REVIEW

@HomeTutor
classzone.com
- Multi-Language Glossary
- Vocabulary practice

REVIEW KEY VOCABULARY

- monomial, *p. 554*
- degree of a monomial, *p. 554*
- polynomial, *p. 554*
- degree of a polynomial, *p. 554*
- leading coefficient, *p. 554*
- binomial, *p. 555*
- trinomial, *p. 555*
- roots, *p. 575*
- vertical motion model, *p. 577*
- perfect square trinomial, *p. 601*
- factor by grouping, *p. 606*
- factor completely, *p. 607*

VOCABULARY EXERCISES

1. Copy and complete: The greatest degree of the terms in a polynomial is called the _?_. **degree of the polynomial**

2. **WRITING** Is $2x^{-1}$ a monomial? *Explain* why or why not.
No; a monomial cannot have a negative exponent.

3. **WRITING** What does it mean for a polynomial to be factored completely? Give an example of a polynomial that has been factored completely. **See margin.**

In Exercises 4–6, match the polynomial with its classification.

4. $5x - 22$ **B**
5. $-11x^3$ **A**
6. $x^2 + x + 1$ **C**

A. Monomial **B.** Binomial **C.** Trinomial

REVIEW EXAMPLES AND EXERCISES

Use the review examples and exercises below to check your understanding of the concepts you have learned in each lesson of Chapter 9.

9.1 Add and Subtract Polynomials *pp. 554–559*

EXAMPLE

Find the difference $(3x^2 + 2) - (4x^2 - x - 9)$.

Use a vertical format.

$$\begin{array}{r} 3x^2 \quad\quad + 2 \\ -\ (4x^2 - x - 9) \\ \hline \end{array} \quad\longrightarrow\quad \begin{array}{r} 3x^2 \quad\quad + 2 \\ +\ -4x^2 + x + 9 \\ \hline -x^2 + x + 11 \end{array}$$

EXERCISES

EXAMPLES 3 and 4 on pp. 555–556 for Exs. 7–12

Find the sum or difference.

7. $(9x + 6x^3 - 8x^2) + (-5x^3 + 6x)$ **$x^3 - 8x^2 + 15x$**
8. $(7a^3 - 4a^2 - 2a + 1) + (a^3 - 1)$ **$8a^3 - 4a^2 - 2a$**
9. $(11y^5 + 3y^2 - 4) + (y^2 - y + 1)$ **$11y^5 + 4y^2 - y - 3$**
10. $(3n^2 - 4n + 1) - (8n^2 - 4n + 17)$ **$-5n^2 - 16$**
11. $(2s^3 + 8) - (-3s^3 + 7s - 5)$ **$5s^3 - 7s + 13$**
12. $(-k^2 + 7k + 5) - (2k^4 - 3k^3 - 6)$ **$-2k^4 + 3k^3 - k^2 + 7k + 11$**

@HomeTutor
classzone.com
Chapter Review Practice

9.2 Multiply Polynomials

pp. 562–568

EXAMPLE

Find the product.

a. $(x^2 + 4x - 5)(2x - 1)$

b. $(5y + 6)(y - 3)$

Solution

a. Use a horizontal format.

$(x^2 + 4x - 5)(2x - 1)$ **Write product.**

$= x^2(2x - 1) + 4x(2x - 1) - 5(2x - 1)$ **Distributive property**

$= 2x^3 - x^2 + 8x^2 - 4x - 10x + 5$ **Distributive property**

$= 2x^3 + 7x^2 - 14x + 5$ **Combine like terms.**

b. Use a vertical format.

STEP 1 **Multiply** by −3.

$$\begin{array}{r} 5y + 6 \\ \times \quad y - 3 \\ \hline -15y - 18 \end{array}$$

STEP 2 **Multiply** by y.

$$\begin{array}{r} 5y + 6 \\ \times \quad y - 3 \\ \hline -15y - 18 \\ 5y^2 + 6y \quad \end{array}$$

STEP 3 **Add** products.

$$\begin{array}{r} 5y + 6 \\ \times \quad y - 3 \\ \hline -15y - 18 \\ 5y^2 + 6y \quad \\ \hline 5y^2 - 9y - 18 \end{array}$$

EXERCISES

EXAMPLES 1, 2, 3, and 4 on pp. 562–563 for Exs. 13–21

Find the product.

13. $(x^2 - 2x + 1)(x - 3)$ $x^3 - 5x^2 + 7x - 3$

14. $(y^2 + 5y + 4)(3y + 2)$ $3y^3 + 17y^2 + 22y + 8$

15. $(x - 4)(x + 2)$ $x^2 - 2x - 8$

16. $(5b^2 - b - 7)(b + 6)$ $5b^3 + 29b^2 - 13b - 42$

17. $(z + 8)(z - 11)$ $z^2 - 3z - 88$

18. $(2a - 1)(a - 3)$ $2a^2 - 7a + 3$

19. $(6n + 7)(3n + 1)$ $18n^2 + 27n + 7$

20. $(4n - 5)(7n - 3)$ $28n^2 - 47n + 15$

21. $(3x - 2)(x + 4)$ $3x^2 + 10x - 8$

9.3 Find Special Products of Polynomials

pp. 569–574

EXAMPLE

Find the product $(3x + 2)(3x - 2)$.

$(3x + 2)(3x - 2) = (3x)^2 - 2^2$ **Sum and difference pattern**

$= 9x^2 - 4$ **Simplify.**

EXERCISES

EXAMPLES 1 and 2 on pp. 569–570 for Exs. 22–27

Find the product.

22. $(x + 11)^2$ $x^2 + 22x + 121$

23. $(6y + 1)^2$ $36y^2 + 12y + 1$

24. $(2x - y)^2$ $4x^2 - 4xy + y^2$

25. $(4a - 3)^2$ $16a^2 - 24a + 9$

26. $(k + 7)(k - 7)$ $k^2 - 49$

27. $(3s + 5)(3s - 5)$ $9s^2 - 25$

Extra Example 9.2

Find the product.

a. $(5y + 4)(y - 2)$ $5y^2 - 6y - 8$

b. $(s^2 + 3s - 6)(4s - 2)$ $4s^3 + 10s^2 - 30s + 12$

Extra Example 9.3

Find the product $(4x + 3)^2$. $16x^2 + 24x + 9$

Extra Example 9.4

Solve $4x^2 = 18x$. $0, \frac{9}{2}$

Extra Example 9.5

Factor $x^2 - 3x - 54$.
$(x + 6)(x - 9)$

9 CHAPTER REVIEW

9.4 Solve Polynomial Equations in Factored Form

pp. 575–580

EXAMPLE

Solve $6x^2 + 42x = 0$.

$6x^2 + 42x = 0$	**Write original equation.**
$6x(x + 7) = 0$	**Factor left side.**
$6x = 0$ *or* $x + 7 = 0$	**Zero-product property**
$x = 0$ *or* $x = -7$	**Solve for *x*.**

▶ The solutions of the equation are 0 and −7.

EXERCISES

EXAMPLES 3 and 4 on p. 576 for Exs. 28–33

Solve the equation.

28. $2a^2 + 26a = 0$ $0, -13$

29. $3t^2 - 33t = 0$ $0, 11$

30. $8x^2 - 4x = 0$ $0, \frac{1}{2}$

31. $m^2 = 9m$ $0, 9$

32. $5y^2 = -50y$ $0, -10$

33. $21h^2 = 7h$ $0, \frac{1}{3}$

9.5 Factor $x^2 + bx + c$

pp. 583–589

EXAMPLE

Factor $x^2 + 2x - 63$.

Find two factors of −63 whose sum is 2. One factor will be positive, and the other will be negative. Make an organized list of factors.

Factors of −63	Sum of factors	
1, −63	1 + (−63) = −62	✗
−1, 63	−1 + 63 = 62	✗
3, −21	3 + (−21) = −18	✗
−3, 21	−3 + 21 = 18	✗
9, −7	9 + (−7) = 2	← **Correct sum**
−9, 7	−9 + 7 = −2	✗

▶ $x^2 + 2x - 63 = (x + 9)(x - 7)$

EXERCISES

EXAMPLES 1,2 and 3 on pp. 583–584 for Exs. 34–42

Factor the trinomial.

34. $n^2 + 15n + 26$ $(n + 13)(n + 2)$

35. $s^2 + 10s - 11$ $(s + 11)(s - 1)$

36. $b^2 - 5b - 14$ $(b - 7)(b + 2)$

37. $a^2 + 5a - 84$ $(a + 12)(a - 7)$

38. $t^2 - 24t + 135$ $(t - 9)(t - 15)$

39. $x^2 + 4x - 32$ $(x + 8)(x - 4)$

40. $p^2 + 9p + 14$ $(p + 7)(p + 2)$

41. $c^2 + 8c + 15$ $(c + 5)(c + 3)$

42. $y^2 - 10y + 21$ $(y - 7)(y - 3)$

@HomeTutor
classzone.com
Chapter Review Practice

9.6 Factor $ax^2 + bx + c$

pp. 593–599

EXAMPLE

THROWN BALL You throw a ball up into the air. At 4 feet above the ground, the ball leaves your hand with an initial vertical velocity of 30 feet per second.

a. Write an equation that gives the height (in feet) of the ball as a function of the time (in seconds) since it left your hand.

b. After how many seconds does the ball land on the ground?

Solution

a. Use the vertical motion model $h = -16t^2 + vt + s$ to write an equation for the height h (in feet) of the ball as a function of the time t (in seconds). In this case, $v = 30$ and $s = 4$.

$h = -16t^2 + vt + s$ **Vertical motion model**

$h = -16t^2 + 30t + 4$ **Substitute 30 for *v* and 4 for *s*.**

b. When the ball lands on the ground, its height is 0 feet. Substitute 0 for h and solve the equation for t.

$0 = -16t^2 + 30t + 4$ **Substitute 0 for *h*.**

$0 = -2(8t^2 - 15t - 2)$ **Factor out −2.**

$0 = -2(8t + 1)(t - 2)$ **Factor the trinomial. Find factors of 8 and −2 that produce a middle term with a coefficient of −15.**

$8t + 1 = 0$ *or* $t - 2 = 0$ **Zero-product property**

$t = -\frac{1}{8}$ *or* $t = 2$ **Solve for *t*.**

The solutions of the equation are $-\frac{1}{8}$ and 2. A negative solution does not make sense in this situation, so disregard $-\frac{1}{8}$.

▶ The ball lands on the ground after 2 seconds.

EXERCISES

EXAMPLES 1, 2, 3, and 4 on pp. 593–595 for Exs. 43–50

Solve the equation.

43. $7x^2 - 8x = -1$ $\frac{1}{7}, 1$

44. $4n^2 + 3 = 7n$ $\frac{3}{4}, 1$

45. $3s^2 + 4s + 4 = 8$ $\frac{2}{3}, -2$

46. $6z^2 + 13z = 5$ $\frac{1}{3}, -\frac{5}{2}$

47. $-4r^2 = 18r + 18$ $-\frac{3}{2}, -3$

48. $9a^2 = 6a + 24$ $-\frac{4}{3}, 2$

49. **THROWN BALL** You throw a ball up into the air with an initial vertical velocity of 46 feet per second. The ball leaves your hand when it is 6 feet above the ground. After how many seconds does the ball land on the ground? 3 sec

50. **GEOMETRY** The length of a rectangle is 1 inch less than twice the width. The area of the rectangle is 21 square inches. What is the length of the rectangle? 6 in.

Extra Example 9.6

You throw a ball up into the air with an initial velocity of 38 feet per second. The ball leaves your hand at 5 feet above the ground.

a. Write an equation that gives the height (in feet) of the ball as a function of the time (in seconds) since it left your hand. $h = -16t^2 + 38t + 5$

b. After how many seconds does the ball land on the ground? 2.5 sec

Extra Example 9.7

Factor the polynomial.

a. $a^2 - 36y^2$ $(a - 6y)(a + 6y)$

b. $9x^2 + 12x + 4$ $(3x + 2)^2$

Extra Example 9.8

Factor the polynomial completely.

a. $c^3 - 7c^2 + 3c - 21$ $(c - 7)(c^2 + 3)$

b. $4y^3 + 24y^2 + 36y$ $4y(y + 3)^2$

9 CHAPTER REVIEW

9.7 Factor Special Products

pp. 600–605

EXAMPLE

Factor the polynomial.

a. $100x^2 - y^2$

b. $4x^2 - 36x + 81$

Solution

a. $100x^2 - y^2 = (10x)^2 - y^2$ Write as $a^2 - b^2$.

$= (10x + y)(10x - y)$ Difference of two squares pattern

b. $4x^2 - 36x + 81 = (2x)^2 - 2(2x \cdot 9) + 9^2$ Write as $a^2 - 2ab + b^2$.

$= (2x - 9)^2$ Perfect square trinomial pattern

EXERCISES

EXAMPLES 1, 2, 3, 4, and 6 on pp. 600–602 for Exs. 51–57

Factor the polynomial.

51. $z^2 - 225$ $(z - 15)(z + 15)$

52. $a^2 - 16y^2$ $(a - 4y)(a + 4y)$

53. $12 - 48n^2$ $12(1 - 2n)(1 + 2n)$

54. $x^2 + 20x + 100$ $(x + 10)^2$

55. $16p^2 - 8p + 1$ $(4p - 1)^2$

56. $-2y^2 + 32y - 128$ $-2(y - 8)^2$

57. **DROPPED OBJECT** You drop a penny from a height of 16 feet. After how many seconds does the penny land on the ground? 1 sec

9.8 Factor Polynomials Completely

pp. 606–613

EXAMPLE

Factor the polynomial completely.

a. $y^3 - 4y^2 + 8y - 32$

b. $5x^3 - 40x^2 + 80x$

Solution

a. $y^3 - 4y^2 + 8y - 32 = (y^3 - 4y^2) + (8y - 32)$ Group terms.

$= y^2(y - 4) + 8(y - 4)$ Factor each group.

$= (y - 4)(y^2 + 8)$ Distributive property

b. $5x^3 - 40x^2 + 80x = 5x(x^2 - 8x + 16)$ Factor out $5x$.

$= 5x(x - 4)^2$ Perfect square trinomial pattern

EXERCISES

EXAMPLE 4 on p. 608 for Exs. 58–66

Factor the polynomial completely.

58. $a^3 + 6a - 5a^2 - 30$ $(a^2 + 6)(a - 5)$

59. $y^2 + 3y + yx + 3x$ $(y + 3)(y + x)$

60. $x^3 - 11x^2 - x + 11$ $(x - 11)(x - 1)(x + 1)$

61. $5s^4 - 125s^2$ $5s^2(s - 5)(s + 5)$

62. $147n^5 - 3n^3$ $3n^3(7n - 1)(7n + 1)$

63. $2z^3 + 2z^2 - 60z$ $2z(z + 6)(z - 5)$

64. $x^3 + 5x^2 - x - 5$ $(x + 5)(x + 1)(x - 1)$

65. $2b^3 + 3b^2 - 8b - 12$ $(2b + 3)(b - 2)(b + 2)$

66. $x^3 + x^2 - 6x - 6$ $(x + 1)(x^2 - 6)$

9 CHAPTER TEST

Find the sum or difference.

1. $(a^2 - 4a + 6) + (-3a^2 + 13a + 1)$ $-2a^2 + 9a + 7$
2. $(5x^2 - 2) + (8x^3 + 2x^2 - x + 9)$ $8x^3 + 7x^2 - x + 7$
3. $(15n^2 + 7n - 1) - (4n^2 - 3n - 8)$ $11n^2 + 10n + 7$
4. $(9c^3 - 11c^2 + 2c) - (-6c^2 - 3c + 11)$ $9c^3 - 5c^2 + 5c - 11$

Find the product.

5. $(2z + 9)(z - 7)$ $2z^2 - 5z - 63$
6. $(5m - 8)(5m - 7)$ $25m^2 - 75m + 56$
7. $(b + 2)(-b^2 + 4b - 3)$ $-b^3 + 2b^2 + 5b - 6$
8. $(5 + 7y)(1 - 9y)$ $5 - 38y - 63y^2$
9. $(2x^2 - 3x + 5)(x - 4)$ $2x^3 - 11x^2 + 17x - 20$
10. $(5p - 6)(5p + 6)$ $25p^2 - 36$
11. $(12 - 3g)^2$ $144 - 72g + 9g^2$
12. $(2s + 9t)^2$ $4s^2 + 36st + 81t^2$
13. $(11a - 4b)(11a + 4b)$ $121a^2 - 16b^2$

Factor the polynomial.

14. $x^2 + 8x + 7$ $(x + 7)(x + 1)$
15. $2n^2 - 11n + 15$ $(2n - 5)(n - 3)$
16. $-12r^2 + 5r + 3$ $-(3r + 1)(4r - 3)$
17. $t^2 - 10t + 25$ $(t - 5)^2$
18. $-3n^2 + 75$ $-3(n - 5)(n + 5)$
19. $3x^2 + 29x - 44$ $(3x - 4)(x + 11)$
20. $x^2 - 49$ $(x - 7)(x + 7)$
21. $2a^4 + 21a^3 + 49a^2$ $a^2(2a + 7)(a + 7)$
22. $y^3 + 2y^2 - 81y - 162$ $(y + 2)(y - 9)(y + 9)$

Solve the equation.

23. $25a = 10a^2$ $0, \frac{5}{2}$
24. $21z^2 + 85z - 26 = 0$ $-\frac{13}{3}, \frac{2}{7}$
25. $x^2 - 22x = -121$ 11
26. $a^2 - 11a + 24 = 0$ $3, 8$
27. $t^2 + 7t = 60$ $-12, 5$
28. $4x^2 = 22x + 42$ $-\frac{3}{2}, 7$
29. $56b^2 + b = 1$ $\frac{1}{8}, -\frac{1}{7}$
30. $n^3 - 121n = 0$ $0, \pm 11$
31. $a^3 + a^2 = 64a + 64$ $-1, \pm 8$

32. **VERTICAL MOTION** A cricket jumps off the ground with an initial vertical velocity of 4 feet per second.
    a. Write an equation that gives the height (in feet) of the cricket as a function of the time (in seconds) since it jumps. $h = -16t^2 + 4t$
    b. After how many seconds does the cricket land on the ground? 0.25 sec

33. **POSTER AREA** Two posters have the lengths and widths shown. The posters have the same area.
    a. Write an equation that relates the areas of the two posters. $3w^2 = 2w(w + 2)$
    b. Find the length and width of each poster. 12 ft, 4 ft; 8 ft, 6 ft

34. **CONSTRUCTION** A construction worker is working on the roof of a building. A drop of paint falls from a rafter that is 225 feet above the ground. After how many seconds does the paint hit the ground? 3.75 sec

35. **BOX DIMENSIONS** A cardboard box that is a rectangular prism has the dimensions shown.
    a. Write a polynomial that represents the volume of the box. $x^3 + 3x^2 - 16x + 12$
    b. The volume of the box is 60 cubic inches. What are the length, width, and height of the box? 10 in., 2 in., 3 in.

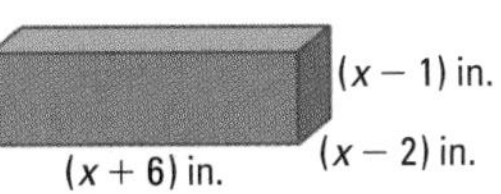

Additional Resources

Assessment Book

- Chapter Test, Levels A, B, C, pp. 127–132
- Standardized Chapter Test, pp. 133–134
- SAT/ACT Chapter Test, pp. 135–136
- Alternative Assessment, pp. 137–138

Test Generator CD-ROM

Chapter Test

Easily-readable reduced copies (with answers) of Chapter Test B, the Standardized Chapter Test, and the Alternative Assessment from the Assessment Book can be found on pp. 552E–552F.

MULTIPLE CHOICE QUESTIONS

If you have difficulty solving a multiple choice problem directly, you may be able to use another approach to eliminate incorrect answer choices and obtain the correct answer.

PROBLEM 1

What are the solutions of the equation $x^2 + 5x = -6$?

A. 3 and 2 **B.** −3 and −2 **C.** −6 and 1 **D.** 6 and −1

Method 1

SOLVE DIRECTLY

STEP 1 **Write** in standard form.

$x^2 + 5x + 6 = 0$

STEP 2 **Factor** the equation.

The factors of 6 are 1, 2, 3, and 6.

Ask yourself, "What two factors of 6 have a sum of 5?"

$3 \times 2 = 6$ and $3 + 2 = 5$

The factored equation is

$(x + 3)(x + 2) = 0$.

STEP 3 **Find** the solutions.

Set each binomial equal to 0 and solve for x.

$x + 3 = 0$ and $x + 2 = 0$

$x = -3$ $x = -2$

The solutions are −3 and −2.

The answer is **B**.

Method 2

ELIMINATE CHOICES Solve a portion of the equation. Then check to see if choices can be eliminated.

STEP 1 **Write** in standard form.

$x^2 + 5x + 6 = 0$

You know 2 factors must multiply to equal 6. Therefore, both factors must be positive, or both factors must be negative. So you can eliminate Choices **C** and **D**.

STEP 2 **Substitute** solutions given in choices **A** and **B**.

Choice A: 3 and 2

$x^2 + 5x = -6$

$(3)^2 + 5(3) \stackrel{?}{=} -6$

$24 \stackrel{?}{=} -6$ ✗

Because 3 is not a solution, you may eliminate Choice **A**.

Choice B: −3 and −2

$x^2 + 5x = -6$

$(-3)^2 + 5(-3) = -6$

$-6 = -6$ ✓

$(-2)^2 + 5(-2) = -6$

$-6 = -6$ ✓

The solutions are −3 and −2.

The answer is **B**.

Illinois Test Practice

1. D
2. J
3. A

PROBLEM 2

The width of a rectangle measures x. The length measures $x + 5$. The area of the rectangle is 150 square feet. Which of the following will help you find the length and width of the rectangle?

F. $(x + 15)(x - 10) = 0$ **H.** $(x + 15)(x + 10) = 0$

G. $(x - 15)(x + 10) = 0$ **J.** $(x + 30)(x + 5) = 0$

Method 1

SOLVE DIRECTLY

STEP 1 **Write** an equation for the area.

$x(x + 5) = 150$

STEP 2 **Write** the equation in standard form.

$x(x + 5) = 150$	
$x^2 + 5x = 150$	Distribute the x.
$x^2 + 5x - 150 = 0$	Subtract 150 from both sides.
$(x + 15)(x - 10) = 0$	Factor the equation.

The answer is **F.**

Method 2

ELIMINATE CHOICES Substitute the possible solutions for x in the answer choices into the equation.

STEP 1 **Write** an equation for the area.

$x(x + 5) = 150$

STEP 2 **Eliminate** possible values of x. Because x must be a positive number, we can eliminate any choices that yield only negative solutions.

Choice H has solutions of -15 and -10.
Choice J has solution of -30 and -5.

Eliminate Choices **H** and **J.**

STEP 3 **Check** the remaining solutions.

Choice F: $(x + 15)(x - 10) = 0$

The solutions are -15 and 10. Check 10. $10(10 + 5) = 150$. So 10 is a solution.

The answer is **F.**

PRACTICE

1. Which is the correct factorization of $25x^2 - 144$?

   A. $(5x + 9)(5x - 16)$ **C.** $(5x + 18)(5x - 8)$

   B. $(5x - 12)^2$ **D.** $(5x - 12)(5x + 12)$

2. What are the solutions of the equation $(x + 4)(x - 12) = 0$?

   F. 4 and -12 **G.** 4 and 12 **H.** -4 and -12 **J.** -4 and 12

3. What are the solutions of the equation $x^2 - 26 = 11x$?

   A. -2 and 13 **B.** 2 and 13 **C.** -2 and -13 **D.** 2 and -13

TEST PREPARATION

Illinois Test Practice

1. D
2. J
3. A
4. H
5. A
6. F
7. C
8. G
9. A
10. J
11. D
12. G
13. D
14. H
15. D
16. G
17. D
18. H
19. C
20. G

Illinois Test Practice

1. Which of the following is a solution of the equation $m^2 + 3m - 108 = 0$?

A. -18

B. -6

C. 5

D. 9

2. What are the solutions of the equation $-4x^2 + 2x + 12 = 0$?

F. -2 and 3

G. 2 and -3

H. -2 and $\frac{3}{2}$

J. 2 and $-\frac{3}{2}$

3. What are the solutions of the equation $x^2 - x - 6 = 0$?

A. -2 and 3

B. 2 and -3

C. -1 and 5

D. 5 and 1

4. Classify $-2x - 11 - 3x^3$ by degree and by the number of terms.

F. cubic binomial

G. quadratic polynomial

H. cubic trinomial

J. quadratic trinomial

5. Which of the following is equal to $(9 + 3x^2 + 4x^3 + 3x) + (5x^3 - 3x^2 - 4)$?

A. $9x^3 + 3x + 5$

B. $5x^3 + 5x^2 + 5$

C. $x^3 - 3x^2 - 6x + 4$

D. $3x^3 - 5x^2 - 5$

6. Which of the following is equal to $(4x^3 + x^2 - 12) - (3x^3 - 2x^2 + 4x - 6)$?

F. $x^3 + 3x^2 - 4x - 6$

G. $7x^3 + 3x^2 - 4x + 6$

H. $3x^3 + 3x^2 - 4x + 6$

J. $-x^3 + 3x^2 - 4x - 6$

7. The base of a triangular roof is $\frac{1}{3}(2x + 2)$ feet and its height is $(6x - 3)$ feet. Which expression represents the roof's area?

A. $3x^2 + x - 3$

B. $x^2 + x - 1$

C. $2x^2 + x - 1$

D. $6x^2 + x + 3$

8. Which of the following is equal to $(x - 5)(2 + 3x)$?

F. $5x^2 - 17x - 2$

G. $3x^2 - 13x - 10$

H. $3x^2 - 13x + 10$

J. $3x^2 + 17x + 10$

9. If 3 is a solution of $4x^2 - 5x + p = 5$ then what is the value of p?

A. -16

B. -6

C. 3

D. 16

10. Which of the following is equal to $(3x - 2)^2$?

F. $3x^2 - 12x + 4$

G. $9x^2 - 12x - 4$

H. $9x^2 + 12x + 4$

J. $9x^2 - 12x + 4$

11. Which of the following is one solution of the equation $2x^2 - 15x = -25$?

A. -3

B. -2

C. 3

D. 5

12. Which of the following is a correct factorization of $16x^2 - 24x + 9$?

F. $(6x - 3)^2$

G. $(4x - 3)^2$

H. $(4x + 3)^2$

J. $(4x - 2)^2$

13. The floor of a rectangular room has an area given by $A = x^2 - 9x + 110$, where x is the length of one of the sides. The area of the floor is 132 square feet. Which of these could represent the dimensions of this floor?

A. 2 ft by 66 ft

B. 4 ft by 33 ft

C. 6 ft by 22 ft

D. 11 ft by 12 ft

14. What is a simplified form of $(-x^2 + 4x - 9) - (x^2 - 4x - 9)$?

F. 0

G. $8x - 18$

H. $-2x^2 + 8x$

J. $2x^2 + 8x + 18$

15. Find the product of $(b - 8)^2$.

A. $b^2 + 64$

B. $b^2 - 64$

C. $b^2 - 16b - 64$

D. $b^2 - 16b + 64$

16. What is a factored form of the expression $4x^2 - 36$?

F. $(2x - 6)(2x - 6)$

G. $4(x + 3)(x - 3)$

H. $(2x - 4)(2x - 9)$

J. $4(x - 6)(x - 6)$

17. What is a factored form of the expression $n^2 - 14n + 49$?

A. $(n + 7)(n - 7)$

B. $(n + 7)(n + 7)$

C. $n(n - 14 + 49)$

D. $(n - 7)(n - 7)$

18. Classify $5x^2 - 6x + 21 - 7x^3$ by degree and by the number of terms.

F. cubic binomial

G. quadratic trinomial

H. cubic polynomial

J. quadratic polynomial

19. Which of the following is one solution of the equation $x^2 - 15x = -50$?

A. -15

B. -5

C. 5

D. 15

20. Which of the following is a correct factorization of $-12x^2 + 12x - 3$?

F. $12(2x - 1)^2$

G. $-3(2x - 1)^2$

H. $-4(2x + 1)^2$

J. $-3(2x + 1)^2$

TEST PRACTICE

Illinois Resources Guide

Pacing and Assignment Guide

REGULAR SCHEDULE

Pre-AP For pacing and assignments for a Pre-AP course, see the *Algebra 1 Toolkit.*

Lesson	Les. Day	BASIC	AVERAGE	ADVANCED
10.1 8.11.08	Day 1	EP p. 941 Exs. 56–59; pp. 632–634 Exs. 1–23	pp. 632–634 Exs. 1–5, 10–23, 52–57	pp. 632–634 Exs. 1–5, 12–23, 45*, 52–57
	Day 2	pp. 632–634 Exs. 24–35, 40–42, 46–57	pp. 632–634 Exs. 26–36, 40–44, 46–51	pp. 632–634 Exs. 28–44*, 46–51
10.2 8.11.08	Day 1	pp. 638–640 Exs. 1, 2, 3–11 odd, 12–20, 27–32, 37, 40–43, 46, 49, 51, 55	pp. 638–640 Exs. 1, 2, 6–14 even, 20–27, 31–38, 40–44, 47, 52, 56	pp. 638–640 Exs. 1, 8–12, 20–27, 32–45*, 48, 53, 54, 58
10.3 8.11.19	Day 1	EP p. 944 Exs. 1–4; pp. 647–649 Exs. 1–21	pp. 647–649 Exs. 1, 2, 5–21, 47, 48, 59–63 odd	pp. 647–649 Exs. 1, 2, 6–20, 47–49*, 60–64 even
	Day 2	pp. 647–649 Exs. 22–36 even, 37–41, 50–53, 56–64	pp. 647–649 Exs. 24–46, 50–54, 56–58	pp. 647–649 Exs. 25–46, 50–56*, 58
10.4 8.11.19	Day 1	pp. 655–658 Exs. 1–11, 15–25, 29	pp. 655–658 Exs. 1, 2, 7–16, 21–29, 47–49	pp. 655–658 Exs. 1, 2, 8–16, 23–29, 47–52
	Day 2	pp. 655–658 Exs. 30–46, 56–60, 64–73	pp. 655–658 Exs. 30–46, 50–52, 56–62, 64–72 even	pp. 655–658 Exs. 32–46, 53–63*, 66, 70, 73
10.5 8.11.19	Day 1	EP p. 946 Exs. 13–18; pp. 666–668 Exs. 1–23	pp. 666–668 Exs. 1, 2, 5–11, 15–23, 28–33	pp. 666–668 Exs. 1, 7–11, 18–25, 28–36
	Day 2	pp. 666–668 Exs. 24–33, 45–48, 52–64 even	pp. 666–668 Exs. 24–27, 34–42, 45–50, 55–58, 62	pp. 666–668 Exs. 37–51*, 56, 57, 60, 63, 64
10.6 8.11.08	Day 1	pp. 674–676 Exs. 1–8, 12–21, 25–27	pp. 674–676 Exs. 1, 2, 6–12, 16–27	pp. 674–676 Exs. 1, 2, 6–12, 16–25
	Day 2	pp. 674–676 Exs. 28–38, 46–49, 52–61	pp. 674–676 Exs. 28–44, 46–50, 52–60 even	pp. 674–676 Exs. 28–51*, 53–61 odd
10.7	Day 1	pp. 681–683 Exs. 1–11, 18–26, 31–35, 45–48, 51, 54, 57, 60, 63	pp. 681–683 Exs. 1, 2, 11–21, 27–41, 45–49, 52, 58, 64	pp. 681–683 Exs. 1, 2, 13–19, 28–50*, 56, 62, 65
10.8 8.11.14	Day 1	pp. 688–691 Exs. 1–11, 35–43	pp. 688–691 Exs. 1–11, 35–43	pp. 688–691 Exs. 1–11, 35–43
	Day 2	pp. 688–691 Exs. 12–20, 23–26, 29–34	pp. 688–691 Exs. 14–21, 23–27, 29–34	pp. 688–691 Exs. 15–18, 20–34*
Review	Day 1	pp. 696–700 Exs. 1–38	pp. 696–700 Exs. 1–38	pp. 696–700 Exs. 1–38
Assess	Day 1	Chapter 10 Test	Chapter 10 Test	Chapter 10 Test

Yearly Pacing Chapter 10 Total – 16 days Chapters 1–10 Total – 122 days Remaining – 38 days

*Challenge Exercises EP = Extra Practice SRH = Skills Review Handbook

BLOCK SCHEDULE

DAY 1	DAY 2	DAY 3	DAY 4	DAY 5	DAY 6	DAY 7	DAY 8
10.1	**10.2**	**10.3 (CONT.)**	**10.4 (CONT.)**	**10.5 (CONT.)**	**10.6 (CONT.)**	**10.8**	**REVIEW**
pp. 632–634 Exs. 1–5, 10–23, 26–37, 40–44, 46–57	pp. 638–640 Exs. 1, 2, 6–14 even, 20–27, 31–38, 40–44, 47, 52, 56	pp. 647–649 Exs. 24–46, 50–54, 56–58	pp. 655–658 Exs. 30–46, 50–52, 56–62, 64–72 even	pp. 666–668 Exs. 24–27, 34–42, 45–50, 55–58, 62	pp. 674–676 Exs. 28–44, 46–50, 52–60 even	pp. 688–691 Exs. 1–11, 14–21, 23–27, 29–43	pp. 696–700 Exs. 1–38
	10.3	**10.4**	**10.5**	**10.6**	**10.7**		**ASSESS**
	pp. 647–649 Exs. 1, 2, 5–21, 47, 48, 59–63 odd	pp. 655–658 Exs. 1, 2, 7–16, 21–29, 47–49	pp. 666–668 Exs. 1, 2, 5–11, 15–23, 28–33	pp. 674–676 Exs. 1, 2, 6–12, 16–27	pp. 681–683 Exs. 1, 2, 11–21, 27–41, 45–49, 52, 58, 64		Chapter 10 Test

Yearly Pacing Chapter 10 Total – 8 days Chapters 1–10 Total – 61 days Remaining – 19 days

Chapter Resource Guide

Chapter Resource Book

CHAPTER SUPPORT

Parents as Partners (Chapter Overview with home involvement exercises and activity)							p. 1	
LESSON SUPPORT	**10.1**	**10.2**	**10.3**	**10.4**	**10.5**	**10.6**	**10.7**	**10.8**
Standard	**8.11.08**	**8.11.08**	**8.11.19**	**8.11.19**	**8.11.19**	**8.11.08**		**8.11.14**
Teaching Guide/Lesson Plan	p. 3	p. 17	p. 32	p. 46	p. 58	p. 69	p. 79	p. 89
Activity Masters	p. 5			p. 48				
Technology Activities & Keystrokes		p. 19	p. 34					p. 91
Activity Support Masters					p. 60			
Practice (3 levels)	p. 6	p. 21	p. 35	p. 49	p. 61	p. 71	p. 81	p. 92
Study Guide	p. 12	p. 27	p. 41	p. 52	p. 64	p. 74	p. 84	p. 98
Catch-Up for Absent Students	p. 14	p. 29	p. 43	p. 54	p. 66	p. 76	p. 86	p. 100
Problem Solving/Application	p. 15	p. 30	p. 44	p. 55	p. 67	p. 77	p. 87	p. 101
Challenge Practice	p. 16	p. 31	p. 45	p. 57	p. 68	p. 78	p. 88	p. 102

REVIEW

Chapter Review Games and Activities	p. 103	Cumulative Practice	p. 106
Project with Rubric	p. 104	Resource Book Answers	A1

Transparencies	*10.1*	*10.2*	*10.3*	*10.4*	*10.5*	*10.6*	*10.7*	*10.8*
Warm-Up/Daily Homework Quiz	✔	✔	✔	✔	✔	✔	✔	✔
Notetaking Guide	✔	✔	✔	✔	✔	✔	✔	✔
Teacher Support	✔	✔	✔		✔			✔
Answer Transparencies	✔	✔	✔	✔	✔	✔	✔	✔

ASSESSMENT BOOK

Quizzes	p. 139	SAT/ACT Chapter Test	p. 150
Chapter Tests (3 levels)	p. 142	Alternative Assessment with Rubric	p. 152
Standardized Chapter Test	p. 148		

TECHNOLOGY

- Easy Planner
- Test and Practice Generator
- Power Presentations
- @HomeTutor
- Activity Generator
- Animated Algebra
- Classzone.com
- eEdition Plus Online
- eWorkbook Plus Online
- ML Assessment System

ADDITIONAL RESOURCES

Illinois Additional Lessons

- Worked-Out Solution Key
- Notetaking Guide
- Practice Workbook
- Algebra 1 Toolkit
- Benchmark Tests
- Reteaching and Remediation
- Spanish Study Guide
- Spanish Assessment Book
- Spanish Resources in Spanish
- Multi-Language Visual Glossary

LESSON 10.1 Practice B
For use with pages 628–634

Use the quadratic function to complete the table of values.

1. $y = 9x^2$

x	−2	−1	0	1	2
y	36	9	0	9	36

2. $y = -5x^2$

x	−2	−1	0	1	2
y	−20	−5	0	−5	−20

3. $y = \frac{5}{2}x^2 + 1$

x	−4	−2	0	2	4
y	41	11	1	11	41

4. $y = -\frac{1}{8}x^2 - 2$

x	−16	−8	0	8	16
y	−34	−10	−2	−10	−34

5. $y = -4x^2 + 3$

x	−2	−1	0	1	2
y	−13	−1	3	−1	−13

6. $y = 6x^2 - 5$

x	−2	−1	0	1	2
y	19	1	−5	1	19

Match the function with its graph.

7. $y = -4x^2 + 3$ F
8. $y = 3x^2 + 4$ A
9. $y = \frac{1}{3}x^2 - 4$ D
10. $y = \frac{1}{4}x^2 - 3$ B
11. $y = -3x^2 + 4$ C
12. $y = 4x^2 + 3$ E

A. 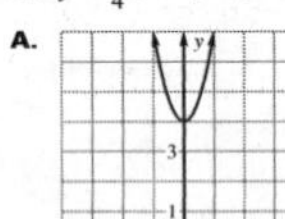

B. 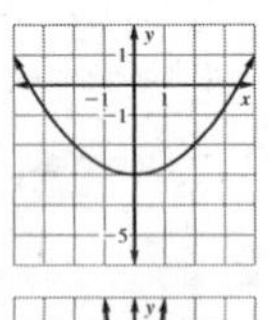

C. 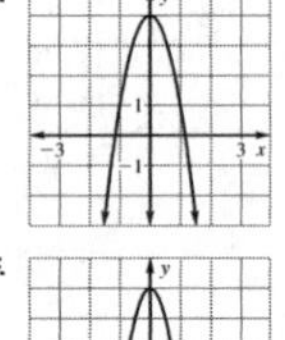

D.

E.

F.

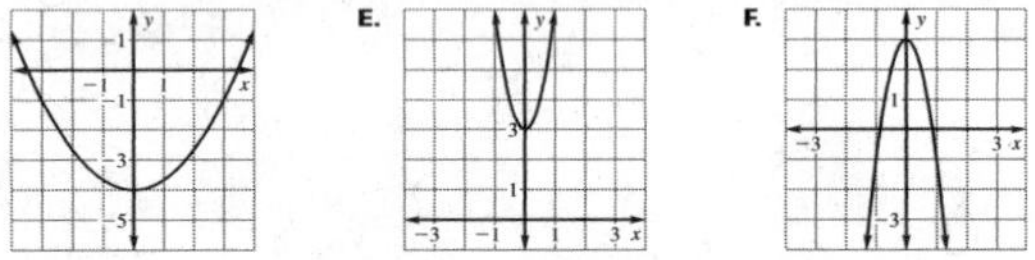

Describe how you can use the graph of $y = x^2$ to graph the given function.

13. $y = x^2 - 8$ See above.
14. $y = -x^2 + 4$ See above.
15. $y = 2x^2 + 3$ See above.
16. $y = -5x^2 + 1$ See above.
17. $y = \frac{1}{2}x^2 - 2$
18. $y = -\frac{3}{4}x^2 + 5$

13. shift the graph 8 units down
14. shift the graph 4 units up and reflect over x-axis
15. stretch vertically by a factor of 2 and shift 3 units up
16. stretch vertically by a factor of 5, reflect in x-axis, and shift 1 unit up
17. shrink vertically by a factor of $\frac{1}{2}$ and shift 2 units down
18. shrink vertically by a factor of $\frac{3}{4}$, reflect over x-axis, and shift 5 units up

LESSON 10.1 Practice B *continued*
For use with pages 628–634

Graph the function and identify its domain and range. Compare the graph with the graph of $y = x^2$.

19. $y = x^2 + 9$ See above.
20. $y = -\frac{1}{5}x^2$ See above.
21. $y = -\frac{3}{2}x^2$ See below.

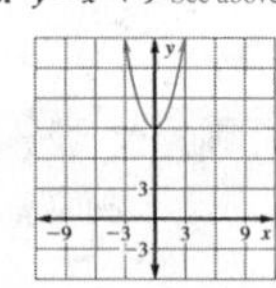

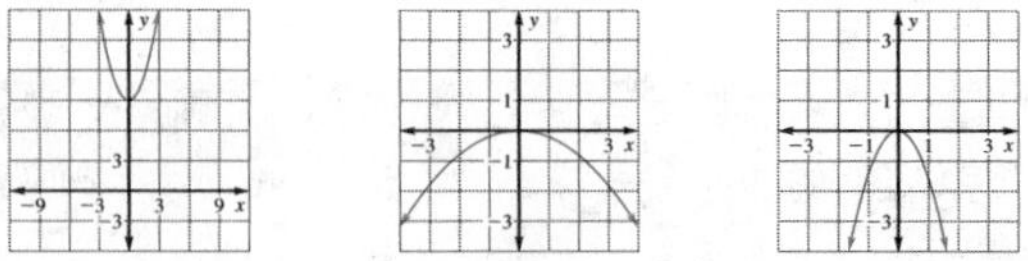

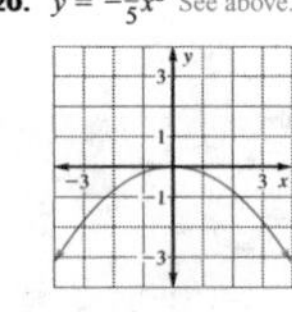

22. $y = x^2 - 3.5$ See below.
23. $y = 2x^2 - 9$ See below.
24. $y = -5x^2 + 2$ See below.

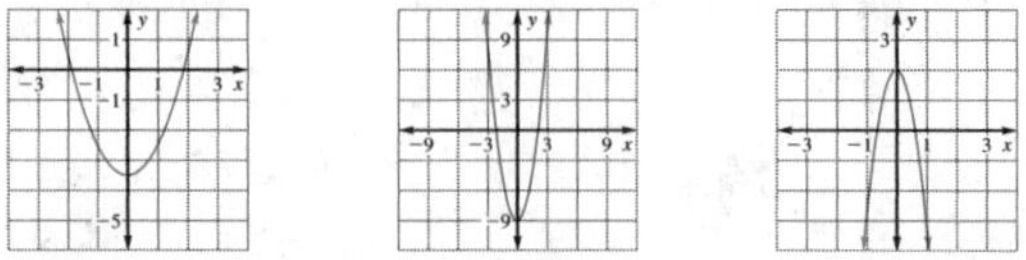

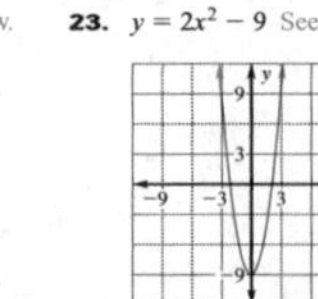

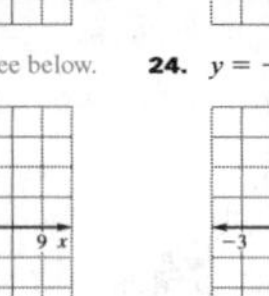

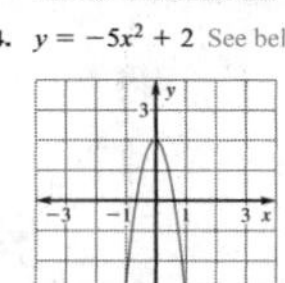

19. domain: all reals; range: $y \geq 9$; vertical shift 9 units up
20. domain: all reals; range: $y \leq 0$; vertical shrink by a factor of $\frac{1}{5}$ and reflection in x-axis

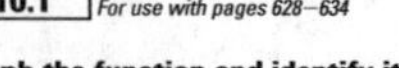

25. **Serving Plate** The top view of a freeform serving plate you made in a ceramics class is shown in the graph. One edge of the plate can be modeled by the graph of the function $y = -\frac{5}{81}x^2 + 20$ where x and y are measured in inches.
 a. Find the domain of the function in this situation. $-18 \leq x \leq 18$
 b. Find the range of the function in this situation. $-4 \leq y \leq 20$

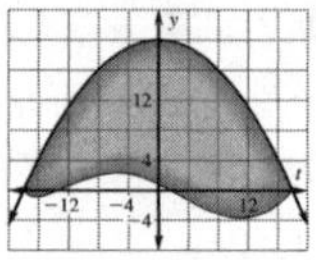

26. **Roof Shingle** A roof shingle is dropped from a rooftop that is 100 feet above the ground. The height y (in feet) of the dropped roof shingle is given by the function $y = -16t^2 + 100$ where t is the time (in seconds) since the shingle is dropped.
 a. Graph the function.
 b. Identify the domain and range of the function in this situation.
 c. Use the graph to estimate the shingle's height at 1 second. 84 ft
 d. Use the graph to estimate when the shingle is at a height of 50 feet.
 e. Use the graph to estimate when the shingle is at a height of 0 feet. 2.5 sec

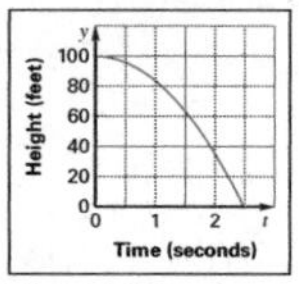

26. b. $0 \leq t \leq 2.5$; $0 \leq y \leq 100$
 d. about 1.8 sec

21. domain: all reals; range: $y \leq 0$; vertical stretch by a factor of $\frac{3}{2}$ and reflection in x-axis
22. domain: all reals; range: $y \geq -3.5$; vertical shift 3.5 units down
23. domain: all reals; range: $y \geq -9$; vertical stretch by a factor of 2 and shift 9 units down
24. domain: all reals; range: $y \leq 2$; vertical stretch by a factor of 5, reflection in x-axis, and vertical shift 2 units up

LESSON 10.2 Practice B
For use with pages 635–640

Identify the values of a, b, and c in the quadratic function.

1. $y = 6x^2 + 3x + 5$
2. $y = \frac{3}{2}x^2 - x + 8$
3. $y = 7x^2 - 3x - 1$
4. $y = -2x^2 + 9x$
5. $y = \frac{3}{4}x^2 - 10$
6. $y = -8x^2 + 3x - 7$

1. $a = 6, b = 3, c = 5$
2. $a = \frac{3}{2}, b = -1, c = 8$
3. $a = 7, b = -3, c = -1$
4. $a = -2, b = 9, c = 0$
5. $a = \frac{3}{4}, b = 0, c = -10$
6. $a = -8, b = 3, c = -7$

Tell whether the graph opens upward or downward. Then find the axis of symmetry and vertex of the graph of the function. See below.

7. $y = x^2 - 5$
8. $y = -x^2 + 9$
9. $y = -2x^2 + 6x + 7$
10. $y = 3x^2 - 12x + 1$
11. $y = 3x^2 + 6x - 2$
12. $y = -2x^2 + 7x - 21$
13. $y = \frac{1}{2}x^2 + 5x - 4$
14. $y = -\frac{1}{4}x^2 - 24$
15. $y = -3x^2 + 9x - 8$
16. $y = 3x^2 - 2x + 3$
17. $y = -2x^2 + 7x + 1$
18. $y = 3x^2 + 2x - 5$

Find the vertex of the graph of the function. Make a table of values using x-values to the left and right of the vertex.

19. $y = x^2 - 10x + 3$

x	3	4	5	6	7
y	−18	−21	−22	−21	−18

20. $y = -x^2 + 6x - 2$

x	1	2	3	4	5
y	3	6	7	6	3

21. $y = \frac{1}{2}x^2 - x + 7$

x	−1	0	1	2	3
y	$\frac{17}{2}$	7	$\frac{13}{2}$	7	$\frac{17}{2}$

22. $y = \frac{1}{3}x^2 - 2x + 3$

x	1	2	3	4	5
y	$\frac{4}{3}$	$\frac{1}{3}$	0	$\frac{1}{3}$	$\frac{4}{3}$

Graph the function. Label the vertex and axis of symmetry.

23. $y = -x^2 - 10$
24. $y = 2x^2 + 3$
25. $y = -2x^2 + 2x + 1$

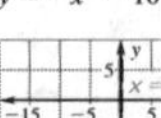

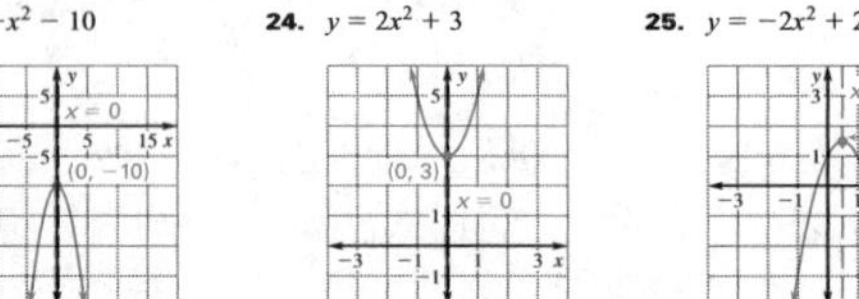

7. upward; $x = 0$; $(0, -5)$
8. downward; $x = 0$; $(0, 9)$
9. downward; $x = \frac{3}{2}$; $\left(\frac{3}{2}, \frac{23}{2}\right)$
10. upward; $x = 2$; $(2, -11)$
11. upward; $x = -1$; $(-1, -5)$
12. downward; $x = \frac{7}{4}$; $\left(\frac{7}{4}, -\frac{119}{8}\right)$
13. upward; $x = -5$; $\left(-5, -\frac{33}{2}\right)$
14. downward; $x = 0$; $(0, -24)$
15. downward; $x = \frac{3}{2}$; $\left(\frac{3}{2}, -\frac{5}{4}\right)$
16. upward; $x = \frac{1}{3}$; $\left(\frac{1}{3}, \frac{8}{3}\right)$
17. downward; $x = \frac{7}{4}$; $\left(\frac{7}{4}, \frac{57}{8}\right)$
18. upward; $x = -\frac{1}{3}$; $\left(-\frac{1}{3}, -\frac{16}{3}\right)$

LESSON 10.2 Practice B *continued*
For use with pages 635–640

26. $y = 5x^2 + 2x$
27. $y = -2x^2 + x - 4$
28. $y = x^2 - 8x + 5$

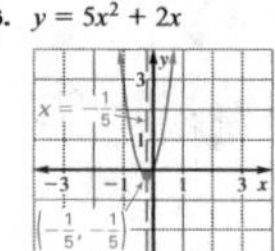

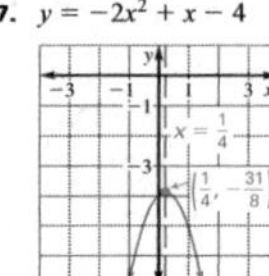

29. $y = -\frac{1}{2}x^2 - 8x + 3$
30. $y = \frac{1}{4}x^2 + 3x - 1$
31. $y = -\frac{3}{4}x^2 - 2x + 2$

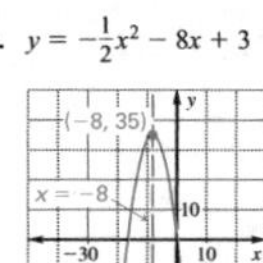

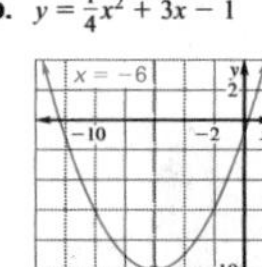

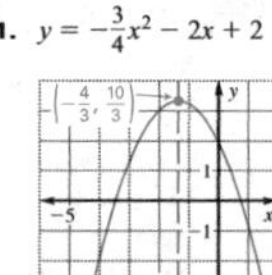

Tell whether the function has a *minimum value* or a *maximum value*. Then find the minimum or maximum value.

32. $f(x) = 8x^2 - 40$ minimum; $(0, -40)$
33. $f(x) = -5x^2 + 10x - 2$ maximum; $(1, 3)$
34. $f(x) = 8x^2 - 4x + 4$ minimum; $\left(\frac{1}{4}, \frac{7}{2}\right)$

35. **Storage Building** The storage building shown can be modeled by the graph of the function $y = -0.12x^2 + 2.4x$ where x and y are measured in feet. What is the height h at the highest point of the building as shown in the diagram? 12 ft

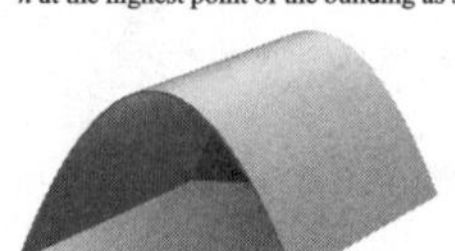

36. **Velvet Rope** A parabola is formed by a piece of velvet rope found around a museum display as shown. This parabola can be modeled by the graph of the function $y = \frac{4}{225}x^2 - \frac{16}{15}x + 40$ where x and y are measured in inches and y represents the number of inches the parabola is above the ground. How far above the ground is the lowest point on the rope? 24 in.

LESSON 10.3 Practice B
For use with pages 643–649

Determine whether the given value is a solution of the equation.

1. $x^2 - 2x + 15 = 0; 3$
2. $x^2 - 4x - 12 = 0; 2$
3. $-x^2 - 5x - 6 = 0; 3$
4. $x^2 + 3x - 4 = 0; 1$
5. $2x^2 + 9x - 5 = 0; -2$
6. $3x^2 - 5x - 2 = 0; 2$

1. not a solution 2. not a solution 3. not a solution 4. solution 5. not a solution 6. solution

Use the graph to find the solutions of the given equation.

7. $x^2 + 8x + 16 = 0$ −4
8. $-x^2 + 36 = 0$ −6, 6
9. $x^2 + 5x - 24 = 0$ −8, 3

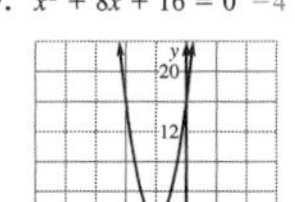
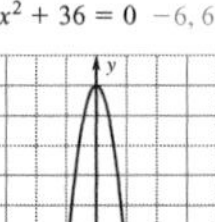
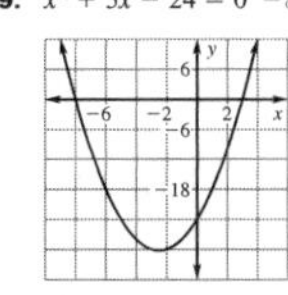

10. $x^2 + 11x + 30 = 0$ −6, −5
11. $x^2 - 25 = 0$ −5, 5
12. $x^2 + 7 = 0$ no solution

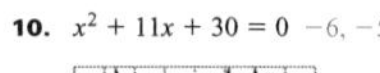
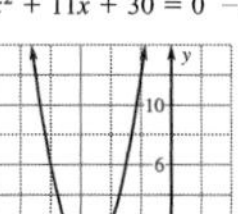
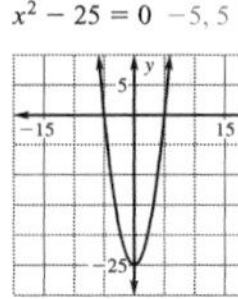
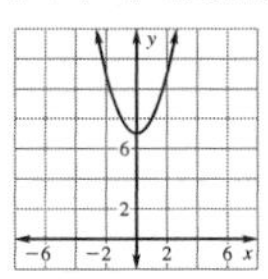

Solve the equation by graphing.

13. $-x^2 - 6x = 0$ −6, 0
14. $2x^2 = 2$ −1, 1
15. $x^2 - 7x + 10 = 0$ 2, 5

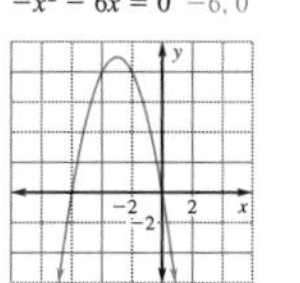
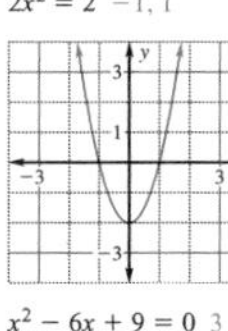
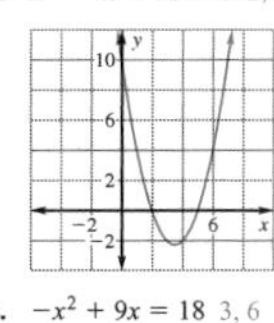

16. $x^2 = 10x$ 0, 10
17. $x^2 - 6x + 9 = 0$ 3
18. $-x^2 + 9x = 18$ 3, 6

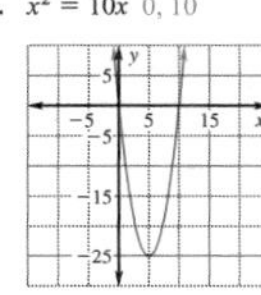
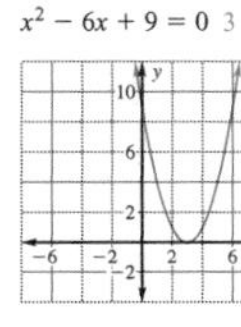
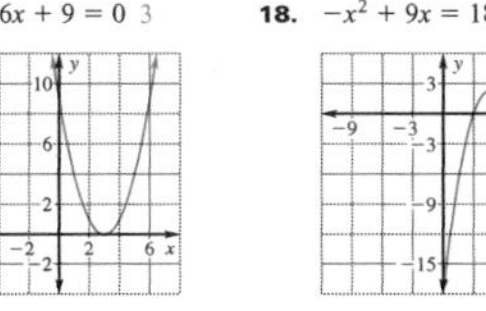

LESSON 10.3

LESSON 10.3 Practice B
For use with pages 643–649

Find the zeros of the function by graphing.

19. $f(x) = -x^2 - 5x - 10$ no zeros
20. $f(x) = x^2 + 12x + 36$ −6
21. $f(x) = 2x^2 + 24x$ −12, 0

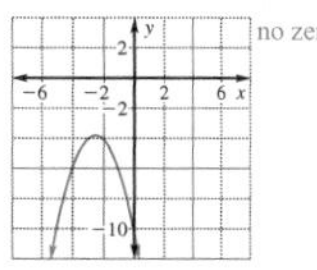
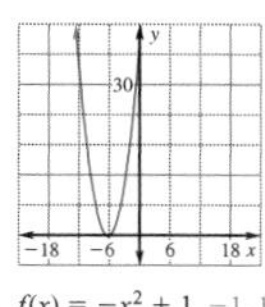

22. $f(x) = x^2 - 49$ −7, 7
23. $f(x) = -x^2 + 1$ −1, 1
24. $f(x) = 3x^2 + 12x$ −4, 0

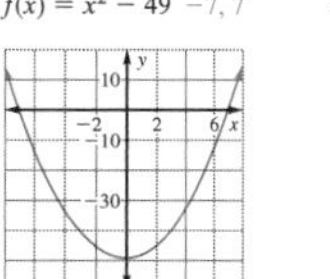
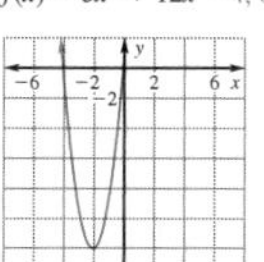

25. **Stunt Double** A movie stunt double jumps from the top of a building 50 feet above the ground onto a pad on the ground below. The stunt double jumps with an initial vertical velocity of 10 feet per second.
    a. Write and graph a function that models the height h (in feet) of the stunt double t seconds after she jumps.
    b. How long does it take the stunt double to reach the ground? about 2.1 sec

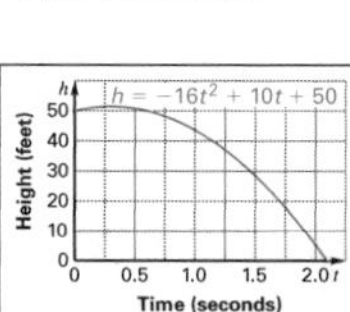

26. **Wastebasket** You throw a wad of used paper towards a wastebasket from a height of about 1.3 feet above the floor with an initial vertical velocity of 3 feet per second.
    a. Write and graph a function that models the height h (in feet) of the paper t seconds after it is thrown.
    b. If you miss the wastebasket and the paper hits the floor, how long does it take for the ball of paper to reach the floor? about 0.4 sec
    c. If the ball of paper hits the rim of the wastebasket one-half foot above the ground, how long was the ball in the air? about 0.34 sec

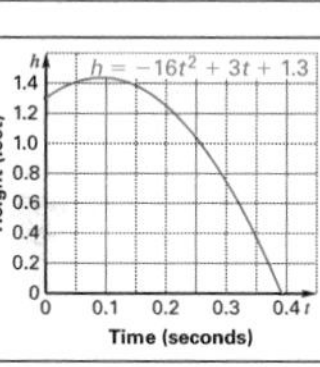

LESSON 10.3

LESSON 10.4 Practice B
For use with pages 652–658

LESSON 10.4

Solve the equation.

1. $6x^2 - 24 = 0$ −2, 2
2. $8x^2 - 128 = 0$ −4, 4
3. $x^2 - 13 = 23$ −6, 6
4. $3x^2 - 60 = 87$ −7, 7
5. $2x^2 - 33 = 17$ −5, 5
6. $5x^2 - 200 = 205$ −9, 9
7. $4x^2 - 125 = -25$ −5, 5
8. $7x^2 - 50 = 13$ −3, 3
9. $\frac{1}{2}x^2 - \frac{1}{2} = 0$ −1, 1

Solve the equation. Round the solutions to the nearest hundredth.

10. $x^2 + 15 = 23$ −2.83, 2.83
11. $x^2 - 16 = -13$ −1.73, 1.73
12. $12 - x^2 = 17$ no solution
13. $3x^2 - 8 = 7$ −2.24, 2.24
14. $9 - x^2 = 9$ 0
15. $4 + 5x^2 = 34$ −2.45, 2.45
16. $48 = 14 + 2x^2$ −4.12, 4.12
17. $8x^2 = 50$ −2.5, 2.5
18. $3x^2 + 23 = 18$ no solution
19. $(x - 3)^2 = 5$ 0.76, 5.24
20. $(x + 2)^2 = 10$ −5.16, 1.16
21. $3(x - 4)^2 = 18$ 1.55, 6.45

Use the given area *A* of the circle to find the radius *r* or the diameter *d* of the circle. Round the answer to the nearest hundredth, if necessary.

22. $A = 169\pi$ m² 13 m
23. $A = 38\pi$ in.² about 6.16 in.
24. $A = 45\pi$ cm² about 13.42 cm

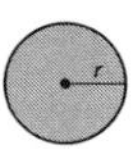
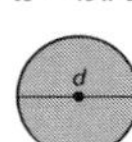

25. **Flower Seed** A manufacturer is making a cylindrical can that will hold and dispense flower seeds through small holes in the top of the can. The manufacturer wants the can to have a volume of 42 cubic inches and be 6 inches tall. What should the diameter of the can be? (*Hint:* Use the formula for volume, $V = \pi r^2 h$, where V is the volume, r is the radius, and h is the height.) Round your answer to the nearest inch. about 3 in.

26. **Stockpile** You can find the diameter D (in feet) of a conical pile of sand, dirt, etc. by using the formula $V = 0.2618hD^2$ where h is the height of the pile (in feet) and V is the volume of the pile (in cubic feet). Find the diameter of each stockpile in the table. Round your answers to the nearest foot. 5 ft, 8 ft, 10 ft

Stockpile	Height (ft)	Diameter (ft)	Volume (ft³)
A	10	?	68
B	15	?	230
C	20	?	545

LESSON 10.5 Practice B
For use with pages 663–668

Find the value of *c* that makes the expression a perfect square trinomial. Then write the expression as a square of a binomial.

1. $x^2 + 12x + c$ 36; $(x + 6)^2$
2. $x^2 + 50x + c$ 625; $(x + 25)^2$
3. $x^2 - 26x + c$ 169; $(x - 13)^2$
4. $x^2 - 18x + c$ 81; $(x - 9)^2$
5. $x^2 + 13x + c$ $\frac{169}{4}$; $\left(x + \frac{13}{2}\right)^2$
6. $x^2 - 9x + c$ $\frac{81}{4}$; $\left(x - \frac{9}{2}\right)^2$
7. $x^2 - 11x + c$ $\frac{121}{4}$; $\left(x - \frac{11}{2}\right)^2$
8. $x^2 + \frac{1}{2}x + c$ $\frac{1}{16}$; $\left(x + \frac{1}{4}\right)^2$
9. $x^2 - \frac{6}{5}x + c$ $\frac{9}{25}$; $\left(x - \frac{3}{5}\right)^2$

Solve the equation by completing the square. Round your solutions to the nearest hundredth, if necessary.

10. $x^2 + 6x = 1$ −6.16, 0.16
11. $x^2 + 4x = 13$ −6.12, 2.12
12. $x^2 - 10x = 15$ −1.32, 11.32
13. $x^2 + 8x = 10$ −9.10, 1.10
14. $x^2 - 2x - 7 = 0$
15. $x^2 - 12x - 21 = 0$
16. $x^2 + 3x - 2 = 0$
17. $x^2 + 5x - 3 = 0$
18. $x^2 - x = 1$ −0.62, 1.62

14. −1.83, 3.83 15. −1.55, 13.55 16. −3.56, 0.56 17. −5.54, 0.54

LESSON 10.5

Find the value of *x*. Round your answer to the nearest hundredth, if necessary.

19. Area of triangle = 30 ft² 6

x ft
(*x* + 4) ft

20. Area of rectangle = 140 in.² 5

2*x* in.
(3*x* − 1) in.

21. **Colorado** The state of Colorado is almost perfectly rectangular, with its north border is 111 miles longer than its west border. If the state encompasses 104,000 square miles, estimate the dimensions of Colorado. Round your answer to the nearest mile. about 272 mi by about 383 mi

22. **Baseball** After a baseball is hit, the height h (in feet) of the ball above the ground t seconds after it is hit can be approximated by the equation $h = -16t^2 + 65t + 3$. Determine how long it will take for the ball to hit the ground. Round your answer to the nearest hundredth. about 4.11 sec

23. **Fenced-In Yard** You have 60 feet of fencing to fence in part of your backyard for your dog. You want to make sure that your dog has 400 square feet of space to run around in. The back of your house will be used as one side of the enclosure as shown.
    a. Write equations for the perimeter and area of the enclosure.
    b. Use substitution to solve the system of equations from part (a). What are the possible lengths and widths of the enclosure? 20 ft by 20 ft, 40 ft by 10 ft

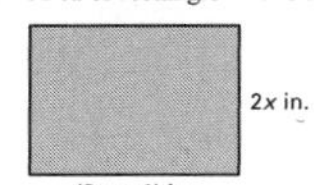

23. a. $\ell + 2w = 60$; $\ell w = 400$

Lesson Practice Level B

LESSON 10.6 **Practice B** *For use with pages 671–676*

13. *Sample answer:* Use finding square roots because the equation can be written in the form $x^2 = d$.
14. *Sample answer:* Use finding square roots because the equation can be written in the form $x^2 = d$.

Use the quadratic formula to solve the equation. Round your solutions to the nearest hundredth, if necessary.

1. $x^2 + 7x - 80 = 0$ $-13.10, 6.10$ **2.** $3x^2 - x - 16 = 0$ $-2.15, 2.48$

3. $8x^2 - 2x - 30 = 0$ $-1.82, 2.07$ **4.** $x^2 + 4x + 1 = 0$ $-3.73, -0.27$

5. $-x^2 + x + 12 = 0$ $-3, 4$ **6.** $-3x^2 - 4x + 10 = 0$ N$-2.61, 1.28$

7. $5x^2 + 30x + 32 = 0$ $-4.61, -1.39$ **8.** $x^2 + 6x - 100 = 0$ $-13.44, 7.44$

9. $4x^2 - x - 20 = 0$ $-2.11, 2.36$ **10.** $5x^2 + x - 9 = 0$ $-1.45, 1.25$

11. $6x^2 + 7x - 3 = 0$ $-\frac{3}{2}, \frac{1}{3}$ **12.** $10x^2 - 7x + 5 = 0$ no solution

Tell which method(s) you would use to solve the quadratic equation. *Explain* your choice(s).

13. $6x^2 - 216 = 0$ See above. **14.** $8x^2 = 56$ See above. **15.** $5x^2 - 10x = 0$ See below.

16. $x^2 + 8x + 7 = 0$ See below. **17.** $x^2 - 6x + 1 = 0$ See below. **18.** $-9x^2 + 10x = 5$ See below.

Solve the quadratic equation using any method. Round your solutions to the nearest hundredth, if necessary.

19. $-10x^2 = -50$ $-2.24, 2.24$ **20.** $x^2 - 16x = -64$ 8 **21.** $x^2 + 3x - 8 = 0$ $-4.70, 1.70$

22. $x^2 = 14x - 49$ 7 **23.** $x^2 + 6x = 14$ $-7.80, 1.80$ **24.** $-5x^2 + x = 13$ no solution

15. *Sample answer:* Use factoring because the equation is easily factored.
16. *Sample answer:* Use factoring because the equation is easily factored.

25. Pasta For the period 1990–2003, the amount of biscuits, pasta, and noodles y (in thousands of metric tons) imported into the United States can be modeled by the function $y = 1.36x^2 + 27.8x + 304$ where x is the number of years since 1990.

a. Write and solve an equation that you can use to approximate the year in which 500 million pounds of biscuits, pasta, and noodles were imported. See below.

b. Write and solve an equation that you can use to approximate the year in which 575 million pounds of biscuits, pasta, and noodles were imported. See below.

26. Eggs For the period 1997–2003, the number of eggs y (in billions) produced in the United States can be modeled by the function $y = -0.27x^2 + 3.3x + 77$ where x is the number of years since 1997.

a. Write and solve an equation that you can use to approximate the year(s) in which 80 billion eggs were produced. $80 = -0.27x^2 + 3.3x + 77$; 1998

b. Graph the function on a graphing calculator. Use the *trace* feature to find the year when 80 billion eggs were produced. Use the graph to check your answer from part (a).

Number of eggs (billions)
95 90 85 80 75 70 65
X=1.0425532 Y=80.146958
0 1 2 3 4 5 6 7
Years since 1997

17. *Sample answer:* Use the quadratic formula because it cannot be factored easily.
18. *Sample answer:* Use the quadratic formula because it cannot be factored easily.

25. a. $500 = 1.36x^2 + 27.8x + 304$; between 1995 and 1996
b. $575 = 1.36x^2 + 27.8x + 304$; 1997

LESSON 10.7 **Practice B** *For use with pages 678–683*

2. two solutions **3.** two solutions
4. no solution **5.** two solutions

Tell whether the equation has *two solutions, one solution,* or *no solution.*

1. $x^2 + x + 3 = 0$ no solution **2.** $2x^2 - 4x - 5 = 0$ **3.** $-2x^2 + 10x - 5 = 0$

4. $3x^2 - 9x + 8 = 0$ **5.** $10x^2 - 8x + 1 = 0$ **6.** $-4x^2 + 9 = 0$ two solutions

7. $36x^2 - 9x = 0$ two solutions **8.** $3x^2 + 2 = 4x$ no solution **9.** $12 = x^2 - 6x$ two solutions

10. $\frac{1}{6}x^2 + 3 = x$ no solution **11.** $-8x^2 - 9x = \frac{2}{3}$ two solutions **12.** $8x^2 + 12x + 2 = 4x$ one solution

Find the number of *x*-intercepts that the graph of the function has.

13. $y = x^2 - 6x - 3$ two **14.** $y = 5x^2 - x - 1$ two **15.** $y = 6x^2 - 6x + 1$ two

16. $y = x^2 + x + 6$ none **17.** $y = -4x^2 + x + 1$ two **18.** $y = 4x^2 + 5x - 1$ two

19. $y = 2x^2 - 4x + 2$ one **20.** $y = 10x^2 - 5x + 1$ none **21.** $y = 8x^2 + x + 4$ none

22. $y = -15x^2 + 3x + 5$ two **23.** $y = \frac{1}{2}x^2 - 4x + 8$ one **24.** $y = \frac{2}{3}x^2 - 5x + 2$ two

Give a value of *c* for which the equation has (a) two solutions, (b) one solution, and (c) no solution.

25. $x^2 + 10x + c = 0$ **26.** $x^2 - 4x + c = 0$ **27.** $25x^2 + 10x + c = 0$

28. $49x^2 - 14x + c = 0$ **29.** $2x^2 + 4x + c = 0$ **30.** $3x^2 - 18x + c = 0$

25–30. Answers will vary.

31. Playhouse You want to build a playhouse for your sister in your backyard. You have blueprints which show that the playhouse is 12 feet long and 13 feet wide. You want to change the dimensions as shown. The new area can be modeled by the function $y = -x^2 + x + 156$.

12 ft
x
13 ft
13 − x

a. Write an equation that you can use to determine if there is a value of x that gives an area of 150 square feet.

b. Use the discriminant of your equation from part (a) to show that it is possible to find a value of x for which the area is 150 square feet. discriminant: $25 > 0$

c. Find the value(s) of x for which the area is 150 square feet. 3

31. a. $150 = -x^2 + x + 156$

32. Tennis You and your friend are walking around the exterior of a tennis court that has a 12-foot high fence around it. You pick up a ball and try to throw it from a height of 5 feet over the fence. You throw it with an initial vertical velocity of 20 feet per second. Did the ball make it over the fence? no

LESSON 10.8

Practice B

For use with pages 684–691

LESSON 10.8

Match the function with the graph it represents.

1. Linear function B **2.** Exponential function C **3.** Quadratic function A

A.

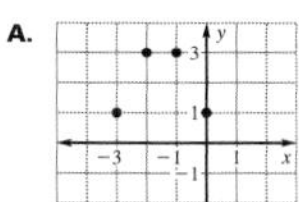

B.

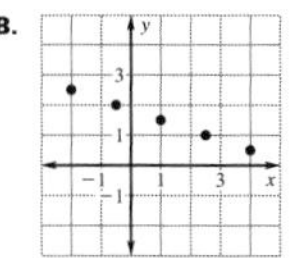

C.

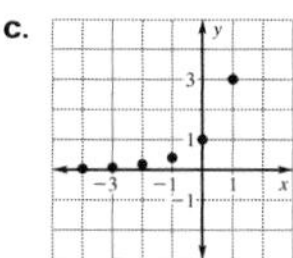

Use a graph to tell whether the ordered pairs represent a linear function, an exponential function, or a quadratic function.

4. $(-2, 16), (-1, 8), (0, 4), (1, 2), (2, 1)$ exponential

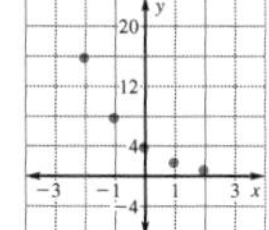

5. $(-3, 4), (-2, 0), (-1, -2), (0, -2), (1, 0)$ quadratic

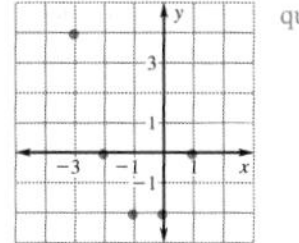

6. $(-4, 17), (-2, 11), (0, 5), (2, -1), (4, -7)$ linear

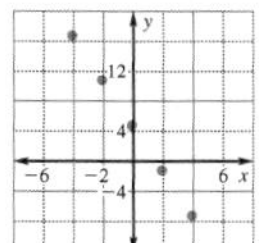

7. $(-9, -1), (-6, -2), (-3, -3), (0, -4), (3, -5)$ linear

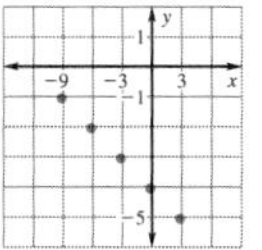

8. $\left(-2, \frac{1}{9}\right), \left(-1, \frac{1}{3}\right), (0, 1), (1, 3), (2, 9)$ exponential

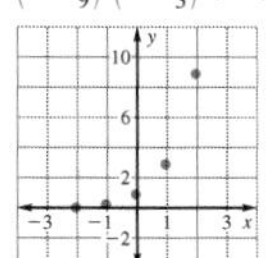

9. $(2, 5), (3, 2), (4, 1), (5, 2), (6, 5)$ quadratic

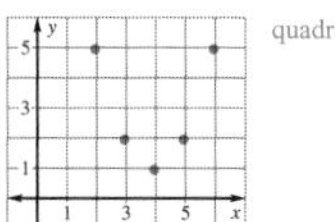

LESSON 10.8

Practice B *continued*

For use with pages 684–691

LESSON 10.8

Tell whether the table of values represents a linear function, an exponential function, or a quadratic function.

10. exponential

x	0	1	2	3	4
y	1	5	25	125	625

11. linear

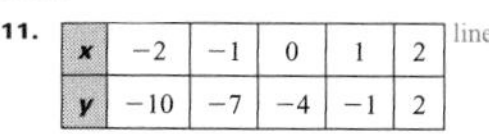

x	−2	−1	0	1	2
y	−10	−7	−4	−1	2

12. quadratic

x	−1	0	1	2	3
y	4	1	0	1	4

13. linear

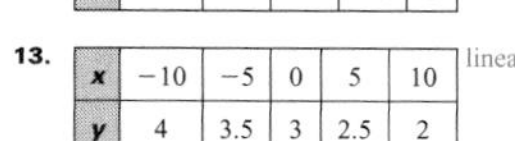

x	−10	−5	0	5	10
y	4	3.5	3	2.5	2

14. exponential

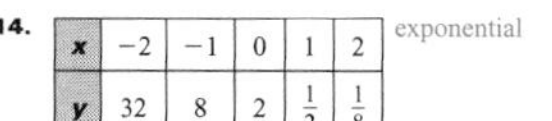

x	−2	−1	0	1	2
y	32	8	2	$\frac{1}{2}$	$\frac{1}{8}$

15. quadratic

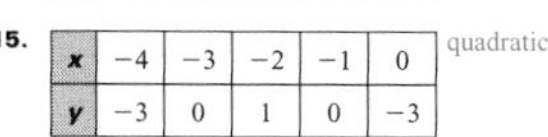

x	−4	−3	−2	−1	0
y	−3	0	1	0	−3

16. linear

x	−2	−1	0	1	2
y	1	3	5	7	9

17. exponential

x	−3	−2	−1	0	1
y	27	9	3	1	$\frac{1}{3}$

18. Use the graph shown.

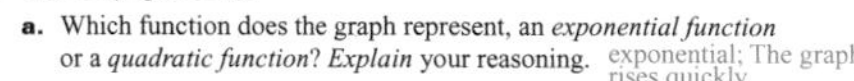

a. Which function does the graph represent, an *exponential function* or a *quadratic function*? *Explain* your reasoning. exponential; The graph rises quickly.

b. Make a table of values for the points on the graph. Then use differences or ratios to check your answer in part (a).

c. Write an equation for the function that the table of values from part (b) represents. $y = 4^x$

b.

x	0	1	2	3	4
y	1	4	16	64	256

19. Pleasure Boats The graph shows total amount of sales (in millions of dollars) of pleasure boats in the United States for the period 1990–2002. Tell whether the data should be modeled by a *linear function*, an *exponential function*, or a *quadratic function*. *Explain* your reasoning. Answers will vary.

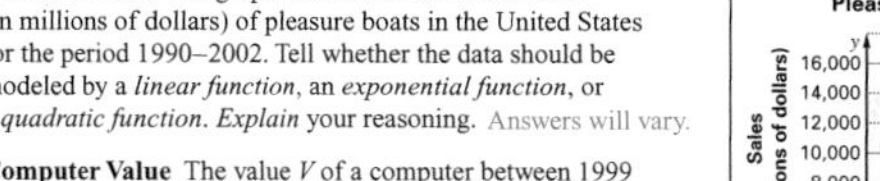

20. Computer Value The value V of a computer between 1999 and 2003 is given in the table. Tell whether the data should be modeled by a *linear function*, an *exponential function*, or a *quadratic function*. Then write an equation for the function. linear; $V = -75t + 800$

Years since 1999, t	0	1	2	3	4
Value, V (dollars)	800	725	650	575	500

10 Assessment

CHAPTER 10 **Quiz 1**
For use after Lessons 10.1–10.3

Graph the function. Compare the graph with the graph of $y = x^2$.

1. $y = \frac{2}{5}x^2$
2. $y = -3x^2 + 2$

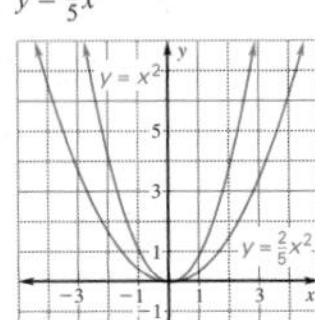
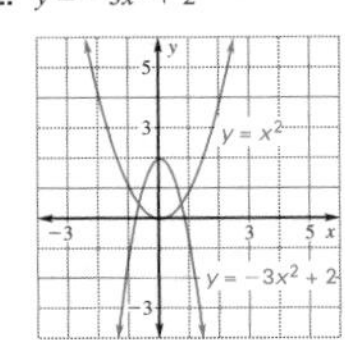

Graph the function. Label the vertex and axis of symmetry.

3. $y = x^2 + 2x + 3$
4. $y = -2x^2 + 8x - 5$

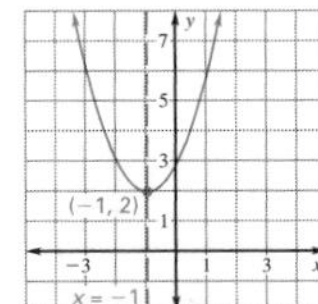
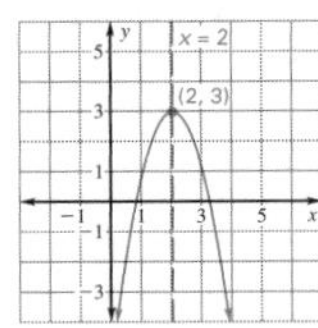

Solve the equation by graphing.

5. $x^2 - 5x + 6 = 0$
6. $x^2 - 8x = -12$

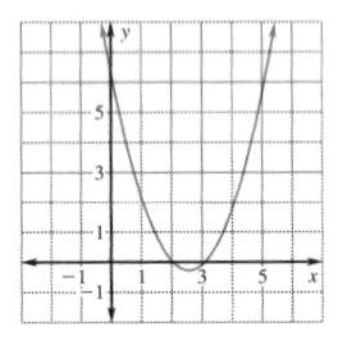
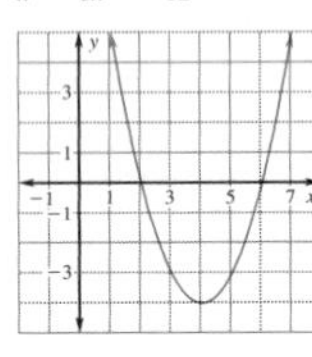

Find the zeros of the function.

7. $y = x^2 - 7x + 12$
8. $y = -x^2 - 6x - 5$

Answers

1. See left. The graph of $y = \frac{2}{5}x^2$ is a vertical shrink (by a factor of $\frac{2}{5}$) of the graph of $y = x^2$.
2. See left. The graph of $y = -3x^2 + 2$ is a reflection in the x-axis and a vertical translation (of 2 units up) of the graph of $y = x^2$.
3. See left.
4. See left.
5. See left. 2, 3
6. See left. 2, 6
7. 3, 4
8. $-5, -1$

CHAPTER 10 **Quiz 2**
For use after Lessons 10.4–10.6

Solve the equation using square roots.

1. $5x^2 = 45$
2. $x^2 - 3 = 4$

Solve the equation by completing the square.

3. $x^2 + 4x - 5 = 0$
4. $x^2 - 10x + 24 = 0$
5. $x^2 - 8x + 12 = 0$
6. $x^2 - 2x = 10$
7. $x^2 + 6x + 2 = 0$
8. $x^2 + 8x = -4$

Solve the equation by using the quadratic formula.

9. $3x^2 - 5x - 2 = 0$
10. $x^2 - 2x - 15 = 0$
11. $x^2 + 6x + 9 = 0$
12. $2x^2 - 7x = -3$

Answers

1. $-3, 3$
2. $-\sqrt{7}, \sqrt{7}$
3. $-5, 1$
4. 4, 6
5. 2, 6
6. $1 - \sqrt{11}, 1 + \sqrt{11}$
7. $-3 - \sqrt{7}, -3 + \sqrt{7}$
8. $-4 - 2\sqrt{3}, -4 + 2\sqrt{3}$
9. $-\frac{1}{3}, 2$
10. $-3, 5$
11. -3
12. $\frac{1}{2}, 3$

CHAPTER 10 **Quiz 3**
For use after Lessons 10.7–10.8

Tell whether the equation has *two solutions, one solution,* or *no solution.*

1. $2x^2 + x + 2 = 0$
2. $3x^2 - 4x + 1 = 0$

Find the number of x-intercepts of the graph of the function.

3. $y = 4x^2 - 12x + 9$
4. $y = x^2 + x - 20$

Tell whether the table of values represents a *linear function*, an *exponential function*, or a *quadratic function*. Then write an equation for the function.

5.

x	-2	-1	0	1	2
y	-5	-3	-1	1	3

6.

x	-2	-1	0	1	2
y	-3	0	1	0	-3

Answers

1. no solution
2. two solutions
3. one x-intercept
4. two x-intercepts
5. linear function $y = 2x - 1$
6. quadratic function $y = 2x^2 + 1$

CHAPTER 10 **Chapter Test B**
For use after Chapter 10

Graph the function. Compare the graph with the graph of $y = x^2$.

1. $y = \frac{1}{4}x^2 - 1$
2. $y = -x^2 + 5$

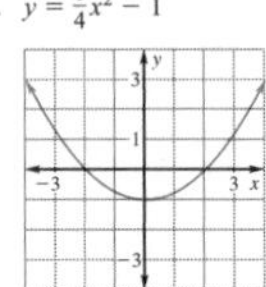
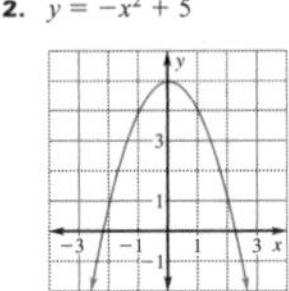

3. A cross section of the parabolic glass mirror of the Hubble space telescope shown can be modeled by the graph of the function $y = 0.0043x^2$ where x and y are measured in meters. Find the domain and range of the function in this situation.

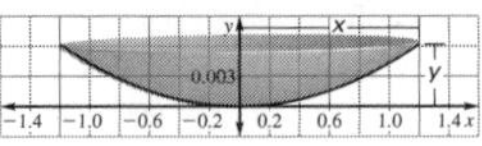

Find the axis of symmetry and the vertex of the graph of the function. Then tell whether the function has a *maximum value* or a *minimum value*.

4. $y = -2x^2 + 8x + 3$
5. $y = \frac{1}{2}x^2 - 2x + 5$
6. $y = 6x^2 + 7$
7. An arch of balloons decorates the entrance to a high school prom. The balloons are tied to a frame. The shape of the frame can be modeled by the graph of the equation $y = -\frac{1}{4}x^2 + 3x$ where x and y are measured in feet. What is the maximum height of the arch of balloons?

Solve the equation by graphing.

8. $x^2 + 5x - 14 = 0$
9. $-x^2 + 3x + 4 = 0$

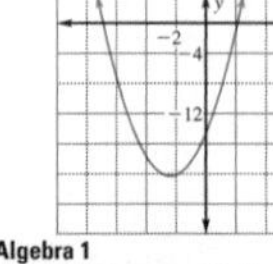
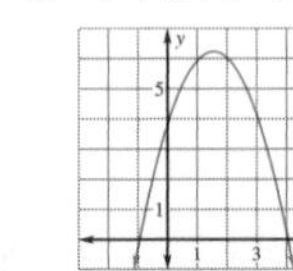
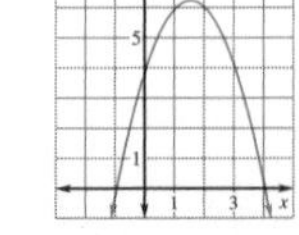

Answers

1. See left. The graph is a vertical shrink and downward translation of the graph of $y = x^2$.
2. See left. The graph is a reflection in the x-axis and an upward translation of the graph of $y = x^2$.
3. $-1.2 \le x \le 1.2$; $0 \le y \le 0.006$
4. $x = 2$; (2, 11) maximum value
5. $x = 2$; (2, 3) minimum value
6. $x = 0$; (0, 7) minimum value
7. 6 ft
8. See left. $-7, 2$
9. See left. $-1, 4$

CHAPTER 10

Chapter Test B *continued*

For use after Chapter 10

Solve the equation. Round the solutions to the nearest hundredth, if necessary.

10. $16t^2 - 9 = 0$ **11.** $2(x - 6)^2 = 24$ **12.** $4n^2 - 13 = -20$

13. Sailors need to consider the speed of the wind when adjusting the sails on their boat. The force F (in pounds per square foot) on a sail when the wind is blowing perpendicular to the sail can be modeled by the function $F = 0.004v^2$ where v is the wind speed (in knots). Find the wind speed that will produce a force of 2.5 pounds per square foot on a sail.

14. Complete the steps to solve the equation $x^2 - 8x - 3 = 0$ by completing the square.

$x^2 - 8x = \underline{?}$

$x^2 - 8x + \underline{?} = 19$

$(x - \underline{?})^2 = 19$

$x - \underline{?} = \underline{?}$

$x = \underline{?}$

Use the quadratic formula to solve the equation. Round the solutions to the nearest hundredth, if necessary.

15. $p^2 + 8p - 15 = 0$ **16.** $2y^2 - 7y = 10$ **17.** $9z^2 + 12z + 4 = 0$

18. During the period 1998–2002, the number y (in millions) of juvenile books shipped to bookstores can be modeled by the equation $y = -15x^2 + 64x + 360$ where x is the number of years since 1998. In what year were there 400 million juvenile books shipped to bookstores?

Find the number of *x*-intercepts that the graph of the function has.

19. $f(x) = 3x^2 - 3x + 4$

20. $f(x) = 4x^2 - 2x - 1$

21. $f(x) = 4x^2 + 12x + 9$

Tell whether the ordered pairs represent a *linear function*, an *exponential function*, or a *quadratic function*.

22. (–2, –13), (–1, –8), (0, –3), (1, 2), (2, 7)

23. (–2, 0), (–1, –3), (0, –4), (1, –3), (2, 0)

24. $\left(-2, \frac{1}{9}\right), \left(-1, \frac{1}{3}\right), (0, 1), (1, 3), (2, 9)$

Answers

10. ± 0.75

11. 2.54, 9.46

12. no solution

13. 25 knots

14. $3; 16; 4; 4; \pm\sqrt{19}$

$4 \pm \sqrt{19}$

15. –9.57, 1.57

16. –1.09, 4.59

17. –0.67

18. 2001

19. none

20. two

21. one

22. linear function

23. quadratic function

24. exponential function

CHAPTER 10

Standardized Test

For use after Chapter 10

Multiple Choice

1. What is the vertex of the graph of the function $y = -\frac{2}{3}x^2 + 5$? A

Ⓐ (0, 5) Ⓑ (5, 0)
Ⓒ (0, –5) Ⓓ (–5, 0)

2. How would the graph of the function $y = x^2 - 3$ be affected if the function were changed to $y = x^2 + 2$? B

Ⓐ The graph would shift 2 units up.
Ⓑ The graph would shift 5 units up.
Ⓒ The graph would shift 2 units to the right.
Ⓓ The graph would shift 5 unit down.

3. What is the vertex of the graph of the function $y = -2x^2 + 16x - 15$? D

Ⓐ (–4, –111) Ⓑ (–4, –81)
Ⓒ (4, –47) Ⓓ (4, 17)

4. What is the axis of symmetry of the function $y = -x^2 + 6x - 8$? B

Ⓐ $x = -3$ Ⓑ $x = 3$
Ⓒ $x = -8$ Ⓓ $x = 8$

5. What are the solutions of the equation shown? C

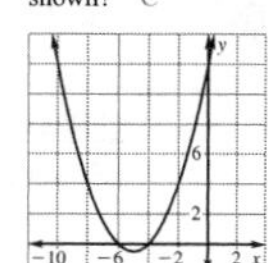

Ⓐ 4 and 6 Ⓑ 4 and –6
Ⓒ –4 and –6 Ⓓ –4 and 6

6. Which function has a zero between 7 and 8? C

Ⓐ $f(x) = \frac{1}{2}x^2 + 5x + 12$
Ⓑ $f(x) = -4x^2 + 6x + 5$
Ⓒ $f(x) = 3x^2 - 24x + 12$
Ⓓ $f(x) = \frac{1}{2}x^2 + 12$

7. What are the approximate zeros of the function $y = -x^2 - 5x + 5$ to the nearest tenth? D

Ⓐ 1.4 and 3.6 Ⓑ –0.9 and 5.9
Ⓒ –3.6 and –1.4 Ⓓ –5.9 and 0.9

8. Which of the following is a solution of the equation $107 - 5x^2 = -18$? B

Ⓐ –25 Ⓑ –5 Ⓒ 15 Ⓓ 25

9. Which of the following is a solution of the equation $2x^2 - 5 = -4\frac{1}{2}$? A

Ⓐ $-\frac{1}{2}$ Ⓑ $-\frac{1}{4}$ Ⓒ 1 Ⓓ $\frac{3}{4}$

10. What are the solutions of $4x^2 + 40x = -91$? A

Ⓐ $-\frac{13}{2}, -\frac{7}{2}$ Ⓑ $-\frac{13}{2}, \frac{7}{2}$
Ⓒ $\frac{13}{2}, -\frac{7}{2}$ Ⓓ $\frac{13}{2}, \frac{7}{2}$

11. What are the solutions of $4x^2 + 48x + 20 = 0$? D

Ⓐ $6 \pm \sqrt{41}$ Ⓑ $6 \pm \sqrt{31}$
Ⓒ $-6 \pm \sqrt{41}$ Ⓓ $-6 \pm \sqrt{31}$

12. What are the solutions of $4x^2 - 16x = 16x - 39$? D

Ⓐ $-\frac{13}{2}, -\frac{3}{2}$ Ⓑ $-\frac{13}{2}, \frac{3}{2}$
Ⓒ $\frac{13}{2}, -\frac{3}{2}$ Ⓓ $\frac{13}{2}, \frac{3}{2}$

CHAPTER 10

Standardized Test *continued*

For use after Chapter 10

13. What is the value of the discriminant of the equation $6x^2 - 5x - 3 = 0$? C

Ⓐ –47 Ⓑ 24 Ⓒ 97 Ⓓ 115

14. How many solutions does $5x^2 - 2x + 3$ have? A

Ⓐ None Ⓑ One
Ⓒ Two Ⓓ Three

15. Which function is represented by the following ordered pairs: (–5, 50), (–2, 8), (0, 0), (1, 2), (3, 18)? C

Ⓐ $y = 2^x$ Ⓑ $y = 2x$
Ⓒ $y = 2x^2$ Ⓓ $y = 0.5x^2$

16. The graph represents what kind of function? B

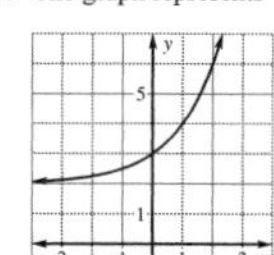

Ⓐ absolute value function
Ⓑ exponential function
Ⓒ linear function
Ⓓ quadratic function

Gridded Answer

17. The value of the discriminant of the equation $2x^2 - x - c = 2$ is 49. What is the value of c?

(Grid answer: 4)

Short Response

18. The science club wants to have fliers made to advertise their upcoming science fair. The table shows the cost y (in dollars) for x fliers.

Fliers, x	75	125	175	225
Cost (dollars), y	17	23	29	35

a. Tell whether the data can be modeled by a *linear function*, an *exponential function*, or a *quadratic function*. Then write an equation for the function.

b. If the number of fliers printed is tripled, does the price triple? *Explain.* See below.

Extended Response

19. The Art Club is selling scrapbooks to raise money for supplies. Last year, when the students charged \$10 per scrapbook, they sold 250 scrapbooks. The students want to increase the cost per scrapbook. They estimate that they will lose 5 sales for each \$1 increase in the cost per package. The revenue R (in dollars) generated by selling the scrapbooks is given by the function $R = (10 + n)(250 - 5n)$ where n is the number of \$1 increases.

a. Write the function in standard form. See below.

b. Find the maximum value of the function. 4500

c. At what price should the scrapbooks be sold to generate the most revenue? *Explain* your reasoning. \$30; According to the function, the maximum amount of revenue is \$4500. The maximum amount of revenue is made when n is 20. This means they can increase their price by \$20 to make their maximum amount of revenue. So, the new selling price would be \$30.

18. a. Linear function; $y = \frac{3}{25}x + 8$ **b.** No, if the number of fliers printed is tripled, the price is not tripled. The price increases exponentially.

19. a. $R = -5n^2 + 200n + 2500$

CHAPTER 10

Alternative Assessment and Math Journal

For use after Chapter 10

Journal **1.** Discuss the behavior of successive y-values for linear, exponential, and quadratic functions given that the increments between successive x-values are all equal. Give an example of an equation for each type of function.

Multi-Step Problem **2.** During a halftime show, a baton twirler releases her baton from a point 4 feet above the ground with an initial vertical velocity of 25 feet per second.

a. Use the vertical motion model to write a function for the height h (in feet) of the baton after t seconds.

b. Graph the function in part (a). Label the vertex of the graph.

c. How high does the baton go? Round your answer to the nearest tenth.

d. How long after the baton is released does it reach its maximum height?

e. At what moments is the baton at a height of 10 feet? Round your answer to the nearest hundredth.

f. How much time does the twirler have if she plans to catch the baton on its way down at a height of 5 feet? Round your answer to the nearest hundredth.

1. Complete answers should include: an explanation that the differences in successive y-values will be equal for linear functions; an explanation that the ratios in successive y-values will be equal for exponential functions; an explanation that the differences in successive first differences in y-values will be equal for quadratic functions; an example of an equation for each type of function.

2. a. $h = -16t^2 + 25t + 4$

b.

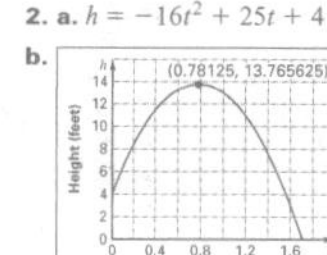

c. 13.8 ft **d.** 0.78125 sec **e.** 0.30 sec and 1.27 sec after release **f.** 1.52 sec

PLAN AND PREPARE

Main Ideas

In Chapter 10, students graph quadratic functions and compare them to the parent graph. They find the axis of symmetry, the vertex, and minimum or maximum values. They solve quadratic equations by factoring, graphing, using square roots, completing the square, and using the quadratic formula. Students use the discriminant to determine the number and type of solutions of a quadratic equation. Finally, students determine whether a linear, exponential, or quadratic function best models a set of data.

Prerequisite Skills

- Reflecting points in a line
- Finding square roots

Additional resources for reviewing prerequisite skills are:

- Skills Review Handbook, pp.909–937
- @HomeTutor

10 Quadratic Equations and Functions

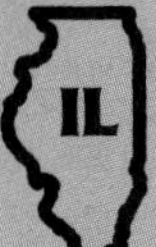

Before

In previous chapters, you learned the following skills, which you'll use in Chapter 10: reflecting points in a line and finding square roots.

Prerequisite Skills

VOCABULARY CHECK

Copy and complete the statement.

1. The x-coordinate of a point where a graph crosses the x-axis is a(n) __?__. **x-intercept**
2. A(n) __?__ is a function of the form $y = a \cdot b^x$ where $a \neq 0$, $b > 0$, and $b \neq 1$. **exponential function**

SKILLS CHECK

Draw the blue figure. Then draw its image after a reflection in the red line. *(Review p. 922 for 10.1–10.3.)* 3–5. See margin.

3. 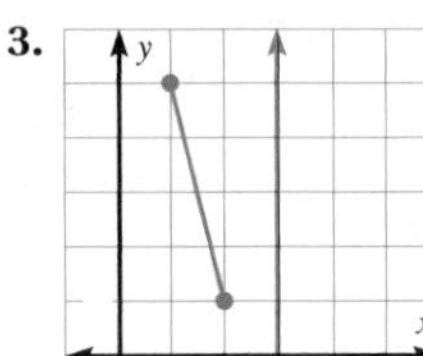

4. 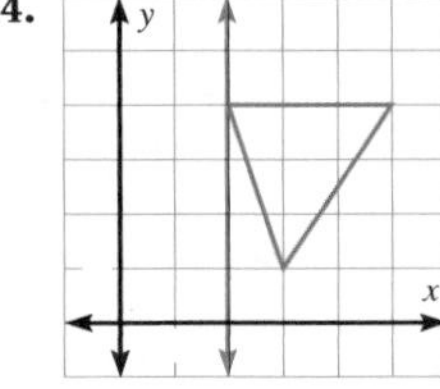

5. 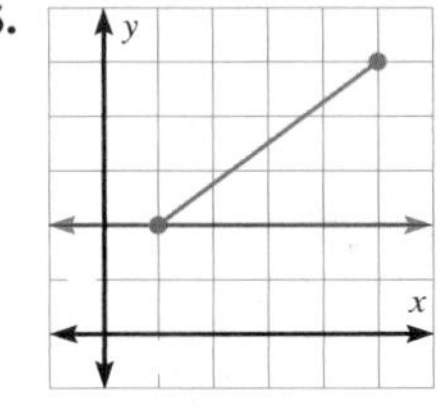

Evaluate the expression. *(Review p. 110 for 10.4–10.6.)*

6. $\sqrt{81}$ **9**
7. $-\sqrt{25}$ **−5**
8. $\sqrt{1}$ **1**
9. $\pm\sqrt{64}$ **±8**

@HomeTutor Prerequisite skills practice at classzone.com

626

Chapter Planning Guide

Chapter 10 Resource Book

- Teaching Guide/Lesson Plan (pp. 3, 17, 32, 46, 58, 69, 79, 89)
- Project with Rubric (p. 104)

Assessment and Intervention

- Assessment Book (pp. 139–153)
- Benchmark Tests
- Reteaching and Remediation Book

Interactive Technology

- Easy Planner
- Power Presentations CD-ROM
- Activity Generator CD-ROM
- Animated Algebra
- Test Generator CD-ROM
- Online Quizzes
- eWorkbook
- eEdition
- @HomeTutor

Resources for English Learners

- Quick Reference for English Learners
- Spanish Study Guide
- Multi-Language Visual Glossary
- Student Resources in Spanish

Now

In Chapter 10, you will apply the big ideas listed below and reviewed in the Chapter Summary on page 695. You will also use the key vocabulary listed below.

Big Ideas

1. **Graphing quadratic functions**
2. **Solving quadratic equations**
3. **Comparing linear, exponential, and quadratic models**

KEY VOCABULARY

- quadratic function, *p. 628*
- parabola, *p. 628*
- parent quadratic function, *p. 628*
- vertex, *p. 628*
- axis of symmetry, *p. 628*
- minimum value, *p. 636*
- maximum value, *p. 636*
- quadratic equation, *p. 643*
- completing the square, *p. 663*
- quadratic formula, *p. 671*
- discriminant, *p. 678*

Why?

You can use a quadratic model for real-world situations involving vertical motion. For example, you can write and solve a quadratic equation to find the time a snowboarder is in the air during a jump.

Animated Algebra

The animation illustrated below for Exercise 50 on page 668 helps you answer this question: How many seconds is the snowboarder in the air during a jump?

You need to find the time that the snowboarder is in the air.

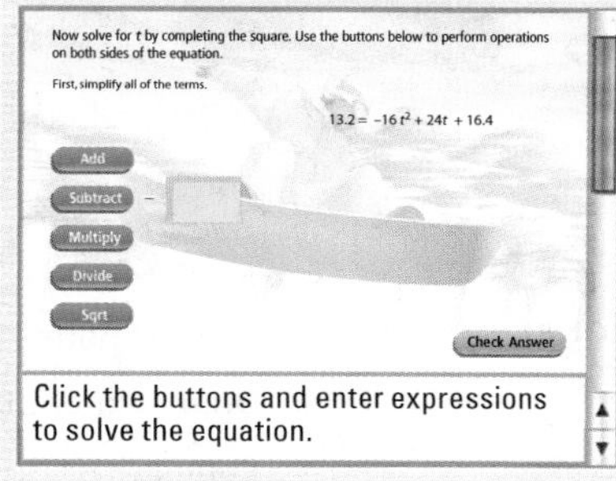

Now solve for t by completing the square. Use the buttons below to perform operations on both sides of the equation.
First, simplify all of the terms.
13.2 = −16t² + 24t + 16.4
Add
Subtract
Multiply
Divide
Sqrt
Check Answer

Click the buttons and enter expressions to solve the equation.

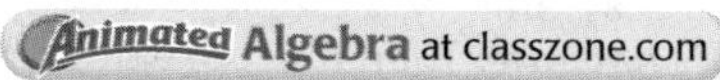

Other animations for Chapter 10: pages 634, 636, 642, 662, 668, 672, 684, and 695

627

Algebra 1 Toolkit

- Reading Strategies for Chapter 10, pp. 27–28
- Differentiated Instruction Notes, pp. 77–80
- English Learners Notes, pp. 115–116
- Inclusion Notes, pp. 147–148
- Teaching Strategies with Sample Worksheets, pp. 155–178
- Using Technology in the Classroom, pp. 179–184
- Tips for New Teachers, pp. 203–204
- Math Background Notes, pp. 229–230
- Pre-AP Strategies and Copymasters, pp. 296–297, 427–452
- Teacher Survival Activities, pp. 573–574, 599–600
- Bulletin Board Idea, p. 616
- Teacher Tool Transparencies, following p.620

3. 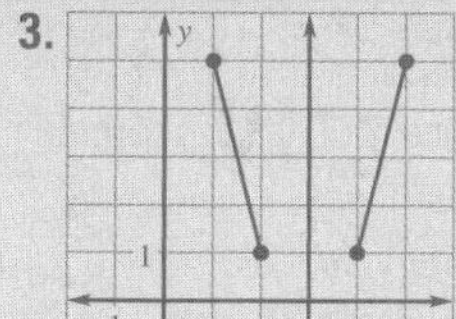

4. 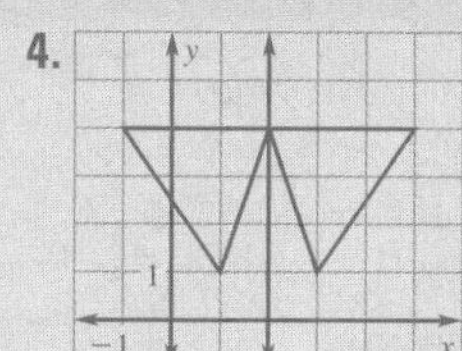

5. 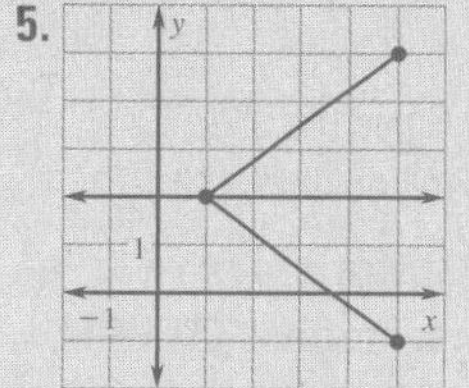

10.1 Graph $y = ax^2 + c$

8.11.08 Recognize and describe the general shape and properties of functions from graphs, tables or equations (e.g., . . . quadratic . . .).

Before You graphed linear and exponential functions.

Now You will graph simple quadratic functions.

Why? So you can solve a problem involving an antenna, as in Ex. 40.

1 PLAN AND PREPARE

Warm-Up Exercises

Transparency Available

1. Graph the function $y = 2^x$.

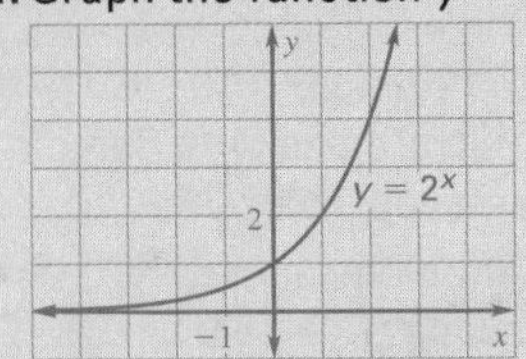

2. Identify the domain and range of your graph in Exercise 1. **domain: all real numbers; range: all positive real numbers**

Notetaking Guide

Transparency Available

Promotes interactive learning and notetaking skills, pp. 220–223.

Pacing

Basic: 2 days
Average: 2 days
Advanced: 2 days
Block: 1 block

- See *Teaching Guide/Lesson Plan.*

2 FOCUS AND MOTIVATE

Essential Question

Big Idea 1, p. 627

How do you graph a quadratic function? **Tell students they will learn how to answer this question by drawing a smooth curve through points from a table of values.**

Key Vocabulary
- quadratic function
- parabola
- parent quadratic function
- vertex
- axis of symmetry

A **quadratic function** is a nonlinear function that can be written in the **standard form** $y = ax^2 + bx + c$ where $a \neq 0$. Every quadratic function has a U-shaped graph called a **parabola**. In this lesson, you will graph quadratic functions where $b = 0$.

KEY CONCEPT *For Your Notebook*

Parent Quadratic Function

The most basic quadratic function in the family of quadratic functions, called the **parent quadratic function**, is $y = x^2$. The graph of $y = x^2$ is shown below.

The lowest or highest point on a parabola is the **vertex**. The vertex of the graph of $y = x^2$ is (0, 0).

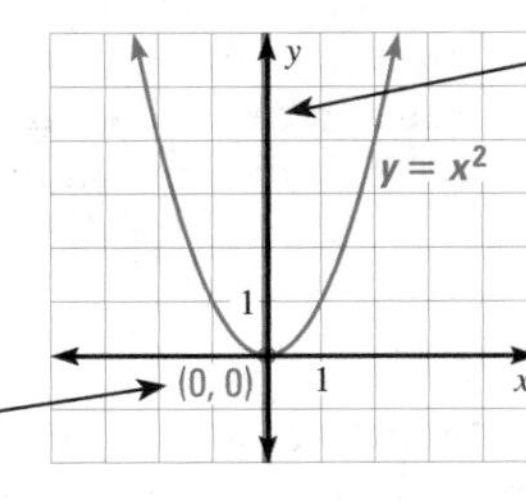

The line that passes through the vertex and divides the parabola into two symmetric parts is called the **axis of symmetry**. The axis of symmetry for the graph of $y = x^2$ is the y-axis, $x = 0$.

EXAMPLE 1 Graph $y = ax^2$ where $|a| > 1$

STEP 1 **Make** a table of values for $y = 3x^2$.

x	−2	−1	0	1	2
y	12	3	0	3	12

STEP 2 **Plot** the points from the table.

STEP 3 **Draw** a smooth curve through the points.

STEP 4 **Compare** the graphs of $y = 3x^2$ and $y = x^2$. Both graphs open up and have the same vertex, (0, 0), and axis of symmetry, $x = 0$. The graph of $y = 3x^2$ is narrower than the graph of $y = x^2$ because the graph of $y = 3x^2$ is a vertical stretch (by a factor of 3) of the graph of $y = x^2$.

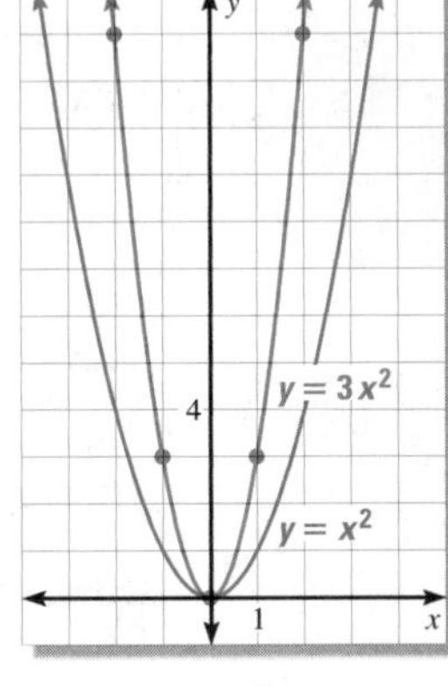

PLOT ADDITIONAL POINTS
If you are having difficulty seeing the shape of the parabola, plot additional points.

Resource Planning Guide

Chapter Resource Book
- Teaching Guide/Lesson Plan (pp. 3–4)
- Activity Master (p. 5)
- Practice levels A, B, C (pp. 6–11)
- Study Guide (pp. 12–13)
- Catch-up for Absent Students (p. 14)
- Application (p. 15)
- Challenge (p. 16)

Workbooks
- Notetaking Guide (pp. 220–223)
- Practice Workbook (pp. 149–151)

Teaching Options
- **Power Presentations CD-ROM** provides dynamic electronic teaching resources for the classroom.
- **Activity Generator CD-ROM** provides editable activities for all ability levels.

Interactive Technology
- Easy Planner
- Power Presentations CD-ROM
- Activity Generator CD-ROM
- Animated Algebra
- Test Generator CD-ROM
- Online Quiz
- eWorkbook
- eEdition
- @HomeTutor

Resources for English Learners
- Quick Reference for English Learners
- Spanish Study Guide
- Multi-Language Visual Glossary
- Student Resources in Spanish

See also the *Algebra 1 Toolkit* for more strategies for meeting individual needs.

EXAMPLE 2 Graph $y = ax^2$ where $|a| < 1$

Graph $y = -\frac{1}{4}x^2$. Compare the graph with the graph of $y = x^2$.

STEP 1 **Make** a table of values for $y = -\frac{1}{4}x^2$.

MAKE A TABLE
To make the calculations easier, choose values of x that are multiples of 2.

x	−4	−2	0	2	4
y	−4	−1	0	−1	−4

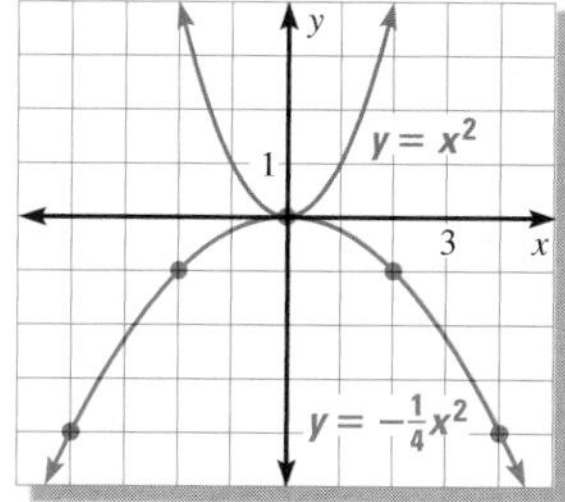

STEP 2 **Plot** the points from the table.

STEP 3 **Draw** a smooth curve through the points.

STEP 4 **Compare** the graphs of $y = -\frac{1}{4}x^2$ and $y = x^2$. Both graphs have the same vertex (0, 0), and the same axis of symmetry, $x = 0$. However, the graph of $y = -\frac{1}{4}x^2$ is wider than the graph of $y = x^2$ and it opens down. This is because the graph of $y = -\frac{1}{4}x^2$ is a vertical shrink $\left(\text{by a factor of } \frac{1}{4}\right)$ with a reflection in the x-axis of the graph of $y = x^2$.

GRAPHING QUADRATIC FUNCTIONS Examples 1 and 2 suggest the following general result: a parabola opens up when the coefficient of x^2 is positive and opens down when the coefficient of x^2 is negative.

EXAMPLE 3 Graph $y = x^2 + c$

Graph $y = x^2 + 5$. Compare the graph with the graph of $y = x^2$.

STEP 1 **Make** a table of values for $y = x^2 + 5$.

x	−2	−1	0	1	2
y	9	6	5	6	9

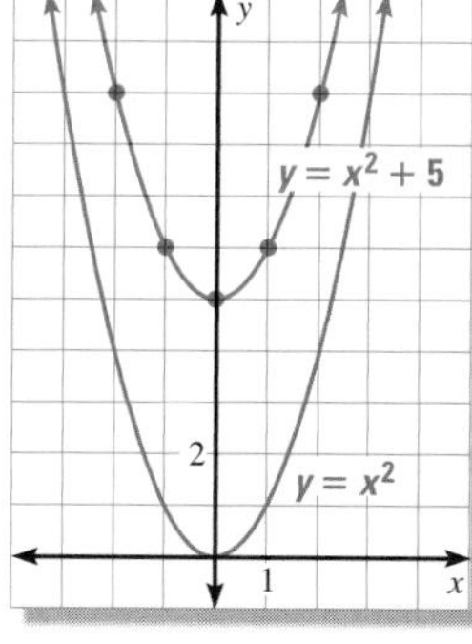

STEP 2 **Plot** the points from the table.

STEP 3 **Draw** a smooth curve through the points.

STEP 4 **Compare** the graphs of $y = x^2 + 5$ and $y = x^2$. Both graphs open up and have the same axis of symmetry, $x = 0$. However, the vertex of the graph of $y = x^2 + 5$, (0, 5), is different than the vertex of the graph of $y = x^2$, (0, 0), because the graph of $y = x^2 + 5$ is a vertical translation (of 5 units up) of the graph of $y = x^2$.

✓ **GUIDED PRACTICE** for Examples 1, 2, and 3

Graph the function. Compare the graph with the graph of $y = x^2$. 1–3. See margin.

1. $y = -4x^2$ **2.** $y = \frac{1}{3}x^2$ **3.** $y = x^2 + 2$

Motivating the Lesson

You see that your neighbors have a satellite dish on the roof of their house. You notice that the face of the dish is curved. In this lesson you will learn about that curve, called a parabola, and learn how to solve problems involving parabolas.

3 TEACH

Extra Example 1

Graph $y = 2x^2$. Compare the graph with the graph of $y = x^2$.

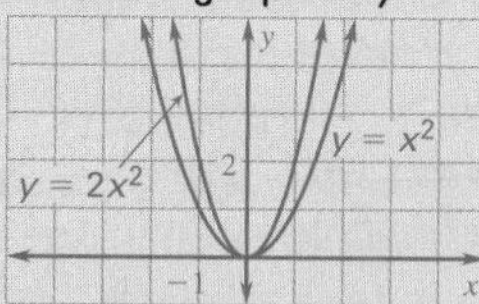

Both graphs open up and have the same vertex, (0, 0), and the same axis of symmetry, $x = 0$. The graph of $y = 2x^2$ is narrower than the graph of $y = x^2$ because it is a vertical stretch (by a factor of 2) of the parent graph.

Extra Example 2

Graph $y = -\frac{1}{2}x^2$. Compare the graph with the graph of $y = x^2$.

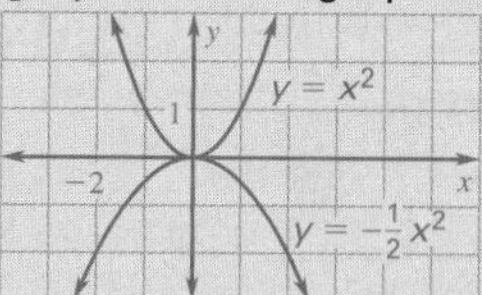

Both graphs have the same vertex, (0, 0), and the same axis of symmetry, $x = 0$. The graph of $y = -\frac{1}{2}x^2$ opens down. Also, the graph of $y = -\frac{1}{2}x^2$ is a reflection in the x-axis of $y = x^2$ after a vertical shrink $\left(\text{by a factor of } \frac{1}{2}\right)$.

1–3. See Additional Answers beginning on p. AA1.

Differentiated Instruction

English Learners The parent quadratic function $y = x^2$ produces the family of quadratic functions $y = ax^2 + bx + c$. Students may notice the analogy with a parent linear function producing a family of linear functions (Section 4.7).

See also the *Algebra 1 Toolkit* for more strategies.

EXAMPLE 4 Graph $y = ax^2 + c$

Graph $y = \frac{1}{2}x^2 - 4$. Compare the graph with the graph of $y = x^2$.

STEP 1 **Make** a table of values for $y = \frac{1}{2}x^2 - 4$.

x	−4	−2	0	2	4
y	4	−2	−4	−2	4

STEP 2 **Plot** the points from the table.

STEP 3 **Draw** a smooth curve through the points.

STEP 4 **Compare** the graphs of $y = \frac{1}{2}x^2 - 4$ and $y = x^2$. Both graphs open up and have the same axis of symmetry, $x = 0$. However, the graph of $y = \frac{1}{2}x^2 - 4$ is wider and has a lower vertex than the graph of $y = x^2$ because the graph of $y = \frac{1}{2}x^2 - 4$ is a vertical shrink and a vertical translation of the graph of $y = x^2$.

✓ GUIDED PRACTICE for Example 4

Graph the function. Compare the graph with the graph of $y = x^2$. 4–6. See margin.

4. $y = 3x^2 - 6$
5. $y = -5x^2 + 1$
6. $y = \frac{3}{4}x^2 - 2$

KEY CONCEPT *For Your Notebook*

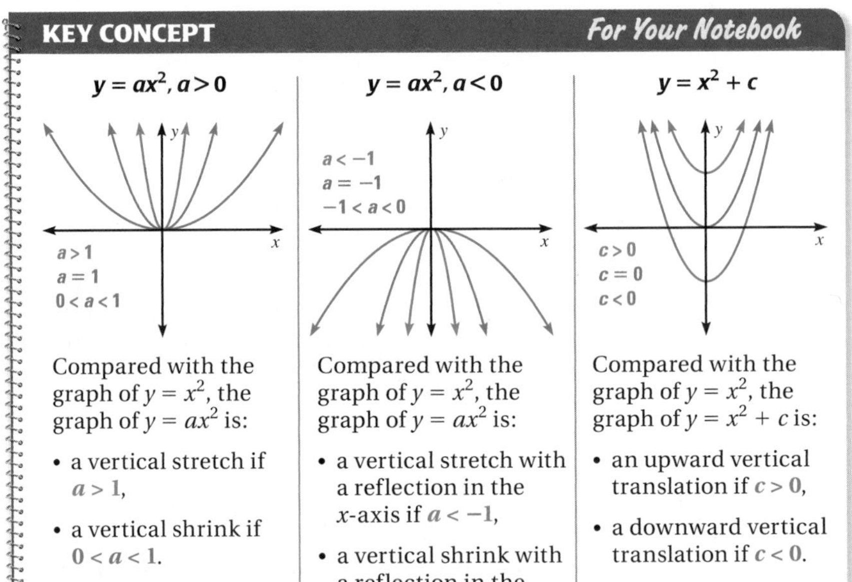

$y = ax^2, a > 0$

Compared with the graph of $y = x^2$, the graph of $y = ax^2$ is:

- a vertical stretch if $a > 1$,
- a vertical shrink if $0 < a < 1$.

$y = ax^2, a < 0$

Compared with the graph of $y = x^2$, the graph of $y = ax^2$ is:

- a vertical stretch with a reflection in the x-axis if $a < -1$,
- a vertical shrink with a reflection in the x-axis if $-1 < a < 0$.

$y = x^2 + c$

Compared with the graph of $y = x^2$, the graph of $y = x^2 + c$ is:

- an upward vertical translation if $c > 0$,
- a downward vertical translation if $c < 0$.

Extra Example 3

Graph $y = x^2 + 1$. Compare the graph with the graph of $y = x^2$.

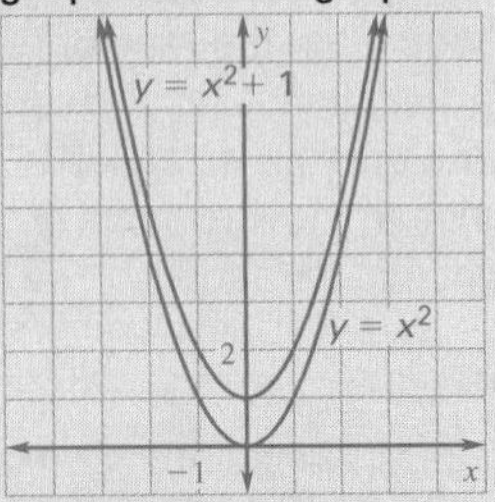

Both graphs open up and have the same axis of symmetry, $x = 0$. The vertex of the graph of $y = x^2 + 1$, which is (0, 1), is different that the vertex of the graph of $y = x^2$, which is (0, 0), because the graph of $y = x^2 + 1$ is a vertical translation (of 1 unit up) of the graph of $y = x^2$.

Key Questions to Ask for Example 3

- Why does the parabola open up? The coefficient of x^2 is positive.
- How can you tell that the parabola is shifted a positive number of units? The value of c in $y = x^2 + c$ is positive.

Extra Example 4

Graph $y = \frac{3}{2}x^2 - 2$. Compare the graph with the graph of $y = x^2$.

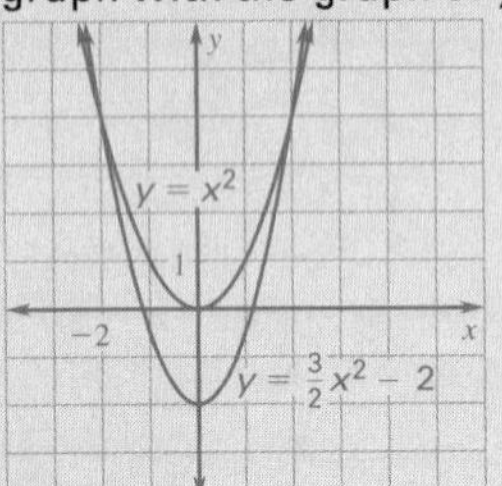

Both graphs open up and have the same axis of symmetry, $x = 0$. The graph of $y = \frac{3}{2}x^2 - 2$ is narrower and has a lower vertex than the graph of $y = x^2$ because it is a vertical stretch and a vertical translation of the graph of $y = x^2$.

4. 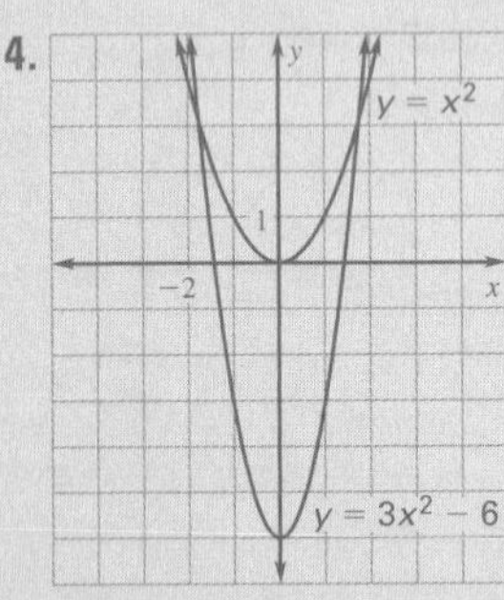

The graph is a vertical stretch (by a factor of 3) with a vertical translation (of 6 units down) of the graph of $y = x^2$.

5. 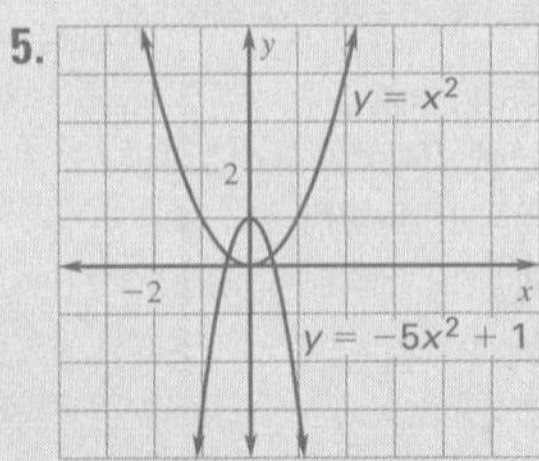

The graph is a vertical stretch (by a factor of 5) with a vertical translation (of 1 unit up) and a reflection in the x-axis of the graph of $y = x^2$.

EXAMPLE 5 Standardized Test Practice

How would the graph of the function $y = x^2 + 6$ be affected if the function were changed to $y = x^2 + 2$?

Ⓐ The graph would shift 2 units up.

Ⓑ The graph would shift 4 units up.

Ⓒ The graph would shift 4 units down.

Ⓓ The graph would shift 4 units to the left.

ELIMINATE CHOICES You can eliminate choice D because changing the value of c in a function of the form $y = x^2 + c$ translates the graph up or down.

Solution

The vertex of the graph of $y = x^2 + 6$ is 6 units above the origin, or (0, 6). The vertex of the graph of $y = x^2 + 2$ is 2 units above the origin, or (0, 2). Moving the vertex from (0, 6) to (0, 2) translates the graph 4 units down.

▶ The correct answer is C. Ⓐ Ⓑ Ⓒ Ⓓ

EXAMPLE 6 Use a graph

SOLAR ENERGY A solar trough has a reflective parabolic surface that is used to collect solar energy. The sun's rays are reflected from the surface toward a pipe that carries water. The heated water produces steam that is used to produce electricity.

The graph of the function $y = 0.09x^2$ models the cross section of the reflective surface where x and y are measured in meters. Use the graph to find the domain and range of the function in this situation.

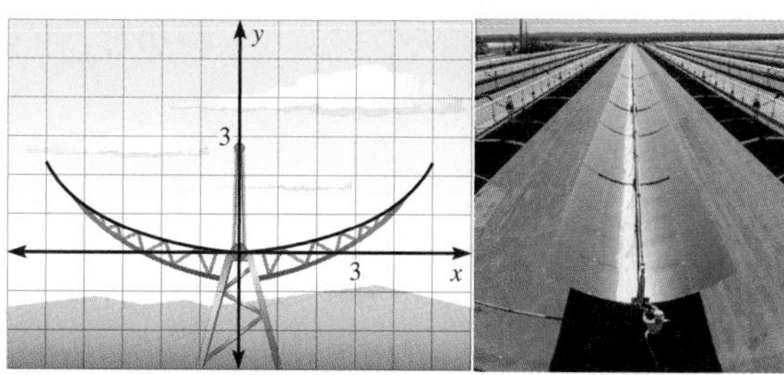

Solution

STEP 1 **Find** the domain. In the graph, the reflective surface extends 5 meters on either side of the origin. So, the domain is $-5 \le x \le 5$.

STEP 2 **Find** the range using the fact that the lowest point on the reflective surface is (0, 0) and the highest point, 5, occurs at each end.

$y = 0.09(5)^2 = 2.25$ **Substitute 5 for x. Then simplify.**

The range is $0 \le y \le 2.25$.

GUIDED PRACTICE for Examples 5 and 6

7. *Describe* how the graph of the function $y = x^2 + 2$ would be affected if the function were changed to $y = x^2 - 2$.
The graph would be translated 4 units down.

8. **WHAT IF?** In Example 6, suppose the reflective surface extends just 4 meters on either side of the origin. Find the domain and range of the function in this situation. **$-4 \le x \le 4$, $0 \le y \le 1.44$**

Extra Example 5

How would the graph of the function $y = x^2 - 3$ be affected if the function were changed to $y = x^2 - 2$? **B**

Ⓐ The graph would shift 2 units up.

Ⓑ The graph would shift 1 unit up.

Ⓒ The graph would shift 1 unit down.

Ⓓ The graph would shift 2 units down.

Extra Example 6

This graph shows a large parabolic umbrella. The graph of the function $y = -0.25x^2$ models the cross section of the surface, where x and y are measured in meters. Use the graph to find the domain and range of the function.

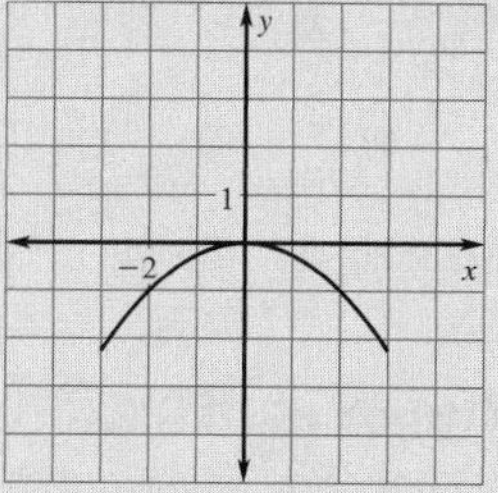

domain: $-3 \le x \le 3$
range: $-2.25 \le y \le 0$

Closing the Lesson

Have students summarize the major points of the lesson and answer the Essential Question: How do you graph a quadratic function?

- **The parent quadratic function is $y = x^2$.**
- **The vertex is the lowest or highest point on a parabola. The axis of symmetry passes through the vertex.**

Make a table of values for the function. Since a parabola is U-shaped, include values to the left and right of the vertex. Plot the points from the table and then draw a smooth curve through the points.

6. $y = x^2$; $y = \frac{3}{4}x^2 - 2$

The graph is a vertical shrink (by a factor of $\frac{3}{4}$) with a vertical translation (of 2 units down) of the graph of $y = x^2$.

10.1 EXERCISES

HOMEWORK KEY
○ = **WORKED-OUT SOLUTIONS** on p. WS23 for Exs. 7 and 41
★ = **STANDARDIZED TEST PRACTICE** Exs. 2, 22, 33, 43, and 44

4 PRACTICE AND APPLY

Assignment Guide

Answer Transparencies available for all exercises

Basic:
Day 1: EP p. 941 Exs. 56–59
pp. 632–634
Exs. 1–23
Day 2: pp. 632–634
Exs. 24–35, 40–42, 46–57

Average:
Day 1: pp. 632–634
Exs. 1–5, 10–23, 52–57
Day 2: pp. 632–634
Exs. 26–36, 40–44, 46–51

Advanced:
Day 1: pp. 632–634
Exs. 1–5, 12–23, 45*, 52–57
Day 2: pp. 632–634
Exs. 28–44*, 46–51

Block:
pp. 632–634
Exs. 1–5, 10–23, 26–37, 40–44, 46–57

Differentiated Instruction

See *Algebra 1 Best Practices Toolkit* for suggestions on addressing the needs of a diverse classroom.

Homework Check

For a quick check of student understanding of key concepts, go over the following exercises:

Basic: 8, 16, 26, 34, 40
Average: 12, 18, 28, 35, 40
Advanced: 15, 20, 31, 36, 41

Extra Practice

- Student Edition, p. 947
- Chapter 10 Resource Book: Practice levels A, B, C, pp. 6–11

Practice Worksheet

An easily-readable reduced practice page (with answers) for this lesson can be found on p. 626C.

6–21. See Additional Answers beginning on p. AA1.

SKILL PRACTICE

A

1. **VOCABULARY** Copy and complete: Every quadratic function has a U-shaped graph called a(n) __?__. parabola

2. ★ **WRITING** *Explain* how you can tell whether the graph of a quadratic function opens up or down. The graph of the quadratic function $y = ax^2 + bx + c$ opens up if $a > 0$ and opens down if $a < 0$.

MATCHING **Match the quadratic function with its graph.**

3. $y = \frac{1}{2}x^2 - 4$ C
4. $y = \frac{1}{2}x^2 - 2$ A
5. $y = -\frac{1}{2}x^2 + 2$ B

A. 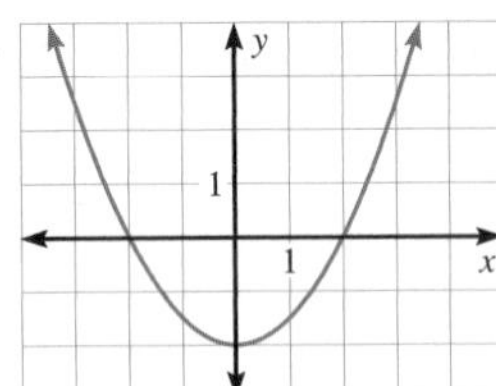

B. 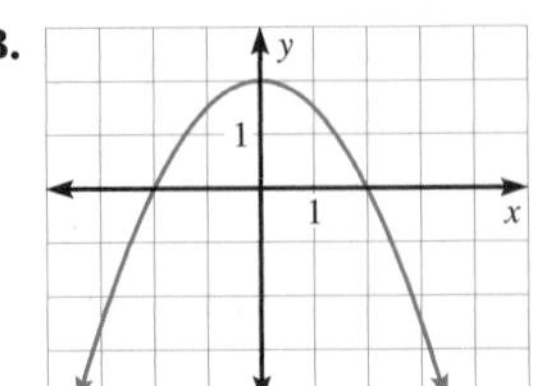

C. 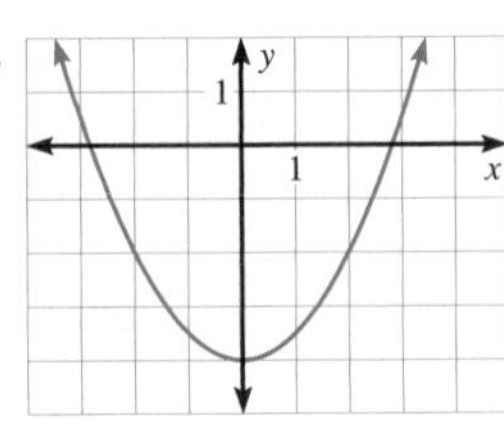

EXAMPLES 1, 2, and 3 on pp. 628–629 for Exs. 6–23

GRAPHING QUADRATIC FUNCTIONS **Graph the function. Compare the graph with the graph of $y = x^2$.** 6–21. See margin.

6. $y = 8x^2$
7. $y = -2x^2$
8. $y = -3x^2$
9. $y = 5x^2$
10. $y = \frac{11}{2}x^2$
11. $y = \frac{2}{3}x^2$
12. $y = -\frac{3}{4}x^2$
13. $y = -\frac{1}{9}x^2$
14. $y = \frac{3}{8}x^2$
15. $y = -\frac{1}{5}x^2$
16. $y = x^2 - 7$
17. $y = x^2 + 9$
18. $y = x^2 + 6$
19. $y = x^2 - 4$
20. $y = x^2 - 1$
21. $y = x^2 + \frac{7}{4}$

22. ★ **MULTIPLE CHOICE** What is the vertex of the graph of the function $y = -\frac{3}{4}x^2 + 7$? C

Ⓐ (−7, 0) Ⓑ (0, −7) Ⓒ (0, 7) Ⓓ (7, 0)

23. **ERROR ANALYSIS** *Describe* and correct the error in drawing and comparing the graphs of $y = x^2$ and $y = x^2 - 2$. The graph of $y = x^2 - 2$ should be shifted 2 units down, not 2 units up. The vertex should be at (0, −2); see margin for art.

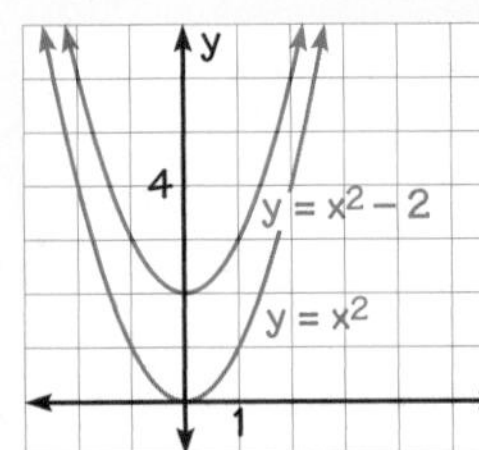

Both graphs open up and have the same axis of symmetry. However, the vertex of the graph of $y = x^2 - 2$, (0, 2), is 2 units above the vertex of the graph of $y = x^2$, (0, 0).

23. 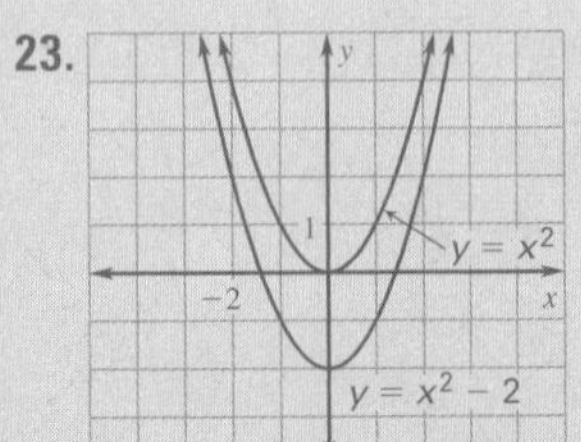

EXAMPLE 4 on p. 630 for Exs. 24–32

GRAPHING QUADRATIC FUNCTIONS Graph the function. Compare the graph with the graph of $y = x^2$. 24–32. See margin.

24. $y = 7x^2 + 7$ **25.** $y = -x^2 + 5$ **26.** $y = 2x^2 - 12$

27. $y = -2x^2 - 1$ **28.** $y = -3x^2 - 2$ **29.** $y = \frac{3}{4}x^2 - 3$

30. $y = \frac{1}{5}x^2 + 10$ **31.** $y = \frac{1}{2}x^2 - 5$ **32.** $y = -\frac{2}{3}x^2 + 9$

EXAMPLE 5 on p. 631 for Exs. 33–36

33. ★ **MULTIPLE CHOICE** How would the graph of the function $y = x^2 + 3$ be affected if the function were changed to $y = x^2 + 9$? B

Ⓐ The graph would shift 9 units to the right.

Ⓑ The graph would shift 6 units up.

Ⓒ The graph would shift 9 units up.

Ⓓ The graph would shift 6 units down.

B **COMPARING GRAPHS Tell how you can obtain the graph of g from the graph of f using transformations.** 34–36. See margin.

34. $f(x) = x^2 - 5$, $g(x) = x^2 + 8$ **35.** $f(x) = 3x^2 - 11$, $g(x) = 3x^2 - 16$ **36.** $f(x) = 4x^2$, $g(x) = 2x^2$

C **CHALLENGE Write a function of the form $y = ax^2 + c$ whose graph passes through the two given points.**

37. $(-1, 9), (0, 3)$ $y = 6x^2 + 3$ **38.** $(2, 1), (5, -20)$ $y = -x^2 + 5$ **39.** $(-2, -16.5), (1, 4.5)$ $y = -7x^2 + 11.5$

PROBLEM SOLVING

GRAPHING CALCULATOR You may wish to use a graphing calculator to complete the following Problem Solving exercises.

EXAMPLE 6 on p. 631 for Exs. 40–41

A **40. ASTRONOMY** A cross section of the parabolic surface of the antenna shown can be modeled by the graph of the function $y = 0.012x^2$ where x and y are measured in meters.

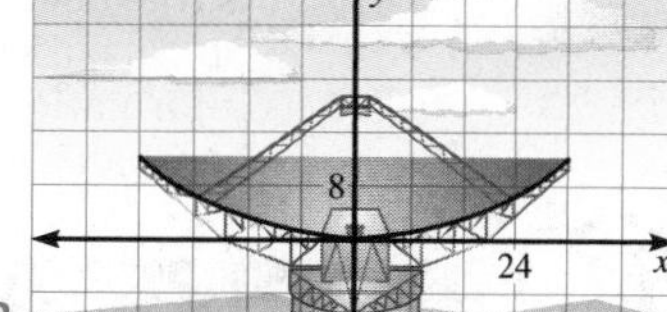

a. Find the domain of the function in this situation. $-32 \le x \le 32$

b. Find the range of the function in this situation. $0 \le y \le 12.288$

@HomeTutor for problem solving help at classzone.com

41. SAILING Sailors need to consider the speed of the wind when adjusting the sails on their boat. The force F (in pounds per square foot) on a sail when the wind is blowing perpendicular to the sail can be modeled by the function $F = 0.004v^2$ where v is the wind speed (in knots).

a. Graph the function for wind speeds from 0 knots to 50 knots. See margin for art.

b. Use the graph to estimate the wind speed that will produce a force of 1 pound per square foot on a sail. about 16 knots

c. Estimate the wind speed that will produce a force of 5 pounds per square foot on a sail. about 35 knots

@HomeTutor for problem solving help at classzone.com

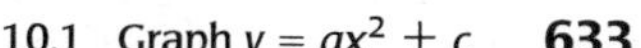

Avoiding Common Errors

Exercises 6–21, 24–32 Watch for students who do not graph points on both side of the vertex of the parabola. Remind these students that a parabola is U-shaped and symmetric, and they can use that symmetry to locate points on both sides of the vertex.

Graphing Calculator

Exercises 40–45 A graphing calculator will help students find approximate values for these exercises. Tell students to use the same steps to graph quadratic functions as they use to graph any other function.

An **Animated Algebra** activity is available on-line for **Exercise 44**. This activity is also available on the **Power Presentations CD-ROM**.

24–32. See Additional Answers beginning on p. AA1.

34. Translate the graph of f 13 units up.

35. Translate the graph of f 5 units down.

36. Shrink the graph of f by a factor of $\frac{1}{2}$.

41a.

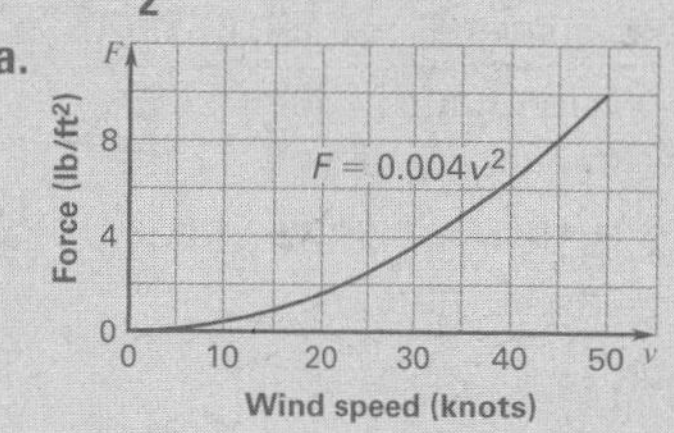

5 ASSESS AND RETEACH

Daily Homework Quiz

Transparency Available

1. Graph $y = -0.5x^2 + 2$.

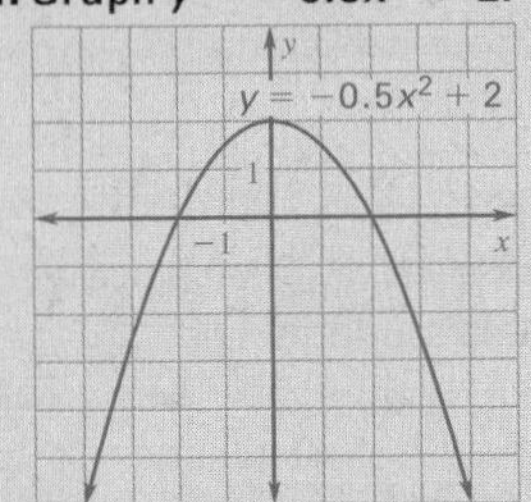

2. How would the graph of the function $y = -2x^2 + 3$ be affected if the function were changed to $y = -2x^2 - 3$? It would be shifted down 6 units.

3. A pinecone falls about 50 feet from the branch of a pine tree. Its height (in feet) can be modeled by the function $h(t) = -16t^2 + 50$, where t is the time in seconds. How long does it take to land on the ground? about 1.8 sec

Available at **classzone.com**

Diagnosis/Remediation

- Practice A, B, C in Chapter 10 Resource Book, pp. 6–11
- Study Guide in Chapter 10 Resource Book, pp. 12–13
- Practice Workbook, pp. 149–151
- @HomeTutor

Challenge

Additional challenge is available in the Chapter 10 Resource Book, p. 16.

43a–b, 44a–c. See Additional Answers beginning on p. AA1.

45.

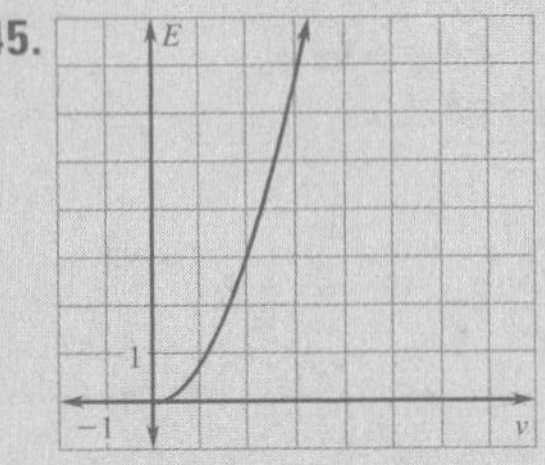

REVIEW VERTICAL MOTION

For help with the vertical motion model, see p. 575.

42b. *Sample answer:* The graph of $h = -16t^2 + 45$ is a vertical translation (of 13 units up) of the graph of $h = -16t^2 + 32$.

B

42. **FALLING OBJECTS** Two acorns drop from an oak tree. One falls 45 feet, while the other falls 32 feet.

 a. For each acorn, write an equation that gives the height h (in feet) of the acorn as a function of the time t (in seconds) it has fallen. $h = -16t^2 + 45$, $h = -16t^2 + 32$

 b. *Describe* how the graphs of the two equations are related.

43. ★ **SHORT RESPONSE** The breaking strength w (in pounds) of a manila rope can be modeled by the function $w = 8900d^2$ where d is the diameter (in inches) of the rope.

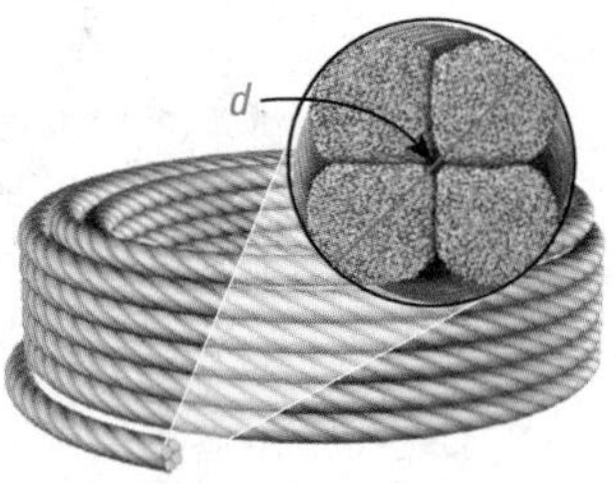

 a. Graph the function. a–b. See margin.

 b. If a manila rope has 4 times the breaking strength of another manila rope, does the rope have 4 times the diameter of the other rope? *Explain.*

44. ★ **EXTENDED RESPONSE** For an engineering contest, you have to create a container for an egg so that the container can be dropped from a height of 30 feet without breaking the egg.

 a. The distance y (in feet) that the container falls is given by the function $y = 16t^2$ where t is the time (in seconds) the container has fallen. Graph the function. a–c. See margin.

 b. The height y (in feet) of the dropped container is given by the function $y = -16t^2 + 30$ where t is the time (in seconds) since the container is dropped. Graph the function.

 c. How are the graphs from part (a) and part (b) related? *Explain* how you can use each graph to find the number of seconds after which the container has fallen 10 feet.

 Animated Algebra at classzone.com

C

45. **CHALLENGE** The kinetic energy E (in joules) of an object in motion is given by $E = \frac{1}{2}mv^2$ where m is the object's mass (in kilograms) and v is the object's velocity (in meters per second). Suppose a baseball has 918.75 joules of energy when traveling 35 meters per second. Use this information to write and graph an equation that gives the energy E of the baseball as a function of its velocity v. $E = 0.75v^2$; see margin for art.

ILLINOIS MIXED REVIEW

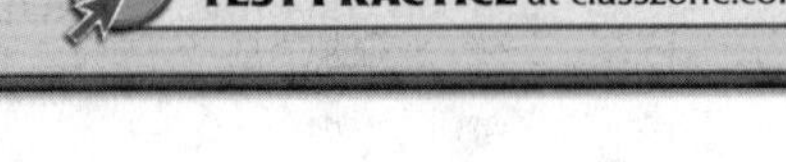

46. A fence that measures 72 feet in length encloses a rectangular patch of grass. The patch of grass has an area of 300 square feet. Which system of equations can be used to find ℓ, the length in feet of the patch of grass, and w, the width in feet of the patch of grass?

 Ⓐ $2\ell + 2w = 144$, $\ell w = 300$ C

 Ⓑ $2\ell + 2w = 72$, $300\ell = w$

 Ⓒ $2\ell + 2w = 72$, $\ell w = 300$

 Ⓓ $2\ell + 2w = 144$, $4\ell w = 300$

10.2 Graph $y = ax^2 + bx + c$

8.11.08 Recognize and describe the general shape and properties of functions from graphs, tables or equations (e.g., . . . quadratic . . .).

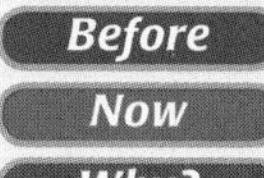

Before You graphed simple quadratic functions.

Now You will graph general quadratic functions.

Why? So you can investigate a cable's height, as in Example 4.

Key Vocabulary
- **minimum value**
- **maximum value**

You can use the properties below to graph any quadratic function. You will justify the formula for the axis of symmetry in Exercise 38 on page 639.

KEY CONCEPT *For Your Notebook*

Properties of the Graph of a Quadratic Function

The graph of $y = ax^2 + bx + c$ is a parabola that:

- opens up if $a > 0$ and opens down if $a < 0$.
- is narrower than the graph of $y = x^2$ if $|a| > 1$ and wider if $|a| < 1$.
- has an axis of symmetry of $x = -\frac{b}{2a}$.
- has a vertex with an x-coordinate of $-\frac{b}{2a}$.
- has a y-intercept of c. So, the point $(0, c)$ is on the parabola.

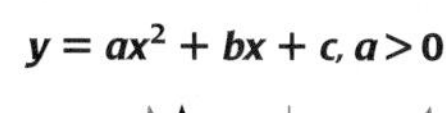

$y = ax^2 + bx + c, a > 0$

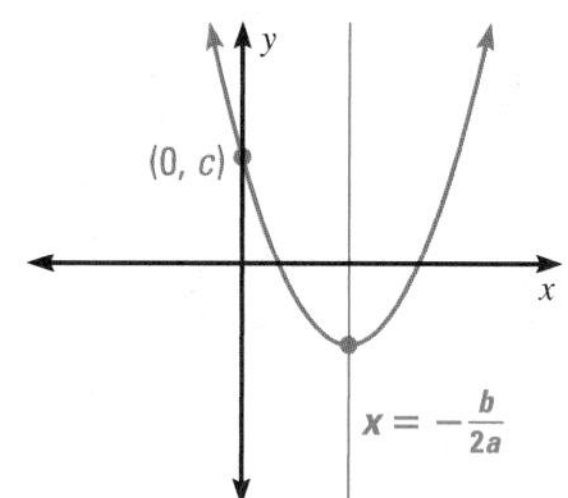

EXAMPLE 1 Find the axis of symmetry and the vertex

Consider the function $y = -2x^2 + 12x - 7$.

a. Find the axis of symmetry of the graph of the function.

b. Find the vertex of the graph of the function.

Solution

a. For the function $y = -2x^2 + 12x - 7$, $a = -2$ and $b = 12$.

$x = -\frac{b}{2a} = -\frac{12}{2(-2)} = 3$ **Substitute −2 for *a* and 12 for *b*. Then simplify.**

IDENTIFY THE VERTEX
Because the vertex lies on the axis of symmetry, $x = 3$, the x-coordinate of the vertex is 3.

b. The x-coordinate of the vertex is $-\frac{b}{2a}$, or 3.

To find the y-coordinate, substitute 3 for x in the function and find y.

$y = -2(3)^2 + 12(3) - 7 = 11$ **Substitute 3 for *x*. Then simplify.**

▶ The vertex is (3, 11).

1 PLAN AND PREPARE

Warm-Up Exercises

Transparency Available

Evaluate the expression.

1. $x^2 - 2$ when $x = 3$ **7**

2. $2x^2 + 9$ when $x = 2$ **17**

3. Martin is replacing a square patch of counter top. The area of the patch is represented by $A = s^2$. What is the area of the patch if the side length is 2.5 inches? **6.25 in.²**

Notetaking Guide

Transparency Available

Promotes interactive learning and notetaking skills, pp. 224–226.

Pacing

Basic: 1 day
Average: 1 day
Advanced: 1 day
Block: 0.5 block with 10.3
- See *Teaching Guide/Lesson Plan.*

2 FOCUS AND MOTIVATE

Essential Question

Big Idea 1, p. 627

How do you graph a quadratic function of the form $y = ax^2 + bx + c$? **Tell students they will learn how to answer this question by finding the axis of symmetry, finding the vertex, and using symmetry to plot several points.**

Resource Planning Guide

Chapter Resource Book
- Teaching Guide/Lesson Plan (pp. 17–18)
- Activity Master (p. 19)
- Practice levels A, B, C (pp. 21–26)
- Study Guide (pp. 27–28)
- Catch-up for Absent Students (p. 29)
- Problem Solving Workshop (p. 30)
- Challenge (p. 31)

Workbooks
- Notetaking Guide (pp. 224–226)
- Practice Workbook (pp. 152–154)

Teaching Options
- **Power Presentations CD-ROM** provides dynamic electronic teaching resources for the classroom.
- **Activity Generator CD-ROM** provides editable activities for all ability levels.

Interactive Technology
- Easy Planner
- Power Presentations CD-ROM
- Activity Generator CD-ROM
- Animated Algebra
- Test Generator CD-ROM
- Online Quiz
- eWorkbook
- eEdition
- @HomeTutor

Resources for English Learners
- Quick Reference for English Learners
- Spanish Study Guide
- Multi-Language Visual Glossary
- Student Resources in Spanish

See also the *Algebra 1 Toolkit* for more strategies for meeting individual needs.

Motivating the Lesson

As you pass over a suspension bridge, you notice that the cables form a parabola. You also notice, as you pass beneath a bridge, that arches in the shape of a parabola support the bridge. In this lesson you will learn how to find maximum and minimum points on a parabola and how to use that information to find the highest and lowest points of suspension cables and support arches.

3 TEACH

Extra Example 1

Consider the function $y = 3x^2 + 12x - 8$.

a. Find the axis of symmetry of the graph of the function. $x = -2$

b. Find the vertex of the graph of the function. $(-2, -20)$

Extra Example 2

Graph $y = 2x^2 - 8x + 7$.

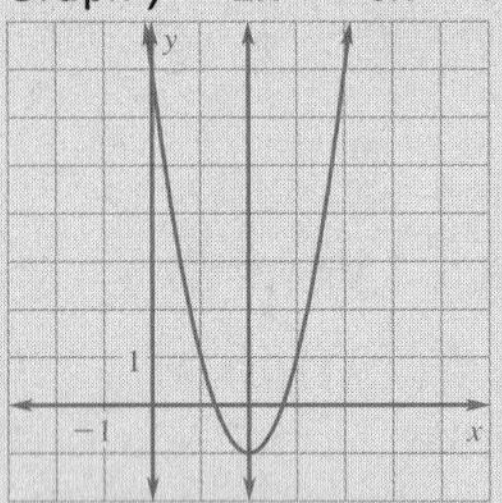

Key Question to Ask for Example 2

- In Step 4, why do you find two x-values less than the x-coordinate of the vertex? The parabola is U-shaped, so after you find two points to the left of the vertex you can use symmetry to locate corresponding points to the right of the vertex.

EXAMPLE 2 Graph $y = ax^2 + bx + c$

Graph $y = 3x^2 - 6x + 2$.

STEP 1 **Determine** whether the parabola opens up or down. Because $a > 0$, the parabola opens up.

AVOID ERRORS
Be sure to include the negative sign before the fraction when calculating the axis of symmetry.

STEP 2 **Find** and draw the axis of symmetry: $x = -\frac{b}{2a} = -\frac{-6}{2(3)} = 1$.

STEP 3 **Find** and plot the vertex.

The x-coordinate of the vertex is $-\frac{b}{2a}$, or 1.

To find the y-coordinate, substitute 1 for x in the function and simplify.

$y = 3(1)^2 - 6(1) + 2 = -1$

So, the vertex is $(1, -1)$.

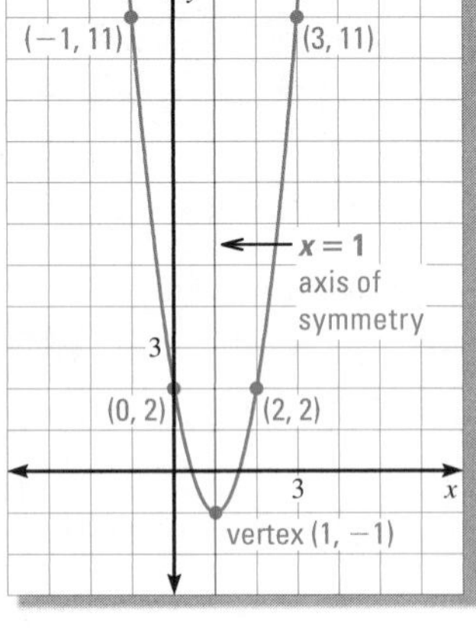

STEP 4 **Plot** two points. Choose two x-values less than the x-coordinate of the vertex. Then find the corresponding y-values.

x	0	−1
y	2	11

REVIEW REFLECTIONS
For help with reflections, see p. 922.

STEP 5 **Reflect** the points plotted in Step 4 in the axis of symmetry.

STEP 6 **Draw** a parabola through the plotted points.

Animated Algebra at classzone.com

GUIDED PRACTICE for Examples 1 and 2

1. Find the axis of symmetry and the vertex of the graph of the function $y = x^2 - 2x - 3$. $x = 1, (1, -4)$

2. Graph the function $y = 3x^2 + 12x - 1$. Label the vertex and axis of symmetry. See margin.

KEY CONCEPT — For Your Notebook

Minimum and Maximum Values

For $y = ax^2 + bx + c$, the y-coordinate of the vertex is the **minimum value** of the function if $a > 0$ or the **maximum value** of the function if $a < 0$.

$y = ax^2 + bx + c, a > 0$ **$y = ax^2 + bx + c, a < 0$**

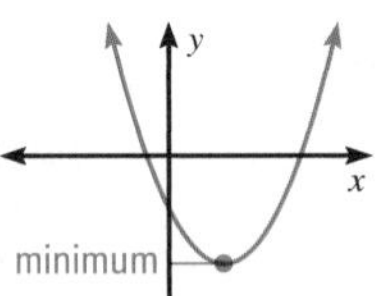

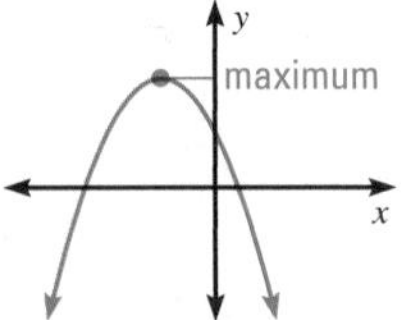

Differentiated Instruction

Visual Learners Show students that the Key Concept in Lesson 10.1 on p. 630 shows the special cases of the function $y = ax^2 + bx + c$ when $b = 0$ and when $b = c = 0$.

See also the *Algebra 1 Toolkit* for more strategies.

EXAMPLE 3 Find the minimum or maximum value

Tell whether the function $f(x) = -3x^2 - 12x + 10$ has a *minimum value* or a *maximum value*. Then find the minimum or maximum value.

Solution

Because $a = -3$ and $-3 < 0$, the parabola opens down and the function has a maximum value. To find the maximum value, find the vertex.

$x = -\frac{b}{2a} = -\frac{-12}{2(-3)} = -2$ The x-coordinate is $-\frac{b}{2a}$.

$f(-2) = -3(-2)^2 - 12(-2) + 10 = 22$ Substitute −2 for x. Then simplify.

▶ The maximum value of the function is $f(-2) = 22$.

EXAMPLE 4 Find the minimum value of a function

SUSPENSION BRIDGES The suspension cables between the two towers of the Mackinac Bridge in Michigan form a parabola that can be modeled by the graph of $y = 0.000097x^2 - 0.37x + 549$ where x and y are measured in feet. What is the height of the cable above the water at its lowest point?

Solution

The lowest point of the cable is at the vertex of the parabola. Find the x-coordinate of the vertex. Use $a = 0.000097$ and $b = -0.37$.

$x = -\frac{b}{2a} = -\frac{-0.37}{2(0.000097)} \approx 1910$ Use a calculator.

Substitute 1910 for x in the equation to find the y-coordinate of the vertex.

$y \approx 0.000097(1910)^2 - 0.37(1910) + 549 \approx 196$

▶ The cable is about 196 feet above the water at its lowest point.

✓ **GUIDED PRACTICE** for Examples 3 and 4

3. minimum value; $-\frac{1}{2}$

3. Tell whether the function $f(x) = 6x^2 + 18x + 13$ has a *minimum value* or a *maximum value*. Then find the minimum or maximum value.

4. **SUSPENSION BRIDGES** The cables between the two towers of the Takoma Narrows Bridge form a parabola that can be modeled by the graph of the equation $y = 0.00014x^2 - 0.4x + 507$ where x and y are measured in feet. What is the height of the cable above the water at its lowest point? Round your answer to the nearest foot. 221 ft

2.

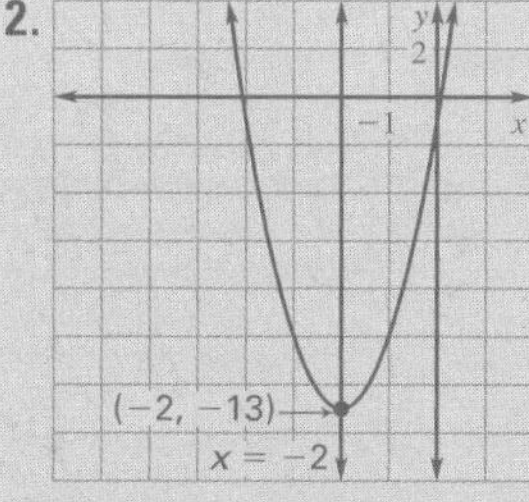

An **Animated Algebra** activity is available on-line for **Example 2**. This activity is also available on the **Power Presentations CD-ROM**.

Extra Example 3

Tell whether the function $f(x) = 2x^2 - 16x + 4$ has a *minimum value* or a *maximum value*. Then find the minimum or maximum value. The graph opens up, so it has a minimum value. The minimum value is $f(4) = -28$.

Extra Example 4

The cables between two telephone poles can be modeled by the equation $y = 0.0024x^2 - 0.1x + 24$, where x and y are measured in feet. To the nearest foot, what is the height of the cable above the ground at its lowest point? 23 ft

Closing the Lesson

Have students summarize the major points of the lesson and answer the Essential Question: How do you graph a quadratic function of the form $y = ax^2 + bx + c$?

- The graph of a quadratic function is a parabola that opens up if $a > 0$ and opens down if $a < 0$.
- An equation for the axis of symmetry of a quadratic function is $x = -\frac{b}{2a}$.
- The x-coordinate of the vertex is $-\frac{b}{2a}$.

Determine whether the graph opens up or opens down. Then find and draw the axis of symmetry by substituting values for a and b in the equation $x = -\frac{b}{2a}$. Substitute that x-value into the function and simplify to find the y-coordinate of the vertex. Choose two x-values less than the x-coordinate of the vertex and plot the points. Reflect the points in the axis of symmetry. Draw a parabola through the points.

10.2 EXERCISES

HOMEWORK KEY
○ = **WORKED-OUT SOLUTIONS** on p. WS23 for Exs. 9 and 41
★ = **STANDARDIZED TEST PRACTICE** Exs. 2, 12, 27, 37, 42, and 44

4 PRACTICE AND APPLY

Assignment Guide

Answer Transparencies available for all exercises

Basic:
Day 1: pp. 638–640
Exs. 1, 2, 3–11 odd, 12–20, 27–32, 37, 40–43, 46, 49, 51, 55

Average:
Day 1: pp. 638–640
Exs. 1, 2, 6–14 even, 20–27, 31–38, 40–44, 47, 52, 56

Advanced:
Day 1: pp. 638–640
Exs. 1, 8–12, 20–27, 32–45*, 48, 53, 54, 58

Block:
pp. 638–640
Exs. 1, 2, 6–14 even, 20–27, 31–38, 40–44, 47, 52, 56 (with 10.3)

Differentiated Instruction

See *Algebra 1 Best Practices Toolkit* for suggestions on addressing the needs of a diverse classroom.

Homework Check

For a quick check of student understanding of key concepts, go over the following exercises:
Basic: 5, 17, 20, 30, 40
Average: 8, 22, 24, 33, 41
Advanced: 10, 24, 25, 35, 42

Extra Practice

- Student Edition, p. 947
- Chapter 10 Resource Book: Practice levels A, B, C, pp. 21–26

Practice Worksheet

An easily-readable reduced practice page (with answers) for this lesson can be found on p. 626C.

SKILL PRACTICE

A

1. **VOCABULARY** *Explain* how you can tell whether a quadratic function has a maximum value or minimum value without graphing the function. See margin.

2. ★ **WRITING** *Describe* the steps you would take to graph a quadratic function in standard form. See margin.

EXAMPLE 1 on p. 635 for Exs. 3–14

FINDING AXIS OF SYMMETRY AND VERTEX Find the axis of symmetry and the vertex of the graph of the function.

3. $y = 2x^2 - 8x + 6$
4. $y = x^2 - 6x + 11$
5. $y = -3x^2 + 24x - 22$
6. $y = -x^2 - 10x$
7. $y = 6x^2 + 6x$
8. $y = 4x^2 + 7$
9. $y = -\frac{2}{3}x^2 - 1$
10. $y = \frac{1}{2}x^2 + 8x - 9$
11. $y = -\frac{1}{4}x^2 + 3x - 2$

Answers: 3. $x = 2$, $(2, -2)$ 4. $x = 3$, $(3, 2)$ 5. $x = 4$, $(4, 26)$ 6. $x = -5$, $(-5, 25)$ 7. $x = -\frac{1}{2}$, $\left(-\frac{1}{2}, -\frac{3}{2}\right)$ 8. $x = 0$, $(0, 7)$ 9. $x = 0$, $(0, -1)$ 10. $x = -8$, $(-8, -41)$ 11. $x = 6$, $(6, 7)$

12. ★ **MULTIPLE CHOICE** What is the vertex of the graph of the function $y = -3x^2 + 18x - 13$? D

Ⓐ $(-3, -94)$ Ⓑ $(-3, -14)$ Ⓒ $(3, -13)$ Ⓓ $(3, 14)$

ERROR ANALYSIS *Describe* **and correct the error in finding the axis of symmetry of the graph of the given function.** 13, 14. See margin.

13. $y = 2x^2 + 16x - 1$

$x = \frac{b}{2a} = \frac{16}{2(2)} = 4$
The axis of symmetry is x = 4.

14. $y = -\frac{3}{2}x^2 + 18x - 5$

$x = -\frac{b}{2a} = -\frac{18}{2\left(\frac{3}{2}\right)} = -6$
The axis of symmetry is x = −6.

EXAMPLE 2 on p. 636 for Exs. 15–27

GRAPHING QUADRATIC FUNCTIONS Graph the function. Label the vertex and axis of symmetry. 15–26. See margin for art.

15. $y = x^2 + 6x + 2$
16. $y = x^2 + 4x + 8$
17. $y = 2x^2 + 7x + 21$
18. $y = 5x^2 + 10x - 3$
19. $y = 4x^2 + x - 32$
20. $y = -4x^2 + 4x + 8$
21. $y = -3x^2 - 2x - 5$
22. $y = -8x^2 - 12x + 1$
23. $y = -x^2 + \frac{1}{4}x + \frac{1}{2}$
24. $y = \frac{1}{3}x^2 + 6x - 9$
25. $y = -\frac{1}{2}x^2 + 6x + 3$
26. $y = -\frac{1}{4}x^2 - x + 1$

13. The equation of the axis of symmetry is $x = -\frac{b}{2a}$, not $x = \frac{b}{2a}$; $x = -\frac{b}{2a} = -\frac{16}{2(2)}$, $x = -4$.

14. $-\frac{3}{2}$ should be substituted for a; $x = -\frac{18}{2\left(-\frac{3}{2}\right)}$, $x = 6$.

27. ★ **MULTIPLE CHOICE** Which function has the graph shown? B

Ⓐ $y = -2x^2 + 8x + 3$
Ⓑ $y = -\frac{1}{2}x^2 + 2x + 3$
Ⓒ $y = \frac{1}{2}x^2 + 2x + 3$
Ⓓ $y = 2x^2 + 8x + 3$

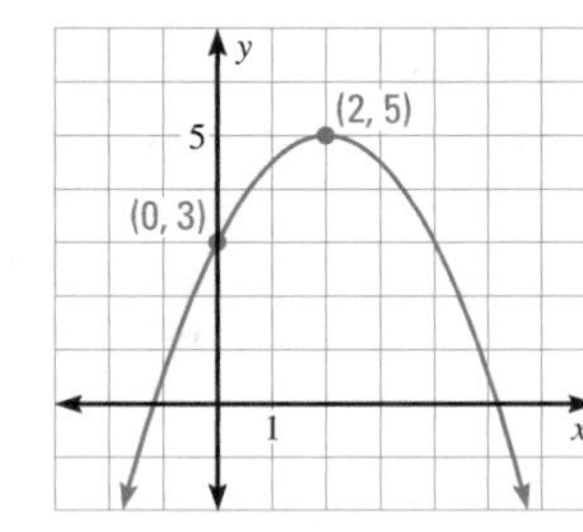

1. When the function is in standard form, $y = ax^2 + bx + c$, it will have a minimum value if $a > 0$ and a maximum value if $a < 0$.

2. Use the sign of a to tell if the parabola opens up or down. Find the axis of symmetry, $x = -\frac{b}{2a}$, which also gives the x-coordinate of the vertex. Substitute $-\frac{b}{2a}$ for x in the function to find the y-coordinate of the vertex. Calculate y-values for two x-values on one side of the vertex. Plot the vertex and the two points; then reflect the two points through the axis of symmetry to locate two more points. Draw a parabola through the plotted points.
15–26. See Additional Answers beginning on p. AA1.

EXAMPLE 3
on p. 637
for Exs. 28–36

MAXIMUM AND MINIMUM VALUES ***Tell whether the function has a minimum value or a maximum value. Then find the minimum or maximum value.***

28. $f(x) = x^2 - 6$
29. $f(x) = -5x^2 + 7$
30. $f(x) = 4x^2 + 32x$
31. $f(x) = -3x^2 + 12x - 20$
32. $f(x) = x^2 + 7x + 8$
33. $f(x) = -2x^2 - x + 10$
34. $f(x) = \frac{1}{2}x^2 - 2x + 5$
35. $f(x) = -\frac{3}{8}x^2 + 9x$
36. $f(x) = \frac{1}{4}x^2 + 7x + 11$

28. minimum value; -6
29. maximum value; 7
30. minimum value; -64
31. maximum value; -8
32. minimum value; $-\frac{17}{4}$
33. maximum value; $\frac{81}{8}$
34. minimum value; 3
35. maximum value; 54
36. minimum value; -38

B

37. ★ **WRITING** Compare the graph of $y = x^2 + 4x + 1$ with the graph of $y = x^2 - 4x + 1$. **The graph of $y = x^2 + 4x + 1$ is a horizontal translation (of 4 units left) of the graph $y = x^2 - 4x + 1$.**

38. **REASONING** Follow the steps below to justify the equation for the axis of symmetry for the graph of $y = ax^2 + bx + c$. Because the graph of $y = ax^2 + bx + c$ is a vertical translation of the graph of $y = ax^2 + bx$, the two graphs have the same axis of symmetry. Use the function $y = ax^2 + bx$ in place of $y = ax^2 + bx + c$.
   a. Find the x-intercepts of the graph of $y = ax^2 + bx$. (You can do this by finding the zeros of the function $y = ax^2 + bx$ using factoring.) **$0, -\frac{b}{a}$**
   b. Because a parabola is symmetric about its axis of symmetry, the axis of symmetry passes through a point halfway between the x-intercepts of the parabola. Find the x-coordinate of this point. What is an equation of the vertical line through this point? **$-\frac{b}{2a}$; $x = -\frac{b}{2a}$**

C

39. **CHALLENGE** Write a function of the form $y = ax^2 + bx$ whose graph contains the points (1, 6) and (3, 6). ***Sample answer:*** **$y = -2x^2 + 8x$**

PROBLEM SOLVING

GRAPHING CALCULATOR **You may wish to use a graphing calculator to complete the following Problem Solving exercises.**

EXAMPLE 4
on p. 637
for Exs. 40–42

A

40. **SPIDERS** Fishing spiders can propel themselves across water and leap vertically from the surface of the water. During a vertical jump, the height of the body of the spider can be modeled by the function $y = -4500x^2 + 820x + 43$ where x is the duration (in seconds) of the jump and y is the height (in millimeters) of the spider above the surface of the water. After how many seconds does the spider's body reach its maximum height? What is the maximum height? **about 0.091 sec; about 80 mm**

@HomeTutor for problem solving help at classzone.com

41. **ARCHITECTURE** The parabolic arches that support the roof of the Dallas Convention Center can be modeled by the graph of the equation $y = -0.0019x^2 + 0.71x$ where x and y are measured in feet. What is the height h at the highest point of the arch as shown in the diagram? **about 66 ft**

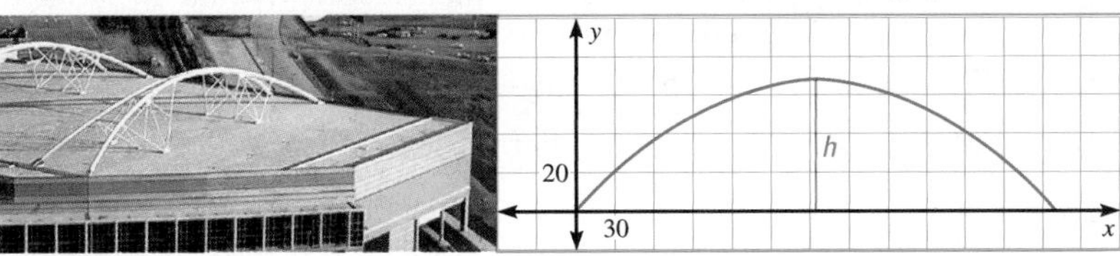

@HomeTutor for problem solving help at classzone.com

Avoiding Common Errors

Exercises 3–11, 15–26 Some students may overlook the negative sign in $-\frac{b}{2a}$ when calculating the axis of symmetry. Suggest that students double check that they included the negative sign before finding the vertex of the graph.

Teaching Strategy

Exercises 27, 28–36 Before students begin these exercises, have a class discussion about whether each has a minimum or maximum value. This will help students focus on the sign of a in the quadratic function. Point out that, in Exercise 27, students can use this method to eliminate two of the answer choices.

Study Strategy

Exercise 40 Suggest to students that they make a note on what the values of x and y represent before they work the problem. This can help them identify the values for height and time.

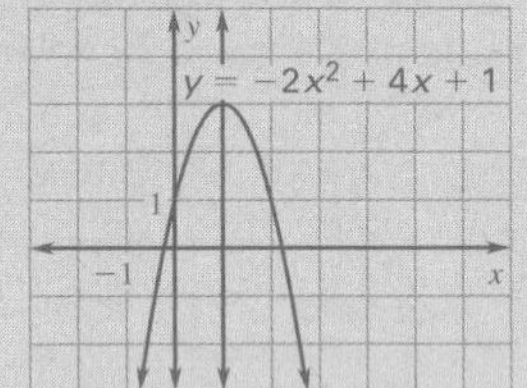

5 ASSESS AND RETEACH

Daily Homework Quiz

Transparency Available

1. Find the axis of symmetry and the vertex of the graph of the function $y = -4x^2 + 8x - 9$. $x = 1$; $(1, -5)$
2. Graph $y = -2x^2 + 4x + 1$.
3. An arch to the entrance of the library can be modeled by $y = -0.13x^2 + 2.5x$, where x and y are measured in feet. To the nearest foot, what is the height of the highest point of the arch? 12 ft

Online Quiz

Available at **classzone.com**

Diagnosis/Remediation

- Practice A, B, C in Chapter 10 Resource Book, pp. 21–26
- Study Guide in Chapter 10 Resource Book, pp. 27–28
- Practice Workbook, pp. 152–154
- @HomeTutor

Challenge

Additional challenge is available in the Chapter 10 Resource Book, p. 31.

43. See Additional Answers beginning on p. AA1.

44. No; the maximum value of the function $S = 332 + 132t - 10.4t^2$ occurs when $t = -\frac{132}{2(-10.4)} \approx 6.35$. Because the function S makes sense only for integer values of t, the maximum value of S occurs at either $t = 6$ or $t = 7$. These t-values correspond to 1996 and 1997, so the greatest number of tickets for Broadway tours was sold after 1995.

42c. $10; the maximum value of $1000 occurs when $n = 5$, so the students should charge 5 $1 increases, or $5 + $5 = $10 in order to generate the most sales revenue.

42. ★ **EXTENDED RESPONSE** Students are selling packages of flower bulbs to raise money for a class trip. Last year, when the students charged $5 per package, they sold 150 packages. The students want to increase the cost per package. They estimate that they will lose 10 sales for each $1 increase in the cost per package. The sales revenue R (in dollars) generated by selling the packages is given by the function $R = (5 + n)(150 - 10n)$ where n is the number of $1 increases.

    a. Write the function in standard form. $R = -10n^2 + 100n + 750$

    b. Find the maximum value of the function. $1000

    c. At what price should the packages be sold to generate the most sales revenue? *Explain* your reasoning.

B

43. **AIRCRAFT** An aircraft hangar is a large building where planes are stored. The opening of one airport hangar is a parabolic arch that can be modeled by the graph of the equation $y = -0.007x^2 + 1.7x$ where x and y are measured in feet. Graph the function. Use the graph to determine how wide the hangar is at its base. See margin for art; about 243 ft.

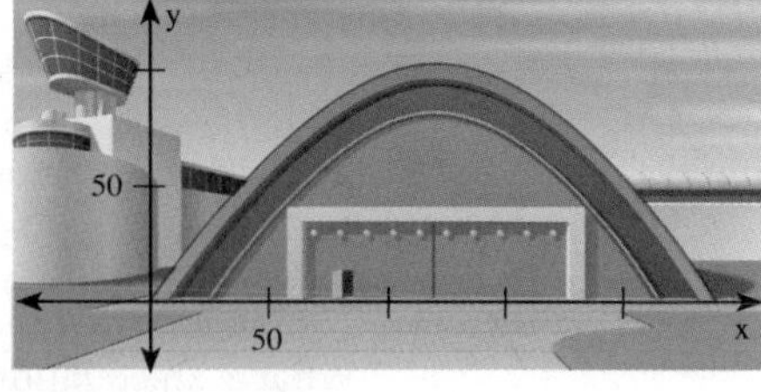

44. ★ **SHORT RESPONSE** The casts of some Broadway shows go on tour, performing their shows in cities across the United States. For the period 1990–2001, the number of tickets sold S (in millions) for Broadway road tours can be modeled by the function $S = 332 + 132t - 10.4t^2$ where t is the number of years since 1990. Was the greatest number of tickets for Broadway road tours sold in 1995? *Explain.* See margin.

C

45. **CHALLENGE** During an archery competition, an archer shoots an arrow from 1.5 meters off of the ground. The arrow follows the parabolic path shown and hits the ground in front of the target 90 meters away. Use the y-intercept and the points on the graph to write an equation for the graph that models the path of the arrow. $y = -0.00031x^2 + 0.011x + 1.5$

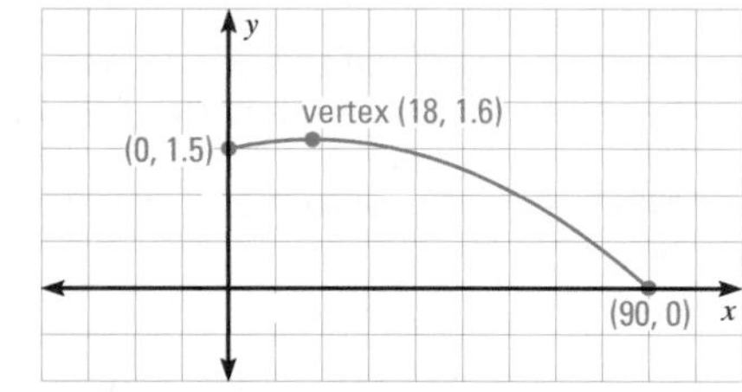

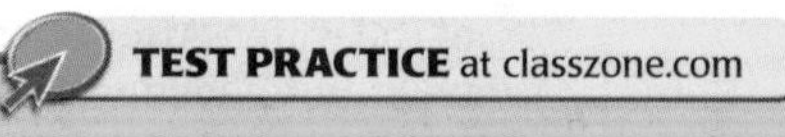

ILLINOIS MIXED REVIEW

46. Simplify the algebraic expression $2(1 - a) - 5a$. B

    (A) $-7a - 2$ (B) $-7a + 2$ (C) $-2a + 2$ (D) $3a + 2$

47. A 3-dimensional solid is shown. Which best represents the shape of the solid when viewed from the top?

    (A) Pentagon (B) Hexagon B

    (C) Octagon (D) Not here

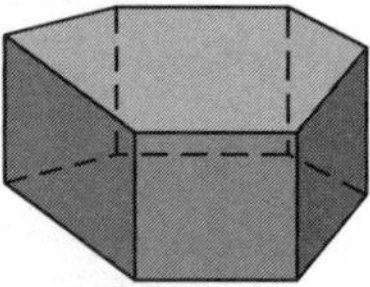

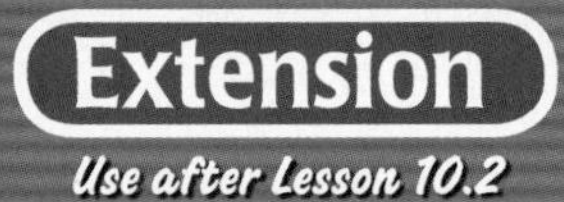

Graph Quadratic Functions in Intercept Form

GOAL Graph quadratic functions in intercept form.

Key Vocabulary
- **intercept form**

In Lesson 10.2 you graphed quadratic functions written in standard form. Quadratic functions can also be written in **intercept form**, $y = a(x - p)(x - q)$ where $a \neq 0$. In this form, the x-intercepts of the graph can easily be determined.

KEY CONCEPT *For Your Notebook*

Graph of Intercept Form $y = a(x - p)(x - q)$

Characteristics of the graph of $y = a(x - p)(x - q)$:

- The x-intercepts are p and q.
- The axis of symmetry is halfway between $(p, 0)$ and $(q, 0)$. So, the axis of symmetry is $x = \frac{p+q}{2}$.
- The parabola opens up if $a > 0$ and opens down if $a < 0$.

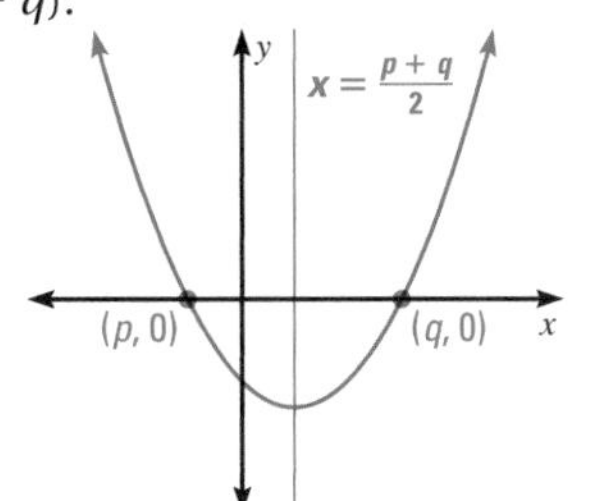

EXAMPLE 1 Graph a quadratic function in intercept form

Graph $y = -(x + 1)(x - 5)$.

Solution

FIND ZEROS OF A FUNCTION
Notice that the x-intercepts of the graph are also the zeros of the function:
$0 = -(x + 1)(x - 5)$
$x + 1 = 0$ *or* $x - 5 = 0$
$x = -1$ *or* $x = 5$

STEP 1 **Identify** and plot the x-intercepts. Because $p = -1$ and $q = 5$, the x-intercepts occur at the points $(-1, 0)$ and $(5, 0)$.

STEP 2 **Find** and draw the axis of symmetry.

$$x = \frac{p+q}{2} = \frac{-1+5}{2} = 2$$

STEP 3 **Find** and plot the vertex.

The x-coordinate of the vertex is 2.

To find the y-coordinate of the vertex, substitute 2 for x and simplify.

$$y = -(2 + 1)(2 - 5) = 9$$

So, the vertex is $(2, 9)$.

STEP 4 **Draw** a parabola through the vertex and the points where the x-intercepts occur.

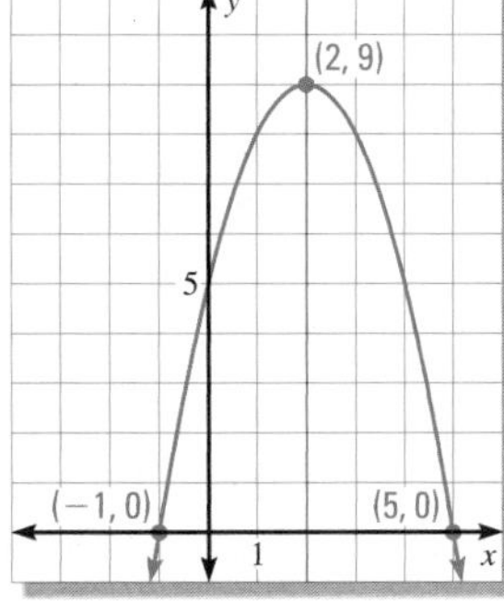

1 PLAN AND PREPARE

Warm-Up Exercises

1. Find the axis of symmetry and the vertex of the graph of the function $y = x^2 + 2x - 15$. $x = -1$; $(-1, -16)$
2. Graph $y = 3x^2 - 6x + 1$.

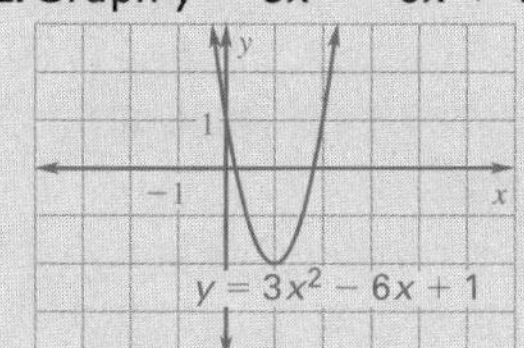

2 FOCUS AND MOTIVATE

Essential Question

Big Idea 1, p. 627

How do you graph a quadratic function in intercept form? **Tell students they will learn how to answer this question by identifying and plotting the x-intercepts, the axis of symmetry, and the vertex of the function.**

3 TEACH

Extra Example 1

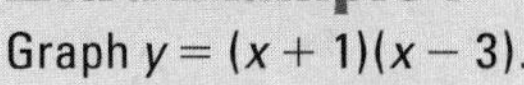

Graph $y = (x + 1)(x - 3)$.

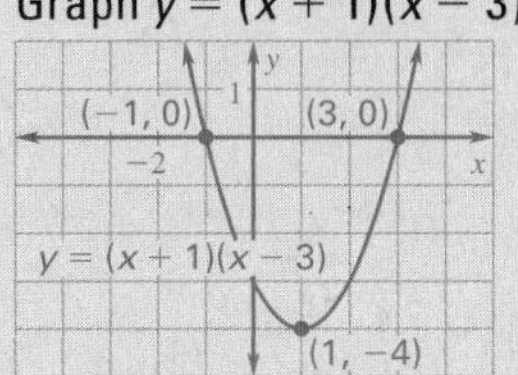

NCTM STANDARDS

Standard 2: Analyze situations using algebraic symbols

Standard 3: Use symmetry to analyze math situations

Extra Example 2

Graph $y = 2x^2 - 2$.

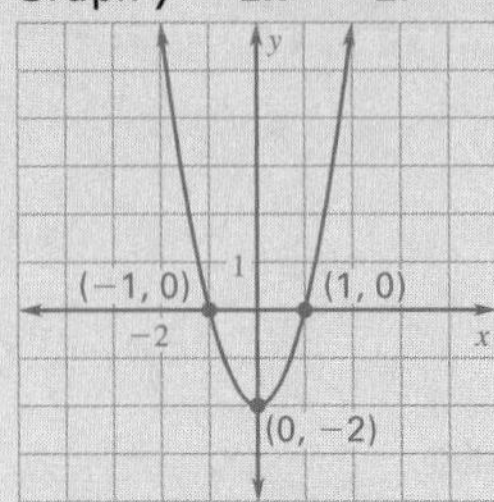

Key Question to Ask for Example 2

- What is the relationship between the x-intercepts of the graph and the zeros of the function? **The x-intercepts of the graph are the zeros of the function.**

An **Animated Algebra** activity is available on-line for **Example 2**. This activity is also available on the **Power Presentations CD-ROM**.

Closing the Lesson

Have students summarize the major points of the lesson and answer the Essential Question: How do you graph a quadratic function in intercept form?

- **The intercept form of a quadratic function is $y = a(x - p)(x - q)$. The x-intercepts are p and q.**
- **The axis of symmetry is $x = \frac{p+q}{2}$.**

Identify and plot the x-intercepts. Find and plot the axis of symmetry. Find and plot the vertex and another point on each side of the vertex. Draw a parabola through those points.

4 PRACTICE AND APPLY

Avoiding Common Errors

Exercises 4–9 When finding the y-coordinate of the vertex, some students may forget to multiply by the coefficient of the factored terms. Tell students they can avoid this error by using *all* the terms of the function when calculating the value of the y-coordinate of the vertex.

EXAMPLE 2 Graph a quadratic function

Graph $y = 2x^2 - 8$.

Solution

STEP 1 **Rewrite** the quadratic function in intercept form.

$y = 2x^2 - 8$	**Write original function.**
$= 2(x^2 - 4)$	**Factor out common factor.**
$= 2(x + 2)(x - 2)$	**Difference of two squares pattern**

STEP 2 **Identify** and plot the x-intercepts. Because $p = -2$ and $q = 2$, the x-intercepts occur at the points $(-2, 0)$ and $(2, 0)$.

STEP 3 **Find** and draw the axis of symmetry.

$$x = \frac{p+q}{2} = \frac{-2+2}{2} = 0$$

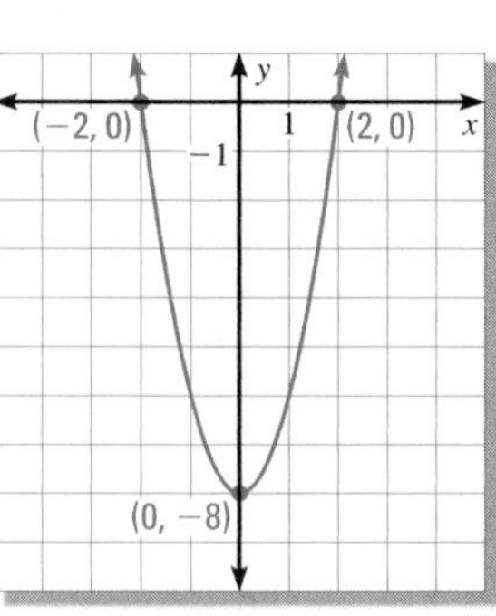

STEP 4 **Find** and plot the vertex.

The x-coordinate of the vertex is 0.

The y-coordinate of the vertex is:

$y = 2(0)^2 - 8 = -8$

So, the vertex is $(0, -8)$.

STEP 5 **Draw** a parabola through the vertex and the points where the x-intercepts occur.

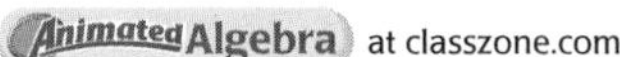

at classzone.com

PRACTICE

EXAMPLE 1 on p. 641 for Exs. 1–9

Graph the quadratic function. Label the vertex, axis of symmetry, and x-intercepts. **1–15. See margin for art.**

1. $y = (x + 2)(x - 3)$
2. $y = (x + 5)(x + 2)$
3. $y = (x + 9)^2$
4. $y = -2(x - 5)(x + 1)$
5. $y = -5(x + 7)(x + 2)$
6. $y = 3(x - 6)(x - 3)$
7. $y = -\frac{1}{2}(x + 4)(x - 2)$
8. $y = (x - 7)(2x - 3)$
9. $y = 2(x + 10)(x - 3)$

EXAMPLE 2 on p. 642 for Exs. 10–15

10. $y = -x^2 + 8x - 16$
11. $y = -x^2 - 9x - 18$
12. $y = 12x^2 - 48$
13. $y = -6x^2 + 294$
14. $y = 3x^2 - 24x + 36$
15. $y = 20x^2 - 6x - 2$

16. Follow the steps below to write an equation of the parabola shown.

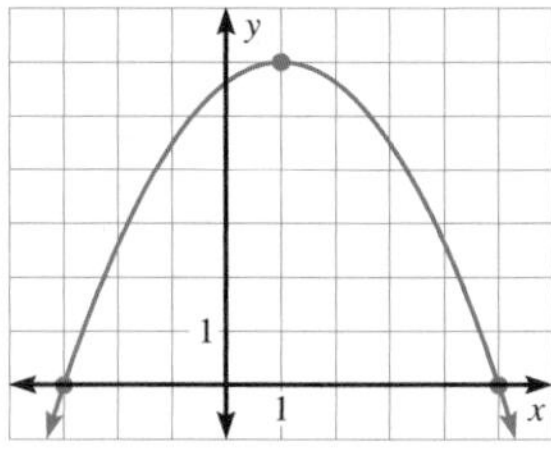

   a. Find the x-intercepts. **−3, 5**

   b. Use the values of p and q and the coordinates of the vertex to find the value of a in the equation $y = a(x - p)(x - q)$. $-\frac{3}{8}$

   c. Write a quadratic equation in intercept form. $y = -\frac{3}{8}(x + 3)(x - 5)$

1–15. See Additional Answers beginning on p. AA1.

10.3 Solve Quadratic Equations by Graphing

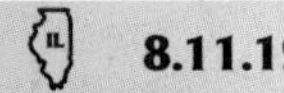 **8.11.19** Solve problems that include nonlinear functions, including selecting and evaluating formulas . . .

Before You solved quadratic equations by factoring.

Now You will solve quadratic equations by graphing.

Why? So you can solve a problem about sports, as in Example 6.

Key Vocabulary
- **quadratic equation**
- ***x*-intercept,** *p. 225*
- **roots,** *p. 575*
- **zero of a function,** *p. 337*

A **quadratic equation** is an equation that can be written in the **standard form** $ax^2 + bx + c = 0$ where $a \neq 0$.

In Chapter 9, you used factoring to solve a quadratic equation. You can also use graphing to solve a quadratic equation. Notice that the solutions of the equation $ax^2 + bx + c = 0$ are the *x*-intercepts of the graph of the related function $y = ax^2 + bx + c$.

Solve by Factoring

$x^2 - 6x + 5 = 0$

$(x - 1)(x - 5) = 0$

$x = 1$ *or* $x = 5$

Solve by Graphing

To solve $x^2 - 6x + 5 = 0$, graph $y = x^2 - 6x + 5$. From the graph you can see that the *x*-intercepts are 1 and 5.

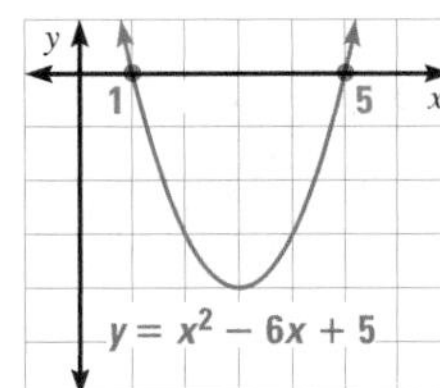

READING
In this course, *solutions* refers to real-number solutions.

To solve a quadratic equation by graphing, first write the equation in standard form, $ax^2 + bx + c = 0$. Then graph the related function $y = ax^2 + bx + c$. The *x*-intercepts of the graph are the solutions, or roots, of $ax^2 + bx + c = 0$.

EXAMPLE 1 Solve a quadratic equation having two solutions

Solve $x^2 - 2x = 3$ by graphing.

Solution

STEP 1 **Write** the equation in standard form.

$x^2 - 2x = 3$ **Write original equation.**

$x^2 - 2x - 3 = 0$ **Subtract 3 from each side.**

STEP 2 **Graph** the function $y = x^2 - 2x - 3$. The *x*-intercepts are -1 and 3.

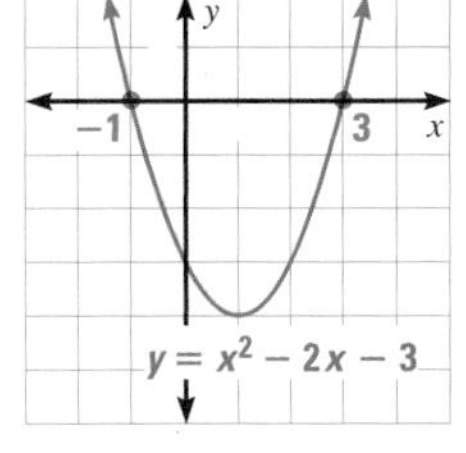

▸ The solutions of the equation $x^2 - 2x = 3$ are -1 and 3.

CHECK You can check -1 and 3 in the original equation.

$x^2 - 2x = 3$	$x^2 - 2x = 3$	**Write original equation.**
$(-1)^2 - 2(-1) \stackrel{?}{=} 3$	$(3)^2 - 2(3) \stackrel{?}{=} 3$	**Substitute for *x*.**
$3 = 3$ ✓	$3 = 3$ ✓	**Simplify. Each solution checks.**

1 PLAN AND PREPARE

Warm-Up Exercises

Transparency Available

Find the zeros of the polynomial function.

1. $f(x) = x^2 + 5x - 36$ **−9, 4**
2. $f(x) = x^2 - 9x + 20$ **4, 5**
3. You are making a rectangular flag for your school team. The number of square inches in the area of the flag is $9x + 108$. The number of inches in the length of the flag is $x + 12$. What is the width of the flag? **9 in.**

Notetaking Guide

Transparency Available

Promotes interactive learning and notetaking skills, pp. 227–229.

Pacing

Basic: 2 days
Average: 2 days
Advanced: 2 days
Block: 0.5 block with 10.2
0.5 block with 10.4
- See *Teaching Guide/Lesson Plan*.

2 FOCUS AND MOTIVATE

Essential Question

Big Idea 2, p. 627

How do you solve a quadratic equation by graphing? **Tell students they will learn how to answer this question by finding the *x*-intercepts of the related function.**

Resource Planning Guide

Chapter Resource Book
- Teaching Guide/Lesson Plan (pp. 32–33)
- Practice levels A, B, C (pp. 35–40)
- Study Guide (pp. 41–42)
- Catch-up for Absent Students (p. 43)
- Application (p. 44)
- Challenge (p. 45)

Workbooks
- Notetaking Guide (pp. 227–229)
- Practice Workbook (pp. 155–157)

Teaching Options
- **Power Presentations CD-ROM** provides dynamic electronic teaching resources for the classroom.
- **Activity Generator CD-ROM** provides editable activities for all ability levels.

Interactive Technology
- Easy Planner
- Power Presentations CD-ROM
- Activity Generator CD-ROM
- Animated Algebra
- Test Generator CD-ROM
- Online Quiz
- eWorkbook
- eEdition
- @HomeTutor

Resources for English Learners
- Quick Reference for English Learners
- Spanish Study Guide
- Multi-Language Visual Glossary
- Student Resources in Spanish

See also the *Algebra 1 Toolkit* for more strategies for meeting individual needs.

Motivating the Lesson

In soccer, the path of the ball depends on the velocity of the kick and the height of the ball when it is kicked. In this lesson, you will learn how to use the vertical motion model to determine how high and how far a kicked soccer ball will go.

3 TEACH

Extra Example 1

Solve $x^2 + 4x = 5$ by graphing. $-5, 1$

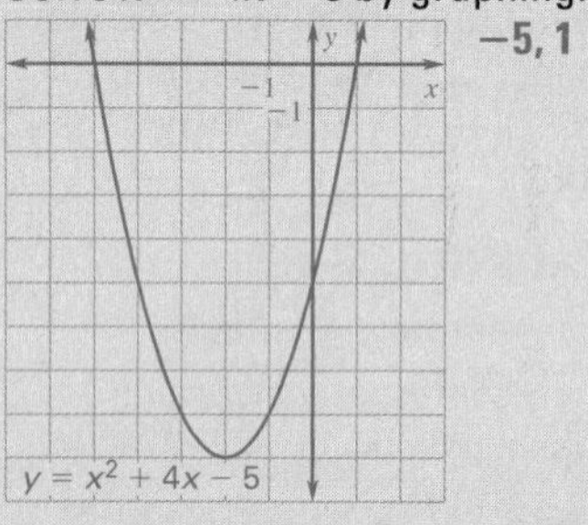

Extra Example 2

Solve $-x^2 - 6x = 9$ by graphing. -3

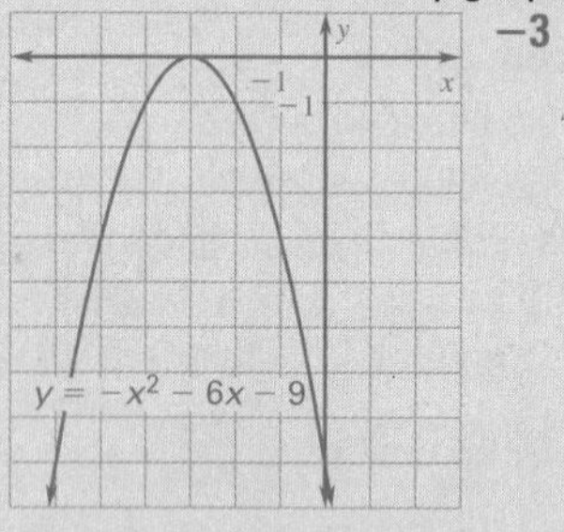

Extra Example 3

Solve $x^2 + 4x = -6$ by graphing. no solutions

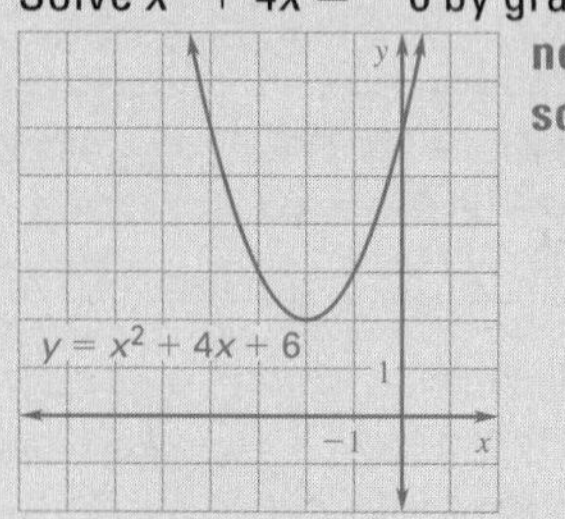

EXAMPLE 2 Solve a quadratic equation having one solution

Solve $-x^2 + 2x = 1$ by graphing.

Solution

STEP 1 **Write** the equation in standard form.

$-x^2 + 2x = 1$ **Write original equation.**

$-x^2 + 2x - 1 = 0$ **Subtract 1 from each side.**

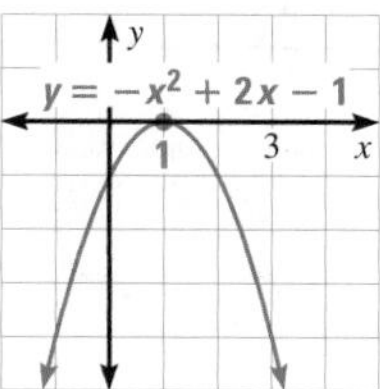

STEP 2 **Graph** the function $y = -x^2 + 2x - 1$. The x-intercept is 1.

▶ The solution of the equation $-x^2 + 2x = 1$ is 1.

EXAMPLE 3 Solve a quadratic equation having no solution

Solve $x^2 + 7 = 4x$ by graphing.

Solution

AVOID ERRORS
Do not confuse y-intercepts and x-intercepts. Although the graph has a y-intercept, it does not have any x-intercepts.

STEP 1 **Write** the equation in standard form.

$x^2 + 7 = 4x$ **Write original equation.**

$x^2 - 4x + 7 = 0$ **Subtract 4x from each side.**

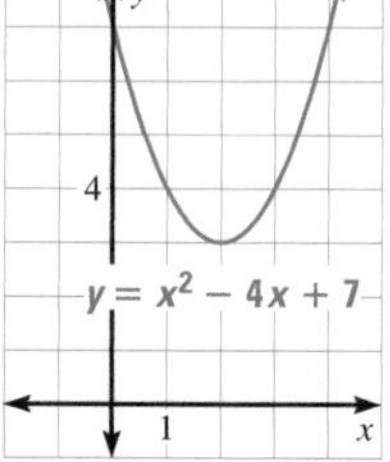

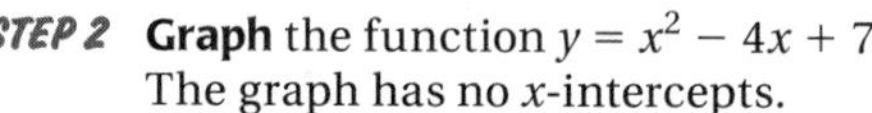

STEP 2 **Graph** the function $y = x^2 - 4x + 7$. The graph has no x-intercepts.

▶ The equation $x^2 + 7 = 4x$ has no solution.

✓ GUIDED PRACTICE for Examples 1, 2, and 3

Solve the equation by graphing.

1. $x^2 - 6x + 8 = 0$ 2, 4
2. $x^2 + x = -1$ no solution
3. $-x^2 + 6x = 9$ 3

KEY CONCEPT — *For Your Notebook*

Number of Solutions of a Quadratic Equation

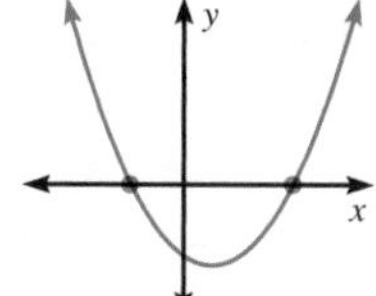

A quadratic equation has **two solutions** if the graph of its related function has **two x-intercepts.**

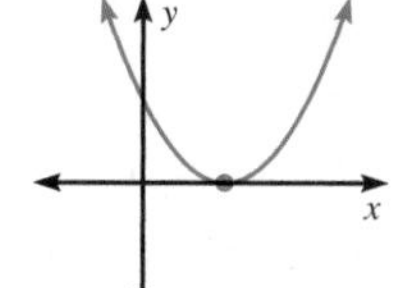

A quadratic equation has **one solution** if the graph of its related function has **one x-intercept.**

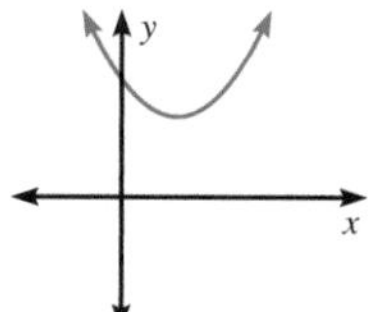

A quadratic equation has **no real solution** if the graph of its related function has **no x-intercepts.**

FINDING ZEROS Because a zero of a function is an x-intercept of the function's graph, you can use the function's graph to find the zeros of a function.

EXAMPLE 4 Find the zeros of a quadratic function

Find the zeros of $f(x) = x^2 + 6x - 7$.

ANOTHER WAY
You can find the zeros of a function by factoring:
$f(x) = x^2 + 6x - 7$
$0 = x^2 + 6x - 7$
$0 = (x + 7)(x - 1)$
$x = -7$ or $x = 1$

Solution

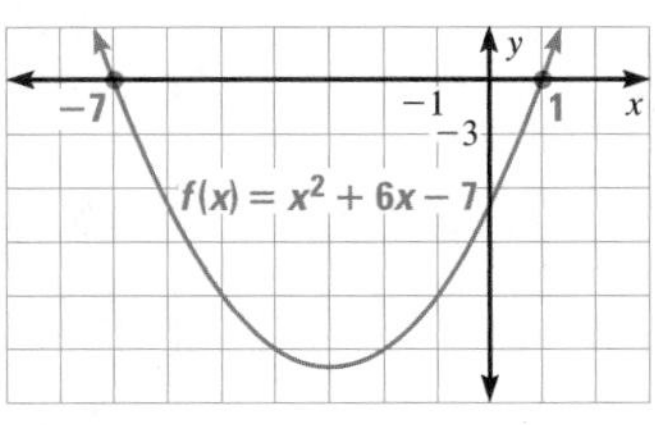

Graph the function $f(x) = x^2 + 6x - 7$. The x-intercepts are -7 and 1.

▶ The zeros of the function are -7 and 1.

CHECK Substitute -7 and 1 in the original function.

$f(-7) = (-7)^2 + 6(-7) - 7 = 0$ ✓

$f(1) = (1)^2 + 6(1) - 7 = 0$ ✓

APPROXIMATING ZEROS The zeros of a function are not necessarily integers. To approximate zeros, look at the signs of the function values. If two function values have opposite signs, then a zero falls between the x-values that correspond to the function values.

EXAMPLE 5 Approximate the zeros of a quadratic function

Approximate the zeros of $f(x) = x^2 + 4x + 1$ to the nearest tenth.

Solution

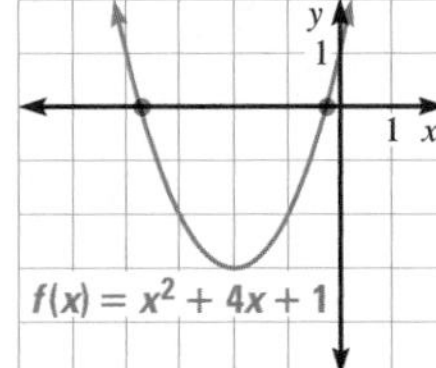

STEP 1 **Graph** the function $f(x) = x^2 + 4x + 1$. There are two x-intercepts: one between -4 and -3 and another between -1 and 0.

STEP 2 **Make** a table of values for x-values between -4 and -3 and between -1 and 0 using an increment of 0.1. Look for a change in the signs of the function values.

INTERPRET FUNCTION VALUES
The function value that is closest to 0 indicates the x-value that best approximates a zero of the function.

x	−3.9	−3.8	−3.7	−3.6	−3.5	−3.4	−3.3	−3.2	−3.1
$f(x)$	0.61	0.24	−0.11	−0.44	−0.75	−1.04	−1.31	−1.56	−1.79

x	−0.9	−0.8	−0.7	−0.6	−0.5	−0.4	−0.3	−0.2	−0.1
$f(x)$	−1.79	−1.56	−1.31	−1.04	−0.75	−0.44	−0.11	0.24	0.61

▶ In each table, the function value closest to 0 is -0.11. So, the zeros of $f(x) = x^2 + 4x + 1$ are about -3.7 and about -0.3.

✓ **GUIDED PRACTICE** for Examples 4 and 5

4. Find the zeros of $f(x) = x^2 + x - 6$. $-3, 2$
5. Approximate the zeros of $f(x) = -x^2 + 2x + 2$ to the nearest tenth. $-0.7, 2.7$

Extra Example 4

Use a graph to find the zeros of $f(x) = x^2 + 7x + 6$. $-6, -1$

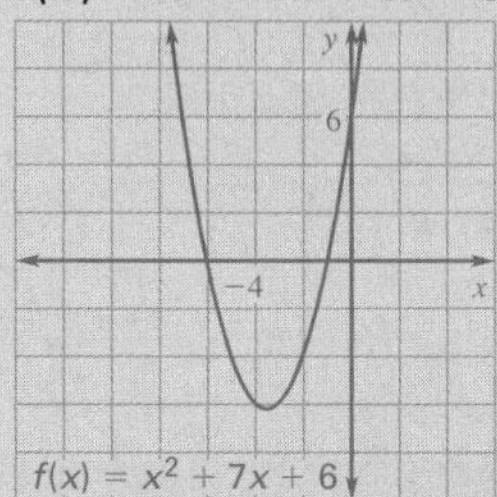

Key Question to Ask for Example 4

- Does every quadratic function have two zeros? Explain. The zeros of a function occur when the graph of the function crosses or touches the x-axis. The graph of a quadratic function can touch the x-axis once, which indicates two solutions that are the same; it can cross the x-axis twice, which indicates two distinct solutions; or it can lie completely above or completely below the x-axis, which indicates no real-number solutions.

Extra Example 5

Approximate the zeros of $f(x) = x^2 + 2x - 4$ to the nearest tenth. $-3.2, 1.2$

Key Question to Ask for Example 5

- Can $x^2 + 4x + 1$ be factored? Explain. No, $x^2 + 4x + 4$ can be factored and $x^2 + 2x + 1$ can be factored, so the trinomial $x^2 + 4x + 1$ cannot be factored.

Differentiated Instruction

Below Level Have students work in pairs to approximate the zeros of the function in **Guided Practice Exercise 5**. Suggest that they use a step-by-step process and have you confirm that they have completed each step correctly. Check that their graphs are correct, that the calculations in their tables are correct, and that they have chosen the values in the tables for which $f(x)$ is closest to 0. After they have successfully worked through the example, have them write a summary of the steps they used.

See also the *Algebra 1 Toolkit* for more strategies.

Extra Example 6

A baseball player throws a ball into the air with an initial vertical velocity of 32 feet per second. The ball is released at a height of 5 feet.

a. Write an equation that models the height h (in feet) of the ball as a function of the time t (in seconds) after it is thrown. $h = -16t^2 + 32t + 5$

b. Use the equation to find the time that the ball is in the air if the player lets the ball drop to the ground. about 2.1 sec

Key Question to Ask for Example 6

- What do the x- and y-axes on the graphing calculator display represent? The x-axis represents time in seconds and the y-axis represents height in feet.

Closing the Lesson

Have students summarize the major points of the lesson and answer the Essential Question: How do you solve a quadratic equation by graphing?

- The standard form of a quadratic equation is $ax^2 + bx + c = 0$.
- A quadratic equation can have one real solution, two real solutions, or no real solutions.

To solve a quadratic equation by graphing, write it in standard form and graph the related function. The x-intercepts are the solutions of the equation. Check the solutions in the original equation.

EXAMPLE 6 Solve a multi-step problem

SPORTS An athlete throws a shot put with an initial vertical velocity of 40 feet per second as shown.

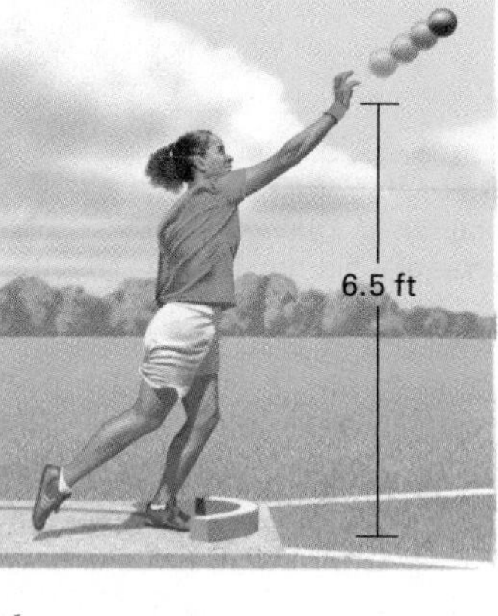

a. Write an equation that models the height h (in feet) of the shot put as a function of the time t (in seconds) after it is thrown.

b. Use the equation to find the time that the shot put is in the air.

Solution

a. Use the initial vertical velocity and the release height to write a vertical motion model.

$h = -16t^2 + vt + s$ — Vertical motion model

$h = -16t^2 + 40t + 6.5$ — Substitute 40 for v and 6.5 for s.

b. The shot put lands when $h = 0$. To find the time t when $h = 0$, solve $0 = -16t^2 + 40t + 6.5$ for t.

USE A GRAPHING CALCULATOR
When entering $h = -16t^2 + 40t + 6.5$ in a graphing calculator, use y instead of h and x instead of t.

To solve the equation, graph the related function $h = -16t^2 + 40t + 6.5$ on a graphing calculator. Use the *trace* feature to find the t-intercepts.

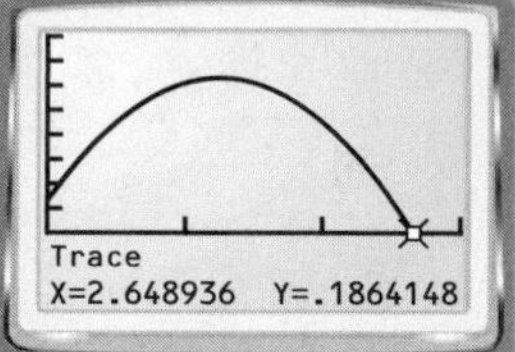

▶ There is only one positive t-intercept. The shot put is in the air for about 2.6 seconds.

✓ GUIDED PRACTICE for Example 6

6. WHAT IF? In Example 6, suppose the initial vertical velocity is 30 feet per second. Find the time that the shot put is in the air. about 2.1 sec

CONCEPT SUMMARY — *For Your Notebook*

Relating Solutions of Equations, x-Intercepts of Graphs, and Zeros of Functions

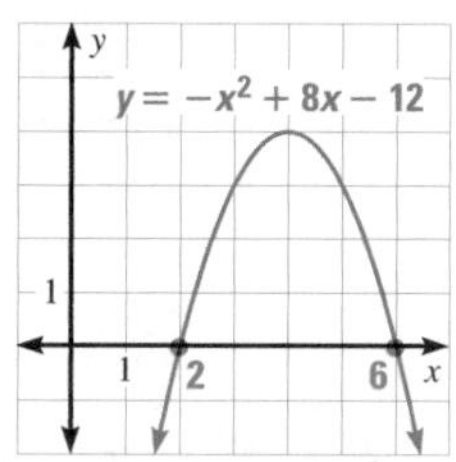

Solutions of an Equation
The solutions of the equation $-x^2 + 8x - 12 = 0$ are 2 and 6.

x-Intercepts of a Graph
The x-intercepts of the graph of $y = -x^2 + 8x - 12$ occur where $y = 0$, so the x-intercepts are 2 and 6, as shown.

Zeros of a Function
The zeros of the function $f(x) = -x^2 + 8x - 12$ are the values of x for which $f(x) = 0$, so the zeros are 2 and 6.

Differentiated Instruction

Auditory Learners When discussing **Example 6**, ask students how the time the shot put is in air changes as the velocity increases and decreases. Engage in discussion first. Students should propose that as velocity increases, the time in the air increases, and as velocity decreases, the time in the air decreases. Then work out examples using different values of v near 40.

See also the *Algebra 1 Toolkit* for more strategies.

10.3 EXERCISES

HOMEWORK KEY ○ = WORKED-OUT SOLUTIONS on p. WS24 for Exs. 5 and 51
★ = STANDARDIZED TEST PRACTICE Exs. 2, 46, 53, and 54

SKILL PRACTICE

A

1. **VOCABULARY** Write $2x^2 + 11 = 9x$ in standard form. $2x^2 - 9x + 11 = 0$

2. ★ **WRITING** Is $3x^2 - 2 = 0$ a quadratic equation? *Explain.*

2. Yes; $3x^2 - 2 = 0$ is a quadratic equation in the standard form $ax^2 + bx + c = 0$, where $a = 3$, $b = 0$, and $c = -2$: $3x^2 + 0x + (-2) = 0$ or $3x^2 - 2 = 0$.

SOLVING EQUATIONS Solve the equation by graphing.

EXAMPLES 1, 2, and 3 on pp. 643–644 for Exs. 3–21

3. $x^2 - 5x + 4 = 0$ 4, 1
4. $x^2 + 5x + 6 = 0$ −3, −2
5. $x^2 + 6x = -8$ −4, −2
6. $x^2 - 4x = 5$ 5, −1
7. $x^2 - 16 = 6x$ 8, −2
8. $x^2 - 12x = -35$ 7, 5
9. $x^2 - 6x + 9 = 0$ 3
10. $x^2 + 8x + 16 = 0$ −4
11. $x^2 + 10x = -25$ −5
12. $x^2 + 81 = 18x$ 9
13. $-x^2 - 14x = 49$ −7
14. $-x^2 + 16x = 64$ 8
15. $x^2 - 5x + 7 = 0$ no solution
16. $x^2 - 2x + 3 = 0$ no solution
17. $x^2 + x = -2$ no solution
18. $\frac{1}{5}x^2 - 5 = 0$ ±5
19. $\frac{1}{2}x^2 + 2x = 6$ −6, 2
20. $-\frac{1}{4}x^2 - 8 = x$ no solution

21. **ERROR ANALYSIS** The graph of the function related to the equation $0 = x^2 - 4x + 4$ is shown. *Describe* and correct the error in solving the equation. See margin.

> The only solution of the equation $0 = x^2 - 4x + 4$ is 4.

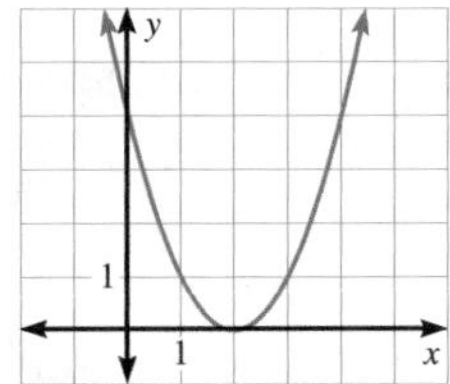

FINDING ZEROS Find the zeros of the function.

EXAMPLE 4 on p. 645 for Exs. 22–30

22. $f(x) = x^2 + 4x - 5$ −5, 1
23. $f(x) = x^2 - x - 12$ −3, 4
24. $f(x) = x^2 - 5x - 6$ −1, 6
25. $f(x) = x^2 + 3x - 10$ −5, 2
26. $f(x) = -x^2 + 8x + 9$ −1, 9
27. $f(x) = x^2 + x - 20$ −5, 4
28. $f(x) = -x^2 - 7x + 8$ −8, 1
29. $f(x) = x^2 - 12x + 11$ 1, 11
30. $f(x) = -x^2 + 4x + 12$ −2, 6

B

SOLVING EQUATIONS Solve the equation by graphing.

31. $2x^2 + x = 3$ $-1\frac{1}{2}, 1$
32. $4x^2 - 5 = 8x$ $-\frac{1}{2}, 2\frac{1}{2}$
33. $4x^2 - 4x + 1 = 0$ $\frac{1}{2}$
34. $x^2 + x = -\frac{1}{4}$ $-\frac{1}{2}$
35. $3x^2 + 1 = 2x$ no solution
36. $5x^2 + x + 3 = 0$ no solution

APPROXIMATING ZEROS Approximate the zeros of the function to the nearest tenth.

EXAMPLE 5 on p. 645 for Exs. 37–46

40. −3.8, 0.8
41. 0.8, 6.2
42. −4.6, −0.4

37. $f(x) = x^2 + 4x + 2$ −3.4, −0.6
38. $f(x) = x^2 - 5x + 3$ 0.7, 4.3
39. $f(x) = x^2 - 2x - 5$ −1.4, 3.4
40. $f(x) = -x^2 - 3x + 3$
41. $f(x) = -x^2 + 7x - 5$
42. $f(x) = -x^2 - 5x - 2$
43. $f(x) = 2x^2 + x - 2$ −1.3, 0.8
44. $f(x) = -3x^2 + 8x - 2$ 0.3, 2.4
45. $f(x) = 5x^2 + 30x + 30$ −4.7, −1.3

46. ★ **MULTIPLE CHOICE** Which function has a zero between −3 and −2? C

Ⓐ $f(x) = -3x^2 + 4x + 11$ Ⓑ $f(x) = 4x^2 - 3x - 11$

Ⓒ $f(x) = 3x^2 + 4x - 11$ Ⓓ $f(x) = 3x^2 + 11$

21. Any solution of a quadratic equation is an x-intercept of the graph of the related quadratic function. The x-intercept of the function shown in the graph is 2, not 4; the only solution of the equation is 2.

4 PRACTICE AND APPLY

Assignment Guide

Answer Transparencies available for all exercises

Basic:
Day 1: EP p. 944 Exs. 1–4
pp. 647–649
Exs. 1–21
Day 2: pp. 647–649
Exs. 22–36 even, 37–41, 50–53, 56–64

Average:
Day 1: pp. 647–649
Exs. 1, 2, 5–21, 47, 48, 59–63 odd
Day 2: pp. 647–649
Exs. 24–46, 50–54, 56–58

Advanced:
Day 1: pp. 647–649
Exs. 1, 2, 6–20, 47–49*, 60–64 even
Day 2: pp. 647–649
Exs. 25–46, 50–56*, 58

Block:
pp. 647–649
Exs. 1, 2, 5–21, 47, 48, 59–63 odd (with 10.2)
pp. 647–649
Exs. 24–46, 50–54, 56–58 (with 10.4)

Differentiated Instruction

See *Algebra 1 Best Practices Toolkit* for suggestions on addressing the needs of a diverse classroom.

Homework Check

For a quick check of student understanding of key concepts, go over the following exercises:

Basic: 6, 9, 24, 38, 50
Average: 10, 16, 26, 41, 51
Advanced: 12, 17, 29, 44, 52

Extra Practice

- Student Edition, p. 947
- Chapter 10 Resource Book: Practice levels A, B, C, pp. 35–40

Practice Worksheet

An easily-readable reduced practice page (with answers) for this lesson can be found on p. 626C.

Avoiding Common Errors

Exercises 5–20 Some students may attempt to graph an equation without first writing it in standard form. Suggest that students go through the exercises and write each of the equations in standard form before they solve the equations by graphing.

Mathematical Reasoning

Exercises 50–52 To help students make a connection between the real life situations in these problems and visual and algebraic representations of them, you may want to discuss how the values of x and y in these exercises are similar to the variable values in Example 6, and how they are different.

Study Strategy

Exercise 54 Point out to students that they must solve part (a) of the problem before they can solve parts (b) or (c). If students are confused by part (c), ask how many times the ball reaches a height of 5.5 feet. Then suggest that they examine the graph in terms of x and y to determine which point they should use to solve part (c).

53. 16 ft; the distance from the nozzle to the circle is the distance between the x-intercepts of $y = -0.75x^2 + 6x$. Substitute 0 for y and solve for x: $0 = -0.75x^2 + 6x$ has solutions 0 and 8. The radius of the display circle is 8 feet, so the diameter is 16 feet.

54c. 2.5 sec; the two points on the graph of $h = -16t^2 + 40t + 5.5$ that correspond to a height of 5.5 feet are the two points with h-coordinate 5.5. These points are reflections of each other in the parabola's axis of symmetry, $t = 1.25$. Because one point with h-coordinate 5.5 is (0, 5.5), the t-coordinate of the other point with h-coordinate 5.5 is $2(1.25) = 2.5$. So, after 2.5 seconds, the ball is again at a height of 5.5 feet.

C **CHALLENGE** **Use the given surface area S of the cylinder to find the radius r to the nearest tenth. (Use 3.14 for π.)**

47. $S = 251 \text{ ft}^2$ 4.0 ft

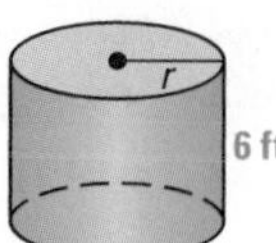

48. $S = 716 \text{ m}^2$ 6.0 m

13 m

49. $S = 1074 \text{ cm}^2$ 9.0 cm

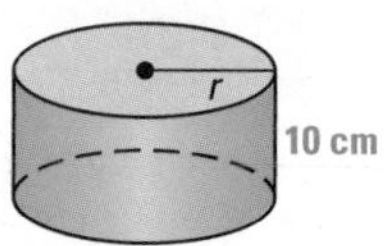

PROBLEM SOLVING

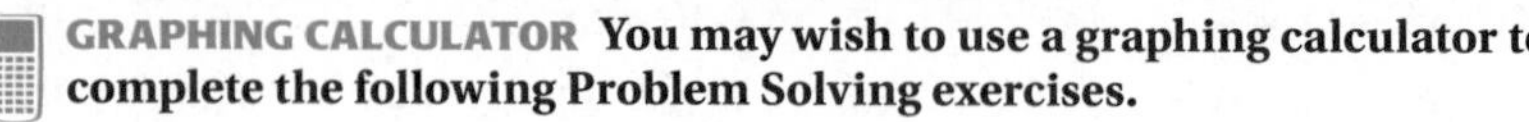

GRAPHING CALCULATOR **You may wish to use a graphing calculator to complete the following Problem Solving exercises.**

EXAMPLE 6 on p. 646 for Exs. 50–52

A **50. SOCCER** The height y (in feet) of a soccer ball after it is kicked can be modeled by the graph of the equation $y = -0.04x^2 + 1.2x$ where x is the horizontal distance (in feet) that the ball travels. The ball is not touched, and it lands on the ground. Find the distance that the ball was kicked. 30 ft

@HomeTutor for problem solving help at classzone.com

51. SURVEYING To keep water off a road, the road's surface is shaped like a parabola as in the cross section below. The surface of the road can be modeled by the graph of $y = -0.0017x^2 + 0.041x$ where x and y are measured in feet. Find the width of the road to the nearest tenth of a foot. 24.1 ft

@HomeTutor for problem solving help at classzone.com

52. DIVING During a cliff diving competition, a diver begins a dive with his center of gravity 70 feet above the water. The initial vertical velocity of his dive is 8 feet per second.

a. Write an equation that models the height h (in feet) of the diver's center of gravity as a function of time t (in seconds). $h = -16t^2 + 8t + 70$

b. How long after the diver begins his dive does his center of gravity reach the water? about 2.4 sec

B **53. ★ SHORT RESPONSE** An arc of water sprayed from the nozzle of a fountain can be modeled by the graph of $y = -0.75x^2 + 6x$ where x is the horizontal distance (in feet) from the nozzle and y is the vertical distance (in feet). The diameter of the circle formed by the arcs on the surface of the water is called the display diameter. Find the display diameter of the fountain. *Explain* your reasoning. See margin.

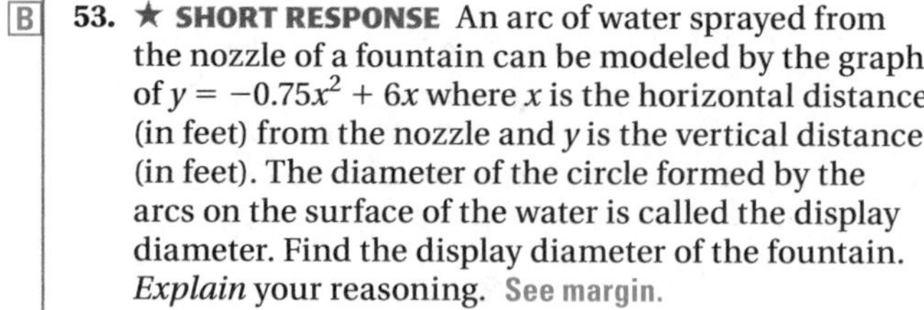

○ = WORKED-OUT SOLUTIONS on p. WS1 ★ = STANDARDIZED TEST PRACTICE

54. ★ **EXTENDED RESPONSE** Two softball players are practicing catching fly balls. One player throws a ball to the other. She throws the ball upward from a height of 5.5 feet with an initial vertical velocity of 40 feet per second for her teammate to catch.

a. Write an equation that models the height h (in feet) of the ball as a function of time t (in seconds) after it is thrown. $h = -16t^2 + 40t + 5.5$

b. If her teammate misses the ball and it lands on the ground, how long was the ball in the air? about 2.6 sec

c. If her teammate catches the ball at a height of 5.5 feet, how long was the ball in the air? *Explain* your reasoning. See margin.

C 55. **CHALLENGE** A stream of water from a fire hose can be modeled by the graph of $y = -0.003x^2 + 0.58x + 3$ where x and y are measured in feet. A firefighter is holding the hose 3 feet above the ground, 137 feet from a building. Will the stream of water pass through a window if the top of the window is 26 feet above the ground? *Explain*. No; the height of the water at the point 137 feet from the firefighter is $-0.003(137)^2 + 0.58(137) + 3 \approx 26.2$ feet. The water will hit the building just above the window.

ILLINOIS MIXED REVIEW

TEST PRACTICE at classzone.com

56. How would the graph of the function $y = x^2 - 6$ be affected if the function were changed to $y = x^2 - 3$? C

Ⓐ The graph would shift 3 units to the right.

Ⓑ The graph would shift 3 units to the left.

Ⓒ The graph would shift 3 units up.

Ⓓ The graph would shrink vertically.

QUIZ for Lessons 10.1–10.3

Graph the function. Compare the graph with the graph of $y = x^2$. *(p. 628)* 1–3. See margin.

1. $y = -\frac{1}{2}x^2$
2. $y = 2x^2 - 5$
3. $y = -x^2 + 3$

Graph the function. Label the vertex and axis of symmetry. 4–9. See margin.

4. $y = x^2 + 5$ *(p. 628)*
5. $y = -5x^2 + 1$ *(p. 628)*
6. $y = x^2 + 4x - 2$ *(p. 635)*
7. $y = 2x^2 - 12x + 5$ *(p. 635)*
8. $y = -\frac{1}{2}x^2 + 2x - 5$ *(p. 635)*
9. $y = -4x^2 - 10x + 2$ *(p. 635)*

Solve the equation by graphing. *(p. 643)*

10. $x^2 - 7x = 8$ −1, 8
11. $x^2 + 6x + 9 = 0$ −3
12. $x^2 + 10x = 11$ −11, 1
13. $x^2 - 7 = -6x$ −7, 1
14. $-x^2 + x - 1 = 0$ no solution
15. $x^2 - 4x + 9 = 0$ no solution

Find the zeros of the function. *(p. 643)*

16. $f(x) = x^2 + 3x - 10$ −5, 2
17. $f(x) = x^2 - 8x + 12$ 2, 6
18. $f(x) = -x^2 + 5x + 14$ −2, 7

EXTRA PRACTICE for Lesson 10.3, p. 947

ONLINE QUIZ at classzone.com

5 ASSESS AND RETEACH

Daily Homework Quiz

Transparency Available

1. Solve $x^2 + 6x + 8$ by graphing.

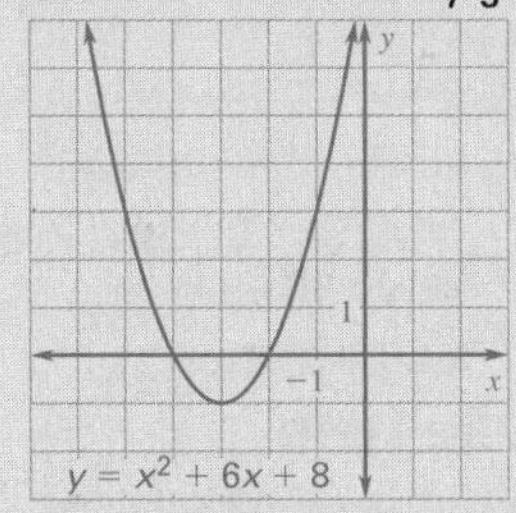

−4, −2

Find the number of solutions for each equation.

2. $x^2 + 6x = -10$ none
3. $x^2 + 6x = -9$ one
4. Find the zeros of $f(x) = -x^2 + 2x + 3$. −1, 3
5. Approximate the zeros of $f(x) = x^2 + x - 3$ to the nearest tenth. −2.3, 1.3
6. Maria throws a shot put with an initial velocity of 25 feet per second. She releases it at a height of 5 feet. Find the time the shot put in the air. about 1.7 sec

Online Quiz

Available at **classzone.com**

Diagnosis/Remediation

- Practice A, B, C in Chapter 10 Resource Book, pp. 35–40
- Study Guide in Chapter 10 Resource Book, pp. 41–42
- Practice Workbook, pp. 155–157
- @HomeTutor

Challenge

Additional challenge is available in the Chapter 10 Resource Book, p. 45.

Quiz

An easily-readable reduced copy of the quiz (with answers) on Lessons 10.1–10.3 from the Assessment Book can be found on p. 626G.

Quiz 1–9. See Additional Answers beginning on p. AA1.

1 PLAN AND PREPARE

Learn the Method

- Students will find the maximum or minimum value and approximate the zeros of a quadratic function using their graphing calculators.
- After the activity, students can use a graphing calculator to check their solutions in Lesson 10.3, Exercises 3–46.

Keystroke Help

Keystrokes for several models of calculators are available in blackline format in the *Chapter 10 Resource Book.*

2 TEACH

Tips for Success

In Example 1, point out to students that the lower right calculator screen indicates the maximum value of the function: Y = 11.5. In Example 2, make sure that students understand that they will need to give lower and upper bounds on one of the zeros at a time, not both. For the lower bound they need a number to the left of the x-intercept, and for the upper bound they need a number to the right of the x-intercept.

Extra Example 1

Find the minimum value of $y = 3x^2 + 9x - 2$. **−8.75**

10.3 Find Minimum and Maximum Values and Zeros

QUESTION How can you find the minumum or maximum value and the zeros of a quadratic function using a graphing calculator?

EXAMPLE 1 Find the maximum value of a function

Find the maximum value of the function $y = -2x^2 - 6x + 7$.

STEP 1 ***Enter the function***

Press Y= and enter the function $y = -2x^2 - 6x + 7$.

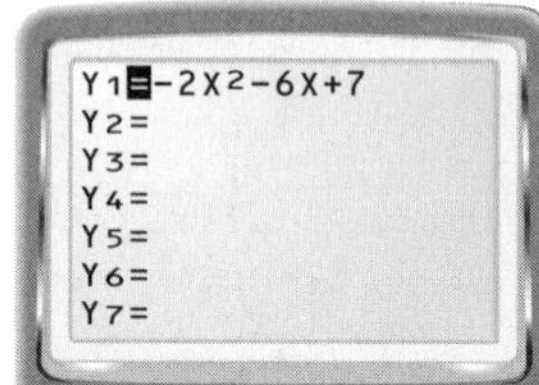

STEP 2 ***Adjust the window***

Display the graph. Adjust the viewing window as needed so that the vertex of the parabola is visible.

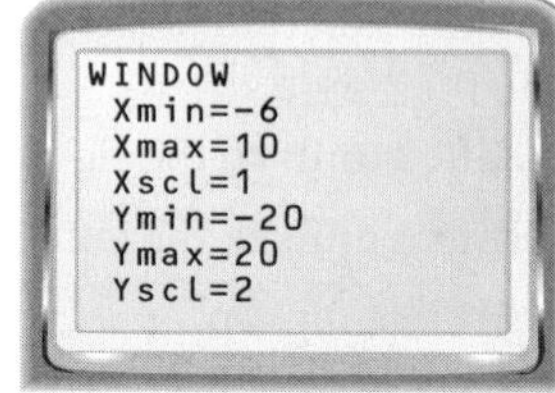

STEP 3 ***Use the maximum feature***

The *maximum* feature is located under the CALCULATE menu.

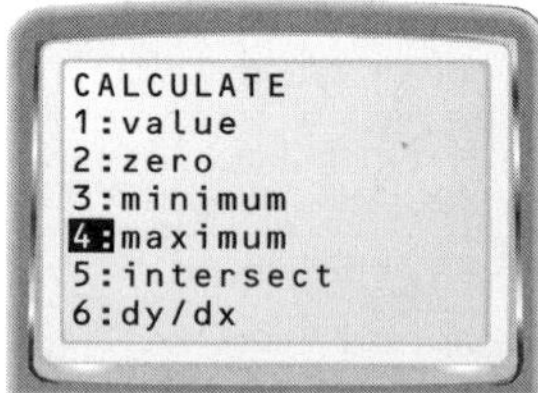

STEP 4 ***Find the maximum value***

Follow the graphing calculator's procedure to find the maximum of the function.

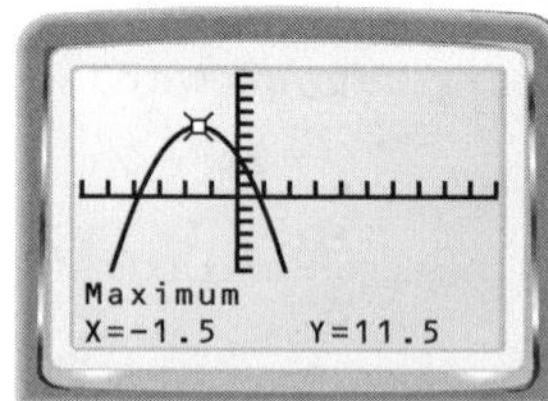

▶ The maximum value of the function $y = -2x^2 - 6x + 7$ is 11.5.

PRACTICE

Find the maximum or minimum value of the function.

1. $y = 3x^2 - 8x + 7$ $1\frac{2}{3}$
2. $y = -x^2 + 3x + 10$ 12.25
3. $y = -4x^2 - 6x - 6$ −3.75
4. $y = 5x^2 + 10x - 8$ −13
5. $y = -1.4x^2 + 3.8x - 6.1$ about −3.5
6. $y = 2.57x^2 - 8.45x - 5.04$ about −12

@HomeTutor classzone.com Keystrokes

EXAMPLE 2 Approximate the zeros of a function

Approximate the zeros of the function $y = 3x^2 + 2x - 4$.

STEP 1 *Enter the function*

Press Y= and enter the function $y = 3x^2 + 2x - 4$.

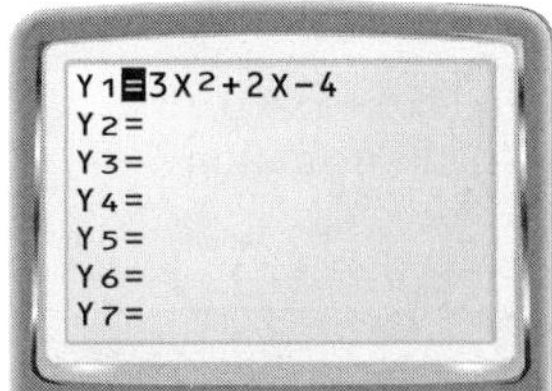

STEP 2 *Adjust the window*

Display the graph. Adjust the viewing window as needed so that the x-intercepts of the parabola are visible.

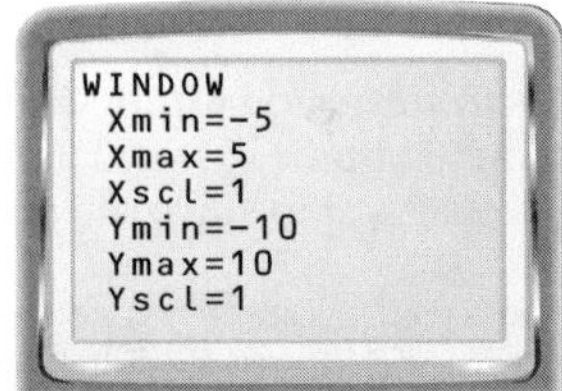

STEP 3 *Use the zero feature*

The *zero* feature is under the CALCULATE menu.

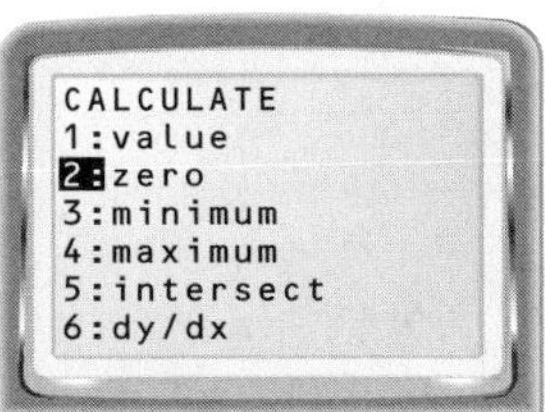

STEP 4 *Find the zeros*

Follow the graphing calculator's procedure to find a zero of the function. Then repeat the process to find the other zero.

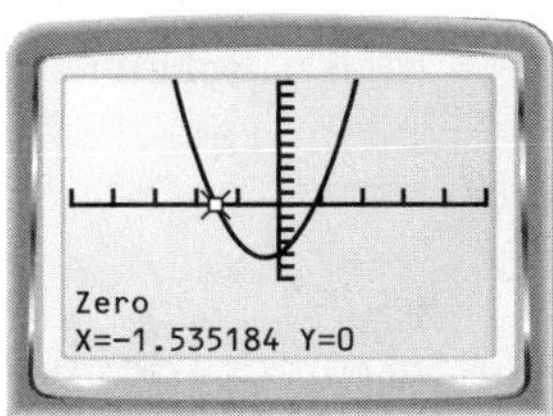

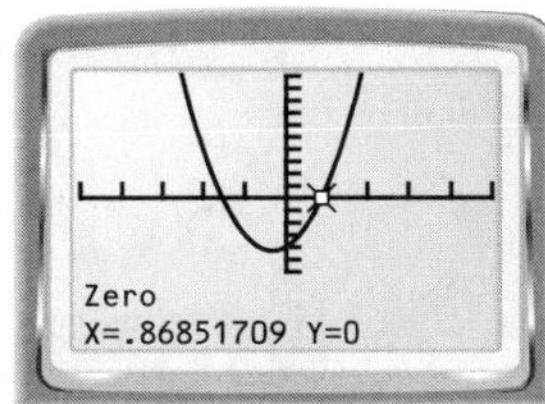

▶ The zeros are about −1.54 and about 0.87.

PRACTICE

Approximate the zeros of the quadratic function to the nearest hundredth.

7. $y = 2x^2 - 5x - 8$ −1.11, 3.61
8. $y = -3x^2 + 6x - 2$ 0.42, 1.58
9. $y = -x^2 + 4x + 9$ −1.61, 5.61
10. $y = 4x^2 - 7x + 1$ 0.16, 1.59
11. $y = -2.5x^2 + 7.7x - 4.9$ 0.90, 2.18
12. $y = 1.56x^2 - 5.19x - 2.25$ −0.39, 3.72
13. $y = -0.82x^2 - 4x + 12.4$ −7.03, 2.15
14. $y = 5.36x^2 + 17x + 2.67$ −3.01, −0.17

DRAW CONCLUSIONS

15. If a quadratic function has only one zero, what is the maximum or minimum value of the function? *Explain.* See margin.
16. If a quadratic function has a maximum value that is greater than 0, how many zeros does the function have? *Explain.* See margin.

Extra Example 2

Approximate the zeros of the function $y = -2x^2 + 5x + 6$. −0.89, 3.39

3 ASSESS AND RETEACH

1. If a quadratic function has a minimum value less than 0, how many zeros does the function have? Explain. Two zeros; a minimum value means the parabola opens upward, and if it opens upward from a negative y-value, it must cross the x-axis in two points.
2. If a quadratic function has a minimum value greater than 0, how many zeros does the function have? Explain. No zeros; a minimum value means the parabola opens upward, and if it opens upward from a positive y-value, it does not cross the x-axis.

15. 0; the maximum or minimum value of a quadratic function occurs at the vertex of the parabola that is the graph of the function. When a quadratic function has only one zero, its graph has only one x-intercept, which must also be the x-coordinate of the vertex of the parabola. Then the y-coordinate of the vertex is 0, so the maximum or minimum value of the function is 0.

16. 2; the graph of a quadratic function with a maximum value must open down. Because the maximum is greater than 0, the vertex of the parabola is above the x-axis; then, because the parabola opens down, it must cross the x-axis in two points. The two x-intercepts are the two zeros of the function.

1 PLAN AND PREPARE

Warm-Up Exercises

Transparency Available

Evaluate the expression.

1. $-\sqrt{49}$ -7
2. $\sqrt{200}$ about 14.1
3. $\pm\sqrt{121}$ ± 11
4. A ball is dropped from a height 9 feet above the ground. How long does it take the ball to hit the ground? 0.75 sec

Notetaking Guide

Transparency Available

Promotes interactive learning and notetaking skills, pp. 230–232.

Pacing

Basic: 2 days
Average: 2 days
Advanced: 2 days
Block: 0.5 block with 10.3
0.5 block with 10.5

- See *Teaching Guide/Lesson Plan.*

2 FOCUS AND MOTIVATE

Essential Question

Big Idea 2, p. 627

How do you solve a quadratic equation by finding square roots? Tell students they will learn how to answer this question for equations that can be written in the form $ax^2 + c = 0$.

10.4 Use Square Roots to Solve Quadratic Equations

 **8.11.19** Solve problems that include nonlinear functions, including selecting and evaluating formulas . . .

Before You solved a quadratic equation by graphing.

Now You will solve a quadratic equation by finding square roots.

Why? So you can solve a problem about a falling object, as in Example 5.

Key Vocabulary
- **square root,** *p. 110*
- **perfect square,** *p. 111*

To use square roots to solve a quadratic equation of the form $ax^2 + c = 0$, first isolate x^2 on one side to obtain $x^2 = d$. Then use the following information about the solutions of $x^2 = d$ to solve the equation.

READING Recall that in this course, *solutions* refers to real-number solutions.

KEY CONCEPT *For Your Notebook*

Solving $x^2 = d$ by Taking Square Roots

- If $d > 0$, then $x^2 = d$ has two solutions: $x = \pm\sqrt{d}$.
- If $d = 0$, then $x^2 = d$ has one solution: $x = 0$.
- If $d < 0$, then $x^2 = d$ has no solution.

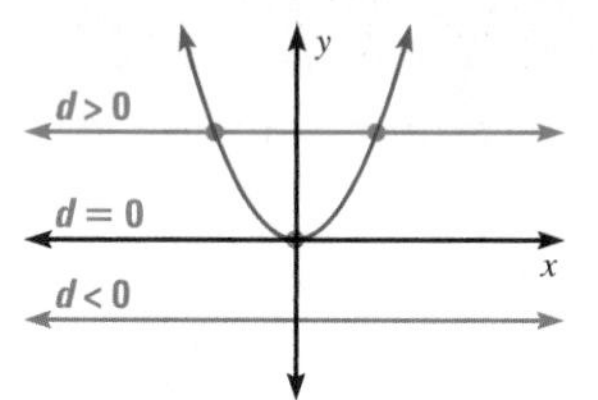

EXAMPLE 1 Solve quadratic equations

Solve the equation.

a. $2x^2 = 8$ **b.** $m^2 - 18 = -18$ **c.** $b^2 + 12 = 5$

Solution

ANOTHER WAY You can also use factoring to solve $2x^2 - 8 = 0$:
$2x^2 - 8 = 0$
$2(x^2 - 4) = 0$
$2(x - 2)(x + 2) = 0$
$x = 2$ *or* $x = -2$

a. $2x^2 = 8$ Write original equation.
$x^2 = 4$ Divide each side by 2.
$x = \pm\sqrt{4} = \pm 2$ Take square roots of each side. Simplify.

▶ The solutions are -2 and 2.

b. $m^2 - 18 = -18$ Write original equation.
$m^2 = 0$ Add 18 to each side.
$m = 0$ The square root of 0 is 0.

▶ The solution is 0.

c. $b^2 + 12 = 5$ Write original equation.
$b^2 = -7$ Subtract 12 from each side.

▶ Negative real numbers do not have real square roots. So, there is no solution.

Resource Planning Guide

Chapter Resource Book
- Teaching Guide/Lesson Plan (pp. 46–47)
- Activity Master (p. 48)
- Practice levels A, B, C (pp. 49–51)
- Study Guide (pp. 52–53)
- Catch-up for Absent Students (p. 54)
- Problem Solving Workshop (p. 55)
- Challenge (p. 57)

Workbooks
- Notetaking Guide (pp. 230–232)
- Practice Workbook (pp. 158–159)

Teaching Options
- **Power Presentations CD-ROM** provides dynamic electronic teaching resources for the classroom.
- **Activity Generator CD-ROM** provides editable activities for all ability levels.

Interactive Technology
- Easy Planner
- Power Presentations CD-ROM
- Activity Generator CD-ROM
- Animated Algebra
- Test Generator CD-ROM
- Online Quiz
- eWorkbook
- eEdition
- @HomeTutor

Resources for English Learners
- Quick Reference for English Learners
- Spanish Study Guide
- Multi-Language Visual Glossary
- Student Resources in Spanish

See also the *Algebra 1 Toolkit* for more strategies for meeting individual needs.

SIMPLIFYING SQUARE ROOTS In cases where you need to take the square root of a fraction whose numerator and denominator are perfect squares, the radical can be written as a fraction. For example, $\sqrt{\frac{16}{25}}$ can be written as $\frac{4}{5}$ because $\left(\frac{4}{5}\right)^2 = \frac{16}{25}$.

EXAMPLE 2 Take square roots of a fraction

Solve $4z^2 = 9$.

Solution

$4z^2 = 9$	Write original equation.
$z^2 = \frac{9}{4}$	Divide each side by 4.
$z = \pm\sqrt{\frac{9}{4}}$	Take square roots of each side.
$z = \pm\frac{3}{2}$	Simplify.

▶ The solutions are $-\frac{3}{2}$ and $\frac{3}{2}$.

APPROXIMATING SQUARE ROOTS In cases where d in the equation $x^2 = d$ is not a perfect square or a fraction whose numerator and denominator are not perfect squares, you need to approximate the square root. A calculator can be used to find an approximation.

EXAMPLE 3 Approximate solutions of a quadratic equation

Solve $3x^2 - 11 = 7$. Round the solutions to the nearest hundredth.

Solution

$3x^2 - 11 = 7$	Write original equation.
$3x^2 = 18$	Add 11 to each side.
$x^2 = 6$	Divide each side by 3.
$x = \pm\sqrt{6}$	Take square roots of each side.
$x \approx \pm 2.45$	Use a calculator. Round to the nearest hundredth.

▶ The solutions are about −2.45 and about 2.45.

✓ GUIDED PRACTICE for Examples 1, 2, and 3

Solve the equation.

1. $c^2 - 25 = 0$ ± 5
2. $5w^2 + 12 = -8$ no solution
3. $2x^2 + 11 = 11$ 0
4. $25x^2 = 16$ $\pm\frac{4}{5}$
5. $9m^2 = 100$ $\pm\frac{10}{3}$
6. $49b^2 + 64 = 0$ no solution

Solve the equation. Round the solutions to the nearest hundredth.

7. $x^2 + 4 = 14$ ± 3.16
8. $3k^2 - 1 = 0$ ± 0.58
9. $2p^2 - 7 = 2$ ± 2.12

Motivating the Lesson

Tell students that if an object is dropped from a known height, they can calculate how long the object is in the air. For example, if you are standing on a balcony 12 feet above the ground and you drop a key to a friend who catches it at a height of 4 feet, you can use the vertical motion model to find how long the key is in the air.

3 TEACH

Extra Example 1

Solve the equation.

a. $3x^2 = 27$ −3, 3
b. $p^2 + 12 = 12$ 0
c. $a^2 - 3 = -4$ no solution

Extra Example 2

Solve $25s^2 = 49$. $-\frac{7}{5}, \frac{7}{5}$

Key Question to Ask for Example 2

- Why do you get two solutions when you take the square root of each side of the equation? The square root of a positive number has two values, one positive and one negative.

Extra Example 3

Solve $2x^2 - 10 = 6$. Round the solutions to the nearest hundredth. −2.83, 2.83

Differentiated Instruction

Visual Learners Use **Example 3** to provide students with another way to see square roots. First graph $y = x^2$ and then graph $y = 6$. The intersections of the two graphs occur when $x = \pm\sqrt{6}$. This gives a concrete example of the sketch in the Key Concept on p. 652 and illustrates one way to visualize the square roots of 6.

See also the *Algebra 1 Toolkit* for more strategies.

Extra Example 4

Solve $4(x+6)^2 = 32$. Round the solutions to the nearest hundredth.
$-6+\sqrt{8} \approx -3.17, -6-\sqrt{8} \approx -8.83$

Extra Example 5

You drop a towel from a balcony 18 feet above your den onto a table that is 3 feet above the ground. How long is the towel in the air?
about 0.97 sec

Closing the Lesson

Have students summarize the major points of the lesson and answer the Essential Question: How do you solve a quadratic equation by finding square roots?

- If a quadratic equation is in the form $ax^2 + c = 0$, rewrite it in the form $x^2 = d$.
- If $d > 0$, then $x^2 = d$ has two solutions. If $d = 0$, there is one solution, 0. If $d < 0$, there is no real-number solution.

You can use square roots to solve a quadratic equation if you can write it as $x^2 = d$. If $d > 0$ and d is not a perfect square, approximate the values of d using a calculator.

EXAMPLE 4 Solve a quadratic equation

Solve $6(x-4)^2 = 42$. Round the solutions to the nearest hundredth.

$6(x-4)^2 = 42$	Write original equation.
$(x-4)^2 = 7$	Divide each side by 6.
$x - 4 = \pm\sqrt{7}$	Take square roots of each side.
$x = 4 \pm \sqrt{7}$	Add 4 to each side.

▶ The solutions are $4 + \sqrt{7} \approx 6.65$ and $4 - \sqrt{7} \approx 1.35$.

CHECK To check the solutions, first write the equation so that 0 is on one side as follows: $6(x-4)^2 - 42 = 0$. Then graph the related function $y = 6(x-4)^2 - 42$. The x-intercepts appear to be about 6.6 and about 1.3. So, each solution checks.

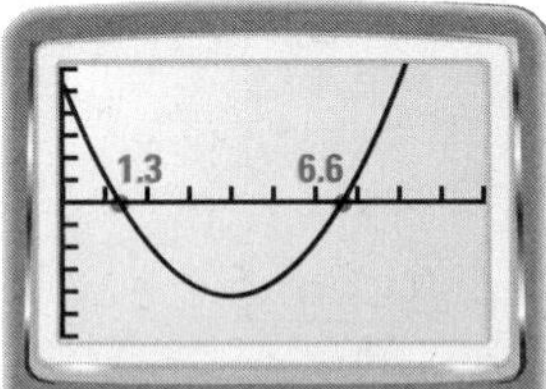

EXAMPLE 5 Solve a multi-step problem

ANOTHER WAY
For alternative methods for solving the problem in Example 5, turn to page 659 for the **Problem Solving Workshop**.

SPORTS EVENT During an ice hockey game, a remote-controlled blimp flies above the crowd and drops a numbered table-tennis ball. The number on the ball corresponds to a prize. Use the information in the diagram to find the amount of time that the ball is in the air.

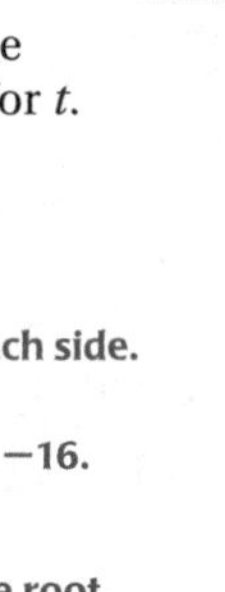

Not drawn to scale

Solution

STEP 1 **Use** the vertical motion model to write an equation for the height h (in feet) of the ball as a function of time t (in seconds).

DETERMINE VELOCITY
When an object is dropped, it has an initial vertical velocity of 0 feet per second.

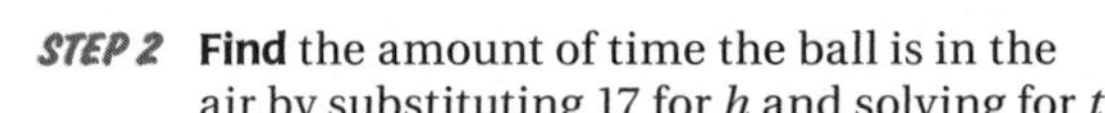

$h = -16t^2 + vt + s$	Vertical motion model
$h = -16t^2 + 0t + 45$	Substitute for v and s.

STEP 2 **Find** the amount of time the ball is in the air by substituting 17 for h and solving for t.

$h = -16t^2 + 45$	Write model.
$17 = -16t^2 + 45$	Substitute 17 for h.
$-28 = -16t^2$	Subtract 45 from each side.
$\frac{28}{16} = t^2$	Divide each side by -16.
$\sqrt{\frac{28}{16}} = t$	Take positive square root.
$1.32 \approx t$	Use a calculator.

INTERPRET SOLUTION
Because the time cannot be a negative number, ignore the negative square root.

▶ The ball is in the air for about 1.32 seconds.

Differentiated Instruction

Below Level Real world situations often motivate students to learn mathematical concepts, so have students work with a partner to create and solve a real world situation based on **Example 5**. Explain that they want a situation in which a dropped object is caught or interrupted in its fall before it hits the ground. Have students develop stepped-out solutions for their problems, which they can use as a guide for future work. See also the *Algebra 1 Toolkit* for more strategies.

GUIDED PRACTICE for Examples 4 and 5

Solve the equation. Round the solutions to the nearest hundredth, if necessary.

10. $2(x-2)^2 = 18$ −1, 5 **11.** $4(q-3)^2 = 28$ 0.35, 5.65 **12.** $3(t+5)^2 = 24$ −7.83, −2.17

13. WHAT IF? In Example 5, suppose the table-tennis ball is released 58 feet above the ground and is caught 12 feet above the ground. Find the amount of time that the ball is in the air. Round your answer to the nearest hundredth of a second. 1.70 sec

10.4 EXERCISES

HOMEWORK KEY

○ = **WORKED-OUT SOLUTIONS** on p. WS24 for Exs. 25 and 59

★ = **STANDARDIZED TEST PRACTICE** Exs. 2, 15, 16, 29, 51, 52, 57, and 60

◆ = **MULTIPLE REPRESENTATIONS** Ex. 62

SKILL PRACTICE

A

1. VOCABULARY Copy and complete: If $b^2 = a$, then b is a(n) _?_ of a. square root

2. ★ WRITING *Describe* two methods for solving a quadratic equation of the form $ax^2 + c = 0$. (1) Graph the parabola $y = ax^2 + c$ and find its x-intercepts. (2) Write the equation in the form $x^2 = -\frac{c}{a}$ and take the square roots of each side.

EXAMPLES 1 and 2 on pp. 652–653 for Exs. 3–16

SOLVING EQUATIONS **Solve the equation.**

3. $3x^2 - 3 = 0$ ±1 **4.** $2x^2 - 32 = 0$ ±4 **5.** $4x^2 - 400 = 0$ ±10

6. $2m^2 - 42 = 8$ ±5 **7.** $15d^2 = 0$ 0 **8.** $a^2 + 8 = 3$ no solution

9. $4g^2 + 10 = 11$ $\pm\frac{1}{2}$ **10.** $2w^2 + 13 = 11$ no solution **11.** $9q^2 - 35 = 14$ $\pm\frac{7}{3}$

12. $25b^2 + 11 = 15$ $\pm\frac{2}{5}$ **13.** $3z^2 - 18 = -18$ 0 **14.** $5n^2 - 17 = -19$ no solution

15. ★ MULTIPLE CHOICE Which of the following is a solution of the equation $61 - 3n^2 = -14$? A

Ⓐ 5 Ⓑ 10 Ⓒ 25 Ⓓ 625

16. ★ MULTIPLE CHOICE Which of the following is a solution of the equation $13 - 36x^2 = -12$? C

Ⓐ $-\frac{6}{5}$ Ⓑ $\frac{1}{6}$ Ⓒ $\frac{5}{6}$ Ⓓ 5

EXAMPLE 3 on p. 653 for Exs. 17–29

APPROXIMATING SQUARE ROOTS **Solve the equation. Round the solutions to the nearest hundredth.**

17. $x^2 + 6 = 13$ ±2.65 **18.** $x^2 + 11 = 24$ ±3.61 **19.** $14 - x^2 = 17$ no solution

20. $2a^2 - 9 = 11$ ±3.16 **21.** $4 - k^2 = 4$ 0 **22.** $5 + 3p^2 = 38$ ±3.32

23. $53 = 8 + 9m^2$ ±2.24 **24.** $-21 = 15 - 2z^2$ ±4.24 **(25.)** $7c^2 = 100$ ±3.78

26. $5d^2 + 2 = 6$ ±0.89 **27.** $4b^2 - 5 = 2$ ±1.32 **28.** $9n^2 - 14 = -3$ ±1.11

29. ★ MULTIPLE CHOICE The equation $17 - \frac{1}{4}x^2 = 12$ has a solution between which two integers? D

Ⓐ 1 and 2 Ⓑ 2 and 3 Ⓒ 3 and 4 Ⓓ 4 and 5

4 PRACTICE AND APPLY

Assignment Guide

Answer Transparencies available for all exercises

Basic:
Day 1: pp. 655–658
Exs. 1–11, 15–25, 29
Day 2: pp. 655–658
Exs. 30–46, 56–60, 64–73

Average:
Day 1: pp. 655–658
Exs. 1, 2, 7–16, 21–29, 47–49
Day 2: pp. 655–658
Exs. 30–46, 50–52, 56–62, 64–72 even

Advanced:
Day 1: pp. 655–658
Exs. 1, 2, 8–16, 23–29, 47–52
Day 2: pp. 655–658
Exs. 32–46, 53–63*, 66, 70, 73

Block:
pp. 655–658
Exs. 1, 2, 7–16, 21–29, 47–49 (with 10.3)
pp. 655–658
Exs. 30–46, 50–52, 56–62, 64–72 even (with 10.5)

Differentiated Instruction

See *Algebra 1 Best Practices Toolkit* for suggestions on addressing the needs of a diverse classroom.

Homework Check

For a quick check of student understanding of key concepts, go over the following exercises:

Basic: 6, 11, 20, 33, 56
Average: 7, 12, 24, 36, 56
Advanced: 8, 13, 27, 38, 57

Extra Practice

- Student Edition, p. 947
- Chapter 10 Resource Book: Practice levels A, B, C, pp. 49–51

Practice Worksheet

An easily-readable reduced practice page (with answers) for this lesson can be found on p. 626C.

Avoiding Common Errors

Exercises 3–14, 17–28, 32–46 Students often indicate only one solution to a quadratic equation. Remind students that there may be zero, one, or two real-number solutions to a quadratic equation.

Graphing Calculator

Exercises 17–28, 32–40 Encourage students to use their graphing calculators to check their solutions. To do so, they need to write the equation so that 0 is on one side. Tell students they can also use the CALCULATE menu to find the zeros of a function. Encourage students to get familiar with all the methods and decide which one is quickest and easiest for them.

51. $\pm\frac{6}{5}$, or ± 1.2. *Sample answer:* Rewrite the decimal as a fraction and then take square roots of each side of the equation: $x^2 = \frac{100}{144}$, so $x = \pm\sqrt{\frac{144}{100}} = \pm\frac{12}{10} = \pm\frac{6}{5}$, or ± 1.2.

30. 36 has two square roots, 6 and −6, so both numbers should be given as solutions of the equation; $x = \pm\sqrt{36}$, $x = \pm 6$; the solutions are −6 and 6.

31. Negative numbers do not have real number square roots, so $\pm\sqrt{-\frac{11}{7}}$ are not real numbers; there is no solution.

ERROR ANALYSIS *Describe* and correct the error in solving the equation.

30. $2x^2 - 54 = 18$

$2x^2 - 54 = 18$
$2x^2 = 72$
$x^2 = 36$
$x = \sqrt{36}$
$x = 6$
The solution is 6.

31. $7d^2 - 6 = -17$

$7d^2 - 6 = -17$
$7d^2 = -11$
$d^2 = -\frac{11}{7}$
$d \approx \pm 1.25$
The solutions are about −1.25 and about 1.25.

EXAMPLE 4 on p. 654 for Exs. 32–40

SOLVING EQUATIONS Solve the equation. Round the solutions to the nearest hundredth.

32. $(x - 7)^2 = 6$ 4.55, 9.45
33. $7(x - 3)^2 = 35$ 0.76, 5.24
34. $6(x + 4)^2 = 18$ −5.73, −2.27
35. $20 = 2(m + 5)^2$ −8.16, −1.84
36. $5(a - 2)^2 = 70$ −1.74, 5.74
37. $21 = 3(z + 14)^2$ −16.65, −11.35
38. $\frac{1}{2}(c - 8)^2 = 3$ 5.55, 10.45
39. $\frac{3}{2}(n + 1)^2 = 33$ −5.69, 3.69
40. $\frac{4}{3}(k - 6)^2 = 20$ 2.13, 9.87

B

SOLVING EQUATIONS Solve the equation. Round the solutions to the nearest hundredth, if necessary.

41. $3x^2 - 35 = 45 - 2x^2$ ±4
42. $42 = 3(x^2 + 5)$ ±3
43. $11x^2 + 3 = 5(4x^2 - 3)$ ±1.41
44. $\left(\frac{t - 5}{3}\right)^2 = 49$ −16, 26
45. $11\left(\frac{w - 7}{2}\right)^2 - 20 = 101$ 0.37, 13.63
46. $(4m^2 - 6)^2 = 81$ ±1.94

GEOMETRY Use the given area A of the circle to find the radius r or the diameter d to the nearest hundredth.

47. $A = 144\pi$ in.^{2} 12 in.

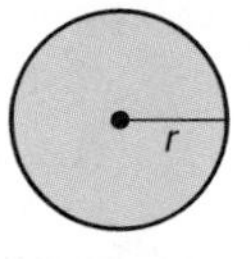

48. $A = 21\pi$ m^2 4.58 m

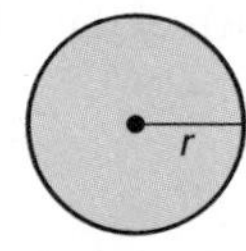

49. $A = 34\pi$ ft^2 11.66 ft

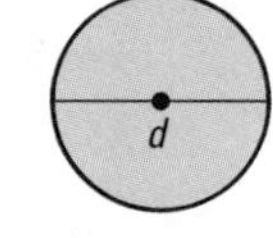

50. **REASONING** An equation of the graph shown is $y = \frac{1}{2}(x - 2)^2 + 1$. Two points on the parabola have y-coordinates of 9. Find the x-coordinates of these points. −2, 6

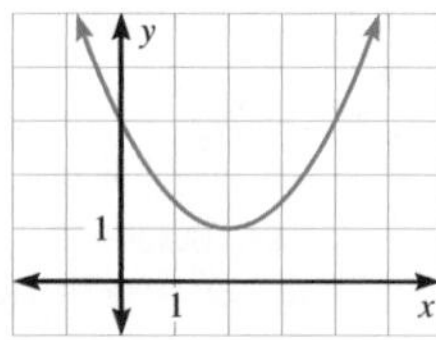

51. ★ **SHORT RESPONSE** Solve $x^2 = 1.44$ without using a calculator. *Explain* your reasoning. See margin.

52. ★ **OPEN-ENDED** Give values for a and c so that $ax^2 + c = 0$ has (a) two solutions, (b) one solution, and (c) no solution. Sample answers are given. (a) 5, −1; (b) 3, 0; (c) 2, 4

C

CHALLENGE Solve the equation without graphing.

53. $x^2 - 12x + 36 = 64$ −2, 14
54. $x^2 + 14x + 49 = 16$ −11, −3
55. $x^2 + 18x + 81 = 25$ −4, −14

○ = WORKED-OUT SOLUTIONS on p. WS1 ★ = STANDARDIZED TEST PRACTICE

PROBLEM SOLVING

EXAMPLE 5 A on p. 654 for Exs. 56–57

56. FALLING OBJECT Fenway Park is a Major League Baseball park in Boston, Massachusetts. The park offers seats on top of the left field wall. A person sitting in one of these seats accidentally drops his sunglasses on the field. The height h (in feet) of the sunglasses can be modeled by the function $h = -16t^2 + 38$ where t is the time (in seconds) since the sunglasses were dropped. Find the time it takes for the sunglasses to reach the field. Round your answer to the nearest hundredth of a second. **1.54 sec**

@HomeTutor for problem solving help at classzone.com

57. ★ MULTIPLE CHOICE Which equation can be used to find the time it takes for an object to hit the ground after it was dropped from a height of 68 feet? **C**

Ⓐ $-16t^2 = 0$ Ⓑ $-16t^2 - 68 = 0$ Ⓒ $-16t^2 + 68 = 0$ Ⓓ $-16t^2 = 68$

@HomeTutor for problem solving help at classzone.com

58. INTERNET USAGE For the period 1995–2001, the number y (in thousands) of Internet users worldwide can be modeled by the function $y = 12{,}697x^2 + 55{,}722$ where x is the number of years since 1995. Between which two years did the number of Internet users worldwide reach 100,000,000? **1996 and 1997**

59. GEMOLOGY To find the weight w (in carats) of round faceted gems, gemologists use the formula $w = 0.0018D^2ds$ where D is the diameter (in millimeters) of the gem, d is the depth (in millimeters) of the gem, and s is the specific gravity of the gem. Find the diameter to the nearest tenth of a millimeter of each round faceted gem in the table.

	Gem	Weight (carats)	Depth (mm)	Specific gravity	Diameter (mm)	
a.	Amethyst	1	4.5	2.65	?	6.8 mm
b.	Diamond	1	4.5	3.52	?	5.9 mm
c.	Ruby	1	4.5	4.00	?	5.6 mm

B **60. ★ SHORT RESPONSE** In deep water, the speed s (in meters per second) of a series of waves and the wavelength L (in meters) of the waves are related by the equation $2\pi s^2 = 9.8L$.

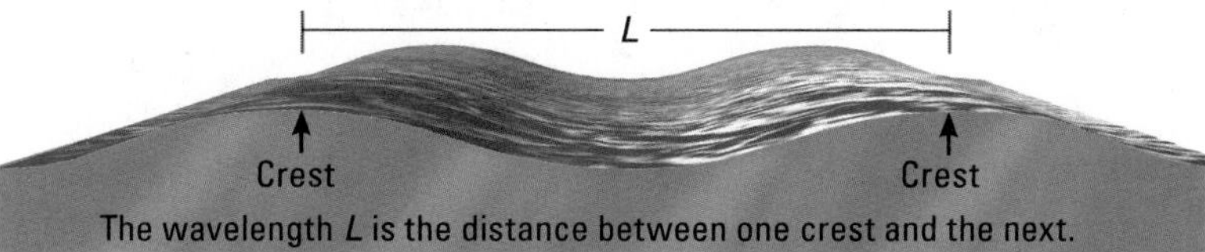

The wavelength L is the distance between one crest and the next.

a. Find the speed to the nearest hundredth of a meter per second of a series of waves with the following wavelengths: 6 meters, 10 meters, and 25 meters. (Use 3.14 for π.) **3.06 m/sec, 3.95 m/sec, 6.25 m/sec**

b. Does the speed of a series of waves increase or decrease as the wavelength of the waves increases? *Explain.* **Increase; as the wavelength in part (a) increased, respective speeds increased.**

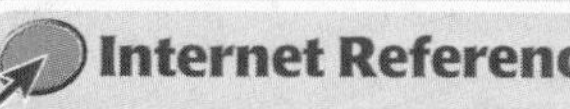

Exercise 56 Additional information about Fenway Park can be found at redsox.mlb.com/NASApp/mlb/bos/ballpark/bos_ballpark_history.jsp

Teaching Strategy

Exercises 56–57 Before assigning these exercises, you may want to discuss how they are similar. Ask students to identify the value of h in Exercise 56 and explain what "+ 38" represents in the function. Then have them identify similar values in Exercise 57. Ask students how they can use these similarities to identify the correct solution to Exercise 57.

5 ASSESS AND RETEACH

Daily Homework Quiz

Transparency Available

Solve the equation. Round solutions to the nearest hundredth, if necessary.

1. $4b^2 - 13 = 3$ $-2, 2$
2. $9x^2 = 25$ $-\frac{5}{3}, \frac{5}{3}$
3. $3n^2 - 18 = 12$ $-3.16, 3.16$
4. At a football game you are sitting 32 feet above the ground. If your hat comes off and falls to the ground, how long will it be in the air? about 1.41 sec

Online Quiz

Available at **classzone.com**

Diagnosis/Remediation

- Practice A, B, C in Chapter 10 Resource Book, pp. 49–51
- Study Guide in Chapter 10 Resource Book, pp. 52–53
- Practice Workbook, pp. 158–159
- @HomeTutor

Challenge

Additional challenge is available in the Chapter 10 Resource Book, p. 57.

62b.

Time of free fall, t (sec)	Height, h (ft)
0	250
1	234
2	186
3	106
4	−6

61. MULTI-STEP PROBLEM The Doyle log rule is a formula used to estimate the amount of lumber that can be sawn from logs of various sizes. The amount of lumber V (in board feet) is given by $V = \frac{L(D-4)^2}{16}$ where L is the length (in feet) of a log and D is the small-end diameter (in inches) of the log.

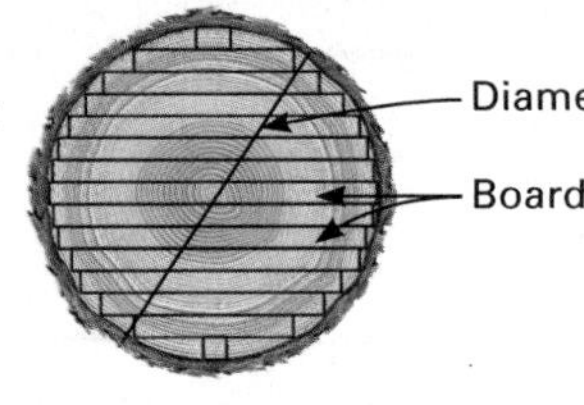

a. Solve the formula for D. $D = 4 \pm \sqrt{\frac{16V}{L}}$

b. Use the rewritten formula to find the diameters, to the nearest tenth of a foot, of logs that will yield 50 board feet and have the following lengths: 16 feet, 18 feet, 20 feet, and 22 feet. 11.1 ft, 10.7 ft, 10.3 ft, 10.0 ft

62. MULTIPLE REPRESENTATIONS A ride at an amusement park lifts seated riders 250 feet above the ground. Then the riders are dropped. They experience free fall until the brakes are activated at 105 feet above the ground.

a. Writing an Equation Use the vertical motion model to write an equation for the height h (in feet) of the riders as a function of the time t (in seconds) into the free fall. $h = -16t^2 + 250$

b. Making a Table Make a table that shows the height of the riders after 0, 1, 2, 3, and 4 seconds. Use the table to estimate the amount of time the riders experience free fall. See margin for table; about 3 sec.

c. Solving an Equation Use the equation to find the amount of time, to the nearest tenth of a second, that the riders experience free fall. 3.0 sec

C **63. CHALLENGE** The height h (in feet) of a dropped object on any planet can be modeled by $h = -\frac{g}{2}t^2 + s$ where g is the acceleration (in feet per second per second) due to the planet's gravity, t is the time (in seconds) after the object is dropped, and s is the initial height (in feet) of the object. Suppose the same object is dropped from the same height on Earth and Mars. Given that g is 32 feet per second per second on Earth and 12 feet per second per second on Mars, on which planet will the object hit the ground first? *Explain.* See margin.

ILLINOIS MIXED REVIEW

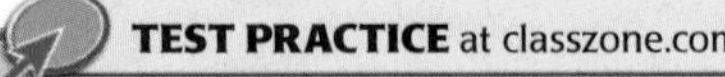

TEST PRACTICE at classzone.com

64. Which equation describes a line that has a slope of −9 and a y-intercept of 11? B

(A) $y = -9(x + 11)$ (B) $y = -9x + 11$

(C) $y = 11x - 9$ (D) $y = 11(x - 9)$

65. Two houses are each built on a square lot. The first lot has a perimeter that is 150% of the perimeter of the second lot. How much greater is the area of the first lot than the area of the second lot? D

(A) 36.5% (B) 75% (C) 150% (D) 225%

Using ALTERNATIVE METHODS

Another Way to Solve Example 5, page 654

MULTIPLE REPRESENTATIONS In Example 5 on page 654, you saw how to solve a problem about a dropped table-tennis ball by using a square root. You can also solve the problem by using factoring or by using a table.

PROBLEM

SPORTS EVENT During an ice hockey game, a remote-controlled blimp flies above the crowd and drops a numbered table-tennis ball. The number on the ball corresponds to a prize. Use the information in the diagram to find the amount of time that the ball is in the air.

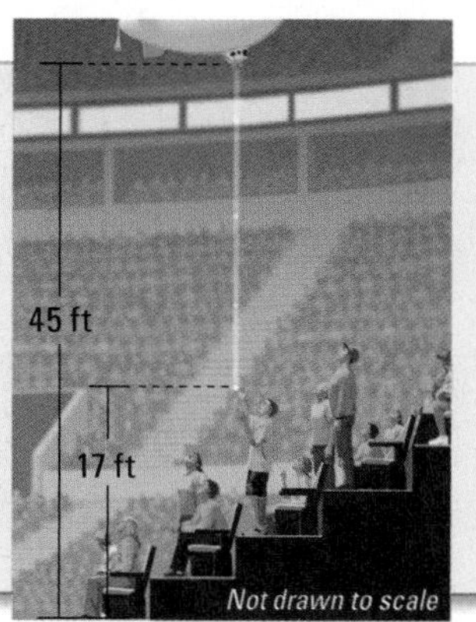

METHOD 1

Using Factoring One alternative approach is to use factoring.

STEP 1 **Write** an equation for the height h (in feet) of the ball as a function of time t (in seconds) after it is dropped using the vertical motion model.

$h = -16t^2 + vt + s$	Vertical motion model
$h = -16t^2 + 0t + 45$	Substitute 0 for v and 45 for s.

STEP 2 **Substitute** 17 for h to find the time it takes the ball to reach a height of 17 feet. Then write the equation so that 0 is on one side.

$17 = -16t^2 + 45$	Substitute 17 for h.
$0 = -16t^2 + 28$	Subtract 17 from each side.

STEP 3 **Solve** the equation by factoring. Replace 28 with the closest perfect square, 25, so that the right side of the equation is factorable as a difference of two squares.

$0 = -16t^2 + 25$	Use 25 as an approximation for 28.
$0 = -(16t^2 - 25)$	Factor out -1.
$0 = -(4t - 5)(4t + 5)$	Difference of two squares pattern
$4t - 5 = 0$ *or* $4t + 5 = 0$	Zero-product property
$t = \frac{5}{4}$ *or* $t = -\frac{5}{4}$	Solve for t.

USE AN APPROXIMATION
By replacing 28 with 25, you will obtain an answer that is an approximation of the amount of time that the ball is in the air.

▶ The ball is in the air about $\frac{5}{4}$, or 1.25, seconds.

Alternative Strategy

Example 5 on page 654 can be solved by using factoring or by using a table. You may want to point out that these alternative strategies do not give the same exact result as the vertical motion model, though the results are close for all three methods. Stress that all three methods give an approximation, and that they all round to 1.3 seconds. Point out that each strategy can be used to check a solution found by using a different strategy.

Avoiding Common Errors

In Method 1, watch for students who use a perfect square that is not closest to 28. Suggest that students list the perfect squares on each side of 28 to make sure they choose the closest one.

p. 658

63. Earth; on Earth the fraction $-\frac{g}{2}$ is $-\frac{32}{2} = -16$, and on Mars the fraction $-\frac{g}{2}$ is $-\frac{12}{2} = -6$; so, on Earth the height of the object is modeled by $h = -16t^2 + s$ and on Mars the height of the object is modeled by $h = -6t^2 + s$. To compare how long it takes the same object dropped from the same height s to hit the ground on each planet, substitute 0 for h in each equation and solve for t in terms of s (disregard any negative solutions). Earth's equation: $0 = -16t^2 + s$; $16t^2 = s$; $t^2 = \frac{s}{16}$; $t = \sqrt{\frac{s}{16}} = \frac{\sqrt{s}}{\sqrt{16}}$, or $t = \frac{\sqrt{s}}{4}$. Mars's equation: $0 = -6t^2 + s$; $6t^2 = s$; $t^2 = \frac{s}{6}$; $t = \sqrt{\frac{s}{6}} = \frac{\sqrt{s}}{\sqrt{6}}$, or $t \approx \frac{\sqrt{s}}{2.45}$. Because $4 > 2.45$, $\frac{1}{4} < \frac{1}{2.45}$, and $\frac{\sqrt{s}}{4} < \frac{\sqrt{s}}{2.45}$; thus, it takes less time for the object to hit the ground on Earth than on Mars.

Teaching Strategy

Emphasize to students the usefulness of using two tables. Point out that the first table gives the time in increments of 1 second, which is fairly easy to calculate, and narrows the focus to a time between 1 and 2 seconds. Then they can calculate in tenths of a second beginning with 1.0 second.

1. See Additional Answers beginning on p. AA1.

2. *Sample answer:* A bird flying 50 feet above the ground drops a twig it was carrying in its beak. How many seconds does it take the twig to reach a height of 15 feet off the ground? The height (in feet) of the twig t seconds after it falls is modeled by $h = -16t^2 + 50$. To find the time it takes the twig to reach a height of 15 feet, substitute 15 for h and solve for t: $15 = -16t^2 + 50$, or $0 = -16t^2 + 35$. Replace 35 with the closest perfect square and factor: $0 = -16t^2 + 36$; $0 = -(4t + 6)(4t - 6)$; $4t + 6 = 0$ *or* $4t - 6 = 0$; $t = -\frac{3}{2}$ *or* $t = \frac{3}{2}$. The time cannot be negative, so disregard the negative solution; the twig is at a height of 15 feet after about $\frac{3}{2}$, or 1.5 seconds.

3b, 3c. See Additional Answers beginning on p. AA1.

4. About 1.73 sec. *Sample answer:* Use factoring. The height h (in feet) of the shoe t seconds after it falls is modeled by $h = -16t^2 + 54$. To find the time it takes the shoe to reach a height of 6 feet, substitute 6 for h and solve for t: $6 = -16t^2 + 54$, or $0 = -16t^2 + 48$. Replace 48 with the closest perfect square and factor: $0 = -16t^2 + 49$; $0 = -(16t^2 - 49)$; $0 = -(4t + 7)(4t - 7)$; $4t + 7 = 0$ *or* $4t - 7 = 0$; $t = -\frac{7}{4}$ *or* $t = \frac{7}{4}$. The time cannot be negative, so disregard the negative solution; the shoe hits the net in about $\frac{7}{4}$, or 1.75 seconds.

METHOD 2 **Using a Table** Another approach is to make and use a table.

STEP 1 **Make** a table that shows the height h (in feet) of the ball by substituting values for time t (in seconds) in the function $h = -16t^2 + 45$. Use increments of 1 second.

Time t (seconds)	Height h (feet)
0	45
1	29
2	−19

STEP 2 **Identify** the time interval in which the height of the ball is 17 feet. This happens between 1 and 2 seconds.

STEP 3 **Make** a second table using increments of 0.1 second to get a closer approximation.

Time t (seconds)	Height h (feet)
1.0	29.00
1.1	25.64
1.2	21.96
1.3	17.96
1.4	13.64

▶ The ball is in the air about 1.3 seconds.

PRACTICE

1. **WHAT IF?** In the problem on page 659, suppose the ball is caught at a height of 10 feet. For how many seconds is the ball in the air? Solve this problem using two different methods. See margin.

2. **OPEN-ENDED** *Describe* a problem about a dropped object. Then solve the problem and explain what your solution means in this situation. See margin.

3. **GEOMETRY** The box below is a rectangular prism with the dimensions shown.

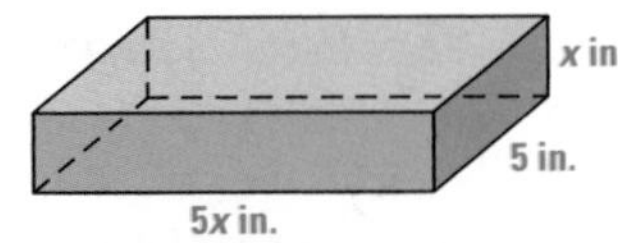

a. Write an equation that gives the volume V (in cubic inches) of the box as a function of x. $V = 25x^2$

b. The volume of the box is 83 cubic inches. Find the dimensions of the box. Use factoring to solve the problem. b–c. See margin.

c. Make a table to check your answer from part (b).

4. **TRAPEZE** You are learning how to perform on a trapeze. While hanging from a still trapeze bar, your shoe comes loose and falls to a safety net that is 6 feet off the ground. If your shoe falls from a height of 54 feet, how long does it take your shoe to hit the net? Choose any method for solving the problem. Show your steps. See margin.

5. **ERROR ANALYSIS** A student solved the problem in Exercise 4 as shown below. *Describe* and correct the error. See margin.

> Let t be the time (in seconds) that the shoe is in the air.
>
> $6 = -16t^2 + 54$
>
> $0 = -16t^2 + 60$
>
> Replace 60 with the closest perfect square, 64.
>
> $0 = -16t^2 + 64$
>
> $0 = -16(t - 2)(t + 2)$
>
> $t = 2$ or $t = -2$
>
> It takes about 2 seconds.

5. To rewrite the equation $6 = -16t^2 + 54$ so that one side is 0, you must subtract 6 from each side; $0 = -16t^2 + 48$, replace 48 with the closest perfect square, 49. $0 = -16t^2 + 49 = -(16t^2 - 49) = -(4t + 7)(4t - 7)$, so the approximate solutions of this equation are $\pm\frac{7}{4}$. Disregard the negative solution because time cannot be negative; so, it takes about $\frac{7}{4}$, or 1.75, seconds for the shoe to hit the net.

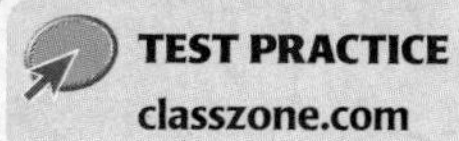
TEST PRACTICE
classzone.com

Lessons 10.1–10.4

1. **BUSINESS** A company's yearly profits from 1996 to 2006 can be modeled by the function $y = x^2 - 8x + 80$ where y is the profit (in thousands of dollars) and x is the number of years since 1996. What was the company's least yearly profit during the time period?

   A. \$4,000 **C.** \$64,000
   B. \$48,000 **D.** \$80,000

2. **LACROSSE** During a game of lacrosse, you throw a ball twice using a lacrosse stick. In the first throw, the ball is released 8 feet above the ground with an initial vertical velocity of 35 feet per second. In the second throw, the ball is released 8 feet above the ground with an initial vertical velocity of 42 feet per second. Which statement correctly compares the two throws if no one catches either throw?

   F. The second throw is in the air longer.
   G. The first throw reaches a greater height.
   H. The two throws have the same maximum height.
   J. The first throw travels 7 feet farther.

3. **FALLING OBJECTS** In a science experiment, two balls are dropped from a building at the same time, one from a window 40 feet above the ground and the other from the roof 80 feet above the ground. What is the height of the ball dropped from the roof when the other ball hits the ground?

   A. 5 ft **C.** 30 ft
   B. 20 ft **D.** 40 ft

4. **FENCING** You want to enclose a rectangular area with 48 feet of fencing. What is the greatest possible area that you can enclose with the fence?

   F. 119 ft^2 **H.** 144 ft^2
   G. 140 ft^2 **J.** 576 ft^2

5. **FOOTBALL** A football player attempts a field goal. The path of the kicked football can be modeled by $y = -0.03x^2 + 1.8x$ where x is the horizontal distance (in yards) traveled by the football and y is the corresponding height (in yards) of the football. How high will the football be after it has traveled 45 yards?

   A. 20.25 yd **C.** 60.75 yd
   B. 30 yd **D.** None of the above

6. **TUNNEL** The opening of the tunnel shown can be modeled by the graph of the equation $y = -0.18x^2 + 4.4x - 12$ where x and y are measured in feet. Which is the maximum height of the tunnel?

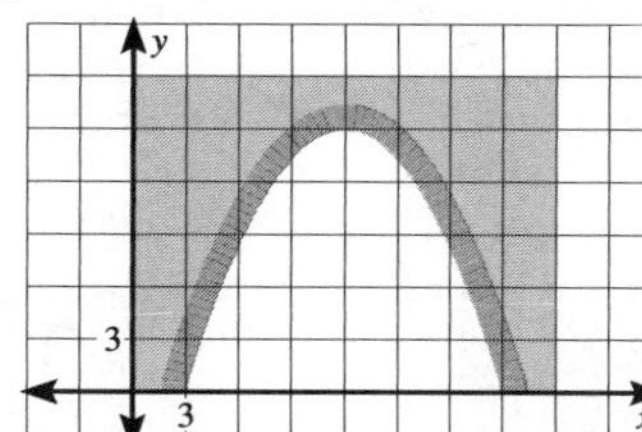

   F. 12.22 ft **H.** 14.89 ft
   G. 14.62 ft **J.** 26.89 ft

7. **SUBWAY** The force F (in newtons) that a passenger feels when a subway train goes around a curve is given by $F = \frac{mv^2}{r}$ where m is the mass (in kilograms) of the passenger, v is the velocity (in meters per second) of the train, and r is the radius (in meters) of the curve. A passenger who has a mass of 75 kilograms experiences a force of 18,150 newtons while going around a curve that has a radius of 8 meters. Find the velocity of the train in meters per second.

   A. 5.5 m/s **C.** 44 m/s
   B. 30.3 m/s **D.** 88 m/s

Illinois Mixed Review

1. C
2. F
3. D
4. H
5. A
6. H
7. C

Animated Algebra classzone.com

10.5 Completing the Square Using Algebra Tiles

MATERIALS • algebra tiles

QUESTION How can you use algebra tiles to complete the square?

For an expression of the form $x^2 + bx$, you can add a constant c to the expression so that the expression $x^2 + bx + c$ is a perfect square trinomial. This process is called *completing the square.*

EXPLORE Complete the square

Find the value of c that makes $x^2 + 4x + c$ a perfect square trinomial.

***STEP 1* Model expression**
Use algebra tiles to model the expression $x^2 + 4x$. You will need one x^2-tile and four x-tiles for this expression.

***STEP 2* Rearrange tiles**
Arrange the tiles to form a square. The arrangement will be incomplete in one of the corners.

***STEP 3* Complete the square**
Determine the number of 1-tiles needed to complete the square. The number of 1-tiles is the value of c. So, the perfect square trinomial is $x^2 + 4x + 4$ or $(x + 2)^2$.

DRAW CONCLUSIONS Use your observations to complete these exercises

1. Copy and complete the table using algebra tiles.

Expression	Number of 1-tiles needed to complete the square	Expression written as a square
$x^2 + 4x$	4	$x^2 + 4x + 4 = (x + 2)^2$
$x^2 + 6x$	? 9	?
$x^2 + 8x$	? 16	?
$x^2 + 10x$	? 25	?

$x^2 + 6x + 9 = (x + 3)^2$
$x^2 + 8x + 16 = (x + 4)^2$
$x^2 + 10x + 25 = (x + 5)^2$

2. In the statement $x^2 + bx + c = (x + d)^2$, how are b and d related? How are c and d related? $b = 2d$; $c = d^2$

3. Use your answer to Exercise 2 to predict the number of 1-tiles you would need to add to complete the square for the expression $x^2 + 18x$. 81 1–tiles

1 PLAN AND PREPARE

Explore the Concept

- Students will use algebra tiles to complete the square.
- This activity leads into the study of completing the square in Lesson 10.5, Example 1.

Materials

Each student will need:

- algebra tiles
- Activity Support Master (*Chapter 10 Resource Book*, p. 60)

Recommended Time

Work activity: 10 min

Discuss results: 5 min

Grouping

Students should work individually.

2 TEACH

Tips for Success

Make sure that the tiles in Step 2 are arranged to form a square.

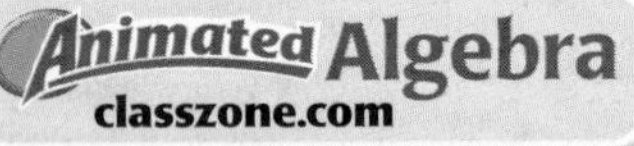

An **Animated Algebra** activity is available on-line. This activity is also available on the **Power Presentations CD-ROM**.

Key Discovery

You can complete the square for an expression in the form of $x^2 + bx$ by adding the square of one-half the value of b.

3 ASSESS AND RETEACH

Predict the number of 1-tiles needed to complete the square for each expression.

1. $x^2 + 2x$ 1

2. $x^2 + 12x$ 36

10.5 Solve Quadratic Equations by Completing the Square

8.11.19 Solve problems that include nonlinear functions, including selecting and evaluating formulas . . .

Before You solved quadratic equations by finding square roots.

Now You will solve quadratic equations by completing the square.

Why? So you can solve a problem about snowboarding, as in Ex. 50.

Key Vocabulary
- **completing the square**
- **perfect square trinomial,** *p. 601*

For an expression of the form $x^2 + bx$, you can add a constant c to the expression so that the expression $x^2 + bx + c$ is a perfect square trinomial. This process is called **completing the square**.

KEY CONCEPT *For Your Notebook*

Completing the Square

Words To complete the square for the expression $x^2 + bx$, add the square of half the coefficient of the term bx.

Algebra $x^2 + bx + \left(\frac{b}{2}\right)^2 = \left(x + \frac{b}{2}\right)^2$

EXAMPLE 1 Complete the square

Find the value of c that makes the expression $x^2 + 5x + c$ a perfect square trinomial. Then write the expression as the square of a binomial.

STEP 1 **Find** the value of c. For the expression to be a perfect square trinomial, c needs to be the square of half the coefficient of bx.

$c = \left(\frac{5}{2}\right)^2 = \frac{25}{4}$ Find the square of half the coefficient of bx.

STEP 2 **Write** the expression as a perfect square trinomial. Then write the expression as the square of a binomial.

$x^2 + 5x + c = x^2 + 5x + \frac{25}{4}$ Substitute $\frac{25}{4}$ for c.

$= \left(x + \frac{5}{2}\right)^2$ Square of a binomial

GUIDED PRACTICE for Example 1

Find the value of c that makes the expression a perfect square trinomial. Then write the expression as the square of a binomial.

1. $x^2 + 8x + c$ $16; (x + 4)^2$
2. $x^2 - 12x + c$ $36; (x - 6)^2$
3. $x^2 + 3x + c$ $\frac{9}{4}; \left(x + \frac{3}{2}\right)^2$

1 PLAN AND PREPARE

Warm-Up Exercises

Transparency Available

Evaluate the expression.

1. $\left(\frac{2}{3}\right)^2$ $\frac{4}{9}$
2. $\left(\frac{7}{5}\right)^2$ $\frac{49}{25}$
3. An acorn falls to the ground from a height of 25 feet. How long was the acorn in the air? 1.25 sec

Notetaking Guide

Transparency Available

Promotes interactive learning and notetaking skills, pp. 233–235.

Pacing

Basic: 2 days
Average: 2 days
Advanced: 2 days
Block: 0.5 block with 10.4
0.5 block with 10.6
- See *Teaching Guide/Lesson Plan.*

2 FOCUS AND MOTIVATE

Essential Question

Big Idea 2, p. 627

How do you solve a quadratic equation by completing the square? **Tell students they will learn how to answer this question by adding a value to each side of the equation so one side is a perfect square trinomial.**

Resource Planning Guide

Chapter Resource Book
- Teaching Guide/Lesson Plan (pp. 58–59)
- Practice levels A, B, C (pp. 61–63)
- Study Guide (pp. 64–65)
- Catch-up for Absent Students (p. 66)
- Application (p. 67)
- Challenge (p. 68)

Workbooks
- Notetaking Guide (pp. 233–235)
- Practice Workbook (pp. 160–161)

Teaching Options
- **Power Presentations CD-ROM** provides dynamic electronic teaching resources for the classroom.
- **Activity Generator CD-ROM** provides editable activities for all ability levels.

Interactive Technology
- Easy Planner
- Power Presentations CD-ROM
- Activity Generator CD-ROM
- Animated Algebra
- Test Generator CD-ROM
- Online Quiz
- eWorkbook
- eEdition
- @HomeTutor

Resources for English Learners
- Quick Reference for English Learners
- Spanish Study Guide
- Multi-Language Visual Glossary
- Student Resources in Spanish

See also the *Algebra 1 Toolkit* for more strategies for meeting individual needs.

Motivating the Lesson

You want to put a mat frame around a photograph. You know the outside dimensions of the mat and you know the area of the photograph. You can write an equation to model this situation, and solve it to find the width of the mat frame.

3 TEACH

Extra Example 1

Find the value of c that makes the expression $x^2 + 7x + c$ a perfect square trinomial. Then write the expression as the square of a binomial. $\frac{49}{4}$; $\left(x + \frac{7}{2}\right)^2$

Key Question to Ask for Example 1

- What is a perfect square trinomial? A perfect square trinomial can be written in the form of $(a + b)^2$ or $(a - b)^2$.

Extra Example 2

Solve $x^2 + 6x = 7$ by completing the square. $(x + 3)^2 = 16$; $-7, 1$

Key Question to Ask for Example 2

- What is the value of $\left(\frac{b}{2}\right)^2$? 64

Extra Example 3

Solve $3x^2 + 12x - 18 = 0$ by completing the square. $(x + 2)^2 = 10$; $-2 + \sqrt{10} \approx 1.16$, $-2 - \sqrt{10} \approx -5.16$

SOLVING EQUATIONS The method of completing the square can be used to solve any quadratic equation. To use completing the square to solve a quadratic equation, you must write the equation in the form $x^2 + bx = d$.

EXAMPLE 2 Solve a quadratic equation

AVOID ERRORS
When completing the square to solve an equation, be sure you add the term $\left(\frac{b}{2}\right)^2$ to both sides of the equation.

Solve $x^2 - 16x = -15$ by completing the square.

Solution

$x^2 - 16x = -15$	Write original equation.
$x^2 - 16x + (-8)^2 = -15 + (-8)^2$	Add $\left(\frac{-16}{2}\right)^2$, or $(-8)^2$, to each side.
$(x - 8)^2 = -15 + (-8)^2$	Write left side as the square of a binomial.
$(x - 8)^2 = 49$	Simplify the right side.
$x - 8 = \pm 7$	Take square roots of each side.
$x = 8 \pm 7$	Add 8 to each side.

▶ The solutions of the equation are $8 + 7 = 15$ and $8 - 7 = 1$.

CHECK You can check the solutions in the original equation.

If $x = 15$:	If $x = 1$:
$(15)^2 - 16(15) \stackrel{?}{=} -15$	$(1)^2 - 16(1) \stackrel{?}{=} -15$
$-15 = -15$ ✓	$-15 = -15$ ✓

EXAMPLE 3 Solve a quadratic equation in standard form

AVOID ERRORS
Be sure that the coefficient of x^2 is 1 before you complete the square.

Solve $2x^2 + 20x - 8 = 0$ by completing the square.

Solution

$2x^2 + 20x - 8 = 0$	Write original equation.
$2x^2 + 20x = 8$	Add 8 to each side.
$x^2 + 10x = 4$	Divide each side by 2.
$x^2 + 10x + 5^2 = 4 + 5^2$	Add $\left(\frac{10}{2}\right)^2$, or 5^2, to each side.
$(x + 5)^2 = 29$	Write left side as the square of a binomial.
$x + 5 = \pm\sqrt{29}$	Take square roots of each side.
$x = -5 \pm \sqrt{29}$	Subtract 5 from each side.

▶ The solutions are $-5 + \sqrt{29} \approx 0.39$ and $-5 - \sqrt{29} \approx -10.39$.

✓ **GUIDED PRACTICE** for Examples 2 and 3

Solve the equation by completing the square. Round your solutions to the nearest hundredth, if necessary.

4. $x^2 - 2x = 3$ $-1, 3$
5. $m^2 + 10m = -8$ $-9.12, -0.88$
6. $3g^2 - 24g + 27 = 0$ $1.35, 6.65$

Differentiated Instruction

Below Level The exercises in this lesson provides numerous places where students can make calculation errors, so encourage them to use their graphing calculators to check their solutions. After they enter and graph an equation, have them check the x-intercepts or the zeros of the function. If the solutions do not check, have them go over their calculations to discover and correct the error. Encourage students to think of their graphing calculators as a way to check their answers and to find and correct errors. See also the *Algebra 1 Toolkit* for more strategies.

EXAMPLE 4 Solve a multi-step problem

CRAFTS You decide to use chalkboard paint to create a chalkboard on a door. You want the chalkboard to have a uniform border as shown. You have enough chalkboard paint to cover 6 square feet. Find the width of the border to the nearest inch.

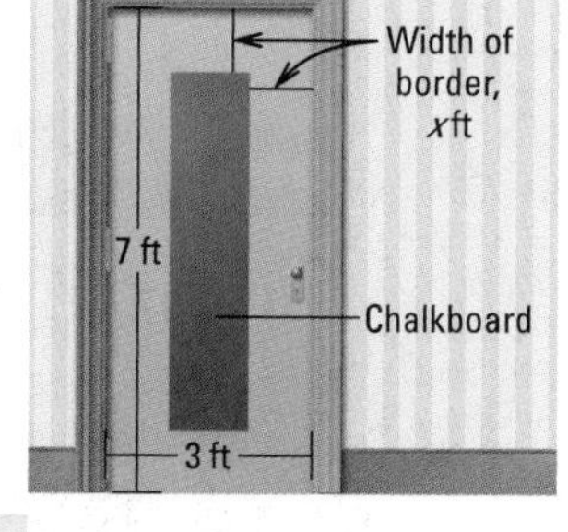

Solution

STEP 1 **Write** a verbal model. Then write an equation. Let x be the width (in feet) of the border.

Area of chalkboard (square feet)	=	Length of chalkboard (feet)	•	Width of chalkboard (feet)
6	=	$(7 - 2x)$	•	$(3 - 2x)$

WRITE EQUATION
The width of the border is subtracted twice because it is at the top and the bottom of the door, as well as at the left and the right.

STEP 2 **Solve** the equation.

$6 = (7 - 2x)(3 - 2x)$ Write equation.

$6 = 21 - 20x + 4x^2$ Multiply binomials.

$-15 = 4x^2 - 20x$ Subtract 21 from each side.

$-\frac{15}{4} = x^2 - 5x$ Divide each side by 4.

$-\frac{15}{4} + \frac{25}{4} = x^2 - 5x + \frac{25}{4}$ Add $\left(-\frac{5}{2}\right)^2$, or $\frac{25}{4}$, to each side.

$-\frac{15}{4} + \frac{25}{4} = \left(x - \frac{5}{2}\right)^2$ Write right side as the square of a binomial.

$\frac{5}{2} = \left(x - \frac{5}{2}\right)^2$ Simplify left side.

$\pm\sqrt{\frac{5}{2}} = x - \frac{5}{2}$ Take square roots of each side.

$\frac{5}{2} \pm \sqrt{\frac{5}{2}} = x$ Add $\frac{5}{2}$ to each side.

The solutions of the equation are $\frac{5}{2} + \sqrt{\frac{5}{2}} \approx 4.08$ and $\frac{5}{2} - \sqrt{\frac{5}{2}} \approx 0.92$.

It is not possible for the width of the border to be 4.08 feet because the width of the door is 3 feet. So, the width of the border is 0.92 foot. Convert 0.92 foot to inches.

$0.92 \text{ ft} \cdot \frac{12 \text{ in.}}{1 \text{ ft}} = 11.04 \text{ in.}$ Multiply by conversion factor.

▶ The width of the border should be about 11 inches.

✓ GUIDED PRACTICE for Example 4

7. **WHAT IF?** In Example 4, suppose you have enough chalkboard paint to cover 4 square feet. Find the width of the border to the nearest inch. **13 in.**

Extra Example 4

You are designing an herb garden with a uniform border of ornamental grass around it as shown. Your design includes 10 square feet for the herb garden. Find the width of the grass border to the nearest inch. **20 in.**

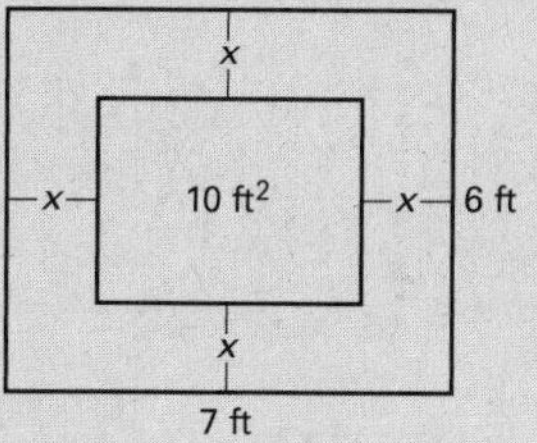

Key Questions to Ask for Example 4

- Why do you divide each side of the equation by 4? **You want the leading coefficient to be 1.**
- How can you check that your solution is correct? **You can substitute the solution for x in the original equation.**

Closing the Lesson

Have students summarize the major points of the lesson and answer the Essential Question: How do you solve a quadratic equation by completing the square?

- **Starting with an expression in the form $x^2 + bx$, you can add a constant $c = \left(\frac{b}{2}\right)^2$ to the expression so that $x^2 + bx + c$ is a perfect square trinomial.**

To complete the square, write the equation in the form $x^2 + bx = d$. Add $\left(\frac{b}{2}\right)^2$ to each side so that one side is $x^2 + bx + \left(\frac{b}{2}\right)^2$ or $\left(x + \frac{b}{2}\right)^2$. Then take the square root of each side and solve for x.

Differentiated Instruction

Kinesthetic Learners As you begin **Example 4**, have students sketch scale models of the chalkboard using 1 inch equal to 1 foot. Then have them vary the width of the border and calculate the corresponding areas. This will help students get an idea of what the width of the border should be.

See also the *Algebra 1 Toolkit* for more strategies.

4 PRACTICE AND APPLY

Assignment Guide

Answer Transparencies available for all exercises

Basic:
Day 1: EP p. 946 Exs. 13–18
pp. 666–668
Exs. 1–23
Day 2: pp. 666–668
Exs. 24–33, 45–48, 52–64 even

Average:
Day 1: pp. 666–668
Exs. 1, 2, 5–11, 15–23, 28–33
Day 2: pp. 666–668
Exs. 24–27, 34–42, 45–50, 55–58, 62

Advanced:
Day 1: pp. 666–668
Exs. 1, 7–11, 18–25, 28–36
Day 2: pp. 666–668
Exs. 37–51*, 56, 57, 60, 63, 64

Block:
pp. 666–668
Exs. 1, 2, 5–11, 15–23, 28–33 (with 10.4)
pp. 666–668
Exs. 24–27, 34–42, 45–50, 55–58, 62 (with 10.6)

Differentiated Instruction

See *Algebra 1 Best Practices Toolkit* for suggestions on addressing the needs of a diverse classroom.

Homework Check

For a quick check of student understanding of key concepts, go over the following exercises:
Basic: 6, 14, 17, 28, 45
Average: 8, 18, 21, 34, 46
Advanced: 10, 20, 22, 38, 46

Extra Practice

- Student Edition, p. 947
- Chapter 10 Resource Book: Practice levels A, B, C, pp. 61–63

Practice Worksheet

An easily-readable reduced practice page (with answers) for this lesson can be found on p. 626C.

10.5 EXERCISES

HOMEWORK KEY
○ = **WORKED-OUT SOLUTIONS** on p. WS24 for Exs. 19 and 47
★ = **STANDARDIZED TEST PRACTICE** Exs. 2, 24, 25, 42, and 49
◆ = **MULTIPLE REPRESENTATIONS** Ex. 47

SKILL PRACTICE

A

1. **VOCABULARY** Copy and complete: The process of writing an expression of the form $x^2 + bx$ as a perfect square trinomial is called _?_. completing the square

2. ★ **WRITING** Give an example of an expression that is a perfect square trinomial. *Explain* why the expression is a perfect square trinomial.
Sample answer: $x^2 + 14x + 49$; when factored, it is the square of a binomial: $(x + 7)^2$.

EXAMPLE 1 on p. 663 for Exs. 3–11

COMPLETING THE SQUARE Find the value of *c* that makes the expression a perfect square trinomial. Then write the expression as the square of a binomial.

3. $x^2 + 6x + c$ $9; (x+3)^2$
4. $x^2 + 12x + c$ $36; (x+6)^2$
5. $x^2 - 4x + c$ $4; (x-2)^2$
6. $x^2 - 8x + c$ $16; (x-4)^2$
7. $x^2 - 3x + c$ $\frac{9}{4}; \left(x - \frac{3}{2}\right)^2$
8. $x^2 + 5x + c$ $\frac{25}{4}; \left(x + \frac{5}{2}\right)^2$
9. $x^2 + 2.4x + c$ $1.44; (x+1.2)^2$
10. $x^2 - \frac{1}{2}x + c$ $\frac{1}{16}; \left(x - \frac{1}{4}\right)^2$
11. $x^2 - \frac{4}{3}x + c$ $\frac{4}{9}; \left(x - \frac{2}{3}\right)^2$

EXAMPLES 2 and 3 on p. 664 for Exs. 12–27

SOLVING EQUATIONS Solve the equation by completing the square. Round your solutions to the nearest hundredth, if necessary.

12. $x^2 + 2x = 3$ $-3, 1$
13. $x^2 + 10x = 24$ $-12, 2$
14. $c^2 - 14c = 15$ $-1, 15$
15. $n^2 - 6n = 72$ $-6, 12$
16. $a^2 - 8a + 15 = 0$ $3, 5$
17. $y^2 + 4y - 21 = 0$ $-7, 3$
18. $w^2 - 5w = \frac{11}{4}$ $-0.5, 5.5$
19. $z^2 + 11z = -\frac{21}{4}$ $-10.5, -0.5$
20. $g^2 - \frac{2}{3}g = 7$ $-2.33, 3$
21. $k^2 - 8k - 7 = 0$ $-0.80, 8.80$
22. $v^2 - 7v + 1 = 0$ $0.15, 6.85$
23. $m^2 + 3m + \frac{5}{4} = 0$ $-2.5, -0.5$

24. ★ **MULTIPLE CHOICE** What are the solutions of $4x^2 + 16x = 9$? C

Ⓐ $-\frac{1}{2}, -\frac{9}{2}$ Ⓑ $-\frac{1}{2}, \frac{9}{2}$ Ⓒ $\frac{1}{2}, -\frac{9}{2}$ Ⓓ $\frac{1}{2}, \frac{9}{2}$

25. ★ **MULTIPLE CHOICE** What are the solutions of $x^2 + 12x + 10 = 0$? B

Ⓐ $-6 \pm \sqrt{46}$ Ⓑ $-6 \pm \sqrt{26}$ Ⓒ $6 \pm \sqrt{26}$ Ⓓ $6 \pm \sqrt{46}$

ERROR ANALYSIS *Describe* and correct the error in solving the given equation. 26, 27. See margin.

26. $x^2 - 14x = 11$

$$x^2 - 14x = 11$$
$$x^2 - 14x + 49 = 11$$
$$(x - 7)^2 = 11$$
$$x - 7 = \pm\sqrt{11}$$
$$x = 7 \pm \sqrt{11}$$

27. $x^2 - 2x - 4 = 0$

$$x^2 - 2x - 4 = 0$$
$$x^2 - 2x = 4$$
$$x^2 - 2x + 1 = 4 + 1$$
$$(x + 1)^2 = 5$$
$$x + 1 = \pm\sqrt{5}$$
$$x = 1 \pm \sqrt{5}$$

26. When completing the square, you must add the same number to each side of the equation, not just to the side of the equation for which you complete the square; $x^2 - 14x + 49 = 11 + 49$, $(x - 7)^2 = 60$, $x - 7 = \pm\sqrt{60}$, $x = 7 \pm \sqrt{60}$.
27. The perfect square trinomial $x^2 - 2x + 1$ factors as $(x - 1)^2$ not $(x + 1)^2$; $(x - 1)^2 = 5$, $x - 1 = \pm\sqrt{5}$, $x = 1 \pm \sqrt{5}$.

B **SOLVING EQUATIONS** **Solve the equation by completing the square. Round your solutions to the nearest hundredth, if necessary.**

31. −1.91, 0.91
32. −3.67, −0.33
33. −0.96, 6.96
34. −0.30, 12.30
35. 0.79, 2.21
36. −0.65, 4.65

28. $2x^2 - 8x - 14 = 0$ −1.32, 5.32 **29.** $2x^2 + 24x + 10 = 0$ −11.57, −0.43 **30.** $3x^2 - 48x + 39 = 0$ 0.86, 15.14

31. $4y^2 + 4y - 7 = 0$ **32.** $9n^2 + 36n + 11 = 0$ **33.** $3w^2 - 18w - 20 = 0$

34. $3p^2 - 30p - 11 = 6p$ **35.** $3a^2 - 12a + 3 = -a^2 - 4$ **36.** $15c^2 - 51c - 30 = 9c + 15$

37. $7m^2 + 24m - 2 = m^2 - 9$ −3.68, −0.32 **38.** $g^2 + 2g + 0.4 = 0.9g^2 + g$ −9.58, −0.42 **39.** $11z^2 - 10z - 3 = -9z^2 + \frac{3}{4}$ −0.25, 0.75

GEOMETRY **Find the value of x. Round your answer to the nearest hundredth, if necessary.**

40. Area of triangle = 108 m^2 12

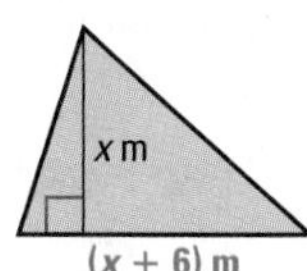

41. Area of rectangle = 288 $in.^2$ 4.87

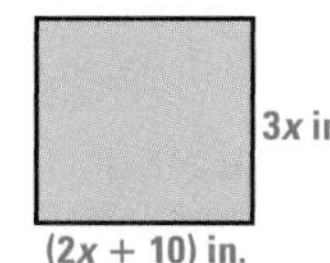

42. ★ **WRITING** How many solutions does $x^2 + bx = c$ have if $c < -\left(\frac{b}{2}\right)^2$? *Explain.* See margin.

C **43. CHALLENGE** The product of two consecutive negative integers is 210. Find the integers. −15, −14

44. CHALLENGE The product of two consecutive positive even integers is 288. Find the integers. 16, 18

PROBLEM SOLVING

EXAMPLE 4 **A** on p. 665 for Exs. 45–46

45. LANDSCAPING You are building a rectangular brick patio surrounded by crushed stone in a rectangular courtyard as shown. The crushed stone border has a uniform width x (in feet). You have enough money in your budget to purchase patio bricks to cover 140 square feet. Solve the equation $140 = (20 - 2x)(16 - 2x)$ to find the width of the border. 3 ft

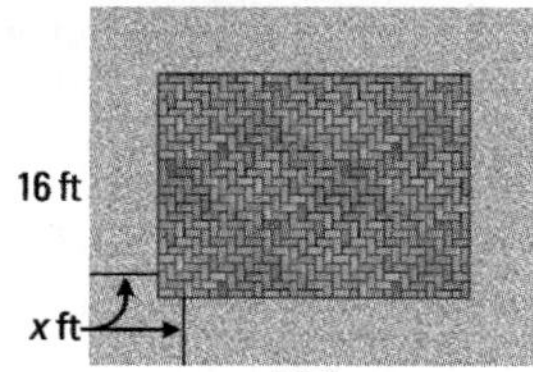

@HomeTutor for problem solving help at classzone.com

46. TRAFFIC ENGINEERING The distance d (in feet) that it takes a car to come to a complete stop on dry asphalt can be modeled by $d = 0.05s^2 + 1.1s$ where s is the speed of the car (in miles per hour). A car has 78 feet to come to a complete stop. Find the maximum speed at which the car can travel. 30 mi/h

@HomeTutor for problem solving help at classzone.com

47. ◆ **MULTIPLE REPRESENTATIONS** For the period 1985–2001, the average salary y (in thousands of dollars) per season of a Major League Baseball player can be modeled by $y = 7x^2 - 4x + 392$ where x is the number of years since 1985.

a. Solving an Equation Write and solve an equation to find the year when the average salary was \$1,904,000. $1904 = 7x^2 - 4x + 392$, 2000

b. Drawing a Graph Use a graph to check your solution to part (a). See margin.

Avoiding Common Errors

Exercises 12–25, 28–39 Watch for students who add the term $\left(\frac{b}{2}\right)^2$ to one side of the equation only. Stress to students that they must add the term to each side in order to write an equivalent equation.

An **Animated Algebra** activity is available on-line for **Exercise 50.** This activity is also available on the **Power Presentations CD-ROM**.

Study Strategy

Exercise 51 Suggest to students that they draw a diagram to help them visualize the solution to this problem.

42. Zero; $\left(\frac{b}{2}\right)^2$ is always positive, so if $c < -\left(\frac{b}{2}\right)^2$, c must be a negative number whose absolute value is greater than $\left(\frac{b}{2}\right)^2$. Then $c + \left(\frac{b}{2}\right)^2$ will simplify to a negative number, implying that $\left(x + \frac{b}{2}\right)^2 = c + \left(\frac{b}{2}\right)^2$ has no solution.

47b.

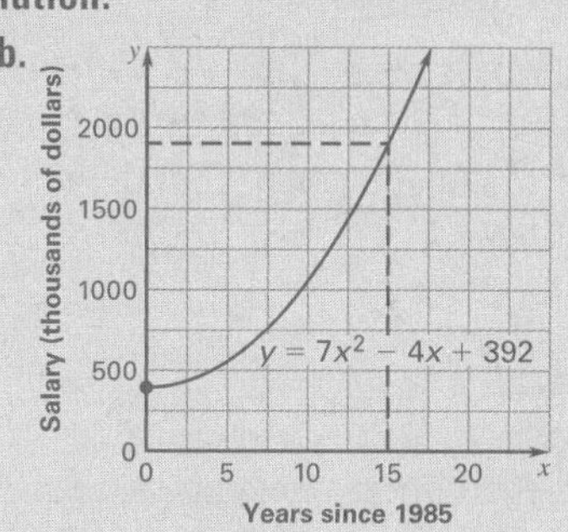

When $y \approx 1904$, the value of x is about 15. So, the year 2000 (1985 + 15) found in part (a) is correct.

5 ASSESS AND RETEACH

Daily Homework Quiz

Transparency Available

Solve the equation by completing the square. Round to the nearest hundredth, if necessary.

1. $x^2 + 12x = 28$ −14, 2

2. $m^2 - 8m = 12$ −1.29, 9.29

3. What is the width of the border that surrounds this poster? 1 in.

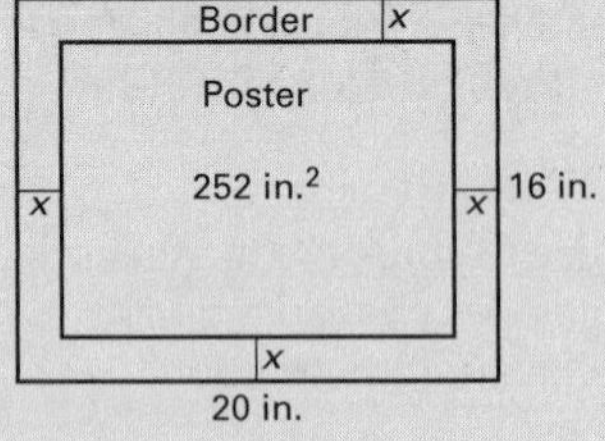

Online Quiz

Available at **classzone.com**

Diagnosis/Remediation

- Practice A, B, C in Chapter 10 Resource Book, pp. 61–63
- Study Guide in Chapter 10 Resource Book, pp. 64–65
- Practice Workbook, pp. 160–161
- @HomeTutor

Challenge

Additional challenge is available in the Chapter 10 Resource Book, p. 68.

49. Yes; to find the number of days x after which the stock price was \$23.50 per share, substitute 23.5 for y and solve for x by completing the square to find that the solutions are 10 and 30. You could have sold the stock for \$23.50 per share 10 days after you purchased it.

B

48. MULTI-STEP PROBLEM You have 80 feet of fencing to make a rectangular horse pasture that covers 750 square feet. A barn will be used as one side of the pasture as shown.

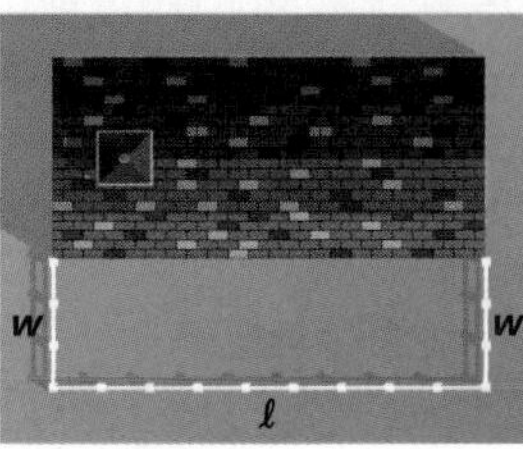

a. Write equations for the perimeter and area of the pasture. $\ell + 2w = 80, \ell w = 750$

b. Use substitution to solve the system of equations from part (a). What are the possible dimensions of the pasture? length: 50 ft, width: 15 ft; length: 30 ft, width: 25 ft

49. ★ SHORT RESPONSE You purchase stock for \$16 per share, and you sell the stock 30 days later for \$23.50 per share. The price y (in dollars) of a share during the 30 day period can be modeled by $y = -0.025x^2 + x + 16$ where x is the number of days after the stock is purchased. Could you have sold the stock earlier for \$23.50 per share? *Explain.* See margin.

50. SNOWBOARDING During a "big air" competition, snowboarders launch themselves from a half pipe, perform tricks in the air, and land back in the half pipe.

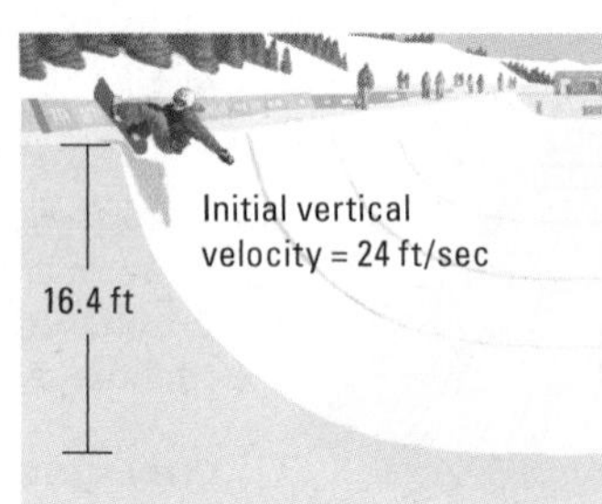

Cross section of a half pipe

a. Model Use the vertical motion model to write an equation that models the height h (in feet) of a snowboarder as a function of the time t (in seconds) she is in the air. $h = -16t^2 + 24t + 16.4$

b. Apply How long is the snowboarder in the air if she lands 13.2 feet above the base of the half pipe? Round your answer to the nearest tenth of a second. about 1.6 sec

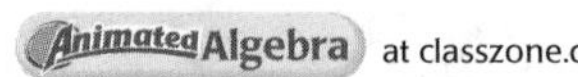 at classzone.com

C

51. CHALLENGE You are knitting a rectangular scarf. The pattern you have created will result in a scarf that has a length of 60 inches and a width of 4 inches. However, you happen to have enough yarn to cover an area of 480 square inches. You decide to increase the dimensions of the scarf so that all of your yarn will be used. If the increase in the length is 10 times the increase in the width, what will the dimensions of the scarf be? length: 80 in., width: 6 in.

ILLINOIS MIXED REVIEW

TEST PRACTICE at classzone.com

52. When graphed, which function would appear to be shifted 2 units up from the graph of $y = x^2 + 1$? D

Ⓐ $y = x^2 - 1$ Ⓑ $y = 2x^2 + 1$

Ⓒ $y = (x + 2)^2 + 1$ Ⓓ Not here

53. Pedro has 6 more DVDs than Matt has. Laura has twice as many DVDs as Pedro has. Altogether they have 73 DVDs. Which equation can be used to find how many DVDs each person has? C

Ⓐ $6x + 2x + x = 73$ Ⓑ $x + (x + 6) + 2x = 73$

Ⓒ $x + (x + 6) + 2(x + 6) = 73$ Ⓓ $x + 2(6x) + 6x = 73$

Use after Lesson 10.5

Graph Quadratic Functions in Vertex Form

GOAL Graph quadratic functions in vertex form.

Key Vocabulary
- **vertex form**

In Lesson 10.2, you graphed quadratic functions in standard form. Quadratic functions can also be written in **vertex form**, $y = a(x - h)^2 + k$ where $a \neq 0$. In this form, the vertex of the graph can be easily determined.

KEY CONCEPT *For Your Notebook*

Graph of Vertex Form $y = a(x - h)^2 + k$

The graph of $y = a(x - h)^2 + k$ is the graph of $y = ax^2$ translated h units horizontally and k units vertically.

Characteristics of the graph of $y = a(x - h)^2 + k$:

- The vertex is (h, k).
- The axis of symmetry is $x = h$.
- The graph opens up if $a > 0$, and the graph opens down if $a < 0$.

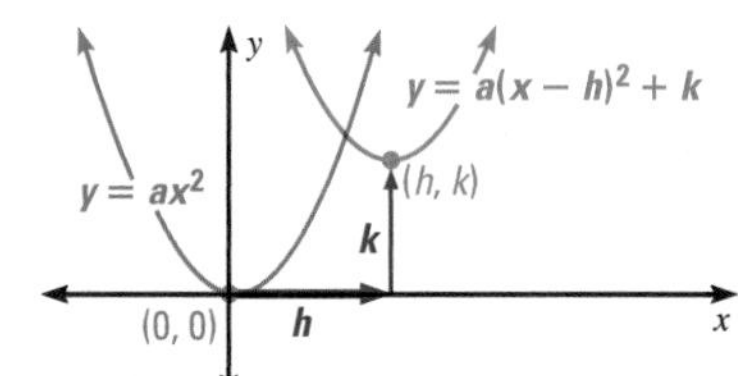

EXAMPLE 1 Graph a quadratic function in vertex form

Graph $y = -(x + 2)^2 + 3$.

Solution

STEP 1 **Identify** the values of a, h, and k: $a = -1$, $h = -2$, and $k = 3$. Because $a < 0$, the parabola opens down.

STEP 2 **Draw** the axis of symmetry, $x = -2$.

STEP 3 **Plot** the vertex $(h, k) = (-2, 3)$.

STEP 4 **Plot** four points. Evaluate the function for two x-values less than the x-coordinate of the vertex.

$x = -3$: $y = -(-3 + 2)^2 + 3 = 2$

$x = -5$: $y = -(-5 + 2)^2 + 3 = -6$

Plot the points $(-3, 2)$ and $(-5, -6)$ and their reflections, $(-1, 2)$ and $(1, -6)$, in the axis of symmetry.

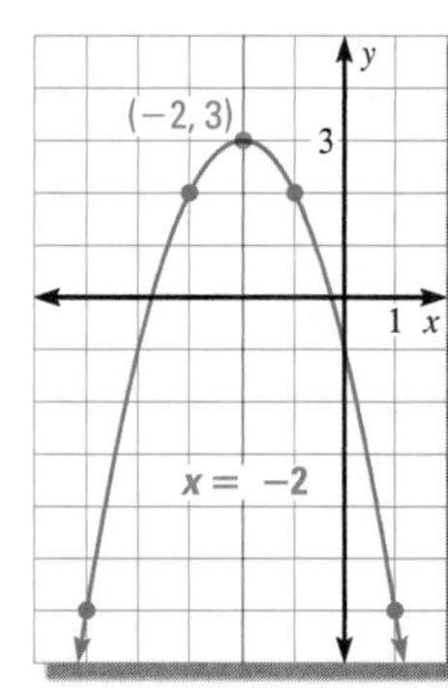

STEP 5 **Draw** a parabola through the plotted points.

1 PLAN AND PREPARE

Warm-Up Exercises

1. Find the axis of symmetry and vertex of the graph of $y = -x^2 + 2x + 1$. $x = 1$; $(1, 2)$
2. Graph $y = -2x^2 + 4x + 1$.

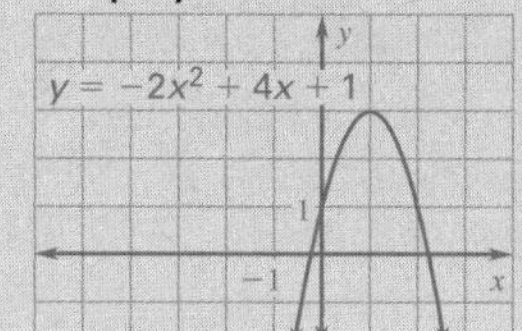

2 FOCUS AND MOTIVATE

Essential Question

Big Idea 1, p. 627

How do you graph a quadratic function in vertex form? Tell students they will learn how to answer this question by using the vertex form of a quadratic to identify the axis of symmetry, the vertex, and other points.

3 TEACH

Extra Example 1

Graph $y = (x + 1)^2 - 1$.

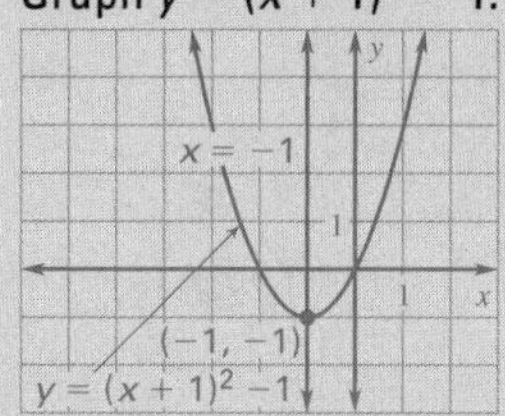

NCTM STANDARDS

Standard 2: Analyze situations using algebraic symbols

Standard 3: Use symmetry to analyze math situations

Extra Example 2

Graph $y = x^2 - 6x + 5$ by writing it in vertex form. $y = (x - 3)^2 - 4$

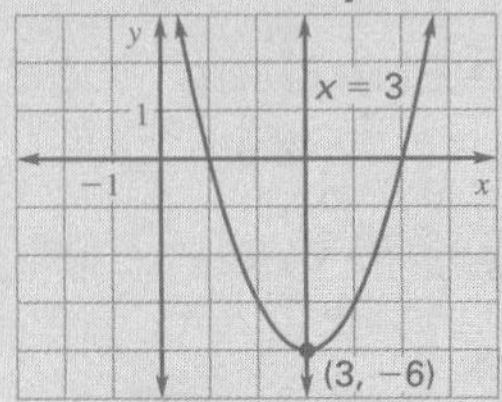

Key Question to Ask for Example 2

- Why is $h = 4$? Why is $k = 5$? Comparing $y = (x - h)^2 + k$ and $y = (x - 4)^2 - 5$, you get $h = 4$ and $k = -5$.

Closing the Lesson

Have students summarize the major points of the lesson and answer the Essential Question: How do you graph a quadratic function in intercept form?

- The vertex form of a quadratic function is $y = a(x - h)^2 + k$. The vertex is (h, k). The axis of symmetry is $x = h$.

If necessary, use the method of completing the square to write the function in vertex form. Determine whether the parabola opens up or down. Use the value of h to draw the axis of symmetry, and use the values of h and k to plot the vertex. Evaluate the function for two x-values to the left of the vertex, and use symmetry to find corresponding points to the right of the vertex. Draw a parabola through the points.

4 PRACTICE AND APPLY

Avoiding Common Errors

Exercises 1–12 Some students forget to use the sign of the leading coefficient. Remind students that if $a < 0$ the parabola opens down, and if $a > 0$ the parabola opens up.

1–12. See Additional Answers beginning on p. AA1.

EXAMPLE 2 Graph a quadratic function

Graph $y = x^2 - 8x + 11$.

Solution

STEP 1 **Write** the function in vertex form by completing the square.

$y = x^2 - 8x + 11$	Write original function.
$y + \square = (x^2 - 8x + \square) + 11$	Prepare to complete the square.
$y + 16 = (x^2 - 8x + 16) + 11$	Add $\left(\frac{-8}{2}\right)^2 = (-4)^2 = 16$ to each side.
$y + 16 = (x - 4)^2 + 11$	Write $x^2 - 8x + 16$ as a square of a binomial.
$y = (x - 4)^2 - 5$	Subtract 16 from each side.

STEP 2 **Identify** the values of a, h, and k: $a = 1$, $h = 4$, and $k = -5$. Because $a > 0$, the parabola opens up.

STEP 3 **Draw** the axis of symmetry, $x = 4$.

STEP 4 **Plot** the vertex $(h, k) = (4, -5)$.

STEP 5 **Plot** four more points. Evaluate the function for two x-values less than the x-coordinate of the vertex.

$x = 3$: $y = (3 - 4)^2 - 5 = -4$
$x = 1$: $y = (1 - 4)^2 - 5 = 4$

Plot the points $(3, -4)$ and $(1, 4)$ and their reflections, $(5, -4)$ and $(7, 4)$, in the axis of symmetry.

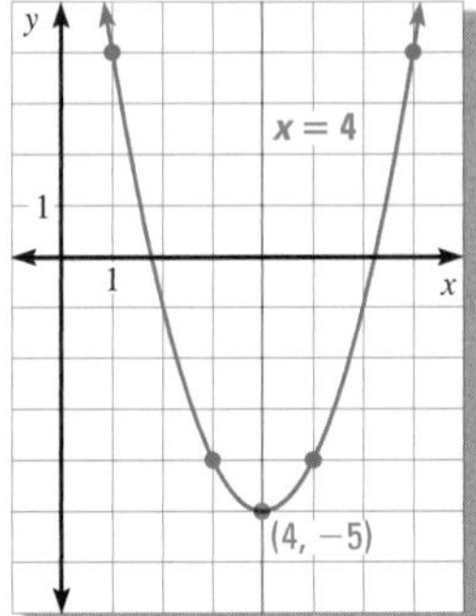

STEP 6 **Draw** a parabola through the plotted points.

PRACTICE

EXAMPLE 1 on p. 669 for Exs. 1–6

Graph the quadratic function. Label the vertex and axis of symmetry. 1–6. See margin.

1. $y = (x + 2)^2 - 5$
2. $y = -(x - 4)^2 + 1$
3. $y = x^2 + 3$
4. $y = 3(x - 1)^2 - 2$
5. $y = -2(x + 5)^2 - 2$
6. $y = -\frac{1}{2}(x + 4)^2 + 4$

EXAMPLE 2 on p. 670 for Exs. 7–12

Write the function in vertex form, then graph the function. Label the vertex and axis of symmetry. 7–12. See margin.

7. $y = x^2 - 12x + 36$
8. $y = x^2 + 8x + 15$
9. $y = -x^2 + 10x - 21$
10. $y = 2x^2 - 12x + 19$
11. $y = -3x^2 - 6x - 1$
12. $y = -\frac{1}{2}x^2 - 6x - 21$

13. Write an equation in vertex form of the parabola shown. Use the coordinates of the vertex and the coordinates of a point on the graph to write the equation.
$y = \frac{1}{4}(x + 6)^2 + 1$

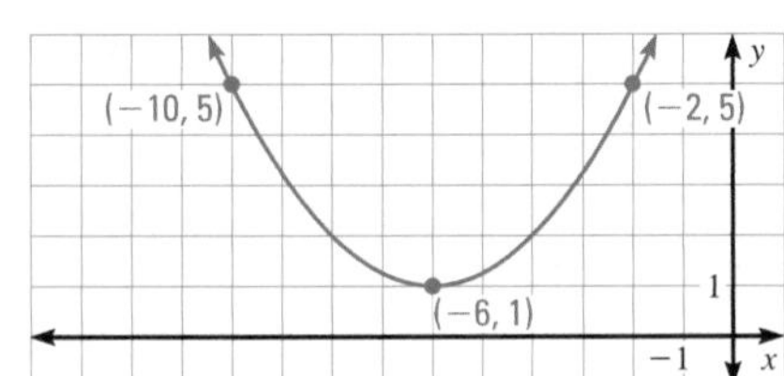

10.6 Solve Quadratic Equations by the Quadratic Formula

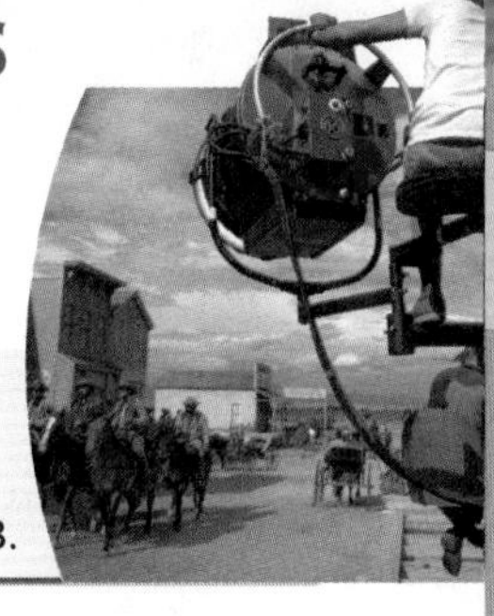

 **8.11.08** Recognize and describe the general shape and properties of functions from graphs, tables or equations (e.g., . . . quadratic . . .).

Before You solved quadratic equations by completing the square.

Now You will solve quadratic equations using the quadratic formula.

Why? So you can solve a problem about film production, as in Example 3.

Key Vocabulary
- **quadratic formula**

By completing the square for the quadratic equation $ax^2 + bx + c = 0$, you can develop a formula that gives the solutions of any quadratic equation in standard form. This formula is called the **quadratic formula**. (The quadratic formula is developed on page 727.)

KEY CONCEPT *For Your Notebook*

The Quadratic Formula

The solutions of the quadratic equation $ax^2 + bx + c = 0$ are

$x = \frac{-b \pm \sqrt{b^2 - 4ac}}{2a}$ where $a \neq 0$ and $b^2 - 4ac \geq 0$.

 **EXAMPLE 1** **Standardized Test Practice**

What are the solutions of $3x^2 + 5x = 8$?

Ⓐ -1 and $-\frac{8}{3}$ Ⓑ -1 and $\frac{8}{3}$ Ⓒ 1 and $-\frac{8}{3}$ Ⓓ 1 and $\frac{8}{3}$

ANOTHER WAY
Instead of solving the equation, you can check the answer choices in the equation.

Solution

$3x^2 + 5x = 8$ **Write original equation.**

$3x^2 + 5x - 8 = 0$ **Write in standard form.**

$x = \frac{-b \pm \sqrt{b^2 - 4ac}}{2a}$ **Quadratic formula**

$x = \frac{-5 \pm \sqrt{5^2 - 4(3)(-8)}}{2(3)}$ **Substitute values in the quadratic formula: $a = 3$, $b = 5$, and $c = -8$.**

$= \frac{-5 \pm \sqrt{121}}{6}$ **Simplify.**

$= \frac{-5 \pm 11}{6}$ **Simplify the square root.**

The solutions of the equation are $\frac{-5 + 11}{6} = 1$ and $\frac{-5 - 11}{6} = -\frac{8}{3}$.

▶ The correct answer is C. Ⓐ Ⓑ Ⓒ Ⓓ

1 PLAN AND PREPARE

Warm-Up Exercises

Transparency Available

Evaluate the expression for the given value of x.

1. $15 - (-x) + 9$; $x = -2$ 22

2. $14 - x + 3$; $x = 8$ 9

3. A basketball is thrown in the air from a height of 6 feet with an initial velocity of 40 feet per second. What is the height (in feet) of the ball after 2 seconds? 22 ft

Notetaking Guide

Transparency Available

Promotes interactive learning and notetaking skills, pp. 236–238.

Pacing

Basic: 2 days
Average: 2 days
Advanced: 2 days
Block: 0.5 block with 10.5
0.5 block with 10.7
- See *Teaching Guide/Lesson Plan.*

2 FOCUS AND MOTIVATE

Essential Question

Big Idea 2, p. 627

How do you solve a quadratic equation using the quadratic formula? **Tell students they will learn how to answer this question by substituting values in the quadratic formula and then simplifying.**

Resource Planning Guide

Chapter Resource Book
- Teaching Guide/Lesson Plan (pp. 69–70)
- Practice levels A, B, C (pp. 71–73)
- Study Guide (pp. 74–75)
- Catch-up for Absent Students (p. 76)
- Problem Solving Workshop (p. 77)
- Challenge (p. 78)

Workbooks
- Notetaking Guide (pp. 236–238)
- Practice Workbook (pp. 162–163)

Teaching Options
- **Power Presentations CD-ROM** provides dynamic electronic teaching resources for the classroom.
- **Activity Generator CD-ROM** provides editable activities for all ability levels.

Interactive Technology
- Easy Planner
- Power Presentations CD-ROM
- Activity Generator CD-ROM
- Animated Algebra
- Test Generator CD-ROM
- Online Quiz
- eWorkbook
- eEdition
- @HomeTutor

Resources for English Learners
- Quick Reference for English Learners
- Spanish Study Guide
- Multi-Language Visual Glossary
- Student Resources in Spanish

See also the *Algebra 1 Toolkit* for more strategies for meeting individual needs.

Motivating the Lesson

Ask students how they would solve a quadratic equation such as $0.5x^2 - 1.25x - 7.5 = 0$. Tell them that in this lesson they will learn how to use a formula to solve *any* quadratic equation.

3 TEACH

Extra Example 1

What are the solutions of $2x^2 + 7x = 9$? B

Ⓐ -1 and $-\frac{9}{2}$ Ⓑ 1 and $-\frac{9}{2}$

Ⓒ -1 and $\frac{9}{2}$ Ⓓ 1 and $\frac{9}{2}$

Extra Example 2

Use the quadratic formula to solve $3x^2 - 1 = x$. $a = 3, b = -1, c = -1$; $\frac{1 + \sqrt{13}}{6} \approx 0.77, \frac{1 - \sqrt{13}}{6} \approx -0.43$

An **Animated Algebra** activity is available on-line for **Example 2**. This activity is also available on the **Power Presentations CD-ROM**.

Extra Example 3

For the period 1990–2003, the number of book titles published by a small publishing company can be modeled by the function $y = 0.5x^2 + 4x + 19$, where x is the number of years since 1990. In what year did the company publish 80 books? almost 8 years after 1990, or during 1997

EXAMPLE 2 Solve a quadratic equation

Solve $2x^2 - 7 = x$.

$2x^2 - 7 = x$ Write original equation.

$2x^2 - x - 7 = 0$ Write in standard form.

$x = \frac{-b \pm \sqrt{b^2 - 4ac}}{2a}$ Quadratic formula

$= \frac{-(-1) \pm \sqrt{(-1)^2 - 4(2)(-7)}}{2(2)}$ Substitute values in the quadratic formula: $a = 2$, $b = -1$, and $c = -7$.

$= \frac{1 \pm \sqrt{57}}{4}$ Simplify.

▶ The solutions are $\frac{1 + \sqrt{57}}{4} \approx 2.14$ and $\frac{1 - \sqrt{57}}{4} \approx -1.64$.

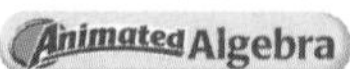 at classzone.com

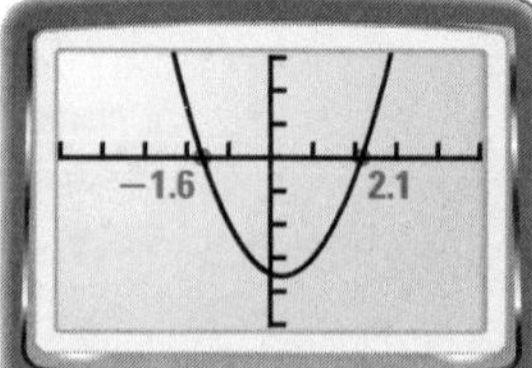

CHECK Write the equation in standard form, $2x^2 - x - 7 = 0$. Then graph the related function $y = 2x^2 - x - 7$. The x-intercepts are about -1.6 and 2.1. So, each solution checks.

✓ GUIDED PRACTICE for Examples 1 and 2

Use the quadratic formula to solve the equation. Round your solutions to the nearest hundredth, if necessary.

1. $x^2 - 8x + 16 = 0$ 4
2. $3n^2 - 5n = -1$ 0.23, 1.43
3. $4z^2 = 7z + 2$ -0.25, 2

EXAMPLE 3 Use the quadratic formula

FILM PRODUCTION For the period 1971–2001, the number y of films produced in the world can be modeled by the function $y = 10x^2 - 94x + 3900$ where x is the number of years since 1971. In what year were 4200 films produced?

Solution

$y = 10x^2 - 94x + 3900$ Write function.

$4200 = 10x^2 - 94x + 3900$ Substitute 4200 for y.

$0 = 10x^2 - 94x - 300$ Write in standard form.

$x = \frac{-(-94) \pm \sqrt{(-94)^2 - 4(10)(-300)}}{2(10)}$ Substitute values in the quadratic formula: $a = 10$, $b = -94$, and $c = -300$.

$= \frac{94 \pm \sqrt{20{,}836}}{20}$ Simplify.

The solutions of the equation are $\frac{94 + \sqrt{20{,}836}}{20} \approx 12$ and $\frac{94 - \sqrt{20{,}836}}{20} \approx -3$.

▶ There were 4200 films produced about 12 years after 1971, or in 1983.

INTERPRET SOLUTIONS
The solution -3 can be ignored because -3 represents the year 1968, which is not in the given time period.

Differentiated Instruction

Visual Learners Students may find the quadratic formula easier to memorize by visualizing the graph of the quadratic function $y = ax^2 + bx + c$. Write the quadratic formula as $x = -\frac{b}{2a} \pm \frac{\sqrt{b^2 - 4ac}}{2a}$. Point out that $x = -\frac{b}{2a}$ is the axis of symmetry for the function $y = ax^2 + bx + c$ and the x-intercepts of the function are $\frac{\sqrt{b^2 - 4ac}}{2a}$ units to the left and right of the axis of symmetry.

See also the *Algebra 1 Toolkit* for more strategies.

GUIDED PRACTICE for Example 3

4. **WHAT IF?** In Example 3, find the year when 4750 films were produced. 1986

CONCEPT SUMMARY *For Your Notebook*

Methods for Solving Quadratic Equations

Method	Lesson(s)	When to Use
Factoring	9.4–9.8	Use when a quadratic equation can be factored easily.
Graphing	10.3	Use when approximate solutions are adequate.
Finding square roots	10.4	Use when solving an equation that can be written in the form $x^2 = d$.
Completing the square	10.5	Can be used for *any* quadratic equation $ax^2 + bx + c = 0$ but is simplest to apply when $a = 1$ and b is an even number.
Quadratic formula	10.6	Can be used for *any* quadratic equation.

EXAMPLE 4 Choose a solution method

Tell what method you would use to solve the quadratic equation. *Explain* your choice(s).

a. $10x^2 - 7 = 0$ **b.** $x^2 + 4x = 0$ **c.** $5x^2 + 9x - 4 = 0$

Solution

a. The quadratic equation can be solved using square roots because the equation can be written in the form $x^2 = d$.

b. The equation can be solved by factoring because the expression $x^2 + 4x$ can be factored easily. Also, the equation can be solved by completing the square because the equation is of the form $ax^2 + bx + c = 0$ where $a = 1$ and b is an even number.

c. The quadratic equation cannot be factored easily, and completing the square will result in many fractions. So, the equation can be solved using the quadratic formula.

GUIDED PRACTICE for Example 4

Tell what method you would use to solve the quadratic equation. *Explain* your choice(s). 5–7. See margin.

5. $x^2 + x - 6 = 0$ **6.** $x^2 - 9 = 0$ **7.** $x^2 + 6x = 5$

Key Question to Ask for Example 3

- Can you use the model to approximate the number of films for any particular year? Explain. **The model is based on data from 1971 through 2001. It may not be accurate for years prior to 1971 or after 2001.**

Extra Example 4

Tell what method you would use to solve the quadratic equation. *Explain* your choice(s).

a. $3x^2 + 14x + 13 = 0$

b. $9x^2 - 3 = 0$

c. $x^2 + 8x = 0$

a. The quadratic formula is best since the equation cannot be factored easily and completing the square would result in too many fractions.

b. The equation can be written in the form $x^2 = d$, so the easiest method is finding square roots.

c. You could use factoring because it can be factored easily, or you can use completing the square since a is 1 and b is even.

Closing the Lesson

Have students summarize the major points of the lesson and answer the Essential Question: How do you solve a quadratic equation using the quadratic formula?

- **For the general quadratic equation $ax^2 + bx + c = 0$, the quadratic formula is $x = \frac{-b \pm \sqrt{b^2 - 4ac}}{2a}$. Substitute values for a, b, and c into the quadratic formula, and then simplify.**

5. *Sample answer:* Factoring, the expression $x^2 + x - 6$ factors easily.

6. *Sample answer:* Factoring, the expression $x^2 - 9$ factors easily; or using square roots, the equation can be written in the form $x^2 = d$.

7. *Sample answer:* Completing the square, the equation is of the form $ax^2 + bx = c$ where $a = 1$ and b is an even number; or quadratic formula, the equation does not factor easily.

10.6 EXERCISES

HOMEWORK KEY

○ = **WORKED-OUT SOLUTIONS** on p. WS25 for Exs. 19 and 47

★ = **STANDARDIZED TEST PRACTICE** Exs. 2, 12, 25, and 50

◆ = **MULTIPLE REPRESENTATIONS** Ex. 49

SKILL PRACTICE

A

1. **VOCABULARY** What formula can be used to solve any quadratic equation? quadratic formula

2. ★ **WRITING** What method(s) would you use to solve $-x^2 + 8x = 1$? *Explain* your choice(s). See margin.

EXAMPLES 1 and 2 on pp. 671–672 for Exs. 3–27

2. *Sample answer:* Completing the square, the equation can be put in the form $ax^2 + bx = c$ where $a = 1$ and b is an even number; or quadratic formula, the equation does not factor easily.

SOLVING QUADRATIC EQUATIONS **Use the quadratic formula to solve the equation. Round your solutions to the nearest hundredth, if necessary.**

3. $x^2 + 5x - 104 = 0$ −13, 8
4. $4x^2 - x - 18 = 0$ −2, 2.25
5. $6x^2 - 2x - 28 = 0$ −2, 2.33
6. $m^2 + 3m + 1 = 0$ −2.62, −0.38
7. $-z^2 + z + 14 = 0$ −3.27, 4.27
8. $-2n^2 - 5n + 16 = 0$ −4.34, 1.84
9. $4w^2 + 20w + 25 = 0$ −2.5
10. $2t^2 + 3t - 11 = 0$ −3.21, 1.71
11. $-6g^2 + 9g + 8 = 0$ −0.63, 2.13

12. ★ **MULTIPLE CHOICE** What are the solutions of $10x^2 - 3x - 1 = 0$? B

Ⓐ $-\frac{1}{5}$ and $-\frac{1}{2}$ Ⓑ $-\frac{1}{5}$ and $\frac{1}{2}$ Ⓒ $\frac{1}{5}$ and $-\frac{1}{2}$ Ⓓ $\frac{1}{5}$ and $\frac{1}{2}$

SOLVING QUADRATIC EQUATIONS **Use the quadratic formula to solve the equation. Round your solutions to the nearest hundredth, if necessary.**

13. $x^2 - 5x = 14$ −2, 7
14. $3x^2 - 4 = 11x$ −0.33, 4
15. $9 = 7x^2 - 2x$ −1, 1.29
16. $2m^2 + 9m + 7 = 3$ −4, −0.5
17. $-10 = r^2 - 10r + 12$ 3.27, 6.73
18. $3g^2 - 6g - 14 = 3g$ −1.13, 4.13
19. $6z^2 = 2z^2 + 7z + 5$ −0.54, 2.29
20. $8h^2 + 8 = 6 - 9h$ −0.82, −0.30
21. $4t^2 - 3t = 5 - 3t^2$ −0.66, 1.09
22. $-4y^2 - 3y + 3 = 2y + 4$ −1, −0.25
23. $7n + 5 = -3n^2 + 2$ −1.77, −0.57
24. $5w^2 + 4 = w + 6$ −0.54, 0.74

25. ★ **MULTIPLE CHOICE** What are the solutions of $x^2 + 14x = 2x - 11$? B

Ⓐ −2 and −22 Ⓑ −1 and −11 Ⓒ 1 and 11 Ⓓ 2 and 22

ERROR ANALYSIS ***Describe*** **and correct the error in solving the equation.** 26–27. See margin.

26. $7x^2 - 5x - 1 = 0$

$$x = \frac{-5 \pm \sqrt{(-5)^2 - 4(7)(-1)}}{2(7)}$$
$$= \frac{-5 \pm \sqrt{53}}{14}$$
$x \approx -0.88$ and $x \approx 0.16$ ✗

27. $-2x^2 + 3x = 1$

$$x = \frac{-3 \pm \sqrt{3^2 - 4(-2)(1)}}{2(-2)}$$
$$= \frac{-3 \pm \sqrt{17}}{-4}$$
$x \approx -0.28$ and $x \approx 1.78$ ✗

EXAMPLE 4 on p. 673 for Exs. 28–33

CHOOSING A METHOD **Tell what method(s) you would use to solve the quadratic equation.** ***Explain*** **your choice(s).** 28–33. See margin.

28. $3x^2 - 27 = 0$
29. $5x^2 = 25$
30. $2x^2 - 12x = 0$
31. $m^2 + 5m + 6 = 0$
32. $z^2 - 4z + 1 = 0$
33. $-10g^2 + 13g = 4$

4 PRACTICE AND APPLY

Assignment Guide

Answer Transparencies available for all exercises

Basic:
Day 1: pp. 674–676
Exs. 1–8, 12–21, 25–27
Day 2: pp. 674–676
Exs. 28–38, 46–49, 52–61

Average:
Day 1: pp. 674–676
Exs. 1, 2, 6–12, 16–27
Day 2: pp. 674–676
Exs. 28–44, 46–50, 52–60 even

Advanced:
Day 1: pp. 674–676
Exs. 1, 2, 6–12, 16–25
Day 2: pp. 674–676
Exs. 28–51*, 53–61 odd

Block:
pp. 674–676
Exs. 1, 2, 6–12, 16–27 (with 10.5)
pp. 674–676
Exs. 28–44, 46–50, 52–60 even (with 10.7)

Differentiated Instruction

See *Algebra 1 Best Practices Toolkit* for suggestions on addressing the needs of a diverse classroom.

Homework Check

For a quick check of student understanding of key concepts, go over the following exercises:

Basic: 8, 12, 28, 32, 46

Average: 12, 16, 31, 36, 46

Advanced: 20, 25, 33, 40, 47

Extra Practice

- Student Edition, p. 947
- Chapter 10 Resource Book: Practice levels A, B, C, pp. 71–73

Practice Worksheet

An easily-readable reduced practice page (with answers) for this lesson can be found on p. 626C.

26. The first term of the numerator of the quadratic formula is $-b$, so the first term of the numerator of the answer should be $-(-5) = 5$; $x = \frac{5 \pm \sqrt{(-5)^2 - 4(7)(-1)}}{2(7)}$, $x = \frac{5 \pm \sqrt{53}}{14}$, $x \approx -0.16$ and $x \approx 0.88$.

27. Before identifying the values of a, b, and c, the equation must be written in standard form $ax^2 + bx + c = 0$; $-2x^2 + 3x - 1 = 0$, so $c = -1$, not 1; $x = \frac{-3 \pm \sqrt{3^2 - 4(-2)(-1)}}{2(-2)}$, $x = \frac{-3 \pm \sqrt{1}}{-4}$, $x = \frac{1}{2}$ and $x = 1$.

B **SOLVING QUADRATIC EQUATIONS** **Solve the quadratic equation using any method. Round your solutions to the nearest hundredth, if necessary.**

34. $-2x^2 = -32$ ±4

35. $x^2 - 8x = -16$ 4

36. $x^2 + 2x - 6 = 0$ −3.65, 1.65

37. $x^2 = 12x - 36$ 6

38. $x^2 + 4x = 9$ −5.61, 1.61

39. $-4x^2 + x = -17$ −1.94, 2.19

40. $11x^2 - 1 = 6x^2 + 2$ ±0.77

41. $-2x^2 + 5 = 3x^2 - 10x$ −0.41, 2.41

42. $(x + 13)^2 = 25$ −18, −8

GEOMETRY **Use the given area A of the rectangle to find the value of x. Then give the dimensions of the rectangle.**

43. $A = 91\text{ m}^2$ 5; 13 m by 7 m

(x + 2) m

(2x + 3) m

44. $A = 209\text{ ft}^2$ 4; 19 ft by 11 ft

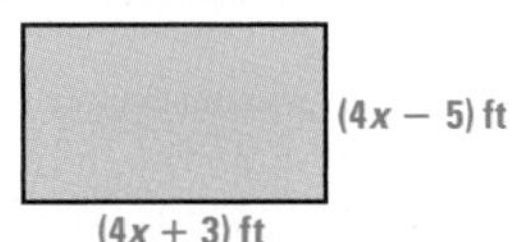

C **45. CHALLENGE** The solutions of the quadratic equation $ax^2 + bx + c = 0$ are $x = \frac{-b + \sqrt{b^2 - 4ac}}{2a}$ and $x = \frac{-b - \sqrt{b^2 - 4ac}}{2a}$. Find the mean of the solutions. How is the mean of the solutions related to the graph of $y = ax^2 + bx + c$? *Explain.* See margin.

PROBLEM SOLVING

EXAMPLE 3 **A** on p. 672 for Exs. 46–47

46. ADVERTISING For the period 1990–2000, the amount of money y (in billions of dollars) spent on advertising in the U.S. can be modeled by the function $y = 0.93x^2 + 2.2x + 130$ where x is the number of years since 1990. In what year was 164 billion dollars spent on advertising? 1995

@HomeTutor for problem solving help at classzone.com

(47.) CELL PHONES For the period 1985–2001, the number y (in millions) of cell phone service subscribers in the U.S. can be modeled by the function $y = 0.7x^2 - 4.3x + 5.5$ where x is the number of years since 1985. In what year were there 16,000,000 cell phone service subscribers? 1993

@HomeTutor for problem solving help at classzone.com

48. MULTI-STEP PROBLEM A football is punted from a height of 2.5 feet above the ground and with an initial vertical velocity of 45 feet per second.

a. Use the vertical motion model to write an equation that gives the height h (in feet) of the football as a function of the time t (in seconds) after it has been punted. $h = -16t^2 + 45t + 2.5$

b. The football is caught 5.5 feet above the ground as shown in the diagram. Find the amount of time that the football is in the air. about 2.7 sec

Avoiding Common Errors

Exercises 3–25 Students often make calculation errors when using the quadratic formula, especially when substituting values with negative signs. For each exercise, prior to doing any calculations they should write the values of a, b, and c and then rewrite the formula using those values.

Graphing Calculator

Exercises 3–25 Suggest that students use their graphing calculators to check their solutions.

Study Strategy

Exercise 47 Point out to students that this exercise has a worked-out solution. Recommend that they attempt a solution first. Then they can use the worked-out solution to check their results and compare solution methods.

Exercise 50 For additional information about NASA's weightless environment, visit liftoff.msfc.nasa.gov/academy/astronauts/training.html

32. Completing the square, the equation is in the form $ax^2 + bx + c = 0$ where $a = 1$ and b is an even number; or quadratic formula, the equation does not factor easily.

33. Quadratic formula, the equation does not factor easily.

45. $-\frac{b}{2a}$; $x = -\frac{b}{2a}$ is the equation of the axis of symmetry of the parabola $y = ax^2 + bx + c$, and $-\frac{b}{2a}$ is the x-coordinate of the vertex of the parabola; the axis of symmetry of $y = ax^2 + bx + c$ is located half-way between the x-intercepts, and the x-intercepts are the solutions of $ax^2 + bx + c = 0$, so the mean of the solutions is the equation of the axis of symmetry; the equation of the axis of symmetry gives the x-coordinate of the vertex of the parabola.

28–33. Sample answers are given.

28. Factoring, the expression $3x^2 - 27$ factors easily; or using square roots, the equation can be written in the form $x^2 = d$.

29. Using square roots, the equation can be written in the form $x^2 = d$.

30. Factoring, the expression $2x^2 - 12x$ factors easily; or using square roots, the equation can be written in the form $x^2 = d$; completing the square, the equation is of the form $ax^2 + bx = c$ where $a = 1$ and b is an even number.

31. Factoring, the expression $m^2 + 5m + 6$ factors easily.

5 ASSESS AND RETEACH

Daily Homework Quiz

Transparency Available

Use the quadratic formula to solve the equation. Round your solutions to the nearest hundredth, if necessary.

1. $6x^2 - 6 = -5x$ $-\frac{3}{2}, \frac{2}{3}$
2. $2x^2 + 3x - 8 = 0$ $-2.87, 1.39$
3. $3m^2 - m + 9 = 12$ $-0.85, 1.18$
4. You have seen that the function $y = 10x^2 - 94x + 3900$ models the number y of films produced in the world, where x is the number of years since 1971. In what year were 10,000 films produced? about 29.8 years after 1971, or during the year 2000

Online Quiz

Available at **classzone.com**

Diagnosis/Remediation

- Practice A, B, C in Chapter 10 Resource Book, pp. 71–73
- Study Guide in Chapter 10 Resource Book, pp. 74–75
- Practice Workbook, pp. 162–163
- @HomeTutor

Challenge

Additional challenge is available in the Chapter 10 Resource Book, p. 78.

Quiz

An easily-readable reduced copy of the quiz (with answers) on Lessons 10.4–10.6 from the Assessment Book can be found on p. 626G.

49b.

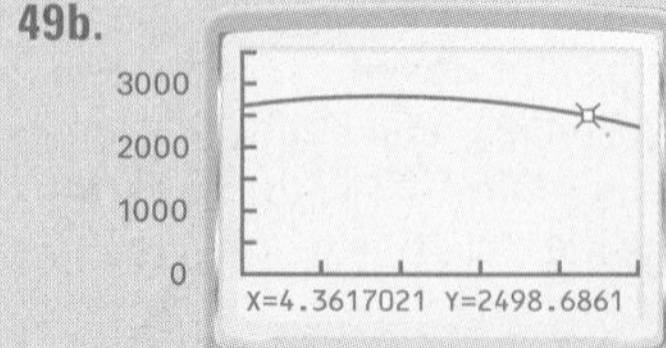

B

49. **MULTIPLE REPRESENTATIONS** For the period 1997–2002, the number y (in thousands) of 16- and 17-year-olds employed in the United States can be modeled by the function $y = -46.7x^2 + 169x + 2650$ where x is the number of years since 1997.

 a. **Solving an Equation** Write and solve an equation to find the year during which 2,500,000 16- and 17-year-olds were employed. 2001

 b. **Drawing a Graph** Graph the function on a graphing calculator. Use the *trace* feature to find the year when 2,500,000 16- and 17-year-olds were employed. Use the graph to check your answer from part (a). See margin.

50. ★ **SHORT RESPONSE** NASA creates a weightless environment by flying a plane in a series of parabolic paths. The height h (in feet) of a plane after t seconds in a parabolic flight path can be modeled by the graph of $h = -11t^2 + 700t + 21{,}000$. The passengers experience a weightless environment when the height of the plane is greater than or equal to 30,800 feet. Find the period of weightlessness on such a flight. *Explain.* about 22 sec

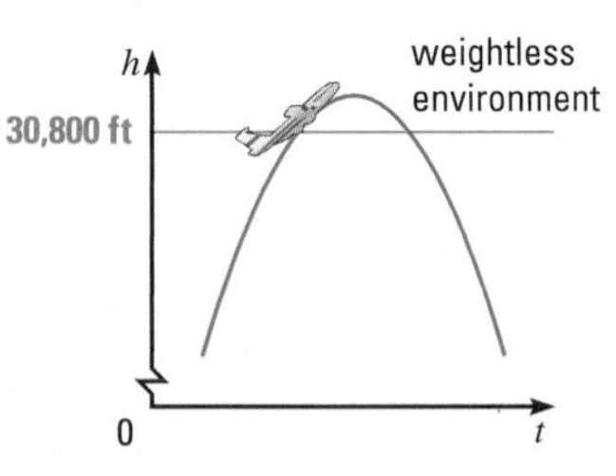

C

51. **CHALLENGE** Mineral deposits have formed a uniform coating that is 4 millimeters thick on the inside of a water pipe. The cross-sectional area of the pipe has decreased by 10%. What was the original diameter of the pipe (to the nearest tenth of a millimeter)? about 156.0 mm

ILLINOIS MIXED REVIEW

TEST PRACTICE at classzone.com

52. Which expression is equivalent to $0.5((2x)^3)^2$? C

 Ⓐ $32x^3$ Ⓑ $16x^5$ Ⓒ $32x^6$ Ⓓ $256x^9$

53. A scale model of a house has a scale of 1 foot : 13.5 feet. If the actual house is 36 feet tall, how tall is the scale model? B

 Ⓐ 30 in. Ⓑ 32 in. Ⓒ 36 in. Ⓓ 486 in.

QUIZ *for Lessons 10.4–10.6*

Solve the equation using square roots. *(p. 652)*

1. $3x^2 - 48 = 0$ ± 4
2. $-6x^2 = -24$ ± 2
3. $x^2 + 5 = 16$ about ± 3.32

Solve the equation by completing the square. *(p. 663)*

4. $x^2 + 2x + 6 = 0$ no solution
5. $x^2 + 10x - 12 = 0$ $-11.08, 1.08$
6. $x^2 - 8x = -6$ $0.84, 7.16$
7. $x^2 - 12x = 30$ $-2.12, 14.12$
8. $x^2 - 5x = -\frac{9}{4}$ $0.5, 4.5$
9. $x^2 + x = -7.75$ no solution

Solve the equation using the quadratic formula. *(p. 671)*

10. $x^2 + 4x + 1 = 0$ $-3.73, -0.27$
11. $-3x^2 + 3x = -1$ $-0.26, 1.26$
12. $4x^2 - 11x = 3$ $-0.25, 3$

EXTRA PRACTICE for Lesson 10.6, p. 947   **ONLINE QUIZ** at classzone.com

10.7 The Discriminant

QUESTION How can you determine the number of solutions of a quadratic equation?

In the quadratic formula, $x = \frac{-b \pm \sqrt{b^2 - 4ac}}{2a}$, the expression $b^2 - 4ac$ is called the *discriminant.*

EXPLORE Determine how the discriminant is related to the number of solutions of a quadratic equation

STEP 1 ***Find the number of solutions*** See Step 3.
Find the number of solutions of the equations below by finding the number of x-intercepts of the graphs of the related functions.

$0 = x^2 - 6x - 7$
$0 = x^2 - 6x + 9$
$0 = x^2 - 6x + 12$

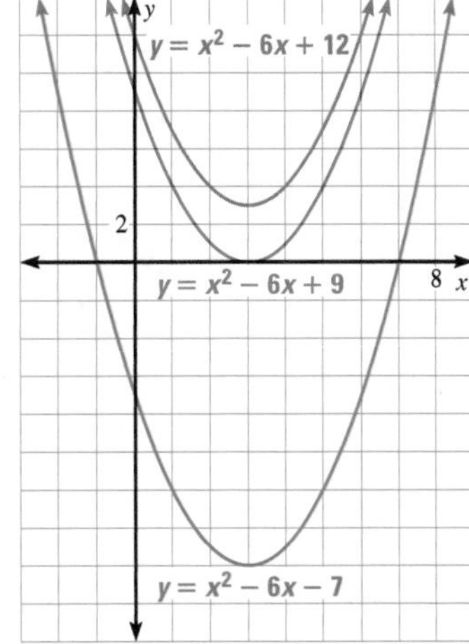

STEP 2 ***Find the value of $b^2 - 4ac$*** See Step 3.
For each equation in Step 1, determine whether the value of $b^2 - 4ac$ is positive, negative, or zero.

STEP 3 ***Make a table***
Organize your results from Steps 1 and 2 in a table as shown.

Equation	Number of solutions	Value of $b^2 - 4ac$
$0 = x^2 - 6x - 7$	? 2	? 64
$0 = x^2 - 6x + 9$	? 1	? 0
$0 = x^2 - 6x + 12$	? 0	? −12

STEP 4 ***Make a conjecture***
Make a generalization about the value of the discriminant and the number of solutions of a quadratic equation.
The number of solutions of a quadratic equation $ax^2 + bx + c = 0$ is 2 if $b^2 - 4ac > 0$, is 1 if $b^2 - 4ac = 0$, and is 0 if $b^2 - 4ac < 0$.

DRAW CONCLUSIONS Use your observations to complete these exercises
1, 2. See margin.

1. Repeat Steps 1–3 using the following equations: $x^2 + 4x - 5 = 0$, $x^2 + 4x + 4 = 0$, and $x^2 + 4x + 6 = 0$. Is your conjecture still true?
2. Notice that the expression $b^2 - 4ac$ is under the radical sign in the quadratic formula. Use this observation to explain why the value of $b^2 - 4ac$ determines the number of solutions of a quadratic equation.

1 PLAN AND PREPARE

Explore the Concept

- Students will determine how the discriminant is related to the number of solutions of a quadratic formula.
- This activity leads into the study of using the discriminant in Lesson 10.7, Example 1.

Recommended Time

Work activity: 10 min
Discuss results: 5 min

Grouping

Students should work individually.

2 TEACH

Tips for Success

Caution students to make sure that they are using the correct graphs to find the number of x-intercepts and record the number of solutions. Remind students that the number of solutions is the same as the number of x-intercepts.

Key Discovery

If the value of the discriminant is positive, there are two solutions. If the value is 0, there is one solution. If the value is negative, there is no real-number solution.

3 ASSESS AND RETEACH

Use the discriminant to find the number of x-intercepts of the graph of $5x^2 + 14x = 7$.
$b^2 - 4ac = 14^2 - 4(5)(-7) = 336$; $336 > 0$, so there are 2 x-intercepts.

1.

Equation	Number of solutions	Value of $b^2 - 4ac$
$x^2 + 4x - 5 = 0$	2	36
$x^2 + 4x + 4 = 0$	1	0
$x^2 + 4x + 6 = 0$	0	−8

yes

2. See Additional Answers beginning on p. AA1.

1 PLAN AND PREPARE

Warm-Up Exercises

Transparency Available

Evaluate the expression.

1. $8x^2$ when $x = 4$ 128
2. $-4 + \sqrt{x}$ when $x = 9$ -1
3. A ball is kicked into the air from a height of 4.5 feet with an initial velocity of 30 feet per second. What is the height of the ball after 1 second? 18.5 ft

Notetaking Guide

Transparency Available

Promotes interactive learning and notetaking skills, pp. 239–241.

Pacing

Basic: 1 day
Average: 1 day
Advanced: 1 day
Block: 0.5 block with 10.6
• See *Teaching Guide/Lesson Plan.*

2 FOCUS AND MOTIVATE

Essential Question

Big Idea 2, p. 627

How do you use the value of the discriminant? Tell students they will learn how to answer this question by using the discriminant to find the number of solutions of a quadratic equation.

10.7 Interpret the Discriminant

Before You used the quadratic formula.
Now You will use the value of the discriminant.
Why? So you can solve a problem about gymnastics, as in Ex. 49.

Key Vocabulary
• discriminant

In the quadratic formula, the expression $b^2 - 4ac$ is called the **discriminant** of the associated equation $ax^2 + bx + c = 0$.

$$x = \frac{-b \pm \sqrt{b^2 - 4ac}}{2a} \quad \longleftarrow \text{discriminant}$$

Because the discriminant is under the radical symbol, the value of the discriminant can be used to determine the number of solutions of a quadratic equation and the number of x-intercepts of the graph of the related function.

READING Recall that in this course, *solutions* refers to real-number solutions.

KEY CONCEPT *For Your Notebook*

Using the Discriminant of $ax^2 + bx + c = 0$

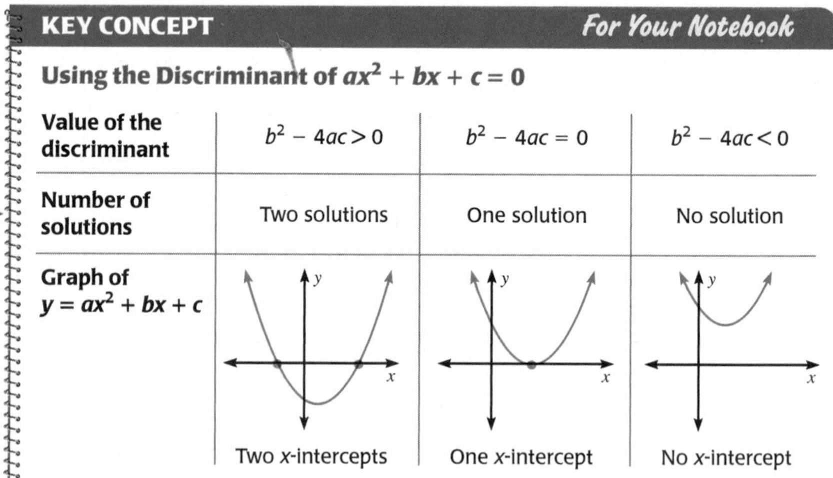

Value of the discriminant	$b^2 - 4ac > 0$	$b^2 - 4ac = 0$	$b^2 - 4ac < 0$
Number of solutions	Two solutions	One solution	No solution
Graph of $y = ax^2 + bx + c$	Two x-intercepts	One x-intercept	No x-intercept

EXAMPLE 1 Use the discriminant

	Equation $ax^2 + bx + c = 0$	Discriminant $b^2 - 4ac$	Number of solutions
a.	$2x^2 + 6x + 5 = 0$	$6^2 - 4(2)(5) = -4$	No solution
b.	$x^2 - 7 = 0$	$0^2 - 4(1)(-7) = 28$	Two solutions
c.	$4x^2 - 12x + 9 = 0$	$(-12)^2 - 4(4)(9) = 0$	One solution

Resource Planning Guide

Chapter Resource Book
• Teaching Guide/Lesson Plan (pp. 79–80)
• Practice levels A, B, C (pp. 81–83)
• Study Guide (pp. 84–85)
• Catch-up for Absent Students (p. 86)
• Application (p. 87)
• Challenge (p. 88)

Workbooks
• Notetaking Guide (pp. 239–241)
• Practice Workbook (pp. 164–165)

Teaching Options
• **Power Presentations CD-ROM** provides dynamic electronic teaching resources for the classroom.
• **Activity Generator CD-ROM** provides editable activities for all ability levels.

Interactive Technology
• Easy Planner
• Power Presentations CD-ROM
• Activity Generator CD-ROM
• Animated Algebra
• Test Generator CD-ROM
• Online Quiz
• eWorkbook
• eEdition
• @HomeTutor

Resources for English Learners
• Quick Reference for English Learners
• Spanish Study Guide
• Multi-Language Visual Glossary
• Student Resources in Spanish

See also the *Algebra 1 Toolkit* for more strategies for meeting individual needs.

EXAMPLE 2 Find the number of solutions

Tell whether the equation $3x^2 - 7 = 2x$ has *two solutions, one solution,* or *no solution.*

Solution

STEP 1 **Write** the equation in standard form.

$3x^2 - 7 = 2x$ Write equation.

$3x^2 - 2x - 7 = 0$ Subtract $2x$ from each side.

STEP 2 **Find** the value of the discriminant.

$b^2 - 4ac = (-2)^2 - 4(3)(-7)$ Substitute 3 for a, −2 for b, and −7 for c.

$= 88$ Simplify.

▶ The discriminant is positive, so the equation has two solutions.

GUIDED PRACTICE for Examples 1 and 2

Tell whether the equation has *two solutions, one solution,* or *no solution.*

1. $x^2 + 4x + 3 = 0$ two solutions
2. $2x^2 - 5x + 6 = 0$ no solution
3. $-x^2 + 2x = 1$ one solution

EXAMPLE 3 Find the number of x-intercepts

Find the number of x-intercepts of the graph of $y = x^2 + 5x + 8$.

Solution

Find the number of solutions of the equation $0 = x^2 + 5x + 8$.

$b^2 - 4ac = (5)^2 - 4(1)(8)$ Substitute 1 for a, 5 for b, and 8 for c.

$= -7$ Simplify.

▶ The discriminant is negative, so the equation has no solution. This means that the graph of $y = x^2 + 5x + 8$ has no x-intercepts.

CHECK You can use a graphing calculator to check the answer. Notice that the graph of $y = x^2 + 5x + 8$ has no x-intercepts.

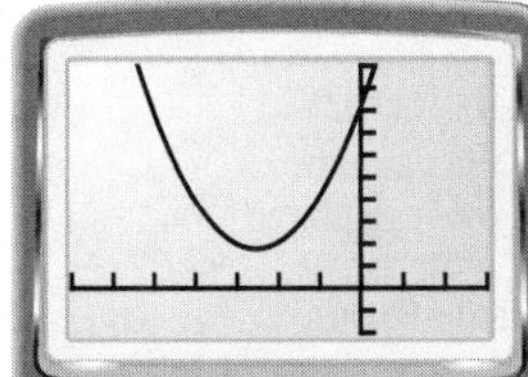

GUIDED PRACTICE for Example 3

Find the number of x-intercepts of the graph of the function.

4. $y = x^2 + 10x + 25$ 1
5. $y = x^2 - 9x$ 2
6. $y = -x^2 + 2x - 4$ 0

Motivating the Lesson

You are helping a friend's family move to a new house. On the drive to the new house, the truck has to pass under an overpass that has an arch in the shape of a parabola. You can model the situation with a quadratic equation and then use the discriminant to determine whether the truck will fit under the overpass.

3 TEACH

Extra Example 1

Use the discriminant to find the number of solutions of each equation.

a. $3x^2 + 8x + 7 = 0$ Discriminant is −20; no solution

b. $x^2 + 2x - 3 = 0$ Discriminant is 16; two solutions

c. $4x^2 + 20x + 25 = 0$ Discriminant is 0; one solution

Key Question to Ask for Example 1

- Can you tell how many x-intercepts each of the equations has? Explain. Each x-intercept of the graph of the equation represents a solution of the equation, so the number of x-intercepts of the graph is the same as the number of solutions of the equation.

Extra Example 2

Use the discriminant to tell whether the equation $4x^2 + 1 = -4x$ has *two solutions, one solution,* or *no solution.* Discriminant is 0; one solution

Extra Example 3

Use the discriminant to find the number of x-intercepts of the graph of $y = x^2 + 7x - 2$. Discriminant is 57; that is positive, so the graph has two x-intercepts.

Differentiated Instruction

Inclusion Students who have difficulty memorizing the rules for the discriminant should think of how the square root of the discriminant is used in the quadratic formula. For a positive discriminant, the square root has two real values; for a zero discriminant, the square root has one real value; and for a negative discriminant, the square root has no real values.

See also the *Algebra 1 Toolkit* for more strategies.

Extra Example 4

The arc of a baseball hit into the outfield can be modeled by the function $y = -0.005x^2 + 1.2x + 3$, where x is the horizontal distance (in feet) that the baseball travels and y is the height of the baseball. Does the baseball reach a height of 50 feet? If it does, about how far has it traveled horizontally from the hitter? **The ball reaches a height of 50 feet twice. The first time it reaches a height of 50 feet (on its way up), it is at a horizontal distance of 49 feet from the hitter. The second time (on its way down), it is at a horizontal distance of 191 feet from the hitter.**

Closing the Lesson

Have students summarize the major points of the lesson and answer the Essential Question: How do you use the value of the discriminant?

- **The discriminant is $b^2 - 4ac$, where a, b, and c are the values when the equation is written in the form $ax^2 + bx + c = 0$.**

If the value of the discriminant is positive, there are two solutions. If the value is negative, there are no real-number solutions. If the value is 0, there is one solution.

EXAMPLE 4 Solve a multi-step problem

FOUNTAINS The Centennial Fountain in Chicago shoots a water arc that can be modeled by the graph of the equation $y = -0.006x^2 + 1.2x + 10$ where x is the horizontal distance (in feet) from the river's north shore and y is the height (in feet) above the river. Does the water arc reach a height of 50 feet? If so, about how far from the north shore is the water arc 50 feet above the water?

Solution

STEP 1 **Write** a quadratic equation. You want to know whether the water arc reaches a height of 50 feet, so let $y = 50$. Then write the quadratic equation in standard form.

$y = -0.006x^2 + 1.2x + 10$	**Write given equation.**
$50 = -0.006x^2 + 1.2x + 10$	**Substitute 50 for y.**
$0 = -0.006x^2 + 1.2x - 40$	**Subtract 50 from each side.**

STEP 2 **Find** the value of the discriminant of $0 = -0.006x^2 + 1.2x - 40$.

$b^2 - 4ac = (1.2)^2 - 4(-0.006)(-40)$	**$a = -0.006$, $b = 1.2$, $c = -40$**
$= 0.48$	**Simplify.**

STEP 3 **Interpret** the discriminant. Because the discriminant is positive, the equation has two solutions. So, the water arc reaches a height of 50 feet at two points on the water arc.

STEP 4 **Solve** the equation $0 = -0.006x^2 + 1.2x - 40$ to find the distance from the north shore where the water arc is 50 feet above the water.

$x = \dfrac{-b \pm \sqrt{b^2 - 4ac}}{2a}$	**Quadratic formula**
$= \dfrac{-1.2 \pm \sqrt{0.48}}{2(-0.006)}$	**Substitute values in the quadratic formula.**
$x \approx 42$ *or* $x \approx 158$	**Use a calculator.**

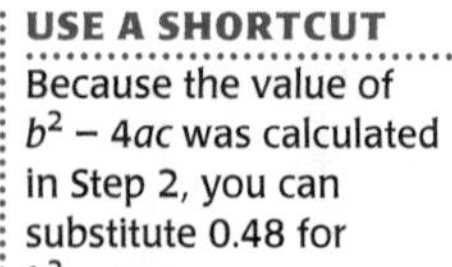
USE A SHORTCUT
Because the value of $b^2 - 4ac$ was calculated in Step 2, you can substitute 0.48 for $b^2 - 4ac$.

▶ The water arc is 50 feet above the water about 42 feet from the north shore and about 158 feet from the north shore.

GUIDED PRACTICE for Example 4

7. **WHAT IF?** In Example 4, does the water arc reach a height of 70 feet? If so, about how far from the north shore is the water arc 70 feet above the water? **yes; 100 ft**

Differentiated Instruction

Below Level Have students, working with partners, look at Example 4 and determine whether the water arc reaches a height of 100 feet. (It does not.) Then challenge the students to determine the greatest height of the arc. (It is 70 feet.) Have them check their results by graphing the function on their graphing calculators. Then have them write a brief summary of what they discovered.

See also the *Algebra 1 Toolkit* for more strategies.

10.7 EXERCISES

HOMEWORK KEY
○ = **WORKED-OUT SOLUTIONS** on p. WS25 for Exs. 9 and 47
★ = **STANDARDIZED TEST PRACTICE** Exs. 2, 18, 19, 40, 41, and 47

SKILL PRACTICE

A

1. **VOCABULARY** Write the quadratic formula and circle the expression that represents the discriminant. $x = \frac{-b \pm \sqrt{b^2 - 4ac}}{2a}$, $b^2 - 4ac$ should be circled.

2. ★ **WRITING** *Explain* how the discriminant of $ax^2 + bx + c = 0$ is related to the graph of $y = ax^2 + bx + c$. See margin.

EXAMPLES 1 and 2 on pp. 678–679 for Exs. 3–21

USING THE DISCRIMINANT **Tell whether the equation has *two solutions, one solution,* or *no solution.***

3. $x^2 + x + 1 = 0$ no solution
4. $2x^2 - 5x - 6 = 0$ two solutions
5. $-2x^2 + 8x - 4 = 0$ two solutions
6. $3m^2 - 6m + 7 = 0$ no solution
7. $9v^2 - 6v + 1 = 0$ one solution
8. $-3q^2 + 8 = 0$ two solutions
9. $25p^2 - 16p = 0$ two solutions
10. $2h^2 + 3 = 4h$ no solution
11. $10 = x^2 - 5x$ two solutions
12. $\frac{1}{4}z^2 + 2 = z$ no solution
13. $-3g^2 - 4g = \frac{4}{3}$ one solution
14. $8r^2 + 10r - 1 = 4r$ two solutions
15. $3n^2 + 3 = 10n - 3n^2$ two solutions
16. $8x^2 + 9 = 4x^2 - 4x + 8$ one solution
17. $w^2 - 7w + 29 = 4 - 7w$ no solution

18. ★ **MULTIPLE CHOICE** What is the value of the discriminant of the equation $5x^2 - 7x - 2 = 0$? D

Ⓐ −9 Ⓑ 9 Ⓒ 59 Ⓓ 89

19. ★ **MULTIPLE CHOICE** How many solutions does $-x^2 + 4x = 8$ have? A

Ⓐ None Ⓑ One Ⓒ Two Ⓓ Three

ERROR ANALYSIS ***Describe*** **and correct the error in finding the number of solutions of the equation.** 20–21. See margin.

20. $4x^2 + 12x + 9 = 0$

$b^2 - 4ac = 12^2 - 4(4)(9)$
$= 144 - 144$
$= 0$
The equation has two solutions.

21. $3x^2 - 7x - 4 = -9$

$b^2 - 4ac = (-7)^2 - 4(3)(-4)$
$= 49 - (-48)$
$= 97$
The equation has two solutions.

EXAMPLE 3 on p. 679 for Exs. 22–30

FINDING THE NUMBER OF *x*-INTERCEPTS **Find the number of *x*-intercepts of the graph of the function.**

22. $y = x^2 - 2x - 4$ 2
23. $y = 2x^2 - x - 1$ 2
24. $y = 4x^2 + 4x + 1$ 1
25. $y = 2x^2 - 5x + 5$ 0
26. $y = x^2 - 6x + 9$ 1
27. $y = 6x^2 + x + 2$ 0
28. $y = -13x^2 + 2x + 6$ 2
29. $y = \frac{1}{4}x^2 - 3x + 9$ 1
30. $y = \frac{2}{3}x^2 - 5x + 12$ 0

B

REASONING **Give a value of *c* for which the equation has (a) two solutions, (b) one solution, and (c) no solution.** 31–33. Sample answers are given for parts (a) and (c).

31. $x^2 - 2x + c = 0$ (a) 0, (b) 1, (c) 2
32. $x^2 - 8x + c = 0$ (a) 15, (b) 16, (c) 17
33. $4x^2 + 12x + c = 0$ (a) 8, (b) 9, (c) 10

4 PRACTICE AND APPLY

Assignment Guide

Answer Transparencies available for all exercises

Basic:
Day 1: pp. 681–683
Exs. 1–11, 18–26, 31–35, 45–48, 51, 54, 57, 60, 63

Average:
Day 1: pp. 681–683
Exs. 1, 2, 11–21, 27–41, 45–49, 52, 58, 64

Advanced:
Day 1: pp. 681–683
Exs. 1, 2, 13–19, 28–50*, 56, 62, 65

Block:
pp. 681–683
Exs. 1, 2, 11–21, 27–41, 45–49, 52, 58, 64 (with 10.6)

Differentiated Instruction

See *Algebra 1 Best Practices Toolkit* for suggestions on addressing the needs of a diverse classroom.

Homework Check

For a quick check of student understanding of key concepts, go over the following exercises:
Basic: 6, 10, 23, 26, 45
Average: 12, 14, 28, 31, 45
Advanced: 15, 17, 30, 32, 46

Extra Practice

- Student Edition, p. 947
- Chapter 10 Resource Book: Practice levels A, B, C, pp. 81–83

Practice Worksheet

An easily-readable reduced practice page (with answers) for this lesson can be found on p. 626C.

2. The value of the discriminant (positive, zero, or negative) determines the number of solutions of the equation $ax^2 + bx + c = 0$, which is the same as the number of x-intercepts of the graph of $y = ax^2 + bx + c$.

20. The discriminant, 0, was interpreted incorrectly; the equation has one solution.

21. Before calculating the discriminant, the equation must be written in standard form: $3x^2 - 7x + 5$. Thus, c is 5, not 9, so $b^2 - 4ac = (-7)^2 - 4(3)(5) = 49 - 60 = -11$, the equation has no solution.

Avoiding Common Errors

Exercises 3–19, 22–30 A common error students make is equating a discriminant of 0 with no solution. Remind these students that when the discriminant is zero, then the quadratic formula simplifies to $x = \frac{-b \pm \sqrt{0}}{2a} = -\frac{b}{2a}$, so there is one solution to the quadratic equation.

Mathematical Reasoning

Exercises 34–39 Before students attempt these exercises, you may want to ask them to describe when the graph of an opening-upward parabola has and does not have solutions, and when the graph of an opening-downward parabola has and does not have solutions.

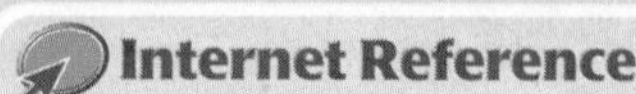

Exercise 49 For more information about trampoline competitions, visit the USA Gymnastics' site at www.usa-gymnastics.org/tt/about-tt.html

34. Below; $a > 0$, so the graph opens up. The value of the discriminant is $(-3)^2 - 4(1)(2) = 1 > 0$, so the graph has two x-intercepts; a parabola that opens up and has two x-intercepts must have its vertex below the x-axis.

35. On; the value of the discriminant is $(-6)^2 - 4(3)(3) = 0$, so the graph has exactly one x-intercept. A parabola that has exactly one x-intercept must have its vertex on the x-axis.

36. Above; $a > 0$, so the graph opens up. The value of the discriminant is $(-2)^2 - 4(6)(4) = -60 < 0$, so the graph has no x-intercepts; a parabola that opens up and has no x-intercepts must have its vertex above the x-axis.

37. Below; $a < 0$, so the graph opens down. The value of the discriminant is $(10)^2 - 4(-15)(-25) = -1400 < 0$, so the graph has no x-intercepts; a parabola that opens down and has no x-intercepts must have its vertex below the x-axis.

USING THE DISCRIMINANT Tell whether the vertex of the graph of the function lies above, below, or on the x-axis. *Explain* your reasoning. 34–39. See margin.

34. $y = x^2 - 3x + 2$ **35.** $y = 3x^2 - 6x + 3$ **36.** $y = 6x^2 - 2x + 4$

37. $y = -15x^2 + 10x - 25$ **38.** $y = -3x^2 - 4x + 8$ **39.** $y = 9x^2 - 24x + 16$

40. ★ **OPEN-ENDED** Write a function of the form $y = ax^2 + bx + c$ whose graph has one x-intercept. *Sample answer:* $y = x^2 + 14x + 49$

41. ★ **EXTENDED RESPONSE** Use the rectangular prism shown.

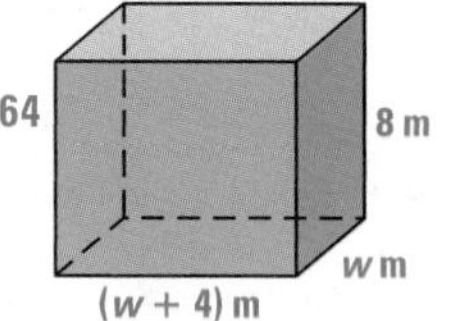

a. The surface area of the prism is 314 square meters. Write an equation that you can solve to find the value of w. $314 = 2w^2 + 40w + 64$

b. Use the discriminant to determine the number of values of w in the equation from part (a). 2

c. Solve the equation. Do the value(s) of w make sense in the context of the problem? *Explain.* See margin.

C **CHALLENGE Find all values of k for which the equation has (a) two solutions, (b) one solution, and (c) no solution.** See margin.

42. $2x^2 + x + 3k = 0$ **43.** $x^2 - 4kx + 36 = 0$ **44.** $kx^2 + 5x - 16 = 0$

PROBLEM SOLVING

EXAMPLE 4 A on p. 680 for Exs. 45–46

45. BIOLOGY The amount y (in milliliters per gram of body mass per hour) of oxygen consumed by a parakeet during flight can be modeled by the function $y = 0.06x^2 - 4x + 87$ where x is the speed (in kilometers per hour) of the parakeet.

a. Use the discriminant to show that it is possible for a parakeet to consume 25 milliliters of oxygen per gram of body mass per hour. See margin.

b. Find the speed(s) at which the parakeet consumes 25 milliliters of oxygen per gram of body mass per hour. Round your solution(s) to the nearest tenth. 24.5 km/h and 42.2 km/h

@HomeTutor for problem solving help at classzone.com

46. FOOD For the period 1950–1999, the average amount y (in pounds per person per year) of butter consumed in the United States can be modeled by $y = 0.0051x^2 - 0.37x + 11$ where x is the number of years since 1950. According to the model, did the butter consumption in the United States ever reach 5 pounds per person per year? If so, in what year(s)? yes; 1974 and 1998

@HomeTutor for problem solving help at classzone.com

(47.) ★ **SHORT RESPONSE** The frame of the tent shown is defined by a rectangular base and two parabolic arches that connect the opposite corners of the base. The graph of $y = -0.18x^2 + 1.6x$ models the height y (in feet) of one of the arches x feet along the diagonal of the base. Can a child that is 4 feet tall walk under one of the arches without having to bend over? *Explain.* See margin.

○ = WORKED-OUT SOLUTIONS on p. WS1 ★ = STANDARDIZED TEST PRACTICE

38. Above; $a < 0$, so the graph opens down. The value of the discriminant is $(-4)^2 - 4(-3)(8) = 112 > 0$, so the graph has two x-intercepts; a parabola that opens down and has two x-intercepts must have its vertex above the x-axis.

39. On; the value of the discriminant is $(-24)^2 - 4(9)(16) = 0$, so the graph has exactly one x-intercept; a parabola that has exactly one x-intercept must have its vertex on the x-axis.

41c, 42–44, 45a, 47. See Additional Answers beginning on p. AA1.

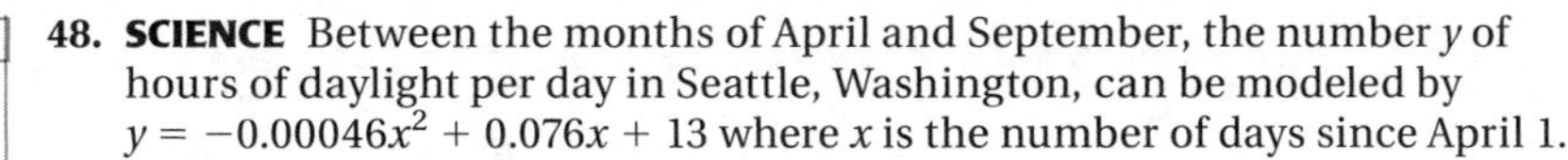

B **48. SCIENCE** Between the months of April and September, the number y of hours of daylight per day in Seattle, Washington, can be modeled by $y = -0.00046x^2 + 0.076x + 13$ where x is the number of days since April 1.

a. Do any of the days between April and September in Seattle have 17 hours of daylight? If so, how many? **no**

b. Do any of the days between April and September in Seattle have 14 hours of daylight? If so, how many? **yes; 2**

49. MULTI-STEP PROBLEM During a trampoline competition, a trampolinist leaves the mat when her center of gravity is 6 feet above the ground. She has an initial vertical velocity of 32 feet per second.

a. Use the vertical motion model to write an equation that models the height h (in feet) of the center of gravity of the trampolinist as a function of the time t (in seconds) into her jump. $h = -16t^2 + 32t + 6$

b. Does her center of gravity reach a height of 24 feet during the jump? If so, at what time(s)? **no**

c. On another jump, the trampolinist leaves the mat when her center of gravity is 6 feet above the ground and with an initial vertical velocity of 35 feet per second. Does her center of gravity reach a height of 24 feet on this jump? If so, at what time(s)? **yes; about 0.8 sec and about 1.4 sec**

C **50. CHALLENGE** Last year, a manufacturer sold backpacks for $24 each. At this price, the manufacturer sold about 1000 backpacks per week. A marketing analyst predicts that for every $1 reduction in the price of the backpack, the manufacturer will sell 100 more backpacks per week.

a. Write a function that models the weekly revenue R (in dollars) that the manufacturer will receive for x reductions of $1 in the price of the backpack. $R = -100x^2 + 1400x + 24{,}000$

b. Is it possible for the manufacturer to receive a weekly revenue of $28,000? $30,000? What is the maximum weekly revenue that the manufacturer can receive? *Explain* your answers using the discriminants of quadratic equations. **See margin.**

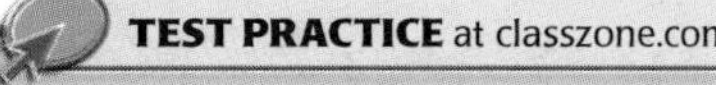

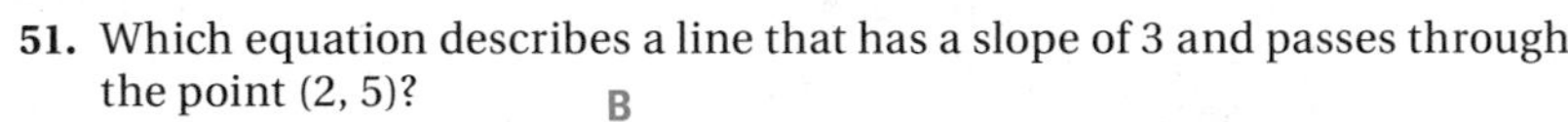

ILLINOIS MIXED REVIEW

51. Which equation describes a line that has a slope of 3 and passes through the point (2, 5)? **B**

Ⓐ $y = 3x - 13$ Ⓑ $y = 3x - 1$ Ⓒ $y = 3x + 11$ Ⓓ $y = 5x + 3$

52. The first five numbers in a sequence are $\frac{2}{5}$, 1, $\frac{5}{2}$, $\frac{25}{4}$, and $\frac{125}{8}$. If this pattern continues, what is the seventh number in the sequence? **C**

Ⓐ $\frac{625}{32}$ Ⓑ $\frac{625}{16}$ Ⓒ $\frac{3125}{32}$ Ⓓ $\frac{3125}{16}$

5 ASSESS AND RETEACH

Daily Homework Quiz

Transparency Available

Tell whether the equation has *two solutions, one solution,* or *no solutions.*

1. $4b^2 + 2b - 5 = 0$ **two solutions**
2. $2g^2 + 8g = -11$ **no solution**

Find the number of x-intercepts of the graph of the equation.

3. $y = x^2 + 14x + 49$ **one**
4. $y = x^2 + 14x + 50$ **none**
5. The graph of $y = -0.2x^2 + 3.5x$ models the height of one of the arches at the entrance to a parking structure. Can a truck that is 20 feet high fit under the arch? **The value of the discriminant of $0 = -0.2x^2 + 3.5x - 20$ is negative, so there is no solution. The truck will not fit under the arch.**

Online Quiz

Available at **classzone.com**

Diagnosis/Remediation

- Practice A, B, C in Chapter 10 Resource Book, pp. 81–83
- Study Guide in Chapter 10 Resource Book, pp. 84–85
- Practice Workbook, pp. 164–165
- @HomeTutor

Challenge

Additional challenge is available in the Chapter 10 Resource Book, p. 88.

50b. See Additional Answers beginning on p. AA1.

10.8 Compare Linear, Exponential, and Quadratic Models

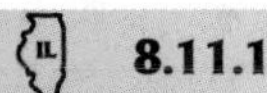

8.11.14 Model problems using mathematical functions and relations (e.g., linear, non-linear).

Before You graphed linear, exponential, and quadratic functions.

Now You will compare linear, exponential, and quadratic models.

Why? So you can solve a problem about biology, as in Ex. 23.

Key Vocabulary
- **linear function,** *p. 217*
- **exponential function,** *p. 520*
- **quadratic function,** *p. 628*

So far you have studied linear functions, exponential functions, and quadratic functions. You can use these functions to model data.

KEY CONCEPT *For Your Notebook*

Linear, Exponential, and Quadratic Functions

Linear Function	Exponential Function	Quadratic Function
$y = mx + b$	$y = ab^x$	$y = ax^2 + bx + c$

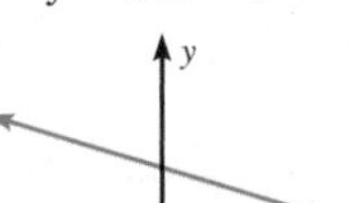
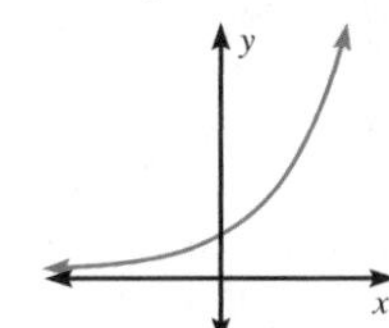
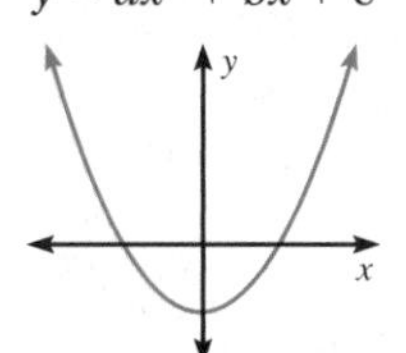

EXAMPLE 1 Choose functions using sets of ordered pairs

Use a graph to tell whether the ordered pairs represent a *linear function*, an *exponential function*, or a *quadratic function*.

a. $\left(-4, \frac{1}{32}\right), \left(-2, \frac{1}{8}\right), \left(0, \frac{1}{2}\right), (2, 2), (4, 8)$

b. $(-4, 1), (-2, 2), (0, 3), (2, 4), (4, 5)$

c. $(-4, 5), (-2, 2), (0, 1), (2, 2), (4, 5)$

Solution

a.
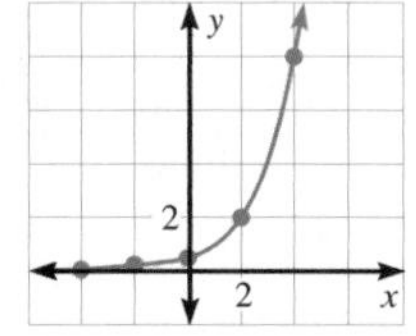
Exponential function

b.
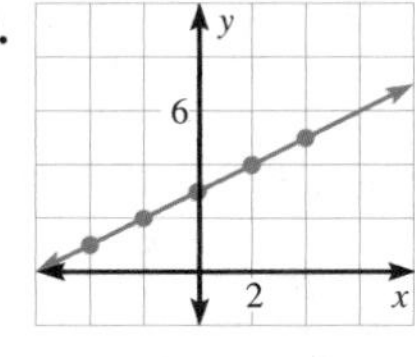
Linear function

c.
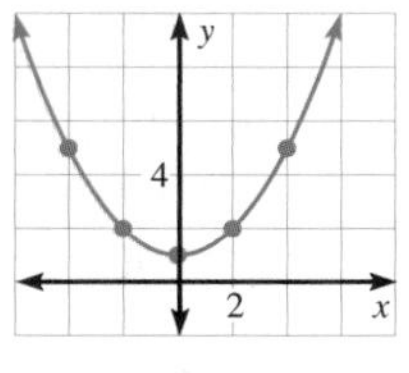
Quadratic function

Animated Algebra at classzone.com

1 PLAN AND PREPARE

Warm-Up Exercises

Transparency Available

1. Graph $y = 3^x$.

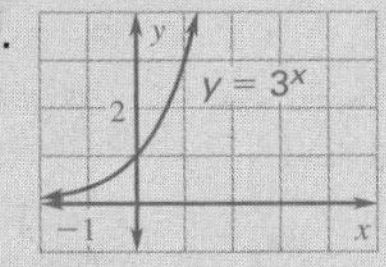

2. Tell whether the ordered pairs (0, 0), (1, 2), (2, 4), and (3, 6) represent a linear function. yes
3. For $y = x^2 - 3x - 5$, find corresponding y-values for the x-values -2, 1, and 3. 5, -7, -5

Notetaking Guide

Transparency Available

Promotes interactive learning and notetaking skills, pp. 242–244.

Pacing

Basic: 2 days
Average: 2 days
Advanced: 2 days
Block: 1 block
- See *Teaching Guide/Lesson Plan.*

2 FOCUS AND MOTIVATE

Essential Question

Big Idea 3, p. 627

How do you decide whether a linear, exponential, or quadratic model best represents data? **Tell students they will learn how to answer this question by making comparisons between the models.**

Resource Planning Guide

Chapter Resource Book
- Teaching Guide/Lesson Plan (pp. 89–90)
- Practice levels A, B, C (pp. 92–97)
- Study Guide (pp. 98–99)
- Catch-up for Absent Students (p. 100)
- Problem Solving Workshop (p. 101)
- Challenge (p. 102)

Workbooks
- Notetaking Guide (pp. 242–244)
- Practice Workbook (pp. 166–168)

Teaching Options
- **Power Presentations CD-ROM** provides dynamic electronic teaching resources for the classroom.
- **Activity Generator CD-ROM** provides editable activities for all ability levels.

Interactive Technology
- Easy Planner
- Power Presentations CD-ROM
- Activity Generator CD-ROM
- Animated Algebra
- Test Generator CD-ROM
- Online Quiz
- eWorkbook
- eEdition
- @HomeTutor

Resources for English Learners
- Quick Reference for English Learners
- Spanish Study Guide
- Multi-Language Visual Glossary
- Student Resources in Spanish

See also the *Algebra 1 Toolkit* for more strategies for meeting individual needs.

DIFFERENCES AND RATIOS A table of values represents a linear function if the *differences* of successive y-values are all equal. A table of values represents an exponential function if the *ratios* of successive y-values are all equal. In both cases, the increments between successive x-values need to be equal.

Linear function: $y = 3x + 5$

x	−1	0	1	2
y	2	5	8	11

Differences: $5 - 2 = 3$ 3 3

Exponential function: $y = 0.5(2)^x$

x	−1	0	1	2
y	0.25	0.5	1	2

Ratios: $\frac{0.5}{0.25} = 2$ 2 2

You can use differences to tell whether a table of values represents a quadratic function, as shown.

CHECK VALUES OF x
When deciding what function is represented by a table of values, be sure that the values of x are increasing by the same amount.

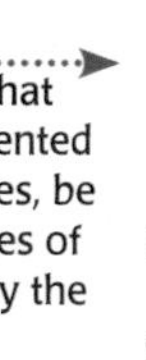

Quadratic function: $y = x^2 - 2x + 2$

x	−1	0	1	2	3
y	5	2	1	2	5

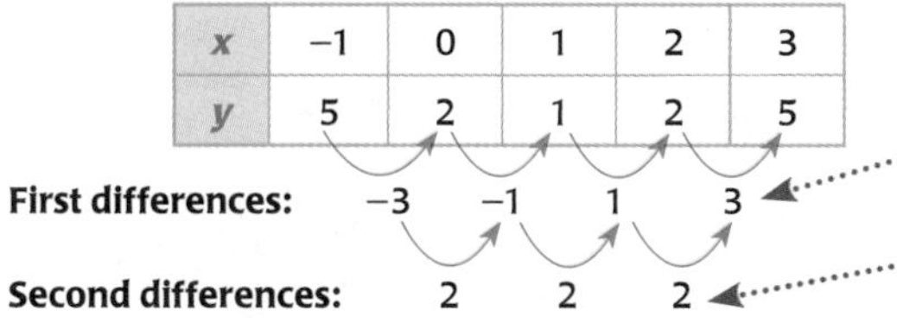

First differences: −3 −1 1 3 ← First find the differences of successive y-values, or *first differences.*

Second differences: 2 2 2 ← Then find the differences of successive first differences, or *second differences.*

The table of values represents a quadratic function if the second differences are all equal.

EXAMPLE 2 Identify functions using differences or ratios

Use differences or ratios to tell whether the table of values represents a *linear function*, an *exponential function*, or a *quadratic function*.

a.

x	−2	−1	0	1	2
y	−6	−6	−4	0	6

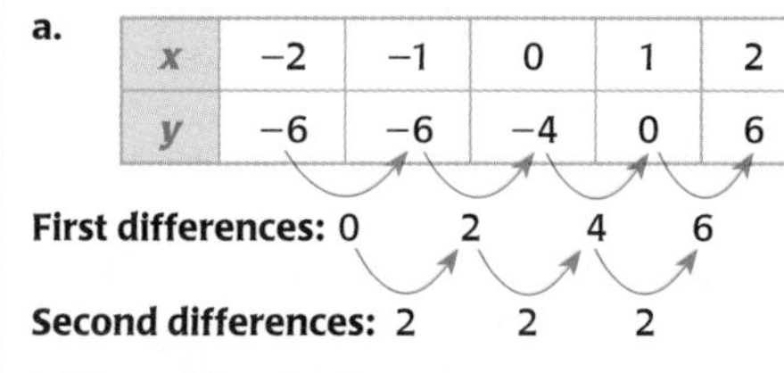

First differences: 0 2 4 6

Second differences: 2 2 2

▶ The table of values represents a quadratic function.

b.

x	−2	−1	0	1	2
y	−2	1	4	7	10

Differences: 3 3 3 3

▶ The table of values represents a linear function.

✓ **GUIDED PRACTICE** for Examples 1 and 2

1. Tell whether the ordered pairs represent a *linear function*, an *exponential function*, or a *quadratic function*: (0, −1.5), (1, −0.5), (2, 2.5), (3, 7.5). quadratic function
2. Tell whether the table of values represents a *linear function*, an *exponential function*, or a *quadratic function*. exponential function

x	−2	−1	0	1
y	0.08	0.4	2	10

Motivating the Lesson

You create T-shirts with designs and slogans. You want to examine your sales for the past year to determine whether you should increase the price of the T-shirts, decrease the price, or keep the price the same. By knowing how to choose a linear, exponential, or quadratic model that fits the data, you can model the situation and determine the best price for your T-shirts.

3 TEACH

Extra Example 1

Use a graph to tell whether the ordered pairs represent a *linear function*, an *exponential function*, or a *quadratic function.*

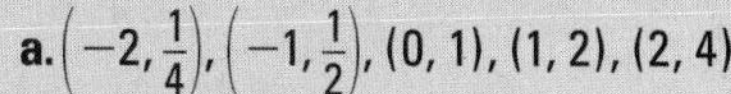

a. $\left(-2, \frac{1}{4}\right)$, $\left(-1, \frac{1}{2}\right)$, (0, 1), (1, 2), (2, 4)

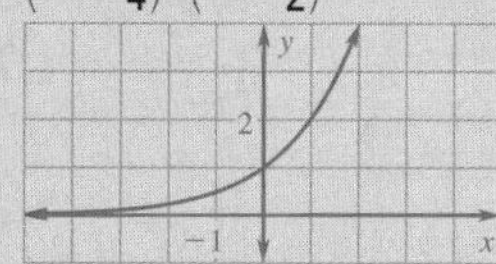

exponential function

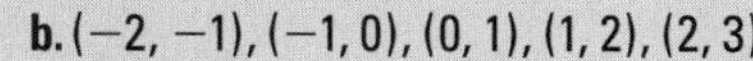

b. (−2, −1), (−1, 0), (0, 1), (1, 2), (2, 3)

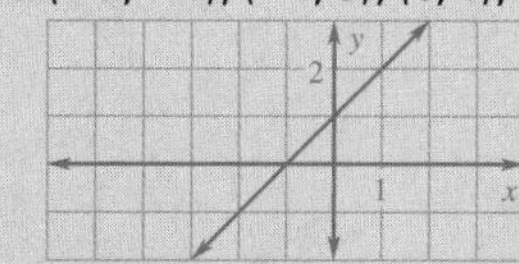

linear function

c. (−2, 5), (−1, 2), (0, 1), (1, 2), (2, 5)

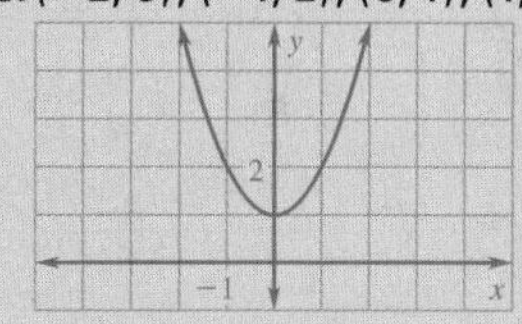

quadratic function

Animated Algebra classzone.com

An **Animated Algebra** activity is available on-line for **Example 1.** This activity is also available on the **Power Presentations CD-ROM.**

Differentiated Instruction

Inclusion Some students may find a table of differences difficult to write because the alignment of the columns must be precise. One method is to align a page of ruled notebook paper so that the lines are vertical. Each ordered pair (x, y) occupies one column.

See also the *Algebra 1 Toolkit* for more strategies.

Extra Example 2

Use differences or ratios to tell whether the table of values represents a *linear function*, an *exponential function*, or a *quadratic function*.

a.

x	−2	−1	0	1	2
y	9	4	1	0	1

The second differences are constant, so the table represents a quadratic function.

b.

x	−2	−1	0	1	2
y	4	2	1	0.5	0.25

The ratio of successive y-values are equal, so the table represents an exponential function.

Key Questions to Ask for Example 2

- How do you know that the table of values in part (b) represents a linear function? **The differences of successive y-values are equal.**
- How is a table of values for a quadratic function different from a table of values for a linear function? **In a table for a linear function, the first differences are constant; in a table for a quadratic function, the first differences are not constant but the second differences are.**

Extra Example 3

Tell whether the table of values represents a *linear function*, an *exponential function*, or a *quadratic function*. Then write an equation for the function.

x	−2	−1	0	1	2
y	8	4	2	1	0.5

Ratios of successive y-values are equal, so the table represents an exponential function; $y = 2(0.5)^x$.

3. linear function; $y = 2x - 1$
4. quadratic function; $y = 2x^2$

WRITING AN EQUATION When you decide that a set of ordered pairs represents a linear, an exponential, or a quadratic function, you can write an equation for the function. In this lesson, when you write an equation for a quadratic function, the equation will have the form $y = ax^2$.

EXAMPLE 3 Write an equation for a function

Tell whether the table of values represents a *linear function*, an *exponential function*, or a *quadratic function*. Then write an equation for the function.

x	−2	−1	0	1	2
y	2	0.5	0	0.5	2

Solution

STEP 1 **Determine** which type of function the table of values represents.

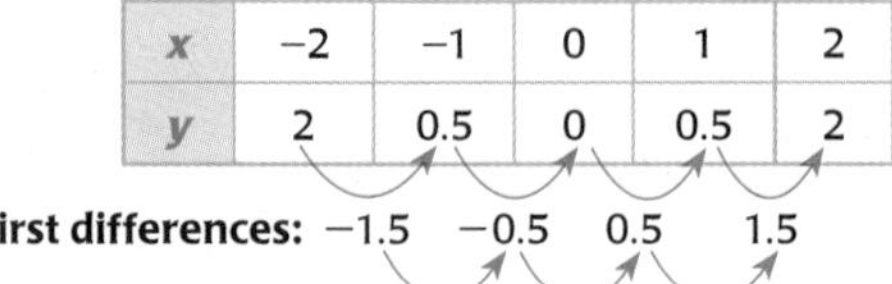

x	−2	−1	0	1	2
y	2	0.5	0	0.5	2

First differences: −1.5 −0.5 0.5 1.5

Second differences: 1 1 1

The table of values represents a quadratic function because the second differences are equal.

STEP 2 **Write** an equation for the quadratic function. The equation has the form $y = ax^2$. Find the value of a by using the coordinates of a point that lies on the graph, such as (1, 0.5).

$y = ax^2$ **Write equation for quadratic function.**

$0.5 = a(1)^2$ **Substitute 1 for *x* and 0.5 for *y*.**

$0.5 = a$ **Solve for *a*.**

AVOID ERRORS
In Example 3, do not use (0, 0) to find the value of a, even though (0, 0) lies on the graph of $y = ax^2$. If you do, you will obtain an undefined value for a.

▸ The equation is $y = 0.5x^2$.

CHECK Plot the ordered pairs from the table. Then graph $y = 0.5x^2$ to see that the graph passes through the plotted points.

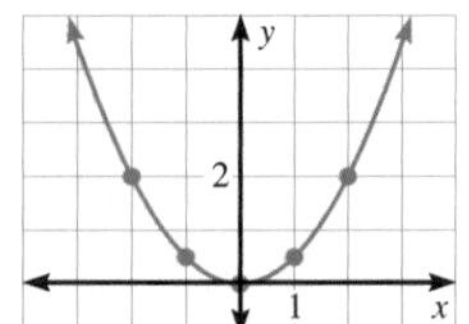

✓ GUIDED PRACTICE for Example 3

Tell whether the table of values represents a *linear function*, an *exponential function*, or a *quadratic function*. Then write an equation for the function.

3.

x	−3	−2	−1	0	1
y	−7	−5	−3	−1	1

4.

x	−2	−1	0	1	2
y	8	2	0	2	8

3, 4. See margin.

EXAMPLE 4 Solve a multi-step problem

CYCLING The table shows the breathing rates y (in liters of air per minute) of a cyclist traveling at different speeds x (in miles per hour). Tell whether the data can be modeled by a *linear function*, an *exponential function*, or a *quadratic function*. Then write an equation for the function.

Speed of cyclist, x (mi/h)	20	21	22	23	24	25
Breathing rate, y (L/min)	51.4	57.1	63.3	70.3	78.0	86.6

Solution

STEP 1 **Graph** the data. The graph has a slight curve. So, a linear function does not appear to model the data.

STEP 2 **Decide** which function models the data.

In the table below, notice that $\frac{57.1}{51.4} \approx 1.11$, $\frac{63.3}{57.1} \approx 1.11$, $\frac{70.3}{63.3} \approx 1.11$, $\frac{78.0}{70.3} \approx 1.11$, and $\frac{86.6}{78.0} \approx 1.11$. So, the ratios are all approximately equal. An exponential function models the data.

Speed of cyclist, x (mi/h)	20	21	22	23	24	25
Breathing rate, y (L/min)	51.4	57.1	63.3	70.3	78.0	86.6

Ratios: 1.11 1.11 1.11 1.11 1.11

STEP 3 **Write** an equation for the exponential function. The breathing rate increases by a factor of 1.11 liters per minute, so $b = 1.11$. Find the value of a by using one of the data pairs, such as (20, 51.4).

$y = ab^x$ Write equation for exponential function.

$51.4 = a(1.11)^{20}$ Substitute 1.11 for b, 20 for x, and 51.4 for y.

$\frac{51.4}{(1.11)^{20}} = a$ Solve for a.

$6.38 \approx a$ Use a calculator.

▶ The equation is $y = 6.38(1.11)^x$.

REVIEW EXPONENTIAL FUNCTIONS
For help with writing an equation for an exponential function, see p. 520.

GUIDED PRACTICE for Example 4

5. In Example 4, suppose the cyclist is traveling at 15 miles per hour. Find the breathing rate of the cyclist at this speed. about 30.5 liters of air per minute

Extra Example 4

The table shows the cost to run an ad in a magazine. Tell whether the data can be modeled by a *linear function*, an *exponential function*, or a *quadratic function*. Then write an equation for the function.

Number of lines, x	Total cost, y
4	\$10.40
5	\$12.25
6	\$14.10
7	\$15.95
8	\$17.80
9	\$19.65

The equation can be modeled by a linear function; $y = 1.85x + 3$

Closing the Lesson

Have students summarize the major points of the lesson and answer the Essential Question: How do you decide whether a linear, exponential, or quadratic model best describes data?

- A table of values represents a linear function if the differences of successive y-values are equal.
- A table of values represents an exponential function if the ratios of successive y-values are equal.
- A table of values represents a quadratic function if the second differences of successive y-values are equal.

To identify whether a function is linear, exponential, or quadratic, plot points, draw the graph, and then identify the function from the graph. If given a table of values, use differences and ratios to identify the type of function.

4 PRACTICE AND APPLY

Assignment Guide

Answer Transparencies available for all exercises

Basic:
Day 1: pp. 688–691
Exs. 1–11, 35–43
Day 2: pp. 688–691
Exs. 12–20, 23–26, 29–34

Average:
Day 1: pp. 688–691
Exs. 1–11, 35–43
Day 2: pp. 688–691
Exs. 14–21, 23–27, 29–34

Advanced:
Day 1: pp. 688–691
Exs. 1–11, 35–43
Day 2: pp. 688–691
Exs. 15–18, 20–34*

Block:
pp. 688–691
Exs. 1–11, 14–21, 23–27, 29–43

Differentiated Instruction

See *Algebra 1 Best Practices Toolkit* for suggestions on addressing the needs of a diverse classroom.

Homework Check

For a quick check of student understanding of key concepts, go over the following exercises:

Basic: 4, 6, 12, 15, 23
Average: 3, 8, 15, 20, 24
Advanced: 10, 16, 20, 25, 26

Extra Practice

- Student Edition, p. 947
- Chapter 10 Resource Book: Practice levels A, B, C, pp. 92–97

Practice Worksheet

An easily-readable reduced practice page (with answers) for this lesson can be found on p. 626C.

10.8 EXERCISES

HOMEWORK KEY
○ = **WORKED-OUT SOLUTIONS** on p. WS25 for Exs. 7, 13, and 25
★ = **STANDARDIZED TEST PRACTICE** Exs. 2, 18, 26, and 27
◆ = **MULTIPLE REPRESENTATIONS** Ex. 25

SKILL PRACTICE

A

1. VOCABULARY Copy and complete: A function that is of the form $y = ab^x$ is a(n) __?__. exponential function

2. ★ WRITING *Describe* how you can tell whether a table of values represents a quadratic function. See margin.

EXAMPLE 1 on p. 684 for Exs. 3–11

MATCHING **Match the function with the graph that the function represents.**

3. Linear function B

4. Exponential function C

5. Quadratic function A

A.
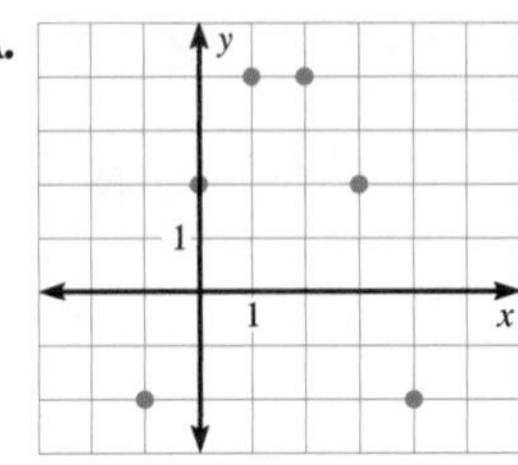

B.
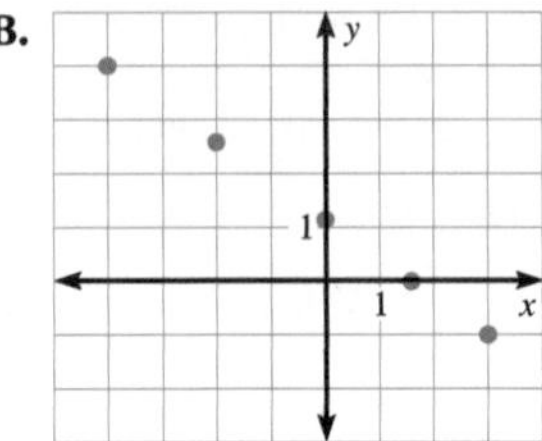

C.
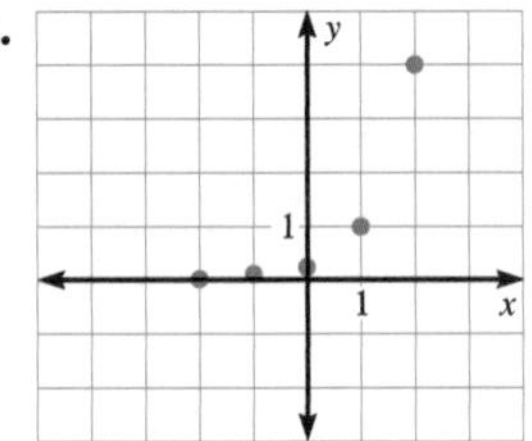

USING A GRAPH **Use a graph to tell whether the ordered pairs represent a *linear function*, an *exponential function*, or a *quadratic function*.**

6. $(-4, -7), (-2, -1), (0, 1), (2, -1), (4, -7)$ quadratic function

7. $(-5, -1), (-3, 0), (-1, 1), (1, 2), (3, 3)$ linear function

8. $\left(-1, \frac{1}{16}\right), \left(0, \frac{1}{4}\right), (1, 1), (2, 4), (3, 16)$ exponential function

9. $(-1, 8), (1, 2), \left(3, \frac{1}{2}\right), \left(5, \frac{1}{8}\right), \left(7, \frac{1}{32}\right)$ exponential function

10. $(-4, -4), (-2, -3.5), (0, -3), (2, -2.5)$ linear function

11. $(-1, 0.5), (0, -0.5), (1, 0.5), (2, 3.5)$ quadratic function

EXAMPLES 2 and 3 on p. 685–686 for Exs. 12–19

USING DIFFERENCES AND RATIOS **Tell whether the table of values represents a *linear function*, an *exponential function*, or a *quadratic function*. Then write an equation for the function.**

12.
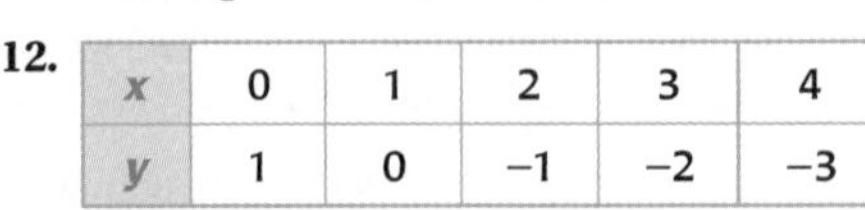

x	0	1	2	3	4
y	1	0	−1	−2	−3

linear function; $y = -x + 1$

13.

x	−2	−1	0	1	2
y	−4	−1	0	−1	−4

quadratic function; $y = -x^2$

14.

x	−3	−2	−1	0	1
y	13.5	6	1.5	0	1.5

quadratic function; $y = 1.5x^2$

15.
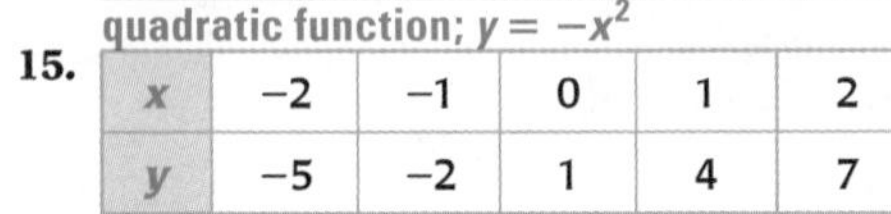

x	−2	−1	0	1	2
y	−5	−2	1	4	7

linear function; $y = 3x + 1$

16.

x	−2	−1	0	1	2
y	$\frac{1}{9}$	$\frac{1}{3}$	1	3	9

exponential function; $y = 3^x$

17.
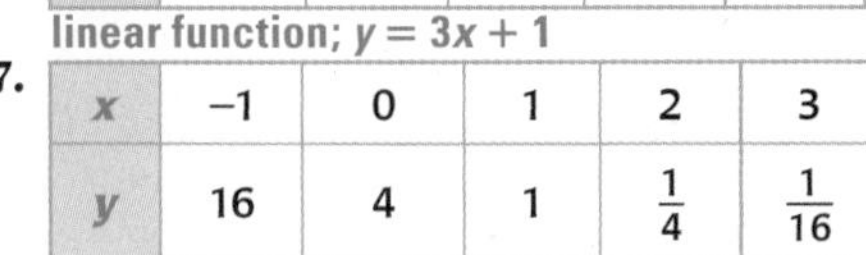

x	−1	0	1	2	3
y	16	4	1	$\frac{1}{4}$	$\frac{1}{16}$

exponential function; $y = 4\left(\frac{1}{4}\right)^x$

18. ★ MULTIPLE CHOICE Which function is represented by the following ordered pairs: $(-1, 4), (0, 0), (1, 4), (2, 16), (3, 36)$? C

Ⓐ $y = 0.25x^2$ Ⓑ $y = 4^x$ Ⓒ $y = 4x^2$ Ⓓ $y = 4x$

2. Find the differences of successive *y*-values, called the first differences. If they are not equal, then find the differences of successive first differences, called second differences. If the second differences are equal, then the table of values represents a quadratic function.

19. **ERROR ANALYSIS** *Describe* and correct the error in writing an equation for the function represented by the ordered pairs. See margin.

(0, 0), (1, 2.5), (2, 10), (3, 22.5), (4, 40)

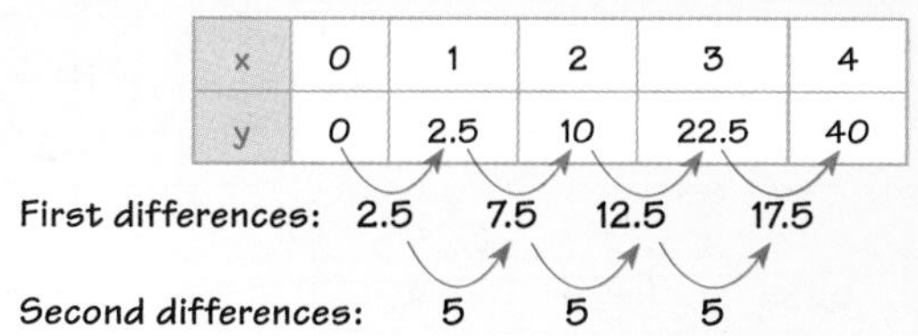

x 0 1 2 3 4
y 0 2.5 10 22.5 40
First differences: 2.5 7.5 12.5 17.5
Second differences: 5 5 5

The ordered pairs represent a quadratic function.

$y = ax^2$

$2 = a(10)^2$

$0.02 = a$

So, the equation is $y = 0.02x^2$.

B 20. **REASONING** Use the graph shown.

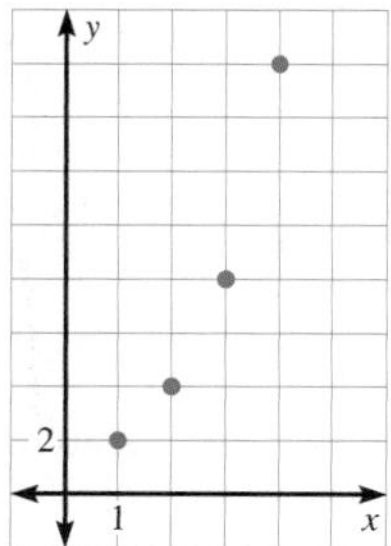

a. Tell whether the graph represents an *exponential function* or a *quadratic function* by looking at the graph. exponential function

b. Make a table of values for the points on the graph. Then use differences or ratios to check your answer in part (a). See margin.

c. Write an equation for the function that the table of values from part (b) represents. $y = 2^x$

21. **GEOMETRY** The table shows the area A (in square centimeters) of an equilateral triangle for various side lengths s (in centimeters). Write an equation for the function that the table of values represents. Then find the area of an equilateral triangle that has a side length of 10 centimeters.

Side length, s (cm)	1	2	3	4	5
Area, A (cm²)	$0.25\sqrt{3}$	$\sqrt{3}$	$2.25\sqrt{3}$	$4\sqrt{3}$	$6.25\sqrt{3}$

$A = \left(\frac{\sqrt{3}}{4}\right)s^2$; $25\sqrt{3}$ cm²

C 22. **CHALLENGE** In the ordered pairs below, the y-values are given in terms of m. Tell whether the ordered pairs represent a *linear function*, an *exponential function*, or a *quadratic function*.

(1, $3m - 1$), (2, $10m + 2$), (3, $26m$), (4, $51m - 7$), (5, $85m - 19$) quadratic function

PROBLEM SOLVING

EXAMPLE 4 A on p. 687 for Exs. 23–25

23. **LIZARDS** The table shows the body temperature B (in degrees Celsius) of a desert spiny lizard at various air temperatures A (in degrees Celsius). Tell whether the data can be modeled by a *linear function*, an *exponential function*, or a *quadratic function*. Then write an equation for the function.

Air temperature, A (°C)	26	27	28	29	30
Body temperature, B (°C)	33.44	33.78	34.12	34.46	34.80

@HomeTutor for problem solving help at classzone.com

linear function; $y = 0.34x + 24.6$

Avoiding Common Errors

Exercises 6–11, 12–17 A common error arises out of trying to identify a function by looking at a table of values or ordered pairs without graphing the ordered pairs or checking for differences or ratios in the table of values. Encourage students to plot points and calculate differences and ratios.

Graphing Calculator

Exercises 12–17 Encourage students to use their graphing calculators to check their equations.

Internet Reference

Exercise 23 More information about desert spiny lizards can be found at www.werc.usgs.gov/fieldguide/scma.htm

19. The x- and y-values were reversed when substituting the coordinates of the ordered pair (2, 10) into the equation $y = ax^2$. Substituting 2 for x and 10 for y gives $10 = a(2)^2$, $a = 2.5$; so, the equation is $y = 2.5x^2$.

20b.

x	1	2	3	4
y	2	4	8	16
Ratios of successive y-values	$\frac{2}{1} = 2$	$\frac{4}{2} = 2$	$\frac{8}{4} = 2$	$\frac{16}{8} = 2$

The ratios are the same, so the table of values and the graph represent an exponential function.

Study Strategy

Exercises 24–27 Remind students that for data modeled by exponential functions, the ratios may be approximately equal, not exact. Students should also keep in mind that for quadratic functions, second difference are equal and first differences are not.

25b.

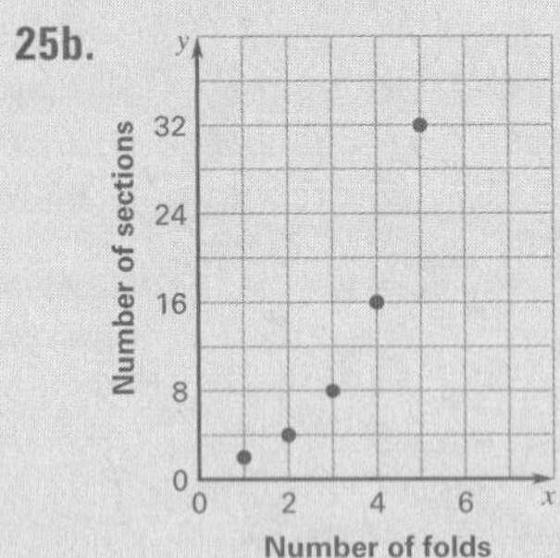

27c. The period decreases by about 71%. For example, consider $t = 4$ for $d = 13.12$. To find t for 50% of d, solve $0.5(13.12) = 0.82t^2$; $t \approx 2.83$, and $\frac{2.83}{4} = 0.708$, so the period decreased by about 71%. Consider $t = 2$ for $d = 3.28$. To find t for 50% of d, solve $0.5(3.28) = 0.82t^2$; $t \approx 1.41$, and $\frac{1.41}{2} = 0.705$, so the period decreased by about 71%. Consider $t = 1$ for $d = 0.82$. To find t for 50% of d, solve $0.5(0.82) = 0.82t^2$; $t \approx 0.707$, and $\frac{0.707}{1} = 0.707$, so the period decreased by about 71%.

24. **NAUTILUS** A chambered nautilus is a marine animal that lives in the outermost chamber of its shell. When the nautilus outgrows a chamber, it adds a new, larger chamber to its shell. The table shows the volumes (in cubic centimeters) of consecutive chambers of a nautilus. Tell whether the data can be modeled by a *linear function*, an *exponential function*, or a *quadratic function*. Then write an equation for the function. **exponential function; $y = 0.789(1.06)^x$**

Chamber	1	2	3	4	5	6
Volume (cm^3)	0.836	0.889	0.945	1.005	1.068	1.135

@HomeTutor for problem solving help at classzone.com

25. ◆ **MULTIPLE REPRESENTATIONS** Fold a rectangular piece of paper in half. Open the paper and record the number of folds and the number of sections created. Repeat by increasing the number of folds by 1 fold each time.

a. **Making a Table** Copy and complete the table.

Folds	1	2	3	4	5
Sections	? 2	? 4	? 8	? 16	? 32

b. **Drawing a Graph** Graph the data in part (a). Use the graph and the table to tell whether the data can be modeled by a *linear function*, an *exponential function*, or a *quadratic function*. **See margin for art; exponential function.**

c. **Writing a Model** Write an equation for the function that models the data. Then find the number of sections that are created by 7 folds. **$y = 2^x$; 128 sections**

B

26. ★ **MULTIPLE CHOICE** The table shows the cost of a custom circular rug for various diameters (in feet). What is the approximate cost of a custom circular rug that has a diameter of 8 feet? **C**

Diameter (ft)	2	3	4	5	6
Cost (dollars)	28.40	63.90	113.60	177.50	255.60

(A) \$333.70 (B) \$411.80 (C) \$454.40 (D) \$908.80

27. ★ **EXTENDED RESPONSE** The time it takes for a clock's pendulum to swing from one side to the other and back again, as shown in the back view of the clock, is called the pendulum's period. The table shows the period t (in seconds) of a pendulum of length ℓ (in feet).

Period, t (sec)	1	2	3	4	5
Length, ℓ (ft)	0.82	3.28	7.38	13.12	20.5

a. **Model** Tell whether the data can be modeled by a *linear function*, an *exponential function*, or a *quadratic function*. Then write an equation for the function. **quadratic function; $\ell = 0.82t^2$**

b. **Apply** Find the length of a pendulum that has a period of 0.5 second. **0.205 ft**

c. **Analyze** How does decreasing the length of the pendulum by 50% change the period? *Justify* your answer using several examples. **See margin.**

C **28. CHALLENGE** The table shows the height h (in feet) that a pole vaulter's center of gravity reaches for various running speeds s (in feet per second) at the moment the pole vaulter launches himself into the air.

Running speed, s (ft/sec)	30	31	32	33	34
Height of center of gravity, h (ft)	$14\frac{1}{16}$	$15\frac{1}{64}$	16	$17\frac{1}{64}$	$18\frac{1}{16}$

a. A pole vaulter is running at $31\frac{1}{2}$ feet per second when he launches himself into the air. Find the height that the pole vaulter's center of gravity reaches. about 15.5 ft

b. Find the speed at which the pole vaulter needs to be running when he launches himself into the air in order for his center of gravity to reach a height of 19 feet. Round your answer to the nearest foot per second. about 35 ft/sec

ILLINOIS MIXED REVIEW

TEST PRACTICE at classzone.com

29. $\triangle TUV$ is shown at the right. Find the coordinates of the vertices of the image of $\triangle TUV$ reflected across the y-axis.

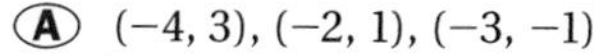

Ⓐ (−4, 3), (−2, 1), (−3, −1) C

Ⓑ (−3, −4), (−1, 2), (1, 3)

Ⓒ (3, −4), (1, −2), (−1, −3)

Ⓓ (4, −3), (2, −1), (3, 1)

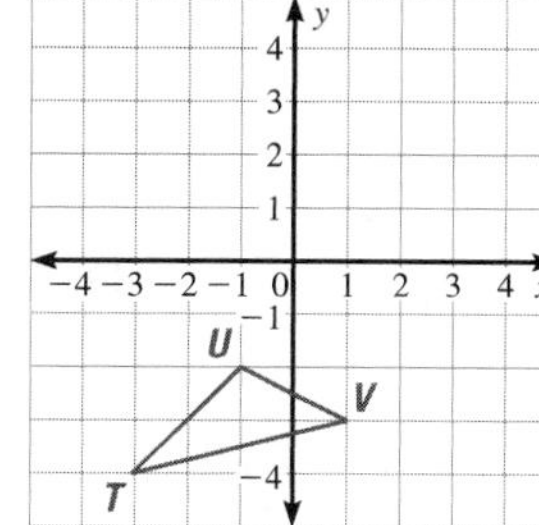

QUIZ *for Lessons 10.7–10.8*

Tell whether the equation has *two solutions, one solution,* or *no solution.* *(p. 678)*

1. $x^2 + x + 5 = 0$ no solution

2. $5x^2 + 4x - 1 = 0$ two solutions

Find the number of x-intercepts of the graph of the function. *(p. 678)*

3. $y = -3x^2 + 4x - 2$ 0

4. $y = \frac{4}{9}x^2 + 4x + 9$ 1

Tell whether the table of values represents a *linear function*, an *exponential function*, or a *quadratic function*. Then write an equation for the function. *(p. 684)*

5. quadratic function; $y = -0.25x^2$

x	−6	−3	0	3	6
y	−9	−2.25	0	−2.25	−9

6. exponential function; $y = 25\left(\frac{1}{5}\right)^x$

x	1	2	3	4	5
y	5	1	$\frac{1}{5}$	$\frac{1}{25}$	$\frac{1}{125}$

5 ASSESS AND RETEACH

Daily Homework Quiz

Transparency Available

1. Tell whether the data can be modeled by a *linear function*, an *exponential function*, or a *quadratic function.* quadratic

x	−2	−1	0	1	2
y	7	1	−1	1	7

2. Tell whether the data can be modeled by a *linear function*, an *exponential function*, or a *quadratic function*. Then write an equation for the function.

x	1	2	3	4	5
y	0.05	0.1	0.2	0.4	0.8

exponential; $y = 0.025(2)^x$

Available at **classzone.com**

Diagnosis/Remediation

- Practice A, B, C in Chapter 10 Resource Book, pp. 92–97
- Study Guide in Chapter 10 Resource Book, pp. 98–99
- Practice Workbook, pp. 166–168
- @HomeTutor

Challenge

Additional challenge is available in the Chapter 10 Resource Book, p. 102.

Quiz

An easily-readable reduced copy of the quiz (with answers) on Lessons 10.7–10.8 from the Assessment Book can be found on p. 626G.

1 PLAN AND PREPARE

Learn the Method

- Students will use a graphing calculator to find models for data.
- After the activity, students can use a graphing calculator to check their solutions in Lesson 10.8, Exercises 23–27.

Keystroke Help

Keystrokes for several models of calculators are available in blackline format in the *Chapter 10 Resource Book*.

2 TEACH

Tips for Success

For both examples, encourage students to check that they entered the data correctly.

Extra Example 1

The table shows the shipment (in millions of units) of DVD videos in the U.S. each year for the period 1998–2003. Find an exponential model for the data.

Year	Shipments (millions of units)
1998	0.5
1999	2.5
2000	3.3
2001	7.9
2002	10.7
2003	17.5

$y = 0.83(1.9)^x$

10.8 Perform Regressions

QUESTION How can you use a graphing calculator to find models for data?

On page 335, you used a graphing calculator to perform linear regression on data to find a linear model for the data. A graphing calculator can also be used to perform exponential regression and quadratic regression.

EXAMPLE 1 Use exponential regression to find a model

The table shows the sales (in millions of dollars) of organic milk, organic half and half, and organic cream in the U.S. each year for the period 1996–2000. Find an exponential model for the data.

Year	1996	1997	1998	1999	2000
Sales (millions of dollars)	15.8	30.7	46	75.7	104

STEP 1 *Enter data*

Enter the data into two lists. Let $x = 0$ represent 1996.

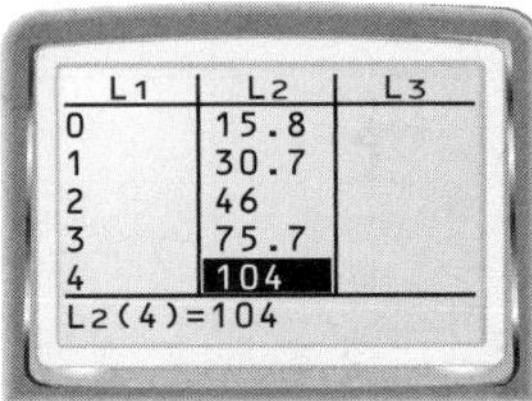

STEP 2 *Make scatter plot*

Make a scatter plot of the data. Notice that the points show an exponential trend.

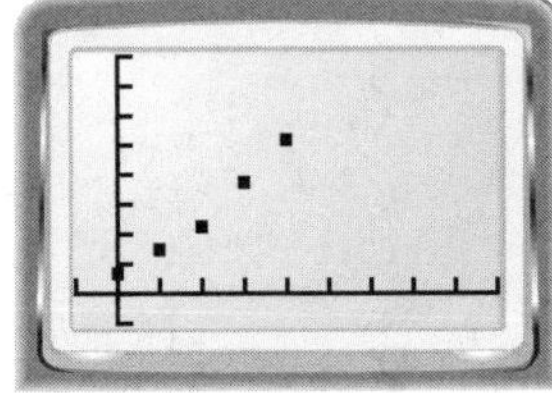

STEP 3 *Perform regression*

Use the exponential regression feature to obtain the model $y = 17.5(1.6)^x$.

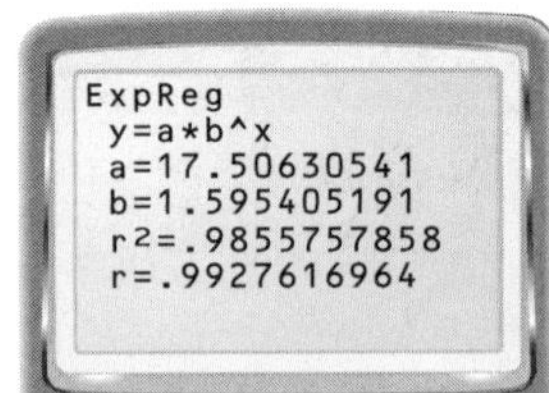

STEP 4 *Check model*

Check how well the model fits the data by graphing the model and the data.

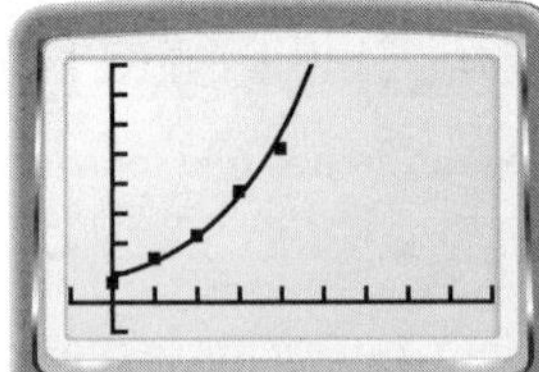

PRACTICE

1. The table shows the value (in dollars) of a car over time. Find an exponential model for the data in the table. $y = 15{,}600(0.866)^x$

Age of car (years)	0	1	2	3	4	5
Value (dollars)	15,600	13,510	11,700	10,132	8774	7598

@HomeTutor
classzone.com
Keystrokes

EXAMPLE 2 Use quadratic regression to find a model

In September 2001, the first U.S. digital satellite radio station was launched. The table shows the number of subscribers of the service for various months after its launch. Find a quadratic model for the data.

Months after launch	0	3	6	9	12	15
Subscribers	500	31,000	76,000	135,500	201,500	360,000

STEP 1 ***Make scatter plot***

Enter the data into two lists and make a scatter plot of the data. Notice that the points show a quadratic trend.

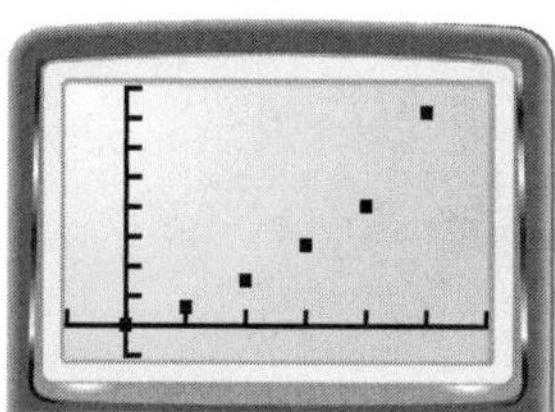

STEP 2 ***Perform regression***

Use the quadratic regression feature to obtain the model $y = 1440x^2 + 1010x + 8000$.

STEP 3 ***Check model***

Check how well the model fits the data by graphing the model and the data.

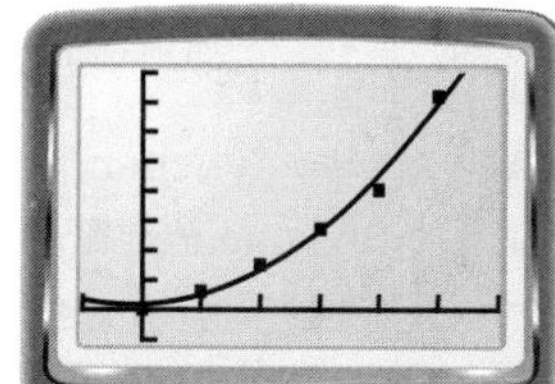

PRACTICE

2. The table shows the maximum weight (in pounds) that can be supported by a 16 foot floor beam of different depths. Find a quadratic model for the data. $y = 10.2x^2 - 96.8x + 285.4$

Depth (inches)	6	7.5	9	10.5	12	13.5
Weight (pounds)	68	137	242	389	586	838

DRAW CONCLUSIONS

3. The table shows the temperature (in degrees Fahrenheit) of a cup of hot chocolate over time. Find an exponential model and a quadratic model for the data. Make a scatter plot of the data and graph both models. Which model fits the data better? *Explain.* See margin.

Time (minutes)	0	10	20	30	40	50	60
Temperature (°F)	200	157	128	109	99	92	90

Extra Example 2

The table shows the number (in thousands) of basic cable television subscribers in the U.S. from 1997–2002. Find a quadratic model for the data.

Year	Number of Subscribers (in hundred thousands)
1997	636
1998	646.5
1999	855
2000	862.5
2001	667.32
2002	664.72

$y = -30x^2 + 156x + 607$

3 ASSESS AND RETEACH

The table shows the time it takes Nikki to keyboard 200 words each week with practice. Find an exponential and a quadratic model for the data. Does an exponential or the quadratic model fit the data better? *Explain.*

Week	Number of Minutes to Keyboard 200 Words
1	6
2	5.7
3	4.7
4	4.5
5	3.9
6	3.7

The quadratic model is $y = 0.038x^2 - 0.75x + 6.8$ and the exponential model is $y = 6.07(0.9)^x$. Both models fit the data, so one model is not better than the other.

3. $y = 179(0.987)^x$,
$y = 0.040x^2 - 4.13x + 197$

The exponential model; although the quadratic model appears to fit the given data points more closely than the exponential model does, the graph shows that after the last data point, (60, 90), the quadratic model implies increasing temperatures as time goes on, while the exponential model shows gradually decreasing temperatures as time goes on; the exponential model is a more accurate model of what will happen as the hot chocolate continues to cool.

Illinois Mixed Review

1. A
2. F
3. B
4. F
5. C
6. G
7. C

Illinois Mixed Review

Lessons 10.5–10.8

1. **SPRINGS** Different masses (in kilograms) are hung from a spring. The distances (in centimeters) that the spring stretches are shown in the table.

Mass (kilograms)	Distance (centimeters)
1	2.6
2	5.2
3	7.8
4	10.4
5	13.0

Which type of function can be used to model the data?

A. A linear function
B. An exponential function
C. A quadratic function
D. None of the above

2. **CHEERLEADING** A cheerleading routine involves throwing a flyer straight up into the air and catching her on the way down. The flyer begins this stunt with her center of gravity 4.5 feet above the ground, and she is thrown with an initial vertical velocity of 30 feet per second. How many seconds after she is thrown will the cheerleader's center of gravity be 15 feet high?

F. After about 0.5 second
G. After about 1.2 seconds
H. After about 0.5 second and 1.4 seconds
J. After about 0.1 second and 1.8 seconds

3. **WHAT IF?** In Exercise 2, suppose the flyer wants to have her center of gravity reach a height of 25 feet above the ground at its peak. Which initial vertical velocity will accomplish this?

A. 18.1 ft/sec
B. 36.2 ft/sec
C. 42.2 ft/sec
D. 50 ft/sec

4. **MOSAIC** You are making a tiled tabletop with a uniform mosaic tile border as shown

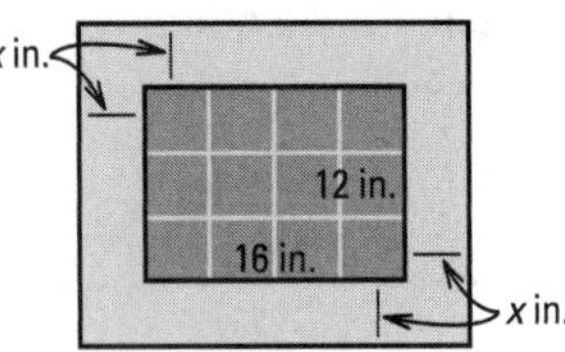

You have enough mosaic tiles to cover 130 square inches. To the nearest inch, what should the width of the border be?

F. 2 in. **H.** 8 in.
G. 4 in. **J.** 11 in.

5. **SOFTBALL** In slow-pitch softball, the ball is pitched in an underhand motion. A batter in a softball game is pitched a ball whose height h (in feet) can be modeled by $h = -16t^2 + 35t + 2$ where t is the time (in seconds) since the ball was pitched. The batter hits the ball when it is 2.5 feet above the ground. About how long after the ball is pitched is the ball hit?

A. 0.5 sec **C.** 2.2 sec
B. 1.1 sec **D.** None of the above

6. **TRAPEZOID** The trapezoid shown has an area of 54 square inches. What is the value of x?

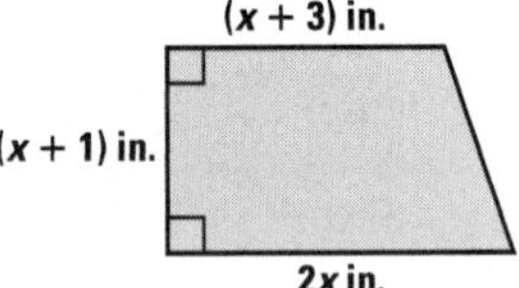

F. 2.5 in. **H.** 10 in.
G. 5 in. **J.** 13 in.

7. **BUSINESS** For the period 1990–2000, the sales y (in billions of dollars) of computers, computer accessories, and computer software can be modeled by the function $y = -0.05x^2 + 2.2x + 7$ where x is the number of years since 1990. In which year during the period 1990–2000 did the sales reach \$24 billion?

A. 1991 **C.** 2000
B. 1994 **D.** 2001

10 CHAPTER SUMMARY

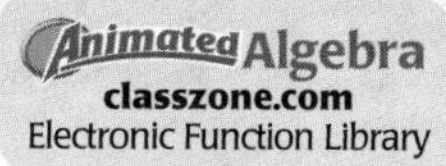

BIG IDEAS

For Your Notebook

Big Idea 1

Graphing Quadratic Functions

You can use the properties below to graph any quadratic function.

The graph of $y = ax^2 + bx + c$ is a parabola that:

- opens up if $a > 0$ and opens down if $a < 0$.
- is narrower than the graph of $y = x^2$ if $|a| > 1$ and wider if $|a| < 1$.
- has an axis of symmetry of $x = -\frac{b}{2a}$.
- has a vertex with an x-coordinate of $-\frac{b}{2a}$.
- has a y-intercept of c. So, the point $(0, c)$ is on the parabola.

$y = ax^2 + bx + c, a > 0$

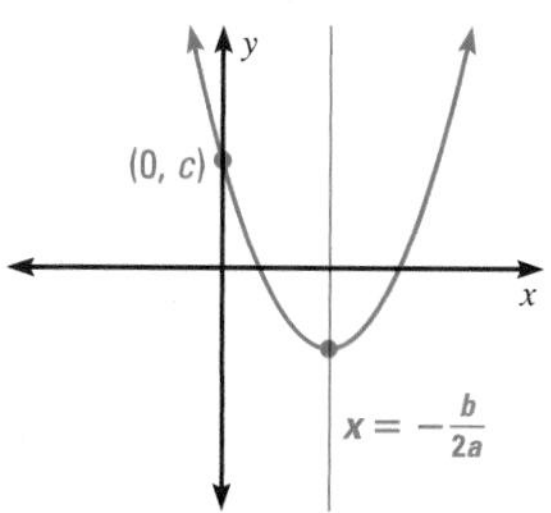

Big Idea 2

Solving Quadratic Equations

You can use the following methods to solve a quadratic equation. Sometimes it is easier to use one method instead of another.

Method	Lesson	When to use
Graphing	10.3	Use when approximate solutions are adequate.
Finding square roots	10.4	Use when solving an equation that can be written in the form $x^2 = d$.
Completing the square	10.5	Can be used for *any* quadratic equation $y = ax^2 + bx + c$ but is simplest to apply when $a = 1$ and b is an even number.
Quadratic formula	10.6	Can be used for *any* quadratic equation

Big Idea 3

Comparing Linear, Exponential, and Quadratic Models

You can use linear, exponential, and quadratic functions to model data.

Function	Example	x- and y-values
Linear	$y = 5x + 1$	If the increments between successive x-values are equal, the differences of successive y-values are all equal.
Exponential	$y = 3(2)^x$	If the increments between successive x-values are equal, the ratios of successive y-values are all equal.
Quadratic	$y = x^2 - 4x + 6$	If the increments between successive x-values are equal, the differences of successive first differences of y-values are all equal.

Additional Resources

The following resources are available to help review the materials in this chapter.

Chapter 10 Resource Book
- Chapter Review Games and Activities, p. 103
- Cumulative Practice, Chs. 1–10, pp. 106–107

Student Resources in Spanish

eWorkbook

@HomeTutor

Vocabulary Practice

Vocabulary practice is available at **classzone.com**

Extra Example 10.1

Graph $y = -x^2 + 1$. Compare the graph with the graph of $y = x^2$.

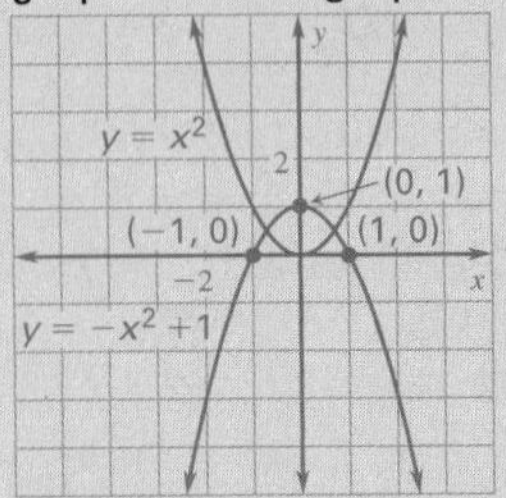

Both graphs have the same line of symmetry, $x = 0$. The graph of $y = -x^2 + 1$ is a reflection in the x-axis of $y = x^2$ and then a vertical translation (of 1 unit up).

5.

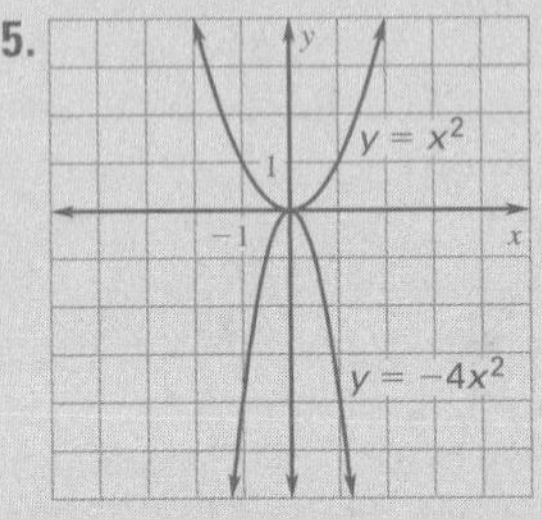

The graph is a vertical stretch (by a factor of 4) with a reflection in the x-axis of the graph of $y = x^2$.

6.

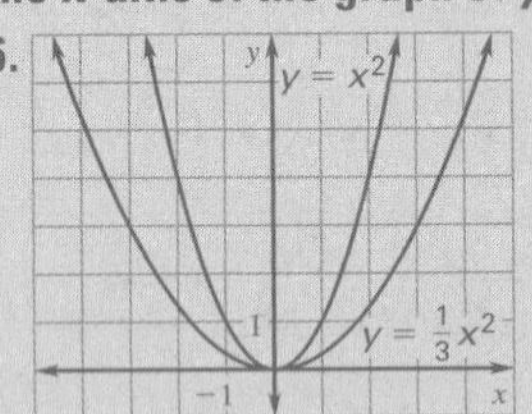

The graph is a vertical shrink $\left(\text{by a factor of } \frac{1}{3}\right)$ of the graph of $y = x^2$.

7.

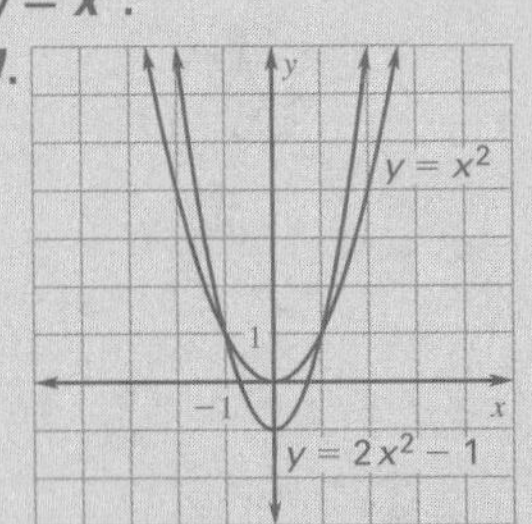

The graph is a vertical stretch (by a factor of 2) with a vertical translation (of 1 unit down) of the graph of $y = x^2$.

10 CHAPTER REVIEW

@HomeTutor
classzone.com
- Multi-Language Glossary
- Vocabulary practice

REVIEW KEY VOCABULARY

- quadratic function, *p. 628*
- standard form of a quadratic function, *p. 628*
- parabola, *p. 628*
- parent quadratic function, *p. 628*
- vertex of a parabola, *p. 628*
- axis of symmetry, *p. 628*
- minimum value, *p. 636*
- maximum value, *p. 636*
- intercept form of a quadratic function, *p. 641*
- quadratic equation, *p. 643*
- standard form of a quadratic equation, *p. 643*
- completing the square, *p. 663*
- vertex form of a quadratic function, *p. 669*
- quadratic formula, *p. 671*
- discriminant, *p. 678*

VOCABULARY EXERCISES

1. Copy and complete: The line that passes through the vertex and divides a parabola into two symmetric parts is called the _?_. **axis of symmetry**

Tell whether the function has a *minimum value* or a *maximum value*.

2. $f(x) = 5x^2 - 4x$ **minimum**
3. $f(x) = -x^2 + 6x + 2$ **maximum**
4. $f(x) = 0.3x^2 - 7.7x + 1.8$ **minimum**

REVIEW EXAMPLES AND EXERCISES

Use the review examples and exercises below to check your understanding of the concepts you have learned in each lesson of Chapter 10.

10.1 Graph $y = ax^2 + c$ *pp. 628–634*

EXAMPLE

Graph $y = -x^2 + 3$. Compare the graph with the graph of $y = x^2$.

Make a table of values for $y = -x^2 + 3$. Then plot the points from the table and draw a smooth curve through the points.

x	−2	−1	0	1	2
y	−1	2	3	2	−1

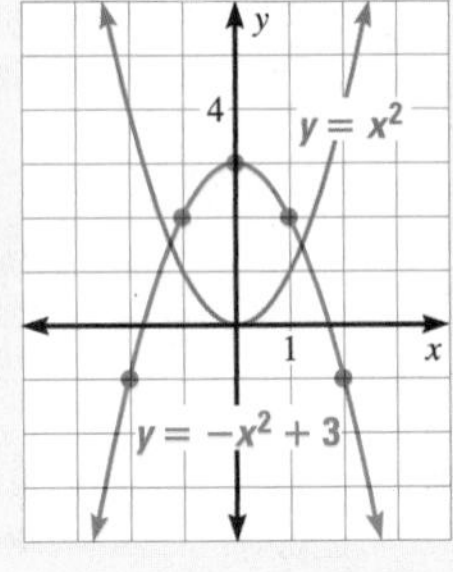

Both graphs have the same axis of symmetry, $x = 0$. However, the graph of $y = -x^2 + 3$ has a different vertex than the graph of $y = x^2$, and it opens down. This is because the graph of $y = -x^2 + 3$ is a vertical translation (of 3 units up) and a reflection in the x-axis of the graph of $y = x^2$.

EXAMPLES 1, 2, and 4 on pp. 628–630 for Exs. 5–7

EXERCISES

Graph the function. Compare the graph with the graph of $y = x^2$. **5–7. See margin.**

5. $y = -4x^2$
6. $y = \frac{1}{3}x^2$
7. $y = 2x^2 - 1$

@HomeTutor
classzone.com
Chapter Review Practice

10.2 Graph $y = ax^2 + bx + c$ *pp. 635–640*

EXAMPLE

Graph $y = -x^2 + 2x + 1$.

STEP 1 **Determine** whether the parabola opens up or down. Because $a < 0$, the parabola opens down.

STEP 2 **Find** and draw the axis of symmetry:

$$x = -\frac{b}{2a} = -\frac{2}{2(-1)} = 1$$

STEP 3 **Find** and plot the vertex. The x-coordinate of the vertex is $-\frac{b}{2a}$, or 1. The y-coordinate of the vertex is $y = -(1)^2 + 2(1) + 1 = 2$.

STEP 4 **Plot** four more points. Evaluating the function for $x = 0$ and $x = -1$ gives the points (0, 1) and (−1, −2). Plot these points and their reflections in the axis of symmetry.

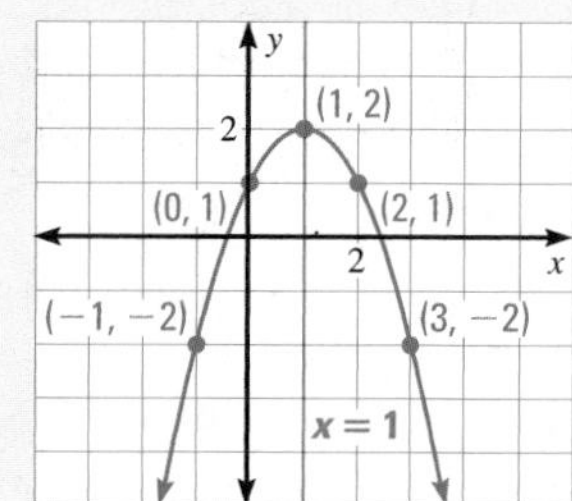

STEP 5 **Draw** a parabola through the plotted points.

EXERCISES

EXAMPLE 2 on p. 636 for Exs. 8–10

Graph the function. Label the vertex and axis of symmetry. 8–10. See margin.

8. $y = x^2 + 4x + 1$ **9.** $y = 2x^2 - 4x - 3$ **10.** $y = -2x^2 + 8x + 5$

10.3 Solve Quadratic Equations by Graphing *pp. 643–649*

EXAMPLE

Solve $x^2 - 7x = -12$ by graphing.

STEP 1 **Write** the equation in standard form.

$x^2 - 7x = -12$ **Write original equation.**

$x^2 - 7x + 12 = 0$ **Add 12 to each side.**

STEP 2 **Graph** the related function $y = x^2 - 7x + 12$. The x-intercepts of the graph are 3 and 4.

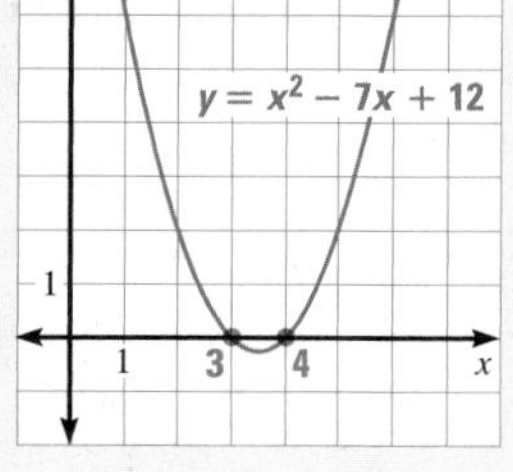

▶ The solutions of the equation $x^2 - 7x + 12 = 0$ are 3 and 4.

EXERCISES

EXAMPLES 1, 2, and 3 on pp. 643–644 for Exs. 11–13

Solve the equation by graphing.

11. $4x^2 + x + 3 = 0$ no solution **12.** $x^2 + 2x = -1$ −1 **13.** $-x^2 + 8 = 7x$ −8, 1

Extra Example 10.2

Graph $y = x^2 + 4x + 4$.

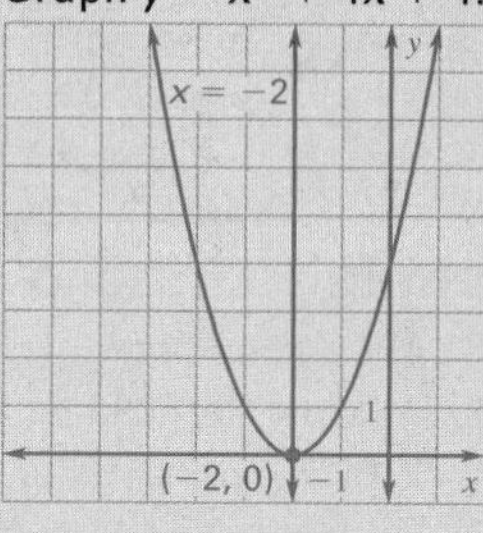

Extra Example 10.3

Solve $x^2 - 5x = -4$ by graphing. **1, 4**

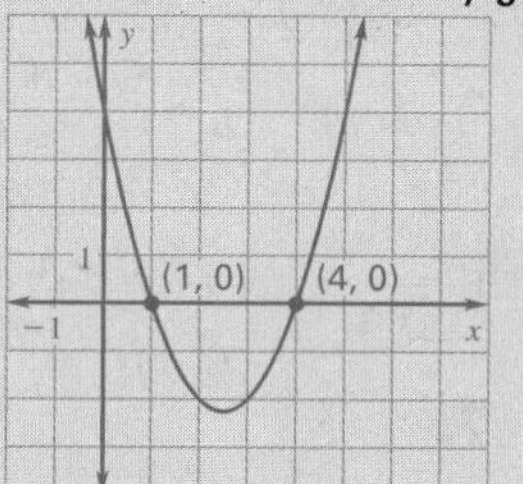

8.

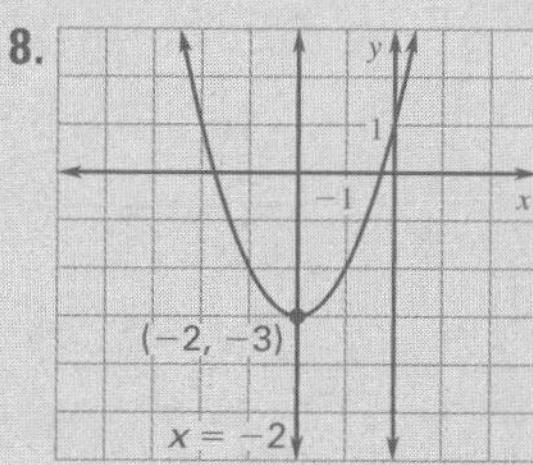

9.

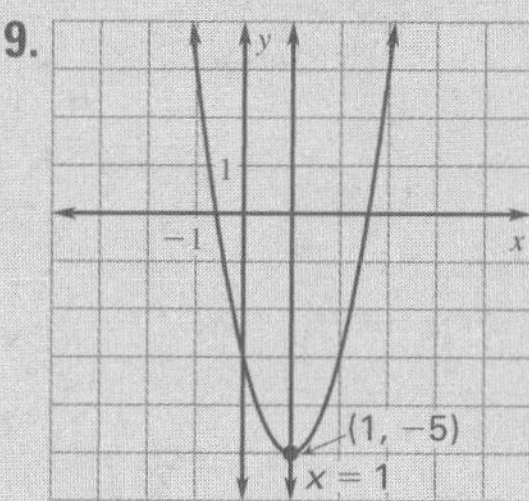

10.

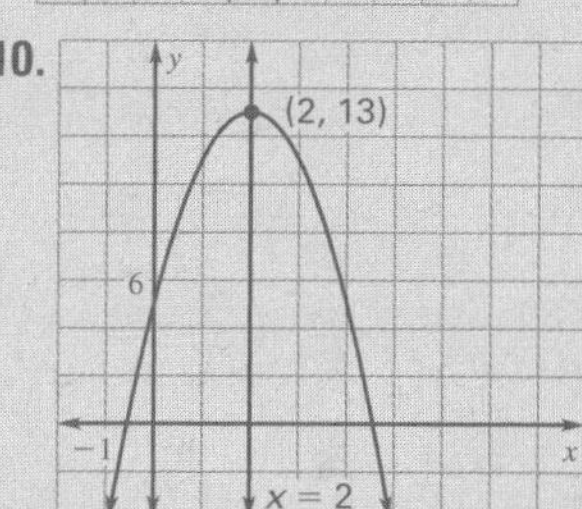

Extra Example 10.4

Solve $2(x-1)^2 = 10$. Round your solutions to the nearest hundredth.

$(x-1)^2 = 5$; $1+\sqrt{5} \approx 3.24$, $1-\sqrt{5} \approx -1.24$

Extra Example 10.5

Solve $2x^2 + 8x = 6$ by completing the square. Round your solutions to the nearest hundredth, if necessary.

$(x+2)^2 = 7$; $-2+\sqrt{7} \approx 0.65$, $-2-\sqrt{7} \approx -4.65$

10 CHAPTER REVIEW

10.4 Use Square Roots to Solve Quadratic Equations

pp. 652–658

EXAMPLE

Solve $5(x-6)^2 = 30$. Round the solutions to the nearest hundredth.

$5(x-6)^2 = 30$	**Write original equation.**
$(x-6)^2 = 6$	**Divide each side by 5.**
$x-6 = \pm\sqrt{6}$	**Take square roots of each side.**
$x = 6 \pm \sqrt{6}$	**Add 6 to each side.**

▸ The solutions of the equation are $6+\sqrt{6} \approx 8.45$ and $6-\sqrt{6} \approx 3.55$.

CHECK To check the solutions, first rewrite the equation so that 0 is on the one side as follows: $5(x-6)^2 - 30 = 0$. Then graph the related function $y = 5(x-6)^2 - 30$. The x-intercepts are about 8.4 and about 3.5. So, each solution checks.

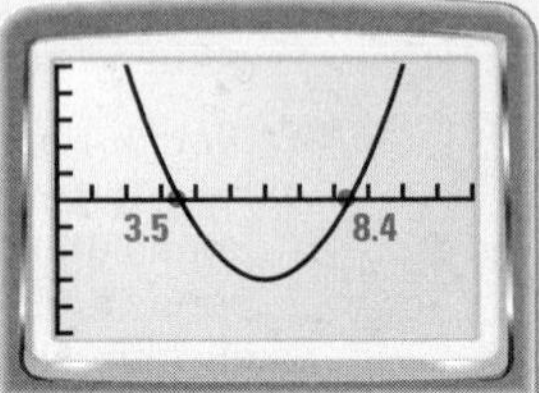

EXERCISES

Solve the equation. Round your solutions to the nearest hundredth, if necessary.

EXAMPLES 1–4 on p. 652–654 for Exs. 14–19

14. $6x^2 - 54 = 0$ ± 3

15. $3x^2 + 7 = 4$ no solution

16. $g^2 + 11 = 24$ ± 3.61

17. $7n^2 + 5 = 9$ ± 0.76

18. $2(a+7)^2 = 34$ $-11.12, -2.88$

19. $3(w-4)^2 = 5$ $2.71, 5.29$

10.5 Solve Quadratic Equations by Completing the Square

pp. 663–668

EXAMPLE

Solve $3x^2 + 12x = 18$ by completing the square.

$3x^2 + 12x = 18$	**Write original equation.**
$x^2 + 4x = 6$	**Divide each side by 3.**
$x^2 + 4x + 2^2 = 6 + 2^2$	**Add $\left(\frac{4}{2}\right)^2$, or 2^2, to each side.**
$(x+2)^2 = 10$	**Write left side as the square of a binomial.**
$x+2 = \pm\sqrt{10}$	**Take square roots of each side.**
$x = -2 \pm \sqrt{10}$	**Subtract 2 from each side.**

▸ The solutions of the equation are $-2+\sqrt{10} \approx 1.16$ and $-2-\sqrt{10} \approx -5.16$.

@HomeTutor
classzone.com
Chapter Review Practice

EXERCISES

EXAMPLES 2 and 3 on p. 664 for Exs. 20–23

Solve the equation by completing the square. Round your solutions to the nearest hundredth, if necessary.

20. $x^2 - 14x = 51$ −3, 17
21. $2a^2 + 12a - 4 = 0$ 0.32, −6.32
22. $2n^2 + 4n + 1 = 10n + 9$ −1, 4
23. $5g^2 - 3g + 6 = 2g^2 + 9$ −0.62, 1.62

Extra Example 10.6

Use the quadratic formula to solve $x^2 + 11x = -30$. $a = 1, b = 11, c = 30; \frac{-11+1}{2} = -5, \frac{-11-1}{2} = -6$

10.6 Solve Quadratic Equations by the Quadratic Formula

pp. 671–676

EXAMPLE

Solve $4x^2 + 3x = 1$.

$4x^2 + 3x = 1$	Write original equation.
$4x^2 + 3x - 1 = 0$	Write in standard form.
$x = \frac{-b \pm \sqrt{b^2 - 4ac}}{2a}$	Quadratic formula
$= \frac{-3 \pm \sqrt{3^2 - 4(4)(-1)}}{2(4)}$	Substitute values in the quadratic formula: $a = 4$, $b = 3$, and $c = -1$.
$= \frac{-3 \pm \sqrt{25}}{8}$	Simplify.
$= \frac{-3 \pm 5}{8}$	Simplify the square root.

▶ The solutions of the equation are $\frac{-3+5}{8} = \frac{1}{4}$ and $\frac{-3-5}{8} = -1$.

CHECK You can check the solutions in the original equation.

If $x = \frac{1}{4}$:	If $x = -1$:
$4x^2 + 3x = 1$	$4x^2 + 3x = 1$
$4\left(\frac{1}{4}\right)^2 + 3\left(\frac{1}{4}\right) \stackrel{?}{=} 1$	$4(-1)^2 + 3(-1) \stackrel{?}{=} 1$
$1 = 1$ ✓	$1 = 1$ ✓

EXERCISES

EXAMPLES 1, 2, and 3 on p. 671–672 for Exs. 24–30

Use the quadratic formula to solve the equation. Round your solutions to the nearest hundredth, if necessary.

24. $x^2 - 2x - 15 = 0$ −3, 5
25. $2m^2 + 7m - 3 = 0$ −3.89, 0.39
26. $-w^2 + 5w = 3$ 0.70, 4.30
27. $5n^2 - 7n = -1$ 0.16, 1.24
28. $t^2 - 4 = 6t + 8$ −1.58, 7.58
29. $2h - 1 = 10 - 9h^2$ −1.22, 1

30. The area A of the rectangle shown is 500 square meters. Find the value of x. Then give the dimensions of the rectangle. 7; 25 m by 20 m

$(2x + 6)$ m

$(4x - 3)$ m

10 CHAPTER REVIEW

Extra Example 10.7

Use the discriminant to find the number of solutions for each equation.

a. $4x^2 + 12x + 9 = 0$ one solution

b. $8x^2 + 2x + 2 = 0$ no solution

c. $x^2 + 5x = 0$ two solutions

Extra Example 10.8

Use differences or ratios to tell whether the table of values represents a *linear function*, an *exponential function*, or a *quadratic function*.

a.

x	−1	0	1	2	3
y	2	6	12	20	30

Second differences are constant; quadratic function.

b.

x	−1	0	1	2	3
y	8	4	2	1	0.5

Ratios of successive y-values are equal; exponential function.

10.7 Interpret the Discriminant
pp. 678–683

EXAMPLE

	Equation $ax^2 + bx + c = 0$	Discriminant $b^2 - 4ac$	Number of solutions
a.	$-16x^2 + 8x - 1 = 0$	$8^2 - 4(-16)(-1) = 0$	One solution
b.	$4x^2 - 5x + 2 = 0$	$(-5)^2 - 4(4)(2) = -7$	No solution
c.	$x^2 + 3x = 0$	$3^2 - 4(1)(0) = 9$	Two solutions

EXERCISES

EXAMPLES 1 and 2 on pp. 678–679 for Exs. 31–36

Tell whether the equation has *two solutions, one solution,* or *no solution.*

31. $x^2 - 2x + 2 = 0$ no solution

32. $4g^2 + 12g + 9 = 0$ one solution

33. $5w^2 - 4w - 1 = 0$ two solutions

34. $\frac{1}{8}v^2 - 6 = 0$ two solutions

35. $n^2 - 3n = 4 - 2n^2$ two solutions

36. $2q^2 + 1 = 3q - 5$ no solution

10.8 Compare Linear, Exponential, and Quadratic Models
pp. 684–691

EXAMPLE

Use differences or ratios to tell whether the table of values represents a *linear function*, an *exponential function*, or a *quadratic function*.

a.

x	−1	0	1	2
y	5	3	1	−1

Differences: −2 −2 −2

▶ The table of values represents a linear function.

b.

x	−1	0	1	2
y	4	5	4	1

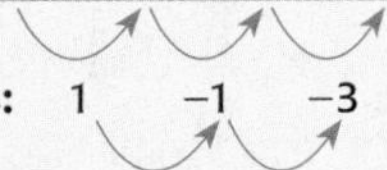

First differences: 1 −1 −3

Second differences: −2 −2

▶ The table of values represents a quadratic function.

EXERCISES

EXAMPLE 2 on pp. 685 for Exs. 37–38

Tell whether the table of values represents a *linear function*, an *exponential function*, or a *quadratic function*.

37.

x	1	2	3	4	5	6
y	1	2	4	8	16	32

exponential function

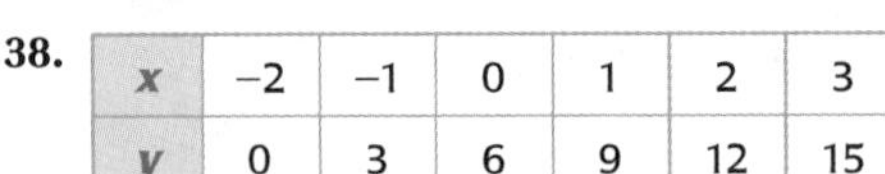

38.

x	−2	−1	0	1	2	3
y	0	3	6	9	12	15

linear function

10 CHAPTER TEST

Match the quadratic function with its graph.

1. $y = x^2 - 2$ C
2. $y = x^2 + 2$ A
3. $y = -2x^2$ B

A. 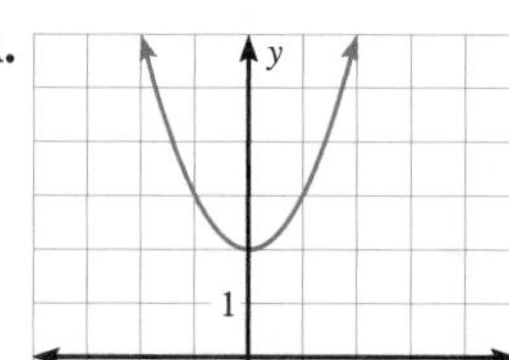

B. 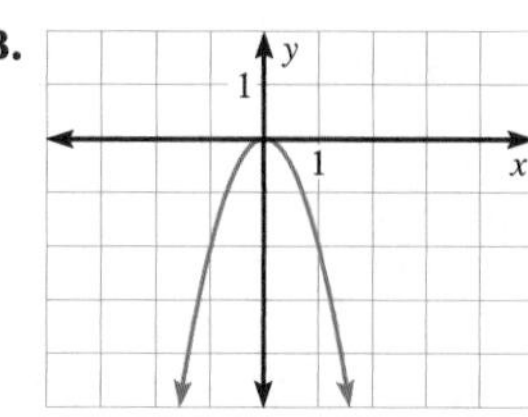

C. 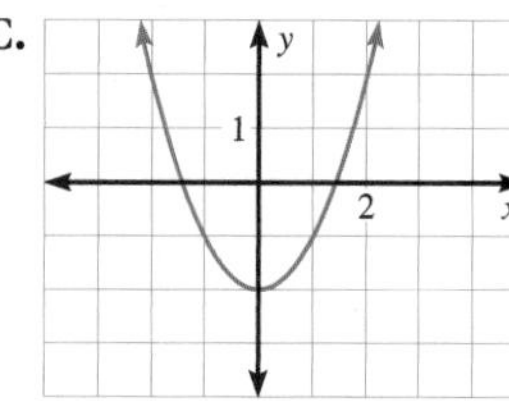

Graph the function. Label the vertex and axis of symmetry. 4–6. See margin.

4. $y = 2x^2 + 6x - 5$
5. $y = -4x^2 - 8x + 25$
6. $y = \frac{1}{4}x^2 - x - 7$

Approximate the zeros of the function to the nearest tenth.

7. $f(x) = x^2 + 5x + 1$ $-4.8, -0.2$
8. $f(x) = x^2 - 8x + 3$ 0.4, 7.6
9. $f(x) = -3x^2 - 2x + 5$ $-1.7, 1$

Solve the equation. Round your solutions to the nearest hundredth, if necessary.

10. $3x^2 = 108$ ± 6
11. $-5w^2 + 51 = 6$ ± 3
12. $-p^2 + 2p + 3 = 0$ $-1, 3$
13. $-2t^2 + 6t + 9 = 0$ $-1.10, 4.10$
14. $5m^2 - m = 5$ $-0.90, 1.10$
15. $2x^2 - 12x - 1 = -7x + 6$ $-1, 3.5$

Tell whether the equation has *two solutions, one solution,* or *no solution.*

16. $3x^2 - 4x + 9 = 0$ no solution
17. $4g^2 - 12g + 11 = 0$ no solution
18. $-2n^2 + 7n - 1 = 0$ two solutions
19. $-m^2 - 17m = 0$ two solutions
20. $-6x^2 - x - 5 = 0$ no solution
21. $10x^2 - 13 = 0$ two solutions

Tell whether the table of values represents a *linear function,* an *exponential function,* or a *quadratic function.* Then write an equation for the function.

22.

x	−3	−2	−1	0	1	2
y	18	8	2	0	2	8

quadratic function; $y = 2x^2$

23.

x	−4	0	4	8	12	16
y	1	2	3	4	5	6

linear function; $y = \frac{1}{4}x + 2$

24. **TENNIS** You are playing tennis with a friend. The path of the tennis ball after you hit the ball can be modeled by the graph of the equation $y = -0.005x^2 + 0.17x + 3$ where x is the horizontal distance (in feet) from where you hit the ball and y is the height of the ball (in feet) above the court.

    a. What is the maximum height reached by the tennis ball? Round your answer to the nearest tenth of a foot. 4.4 ft

    b. Suppose you are standing 30 feet from the net, which has a height of 3 feet. Will the ball clear the net? *Explain* your reasoning. See margin.

    c. If your friend does not hit the ball back to you, how far from you does the ball strike the ground? about 47 ft

Additional Resources

Assessment Book

- Chapter Test, Levels A, B, C, pp. 142–147
- Standardized Chapter Test, pp. 148–149
- SAT/ACT Chapter Test, pp. 150–151
- Alternative Assessment, pp. 152–153

Test Generator CD-ROM

Chapter Test

Easily-readable reduced copies (with answers) of Chapter Test B, the Standardized Chapter Test, and the Alternative Assessment from the Assessment Book can be found on pp. 626G–626H.

4. 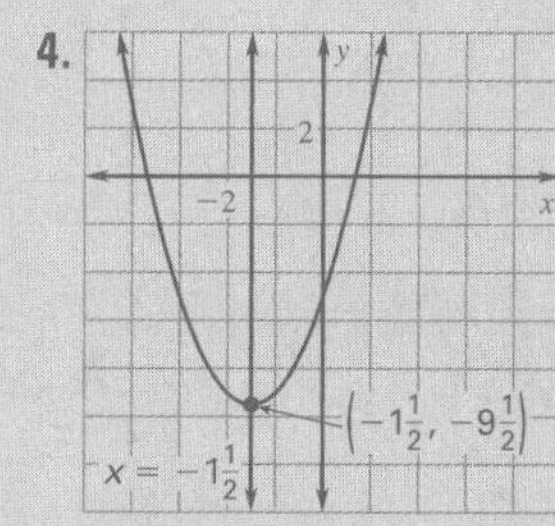

5. 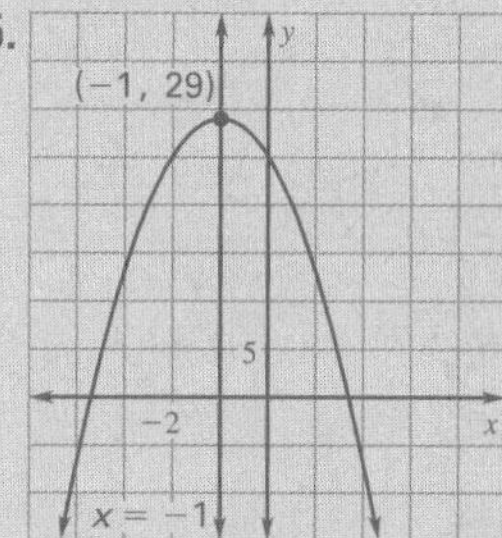

6. 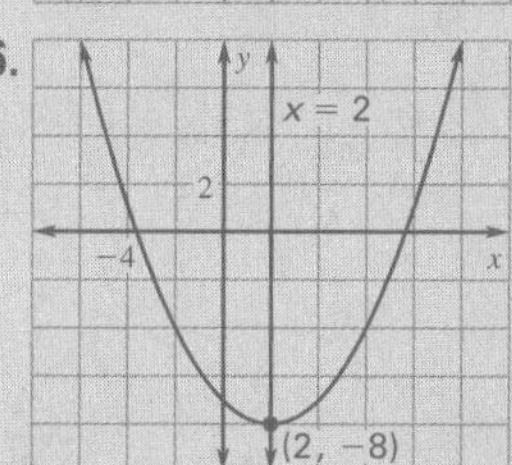

24b. Yes; to find the height of the ball 30 feet from where you hit it, evaluate y when x is 30: $y = -0.005(30)^2 + 0.17(30) + 3 = 3.6$ feet. The height of the ball is greater than the height of the net, so the ball will go over the net.

MULTIPLE CHOICE QUESTIONS

Some of the information you need to solve a multiple choice question may appear in a table, a diagram, or a graph.

PROBLEM 1

A model rocket is launched. Its height above the ground is given by the equation $h = -16t^2 + 48t + 4$, where h is the height in feet and t is the time in seconds after the launch. The graph of the equation is shown at right. What is the maximum height of the rocket and when does it occur?

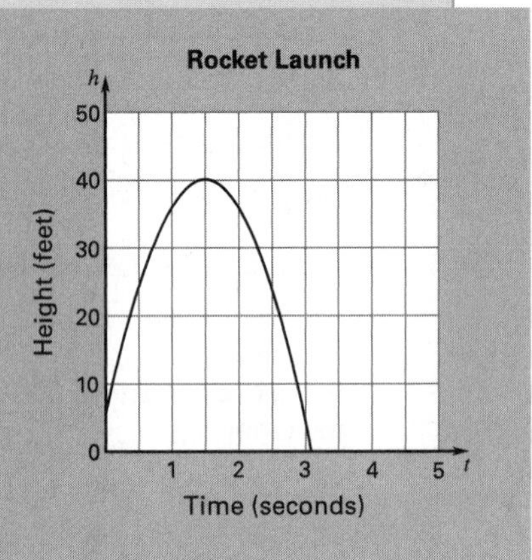

A. maximum height is 50 feet at 1.5 seconds

B. maximum height is 40 feet at 1.5 seconds

C. maximum height is 1.5 feet at 50 seconds

D. maximum height is 1.5 feet at 40 seconds

Plan

INTERPRET THE GRAPH Locate the vertex. The first coordinate represents the time and the second coordinate represents the height

Solution

STEP 1 Find the vertex of the graph.

Locate the highest point on the graph, where the height h is at its maximum. The point is (1.5, 40).

STEP 2 Explain the meaning of the vertex.

The maximum height is 40 feet. It occurs 1.5 seconds after the launch.

The correct answer is **B**.

PROBLEM 2

Veronica makes a model suspension bridge for a science project. The equation $h = 0.05(d - 11)^2 + 1$ models the position of the suspension cable, where h is the height above the "road" in inches, and d is the distance from the first "tower" in inches. What is the height of the lowest point of the cable?

F. 0 **H.** 7

G. 1 **J.** 11

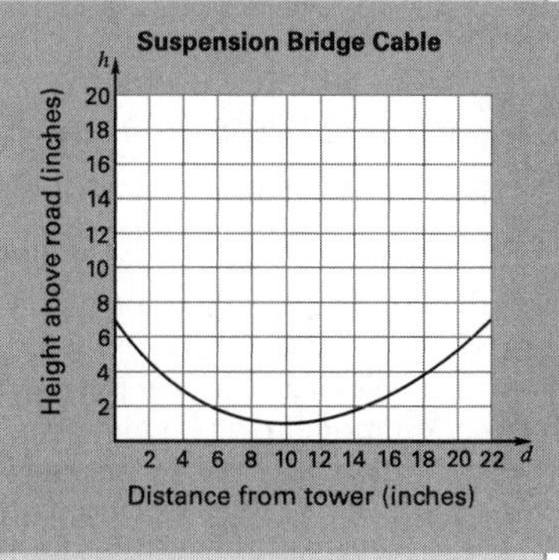

Plan

INTERPRET THE INFORMATION Locate the vertex of the graph. Then find the coordinates.

Solution

STEP 1 Find the vertex of the graph.

Locate the lowest point on the graph where height h is at its minimum. The point is (11, 1).

STEP 2 Explain the meaning of the vertex.

The first coordinate, 11, represents the distance from the tower. The second coordinate, 1, represents the height of the cable above the road.

The correct answer is **G**.

PRACTICE

The path of a bouncing table tennis ball between its first and second bounce is given by the equation $y = -0.5x^2 + 6x$, where y is the height and x is the horizontal distance in inches.

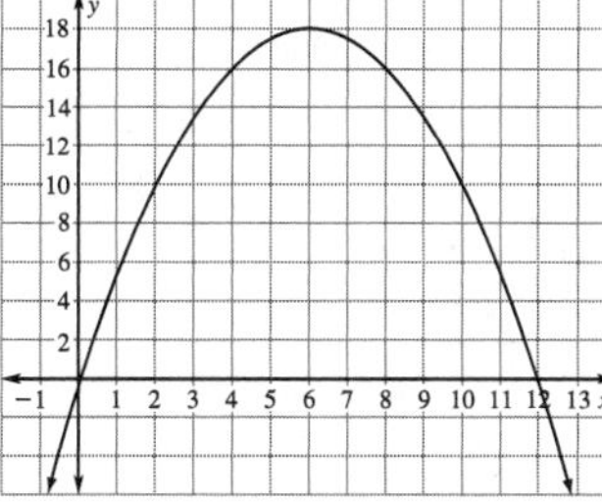

1. What is the horizontal distance when the ball reaches its maximum height?

   A. 6 inches **C.** 12 inches

   B. 8 inches **D.** 18 inches

TEST PREPARATION

Illinois Test Practice

1. A

Illinois Test Practice

1. D
2. J
3. C
4. J
5. B
6. H
7. C
8. H
9. B
10. H
11. C
12. F
13. C
14. F
15. A
16. J
17. C
18. J
19. B

Illinois Test Practice

1. How would the graph of the function $y = 3x^2 + 6$ be affected if the function were changed to $y = 3x^2 - 1$?
   A. The graph would shift 5 units up.
   B. The graph would shift 5 units down.
   C. The graph would shift 7 units up.
   D. The graph would shift 7 units down.

2. A volleyball player serves the ball from a height of 6.5 feet above the ground with an initial vertical velocity of 21 feet per second. Which function models the height h (in feet) of the ball in t seconds after it is served?
   F. $h = -21t - t^2 + 6.5$
   G. $h = -16t^2 + 6.5$
   H. $h = 16t^2 + 21t + 6.5$
   J. $h = 6.5 + 21t - 16t^2$

3. A house painter charges a fixed rate for each square meter painted. Which graph best represents the relationship between the amount the painter charges and the area painted?
   A.
   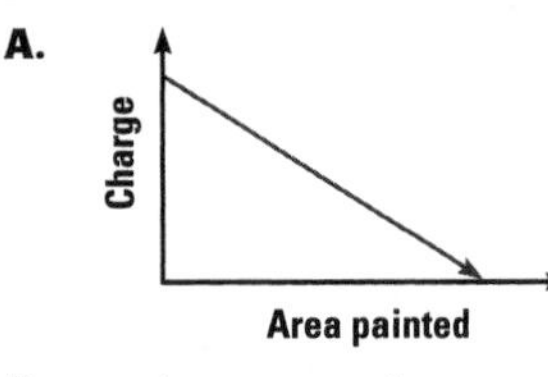

   B.
   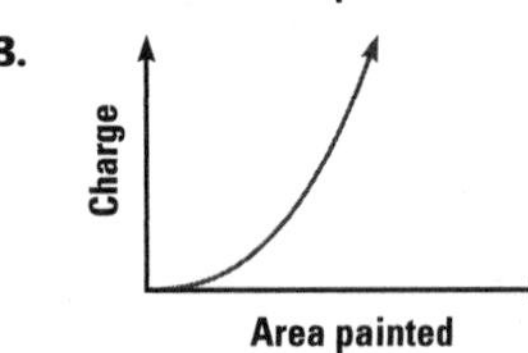

   C.
   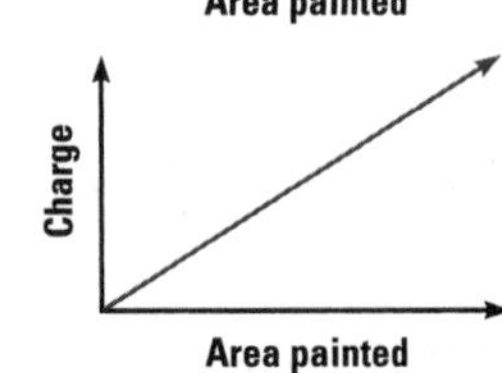

   D.
   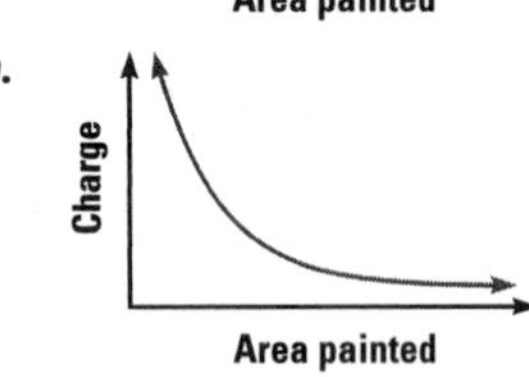

4. How would the graph of the function $y = 2x^2 - 6$ be affected if it were changed to $y = 2x^2 - 1$?
   F. The graph would shift 5 units down.
   G. The graph would shift 6 units to the right.
   H. The graph would shift 6 units to the left.
   J. The graph would shift 5 units up.

5. Which is the best representation of the function $y = x^2$?
   A.
   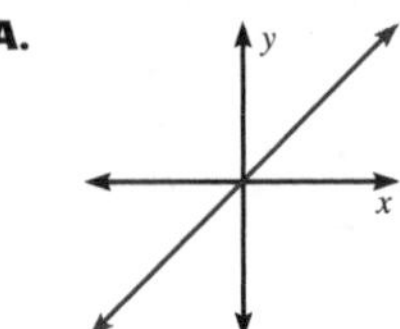

   B.
   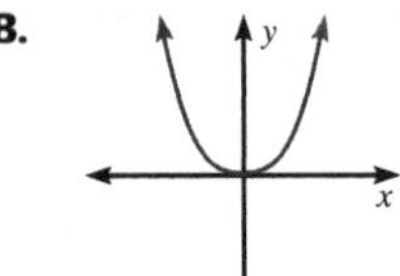

   C.
   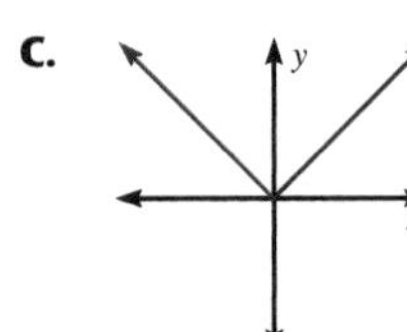

   D.
   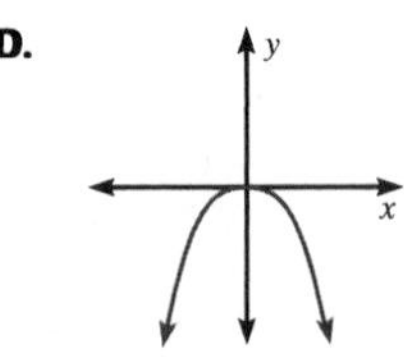

6. Which of the following is *not* a quadratic function?
   F. $y = 3x^2 - 4x + 19$
   G. $y = -7x(x + 2) + 3$
   H. $y = 5x - 21$
   J. $y = -2x^2 - 4x + 9$

7. A rock is released from a height of 676 feet above the ground. In how manyseconds, t, will the rock hit the ground? $(h = -16t^2 + s)$

A. 1.6 seconds **C.** 6.5 seconds

B. 3.3 seconds **D.** 21.1 seconds

8. What is the x-coordinate of the vertex of the graph of the equation below?

$y = -3x^2 + 12x + 19$

F. −3 **H.** 2

G. −2 **J.** 3

9. What are the solutions of the equation $2x^2 + 3x - 9 = 0$?

A. $-\frac{3}{2}$ and 3 **C.** −3 and 3

B. −3 and $\frac{3}{2}$ **D.** 0 and 9

10. What is the discriminant of the equation $5x^2 - 20x + 16 = 0$?

F. −80 **H.** 80

G. −60 **J.** 720

11. Which is a solution to the equation $(x - 1)^2 = 5$?

A. 6 **C.** $1 + \sqrt{5}$

B. 36 **D.** $-1 + \sqrt{5}$

12. Which of the following is a zero of the function $f(x) = \frac{7}{4}x^2 - 28$?

F. −4 **H.** 28

G. −1 **J.** 49

13. Paula correctly solves the equation $x^2 + 2x + 1 = 25$ by completing the square. Which of the following shows her first step?

A. $x^2 + 2x - 24 = 0$

B. $x(x + 2) = 24$

C. $(x + 1)^2 = 25$

D. $(x + 2)^2 = 25$

14. Craig wants to solve the equation $2x^2 - x + 6 = 0$ using the quadratic formula. Which shows the correct use of the quadratic formula?

F. $x = \frac{-(-1) \pm \sqrt{(-1)^2 - 4(2)(6)}}{2(2)}$

G. $x = \frac{-(1) \pm \sqrt{(1)^2 - 4(2)(6)}}{2(2)}$

H. $x = \frac{-(2) \pm \sqrt{(2)^2 - 4(-1)(6)}}{2(-1)}$

J. $x = \frac{-(6) \pm \sqrt{(6)^2 - 4(2)(-1)}}{2(2)}$

15. What is the y-coordinate of the vertex of the graph of the equation below?
$y = 4x^2 + 8x - 3$

A. −7 **C.** 57

B. 9 **D.** 137

16. Which quadratic function contains the point (−1, 2)?

F. $y = -2x^2 + 1$ **H.** $y = x^2 - 2x + 4$

G. $y = -2x^2 + 11x$ **J.** $y = x^2 - 2x - 1$

17. A quadratic function has discriminant $D = 3$. How many x-intercepts does the graph have?

A. 0 **B.** 1 **C.** 2 **D.** 3

18. What is the value of c that makes $x^2 + 6x + c$ a perfect square trinomial?

F. 3 **G.** 6 **H.** 8 **J.** 9

19. Which table of values represents an *exponential function?*

A.

x	0	1	2	3
y	6	4	2	0

B.

x	0	1	2	3
y	−1	0	3	8

C.

x	−1	0	1	2
y	16	8	4	2

D.

x	−1	0	1	2
y	5	4	5	6

TEST PRACTICE

CUMULATIVE REVIEW Chapters 1–10

Additional Resources

The following resources are available to help review the materials in Chapters 1–10.

Chapter Resource Books

- Chapter 8 CRB, Cumulative Review, pp. 80–81
- Chapter 9 CRB, Cumulative Review, pp. 95–96
- Chapter 10 CRB, Cumulative Review, pp. 106–107

7. 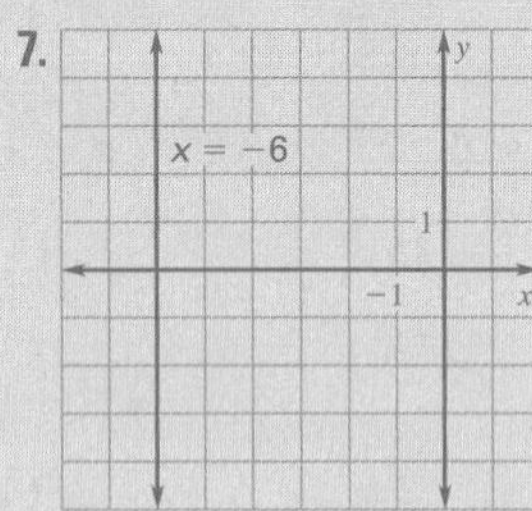

8. 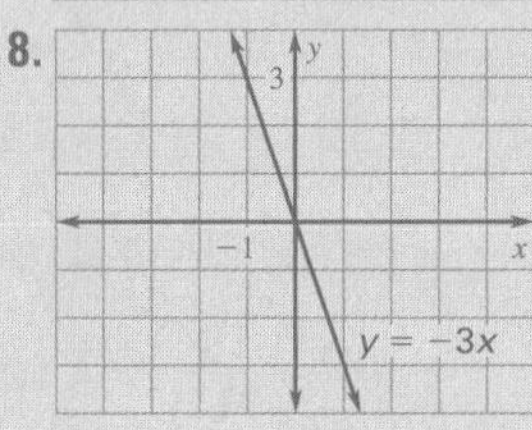

9. 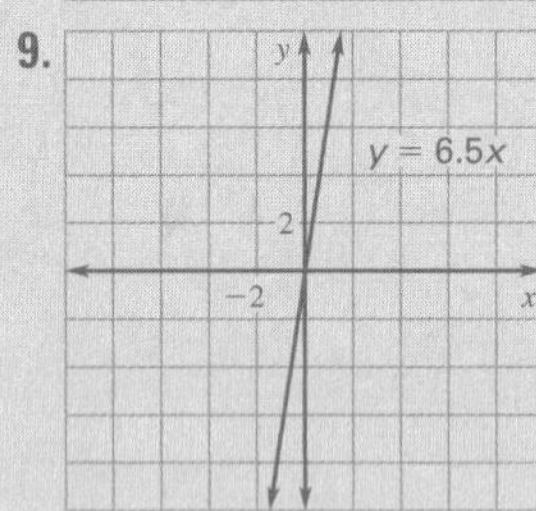

10. 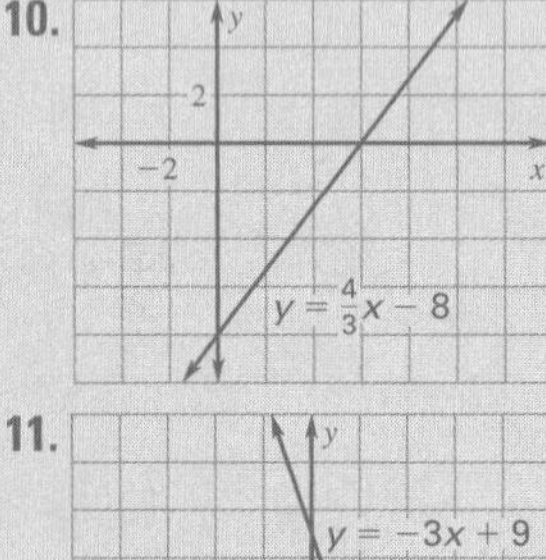

11. 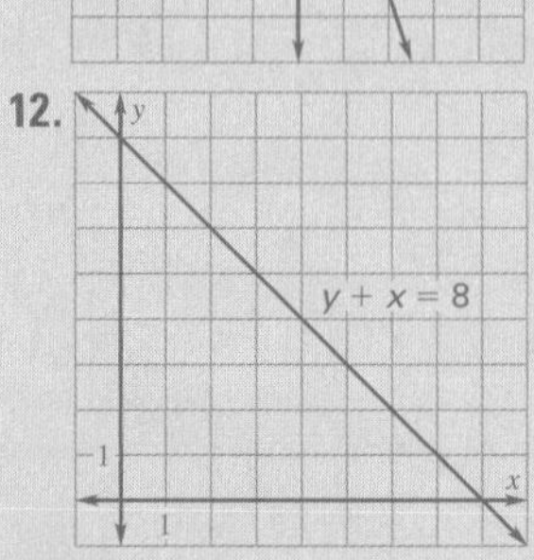

12. y + x = 8

13. 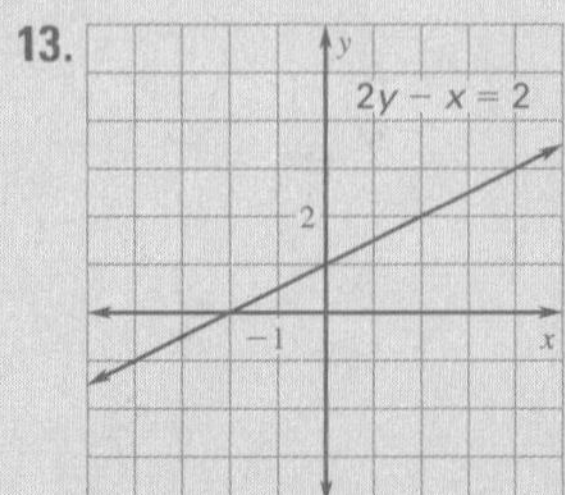

14. 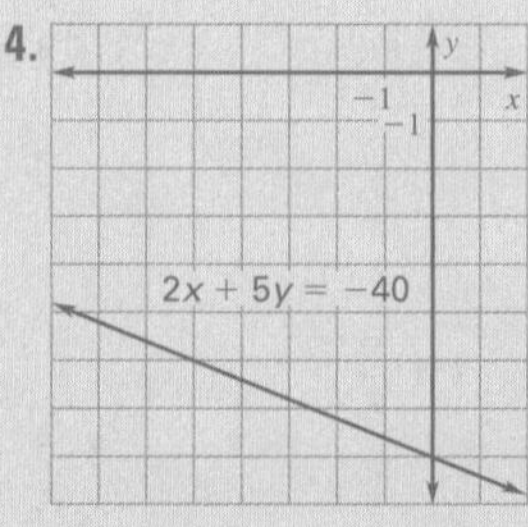

18–23. See Additional Answers beginning on p. AA1.

Evaluate the expression for the given value of *x*. *(p. 64)*

1. $-|x| + 9$ when $x = -6$ 3
2. $|-x| + 2.6$ when $x = 2$ 4.6
3. $0.7 - |x|$ when $x = -0.5$ 0.2

Solve the equation.

4. $5 - 2a = 13$ *(p. 141)* −4
5. $13y + 16 - y = 4$ *(p. 148)* −1
6. $-(w + 1) = w + 3$ *(p. 154)* −2

Graph the equation. *(pp. 215, 225, 244, 253)* 7–14. See margin.

7. $x = -6$
8. $y = -3x$
9. $y = 6.5x$
10. $y = \frac{4}{3}x - 8$
11. $y = -3x + 9$
12. $y + x = 8$
13. $2y - x = 2$
14. $2x + 5y = -40$

Write an equation of the line that passes through the given point and is perpendicular to the given line. *(p. 319)*

15. $(0, 3)$, $y = -5x + 2$ $y = \frac{1}{5}x + 3$
16. $(2, 2)$, $y = -x - 7$ $y = x$
17. $(8, 3)$, $y = \frac{1}{2}x + 2$ $y = -2x + 19$

Solve the inequality. Then graph the solution. 18–23. See margin for art.

18. $m - 8 < -15$ *(p. 356)* $m < -7$
19. $\frac{x}{-3} > 12$ *(p. 363)* $x < -36$
20. $1 - 4n < -11$ *(p. 369)* $n > 3$
21. $5b - 7 \le 7b - 5$ *(p. 369)* $b \ge -1$
22. $12 < z + 9 \le 16$ *(p. 380)* $3 < z \le 7$
23. $4 \le 2c + 7 \le 21$ *(p. 380)* $-\frac{3}{2} \le c \le 7$

Solve the linear system. *(pp. 427, 435, 444, 451, 459)*

24. $y = 5x - 4$, $-4x + y = -2$ (2, 6)
25. $x - 4y = -44$, $-3x + 12y = 132$ all real numbers
26. $-4x + 7y = -33$, $-3x + 2y = -15$ (3, −3)

Simplify the expression.

27. $(-9r)^3$ *(p. 489)* $-729r^3$
28. $(2p^4)^3 \cdot p^7$ *(p. 489)* $8p^{19}$
29. $\frac{(3x)^4y}{xy^3}$ *(p. 495)* $\frac{81x^3}{y^2}$

Graph the function. 30–32. See margin.

30. $y = (2.5)^x$ *(p. 520)*
31. $y = (0.8)^x$ *(p. 531)*
32. $y = \frac{1}{2} \cdot \left(\frac{1}{4}\right)^x$ *(p. 531)*

Find the sum or difference. *(p. 554)*

33. $(x^2 - 3x + 8) + (-2x^2 + 15x + 4)$ $-x^2 + 12x + 12$
34. $(5m^2 - 6) - (8m^3 + m^2 - 2m + 11)$ $-8m^3 + 4m^2 + 2m - 17$

Find the product.

35. $(z + 9)(2z - 7)$ *(p. 562)* $2z^2 + 11z - 63$
36. $(5b - 2)(8b - 7)$ *(p. 562)* $40b^2 - 51b + 14$
37. $(q + 2)(-3q^2 + 6q - 1)$ *(p. 562)* $-3q^3 + 11q - 2$
38. $(7 + y)^2$ *(p. 569)* $49 + 14y + y^2$
39. $(2k - 11)^2$ *(p. 569)* $4k^2 - 44k + 121$
40. $(12w - 5)(12w + 5)$ *(p. 569)* $144w^2 - 25$

Factor the expression.

41. $x^2 + 6x - 72$ *(p. 583)* $(x + 12)(x - 6)$
42. $2m^2 - 5mn - 3n^2$ *(p. 593)* $(2m + n)(m - 3n)$
43. $25d^2 + 60d + 36$ *(p. 600)* $(5d + 6)^2$
44. $-2a^2 + 50b^2$ *(p. 600)* $-2(a + 5b)(a - 5b)$
45. $z^2(z - 6) + 4(6 - z)$ *(p. 606)* $(z - 6)(z + 2)(z - 2)$
46. $y^3 + 8y^2 - 9y - 72$ *(p. 606)* $(y + 8)(y + 3)(y - 3)$

Graph the function. Label the vertex and axis of symmetry. ***(p. 635)*** 47–49. See margin.

47. $y = x^2 - 4x + 1$ **48.** $y = 3x^2 + 6x + 4$ **49.** $y = -x^2 - 4x + 10$

Solve the equation. Round your solutions to the nearest hundredth, if necessary. ***(pp. 643, 652, 663, 671)***

50. $5x^2 = 720$ ±12

51. $-x^2 + 12 = 1$ ±3.32

52. $x^2 + 6x - 13 = 0$ −7.69, 1.69

53. $-2x^2 + 7x - 3 = 0$ 0.5, 3

54. $4x^2 - 9x = 9$ −0.75, 3

55. $-7x^2 + 7x + 3 = 4x - 1$ −0.57, 1

56. SPORTS The Pan American Games is a sports event that is held every four years. Athletes from countries in North America, Central America, and South America compete in the games. The table shows the number c of countries that participated in each Pan American Games as a function of the time t (in years) since 1951. Graph the function. ***(p. 43)*** See margin.

Years since 1951, *t*	0	4	8	12	16	20	24	28	32
Countries, *c*	21	22	25	22	29	32	33	34	36

57. INCOME A salesperson earns a 5% commission on the sales of computers. If the salesperson's computer sales total \$9500, how much is the commission? ***(p. 176)*** \$475

58. CUSTOM PRINTING You create a design for a T-shirt. The table shows the cost for printing your design on T-shirts at a printing company. The printing company requires that your design be printed on a minimum of 6 T-shirts. ***(p. 302)***

T-shirts	6	7	8	9	10
Cost (dollars)	78	81	84	87	90

a. *Explain* why the situation can be modeled by a linear equation. See margin.

b. Write an equation in point-slope form that gives the cost of the T-shirts as a function of the number of T-shirts printed. *Sample answer:* $y - 78 = 3(x - 6)$

59. GEOMETRY A rectangle has a perimeter of 54 inches. Its length is 3 more than twice its width. Find the dimensions of the rectangle. ***(p. 435)*** length 19 in., width: 8 in.

60. SCHOOL ENROLLMENT In 1990, 5000 students were enrolled at a school. The number of students enrolled at the school increased by about 2% per year from 1990 to 2005. Write a model for the number of students enrolled at the school over time. According to the model, how many students were enrolled at the school in 2005? ***(p. 520)*** $y = 5000(1.02)^x$; about 6730 students

61. LANDSCAPING An arc of water sprayed from a lawn sprinkler can be modeled by the graph of the equation $y = -0.05x^2 + 0.9x$ where x is the distance (in feet) from the sprinkler and y is the height (in feet) of the arc.

a. Graph the function. Label the vertex and axis of symmetry. ***(p. 635)*** See margin.

b. How far from the sprinkler does the water hit the ground? ***(p. 643)*** 18 ft

47.

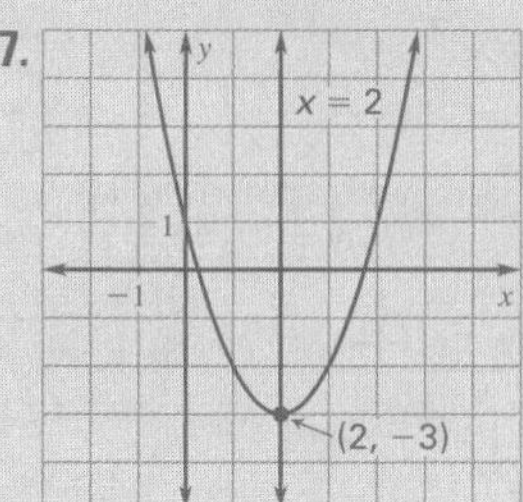

48.

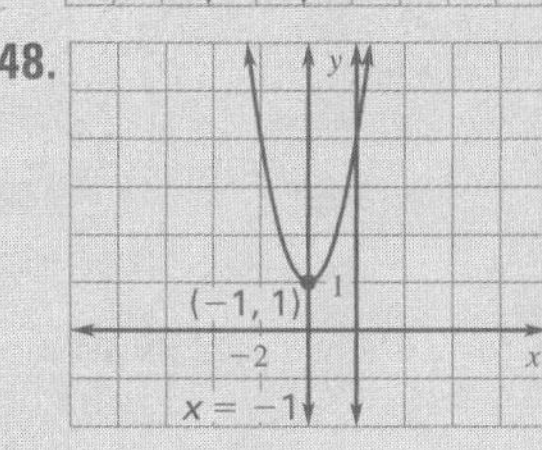

49.

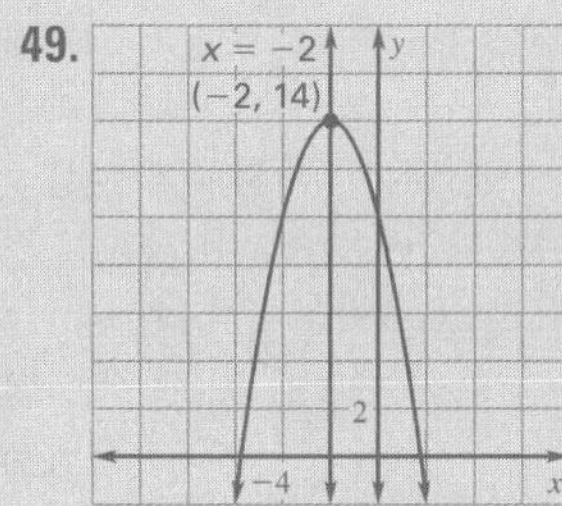

56.

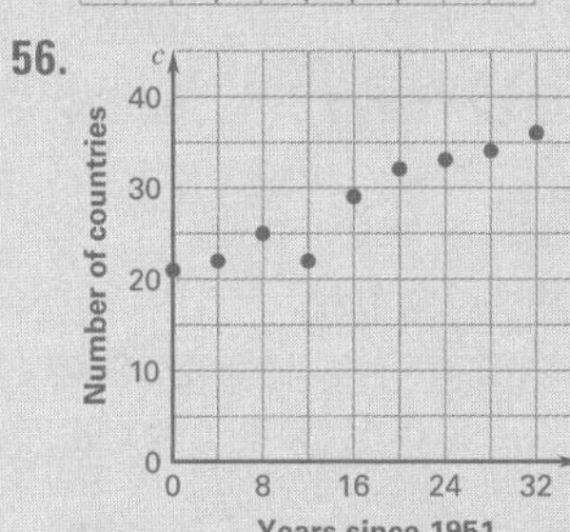

58a. Each time the number of T-shirts increases by 1, the cost increases by \$3, so the rate of change is \$3 per T-shirt.

61a.

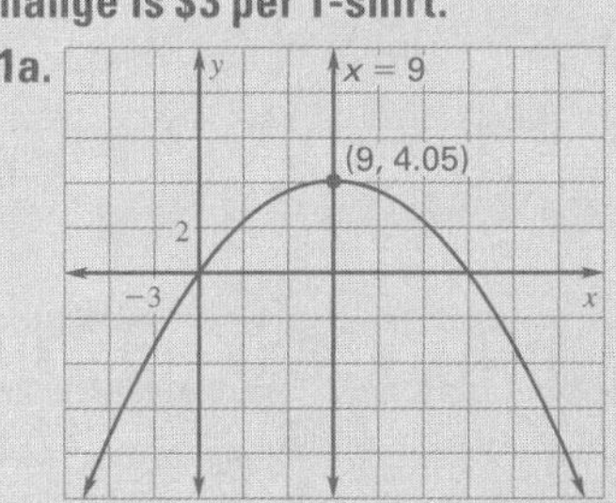

30.

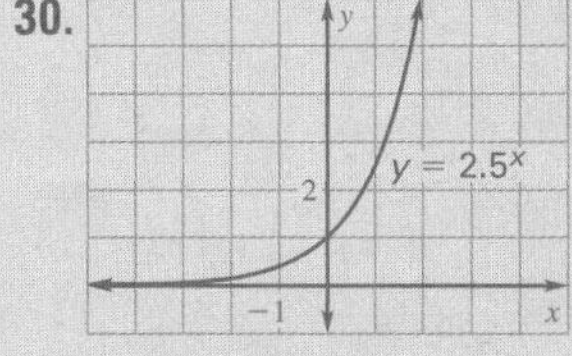

31.

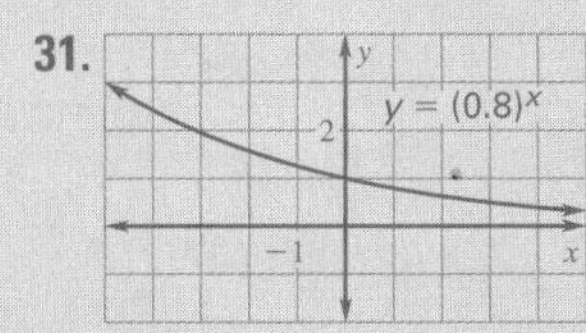

32.

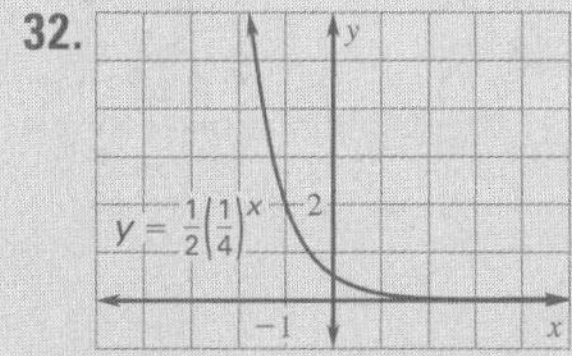

Illinois Resources Guide

Pacing and Assignment Guide

REGULAR SCHEDULE

Pre-AP For pacing and assignments for a Pre-AP course, see the *Algebra 1 Toolkit.*

Lesson	Les. Day	BASIC	AVERAGE	ADVANCED
11.1 8.11.08	Day 1	EP p. 947 Exs. 1–7 odd; pp. 713–716 Exs. 1–22	pp. 713–716 Exs. 1, 2, 5–22, 41	pp. 713–716 Exs. 1, 2, 6–22, 41, 42*
	Day 2	pp. 713–716 Exs. 23–34, 43–46, 50–66 even	pp. 713–716 Exs. 25–40, 43–47, 51–67 odd	pp. 713–716 Exs. 26–40, 43–49*, 50–66 even
11.2 8.11.01	Day 1	EP p. 946 Exs. 7–12; pp. 723–726 Exs. 1–25	pp. 723–726 Exs. 1, 2, 4–22 even, 23–32, 55–58	pp. 723–726 Exs. 1, 15–23, 25–33, 55–62
	Day 2	pp. 723–726 Exs. 26–50 even, 67–70, 73–93 odd	pp. 723–726 Exs. 35–53 odd, 59–63, 67–71, 74, 77, 80, 82, 84, 87, 90, 93	pp. 723–726 Exs. 34–54 even, 59–72*, 78, 81, 88, 94
11.3 8.11.19	Day 1	EP p. 946 Exs. 19–24; pp. 732–734 Exs. 1–21	pp. 732–734 Exs. 1, 2, 5–21, 31, 32	pp. 732–734 Exs. 1, 6–21, 31–34
	Day 2	pp. 732–734 Exs. 22–26, 36–39, 42–49	pp. 732–734 Exs. 22–30, 36–40, 42–48 even	pp. 732–734 Exs. 22–30, 35–41*, 43–47 odd
11.4 9.11.01	Day 1	pp. 740–742 Exs. 1, 2, 3–15 odd, 16–30, 33–36, 39–49 odd	pp. 740–742 Exs. 1, 2, 9–22, 26–31, 33–37, 40–50 even	pp. 740–742 Exs. 1, 10–15, 17–22, 26–32*, 34–38*, 44–46, 48, 50
11.5 9.11.09	Day 1	pp. 747–750 Exs. 1, 2, 3–33 odd, 34–38, 47–50, 53–63 odd	pp. 747–750 Exs. 1, 2, 10–15, 19–21, 30–44, 48–51, 54–64 even	pp. 747–750 Exs. 1, 11–15, 20, 21, 31–46*, 49–52*, 56, 58, 62, 64
Review	Day 1	pp. 754–756 Exs. 1–36	pp. 754–756 Exs. 1–36	pp. 754–756 Exs. 1–36
Assess	Day 1	Chapter 11 Test	Chapter 11 Test	Chapter 11 Test
Yearly Pacing		Chapter 11 Total – 10 days	Chapters 1–11 Total – 132 days	Remaining – 28 days

*Challenge Exercises EP = Extra Practice SRH = Skills Review Handbook

BLOCK SCHEDULE

DAY 1	DAY 2	DAY 3	DAY 4	DAY 5
11.1	11.2	11.3	11.4	Review
pp. 713–716 Exs. 1, 2, 5–22, 25–41, 43–47, 51–67 odd	pp. 723–726 Exs. 1, 2, 4–22 even, 23–32, 35–53 odd, 55–63, 67–71, 74, 77, 80, 82, 84, 87, 90, 93	pp. 732–734 Exs. 1, 2, 5–32, 36–40, 42–48 even	pp. 740–742 Exs. 1, 2, 9–22, 26–31, 33–37, 40–50 even	pp. 754–756 Exs. 1–36
			11.5	Assess
			pp. 747–750 Exs. 1, 2, 10–15, 19–21, 30–44, 48–51, 54–64 even	Chapter 11 Test
Yearly Pacing	Chapter 11 Total – 5 days	Chapters 1–11 Total – 66 days	Remaining – 14 days	

Chapter Resource Guide

Chapter Resource Book					
CHAPTER SUPPORT					
Parents as Partners (Chapter Overview with home involvement exercises and activity)					p. 1
LESSON SUPPORT Standard	**11.1** 8.11.08	**11.2** 8.11.01	**11.3** 8.11.19	**11.4** 9.11.01	**11.5** 9.11.09
Teaching Guide/Lesson Plan	p. 3	p. 18	p. 29	p. 42	p. 52
Activity Masters	p. 5				
Technology Activities & Keystrokes	p. 6		p. 31		
Activity Support Masters		p. 20			
Practice (3 levels)	p. 7	p. 21	p. 33	p. 44	p. 54
Study Guide	p. 13	p. 24	p. 36	p. 47	p. 57
Catch-Up for Absent Students	p. 15	p. 26	p. 38	p. 49	p. 59
Problem Solving/Application	p. 16	p. 27	p. 39	p. 50	p. 60
Challenge Practice	p. 17	p. 28	p. 41	p. 51	p. 61
REVIEW					
Chapter Review Games and Activities		p. 62	Cumulative Practice		p. 65
Project with Rubric		p. 63	Resource Book Answers		A1

Transparencies	11.1	11.2	11.3	11.4	11.5
Warm-Up/Daily Homework Quiz	✔	✔	✔	✔	✔
Notetaking Guide	✔	✔	✔	✔	✔
Teacher Support	✔				
Answer Transparencies	✔	✔	✔	✔	✔

ASSESSMENT BOOK

Quizzes	p. 154	SAT/ACT Chapter Test	p. 164
Chapter Tests (3 levels)	p. 156	Alternative Assessment with Rubric	p. 166
Standardized Chapter Test	p. 162		

TECHNOLOGY

- Easy Planner
- Test and Practice Generator
- Power Presentations
- @HomeTutor
- Activity Generator
- Animated Algebra
- Classzone.com
- eEdition Plus Online
- eWorkbook Plus Online
- ML Assessment System

ADDITIONAL RESOURCES

Illinois Additional Lessons

- Additional Lesson C Special Right Triangles
- Additional Lesson D Triangle Inequalities
- Additional Lesson E The Tangent Ratio
- Additional Lesson F The Sine and Cosine Ratio
- Worked-Out Solution Key
- Notetaking Guide
- Practice Workbook
- Algebra 1 Toolkit
- Benchmark Tests
- Reteaching and Remediation
- Spanish Study Guide
- Spanish Assessment Book
- Spanish Resources in Spanish
- Multi-Language Visual Glossary

11 Lesson Practice Level B

LESSON 11.1 **Practice B**
For use with pages 710–716

1. domain: $x \ge 0$; range: $y \ge 0$; vertical stretch by a factor of 7
2. domain: $x \ge 0$; range: $y \ge 0$; vertical shrink by a factor of $\frac{1}{5}$
3. domain: $x \ge 0$; range: $y \le 0$; vertical stretch by a factor of 4 and reflection in x-axis

Graph the function and identify its domain and range. Compare the graph with the graph of $y = \sqrt{x}$.

1. $y = 7\sqrt{x}$ **2.** $y = \frac{1}{5}\sqrt{x}$ **3.** $y = -4\sqrt{x}$

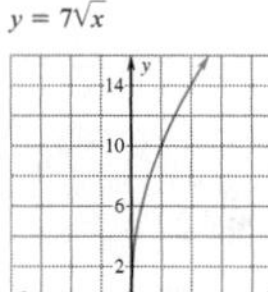

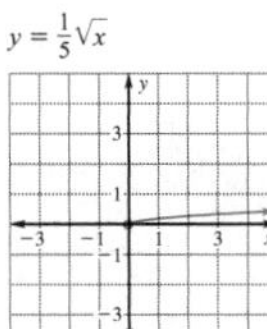

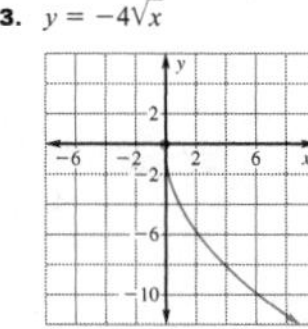

Describe how you would graph the function by using the graph of $y = \sqrt{x}$.

4. $y = \sqrt{x - 8}$ **5.** $y = \sqrt{x} + 3$ **6.** $y = \sqrt{x + 7}$

7. $y = \sqrt{x} - 5$ **8.** $y = \sqrt{x} + 3.5$ **9.** $y = \sqrt{x - \frac{1}{2}}$

4. translate graph of $y = \sqrt{x}$ horizontally 8 units right 5. translate graph of $y = \sqrt{x}$ vertically 3 units up

Match the function with its graph.

10. $y = \sqrt{x + 4} - 3$ E **11.** $y = \sqrt{x - 3} + 4$ C **12.** $y = \sqrt{x - 4} + 3$ A

13. $y = \sqrt{x - 4} - 3$ F **14.** $y = \sqrt{x + 3} - 4$ B **15.** $y = \sqrt{x + 3} + 3$ D

A. 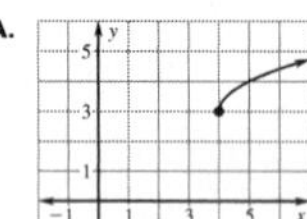

B. 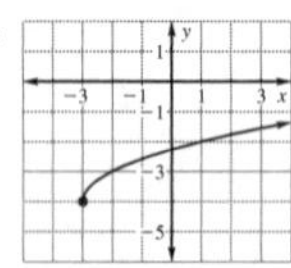

C. 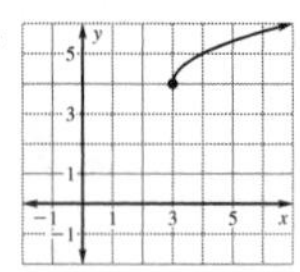

D. 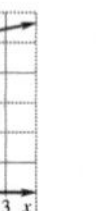

E. 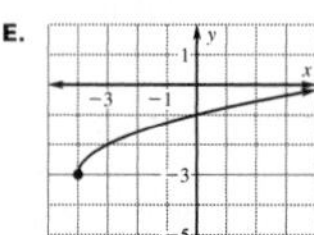

F. 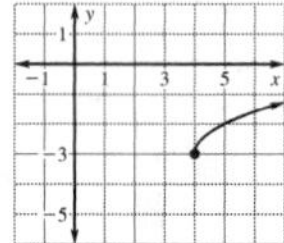

6. translate graph of $y = \sqrt{x}$ horizontally 7 units left
7. translate graph of $y = \sqrt{x}$ vertically 5 units down
8. translate graph of $y = \sqrt{x}$ vertically 3.5 units up
9. translate graph of $y = \sqrt{x}$ horizontally $\frac{1}{2}$ unit right

LESSON 11.1

LESSON 11.1 **Practice B** *continued*
For use with pages 710–716

16. domain: $x \ge -4$; range: $y \ge -4$; vertical translation 4 units down and horizontal translation 4 units left
17. domain: $x \ge -5$; range: $y \ge 1$; vertical translation 1 unit up and horizontal translation 5 units left

Graph the function and identify its domain and range. Compare the graph with the graph of $y = \sqrt{x}$.

16. $y = \sqrt{x + 4} - 4$ **17.** $y = \sqrt{x + 5} + 1$ **18.** $y = \sqrt{x - 6} + 4$ See below.

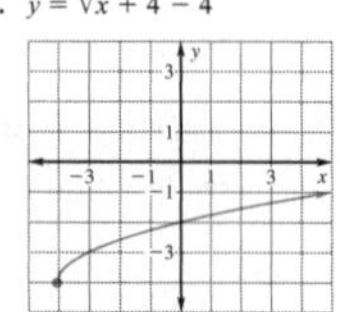

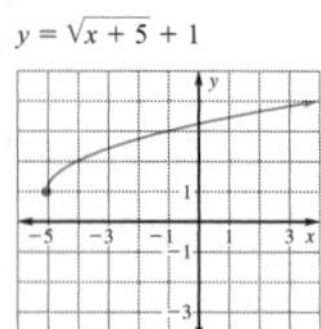

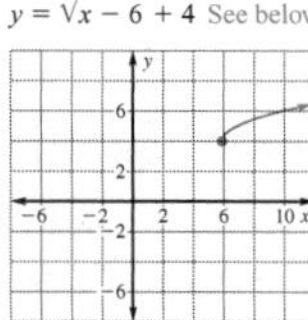

19. $y = \sqrt{x - 5} - 7$ See below. **20.** $y = \sqrt{x - 1} + 2$ See below. **21.** $y = \sqrt{x + 5} - 4$ See below.

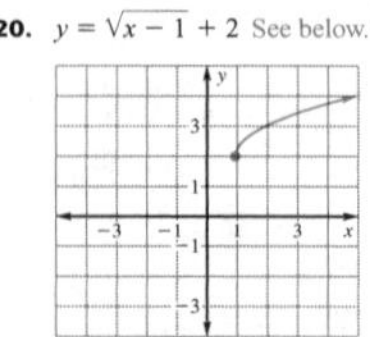

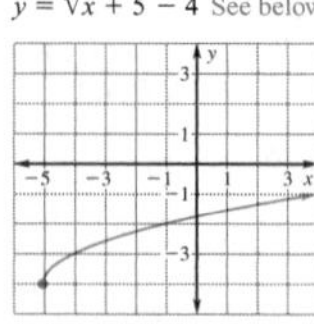

18. domain: $x \ge 6$; range: $y \ge 4$; vertical translation 4 units up and horizontal translation 6 units right

22. Box Design You are designing a box with a square base that will hold popcorn. The box must be 9 inches tall. The side length x (in inches) of the box is given by the function $x = \frac{1}{3}\sqrt{V}$ where V is the volume (in cubic inches) of the box. domain: $V > 0$; range: $x > 0$

a. Graph the function and identify its domain and range.

b. What is the volume of a box with a side length of 5 inches? 225 in.³

c. What is the volume of a box with a side length of 8 inches? 576 in.³

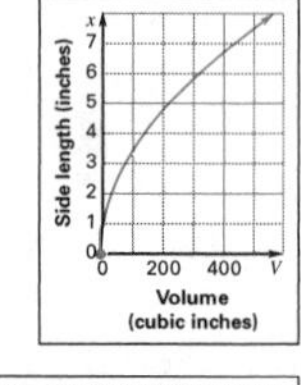

19. domain: $x \ge 5$; range: $y \ge -7$; vertical translation 7 units down and horizontal translation 5 units right
20. domain: $x \ge 1$; range: $y \ge 2$; vertical translation 2 units up and horizontal translation 1 unit right

23. Steel Pipe The inside diameter d of a steel pipe (in inches) and the weight w of water in the pipe (in pounds) are related by the function $d = 1.71\sqrt{w}$. domain: $w \ge 0$; range: $d \ge 0$

a. Graph the function and identify its domain and range.

b. What does the water weigh in a pipe with an inside diameter of 17 inches? Round your answer to the nearest pound. about 99 lb

c. What does the water weigh in a pipe with an inside diameter of 3.5 inches? Round your answer to the nearest pound. about 4 lb

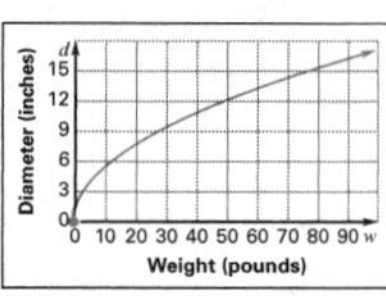

21. domain: $x \ge -5$; range: $y \ge -4$; vertical translation 4 units down and horizontal translation 5 units left

LESSON 11.1

LESSON 11.2 **Practice B**
For use with pages 719–726

Simplify the expression.

1. $\sqrt{200}$ $10\sqrt{2}$ **2.** $\sqrt{45}$ $3\sqrt{5}$ **3.** $\sqrt{112}$ $4\sqrt{7}$

4. $\sqrt{400d}$ $20\sqrt{d}$ **5.** $\sqrt{9y^2}$ $3|y|$ **6.** $\sqrt{25n^3}$ $5|n|\sqrt{n}$

7. $\sqrt{3} \cdot \sqrt{21}$ $3\sqrt{7}$ **8.** $\sqrt{20} \cdot \sqrt{15}$ $10\sqrt{3}$ **9.** $\sqrt{10x} \cdot \sqrt{2x}$ $2|x|\sqrt{5}$

10. $\sqrt{\frac{16}{81}}$ $\frac{4}{9}$ **11.** $\sqrt{\frac{5}{49}}$ $\frac{\sqrt{5}}{7}$ **12.** $\sqrt{\frac{x^2}{144}}$ $\frac{|x|}{12}$

Simplify the expression by rationalizing the denominator.

13. $\frac{4}{\sqrt{5}}$ $\frac{4\sqrt{5}}{5}$ **14.** $\sqrt{\frac{3}{50}}$ $\frac{\sqrt{6}}{10}$ **15.** $\sqrt{\frac{9}{75}}$ $\frac{\sqrt{3}}{5}$

16. $\frac{2}{\sqrt{p}}$ $\frac{2\sqrt{p}}{|p|}$ **17.** $\frac{1}{\sqrt{3y}}$ $\frac{\sqrt{3y}}{3|y|}$ **18.** $\frac{9}{\sqrt{2x}}$ $\frac{9\sqrt{2x}}{2|x|}$

Simplify the expression.

19. $10\sqrt{7} + 3\sqrt{7}$ $13\sqrt{7}$ **20.** $4\sqrt{5} - 7\sqrt{5}$ $-3\sqrt{5}$ **21.** $\sqrt{7}(4 - \sqrt{7})$ $-7 + 4\sqrt{7}$

22. $\sqrt{5}(8\sqrt{10} + 1)$ $40\sqrt{2} + \sqrt{5}$ **23.** $(2\sqrt{3} + 5)^2$ $37 + 20\sqrt{3}$ **24.** $(6 + \sqrt{3})(6 - \sqrt{3})$ 33

25. Water Flow You can measure the speed of water by using an L-shaped tube. The speed V of the water (in miles per hour) is given by the function $V = \sqrt{\frac{5}{2}h}$ where h is the height of the column of water above the surface (in inches).

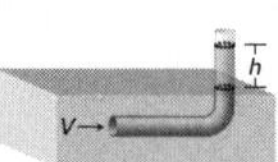

a. If you use the tube in a river and find that h is 6 inches, what is the speed of the water? Round your answer to the nearest hundredth. about 3.87 mi/h

b. If you use the tube in a river and find that h is 8.5 inches, what is the speed of the water? Round your answer to the nearest hundredth. about 4.61 mi/h

26. Walking Speed The maximum walking speed S (in feet per second) of an animal is given by the function $S = \sqrt{gL}$ where g is 32 feet per second squared and L is the length of the animal's leg (in feet).

a. How fast can an animal whose legs are 9 inches long walk? Round your answer to the nearest hundredth. about 4.90 fps

b. How fast can an animal whose legs are 3 feet long walk? Round your answer to the nearest hundredth. about 9.80 fps

LESSON 11.2

LESSON 11.3 **Practice B**
For use with pages 729–734

7. Add 5 to each side, then square each side, subtract 3 from each side, and divide each side by 7.
8. Add 3 to each side, divide each side by 6, square each side and solve the linear equation for x.

Determine whether the given value is a solution of the equation.

1. $4\sqrt{2x} - 3 = 12$; 2 not a solution **2.** $2\sqrt{9x} - 1 = 20$; 7 not a solution

3. $\sqrt{4x + 8} = \sqrt{6 + 2x}$; -1 solution **4.** $\sqrt{7x - 2} = \sqrt{8 - 3x}$; -1 not a solution

5. $x = \sqrt{4x - 3}$; 3 solution **6.** $\sqrt{4x - 3} = x - 2$; 7 solution

Describe the steps you would use to solve the equation. Do not solve the equation.

9. Square each side and solve the resulting linear equation for x.
10. Divide each side by 2, square each side, and solve the resulting linear equation for x.

7. $\sqrt{7x + 3} - 5 = 2$ **8.** $6\sqrt{4 - x} - 3 = 1$

9. $\sqrt{12x - 7} = \sqrt{9x + 3}$ **10.** $10\sqrt{6 - x} = 2\sqrt{x + 4}$

11. $\sqrt{5x - 3} - \sqrt{10 - 4x} = 0$ See below. **12.** $\sqrt{9x + 1} - 2 = x$ See below.

Solve the equation. Check for extraneous solutions.

13. $8\sqrt{x} - 32 = 0$ 16 **14.** $\sqrt{5x} - 4 = 16$ 80 **15.** $\sqrt{x + 3} + 8 = 15$ 46

16. $\sqrt{x - 6} - 2 = 4$ 42 **17.** $\sqrt{x + 9} - 5 = 2$ 40 **18.** $\sqrt{8 - 3x} + 5 = 6$ $\frac{7}{3}$

19. $\sqrt{5x + 4} - 12 = -6$ $\frac{32}{5}$ **20.** $3\sqrt{x + 5} - 3 = 6$ 4 **21.** $4\sqrt{2x + 1} - 7 = 1$ $\frac{3}{2}$

22. $\sqrt{x} = \sqrt{5x - 1}$ $\frac{1}{4}$ **23.** $\sqrt{7x - 6} = \sqrt{x}$ 1 **24.** $\sqrt{6x - 8} = \sqrt{4x - 10}$

25. $\sqrt{7x - 5} = \sqrt{3x + 19}$ 6 **26.** $\sqrt{x - 15} - \sqrt{x - 7} = 0$ **27.** $\sqrt{10x - 3} - \sqrt{8x - 11} = 0$

28. $\sqrt{5x - 6} = x$ 2, 3 **29.** $x = \sqrt{2x + 24}$ 6 **30.** $\sqrt{2x - 15} = x$ no solution

24. no solution 26. no solution 27. no solution

31. Market Research A marketing department determines that the price of a magazine subscription and the demand to subscribe are related by the function $P = 40 - \sqrt{0.0004x + 1}$ where P is the price per subscription and x is the number of subscriptions sold.

a. If the subscription price is set at \$25, how many subscriptions would be sold? Round your answer to the nearest whole subscription. about 560,000 subscriptions

b. If the subscription price is set at \$30, how many more subscriptions are sold in part (a) than when the price is \$30. Round your answer to the nearest whole subscription. 312,500 subscriptions

32. Awning The area A of a portion of a circle bounded by two radii r and angle t of a sector of a circle are related by the function

$$r = \sqrt{\frac{2A}{t}}.$$

The length of a side (radius) of the top view of the awning shown at the right is 6 feet and the angle that is formed by the awning is $\frac{5\pi}{3}$. Find the area of the awning. Round your answer to the nearest hundredth. about 94.25 ft

11. Add the second radical expression to each side, square each side, and solve the resulting linear equation for x.
12. Add 2 to each side, square each side, and then solve the resulting quadratic equation for x.

LESSON 11.3

LESSON 11.4

Practice B

For use with pages 737–742

Let *a* and *b* represent the lengths of the legs of a right triangle, and let *c* represent the length of the hypotenuse. Find the unknown length.

1. $a = 1, b = 5$ $\sqrt{26}$
2. $b = 4, c = 9$ $\sqrt{65}$
3. $a = 6, b = 6$ $6\sqrt{2}$
4. $b = 7, c = 12$ $\sqrt{95}$
5. $a = 2, b = 8$ $2\sqrt{17}$
6. $a = 6, b = 30$ $6\sqrt{26}$
7. $a = 4, b = 15$ $\sqrt{241}$
8. $b = 7, c = 11$ $6\sqrt{2}$
9. $a = 10, b = 20$ $10\sqrt{5}$
10. $a = 30, b = 40$ 50
11. $a = 15, c = 25$ 20
12. $a = 11, b = 22$ $11\sqrt{5}$

Find the unknown lengths.

13. x, $x - 6$, $2\sqrt{17}$

2, 8

14.

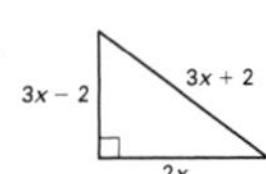

12, 16, 20

15.

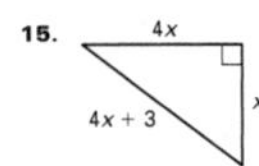

9, 12, 15 or 15, 36, 39

16. A right triangle has one leg that is 3 inches longer than the other leg. The hypotenuse is $\sqrt{65}$ inches. Find the lengths of the legs. 4 in., 7 in.

Tell whether the triangle with the given side lengths is a right triangle.

17. 4, 5, 6 not a right triangle
18. 15, 20, 25 right triangle
19. 9, 15, 20 not a right triangle

20. **Shuffleboard** The playing bed of a shuffleboard table is in the shape of a rectangle. If the playing bed measures 154 inches by 20 inches, what is the length of the diagonal from one corner of the playing bed to the opposite corner? Round your answer to the nearest inch. about 155 in.

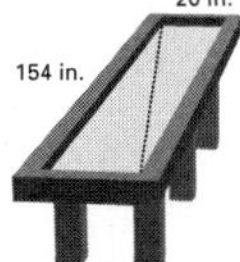

21. **Indirect Measurement** You are trying to determine the distance across a pond. You put posts into the ground at A, B, and C so that angle B is a right angle. You measure and find that the length of AB is 18 feet and the length of CB is 28 feet. How wide is the pond from A to C? Round your answer to the nearest foot. about 33 ft

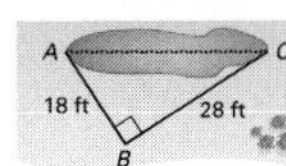

22. **Badminton** You are setting up a badminton net. To keep each pole standing straight, you use two ropes and two stakes as shown. How long is each piece of rope? Round your answer to the nearest tenth. about 9.2 ft

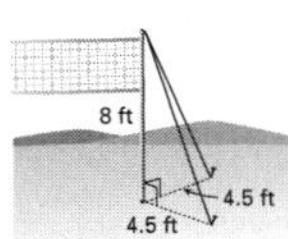

LESSON 11.4

LESSON 11.5

Practice B

For use with pages 744–750

Find the distance between the two points.

1. (8, 3), (10, 4) $\sqrt{5}$
2. (2, 7), (5, 6) $\sqrt{10}$
3. (9, 6), (4, 1) $5\sqrt{2}$
4. (0, 4), (8, −2) 10
5. (−5, 3), (1, 2) $\sqrt{37}$
6. (1, −6), (−2, 4) $\sqrt{109}$
7. (8, −7), (4, −3) $4\sqrt{2}$
8. (−10, −2), (6, 5) $\sqrt{305}$
9. (−1, −8), (−5, −2) $2\sqrt{13}$

The distance *d* between two points is given. Find the value of *b*.

10. $(b, 4), (2, -1); d = 5$ 2
11. $(-3, 2), (7, b); d = 10$ 2
12. $(3, 2), (b, -9); d = 11$ 3
13. $(4, 1), (5, b); d = \sqrt{17}$ −3, 5
14. $(b, 2), (3, -1); d = \sqrt{58}$ −4, 10
15. $(-4, b), (5, -2); d = \sqrt{106}$ −7, 3

Find the midpoint of the line segment with the given endpoints.

16. (2, 5), (4, 12) $\left(3, \frac{17}{2}\right)$
17. (−7, 2), (−10, 14) $\left(-\frac{17}{2}, 8\right)$
18. (−9, −5), (7, −14) $\left(-1, -\frac{19}{2}\right)$
19. (8, −8), (3, 5) $\left(\frac{11}{2}, -\frac{3}{2}\right)$
20. (20, 5), (30, −5) (25, 0)
21. (−11, 7), (8, −3) $\left(-\frac{3}{2}, 2\right)$

Use the distance formula and the converse of the Pythagorean theorem to determine whether the points are vertices of a right triangle. See below.

22. (1, 1), (4, 4), (1, 4)
23. (6, 0), (6, 4), (2, 4)
24. (−2, 1), (3, 5), (6, −2)
25. (6, 4), (−1, −2), (−4, 3)
26. (5, 3), (4, −2), (10, 2)
27. (2, −4), (2, −3), (6, 1)

28. **Walking Trail** A walking trail follows the path shown on the map. The distance between consecutive grid lines is 1 mile. Find the total distance of the trail from start to finish. Round your answer to the nearest mile. 15 mi

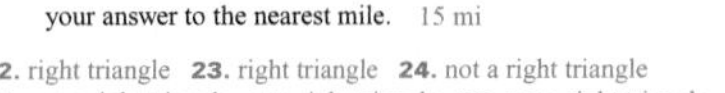

22. right triangle 23. right triangle 24. not a right triangle
25. not a right triangle 26. right triangle 27. not a right triangle

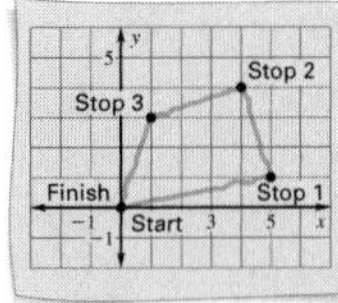

29. **Amusement Park** An amusement park designer wants to place a Ferris wheel midway between the two largest coasters. The distance between consecutive grid lines is 500 feet. (1750, 2000)
    a. Determine the coordinates of where the Ferris wheel should be.
    b. How far will the Ferris wheel be from each of the coasters? Round your answer to the nearest foot. 1953 ft

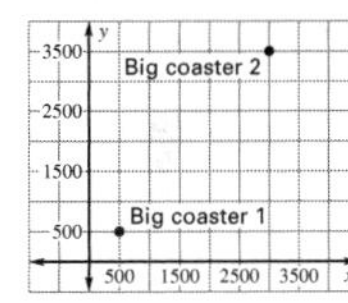

30. **Reading** You have 30 days left to read the books on your summer reading list. As of today, you have read 5 books. By the end of the 30 days, you have to have read 12 books. Assume that the books are all approximately the same length and you read at a relatively constant pace. After 15 days, how many books should you have read? 8.5 books

LESSON 11.5

CHAPTER 11 Quiz 1
For use after Lessons 11.1–11.3

1. Graph the function $y = \sqrt{x - 2}$ and identify its domain and range. Compare the graph with the graph of $y = \sqrt{x}$.

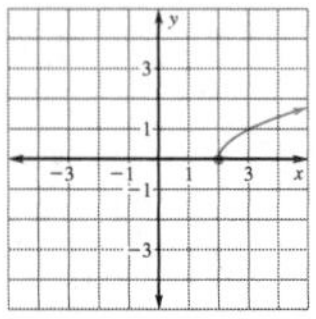

Simplify the expression.

2. $\sqrt{90}$
3. $\sqrt{12} \cdot \sqrt{3y^2}$
4. $(\sqrt{3} + 4)(\sqrt{3} - 1)$
5. $\frac{10}{\sqrt{5}}$
6. $\sqrt{\frac{125}{x^4}}$
7. $\sqrt{\frac{72k^6}{6g^2}}$

Solve the equation. Check for extraneous solutions.

8. $\sqrt{x} - 9 = 0$
9. $\sqrt{4x + 3} = \sqrt{3x + 4}$
10. $\sqrt{4x - 3} = x$
11. $\sqrt{x - 6} + 4 = 9$

Answers

1. See left. The domain is $x \geq 2$. The range is $y \geq 0$. The graph of $y = \sqrt{x - 2}$ is a horizontal translation (of 2 units to the right) of the graph of $y = \sqrt{x}$.
2. $3\sqrt{10}$
3. $6y$
4. $3\sqrt{3} - 1$
5. $2\sqrt{5}$
6. $\frac{5\sqrt{5}}{x^2}$
7. $\frac{2\sqrt{3}k^3}{g}$
8. 81
9. 1
10. 1, 3
11. 31

CHAPTER 11 Quiz 2
For use after Lessons 11.4–11.5

Let *a* and *b* represent the lengths of the legs of a right triangle, and let *c* represent the length of the hypotenuse. Find the unknown length.

1. $a = 8, b = 15$
2. $b = 3, c = 7$
3. $a = 5, c = 10$
4. $a = 6, b = 6$

Find the unknown lengths.

5.

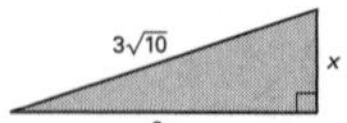

6.

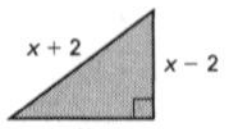

Find the distance between the two points.

7. (4, −5), (0, −5)
8. (3, 2), (3, −4)

Find the midpoint of the line segment with the given endpoints.

9. (0, 4), (14, 2)
10. (6, −2), (4, −8)

Answers

1. $c = 17$
2. $a = 2\sqrt{10}$
3. $b = 5\sqrt{3}$
4. $c = 6\sqrt{2}$
5. $x = 3, 3x = 9$
6. $x = 8, x - 2 = 6, x + 2 = 10$
7. 4
8. 6
9. (7, 3)
10. (5, −5)

CHAPTER 11 Chapter Test B
For use after Chapter 11

Graph the function and identify the domain and range. Then compare the graph with the graph of $y = \sqrt{x}$.

1. $y = \frac{1}{2}\sqrt{x} - 3$
2. $y = -\sqrt{x + 2}$

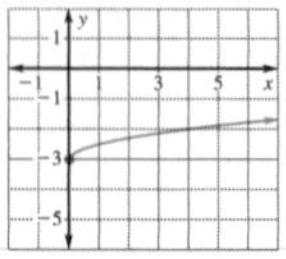

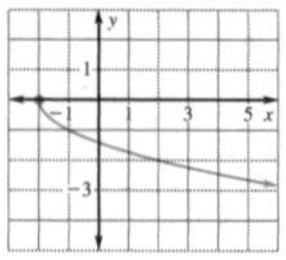

Simplify the expression.

3. $\sqrt{72a^5}$
4. $5\sqrt{2} - 3\sqrt{2} + 12\sqrt{2}$
5. $3\sqrt{12} - 5\sqrt{27}$
6. $\frac{6}{\sqrt{3b}}$
7. $\sqrt{\frac{4p^2}{q^6}}$
8. $(2\sqrt{7} + 4)^2$

In Exercises 9 and 10, use the following information.

The time t (in seconds) it takes an object dropped from a height h (in feet) to reach the ground is given by the equation $t = \sqrt{\frac{h}{16}}$.

9. Write the equation in simplified form.
10. Find the exact time it takes a stone to reach the ground if it is dropped from a bridge that is 200 feet high.

Solve the equation. Check for extraneous solutions.

11. $\sqrt{4x} + 5 = 2$
12. $\sqrt{3x + 4} = \sqrt{12x - 14}$
13. $\sqrt{6x + 7} + 3 = x + 5$

Answers

1. See left. domain: $x \geq 0$; range: $y \geq -3$; The graph is a vertical shrink and a shift 3 units down from the graph of $y = \sqrt{x}$.
2. See left. domain: $x \geq -2$; range: $y \leq 0$; The graph is a reflection in the x-axis and a shift 2 units to the left of the graph of $y = \sqrt{x}$.
3. $6a^2\sqrt{2a}$
4. $14\sqrt{2}$
5. $-9\sqrt{3}$
6. $\frac{2\sqrt{3b}}{b}$
7. $\frac{2p}{q^3}$
8. $44 + 16\sqrt{7}$
9. $t = \frac{\sqrt{h}}{4}$
10. $\frac{5\sqrt{2}}{2}$ sec
11. no solution
12. 2
13. −1, 3

CHAPTER 11 Chapter Test B *continued*
For use after Chapter 11

14. A person's maximum running speed s (in meters per second) can be approximated by the function $s = \pi\sqrt{\frac{9.8\ell}{6}}$ where ℓ is the person's leg length (in meters). To the nearest tenth of a meter, what is the leg length of a person whose maximum running speed is about 3.4 meters per second?

Find the unknown lengths.

15. A right triangle has one leg that is twice as long as the other leg. The hypotenuse is $2\sqrt{5}$ inches.
16. A right triangle has a hypotenuse that is 3 feet longer than one leg. The other leg is 4 feet.

Find the midpoint of the line segment with the given endpoints.

17. (5, 4), (1, 1)
18. (−1, 1), (−4, −3)
19. (9, −2), (3, −2)

In Exercises 20 and 21, use the following graph.

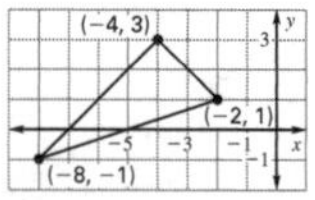

20. Find the length of each line segment.
21. Use the converse of the Pythagorean theorem to determine whether the points are the vertices of a right triangle.

The distance *d* between two points is given. Find the value of *b*.

22. $(b, -2), (6, 1); d = 5$
23. $(5, 1), (0, b); d = \sqrt{29}$

24. A fire is sighted in the forest from a helicopter. The forest ranger can send a crew from one of the two towers, as shown on the map. The distance between consecutive grid lines represents 0.5 mile. Which tower is closer to the fire?

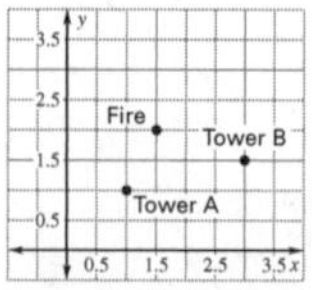

Answers

14. 0.7 m
15. 4 in., 2 in.
16. $\frac{7}{6}$ ft, $\frac{25}{6}$ ft
17. $\left(3, \frac{5}{2}\right)$
18. $\left(-\frac{5}{2}, -1\right)$
19. (6, −2)
20. $2\sqrt{2}, 2\sqrt{10}, 4\sqrt{2}$
21. yes
22. 2 or 10
23. 3 or −1
24. Tower A

CHAPTER 11 Standardized Test

For use after Chapter 11

Multiple Choice

1. The graph of which function is a vertical stretch of the graph $y = \sqrt{x}$? C

Ⓐ $y = \frac{1}{2}\sqrt{x}$ Ⓑ $y = 5 + \sqrt{x}$

Ⓒ $y = 4\sqrt{x}$ Ⓓ $y = \sqrt{x + 3}$

2. The graph of which function is a horizontal translation of 2 units to the left of the graph $y = \sqrt{x}$? D

Ⓐ $y = \sqrt{x} - 2$ Ⓑ $y = \sqrt{x} + 2$

Ⓒ $y = \sqrt{x - 2}$ Ⓓ $y = \sqrt{x + 2}$

3. The graph of which function is shown? A

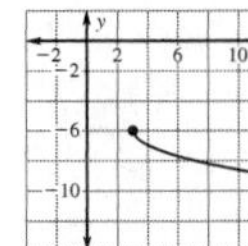

Ⓐ $y = -\sqrt{x - 3} - 6$

Ⓑ $y = -\sqrt{x + 3} + 6$

Ⓒ $y = -\sqrt{x - 3} + 6$

Ⓓ $y = -\sqrt{x + 3} - 6$

4. How is the graph of $f(x) = \sqrt{x} + 5$ related to the graph of $g(x) = \sqrt{x} - 5$. B

Ⓐ It is a vertical translation of 5 units down of the graph of g.

Ⓑ It is a vertical translation of 10 units down of the graph of g.

Ⓒ It is a horizontal translation of 5 units to the right of the graph of g.

Ⓓ It is a horizontal translation of 10 units to the right of the graph of g.

5. Which expression is equivalent to $\sqrt{72}$? B

Ⓐ $\sqrt{70} + \sqrt{2}$ Ⓑ $6\sqrt{2}$

Ⓒ 12 Ⓓ 36

6. Which expression is equivalent to $\sqrt{24} \cdot \sqrt{2}$ in its simplest form? A

Ⓐ $4\sqrt{3}$ Ⓑ $16\sqrt{3}$

Ⓒ $2\sqrt{12}$ Ⓓ $12\sqrt{2}$

7. Which expression is equivalent to $\sqrt{\frac{16x}{49}}$? C

Ⓐ $\frac{4x}{7}$ Ⓑ $\frac{4\sqrt{x}}{49}$

Ⓒ $\frac{4\sqrt{x}}{7}$ Ⓓ $\frac{\sqrt{4x}}{7}$

8. Which expression is equivalent to $\sqrt{\frac{9}{32}}$ in its simplest form? D

Ⓐ $\frac{3}{\sqrt{32}}$ Ⓑ $\frac{3}{4\sqrt{2}}$

Ⓒ $\frac{3\sqrt{2}}{4}$ Ⓓ $\frac{3\sqrt{2}}{8}$

9. Which expression is equivalent to $\sqrt{\frac{5x^2}{6}}$ in its simplest form? D

Ⓐ $\frac{x\sqrt{5}}{\sqrt{6}}$ Ⓑ $\frac{30\sqrt{x}}{6}$

Ⓒ $\frac{x\sqrt{5}}{6}$ Ⓓ $\frac{x\sqrt{30}}{6}$

10. Which expression is equivalent to $\sqrt{24} + 5\sqrt{6} - \sqrt{54}$? B

Ⓐ $10\sqrt{2}$ Ⓑ $4\sqrt{6}$

Ⓒ $5 - \sqrt{24}$ Ⓓ $10\sqrt{6}$

11. Which expression is equivalent to $(3\sqrt{5} - 2)^2$? A

Ⓐ $49 - 12\sqrt{5}$ Ⓑ $4 - 3\sqrt{5}$

Ⓒ $30 - 12\sqrt{5}$ Ⓓ $-4 - 3\sqrt{5}$

12. Which expression is equivalent to $\frac{5r}{\sqrt{r}} - \frac{2}{\sqrt{r}}$ in its simplest form? C

Ⓐ $\frac{3r}{r}$ Ⓑ $\frac{5r - 2}{r^2}$

Ⓒ $\frac{3\sqrt{r}}{r}$ Ⓓ $\frac{3}{\sqrt{r}}$

13. Which expression is equivalent to $\frac{15}{\sqrt{6} - \sqrt{3}}$ in its simplest form? B

Ⓐ $-\frac{15\sqrt{9}}{3}$ Ⓑ $5\sqrt{6} + 5\sqrt{3}$

Ⓒ $-\frac{15\sqrt{6} + 15\sqrt{3}}{3}$ Ⓓ $15\sqrt{3}$

14. What is the solution of the equation $6\sqrt{x + 2} + 5 = 35$? C

Ⓐ $\sqrt{3}$ Ⓑ 3 Ⓒ 23 Ⓓ 25

15. Given a right triangle with side lengths 7 and 24, what is the length of the hypotenuse? A

Ⓐ 25 Ⓑ 31 Ⓒ 62 Ⓓ 625

16. Which of the triangles with the given side lengths is *not* a right triangle? D

Ⓐ 3, 4, 5 Ⓑ 11, 60, 61

Ⓒ 15, 20, 25 Ⓓ 9, 39, 41

17. What is the midpoint of the line segment with endpoints $(-3, -2)$ and $(5, -4)$? A

Ⓐ $(1, -3)$ Ⓑ $(-4, -1)$

Ⓒ $(-1, 3)$ Ⓓ $(4, 1)$

18. What is the distance between (5, 3.5) and $(-2, -2.5)$? C

Ⓐ 2 Ⓑ $\sqrt{13}$

Ⓒ $\sqrt{85}$ Ⓓ 13

21. a. Twenty-four steps are needed. The height from floor to ceiling is 12 feet or 144 inches. If the riser of each step is 6 inches, you would need 24 steps to reach the second floor. **b.** 24 ft; Each step has a tread of 12 inches and there are 24 steps, so the linear distance would be 288 inches or 24 feet. **c.** A 322 inch rail is needed.

Gridded Answer

19. What is the value of x in the equation $4\sqrt{x + 5} + 2 = 18$?

Answer: 11

20. You would meet at the fountain. The midpoint between the two locations is the point (4, 3). The two locations closest to this point are the school and the library. You can use either the distance formula or your knowledge of right triangles to determine that the fountain is closest.

Short Response

20. A map of your town is shown. See above.

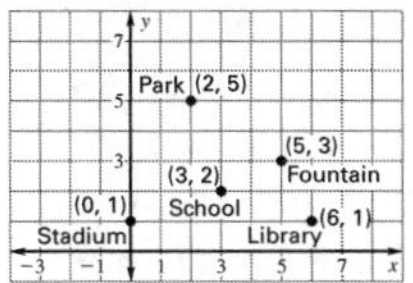

You are at the library. Your friend is at the park. You want to meet at the place that is closest to the midpoint of your locations. At which location should you meet? *Explain.*

Extended Response

21. The vertical distance from the first floor of a house to the second floor is 12 feet. The tread of each step is 12 inches and the riser is 6 inches. See left.

a. How many steps are needed? *Explain.*

b. What is the linear distance (in feet) needed for the staircase? *Explain.*

c. If a railing is installed from the edge of the bottom step to the edge of the top step, how long of a rail is needed? Round your answer to the nearest inch.

CHAPTER 11 Alternative Assessment and Math Journal

For use after Chapter 11

Journal

1. State and explain the product and quotient properties of radicals for $a \geq 0$ and $b \geq 0$. Use examples to illustrate why there are not sum or difference properties of radicals.

Multi-Step Problem

2. The function $t = \frac{1}{4}\sqrt{36 - h}$ represents the time t (in seconds) it takes an object to fall to a height h (in feet) after being dropped from an initial height of 36 feet.

a. Graph the function and state the domain.

b. Identify the intercepts of this function and explain what each conveys about the position of the object.

c. Determine the distance between the intercepts. Round your answer to the nearest hundredth.

d. What is the height of the object after $\frac{1}{2}$ second?

e. What is the height of the object after 1 second?

f. How long does it take for the object to travel halfway to the ground? Round your answer to the nearest hundredth.

g. Does the second half of the object's fall take more or less time than the first half? Explain your reasoning.

1. Complete answers should include: an explanation of each property of radicals; an example illustrating why there is no sum property of radicals; an example illustrating why there is no difference property of radicals.

2. a.

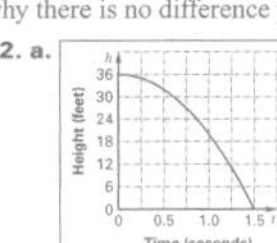

Domain: $0 \leq h \leq 36$

b. (1.5, 0), (0, 36); 1.5 seconds after the object is dropped it has a height of 0 feet; the object is at a height of 36 feet right before it is released.
c. 36.03 units **d.** 32 ft **e.** 20 ft **f.** 1.06 sec
g. Less time; The object is in the air for a total of 1.5 seconds, and it takes just over 1 second to fall the first 18 feet, which means it takes less than 0.5 second to fall the second 18 feet.

Journal Solution

1. Complete answers should include:

- an explanation of each property of radicals.
- an example illustrating why there is no sum property of radicals.
- an example illustrating why there is no difference property of radicals.

Multi-Step Problem Solution

2. a.

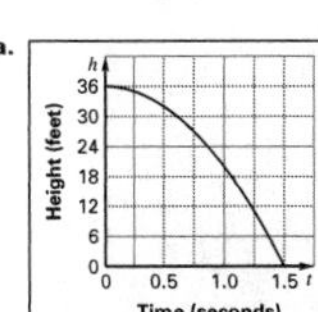

Domain: $0 \leq h \leq 36$

b. x-intercept: (1.5, 0), y-intercept: (0, 36); 1.5 seconds after the object is dropped it has a height of 0 feet; the object is at a height of 36 feet right before it is released.

c. 36.03 units

d. 32 feet

e. 20 feet

f. 1.06 seconds

g. Less time; The object is in the air for a total of 1.5 seconds, and it takes just over 1 second to fall the first 18 feet, which means it takes less than 0.5 second to fall the second 18 feet.

Multi-Step Problem Rubric

4 The student answers all parts of the problem correctly and completely. The student shows all work. The student's work is neat.

3 The student answers all parts of the problem. The student's work may contain one or two errors in the calculations, graph, or equations. The student shows most work. The student's work is neat.

2 The student answers all parts of the problem, but there are more than two errors in the calculations, graph, or equations. The student shows some work. The student's work is sloppy.

1 The student does not complete all parts of the problem. The student's work has several errors in the calculations, graph, and equations. The student's work is sloppy, or no work is shown.

PLAN AND PREPARE

Main Ideas

In Chapter 11, students graph square root functions. They use properties to simplify radical expressions, including rationalizing the denominator. They add, subtract, and multiply radicals. They solve radical equations, including equations with extraneous solutions. They apply the Pythagorean theorem and its converse to find missing lengths and to determine whether triangles are right triangles. They apply the distance and midpoint formulas to find the distance between two points and to find missing coordinates.

Prerequisite Skills

- Comparing graphs of functions with graphs of parent functions
- Evaluating square roots
- Using the distributive property
- Factoring trinomials
- Evaluating expressions

Additional resources for reviewing prerequisite skills are:

- Skills Review Handbook, pp. 909–937
- @HomeTutor

3.

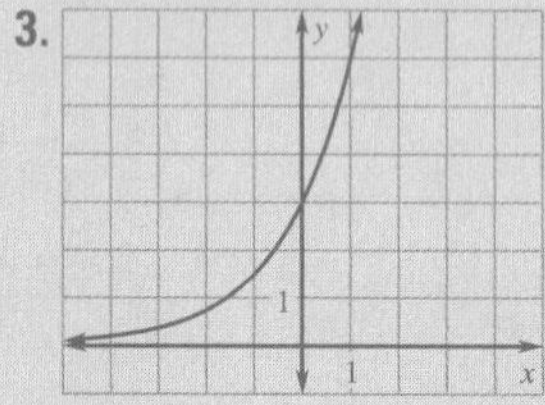

11 Radicals and Geometry Connections

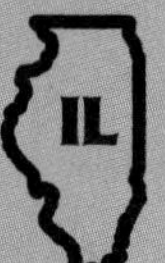

Before

In previous chapters, you learned the following skills, which you'll use in Chapter 11: comparing the graphs of functions with the graphs of parent functions, evaluating square roots, using the distributive property, factoring trinomials, and evaluating expressions.

Prerequisite Skills

VOCABULARY CHECK

Copy and complete the statement.

1. The number or expression inside a radical symbol is called the __?__. radicand
2. If $b^2 = a$, then b is a(n) __?__ of a. square root

SKILLS CHECK

3. Graph $y = 3 \cdot 2^x$. Compare the graph with the graph of $y = 2^x$. *(Review p. 520 for 11.1.)* See margin for art; the graph is a vertical stretch of $y = 2^x$.

Evaluate the expression. *(Review p. 110 for 11.2.)*

4. $\sqrt{81}$ 9
5. $-\sqrt{64}$ -8
6. $\pm\sqrt{100}$ ± 10
7. $-\sqrt{121}$ -11

Use the distributive property to write an equivalent expression. *(Review p. 96 for 11.2.)*

8. $4(y - 3)$ $4y - 12$
9. $2(x - 2)$ $2x - 4$
10. $-x(x + 11)$ $-x^2 - 11x$
11. $4x(x - 9)$ $4x^2 - 36x$

Factor the trinomial. *(Review p. 583 for 11.3.)*

12. $x^2 + 4x + 4$ $(x + 2)^2$
13. $m^2 + 9m + 8$ $(m + 8)(m + 1)$
14. $r^2 + 8r + 7$ $(r + 7)(r + 1)$
15. $b^2 + 10b + 16$ $(b + 8)(b + 2)$
16. Evaluate a^2 when $a = 7$. *(Review p. 2 for 11.4–11.5.)* 49

@HomeTutor Prerequisite skills practice at classzone.com

708

Chapter Planning Guide

Chapter 11 Resource Book
- Teaching Guide/Lesson Plan (pp. 3, 18, 29, 42, 52)
- Project with Rubric (p. 63)

Assessment and Intervention
- Assessment Book (pp. 154–167)
- Benchmark Tests
- Reteaching and Remediation Book

Interactive Technology
- Easy Planner
- Power Presentations CD-ROM
- Activity Generator CD-ROM
- Animated Algebra
- Test Generator CD-ROM
- Online Quizzes
- eWorkbook
- eEdition
- @HomeTutor

Resources for English Learners
- Quick Reference for English Learners
- Spanish Study Guide
- Multi-Language Visual Glossary
- Student Resources in Spanish

Now

In Chapter 11, you will apply the big ideas listed below and reviewed in the Chapter Summary on page 753. You will also use the key vocabulary listed below.

Big Ideas

1. **Graphing square root functions**
2. **Using properties of radicals in expressions and equations**
3. **Working with radicals in geometry**

KEY VOCABULARY

- radical expression, *p. 710*
- radical function, *p. 710*
- square root function, *p. 710*
- parent square root function, *p. 710*
- simplest form of a radical expression, *p. 719*
- rationalizing the denominator, *p. 721*
- radical equation, *p. 729*
- extraneous solution, *p. 730*
- hypotenuse, *p. 737*
- legs of a right triangle, *p. 737*
- Pythagorean theorem, *p. 737*
- distance formula, *p. 744*
- midpoint, *p. 745*
- midpoint formula, *p. 745*

Why?

You can use radical equations to solve real-world problems. For example, you can find the length of a sailboat's waterline given the hull speed of the sailboat.

Animated Algebra

The animation illustrated below for Example 5 on page 731 helps you answer this question: What is the length of a sailboat's waterline if the sailboat has a hull speed of 8 nautical miles per hour?

Start
You need to find the length of the sailboat's waterline.

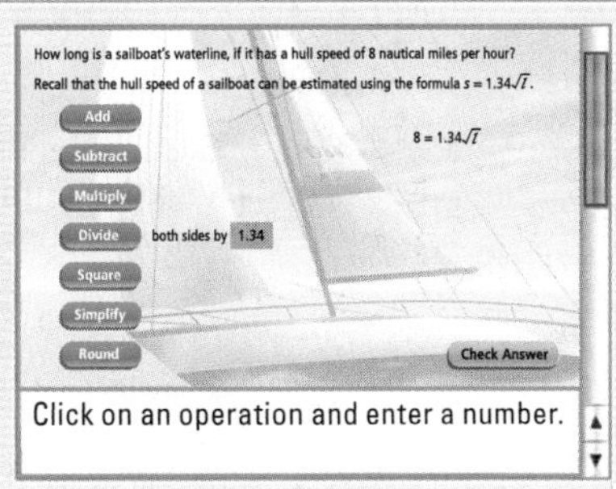

Click on an operation and enter a number.

Animated Algebra at classzone.com

Other animations for Chapter 11: pages 711, 719, 722, 737, 746, and 753

Algebra 1 Toolkit

- Reading Strategies for Chapter 11, pp. 29–30
- Differentiated Instruction Notes, pp. 81–84
- English Learners Notes, pp. 117–118
- Inclusion Notes, pp. 149–150
- Teaching Strategies with Sample Worksheets, pp. 155–178
- Using Technology in the Classroom, pp. 179–184
- Tips for New Teachers, pp. 205–206
- Math Background Notes, pp. 231–232
- Pre-AP Strategies and Copymasters, pp. 298–299, 453–481
- Teacher Survival Activities, pp. 575–576, 601–602
- Bulletin Board Idea, p. 617
- Teacher Tool Transparencies, following p. 620

1 PLAN AND PREPARE

Warm-Up Exercises

Transparency Available

1. Graph the function $y = 2^x$.

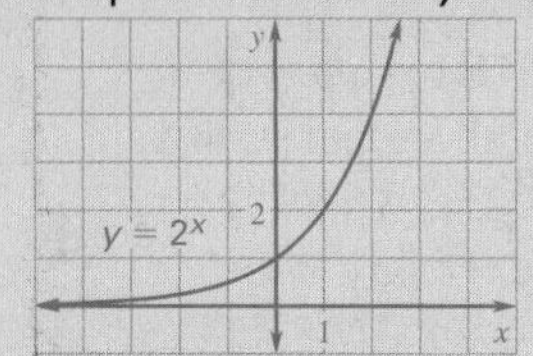

2. Evaluate $3\sqrt{x}$ when $x = 4$. 6
3. Evaluate $\sqrt{x + 5}$ when $x = 11$. 4

Notetaking Guide

Transparency Available

Promotes interactive learning and notetaking skills, pp. 274–250.

Pacing

Basic: 2 days
Average: 2 days
Advanced: 2 days
Block: 1 block
• See *Teaching Guide/Lesson Plan.*

2 FOCUS AND MOTIVATE

Essential Question

Big Idea 1, p. 709

How do you graph square root functions? **Tell students they will learn how to answer this question by making tables, plotting points, and then connecting the points.**

11.1 Graph Square Root Functions

8.11.08 Recognize and describe the general shape and properties of functions from graphs, tables or equations . . .

Before You graphed linear, exponential, and quadratic functions.

Now You will graph square root functions.

Why? So you can analyze the speed of an athlete, as in Ex. 45.

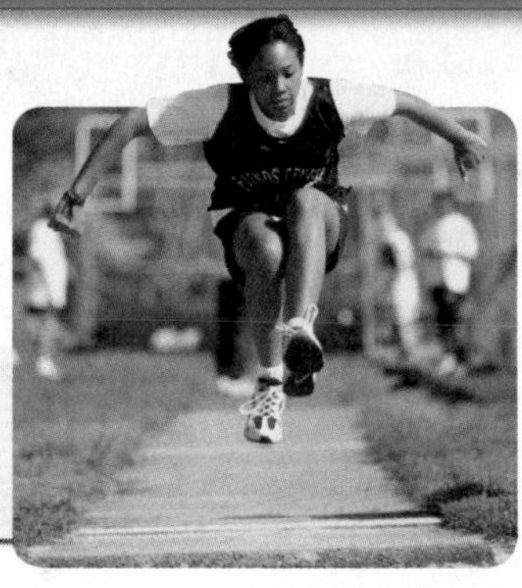

Key Vocabulary
• radical expression
• radical function
• square root function
• parent square root function

A **radical expression** is an expression that contains a radical, such as a square root, cube root, or other root. A **radical function** contains a radical expression with the independent variable in the radicand. For example, $y = \sqrt[3]{2x}$ and $y = \sqrt{x + 2}$ are radical functions. If the radical is a square root, then the function is called a **square root function**.

KEY CONCEPT *For Your Notebook*

Parent Function for Square Root Functions

The most basic square root function in the family of all square root functions, called the **parent square root function**, is:

$$y = \sqrt{x}$$

The graph of the parent square root function is shown.

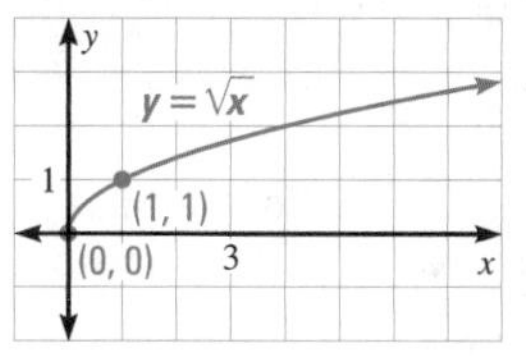

EXAMPLE 1 Graph a function of the form $y = a\sqrt{x}$

Graph the function $y = 3\sqrt{x}$ and identify its domain and range. Compare the graph with the graph of $y = \sqrt{x}$.

REVIEW SQUARE ROOTS
For help with square roots, see p. 110.

Solution

STEP 1 **Make** a table. Because the square root of a negative number is undefined, x must be nonnegative. So, the domain is $x \geq 0$.

x	0	1	2	3	4
y	0	3	4.2	5.2	6

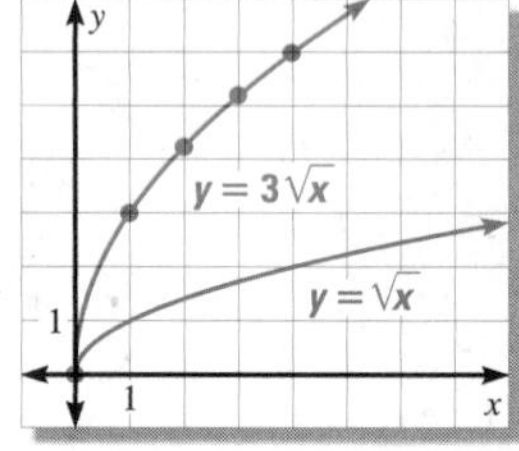

STEP 2 **Plot** the points.

STEP 3 **Draw** a smooth curve through the points. From either the table or the graph, you can see the range of the function is $y \geq 0$.

STEP 4 **Compare** the graph with the graph of $y = \sqrt{x}$. The graph of $y = 3\sqrt{x}$ is a vertical stretch (by a factor of 3) of the graph of $y = \sqrt{x}$.

Resource Planning Guide

Chapter Resource Book
• Teaching Guide/Lesson Plan (pp. 3–4)
• Activity Master (p. 5)
• Practice levels A, B, C (pp. 7–12)
• Study Guide (pp. 13–14)
• Catch-up for Absent Students (p. 15)
• Problem Solving Workshop (p. 16)
• Challenge (p. 17)

Workbooks
• Notetaking Guide (pp. 247–250)
• Practice Workbook (pp. 169–171)

Teaching Options
• **Power Presentations CD-ROM** provides dynamic electronic teaching resources for the classroom.
• **Activity Generator CD-ROM** provides editable activities for all ability levels.

Interactive Technology
• Easy Planner
• Power Presentations CD-ROM
• Activity Generator CD-ROM
• Animated Algebra
• Test Generator CD-ROM
• Online Quiz
• eWorkbook
• eEdition
• @HomeTutor

Resources for English Learners
• Quick Reference for English Learners
• Spanish Study Guide
• Multi-Language Visual Glossary
• Student Resources in Spanish

See also the *Algebra 1 Toolkit* for more strategies for meeting individual needs.

EXAMPLE 2 Graph a function of the form $y = a\sqrt{x}$

Graph the function $y = -0.5\sqrt{x}$ and identify its domain and range. Compare the graph with the graph of $y = \sqrt{x}$.

Solution

To graph the function, make a table, plot the points, and draw a smooth curve through the points. The domain is $x \geq 0$.

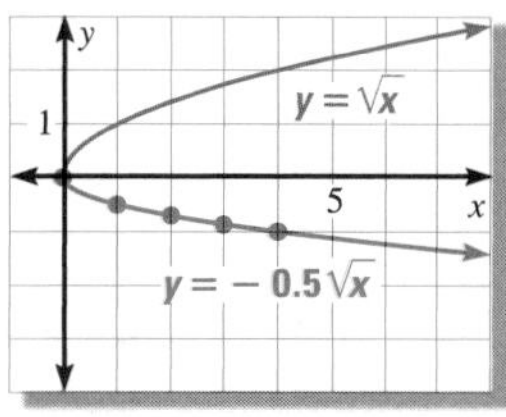

x	0	1	2	3	4
y	0	−0.5	−0.7	−0.9	−1

The range is $y \leq 0$. The graph of $y = -0.5\sqrt{x}$ is a vertical shrink (by a factor of 0.5) with a reflection in the x-axis of the graph of $y = \sqrt{x}$.

GRAPHS OF SQUARE ROOT FUNCTIONS Examples 1 and 2 illustrate the following:

- When $|a| > 1$, the graph of $y = a\sqrt{x}$ is a vertical stretch of the graph of $y = \sqrt{x}$. When $0 < |a| < 1$, the graph of $y = a\sqrt{x}$ is a vertical shrink of the graph of $y = \sqrt{x}$.
- When $a < 0$, the graph of $y = a\sqrt{x}$ is the reflection in the x-axis of the graph of $y = |a|\sqrt{x}$.

EXAMPLE 3 Graph a function of the form $y = \sqrt{x} + k$

Graph the function $y = \sqrt{x} + 2$ and identify its domain and range. Compare the graph with the graph of $y = \sqrt{x}$.

Solution

To graph the function, make a table, then plot and connect the points. The domain is $x \geq 0$.

x	0	1	2	3	4
y	2	3	3.4	3.7	4

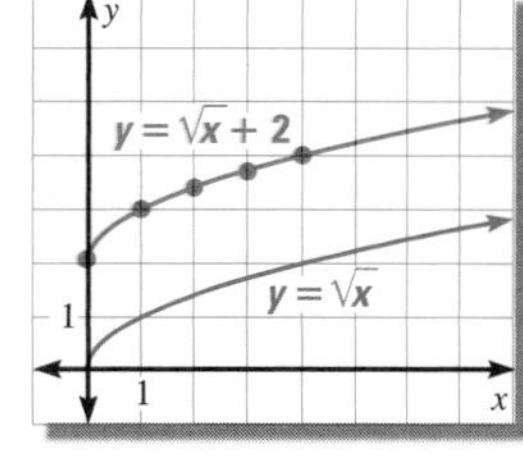

The range is $y \geq 2$. The graph of $y = \sqrt{x} + 2$ is a vertical translation (of 2 units up) of the graph of $y = \sqrt{x}$.

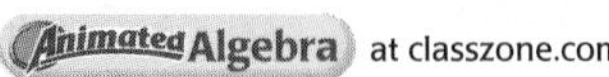

at classzone.com

GUIDED PRACTICE for Examples 1, 2, and 3

Graph the function and identify its domain and range. Compare the graph with the graph of $y = \sqrt{x}$. 1–4. See margin.

1. $y = 2\sqrt{x}$ **2.** $y = -2\sqrt{x}$ **3.** $y = \sqrt{x} - 1$ **4.** $y = \sqrt{x} + 3$

Motivating the Lesson

Tell students that if they know how long two skydivers are in freefall and they know how to use a square root function, they can determine how far the skydivers fall before they open their parachutes.

3 TEACH

Extra Example 1

Graph the function $y = 0.5\sqrt{x}$ and identify its domain and range. Compare the graph with the graph of $y = \sqrt{x}$.

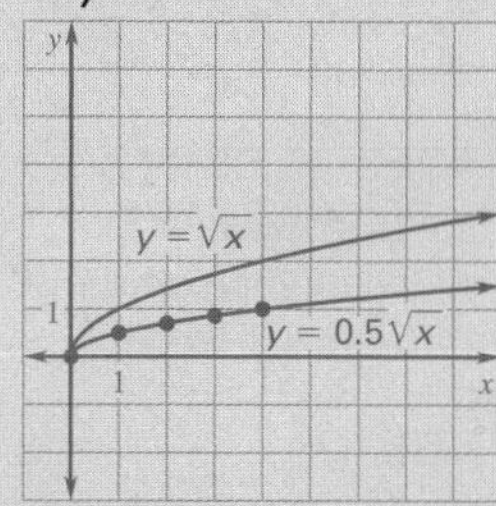

Domain: $x \geq 0$; range: $y \geq 0$; the graph is a vertical shrink (by a factor of 0.5) of the graph of $y = \sqrt{x}$.

Extra Example 2

Graph the function $y = -1.5\sqrt{x}$ and identify its domain and range. Compare the graph with the graph of $y = \sqrt{x}$.

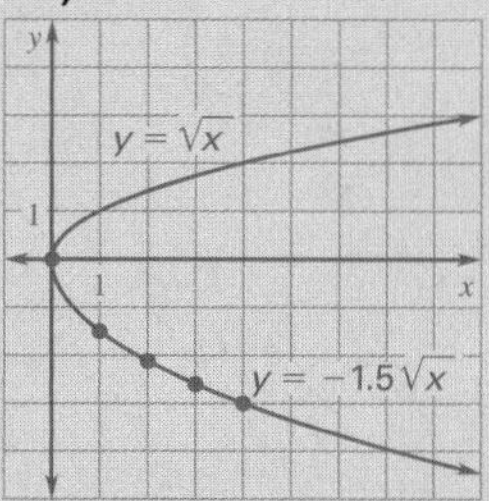

Domain: $x \geq 0$; range: $y \leq 0$; the graph is a vertical stretch (by a factor of 1.5) and a reflection in the x-axis of the graph of $y = \sqrt{x}$.

1–4. See Additional Answers beginning on p. AA1.

Differentiated Instruction

Below Level Some students may find it easier to graph the parent function and to compare graphs if they first make a table for $y = \sqrt{x}$. Suggest that they use five x-values to help them draw a smooth curve. Show students they can check the factor of the vertical stretch or shrink in Examples 1 and 2 by multiplying the y-value of the parent graph by the factor of the stretch or shrink. Compare this to Example 3 where they check that the translation is 2 units up by adding 2 to the y-value of the parent graph, rather than multiplying.

See also the *Algebra 1 Toolkit* for more strategies.

EXAMPLE 4 Graph a function of the form $y = \sqrt{x - h}$

Graph the function $y = \sqrt{x - 4}$ and identify its domain and range. Compare the graph with the graph of $y = \sqrt{x}$.

Solution

To graph the function, make a table, then plot and connect the points. To find the domain, find the values of x for which the radicand, $x - 4$, is nonnegative. The domain is $x \geq 4$.

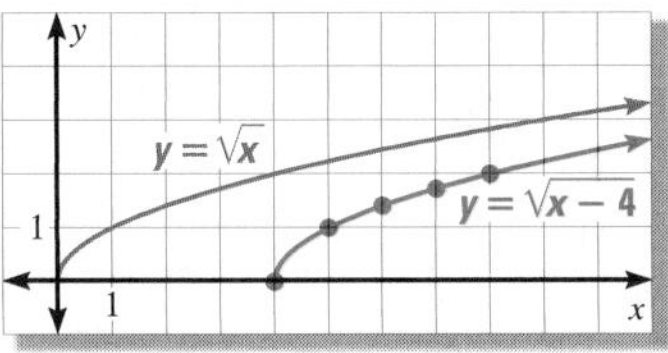

x	4	5	6	7	8
y	0	1	1.4	1.7	2

The range is $y \geq 0$. The graph of $y = \sqrt{x - 4}$ is a horizontal translation (of 4 units to the right) of the graph of $y = \sqrt{x}$.

KEY CONCEPT — *For Your Notebook*

Graphs of Square Root Functions

To graph a function of the form $y = a\sqrt{x - h} + k$, you can follow these steps.

STEP 1 **Sketch** the graph of $y = a\sqrt{x}$. The graph of $y = a\sqrt{x}$ starts at the origin and passes through the point $(1, a)$.

STEP 2 **Shift** the graph $|h|$ units horizontally (to the right if h is positive and to the left if h is negative) and $|k|$ units vertically (up if k is positive and down if k is negative).

EXAMPLE 5 Graph a function of the form $y = a\sqrt{x - h} + k$

Graph the function $y = 2\sqrt{x + 4} - 1$.

STEP 1 **Sketch** the graph of $y = 2\sqrt{x}$.

STEP 2 **Shift** the graph $|h|$ units horizontally and $|k|$ units vertically. Notice that

$$y = 2\sqrt{x + 4} - 1 = 2\sqrt{x - (-4)} + (-1).$$

So, $h = -4$ and $k = -1$. Shift the graph left 4 units and down 1 unit.

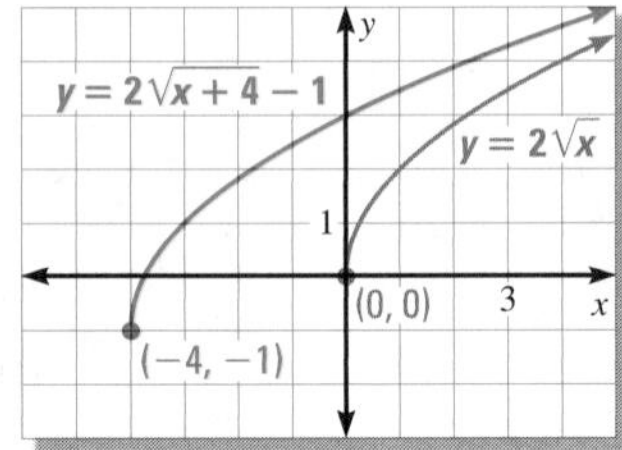

✓ GUIDED PRACTICE for Examples 4 and 5

5. Graph the function $y = \sqrt{x + 3}$ and identify its domain and range. Compare the graph with the graph of $y = \sqrt{x}$.
See margin for art; domain: $x \geq -3$, range: $y \geq 0$; horizontal translation 3 units to the left.

6. Identify the domain and range of the function in Example 5.
domain: $x \geq -4$, range: $y \geq -1$

Extra Example 3

Graph the function $y = \sqrt{x} - 2$ and identify its domain and range. Compare the graph with the graph of $y = \sqrt{x}$.

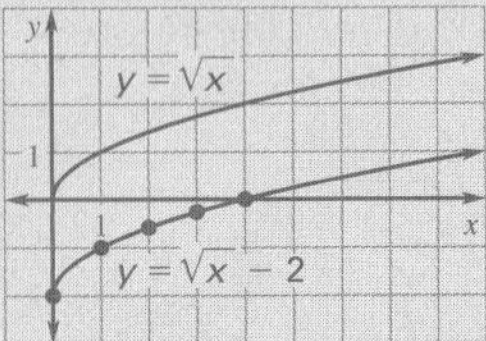

Domain: $x \geq 0$; range: $y \geq -2$; the graph is a translation 2 units down of the graph of $y = \sqrt{x}$.

An **Animated Algebra** activity is available on-line for **Example 3**. This activity is also available on the **Power Presentations CD-ROM**.

Extra Example 4

Graph the function $y = \sqrt{x + 2}$ and identify its domain and range. Compare the graph with the graph of $y = \sqrt{x}$.

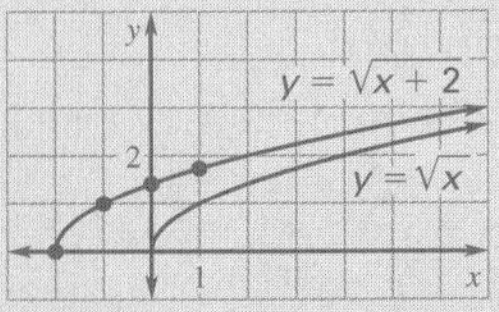

Domain: $x \geq -2$; range: $y \geq 0$; the graph is a horizontal translation 2 units to the left of $y = \sqrt{x}$.

Extra Example 5

Graph the function $y = 2\sqrt{x - 1} + 2$.

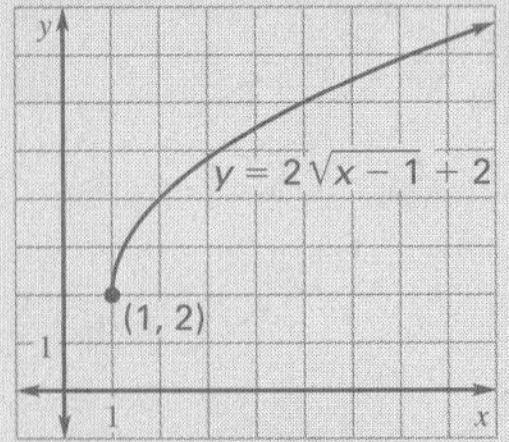

Key Question to Ask for Example 5

- What are the domain and range of $y = 2\sqrt{x + 4} - 1$? **The domain is $x \geq -4$ and the range is $y \geq -1$.**

5.

Differentiated Instruction

Visual Learners Some students may notice that the graph of the parent function $y = \sqrt{x}$ is the right half of the graph of $y = x^2$ flipped onto its side. Explain that such a transformation of a graph is a result of switching the variables x and y. That is, switching x and y in $y = x^2$ gives $x = y^2$. Taking the square root of both sides gives $\sqrt{x} = y$, or $y = \sqrt{x}$.

See also the *Algebra 1 Toolkit* for more strategies.

EXAMPLE 6 Solve a real-world problem

MICROPHONE SALES For the period 1988–2002, the amount of sales y (in millions of dollars) of microphones in the United States can be modeled by the function $y = 93\sqrt{x} + 2.2$ where x is the number of years since 1988. Graph the function on a graphing calculator. In what year were microphone sales about $325 million?

ANOTHER WAY
You can graph $y = 93\sqrt{x} + 2.2$ and $y = 325$. The x-coordinate of the point where the graphs intersect represents the year in which sales were about $325 million.

Solution

The graph of the function is shown.

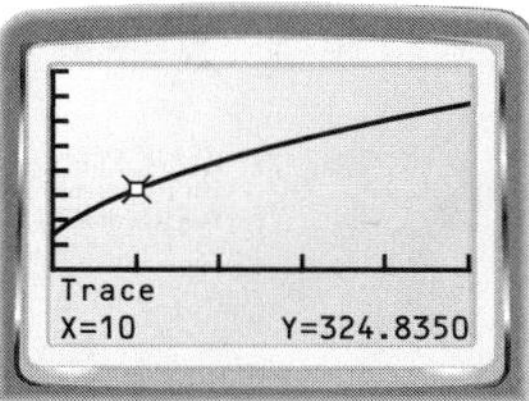

Using the *trace* feature, you can see that $y \approx 325$ when $x = 10$. So, microphone sales were about $325 million 10 years after 1988, or in 1998.

✓ GUIDED PRACTICE for Example 6

7. **MICROPHONE SALES** Use the function in Example 6 to find the year in which microphone sales were about $250 million. 1993

11.1 EXERCISES

HOMEWORK KEY
○ = **WORKED-OUT SOLUTIONS** on p. WS26 for Exs. 7, 23, and 45
★ = **STANDARDIZED TEST PRACTICE** Exs. 2, 15, 16, 29, 39, 41, and 48

SKILL PRACTICE

A

1. **VOCABULARY** Copy and complete: A function containing a radical expression with the independent variable in the radicand is called a(n) __?__. radical function

2. ★ **WRITING** Is the graph of $y = 1.25\sqrt{x}$ a vertical stretch or a vertical shrink of the graph of $y = \sqrt{x}$? *Explain* your answer.
Vertical stretch. *Sample answer*: Since $|1.25| > 1$, the graph is a vertical stretch.

EXAMPLES 1 and 2 on pp. 710–711 for Exs. 3–16

GRAPHING FUNCTIONS **Graph the function and identify its domain and range. Compare the graph with the graph of $y = \sqrt{x}$.** 3–14. See margin.

3. $y = 4\sqrt{x}$
4. $y = 5\sqrt{x}$
5. $y = 0.5\sqrt{x}$
6. $y = 0.25\sqrt{x}$

7. $y = \frac{3}{2}\sqrt{x}$
8. $y = \frac{1}{3}\sqrt{x}$
9. $y = -3\sqrt{x}$
10. $y = -6\sqrt{x}$
11. $y = -0.8\sqrt{x}$
12. $y = -0.75\sqrt{x}$
13. $y = -\frac{1}{4}\sqrt{x}$
14. $y = -\frac{5}{2}\sqrt{x}$

15. ★ **MULTIPLE CHOICE** The graph of which function is a vertical shrink of the graph of $y = \sqrt{x}$? C

Ⓐ $y = -5\sqrt{x}$ Ⓑ $y = -\sqrt{x}$ Ⓒ $y = \frac{1}{2}\sqrt{x}$ Ⓓ $y = 8\sqrt{x}$

16. ★ **WRITING** The range of the function $y = a\sqrt{x}$ is $y \le 0$. What can you conclude about the value of a? How do you know? See margin.

Extra Example 6

For the period 1990–2004, the amount of sales y (in thousands of dollars) of bicycles at a shop can be modeled by the function $y = 24\sqrt{x} + 4.6$, where x is the number of years since 1990. Graph the function on a graphing calculator. In what year were bicycle sales about $95 thousand? 2001

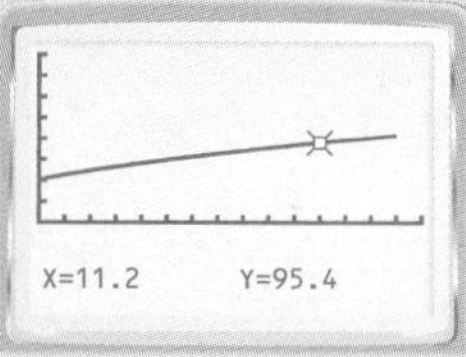

Closing the Lesson

Have students summarize the major points of the lesson and answer the Essential Question: How do you graph square root functions?

- The parent square root function is $y = \sqrt{x}$. A vertical stretch of the parent function results when $|a|$ in the equation $y = a\sqrt{x}$ is greater than 1. If $|a|$ is between 0 and 1, a vertical shrink results. A reflection in the x-axis results when $a < 0$.
- Vertical and horizontal translations of $y = a\sqrt{x}$ result when h and k in the equation $y = a\sqrt{x - h} + k$ are replaced by real numbers.

To graph square root functions, make a table of values, plot the points, and then draw a smooth curve through the points. The radicand must be nonnegative, so values of x in the radicand must result in nonnegative numbers.

3–14. See Additional Answers beginning on p. AA1.

16. $a < 0$; *Sample answer:* If $a > 0$, the range of the function would include positive numbers, so a cannot be greater than 0. If a were 0, y would always be 0.

4 PRACTICE AND APPLY

Assignment Guide

Answer Transparencies available for all exercises

Basic:
Day 1: EP p. 947 Exs. 1–7 odd
pp. 713–716
Exs. 1–22
Day 2: pp. 713–716
Exs. 23–34, 43–46, 50–66 even

Average:
Day 1: pp. 713–716
Exs. 1, 2, 5–22, 41
Day 2: pp. 713–716
Exs. 25–40, 43–47, 51–67 odd

Advanced:
Day 1: pp. 713–716
Exs. 1, 2, 6–22, 41, 42*
Day 2: pp. 713–716
Exs. 26–40, 43–49*, 50–66 even

Block:
pp. 713–716
Exs. 1, 2, 5–22, 25–41, 43–47, 51–67 odd

Differentiated Instruction

See *Algebra 1 Best Practices Toolkit* for suggestions on addressing the needs of a diverse classroom.

Homework Check

For a quick check of student understanding of key concepts, go over the following exercises:

Basic: 6, 18, 24, 31, 43

Average: 10, 20, 25, 34, 44

Advanced: 13, 21, 26, 36, 45

Extra Practice

- Student Edition, p. 948
- Chapter 11 Resource Book: Practice levels A, B, C, pp. 7–12

Practice Worksheet

An easily-readable reduced practice page (with answers) for this lesson can be found on p.708C.

17–28, 30–38. See Additional Answers beginning on p. AA1.

EXAMPLES 3 and 4 on pp. 711–712 for Exs. 17–29

GRAPHING FUNCTIONS Graph the function and identify its domain and range. Compare the graph with the graph of $y = \sqrt{x}$. 17–28. See margin.

17. $y = \sqrt{x} + 1$ **18.** $y = \sqrt{x} + 5$ **19.** $y = \sqrt{x} - 3$

20. $y = \sqrt{x} - 4$ **21.** $y = \sqrt{x} + \frac{3}{4}$ **22.** $y = \sqrt{x} - 4.5$

(23.) $y = \sqrt{x - 1}$ **24.** $y = \sqrt{x - 6}$ **25.** $y = \sqrt{x + 2}$

26. $y = \sqrt{x + 4}$ **27.** $y = \sqrt{x + 1.5}$ **28.** $y = \sqrt{x - \frac{1}{2}}$

29. ★ **MULTIPLE CHOICE** The graph of which function is a horizontal translation of 3 units to the right of the graph of $y = \sqrt{x}$? D

(A) $y = \sqrt{x} + 3$ (B) $y = \sqrt{x} - 3$

(C) $y = \sqrt{x + 3}$ (D) $y = \sqrt{x - 3}$

EXAMPLE 5 on p. 712 for Exs. 30–39

B

GRAPHING FUNCTIONS Graph the function. 30–38. See margin.

30. $y = \sqrt{x + 3} - 2$ **31.** $y = \sqrt{x - 2} + 5$ **32.** $y = 2\sqrt{x} + 1$

33. $y = -\sqrt{x + 1} + 2$ **34.** $y = -3\sqrt{x + 2} - 6$ **35.** $y = 4\sqrt{x + 4} - 4$

36. $y = \frac{1}{2}\sqrt{x - 5} - 3$ **37.** $y = -\frac{3}{2}\sqrt{x - 1} - 5$ **38.** $y = -\frac{3}{4}\sqrt{x + 8} - 3$

39. ★ **MULTIPLE CHOICE** The graph of which function is shown? A

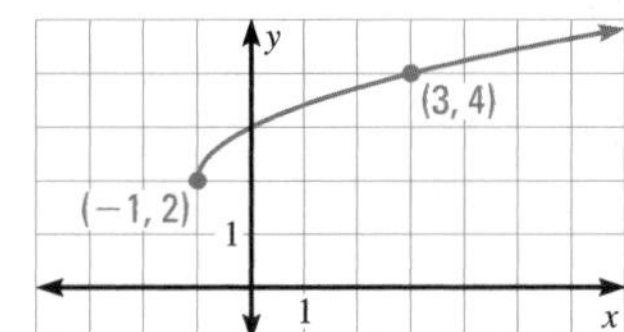

(A) $y = \sqrt{x + 1} + 2$

(B) $y = \sqrt{x - 1} + 2$

(C) $y = \sqrt{x + 1} - 2$

(D) $y = \sqrt{x - 1} - 2$

40. **ERROR ANALYSIS** *Describe* and correct the error in explaining how to graph the function $y = -5\sqrt{x - 9} - 10$.

The discussion about shifting the graph is incorrect. It should say "Then shift the graph 9 units to the right and 10 units down."

> To graph $y = -5\sqrt{x - 9} - 10$, sketch the graph of $y = -5\sqrt{x}$. Then shift the graph 9 units to the left and 10 units down.

C

41. ★ **MULTIPLE CHOICE** How is the graph of $g(x) = 4\sqrt{x} - 3$ related to the graph of $h(x) = 4\sqrt{x} + 3$? C

(A) It is a vertical stretch by a factor of 3 of the graph of h.

(B) It is a vertical translation of 3 units down of the graph of h.

(C) It is a vertical translation of 6 units down of the graph of h.

(D) It is a horizontal translation of 6 units to the left of the graph of h.

42. **CHALLENGE** Write a rule for a radical function that has a domain of all real numbers greater than or equal to −5 and a range of all real numbers less than or equal to 3. $y = -\sqrt{x + 5} + 3$

○ = WORKED-OUT SOLUTIONS on p. WS1 ★ = STANDARDIZED TEST PRACTICE

PROBLEM SOLVING

EXAMPLE 6 A on p. 713 for Exs. 43–45

GRAPHING CALCULATOR **You may wish to use a graphing calculator to complete the following Problem Solving exercises.**

43. SUSPENSION BRIDGE The time t (in seconds) it takes an object dropped from a height h (in feet) to reach the ground is given by the function $t = \frac{1}{4}\sqrt{h}$.

a. Graph the function and identify its domain and range. See margin for art; domain: $x \geq 0$, range: $y \geq 0$.

b. The Royal Gorge Bridge in Colorado is the world's highest suspension bridge. It takes about 8 seconds for a stone dropped from the bridge to reach the gorge below. About how high is the bridge?

43b. about 1024 ft

@HomeTutor for problem solving help at classzone.com

44. OCEANOGRAPHY Ocean waves can be shallow water, intermediate depth, or deep water waves. The speed s (in meters per second) of a shallow water wave can be modeled by the function $s = 3.13\sqrt{d}$ where d is the depth (in meters) of the water over which the wave is traveling.

a. Graph the function and identify its domain and range. See margin for art; domain: $x \geq 0$, range: $y \geq 0$.

b. A tsunami is a type of shallow water wave. Suppose a tsunami has a speed of 200 meters per second. Over approximately what depth of water is the tsunami traveling? about 4083 m

@HomeTutor for problem solving help at classzone.com

45. LONG JUMP A function for the speed at which a long jumper is running before jumping is $s = 10.9\sqrt{h}$ where s and h are defined in the diagram. Graph the function and identify its domain and range. To the nearest tenth, approximate the maximum height reached when the long jumper's speed before jumping is 10.25 meters per second.

See margin for art; domain: $x \geq 0$, range: $y \geq 0$; about 0.9 m.

46. MULTI-STEP PROBLEM The reading age of written materials is the age at which an average person can read and understand the materials. A function that is sometimes used to identify the reading age r (in years) of written materials is $r = \sqrt{w} + 8$ where w is the average number of words with 3 or more syllables in samples taken from the written materials.

a. Graph the function and identify its domain and range. See margin for art; domain: $x \geq 0$, range: $y \geq 8$.

b. What is the average number of words with 3 or more syllables in samples taken from material that can be read and understood by a 10-year-old? 4 words

Avoiding Common Errors

Exercises 17–22 Watch for students who treat a number added to the radical expression as part of the radicand. You may want to remind these students that the graphs in these exercises are vertical translations.

Study Strategy

Exercises 30–38 Tell students that it may be helpful to go through each of the functions before they begin to graph them to determine the general form of the graph of the function. This will help them to start focusing on whether the graph is a vertical stretch or shrink, a reflection, or a translation of the parent function. Suggest that they make short notes next to the exercises and then check their graphs against these notes to see whether they have a good grasp of the concepts.

Mathematical Reasoning

Exercises 23–28, 30–31, 33–38 Some students may wonder why the radicand must be a nonnegative number. You may want to ask what would be the square root of −9, leading students to see that square root functions are limited to real numbers and therefore the radicand cannot be a negative number.

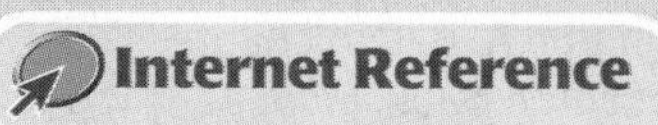

Exercise 44 For more information about tsunamis, visit the National Oceanic and Atmospheric Administration website at www.tsunami.noaa.gov/tsunami_story.html

43a.
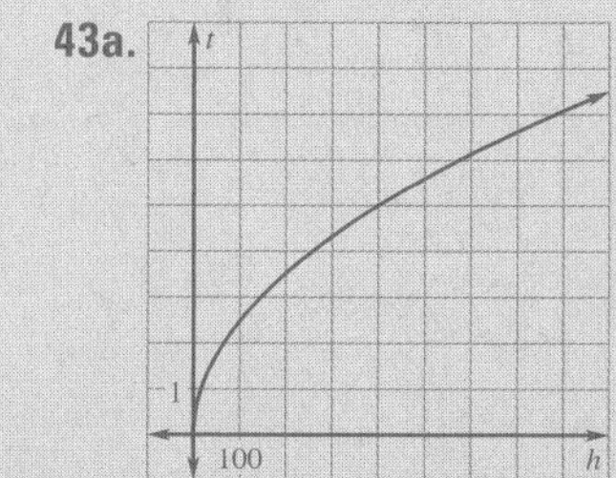

44a.
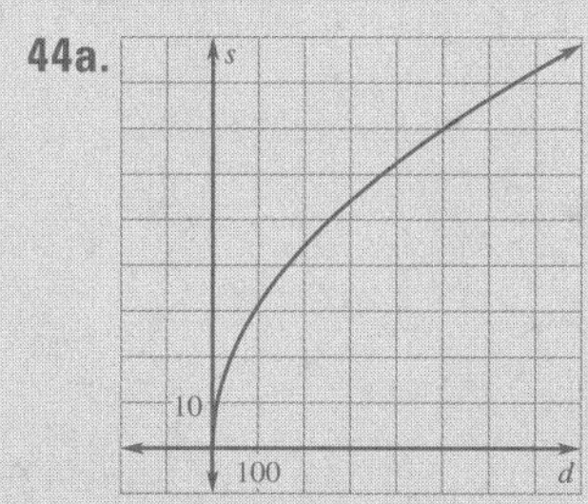

45.

46a.
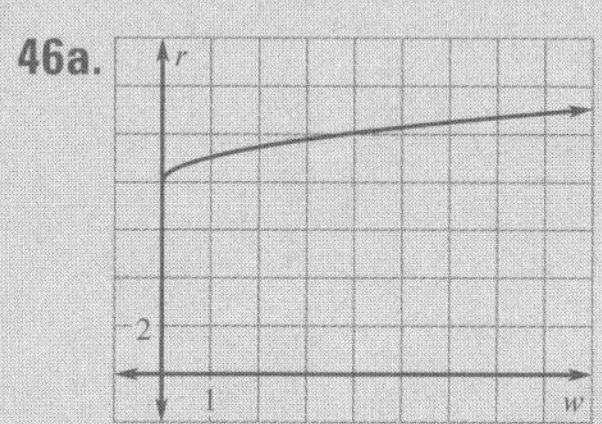

5 ASSESS AND RETEACH

Daily Homework Quiz

Transparency Available

1. Graph the function $y = 2\sqrt{x} + 1$.

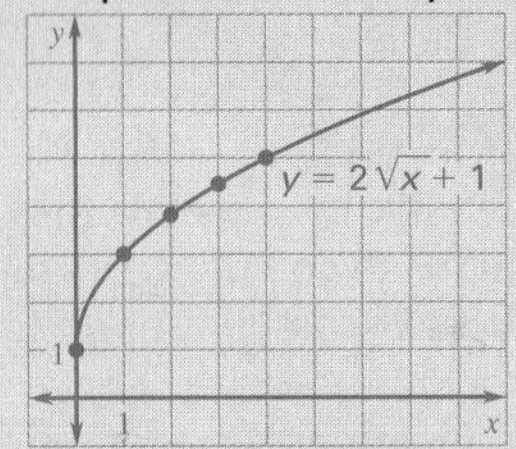

2. Graph the function

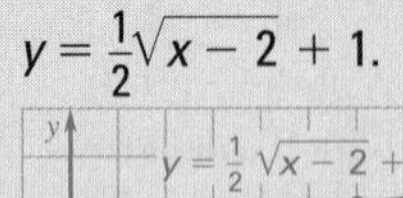

$y = \frac{1}{2}\sqrt{x - 2} + 1$.

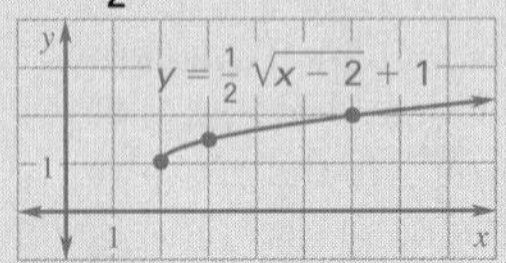

3. Use the function $t = \frac{1}{4}\sqrt{h}$, where t is time (in seconds) and h is distance (in feet) to model a sky diver's freefall. How many feet did a sky diver freefall if the freefall lasted 9 seconds?
1296 ft

Available at **classzone.com**

Diagnosis/Remediation

- Practice A, B, C in Chapter 11 Resource Book, pp. 7–12
- Study Guide in Chapter 11 Resource Book, pp. 13–14
- Practice Workbook, pp. 169–171
- @HomeTutor

Challenge

Additional challenge is available in the Chapter 11 Resource Book, p. 17.

47a, 48a, 48c. See Additional Answers beginning on p. AA1.

B **47. BIOLOGY** Biologists studied two types of duck in the northern Great Plains of the United States from 1987 to 1990. The biologists found functions, given below, that model the number y of breeding pairs of each type of duck in wetlands with area x (in hectares).

Blue-winged teal: $y = 0.7\sqrt{x}$

Northern pintail: $y = 0.2\sqrt{x}$

a. Graph the functions in the same coordinate plane. Identify the domain and range of each function. **See margin.**

b. Find the area (to the nearest hectare) for 1 breeding pair of each type of duck. **blue-winged teal: about 2 hectares, northern pintail: 25 hectares**

C **48. ★ EXTENDED RESPONSE** The amount of mozzarella cheese y (in pounds per person) consumed in the United States for the period 1980–2001 can be modeled by $y = 2\sqrt{x + 1}$ where x is the number of years since 1980.

a. Graph Graph the function and identify its domain and range. **See margin for art; domain: $x \ge -1$, range: $y \ge 0$.**

b. Apply In what year was the amount of mozzarella cheese consumed equal to 2 pounds per person? **1980**

c. Explain In what year was the amount of mozzarella cheese consumed per person double the amount consumed per person in 1980? *Explain.* **See margin.**

49. CHALLENGE The flow rate r (in gallons per minute) of water through a high-pressure water hose is given by $r = 29.7d^2\sqrt{p}$ where d is the nozzle diameter (in inches) and p is the nozzle pressure (in pounds per square inch). For what value of d would the graph of the function be identical to the graph of the parent square root function? For what values of d would the graph be a vertical stretch? a vertical shrink? $\frac{1}{\sqrt{29.7}}$; $d > \frac{1}{\sqrt{29.7}}$; $0 < d < \frac{1}{\sqrt{29.7}}$

ILLINOIS MIXED REVIEW

50. The area of a rectangle is given by $3\ell^2 + 11\ell = 20$, in which ℓ is the rectangle's length. What is the length of the rectangle? **B**

Ⓐ $\frac{1}{3}$ Ⓑ $\frac{4}{3}$ Ⓒ 4 Ⓓ 5

51. $\triangle JKL$ is similar to $\triangle MNL$. What is x? **C**

Ⓐ 7.47 Ⓑ 19.6

Ⓒ 26.25 Ⓓ Not here

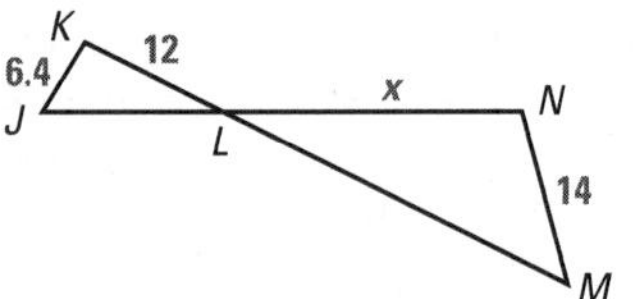

Graphing Calculator **ACTIVITY** *Use after Lesson 11.1*

@HomeTutor
classzone.com
Keystrokes

11.1 Graph Square Root Functions

QUESTION How can you use a graphing calculator to graph square root functions?

EXAMPLE Graph the function $y = \sqrt{2x + 3}$ and describe its domain and range

STEP 1 *Enter the function*
Enter the function into a graphing calculator. Use parentheses around the radicand.

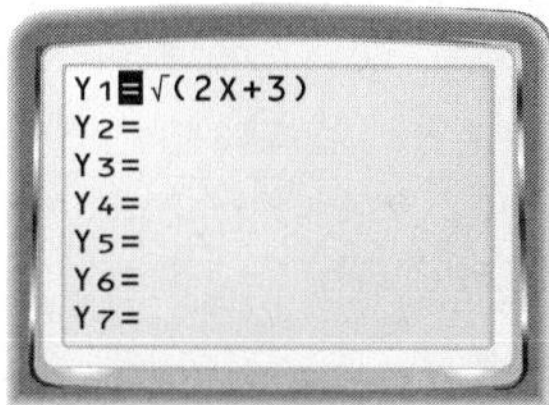

STEP 2 *Graph the function*
Graph the function. Adjust the viewing window if necessary.

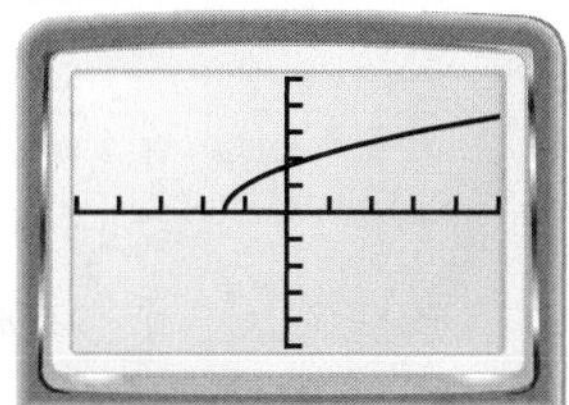

STEP 3 *Describe the domain and range*
From the graph, you can see that the domain is all real numbers greater than or equal to -1.5, or $x \geq -1.5$. The range is all nonnegative numbers, or $y \geq 0$.

PRACTICE

Graph the function using a graphing calculator. Then describe the domain and range of the function. 1–12. See margin.

1. $y = \sqrt{4x}$
2. $y = \sqrt{9x}$
3. $y = \sqrt{7x}$
4. $y = -\sqrt{10x}$
5. $y = -3\sqrt{x}$
6. $y = 1.5\sqrt{3x}$
7. $y = 4.4\sqrt{8x}$
8. $y = \sqrt{2x + 8}$
9. $y = \sqrt{3x + 4}$
10. $y = -\sqrt{2x - 5}$
11. $y = -\sqrt{4x - 6}$
12. $y = \frac{1}{2}\sqrt{6 - 5x}$

13. **ROLLER COASTER** If friction is ignored, the velocity v (in meters per second) of a roller coaster when it reaches the bottom of a hill can be calculated using the formula $v = \sqrt{19.6h}$ where h (in meters) is the height of the hill.
    a. Graph the function and describe its domain and range. See margin for art; domain: $x \geq 0$, range: $y \geq 0$.
    b. Use the graph to find the height of a hill if the velocity of the roller coaster at the bottom of the hill is 55 meters per second. about 154.3 m

1–12. See Additional Answers beginning on p. AA1.

13a.

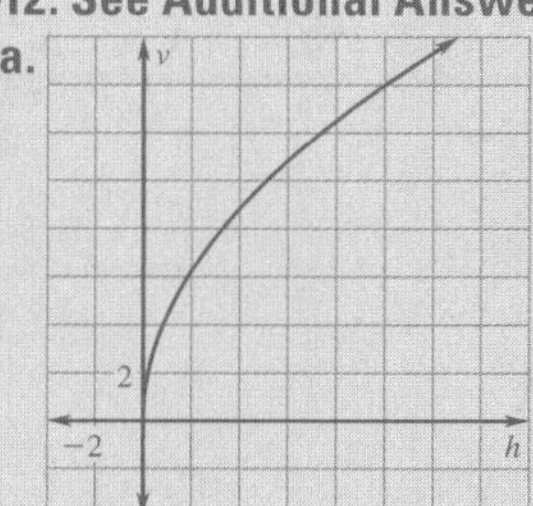

1 PLAN AND PREPARE

Learn the Method

- Students will graph square root functions.
- After the activity, students can use a graphing calculator to check their solutions in Exercises 3–14, 17–28, and 30–38 in Lesson 11.1.

Keystroke Help

Keystrokes for several models of calculators are available in blackline format in the *Chapter 11 Resource Book*.

2 TEACH

Tips for Success

In Step 3, students can use the *trace* feature if they are unsure of the domain.

Extra Example

Graph the function $y = \sqrt{2x - 5}$ and describe its domain and range.
Domain: $x \geq 2.5$, Range: $y \geq 0$.

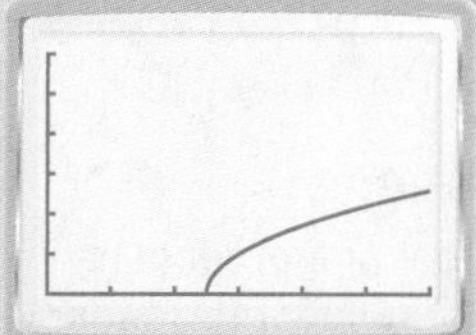

3 ASSESS AND RETEACH

The velocity v (in feet per second) of an object dropped from a height can be found using the formula $v = \sqrt{64d}$, where d (in feet) is the distance the object is dropped. Explain how to use your graphing calculator to find the velocity of an object that that has fallen 80 feet. **Graph the function using x for distance and y for velocity. Use the trace feature to find the value of y when $x = 80$.**

1 PLAN AND PREPARE

Explore the Concept

- Students will simplify products and quotients of square roots.
- This activity leads into the study of using the product property of radicals in Example 1 in Lesson 11.2.

Materials

Each student will need:

- calculator
- Activity Support Master (*Chapter 11 Resource Book*, p. 20)

Recommended Time

Work activity: 10 min

Discuss results: 5 min

Grouping

Students should work individually.

2 TEACH

Key Question

- How are the examples in Step 1 different from those in Step 2? The factors are perfect squares in Step 1 but not in Step 2.

Key Discovery

The square root of a product is equal to the product of the square roots of the factors. The square root of a quotient is equal to the quotient of the square roots of the numerator and denominator.

3 ASSESS AND RETEACH

1. Write an equivalent expression for $\sqrt{6b}$. $\sqrt{6} \cdot \sqrt{b}$
2. Write an equivalent expression for $\sqrt{\frac{7}{a}}$. $\frac{\sqrt{7}}{\sqrt{a}}$

Investigating Algebra ACTIVITY *Use before Lesson 11.2*

11.2 Properties of Radicals

MATERIALS • calculator

QUESTION How can you simplify products and quotients of square roots?

EXPLORE Simplify products and quotients of square roots

STEP 1 ***Find products of square roots***

Copy and complete the table without using a calculator. Compare the values in the second and third columns.

Values of a and b	Value of $\sqrt{a} \cdot \sqrt{b}$	Value of $\sqrt{ab}$
$a = 4, b = 9$	? 6	? 6
$a = 9, b = 16$	? 12	? 12
$a = 25, b = 4$	? 10	? 10
$a = 16, b = 36$	? 24	? 24

STEP 2 ***Find products of square roots***

Use a calculator to copy and complete the table. Compare the values in the second and third columns.

Values of a and b	Value of $\sqrt{a} \cdot \sqrt{b}$	Value of $\sqrt{ab}$
$a = 2, b = 3$	? 2.45	? 2.45
$a = 10, b = 5$	? 7.07	? 7.07
$a = 7, b = 11$	? 8.77	? 8.77
$a = 13, b = 6$	? 8.83	? 8.83

STEP 3 ***Find quotients of square roots***

Copy and complete the table without using a calculator. Compare the values in the second and third columns.

Values of a and b	Value of $\frac{\sqrt{a}}{\sqrt{b}}$	Value of $\sqrt{\frac{a}{b}}$
$a = 4, b = 16$	? $\frac{1}{2}$	? $\frac{1}{2}$
$a = 9, b = 25$	? $\frac{3}{5}$	? $\frac{3}{5}$
$a = 36, b = 4$	? 3	? 3
$a = 4, b = 49$	? $\frac{2}{7}$	? $\frac{2}{7}$

STEP 4 ***Find quotients of square roots***

Use a calculator to copy and complete the table. Compare the values in the second and third columns.

Values of a and b	Value of $\frac{\sqrt{a}}{\sqrt{b}}$	Value of $\sqrt{\frac{a}{b}}$
$a = 1, b = 2$	? 0.71	? 0.71
$a = 3, b = 8$	? 0.61	? 0.61
$a = 12, b = 7$	? 1.31	? 1.31
$a = 6, b = 11$	? 0.74	? 0.74

DRAW CONCLUSIONS Use your observations to complete these exercises

In Exercises 1 and 2, copy and complete the statement.

1. The product of two square roots is equal to __?__. the square root of the product of the radicands
2. The quotient of a square root and a nonzero square root is equal to __?__. the square root of the quotient of the radicands
3. **REASONING** Do you think that $\sqrt{a} + \sqrt{b} = \sqrt{a + b}$ for any $a \ge 0$ and any $b \ge 0$? *Justify* your answer. No. *Sample answer*: If $a = 1$ and $b = 4$, then $\sqrt{a} + \sqrt{b} = 1 + 2 = 3$, which does not equal $\sqrt{a + b} = \sqrt{1 + 2} = \sqrt{3}$.

11.2 Simplify Radical Expressions

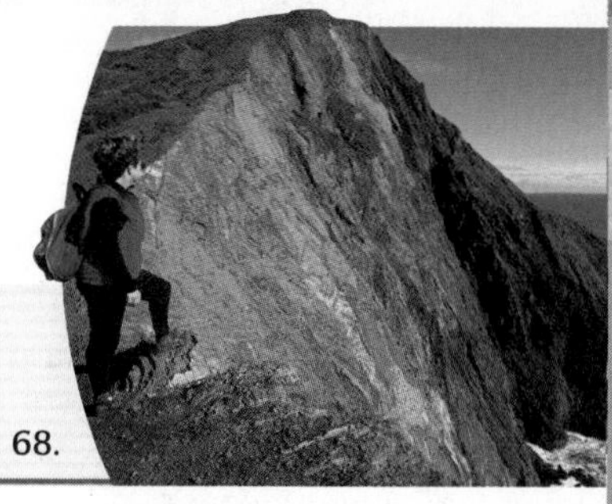

8.11.01 Simplify or identify equivalent algebraic expressions (e.g., exponential, rational, logarithmic, factored, polynomial).

Before You found square roots.

Now You will simplify radical expressions.

Why? So you can find the distance to the horizon, as in Ex. 68.

Key Vocabulary
- **simplest form of a radical expression**
- **rationalizing the denominator**

A radical expression is in **simplest form** if the following conditions are true:

- No perfect square factors other than 1 are in the radicand.
- No fractions are in the radicand.
- No radicals appear in the denominator of a fraction.

You can use the following property to simplify radical expressions.

KEY CONCEPT *For Your Notebook*

Product Property of Radicals

Words The square root of a product equals the product of the square roots of the factors.

Algebra $\sqrt{ab} = \sqrt{a} \cdot \sqrt{b}$ where $a \geq 0$ and $b \geq 0$

Example $\sqrt{4x} = \sqrt{4} \cdot \sqrt{x} = 2\sqrt{x}$

You can also use the fact that $\sqrt{a^2} = a$, where $a \geq 0$, to simplify radical expressions. In this lesson, whenever a variable appears in the radicand *assume that it has only nonnegative values.*

REVIEW SQUARE ROOTS
For help finding square roots of perfect squares, see p. 110.

EXAMPLE 1 Use the product property of radicals

a. $\sqrt{32} = \sqrt{16 \cdot 2}$ Factor using perfect square factor.

$= \sqrt{16} \cdot \sqrt{2}$ Product property of radicals

$= 4\sqrt{2}$ Simplify.

b. $\sqrt{9x^3} = \sqrt{9 \cdot x^2 \cdot x}$ Factor using perfect square factors.

$= \sqrt{9} \cdot \sqrt{x^2} \cdot \sqrt{x}$ Product property of radicals

$= 3x\sqrt{x}$ Simplify.

Animated Algebra at classzone.com

GUIDED PRACTICE for Example 1

1. Simplify (**a**) $\sqrt{24}$ and (**b**) $\sqrt{25x^2}$. (a) $2\sqrt{6}$; (b) $5x$

1 PLAN AND PREPARE

Warm-Up Exercises

Transparency Available

Use the distributive property to write an equivalent expression.

1. $2(x + 6)$ $2x + 12$

2. $x(x^2 + 2)$ $x^3 + 2x$

3. $(x + x^2)(-3)$ $-3x - 3x^2$

4. $0.1(6 + 10x)$ $0.6 + x$

5. The area of a square field is 148 square meters. What is the side length of the field? about 12.2 m

Notetaking Guide

Transparency Available

Promotes interactive learning and notetaking skills, pp. 251–255.

Pacing

Basic: 2 days
Average: 2 days
Advanced: 2 days
Block: 1 block
- See *Teaching Guide/Lesson Plan.*

2 FOCUS AND MOTIVATE

Essential Question

Big Idea 2, p. 709

How do you simplify radical expressions? Tell students they will learn how to answer this question by using properties of radicals.

Resource Planning Guide

Chapter Resource Book
- Teaching Guide/Lesson Plan (pp. 18–19)
- Practice levels A, B, C (pp. 21–23)
- Study Guide (pp. 24–25)
- Catch-up for Absent Students (p. 26)
- Application (p. 27)
- Challenge (p. 28)

Workbooks
- Notetaking Guide (pp. 251–255)
- Practice Workbook (pp. 172–173)

Teaching Options
- **Power Presentations CD-ROM** provides dynamic electronic teaching resources for the classroom.
- **Activity Generator CD-ROM** provides editable activities for all ability levels.

Interactive Technology
- Easy Planner
- Power Presentations CD-ROM
- Activity Generator CD-ROM
- Animated Algebra
- Test Generator CD-ROM
- Online Quiz
- eWorkbook
- eEdition
- @HomeTutor

Resources for English Learners
- Quick Reference for English Learners
- Spanish Study Guide
- Multi-Language Visual Glossary
- Student Resources in Spanish

See also the *Algebra 1 Toolkit* for more strategies for meeting individual needs.

Motivating the Lesson

Ask students if they have ever wondered how far away the horizon is from a height of 32,000 feet in an airplane. Tell them that a formula containing a radical expression can help them estimate the distance.

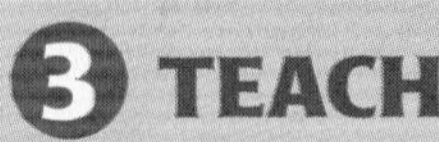

3 TEACH

Extra Example 1

Simplify.

a. $\sqrt{48}$ $4\sqrt{3}$

b. $\sqrt{25x^5}$ $5x^2\sqrt{x}$

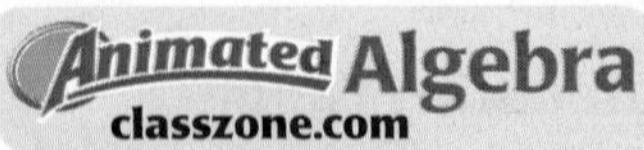

An **Animated Algebra** activity is available on-line for **Example 1**. This activity is also available on the **Power Presentations CD-ROM**.

Extra Example 2

Simplify.

a. $\sqrt{7} \cdot \sqrt{7}$ 7

b. $3\sqrt{b} \cdot \sqrt{2b^3}$ $3b^2\sqrt{2}$

c. $2\sqrt{mn^2} \cdot \sqrt{5m^2}$ $2mn\sqrt{5m}$

Extra Example 3

Simplify.

a. $\sqrt{\frac{5}{49}}$ $\frac{\sqrt{5}}{7}$

b. $\sqrt{\frac{11}{d^4}}$ $\frac{\sqrt{11}}{d^2}$

Key Question to Ask for Example 3

- In part b, why does the numerator remain the same but the denominator simplifies? The radicand in the numerator has no perfect squares other than 1, but the radicand in the denominator can be simplified since x^2 is the product of $x \cdot x$.

EXAMPLE 2 Multiply radicals

a. $\sqrt{6} \cdot \sqrt{6} = \sqrt{6 \cdot 6}$ — Product property of radicals

$= \sqrt{36}$ — Multiply.

$= 6$ — Simplify.

b. $\sqrt{3x} \cdot 4\sqrt{x} = 4\sqrt{3x \cdot x}$ — Product property of radicals

$= 4\sqrt{3x^2}$ — Multiply.

$= 4 \cdot \sqrt{3} \cdot \sqrt{x^2}$ — Product property of radicals

$= 4x\sqrt{3}$ — Simplify.

WRITE RADICALS
When writing a product involving a radical, write the radical last to avoid confusion. For instance, if you write the product of x and $\sqrt{2}$ as $\sqrt{2}x$, it might be read as $\sqrt{2x}$.

c. $\sqrt{7xy^2} \cdot 3\sqrt{x} = 3\sqrt{7xy^2 \cdot x}$ — Product property of radicals

$= 3\sqrt{7x^2y^2}$ — Multiply.

$= 3 \cdot \sqrt{7} \cdot \sqrt{x^2} \cdot \sqrt{y^2}$ — Product property of radicals

$= 3xy\sqrt{7}$ — Simplify.

KEY CONCEPT — *For Your Notebook*

Quotient Property of Radicals

Words The square root of a quotient equals the quotient of the square roots of the numerator and denominator.

Algebra $\sqrt{\frac{a}{b}} = \frac{\sqrt{a}}{\sqrt{b}}$ where $a \geq 0$ and $b > 0$

Example $\sqrt{\frac{16}{25}} = \frac{\sqrt{16}}{\sqrt{25}} = \frac{4}{5}$

EXAMPLE 3 Use the quotient property of radicals

a. $\sqrt{\frac{13}{100}} = \frac{\sqrt{13}}{\sqrt{100}}$ — Quotient property of radicals

$= \frac{\sqrt{13}}{10}$ — Simplify.

b. $\sqrt{\frac{7}{x^2}} = \frac{\sqrt{7}}{\sqrt{x^2}}$ — Quotient property of radicals

$= \frac{\sqrt{7}}{x}$ — Simplify.

✓ GUIDED PRACTICE for Examples 2 and 3

2. Simplify (**a**) $\sqrt{2x^3} \cdot \sqrt{x}$ and (**b**) $\sqrt{\frac{1}{y^2}}$. (a) $x^2\sqrt{2}$; (b) $\frac{1}{y}$

Differentiated Instruction

Below Level Until students develop facility in simplifying square roots, it may help if they write out notecards or make charts listing some of the multiples of perfect squares such as $16 \cdot 2 = 32$, $25 \cdot 2 = 50$, $36 \cdot 2 = 72$ and so on up to 100. Encourage students to make organized lists so it is easy to find the factors of a product.

See also the *Algebra 1 Toolkit* for more strategies.

RATIONALIZING THE DENOMINATOR Example 4 shows how to eliminate a radical from the denominator of a radical expression by multiplying the expression by an appropriate form of 1. The process of eliminating a radical from an expression's denominator is called **rationalizing the denominator.**

EXAMPLE 4 Rationalize the denominator

MULTIPLY BY 1
In part (a), notice that $\frac{\sqrt{7}}{\sqrt{7}}$ is equal to 1, so multiplying by it does not change the value of the expression.

a. $\frac{5}{\sqrt{7}} = \frac{5}{\sqrt{7}} \cdot \frac{\sqrt{7}}{\sqrt{7}}$ Multiply by $\frac{\sqrt{7}}{\sqrt{7}}$.

$= \frac{5\sqrt{7}}{\sqrt{49}}$ Product property of radicals

$= \frac{5\sqrt{7}}{7}$ Simplify.

b. $\frac{\sqrt{2}}{\sqrt{3b}} = \frac{\sqrt{2}}{\sqrt{3b}} \cdot \frac{\sqrt{3b}}{\sqrt{3b}}$ Multiply by $\frac{\sqrt{3b}}{\sqrt{3b}}$.

$= \frac{\sqrt{6b}}{\sqrt{9b^2}}$ Product property of radicals

$= \frac{\sqrt{6b}}{\sqrt{9} \cdot \sqrt{b^2}}$ Product property of radicals

$= \frac{\sqrt{6b}}{3b}$ Simplify.

SUMS AND DIFFERENCES You can use the distributive property to simplify sums and differences of radical expressions when the expressions have the same radicand.

EXAMPLE 5 Add and subtract radicals

a. $4\sqrt{10} + \sqrt{13} - 9\sqrt{10} = 4\sqrt{10} - 9\sqrt{10} + \sqrt{13}$ Commutative property

$= (4 - 9)\sqrt{10} + \sqrt{13}$ Distributive property

$= -5\sqrt{10} + \sqrt{13}$ Simplify.

b. $5\sqrt{3} + \sqrt{48} = 5\sqrt{3} + \sqrt{16 \cdot 3}$ Factor using perfect square factor.

$= 5\sqrt{3} + \sqrt{16} \cdot \sqrt{3}$ Product property of radicals

$= 5\sqrt{3} + 4\sqrt{3}$ Simplify.

$= (5 + 4)\sqrt{3}$ Distributive property

$= 9\sqrt{3}$ Simplify.

GUIDED PRACTICE for Examples 4 and 5

Simplify the expression.

3. $\frac{1}{\sqrt{3}}$ $\frac{\sqrt{3}}{3}$

4. $\frac{1}{\sqrt{x}}$ $\frac{\sqrt{x}}{x}$

5. $\frac{3}{\sqrt{2x}}$ $\frac{3\sqrt{2x}}{2x}$

6. $2\sqrt{7} + 3\sqrt{63}$ $11\sqrt{7}$

Extra Example 4

Rationalize the denominator.

a. $\frac{7}{\sqrt{6}}$ $\frac{7\sqrt{6}}{6}$

b. $\frac{\sqrt{3}}{\sqrt{5a}}$ $\frac{\sqrt{15a}}{5a}$

Key Question to Ask for Example 4

- Could you multiply the expression in part a by $\frac{5}{\sqrt{7}}$ to rationalize the denominator? Explain. No; it would change the value of the expression.

Extra Example 5

Add and subtract radicals.

a. $7\sqrt{14} + \sqrt{21} - 4\sqrt{14}$ $3\sqrt{14} + \sqrt{21}$

b. $2\sqrt{7} + \sqrt{28}$ $4\sqrt{7}$

Key Question to Ask for Example 5

- Why do you use the commutative property in part a? You want to arrange the terms so that you can combine like terms.

Differentiated Instruction

Auditory Learners Phrases which have parallel structure are easier to learn for some students. The product property of radicals, when abridged slightly to read, "The square root of a product is the product of the square roots", has a parallel structure which is easy for students to remember. Show students that the quotient property of radicals follows from the product property by changing b to $\frac{1}{b}$.

See also the *Algebra 1 Toolkit* for more strategies.

Extra Example 6

Multiply radical expressions.

a. $\sqrt{3}(2+\sqrt{12})$ $2\sqrt{3}+6$

b. $(\sqrt{2}+\sqrt{5})(\sqrt{2}-3\sqrt{5})$ $-13-2\sqrt{10}$

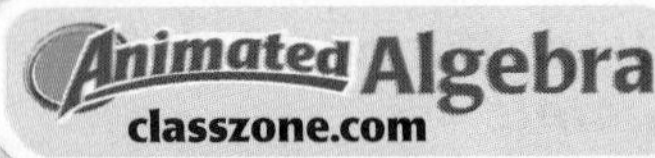

An **Animated Algebra** activity is available on-line for **Example 6**. This activity is also available on the **Power Presentations CD-ROM**.

Extra Example 7

An investigator can determine the speed S (in miles per hour) of a car by using the formula $S=\sqrt{27\ell}$, where ℓ is the length (in feet) of the car's skid mark.

a. Simplify the formula. $S=3\sqrt{3\ell}$

b. A skid mark is 96 feet long. What was the speed of the car? about 51 mi/h

Closing the Lesson

Have students summarize the major points of the lesson and answer the Essential Question: How do you simplify radical expressions?

- When simplifying radical expressions, look for perfect square factors in the radicand, eliminate radicals in the denominator of a fraction, and eliminate fractions in the radicand.

Simplify after you factor out perfect squares and eliminate fractions in the radicand. If the denominator of a fraction contains a radical, eliminate the radical by rationalizing the denominator.

8. No. *Sample answer:* Neptune's orbital period is $(6\cdot 5)\sqrt{6\cdot 5}=6\cdot 5\cdot\sqrt{6}\cdot\sqrt{5}=6\sqrt{6}\cdot 5\sqrt{5}$. Thus, Neptune's orbital period is $6\sqrt{6}$ times the orbital period of Jupiter.

EXAMPLE 6 Multiply radical expressions

a. $\sqrt{5}(4-\sqrt{20})=4\sqrt{5}-\sqrt{5}\cdot\sqrt{20}$ **Distributive property**

$=4\sqrt{5}-\sqrt{100}$ **Product property of radicals**

$=4\sqrt{5}-10$ **Simplify.**

b. $(\sqrt{7}+\sqrt{2})(\sqrt{7}-3\sqrt{2})$

$=(\sqrt{7})^2+\sqrt{7}(-3\sqrt{2})+\sqrt{2}\cdot\sqrt{7}+\sqrt{2}(-3\sqrt{2})$ **Multiply.**

$=7-3\sqrt{7\cdot 2}+\sqrt{7\cdot 2}-3(\sqrt{2})^2$ **Product property of radicals**

$=7-3\sqrt{14}+\sqrt{14}-6$ **Simplify.**

$=1-2\sqrt{14}$ **Simplify.**

REVIEW FOIL METHOD
For help with the FOIL method, see p. 562.

Animated Algebra at classzone.com

EXAMPLE 7 Solve a real-world problem

ASTRONOMY The orbital period of a planet is the time that it takes the planet to travel around the sun. You can find the orbital period P (in Earth years) using the formula $P=\sqrt{d^3}$ where d is the average distance (in astronomical units, abbreviated AU) of the planet from the sun.

a. Simplify the formula.

b. Jupiter's average distance from the sun is shown in the diagram. What is Jupiter's orbital period?

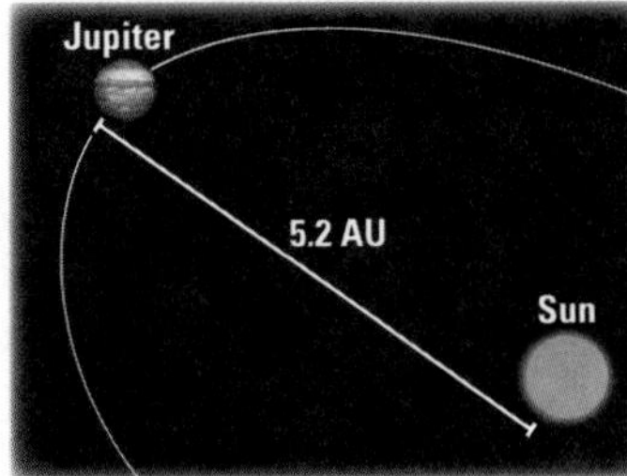

Not drawn to scale

Solution

a. $P=\sqrt{d^3}$ **Write formula.**

$=\sqrt{d^2\cdot d}$ **Factor using perfect square factor.**

$=\sqrt{d^2}\cdot\sqrt{d}$ **Product property of radicals**

$=d\sqrt{d}$ **Simplify.**

b. Substitute 5.2 for d in the simplified formula.

$P=d\sqrt{d}=5.2\sqrt{5.2}$

 The orbital period of Jupiter is $5.2\sqrt{5.2}$, or about 11.9, Earth years.

✓ GUIDED PRACTICE for Examples 6 and 7

7. Simplify the expression $(4-\sqrt{5})(1-\sqrt{5})$. $9-5\sqrt{5}$

8. **ASTRONOMY** Neptune's average distance from the sun is about 6 times Jupiter's average distance from the sun. Is the orbital period of Neptune 6 times the orbital period of Jupiter? *Explain.* See margin.

11.2 EXERCISES

HOMEWORK KEY

○ = **WORKED-OUT SOLUTIONS** on p. WS26 for Exs. 9, 37, and 69
★ = **STANDARDIZED TEST PRACTICE** Exs. 2, 23, 25, 64, and 71
◆ = **MULTIPLE REPRESENTATIONS** Ex. 70

SKILL PRACTICE

A

1. **VOCABULARY** Copy and complete: The process of eliminating a radical from the denominator of a radical expression is called _?_. rationalizing the denominator

2. ★ **WRITING** Is the expression $\sqrt{\frac{2x}{9}}$ written in simplest form? *Explain* why or why not.
No. *Sample answer*: An expression is not in simplest form if there is a fraction in the radicand.

EXAMPLES 1, 2, and 3 on pp. 719–720 for Exs. 3–25

USING PRODUCT AND QUOTIENT PROPERTIES **Simplify the expression.**

3. $\sqrt{20}$ $2\sqrt{5}$
4. $\sqrt{48}$ $4\sqrt{3}$
5. $\sqrt{96}$ $4\sqrt{6}$
6. $\sqrt{72}$ $6\sqrt{2}$
7. $\sqrt{125b}$ $5\sqrt{5b}$
8. $\sqrt{4x^2}$ $2x$
9. $\sqrt{81m^3}$ $9m\sqrt{m}$
10. $\sqrt{32m^5}$ $4m^2\sqrt{2m}$
11. $\sqrt{5} \cdot \sqrt{30}$ $5\sqrt{6}$
12. $\sqrt{50} \cdot \sqrt{18}$ 30
13. $\sqrt{14x} \cdot \sqrt{2x}$ $2x\sqrt{7}$
14. $\sqrt{3b^3} \cdot \sqrt{18b}$ $3b^2\sqrt{6}$
15. $2\sqrt{a^4b^5}$ $2a^2b^2\sqrt{b}$
16. $\sqrt{64s^4t^3}$ $8s^2t\sqrt{t}$
17. $\sqrt{m^2n} \cdot \sqrt{n}$ mn
18. $\sqrt{75xy} \cdot \sqrt{2x^3}$ $5x^2\sqrt{6y}$
19. $\sqrt{\frac{4}{49}}$ $\frac{2}{7}$
20. $\sqrt{\frac{7}{81}}$ $\frac{\sqrt{7}}{9}$
21. $\sqrt{\frac{a^3}{121}}$ $\frac{a\sqrt{a}}{11}$
22. $\sqrt{\frac{100}{4x^2}}$ $\frac{5}{x}$

23. ★ **MULTIPLE CHOICE** Which expression is equivalent to $\sqrt{\frac{9x}{16}}$? B

Ⓐ $\frac{\sqrt{3x}}{4}$ Ⓑ $\frac{3\sqrt{x}}{4}$ Ⓒ $\frac{3\sqrt{x}}{16}$ Ⓓ $\frac{3x}{4}$

24. **ERROR ANALYSIS** *Describe* and correct the error in simplifying the expression $\sqrt{72}$.
Sample answer: The answer is not simplified completely. $2\sqrt{18}$ can be written as $2\sqrt{2} \cdot \sqrt{9} = 6\sqrt{2}$.

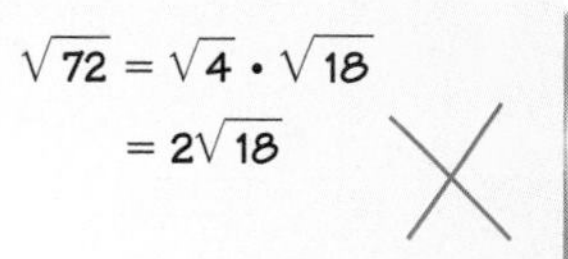

25. ★ **WRITING** *Describe* two different sequences of steps you could take to simplify the expression $\sqrt{45} \cdot \sqrt{5}$. *Sample answer*: Simplify $\sqrt{45}$ to $\sqrt{9} \cdot \sqrt{5} = 3\sqrt{5}$. Then multiply $3\sqrt{5} \cdot \sqrt{5} = 3 \cdot 5 = 15$. Or, combine the expressions to create $\sqrt{45 \cdot 5} = \sqrt{225} = 15$.

EXAMPLE 4 on p. 721 for Exs. 26–33

RATIONALIZING THE DENOMINATOR **Simplify the expression.**

26. $\frac{2}{\sqrt{2}}$ $\sqrt{2}$
27. $\frac{4}{\sqrt{3}}$ $\frac{4\sqrt{3}}{3}$
28. $\sqrt{\frac{5}{48}}$ $\frac{\sqrt{15}}{12}$
29. $\sqrt{\frac{4}{52}}$ $\frac{\sqrt{13}}{13}$
30. $\frac{3}{\sqrt{a}}$ $\frac{3\sqrt{a}}{a}$
31. $\frac{1}{\sqrt{2x}}$ $\frac{\sqrt{2x}}{2x}$
32. $\sqrt{\frac{2x^2}{5}}$ $\frac{x\sqrt{10}}{5}$
33. $\sqrt{\frac{8}{3n^3}}$ $\frac{2\sqrt{6n}}{3n^2}$

EXAMPLES 5 and 6 on pp. 721–722 for Exs. 34–45

38. $8\sqrt{3} + 2\sqrt{6}$

39. $7\sqrt{7} - 5\sqrt{14}$

PERFORMING OPERATIONS ON RADICALS **Simplify the expression.**

34. $2\sqrt{2} + 6\sqrt{2}$ $8\sqrt{2}$
35. $\sqrt{5} - 6\sqrt{5}$ $-5\sqrt{5}$
36. $2\sqrt{6} - 5\sqrt{54}$ $-13\sqrt{6}$
37. $9\sqrt{32} + \sqrt{2}$ $37\sqrt{2}$
38. $\sqrt{12} + 6\sqrt{3} + 2\sqrt{6}$
39. $3\sqrt{7} - 5\sqrt{14} + 2\sqrt{28}$
40. $\sqrt{5}(5 - \sqrt{5})$ $5\sqrt{5} - 5$
41. $\sqrt{6}(7\sqrt{3} + 6)$ $21\sqrt{2} + 6\sqrt{6}$
42. $\sqrt{3}(6\sqrt{2} - 4\sqrt{3})$ $6\sqrt{6} - 12$
43. $(4 - \sqrt{2})(5 + \sqrt{2})$ $18 - \sqrt{2}$
44. $(2\sqrt{5} + 7)^2$ $69 + 28\sqrt{5}$
45. $(\sqrt{7} + \sqrt{3})(6 + \sqrt{8})$ $6\sqrt{7} + 6\sqrt{3} + 2\sqrt{14} + 2\sqrt{6}$

4 PRACTICE AND APPLY

Assignment Guide

Answer Transparencies available for all exercises

Basic:
Day 1: EP p. 946 Exs. 7–12
pp. 723–726
Exs. 1–25
Day 2: pp. 723–726
Exs. 26–50 even, 67–70, 73–93 odd

Average:
Day 1: pp. 723–726
Exs. 1, 2, 4–22 even, 23–32, 55–58
Day 2: pp. 723–726
Exs. 35–53 odd, 59–63, 67–71, 74, 77, 80, 82, 84, 87, 90, 93

Advanced:
Day 1: pp. 723–726
Exs. 1, 15–23, 25–33, 55–62
Day 2: pp. 723–726
Exs. 34–54 even, 59–72*, 78, 81, 88, 94

Block:
pp. 723–726
Exs. 1, 2, 4–22 even, 23–32, 35–53 odd, 55–63, 67–71, 74, 77, 80, 82, 84, 87, 90, 93

Differentiated Instruction

See *Algebra 1 Best Practices Toolkit* for suggestions on addressing the needs of a diverse classroom.

Homework Check

For a quick check of student understanding of key concepts, go over the following exercises:
Basic: 14, 28, 36, 42, 67
Average: 18, 30, 35, 43, 67
Advanced: 21, 32, 38, 44, 68

Extra Practice

- Student Edition, p. 948
- Chapter 11 Resource Book: Practice levels A, B, C, pp. 21–23

Practice Worksheet

An easily-readable reduced practice page (with answers) for this lesson can be found on p. 708C.

Avoiding Common Errors

Exercises 3–22 Some students may factor a perfect square in a radicand and then simplify without checking to see if there is more than one perfect square factor. It may help some students to use prime factorization or a factor tree to avoid missing perfect square factors.

Teaching Strategy

Exercises 43–45 Recommend that students use the FOIL pattern to multiply the expressions. Some students may find it easier to multiply each term on a separate line. If they use this method, remind them to combine like terms after they have multiplied.

Exercises 55–62 You may want to offer students an additional example before they begin these exercises. One example is $\frac{2}{3 + \sqrt{5}}$. Ask students to identify the conjugate $3 - \sqrt{5}$ and then continue asking them to describe the next step as you work the example on the board.

66. Odd values of m; even values of m. *Sample answer:* When m is even, the expression can be divided evenly into groups of $\sqrt{m^2}$, which all simplify to m, but when m is odd, it cannot be divided evenly into groups of $\sqrt{m^2}$.

57. $\frac{7\sqrt{10} + 2\sqrt{5}}{47}$

60. $\frac{11\sqrt{11} + 11\sqrt{7}}{4}$

B **SIMPLIFYING RADICAL EXPRESSIONS** **Simplify the expression.**

46. $\sqrt{75m^2np^4}$ $5mp^2\sqrt{3n}$ **47.** $\sqrt{512rs^6} \cdot \sqrt{t^3}$ $16s^3t\sqrt{2rt}$ **48.** $\sqrt{\frac{600a}{4b^3}}$ $\frac{5\sqrt{6ab}}{b^2}$

49. $\sqrt{\frac{50gh^2}{125f^3}}$ $\frac{h\sqrt{10gf}}{5f^2}$ **50.** $\frac{4}{\sqrt{3}} + \frac{7}{\sqrt{12}}$ $\frac{5\sqrt{3}}{2}$ **51.** $\frac{2\sqrt{6}}{\sqrt{30}} - \frac{3}{\sqrt{20}}$ $\frac{\sqrt{5}}{10}$

52. $\frac{7}{\sqrt{x}} + \frac{3}{2\sqrt{x}}$ $\frac{17\sqrt{x}}{2x}$ **53.** $\frac{3}{\sqrt{x^3}} + \frac{4}{\sqrt{x}}$ $\frac{3\sqrt{x} + 4x\sqrt{x}}{x^2}$ **54.** $\frac{6m}{\sqrt{m^3}} - \frac{8}{\sqrt{m}}$ $\frac{-2\sqrt{m}}{m}$

CONJUGATES **In Exercises 55–62, use the example to simplify the expression.**

EXAMPLE **Rationalize the denominator using conjugates**

Simplify $\frac{9}{2 - \sqrt{3}}$.

Solution

The binomials $a\sqrt{b} + c\sqrt{d}$ and $a\sqrt{b} - c\sqrt{d}$ are called *conjugates*. They differ only by the sign of one term. The product of two conjugates $a\sqrt{b} + c\sqrt{d}$ and $a\sqrt{b} - c\sqrt{d}$ does not contain a radical: $(2 + \sqrt{3})(2 - \sqrt{3}) = 2^2 - (\sqrt{3})^2 = 4 - 3 = 1$. You can use conjugates to simplify the expression.

$\frac{9}{2 - \sqrt{3}} = \frac{9}{2 - \sqrt{3}} \cdot \frac{2 + \sqrt{3}}{2 + \sqrt{3}}$ **Multiply the numerator and denominator by the conjugate of the denominator.**

$= \frac{9(2 + \sqrt{3})}{(2 - \sqrt{3})(2 + \sqrt{3})}$ **Multiply fractions.**

$= \frac{18 + 9\sqrt{3}}{4 - 3}$ **Simplify numerator and denominator.**

$= 18 + 9\sqrt{3}$ **Simplify.**

55. $\frac{1}{\sqrt{7} + 1}$ $\frac{\sqrt{7} - 1}{6}$ **56.** $\frac{2}{5 - \sqrt{3}}$ $\frac{5 + \sqrt{3}}{11}$ **57.** $\frac{\sqrt{10}}{7 - \sqrt{2}}$ **58.** $\frac{\sqrt{5}}{6 + \sqrt{5}}$ $\frac{6\sqrt{5} - 5}{31}$

59. $\frac{3}{\sqrt{7} + \sqrt{6}}$ $3\sqrt{7} - 3\sqrt{6}$ **60.** $\frac{11}{\sqrt{11} - \sqrt{7}}$ **61.** $\frac{\sqrt{6}}{\sqrt{2} - \sqrt{3}}$ $-2\sqrt{3} - 3\sqrt{2}$ **62.** $\frac{\sqrt{7} + 1}{\sqrt{7} + \sqrt{2}}$

$\frac{7 + \sqrt{7} - \sqrt{14} - \sqrt{2}}{5}$

C **63.** **REASONING** Multiply the binomials $a\sqrt{b} + c\sqrt{d}$ and $a\sqrt{b} - c\sqrt{d}$ to show that the product does not contain a radical.
$(a\sqrt{b} + c\sqrt{d})(a\sqrt{b} - c\sqrt{d}) = a^2b - ac\sqrt{bd} + ac\sqrt{bd} - c^2d = a^2b - c^2d$

64. ★ **WRITING** According to the definition of square root, a number b is a square root of a number a if $b^2 = a$. How can you use the definition to show that $\sqrt{x^2} = x$? *Explain.* *Sample answer*: The expression $\sqrt{x^2} = x$ is true if x is a square root of x^2. You know x is a square root of x^2 because the square of $x = x^2$.

65. **MULTIPLYING FUNCTIONS** Let $f(x) = \sqrt{x} - \sqrt{4x}$, and let $g(x) = \sqrt{x}$. Find $h(x) = f(x) \cdot g(x)$. $-x$

66. **CHALLENGE** Consider the expression $\sqrt{2^m}$. Assume m is a positive integer. For what values of m will the expression contain a radical when simplified? For what values of m will the expression contain no radical when simplified? *Explain.* See margin.

○ = **WORKED-OUT SOLUTIONS on p. WS1** ★ = **STANDARDIZED TEST PRACTICE** ◆ = **MULTIPLE REPRESENTATIONS**

PROBLEM SOLVING

EXAMPLE 7 A on p. 722 for Exs. 67, 68

67. **FINANCE** You invest \$225 in a savings account for two years. The account has an annual interest rate that changes from year to year. You can find the average annual interest rate r that the account earned over two years using the formula $r = \sqrt{\frac{V_2}{V_0}} - 1$ where V_0 is the initial investment and V_2 is the amount in the account after two years. At the end of two years, you have \$270 in the account. What was the average annual interest rate (written as a percent) the account earned over two years? **about 9.54%**

@HomeTutor for problem solving help at classzone.com

68. **DISTANCE TO THE HORIZON** The distance d (in miles) that a person can see to the horizon is given by the formula $d = \sqrt{\frac{3h}{2}}$ where h is the person's eye level (in feet) above the water. To the nearest mile, find the distance that the person shown can see to the horizon. **12 mi**

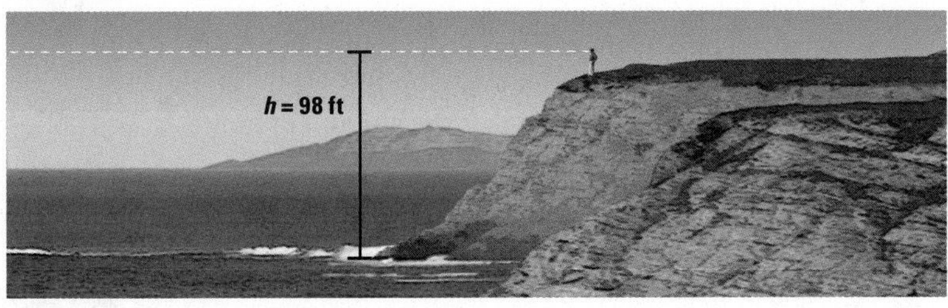

@HomeTutor for problem solving help at classzone.com

69. **MULTI-STEP PROBLEM** You are making a cube-shaped footrest. You want to cover the footrest with fabric. At a fabric store, you choose fabric that costs \$6 per square yard.
   a. You have \$30 to spend on fabric. How much fabric can you buy? **5 yd^2**
   b. The edge length s (in yards) of the largest footrest you can cover can be found using the formula $s = \sqrt{\frac{S}{6}}$ where S is the surface area of the footrest (in square yards). Use unit analysis to check the units in the formula. **The side length s is in yd, and $\sqrt{\frac{S}{6}}$ is $\sqrt{yd^2}$ = yd.**
   c. Find the edge length of the largest footrest you can cover to the nearest tenth of a yard. **0.9 yd**

B 70. ◆ **MULTIPLE REPRESENTATIONS** The velocity v (in feet per second) of an object that has been dropped can be found using the equation $v = \sqrt{64d}$ where d is the distance the object falls (in feet) before hitting the ground.
   a. **Writing an Equation** Write the equation in simplified form. **$v = 8\sqrt{d}$**
   b. **Drawing a Graph** Graph the equation. For what value of d is the velocity about 16 feet per second? **See margin for art; 4 ft.**
   c. **Solving an Equation** Use the equation from part (a) to find the exact value of d when the velocity is 16 feet per second. **4 ft**

Study Strategy

Exercises 67–69 Point out to students that these exercises contain fractions in the radicand and that they will need to rationalize the denominator after they use the quotient property of radicals. Suggest that they simplify the formulas before substituting values for the variables.

Vocabulary

Exercise 72 Tell students that the *coefficient of friction* is a ratio of resistive forces that apply when two objects come in contact.

70b.

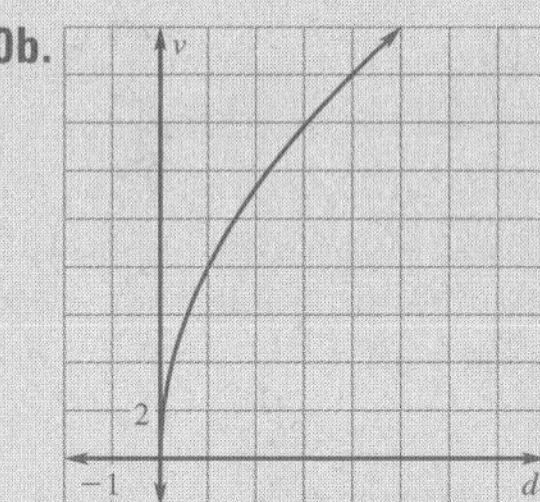

5 ASSESS AND RETEACH

Daily Homework Quiz

Transparency Available

Simplify the expression.

1. $\sqrt{56a^2}$ $2a\sqrt{14}$

2. $\sqrt{\frac{b}{64}}$ $\frac{\sqrt{b}}{8}$

3. $5\sqrt{2} - 2\sqrt{8} + \sqrt{6}$ $\sqrt{2} + \sqrt{6}$

4. A person is standing on a cliff, with an eye level at 60 feet, looking out across the ocean. Use the formula $d = \sqrt{\frac{3h}{2}}$ where d (in miles) is the distance a person can see to the horizon and h (in feet) is the person's eye level above the water to find the number of miles the person can see to the horizon. about 9.5 mi

Available at **classzone.com**

Diagnosis/Remediation

- Practice A, B, C in Chapter 11 Resource Book, pp. 21–23
- Study Guide in Chapter 11 Resource Book, pp. 24–25
- Practice Workbook, pp. 172–173
- @HomeTutor

Challenge

Additional challenge is available in the Chapter 11 Resource Book, p. 28.

---

71. ★ **SHORT RESPONSE** Physicians can calculate the body surface area S (in square meters) of an adult using the formula $S = \sqrt{\frac{hw}{3600}}$ where h is the adult's height (in centimeters) and w is the adult's mass (in kilograms).

   a. Simplify the formula. $S = \frac{\sqrt{hw}}{60}$

   b. Does an adult who is 1.7 meters tall and has a mass of 70 kilograms have a greater body surface area than an adult who is 1.5 meters tall and has a mass of 70 kilograms? *Explain* what effect height has on surface area if two people have the same mass. Yes. *Sample answer*: If the mass stays the same, then the greater the height the greater the body surface area will be.

C 72. **CHALLENGE** The speed s (in miles per hour) at which a vehicle is traveling before an accident is given by $s = \sqrt{30df}$ where d is the length of the skid mark (in feet) and f is the coefficient of friction. The coefficient of friction varies depending on the type of road surface and on the road conditions.

   a. A driver is traveling on a newly paved road with a coefficient of friction of 0.80. The driver sees a hazard in the road and is forced to brake. The car skids to a halt leaving a skid mark that is 100 feet long. At what speed was the car traveling when the driver applied the brakes? about 49.0 mi/h

   b. A perception-reaction time is the amount of time it takes for a person to react to a situation after perceiving it, such as applying the brakes after seeing a hazard in the road. The driver in part (a) has a perception-reaction time of 1.5 seconds. How many feet does the car travel before the driver applies the brakes? *Explain* how you found your answer.

   c. What is the total distance (in feet) traveled from the time the driver in part (a) sees the hazard until the time the car skids to a halt? 207.8 ft

72b. about 107.8 ft. *Sample answer*: First, convert 49 miles per hour from part (a) to feet per second $\frac{49 \cdot 5280}{60 \cdot 60} =$ 71.0867 feet per second. Then multiply by 1.5 seconds.

ILLINOIS MIXED REVIEW

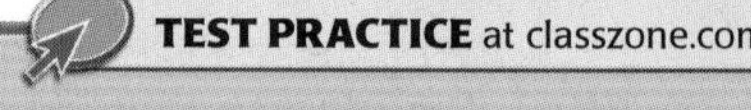

73. The area of a rectangle is given by $2x - 32$. Which of the following represents possible values of x? C

   Ⓐ $x \geq 16$ Ⓑ $x > -16$ Ⓒ $x > 16$ Ⓓ $-16 < x < 16$

74. A scientist examines 100 randomly selected frogs from a wetland for evidence of a particular trait. The scientist finds that 12 of the frogs have the trait. If there is a total of 750 frogs in the wetland, how many frogs can the scientist expect to have the trait? C

   Ⓐ 62 Ⓑ 75 Ⓒ 90 Ⓓ 105

75. Which equation describes a line having a slope of $-\frac{2}{3}$ and a y-intercept of $\frac{3}{5}$? B

   Ⓐ $10x + 15y = -9$ Ⓑ $10x + 15y = 9$

   Ⓒ $15x + 10y = 9$ Ⓓ $15x + 10y = -9$

Derive the Quadratic Formula

GOAL Solve quadratic equations and check solutions.

In Lesson 10.6, you learned how to find solutions of quadratic equations using the quadratic formula. You can use the method of completing the square and the quotient property of radicals to derive the quadratic formula.

$ax^2 + bx + c = 0$	**Write standard form of a quadratic equation.**
$ax^2 + bx = -c$	**Subtract c from each side.**
$x^2 + \frac{b}{a}x = -\frac{c}{a}$	**Divide each side by a, $a \neq 0$.**
$x^2 + \frac{b}{a}x + \left(\frac{b}{2a}\right)^2 = -\frac{c}{a} + \left(\frac{b}{2a}\right)^2$	**Add $\left(\frac{b}{2a}\right)^2$ to each side to complete the square.**
$\left(x + \frac{b}{2a}\right)^2 = -\frac{c}{a} + \frac{b^2}{4a^2}$	**Write left side as the square of a binomial.**
$\left(x + \frac{b}{2a}\right)^2 = \frac{b^2 - 4ac}{4a^2}$	**Simplify right side.**
$x + \frac{b}{2a} = \pm\sqrt{\frac{b^2 - 4ac}{4a^2}}$	**Take square roots of each side.**
$x + \frac{b}{2a} = \frac{\pm\sqrt{b^2 - 4ac}}{2a}$	**Quotient property of radicals**
$x = \frac{-b \pm \sqrt{b^2 - 4ac}}{2a}$	**Subtract $\frac{b}{2a}$ from each side.**

SOLVING QUADRATIC EQUATIONS You can use the quadratic formula and properties of radicals to solve quadratic equations.

EXAMPLE 1 Solve an equation

Solve $x^2 - 6x + 3 = 0$.

Solution

$x^2 - 6x + 3 = 0$	**Identify $a = 1$, $b = -6$, and $c = 3$.**
$x = \frac{-(-6) \pm \sqrt{(-6)^2 - 4(1)(3)}}{2(1)}$	**Substitute values in the quadratic formula.**
$= \frac{6 \pm \sqrt{24}}{2}$	**Simplify.**
$= \frac{6 \pm \sqrt{4 \cdot 6}}{2}$	**Product property of radicals**
$= \frac{6 \pm 2\sqrt{6}}{2} = 3 \pm \sqrt{6}$	**Simplify.**

▶ The solutions of the equation are $3 + \sqrt{6}$ and $3 - \sqrt{6}$.

1 PLAN AND PREPARE

Warm-Up Exercises

Solve the equation.

1. $x^2 + 3x - 4 = 0$ 1, −4
2. $x^2 - 6x + 2 = 0$ $3 \pm \sqrt{7}$
3. $2x^2 + 3x - 5 = 0$ 1, −2.5
4. A ball is thrown upward in the air from a height of 5 feet and with an initial velocity of 15 feet per second. After how many seconds does the ball hit the ground? about 1.2 sec

2 FOCUS AND MOTIVATE

Essential Question

Big Idea 2, p. 709

How do you solve quadratic equations? Tell students they will learn how to answer this question by using the quadratic formula.

3 TEACH

Extra Example 1

Solve $x^2 + 8x + 1 = 0$. $-4 \pm \sqrt{15}$

Key Question to Ask for Example 1

- Why are there two solutions of the equation? The discriminant is positive, so the equation has two real solutions.

NCTM STANDARDS

Standard 2: Analyze situations using algebraic symbols

Standard 7: Develop mathematical arguments and proofs

Extra Example 2

Check the solutions of the equation from Extra Example 1. **The solutions check when you substitute them into the original equation.**

Closing the Lesson

Have students summarize the major points of the lesson and answer the Essential Question: How do you solve quadratic equations?

- **The quadratic formula is $x = \frac{-b \pm \sqrt{b^2 - 4ac}}{2a}$. When using the quadratic formula, first identify the values of *a*, *b*, and *c*. Then substitute the values into the formula and simplify. Check the solutions by substituting each into the original equation.**

4 PRACTICE AND APPLY

Avoiding Common Errors

Exercises 1–18 Urge students to use caution when substituting values into the quadratic formula to avoid calculation errors. Places to be especially careful include replacing *b* with a negative number and remembering that the denominator is 2 • *a*, not 2 or *a*.

Graphing Calculator

Exercises 1–18 Students may want to check their solutions by graphing the equations. They can use the *zero* feature to check the solutions.

EXAMPLE 2 Check the solutions of an equation

Check the solutions of the equation from Example 1.

Solution

The solutions of $x^2 - 6x + 3 = 0$ are $3 + \sqrt{6}$ and $3 - \sqrt{6}$. You can check each solution by substituting it into the original equation.

Check $x = 3 + \sqrt{6}$:

$x^2 - 6x + 3 = 0$	Write original equation.
$(3 + \sqrt{6})^2 - 6(3 + \sqrt{6}) + 3 \stackrel{?}{=} 0$	Substitute $3 + \sqrt{6}$ for *x*.
$9 + 6\sqrt{6} + 6 - 18 - 6\sqrt{6} + 3 \stackrel{?}{=} 0$	Multiply.
$0 = 0$ ✓	Solution checks.

Check $x = 3 - \sqrt{6}$:

$x^2 - 6x + 3 = 0$	Write original equation.
$(3 - \sqrt{6})^2 - 6(3 - \sqrt{6}) + 3 \stackrel{?}{=} 0$	Substitute $3 - \sqrt{6}$ for *x*.
$9 - 6\sqrt{6} + 6 - 18 + 6\sqrt{6} + 3 \stackrel{?}{=} 0$	Multiply.
$0 = 0$ ✓	Solution checks.

PRACTICE

EXAMPLES 1 and 2 on pp. 727–728 for Exs. 1–18

Solve the equation using the quadratic formula. Check the solution. 1–18. See margin.

1. $x^2 + 4x + 2 = 0$
2. $x^2 + 6x - 1 = 0$
3. $x^2 + 8x + 8 = 0$
4. $x^2 - 7x + 1 = 0$
5. $3x^2 + 6x - 1 = 0$
6. $2x^2 - 4x - 3 = 0$
7. $5x^2 - 2x - 2 = 0$
8. $4x^2 + 10x + 3 = 0$
9. $x^2 - x - 3 = 0$
10. $x^2 - 2x - 8 = 0$
11. $-x^2 + 7x + 3 = 0$
12. $x^2 + 3x - 9 = 0$
13. $-\frac{5}{2}x^2 + 10x - 5 = 0$
14. $\frac{1}{2}x^2 + 3x - 9 = 0$
15. $3x^2 - 2 = 0$
16. $-2x^2 - 7x = 0$
17. $3x^2 + x = 6$
18. $x^2 - 4x = -2$
19. Show that $\frac{-b + \sqrt{b^2 - 4ac}}{2a}$ and $\frac{-b - \sqrt{b^2 - 4ac}}{2a}$ are solutions of $ax^2 + bx + c = 0$ by substituting. See margin.
20. Derive a formula to find solutions of equations that have the form $ax^2 + x + c = 0$. Use your formula to find solutions of $-2x^2 + x + 8 = 0$. See margin.
21. Find the sum and product of $\frac{-b + \sqrt{b^2 - 4ac}}{2a}$ and $\frac{-b - \sqrt{b^2 - 4ac}}{2a}$. Write a quadratic expression whose solutions have a sum of 2 and a product of $\frac{1}{2}$. See margin.
22. What values can *a* have in the equation $ax^2 + 12x + 3 = 0$ in order for the equation to have one or two real solutions? *Explain.* See margin.

1. $-2 - \sqrt{2}, -2 + \sqrt{2}$
2. $-3 - \sqrt{10}, -3 + \sqrt{10}$
3. $-4 - 2\sqrt{2}, -4 + 2\sqrt{2}$
4. $\frac{7}{2} - \frac{5\sqrt{5}}{2}, \frac{7}{2} + \frac{5\sqrt{5}}{2}$
5. $-1 - \frac{2\sqrt{3}}{3}, -1 + \frac{2\sqrt{3}}{3}$
6. $1 - \frac{\sqrt{10}}{2}, 1 + \frac{\sqrt{10}}{2}$
7. $\frac{1}{5} - \frac{\sqrt{11}}{5}, \frac{1}{5} + \frac{\sqrt{11}}{5}$
8. $-\frac{5}{4} - \frac{\sqrt{13}}{4}, -\frac{5}{4} + \frac{\sqrt{13}}{4}$
9. $\frac{1}{2} - \frac{\sqrt{13}}{2}, \frac{1}{2} + \frac{\sqrt{13}}{2}$
10. 4, −2
11. $\frac{7}{2} - \frac{\sqrt{61}}{2}, \frac{7}{2} + \frac{\sqrt{61}}{2}$
12. $-\frac{3}{2} - \frac{3\sqrt{5}}{2}, -\frac{3}{2} + \frac{3\sqrt{5}}{2}$
13. $2 - \sqrt{2}, 2 + \sqrt{2}$
14. $-3 - 3\sqrt{3}, -3 + 3\sqrt{3}$
15. $-\frac{\sqrt{6}}{3}, \frac{\sqrt{6}}{3}$
16. $-\frac{7}{4} - \sqrt{57}, -\frac{7}{4} + \sqrt{57}$
17. $-\frac{1}{6} - \frac{\sqrt{73}}{6}, -\frac{1}{6} + \frac{\sqrt{73}}{6}$,
18. $2 - \sqrt{2}, 2 + \sqrt{2}$
19. See Additional Answers beginning on p. AA1.
20. $\frac{-1 \pm \sqrt{1 - 4ac}}{2a}, \frac{1}{4} \pm \frac{\sqrt{65}}{4}$
21. Sum: $-\frac{b}{a}$, product: $\frac{c}{a}$. *Sample answer:* $y = 2x^2 - 4x + 1$
22. See Additional Answers beginning on p. AA1.

11.3 Solve Radical Equations

 **8.11.19** Solve problems that include nonlinear functions, including selecting and evaluating formulas . . .

Before You solved linear, quadratic, and exponential equations.

Now You will solve radical equations.

Why? So you can use scientific formulas to study animals, as in Ex. 39.

Key Vocabulary
- **radical equation**
- **extraneous solution**

An equation that contains a radical expression with a variable in the radicand is a **radical equation.** To solve a radical equation, you need to isolate the radical on one side and then square both sides of the equation.

KEY CONCEPT *For Your Notebook*

Squaring Both Sides of an Equation

Words If two expressions are equal, then their squares are equal.

Algebra If $a = b$, then $a^2 = b^2$. **Example** If $\sqrt{x} = 3$, then $(\sqrt{x})^2 = 3^2$.

EXAMPLE 1 **Solve a radical equation**

Solve $2\sqrt{x} - 8 = 0$.

Solution

$2\sqrt{x} - 8 = 0$ Write original equation.

$2\sqrt{x} = 8$ Add 8 to each side.

$\sqrt{x} = 4$ Divide each side by 2.

$(\sqrt{x})^2 = 4^2$ Square each side.

$x = 16$ Simplify.

▸ The solution is 16.

CHECK Check the solution by substituting it in the original equation.

$2\sqrt{x} - 8 = 0$ Write original equation.

$2\sqrt{16} - 8 \stackrel{?}{=} 0$ Substitute 16 for x.

$2 \cdot 4 - 8 \stackrel{?}{=} 0$ Simplify.

$0 = 0$ ✓ Solution checks.

 **GUIDED PRACTICE** for Example 1

1. Solve (a) $\sqrt{x} - 7 = 0$ and (b) $12\sqrt{x} - 3 = 0$. a. 49 b. $\frac{1}{16}$

1 PLAN AND PREPARE

Warm-Up Exercises

Transparency Available

Solve the equation.

1. $2x + 3 = 13$ $x = 5$
2. $3x - 8 = 16$ $x = 8$
3. $4x^2 - 16 = 0$ $x = -2, x = 2$
4. $x^2 - x = 12$ $x = -3, x = 4$
5. You put $250 in a savings account that earns 3% interest compounded yearly. If you make no deposits and no withdrawals, how much will your savings be worth in 5 years? about $290

Notetaking Guide

Transparency Available

Promotes interactive learning and notetaking skills, pp. 256–258.

Pacing

Basic: 2 days
Average: 2 days
Advanced: 2 days
Block: 1 block
- See *Teaching Guide/Lesson Plan.*

2 FOCUS AND MOTIVATE

Essential Question

Big Idea 2, p. 709

How do you solve radical equations? Tell students they will learn how to answer this question by squaring both sides of the equation and checking for extraneous solutions.

Resource Planning Guide

Chapter Resource Book
- Teaching Guide/Lesson Plan (pp. 29–30)
- Activity Master (p. 31)
- Practice levels A, B, C (pp. 33–35)
- Study Guide (pp. 36–37)
- Catch-up for Absent Students (p. 38)
- Problem Solving Workshop (p. 39)
- Challenge (p. 41)

Workbooks
- Notetaking Guide (pp. 256–258)
- Practice Workbook (pp. 174–175)

Teaching Options
- **Power Presentations CD-ROM** provides dynamic electronic teaching resources for the classroom.
- **Activity Generator CD-ROM** provides editable activities for all ability levels.

Interactive Technology
- Easy Planner
- Power Presentations CD-ROM
- Activity Generator CD-ROM
- Animated Algebra
- Test Generator CD-ROM
- Online Quiz
- eWorkbook
- eEdition
- @HomeTutor

Resources for English Learners
- Quick Reference for English Learners
- Spanish Study Guide
- Multi-Language Visual Glossary
- Student Resources in Spanish

See also the *Algebra 1 Toolkit* for more strategies for meeting individual needs.

Motivating the Lesson

Ask students to describe some of their favorite rides at recreational parks. Tell them that solving radical equations will give them information about rides, such as the speeds of roller coasters or the forces acting on rides that spin.

3 TEACH

Extra Example 1

Solve $3\sqrt{x} - 6 = 0$. $x = 4$

Key Question to Ask for Example 1

- What is the first step in solving a radical equation? Isolate the radical.
- What is the next step? Square each side of the equation.

Extra Example 2

Solve $2\sqrt{x + 6} + 9 = 21$. $x = 30$

Extra Example 3

Solve $\sqrt{4x - 12} = \sqrt{x + 3}$. $x = 5$

Key Question to Ask for Example 3

- How is Example 3 different from Examples 1 and 2? In the previous examples, you isolate the radical and then square each side. In this example, you square each side first since each side contains a radical, and then you isolate the variable.

EXAMPLE 2 Solve a radical equation

Solve $4\sqrt{x-7} + 12 = 28$.

Solution

$4\sqrt{x-7} + 12 = 28$	Write original equation.
$4\sqrt{x-7} = 16$	Subtract 12 from each side.
$\sqrt{x-7} = 4$	Divide each side by 4.
$(\sqrt{x-7})^2 = 4^2$	Square each side.
$x - 7 = 16$	Simplify.
$x = 23$	Add 7 to each side.

▶ The solution is 23.

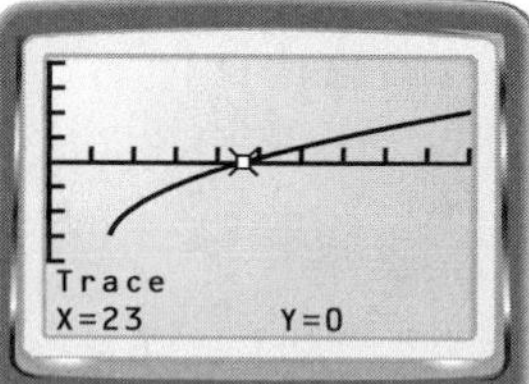

CHECK To check the solution using a graphing calculator, first rewrite the equation so that one side is 0: $4\sqrt{x-7} - 16 = 0$. Then graph the related equation $y = 4\sqrt{x-7} - 16$. You can see that the graph crosses the x-axis at $x = 23$.

EXAMPLE 3 Solve an equation with radicals on both sides

Solve $\sqrt{3x - 17} = \sqrt{x + 21}$.

Solution

SOLVE EQUATIONS To solve a radical equation that contains two radical expressions, be sure that each side of the equation has only one radical expression before squaring each side.

$\sqrt{3x-17} = \sqrt{x+21}$	Write original equation.
$(\sqrt{3x-17})^2 = (\sqrt{x+21})^2$	Square each side.
$3x - 17 = x + 21$	Simplify.
$2x - 17 = 21$	Subtract x from each side.
$2x = 38$	Add 17 to each side.
$x = 19$	Divide each side by 2.

▶ The solution is 19. Check the solution.

✓ GUIDED PRACTICE for Examples 2 and 3

Solve the equation.

2. $\sqrt{x-5} + 7 = 12$ 30
3. $\sqrt{x+4} = \sqrt{2x-1}$ 5
4. $\sqrt{4x-3} - \sqrt{x} = 0$ 1

EXTRANEOUS SOLUTIONS Squaring both sides of the equation $a = b$ can result in a solution of $a^2 = b^2$ that is *not* a solution of the original equation. Such a solution is called an **extraneous solution.** When you square both sides of an equation, check each solution in the original equation to be sure there are no extraneous solutions.

Differentiated Instruction

English Learners The vocabulary of mathematics can sometimes be more difficult than the mathematics itself. Explain that an extraneous solution as an *extra* solution which is to be discarded. Point out that in words such as *extracurricular* or *extraordinary*, the prefix "extra-" means *outside*. Suggest that students remember the term extraneous solution as meaning outside of the set of solutions.

See also the *Algebra 1 Toolkit* for more strategies.

EXAMPLE 4 Solve an equation with an extraneous solution

Solve $\sqrt{6 - x} = x$.

$\sqrt{6 - x} = x$	**Write original equation.**
$(\sqrt{6 - x})^2 = x^2$	**Square each side.**
$6 - x = x^2$	**Simplify.**
$0 = x^2 + x - 6$	**Write in standard form.**
$0 = (x - 2)(x + 3)$	**Factor.**
$x - 2 = 0$ *or* $x + 3 = 0$	**Zero-product property**
$x = 2$ *or* $x = -3$	**Solve for *x*.**

REVIEW FACTORING
For help with factoring, see pp. 583, 593, 600, and 606.

CHECK Check 2 and −3 in the original equation.

If $x = 2$: $\sqrt{6 - 2} \stackrel{?}{=} 2$ **If $x = -3$:** $\sqrt{6 - (-3)} \stackrel{?}{=} -3$

$2 = 2$ ✓ $3 = -3$ ✗

▶ Because −3 does not check in the original equation, it is an extraneous solution. The only solution of the equation is 2.

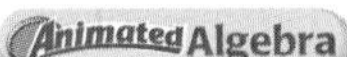
at classzone.com

EXAMPLE 5 Solve a real-world problem

SAILING The hull speed s (in nautical miles per hour) of a sailboat can be estimated using the formula $s = 1.34\sqrt{\ell}$ where ℓ is the length (in feet) of the sailboat's waterline, as shown. Find the length (to the nearest foot) of the sailboat's waterline if it has a hull speed of 8 nautical miles per hour.

Solution

$s = 1.34\sqrt{\ell}$	**Write original equation.**
$8 = 1.34\sqrt{\ell}$	**Substitute 8 for *s*.**
$\frac{8}{1.34} = \sqrt{\ell}$	**Divide each side by 1.34.**
$\left(\frac{8}{1.34}\right)^2 = (\sqrt{\ell})^2$	**Square each side.**
$35.6 \approx \ell$	**Simplify.**

▶ The sailboat has a waterline length of about 36 feet.

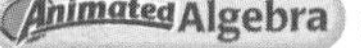
at classzone.com

GUIDED PRACTICE for Examples 4 and 5

5. Solve $\sqrt{3x + 4} = x$. 4
6. **WHAT IF?** In Example 5, suppose the sailboat's hull speed is 6.5 nautical miles per hour. Find the sailboat's waterline length to the nearest foot. 24 ft

Extra Example 4

Solve $\sqrt{20 - x} = x$. $x = 4$

An **Animated Algebra** activity is available on-line for **Example 4**. This activity is also available on the **Power Presentations CD-ROM**.

Extra Example 5

If friction is ignored, the velocity v (in feet per second) of a roller coaster when it reaches the bottom of a hill, can be found by using the formula $v = \sqrt{64h}$, where h is the height (in feet) of the hill. The approximate velocity of one of the fastest roller coasters in the world is 176 feet per second. Find the height of the hill. about 484 ft

An **Animated Algebra** activity is available on-line for **Example 5**. This activity is also available on the **Power Presentations CD-ROM**.

Closing the Lesson

Have students summarize the major points of the lesson and answer the Essential Question: How do you solve radical equations?

- **If two expressions are equal, their squares are equal.**
- **Squaring both sides of an equation can result in an extraneous solution.**

Isolate the radical on one side of the equation, square both sides, and then solve for the variable. If there are radicals on both sides of the equation, square both sides, isolate the variable, and then solve. Always check both solutions in the original equation to rule out an extraneous solution.

4 PRACTICE AND APPLY

Assignment Guide

Answer Transparencies available for all exercises

Basic:
Day 1: EP p. 946 Exs. 19–24
pp. 732–734
Exs. 1–21
Day 2: pp. 732–734
Exs. 22–26, 36–39, 42–49

Average:
Day 1: pp. 732–734
Exs. 1, 2, 5–21, 31, 32
Day 2: pp. 732–734
Exs. 22–30, 36–40, 42–48 even

Advanced:
Day 1: pp. 732–734
Exs. 1, 6–21, 31–34
Day 2: pp. 732–734
Exs. 22–30, 35–41*, 43–47 odd

Block:
pp. 732–734
Exs. 1, 2, 5–32, 36–40, 42–48 even

Differentiated Instruction

See *Algebra 1 Best Practices Toolkit* for suggestions on addressing the needs of a diverse classroom.

Homework Check

For a quick check of student understanding of key concepts, go over the following exercises:

Basic: 4, 10, 14, 22, 36
Average: 5, 12, 16, 24, 37
Advanced: 6, 13, 18, 26, 38

Extra Practice

- Student Edition, p. 948
- Chapter 11 Resource Book: Practice levels A, B, C, pp. 33–35

Practice Worksheet

An easily-readable reduced practice page (with answers) for this lesson can be found on p.708C.

11.3 EXERCISES

HOMEWORK KEY
○ = **WORKED-OUT SOLUTIONS** on p. WS27 for Exs. 11 and 37
★ = **STANDARDIZED TEST PRACTICE** Exs. 2, 21, 34, and 40

SKILL PRACTICE

A

1. **VOCABULARY** Copy and complete: To find the solution of $\sqrt{12-x} = x$, you square both sides of the equation and solve. The solutions of $(\sqrt{12-x})^2 = x^2$ are -4 and 3, but -4 is a(n) _?_ of $\sqrt{12-x} = x$. extraneous solution

2. ★ **WRITING** Is $x + x\sqrt{2} = 4$ a radical equation? *Explain* why or why not. No. *Sample answer:* It does not contain a variable in a radicand.

EXAMPLES 1, 2, and 3 on pp. 729–730 for Exs. 3–21, 28

SOLVING EQUATIONS Solve the equation. Check for extraneous solutions.

3. $3\sqrt{x} - 6 = 0$ 4
4. $2\sqrt{x} - 9 = 0$ $\frac{81}{4}$
5. $\sqrt{3x} + 4 = 16$ 48
6. $\sqrt{5x} + 5 = 0$ no real solutions
7. $\sqrt{x+7} + 5 = 11$ 29
8. $\sqrt{x-8} - 4 = -2$ 12
9. $2\sqrt{x-4} - 2 = 2$ 8
10. $3\sqrt{x-1} - 5 = 5$ $\frac{109}{9}$
11. $\sqrt{6-2x} + 12 = 21$ $-\frac{75}{2}$
12. $5\sqrt{x-3} + 4 = 14$ 7
13. $2\sqrt{x-11} - 8 = 4$ 47
14. $\sqrt{3x-2} = \sqrt{x}$ 1
15. $\sqrt{7-2x} = \sqrt{9-x}$ -2
16. $\sqrt{3x+8} = \sqrt{x+4}$ -2
17. $\sqrt{9x-30} = \sqrt{4x+5}$ 7
18. $\sqrt{21-x} - \sqrt{1-x} = 0$ no real solutions
19. $\sqrt{x-12} - \sqrt{x-8} = 0$ no real solutions
20. $\sqrt{\frac{1}{2}x-2} - \sqrt{x-8} = 0$ 12

21. ★ **MULTIPLE CHOICE** Which is the solution of the equation $10\sqrt{x+3} + 3 = 18$? B

Ⓐ $-\frac{3}{2}$ Ⓑ $-\frac{3}{4}$ Ⓒ $\frac{3}{4}$ Ⓓ $\frac{3}{2}$

EXAMPLE 4 B on p. 731 for Exs. 22–27, 29

SOLVING EQUATIONS Solve the equation. Check for extraneous solutions.

22. $x = \sqrt{42-x}$ 6
23. $\sqrt{4-3x} = x$ 1
24. $\sqrt{11x-24} = x$ 3, 8
25. $\sqrt{14x-3} = 4x$ $\frac{3}{8}, \frac{1}{2}$
26. $2x = \sqrt{1-3x}$ $\frac{1}{4}$
27. $\sqrt{2-x} = x + 4$ -2

ERROR ANALYSIS *Describe* and correct the error in solving the equation.

28.

$\sqrt{3x} + 9 = 0$
$\sqrt{3x} = -9$
$3x = 81$
$x = 27$ ✗

Sample answer: The solution $x = 27$ does not check in the original equation, so it is an extraneous solution. There are no real solutions to this equation.

29.

$x = \sqrt{18-7x}$
$x^2 = 18 - 7x$
$x^2 + 7x - 18 = 0$
$(x-2)(x+9) = 0$
$x - 2 = 0$ or $x + 9 = 0$
$x = 2$ or $x = -9$ ✗

29. *Sample answer*: The solution $x = -9$ does not check in the original equation, so it is an extraneous solution. The only real solution is $x = 2$.

30. **GEOMETRY** The formula for the slant height s (in inches) of a cone is $s = \sqrt{h^2 + r^2}$ where h is the height of the cone (in inches) and r is the radius of its base (in inches), as shown. Find the height of the cone if you know the slant height is 4 inches and the radius is 2 inches. $2\sqrt{3}$ in. or about 3.5 in.

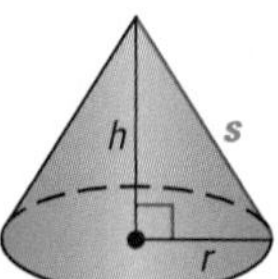

C **SOLVING EQUATIONS** **Solve the equation. Check for extraneous solutions.**

31. $\sqrt{x} + 2 = \sqrt{x - 1}$ no real solutions

32. $2 - \sqrt{x + 1} = \sqrt{x + 3}$ $-\frac{3}{4}$

33. $\sqrt{5x + 9} + \sqrt{5x} = 9$ $\frac{16}{5}$

34. ★ **WRITING** A student solves the equation $\sqrt{x + 2} = x$ and finds that $x = 2$ or $x = -1$. Without checking by substituting into the equation, which is the extraneous solution, 2 or -1? How do you know? -1; since in the equation x is equal to a radical expression, x cannot be a negative number.

35. **CHALLENGE** Write a radical equation that has 3 and 4 as solutions. *Sample answer*: $\sqrt{7x - 12} = x$

Problem Solving

EXAMPLE 5 A on p. 731 for Exs. 36–38

36. **FORESTS** The dark green areas on the image shown represent regions with heavy foliage. In Texas, the area of land y (in millions of acres) that was covered by forest during the period 1907–2002 can be modeled by the function $y = 2.5\sqrt{143 - x}$ where x is the number of years since 1907. In what year were about 20 million acres of land covered by forest in Texas? 1986

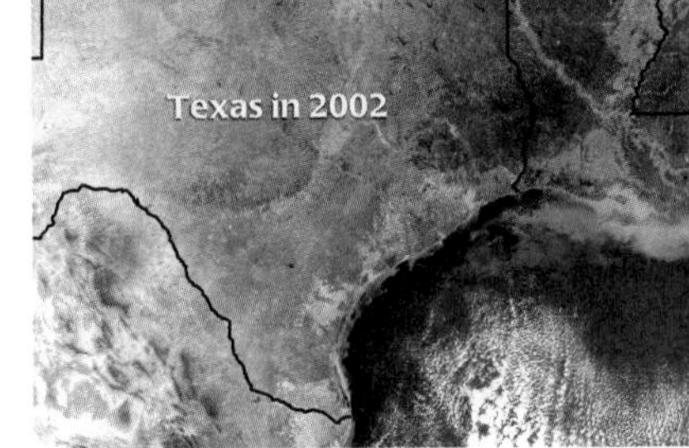

@HomeTutor for problem solving help at classzone.com

37. **PER CAPITA CONSUMPTION** The annual banana consumption y (in pounds per person) in the United States for the period 1970–2000 can be modeled by the function $y = \sqrt{18x + 272}$ where x is the number of years since 1970. In what year were about 20 pounds of bananas consumed per person? 1977

@HomeTutor for problem solving help at classzone.com

38. **MULTI-STEP PROBLEM** The velocity v (in meters per second) at which a trapeze performer swings can be modeled by the function $v = \sqrt{19.6d}$ where d is the difference (in meters) between the highest and lowest position of the performer's center of gravity during the swing.

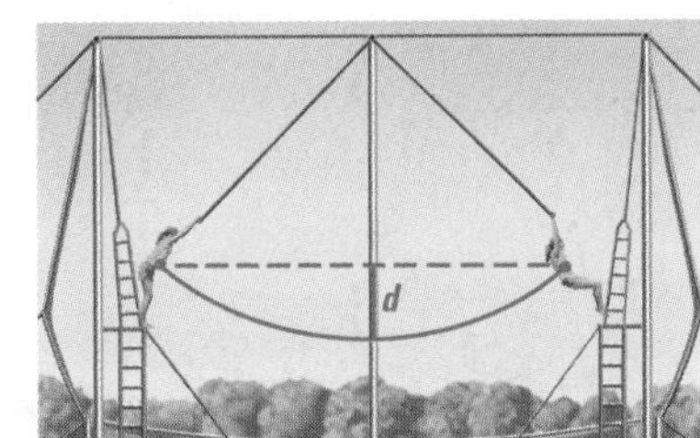

a. A trapeze performer swings at a velocity of 5 meters per second. What is the value of d? about 1.28 m

b. Suppose the performer jumps straight up off the starting board, increasing the velocity of the swing by 0.4 meter per second. By how many meters does the value of d increase? about 0.21 m

B 39. **BIOLOGY** A bushbaby is a small animal that can perform standing jumps of over 2 meters. Scientists found that the time t (in seconds) in which a bushbaby must extend its legs in order to jump to a height h (in meters) is given by the function $t = 0.45\ell\sqrt{\frac{1}{h}}$ where ℓ is the length of the bushbaby's legs (in meters). A particular bushbaby has a leg length of 0.16 meter. The bushbaby can extend its legs in 0.05 second. About how high does the bushbaby jump? Round your answer to the nearest tenth of a meter. 2.1 m

Avoiding Common Errors

Exercises 3–13 Students often fail to isolate the radical before they square both sides. Remind students that they first use properties of equality to isolate the radical on one side of the equation in the same way that they isolate the variable on one side of a linear equation.

Study Strategy

Exercise 35 Suggest to students that they use a strategy of working backward to solve this challenge. They could start by asking what two binomials they would need to multiply to get solutions of 3 and 4.

Graphing Calculator

Exercises 36–41 Students may want to use their calculators for these problems so they can concentrate on problem-solving strategies rather than calculations.

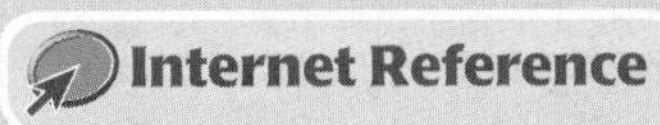

Internet Reference

Exercise 39 Additional information about bushbabies can be found at the African Wildlife Foundation website at www.awf.org/wildlives/7

5 ASSESS AND RETEACH

Daily Homework Quiz

 **Transparency Available**

Solve the equation. Check for extraneous solutions.

1. $2\sqrt{x+11} - 4 = 10$ $x = 38$
2. $\sqrt{2x-29} = \sqrt{x-11}$ $x = 18$
3. $\sqrt{3+2x} = x$ $x = 3$
4. Find the length (to the nearest foot) of a sailboat's waterline if it has a hull speed of 10 nautical miles per hour. Use the formula $s = 1.34\sqrt{\ell}$ where s is hull speed (in nautical miles per hour) and ℓ is the length (in feet) of the sailboat's waterline. about 56 feet

Online Quiz

Available at **classzone.com**

Diagnosis/Remediation

- Practice A, B, C in Chapter 11 Resource Book, pp. 33–35
- Study Guide in Chapter 11 Resource Book, pp. 36–37
- Practice Workbook, pp. 174–175
- @HomeTutor

Challenge

Additional challenge is available in the Chapter 11 Resource Book, p. 41.

Quiz

An easily-readable reduced copy of the quiz (with answers) on Lessons 11.1–11.3 from the Assessment Book can be found on p. 708E.

Quiz

1. 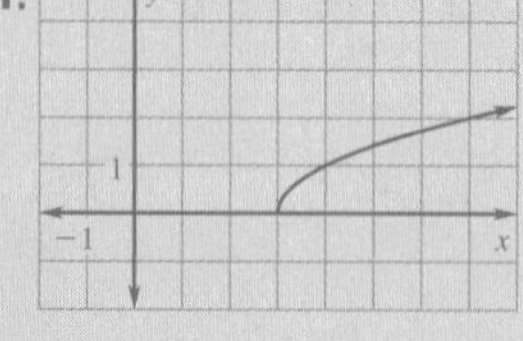

40b. Increase. Sample answer: The greater the value of ℓ, the greater the value of the radicand, and the greater the value of t.

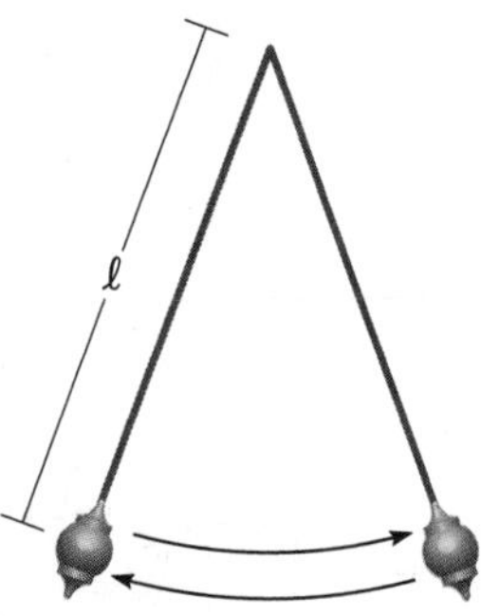

40. ★ **SHORT RESPONSE** The amount of time t (in seconds) it takes a simple pendulum to complete one full swing is called the period of the pendulum and is given by $t = 2\pi\sqrt{\frac{\ell}{32}}$ where ℓ is the length of the pendulum (in feet).

a. **Apply** A visitor at a museum notices that a pendulum on display has a period of about 11 seconds. About how long is the pendulum? Use 3.14 for π and round your answer to the nearest foot. 98 ft

b. **Explain** Does increasing the length of a pendulum increase or decrease its period? *Explain.*

C **41.** **CHALLENGE** The frequency f (in cycles per second) of a string of an electric guitar is given by the equation $f = \frac{1}{2\ell}\sqrt{\frac{T}{m}}$ where ℓ is the length of the string (in meters), T is the string's tension (in newtons), and m is the string's mass per unit length (in kilograms per meter). The high E string of a particular electric guitar is 0.64 meter long with a mass per unit length of 0.000401 kilogram per meter. How much tension is required to produce a frequency of about 330 cycles per second? Would you need more or less tension if you want to create the same frequency on a string with greater mass per unit length? *Explain.* About 71.5 N; more. Sample answer: If the mass increased then the tension would have to increase to create the same value in the radicand. If the radicand has the same value and the length is constant, the frequency will stay the same.

ILLINOIS MIXED REVIEW

 **TEST PRACTICE** at classzone.com

42. The scatter plot represents the cost of several bus trips as a function of the distance, in miles, traveled during each trip. Which additional point would be most surprising given the existing data? C

Ⓐ (40, 17) Ⓑ (70, 28)

Ⓒ (95, 48) Ⓓ (125, 50)

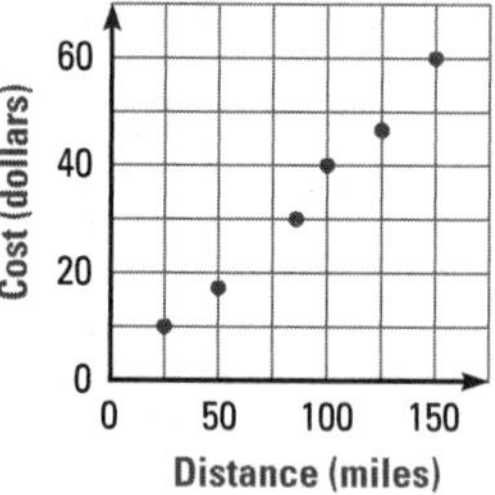

QUIZ for Lessons 11.1–11.3

1. Graph the function $y = \sqrt{x-3}$ and identify its domain and range. Compare the graph with the graph of $y = \sqrt{x}$. *(p. 710)* See margin for art; domain: $x \geq 3$, range: $y \geq 0$; the graph is a horizontal translation 3 units to the right.

Simplify the expression. *(p. 719)*

2. $\sqrt{150}$ $5\sqrt{6}$
3. $\sqrt{2c^2} \cdot \sqrt{8c}$ $4c\sqrt{c}$
4. $(7+\sqrt{5})(2-\sqrt{5})$ $9-5\sqrt{5}$
5. $\frac{14}{\sqrt{2}}$ $7\sqrt{2}$
6. $\sqrt{\frac{98}{x^6}}$ $\frac{7\sqrt{2}}{x^3}$
7. $\sqrt{\frac{80x^3}{5y}}$ $\frac{4x\sqrt{xy}}{y}$

Solve the equation. Check for extraneous solutions. *(p. 729)*

8. $\sqrt{x} - 15 = 0$ 225
9. $\sqrt{4x-7} = \sqrt{2x+19}$ 13
10. $\sqrt{6x-5} = x$ 1, 5

EXTRA PRACTICE for Lesson 11.3, p. 948  **ONLINE QUIZ** at classzone.com

Illinois Mixed Review

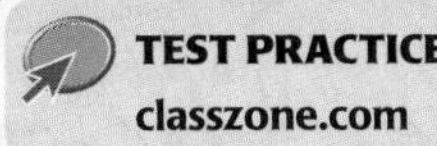

Lessons 11.1–11.3

1. **STOCKS** The number y of companies listed on the New York Stock Exchange for the period 1999–2002 can be modeled by the function $y = 3018 - 146\sqrt{x}$ where x is the number of years since 1999. About how many more companies were listed on the New York Stock Exchange in 1999 than in 2001?

   A. 73
   B. 146
   C. 206
   D. 292

2. **RUNNING SPEED** A person's maximum running speed s (in meters per second) as a function of the person's leg length l (in meters) is graphed below. To the nearest tenth of a meter, what is the leg length of a person whose maximum running speed is about 3.6 meters per second?

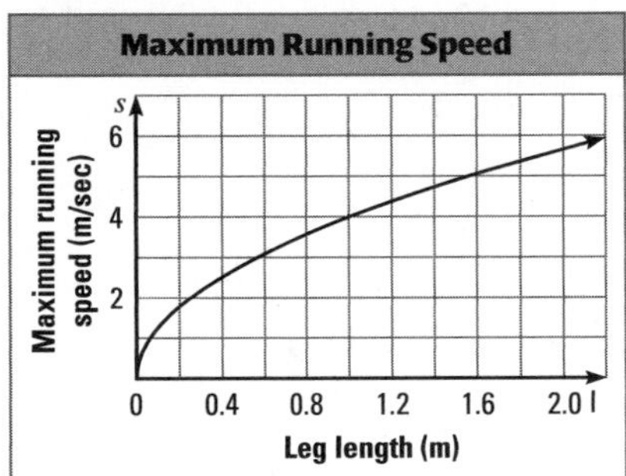

   F. 0.6 **H.** 6.6
   G. 0.8 **J.** 7.4

3. **AMPLIFIER** The voltage V (in volts) of an amplifier is given by the function $V = \sqrt{PR}$ where P is the power (in watts) and R is the resistance (in ohms). A particular amplifier uses 10 amperes and has a resistance of 4 ohms. How many watts are produced by the amplifier?

   A. 2.5
   B. 5
   C. 25
   D. 40

4. **CORN** For the period 1994–2001, the annual consumption (in pounds per person) of corn products y in the United States can be modeled by the function $y = 6.1\sqrt{x + 15.8}$ where x is the number of years since 1994. In what year were about 25 pounds of corn products consumed per person?

   F. 1995
   G. 1996
   H. 1997
   J. 1998

5. **CARS** The velocity v (in meters per second) of a car moving in a circular path that has a radius r (in meters) is given by $v = \sqrt{\frac{Fr}{m}}$ where F is the force (in newtons) pulling the car toward the center of the circle and m is the mass of the car (in kilograms). A 1600 kilogram car is traveling in a circular path with a radius of 175 meters. The force is 200 newtons. What is the velocity (in meters per second) of the car?

   A. $\frac{1}{4}\sqrt{7}$ **C.** $\frac{5}{4}\sqrt{14}$
   B. $\frac{5}{8}\sqrt{7}$ **D.** $2000\sqrt{14}$

6. **SOUND** Near Earth's surface, the speed s (in meters per second) of sound through air is given by $s = 20\sqrt{T + 273}$ where T is the air temperature (in degrees Celsius). Suppose that a ship is 1000 meters from a loud foghorn and that the air temperature is 16°C. About how many seconds will it take for the sound to travel to the ship? Round your answer to the nearest tenth of a second.

   F. 44.6
   G. 33.7
   H. 3.1
   J. 2.9

Illinois Mixed Review

1. C
2. G
3. C
4. F
5. C
6. J

11.4 The Pythagorean Theorem

MATERIALS • graph paper • scissors

QUESTION How are the lengths of the sides of a right triangle related to each other?

EXPLORE Examine the relationship among the lengths of the sides of a right triangle

STEP 1 *Make right triangles*

Cut a right triangle out of graph paper. Make three copies of it.

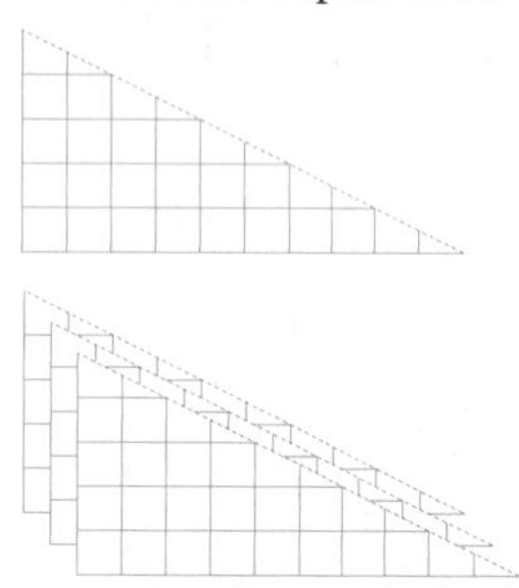

STEP 2 *Arrange as a square*

Arrange the right triangles to form a square within a square, as shown.

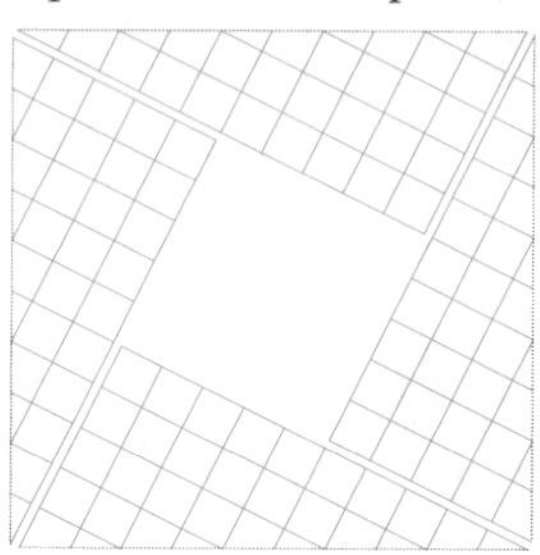

DRAW CONCLUSIONS Use your observations to complete these exercises

1. How are the areas of the triangles and inner square related to the area of the outer square? The sum of the areas of the triangles and the inner square is equal to the area of the outer square.

In Exercises 2–4, let *a*, *b*, and *c* be the lengths of the sides of a right triangle with $a < b < c$, as shown. Write an expression for the area of the figure described below.

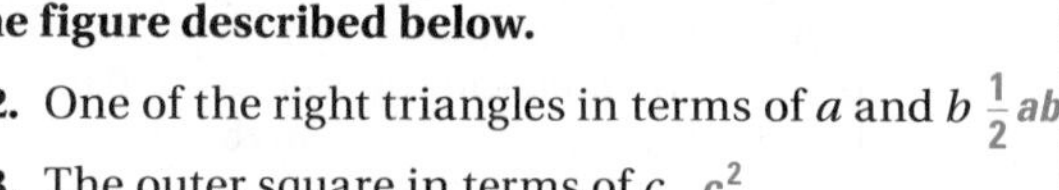

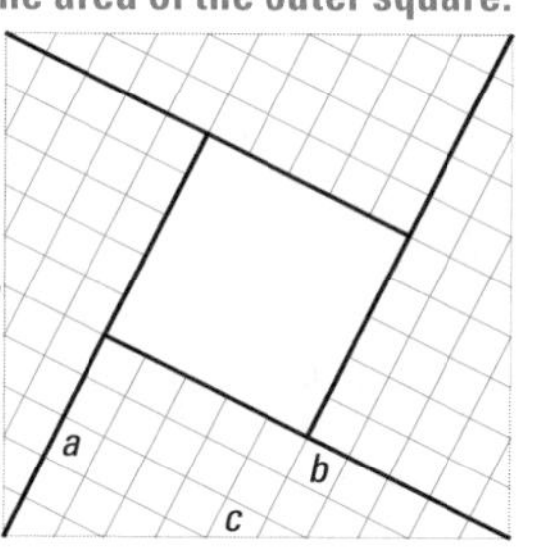

2. One of the right triangles in terms of *a* and *b* $\frac{1}{2}ab$
3. The outer square in terms of *c* c^2
4. The inner square in terms of *a* and *b* $(b - a)^2$
5. Use the relationship you determined in Exercise 1 and your results from Exercises 2–4 to write an equation that relates *a*, *b*, and *c*. Simplify the equation. $c^2 = 4 \cdot \frac{1}{2} \cdot ab + (b - a)^2 = 2ab + b^2 - 2ab + a^2 = b^2 + a^2$
6. **REASONING** The triangle shown is a right triangle. Find the value of *x*. *Explain* how you found your answer. 26. *Sample answer*: Use the equation found in Exercise 5, and let $a = 10$, $b = 24$, and $c = x$. Solve for *x*.

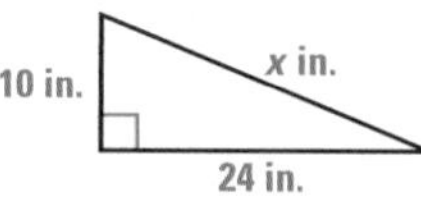

1 PLAN AND PREPARE

Explore the Concept

- Students will examine the relationship among the lengths of the sides of a right triangle.
- This activity leads into the study of the Pythagorean theorem in Example 1 in Lesson 11.4.

Materials

Each student will need:

- graph paper
- scissors

Recommended Time

Work activity: 10 min

Discuss results: 5 min

Grouping

Students should work individually.

2 TEACH

Tips for Success

Make sure students relate the total areas of the four triangles and the inner square to the area of the outer square.

Key Discovery

The relationship between side lengths of a right triangle with side lengths *a*, *b*, and *c* is $a^2 + b^2 = c^2$, where *c* is the longest side length.

3 ASSESS AND RETEACH

The longest side length of a right triangle is 15 inches. One of the other side lengths is 9 inches. What is the unknown side length? Justify your answer. 12 inches; Using $a^2 + b^2 = c^2$ results in $9^2 + x^2 = 15^2$ or $81 + x^2 = 225$. Solving for *x* gives $x = 12$.

11.4 Apply the Pythagorean Theorem and Its Converse

9.11.01 Apply the Pythagorean theorem.

Before You solved radical equations.

Now You will use the Pythagorean theorem and its converse.

Why? So you can examine angles in architecture, as in Ex. 35.

Key Vocabulary
- hypotenuse
- legs of a right triangle
- Pythagorean theorem

The **hypotenuse** of a right triangle is the side opposite the right angle. It is the longest side of a right triangle. The **legs** are the two sides that form the right angle.

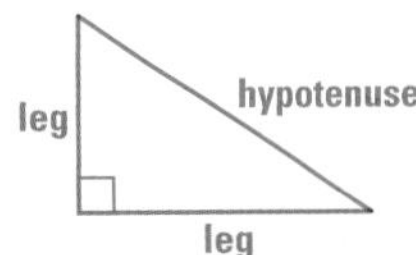

A *theorem* is a statement that can be proved true. The **Pythagorean theorem** states the relationship among the lengths of the sides of a right triangle.

KEY CONCEPT *For Your Notebook*

The Pythagorean Theorem

Words If a triangle is a right triangle, then the sum of the squares of the lengths of the legs equals the square of the length of the hypotenuse.

Algebra $a^2 + b^2 = c^2$

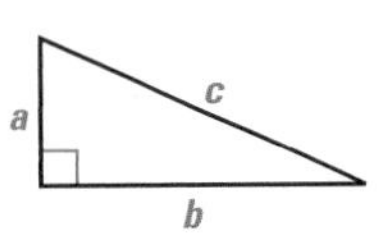

EXAMPLE 1 Use the Pythagorean theorem

Find the unknown length for the triangle shown.

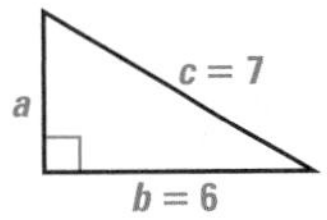

(Triangle with legs a and $b = 6$, hypotenuse $c = 7$)

Solution

$a^2 + b^2 = c^2$	Pythagorean theorem
$a^2 + 6^2 = 7^2$	Substitute 6 for b and 7 for c.
$a^2 + 36 = 49$	Simplify.
$a^2 = 13$	Subtract 36 from each side.
$a = \sqrt{13}$	Take positive square root of each side.

▶ The side length a is $\sqrt{13}$.

 at classzone.com

REVIEW QUADRATIC EQUATIONS
For help with solving quadratic equations by using square roots, see p. 652.

GUIDED PRACTICE for Example 1

1. The lengths of the legs of a right triangle are $a = 5$ and $b = 12$. Find c. 13

1 PLAN AND PREPARE

Warm-Up Exercises

Transparency Available

Solve the equation.

1. $\sqrt{x-5} + 2 = 7$ $x = 30$
2. $2\sqrt{x} + 9 = 9$ $x = 0$
3. $\sqrt{x+11} - 3 = 5$ $x = 53$
4. Use the equation $v = \sqrt{64d}$, where v is velocity (in feet per second) and d is the distance (in feet) an object falls to find how far an object has dropped when its velocity is about 24 feet per second. 9 ft

Notetaking Guide

Transparency Available

Promotes interactive learning and notetaking skills, pp. 259–261.

Pacing

Basic: 1 day
Average: 1 day
Advanced: 1 day
Block: 0.5 block with 11.5
- See *Teaching Guide/Lesson Plan.*

2 FOCUS AND MOTIVATE

Essential Question

Big Idea 3, p. 709

How do you use the Pythagorean theorem and its converse? Tell students they will learn how to answer this question by using known side lengths of right triangles to find unknown lengths.

Resource Planning Guide

Chapter Resource Book
- Teaching Guide/Lesson Plan (pp. 42–43)
- Practice levels A, B, C (pp. 44–46)
- Study Guide (pp. 47–48)
- Catch-up for Absent Students (p. 49)
- Application (p. 50)
- Challenge (p. 51)

Workbooks
- Notetaking Guide (pp. 259–261)
- Practice Workbook (pp. 176–177)

Teaching Options
- **Power Presentations CD-ROM** provides dynamic electronic teaching resources for the classroom.
- **Activity Generator CD-ROM** provides editable activities for all ability levels.

Interactive Technology
- Easy Planner
- Power Presentations CD-ROM
- Activity Generator CD-ROM
- Animated Algebra
- Test Generator CD-ROM
- Online Quiz
- eWorkbook
- eEdition
- @HomeTutor

Resources for English Learners
- Quick Reference for English Learners
- Spanish Study Guide
- Multi-Language Visual Glossary
- Student Resources in Spanish

See also the *Algebra 1 Toolkit* for more strategies for meeting individual needs.

Motivating the Lesson

You are shopping for an entertainment center and you find one that you like. If you know the dimensions of the entertainment center and the dimensions of your television screen, you can use the Pythagorean theorem to determine whether your television set will fit in the entertainment center.

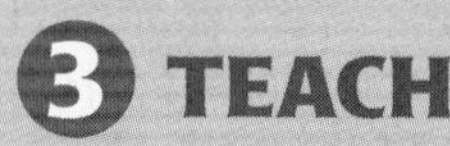

3 TEACH

Extra Example 1

Find the unknown length for the triangle shown. $\sqrt{65}$

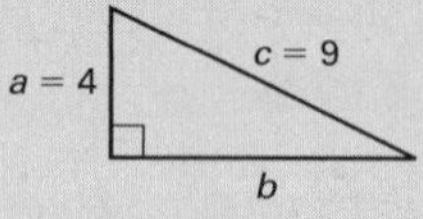

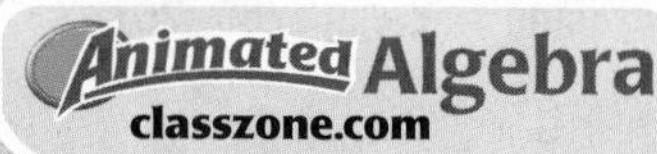

An **Animated Algebra** activity is available on-line for **Example 1**. This activity is also available on the **Power Presentations CD-ROM**.

Extra Example 2

A right triangle has one leg that is 1 foot longer than the other leg. The hypotenuse is $\sqrt{13}$ feet. Find the unknown lengths. 2 ft and 3 ft

Extra Example 3

A person at A in the diagram throws a flying disc to a person at C. To the nearest foot, how far does the person throw the flying disc? D

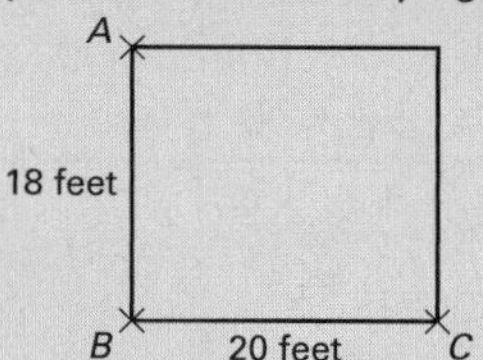

Ⓐ 6 feet Ⓑ 19 feet
Ⓒ 22 feet Ⓓ 27 feet

EXAMPLE 2 Use the Pythagorean theorem

A right triangle has one leg that is 2 inches longer than the other leg. The length of the hypotenuse is $\sqrt{10}$ inches. Find the unknown lengths.

Solution

Sketch a right triangle and label the sides with their lengths. Let x be the length of the shorter leg.

$a^2 + b^2 = c^2$	Pythagorean theorem
$x^2 + (x + 2)^2 = (\sqrt{10})^2$	Substitute.
$x^2 + x^2 + 4x + 4 = 10$	Simplify.
$2x^2 + 4x - 6 = 0$	Write in standard form.
$2(x - 1)(x + 3) = 0$	Factor.
$x - 1 = 0$ *or* $x + 3 = 0$	Zero-product property
$x = 1$ *or* $x = -3$	Solve for x.

▶ Because length is nonnegative, the solution $x = -3$ does not make sense. The legs have lengths of 1 inch and $1 + 2 = 3$ inches.

EXAMPLE 3 Standardized Test Practice

A soccer player makes a corner kick to another player, as shown. To the nearest yard, how far does the player kick the ball?

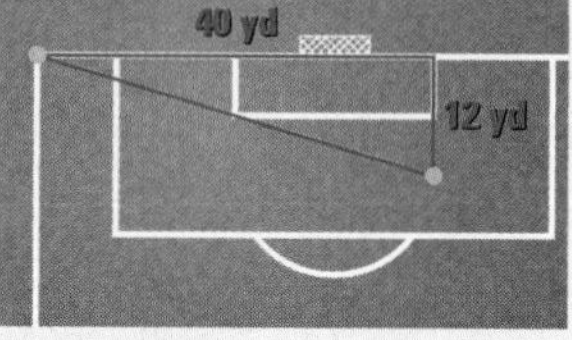

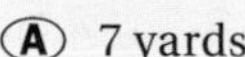

Ⓐ 7 yards Ⓑ 38 yards
Ⓒ 42 yards Ⓓ 52 yards

ELIMINATE CHOICES
The hypotenuse is the longest side of the triangle, so the length must be greater than 40 yards. Eliminate choices A and B.

Solution

The path of the kicked ball is the hypotenuse of a right triangle. The length of one leg is 12 yards, and the length of the other leg is 40 yards.

$c^2 = a^2 + b^2$	Pythagorean theorem
$c^2 = 12^2 + 40^2$	Substitute 12 for a and 40 for b.
$c^2 = 1744$	Simplify.
$c = \sqrt{1744} \approx 42$	Take positive square root of each side.

▶ The correct answer is C. Ⓐ Ⓑ Ⓒ Ⓓ

GUIDED PRACTICE for Examples 2 and 3

2. A right triangle has one leg that is 3 inches longer than the other leg. The length of the hypotenuse is 15 inches. Find the unknown lengths. 9 in. and 12 in.

3. **SWIMMING** A rectangular pool is 30 feet wide and 60 feet long. You swim diagonally across the pool. To the nearest foot, how far do you swim? 67 ft

Differentiated Instruction

English Learners The word *hypotenuse* comes from the Greek *hypo* meaning under and *teinein* meaning tension. Thus, the word could be translated as "under tension." Looking at a triangle such as the one in **Example 2**, the hypotenuse can be envisioned as a wire stretched from one side of the triangle to the other, with the wire being under tension.

See also the *Algebra 1 Toolkit* for more strategies.

REVIEW REASONING
For help with if-then statements and converses, see pp. 64, 110, and 319.

CONVERSE OF THE PYTHAGOREAN THEOREM Recall that when you reverse the hypothesis and conclusion of an if-then statement, the new statement is called the converse. Although not all converses of true statements are true, the converse of the Pythagorean theorem is true.

KEY CONCEPT *For Your Notebook*

Converse of the Pythagorean Theorem

If a triangle has side lengths a, b, and c such that $a^2 + b^2 = c^2$, then the triangle is a right triangle.

EXAMPLE 4 Determine right triangles

Tell whether the triangle with the given side lengths is a right triangle.

a. 8, 15, 17

$8^2 + 15^2 \stackrel{?}{=} 17^2$

$64 + 225 \stackrel{?}{=} 289$

$289 = 289$ ✓

▶ The triangle is a right triangle.

b. 5, 8, 9

$5^2 + 8^2 \stackrel{?}{=} 9^2$

$25 + 64 \stackrel{?}{=} 81$

$89 = 81$ ✗

▶ The triangle is *not* a right triangle.

EXAMPLE 5 Use the converse of the Pythagorean theorem

CONSTRUCTION A construction worker is making sure one corner of the foundation of a house is a right angle. To do this, the worker makes a mark 8 feet from the corner along one wall and another mark 6 feet from the same corner along the other wall. The worker then measures the distance between the two marks and finds the distance to be 10 feet. Is the corner a right angle?

Solution

$8^2 + 6^2 \stackrel{?}{=} 10^2$	Check to see if $a^2 + b^2 = c^2$ when $a = 8$, $b = 6$, and $c = 10$.
$64 + 36 \stackrel{?}{=} 100$	Simplify.
$100 = 100$ ✓	Add.

▶ Because the sides that the construction worker measured form a right triangle, the corner of the foundation is a right angle.

GUIDED PRACTICE for Examples 4 and 5

Tell whether the triangle with the given side lengths is a right triangle.

4. 7, 11, 13 not a right triangle **5.** 15, 36, 39 right triangle **6.** 15, 112, 113 right triangle

7. WINDOW DESIGN A window has the shape of a triangle with side lengths of 120 centimeters, 120 centimeters, and 180 centimeters. Is the window a right triangle? *Explain.*

7. No. *Sample answer:* $120^2 + 120^2 \neq 180^2$, so it cannot be a right triangle.

Extra Example 4

Tell whether the triangle with the given side lengths is a right triangle.

a. 7, 23, 24 no

b. 5, 12, 13 yes

Key Question to Ask for Example 4

- Which side length in part a is the hypotenuse of the triangle? 17

Extra Example 5

A real estate lot is in the shape of a triangle. The side lengths are 48 feet, 55 feet, and 73 feet. The real estate agent told a potential buyer that one of the corners forms a right angle. Is the real estate agent correct? yes

Closing the Lesson

Have students summarize the major points of the lesson and answer the Essential Question: How do you use the Pythagorean theorem and its converse?

- The Pythagorean theorem is $a^2 + b^2 = c^2$, where a and b are leg lengths of a right triangle and c is the length of the hypotenuse.

To find an unknown length in a right triangle, use the Pythagorean theorem and substitute values for either the hypotenuse and one leg or both legs, and solve by isolating the variable and then taking the positive square root of each side. The hypotenuse is always side with length c. Use the converse of the Pythagorean theorem to determine whether a triangle is a right triangle by checking to see if the sum of the squares of the shorter lengths is equal to the square of the longest length.

4 PRACTICE AND APPLY

Assignment Guide

Answer Transparencies available for all exercises

Basic:
Day 1: pp. 740–742
Exs. 1, 2, 3–15 odd, 16–30, 33–36, 39–49 odd

Average:
Day 1: pp. 740–742
Exs. 1, 2, 9–22, 26–31, 33–37, 40–50 even

Advanced:
Day 1: pp. 740–742
Exs. 1, 10–15, 17–22, 26–32*, 34–38*, 44–46, 48, 50

Block:
pp. 740–742
Exs. 1, 2, 9–22, 26–31, 33–37, 40–50 even (with 11.5)

Differentiated Instruction

See *Algebra 1 Best Practices Toolkit* for suggestions on addressing the needs of a diverse classroom.

Homework Check

For a quick check of student understanding of key concepts, go over the following exercises:

Basic: 7, 18, 24, 33, 34
Average: 11, 20, 26, 33, 35
Advanced: 14, 22, 28, 34, 35

Extra Practice

- Student Edition, p. 948
- Chapter 11 Resource Book: Practice levels A, B, C, pp. 44–46

Practice Worksheet

An easily-readable reduced practice page (with answers) for this lesson can be found on p.708C.

11.4 EXERCISES

HOMEWORK KEY
○ = WORKED-OUT SOLUTIONS on p. WS27 for Exs. 9, 23, and 35
★ = STANDARDIZED TEST PRACTICE Exs. 2, 15, 29, 30, and 37

SKILL PRACTICE

A

1. **VOCABULARY** Copy and complete: In a right triangle, the side opposite the right angle is called the __?__. hypotenuse

2. ★ **WRITING** *Explain* how you can tell whether a triangle with side lengths of 9, 12, and 15 is a right triangle. If the sum of 9 squared and 12 squared is 15 squared, then it is a right triangle. If they are not equal, then it is not a right triangle.

EXAMPLE 1 on p. 737 for Exs. 3–16

USING THE PYTHAGOREAN THEOREM **Let a and b represent the lengths of the legs of a right triangle, and let c represent the length of the hypotenuse. Find the unknown length.**

3. $a = 3, c = 5$ $b = 4$
4. $b = 3, c = 7$ $a = 2\sqrt{10}$
5. $a = 5, b = 6$ $c = \sqrt{61}$
6. $b = 5, c = 10$ $a = 5\sqrt{3}$
7. $a = 8, b = 8$ $c = 8\sqrt{2}$
8. $a = 5, b = 12$ $c = 13$
9. $a = 8, b = 12$ $c = 4\sqrt{13}$
10. $a = 7, c = 25$ $b = 24$
11. $b = 15, c = 17$ $a = 8$
12. $a = 9, c = 41$ $b = 40$
13. $b = 3, c = 3.4$ $a = 1.6$
14. $a = 1.2, c = 3.7$ $b = 3.5$

15. ★ **MULTIPLE CHOICE** A tennis court is 36 feet by 78 feet. What is the length of a diagonal? Round your answer to the nearest tenth of a foot. C

Ⓐ 42.0 feet Ⓑ 69.2 feet Ⓒ 85.9 feet Ⓓ 114.0 feet

16. **ERROR ANALYSIS** *Describe* and correct the error in finding the unknown length.

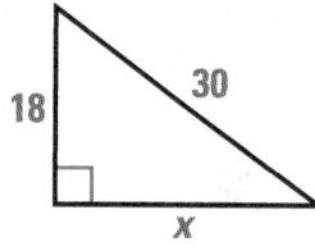

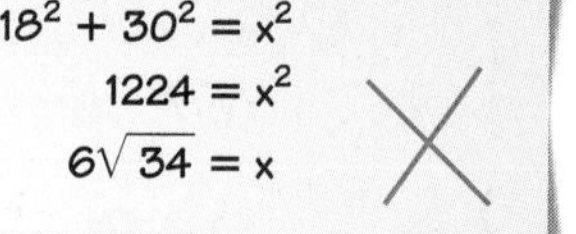

The side with length 30 is the hypotenuse, and should be substituted for c in the Pythagorean theorem, not b; $18^2 + x^2 = 30^2$, $324 + x^2 = 900$, $x^2 = 576$, $x = 24$.

EXAMPLE 2 on p. 738 for Exs. 17–22

USING THE PYTHAGOREAN THEOREM **Find the unknown lengths.**

17.
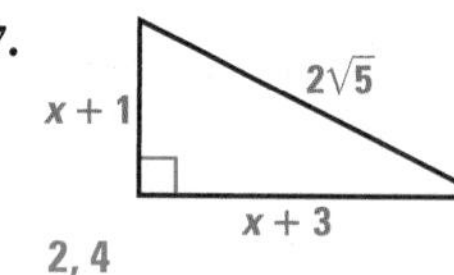

2, 4

18.
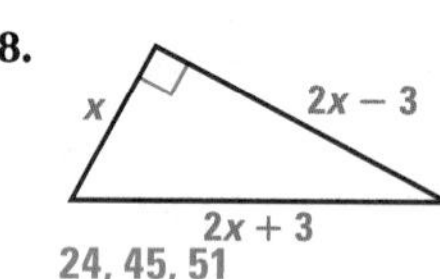

24, 45, 51

19.
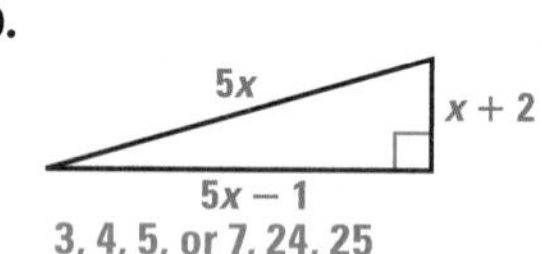

3, 4, 5, or 7, 24, 25

20. A right triangle has one leg that is 2 inches longer than the other leg. The length of the hypotenuse is $\sqrt{130}$ inches. Find the lengths of the legs. 7 in., 9 in.

21. A right triangle has one leg that is 3 times as long as the other leg. The length of the hypotenuse is $\sqrt{40}$ inches. Find the lengths of the legs. 2 in., 6 in.

22. A right triangle has one leg that is $\frac{1}{2}$ of the length of the other leg. The length of the hypotenuse is $6\sqrt{5}$ inches. Find the lengths of the legs. 6 in., 12 in.

EXAMPLE 4 on p. 739 for Exs. 23–28

DETERMINING RIGHT TRIANGLES **Tell whether the triangle with the given side lengths is a right triangle.**

23. 2, 3, 4 not a right triangle
24. 9, 12, 15 right triangle
25. 8, 16, 18 not a right triangle
26. 9, 21, 24 not a right triangle
27. 11, 60, 61 right triangle
28. 24, 143, 145 right triangle

29. ★ **MULTIPLE CHOICE** What is the area of the largest square in the coordinate plane shown? A

Ⓐ 100 square units

Ⓑ 64 square units

Ⓒ 36 square units

Ⓓ 25 square units

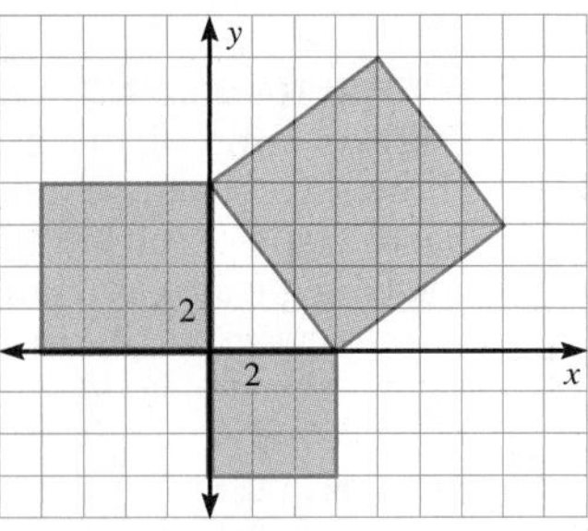

30. No. *Sample answer:* The unknown side might be the hypotenuse, or it might be a leg of the triangle. Each case would give a different answer.

B

30. ★ **WRITING** Given that two side lengths of a right triangle are 11 inches and 6 inches, is it possible to find the length of the third side? *Explain.*

31. **REASONING** A *Pythagorean triple* is a group of integers a, b, and c that represent the side lengths of a right triangle. For example, the integers 3, 4, and 5 form a Pythagorean triple. Choose any two positive integers m and n such that $m < n$. Then find a, b, and c as follows: $a = n^2 - m^2$, $b = 2mn$, and $c = n^2 + m^2$. Show that the numbers you generated form a Pythagorean triple. Then use the converse of the Pythagorean theorem to show that the equations for a, b, and c always generate Pythagorean triples. See margin.

C

32. **CHALLENGE** The edge length of the cube is 7 inches.

a. Find the value of x. $7\sqrt{2}$

b. Find the value of y. $7\sqrt{3}$

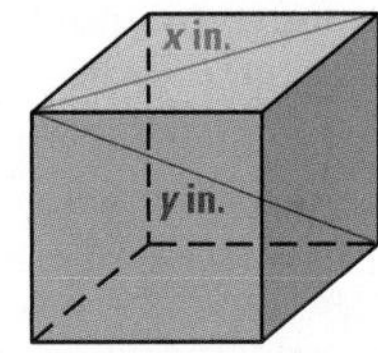

Problem Solving

EXAMPLES 3 and 5 on pp. 738–739 for Exs. 33–35

A

33. **ARCHITECTURE** An earthquake-resistant building has dampers built into its structure to help minimize damage caused by an earthquake. A section of the structural frame of such a building is shown. What is the length of the damper? Round your answer to the nearest foot. 16 ft

@HomeTutor for problem solving help at classzone.com

34. No; the sum of the squares of the two shorter sides is not equal to the square of the longer side.

34. **SAILS** A sail has the shape of a triangle. The side lengths are 146 inches, 131 inches, and 84 inches. Is the sail a right triangle? *Explain.*

@HomeTutor for problem solving help at classzone.com

Avoiding Common Errors

Exercises 3–14 Some students may forget to take the square of both sides when finding a leg or hypotenuse length. Suggest that students substitute the side lengths into the Pythagorean theorem to make sure that their answers make sense.

Mathematical Reasoning

Exercises 17–22 Point out to students that if they find that one or both of the legs of the triangle are longer than the hypotenuse, given that the hypotenuse is the longest side of the triangle, then they know that they need to recalculate the side lengths of the triangle.

Reading Strategy

Exercise 29 Draw students' attention to the diagram and note that the 2 on the grid indicates the length of one unit on the grid, not the length of the sides of the squares.

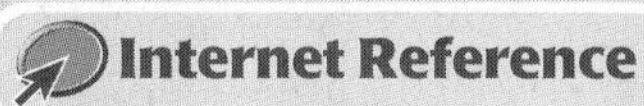

Internet Reference

Exercise 33 For more information about earthquake-resistant structures, visit the United States Geological Survey website at quake.wr.usgs.gov/prepare/factsheets/SaferStructures

31. *Sample answer:* Let $m = 3$ and $n = 6$. Then $a = 6^2 - 3^2 = 27$, $b = 2(3)(6) = 36$, $c = 6^2 + 3^2 = 45$; substitute the values from the equation for a, b, and c in the Pythagorean theorem: $(n^2 - m^2)^2 + (2mn)^2 = (n^2 + m^2)^2$. Simplify to $n^4 - 2m^2n^2 + m^4 + 4m^2n^2 = n^4 + 2m^2n^2 + m^4$; $-2m^2n^2 + 4m^2n^2 = 2m^2n^2$; $2 = 2$. The equations are equal, so by the converse of the Pythagorean theorem, the lengths a, b, and c are a Pythagorean triple.

5 ASSESS AND RETEACH

Daily Homework Quiz

Transparency Available

Let a and b represent the lengths of the legs of a right triangle, and let c represent the length of the hypotenuse. Find the unknown length.

1. $a = 4$, $c = 8$ $b = \sqrt{48}$ or $4\sqrt{3}$

2. $a = 5$, $b = 7$ $c = \sqrt{74}$

3. $b = 15$, $c = 21$ $a = \sqrt{216}$ or $6\sqrt{6}$

4. $a = 3$, $c = 11$ $b = \sqrt{112}$ or $4\sqrt{7}$

5. A triangular garden has side lengths of 5 feet, 12 feet, and 14 feet. Is the garden in the shape of a right triangle? no

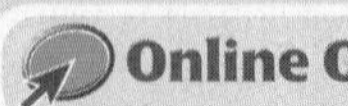

Available at **classzone.com**

Diagnosis/Remediation

- Practice A, B, C in Chapter 11 Resource Book, pp. 44–46
- Study Guide in Chapter 11 Resource Book, pp. 47–48
- Practice Workbook, pp. 176–177
- @HomeTutor

Challenge

Additional challenge is available in the Chapter 11 Resource Book, p. 51.

35. **FLATIRON BUILDING** A top view of the Flatiron Building in New York City is shown. The triangle indicates the basic shape of the building's roof. Is the triangle a right triangle? *Explain.* No; the sum of the squares of the two shorter sides is not equal to the square of the longer side.

B **36.** **SCREEN SIZES** The size of a television is indicated by the length of a diagonal of the television screen. The aspect ratio of a television screen is the ratio of the length of the screen to the width of the screen. The size of a particular television is 30 inches, and its aspect ratio is 4 : 3. What are the width and the length of the television screen? 18 in., 24 in.

37. ★ **EXTENDED RESPONSE** The *Wheel of Theodorus* is a figure formed by a chain of right triangles with consecutive triangles sharing a common side. The hypotenuse of one triangle becomes a leg of the next, as shown.

a. **Calculate** What is the length of the longest hypotenuse in the diagram? $\sqrt{6}$

b. **Extend** Extend the diagram to include two more triangles. What is the length of the longest hypotenuse in the new diagram? $\sqrt{8}$

c. **Analyze** Find a formula for the length of the hypotenuse of the nth triangle. *Explain* how you found your answer. $c_n = \sqrt{n+1}$; *Sample answer*: A list of the hypotenuse's for the first few triangles is $\sqrt{2}, \sqrt{3}, \sqrt{4}, \sqrt{5}, \ldots$. A general formula for this series is $c_n = \sqrt{n+1}$.

C **38.** **CHALLENGE** A baseball diamond has the shape of a square with side lengths of 90 feet. A catcher wants to get a player running from first base to second base out, so the catcher must throw the ball to second base before the runner reaches second base.

a. The catcher is 5 feet behind home plate. How far does the catcher have to throw the ball to reach second base? Round your answer to the nearest foot. 132 ft

b. The catcher throws the ball at a rate of 90 feet per second when the player is 30 feet away from second base. Will the catcher get the player out if the player is running at a rate of 22 feet per second? *Explain.*

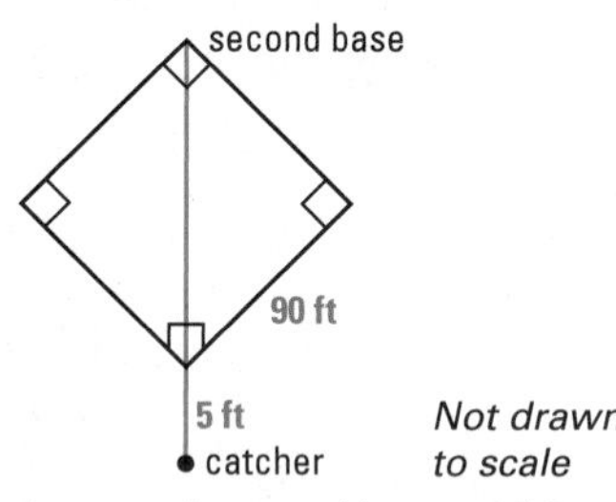

No. *Sample answer*: The ball will take about 1.47 seconds to reach second base, and the player will reach the base in about 1.36 seconds.

ILLINOIS MIXED REVIEW

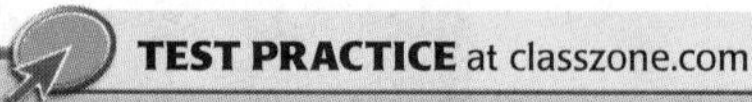

39. $\triangle ABC$ is shown in the graph at the right. Find the coordinates of point C if $\triangle ABC$ is translated 3 units to the right and 2 units down.

Ⓐ (3, 0) Ⓑ (−3, 4) C

Ⓒ (3, −4) Ⓓ (−3, 0)

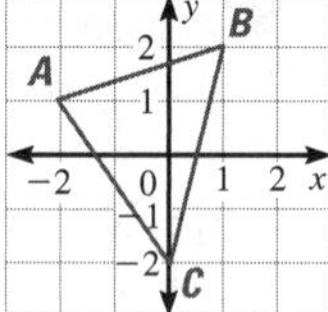

Investigating Algebra ACTIVITY *Use before Lesson 11.5*

11.5 Distance in The Coordinate Plane

MATERIALS • graph paper

QUESTION **How can you find the distance between two points?**

EXPLORE **Find the distance between points $A(-3, -2)$ and $B(4, -2)$**

STEP 1 ***Plot points***

Plot the points $A(-3, -2)$ and $B(4, -2)$ in the same coordinate plane.

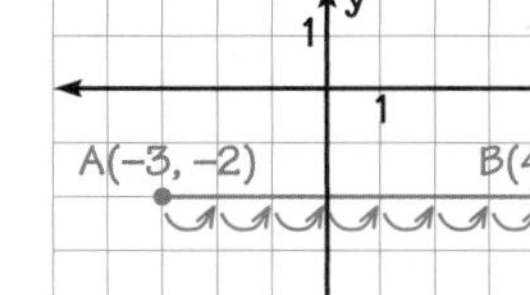

STEP 2 ***Find distance***

Find the distance between the points by counting the grid spaces between them. **7 units**

STEP 3 ***Find distance***

Find the distance by subtracting the x-coordinate of point A from the x-coordinate of point B. **7 units**

STEP 4 ***Compare results***

How does your result from Step 2 compare with your result from Step 3? **They are the same.**

DRAW CONCLUSIONS **Use your observations to complete these exercises**

1. Subtract the x-coordinate of point B from the x-coordinate of point A. How is the value different from the values found in Steps 2 and 3 above? How could you make them the same? **−7; it is the opposite of the value in Step 2 and 3; take the absolute value.**
2. Assume points $C(x_1, y_1)$ and $D(x_2, y_2)$ lie on the same horizontal line. Write an expression that can be used to find the distance between the points. $|x_2 - x_1|$ **or** $|x_1 - x_2|$
3. Assume points $C(x_1, y_1)$ and $D(x_2, y_2)$ lie on the same vertical line. Write an expression that can be used to find the distance between the points. Check your expression using $(-2, 4)$ and $(-2, -3)$. $|y_2 - y_1|$ **or** $|y_1 - y_2|$; **7**

In Exercises 4–12, find the distance between the two points.

4. (2, 3), (−5, 3) 7	**5.** (0, −4), (7, −4) 7	**6.** (−1, 5), (2, 5) 3
7. (4, −6), (6, −6) 2	**8.** (−5, −4), (−2, −4) 3	**9.** (2, 8), (2, 3) 5
10. (5, −6), (5, −2) 4	**11.** (0, −4), (0, 2) 6	**12.** (−3, 0), (−3, 6) 6

13. **REASONING** Plot the points $A(6, 5)$, $B(2, 5)$, and $C(6, 2)$. Find the distance between points A and B. Find the distance between points A and C. Use the distances and the Pythagorean theorem to find the distance between points B and C. **See margin for art; 4; 3; 5.**

1 PLAN AND PREPARE

Explore the Concept

- Students will find the distance between two points on a coordinate plane.
- This activity leads into the study of the distance formula in Example 1 in Lesson 11.5.

Materials

Each student will need graph paper.

Recommended Time

Work activity: 10 min

Discuss results: 5 min

Grouping

Students should work individually.

2 TEACH

Tips for Success

In Step 3, watch for students who subtract the y-coordinate of point A from the x-coordinate of point B. Point out that the red arrows on the diagram refer to the number of grid lines between the points, not to the coordinates of the points.

Key Discovery

On a coordinate plane, find the horizontal distance between two points by subtracting the x-coordinates and find the vertical distance by subtracting the y-coordinates.

3 ASSESS AND RETEACH

Show how to find the vertical distance between points (x_1, y_1) and (x_2, y_2) for (6, 4) and (8, 9). **Use $y_2 - y_1$, or $9 - 4$, to find a vertical distance of 5 units.**

13.

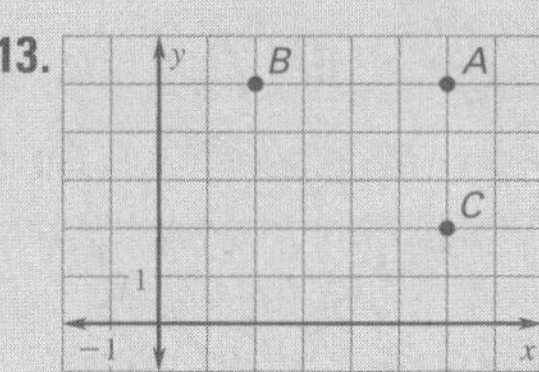

11.5 Apply the Distance and Midpoint Formulas

 9.11.09 Solve problems that involve calculating distance, midpoint, and slope using coordinate geometry.

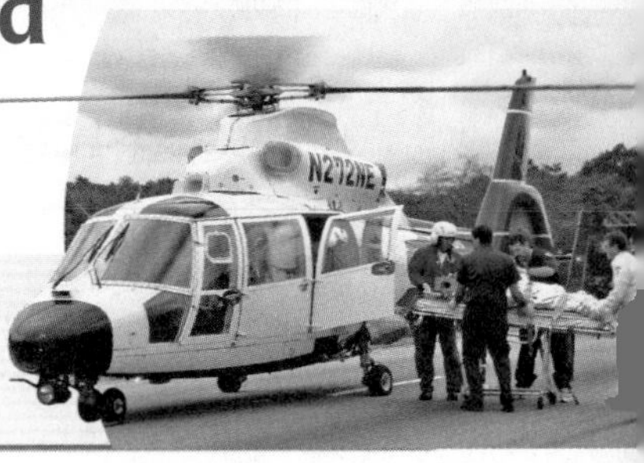

Before You used the Pythagorean theorem and its converse.

Now You will use the distance and midpoint formulas.

Why? So you can calculate distances traveled, as in Ex. 47.

1 PLAN AND PREPARE

Warm-Up Exercises

Transparency Available

1. Is a triangle with side lengths 9, 40, 41 a right triangle? yes
2. A triangular window is 14 inches wide and 18 inches high. The length and width of the window meet at a right angle. What is the length of the other side to the nearest whole number? 23 in.

Notetaking Guide

Transparency Available

Promotes interactive learning and notetaking skills, pp. 262–264.

Pacing

Basic: 1 day
Average: 1 day
Advanced: 1 day
Block: 0.5 block with 11.4
- See *Teaching Guide/Lesson Plan.*

2 FOCUS AND MOTIVATE

Essential Question

Big Idea 3, p. 709

How do you use the distance and midpoint formulas? Tell students they will learn how to answer this question by using coordinates to find the distance between two points and the midpoint of two points.

Key Vocabulary
- **distance formula**
- **midpoint**
- **midpoint formula**

To find the distance between the points $A(-2, -1)$ and $B(3, 2)$, draw a right triangle, as shown. The lengths of the legs of the right triangle are as follows.

$AC = |3 - (-2)| = 5$

$BC = |-1 - 2| = 3$

You can use the Pythagorean theorem to find AB, the length of the hypotenuse of the right triangle.

$(AB)^2 = (AC)^2 + (BC)^2$ **Pythagorean theorem**

$AB = \sqrt{(AC)^2 + (BC)^2}$ **Take positive square root of each side.**

$AB = \sqrt{5^2 + 3^2} = \sqrt{34}$ **Substitute 5 for *AC* and 3 for *BC* and simplify.**

This example suggests that you can find the distance between two points in a coordinate plane using the following formula, called the **distance formula**.

KEY CONCEPT *For Your Notebook*

The Distance Formula

The distance d between any two points (x_1, y_1) and (x_2, y_2) is

$$d = \sqrt{(x_2 - x_1)^2 + (y_2 - y_1)^2}.$$

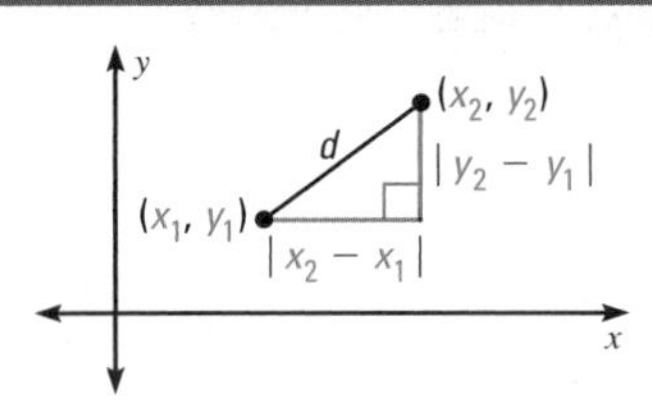

EXAMPLE 1 Find the distance between two points

Find the distance between (−1, 3) and (5, 2).

Let $(x_1, y_1) = (-1, 3)$ and $(x_2, y_2) = (5, 2)$.

$d = \sqrt{(x_2 - x_1)^2 + (y_2 - y_1)^2}$ **Distance formula**

$= \sqrt{(5 - (-1))^2 + (2 - 3)^2}$ **Substitute.**

$= \sqrt{6^2 + (-1)^2} = \sqrt{37}$ **Simplify.**

▶ The distance between the points is $\sqrt{37}$ units.

Resource Planning Guide

Chapter Resource Book
- Teaching Guide/Lesson Plan (pp. 52–53)
- Practice levels A, B, C (pp. 54–56)
- Study Guide (pp. 57–58)
- Catch-up for Absent Students (p. 59)
- Problem Solving Workshop (p. 60)
- Challenge (p. 61)

Workbooks
- Notetaking Guide (pp. 262–264)
- Practice Workbook (pp. 178–179)

Teaching Options
- **Power Presentations CD-ROM** provides dynamic electronic teaching resources for the classroom.
- **Activity Generator CD-ROM** provides editable activities for all ability levels.

Interactive Technology
- Easy Planner
- Power Presentations CD-ROM
- Activity Generator CD-ROM
- Animated Algebra
- Test Generator CD-ROM
- Online Quiz
- eWorkbook
- eEdition
- @HomeTutor

Resources for English Learners
- Quick Reference for English Learners
- Spanish Study Guide
- Multi-Language Visual Glossary
- Student Resources in Spanish

See also the *Algebra 1 Toolkit* for more strategies for meeting individual needs.

EXAMPLE 2 Find a missing coordinate

The distance between (3, −5) and (7, b) is 5 units. Find the value of b.

Solution

Use the distance formula with $d = 5$. Let $(x_1, y_1) = (3, -5)$ and $(x_2, y_2) = (7, b)$. Then solve for b.

$d = \sqrt{(x_2 - x_1)^2 + (y_2 - y_1)^2}$	Distance formula
$5 = \sqrt{(7 - 3)^2 + (b - (-5))^2}$	Substitute.
$5 = \sqrt{16 + b^2 + 10b + 25}$	Multiply.
$5 = \sqrt{b^2 + 10b + 41}$	Simplify.
$25 = b^2 + 10b + 41$	Square each side.
$0 = b^2 + 10b + 16$	Write in standard form.
$0 = (b + 2)(b + 8)$	Factor.
$b + 2 = 0$ *or* $b + 8 = 0$	Zero-product property
$b = -2$ *or* $b = -8$	Solve for b.

▶ The value of b is −2 or −8.

INTERPRET GEOMETRICALLY

The point (7, b) lies on the line $x = 7$. If you let the point (3, −5) be the center of a circle with radius 5, you will see that the circle crosses the line at (7, −2) and (7, −8).

✓ GUIDED PRACTICE for Examples 1 and 2

Find the distance between the points.

1. (3, 0), (3, 6) 6
2. (−2, 1), (2, 5) $4\sqrt{2}$
3. (6, −2), (−4, 7) $\sqrt{181}$
4. The distance between (1, a) and (4, 2) is 3 units. Find the value of a. 2

MIDPOINT The **midpoint** of a line segment is the point on the segment that is equidistant from the endpoints. You can find the coordinates of the midpoint of a line segment using the following formula, called the **midpoint formula**.

KEY CONCEPT *For Your Notebook*

The Midpoint Formula

The midpoint M of the line segment with endpoints $A(x_1, y_1)$ and $B(x_2, y_2)$ is

$$M\left(\frac{x_1 + x_2}{2}, \frac{y_1 + y_2}{2}\right).$$

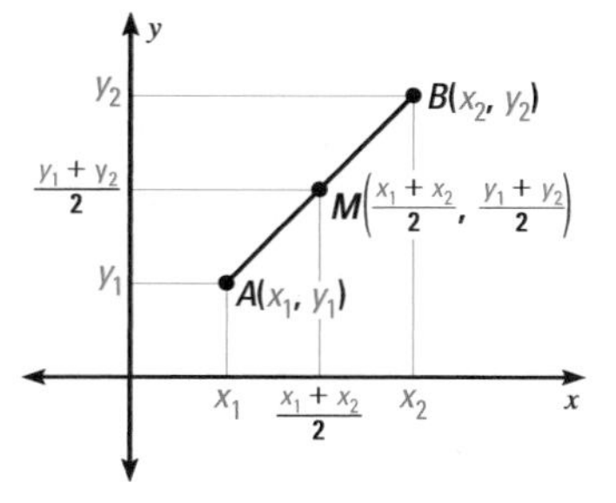

Motivating the Lesson

You are trying to find a place to meet a friend who lives in a different part of the city. By superimposing a coordinate grid over a map, you can use coordinates and the midpoint formula to find a meeting place that is about halfway for both of you.

3 TEACH

Extra Example 1

Find the distance between (−3, 1) and (2, 3). $\sqrt{29}$ units

Key Questions to Ask for Example 1

- Can either addend in the radicand be negative? Explain. No; if you obtain a negative value by subtracting two coordinates, the value is squared and a squared value is always positive.
- Does it matter which ordered pair is first when using the distance formula? Explain. No, either ordered pair can be first since the distance between the two points is the same no matter the order.
- Is the distance between the two points one of the legs of the right triangle or the hypotenuse?. The distance between the points represents the hypotenuse of the triangle.

Extra Example 2

The distance between (4, a) and (1, 6) is 5 units. Find the value of a. The value of a is 2 or 10.

Differentiated Instruction

Kinesthetic Learners Students may learn the distance formula more easily by first doing a few examples involving plotting two points, drawing a related right triangle, and applying the properties of a right triangle. For **Example 1**, students would construct a triangle with side lengths 6 and 1 and then apply the Pythagorean theorem. This should help students see the relationship between the horizontal and vertical distances between the two points and the side lengths of the right triangle.

See also the *Algebra 1 Toolkit* for more strategies.

Extra Example 3

What is the midpoint of the line segment with endpoints $(-3, -1)$ and $(7, -5)$? B

Ⓐ $(-3, 2)$ Ⓑ $(2, -3)$

Ⓒ $(-3, 5)$ Ⓓ $(5, -3)$

An **Animated Algebra** activity is available on-line for **Example 3**. This activity is also available on the **Power Presentations CD-ROM**.

Extra Example 4

The grid shows the locations of several buildings in a town. Which building is closest to the midpoint of the library and fire station? the bank

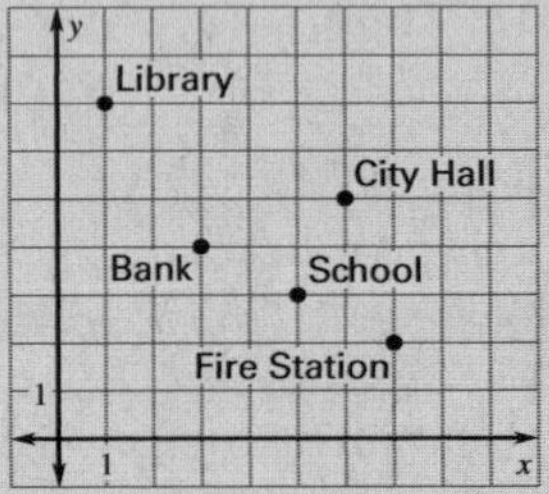

Closing the Lesson

Have students summarize the major points of the lesson and answer the Essential Question: How do you use the distance and midpoint formulas?

- The distance formula is $d = \sqrt{(x_2 - x_1)^2 + (y_2 - y_1)^2}$.
- The midpoint formula is $M\left(\frac{x_1 + x_2}{2}, \frac{y_1 + y_2}{2}\right)$.

To find the distance between two points, substitute coordinates in the distance formula and simplify. To find the coordinates of the midpoint of two points, substitute the endpoint coordinates in the midpoint formula and simplify.

EXAMPLE 3 Standardized Test Practice

What is the midpoint of the line segment with endpoints $(-1, -2)$ and $(3, -4)$?

Ⓐ $(2, -1)$ Ⓑ $(1, -3)$ Ⓒ $(-2, 1)$ Ⓓ $(-3, 1)$

ELIMINATE CHOICES

The *y*-coordinate of the midpoint has to be negative because it is an average of the *y*-coordinates of the endpoints of the line segment. Eliminate choices C and D.

Solution

Let $(x_1, y_1) = (-1, -2)$ and $(x_2, y_2) = (3, -4)$.

$$\left(\frac{x_1 + x_2}{2}, \frac{y_1 + y_2}{2}\right) = \left(\frac{-1 + 3}{2}, \frac{-2 + (-4)}{2}\right) \quad \text{Substitute.}$$

$$= (1, -3) \quad \text{Simplify.}$$

▶ The correct answer is B. Ⓐ Ⓑ Ⓒ Ⓓ

Animated Algebra at classzone.com

EXAMPLE 4 Solve a real-world problem

ANOTHER WAY

For alternative methods for solving Example 4, turn to page 751 for the **Problem Solving Workshop**.

SIGHTSEEING You and a friend are sightseeing in Washington, D.C. You are at the National Gallery of Art, and your friend is at the Washington Monument, as shown on the map. You want to meet at the landmark that is closest to the midpoint of your locations. At which landmark should you meet?

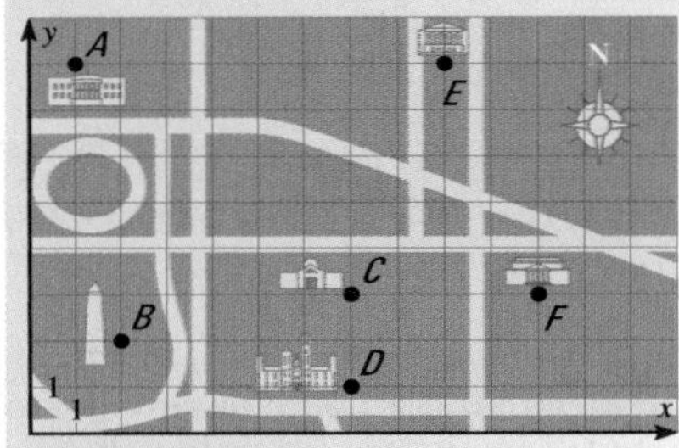

SIGHTS IN WASHINGTON, D.C.

A) White House
B) Washington Monument
C) Natural History Museum
D) Smithsonian Institution
E) National Portrait Gallery
F) National Gallery of Art

Solution

Your coordinates are $(11, 3)$, and your friend's coordinates are $(2, 2)$. First, find the midpoint of your locations, which is

$$\left(\frac{x_1 + x_2}{2}, \frac{y_1 + y_2}{2}\right) = \left(\frac{11 + 2}{2}, \frac{3 + 2}{2}\right) = (6.5, 2.5).$$

Next, find the distance from the midpoint to the Smithsonian Institution, located at $(7, 1)$, and to the Natural History Museum, located at $(7, 3)$.

Distance to Smithsonian Institution: $d = \sqrt{(6.5 - 7)^2 + (2.5 - 1)^2} \approx 1.58$ units

Distance to Natural History Museum: $d = \sqrt{(6.5 - 7)^2 + (2.5 - 3)^2} \approx 0.71$ unit

▶ You should meet at the Natural History Museum.

GUIDED PRACTICE for Examples 3 and 4

5. Find the midpoint of the line segment with endpoints (4, 3) and (2, 5). (3, 4)

6. **WHAT IF?** In Example 4, suppose you are at the Smithsonian and your friend is at the National Portrait Gallery. Which landmark on the map is closest to the midpoint of your locations? Natural History Museum

11.5 EXERCISES

HOMEWORK KEY

 = **WORKED-OUT SOLUTIONS** on p. WS27 for Exs. 7, 23, and 49

★ = **STANDARDIZED TEST PRACTICE** Exs. 2, 15, 34, 37, 45, and 50

SKILL PRACTICE

A

1. **VOCABULARY** Copy and complete: The point on a line segment that is equidistant from its endpoints is called the _?_ of the line segment. midpoint

2. ★ **WRITING** You want to know the distance between the points (3, 2) and (6, 8). Does it matter which point represents (x_1, y_1) and which point represents (x_2, y_2)? *Explain.* No. *Sample answer*: Since the absolute value is taken, the points can be interchanged without affecting the distance.

EXAMPLE 1 on p. 744 for Exs. 3–15

FINDING DISTANCE **Find the distance between the two points.**

3. (4, 8), (4, 7) 1
4. (5, −9), (8, −9) 3
5. (2, −2), (6, 1) 5
6. (5, 1), (0, 3) $\sqrt{29}$
7. (−4, 1), (3, −1) $\sqrt{53}$
8. (2, 4), (−5, 0) $\sqrt{65}$
9. (−6, 7), (2, 9) $2\sqrt{17}$
10. (−10, 8), (2, −3) $\sqrt{265}$
11. (7, 5), (−12, −1) $\sqrt{397}$
12. (4, 2.5), (2.5, −3) $\frac{\sqrt{130}}{2}$
13. $\left(5, -\frac{1}{2}\right), \left(-3, \frac{5}{2}\right)$ $\sqrt{73}$
14. $\left(-\frac{3}{4}, \frac{7}{2}\right), \left(\frac{5}{4}, \frac{1}{4}\right)$ $\frac{\sqrt{233}}{4}$

15. ★ **MULTIPLE CHOICE** What is the distance between (4.5, 1) and (−2.5, −5)? D

Ⓐ $\sqrt{13}$ Ⓑ $\sqrt{24}$ Ⓒ $\sqrt{68.5}$ Ⓓ $\sqrt{85}$

EXAMPLE 2 on p. 745 for Exs. 16–21

FINDING MISSING COORDINATES **The distance *d* between two points is given. Find the value of *b*.**

16. (0, *b*), (3, 1); *d* = 5 −3, 5
17. (13, −3), (*b*, 2); *d* = 13 1, 25
18. (−9, −2), (*b*, 5); *d* = 7 −9
19. (*b*, −6), (−5, 2); *d* = 10 −11, 1
20. (−6, 8), (−1, *b*); $d = \sqrt{29}$ 6, 10
21. (*b*, −4), (4, 7); $d = 11\sqrt{2}$ −7, 15

EXAMPLE 3 on p. 746 for Exs. 22–34

FINDING THE MIDPOINT **Find the midpoint of the line segment with the given endpoints.**

22. (0, 1), (8, 3) (4, 2)
23. (6, −3), (4, −7) (5, −5)
24. (−5, 0), (1, 14) (−2, 7)
25. (11, −4), (−9, −4) (1, −4)
26. (−6, 6), (4, −4) (−1, 1)
27. (−17, −8), (−5, −4)
28. (2, 7), (5, 3) (3.5, 5)
29. (−2, 3), (−2, −3) (−2, 0)
30. (12, −5), (−12, 4) (0, −0.5)
31. (−15, −8), (−1, −1) (−8, −4.5)
32. (18, −17), (12, −7) (15, −12)
33. (−50, −75), (8, 9) (−21, −33)

27. (−11, −6)

34. ★ **MULTIPLE CHOICE** What is the midpoint of the line segment with endpoints (2, 1) and (4, 7)? C

Ⓐ (1, 3) Ⓑ (1.5, 5.5) Ⓒ (3, 4) Ⓓ (4, 3)

4 PRACTICE AND APPLY

Assignment Guide

Answer Transparencies available for all exercises

Basic:
Day 1: pp. 747–750
Exs. 1, 2, 3–33 odd, 34–38, 47–50, 53–63 odd

Average:
Day 1: pp. 747–750
Exs. 1, 2, 10–15, 19–21, 30–44, 48–51, 54–64 even

Advanced:
Day 1: pp. 747–750
Exs. 1, 11–15, 20, 21, 31–46*, 49–52*, 56, 58, 62, 64

Block:
pp. 747–750
Exs. 1, 2, 10–15, 19–21, 30–44, 48–51, 54–64 even (with 11.4)

Differentiated Instruction

See *Algebra 1 Best Practices Toolkit* for suggestions on addressing the needs of a diverse classroom.

Homework Check

For a quick check of student understanding of key concepts, go over the following exercises:

Basic: 9, 17, 27, 47, 48
Average: 12, 20, 32, 48, 49
Advanced: 14, 21, 32, 49, 50

Extra Practice

- Student Edition, p. 948
- Chapter 11 Resource Book: Practice levels A, B, C, pp. 54–56

Practice Worksheet

An easily-readable reduced practice page (with answers) for this lesson can be found on p. 708C.

Avoiding Common Errors

Exercises 16–21 Remind students that there are often two values for the missing coordinate. Encourage them to check both values against the distance formula to confirm that both result in the same distance.

Study Strategy

Exercises 38–40 Suggest that students plot the points in the coordinate plane. This will help them visualize the solution.

35. *Sample answer:* The square of the difference in the x values and the square of the difference in the y values should be added, not subtracted; $d = \sqrt{(3-(-17))^2 + (8-(-2))^2} = \sqrt{400 + 100} = \sqrt{500} = 10\sqrt{5}$.

36. *Sample answer:* The x terms should be added, not subtracted, as should the y terms; $\left(\frac{3+(-17)}{2}, \frac{8+(-2)}{2}\right) = \left(\frac{-14}{2}, \frac{6}{3}\right) = (-7, 3)$.

46. *Sample answer:* (0, 1) and (0, −1), (1, 0) and (−1, 0), $\left(\frac{\sqrt{2}}{2}, \frac{\sqrt{2}}{2}\right)$, and $\left(-\frac{\sqrt{2}}{2}, -\frac{\sqrt{2}}{2}\right)$; since (0, 0) is the midpoint, the x-coordinates must be opposites as well as the y-coordinates. Choose 3 lines that go through the origin; $x = 0$, $y = 0$, and $y = x$. For $x = 0$, start at the origin and move 1 unit up and 1 unit down to find the points (0, 1) and (0, −1). For $y = 0$, start at the origin and move 1 unit right and 1 unit left to find the points (1, 0) and (−1, 0). For $y = x$, the points must be in the forms (a, a) and $(-a, -a)$. Use the distance formula to find a. $2 = \sqrt{(2a)^2 + (2a)^2}$, $2 = \sqrt{8a^2}$, $4 = 8a^2$, $\frac{1}{2} = a^2$, $a = \frac{\sqrt{2}}{2}$; so $-a = -\frac{\sqrt{2}}{2}$, giving the points $\left(\frac{\sqrt{2}}{2}, \frac{\sqrt{2}}{2}\right)$ and $\left(-\frac{\sqrt{2}}{2}, -\frac{\sqrt{2}}{2}\right)$.

B **ERROR ANALYSIS** ***Describe* and correct the error in finding the distance between (−17, −2) and (3, 8), and the midpoint of the line segment with endpoints (−17, −2) and (3, 8).** 35, 36. See margin.

35.

Distance:

$d = \sqrt{(3-(-17))^2 - (8-(-2))^2}$

$= \sqrt{400 - 100}$

$= \sqrt{300} = 10\sqrt{3}$

36.

Midpoint:

$\left(\frac{3-(-17)}{2}, \frac{8-(-2)}{2}\right) = \left(\frac{20}{2}, \frac{10}{2}\right)$

$= (10, 5)$

37. ★ **MULTIPLE CHOICE** What is the distance between point A and the midpoint of the line segment that joins points A and B? A

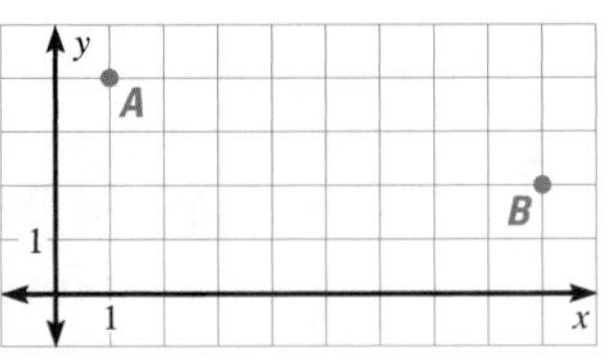

Ⓐ $\sqrt{17}$ units Ⓑ $3\sqrt{5}$ units

Ⓒ $2\sqrt{17}$ units Ⓓ $\sqrt{117}$ units

FINDING ENDPOINTS **The midpoint and an endpoint of a line segment are given. Find the other endpoint.**

38. endpoint: (1, 2)
midpoint: (−6, 4)
(−13, 6)

39. endpoint: (−2, −4)
midpoint: (3, −3)
(8, −2)

40. endpoint: (7, 5)
midpoint: (1, 0.5)
(−5, −4)

RIGHT TRIANGLES **Use the distance formula and the converse of the Pythagorean theorem to determine whether the points are vertices of a right triangle.**

41. (3, 5), (3, −1), (−2, −1) right triangle

42. (3, −1), (1, 4), (−3, 0) not a right triangle

43. (−5, −2), (0, −4), (−2, 3) not a right triangle

44. (−2, 1), (−4, 3), (−8, −1) right triangle

45. *Sample answer:* Use the distance formula to find the distance between the midpoint and each of the endpoints. If they are equal, the midpoint is equidistant from each endpoint.

C **45.** ★ **WRITING** *Explain* how you can use the distance formula to verify that the midpoint of a line segment is equidistant from its endpoints.

46. **CHALLENGE** The midpoint of a line segment is (0, 0). The line segment has a length of 2 units. Give three possible sets of endpoints for the line segment. *Explain* how you found your answer. See margin.

PROBLEM SOLVING

EXAMPLE 4 on p. 746 for Exs. 47–50

A **47.** **MULTI-STEP PROBLEM** A rescue helicopter and an ambulance are both traveling from the dispatch center to the scene of an accident. The distance between consecutive grid lines represents 1 mile.

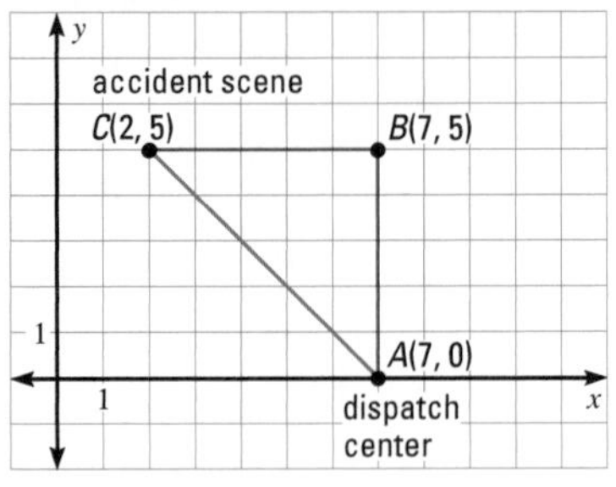

a. Find the distance that the ambulance traveled (red route). 10 mi

b. How many times greater is the distance that the ambulance traveled than the distance that the helicopter traveled (blue route)?

47b. $\sqrt{2}$ times greater

@HomeTutor for problem solving help at classzone.com

○ = WORKED-OUT SOLUTIONS on p. WS1 ★ = STANDARDIZED TEST PRACTICE

48. SUBWAY A student is taking the subway to the public library. The student can get off the subway at one of two stops, as shown in the map. The distance between consecutive grid lines represents 0.25 mile. Which stop is closer to the library? **stop 2**

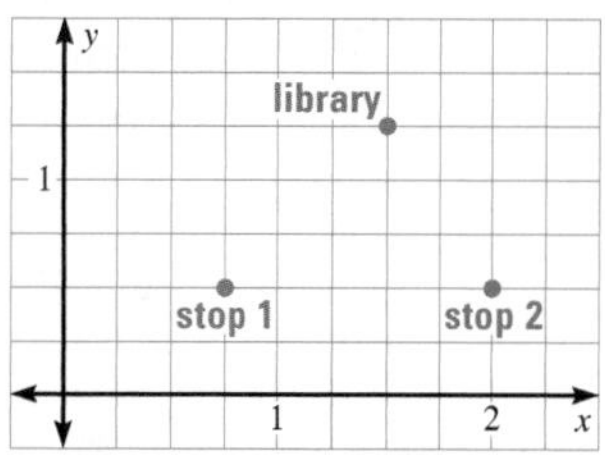

@HomeTutor for problem solving help at classzone.com

49. ARCHAEOLOGY Underwater archaeologists sometimes lay survey grids of the site they are studying. A sample survey grid is shown. The distance between consecutive grid lines represents 50 feet.

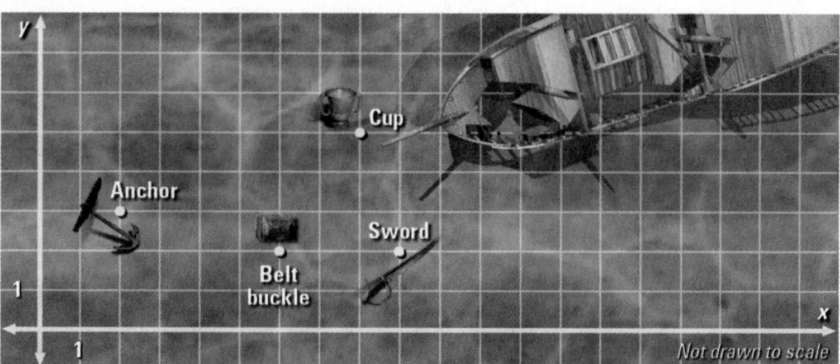

a. Which is shorter, the distance between the anchor and the sword or the distance between the anchor and the cup? **the anchor and the cup**

b. Which two objects are closest together? Which two objects are farthest apart? **the belt buckle and the sword; the anchor and the sword**

B **50. ★ SHORT RESPONSE** The point of no return in aviation is the farthest point to which a plane can fly and still have enough fuel to return to its starting place or to fly to an alternative landing destination. After a plane passes the point of no return, it must fly to its planned destination. The distance between consecutive grid lines represents 50 nautical miles.

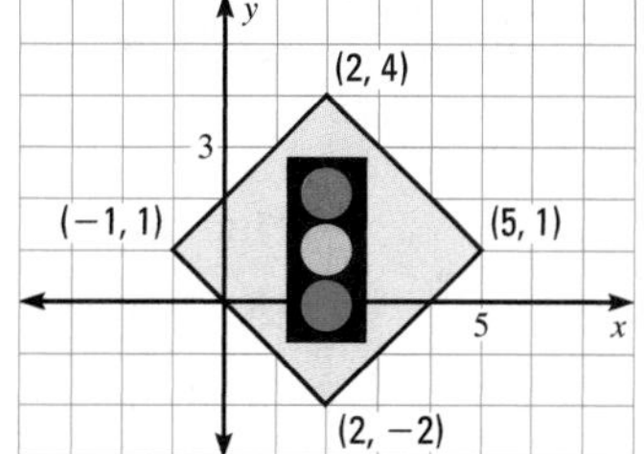

a. The flight path of a plane is from airport A to airport B. The plane is currently at the midpoint of the flight path. How far away is the plane from airport A? Round your answer to the nearest nautical mile. **168 mi**

b. The plane's point of no return is calculated to be 200 nautical miles. Has the plane reached its point of no return? *Explain.*
No. ***Sample answer*****: The plane has only traveled about 168 miles.**

REVIEW GEOMETRY
For help with classifying quadrilaterals, see p. 919.

51. ROAD SIGN Describe the quadrilateral formed by the sides of the road sign shown by answering the following questions.

- Are opposite sides parallel? **yes**
- Do the sides form right angles? **yes**
- Which sides, if any, are congruent? **all of them**

The quadrilateral is a square.

y
(2, 4)
3
(−1, 1)
(5, 1)
5
x
(2, −2)

Avoiding Common Errors

Exercises 48–50 Remind students that they need to multiply the total units by the appropriate value.

Exercises 50–51 Caution students to use care when using the midpoint formula. They often confuse the midpoint formula with the distance formula and subtract the coordinates rather than add them. Tell students to think of the coordinates of the midpoint as the "average" of the coordinates of the endpoints.

5 ASSESS AND RETEACH

Daily Homework Quiz

Transparency Available

1. Find the distance between $(-4, 3)$ and $(5, 4)$. $\sqrt{82}$ **units**
2. The distance between $(4, -1)$ and $(a, 5)$ is 10 units. Find the value of a. -4 **or 12**
3. Find the coordinates of the midpoint of the line segment with endpoints $(6, -1)$ and $(-4, -5)$. $(1, -3)$
4. Each unit of distance on the map represents 1.5 miles. What is the distance between High Point and Big Rock? **about 6.7 mi**

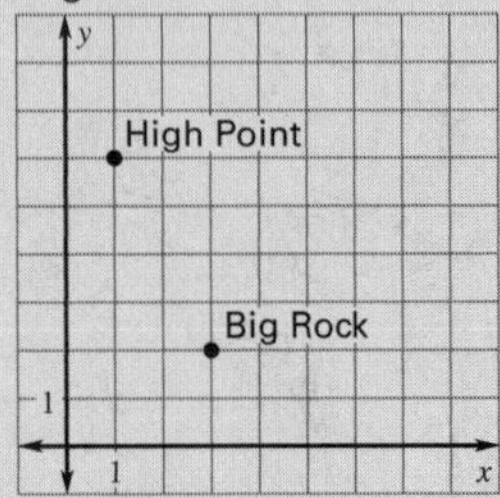

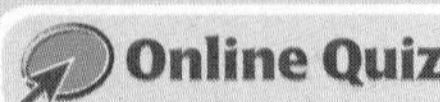

Available at **classzone.com**

Diagnosis/Remediation

- Practice A, B, C in Chapter 11 Resource Book, pp. 54–56
- Study Guide in Chapter 11 Resource Book, pp. 57–58
- Practice Workbook, pp. 178–179
- @HomeTutor

Challenge

Additional challenge is available in the Chapter 11 Resource Book, p. 61.

Quiz

An easily-readable reduced copy of the quiz (with answers) on Lessons 11.4–11.5 from the Assessment Book can be found on p. 708E.

C **52. CHALLENGE** A computer programmer is creating a baseball player's strike zone for a video game, as shown. The strike zone is a rectangular region over home plate through which a ball must pass to be called a strike. In the animation, $\overline{AB}$ is the top of the strike zone and lies on a horizontal line that passes through the midpoint of $\overline{XY}$. The distance between grid lines represents 1 foot.

a. If the coordinates of X are (4, 5.5) and the coordinates of Y are (4, 3.5), what is the midpoint of $\overline{XY}$? **(4, 4.5)**

b. The coordinates of C are (7, 2) and the coordinates of D are (8.5, 2). Find the coordinates of point A and point B. **A: (7, 4.5), B: (8.5, 4.5)**

c. What is the area of the strike zone in the animation? **3.75 ft²**

ILLINOIS MIXED REVIEW

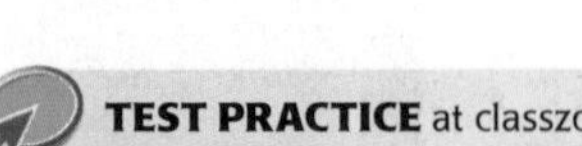

53. How would the graph of $y = x^2 + 5$ be affected if it were changed to $y = x^2 + 3$? **D**

Ⓐ The graph would shift 2 units to the left.

Ⓑ The graph would shift 2 units to the right.

Ⓒ The graph would shift 2 units up.

Ⓓ The graph would shift 2 units down.

QUIZ for Lessons 11.4–11.5

Let a and b represent the lengths of the legs of a right triangle, and let c represent the length of the hypotenuse. Find the unknown length. *(p. 737)*

1. $a = 6, c = 10$ $b = 8$ **2.** $b = 2, c = 6$ $a = 4\sqrt{2}$ **3.** $a = 4, b = 7$ $c = \sqrt{65}$

Find the unknown lengths. *(p. 737)*

4.

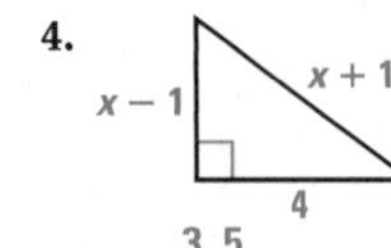

3, 5

5. 2x, x, $2\sqrt{5}$ — 2, 4

6. 2x + 2, x, 3x − 2 — 5, 12, 13

Find the distance between the two points. *(p. 744)*

7. (7, 2), (7, 5) 3 **8.** (−1, −3), (4, −3) 5 **9.** (0, 0), (−6, 9) $3\sqrt{13}$

Find the midpoint of the line segment with the given endpoints. *(p. 744)*

10. (0, 5), (−6, 3) (−3, 4) **11.** (8, −1), (2, −7) (5, −4) **12.** (−5, −3), (5, −3) (0, −3)

13. (0, 6), (1.5, 4) (0.75, 5) **14.** (2.5, −3), (0.5, 6) (1.5, 1.5) **15.** $\left(-\frac{1}{4}, \frac{3}{4}\right), \left(\frac{1}{4}, \frac{5}{4}\right)$ (0, 1)

EXTRA PRACTICE for Lesson 11.5, p. 948 ONLINE QUIZ at classzone.com

PROBLEM SOLVING WORKSHOP
LESSON 11.5

Using ALTERNATIVE METHODS

Another Way to Solve Example 4, page 746

MULTIPLE REPRESENTATIONS In Example 4 on page 746, you saw how to solve a problem about finding a meeting place by using the midpoint and distance formulas. You can also solve the problem by folding a map and using a compass.

PROBLEM

SIGHTSEEING You and a friend are sightseeing in Washington, D.C. You are at the National Gallery of Art, and your friend is at the Washington Monument, as shown on the map. You want to meet at the landmark that is closest to the midpoint of your locations. At which landmark should you meet?

METHOD 1

Folding a map and using a compass An alternative approach is to fold a map and use a compass. First, draw a line connecting your location to your friend's location. Then fold the map so that your locations coincide. The point where the line connecting your locations is folded represents the midpoint. Place the point of your compass at the midpoint. Adjust the opening of the compass to match the distance between the midpoint and the apparent closest landmark. Swing the compass to see if the other landmark is closer.

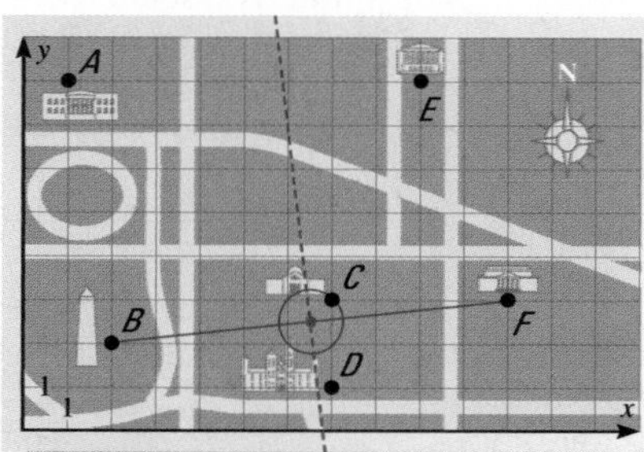

SIGHTS IN WASHINGTON, D.C.
A) White House
B) Washington Monument
C) Natural History Museum
D) Smithsonian Institution
E) National Portrait Gallery
F) National Gallery of Art

▶ Because the Smithsonian lies outside the circle, the Natural History Museum is closer to the midpoint of your locations.

PRACTICE

1. **WHAT IF?** In the problem above, suppose your friend is at the White House.
   a. At which landmark should you meet? Natural History Museum
   b. Suppose you can walk directly to the landmark in part (a). If the distance between consecutive grid lines represents 0.06 mile, how far do you have to walk? 0.24 mi

2. **MAPS** A student makes a map of a town in which the student's house is located at (1, 2) and a friend's house is located at (8, 5). A grocery store is located at (5, 3), and a shoe store is located at (3, 4). The student and the friend want to meet at the store that is closer to the midpoint between their houses. At which store should they meet? Solve this problem using two methods. grocery store

Alternative Strategy

Example 4 on page 746 can be solved by folding a map and using a compass. This strategy will appeal to students who prefer a hands-on approach to solving problems. It is also a good method to use in the field when coordinate grids are scarce. Even if students do not have a compass handy when using a map, they can still fold the map to find a midpoint.

Avoiding Common Errors

Students should make sure that the locations coincide when they fold their maps or the midpoint will be off. Students should also make sure that their compasses are stable so that when they swing the compass, it does not change calibration.

1. D
2. J
3. A
4. H
5. B
6. H

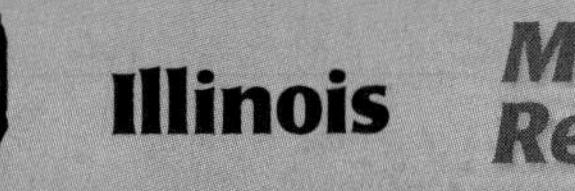

Illinois Mixed Review

Lessons 11.4–11.5

1. **STAIRCASE** A drawing of a staircase is shown. What is the distance d between the edges of two consecutive steps?

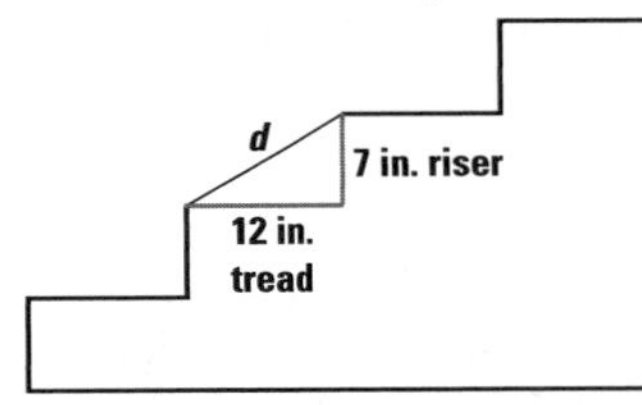

A. $\sqrt{19}$ **C.** 19

B. $\sqrt{95}$ **D.** None of the above

2. **FOOTBALL** At the start of a football game, the kicker on one team must kick the ball to the opposing team. To position himself for the starting kick, the kicker places a football on a tee, walks 8 yards behind the tee, then 6 yards to the left. What is the kicker's distance from the football?

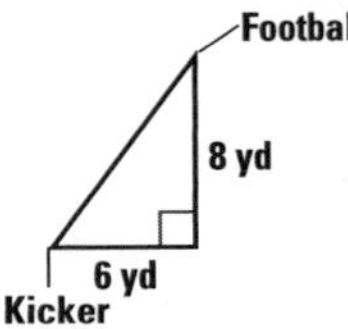

F. $\sqrt{14}$ yards **H.** $3\sqrt{10}$ yards

G. $2\sqrt{7}$ yards **J.** 10 yards

3. **CITY BLOCK** Three streets in the downtown area of a city form a right triangle with the lengths shown. Find the area of the triangle to the nearest 100 square feet.

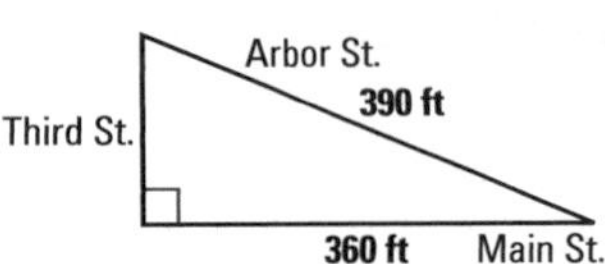

A. 27,000 ft^2 **C.** 152,100 ft^2

B. 117,100 ft^2 **D.** 95,500 ft^2

4. **FERRY** A ferry travels from a city to an island and then to another island before returning to the city, as shown below. The distance between consecutive grid lines represents 1 mile. The ferry travels at an average rate of 20 miles per hour and leaves the city at 10 A.M. At what time does the ferry return?

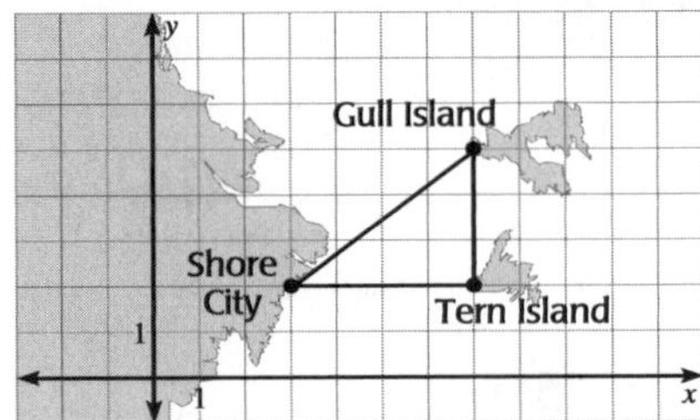

F. 10:15 A.M. **H.** 10:36 A.M.

G. 10:24 A.M. **J.** 11:40 A.M.

5. **MAP** A map of a town is shown. The distance between consecutive grid lines is 1 mile. A student leaves the school and goes directly to the library. From the library, the student goes directly to the stadium. How many miles did the student travel?

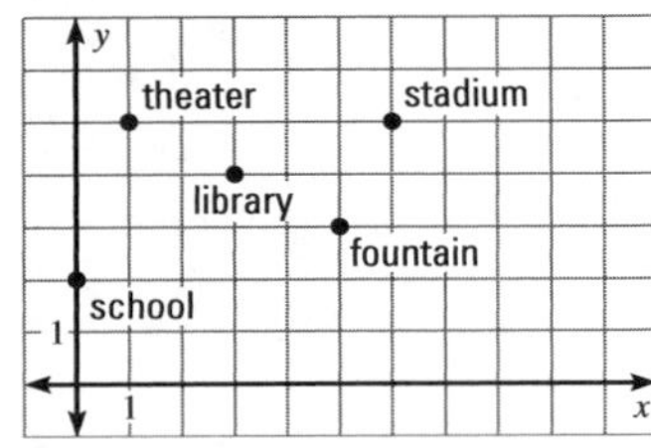

A. $2\sqrt{5}$ **C.** $\sqrt{23}$

B. $\sqrt{13} + \sqrt{10}$ **D.** $\sqrt{39}$

6. **HIKING** You go on a hiking trip. You walk 2 miles directly east and then 4 miles directly north. If you could walk in a straight path back to your starting point, how many miles would you have to walk? Round your answer to the nearest tenth of a mile.

F. 2.8 **H.** 4.5

G. 4.2 **J.** 6.0

CHAPTER SUMMARY

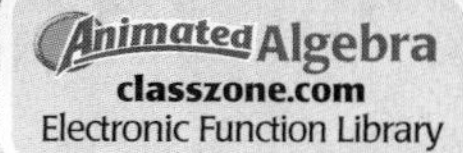
classzone.com
Electronic Function Library

BIG IDEAS *For Your Notebook*

Big Idea 1

Graphing Square Root Functions

You can graph a square root function $y = a\sqrt{x - h} + k$ and compare its graph with the graph of the parent function, $y = \sqrt{x}$, based on the constants a, h, and k.

Constant	Comparison of graphs
a	• When $a > 0$, the graph is a vertical stretch or shrink of the parent graph. • When $a < 0$, the graph is a vertical stretch or shrink with a reflection in the x-axis of the parent graph.
h	The graph is a horizontal translation of the parent graph.
k	The graph is a vertical translation of the parent graph.

Big Idea 2

Using Properties of Radicals in Expressions and Equations

You can use the properties of radicals to simplify radical expressions and to solve radical equations.

Product property of radicals	$\sqrt{ab} = \sqrt{a} \cdot \sqrt{b}$ where $a \geq 0$ and $b \geq 0$
Quotient property of radicals	$\sqrt{\frac{a}{b}} = \frac{\sqrt{a}}{\sqrt{b}}$ where $a \geq 0$ and $b > 0$

Big Idea 3

Working with Radicals in Geometry

You can use radicals to solve problems involving the following geometric theorems and formulas.

Pythagorean theorem	If a triangle is a right triangle, then the sum of the squares of the lengths of the legs, a and b, equals the square of the length of the hypotenuse c. $a^2 + b^2 = c^2$
Converse of Pythagorean theorem	If a triangle has side lengths a, b, and c such that $a^2 + b^2 = c^2$, then the triangle is a right triangle.
Distance formula	$d = \sqrt{(x_2 - x_1)^2 + (y_2 - y_1)^2}$
Midpoint formula	$M\left(\frac{x_1 + x_2}{2}, \frac{y_1 + y_2}{2}\right)$

Additional Resources

The following resources are available to help review the materials in this chapter.

Chapter 11 Resource Book

- Chapter Review Games and Activities, p. 62
- Cumulative Practice, Chs. 1–11, pp. 65–66

Student Resources in Spanish

eWorkbook

@HomeTutor

Vocabulary Practice

Vocabulary practice is available at **classzone.com**

11 CHAPTER REVIEW

@HomeTutor
classzone.com
- Multi-Language Glossary
- Vocabulary practice

Extra Example 11.1

Graph the function $3\sqrt{x} + 1$ and identify its domain and range. Compare the graph with the graph of $y = \sqrt{x}$.

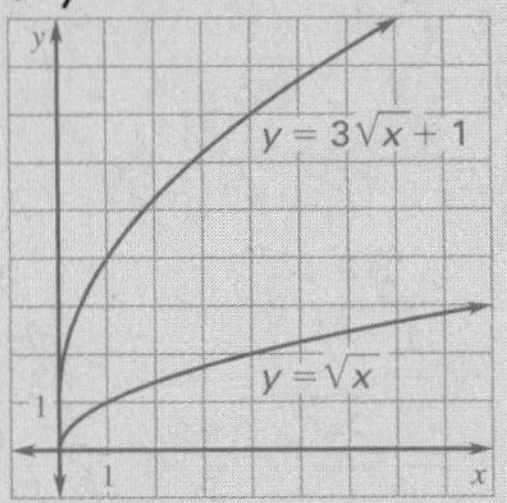

Domain: $x \ge 0$, range: $y \ge 1$; the graph of $y = 3\sqrt{x} + 1$ is a vertical stretch (by a factor of 3) and a translation 1 unit up of the graph of $y = \sqrt{x}$.

2. *Sample answer:* To rationalize the denominator of a radical expression, multiply the fraction by the denominator over itself. This will not change the value of the expression and will remove the radical from the denominator. If the denominator is a binomial that contains a radical, multiply by the conjugate of the binomial over itself.

5.

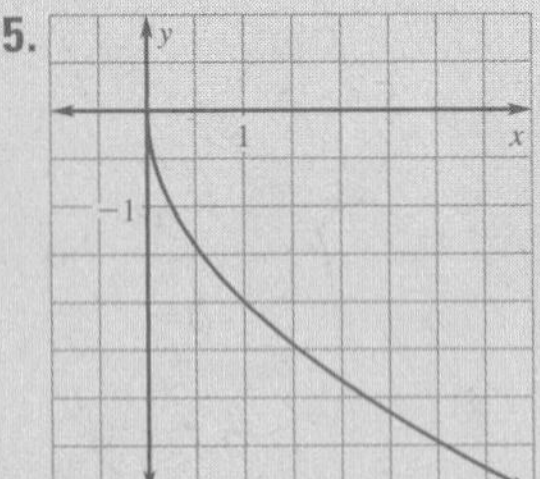

domain: $x \ge 0$, range: $y \le 0$; vertical stretch by a factor of 2 with a reflection in the x-axis

6.

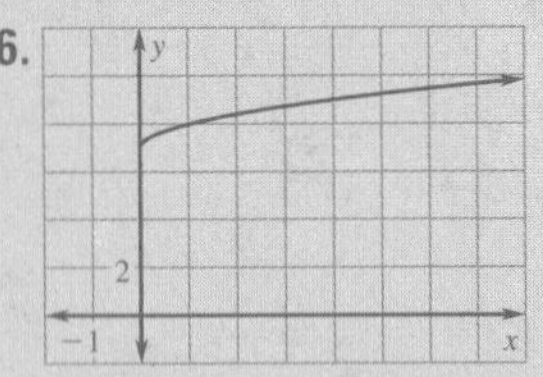

domain: $x \ge 0$, range: $y \ge 7$; vertical translation of 7 units up

REVIEW KEY VOCABULARY

- radical expression, *p. 710*
- radical function, *p. 710*
- square root function, *p. 710*
- parent square root function, *p. 710*
- simplest form of a radical expression, *p. 719*
- rationalizing the denominator, *p. 721*
- radical equation, *p. 729*
- extraneous solution, *p. 730*
- hypotenuse, legs of a right triangle, *p. 737*
- Pythagorean theorem, *p. 737*
- distance formula, *p. 744*
- midpoint, midpoint formula, *p. 745*

VOCABULARY EXERCISES

1. *Describe* how the graph of the function $y = 3\sqrt{x}$ compares with the graph of the parent square root function. **It is a vertical stretch by a factor of 3.**
2. *Describe* the steps you would take to rationalize the denominator of a radical expression. **See margin.**

Tell which theorem or formula you would use to complete the exercise.

3. Tell whether a triangle with side lengths 2, 4, and 6 is a right triangle. **converse of the Pythagorean theorem**
4. The point $(b, 4)$ is 10 units away from the point $(5, 10)$. Find b. **distance formula**

REVIEW EXAMPLES AND EXERCISES

Use the review examples and exercises below to check your understanding of the concepts you have learned in each lesson of Chapter 11.

11.1 Graph Square Root Functions *pp. 710–716*

EXAMPLE

Graph the function $y = \sqrt{x - 3}$ and identify its domain and range. Compare the graph with the graph of $y = \sqrt{x}$.

To graph the function, make a table, plot the points, and draw a smooth curve through the points. The domain is $x \ge 3$.

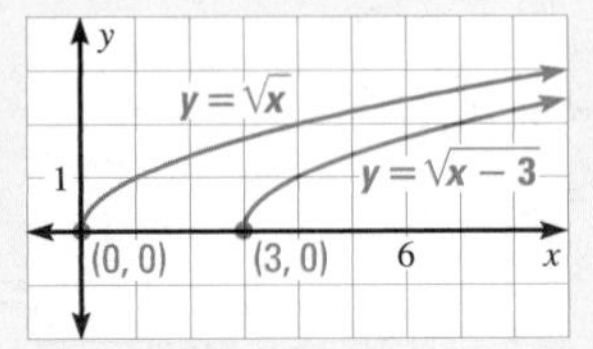

x	3	4	5	6
y	0	1	1.4	1.7

The range is $y \ge 0$. The graph of $y = \sqrt{x - 3}$ is a horizontal translation (of 3 units to the right) of the graph of $y = \sqrt{x}$.

EXERCISES

EXAMPLES 2, 3, and 4 on pp. 711–712 for Exs. 5–7

Graph the function and identify its domain and range. Compare the graph with the graph of $y = \sqrt{x}$. **5–7. See margin.**

5. $y = -2\sqrt{x}$
6. $y = \sqrt{x} + 7$
7. $y = \sqrt{x + 7}$

7.

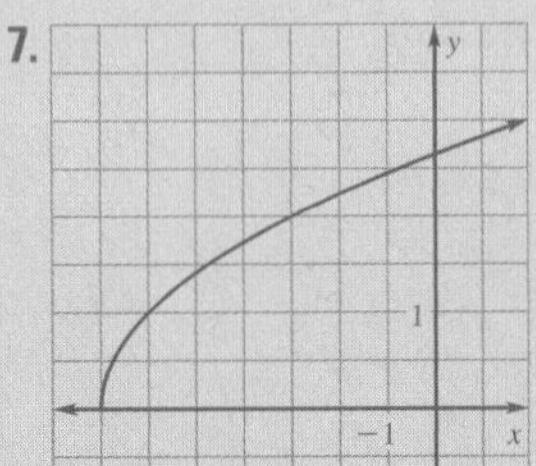

domain: $x \ge -7$, range: $y \ge 0$; horizontal translation of 7 units to the left

@HomeTutor
classzone.com
Chapter Review Practice

11.2 Simplify Radical Expressions

pp. 719–726

EXAMPLE

Simplify $7\sqrt{5} - \sqrt{45}$.

$$7\sqrt{5} - \sqrt{45} = 7\sqrt{5} - \sqrt{9 \cdot 5}$$ **Factor using perfect square factor.**

$$= 7\sqrt{5} - \sqrt{9} \cdot \sqrt{5}$$ **Product property of radicals**

$$= 7\sqrt{5} - 3\sqrt{5}$$ **Simplify.**

$$= (7 - 3)\sqrt{5}$$ **Distributive property**

$$= 4\sqrt{5}$$ **Simplify.**

EXERCISES

EXAMPLES 1–7 on pp. 719–722 for Exs. 8–16

Simplify the expression.

8. $\sqrt{98}$ $7\sqrt{2}$

9. $\sqrt{121x^3}$ $11x\sqrt{x}$

10. $\sqrt{7} \cdot \sqrt{21}$ $7\sqrt{3}$

11. $\sqrt{7x} \cdot 7\sqrt{x}$ $7x\sqrt{7}$

12. $\sqrt{\frac{5}{x^2}}$ $\frac{\sqrt{5}}{x}$

13. $\frac{2}{\sqrt{5}}$ $\frac{2\sqrt{5}}{5}$

14. $3\sqrt{2} - \sqrt{128}$ $-5\sqrt{2}$

15. $\sqrt{2}(7 - \sqrt{6})$ $7\sqrt{2} - 2\sqrt{3}$

16. GEOMETRY The lateral surface area L of a square pyramid with height h and base length ℓ is given by $L = 2\ell\sqrt{0.25\ell^2 + h^2}$. Find L (in square feet) for a square pyramid that has a height of 4 feet and a base length of 4 feet. $16\sqrt{5}$ ft^2

11.3 Solve Radical Equations

pp. 729–734

EXAMPLE

Solve $\sqrt{x + 90} = x$.

$$\sqrt{x + 90} = x$$ **Write original equation.**

$$\left(\sqrt{x + 90}\right)^2 = x^2$$ **Square each side.**

$$x + 90 = x^2$$ **Simplify.**

$$0 = x^2 - x - 90$$ **Write in standard form.**

$$0 = (x - 10)(x + 9)$$ **Factor.**

$$x - 10 = 0 \quad or \quad x + 9 = 0$$ **Zero-product property**

$$x = 10 \quad or \quad x = -9$$ **Solve for x.**

▶ Checking 10 and −9 in the original equation shows that −9 is an extraneous solution. The only solution of the equation is 10.

EXERCISES

EXAMPLES 1, 2, 3, and 4 on pp. 729–731 for Exs. 17–22

Solve the equation. Check for extraneous solutions.

17. $\sqrt{x} - 28 = 0$ 784

18. $8\sqrt{x - 5} + 34 = 58$ 14

19. $\sqrt{5x - 3} = \sqrt{x + 17}$ 5

20. $\sqrt{5x} + 6 = 5$ no real solutions

21. $\sqrt{x} + 36 = 0$ no real solutions

22. $x = \sqrt{2 - x}$ 1

Extra Example 11.2

Simplify $6\sqrt{7} + \sqrt{28}$. $8\sqrt{7}$

Extra Example 11.3

Solve $\sqrt{6x} + 5 = 11$. 6

11 CHAPTER REVIEW

Extra Example 11.4

Find the unknown length.

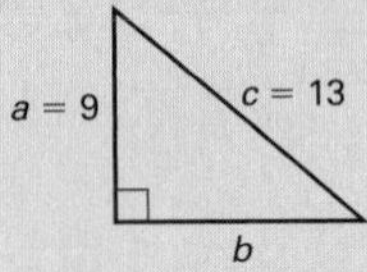

$\sqrt{88}$ or $2\sqrt{22}$

Extra Example 11.5

Find the midpoint of the line segment with endpoints (−2, 7) and (4, −5).
(1, 1)

11.4 Apply the Pythagorean Theorem and Its Converse *pp. 737–742*

EXAMPLE

Find the unknown length for the triangle shown.

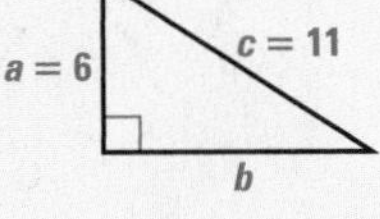

$a^2 + b^2 = c^2$	Pythagorean theorem
$6^2 + b^2 = 11^2$	Substitute 6 for *a* and 11 for *c*.
$36 + b^2 = 121$	Simplify.
$b^2 = 85$	Subtract 36 from each side.
$b = \sqrt{85}$	Take positive square root of each side.

EXERCISES

EXAMPLES 1 and 4 on pp. 737, 739 for Exs. 23–29

Let *a* and *b* represent the lengths of the legs of a right triangle, and let *c* represent the length of the hypotenuse. Find the unknown length.

23. $a = 7, b = 13$ $c = \sqrt{218}$ **24.** $a = 10, c = 21$ $b = \sqrt{341}$ **25.** $a = 8, c = 11$ $b = \sqrt{57}$

26. $a = 9, b = 17$ $c = \sqrt{370}$ **27.** $b = 4, c = 15$ $a = \sqrt{209}$ **28.** $b = 6, c = 6.5$ $a = 2.5$

29. REFLECTING POOL The Reflecting Pool in front of the Lincoln Memorial in Washington, D.C., is rectangular with a length of 2029 feet and a width of 167 feet. To the nearest foot, what is the length of a diagonal of the Reflecting Pool? 2036 ft

11.5 Apply the Distance and Midpoint Formulas *pp. 744–750*

EXAMPLE

Find the distance between (−3, 8) and (5, −12).

Let $(x_1, y_1) = (-3, 8)$ and $(x_2, y_2) = (5, -12)$.

$d = \sqrt{(x_2 - x_1)^2 + (y_2 - y_1)^2}$	Distance formula
$= \sqrt{(5 - (-3))^2 + (-12 - 8)^2}$	Substitute.
$= \sqrt{464} = 4\sqrt{29}$	Simplify.

EXERCISES

EXAMPLES 1, 3, and 4 on pp. 744, 746 for Exs. 30–36

Find the distance between the two points.

30. (−1, −3), (9, −13) $10\sqrt{2}$ **31.** (−8, −4), (0, 2) 10 **32.** (7, 1), (4, −0.25) 3.25

Find the midpoint of the line segment with the given endpoints.

33. (−2, −4), (9, −4) (3.5, −4) **34.** (−8, 0), (−8, 2) (−8, 1) **35.** (6, 1), (4, −5) (5, −2)

36. ISLANDS On a coordinate grid, an island is located at (1, 6). Another island is located at (4, 9). What is the distance between the islands if the distance between consecutive grid lines represents 2 miles? $6\sqrt{2}$ mi

11 CHAPTER TEST

Graph the function and identify its domain and range. Compare the graph with the graph of $y = \sqrt{x}$. 1–4. See margin.

1. $y = 3\sqrt{x}$ **2.** $y = -\sqrt{x}$ **3.** $y = \sqrt{x - 5}$ **4.** $y = -\sqrt{x - 1} + 4$

Simplify the expression.

5. $\sqrt{72m^6}$ $6m^3\sqrt{2}$ **6.** $\sqrt{8z^3} \cdot \sqrt{6z^3}$ $4z^3\sqrt{3}$ **7.** $\sqrt{\frac{20}{3n^3}}$ $\frac{2\sqrt{15n}}{3n^2}$

8. $7\sqrt{6} - 2\sqrt{12} + \sqrt{24}$ $9\sqrt{6} - 4\sqrt{3}$ **9.** $\sqrt{3}(7 - \sqrt{15})$ $7\sqrt{3} - 3\sqrt{5}$ **10.** $(8 - \sqrt{7})(1 + \sqrt{7})$ $1 + 7\sqrt{7}$

Solve the equation. Check for extraneous solutions.

11. $\sqrt{x} = 8$ 64 **12.** $\sqrt{x + 5} - 6 = -2$ 11 **13.** $-4\sqrt{3x} - 6 = 30$ no real solutions

14. $\sqrt{5x - 11} = \sqrt{x}$ $\frac{11}{4}$ **15.** $\sqrt{x + 7} = \sqrt{2x - 3}$ 10 **16.** $x = \sqrt{12 - x}$ 3

Find the unknown lengths.

17.

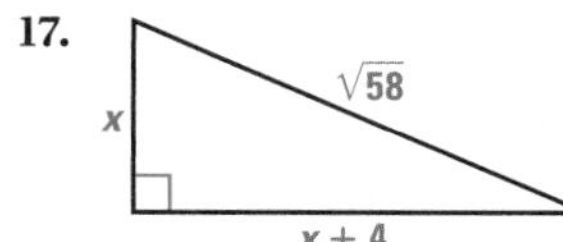

3, 7

18.

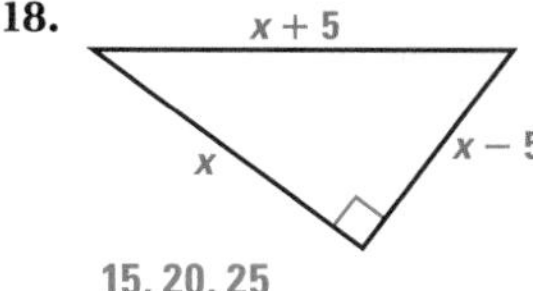

15, 20, 25

19.

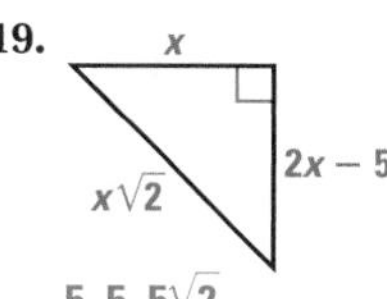

5, 5, $5\sqrt{2}$

Tell whether the triangle with the given side lengths is a right triangle.

20. 8, 16, 20 not a right triangle **21.** 11, 60, 61 right triangle **22.** 7.5, 10, 12.5 right triangle

Find the distance between the given points. Then find the midpoint of the line segment whose endpoints are the given points.

23. (6, 6), (9, 10) 5; (7.5, 8) **24.** (−8, 7), (4, 3) $4\sqrt{10}$; (−2, 5) **25.** $\left(5, -\frac{3}{2}\right), \left(-2, \frac{9}{2}\right)$ $\sqrt{85}$; $\left(1\frac{1}{2}, 1\frac{1}{2}\right)$

26. LADDERS A ladder that is 25 feet long is placed against a house. The bottom of the ladder is 10 feet from the base of the house. How far up the house does the ladder reach? Round your answer to the nearest tenth of a foot. 22.9 ft

27. BIRD HOUSES The front view of a bird house is shown. Find the height of the house to the nearest tenth of a foot. 1.9 ft

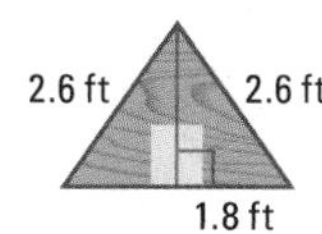

28. LACROSSE Two lacrosse players are playing on a field, as shown. The distance between consecutive grid lines represents 2 meters.

a. How far is each player from the ball? Round your answer to the nearest tenth of a meter. player A: 8.2 m; player B: 10.8 m

b. Both players start running toward the ball. Player A can run at a rate of 6 meters per second. Player B can run at a rate of 7 meters per second. Who will reach the ball first? player A

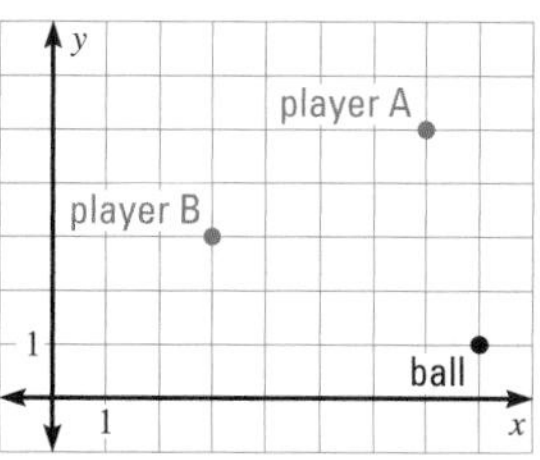

Additional Resources

Assessment Book

- Chapter Test, Levels A, B, C, pp. 156–161
- Standardized Chapter Test, pp. 162–163
- SAT/ACT Chapter Test, pp. 164–165
- Alternative Assessment, pp. 166–167

Test Generator CD-ROM

Chapter Test

Easily-readable reduced copies (with answers) of Chapter Test B, the Standardized Chapter Test, and the Alternative Assessment from the Assessment Book can be found on pp. 708E–708F.

1.

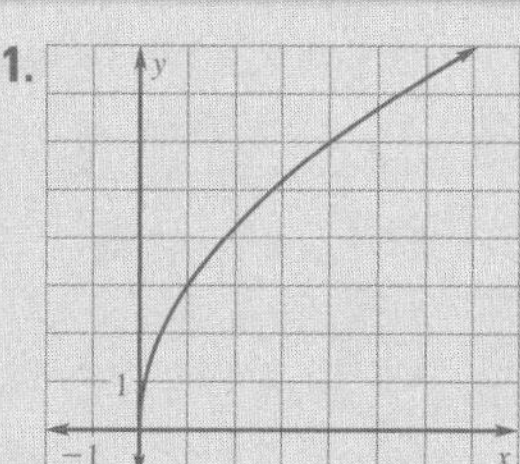

domain: $x \geq 0$, range: $y \geq 0$; vertical stretch by a factor of 3

2.

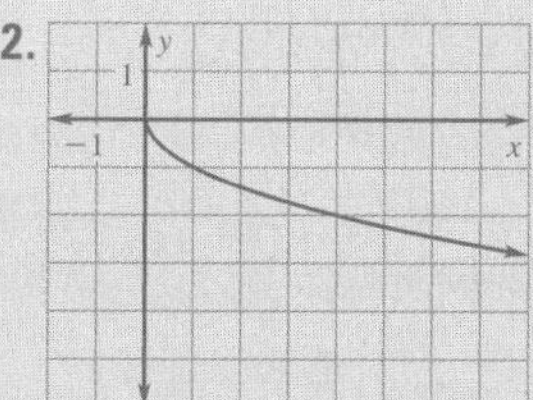

domain: $x \geq 0$, range: $y \leq 0$; reflection in the x-axis

3.

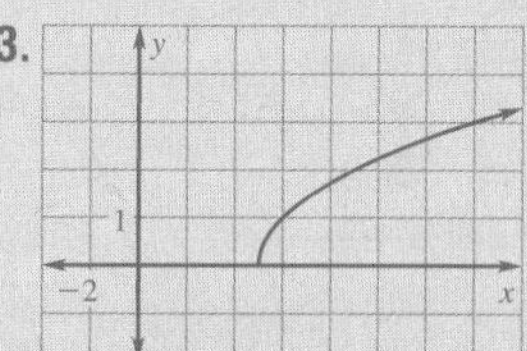

domain: $x \geq 5$, range: $y \geq 0$; horizontal translation of 5 units to the right

4.

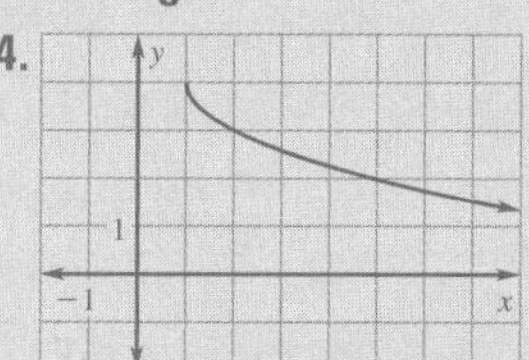

domain: $x \geq 1$, range: $y \leq 4$; horizontal translation of 1 unit to the right with a reflection in the x-axis and a translation vertically 4 units up

MULTIPLE CHOICE QUESTIONS

If you have difficulty solving a multiple choice problem directly, you may be able to use another approach to eliminate incorrect answer choices and obtain the correct answer.

PROBLEM 1

What is the solution of the equation $\sqrt{3 - x} = 2x$?

A. $1, -\frac{3}{4}$ **B.** $-1, \frac{3}{4}$ **C.** -1 **D.** $\frac{3}{4}$

METHOD 1

SOLVE DIRECTLY Solve the radical equation and check for extraneous solutions.

STEP 1 **Solve** the radical equation.

$$\sqrt{3 - x} = 2x$$
$$3 - x = 4x^2$$
$$0 = 4x^2 + x - 3$$
$$0 = (4x - 3)(x + 1)$$
$$4x - 3 = 0 \text{ or } x + 1 = 0$$
$$x = \frac{3}{4} \text{ or } \quad x = -1$$

STEP 2 **Check** $\frac{3}{4}$ and -1 in the original equation.

Check $\frac{3}{4}$: $\sqrt{3 - \frac{3}{4}} \stackrel{?}{=} 2\left(\frac{3}{4}\right)$

$$\frac{3}{2} = \frac{3}{2} \checkmark$$

Solution checks.

Check -1: $\sqrt{3 - (-1)} \stackrel{?}{=} 2(-1)$

$$2 = -2 \times$$

Solution does not check.

The only solution is $\frac{3}{4}$.

The correct answer is **D**.

METHOD 2

ELIMINATE CHOICES Substitute the values given in each answer choice for x in the equation.

Choice A: $1, -\frac{3}{4}$

$\sqrt{3 - 1} \stackrel{?}{=} 2(1)$ | $\sqrt{3 - \left(-\frac{3}{4}\right)} \stackrel{?}{=} -\frac{3}{4}$

$\sqrt{2} = 2 \times$ | $\frac{\sqrt{15}}{2} = -\frac{3}{4} \times$

The values do not check, so choice A can be eliminated.

Choice B: $-1, \frac{3}{4}$

$\sqrt{3 - (-1)} \stackrel{?}{=} 2(-1)$ | $\sqrt{3 - \frac{3}{4}} \stackrel{?}{=} 2\left(\frac{3}{4}\right)$

$2 = -2 \times$ | $\frac{3}{2} = \frac{3}{2} \checkmark$

Because -1 does not check, both choice B and choice C can be eliminated.

Choice D: $\frac{3}{4}$

You know that $\frac{3}{4}$ is a solution from checking the values in choice B.

The only solution is $\frac{3}{4}$.

The correct answer is **D**.

PROBLEM 2

A carpenter is building a wooden bench and wants to be sure that the back and the seat make a right angle. The back is 24 inches tall, and the seat is 18 inches deep. What should the distance from the front of the seat to the top of the back be?

F. 6 inches **G.** 15.9 inches **H.** 30 inches **J.** 42 inches

METHOD 1

SOLVE DIRECTLY Use the Pythagorean theorem to find the unknown distance.

STEP 1 **Identify** the known values by drawing a diagram.

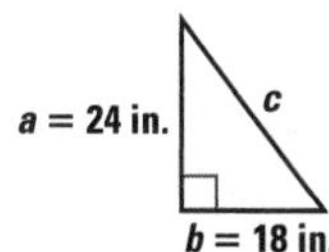

STEP 2 **Substitute** the values of a and b and solve for c.

$$a^2 + b^2 = c^2$$
$$18^2 + 24^2 = c^2$$
$$900 = c^2$$
$$\sqrt{900} = c$$
$$30 = c$$

The distance from the front of the seat to the top of the back should be 30 inches.

The correct answer is **H**.

METHOD 2

ELIMINATE CHOICES You can eliminate choices either by using the fact that the hypotenuse is the longest side of a right triangle or by using the converse of the Pythagorean theorem. Check to see if the value given in each answer choice could represent the length of the hypotenuse of a right triangle with leg lengths of 18 and 24 inches.

Choice F: 6 inches

$6 < 18$ ✗

Choice G: 15.9 inches

$15.9 < 18$ ✗

Choice H: 30 inches

$30 > 24$, so use the converse of the Pythagorean theorem.

$18^2 + 24^2 \stackrel{?}{=} 30^2$

$900 = 900$ ✓

The correct answer is **H**.

PRACTICE

Explain why you can eliminate the highlighted answer choice.

1. What is the solution of the equation $\sqrt{20 - x} = x$?

   A. 4, −5 **B.** −4, 5 **C.** ✗ −5 **D.** 4

2. Which of the following represents the side lengths of a right triangle?

   F. 1, 2, 3 **G.** ✗ 6, 8, 14 **H.** 12, 13, 15 **J.** 8, 15, 17

3. A side view of a wheelchair ramp can be represented by the hypotenuse of a right triangle. The triangle has a length of 24 feet and a height of 2 feet. To the nearest tenth, how long is the ramp?

   A. ✗ 22 feet **B.** 23.9 feet **C.** 24.1 feet **D.** 26 feet

TEST PREPARATION

Illinois Test Practice

1. ***Sample answer***: **The answer $x = -5$ does not check in the original equation, so you can eliminate both A and C as answer choices.**
2. ***Sample answer:*** **$6^2 + 8^2 \neq 14^2$, so you can eliminate choice G.**
3. ***Sample answer***: **The square of the length of the ramp should equal the sum of the squares of 24 and 2; $24^2 + 2^2 = 580$. Since $22^2 \neq 580$, you can eliminate choice A.**

Illinois Test Practice

1. D
2. G
3. B
4. G
5. C
6. H
7. A
8. H
9. B
10. J
11. D
12. G
13. C
14. G
15. C
16. J
17. C
18. F
19. C
20. H

Illinois Test Practice

1. What is the solution of the equation $\sqrt{2x+8} = x$?

A. $-2, 4$ **C.** -2
B. $24, 2$ **D.** 4

2. Which expression is equivalent to $\sqrt{4x^2y} \cdot \sqrt{y}$?

F. $4xy$ **H.** $2x\sqrt{y}$
G. $2xy$ **J.** $4x\sqrt{y}$

3. The graph of which function is shown?

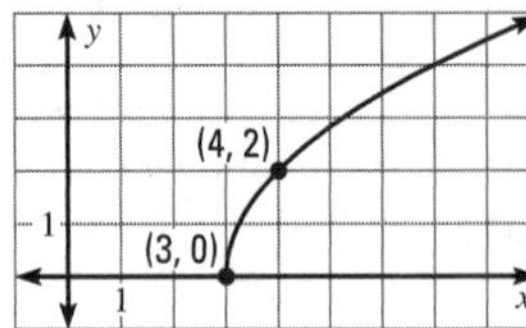

A. $y = \sqrt{x-3}$ **C.** $y = 2\sqrt{x+3}$
B. $y = 2\sqrt{x-3}$ **D.** $y = 2\sqrt{x} - 3$

4. How does the graph of $y = \sqrt{x} + 3$ compare with the graph of $y = \sqrt{x}$?

F. It is a vertical stretch by a factor of 3 of the graph of $y = \sqrt{x}$.
G. It is a vertical translation of 3 units up of the graph of $y = \sqrt{x}$.
H. It is a vertical translation of 3 units down of the graph of $y = \sqrt{x}$.
J. It is a horizontal translation of 3 units to the right of the graph of $y = \sqrt{x}$.

5. Which expression represents the length of a diagonal of the rectangle?

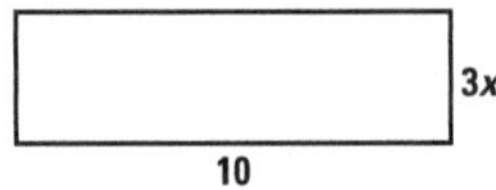

A. $3x^2 + 100$
B. $9x^2 + 100$
C. $\sqrt{9x^2 + 100}$
D. $\sqrt{3x^2 + 100}$

6. What is the solution of the equation $\sqrt{x+3} = x - 9$?

F. $-13, -6$ **H.** 13
G. $13, 6$ **J.** 6

7. The table below represents which function?

x	4	5	8	13
y	5	8	11	14

A. $y = 3\sqrt{x-4} + 5$
B. $y = 3\sqrt{x-3} + 8$
C. $y = 3\sqrt{x-4} + 8$
D. $y = 3\sqrt{x-3} + 5$

In Exercises 8 and 9, use the map of the college campus shown.

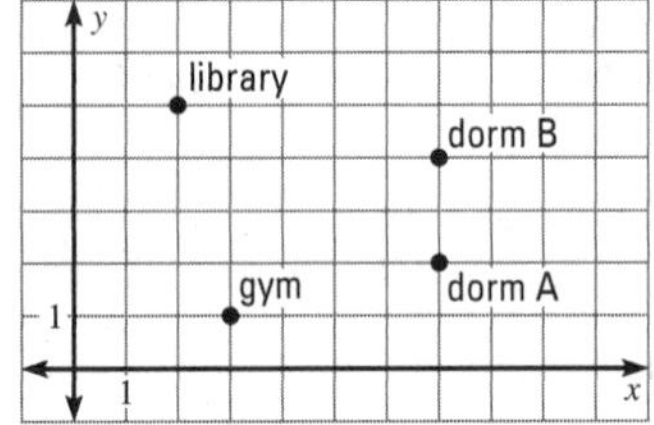

8. Which of the following pairs of buildings are closest together?

F. Dorm A and the library
G. Dorm B and the gym
H. The gym and the library
J. Dorm B and the library

9. A student who lives in dorm A forgets a book at the library. The student jogs at a rate of 6 miles per hour from the dorm straight to the library and back. The distance between consecutive grid lines represents 0.1 mile. To the nearest tenth of an hour, how long does it take the student to jog to the library and back?

A. 0.1 hour **C.** 0.3 hour
B. 0.2 hour **D.** 0.4 hour

10. Line segment d is a diagonal in each polygon shown below. Which drawing shows enough information to find the length of line segment d?

F.

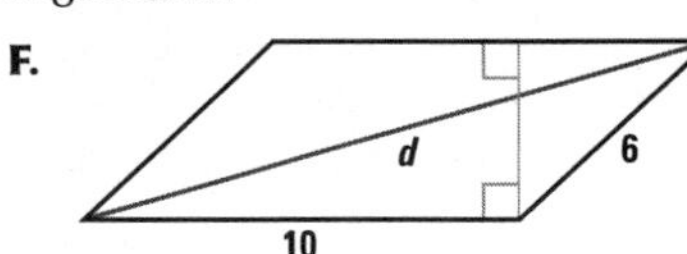

G.

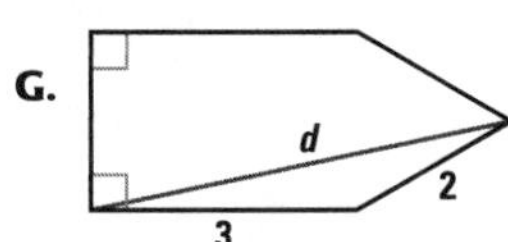

H.

J.

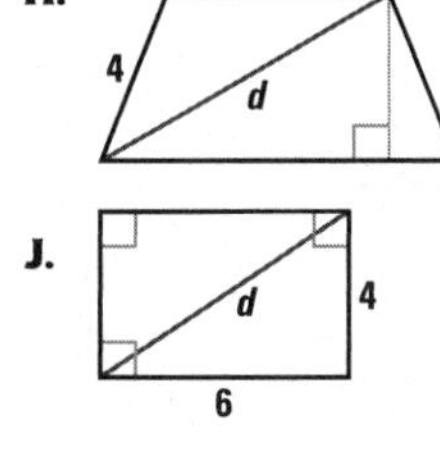

11. Which expression is $\sqrt{\frac{12n}{25}}$ in simplest form?

A. $\frac{\sqrt{12n}}{5}$ **C.** $\frac{2n\sqrt{3}}{5}$

B. $\frac{4\sqrt{3n}}{5}$ **D.** $\frac{2\sqrt{3n}}{5}$

12. What is the simplified form of $5\sqrt{128} - 3\sqrt{32} + 3\sqrt{8} - 7\sqrt{18}$

F. $12\sqrt{2}$

G. $13\sqrt{2}$

H. $21\sqrt{2}$

J. $33\sqrt{2}$

13. What is the midpoint between $(-5, 7)$ and $(11, 13)$?

A. $(20, 6)$ **C.** $(3, 10)$

B. $(6, 20)$ **D.** $(10, 3)$

14. Which of the following is the simplified expression of $(2 - \sqrt{3})^2$?

F. $7 + 4\sqrt{3}$ **H.** 7

G. $7 - 4\sqrt{3}$ **J.** $4\sqrt{3} - 7$

15. What is the solution of the equation $\sqrt{x - 5} = x - 7$?

A. 4 **C.** 9

B. 5 **D.** 12

16. What is the length of the unknown side of the right triangle?

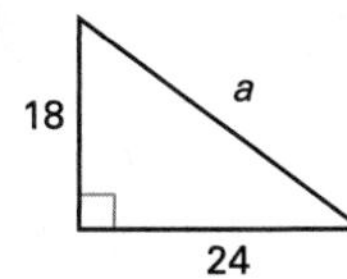

F. 12 **H.** 20

G. 15 **J.** 30

17. What is the distance between $(-2, 3)$ and $(3, 2)$?

A. 26 **C.** $\sqrt{26}$

B. 13 **D.** $\sqrt{24}$

18. What is the domain of the function $y = \sqrt{1 - x} + x + 1$?

F. $x \leq 1$

G. $x = 1$

H. $x = -1$

J. $x \geq 1$

19. Which of the following equations has no solution?

A. $2\sqrt{x} - 28 = 4$

B. $\sqrt{3x} - 39 = 0$

C. $\sqrt{x} + 12 = 9$

D. $\sqrt{x} - 14 = 0$

20. What is the midpoint between the points $(4, 9)$ and $(6, 7)$?

F. $(1, 1)$

G. $(-1, -1)$

H. $(5, 8)$

J. $(10, 16)$

TEST PRACTICE

Illinois Resources Guide

Pacing and Assignment Guide

REGULAR SCHEDULE

Pre-AP For pacing and assignments for a Pre-AP course, see the *Algebra 1 Toolkit*.

Lesson	Les. Day	BASIC	AVERAGE	ADVANCED
12.1 6.11.19	Day 1	pp. 769–772 Exs. 1–26	pp. 769–772 Exs. 1, 2, 6–26, 49–51	pp. 769–772 Exs. 1, 2, 7–26, 49–51
	Day 2	pp. 769–772 Exs. 27–43 odd, 44–49, 54–59, 62–74 even	pp. 769–772 Exs. 27, 35–48, 54–60, 63–73 odd	pp. 769–772 Exs. 37–48, 52–61*, 62–74 even
12.2 8.11.08	Day 1	EP p. 948 Exs. 1–9 odd; pp. 779–782 Exs. 1–17, 52–60	pp. 779–782 Exs. 1, 2, 6–17, 37, 52–60	pp. 779–782 Exs. 1, 6–17, 37, 52–60
	Day 2	pp. 779–782 Exs. 18–33, 39–43, 46–51	pp. 779–782 Exs. 18–28 even, 29–36, 39–44, 46–51	pp. 779–782 Exs. 18, 24–36, 38–45*, 46–50 even
12.3 8.11.01	Day 1	EP p. 946 Exs. 3–6; pp. 788–791 Exs. 1–12, 19–21, 51–59	pp. 788–791 Exs. 1, 2, 5–12, 19–21, 35–37, 51–59	pp. 788–791 Exs. 1, 2, 4–12 even, 19, 35–41*, 51–59
	Day 2	pp. 788–791 Exs. 13–18, 23–29 odd, 31–34, 42–47, 60–65	pp. 788–791 Exs. 13–18, 22–30 even, 31–34, 38, 42–49, 60–64 even	pp. 788–791 Exs. 13–18, 22–30 even, 31–34, 42–50*, 60–64 even
12.4 8.11.01	Day 1	EP p. 946 Exs. 25–30; pp. 797–800 Exs. 1–12, 13–33 odd, 34–36, 40–44, 48, 52, 55, 58	pp. 797–800 Exs. 1, 2, 7–12, 14–32 even, 33–38, 40–45, 49, 53, 56, 59	pp. 797–800 Exs. 1, 8–11, 14–32 even, 33–46*, 50, 54, 57, 60
12.5 8.11.01	Day 1	EP p. 946 Exs. 49–57 odd; pp. 806–809 Exs. 1–10, 12, 22, 23, 47–52	pp. 806–809 Exs. 1, 2, 4–10, 12, 22, 23, 29, 47–52	pp. 806–809 Exs. 1, 4–10, 22, 23, 29–31*, 47–52
	Day 2	pp. 806–809 Exs. 11, 13–21, 24–26, 33–36, 39–46	pp. 806–809 Exs. 11, 13–21, 24–28, 30, 33–37, 39–45 odd	pp. 806–809 Exs. 13–21, 24–28, 32–38*, 40–46 even
12.6 8.11.01	Day 1	pp. 816–819 Exs. 1–17, 19–21, 25, 26, 58–62	pp. 816–819 Exs. 1, 2, 7–17, 19–21, 25, 26, 29, 30, 35, 36, 58–62	pp. 816–819 Exs. 1, 2, 7–17, 19–21, 25, 26, 35, 36, 58–62
	Day 2	pp. 816–819 Exs. 18, 22–24, 27–35, 42–47, 50–57	pp. 816–819 Exs. 18, 22–24, 27–34, 37–40, 42–48, 50–56 even	pp. 816–819 Exs. 22–24, 27, 28, 31–34, 37, 41–49*, 51–57 odd
12.7 8.11.19	Day 1	EP p. 946 Exs. 43–48; pp. 823–826 Exs. 1–8, 12–19, 24–26, 31–35, 39–53 odd	pp. 823–826 Exs. 1, 2, 7–13, 19–29, 31–37, 40–52 even	pp. 823–826 Exs. 1, 2, 8–11, 20–38*, 40–52 even
Review	Day 1	pp. 831–834 Exs. 1–31	pp. 831–834 Exs. 1–31	pp. 831–834 Exs. 1–31
Assess	Day 1	Chapter 12 Test	Chapter 12 Test	Chapter 12 Test

Yearly Pacing Chapter 12 Total – 14 days Chapters 1–12 Total – 146 days Remaining – 14 days

*Challenge Exercises EP = Extra Practice SRH = Skills Review Handbook

BLOCK SCHEDULE

DAY 1	DAY 2	DAY 3	DAY 4	DAY 5	DAY 6	DAY 7
12.1	**12.2**	**12.3**	**12.4**	**12.5 (CONT.)**	**12.6 (CONT.)**	**REVIEW**
pp. 769–772 Exs. 1, 2, 6–27, 35–51, 54–60, 63–73 odd	pp. 779–782 Exs. 1, 2, 6–17, 18–28 even, 29–37, 39–44, 46–60	pp. 788–791 Exs. 1, 2, 5–21, 22–30 even, 31–38, 42–49, 51–59, 60–64 even	pp. 797–800 Exs. 1, 2, 7–12, 14–32 even, 33–38, 40–45, 49, 53, 56, 59	pp. 806–809 Exs. 11, 13–21, 24–28, 30, 33–37, 39–45 odd	pp. 816–819 Exs. 18, 22–24, 27–34, 37–40, 42–48, 50–56 even	pp. 831–834 Exs. 1–31
			12.5	**12.6**	**12.7**	**ASSESS**
			pp. 806–809 Exs. 1, 2, 4–10, 12, 22, 23, 29, 47–52	pp. 816–819 Exs. 1, 2, 7–17, 19–21, 25, 26, 29, 30, 35, 36, 58–62	pp. 823–826 Exs. 1, 2, 7–13, 19–29, 31–37, 40–52 even	Chapter 12 Test

Yearly Pacing Chapter 12 Total – 7 days Chapters 1–12 Total – 73 days Remaining – 7 days

12 Chapter Resource Guide

Chapter Resource Book							
CHAPTER SUPPORT							
Parents as Partners (Chapter Overview with home involvement exercises and activity)						p. 1	
LESSON SUPPORT	12.1	12.2	12.3	12.4	12.5	12.6	12.7
Standard	**6.11.19**	**8.11.08**	**8.11.01**	**8.11.01**	**8.11.01**	**8.11.01**	**8.11.19**
Teaching Guide/Lesson Plan	p. 3	p. 17	p. 30	p. 42	p. 54	p. 66	p. 77
Activity Masters				p. 44		p. 68	
Technology Activities & Keystrokes			p. 33		p. 56		
Activity Support Masters	p. 5		p. 32				
Practice (3 levels)	p. 6	p. 19	p. 34	p. 45	p. 58	p. 69	p. 79
Study Guide	p. 12	p. 25	p. 37	p. 48	p. 61	p. 72	p. 82
Catch-Up for Absent Students	p. 14	p. 27	p. 39	p. 50	p. 63	p. 74	p. 84
Problem Solving/Application	p. 15	p. 28	p. 40	p. 51	p. 64	p. 75	p. 85
Challenge Practice	p. 16	p. 29	p. 41	p. 53	p. 65	p. 76	p. 86
REVIEW							
Chapter Review Games and Activities		p. 87		Cumulative Practice		p. 90	
Project with Rubric		p. 88		Resource Book Answers		A1	

Transparencies	12.1	12.2	12.3	12.4	12.5	12.6	12.7
Warm-Up/Daily Homework Quiz	✔	✔	✔	✔	✔	✔	✔
Notetaking Guide	✔	✔	✔	✔	✔	✔	✔
Teacher Support	✔	✔	✔				
Answer Transparencies	✔	✔	✔	✔	✔	✔	✔

ASSESSMENT BOOK

Quizzes	p. 168	SAT/ACT Chapter Test	p. 179
Chapter Tests (3 levels)	p. 171	Alternative Assessment with Rubric	p. 181
Standardized Chapter Test	p. 177		

TECHNOLOGY

- Easy Planner
- Test and Practice Generator
- Power Presentations
- @HomeTutor
- Activity Generator
- Animated Algebra
- Classzone.com
- eEdition Plus Online
- eWorkbook Plus Online
- ML Assessment System

ADDITIONAL RESOURCES

Illinois Additional Lessons

- Worked-Out Solution Key
- Notetaking Guide
- Practice Workbook
- Algebra 1 Toolkit
- Benchmark Tests
- Reteaching and Remediation
- Spanish Study Guide
- Spanish Assessment Book
- Spanish Resources in Spanish
- Multi-Language Visual Glossary

12 Lesson Practice Level B

LESSON 12.1 Practice B
For use with pages 765–772

Tell whether the equation represents *direct variation, inverse variation,* or *neither*.

1. $y = -11x$ direct variation
2. $xy = -5$ inverse variation
3. $y = x - 4$ neither
4. $x = \frac{-8}{y}$ inverse variation
5. $xy = 14$ inverse variation
6. $\frac{y}{x} = 13$ direct variation
7. $2x + y = 8$ neither
8. $3y = \frac{9}{x}$ inverse variation
9. $4x - 4y = 0$ direct variation

Graph the inverse variation equation.

10. $xy = 12$
11. $xy = -6$
12. $xy = 7$

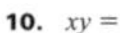

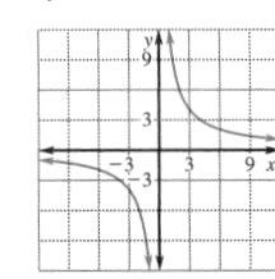

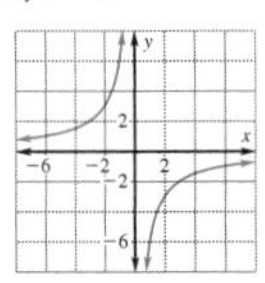

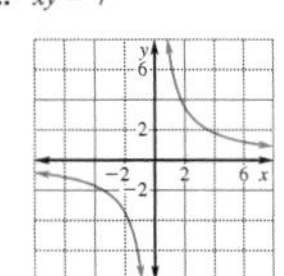

13. $y = \frac{-8}{x}$
14. $y = \frac{15}{x}$
15. $y = \frac{14}{x}$

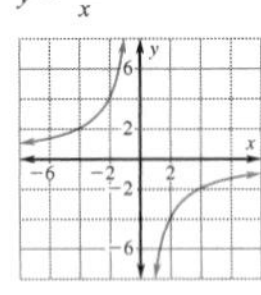

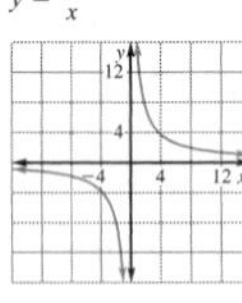

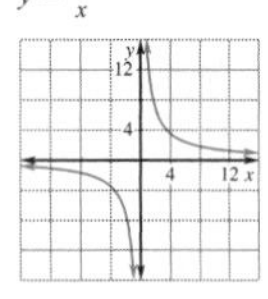

16. $y = \frac{-9}{x}$
17. $y = \frac{-12}{x}$
18. $y = \frac{5}{x}$

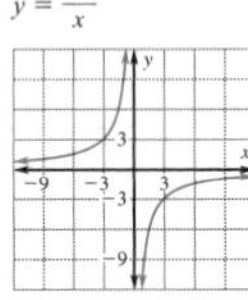

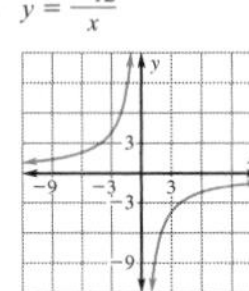

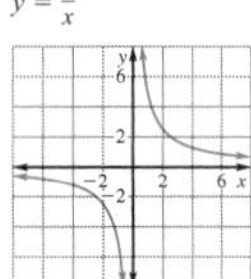

LESSON 12.1 Practice B *continued*
For use with pages 765–772

22. $y = \frac{-11}{x}; -\frac{11}{2}$ 23. $y = \frac{144}{x}; 72$ 26. $y = \frac{-28}{x}; -14$ 28. $y = \frac{-36}{x}; -18$ 29. $y = \frac{-200}{x}; -100$

Given that *y* varies inversely with *x*, use the specified values to write an inverse variation equation that relates *x* and *y*. Then find the value of *y* when $x = 2$.

19. $x = 7, y = 2$ $y = \frac{14}{x}; 7$
20. $x = 3, y = 9$ $y = \frac{27}{x}; \frac{27}{2}$
21. $x = -3, y = 1$ $y = \frac{-3}{x}; -\frac{3}{2}$
22. $x = 11, y = -1$
23. $x = -12, y = -12$
24. $x = -18, y = -4$ $y = \frac{72}{x}; 36$
25. $x = 10, y = 5$ $y = \frac{50}{x}; 25$
26. $x = 7, y = -4$
27. $x = 6, y = 6$ $y = \frac{36}{x}; 18$
28. $x = -3, y = 12$
29. $x = -5, y = 40$
30. $x = -5, y = -11$ $y = \frac{55}{x}; \frac{55}{2}$

Tell whether the table represents inverse variation. If so, write the inverse variation equation.

31. no

x	2	4	6	8	10
y	11	21	31	41	51

32. yes; $y = \frac{20}{x}$

x	−5	−4	1	2	10
y	−4	−5	20	10	2

33. no

x	10	23	25	28	50
y	160	368	400	448	800

34. yes; $y = \frac{18}{x}$

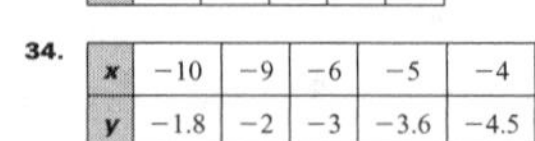

x	−10	−9	−6	−5	−4
y	−1.8	−2	−3	−3.6	−4.5

35. **Catalog Orders** A clothing company allows customers to place orders on the Internet or by phone. The orders must be entered into the computer inventory system. The number of orders *n* entered into the system varies inversely with the number *p* of people working. The company estimates that 10 people working during a shift can get 960 orders entered.
    a. Write an inverse variation equation that relates *n* and *p*. $n = \frac{9600}{p}$
    b. Find the number of orders entered during a shift if 20 people are working. 480 orders
    c. Find the number of orders entered during a shift if 8 people are working. 1200 orders

36. **Volume and Pressure** The volume *V* of a gas at a constant temperature varies inversely with the pressure *P*. When the volume is 125 cubic inches, the pressure is 20 pounds per cubic inch.
    a. Write the inverse variation equation that relates *P* and *V*. $V = \frac{2500}{P}$
    b. Find the pressure of a gas with a volume of 250 cubic inches. 10 pounds per in.^{3}

37. **Running** Every other day, weather permitting, you run 5 miles. Write and graph an equation that relates your average running speed *s* (in miles per hour) and the time *t* (in hours) that it takes for you to complete the run. Is the equation an inverse variation equation? *Explain.* yes; Answers will vary.

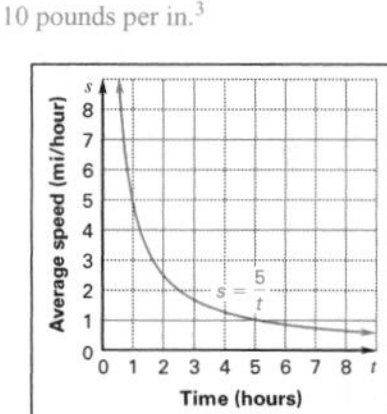

LESSON 12.2 Practice B
For use with pages 775–782

1. domain: all reals except 3; range: all reals except 1
2. domain: all reals except 4; range: all reals except 3
3. domain: all reals except −6; range: all reals except −4
4. domain: all reals except −6; range: all reals except −8

Identify the domain and range of the function from its graph.

1.

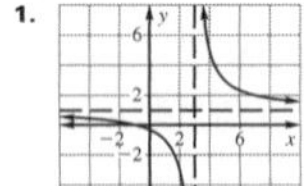

2.

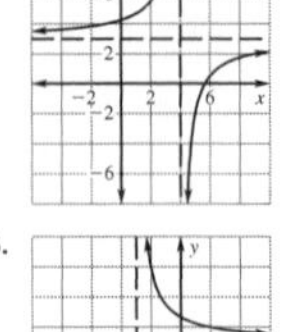

3.

4.

5.

6.

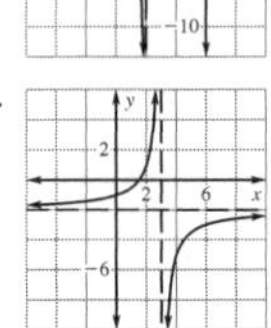

Graph the function and identify its domain and range. Then compare the graph with the graph of $y = \frac{1}{x}$.

5. domain: all reals except −3; range: all reals except 3
6. domain: all reals except 3; range: all reals except −2

7. $y = \frac{8}{x}$
8. $y = \frac{1}{6x}$
9. $y = \frac{-3}{2x}$

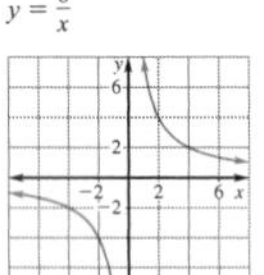

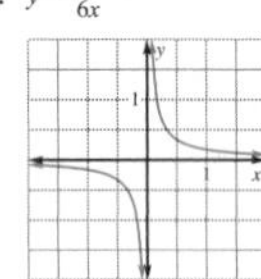

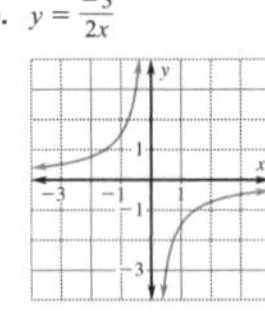

10. $y = \frac{1}{x} - 7$
11. $y = \frac{1}{x} + 10$
12. $y = \frac{1}{x - 4}$

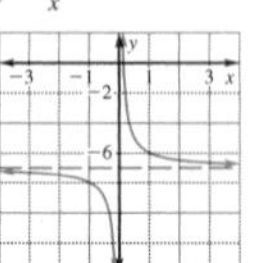

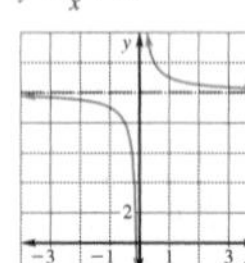

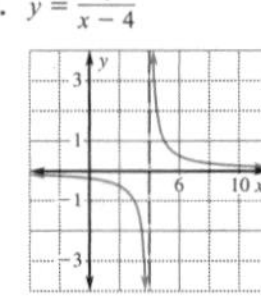

7. domain: all reals except 0; range: all reals except 0; vertical stretch
8. domain: all reals except 0; range: all reals except 0; vertical shrink
9. domain: all reals except 0; range: all reals except 0; vertical stretch and reflection in *x*-axis
10. domain: all reals except 0; range: all reals except −7; vertical translation 7 units down
11. domain: all reals except 0; range: all reals except 10; vertical translation 10 units up
12. domain: all reals except 4; range: all reals except 0; horizontal translation 4 units right

LESSON 12.2 Practice B *continued*
For use with pages 775–782

13. $x = 6, y = 4$ 14. $x = -5, y = -6$
15. $x = 3, y = -8$ 16. $x = -7, y = 7$
17. $x = 8, y = 12$ 18. $x = -5, y = 10$

Determine the asymptotes of the graph of the function.

13. $y = \frac{10}{x - 6} + 4$
14. $y = \frac{-8}{x + 5} - 6$
15. $y = \frac{14}{x - 3} - 8$
16. $y = \frac{12}{x + 7} + 7$
17. $y = \frac{-4}{x - 8} + 12$
18. $y = \frac{9}{x + 5} + 10$
19. $y = \frac{14}{x - 14} + 1$ $x = 14, y = 1$
20. $y = \frac{-12}{x + 12} - 3$ $x = -12, y = -3$
21. $y = \frac{7}{x - 5} - 14$ $x = 5, y = -14$

Graph the function.

22. $y = \frac{2}{x} + 5$
23. $y = \frac{1}{x - 4} + 2$
24. $y = \frac{-3}{x + 6} - 1$

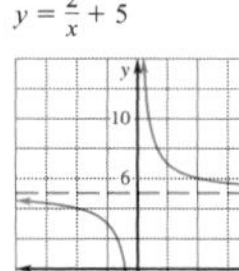

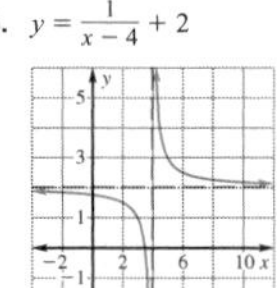

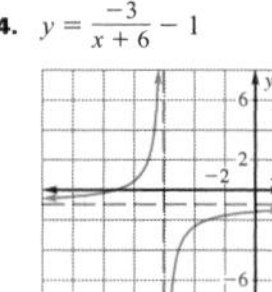

25. **Baseball Hall of Fame** Your baseball team is planning a bus trip to the National Baseball Hall of Fame. The cost for renting a bus is $515, and the cost will be divided equally among the people who are going on the trip. One admission costs $14.50.
    a. Write an equation that gives the cost *C* (in dollars per person) of the trip as a function of the number *p* of people going on the trip. $C = \frac{515}{p} + 14.5$
    b. Graph the equation.
    c. What would the cost per person be if 20 people go on the trip? $40.25

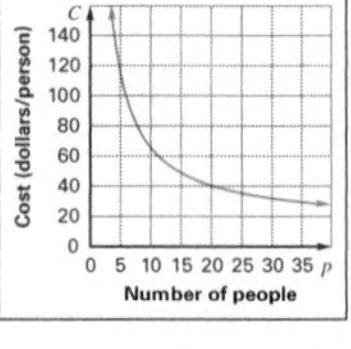

26. **Fundraiser** A pizza shop makes pizzas that organizations sell for fundraisers. One organization has placed an order for 450 pizzas. Currently, 4 people are scheduled to put together the pizzas. The owner of the shop hopes to call in some extra workers to complete all of the pizzas.
    a. Write an equation that gives the average number *n* of pizzas made per person as a function of the number *p* of extra workers that can come in and help complete the work. $n = \frac{450}{4 + p}$
    b. Graph the equation.
    c. If 2 people come in to help out, what is the average number of pizzas made person? 75 pizzas

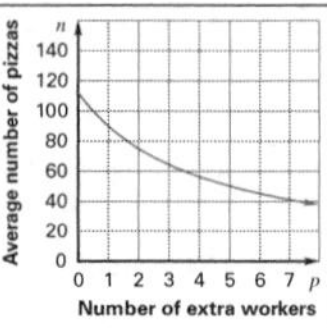

LESSON 12.3 Practice B

For use with pages 784–791

Divide.

1. $(18x^3 - 24x^2 + 12x) \div 6x$ $3x^2 - 4x + 2$
2. $(-5x^3 + 15x^2 - 30x) \div (-5x)$ $x^2 - 3x + 6$
3. $(22x^4 - 18x^2 + 6x) \div (-2x)$ $-11x^3 + 9x - 3$
4. $(x^2 + 6x + 5) \div (x + 5)$ $x + 1$
5. $(5x^2 + 7x - 6) \div (x + 2)$ $5x - 3$
6. $(4x^2 + x - 5) \div (x - 1)$ $4x + 5$
7. $(6x^2 + 22x - 8) \div (x + 4)$ $6x - 2$
8. $(4x^2 + x - 8) \div (x - 2)$ $4x + 9 + \frac{10}{x - 2}$
9. $(9x^2 + 5x - 6) \div (x + 1)$ $9x - 4 - \frac{2}{x + 1}$
10. $(3x^2 - 7x + 14) \div (3x + 2)$ $x - 3 + \frac{20}{3x + 2}$

Graph the function.

11. $y = \frac{x + 8}{x}$

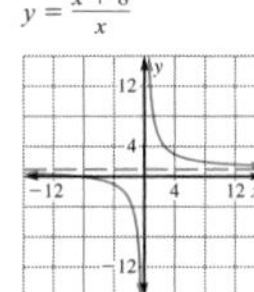

12. $y = \frac{3x - 5}{x}$

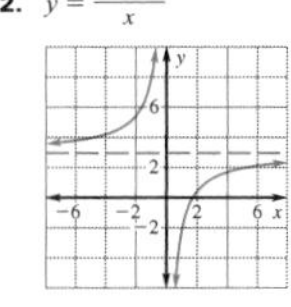

13. $y = \frac{x + 5}{x - 2}$

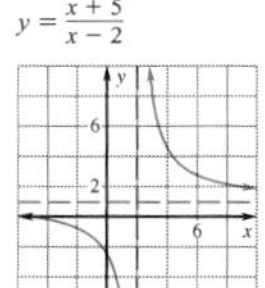

14. **Scootcar Rental** A resort area offers rentals of scootcars (a cross between a scooter and a small car) for \$40 per hour plus a \$4.50 gasoline fill-up fee.
   a. Write an equation that gives the average cost C per hour as a function of the number h of hours the scootcar is rented.
   b. Graph the equation. $C = \frac{40h + 4.5}{h}$

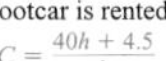

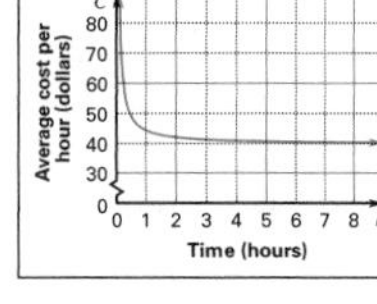

15. **Juice Bar** Between 1995 and 2004, the number D of drinks (in thousands) sold at a juice bar can be modeled by $D = 4t + 18$ where t is the number of years since 1995. The number F of drinks (in thousands) made from fruit juice rather than vegetable juice can be modeled by $F = 2t + 32$.
   a. Use long division to find a model for the ratio R of the number of fruit drinks sold to the total number of drinks sold. $R = \frac{1}{2} + \frac{23}{2(2t + 9)}$
   b. Graph the model.

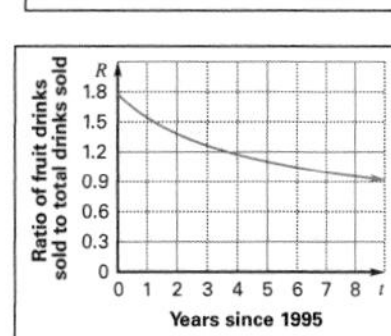

LESSON 12.3

LESSON 12.4 Practice B

For use with pages 794–800

LESSON 12.4

Find the excluded values, if any, of the expression.

1. $\frac{14}{3x}$ $x = 0$
2. $\frac{-8}{x - 5}$ $x = 5$
3. $\frac{5x}{x + 10}$ $x = -10$
4. $\frac{-x}{4x - 8}$ $x = 2$
5. $\frac{3x}{7x + 21}$ $x = -3$
6. $\frac{x + 1}{3x + 7}$ $x = -\frac{7}{3}$
7. $\frac{x + 6}{x^2 - 2x + 1}$ $x = 1$
8. $\frac{8}{x^2 + 4x - 12}$ $x = -6, 2$
9. $\frac{7x}{x^2 - 25}$ $x = -5, 5$

Simplify the rational expression, if possible. Find the excluded values.

10. $\frac{-36x^2}{18x}$ $-2x; x = 0$
11. $\frac{6x - 24}{x - 4}$ $6; x = 4$
12. $\frac{4x - 12}{3 - x}$ $-4; x = 3$
13. $\frac{x + 11}{x^2 - 121}$ $\frac{1}{x - 11}; x = -11, 11$
14. $\frac{x + 3}{x^2 + 10x + 21}$ $\frac{1}{x + 7}; x = -3, -7$
15. $\frac{x - 4}{x^2 + 11x + 24}$ in simplest form; $x = -3, -8$

Write and simplify a rational expression for the ratio of the perimeter to the area of the given figure.

16. Square $\frac{1}{2x}$

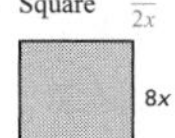

17. Rectangle $\frac{3x + 5}{x(x + 5)}$

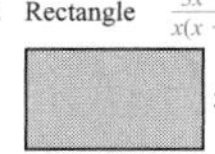

18. Triangle $\frac{3x + 2}{x(x + 1)}$

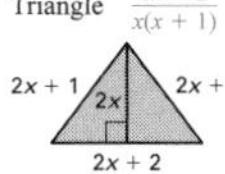

19. **Zoo Exhibit** The directors of a zoo have drawn up preliminary plans for a rectangular exhibit. They have decided on dimensions that are related as shown.
   a. Write a rational expression for the ratio of the perimeter to the area of the exhibit.
   b. Simplify your expression from part (a).

19. a. $\frac{2(4x + 3) + 2(4x - 2)}{(4x + 3)(4x - 2)}$ b. $\frac{8x + 1}{(4x + 3)(2x - 1)}$

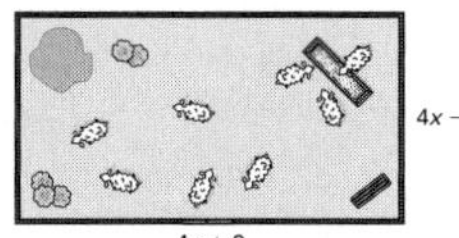

20. **Materials Used** The material consumed M (in thousands of pounds) by a plastic injection molding machine per year between 1995 and 2004 can be modeled by

$$M = \frac{8t^2 + 66t + 70}{(3 - 0.2t + 0.1t^2)(t + 7)}$$

where t is the number of years since 1995. Simplify the model and approximate the number of pounds consumed in 2000.

$\frac{2(4t + 5)}{0.1t^2 - 0.2t + 3}$; about 11 thousand pounds

LESSON 12.5 Practice B

For use with pages 802–809

5. $\frac{1}{2(x + 5)}$ 7. $\frac{x(x + 3)}{3(2x - 1)}$ 9. $3(x + 5)$

Find the product.

1. $\frac{4x^2}{15} \cdot \frac{5}{8x^5}$ $\frac{1}{6x^3}$
2. $\frac{24}{7x^2} \cdot \frac{14x^6}{40}$ $\frac{6x^4}{5}$
3. $\frac{21}{2x + 12} \cdot \frac{4x + 24}{15}$ $\frac{14}{5}$
4. $\frac{5x + 10}{2x - 6} \cdot \frac{x - 3}{10x + 20}$ $\frac{1}{4}$
5. $\frac{x - 3}{2x + 8} \cdot \frac{x + 4}{x^2 + 2x - 15}$
6. $\frac{x^2 + 4x - 12}{x^2 + 7x + 10} \cdot \frac{x + 5}{2x - 4}$ $\frac{x + 6}{2(x + 2)}$
7. $\frac{6x}{4x^2 - 1} \cdot \frac{2x^2 + 7x + 3}{18}$
8. $\frac{x^4}{x^4 + 5x^3} \cdot (x + 5)$ x
9. $\frac{3x - 6}{x^2 - x - 2} \cdot (x^2 + 6x + 5)$

Find the quotient.

10. $\frac{24}{5x^3} \div \frac{6}{25x^2}$ $\frac{20}{x}$
11. $\frac{11x^4}{18} \div \frac{22}{9x^2}$ $\frac{x^6}{4}$
12. $\frac{7x + 21}{30} \div \frac{21x + 63}{20}$ $\frac{2}{9}$
13. $\frac{4x - 24}{3x + 15} \div \frac{12x - 72}{x + 5}$ $\frac{1}{9}$
14. $\frac{x + 2}{3x - 3} \div \frac{x^2 + 11x + 18}{x - 1}$ $\frac{1}{3(x + 9)}$
15. $\frac{x^2 + 4x}{4x} \div \frac{x^2 + x - 12}{x - 3}$ $\frac{1}{4}$
16. $\frac{2x + 10}{x^2 - 25} \div \frac{4x^2}{2x^2 - 10x}$ $\frac{1}{x}$
17. $\frac{2x - 14}{x^2 - 4x - 21} \div (x + 3)$ $\frac{2}{(x + 3)^2}$

LESSON 12.5

18. **Wall Art** You want to create a rectangular picture from 2-inch by 3-inch tiles. You want the picture's dimensions to be related as shown.
   a. Write and simplify an expression that you can use to determine the number of 2-inch by 3-inch tiles that will be needed for the picture. $4x^2$
   b. If $x = 5$, how many tiles will you need? 100 tiles

6x
4x
2 in.
3 in.

19. **Profit** The total profit P (in millions of dollars) earned by a company from 1995 to 2004 can be modeled by

$$P = \frac{3500 + 500t}{98 - t}$$

where t is the number of years since 1995. The number N (in hundreds of thousands) of units sold can be modeled by

$$N = \frac{(t + 7)(3000 - 20t)}{490 - 5t}$$

where t is the number of years since 1995. Write a model that gives the profit earned per unit per year. Then approximate the profit per unit in 2002.

$\frac{125}{150 - t}$; about \$8.74 per unit

12 Lesson Practice Level B

LESSON 12.6 Practice B

For use with pages 812–819

Find the sum or difference.

1. $\frac{8}{x+5} + \frac{x}{x+5}$ $\frac{x+8}{x+5}$
2. $\frac{10x}{x-4} - \frac{6x}{x-4}$ $\frac{4x}{x-4}$
3. $\frac{x+3}{x-9} + \frac{5x}{x-9}$ $\frac{3(2x+1)}{x-9}$
4. $\frac{x-5}{x+2} - \frac{x+6}{x+2}$ $\frac{-11}{x+2}$
5. $\frac{3x-4}{x^2-9} + \frac{7x-3}{x^2-9}$ $\frac{10x-7}{x^2-9}$
6. $\frac{2x+4}{3x^2} - \frac{x-1}{3x^2}$ $\frac{x+5}{3x^2}$

Find the LCD of the rational expressions.

7. $\frac{6}{5x^3}, \frac{7}{15x}$ $15x^3$
8. $\frac{10}{x}, \frac{9x}{x+7}$ $x(x+7)$
9. $\frac{3x+1}{x-4}, \frac{x-4}{x+6}$ $(x-4)(x+6)$
10. $\frac{x+5}{2x-4}, \frac{4x}{x-2}$ $2(x-2)$
11. $\frac{1}{x^2-5x}, \frac{8}{x^2-3x-10}$ $x(x-5)(x+2)$
12. $\frac{3}{x^2+5x+4}, \frac{4x}{x^2+2x+1}$ $(x+1)^2(x+4)$

Find the sum or difference.

13. $\frac{11}{2x} + \frac{4}{7x}$ $\frac{85}{14x}$
14. $\frac{8}{3x^3} - \frac{5}{12x}$ $\frac{32-5x^2}{12x^3}$
15. $\frac{8x}{x-5} - \frac{3x}{x+2}$ $\frac{x(5x+31)}{(x-5)(x+2)}$
16. $\frac{x}{6x-5} + \frac{1}{5x-3}$
17. $\frac{4}{x^2-7x} - \frac{3}{x}$ $\frac{25-3x}{x(x-7)}$
18. $\frac{5}{x^2} + \frac{x+3}{x-1}$ $\frac{x^3+3x^2+5x-5}{x^2(x-1)}$
19. $\frac{x+3}{x-1} + \frac{x+2}{x+1}$ $\frac{2x^2+5x+1}{(x-1)(x+1)}$
20. $\frac{2x}{x^2-3x} + \frac{x+4}{x-3}$ $\frac{x(x+6)}{x(x-3)}$
21. $\frac{1}{x^2+5x+4} - \frac{1}{x^2-16}$ $\frac{-5}{(x+1)(x+4)(x-4)}$

16. $\frac{5x^2+3x-5}{(6x-5)(5x-3)}$

22. **Paddle Boat** You paddle boat 8 miles upstream (against the current) and 8 miles downstream (with the current). The speed of the current is 1 mile per hour.
    a. Write an equation that gives the total travel time t (in hours) as a function of your average speed r (in miles per hour) in still water. $t = \frac{8}{r-1} + \frac{8}{r+1}$
    b. Find your total travel time if your average speed in still water is 3 miles per hour. 6 h
    c. How much faster is your total travel time if you increased your average speed in still water to 3.5 miles per hour? Round your answer to the nearest tenth. about 1 h

23. **Bike Ride** You bike 50 miles from home. On your way back home, your average speed increases by 3 miles per hour.
    a. Write an equation that gives the total biking time t (in hours) as a function of your average speed r (in miles per hour) when you are biking away from home. $t = \frac{50}{r} + \frac{50}{r+3}$
    b. Find the total biking time if you bike away from your home at an average speed of 15 miles per hour. Round your answer to the nearest tenth. about 6.1 h
    c. How much longer is your total biking time if you bike away from your home at an average speed of 12 miles per hour? about 1.4 h

LESSON 12.6

LESSON 12.7 Practice B

For use with pages 820–826

Solve the equation. Check your solution.

1. $\frac{x}{27} = \frac{3}{x}$ $-9, 9$
2. $\frac{3}{x} = \frac{2}{x+4}$ -12
3. $\frac{4}{x-7} = \frac{2}{x}$ -7
4. $\frac{10}{x+2} = \frac{7}{x-4}$ 18
5. $\frac{-5}{x+4} = \frac{x}{x+4}$ -5
6. $\frac{8}{x+8} = \frac{x}{x+2}$ $-4, 4$
7. $\frac{-1}{x+2} = \frac{x}{x+2}$ -1
8. $\frac{2}{3x} = \frac{x+3}{2x-5}$ no solution
9. $\frac{6x}{x+2} = \frac{-2}{x+2}$ $-\frac{1}{3}$

Find the LCD of the rational expressions in the equation.

10. $\frac{7x}{x-3} + 4 = \frac{x+1}{x-3}$ $x-3$
11. $\frac{3}{2x-2} + 4 = \frac{7x}{x-1}$ $2(x-1)$
12. $\frac{7}{x-2} + 1 = \frac{4}{x-3}$ $(x-2)(x-3)$

Solve the equation. Check your solution.

13. $\frac{3x}{x+4} - 3 = \frac{-12}{x+4}$ 0
14. $\frac{3}{x+2} + 5 = \frac{4}{x+2}$ $-\frac{9}{5}$
15. $\frac{2x}{x-1} + 2 = \frac{10}{x+2}$ no solution
16. $\frac{x-1}{x+5} + 6 = \frac{-2}{x+2}$ $-4, -\frac{17}{7}$
17. $\frac{4x}{x-5} + 1 = \frac{9}{x-1}$ no solution
18. $\frac{x}{x-4} - \frac{5x}{x-2} = \frac{-18}{x-2}$ $3, 6$

19. **Stain Mixing** You are staining a coffee table you just made. After testing some sample pieces of wood, you decide that you want a mix of a yellow stain and a red stain. You estimate that you want a mix that contains 75% of the yellow stain. You only have 1-pint that is made up of equal parts of the stain. How many pints of the yellow stain do you have to add to the current mixture? 1 pt

20. **Wallpaper** Working together an expert wallpaper hanger and an assistant can hang the wallpaper in a room in 3 hours. The assistant can hang the wallpaper in one and one-half times the time it takes the expert wallpaper hanger to hang the wallpaper alone. Let x represent the time (in hours) that the assistant can hang the wallpaper alone.
    a. Copy and complete the table.

Person	Fraction of room papered each hour	Time (hours)	Fraction of room papered
Assistant	$\frac{1}{x}$	3	$\frac{3}{x}$
Expert	$\frac{3}{2x}$	3	$\frac{9}{2x}$

    b. *Explain* why the sum of the expressions in the last column must be 1. Answers will vary.
    c. Write a rational equation that you can use to find the amount of time it takes the assistant to wallpaper the room alone. Then solve the equation. $\frac{3}{x} + \frac{9}{2x} = 1$; 7.5 h

LESSON 12.7

CHAPTER 12 Quiz 1
For use after Lessons 12.1–12.2

Tell whether the equation represents *direct variation, inverse variation,* or *neither.*

1. $y = 3x$
2. $xy = -2$
3. $2x + y = 7$

Given that *y* varies inversely with *x*, use the specified values to write an inverse equation that relates *x* and *y*. Then find the value of *y* when *x* = 2.

4. $x = 7, y = 5$
5. $x = 3, y = -8$
6. $x = \frac{1}{2}, y = 14$

Graph the function and identify its domain and range.

7. $y = \frac{7}{x}$

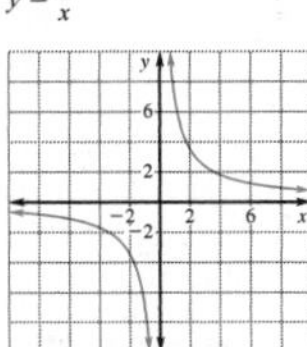

8. $y = \frac{-1}{x}$

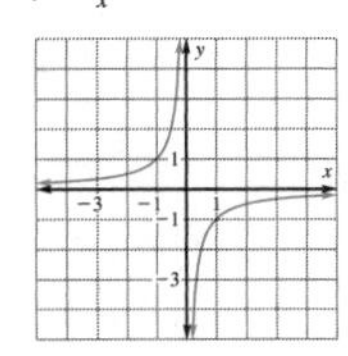

9. $y = \frac{-2}{x+1}$

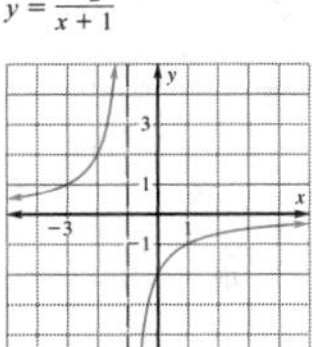

Answers

1. direct variation
2. inverse variation
3. neither
4. $y = \frac{35}{x}; \frac{35}{2}$
5. $y = \frac{-24}{x}; -12$
6. $y = \frac{7}{x}; \frac{7}{2}$
7. See left. The domain and range are all nonzero real numbers.
8. See left. The domain and range are all nonzero real numbers.
9. See left. The domain is all real numbers except $x = -1$. The range is all real numbers except $y = 0$.

CHAPTER 12 Quiz 2
For use after Lessons 12.3–12.4

Divide.

1. $(x^2 - 8x + 15) \div (x - 5)$
2. $(x^2 + 7x - 18) \div (x - 2)$

Graph the function.

3. $y = \frac{x+5}{x-6}$

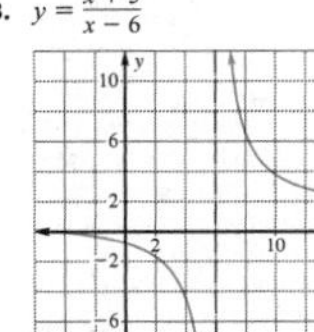

4. $y = \frac{3x+4}{x+3}$

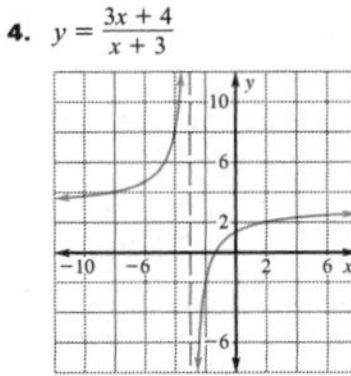

Simplify the rational expression, if possible. Find the excluded values.

5. $\frac{x-1}{x^2-1}$
6. $\frac{4x^3 - 12x^2}{8x^2}$
7. $\frac{132x^4}{55x}$
8. $\frac{x^2 - 2x - 15}{x^2 - 9}$

Answers

1. $x - 3$
2. $x + 9$
3. See left.
4. See left.
5. $\frac{1}{x+1}$; The excluded values are -1 and 1.
6. $\frac{x-3}{2}$; The excluded value is 0.
7. $\frac{12x^3}{5}$; The excluded value is 0.
8. $\frac{x-5}{x-3}$; The excluded values are -3 and 3.

CHAPTER 12 Quiz 3
For use after Lessons 12.5–12.7

Find the product or quotient.

1. $\frac{6x^3}{5} \cdot \frac{7}{18x^4}$
2. $\frac{20 - 4x}{25 - x^2} \div \frac{x}{5 + x}$

Find the sum or difference.

3. $\frac{3x+5}{x-6} - \frac{x-4}{x-6}$
4. $\frac{x}{x^2 + 9x + 8} + \frac{7}{x+8}$

Solve the equation. Check your solution.

5. $\frac{3x}{x+4} = \frac{x}{x-2}$
6. $\frac{3}{x+1} + \frac{1}{x-1} = 2$
7. Jeremy and Paul can plant a garden in 4 hours if they work together. If each worked alone, it would take Jeremy 6 hours longer than Paul to plant the garden. How long would it take Jeremy to plant the garden if he worked alone?

Answers

1. $\frac{7}{15x}$
2. $\frac{4}{x}$
3. $\frac{2x+9}{x-6}$
4. $\frac{8x+7}{(x+8)(x+1)}$
5. 0 and 5
6. 0 and 2
7. 12 h

12 Assessment

CHAPTER 12 Chapter Test B
For use after Chapter 12

Tell whether the table represents inverse variation. If so, write the inverse variation equation.

1.

x	−10	−5	5	10	15
y	−40	−20	20	40	60

2.

x	−8	−1	12	32	64
y	−6	−48	4	1.5	0.5

In Exercises 3 and 4, use the following information.

In chemistry, Boyle's law states that at a constant temperature, the volume V of a gas varies inversely with the pressure P. For a certain gas, the pressure is 5 when the volume is 20.

3. Write the inverse variation equation that relates V and P.

4. Find the volume of the gas when the pressure is 10.

Graph the function and identify its domain and range. Then compare the graph with the graph of $y = \frac{1}{x}$.

5. $y = \frac{2}{x+3}$

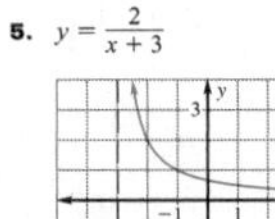

6. $y = \frac{-1}{x} + 2$

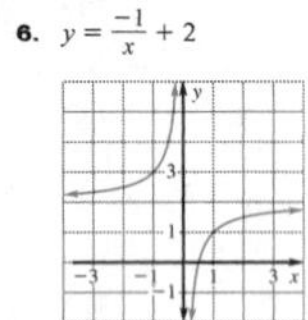

Write a function whose graph is a hyperbola that has the asymptotes and passes through the point.

7. $x = 5, y = 6$; $(4, 2)$

8. $x = -1, y = -3$; $(1, -2)$

Divide.

9. $(x^2 + 3x - 6) \div (x + 1)$

10. $(6x^2 - 3x + 5) \div (2x - 3)$

Simplify the expression, if possible. Find the excluded values.

11. $\frac{-35x^6}{25x^2}$

12. $\frac{2x - 18}{9 - x}$

13. $\frac{2x^2 - x - 15}{x^2 + x - 12}$

14. Write and simplify a rational expression for the ratio of the surface area to the volume of the rectangular solid.

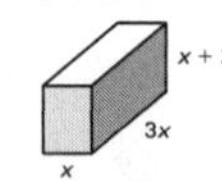

Answers

1. no
2. yes; $y = \frac{48}{x}$
3. $V = \frac{100}{P}$
4. 10
5. See left. domain: all real numbers except −3; range: all real numbers except 0; The graph is a vertical stretch and horizontal shift (of 3 units to the left) of the graph of $y = \frac{1}{x}$.
6. See left. domain: all real numbers except 0; range: all real numbers except 2; The graph is a reflection in the x-axis and a vertical shift (of 2 units up) of the graph of $y = \frac{1}{x}$.
7. $y = \frac{4}{x-5} + 6$
8. $y = \frac{2}{x+1} - 3$
9. $x + 2 + \frac{-8}{x+1}$
10. $3x + 3 + \frac{14}{2x-3}$
11. $\frac{-7x^4}{5}$; 0
12. −2; 9
13. $\frac{2x+5}{x+4}$; −4, 5
14. $\frac{2(7x+8)}{3x(x+2)}$

CHAPTER 12 Chapter Test B *continued*
For use after Chapter 12

15. The percent p of salt in a saltwater solution can be modeled by $p = \frac{100x + 100}{x + 10}$ where x is the number of grams of salt that are added to the solution. Write the model in the form $y = \frac{a}{x - h} + k$. Then graph the equation.

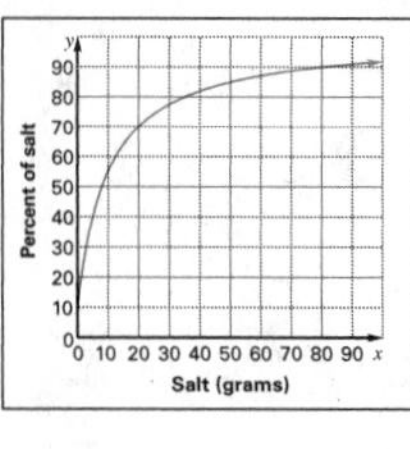

Find the product or quotient.

16. $\frac{18x^4}{25x^2} \cdot \frac{50x^5}{27x^6}$

17. $\frac{20}{x^3} \div \frac{30}{x^5}$

18. $\frac{x^2 - 9}{x + 3} \cdot \frac{1}{6 - 2x}$

19. $\frac{x^2 - 25}{x^2 - 4x - 5} \div \frac{2x + 10}{x^2 - 1}$

In Exercises 20 and 21, use the following information.

For the period of 1990-2002, the number Y of rushing yards gained by Emmitt Smith can be modeled by $Y = \frac{860 + 1800x}{1 + 0.024x}$ where x is the number of years since 1990.

20. Rewrite the model so that it has only whole number coefficients. Then simplify the model.

21. Approximate the number of rushing yards Smith gained in 1999.

Find the sum or difference.

22. $\frac{x - 2}{x + 3} + \frac{x + 8}{x + 3}$

23. $\frac{1}{3x^2} - \frac{2}{9x}$

24. $\frac{x}{x - 1} + \frac{2x + 3}{x^2 - 1}$

Solve the equation. Check your solutions.

25. $\frac{8}{x + 3} = \frac{4}{x}$

26. $\frac{3x}{x - 4} = 5 + \frac{12}{x - 4}$

27. The body mass index expresses the relationship between a person's height and weight by the equation $B = \frac{705W}{H^2}$ where H is the height (in inches) and W is the weight (in pounds). A woman weighs 160 pounds and is 5 feet 4 inches tall. How many pounds must the woman lose to lower her BMI to 25?

Answers

15. $y = \frac{-900}{x + 10} + 100$; See left.
16. $\frac{4x}{3}$
17. $\frac{2x^2}{3}$
18. $-\frac{1}{2}$
19. $\frac{x - 1}{2}$
20. $Y = \frac{860{,}000 + 1{,}800{,}000x}{1000 + 24x}$; $Y = \frac{107{,}500 + 225{,}000x}{125 + 24x}$
21. 14,030 yd
22. 2
23. $\frac{3 - 2x}{9x^2}$
24. $\frac{x^2 + 3x + 3}{(x - 1)(x + 1)}$
25. 3
26. no solution
27. about 15 pounds

CHAPTER 12 Standardized Test
For use after Chapter 12

Multiple Choice

1. Suppose that y varies inversely with x, and $y = 8$ when $x = 9$. What is the constant of variation? C

Ⓐ $\frac{9}{8}$ Ⓑ 8 Ⓒ 9 Ⓓ 72

2. Which equation represents the given graph? D

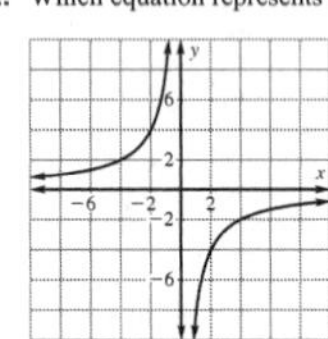

Ⓐ $y = \frac{2}{x}$ Ⓑ $y = -\frac{2}{x}$

Ⓒ $y = \frac{8}{x}$ Ⓓ $y = -\frac{8}{x}$

3. What are the vertical and horizontal asymptotes of the graph shown? B

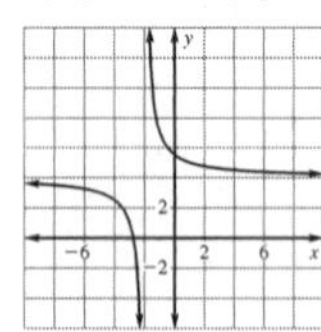

Ⓐ $x = 4, y = -2$ Ⓑ $x = -2, y = 4$

Ⓒ $x = -4, y = 2$ Ⓓ $x = 2, y = -4$

4. What is the range of the equation $y = \frac{a}{x - 2} - 5$? B

Ⓐ All real numbers except $y = 5$

Ⓑ All real numbers except $y = -5$

Ⓒ All real numbers except $x = 2$

Ⓓ All real numbers except $x = -2$

5. Which equation represents the given graph? C

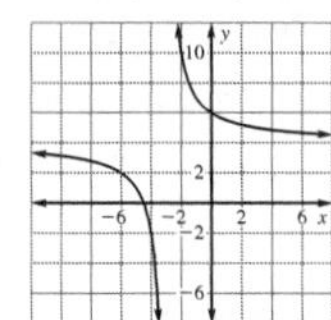

Ⓐ $y = \frac{6}{x + 3} - 4$ Ⓑ $y = \frac{6}{x - 3} - 4$

Ⓒ $y = \frac{6}{x + 3} + 4$ Ⓓ $y = \frac{6}{x - 3} + 4$

6. What is the remainder when you divide $5x^2 + 4x - 40$ by $x - 4$? D

Ⓐ $-\frac{15}{x - 4}$ Ⓑ $-\frac{24}{x - 4}$

Ⓒ $\frac{24}{x - 4}$ Ⓓ $\frac{56}{x - 4}$

7. What is the vertical asymptote of the graph of $y = \frac{bx + c}{x} + k$? A

Ⓐ $y = b$ Ⓑ $y = c$

Ⓒ $y = k$ Ⓓ $y = 0$

CHAPTER 12 Standardized Test *continued*
For use after Chapter 12

8. The expression $\frac{a}{x^2 - 9x + 20}$ simplifies to $\frac{x + 2}{x - 4}$. What is the value of a? C

Ⓐ $x^2 + 5x - 6$ Ⓑ $x^2 - 8x + 15$

Ⓒ $x^2 - 3x - 10$ Ⓓ $x^2 + 7x + 12$

9. What is the quotient $\frac{x^2 - 9}{-(x + 3)} \div (x - 3)$? A

Ⓐ −1 Ⓑ 0

Ⓒ 1 Ⓓ $-(x^2 - 9)$

10. Which is a factor of the LCD of $\frac{x - 5}{x^2 + 8x + 15}$ and $\frac{x - 2}{x^2 - 4x - 21}$? D

Ⓐ $x - 5$ Ⓑ $x - 2$

Ⓒ $x + 7$ Ⓓ $x - 7$

11. What is the solution of $\frac{4}{x - 5} = \frac{2}{x + 5} + \frac{20}{x^2 - 25}$? B

Ⓐ −10 Ⓑ −5 Ⓒ 0 Ⓓ 5

12. If the solution to the equation $\frac{6}{x - n} = \frac{10}{x + n} - \frac{4}{x^2 - n^2}$ is 9, what is the value of n? C

Ⓐ −2 Ⓑ 0 Ⓒ 2 Ⓓ 4

Gridded Answer

13. What value of x makes the expression $\frac{6}{x - 5} - 8$ undefined?

14. a. $t = \frac{300}{r} + 0.75$;

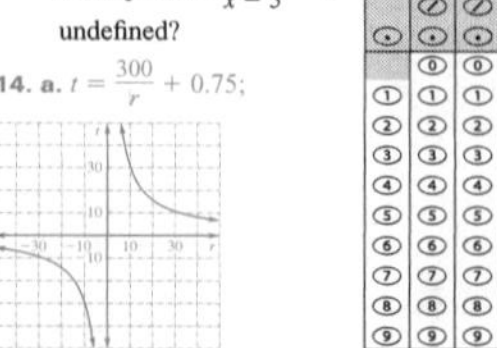

b. The graph shifts 5 units to the right and 0.25 unit down.

Short Response

14. Your aunt is driving 300 miles to your house. On her way, she takes a 45 minute lunch break. See below.

a. Write and graph an equation that gives the total time t (in hours) of your aunt's trip as a function of her average driving speed r (in miles per hour).

b. Your aunt drives to your house again. This time her average speed is 5 miles per hour less than her average driving speed in part (a), and she takes a 30 minute lunch break. *Explain* how the graph would change.

Extended Response

15. A gift wrap company offers you the opportunity to sell its gift wrap packages, but you must pay the company a one-time fee of \$350 plus \$3 for each package that you plan to sell.

a. Write an equation that gives the average cost C per package (including the fee) as a function of the number of packages p that you plan to sell.

b. You want to sell enough gift wrap packages so that the average cost C per package (including the fee) decreases to \$4. Write and solve an equation to find the number of packages you need to sell.

c. Is it possible for you to sell enough packages so that the average cost per package drops to \$2.25? *Explain* your answer. No; If you were to substitute \$2.25 for C in the equation, you would get a negative answer for p. It is not possible to sell a negative number of packages.

15. a. $C = \frac{350 + 3p}{p}$ **b.** $p = \frac{350}{C - 3}$; You would need to sell 350 packages to reduce the cost of each package to \$4.

CHAPTER 12

Alternative Assessment and Math Journal

For use after Chapter 12

Journal 1. Explain and show how to add, subtract, multiply, and divide the rational expressions $\frac{5+x}{x^2+1}$ and $\frac{4}{x-3}$.

Multi-Step Problem 2. Your family is planning a big reunion picnic at a local park. The cost to reserve a pavilion for a day is $400. It is a potluck-style picnic, but your family has agreed to purchase all of the beverages and accessories (i.e., plates, napkins, cups) for the entire group. It has been determined that the cost for these items is $4.75 per person.

a. Write a function C for the average cost (including pavilion) per person attending the picnic.

b. Graph the function in part (a).

c. If 50 people attend the picnic, what is the average cost per person?

d. How many people need to attend to get the average cost per person below $6?

e. What is the domain of this function? What is the range?

f. Describe the values for the average cost per person as the number of people increases.

g. Will the average cost per person ever go below $4.75? Explain.

1. Complete answers should include: work showing each operation being carried out; explanations of the steps being used to carry out each operation.

2. a. $C = \frac{400 + 4.75x}{x}$

b.

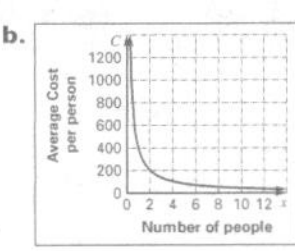

c. $12.75 **d.** over 320 people **e.** $x > 0$; $C > 4.75$ **f.** The average cost per person decreases toward 4.75 as the number of people increases. The decreases are rapid at first, but become more gradual. **g.** No, the average cost per person cannot go below $4.75. This value is a horizontal asymptote for the function. Because the extra items cost $4.75 per person and a portion of the pavilion cost will be added to this amount, the average cost per person will never drop below this amount.

CHAPTER 12

Alternative Assessment Rubric *continued*

For use after Chapter 12

Journal Solution 1. Complete answers should include:

- work showing each operation being carried out.
- explanations of the steps being used to carry out each operation.

Multi-Step Problem Solution 2. **a.** $C = \frac{400 + 4.75x}{x}$

b.

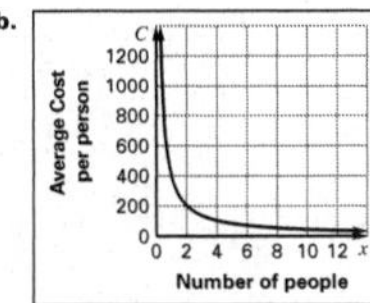

c. $12.75

d. over 320 people

e. $x > 0$; $C > 4.75$

f. The average cost per person decreases toward 4.75 as the number of people increases. The decreases are rapid at first, but become more gradual.

g. No, the average cost per person cannot go below $4.75. This value is a horizontal asymptote for the function. Because the extra items cost $4.75 per person and a portion of the pavilion cost will be added to this amount, the average cost per person will never drop below this amount.

Multi-Step Problem Rubric

4 The student answers all parts of the problem correctly and completely. The student shows all work. The student's work is neat.

3 The student answers all parts of the problem. The student's work may contain one or two errors in the calculations, graph, or equation. The student shows most work. The student's work is neat.

2 The student answers all parts of the problem, but there are more than two errors in the calculations, graph, or equation. The student shows some work. The student's work is sloppy.

1 The student does not complete all parts of the problem. The student's work has several errors in the calculations, graph, and equation. The student's work is sloppy, or no work is shown.

PLAN AND PREPARE

Main Ideas

In Chapter 12, students model inverse variation by writing and graphing inverse equations. Students graph rational equations and compare them to the parent function. They divide polynomials and then use this skill to graph rational functions. Students simplify rational expressions, stating any excluded values. They multiply, divide, add, and subtract rational expressions and then use these operations to solve rational equations.

Prerequisite Skills

- Performing operations on numerical fractions
- Solving equations
- Factoring polynomials

Additional resources for reviewing prerequisite skills are:

- Skills Review Handbook, pp. 909–937
- @HomeTutor

12 Rational Equations and Functions

Before

In previous chapters and courses, you learned the following skills, which you'll use in Chapter 12: performing operations on numerical fractions, solving equations, and factoring polynomials.

Prerequisite Skills

VOCABULARY CHECK

1. What is the **least common denominator** of $\frac{3}{8}$ and $\frac{7}{10}$? 40
2. Which equation is a **direct variation** equation, $\frac{y}{5} = x$ or $\frac{5}{y} = x$? $\frac{y}{5} = x$
3. What is the **degree** of the polynomial $4x - 2 + 5x^2$? 2
4. Identify the **extraneous solution** when solving $\sqrt{x + 2} = x$. -1

SKILLS CHECK

Factor the polynomial. *(Review pp. 583, 600, 606 for 12.4–12.6.)*

5. $x^2 - 2x - 15$ $(x - 5)(x + 3)$
6. $2x^2 - 8x + 6$ $2(x - 3)(x - 1)$
7. $9x^2 - 25$ $(3x + 5)(3x - 5)$
8. $3x^3 - 48x$ $3x(x + 4)(x - 4)$

Add, subtract, multiply, or divide. *(Review pp. 914, 915 for 12.5–12.6.)*

9. $\frac{1}{3} + \frac{3}{4}$ $1\frac{1}{12}$
10. $\frac{7}{8} - \frac{2}{5}$ $\frac{19}{40}$
11. $\frac{5}{9} \times \frac{3}{5}$ $\frac{1}{3}$
12. $\frac{3}{10} \div \frac{6}{25}$ $1\frac{1}{4}$

Solve the equation or proportion. *(Review pp. 134, 162, 583, 729 for 12.7.)*

13. $4x = 9$ $\frac{9}{4}$
14. $\frac{x}{10} = \frac{3}{5}$ 6
15. $x^2 + x = 6$ $-3, 2$
16. $\sqrt{x - 9} = 2$ 13

@HomeTutor Prerequisite skills practice at classzone.com

Chapter Planning Guide

Chapter 12 Resource Book
- Teaching Guide/Lesson Plan (pp. 3, 17, 30, 42, 54, 66, 77)
- Project with Rubric (p. 88)

Assessment and Intervention
- Assessment Book (pp. 168–182)
- Benchmark Tests
- Reteaching and Remediation Book

Interactive Technology
- Easy Planner
- Power Presentations CD-ROM
- Activity Generator CD-ROM
- Animated Algebra
- Test Generator CD-ROM
- Online Quizzes
- eWorkbook
- eEdition
- @HomeTutor

Resources for English Learners
- Quick Reference for English Learners
- Spanish Study Guide
- Multi-Language Visual Glossary
- Student Resources in Spanish

Now

In Chapter 12, you will apply the big ideas listed below and reviewed in the Chapter Summary on page 830. You will also use the key vocabulary listed below.

Big Ideas

1. **Graphing rational functions**
2. **Performing operations on rational expressions**
3. **Solving rational equations**

KEY VOCABULARY

- inverse variation, *p. 765*
- constant of variation, *p. 765*
- hyperbola, *p. 767*
- branches, asymptotes of a hyperbola, *p. 767*
- rational function, *p. 775*
- rational expression, *p. 794*
- excluded value, *p. 794*
- simplest form of a rational expression, *p. 795*
- least common denominator (LCD) of rational expressions, *p. 813*
- rational equation, *p. 820*

Why?

You can use rational functions to solve problems in biology. For example, you can graph a rational function to describe how a microorganism's efficiency at performing metabolic tasks changes as its dimensions change.

Animated Algebra

The animation illustrated below for Exercise 49 on page 791 helps you answer this question: How does changing one dimension of a cylindrical microorganism change the ratio of the cylinder's surface area to its volume?

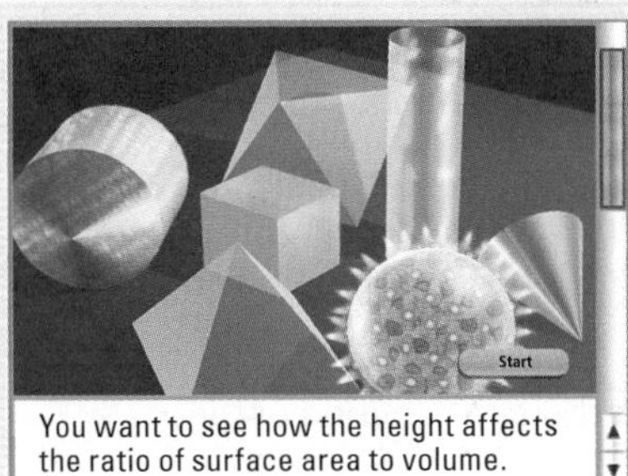

You want to see how the height affects the ratio of surface area to volume.

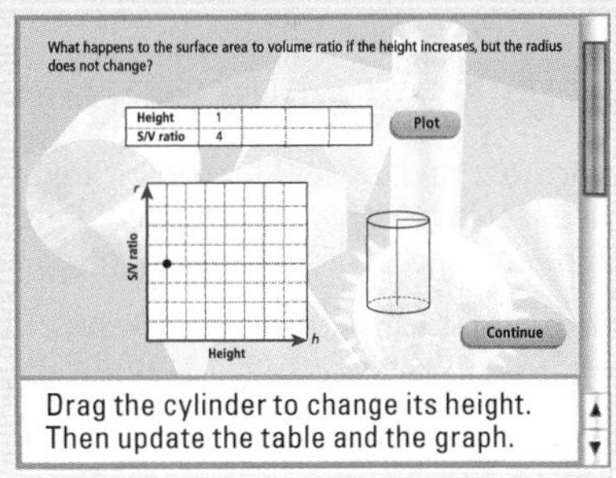

Drag the cylinder to change its height. Then update the table and the graph.

Animated Algebra at classzone.com

Other animations for Chapter 12: pages 766, 777, 783, 804, 814, and 830

763

Algebra 1 Toolkit

- Reading Strategies for Chapter 12, pp. 31–32
- Differentiated Instruction Notes, pp. 85–88
- English Learners Notes, pp. 119–120
- Inclusion Notes, pp. 151–152
- Teaching Strategies with Sample Worksheets, pp. 155–178
- Using Technology in the Classroom, pp. 179–184
- Tips for New Teachers, pp. 207–208
- Math Background Notes, pp. 233–234
- Pre-AP Strategies and Copymasters, pp. 300–301, 482–511
- Teacher Survival Activities, pp. 577–578, 603–604
- Bulletin Board Idea, p. 618
- Teacher Tool Transparencies, following p. 620

1 PLAN AND PREPARE

Explore the Concept

- Students will graph the relationship between the dimensions of a rectangle.
- This activity leads into the study of inverse variation in Lesson 12.1, Example 1.

Materials

Each student will need:

- 12 square tiles
- Activity Support Master (*Chapter 12 Resource Book*, p. 5)

Recommended Time

Work activity: 10 min

Discuss results: 5 min

Grouping

Students should work individually.

2 TEACH

Tips for Success

You may want to recommend that students form rectangles in sequence beginning with 1 column of 12 tiles, then 2 columns of 6 tiles, and so on so that they form all possible rectangles.

Key Discovery

If the product of two variables is constant, then as one variable increases the other variable decreases. Such variables are inversely related.

3 ASSESS AND RETEACH

Let A = the area of a rectangle. For $A = 48$, write an equation that gives y as a function of x. If the horizontal length x is 12, what is the vertical length y? $y = \frac{48}{x}$; 4

12.1 Relationships Between Dimensions of a Rectangle

MATERIALS • 12 square tiles

QUESTION **Given a rectangle with a fixed area, how is one dimension related to the other?**

EXPLORE **Graph the relationship between the dimensions of a rectangle**

STEP 1 ***Form rectangle***

Draw the x- and y-axes on a sheet of paper as shown. Use all of the tiles to form a rectangle in Quadrant I with the lower left vertex on the origin. Then label the upper right vertex with the coordinates (x, y) where x is the horizontal length of the rectangle and y is the vertical length.

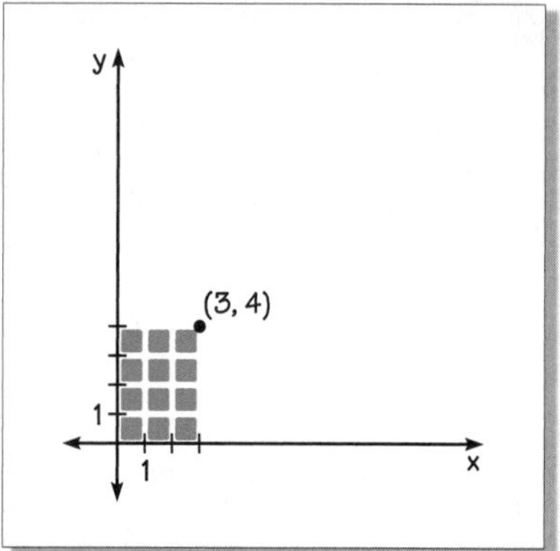

STEP 2 ***Draw curve***

Repeat Step 1 for all possible rectangles that can be formed with the tiles. Then connect the points by drawing a smooth curve through them.

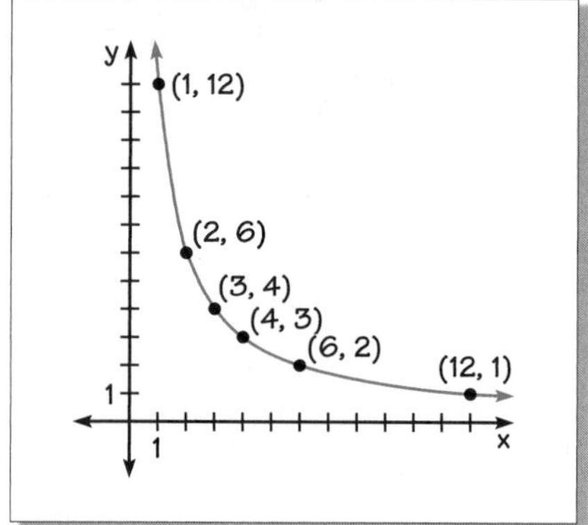

DRAW CONCLUSIONS **Use your observations to complete these exercises**

1. *Describe* how the vertical length changes as the horizontal length increases. *Describe* how the vertical length changes as the horizontal length decreases. **The vertical length decreases; the vertical length increases.**
2. Does the graph cross the axes? *Explain* your reasoning. **No; for the graph to cross an axis, one coordinate would have to be zero, but neither x nor y can be zero if their product is 12.**
3. Write an equation that gives the vertical length y as a function of the horizontal length x. $y = \frac{12}{x}$
4. Let A represent the area of a rectangle. For $A = 40$, write an equation that gives y as a function of x. Then graph the equation. $y = \frac{40}{x}$; **see margin for art.**
5. *Compare* the graph of the equation that you wrote in Exercise 4 with the graph of the equation that you wrote in Exercise 3. **See margin.**

4. 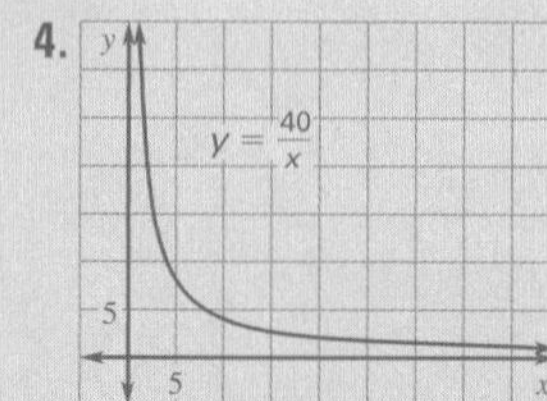

5. The two graphs have the same general shape: a wide curve in the first quadrant; the curve approaches both axes, but does not cross them.

12.1 Model Inverse Variation

 **6.11.19** Set up, evaluate, or solve problems stated in terms of direct and inverse variation of simple quantities.

Before You wrote and graphed direct variation equations.

Now You will write and graph inverse variation equations.

Why? So you can find a person's work time, as in Example 6.

Key Vocabulary
- **inverse variation**
- **constant of variation**
- **hyperbola**
- **branches of a hyperbola**
- **asymptotes of a hyperbola**

Recall that two variables x and y show direct variation if $y = ax$ and $a \neq 0$. The variables x and y show **inverse variation** if $y = \frac{a}{x}$ and $a \neq 0$. The nonzero number a is the **constant of variation**, and y is said to *vary inversely* with x.

EXAMPLE 1 Identify direct and inverse variation

Tell whether the equation represents *direct variation, inverse variation,* or *neither.*

a. $xy = 4$ **b.** $\frac{y}{2} = x$ **c.** $y = 2x + 3$

Solution

a. $xy = 4$ Write original equation.

$y = \frac{4}{x}$ Divide each side by x.

Because $xy = 4$ can be written in the form $y = \frac{a}{x}$, $xy = 4$ represents inverse variation. The constant of variation is 4.

b. $\frac{y}{2} = x$ Write original equation.

$y = 2x$ Multiply each side by 2.

Because $\frac{y}{2} = x$ can be written in the form $y = ax$, $\frac{y}{2} = x$ represents direct variation.

c. Because $y = 2x + 3$ cannot be written in the form $y = \frac{a}{x}$ or $y = ax$, $y = 2x + 3$ does not represent either direct variation or inverse variation.

 **GUIDED PRACTICE** for Example 1

Tell whether the equation represents *direct variation, inverse variation,* or *neither.*

1. $y = \frac{2}{x}$ inverse variation **2.** $4y = 3x$ direct variation **3.** $5x - y = 3$ neither **4.** $xy = \frac{1}{2}$ inverse variation

1 PLAN AND PREPARE

Warm-Up Exercises

Transparency Available

1. Rewrite $2x - 5y = 0$ as a direct variation equation. $y = \frac{2}{5}x$

2. The number of words w you type on a keyboard varies directly with the number of minutes m that you type. You can type 360 words in 8 minutes. How many words can you type in 12 minutes? 540 words

Notetaking Guide

Transparency Available

Promotes interactive learning and notetaking skills, pp. 267–270.

Pacing

Basic: 2 days
Average: 2 days
Advanced: 2 days
Block: 1 block
- See *Teaching Guide/Lesson Plan.*

2 FOCUS AND MOTIVATE

Essential Question

Big Idea 1, p. 763

How do you graph and solve inverse variation equations? Tell students they will learn how to answer this question by using tables to graph equations and by using x- and y-values to write equations.

Resource Planning Guide

Chapter Resource Book
- Teaching Guide/Lesson Plan (pp. 3–4)
- Practice levels A, B, C (pp. 6–11)
- Study Guide (pp. 12–13)
- Catch-up for Absent Students (p. 14)
- Application (p. 15)
- Challenge (p. 16)

Workbooks
- Notetaking Guide (pp. 267–270)
- Practice Workbook (pp. 180–182)

Teaching Options
- **Power Presentations CD-ROM** provides dynamic electronic teaching resources for the classroom.
- **Activity Generator CD-ROM** provides editable activities for all ability levels.

Interactive Technology
- Easy Planner
- Power Presentations CD-ROM
- Activity Generator CD-ROM
- Animated Algebra
- Test Generator CD-ROM
- Online Quiz
- eWorkbook
- eEdition
- @HomeTutor

Resources for English Learners
- Quick Reference for English Learners
- Spanish Study Guide
- Multi-Language Visual Glossary
- Student Resources in Spanish

See also the *Algebra 1 Toolkit* for more strategies for meeting individual needs.

Motivating the Lesson

You are part of a crew that is cleaning up after a football game. By knowing how to write and solve an inverse variation equation, you can determine how long it will take to clean the grounds depending on whether there are 2, 3, 4 or more students in the cleaning crew.

3 TEACH

Extra Example 1

Tell whether the equation represents *direct variation*, *inverse variation*, or *neither*.

a. $xy = 7$ inverse variation

b. $\frac{x}{y} = 2$ direct variation

c. $3x - y = 5$ neither

Extra Example 2

Graph $y = \frac{2}{x}$.

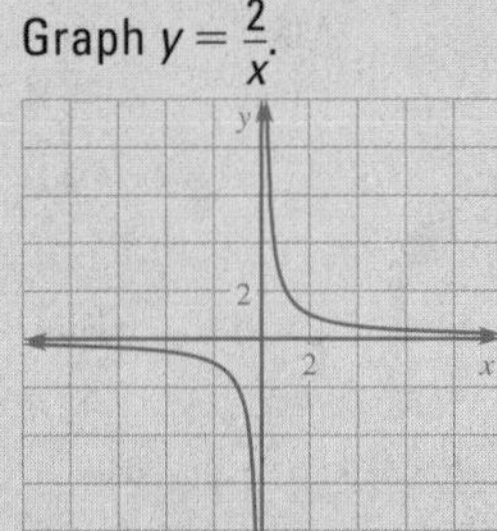

Key Question to Ask for Example 2

- How is the graph of an inverse variation equation different from the graph of a direct variation equation? The graph of an inverse variation equation is a two-part curve and it does not cross the *x*- or *y*-axis. The graph of a direct variation equation is a line and it passes through the origin.

EXAMPLE 2 Graph an inverse variation equation

Graph $y = \frac{4}{x}$.

Solution

STEP 1 **Make** a table by choosing several integer values of x and finding the values of y. Then plot the points. To see how the function behaves for values of x very close to 0 and very far from 0, make a second table for such values and plot the points.

AVOID ERRORS
Note that y is undefined when $x = 0$. There is no point $(0, y)$ on the graph of $y = \frac{4}{x}$.

x	y
−4	−1
−2	−2
−1	−4
0	undefined
1	4
2	2
4	1

x	y
−10	−0.4
−5	−0.8
−0.5	−8
−0.4	−10
0.4	10
0.5	8
5	0.8
10	0.4

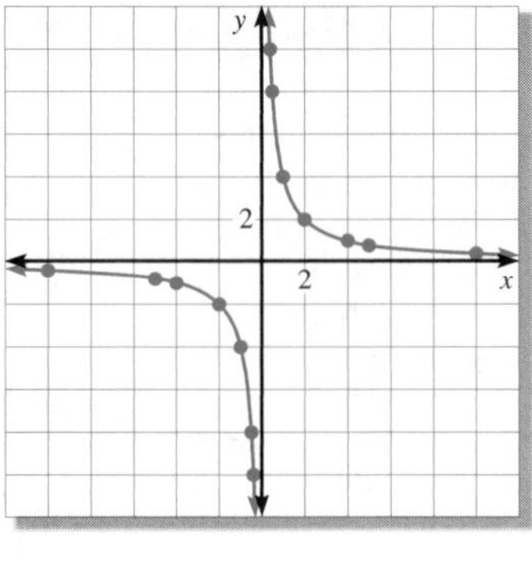

STEP 2 **Connect** the points in Quadrant I by drawing a smooth curve through them. Repeat for the points in Quadrant III.

GRAPHS OF INVERSE VARIATION As shown in Example 2, as you move away from the origin along the x-axis, the graph of an inverse variation equation approaches the x-axis without crossing it. As you move away from the origin along the y-axis, the graph approaches the y-axis without crossing it.

EXAMPLE 3 Graph an inverse variation equation

Graph $y = \frac{-4}{x}$.

Solution

COMPARE GRAPHS
The graph of an inverse variation equation lies in Quadrants I and III if $a > 0$, and the graph lies in Quadrants II and IV if $a < 0$.

Notice that $y = \frac{-4}{x} = -1 \cdot \frac{4}{x}$. So, for every nonzero value of x, the value of y in $y = \frac{-4}{x}$ is the opposite of the value of y in $y = \frac{4}{x}$. You can graph $y = \frac{-4}{x}$ by reflecting the graph of $y = \frac{4}{x}$ (see Example 2) in the x-axis.

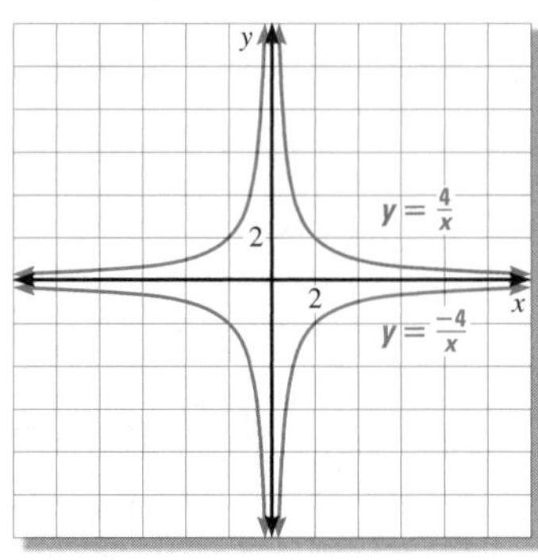

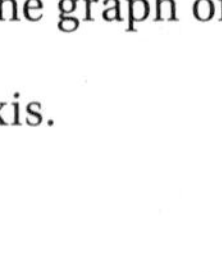
at classzone.com

CONCEPT SUMMARY *For Your Notebook*

Graphs of Direct Variation and Inverse Variation Equations

Direct variation		Inverse variation	
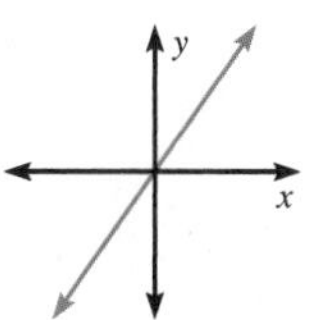	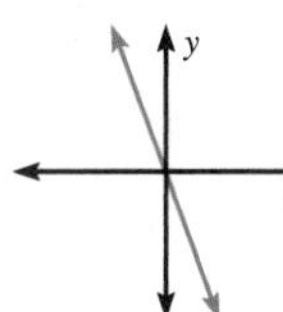	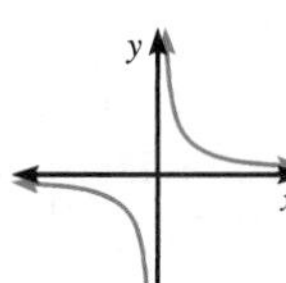	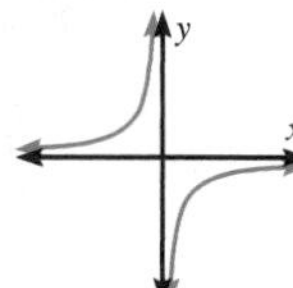
$y = ax, a > 0$	$y = ax, a < 0$	$y = \frac{a}{x}, a > 0$	$y = \frac{a}{x}, a < 0$

HYPERBOLAS The graph of the inverse variation equation $y = \frac{a}{x}$ $(a \neq 0)$ is a **hyperbola**. The two symmetrical parts of a hyperbola are called the **branches of the hyperbola**. The lines that the hyperbola approaches but doesn't intersect are called the **asymptotes of the hyperbola**. The asymptotes of the graph of $y = \frac{a}{x}$ are the x-axis and the y-axis.

EXAMPLE 4 Use an inverse variation equation

The variables x and y vary inversely, and $y = 6$ when $x = -3$.

a. Write an inverse variation equation that relates x and y.

b. Find the value of y when $x = 4$.

Solution

a. Because y varies inversely with x, the equation has the form $y = \frac{a}{x}$.

Use the fact that $x = -3$ and $y = 6$ to find the value of a.

$y = \frac{a}{x}$ Write inverse variation equation.

$6 = \frac{a}{-3}$ Substitute -3 for x and 6 for y.

$-18 = a$ Multiply each side by -3.

An equation that relates x and y is $y = \frac{-18}{x}$.

b. When $x = 4$, $y = \frac{-18}{4} = -\frac{9}{2}$.

✓ GUIDED PRACTICE for Examples 2, 3, and 4

5. Graph **(a)** $y = \frac{3}{x}$ and **(b)** $y = \frac{-3}{x}$. See margin.

6. The variables x and y vary inversely, and $y = -2$ when $x = 12$. Write an inverse variation equation that relates x and y. Then find the value of y when $x = -3$. $y = \frac{-24}{x}$; 8

Extra Example 3

Graph $y = \frac{-2}{x}$.

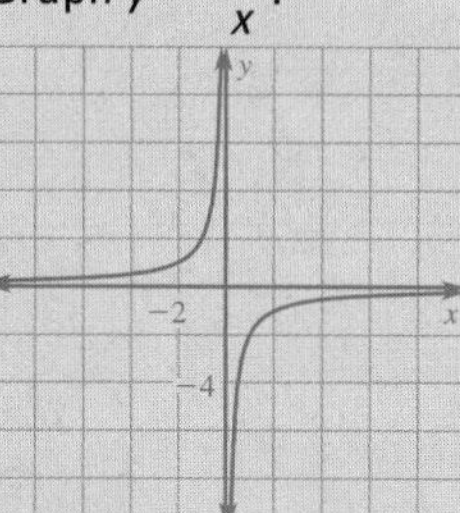

Key Questions to Ask for Example 3

- In which quadrants is the graph of the equation $y = \frac{-4}{x}$? II and IV
- What would happen if you reflected the graph of $y = \frac{-4}{x}$ in the x-axis? The new graph represents $y = \frac{4}{x}$ and lies in quadrants I and III.

An **Animated Algebra** activity is available on-line for **Example 3**. This activity is also available on the **Power Presentations CD-ROM**.

Extra Example 4

The variables x and y vary inversely, and $y = 2$ when $x = -6$.

a. Write an inverse variation equation that relates x and y. $y = \frac{-12}{x}$

b. Find the value of y when $x = 8$. $-\frac{3}{2}$

Key Questions to Ask for Example 4

- What is the constant of the inverse variation equation in part (a)? −18
- If you graph the equation in part (a), in which quadrants is it? II and IV

Differentiated Instruction

Inclusion Some students may confuse direct and inverse variation. For problems similar to **Example 4**, give additional practice by having students find the direct variation equation under the same conditions. Then have students graph both the inverse variation and direct variation equations on the same graph.

See also the *Algebra 1 Toolkit* for more strategies.

5a.

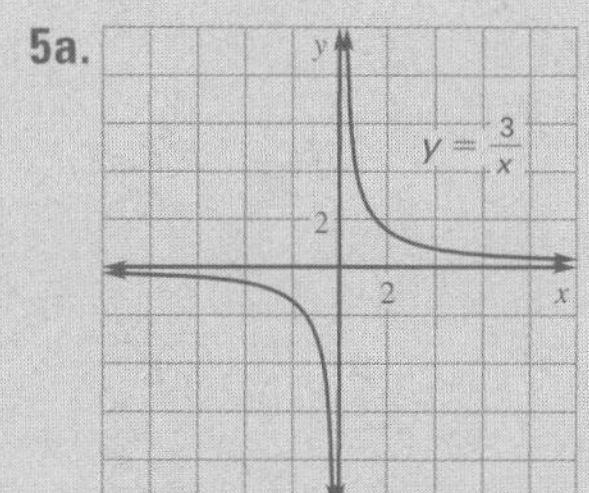

5b.

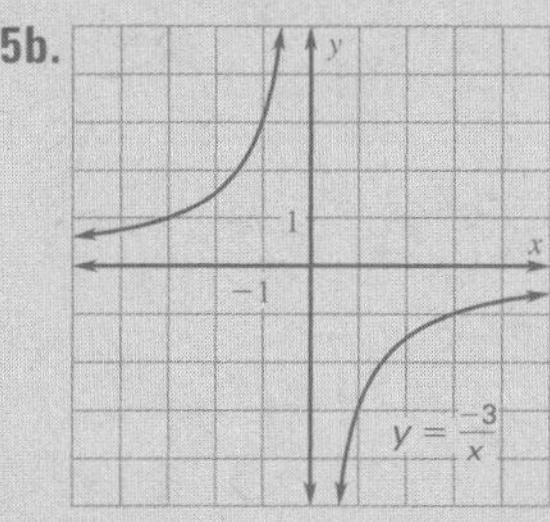

PRODUCTS By multiplying both sides of $y = \frac{a}{x}$ by x, you can write the equation as $xy = a$. This means that a set of ordered pairs (x, y) shows inverse variation if all the products xy are constant.

EXAMPLE 5 Write an inverse variation equation

Tell whether the table represents inverse variation. If so, write the inverse variation equation.

x	−5	−3	4	8	24
y	2.4	4	−3	−1.5	−0.5

Solution

Find the products xy for all pairs (x, y):

$-5(2.4) = -12 \quad -3(4) = -12 \quad 4(-3) = -12 \quad 8(-1.5) = -12 \quad 24(-0.5) = -12$

The products are equal to the same number, −12. So, y varies inversely with x.

▶ The inverse variation equation is $xy = -12$, or $y = \frac{-12}{x}$.

EXAMPLE 6 Solve a multi-step problem

THEATER A theater company plans to hire people to build a stage set. The work time t (in hours per person) varies inversely with the number p of people hired. The company estimates that 25 people working for 300 hours each can complete the job. Find the work time per person if the company hires 30 people.

Solution

STEP 1 **Write** the inverse variation equation that relates p and t.

$t = \frac{a}{p}$ — **Write inverse variation equation.**

$300 = \frac{a}{25}$ — **Substitute 25 for p and 300 for t.**

$7500 = a$ — **Multiply each side by 25.**

The inverse variation equation is $t = \frac{7500}{p}$.

STEP 2 **Find** t when $p = 30$: $t = \frac{7500}{p} = \frac{7500}{30} = 250$.

▶ If 30 people are hired, the work time per person is 250 hours.

GUIDED PRACTICE for Examples 5 and 6

7. Tell whether the ordered pairs (−5, 2), (−4, 2.5), (8, −1.25), and (20, −0.5) represent inverse variation. If so, write the inverse variation equation. **inverse variation; $y = \frac{-10}{x}$**

8. **WHAT IF?** In Example 6, suppose the theater company estimates that 20 people working for 270 hours each can complete the job. Find the work time per person if the company hires 30 people. **180 hours per person**

Extra Example 5

Tell whether the table represents inverse variation. If so, write the inverse variation equation. **yes; $xy = 8$ or $y = \frac{8}{x}$**

x	−5	−2	4	10	16
y	−1.6	−4	2	0.8	0.5

Extra Example 6

The coaches of a youth baseball league estimate that 15 adults working for 25 hours each can repaint all of the bleachers in time for the baseball season. The work time t (in hours) varies inversely with the number of adults a who volunteer to repaint the bleachers. Find the total work time per person if there are 75 adult volunteers. **5 h**

Closing the Lesson

Have students summarize the major points of the lesson and answer the Essential Question: How do you graph and solve inverse variation equations?

- **Write an inverse variation equation in the form $y = \frac{a}{x}$, where a is the constant of variation.**
- **The graph of an inverse variation equation is a hyperbola. The hyperbola approaches the x- and y-axes, but does not intersect the axes.**

To graph an inverse variation equation, make a table of positive and negative values of x, some close to 0 and some far away from 0. Plot and connect the points. The resulting curve is a hyperbola. Write an inverse variation equation by substituting values for y and x in the form $y = \frac{a}{x}$ and then solving for a.

15–26. See Additional Answers beginning on p. AA1.

28. $y = \frac{10}{x}$; 5

29. $y = \frac{21}{x}$; 10.5

30. $y = \frac{-20}{x}$; −10

12.1 EXERCISES

HOMEWORK KEY

○ = **WORKED-OUT SOLUTIONS** on p. WS28 for Exs. 17, 33, and 57

★ = **STANDARDIZED TEST PRACTICE** Exs. 2, 43, 59, and 60

◆ = **MULTIPLE REPRESENTATIONS** Ex. 58

SKILL PRACTICE

A

1. **VOCABULARY** Identify the constant of variation in the equation $y = \frac{-3}{x}$. −3

2. ★ **WRITING** *Describe* the difference between a direct variation equation and an inverse variation equation. In direct variation, y is the product of x and the constant of variation; in inverse variation, y is the quotient of the constant of variation and x.

EXAMPLE 1 on p. 765 for Exs. 3–14, 43

DESCRIBING EQUATIONS Tell whether the equation represents *direct variation, inverse variation,* or *neither.*

3. $y = -2x$ direct variation	4. $xy = 1$ inverse variation	5. $y = x + 5$ neither	6. $x = \frac{-1}{y}$ inverse variation
7. $xy = 5$ inverse variation	8. $\frac{y}{x} = 4$ direct variation	9. $x = 7y$ direct variation	10. $2x + y = 6$ neither
11. $2x = \frac{8}{y}$ inverse variation	12. $x = -7$ neither	13. $3x - 3y = 0$ direct variation	14. $3xy = 20$ inverse variation

EXAMPLES 2 and 3 on p. 766 for Exs. 15–26

GRAPHING EQUATIONS Graph the inverse variation equation. 15–26. See margin.

15. $y = \frac{2}{x}$	16. $y = \frac{-1}{x}$	(17.) $y = \frac{-7}{x}$	18. $y = \frac{10}{x}$
19. $y = \frac{-5}{x}$	20. $y = \frac{18}{x}$	21. $y = \frac{9}{x}$	22. $y = \frac{-2}{x}$
23. $y = \frac{15}{x}$	24. $y = \frac{6}{x}$	25. $y = \frac{-12}{x}$	26. $y = \frac{-8}{x}$

EXAMPLE 4 on p. 767 for Exs. 27–42

27. An inverse variation equation has the form $y = \frac{a}{x}$, not $y = ax$; $8 = \frac{a}{2}$, $16 = a$, so $y = \frac{16}{x}$.

27. **ERROR ANALYSIS** The variables x and y vary inversely, and $y = 8$ when $x = 2$. *Describe* and correct the error in writing an inverse variation equation that relates x and y.

$y = ax$
$8 = a(2)$
$4 = a$
So, $y = 4x$.

USE INVERSE VARIATION Given that y varies inversely with x, use the specified values to write an inverse variation equation that relates x and y. Then find the value of y when $x = 2$. 28–42. See margin.

28. $x = 5, y = 2$	29. $x = 3, y = 7$	30. $x = -5, y = 4$
31. $x = 13, y = -1$	32. $x = -15, y = -15$	(33.) $x = -22, y = -6$
34. $x = 8, y = 3$	35. $x = 9, y = -2$	36. $x = 3, y = 3$
37. $x = -2, y = -10$	38. $x = -3, y = 40$	39. $x = -7, y = -10$
40. $x = -17, y = 8$	41. $x = 6, y = 11$	42. $x = -12, y = -13$

43. ★ **MULTIPLE CHOICE** The variables x and y vary inversely, and $y = 6$ when $x = 4$. What is the constant of variation? D

(A) 1.5 (B) 4 (C) 6 (D) 24

31. $y = \frac{-13}{x}$; −6.5	35. $y = \frac{-18}{x}$; −9	39. $y = \frac{70}{x}$; 35
32. $y = \frac{225}{x}$; 112.5	36. $y = \frac{9}{x}$; 4.5	40. $y = \frac{-136}{x}$; −68
33. $y = \frac{132}{x}$; 66	37. $y = \frac{20}{x}$; 10	41. $y = \frac{66}{x}$; 33
34. $y = \frac{27}{x}$; 12	38. $y = \frac{-120}{x}$; −60	42. $y = \frac{156}{x}$; 78

4 PRACTICE AND APPLY

Assignment Guide

Answer Transparencies available for all exercises

Basic:
Day 1: pp. 769–772
Exs. 1–26
Day 2: pp. 769–772
Exs. 27–43 odd, 44–49, 54–59, 62–74 even

Average:
Day 1: pp. 769–772
Exs. 1, 2, 6–26, 49–51
Day 2: pp. 769–772
Exs. 27, 35–48, 54–60, 63–73 odd

Advanced:
Day 1: pp. 769–772
Exs. 1, 2, 7–26, 49–51
Day 2: pp. 769–772
Exs. 37–48, 52–61*, 62–74 even

Block:
pp. 769–772
Exs. 1, 2, 6–27, 35–51, 54–60, 63–73 odd

Differentiated Instruction

See *Algebra 1 Best Practices Toolkit* for suggestions on addressing the needs of a diverse classroom.

Homework Check

For a quick check of student understanding of key concepts, go over the following exercises:

Basic: 8, 18, 31, 44, 55
Average: 11, 22, 38, 54, 55
Advanced: 13, 23, 40, 56, 57

Extra Practice

- Student Edition, p. 946
- Chapter 12 Resource Book: Practice levels A, B, C, pp. 6–11

Practice Worksheet

An easily-readable reduced practice page (with answers) for this lesson can be found on p. 762C.

Avoiding Common Errors

Exercises 28–42, 43 Watch for students who use the direct variation form of an equation rather than the inverse variation form. Suggest that students examine the values of x and y to make sure that the value of one variable increases as the value of the other variable decreases.

Study Strategy

Exercise 55 Encourage students to use two steps to solve this problem, using Example 6 as a model.

48. Divided by 2; divided by 3. *Sample answer:* Let $x = 2$ in the inverse variation equation $y = \frac{12}{x}$, then $y = \frac{12}{2} = 6$. If x is doubled, then $x = 2(2) = 4$ and $y = \frac{12}{4} = 3 = \frac{6}{2}$, so y is divided by 2. If x is tripled, then $x = 3(2) = 6$ and $y = \frac{12}{6} = 2 = \frac{6}{3}$, so y is divided by 3.

56. $t = \frac{200}{r}$;

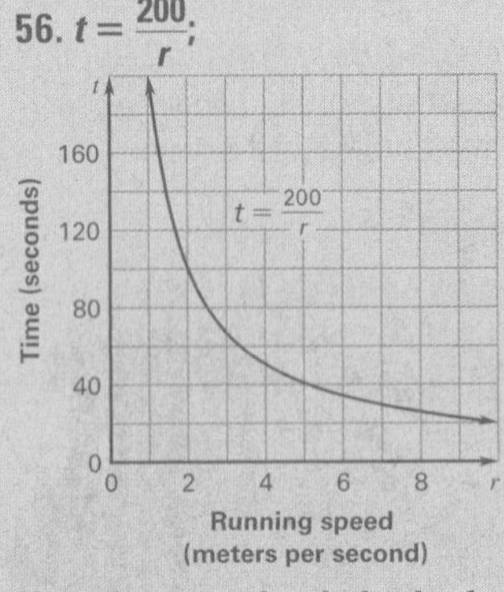

Yes; the equation is in the form $y = \frac{a}{x}$.

57a.

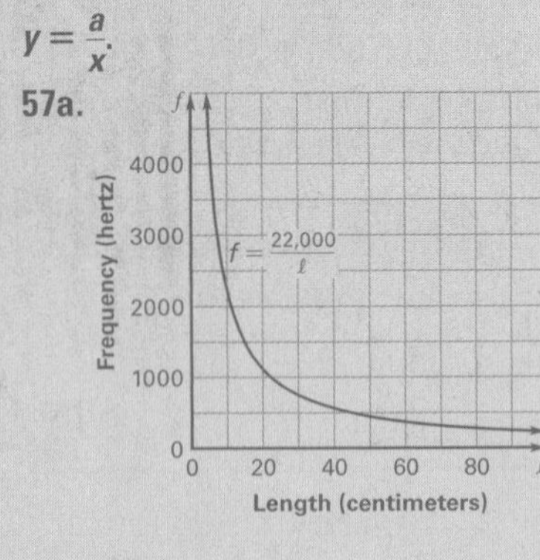

EXAMPLE 5 on p. 768 for Exs. 44–47

WRITING EQUATIONS **Tell whether the table represents inverse variation. If so, write the inverse variation equation.**

44.

x	4	8	12	16	20
y	1	2	3	4	5

not inverse variation

45.

x	−20	−5	14	32	50
y	−80	−20	56	128	200

not inverse variation

46.

x	−10	−5	15	20	40
y	−30	−60	20	15	7.5

inverse variation; $y = \frac{300}{x}$

47.

x	−12	−10	−8	−5	−4
y	2	2.4	3	4.8	6

inverse variation; $y = \frac{-24}{x}$

B

48. REASONING The variables x and y vary inversely. How does the value of y change if the value of x is doubled? tripled? Give examples. See margin.

GEOMETRY **Translate the verbal sentence into an equation using the appropriate geometric formula. Then tell whether the equation represents *direct variation, inverse variation,* or *neither.***

49. The circumference of a circle with radius r units is C units. $2\pi r = C$; direct variation

50. The perimeter of a rectangle with length ℓ units and width w units is 27 units. $2\ell + 2w = 27$; neither

51. The volume of a rectangular prism with base B square units and height h units is 400 cubic units. $Bh = 400$; inverse variation

C

52. CHALLENGE The variables x and y vary inversely with constant of variation a. The variables y and z vary inversely with constant of variation b. Write an equation that gives z as a function of x. Then tell whether x and z vary *directly* or *inversely*. $z = \frac{b}{a} \cdot x$; directly

53. CHALLENGE The points $(3, a^2 - 7a + 10)$ and $(3a + 1, a + 2)$ lie on the graph of an inverse variation equation. Find the coordinates of the points. (3, 4), (4, 3)

Problem Solving

EXAMPLE 5 on p. 768 for Exs. 54, 57

A

54. BICYCLES The table shows the bicycle speed s (in miles per hour) for various pedaling speeds p (in pedal rotations per mile). Tell whether the table represents inverse variation. If so, write the inverse variation equation that relates p and s.

54. inverse variation; $s = \frac{3600}{p}$

Pedaling speed, p (pedal rotations/mi)	831	612	420	305
Bicycle speed, s (mi/h)	4.33	5.88	8.57	11.8

@HomeTutor for problem solving help at classzone.com

EXAMPLE 6 on p. 768 for Exs. 55–56, 58

55. ECONOMICS The owner of an electronics store determines that the monthly demand d (in units) for a computer varies inversely with the price p (in dollars) of the computer. When the price is \$700, the monthly demand is 250 units. Write the inverse variation equation that relates p and d. Then find the monthly demand when the price is \$500. $d = \frac{175{,}000}{p}$; 350 units

@HomeTutor for problem solving help at classzone.com

○ = WORKED-OUT SOLUTIONS on p. WS1 ★ = STANDARDIZED TEST PRACTICE ◆ = MULTIPLE REPRESENTATIONS

56. SPORTS An athlete is running a 200 meter dash. Write and graph an equation that relates the athlete's average running speed r (in meters per second) and the time t (in seconds) that the athlete will take to finish the race. Is the equation an inverse variation equation? *Explain.* **See margin.**

57. MULTI-STEP PROBLEM The table shows the vibration frequencies f (in hertz) for various lengths ℓ (in centimeters) of strings on a stringed instrument.

Length of string, ℓ (cm)	42.1	37.5	33.4	31.5
Frequency, f (Hz)	523	587	659	698

a. **Decide** Tell whether an inverse variation equation can be used to model the data. If so, write and graph the inverse variation equation.

b. **Calculate** Find the frequency of a string with a length of 29.4 centimeters. **about 748 Hz**

c. **Describe** *Describe* the change in the frequency as the length of the string decreases. Does your answer in part (b) support your description? **The frequency increases; yes.**

57a. Yes; $f = \frac{22{,}000}{\ell}$; see margin for art.

58. MULTIPLE REPRESENTATIONS You plan to save the same amount of money each month to pay for a summer sports camp that costs $1200.

a. **Making a Table** Let a represent the amount (in dollars) that you plan to save each month. Make a table that shows the number m of months that you need to save money for the following values of a: 75, 100, 120, 150, 200, and 240. *Describe* how the number of months changes as the amount of money that you save each month increases. **a, b. See margin.**

b. **Drawing a Graph** Use the values in the table to draw a graph of the situation. Does the graph suggest a situation that represents *direct variation* or *inverse variation*? *Explain* your choice.

c. **Writing an Equation** Write the equation that relates a and m. $m = \frac{1200}{a}$

B

59. ★ SHORT RESPONSE As shown in the diagram, the focal length of a camera lens is the distance between the lens and the point at which light rays meet after passing through the aperture, or opening, in the lens. The f-stop s is the ratio of the focal length f (in millimeters) to the diameter a (in millimeters) of the aperture.

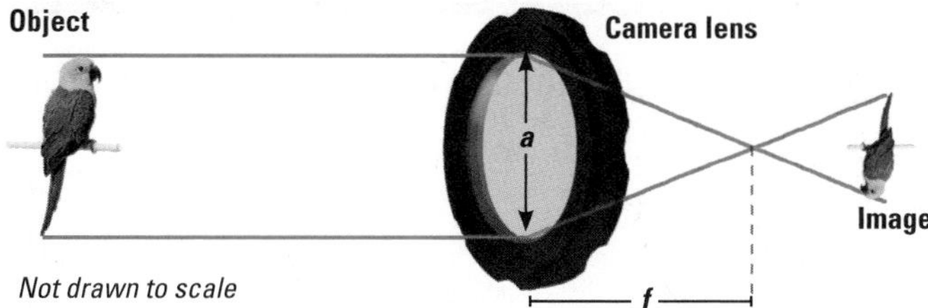

a. **Model** A photographer has a camera with a focal length of 35 millimeters. Write and graph an equation that relates a and s. Tell whether the equation represents inverse variation.

b. **Compare** The greater the diameter of the aperture, the more light that passes through the aperture. For the camera in part (a), does more light pass through the aperture when the f-stop is 4 or when the f-stop is 8? *Explain.*

59a. $s = \frac{35}{a}$, see margin for art, inverse variation.

59b. 4; when $s = 4$, the diameter of the aperture is $a = \frac{35}{4} =$ 8.75 millimeters, and when $s = 8$, the diameter of the aperture is $a = \frac{35}{8} =$ 4.375 millimeters.

Avoiding Common Errors

Exercise 56 Some students may think that 200 meters represents a variable in the inverse variation equation. Ask them if 200 meters is constant or if it varies, leading them to the idea that, for this exercise, d is constant and r and t are the variables.

Mathematical Reasoning

Exercise 58 In part (b), have students use 5 to 7 values, with increments of 10 or 20, so that their graphs clearly show the Quadrant-I branch of a hyperbola.

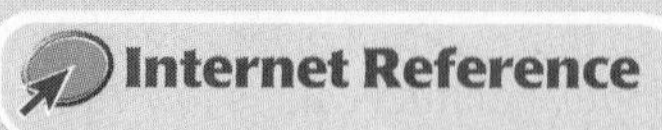

Exercise 60 More information about the aspect ratio of a wing can be found at www.grc.nasa.gov/WWW/K-12/airplane/geom.html

58b.

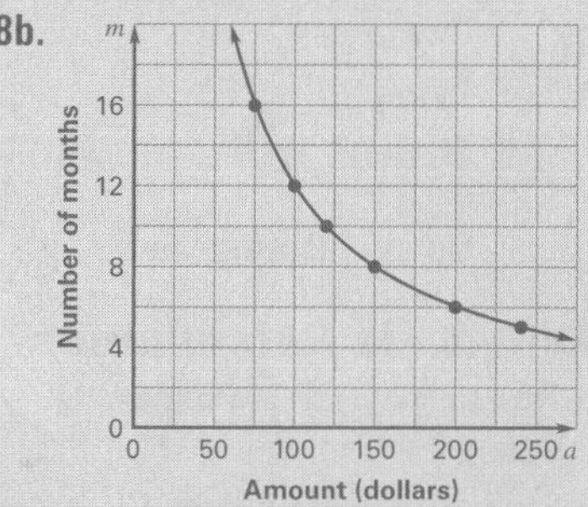

Inverse variation; the points (a, m) appear to lie on a hyperbola.

59a.

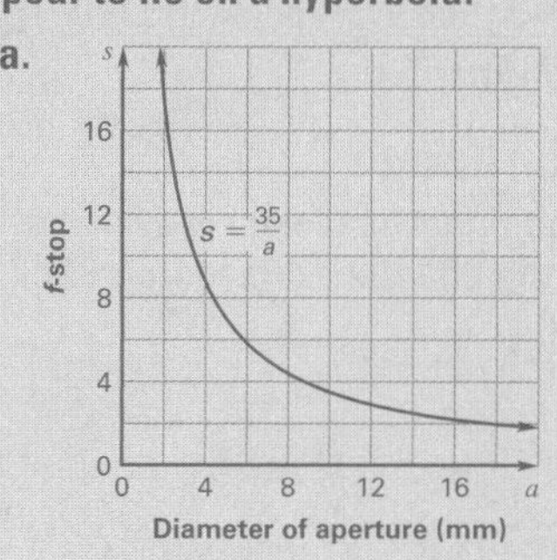

58a.

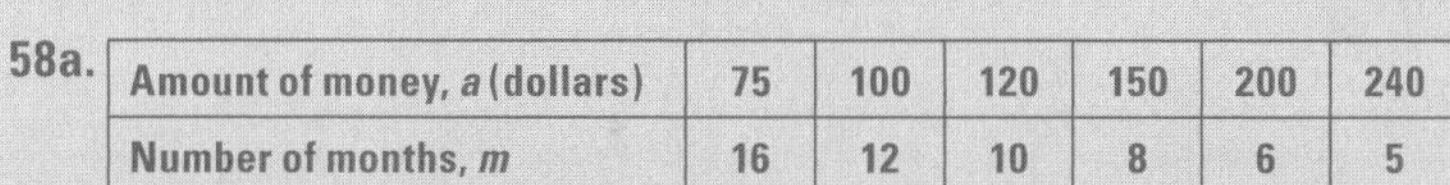

Amount of money, a (dollars)	75	100	120	150	200	240
Number of months, m	16	12	10	8	6	5

The number of months decreases.

5 ASSESS AND RETEACH

Daily Homework Quiz

Transparency Available

1. Graph $y = \frac{-6}{x}$.

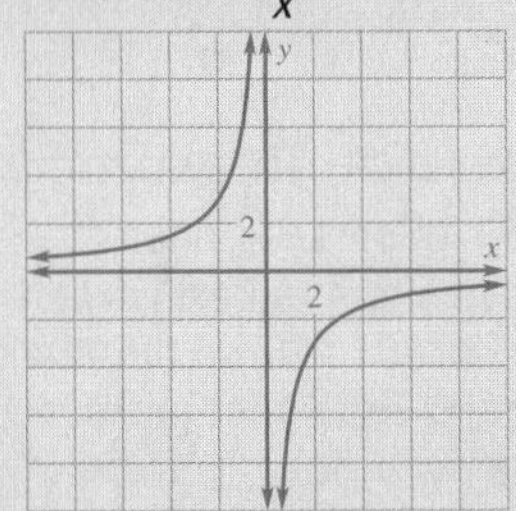

Given that y varies inversely with x, use the specified values to write an inverse variation equation that relates x and y. Then find the value of y when $x = 3$.

2. $x = -6, y = 5$ $y = -\frac{30}{x}$; -10

3. $x = 12, y = 7$ $y = \frac{84}{x}$; 28

Available at **classzone.com**

Diagnosis/Remediation

- Practice A, B, C in Chapter 12 Resource Book, pp. 6–11
- Study Guide in Chapter 12 Resource Book, pp. 12–13
- Practice Workbook, pp. 180–182
- @HomeTutor

Challenge

Additional challenge is available in the Chapter 12 Resource Book, p. 16.

60c. $0 < c < 6$; substituting $\frac{20}{3}$ for r and 40 for s in the formula $r = \frac{s}{c}$ gives a value of $c = 6$ feet for the chord of a wing of the Wright brothers' airplane. The aspect ratio $r = \frac{40}{c}$ gets larger when the denominator c gets smaller; so, $0 < c < 6$ are the values of c for which the plane would have glided more easily.

60. ★ **EXTENDED RESPONSE** The photo below shows a replica of an airplane designed by Orville and Wilbur Wright, who were aviation pioneers in the early 20th century. The aspect ratio r of a wing from similar airplanes is given by the formula $r = \frac{s^2}{A}$ where s is the span, or the distance (in feet) between the wing tips, and A is the area (in square feet) of the wing.

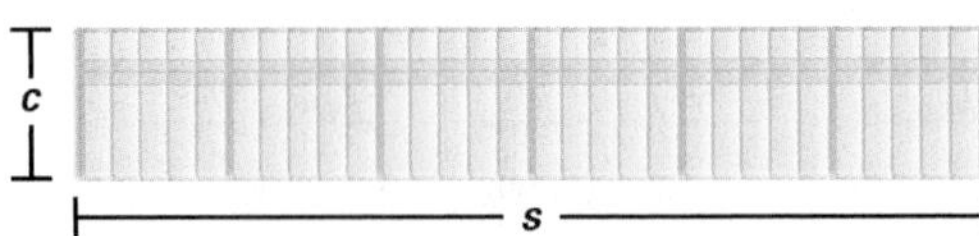

a. **Model** The length c of the chord of a wing is the distance (in feet) between the front and the back of the wing. For the rectangular wing shown, rewrite the formula for r in terms of c and s. $r = \frac{s}{c}$

b. **Analyze** How does the value of r change when s is constant and c increases? when c is constant and s increases? r decreases; r increases.

c. **Interpret** The greater the aspect ratio, the easier it is for an airplane to glide. Orville and Wilbur Wright designed an airplane with two rectangular wings that each had an aspect ratio of $\frac{20}{3}$ and a span of 40 feet. For what values of c would the airplane have glided more easily? *Explain.* See margin.

61. **CHALLENGE** A fulcrum is placed under the center of a board. In order for two objects to balance on the board, the distance (in feet) of each object from the center of the board must vary inversely with its weight (in pounds). In the diagram shown, what is the distance of each animal from the center of the board? The dog is 1.875 feet from the fulcrum and the cat is 3.125 feet from the fulcrum.

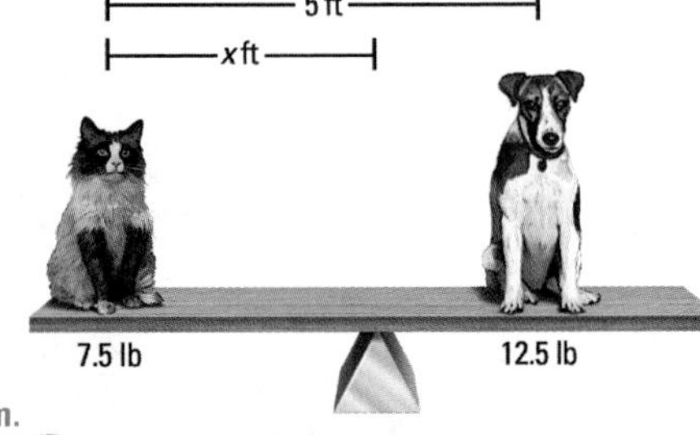

ILLINOIS MIXED REVIEW

TEST PRACTICE at classzone.com

62. If $y = -2x^2$, what is equivalent to $2y^3$? C

(A) $-16x^8$ (B) $-4x^8$ (C) $-16x^6$ (D) $-4x^6$

63. What is the area of the largest square in the diagram?

(A) $\sqrt{10}$ units^2

(B) 4 units^2

(C) 10 units^2

(D) 12 units^2

C

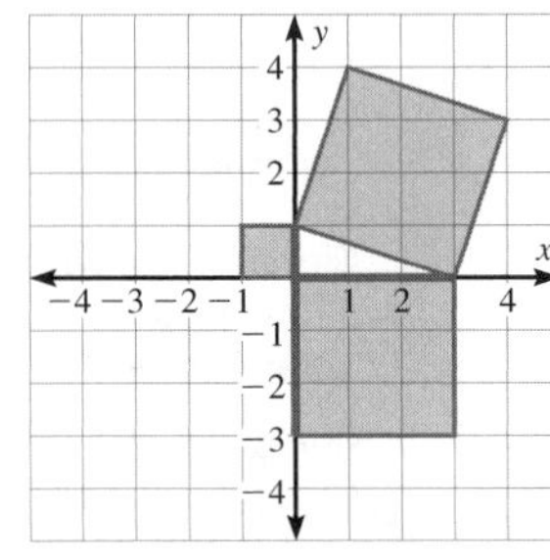

12.2 Graphing $y = \frac{a}{x - h} + k$

MATERIALS • graph paper • graphing calculator

QUESTION What characteristics does the graph of $y = \frac{a}{x - h} + k$ have?

EXPLORE 1 Use tables to graph a function

Graph $y = \frac{2}{x - 3} + 4$ using a table.

***STEP 1* Use a table**

Make a table of values for $y = \frac{2}{x - 3} + 4$ by choosing several integer values of x. Round the values of y, if necessary. Then plot the points.

x	0	1	2	3	4	5	6
y	3.3	3	2	undefined	6	5	4.7

***STEP 2* Check close to and far from 3**

To see how the function behaves for values of x closer to 3 and farther from 3, make tables for such values and plot the points.

x	2.2	2.4	2.6	2.8	3.2	3.4	3.6
y	1.5	0.7	−1	−6	14	9	7.3

x	−4	−3	−2	−1	7	8	9
y	3.71	3.66	3.6	3.5	4.5	4.4	4.3

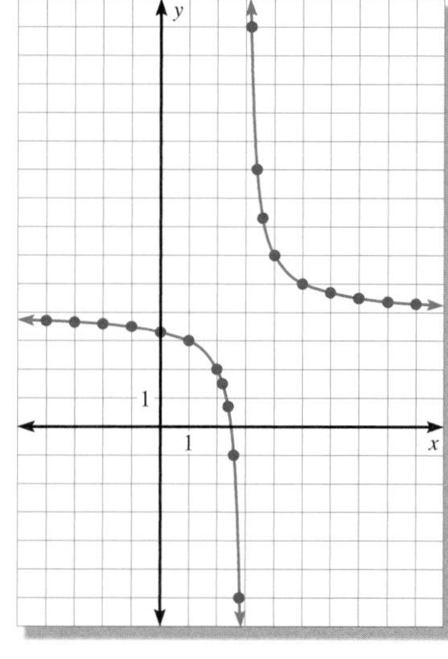

***STEP 3* Draw a graph**

Draw a smooth curve through the points (x, y) where $x > 3$. Repeat for the points (x, y) where $x < 3$.

PRACTICE

1. *Describe* how the values of y change as the values of x get close to 3. What is the equation of the vertical asymptote? **See margin.**
2. *Describe* how the values of y change as the values of x get far from 3. What is the equation of the horizontal asymptote? **As the absolute value of x becomes greater and greater, the value of y approaches 4; $y = 4$.**

Graph the function using a table.
3–5. See margin.

3. $y = \frac{5}{x - 4} - 6$
4. $y = \frac{-10}{x + 3} - 1$
5. $y = \frac{-11}{x + 13} + 9$

1 PLAN AND PREPARE

Explore the Concept

- Students will use tables and a graphing calculator to graph functions.
- This activity leads into the discussion in Lesson 12.2, Example 4, of how to transform the graph of $y = \frac{1}{x}$ into the graph of $y = \frac{a}{x - h} + k$.

Materials

Each student will need:
- graph paper
- graphing calculator

Recommended Time

Work activity: 15 min
Discuss results: 5 min

Grouping

Students should work individually.

2 TEACH

Key Questions

- In Explore 1, why is the value of y undefined when $x = 3$? **The expression $x - 3$ appears in a denominator of the equation. If $x = 3$ the denominator is zero, and division by zero is undefined.**
- In Explore 2, why do you think that the vertical line connecting the two branches of the hyperbola is $x = -1.7$? **The expression $x + 1.7$ appears in a denominator, so the line at $x = -1.7$, which would make the denominator equal zero, is the vertical asymptote.**

Key Discovery

In the graph of $y = \frac{a}{x - h} + k$, the horizontal asymptote is $y = k$ and the vertical asymptote is $x = h$.

1. As the value of x approaches 3 through numbers less than 3, the value of y becomes a smaller and smaller negative number (larger and larger in absolute value); as the value of x approaches 3 through numbers greater than 3, the value of y becomes a larger and larger positive number; $x = 3$.

3. 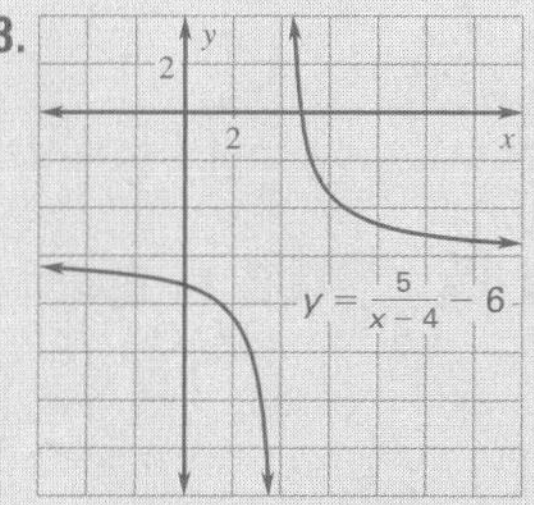

4. 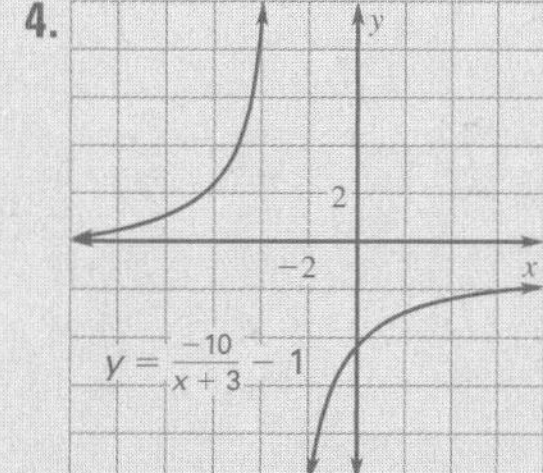

5. 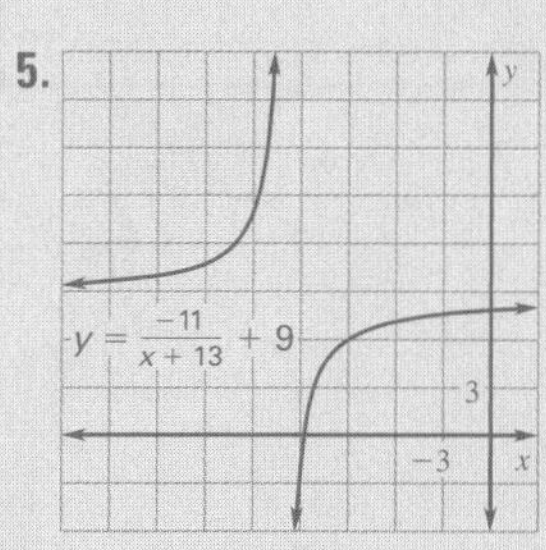

3 ASSESS AND RETEACH

1. Identify the horizontal and vertical asymptotes of the graph of $y = \frac{-8}{x+5} - 3$. **The horizontal asymptote is $y = -3$ and the vertical asymptote is $x = -5$.**

2. Using the form of $y = \frac{a}{x-h} + k$, write an equation of a graph that has a horizontal asymptote of $y = 3$ and a vertical asymptote of $x = 2$. ***Sample answer:*** $y = \frac{2}{x-2} + 3$

6. As the value of x approaches -1.7 through numbers less than -1.7, the value of y becomes a smaller and smaller negative number (larger and larger in absolute value); as the value of x approaches -1.7 through numbers greater than -1.7, the value of y becomes a larger and larger positive number; $x = -1.7$.

8.

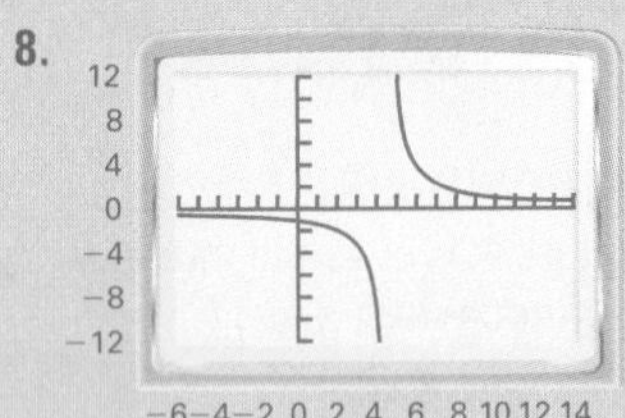

9.

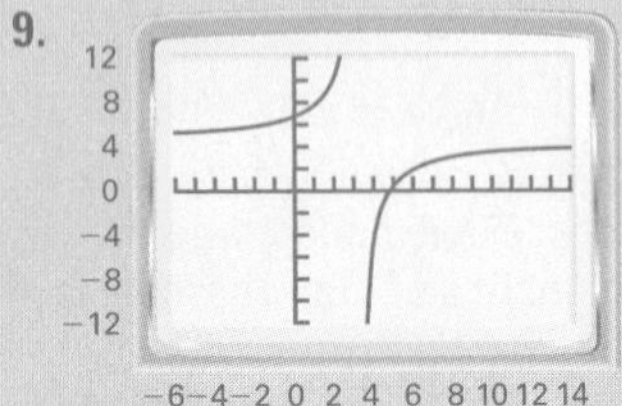

10.

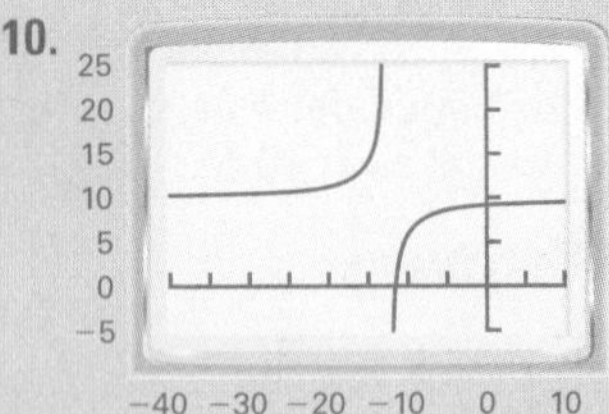

EXPLORE 2 Use a graphing calculator to graph a function

Graph $y = \frac{-3.4}{x+1.7} - 2.8$ using a graphing calculator.

Enter $y_1 = \frac{-3.4}{x+1.7} - 2.8$ into your graphing calculator. Press MODE and select either connected mode or dot mode. Then graph the function.

Connected mode

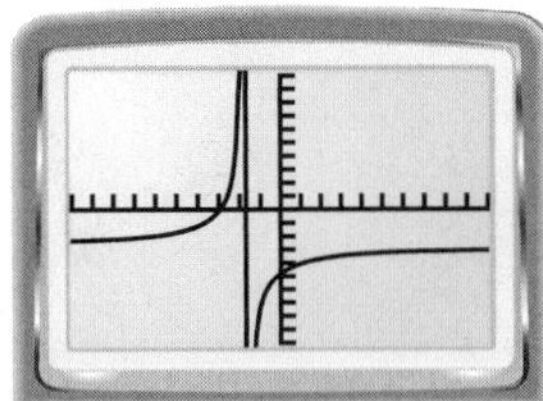

Dot mode

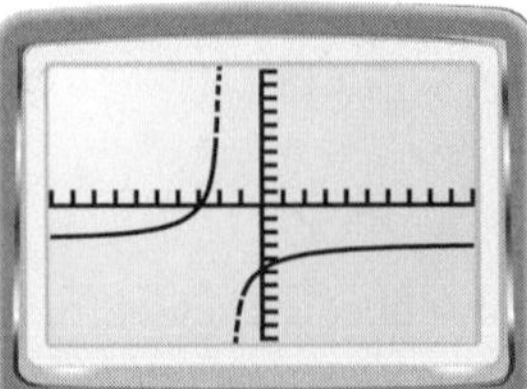

In connected mode, the screen appears to show the line $x = -1.7$. This line is *not* part of the graph. The calculator is instead connecting the two branches of the hyperbola. In dot mode, the screen does not show the line, but the points that are plotted are not connected by a smooth curve.

PRACTICE

6. *Describe* how the value of y changes as the value of x gets closer to -1.7. Use the *trace* feature of the graphing calculator to find the equation of the vertical asymptote. **See margin.**

7. *Describe* how the value of y changes as the value of x gets farther from -1.7. Use the *trace* feature of the graphing calculator to find the equation of the horizontal asymptote. **As the absolute value of x becomes greater and greater, the value of y approaches -2.8; $y = -2.8$.**

Graph the function using a graphing calculator.
8–10. See margin.

8. $y = \frac{5.3}{x-4.6} - 1.2$
9. $y = \frac{-7.1}{x-3.2} + 4.5$
10. $y = \frac{-10.2}{x+12.4} + 9.8$

DRAW CONCLUSIONS Use your observations to complete these exercises

11. How are the constants in the equations of the asymptotes in Exercises 1 and 2 related to the constants in the function $y = \frac{2}{x-3} + 4$? **See margin.**

12. How are the constants in the equations of the asymptotes in Exercises 6 and 7 related to the constants in the function $y = \frac{-3.4}{x+1.7} - 2.8$? **See margin.**

13. **CONJECTURE** Copy and complete: The graph of $y = \frac{a}{x-h} + k$ has a vertical asymptote of $x =$ __?__ and a horizontal asymptote of $y =$ __?__. ***h, k***

11. The constant in the equation of the vertical asymptote is the same as the constant that is subtracted from x in the function. The constant in the equation of the horizontal asymptote is the same as the constant term of the function.

12. The constant in the equation of the vertical asymptote is the opposite of the constant that is added to x in the function. The constant in the equation of the horizontal asymptote is the same as the constant term of the function.

12.2 Graph Rational Functions

8.11.08 Recognize and describe the general shape and properties of functions from graphs, tables or equations . . .

Before You graphed inverse variation equations.

Now You will graph rational functions.

Why? So you can find the cost of a group trip, as in Ex. 39.

Key Vocabulary
- **rational function**
- **hyperbola,** *p. 767*
- **branches of a hyperbola,** *p. 767*
- **asymptotes of a hyperbola,** *p. 767*

The inverse variation equation $y = \frac{a}{x}$ $(a \neq 0)$ is a type of *rational function.*

A **rational function** has a rule given by a fraction whose numerator and denominator are polynomials and whose denominator is not 0.

KEY CONCEPT *For Your Notebook*

Parent Rational Function

The function $y = \frac{1}{x}$ is the parent function for any rational function whose numerator has degree 0 or 1 and whose denominator has degree 1. The function and its graph have the following characteristics:

- The domain and range are all nonzero real numbers.
- The horizontal asymptote is the x-axis. The vertical asymptote is the y-axis.

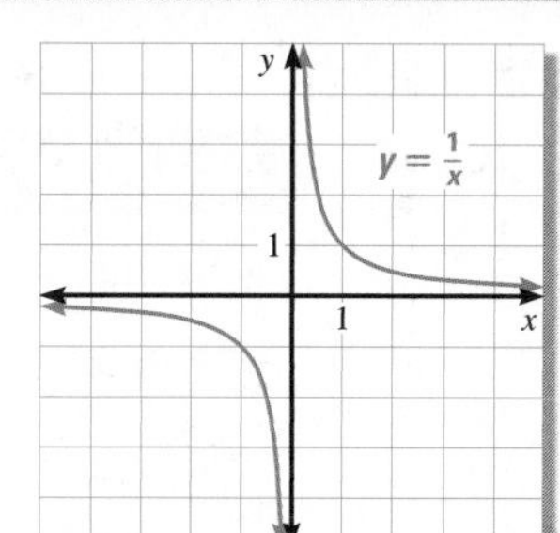

EXAMPLE 1 **Compare graph of $y = \frac{a}{x}$ with graph of $y = \frac{1}{x}$**

REWRITE FUNCTION

In the function $y = \frac{1}{3x}$, the value of a is $\frac{1}{3}$ as shown:

$$y = \frac{1}{3x} = \frac{1}{3} \cdot \frac{1}{x} = \frac{\frac{1}{3}}{x}$$

a. The graph of $y = \frac{-2}{x}$ is a vertical stretch with a reflection in the x-axis of the graph of $y = \frac{1}{x}$.

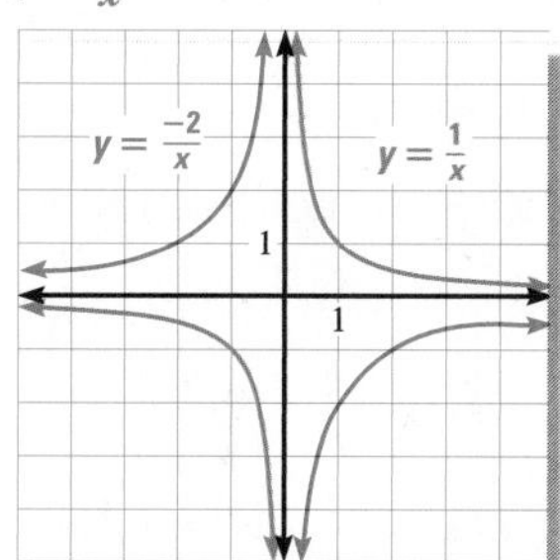

b. The graph of $y = \frac{1}{3x}$ is a vertical shrink of the graph of $y = \frac{1}{x}$.

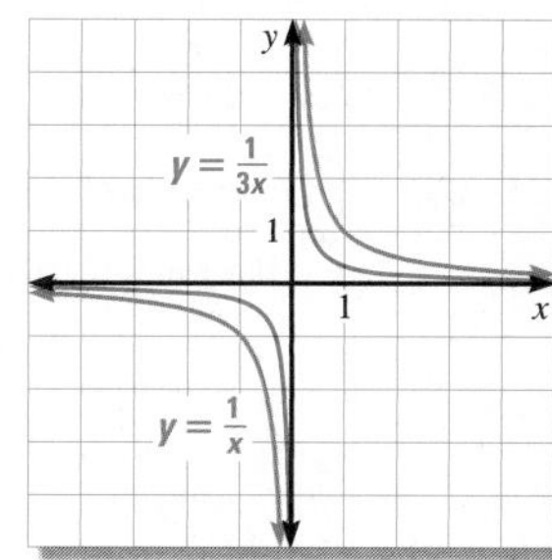

1 PLAN AND PREPARE

Warm-Up Exercises

Transparency Available

1. Graph $y = \frac{5}{x}$.

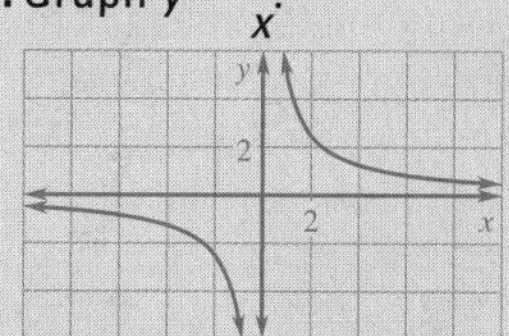

2. It takes a crew of 8 construction workers 150 hours to frame a house. How long will it take a crew of 12 workers? **100 h**

Notetaking Guide

Transparency Available

Promotes interactive learning and notetaking skills, pp. 271–275.

Pacing

Basic: 2 days
Average: 2 days
Advanced: 2 days
Block: 1 block
- See *Teaching Guide/Lesson Plan.*

2 FOCUS AND MOTIVATE

Essential Question

Big Idea 1, p. 763

How do you graph a rational function? **Tell students they will learn how to answer this question by using the parent function $y = \frac{1}{x}$ and the values of the constants to graph a rational function.**

Resource Planning Guide

Chapter Resource Book
- Teaching Guide/Lesson Plan (pp. 17–18)
- Practice levels A, B, C (pp. 19–24)
- Study Guide (pp. 25–26)
- Catch-up for Absent Students (p. 27)
- Application (p. 28)
- Challenge (p. 29)

Workbooks
- Notetaking Guide (pp. 271–275)
- Practice Workbook (pp. 183–185)

Teaching Options
- **Power Presentations CD-ROM** provides dynamic electronic teaching resources for the classroom.
- **Activity Generator CD-ROM** provides editable activities for all ability levels.

Interactive Technology
- Easy Planner
- Power Presentations CD-ROM
- Activity Generator CD-ROM
- Animated Algebra
- Test Generator CD-ROM
- Online Quiz
- eWorkbook
- eEdition
- @HomeTutor

Resources for English Learners
- Quick Reference for English Learners
- Spanish Study Guide
- Multi-Language Visual Glossary
- Student Resources in Spanish

See also the *Algebra 1 Toolkit* for more strategies for meeting individual needs.

Motivating the Lesson

You purchase a swimming pass at a community pool for the summer. The pass allows you to use the pool as many times as you want during the season. You would like the average cost per use to be $3 or less. By writing an equation that models the situation, you can use the equation to determine how many times you need to use the pass so that the average cost is $3 or less.

3 TEACH

Extra Example 1

a. Compare the graph of $y = \frac{4}{x}$ with the graph of $y = \frac{1}{x}$.

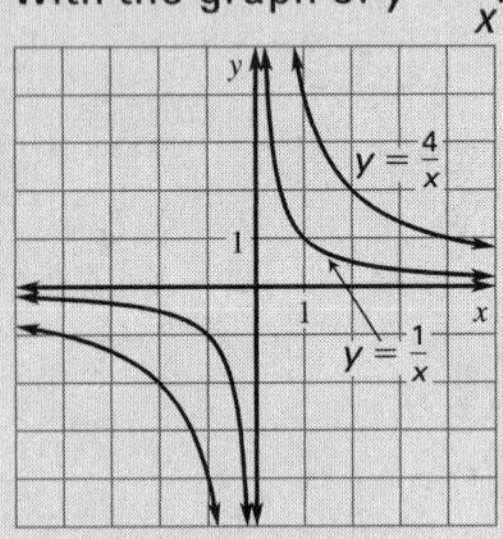

vertical stretch of the graph of $y = \frac{1}{x}$

b. Compare the graph of $y = \frac{-1}{2x}$ with the graph of $y = \frac{1}{x}$.

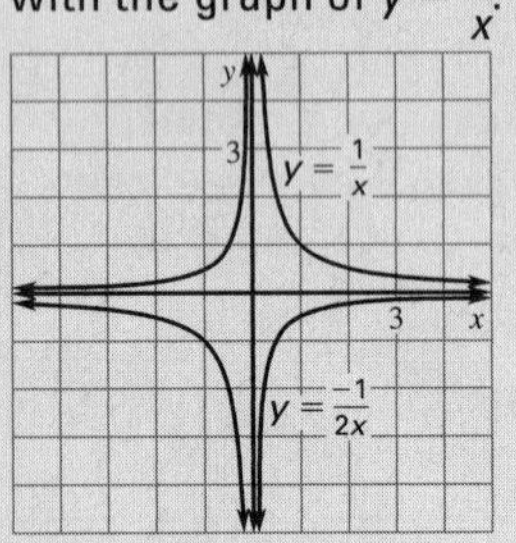

vertical shrink of $y = \frac{1}{x}$, and reflection in the x-axis

1–4. See Additional Answers beginning on p. AA1.

EXAMPLE 2 Graph $y = \frac{1}{x} + k$

Graph $y = \frac{1}{x} + 3$ and identify its domain and range. Compare the graph with the graph of $y = \frac{1}{x}$.

Solution

Graph the function using a table of values.

The domain is all real numbers except 0. The range is all real numbers except 3.

The graph of $y = \frac{1}{x} + 3$ is a vertical translation (of 3 units up) of the graph of $y = \frac{1}{x}$.

x	y
−2	2.5
−1	2
−0.5	1
0	undefined
0.5	5
1	4
2	3.5

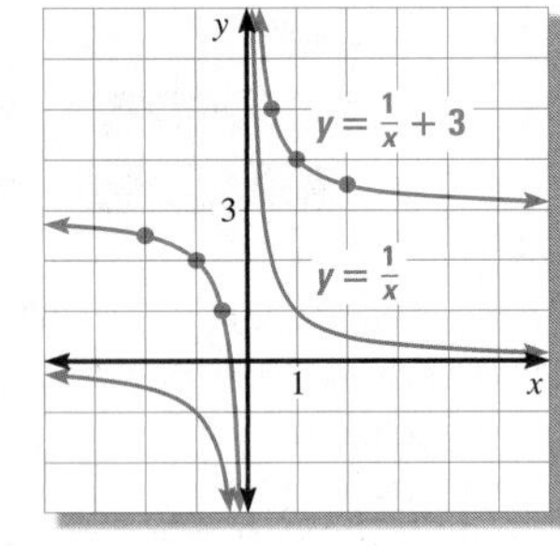

EXAMPLE 3 Graph $y = \frac{1}{x - h}$

Graph $y = \frac{1}{x - 2}$ and identify its domain and range. Compare the graph with the graph of $y = \frac{1}{x}$.

Solution

Graph the function using a table of values.

The domain is all real numbers except 2. The range is all real numbers except 0.

The graph of $y = \frac{1}{x - 2}$ is a horizontal translation (of 2 units to the right) of the graph of $y = \frac{1}{x}$.

x	y
0	−0.5
1	−1
1.5	−2
2	undefined
2.5	2
3	1
4	0.5

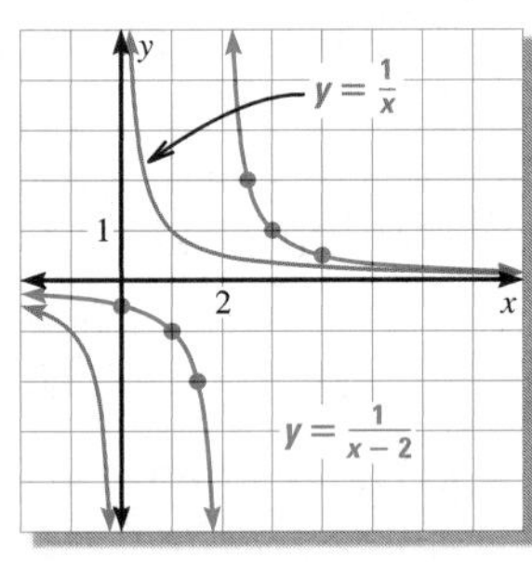

✓ **GUIDED PRACTICE** for Examples 1, 2, and 3

Graph the function and identify its domain and range. *Compare* the graph with the graph of $y = \frac{1}{x}$. 1–3. See margin.

1. $y = \frac{-4}{x}$ **2.** $y = \frac{1}{x} - 4$ **3.** $y = \frac{1}{x + 5}$

4. *Describe* how the graph of $y = \frac{1}{x + 3}$ is related to the graph of $y = \frac{1}{x}$. See margin.

Differentiated Instruction

English Learners When reading mathematics, students should learn to always see the word *ratio* as part of *rational*. This will help them to remember that a rational number is a ratio of two integers (as in Lesson 3.5), and a rational function is a ratio of two polynomials.

See also the *Algebra 1 Toolkit* for more strategies.

GRAPHING RATIONAL FUNCTIONS You can graph a rational function of the form $y = \frac{a}{x-h} + k$ $(a \neq 0)$ by using the values of a, k, and h.

KEY CONCEPT — *For Your Notebook*

Graph of $y = \frac{a}{x-h} + k$

The graph of $y = \frac{a}{x-h} + k$ is a hyperbola that has the following characteristics:

- If $|a| > 1$, the graph is a vertical stretch of the graph of $y = \frac{1}{x}$. If $0 < |a| < 1$, the graph is a vertical shrink of the graph of $y = \frac{1}{x}$. If $a < 0$, the graph is a reflection in the x-axis of the graph of $y = \frac{1}{x}$.
- The horizontal asymptote is $y = k$. The vertical asymptote is $x = h$.

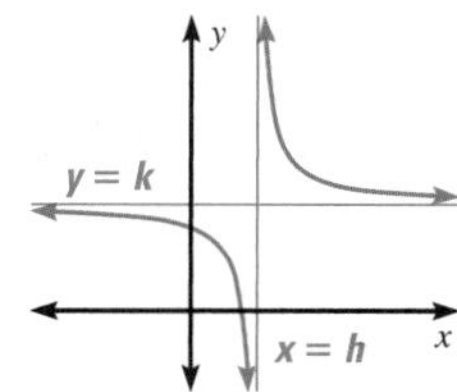

The domain of the function is all real numbers except $x = h$. The range is all real numbers except $y = k$.

EXAMPLE 4 Graph $y = \frac{a}{x-h} + k$

Graph $y = \frac{2}{x+1} - 3$.

Solution

AVOID ERRORS
The asymptotes are used to help you draw a hyperbola. They are *not* part of the hyperbola.

STEP 1 **Identify** the asymptotes of the graph. The vertical asymptote is $x = -1$. The horizontal asymptote is $y = -3$.

STEP 2 **Plot** several points on each side of the vertical asymptote.

STEP 3 **Graph** two branches that pass through the plotted points and approach the asymptotes.

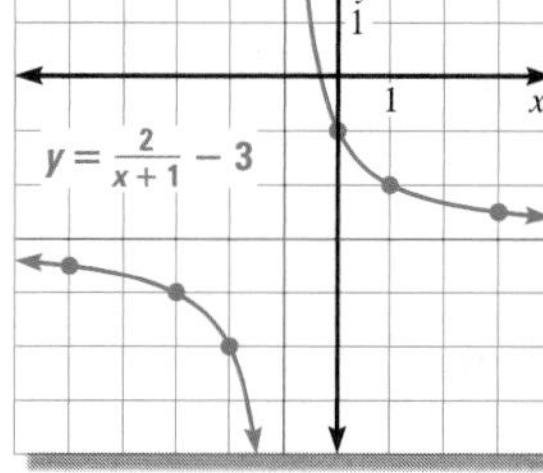

Animated Algebra at classzone.com

✓ GUIDED PRACTICE for Example 4

5. Graph $y = \frac{4}{x-5} + 6$. See margin.

6. For which function is the domain all real numbers except -3 and the range all real numbers except 7? C

(A) $y = \frac{2}{x-3} + 7$ (B) $y = \frac{2}{x-3} - 7$ (C) $y = \frac{2}{x+3} + 7$ (D) $y = \frac{2}{x+3} - 7$

5.

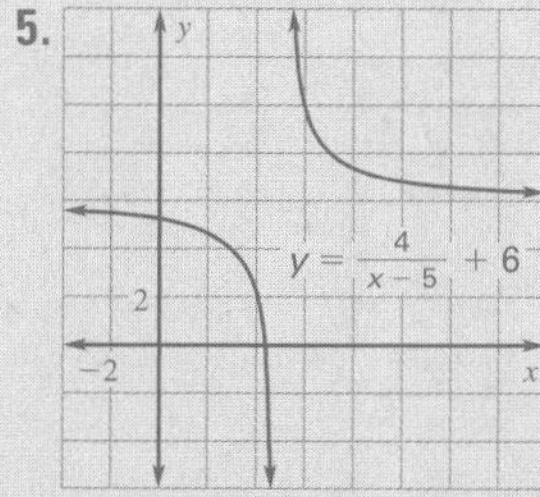

Extra Example 2

Graph $y = \frac{1}{x} - 1$ and identify its domain and range. Compare the graph with the graph of $y = \frac{1}{x}$.

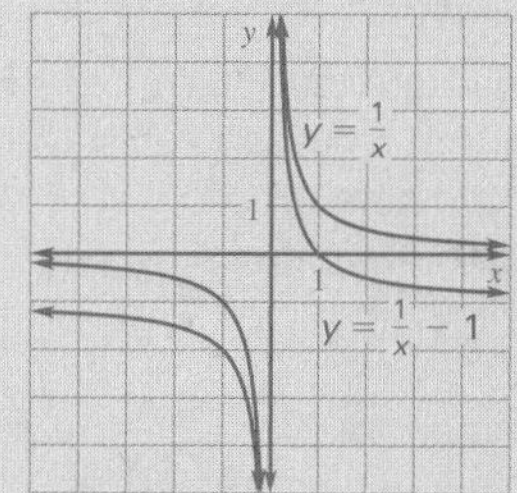

Domain: all real numbers except 0; range: all real numbers except −1; vertical translation of $y = \frac{1}{x}$, 1 unit down

Extra Example 3

Graph $y = \frac{1}{x+2}$ and identify its domain and range. Compare the graph with the graph of $y = \frac{1}{x}$.

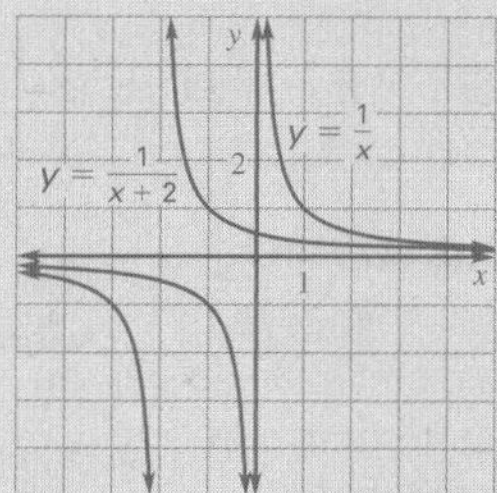

Domain: all real numbers except −2; range: all real numbers except 0; the graph of $y = \frac{1}{x+2}$ is a horizontal translation of $y = \frac{1}{x}$, 2 units left.

Extra Example 4

Graph $y = \frac{3}{x+2} + 1$.

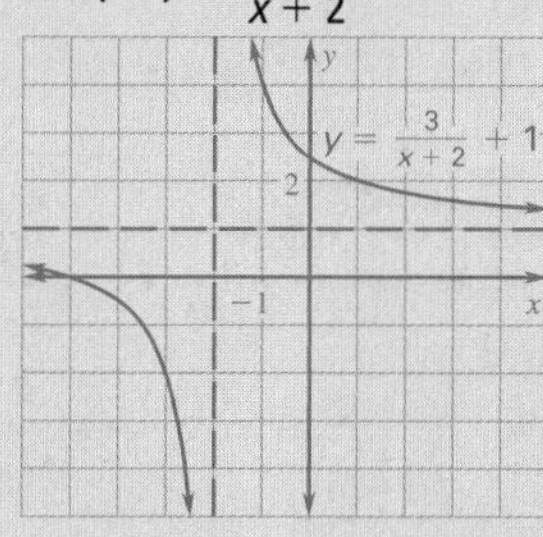

Animated Algebra classzone.com

An **Animated Algebra** activity is available on-line for **Example 4**. This activity is also available on the **Power Presentations CD-ROM**.

EXAMPLE 5 Solve a multi-step problem

TRIP EXPENSES Your art club is planning a bus trip to an art museum. The cost for renting a bus is $495, and the cost will be divided equally among the people who are going on the trip. A museum ticket costs $12.50 per person.

- Write an equation that gives the cost C (in dollars per person) of the trip as a function of the number p of people going on the trip.
- Graph the equation. *Describe* the change in the cost as the number of people increases.
- Use the graph to approximate the number of people who need to go on the trip so that the cost is about $25 per person.

San Francisco Art Museum

Solution

STEP 1 **Write** a verbal model. Then write an equation.

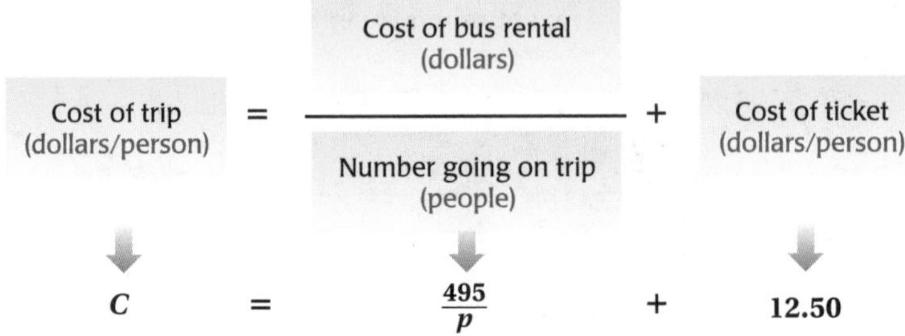

$$C = \frac{495}{p} + 12.50$$

STEP 2 **Graph** $C = \frac{495}{p} + 12.50$ on a graphing calculator. The vertical asymptote is $p = 0$. The horizontal asymptote is $C = 12.5$. As the number of people increases, the cost decreases.

STEP 3 **Approximate** the number of people needed in order for the cost to be about $25. When $C \approx 25$, the value of p is about 40. So, if about 40 people go on the trip, each person will pay about $25.

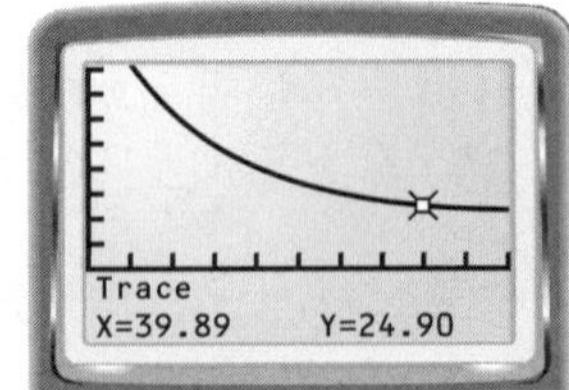

✓ GUIDED PRACTICE for Example 5

7. **WHAT IF?** In Example 5, suppose the club rents a larger bus for $610. Write and graph an equation that gives the cost C (in dollars per person) of the trip as a function of the number p of people going on the trip. Then approximate the number of people who need to go on the trip so that the cost is about $25 per person. $C = \frac{610}{p} + 12.50$; see margin for art; 49 people.

Extra Example 5

A ski club rented a cabin for $750. The club also purchased ski lift tickets for $22.50 each. The cost will be divided equally among all who use the cabin.

- Write an equation that gives the cost C for each person as a function of the number p of people renting the cabin. $C = \frac{750}{p} + 22.50$
- Graph the equation. *Describe* the change in the cost as the number of people increases.

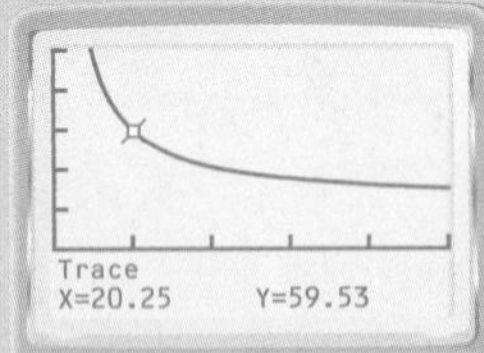

As the number of people increases, the cost decreases.

- Use the graph to approximate the number of people who need to rent the cabin so that the cost is $60 per person. 20 people

Closing the Lesson

Have students summarize the major points of the lesson and answer the Essential Question: How do you graph a rational function?

- The parent function for a rational function is $y = \frac{1}{x}$.
- For the graph of $y = \frac{a}{x-h} + k$, the horizontal asymptote is $y = k$ and the vertical asymptote is $x = h$.

Use the value of a to determine whether the graph of a rational function is a vertical stretch, vertical shrink, and/or reflection in the x-axis of the parent graph. Use the value of k to determine the value of the vertical translation, and use the value of h to determine the value of the horizontal translation. You can also use the asymptotes $y = k$ and $x = h$ to graph the function.

7.

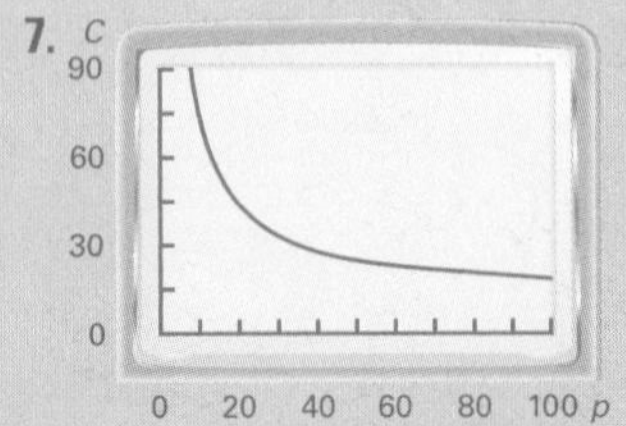

12.2 EXERCISES

HOMEWORK KEY

 = **WORKED-OUT SOLUTIONS** on p. WS28 for Exs. 7, 21, and 41

★ = **STANDARDIZED TEST PRACTICE** Exs. 2, 18, 28, 29, 36, 42, and 44

◆ = **MULTIPLE REPRESENTATIONS** Ex. 41

SKILL PRACTICE

A

1. **VOCABULARY** Identify the vertical asymptote and horizontal asymptote of the graph of $y = \frac{1}{x-3} - 6$. $x = 3, y = -6$

2. ★ **WRITING** *Describe* the difference between the graph of $y = \frac{1}{x+2}$ and the graph of $y = \frac{1}{x}$. The graph of $y = \frac{1}{x+2}$ is the graph of $y = \frac{1}{x}$ translated 2 units to the left.

EXAMPLES 1, 2, and 3 on pp. 775–776 for Exs. 3–17

GRAPHING FUNCTIONS **Graph the function and identify its domain and range.** ***Compare*** **the graph with the graph of $y = \frac{1}{x}$.** 3–17. See margin.

3. $y = \frac{3}{x}$
4. $y = \frac{1}{2x}$
5. $y = \frac{-3}{x}$
6. $y = \frac{-2}{3x}$
7. $y = \frac{-1}{4x}$
8. $y = \frac{1}{x} + 7$
9. $y = \frac{1}{x} - 5$
10. $y = \frac{1}{x} + 4$
11. $y = \frac{1}{x} + 8$
12. $y = \frac{1}{x} - 6$
13. $y = \frac{1}{x+3}$
14. $y = \frac{1}{x-7}$
15. $y = \frac{1}{x+8}$
16. $y = \frac{1}{x-1}$
17. $y = \frac{1}{x-6}$

EXAMPLE 4 on p. 777 for Exs. 18–31

18. ★ **MULTIPLE CHOICE** For which function is the domain all real numbers except −5 and the range all real numbers except 0? C

(A) $y = \frac{5}{x}$ (B) $y = \frac{5}{x-5}$ (C) $y = \frac{5}{x+5}$ (D) $y = \frac{-5}{x-5}$

GRAPHING FUNCTIONS **Graph the function.** 19–27. See margin.

19. $y = \frac{1}{x-2} - 8$
20. $y = \frac{2}{x-6} + 3$
21. $y = \frac{4}{x+7} + 5$
22. $y = \frac{-3}{x+3} - 4$
23. $y = \frac{-1}{x+5} + 6$
24. $y = \frac{2}{x-1} + 2$
25. $y = \frac{1}{x-4} + 2$
26. $y = \frac{4}{x-3} - 1$
27. $y = \frac{-5}{x-1} - 4$

28. ★ **MULTIPLE CHOICE** The graph of which function has the same horizontal asymptote as the graph of $y = \frac{1}{x}$? C

(A) $y = \frac{2}{x} + 3$ (B) $y = \frac{1}{x} - 1$ (C) $y = \frac{-10}{x}$ (D) $y = \frac{-10}{x-1} + 1$

29. ★ **OPEN-ENDED** Write an equation whose graph is a hyperbola that has the following characteristics: *Sample answer:* $y = \frac{1}{x+1} + 2$
- The vertical asymptote is $x = -1$.
- The horizontal asymptote is $y = 2$.

4 PRACTICE AND APPLY

Assignment Guide

Answer Transparencies available for all exercises

Basic:
Day 1: EP p. 948 Exs. 1–9 odd
pp. 779–782
Exs. 1–17, 52–60
Day 2: pp. 779–782
Exs. 18–33, 39–43, 46–51

Average:
Day 1: pp. 779–782
Exs. 1, 2, 6–17, 37, 52–60
Day 2: pp. 779–782
Exs. 18–28 even, 29–36, 39–44, 46–51

Advanced:
Day 1: pp. 779–782
Exs. 1, 6–17, 37, 52–60
Day 2: pp. 779–782
Exs. 18, 24–36, 38–45*, 46–50 even

Block:
pp. 779–782
Exs. 1, 2, 6–17, 18–28 even, 29–37, 39–44, 46–60

Differentiated Instruction

See *Algebra 1 Best Practices Toolkit* for suggestions on addressing the needs of a diverse classroom.

Homework Check

For a quick check of student understanding of key concepts, go over the following exercises:

Basic: 4, 10, 14, 22, 39
Average: 6, 11, 15, 24, 40
Advanced: 7, 12, 16, 26, 41

Extra Practice

- Student Edition, p. 946
- Chapter 12 Resource Book: Practice levels A, B, C, pp. 19–24

Practice Worksheet

An easily-readable reduced practice page (with answers) for this lesson can be found on p. 762C.

3–17, 19–27. See Additional Answers beginning on p. AA1.

ERROR ANALYSIS ***Describe*** **and correct the error in identifying the asymptotes of the graph of the given rational function.** 30–31. See margin.

30. $y = \frac{3}{x+1} - 4$

Vertical asymptote: x = 1
Horizontal asymptote: y = −4

31. $y = \frac{-2}{x-6} + 7$

Vertical asymptote: x = 6
Horizontal asymptote: y = −7

B **WRITING EQUATIONS** **Write an equation whose graph is a hyperbola that has the given asymptotes and passes through the given point.**

32. $x = 7, y = 8; (-6, 0)$ $y = \frac{104}{x-7} + 8$

33. $x = -2, y = 5; (0, -9)$ $y = \frac{-28}{x+2} + 5$

34. $x = 3, y = -2; (5, -1)$ $y = \frac{2}{x-3} - 2$

35. $x = -4, y = -4; (-8, 3)$ $y = \frac{-28}{x+4} - 4$

36. ★ **WRITING** Let f be a function of the form $f(x) = \frac{a}{x-h} + k$. Can you graph f if you know only two points on the graph? *Explain.* No; two points do not provide enough information to determine the three unknown values, *a*, *h*, and *k*.

37. **GEOMETRY** The height h of a trapezoid is given by the formula

$$h = \frac{2A}{b_1 + b_2}$$

where A is the area and b_1 and b_2 are the bases.

a. Let $A = 50$ and $b_1 = 4$. Write h as a function of b_2. Then graph the function and identify its domain and range. See margin.

b. Use the graph to approximate the value of b_2 when $h = 6$. about 13

C **38.** **CHALLENGE** *Describe* how to find the asymptotes of the graph of $g(x) = \frac{3}{2x-4} + 8$. Then graph the function. See margin.

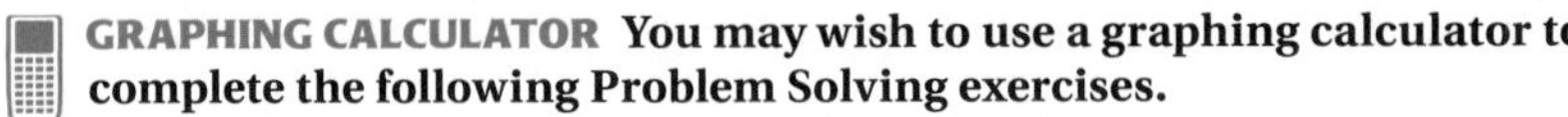

PROBLEM SOLVING

GRAPHING CALCULATOR **You may wish to use a graphing calculator to complete the following Problem Solving exercises.**

EXAMPLE 5 A on p. 778 for Exs. 39–42

39. **TEAM SPORTS** A figure skating troupe is planning an out-of-town trip. The expenses for the trip are shown in the flyer. Write an equation that gives the cost C (in dollars per person) as a function of the number p of people going on the trip. Then graph the equation.

Trip Expenses

Bus rental $900
Food and lodging (per person) $400

39. $C = \frac{900}{p} + 400$; see margin for art.

@HomeTutor for problem solving help at classzone.com

40. **CHARITY EVENTS** A committee of 5 people is responsible for making 500 sandwiches for a charity picnic. The committee hopes to recruit extra people for the task. Write an equation that gives the average number s of sandwiches made per person as a function of the number p of extra people recruited for the task. Then graph the equation. $s = \frac{500}{5+p}$; see margin for art.

@HomeTutor for problem solving help at classzone.com

○ = WORKED-OUT SOLUTIONS on p. WS1 ★ = STANDARDIZED TEST PRACTICE ◆ = MULTIPLE REPRESENTATIONS

Avoiding Common Errors

Exercises 3–17 Watch for students who confuse vertical and horizontal translations. Remind students that in the equation $y = \frac{a}{x-h} + k$, the value of h determines the horizontal translation and the value of k determines the vertical translation.

Study Strategy

Exercises 3–17 Suggest that students draw the graph of $y = \frac{1}{x}$ and then use it as a guide to make comparisons with the graph for each exercise.

Teaching Strategy

Exercises 19–27 Before students begin these exercises, you may want to ask them to identify the horizontal and vertical asymptote of each function. This will serve as a quick check that they understand the concept, and they can use the asymptotes to graph the functions.

30. To identify the asymptotes $x = h$ and $y = k$ of the hyperbola, write its equation in the form $y = \frac{a}{x-h} + k$: $y = \frac{3}{x-(-1)} + (-4)$; thus the vertical asymptote is $x = -1$, not $x = 1$.

31. To identify the asymptotes of the hyperbola, write its equation in the form $y = \frac{a}{x-h} + k$: $y = \frac{-2}{x-6} + 7$; thus the horizontal asymptote is $y = 7$, not $y = -7$.

37a. $h = \frac{100}{b_2 + 4}$;

Height; Base length; $h = \frac{100}{b_2+4}$

domain: $b_2 > 0$, range: $0 < h < 25$

38. To write the equation in the form $y = \frac{a}{x-h} + k$, divide the numerator and denominator of $\frac{3}{2x-4}$ by 2: $y = \frac{\frac{3}{2}}{x-2} + 8$; so, the asymptotes are $x = 2$ and $y = 8$.

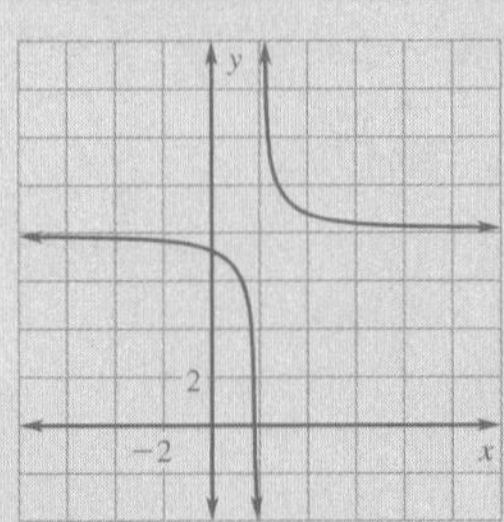

41. ◆ **MULTIPLE REPRESENTATIONS** Your movie rental membership lets you rent any number of movies for \$22 per month. You rent at least 2 movies per month.

a. **Writing an Equation** Write an equation that gives the average cost C (in dollars per rental) as a function of the number r of additional rentals beyond 2 rentals. $C = \frac{22}{r+2}$

b. **Drawing a Graph** Graph the equation from part (a). Then use the graph to approximate the number of additional rentals needed per month so that the average cost is \$1.50 per rental.
See margin for art; 13 additional rentals.

42. ★ **SHORT RESPONSE** The Mount Washington Auto Road in New Hampshire is a 7.6 mile uphill road that leads to the mountain's 6288 foot peak. The year's fastest time t (in seconds) for driving up the road during the period 1904–1998 can be modeled by

$$t = \frac{56{,}000}{x + 40}$$

where x is the number of years since 1904. Graph the function. *Describe* how the fastest times changed during the period. Was the *change* in the fastest time from year to year *increasing* or *decreasing*? *Explain.* **See margin.**

B

43. **See margin for art; domain: $d \geq 32.8$, range: $0 \leq p < 0.859$; the percent of time gliding increases.**

43. **DIVING DEPTHS** The percent p (in decimal form) of time that an elephant seal spends gliding through the water while diving can be modeled by

$$p = \frac{-28.2}{d} + 0.859$$

where d is the depth (in meters) of the dive. Graph the equation and identify its domain and range. *Describe* how the percent of time gliding changes as the depth increases.

44. ★ **EXTENDED RESPONSE** Oxygen cost is a measure of a person's walking efficiency. The models below give the oxygen cost c (in millimeters per kilogram of body mass per meter) as a function of the walking speed v (in meters per minute) for various age groups.

Ages 6–12	Ages 13–19	Ages 20–59

$c = \frac{2.61}{v} + 0.188$	$c = \frac{1.68}{v} + 0.147$	$c = \frac{2.60}{v} + 0.129$

a. **Graph** Normal walking speeds range from 40 meters per minute to 100 meters per minute. Graph the models in the same coordinate plane. Use the domain $40 \leq v \leq 100$. **See margin.**

b. **Interpret** The greater the oxygen cost, the less efficient the person is while walking. Use the graphs to tell whether a person is *more efficient* or *less efficient* while walking as the person's speed increases. **more efficient**

c. **Compare** Which age group has the least efficient walkers at the speeds given in part (a)? *Justify* your choice.

44c. Ages 6–12; the graph for the 6–12 year old age group is above the graphs for the other two age groups for all values of v in the given domain. This means the oxygen cost c is greater for the 6–12 year old age group for all values of v in the given domain.

Avoiding Common Errors

Exercises 42–44 Some students confuse variables when discussing inverse relations. Caution students to make sure that their descriptions, explanations, and justifications refer to the correct relationship between specific variables.

Internet Reference

Exercise 43 Addition information about elephant seals can be found at www.marinemammalcenter.org/learning/education/pinnipeds/noelephseal.asp

42.
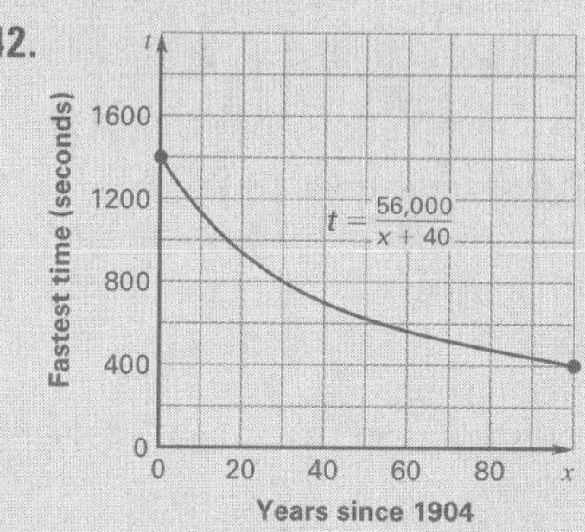

The fastest time decreased. The change in the fastest time was decreasing; the graph is steeper for the years near the beginning of the time period and then gradually becomes less steep, implying that the p-value changed more between two successive years near the beginning of the time period than it changed between two successive years near the end of the time period.

43.
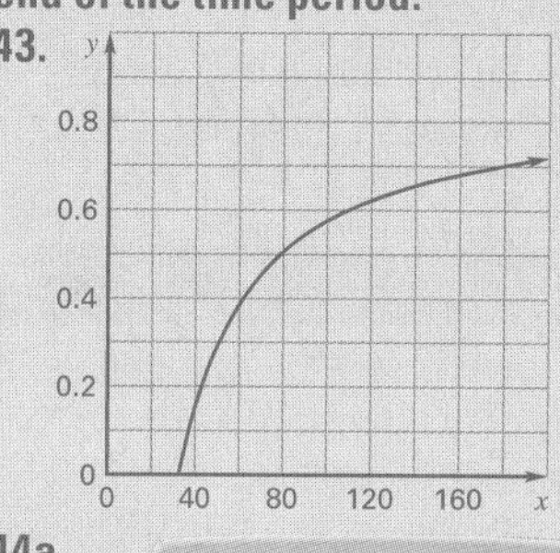

44a.
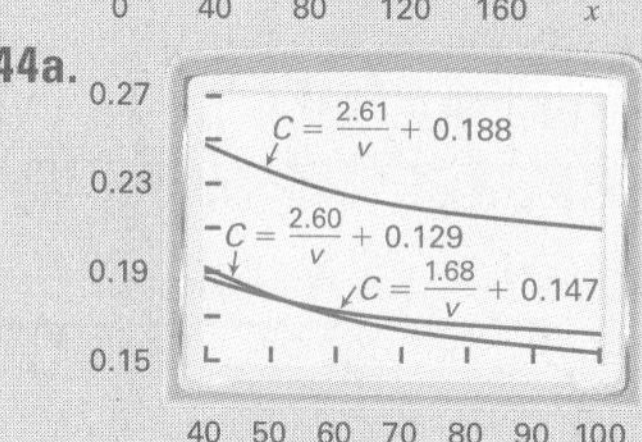

39.
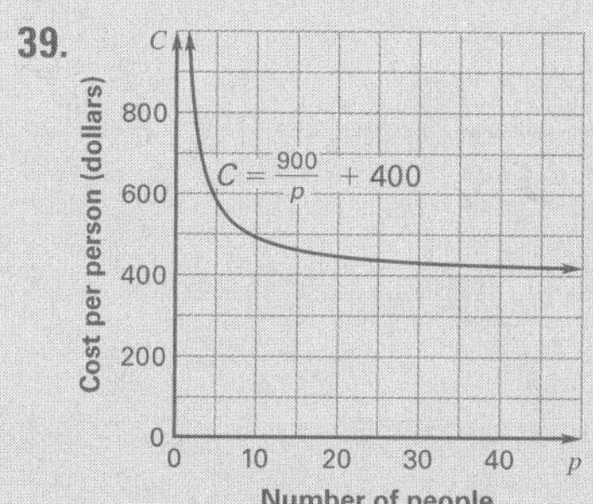

40.
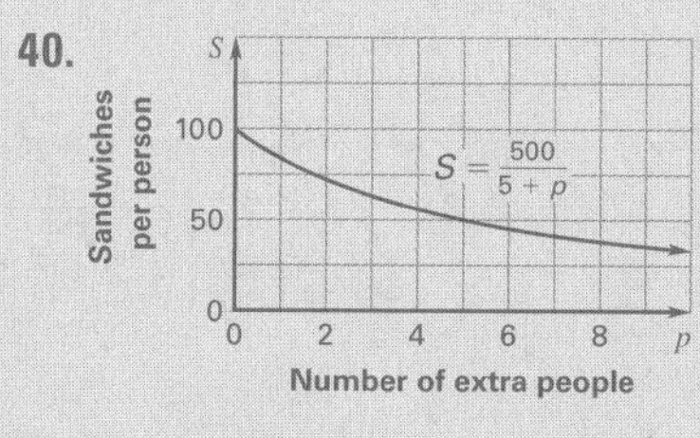

41b.
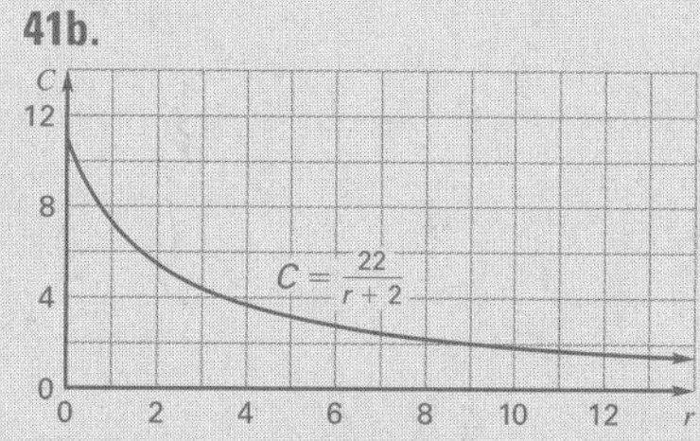

5 ASSESS AND RETEACH

Daily Homework Quiz

Transparency Available

1. Graph $y = \frac{1}{x+3} + 2$.

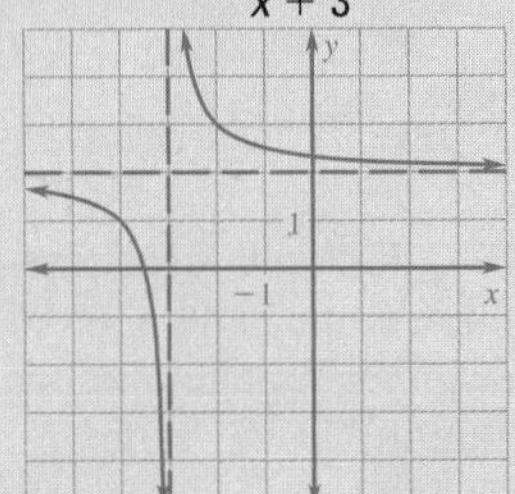

2. The cost per person C for a chartered boat can be modeled by $C = \frac{850}{p} + 12$, where p is the number of people who charter the boat. Find the least number of people who need to charter the boat so the cost is less than \$80 per person. **13 people**

Available at **classzone.com**

Diagnosis/Remediation

- Practice A, B, C in Chapter 12 Resource Book, pp. 19–24
- Study Guide in Chapter 12 Resource Book, pp. 25–26
- Practice Workbook, pp. 183–185
- @HomeTutor

Challenge

Additional challenge is available in the Chapter 12 Resource Book, p. 29.

Quiz

An easily-readable reduced copy of the quiz (with answers) on Lessons 12.1–12.2 from the Assessment Book can be found on p. 762F.

45a, Quiz 7–9. See Additional Answers beginning on p. AA1.

C **45. CHALLENGE** To decide whether a person qualifies for a loan to buy a house, a lender uses the ratio r of the person's expected monthly housing expenses to monthly income. Suppose the person has a monthly income of \$4150 and expects to pay \$1200 per month in housing expenses. The person also expects to receive a raise of x dollars this month.

a. Write and graph an equation that gives r as a function of x. $r = \frac{1200}{4150 + x}$; see margin for art.

b. The person will qualify for a loan if the ratio is 0.28. What must the amount of the raise be in order for the person to qualify for a loan? **about \$136**

ILLINOIS MIXED REVIEW

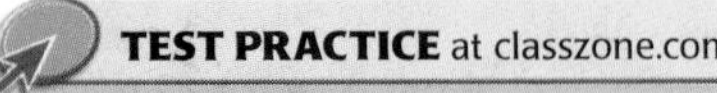

46. Which of the following can NOT be modeled using a linear equation? **A**

Ⓐ Julia deposits \$5000 in a savings account that earns 5% interest compounded annually. Predict the amount of money in the account in x years.

Ⓑ A store sells 5 oranges for \$2. How many oranges can you buy for x dollars?

Ⓒ You have \$12 more than your friend, who has x dollars. How much do you have?

Ⓓ Leonard's current salary is \$40,000, and every year he gets a raise of \$1000. Predict his salary in x years.

47. Find the surface area of the cylinder shown. **B**

Ⓐ $205\pi \text{ cm}^2$

Ⓑ $230\pi \text{ cm}^2$

Ⓒ $450\pi \text{ cm}^2$

Ⓓ $900\pi \text{ cm}^2$

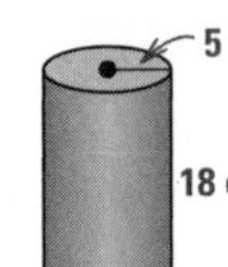

QUIZ for Lessons 12.1–12.2

Tell whether the equation represents *direct variation, inverse variation,* or *neither.* (p. 765)

1. $\frac{1}{5}xy = 1$ **inverse variation** **2.** $y = -9x$ **direct variation** **3.** $5x + y = 3$ **neither**

Given that y varies inversely with x, use the specified values to write an inverse variation equation that relates x and y. Then find the value of y when $x = 3$. (p. 765)

4. $x = 6, y = 4$ $y = \frac{24}{x}$; 8 **5.** $x = -3, y = 7$ $y = \frac{-21}{x}$; −7 **6.** $x = \frac{5}{2}, y = 2$ $y = \frac{5}{x}$; $\frac{5}{3}$

Graph the function. Identify its domain and range. (p. 775) **7–9. See margin.**

7. $y = \frac{4}{x}$ **8.** $y = \frac{-2}{x - 6}$ **9.** $y = \frac{3}{x + 2} - 5$

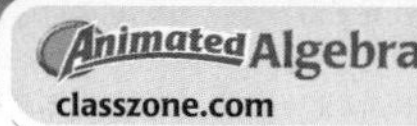

12.3 Dividing Polynomials Using Algebra Tiles

MATERIALS • algebra tiles

QUESTION How can you divide polynomials using algebra tiles?

In the equation $36 \div 5 = 7\frac{1}{5}$, the dividend is 36, the divisor is 5, the quotient is 7, and the remainder is 1. This equation illustrates the following rule:

$$\text{Dividend} \div \text{Divisor} = \text{Quotient} + \frac{\text{Remainder}}{\text{Divisor}}$$

This rule can also be applied when dividing polynomials.

EXPLORE Divide polynomials

Divide $2x^2 + 3x + 5$ by $x + 1$.

STEP 1 ***Model using algebra tiles***
Think of $2x^2 + 3x + 5$ as the area of a figure. Try to arrange the tiles to form a rectangle with $x + 1$ as one of the side lengths.

Notice that the other side length is $2x + 1$, but there are four 1-tiles remaining.

STEP 2 ***Write equation***
The divisor is $x + 1$, the quotient is $2x + 1$, and the remainder is 4.
So, $(2x^2 + 3x + 5) \div (x + 1) = 2x + 1 + \frac{4}{x + 1}$.

DRAW CONCLUSIONS Use your observations to complete these exercises

1. To check that $36 \div 5 = 7\frac{1}{5}$, you can evaluate $5 \cdot 7 + 1$ to obtain 36. Use this method to check the division equation in Step 2 above. $(x + 1)(2x + 1) + 4 = 2x^2 + 3x + 1 + 4 = 2x^2 + 3x + 5$

Use algebra tiles to divide the polynomials. Include a drawing of your model. 2–7. See margin.

2. $(2x^2 + 7x + 6) \div (x + 2)$
3. $(2x^2 + 9x + 10) \div (x + 3)$
4. $(4x^2 + 4x + 5) \div (2x + 1)$
5. $(2x^2 + 5x + 7) \div (2x + 3)$
6. $(3x^2 + 7x + 3) \div (x + 2)$
7. $(4x^2 + 6x + 5) \div (x + 1)$
8. **REASONING** For which of the division problems in Exercises 2–7 is the divisor a factor of the dividend? How do you know? Exercise 2; the remainder is zero so it is a factor.

2–7. See Additional Answers beginning on p. AA1.

1 PLAN AND PREPARE

Explore the Concept
- Students will divide polynomials using algebra tiles.
- This activity leads into the study of dividing a polynomial by a binomial in Lesson 12.3, Example 2.

Materials
Each student will need:
- algebra tiles
- Activity Support Master (*Chapter 12 Resource Book*, p. 32)

Recommended Time
Work activity: 10 min
Discuss results: 5 min

Grouping
Students should work individually.

2 TEACH

Tips for Success
Encourage students to use the divisor as the length of one side of the rectangle.

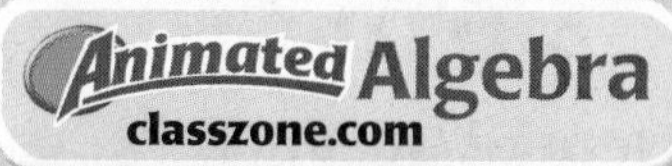

An **Animated Algebra** activity is available on-line. This activity is also available on the **Power Presentations CD-ROM**.

Key Discovery
When dividing polynomials, represent the remainder as a fraction, using the divisor as the denominator of the fraction.

3 ASSESS AND RETEACH

Explain how to check the division equation $(2x^2 + 10x + 12) \div (x + 4) = 2x + 2 + \frac{4}{x + 2}$. Find the product of the divisor and the quotient. Add the numerator of the fraction to the product, and compare the result with the original dividend.

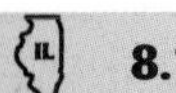

12.3 Divide Polynomials

8.11.01 Simplify or identify equivalent algebraic expressions (e.g., exponential, rational, logarithmic, factored, polynomial).

Before You multiplied polynomials.

Now You will divide polynomials.

Why? So you can describe an average cost, as in Ex. 43.

1 PLAN AND PREPARE

Warm-Up Exercises

Transparency Available

Find the product.

1. $2x(x^2 + 3x + 5)$ $2x^3 + 6x^2 + 10x$
2. $(x + 4)(x - 5)$ $x^2 - x - 20$
3. $(x - 3)(2x + 1)$ $2x^2 - 5x - 3$
4. $(3x + 1)(2x + 3)$ $6x^2 + 11x + 3$
5. The dimensions of a rectangle are $x + 3$ and $2x - 5$. Write an expression to represent the number of units for the area of the rectangle. $2x^2 + x - 15$

Notetaking Guide

Transparency Available

Promotes interactive learning and notetaking skills, pp. 276–279.

Pacing

Basic: 2 days

Average: 2 days

Advanced: 2 days

Block: 1 block

- See *Teaching Guide/Lesson Plan.*

2 FOCUS AND MOTIVATE

Essential Question

Big Idea 2, p. 763

How do you divide polynomials? Tell students they will learn how to answer this question by using a method similar to long division.

Key Vocabulary
- **monomial,** *p. 554*
- **polynomial,** *p. 554*
- **binomial,** *p. 555*
- **rational function,** *p. 775*

Just as you can find the product of two polynomials, you can divide the product by one of the polynomials to obtain the other polynomial. For example, $x^2 + 5x + 6 = (x + 2)(x + 3)$ is equivalent to $\frac{x^2 + 5x + 6}{x + 2} = x + 3$.

EXAMPLE 1 Divide a polynomial by a monomial

Divide $4x^3 + 8x^2 + 10x$ by $2x$.

Solution

Method 1: Write the division as a fraction.

$$(4x^3 + 8x^2 + 10x) \div 2x = \frac{4x^3 + 8x^2 + 10x}{2x}$$ **Write as fraction.**

$$= \frac{4x^3}{2x} + \frac{8x^2}{2x} + \frac{10x}{2x}$$ **Divide each term by $2x$.**

$$= 2x^2 + 4x + 5$$ **Simplify.**

Method 2: Use long division.

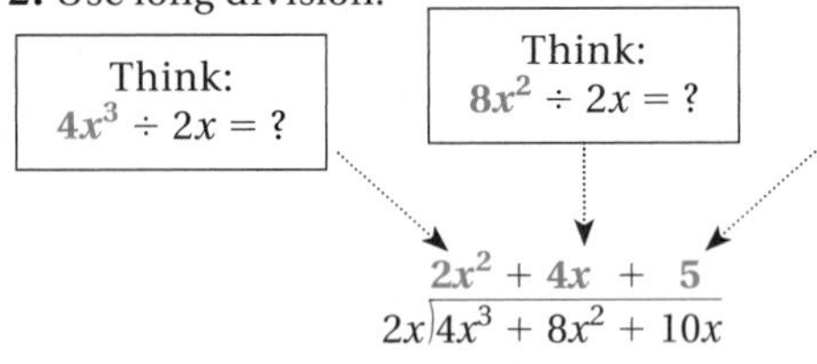

Think: $4x^3 \div 2x = ?$
Think: $8x^2 \div 2x = ?$
Think: $10x \div 2x = ?$
$2x^2 + 4x + 5$
$2x\overline{)4x^3 + 8x^2 + 10x}$

▶ $(4x^3 + 8x^2 + 10x) \div 2x = 2x^2 + 4x + 5$

CHECK

$$2x(2x^2 + 4x + 5) \stackrel{?}{=} 4x^3 + 8x^2 + 10x$$

$$2x(2x^2) + 2x(4x) + 2x(5) \stackrel{?}{=} 4x^3 + 8x^2 + 10x$$

$$4x^3 + 8x^2 + 10x = 4x^3 + 8x^2 + 10x \checkmark$$

✓ GUIDED PRACTICE for Example 1

Divide.

1. $(6x^3 + 3x^2 - 12x) \div 3x$ $2x^2 + x - 4$
2. $(12y^4 - 16y^3 + 20y^2) \div 4y$ $3y^3 - 4y^2 + 5y$

Resource Planning Guide

Chapter Resource Book
- Teaching Guide/Lesson Plan (pp. 30–31)
- Activity Master (p. 33)
- Practice levels A, B, C (pp. 34–36)
- Study Guide (pp. 37–38)
- Catch-up for Absent Students (p. 39)
- Application (p. 40)
- Challenge (p. 41)

Workbooks
- Notetaking Guide (pp. 276–279)
- Practice Workbook (pp. 186–187)

Teaching Options
- **Power Presentations CD-ROM** provides dynamic electronic teaching resources for the classroom.
- **Activity Generator CD-ROM** provides editable activities for all ability levels.

Interactive Technology
- Easy Planner
- Power Presentations CD-ROM
- Activity Generator CD-ROM
- Animated Algebra
- Test Generator CD-ROM
- Online Quiz
- eWorkbook
- eEdition
- @HomeTutor

Resources for English Learners
- Quick Reference for English Learners
- Spanish Study Guide
- Multi-Language Visual Glossary
- Student Resources in Spanish

See also the *Algebra 1 Toolkit* for more strategies for meeting individual needs.

DIVIDING BY A BINOMIAL As shown in Example 1, you can use two methods when dividing a polynomial by a monomial. To divide a polynomial by a binomial, use long division.

EXAMPLE 2 Divide a polynomial by a binomial

Divide $x^2 + 2x - 3$ by $x - 1$.

Solution

STEP 1 **Divide** the first term of $x^2 + 2x - 3$ by the first term of $x - 1$.

$$\begin{array}{r|l} & x \\ x - 1 & \overline{x^2 + 2x - 3} \\ & \underline{x^2 - x} \\ & 3x \end{array}$$

Think: $x^2 \div x = ?$

Multiply x and $x - 1$.

Subtract $x^2 - x$ from $x^2 + 2x$.

AVOID ERRORS
Be sure to *subtract* $x^2 - x$ from $x^2 + 2x$ in order to obtain $3x$. Do *not* add the expressions.

STEP 2 **Bring** down -3. Then divide the first term of $3x - 3$ by the first term of $x - 1$.

$$\begin{array}{r|l} & x + 3 \\ x - 1 & \overline{x^2 + 2x - 3} \\ & \underline{x^2 - x} \\ & 3x - 3 \\ & \underline{3x - 3} \\ & 0 \end{array}$$

Think: $3x \div x = ?$

Multiply 3 and $x - 1$.

Subtract $3x - 3$ from $3x - 3$.

▶ $(x^2 + 2x - 3) \div (x - 1) = x + 3$

NONZERO REMAINDERS In Example 2, if the dividend had been $x^2 + 2x - 2$, the remainder would have been 1. When you obtain a nonzero remainder, you can apply the following rule: Dividend ÷ Divisor = Quotient + $\frac{\text{Remainder}}{\text{Divisor}}$.

EXAMPLE 3 Divide a polynomial by a binomial

Divide $2x^2 + 11x - 9$ by $2x - 3$.

$$\begin{array}{r|l} & x + 7 \\ 2x - 3 & \overline{2x^2 + 11x - 9} \\ & \underline{2x^2 - 3x} \\ & 14x - 9 \\ & \underline{14x - 21} \\ & 12 \end{array}$$

Multiply x and $2x - 3$.

Subtract $2x^2 - 3x$. Bring down -9.

Multiply 7 and $2x - 3$.

Subtract $14x - 21$.

▶ $(2x^2 + 11x - 9) \div (2x - 3) = x + 7 + \frac{12}{2x - 3}$

CHECK DIVISION
To check your answer, multiply the quotient by the divisor, then add the remainder to the product.

✓ **GUIDED PRACTICE** for Examples 2 and 3

3. Divide: $(a^2 + 3a - 4) \div (a + 1)$
$a + 2 + \frac{-6}{a + 1}$

4. Divide: $(9b^2 + 6b + 8) \div (3b - 4)$
$3b + 6 + \frac{32}{3b - 4}$

Motivating the Lesson

Before you join a teen bowling league, you want to know what your costs will be. If you know the cost to join the league and the cost per game, you can write an equation that models the situation and gives your total cost as a function of the number of games that you bowl.

3 TEACH

Extra Example 1

Divide $6x^3 - 12x^2 + 9x$ by $3x$.
$2x^2 - 4x + 3$

Key Question to Ask for Example 1

- In Method 2, how can you check each step as you solve the problem? **Multiply each term in the quotient by the divisor to see if you get each term in the dividend.**

Extra Example 2

Divide $x^2 + x - 6$ by $x + 3$. $x - 2$

Key Questions to Ask for Example 2

- In Step 1, why do you place the quotient term x over the dividend term $2x$? **When you multiply x and $x - 1$, each term in the product will be aligned under the like term in the dividend.**
- How do you subtract $x^2 - x$ from $x^2 + 2x$? **For each term in $x^2 - x$, add its opposite by multiplying that term by -1.**

Extra Example 3

Divide $3x^2 + 17x + 13$ by $3x + 2$.
$x + 5 + \frac{3}{3x + 2}$

REWRITING POLYNOMIALS When dividing polynomials, you may first need to rewrite the polynomials so that the exponents decrease from left to right. When rewriting polynomials, insert any missing terms using zero coefficients. For example, $8 + 3x^2$ should be rewritten as $3x^2 + 0x + 8$.

EXAMPLE 4 Rewrite polynomials

Divide $5y + y^2 + 4$ by $2 + y$.

REVIEW POLYNOMIALS
For help with rewriting a polynomial, see p. 554.

$$\begin{array}{r l}
y + 3 & \\
y + 2\,\overline{)\,y^2 + 5y + 4} & \text{Rewrite polynomials.} \\
\underline{y^2 + 2y} & \text{Multiply } y \text{ and } y + 2. \\
3y + 4 & \text{Subtract } y^2 + 2y. \text{ Bring down 4.} \\
\underline{3y + 6} & \text{Multiply 3 and } y + 2. \\
-2 & \text{Subtract } 3y + 6.
\end{array}$$

▶ $(5y + y^2 + 4) \div (2 + y) = y + 3 + \frac{-2}{y + 2}$

EXAMPLE 5 Insert missing terms

Divide $13 + 4m^2$ by $-1 + 2m$.

$$\begin{array}{r l}
2m + 1 & \\
2m - 1\,\overline{)\,4m^2 + 0m + 13} & \text{Rewrite polynomials. Insert missing term.} \\
\underline{4m^2 - 2m} & \text{Multiply } 2m \text{ and } 2m - 1. \\
2m + 13 & \text{Subtract } 4m^2 - 2m. \text{ Bring down 13.} \\
\underline{2m - 1} & \text{Multiply 1 and } 2m - 1. \\
14 & \text{Subtract } 2m - 1.
\end{array}$$

▶ $(13 + 4m^2) \div (-1 + 2m) = 2m + 1 + \frac{14}{2m - 1}$

EXAMPLE 6 Rewrite and graph a rational function

Graph $y = \frac{2x - 1}{x - 2}$.

Solution

USE ASYMPTOTES
Use the graphing technique in Lesson 12.2 to graph the function. For instance, the lines $x = 2$ and $y = 2$ are asymptotes of the graph.

STEP 1 **Rewrite** the rational function in the form $y = \frac{a}{x - h} + k$.

$$\begin{array}{r}
2 \\
x - 2\,\overline{)\,2x - 1} \\
\underline{2x - 4} \\
3
\end{array}$$

So, $y = \frac{3}{x - 2} + 2$.

STEP 2 **Graph** the function.

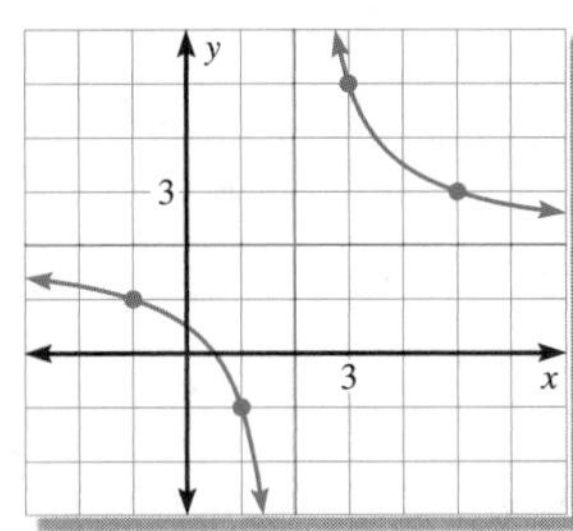

Extra Example 4

Divide $-3n + n^2 - 21$ by $3 + n$.

$n - 6 + \frac{-3}{n + 3}$

Key Questions to Ask for Example 4

- How can you check your answer? Find the product of the divisor and the quotient. Then add the numerator of the fraction. The result should be the original dividend.
- What is the remainder? What is the entire quotient? -2, $y + 3 + \frac{-2}{y + 2}$

Extra Example 5

Divide $-12 + 4y^2$ by $-1 + 2y$.

$2y + 1 + \frac{-11}{2y - 1}$

Key Questions to Ask for Example 5

- Why do you insert missing terms using zero coefficients? The dividend has no m-term, and the long-division process requires a place for m-terms.
- What is the purpose of inserting missing terms? Missing terms, with 0 coefficients, serve as placeholders in the long-division process.

Extra Example 6

Graph $y = \frac{2x + 1}{x - 1}$.

$y = \frac{2x + 1}{x - 1}$

7.

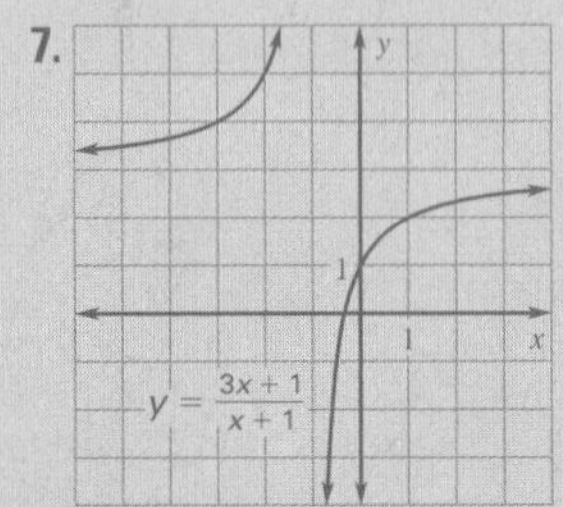

8.

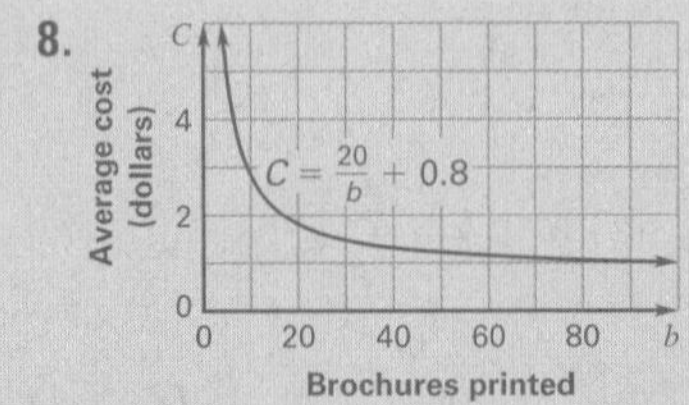

Differentiated Instruction

Inclusion Students may forget to organize the exponents in descending order before performing the long division as shown in **Examples 4 and 5**. It may help to show them the similarity to long division done in arithmetic. When they divide $23\overline{)648}$ for example, the highest powers (of 10) also appear first.

$$2.3 \times 10^1 + 3 \times 10^0\,\overline{)\,6 \times 10^2 + 4 \times 10^1 + 8 \times 10^0}$$

See also the *Algebra 1 Toolkit* for more strategies.

GUIDED PRACTICE for Examples 4, 5, and 6

5. Divide: $(8m - 7 + 4m^2) \div (5 + 2m)$ $\quad 2m - 1 + \frac{-2}{2m + 5}$

6. Divide: $(n^2 - 6) \div (-3 + n)$ $\quad n + 3 + \frac{3}{n - 3}$

7. Graph $y = \frac{3x + 1}{x + 1}$.
See margin.

EXAMPLE 7 Solve a multi-step problem

PRINTING COSTS You are creating brochures that promote your school's sports events. You pay \$20 for computer time. The cost of printing a brochure is \$.60. Write and graph an equation that gives the average cost C (in dollars per brochure) as a function of the number b of brochures printed.

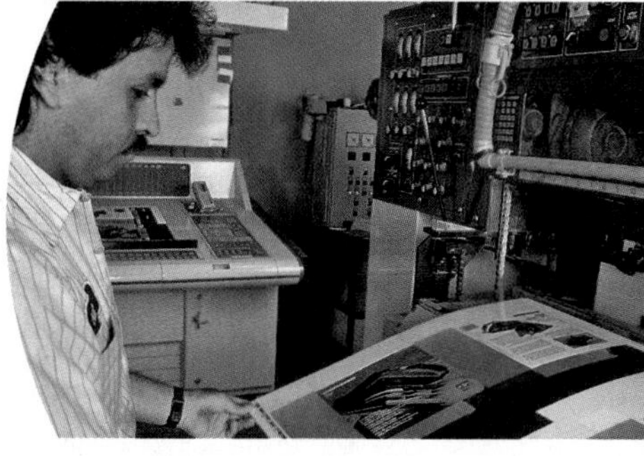

Solution

STEP 1 **Write** a verbal model. Then write an equation.

$$\text{Average cost (dollars/brochure)} = \frac{\text{Cost of computer time (dollars)} + \text{Printing cost (dollars/brochure)} \cdot \text{Number printed (brochures)}}{\text{Number printed (brochures)}}$$

$$C = \frac{20 + 0.6b}{b}$$

STEP 2 **Rewrite** the rational function.

$$C = \frac{20 + 0.6b}{b} = \frac{20}{b} + \frac{0.6b}{b} = \frac{20}{b} + 0.6$$

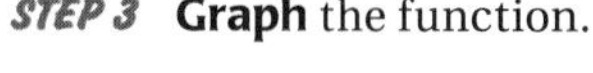

STEP 3 **Graph** the function.

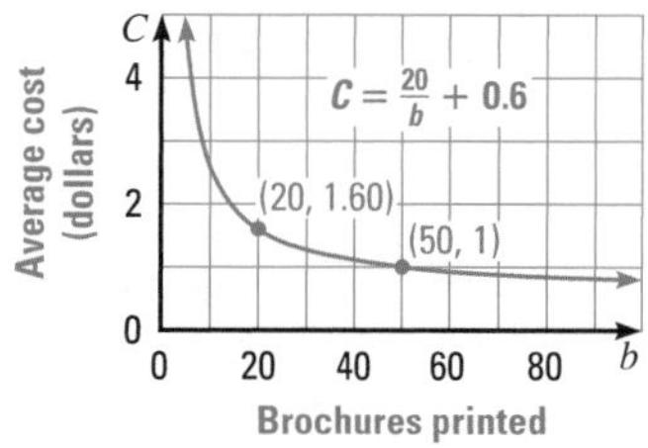

GUIDED PRACTICE for Example 7

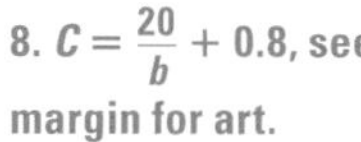

8. $C = \frac{20}{b} + 0.8$, see margin for art.

9. $C = \frac{100}{m} + 45$, see margin for art.

8. **WHAT IF?** In Example 7, suppose the cost of printing a brochure is \$.80. Write and graph an equation that gives the average cost C (in dollars per brochure) as a function of the number b of brochures printed.

9. **INTERNET COSTS** A cable Internet service provider charges an installation fee of \$100 and a monthly service charge of \$45. Write and graph an equation that gives the average cost C (in dollars per month) as a function of the number m of months of Internet service.

Extra Example 7

You pay \$50 for an annual park permit and \$5 per day for camping fees. Write and graph an equation that gives the average cost per day C of camping as a function of the number of d days that you camp.

$C = \frac{50}{d} + 5$

Average cost (dollars): 0, 10, 20, 30, 40; Days of camping: 0, 10, 20, 30, 40, d; $C = \frac{50}{d} + 5$

Closing the Lesson

Have students summarize the major points of the lesson and answer the Essential Question: How do you divide polynomials?

- **Write the problem as long division, using placeholders with a zero coefficient for missing terms.**
- **Write the result of dividing as: Dividend ÷ Divisor = Quotient + $\frac{\text{Remainder}}{\text{Divisor}}$.**
- **To check, find the product of the quotient and the divisor. Then add the numerator of the fraction. The result should be the original dividend.**

When dividing a polynomial by a monomial, write the division as a fraction and simplify, or use long division. Use long division when dividing a polynomial by a binomial. Write the polynomials so that the exponents decrease from left to right.

9.

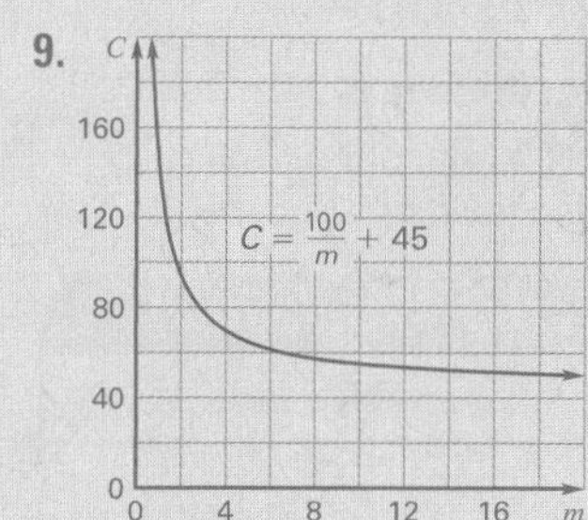

Differentiated Instruction

Below Level For **Example 7**, have students find the cost to print 5, 15, 25, 70, and 80 brochures. Ask them to find those costs two ways: by substituting values for b in the equation, and by using the graph. Then ask them to compare and contrast the two methods.

Advanced For **Example 7**, have students research several local printing stores to find what they charge for computer time and for printing brochures. Ask them to do a comparison analysis of the costs by writing equations for all of the stores and then graphing them in the same coordinate plane.

See also the *Algebra 1 Toolkit* for more strategies.

4 PRACTICE AND APPLY

Assignment Guide

Answer Transparencies available for all exercises

Basic:
Day 1: EP p. 946 Exs. 3–6
pp. 788–791
Exs. 1–12, 19–21, 51–59
Day 2: pp. 788–791
Exs. 13–18, 23–29 odd, 31–34, 42–47, 60–65

Average:
Day 1: pp. 788–791
Exs. 1, 2, 5–12, 19–21, 35–37, 51–59
Day 2: pp. 788–791
Exs. 13–18, 22–30 even, 31–34, 38, 42–49, 60–64 even

Advanced:
Day 1: pp. 788–791
Exs. 1, 2, 4–12 even, 19, 35–41*, 51–59
Day 2: pp. 788–791
Exs. 13–18, 22–30 even, 31–34, 42–50*, 60–64 even

Block:
pp. 788–791
Exs. 1, 2, 5–21, 22–30 even, 31–38, 42–49, 51–59, 60–64 even

Differentiated Instruction

See *Algebra 1 Best Practices Toolkit* for suggestions on addressing the needs of a diverse classroom.

Homework Check

For a quick check of student understanding of key concepts, go over the following exercises:

Basic: 6, 9, 17, 24, 42
Average: 8, 10, 18, 26, 43
Advanced: 12, 16, 18, 28, 44

Extra Practice

- Student Edition, p. 946
- Chapter 12 Resource Book: Practice levels A, B, C, pp. 34–36

Practice Worksheet

An easily-readable reduced practice page (with answers) for this lesson can be found on p. 762C.

12.3 EXERCISES

HOMEWORK KEY
○ = **WORKED-OUT SOLUTIONS** on p. WS29 for Exs. 7, 25, and 45
★ = **STANDARDIZED TEST PRACTICE** Exs. 2, 19, 33, 34, 38, 47, 48, and 49
◆ = **MULTIPLE REPRESENTATIONS** Ex. 46

SKILL PRACTICE

A

1. VOCABULARY Copy and complete: To divide a polynomial by a(n) __?__, you can either write the division as a fraction or use long division. monomial

2. ★ WRITING *Describe* the steps you would take in graphing the rational function $f(x) = \frac{3x - 2}{x + 6}$. See margin.

EXAMPLES 1, 2, 3, 4, and 5 on pp. 784–786 for Exs. 3–21

DIVIDING POLYNOMIALS Divide.

3. $(8x^3 - 12x^2 + 16x) \div 4x$ $2x^2 - 3x + 4$

4. $(10y^3 + 20y^2 + 55y) \div 5y$ $2y^2 + 4y + 11$

5. $(12r^4 - 30r^2 - 72r) \div (-6r)$ $-2r^3 + 5r + 12$

6. $(21s^4 + 49s^3 - 35s^2) \div (-7s)$ (6. $-3s^3 - 7s^2 + 5s$)

7. $(3v^2 - v - 10) \div (v - 2)$ $3v + 5$

8. $(7w^2 + 3w - 4) \div (w + 1)$ $7w - 4$

9. $(2m^2 - 5m - 12) \div (2m + 3)$ $m - 4$

10. $(6n^2 + 7n - 3) \div (3n - 1)$ $2n + 3$

11. $(a^2 - 5a + 3) \div (a - 1)$ $a - 4 + \frac{-1}{a - 1}$

12. $(c^2 - 2c - 4) \div (c + 4)$ $c - 6 + \frac{20}{c + 4}$

13. $(-21 - 4p + 3p^2) \div (3 + p)$ (13. $3p - 13 + \frac{18}{3 + p}$)

14. $(8q + q^2 + 7) \div (7 + q)$ $q + 1$

15. $(9x + x^2 + 6) \div (6 + x)$ $x + 3 + \frac{-12}{6 + x}$

16. $(4y^2 - 5) \div (2y + 5)$ $2y - 5 + \frac{20}{2y + 5}$

17. $(5 - t^2) \div (t - 3)$ $-t - 3 + \frac{-4}{t - 3}$

18. $(7 - 8x^2) \div (3 + 2x)$ $-4x + 6 + \frac{-11}{3 + 2x}$

19. ★ MULTIPLE CHOICE What is the remainder when you divide $x^2 + 4x + 9$ by $x - 4$? B

Ⓐ $x - 4$ Ⓑ 41 Ⓒ $x + 8$ Ⓓ $\frac{41}{x - 4}$

ERROR ANALYSIS ***Describe* and correct the error in dividing the polynomials.** 20, 21. See margin.

20. $(5x + 6) \div (x + 2)$

$$\begin{array}{r} 5 \\ x + 2\overline{)5x + 6} \\ 5x + 10 \\ \hline -4 \end{array}$$

$(5x + 6) \div (x + 2) = 5 + \frac{-4}{5x + 6}$

21. $(8x - 9) \div (x - 3)$

$$\begin{array}{r} 8 \\ x - 3\overline{)8x - 9} \\ 8x - 24 \\ \hline -33 \end{array}$$

$(8x - 9) \div (x - 3) = 8 + \frac{-33}{x - 3}$

EXAMPLE 6 on p. 786 for Exs. 22–30

GRAPHING FUNCTIONS Graph the function. 22–30. See margin.

22. $y = \frac{x + 10}{x}$

23. $y = \frac{2x - 7}{x}$

24. $y = \frac{x + 4}{x - 3}$

25. $y = \frac{2x - 4}{x - 1}$

26. $y = \frac{5x + 2}{x + 3}$

27. $y = \frac{6x - 4}{x + 5}$

28. $y = \frac{2 - x}{x + 9}$

29. $y = \frac{2 + 4x}{x - 3}$

30. $y = \frac{7 - 10x}{x + 7}$

2. *Sample answer:* Use long division to divide $3x - 2$ by $x + 6$, thus rewriting the function in the form $f(x) = \frac{a}{x - h} + k$. Then identify the asymptotes of the function, plot several points on each side of the vertical asymptote, and sketch the hyperbola.

20. The remainder, -4, should be placed over the divisor, $x + 2$, the dividend, $5x + 6$; $(5x + 6) \div (x + 2) = 5 + \frac{-4}{x + 2}$.

 **GEOMETRY Divide the surface area of the rectangular prism by its volume.**

31. 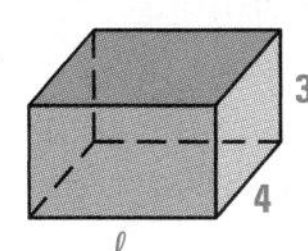 $\frac{7}{6} + \frac{2}{\ell}$

32. 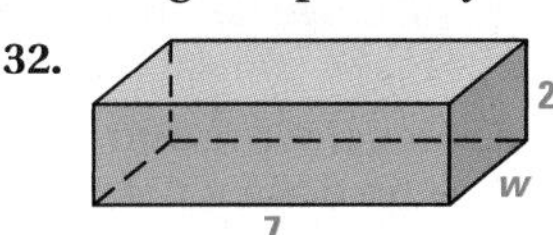 $\frac{9}{7} + \frac{2}{w}$

33. ★ **MULTIPLE CHOICE** What is the horizontal asymptote of the graph of $y = \frac{bx + c}{x - d}$? A

Ⓐ $y = b$ Ⓑ $y = c$ Ⓒ $y = d$ Ⓓ $y = 0$

34. ★ **MULTIPLE CHOICE** The graph of which function is shown? C

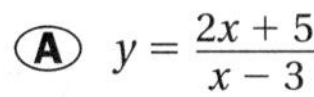

Ⓐ $y = \frac{2x + 5}{x - 3}$ Ⓑ $y = \frac{2x + 5}{x + 3}$

Ⓒ $y = \frac{2x - 5}{x - 3}$ Ⓓ $y = \frac{2x - 5}{x + 3}$

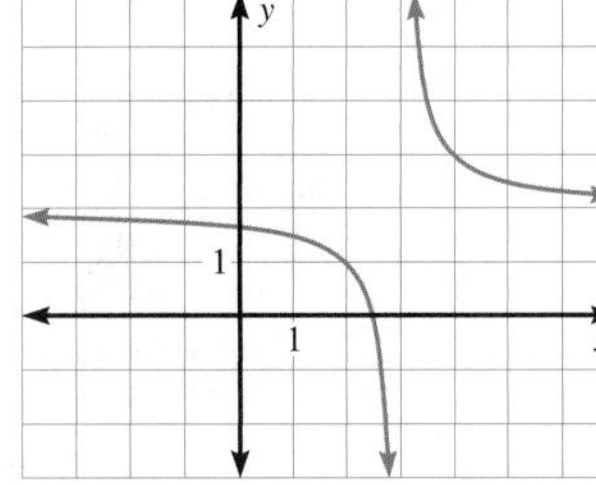

REASONING In Exercises 35–37, find the value of *k* using the given information.

35. When $8x^2 + 26x + k$ is divided by $x + 3$, the remainder is 4. 10

36. When $100x^2 + k$ is divided by $5x + 2$, the remainder is 0. −16

37. The graph of $y = \frac{kx + 4}{x - 6}$ has $y = -5$ as its horizontal asymptote. −5

38. ★ **OPEN-ENDED** Write a function of the form $f(x) = \frac{bx + c}{x - h}$ such that the graph of the function has $x = 4$ and $y = 6$ as its asymptotes. *Sample answer:* $\frac{6x + 1}{x - 4}$

 **CHALLENGE Graph the function.** 39–41. See margin.

39. $y = \frac{6x + 10}{3x + 6}$ **40.** $y = \frac{12x - 7}{4x - 8}$ **41.** $y = \frac{10x + 3}{2x - 6}$

PROBLEM SOLVING

EXAMPLE 7 on p. 787 for Exs. 42–45

A **42. MOVIE RENTALS** You order movie rental coupons from a website for \$3 each. The total cost of your order includes a \$4 shipping fee. Write an equation that gives the average cost *C* (in dollars per coupon) as a function of the number *r* of coupons ordered. Then graph the function.

@HomeTutor for problem solving help at classzone.com $C = \frac{4 + 3r}{r}$; see margin for art.

43. MEMBERSHIP FEES You pay \$80 for an annual membership to a dance club and pay \$3 per dance class. Write an equation that gives the average cost *C* (in dollars per class) as a function of the number *d* of dance classes that you take. Then graph the function. $C = \frac{80 + 3d}{d}$; see margin for art.

@HomeTutor for problem solving help at classzone.com

Avoiding Common Errors

Exercises 3–18 Some students may write the remainder fraction using the dividend as the fraction's denominator, rather than the divisor. Suggest that students write the following rule on a notecard and use it to check the form of their answers: Dividend ÷ Divisor = Quotient + $\frac{\text{Remainder}}{\text{Divisor}}$.

Teaching Strategy

Exercises 22–30 Before students graph the functions, ask for one or two volunteers to rewrite each function in the form $y = \frac{a}{x - h} + k$ on the chalkboard. Ask students to identify the asymptotes for each example and to explain how the asymptotes are related to the graph of the function.

41. 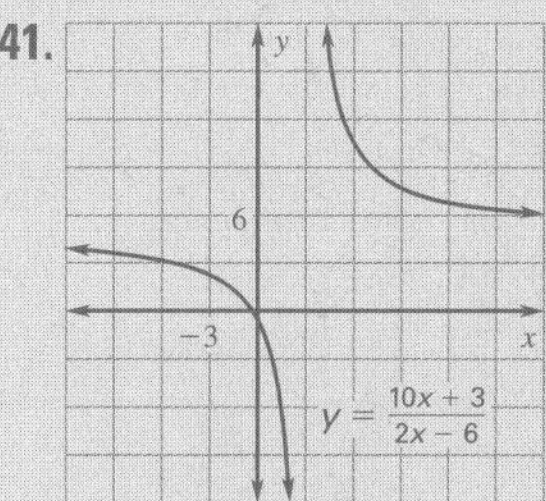

42. 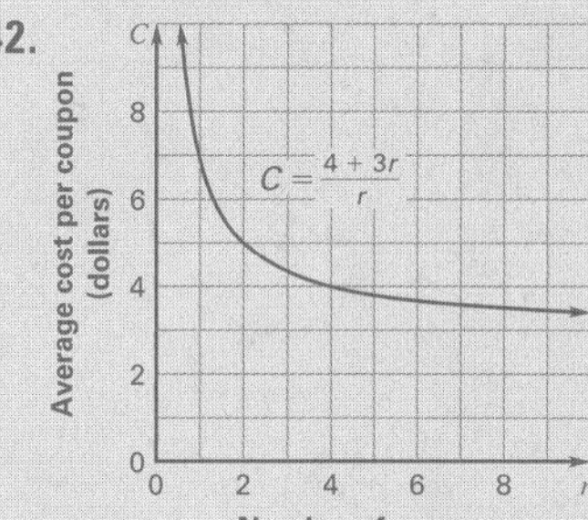

43. 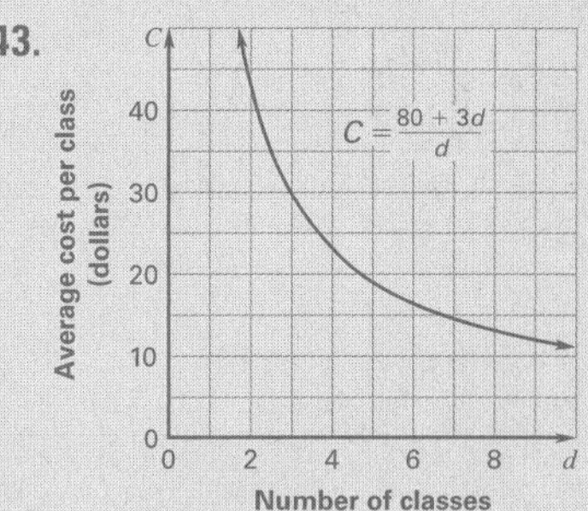

21. When subtracting $8x - 24$ from $8x - 9$, the result is $-9 - (-24) = -9 + 24 = 15$; $(8x - 9) \div (x - 3) = 8 + \frac{15}{x - 3}$.

22–30. See Additional Answers beginning on p. AA1.

39. 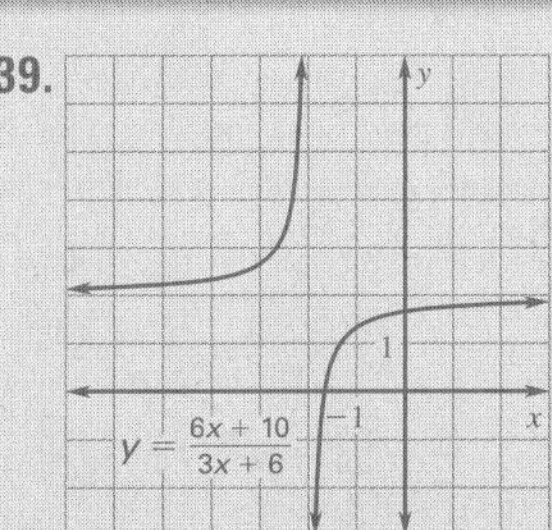

40. 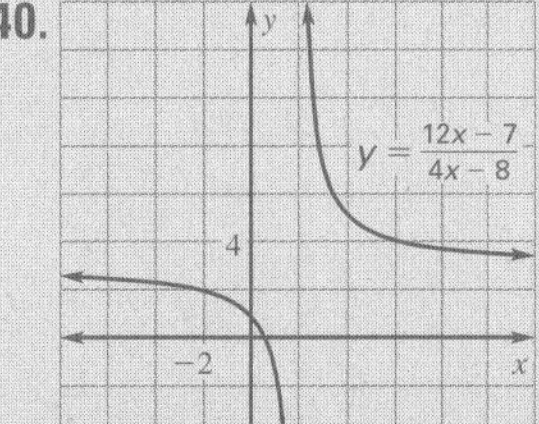

Mathematical Reasoning

Exercise 46 For part (a), review scatterplots and lines of fit before students attempt this exercise. For part (b), make sure students understand how to calculate what percent is represented by a specific tip.

An **Animated Algebra** activity is available on-line for **Exercise 49**. This activity is also available on the **Power Presentations CD-ROM**.

44a.

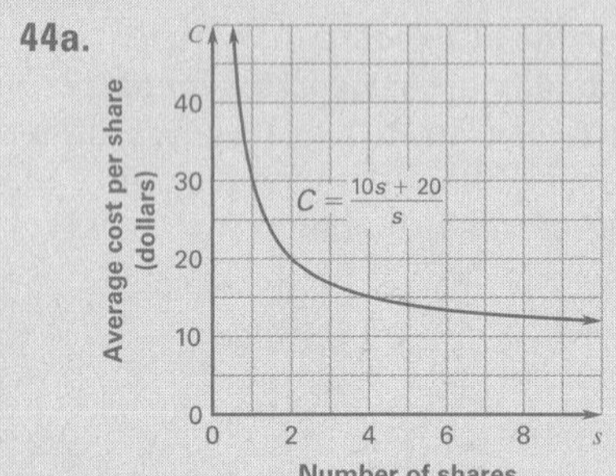

45b.

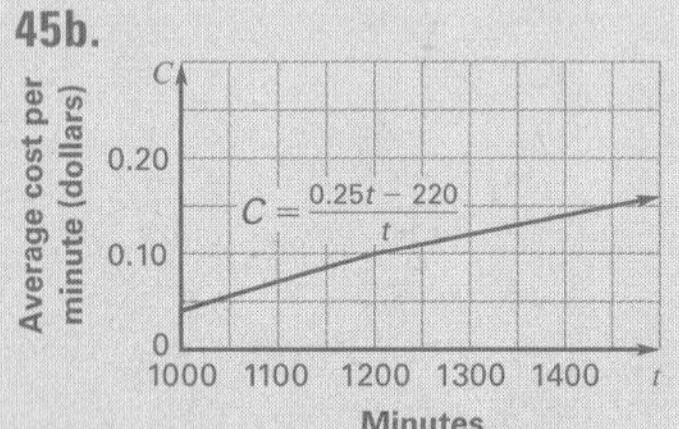

46a.

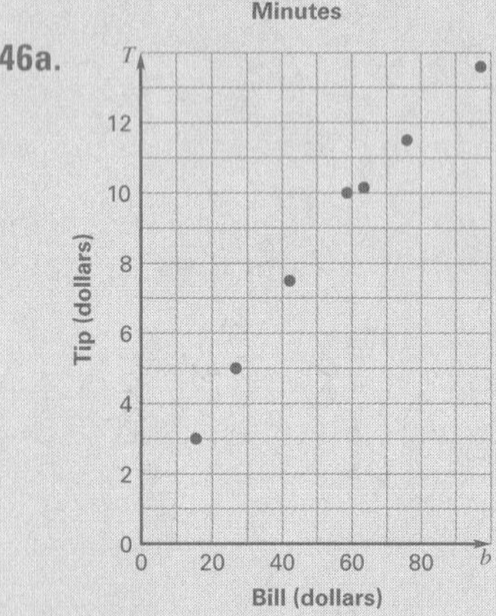

46c.

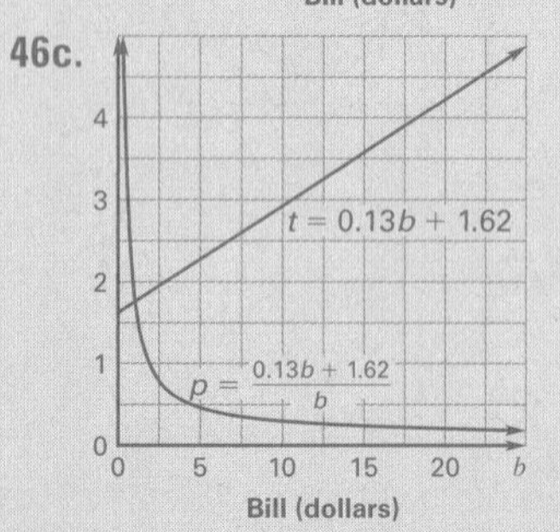

44. INVESTING An investor plans to purchase shares of a stock through a brokerage company. Each share costs $10, and the company charges a transaction fee of $20.

a. **Model** Write and graph an equation that gives the average cost C (in dollars per share) as a function of the number s of shares that the investor purchases. $C = \frac{10s + 20}{s}$; see margin for art.

b. **Approximate** Use the graph to approximate the number of shares purchased if the average cost is $12 per share. 10 shares

45. CELL PHONE PLAN You are thinking about subscribing to the cell phone plan described in the advertisement below.

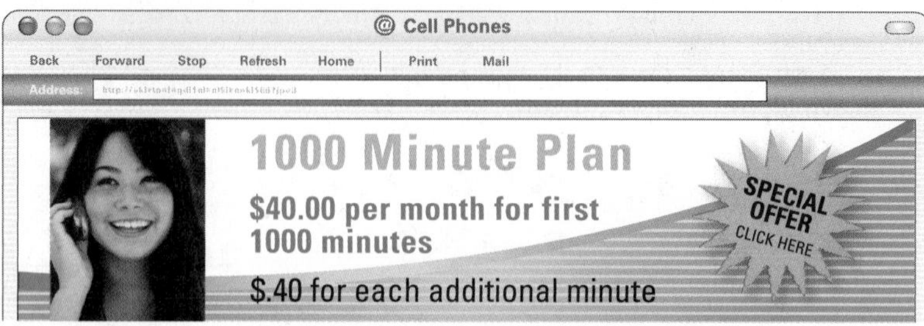

Cell Phones
Back Forward Stop Refresh Home Print Mail
Address:
1000 Minute Plan
$40.00 per month for first 1000 minutes
$.40 for each additional minute
SPECIAL OFFER
CLICK HERE

a. **Model** Write an equation that gives the average cost C (in dollars per minute) as a function of the time t (in minutes) of cell phone use for 1000 or more minutes. $C = \frac{0.4t - 360}{t}$

b. **Describe** Graph the function. *Describe* how the average cost per minute changes as time increases.

45b. See margin for art; the average cost increases.

c. **Approximate** Use the graph to approximate the number of minutes used if the average cost is $.05 per minute. about 1030 min

B

46. MULTIPLE REPRESENTATIONS The table shows several restaurant bills and their corresponding tips.

Bill, b (dollars)	15.42	26.75	42.18	58.66	63.48	75.89	97.14
Tip, t (dollars)	3.00	5.00	7.50	10.00	10.15	11.50	13.60

a. **Writing an Equation** Make a scatter plot of the data. Then write a linear equation that models the tip t as a function of the bill b. $t = 0.13b + 1.62$; see margin for art.

b. **Writing an Equation** Write an equation that gives the percent tip p (in decimal form) as a function of the bill b. $p = \frac{0.13b + 1.62}{b}$

c. **Drawing Graphs** Draw the graphs of both equations in the same coordinate plane. *Compare* how the tip changes with how the percent tip changes as the bill increases. See margin for art; the tip increases, but the percent tip decreases.

47. ★ SHORT RESPONSE The number y (in millions) of households that owned VCRs during the period 1984–2000 can be modeled by

$$y = \frac{60 + 120x}{7 + x}$$

where x is the number of years since 1984.

a. **Describe** Graph the model. *Describe* how the number of households that owned VCRs changed during this period.

47a. See margin for art; the number of households with VCRs increased.

b. **Justify** Do you expect that the number of households that own VCRs will ever exceed 150 million? *Justify* your answer. See margin.

○ = WORKED-OUT SOLUTIONS on p. WS1 ★ = STANDARDIZED TEST PRACTICE

= MULTIPLE REPRESENTATIONS

47a.

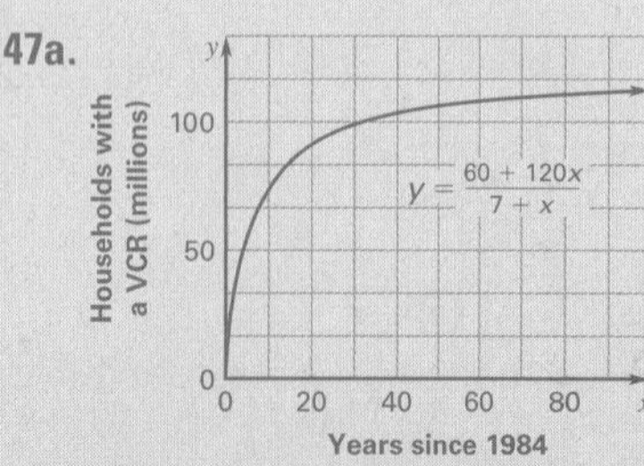

47b. No; as x increases, the graph of the function approaches its horizontal asymptote $y = 120$ from below, so the value of y will never exceed 120 million if this model applies to years beyond 2000.

48. ★ **MULTIPLE CHOICE** A building's ratio y of surface area to volume is a measure of how well the building minimizes heat loss. A company plans to build a store in the shape of a rectangular prism. The store will have a length of 500 feet and a width of 300 feet, but the company hasn't decided on a height h (in feet). Which equation gives the ratio y as a function of the height h? **A**

Ⓐ $y = \frac{4}{375} + \frac{2}{h}$ Ⓑ $y = 1600 + \frac{1}{150{,}000h}$

Ⓒ $y = 1600 + \frac{2}{h}$ Ⓓ $y = 300 + \frac{500}{h}$

49. ★ **EXTENDED RESPONSE** The ratio of a microorganism's surface area to its volume is a measure of how efficiently the microorganism can perform certain metabolic tasks. Suppose a microorganism is shaped approximately like a cylinder and grows by increasing its length but not its radius. **a–c. See margin.**

a. **Model and Graph** Write an equation that gives the ratio y of surface area to volume in terms of the length ℓ (in micrometers) and the radius r (in micrometers). Then graph the equation for a microorganism whose radius is 50 micrometers.

b. **Interpret** The greater the ratio, the less efficiently a microorganism performs metabolic tasks. As the microorganism's length increases, is the microorganism *more efficient* or *less efficient* at performing metabolic tasks? *Explain* your choice.

c. **Explain** How would the microorganism's efficiency change if the length remained constant but the radius increased? *Explain.*

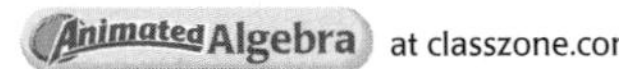

at classzone.com

50. No; the effective tax rate e for total income I is given by the function $e(I) = \frac{-600}{I} + 0.06$. As seen in the graph, the value of $e(I)$ approaches 0.06 from below but never actually takes on the value 0.06; see margin for art.

50. **CHALLENGE** The effective tax rate is the percent of total income that a worker pays in taxes. Suppose that a worker doesn't pay taxes on income up to \$10,000 and pays taxes of 6% on total income that exceeds \$10,000. Will the effective tax rate be 6% for any amount of total income? *Justify* your answer graphically. C

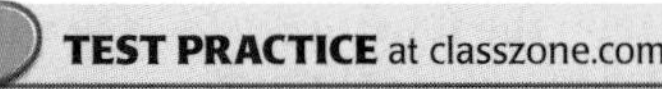

TEST PRACTICE at classzone.com

ILLINOIS MIXED REVIEW

51. How would the graph of the function $y = x^2 - 3$ be affected if the function were changed to $y = x^2 + 3$? **C**

Ⓐ The graph would shift 6 units to the left.

Ⓑ The graph would shift 6 units to the right.

Ⓒ The graph would shift 6 units up.

Ⓓ The graph would shift 6 units down.

52. If the variables x and y are related so that $xy = 60$, which statement must be true? **B**

Ⓐ Both x and y are less than 60. Ⓑ If x is negative, y is negative.

Ⓒ As x decreases, y decreases. Ⓓ Both x and y are greater than 1.

5 ASSESS AND RETEACH

Daily Homework Quiz

Transparency Available

Divide.

1. $(6x^3 - 4x^2 + 18x) \div 2x$ $3x^2 - 2x + 9$
2. $(3x^2 - x - 2) \div (x - 1)$ $3x + 2$
3. $(-20 + 4x^2) \div (5 + 2x)$ $2x - 5 + \frac{5}{2x + 5}$
4. A print shop charges \$15 plus \$.12 per page to copy and bind reports. Write an equation that gives the average cost C per page as a function of the number of pages p that are copied. $C = \frac{15}{p} + 0.12$

Available at **classzone.com**

Diagnosis/Remediation

- Practice A, B, C in Chapter 12 Resource Book, pp. 34–36
- Study Guide in Chapter 12 Resource Book, pp. 37–38
- Practice Workbook, pp. 186–187
- @HomeTutor

Challenge

Additional challenge is available in the Chapter 12 Resource Book, p. 41.

49a–c. See Additional Answers beginning on p. AA1.

50.

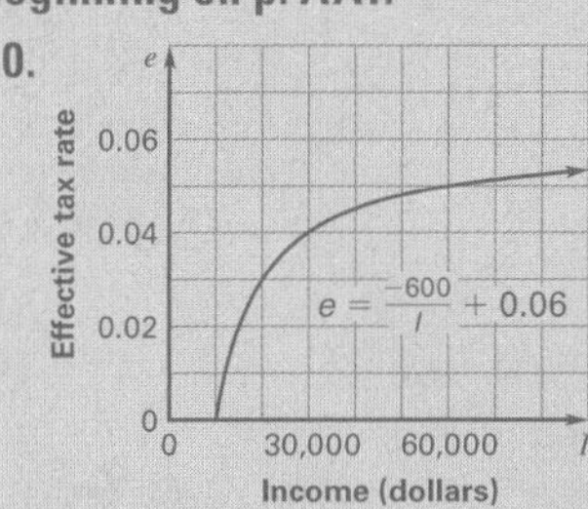

1 PLAN AND PREPARE

Learn the Method

- Students will use graphing calculators to find the asymptotes of the graph of a rational function.
- After the activity, students can use a graphing calculator to check their solutions in Lesson 12.3, Exercises 22–30, 33–34, and 39–41.

Keystroke Help

Keystrokes for several models of calculators are available in blackline format in the *Chapter 12 Resource Book*.

2 TEACH

Tips for Success

When students enter a rational function into a graphing calculator, make sure they use parentheses around the numerator and around the denominator.

Extra Example 1

Graph $y = \frac{x+1}{x^2 - 6x + 9}$ using a graphing calculator. Identify any vertical or horizontal asymptotes.

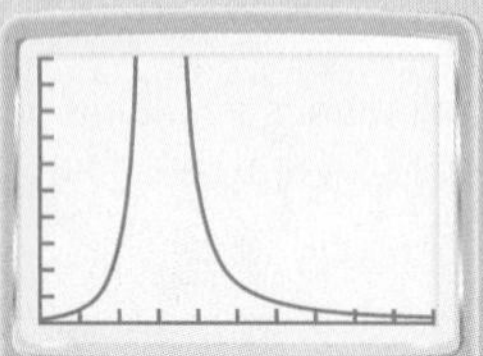

$y = 0$ is a horizontal asymptote and $x = 3$ is a vertical asymptote.

Graphing Calculator ACTIVITY *Use after Lesson 12.3*

12.3 Find Asymptotes of Graphs

QUESTION How can you find the asymptotes of the graph of a rational function?

EXAMPLE 1 Graph a rational function

Graph $y = \frac{2x+1}{3x^2 - 4x + 5}$ using a graphing calculator. Identify any vertical or horizontal asymptotes.

STEP 1 *Enter function*
Press Y= and enter the function as shown.

```
Y1=(2X+1)/(3X2-4X+5)
Y2=
Y3=
Y4=
Y5=
Y6=
Y7=
```

STEP 2 *Identify asymptotes*
Graph the function. Use the *trace* feature to identify the asymptotes.

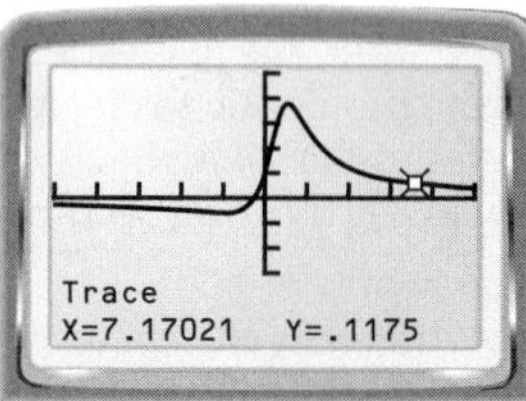

The graph doesn't approach a vertical line. So, the graph doesn't have a vertical asymptote. The graph approaches the x-axis. So, $y = 0$ is a horizontal asymptote.

PRACTICE

Graph the function using a graphing calculator. Identify any vertical or horizontal asymptotes. 1–6. See margin.

1. $y = \frac{8}{x-2}$
2. $y = \frac{4}{6x-7}$
3. $y = \frac{x-9}{x^2+1}$
4. $y = \frac{x+5}{x^2+4x+4}$
5. $y = \frac{x+1}{4x^2-36}$
6. $y = \frac{5}{10x^2+9}$
7. Make a table that shows the following information for each function in Exercises 1–6: See margin.
   - vertical asymptotes, if any
   - values, if any, of x that make the function undefined
   - horizontal asymptotes, if any
   - degree of numerator
   - degree of denominator

1.
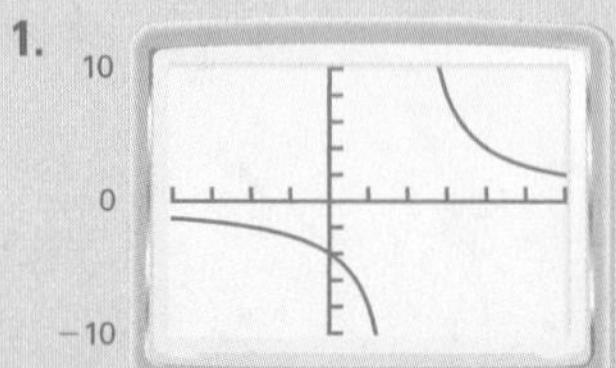

vertical: $x = 2$, horizontal: $y = 0$

2.
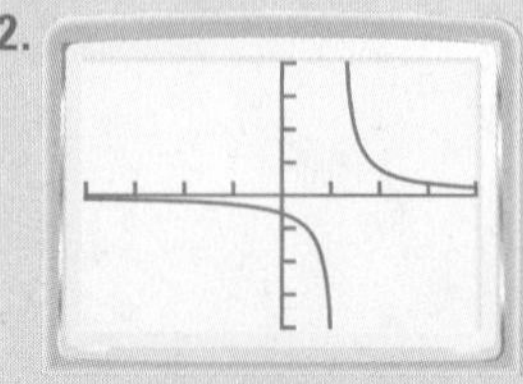
vertical: $x = \frac{7}{6}$, horizontal: $y = 0$

3.
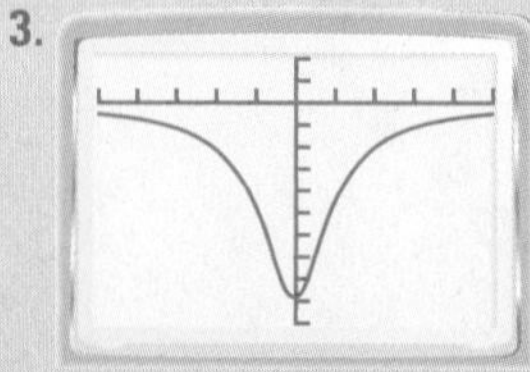
vertical: none, horizontal: $y = 0$

4.
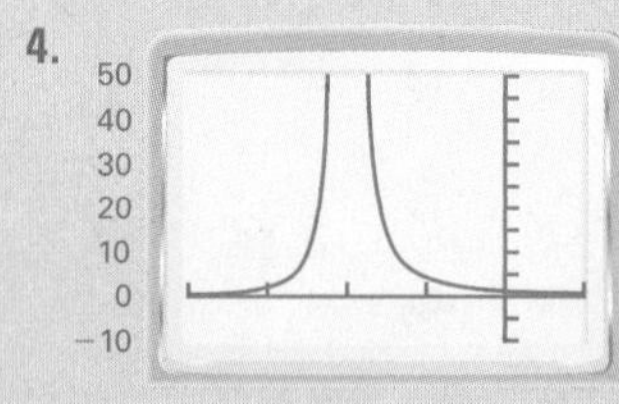

vertical: $x = -2$, horizontal: $y = 0$

@HomeTutor
classzone.com
Keystrokes

EXAMPLE 2 Graph a rational function

Graph $y = \frac{2x^2 + 1}{x^2 - 9}$ using a graphing calculator. Identify any vertical or horizontal asymptotes.

STEP 1 *Enter function*

Press Y= and enter the function as shown.

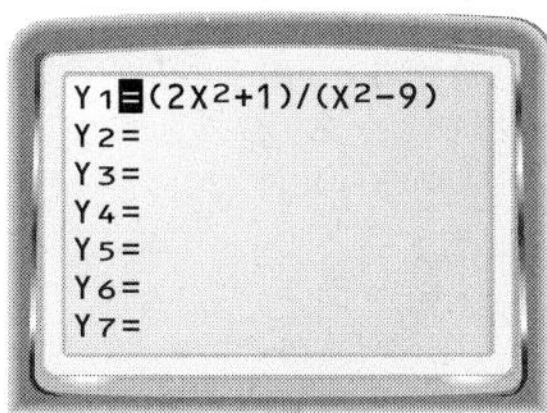

STEP 2 *Identify asymptotes*

Graph the function. Use the *trace* feature to identify the asymptotes.

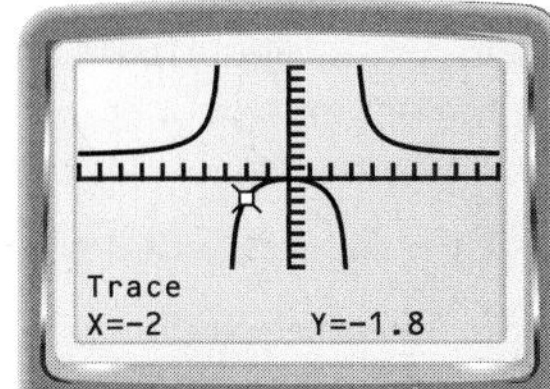

The graph approaches one of two vertical lines, $x = -3$ and $x = 3$. So, $x = -3$ and $x = 3$ are vertical asymptotes. The graph also approaches the line $y = 2$. So, $y = 2$ is a horizontal asymptote.

PRACTICE

Graph the function using a graphing calculator. Identify any vertical or horizontal asymptotes. 8–13. See margin.

8. $y = \frac{-6x}{x + 9}$
9. $y = \frac{5x - 12}{x - 1}$
10. $y = \frac{10x}{2x - 9}$
11. $y = \frac{12x^2 - 7}{4x^2 + 2}$
12. $y = \frac{27x^2 - x}{9x^2 - 16}$
13. $y = \frac{18x^2 - 1}{6x^2 - 6}$
14. Repeat Exercise 7 for the functions in Exercises 8–13. For each function, include in your table the quotient of the leading coefficient of the numerator and the leading coefficient of the denominator. See margin.

DRAW CONCLUSIONS

15. What vertical asymptotes, if any, does the graph of a rational function whose numerator and denominator do not have any common factors have? Vertical lines $x = a$, where a is an x-value that makes the denominator of the rational function equal to 0.
16. If the degree of the numerator of a rational function is less than the degree of the denominator, what is a horizontal asymptote of the graph? $y = 0$
17. If the degree of the numerator of a rational function equals the degree of the denominator, what is a horizontal asymptote of the graph? $y = a$, where a is the quotient of the leading coefficient of the numerator and the leading coefficient of the denominator.
18. **CONJECTURE** Suppose the degree of the numerator of a rational function is greater than the degree of the denominator. Does the graph of the function have a horizontal asymptote? Give examples. See margin.

5. vertical: $x = -3$, $x = 3$, horizontal: $y = 0$

6. vertical: none, horizontal: $y = 0$

7–14. See Additional Answers beginning on p. AA1.

Extra Example 2

Graph $y = \frac{x^2 + 4}{x^2 - 1}$ using a graphing calculator. Identify any vertical or horizontal asymptotes.

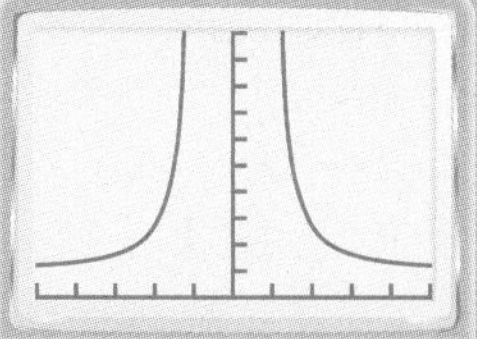

$y = 1$ is a horizontal asymptote and $x = 1$ and $x = -1$ are vertical asymptotes.

3 ASSESS AND RETEACH

Without graphing the following functions, explain whether they have a horizontal asymptote.

1. $y = \frac{x + 2}{x^2 + 6x + 8}$ There is a horizontal asymptote (it is $y = 0$) since the degree of the denominator is greater than the degree of the numerator.
2. $y = \frac{x + 4}{2x + 1}$ There is a horizontal asymptote $\left(\text{it is } y = \frac{1}{2}\right)$ since the degree of the denominator and the degree of the numerator are the same.

18. No. *Sample answer:* For example, a linear equation, such as $y = 2x$, can be written as a rational equation, $y = \frac{2x}{1}$, where the degree of the numerator is 1 and the degree of the denominator is 0. The graph of a linear equation is a straight line, which has no horizontal asymptote. A quadratic equation, such as $y = x^2$, can also be written as a rational equation, $y = \frac{x^2}{1}$, where the degree of the numerator is 2 and the degree of the denominator is 0. The graph of a quadratic equation is a parabola, which has no horizontal asymptote.

1 PLAN AND PREPARE

Warm-Up Exercises

Transparency Available

Factor the polynomial.

1. $x^2 + 8x + 15$ $(x + 3)(x + 5)$
2. $2x^2 + 15x - 8$ $(x + 8)(2x - 1)$
3. You pay $20 to join an aerobics center and pay $4 per class session. Write an equation that gives the average cost C per session as a function of the number a of aerobics sessions that you take. $C = \frac{20}{a} + 4$

Notetaking Guide

Transparency Available

Promotes interactive learning and notetaking skills, pp. 280–282.

Pacing

Basic: 1 day

Average: 1 day

Advanced: 1 day

Block: 0.5 block with 12.5

- See *Teaching Guide/Lesson Plan.*

2 FOCUS AND MOTIVATE

Essential Question

Big Idea 2, p. 763

How do you simplify a rational expression? Tell students they will learn how to answer this question by factoring, dividing, and finding excluded values.

12.4 Simplify Rational Expressions

8.11.01 Simplify or identify equivalent algebraic expressions (e.g., exponential, rational, logarithmic, factored, polynomial).

Before You simplified polynomials.

Now You will simplify rational expressions.

Why So you can model a cost over time, as in Example 5.

Key Vocabulary
- rational expression
- excluded value
- simplest form of a rational expression

A **rational expression** is an expression that can be written as a ratio of two polynomials where the denominator is not 0. A rational expression is undefined when the denominator is 0. A number that makes a rational expression undefined is called an **excluded value**. For example, $\frac{2}{x-3}$ is undefined when $x = 3$. So, 3 is an excluded value.

EXAMPLE 1 Find excluded values

Find the excluded values, if any, of the expression.

a. $\frac{x+8}{10x}$ b. $\frac{5}{2y+14}$ c. $\frac{4v}{v^2-9}$ d. $\frac{7w+2}{8w^2+w+5}$

Solution

a. The expression $\frac{x+8}{10x}$ is undefined when $10x = 0$, or $x = 0$.

▶ The excluded value is 0.

b. The expression $\frac{5}{2y+14}$ is undefined when $2y + 14 = 0$, or $x = -7$.

▶ The excluded value is -7.

c. The expression $\frac{4v}{v^2-9}$ is undefined when $v^2 - 9 = 0$, or $(v + 3)(v - 3) = 0$. The solutions of the equation are -3 and 3.

▶ The excluded values are -3 and 3.

d. The expression $\frac{7w+2}{8w^2+w+5}$ is undefined when $8w^2 + w + 5 = 0$. The discriminant is $b^2 - 4ac = 1^2 - 4(8)(5) < 0$. So, the quadratic equation has no real roots.

▶ There are no excluded values.

REVIEW DISCRIMINANT
For help with finding the discriminant of a quadratic equation, see p. 678.

GUIDED PRACTICE for Example 1

Find the excluded values, if any, of the expression.

1. $\frac{x+2}{3x-5}$ $\frac{5}{3}$ 2. $\frac{2}{5y^2+2y+3}$ none 3. $\frac{n-6}{2n^2-5n-12}$ $-\frac{3}{2}, 4$ 4. $\frac{2m}{m^2-4}$ $-2, 2$

Resource Planning Guide

Chapter Resource Book
- Teaching Guide/Lesson Plan (pp. 42–43)
- Activity Master (p. 44)
- Practice levels A, B, C (pp. 45–47)
- Study Guide (pp. 48–49)
- Catch-up for Absent Students (p. 50)
- Problem Solving Workshop (p. 51)
- Challenge (p. 53)

Workbooks
- Notetaking Guide (pp. 280–282)
- Practice Workbook (pp. 188–189)

Teaching Options
- **Power Presentations CD-ROM** provides dynamic electronic teaching resources for the classroom.
- **Activity Generator CD-ROM** provides editable activities for all ability levels.

Interactive Technology
- Easy Planner
- Power Presentations CD-ROM
- Activity Generator CD-ROM
- Animated Algebra
- Test Generator CD-ROM
- Online Quiz
- eWorkbook
- eEdition
- @HomeTutor

Resources for English Learners
- Quick Reference for English Learners
- Spanish Study Guide
- Multi-Language Visual Glossary
- Student Resources in Spanish

See also the *Algebra 1 Toolkit* for more strategies for meeting individual needs.

SIMPLIFYING A RATIONAL EXPRESSION To simplify a rational expression, you factor the numerator and denominator and then divide out any common factors. A rational expression is in **simplest form** if the numerator and denominator have no factors in common other than 1.

KEY CONCEPT *For Your Notebook*

Simplifying Rational Expressions

Let a, b, and c be polynomials where $b \neq 0$ and $c \neq 0$.

Algebra $\frac{ac}{bc} = \frac{a \cdot \cancel{c}}{b \cdot \cancel{c}} = \frac{a}{b}$

Example $\frac{2x+4}{3x+6} = \frac{2\cancel{(x+2)}}{3\cancel{(x+2)}} = \frac{2}{3}$

EXAMPLE 2 Simplify expressions by dividing out monomials

Simplify the rational expression, if possible. State the excluded values.

a. $\frac{r}{2r}$ **b.** $\frac{5x}{5(x+2)}$ **c.** $\frac{6m^3 - 12m^2}{18m^2}$ **d.** $\frac{y}{7-y}$

Solution

AVOID ERRORS
When finding excluded values, be sure to use the original expression, not the simplified expression.

a. $\frac{r}{2r} = \frac{\cancel{r}}{2\cancel{r}}$ Divide out common factor.

$= \frac{1}{2}$ Simplify.

▶ The excluded value is 0.

b. $\frac{5x}{5(x+2)} = \frac{\cancel{5} \cdot x}{\cancel{5} \cdot (x+2)}$ Divide out common factor.

$= \frac{x}{x+2}$ Simplify.

▶ The excluded value is −2.

c. $\frac{6m^3 - 12m^2}{18m^2} = \frac{6m^2(m-2)}{6 \cdot 3 \cdot m^2}$ Factor numerator and denominator.

$= \frac{\cancel{6m^2}(m-2)}{\cancel{6} \cdot 3 \cdot \cancel{m^2}}$ Divide out common factors.

$= \frac{m-2}{3}$ Simplify.

▶ The excluded value is 0.

d. The expression $\frac{y}{7-y}$ is already in simplest form.

▶ The excluded value is 7.

GUIDED PRACTICE for Example 2

Simplify the rational expression, if possible. State the excluded values.

5. $\frac{4a^3}{22a^6}$ $\frac{2}{11a^3}$; 0 **6.** $\frac{2c}{c+5}$ $\frac{2c}{c+5}$; −5 **7.** $\frac{2s^2 + 8s}{3s + 12}$ $\frac{2s}{3}$; −4 **8.** $\frac{8x}{8x^3 + 16x^2}$ $\frac{1}{x^2 + 2x}$; 0, −2

Motivating the Lesson

You are thinking about switching to a different Internet Service Provider and you would like to analyze the average monthly costs of several providers over the past 10 years. By knowing how to use and simplify models of real world situations, you can analyze and compare costs to help make a decision.

3 TEACH

Extra Example 1

Find the excluded values, if any, of the expression.

a. $\frac{x+6}{4x}$ 0

b. $\frac{7}{3x-9}$ 3

c. $\frac{2x}{x^2-16}$ −4, 4

d. $\frac{5x+3}{x^2+4x+5}$ no excluded values

Key Question to Ask for Example 1

- In part (b), why is −7 the excluded value? The value $x = -7$ would give a zero denominator.

Extra Example 2

Simplify the rational expression, if possible. State the excluded values.

a. $\frac{2x}{3x}$ $\frac{2}{3}$; 0

b. $\frac{6x}{6(x+5)}$ $\frac{x}{x+5}$; −5

c. $\frac{8b^2 + 16b}{32b}$ $\frac{b+2}{4}$; 0

d. $\frac{a}{1-a}$ simplest form; 1

Key Question to Ask for Example 2

- How do you determine the excluded value in part (b)? The denominator is $5(x+2)$, and the value $x = -2$ would give a zero denominator.

Extra Example 3

Simplify $\frac{x^2 + x - 12}{x^2 - x - 6}$. State the excluded values. $\frac{x + 4}{x + 2}$; $-2, 3$

Key Questions to Ask for Example 3

- What step makes it easier to determine excluded values? **If you factor the denominator, you can more easily tell what values would give a zero denominator.**
- Why is -2 an excluded value if the expression simplifies to $\frac{x - 5}{x - 4}$? **You use the original expression to find excluded values. In the original expression, -2 is an excluded value.**

Extra Example 4

Simplify $\frac{x^2 - 7x + 10}{25 - x^2}$. State the excluded values. $-\frac{x - 2}{x + 5}$; $-5, 5$

Key Question to Ask for Example 4

- Why can't you rewrite $(4 - x)$ as $(x - 4)$? **$(4 - x)$ is the opposite of $(x - 4)$.**

EXAMPLE 3 Simplify an expression by dividing out binomials

Simplify $\frac{x^2 - 3x - 10}{x^2 + 6x + 8}$. State the excluded values.

$\frac{x^2 - 3x - 10}{x^2 + 6x + 8} = \frac{(x - 5)(x + 2)}{(x + 4)(x + 2)}$ **Factor numerator and denominator.**

$= \frac{(x - 5)\cancel{(x + 2)}}{(x + 4)\cancel{(x + 2)}}$ **Divide out common factor.**

$= \frac{x - 5}{x + 4}$ **Simplify.**

▸ The excluded values are -4 and -2.

CHECK In the graphing calculator activity on page 560, you saw how to use a graph to check a sum or difference of polynomials.

Check your simplification using a graphing calculator.

Graph $y_1 = \frac{x^2 - 3x - 10}{x^2 + 6x + 8}$ and $y_2 = \frac{x - 5}{x + 4}$.

The graphs coincide. So, the expressions are equivalent for all values of x other than the excluded values (-4 and -2).

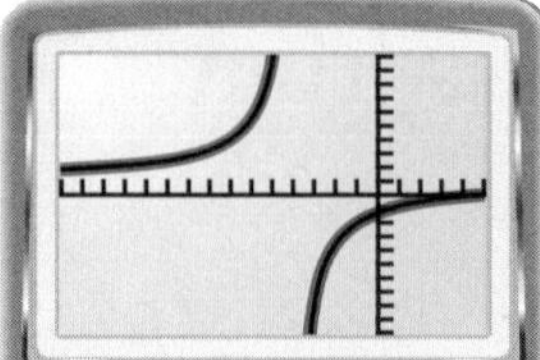

INTERPRET THE GRAPH

Although the graphs of y_1 and y_2 appear to pass through $(-2, -3.5)$, the point is not on either graph because -2 is an excluded value of both y_1 and y_2.

OPPOSITES When simplifying a rational expression, look for factors that are opposites of each other. For example, $x - 1$ and $1 - x$ are opposites, because $x - 1 = -(1 - x)$.

EXAMPLE 4 Recognize opposites

Simplify $\frac{x^2 - 7x + 12}{16 - x^2}$. State the excluded values.

$\frac{x^2 - 7x + 12}{16 - x^2} = \frac{(x - 3)(x - 4)}{(4 - x)(4 + x)}$ **Factor numerator and denominator.**

$= \frac{(x - 3)(x - 4)}{-(x - 4)(4 + x)}$ **Rewrite $4 - x$ as $-(x - 4)$.**

$= \frac{(x - 3)\cancel{(x - 4)}}{-\cancel{(x - 4)}(4 + x)}$ **Divide out common factor.**

$= \frac{x - 3}{-(4 + x)} = -\frac{x - 3}{x + 4}$ **Simplify.**

▸ The excluded values are -4 and 4.

✓ GUIDED PRACTICE for Examples 3 and 4

Simplify the rational expression. State the excluded values.

9. $\frac{x^2 + 3x + 2}{x^2 + 7x + 10}$ $\frac{x + 1}{x + 5}$; $-2, -5$
10. $\frac{y^2 - 64}{y^2 - 16y + 64}$ $\frac{y + 8}{y - 8}$; 8
11. $\frac{5 + 4z - z^2}{z^2 - 3z - 10}$ $-\frac{z + 1}{z + 2}$; $5, -2$

EXAMPLE 5 Simplify a rational model

CELL PHONE COSTS The average cost C (in dollars per minute) for cell phone service in the United States during the period 1991–2000 can be modeled by

$$C = \frac{46 - 2.2x}{100 - 18x + 2.2x^2}$$

where x is the number of years since 1991. Rewrite the model so that it has only whole number coefficients. Then simplify the model.

1991 cell phone

Solution

$C = \frac{46 - 2.2x}{100 - 18x + 2.2x^2}$ **Write model.**

$= \frac{460 - 22x}{1000 - 180x + 22x^2}$ **Multiply numerator and denominator by 10.**

$= \frac{2(230 - 11x)}{2(500 - 90x + 11x^2)}$ **Factor numerator and denominator.**

$= \frac{\cancel{2}(230 - 11x)}{\cancel{2}(500 - 90x + 11x^2)}$ **Divide out common factor.**

$= \frac{230 - 11x}{500 - 90x + 11x^2}$ **Simplify.**

GUIDED PRACTICE for Example 5

12. In Example 5, approximate the average cost per minute in 2000. about $.23/min

12.4 EXERCISES

HOMEWORK KEY
○ = **WORKED-OUT SOLUTIONS** on p. WS29 for Exs. 9, 23, and 43
★ = **STANDARDIZED TEST PRACTICE** Exs. 2, 33, 34, 35, and 45

SKILL PRACTICE

A

1. **VOCABULARY** Copy and complete: A value that makes a rational expression undefined is called a(n) __?__. excluded value

2. ★ **WRITING** Is $\frac{(x + 3)(x - 6)}{(x - 3)(6 - x)}$ in simplest form? *Explain.* See margin.

EXAMPLE 1 on p. 794 for Exs. 3–10

FINDING EXCLUDED VALUES **Find the excluded values, if any, of the expression.**

3. $\frac{4x}{20}$ none
4. $\frac{13}{2y}$ 0
5. $\frac{5}{r + 1}$ -1
6. $\frac{-s}{3s + 4}$ $-\frac{4}{3}$
7. $\frac{-m}{4m^2 - 3m + 9}$ none
8. $\frac{n + 2}{n^2 - 64}$ $-8, 8$
9. $\frac{-3}{2p^2 - p}$ $0, \frac{1}{2}$
10. $\frac{5q}{q^2 - 6q + 9}$ 3

Extra Example 5

The average amount of a customer's purchase P applied to a credit card account at a toy store during the period 1998–2004 can be modeled by $P = \frac{24 + 0.8x^2}{0.5 + 0.02x^2}$, where x is the number of years since 1998. Rewrite the model so that it has only whole number coefficients. Then simplify the model. $P = \frac{2400 + 80x^2}{50 + 2x^2}$; $\frac{1200 + 40x^2}{25 + x^2}$

Key Questions to Ask for Example 5

- How do you approximate the average cost for cell phone service in 2000? **Since 2000 is 9 years since 1991, evaluate the model for $x = 9$.**
- Do you have to use the simplified model to approximate the cost for a particular year? Explain. **Either model will give the same value, but it may be easier to calculate with the simplified model.**

Closing the Lesson

Have students summarize the major points of the lesson and answer the Essential Question: How do you simplify a rational expression?

- **Exclude values that would result in a zero denominator.**
- **Some rational expressions can be simplified by factoring and dividing.**

To simplify a rational expression, factor the numerator and denominator, divide out the common factors, and note excluded values. When factoring, watch for expressions that are opposites.

2. No, after rewriting $6 - x$ in the denominator as $-1(x - 6)$, you can divide out the common factor of $x - 6$ from the numerator and denominator.

Differentiated Instruction

Visual Learners Show students that an excluded value can be represented on a graph by an open circle or dashed vertical line. For **Example 3**, plot the graph of $y = \frac{x - 5}{x + 4}$ and place an open circle at the point $(-2, -3.5)$. The other excluded value can be illustrated by a dashed vertical line at $x = -4$.

See also the *Algebra 1 Toolkit* for more strategies.

4 PRACTICE AND APPLY

Assignment Guide

Answer Transparencies available for all exercises

Basic:
Day 1: EP p. 946 Exs. 25–30
pp. 797–800
Exs. 1–12, 13–33 odd, 34–36, 40–44, 48, 52, 55, 58

Average:
Day 1: pp. 797–800
Exs. 1, 2, 7–12, 14–32 even, 33–38, 40–45, 49, 53, 56, 59

Advanced:
Day 1: pp. 797–800
Exs. 1, 8–11, 14–32 even, 33–46*, 50, 54, 57, 60

Block:
pp. 797–800
Exs. 1, 2, 7–12, 14–32 even, 33–38, 40–45, 49, 53, 56, 59 (with 12.5)

Differentiated Instruction

See *Algebra 1 Best Practices Toolkit* for suggestions on addressing the needs of a diverse classroom.

Homework Check

For a quick check of student understanding of key concepts, go over the following exercises:

Basic: 4, 15, 19, 28, 40
Average: 10, 16, 24, 30, 41
Advanced: 8, 16, 26, 32, 42

Extra Practice

- Student Edition, p. 946
- Chapter 12 Resource Book: Practice levels A, B, C, pp. 45–47

Practice Worksheet

An easily-readable reduced practice page (with answers) for this lesson can be found on p. 762C.

23. $\frac{1}{h-4}$; −3, 4
24. $\frac{1}{j-4}$; 2, 4
25. $\frac{-6}{2w-5}$; 0, $\frac{5}{2}$
26. $\frac{2y^3}{2y+3}$; 0, $-\frac{3}{2}$
27. 3; 0, 4
28. $\frac{7x}{x-1}$; 1, $-\frac{3}{2}$
29. $\frac{s+8}{s-1}$; 1, −8
30. $\frac{t+5}{2t-3}$; 9, $\frac{3}{2}$
31. $\frac{1}{m^2+5m}$; 0, −5
32. $-\frac{1}{3n}$; −7, 0, 4

EXAMPLES 2, 3, and 4 on pp. 795–796 for Exs. 11–33

ERROR ANALYSIS *Describe* and correct the error in simplifying the rational expression or in stating the excluded values. 11, 12. See margin.

11. $\frac{2x^2 - x - 3}{2x^2 - 11x + 12}$

$$\frac{2x^2 - x - 3}{2x^2 - 11x + 12} = \frac{(x+1)(2x-3)}{(2x-3)(x-4)} = \frac{(x+1)\cancel{(2x-3)}}{\cancel{(2x-3)}(x-4)} = \frac{x+1}{x-4}$$

The excluded value is 4. ✗

12. $\frac{2(x-5)}{(x-5)(x+2)}$

$$\frac{2(x-5)}{(x-5)(x+2)} = \frac{2\cancel{(x-5)}}{\cancel{(x-5)}(x+2)} = \frac{2}{x+2} = \frac{\cancel{2}}{x+\cancel{2}} = \frac{1}{x+1}$$

The excluded values are −2 and 5. ✗

SIMPLIFYING EXPRESSIONS **Simplify the rational expression, if possible. State the excluded values.**

13. $\frac{10x}{25}$ $\frac{2x}{5}$; none
14. $\frac{63}{18y}$ $\frac{7}{2y}$; 0
15. $\frac{-48a^2}{16a}$ $-3a$; 0
16. $\frac{27b^2}{30b^5}$ $\frac{9}{10b^3}$; 0
17. $\frac{3c+33}{c+11}$ 3; −11
18. $\frac{d+8}{d-8}$ $\frac{d+8}{d-8}$; 8
19. $\frac{2u-6}{3-u}$ −2; 3
20. $\frac{v+2}{v^2-4}$ $\frac{1}{v-2}$; ±2
21. $\frac{2}{f^2-9}$ $\frac{2}{f^2-9}$; ±3
22. $\frac{g+4}{g^2-16}$ $\frac{1}{g-4}$; ±4
23. $\frac{h+3}{h^2-h-12}$
24. $\frac{j-2}{j^2-6j+8}$
25. $\frac{-48w}{16w^2-40w}$
26. $\frac{12y^4}{12y^2+18y}$
27. $\frac{6z^2-24z}{2z^2-8z}$
28. $\frac{14x^2+21x}{2x^2+x-3}$
29. $\frac{s^2+16s+64}{s^2+7s-8}$
30. $\frac{t^2-4t-45}{2t^2-21t+27}$
31. $\frac{m+5}{m^3+10m^2+25m}$
32. $\frac{-n^2-3n+28}{3n^3+9n^2-84n}$

33. ★ **WRITING** Are the rational expressions $\frac{x^2+x}{x^2-1}$ and $\frac{x^2}{x^2-x}$ equivalent? *Explain* how you know. What are the excluded values, if any, of the rational expressions? See margin.

B 34. ★ **OPEN-ENDED** Write a rational expression whose excluded values are −3 and −5. *Sample answer:* $\frac{1}{x^2+8x+15}$

35. ★ **MULTIPLE CHOICE** The expression $\frac{a}{x^2+5x-6}$ simplifies to $\frac{2x+5}{x+6}$. What is a? C

Ⓐ $2x^2+7x+5$ Ⓑ $2x^2+5x-1$ Ⓒ $2x^2+3x-5$ Ⓓ $2x^2+7x-5$

GEOMETRY **Write and simplify a rational expression for the ratio of the perimeter of the given figure to its area.**

36. Square $\frac{4}{5x}$
37. Rectangle $\frac{3(x+2)}{x(x+6)}$
38. Triangle $\frac{3}{x}$

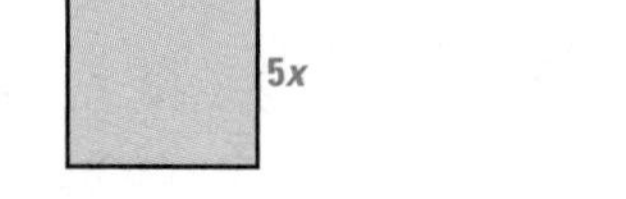

C 39. **CHALLENGE** Find two polynomials whose ratio simplifies to $\frac{3x-1}{2x+1}$ and whose sum is $5x^2+20x$. *Describe* your steps. See margin.

○ = WORKED-OUT SOLUTIONS on p. WS1 ★ = STANDARDIZED TEST PRACTICE

11. When finding the excluded values you must find the values for which the denominator of the original expression, $2x^2 - 11x + 12$, is 0; the excluded values are $\frac{3}{2}$ and 4.

12. 2 cannot be divided out of the numerator and denominator of $\frac{2}{x+2}$ because 2 is not a factor of the denominator, $x + 2$; $\frac{2}{x+2}$.

33. No; the two expressions do not have the same excluded values; the excluded values for $\frac{x^2+x}{x^2-1}$ are ±1, while the excluded values for $\frac{x^2}{x^2-x}$ are 0 and 1. The expressions are not equivalent for $x = 0$ and for $x = -1$.

PROBLEM SOLVING

EXAMPLE 5 A on p. 797 for Exs. 40–43

40. **CREDIT CARD FEES** The average late payment fee F (in dollars) on a credit card account during the period 1994–2003 can be modeled by

$$F = \frac{12 + 1.6x^2}{1 + 0.04x^2}$$

where x is the number of years since 1994. Rewrite the model so that it has only whole number coefficients. Then simplify the model and approximate the average late payment fee in 2003.

@HomeTutor for problem solving help at classzone.com

$F = \frac{300 + 40x^2}{25 + x^2}$; \$33.40

41. **TELEVISION** For the period 1980–2003, the percent p (in decimal form) of non-network television commercials in the United States that lasted 15 seconds can be modeled by

$$p = \frac{0.12x^2 - 0.48}{0.88x^2 + 100}$$

where x is the number of years since 1980. Rewrite the model so that it has only whole number coefficients. Then simplify the model and approximate the percent of non-network television commercials in 2003 that lasted 15 seconds.

@HomeTutor for problem solving help at classzone.com

$p = \frac{3x^2 - 12}{22x^2 + 2500}$; about 11%

42. **CAR RADIOS** A company forecasts that the number R (in thousands) of digital car radios sold annually and the sales S (in millions of dollars) of digital car radios during the period 2004–2007 can be modeled by

$$R = 190x^2 + 55x + 140 \quad \text{and} \quad S = 170x + 60$$

where x is the number of years since 2004. Write and simplify a model that gives the average price P (in thousands of dollars) of a digital car radio as a function of x. Then predict the average price in 2007.

$P = \frac{34x + 12}{38x^2 + 11x + 28}$; about \$280

43. **HOUSES** The total number H of new single-family houses and the number W of new single-family wood houses in the United States during the period 1990–2002 can be modeled by

$$H = 34{,}500x + 913{,}000$$
$$\text{and } W = -20{,}200x + 366{,}000$$

where x is the number of years since 1990. Write and simplify a model that gives the percent p (in decimal form) of the houses that were wood houses as a function of x. *Describe* how the percent that were wood houses changed during the period 1990–2002.

$p = \frac{-202x + 3660}{345x + 9130}$; the percent of wood houses decreased.

B 44. **AIRPORTS** The total number A of airports and the number P of private airports in the United States during the period 1989–2002 can be modeled by

$$A = 0.18x^3 + 140x + 17{,}000 \quad \text{and} \quad P = 0.16x^3 + 120x + 12{,}000$$

where x is the number of years since 1989. Using only whole number coefficients, write a model that gives the percent p (in decimal form) of all airports that were private airports. Simplify the model and approximate the percent of airports in 2002 that were private airports.

$p = \frac{8x^3 + 6000x + 600{,}000}{9x^3 + 7000x + 850{,}000}$; about 72%

Avoiding Common Errors

Exercises 13–32 Some students start to identify excluded values after expressions are simplified. Remind them to use the original expression. If they are in doubt about the excluded values, suggest they check whether the values would give a zero denominator.

Graphing Calculator

Exercises 13–32 Suggest that students use their graphing calculators to check their simplified expressions. They can use the check in Example 3, page 796, as a guide.

Reading Strategy

Exercises 40–41, 44–45 Encourage students to look carefully at each of the models in these exercises. Suggest that when they rewrite the models using only whole number coefficients, they pay close attention to place value.

39. $3x^2 + 11x - 4$, $2x^2 + 9x + 4$; if the ratio of the polynomials simplifies to $\frac{3x - 1}{2x + 1}$, then find a value a such that the ratio of the polynomials can be written in the form $\frac{(x + a)(3x - 1)}{(x + a)(2x + 1)}$. To solve for a, multiply out the factored polynomials, find their sum, and set the sum equal to $5x^2 + 20x$. Then solve for a. Substitute the value of a into the expressions for the polynomials and simplify.

5 ASSESS AND RETEACH

Daily Homework Quiz

Transparency Available

Simplify the rational expression, if possible. Find the excluded values.

1. $\frac{12x^3}{18x^5}$ $\frac{2}{3x^2}$; 0
2. $\frac{2x - 14}{x^2 - 9x + 14}$ $\frac{2}{x - 2}$; 2, 7
3. The average cost C (in dollars per hour) for a cleaning service during the period 1994–2003 can be modeled by $C = \frac{52 - 1.4x}{10 - 14x + 2.1x^2}$, where x is the number of years since 1994. Rewrite the model so that it has only whole number coefficients. Then simplify the model, if possible. $C = \frac{520 - 14x}{100 - 140x + 21x^2}$

Available at **classzone.com**

Diagnosis/Remediation

- Practice A, B, C in Chapter 12 Resource Book, pp. 45–47
- Study Guide in Chapter 12 Resource Book, pp. 48–49
- Practice Workbook, pp. 188–189
- @HomeTutor

Challenge

Additional challenge is available in the Chapter 12 Resource Book, p. 53.

Quiz

An easily-readable reduced copy of the quiz (with answers) on Lessons 12.3–12.4 from the Assessment Book can be found on p. 762F.

45b, Quiz 3, 4. See Additional Answers beginning on p. AA1.

45a. $R = \frac{37,500 + 2500x}{125 + x}$; about $522 million

45c. No; if the price per copy of printed music went up during the period 1988–2002, then the revenue may have increased without the number of copies sold increasing.

45. ★ **EXTENDED RESPONSE** The revenue R (in millions of dollars) from sales of printed music in the United States during the period 1988–2002 can be modeled by

$$R = \frac{300 + 20x}{1 + 0.008x}$$

where x is the number of years since 1988.

a. **Model and Calculate** Rewrite the model so that it has only whole number coefficients. Then simplify the model and approximate the revenue from sales of printed music in 2002.

b. **Graph** Graph the model. *Describe* how revenue changed during the period. See margin for art; revenue increased.

c. **Decide** Can you use the model to conclude that the number of copies of printed music sold increased over time? *Explain.*

C 46. **CHALLENGE** The average annual expenses E (in dollars) of a middle income family and the average annual amount T (in dollars) spent on telephone service during the period 1992–2001 can be modeled by

$$E = 1240x + 24,800 \quad \text{and} \quad T = 31x + 620$$

where x is the number of years since 1992. Write and simplify a model to show that the average annual amount spent on telephone service was 2.5% of the average annual expenses during the period.
$\frac{T}{E} = \frac{31x + 620}{1240x + 24,800} = \frac{31(x + 20)}{1240(x + 20)} = \frac{31}{1240} = 0.025$. Thus, $T = 0.025E$, so T is 2.5% of E.

ILLINOIS MIXED REVIEW

TEST PRACTICE at classzone.com

47. The area of a rectangle is $42s^6t^4$ square units. If the width of the rectangle is $14s^2t$ units, how many units long is the rectangle? ($s \neq 0$ and $t \neq 0$) D

Ⓐ $3s^3t^2$ Ⓑ $3s^3t^3$ Ⓒ $3s^4t^2$ Ⓓ $3s^4t^3$

48. A school has a rectangular courtyard that is 32 feet by 24 feet. The school builds a walkway along a diagonal of the rectangle. To the nearest foot, how long is the walkway? C

Ⓐ 28 ft Ⓑ 35 ft Ⓒ 40 ft Ⓓ 56 ft

QUIZ *for Lessons 12.3–12.4*

Divide. *(p. 784)*

1. $(y^2 - 5y + 6) \div (y - 3)$ $y - 2$
2. $(x^2 + 3x - 28) \div (x - 6)$ $x + 9 + \frac{26}{x - 6}$

Graph the function. *(p. 784)* 3–4. See margin.

3. $y = \frac{x + 3}{x - 4}$
4. $y = \frac{2x - 1}{x + 3}$

Simplify the rational expression, if possible. State the excluded values. *(p. 794)*

5. $\frac{w + 10}{w^2 - 100}$ $\frac{1}{w - 10}$; ±10
6. $\frac{250x^3}{14x}$ $\frac{125x^2}{7}$; 0
7. $\frac{y + 7}{y - 7}$ $\frac{y + 7}{y - 7}$; 7
8. $\frac{z^2 - 4z - 45}{3z^2 + 25z + 50}$ $\frac{z - 9}{3z + 10}$; $-\frac{10}{3}$, −5

EXTRA PRACTICE for Lesson 12.4, p. 949

ONLINE QUIZ at classzone.com

 Illinois Mixed Review

 TEST PRACTICE classzone.com

Lessons 12.1–12.4

1. **PACKAGING** A retail company is designing a package in the shape of a rectangular prism whose base is 3 feet by 2 feet. The company is trying to decide the height of the package by considering the ratio of the package's surface area to volume. Which graph represents the ratio r as a function of the height h?

A. 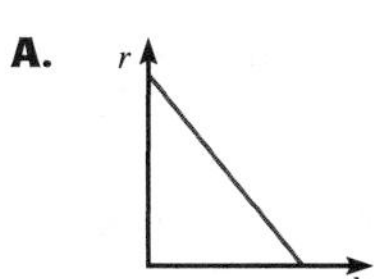

C. 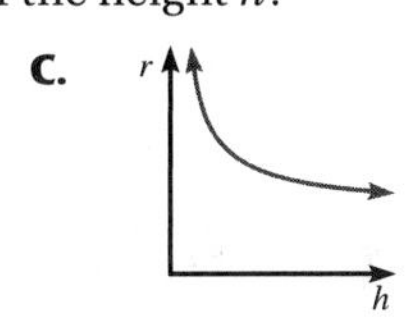

B. 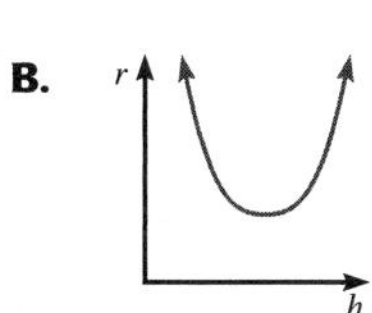

D. 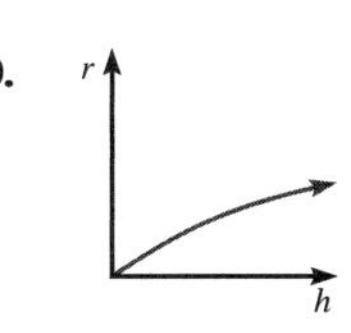

2. **SEAFOOD** The average amount A (in pounds per person) of fish and shellfish consumed in the United States during the period 1992–2001 can be modeled by

$$A = \frac{52x + 3800}{3.2x + 260}$$

where x is the number of years since 1992. What was the approximate average number of pounds of fish and shellfish consumed per person in 2001?

F. 15

G. 16

H. 1142

J. 11,416

3. **TRIP EXPENSES** You and some friends are taking a car trip to an amusement park. Admission costs \$50 per person, and everyone will share the combined cost of gas and parking, which is \$30. How much more will one person pay (in dollars) if 4 people go on the trip than if 5 people go?

A. \$1.50 **C.** \$11.50

B. \$4 **D.** \$56

4. **SHIPMENTS** A truck is traveling to a town 250 miles away to pick up a shipment. When the truck arrives in the town, the driver will take 4 hours to load the truck. The truck will then return with the shipment. Suppose you graph the time t (in hours) of the entire trip as a function of the average rate r (in miles per hour) the truck travels. How would the graph change if the truck is loaded in 3 hours instead of 4 hours?

F. The graph would be a horizontal translation 1 unit to the right.

G. The graph would be a vertical translation 1 unit down.

H. The graph would be a vertical stretch.

J. The graph would be a vertical shrink.

5. **GAS** The table shows the relationship between the volume (in liters) and the pressure (in kilopascals) of a certain gas in a container. Which equation models the relationship between the volume V of the gas and the pressure P?

Volume (L)	20	5	2.5	1.6	0.4
Pressure (kPa)	1	4	8	12.5	50

A. $V = 20P$ **C.** $20 = \frac{1}{V + P}$

B. $V = \frac{20}{P}$ **D.** None of the above

6. **POPULATION** A town's population density (in people per square mile) is the ratio of the population of the town to the area (in square miles) of the town. Suppose a town has a population of 30,000 people and an area of 120 square miles. How many people would need to move into the area before the town's population density is 275 people per square mile?

F. 3300 **H.** 300

G. 3000 **J.** 25

Illinois Mixed Review

1. C
2. F
3. A
4. G
5. B
6. G

1 PLAN AND PREPARE

Warm-Up Exercises

Transparency Available

Factor the polynomial.

1. $x^2 + 3x - 18$ $(x - 3)(x + 6)$
2. $2x^2 - 4x - 16$ $(x - 4)(2x + 4)$
3. $2x^2 + 8x - 10$ $(x + 5)(2x - 2)$
4. A golf clinic charges a $30 enrollment fee and $5 per session. What is the average cost per session if you attend 8 sessions? $8.75

Notetaking Guide

Transparency Available

Promotes interactive learning and notetaking skills, pp. 283–286.

Pacing

Basic: 2 days
Average: 2 days
Advanced: 2 days
Block: 0.5 block with 12.4
0.5 block with 12.6

- See *Teaching Guide/Lesson Plan*.

2 FOCUS AND MOTIVATE

Essential Question

Big Idea 2, p. 763

How do you multiply and divide rational expressions? Tell students they will learn how to answer this question by using processes that are similar to multiplying and dividing fractions.

12.5 Multiply and Divide Rational Expressions

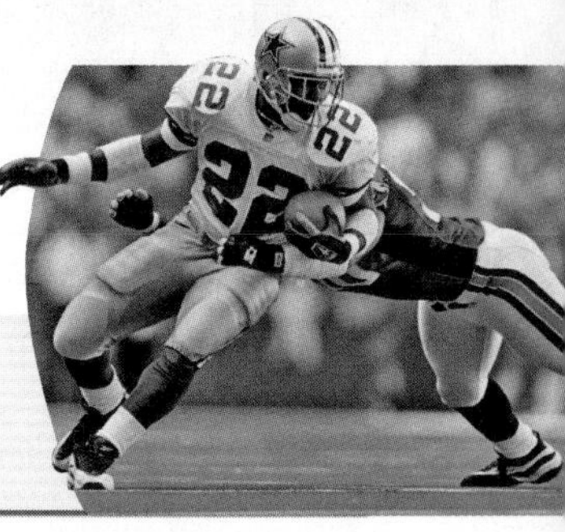

8.11.01 Simplify or identify equivalent algebraic expressions (e.g., exponential, rational, logarithmic, factored, polynomial).

Before You multiplied and divided polynomials.

Now You will multiply and divide rational expressions.

Why? So you can describe football data, as in Ex. 35.

Key Vocabulary
- **multiplicative inverse,** *p. 103*
- **polynomial,** *p. 554*
- **rational expression,** *p. 794*

Multiplying and dividing rational expressions is similar to multiplying and dividing numerical fractions.

KEY CONCEPT — *For Your Notebook*

Multiplying and Dividing Rational Expressions

Let a, b, c, and d be polynomials.

Algebra $\frac{a}{b} \cdot \frac{c}{d} = \frac{ac}{bd}$ where $b \neq 0$ and $d \neq 0$

$\frac{a}{b} \div \frac{c}{d} = \frac{a}{b} \cdot \frac{d}{c} = \frac{ad}{bc}$ where $b \neq 0$, $c \neq 0$, and $d \neq 0$

Examples $\frac{x+2}{x} \cdot \frac{3}{x^2} = \frac{3(x+2)}{x^3}$ $\qquad \frac{x}{x-1} \div \frac{4}{x} = \frac{x}{x-1} \cdot \frac{x}{4} = \frac{x^2}{4(x-1)}$

EXAMPLE 1 Multiply rational expressions involving monomials

Find the product $\frac{2x^2}{3x} \cdot \frac{6x^2}{12x^3}$.

$$\frac{2x^2}{3x} \cdot \frac{6x^2}{12x^3} = \frac{(2x^2)(6x^2)}{(3x)(12x^3)} \quad \text{Multiply numerators and denominators.}$$

$$= \frac{12x^4}{36x^4} \quad \text{Product of powers property}$$

$$= \frac{\cancel{12} \cdot \cancel{x^4}}{3 \cdot \cancel{12} \cdot \cancel{x^4}} \quad \text{Factor and divide out common factors.}$$

$$= \frac{1}{3} \quad \text{Simplify.}$$

APPLY EXCLUDED VALUES
When performing operations with rational expressions, remember that the answer may have excluded values. In Example 1, the excluded value is 0.

GUIDED PRACTICE for Example 1

Find the product.

1. $\frac{2y^3}{5y} \cdot \frac{15y^3}{8y^5}$ $\frac{3}{4}$

2. $\frac{7z^2}{4z^3} \cdot \frac{z^3}{14z}$ $\frac{z}{8}$

Resource Planning Guide

Chapter Resource Book
- Teaching Guide/Lesson Plan (pp. 54–55)
- Activity Master (p. 56)
- Practice levels A, B, C (pp. 58–60)
- Study Guide (pp. 61–62)
- Catch-up for Absent Students (p. 63)
- Application (p. 64)
- Challenge (p. 65)

Workbooks
- Notetaking Guide (pp. 283–286)
- Practice Workbook (pp. 190–191)

Teaching Options
- **Power Presentations CD-ROM** provides dynamic electronic teaching resources for the classroom.
- **Activity Generator CD-ROM** provides editable activities for all ability levels.

Interactive Technology
- Easy Planner
- Power Presentations CD-ROM
- Activity Generator CD-ROM
- Animated Algebra
- Test Generator CD-ROM
- Online Quiz
- eWorkbook
- eEdition
- @HomeTutor

Resources for English Learners
- Quick Reference for English Learners
- Spanish Study Guide
- Multi-Language Visual Glossary
- Student Resources in Spanish

See also the *Algebra 1 Toolkit* for more strategies for meeting individual needs.

EXAMPLE 2 Multiply rational expressions involving polynomials

Find the product $\frac{3x^2 + 3x}{4x^2 - 24x + 36} \cdot \frac{x^2 - 4x + 3}{x^2 - x}$.

$\frac{3x^2 + 3x}{4x^2 - 24x + 36} \cdot \frac{x^2 - 4x + 3}{x^2 - x}$

$= \frac{(3x^2 + 3x)(x^2 - 4x + 3)}{(4x^2 - 24x + 36)(x^2 - x)}$ **Multiply numerators and denominators.**

$= \frac{3x(x + 1)\cancel{(x - 3)}\cancel{(x - 1)}}{4\cancel{x}\cancel{(x - 3)}(x - 3)\cancel{(x - 1)}}$ **Factor and divide out common factors.**

$= \frac{3(x + 1)}{4(x - 3)}$ **Simplify.**

CHECK Check your simplification using a graphing calculator.

Graph $y_1 = \frac{3x^2 + 3x}{4x^2 - 24x + 36} \cdot \frac{x^2 - 4x + 3}{x^2 - x}$

and $y_2 = \frac{3(x + 1)}{4(x - 3)}$.

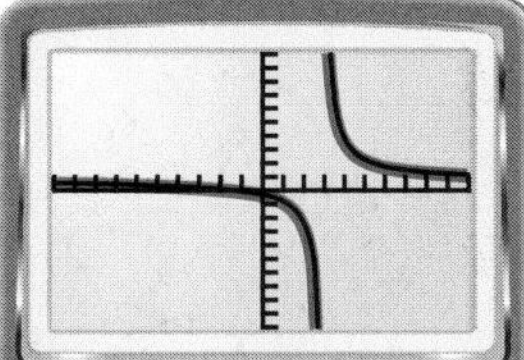

The graphs coincide. So, the expressions are equivalent for all values of x other than the excluded values (0, 1, and 3).

MULTIPLYING BY A POLYNOMIAL When you multiply a rational expression by a polynomial, first write the polynomial as a fraction with a denominator of 1.

EXAMPLE 3 Multiply a rational expression by a polynomial

Find the product $\frac{5x}{x^2 + 5x + 6} \cdot (x + 3)$.

$\frac{5x}{x^2 + 5x + 6} \cdot (x + 3)$

$= \frac{5x}{x^2 + 5x + 6} \cdot \frac{x + 3}{1}$ **Rewrite polynomial as a fraction.**

$= \frac{5x(x + 3)}{x^2 + 5x + 6}$ **Multiply numerators and denominators.**

$= \frac{5x\cancel{(x + 3)}}{(x + 2)\cancel{(x + 3)}}$ **Factor and divide out common factor.**

$= \frac{5x}{x + 2}$ **Simplify.**

GUIDED PRACTICE for Examples 2 and 3

Find the product.

3. $\frac{x^2 + x - 2}{x^2 + 2x} \cdot \frac{2x^2 + 2x}{5x^2 - 15x + 10}$ $\frac{2(x + 1)}{5(x - 2)}$

4. $\frac{2w^2}{w^2 - 7w + 12} \cdot (w - 4)$ $\frac{2w^2}{w - 3}$

Motivating the Lesson

A local basketball association wants to report some statistics for a brochure. They have expressions that model the total number of points per game and the total number of free throw points per game for the past 6 years. By learning how to divide rational expressions, you can determine what percent of the total points scored were free throws.

3 TEACH

Extra Example 1

Find the product $\frac{3x^2}{2x} \cdot \frac{8x^3}{15x}$. $\frac{4x^3}{5}$

Key Question to Ask for Example 1

- What is the product of powers property? $a^m \cdot a^n = a^{m+n}$

Extra Example 2

Find the product $\frac{3x + 6}{3x^2 + 18x + 27} \cdot \frac{x^2 - x - 12}{x^2 - 4}$. $\frac{x - 4}{(x + 3)(x - 2)}$

Extra Example 3

Find the product $\frac{4x^2}{x^2 + 3x - 10} \cdot (x - 2)$. $\frac{4x^2}{x + 5}$

Key Question to Ask for Example 3

- Are there any excluded values in the expression? Explain. The two excluded values are −3 and −2, even though −3 is not an excluded value for the simplified product.

Differentiated Instruction

Below Level It may help students to see that the original expressions and the simplified expressions in **Examples 1–3** are equivalent if they substitute values for the variables. Have students substitute 2 for x in the original expression in Example 1 and then compare it to the simplified expression. Have them do the same for Examples 2 and 3. To make sure that they understand the concept, have them substitute 3 for x in Example 2 and ask them to explain the results.

See also the *Algebra 1 Toolkit* for more strategies.

Extra Example 4

Find the quotient $\frac{x^2-9}{x^2+5x+6} \div \frac{4x^2-12x}{x^2-2x-8}$. $\frac{x-4}{4x}$

Key Questions to Ask for Example 4

- How do you find the multiplicative inverse of an expression? Switch the numerator and denominator.
- How do you check whether two expressions are multiplicative inverses? Their product is 1.

Extra Example 5

Find the quotient $\frac{3x^2+24x+36}{6x+9} \div (x+2)$. $\frac{x+6}{2x+3}$

Key Questions to Ask for Example 5

- What are the excluded values? 0, −6
- What can you tell about the graph of $y = \frac{2x^2+16x+24}{3x^2} \div (x+6)$ by looking at the expression? A vertical asymptote is $x = 0$.

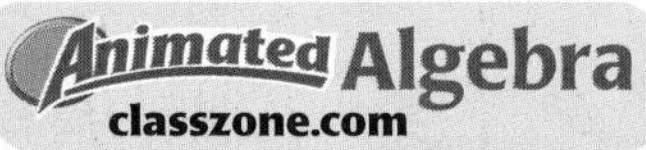

An **Animated Algebra** activity is available on-line for **Example 5**. This activity is also available on the **Power Presentations CD-ROM**.

DIVIDING RATIONAL EXPRESSIONS To divide by a rational expression, multiply by its multiplicative inverse.

EXAMPLE 4 Divide rational expressions involving polynomials

Find the quotient $\frac{7x^2-7x}{x^2+2x-3} \div \frac{x+1}{x^2-7x-8}$.

REVIEW INVERSES For help with finding the multiplicative inverse of a number, see p. 103.

$$\frac{7x^2-7x}{x^2+2x-3} \div \frac{x+1}{x^2-7x-8}$$

$$= \frac{7x^2-7x}{x^2+2x-3} \cdot \frac{x^2-7x-8}{x+1}$$ **Multiply by multiplicative inverse.**

$$= \frac{(7x^2-7x)(x^2-7x-8)}{(x^2+2x-3)(x+1)}$$ **Multiply numerators and denominators.**

$$= \frac{7x(x-1)(x-8)(x+1)}{(x+3)(x-1)(x+1)}$$ **Factor and divide out common factors.**

$$= \frac{7x(x-8)}{x+3}$$ **Simplify.**

DIVIDING BY A POLYNOMIAL When you divide a rational expression by a polynomial, first write the polynomial as a fraction with a denominator of 1. Then multiply by the multiplicative inverse of the polynomial.

EXAMPLE 5 Divide a rational expression by a polynomial

Find the quotient $\frac{2x^2+16x+24}{3x^2} \div (x+6)$.

$$\frac{2x^2+16x+24}{3x^2} \div (x+6)$$

$$= \frac{2x^2+16x+24}{3x^2} \div \frac{x+6}{1}$$ **Rewrite polynomial as fraction.**

$$= \frac{2x^2+16x+24}{3x^2} \cdot \frac{1}{x+6}$$ **Multiply by multiplicative inverse.**

$$= \frac{2x^2+16x+24}{3x^2(x+6)}$$ **Multiply numerators and denominators.**

$$= \frac{2(x+2)(x+6)}{3x^2(x+6)}$$ **Factor and divide out common factor.**

$$= \frac{2(x+2)}{3x^2}$$ **Simplify.**

✓ **GUIDED PRACTICE** for Examples 4 and 5

Find the quotient.

5. $\frac{m^2-4}{2m^2+4m} \div \frac{6m-3m^2}{4m+44}$ $\frac{-2(m+11)}{3m^2}$

6. $\frac{n^2-6n+9}{12n} \div (n-3)$ $\frac{n-3}{12n}$

Differentiated Instruction

Kinesthetic Learners The excluded values of the quotient are the x-values that make the value of any denominator equal to zero. In **Example 4**, the excluded values include not only $x = -3$, but also $x = -1$, 1, and 8. Students can find the excluded values by using the TABLE feature of a calculator. Because the quotient is complicated, let $Y_1 = \frac{7x^2-7x}{x^2+2x-3}$, $Y_2 = \frac{x+1}{x^2-7x-8}$, and $Y_3 = \frac{Y_1}{Y_2}$. Make a TABLE of values for Y_3.

See also the *Algebra 1 Toolkit* for more strategies.

EXAMPLE 6 Solve a multi-step problem

ADVERTISING The amount A (in millions of dollars) spent on all advertising and the amount T (in millions of dollars) spent on television advertising in the United States during the period 1970–2003 can be modeled by

$$A = \frac{13{,}000 + 3700x}{1 - 0.015x} \quad \text{and} \quad T = \frac{1800 + 860x}{1 - 0.016x}$$

where x is the number of years since 1970. Write a model that gives the percent p (in decimal form) of the amount spent on all advertising that was spent on television advertising. Then approximate the percent spent on television advertising in 2003.

Solution

STEP 1 **Write** a verbal model. Then write an equation.

Percent spent on television advertising	=	Amount spent on television advertising	÷	Amount spent on all advertising
p	=	T	÷	A

STEP 2 **Find** the quotient.

$p = T \div A$ **Write equation.**

$= \frac{1800 + 860x}{1 - 0.016x} \div \frac{13{,}000 + 3700x}{1 - 0.015x}$ **Substitute for T and for A.**

$= \frac{1800 + 860x}{1 - 0.016x} \cdot \frac{1 - 0.015x}{13{,}000 + 3700x}$ **Multiply by multiplicative inverse.**

$= \frac{(1800 + 860x)(1 - 0.015x)}{(1 - 0.016x)(13{,}000 + 3700x)}$ **Multiply numerators and denominators.**

$= \frac{\cancel{20}(90 + 43x)(1 - 0.015x)}{(1 - 0.016x)(\cancel{20})(650 + 185x)}$ **Factor and divide out common factor.**

$= \frac{(90 + 43x)(1 - 0.015x)}{(1 - 0.016x)(650 + 185x)}$ **Simplify.**

STEP 3 **Approximate** the percent spent on television advertising in 2003. Because $2003 - 1970 = 33$, $x = 33$. Substitute 33 for x in the model and use a calculator to evaluate.

$$p = \frac{(90 + 43 \cdot 33)(1 - 0.015 \cdot 33)}{(1 - 0.016 \cdot 33)(650 + 185 \cdot 33)} \approx 0.239$$

▶ About 24% of the amount spent on all advertising was spent on television advertising in 2003.

GUIDED PRACTICE for Example 6

7. In Example 6, find the values of T and of A separately when $x = 33$. Then divide the value of T by the value of A. *Compare* your answer with the answer in Step 3 above.

7. About $63,941 million, about $267,525 million; about 0.239; the answers are the same.

Extra Example 6

The average amount T of gross revenue (in thousands of dollars) from toys sold at a toy store and the average amount G (in thousands of dollars) of gross revenue from games sold at the toy store during the period 1995–2003 can be modeled by $T = \frac{1950 - 30x}{1 - 0.03x}$ and $G = \frac{1010 + 70x}{1 - 0.007x}$ where x is the number of years since 1995. Write a model that gives the percent p (in decimal form) of the amount of gross revenue from toys that was gross revenue from games. Then approximate the percent of gross revenue from games in 2003.

$p = \frac{(101 + 7x) \cdot (1 - 0.03x)}{(1 - 0.007x) \cdot (195 - 3x)}$; in 2003, about 74% of the gross revenue of toys was games.

Closing the Lesson

Have students summarize the major points of the lesson and answer the Essential Question: How do you multiply and divide rational expressions?

- **Rational expressions can be multiplied and divided using the rules for multiplying and dividing rational numbers.**
- **Check for excluded values when performing operations with rational expressions.**

When multiplying rational expressions, factor and divide out common factors, multiply numerators and multiply denominators, then simplify. When multiplying by a polynomial, write the polynomial as a fraction with a denominator of 1. When dividing polynomials, multiply by the multiplicative inverse.

4 PRACTICE AND APPLY

Assignment Guide

Answer Transparencies available for all exercises

Basic:
Day 1: EP p. 946 Exs. 49–57 odd
pp. 806–809
Exs. 1–10, 12, 22, 23, 47–52
Day 2: pp. 806–809
Exs. 11, 13–21, 24–26, 33–36, 39–46

Average:
Day 1: pp. 806–809
Exs. 1, 2, 4–10, 12, 22, 23, 29, 47–52
Day 2: pp. 806–809
Exs. 11, 13–21, 24–28, 30, 33–37, 39–45 odd

Advanced:
Day 1: pp. 806–809
Exs. 1, 4–10, 22, 23, 29–31*, 47–52
Day 2: pp. 806–809
Exs. 13–21, 24–28, 32–38*, 40–46 even

Block:
pp. 806–809
Exs. 1, 2, 4–10, 12, 22, 23, 29, 47–52 (with 12.4)
pp. 806–809
Exs. 11, 13–21, 24–28, 30, 33–37, 39–45 odd (with 12.6)

Differentiated Instruction

See *Algebra 1 Best Practices Toolkit* for suggestions on addressing the needs of a diverse classroom.

Homework Check

For a quick check of student understanding of key concepts, go over the following exercises:

Basic: 4, 8, 14, 16, 33
Average: 6, 9, 17, 19, 34
Advanced: 7, 10, 18, 20, 35

Extra Practice

- Student Edition, p. 946
- Chapter 12 Resource Book: Practice levels A, B, C, pp. 58–60

Practice Worksheet

An easily-readable reduced practice page (with answers) for this lesson can be found on p. 762C.

12.5 EXERCISES

HOMEWORK KEY
○ = **WORKED-OUT SOLUTIONS** on p. WS30 for Exs. 5, 15, and 35
★ = **STANDARDIZED TEST PRACTICE** Exs. 2, 21, 26, 27, 28, 36, and 37
◆ = **MULTIPLE REPRESENTATIONS** Ex. 35

SKILL PRACTICE

A

1. **VOCABULARY** Copy and complete: To divide by a rational expression, multiply by its __?__. multiplicative inverse

2. ★ **WRITING** *Describe* how to multiply a rational expression by a polynomial. See margin.

EXAMPLES 1, 2, and 3 on pp. 802–803 for Exs. 3–10, 12

MULTIPLYING EXPRESSIONS Find the product.

3. $\frac{9p^2}{7} \cdot \frac{5}{6p^4}$ $\frac{15}{14p^2}$

4. $\frac{5}{8q^6} \cdot \frac{4q^5}{3}$ $\frac{5}{6q}$

5. $\frac{v^2 + v - 12}{5v + 10} \cdot \frac{-v - 2}{v^2 + 5v + 4}$ $\frac{-(v-3)}{5(v+1)}$

6. $\frac{y - 2}{-2y^2 - 10y} \cdot \frac{4y^2 + 20y}{y^2 - 4}$ $\frac{-2}{y+2}$

7. $\frac{5x}{2x^3 - 17x^2 - 9x} \cdot \frac{4x^2 - 20x - 144}{20}$ $\frac{x+4}{2x+1}$

8. $\frac{r^5}{7r^3 + 56r} \cdot (r^2 + 8)$ $\frac{r^4}{7}$

9. $\frac{-3m}{m^2 - 7m + 10} \cdot (m - 5)$ $\frac{-3m}{m-2}$

10. $\frac{2n - 6}{3n^2 - 7n - 6} \cdot (3n^2 + 14n + 8)$ $2(n + 4)$

EXAMPLES 4 and 5 on p. 804 for Exs. 11, 13–21

ERROR ANALYSIS *Describe* and correct the error in finding the product or quotient. 11–12. See margin.

11. $\frac{x^3}{5} \div \frac{15x^3}{2}$

$$\frac{x^3}{5} \div \frac{15x^3}{2} = \frac{5}{x^3} \cdot \frac{15x^3}{2} = \frac{75x^3}{2x^3} = \frac{75}{2}$$

12. $\frac{x - 2}{x + 5} \cdot \frac{x}{2 - x}$

$$\frac{x-2}{x+5} \cdot \frac{x}{2-x} = \frac{(x-2)x}{(x+5)(2-x)} = \frac{(x-2)x}{(x+5)(2-x)} = \frac{x}{x+5}$$

DIVIDING EXPRESSIONS Find the quotient.

13. $\frac{16r^2}{3} \div \frac{12}{5r}$ $\frac{20r^3}{9}$

14. $\frac{25s^{12}}{18} \div \frac{5s^6}{2}$ $\frac{5s^6}{9}$

15. $\frac{2w^2 + 5w}{w^2 - 81} \div \frac{w^2}{w + 9}$ $\frac{2w+5}{w(w-9)}$

16. $\frac{c^2 + c}{c^2 + c - 30} \div \frac{c - 6}{c^2 - 11c + 30}$ $\frac{c(c+1)}{c+6}$

17. $\frac{a^2 + 3a - 10}{a^2 + 6a - 7} \div \frac{9a^3 - 18a^2}{3a^2 + 18a - 21}$ $\frac{a+5}{3a^2}$

18. $\frac{2x^2 - 9x + 9}{35x + 14} \div \frac{-3x^2 + 13x - 12}{15x^2 - 14x - 8}$ $\frac{3-2x}{7}$

19. $\frac{4k^2 + 4k - 15}{2k - 3} \div (2k + 5)$ 1

20. $\frac{t^2 - 9t - 22}{5t - 1} \div (5t^2 + 9t - 2)$ $\frac{t-11}{(5t-1)^2}$

21. ★ **MULTIPLE CHOICE** What common factor do you divide out when finding the quotient $\frac{x^2 - 3x + 2}{x^2 - 2x - 3} \div \frac{x^2 + 4x + 3}{x^2 - 7x + 12}$? B

Ⓐ $x - 1$ Ⓑ $x - 3$ Ⓒ $x + 1$ Ⓓ $x + 3$

2. First write the polynomial as a fraction with a denominator of 1. Then write the product of the numerators over the product of the denominators, leaving the products in factored form. Factor the numerator and denominator completely and divide out any common factors.

11. To divide by the rational expression $\frac{15x^3}{2}$, you must multiply by its multiplicative inverse, $\frac{2}{15x^3}$; $\frac{x^3}{5} \cdot \frac{2}{15x^3} = \frac{2x^3}{75x^3} = \frac{2}{75}$.

B **TRANSLATING PHRASES** **Translate the verbal phrase into a product or quotient of rational expressions. Then find the product or quotient.**

22. The product of $x + 3$ and the ratio of $x + 5$ to $x^2 - 9$ $(x+3) \cdot \frac{x+5}{x^2-9}; \frac{x+5}{x-3}$

23. The product of $8x^2$ and the multiplicative inverse of $2x^3$ $8x^2 \cdot \frac{1}{2x^3}; \frac{4}{x}$

24. $(x^2 + 3x - 18) \div \frac{x+6}{2}$; $2(x-3)$

24. The quotient of $x^2 + 3x - 18$ and the ratio of $x + 6$ to 2

25. The quotient of the multiplicative inverse of $x^2 - 3x - 4$ and twice the multiplicative inverse of $x^2 - 1$ $\frac{1}{x^2-3x-4} \div \frac{2}{x^2-1}; \frac{x-1}{2(x-4)}$

26. ★ **MULTIPLE CHOICE** What is the quotient $\frac{x^2-1}{-(x+1)} \div (x-1)$? A

Ⓐ -1 Ⓑ 0 Ⓒ 1 Ⓓ $x^2 - 1$

★ **OPEN-ENDED** **Let a, b, c, and d be different polynomials. Find two rational expressions $\frac{a}{b}$ and $\frac{c}{d}$ that satisfy the given conditions.**

27. The product of the rational expressions is $\frac{x-3}{x+2}$, and the excluded values are -2, -1, 4, and 5. *Sample answer:* $\frac{x^2-2x-3}{x^2-2x-8}, \frac{x^2-9x+20}{x^2-4x-5}$

28. The quotient of the rational expressions is $\frac{x-6}{x+4}$, and the excluded values are -4, -2, 3, and 6. *Sample answer:* $\frac{x^2-4x-12}{x^2-2x-24}, \frac{x^2-x-6}{x^2-9x+18}$

GEOMETRY **Write an expression for the area of the figure. Find a value of x less than 5 for which the given dimensions and the area are positive.**

29. Rectangle

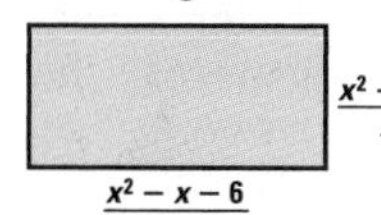

$(x-1)(x-3)$. *Sample answer:* 0

30. Triangle

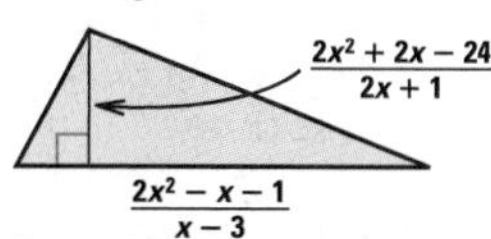

$(x-1)(x+4)$. *Sample answer:* 4

C **CHALLENGE** **Let a be a polynomial in the given equation. Find a.**

31. $\frac{a}{x+2} \cdot \frac{3x^2+5x-2}{x-4} = 6x^2 + 7x - 3$
$2x^2 - 5x - 12$

32. $\frac{8x^2-2x-3}{x-5} \div \frac{2x+1}{a} = 12x^2 - x - 6$
$3x^2 - 13x - 10$

PROBLEM SOLVING

EXAMPLE 6 on p. 805 for Exs. 33–35

A **33. VEHICLES** The total distance M (in billions of miles) traveled by all motor vehicles and the distance T (in billions of miles) traveled by trucks in the United States during the period 1980–2002 can be modeled by

$$M = 1500 + 63x \qquad \text{and} \qquad T = \frac{100 + 2.2x}{1 - 0.014x}$$

where x is the number of years since 1980. Write a model that gives the percent p (in decimal form) of the total motor vehicle distance that was traveled by trucks as a function of x. Then approximate the percent traveled by trucks in 2002. See margin.

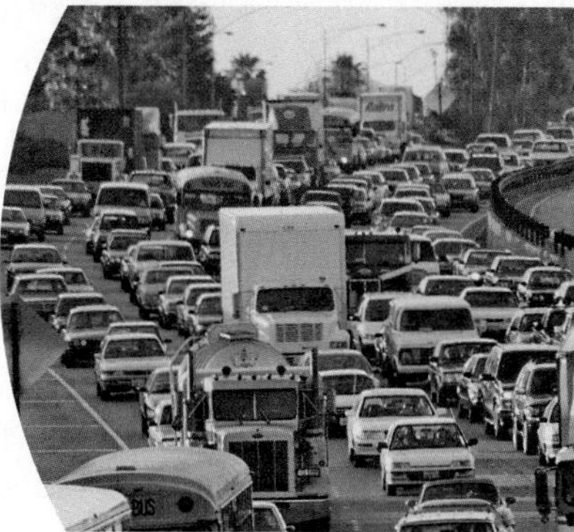

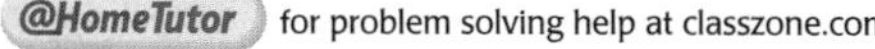
@HomeTutor for problem solving help at classzone.com

Avoiding Common Errors

Exercises 13–21 Watch for students who do not rewrite division as multiplication. Remind students that when they see a division symbol, they should multiply by the reciprocal.

Reading Strategy

Exercises 5, 15, 35 Point out to students that each of these exercises is circled in red, which means that there is a worked-out solution. Encourage them to solve the problem first and then check their solutions against the worked-out solutions.

12. Before dividing out the common factor $(x-2)$, you must first rewrite the factor $(2-x)$ in the denominator as $-1(x-2)$, leaving a factor of -1 in the denominator; $\frac{(x-2)x}{-1(x+5)(x-2)} = \frac{-x}{x+5}$.

33. $p = \frac{100 + 2.2x}{(1 - 0.014x)(1500 + 63x)}$; about 7%

34. CONSUMER SPENDING The average annual amount T (in dollars) spent on reading and entertainment and the average annual amount E (in dollars) spent on entertainment by consumers in the United States during the period 1985–2002 can be modeled by

$$T = \frac{1300 + 84x}{1 + 0.015x} \quad \text{and} \quad E = \frac{1100 + 64x}{1 + 0.0062x}$$

where x is the number of years since 1985. Write a model that gives the percent p (in decimal form) of the amount spent on reading and entertainment that was spent on entertainment as a function of x. Then approximate the percent spent on entertainment in 2000.

@HomeTutor for problem solving help at classzone.com

$p = \frac{(275 + 16x)(1 + 0.015x)}{(1 + 0.0062x)(325 + 21x)}$; about 90%

35. ◆ **MULTIPLE REPRESENTATIONS** Football player Emmitt Smith's career number Y of rushing yards gained and his career number A of rushing attempts from 1990 (when he started playing professional football) through the 2002 football season can be modeled by

$$Y = \frac{860 + 1800x}{1 + 0.024x} \quad \text{and} \quad A = \frac{230 + 380x}{1 + 0.014x}$$

where x is the number of years since 1990.

a. **Writing an Equation** A football player's rushing average is the number of rushing yards gained divided by the number of rushing attempts. Write a model that gives Smith's career rushing average R as a function of x for the period 1990–2002. $R = \frac{(86 + 180x)(1 + 0.014x)}{(1 + 0.024x)(23 + 38x)}$

b. **Making a Table** Make a table that shows Smith's approximate career rushing average (rounded to the nearest hundredth) for each year during the period. *Describe* how the career rushing average changed over time. See margin for table; Smith's career rushing average increased for the first several years and then began to decrease.

B **36.** ★ **SHORT RESPONSE** Baseball player Hank Aaron's career number B of times at bat and career number H of hits during the period 1954–1976 can be modeled by

$$B = \frac{300 + 700x}{1 + 0.01x} \quad \text{and} \quad H = \frac{62 + 240x}{1 + 0.017x}$$

where x is the number of years since 1954.

a. **Model** A baseball player's batting average is the number of hits divided by the number of times at bat. Write a model that gives Hank Aaron's career batting average A as a function of x. See margin.

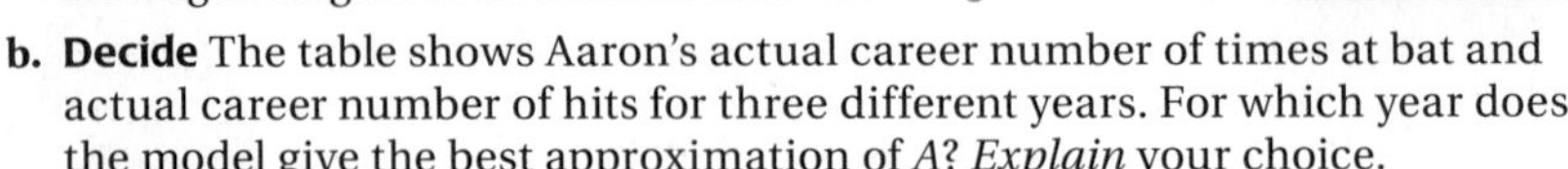

b. **Decide** The table shows Aaron's actual career number of times at bat and actual career number of hits for three different years. For which year does the model give the best approximation of A? *Explain* your choice.

Year	1954	1959	1976
Career times at bat	468	3524	12,364
Career hits	131	1137	3771

1959; using the values in the table to calculate the ratio $\frac{H}{B}$ for the three given years gives batting averages A of 0.280 in 1954, 0.323 in 1959, and 0.305 in 1976. Calculating A using the model from part (a) for $x = 0$, 5, and 22 gives batting averages of 0.207 in 1954, 0.321 in 1959, and 0.302 in 1976.

○ = WORKED-OUT SOLUTIONS on p. WS1 ★ = STANDARDIZED TEST PRACTICE

◆ = MULTIPLE REPRESENTATIONS

35b.

x	1990	1991	1992	1993	1994	1995	1996
R	3.74	4.32	4.42	4.44	4.44	4.42	4.40

x	1997	1998	1999	2000	2001	2002
R	4.38	4.35	4.33	4.30	4.28	4.25

Study Strategy

Exercise 34 Suggest that students write a stepped-out solution to this problem using the model from Example 6, page 805. Encourage them to model each step of Example 6, including Step 1.

Avoiding Common Errors

Exercises 35–38 Tell students that writing a verbal model of an equation can help them avoid confusion between which expression is the dividend and which is the divisor.

Internet Reference

Exercise 36 For more information about Hank Aaron, go to www.baseballhalloffame.org and do a search for "Hank Aaron."

35b. See below.

36a. $A = \frac{(31 + 120x)(1 + 0.01x)}{(1 + 0.017x)(150 + 350x)}$

37a. $T = \frac{4700 - 74x}{(1 - 0.053x)(0.015x^2 + 4.1)}$

37b.

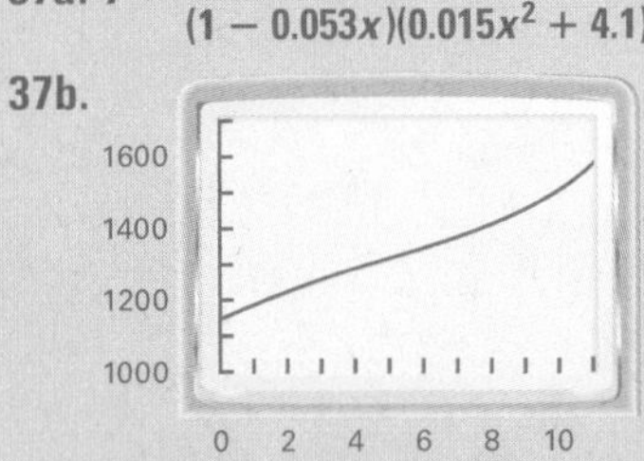

The number of tickets increased. No; the graph only shows how the *ratio* of the gross revenue and the ticket prices changed. R and P could go up and/or down while their ratio increases.

37c.

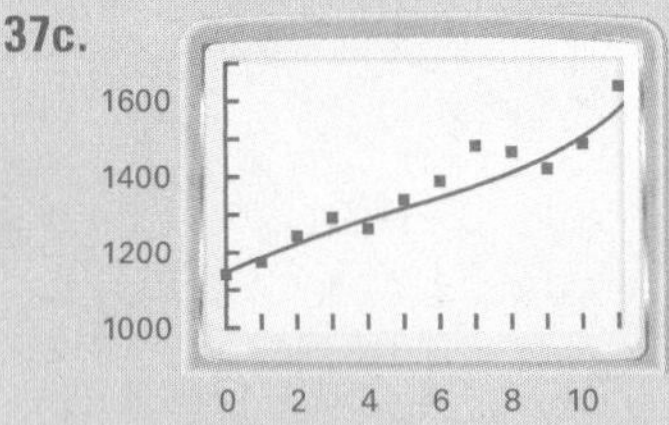

The points of the scatter plot are very close to the graph of the model for all years except 1998, 1999, and 2002.

37. ★ **EXTENDED RESPONSE** The gross revenue R (in millions of dollars) from movie tickets sold and the average movie ticket price P (in dollars) in the United States during the period 1991–2002 can be modeled by

$$R = \frac{4700 - 74x}{1 - 0.053x} \quad \text{and} \quad P = 0.015x^2 + 4.1$$

where x is the number of years since 1991. a–c. See margin.

a. **Model** Write a model that gives the number T of movie tickets sold (in millions) as a function of x.

b. **Describe** Graph the model on a graphing calculator and describe how the number of tickets sold changed over time. Can you use the graph to describe how the gross revenue and ticket prices changed over time? *Explain* your reasoning.

c. **Compare** The table shows the actual number of tickets sold for each year during the period. Make a scatter plot of the data on the same screen as the graph of the model in part (b). *Compare* the scatter plot with the graph of the model.

Year	1991	1992	1993	1994	1995	1996
Tickets (millions)	1141	1173	1244	1292	1263	1339

Year	1997	1998	1999	2000	2001	2002
Tickets (millions)	1388	1481	1465	1421	1487	1639

C 38. **CHALLENGE** The total amount F (in billions of dollars) spent on food other than groceries and the amount E (in billions of dollars) spent at restaurants in the U.S. during the period 1977–2003 can be modeled by

$$F = \frac{88 + 9.2x}{1 - 0.0097x} \quad \text{and} \quad E = \frac{54 + 6.5x}{1 - 0.012x}$$

where x is the number of years since 1977. Write a model that gives the percent p (in decimal form) of the amount spent on food other than groceries that was spent at restaurants as a function of x. Approximate the percent that was spent at locations other than restaurants in 2002.

$p = \frac{(54 + 6.5x)(1 - 0.0097x)}{(1 - 0.012x)(88 + 9.2x)}$; about 26%

TEST PRACTICE at classzone.com

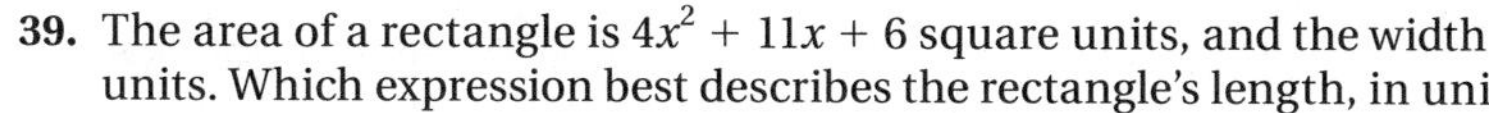

ILLINOIS MIXED REVIEW

39. The area of a rectangle is $4x^2 + 11x + 6$ square units, and the width is $x + 2$ units. Which expression best describes the rectangle's length, in units? C

Ⓐ $x + 4$ Ⓑ $2x + 3$ Ⓒ $4x + 3$ Ⓓ $4x + 2$

40. A cylindrical tank has a radius of 2 feet and a height of 8.5 feet. The tank is filled with water to the top. If water can be pumped out of the tank at a rate of 36 cubic feet per minute, about how long will it take to empty the tank? B

Ⓐ 1 min Ⓑ 3 min Ⓒ 5 min Ⓓ 22 min

5 ASSESS AND RETEACH

Daily Homework Quiz

Transparency Available

1. Find the product $\frac{3x}{x^2 - 3x - 10} \cdot (x + 2)$. $\frac{3x}{x - 5}$

2. Find the quotient $(2x^3 + 11x^2 + 11x - 4) \div (x + 4)$. $2x^2 + 3x - 1$

3. The average total revenue (in thousands of dollars) of books B sold at a used bookstore and the average revenue of paperback books P sold at the store during 1990–2004 can be represented by $B = \frac{824 + 12x}{1 - 0.02x}$ and $P = \frac{720 - 36x}{1 - 0.017x}$ where x is the number of years since 1990. Approximate the percent of the total revenue of books from paperback sales in 2004. about 21%

Online Quiz

Available at **classzone.com**

Diagnosis/Remediation

- Practice A, B, C in Chapter 12 Resource Book, pp. 58–60
- Study Guide in Chapter 12 Resource Book, pp. 61–62
- Practice Workbook, pp. 190–191
- @HomeTutor

Challenge

Additional challenge is available in the Chapter 12 Resource Book, p. 65.

1 PLAN AND PREPARE

Warm-Up Exercises

Find the quotient.

1. $\frac{5x}{3} \div 5x^2$ $\frac{1}{3x}$

2. $\frac{x^2 - 10x + 16}{2x} \div (x - 2)$ $\frac{x - 8}{2x}$

2 FOCUS AND MOTIVATE

Essential Question

Big Idea 2, p. 736

How do you simplify a complex fraction? Tell students they will learn how to answer this question by treating a complex fraction as division of two rational expressions.

3 TEACH

Extra Example 1

Simplify the complex fraction.

a. $\frac{\frac{8x^2}{5}}{-2x}$ $-\frac{4x}{5}$

b. $\frac{\frac{x-4}{x+4}}{x^2 - 16}$ $\frac{1}{(x+4)^2}$

Key Question to Ask for Example 1

- In part (b), how can you tell which expression represents the complex fraction's numerator? The longest fraction bar separates the numerator and denominator of the complex fraction.

NCTM STANDARDS

Standard 1: Understand how operations are related

Standard 2: Analyze situations using algebraic symbols

Extension Simplify Complex Fractions

Use after Lesson 12.5

GOAL Simplify complex fractions.

Key Vocabulary
- **complex fraction**

A **complex fraction** is a fraction that contains a fraction in its numerator, denominator, or both. To simplify a complex fraction, divide its numerator by its denominator.

READING
The widest fraction bar separates the numerator of a complex fraction from the denominator.

KEY CONCEPT *For Your Notebook*

Simplifying a Complex Fraction

Let a, b, c, and d be polynomials where $b \neq 0$, $c \neq 0$, and $d \neq 0$.

Algebra $\frac{\frac{a}{b}}{\frac{c}{d}} = \frac{a}{b} \div \frac{c}{d} = \frac{a}{b} \cdot \frac{d}{c}$

Example $\frac{\frac{x}{2}}{\frac{x}{3}} = \frac{x}{2} \div \frac{x}{3} = \frac{x}{2} \cdot \frac{3}{x} = \frac{3x}{2x} = \frac{3}{2}$

EXAMPLE 1 Simplify a complex fraction

Simplify the complex fraction.

a. $\frac{\frac{3x}{2}}{-6x^3} = \frac{3x}{2} \div (-6x^3)$ — **Write fraction as quotient.**

$= \frac{3x}{2} \cdot \frac{1}{-6x^3}$ — **Multiply by multiplicative inverse.**

$= \frac{3x}{-12x^3}$ — **Multiply numerators and denominators.**

$= -\frac{1}{4x^2}$ — **Simplify.**

b. $\frac{x^2 - 1}{\frac{x+1}{x-1}} = (x^2 - 1) \div \frac{x+1}{x-1}$ — **Write fraction as quotient.**

$= (x^2 - 1) \cdot \frac{x-1}{x+1}$ — **Multiply by multiplicative inverse.**

$= \frac{(x^2 - 1)(x - 1)}{x + 1}$ — **Multiply numerators and denominators.**

$= \frac{\cancel{(x+1)}(x-1)(x-1)}{\cancel{x+1}}$ — **Factor and divide out common factor.**

$= (x - 1)^2$ — **Simplify.**

EXAMPLE 2 Simplify a complex fraction

Simplify $\dfrac{\frac{2x^2 - 8x}{x^2 + 4x + 4}}{\frac{x^3 - 16x}{x + 2}}$.

$\dfrac{\frac{2x^2 - 8x}{x^2 + 4x + 4}}{\frac{x^3 - 16x}{x + 2}} = \dfrac{2x^2 - 8x}{x^2 + 4x + 4} \div \dfrac{x^3 - 16x}{x + 2}$ **Write fraction as quotient.**

$= \dfrac{2x^2 - 8x}{x^2 + 4x + 4} \cdot \dfrac{x + 2}{x^3 - 16x}$ **Multiply by multiplicative inverse.**

$= \dfrac{(2x^2 - 8x)(x + 2)}{(x^2 + 4x + 4)(x^3 - 16x)}$ **Multiply numerators and denominators.**

$= \dfrac{2x\cancel{(x-4)}\cancel{(x+2)}}{\cancel{(x+2)}(x+2)x(x+4)\cancel{(x-4)}}$ **Factor and divide out common factors.**

$= \dfrac{2}{(x + 2)(x + 4)}$ **Simplify.**

PRACTICE

EXAMPLES 1 and 2 on pp. 810–811 for Exs. 1–9

Simplify the complex fraction.

1. $\dfrac{\frac{-9x^5}{7}}{-12x^2}$ $\frac{3x^3}{28}$

2. $\dfrac{\frac{-2}{11x^4}}{18x^4}$ $\frac{-1}{99x^8}$

3. $\dfrac{\frac{x^2 + 7x}{2x - 6}}{x^2 - 49}$ $\frac{x}{2(x-3)(x-7)}$

4. $\dfrac{-24x^4}{\frac{8x^2}{-4x^3}}$ $12x^5$

5. $\dfrac{\frac{x^2 + 4x}{x + 4}}{x^2 - x}$ $x^2(x-1)$

6. $\dfrac{2x^2 + 5x - 3}{\frac{x^2 + 4x + 3}{15x}}$ $\frac{15x(2x-1)}{x+1}$

7. $\dfrac{\frac{x^2 - x - 20}{4}}{\frac{x - 5}{10}}$ $\frac{5(x+4)}{2}$

8. $\dfrac{\frac{x^2 - 2x - 8}{6x - 3x^2}}{\frac{x^3 + 4x^2}{x^2 - 4}}$ $-\frac{(x-4)(x+2)^2}{3x^3(x+4)}$

9. $\dfrac{\frac{2x^2 + 5x - 3}{3x^2 + 4x + 1}}{\frac{10x^2 - 5x}{2x^3 - 2x}}$ $\frac{2(x+3)(x-1)}{5(3x+1)}$

GEOMETRY Write a rational expression for the ratio of the surface area S of the given solid to its volume V.

10. Sphere $\frac{3}{r}$

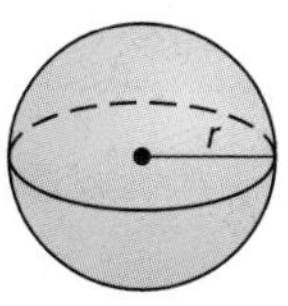

$S = 4\pi r^2$

$V = \dfrac{4\pi r^3}{3}$

11. Cone $\frac{3(r+\ell)}{rh}$

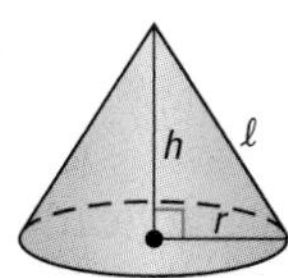

$S = \pi r^2 + \pi r\ell$

$V = \dfrac{\pi r^2 h}{3}$

12. Pyramid with a square base $\frac{3(s+2\ell)}{sh}$

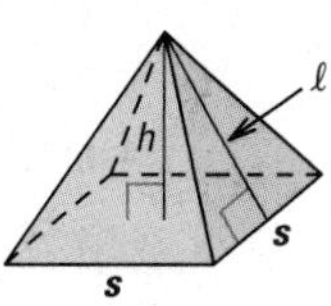

$S = s^2 + 2s\ell$

$V = \dfrac{s^2 h}{3}$

13. Are the complex fractions $\dfrac{\frac{a}{b}}{c}$ and $\dfrac{a}{\frac{b}{c}}$ equivalent? *Explain* your answer. See margin.

Extra Example 2

Simplify $\dfrac{\frac{3x - 18}{2x^2 + 16x + 30}}{\frac{x - 6}{x^2 + 2x - 15}}$. $\frac{3(x-3)}{2(x+3)}$

Key Questions to Ask for Example 2

- How many fractions make up the complex fraction? two; one in the numerator and one in the denominator
- For which fraction do you find the multiplicative inverse? the one in the denominator

Closing the Lesson

Have students summarize the major points of the lesson and answer the Essential Question: How do you simplify a complex fraction?

- A complex fraction contains a fraction in its numerator, denominator, or both.

To simplify a complex fraction, first write the fraction as a quotient. Then use the reciprocal of the divisor to rewrite the expression as a product. Factor numerators and/or denominators, divide out common factors, and simplify.

4 PRACTICE AND APPLY

Avoiding Common Errors

Exercises 1–9 Watch for students who separate the complex fraction incorrectly, using part of the numerator as the denominator or vice versa. Remind these students that the longest fraction bar indicates how to rewrite the complex fraction as the division of two rational expressions.

13. No; $\dfrac{\frac{a}{b}}{c} = \frac{a}{b} \div c = \frac{a}{b} \cdot \frac{1}{c} = \frac{a}{bc}$ and $\dfrac{a}{\frac{b}{c}} = a \div \frac{b}{c} = \frac{a}{1} \cdot \frac{c}{b} = \frac{ac}{b}$. Thus, $\dfrac{\frac{a}{b}}{c} \neq \dfrac{a}{\frac{b}{c}}$.

1 PLAN AND PREPARE

Warm-Up Exercises

Transparency Available

1. Find $\frac{1}{4} + \frac{2}{3}$. $\frac{11}{12}$
2. Find $\frac{7}{8} - \frac{5}{6}$. $\frac{1}{24}$
3. A boat travels 8 miles upstream (against the current) in 4 hours, and 8 miles downstream (with the current) in 3.2 hours. What is the average speed of the boat in still water? **2.25 mi/h**

Notetaking Guide

Transparency Available

Promotes interactive learning and notetaking skills, pp. 287–290.

Pacing

Basic: 2 days
Average: 2 days
Advanced: 2 days
Block: 0.5 block with 12.5
0.5 block with 12.7

- See *Teaching Guide/Lesson Plan.*

2 FOCUS AND MOTIVATE

Essential Question

Big Idea 2, p. 736

How do you add or subtract rational expressions? **Tell students they will learn how to answer this question by using processes similar to adding or subtracting fractions.**

12.6 Add and Subtract Rational Expressions

 **8.11.01** Simplify or identify equivalent algebraic expressions (e.g., exponential, rational, logarithmic, factored, polynomial).

Before You multiplied and divided rational expressions.

Now You will add and subtract rational expressions.

Why? So you can solve work problems, as in Ex. 49.

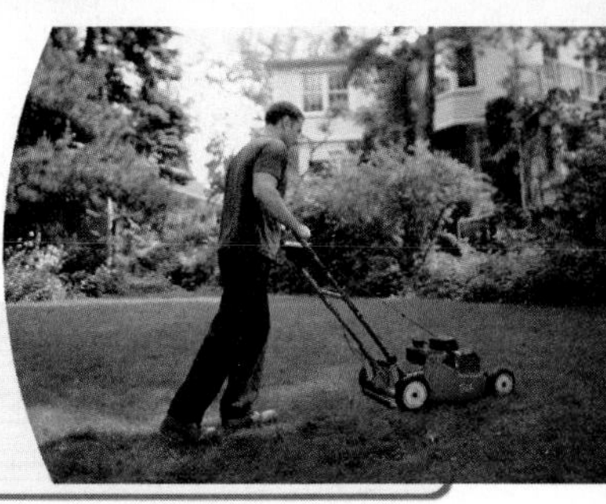

Key Vocabulary
- **least common denominator (LCD) of rational expressions**

Adding and subtracting rational expressions with the same denominator is similar to adding and subtracting numerical fractions with the same denominator.

KEY CONCEPT *For Your Notebook*

Adding and Subtracting Rational Expressions with the Same Denominator

Let a, b, and c be polynomials where $c \neq 0$.

Algebra $\frac{a}{c} + \frac{b}{c} = \frac{a+b}{c}$ $\qquad$ $\frac{a}{c} - \frac{b}{c} = \frac{a-b}{c}$

Examples $\frac{2}{x} + \frac{3}{x} = \frac{2+3}{x} = \frac{5}{x}$ $\qquad$ $\frac{5}{4x} - \frac{2}{4x} = \frac{5-2}{4x} = \frac{3}{4x}$

EXAMPLE 1 **Add and subtract with the same denominator**

a. $\frac{5}{3x} + \frac{7}{3x} = \frac{12}{3x}$ **Add numerators.**

$= \frac{\cancel{3} \cdot 4}{\cancel{3} \cdot x}$ **Factor and divide out common factor.**

$= \frac{4}{x}$ **Simplify.**

b. $\frac{3x}{x-1} - \frac{x+5}{x-1} = \frac{3x-(x+5)}{x-1}$ **Subtract numerators.**

$= \frac{2x-5}{x-1}$ **Simplify.**

CHECK Check your simplification using a graphing calculator. For part (b), graph $y_1 = \frac{3x}{x-1} - \frac{x+5}{x-1}$ and $y_2 = \frac{2x-5}{x-1}$. The graphs coincide. So, the expressions are equivalent for all values of x other than the excluded value of 1.

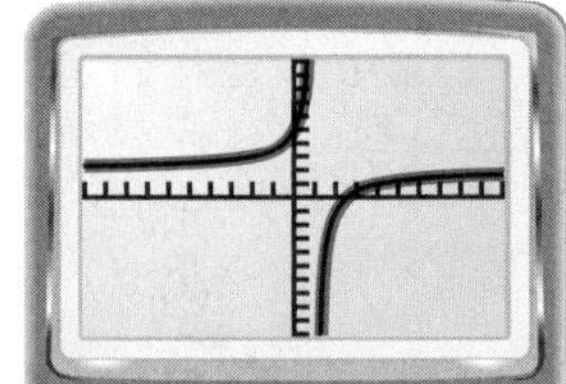

Resource Planning Guide

Chapter Resource Book
- Teaching Guide/Lesson Plan (pp. 66–67)
- Activity Master (p. 68)
- Practice levels A, B, C (pp. 69–71)
- Study Guide (pp. 72–73)
- Catch-up for Absent Students (p. 74)
- Problem Solving Workshop (p. 75)
- Challenge (p. 76)

Workbooks
- Notetaking Guide (pp. 287–290)
- Practice Workbook (pp. 192–193)

Teaching Options
- **Power Presentations CD-ROM** provides dynamic electronic teaching resources for the classroom.
- **Activity Generator CD-ROM** provides editable activities for all ability levels.

Interactive Technology
- Easy Planner
- Power Presentations CD-ROM
- Activity Generator CD-ROM
- Animated Algebra
- Test Generator CD-ROM
- Online Quiz
- eWorkbook
- eEdition
- @HomeTutor

Resources for English Learners
- Quick Reference for English Learners
- Spanish Study Guide
- Multi-Language Visual Glossary
- Student Resources in Spanish

See also the *Algebra 1 Toolkit* for more strategies for meeting individual needs.

GUIDED PRACTICE for Example 1

Find the sum or difference.

1. $\frac{2}{y} + \frac{y+1}{y}$ $\frac{y+3}{y}$

2. $\frac{4x+1}{2x-1} - \frac{2x-3}{2x-1}$ $\frac{2x+4}{2x-1}$

LEAST COMMON DENOMINATOR The **least common denominator (LCD)** of two or more rational expressions is the product of the factors of the denominators of the rational expressions with each common factor used only once.

EXAMPLE 2 Find the LCD of rational expressions

Find the LCD of the rational expressions.

a. $\frac{1}{4r}, \frac{r+3}{10r^2}$ **b.** $\frac{5}{(x-3)^2}, \frac{3x+4}{x^2-x-6}$ **c.** $\frac{3}{c-2}, \frac{c+8}{2c+7}$

Solution

a. Find the least common multiple (LCM) of $4r$ and $10r^2$.

$$4r = 2 \cdot 2 \cdot r$$ ← **The common factors are circled.**

$$10r^2 = 2 \cdot 5 \cdot r \cdot r$$

AVOID ERRORS
When finding the LCD, be sure to use the common factors only once.

$$\text{LCM} = 2 \cdot r \cdot 2 \cdot 5 \cdot r = 20r^2$$

▶ The LCD of $\frac{1}{4r}$ and $\frac{r+3}{10r^2}$ is $20r^2$.

b. Find the least common multiple (LCM) of $(x-3)^2$ and $x^2 - x - 6$.

$$(x-3)^2 = (x-3) \cdot (x-3)$$

$$x^2 - x - 6 = (x-3) \cdot (x+2)$$

$$\text{LCM} = (x-3) \cdot (x-3) \cdot (x+2) = (x-3)^2(x+2)$$

▶ The LCD of $\frac{5}{(x-3)^2}$ and $\frac{3x+4}{x^2-x-6}$ is $(x-3)^2(x+2)$.

c. Find the least common multiple of $c - 2$ and $2c + 7$.

Because $c - 2$ and $2c + 7$ cannot be factored, they don't have any factors in common. The least common multiple is their product, $(c-2)(2c+7)$.

▶ The LCD of $\frac{3}{c-2}$ and $\frac{c+8}{2c+7}$ is $(c-2)(2c+7)$.

GUIDED PRACTICE for Example 2

Find the LCD of the rational expressions.

3. $\frac{1}{28m}, \frac{m+1}{7m^3}$ $28m^3$

4. $\frac{2}{x^2+4x-5}, \frac{x^2+2}{x^2+7x+10}$ $(x+5)(x-1)(x+2)$

5. $\frac{5a}{a+3}, \frac{a+6}{a-4}$ $(a+3)(a-4)$

DIFFERENT DENOMINATORS To add or subtract rational expressions that have different denominators, use the LCD to write equivalent rational expressions that have the same denominator just as you would for numerical fractions.

Motivating the Lesson

You are planning a 500-mile trip to the Grand Canyon. You estimate that your average speed driving to the Canyon will be greater than your average speed returning home. In this lesson you will learn how to write an equation to model this situation and how to use the model to determine your average speed for the entire trip to and from the Grand Canyon.

3 TEACH

Extra Example 1

Add or subtract.

a. $\frac{2x}{x+2} + \frac{x+1}{x+2}$ $\frac{3x+1}{x+2}$

b. $\frac{4x+1}{5x} - \frac{x+3}{5x}$ $\frac{3x-2}{5x}$

Extra Example 2

Find the LCD of the rational expressions.

a. $\frac{1}{12x}, \frac{x+7}{4x^2}$ $12x^2$

b. $\frac{4}{x^2-x-6}, \frac{3x^2}{(x+2)^2}$ $(x+2)^2(x-3)$

c. $\frac{2x}{x-8}, \frac{3x+15}{x+1}$ $(x-8)(x+1)$

Key Question to Ask for Example 2

- If two denominators have repeated factors, such as $2 \cdot 2 \cdot 2 \cdot x$ and $2 \cdot 2 \cdot x \cdot x$, how many times does each factor appear in the LCD? In the LCD, use the greater number of times it occurs. For these denominators, the LCD is $2 \cdot 2 \cdot 2 \cdot x \cdot x$ or $8x^2$.

Extra Example 3

Find the sum $\frac{6}{18x} + \frac{4}{6x^2}$. $\frac{x+2}{3x^2}$

Key Question to Ask for Example 3

- How did you determine the LCD? The denominators are $2 \cdot 2 \cdot 2 \cdot x \cdot x$ and $2 \cdot 2 \cdot 3 \cdot x \cdot x \cdot x$. Taking each factor the greater number of times, the LCD is $2 \cdot 2 \cdot 2 \cdot 3 \cdot x \cdot x \cdot x$, or $24x^3$.

Extra Example 4

Find the difference $\frac{5}{2x} - \frac{3x}{x-1}$.

$\frac{-6x^2+5x-5}{2x(x-1)}$

Key Question to Ask for Example 4

- In the second step of the example, can you divide out the common factor of $(x+2)$ on the right side of the equation? Explain. No; $(x+2)$ does not appear in the numerator of one of the terms.

Extra Example 5

Find the difference

$\frac{x+3}{x^2-8x+15} - \frac{x+6}{x^2-x-20}$.

$\frac{4x+30}{(x-3)(x-5)(x+4)}$

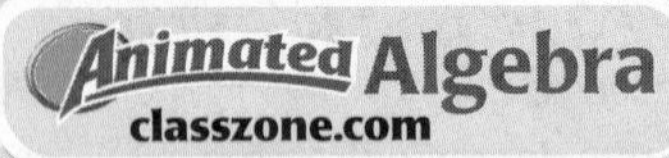

An **Animated Algebra** activity is available on-line for **Example 5**. This activity is also available on the **Power Presentations CD-ROM**.

EXAMPLE 3 Add expressions with different denominators

Find the sum $\frac{9}{8x^2} + \frac{5}{12x^3}$.

$$\frac{9}{8x^2} + \frac{5}{12x^3} = \frac{9 \cdot 3x}{8x^2 \cdot 3x} + \frac{5 \cdot 2}{12x^3 \cdot 2}$$ Rewrite fractions using LCD, $24x^3$.

$$= \frac{27x}{24x^3} + \frac{10}{24x^3}$$ Simplify numerators and denominators.

$$= \frac{27x+10}{24x^3}$$ Add fractions.

EXAMPLE 4 Subtract expressions with different denominators

Find the difference $\frac{10}{3x} - \frac{7x}{x+2}$.

$$\frac{10}{3x} - \frac{7x}{x+2} = \frac{10(x+2)}{3x(x+2)} - \frac{7x(3x)}{(x+2)(3x)}$$ Rewrite fractions using LCD, $3x(x+2)$.

$$= \frac{10(x+2) - 7x(3x)}{3x(x+2)}$$ Subtract fractions.

$$= \frac{-21x^2+10x+20}{3x(x+2)}$$ Simplify numerator.

EXAMPLE 5 Subtract expressions with different denominators

Find the difference $\frac{x+4}{x^2+3x-10} - \frac{x-1}{x^2+2x-8}$.

$$\frac{x+4}{x^2+3x-10} - \frac{x-1}{x^2+2x-8}$$

$$= \frac{x+4}{(x-2)(x+5)} - \frac{x-1}{(x+4)(x-2)}$$ Factor denominators.

$$= \frac{(x+4)(x+4)}{(x-2)(x+5)(x+4)} - \frac{(x-1)(x+5)}{(x+4)(x-2)(x+5)}$$ Rewrite fractions using LCD, $(x-2)(x+5)(x+4)$.

$$= \frac{(x+4)(x+4) - (x-1)(x+5)}{(x-2)(x+5)(x+4)}$$ Subtract fractions.

$$= \frac{x^2+8x+16-(x^2+4x-5)}{(x-2)(x+5)(x+4)}$$ Find products in numerator.

$$= \frac{4x+21}{(x-2)(x+5)(x+4)}$$ Simplify.

AVOID ERRORS
Because you are subtracting $x^2 + 4x - 5$ in the numerator, you need to add the opposite of *every* term in $x^2 + 4x - 5$.

Animated Algebra at classzone.com

✓ GUIDED PRACTICE for Examples 3, 4, and 5

Find the sum or difference.

6. $\frac{3}{2x} + \frac{7}{5x^4}$ $\frac{15x^3+14}{10x^4}$

7. $\frac{y}{y+1} + \frac{3}{y+2}$ $\frac{y^2+5y+3}{(y+1)(y+2)}$

8. $\frac{2z-1}{z^2+2z-8} - \frac{z+1}{z^2-4}$ $\frac{z^2-2z-6}{(z+4)(z-2)(z+2)}$

Differentiated Instruction

Auditory Learners Students may find other methods of adding and subtracting fractions easier to recall. In **Example 3**, students can "cross-multiply" to get a numerator of $9 \cdot 12x^3 + 5 \cdot 8x^2$ and then multiply the denominators to get $96x^5$. Students can conclude by simplifying the resulting rational expression, $\frac{9 \cdot 12x^3 + 5 \cdot 8x^2}{96x^5}$, as $\frac{27x+10}{24x^3}$.

See also the *Algebra 1 Toolkit* for more strategies.

EXAMPLE 6 Solve a multi-step problem

BOAT TRAVEL A boat travels 24 kilometers upstream (against the current) and 24 kilometers downstream (with the current) as shown in the diagram. Write an equation that gives the total travel time t (in hours) as a function of the boat's average speed r (in kilometers per hour) in still water. Find the total travel time if the boat's average speed in still water is 10 kilometers per hour.

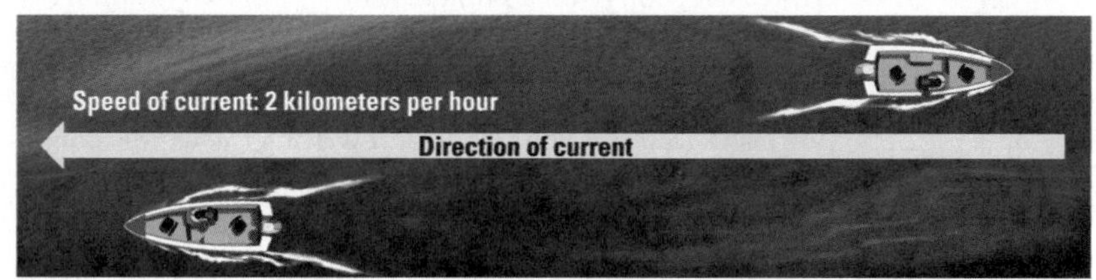

Solution

STEP 1 **Write** a verbal model. Then write an equation.

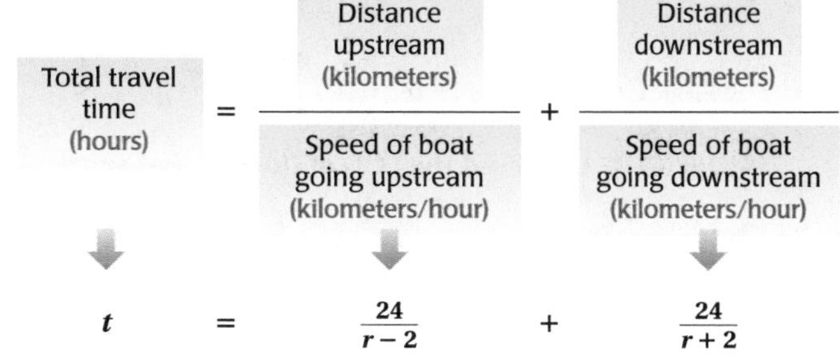

Total travel time (hours)
=
Distance upstream (kilometers)
Speed of boat going upstream (kilometers/hour)
+
Distance downstream (kilometers)
Speed of boat going downstream (kilometers/hour)

$$t = \frac{24}{r-2} + \frac{24}{r+2}$$

COMBINE SPEEDS When you go upstream, you subtract the speed of the current from the speed at which you travel in still water. When you go downstream, you add the speeds.

STEP 2 **Find** the sum of the expressions on the right side of the equation.

$t = \frac{24}{r-2} + \frac{24}{r+2}$ **Write equation.**

$= \frac{24(r+2)}{(r-2)(r+2)} + \frac{24(r-2)}{(r+2)(r-2)}$ **Rewrite fractions using LCD, $(r-2)(r+2)$.**

$= \frac{24(r+2) + 24(r-2)}{(r-2)(r+2)}$ **Add fractions.**

$= \frac{48r}{(r-2)(r+2)}$ **Simplify.**

STEP 3 **Calculate** the value of t when $r = 10$.

$$t = \frac{48(10)}{(10-2)(10+2)} = \frac{480}{(8)(12)} = \frac{480}{96} = 5$$

▶ The total travel time is 5 hours.

✓ **GUIDED PRACTICE** for Example 6

9. **WHAT IF?** In Example 6, suppose the speed of the current is 3 kilometers per hour. Find the total travel time. about 5.3 h

Extra Example 6

A rowing crew rows a boat 18 miles upstream (against the current) and 18 miles downstream (with the current). The speed of the current is 3 miles per hour. Write an equation that gives the boat's average speed r (in miles per hour) in still water. Find the total travel time if the boat's average speed in still water is 5 miles per hour. $t = \frac{18}{r-3} + \frac{18}{r+3}$; 11.25 h

Closing the Lesson

Have students summarize the major points of the lesson and answer the Essential Question: How do you add or subtract rational expressions?

- Rational expressions can be added or subtracted by using the rules for adding and subtracting rational numbers.
- To find the least common denominator (LCD) of two rational expressions, find the product of the factors of each denominator. If the denominators have a common factor, use it just once. If either denominator has repeated factors, the LCD also will have repeated factors.

When adding or subtracting rational expressions with the same denominator, write the sum or difference of the numerators over the common denominator and simplify. When adding or subtracting rational expressions with different denominators, start by using the LCD to write equivalent rational expressions.

12.6 EXERCISES

HOMEWORK KEY ◯ = **WORKED-OUT SOLUTIONS** on p. WS30 for Exs. 7, 29, and 45
★ = **STANDARDIZED TEST PRACTICE** Exs. 2, 32, 44, and 48

SKILL PRACTICE

A

1. **VOCABULARY** Copy and complete: The _?_ of two rational expressions is the product of the factors of their denominators with each common factor used only once. least common denominator

2. ★ **WRITING** *Describe* your steps in rewriting the expressions $\frac{1}{x+2}$ and $\frac{2x}{x^2-4}$ so that they have the same denominator. See margin.

EXAMPLE 1 on p. 812 for Exs. 3–11

ADDING AND SUBTRACTING EXPRESSIONS Find the sum or difference.

3. $\frac{2}{5x}+\frac{3}{5x}$ $\frac{1}{x}$
4. $\frac{y+1}{2y}+\frac{5}{2y}$ $\frac{y+6}{2y}$
5. $\frac{6z}{z^2}-\frac{2z}{z^2}$ $\frac{4}{z}$
6. $\frac{7}{a+2}-\frac{3a}{a+2}$ $\frac{7-3a}{a+2}$
7. $\frac{b}{b-3}+\frac{b+1}{b-3}$ $\frac{2b+1}{b-3}$
8. $\frac{c+2}{c-9}+\frac{c+5}{c-9}$ $\frac{2c+7}{c-9}$
9. $\frac{7}{m^2+1}-\frac{8}{m^2+1}$ $\frac{-1}{m^2+1}$
10. $\frac{2n+1}{n^2-16}-\frac{n}{n^2-16}$ $\frac{n+1}{n^2-16}$
11. $\frac{3r}{r^2+r-7}+\frac{1}{r^2+r-7}$ $\frac{3r+1}{r^2+r-7}$

EXAMPLE 2 on p. 813 for Exs. 12–17, 32

FINDING THE LCD Find the LCD of the rational expressions.

12. $\frac{1}{24x}, \frac{x+2}{6x^3}$ $24x^3$
13. $\frac{3}{15v^2}, \frac{v^2-4}{20v^3}$ $60v^3$
14. $\frac{4w}{w+5}, \frac{w+3}{w-2}$ $(w+5)(w-2)$
15. $\frac{s-1}{s+2}, \frac{s+2}{s-1}$ $(s+2)(s-1)$
16. $\frac{1}{t^2-4t}, \frac{6}{t^2-2t-8}$ $t(t+2)(t-4)$
17. $\frac{u+9}{u^2+8u+7}, \frac{-3}{u^2-2u-3}$ $(u+7)(u+1)(u-3)$

EXAMPLES 3, 4, and 5 on p. 814 for Exs. 18–31

ERROR ANALYSIS *Describe* and correct the error in finding the sum or difference. 18, 19. See margin.

18. $\frac{8}{2x+3}-\frac{4x}{x+2}$

$$\frac{8}{2x+3}-\frac{4x}{x+2}=\frac{8-4x}{2x+3-(x+2)}=\frac{8-4x}{2x+3-x-2}=\frac{8-4x}{x+1}$$

19. $\frac{5x}{x-4}+\frac{2}{x+3}$

$$\frac{5x}{x-4}+\frac{2}{x+3}=\frac{5x(x-4)+2(x+3)}{(x-4)(x+3)}=\frac{5x^2-20x+2x+6}{(x-4)(x+3)}=\frac{5x^2-18x+6}{(x-4)(x+3)}$$

ADDING AND SUBTRACTING EXPRESSIONS Find the sum or difference. 20–31. See margin.

20. $\frac{5x}{4}+\frac{2}{5x}$
21. $\frac{13}{3y}+\frac{2}{11y}$
22. $\frac{7}{2z}-\frac{2}{3z^2}$
23. $\frac{7r}{r-2}-\frac{2r}{r-3}$
24. $\frac{s}{5s-2}-\frac{1}{4s+1}$
25. $\frac{c+3}{c-6}+\frac{c}{3c+10}$
26. $\frac{d-5}{d+7}+\frac{d-5}{4d}$
27. $\frac{f+3}{7f}-\frac{3f}{f+4}$
28. $\frac{1}{g^2+5g+6}-\frac{1}{g^2-4}$
29. $\frac{2j}{j^2-1}+\frac{j-1}{j^2-7j+6}$
30. $\frac{k+7}{k^2+6k+9}+\frac{k-5}{k^2-5k-24}$
31. $\frac{v+2}{2v^2-v-15}-\frac{v-2}{v^2+2v-15}$

4 PRACTICE AND APPLY

Assignment Guide

Answer Transparencies available for all exercises

Basic:
Day 1: pp. 816–819
Exs. 1–17, 19–21, 25, 26, 58–62
Day 2: pp. 816–819
Exs. 18, 22–24, 27–35, 42–47, 50–57

Average:
Day 1: pp. 816–819
Exs. 1, 2, 7–17, 19–21, 25, 26, 29, 30, 35, 36, 58–62
Day 2: pp. 816–819
Exs. 18, 22–24, 27–34, 37–40, 42–48, 50–56 even

Advanced:
Day 1: pp. 816–819
Exs. 1, 2, 7–17, 19–21, 25, 26, 35, 36, 58–62
Day 2: pp. 816–819
Exs. 22–24, 27, 28, 31–34, 37, 41–49*, 51–57 odd

Block:
pp. 816–819
Exs. 1, 2, 7–17, 19–21, 25, 26, 29, 30, 35, 36, 58–62 (with 12.5)
pp. 816–819
Exs. 18, 22–24, 27–34, 37–40, 42–48, 50–56 even (with 12.7)

Differentiated Instruction

See *Algebra 1 Best Practices Toolkit* for suggestions on addressing the needs of a diverse classroom.

Homework Check

For a quick check of student understanding of key concepts, go over the following exercises:

Basic: 8, 20, 23, 25, 42
Average: 10, 21, 24, 26, 44
Advanced: 11, 22, 26, 31, 46

Extra Practice

- Student Edition, p. 946
- Chapter 12 Resource Book: Practice levels A, B, C, pp. 69–71

Practice Worksheet

An easily-readable reduced practice page (with answers) for this lesson can be found on p. 762C.

2. Write each denominator in factored form: $(x+2)$ and $(x+2)(x-2)$. The least common denominator (LCD) will have all the factors of both denominators, using any common factor only once: the denominator of the second fraction, $(x+2)(x-2)$, is the LCD. Write the first fraction with the LCD by multiplying its numerator and its denominator by $(x-2)$: $\frac{x-2}{(x+2)(x-2)}$.

32. ★ **MULTIPLE CHOICE** Which is a factor of the LCD of $\frac{3}{x^2 - 4x}$ and $\frac{4x}{x + 2}$? B

Ⓐ 3　　Ⓑ $x - 4$　　Ⓒ $4x$　　Ⓓ $x - 2$

B 33. **GEOMETRY** The height h of a rectangular prism is given by

$$h = \frac{S}{2(\ell + w)} - \frac{\ell w}{\ell + w}$$

where S is the surface area, ℓ is the length, and w is the width. Find the difference of the expressions on the right side of the equation. $\frac{S - 2\ell w}{2(\ell + w)}$

USING ORDER OF OPERATIONS Use the order of operations to write the expression as a single rational expression.

34. $2\left(\frac{x}{x+1}\right) - 3\left(\frac{x-4}{x+2}\right)$ $\frac{-x^2 + 13x + 12}{(x + 1)(x + 2)}$

35. $5\left(\frac{3x}{x-2} + \frac{4}{x^2 + 6x - 16}\right)$ $\frac{15x^2 + 120x + 20}{(x - 2)(x + 8)}$

36. $\frac{x - 3}{x^2 + 9x + 20} + \frac{5x}{x + 2} \cdot \frac{12}{x + 4}$ $\frac{61x^2 + 299x - 6}{(x + 5)(x + 4)(x + 2)}$

37. $\frac{x + 5}{x - 9} - \frac{3x^2 + 2x - 1}{x + 4} \div \frac{x^2 - 3x - 4}{x^2 - 16}$ $\frac{-3x^2 + 29x - 4}{x - 9}$

WRITING EQUATIONS For the given hyperbola, write an equation of the form $y = \frac{a}{b}$ where a and b are first-degree polynomials.

38. $y = \frac{2x + 4}{x - 1}$

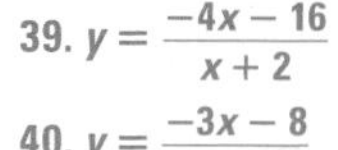

39. $y = \frac{-4x - 16}{x + 2}$

40. $y = \frac{-3x - 8}{x + 6}$

38.

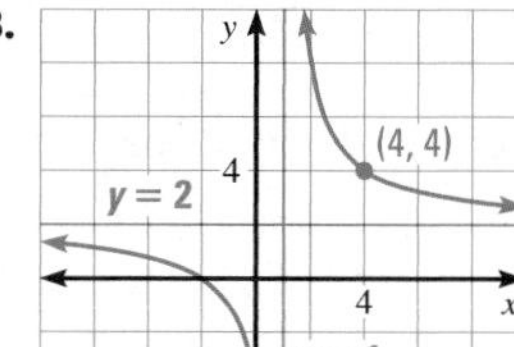

39.

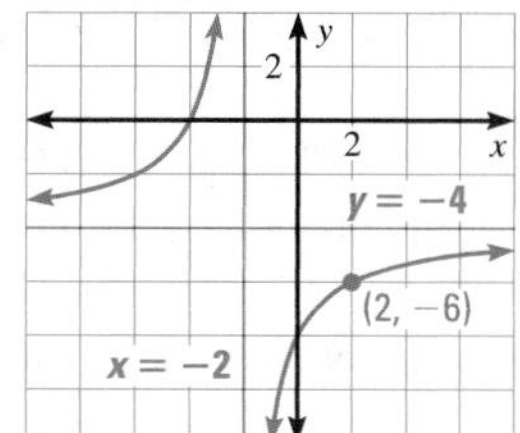

40.

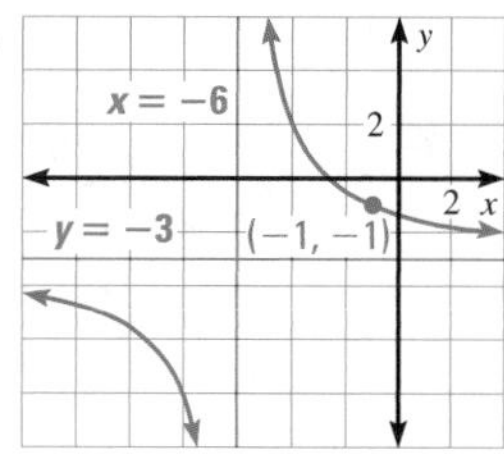

41. **CHALLENGE** Let a, b, c, and d be first-degree polynomials. Find two rational expressions $\frac{a}{b}$ and $\frac{c}{d}$ such that $\frac{a}{b} - \frac{c}{d} = \frac{5x + 7}{(x + 2)(x + 3)}$.
Sample answer: $\frac{-3}{x + 2}, \frac{-8}{x + 3}$

PROBLEM SOLVING

EXAMPLE 6 A on p. 815 for Exs. 42–46

42. **CANOEING** A canoeist travels 16 miles upstream (against the current) and 16 miles downstream (with the current). The speed of the current is 1 mile per hour. Write an equation that gives the total travel time t (in hours) as a function of the canoeist's average speed r (in miles per hour) in still water. Then find the total travel time if the canoeist's average speed in still water is 6 miles per hour. $t = \frac{32r}{(r - 1)(r + 1)}$; about 5.5 h

@HomeTutor for problem solving help at classzone.com

43. **DRIVING** Matt drives 200 miles to another city. On the drive back home, his average speed decreases by 5 miles per hour. Write an equation that gives the total driving time t (in hours) as a function of his average speed r (in miles per hour) when driving to the city. Then find the total driving time if he drives to the city at an average speed of 50 miles per hour. $t = \frac{400r - 1000}{r(r - 5)}$; about 8.4 h

@HomeTutor for problem solving help at classzone.com

18. Rational expressions are not subtracted by subtracting their numerators and subtracting their denominators. Instead, you must write the expressions with a common denominator and then subtract the numerators over the common denominator; $\frac{8}{2x + 3} - \frac{4x}{x + 2} = \frac{8(x + 2)}{(2x + 3)(x + 2)} - \frac{4x(2x + 3)}{(2x + 3)(x + 2)} = \frac{8x + 16 - 8x^2 - 12x}{(2x + 3)(x + 2)} = \frac{-8x^2 - 4x + 16}{(2x + 3)(x + 2)}$.

19. See Additional Answers beginning on p. AA1.

Avoiding Common Errors

Exercises 3–11, 20–31 Watch for students who divide out common factors before adding or subtracting. Remind students that they must combine the expressions before they look for common factors in the numerator and denominator.

Exercises 20–31 Students sometimes find the correct LCD but calculate an incorrect numerator for the equivalent rational expression. Suggest that students check their calculations for this type of error.

Teaching Strategy

Exercises 34–37 Before students begin these exercises, you may want to ask them to describe the steps they will take to rewrite each of the exercises. Make sure students know that they must distribute the factor outside the parentheses to each term inside the parentheses.

20. $\frac{25x^2 + 8}{20x}$

21. $\frac{149}{33y}$

22. $\frac{21z - 4}{6z^2}$

23. $\frac{5r^2 - 17r}{(r - 2)(r - 3)}$

24. $\frac{4s^2 - 4s + 2}{(5s - 2)(4s + 1)}$

25. $\frac{4c^2 + 13c + 30}{(c - 6)(3c + 10)}$

26. $\frac{5d^2 - 18d - 35}{4d(d + 7)}$

27. $\frac{-20f^2 + 7f + 12}{7f(f + 4)}$

28. $\frac{-5}{(g + 2)(g + 3)(g - 2)}$

29. $\frac{3j^2 - 12j - 1}{(j - 1)(j + 1)(j - 6)}$

30. $\frac{2k^2 - 3k - 71}{(k - 8)(k + 3)^2}$

31. $\frac{-v^2 + 6v + 20}{(2v + 5)(v - 3)(v + 5)}$

Study Strategy

Exercises 44, 48 Point out to students that these exercises mimic a type of question often found on standardized tests. Tell them that a useful strategy for these questions is to read all of the parts before starting to answer. For each part, they may want to write a note about how to answer it.

Vocabulary

Exercises 46, 47 You may want to ask students who are familiar with the concepts of resistance and ohms in parallel circuits and with amplitude modulation and frequency modulation in radio broadcasting to explain these concepts in class.

44a. $t = \frac{420{,}000}{(300 - w)(300 + w)}$; 4.7 h

44b. 0; the flying time one way will be half the total flying time only when the flying time against the wind, which is $\frac{700}{300 + w}$, and the flying time with the wind, which is $\frac{700}{300 - w}$, are equal. Because these two rational expressions have equal numerators, they can only be equal if they also have equal denominators: $300 + w = 300 - w$, so $2w = 0$, and $w = 0$.

45a. $\frac{2A^2 + 200A}{3}$; $\frac{7A^2 + 18{,}750A - 250{,}050}{150}$

44. ★ **SHORT RESPONSE** An airplane makes a round trip between two destinations as shown in the diagram. The airplane flies against the wind when traveling west and flies with the wind when traveling east. Assume that the speed of the wind remains constant during each flight.

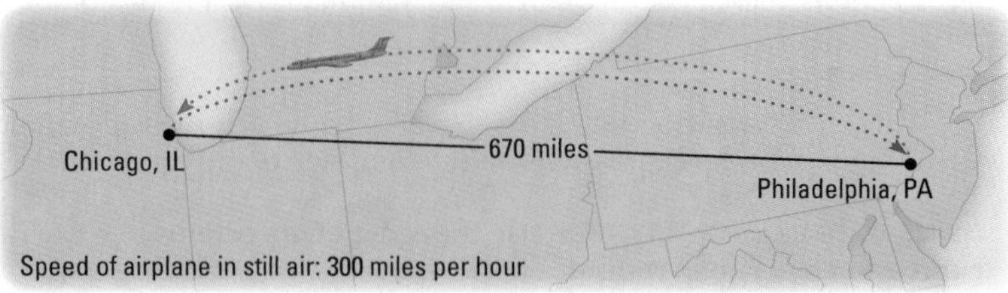

a. **Model** Write an equation that gives the total flying time t (in hours) as a function of the speed w (in miles per hour) of the wind. Then find the total flying time if the speed of the wind is 15 miles per hour. a, b. See margin.

b. **Decide** For what value of w does the flying time one way take half as long as the total flying time? *Explain* your reasoning.

(45.) **ELEVATORS** According to the law in one state, the minimum weight W (in pounds) that a passenger elevator must hold is given by

$$W = \frac{2A^2}{3} + \frac{200A}{3} \text{ if } A \le 50 \qquad \text{and} \qquad W = \frac{7A^2}{150} + (125A - 1367) \text{ if } A > 50$$

where A represents the area (in square feet) of the elevator platform.

a. Write the right side of each equation as a single rational expression. See margin.

b. What is the minimum weight that an elevator must hold if the area of the platform is 30 square feet? 60 square feet? 2600 lb; 6301 lb

46. **MULTI-STEP PROBLEM** A parallel electric circuit consists of a power source and several parallel resistors through which electricity can flow. For a parallel circuit with two resistors, let r_1 represent the resistance (in ohms) of one resistor, and let r_2 represent the resistance (in ohms) of the other resistor.

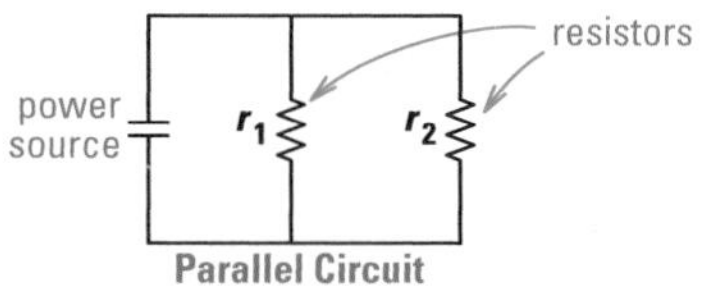

a. **Model** The total resistance r_T is equal to the multiplicative inverse of $\frac{1}{r_1} + \frac{1}{r_2}$. Write $\frac{1}{r_1} + \frac{1}{r_2}$ as a single rational expression. Then write an equation that gives r_T in terms of r_1 and r_2. $\frac{r_2 + r_1}{r_1 r_2}$; $r_T = \frac{r_1 r_2}{r_2 + r_1}$

b. **Calculate** Find the total resistance when one resistor has a resistance of 2 ohms and the other resistor has a resistance of 6 ohms. 1.5 ohms

B **47.** **RADIO STATIONS** Radio stations use either amplitude modulation (AM) broadcasting or frequency modulation (FM) broadcasting. The percent a (in decimal form) of commercial radio stations that used AM broadcasting during the period 1990–2003 can be modeled by

$$a = \frac{2.8 + 0.085x}{5.3 + 0.30x}$$

where x is the number of years since 1990. Write a model that gives the percent f (in decimal form) of commercial radio stations that used FM broadcasting as a function of x. Then approximate the value of f in 2003. $f = \frac{2.5 + 0.215x}{5.3 + 0.30x}$; about 58%

◯ = WORKED-OUT SOLUTIONS on p. WS1 ★ = STANDARDIZED TEST PRACTICE

48. ★ **EXTENDED RESPONSE** The axle load for a tow vehicle is the weight (in pounds) that an axle on the vehicle supports. The rear axle load R and the front axle load F are given by the formulas

$$R = \frac{t(w + h)}{w} \quad \text{and} \quad F = \frac{th}{w}$$

where t represents the weight (in pounds) that presses down on the hitch by a trailer and w and h represent the distances (in feet) shown.

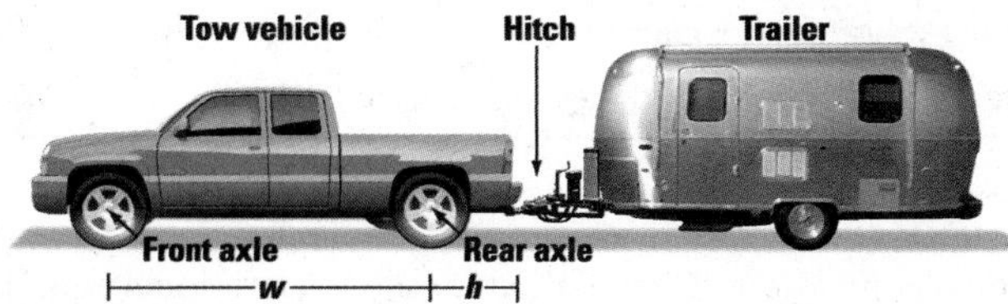

a. **Calculate** For a certain tow vehicle, $t = 300$, $w = 9$, and $h = 3.5$. Find the rear axle load and the front axle load. $416\frac{2}{3}$ lb, $116\frac{2}{3}$ lb

b. **Compare** Find the difference of the rear axle load and the front axle load found in part (a). *Compare* your answer with the given value of t. 300 lb; the answers are the same.

c. **Model** Write an equation that gives t in terms of R and F. *Justify* your answer algebraically. $t = R - F$; $R - F = \frac{t(w+h)}{w} - \frac{th}{w} = \frac{tw + th - th}{w} = \frac{tw}{w} = t$

C 49. **CHALLENGE** You and your friend plan to spend 10 minutes mowing your family's lawn together. You can mow the entire lawn alone in 30 minutes.

a. Write an equation that gives the fraction y of the lawn that you and your friend can mow in 10 minutes as a function of the time t (in minutes) in which your friend can mow the entire lawn alone. $y = \frac{t + 30}{3t}$

b. Suppose your friend can mow the entire lawn alone in 20 minutes. Can the entire lawn be mowed if you and your friend work together for 10 minutes? *Explain.* No; to find the fraction of the lawn that you and your friend can mow in 10 minutes, find the value of y when $t = 20$ in the equation in part (a): $y = \frac{20 + 30}{3(20)} = \frac{50}{60} = \frac{5}{6}$. You and your friend can mow only $\frac{5}{6}$ of the lawn in 10 minutes.

TEST PRACTICE at classzone.com

ILLINOIS MIXED REVIEW

50. Simplify the algebraic expression $(x + 2)[(2x - 3) - (x - 1)]$. C

Ⓐ $x^2 - 4x - 4$ Ⓑ $x^2 - 2x - 8$ Ⓒ $x^2 - 4$ Ⓓ $2x^2 - 3x - 7$

51. Segment PR was transformed to create segment $P'R'$, as shown in the graph. What transformation was used?

Ⓐ Translation of 2 units to the right C

Ⓑ Translation of 6 units to the right

Ⓒ Reflection across the y-axis

Ⓓ Reflection across the x-axis

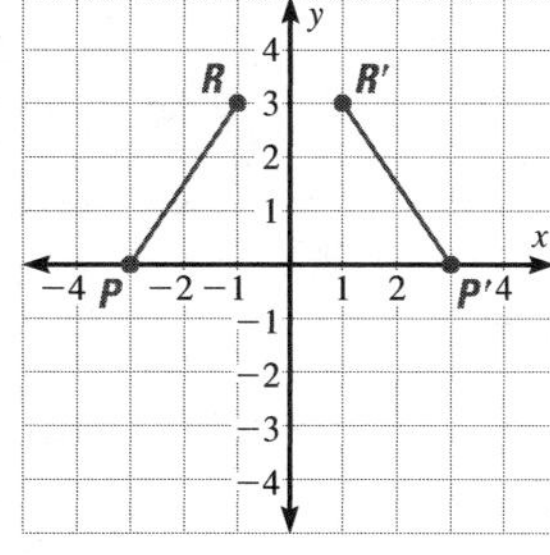

5 ASSESS AND RETEACH

Daily Homework Quiz

Transparency Available

Find the sum or difference.

1. $\frac{4}{2x} + \frac{x+1}{3}$ $\frac{x^2 + x + 6}{3x}$

2. $\frac{x-6}{x-1} - \frac{x-1}{3x}$ $\frac{2x^2 - 16x - 1}{(x-1)(3x)}$

3. $\frac{2x}{x^2 + 6x - 16} + \frac{x+3}{x^2 - 3x + 2}$ $\frac{3x^2 + 9x + 24}{(x+8)(x-2)(x-1)}$

4. You hike 4 miles up a hill and then 4 miles back down the hill. Your speed hiking up the hill is 1.5 miles per hour less than your speed hiking back down. Find the total time of your hike if you hiked 2.5 miles per hour up the hill. 2.6 h

Online Quiz

Available at **classzone.com**

Diagnosis/Remediation

- Practice A, B, C in Chapter 12 Resource Book, pp. 69–71
- Study Guide in Chapter 12 Resource Book, pp. 72–73
- Practice Workbook, pp. 192–193
- @HomeTutor

Challenge

Additional challenge is available in the Chapter 12 Resource Book, p. 76.

1 PLAN AND PREPARE

Warm-Up Exercises

Transparency Available

Solve the equation or proportion.

1. $3x + 7 = 22$ 5

2. $\frac{6}{m} = \frac{3}{7}$ 14

3. Daniel mixes 5 measures of Kenyan beans to every 7 measures of Jamaican beans to make a blend. If he uses 21 measures of Jamaican beans, how many measures of Kenyan beans should he use? 15 measures

Notetaking Guide

Transparency Available

Promotes interactive learning and notetaking skills, pp. 291–293.

Pacing

Basic: 1 day

Average: 1 day

Advanced: 1 day

Block: 0.5 block with 12.6

- See *Teaching Guide/Lesson Plan.*

2 FOCUS AND MOTIVATE

Essential Question

Big Idea 3, p. 763

How do you solve a rational equation? Tell students they will learn how to answer this question by using cross products and the LCD.

12.7 Solve Rational Equations

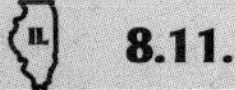

8.11.19 Solve problems that include nonlinear functions, including selecting and evaluating formulas . . .

Before You simplified rational expressions.

Now You will solve rational equations.

Why? So you can calculate a hockey statistic, as in Ex. 31.

Key Vocabulary
- **rational equation**
- **cross product,** *p. 168*
- **extraneous solution,** *p. 730*
- **least common denominator (LCD) of rational expressions,** *p. 813*

A **rational equation** is an equation that contains one or more rational expressions. One method for solving a rational equation is to use the cross products property. You can use this method when both sides of the equation are single rational expressions.

REVIEW CROSS PRODUCTS
For help with using the cross products property, see p. 168.

EXAMPLE 1 Use the cross products property

Solve $\frac{6}{x+4} = \frac{x}{2}$. Check your solution.

$\frac{6}{x+4} = \frac{x}{2}$	Write original equation.
$12 = x^2 + 4x$	Cross products property
$0 = x^2 + 4x - 12$	Subtract 12 from each side.
$0 = (x + 6)(x - 2)$	Factor polynomial.
$x + 6 = 0$ *or* $x - 2 = 0$	Zero-product property
$x = -6$ *or* $x = 2$	Solve for *x*.

▶ The solutions are −6 and 2.

CHECK **If $x = -6$:** $\frac{6}{-6+4} \stackrel{?}{=} \frac{-6}{2}$, $-3 = -3$ ✓ **If $x = 2$:** $\frac{6}{2+4} \stackrel{?}{=} \frac{2}{2}$, $1 = 1$ ✓

GUIDED PRACTICE for Example 1

Solve the equation. Check your solution.

1. $\frac{5}{y-2} = \frac{y}{3}$ −3, 5

2. $\frac{2}{z+5} = \frac{z}{7}$ −7, 2

USING THE LCD Given an equation with fractional coefficients such as $\frac{2}{3}x + \frac{1}{6} = \frac{3}{4}$, you can multiply each side by the least common denominator (LCD), 12. The equation becomes $8x + 2 = 9$, which you may find easier to solve than the original equation. You can use this method to solve a rational equation.

Resource Planning Guide

Chapter Resource Book
- Teaching Guide/Lesson Plan (pp. 77–78)
- Practice levels A, B, C (pp. 79–81)
- Study Guide (pp. 82–83)
- Catch-up for Absent Students (p. 84)
- Problem Solving Workshop (p. 85)
- Challenge (p. 86)

Workbooks
- Notetaking Guide (pp. 291–293)
- Practice Workbook (pp. 194–195)

Teaching Options
- **Power Presentations CD-ROM** provides dynamic electronic teaching resources for the classroom.
- **Activity Generator CD-ROM** provides editable activities for all ability levels.

Interactive Technology
- Easy Planner
- Power Presentations CD-ROM
- Activity Generator CD-ROM
- Animated Algebra
- Test Generator CD-ROM
- Online Quiz
- eWorkbook
- eEdition
- @HomeTutor

Resources for English Learners
- Quick Reference for English Learners
- Spanish Study Guide
- Multi-Language Visual Glossary
- Student Resources in Spanish

See also the *Algebra 1 Toolkit* for more strategies for meeting individual needs.

EXAMPLE 2 Multiply by the LCD

Solve $\frac{x}{x-2} + \frac{1}{5} = \frac{2}{x-2}$. Check your solution.

$\frac{x}{x-2} + \frac{1}{5} = \frac{2}{x-2}$ Write original equation.

$\frac{x}{x-2} \cdot 5(x-2) + \frac{1}{5} \cdot 5(x-2) = \frac{2}{x-2} \cdot 5(x-2)$ Multiply by LCD, $5(x-2)$.

$\frac{x \cdot 5\cancel{(x-2)}}{\cancel{x-2}} + \frac{\cancel{5}(x-2)}{\cancel{5}} = \frac{2 \cdot 5\cancel{(x-2)}}{\cancel{x-2}}$ Multiply and divide out common factors.

$5x + x - 2 = 10$ Simplify.

$6x - 2 = 10$ Combine like terms.

$6x = 12$ Add 2 to each side.

$x = 2$ Divide each side by 6.

AVOID ERRORS
Be sure to identify the excluded values for the rational expressions in the original equation.

The solution appears to be 2, but the expressions $\frac{x}{x-2}$ and $\frac{2}{x-2}$ are undefined when $x = 2$. So, 2 is an extraneous solution.

▶ There is no solution.

EXAMPLE 3 Factor to find the LCD

Solve $\frac{3}{x-7} + 1 = \frac{8}{x^2 - 9x + 14}$. Check your solution.

Solution

Write each denominator in factored form. The LCD is $(x-2)(x-7)$.

$$\frac{3}{x-7} + 1 = \frac{8}{(x-2)(x-7)}$$

$$\frac{3}{x-7} \cdot (x-2)(x-7) + 1 \cdot (x-2)(x-7) = \frac{8}{(x-2)(x-7)} \cdot (x-2)(x-7)$$

$$\frac{3(x-2)\cancel{(x-7)}}{\cancel{x-7}} + (x-2)(x-7) = \frac{8\cancel{(x-2)(x-7)}}{\cancel{(x-2)(x-7)}}$$

$$3(x-2) + (x^2 - 9x + 14) = 8$$

$$x^2 - 6x + 8 = 8$$

$$x^2 - 6x = 0$$

$$x(x-6) = 0$$

$$x = 0 \text{ or } x - 6 = 0$$

$$x = 0 \text{ or } \quad x = 6$$

▶ The solutions are 0 and 6.

CHECK **If $x = 0$:**

$\frac{3}{0-7} + 1 \stackrel{?}{=} \frac{8}{0^2 - 9 \cdot 0 + 14}$

$\frac{4}{7} = \frac{4}{7}$ ✓

If $x = 6$:

$\frac{3}{6-7} + 1 \stackrel{?}{=} \frac{8}{6^2 - 9 \cdot 6 + 14}$

$-2 = -2$ ✓

Motivating the Lesson

You and a friend work together during the summer to mow and trim lawns. You know that you can finish the work alone twice as fast as when your friend works alone. If you know the time it takes the two of you to complete a job together, you can write an equation to find the amount of time it would take you to do the job alone.

3 TEACH

Extra Example 1

Solve $\frac{8}{x+6} = \frac{x}{2}$. Check your solution. -8 and 2; both solutions check.

Key Question to Ask for Example 1

- When is it appropriate to use cross products to solve a rational equation? Use cross products if both sides of the equation are single rational expressions.

Extra Example 2

Solve $\frac{2x}{x+3} + \frac{1}{3} = \frac{-6}{x+3}$. Check your solution. There is no solution. The solution appears to be -3, but the expressions $\frac{2x}{x+3}$ and $\frac{-6}{x+3}$ are undefined when $x = -3$.

Extra Example 3

Solve $\frac{4}{x-1} + 1 = \frac{-10}{x^2 - 9x + 8}$. Check your solution. -2 and 7; both solutions check.

Differentiated Instruction

Visual Learners Teach students to use the factored form as a way to visualize the solution. In **Example 3**, first visualize $x^2 - 9x + 14$ in the factored form $(x-2)(x-7)$. Next visualize $\frac{3}{x-7}$ as $\frac{3}{x-7} \cdot 1$, or $\frac{3}{x-7} \cdot \frac{x-2}{x-2}$. Finally, the constant 1 is the fraction $\frac{(x-2)(x-7)}{(x-2)(x-7)}$. Now that all of the fractions have the same denominator, the numerators can be used to write the equation $3(x-2) + (x-2)(x-7) = 8$ which can be solved for x.

See also the *Algebra 1 Toolkit* for more strategies.

Extra Example 4

You are mixing a bug repellent solution for your plants. Your mixture contains 12 units of jojoba oil and water in equal parts. You want to make a solution that is 70% jojoba oil. How many units of jojoba oil do you need to add to the solution? 8 units

Key Questions to Ask for Example 4

- Why do you write the verbal model with the number of pints of yellow paint in the mixture as the numerator of the expression and the number of total pints in the paint mixture as the denominator of the expression? You need to compare the amount of yellow paint in the mixture to the total amount of paint in the mixture since you want the total mixture to be 80% yellow.

Closing the Lesson

Have students summarize the major points of the lesson and answer the Essential Question: How do you solve a rational equation?

- Use cross products and the LCD to solve rational equations.
- Check for excluded values.

If both sides of an equation are single rational expressions, use cross products and then solve for the variable. If an equation has fractional coefficients, multiply each term on each side of the equation by the LCD. Then solve the resulting equation for the variable. If the result is an excluded value, it is extraneous and not a solution.

EXAMPLE 4 Solve a multi-step problem

PAINT MIXING You have an 8 pint mixture of paint that is made up of equal amounts of yellow paint and blue paint. To create a certain shade of green, you need a paint mixture that is 80% yellow. How many pints of yellow paint do you need to add to the mixture?

ANOTHER WAY
For an alternative method for solving the problem in Example 4, turn to page 827 for the **Problem Solving Workshop**.

Solution

Because the amount of yellow paint equals the amount of blue paint, the mixture has 4 pints of yellow paint. Let p represent the number of pints of yellow paint that you need to add.

STEP 1 **Write** a verbal model. Then write an equation.

$$\frac{\text{Pints of yellow paint in mixture} + \text{Pints of yellow paint needed}}{\text{Pints of paint in mixture} + \text{Pints of yellow paint needed}} = \text{Desired percent yellow in mixture}$$

$$\frac{4+p}{8+p} = 0.8$$

STEP 2 **Solve** the equation.

$\frac{4+p}{8+p} = 0.8$	**Write equation.**
$4 + p = 0.8(8 + p)$	**Cross products property**
$4 + p = 6.4 + 0.8p$	**Distributive property**
$0.2p = 2.4$	**Rewrite equation.**
$p = 12$	**Solve for p.**

▶ You need to add 12 pints of yellow paint.

CHECK	$\frac{4+p}{8+p} = 0.8$	**Write original equation.**
	$\frac{4+12}{8+12} \stackrel{?}{=} 0.8$	**Substitute 12 for p.**
	$\frac{16}{20} \stackrel{?}{=} 0.8$	**Simplify numerator and denominator.**
	$0.8 = 0.8$ ✓	**Write fraction as decimal. Solution checks.**

GUIDED PRACTICE for Examples 2, 3, and 4

Solve the equation. Check your solution.

3. $\frac{a}{a+4} + \frac{1}{3} = \frac{-12}{a+4}$ -10

4. $\frac{n}{n-11} - 1 = \frac{22}{n^2 - 5n - 66}$ -4

5. WHAT IF? In Example 4, suppose you need a paint mixture that is 75% yellow. How many pints of yellow paint do you need to add to the mixture? 8 pints

12.7 EXERCISES

HOMEWORK KEY

○ = **WORKED-OUT SOLUTIONS** on p. WS31 for Exs. 7, 15, and 33

★ = **STANDARDIZED TEST PRACTICE** Exs. 2, 24, 28, and 35

SKILL PRACTICE

A

1. **VOCABULARY** The equation $\frac{3}{x-1} = \frac{7}{x} + 4$ is an example of a(n) __?__. rational equation

2. ★ **WRITING** *Describe* two methods for solving a rational equation. Which method can you use to solve any kind of rational equation? *Explain.* See margin.

EXAMPLE 1 on p. 820 for Exs. 3–13, 24

SOLVING EQUATIONS Solve the equation. Check your solution.

3. $\frac{5}{r} = \frac{r}{20}$ ±10

4. $\frac{3}{s-13} = \frac{s}{10}$ −2, 15

5. $\frac{2}{t} = \frac{10}{t-6}$ $-1\frac{1}{2}$

6. $\frac{2}{c+3} = \frac{-5}{c-1}$ $-1\frac{6}{7}$

7. $\frac{2m}{m+4} = \frac{3}{m-1}$ $-1\frac{1}{2}$, 4

8. $\frac{n-3}{n-6} = \frac{n+1}{n+5}$ $1\frac{2}{7}$

9. $\frac{w}{2} = \frac{15}{w+1}$ −6, 5

10. $\frac{2x}{4-x} = \frac{x}{x-4}$ 0

11. $\frac{2y}{y-3} = \frac{24}{y}$ 6

ERROR ANALYSIS *Describe* and correct the error in solving the equation. 12, 13. See margin.

12. $\frac{x+1}{2x+2} = \frac{3}{2x}$

$\frac{x+1}{2x+2} = \frac{3}{2x}$

$(x+1)2x = 3(2x+2)$

$2x^2 + 2x = 6x + 6$

$2x^2 - 4x - 6 = 0$

$2(x-3)(x+1) = 0$

$x - 3 = 0$ or $x + 1 = 0$

$x = 3$ or $x = -1$

The solutions are 3 and −1.

13. $\frac{4x+1}{8x-1} = \frac{3}{5}$

$\frac{4x+1}{8x-1} = \frac{3}{5}$

$5(4x+1) = 3(8x-1)$

$20x + 1 = 24x - 3$

$1 = 4x - 3$

$4 = 4x$

$1 = x$

The solution is 1.

EXAMPLES 2 and 3 on p. 821 for Exs. 14–23

SOLVING EQUATIONS Solve the equation. Check your solution.

14. $\frac{6x}{x-11} + 1 = \frac{3}{x-11}$ 2

15. $\frac{z}{z+7} - 3 = \frac{-1}{z+7}$ −10

16. $\frac{a+7}{a+4} - 1 = \frac{a+10}{2a+8}$ no solution

17. $\frac{1}{b+3} + 2 = \frac{b^2-3}{b^2+12b+27}$ −22

18. $\frac{m}{m-2} - \frac{3m}{m-4} = \frac{-2m+2}{m^2-6m+8}$ 1

19. $\frac{3n}{n+1} = \frac{12}{n^2-1} + \frac{n+4}{n-1}$ $2 \pm 2\sqrt{3}$

20. $\frac{3}{p-1} - \frac{2}{p-1} = \frac{-6}{p^2-3p+2}$ −4

21. $\frac{5}{q+4} = \frac{q}{q-3} + \frac{2q-27}{q^2+q-12}$ no solution

22. $\frac{r+2}{r^2+6r-7} = \frac{8}{r^2+3r-4}$ −6, 8

23. $\frac{9}{s^2-4} = \frac{4-5s}{s-2}$ $-\frac{1}{5}$, −1

24. ★ **OPEN-ENDED** Write a rational equation that can be solved using the cross products property. Then solve the equation. *Sample answer:* $\frac{x}{x+1} = \frac{2}{x+3}$; −2, 1

4 PRACTICE AND APPLY

Assignment Guide

Answer Transparencies available for all exercises

Basic:
Day 1: EP p. 946 Exs. 43–48
pp. 823–826
Exs. 1–8, 12–19, 24–26, 31–35, 39–53 odd

Average:
Day 1: pp. 823–826
Exs. 1, 2, 7–13, 19–29, 31–37, 40–52 even

Advanced:
Day 1: pp. 823–826
Exs. 1, 2, 8–11, 20–38*, 40–52 even

Block:
pp. 823–826
Exs. 1, 2, 7–13, 19–29, 31–37, 40–52 even (with 12.6)

Differentiated Instruction

See *Algebra 1 Best Practices Toolkit* for suggestions on addressing the needs of a diverse classroom.

Homework Check

For a quick check of student understanding of key concepts, go over the following exercises:

Basic: 6, 14, 18, 31, 32
Average: 8, 20, 22, 32, 33
Advanced: 10, 21, 23, 33, 34

Extra Practice

- Student Edition, p. 946
- Chapter 12 Resource Book: Practice levels A, B, C, pp. 79–81

Practice Worksheet

An easily-readable reduced practice page (with answers) for this lesson can be found on p. 762C.

2. Method 1: Use the cross products property, Method 2: Multiply each side of the equation by the LCD of all the rational expressions in the equation. Method 2 can be used for any rational equation, but Method 1 can be used only for rational equations for which both sides are single rational expressions.

12. The solutions must be checked in the original equation. The solution $x = -1$ is extraneous because it is an excluded value for the original equation. The correct solution is 3.

13. The distributive property must be used to find the product of 5 and $(4x + 1)$; $5(4x + 1) = 3(8x - 1)$, $20x + 5 = 24x - 3$, $8 = 4x$, $2 = x$. The solution is 2.

B **25. REASONING** Consider the equation $\frac{2}{x-a} = \frac{x}{x-a}$ where a is a real number. For what value(s) of a does the equation have exactly one solution? no solution? *Explain* your answers. **See margin.**

26. USING ANOTHER METHOD Another way to solve a rational equation is to write each side of the equation as a single rational expression and then use the cross products property. Use this method to solve the equation $\frac{x}{x+1} + \frac{x-2}{2} = \frac{2x-1}{4}$. **3**

27. SOLVING SYSTEMS OF EQUATIONS Consider the following system:

$$y = 3x + 1$$

$$y = \frac{-5}{x-3} - 6$$

a. Solve the system algebraically. $\left(\frac{8}{3}, 9\right), (-2, -5)$

b. Check your solution by graphing the equations. **See margin.**

28. ★ MULTIPLE CHOICE Let a be a real number. How many solutions does the equation $\frac{2}{x-a} = \frac{1}{x+a} + \frac{2a}{x^2-a^2}$ have? **A**

Ⓐ Zero Ⓑ One Ⓒ Two Ⓓ Infinitely many

29. REASONING Is the expression $\frac{x+a}{x+1+a}$ ever equivalent to $\frac{x}{x+1}$ for some nonzero value of a? *Justify* your answer algebraically. **See margin.**

C **30. CHALLENGE** Let a and b be real numbers. The solutions of the equation $ax + b = \frac{30}{x+2} - 1$ are -8 and 8. What are the values of a and b? *Explain* your answer.

$a = \frac{1}{2}$, $b = -2$. *Sample answer:* Replacing x in the equation with -8 and then again with 8 gives two equations in two variables, a and b. Solving this system of two equations yields $a = \frac{1}{2}$ and $b = -2$.

PROBLEM SOLVING

EXAMPLE 4 on p. 822 for Exs. 31–34

A **31. ICE HOCKEY** In ice hockey, a goalie's save percentage (in decimal form) is the number of shots blocked by a goalie divided by the number of shots made by an opposing team. Suppose a goalie has blocked 160 out of 200 shots. How many consecutive shots does the goalie need to block in order to raise the save percentage to 0.840? **50 consecutive shots**

@HomeTutor for problem solving help at classzone.com

32. RUNNING TIMES You are running a 6000 meter charity race. Your average speed in the first half of the race is 50 meters per minute faster than your average speed in the second half. You finish the race in 27 minutes. What is your average speed in the second half of the race? **200 m/min**

@HomeTutor for problem solving help at classzone.com

○ = WORKED-OUT SOLUTIONS on p. WS1   ★ = STANDARDIZED TEST PRACTICE

Avoiding Common Errors

Exercises 3–11 Some students may multiply the numerators and multiply the denominators of the two expressions rather than find the cross products. Discuss with students when they multiply pairs of numerators and pairs of denominators and when they find cross products.

Exercises 14–21 Remind students that they must multiply the LCD by each term on both sides of an equation.

Teaching Strategy

Exercise 26 To get students started on this exercise, ask them how they can write the left side of the equation as a single rational expression.

25. All real numbers except 2; 2; two fractions with equal denominators must also have equal numerators, so $x = 2$, and the denominator of both fractions is $2 - a$. The equation has this one solution as long as the denominator $2 - a$ is not 0; so, the equation has no solution when $a = 2$.

27b.

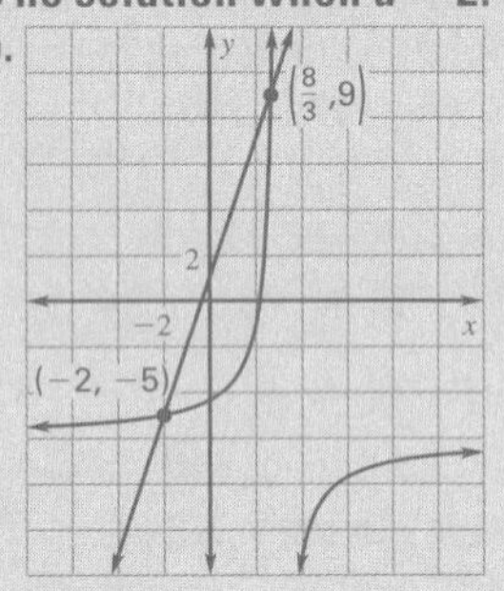

29. No; suppose that $\frac{x+a}{x+1+a} = \frac{x}{x+1}$. Then, using the cross products property, $(x+1)(x+a) = x(x+1+a)$; $x^2 + xa + x + a = x^2 + x + xa$; $x^2 + x(a+1) + a = x^2 + x(1+a)$. Then, subtracting $x^2 + x(1+a)$ from both sides gives the result $a = 0$; so, the only value of a for which the equation is true is 0.

33. **CLEANING SOLUTIONS** You have a cleaning solution that consists of 2 cups of vinegar and 7 cups of water. You need a cleaning solution that consists of 5 parts water and 1 part vinegar in order to clean windows. How many cups of water do you need to add to your cleaning solution so that you can use it to clean windows? **3 c**

34. **MULTI-STEP PROBLEM** Working together, a painter and an assistant can paint a certain room in 2 hours. The painter can paint the room alone in half the time it takes the assistant to paint the room alone. Let t represent the time (in hours) that the painter can paint the room alone.

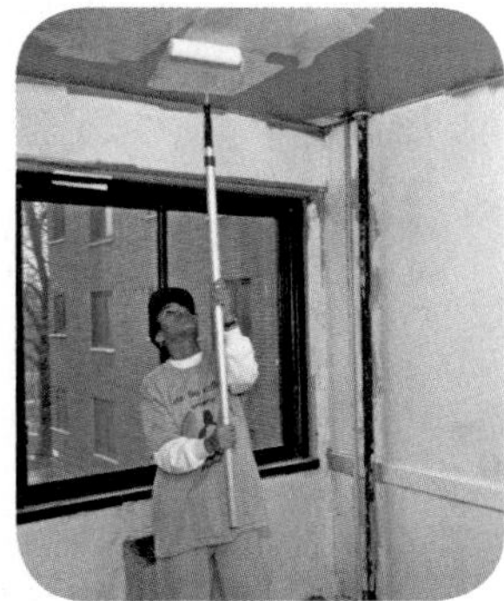

a. Copy and complete the table.

Person	Fraction of room painted each hour	Time (hours)	Fraction of room painted
Painter	$\frac{1}{t}$	2	? $\frac{2}{3}$
Assistant	? $\frac{1}{2t}$	2	? $\frac{1}{3}$

b. *Explain* why the sum of the expressions in the fourth column of the table must be 1. **See margin.**

c. Write a rational equation that you can use to find the time that the painter takes to paint the room alone. Then solve the equation. $\frac{2}{t} + \frac{1}{t} = 1$; **3 h**

d. How long does the assistant take to paint the room alone? **6 h**

B 35. ★ **EXTENDED RESPONSE** You and your sister can rake a neighbor's front lawn together in 30 minutes. Your sister takes 1.5 times as long as you to rake the lawn by herself.

a. **Solve** Write an equation that you can use to find the time t (in minutes) you take to rake the lawn by yourself. Then solve the equation. $\frac{30}{t} + \frac{30}{1.5t} = 1$; **50 min**

b. **Compare** With more experience, both of you can now rake the lawn together in 20 minutes, and your sister can rake the lawn alone in the same amount of time as you. Tell how you would change the equation in part (a) in order to describe this situation. Then solve the equation. **Change each 30 to 20, and change 1.5 to 1; 40 min.**

c. **Explain** *Explain* why your solution of the equation in part (b) makes sense. Then justify your explanation algebraically for any given amount of time that both of you rake the lawn together. **See margin.**

36. **TELEVISION** The average time t (in minutes) that a person in the United States watched television per day during the period 1950–2000 can be modeled by

$$t = \frac{265 + 8.85x}{1 + 0.0114x}$$

where x is the number of years since 1950.

a. Approximate the year in which a person watched television for an average of 6 hours per day. **1970**

b. About how many years had passed when the average time a person spent watching television per day increased from 5 hours to 7 hours? **about 32 yr**

Study Strategy

Exercise 33 Some students may prefer one of the alternative methods, shown on pages 827–828, for solving this problem. Suggest that students make themselves familiar with the three methods (Example 4 on page 822 and the two alternative methods), and identify which method they prefer.

34b. The expressions in the fourth column represent the fractions of the room painted by each person in 2 hours. Because the painter and assistant can paint the whole room in 2 hours, the sum of the fractions must be 1 (one whole room).

35c. Because you now both rake at the same rate, whenever you work together, the time it takes to rake a portion of the lawn will be half the time it takes either of you to rake that portion alone. Suppose you rake together for m minutes. Then you each rake $\frac{m}{40}$ of the lawn, and together you rake $\frac{m}{40} + \frac{m}{40} = \frac{2m}{40} = \frac{m}{20}$ of the lawn. To rake $\frac{m}{20}$ of the lawn alone would take you $2m$ minutes.

5 ASSESS AND RETEACH

Daily Homework Quiz

Transparency Available

Solve the equation.

1. $\frac{7}{x-4} = \frac{x}{3}$ **−3 and 7**
2. $\frac{x+9}{x+6} - 2 = \frac{x+12}{2x+12}$ **no solution**
3. $\frac{3}{x-2} + 1 = \frac{8}{x^2+x-6}$ **−5 and 1**
4. You have a 6-ounce spice blend that is made up of equal parts of basil and oregano. A recipe calls for a blend that is 60% basil. How many ounces of basil do you need to add to the blend? **1.5 oz**

Available at **classzone.com**

Diagnosis/Remediation

- Practice A, B, C in Chapter 12 Resource Book, pp. 79–81
- Study Guide in Chapter 12 Resource Book, pp. 82–83
- Practice Workbook, pp. 194–195
- @HomeTutor

Challenge

Additional challenge is available in the Chapter 12 Resource Book, p. 86.

Quiz

An easily-readable reduced copy of the quiz (with answers) on Lessons 12.5–12.7 from the Assessment Book can be found on p. 762F.

37. From 8 psi to 7 psi; substitute the given psi values for p in the given equation and then solve for a: for $p = 10$, $a \approx 10{,}722$; for $p = 9$, $a \approx 13{,}536$; for $p = 8$, $a \approx 16{,}600$; for $p = 7$, $a \approx 19{,}948$. The change in altitude when the atmospheric pressure changes from 10 psi to 9 psi is about $13{,}536 - 10{,}722 = 2814$, and the change in altitude when the atmospheric pressure changes from 8 psi to 7 psi is about $19{,}948 - 16{,}600 = 3348$.

37. **SCIENCE** Atmospheric pressure, measured in pounds per square inch (psi), is the pressure exerted on an object by the weight of the atmosphere above the object. The atmospheric pressure p (in psi) can be modeled by

$$p = \frac{14.55(56{,}267 - a)}{55{,}545 + a}$$

where a is the altitude (in feet). Is the change in altitude greater when the atmospheric pressure changes from 10 psi to 9 psi or from 8 psi to 7 psi? *Explain* your answer. **See margin.**

C 38. **CHALLENGE** Butterfat makes up about 1% of the volume of milk in 1% milk. Butterfat can make up no more than 0.2% of the volume of milk in skim milk. A container holds 15 fluid ounces of 1% milk. How many fluid ounces of butterfat must be removed in order for the milk to be considered skim milk? Round your answer to the nearest hundredth. **0.12 fl oz**

ILLINOIS MIXED REVIEW

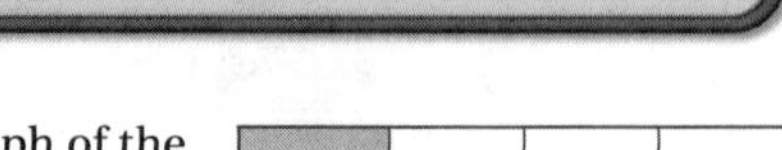

39. The table shows three points that lie on the graph of the linear function $f(x)$. What is the slope of the graph of $f(x)$?

x	2	4	7
$f(x)$	9	12	16.5

Ⓐ $\frac{3}{2}$ Ⓑ 2 Ⓒ 3 Ⓓ $\frac{9}{2}$ **A**

40. Given the set of data {32, 27, 22, 32, 27, 22, 32, 32, 62}, which statement best interprets the data?

Ⓐ Of the mean, median, and mode, only the mean is 32.

Ⓑ The range of the set of data is 32.

Ⓒ The mean, median, and mode are all 32.

Ⓓ The mode and median are not the same.

C

QUIZ *for Lessons 12.5–12.7*

Find the product or quotient. *(p. 802)*

1. $\frac{5}{8x^2} \cdot \frac{4x^3}{15}$ **$\frac{x}{6}$**
2. $\frac{3y^2+6y}{y^2-16} \div \frac{y^2}{y-4}$ **$\frac{3(y+2)}{y(y+4)}$**

Find the sum or difference. *(p. 812)*

3. $\frac{8a}{a+11} - \frac{5a-1}{a+11}$ **$\frac{3a+1}{a+11}$**
4. $\frac{6n}{n+3} + \frac{n-1}{n^2+5n+6}$ **$\frac{6n^2+13n-1}{(n+3)(n+2)}$**

Solve the equation. Check your solution. *(p. 820)*

5. $\frac{2z}{z+5} = \frac{z}{z-3}$ **0, 11**
6. $\frac{2x}{x} + \frac{3-x}{x+1} = \frac{-4}{x^2+x}$ **−4**
7. **BATTING AVERAGES** A softball player's batting average is the number of hits divided by the number of times at bat. A softball player has a batting average of .200 after 90 times at bat. How many consecutive hits does the player need in order to raise the batting average to .250? *(p. 820)* **6 hits**

EXTRA PRACTICE for Lesson 12.7, p. 949

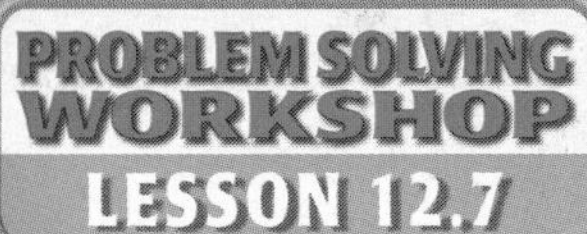

Using ALTERNATIVE METHODS

Another Way to Solve Example 4, page 822

MULTIPLE REPRESENTATIONS In Example 4 on page 822, you saw how to solve a problem about mixing paint by using a rational equation. You can also solve the problem by using a table or by reinterpreting the problem.

PROBLEM

PAINT MIXING You have an 8 pint mixture of paint that is made up of equal amounts of yellow paint and blue paint. To create a certain shade of green, you need a paint mixture that is 80% yellow. How many pints of yellow paint do you need to add to the mixture?

METHOD 1

Use a Table One alternative approach is to use a table.

The mixture has 8 pints of paint. Because the mixture has an equal amount of yellow paint and blue paint, the mixture has $8 \div 2 = 4$ pints of yellow paint.

STEP 1 **Make** a table that shows the percent of the mixture that is yellow paint after you add various amounts of yellow paint.

Yellow paint (pints)	Paint in mixture (pints)	Percent of mixture that is yellow paint
4	8	$\frac{4}{8} = 50\%$
6	10	$\frac{6}{10} = 60\%$
8	12	$\frac{8}{12} \approx 67\%$
10	14	$\frac{10}{14} \approx 71\%$
12	16	$\frac{12}{16} = 75\%$
14	18	$\frac{14}{18} \approx 78\%$
15	19	$\frac{15}{19} \approx 79\%$
16	20	$\frac{16}{20} = 80\%$

A mixture with 6 pints of yellow paint is the result of adding 2 pints of yellow paint to the mixture.

This amount of yellow paint gives you the percent yellow you want.

STEP 2 **Find** the number of pints of yellow paint needed. Subtract the number of pints of yellow paint already in the mixture from the total number of pints of yellow paint you have: $16 - 4 = 12$.

▶ You need to add 12 pints of yellow paint.

Alternative Strategy

Example 4 on page 822 can be solved by using a table or by reinterpreting the problem. When using a table, students should be careful to organize the table to include all existing data and to show all of the data they need to solve the problem. Reinterpreting the problem as a ratio allows students to write an equation whose solution has fewer steps than solving a rational equation.

Avoiding Common Errors

In Method 1, some students may forget to perform Step 2 after they have found the percent of the mixture that is yellow paint. Remind students that the original mixture already contains some yellow paint, and that they need to subtract this amount from the total amount needed.

Avoiding Common Errors

In Step 1, some students may think that $\frac{4}{5}$ to $\frac{1}{5}$ means the ratio is 4:5. It may help these students to ask how many pints of yellow paint would be in a mixture that contains 5 pints of yellow and blue paint, given the ratio of 4 pints of yellow paint to 1 pint of blue paint.

1. See Additional Answers beginning on p. AA1.
2. Because Jill already has $1000 in the mutual fund she only needs to add $2250 − $1000 = $1250 to the account.
3, 5. See Additional Answers beginning on p. AA1.

METHOD 2 **Reinterpret Problem** Another alternative approach is to reinterpret the problem.

STEP 1 **Reinterpret** the problem. A mixture with 80% yellow paint means that $\frac{4}{5}$ of the mixture is yellow and $\frac{1}{5}$ of the mixture is blue. So, the ratio of yellow paint to blue paint needs to be 4 : 1. You need 4 times as many pints of yellow paint as pints of blue paint.

STEP 2 **Write** a verbal model. Then write an equation. Let p represent the number of pints of yellow paint that you need to add.

Pints of yellow paint already in mixture	+	Pints of yellow paint you need to add	= 4 •	Pints of blue paint in mixture
↓		↓		↓
4	+	p	= 4 •	4

STEP 3 **Solve** the equation.

$4 + p = 4 \cdot 4$ Write equation.

$4 + p = 16$ Multiply.

$p = 12$ Subtract 4 from each side.

▶ You need to add 12 pints of yellow paint to the mixture.

PRACTICE

1. **INVESTING** Jill has $10,000 in various investments, including $1000 in a mutual fund. Jill wants the amount in the mutual fund to make up 20% of the amount in all of her investments. How much money should she add to the mutual fund? Solve this problem using two different methods. See margin.

2. **ERROR ANALYSIS** *Describe* and correct the error in solving Exercise 1. See margin.

Amount in mutual fund	Amount in all investments	Percent in mutual fund
1000	10,000	10%
1400	10,400	About 13%
1800	10,800	About 17%
2250	11,250	20%

Jill needs to add $2250 to her mutual fund. ✗

3. **BASKETBALL** A basketball player has made 40% of 30 free throw attempts so far. How many consecutive free throws must the player make in order to increase the percent of free throw attempts made to 50%? Solve this problem using two different methods. See margin.

4. **WHAT IF?** In Exercise 3, suppose the basketball player instead wants to increase the percent of free throw attempts made to 60%. How many consecutive free throws must the player make? 15 free throws

5. **SNOW SHOVELING** You and your friend are shoveling snow out of a driveway. You can shovel the snow alone in 50 minutes. Both of you can shovel the snow in 30 minutes when working together. How many minutes will your friend take to shovel the snow alone? Solve this problem using two different methods. See margin.

Illinois Mixed Review

Lessons 12.5–12.7

1. **REVENUE** For the period 1991–2002, the average total revenue T (in dollars per admission) that a U.S. movie theater earned and the average revenue C (in dollars per admission) that a U.S. movie theater earned from concessions can be modeled by

$$T = \frac{0.018x^2 + 5.4}{1 - 0.0011x^2} \quad \text{and} \quad C = \frac{0.013x^2 + 1.1}{0.0011x^2 + 1}$$

where x is the number of years since 1991. Which equation gives the percent p (in decimal form) of the average total revenue per admission that came from concessions as a function of x?

A. $p = \frac{(1 - 0.0011x^2)(0.013x^2 + 1.1)}{(0.018x^2 + 5.4)(0.0011x^2 + 1)}$

B. $p = \frac{(0.018x^2 + 5.4)(0.0011x^2 + 1)}{(1 - 0.0011x^2)(0.013x^2 + 1.1)}$

C. $p = \frac{(0.018x^2 + 5.4)(0.013x^2 + 1.1)}{(1 - 0.0011x^2)(0.0011x^2 + 1)}$

D. $p = \frac{(1 - 0.0011x^2)(0.0011x^2 + 1)}{(0.018x^2 + 5.4)(0.013x^2 + 1.1)}$

2. **ROWERS** A rower travels 5 miles upstream (against the current) and 5 miles downstream (with the current). The speed of the current is 1 mile per hour. Which equation gives the total travel time t (in hours) as a function of the rower's average speed r (in miles per hour) in still water?

F. $t = \frac{10r}{r^2 - 1}$

G. $t = \frac{2r}{5}$

H. $t = \frac{25}{r^2 - 1}$

J. $t = \frac{10}{r}$

3. **COLLEGE DEGREES** The number D (in thousands) of all college degrees earned and the number M (in thousands) of master's degrees earned in the United States during the period 1984–2001 can be modeled by

$$D = \frac{17x^2 + 1800}{1 + 0.0062x^2} \quad \text{and} \quad M = \frac{2.5x^2 + 280}{1 + 0.0040x^2}$$

where x is the number of years since 1984. Which equation gives the number C of college degrees that were *not* master's degrees as a function of x?

A. $C = \frac{17x^2 + 1800 + 2.5x^2 + 280}{(1 + 0.0062x^2)(1 + 0.0040x^2)}$

B. $C = \frac{17x^2 + 1800}{1 + 0.0062x^2} - \frac{2.5x^2 + 280}{1 + 0.0040x^2}$

C. $C = \frac{17x^2 + 1800}{1 + 0.0062x^2} + \frac{2.5x^2 + 280}{1 + 0.0040x^2}$

D. $C = \frac{(17x^2 + 1800)(2.5x^2 + 280)}{(1 + 0.0062x^2)(1 + 0.0040x^2)}$

4. **WEIGHT CAPACITY** The diagram below shows the distance between the first axle and the last axle for a group of consecutive axles on a truck.

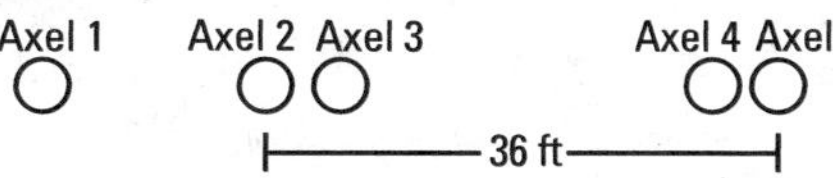

The maximum weight W (to the nearest 500 pounds) that a truck on a highway can carry on a group of consecutive axles is given by the formula

$$W = 500\left(\frac{d}{n - 1} + 12n + 36\right)$$

where d is the distance between the first axle and the last axle of the group and n is the number of axles in the group. How many thousands of pounds can the truck carry on axles 2–5?

F. 45 **H.** 45,000

G. 48 **J.** 48,000

Illinois Mixed Review

1. A
2. F
3. B
4. G

12 CHAPTER SUMMARY

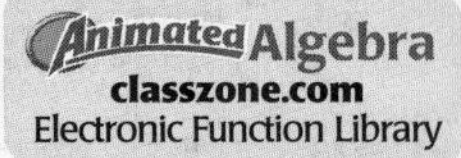

Additional Resources

The following resources are available to help review the materials in this chapter.

Chapter 12 Resource Book

- Chapter Review Games and Activities, p. 87
- Cumulative Practice, Chs. 1–12, pp. 90–91

Student Resources in Spanish

eWorkbook

@HomeTutor

Vocabulary Practice

Vocabulary practice is available at **classzone.com**

BIG IDEAS — For Your Notebook

Big Idea 1

Graphing Rational Functions

The graphs of $y = \frac{a}{x}$ $(a \neq 0)$ and $y = \frac{a}{x - h} + k$ $(a \neq 0)$ are hyperbolas that have two symmetrical branches. The characteristics of the functions and their graphs are given below. To graph a rational function whose numerator and denominator are first-degree polynomials, you can first use long division to rewrite the function so that it has the form $y = \frac{a}{x - h} + k$.

Function	Vertical asymptote	Horizontal asymptote	Domain	Range
$y = \frac{a}{x}$	$x = 0$	$y = 0$	All real numbers except $x = 0$	All real numbers except $y = 0$
$y = \frac{a}{x - h} + k$	$x = h$	$y = k$	All real numbers except $x = h$	All real numbers except $y = k$

Big Idea 2

Performing Operations on Rational Expressions

Performing operations on rational expressions is similar to performing operations on numerical fractions. Any common factors in the numerator and denominator should be divided out, and the original expression should be used when finding excluded values.

Operation	Rule
Multiplication	$\frac{a}{b} \cdot \frac{c}{d} = \frac{ac}{bd}$ where $b \neq 0$ and $d \neq 0$
Division	$\frac{a}{b} \div \frac{c}{d} = \frac{a}{b} \cdot \frac{d}{c}$ where $b \neq 0$, $c \neq 0$, and $d \neq 0$
Addition	Same denominator: $\frac{a}{c} + \frac{b}{c} = \frac{a + b}{c}$ where $c \neq 0$ Different denominators: Use LCD of rational expressions.
Subtraction	Same denominator: $\frac{a}{c} - \frac{b}{c} = \frac{a - b}{c}$ where $c \neq 0$ Different denominators: Use LCD of rational expressions.

Big Idea 3

Solving Rational Equations

You can use the following steps to solve a rational equation.

1. Rewrite the rational equation by using the cross products property or by multiplying each side by the least common denominator (LCD) of the rational expressions in the equation.
2. Solve the rewritten equation.
3. Check for extraneous solutions.

12 CHAPTER REVIEW

@HomeTutor
classzone.com
• Multi-Language Glossary
• Vocabulary practice

REVIEW KEY VOCABULARY

- inverse variation, *p. 765*
- constant of variation, *p. 765*
- hyperbola, branches of a hyperbola, asymptotes of a hyperbola, *p. 767*
- rational function, *p. 775*
- rational expression, *p. 794*
- excluded value, *p. 794*
- simplest form of a rational expression, *p. 795*
- least common denominator (LCD) of rational expressions, *p. 813*
- rational equation, *p. 820*

VOCABULARY EXERCISES

1. Copy and complete: A(n) _?_ of a hyperbola is a line that the hyperbola approaches but doesn't intersect. asymptote
2. **WRITING** *Explain* how you can use an LCD to solve a rational equation. See margin.
3. Identify the vertical asymptote and horizontal asymptote of the graph of $y = \frac{-5}{x+2} - 4$. $x = -2, y = -4$

REVIEW EXAMPLES AND EXERCISES

Use the review examples and exercises below to check your understanding of the concepts you have learned in each lesson of Chapter 12.

12.1 Model Inverse Variation pp. 765–772

EXAMPLE

The variables x and y vary inversely, and $y = 14$ when $x = 4$. Write the inverse variation equation that relates x and y. Then find the value of y when $x = 7$.

$y = \frac{a}{x}$ — **Write inverse variation equation.**

$14 = \frac{a}{4}$ — **Substitute 4 for x and 14 for y.**

$56 = a$ — **Simplify.**

▶ The inverse variation equation is $y = \frac{56}{x}$. When $x = 7$, $y = \frac{56}{7} = 8$.

EXERCISES

EXAMPLES 4 and 5 on pp. 767–768 for Exs. 4–7

Given that y varies inversely with x, use the specified values to write an inverse variation equation that relates x and y. Then find y when $x = 5$.

4. $x = 9, y = 2$ $y = \frac{18}{x}$, 3.6
5. $x = 3, y = 21$ $y = \frac{63}{x}$, 12.6
6. $x = -6, y = 6$ $y = \frac{-36}{x}$, −7.2
7. Tell whether the ordered pairs (−10, 0.8), (−4, 2), (5, −1.6), and (16, −0.5) represent inverse variation. If so, write the inverse variation equation. See margin.

Extra Example 12.1

The variables x and y vary inversely, and $y = 8$ when $x = 3$. Write the inverse variation equation that relates x and y. Then find the value of y when $x = 12$. $y = \frac{24}{x}$; 2

2. Multiply each side of the equation by the least common denominator of all the rational expressions in the equation. This will make all the denominators in the equation equal to 1 and allow you to identify the equation as linear or quadratic in form.

7. inverse variation; $y = \frac{-8}{x}$

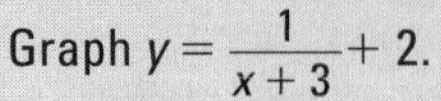

CHAPTER REVIEW

Extra Example 12.2

Graph $y = \frac{1}{x+3} + 2$.

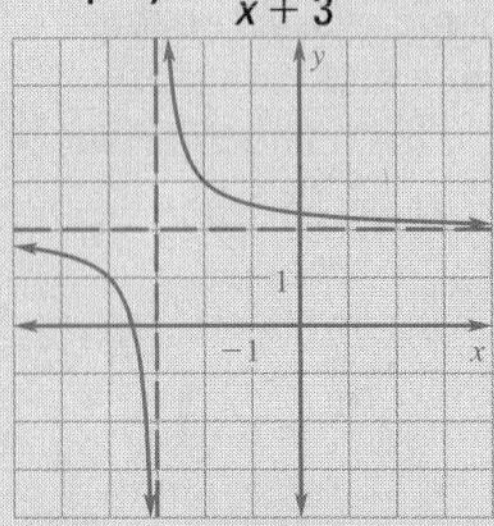

Extra Example 12.3

Divide $x^2 + 4x + 8$ by $x + 2$.

$x + 2 + \frac{4}{x+2}$

8.

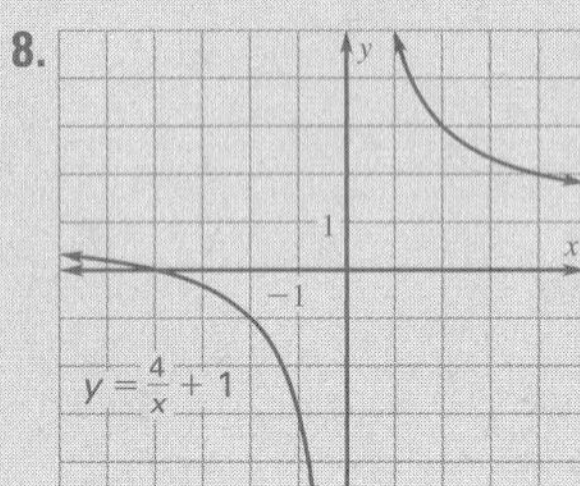

9.

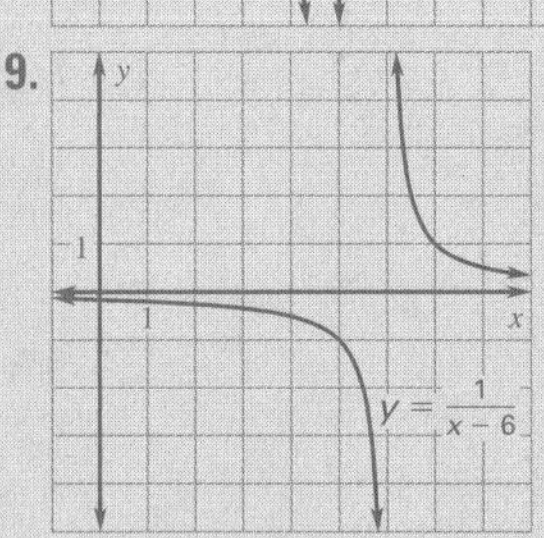

10.

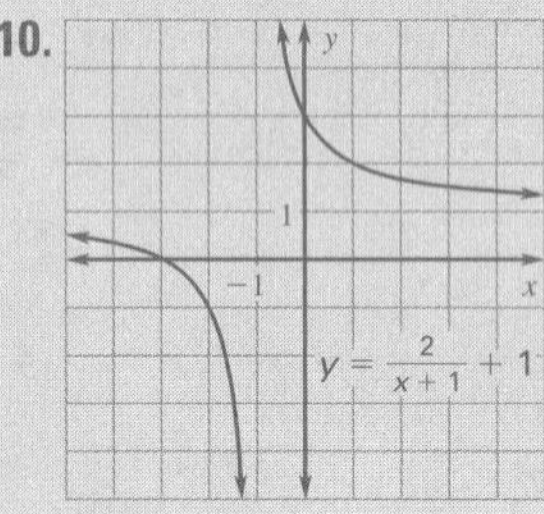

15.

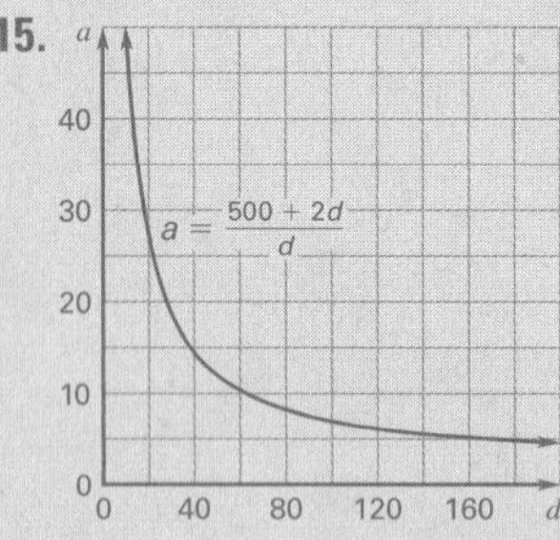

12.2 Graph Rational Functions

pp. 775–782

EXAMPLE

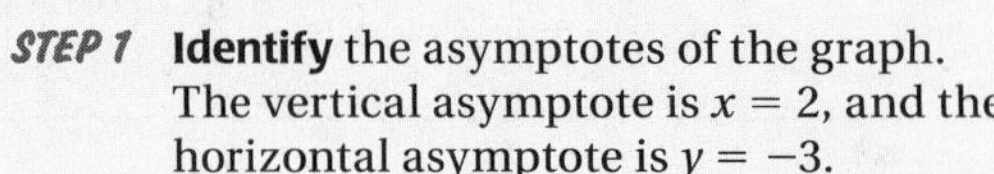

Graph $y = \frac{-1}{x-2} - 3$.

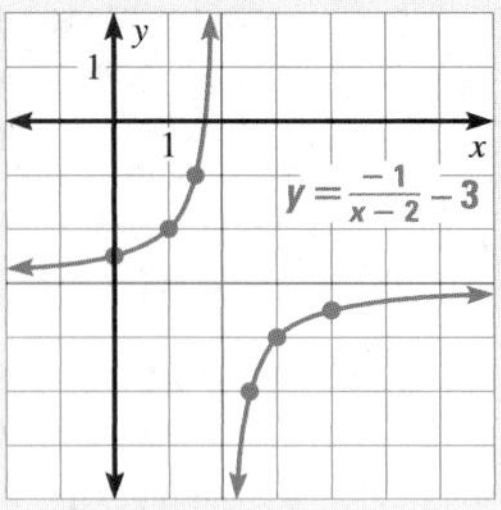

STEP 1 **Identify** the asymptotes of the graph. The vertical asymptote is $x = 2$, and the horizontal asymptote is $y = -3$.

STEP 2 **Plot** several points on each side of the vertical asymptote.

STEP 3 **Graph** two branches that pass through the plotted points and approach the asymptotes.

EXERCISES

EXAMPLES 2, 3, and 4 on pp. 776–777 for Exs. 8–10

Graph the function. 8–10. See margin.

8. $y = \frac{4}{x} + 1$

9. $y = \frac{1}{x-6}$

10. $y = \frac{2}{x+1} + 1$

12.3 Divide Polynomials

pp. 784–791

EXAMPLE

Divide $x^2 + 7x - 2$ by $x - 2$.

$$\begin{array}{r l} x + 9 & \\ x - 2\,\overline{)\,x^2 + 7x - 2} & \\ \underline{x^2 - 2x} & \text{Multiply } x \text{ and } x - 2. \\ 9x - 2 & \text{Subtract } x^2 - 2x. \text{ Bring down } -2. \\ \underline{9x - 18} & \text{Multiply 9 and } x - 2. \\ 16 & \text{Subtract } 9x - 18. \end{array}$$

▶ $(x^2 + 7x - 2) \div (x - 2) = x + 9 + \frac{16}{x-2}$

EXERCISES

EXAMPLES 2, 3, 4, 5, and 7 on pp. 785–787 for Exs. 11–15

Divide.

11. $(x^2 + 12x + 35) \div (x + 7)$ $x + 5$

12. $(y^2 - 5y - 8) \div (y - 3)$ $y - 2 + \frac{-14}{y-3}$

13. $(4z + z^2 - 1) \div (5 + z)$ $z - 1 + \frac{4}{z+5}$

14. $(3a^2 - 2) \div (3 + 3a)$ $a - 1 + \frac{1}{3+3a}$

15. **CHARITY DONATIONS** Sean intends to collect $500 in individual donations for a charity. His company will contribute $2 for every donation collected. Write and graph an equation that gives the average amount a (including the company contribution) that the charity will receive per individual donation as a function of the number d of donations. $a = \frac{500 + 2d}{d}$; see margin for art.

@HomeTutor
classzone.com
Chapter Review Practice

12.4 Simplify Rational Expressions

pp. 794–800

EXAMPLE

Simplify $\frac{x^2 - 3x - 18}{x^2 + 11x + 24}$. State the excluded values.

$$\frac{x^2 - 3x - 18}{x^2 + 11x + 24} = \frac{(x + 3)(x - 6)}{(x + 3)(x + 8)}$$ **Factor numerator and denominator.**

$$= \frac{\cancel{(x + 3)}(x - 6)}{\cancel{(x + 3)}(x + 8)}$$ **Divide out common factor.**

$$= \frac{x - 6}{x + 8}$$ **Simplify.**

▶ The excluded values are −8 and −3.

EXERCISES

EXAMPLES 1, 2, 3, and 4 on pp. 794–796 for Exs. 16–21

Find the excluded values, if any, of the expression.

16. $\frac{x + 3}{2x - 4}$ 2

17. $\frac{3}{y^2 - 4y - 12}$ −2, 6

18. $\frac{8z}{9z^2 - 1}$ $\pm\frac{1}{3}$

Simplify the expression, if possible. State the excluded values.

19. $\frac{5m^3 - 15m^2}{20m^2}$ $\frac{m - 3}{4}$; 0

20. $\frac{3n^2 - n - 2}{2n^2 - 3n + 1}$ $\frac{3n + 2}{2n - 1}$; $\frac{1}{2}$, 1

21. $\frac{4 - r^2}{r^2 - r - 2}$ $\frac{-(r + 2)}{r + 1}$; −1, 2

12.5 Multiply and Divide Rational Expressions

pp. 802–809

EXAMPLE

Find the quotient $\frac{5x^2 + 3x - 2}{4x} \div (5x - 2)$.

$$\frac{5x^2 + 3x - 2}{4x} \div (5x - 2) = \frac{5x^2 + 3x - 2}{4x} \div \frac{5x - 2}{1}$$ **Rewrite polynomial as fraction.**

$$= \frac{5x^2 + 3x - 2}{4x} \cdot \frac{1}{5x - 2}$$ **Multiply by multiplicative inverse.**

$$= \frac{5x^2 + 3x - 2}{4x(5x - 2)}$$ **Multiply numerators and denominators.**

$$= \frac{\cancel{(5x - 2)}(x + 1)}{4x\cancel{(5x - 2)}}$$ **Factor and divide out common factor.**

$$= \frac{x + 1}{4x}$$ **Simplify.**

EXERCISES

EXAMPLES 3 and 4 on pp. 803–804 for Exs. 22–24

Find the product or quotient.

22. $\frac{-x^3}{x^2 + 5x - 14} \cdot (2 - x)$ $\frac{x^3}{x + 7}$

23. $\frac{6v^8}{2v^5} \div \frac{8v}{14v^5}$ $\frac{21v^7}{4}$

24. $\frac{w^2 - 9}{2w + 1} \div \frac{w + 3}{4w^2 - 1}$ $(w - 3)(2w - 1)$

Extra Example 12.4

Simplify $\frac{x^2 - 6x - 16}{x^2 + 8x + 12}$. State the excluded values. $\frac{x - 8}{x + 6}$; −6, −2

Extra Example 12.5

Find the product $\frac{2x}{x^2 + 3x - 4} \cdot (x + 4)$. $\frac{2x}{x - 1}$

Extra Example 12.6

Find the sum $\frac{5x}{x+2} + \frac{4}{x-3}$.

$\frac{5x^2 - 11x + 8}{(x+2)(x-3)}$

Extra Example 12.7

Solve $\frac{8}{x+5} + \frac{3}{4} = \frac{2}{x+5}$. -13

12 CHAPTER REVIEW

12.6 Add and Subtract Rational Expressions

pp. 812–819

EXAMPLE

Find the difference $\frac{x}{x-4} - \frac{5}{x+3}$.

$$\frac{x}{x-4} - \frac{5}{x+3} = \frac{x(x+3)}{(x-4)(x+3)} - \frac{5(x-4)}{(x+3)(x-4)}$$ **Rewrite fractions using LCD, $(x-4)(x+3)$.**

$$= \frac{x(x+3) - 5(x-4)}{(x-4)(x+3)}$$ **Subtract fractions.**

$$= \frac{x^2 - 2x + 20}{(x-4)(x+3)}$$ **Simplify numerator.**

EXERCISES

EXAMPLES 1, 3, 5, and 6 on pp. 812–815 for Exs. 25–28

Find the sum or difference.

25. $\frac{x+13}{5x-3} - \frac{9x-20}{5x-3}$ $\frac{-8x+33}{5x-3}$

26. $\frac{5}{6a} + \frac{1}{9a^3}$ $\frac{15a^2+2}{18a^3}$

27. $\frac{6}{c+1} - \frac{c}{c^2-2c-8}$ $\frac{5c^2-13c-48}{(c+1)(c-4)(c+2)}$

28. BICYCLING You ride your bike to a beach that is 15 miles away. Your average speed on the way home is 5 miles per hour less than your average speed on the way to the beach. Write an equation that gives the total travel time t (in hours) as a function of your average speed r (in miles per hour) on the way to the beach. Then find the total travel time if you biked to the beach at an average speed of 15 miles per hour. $t = \frac{30r - 75}{r(r-5)}$; 2.5 h

12.7 Solve Rational Equations

pp. 820–826

EXAMPLE

Solve $\frac{2x}{x-1} + \frac{2}{3} = \frac{10}{x-1}$.

$$\frac{2x}{x-1} + \frac{2}{3} = \frac{10}{x-1}$$ **Write original equation.**

$$\frac{2x}{x-1} \cdot 3(x-1) + \frac{2}{3} \cdot 3(x-1) = \frac{10}{x-1} \cdot 3(x-1)$$ **Multiply each expression by LCD, $3(x-1)$.**

$$\frac{2x \cdot 3(x-1)}{(x-1)} + \frac{2 \cdot 3(x-1)}{3} = \frac{10 \cdot 3(x-1)}{(x-1)}$$ **Divide out common factors.**

$$6x + 2x - 2 = 30$$ **Simplify.**

$$8x - 2 = 30$$ **Combine like terms.**

$$x = 4$$ **Solve for x.**

EXERCISES

EXAMPLES 1, 2, and 3 on pp. 820–821 for Exs. 29–31

Solve the equation. Check your solution.

29. $\frac{18}{x-3} = \frac{x}{3}$ $-6, 9$

30. $\frac{4}{y+6} - 2 = \frac{20}{y^2+3y-18}$ $-2, 1$

31. $\frac{1}{z+3} - \frac{5}{6} = \frac{2}{z+3}$ $\frac{-21}{5}$

12 CHAPTER TEST

Given that y varies inversely with x, use the specified values to write an inverse variation equation that relates x and y. Then find y when $x = 3$.

1. $x = 2, y = 5$ $y = \frac{10}{x}, \frac{10}{3}$
2. $x = 9, y = 9$ $y = \frac{81}{x}, 27$
3. $x = \frac{9}{2}, y = 4$ $y = \frac{18}{x}, 6$

4. Tell whether the table represents inverse variation. If so, write the inverse variation equation. inverse variation; $y = \frac{-5}{x}$

x	−10	−2	4	5	20
y	0.5	2.5	−1.25	−1	−0.25

Graph the function. 5–7. See margin.

5. $y = \frac{-6}{x}$
6. $y = \frac{2}{x-5} + 2$
7. $y = \frac{3x-1}{x+4}$

Divide.

8. $(v^2 - 16v + 49) \div (v - 8)$ $v - 8 + \frac{-15}{v-8}$
9. $(8w - 2w^2 - 6) \div (w - 1)$ $-2w + 6$
10. $(6x^2 + x) \div (2x + 1)$ $3x - 1 + \frac{1}{2x+1}$

Simplify the expression, if possible. State the excluded values.

11. $\frac{42x^4}{3x^2}$ $14x^2$; 0
12. $\frac{2y-8}{4-y}$ −2; 4
13. $\frac{z^2 - 4z - 77}{z^2 - 13z + 22}$ $\frac{z+7}{z-2}$; 2, 11

Find the sum, difference, product, or quotient. 14–19. See margin.

14. $\frac{r^2 - 9r + 18}{r^2 + 11r + 30} \cdot \frac{r+5}{r^2 - 36}$
15. $\frac{s^2 + 3s - 10}{s^2 - 9} \div \frac{s-2}{s+3}$
16. $\frac{x^2 - 9x}{x+3} \div (x^2 - 6x - 27)$
17. $\frac{4}{m+2} - \frac{3m}{m-3}$
18. $\frac{2n+7}{n-1} - \frac{8n}{n+5}$
19. $\frac{p+1}{p^2 - 49} + \frac{p-1}{p^2 + 10p + 21}$

Solve the equation. Check your solution.

20. $\frac{7}{u+1} = \frac{4}{u+4}$ −8
21. $\frac{t+11}{t-11} = \frac{11t + 121}{t^2 - 6t - 55}$ 6, −11
22. $\frac{8}{x+4} = \frac{5x}{x^2 - 2x - 24} - 1$ −9, 8

23. **GOLF** Your local golf club offers two payment options to anyone who wants to use its course. For the first option, you pay a one-time fee of \$750 to join for the season plus \$25 each time you use the golf course. For the second option, you instead pay \$45 each time you use the golf course.
    a. Using the first option, write an equation that gives your average cost C (in dollars) per use of the golf course as a function of the number g of times you use the golf course. Then graph the equation. See margin.
    b. Use the graph to approximate the number of times you need to use the golf course before the average cost is less than \$45. 38 times

24. **CLEANING** You and your brother start a house cleaning business for the summer. Your brother needs twice the time you need to clean a certain room. Working together, the two of you need 60 minutes to clean the room.
    a. Write an equation that you can use to find the time t (in minutes) you need to clean the room by yourself. Then solve the equation. $\frac{60}{t} + \frac{60}{2t} = 1$; 90
    b. How long will each of you need to clean the room individually? You need 90 minutes and your brother needs 180 minutes.

Additional Resources

Assessment Book

- Chapter Test, Levels A, B, C, pp. 171–176
- Standardized Chapter Test, pp. 177–178
- SAT/ACT Chapter Test, pp. 179–180
- Alternative Assessment, pp. 181–182

Test Generator CD-ROM

Chapter Test

Easily-readable reduced copies (with answers) of Chapter Test B, the Standardized Chapter Test, and the Alternative Assessment from the Assessment Book can be found on pp. 762G–762H.

14. $\frac{r-3}{(r+6)^2}$

15. $\frac{s+5}{s-3}$

16. $\frac{x}{(x+3)^2}$

17. $\frac{-3m^2 - 2m - 12}{(m+2)(m-3)}$

18. $\frac{-6n^2 + 25n + 35}{(n-1)(n+5)}$

19. $\frac{2p^2 - 4p + 10}{(p-7)(p+7)(p+3)}$

23a. $C = \frac{750 + 25g}{g}$;

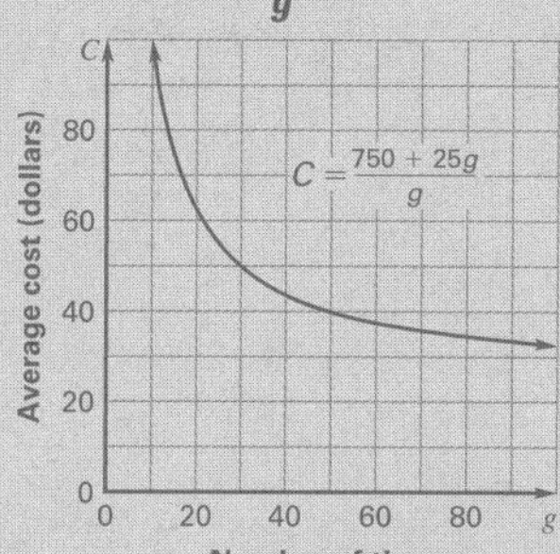

5.

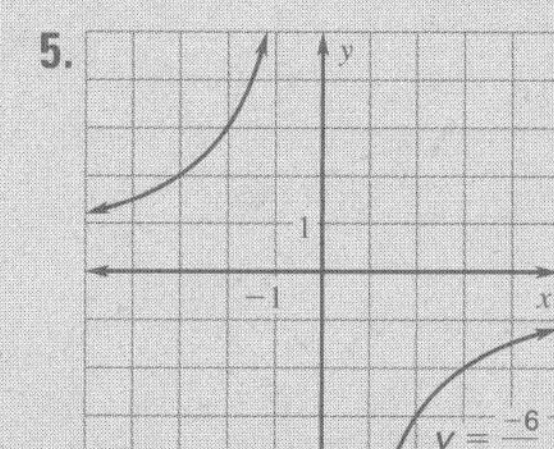

6.

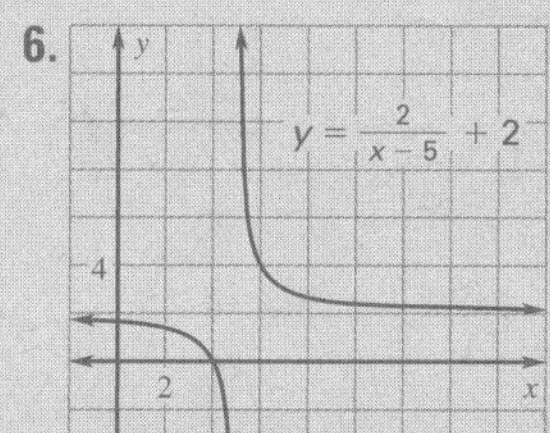

7.

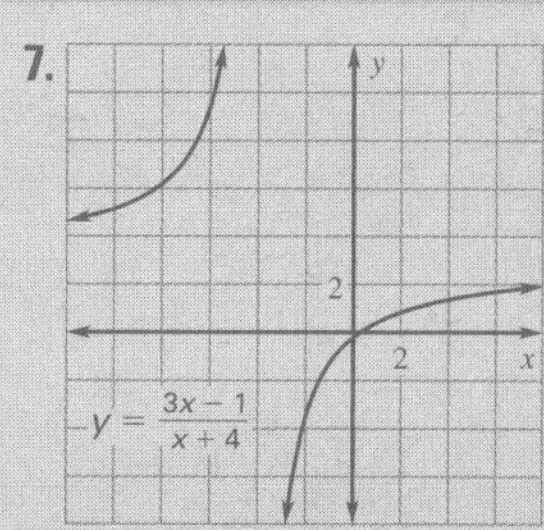

MULTIPLE CHOICE QUESTIONS

Some of the information you need to solve a multiple choice question may appear in a table, a diagram, or a graph.

PROBLEM 1

Gary competes in the triathlon described in the flyer. His average biking speed is 8 times his average swimming speed. His average running speed is 4 times his average swimming speed. He takes 0.75 minute to transition from swimming to biking and 0.25 minute to transition from biking to running. He finishes the triathlon in 2 hours 25 minutes. What is his average swimming speed?

OAK CITY TRIATHLON

July 29, 8 A.M.

Swim: 1.5 kilometers
Bike: 40 kilometers
Run: 10 kilometers

A. 0.0625 kilometer per minute

B. 0.125 kilometer per minute

C. 0.25 kilometer per minute

D. 0.5 kilometer per minute

Plan

INTERPRET THE INFORMATION Use the distance for each stage of the triathlon and Gary's average speed for each stage to write a rational equation that describes the situation. Then solve the equation to find his average swimming speed.

Solution

STEP 1 Use the information in the problem to write an equation that describes the situation.

The time that Gary takes to complete each stage of the triathlon is the distance of the stage divided by the average speed for that stage. The sum of the times of each stage and the transition times equals 2 hours 25 minutes, or 145 minutes. Let x represent Gary's average swimming speed (in kilometers per minute).

$$\frac{1.5}{x} + \frac{40}{8x} + \frac{10}{4x} + 0.75 + 0.25 = 145$$

STEP 2 Solve the equation to find Gary's average swimming speed.

$$\frac{1.5}{x} \cdot \mathbf{8x} + \frac{40}{8x} \cdot \mathbf{8x} + \frac{10}{4x} \cdot \mathbf{8x} + 0.75 \cdot \mathbf{8x} + 0.25 \cdot \mathbf{8x} = 145 \cdot \mathbf{8x}$$

$$\frac{1.5 \cdot 8\cancel{x}}{\cancel{x}} + \frac{40 \cdot \cancel{8x}}{\cancel{8x}} + \frac{10 \cdot 8\cancel{x}}{4\cancel{x}} + 0.75 \cdot 8x + 0.25 \cdot 8x = 145 \cdot 8x$$

$$12 + 40 + 20 + 6x + 2x = 1160x$$

$$72 + 8x = 1160x$$

$$0.0625 = x$$

Gary's average swimming speed is 0.0625 kilometer per minute.

The correct answer is **A**.

Illinois Test Practice

1. B
2. F

PROBLEM 2

The graph of which function is shown?

F. $y = \frac{2}{x-3} + 4$ **H.** $y = \frac{1}{x+3} + 4$

G. $y = \frac{2}{x+3} + 4$ **J.** $y = \frac{1}{x+4} - 3$

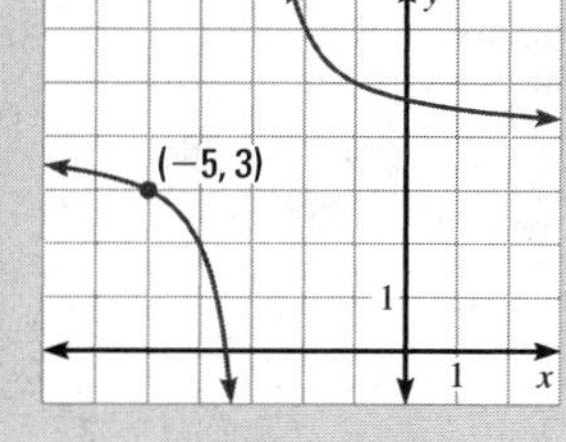

Plan

INTERPRET THE GRAPH The graph is a hyperbola that represents a rational function of the form $y = \frac{a}{x-h} + k$. Use the asymptotes and the fact that $(-5, 3)$ lies on the graph to find the function.

Solution

STEP 1 Find the values of *h* and *k*.

The hyperbola has a vertical asymptote of $x = -3$ and a horizontal asymptote of $y = 4$. So, the function has the form $y = \frac{a}{x-(-3)} + 4$, or $y = \frac{a}{x+3} + 4$.

STEP 2 Find the value of *a*.

To find the value of a, substitute the coordinates of $(-5, 3)$ into the function.

$3 = \frac{a}{-5+3} + 4$ **Substitute −5 for *x* and 3 for *y*.**

$2 = a$ **Solve for *a*.**

The function is $y = \frac{2}{x+3} + 4$. The correct answer is **G.**

TEST PREPARATION

PRACTICE

1. A community service club is recruiting volunteers to work at a charity event. The table shows the number of hours that each volunteer needs to work for various numbers of volunteers that the club recruits. If the club recruits 50 volunteers, how many hours does each volunteer need to work?

Volunteers	Work time (hours/person)
20	4
25	3.2
32	2.5

A. 1 hour **B.** 1.6 hours **C.** 2 hours **D.** 2.8 hours

2. What is the area of the right triangle shown?

F. $\frac{x^2 - 12x + 35}{2}$ **H.** $\frac{x^2 + 12x - 35}{4}$

G. $\frac{x^2 + 12x - 35}{2}$ **J.** $x^2 - 12x + 35$

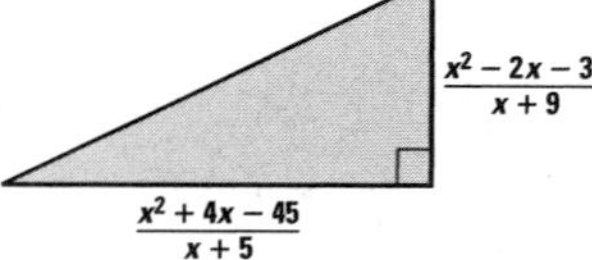

Illinois Test Practice

1. D
2. G
3. C
4. F
5. D
6. G
7. B
8. G
9. B
10. F
11. A
12. H
13. B
14. G
15. B
16. G
17. D
18. F
19. D
20. F

Illinois Test Practice

In Exercises 1–3, use the following information. The length of a string on a stringed instrument varies inversely with the frequency of vibration. The table gives several notes and their approximate frequencies (in hertz).

Note	Frequency (Hz)
C	65.4
D	73.4
E	82.4
F	87.3
G	98.0

1. The string corresponding to which note has the shortest length?

   A. C note **B.** D note **C.** E note **D.** G note

2. If the string that produces the C note has a length of 42 centimeters, what is the approximate length of the string that produces the F note?

   F. 28 cm **G.** 31 cm **H.** 35 cm **J.** 46 cm

3. If the string that produces the D note has a length of 56 centimeters, what is the approximate length of the string that produces the G note?

   A. 31 cm **B.** 35 cm **C.** 42 cm **D.** 65 cm

4. Which equation gives the ratio r of the surface area of the rectangular prism to its volume as a function of the height h?

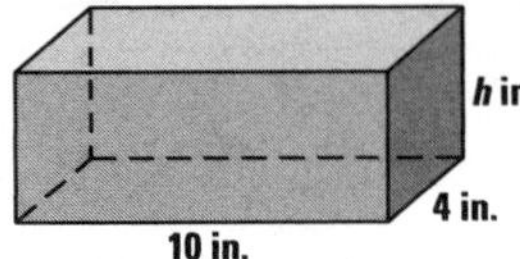

   F. $r = \frac{2}{h} + 0.7$ **G.** $r = \frac{1}{20h} + 0.7$ **H.** $r = \frac{1}{20h} + 28$ **J.** $r = \frac{2}{h} + 0.05$

5. Which point lies on the hyperbola shown?

   A. $(-7, 2.5)$ **B.** $(-9, 2.6)$ **C.** $(9, 3.4)$ **D.** $(11, 3.2)$

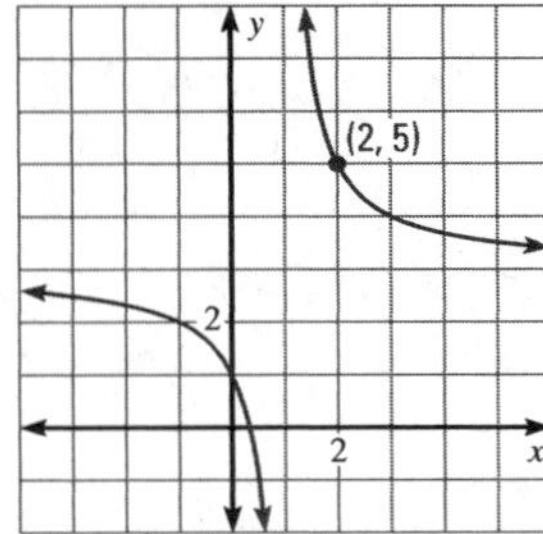

In Exercises 6–8, use the following information.

Jan is hiking a trail and plans to rest for 2 hours along the way. The hyperbola shown is the graph of her combined time t (in hours) for hiking and resting as a function of her average hiking speed r (in miles per hour).

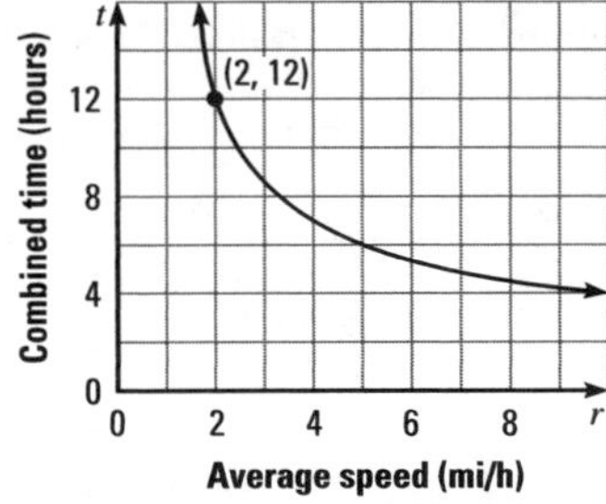

6. If $r = 5$, what is the value of t?

   F. 5 **G.** 6 **H.** 7 **J.** 10

7. What is the length of the trail?

   A. 10 miles **B.** 20 miles **C.** 30 miles **D.** 40 miles

8. Suppose Jan's combined time for hiking and resting is 8 hours 15 minutes. What is her average hiking speed?

   F. 3 mi/h **G.** 3.2 mi/h **H.** 3.4 mi/h **J.** 3.6 mi/h

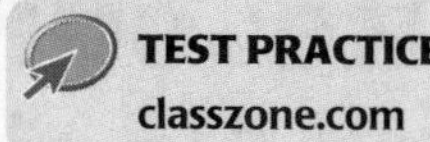

9. Which of the following equations models inverse variation?

A. $y = -4x$

B. $y = \frac{4}{x}$

C. $x + 3y = 0$

D $x - 3y = 0$

10. The variables x and y vary directly. When $x = -4$, $y = 12$. What is the value of y when $x = 5$?

F. –15

G. –12

H. 12

J. 15

11. What is the LCD of $\frac{x}{4x^2 - 1}$ and $\frac{x - 5}{2x^2 + x - 1}$?

A. $(2x - 1)(2x + 1)(x + 1)$

B. $(2x + 1)(x + 1)(x - 1)$

C. $(x + 2)(x - 2)(2x + 3)$

D. $(x + 3)(x - 2)(2x - 1)$

12. Which of the following is true if $\frac{a - 1}{b} = \frac{b - 1}{a + 1}$?

F. $a + 1 = b - 1$

G. $a - 1 = b + 1$

H. $a^2 - 1 = b^2 - b$

J. $a^2 - 1 = b^2 + b$

13. What is the solution of the equation $\frac{15}{2t - 7} = \frac{20}{3t - 11}$?

A. –5 **C.** 20

B. 5 **D.** 25

14. Which of the following equations models direct variation?

F. $xy = 5$

G. $y = 5x$

H. $x + y = 5$

J. $x - y = 5$

15. The variables x and y vary inversely. When $x = 3$, $y = 30$. If $x = 15$, what is the value of y?

A. 5 **C.** 12

B. 6 **D.** 150

16. What is the simplified form of the expression $\frac{x^3 + 3x^2 + 2x}{x^2 + 4x + 3}$?

F. $\frac{x + 2}{x + 3}$

G. $\frac{x(x + 2)}{x + 3}$

H. $\frac{x(x + 2)}{x + 1}$

J. $\frac{x(x + 1)}{x + 3}$

17. Subtract: $\frac{5}{3x} - \frac{1}{2x}$.

A. $\frac{2}{3x}$ **C.** $\frac{7}{x}$

B. $\frac{4}{x}$ **D.** $\frac{7}{6x}$

18. Multiply: $\frac{2x}{x^2 - 49} \cdot (7 + x)$.

F. $\frac{2x}{x - 7}$

G. $\frac{2x}{x + 7}$

H. $\frac{14x}{x^2 - 49}$

J. $\frac{14x + x^2}{x^2 - 49}$

19. What is the remainder when $2x^2 + 7x + 11$ is divided by $x - 1$?

A. –3 **C.** 14

B. –6 **D.** 20

20. What is the solution of the equation $\frac{1}{2} + \frac{1}{x} = \frac{3}{x}$?

F. 4 **H.** –1

G. 2 **J.** –6

TEST PRACTICE

839

Illinois Resources Guide

Pacing and Assignment Guide

REGULAR SCHEDULE

Pre-AP For pacing and assignments for a Pre-AP course, see the *Algebra 1 Toolkit*.

Lesson	Les. Day	BASIC	AVERAGE	ADVANCED
13.1 10.11.01	Day 1	SRH p. 932 Exs. 4–8; pp. 846–848 Exs. 1–15, 19–21, 24–26	pp. 846–848 Exs. 1, 2–12 even, 13–17, 19–22, 24–26	pp. 846–848 Exs. 1, 2–6 even, 10, 12, 13–26*
13.2 10.11.10	Day 1	pp. 853–855 Exs. 1–19	pp. 853–855 Exs. 1–19	pp. 853–855 Exs. 1–19
	Day 2	pp. 853–855 Exs. 20–29, 32–36, 40–43	pp. 853–855 Exs. 22–30, 32–38, 40–43	pp. 853–855 Exs. 24–43*
13.3 10.11.10	Day 1	pp. 858–859 Exs. 1–17, 23–25, 28–33	pp. 858–859 Exs. 1–5, 6–14 even, 15–20, 23–26, 28–33	pp. 858–859 Exs. 1–3, 10–33*
13.4 10.11.08	Day 1	SRH p. 915 Exs. 1, 2, 6, 7; pp. 864–867 Exs. 1–8, 30–34	pp. 864–867 Exs. 1, 2, 5–8, 18, 19, 30–34	pp. 864–867 Exs. 1, 2, 6–8, 18, 19, 21*, 30–34
	Day 2	pp. 864–867 Exs. 9–17, 22–25, 28, 29	pp. 864–867 Exs. 11–17, 20, 22–26, 28, 29	pp. 864–867 Exs. 11–17, 20, 22–29*
13.5	Day 1	pp. 873–874 Exs. 1–10, 13–16, 19–27	pp. 873–874 Exs. 1, 2, 4–11, 13–17, 19–27	pp. 873–874 Exs. 1, 2, 5–27*
13.6 10.11.05	Day 1	pp. 877–878 Exs. 1–14, 19–21, 24	pp. 877–878 Exs. 1, 2, 4–10, 13–17, 19–22, 24	pp. 877–878 Exs. 1, 5–9, 13–24*
13.7 10.11.01	Day 1	pp. 883–885 Exs. 1–9, 17, 20	pp. 883–885 Exs. 1, 2, 4–9, 17, 20, 21	pp. 883–885 Exs. 1, 4–9, 17, 20, 21
	Day 2	pp. 883–885 Exs. 10–13, 18, 19, 23–27	pp. 883–885 Exs. 10–15, 18, 19, 23–27	pp. 883–885 Exs. 11–16*, 18, 19, 22–27*
13.8 10.11.01	Day 1	pp. 889–892 Exs. 1–7, 15, 16	pp. 889–892 Exs. 1, 2, 4–7, 15, 16, 21, 22	pp. 889–892 Exs. 1, 2, 4–6, 15, 16, 21, 22
	Day 2	pp. 889–892 Exs. 8–12, 17–19, 21–24	pp. 889–892 Exs. 8–13, 17–19, 23, 24	pp. 889–892 Exs. 8–14*, 17–20*, 23, 24
Review	Day 1	pp. 896–900 Exs. 1–25	pp. 896–900 Exs. 1–25	pp. 896–900 Exs. 1–25
Assess	Day 1	Chapter 13 Test	Chapter 13 Test	Chapter 13 Test
Yearly Pacing		Chapter 13 Total – 14 days	Chapters 1–13 Total – 160 days	Remaining – 0 days

*Challenge Exercises EP = Extra Practice SRH = Skills Review Handbook

BLOCK SCHEDULE

DAY 1	DAY 2	DAY 3	DAY 4	DAY 5	DAY 6	DAY 7
13.1	**13.2 (CONT.)**	**13.4**	**13.5**	**13.7**	**13.8**	**REVIEW**
pp. 846–848 Exs. 1, 2–12 even, 13–17, 19–22, 24–26	pp. 853–855 Exs. 22–30, 32–38, 40–43	pp. 864–867 Exs. 1, 2, 5–8, 11–20, 22–26, 28–34	pp. 873–874 Exs. 1, 2, 4–11, 13–17, 19–27	pp. 883–885 Exs. 1, 2, 4–15, 17–21, 23–27	pp. 889–892 Exs. 1, 2, 4–13, 15–19, 21–24	pp. 896–900 Exs. 1–25
13.2	**13.3**		**13.6**			**ASSESS**
pp. 853–855 Exs. 1–19	pp. 858–859 Exs. 1–5, 6–14 even, 15–20, 23–26, 28–33		pp. 877–878 Exs. 1, 2, 4–10, 13–17, 19–22, 24			Chapter 13 Test

Yearly Pacing Chapter 13 Total – 7 days Chapters 1–13 Total – 80 days Remaining – 0 days

13

Chapter Resource Guide

Chapter Resource Book

CHAPTER SUPPORT								
Parents as Partners (Chapter Overview with home involvement exercises and activity)							p. 1	
LESSON SUPPORT **Standard**	13.1 **10.11.01**	13.2 **10.11.10**	13.3 **10.11.10**	13.4 **10.11.08**	13.5	13.6 **10.11.05**	13.7 **10.11.01**	13.8 **10.11.01**
Teaching Guide/Lesson Plan	p. 3	p. 14	p. 24	p. 36	p. 48	p. 58	p. 71	p. 85
Activity Masters			p. 26	p. 38				
Technology Activities & Keystrokes	p. 5		p. 27			p. 60	p. 73	p. 87
Activity Support Masters								
Practice (3 levels)	p. 6	p. 16	p. 28	p. 39	p. 50	p. 63	p. 74	p. 88
Study Guide	p. 9	p. 19	p. 31	p. 42	p. 53	p. 66	p. 80	p. 94
Catch-Up for Absent Students	p. 11	p. 21	p. 33	p. 44	p. 55	p. 68	p. 82	p. 96
Problem Solving/Application	p. 12	p. 22	p. 34	p. 45	p. 56	p. 69	p. 83	p. 97
Challenge Practice	p. 13	p. 23	p. 35	p. 47	p. 57	p. 70	p. 84	p. 98

REVIEW			
Chapter Review Games and Activities	p. 99	Cumulative Practice	p. 102
Project with Rubric	p. 100	Resource Book Answers	A1

Transparencies	13.1	13.2	13.3	13.4	13.5	13.6	13.7	13.8
Warm-Up/Daily Homework Quiz	✔	✔	✔	✔	✔	✔	✔	✔
Notetaking Guide	✔	✔	✔	✔	✔	✔	✔	✔
Teacher Support	✔			✔				✔
Answer Transparencies	✔	✔	✔	✔	✔	✔	✔	✔

ASSESSMENT BOOK

Quizzes	p. 183	SAT/ACT Chapter Test	p. 193
Chapter Tests (3 levels)	p. 185	Alternative Assessment with Rubric	p. 195
Standardized Chapter Test	p. 191	Cumulative Test	p. 197

TECHNOLOGY

- Easy Planner
- Test and Practice Generator
- Power Presentations
- @HomeTutor
- Activity Generator
- Animated Algebra
- Classzone.com
- eEdition Plus Online
- eWorkbook Plus Online
- ML Assessment System

ADDITIONAL RESOURCES

Illinois Additional Lessons

- Additional Lesson I
  Introduction to Recursive Functions for Sequences
- Additional Lesson K
  Two-Way Tables of Probability
- Additional Lesson L
  Quantitative vs. Qualitative Data
- Additional Lesson M
  Causation vs. Correlation
- Additional Lesson N
  Misleading Data Displays
- Worked-Out Solution Key
- Notetaking Guide
- Practice Workbook
- Algebra 1 Toolkit
- Benchmark Tests
- Reteaching and Remediation
- Spanish Study Guide
- Spanish Assessment Book
- Spanish Resources in Spanish
- Multi-Language Visual Glossary

Lesson Practice Level B

LESSON 13.1 Practice B

For use with pages 843–848

3. 36; 1, 1; 1, 2; 1, 3; 1, 4; 1, 5; 1, 6; 2, 1; 2, 2; 2, 3; 2, 4; 2, 5; 2, 6; 3, 1; 3, 2; 3, 3; 3, 4; 3, 5; 3, 6; 4, 1; 4, 2; 4, 3; 4, 4; 4, 5; 4, 6; 5, 1; 5, 2; 5, 3; 5, 4; 5, 5; 5, 6; 6, 1; 6, 2; 6, 3; 6, 4; 6, 5; 6, 6

Find the number of possible outcomes in the sample space. Then list the possible outcomes.

1. A bag contains 6 blue cards numbered 1–6 and 8 red cards numbered 1–8. You choose a card at random. 14; blue 1; blue 2; blue 3; blue 4; blue 5; blue 6; red 1; red 2; red 3; red 4; red 5; red 6; red 7; red 8
2. You roll one 3-sided number cube and toss two coins. **2.** 12; 1, H, H; 1, H, T; 1, T, H; 1, T, T; 2, H, H; 2, H, T; 2, T, H; 2, T, T; 3, H, H; 3, H, T; 3, T, H; 3, T, T
3. You roll two number cubes. See above.

In Exercises 4–9, refer to the spinner shown. The spinner is divided into sections with the same area.

4. What is the probability that the spinner stops on an even number? $\frac{4}{9}$
5. What is the probability that the spinner stops on an odd number? $\frac{5}{9}$
6. You spin the spinner 24 times. It stops on 27 twice. What is the experimental probability of stopping on 27? $\frac{1}{12}$
7. You spin the spinner 30 times. It stops on a multiple of 3 five times. What is the experimental probability of stopping on a multiple of 3? $\frac{1}{6}$
8. What are the odds in favor of stopping on a multiple of 4? $\frac{1}{3}$
9. What are the odds against stopping on a multiple of 6? $\frac{7}{2}$

10. **Favorite Spectator Sport** A survey asked a total of 180 students in your school about their favorite spectator sports. The table shows the results of the survey.

Sport	Basketball	Soccer	Football	Baseball	Volleyball	Wrestling	Hockey
Number of students	40	20	45	20	16	18	21

   a. What is the probability that a randomly selected student who participated in this survey chose football as his or her favorite spectator sport? $\frac{1}{4}$
   b. What is the probability that a randomly selected student who participated in this survey chose wrestling or hockey as his or her favorite spectator sport? $\frac{13}{60}$
   c. What are the odds in favor of a randomly selected student who participated in this survey choosing basketball as his or her favorite spectator sport? $\frac{2}{7}$

11. **Movies** A local movie theater did a survey of students to determine their favorite types of movies. The circle graph shows the results of the survey.
   a. What is the probability that a randomly selected student chose science fiction as his or her favorite type of movie?
   b. What is the probability that a randomly selected student chose drama or comedy as his or her favorite type of movie? **11. a.** $\frac{9}{100}$ **b.** $\frac{37}{50}$

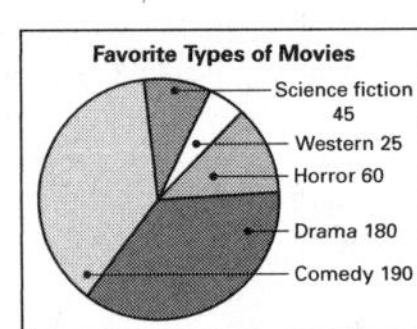

LESSON 13.1

LESSON 13.2 Practice B

For use with pages 851–855

4. the number of permutations of 14 objects taken 3 at a time
5. the number of permutations of 24 objects taken 10 at a time
6. the number of permutations of 30 objects taken 20 at a time

Find the number of ways you can arrange (a) all of the letters in the given word and (b) 2 of the letters in the word.

1. TACK **a.** 24 **b.** 12
2. MAR **a.** 6 **b.** 6
3. GAMER **a.** 120 **b.** 20

Write the meaning of the notation in words. See above.

4. $_{14}P_3$
5. $_{24}P_{10}$
6. $_{30}P_{20}$

Evaluate the expression.

7. 6! 720
8. 9! 362,880
9. 11! 39,916,800
10. $\frac{8!}{3!}$ 6720
11. $\frac{12!}{9!}$ 1320
12. $\frac{15!}{14!}$ 15
13. $_6P_3$ 120
14. $_4P_4$ 24
15. $_{15}P_3$ 2730
16. $_8P_7$ 40,320
17. $_{10}P_6$ 151,200
18. $_5P_0$ 1

Complete the statement using >, <, or =.

19. $_6P_4$? $_4P_1$ >
20. $_8P_6$? $_{10}P_8$ <
21. $_3P_0$? $_6P_5$ <
22. $_6P_3$? $_4P_1$ >
23. $_{24}P_1$? $_4P_4$ =
24. $_7P_5$? $_{12}P_3$ >

25. **Summer Reading List** At the beginning of the summer, you have 6 books to read. In how many orders can you read the books? 720
26. **Air Conditioning Repair** An air conditioner repair person has repairs to make at 7 different homes. The destinations are all so close, it doesn't matter the order in which the repairs are made. In how many orders can the repairs be made? 5040
27. **Boat Racing** You are in a boat racing competition. In each heat, 4 boats race and the positions of the boats are randomly assigned.
   a. In how many ways can a position be assigned? 24
   b. What is the probability that you are chosen to be in the last position? *Explain* how you found your answer.
   c. What is the probability that you are chosen to be in the first or second position of the heat that you are racing in? *Explain* how you found your answer.
   d. What is the probability that you are chosen to be in the second or third position of the heat that you are racing in? *Compare* your answer with that in part (c).
28. **Math Exam** On an exam, you are asked to list the 6 steps to solving a particular kind of problem in order. You guess the order of the steps at random. What is the probability that you choose the correct order? $\frac{1}{720}$

27. b. $\frac{1}{4}$; The number of ways to be chosen to be in last position is given by 3!. The total number of ways a position is chosen is 4! = 24. So, the probability is $\frac{3!}{4!} = \frac{1}{4}$. **c.** $\frac{1}{2}$; You can be chosen to be in the first position 6 out of 24 ways and you can be chosen to be in the second position 6 out of 24 ways, so you can be chosen to be in the first or second position 12 out of 24 ways. **d.** $\frac{1}{2}$; You can be chosen to be in the second position 6 out of 24 ways and you can be chosen to be in the third position 6 out of 24 ways, so you can be chosen to be in the second or third position 12 out of 24 ways. The answers are the same.

LESSON 13.2

LESSON 13.3 Practice B

For use with pages 856–859

Evaluate the expression.

1. $_8C_4$ 70
2. $_5C_5$ 1
3. $_{12}C_0$ 1
4. $_7C_1$ 7
5. $_{15}C_{11}$ 1365
6. $_{10}C_3$ 120
7. $_6C_5$ 6
8. $_4C_2$ 6
9. $_{16}C_8$ 12,870

Complete the statement using >, <, or =.

10. $_{10}C_6$? $_8C_5$ >
11. $_{22}C_3$? $_{18}C_4$ <
12. $_9C_6$? $_9C_3$ =
13. $_8C_2$? $_{15}C_{14}$ >
14. $_7C_7$? $_{14}C_{14}$ =
15. $_5C_3$? $_8C_3$ <

In Exercises 16–18, tell whether the question can be answered using *combinations* or *permutations*. *Explain* your choice, then answer the question.

16. Five students from the 90 students in your class not running for class president will be selected to count the ballots for the vote for class president. In how many ways can the 5 students be selected? combinations; Answers will vary. 43,949,268
17. Twenty students are running for 3 different positions on student council. In how many ways can the 3 positions be filled? permutations; Answers will vary. 6840
18. To complete a quiz, you must answer 3 questions from a list of 6 questions. In how many ways can you complete the quiz? combinations; Answers will vary. 20
19. **Sweaters** The buyer for a retail store must decide which sweaters to stock for the upcoming fall season. A sweater from one manufacturer comes in 5 different colors and 3 different textures. The buyer decides that the store will stock the sweater in 3 different colors and 2 different textures. How many different sweaters are possible? 30
20. **Greeting Cards** A greeting card company packages 4 different cards together that are randomly selected from 10 different cards with a different animal on each card. What is the probability that one of the cards in a package is the card that has a dog on it? $\frac{2}{5}$
21. **Open-Mike Night** A coffee shop offers an open-mike night for poetry. Tonight, 15 people would like to read, but there is only enough time to have 7 people read.
   a. Seven of the 15 people that would like to read are randomly chosen. How many combinations of 7 readers from the group of people that would like to read are possible? 6435
   b. You and your friend are part of the group that would like to read. What is the probability that you and your friend are chosen? What is the probability that you are chosen first and your friend is chosen second? Which event is more likely to occur? $\frac{1}{5}$; $\frac{1}{5}$; They are equally likely to occur.

LESSON 13.3

LESSON 13.4

Practice B
For use with pages 861–867

In Exercises 1–4, you draw a card from a bag that contains 4 yellow cards numbered 1–4 and 5 blue cards numbered 1–5. Tell whether the events A *and* B are *mutually exclusive* or *overlapping*. Then find *P*(A *or* B).

1. **Event A:** You choose a card with an even number.
   Event B: You choose a number 4 card.
   overlapping; $\frac{4}{9}$

2. **Event A:** You choose a yellow card.
   Event B: You choose a number 5 card.
   mutually exclusive; $\frac{5}{9}$

3. **Event A:** You choose a blue number 3 card.
   Event B: You choose a blue card.
   overlapping; $\frac{5}{9}$

4. **Event A:** You choose a card with an odd number.
   Event B: You choose a blue card.
   overlapping; $\frac{7}{9}$

In Exercises 5 and 6, tell whether the events A *and* B are *dependent* or *independent*. Then find *P*(A *and* B).

5. A bag contains 6 red balls and 5 green balls. You randomly draw one ball, replace it, and randomly draw a second ball.
   Event A: The first ball is green.
   Event B: The second ball is green. independent; $\frac{25}{121}$

6. You write each of the letters of the word BRILLIANT on pieces of paper and place them in a bag. You randomly draw one letter, do not replace it, then randomly draw a second letter.
   Event A: The first letter is an L.
   Event B: The second letter is a T. dependent; $\frac{1}{36}$

7. **Eating Habits** A survey of 500 students in a school found that about 100 households consist of only vegetarians, 240 consist of vegetarians and non-vegetarians, and 160 consist of non-vegetarians.
   a. What is the probability that one of the households surveyed, chosen at random, consists of vegetarians or non-vegetarians? $\frac{13}{25}$
   b. What is the probability that one of the households surveyed, chosen at random, consists of vegetarians and non-vegetarians? $\frac{12}{25}$
   c. *Explain* how your answers to parts (a) and (b) are related. The sum of the probabilities is 1.

8. **Coordinating Time** You study with a group for an upcoming math competition on Mondays, Tuesdays, and Thursdays. You volunteer at a hospital on Mondays, Wednesdays, and Thursdays.
   a. Make a Venn diagram that shows the days of the week that you participate in each activity.
   b. Your class is taking a field trip that could be scheduled for any day of the week (Monday through Friday). Find the probability that it is scheduled for a day when you are studying with your group or are volunteering. $\frac{4}{5}$

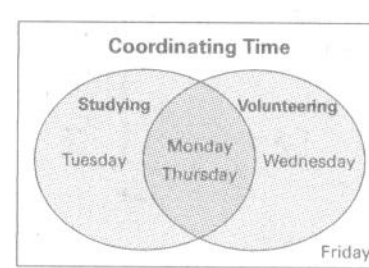

LESSON 13.5

Practice B
For use with pages 871–874

1. music store customers; self-selected sample
3. likely to result in a biased sample
4. not likely to result in a biased sample

In Exercises 1 and 2, identify the population and classify the sampling method.

1. The manager of a music store wants to evaluate how customers rate the selection of music the store has in stock. Customers are given comment cards with their receipts.
2. Your school's administrators want to know if students are satisfied with the choices of activities for activity period. In each grade, every seventh student in alphabetical order is surveyed. all students in school; systematic sample

Tell whether the survey method used is likely to result in a biased sample.

3. A bicycling club wants to gather information about biking conditions throughout a city. A survey for bicycle riders is posted on the club's website.
4. A management company that owns several apartment buildings wants to gather information about tenant satisfaction with the condition of the apartments. They send a survey to 30 random tenants in each of the buildings.

In Exercises 5 and 6, tell whether the question is potentially biased. *Explain* your answer.

5. Don't you think that the lunch menu should include grilled chicken rather than pizza because grilled chicken is healthier for you? See below.
6. Do you think that the city's excess revenue should be spent on road repairs or building a new sports stadium? See below.

In Exercises 7–9, explain why the question is biased. Then rewrite it so that it is not.

7. Don't you agree that it is better to offer an accounting class as an elective rather than a computer programming class? See below.
8. Don't you agree that a science center would be more fun to go to than a planetarium? See below.
9. Would you pay even higher taxes to fund a new highway? biased because it suggests that taxes are already high; Would you use your taxes to fund a new highway?
10. **Bus Stop Conditions** A newspaper does a report on the condition of the bus stops in a large city. Part of the report includes a survey of people living in the area. The survey is done by asking people at a mall what they think of local bus stops. Is the sample likely to be biased? *Explain.* Answers will vary.
11. **After-School Activities** You plan a report on the participation of students at your school in after-school activities for your school's website. *Describe* how you could choose a representative sample. *Justify* your sampling method. Answers will vary.

5. biased because it suggests that grilled chicken is healthier than pizza
6. not biased because a particular response is not encouraged
7. biased because it suggests that accounting class is better than a computer programming class; Which class should your school offer as an elective, an accounting class or a computer programming class?
8. biased because it suggests that going to a science center is more fun than going to a planetarium; Where would you like to go, to a science center or to a planetarium?

LESSON 13.6

Practice B
For use with pages 875–878

1. mean: 5; median: 5; modes: 1, 5
2. mean: 68; median: 67.5; mode: 81
3. mean: 19; median: 22; mode: 25
4. mean: 16; median: 13.5; modes: 8, 28

Find the mean, median, and mode(s) of the data.

1. 6, 1, 3, 8, 5, 11, 1, 5
2. 60, 81, 52, 75, 59, 81
3. 15, 27, 10, 25, 9, 22, 25
4. 23, 6, 8, 14, 28, 8, 13, 28
5. 16, 11, 14, 30, 22, 9, 19, 15
   mean: 17; median: 15.5; mode: none
6. 4.2, 2.2, 3.7, 2.8, 1.1
   mean: 2.8; median: 2.8; mode: none

For the set of data, determine which measure of central tendency best represents the data.

7. 89, 86, 96, 87, 100, 86 median
8. 38, 35, 40, 36, 36, 33, 42, 37, 39, 34 median
9. 50, 47, 48, 49, 72, 47, 54, 50 median
10. 115, 112, 127, 116, 123, 113 median
11. 87, 77, 151, 105, 65, 141, 104, 166 mean
12. 100, 106, 180, 41, 161, 292, 116, 213 mean

Find the range and mean absolute deviation of the data. Round to the nearest hundredth, if necessary.

13. range: 6; mean absolute deviation: 1.68
14. range: 10; mean absolute deviation: 2.88
15. range: 13; mean absolute deviation: 4.67
16. range: 8; mean absolute deviation: 2.25

13. 10, 7, 13, 10, 8
14. 110, 114, 104, 108, 106
15. 87, 75, 85, 77, 74, 82
16. 15, 17, 15, 17, 21, 17, 15, 23
17. 40, 46, 41, 46, 49, 49, 46, 44, 44
    range: 9; mean absolute deviation: 2.44
18. 50.8, 51.6, 51.9, 52, 52.5, 52.8, 53.1
    range: 2.3; mean absolute deviation: 0.6
19. **Bean Plants** The heights (in inches) of eight bean plants are 28, 36, 41, 50, 35, 42, 46, and 52.
    a. What is the range of the bean plant heights? 24
    b. Find the mean, median, and mode(s) of the bean plant heights.
    c. Which measure of central tendency best represents the data? *Explain.*

    b. mean: 41.25; median: 41.5; mode: none
    c. either the mean or the median because they are both close to all of the data
20. **Hotel Stay** You are planning a trip to Washington, D.C. and are looking up hotel room rates. On the Internet, you find the following rates for a one-night stay in a hotel in Washington, D.C.
    $109, $126.50, $175.95, $139, $77.50, $145, $162.35, $173, $181.50, $105
    a. Find the mean, median, and mode(s) of the rates. mean: 139.48; median: 142; mode: none
    b. Which measure of central tendency best represents the data? *Explain.*

    20. b. mean; because it is closer to all of the data
21. **Temperature** The high and low temperatures for the last seven days are given.
    High temperatures: 81°F, 78°F, 83°F, 89°F, 90°F, 87°F, 89°F
    Low temperatures: 64°F, 53°F, 62°F, 66°F, 68°F, 69°F, 67°F
    a. Find the mean, median, and mode of each data set. Round your answers to the nearest tenth. highs: mean: 85.3; median: 87; mode: 89; lows: mean: 64.1; median: 66; mode: none
    b. For each data set, determine which measure of central tendency best represents the data. *Explain.* both the medians because they are closer to all of the data
    c. *Compare* the spreads of data by using the range.
    d. *Compare* the spreads of data by using the mean absolute deviation. Round your answers to the nearest hundredth. The mean absolute deviation of the highs is greater, so the average variation from the mean is greater for the highs than the lows.

    21. c. The range of the lows is greater than the range of the highs, so the lows cover a wider interval than the highs.

13 Lesson Practice Level B

LESSON 13.7

Practice B
For use with pages 881–885

Give two possible keys for the stem-and-leaf plot.

1.
4 | 1 1 5
5 | 0 2 7 8
6 | 3 9
7 | 4 5 6 9
8 | 0 1 3

4 | 1 = 41; 4 | 1 = 4.1

2.
0 | 0 2 3 8 9
1 | 0 2 5 5 8
2 | 4 6 8
3 | 3 3 4 5
4 | 6 7

1 | 0 = 10; 1 | 0 = 1.0

Make a stem-and-leaf plot of the data.

3. 21, 10, 14, 26, 8, 30, 17, 15, 34, 27, 36, 20, 7, 19, 25, 33, 19, 32, 12, 25

0 | 7 8
1 | 0 2 4 5 7 9 9
2 | 0 1 5 5 6 7
3 | 0 2 3 4 6

Key: 1 | 0 = 10

4. 52, 66, 61, 82, 51, 60, 62, 54, 73, 70, 89, 85, 74, 53, 61, 75, 89, 85, 77, 55

5 | 1 2 3 4 5
6 | 0 1 1 2 6
7 | 0 3 4 5 7
8 | 2 5 5 9 9

Key: 5 | 1 = 51

5. 3, 5, 11, 34, 28, 19, 4, 6, 14, 17, 22, 30, 1, 1, 9, 10, 24, 27, 33, 20, 9, 4

0 | 1 1 3 4 4 5 6 9 9
1 | 0 1 4 7 9
2 | 0 2 4 7 8
3 | 0 3 4

Key: 1 | 0 = 10

6. 0.1, 3.6, 2.2, 1.0, 2.1, 1.1, 0.2, 3.5, 3.1, 2.4, 0.3, 1.5, 2.3, 0.5, 1.2

0 | 1 2 3 5
1 | 0 1 2 5
2 | 1 2 3 4
3 | 1 5 6

Key: 0 | 1 = 0.1

Make a histogram of the data.

7. 78, 96, 72, 108, 82, 108, 99, 118, 94, 100, 86, 74

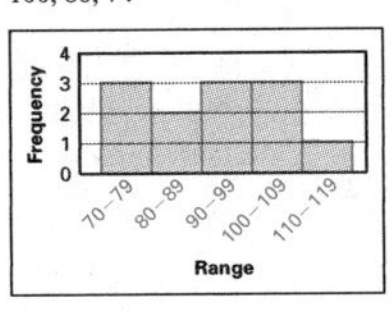

8. 58, 55, 65, 69, 66, 53, 60, 68, 61, 52, 66, 51

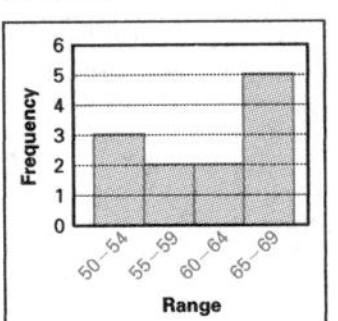

LESSON 13.7

Practice B *continued*
For use with pages 881–885

9. 4, 2.7, 3.2, 3, 3.7, 2.9, 3.1, 2.6, 3.4, 3, 3.6, 2.9

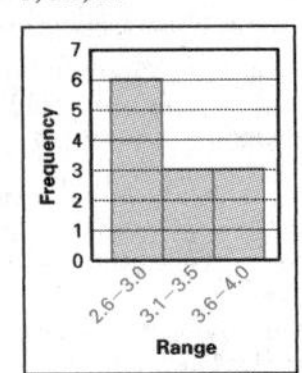

10. 18, 17.1, 15.5, 16.3, 15.2, 17.4, 16.6, 17.2, 15.1

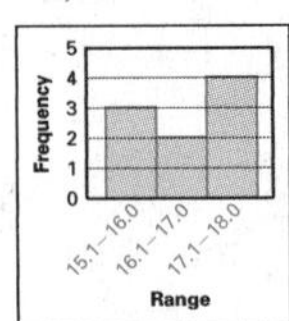

11. Mountains The table shows the heights of the world's 14 tallest mountains (in thousands of meters). Make a stem-and-leaf plot of the data.

Mountain	Height	Mountain	Height
Aconagua	7.0	Mt. Damavand	5.8
Annapurna	8.1	Mt. Everest	8.8
Cotopoxi	5.9	Mt. Godwin Austen (K-2)	8.6
Illampu	6.6	Mt. Logan	6.1
Kanchenjuga	8.6	Mt. Makalu	8.5
Kilimanjaro	5.9	Mt. McKinley	6.2
Lenin	7.1	Orizaba	5.7

5 | 7 8 9 9
6 | 1 2 6
7 | 0 1
8 | 1 5 6 6 8

Key: 5 | 7 = 5.7

12. Books A survey asked people how many books they have read in the last month. The results are shown in the table.

Books	0–5	6–11	12–17	18–23
Frequency	12	4	3	1

a. Make a histogram of the data.

b. What is the probability that a person surveyed, chosen at random, has read 0–5 books in the last month? $\frac{3}{5}$

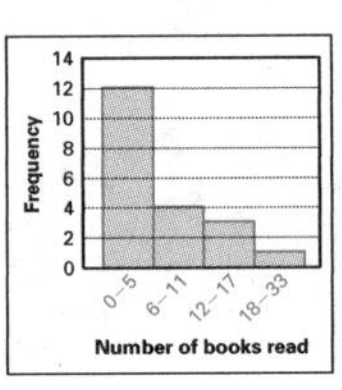

LESSON 13.8

Practice B
For use with pages 887–892

Identify the median, quartiles, and interquartile range of the data from the box-and-whisker plot. See below.

1.

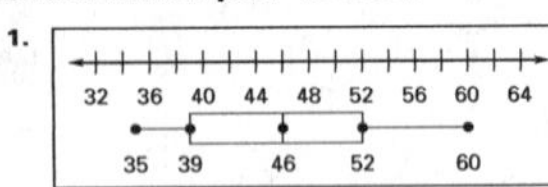

2.

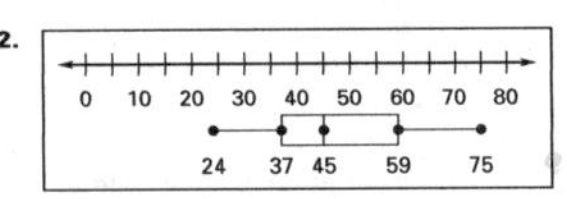

3.

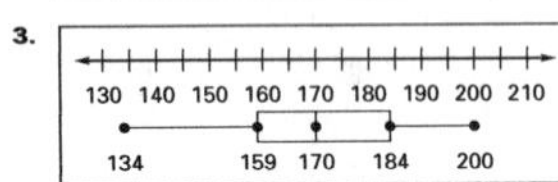

4.

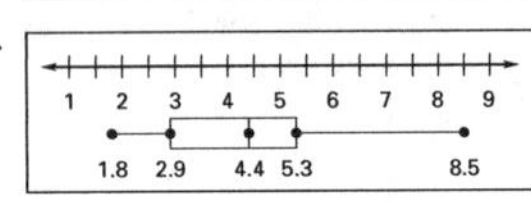

Make a box-and-whisker plot of the data.

5. 11, 33, 39, 27, 25, 31, 28, 33, 31, 49

10 15 20 25 30 35 40 45 50
11 27 31 33 49

6. 10, 16, 18, 10, 13, 7, 10, 13, 2, 48

0 5 10 15 20 25 30 35 40 45 50
2 10 11.5 16 48

7. 108, 124, 92, 110, 117, 102, 100, 98, 120

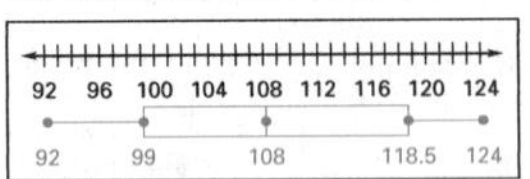

8. 350, 225, 300, 314, 210, 321, 275, 290, 310

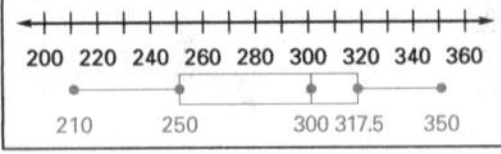

In Exercises 9 and 10, use the box-and-whisker plot.

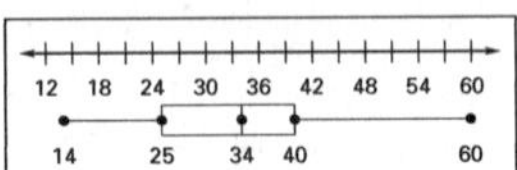

9. About what percent of the data are greater than 25? 75%

10. About what percent of the data are less than 34? 50%

1. median: 46; lower quartile: 39; upper quartile: 52; interquartile range: 13
2. median: 45; lower quartile: 37; upper quartile: 59; interquartile range: 22
3. median: 170; lower quartile: 159; upper quartile: 184; interquartile range: 25
4. median: 4.4; lower quartile: 2.9; upper quartile: 5.3; interquartile range: 2.4

LESSON 13.8

Practice B *continued*
For use with pages 887–892

Make a box-and-whisker plot of the data. Identify any outliers.

11. 17, 38, 22, 15, 13, 24, 18, 10, 20, 13, 17, 12

10 15 20 25 30 35 40
10 13 17 21 38

38 is an outlier

12. 134, 115, 105, 100, 115, 134, 200, 310, 124

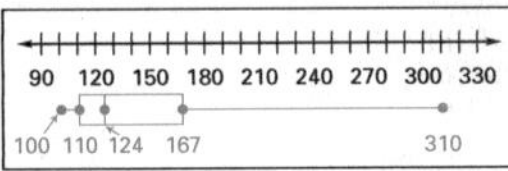

310 is an outlier

13. 45, 30, 30, 17, 15, 27, 23, 25, 26, 30, 33, 30

10 15 20 25 30 35 40 45 50
15 24 28.5 30 45

45 is an outlier

14. 730, 640, 500, 719, 620, 645, 740, 703, 690

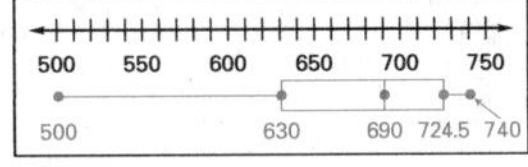

no outliers

15. Gas Prices The prices of a gallon of gasoline (in dollars) for selected countries in 2003 are listed below.

Australia: $2.20 Canada: $2.02
Germany: $4.58 Japan: $3.47
Mexico: $2.09 Taiwan: $2.16
United States: $1.59

a. Make a box-and-whisker plot of the gasoline prices.

b. Which countries, if any, had gasoline prices that can be considered outliers? no outliers

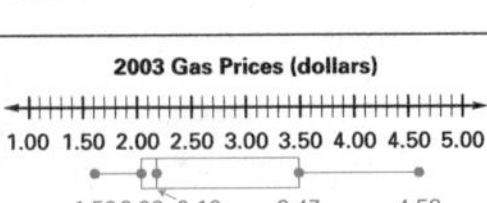

16. Supreme Court Justices The stem-and-leaf plot shows the lengths of the terms (in years) of Supreme Court justices appointed from 1902 until 1986.

Stems	Leaves
0	1 3 3 4 4 5 5 5 5 5 6 6 7 7 7 8 9
1	0 0 1 2 3 5 5 5 6 6 6 6 6 7 8 9 9
2	2 3 3 4 4 6 6 9
3	1 3 4 6

Key: 1 | 5 = 15

Term Lengths of Supreme Court Justices (years)
0 5 10 15 20 25 30 35 40
1 6 15 22 36

a. Make a box-and-whisker plot of the lengths of the terms.

b. William Douglas has served the longest so far with a term of 36 years. Can his term be considered an outlier? *Explain* why or why not. no, because 36 < 22 + 1.5(6)

13 Assessment

CHAPTER 13 Quiz 1

For use after Lessons 13.1–13.4

In Exercises 1 and 2, use the following information.

A box contains 10 green balls and 6 red balls. You choose a ball at random.

1. What is the probability that you select a green ball?
2. What is the probability that you select a red ball?

In Exercises 3 and 4, use the following information.

A bucket contains 10 balls numbered as follows: 1, 2, 2, 3, 3, 3, 3, 4, 4, 5. A single ball is randomly chosen from the bucket.

3. What is the probability of drawing a ball numbered 3?
4. What is the probability of drawing a ball with a number greater than 3?
5. Consider the number of permutations of the letters in the word BOATS. In how many ways can you arrange all of the letters?

Evaluate the expression.

6. ${}_4P_2$
7. ${}_5P_3$
8. ${}_5C_2$
9. ${}_6C_3$

Answers

1. $\frac{5}{8}$
2. $\frac{3}{8}$
3. $\frac{2}{5}$
4. $\frac{3}{10}$
5. 120
6. 12
7. 60
8. 10
9. 20

CHAPTER 13 Quiz 2

For use after Lessons 13.5–13.8

In Exercises 1 and 2, use the following information.

A community hospital conducts a survey to determine patient satisfaction. One hundred patients are randomly selected to complete the survey.

1. Identify the population.
2. Classify the sampling method.

In Exercises 3 and 4, find the range and mean absolute deviation of the data. Round to the nearest hundredth, if necessary.

3. 13, 21, 17, 8, 19, 18
4. 83, 90, 49, 57, 74, 63, 32
5. Make a histogram of the data: 1.4, 2.5, 1.7, 2.0, 1.6, 2.2, 2.7, 1.5, 2.3.

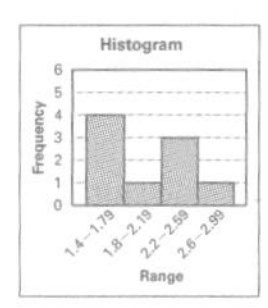

6. Make a stem-and-leaf plot of the data: 24, 12, 6, 31, 8, 17, 35, 15.

0	6 8
1	2 5 7
2	4
3	1 5

Key: 1|2 = 12

In Exercises 7 and 8, use the following information.

The ages of senior citizens who play on a chess team are given in years: 77, 65, 78, 70, 71, 86, 73, 65, 75, 69, 68.

7. Make a box-and-whisker plot of the data.

Age of Senior Citizens (years)

60 64 68 72 76 80 84 88 92

65 68 71 77 86

8. Identify any outliers.

Answers

1. all selected patients
2. random sample
3. 13; 3.67
4. 58; 15.71
5. See left.
6. See left.
7. See left.
8. 86

CHAPTER 13 Chapter Test B

For use after Chapter 13

In Exercises 1–3, use the following information.

Cystic fibrosis is an inherited disease that effects the functioning of the glands. F is the normal gene and f is the mutant gene. Any gene combination with an F results in healthy offspring. Suppose each parent has the same gene combination Ff.

1. Use a Punnett square to list the possible outcomes for their offspring.
2. What is the probability that a child will have cystic fibrosis?
3. What are the odds against a child being a carrier of cystic fibrosis?
4. The table shows the data collected from a citizen's group concerned about the safety of three intersections in their community. Find the probability that a randomly chosen vehicle will be involved in an accident at each intersection. Which intersection is the most dangerous? Explain.

Intersection	1	2	3
Number of vehicles (per day)	8330	25,250	3640
Number of accidents (per year)	110	175	45

Evaluate the expression.

5. 0!
6. ${}_{10}P_4$
7. ${}_7C_3$

Tell whether the question can be answered using *combinations* or *permutations*. Explain your choice, then answer the question.

8. On a sailboat there are 6 signal flags. The order the flags are strung on the mast determines the signal being sent. How many 3-flag signals can the captain send?
9. You are taking an online algebra quiz in which 6 questions are randomly selected from a test bank containing 50 questions. How many versions of the quiz are possible?

In Exercises 10 and 11, refer to a bag containing 13 red balls numbered 1–13 and 5 green balls numbered 14–18.

10. You choose a ball at random. What is the probability that you choose a red or an even numbered ball?
11. You randomly choose 2 balls from the bag at the same time. What is the probability that you choose a red ball and a green ball?

Answers

1. FF, Ff, Ff, ff
2. $\frac{1}{4}$
3. 1 : 1
4. $\frac{11}{833}, \frac{7}{1010}, \frac{9}{728}$ Intersection #1 because the probability is the highest.
5. 1
6. 5040
7. 35
8. permutations; the order of the flags is important; 120
9. combinations; the order of the questions is not important; 15,890,700
10. $\frac{8}{9}$
11. $\frac{65}{306}$

CHAPTER 13 Chapter Test B *continued*

For use after Chapter13

In Exercises 12–14, use the following information.

A manager of a buffet-style restaurant wants to gather information about his customers' perceptions of the cleanliness of the restaurant. The first 25 people leaving the restaurant are briefly interviewed.

12. Identify the population.
13. Classify the sampling method.
14. Tell whether the survey method used is likely to result in a biased sample.

Find the mean, median, and mode(s) of the data.

15. 1, 2, 5, 7, 8, 18, 22
16. 14, 12, 17, 15, 11, 12, 11, 13

Find the range and mean absolute deviation of the data. Round to the nearest hundredth, if necessary.

17. 48, 93, 87, 93, 59, 70
18. 1, 3, 6, 7, 5

In Exercises 19–21, use the following information.

A survey asked people how many minutes they talked during a long-distance phone call. The results are: 15, 7, 25, 10, 18, 10, 10, 23, 4, 12, 8, 6.

19. Make a stem-and-leaf plot of the data.

20. Make a histogram of the data.

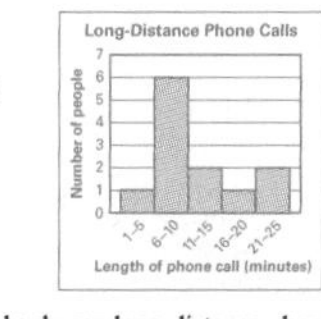

21. What is the probability that a randomly chosen long-distance phone call was more than 15 minutes?

In Exercises 22–24, use the box-and-whisker plot.

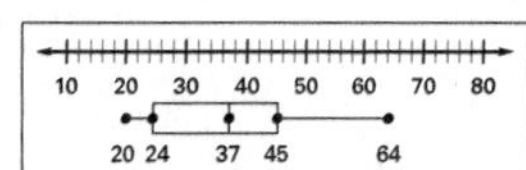

22. About what percent of the data are less than 45?
23. About what percent of the data are greater than 37?
24. Which value, if any, is an outlier?

Answers

12. all patrons of the restaurant
13. convenience sample
14. The restaurant may lack cleanliness later in the day or during other shifts, so the method may result in a biased sample.
15. 9; 7; none
16. 13; 12.5; 12 and 11
17. 45; 16
18. 6; 1.92
19. See left.
20. See left.
21. $\frac{1}{4}$
22. 75%
23. 50%
24. 64

CHAPTER 13
Standardized Test
For use after Chapter 13

Multiple Choice

1. How many possible outcomes are there when you roll two number cubes and toss one coin? C

Ⓐ 13 Ⓑ 36 Ⓒ 72 Ⓓ 144

2. The probability of an event occurring is 7 : 10. What are the odds against the event? A

Ⓐ 3 : 10 Ⓑ 10 : 3
Ⓒ 3 : 17 Ⓓ 10 : 7

3. According to a meteorologist, there is a 60% chance of thunderstorms today. What are the odds that it will *not* storm? C

Ⓐ 3 : 5 Ⓑ 2 : 3
Ⓒ 2 : 5 Ⓓ 1 : 25

4. How many ways can you arrange all the letters in the word MATH? D

Ⓐ 4 Ⓑ 6 Ⓒ 12 Ⓓ 24

5. The judges of the science fair will be awarding ribbons for first, second, and third place, plus a ribbon for honorable mention out of 15 entries. Which expression gives the number of ways the judges can award first place, second place, third place, and honorable mention? B

Ⓐ $\frac{4!}{11!}$ Ⓑ $\frac{15!}{11!}$ Ⓒ $\frac{11!}{15!}$ Ⓓ $\frac{11!}{4!}$

6. You need to go to the library, grocery store, and pharmacy. In how many orders can you visit these places? B

Ⓐ 3 Ⓑ 6 Ⓒ 9 Ⓓ 12

7. What is the value of ${}_8P_5$? C

Ⓐ 56 Ⓑ 120
Ⓒ 6720 Ⓓ 40,320

8. What is the value of ${}_6C_3$? A

Ⓐ 20 Ⓑ 120 Ⓒ 240 Ⓓ 1200

9. How many combinations of 3 letters can you make from the list A, B, C, D, and E? A

Ⓐ 10 Ⓑ 20 Ⓒ 30 Ⓓ 60

10. You are ordering a 3-topping pizza from a pizzeria. You have 10 topping choices. How many different pizzas are possible? B

Ⓐ 60 Ⓑ 120 Ⓒ 720 Ⓓ 5040

11. You roll a number cube. What is the probability that you will roll an even number *or* a number greater than 4? C

Ⓐ $0.1\overline{6}$ Ⓑ 0.5 Ⓒ $0.\overline{6}$ Ⓓ $0.8\overline{3}$

12. You flip a coin and roll a number cube. What is the probability that the coin shows tails and the number cube shows a 3? D

Ⓐ $\frac{2}{3}$ Ⓑ $\frac{1}{2}$ Ⓒ $\frac{1}{6}$ Ⓓ $\frac{1}{12}$

13. A jar contains 6 red marbles, 5 blue marbles, and 9 green marbles. What is the probability of randomly choosing a blue marble and then another blue marble if the first marble is not replaced? B

Ⓐ $\frac{1}{20}$ Ⓑ $\frac{1}{19}$ Ⓒ $\frac{1}{18}$ Ⓓ $\frac{1}{16}$

14. Which of the following statements is *not* potentially biased? C

Ⓐ Do you prefer creamy macaroni and cheese or bland rice?

Ⓑ Don't you feel the city is wasting money by building that new stadium?

Ⓒ Do you prefer shopping online or in the stores?

Ⓓ Don't you agree that the driving age should be raised to 18 so as to decrease the number of accidents?

CHAPTER 13
Standardized Test *continued*
For use after Chapter 13

15. What is the mean absolute deviation of the data? Round your answer to the nearest hundredth if necessary. D

36.2, 3.4, 76.4, 5.5, 2.8, 84.8

Ⓐ 22.54 Ⓑ 28.72
Ⓒ 32.6 Ⓓ 30.95

In Exercises 16 and 17, use the stem-and-leaf plot.

Set A		Set B
2 0	1	2 5 7 8 8
8 7 4 1	2	1 3 4 6
9 5 3 1 0	3	
8 7 4 1 1	4	2 5 8 9 9

16. What is the range of data set A? C

Ⓐ 36 Ⓑ 37 Ⓒ 38 Ⓓ 48

17. What is the mean of data set B? Round your answer to the nearest hundredth if necessary. D

Ⓐ 24.89 Ⓑ 25.48
Ⓒ 27.32 Ⓓ 29.07

18. In a box-and-whisker plot, each whisker represents about what percent of the data? A

Ⓐ 25% Ⓑ 50% Ⓒ 75% Ⓓ 100%

Gridded Answer

19. What is the median of the following data set?

0.2, 0.5, 0.2, 1.2, 0.8, 1.4, 0.6, 1.8

	0	.	7

Short Response

20. The stem-and-leaf plot shows the number of years spent teaching by teachers in your school.

0	0 3 5 5 8 8 9
1	0 1 2 2 4 5 7
2	0 1 7 9
3	6

a. Make a box-and-whisker plot of the data. See above.

b. Mrs. Smith has been teaching for 36 years. Can the number of years she has spent teaching be considered an outlier? *Explain* your reasoning.

20. a. Number of Years Spent Teaching (−5 to 40): 0, 8, 12, 20, 36

20. b. Yes, 36 would be considered an outlier because it is more than 1.5 times the upperquartile.

Extended Response

21. The table shows last season's 3-point shot statistics for your school's star basketball player.

	Point Difference at end of game		
	0–7 points	**8–14 points**	**≥ 15 points**
3-point shots attempted	12	7	3
3-point shots made	8	3	1

a. During last season, what was the probability that your school's star basketball player would make an attempted 3-point shot, regardless of the point difference? Write your answer in fraction form. See left.

b. Find the probabilities that the star player made an attempted 3-point shot when the point difference at the end of the game was 0–7 points, 8–14 points, and at least 15 points. Write your answers in fraction form. See left.

c. During what kind of games is the star player most likely to make attempted 3-point shots. *Justify* your conclusion. See left.

21. a. $\frac{6}{11}$ **b.** $\frac{2}{3}$; $\frac{3}{7}$; $\frac{1}{3}$

c. The star player is most likely to make attempted 3-point shots during games with a point difference of 0–7 points at the end of the game because the probability of the player making them is $\frac{2}{3}$, rather than $\frac{3}{7}$ and $\frac{1}{3}$.

CHAPTER 13

Alternative Assessment and Math Journal

For use after Chapter 13

Journal

1. Write a survey question that is biased in some way and explain the reason. Rewrite the question so that it is no longer biased.

Multi-Step Problem

2. The data given represent the heights (in inches) of a class of ninth grade students. The first row are the heights of the girls in the class and the second row are the heights of the boys.

Girls: 60, 58, 63, 54, 65, 66, 65, 67, 64, 59

Boys: 62, 65, 60, 69, 70, 68, 61, 65, 71, 67

a. A student is randomly selected from the class, what is the probability that the student is over 60 inches tall?

b. A student is randomly selected from the class, what is the probability that the student is a girl and over 60 inches tall?

c. A student is randomly selected from the class, what is the probability that the student is a boy or over 60 inches tall?

d. Determine the mean, median, and mode(s) of the students' heights.

e. Compare the spread of the data for the girls and boys heights using the range and the mean absolute deviation.

f. Make a stem-and-leaf plot of the entire set of data.

g. Make a box-and-whisker plot of the data for each group.

1. Complete answers should include: a survey question that is biased; an explanation of the reason for the bias; an edited survey question that is no longer biased.

2. a. $\frac{3}{4} = 0.75$ **b.** $\frac{3}{10} = 0.3$ **c.** $\frac{4}{5} = 0.8$ **d.** 63.95; 65; 65

e. Girls: range = 13, mean absolute deviation = 3.48; Boys: range = 11, mean absolute deviation = 3.2

f. Students' Heights

Girls		Boys
9 8 4	5	
7 6 5 5 4 3 0	6	0 1 2 5 5 7 8 9
	7	0 1

g.

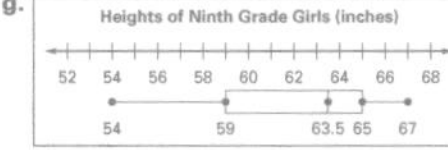

Heights of Ninth Grade Boys (inches)

58 60 62 64 66 68 70 72 74

60 62 66 69 71

CHAPTER 13

Alternative Assessment Rubric *continued*

For use after Chapter 13

Journal Solution

1. Complete answers should include:

- a survey question that is biased.
- an explanation of the reason for the bias.
- an edited survey question that is no longer biased.

Multi-Step Problem Solution

2. a. $\frac{3}{4} = 0.75$ **b.** $\frac{3}{10} = 0.3$ **c.** $\frac{4}{5} = 0.8$ **d.** 63.95; 65; 65

e. Girls: range = 13, mean absolute deviation = 3.48; Boys: range = 11, mean absolute deviation = 3.2

f. Students' Heights

Girls		Boys
9 8 4	5	
7 6 5 5 4 3 0	6	0 1 2 5 5 7 8 9
	7	0 1

g.

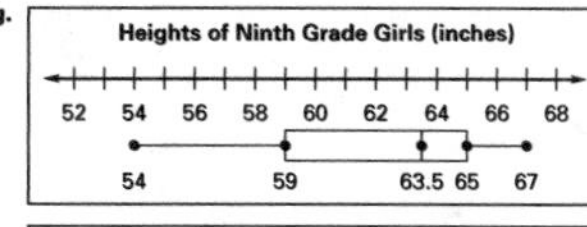

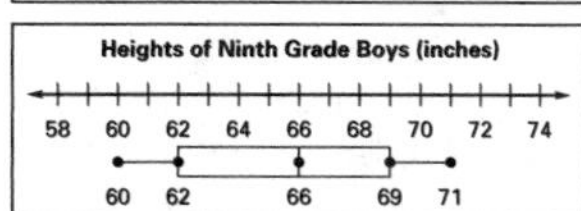

Multi-Step Problem Rubric

4 The student answers all parts of the problem correctly and completely. The student shows all work. The student's work is neat.

3 The student answers all parts of the problem. The student's work may contain one or two errors in the calculations or plots. The student shows most work. The student's work is neat.

2 The student answers all parts of the problem, but there are more than two errors in the calculations or plots. The student shows some work. The student's work is sloppy.

1 The student does not complete all parts of the problem. The student's work has several errors in the calculations and plots. The student's work is sloppy, or no work is shown.

PLAN AND PREPARE

Main Ideas

In Chapter 13, students use sample spaces to calculate probabilities and odds. They identify and use the number of permutations or the number of combinations in a set of objects to calculate the probability of an event. They find the probability of compound events by identifying whether the events are mutually exclusive or overlapping, or whether the events are dependent or independent. Students analyze data by identifying sampling methods and potentially biased samples and questions. They compare measures of central tendency: the mean, median, and mode; and they compare measures of dispersion: the range and mean absolute deviation. They analyze and display data in stem-and-leaf plots, histograms, and box-and-whisker plots.

Prerequisite Skills

- Finding the mean, median, and mode(s) of data
- Using a display to analyze data

Additional resources for reviewing prerequisite skills are:

- Skills Review Handbook, pp. 909–937
- @HomeTutor

13 Probability and Data Analysis

Before

In previous courses, you learned the following skills, which you'll use in Chapter 13: finding the mean, median, and mode(s) of data and using a display to analyze data.

Prerequisite Skills

VOCABULARY CHECK

1. Copy and complete: The _?_ of a numerical data set is the middle number when the values are written in numerical order. median

SKILLS CHECK

Find the mean, median, and mode(s) of the data. *(Review p. 918 for 13.6.)*

2. 0.2, 1.3, 0.9, 1.5, 2.1, 1.8, 0.6
1.2, 1.3, no mode

3. 103, 121, 111, 194, 99, 160, 134, 160
135.25, 127.5, 160

In Exercises 4 and 5, use the bar graph, which shows the numbers of adults who participate in leisure activities, according to the results of a survey. *(Review p. 933 for 13.7.)*

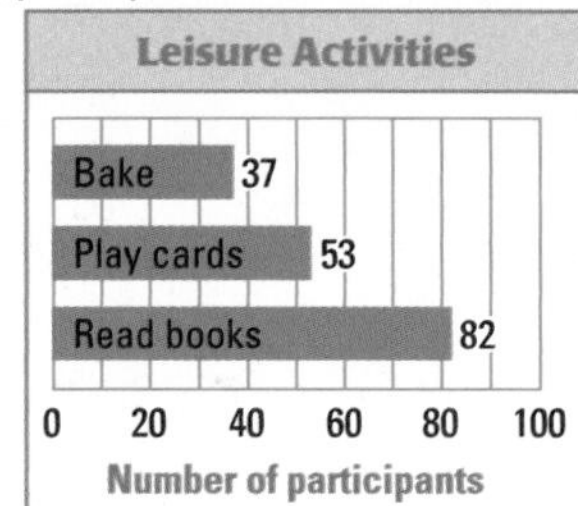

4. Which activities have fewer than 60 participants? baking, playing cards

5. Of those surveyed, how many more read books than play cards? 29 people

@HomeTutor Prerequisite skills practice at classzone.com

840

Chapter Planning Guide

Chapter 13 Resource Book
- Teaching Guide/Lesson Plan (pp. 3, 14, 24, 36, 48, 58, 71, 85)
- Project with Rubric (p. 100)

Assessment and Intervention
- Assessment Book (pp. 183–196)
- Benchmark Tests
- Reteaching and Remediation Book

Interactive Technology
- Easy Planner
- Power Presentations CD-ROM
- Activity Generator CD-ROM
- Animated Algebra
- Test Generator CD-ROM
- Online Quizzes
- eWorkbook
- eEdition
- @HomeTutor

Resources for English Learners
- Quick Reference for English Learners
- Spanish Study Guide
- Multi-Language Visual Glossary
- Student Resources in Spanish

Now

In Chapter 13, you will apply the big ideas listed below and reviewed in the Chapter Summary on page 895. You will also use the key vocabulary listed below.

Big Ideas

1. **Finding probabilities of simple and compound events**
2. **Analyzing sets of data**
3. **Making and interpreting data displays**

KEY VOCABULARY

- outcome, *p. 843*
- event, *p. 843*
- probability, *p. 843*
- odds, *p. 845*
- permutation, *p. 851*
- combination, *p. 856*
- compound event, *p. 861*
- survey, *p. 871*
- sample, *p. 871*
- measure of dispersion, *p. 876*
- range, *p. 876*
- stem-and-leaf plot, *p. 881*
- frequency, *p. 882*
- histogram, *p. 882*
- box-and-whisker plot, *p. 887*
- interquartile range, *p. 888*
- outlier, *p. 889*

Why?

You can use probability and data analysis to make predictions. For example, you can use data about a kicker's past successes in football games to find the chance of his success in the future.

Animated Algebra

The animation illustrated below for Exercise 22 on page 848 helps you to answer this question: What is the probability that the kicker makes an attempted field goal?

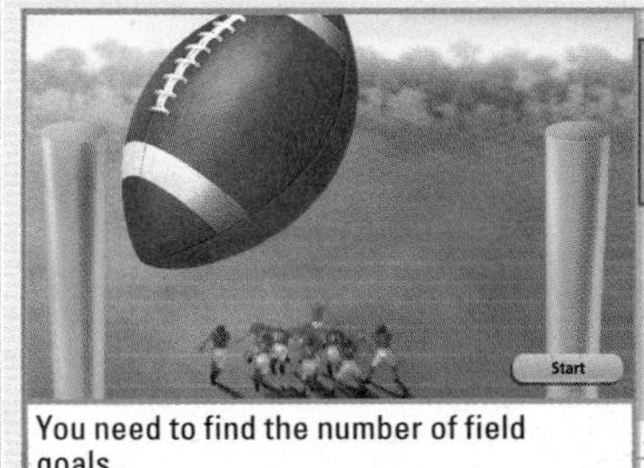

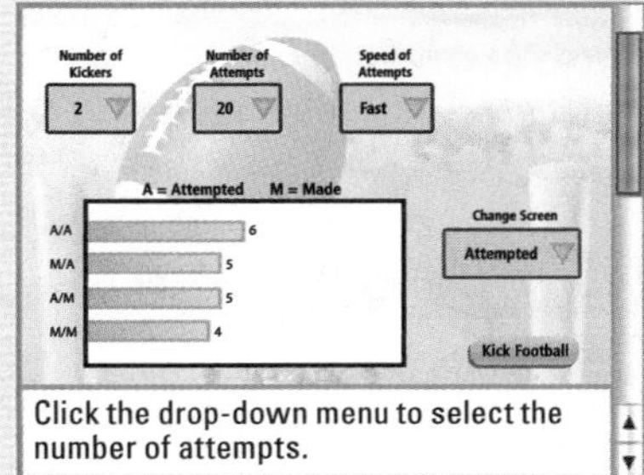

Animated Algebra at classzone.com

Other animations for Chapter 13: pages 845, 856, 875, and 887

Algebra 1 Toolkit

- Reading Strategies for Chapter 13, pp. 33–34
- Differentiated Instruction Notes, pp. 89–92
- English Learners Notes, pp. 121–122
- Inclusion Notes, pp. 153–154
- Teaching Strategies with Sample Worksheets, pp. 155–178
- Using Technology in the Classroom, pp. 179–184
- Tips for New Teachers, pp. 209–210
- Math Background Notes, pp. 235–236
- Pre-AP Strategies and Copymasters, pp. 302–303, 512–533
- Teacher Survival Activities, pp. 579–580, 605–606
- Bulletin Board Idea, p. 619
- Teacher Tool Transparencies, following p. 620

1 PLAN AND PREPARE

Explore the Concept

- Students will perform an experiment and record the results to find the likelihood of selecting the first initial, the last initial, or both first and last initials of students in the class.
- This activity leads into the study of experimental probability in Example 3 in Lesson 13.1.

Materials

Each student or group of students will need a paper bag.

Recommended Time

Work activity: 10 min

Discuss results: 5 min

Grouping

Students can work individually or in pairs. If students work in pairs, one student can draw a letter at random and the other student can record the result.

2 TEACH

Tips for Success

Tell students to make both selections before they put any tally marks in their table so that they do not end up with too many tally marks.

Key Discovery

You can use the outcomes of an experiment to predict the likelihood of an event.

3 ASSESS AND RETEACH

How many times would you expect to select the first initial of a student after 60 experiments? Answers will vary.

13.1 Find a Probability

MATERIALS • paper bag

QUESTION What is the chance that you would select the initials of a student in your class from a bag of letters?

You can perform an experiment and record the results to approximate the likelihood of selecting the initials of a student in your class.

EXPLORE Perform an experiment

STEP 1 ***Select letters***

Write each of the 26 letters of the alphabet on separate pieces of paper. Put all of the letters into a bag. Select a letter at random (without looking into the bag). Replace the letter and select a second letter at random.

STEP 2 ***Record the results***

Record the results of the selections in a table like the one shown.

- If the first letter is the first initial of any student in your class, put a tally mark in the "first initial" column.
- If the second letter is the last initial of any student in your class, put a tally mark in the "last initial" column.
- If the two letters are the first and last initials of any student in your class, put a tally mark in the "both initials" column, but do not put a tally mark in the other columns.

Perform this experiment 30 times.

	First initial	Last initial	Both initials
Tally	𝍸	𝍸 II	I
Frequency	?	?	?

STEP 3 ***Record the frequencies***

Record the *frequency*, the total number of tally marks, of each possible result.

DRAW CONCLUSIONS Use your observations to complete these excercises

1–3. Answers may vary.

1. For what fraction of the times that you performed the experiment did you select the first initial of a student in your class? the last initial? both?
2. Which of these results do you think is least likely to happen if you repeat the experiment 30 more times? *Explain* your choice.
3. **REASONING** You perform the experiment 90 times. How many times do you expect to select both the first and last initials of a student in your class? *Explain* how you made your prediction.

13.1 Find Probabilities and Odds

10.11.01 Read, interpret, predict, interpolate, extrapolate, and use information from a variety of graphs, charts, and tables.

Before You made organized lists and tree diagrams.

Now You will find sample spaces and probabilities.

Why? So you can find the likelihood of an event, as in Example 2.

Key Vocabulary
- outcome
- event
- sample space
- probability
- odds

A possible result of an experiment is an **outcome**. For instance, when you roll a number cube there are 6 possible outcomes: a 1, 2, 3, 4, 5, or 6. An **event** is an outcome or a collection of outcomes, such as rolling an odd number. The set of all possible outcomes is called a **sample space**.

EXAMPLE 1 Find a sample space

You flip a coin and roll a number cube. How many possible outcomes are in the sample space? List the possible outcomes.

REVIEW TREE DIAGRAMS
For help with tree diagrams, see p. 931.

Solution

Use a tree diagram to find the outcomes in the sample space.

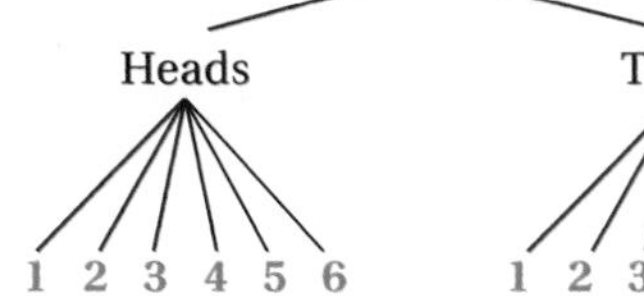

The sample space has 12 possible outcomes. They are listed below.

Heads, 1 Heads, 2 Heads, 3 Heads, 4 Heads, 5 Heads, 6
Tails, 1 Tails, 2 Tails, 3 Tails, 4 Tails, 5 Tails, 6

✓ GUIDED PRACTICE for Example 1

1. You flip 2 coins and roll a number cube. How many possible outcomes are in the sample space? List the possible outcomes.
24 outcomes; HH1, HH2, HH3, HH4, HH5, HH6, HT1, HT2, HT3, HT4, HT5, HT6, TH1, TH2, TH3, TH4, TH5, TH6, TT1, TT2, TT3, TT4, TT5, TT6

PROBABILITY The **probability of an event** is a measure of the likelihood, or chance, that the event will occur. Probability is a number from 0 to 1 and can be expressed as a decimal, fraction, or percent.

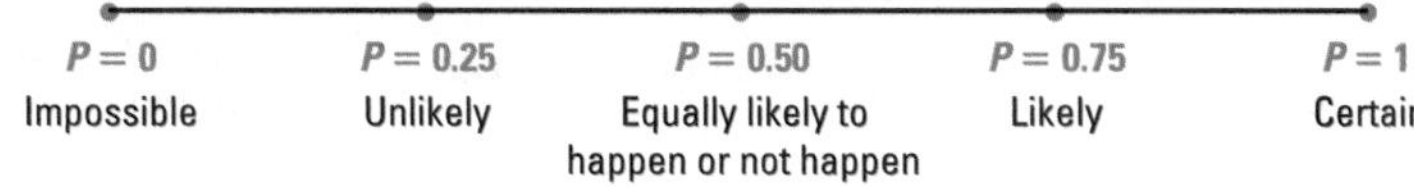

1 PLAN AND PREPARE

Warm-Up Exercises

Transparency Available

1. Use a tree diagram to find the number of possible outfits you can make using one shirt and one pair of shorts if you have 3 shirts and 4 pairs of shorts. 12 outfits
2. Use an organized list to find the number of possible ways to travel to and from Chicago if you can travel by car, bus, train, or airplane. 16 ways

Notetaking Guide

Transparency Available

Promotes interactive learning and notetaking skills, pp. 296–298.

Pacing

Basic: 1 day
Average: 1 day
Advanced: 1 day
Block: 0.5 block with 13.2
- See *Teaching Guide/Lesson Plan.*

2 FOCUS AND MOTIVATE

Essential Question

Big Idea 1, p. 841

How do you find the probability an event? **Tell students they will learn how to answer this question by comparing favorable and possible outcomes in a theoretical situation and successes and trials in an experimental situation.**

Resource Planning Guide

Chapter Resource Book
- Teaching Guide/Lesson Plan (pp. 3–4)
- Practice levels A, B, C (pp. 6–8)
- Study Guide (pp. 9–10)
- Catch-up for Absent Students (p. 11)
- Application (p. 12)
- Challenge (p. 13)

Workbooks
- Notetaking Guide (pp. 296–298)
- Practice Workbook (pp. 196–197)

Teaching Options
- **Power Presentations CD-ROM** provides dynamic electronic teaching resources for the classroom.
- **Activity Generator CD-ROM** provides editable activities for all ability levels.

Interactive Technology
- Easy Planner
- Power Presentations CD-ROM
- Activity Generator CD-ROM
- Animated Algebra
- Test Generator CD-ROM
- Online Quiz
- eWorkbook
- eEdition
- @HomeTutor

Resources for English Learners
- Quick Reference for English Learners
- Spanish Study Guide
- Multi-Language Visual Glossary
- Student Resources in Spanish

See also the *Algebra 1 Toolkit* for more strategies for meeting individual needs.

THEORETICAL PROBABILITY The outcomes for a specified event are called *favorable outcomes.* When all outcomes are equally likely, the **theoretical probability** of the event can be found using the following:

$$\textbf{Theoretical probability} = \frac{\textbf{Number of favorable outcomes}}{\textbf{Total number of outcomes}}$$

The probability of event A is written as $P(A)$.

EXAMPLE 2 Find a theoretical probability

T-SHIRTS You and your friends designed T-shirts with silk screened emblems, and you are selling the T-shirts to raise money. The table below shows the number of T-shirts you have in each design. A student chooses a T-shirt at random. What is the probability that the student chooses a red T-shirt?

	Gold emblem	Silver emblem
Green T-shirt	10	8
Red T-shirt	6	6

Solution

You and your friends have a total of $10 + 6 + 8 + 6 = 30$ T-shirts. So, there are 30 possible outcomes. Of all the T-shirts, 12 T-shirts are red. There are 12 favorable outcomes.

$$P(\text{red T-shirt}) = \frac{\text{Number of favorable outcomes}}{\text{Total number of outcomes}}$$

$$= \frac{\text{Number of red T-shirts}}{\text{Total number of T-shirts}}$$

$$= \frac{12}{30}$$

$$= \frac{2}{5}$$

GUIDED PRACTICE for Example 2

2. **T-SHIRTS** In Example 2, what is the probability that the student chooses a T-shirt with a gold emblem? $\frac{8}{15}$
3. You toss a coin and roll a number cube. What is the probability that the coin shows tails and the number cube shows 4? $\frac{1}{12}$

EXPERIMENTAL PROBABILITY An **experimental probability** is based on repeated *trials* of an experiment. The number of trials is the number of times the experiment is performed. Each trial in which a favorable outcome occurs is called a *success.*

$$\textbf{Experimental probability} = \frac{\textbf{Number of successes}}{\textbf{Number of trials}}$$

Motivating the Lesson

In a contest on a local radio station, one female and one male teen will be chosen at random to be on the air for an hour with a disc jockey. If you enter the contest and you know the number of other teens of your gender who entered the contest, you can determine the likelihood that you will be chosen as one of the teen disc jockeys.

3 TEACH

Extra Example 1

You flip a coin twice. How many possible outcomes are in the sample space? List the possible outcomes. The sample space has 4 outcomes. heads, heads; heads, tails; tails, heads; tails, tails

Key Question to Ask for Example 1

- Does the sample space change if you flip the coin first and then roll the number cube? Explain. No; each number on the number cube will still be paired with heads and also with tails.

Extra Example 2

A department store is offering a discount on sunglasses. The table shows the number of each type of discounted sunglasses. You choose a pair at random. What is the probability that the pair you choose is polarized? $\frac{3}{7}$

	Green Lens	Brown Lens
Polarized	8	4
Mirrored	7	9

Differentiated Instruction

Below Level Ask students to find the probability of choosing a T-shirt for each of the four designs. Then ask which design is most likely to be chosen at random and which design is least likely to be chosen. Have them support their answers using the probabilities they found for each of the designs. Then have them reproduce the probability line on page 843 and insert the probabilities for each T-shirt design on the line. Suggest that they include the probability of choosing a T-shirt that is red, that is green, that has a gold emblem, and that has a silver emblem. See also the *Algebra 1 Toolkit* for more strategies.

EXAMPLE 3 Standardized Test Practice

Each section of the spinner shown has the same area. The spinner was spun 20 times. The table shows the results. For which color is the experimental probability of stopping on the color the same as the theoretical probability?

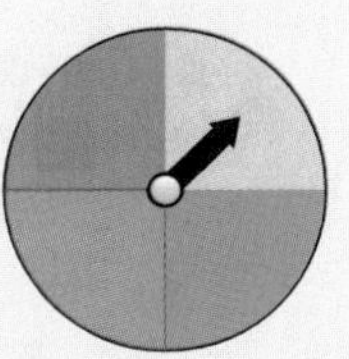

Spinner Results			
Red	Green	Blue	Yellow
5	9	3	3

(A) Red (B) Green (C) Blue (D) Yellow

Solution

The theoretical probability of stopping on each of the four colors is $\frac{1}{4}$. Use the outcomes in the table to find the experimental probabilities.

$P(\text{red}) = \frac{5}{20} = \frac{1}{4}$ $P(\text{green}) = \frac{9}{20}$ $P(\text{blue}) = \frac{3}{20}$ $P(\text{yellow}) = \frac{3}{20}$

▶ The correct answer is A. (A) (B) (C) (D)

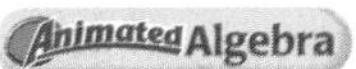 at classzone.com

ODDS The odds of an event compare the number of favorable and unfavorable outcomes when all outcomes are equally likely.

$$\textbf{Odds in favor} = \frac{\text{Number of favorable outcomes}}{\text{Number of unfavorable outcomes}}$$

$$\textbf{Odds against} = \frac{\text{Number of unfavorable outcomes}}{\text{Number of favorable outcomes}}$$

EXAMPLE 4 Find the odds

READING
Odds are read as the ratio of one number to another. For instance, the odds $\frac{3}{1}$ are read as "three to one." Odds are usually written as *a* : *b*.

SPINNER In Example 3, find the odds against stopping on green.

Solution

The 4 possible outcomes are all equally likely. Green is the 1 favorable outcome. The other 3 colors are unfavorable outcomes.

$$\text{Odds against green} = \frac{\text{Number of unfavorable outcomes}}{\text{Number of favorable outcomes}} = \frac{3}{1} \text{ or } 3:1.$$

GUIDED PRACTICE for Examples 3 and 4

4. In Example 3, for which color is the experimental probability of stopping on the color greater than the theoretical probability? green
5. In Example 3, what are the odds in favor of stopping on blue? $\frac{1}{3}$ or 1 : 3

Extra Example 3

A bag contains one blue, one green, one yellow, and one red ball. A ball is drawn at random from the bag and then replaced. The table shows the results for 24 drawings. For which color of ball is the experimental probability of drawing the color the same as the theoretical probability?

Random Drawing Results			
Blue	Green	Yellow	Red
4	6	9	5

(A) Blue (B) Green
(C) Red (D) Yellow

The correct answer is B.

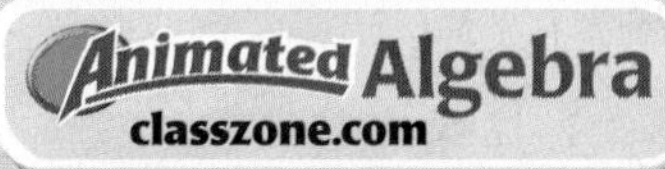

An **Animated Algebra** activity is available on-line for **Example 3.** This activity is also available on the **Power Presentations CD-ROM**.

Extra Example 4

In Extra Example 3, find the odds in favor of drawing a yellow ball. 1:3

Closing the Lesson

Have students summarize the major points of the lesson and answer the Essential Question: How do you find the probability of an event?

- Theoretical probability is based on all possible outcomes being equally likely.
- Experimental probability is based on repeated trials, which is the number of times the experiment is performed.

The theoretical probability of an event is the ratio of the number of favorable outcomes to the total number of outcomes. The experimental probability of an event is the ratio of the number of successes of the experiment to the number of trials.

13.1 EXERCISES

HOMEWORK KEY
○ = **WORKED-OUT SOLUTIONS** on p. WS31 for Exs. 3 and 21
★ = **STANDARDIZED TEST PRACTICE** Exs. 2, 14–16, 21, and 22

4 PRACTICE AND APPLY

Assignment Guide

Answer Transparencies available for all exercises

Basic:
Day 1: SaRH p. 932 Exs. 4–8
pp. 846–848
Exs. 1–15, 19–21, 24–26

Average:
Day 1: pp. 846–848
Exs. 1, 2–12 even, 13–17, 19–22, 24–26

Advanced:
Day 1: pp. 846–848
Exs. 1, 2–6 even, 10, 12, 13–26*

Block:
pp. 846–848
Exs. 1, 2–12 even, 13–17, 19–22, 24–26 (with 13.2)

Differentiated Instruction

See *Algebra 1 Best Practices Toolkit* for suggestions on addressing the needs of a diverse classroom.

Homework Check

For a quick check of student understanding of key concepts, go over the following exercises:

Basic: 4, 7, 9, 11, 21
Average: 4, 10, 12, 19, 21
Advanced: 6, 10, 14, 20, 21

Extra Practice

- Student Edition, p. 950
- Chapter 13 Resource Book: Practice levels A, B, C, pp. 6–8

Practice Worksheet

An easily-readable reduced practice page (with answers) for this lesson can be found on p. 840C.

SKILL PRACTICE

A

1. **VOCABULARY** Copy and complete: A number that describes the likelihood of an event is the _?_ of the event. probability

2. ★ **WRITING** *Explain* how the probability of an event differs from the odds in favor of the event when all outcomes are equally likely. See margin.

EXAMPLE 1 on p. 843 for Exs. 3–6

SAMPLE SPACE In Exercises 3–6, find the number of possible outcomes in the sample space. Then list the possible outcomes.

3. A bag contains 4 red cards numbered 1–4, 4 white cards numbered 1–4, and 4 black cards numbered 1–4. You choose a card at random. 12 outcomes; R1, R2, R3, R4, W1, W2, W3, W4, B1, B2, B3, B4

4. You toss two coins. 4 outcomes; HH, TT, HT, TH

5. You roll a number cube and toss three coins. See margin.

6. You roll two number cubes. See margin.

EXAMPLE 2 on p. 844 for Exs. 7–8

PROBABILITY AND ODDS In Exercises 7–13, refer to the spinner shown. The spinner is divided into sections with the same area.

7. What is the probability that the spinner stops on a multiple of 3? $\frac{9}{10}$

8. **ERROR ANALYSIS** *Describe* and correct the error in finding the probability of stopping on a multiple of 9.

$$\frac{\text{Number of favorable outcomes}}{\text{Total number of outcomes}} = \frac{2}{10} = \frac{1}{5}$$

There are 3 favorable outcomes (landing on 9, 18, and 27); $\frac{3}{10}$.

EXAMPLE 3 on p. 845 for Exs. 9–10

9. You spin the spinner 30 times. It stops on 12 three times. What is the experimental probability of stopping on 12? $\frac{1}{10}$

10. You spin the spinner 10 times. It stops on an even number 6 times. What is the experimental probability of stopping on an even number? $\frac{3}{5}$

EXAMPLE 4 on p. 845 for Exs. 11–14

11. What are the odds in favor of stopping on a multiple of 4? $\frac{3}{7}$ or 3 : 7

12. What are the odds against stopping on a number less than 12? $\frac{7}{3}$ or 7 : 3

13. **ERROR ANALYSIS** *Describe* and correct the error in finding the odds in favor of stopping on a multiple of 3. See margin.

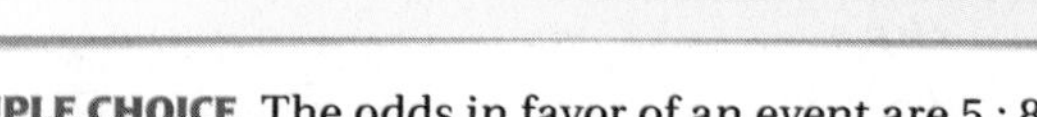

$$\text{Odds in favor of a multiple of 3} = \frac{\text{Number of favorable outcomes}}{\text{Total number of outcomes}} = \frac{9}{10} \text{ or } 9:10$$

B

14. ★ **MULTIPLE CHOICE** The odds in favor of an event are 5 : 8. What are the odds against the event? D

(A) 3 : 8 (B) 8 : 3 (C) 5 : 8 (D) 8 : 5

15. ★ **OPEN-ENDED** *Describe* a real-world event whose probability is 0. *Describe* another real-world event whose probability is 1. *Sample answer:* Rolling a standard number cube and getting a 0, flipping a coin and getting heads or tails.

2. *Sample answer:* The probability of an event is the number of favorable outcomes divided by the number of possible outcomes, while the odds in favor of an event is the number of favorable outcomes divided by the number of unfavorable outcomes.

5. 48; HHH1, HHH2, HHH3, HHH4, HHH5, HHH6, HHT1, HHT2, HHT3, HHT4, HHT5, HHT6, HTH1, HTH2, HTH3, HTH4, HTH5, HTH6, HTT1, HTT2, HTT3, HTT4, HTT5, HTT6, THH1, THH2, THH3, THH4, THH5, THH6, THT1, THT2, THT3, THT4, THT5, THT6, TTH1, TTH2, TTH3, TTH4, TTH5, TTH6, TTT1, TTT2, TTT3, TTT4, TTT5, TTT6

6. 36 outcomes; 1-1, 1-2, 1-3, 1-4, 1-5, 1-6, 2-1, 2-2, 2-3, 2-4, 2-5, 2-6, 3-1, 3-2, 3-3, 3-4, 3-5, 3-6, 4-1, 4-2, 4-3, 4-4, 4-5, 4-6, 5-1, 5-2, 5-3, 5-4, 5-5, 5-6, 6-1, 6-2, 6-3, 6-4, 6-5, 6-6

13. See Additional Answers beginning on p. AA1.

16. ★ **MULTIPLE CHOICE** According to a meteorologist, there is a 40% chance that it will rain today. What are the odds in favor of rain? B

Ⓐ 2 : 5 Ⓑ 2 : 3 Ⓒ 3 : 2 Ⓓ 4 : 1

17. **NUMBER CUBES** Make a table showing all of the possible sums that result from rolling two number cubes. (Columns represent the possible outcomes of the first number cube. Rows represent the possible outcomes of the second number cube. The cells of the table represent the sums of the two outcomes.) Then find the probability of rolling each sum. See margin.

C 18. **CHALLENGE** A bag holds red, white, and blue marbles. You randomly draw a marble from the bag. The odds against drawing a white marble are 47 : 3.

a. There are fewer than 100 marbles in the bag. How many marbles are in the bag? *Justify* your answer. See margin.

b. The probability of drawing a red marble is 0.5. What is the probability of drawing a blue marble? *Explain* how you found your answer. See margin.

PROBLEM SOLVING

EXAMPLE 2 A on p. 844 for Exs. 19–20

19. **MUSIC PROGRAM** You have created a playlist of 7 songs on your MP3 player. You play these songs in a random shuffle, where each song has an equally likely chance of being played. What is the probability that the second song on the list will be played first? $\frac{1}{7}$

@HomeTutor for problem solving help at classzone.com

20. **SURVEY** A survey asked a total of 600 students (100 male students and 100 female students who were 11, 13, and 15 years old) about their exercise habits. The table shows the numbers of students who said they exercise 2 hours or more each week.

	11 years	13 years	15 years
Female	53	57	51
Male	65	68	67

a. What is the probability that a randomly selected female student who participated in this survey exercises 2 hours or more each week? $\frac{161}{300}$

b. What is the probability that a randomly selected 15-year-old student who participated in this survey exercises 2 hours or more each week? $\frac{59}{100}$

c. What is the probability that a randomly selected student who participated in this survey exercises 2 hours or more each week? $\frac{361}{600}$

@HomeTutor for problem solving help at classzone.com

EXAMPLES 2 and 4 on pp. 844–845 for Ex. 21

21. ★ **SHORT RESPONSE** Suppose there are 15 girls and 12 boys in your homeroom. The teacher chooses one student representative at random. What is the probability that a boy is chosen? What are the odds in favor of choosing a boy? *Explain* how the probablity and odds are related. See margin.

Avoiding Common Errors

Exercises 7, 9–14 Students often confuse probabilities and odds and experimental and theoretical probability. Remind students that experimental probabilities are based on the number of trials or experiments, and that theoretical probability and odds are based on equally likely outcomes. Suggest that students check each of their answers against the respective formulas for probabilities and odds.

Study Strategy

Exercise 16 Suggest that students ask themselves what the chances are that it will not rain and then compare favorable chances to unfavorable chances to find the odds.

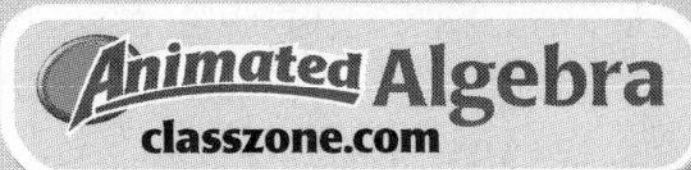

An **Animated Algebra** activity is available on-line for **Exercise 22**. This activity is also available on the **Power Presentations CD-ROM**.

18a. 50 marbles. *Sample answer:* The odds against picking a white marble says that the number of non-white marbles to white marbles must be 47 : 3. The only pair of numbers that simplifies to this ratio and whose sum is less than 100 total marbles is 47 and 3. There are 47 non-white marbles and 3 white marbles, for a total of 50 marbles.

18b. 0.44. *Sample answer:* There are 50 marbles in the bag, and half of them are blue. So there are 25 blue marbles and 3 white marbles. The rest are red, so there are 22 red marbles. The probability that a red marble is drawn is $\frac{22}{50} = 0.44$.

21. See Additional Answers beginning on p. AA1.

17.

	1	2	3	4	5	6
1	2	3	4	5	6	7
2	3	4	5	6	7	8
3	4	5	6	7	8	9
4	5	6	7	8	9	10
5	6	7	8	9	10	11
6	7	8	9	10	11	12

$P(2) = \frac{1}{36}$; $P(3) = \frac{1}{18}$; $P(4) = \frac{1}{12}$; $P(5) = \frac{1}{9}$; $P(6) = \frac{5}{36}$; $P(7) = \frac{1}{6}$; $P(8) = \frac{5}{36}$; $P(9) = \frac{1}{9}$; $P(10) = \frac{1}{12}$; $P(11) = \frac{1}{18}$; $P(12) = \frac{1}{36}$

5 ASSESS AND RETEACH

Daily Homework Quiz

Transparency Available

1. The table shows the number of students in your history class. Your teacher chooses one student at random to give an oral report. What is the probability the student is female? $\frac{7}{15}$

	9th Grade	10th Grade
Male	12	4
Female	8	6

2. A bag contains 8 white marbles, 6 red marbles, and 12 blue marbles. Find the odds against choosing a white marble. 9:4

Online Quiz

Available at **classzone.com**

Diagnosis/Remediation

- Practice A, B, C in Chapter 13 Resource Book, pp. 6–8
- Study Guide in Chapter13 Resource Book, pp. 9–10
- Practice Workbook, pp. 196–197
- @HomeTutor

Challenge

Additional challenge is available in the Chapter 13 Resource Book, p. 13.

B **22.** ★ **EXTENDED RESPONSE** The table shows the 2003 regular season field goal statistics for kicker Adam Vinatieri.

	Point difference at end of game		
	0–7 points	8–14 points	≥ 15 points
Field goals attempted	20	11	3
Field goals made	16	7	2

a. During the 2003 regular season, what was the probability that Adam Vinatieri would make an attempted field goal, regardless of the point difference? $\frac{25}{34}$

b. Find the probabilities that Vinatieri made an attempted field goal when the point difference at the end of the game was 0–7 points, 8–14 points, and at least 15 points.

c. During what kinds of games was Adam Vinatieri most likely to make attempted field goals? *Justify* your answer.

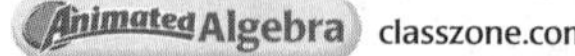
classzone.com

22b. 0–7: $\frac{4}{5}$, 8–14: $\frac{7}{11}$, ≥ 15: $\frac{2}{3}$

22c. Games where the point difference is 0–7. *Sample answer:* In these games he mades 80% of his field goals, while during his other games he made about 64%.

C **23.** **CHALLENGE** The table shows the results of Congressional elections that involved incumbent candidates (representatives or senators who ran for re-election) during the period 1980–2000.

	Incumbent representatives		Incumbent senators	
	Ran	Re-elected	Ran	Re-elected
Presidential election year	2373	2235	163	130
Midterm election year	1984	1873	145	130

a. Did a representative or a senator have a better chance of being re-elected? *Justify* your answer using the data in the table.

b. Did a member of Congress have a better chance of being re-elected during a presidential election year than during a midterm election year? *Justify* your answer.

23a. A representative. *Sample answer:* The data in the table show that about 94% of representatives that ran for re-election were re-elected, while only about 84% of senators running for re-election were re-elected.

23b. No. *Sample answer:* Members of Congress have about a 94% chance of being re-elected during midterm election years, and about a 93% chance in presidential election years.

ILLINOIS MIXED REVIEW

TEST PRACTICE at classzone.com

24. A bag of jelly beans contains 23% green, 36% blue, 22% red, and 19% yellow jelly beans. Carl put 350 of the mixed jelly beans in a bowl. Which proportion can be used to find r, the total number of red jelly beans in the bowl?

Ⓐ $\frac{350}{r} = \frac{22}{100}$ Ⓑ $\frac{22}{100} = \frac{r}{350}$ B

Ⓒ $\frac{100}{350} = \frac{r}{22}$ Ⓓ $\frac{22}{100} = \frac{350}{r}$

Perform Simulations

Extension — *Use after Lesson 13.1*

GOAL Perform simulations to make predictions.

Key Vocabulary
- **simulation**

A **simulation** is an experiment that you can perform to make predictions about real-world situations.

EXAMPLE 1 Perform a simulation

CONCESSION PRIZES Each time you buy an item from the concession stand at a baseball stadium, you receive a prize coupon, chosen at random. There is an equal chance of winning each prize from the following list: hot dog, popcorn, peanuts, pretzel, ice cream, and small drink. About how many times must you buy an item from the concession stand before you win each prize at least once?

Solution

You can perform a simulation to answer the question.

STEP 1 **Write** each prize on a separate piece of paper. Put the pieces of paper in a container.

STEP 2 **Draw** a piece of paper from the container at random. Record the result in a table like the one shown. Put the piece of paper back in the container. Repeat until you put a tally mark in the last empty cell of the table.

Prize	Hot dog	Popcorn	Peanuts	Pretzel	Ice cream	Small drink
Tally	I	IIII	II	~~IIII~~	~~IIII~~ I	II

The sum of all of the tally marks is the number of times you must buy an item from the concession stand before you win each prize at least once.

▶ In this simulation, you must buy an item from the concession stand 20 times.

USING A GRAPHING CALCULATOR You can also use the random integer generator on a graphing calculator to perform simulations.

The random integer generator is found by pressing the MATH key and selecting the PRB menu. It is the fifth item on the list and is displayed as randInt(.

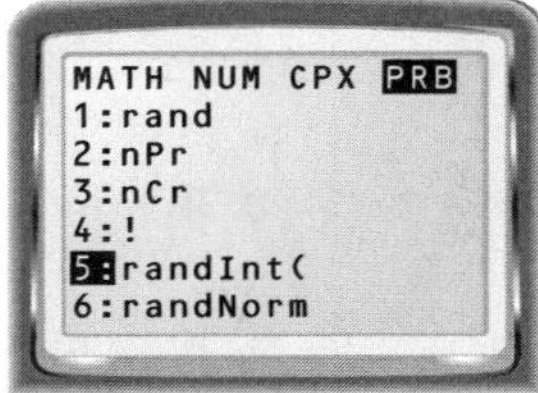

1 PLAN AND PREPARE

Warm-Up Exercises

1. You bought 4 raffle tickets for a weekend trip for two in New York City. If 120 tickets were sold, what is the probability you will win the raffle? $\frac{1}{30}$
2. A sports store is giving away 4 basketballs, 6 footballs, and 8 soccer balls in a random drawing. If you are the first to draw a winning ticket, what is the probability you will win a football? $\frac{1}{3}$

2 FOCUS AND MOTIVATE

Essential Question

Big Idea 1, p.841

How do you perform simulations to make predictions? **Tell students they will learn how to answer this question by using the results of experiments to make predictions.**

3 TEACH

Extra Example 1

Each time you buy an item at a movie store, you receive one of eight prize coupons chosen at random. There is an equal chance of winning each prize. Perform a simulation to predict the number of items you must buy before you win each prize at least once. **Answers will vary.**

NCTM STANDARDS

Standard 5: Understand basic concepts of probability

Standard 10: Use representations to solve problems

Extra Example 2

An electronics store offers a game card for each purchase of $100 or more. Each card has one circle to scratch. There is a $\frac{1}{2}$ chance that the scratched circle will show "Try Again," a $\frac{1}{12}$ chance that it will show a digital camera, a $\frac{1}{6}$ chance that it will show a DVD, and a $\frac{1}{4}$ chance that it will show a computer mouse. Use a calculator simulation to predict the number of game cards must you scratch before you win a digital camera. Answers will vary.

Closing the Lesson

Have students summarize the major points of the lesson and answer the Essential Question: How do you perform simulations to make predictions?

- A simulation is an experiment that you can perform to make a prediction about a real-world situation.
- Two simulations of the same event can have different results.

One way to perform a simulation is to write each possible outcome on a slip of paper, place the slips of paper in a container, and then randomly draw a slip and record the results until you have satisfied the goal of the experiment. Another way to perform a simulation is to use the random integer generator on a graphing calculator.

4 PRACTICE AND APPLY

Avoiding Common Errors

Exercise 1 Students may think that the number of drawings increases by one because the number of items increases by one. Remind students that the probability of selecting each item is equal, so each item must be present at the start of the simulation.

EXAMPLE 2 Perform a simulation using technology

GAME CARDS You receive a game card with every purchase at a sandwich shop. Each card has two circles to scratch. One circle reveals a prize, and the other says "Not a Winner." You cannot claim a prize if you scratch both circles. There is a $\frac{1}{6}$ chance that a card is for a CD, a $\frac{1}{2}$ chance that it is for a drink, and a $\frac{1}{3}$ chance that it is for a sandwich. About how many game cards must you scratch before you win a CD?

Solution

STEP 1 **Use** List 1 to show whether you scratch the circle with the prize. Generate a list of 50 random 1s and 0s. Each 1 means that you scratch the circle with the prize, and each 0 means that you scratch "Not a Winner."

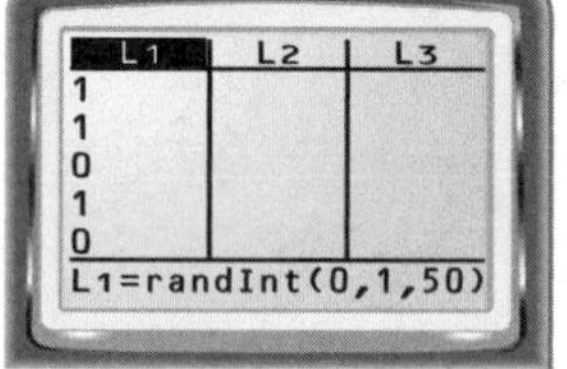

Press STAT and select Edit. Highlight L_1. Enter randInt(0,1,50).

STEP 2 **Use** List 2 to show whether your game card contains the CD as the prize. Generate a list of 50 random integers from 1 to 6. Each 1 represents a prize card with a CD.

Highlight L_2. Enter randInt(1,6,50).

STEP 3 **Compare** the results of your two lists using List 3. Multiply the numbers from List 1 and List 2. Each 0 in List 3 means that you chose the wrong circle, so the prize does not matter. Because $1 \cdot 1 = 1$, you chose the correct circle *and* your card contains the CD prize when you see a 1 in L_3.

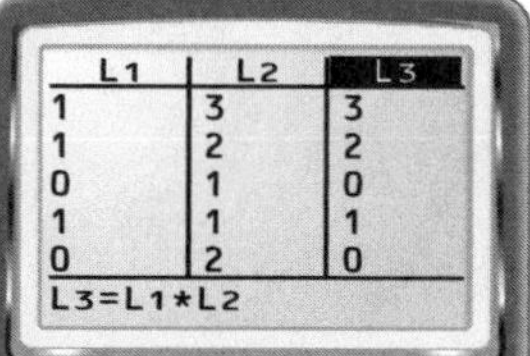

Highlight L_3. Enter $L_1 * L_2$.

STEP 4 **Find** the first occurrence of a 1 in List 3. In this simulation, you can see that the first occurrence of a 1 in List 3 happens after 4 trials.

▶ For this simulation, you must scratch 4 game cards before you win a CD.

PRACTICE

EXAMPLE 1 on p. 849 for Exs. 1–3

1. In Example 1, suppose you can receive a prize coupon for nachos in addition to the items listed in the example. About how many times must you buy an item from the concession stand before you win each prize at least once? *Explain* how you found your answer. Answers will vary.

EXAMPLE 2 on p. 850 for Exs. 2–3

2. In Example 2, about how many game cards must you scratch before you win one of each prize? *Explain* how you found your answer. Answers will vary.
3. In Example 2, there are 3 prizes. *Explain* why the results of the simulation would be inaccurate if you generated random integers from 1 to 3. See margin.

3. *Sample answer:* There are 3 prizes to win, but since the prizes do not have an equal likelihood of being won, generating a list of random integers from 1 to 3 wouldn't represent the situation. The probability of winning a CD is $\frac{1}{6}$, so if there were only 3 possible outcomes in the simulation you couldn't represent winning a CD properly.

13.2 Find Probabilities Using Permutations

10.11.10 Apply counting techniques (e.g., permutations, combinations, Fundamental Counting Principle).

Before You used the counting principle.

Now You will use the formula for the number of permutations.

Why? So you can find the number of possible arrangements, as in Ex. 38.

Key Vocabulary
- **permutation**
- ***n* factorial**

A **permutation** is an arrangement of objects in which order is important. For instance, the 6 possible permutations of the letters A, B, and C are shown.

ABC ACB BAC BCA CAB CBA

EXAMPLE 1 Count permutations

Consider the number of permutations of the letters in the word JULY.

a. In how many ways can you arrange all of the letters?

b. In how many ways can you arrange 2 of the letters?

Solution

a. Use the counting principle to find the number of permutations of the letters in the word JULY.

Number of permutations	=	Choices for 1st letter	•	Choices for 2nd letter	•	Choices for 3rd letter	•	Choices for 4th letter
	=	**4**	•	**3**	•	**2**	•	**1**
	= **24**							

▶ There are 24 ways you can arrange all of the letters in the word JULY.

b. When arranging 2 letters of the word JULY, you have 4 choices for the first letter and 3 choices for the second letter.

Number of permutations = Choices for 1st letter • Choices for 2nd letter

$= 4 \cdot 3$

$= 12$

▶ There are 12 ways you can arrange 2 of the letters in the word JULY.

REVIEW COUNTING PRINCIPLE
For help with using the counting principle, see p. 931.

GUIDED PRACTICE for Example 1

1. In how many ways can you arrange the letters in the word MOUSE? 120 ways
2. In how many ways can you arrange 3 of the letters in the word ORANGE? 120 ways

1 PLAN AND PREPARE

Warm-Up Exercises

Transparency Available

1. There are 8 football teams in your district and 7 teams in a neighboring district. How many teams can you match up for games? 56
2. A padlock has 9 numbers and uses 3 of them in sequence to open the lock. If you randomly choose 3 numbers, what is the probability that you choose the correct sequence? $\frac{1}{729}$

Notetaking Guide

Transparency Available

Promotes interactive learning and notetaking skills, pp. 299–301.

Pacing

Basic: 2 days
Average: 2 days
Advanced: 2 days
Block: 0.5 block with 13.1
0.5 block with 13.3
- See *Teaching Guide/Lesson Plan.*

2 FOCUS AND MOTIVATE

Essential Question

Big Idea 1, p. 841

How do you use the formula for permutations? Tell students they will learn how to answer this question by finding the number of arrangements of *n* objects.

Resource Planning Guide

Chapter Resource Book
- Teaching Guide/Lesson Plan (pp. 14–15)
- Practice levels A, B, C (pp. 16–18)
- Study Guide (pp. 19–20)
- Catch-up for Absent Students (p. 21)
- Problem Solving Workshop (p. 22)
- Challenge (p. 23)

Workbooks
- Notetaking Guide (pp. 299–301)
- Practice Workbook (pp. 198–199)

Teaching Options
- **Power Presentations CD-ROM** provides dynamic electronic teaching resources for the classroom.
- **Activity Generator CD-ROM** provides editable activities for all ability levels.

Interactive Technology
- Easy Planner
- Power Presentations CD-ROM
- Activity Generator CD-ROM
- Animated Algebra
- Test Generator CD-ROM
- Online Quiz
- eWorkbook
- eEdition
- @HomeTutor

Resources for English Learners
- Quick Reference for English Learners
- Spanish Study Guide
- Multi-Language Visual Glossary
- Student Resources in Spanish

See also the *Algebra 1 Toolkit* for more strategies for meeting individual needs.

Motivating the Lesson

You want to photograph five of your friends. If you know how to calculate permutations, you can find the number of ways you can arrange them in a row for a photograph.

3 TEACH

Extra Example 1

Consider the number of permutations of the letters in the word BRIGHTEN.

a. In how many ways can you arrange all of the letters? 40,320 ways

b. In how many ways can you arrange 2 of the letters? 56 ways

Key Questions to Ask for Example 1

- How can you tell that order is important for this exercise? The word "arrange" means to put in order, so order is important.
- Why are there 3 choices for the second letter? There are 4 letters in the word *July.* Once one has been chosen for the first letter, there are 3 letters left from which to choose the second letter.

Extra Example 2

You have 14 CDs. You can arrange 12 of the 14 in a CD wallet. In how many ways can you arrange the CDs in the CD wallet? 43,589,145,600 ways

Key Questions to Ask for Example 2

- What permutations formula would you use to find the number of ways the band might arrange 10 of the 12 songs? ${}_{12}P_{10} = \frac{12!}{2!}$

FACTORIAL In Example 1, you evaluated the expression $4 \cdot 3 \cdot 2 \cdot 1$. This expression can be written as 4! and is read "4 *factorial.*" For any positive integer n, the product of the integers from 1 to n is called ***n* factorial** and is written as $n!$. The value of 0! is defined to be 1.

$$n! = n \cdot (n-1) \cdot (n-2) \cdot \ldots \cdot 3 \cdot 2 \cdot 1 \text{ and } 0! = 1$$

In Example 1, you also found the permutations of four objects taken two at a time. You can find the number of permutations using the formulas below.

KEY CONCEPT *For Your Notebook*

Permutations

Formulas	**Examples**
The number of permutations of n objects is given by: $_nP_n = n!$	The number of permutations of 4 objects is: $_4P_4 = 4! = 4 \cdot 3 \cdot 2 \cdot 1 = 24$
The number of permutations of n objects taken r at a time, where $r \le n$, is given by: $_nP_r = \frac{n!}{(n-r)!}$	The number of permutations of 4 objects taken 2 at a time is: $_4P_2 = \frac{4!}{(4-2)!} = \frac{4 \cdot 3 \cdot \cancel{2!}}{\cancel{2!}} = 12$

EXAMPLE 2 Use a permutations formula

CD RECORDING Your band has written 12 songs and plans to record 9 of them for a CD. In how many ways can you arrange the songs on the CD?

Solution

To find the number of permutations of 9 songs chosen from 12, find $_{12}P_9$.

$$_{12}P_9 = \frac{12!}{(12-9)!} \quad \text{Permutations formula}$$

$$= \frac{12!}{3!} \quad \text{Subtract.}$$

$$= \frac{12 \cdot 11 \cdot 10 \cdot 9 \cdot 8 \cdot 7 \cdot 6 \cdot 5 \cdot 4 \cdot \cancel{3!}}{\cancel{3!}} \quad \text{Expand factorials. Divide out common factor, 3!.}$$

$$= 79{,}833{,}600 \quad \text{Multiply.}$$

▶ There are 79,833,600 ways to arrange 9 songs out of 12.

DIVIDE COMMON FACTORS
When you divide out common factors, remember that 3! is a factor of 12!.

GUIDED PRACTICE for Example 2

3. **WHAT IF?** In Example 2, suppose your band has written 15 songs. You will record 9 of them for a CD. In how many ways can you arrange the songs on the CD? 1,816,214,400 ways

Differentiated Instruction

Below Level Have students work in pairs to confirm that the permutations formula works. Suggest that they make a list of the number of ways the letters in the word SAID can be arranged and then find the arrangements using the permutations formula. Ask them to make a similar list for two of the letters in the word. Then lead students to see the usefulness of the permutations formula by having them examine what happens to the number of permutations as the number of letters in a word increases.

See also the *Algebra 1 Toolkit* for more strategies.

EXAMPLE 3 Find a probability using permutations

PARADE For a town parade, you will ride on a float with your soccer team. There are 12 floats in the parade, and their order is chosen at random. Find the probability that your float is first and the float with the school chorus is second.

Solution

STEP 1 **Write** the number of possible outcomes as the number of permutations of the 12 floats in the parade. This is ${}_{12}P_{12} = 12!$.

STEP 2 **Write** the number of favorable outcomes as the number of permutations of the other floats, given that the soccer team is first and the chorus is second. This is ${}_{10}P_{10} = 10!$.

STEP 3 **Calculate** the probability.

$$P\left(\begin{matrix}\text{soccer team is first} \\ \text{chorus is second}\end{matrix}\right) = \frac{10!}{12!}$$ **Form a ratio of favorable to possible outcomes.**

$$= \frac{\cancel{10!}}{12 \cdot 11 \cdot \cancel{10!}}$$ **Expand factorials. Divide out common factor, 10!.**

$$= \frac{1}{132}$$ **Simplify.**

 GUIDED PRACTICE for Example 3

4. **WHAT IF?** In Example 3, suppose there are 14 floats in the parade. Find the probability that the soccer team is first and the chorus is second. $\frac{1}{182}$

13.2 EXERCISES

HOMEWORK KEY
- ○ = **WORKED-OUT SOLUTIONS** on p. WS32 for Exs. 21 and 35
- ★ = **STANDARDIZED TEST PRACTICE** Exs. 2, 11, 30, 33, and 35
- ◆ = **MULTIPLE REPRESENTATIONS** Ex. 34

SKILL PRACTICE

1. **VOCABULARY** Copy and complete: An arrangement of objects in which order is important is called a(n) _?_. permutation

2. ★ **WRITING** *Explain* what the notation ${}_9P_2$ means. What is the value of this expression? The number of permutations containing 2 items chosen from a group of 9 possible items; 72

EXAMPLES 1 and 2 on pp. 851–852 for Exs. 3–11

COUNTING PERMUTATIONS Find the number of ways you can arrange (a) all of the letters in the given word and (b) 2 of the letters in the word.

3. AT a. 2 ways; b. 2 ways
4. TRY a. 6 ways; b. 6 ways
5. GAME a. 24 ways; b. 12 ways
6. CAT a. 6 ways; b. 6 ways
7. WATER a. 120 ways; b. 20 ways
8. ROCK a. 24 ways; b. 12 ways
9. APRIL a. 120 ways; b. 20 ways
10. FAMILY a. 720 ways; b. 30 ways

11. ★ **OPEN-ENDED** *Describe* a real-world situation where the number of possibilities is given by ${}_5P_2$. *Sample answer:* 5 people are running in a race. How many different results can there be for first and second place?

Extra Example 3

Ten students in your science class are giving reports on endangered animals. The order of the reports is chosen at random. Find the probability that your report on the humpback whale is first and your friend's report on the American crocodile is second. $\frac{1}{90}$

Closing the Lesson

Have students summarize the major points of the lesson and answer the Essential Question: How do you use the formula for permutations?

- A permutation is an arrangement of objects in which order is important.
- The product of positive integers from 1 to n is called n factorial ($n!$). 4! is $4 \cdot 3 \cdot 2 \cdot 1$ or 24.

Use the formula ${}_nP_n = n!$ to find the arrangement of n objects. You can arrange 5 objects in ${}_5P_5 = 5!$ ways, or $5 \cdot 4 \cdot 3 \cdot 2 \cdot 1 = 120$ ways.
Use the permutations formula ${}_nP_r = \frac{n!}{(n-r)!}$ to find the number of permutations of n objects taken r at a time. You can arrange 2 of 5 objects in $\frac{5!}{(5-2)!} = \frac{5!}{3!}$, or 20 ways.

To find a probability using permutations, use formulas to write a ratio of favorable to possible outcomes.

Differentiated Instruction

Visual Learners For Step 2 in **Example 3**, draw a simple diagram to show why the number of outcomes is 10!.

1st	2nd	
soccer team	chorus	remaining 10 floats

The number of permutations of the remaining 10 floats is given by ${}_{10}P_{10} = 10!$.

See also the *Algebra 1 Toolkit* for more strategies.

4 PRACTICE AND APPLY

Assignment Guide

Answer Transparencies available for all exercises

Basic:
Day 1: pp. 853–855
Exs. 1–19
Day 2: pp. 853–855
Exs. 20–29, 32–36, 40–43

Average:
Day 1: pp. 853–855
Exs. 1–19
Day 2: pp. 853–855
Exs. 22–30, 32–38, 40–43

Advanced:
Day 1: pp. 853–855
Exs. 1–19
Day 2: pp. 853–855
Exs. 24–43*

Block:
pp. 853–855
Exs. 1–19 (with 13.1)
pp. 853–855
Exs. 22–30, 32–38, 40–43 (with 13.3)

Differentiated Instruction

See *Algebra 1 Best Practices Toolkit* for suggestions on addressing the needs of a diverse classroom.

Homework Check

For a quick check of student understanding of key concepts, go over the following exercises:

Basic: 6, 13, 22, 32, 34
Average: 8, 15, 24, 33, 35
Advanced: 10, 17, 26, 36, 37

Extra Practice

- Student Edition, p. 950
- Chapter 13 Resource Book: Practice levels A, B, C, pp. 16–18

Practice Worksheet

An easily-readable reduced practice page (with answers) for this lesson can be found on p. 840C.

EXAMPLE 2 on p. 852 for Exs. 12–30

FACTORIALS AND PERMUTATIONS **Evaluate the expression.**

12. 1! 1 **13.** 3! 6 **14.** 0! 1 **15.** 5! 120

16. 8! 40,320 **17.** 10! 3,628,800 **18.** 12! 479,001,600 **19.** 13! 6,227,020,800

20. ${}_5P_2$ 20 **21.** ${}_7P_3$ 210 **22.** ${}_9P_1$ 9 **23.** ${}_6P_5$ 720

24. ${}_8P_8$ 40,320 **25.** ${}_{12}P_0$ 1 **26.** ${}_{30}P_2$ 870 **27.** ${}_{25}P_5$ 6,375,600

B **ERROR ANALYSIS** ***Describe*** **and correct the error in evaluating the expression.**

28. $${}_{11}P_7 = \frac{11!}{(11-7)} = \frac{11!}{4} = 9{,}979{,}200 \quad ✗$$

29. $${}_5P_3 = \frac{5!}{3!} = \frac{5 \cdot 4 \cdot \cancel{3!}}{\cancel{3!}} = 20 \quad ✗$$

28. The denominator of the fraction should be (11 − 7)!, not (11 − 7); $\frac{11!}{(11-7)!} = \frac{11!}{4!} =$ 1,663,200.

29. The denominator of the fraction should be (5 − 3)!, not 3!; $\frac{5!}{(5-3)!} = \frac{5!}{2!} =$ 60.

30. ★ **MULTIPLE CHOICE** The judges in an art contest award prizes for first, second, and third place out of 11 entries. Which expression gives the number of ways the judges can award first, second, and third place? C

Ⓐ $\frac{3!}{11!}$ Ⓑ $\frac{8!}{11!}$ Ⓒ $\frac{11!}{8!}$ Ⓓ $\frac{11!}{3!}$

C **31. CHALLENGE** Consider a set of 4 objects and a set of n objects.

a. Are there more permutations of all 4 of the objects or of 3 of the 4 objects? *Justify* your answer using an organized list. a–b. See margin.

b. In general, are there more permutations of n objects taken n at a time or of n objects taken $n - 1$ at a time? *Justify* your answer using the formula for the number of permutations.

PROBLEM SOLVING

EXAMPLE 2 on p. 852 for Exs. 32–33

A **32. MOVIES** Six friends go to a movie theater. In how many different ways can they sit together in a row of 6 empty seats? 720 ways

@HomeTutor for problem solving help at classzone.com

33. ★ **MULTIPLE CHOICE** You plan to visit 4 stores during a shopping trip. In how many orders can you visit these stores? C

Ⓐ 4 Ⓑ 16 Ⓒ 24 Ⓓ 256

@HomeTutor for problem solving help at classzone.com

EXAMPLE 3 on p. 853 for Exs. 34–38

34. ◆ **MULTIPLE REPRESENTATIONS** You and your friend are two of 4 servers working a shift in a restaurant. The host assigns tables of new diners to the servers in a particular order. This order remains the same, so that all servers are likely to wait on the same number of tables by the end of the shift.

a. Making a List List all the possible orders in which the host can assign tables to the servers. See margin.

b. Using a Formula Use the formula for permutations to find the number of ways in which the host can assign tables to the servers. 24 ways

c. Describe in Words What is the likelihood that you and your friend are assigned the first 2 tables? *Explain* your answer using probability. See margin.

○ = WORKED-OUT SOLUTIONS on p. WS1 ★ = STANDARDIZED TEST PRACTICE ◆ = MULTIPLE REPRESENTATIONS

31a. They are the same; 4 of 4 items: ABCD, ABDC, ACBD, ACDB, ADBC, ADCB, BACD, BADC, BCDA, BCAD, BDAC, BDCA, CABD, CADB, CBAD, CBDA, CDAB, CDBA, DABC, DACB, DBAC, DBCA, DCAB, DCBA; 3 of 4 items: ABC, ABD, ACB, ACD, ADB, ADC, BAC, BAD, BCD, BCA, BDA, BDC, CAB, CAD, CBA, CBD, CDA, CDB, DAB, DAC, DBA, DBC, DCA, DCB.

31b. See Additional Answers beginning on p. AA1.

35a. $\frac{1}{2}$. *Sample answer:* Make a list of possible permutations and count the number in which you are first or second and divide it by the total number of outcomes.

35. ★ **SHORT RESPONSE** Every student in your history class is required to present a project in front of the class. Each day, 4 students make their presentations in an order chosen at random by the teacher. You make your presentation on the first day.

 a. What is the probability that you are chosen to be the first or second presenter on the first day? *Explain* how you found your answer.

 b. What is the probability that you are chosen to be the second or third presenter on the first day? *Compare* your answer with that in part (a). $\frac{1}{2}$; the answers are the same.

B

36. **HISTORY EXAM** On an exam, you are asked to list 5 historical events in the order in which they occurred. You guess the order of the events at random. What is the probability that you choose the correct order? $\frac{1}{120}$

37. **SPIRIT** You make 6 posters to hold up at a basketball game. Each poster has a letter of the word TIGERS. You and 5 friends sit next to each other in a row. The posters are distributed at random. What is the probability that TIGERS is spelled correctly when you hold up the posters? $\frac{1}{720}$

38. **BAND COMPETITION** Seven marching bands will perform at a competition. The order of the performances is determined at random. What is the probability that your school band will perform first, followed by the band from the one other high school in your town? $\frac{1}{42}$

C

39. **CHALLENGE** You are one of 10 students performing in a school talent show. The order of the performances is determined at random. The first five performers go on stage before the intermission, while the remaining five performers go on stage after the intermission.

 a. What is the probability that you are the last performer before the intermission and your rival performs immediately before you? $\frac{1}{90}$

 b. What is the probability that you are *not* the first performer? $\frac{9}{10}$

ILLINOIS MIXED REVIEW

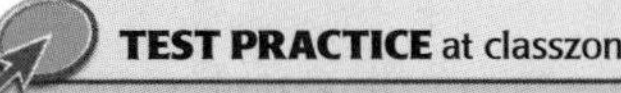

40. A camp counselor buys 4 bottles of water per person for a camping trip. If 35 people are going on the trip and if bottles of water cost $18.09 per case, what other information is needed to find the cost of the bottles of water?

 Ⓐ The number of days of the camping trip D

 Ⓑ The cost of cups and ice

 Ⓒ The number of people who drink water

 Ⓓ The number of bottles of water in a case

5 ASSESS AND RETEACH

Daily Homework Quiz

Transparency Available

1. Find the number of ways you can arrange all of the letters of the word BOUNDARY and then 3 of the letters of the word. 40,320 ways; 336 ways
2. Evaluate ${}_6P_3$. 120
3. Evaluate ${}_{14}P_9$. 726,485,760
4. There are 8 students auditioning for the main role in a school play. The order of the student auditions is chosen at random. Find the probability that you are chosen first to audition and your friend Petra is chosen second. $\frac{1}{56}$

Available at **classzone.com**

Diagnosis/Remediation

- Practice A, B, C in Chapter 13 Resource Book, pp. 16–18
- Study Guide in Chapter13 Resource Book, pp. 19–20
- Practice Workbook, pp. 198–199
- @HomeTutor

Challenge

Additional challenge is available in the Chapter 13 Resource Book, p. 23.

34a. ABCD, ABDC, ACBD, ACDB, ADBC, ADCB, BACD, BADC, BCDA, BCAD, BDAC, BDCA, CABD, CADB, CBAD, CBDA, CDAB, CDBA, DABC, DACB, DBAC, DBCA, DCAB, DCBA

34c. $\frac{1}{6}$. *Sample answer:* Say A and B represent you and your friend. There are 4 permutations in the list from part (a) in which A and B are given the first 2 tables. There are 24 total permutations, so the probability that you and your friend are given the first two tables is $\frac{4}{24} = \frac{1}{6}$.

1 PLAN AND PREPARE

Warm-Up Exercises

Transparency Available

1. Evaluate $_6P_2$. 30
2. Evaluate $_{15}P_8$. 259,459,200
3. You are given the 6 letter tiles, E, K, M, N, O, and Y, face down in no particular order. Find the probability that the letter tiles spell MONKEY as each tile is turned over from left to right. $\frac{1}{720}$

Notetaking Guide

Transparency Available

Promotes interactive learning and notetaking skills, pp. 302–304.

Pacing

Basic: 1 day
Average: 1 day
Advanced: 1 day
Block: 0.5 block with 13.2
• See *Teaching Guide/Lesson Plan.*

2 FOCUS AND MOTIVATE

Essential Question

Big Idea 1, p. 841

How do you use combinations to count possibilities? Tell students they will learn how to answer this question by using a formula to find the numbr of combinations of selected objects.

13.3 Find Probabilities Using Combinations

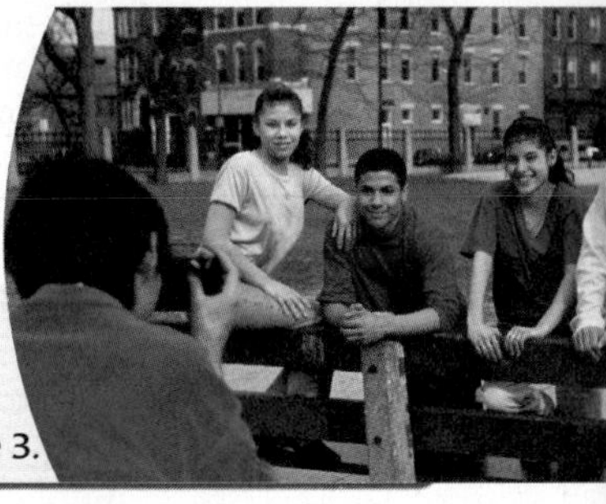

10.11.10 Apply counting techniques (e.g., permutations, combinations, Fundamental Counting Principle).

Before You used permutations to count possibilities.

Now You will use combinations to count possibilities.

Why? So you can find the probability of an event, as in Example 3.

Key Vocabulary
• **combination**

A **combination** is a selection of objects in which order is *not* important. For instance, in a drawing for 3 identical prizes, you would use combinations, because the order of the winners would not matter. If the prizes were different, you would use permutations, because the order would matter.

EXAMPLE 1 Count combinations

Count the combinations of two letters from the list A, B, C, D.

Solution

List all of the permutations of two letters in the list A, B, C, D. Because order is not important in a combination, cross out any duplicate pairs.

AB	AC	AD	~~BA~~	BC	BD
~~CA~~	~~CB~~	CD	~~DA~~	~~DB~~	~~DC~~

BD and DB are the same pair.

▸ There are 6 possible combinations of 2 letters from the list A, B, C, D.

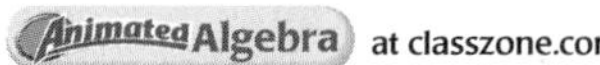 at classzone.com

GUIDED PRACTICE for Example 1

1. Count the combinations of 3 letters from the list A, B, C, D, E. 10 combinations

COMBINATIONS In Example 1, you found the number of combinations of objects by making an organized list. You can also find the number of combinations using the following formula.

KEY CONCEPT *For Your Notebook*

Combinations

Formula

The number of combinations of n objects taken r at a time, where $r \le n$, is given by:

$${}_nC_r = \frac{n!}{(n-r)! \cdot r!}$$

Example

The number of combinations of 4 objects taken 2 at a time is:

$${}_4C_2 = \frac{4!}{(4-2)! \cdot 2!} = \frac{4 \cdot 3 \cdot \cancel{2!}}{\cancel{2!} \cdot (2 \cdot 1)} = 6$$

Resource Planning Guide

Chapter Resource Book
• Teaching Guide/Lesson Plan (pp. 24–25)
• Activity Master (p. 26)
• Practice levels A, B, C (pp. 28–30)
• Study Guide (pp. 31–32)
• Catch-up for Absent Students (p. 33)
• Application (p. 34)
• Challenge (p. 35)

Workbooks
• Notetaking Guide (pp. 302–304)
• Practice Workbook (pp. 200–201)

Teaching Options
• **Power Presentations CD-ROM** provides dynamic electronic teaching resources for the classroom.
• **Activity Generator CD-ROM** provides editable activities for all ability levels.

Interactive Technology
• Easy Planner
• Power Presentations CD-ROM
• Activity Generator CD-ROM
• Animated Algebra
• Test Generator CD-ROM
• Online Quiz
• eWorkbook
• eEdition
• @HomeTutor

Resources for English Learners
• Quick Reference for English Learners
• Spanish Study Guide
• Multi-Language Visual Glossary
• Student Resources in Spanish

See also the *Algebra 1 Toolkit* for more strategies for meeting individual needs.

EXAMPLE 2 Use the combinations formula

LUNCH MENU You order a sandwich at a restaurant. You can choose 2 side dishes from a list of 8. How many combinations of side dishes are possible?

Solution

The order in which you choose the side dishes is not important. So, to find the number of combinations of 8 side dishes taken 2 at a time, find ${}_8C_2$.

$${}_8C_2 = \frac{8!}{(8-2)! \cdot 2!}$$ **Combinations formula**

$$= \frac{8!}{6! \cdot 2!}$$ **Subtract.**

$$= \frac{8 \cdot 7 \cdot \cancel{6!}}{\cancel{6!} \cdot (2 \cdot 1)}$$ **Expand factorials. Divide out common factor, 6!.**

$$= 28$$ **Simplify.**

▶ There are 28 different combinations of side dishes you can order.

EXAMPLE 3 Find a probability using combinations

PHOTOGRAPHY A yearbook editor has selected 14 photos, including one of you and one of your friend, to use in a collage for the yearbook. The photos are placed at random. There is room for 2 photos at the top of the page. What is the probability that your photo and your friend's photo are the two placed at the top of the page?

Solution

STEP 1 **Write** the number of possible outcomes as the number of combinations of 14 photos taken 2 at a time, or ${}_{14}C_2$, because the order in which the photos are chosen is not important.

$${}_{14}C_2 = \frac{14!}{(14-2)! \cdot 2!} = \frac{14!}{12! \cdot 2!} = \frac{14 \cdot 13 \cdot \cancel{12!}}{\cancel{12!} \cdot (2 \cdot 1)} = 91$$

STEP 2 **Find** the number of favorable outcomes. Only one of the possible combinations includes your photo and your friend's photo.

STEP 3 **Calculate** the probability.

P(your photo and your friend's photos are chosen) $= \frac{1}{91}$

GUIDED PRACTICE for Examples 2 and 3

2. **WHAT IF?** In Example 2, suppose you can choose 3 side dishes out of the list of 8 side dishes. How many combinations are possible? **56 combinations**

3. **WHAT IF?** In Example 3, suppose there are 20 photos in the collage. Find the probability that your photo and your friend's photo are the two placed at the top of the page. $\frac{1}{190}$

Motivating the Lesson

You sing in a chorus after school. The director will choose at random 2 songs out of 5 for the chorus to learn to sing. You can use combinations to help find the probability that the director will choose your two favorite songs.

3 TEACH

Extra Example 1

Count the combinations of 2 letters from the list A, B, C, D, E. **10**

An **Animated Algebra** activity is available on-line for **Example 1**. This activity is also available on the **Power Presentations CD-ROM**.

Extra Example 2

You can choose 2 courses out of a list of 6. How many combinations of electives are possible? **15**

Extra Example 3

Your teacher randomly chooses 2 out of 18 students to give an impromptu debate on freedom of the press in high school newspapers. What is the probability that your teacher chooses you and your best friend? $\frac{1}{153}$

Closing the Lesson

Have students summarize the major points of the lesson and answer the Essential Question: How do you use combinations to count possibilities?

- **A combination is a selection of objects in which order is not important.**

Use the formula ${}_nC_r = \frac{n!}{(n-r) \cdot r!}$ to find the number of combinations of n objects taken r at a time.

Differentiated Instruction

Advanced Have students create two situations in which 2 out of 16 objects are selected, with order important in one of the situations and not important in the other. Ask students to use the situations to compare and contrast permutations and combinations, explaining why the number of selections is greater in one than the other, and describing the relationship between the two. Tell students it may be necessary to create several situations in which order is and is not important to be able to describe the relationship between permutations and combinations.

See also the *Algebra 1 Toolkit* for more strategies.

4 PRACTICE AND APPLY

Assignment Guide

Answer Transparencies available for all exercises

Basic:
Day 1: pp. 858–859
Exs. 1–17, 23–25, 28–33

Average:
Day 1: pp. 858–859
Exs. 1–5, 6–14 even, 15–20, 23–26, 28–33

Advanced:
Day 1: pp. 858–859
Exs. 1–3, 10–33*

Block:
pp. 858–859
Exs. 1–5, 6–14 even, 15–20, 23–26, 28–33 (with 13.2)

Differentiated Instruction

See *Algebra 1 Best Practices Toolkit* for suggestions on addressing the needs of a diverse classroom.

Homework Check

For a quick check of student understanding of key concepts, go over the following exercises:

Basic: 3, 8, 16, 23, 24
Average: 4, 10, 17, 24, 25
Advanced: 3, 12, 18, 25, 26

Extra Practice

- Student Edition, p. 950
- Chapter 13 Resource Book: Practice levels A, B, C, pp. 28–30

Practice Worksheet

An easily-readable reduced practice page (with answers) for this lesson can be found on p. 840C.

13.3 EXERCISES

HOMEWORK KEY
○ = WORKED-OUT SOLUTIONS on p. WS32 for Exs. 7 and 25
★ = STANDARDIZED TEST PRACTICE Exs. 2, 14–20, and 25

SKILL PRACTICE

A

1. **VOCABULARY** Copy and complete: A(n) _?_ is a selection of objects in which order is not important. combination

2. ★ **WRITING** *Explain* how a combination differs from a permutation. See margin.

EXAMPLE 1 on p. 856 for Exs. 3, 4

3. **COMBINATIONS** How many combinations of 3 letters from the list A, B, C, D, E, F are possible? 20 combinations

4. **ERROR ANALYSIS** *Describe* and correct the error in listing all of the possible combinations of 2 letters from the list A, B, C. See margin.

AB	BA	CA
AC	BC	CB

✗

EXAMPLE 2 on p. 857 for Exs. 5–15

5. **ERROR ANALYSIS** *Describe* and correct the error in evaluating ${}_9C_4$. See margin.

$${}_9C_4 = \frac{9!}{(9-4)!} = \frac{9!}{5!} = 3024$$ ✗

COMBINATIONS Evaluate the expression.

6. ${}_5C_1$ 5
7. ${}_8C_5$ 56
8. ${}_9C_9$ 1
9. ${}_8C_6$ 28
10. ${}_{12}C_3$ 220
11. ${}_{11}C_4$ 330
12. ${}_{15}C_8$ 6435
13. ${}_{20}C_5$ 15,504

14. ★ **MULTIPLE CHOICE** What is the value of ${}_{10}C_6$? C

(A) 7 (B) 60 (C) 210 (D) 151,200

B

15. ★ **MULTIPLE CHOICE** You have the first season of your favorite television show on a set of DVDs. The set contains 13 episodes. You have time to watch 3 episodes. How many combinations of 3 episodes can you watch? A

(A) 286 (B) 572 (C) 1716 (D) 589,680

★ **SHORT RESPONSE In Exercises 16–19, tell whether the question can be answered using *combinations* or *permutations*. *Explain* your choice, then answer the question.** 16–19. See margin.

16. Four students from your class of 120 students will be selected to organize a fundraiser. How many groups of 4 students are possible?

17. Ten students are auditioning for 3 different roles in a play. In how many ways can the 3 roles be filled?

18. To complete an exam, you must answer 8 questions from a list of 10 questions. In how many ways can you complete the exam?

19. In how many ways can 5 people sit in a car that holds 5 passengers?

20. ★ **WRITING** Which is greater, ${}_6P_r$ or ${}_6C_r$? *Justify* your answer. See margin.

C

21. **REASONING** Write an equation that relates ${}_nP_r$ and ${}_nC_r$. *Explain* your reasoning. See margin.

22. **CHALLENGE** Prove that ${}_nC_r = {}_nC_{n-r}$. *Explain* why this makes sense. See margin.

2. In a combination, the order in which the objects are arranged is not important. In a permutation, the order is important.

4. Each combination is duplicated, since the order of the letters does not matter. AB and BA are the same, as are CA and AC and BC and CB; list: AB, AC, BC.

5. *Sample answer:* The answer given was ${}_9P_4$ not ${}_9C_4$; $\frac{9!}{(9-4)! \cdot 4!} = \frac{9!}{5! \cdot 4!} = 126$.

16. Combinations; the order in which the students are picked for the group does not matter, 8,214,570 groups.

17. Permutations; since the roles are different, the order in which students are selected for the roles matters, 720 ways.

18. Combinations; the order in which you answer the questions does not matter, 45 ways.

19. Permutations; the arrangement of people in the car matters, 120 ways.

20–22. See Additional Answers beginning on p. AA1.

Differentiated Instruction

Kinesthetic Learners Some students may have trouble distinguishing between combinations and permutations. For **Exercises 3 and 4**, have students write single letters on index cards and use the cards to compute combinations and permutations by sorting them. Provide additional exercises to be solved using the cards, such as distinguishing ${}_3C_2 = 3$ from ${}_3P_2 = 6$, and distinguishing ${}_5C_2 = 10$ from ${}_5P_2 = 20$.

See also the *Algebra 1 Toolkit* for more strategies.

PROBLEM SOLVING

EXAMPLE 2 on p. 857 for Ex. 23

A 23. **RESTAURANT** You are ordering a burrito with 2 main ingredients and 3 toppings. The menu below shows the possible choices. How many different burritos are possible? 840 burritos

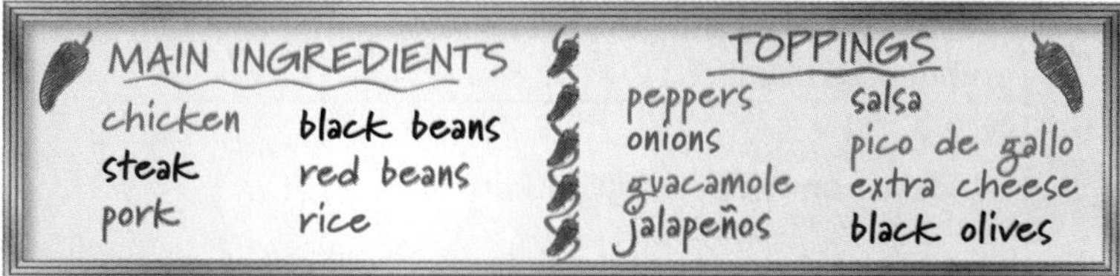

@HomeTutor for problem solving help at classzone.com

EXAMPLE 3 on p. 857 for Exs. 24–26

24. **WORK SCHEDULE** You work 3 evenings each week at a bookstore. Your supervisor assigns you 3 evenings at random from the 7 possibilities. What is the probability that your schedule this week includes working on Friday? $\frac{3}{7}$

@HomeTutor for problem solving help at classzone.com

25. ★ **SHORT RESPONSE** On a television game show, 9 members of the studio audience are randomly selected to be eligible contestants.

a. Six of the 9 eligible contestants are randomly chosen to play a game on the stage. How many combinations of 6 players from the group of eligible contestants are possible? 84 combinations

b. You and your two friends are part of the group of 9 eligible contestants. What is the probability that all three of you are chosen to play the game on stage? *Explain* how you found your answer. See margin.

26. $\frac{1}{435}$; $\frac{1}{870}$; my best friend and I are chosen, regardless of order.

B 26. **REPRESENTATIVES** Your teacher chooses 2 students at random to represent your homeroom. The homeroom has a total of 30 students, including your best friend. What is the probability that you and your best friend are chosen? What is the probability that you are chosen first and your best friend is chosen second? Which event is more likely to occur?

C 27. **CHALLENGE** There are 30 students in your class. Your science teacher will choose 5 students at random to complete a group project. Find the probability that you and your 2 best friends in the science class are chosen to work in the group. *Explain* how you found your answer. See margin.

ILLINOIS MIXED REVIEW

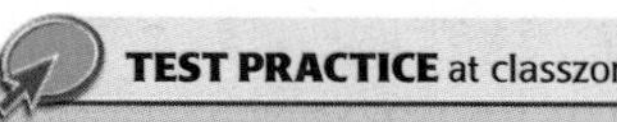

TEST PRACTICE at classzone.com

28. A school newspaper conducts a sports survey of 125 randomly selected students. Of those surveyed, 38 students plan to try out for a sports team next year. If there are a total of 1500 students at the school, how many of them can you expect to try out for a sports team next year?

Ⓐ 304 Ⓑ 456 Ⓒ 475 Ⓓ 570

B

5 ASSESS AND RETEACH

Daily Homework Quiz

Transparency Available

1. You can choose 3 toppings for a pizza out of 14 for no extra charge. How many combinations of pizza toppings are possible? 364 combinations
2. Evaluate ${}_9C_4$. 126
3. Evaluate ${}_{11}C_6$. 462
4. Two out of 10 flag twirlers are randomly chosen to lead the flag twirlers in a school parade. What is the probability that the two flag twirlers are you and your sister? $\frac{1}{45}$

Online Quiz

Available at **classzone.com**

Diagnosis/Remediation

- Practice A, B, C in Chapter 13 Resource Book, pp. 28–30
- Study Guide in Chapter13 Resource Book, pp. 31–32
- Practice Workbook, pp. 200–201
- @HomeTutor

Challenge

Additional challenge is available in the Chapter 13 Resource Book, p. 35.

25b. $\frac{5}{21}$. *Sample answer:* There are 84 possible outcomes of the choice. Find the number of combinations that include you and your 2 friends. After you and your friends are chosen, 3 other contestants from a pool of 6 can be chosen in any combination, so the number of favorable combinations is ${}_6C_3 = 20$. The probability that you and your friends are chosen is $\frac{20}{84} = \frac{5}{21}$.

27. See Additional Answers beginning on p. AA1.

1 PLAN AND PREPARE

Learn the Method

- Students will find combinations and permutations using a graphing calculator.
- After the activity, students can use a graphing calculator to check their solutions in Exercises 6–19 in Lesson 13.3.

Keystroke Help

Keystrokes for several models of calculators are available in blackline format in the *Chapter 13 Resource Book.*

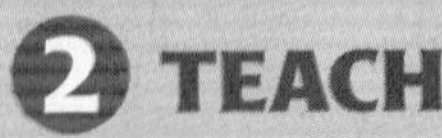

Tips for Success

Make sure that students use the correct sequence of keystrokes, the correct numbers for *n* and *r*, and select the correct item from the PRB menu.

Extra Example 1

Your supervisor at the tutoring center chooses 4 students out of 20 to tutor after school. How many combinations of student tutors are possible? 4845 combinations

Extra Example 2

One student each will tutor reading, algebra, history, and writing. In how many ways can the tutoring roles be assigned using all 20 students? 116,280 ways

3 ASSESS AND RETEACH

For given values of *n* and *r*, which number is greater, $_nC_r$ or $_nP_r$? $_nP_r$, unless $r = 0$ or $r = 1$, in which case $_nC_r = {}_nP_r$

Graphing Calculator ACTIVITY *Use after Lesson 13.3*

@HomeTutor
classzone.com
Keystrokes

13.3 Find Permutations and Combinations

QUESTION How can you find combinations and permutations using a graphing calculator?

EXAMPLE 1 Find the number of combinations

STARTERS There are 15 players on your softball team, but only 9 of them can be the starting players in one game. How many combinations of starting players are possible?

Solution

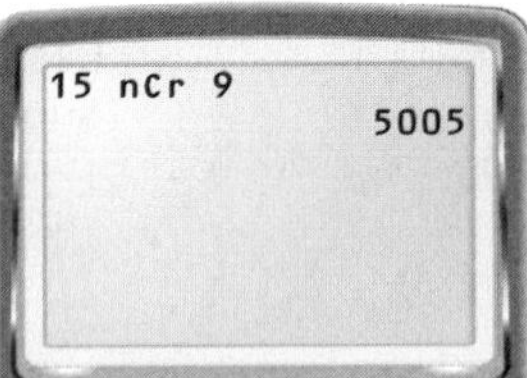

You are finding $_nC_r$ where $n = 15$ and $r = 9$. Enter 15 for n.
Press MATH. Go to the PRB menu and select $_nC_r$.
Then enter 9 for r.

▸ There are 5005 possible combinations of starting players.

EXAMPLE 2 Find the number of permutations

BATTING ORDER Before each softball game, your coach announces the batting order of the 9 starting players. This is the order in which the starting players will bat. How many batting orders can be formed using 9 players on your team of 15 players?

Solution

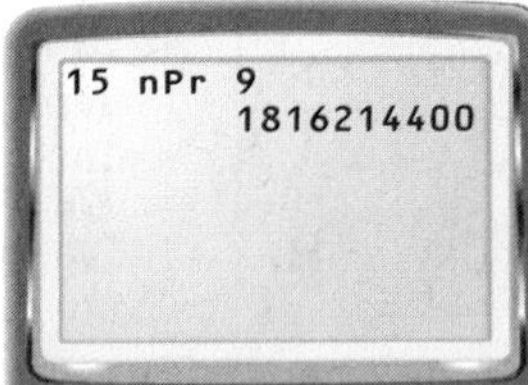

You are finding $_nP_r$ where $n = 15$ and $r = 9$. Enter 15 for n.
Press MATH. Go to the PRB menu and select $_nP_r$.
Then enter 9 for r.

▸ There are 1,816,214,400 possible batting orders.

PRACTICE

Evaluate the expression.

1. $_7C_4$ 35 **2.** $_6C_6$ 1 **3.** $_{10}C_3$ 120 **4.** $_{16}C_8$ 12,870

5. $_9P_5$ 15,120 **6.** $_7P_6$ 5040 **7.** $_{11}P_8$ 6,652,800 **8.** $_{12}P_5$ 95,040

9. GROUP PROJECT Your teacher selects 3 students from a class of 28 students to work on a project in a group. Within the group, one member must be the writer, one must be the researcher, and one must be the presenter.

a. How many different groups of 3 can your teacher select? 3276 groups

b. After the group is formed, in how many ways can the roles in the group be assigned? 6 ways

13.4 Find Probabilities of Compound Events

 **10.11.08** Compute probabilities for compound events.

Before You found the probability of a simple event.

Now You will find the probability of a compound event.

Why? So you can analyze scientific data, as in Ex. 23.

Key Vocabulary
- compound event
- mutually exclusive events
- overlapping events
- independent events
- dependent events

A **compound event** combines two or more events, using the word *and* or the word *or.* To find the probability that either event *A* or event *B* occurs, determine how the events are related. **Mutually exclusive events** have no common outcomes. **Overlapping events** have at least one common outcome.

REVIEW VENN DIAGRAMS For help with using Venn diagrams, see p. 930.

For instance, suppose you roll a number cube.

Mutually Exclusive Events

Event *A*: Roll a 3.

Event *B*: Roll an even number.

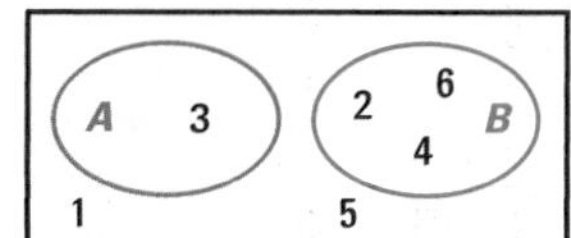

Set *A* has 1 number, and set *B* has 3 numbers.

$P(3 \text{ or even}) = \frac{1}{6} + \frac{3}{6}$

$\boldsymbol{P(A \text{ or } B) = P(A) + P(B)}$

Overlapping Events

Event *A*: Roll an odd number.

Event *B*: Roll a prime number.

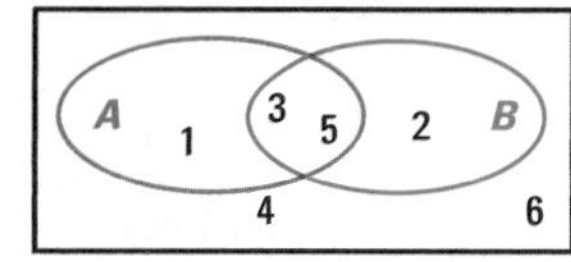

Set *A* has 3 numbers, and set *B* has 3 numbers. There are 2 numbers in both sets.

$P(\text{odd or prime}) = \frac{3}{6} + \frac{3}{6} - \frac{2}{6}$

$\boldsymbol{P(A \text{ or } B) = P(A) + P(B) - P(A \text{ and } B)}$

EXAMPLE 1 **Find the probability of *A* or *B***

You roll a number cube. Find the probability that you roll a 2 or an odd number.

Solution

Because 2 is an even number, rolling a 2 and rolling an odd number are mutually exclusive events.

$$P(2 \text{ or odd}) = P(2) + P(\text{odd}) = \frac{1}{6} + \frac{3}{6} = \frac{4}{6} = \frac{2}{3}$$

1 PLAN AND PREPARE

Warm-Up Exercises

Transparency Available

Find the product.

1. $\frac{2}{5} \cdot \frac{3}{4}$ $\frac{3}{10}$
2. $\frac{7}{8} \cdot \frac{2}{7}$ $\frac{1}{4}$
3. $\frac{12}{15} \cdot \frac{8}{14}$ $\frac{16}{35}$
4. $\frac{18}{52} \cdot \frac{17}{51}$ $\frac{3}{26}$
5. A bag contains 3 green, 5 blue, and 6 yellow marbles. What is the probability of selecting a yellow marble at random? $\frac{3}{7}$

Notetaking Guide

Transparency Available

Promotes interactive learning and notetaking skills, pp. 305–307.

Pacing

Basic: 2 days
Average: 2 days
Advanced: 2 days
Block: 1 block
- See *Teaching Guide/Lesson Plan.*

2 FOCUS AND MOTIVATE

Essential Question

Big Idea 1, p. 841

How do you find the probability of compound events? **Tell students they will learn how to answer this question by finding probabilities of mutually exclusive events or overlapping events and independent or dependent events.**

Resource Planning Guide

Chapter Resource Book
- Teaching Guide/Lesson Plan (pp. 36–37)
- Activity Master (p. 38)
- Practice levels A, B, C (pp. 39–41)
- Study Guide (pp. 42–43)
- Catch-up for Absent Students (p. 44)
- Problem Solving Workshop (p. 45)
- Challenge (p. 47)

Workbooks
- Notetaking Guide (pp. 305–307)
- Practice Workbook (pp. 202–204)

Teaching Options
- **Power Presentations CD-ROM** provides dynamic electronic teaching resources for the classroom.
- **Activity Generator CD-ROM** provides editable activities for all ability levels.

Interactive Technology
- Easy Planner
- Power Presentations CD-ROM
- Activity Generator CD-ROM
- Animated Algebra
- Test Generator CD-ROM
- Online Quiz
- eWorkbook
- eEdition
- @HomeTutor

Resources for English Learners
- Quick Reference for English Learners
- Spanish Study Guide
- Multi-Language Visual Glossary
- Student Resources in Spanish

See also the *Algebra 1 Toolkit* for more strategies for meeting individual needs.

Motivating the Lesson

You are one out of 50 students who will be selected at random to recite a poem or play a song. If you know how to find the probability of compound events, you can determine your chances of being selected for one or the other of these performances.

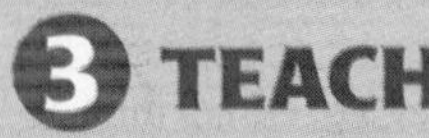

3 TEACH

Extra Example 1

You roll a number cube. Find the probability of rolling a 1 or a number greater than 4. $\frac{1}{2}$

Key Question to Ask for Example 1

- How is a mutually exclusive compound probability similar to a simple probability? Each of the probabilities in a mutually exclusive compound event is represented as the ratio of the number of favorable outcomes to the number of possible outcomes, just as in a simple probability.

Extra Example 2

You roll a number cube. Find the probability of rolling an odd number or a number less than 5. $\frac{5}{6}$

Key Question to Ask for Example 2

- Why do you subtract the probability of the overlapping event in a compound probability? The overlapping event is a subset of both events. You need to subtract its probability so that it is not included twice.

EXAMPLE 2 **Find the probability of *A* or *B***

You roll a number cube. Find the probability that you roll an even number or a prime number.

Solution

Because 2 is both an even number and a prime number, rolling an even number and rolling a prime number are overlapping events. There are 3 even numbers, 3 prime numbers, and 1 number that is both.

$$P(\text{even or prime}) = P(\text{even}) + P(\text{prime}) - P(\text{even and prime})$$

$$= \frac{3}{6} + \frac{3}{6} - \frac{1}{6}$$

$$= \frac{5}{6}$$

✓ **GUIDED PRACTICE** for Examples 1 and 2

1. You roll a number cube. Find the probability that you roll a 2 or a 5. $\frac{1}{3}$
2. You roll a number cube. Find the probability that you roll a number less than 4 or an odd number. $\frac{2}{3}$

INDEPENDENT AND DEPENDENT EVENTS To find the probability that event A and event B both occur, determine how the events are related. Two events are **independent events** if the occurrence of one event has no effect on the occurrence of the other. Two events are **dependent events** if the occurrence of one event affects the occurrence of the other.

For instance, consider the probability of choosing a green marble and then a blue marble from the bag shown. If you choose one marble and replace it before choosing the second, then the events are independent. If you do not replace the first marble, then the sample space has changed, and the events are dependent.

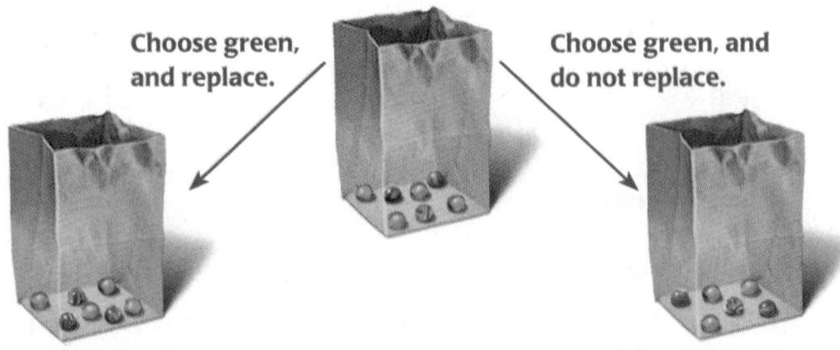
Choose green, and replace.
Choose green, and do not replace.

Independent Events	**Dependent Events**
With replacement:	Without replacement:
$P(\text{green and blue}) = \frac{4}{7} \cdot \frac{1}{7} = \frac{4}{49}$	$P(\text{green and blue}) = \frac{4}{7} \cdot \frac{1}{6} = \frac{2}{21}$
$\mathbf{P(A \text{ and } B) = P(A) \cdot P(B)}$	$\mathbf{P(A \text{ and } B) = P(A) \cdot P(B \text{ given } A)}$

Differentiated Instruction

Inclusion To help students associate *or* with addition, and *and* with multiplication, students can use a simple example. The sample space {H, T} for one toss of a coin gives P(heads *or* tails) = 1. Using addition, P(heads *or* tails) $= \frac{1}{2} + \frac{1}{2} = 1$. So, *or* means addition. Similarly, the sample space {HH, HT, TH, TT} for two tosses of a coin gives P(heads *and* then tails) $= \frac{1}{4}$. By multiplication, P(heads *and* then tails) $= \frac{1}{2} \cdot \frac{1}{2} = \frac{1}{4}$. So, *and* means multiplication. See also the *Algebra 1 Toolkit* for more strategies.

EXAMPLE 3 Find the probability of *A* and *B*

BUS SCHEDULE You take a city bus from your neighborhood to a location within walking distance of your school. The express bus arrives at your neighborhood between 7:30 and 7:36. The local bus arrives at your neighborhood between 7:30 and 7:40. You arrive at the bus stop at 7:33. Find the probability that you have missed both the express bus and the local bus.

ANOTHER WAY
For alternative methods for solving the problem in Example 3, turn to page 868 for the **Problem Solving Workshop**.

Solution

The events are independent. The arrival of one bus does not affect the arrival of the other bus.

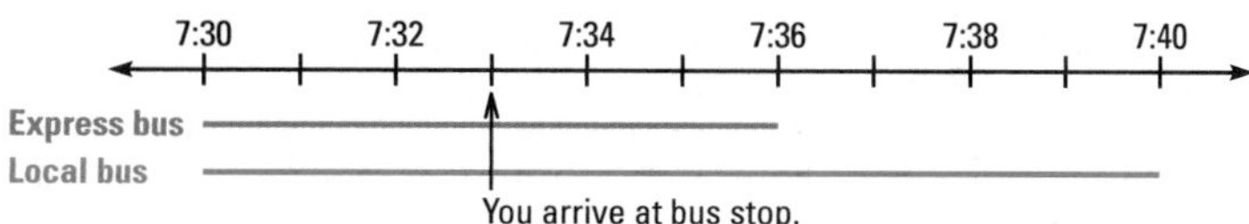

There are 6 minutes when the express bus can arrive. You are not at the bus stop for 3 of those minutes.

$P(\text{you miss express bus}) = \frac{3}{6} = \frac{1}{2}$

There are 10 minutes when the local bus can arrive. You are not at the bus stop for 3 of those minutes.

$P(\text{you miss local bus}) = \frac{3}{10}$

Multiply the probabilities of the two events:

$$P(\text{you miss both buses}) = \frac{1}{2} \cdot \frac{3}{10} = \frac{3}{20}$$

▶ The probability that you miss the express bus and the local bus is $\frac{3}{20}$.

EXAMPLE 4 Find the probability of *A* and *B*

PEN COLORS A box contains 3 blue pens and 5 black pens. You choose one pen at random, do not replace it, then choose a second pen at random. What is the probability that both pens are blue?

Solution

Because you do not replace the first pen, the events are dependent. Before you choose a pen, there are 8 pens, and 3 of them are blue. After you choose a blue pen, there are 7 pens left and 2 of them are blue.

$$P(\text{blue and then blue}) = P(\text{blue}) \cdot P(\text{blue given blue})$$

$$= \frac{3}{8} \cdot \frac{2}{7} = \frac{6}{56} = \frac{3}{28}$$

GUIDED PRACTICE for Examples 3 and 4

3. **MARBLES** A bag contains 4 red, 5 green, and 2 blue marbles. You randomly draw 2 marbles, one at a time. Find the probabililty that both are red if:

   a. you replace the first marble. $\frac{16}{121}$

   b. you do not replace the first marble. $\frac{6}{55}$

Extra Example 3

An acceptable two-digit code, made from the digits 1 through 9, consists of an even number followed by an odd number. You choose two numbers at random. Find the probability that you have chosen an acceptable code. $\frac{20}{81}$

Extra Example 4

A bag contains 4 blue marbles and 8 yellow marbles. You choose one marble at random, do not replace it, and then choose a second marble at random. What is the probability that both marbles are blue? $\frac{1}{11}$

Closing the Lesson

Have students summarize the major points of the lesson and answer the Essential Question: How do you find the probability of compound events?

- A compound event combines two or more events using the word *and* or the word *or.*
- Mutually exclusive events have no common outcomes, while overlapping events have at least one common outcome.
- Independent events are ones in which the occurrence of one event has no effect on the occurrence of the other. Two events are dependent if the occurrence of one event affects the occurrence of the other.

To find the probability that event A *or* event B occurs, determine if the events are mutually exclusive or overlapping. If mutually exclusive, add the probabilities. If overlapping, add the probabilities and subtract the probability of the overlapping event. To find the probability of events A *and* B occurring, multiply the probabilities of the events.

4 PRACTICE AND APPLY

Assignment Guide

Answer Transparencies available for all exercises

Basic:
Day 1: SRH p. 915 Exs. 1, 2, 6, 7
pp. 864–867
Exs. 1–8, 30–34
Day 2: pp. 864–867
Exs. 9–17, 22–25, 28, 29

Average:
Day 1: pp. 864–867
Exs. 1, 2, 5–8, 18, 19, 30–34
Day 2: pp. 864–867
Exs. 11–17, 20, 22–26, 28, 29

Advanced:
Day 1: pp. 864–867
Exs. 1, 2, 6–8, 18, 19, 21*, 30–34
Day 2: pp. 864–867
Exs. 11–17, 20, 22–29*

Block:
pp. 864–867
Exs. 1, 2, 5–8, 11–20, 22–26, 28–34

Differentiated Instruction

See *Algebra 1 Best Practices Toolkit* for suggestions on addressing the needs of a diverse classroom.

Homework Check

For a quick check of student understanding of key concepts, go over the following exercises:

Basic: 4, 8, 10, 22, 24
Average: 5, 11, 23, 24, 25
Advanced: 6, 12, 23, 24, 25

Extra Practice

- Student Edition, p. 950
- Chapter 13 Resource Book: Practice levels A, B, C, pp. 39–41

Practice Worksheet

An easily-readable reduced practice page (with answers) for this lesson can be found on p. 840C.

13.4 EXERCISES

HOMEWORK KEY
○ = WORKED-OUT SOLUTIONS on p. WS32 for Exs. 5 and 23
★ = STANDARDIZED TEST PRACTICE Exs. 2, 8, 13, 20, and 24
◆ = MULTIPLE REPRESENTATIONS Ex. 25

SKILL PRACTICE

A

1. **VOCABULARY** Copy and complete: The probability of __?__ events is found using the formula $P(A \text{ and } B) = P(A) \cdot P(B \text{ given } A)$. dependent

2. ★ **WRITING** *Explain* how overlapping events differ from mutually exclusive events. Overlapping events have one or more outcomes in common, mutually exclusive events do not.

EXAMPLES 1 and 2 on pp. 861–862 for Exs. 3–8

PROBABILITY OF A OR B **In Exercises 3–6, you roll a number cube. Tell whether the events *A* and *B* are *mutually exclusive* or *overlapping*. Then find $P(A \text{ or } B)$.**

3. **Event *A*:** Roll a 6. mutually exclusive; $\frac{2}{3}$
   Event *B*: Roll a prime number.

4. **Event *A*:** Roll an even number.
   Event *B*: Roll a 5. mutually exclusive; $\frac{2}{3}$

5. **Event *A*:** Roll an odd number.
   Event *B*: Roll a number less than 5. overlapping; $\frac{5}{6}$

6. **Event *A*:** Roll a multiple of 3.
   Event *B*: Roll an even number. overlapping; $\frac{2}{3}$

7. **ERROR ANALYSIS** A bag contains 7 yellow marbles, 4 red marbles, and 5 blue marbles. *Describe* and correct the error in finding the probability that you randomly draw a yellow or blue marble. See margin.

$$P(\text{yellow or blue}) = P(\text{yellow}) \cdot P(\text{blue}) = \frac{7}{16} \cdot \frac{5}{16} = \frac{35}{256}$$

7. To find the probability that you draw a yellow *or* a blue marble, the individual probabilities should be added, not multiplied; $\frac{7}{16} + \frac{5}{16} = \frac{12}{16} = \frac{3}{4}$.

8. ★ **MULTIPLE CHOICE** A bag contains tiles with the numbers 1–10 on them. You randomly choose a tile from the bag. What is the probability that you choose an even number or a number less than 5? A

   Ⓐ 0.7 Ⓑ 0.8 Ⓒ 0.9 Ⓓ 1

EXAMPLES 3 and 4 on p. 863 for Exs. 9–12

PROBABILITY OF A AND B **In Exercises 9–12, tell whether the events *A* and *B* are *dependent* or *independent*. Then find $P(A \text{ and } B)$.**

9. You roll two number cubes.
   Event *A*: You roll a 2 first.
   Event *B*: You roll a 5 second. independent; $\frac{1}{36}$

10. You write each of the letters of the word BIOLOGY on pieces of paper and place them in a bag. You randomly draw one letter, do not replace it, then randomly draw a second letter.
    Event *A*: The first letter is O.
    Event *B*: The second letter is B. dependent; $\frac{1}{21}$

11. You flip a coin and roll a number cube.
    Event *A*: The coin shows heads.
    Event *B*: The number cube shows 2. independent; $\frac{1}{12}$

12. A box contains 3 milk chocolates, 3 white chocolates, and 4 dark chocolates. You choose a chocolate at random, eat it, then choose a second chocolate at random.
    Event *A*: You choose a dark chocolate.
    Event *B*: You choose a dark chocolate. dependent; $\frac{2}{15}$

13. ★ **MULTIPLE CHOICE** A vase holds 7 red roses and 5 pink roses. You randomly choose a rose, place it in a different vase, then randomly choose another rose. What is the approximate probability that both the first and second roses are red? B

Ⓐ 0.29 Ⓑ 0.32 Ⓒ 0.34 Ⓓ 0.37

B **CHESS PIECES In Exercises 14–17, consider a bag that contains all of the chess pieces in a set, as shown in the diagram.**

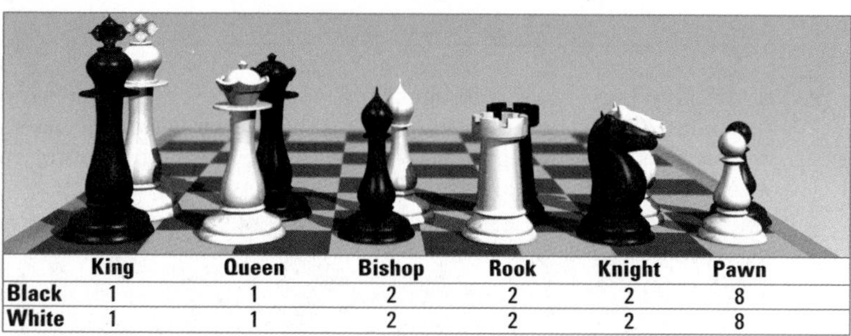

	King	Queen	Bishop	Rook	Knight	Pawn
Black	1	1	2	2	2	8
White	1	1	2	2	2	8

14. You choose one piece at random. Find the probability that you choose a black piece or a queen. $\frac{17}{32}$

15. You choose one piece at random, replace it, then choose a second piece at random. Find the probability that you choose a rook, then a bishop. $\frac{1}{64}$

16. You choose one piece at random, do not replace it, then choose a second piece at random. Find the probability that you choose a king, then a pawn. $\frac{1}{31}$

17. **ERROR ANALYSIS** *Describe* and correct the error in finding the probability that you randomly choose a pawn and a second pawn, without replacement.

$$P(\text{pawn and pawn}) = P(\text{pawn}) \cdot P(\text{pawn}) = \frac{16}{32} \cdot \frac{16}{32} = \frac{1}{4}$$

17. If you first draw a pawn and then do not replace it, the probability of drawing a second pawn is not $\frac{16}{32}$, but $\frac{15}{31}$; $\frac{16}{32} \cdot \frac{15}{31} = \frac{15}{62}$.

In Exercises 18 and 19, use the following information. Two mutually exclusive events for which one or the other must occur are called *complementary* events. If events A and B are complementary events, then $P(A) + P(B) = 1$.

18. **WEATHER** A local meteorologist reports that there is a 70% chance of rain tomorrow. What is the probability that it will *not* rain tomorrow? 30%

19. **BASKETBALL** You make 31% of your attempted 3-point shots. What is the probability that you miss your next attempted 3-point shot? 69%

20. ★ **WRITING** You write the letters of the word WISDOM on pieces of paper and place them in a bag. You randomly choose 2 letters from the bag at the same time. *Explain* whether these events are independent or dependent. What is the probability that you choose the letters S and D?

20. Dependent. *Sample answer*: Even though two pieces of paper are selected at the same time, the selection of one piece of paper affects the selection of the other, so the events are dependent; $\frac{1}{15}$.

C 21. **CHALLENGE** The sections of the spinner shown all have the same area. You spin the spinner.

a. Find the probability that the spinner stops on red *or* a prime number *or* a multiple of 3. You may want to draw a Venn diagram to find the answer. $\frac{7}{8}$

b. Write a general formula for $P(A \text{ or } B \text{ or } C)$ where A, B, and C are overlapping events. *Explain* your reasoning. See margin.

Avoiding Common Errors

Exercises 3–12 Some students may add probabilities when finding $P(\text{A } and \text{ B})$ and multiply probabilities when finding $P(\text{A } or \text{ B})$. Remind these students that they add when the conjunction is *or* and multiply when the conjunction is *and*.

Study Strategy

Exercises 3–8, 9–16 Suggest that students ask themselves key questions when trying to determine whether events are mutually exclusive or overlapping or whether the events are dependent or independent. For example, when finding $P(\text{A } or \text{ B})$, students could ask: *If I choose A, could I also be choosing B?* When finding $P(\text{A } and \text{ B})$, students can ask: *After I find the probability of A, do I then want to find the probability of B or the probability of B given A?*

21b. $P(A) + P(B) + P(C) - P(A \text{ and } B) - P(A \text{ and } C) - P(B \text{ and } C) + P(A \text{ and } B \text{ and } C)$; when $P(A) + P(B) + P(C)$ is added, the overlap of each set is counted twice so it must be subtracted. When you subtract the overlap of each set the overlap of all three sets gets subtracted 3 times, so it must be added one time.

Reading Strategy

Exercises 22–25 Point out to students that these exercises are referenced to examples in the lesson. Encourage students to read through the examples when working on the exercises and to choose the appropriate example as a model for solving the problem.

Internet Reference

Exercise 23 More information about walruses can be found at www.walruses.com/didyouknow.php

Teaching Strategy

Exercises 24, 25 You may want to read these exercises with the class and then discuss the type of compound probability exemplified in each exercise or in each part of the exercise. After the discussion, have students solve the exercises individually and then discuss the solutions as a class. This will help students focus on the processes they should use in learning how to recognize and solve compound probabilities.

25a. See below.

25b.

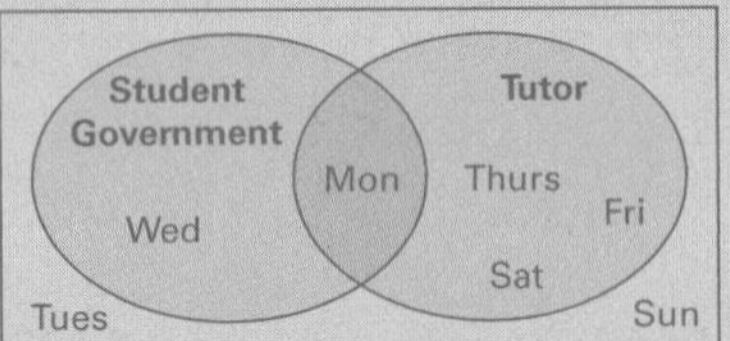

27c. *Sample answer:* You can calculate both the number of favorable outcomes and the number of total outcomes using permutations. There are $_5P_5$ arrangements of the 5 tickets. If you have the aisle seat and your best friend is next to you, there are $_3P_3$ permutations for the remaining seats, which represents the number of favorable outcomes; $\frac{_3P_3}{_5P_5} = \frac{6}{120} = \frac{1}{20}$.

PROBLEM SOLVING

EXAMPLES A **3 and 4** on p. 863 for Exs. 22–23

22. **CONTEST** You can win concert tickets from a radio station if you are the first person to call when the song of the day is played, or if you are the first person to correctly answer the trivia question. The song of the day is played between 5:00 and 5:30 P.M. The trivia question is asked between 5:15 and 5:45 P.M. You begin listening to the radio station at 5:20. Find the probability that you miss the song of the day and the trivia question. $\frac{1}{9}$

@HomeTutor for problem solving help at classzone.com

23. **WALRUS** When a walrus forages for food, it waves its flipper to move sediment 70% of the time. When using the flipper wave technique, a walrus uses its right flipper 89% of the time. Find the probability that a walrus foraging for food uses a flipper and it is the right flipper. 62.3%

@HomeTutor for problem solving help at classzone.com

EXAMPLES **1, 2, 3, and 4** on pp. 861–863 for Ex. 24

24. ★ **SHORT RESPONSE** A survey of 887,403 households found that 270,658 households have a dog, 326,591 have a cat, and 81,641 have both.
    a. What is the probability that one of the households surveyed, chosen at random, has a dog and a cat? about 0.092
    b. What is the probability that one of the households surveyed, chosen at random, has a dog or a cat? 0.58
    c. *Explain* how your answers to parts (a) and (b) are related. See margin.

24c. *Sample answer:* The answer to part b is equal to the sum of the probability of households with dogs and the probability of households with cats, minus the answer to part a.

EXAMPLES B **1 and 2** on pp. 861–862 for Ex. 25

25. ◆ **MULTIPLE REPRESENTATIONS** You have student government meetings on Monday and Wednesday. You tutor in the morning on Monday, Thursday, Friday, and Saturday.
    a. **Making a Table** Make a table that shows your schedule for the week. See margin.
    b. **Drawing a Diagram** Make a Venn diagram that shows the days of the week that you participate in each activity. See margin.
    c. **Using a Formula** Your class is taking a field trip that could be scheduled for any day of the week. Find the probability that it is scheduled for a day when you tutor or have a student government meeting. $\frac{5}{7}$

26. **EARTH SCIENCE** The table shows the ranges of annual mean temperature and precipitation for 57 cities in the U.S. Find the probability that a city in this study has an annual mean temperature in the range 39°F–52°F or an annual precipitation in the range 0–24 inches. $\frac{35}{57}$

Precipitation (inches)	Temperature (degrees Fahrenheit)	
	39–52	**53–66**
0–24	7	7
25–49	21	22

○ = WORKED-OUT SOLUTIONS on p. WS1 ★ = STANDARDIZED TEST PRACTICE ◆ = MULTIPLE REPRESENTATIONS

25a.

Mon	Tues	Wed	Thurs	Fri	Sat	Sun
st. gov.		st. gov.				
tutor			tutor	tutor	tutor	

C **27. CHALLENGE** You have 5 tickets to a play. You invite 4 friends to see the play. You hand out the tickets at random. One ticket is for an aisle seat, and the other tickets are for the next 4 seats in the row.

a. What is the probability that you will get the aisle seat? $\frac{1}{5}$

b. What is the probability that you will get the aisle seat and your best friend will get the ticket for the seat next to you? $\frac{1}{20}$

c. *Explain* how you could solve the problem in part (b) using permutations. See margin.

ILLINOIS MIXED REVIEW

TEST PRACTICE at classzone.com

28. A spinner was spun 32 times. The results are shown in the table below. All sections of the spinner have the same area.

Spinner Results

Yellow	7
Green	11
Red	6
Blue	8

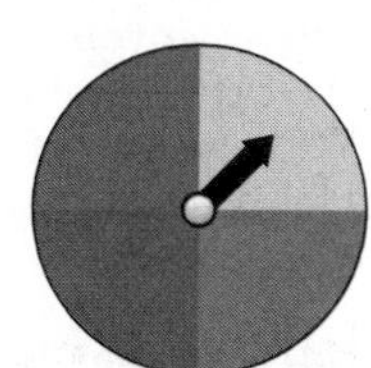

Which color on the spinner has the same experimental probability as theoretical probability?

Ⓐ Yellow Ⓑ Green D Ⓒ Red Ⓓ Blue

QUIZ *for Lessons 13.1–13.4*

1. **MARBLES** A bag contains 16 red marbles and 8 white marbles. You select a marble at random. *(p. 843)*
   a. What is the probability that you select a red marble? $\frac{2}{3}$
   b. What are the odds in favor of selecting a red marble? 2 : 1

2. **PASSWORD** The password for an e-mail account is the word FISH followed by a 3-digit number. The 3-digit number contains the digits 1, 2, and 3. How many different passwords are possible? *(p. 851)* 6

3. **SHUFFLE** A CD plays on random shuffle. The CD has 12 songs on it. Your CD player selects a song at random, plays it, then selects a second song at random. No song is repeated until every song has been played. What is the probability that song 3 is played first and song 1 is played second? *(p. 851)* $\frac{1}{132}$

Evaluate the expression.

4. ${}_5P_4$ *(p. 851)* 120
5. ${}_8P_5$ *(p. 851)* 6720
6. ${}_5C_2$ *(p. 856)* 10
7. ${}_8C_5$ *(p. 856)* 56

8. **NUMBER TILES** Tiles numbered 1–30 are placed in a bag. You select a tile at random. Find the probability that you select an odd number or a prime number. Are the events mutually exclusive or overlapping? *Explain.* *(p. 861)*

8. $\frac{8}{15}$; overlapping. *Sample answer:* The events are overlapping because numbers like 3 and 11 are both odd and prime.

5 ASSESS AND RETEACH

Daily Homework Quiz

Transparency Available

1. A bag contains 4 yellow marbles, 3 blue marbles, and 5 red marbles. You randomly draw a marble, replace it, and draw another marble. What is the probability that you draw a red marble and then a yellow marble? $\frac{5}{36}$

2. A survey of 100 students at your school found that 58 students ride the bus, 22 drive to school, 14 walk, and 6 get a ride from a relative. If one of the students surveyed is chosen at random, what is the probability the student either drives to school or walks? $\frac{9}{25}$

Online Quiz

Available at **classzone.com**

Diagnosis/Remediation

- Practice A, B, C in Chapter 13 Resource Book, pp. 39–41
- Study Guide in Chapter13 Resource Book, pp. 42–43
- Practice Workbook, pp. 202–204
- @HomeTutor

Challenge

Additional challenge is available in the Chapter 13 Resource Book, p. 47.

Quiz

An easily-readable reduced copy of the quiz (with answers) on Lessons 13.1–13.4 from the Assessment Book can be found on p. 840F.

Alternative Strategy

Example 3 on page 863 can be solved by performing a simulation or by using geometry. Point out to students that the simulation in Method 1 gives a probability close to Example 3 on page 863, but not the same as the example. Be sure students realize that different simulations will give different probabilities. Method 2 can help students visualize the relationship between possible and favorable outcomes.

Graphing Calculator

If students need help generating random numbers to perform a simulation, refer them to the directions for the simulations they performed in the extension on page 849.

Teaching Strategy

You may want students to compare their simulations to see how closely they approximate the probability calculated by using the formula in Example 3 in Lesson 13.4 and by using geometry in alternative method 2.

PROBLEM SOLVING WORKSHOP
LESSON 13.4

Using ALTERNATIVE METHODS

Another Way to Solve Example 3, page 863

MULTIPLE REPRESENTATIONS In Example 3 on page 863, you saw how to solve the problem about a bus schedule by using a number line and a formula. You can also solve the problem by performing a simulation or using geometry.

PROBLEM

BUS SCHEDULE You take a city bus from your neighborhood to a location within walking distance of your school. The express bus arrives at your neighborhood between 7:30 and 7:36. The local bus arrives at your neighborhood between 7:30 and 7:40. You arrive at the bus stop at 7:33. Find the probability that you have missed both the express bus and the local bus.

METHOD 1

Performing a Simulation One alternative approach is to perform a simulation.

STEP 1 **Read** the problem. Notice that there is a 6 minute interval when the express bus could arrive and a 10 minute interval when the local bus could arrive. Let 1 represent the first minute, from 7:30 to 7:31, that a bus could arrive. Let 2 represent the second minute, from 7:31 to 7:32, that a bus could arrive. Continue to number the minutes when a bus could arrive.

STEP 2 **Generate** random integers. Use a graphing calculator to generate a random integer from 1 to 6. This number represents the minute that the express bus arrives. Then generate a random integer from 1 to 10. This number represents the minute that the local bus arrives. Perform this simulation 10 times.

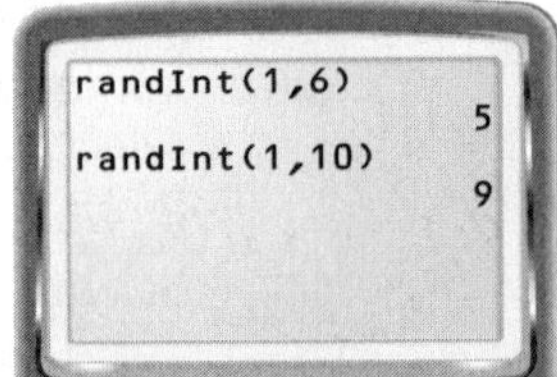

You are not at the bus stop until the fourth minute, so if both numbers that you generate are less than 4, then you miss both buses.

First number	5	4	2	5	2	1	2	3	3	1
Second number	9	1	1	8	4	7	9	10	6	2
Miss both buses?	No	No	Yes	No	No	No	No	No	No	Yes

STEP 3 **Find** the experimental probability that you miss both buses.

$P(\text{miss both buses}) = \frac{2}{10} = \frac{1}{5}$

METHOD 2 **Using Geometry** Another approach is to use geometry. Use the formula for the area of a rectangle to find the number of possible outcomes and the number of favorable outcomes.

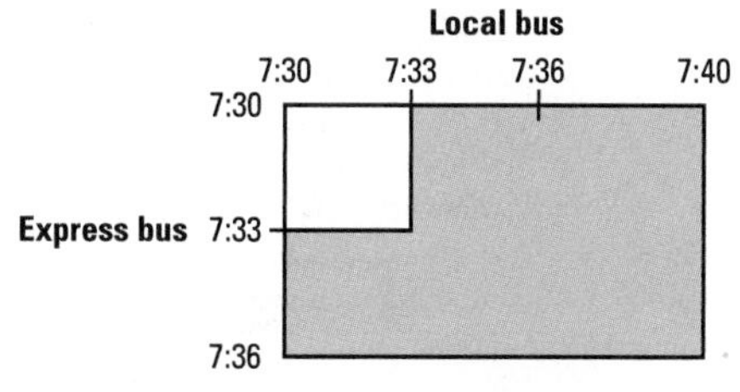

STEP 1 **Draw** a rectangle whose side lengths represent the number of minutes that each bus could arrive.

STEP 2 **Draw** a square within the rectangle to represent the number of minutes that you are *not* at the bus stop.

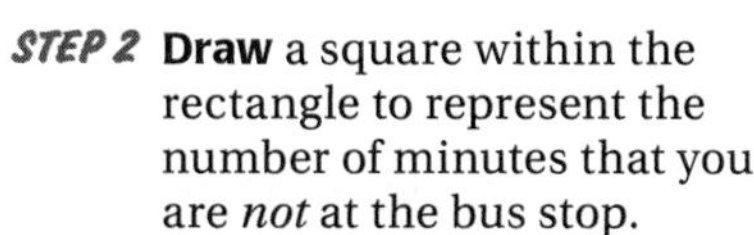

STEP 3 **Calculate** the area of the rectangle that represents the time a bus could arrive. Also calculate the area of the square that represents the time that you are *not* at the bus stop.

Time a bus could arrive: $A = 6 \cdot 10 = 60$

Time you are *not* at bus stop: $A = 3 \cdot 3 = 9$

STEP 4 **Find** the probability that you miss both buses by forming the ratio of the areas from step 2.

$$P(\text{miss both buses}) = \frac{9}{60} = \frac{3}{20}$$

PRACTICE

1. **WHAT IF?** In the problem on page 868, suppose you arrive at 7:34. What is the probability that you miss both buses? $\frac{4}{15}$

2. **VISITING FRIENDS** Two friends are planning to visit you this evening. You expect one friend to arrive at your house between 7:00 and 7:30 P.M. You expect the other friend to arrive between 7:10 and 7:20 P.M. You have to run an errand from 7:00 until 7:15 P.M. What is the probability that you are home when both friends arrive? Solve this problem using two different methods. $\frac{1}{4}$

3. **WHAT IF?** In Exercise 2, suppose a third friend plans to visit you this evening. This friend plans to arrive at your house between 7:00 and 7:20 P.M. What is the probability that you are home when all three of your friends arrive? *Explain* how you found your answer. See margin.

4. **RAFFLE** You enter two different raffles during your neighborhood's street fair. The winner of the first raffle will be announced between 6:00 and 6:30 P.M. The winner of the second raffle will be announced between 6:15 and 6:45 P.M. You leave the fair at 5:00 P.M. and return at 6:20 P.M. What is the probability that you hear the winner of each raffle announced? Solve this problem using two different methods. $\frac{5}{18}$

5. **ERROR ANALYSIS** A student solved the problem in Exercise 4 as shown. *Describe* and correct the error. See margin.

$$P(\text{hear both winners}) = \frac{\text{Favorable time}}{\text{Total time}} = \frac{10 \text{ minutes}}{30 \text{ minutes}} = \frac{1}{3}$$

Avoiding Common Errors

When using simulations in the practice exercises, caution students to generate random numbers that match the minutes which represent the *possible* outcomes of the events.

Study Strategy

Encourage students to rotate the three methods they have learned in solving the problems in the exercises. Tell them that they will gain experience with all three methods and that by trying each method, they will be able to ascertain which method works best for them.

3. $\frac{1}{16}$. *Sample answer:* The third friend can arrive any time in a 20 minute span, and I will be away from the house for 15 of those minutes. The probability is $\frac{1}{4}$ that I will be home when the third friend arrives. Since the three friends arrive independently of each other, you can multiply the probability that you are home when the other two friends arrive by $\frac{1}{4}$ to calculate the probability that you are home when all three friends arrive; $\frac{1}{4} \cdot \frac{1}{4} = \frac{1}{16}$.

5. *Sample answer:* The times at which each raffle is announced are independent, so the two probabilities should be calculated separately and then multiplied; $\frac{10}{30} \cdot \frac{25}{30} = \frac{1}{3} \cdot \frac{5}{6} = \frac{5}{18}$.

Illinois Mixed Review

1. C
2. F
3. A
4. H
5. B
6. H
7. B
8. H

Illinois *Mixed Review*

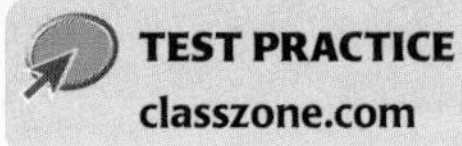

Lessons 13.1–13.4

1. **SURVEY** A study surveyed 100 male and 100 female 13-year-olds, and 100 male and 100 female 15-year-olds. The table shows the numbers of those surveyed who eat fruit every day. For which of the following groups is a randomly selected person most likely to eat fruit every day?

	13-year-olds	15-year-olds
Male	60	53
Female	61	58

A. 15-year-old females
B. 13-year-old males
C. 13-year-olds
D. 15-year-old males

2. **BASKETBALL** In NCAA women's basketball tournaments from 1982 to 2003, the teams seeded, or ranked, number one have won 283 games and lost 71 games in the tournament. Find the probability that a team, chosen at random from all those that have been seeded number one, lost a game in the tournament.

F. $\frac{71}{354}$ **H.** $\frac{212}{283}$
G. $\frac{71}{283}$ **J.** $\frac{283}{354}$

3. **WEATHER** A meteorologist reports that there is a 15% chance of snow tomorrow. What are the odds in favor of snow tomorrow?

A. 3:17 **C.** 20:3
B. 17:3 **D.** 15:1

4. **PRO SPORTS** In the United States, there are 21 states with teams in the National Football League and 17 states with Major League Baseball teams. There are 15 states that have both types of teams. What is the probability that a state chosen at random has either a team in the National Football League or a Major League Baseball team?

F. 23% **H.** 46%
G. 38% **J.** 76%

5. **OMELET** You are ordering an omelet with two ingredients. You can choose your ingredients from the following list: cheese, mushrooms, onions, tomatoes, peppers, sausage, ham, steak. How many possible omelets can you choose?

A. 15 **C.** 56
B. 28 **D.** 64

6. **TALENT SHOW** Your friend is competing in a talent show. There are 5 contestants in the show, and the order of the contestants is determined randomly. You are running late and will miss the first 2 contestants. What is the probability that you will *not* miss your friend's performance?

F. 30% **H.** 60%
G. 36% **J.** 80%

7. **SUNKEN TREASURE** You hear a rumor that there is a sunken treasure located in the ocean within a 2 mile radius of a small island. You buy diving gear and begin to search for the treasure. With one tank of oxygen, you can thoroughly search an area of approximately 0.5 square mile. You have 3 oxygen tanks to use. If the rumor is true, what is the approximate probability that you will find the treasure?

A. 4.0% **C.** 23.9%
B. 11.9% **D.** 75.0%

8. **CD CLUB** A music club gives you 6 free CDs for joining. You would like to own 11 of the free CDs that are offered. How many combinations of 6 CDs from the 11 CDs can you choose?

F. 462 **H.** 332,640
G. 720 **J.** 39,916,800

13.5 Analyze Surveys and Samples

Before You found experimental probabilities.
Now You will identify populations and sampling methods.
Why? So you can analyze surveys of sports fans, as in Ex. 15.

Key Vocabulary
- survey
- population
- sample
- biased sample
- biased question

A **survey** is a study of one or more characteristics of a group. The entire group you want information about is called a **population**. You may find it difficult to survey an entire population. Instead, you can survey a **sample**, which is a part of the population. Five types of samples are listed below.

KEY CONCEPT *For Your Notebook*

Sampling Methods

In a **random sample**, every member of the population has an equal chance of being selected.

In a **stratified random sample**, the population is divided into distinct groups. Members are selected at random from each group.

In a **systematic sample**, a rule is used to select members of the population.

In a **convenience sample**, only members of the population who are easily accessible are selected.

In a **self-selected sample**, members of the population select themselves by volunteering.

EXAMPLE 1 Classify a sampling method

EMPLOYEE SAFETY The owners of a company with several factories conduct a survey to determine whether employees are informed about safety regulations. At each factory, 50 employees are chosen at random to complete the survey. Identify the population and classify the sampling method.

Solution

The population is all company employees. Because the population is divided into distinct groups (individual factories), with employees chosen at random from each group, the sample is a stratified random sample.

GUIDED PRACTICE for Example 1

1. **WHAT IF?** In Example 1, suppose the owners survey each employee whose last name begins with M. Classify the sampling method. systematic

1 PLAN AND PREPARE

Warm-Up Exercises

Transparency Available

A spinner has 5 sections of equal area, with sections numbered 1–5.

1. You toss a coin and spin the spinner. How many outcomes are in the sample space? 10
2. You spin the spinner twice. How many outcomes are in the sample space? 25

Notetaking Guide

Transparency Available

Promotes interactive learning and notetaking skills, pp. 308–310.

Pacing

Basic: 1 day
Average: 1 day
Advanced: 1 day
Block: 0.5 block with 13.6
- See *Teaching Guide/Lesson Plan.*

2 FOCUS AND MOTIVATE

Essential Question

Big Idea 2, p. 841

How do you identify populations and sampling methods? **Tell students they will learn how to answer this question by analyzing surveys and samples.**

Resource Planning Guide

Chapter Resource Book
- Teaching Guide/Lesson Plan (pp. 48–49)
- Practice levels A, B, C (pp. 50–52)
- Study Guide (pp. 53–54)
- Catch-up for Absent Students (p. 55)
- Application (p. 56)
- Challenge (p. 57)

Workbooks
- Notetaking Guide (pp. 308–310)
- Practice Workbook (pp. 204–205)

Teaching Options
- **Power Presentations CD-ROM** provides dynamic electronic teaching resources for the classroom.
- **Activity Generator CD-ROM** provides editable activities for all ability levels.

Interactive Technology
- Easy Planner
- Power Presentations CD-ROM
- Activity Generator CD-ROM
- Animated Algebra
- Test Generator CD-ROM
- Online Quiz
- eWorkbook
- eEdition
- @HomeTutor

Resources for English Learners
- Quick Reference for English Learners
- Spanish Study Guide
- Multi-Language Visual Glossary
- Student Resources in Spanish

See also the *Algebra 1 Toolkit* for more strategies for meeting individual needs.

Motivating the Lesson

You want to know how many students participate in Internet chat rooms. By learning how to identify populations and sampling methods, you can design an unbiased survey.

3 TEACH

Extra Example 1

Owners of a computer store survey customers to see whether they should expand their game selection. They survey customers in the game aisle. Identify the population and classify the sampling method. **Population: store customers; Method: convenience sampling**

Extra Example 2

In Extra Example 1, suppose owners randomly survey all customers at the store on a Saturday. Is the method likely to result in a biased sample? **Saturday customers may reflect different buying attitudes than weekday customers, so the method may result in a biased sample.**

Extra Example 3

Tell whether the question is potentially biased. Explain your answer. *Do you think the city should renovate the library?* **It does not encourage a particular response, so the question is not biased.**

Closing the Lesson

Have students summarize the major points of the lesson and answer the Essential Question: How do you identify populations and sampling methods?

- **A population is the entire group you want information about.**

Identify populations by looking for all members of a group affected by a survey. Identify sampling methods by deciding if they represent the selected population.

BIASED SAMPLES A sample chosen for a survey should be representative of the population. A **biased sample** is a sample that is not representative. In a biased sample, parts of the population may be over-represented or under-represented.

Random samples and stratified random samples (as in Example 1) are the most likely types of samples to be representative. A systematic sample may be representative if the rule used to choose individuals is not biased.

EXAMPLE 2 Identify a potentially biased sample

In Example 1, suppose the owners question 50 workers chosen at random from one factory. Is the method likely to result in a biased sample?

Solution

Workers at other factories may hold significantly different opinions, so the method may result in a biased sample.

BIASED QUESTIONS A question that encourages a particular response is a **biased question**. Survey questions should be worded to avoid bias.

EXAMPLE 3 Identify potentially biased questions

Tell whether the question is potentially biased. Explain your answer. If the question is potentially biased, rewrite it so that it is not.

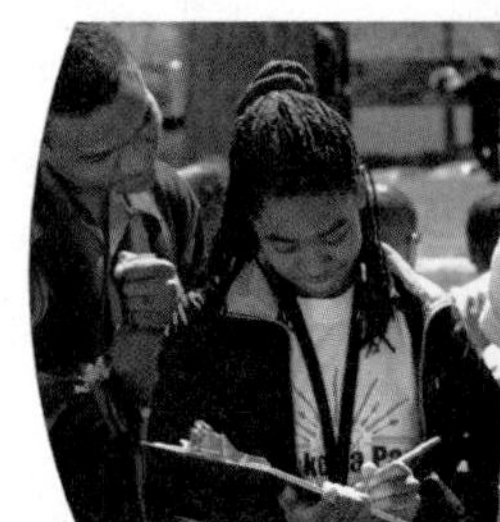

a. Don't you agree that the voting age should be lowered to 16 because many 16-year-olds are responsible and informed?

b. Do you think the city should risk an increase in pollution by allowing expansion of the Northern Industrial Park?

Solution

a. This question is biased because it suggests that lowering the voting age is a good thing to do. An unbiased question is "Do you think the voting age should be lowered to 16?"

b. This question is biased because it suggests that the proposed expansion will be bad for the environment. An unbiased question is "Do you think the city should allow expansion of the Northern Industrial Park?"

✓ GUIDED PRACTICE for Examples 2 and 3

2. **SOCCER** In a survey about Americans' interest in soccer, the first 25 people admitted to a high school soccer game were asked, "How interested are you in the world's most popular sport, soccer?" **a, b. See margin.**
   a. Is the sampling method likely to result in a biased sample? *Explain.*
   b. Is the question potentially biased? *Explain* your answer. If the question is potentially biased, rewrite it so that it is not.

Differentiated Instruction

English Learners Students should be aware that there can be more than one way to rewrite a biased question as an unbiased one. In **Example 3b**, the basic question is biased because it asks if you agree to increasing pollution. An equally valid, unbiased question, would be "Do you think the city will have an increase in pollution by allowing the expansion of the Northern Industrial Park?"

See also the *Algebra 1 Toolkit* for more strategies.

13.5 EXERCISES

HOMEWORK KEY ○ = **WORKED-OUT SOLUTIONS** on p. WS33 for Exs. 3 and 15
★ = **STANDARDIZED TEST PRACTICE** Exs. 2, 6, and 17

SKILL PRACTICE

A

1. **VOCABULARY** Copy and complete: In a(n) _?_ sample, participants are chosen using a rule. systematic

2. ★ **WRITING** *Explain* how a sample is related to a population. A sample is a portion of a population.

POPULATIONS AND SAMPLES In Exercises 3–5, identify the population and classify the sampling method.

EXAMPLE 1 on p. 871 for Exs. 3–6

3. **RESTAURANT SERVICE** A restaurant manager wants to evaluate the restaurant's quality of service. Diners are given mail-in comment cards. people who have eaten at the restaurant, self-selected

4. **EXTRACURRICULAR ACTIVITIES** Your school wants to know if students are satisfied with the school's extracurricular activities. In each grade, every tenth student on an alphabetized list is surveyed. students at your school, systematic

5. **CUSTOMER SATISFACTION** An airline wants to gather information on passenger satisfaction during a flight. A computer randomly selects 30 passengers to complete a survey. passengers of the airline, random

6. ★ **MULTIPLE CHOICE** Scientists wanted to gather information about the birds in a particular region. They chose observation sites and asked bird watchers at those sites to record the number and types of birds they saw in 3 minutes. What population was being studied? A

   Ⓐ Birds Ⓑ Sites Ⓒ Scientists Ⓓ Bird watchers

EXAMPLE 2 on p. 872 for Exs. 7–8

BIASED SAMPLES Tell whether the sampling method used is likely to result in a biased sample. *Explain.*

7. **NEIGHBORHOOD WATCH** A family wants to gather information from other residents on their street about forming a neighborhood watch. They survey every third house on both sides of the street. Not likely. *Sample answer:* The sample should represent the neighborhood.

8. **NURSE SURVEY** The American Nurses Association wanted to gather information about the working environment for nurses in hospitals. A survey for nurses was posted on the association's website. See margin.

EXAMPLE 3 on p. 872 for Exs. 9–11

B

BIASED QUESTIONS In Exercises 9 and 10, tell whether the question is potentially biased. *Explain* your answer. 9, 10. See margin.

9. Do you support the incumbent's tax plan or the challenger's tax plan?

10. Do you prefer the ease of shopping online or the fun of going to a mall?

11. **ERROR ANALYSIS** *Describe* and correct the error in revising the survey question "Don't you think the minimum driving age should be lower?" so that it is not biased. See margin.

Not biased:
Is the minimum driving age too high or too low? ✗

C

12. **CHALLENGE** Two toothpaste manufacturers each claim that 4 out of every 5 dentists use their brand exclusively. Both manufacturers can support their claims with survey results. *Explain* how this is possible.

12. *Sample answer:* Both manufacturers can make this claim if they used biased survey questions, techniques, or samples.

4 PRACTICE AND APPLY

Assignment Guide

Answer Transparencies available for all exercises

Basic:
Day 1: pp. 873–874
Exs. 1–10, 13–16, 19–27

Average:
Day 1: pp. 873–874
Exs. 1, 2, 4–11, 13–17, 19–27

Advanced:
Day 1: pp. 873–874
Exs. 1, 2, 5–27*

Block:
pp. 873–874
Exs. 1, 2, 4–11, 13–17, 19–27
(with 13.6)

Differentiated Instruction

See *Algebra 1 Best Practices Toolkit* for suggestions on addressing the needs of a diverse classroom.

Homework Check

For a quick check of student understanding of key concepts, go over the following exercises:

Basic: 4, 7, 9, 13, 14
Average: 5, 8, 10, 14, 15
Advanced: 6, 8, 11, 15, 16

Extra Practice

- Student Edition, p. 950
- Chapter 13 Resource Book: Practice levels A, B, C, pp. 50–52

Practice Worksheet

An easily-readable reduced practice page (with answers) for this lesson can be found on p. 840C.

10. Potentially biased. *Sample answer:* Even though it presents both choices in a favorable light, the question is not neutral and is likely to affect the survey's results.

11. *Sample answer:* The new question presumes that the driving age should be changed, and does not present the option that it should remain the same; "What do you think about the current driving age?"

p. 872
2a–b. See Additional Answers beginning on p. AA1.

p. 873
8. Likely. *Sample answer:* Since it is a self-selected sample, only the nurses with extreme views are likely to take the time to respond, and the results of the survey will be swayed toward either extreme negative or positive views.

9. Not potentially biased. *Sample answer:* This question simply presents the two choices.

5 ASSESS AND RETEACH

Daily Homework Quiz

Transparency Available

Identify the population and classify the sampling method.

1. You want to know if students would like year-round schools. You survey every fifth student entering first period classes. **Population: all students at a school; systematic sample**
2. A theater owner asks people in line to see a horror movie if they think the theater should show more comedies. Explain whether the survey method is likely to result in a biased survey. **People who go to horror movies may prefer horror to comedy, so the survey may be biased.**

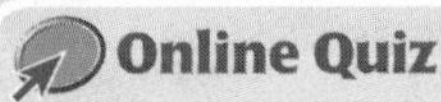

Online Quiz

Available at **classzone.com**

Diagnosis/Remediation

- Practice A, B, C in Chapter 13 Resource Book, pp. 50–52
- Study Guide in Chapter13 Resource Book, pp. 53–54
- Practice Workbook, pp. 204–205
- @HomeTutor

Challenge

Additional challenge is available in the Chapter 13 Resource Book, p. 57.

13. ***Sample answer:*** **This question is phrased to prompt people into agreeing that the athletic field is more important than the science lab; "Which do you think the school needs more: a new athletic field or a new science lab?"**

14. ***Sample answer:*** **This question suggests that prices are already too high, and is likely to make respondents more likely to say no; "Would you pay higher concert ticket prices to finance a new arena?"**

16, 17b, 18. See Additional Answers beginning on p. AA1.

PROBLEM SOLVING

EXAMPLES 2 and 3 on p. 872 for Exs. 13–16 [A]

In Exercises 13 and 14, explain why the question is biased. Then rewrite it so that it is not. 13, 14. See margin.

13. Don't you agree that the school needs a new athletic field more than a new science lab?

@HomeTutor for problem solving help at classzone.com

14. Would you pay even higher concert ticket prices to finance a new arena?

@HomeTutor for problem solving help at classzone.com

15. No. *Sample answer:* Only some of the fans are able to attend games, and those who attend games may have different player preferences than thos who do not attend games.

15. BASEBALL Every Major League Baseball (MLB) season, players are chosen to represent the two leagues in an All-Star game. At each MLB park, fans are given ballots to vote for their favorite players. Are the ballots collected at the Chicago Cubs' park, Wrigley Field, necessarily representative of the opinions of all Chicago Cubs fans? *Explain.*

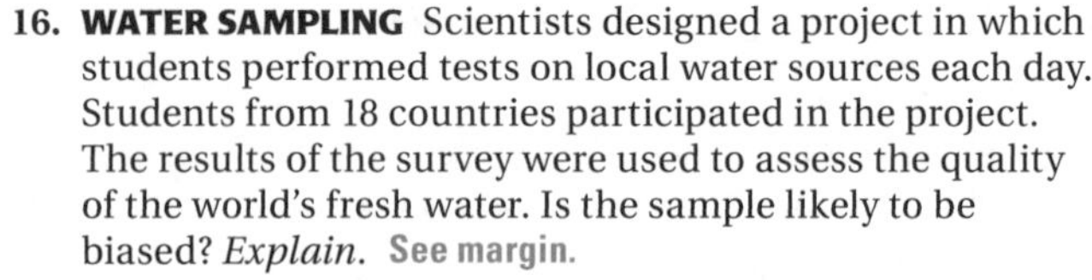

16. WATER SAMPLING Scientists designed a project in which students performed tests on local water sources each day. Students from 18 countries participated in the project. The results of the survey were used to assess the quality of the world's fresh water. Is the sample likely to be biased? *Explain.* See margin.

17a. *Sample answer:* Obtain a list of everyone at the school and select names randomly using a random number generator.

[B] **17. ★ SHORT RESPONSE** You plan to report on the academic performance of students in your school for your school newspaper.

a. *Describe* how you could choose a representative sample.

b. Write an unbiased question you could use to collect information on how many hours per night a student studies. *Explain* why your question is unbiased. See margin.

[C] **18. CHALLENGE** A systematic sample of a population is used for a survey containing unbiased questions. *Explain* how it is possible for the survey to be biased. *Describe* a situation in which this might occur. See margin.

TEST PRACTICE at classzone.com

ILLINOIS MIXED REVIEW

19. Joe has a blue number cube and a red number cube. If joe tosses both cubes, what is the probability that he will get a 3 on the blue cube and an even number on the red cube? A

Ⓐ $\frac{1}{12}$ Ⓑ $\frac{1}{3}$ Ⓒ $\frac{1}{2}$ Ⓓ $\frac{2}{3}$

20. A salesperson knows that about 20% of his conversations with customers will result in a sale. Last week he made 26 sales. About how many customers did he speak with last week? C

Ⓐ 5   Ⓑ 74   Ⓒ 130   Ⓓ 220

EXTRA PRACTICE for Lesson 13.5, p. 950

ONLINE QUIZ at classzone.com

13.6 Use Measures of Central Tendency and Dispersion

10.11.05 Calculate, interpret, and use measures of central tendency and dispersion.

Before You analyzed surveys and samples.

Now You will compare measures of central tendency and dispersion.

Why? So you can analyze and compare data, as in Example 1.

Key Vocabulary
- **measure of dispersion**
- **range**
- **mean absolute deviation**

KEY CONCEPT *For Your Notebook*

Measures of Central Tendency

The **mean**, or *average*, of a numerical data set is denoted by $\bar{x}$, which is read as "*x*-bar." For the data set $x_1, x_2, \ldots, x_n$, the mean is $\bar{x} = \frac{x_1 + x_2 + \ldots + x_n}{n}$.

The **median** of a numerical data set is the middle number when the values are written in numerical order. If the data set has an even number of values, the median is the mean of the two middle values.

The **mode** of a data set is the value that occurs most frequently. There may be one mode, no mode, or more than one mode.

EXAMPLE 1 Compare measures of central tendency

The heights (in feet) of 8 waterfalls in the state of Washington are listed below. Which measure of central tendency best represents the data?

1000, 1000, 1181, 1191, 1200, 1268, 1328, 2584

Solution

$$\bar{x} = \frac{1000 + 1000 + 1181 + 1191 + 1200 + 1268 + 1328 + 2584}{8} = \frac{10,752}{8} = 1344$$

The median is the mean of the two middle values, 1191 and 1200, or 1195.5.

The mode is 1000.

▶ The median best represents the data. The mode is significantly less than most of the data, and the mean is significantly greater than most of the data.

Animated Algebra at classzone.com

✓ **GUIDED PRACTICE** for Example 1

1. **WHAT IF?** In Example 1, suppose you eliminate the greatest data value, 2584. Which measure of central tendency best represents the remaining data? *Explain* your reasoning. *Sample answer:* Median; the median, 1191, is close to the data points.

1 PLAN AND PREPARE

Warm-Up Exercises

Transparency Available

1. Order from least to greatest: 10.14, 11.2, 10.1, 10.08, 11.21 **10.08, 10.1, 10.14, 11.2, 11.21**
2. Jenna scored the following points in her last five basketball games: 28, 18, 24, 22, and 18. What is Jenna's average score for the 5 games? **22 points**

Notetaking Guide

Transparency Available

Promotes interactive learning and notetaking skills, pp. 311–313.

Pacing

Basic: 1 day
Average: 1 day
Advanced: 1 day
Block: 0.5 block with 13.5
- See *Teaching Guide/Lesson Plan.*

2 FOCUS AND MOTIVATE

Essential Question

Big Idea 2, p. 841

How do you compare measures of central tendency and dispersion? **Tell students they will learn how to answer this question by using the mean, median, mode, range, and mean absolute deviation to analyze data.**

Resource Planning Guide

Chapter Resource Book
- Teaching Guide/Lesson Plan (pp. 58–59)
- Activity Master (p. 60)
- Practice levels A, B, C (pp. 63–65)
- Study Guide (pp. 66–67)
- Catch-up for Absent Students (p. 68)
- Problem Solving Workshop (p. 69)
- Challenge (p. 70)

Workbooks
- Notetaking Guide (pp. 311–313)
- Practice Workbook (pp. 206–207)

Teaching Options
- **Power Presentations CD-ROM** provides dynamic electronic teaching resources for the classroom.
- **Activity Generator CD-ROM** provides editable activities for all ability levels.

Interactive Technology
- Easy Planner
- Power Presentations CD-ROM
- Activity Generator CD-ROM
- Animated Algebra
- Test Generator CD-ROM
- Online Quiz
- eWorkbook
- eEdition
- @HomeTutor

Resources for English Learners
- Quick Reference for English Learners
- Spanish Study Guide
- Multi-Language Visual Glossary
- Student Resources in Spanish

See also the *Algebra 1 Toolkit* for more strategies for meeting individual needs.

MEASURES OF DISPERSION A **measure of dispersion** describes the dispersion, or spread, of data. Two such measures are the *range*, which gives the length of the interval containing the data, and the *mean absolute deviation*, which gives the average variation of the data from the mean.

REVIEW ABSOLUTE VALUE

For help with absolute value, see p. 66.

KEY CONCEPT *For Your Notebook*

Measures of Dispersion

The **range** of a numerical data set is the difference of the greatest value and the least value.

The **mean absolute deviation** of the data set $x_1, x_2, \ldots, x_n$ is given by:

$$\text{Mean absolute deviation} = \frac{|x_1 - \overline{x}| + |x_2 - \overline{x}| + \ldots + |x_n - \overline{x}|}{n}$$

EXAMPLE 2 Compare measures of dispersion

RUNNING The top 10 finishing times (in seconds) for runners in two men's races are given. The times in a 100 meter dash are in set A, and the times in a 200 meter dash are in set B. Compare the spread of the data for the two sets using (**a**) the range and (**b**) the mean absolute deviation.

A: 10.62, 10.94, 10.94, 10.98, 11.05, 11.13, 11.15, 11.28, 11.29, 11.32

B: 21.37, 21.40, 22.23, 22.23, 22.34, 22.34, 22.36, 22.60, 22.66, 22.73

Solution

a. A: $11.32 - 10.62 = 0.7$ B: $22.73 - 21.37 = 1.36$

▶ The range of set B is greater than the range of set A. So, the data in B cover a wider interval than the data in A.

b. The mean of set A is 11.07, so the mean absolute deviation is:

$$\frac{|10.62 - 11.07| + |10.94 - 11.07| + \ldots + |11.32 - 11.07|}{10} = 0.164$$

The mean of set B is 22.226, so the mean absolute deviation is:

$$\frac{|21.37 - 22.226| + |21.40 - 22.226| + \ldots + |22.73 - 22.226|}{10} = 0.3364$$

▶ The mean absolute deviation of set B is greater, so the average variation from the mean is greater for the data in B than for the data in A.

REVIEW NEGATIVE NUMBERS

When using the formula for mean absolute deviation, you will encounter negative numbers. For help with negative numbers, see p. 64.

✓ **GUIDED PRACTICE** for Example 2

2. RUNNING The top 10 finishing times (in seconds) for runners in a men's 400 meter dash are 46.89, 47.65, 48.15, 49.05, 49.19, 49.50, 49.68, 51.09, 53.31, and 53.68. *Compare* the spread of the data with that of set A in Example 2 using (**a**) the range and (**b**) the mean absolute deviation.

2a. The range of finishing times for the men's 400 m dash (6.79) is greater than the range for set A (0.7). 2b. The mean absolute deviation is greater for the men's 400 m dash (1.7246) than it is for set A (0.164).

Motivating the Lesson

You follow the career of a baseball player. You can use measures of central tendency and dispersion to analyze and compare statistical data gathered on the player.

3 TEACH

Extra Example 1

The lengths (in miles) of the 10 longest rivers in the U.S. are listed below. Which measure of central tendency best represents the data?

1290, 1310, 1420, 1450, 1460, 1900, 1900, 1980, 2340, 2540

the mean or the median, since both are close to the middle of the data

An **Animated Algebra** activity is available on-line for **Example 1**. This activity is also available on the **Power Presentations CD-ROM**.

Extra Example 2

The top 5 finishing times (in seconds) for swimmers in two women's races are given. Times for the 50-yard free are in set A and for the 100-yard free in set B. Compare the spread of the data for the two sets using (a) the range and (b) the mean absolute deviation.

A: 24.32, 24.34, 24.48, 24.82, 25.02

B: 52.90, 52.96, 52.98, 53.02, 53.24

Data in set A cover a wider interval than data in set B. The average variation from the mean is greater for set A than for set B.

Closing the Lesson

Have students summarize the major points of the lesson and answer the Essential Question: How do you compare measures of central tendency and dispersion?

- **Measures of central tendency are the mean, median, and mode.**
- **Measures of dispersion are range and mean absolute deviation.**

Compare mean, median, and mode to find which measure best represent most of the data. Compare measures of dispersion to find which data set covers a wider interval.

Differentiated Instruction

Auditory Learners Students may have difficulty with relating the mathematical notation in a formula to its meaning. The mean absolute deviation can be verbalized as *the average of all of the distances of the data points from the mean.*

See also the *Algebra 1 Toolkit* for more strategies.

13.6 EXERCISES

HOMEWORK KEY ◯ = WORKED-OUT SOLUTIONS on p. WS33 for Exs. 7 and 19
★ = STANDARDIZED TEST PRACTICE Exs. 2, 9, 17, 19, and 22

SKILL PRACTICE

A

1. **VOCABULARY** Copy and complete: The value that occurs most frequently in a data set is called the _?_ of the data. mode

2. ★ **WRITING** How are measures of central tendency and measures of dispersion used to compare data? See margin.

EXAMPLE 1 on p. 875 for Exs. 3–10

MEASURES OF CENTRAL TENDENCY Find the mean, median, and mode(s) of the data.

3. 1, 1, 1, 2, 3, 3, 5, 5, 6 3, 3, 1
4. 9, 10, 12, 15, 16 12.4, 12, no mode
5. 13, 16, 19, 20, 22, 25, 30, 31 22, 21, no mode
6. 14, 15, 15, 14, 14, 16, 18, 15 15.125, 15, 14 and 15
7. 5.52, 5.44, 3.60, 5.76, 3.80, 7.22 $5.22\overline{3}$, 5.48, no mode
8. 300, 320, 341, 348, 360, 333 $333.\overline{6}$, 337, no mode
9. ★ **MULTIPLE CHOICE** What is the median of the data set? B

   0.7, 0.3, 0.7, 0.8, 0.9, 0.4, 1.0, 1.6, 1.2

   Ⓐ 0.7 Ⓑ 0.8 Ⓒ 0.9 Ⓓ 1.0

10. **ERROR ANALYSIS** *Describe* and correct the error in finding the median of the data set. The list needs to be ordered before you can find the median; 2, 3, 4, 4, 6, 6, 7, 8, 8, the median is 6.

7 4 6 2 4 6 8 8 3

The median is 4.

EXAMPLE 2 on p. 876 for Exs. 11–16

B

MEASURES OF DISPERSION Find the range and mean absolute deviation of the data. Round to the nearest hundredth, if necessary.

11. 30, 35, 20, 85, 60 65, 21.2
12. 111, 135, 115, 120, 145, 130 34, 10.67
13. 30, 45, 52, 48, 100, 45, 42, 45 70, 12.56
14. 505, 510, 480, 550, 495, 500 70, 15.56
15. 1.25, 1.50, 1.70, 0.85, 1.00, 1.25 0.85, 0.23
16. 38.2, 80.1, 2.6, 84.2, 2.5, 5.5 81.7, 31.98
17. ★ **WRITING** *Explain* why the mean absolute deviation of a data set is generally a better measure of dispersion than the range.

17. *Sample answer:* The range only considers the two extreme values, while the mean absolute deviation is affected by all of the values.

C

18. **CHALLENGE** Write a data set that has a mean of 10, a median of 10, and modes of 5 and 8. *Sample answer:* 5, 5, 8 , 8, 10, 11, 13, 14, 16

PROBLEM SOLVING

EXAMPLE 1 on p. 875 for Exs. 19–20

A

19. ★ **SHORT RESPONSE** The weights (in pounds) of ten pumpkins are 22, 21, 24, 24, 5, 24, 5, 23, 24, and 24.
    a. What is the range of the pumpkin weights? 19 lb
    b. Find the mean, median, and mode(s) of the pumpkin weights. 19.6 lb, 23.5 lb, 24 lb
    c. Which measure of central tendency best represents the data? *Explain.* See margin.

@HomeTutor for problem solving help at classzone.com

4 PRACTICE AND APPLY

Assignment Guide

Answer Transparencies available for all exercises

Basic:
Day 1: pp. 877–878
Exs. 1–14, 19–21, 24

Average:
Day 1: pp. 877–878
Exs. 1, 2, 4–10, 13–17, 19–22, 24

Advanced:
Day 1: pp. 877–878
Exs. 1, 5–9, 13–24*

Block:
pp. 877–878
Exs. 1, 2, 4–10, 13–17, 19–22, 24 (with 13.5)

Differentiated Instruction

See *Algebra 1 Best Practices Toolkit* for suggestions on addressing the needs of a diverse classroom.

Homework Check

For a quick check of student understanding of key concepts, go over the following exercises:

Basic: 4, 10, 12, 19, 21
Average: 6, 14, 16, 20, 21
Advanced: 8, 16, 17, 20, 21

Extra Practice

- Student Edition, p. 950
- Chapter 13 Resource Book: Practice levels A, B, C, pp. 63–65

Practice Worksheet

An easily-readable reduced practice page (with answers) for this lesson can be found on p. 840C.

2. *Sample answer:* Measures of central tendency and measures of dispersion are useful in comparing data by providing numbers that represent how spread apart the data are and where the center of the data is. These numbers can be compared for different data sets, providing a picture of the relative position and spread of the data sets.

19c. Median. *Sample answer:* The mode is the greatest data value and the mean is less than 8 of the 10 data values.

5 ASSESS AND RETEACH

Daily Homework Quiz

Transparency Available

1. The list shows the number of e-mails Brennan sent in 8 days. Find the mean, median, and mode(s) of the data. Which measure of central tendency best represents the data?

   45, 25, 38, 42, 51, 52, 24, 51

   Mean: 41, Median: 43.5, Mode: 51; the median best represents the data since the mean is toward the lower end of the data and the mode is toward the upper end.

2. Find the range and mean absolute deviation of the data. Round to the nearest hundredth, if necessary.

   38, 43, 56, 84, 98, 99, 102, 103

   Range: 65; mean absolute deviation: 24.16

Available at **classzone.com**

Diagnosis/Remediation

- Practice A, B, C in Chapter 13 Resource Book, pp. 63–65
- Study Guide in Chapter13 Resource Book, pp. 66–67
- Practice Workbook, pp. 206–207
- @HomeTutor

Challenge

Additional challenge is available in the Chapter 13 Resource Book, p. 70.

22a. Mean: about 67, median: 40. *Sample answer:* The median better represents the data because the mean is highly affected by the Mississippi River, which is substantially higher than the other rivers.

22b. 39.33; yes. *Sample answer:* It is a better representation because the extremely high relative value of the Mississippi river greatly inflated the mean in part (a).

22c, 23b. See Additional Answers beginning on p. AA1.

20. **POPULATION** The population densities (in people per square mile) for each of the 10 most densely populated states in 2003 were 719.0, 418.5, 315.6, 563.6, 820.6, 1164.6, 406.5, 279.3, 275.9, and 1029.9.

a. Find the mean, median, and mode(s) of the data set. **599.35, 491.05, no mode**

b. Which measure of central tendency best represents the data? *Explain.*

@HomeTutor for problem solving help at classzone.com

EXAMPLE 2 B on p. 876 for Ex. 21

20b. Mean and median. *Sample answer:* The mean and median are both close to the center of the data. There is no mode.

21a. The range for Team 2 is 56 and the range for Team 1 is 52, so the scores for Team 2 cover a slightly greater range.

21b. The mean absolute deviation for Team 1 is 15.75 and the mean deviation for Team 2 is 22.5, so the scores for Team 2 are more dispersed.

21. **BOWLING** The average scores of the bowlers on two different bowling teams are given. *Compare* the spreads of the data sets using (**a**) the range and (**b**) the mean absolute deviation.

Team 1: 162, 150, 173, 202 **Team 2:** 140, 153, 187, 196

22. ★ **EXTENDED RESPONSE** The Mississippi River discharges an average of 230 million tons of sediment per year. The average sediment discharges (in millions of tons per year) of the seven U.S. rivers with the greatest discharges are 230, 80, 65, 40, 25, 15, and 11. For parts (a)–(c) below, round your answers to the nearest whole number, if necessary. **a–c. See margin.**

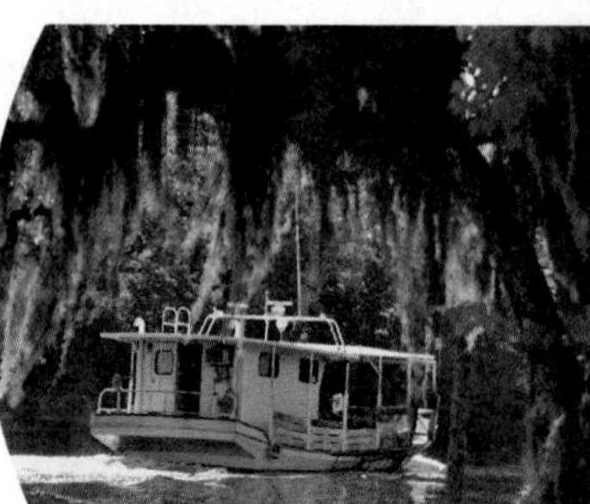

Fishing boat on the Mississippi River

a. Find the mean and median of the data. Which measure represents the data better? *Explain.*

b. Find the mean of the data for the other six rivers, excluding the Mississippi River. Does this mean represent the data better than the mean you found in part (a)? *Explain.*

c. Find the range and mean absolute deviation of the data for all seven rivers. *Describe* what the measures tell you about the dispersion of the data.

C

23. **CHALLENGE** So far, you have scored 84, 92, 76, 88, and 76 on five of the six tests you will take in a particular class. Your goal is to finish the year with a test average of 85 or greater.

a. Let x represent your last test score. Write an expression for the mean of your test scores. Then write and solve an inequality to find the possible scores you can achieve in order to meet your goal. $\frac{416 + x}{6}$; $\frac{416 + x}{6} \geq 85$, $x \geq 94$

b. After the last test, your teacher tells you that the median of your six test scores is 86. Can you tell whether you met your goal? *Explain.* **See margin.**

ILLINOIS MIXED REVIEW

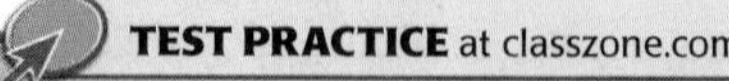

TEST PRACTICE at classzone.com

24. A school's cafeteria surveyed 150 students about their preferred types of fruit. The results are shown in the table. If the cafeteria uses only these data to order fruit, which conclusion best reflects the data collected?

Fruit	Frequency
Apples	66
Bananas	39
Grapes	34
Pears	11

Ⓐ More than half of each order should be apples.

Ⓑ Only apples and bananas should be ordered.

Ⓒ About a quarter of each order should be pears.

Ⓓ About two-thirds of each order should be apples and grapes.

D

Extension
Use after Lesson 13.6

Calculate Variance and Standard Deviation

GOAL Find the variance and standard deviation of a data set.

Key Vocabulary
- **variance**
- **standard deviation**

In addition to range and mean absolute deviation, *variance* and *standard deviation* are also measures of dispersion that can be used to describe the spread of a set of data.

KEY CONCEPT *For Your Notebook*

Variance and Standard Deviation

The **variance** of a numerical data set is denoted by σ^2, which is read as "sigma squared." For the data set $x_1, x_2, \ldots, x_n$, the variance is given by:

$$\sigma^2 = \frac{(x_1 - \overline{x})^2 + (x_2 - \overline{x})^2 + \ldots + (x_n - \overline{x})^2}{n}$$

The **standard deviation** of a numerical data set is denoted by σ, which is read as "sigma." For the data set $x_1, x_2, \ldots, x_n$, the standard deviation is the square root of the variance and is given by:

$$\sigma = \sqrt{\frac{(x_1 - \overline{x})^2 + (x_2 - \overline{x})^2 + \ldots + (x_n - \overline{x})^2}{n}}$$

EXAMPLE 1 Find variance and standard deviation

E-MAIL SIZES The sizes of e-mails (in kilobytes) in your inbox are 1, 2, 2, 7, 4, 1, 10, 3, and 6. Find the variance and standard deviation of the data.

Solution

STEP 1 **Find** the mean.

$$\overline{x} = \frac{1 + 2 + 2 + 7 + 4 + 1 + 10 + 3 + 6}{9} = \frac{36}{9} = 4$$

STEP 2 **Find** the variance.

$$\sigma^2 = \frac{(1 - 4)^2 + (2 - 4)^2 + \ldots + (6 - 4)^2}{9} = \frac{76}{9} = 8.444\ldots$$

STEP 3 **Find** the standard deviation.

$$\sigma = \sqrt{\sigma^2} = \sqrt{8.444\ldots} \approx 2.9$$

▶ The variance is about 8.4, and the standard deviation is about 2.9.

IMPROVE ACCURACY
The more accurate the value of σ^2 you use to calculate σ, the more accurate the value of σ you obtain. In the final answer, both results are rounded.

1 PLAN AND PREPARE

Warm-Up Exercises

1. Find the mean of the data.
12, 18, 17, 6, 10, 15 13
2. Find the range and the mean absolute deviation of the data.
19, 24, 22, 27, 54, 52, 32
35; about 11.51
3. The scores on your English test are 82, 86, 87, 94, and 88. Find the range and the mean absolute deviation of the data. 12; 2.88

2 FOCUS AND MOTIVATE

Essential Question

Big Idea 2, p. 841
How do you find the variance and standard deviation of a data set?
Tell students they will learn how to answer this question by using a formulas based on the mean to find the variance and the standard deviation.

3 TEACH

Extra Example 1

The distances (in miles) that you walked last week are 4, 3, 3, 5, 2, 2, and 4. Find the variance and the standard deviation of the data.
The variance is about 1.06 and the standard deviation is about 1.03.

NCTM STANDARDS

Standard 2: Analyze situations using algebraic symbols

Standard 5: Use proper statistical methods to analyze data

Extra Example 2

The numbers of visitors (in thousands, rounded to the nearest thousand) to Yellowstone National Park for 10 years are given. Find the standard deviation of the data.

3047, 3125, 3012, 2890, 2496, 3131, 2838, 2759, 2943, 3019 **about 183**

Closing the Lesson

Have students summarize the major points of the lesson and answer the Essential Question: How do you find the variance and standard deviation of a data set?

- **Variance and standard deviation are measures of dispersion that can be used to describe the spread of data.**

Find the mean of the data and then substitute the values of the mean and the data in the formula for variance and solve. Find the square root of the variance to find the standard deviation.

4 PRACTICE AND APPLY

Avoiding Common Errors

Exercises 1–7 When using graphing calculators, students should make sure that they use the numbers for standard deviation and not for some other statistic.

Teaching Strategy

Exercises 2, 3, 5, 6 Have students compare the data sets in Exercises 2 and 3 for variance and standard deviation and for standard deviation in Exercises 5 and 6. Have students explain what these measures mean in terms of spread.

USING A CALCULATOR You can use a graphing calculator to find the standard deviation of a data set.

EXAMPLE 2 Find standard deviation

HOUSEHOLDS In 2000 the numbers (in thousands) of households in the 13 states with Atlantic Ocean coastline are given. Find the standard deviation of the data.

299 6338 3006 518 1981 2444 475 3065
7057 3132 408 1534 2699

Solution

STEP 1 **Enter** the data into a graphing calculator. Press STAT and select Edit. Enter the data into List 1 (L_1).

STEP 2 **Calculate** the standard deviation. Press STAT. From the CALC menu select 1-Var Stats.

On this screen, σ_x stands for standard deviation.

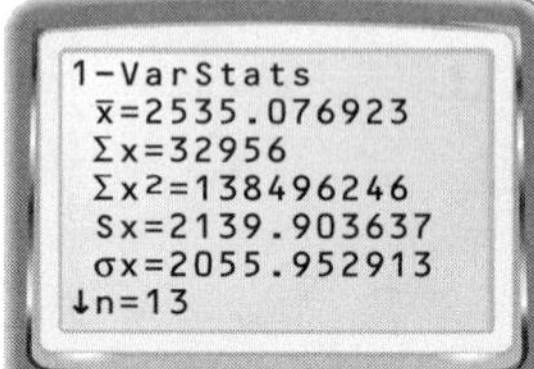

▶ The standard deviation of the data is about 2056.

PRACTICE

EXAMPLE 1 on p. 879 for Exs. 1–3

Use the formulas for variance and standard deviation to find the variance and standard deviation of the data. Round to the nearest tenth, if necessary.

1. 4, 5, 3, 2, 4, 7, 8, 9, 4, 6, 7, 8, 9, 1 **6.3, 2.5**
2. 14, 16, 19, 20, 28, 7, 24, 15, 16, 30, 33, 24 **52.1, 7.2**
3. 110, 205, 322, 608, 1100, 240, 185, 552, 418, 300 **76,656.6, 276.9**

EXAMPLE 2 on p. 880 for Exs. 4–7

7b. *Sample answer:* Since 136 is much greater than the mean, the standard deviation will increase.
7c. 17.7. *Sample answer:* The standard deviation more than tripled, so the prediction was correct.

In Exercises 4–6, use a graphing calculator to find the standard deviation of the data. Round to the nearest tenth, if necessary.

4. 3.5, 3.8, 4.1, 3.0, 3.8, 3.6, 3.3, 4.0, 3.8, 3.9, 3.2, 3.0, 3.3, 4.2, 3.0 **0.4**
5. 66, 43, 9, 28, 7, 5, 90, 9, 78, 6, 69, 55, 28, 43, 10, 54, 13, 88, 21, 4 **29.1**
6. 1002, 1540, 480, 290, 2663, 3800, 690, 1301, 1750, 2222, 4040, 800 **1192.5**
7. **REASONING** The heights (in feet) of 9 pecan trees are 72, 84, 81, 78, 80, 86, 70, 80, and 88. For parts (a)–(c) below, round your answers to the nearest tenth.
   a. Find the standard deviation of the data. **5.6**
   b. Suppose you include a pecan tree with a height of 136 feet. *Predict* the effect of the additional data on the standard deviation of the data set.
   c. Find the standard deviation of the new data set in part (b). *Compare* the results to your prediction in part (b).

13.7 Interpret Stem-and-Leaf Plots and Histograms

10.11.01 Read, interpret, predict, interpolate, extrapolate, and use information from a variety of graphs, charts, and tables.

Before You found measures of central tendency and dispersion.

Now You will make stem-and-leaf plots and histograms.

Why? So you can analyze historical data, as in Ex. 20.

Key Vocabulary
- stem-and-leaf plot
- frequency
- frequency table
- histogram

A **stem-and-leaf plot** is a data display that organizes data based on their digits. Each value is separated into a *stem* (the leading digit(s)) and a *leaf* (the last digit). A stem-and-leaf plot has a key that tells you how to read the data. A stem-and-leaf plot shows how the data are distributed.

EXAMPLE 1 Make a stem-and-leaf plot

BASEBALL The number of home runs hit by the 20 baseball players with the best single-season batting averages in Major League Baseball since 1900 are listed below. Make a stem-and-leaf plot of the data.

14, 25, 8, 8, 7, 7, 19, 37, 39, 18, 42, 23, 4, 32, 14, 21, 3, 12, 19, 41

Solution

STEP 1 **Separate** the data into stems and leaves.

Home Runs

Stem	Leaves
0	8 8 7 7 4 3
1	4 9 8 4 2 9
2	5 3 1
3	7 9 2
4	2 1

Key: 1 | 4 = 14 home runs

STEP 2 **Write** the leaves in increasing order.

Home Runs

Stem	Leaves
0	3 4 7 7 8 8
1	2 4 4 8 9 9
2	1 3 5
3	2 7 9
4	1 2

Key: 1 | 4 = 14 home runs

INTERPRET INTERVALS
Each stem in a stem-and-leaf plot defines an interval. For instance, the stem 2 represents the interval 20–29. The data values in this interval are 21, 23, and 25.

GUIDED PRACTICE for Example 1

1. **U.S. HISTORY** The years in which each of the first 20 states were admitted to the Union are listed below. Make a stem-and-leaf plot of the years. See margin on p. 883.

   1788, 1787, 1788, 1816, 1792, 1812, 1788, 1788, 1817, 1788, 1787, 1788, 1789, 1803, 1787, 1790, 1788, 1796, 1791, 1788

2. **REASONING** In Example 1, describe the distribution of the data on the intervals represented by the stems. Are the data clustered together in a noticeable way? *Explain.*

2. *Sample answer:* The data are clustered from 3–19. Over half of the values are from 3–19.

1 PLAN AND PREPARE

Warm-Up Exercises
Transparency Available

1. The data give the ages of people in an art class. Find the mean, median, and mode of the data.
   38, 15, 13, 32, 13, 17, 29, 43
   mean: 25, median: 23, mode: 13
2. Find the range and the mean absolute deviation of the data.
   8, 3, 3, 8, 9, 2, 3 **7, about 2.73**

Notetaking Guide
Transparency Available

Promotes interactive learning and notetaking skills, pp. 314–316.

Pacing
Basic: 2 days
Average: 2 days
Advanced: 2 days
Block: 1 block
- See *Teaching Guide/Lesson Plan.*

2 FOCUS AND MOTIVATE

Essential Question
Big Idea 3, p. 841

How do you make stem-and-leaf plots and histograms? **Tell students they will learn how to answer this question by organizing the data and then displaying the results in a graph.**

Resource Planning Guide

Chapter Resource Book
- Teaching Guide/Lesson Plan (pp. 71–72)
- Activity Master (p. 73)
- Practice levels A, B, C (pp. 74–79)
- Study Guide (pp. 80–81)
- Catch-up for Absent Students (p. 82)
- Application (p. 83)
- Challenge (p. 84)

Workbooks
- Notetaking Guide (pp. 314–316)
- Practice Workbook (pp. 208–210)

Teaching Options
- **Power Presentations CD-ROM** provides dynamic electronic teaching resources for the classroom.
- **Activity Generator CD-ROM** provides editable activities for all ability levels.

Interactive Technology
- Easy Planner
- Power Presentations CD-ROM
- Activity Generator CD-ROM
- Animated Algebra
- Test Generator CD-ROM
- Online Quiz
- eWorkbook
- eEdition
- @HomeTutor

Resources for English Learners
- Quick Reference for English Learners
- Spanish Study Guide
- Multi-Language Visual Glossary
- Student Resources in Spanish

See also the *Algebra 1 Toolkit* for more strategies for meeting individual needs.

Motivating the Lesson

You volunteer at an animal shelter on the weekends. The director of the shelter wants you to analyze the number of hours volunteers work. By knowing how to organize data in stem-and-leaf plots and histograms, you can display the data in an appropriate graph.

3 TEACH

Extra Example 1

A software developer advertised a position at its home office. The list below shows the number of applications the office received per day. Make a stem-and-leaf plot of the data.

9, 8, 24, 18, 27, 25, 24, 38, 32, 29, 41, 56, 42, 38, 40, 47, 32, 52, 39, 41

Software Applications

Stem	Leaves
0	8 9
1	8
2	4 4 5 7 9
3	2 2 8 8 9
4	0 1 1 2 7
5	2 6

Key: 3 | 2 = 32 applications

Extra Example 2

The back-to-back stem-and-leaf plot shows the ages of participants in two yoga classes. Compare the ages of the participants in the two yoga classes.

Yoga Class Ages

Class 1		Class 2
9	1	8 8 9 9
6 5 4 4 2	2	0 0 1 3
7 4 2 2	3	0 0

Key: 2 | 2 | 0 = 22, 20

Participants in Class 2 are generally younger than participants in Class 1.

EXAMPLE 2 Interpret a stem-and-leaf plot

GYMNASTICS The back-to-back stem-and-leaf plot shows the ages of members of the U.S men's and women's 2004 Olympic gymnastics teams. Compare the ages of the gymnasts on the two teams.

2004 Olympic Gymnast Ages

Men		Women
	1	6 6 8 8
7 4 3 1 1	2	5 6
0	3	

Key: 1 | 2 | 5 = 21, 25

Solution

Consider the distribution of the data. The interval for 10–19 years old contains more than half of the female gymnasts. The interval for 20–29 years old contains more than half of the male gymnasts. The clustering of the data shows that the men's team was generally older than the women's team.

FREQUENCY The **frequency** of an interval is the number of data values in that interval. A stem-and-leaf plot shows the frequencies of intervals determined by the stems. A **frequency table** is also used to group data values into equal intervals, with no gaps between intervals and no intervals overlapping.

A **histogram** is a bar graph that displays data from a frequency table. Each bar represents an interval. Because intervals have equal size, the bars have equal width. A bar's length indicates the frequency. There is no space between bars.

EXAMPLE 3 Make a histogram

SANDWICH PRICES The prices (in dollars) of sandwiches at a restaurant are listed below. Make a histogram of the data.

4.00, 4.00, 4.25, 4.50, 4.75, 4.25, 5.95, 5.50, 5.50, 5.75

Solution

CHOOSE AN INTERVAL SIZE
To choose the interval size for a frequency table, divide the range of the data by the number of intervals you want the table to have. Use the quotient as an approximate interval size.

STEP 1 **Choose** intervals of equal size that cover all of the data values. Organize the data using a frequency table.

Prices	Sandwiches
\$4.00–4.49	||||
\$4.50–4.99	||
\$5.00–5.49	
\$5.50–5.99	||||

STEP 2 **Draw** the bars of the histogram using the intervals from the frequency table.

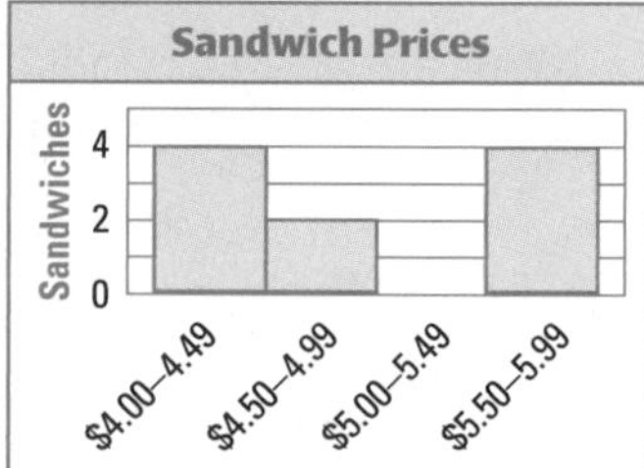

Differentiated Instruction

Kinesthetic Learners Stem-and-leaf plots and histograms place statistical data in equally spaced groups, or "bins." It may be helpful to write numerical data on slips of paper for students to sort and place in small boxes. Then they can construct the appropriate histogram or stem-and-leaf plot, and see how it corresponds to the sorted data.

See also the *Algebra 1 Toolkit* for more strategies.

GUIDED PRACTICE for Examples 2 and 3

3. *Sample answer:* Most of the data for the females is between 10% and 30%, while most of the data for males is between 20% and 40%. There is considerable overlap, but in general the male students watch more television than do the female students.

3. TELEVISION The back-to-back stem-and-leaf plot shows the percents of students in 24 countries who report watching television for 4 or more hours each day. *Compare* the data for female and male students.

Female		Male
9 9 9 8 8 8 6 6 5 4	1	7 8 9
6 6 5 4 3 3 0 0	2	0 1 2 2 4 5 5 6 6 7 7 8
8 3 2 2 1	3	4 6 6 8 8 9
1	4	0 6 6

Key: 4 | 1 | 7 = 14%, 17%

4. PRECIPITATION The average number of days each month with precipitation of 0.01 inch or more in Buffalo, New York, are 20, 17, 16, 14, 13, 11, 10, 10, 11, 12, 16, and 19. Make a histogram of the data. See margin.

13.7 EXERCISES

HOMEWORK KEY

○ = WORKED-OUT SOLUTIONS on p. WS33 for Exs. 3 and 19

★ = STANDARDIZED TEST PRACTICE Exs. 2, 8, 9, 15, and 20

SKILL PRACTICE

A

1. **VOCABULARY** Copy and complete: The number of data values in an interval is the ___?___ of that interval. frequency

2. ★ **WRITING** *Explain* how a histogram differs from a bar graph. *Sample answer:* A histogram displays the frequency of numerical data. A bar graph displays categorical data.

EXAMPLE 1 on p. 881 for Exs. 3–7

STEM-AND-LEAF PLOTS Make a stem-and-leaf plot of the data. 3–6. See margin.

3. 17, 31, 42, 33, 38, 20, 24, 30, 39, 38, 35, 20, 55

4. 2, 8, 17, 7, 14, 20, 32, 5, 33, 6, 6, 8, 11, 9

5. 121, 124, 133, 111, 109, 182, 105, 127, 156, 179, 142

6. 1.23, 1.05, 1.11, 1.29, 1.31, 1.19, 1.45, 1.22, 1.19, 1.35

7. **ERROR ANALYSIS** *Describe* and correct the error in making a stem-and-leaf plot of the following data: 18, 19, 18, 19, 20, 20, 21, 22, 18, 19, 20, 21, 23, 21. There is no key given for the stem-and-leaf plot; Key: 1 | 8 = 18.

1	888999
2	00011123

STEM-AND-LEAF PLOT In Exercises 8 and 9, consider the back-to-back stem-and-leaf plot that shows data sets *A* and *B*.

8. ★ **MULTIPLE CHOICE** What is the median of data set *A*? C

   Ⓐ 21 Ⓑ 32
   Ⓒ 33 Ⓓ 34

9. ★ **MULTIPLE CHOICE** What is the range of data set *B*? C

   Ⓐ 18 Ⓑ 19
   Ⓒ 20 Ⓓ 21

Set *A*		Set *B*
1 1 1	2	
4 3 3 2	3	1 2 2
2 0	4	1 1 3 4
	5	0 1

Key: 2 | 3 | 1 = 32, 31

Extra Example 3

The number of song requests per day for a two week period at a radio station are shown below. Make a histogram of the data.

12, 22, 18, 26, 31, 34, 17, 26, 28, 10, 20, 14, 15, 32

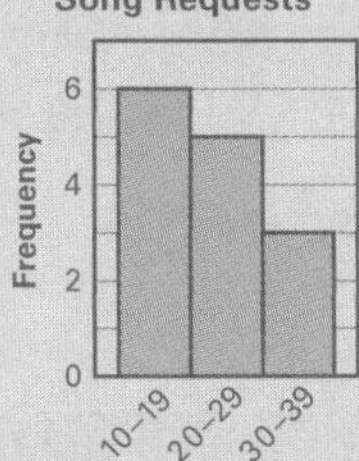

Closing the Lesson

Have students summarize the major points of the lesson and answer the Essential Question: How do you make stem-and-leaf plots and histograms?

- A stem-and-leaf plot organizes data based on their digits, with the leading digit(s) in stems and the last digit in leaves.
- A histogram is a bar graph that displays data from a frequency table, with no space between bars and bars of equal width.

To make a stem-and-leaf plot, separate the data into stems and leaves. Each stem represents an interval, such as 0 represents 0–9. Write the leaves in increasing order and make a key that tells how to read the data. To make a histogram, choose equal intervals that cover all of the data, organize the data using a frequency table, and then use the intervals from the frequency table to draw the bars of the histogram.

p. 881

1.

Stem	Leaves
178	7 7 7 8 8 8 8 8 8 8 8 8 9
179	0 1 2 6
180	3
181	2 6 7

Key: 178 | 7 = 1787

p. 883

3.

Stem	Leaves
1	7
2	0 0 4
3	0 1 3 5 8 8 9
4	2
5	5

Key: 1 | 7 = 17

4.

Stem	Leaves
0	2 5 6 6 7 8 8 9
1	1 4 7
2	0
3	2 3

Key: 0 | 2 = 2

5.

Stem	Leaves
10	5 9
11	1
12	1 4 7
13	3
14	2
15	6
16	
17	9
18	2

Key: 10 | 5 = 105

6.

Stem	Leaves
1.0	5
1.1	1 9 9
1.2	2 3 9
1.3	1 5
1.4	5

Key: 1.0 | 5 = 1.05

p. 883

Guided Practice Ex. 4. See Additional Answers beginning on p. AA1.

4 PRACTICE AND APPLY

Assignment Guide

Answer Transparencies available for all exercises

Basic:
Day 1: pp. 883–885
Exs. 1–9, 17, 20
Day 2: pp. 883–885
Exs. 10–13, 18, 19, 23–27

Average:
Day 1: pp. 883–885
Exs. 1, 2, 4–9, 17, 20, 21
Day 2: pp. 883–885
Exs. 10–15, 18, 19, 23–27

Advanced:
Day 1: pp. 883–885
Exs. 1, 4–9, 17, 20, 21
Day 2: pp. 883–885
Exs. 11–16*, 18, 19, 22–27*

Block:
pp. 883–885
Exs. 1, 2, 4–15, 17–21, 23–27

Differentiated Instruction

See *Algebra 1 Best Practices Toolkit* for suggestions on addressing the needs of a diverse classroom.

Homework Check

For a quick check of student understanding of key concepts, go over the following exercises:

Basic: 4, 10, 17, 18, 20
Average: 5, 12, 17, 18, 20
Advanced: 6, 14, 17, 19, 20

Extra Practice

- Student Edition, p. 950
- Chapter 13 Resource Book: Practice levels A, B, C, pp. 74–79

Practice Worksheet

An easily-readable reduced practice page (with answers) for this lesson can be found on p. 840C.

EXAMPLE 3 on p. 882 for Exs. 10–14

10. ERROR ANALYSIS *Describe* and correct the error in creating a histogram using the frequency table below. See margin.

Ages	0–9	10–19	20–29	30–39
Frequency	III	~~IIII~~ I		IIII

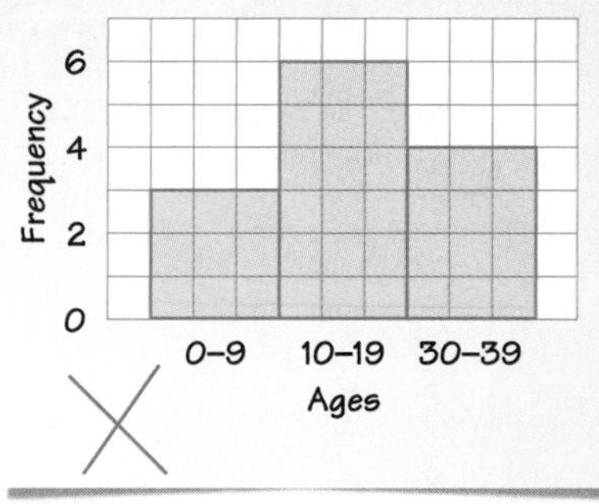

B **HISTOGRAMS** **Make a histogram of the data.**
11–14. See margin.

11. 55, 82, 94, 75, 61, 69, 77, 98, 81, 83, 75, 90, 51

12. 12, 0, 22, 31, 14, 7, 7, 45, 31, 28, 21, 25, 25, 18

13. 0.01, 0.13, 0.09, 1.10, 1.33, 0.99, 0.50, 0.95, 1.05, 1.50, 0.75, 1.01

14. 111, 109, 224, 657, 284, 120, 119, 415, 180, 105, 208, 108

15. ★ **WRITING** *Explain* why a histogram can show the distribution of the data below better than a stem-and-leaf plot. See margin.

15, 21, 18, 10, 12, 11, 17, 18, 16, 12, 20, 12, 17, 16

C **16. CHALLENGE** Create a stem-and-leaf plot that has the same distribution of data as the histogram shown. *Explain* the steps you took to create the stem-and-leaf plot.
See margin for art. *Sample answer:* I created values for each interval of the histogram that would have generated the frequencies shown in the histogram, then plotted the values on a stem-and-leaf plot.

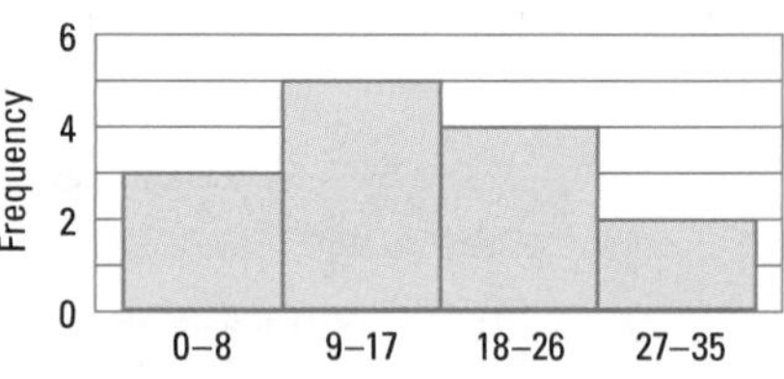

PROBLEM SOLVING

EXAMPLE 1 A on p. 881 for Ex. 17

17. HEIGHTS The heights (in inches) of players on a boys' basketball team are as follows: 80, 76, 81, 69, 81, 78, 74, 68, 78, 74, 81, 72, 69, 81, 70. Make a stem-and-leaf plot of the heights. See margin.

@HomeTutor for problem solving help at classzone.com

EXAMPLE 3 on p. 882 for Exs. 18–19

18. SURVEY A survey asked people how many 8 ounce glasses of water they drink in one day. The results are below. Make a histogram of the data.

3, 0, 9, 1, 4, 2, 11, 5, 3, 6, 0, 5, 7, 8, 5, 2, 9, 6, 10, 2, 4 See margin.

@HomeTutor for problem solving help at classzone.com

19. MEMORY A survey asked people how many phone numbers they have memorized. The results are shown in the table.

Phone numbers	1–5	6–10	11–15	16–20	21–25
Frequency	88	85	50	28	14

a. Make a histogram of the data. See margin.

b. What is the probability that a person surveyed, chosen at random, has 11–25 phone numbers memorized? $\frac{92}{265}$

○ = WORKED-OUT SOLUTIONS on p. WS1   ★ = STANDARDIZED TEST PRACTICE

10–14. See Additional Answers beginning on p. AA1.

15. *Sample answer:* A histogram can show a variety of intervals, but a stem-and-leaf plot can only show intervals that are powers of 10. The given data range from 10 to 20, so a stem-and-leaf plot would place all the data into only two intervals, making it difficult to see trends within the data. The histogram could use an interval of 3 or 4.

16. *Sample:*

Stem	Leaves
0	5 6 7
1	0 1 2 3 4
2	0 1 2 3
3	0 1

Key: 0 | 5 = 5

17, 18, 19a. See Additional Answers beginning on p. AA1.

EXAMPLE 2 on p. 882 for Ex. 20

20c. *Sample answer:* The Senate generally spends more time in session than the House of Representatives and has more variation in the number of days they spend in session.

21c. $\frac{1}{3}$. *Sample answer:* Since 13 of the 39 passengers, or $\frac{1}{3}$ of them, were ages 18–29, we can predict that another passenger about whom we have no information has a $\frac{1}{3}$ probability of being in that age group.

20. ★ **EXTENDED RESPONSE** The back-to-back stem-and-leaf plot shows the numbers of days the House of Representatives and the Senate spent in session each year from 1996 to 2004.

Days in Session

House		Senate
9 0	11	
3 2	12	
7 5 3 2	13	2 3
2	14	1 3 9
	15	3
	16	2 7
	17	3

Key: 2 | 14 | 1 = 142, 141

a. What was the median number of days the House of Representatives spent in session? the Senate? 132 days; 149 days

b. What is the range of the number of days the House of Representatives spent in session? the Senate? 32 days; 41 days

c. *Compare* the data for the House of Representatives and the Senate. What does the distribution of the data tell you?

B

21. **MAYFLOWER** The known ages (in years) of adult male passengers on the *Mayflower* at the time of its departure are listed below.

21, 34, 29, 38, 30, 54, 39, 20, 35, 64, 37, 45, 21, 25, 55, 45, 40, 38, 38, 21, 21, 20, 34, 38, 50, 41, 48, 18, 32, 21, 32, 49, 30, 42, 30, 25, 38, 25, 20

a. Make a stem-and-leaf plot of the ages. See margin.

b. Find the median age and range of the ages. median: 34 yr, range: 46 yr

c. According to one source, the age of passenger Thomas English was unknown at the time of the *Mayflower's* departure. What is the probability that he was 18–29 years old? *Explain* your reasoning.

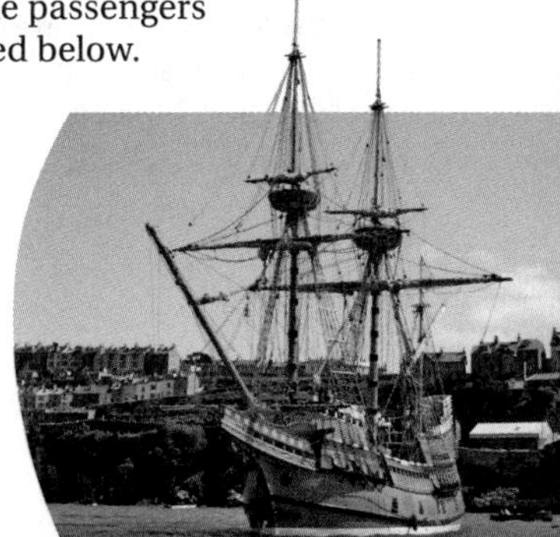

Replica of the *Mayflower*

C

22. **CHALLENGE** Refer to the histogram shown.

a. Find the midpoint of each interval. Multiply each midpoint by the frequency of its interval. Add these products. Divide the sum by the sum of all the frequencies. a, b. See margin.

b. Does the your final result in part (a) best approximate the mean, the median, or the mode of the data? *Explain* your answer.

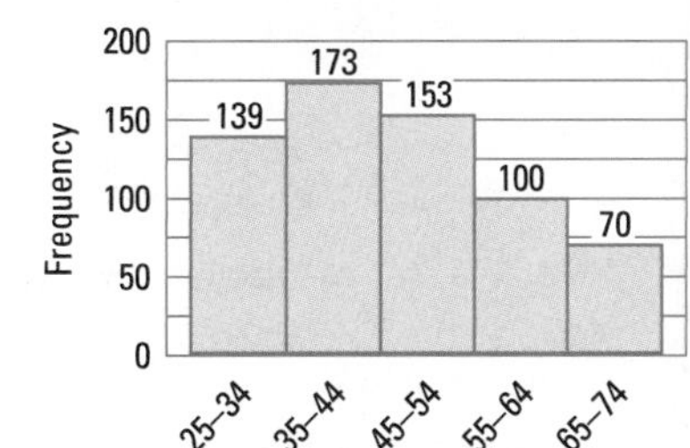

ILLINOIS MIXED REVIEW

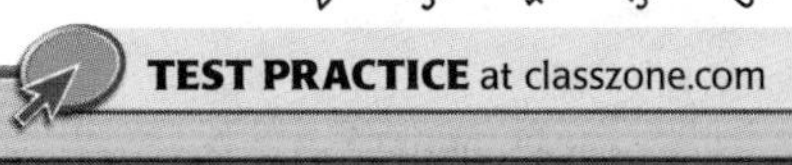

23. Loren purchased 14 boxes of floor tiles. Each box contains 25 square tiles. If Loren wants to tile a floor that is 17 tiles wide and 18 tiles long, which procedure can be used to determine whether there will be enough tiles to complete the job? C

Ⓐ Multiply 17 by 14.

Ⓑ Subtract 17 from 25 and then multiply by 14.

Ⓒ Multiply 14 by 25 and then compare the product with the product of 17 and 18.

Ⓓ Multiply 17 by 18 and then divide the product by 25 and compare the quotient with 14.

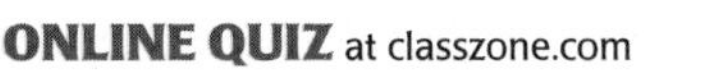

5 ASSESS AND RETEACH

Daily Homework Quiz

Transparency Available

The data show the hours Henry worked at a photo shop over a 10-week period.

21, 2, 10, 4, 12, 4, 10, 9, 8, 9

1. Make a stem-and-leaf plot of the data.

Hours at the Photo Shop

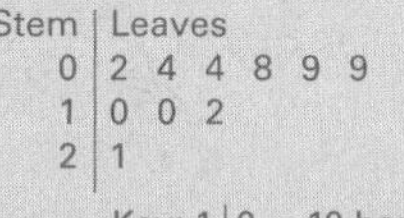

2. Describe the data in the stem-and-leaf plot in Exercise 1. Henry generally works fewer than 10 hours per week.

3. Make a histogram of the data.

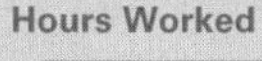

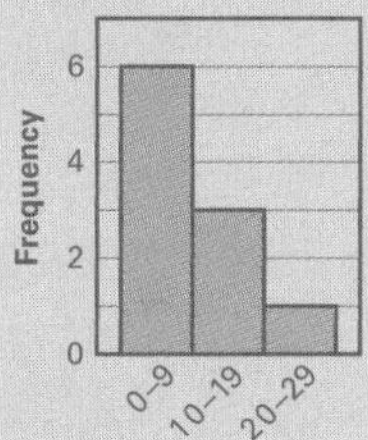

Available at **classzone.com**

Diagnosis/Remediation

- Practice A, B, C in Chapter 13 Resource Book, pp. 74–79
- Study Guide in Chapter13 Resource Book, pp. 80–81
- Practice Workbook, pp. 208–210
- @HomeTutor

Challenge

Additional challenge is available in the Chapter 13 Resource Book, p. 84.

21a, 22a–b. See Additional Answers beginning on p. AA1.

26. *Sample answer:* This question is potentially biased because it encourages the respondent to agree. A better question would be "What do you think of science fiction movies?"

27. *Sample answer:* This question is potentially biased because it assumes that the respondent's ideal vacation is one of the two choices. A less biased question would be "Would you rather take a trip to Florida or Alaska?" or "Tell me about your ideal vacation."

@HomeTutor
classzone.com
Keystrokes

13.7 Draw Histograms

QUESTION How can you use a graphing calculator to make a histogram?

EXAMPLE Make a histogram

POPULATION The populations (in thousands) of metropolitan areas in the states with the greatest metropolitan populations in the United States in 2000 are listed below. Make a histogram of the data.

4527 32,750 14,837 5667 10,542 4390 4911 6101 8169 3795 8414
17,473 5437 9214 10,392 3862 17,692 5528 4899 3640

STEP 1 ***Enter the data***

Go to the STAT menu and choose Edit. Enter the data into List 1.

STEP 2 ***Select histogram***

Go to the STAT PLOT screen. Select Plot 1. Use the settings shown below.

STEP 3 ***Set the viewing window***

Go to the WINDOW screen. Use the settings shown below.

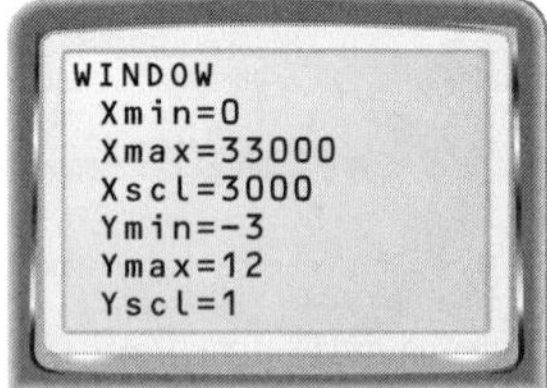

STEP 4 ***Graph***

Press GRAPH. Use the *trace* feature to move from bar to bar.

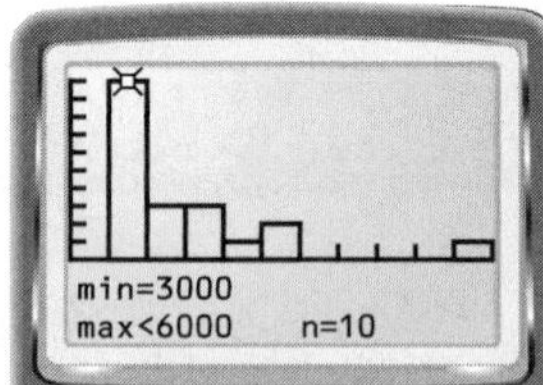

DRAW CONCLUSIONS

1. *Describe* the distribution of the population data in the example above. See margin.
2. **BOWLING** Use a graphing calculator to make a histogram of the following bowling scores: 200, 210, 105, 300, 180, 175, 162, 110, 140, 300, 152, 165, 175, 115, 250, 270, 145, 182, 164, 122, 141, 135, 189, 170, 151, 158. See margin.

1 PLAN AND PREPARE

Learn the Method

- Students will use a graphing calculator to make a histogram.
- After the activity, students can use a graphing calculator to check their solutions in Exercises 11–14 in Lesson 13.7.

Keystroke Help

Keystrokes for several models of calculators are available in blackline format in the *Chapter 13 Resource Book.*

2 TEACH

Tips for Success

In Step 3, have students analyze the data to see how the settings correlate to intervals and frequencies in the graph.

Extra Example

Turtle strandings in North Carolina from 1993–2002 are listed below. Make a histogram of the data.
197, 287, 347, 505, 403, 358, 600, 832, 366, 479

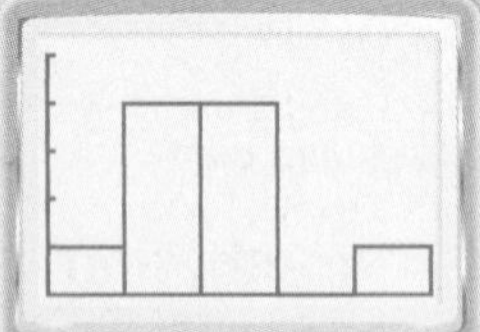

3 ASSESS AND RETEACH

What does each gap in a histogram represent? The gaps represent intervals in which the frequency of the data is 0.

1. *Sample answer:* The majority of the data are at the lower end of the scale, between 3000 and 12,000, with the highest frequency between 3000 and 6000.

2.

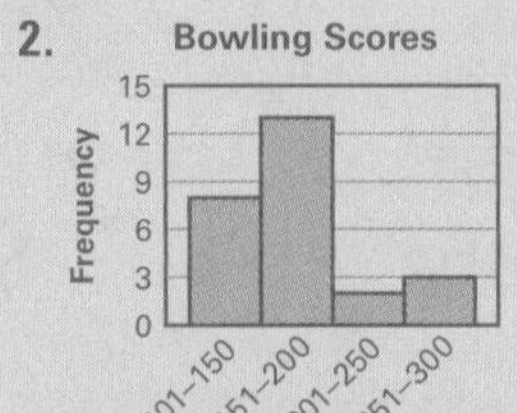

13.8 Interpret Box-and-Whisker Plots

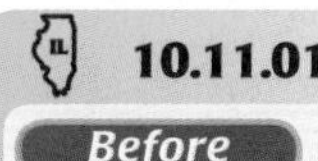

10.11.01 Read, interpret, predict, interpolate, extrapolate, and use information from a variety of graphs, charts, and tables.

Before You made stem-and-leaf plots and histograms.

Now You will make and interpret box-and-whisker plots.

Why? So you can compare sets of scientific data, as in Ex. 19.

Key Vocabulary
- box-and-whisker plot
- quartile
- interquartile range
- outlier

A **box-and-whisker plot** organizes data values into four groups. Ordered data are divided into lower and upper halves by the median. The median of the lower half is the **lower quartile**. The median of the upper half is the **upper quartile**.

EXAMPLE 1 Make a box-and-whisker plot

SONG LENGTHS The lengths of songs (in seconds) on a CD are listed below. Make a box-and-whisker plot of the song lengths.

173, 206, 179, 257, 198, 251, 239, 246, 295, 181, 261

Solution

STEP 1 **Order** the data. Then find the median and the quartiles.

Lower half / Median / Upper half

173, 179, 181, 198, 206, 239, 246, 251, 257, 261, 295

Lower quartile (181) / Upper quartile (257)

STEP 2 **Plot** the median, the quartiles, the maximum value, and the minimum value below a number line.

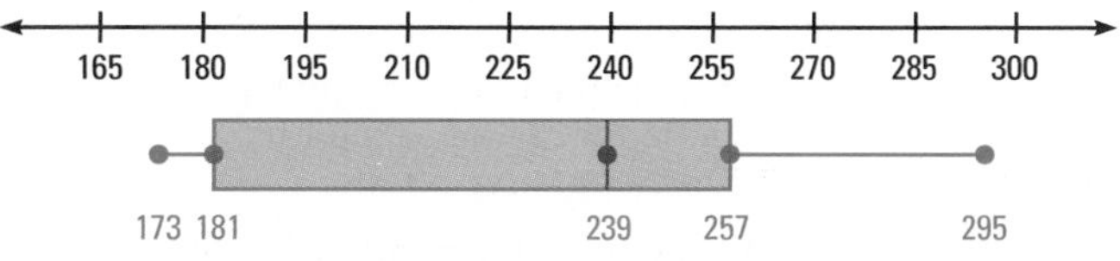

STEP 3 **Draw** a box from the lower quartile to the upper quartile. Draw a vertical line through the median. Draw a line segment (a "whisker") from the box to the maximum and another from the box to the minimum.

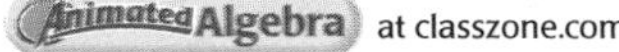

at classzone.com

✓ GUIDED PRACTICE for Example 1

1. Make a box-and-whisker plot of the ages of eight family members: 60, 15, 25, 20, 55, 70, 40, 30. See margin on p. 889.

1 PLAN AND PREPARE

Warm-Up Exercises

Transparency Available

Find the mean, median, and mode(s) of the data.

1. 8, 12, 15, 17, 18, 26 16, 16, no mode
2. 186, 144, 201, 164, 182, 164 173.5, 173, 164
3. The monthly charge for seven dial-up internet service providers are listed. What is the mean price? \$10, \$22, \$17, \$11, \$16, \$23, \$25 about \$17.71

Notetaking Guide

Transparency Available

Promotes interactive learning and notetaking skills, pp. 317–319.

Pacing

Basic: 2 days
Average: 2 days
Advanced: 2 days
Block: 1 block
- See *Teaching Guide/Lesson Plan*.

2 FOCUS AND MOTIVATE

Essential Question

Big Idea 3, p. 841

How do you make and interpret box-and-whisker plots? Tell students they will learn how to answer this question by organizing data values into four groups, each containing 25% of the data.

Resource Planning Guide

Chapter Resource Book
- Teaching Guide/Lesson Plan (pp. 85–86)
- Activity Master (p. 87)
- Practice levels A, B, C (pp. 88–93)
- Study Guide (pp. 94–95)
- Catch-up for Absent Students (p. 96)
- Problem Solving Workshop (p. 97)
- Challenge (p. 98)

Workbooks
- Notetaking Guide (pp. 317–319)
- Practice Workbook (pp. 211–213)

Teaching Options
- **Power Presentations CD-ROM** provides dynamic electronic teaching resources for the classroom.
- **Activity Generator CD-ROM** provides editable activities for all ability levels.

Interactive Technology
- Easy Planner
- Power Presentations CD-ROM
- Activity Generator CD-ROM
- Animated Algebra
- Test Generator CD-ROM
- Online Quiz
- eWorkbook
- eEdition
- @HomeTutor

Resources for English Learners
- Quick Reference for English Learners
- Spanish Study Guide
- Multi-Language Visual Glossary
- Student Resources in Spanish

See also the *Algebra 1 Toolkit* for more strategies for meeting individual needs.

Motivating the Lesson

You want to compare the weather in two cities before your family takes a vacation in one of them. You can easily compare the two places by making box-and-whisker plots to display the weather data from past years.

3 TEACH

Extra Example 1

The prices (in dollars) of 27-inch television sets at an electronics store are given below. Make a box-and-whisker plot of the television prices.

188, 225, 192, 239, 271, 286, 224, 334, 316, 275

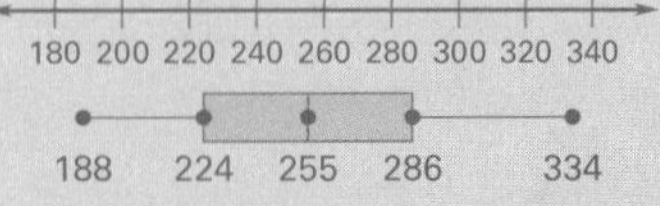

An **Animated Algebra** activity is available on-line for **Example 1**. This activity is also available on the **Power Presentations CD-ROM**.

Extra Example 2

The box-and-whisker plots below show the normal monthly wind speeds (in miles per hour) in Athens and Savannah, Georgia.

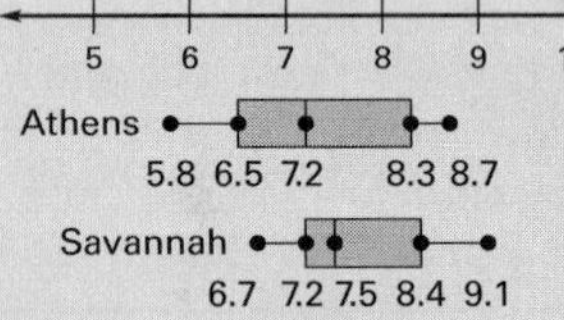

a. For how many months is Athens' wind speed more than 8.3 miles per hour? **3 months**

b. Compare the wind speeds in the two cities. **Wind speed is more variable in Athens, but in general is stronger in Savannah.**

INTERPRET A BOX-AND-WHISKER PLOT A box-and-whisker plot separates data into four groups: the two parts of the box and the two whiskers. Each part contains approximately the same number of data values.

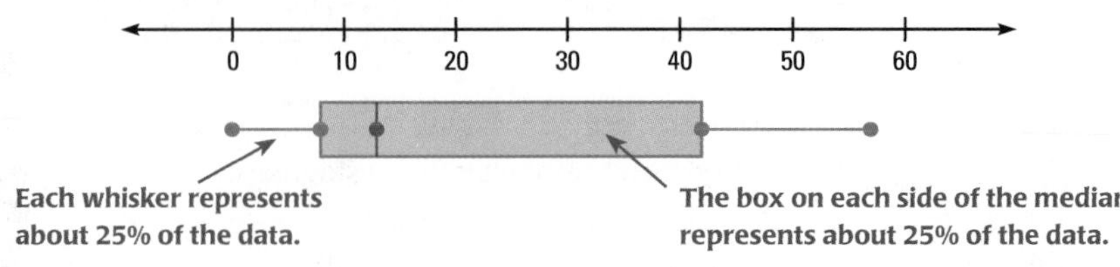

INTERPRET VARIATION

The interquartile range measures the variation in the middle half of the data and ignores the extreme values, whose variation may not be representative of the data.

You know that the range of a data set is the difference of the maximum value and the minimum value. The **interquartile range** of a data set is the difference of the upper quartile and the lower quartile.

EXAMPLE 2 Interpret a box-and-whisker plot

PRECIPITATION The box-and-whisker plots below show the normal precipitation (in inches) each month in Dallas and in Houston, Texas.

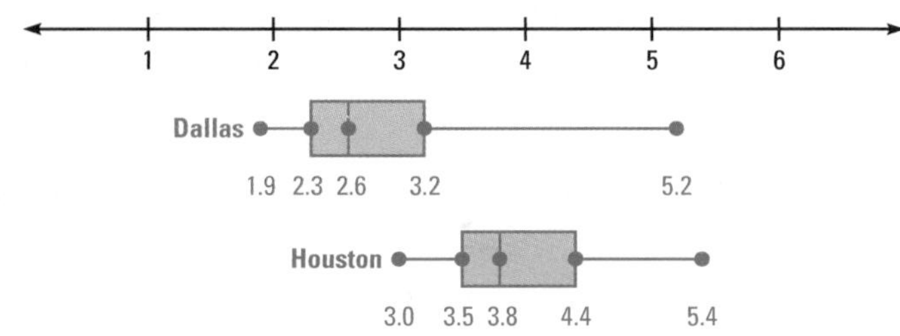

a. For how many months is Houston's precipitation less than 3.5 inches?

b. Compare the precipitation in Dallas with the precipitation in Houston.

Solution

a. For Houston, the lower quartile is 3.5. A whisker represents 25% of the data, so for 25% of 12 months, or 3 months, Houston has less than 3.5 inches of precipitation.

b. The median precipitation for a month in Dallas is 2.6 inches. The median for Houston is 3.8 inches. In general, Houston has more precipitation.

For Dallas, the interquartile range is $3.2 - 2.3$, or 0.9 inch. For Houston, the interquartile range is $4.4 - 3.5 = 0.9$ inch. So, the cities have the same variation in the middle 50% of the data. The range for Dallas is greater than the range for Houson. When all the data are considered, Dallas has more variation in precipitation.

INTERPRET QUARTILES

When the number of data values is a multiple of 4, the median and quartiles will divide the data into four groups of *exactly* the same size.

GUIDED PRACTICE for Example 2

2. **PRECIPITATION** In Example 2, for how many months was the precipitation in Dallas more than 2.6 inches? **6 mo**

Differentiated Instruction

Below Level Have students work with values that are easier to manipulate so that they can concentrate on dividing the data into groups and learning the vocabulary. For example, they could make a box-and-whiskers plot that displays the number of e-mail messages a friend receives. The number of messages could be 6, 9, 12, 8, 6, 4, 5, 10, 8, 9, and 11, with median 8, lower quartile 6, upper quartile 10, minimum value 4, and maximum value 12.

See also the *Algebra 1 Toolkit* for more strategies.

OUTLIERS A value that is widely separated from the rest of the data in a data set is called an **outlier**. Typically, a data value is considered to be an outlier if it is greater than the upper quartile by more than 1.5 times the interquartile range or if it is less than the lower quartile by more than 1.5 times the interquartile range.

EXAMPLE 3 Standardized Test Practice

The normal monthly amounts of precipitation (in inches) in Dallas are: 1.9, 2.4, 3.1, 3.2, 5.2, 3.2, 2.1, 2.0, 2.4, 4.1, 2.6, 2.6. These data were used to create the box-and-whisker plot in Example 2. Which value, if any, is an outlier?

Ⓐ 1.9 Ⓑ 5.2 Ⓒ 1.9 and 5.2 Ⓓ No outlier

Solution

From Example 2, you know the interquartile range of the data is 0.9 inch. Find 1.5 times the interquartile range: $1.5(0.9) = 1.35$.

From Example 2, you also know that the lower quartile is 2.3 and the upper quartile is 3.2. A value less than $2.3 - 1.35 = 0.95$ is an outlier. A value greater than $3.2 + 1.35 = 4.55$, is an outlier. Notice that $5.2 > 4.55$.

▶ The correct answer is B. Ⓐ Ⓑ Ⓒ Ⓓ

✓ GUIDED PRACTICE for Example 3

3. Which value, if any, is an outlier in the data set? D

3.7, 3.0, 3.4, 3.6, 5.2, 5.4, 3.2, 3.8, 4.3, 4.5, 4.2, 3.7

Ⓐ 3.0 Ⓑ 5.4 Ⓒ 3.0 and 5.4 Ⓓ No outlier

13.8 EXERCISES

HOMEWORK KEY
○ = **WORKED-OUT SOLUTIONS** on p. WS33 for Exs. 3 and 17
★ = **STANDARDIZED TEST PRACTICE** Exs. 2, 8, 9, 18, and 19

SKILL PRACTICE

A

1. **VOCABULARY** What is the interquartile range of a data set?
the difference of the upper quartile and the lower quartile

2. ★ **WRITING** *Explain* how you can identify an outlier in a data set. See margin.

EXAMPLE 1 on p. 887 for Exs. 3–7

BOX-AND-WHISKER PLOTS **Make a box-and-whisker plot of the data.** 3–6. See margin.

3. 1, 7, 0, 7, 2, 6, 3, 6, 0, 7, 8
4. 10, 1, 7, 5, 1, 8, 5, 4, 6, 5, 9, 12
5. 52, 20, 24, 45, 35, 32, 39, 42, 23, 64
6. 0.8, 0.4, 0.3, 0.6, 0.7, 0.2, 0.7, 0.9

Extra Example 3

The normal wind speeds (in miles per hour) each month in Savannah are: 8.2, 8.6, 9.1, 8.6, 7.6, 7.4, 6.9, 6.7, 7.2, 7.3, 7.2, 7.6. These data were used to create the box-and-whisker plot in Extra Example 2. Which value, if any, is an outlier? D

Ⓐ 6.7 Ⓑ 9.1 Ⓒ 6.7 and 9.1 Ⓓ No outlier

Closing the Lesson

Have students summarize the major points of the lesson and answer the Essential Question: How do you make and interpret box-and-whisker plots?

- **Each whisker in a box-and-whisker plot represents about 25% of the data.**
- **Each box on each side of the median represents about 25% of the data.**

To make a box-and-whisker plot, order the data from least to greatest, then find the median and the quartiles. The lower quartile is the median of the lower half of the data and the upper quartile is the median of the upper half. Plot the median, the quartiles, and the minimum and maximum values below a number line. Draw a box from the lower to the upper quartile. Draw a vertical line through the median. Draw a horizontal segment from the box to the minimum and another from the box to the maximum. Use median, quartiles, minimum, maximum, and the interquartile range to interpret and compare data.

2. See Additional Answers beginning on p. AA1.

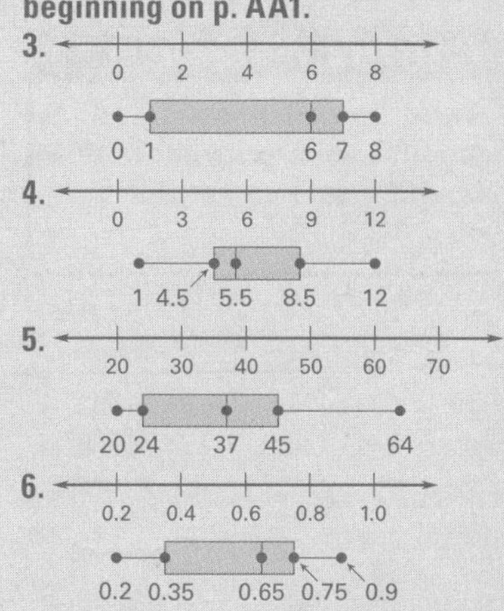

Differentiated Instruction

Kinesthetic Learners Ordering data can be difficult to do on paper. For problems similar to **Example 3**, have students write each data value on a small self-stick note so they can sort the data by moving the self-stick notes on their desk or on a sheet of paper.

See also the *Algebra 1 Toolkit* for more strategies.

p. 887
Guided Practice Ex. 1

15 30 45 60 75

15 22.5 35 57.5 70

4 PRACTICE AND APPLY

Assignment Guide

Answer Transparencies available for all exercises

Basic:
Day 1: pp. 889–892
Exs. 1–7, 15, 16
Day 2: pp. 889–892
Exs. 8–12, 17–19, 21–24

Average:
Day 1: pp. 889–892
Exs. 1, 2, 4–7, 15, 16, 21, 22
Day 2: pp. 889–892
Exs. 8–13, 17–19, 23, 24

Advanced:
Day 1: pp. 889–892
Exs. 1, 2, 4–6, 15, 16, 21, 22
Day 2: pp. 889–892
Exs. 8–14*, 17–20*, 23, 24

Block:
pp. 889–892
Exs. 1, 2, 4–13, 15–19, 21–24

Differentiated Instruction

See *Algebra 1 Best Practices Toolkit* for suggestions on addressing the needs of a diverse classroom.

Homework Check

For a quick check of student understanding of key concepts, go over the following exercises:

Basic: 4, 8, 11, 15, 17
Average: 5, 9, 12, 16, 18
Advanced: 6, 10, 13, 17, 19

Extra Practice

- Student Edition, p. 950
- Chapter 13 Resource Book: Practice levels A, B, C, pp. 88–93

Practice Worksheet

An easily-readable reduced practice page (with answers) for this lesson can be found on p. 840C.

---

7. **ERROR ANALYSIS** *Describe* and correct the error in creating a box-and-whisker plot of the data 0, 2, 4, 0, 6, 10, 8, 12, 5.
Sample answer: The upper quartile is incorrect. The upper quartile should be the median of 8 and 10, or 9; see margin for art.

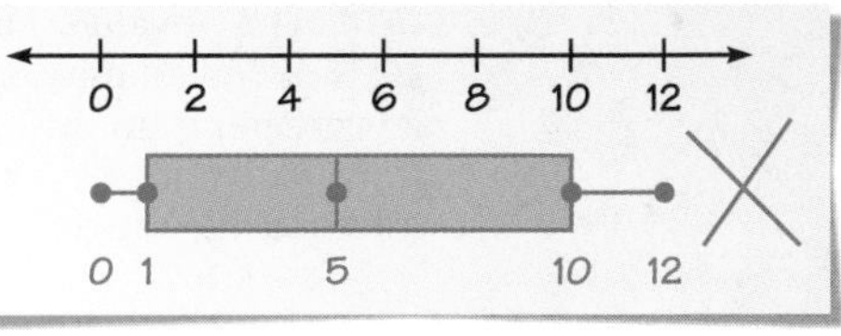

BOX-AND-WHISKER PLOT **In Exercises 8–10, use the box-and-whisker plot.**

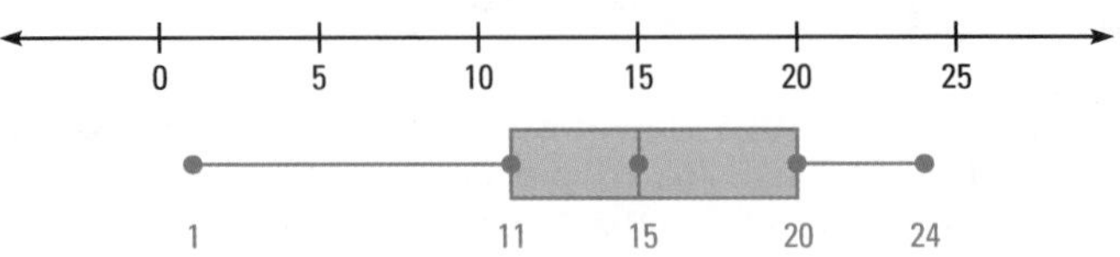

EXAMPLE 2 on p. 888 for Exs. 8–10

8. ★ **MULTIPLE CHOICE** About what percent of the data are greater than 20? A
Ⓐ 25% Ⓑ 50% Ⓒ 75% Ⓓ 100%

9. ★ **MULTIPLE CHOICE** About what percent of the data are less than 15? B
Ⓐ 25% Ⓑ 50% Ⓒ 75% Ⓓ 100%

10. **ERROR ANALYSIS** *Describe* and correct the error in interpreting the box-and-whisker plot.
Sample answer: The box represents 50% of the data values; about 50% of the data values lie between 11 and 20.

About 25% of the data values lie between 11 and 20.

EXAMPLES 1 and 3 on pp. 887, 889 for Exs. 11–13

B **OUTLIERS** **Make a box-and-whisker plot of the data. Identify any outliers.** 11–13. See margin.

11. Hours worked per week: 15, 15, 10, 12, 22, 10, 8, 14, 18, 22, 18, 15, 12, 11, 10
12. Prices of MP3 players: \$124, \$95, \$105, \$110, \$95, \$124, \$300, \$190, \$114
13. Annual salaries: \$30,000, \$35,000, \$48,000, \$68,500, \$32,000, \$38,000

C 14. **CHALLENGE** Two data sets have the same mean, the same interquartile range, and the same range. Is it possible for the box-and-whisker plots of such data sets to be different? *Justify* your answer by creating data sets that fit the situation. Yes. *Sample answer:* A: 0, 2, 4, 6, 8; B: –1, 3, 4, 7, 7

PROBLEM SOLVING

EXAMPLE 1 on p. 887 for Exs. 15–16

A 15. **SEAWAY** The average sailing times to the Atlantic Ocean from several ports on the St. Lawrence Seaway are shown on the map. Make a box-and-whisker plot of the sailing times. See margin.

@HomeTutor for problem solving help at classzone.com

○ = WORKED-OUT SOLUTIONS on p. WS1 ★ = STANDARDIZED TEST PRACTICE

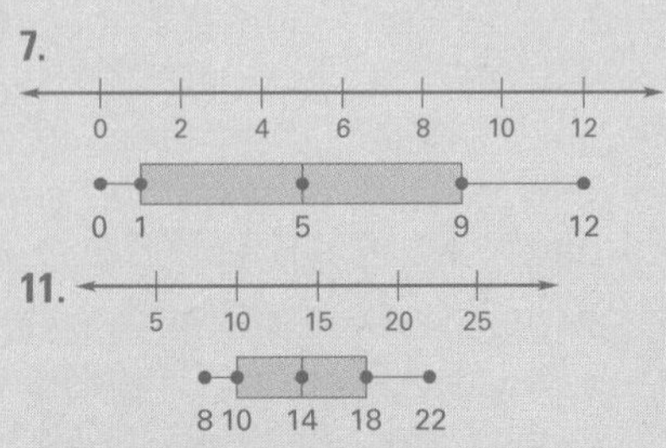

There are no outliers.

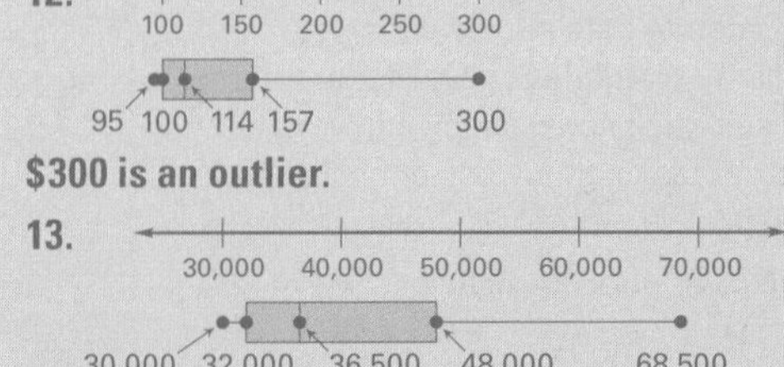

\$300 is an outlier.

There are no outliers.

16. **BASEBALL STATISTICS** In 2004, Ichiro Suzuki scored 101 runs. The numbers of runs he scored against different opposing teams are listed below. Make a box-and-whisker plot of the numbers of runs scored. See margin.

Runs scored: 18, 8, 4, 8, 2, 8, 0, 9, 0, 4, 2, 5, 9, 1, 2, 1, 2, 11, 7

@HomeTutor for problem solving help at classzone.com

EXAMPLES 1 and 3 on pp. 887, 889 for Exs. 17–18

17. **RETAIL SALES** The retail sales (in billions of dollars) of the nine U.S. states with the highest retail sales in 2002 are listed below.

California: $153.1	Florida: $118.2	Georgia: $38.4
Illinois: $52.4	New Jersey: $35.8	New York: $54.7
Ohio: $50.7	Pennsylvania: $49.9	Texas: $107.0

a. Make a box-and-whisker plot of the retail sales. See margin.

b. Which states, if any, had retail sales in 2002 that can be considered outliers? none

18b. Yes. *Sample answer:* Ronald Reagan's age is more than 1.5 times the interquartile range of 7 away from the upper quartile.

18. ★ **SHORT RESPONSE** The stem-and-leaf plot shows the ages of the first 43 presidents of the United States when they first took the oath of office.

Stem	Leaves
4	2 3 6 6 7 8 9 9
5	0 0 1 1 1 1 2 2 4 4 4 4 4 5 5 5 5 6 6 6 7 7 7 7 8
6	0 1 1 1 2 4 4 5 8 9

Key: 4 | 2 = 42 years

a. Make a box-and-whisker plot of the ages. See margin.

b. Ronald Reagan was the oldest United States president, and Theodore Roosevelt was the youngest. Can either of these presidents' ages be considered outliers? *Explain* why or why not.

EXAMPLE 2 B on p. 888 for Ex. 19

19. ★ **EXTENDED RESPONSE** The box-and-whisker plots show the diameters (in kilometers) of craters on Jupiter's moons Callisto and Ganymede.

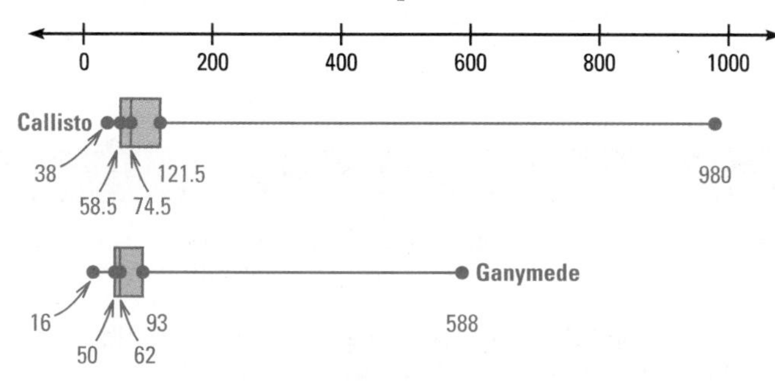

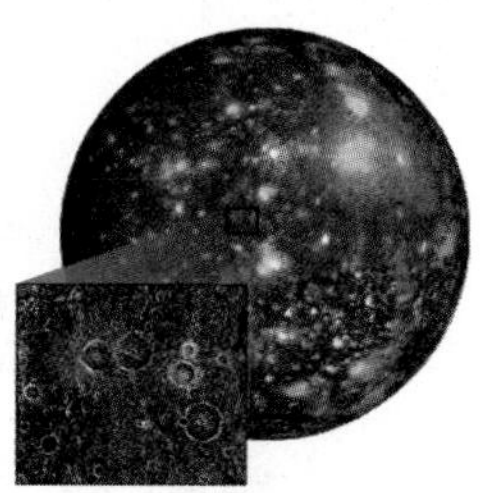
Callisto

a. *Compare* the diameters of craters on Callisto with the diameters of craters on Ganymede. See margin.

b. The largest crater in the United States is the Chesapeake Bay in Virginia, with a diameter of 90 kilometers. *Compare* the diameter of the Chesapeake Bay with diameters of craters on Callisto and Ganymede.

c. The largest crater on Earth is Vredefort in South Africa, with a diameter of 300 kilometers. *Compare* the diameter of Vredefort with the diameter of craters on Callisto and Ganymede.

19b. *Sample answer:* Chesapeake Bay is larger than between 50% and 75% of the craters on both Callisto and Ganymede.

19c. *Sample answer:* Vredefort is larger than at least 75% of the craters on both Callisto and Ganymede.

Avoiding Common Errors

Exercises 3–6, 11–13 Caution students to pay attention to the values they use to determine the median and quartiles. A common error is using the median to determine the quartiles when there is an odd number of values in the data set.

Mathematical Reasoning

Exercise 14 To get students started on this exercise, you may want to ask if two data sets can have the same range and the same mean, but different medians. Ask the students, as a class, to come up with an example.

Exercise 18 For additional information about the presidents of the United States, visit www.whitehouse.gov/history/presidents/index2.html

Teaching Strategy

Exercise 19 You may want to use this exercise to discuss outliers and interquartile range. First have students calculate outliers for Callisto and Ganymede and then point out how the outliers affect the range but not the interquartile range. Ask students to explain whether the range or the interquartile range best describes the spread of the data.

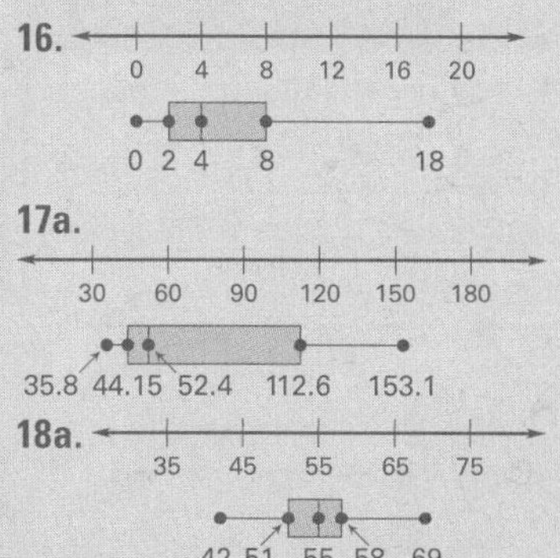

19a. *Sample answer:* The craters on Ganymede are generally smaller than the craters on Callisto. The lower extreme, lower quartile, median, upper quartile, and upper extreme values are all lower for Ganymede than for Callisto.

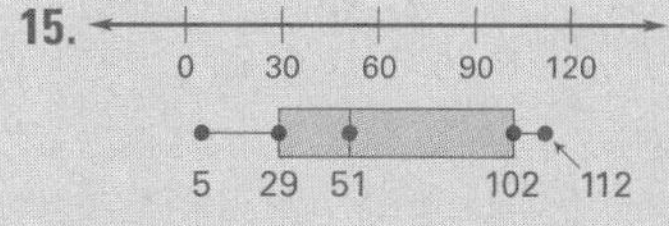

5 ASSESS AND RETEACH

Daily Homework Quiz

Transparency Available

1. Hiking trails (in miles) of moderate difficulty in Arizona's Mazatzal Wilderness Area are listed below. Make a box-and-whisker plot of the data.

   4.2, 5.7, 7, 3.3, 3.1, 3, 3.5, 3, 7.5, 4.2, 7.5, 6.6

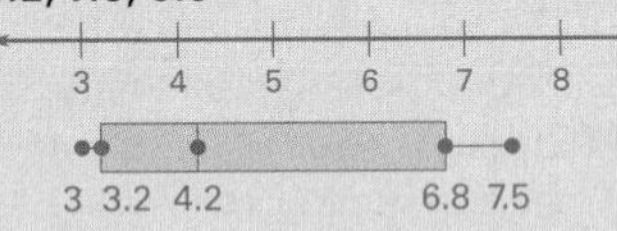

2. About what percent of the trails are greater than 4.2 miles in length? 50%

Available at **classzone.com**

Diagnosis/Remediation

- Practice A, B, C in Chapter 13 Resource Book, pp. 88–93
- Study Guide in Chapter13 Resource Book, pp. 94–95
- Practice Workbook, pp. 211–213
- @HomeTutor

Challenge

Additional challenge is available in the Chapter 13 Resource Book, p. 98.

Quiz

An easily-readable reduced copy of the quiz (with answers) on Lessons 13.5–13.8 from the Assessment Book can be found on p. 840F.

20, Quiz 4–6. See Additional Answers beginning on p. AA1.

C **20. CHALLENGE** The box-and-whisker plots show the heights (in inches) of singers in a chorus, according to their voice parts. A soprano part has the highest pitch, followed by alto, tenor, and bass, respectively. Draw a conclusion about voice parts and heights. *Justify* your conclusion. See margin.

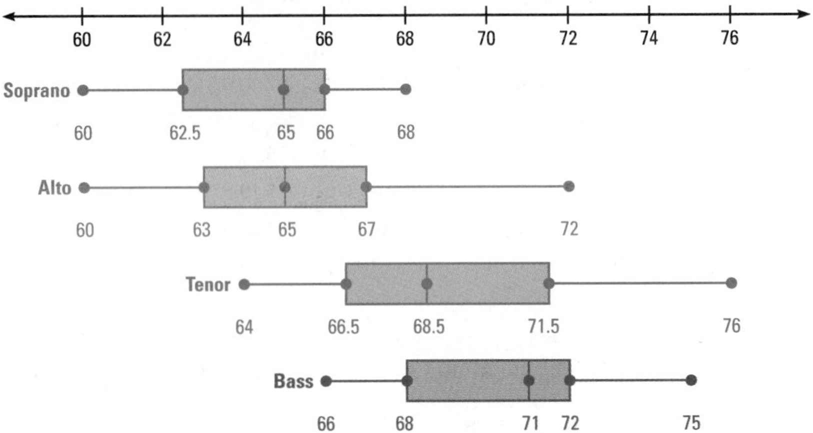

ILLINOIS MIXED REVIEW

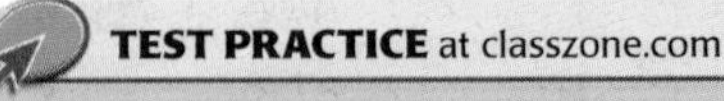

21. For the past 5 years, the yearly rainfall, in inches, at a weather station has been 83, 76, 83, 41, and 70. Which measure of data should a meteorologist use to make the most accurate prediction for next year's rainfall? B

Ⓐ Mean Ⓑ Median Ⓒ Mode Ⓓ Range

22. The probability that a golf ball is defective is $\frac{1}{12}$. About how many balls would be defective in a case of 927 golf balls? C

Ⓐ 8 Ⓑ 12 Ⓒ 77 Ⓓ 93

QUIZ *for Lessons 13.5–13.8*

1. **HOTEL SURVEY** A hotel manager leaves guest comment cards in each room. Identify the population and classify the sampling method. *(p. 871)* all the hotel's guests, self-selected

In Exercises 2 and 3, find the range and mean absolute deviation of the data. Round to the nearest hundredth, if necessary. *(p. 875)*

2. 62, 63, 70, 40, 50, 60 30, 8.33
3. 14, 18, 22, 14, 14, 6, 17 16, 3.43
4. Make a histogram of the data: 44, 52, 60, 47, 65, 40, 49, 45, 32, 68, 39. *(p. 881)* See margin.
5. Make a stem-and-leaf plot of the data: 1.8, 2.2, 1.2, 2.8, 3.6, 3.3, 1.8, 2.2. *(p. 881)* See margin.
6. **TEST SCORES** The scores on a math exam are given below. Make a box-and-whisker plot of the data. Identify any outliers. *(p. 887)* See margin.

   76, 55, 88, 92, 79, 85, 90, 88, 85, 92, 100, 91, 90, 86, 88

Graphing Calculator **ACTIVITY** *Use after Lesson 13.8*

@HomeTutor
classzone.com
Keystrokes

13.8 Draw Box-and-Whisker Plots

QUESTION How can you use a graphing calculator to make a box-and-whisker plot?

EXAMPLE Make a box-and-whisker plot

REPTILE SPECIES The number of known reptile species per 10,000 square kilometers in the countries of Asia (excluding the Middle East) and of Central America, South America, and the Caribbean are listed below. Make box-and-whisker plots of the numbers of species.

Asia: 36, 26, 49, 11, 32, 35, 27, 58, 91, 26, 8, 8, 12, 12, 23, 110, 4, 51, 41, 41, 62, 350, 77, 18, 81, 23, 18, 59

Central America, South America, and the Caribbean: 81, 125, 47, 69, 57, 107, 77, 73, 35, 123, 69, 116, 87, 37, 45, 53, 20, 124, 126, 35, 73, 60, 64

***STEP 1* Enter the data**

Enter the data for Asia into List 1. Enter the data for Central America, South America, and the Caribbean into List 2.

***STEP 2* Select box-and-whisker plot**

Go to the STAT PLOT screen and select the box-and-whisker plot for both Plot 1 and Plot 2. The Xlist for Plot 1 should be L_1, so that it displays the data from List 1. The Xlist for Plot 2 should be L_2, so that it displays the data from List 2. Make sure both plots are on.

***STEP 3* Set the viewing window**

Press ZOOM 9 to set the window so that it shows all of the data.

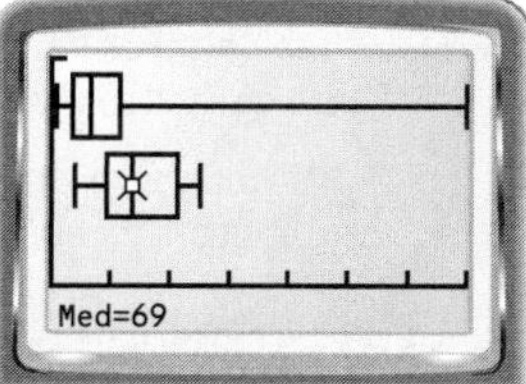

***STEP 4* Graph**

Press GRAPH. Use the trace feature to examine the box-and-whisker plots more closely. Notice that the graphing calculator refers to the lower quartile as Q_1 and the upper quartile as Q_3.

DRAW CONCLUSIONS

1. **REPTILE SPECIES** *Compare* the number of reptile species per 10,000 square kilometers in the countries of Central America, South America, and the Caribbean with the number in Asia. See margin.
2. **BIRD SPECIES** The number of threatened bird species per 10,000 square kilometers in the countries of two regions are listed below. Make box-and-whisker plots of the data and compare the data for the two regions. See margin.

   Middle East and Northern Africa: 13, 8, 11, 14, 12, 8, 4, 3, 5, 2, 11, 5, 11, 7, 6, 14, 4, 13

   North and South America: 5, 50, 41, 27, 103, 18, 64, 53, 3, 26, 64, 2, 11, 22

1. *Sample answer:* Although Asia has an outlier that is greater than any value in Central America, South America, and the Caribbean's data set, in general Asia's data is lower. The lower extreme, lower quartile, median, and upper quartile are all lower for Asia than for Central America, South America, and the Caribbean.

2.

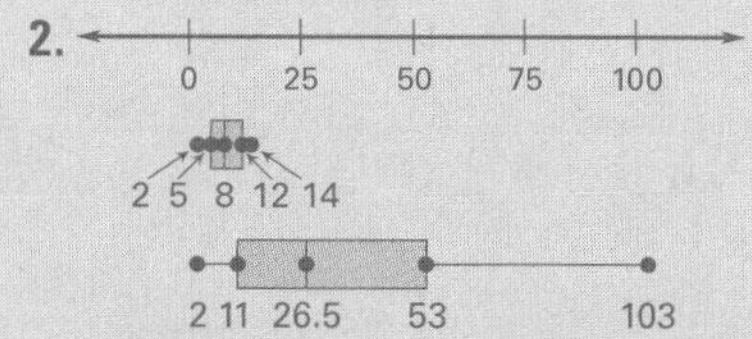

Sample answer: Generally, there are more threatened bird species in North and South America than in the Middle East and Northern Africa. There is also a much greater range of values in North and South America.

1 PLAN AND PREPARE

Learn the Method

- Students will use a graphing calculator to make a box-and-whisker plot.
- After the activity, students can use a graphing calculator to check their solutions in Exercises 3–6 and 11–13 in Lesson 13.8.

Keystroke Help

Keystrokes for several models of calculators are available in blackline format in the *Chapter 13 Resource Book.*

2 TEACH

Tips for Success

If necessary, tell students to adjust Xmin and Xmax in the viewing window so they can clearly see both plots.

Extra Example

The number of recorded green turtle nests and leatherback turtle nests during the years 1996–2004 on a Florida island are listed below. Make box-and-whiskers plots of the number of nests.

Green turtle: 31, 10, 93, 22, 166, 21, 106, 81, 70

Leatherback turtle: 13, 21, 7, 20, 21, 35, 16, 18, 6

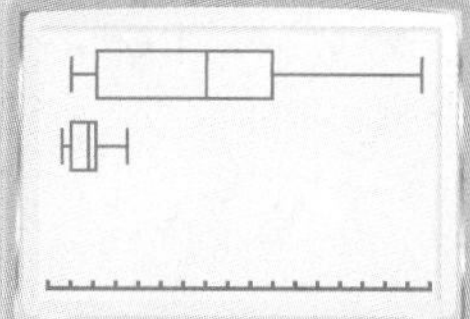

3 ASSESS AND RETEACH

What do the interquartile ranges of the two plots tell you? The interquartile ranges tell you that the number of green turtle nests varied greatly during the 9-year period, while the number of leatherback turtle nests remained fairly consistent.

Illinois Mixed Review

1. C
2. J
3. C
4. A
5. B
6. G

Illinois Mixed Review

TEST PRACTICE
classzone.com

Lessons 13.5–13.8

1. **OFFICE HOURS** A doctor would like to extend her office hours to better accommodate her patients. She wants to choose the day that best suits her patients. Which of the following survey techniques is most likely to generate a representative sample of her patients?

   A. Asking all the patients who come into the office one day

   B. Asking all the patients who come into the office in one week

   C. Alphabetizing all her patients and phoning every tenth one

   D. Leaving surveys in her office for patients to fill out if they choose

2. **SURVEY** A reporter from your school newspaper is considering several questions to ask in a poll. Which of the following is *not* a biased question?

   F. "Don't you think our school is going to win the game this weekend?"

   G. "By how many points do you think our team will win the game this weekend?"

   H. "Do you think our team will be upset in the game this weekend?"

   J. "Which team do you think will win the game this weekend?"

3. **DVD PLAYERS** The prices (in dollars) of portable DVD players at two stores are as follows: 280, 200, 260, 230, 200, 150, 300, 260, 500, 190. Which of the following statements is true of the data?

   A. The median is greater than the mean.

   B. The data set has no outliers.

   C. The interquartile range is $80.

   D. A majority of the data are in the interval $200–$250.

4. **LONG JUMP** The back-to-back stem-and-leaf plot shows the lengths (in meters) of the eight best men's and women's final long jump results in the 2004 Olympics. Based on the data, which of the following statements is true?

   Lengths (in meters) of Long Jump

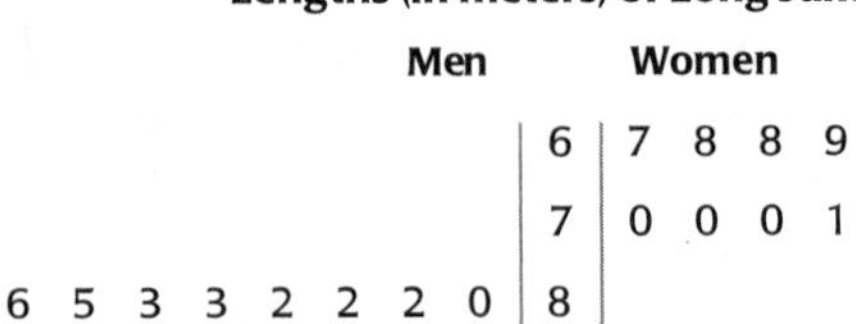

Men		Women
	6	7 8 8 9
	7	0 0 0 1
6 5 3 3 2 2 2 0	8	

Key: 0 | 7 | 1 = 7.0 m, 7.1 m

   F. No woman jumped farther than any man.

   G. The women's jumps had a greater range than the men's jumps.

   H. The median jump for the men was less than 1 meter longer than the median jump for the women.

   J. None of the above

5. **JEANS** A clothing store sells several different styles of jeans for the following prices: $20, $20, $25, $30, $40. Find the mean absolute deviation of the store's jean prices to the nearest ten cents.

   A. $5.50 **C.** $6.50

   B. $6.40 **D.** $32.00

6. **THEATER** The ages (in years) of people who attended an opening reception for a theater production are as follows: 54, 25, 64, 40, 42, 33, 50, 27, 35, 50, 39, 41, 52, 49, 48, 56. Find the interquartile range of the data.

   F. 8

   G. 14

   H. 39

   J. 45

13 CHAPTER SUMMARY

BIG IDEAS

For Your Notebook

Big Idea 1

Finding Probabilities of Simple and Compound Events

To find $P(A)$ when...	
all outcomes are equally likely, use $P(A) = \frac{\text{Number of favorable outcomes}}{\text{Number of possible outcomes}}$	you perform an experiment, use $P(A) = \frac{\text{Number of successes}}{\text{Number of trials}}$

To find $P(A \text{ or } B)$ when...	...use this formula
events A and B have no common outcomes	$P(A \text{ or } B) = P(A) + P(B)$
events A and B have at least one common outcome	$P(A \text{ or } B) = P(A) + P(B) - P(A \text{ and } B)$

To find $P(A \text{ and } B)$ when...	...use this formula
events A and B are independent	$P(A \text{ and } B) = P(A) \cdot P(B)$
events A and B are dependent	$P(A \text{ and } B) = P(A) \cdot P(B \text{ given } A)$

Big Idea 2

Analyzing Sets of Data

You can find values that represent a typical data value using the following measures of central tendency:

mean, median, and mode

You can find values that describe the spread of data using the following measures of dispersion:

range, mean absolute deviation, and interquartile range

Big Idea 3

Making and Interpreting Data Displays

Use an appropriate display to show the distribution of a set of numerical data.

A **stem-and-leaf plot** organizes data based on their digits.

Stem	Leaves
1	0 1 1 2 3
2	0 0 0 2

Key: 1 | 0 = 10

A **histogram** shows the frequency of data on intervals of equal size, with no gaps or overlaps.

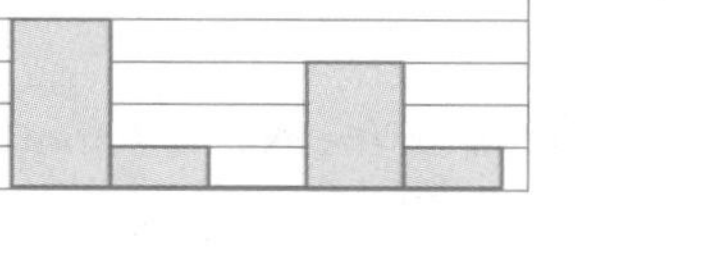

A **box-and-whisker plot** organizes data into four groups of approximately equal size.

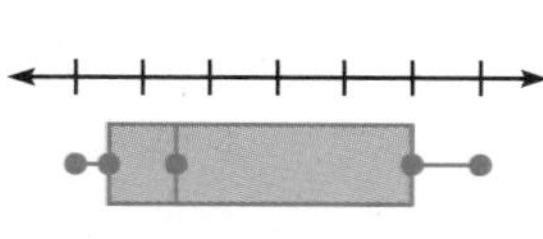

Additional Resources

The following resources are available to help review the materials in this chapter.

Chapter 13 Resource Book

- Chapter Review Games and Activities, p. 99
- Cumulative Practice, Chs. 1–13, pp. 102–103

Student Resources in Spanish

eWorkbook

@HomeTutor

Vocabulary Practice

Vocabulary practice is available at **classzone.com**

Extra Example 13.1

A bag contains 12 green markers, 6 blue markers, and 8 yellow markers. You choose a marker at random. Find the probability you choose a blue marker. $\frac{3}{13}$

13 CHAPTER REVIEW

@HomeTutor
classzone.com
- Multi-Language Glossary
- Vocabulary Practice

REVIEW KEY VOCABULARY

- outcome, event, *p. 843*
- sample space, *p. 843*
- probability of an event, *p. 843*
- theoretical, experimental probability, *p. 844*
- odds in favor, odds against, *p. 845*
- permutation, *p. 851*
- *n* factorial, *p. 852*
- combination, *p. 856*
- compound event, *p. 861*
- mutually exclusive events, *p. 861*
- overlapping events, *p. 861*
- independent events, *p. 862*
- dependent events, *p. 862*
- survey, *p. 871*
- population, *p. 871*
- sample: random, stratified random, systematic, convenience, self-selected, *p. 871*
- biased sample, *p. 872*
- biased question, *p. 872*
- mean, median, mode, *p. 875*
- measure of dispersion, *p. 876*
- range, *p. 876*
- mean absolute deviation, *p. 876*
- stem-and-leaf plot, *p. 881*
- frequency, frequency table, *p. 882*
- histogram, *p. 882*
- box-and-whisker plot, *p. 887*
- lower quartile, upper quartile, *p. 887*
- interquartile range, *p. 888*
- outlier, *p. 889*

VOCABULARY EXERCISES

Copy and complete the statement.

1. An event that combines two or more events is a(n) _?_. compound event
2. A possible result of an experiment is a(n) _?_. outcome
3. **WRITING** *Compare* theoretical probability and experimental probability.
   Sample answer: **Theoretical probability is based on knowing the likelihood of all possible outcomes of an event. Experimental probability is based on the results of an experiment.**

REVIEW EXAMPLES AND EXERCISES

Use the review examples and exercises below to check your understanding of the concepts you have learned in each lesson of Chapter 13.

13.1 Find Probabilities and Odds *pp. 843–848*

EXAMPLE

A bag contains 15 red checkers and 15 black checkers. You choose a checker at random. Find the probability that you choose a black checker.

$$P(\text{black checker}) = \frac{\text{Number of black checkers}}{\text{Total number of checkers}} = \frac{15}{30} = \frac{1}{2}$$

EXERCISES

EXAMPLE 2 on p. 844 for Exs. 4–5

4. **CHECKERS** In the example above, suppose an extra red checker is added to the bag. Find the probability of randomly choosing a black checker. $\frac{15}{31}$
5. **BAG OF LETTERS** A bag contains tiles. Each tile has one letter from the word HAPPINESS on it. You choose a tile at random. What is the probability that you choose a tile with the letter S? $\frac{2}{9}$

@HomeTutor
classzone.com
Chapter Review Practice

13.2 Find Probabilities Using Permutations

pp. 851–855

EXAMPLE

You need to enter a 4 digit code in order to enter the building where you work. The digits are 4 different numbers from 1 to 5. You forgot the code and try to guess it. Find the probability that you guess correctly.

STEP 1 **Write** the number of possible outcomes as the number of permutations of 4 out of the 5 possible digits. This is ${}_5P_4$.

$${}_5P_4 = \frac{5!}{(5-4)!} = \frac{5!}{1!} = 5! = 5 \cdot 4 \cdot 3 \cdot 2 \cdot 1 = 120$$

STEP 2 **Find** the probability. Because only one of the permutations is the correct code, the probability that you guess the correct code is $\frac{1}{120}$.

EXERCISES

EXAMPLE 2 on p. 852 for Exs. 6–10

Evaluate the expression.

6. ${}_7P_6$ 5040
7. ${}_6P_2$ 30
8. ${}_8P_5$ 6720
9. ${}_{13}P_{10}$ 1,037,836,800
10. **MUSIC** You downloaded 6 songs. You randomly choose 4 of these songs to play. Find the probability that you play the first 4 songs you downloaded in the order in which you downloaded them. $\frac{1}{360}$

13.3 Find Probabilities Using Combinations

pp. 856–859

EXAMPLE

For your government class, you must choose 3 states in the United States to research. You may choose your states from the 6 New England states. How many combinations of states are possible?

The order in which you choose the states is not important. So, to find the number of combinations of 6 states taken 3 at a time, find ${}_6C_3$.

$${}_6C_3 = \frac{6!}{(6-3)! \cdot 3!}$$ **Combinations formula**

$$= \frac{6 \cdot 5 \cdot 4 \cdot 3!}{3! \cdot (3 \cdot 2 \cdot 1)}$$ **Expand factorials. Divide out common factor, 3!.**

$$= 20$$ **Simplify.**

EXERCISES

EXAMPLE 2 on p. 857 for Exs. 11–15

Evaluate the expression.

11. ${}_7C_6$ 7
12. ${}_6C_2$ 15
13. ${}_8C_5$ 56
14. ${}_{13}C_{10}$ 286
15. **TICKETS** You win 5 tickets to a concert. In how many ways can you choose 4 friends out of a group of 9 to take with you to the concert? 126 ways

Extra Example 13.2

The coach for the swimming team randomly chooses 2 of the 12 members of the team to talk to local reporters about an upcoming meet. What is the probability that the coach chooses you and your twin brother? $\frac{1}{132}$

Extra Example 13.3

Your dog has 6 puppies. You can choose 2 of the 6 to keep. How many choices of two puppies are possible? 15 choices

13 CHAPTER REVIEW

Extra Examples 13.4

1. You roll a number cube. Find the probability that the number is 2 or an odd number. $\frac{2}{3}$
2. A bag contains 3 red chips, 2 white chips, 4 blue chips, and 6 yellow chips. You choose a chip at random and then return it to the bag. You choose another chip at random. What is the probability that both chips are red? $\frac{1}{25}$

13.4 Find Probabilities of Compound Events

pp. 861–867

EXAMPLE

The sections of the spinner shown all have the same area. You spin the spinner. Find the probability that the spinner stops on red or on an even number.

Because 24 is an even number on a red section, stopping on red and stopping on an even number are overlapping events.

$$P(\text{red or even}) = P(\text{red}) + P(\text{even}) - P(\text{red and even})$$

$$= \frac{3}{8} + \frac{3}{8} - \frac{1}{8}$$

$$= \frac{5}{8}$$

EXERCISES

EXAMPLES 1 and 2 on pp. 861–862 for Exs. 16–19

You spin the spinner shown above. Find the specified probability.

16. P(green or odd) $\frac{7}{8}$
17. P(blue or prime number) $\frac{3}{8}$
18. P(blue or even) $\frac{3}{4}$
19. P(red or multiple of 3) $\frac{5}{8}$

EXAMPLE

A bag contains 5 red marbles, 3 blue marbles, 6 white marbles, and 2 green marbles. You choose one marble at random, put the marble aside, then choose a second marble at random. What is the probability that both marbles are blue?

Because you do not replace the first marble, the events are dependent. Before you choose a marble, there are 16 marbles, and 3 of them are blue. After you choose a blue marble, there are 2 blue marbles among 15 marbles left.

$$P(\text{blue and then blue}) = P(\text{blue}) \cdot P(\text{blue given blue})$$

$$= \frac{3}{16} \cdot \frac{2}{15}$$

$$= \frac{6}{240}$$

$$= \frac{1}{40}$$

EXERCISES

EXAMPLES 3 and 4 on p. 863 for Exs. 20–21

You randomly choose 2 marbles from the bag described in the example above. Find the probability that both are green if:

20. you replace the first marble. $\frac{1}{64}$
21. you don't replace the first marble. $\frac{1}{120}$

@HomeTutor
classzone.com
Chapter Review Practice

13.5 Analyze Surveys and Samples

pp. 871–874

EXAMPLE

You want to determine what type of music is the favorite of students in your grade. You survey every third student from an alphabetical list of students in your grade. You ask each surveyed student, "What is your favorite type of music, classical or country?"

Identify the population and classify the sampling method. Tell whether the question is potentially biased. Explain your answer. If the question is potentially biased, rewrite it so that it is not.

The population is all students in your grade. Because you use the rule "survey every third student," the sample is a systematic sample.

The question is biased, because it does not allow students to choose a type of music other than classical or country. An unbiased question is "What is your favorite type of music?"

EXERCISES

EXAMPLE 1 on p. 871 for Ex. 22

22. **SURVEY** In the example above, suppose you create a questionaire and distribute one to every student in your grade. There is a box in the cafeteria where students can drop off completed questionaires during lunch. Identify the sampling method. self-selected

13.6 Use Measures of Central Tendency and Dispersion

pp. 875–878

EXAMPLE

The amounts of snowfall (in inches) in one town for 8 months of the year are listed below. Find the mean, median, and mode(s) of the data. Which measure of central tendency best represents the data?

0.5, 0.5, 1.5, 2.0, 3.5, 4.5, 16.5, 30.5

$$\bar{x} = \frac{0.5 + 0.5 + 1.5 + 2.0 + 3.5 + 4.5 + 16.5 + 30.5}{8} = \frac{59.5}{8} = 7.4375 \text{ inches}$$

The median is the mean of the two middle values, 2.0 and 3.5, or 2.75 inches.

The mode is 0.5 inch.

The median best represents the data. The mean is greater then most of the data values. The mode is less than most of the data values.

EXERCISES

EXAMPLES 1 and 2 on pp. 875–876 for Ex. 23

23. **BASEBALL STATISTICS** The numbers of home runs hit by baseball player Manny Ramirez against several different opposing teams over 3 seasons are 5, 1, 10, 5, 5, 4, 1, 0, 7, 2, 1, 1, 1, 9, 6, 1, 2, 6, 2, 19, 6, and 17.

    a. Find the mean, median, and mode(s) of the data. about 5.045, 4.5, 1

    b. Which measure of central tendency best represents the data? *Explain.* See margin.

Extra Example 13.5

You want to determine whether the students at your school think the cafeteria serves nutritious food. You randomly choose students standing in the cafeteria line during first period lunch. You ask each student, "Do you think the cafeteria should serve better food?"

Identify the population and classify the sampling method. Tell whether the question is potentially biased. Explain your answer. If the question is potentially biased, rewrite it so that it is not.

The population is all students at your school. The sampling method is convenience.

The question is biased because the word "better" is ambiguous. An unbiased question is "Do you think the cafeteria serves nutritious food?"

Extra Example 13.6

Your test scores for English and science are shown below. Compare the scores using the range and the mean absolute deviation.

English: 82, 76, 84, 82
Science: 91, 84, 88, 90

English: range is 8 and mean absolute deviation is 2.5
Science: range is 7 and mean absolute deviation is 2.25
The range of English test scores is greater. The mean absolute deviation for the English scores is also greater.

23b. Median. *Sample answer:* The mode is much lower than many of the values, and the mean is affected by the two extreme values (17 and 19) that are much greater than the rest of the data. So, the median best represents the data.

13 CHAPTER REVIEW

Extra Example 13.7

The back-to-back stem-and-leaf plot shows the prices (in dollars) of oak trees and maple trees at a nursery. Compare the prices of the two trees at the nursery.

Tree Prices

Oak		Maple
3 1 0	4	0 0 2 3 3
7 5 5	5	1 1 2 3 5 5
8 7 6 5 4	6	0 2 2
8 8 5 5	7	2

Key: 5 | 5 | 1 = \$55, \$51

The median price of oak trees is \$65, while the median price of maple trees is \$52. In general, oak trees cost more than maple trees at the nursery.

Extra Example 13.8

Make a box-and-whisker plot of the prices of oak trees in the extra example above.

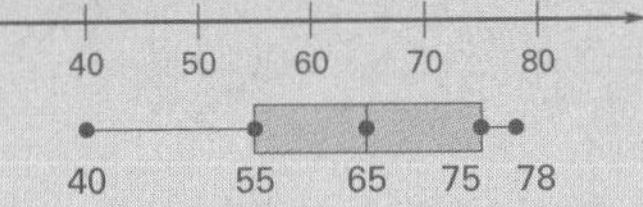

24.

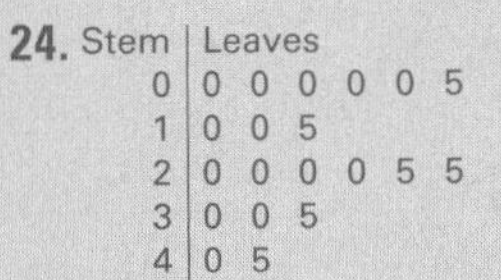

Stem	Leaves
0	0 0 0 0 0 5
1	0 0 5
2	0 0 0 0 5 5
3	0 0 5
4	0 5

Key: 1 | 0 = 10 minutes

25.

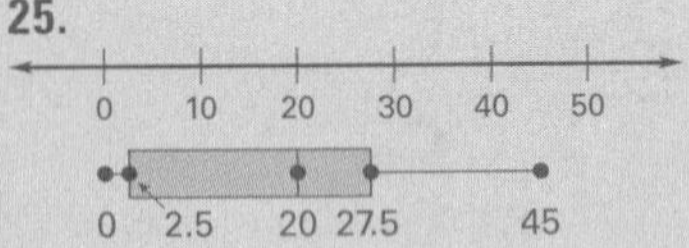

13.7 Interpret Stem-and-Leaf Plots and Histograms *pp. 881–885*

EXAMPLE

The prices (in dollars) of several books are listed below. Make a stem-and-leaf plot of the prices.

14, 15, 9, 19, 21, 29, 12, 25, 10, 8, 15, 13, 15, 20

STEP 1 **Separate** the data into stems and leaves

Book Prices

Stem	Leaves
0	9 8
1	4 5 9 2 0 5 3 5
2	1 9 0 5

Key: 1 | 4 = \$14

STEP 2 **Write** the leaves in increasing order.

Book Prices

Stem	Leaves
0	8 9
1	0 2 3 4 5 5 5 9
2	0 1 5 9

Key: 1 | 4 = \$14

EXERCISES

EXAMPLE 1 on p. 881 for Ex. 24

24. EXERCISING The minutes per day that the students in a class spend exercising are listed below. Make a stem-and-leaf plot of the data. See margin.

20, 25, 0, 10, 0, 30, 35, 20, 45, 25, 40, 0, 0, 0, 5, 10, 20, 15, 20, 30

13.8 Interpret Box-and-Whisker Plots *pp. 887–892*

EXAMPLE

Make a box-and-whisker plot of the book prices in the example above.

Order the data. Then find the median and quartiles.

Upper quartile ↓ 12; Median = 15 ↓; Lower quartile ↓ 20

8 9 10 12 13 14 15 15 15 19 20 21 25 29

Plot the median, the quartiles, the maximum value, and the minimum value below a number line. Draw the box and the whiskers.

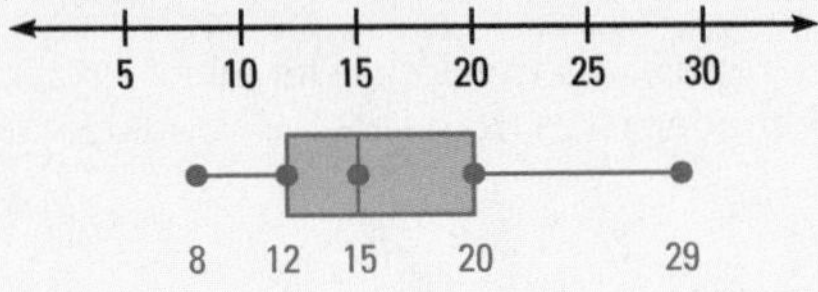

EXERCISES

EXAMPLE 1 on p. 887 for Ex. 25

25. EXERCISING Use the data in Exercise 24 to make a box-and-whisker plot of the minutes per day that the students in the class spend exercising. See margin.

13 CHAPTER TEST

You roll a number cube. Find (a) the probability that the number rolled is as described and (b) the odds in favor of rolling such a number.

1. a 4 a. $\frac{1}{6}$ b. 1 : 5

2. an even number a. $\frac{1}{2}$ b. 1 : 1

3. a number less than 5 a. $\frac{2}{3}$ b. 2 : 1

4. a multiple of 3 a. $\frac{1}{3}$ b. 1 : 2

Evaluate the expression.

5. ${}_7P_2$ 42

6. ${}_8P_3$ 336

7. ${}_6C_3$ 20

8. ${}_{12}C_7$ 792

Tell whether the question can be answered using *combinations* or *permutations*. *Explain* your choice, then answer the question.

9. Permutations; order matters since there are first, second, and third places; 336 ways.

9. Eight swimmers participate in a race. In how many ways can the swimmers finish in first, second, and third place?

10. A restaurant offers 7 different side dishes. In how many different ways can you choose 2 side dishes? Combinations; order does not matter since the side dishes can be selected in either order; 21 ways.

In Exercises 11 and 12, refer to a bag containing 12 tiles numbered 1–12.

11. You choose a tile at random. What is the probability that you choose a number less than 10 or an odd number. $\frac{5}{6}$

12. You choose a tile at random, replace it, and choose a second tile at random. What is the probability that you choose a number greater than 3, then an odd number. $\frac{3}{8}$

13. GOVERNMENT PROJECT City officials want to know whether residents will support construction of a new library. This question appears on the ballot in the citywide election: "Do you support a tax increase to replace the old, deteriorating library with a brand new one?"Is the question potentially biased? *Explain* your answer. If the question is potentially biased, rewrite it so that it is not. See margin.

14. BASKETBALL The back-to-back stem-and-leaf plot shows the heights (in inches) of the players on a high school's basketball teams. a–d. See margin.

Basketball Players' Heights

Girls		Boys
9 7 7 6 6 5 3 3	6	9 9 9
3 2 1 1 0	7	0 0 0 2 4 4 6 6 7 7 7 8

Key: 3 | 6 | 9 = 63 in., 69 in.

a. Find the mean, median, and mode(s) of each data set. Which measure of central tendency best represents each data set? *Explain.*

b. Find the range and mean absolute deviation of each data set. Which team's heights are more spread out? *Explain.*

c. Make a box-and-whisker plot of each data set.

d. *Compare* the boys' heights with the girls' heights.

Additional Resources

Assessment Book

- Chapter Test, Levels A, B, C, pp. 185–190
- Standardized Chapter Test, pp. 191–192
- SAT/ACT Chapter Test, pp. 193–194
- Alternative Assessment, pp. 195–196

Test Generator CD-ROM

Chapter Test

Easily-readable reduced copies (with answers) of Chapter Test B, the Standardized Chapter Test, and the Alternative Assessment from the Assessment Book can be found on pp. 840F–840H.

14a. Girls: mean: about 67.92, median: 67, mode: 66, 67, and 71; Boys: mean: 73.2, median: 74, mode: 69, 70, and 77

14b. Girls: range: 10, mean absolute deviation: 2.84; Boys: range: 9, mean absolute deviation: 3.12. *Sample answer:* Boys; their range is less, but their mean absolute deviation is greater which indicates that, on the average, the heights are farther away from the mean.

14c.

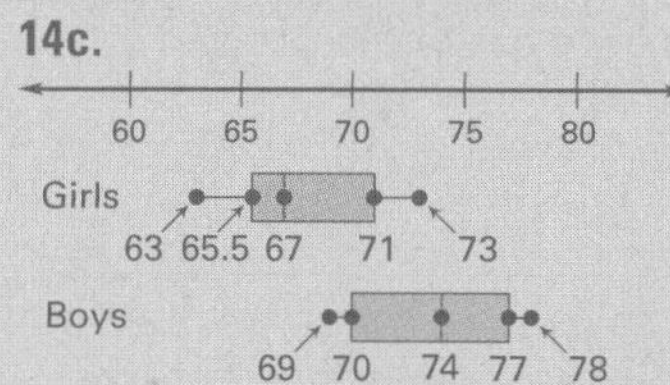

14d. *Sample answer:* Generally, the boys are taller than the girls. 50% of the boys are taller than all of the girls. Each group's data are almost equally dispersed, with the boy's having a slightly greater interquartile range.

13. Yes. *Sample answer:* The question suggests that the current library is old and deteriorating and that a new library would be an improvement; "Are you for or against a tax increase to build a new library to replace the old one?"

MULTIPLE CHOICE QUESTIONS

Some of the information you need to solve a multiple choice question may appear in a table, a diagram, or a graph.

PROBLEM 1

Tommy rolled a number cube 18 times. The results of his experiment are shown.Which of the following statements could *not* be made about Tommy's experiment?

A. The number of ones rolled was greater than the expected number of ones.

B. The number of threes rolled was greater than the expected number of threes.

C. The number of fives rolled was less than the expected number of fives.

D. The number of sixes rolled was less than the expected number of sixes.

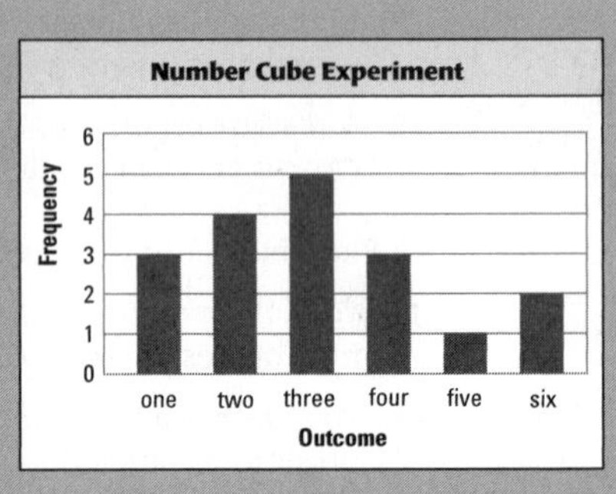

Plan

INTERPRET THE INFORMATION Determine the expected number of rolls for each number on the number cube. Then use the chart to determine the actual rolls. Compare the information.

Solution

STEP 1 Find the expected number of rolls.

The expected rolls for each number on the number cube is $\frac{1}{6}$ of the total number of rolls. Therefore, the expected number of rolls for each number is $\frac{1}{6}(18) = 3$.

For numbers 1 and 4, the number rolled equals the expected. For numbers 2 and 3, the number rolled is greater than the expected. For numbers 5 and 6, the number rolled is less than expected.

STEP 2 Compare expected and actual rolls.

So we CANNOT say that the number of ones rolled was greater than the expected number of ones.

The answer is **A**.

1. C

PROBLEM 2

The stem and leaf plot shows the ages (in years) of members of one family.

What is the median age (in years)?

F. 20 **H.** 42

G. 39 **J.** 43

Stem	Leaves
0	8 9
1	0 4 6 7
2	0
3	9
4	2 3 3 4 5
5	
6	8 9

Key: 0 | 8 = 8 years

Plan

INTERPRET THE GRAPH The median is the middle number of data that has been arranged in order from least to greatest. A stem-and-leaf plot contains all the data in order.

Solution

STEP 1 Find the number of values.

Find the number of values in the stem-and-leaf plot. Then determine the middle value. There are 15 values in the stem-and-leaf plot.

STEP 2 Find the middle value.

The median will be the 8th value. Counting from the first value, you see the 8th value is 39.

The median is 39.

The answer is **G**.

PRACTICE

1. The histogram shown represents the ages of guests who recently stayed at a hotel. Which statement must be true based on the data?

   A. There were 40 guests who stayed at the hotel.

   B. The mean age was 32.

   C. The median age was in the 20's.

   D. The guests were mainly children.

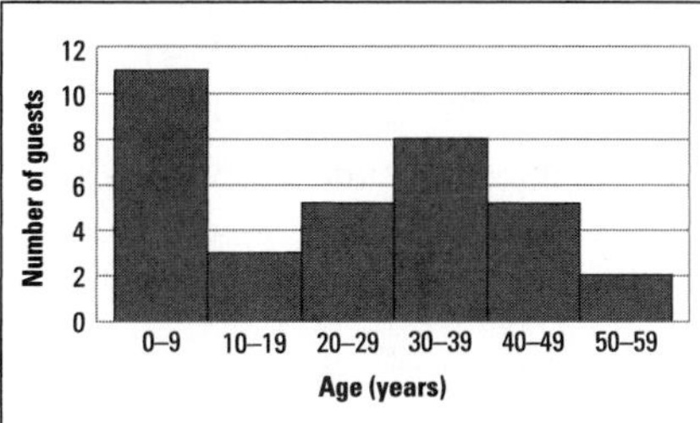

TEST PREPARATION

Illinois Test Practice

1. C
2. H
3. C
4. G
5. D
6. H
7. B
8. G
9. B
10. H
11. B
12. J
13. A
14. C
15. C
16. H
17. C

Illinois Test Preparation

1. A math class includes only sophomores, juniors, and seniors. On one test, the average score for the sophomores was 78, the average score for the juniors was 85, and the average score for the seniors was 82. What information would allow you to determine the average score of the entire class?

A. The total number of students in the class

B. The greatest and least scores on the test

C. The number of sophomores, juniors, and seniors in the class

D. None of the above

2. Five runners are entered in a race. Which expression gives the number of possible arrangements in which the runners can come in first, second, and third place?

F. $3 \times 2 \times 1$

G. $5 + 4 + 3$

H. $5 \times 4 \times 3$

J. 5^3

3. An ice cream store sells a variety of ice cream flavors and toppings. How can you best determine the number of combinations of an ice cream flavor and a single topping that you can choose?

A. Add the number of toppings to the number of flavors.

B. Raise the number of flavors to the power of the number of toppings.

C. Multiply the number of flavors by the number of toppings.

D. None of the above

4. The histogram shows the scores on a recent math test. Which of the following statements is supported by the information in the histogram?

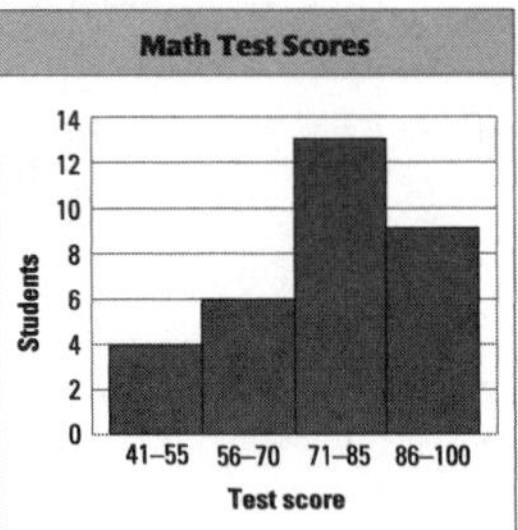

F. More students scored less than 80 than scored greater than 80.

G. More students scored less than 71 than scored greater than 85.

H. A majority of students scored greater than 80.

J. There are 25 students in the class.

5. In an office of 8 employees, 3 need to be chosen for 3 different positions on a committee. From the 8 employees, in how many ways could 3 of them fill the different roles?

A. 8 **B.** 56 **C.** 120 **D.** 336

6. In how many ways could 5 students be arranged in 5 desks in the front row of a classroom?

F. 1 **G.** 25 **H.** 120 **J.** 3,125

7. The odds in favor of an event are 3 : 4. What is the probability of the event?

A. $\frac{1}{4}$

B. $\frac{3}{7}$

C. 75%

D. $\frac{3}{4}$

8. A bag contains 4 red marbles, 3 green marbles, and 5 blue marbles. You randomly choose a marble from the bag. What is the probability that you choose a blue marble?

F. $\frac{1}{5}$

G. $\frac{5}{12}$

H. $\frac{5}{11}$

J. $\frac{5}{7}$

9. The owner of a salon wants to evaluate the salon's customer service. From each of the services offered (hair, nails, facial, massage, etc.), he randomly selects five customers who have been in within the year and asks them to complete a survey. What type of sampling is this?

A. convenience sampling

B. random sampling

C. self-selected sampling

D. stratified random sampling

10. On a three-question "true or false" quiz, you guess on all three questions. What is the probability that you guessed all three correctly?

F. $\frac{1}{2}$ **H.** $\frac{1}{8}$

G. $\frac{1}{3}$ **J.** $\frac{3}{3}$

11. The ages of people at a family reunion are 18, 65, 47, 33, 30, 1, 18, 10, 67, 71, 26, 46, 12, 55, 68, 25, 21, 32, 3, 53, 18, 22, 47, and 8. Which of the following is a true statement about the attendance at this reunion?

A. The median age is 26.

B. 25% of the people are over age 50.

C. The 71-year old represents an outlier in the data.

D. 50% of the people are under age 18.

12. At a small college graduation there were 52 graduates. One was 82 years old, 2 were 42 years old, 3 were 29 years old, 6 were 25 years old, 22 were 22 years old, and 18 were 21 years old. Which of the following measures would best represent the age of the average graduate?

F. mean

G. mode and median

H. mean and mode

J. median and mean

13. Andy has 6 dimes and 10 nickels in his pocket. If he draws two coins without replacing the first coin, what is the probability of drawing a nickel and then a dime?

A. $\frac{1}{4}$ **B.** $\frac{15}{64}$ **C.** $\frac{1}{60}$ **D.** $\frac{3}{5}$

14. This box-and-whisker plot shows scores for students on a biology quiz. According to this plot, which of the following statements is false?

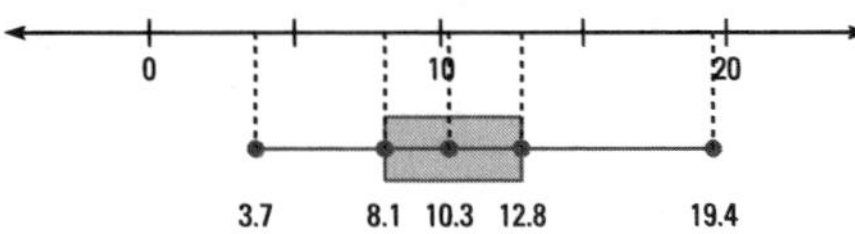

F. The median score was 10.3.

G. More than half of the students scored less than 12.8.

H. Only one student scored above 12.8.

J. The lowest score was 3.7.

15. Josh has a bag of 50 jelly beans. There are 10 yellow, 5 black, 22 red, 8 white, and 5 purple ones. If he draws one jelly bean, does not replace it, and then draws another one, what is the probability that both jelly beans are red?

A. $\frac{11}{25}$ **C.** $\frac{462}{2450}$

B. $\frac{121}{625}$ **D.** $\frac{462}{2500}$

16. Paul has 2 pairs of pants, 4 shirts, and 3 pairs of shoes. How many different outfits does he have?

F. 9 **G.** 16 **H.** 24 **J.** 36

17. If two dice are rolled and the sum is an odd number, what is the probability that the sum is a prime number?

A. $\frac{5}{11}$ **B.** $\frac{2}{3}$ **C.** $\frac{7}{9}$ **D.** $\frac{4}{5}$

TEST PRACTICE

Additional Resources

The following resources are available to help review the materials in Chapters 1–13.

Chapter Resource Books

- Chapter 11 CRB, Cumulative Review, pp. 65–66
- Chapter 12 CRB, Cumulative Review, pp. 90–91
- Chapter 13 CRB, Cumulative Review, pp. 102–103

Assessment Book

- Cumulative Test, Chapters 8–13, pp. 197–200
- Cumulative Test, Chapters 1–13, pp. 201–204

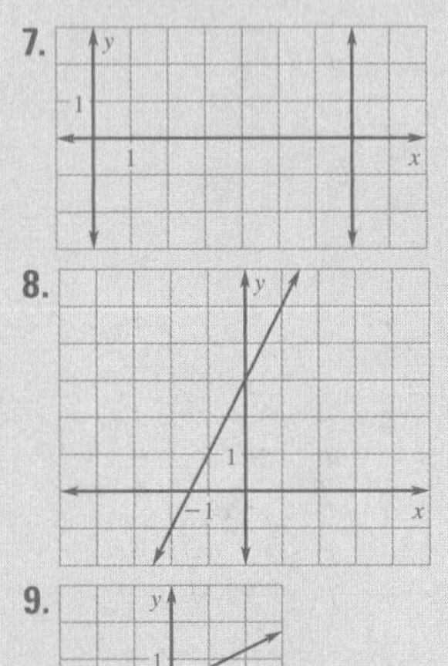

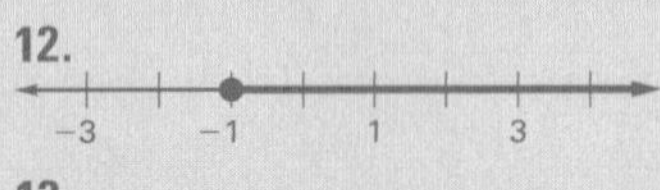

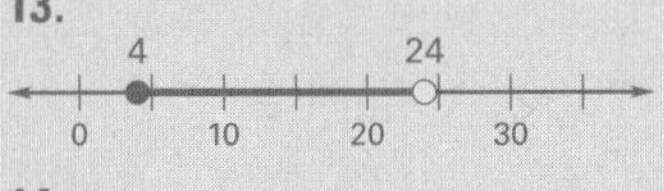

Evaluate the expression.

1. $2^4 \cdot 3 - 16 \div 4$ *(p. 8)* 44
2. $|-125| - 34$ *(p. 80)* 91
3. $\pm\sqrt{2025}$ *(p. 110)* ± 45

Solve the equation.

4. $7 - 2x = 13$ *(p. 141)* -3
5. $-8x + 15 + 5x = 9$ *(p. 148)* 2
6. $5(2x + 3) = 4x$ *(p. 154)* -2.5

Graph the equation. 7–9. See margin.

7. $x = 7$ *(p. 215)*
8. $y = 2x + 3$ *(p. 244)*
9. $4y - 2x = 1$ *(p. 244)*

Write an equation in slope-intercept form of the line with the given characteristics.

10. passes through $(-2, -8)$ and $(3, -5.5)$ *(p. 292)* $y = \frac{1}{2}x - 7$
11. slope: -8; passes through $(1, -5)$ *(p. 292)* $y = -8x + 3$

Solve the inequality. Graph your solution. 12–14. See margin for art.

12. $4x - 6 \le 8x - 2$ *(p. 369)* $x \ge -1$
13. $-2 \le x - 6 < 18$ *(p. 380)* $4 \le x < 24$
14. $2x < 6$ *or* $4x \ge 8$ *(p. 380)* all real numbers

Solve the linear system.

15. $x = 4y + 3$, $2x - 4y = 7$ *(p. 435)* $\left(4, \frac{1}{4}\right)$
16. $3x - 7y = 20$, $-11x + 10y = 5$ *(p. 451)* $(-5, -5)$
17. $-9x + 6y = 0$, $-12x + 8y = 5$ *(p. 451)* no solution

Simplify the expression. Write your answer using only positive exponents.

18. $(2x^3)^4 \cdot x^9$ *(p. 489)* $16x^{21}$
19. $(-9x^3)^2\left(-\frac{1}{4}x^6\right)$ *(p. 489)* $\frac{-81x^{12}}{4}$
20. $\frac{(3x)^{-3}y^3}{x^2y^{-1}}$ *(p. 503)* $\frac{y^4}{27x^5}$

Factor the polynomial.

21. $a^2 - 15a - 54$ *(p. 583)* $(a - 18)(a + 3)$
22. $-3b^2 - 22b - 7$ *(p. 593)* $-(3b + 1)(b + 7)$
23. $4f^2 + 4fg + g^2$ *(p. 600)* $(2f + g)^2$
24. $p^2(p - 5) + 9(5 - p)$ *(p. 606)* $(p - 5)(p - 3)(p + 3)$

Solve the equation.

25. $(x + 7)(x - 3) = 0$ *(p. 575)* $-7, 3$
26. $9x^2 - 28x + 3 = 0$ *(p. 652)* $\frac{1}{9}, 3$
27. $8x^2 + 7 = 36x - 9$ *(p. 661)* $\frac{1}{2}, 4$
28. $\sqrt{x + 8} + 10 = 2$ *(p. 729)* no solution

Find the distance between the two points. *(p. 744)*

29. $(5, 2), (7, 14)$ $2\sqrt{37}$
30. $(-8, 6), (5, 0)$ $\sqrt{205}$
31. $(2.5, 7), (2.5, -8)$ 15

Find the sum, difference, product, or quotient.

32. $\frac{x - 2}{x + 5} \cdot \frac{x + 5}{x - 8}$ *(p. 802)* $\frac{x - 2}{x - 8}$
33. $\frac{x^3 - 16x}{x^2 + 3x} \div (x - 4)$ *(p. 802)* $\frac{x + 4}{x + 3}$
34. $\frac{16}{2x^4} \cdot \frac{7x^3}{2x}$ *(p. 802)* $\frac{28}{x^2}$
35. $\frac{2x}{3 - x} + \frac{x - 9}{3 - x}$ *(p. 812)* -3
36. $\frac{1}{x + 6} + \frac{4x}{x + 6}$ *(p. 812)* $\frac{4x + 1}{x + 6}$
37. $\frac{9}{x^2 - 3x} - \frac{3}{x - 3}$ *(p. 812)* $\frac{9 - 3x}{x^2 - 3x}$

Evaluate the expression.

38. ${}_6P_1$ *(p. 851)* 6
39. ${}_8P_3$ *(p. 851)* 336
40. ${}_7C_3$ *(p. 856)* 35
41. ${}_{10}C_6$ *(p. 856)* 210

42. You roll a number cube. What is the probability that you roll a 5? *(p. 843)* $\frac{1}{6}$

43. You roll a number cube. What is the probability that you roll a 2 or an even number? *(p. 861)* $\frac{1}{2}$

44. You choose a number from 1 to 20 at random. What is the probability that you choose a prime number? *(p. 843)* $\frac{2}{5}$

45. You choose a number from 1 to 20 at random. What is the probability that you choose a multiple of 6? *(p. 843)* $\frac{3}{20}$

46. A bag contains 2 red marbles, 4 green marbles, and 4 blue marbles. You choose one marble at random, put the marble back into the bag, then choose a second marble at random. What is the probability that you choose 2 red marbles? *(p. 861)* $\frac{1}{25}$

47. **MARATHON** Two runners are training for a marathon. When running a practice distance of 26.2 miles, one runner begins running 6 minutes after the other. The speed of the first runner is 11.4 miles per hour. The speed of the second runner is 12 miles per hour. After how many minutes does the second runner pass the first runner? *(p. 435)* ***Sample answer:*** **120 min after the first runner starts**

48. **STONE ARCH** The shape of a stone arch can be modeled by the graph of the equation $y = -0.5x^2 + 4x + 4$ where x is the horizontal distance (in feet) from one end of the arch and y is its height (in feet) above the ground. What is the maximum height of the arch? *Explain* how you found your answer. *(p. 628)* **See margin.**

49. **GUY WIRE** A guy wire supports an antenna tower, as shown at the right. The bottom of the wire is secured in the ground 30 feet from the base of the tower. The top of the wire is secured to the tower at a height of 30 feet above the ground. How long is the wire? Round your answer to the nearest tenth of a foot. *(p. 737)* **42.4 ft**

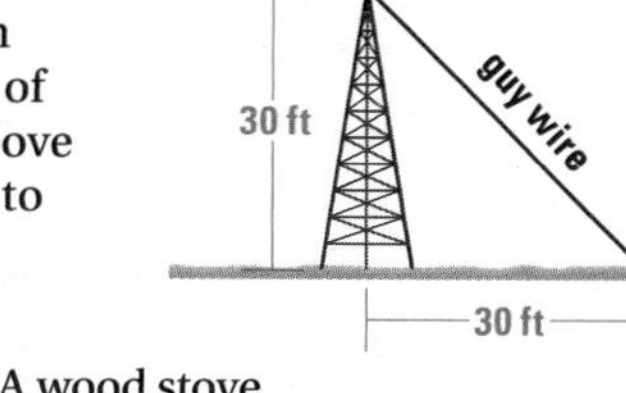

50. **HEATING RATES** An electric heater takes 8 minutes to heat an entire apartment to the desired temperature. A wood stove and an electric heater together take 6 minutes to heat the apartment. How many minutes does it take the wood stove alone to heat the apartment to the desired temperature? *(p. 820)* **24 min**

51. **FLIGHTS** You are traveling from Boston, Massachusetts, to Richmond, Virginia. The prices (in dollars) of airline tickets for different flights between the cities are listed below.

    176, 191, 195, 197, 197, 204, 204, 204, 204,
    204, 206, 206, 206, 206, 206, 217, 217, 221

    a. What is the range of the prices? *(p. 875)* **\$45**

    b. Make a stem-and-leaf plot of the prices. *(p. 881)* **b–d. See margin.**

    c. Make a box-and-whisker plot of the prices. *(p. 887)*

    d. Can any of these prices be considered outliers? *Explain* why or why not. *(p. 887)*

48. 12 ft. ***Sample answer:*** **The graph is a parabola with vertex at $x = -\frac{b}{2a} = 4$. When $x = 4$, the height of the arch is 12 feet.**

51b.

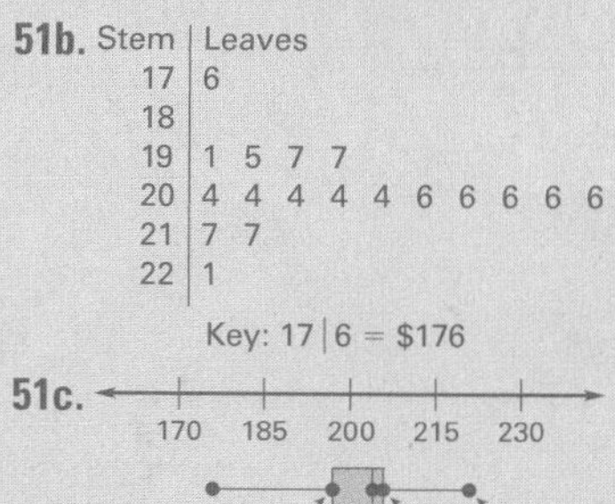

Stem	Leaves
17	6
18	
19	1 5 7 7
20	4 4 4 4 4 6 6 6 6 6
21	7 7
22	1

Key: 17 | 6 = \$176

51c.

51d. Yes. ***Sample answer:*** **The interquartile range is 9, so any data value more than 13.5 less than the lower quartile of 197 or greater than the upper quartile of 206 can be considered outliers. 176 and 221 are both outliers.**

ADDITIONAL LESSONS

ALGEBRA 1

The additional lessons have been written to ensure complete state standard coverage. These lessons provide content addressing material to encompass individual state needs. They are offered to help teach all of the standards or to provide enrichment and challenge opportunities.

Essential Question:

Why is estimation important to know in your daily life? You may not always have tools (paper, pen, calculator, etc.) to solve problems so your best guess may have to work.

Key Question for Ex. 1:

What would happen if you picked different numbers that were higher or lower (i.e. instead of 64 and 81, try 49 and 100)? Would it still work? Generally yes, but the error would be greater.

Extra Example 1:

Estimate $\sqrt{52}$. ≈ 7.2

Common Problem:

Students might be confused on how to set up the proportion.

Closing Question:

Why is it important to know the error associated with measuring? When assembling parts, some tolerances are so tight that if you are even a fraction off, the part will not go together right.

Additional Lesson A Estimation and Accuracy of Measurement

Use after Chapter 1

Key Vocabulary

- **estimation**
- **amount of error**

GOAL Use estimation to determine reasonable solutions and calculate the amount of error with measuring tools.

When solving problems in mathematics, we don't always have a calculator or the appropriate measuring tools available to us. When this happens, we can use estimation as a means of approximating a value. **Estimation** is the process of forming an approximation without actual calculation or measurement. When estimating, there is an **amount of error** that depends on the measuring tool. That is, the determined value will err on either side of the value by the smallest increment on the measuring tool.

EXAMPLE 1 Estimate a reasonable solution

Estimate: $\sqrt{78}$

Find the perfect squares just less than 78 and just greater than 78.

The perfect squares on either side of 78 are 64 and 81. So $\sqrt{78}$ is between $\sqrt{64}$ and $\sqrt{81}$, which means $\sqrt{78}$ is between 8 and 9.

The difference between 64 and 78 is 14, the difference between 64 and 81 is 17, the difference between 8 and $\sqrt{78}$ is "x" and the difference between 8 and 9 is 1. Solve the following proportion.

$$\frac{14}{17} = \frac{x}{1}$$
$$17x = 14$$
$$x = \frac{14}{17}$$
$$x \approx 0.824$$

Therefore $\sqrt{78} = 8 + 0.8$, or 8.8 with accuracy to the tenths place.

EXAMPLE 2 Estimate and determine an amount of error

Estimate the measure of $\angle ABC$ and $\angle DBC$ in the drawing.

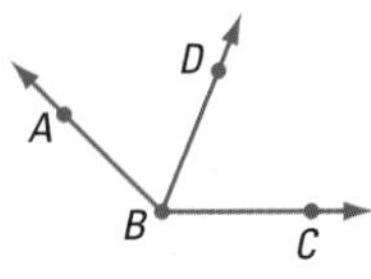

Compare $\angle ABC$ with an angle of known measure such as a right or straight angle.

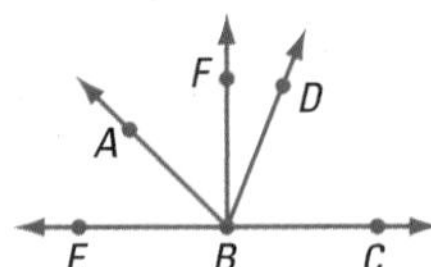

Draw $\angle EBC$ as a straight angle and $\angle FBC$ as a right angle. $\angle ABC$ appears to be approximately $\frac{1}{2}$ of the way between $\angle EBC$ and $\angle FBC$, so $\angle ABC$ is approximately $\frac{(90 + 180)}{2}$, or 135°. $\angle DBC$ is approximately $\frac{1}{2}$ of $\angle ABC$, or approximately 68°, when rounded to the nearest degree.

EXAMPLE 3 Using tools to measure line segments and angles

What is the measure of line segment $\overline{XY}$?

If the ruler being used has increments of tenths of an inch, the measure is approximately $1\frac{9}{10}$ inch, with an error of $\frac{1}{10}$ inch in either direction. That is, the measure is from $1\frac{8}{10}$ inch to 2 inches.

If the ruler is incremented in eighths of an inch, the measure is $1\frac{7}{8}$ inch with an error of $\frac{1}{8}$ of an inch in either direction. That is, the measure is from $1\frac{6}{8}$ inch to 2 inches.

What is the measure of $\angle ABC$?

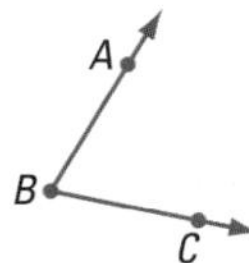

If the protractor being used is incremented every 1°, the angle is about 70°, with an error range of 1° greater or less than 70°. That is, the angle measures from 69° to 71°.

If the protractor being used is incremented every 5°, the angle is about 70°, with an error range of 5° greater or less than 70°. That is, the angle measures from 65° to 75°.

PRACTICE

Complete the following exercises.

Estimate the following square roots.

EXAMPLE 1 for Exs. 1–3

1. $\sqrt{21}$ **2.** $\sqrt{110}$ **3.** $\sqrt{52}$

Use the figure below to answer exercises 4 and 5.

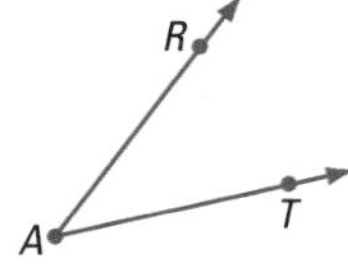

EXAMPLE 2 for Exs. 4–5

4. Estimate the measure of $\angle RAT$.

5. Measure $\angle RAT$.

EXAMPLE 3 for Ex. 6

6. Measure line segment $\overline{PG}$.

Answers to Additional Lessons

1. 4.6
2. 10.5
3. 7.2
4. 45°
5. 40°
6. 1.4 inches

Essential Question:

Why is it important to know conversions? Some professions and other countries use different units for measuring.

Extra Example 1:

Convert 48 inches to meters.

$\approx$ 1.22 meters

Key Question for Ex. 3:

How would you set up the equation if you were given a temperature in °F and wanted to know the temperature in °C?

Subtract 32 then multiply by $\frac{5}{9}$.

Common Problem:

Students will have problems when they have to use more than one conversion.

Closing Question:

Why is it important to know the equivalent temperature in °F when given °C? Often recipes or storage temperatures are given in °C, but most US ovens and refrigerators use °F.

Additional Lesson B

Metric/Customary Conversions

Use after Chapter 1

Key Vocabulary

- **metric system**
- **customary system**

GOAL Use the Metric to Customary Conversion Tables to understand how one unit of measure relates to the other.

History

The **metric system** was developed in France in the late 18th century to replace the various systems that were being used throughout the world at that time. Today, the metric system is referred to as the International System of Units, abbreviated SI. **Customary Systems** grew out of the customs of the area. The system presently used in the United States is the English System and the United States is the only industrial nation using it.

Abbreviations

Customary	Metric
inch = in.	centimeter = cm
foot = ft.	meter = m
mile = mi.	kilometer = km
quart = qt.	liter = l or L
gallon = gal.	Celsius = C
Fahrenheit = F	

CONVERSION TABLES

Into Metric				Into Customary		
Length						
From	**multiply by**	**To**		**From**	**multiply by**	**To**
in.	2.54	cm		m	39.36	in.
ft.	30.48	cm		cm	0.39	in.
mi.	1.61	km		km	0.62	mi.
Volume						
From	**multiply by**	**To**		**From**	**multiply by**	**To**
qt.	.95	L		L	1.06	qt.
gal.	3.79	L		L	0.26	gal.
Temperature						
From		**To**		**From**		**To**
F	subtract 32 then multiply by $\frac{5}{9}$	C		C	multiply by $\frac{9}{5}$ then add 32	F

EXAMPLE 1 Convert from Customary into Metric Units

Convert 9.8 in. to centimeters.

Multiply by 2.54 to change from inches to centimeters.

$$9.8 \times 2.54 = 24.89 \text{ cm}$$

Convert 12 miles to kilometers.

Multiply by 1.61 to change from miles to kilometers.

$$12 \times 1.61 = 19.32 \text{ km}$$

EXAMPLE 2 Convert from Metric into Customary Units

The Granger family is driving a rental car in Canada. They stop and put 45 liters of gas into the car. Determine the number of gallons they put in the car.

To change from liters to gallons, multiply by 0.26.

$$45 \times 0.26 = 11.7 \text{ gallons}$$

The Granger family put 11.7 gallons of gas in the car.

EXAMPLE 3 Convert from Celsius (C) to Fahrenheit (F)

During their drive, the thermometer in the car said that the temperature was 15°. Knowing that Celsius is the unit used in Canada for temperature, what is the Fahrenheit equivalent?

To change from degrees Celsius to degrees Fahrenheit, multiply by $\frac{9}{5}$, and then add 32.

$$15 \times \frac{9}{5} = 27.0$$

$$27.0 + 32 = 59.0°\text{F}$$

The temperature was 59°F.

PRACTICE

Complete the following exercises.

EXAMPLE 1 for Exs. 1, 7
EXAMPLE 2 for Exs. 1, 3, 6
EXAMPLE 3 for Exs. 4–5

1. Convert 16 gal. to liters.
2. Convert 7.5 m to inches.
3. A pediatrician measured a baby's length at 62 cm. What is the baby's length in inches?
4. A friend from Spain tells you that the current temperature is 35°C. Determine the temperature in Fahrenheit.
5. You tell your Spanish friend that the current temperature in your hometown in 77°F. Convert that temperature to °C for your friend.
6. Your friend will be traveling with her family to Barcelona by car next week. The distance is about 300 km from her hometown. What is this distance in miles?
7. You do some research and find that the distance between your hometown in the U.S. and your friend's hometown in Spain is 3,591 miles. How many kilometers is this distance?

Answers to Additional Lessons

1. 60.64 L
2. 295.2 in.
3. 23.79 in.
4. 95°F
5. 25°C
6. 186 mi.
7. 5,781.51 km

Essential Question:

Why are special right triangles good to know? They are easier to solve than other right triangles.

Extra Example 1:

What is the hypotenuse of an isosceles right triangle if the two legs are 18 inches long?
$\approx$ 25.46 inches

Key Question for Ex. 2:

What would happen to the hypotenuse and the horizontal distance if the shorter leg were increased? They both would increase.

Common Problem:

Students will commonly mix up the side length ratios between the two special right triangles.

Closing Question:

Can you show how Pythagorean theorem leads to the ratios for a 45-45-90 triangle?

Pythagorean Theorem: $a^2 + b^2 = c^2$; $2(a^2) = c^2$; $a\sqrt{2} = c$

Additional Lesson C Special Right Triangles

Use after Chapter 11

Key Vocabulary

- **special right triangles**
- **45°-45°-90° triangle**
- **30°-60°-90° triangle**

GOAL Use special right triangles to solve problems.

There are two **special right triangles** that can be used to solve problems quickly. One is a **45°-45°-90° triangle.** This triangle has two angles that are equal, which means it also has two equal sides, therefore the triangle is isosceles. The other special right triangle is the **30°-60°-90° triangle,** which is scalene. There are special relationships among the sides of these triangles that always hold true.

Words In a **45°-45°-90° triangle,** both legs have the same length. The length of the hypotenuse is $\sqrt{2}$ times as long as a leg, a.

Algebra hypotenuse = leg • $\sqrt{2}$ = $a\sqrt{2}$

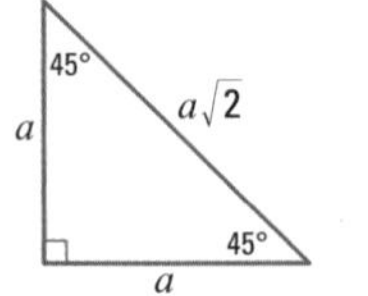

Words Words: In a 30°-60°-90° triangle, the length of the longer leg is $\sqrt{3}$ times as long as the shorter leg, a. The length of the hypotenuse is twice the length of the shorter leg, a.

Algebra longer leg = shorter leg • $\sqrt{3}$ = $a\sqrt{3}$
hypotenuse = 2 • shorter leg = $2a$

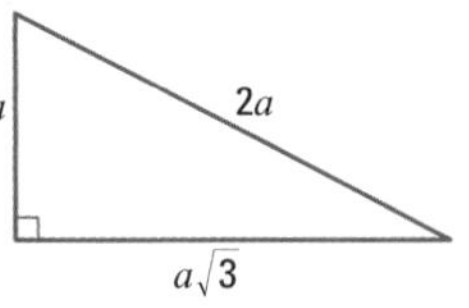

EXAMPLE 1 Using a 45-45°-90° Triangle

A 45°-45°-90° triangle used in a technical drawing has 13-cm legs. Find the length of the hypotenuse to the nearest tenth of a cm.

Solution

hypotenuse = leg • $\sqrt{2}$	Use rule for 45°–45°–90° triangle.
= 13 • $\sqrt{2}$	Substitute 12 for leg.
$\approx$ 18.4	Use a calculator.

The length of the triangle's hypotenuse is about 18.4 centimeters.

EXAMPLE 2 Using a 30°-60°-90° Triangle

A stone stairway going up to the entrance of a museum is 182 feet long and makes a 30° angle with the ground. Find, to the nearest foot, the vertical height of the stairs and the horizontal distance from the base of the stairs to the base of the building.

Solution

Draw a diagram.
This is a 30°-60°-90° triangle.

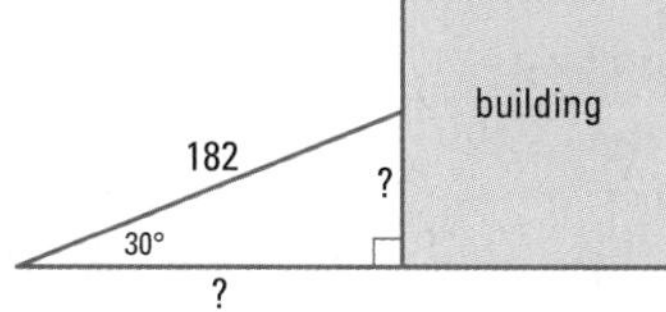

You will need to find the length of the shorter leg (height) first.

1. hypotenuse $= 2 \cdot$ shorter leg — Use rule for 30°-60°-90° triangle.

$182 = 2 \cdot$ shorter leg — Substitute 182 for hypotenuse.

$\frac{182}{2} =$ shorter leg — Divide each side by 2.

$91 =$ shorter leg

Now find the length of longer leg (distance from stairs to building).

2. longer leg $=$ shorter leg $\cdot \sqrt{3}$ — Use rule for 30°-60°-90° triangle.

longer leg $= 91 \cdot \sqrt{3}$ — Substitute 91 for shorter leg.

longer leg ≈ 157.6 — Use a calculator.

The vertical height of the stairs is 91 feet and the distance from the base of the stairs to the base of building is about 157.6 feet.

PRACTICE

Complete the following exercises.

EXAMPLE 1 for Exs. 1, 3

EXAMPLE 2 for Exs. 2, 4–5

1. A 45°-45°-90° triangle has legs that are 7 inches long. Find the length of the hypotenuse to the nearest tenth of an inch.

60°
x
8
30°
y

2. Find the length x of the hypotenuse and the length y of the longer leg of the triangle shown at right.

3. A diagonal is drawn in a square with side length 24mm. What is the length of the diagonal, to the nearest mm?

A skate ramp leading down from the top of a concrete slab is 46 feet long. It forms a 30-degree angle with the ground.

4. What is the vertical height of the ramp?

5. To the nearest foot what is the distance from the bottom of the ramp to the bottom of the concrete slab?

Answers to Additional Lessons

1. **9.9 in.**
2. **$x = 16$ units, $y = 13.9$ units.**
3. **34mm**
4. **23 feet**
5. **40 feet**

Essential Question:

How do you know which angle of the triangle is the largest? It is the angle opposite the longest side.

Key Question for Ex. 1:

Would it work if it were a right triangle? Yes

Extra Example 3:

Given 100, 200, 101; can the side lengths form a triangle? Yes, $101 + 100 > 200$, $100 + 200 > 101$, and $200 + 101 > 100$.

Common Problem:

One angle might appear to look larger or smaller but might not be drawn to scale.

Closing Question:

Is it necessary to add the largest value to the other values to show that the triangle is truly a triangle? No, as long as the smaller values add up to be larger than the largest value.

Additional Lesson D

Triangle Inequalities

Use after Chapter 11

Key Vocabulary

- **Triangle Inequality Theorem**
- **opposite side**

GOAL Use triangle measurements to decide which side is longest and which angle is largest. Determine possible and impossible side lengths of a triangle.

An important relationship exists between the angles of a triangle and their opposite sides. In addition, there is a relationship among the sides of all triangles called the **Triangle Inequality Theorem.** These relationships are summarized below using the triangle shown. Arrows point from each angle to its **opposite side.**

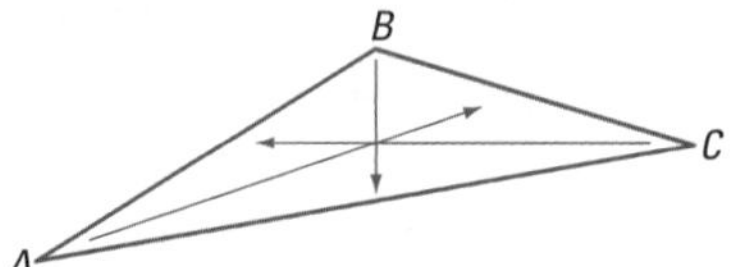

Words	If one side of a triangle is longer than another side, then the angle opposite the longer side is larger than the angle opposite the shorter side.
Symbols	If $AC > BC$, then $m\angle B > m\angle A$.

Words	If one angle of a triangle is larger than another angle, then the side opposite the larger angle is longer than the side opposite the smaller angle.
Symbols	If $m\angle B > m\angle C$, then $AC > AB$.

Words	The **Triangle Inequality Theorem** states that the sum of the lengths of any two sides of a triangle is greater than the length of the third side.
Symbols	$AB + BC > CA$ $BC + CA > AB$ $CA + AB > BC$

EXAMPLE 1 Order Angle Measures

Name the angles from largest to smallest.

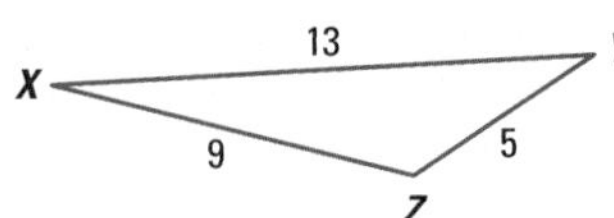

Solution

$XY > XZ$, so $m\angle Z > m\angle Y$.

$XZ > YZ$, so $m\angle Y > m\angle X$.

The order of the angles from largest to smallest is $\angle Z$, $\angle Y$, $\angle X$.

EXAMPLE 2 Order Side Lengths

Name the sides from longest to shortest.

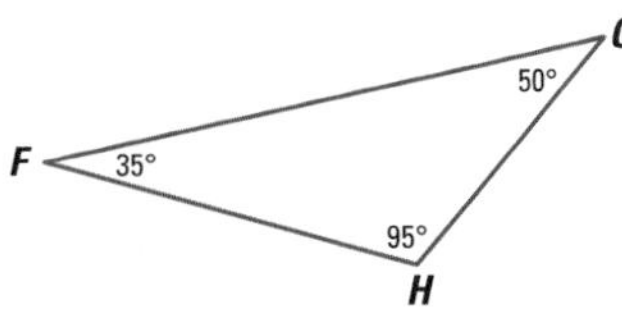

Solution

$m\angle H > m\angle G$, so $\overline{FG} > \overline{FH}$.

$m\angle G > m\angle F$, so $\overline{FH} > \overline{GH}$.

The order of the sides from longest to shortest is $\overline{FG}$, $\overline{FH}$, $\overline{GH}$.

EXAMPLE 3 Use the Triangle Inequality

Can the side lengths form a triangle? Explain.

a. 2, 7, 10 **b.** 2, 7, 9 **c.** 2, 7, 8

Solution

a. These lengths *do not* form a triangle because $2 + 7 < 10$.

b. These lengths *do not* form a triangle because $2 + 7 = 9$.

c. These lengths *do* form a triangle because $2 + 7 > 8$, $2 + 8 > 7$, and $7 + 8 > 2$.

PRACTICE

Complete the following exercises.

EXAMPLE 1 for Exs. 1

1. Name the angles from largest to smallest.

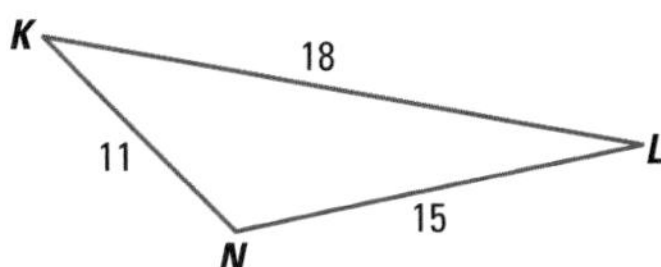

EXAMPLE 2 for Exs. 2

2. Name the sides from longest to shortest.

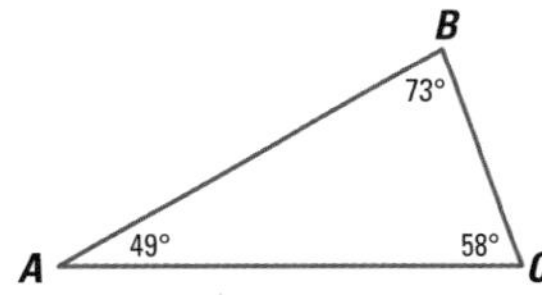

Can the side lengths given form a triangle? Explain.

EXAMPLE 3 for Exs. 3–5

3. 8, 9, 6

4. 12, 8, 21

5. 3, 7, 4

Answers to Additional Lessons

1. $\angle N$, $\angle K$, $\angle L$

2. *AC*, *AB*, *BC*

3. yes; $8 + 9 > 6$, $9 + 6 > 8$, and $6 + 8 > 9$

4. no; $12 + 8 < 21$

5. no; $3 + 4 = 7$

Essential Question:

When would you want to use the tangent ratio? The tangent ratio is used to find the lengths of the sides of a right triangle.

Extra Example 2:

Evaluate: (a) tan 45° (b) tan 90° (c) tan 0°

(a) 1 (b) undefined (c) 0

Key Question for Ex. 3:

What would happen to the height of the tree if the angle at the ground were increased? The height would increase.

Common Problem:

Make sure students have their calculator in degree mode (not radians).

Closing Question:

How would the tangent ratio help you design a roof? By knowing the width of the house you can determine the pitch and height of the roof.

Additional Lesson E

The Tangent Ratio

Use after Chapter 11

GOAL Use the tangent to find side lengths of right triangles.

Key Vocabulary

- **trigonometric ratio**
- **tangent**

Trigonometric ratios are the ratios comparing two sides of a right triangle. They are used to find lengths that are difficult to measure directly. There are three basic trigonometric ratios. In this lesson, we will look at the tangent ratio.

The **tangent** of an acute angle of a right triangle is the ratio of the length of the side opposite the angle to the length of the side adjacent to the angle.

$$\tan A = \frac{\text{side opposite } \angle A}{\text{side adjacent to } \angle A} = \frac{a}{b}$$

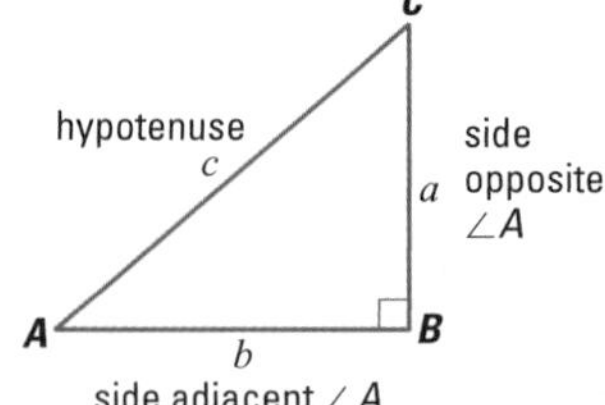

EXAMPLE 1 Finding a Tangent Ratio

a. For $\triangle KLM$, find the tangent $\angle K$.

$$\tan K = \frac{\text{side opposite } \angle K}{\text{side adjacent to } \angle K} = \frac{15}{8}$$

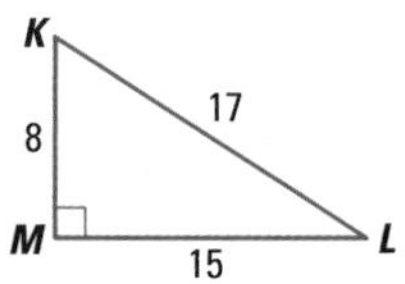

b. For $\triangle KLM$, find the tangent $\angle L$.

$$\tan L = \frac{\text{side opposite } \angle L}{\text{side adjacent to } \angle L} = \frac{8}{15}$$

EXAMPLE 2 Using a Calculator

a. tan 24°

Keystrokes	Display	Answer
tan, 24	tan (24)	.4452286853

b. tan 55°

Keystrokes	Display	Answer
tan, 55	tan (55)	1.428148007

EXAMPLE 3 Using a Tangent Ratio

An arborist walks 25 feet from the base of a tree, and uses surveying equipment to measure the angle from where she stands to the top of the tree. The angle is 52°. Find the height h of the tree to the nearest foot.

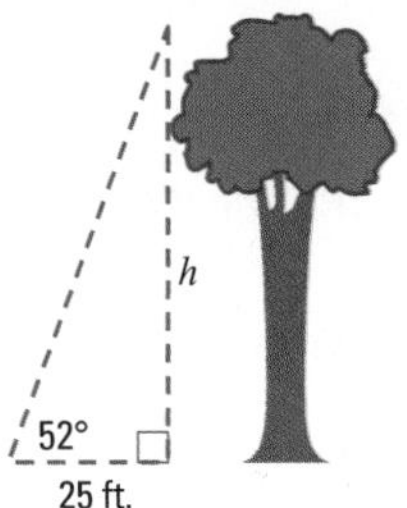

Solution

Since we know the sides opposite and adjacent an angle in a right triangle, we can use the tangent ratio to solve the problem. In the diagram, the length of the leg opposite the 52° angle is h. The length of the adjacent leg is 25 feet.

$\tan \angle = \frac{\text{opposite}}{\text{adjacent}}$ Use the definition of tangent ratio.

$\tan 52° = \frac{h}{25}$ Substitute values from the problem.

$1.28 \approx \frac{h}{25}$ Use a calculator to approximate tan 52°

$32 \approx h$ Multiply each side by 25 to solve for h.

The height of the tree is about 32 feet.

PRACTICE

Complete the following exercises.

EXAMPLE 1 for Exs. 1–2

1. For $\triangle ABC$, find the tangent $\angle A$.

A, B, C; 10, 26, 24

2. For $\triangle ABC$, find the tangent $\angle B$.

Approximate the tangent value to four decimal places.

EXAMPLE 2 for Exs. 3–5

3. tan 10°
4. tan 45°
5. tan 82°

EXAMPLE 3 for Ex 6

6. Find the height h of the flagpole to the nearest foot.

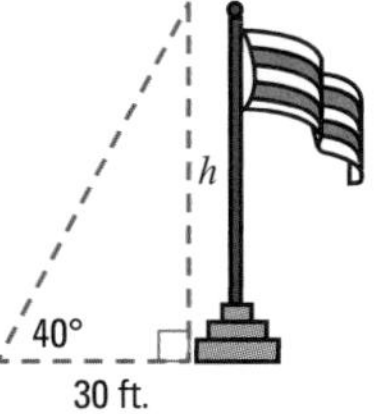

Answers to Additional Lessons

1. $\frac{24}{10} = \frac{12}{5}$
2. $\frac{10}{24} = \frac{5}{12}$
3. 0.1763
4. 1
5. 7.1154
6. 25 feet

Essential Question:

How are the sine and cosine ratios helpful? They allow us to find a side length of a right triangle given one length and an angle measure.

Extra Example 3:

How long would your skateboard ramp be if the pitch is 15° and the vertical height is 2 feet?
≈ 7.7 feet

Common Problem:

Students may forget the corresponding sides with each ratio. Remember *SOHCAHTOA*!

Closing Question:

What would you need to find the length of a roof using the sine method? You would need the pitch and height of the roof.

Additional Lesson F

The Sine and Cosine Ratios

Use after Chapter 11

GOAL Use sine and cosine to find triangle side lengths

Key Vocabulary

- **sine**
- **cosine**

In addition to the tangent ratio, there are two other important trigonometric ratios called the sine ratio and the cosine ratio. They can be used to calculate lengths without measuring directly.

The **sine** of an acute angle of a right triangle is the ratio of the length of the side opposite the angle to the length of the hypotenuse.

$$\sin A = \frac{\text{side opposite } \angle A}{\text{hypotenuse}} = \frac{b}{c}$$

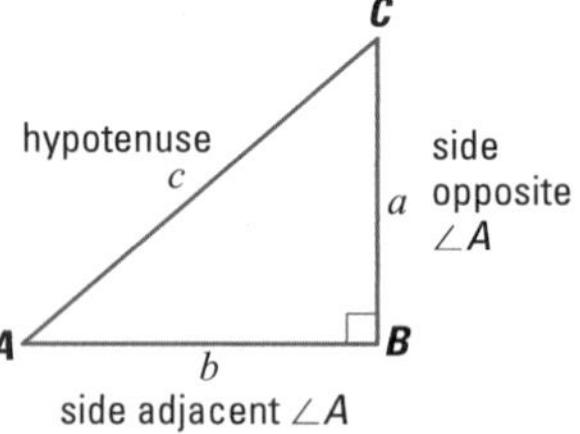

The **cosine** of an acute angle of a right triangle is the ratio of the length of the angle's adjacent side to the length of the hypotenuse.

$$\cos A = \frac{\text{side adjacent } \angle A}{\text{hypotenuse}} = \frac{b}{c}$$

EXAMPLE 1 Finding Sine and Cosine Ratios

a. For △KLM, find the sine ∠*K*.

$$\sin K = \frac{\text{side opposite } \angle K}{\text{hypotenuse}} = \frac{15}{17}$$

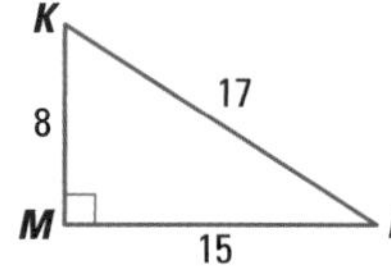

b. For △*KLM*, find the cosine ∠*K*.

$$\cos K = \frac{\text{side opposite } \angle K}{\text{hypotenuse}} = \frac{8}{17}$$

EXAMPLE 2 Using a Calculator

a. sin 60°

Keystrokes	**Display**	**Answer**
Sin, 60	sin (60)	.8660254038

b. cos 45°

Keystrokes	**Display**	**Answer**
Cos, 45	cos (45)	.7071067812

EXAMPLE 3 Using the Sine and Cosine Ratios

Find the value of x in the triangle. Round your answer to the nearest tenth of a unit.

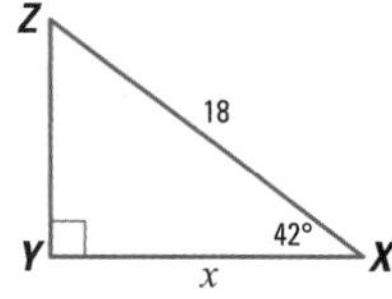

In $\triangle XYZ$, $\overline{XY}$ is adjacent to $\angle X$. Because we know the length of the hypotenuse, we can use cos X and the definition of the cosine ratio to find the value of x.

$\cos \angle = \frac{\text{adjacent}}{\text{hypotenuse}}$ Use the definition of cosine ratio.

$\cos 42° = \frac{x}{18}$ Substitute values from the problem.

$0.7431 \approx \frac{x}{18}$ Use a calculator to approximate cos 39°.

$13.3758 \approx x$ Multiply each side by 18 to solve for x.

$\overline{XY}$ is approximately 13.4 units in length.

PRACTICE

Complete the following exercises.

EXAMPLE 1 for Exs. 1–2

1. For $\triangle ABC$, find the sine $\angle A$.

2. For $\triangle ABC$, find the cosine $\angle A$.

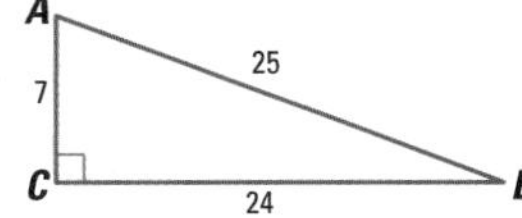

Approximate the sine or cosine value to four decimal places.

EXAMPLE 2 for Exs. 3–5

3. sin 12°
4. cos 60°
5. cos 85°

EXAMPLE 3 for Ex 6

6. The diagonal surface of a ramp used for physics experiments is 8 inches long and makes an angle of 20° with the ground.
   a. To find the height of the ramp, do you need to use a sine or cosine ratio?
   b. To the nearest tenth of an inch, approximate the height of the ramp.

Answers to Additional Lessons

1. $\frac{24}{25}$
2. $\frac{7}{25}$
3. 0.2079
4. 0.5
5. 0.0872
6. a. sine b. 2.7 inches

Essential Question:

Why would you want to use networks and routing when planning a trip? You would do this in order to find the shortest, fastest, and/or most cost effective trip.

Key Question for Ex. 2:

If you lived in Chicago, what would be the most logical route to Madrid? CAM

Extra Example 2: See Below

Common Problem:

The shortest distance may not always be the fastest.

Closing Question:

What is another application of networks and routing? Any type of profession that has to drive a certain route and make various stops, i.e. mail carrier, school bus driver.

Additional Lesson G

Vertex-Edge Graphs, Circuits, Networks, and Routing

Use after Chapter 4

GOAL Apply the characteristics of vertex-edge graphs to circuits and networks. Include using subscripts to name the ordinal position of a vertex.

Key Vocabulary

- **vertex-edge graph**
- **network**
- **vertex**
- **edge**
- **path**
- **adjacent**
- **circuit**
- **route**
- **degree of a vertex**

A **vertex-edge graph** or **network** has a finite number of dots (vertices) and lines (**edges**) connecting them. A **path** through the graph describes a sequence of vertices, all of which are **adjacent,** or next to one another. Vertices of a single graph are sometimes named using the same letter and different subscripts. (Example: M_1, M_2, M_3.) A path that starts and ends at the same vertex and travels over each edge only once is called a **circuit.** A **route** is a path through the graph that yields a particular result, such as shortest, cheapest, fastest, etc.

One way to determine if a particular graph is a circuit is to analyze the degree of the vertices. The **degree of a vertex** is the number of edges that connect to that vertex.

- If a graph has any vertices whose degree is odd-numbered, then it cannot be a circuit.
- Further, if a graph has more than two odd vertices, then it cannot have a path.

EXAMPLE 1 Analyzing a network

Determine whether the graph is a circuit.

a.

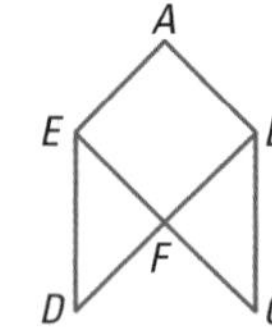

Solution

Analyze the degree of the vertices.

$A = 2$
$B = 3$
$C = 2$
$D = 2$
$E = 3$
$F = 4$

Since the graph has two odd vertices, it is not a circuit, but it does have a path.

b.

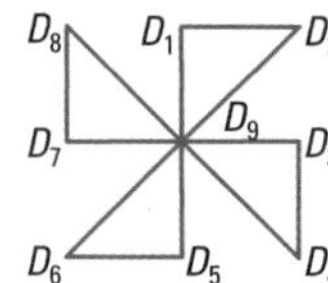

Solution

Analyze the degree of the vertices.

$D_1 = 2$ $D_6 = 2$
$D_2 = 2$ $D_7 = 2$
$D_3 = 2$ $D_8 = 2$
$D_4 = 2$ $D_9 = 8$
$D_5 = 2$

Since the graph has no odd vertices, it is a circuit. Use your finger to trace this path and see that it is a circuit, beginning and ending at the same point, going over each edge only one time:

$D_1, D_2, D_9, D_3, D_4, D_9, D_5, D_6, D_9, D_7, D_8, D_9, D_1$.

Extra Example 2:

You want to travel from Chicago to Honolulu with the least amount of time flying. The table lists the approximate flight times between various cities.

Chicago/ Kansas City	1:25	Kansas City/Okla. City	1:15	Okla. City/ Las Vegas	2:55
Chicago/ St. Louis	1:05	St. Louis/ Okla. City	1:55	Okla. City/ Phoenix	2:30
Chicago/ Omaha	1:45	Omaha/ Denver	1:55	Denver/Las Vegas	2:00
		Las Vegas/ Honolulu	6:30	Phoenix/ Honolulu	7:00

Shortest is Chicago, Kansas City, Oklahoma City, Las Vegas, Honolulu with a total time of 12:05.

EXAMPLE 2 Solving a routing problem

The following network shows several cities and the paths connecting them. The vertices represent cities and the edges indicate nonstop airline routes between them.

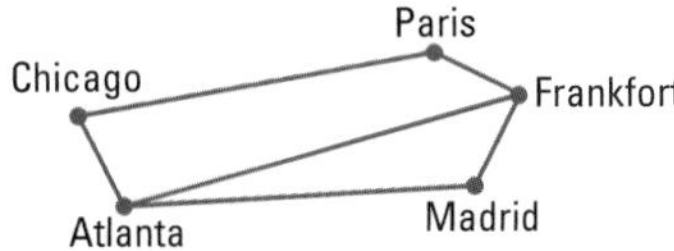

a. List all the paths that describe a trip from Chicago to Frankfort.

Solution Using the first letter of each city, the paths are CPF, CAF, CAMF.

b. If cheapest cost is Javier's greatest concern, which path would you suggest for him to take from Chicago to Frankfort?

Chicago to Paris	$865.00	8 hr. 45 min
Paris to Frankfort	$152.00	1 hr. 20 min.
Layover		3 hr. 10 min.
Chicago to Atlanta	$229.00	3 hr. 05 min.
Atlanta to Frankfort	$1053.00	7 hr. 50 min.
Layover		2 hr. 15 min.
Chicago to Atlanta	$229.00	3 hr. 05 min.
Atlanta to Madrid	$658.00	7 hr. 20 min.
Madrid to Frankfort	$89.00	1 hr. 35 min.
2 Layovers		1 hr. 55 min.

Solution Using the chart, add to find the total cost of each route. The cheapest path is CAMF: Chicago to Atlanta to Madrid to Frankfort.

PRACTICE

Complete the following exercises.

Determine whether the graph is a circuit. If it is, list the path.

EXAMPLE 1 for Exs. 1–2

1.

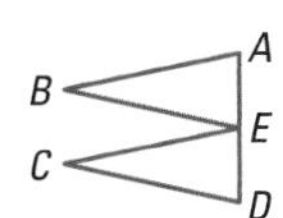

2.

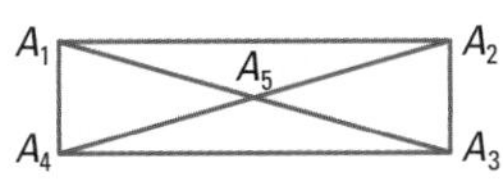

EXAMPLE 2 for Ex 3

3. From Example 2, if shortest time is Javier's greatest concern, which path would you suggest from Chicago to Frankfort?

Answers to Additional Lessons

1. yes; A, B, E, C, D, E, A
2. no
3. CAF: Chicago to Atlanta to Frankfort

Essential Question:

What is a resultant vector? A resultant vector is the sum of two vectors that has a new magnitude and direction.

Key Question for Ex. 1:

What would happen to the magnitude and angle of vector D if it were changed to (−4, 4)? The magnitude would be the same and the angle would increase.

Extra Example:

Add vector A (−1, 3) to B (4, −2) to determine the endpoint of the resultant vector and magnitude.

Endpoint: (3, 1); $|R| = \sqrt{10} \approx 3.2$

Common Problem:

Trying to visualize the angle and direction of the resultant vector.

Closing Question:

How would the resultant vectors be used when playing pool? When a ball gets hit by another ball, the resultant vector will be the path the ball is likely to travel.

Additional Lesson H Introduction to Vectors

Use after Chapter 4

Key Vocabulary

- **vector**
- **initial point**
- **terminal point**
- **magnitude of a vector**
- **direction of a vector**
- **resultant vector**

GOAL Sketch vectors; determine the magnitude and the direction of a resultant vector, and draw vectors with a given bearing.

A **vector** is a directed line segment, with an arrow on the end. Vector AB may be written $\mathbf{AB}$ or $\overline{AB}$, where A is the **initial point** and B is the **terminal point.** If the initial point of a vector is the origin, it can be identified as just one capital letter, set equal to the terminal point. For example, vector A that starts at the origin and ends at (4, 2) can be written $A = (4, 2)$, or just A (4, 2).

There are two characteristics that identify a vector: the magnitude and the direction. The **magnitude of a vector** is the length of the line segment, denoted $\|AB\|$. The **direction of a vector** is the angle, measured counterclockwise in degrees, from the positive x-axis to the vector.

Vectors can be added. The initial point of the two vectors is at the origin. One vector is moved in the same direction and with the same magnitude so that its initial point corresponds to the terminal point of the other vector (see example 2). The sum of two vectors is called the **resultant vector.**

EXAMPLE 1 Sketch vectors and determine their direction and the magnitude

Sketch the vectors C (3, 0) and D (4, 4). Then identify the direction and magnitude of the vectors.

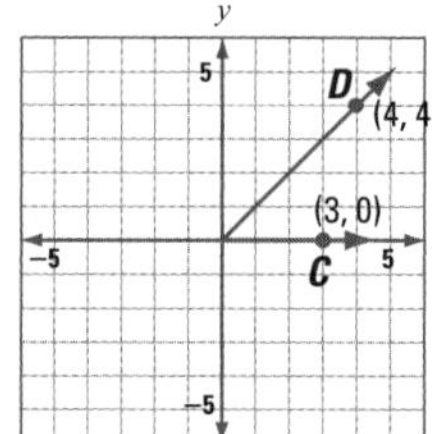

Vector C:
Since vector C is on the x-axis, its direction is 0°.
We can see that its magnitude (length) is 3 units, so $\|C\| = 3$.

Vector D:
The direction of D can be measured using a protractor, starting at the positive x-axis. Its direction is 45°.

We cannot count the units to find the magnitude of vector D, but we can use the Pythagorean Theorem.

$c^2 = a^2 + b^2$

$c = \sqrt{a^2 + b^2}$

$\|D\| = \sqrt{4^2 + 4^2}$

$\|D\| = \sqrt{32} \approx 5.7$

EXAMPLE 2 Add vectors and describe the resultant vector

Add vectors $M(4, 5)$ and $N(-3, -2)$. Identify the endpoint, magnitude, and direction of the resultant vector.

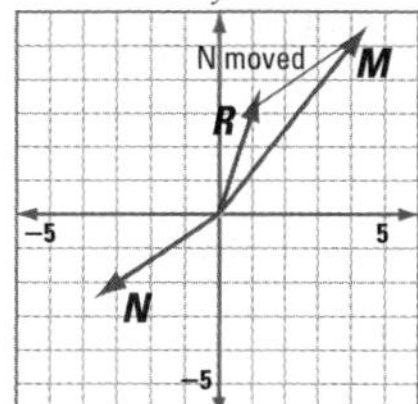

To determine the end point of the resultant vector R, add the coordinates of the two given vectors.

$R(x, y) = M(x_1, y_1) + N(x_2, y_2)$

$R(x, y) = M(4, 5) + N(-3, -2)$

$R(x, y) = (4 + (-3), 5 + (-2) = (1, 3))$

To determine the magnitude of R, use the Pythagorean Theorem.

$\|R\| = \sqrt{1^2 + 3^2} = \sqrt{1 + 9} = \sqrt{10} \approx 3.2$

To determine the direction of R, measure the angle using a protractor. The angle is 70°.

So, the resultant vector $R(1, 3)$ has a magnitude of about 3.2 units and direction 70°.

PRACTICE

Complete the following exercises.

Sketch the vectors and identify their magnitude and direction.

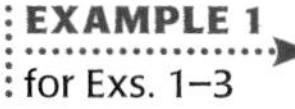

1. $X(0, 4)$

2. $Y(5, 2)$

3. $Z(-1, 3)$

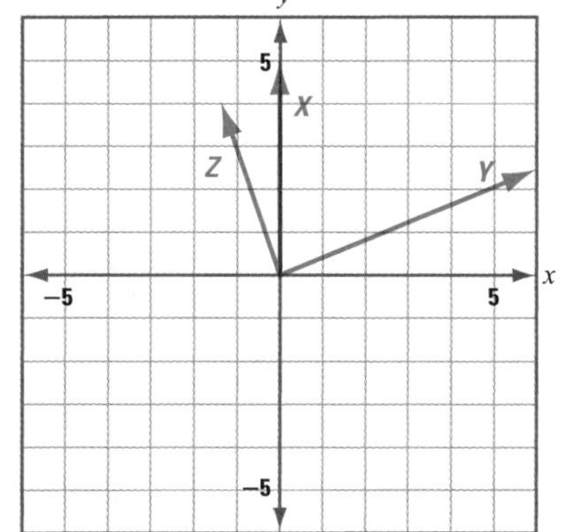

Add the vectors and identify the resultant vector by its endpoint, magnitude, and direction.

EXAMPLE 2
for Exs. 4–5

4. $A(3, 6)$ and $B(-1, -2)$

5. $J(-8, 0)$ and $K(2, 7)$

Answers to Additional Lessons

1. 4 units; 90°
2. $\sqrt{29} \approx 5.4$ units; 20°
3. $\sqrt{10} \approx 3.2$ units; 108°
4. The resultant vector R has endpoint (2, 4). It has a magnitude of $\sqrt{20} \approx 4.5$ units and direction 65°.
5. The resultant vector R has endpoint (−6, 7). It has a magnitude of $\sqrt{85} \approx 9.2$ units and direction 130°.

Essential Question:

When would you use a recursive formula? A recursive formula is used to generate a sequence of numbers.

Key Question for Ex. 1:

How many terms can you generate with the recursive formula? Infinite

Extra Example 2:

Write a recursive formula for the following sequence −1, 2, −7, 20, −61 . . . $t_n = (-3)(t_{n-1}) - 1$

Common Problem:

Students may find it difficult to recognize the pattern in order to write a rule for the sequence.

Closing Question:

Is a function a sequence? Yes

Additional Lesson I

Introduction to Recursive Functions for Sequences

Use after Chapter 13

GOAL Evaluate problems using basic recursive formulas.

Key Vocabulary
- sequence
- term notation
- recursive
- recursive formula

A **sequence** is a set of numbers in a particular order (pattern), such as 2, 4, 6, 8, ...

Sequences can be referred to by using **term notation,** $t_1, t_2, t_3, t_4, \ldots, t_n$. where t_1 is the first term, t_2 is the second term, . . . and t_n is the number nth term. We can also refer to the term after t_n as t_{n+1}, and the previous term, or term before t_n as t_{n-1}.

The word **recursive** means applying the same rule again and again. So a **recursive formula,** given with the first term or several terms of a sequence, is a rule that can be used to determine additional terms.

EXAMPLE 1 Write terms of sequences

a. Write the first 6 terms of the sequence 1, 5, 9, . . . where $t_n = t_{n-1} + 4$, that is, any term is determined by adding 4 to the previous term.

$t_4 = t_3 + 4 \qquad t_4 = 9 + 4 = 13$

$t_5 = t_4 + 4 \qquad t_5 = 13 + 4 = 17$

$t_6 = t_4 + 4 \qquad t_6 = 17 + 4 = 21$

Thus the first 6 terms of this sequence are 1, 5, 9, 13, 17, 21.

b. Write the first 5 terms of the sequence 2, 3, 8 . . . where $t_n = (t_{n-1})^2 - 1$, that is, 1 is subtracted from the square of the previous term.

$t_4 = (t_3)^2 - 1 \qquad t_4 = 8^2 - 1 = 64 - 1 = 63$

$t_5 = (t_4) - 1 \qquad t_5 = 63^2 - 1 = 3969 - 1 = 3968$

Thus the first 5 terms of this sequence are 2, 3, 8, 63, 3968.

EXAMPLE 2 Write a rule for the nth term of a sequence

a. Find the *n*th term, that is, the formula or rule that is used to determine the next term in the sequence 1, 4, 13, 40, 121, . . .

Examine each term. How do you get the second term from the first? How do you get the third term from the second? And so on.

$1 \times 3 + 1 = 4$

$4 \times 3 + 1 = 13$

$13 \times 3 + 1 = 40$

$40 \times 3 + 1 = 121$

The previous term is multiplied by 2 and 1 is added to it.

So, the formula for the nth term is $t_n = 3(t_{n-1}) + 1$.

b. Find the *n*th term, that is, the formula or rule that is used to determine the next term in the sequence 4096, 2048, 1024, 512, 256, 128, . . .

Examine each term. How do you get the second term from the first? How do you get the third term from the second? And so on.

$4096 \div 2 = 2048$

$2048 \div 2 = 1024$

$1024 \div 2 = 512$

$512 \div 2 = 256$

$256 \div 2 = 128$

The previous term is divided by 2.

So, the formula for the *n*th term is $t_n = \frac{t_{n-1}}{2}$.

PRACTICE

Complete the following exercises.

EXAMPLE 1 for Exs. 1–3

1. Write the first 6 terms of the sequence 1, 6, . . . where $t_n = t_{n-1} + 5$.
2. Write the first 5 terms of the sequence 1, 4, . . . where $t_n = (t_{n-1} + 1)^2$.
3. Write the first 7 terms of the sequence 3, 8, . . . where $t_n = 2t_{n-1} + 2$.

Find the *n*th term, that is, the formula for determining the next term for the sequence.

EXAMPLE 2 for Exs. 4–6

4. 1, 4, 7, 10, 13, 16, . . .
5. 1, 5, 25, 125, 525, 2625, . . .
6. 1, 2, 5, 26, 677, 458329, . . .

Answers to Additional Lessons

1. 1, 6, 11, 16, 21, 26
2. 1, 4, 25, 676, 458329
3. 3, 8, 18, 38, 78, 158, 318
4. $t_n = t_{n-1} + 3$
5. $t_n = 5(t_{n-1})$
6. $t_n = (t_{n-1})^2 + 1$

Essential Question:

How is finding the limit similar to weightlifters in the gym? A weightlifter might keep increasing his weight by smaller increments until his maximum weight is desired.

Key Question for Ex. 1:

What is the limit as x approaches 0?

$\lim_{x \to 0} f(x) = 4$

Extra Example 2:

Determine the limit of

$f(x) = \left(\frac{x^3 + x^2 + 3}{x - 4}\right)$

as x approaches 3?

$\lim_{x \to 0} f(x) = 39$

Common Problem:

Students may struggle with the necessity of this topic and ask why they simply can't evaluate the function at the given value. Until they are introduced to a problem where it is undefined at a given value the concept and procedure may not seem needed.

Closing Question:

How is trying to guess a friend's number between 0 and 100 similar to finding a limit? You keep guessing either higher or lower than the correct number, getting closer with each guess, until you get the correct answer.

Additional Lesson J

Introduction to Limits

Use after Chapter 5

Key Vocabulary

- **limit**

GOAL Determine the limit of a function as it approaches a given value.

A **limit** is a point where something ends; the greatest number or value allowed. In mathematics, as x approaches a specific value c, from both sides of c, the value of the function $f(x)$ approaches a unique value L, called the limit. In mathematical symbols, it is written: $\lim_{x \to c} f(x) = L$, and says "the limit of f of x equals L as x approaches c."

EXAMPLE 1 Calculate the limit of a given function choosing values of x as it approaches c from both sides

Determine the limit of $f(x) = x^3 + 4$ as x approaches 2.

This means, determine the value that $f(x)$ gets closer and closer to as x approaches 2.

To do this, chose values of x from both sides of 2, that is, numbers just less than 2 and numbers just greater than 2. Use a calculator to substitute the values into the function and examine the results.

$f(1.5)$	7.35	$f(2.5)$	19.625
$f(1.7)$	8.913	$f(2.3)$	16.167
$f(1.9)$	10.859	$f(2.1)$	13.261
$f(1.99)$	11.881	$f(2.01)$	12.121
$f(1.999)$	11.988	$f(2.001)$	12.012

We can see from the lists that as x gets closer and closer to 2, from either side, $f(x)$ gets closer and closer to 12.Therefore the limit of $f(x)$ as x approaches 2 is 12. Mathematically this is written as $\lim_{x \to 2} f(x) = 12$.

One way to do this on the graphing calculator is to type in the function and use the table. The keystrokes are:

$Y =$, (type the function)
2nd, WINDOW (TBLSET)
(set Indpnt: to Ask)
2nd GRAPH (TABLE)
(type an x-value), ENTER
(type the next x-value), ENTER, etc.

EXAMPLE 2 Calculate the limit of a function as x approaches a given value

Determine the limit of $f(x) = 2x^2 + 2x + 5$ as x approaches 3.

$f(2.5)$	3.75	$f(3.5)$	−0.25
$f(2.7)$	3.11	$f(3.3)$	0.71
$f(2.9)$	2.39	$f(3.1)$	1.59
$f(2.99)$	2.0399	$f(3.01)$	1.9599
$f(2.999)$	2.004	$f(3.001)$	1.996

We can see that the limit of $f(x) = -x^2 + 2x + 5$ as x approaches 3 from either side is 2. This is written mathematically as $\lim_{x \to 3} f(x) = 2$.

PRACTICE

Complete the following exercises.

EXAMPLE 1 for Ex. 1

1. Complete the following table to show that the limit of the function $f(x) = 2x^3$ as x approaches 5 is 250.

$f(4.5)$		$f(5.5)$	
$f(4.7)$		$f(5.3)$	
$f(4.9)$		$f(5.1)$	
$f(4.99)$		$f(5.01)$	
$f(4.999)$		$f(5.001)$	

Find the limits. Write your answer in mathematical symbols.

2. Determine the limit of $f(x) = x^2 + 7$ as x approaches 4.

3. Determine the limit of $f(x) = 5x + 6$ as x approaches 1.

4. Determine the limit of $f(x) = x^3 - 8$ as x approaches 2.

5. Determine the limit of $f(x) = -x^2 + 7x - 3$ as x approaches 5.

6. Determine the limit of $f(x) = \frac{x^2 + 9x - 2}{x + 3}$ as x approaches 2.

Answers to Additional Lessons

1. See Below
2. $\lim_{x \to 4} f(x) = 23$
3. $\lim_{x \to 1} f(x) = 11$
4. $\lim_{x \to 2} f(x) = 0$
5. $\lim_{x \to 5} f(x) = 57$
6. $\lim_{x \to 2} f(x) = 13$

1.

$f(4.5)$	182.25	$f(5.5)$	332.75
$f(4.7)$	207.65	$f(5.3)$	297.75
$f(4.9)$	235.30	$f(5.1)$	265.30
$f(4.99)$	248.50	$f(5.01)$	251.50
$f(4.999)$	249.85	$f(5.001)$	250.15

Essential Question:

Why are two-way tables practical to use? You can compare multiple data sets that relate together.

Extra Example 1:

Out of a group of 500 men and 500 women surveyed on their favorite sport to watch between football, basketball, or neither: 255 men picked football, 195 men picked basketball, 231 women picked football, and 132 women picked basketball. A person is picked at random.

(a) What is the probability that the person would watch neither?
$\approx 0.19 = 19\%$

(b)What is the probability that a woman would not watch football?
$\approx 0.27 = 27\%$

Common Problem:

Students may have a hard time deciding when to include the total number of people versus one group of people in the denominator.

Closing Question:

What jobs would be most inclined to use two-way tables? For example, media, statisticians, etc. All answers are right if given a valid reason.

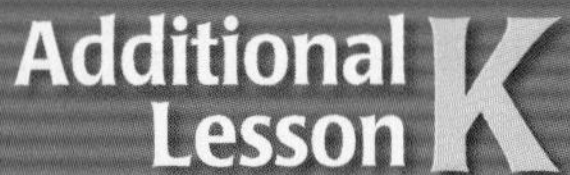

Two-Way Tables of Probability

Use after Chapter 13

Key Vocabulary

- **experiment**
- **outcome**
- **sample space**
- **probability**
- **two-way table**

GOAL Determine the degree of dependence of two quantities specified by a two-way table.

An **experiment** is an activity or process such as rolling a die or flipping a coin. The **outcome** is the result of the experiment, such as rolling a 4 on a die. The **sample space** is the set of all outcomes of an experiment. For example, the sample space for flipping a coin once consists of two outcomes: {heads, tails}. The **probability** of an event is the ratio of times the event occurs to the total number of trials. A **two-way table** is a listing of compound events in multiple rows and columns. It contains information about two categorical variables, which allows for comparisons.

EXAMPLE 1 Use a two-way table to determine probabilities of events

A high school cafeteria surveyed the students for their milk preferences. The following two-way table summarizes the results.

	Do not drink milk	Prefer plain milk	Prefer chocolate milk	Total
Female	32	216	198	446
Male	47	124	283	454
Total	79	340	481	900

A student is selected at random from the group surveyed.

1. What is the probability that a student selected at random drinks plain milk?
$$\frac{\text{total students that prefer plain}}{\text{total number of students}} = \frac{340}{900} \approx 0.38 = 38\%$$

2. What is the probability that a student selected at random is a male that does drink not milk?
$$\frac{\text{total males that do not drink milk}}{\text{total number of students}} = \frac{47}{900} \approx 0.05 = 5\%$$

3. What is the probability that a student selected at random from the males does not drink milk?
$$\frac{\text{total males that do not drink milk}}{\text{total number of males}} = \frac{47}{454} \approx 0.10 = 10\%$$

4. What is the probability that a student selected at random from the females prefers chocolate?
$$\frac{\text{total females that prefer chocolate}}{\text{total number of females}} = \frac{198}{446} \approx 0.44 = 44\%$$

EXAMPLE 1 Use a two-way table to determine probabilities of events *(continued)*

5. Would you be more likely to get a student that prefers chocolate milk when selecting a student at random from the males or from the females? Explain.

In #4, we found that the probability that a female student prefers chocolate milk is 44%. We can find the probability that a male student prefers chocolate and compare.

$$\frac{\text{total males that prefer chocolate}}{\text{total number of males}} = \frac{283}{454} \approx 0.62 = 62\%$$

So there is a better chance of getting a student who prefers chocolate milk, when choosing at random from the male population than from the female population.

PRACTICE

Complete the following exercises.

The birth weight (in ounces) of all the babies born at a hospital in one year is summarized in the table below.

	Weighing below average range	Weighing in the average range	Weighing above the average range	Total
Males	49	115	26	190
Females	34	138	30	202
Total	83	253	56	392

EXAMPLE 1 for Exs. 1–4

1. What is the probability that a baby selected at random weighed below the average birth weight range?

2. What is the probability that a baby selected at random was a female that weighed within the average birth weight range?

3. What is the probability that a baby selected at random from the females weighed above the average birth weight range?

4. Would you be more likely to get a baby that weighed above the average birth weight range is it was selected from the males or from the females? Explain.

Answers to Additional Lessons

1. $\frac{83}{392} \approx 0.21 = 21\%$

2. $\frac{138}{392} \approx 0.35 = 35\%$

3. $\frac{30}{202} \approx 0.15 = 15\%$

4. You would be more likely to get a baby that weighed above the average range if you selected from the females than from the males, because with the females there is a probability of about 15%, and with the males $\frac{26}{190}$, or about 14%.

Essential Question:

What is the difference between qualitative and quantitative data? Quantitative data would be represented with numerals along the x-axis. Qualitative data would be represented with non-numerical categories along the x-axis.

Key Question for Ex. 1:

What might you change to turn the qualitative answers to quantitative answers?

Ask for the ages of the students in a tumbling class.

Extra Example 1:

Classify the following data from college football records as qualitative or quantitative.

(a) Number of National Championships earned by various college teams. Qualitative

(b) Number of yards passing for a given week. Quantitative

(c) Scores from the last ten years for a given team. Quantitative

(d) Given certain receivers, the number passes caught in a given week. Qualitative

Common Problem:

Students may have difficulty deciding what should go on the x-axis.

Closing Question:

Is one type of graph better to use than the other? No, it really depends on the type of data.

Additional Lesson L

Quantitative vs. Qualitative Data

Use after Chapter 13

Key Vocabulary

- **quantitative**
- **qualitative**

GOAL Understand the difference between quantitative and qualitative data.

Two different types of data can be graphed using a bar graph.

Quantitative data is represented by numerical values that can be either single variable (univariate) or a pair of variables (bivariate). That is, the x-axis would be measured in numerals. Examples are voltage, height, SAT scores, number of students arriving late for class, and time to complete a task.

Qualitative data is represented by a set of non-numeric values. That is, the x-axis would be measured in unordered categories. Examples are types of trees, types of compounds, class standing (Fr, So, Jr, Sr), make of a car (Ford, Chevrolet, Nissan), and responses on a questionnaire (disagree, neutral, agree).

EXAMPLE 1 Classify Data

Classify the following data as qualitative or quantitative.

a. Number of infants, toddlers, preschoolers, and kindergarteners in a tumbling class. (Qualitative)

b. Number of students who got each possible score on an end-of-year exam for the seniors in a county school system. (Quantitative)

c. Ages of students in the junior class at a school. (Quantitative)

d. Number of 8th graders who are taking Pre-Algebra, Algebra I, Algebra II, or Geometry. (Qualitative)

EXAMPLE 2 Classify Data Given a Graph

Classify the data shown in the graph as qualitative or quantitative.

a.

(Qualitative)

b.

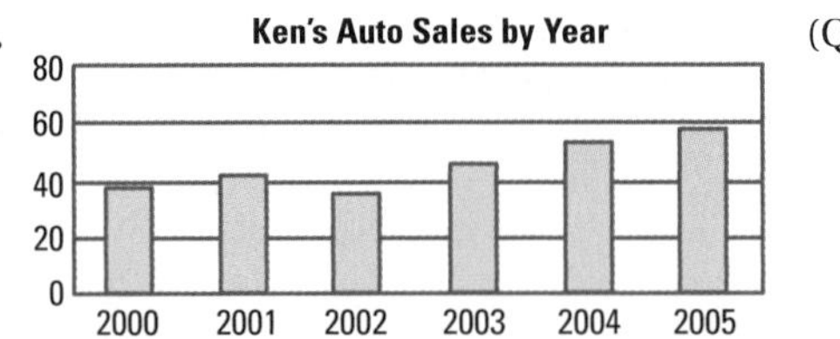

(Quantitative)

PRACTICE

Complete the following exercises.

Classify the following data as qualitative or quantitative.

EXAMPLE 1 for Exs. 1–4

1. Cost of college tuition at a local college for each of 10 years.

2. Number of each type of monkey at a zoo.

3. Percentage of people surveyed who own various pets.

4. Number of books checked out of the library during each hour of the day.

EXAMPLE 2 for Exs. 5–6

Classify the data shown in the graph as qualitative or quantitative.

5. 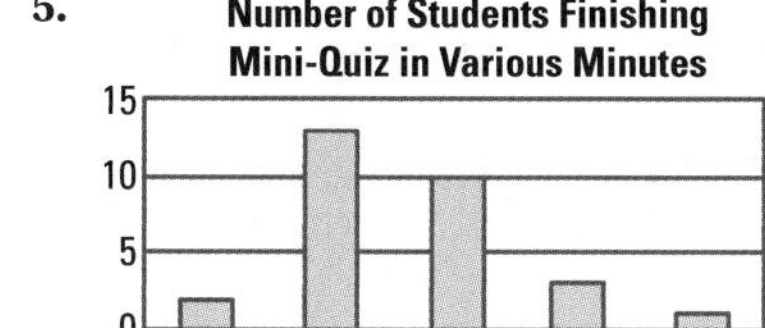

6. 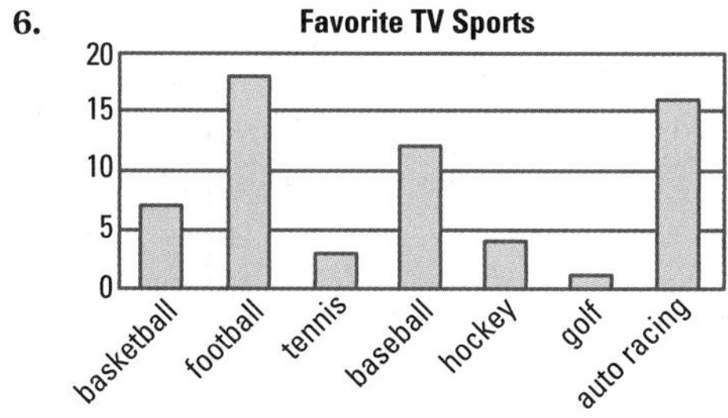

Answers to Additional Lessons

1. **Quantitative**
2. **Qualitative**
3. **Qualitative**
4. **Quantitative**
5. **Qualitative**
6. **Quantitative**

Essential Question:

What would you look for to show that data has a strong correlation? The closer the data appears to be linear, the stronger the correlation.

Key Question for Ex. 1:

Could this also be an example of causation? Yes, of course; as you practice more your speed will increase.

Extra Example:

Would "people who smoke have lung cancer" be causation or correlation? Correlation, the medical data is not enough to prove that everybody who smokes has lung cancer.

Common Problem:

Deciding if something is a true cause and effect.

Closing Question:

Would you consider the following statement to illustrate correlation and/or causation: "people who don't go to the gym will be fat?" Correlation, there is nothing that says being fat is associated with not going to the gym.

Additional Lesson M

Causation vs. Correlation

Use after Chapter 13

GOAL Understand the difference between correlation and causation.

Key Vocabulary
- **correlation**
- **causation**

There is often a relationship between two variables in a set of data. It is easiest to see if the data is graphed in the form of a scatter plot. For data that appears linear, a line of best fit can be drawn.

Correlation describes the relationship or lack thereof, between two variables in a data set, and measures the strength of these linear relationships. With some data, there is also a **causation,** where a change in one variable results in a change in the other. But be careful: a strong correlation between variables in a set of data does not necessarily mean there is a causation between the variables.

EXAMPLE 1 Analyze a set of data to determine a correlation

The following set of data shows the number of hours a student has practiced typing and his typing speed, measured in words per minute. Describe the correlation, if any, between practice time and typing speed.

Hours of Practice	5	6	9	10	12	15	16	17
Typing Speed (WPM)	4	5	12	14	18	20	22	25

Graph the data as a scatter plot on a coordinate grid.

Draw a line of best fit.

As can be seen from the graph, there appears to be a very strong correlation between hours of practice and typing speed.

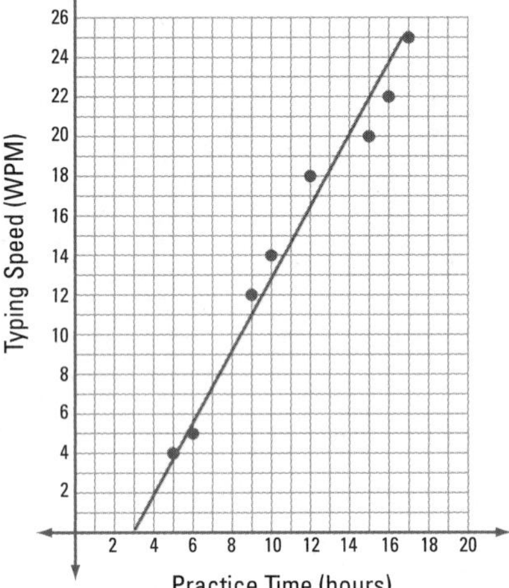

EXAMPLE 2 Analyze a set of data to determine a causation

The following data lists the shoe size and vocabulary size (number of known words) of several children that were studied. Determine if there is a causal relationship between shoe size and vocabulary size.

Graph the data.

Shoe Size	Vocabulary Size (known words)
1	15,000
2	20,000
4	38,000
7	62,000
9	79,000
10	103,000
11	121,000

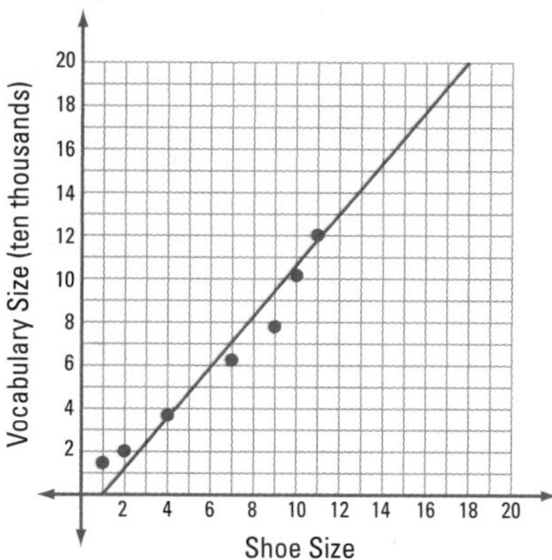

Draw a line of best fit.

There appears to be a strong relationship between shoe size and vocabulary size.

However, this is not a causal relationship.

Larger shoe size does not cause a larger vocabulary. There is a hidden variable at play here, which is age. As children get older, there shoe size and vocabulary size both happen to get larger.

PRACTICE

Complete the following exercises.

For each set of data, describe the correlation, if any, which exists between the variables. Then determine whether or not there is a causal relationship between the variables in the data.

EXAMPLE 1 for Exs. 1–3

1. The data shows the age of a car (number of years old) and its resale value, in dollars.

Age of Car (years)	Resale Value (US $)
1	21,200
2	18,600
5	13,100
8	8,800
10	3,400

2. The data represents the height and IQ (Intelligence Quotient) of six people selected at random.

Height (inches)	53	58	60	62	63	68
IQ	147	128	152	136	131	149

3. The data in the table below represents several approximate house sizes in square feet, and the average amount of money that people who lived in a home of that size spent per week at a coffee shop.

House Size (thousands of sq. ft.)	1	2	3	4	5	6	7
Weekly $ Spent at Coffee Shop	5	128	18	19	27	32	38

Answers to Additional Lessons

1. **strong positive correlation; causation**
2. **no correlation; no causation**
3. **positive correlation; no causation**

Essential Question:

What are some ways you might recognize misleading data displays? Unused or empty space in the graph, grouped data without an even interval.

Key Question for Ex. 1:

What would be a more appropriate range in order for the data to not appear misleading? Range: 20,000 to 40,000 with intervals of 5,000

Extra Example 1:

What would be a good range and interval for the following data: 63, 29, 132, 48, 40, 56, 87, 94, 86, 57, 87, 74, 103, 126? Range 25–135, interval every 10 or 20

Common Problem:

Students may have difficulty recognizing the misleading displays.

Closing Question:

Why are misleading data displays important to know? Media and other people use misleading displays to trick people into believing one thing over another.

Additional Lesson N

Misleading Data Displays

Use after Chapter 13

Key Vocabulary

- **data**
- **display**
- **range**
- **scale**
- **interval**
- **misleading display**

GOAL Determine if and how the data displayed is giving a misleading impression.

Information that is presented in the form of a graph can be misleading. That is, when looking at a graph, one might get the wrong idea, or not see all the information in a clear and accurate way. This can happen for various reasons. Let's first look at some of the components of a graph that can come into play.

Data is a collection of numerical facts. A **display** is a visual representation of data, including bar graphs, circle graphs, line graphs, scatter plots, and other picture displays. The **range** of the data is the difference between the lowest and highest values. The range of the data is used to determine the **scale,** or unit of measure on the horizontal and vertical axes. The difference between every consecutive unit on an axis is called the **interval.** The choices for such things, as the scale and interval, can create a **misleading display,** in which the design of the display may lead to incorrect conclusions. Some reasons for misleading displays include broken scales, intervals that are too large or too small, or unequal intervals.

EXAMPLE 1 Analyze a graph to determine how an incorrect conclusion may be drawn

The line graph shows the change in Grace's annual salary over time. What incorrect conclusion might be drawn from this graph? Explain why it is a misleading display.

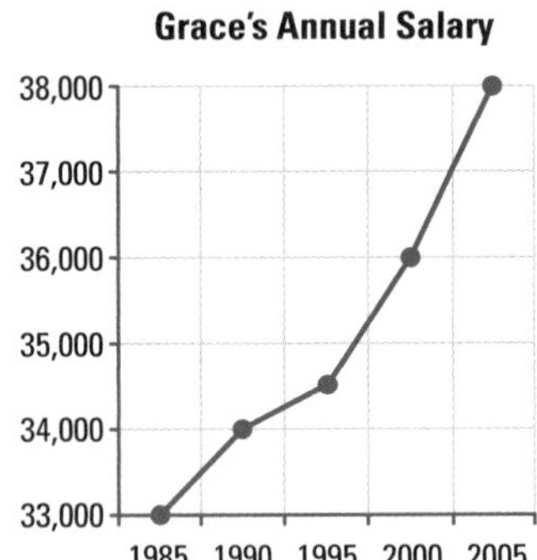

Answer: Someone might conclude that Grace has had drastic increases in her annual salary over time. The y-axis scale goes from \$33,000 to \$38,000, which are the lowest and highest data values. This has the effect of spreading the data points out from the very bottom to the very top of the display, making the changes look more dramatic than if the scale started at 0. The reality is that Grace's salary has only increased a total of \$5,000 over the course of 20 years.

PRACTICE

EXAMPLE 1 for Exs. 1–3

Complete the following exercises.

1. The bar graph shows the number of students that were able to complete a given amount of sit-ups in a one-minute physical fitness test. What incorrect conclusion might be drawn from this graph? Explain why it is a misleading display.

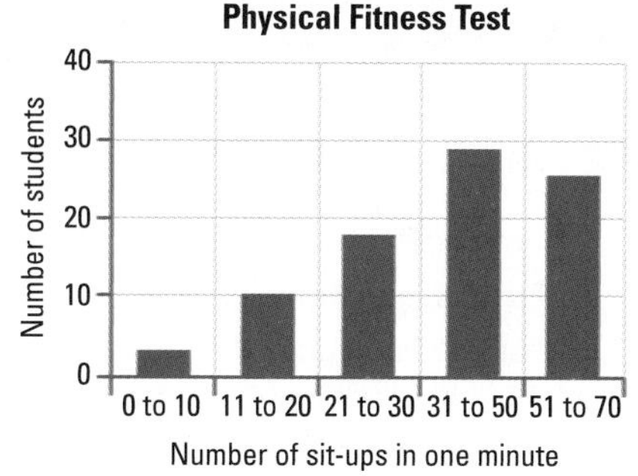

2. The bar graph shows the results of a survey in which teenagers were asked about their favorite leisure time activities. It appears as if twice as many teenagers prefer watching television as playing sports, when asked about their favorite leisure activity. But this is not true. Explain why this graph is misleading.

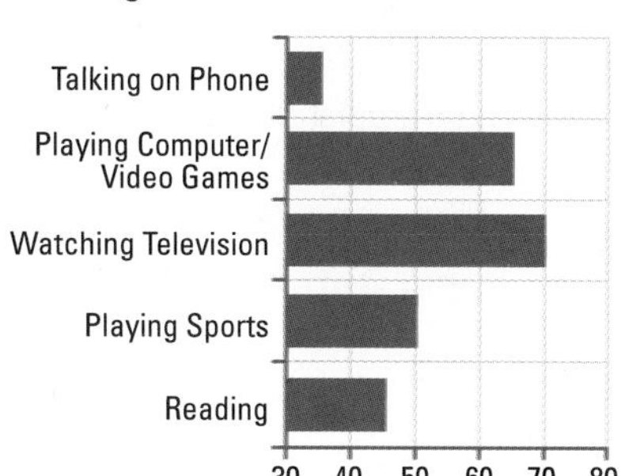

3. The line graph here shows the change in monetary donations given to a charitable organization over the 5 days of a fundraising campaign. What might someone be led to believe from this graph? Explain why it is a misleading display.

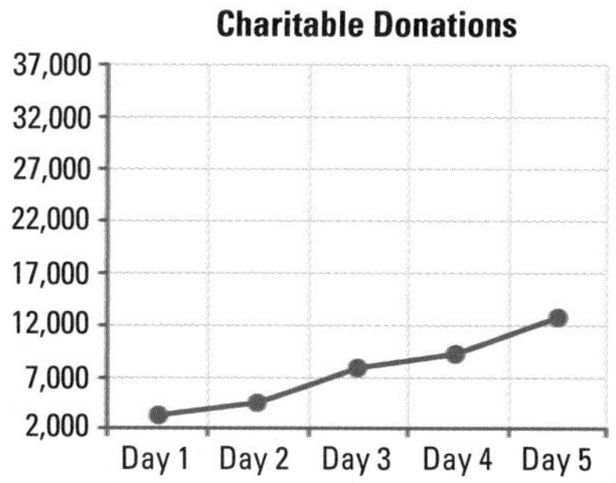

Answers to Additional Lessons

1. **From the graph, it seems that a large majority of kids who took the fitness test were able to do the largest amount of sit-ups, but the size of the intervals is not equal. The last two intervals are both twice as large as all the others. If the intervals were equal, we'd find more equal bar levels.**
2. **It appears that twice as many teenagers prefer watching television as playing sports because the size of the bar for TV is twice as long as the size of the bar for sports. But the scale on the x-axis starts at 30 instead of 0. So the ratio of TV to sports is actually 70 to 50.**
3. **This is a misleading display because the scale on the y-axis goes from \$2,000 up to \$37,000, when the highest donation was about \$12,000. The extra space gives the impression of low values.**

Contents of Student Resources

Comparing and Ordering Decimals

A **number line** is a line whose points are associated with numbers. You can use a number line to compare and order decimals. From left to right, the numbers on a number line appear in order from least to greatest.

EXAMPLE **Copy and complete the statement using <, >, or =.**

a. 9.67 _?_ 9.59

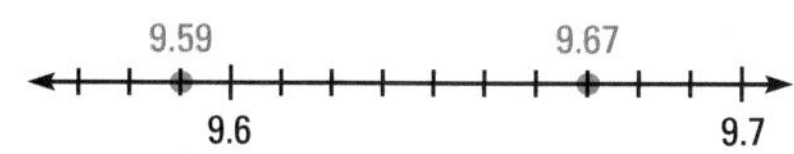

9.67 is to the right of 9.59, so 9.67 is greater than 9.59.

▶ 9.67 > 9.59

b. 0.08 _?_ 0.12

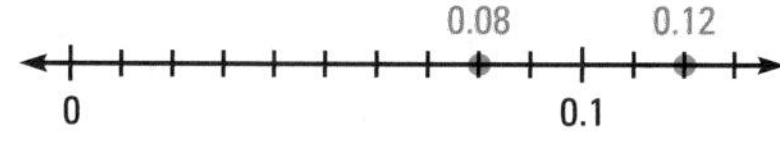

0.08 is to the left of 0.12, so 0.08 is less than 0.012.

▶ 0.08 < 0.012

EXAMPLE **Order the numbers 0.4, 0.56, 0.48, and 0.515 from least to greatest.**

Graph all the numbers on a number line.

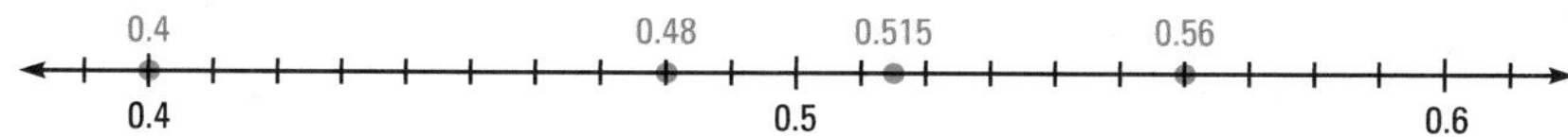

Write the numbers as they appear on the number line from left to right.

▶ The numbers in order from least to greatest are 0.4, 0.48, 0.515, and 0.56.

PRACTICE

Copy and complete the statement using <, >, or =.

1. 1.48 _?_ 1.413 >

2. 0.809 _?_ 0.81 <

3. 5.47 _?_ 5.43 >

4. 0.01 _?_ 0.005 >

5. 35.2 _?_ 35 >

6. 6.24 _?_ 6.2 >

7. 1.674 _?_ 1.678 <

8. 20.05 _?_ 20.3 <

9. 9.018 _?_ 9.017 >

Order the numbers from least to greatest.

10. 2.5, 2.3, 2.45, 2.38
2.3, 2.38, 2.45, 2.5

11. 7.01, 7.13, 7.3, 7.03
7.01, 7.03, 7.13, 7.3

12. 10.19, 10.2, 10, 10.4
10, 10.19, 10.2, 10.4

13. 0.3, 0.47, 0.9, 0.15
0.15, 0.3, 0.47, 0.9

14. 1.3, 1.05, 1.11, 1.0
1.0, 1.05, 1.11, 1.3

15. 12.6, 10.9, 11, 11.9
10.9, 11, 11.9, 12.6

16. 6.1, 6.89, 7.25, 7
6.1, 6.89, 7, 7.25

17. 3.1, 3.3, 0.3, 1.33
0.3, 1.33, 3.1, 3.3

18. 5.46, 5.4, 5.64, 5.6
5.4, 5.46, 5.6, 5.64

SKILLS REVIEW HANDBOOK

Factors and Multiples

A **prime number** is a whole number that is greater than 1 and has exactly two whole number factors, 1 and itself. A **composite number** is a whole number that is greater than 1 and has more than two whole number factors. The table below shows that the first five prime numbers are 2, 3, 5, 7, and 11.

Number	Product(s)	Factor(s)	Prime or composite?
1	1 • 1	1	Neither
2	1 • 2	1, 2	Prime
3	1 • 3	1, 3	Prime
4	1 • 4, 2 • 2	1, 2, 4	Composite
5	1 • 5	1, 5	Prime
6	1 • 6, 2 • 3	1, 2, 3, 6	Composite
7	1 • 7	1, 7	Prime
8	1 • 8, 2 • 4	1, 2, 4, 8	Composite
9	1 • 9, 3 • 3	1, 3, 9	Composite
10	1 • 10, 2 • 5	1, 2, 5, 10	Composite
11	1 • 11	1, 11	Prime
12	1 • 12, 2 • 6, 3 • 4	1, 2, 3, 4, 6, 12	Composite

When you write a composite number as a product of prime numbers, you are writing its **prime factorization**. You can use a **factor tree** to write the prime factorization of a number.

EXAMPLE **Write the prime factorization of 120.**

Write 120 at the top of your factor tree. Draw two branches and write 120 as the product of two factors. Continue to draw branches until all the factors are prime numbers (shown in red). Here are two possible factor trees for 120.

Start with $120 = 2 \cdot 60$.

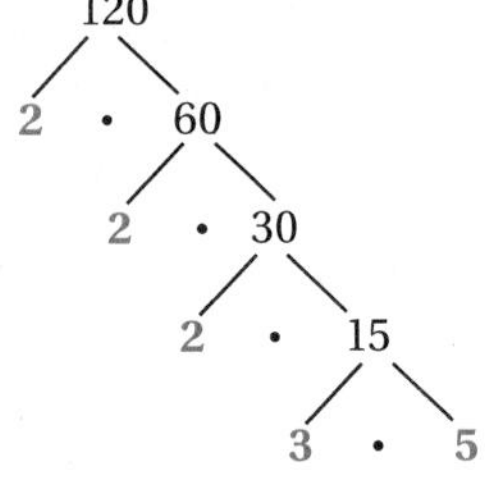

Start with $120 = 10 \cdot 12$.

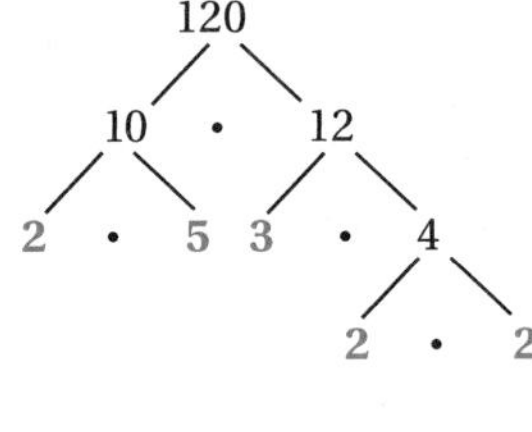

Both factor trees show that $120 = 2 \cdot 2 \cdot 2 \cdot 3 \cdot 5$, or $120 = 2^3 \cdot 3 \cdot 5$.

▶ The prime factorization of 120 is $2^3 \cdot 3 \cdot 5$.

For two or more nonzero whole numbers, a **common factor** is a whole number that is a factor of each number. The **greatest common factor (GCF)** of two or more nonzero whole numbers is the greatest of their common factors.

EXAMPLE **Find the greatest common factor of 30 and 42.**

Write the prime factorization of each number. The greatest common factor is the product of the common prime factors.

$30 = 2 \cdot 3 \cdot 5$ and $42 = 2 \cdot 3 \cdot 7$

The common prime factors are 2 and 3. The GCF is the product $2 \cdot 3 = 6$.

▶ The greatest common factor of 30 and 42 is 6.

A **multiple** of a whole number is the product of the number and any nonzero whole number. A **common multiple** of two or more whole numbers is a multiple of each number. The **least common multiple (LCM)** of two or more whole numbers is the least of their common multiples.

EXAMPLE **Find the least common multiple of 10 and 15.**

Write the prime factorization of each number. The least common multiple is the product of the factors, using each common prime factor only once.

$10 = 2 \cdot 5$ and $15 = 3 \cdot 5$

The common prime factor is 5. The LCM is the product $2 \cdot 3 \cdot 5 = 30$.

▶ The least common multiple of 10 and 15 is 30.

PRACTICE

Write the prime factorization of the number if it is not a prime number. If the number is prime, write *prime*.

1. 28 $2^2 \cdot 7$ **2.** 16 2^4 **3.** 11 prime **4.** 100 $2^2 \cdot 5^2$

5. 81 3^4 **6.** 49 7^2 **7.** 60 $2^2 \cdot 3 \cdot 5$ **8.** 53 prime

9. 180 $2^2 \cdot 3^2 \cdot 5$ **10.** 19 prime **11.** 51 $3 \cdot 17$ **12.** 72 $2^3 \cdot 3^2$

Find the greatest common factor of the pair of numbers.

13. 4, 8 4 **14.** 5, 6 1 **15.** 60, 18 6 **16.** 2, 10 2

17. 36, 27 9 **18.** 15, 21 3 **19.** 12, 16 4 **20.** 24, 108 12

21. 48, 88 8 **22.** 8, 12 4 **23.** 20, 28 4 **24.** 3, 5 1

Find the least common multiple of the pair of numbers.

25. 6, 9 18 **26.** 3, 8 24 **27.** 5, 45 45 **28.** 16, 20 80

29. 10, 65 130 **30.** 12, 15 60 **31.** 9, 30 90 **32.** 8, 9 72

33. 2, 14 14 **34.** 28, 32 224 **35.** 7, 49 49 **36.** 4, 6 12

911

Finding Equivalent Fractions and Simplifying Fractions

A **fraction** is a number of the form $\frac{a}{b}$ where a is the **numerator** and b is the **denominator**. The value of b cannot be 0.

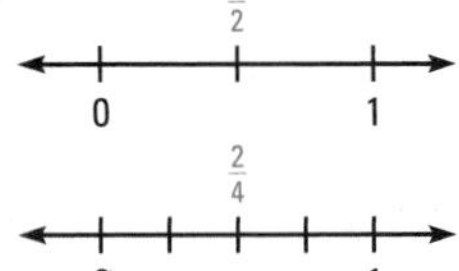

The number lines show the graphs of two fractions, $\frac{1}{2}$ and $\frac{2}{4}$.

These fractions represent the same number. Two fractions that represent the same number are called **equivalent fractions**.

To write equivalent fractions, you can multiply or divide the numerator and the denominator by the same nonzero number.

EXAMPLE **Write two fractions that are equivalent to $\frac{6}{8}$.**

Multiply the numerator and denominator by 3.

$\frac{6}{8} = \frac{6 \times 3}{8 \times 3} = \frac{18}{24}$ **Equivalent fraction**

Divide the numerator and denominator by 2.

$\frac{6}{8} = \frac{6 \div 2}{8 \div 2} = \frac{3}{4}$ **Equivalent fraction**

A fraction is in **simplest form** when its numerator and its denominator have no common factors besides 1.

EXAMPLE **Write the fraction $\frac{10}{15}$ in simplest form.**

Divide the numerator and denominator by 5, the greatest common factor of 10 and 15.

$\frac{10}{15} = \frac{10 \div 5}{15 \div 5} = \frac{2}{3}$ **Simplest form**

PRACTICE

Write two fractions that are equivalent to the given fraction. 1–5. Sample answers are given.

1. $\frac{9}{12}$ $\frac{3}{4}$ and $\frac{18}{24}$ **2.** $\frac{4}{6}$ $\frac{2}{3}$ and $\frac{8}{12}$ **3.** $\frac{1}{2}$ $\frac{2}{4}$ and $\frac{3}{6}$ **4.** $\frac{2}{5}$ $\frac{4}{10}$ and $\frac{6}{15}$ **5.** $\frac{10}{14}$ $\frac{5}{7}$ and $\frac{20}{28}$

Write the fraction in simplest form.

6. $\frac{16}{24}$ $\frac{2}{3}$ **7.** $\frac{3}{12}$ $\frac{1}{4}$ **8.** $\frac{30}{48}$ $\frac{5}{8}$ **9.** $\frac{5}{40}$ $\frac{1}{8}$ **10.** $\frac{8}{20}$ $\frac{2}{5}$

11. $\frac{4}{16}$ $\frac{1}{4}$ **12.** $\frac{64}{72}$ $\frac{8}{9}$ **13.** $\frac{35}{100}$ $\frac{7}{20}$ **14.** $\frac{21}{81}$ $\frac{7}{27}$ **15.** $\frac{44}{55}$ $\frac{4}{5}$

16. $\frac{15}{20}$ $\frac{3}{4}$ **17.** $\frac{12}{28}$ $\frac{3}{7}$ **18.** $\frac{15}{39}$ $\frac{5}{13}$ **19.** $\frac{24}{78}$ $\frac{4}{13}$ **20.** $\frac{60}{96}$ $\frac{5}{8}$

Mixed Numbers and Improper Fractions

A **mixed number** is the sum of a whole number and a fraction. An **improper fraction** is a fraction with a numerator that is greater than or equal to the denominator.

The shaded part of the model at the right represents the mixed number $2\frac{1}{4}$ and the improper fraction $\frac{9}{4}$.

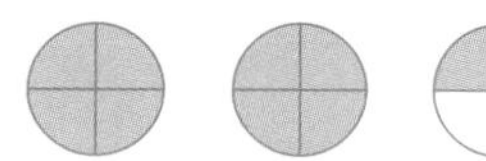

EXAMPLE **Write $5\frac{7}{8}$ as an improper fraction.**

$5\frac{7}{8} = 5 + \frac{7}{8}$	Definition of mixed number
$= \frac{40}{8} + \frac{7}{8}$	1 whole $= \frac{8}{8}$, so 5 wholes $= \frac{40}{8}$.
$= \frac{47}{8}$	Add.

EXAMPLE **Write $\frac{17}{5}$ as a mixed number.**

$$\begin{array}{r} 3 \\ 5\overline{)17} \\ \underline{15} \\ 2 \end{array}$$

Divide the numerator by the denominator: $17 \div 5$.
The quotient is 3 and the remainder is 2.

▸ $\frac{17}{5} = 3\frac{2}{5}$ Write the remainder as a fraction, $\frac{\text{remainder}}{\text{divisor}}$.

PRACTICE

Write the mixed number as an improper fraction.

1. $1\frac{2}{3}$ $\frac{5}{3}$	**2.** $3\frac{1}{4}$ $\frac{13}{4}$	**3.** $10\frac{3}{10}$ $\frac{103}{10}$	**4.** $2\frac{3}{5}$ $\frac{13}{5}$	**5.** $4\frac{1}{2}$ $\frac{9}{2}$
6. $9\frac{1}{3}$ $\frac{28}{3}$	**7.** $1\frac{11}{12}$ $\frac{23}{12}$	**8.** $2\frac{3}{4}$ $\frac{11}{4}$	**9.** $6\frac{5}{8}$ $\frac{53}{8}$	**10.** $5\frac{9}{16}$ $\frac{89}{16}$
11. $8\frac{1}{8}$ $\frac{65}{8}$	**12.** $6\frac{3}{5}$ $\frac{33}{5}$	**13.** $7\frac{2}{9}$ $\frac{65}{9}$	**14.** $2\frac{3}{13}$ $\frac{29}{13}$	**15.** $12\frac{2}{3}$ $\frac{38}{3}$

Write the improper fraction as a mixed number.

16. $\frac{5}{2}$ $2\frac{1}{2}$	**17.** $\frac{12}{5}$ $2\frac{2}{5}$	**18.** $\frac{15}{8}$ $1\frac{7}{8}$	**19.** $\frac{25}{4}$ $6\frac{1}{4}$	**20.** $\frac{37}{3}$ $12\frac{1}{3}$
21. $\frac{7}{4}$ $1\frac{3}{4}$	**22.** $\frac{27}{8}$ $3\frac{3}{8}$	**23.** $\frac{29}{10}$ $2\frac{9}{10}$	**24.** $\frac{69}{16}$ $4\frac{5}{16}$	**25.** $\frac{54}{5}$ $10\frac{4}{5}$
26. $\frac{31}{4}$ $7\frac{3}{4}$	**27.** $\frac{22}{5}$ $4\frac{2}{5}$	**28.** $\frac{13}{3}$ $4\frac{1}{3}$	**29.** $\frac{43}{9}$ $4\frac{7}{9}$	**30.** $\frac{35}{11}$ $3\frac{2}{11}$

Adding and Subtracting Fractions

To add or subtract two fractions with the same denominator, write the sum or difference of the numerators over the denominator.

Sum and Difference Rules ($c \neq 0$)

$$\frac{a}{c} + \frac{b}{c} = \frac{a+b}{c} \qquad \frac{a}{c} - \frac{b}{c} = \frac{a-b}{c}$$

EXAMPLE Add or subtract: **a.** $\frac{1}{10} + \frac{3}{10}$ **b.** $\frac{7}{8} - \frac{3}{8}$

a. $\frac{1}{10} + \frac{3}{10} = \frac{4}{10}$ — **Add numerators.**

$= \frac{2}{5}$ — **Simplify.**

b. $\frac{7}{8} - \frac{3}{8} = \frac{4}{8}$ — **Subtract numerators.**

$= \frac{1}{2}$ — **Simplify.**

The **least common denominator (LCD)** of two fractions is the least common multiple of the denominators. To add or subtract two fractions with different denominators, use the LCD of the fractions to write equivalent fractions that have the same denominator.

EXAMPLE Add: $\frac{1}{4} + \frac{5}{6}$

The LCD of the fractions is 12, so write $\frac{1}{4}$ as $\frac{1 \times 3}{4 \times 3} = \frac{3}{12}$ and $\frac{5}{6}$ as $\frac{5 \times 2}{6 \times 2} = \frac{10}{12}$.

$\frac{1}{4} + \frac{5}{6} = \frac{3}{12} + \frac{10}{12}$ — **Write equivalent fractions.**

$= \frac{13}{12}$ — **Add.**

$= 1\frac{1}{12}$ — **Write as a mixed number.**

PRACTICE

Add or subtract.

1. $\frac{1}{16} + \frac{3}{16}$ $\frac{1}{4}$
2. $\frac{1}{5} + \frac{2}{5}$ $\frac{3}{5}$
3. $\frac{7}{12} - \frac{5}{12}$ $\frac{1}{6}$
4. $\frac{2}{3} - \frac{1}{3}$ $\frac{1}{3}$
5. $\frac{5}{8} + \frac{3}{8}$ 1
6. $\frac{3}{4} + \frac{3}{4}$ $1\frac{1}{2}$
7. $\frac{7}{8} - \frac{3}{8}$ $\frac{1}{2}$
8. $\frac{17}{20} + \frac{9}{20}$ $1\frac{3}{10}$
9. $\frac{7}{10} + \frac{1}{2}$ $1\frac{1}{5}$
10. $\frac{3}{10} + \frac{3}{5}$ $\frac{9}{10}$
11. $\frac{3}{8} - \frac{3}{16}$ $\frac{3}{16}$
12. $\frac{1}{3} + \frac{1}{10}$ $\frac{13}{30}$
13. $\frac{7}{12} - \frac{1}{16}$ $\frac{25}{48}$
14. $\frac{2}{3} - \frac{1}{4}$ $\frac{5}{12}$
15. $\frac{5}{6} + \frac{7}{8}$ $1\frac{17}{24}$
16. $\frac{3}{4} - \frac{5}{8}$ $\frac{1}{8}$
17. $\frac{3}{4} - \frac{1}{5}$ $\frac{11}{20}$
18. $\frac{5}{12} + \frac{2}{3}$ $1\frac{1}{12}$
19. $1 - \frac{1}{5}$ $\frac{4}{5}$
20. $4 - \frac{3}{16}$ $3\frac{13}{16}$
21. $2\frac{5}{8} + 4\frac{1}{8}$ $6\frac{3}{4}$
22. $2\frac{9}{10} - 1\frac{7}{10}$ $1\frac{1}{5}$
23. $1\frac{5}{6} + 3\frac{1}{6}$ 5
24. $2\frac{1}{2} + 2\frac{3}{8}$ $4\frac{7}{8}$
25. $1\frac{3}{4} - \frac{11}{16}$ $1\frac{1}{16}$

Multiplying and Dividing Fractions

To multiply two fractions, write the product of the numerators over the product of the denominators.

Product Rule ($b, d \neq 0$)
$\frac{a}{b} \times \frac{c}{d} = \frac{ac}{bd}$

EXAMPLE **Multiply:** $\frac{3}{5} \times \frac{7}{8}$

$\frac{3}{5} \times \frac{7}{8} = \frac{3 \times 7}{5 \times 8}$ Use product rule.

$= \frac{21}{40}$ Simplify.

Two nonzero numbers whose product is 1 are **reciprocals**. For example, 6 and $\frac{1}{6}$ are reciprocals because $6 \times \frac{1}{6} = 1$. Every number except 0 has a reciprocal.

To divide by a fraction, multiply by its reciprocal.

Quotient Rule ($b, c, d \neq 0$)
$\frac{a}{b} \div \frac{c}{d} = \frac{a}{b} \times \frac{d}{c}$

EXAMPLE **Divide:** $\frac{5}{7} \div \frac{3}{4}$

The reciprocal of $\frac{3}{4}$ is $\frac{4}{3}$ because $\frac{3}{4} \times \frac{4}{3} = 1$, so multiply $\frac{5}{7}$ by $\frac{4}{3}$.

$\frac{5}{7} \div \frac{3}{4} = \frac{5}{7} \times \frac{4}{3}$ Use quotient rule.

$= \frac{20}{21}$ Use product rule.

PRACTICE

Multiply or divide.

1. $\frac{3}{4} \times \frac{2}{3}$ $\frac{1}{2}$ **2.** $\frac{1}{5} \times \frac{5}{8}$ $\frac{1}{8}$ **3.** $\frac{1}{6} \div \frac{1}{3}$ $\frac{1}{2}$ **4.** $\frac{2}{3} \div \frac{2}{3}$ 1 **5.** $\frac{9}{10} \div \frac{4}{5}$ $1\frac{1}{8}$

6. $\frac{1}{12} \times \frac{3}{4}$ $\frac{1}{16}$ **7.** $\frac{3}{8} \times \frac{1}{8}$ $\frac{3}{64}$ **8.** $\frac{5}{6} \div \frac{1}{4}$ $3\frac{1}{3}$ **9.** $\frac{1}{2} \times \frac{1}{4}$ $\frac{1}{8}$ **10.** $\frac{7}{10} \div \frac{5}{8}$ $1\frac{3}{25}$

11. $\frac{3}{4} \div \frac{1}{2}$ $1\frac{1}{2}$ **12.** $\frac{5}{6} \times \frac{3}{10}$ $\frac{1}{4}$ **13.** $\frac{2}{5} \div \frac{4}{5}$ $\frac{1}{2}$ **14.** $\frac{9}{10} \times \frac{1}{3}$ $\frac{3}{10}$ **15.** $\frac{1}{4} \div \frac{7}{8}$ $\frac{2}{7}$

16. $\frac{3}{16} \times \frac{2}{5}$ $\frac{3}{40}$ **17.** $\frac{2}{5} \div 20$ $\frac{1}{50}$ **18.** $18 \times \frac{1}{3}$ 6 **19.** $\frac{1}{10} \times 6$ $\frac{3}{5}$ **20.** $24 \div \frac{3}{8}$ 64

21. $5\frac{1}{2} \times \frac{9}{16}$ $3\frac{3}{32}$ **22.** $8\frac{1}{4} \div \frac{3}{10}$ $27\frac{1}{2}$ **23.** $1\frac{7}{8} \times 2\frac{1}{3}$ $4\frac{3}{8}$ **24.** $3\frac{3}{4} \div 6\frac{1}{2}$ $\frac{15}{26}$ **25.** $2\frac{1}{2} \div 1\frac{7}{8}$ $1\frac{1}{3}$

915

Fractions, Decimals, and Percents

A **percent** is a fraction whose denominator is 100. The symbol for percent is %. In the model at the right, there are 100 squares in all, and 49 of the 100 squares are shaded. You can write the shaded part of the model as a fraction, a decimal, or a percent.

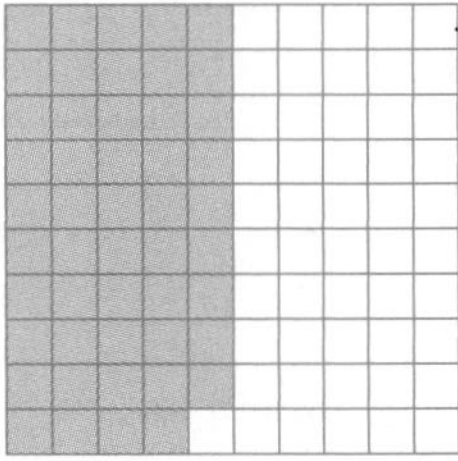

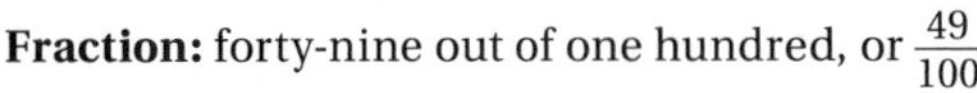

Fraction: forty-nine out of one hundred, or $\frac{49}{100}$

Decimal: forty-nine hundredths, or 0.49

Percent: forty-nine percent, or 49%

EXAMPLE **Write the fraction as a decimal: a. $\frac{1}{8}$ b. $\frac{5}{12}$**

a. $8\overline{)1.000}$ = 0.125 **Divide.**

▸ $\frac{1}{8} = 0.125$

b. $12\overline{)5.00000\ldots}$ = 0.41666. . . **Divide.**

▸ $\frac{5}{12} = 0.41666\ldots = 0.41\overline{6}$

EXAMPLE **Write the decimal as a fraction: a. 0.7 b. 0.32**

a. 0.7 = seven tenths

$= \frac{7}{10}$

b. 0.32 = thirty-two hundredths

$= \frac{32}{100}$

$= \frac{8}{25}$

To write a percent as a decimal, move the decimal point two places to the left and remove the percent sign.

EXAMPLE **Write the percent as a decimal: a. 16% b. 5%**

a. 16% = 16%

= 0.16

b. 5% = 05%

= 0.05

To write a decimal as a percent, move the decimal point two places to the right and write a percent sign.

EXAMPLE **Write the decimal as a percent: a. 0.83 b. 0.195**

a. 0.83 = 0.83

= 83%

b. 0.195 = 0.195

= 19.5%

EXAMPLE Write the percent as a fraction: a. 98% b. 5%

a. $98\% = \frac{98}{100}$ Definition of percent

$= \frac{49}{50}$ Simplify.

b. $5\% = \frac{5}{100}$ Definition of percent

$= \frac{1}{20}$ Simplify.

To write a fraction as a percent, you may be able to rewrite the fraction using a denominator of 100. If the denominator of the fraction is not a factor of 100, you can first write the fraction as a decimal and then as a percent.

EXAMPLE Write the fraction as a percent: a. $\frac{2}{5}$ b. $\frac{5}{8}$

a. $\frac{2}{5} = \frac{2(20)}{5(20)}$ Write as a fraction with denominator 100.

$= \frac{40}{100} = 40\%$ Write as a percent.

b. $\frac{5}{8} = 0.625$ Write as a decimal.

$= 62.5\%$ Write as a percent.

The table below gives commonly used fractions, decimals, and percents written in increasing order.

$\frac{1}{100} = 0.01 = 1\%$	$\frac{1}{16} = 0.0625 = 6.25\%$	$\frac{1}{10} = 0.1 = 10\%$	$\frac{1}{8} = 0.125 = 12.5\%$
$\frac{1}{5} = 0.2 = 20\%$	$\frac{1}{4} = 0.25 = 25\%$	$\frac{1}{3} = 0.\overline{3} \approx 33.3\%$	$\frac{3}{8} = 0.375 = 37.5\%$
$\frac{2}{5} = 0.4 = 40\%$	$\frac{1}{2} = 0.5 = 50\%$	$\frac{3}{5} = 0.6 = 60\%$	$\frac{5}{8} = 0.625 = 62.5\%$
$\frac{2}{3} = 0.\overline{6} \approx 66.7\%$	$\frac{3}{4} = 0.75 = 75\%$	$\frac{4}{5} = 0.8 = 80\%$	$\frac{7}{8} = 0.875 = 87.5\%$

PRACTICE

Write the percent as a decimal and as a fraction.

1. 70% 0.7, $\frac{7}{10}$ **2.** 12% 0.12, $\frac{3}{25}$ **3.** 3% 0.03, $\frac{3}{100}$ **4.** 55% 0.55, $\frac{11}{20}$ **5.** 35% 0.35, $\frac{7}{20}$

6. 9% 0.09, $\frac{9}{100}$ **7.** 110% 1.1, $1\frac{1}{10}$ **8.** 225% 2.25, $2\frac{1}{4}$ **9.** 0.3% 0.003, $\frac{3}{1000}$ **10.** 0.5% 0.005, $\frac{1}{200}$

Write the decimal as a fraction and as a percent.

11. 0.28 $\frac{7}{25}$, 28% **12.** 0.13 $\frac{13}{100}$, 13% **13.** 0.05 $\frac{1}{20}$, 5% **14.** 0.36 $\frac{9}{25}$, 36% **15.** 0.52 $\frac{13}{25}$, 52%

16. 0.004 $\frac{1}{250}$, 0.4% **17.** 0.025 $\frac{1}{40}$, 2.5% **18.** 4 $\frac{4}{1}$, 400% **19.** 1.5 $\frac{3}{2}$, 150% **20.** 2.3 $\frac{23}{10}$, 230%

Write the fraction as a decimal and as a percent. Round decimals to the nearest thousandth. Round percents to the nearest tenth of a percent.

21. $\frac{3}{16}$ 0.188, 18.8% **22.** $\frac{1}{9}$ 0.111, 11.1% **23.** $\frac{61}{100}$ 0.61, 61% **24.** $\frac{3}{20}$ 0.15, 15% **25.** $\frac{19}{100}$ 0.19, 19%

26. $\frac{17}{25}$ 0.68, 68% **27.** $\frac{9}{25}$ 0.36, 36% **28.** $\frac{5}{6}$ 0.833, 83.3% **29.** $\frac{4}{7}$ 0.571, 57.1% **30.** $\frac{5}{12}$ 0.417, 41.7%

Mean, Median, and Mode

Three measures of central tendency are mean, median, and mode.

The **mean** of a data set is the sum of the values divided by the number of values.	The **median** of a data set is the middle value when the values are written in numerical order. If a data set has an even number of values, the median is the mean of the two middle values.	The **mode** of a data set is the value that occurs most often. A data set can have no mode, one mode, or more than one mode.

EXAMPLE **Find the mean, median, and mode(s) of the data in the table.**

Lengths of School Years	
Country	School year (days)
China	251
Korea	222
Taiwan	222
Japan	220
Israel	215
Switzerland	207
Canada	188
United States	178

Mean

Add the values. Then divide by 8, the number of values.

Sum = 251 + 222 + 222 + 220 + 215 + 207 + 188 + 178
= 1703

▸ Mean $= \frac{1703}{8} = 212.875$

Median

Write the values in order from least to greatest.
Then find the middle value(s).

178, 188, 207, 215, 220, 222, 222, 251

Find the mean of the two middle values.

▸ Median $= \frac{215 + 220}{2} = \frac{435}{2} = 217.5$

Mode

Find the value that occurs most often.

▸ Mode = 222

PRACTICE

Find the mean, median, and mode(s) of the data.

1. Test scores: 90, 88, 95, 94, 87, 85, 92, 99, 100, 94 **92.4; 93; 94**
2. Daily high temperatures (°F) for a week: 68, 70, 67, 68, 75, 75, 74 **71°F; 70°F; 68°F and 75°F**
3. Ages of employees: 24, 52, 21, 55, 39, 49, 28, 33, 52, 41, 30, 64, 45 **41 yr; 41 yr; 52 yr**
4. Numbers of students in classes: 21, 24, 27, 28, 25, 18, 22, 25, 26, 22, 27, 20 **23.75; 24.5; 22, 25, and 27**
5. Movie ticket prices: \$6.75, \$7.50, \$7.25, \$6.75, \$6.25, \$7.50, \$7.25, \$6.75, \$7 **\$7; \$7; \$6.75**
6. Hourly rates of pay: \$14.50, \$8.75, \$7, \$11, \$16.50, \$18, \$12, \$10.25 **\$12.25; \$11.50; no mode**
7. Numbers of children in families: 0, 0, 1, 1, 1, 2, 2, 2, 2, 2, 3, 3, 4, 4, 4, 5 **2.25; 2; 2**
8. Ages of students in a high school class: 3 sixteen-year-olds, 10 seventeen-year-olds, and 7 eighteen-year-olds **17.2 yr; 17 yr; 17 yr**

Classifying Triangles and Quadrilaterals

A **polygon** is a closed plane figure whose sides are segments that intersect only at their endpoints. Each endpoint is called a **vertex** of the polygon. Polygons are classified by the number of sides they have.

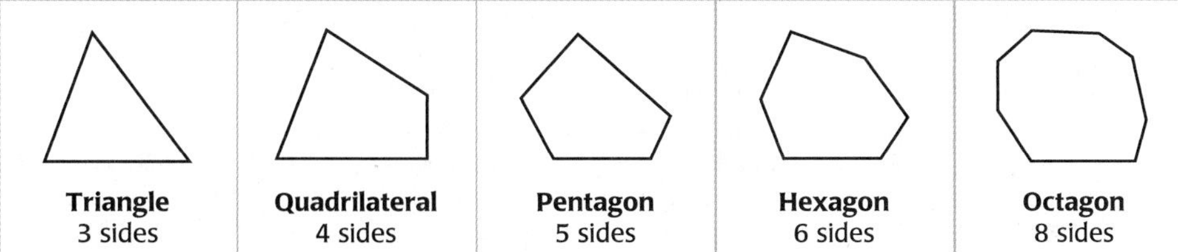

Triangles are classified by their angle measures. If two angles have the same measure, they are **congruent angles**. In a diagram, matching arcs are used to show congruent angles.

A **right angle** measures 90° and is marked by a square corner. An **acute angle** measures less than 90°, and an **obtuse angle** measures more than 90°. The sum of the measures of the angles of a triangle is 180°.

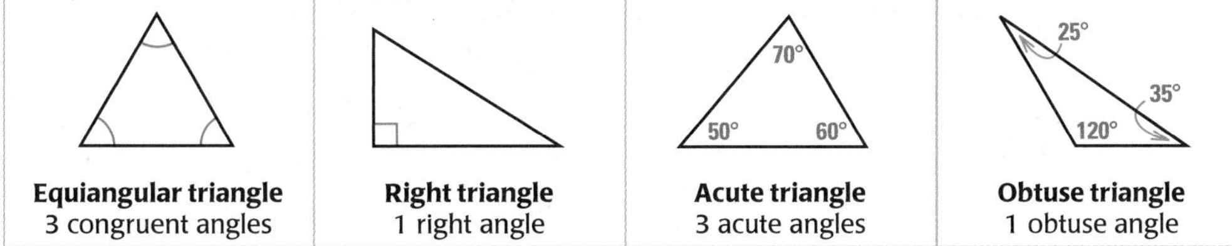

Triangles are also classified by their side lengths. If two sides have the same length, they are **congruent sides**. In a diagram, matching tick marks are used to show congruent sides.

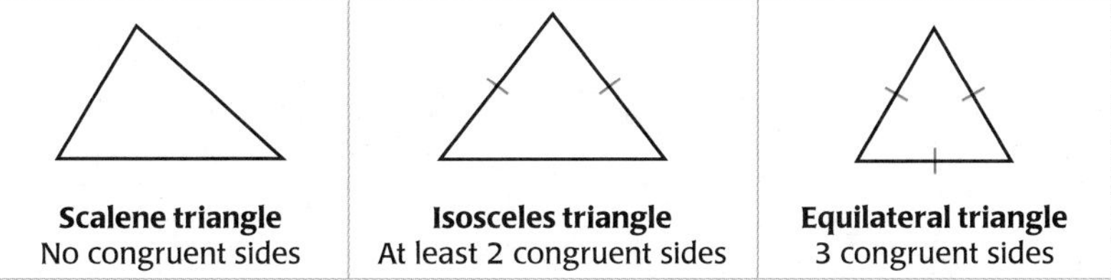

EXAMPLE **Classify the figure using all names that apply.**

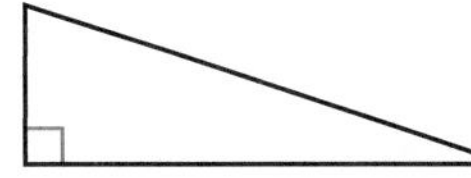

List the characteristics of the figure.

The figure is a polygon with 3 sides, so it is a triangle.

The triangle has no congruent sides, so it is a scalene triangle.

The triangle includes one right angle, so it is a right triangle.

▶ The figure is a scalene right triangle.

SKILLS REVIEW HANDBOOK

Two sides of a figure are parallel if the lines that contain the sides do not intersect. In a diagram, triangles (▶) are used to show parallel sides. Quadrilaterals are classified by whether they have parallel sides, congruent sides, or right angles.

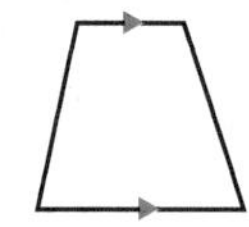		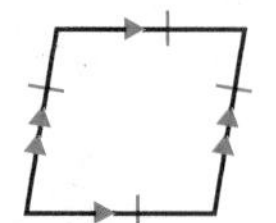	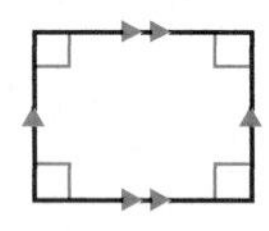	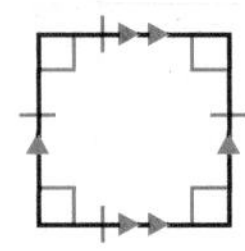
Trapezoid Quadrilateral with exactly one pair of opposite sides parallel	**Parallelogram** Quadrilateral with both pairs of opposite sides parallel	**Rhombus** Parallelogram with 4 congruent sides	**Rectangle** Parallelogram with 4 right angles	**Square** Parallelogram with 4 right angles and 4 congruent sides

EXAMPLE **Classify the figure using all names that apply.**

List the characteristics of the figure.

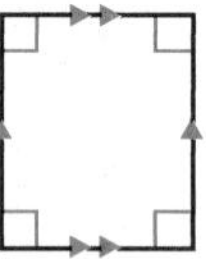

The figure is a polygon with four sides, so it is a quadrilateral.

Both pairs of opposite sides of the quadrilateral are parallel, so the figure is a parallelogram.

The parallelogram has four right angles, so it is a rectangle.

▶ The figure is a quadrilateral, a parallelogram, and a rectangle.

PRACTICE

Classify the figure using all names that apply.

1. 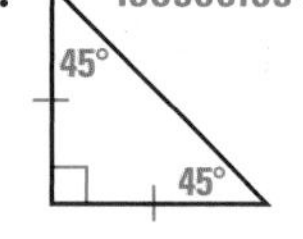

isosceles right triangle

2. 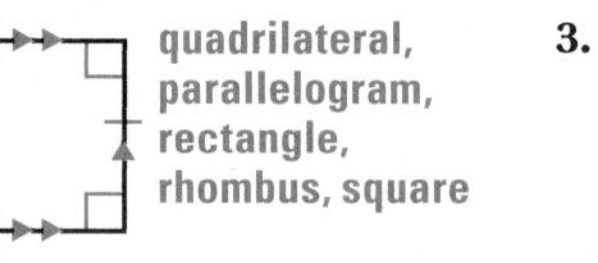
quadrilateral, parallelogram, rectangle, rhombus, square

3. 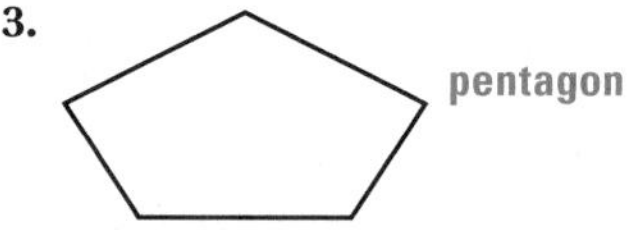
pentagon

4. 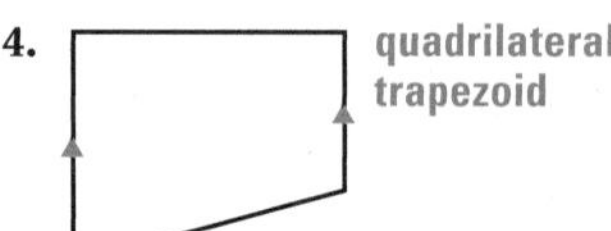
quadrilateral, trapezoid

5. 
hexagon

6. 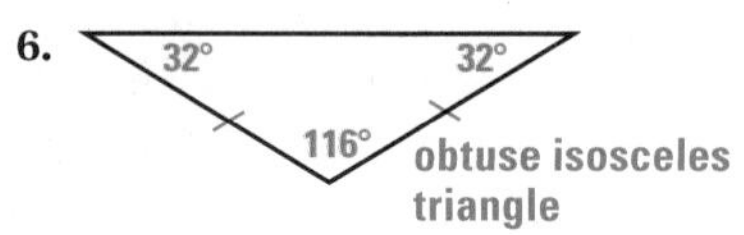

obtuse isosceles triangle

7. 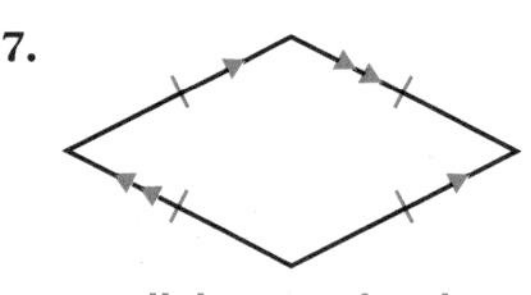
parallelogram, rhombus

8. 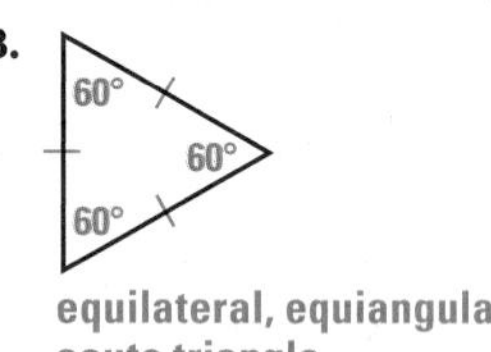

equilateral, equiangular acute triangle

9. 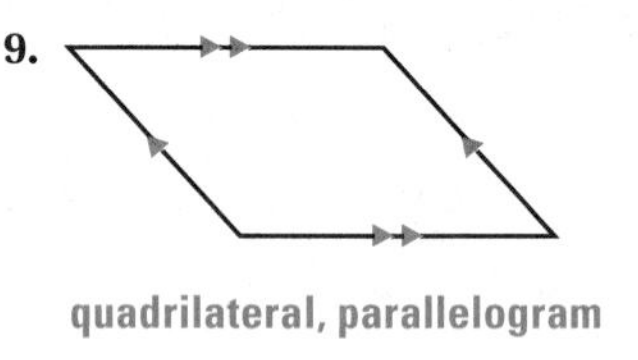
quadrilateral, parallelogram

920

The Coordinate Plane

Just as you use a number line to graph numbers, you use a *coordinate plane* to graph *ordered pairs* of numbers.

A **coordinate plane** has a horizontal ***x*-axis** and a vertical ***y*-axis** that intersect at a point called the **origin**. The origin is labeled *O*.

In an **ordered pair**, the first number is the ***x*-coordinate** and the second number is the ***y*-coordinate**. The coordinates of the origin are (0, 0). The ordered pair (4, 5) is graphed at the right.

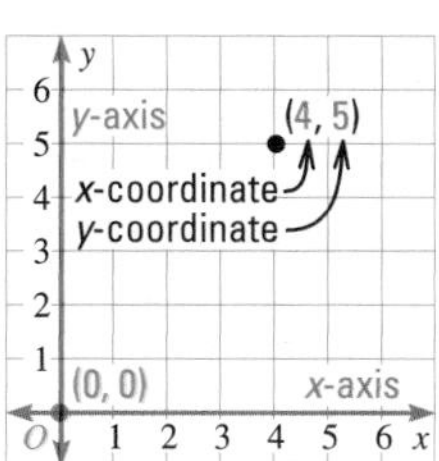

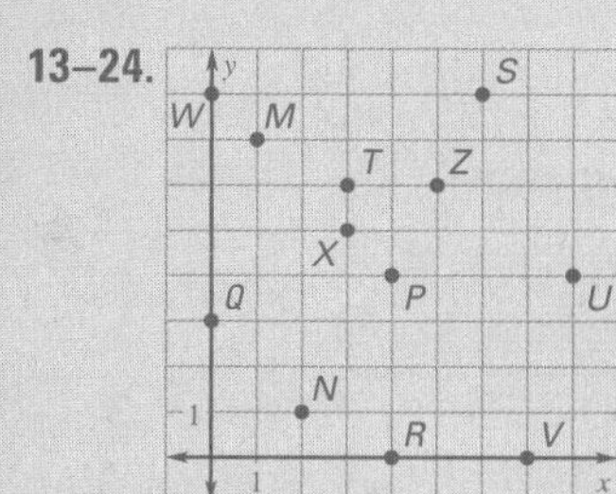

SKILLS REVIEW HANDBOOK

EXAMPLE **Give the coordinates of points *A* and *B*.**

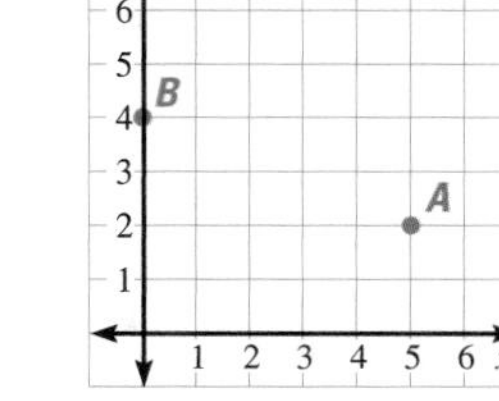

Point *A* is 5 units to the right of the origin and 2 units up, so the *x*-coordinate is 5 and the *y*-coordinate is 2.

▸ The coordinates of point *A* are (5, 2).

Point *B* is 0 units to the right or left of the origin and 4 units up, so the *x*-coordinate is 0 and the *y*-coordinate is 4.

▸ The coordinates of point *B* are (0, 4).

EXAMPLE **Plot the points *C*(1, 3) and *D*(3, 0) in a coordinate plane.**

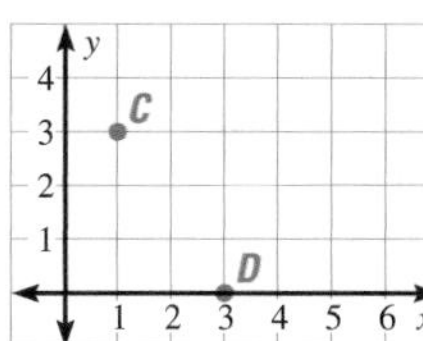

To plot the point *C*(1, 3), begin at the origin and move 1 unit to the right, then 3 units up.

To plot the point *D*(3, 0), begin at the origin and move 3 units right, then 0 units up.

PRACTICE

Give the coordinates of the point.

1. *A* (5, 4) **2.** *B* (0, 1) **3.** *C* (10, 8)

4. *D* (1, 9) **5.** *E* (9, 2) **6.** *F* (7, 0)

7. *G* (2, 6) **8.** *H* (7, 7) **9.** *J* (10, 0)

10. *K* (4, 8) **11.** *L* (0, 5) **12.** *M* (3, 1)

Plot the point in a coordinate plane.

13–24. See margin.

13. *M*(1, 7) **14.** *N*(2, 1) **15.** *P*(4, 4)

16. *Q*(0, 3) **17.** *R*(4, 0) **18.** *S*(6, 8)

19. *T*(3, 6) **20.** *U*(8, 4) **21.** *V*(7, 0)

22. *W*(0, 8) **23.** *X*(3, 5) **24.** *Z*(5, 6)

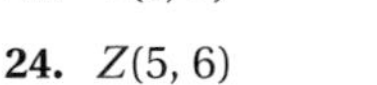

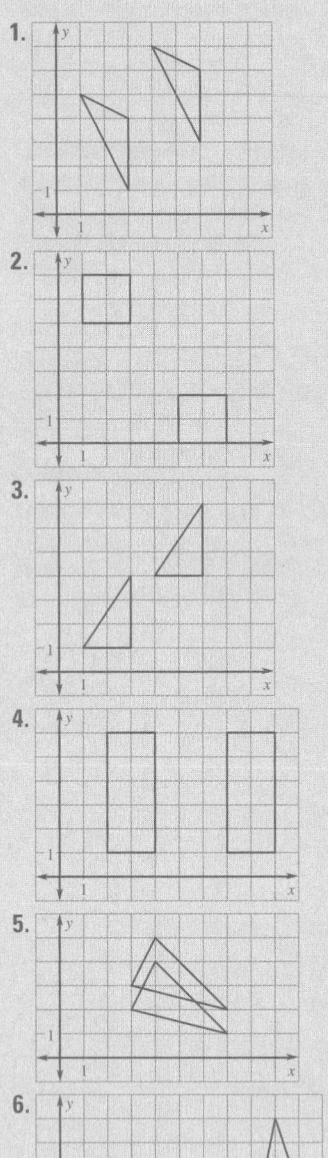

Transformations

A **transformation** is a change made to the location, size, or shape of a figure. The new figure formed by a transformation is called an **image**. In this book, original figures are shown in blue and images in red.

A **translation** is a transformation in which each point of a figure moves the same distance in the same direction. A figure and its translated image are identical in size and shape.

EXAMPLE **Translate the triangle 4 units to the right and 1 unit up.**

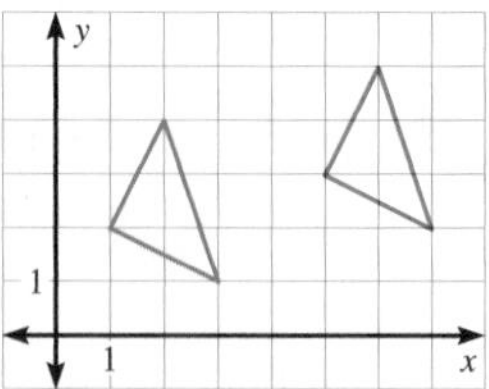

From each vertex of the triangle, move 4 units to the right and 1 unit up to plot the image of the vertex. Draw segments connecting the images of the vertices.

A **reflection** is a transformation in which a figure is reflected, or flipped, in a line, called the *line of reflection*. A figure and its reflected image are identical in size and shape.

EXAMPLE **Reflect the line segment in the given line.**

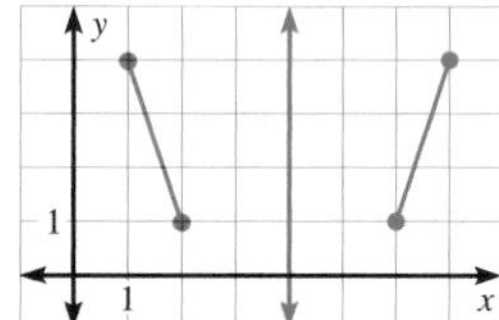

For each endpoint, find the distance from the endpoint to the line of reflection. Move the same distance on the opposite side of the line of reflection and plot the image point. Draw a segment connecting the image points.

A **dilation** is a transformation in which a figure stretches or shrinks with respect to a fixed point called the *center of dilation*. (The examples and exercises below all have the origin as the center of dilation.) A figure and its dilated image have the same shape.

The **scale factor** of a dilation is the ratio of a side length of the image to the corresponding side length of the original figure. A figure *stretches* if its scale factor is greater than 1. A figure *shrinks* if its scale factor is between 0 and 1.

EXAMPLE **Dilate the rectangle using a scale factor of 3.**

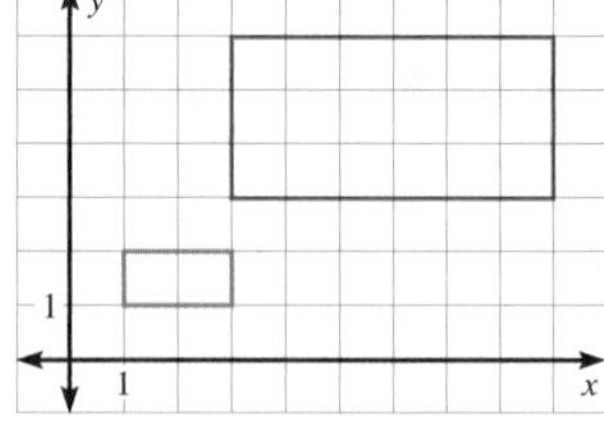

Multiply each coordinate of each vertex by 3 to find the coordinates of the image. Plot the image of each vertex. Connect the image points to form a rectangle.

$(1, 1) \rightarrow (3, 3)$ $\qquad$ $(1, 2) \rightarrow (3, 6)$

$(3, 2) \rightarrow (9, 6)$ $\qquad$ $(3, 1) \rightarrow (9, 3)$

Dilate the triangle using a scale factor of $\frac{1}{2}$.

Multiply each coordinate of each vertex by $\frac{1}{2}$ to find the coordinates of the image. Plot the image of each vertex. Connect the image points to form a triangle.

$(2, 6) \rightarrow (1, 3)$

$(2, 2) \rightarrow (1, 1)$

$(6, 4) \rightarrow (3, 2)$

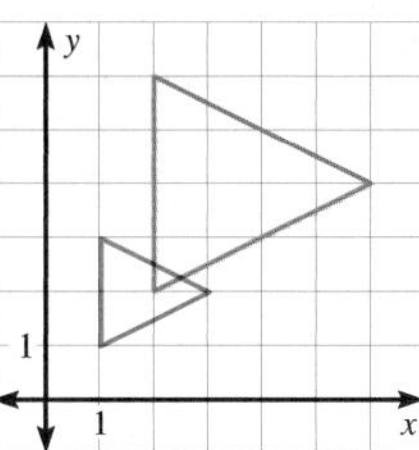

PRACTICE

The coordinates of the vertices of a polygon are given. Draw the polygon. Then find the coordinates of the vertices of the image after the specified translation, and draw the image. 1–5. See margin for art.

1. (1, 5), (3, 4), (3, 1); translate 3 units to the right and 2 units up (4, 7), (6, 6), (6, 3)
2. (5, 0), (7, 0), (7, 2), (5, 2); translate 4 units to the left and 5 units up (1, 5), (3, 5), (3, 7), (1, 7)
3. (4, 4), (6, 4), (6, 7); translate 3 units to the left and 3 units down (1, 1), (3, 1), (3, 4)
4. (2, 1), (4, 1), (4, 6), (2, 6); translate 5 units to the right (7, 1), (9, 1), (9, 6), (7, 6)
5. (4, 5), (7, 2), (3, 3); translate 1 unit down (4, 4), (7, 1), (3, 2)

For the figure shown, find the coordinates of the vertices of the image after a reflection in the given line. Then draw the image. 6–8. See margin for art.

6. 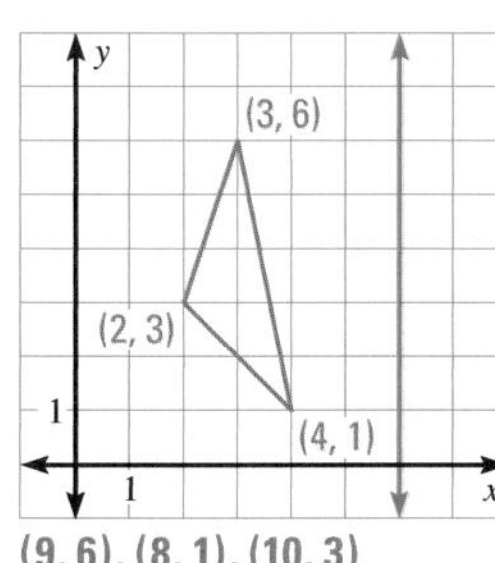

(9, 6), (8, 1), (10, 3)

7. 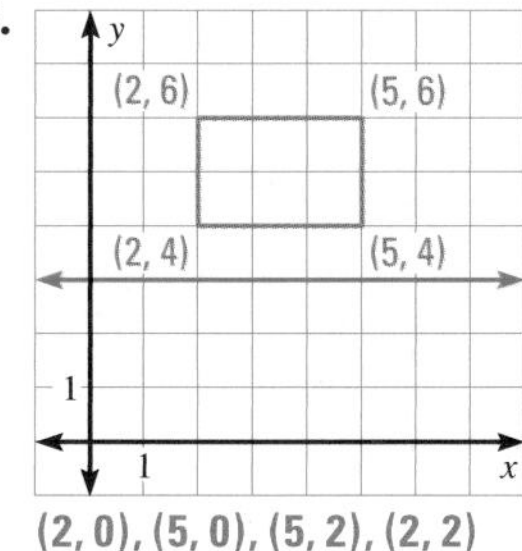

(2, 0), (5, 0), (5, 2), (2, 2)

8. 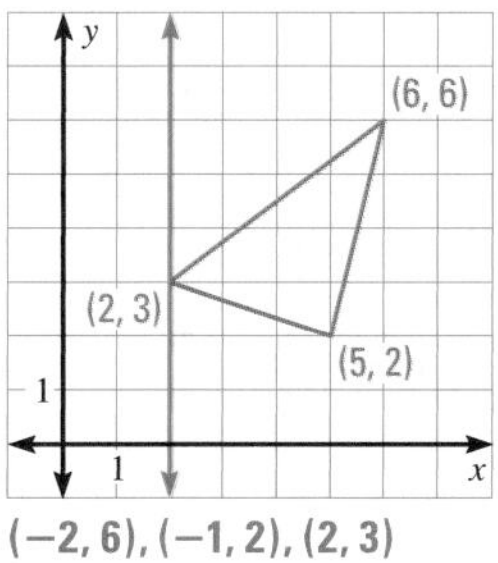

(−2, 6), (−1, 2), (2, 3)

The coordinates of the vertices of a polygon are given. Draw the polygon. Then find the coordinates of the vertices of the image after the specified dilation, and draw the image. 9–13. See margin for art.

9. (1, 2), (2, 4), (5, 3); dilate using a scale factor of 2 (2, 4), (4, 8), (10, 6)
10. (2, 6), (6, 6), (6, 2), (2, 2); dilate using a scale factor of $\frac{1}{2}$ (1, 3), (3, 3), (3, 1), (1, 1)
11. (1, 3), (3, 3), (3, 1), (1, 1); dilate using a scale factor of 4 (4, 12), (12, 12), (12, 4), (4, 4)
12. (3, 9), (6, 9), (6, 3); dilate using a scale factor of $\frac{1}{3}$ (1, 3), (2, 3), (2, 1)
13. (0, 2), (4, 4), (6, 0); dilate using a scale factor of $1\frac{1}{2}$ (0, 3), (6, 6), (9, 0)

SKILLS REVIEW HANDBOOK

8. 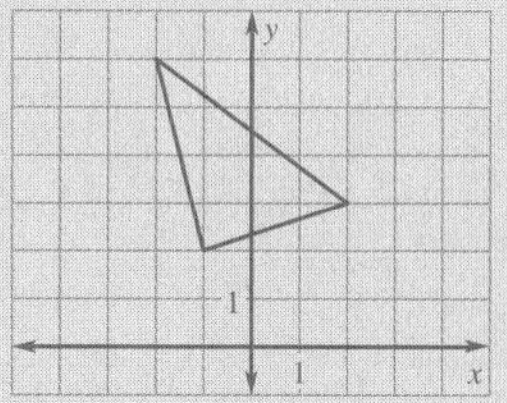
9. 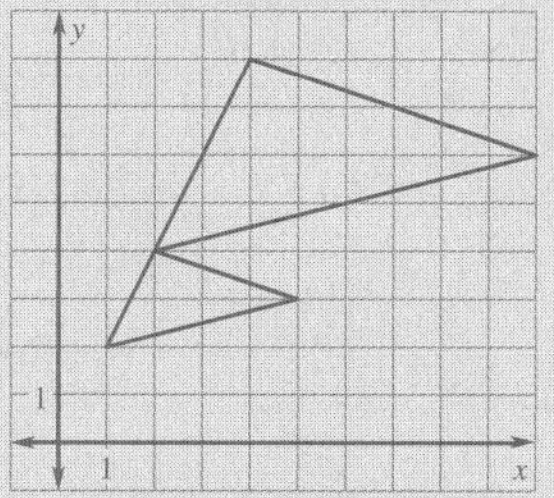
10. 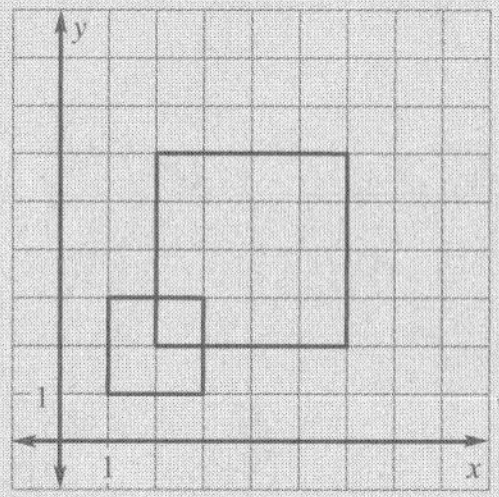
11. 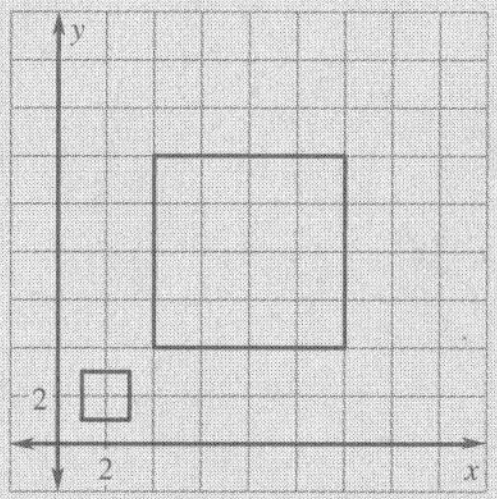
12. 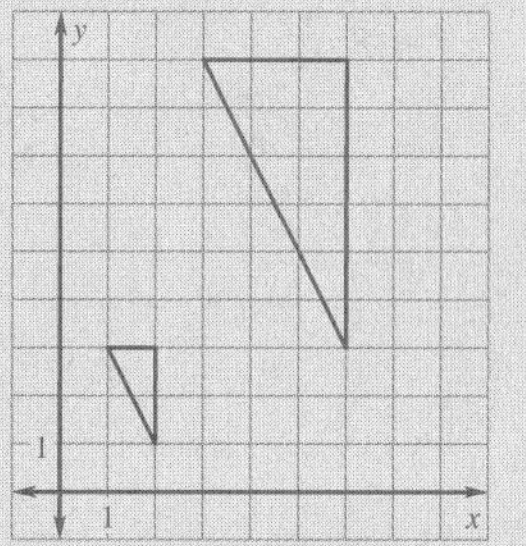
13.

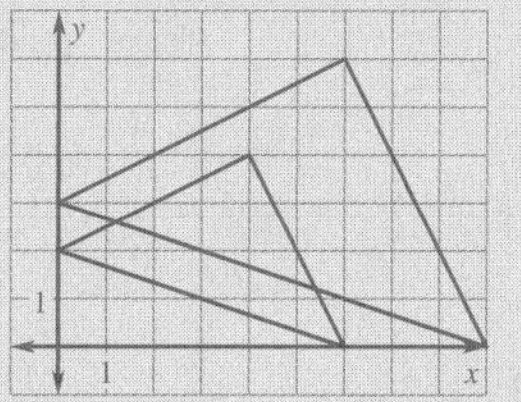

Perimeter and Area

The **perimeter** P of a figure is the distance around it.

Perimeter of a Square	Perimeter of a Rectangle	Perimeter of a Triangle
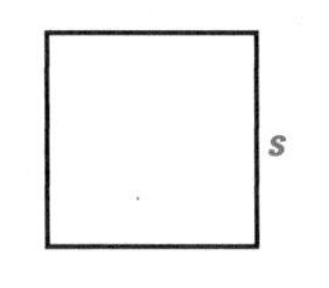	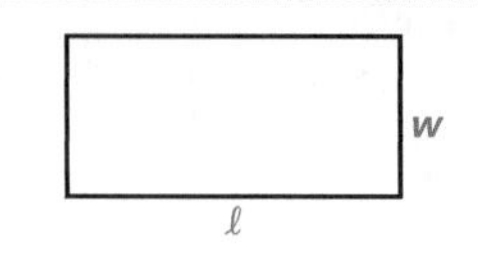	a, b, c
$P = s + s + s + s$ $= 4s$	$P = \ell + w + \ell + w$ $= 2\ell + 2w$	$P = a + b + c$

EXAMPLE **Find the perimeter of the figure.**

a. Square

$P = 4s$

$= 4(9)$

$= 36$ cm

b. Rectangle

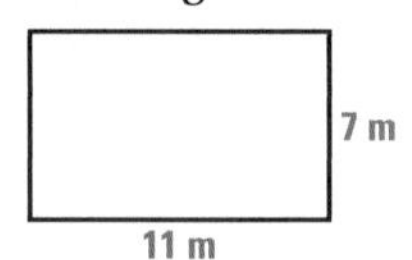

$P = 2\ell + 2w$

$= 2(11) + 2(7)$

$= 22 + 14 = 36$ m

c. Triangle

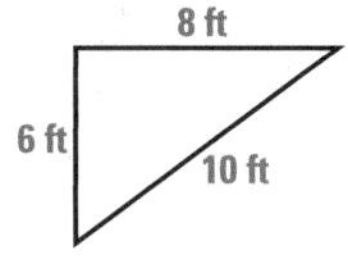

$P = a + b + c$

$= 6 + 8 + 10$

$= 24$ ft

The **area** A of a figure is the number of square units enclosed by the figure.

Area of a Square	Area of a Rectangle	Area of a Parallelogram
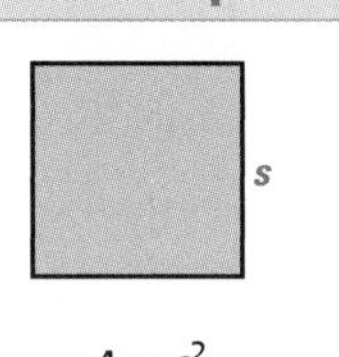	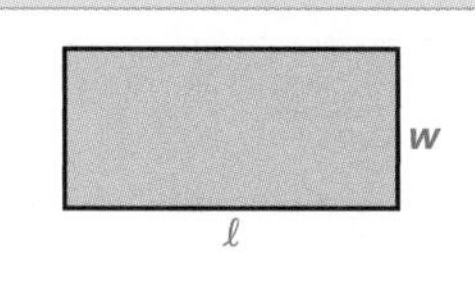	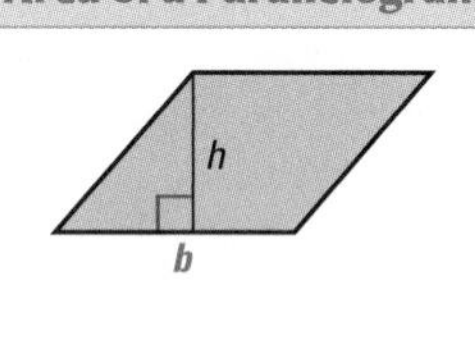
$A = s^2$	$A = \ell w$	$A = bh$

Area of a Triangle	Area of a Trapezoid
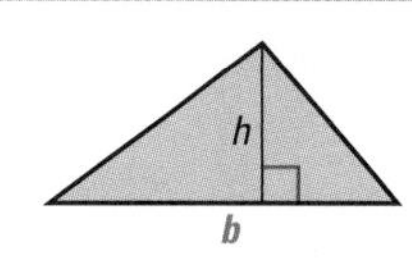	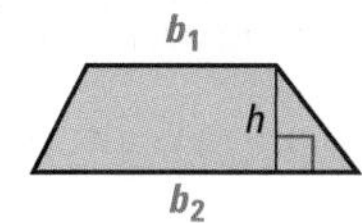
$A = \frac{1}{2}bh$	$P = \frac{1}{2}(b_1 + b_2)h$

924

EXAMPLE **Find the area of the figure.**

a. Rectangle

15 cm

9 cm

$A = \ell w$

$= 9(15)$

$= 135\ \text{cm}^2$

b. Triangle

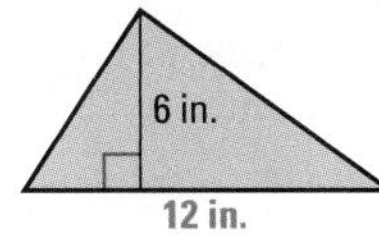

$A = \frac{1}{2}bh$

$= \frac{1}{2}(12)(6)$

$= 36\ \text{in.}^2$

c. Parallelogram

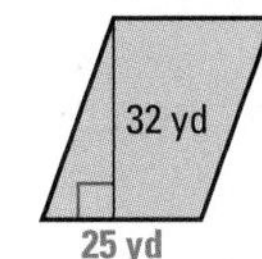

$A = bh$

$= 25(32)$

$= 800\ \text{yd}^2$

PRACTICE

Find the perimeter of the figure.

1. Square 36 ft

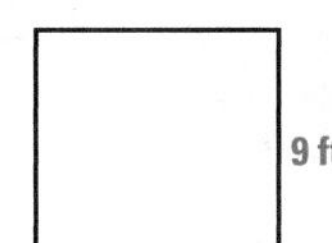

2. Rectangle 28 mm

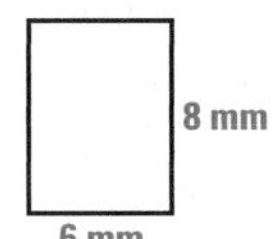

3. Triangle 20 ft

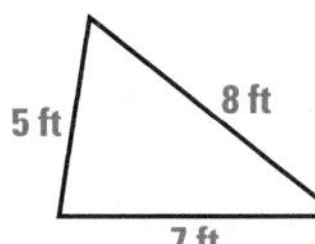

Find the area of the figure.

4. Square 400 in.^{2}

5. Rectangle 66 yd^2

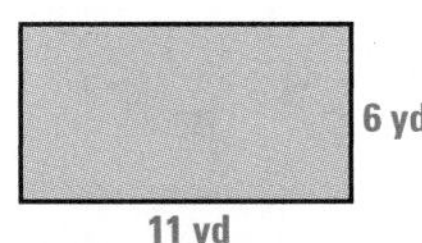

6. Triangle 52 m^2

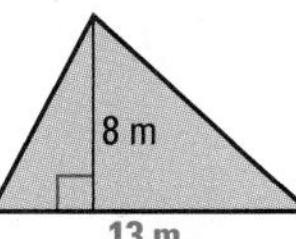

7. Parallelogram 110 in.^{2}

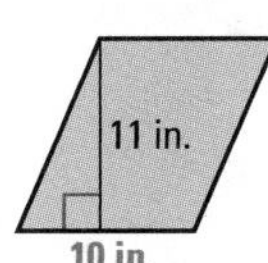

8. Trapezoid 130 m^2

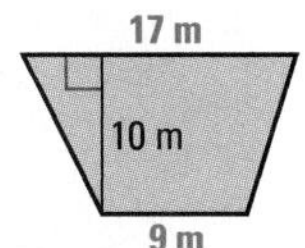
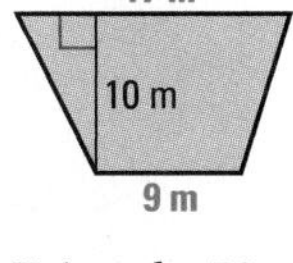

9. Parallelogram 21 ft^2

3 ft

7 ft

10. Trapezoid 234 m^2

24 m

13 m

12 m

11. Triangle 70 yd^2

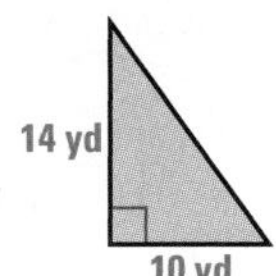

12. Rectangle 144 in.^{2}

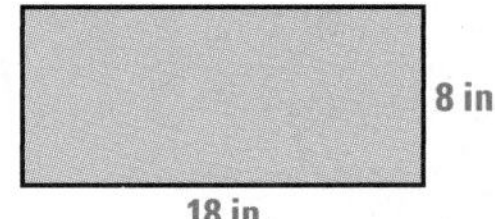

925

Circumference and Area of a Circle

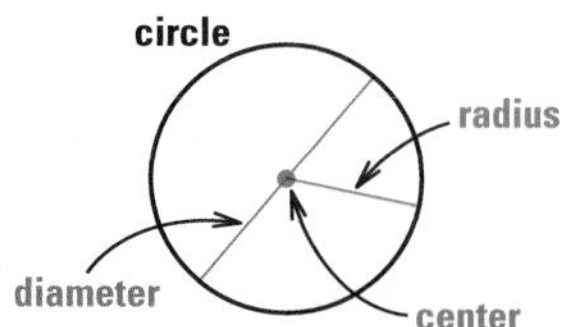

A circle consists of all points in a plane that are the same distance from a fixed point called the **center**.

The distance between the center and any point on the circle is the **radius**. The distance across the circle through the center is the **diameter**. The diameter of a circle is twice its radius.

The **circumference** of a circle is the distance around the circle. For any circle, the ratio of its circumference to its diameter is π (pi), a number that is approximately equal to 3.14 or $\frac{22}{7}$.

Circumference and Area of a Circle

To find the circumference C of a circle with radius r or diameter d, use the formula $C = 2\pi r$ or $C = \pi d$.

To find the area A of a circle with radius r, use the formula $A = \pi r^2$.

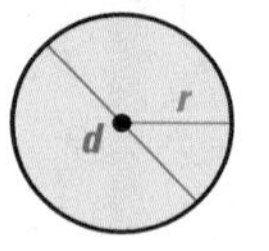

EXAMPLE **Find the circumference and area of the circle. Give your answers in terms of π and as decimals rounded to the nearest tenth.**

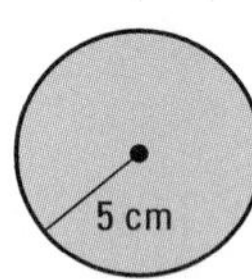

Circumference		**Area**	
$C = 2\pi r$		$A = \pi r^2$	
$= 2\pi(5)$		$= \pi(5^2)$	
$= 10\pi$ cm	Exact answer	$= 25\pi$ cm^2	Exact answer
$\approx 10(3.14)$		$\approx 25(3.14)$	
$= 31.4$ cm	Decimal approximation	$= 78.5$ cm^2	Decimal approximation

PRACTICE

Find the circumference and area of the circle. Give your answers in terms of π and as decimals rounded to the nearest tenth.

1. 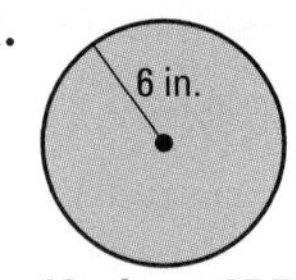

12π in. or 37.7 in., 36π in.^{2} or 113.0 in.^{2}

2. 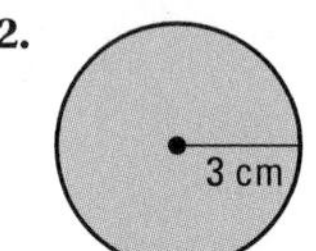

6π cm or 18.8 cm, 9π cm^2 or 28.3 cm^2

3. 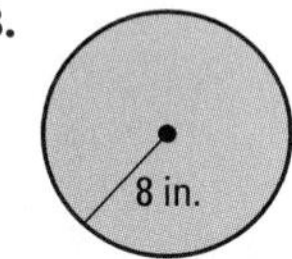

16π in. or 50.2 in., 64π in.^{2} or 201.0 in.^{2}

4. 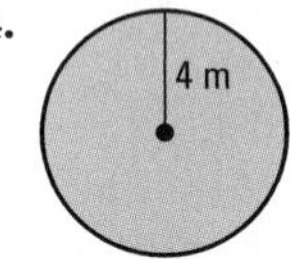

8π m or 25.1 m, 16π m^2 or 50.2 m^2

5. 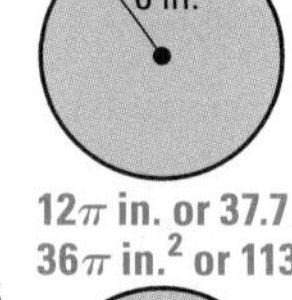

4π ft or 12.6 ft, 4π ft^2 or 12.6 ft^2

6. 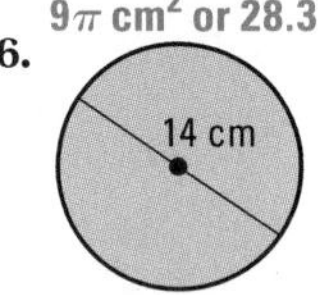

14π cm or 44.0 cm, 49π cm^2 or 153.9 m^2

7. 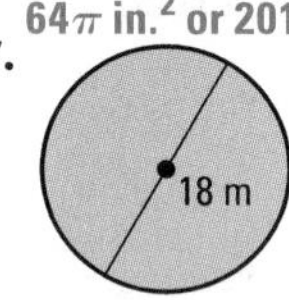

18π m or 56.5 m, 81π m^2 or 254.3 m^2

8. 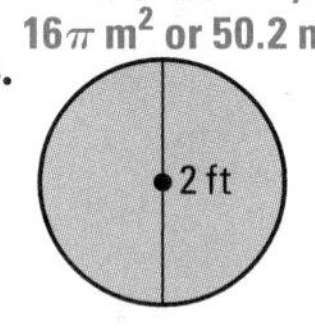

2π ft or 6.3 ft, π ft^2 or 3.1 ft^2

Surface Area and Volume

A **solid** is a three-dimensional figure that encloses part of space. The **surface area** S of a solid is the sum of the areas of all of its surfaces. The **volume** V of a solid is the amount of space that the solid occupies. In the formulas for surface area and volume, the number π (pi) is approximately equal to 3.14 or $\frac{22}{7}$.

Right Rectangular Prism

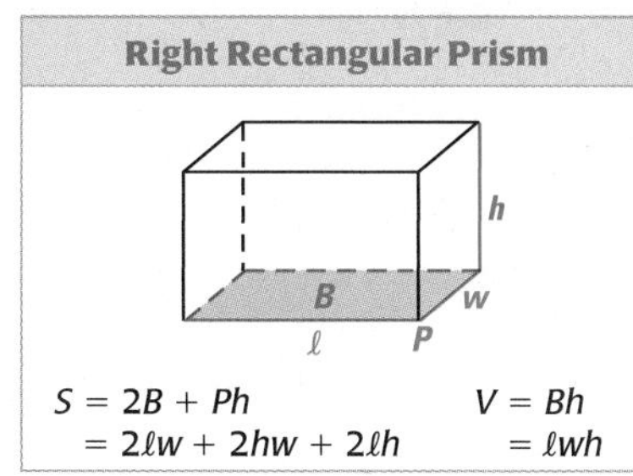

$S = 2B + Ph$
$= 2\ell w + 2hw + 2\ell h$

$V = Bh$
$= \ell wh$

Right Circular Cylinder

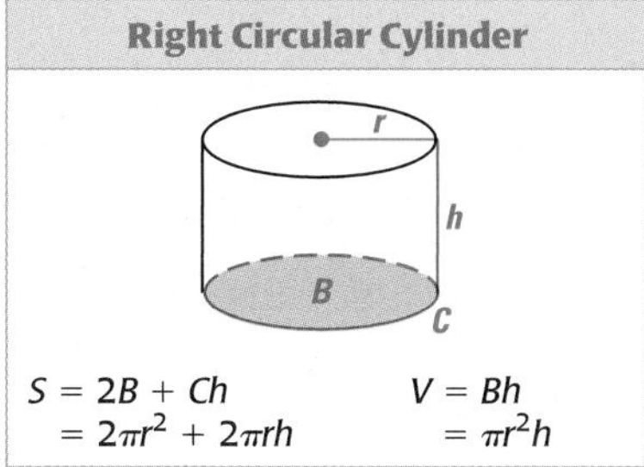

$S = 2B + Ch$
$= 2\pi r^2 + 2\pi rh$

$V = Bh$
$= \pi r^2 h$

Regular Pyramid

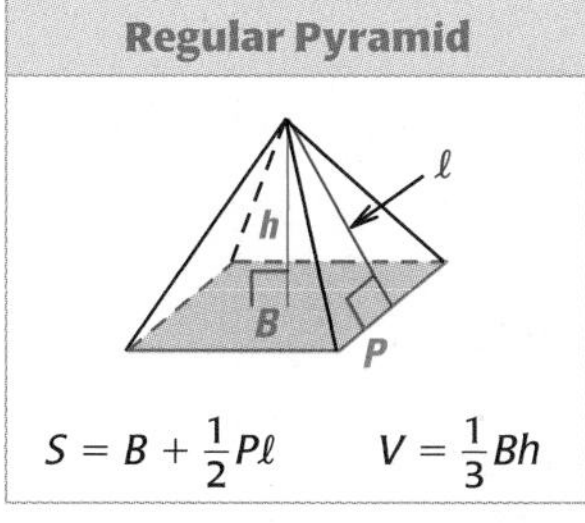

$S = B + \frac{1}{2}P\ell$

$V = \frac{1}{3}Bh$

Right Circular Cone

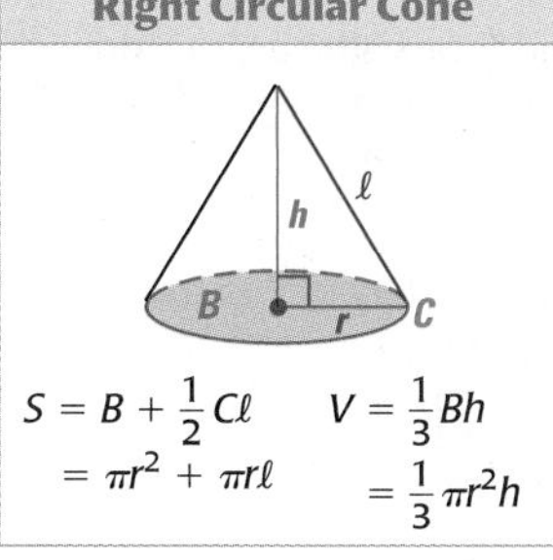

$S = B + \frac{1}{2}C\ell$
$= \pi r^2 + \pi r\ell$

$V = \frac{1}{3}Bh$
$= \frac{1}{3}\pi r^2 h$

Sphere

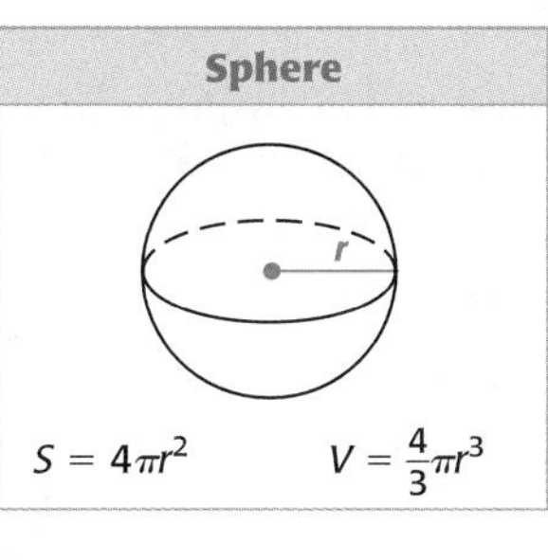

$S = 4\pi r^2$

$V = \frac{4}{3}\pi r^3$

In this book, the adjectives *right* and *circular* will be assumed and therefore will not be used in naming solids.

EXAMPLE **Find the surface area of the solid.**

a. Sphere

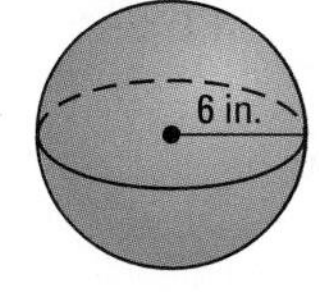

$S = 4\pi r^2$
$= 4\pi(6^2)$
$= 144\pi \text{ in.}^2$
$\approx 144(3.14)$
$\approx 452.2 \text{ in.}^2$

b. Cylinder

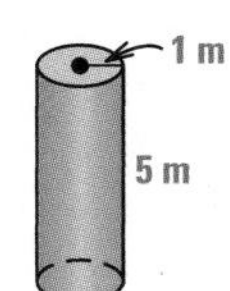

$S = 2\pi r^2 + 2\pi rh$
$= 2\pi(1^2) + 2\pi(1)(5)$
$= 2\pi + 10\pi$
$= 12\pi \text{ m}^2$
$\approx 12(3.14) \approx 37.7 \text{ m}^2$

c. Cone

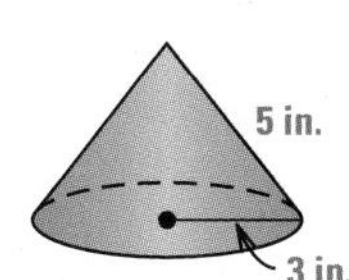

$S = \pi r^2 + \pi r\ell$
$= \pi(3^2) + \pi(3)(5)$
$= 9\pi + 15\pi$
$= 24\pi \text{ in.}^2$
$\approx 24(3.14) \approx 75.4 \text{ in.}^2$

EXAMPLE **Find the volume of the solid.**

a. Rectangular prism

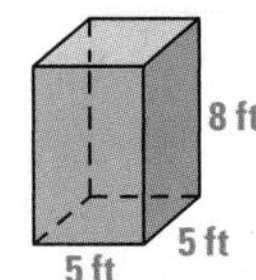

$V = Bh$

$= 25(8)$

$= 200 \text{ ft}^3$

b. Regular pyramid

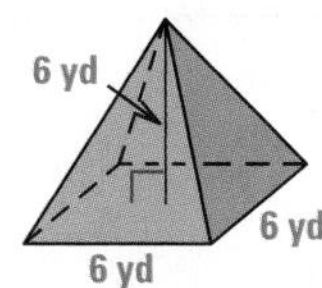

$V = \frac{1}{3}Bh$

$= \frac{1}{3}(36)6$

$= 72 \text{ yd}^3$

c. Cone

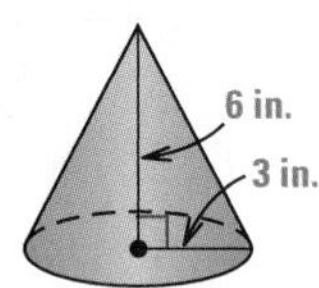

$V = \frac{1}{3}Bh$

$= \frac{1}{3}\pi(3^2)(6)$

$= 18\pi \text{ in.}^3$

$\approx 18(3.14) \approx 56.5 \text{ in.}^3$

PRACTICE

Find the surface area and volume of the solid. For spheres, cylinders, and cones, give your answers in terms of π and as decimals rounded to the nearest tenth.

1. Rectangular prism

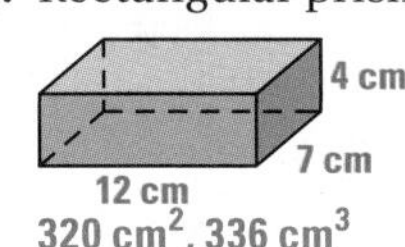

320 cm^2, 336 cm^3

2. Cylinder $72\pi \text{ in.}^2$ or 226.1 in.^2, $80\pi \text{ in.}^3$ or 251.2 in.^3

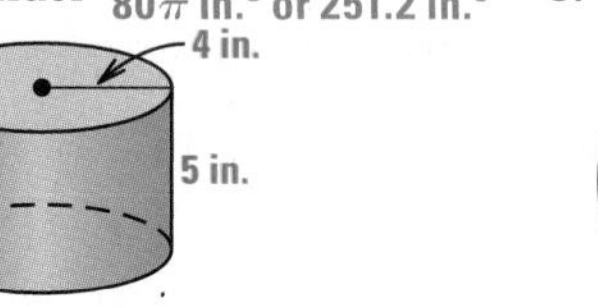

3. Sphere $900\pi \text{ m}^2$ or 2826 m^2, $4500\pi \text{ m}^3$ or $14{,}130 \text{ m}^3$

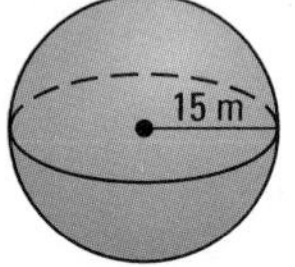

4. Cylinder $136\pi \text{ ft}^2$ or 427.0 ft^2, $208\pi \text{ ft}^3$ or 653.1 ft^3

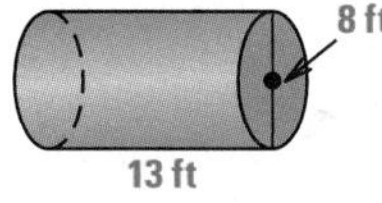

5. Cone $200\pi \text{ in.}^2$ or 628 in.^2, $320\pi \text{ in.}^3$ or 1004.8 in.^3

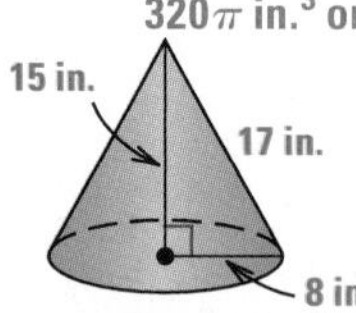

6. Rectangular prism

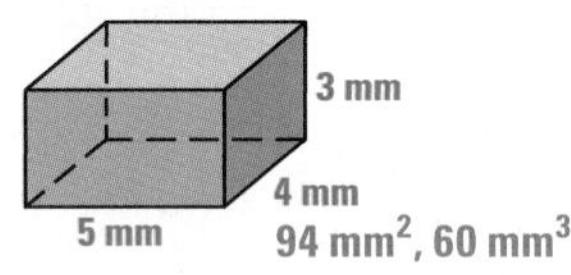

94 mm^2, 60 mm^3

7. Regular pyramid 96 in.^2, 48 in.^3

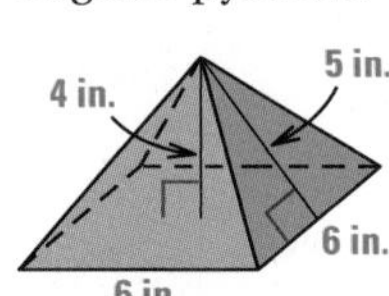

8. Sphere $100\pi \text{ in.}^2$ or 314 in.^2, $166\frac{2}{3}\pi \text{ in.}^3$ or 523.3 in.^3

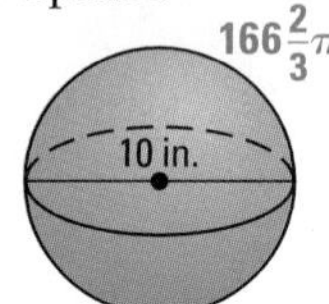

9. Cylinder

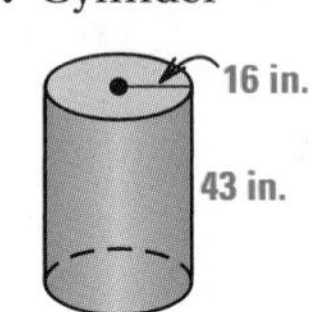

$1888\pi \text{ in.}^2$ or 5928.3 in.^2, $11{,}008\pi \text{ in.}^3$ or $34{,}565.1 \text{ in.}^3$

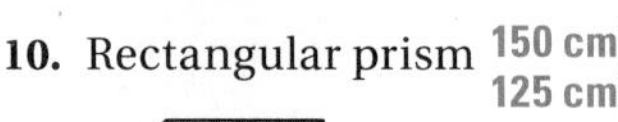

10. Rectangular prism 150 cm^2, 125 cm^3

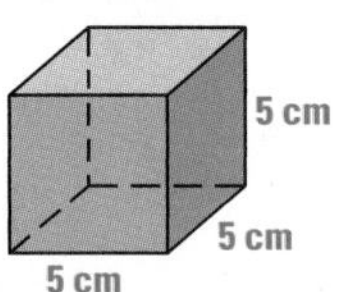

11. Cone $96\pi \text{ m}^2$ or 301.4 m^2, $96\pi \text{ m}^3$ or 301.4 m^3

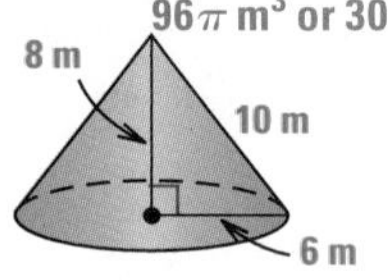

12. Regular pyramid 360 cm^2, 400 cm^3

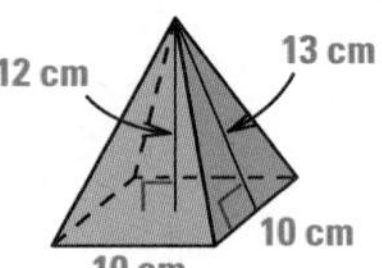

Converting Units of Measurement

The Table of Measures on page 956 gives many statements of equivalent measures. You can write two different conversion factors for each statement, as shown below. Each conversion factor is equal to 1.

Statement of Equivalent Measures	Conversion Factors	
100 cm = 1 m	$\frac{100\text{ cm}}{1\text{ m}} = 1$	$\frac{1\text{ m}}{100\text{ cm}} = 1$

To convert from one unit of measurement to another, multiply by a conversion factor that will eliminate the starting unit and result in the desired unit.

Convert meters to centimeters:

Use $\frac{100\text{ cm}}{1\text{ m}}$.

$3\text{ m} \times \frac{100\text{ cm}}{1\text{ m}} = 300\text{ cm}$

Convert centimeters to meters:

Use $\frac{1\text{ m}}{100\text{ cm}}$.

$400\text{ cm} \times \frac{1\text{ m}}{100\text{ cm}} = 4\text{ m}$

Sometimes you need to use more than one conversion factor.

EXAMPLE **Copy and complete: 2 d = _?_ sec**

STEP 1 **Find** the appropriate statements of equivalent measures.

24 h = 1 d, 60 min = 1 h, and 60 sec = 1 min

STEP 2 **Write** conversion factors.

$\frac{24\text{ h}}{1\text{ d}}, \frac{60\text{ min}}{1\text{ h}}$, and $\frac{60\text{ sec}}{1\text{ min}}$

STEP 3 **Multiply** by conversion factors to convert days to seconds.

$2\text{ d} \times \frac{24\text{ h}}{1\text{ d}} \times \frac{60\text{ min}}{1\text{ h}} \times \frac{60\text{ sec}}{1\text{ min}} = 172{,}800\text{ sec}$

▶ 2 d = 172,800 sec

PRACTICE

Copy and complete.

1. 300 sec = _?_ min 5
2. 2.6 g = _?_ kg 0.0026
3. 64 oz = _?_ lb 4
4. 4 gal = _?_ qt 16
5. 72 in. = _?_ ft 6
6. 94 mm = _?_ cm 9.4
7. 42 ft = _?_ yd 14
8. 5 d = _?_ h 120
9. 3 m = _?_ cm 300
10. 2 yd = _?_ in. 72
11. 70 L = _?_ mL 70,000
12. 10 mi = _?_ ft 52,800
13. 1.5 ton = _?_ lb 3000
14. 4500 mL = _?_ L 4.5
15. 15,000 mg = _?_ g 15
16. 1 mi = _?_ in. 63,360
17. 80 fl oz = _?_ qt 2.5
18. 5 gal = _?_ c 80
19. 1 km = _?_ mm 1,000,000
20. 20 c = _?_ qt 5
21. 8 h = _?_ sec 28,800

1.

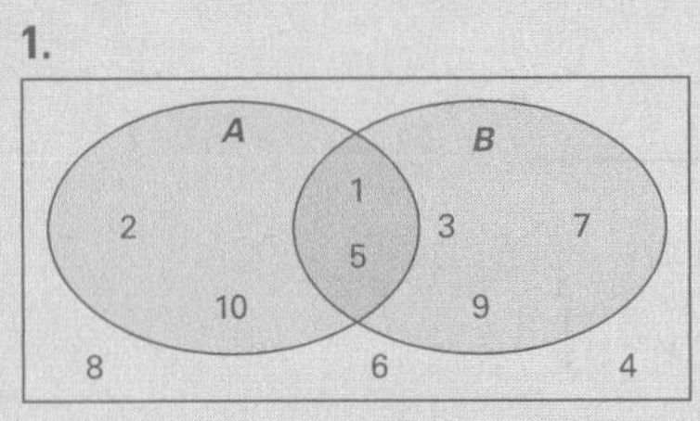

2.

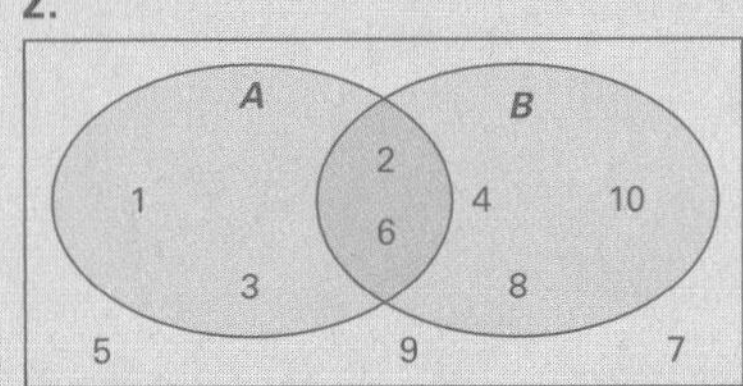

4a. Sometimes; there are whole numbers that are even and less than 10 that are factors of 6 such as 2 and 6, but there are also whole numbers that are even and less than 10 that are not factors of 6 such as 4, 8, and 10.

4b. Sometimes; there are factors of 6 that are less than 10 that are even such as 2 and 6, but there are also factors of 6 that are less than 10 that are odd such as 1 and 3.

SKILLS REVIEW HANDBOOK

Venn Diagrams and Logical Reasoning

A **Venn diagram** uses shapes to show how sets are related.

EXAMPLE **Draw a Venn diagram of the whole numbers less than 10 where set *A* consists of prime numbers and set *B* consists of even numbers.**

Whole numbers less than 10:
0, 1, 2, 3, 4, 5, 6, 7, 8, 9

Set *A*: 2, 3, 5, 7

Set *B*: 0, 2, 4, 6, 8

Both set *A* and set *B*: 2

Neither set *A* nor set *B*: 1, 9

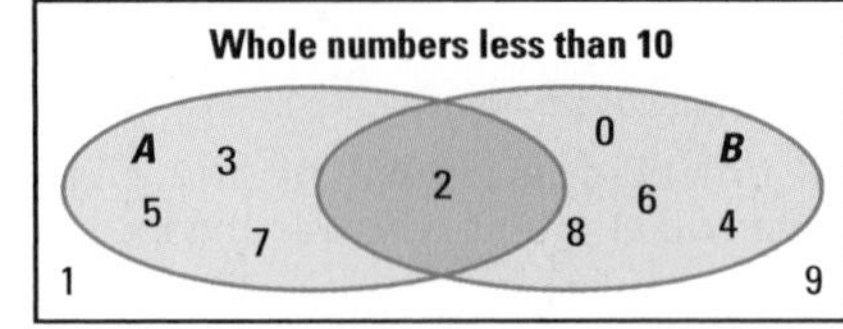

You can use a Venn diagram to answer questions about sets.

EXAMPLE **Use the Venn diagram above to answer the question.**

a. Is the statement below *true* or *false*? Explain.

No whole number less than 10 is prime.

▶ False. The whole number 2 is less than 10 and is prime.

b. Is the statement below *always, sometimes,* or *never* true? Explain.

A whole number less than 10 is either even or prime.

▶ Sometimes. Each of the numbers 0, 2, 3, 4, 5, 6, 7, and 8 are either even or prime, but the numbers 1 and 9 are not even and not prime.

PRACTICE

Draw a Venn diagram of the sets described. 1, 2. See margin.

1. Of the whole numbers less than 10, set *A* consists of factors of 10 and set *B* consists of odd numbers.
2. Of the whole numbers less than 10, set *A* consists of factors of 6 and set *B* consists of even numbers.

Use the Venn diagrams you drew in Exercises 1 and 2 to answer the question.

3. Are the following statements *true* or *false*? Explain.
   a. *If a whole number less than 10 is odd, then it must be a factor of 10.*
   b. *A whole number less than 10 that is a factor of 10 must be odd.*
4. Are the following statements *always, sometimes,* or *never* true? Explain. a, b. See margin.
   a. *A whole number that is even and less than 10 is a factor of 6.*
   b. *A factor of 6 that is less than 10 is even.*

3a. False; there are whole numbers less than 10 that are odd but are not factors of 10, such as 3, 7, and 9.
3b. False; there is a whole number less than 10 that is a factor of 10 but is not odd, 2.

Counting Methods

There are several methods for counting the number of possibilities in a situation.

EXAMPLE **Make a list to find the number of possible lunch specials.**

Lunch Special $6.95	
Choose 1 soup and 1 sandwich.	
Soups	**Sandwiches**
Chicken	Turkey
Tomato	Tuna
	Cheese

Pair each soup with each sandwich.

Chicken soup with turkey sandwich

Chicken soup with tuna sandwich

Chicken soup with cheese sandwich

Tomato soup with turkey sandwich

Tomato soup with tuna sandwich

Tomato soup with cheese sandwich

Count the number of lunch specials in the list.

▶ There are 6 possible lunch specials.

EXAMPLE **Draw a tree diagram to find the number of possible lunch specials given the choices in the example above.**

Arrange the soups and sandwiches in a tree diagram.

Soup	Sandwich	Lunch
Chicken	Turkey	Chicken soup, turkey sandwich
	Tuna	Chicken soup, tuna sandwich
	Cheese	Chicken soup, cheese sandwich
Tomato	Turkey	Tomato soup, turkey sandwich
	Tuna	Tomato soup, tuna sandwich
	Cheese	Tomato soup, cheese sandwich

▶ There are 6 possible lunch specials.

Another way to count the number of possible lunch specials described in the examples above is to multiply. Since there are 2 choices of soup and 3 choices of sandwich, there are $2 \times 3 = 6$ possible lunch specials. This method uses the counting principle.

The Counting Principle

If one event can occur in m ways, and for each of these ways a second event can occur in n ways, then the number of ways that the two events can occur together is $m \cdot n$.

The counting principle can be extended to three or more events.

EXAMPLE **Greta must choose a 4-digit password for her cell phone mailbox. Use the counting principle to find the number of possible 4-digit passwords.**

For each of the 4 digits in the password, there are 10 choices: 0, 1, 2, 3, 4, 5, 6, 7, 8, and 9.

10 choices for first digit × 10 choices for second digit × 10 choices for third digit × 10 choices for fourth digit

$10 \times 10 \times 10 \times 10 = 10{,}000$

▶ There are 10,000 possible 4-digit passwords.

PRACTICE

In Exercises 1–3, use the indicated counting method to answer the question.

1. Andrew, Bettina, and Carl are triplets. In how many different ways can the triplets stand in a row for a photo? (Make a list.) **6 ways**

2. The sign at the right shows the color and size choices for school T-shirts. How many different types of school T-shirts are available? (Draw a tree diagram.) **12 types of T-shirts**

3. A 3-letter monogram consists of the first letter of a person's first name, middle name, and last name. For example, Matthew David Weaver's monogram is MDW. How many different 3-letter monograms are possible? (Use the counting principle.) **17,576 3-letter monograms**

School T-Shirts $9.99	
Choose 1 color and 1 size.	
Colors:	**Sizes:**
Black, Gold, or White	S, M, L, or XL

In Exercises 4–8, answer the question using any counting method you choose.

4. How many different pizzas with 2 different toppings are available for the large pizza special advertised at the right? **28 pizzas**

5. Lance must choose 4 characters for his computer password. Each character can be any letter A–Z or any digit 0–9. How many different computer passwords are possible? **1,679,616 computer passwords**

6. Mia must choose 3 whole numbers less than 50 for her locker combination. The numbers may be repeated. How many different locker combinations are possible? **125,000 locker combinations**

Large Pizza Special	
Any 2 toppings for $12.49	
Pepperoni	Black olive
Sausage	Green pepper
Ground beef	Red onion
Extra cheese	Mushroom

7. A restaurant offers a dinner special. You can choose a main course, a vegetable, and a salad from a choice of 6 main courses, 4 vegetables, and 3 salads. How many different dinners are available? **72 dinners**

8. Each day Scott walks, rides the bus, or gets a ride to school. He has each of the same possibilities for getting home each day. How many combinations of travel to and from school does Scott have? **9 combinations of travel**

Bar Graphs

You can use a **bar graph** to display and compare data that are in categories.

SKILLS REVIEW HANDBOOK

EXAMPLE **Use the bar graph, which shows the medals won by the United States in the 2004 Summer Olympics. (a) Did the United States win more gold medals, silver medals, or bronze medals? (b) How many more silver medals than bronze medals did the United States win?**

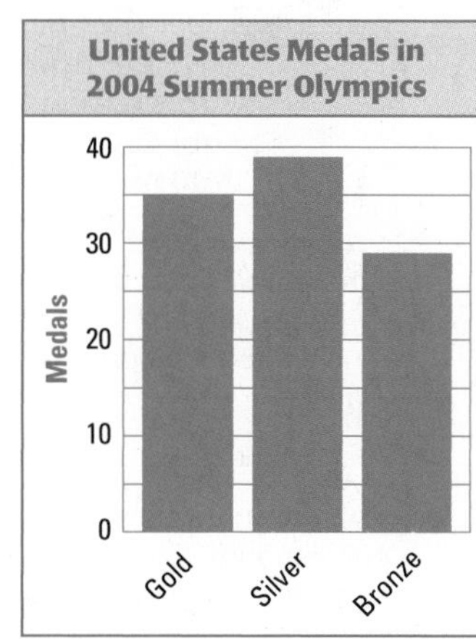

a. The longest bar on the graph is for silver medals won.

▸ The United States won more silver medals than any other type.

b. The bar for silver medals shows 39 silver medals won. The bar for bronze medals shows 29 bronze medals won.

$39 - 29 = 10$

▸ The United States won 10 more silver medals than bronze medals.

PRACTICE

In Exercises 1–3, use the bar graph above.

1. The United States won fewer of which type of medal than any other type? **bronze**
2. How many more silver medals than gold medals did the United States win? **4 more silver medals**
3. How many medals did the United States win altogether? **103 medals**

In Exercises 4–11, use the bar graph below, which shows the top medal-winning countries in the 2002 Winter Olympics.

4. Which country won the most medals? How many medals did it win? **Germany; 37 medals**
5. How many medals did Norway win? **25 medals**
6. Which two countries won 17 medals each? **Canada and Austria**
7. Which country won the same number of medals as France? **Switzerland**
8. How many countries won more than 15 medals? **5 countries**
9. Which country won twice as many medals as Austria? **United States**
10. How many medals did Russia and Italy win altogether? **26 medals**
11. How many medals did the top 3 medal-winning countries win? **96 medals**

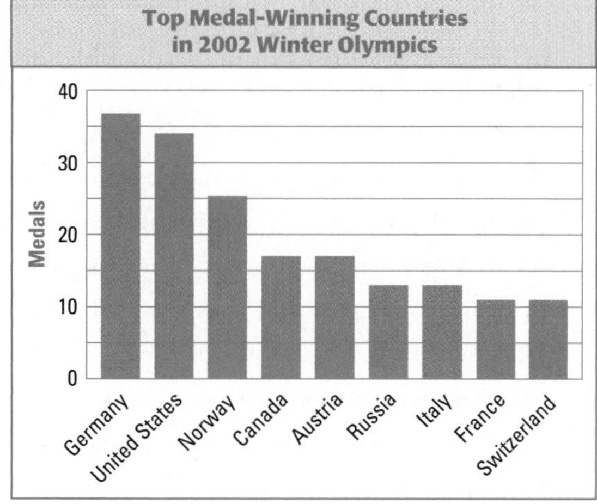

Line Graphs

You can use a **line graph** to show how numerical data change over time.

EXAMPLE **Use the line graph, which shows Charlie's weight from birth to 5 years old. (a) How much weight did Charlie gain in 5 years? (b) At what age did Charlie weigh 30 pounds? (c) In which year did Charlie gain the most weight?**

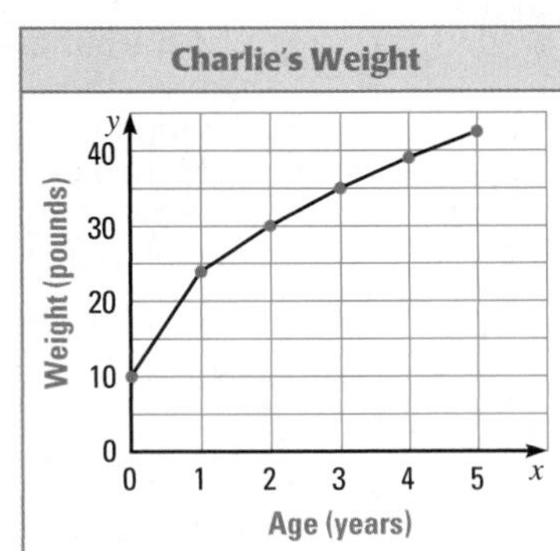

a. The lowest point on the graph shows that Charlie weighed 10 pounds at birth. The highest point on the graph shows he weighed 42.5 pounds at age 5.

$42.5 - 10 = 32.5$

▶ Charlie gained 32.5 pounds in 5 years.

b. The point on the graph to the right of 30 on the weight axis corresponds to an age of 2.

▶ Charlie weighed 30 pounds at age 2.

c. The graph is steepest from birth to age 1.

▶ Charlie gained the most weight in his first year.

PRACTICE

In Exercises 1–5, use the line graph above.

1. How much did Charlie weigh on his first birthday? about 24 lb
2. How old was Charlie when he weighed 40 pounds? about 4.2 years old
3. In which year did Charlie gain the least weight? between ages 4 and 5
4. How much weight did Charlie gain his first year? about 14 lb
5. How much weight did Charlie gain from age 1 to age 4? about 15 lb

In Exercises 6–14, use the line graph, which shows Abby's height from birth to 4 years old.

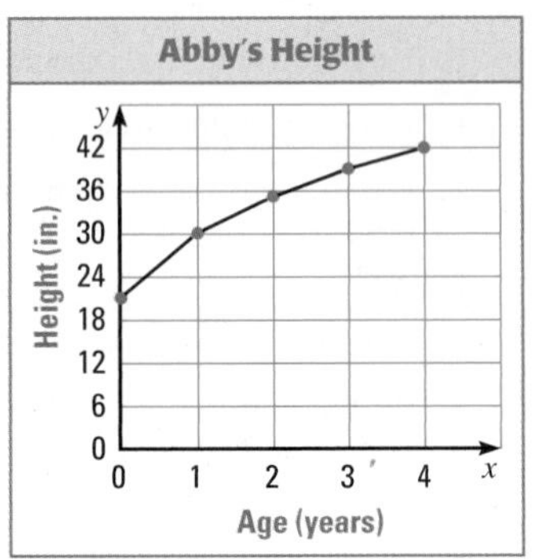

6. How tall was Abby when she was born? about 21 in.
7. How old was Abby when she was 35 inches tall? about 2 years old
8. In which year did Abby grow the most? her first year
9. In which year did Abby grow the least? between ages 3 and 4
10. How many inches did Abby grow from age 3 to age 4? about 3 in.
11. In which year did Abby grow 5 inches? between ages 1 and 2
12. How many inches did Abby grow in 4 years? about 21 in.
13. At what age was Abby's height double her height at birth? about 4 yr
14. If Abby maintains the same growth rate from age 4 to age 5 that she had from age 3 to age 4, how tall will she be when she is 5? about 45 in.

Circle Graphs

You can use a **circle graph** to display data as sections of a circle. The entire circle represents all of the data. The sections of the circle may be labeled using the actual data or the data expressed as fractions, decimals, or percents. When the data are expressed as fractions, decimals, or percents, the sum of the data is 1.

EXAMPLE **Use the circle graph, which shows the string musicians in a college orchestra. (a) What percent of the string musicians in the orchestra play the cello? (b) Which instrument do almost half the string musicians in the orchestra play?**

String Musicians

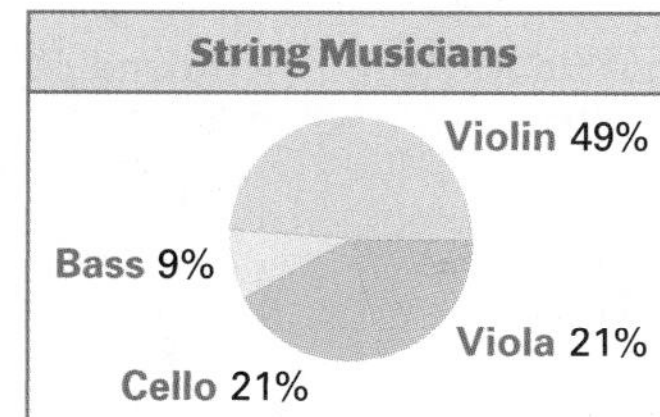

a. The cello section of the circle is labeled 21%.

▶ Of the string musicians in the orchestra, 21% play cello.

b. The violin section of the circle is labeled 49%, which is almost 50%. Also, the violin section of the circle is almost half the total area of the circle.

▶ Almost half of the string musicians in the orchestra play the violin.

PRACTICE

In Exercises 1–4, use the circle graph above.

1. What percent of the string musicians in the orchestra play the bass? 9%
2. How does the number of string musicians who play the viola compare with the number of string musicians who play the cello? They are equal.
3. The violinists are divided evenly into two groups, first violin and second violin. What percent of the string musicians are in each of these groups? 24.5%
4. If there are 57 string musicians in the orchestra, how many musicians play each type of instrument? 28 play violin, 12 play cello, 12 play viola, and 5 play bass

In Exercises 5–10, use the circle graph, which shows the types of instruments played by musicians in a college band.

Band Musicians

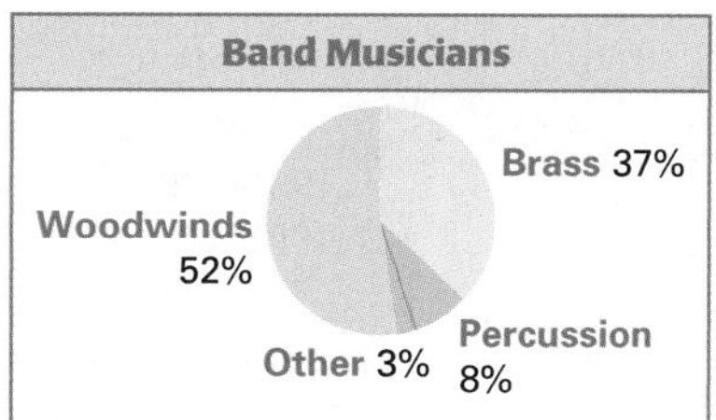

5. What percent of the musicians in the band play a brass instrument? 37%
6. Which type of instrument do 8% of the musicians in the band play? percussion
7. Which type of instrument do more than half of the musicians in the band play? woodwinds

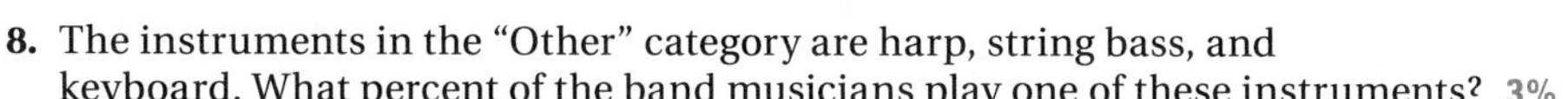

8. The instruments in the “Other” category are harp, string bass, and keyboard. What percent of the band musicians play one of these instruments? 3%
9. In this band, which type of instrument is played by about 5 times as many musicians as play percussion instruments? brass
10. There are 91 musicians in the band. How many more musicians play a woodwind than play a percussion instrument? 40 more musicians

Problem Solving Strategies

The following are strategies that you can use to solve problems.

Strategy	When to use	How to use
Draw a diagram	Draw a diagram when a problem involves any relationships that you can represent visually.	Draw a diagram that shows the given information. Label any unknowns in your diagram and look for relationships between givens and unknowns.
Look for a pattern	Look for a pattern when a problem includes a series of numbers or diagrams that you need to analyze.	Look for a pattern in any given information. Apply, extend, or generalize the pattern to help you solve the problem.
Guess, check, and revise	Guess, check, and revise when you need a place to start or you want to see what happens for a particular number.	Make a reasonable guess. Check to see if your guess solves the problem. If it does not, revise your guess and check again.
Act it out	Act out a problem that involves any relationships that you can represent with physical objects and movement.	Act out the problem, using objects described in the problem or other items that represent those objects.
Make a list or table	Make a list or table when you need to record, generate, or organize information.	Generate a list systematically, accounting for all possibilities. Look for relationships across rows or down columns within a table.
Solve a simpler or related problem	Solve a simpler or related problem when a problem seems difficult and can be made easier by using simpler numbers or conditions.	Think of a way to make the problem easier. Solve the simpler or related problem. Use what you learned to help you solve the original problem.
Work backward	Work backward when a problem gives you an end result and you need to find beginning conditions.	Work backward from the given information until you solve the problem. Work forward through the problem to check your answer.
Break into parts	Break into parts when a problem cannot be solved all at once, but can be solved in parts or stages.	Break the problem into parts and solve each part. Put the answers together to help you solve the original problem.

EXAMPLE **Fletcher baked brownies in a rectangular pan that measures 9 inches by 13 inches. He wants to cut rectangular brownies that are at least 2 inches on each side, with all brownies the same size. What is the greatest number of brownies Fletcher can cut?**

Draw a diagram of the rectangular pan. Label the sides with their lengths. Think about each side of the rectangle.

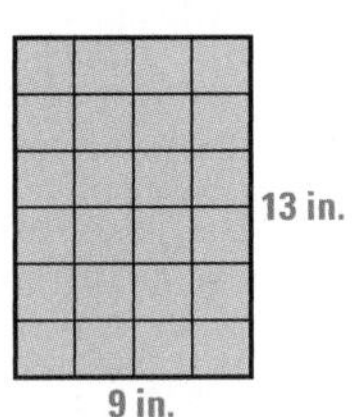

$9 \div 2 = 4.5$, so cut 4 brownies along the 9 inch side.
Check: $9 \div 4 = 2.25$, and $2.25 > 2$.

$13 \div 2 = 6.5$, so cut 6 brownies along the 13 inch side.
Check: $13 \div 6 \approx 2.17$, and $2.17 > 2$.

Use your diagram to count the brownies: $4 \times 6 = 24$.

▸ The greatest number of brownies Fletcher can cut is 24.

PRACTICE

Person	Party expenses
Barb	$11 for drinks
Bonnie	$15 for food
Pam	$6 for invitations
Holly	$8 for decorations

1. Four friends hosted a party. The table shows the amount of money each friend spent. The friends want to share the party expenses equally, and Pam will pay the entire amount she owes to one person. Who owes money to whom? See margin.

2. Six people can be seated at a rectangular table, with one person at each end. How many people can be seated at five of these tables if they are placed end to end? 22 people

3. Bob is 55 years old. In 5 years, Bob will be twice as old as his son. How old is Bob's son? 25 years old

4. Maddie and Rob are sharing a pack of 25 pens. Maddie offers to let Rob have 3 pens for every 2 pens she gets. If they use the entire package of pens, how many pens will each person get? Rob: 15 pens, Maddie: 10 pens

5. In how many different ways can you make $.50 in change using quarters, dimes, and nickels? 10 ways

6. The diagram shows two cuts through the center of a pizza. How many cuts through the center are needed to divide a pizza into 12 equal pieces? 6 cuts

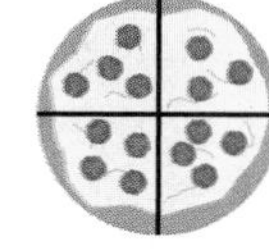

7. Deb is flying to Seattle. Her flight leaves at 4:15 P.M. She wants to arrive at the airport 2 hours early to check in and get through security. The taxi ride from her office to the airport takes about 30 minutes. What time should Deb ask the taxi driver to pick her up at the office? 1:45 P.M.

8. Dan wants to enclose a rectangular area with a fence. He has 12 fence posts to use, and the fence posts will be placed 10 feet apart. The diagram shows a possible shape for the area. Find another shape that would use all the fence posts, placed 10 feet apart, and would increase the area by 100 square feet. a square with 4 posts on each side

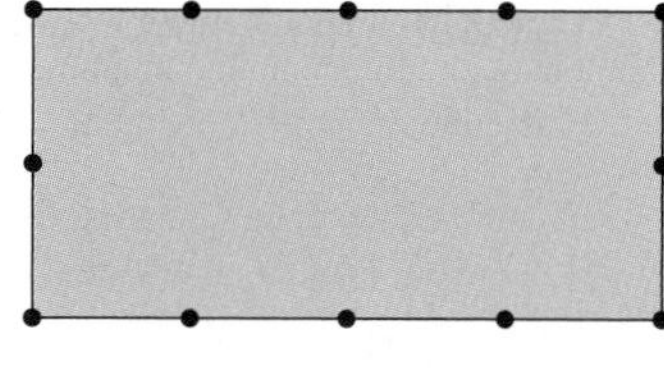

9. A soccer league has a 7 week season, and there are 7 teams in the league. Each team plays a game with every other team once during the season. How many soccer games must be played each week of the season? 3 soccer games per week

10. Julia is setting up a display of cracker boxes at a grocery store. She wants one box in the top row, two boxes in the second row down, three boxes in the third row down, and so on, as shown. Each box is 8 inches tall, and her display will be 6 feet tall. How many cracker boxes will be in the display? 45 cracker boxes

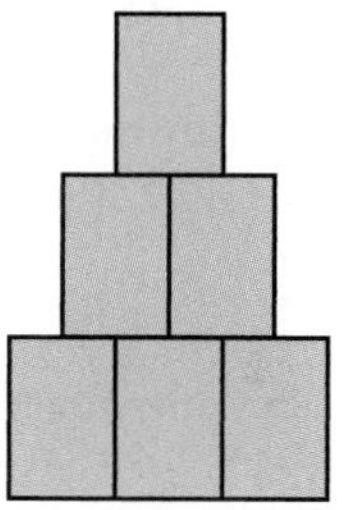

11. Five friends line up for tetherball. William is first in line, Mac is between Quinn and Benjamin, and Nate is next to William and Benjamin. Which friend is last in line? Quinn

12. The 4 members of the Buckner family usually drink 3 gallons of milk altogether each week. For 12 weeks in the summer, they will have a fifth family member staying with them. How many gallons of milk would you expect the 5 family members to drink over the 12 weeks? 45 gal

1. Pam owes $4 that she can pay to Bonnie who is owed a total of $5. Holly should pay both Barb and Bonnie $1.

SKILLS REVIEW HANDBOOK

29. *Sample answer:* You know the temperature in Quito in degrees Celsius and the temperature in Miami in degrees Fahrenheit. You need to find out which one is greater.

30. *Sample answer:* You know the rate and time Katherine walked each day. You need to find out the distance she walked during the 2 days.

32.

Input	2	4	6	8
Output	7.5	10	12.5	15

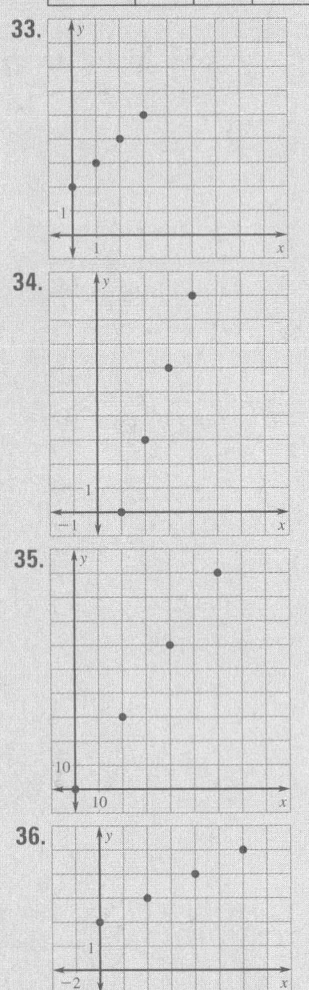

Extra Practice

Chapter 1

Evaluate the expression.

1.1 **1.** $k + 9$ when $k = 7$ 16 **2.** $21 - x$ when $x = 3$ 18 **3.** $3.5 + t$ when $t = 0.9$ 4.4 **4.** $y - \frac{3}{8}$ when $y = \frac{7}{12}$ $\frac{5}{24}$

5. $\frac{m}{4}$ when $m = 9.6$ 2.4 **6.** $1.5t$ when $t = 2.3$ 3.45 **7.** z^3 when $z = \frac{2}{3}$ $\frac{8}{27}$ **8.** p^4 when $p = 0.2$ 0.0016

1.2 **9.** $25 - 7 + 8$ 26 **10.** $67 - 3 \cdot 4$ 55 **11.** $8^2 \div 4 + 12$ 28 **12.** $9 + 6 \div 3$ 11

13. $\frac{3^3 - 7}{2}$ 10 **14.** $\frac{1}{3}(7 - 5.5)^2$ 0.75 **15.** $3 + 4(3 + 24)$ 111 **16.** $\frac{3}{5}[27 - (2 + 5)]^2$ 240

1.3 **Translate the verbal phrase into an expression.**

17. $\frac{3}{4}$ of a number m $\frac{3}{4}m$

18. the quotient of a number x and 7 $\frac{x}{7}$

19. the difference of a number y and 3 $y - 3$

20. 6 more than 3 times a number n $3n + 6$

1.3 **Write an expression for the situation.**

21. Number of minutes left in a 45 minute class after m minutes have gone by $45 - m$

22. Number of meters in c centimeters $\frac{c}{100}$

1.4 **Write an equation or an inequality.**

23. The product of 12 and the difference of a number r and 4 is 72. $12 \cdot (r - 4) = 72$

24. The difference of a number q and 18 is greater than 10 and less than 15. $10 < q - 18 < 15$

1.4 **Solve the equation using mental math.**

25. $d - 13 = 25$ 38 **26.** $12z = 96$ 8 **27.** $23 - m = 7$ 16 **28.** $\frac{k}{6} = 12$ 72

1.5 **In Exercises 29 and 30, identify what you know and what you need to find out. You do *not* need to solve the problem.** 29, 30. See margin.

29. One day the temperature in Quito, Ecuador, was 20°C. The temperature in Miami, Florida was 75°F. Which temperature was higher?

30. On Monday, Katherine walked at a rate of 0.08 mile per minute for 40 minutes. On Tuesday, she walked at a rate of 0.07 mile per minute for 50 minutes. How far did Katherine walk altogether?

1.6 **31.** Identify the domain and range of the function.
domain: 3, 4, 5, 6; range: 9, 11, 13, 15

Input	3	4	5	6
Output	9	11	13	15

1.6 **32.** The domain of the function $y = 1.25x + 5$ is 2, 4, 6, and 8. Make a table for the function. Identify the range of the function.
See margin for table; range: 7.5, 10, 12.5, 15.

1.7 **Graph the function.**
33–36. See margin.

33. $y = x + 2$; domain: 0, 1, 2, and 3

34. $y = 3x - 3$; domain: 1, 2, 3, and 4

35. $y = 1.5x$; domain: 0, 20, 40, and 60

36. $y = \frac{1}{4}x + 2$; domain: 0, 4, 8, and 12

EXTRA PRACTICE

Chapter 2

2.1 Graph the numbers on a number line. Then tell which number is greater. 1–4. See margin for art.

1. 0 and −4 0
2. 2 and −2 2
3. −5 and −3 −3
4. −6 and 4 4

2.1 Tell whether each number in the list is a whole number, an integer, or a rational number. Then order the numbers from least to greatest. 5–7. See margin.

5. $0.25, -\frac{1}{8}, -\frac{1}{10}, -\frac{1}{5}$
6. $-2.5, -3, \frac{5}{2}, -\frac{9}{4}$
7. −4, 3, −5, 0

2.2 Find the sum.

8. $-6 + 10$ 4
9. $-25 + (-36)$ −61
10. $-75 + 58$ −17
11. $8 + (-15) + 7$ 0
12. $-2.8 + 4.3$ 1.5
13. $-8.2 + (-11.5)$ −19.7
14. $3\frac{2}{3} + \left(-5\frac{3}{8}\right)$ $-1\frac{17}{24}$
15. $-12\frac{3}{5} + 8\frac{1}{6}$ $-4\frac{13}{30}$

2.3 Find the difference.

16. $-17 - 20$ −37
17. $16 - (-50)$ 66
18. $-9 - (-12)$ 3
19. $\frac{4}{5} - \frac{1}{2}$ $\frac{3}{10}$
20. $-\frac{1}{2} - \frac{2}{3}$ $-1\frac{1}{6}$
21. $-\frac{1}{3} - \left(-\frac{3}{4}\right)$ $\frac{5}{12}$
22. $-6.4 - 15$ −21.4
23. $-12.8 - (-5.6)$ −7.2

2.3 Evaluate the expression when $x = 1.5$ and $y = -4$.

24. $y - x$ −5.5
25. $-y - (-x)$ 5.5
26. $x - (10 - y)$ −12.5
27. $-7 - (x - y)$ −12.5

2.4 Find the product.

28. $-\frac{2}{3}(-36)$ 24
29. $64\left(-\frac{5}{8}\right)$ −40
30. $-4.1(-3.5)$ 14.35
31. $(1.1)(-0.5)(-4)$ 2.2

2.4 Identify the property illustrated. 32–37. See margin.

32. $(-5)(8)(2) = (-5)(2)(8)$
33. $6 \cdot (7 \cdot 2) = (6 \cdot 7) \cdot 2$
34. $1(mn) = mn$
35. $0 \cdot (134) = 0$
36. $y \cdot (-1) = (-1) \cdot y$
37. $(-1)(-9) = 9$

2.5 Use the distributive property to write an equivalent expression.

38. $8(x + 4)$ $8x + 32$
39. $5(6 - y)$ $30 - 5y$
40. $(m + 7)(-8)$ $-8m - 56$
41. $-3(k - 14)$ $-3k + 42$
42. $\frac{3}{5}(-15r - 5)$ $-9r - 3$
43. $\frac{7}{12}(24s + 12)$ $14s + 7$
44. $(9v - 18)\frac{1}{3}$ $3v - 6$
45. $-\frac{5}{6}(-6w - 30)$ $5w + 25$

2.6 Find the quotient.

46. $-35 \div 7$ −5
47. $-92 \div (-4)$ 23
48. $36 \div \left(-\frac{3}{4}\right)$ −48
49. $-56 \div \left(-\frac{7}{8}\right)$ 64
50. $\frac{5}{9} \div (-5)$ $-\frac{1}{9}$
51. $-\frac{5}{12} \div \frac{1}{2}$ $-\frac{5}{6}$
52. $-\frac{4}{3} \div \frac{4}{3}$ −1
53. $-\frac{5}{6} \div \left(-\frac{6}{5}\right)$ $\frac{25}{36}$

2.7 Evaluate the expression.

54. $-\sqrt{36}$ −6
55. $\pm\sqrt{400}$ ±20
56. $\sqrt{6400}$ 80
57. $\pm\sqrt{144}$ ±12

2.7 Approximate the square root to the nearest integer.

58. $\sqrt{135}$ 12
59. $-\sqrt{75}$ −9
60. $-\sqrt{160}$ −13
61. $\sqrt{250}$ 16

EXTRA PRACTICE

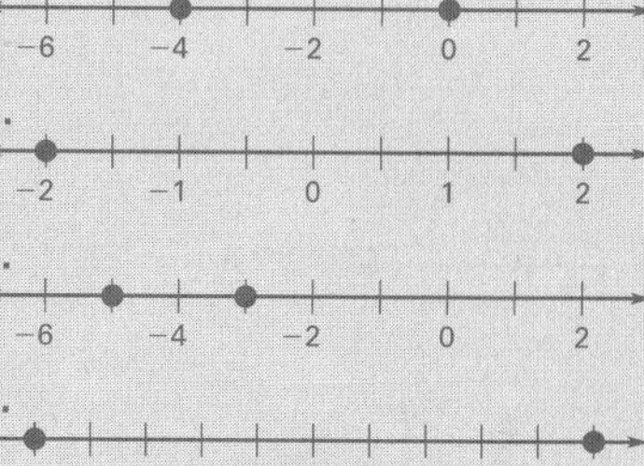

5. Each number is a rational number; $-\frac{1}{5}, -\frac{1}{8}, -\frac{1}{10}, 0.25$.

6. −3 is an integer, the rest are rational numbers; $-3, -2.5, -\frac{9}{4}, \frac{5}{2}$.

7. 3 and 0 are whole numbers, −4 and −5 are integers; −5, −4, 0, 3.

32. Commutative property of multiplication

33. Associative property of multiplication

34. Identity property of multiplication

35. Property of zero

36. Commutative property of multiplication

37. Property of −1

Chapter 4, p. 941

1.

2.

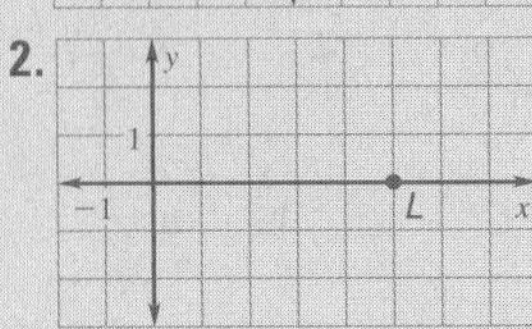

3.

4.

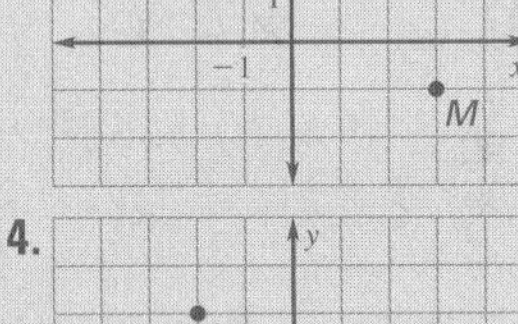

5.

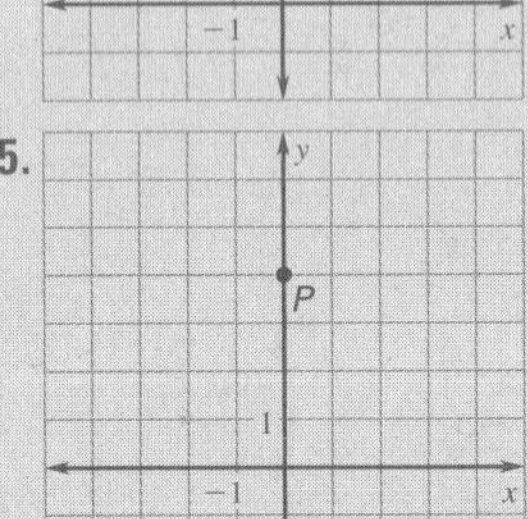

6.

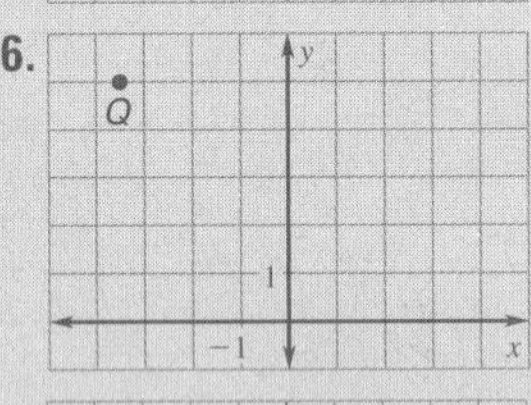

7.

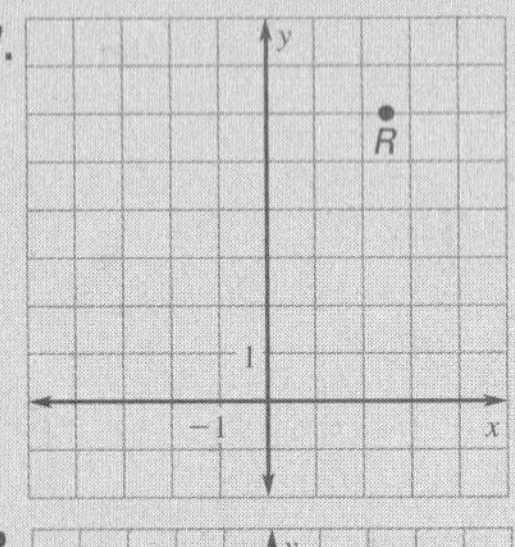

8.

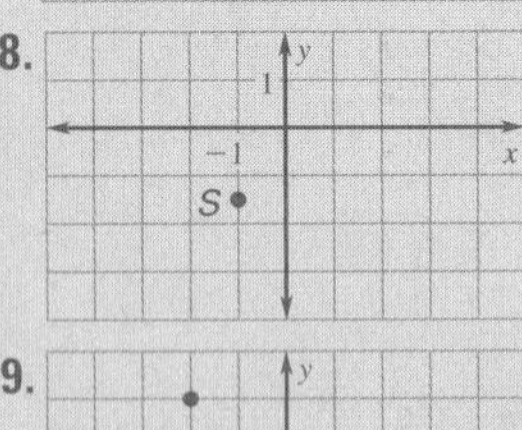

9.

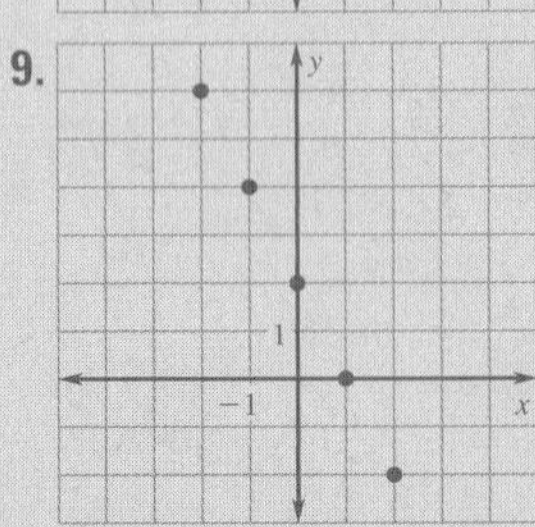

Chapter 3

EXTRA PRACTICE

Solve the equation. Check your solution.

3.1 **1.** $x + 4 = 20$ 16 **2.** $8 = m - 13$ 21 **3.** $t + 2 = -10$ -12 **4.** $z - 8 = -7$ 1

5. $7h = 63$ 9 **6.** $-4t = -44$ 11 **7.** $\frac{b}{4} = 13$ 52 **8.** $\frac{y}{-3} = 8$ -24

3.2 **9.** $4x + 3 = 27$ 6 **10.** $6m - 4 = 14$ 3 **11.** $50 = 7y - 6$ 8

12. $\frac{t}{4} - 3 = 9$ 48 **13.** $\frac{x}{7} + 3 = -2$ -35 **14.** $6p - 2p = 28$ 7

3.3 **15.** $6x + 3x + 8 = 35$ 3 **16.** $12w - 5 - 3w = 40$ 5 **17.** $4d - 3 - 2d = -15$ -6

18. $7m + 3(m + 2) = -24$ -3 **19.** $5x - 3(x - 5) = 13$ -1 **20.** $\frac{3}{4}(2y - 8) = 6$ 8

3.4 **21.** $8x - 4 = 3x + 6$ 2 **22.** $10 - 2x = 3x - 20$ 6 **23.** $5 - 5x = 14 - 8x$ 3

24. $3(2y - 5) = 4y - 7$ 4 **25.** $9 + 4y = 2(3 - y)$ $-\frac{1}{2}$ **26.** $3x - 3 = \frac{3}{4}(2x + 12)$ 8

3.5 **Solve the proportion. Check your solution.**

27. $\frac{7}{2} = \frac{x}{16}$ 56 **28.** $\frac{m}{9} = \frac{6}{27}$ 2 **29.** $\frac{z}{4} = \frac{48}{12}$ 16 **30.** $\frac{30}{50} = \frac{t}{10}$ 6

3.5 **Write the sentence as a proportion. Then solve the proportion.**

31. 5 is to 7 as 15 is to x. $\frac{5}{7} = \frac{15}{x}$; 21 **32.** 9 is to 3 as x is to 12. $\frac{9}{3} = \frac{x}{12}$; 36

33. g is to 9 as 16 is to 12. $\frac{g}{9} = \frac{16}{12}$; 12 **34.** 6 is to 18 as y is to 3. $\frac{6}{18} = \frac{y}{3}$; 1

3.6 **Solve the proportion. Check your solution.**

35. $\frac{12}{x} = \frac{6}{7}$ 14 **36.** $\frac{6x}{4} = \frac{18}{12}$ 1 **37.** $\frac{7}{x + 13} = \frac{4}{12}$ 8 **38.** $\frac{y + 5}{y} = \frac{10}{8}$ 20

39. $\frac{2x + 6}{x} = \frac{7}{2}$ 4 **40.** $\frac{3b}{5b - 7} = \frac{8}{11}$ 8 **41.** $\frac{8}{2x + 12} = \frac{6}{x + 8}$ -2 **42.** $\frac{4.8 - 2x}{8} = \frac{0.4 + x}{10}$ 1.6

3.7 **Use a proportion to answer the question.**

43. What percent of 96 is 12? 12.5% **44.** What number is 35% of 18? 6.3

45. 14 is 40% of what number? 35 **46.** What percent of 125 is 30? 24%

3.7 **Use the percent equation to answer the question.**

47. What number is 250% of 18? 45 **48.** What percent of 58 is 8.7? 15%

49. 30.1 is 35% of what number? 86 **50.** What number is 70% of 250? 175

3.8 **Solve the literal equation for x. Then use the solution to solve the specific equation.**

51. $ax - b = c$; $6x - 5 = 25$ $x = \frac{c + b}{a}$; 5 **52.** $a(b - x) = c$; $2(8 - x) = -6$ $x = b - \frac{c}{a}$; 11

3.8 **Write the equation so that y is a function of x.**

53. $5x + y = 10$ $y = -5x + 10$ **54.** $8x - 2y = 16$ $y = 4x - 8$ **55.** $7x + 3y = 6 - 5x$ $y = -4x + 2$ **56.** $21 = 6x + 7y$ $y = -\frac{6}{7}x + 3$

10.

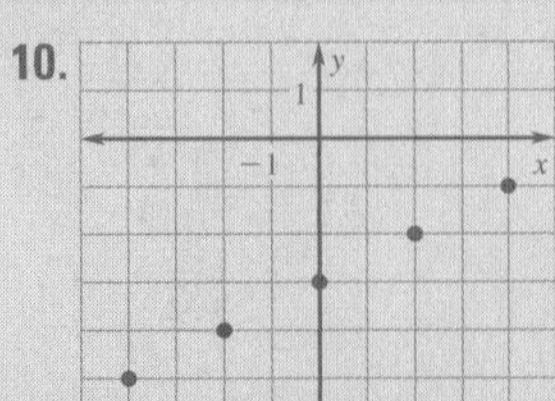

11.

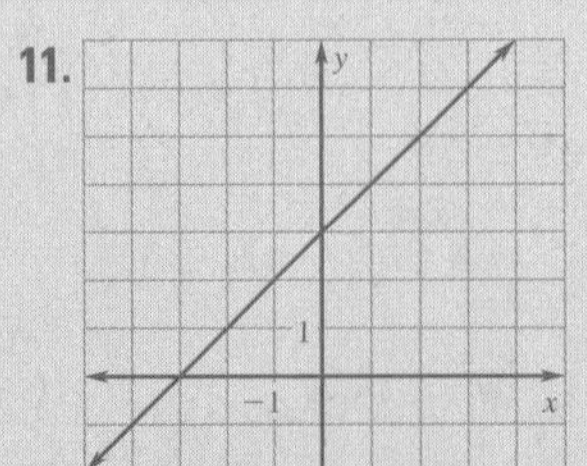

12.

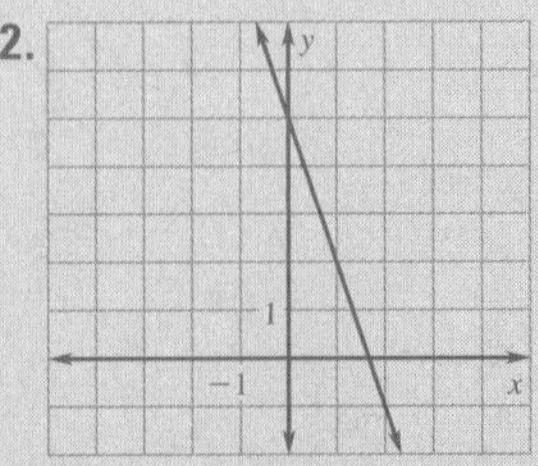

Chapter 4

4.1 Plot the point in a coordinate plane. *Describe* the location of the point. 1–8. See margin for art.

1. $K(-4, -2)$ Quadrant III **2.** $L(5, 0)$ on the x–axis **3.** $M(3, -1)$ Quadrant IV **4.** $N(-2, 2)$ Quadrant II

5. $P(0, 4)$ on the y-axis **6.** $Q(-3.5, 5)$ Quadrant II **7.** $R(2.5, 6)$ Quadrant I **8.** $S(-1, -1.5)$ Quadrant III

4.1 Graph the function with the given domain. Then identify the range of the function. 9, 10. See margin for art.

9. $y = -2x + 2$; domain: $-2, -1, 0, 1, 2$ range: $-2, 0, 2, 4, 6$ **10.** $y = \frac{1}{2}x - 3$; domain: $-4, -2, 0, 2, 4$ range: $-5, -4, -3, -2, -1$

4.2 Graph the equation. 11–18. See margin.

11. $y - x = 3$ **12.** $y + 3x = 5$ **13.** $y - 4x = 10$ **14.** $y = 4$

15. $2x - y = 0$ **16.** $3x + y = 0$ **17.** $3x + 2y = -6$ **18.** $x = 0.5$

4.3 Find the x-intercept and the y-intercept of the graph of the equation. 19–22. See margin.

19. $2x - y = 12$ **20.** $-5x - 2y = 20$ **21.** $-4x + 1.5y = 4$ **22.** $y = \frac{3}{4}x - 15$

4.3 Graph the equation. Label the points where the line crosses the axes. 23–26. See margin.

23. $y = 3x - 6$ **24.** $4x + 5y = -20$ **25.** $\frac{2}{3}x + \frac{1}{2}y = 10$ **26.** $0.3x - y = 6$

4.4 Find the slope of the line that passes through the points.

27. (4, 2) and (6, 8) 3 **28.** (−3, 0) and (2, −5) −1 **29.** (−5, 3) and (−8, 10) $-\frac{7}{3}$

30. (9, 4) and (0, 1) $\frac{1}{3}$ **31.** (−2, 5) and (−2, 10) no slope **32.** (6, −4) and (4, −4) 0

4.5 Identify the slope and y-intercept of the line with the given equation. 33–36. See margin.

33. $y = 7x + 8$ **34.** $y = 10x - 6$ **35.** $y = 3 - 4x$ **36.** $y = x$

4.5 Rewrite the equation in slope-intercept form. Then identify the slope and the y-intercept of the line. 37–40. See margin.

37. $2x + y = 8$ **38.** $10x - y = 20$ **39.** $5x + 2y = 10$ **40.** $-2x - y = 3$

4.5 Graph the equation. 41–44. See margin.

41. $y = 2x - 4$ **42.** $y = -\frac{3}{4}x + 1$ **43.** $2x + y = 1$ **44.** $-2x + 3y = -9$

4.6 Graph the direct variation equation. 45–52. See margin.

45. $y = 2x$ **46.** $y = -x$ **47.** $y = 4x$ **48.** $5x + y = 0$

49. $x - 2y = 0$ **50.** $3x + y = 0$ **51.** $2y = 9x$ **52.** $y - \frac{5}{4}x = 0$

4.7 Find the value of x so that the function has the given value.

53. $f(x) = -7x - 3$; -17 2 **54.** $g(x) = 5x - 4$; 12 $\frac{16}{5}$ **55.** $t(x) = 3x + 1$; -11 −4

4.7 Graph the function. Compare the graph with the graph of $f(x) = x$. 56–59. See margin.

56. $m(x) = x - 2$ **57.** $t(x) = x + 4$ **58.** $z(x) = 6x$ **59.** $h(x) = -2x$

EXTRA PRACTICE

16.
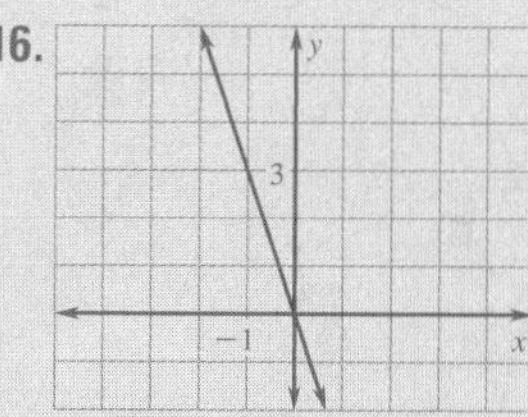

17.
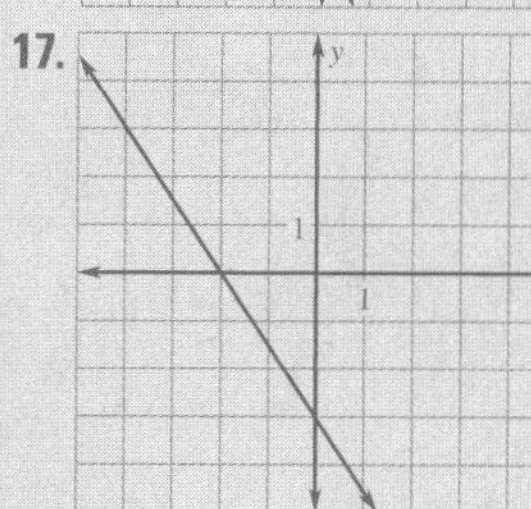

18.
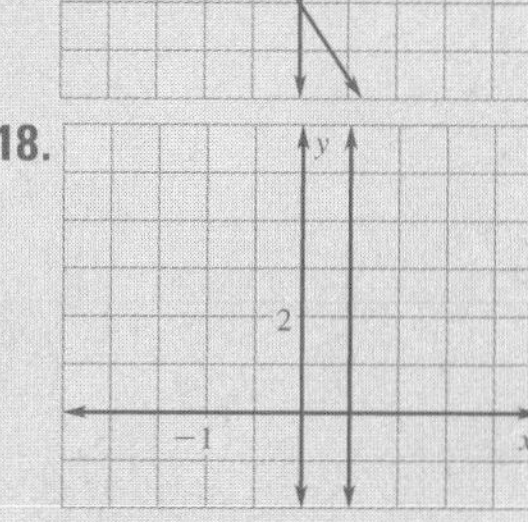

19. x-int: 6, y-int: −12
20. x-int: −4, y-int: −10
21. x-int: −1, y-int: $\frac{8}{3}$
22. x-int: 20, y-int: −15
23–26. See Additional Answers beginning on p. AA1.
33. slope: 7, y-intercept: 8
34. slope: 10, y-intercept: −6
35. slope: −4, y-intercept: 3
36. slope: 1, y-intercept: 0
37. $y = -2x + 8$; slope: −2, y-intercept: 8
38. $y = 10x - 20$; slope: 10, y-intercept: −20
39. $y = -\frac{5}{2}x + 5$; slope: $-\frac{5}{2}$, y-intercept: 5
40. $y = -2x - 3$; slope: −2, y-intercept: −3
41–52, 56–59. See Additional Answers beginning on p. AA1.

13.
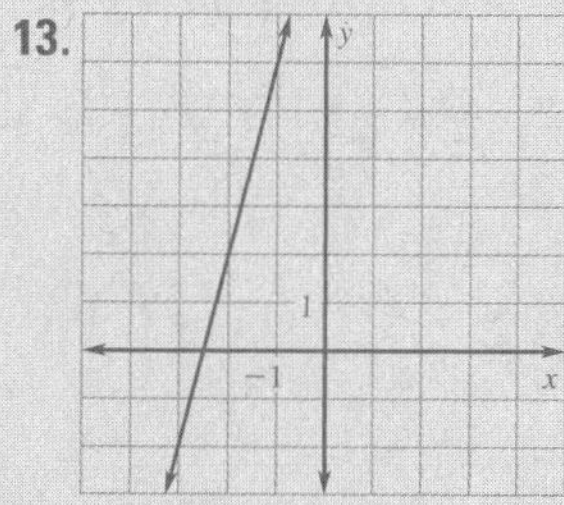

14.
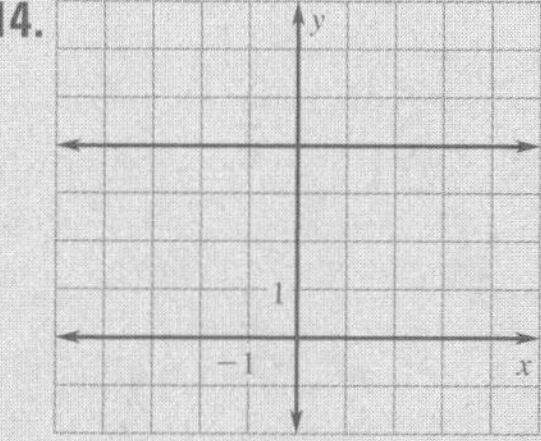

15.
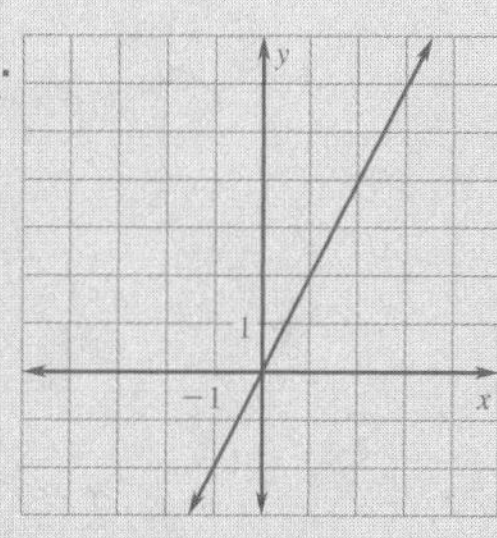

EXTRA PRACTICE

Chapter 5

5.1 Write an equation of the line with the given slope and y-intercept.

1. slope: 3, y-intercept: 6 — $y = 3x + 6$
2. slope: -2, y-intercept: 4 — $y = -2x + 4$
3. slope: 5, y-intercept: -1 — $y = 5x - 1$
4. slope: -1, y-intercept: -3 — $y = -x - 3$
5. slope: $\frac{1}{2}$, y-intercept: -5 — $y = \frac{1}{2}x - 5$
6. slope: $-\frac{7}{10}$, y-intercept: 8 — $y = -\frac{7}{10}x + 8$

5.2 Write an equation of the line that passes through the given point and has the given slope m.

7. $(3, 8)$; $m = 2$ — $y = 2x + 2$
8. $(-1, 5)$; $m = -4$ — $y = -4x + 1$
9. $(-6, 3)$; $m = \frac{2}{3}$ — $y = \frac{2}{3}x + 7$

5.2 Write an equation of the line that passes through the given points.

10. $(2, 4)$, $(5, 13)$ — $y = 3x - 2$
11. $(1, -2)$, $(-2, 13)$ — $y = -5x + 3$
12. $\left(2, \frac{1}{3}\right)$, $(6, 3)$ — $y = \frac{2}{3}x - 1$

5.3 Graph the equation. 13–15. See margin.

13. $y - 3 = -3(x + 4)$
14. $y + 5 = -2(x - 1)$
15. $y - 6 = \frac{2}{3}(x - 3)$

5.3 Write an equation in point-slope form of the line that passes through the given points. 16–18. See margin.

16. $(-4, 2)$, $(-2, 16)$
17. $(3, 9)$, $(-7, 4)$
18. $(10, -2)$, $(12, -6)$

5.4 Write an equation in standard form of the line that passes through the given point and has the given slope m or that passes through the two given points.

19. $(2, 7)$, $m = -4$ — $4x + y = 15$
20. $(5, 11)$, $m = 3$ — $3x - y = 4$
21. $(1, -2)$, $(-2, 4)$ — $2x + y = 0$

5.5 Write an equation of the line that passes through the given point and is parallel to the given line.

22. $(5, 4)$, $y = 3x + 5$ — $y = 3x - 11$
23. $(-3, -7)$, $y = -5x - 2$ — $y = -5x - 22$
24. $(8, -3)$, $y = \frac{3}{4}x + 5$ — $y = \frac{3}{4}x - 9$

5.5 Write an equation of the line that passes through the given point and is perpendicular to the given line.

25. $(-12, -2)$, $y = 3x + 2$ — $y = -\frac{1}{3}x - 6$
26. $(15, -11)$, $y = \frac{3}{5}x - 8$ — $y = -\frac{5}{3}x + 14$
27. $(7, -6)$, $4x + 6y = 7$ — $y = \frac{3}{2}x - \frac{33}{2}$

5.6 Make a scatter plot of the data in the table. Draw a line of fit. Write an equation of the line. 28, 29. See margin for art.

28.

x	1	2	3	3.5	4	4.5	5
y	20	35	40	55	60	45	60

Sample answer: $y = 9.2x + 14.7$

29.

x	10	20	30	40	50	60
y	55	45	45	40	35	20

Sample answer: $y = -0.6x + 61$

5.7 Make a scatter plot of the data. Find the equation of the best-fitting line. Approximate the value of y for $x = 7$. 30–31. See margin for art.

30.

x	0	2	4	6	8
y	0.5	3	4	5.5	7

$y = 0.78x + 0.9$; 6.36

31.

x	0	1	3	6	8
y	5	8	12	15	14

$y = 1.1x + 6.7$; 14.4

942 Student Resources

13.

14.

15.

16–18. Sample answers are given.

16. $y - 2 = 7(x + 4)$

17. $y - 9 = \frac{1}{2}(x - 3)$

18. $y + 2 = -2(x - 10)$

28.

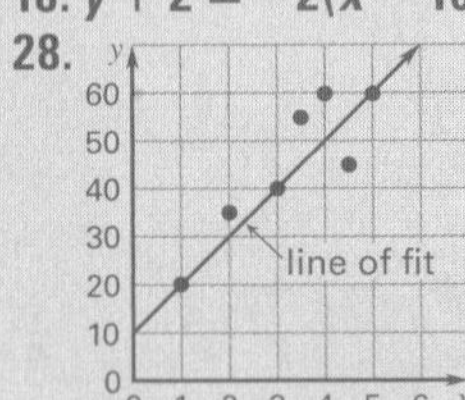

29.

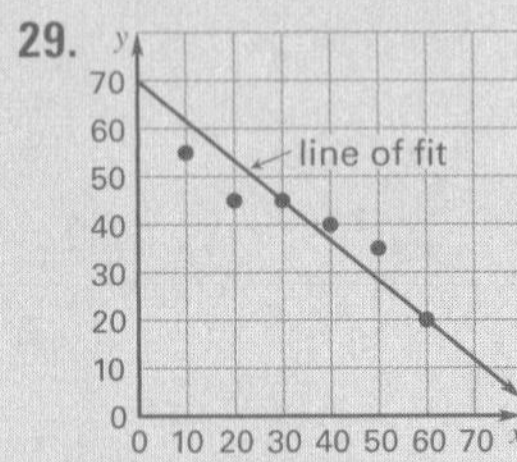

30.

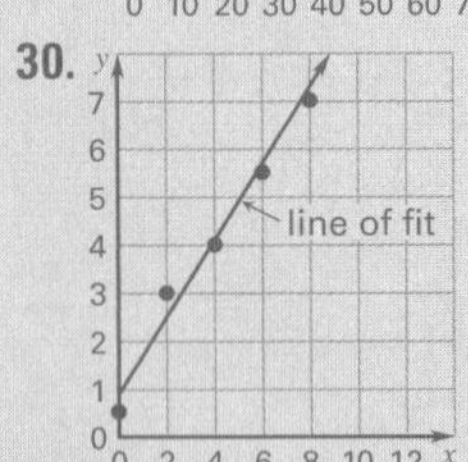

31.

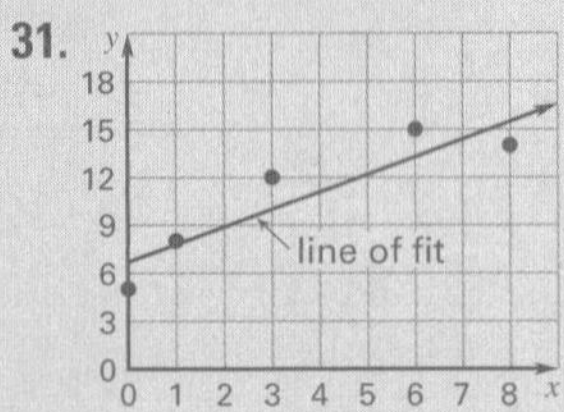

Chapter 6, p. 943

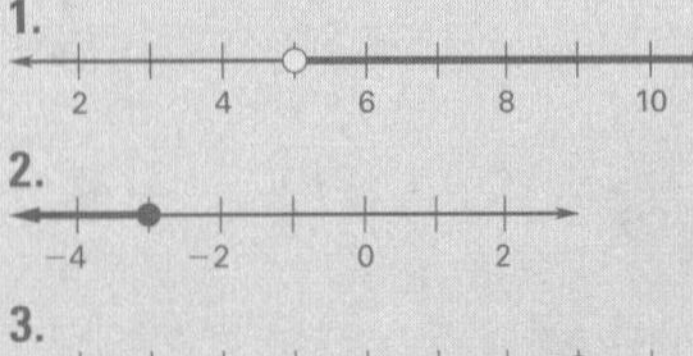

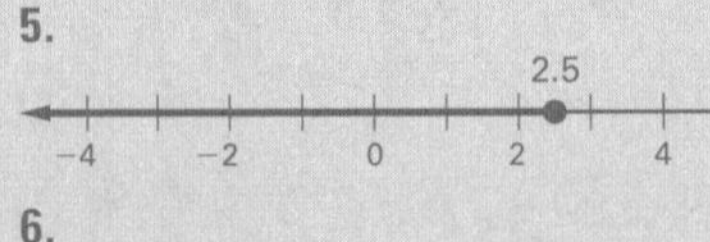

7. $-4\frac{7}{8}$

8. $2\frac{1}{15}$

9. 1.5

Chapter 6

Solve the inequality. Graph your solution. 1–24. See margin for art.

6.1

1. $y - 2 > 3$ — $y > 5$
2. $5 + x \le 2$ — $x \le -3$
3. $4 \ge x - 3$ — $x \le 7$
4. $m + 3 < 2$ — $m < -1$

5. $2 + n \le 4\frac{1}{2}$ — $n \le 2\frac{1}{2}$
6. $2\frac{3}{4} + n < -3\frac{5}{8}$ — $n < -6\frac{3}{8}$
7. $1\frac{7}{8} > 6\frac{3}{4} + z$ — $z < -4\frac{7}{8}$
8. $3\frac{2}{5} \ge 1\frac{1}{3} + k$ — $k \le 2\frac{1}{15}$

9. $-8.5 \le t - 10$ — $t \ge 1.5$
10. $r + 4 < -0.7$ — $r < -4.7$
11. $-6.9 > -1.4 + y$ — $y < -5.5$
12. $1.48 - m \ge -3.13$ — $m \le 4.61$

6.2

13. $3p \le 27$ — $p \le 9$
14. $-13t > 26$ — $t < -2$
15. $\frac{x}{3} \ge 2$ — $x \ge 6$
16. $\frac{y}{-2} < 5$ — $y > -10$

17. $-6m \ge -9$ — $m \le \frac{3}{2}$
18. $-3 \ge \frac{n}{2}$ — $n \le -6$
19. $0.3z \le 2.4$ — $z \le 8$
20. $25 > -2.5s$ — $s > -10$

21. $4.8z \le 3.2$ — $z \le \frac{2}{3}$
22. $0.09d < -1.8$ — $d < -20$
23. $\frac{y}{0.3} > -15$ — $y > -4.5$
24. $-1.8t < 9$ — $t > -5$

6.3 Solve the inequality, if possible. Graph your solution. 25–33. See margin for art.

25. $3x + 5 \ge 20$ — $x \ge 5$
26. $6z - 5 < 13$ — $z < 3$
27. $8(t + 4) > -8$ — $t > -5$

28. $7 - 8n \le 4n - 17$ — $n \ge 2$
29. $8(m + 2) < 4(5 + 2m)$ — all real numbers
30. $6d - 4 - 3d \ge 14$ — $d \ge 6$

31. $\frac{2}{3}y + 28 > 20 + 2y$ — $y < 6$
32. $6(-5 + 3p) \ge 3(6p - 10)$ — all real numbers
33. $\frac{5}{6}(12z - 24) > \frac{2}{5}(25z - 25)$ — no solution

6.4 Solve the inequality. Graph your solution. 34–42. See margin for art.

34. $2 \le y - 4 < 7$ — $6 \le y < 11$
35. $-27 < 9x < 27$ — $-3 < x < 3$
36. $2 < 6z - 10 < 20$ — $2 < z < 5$

37. $15 < \frac{5}{9}(18a - 9) \le 30$ — $2 < a \le 3\frac{1}{2}$
38. $2v > 12$ *or* $v + 2 < 6$ — $v > 6$ or $v < 4$
39. $3r + 7 < -5$ *or* $32 \le 7r + 46$ — $r < -4$ or $r \ge -2$

40. $-4m < 8$ *or* $2m - 2 < -12$ — $m > -2$ or $m < -5$
41. $9t - 20 \ge 4t$ *or* $4 < \frac{1}{-2}t$ — $t \ge 4$ or $t < -8$
42. $-n - 1 > 1$ *or* $2n + 8 > n + 8$ — $n < -2$ or $n > 0$

6.5 Solve the equation, if possible.

43. $|x| = 8$ — ± 8
44. $|y| = -10$ — no solution
45. $|m + 6| = 5$ — $-11, -1$
46. $|4z - 2| = 14$ — $-3, 4$

47. $|t - 7| = 21$ — $-14, 28$
48. $6|z - 4| = 36$ — $-2, 10$
49. $4|6s + 11| = -52$ — no solution
50. $|r + 3| - 16 = -4$ — $-15, 9$

51. $|5r| + 10 = 15$ — $-1, 1$
52. $2|3s + 4| = 14$ — $-3\frac{2}{3}, 1$
53. $-4|7v + 2| = 32$ — no solution
54. $12\left|\frac{5}{6}w - 4\right| - 4 = 8$ — $3\frac{3}{5}, 6$

6.6 Solve the inequality. Graph your solution. 55–66. See margin for art.

55. $|x| \le 3$ — $-3 \le x \le 3$
56. $|y| \ge 5$ — $y \le -5$ or $y \ge 5$
57. $|s| > 1.2$ — $s < -1.2$ or $s > 1.2$
58. $|q| < \frac{2}{5}$ — $-\frac{2}{5} < q < \frac{2}{5}$

59. $|x + 2| > 6$ — $x < -8$ or $x > 4$
60. $|y + 3| \le 5$ — $-8 \le y \le 2$
61. $|8 - m| < 3$ — $5 < m < 11$
62. $|4n - 1| \ge 7$ — $n \le -\frac{3}{2}$ or $n \ge 2$

63. $3|p - 3| \le 12$ — $-1 \le p \le 7$
64. $|3q + 2| - 3 \ge 8$ — $q \le -\frac{13}{3}$ or $q \ge 3$
65. $2|5a - 1| + 3 \le 11$ — $-\frac{3}{5} \le a \le 1$
66. $4\left|\frac{2}{3}c + 2\right| < 64$ — $-27 < c < 21$

6.7 Graph the inequality.
67–78. See margin.

67. $y \ge x + 5$
68. $y < x - 1$
69. $4x + y > 3$
70. $x \le -5$

71. $3(x - 8) \le 6y$
72. $2x - y \ge -2$
73. $y > 8$
74. $2(x - 1) \ge 1 - y$

75. $x - 8 \le y + 2$
76. $2x \ge -2y$
77. $3(y - 8) > x - 9$
78. $2(-x - 1) \ge 4 + y$

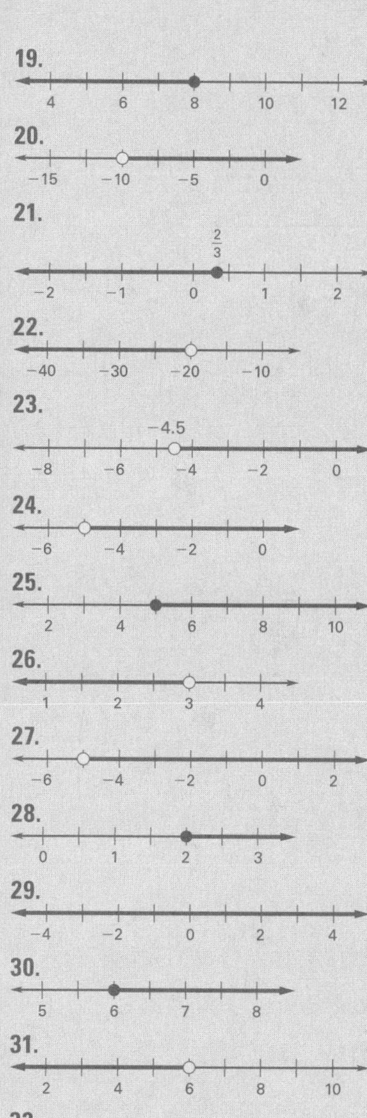

34–42, 55–78. See Additional Answers beginning on p. AA1.

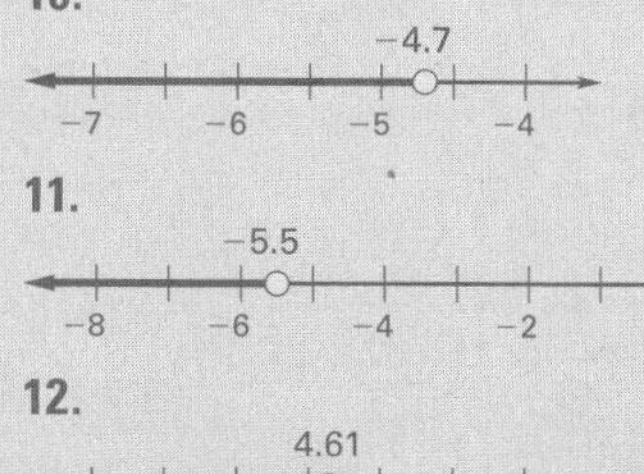

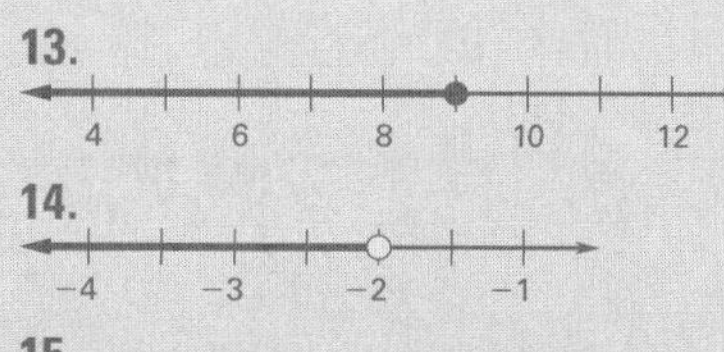

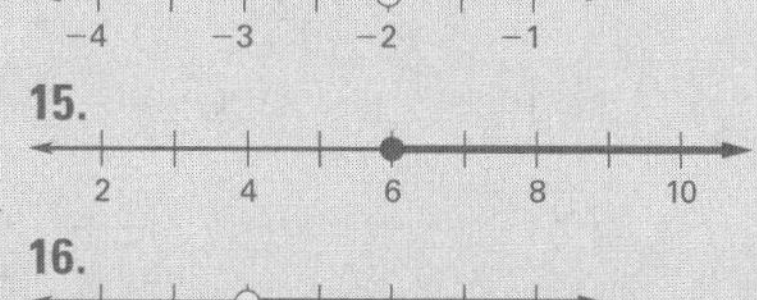

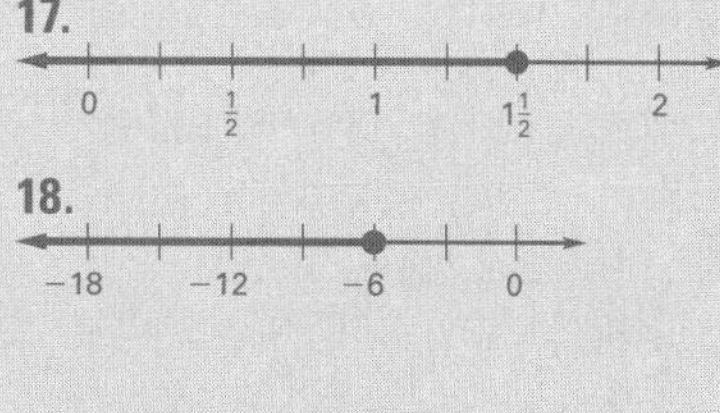

Chapter 7

7.1 Solve the linear system by graphing. Check your solution.

1. $y = x - 1$
   $y = -x + 5$ (3, 2)

2. $y = 3x + 12$
   $y = -4x - 2$ (−2, 6)

3. $x - y = 4$
   $x + y = -2$ (1, −3)

4. $4x - y = 10$
   $x = 4$ (4, 6)

5. $3x - 2y = -5$
   $4x + 3y = -18$ (−3, −2)

6. $\frac{2}{3}x + \frac{1}{3}y = \frac{16}{3}$
   $-\frac{2}{5}x + y = \frac{8}{5}$ (6, 4)

7.2 Solve the linear system using substitution.

7. $y = 2x + 6$
   $x = y - 3$ (−3, 0)

8. $y = 3x + 5$
   $x + y = -1$ $\left(-\frac{3}{2}, \frac{1}{2}\right)$

9. $x = 2y - 5$
   $2x - y = 11$ (9, 7)

10. $2x - y = 0$
    $x + 3y = -56$ (−8, −16)

11. $1.5x - 2.5y = 22$
    $x - y = 10$ (3, −7)

12. $\frac{1}{2}x + \frac{3}{4}y = 5$
    $x - \frac{1}{2}y = 6$ (7, 2)

Solve the linear system using elimination.

7.3

13. $x + 2y = 2$
    $-x + 3y = 13$ (−4, 3)

14. $3x - 4y = -16$
    $x - 4y = -40$ (12, 13)

15. $3x + 2y = -31$
    $5x + 2y = -49$ (−9, −2)

16. $5x + 4y = 6$
    $7x + 4y = 14$ $\left(4, -\frac{7}{2}\right)$

17. $10y - 3x = -41$
    $3x - 5y = 16$ (−3, −5)

18. $4x - 3y = 39$
    $7y = 4x - 79$ $\left(\frac{9}{4}, -10\right)$

7.4

19. $x + y = -3$
    $5x + 7y = -9$ (−6, 3)

20. $5x + 2y = -19$
    $10x - 7y = -16$ (−3, −2)

21. $8x - 3y = 61$
    $2x - 5y = -23$ (11, 9)

22. $4x - 3y = -2$
    $6x + 4y = 31$ $\left(\frac{5}{2}, 4\right)$

23. $5x - 2y = 53$
    $2x + 6y = 11$ $\left(10, -\frac{3}{2}\right)$

24. $15x - 8y = 6$
    $25x - 12y = 16$ $\left(\frac{14}{5}, \frac{9}{2}\right)$

7.5 Graph the linear system. Then use the graph to tell whether the linear system has *one solution*, *no solution*, or *infinitely many solutions*. 25–27. See margin for art.

25. $2x + y = -3$
    $y = -2x + 5$
    no solution

26. $2y - 4x = 10$
    $-2y - 2x = 8$
    one solution

27. $10x + 5y = -15$
    $y = -2x - 3$
    infinitely many solutions

7.5 Solve the linear system using substitution or elimination.

28. $y - 3x = 5$
    $x = y - 5$ (0, 5)

29. $2y - 3x = 36$
    $y = 3x - 12$ (20, 48)

30. $5x + 5y = -32$
    $3x + 3y = 14$ no solution

31. $4x + 6y = 11$
    $y = -\frac{2}{3}x + 7$ no solution

32. $3y - 3x = 12$
    $y = x - 4$ no solution

33. $x + 2y = -30$
    $y = \frac{1}{2}x + 15$ (−30, 0)

7.6 Graph the system of inequalities. 34–39. See margin.

34. $y \geq -5$
    $y \leq -2$

35. $x \geq -3$
    $y < 1$

36. $y < -2x - 3$
    $x - y > -4$

37. $x + 4y \geq -8$
    $y - 4x < 8$
    $x > -1$

38. $x > 3$
    $x < 5$
    $y > -2$
    $y \leq 0$

39. $x + y > 3$
    $x - y > 5$
    $x + 2y \leq 8$
    $x - 5y > 10$

EXTRA PRACTICE

25. $2x + y = -3$; $y = -2x + 5$

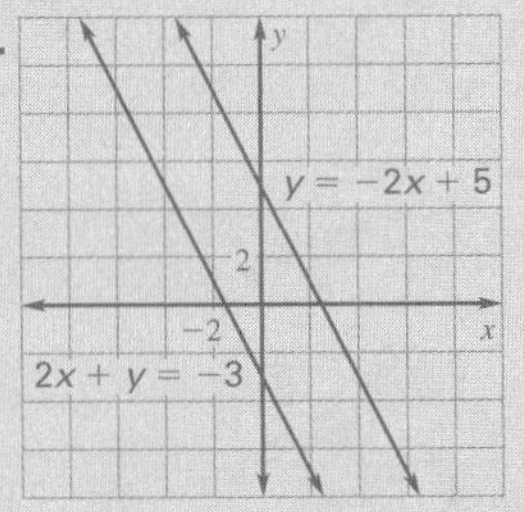

26. $-2y - 2x = 8$; $2y - 4x = 10$

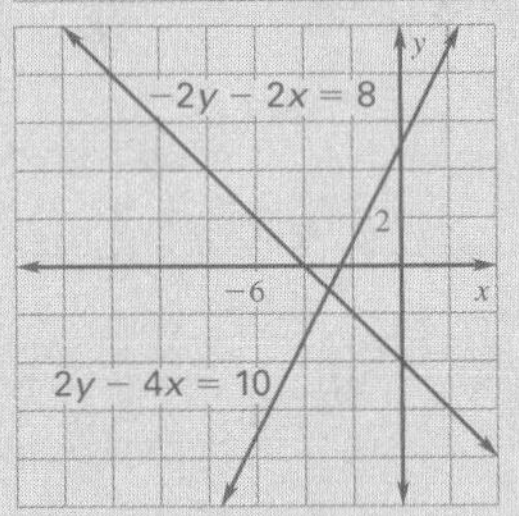

27. $10x + 5y = -15$; $y = -2x - 3$

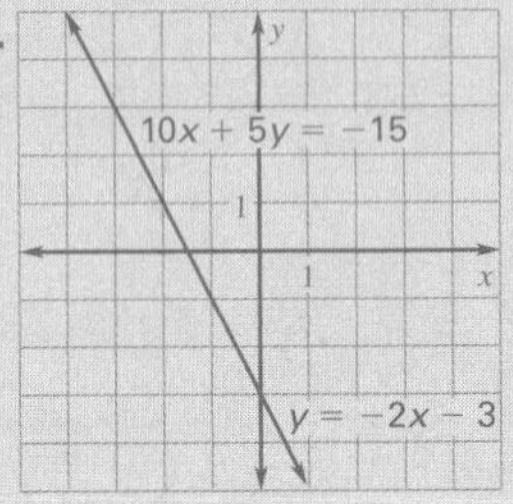

34. $y = -2$; $y = -5$

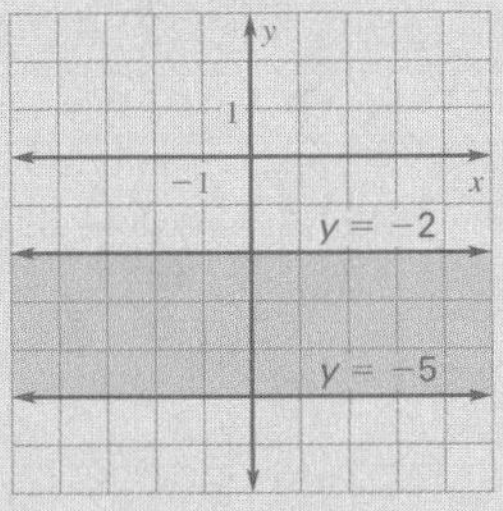

35.

36.
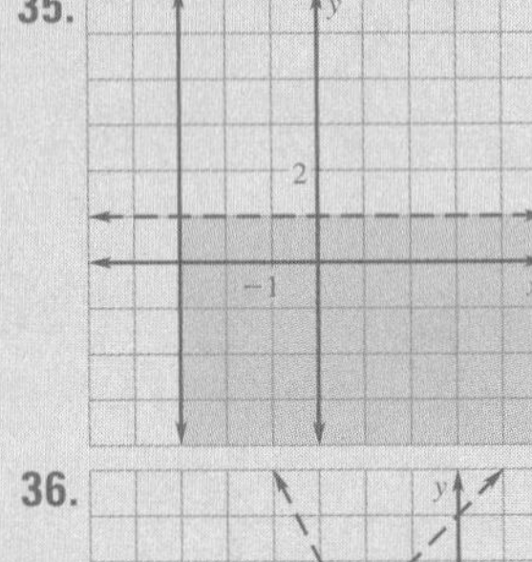

37.
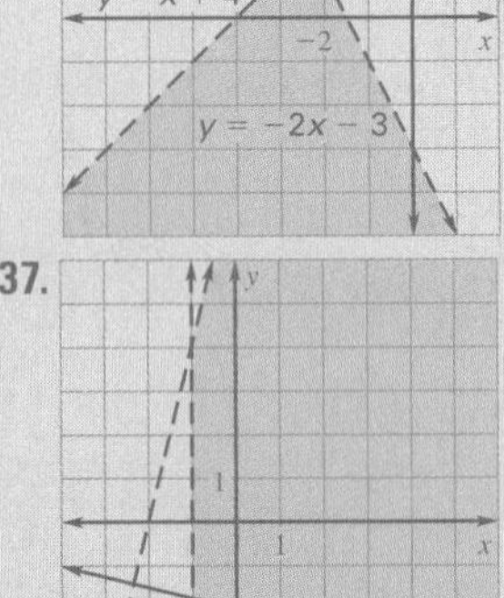

38.
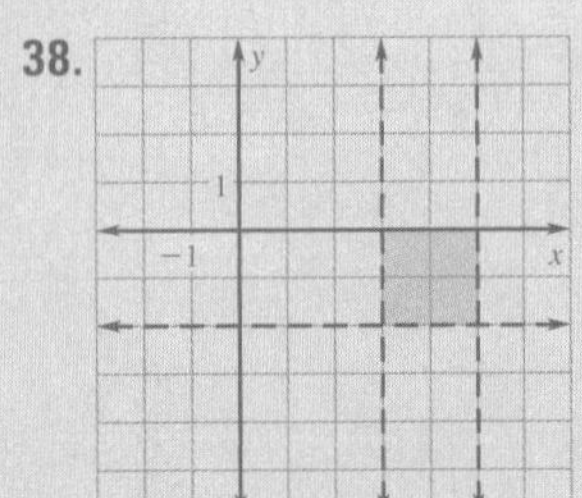

39.
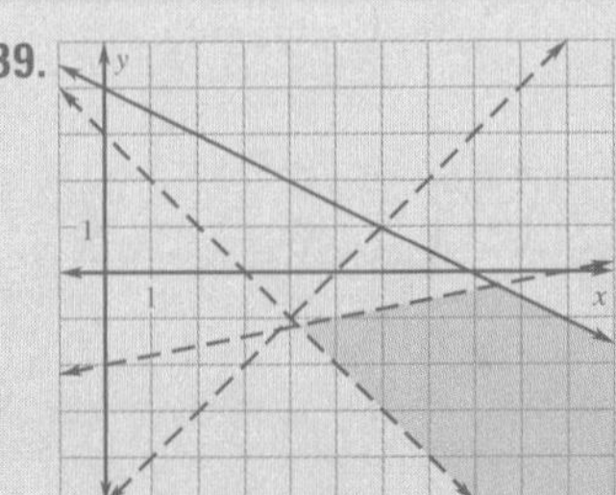

Chapter 8

Simplify the expression. In exercises involving numerical bases only, write your answer using exponents.

8.1 1. $5^3 \cdot 5^4$ 5^7 2. $6 \cdot 6^7$ 6^8 3. $(-2)^3 \cdot (-2)^6$ $(-2)^9$ 4. $(2^8)^2$ 2^{16}

5. $[(-4)^3]^2$ $(-4)^6$ 6. $(8 \cdot 4)^5$ $8^5 \cdot 4^5$ 7. $m^5 \cdot m^2$ m^7 8. $n^2 \cdot n^4 \cdot n^5$ n^{11}

9. $(y^3)^5$ y^{15} 10. $(-2x)^3$ $-8x^3$ 11. $(3d^2)^3 \cdot 2d^2$ $54d^8$ 12. $(-4s^2)^3(2s^3)^6$ $-4096s^{24}$

8.2 13. $\frac{8^7}{8^2}$ 8^5 14. $\frac{4^6 \cdot 4^2}{4^3}$ 4^5 15. $\left(-\frac{2}{3}\right)^5$ $-\frac{2^5}{3^5}$ 16. $10^{12} \cdot \frac{1}{10^7}$ 10^5

17. $7^9 \cdot \left(\frac{1}{7}\right)^4$ 7^5 18. $\frac{1}{t^9} \cdot t^{13}$ t^4 19. $\left(\frac{p}{q}\right)^7$ $\frac{p^7}{q^7}$ 20. $\left(\frac{6x^9}{3y^4}\right)^2$ $\frac{4x^{18}}{y^8}$

21. $\left(\frac{4y^5}{3}\right)^3 \cdot \frac{1}{y^6}$ $\frac{64y^9}{27}$ 22. $\left(\frac{2}{u^2}\right)^3 \cdot \left(\frac{3u^4}{z^2}\right)^4$ $\frac{648u^{10}}{z^8}$ 23. $\left(\frac{5x^3y^4}{2x^2y}\right)^2$ $\frac{25x^2y^6}{4}$ 24. $\frac{6a^4b^5}{ab} \cdot \left(\frac{2ab}{a^2b^2}\right)^3$ $48b$

8.3 Evaluate the expression.

25. 3^{-4} $\frac{1}{81}$ 26. $(-5)^{-3}$ $-\frac{1}{125}$ 27. 7^0 1 28. $4^{-5} \cdot 4^3$ $\frac{1}{16}$

29. $\left(\frac{1}{2}\right)^{-3}$ 8 30. $(3^{-2})^3$ $\frac{1}{729}$ 31. $\frac{1}{2^{-5}}$ 32 32. $\frac{8^{-4}}{8^{-6}}$ 64

8.3 Simplify the expression. Write your answer using only positive exponents.

33. y^{-10} $\frac{1}{y^{10}}$ 34. $(3c)^{-4}$ $\frac{1}{81c^4}$ 35. $10b^{-3}c^5$ $\frac{10c^5}{b^3}$ 36. $(2d^5e^{-2})^{-3}$ $\frac{e^6}{8d^{15}}$

37. $\frac{x^{-4}}{y^{-5}}$ $\frac{y^5}{x^4}$ 38. $\frac{1}{6t^{-5}u^3}$ $\frac{t^5}{6u^3}$ 39. $\frac{3}{(-2z)^{-5}}$ $-96z^5$ 40. $\frac{(2e)^{-4}g^5}{e^5g^{-3}}$ $\frac{g^8}{16e^9}$

8.4 If the number is written in scientific notation, write it in standard form. If the number is written in standard form, write it in scientific notation.

41. 0.87 8.7×10^{-1} 42. 378.4 3.784×10^2 43. 0.000359 3.59×10^{-4} 44. 465,000,000 4.65×10^8

45. 5.3×10^5 530,000 46. 1.67×10^{-4} 0.000167 47. 8×10^{-6} 0.000008 48. 9.0001×10^2 900.01

8.4 Evaluate the expression. Write your answer in scientific notation.

49. $\frac{3 \times 10^2}{8 \times 10^6}$ 3.75×10^{-5} 50. $(8.5 \times 10^{10})(3.7 \times 10^{-5})$ 3.145×10^6 51. $\frac{2.4 \times 10^{-5}}{6 \times 10^{-8}}$ 4×10^2

Graph the function. 52–67. See margin.

8.5 52. $y = 3^x$ 53. $y = 1.25^x$ 54. $y = \left(\frac{9}{4}\right)^x$ 55. $y = 5 \cdot 2^x$

56. $y = \frac{1}{3} \cdot 2^x$ 57. $y = -\frac{1}{2} \cdot 5^x$ 58. $y = -5 \cdot 2^x$ 59. $y = -\frac{1}{3} \cdot 4^x$

8.6 60. $y = \left(\frac{1}{3}\right)^x$ 61. $y = (0.2)^x$ 62. $y = 3 \cdot (0.2)^x$ 63. $y = 2 \cdot \left(\frac{1}{3}\right)^x$

64. $y = 4 \cdot \left(\frac{1}{3}\right)^x$ 65. $y = \frac{1}{2} \cdot \left(\frac{1}{3}\right)^x$ 66. $y = -2 \cdot \left(\frac{1}{3}\right)^x$ 67. $y = -\frac{3}{4} \cdot \left(\frac{1}{3}\right)^x$

8.6 68. Tell whether the table represents an exponential function. If so, write a rule for the function. exponential; $y = 5 \cdot 2^x$

x	−1	0	1	2	3
y	$\frac{5}{2}$	5	10	20	40

52.
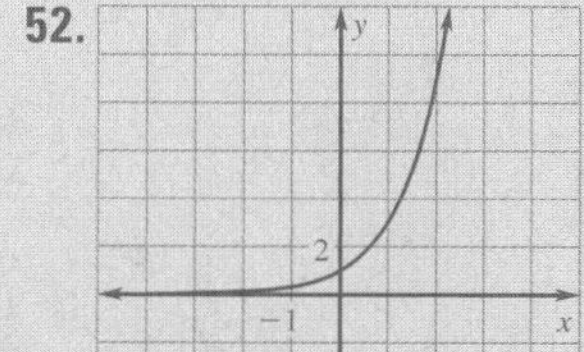

53.
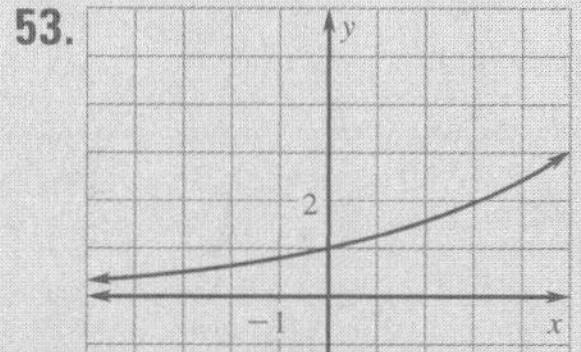

54.
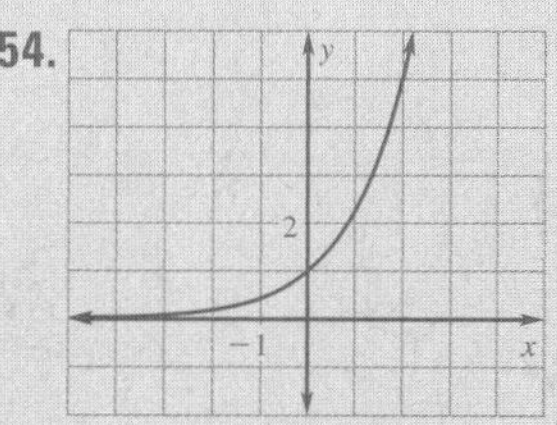

55.
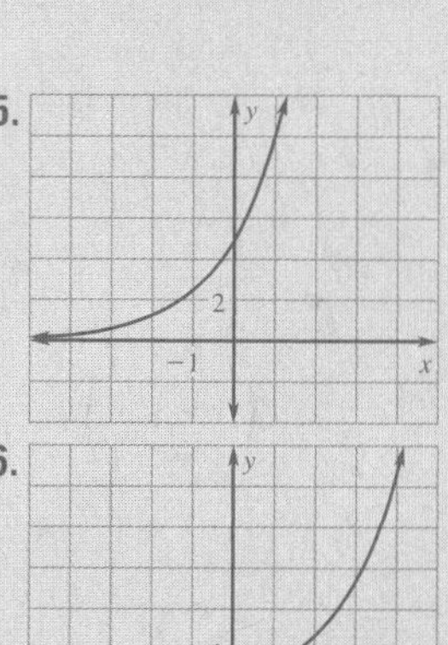

56.
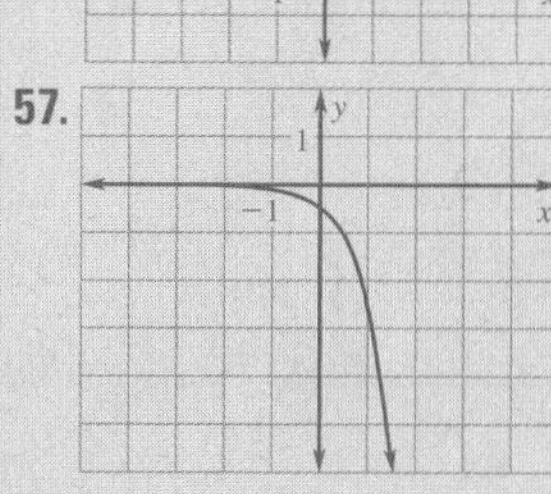

57.
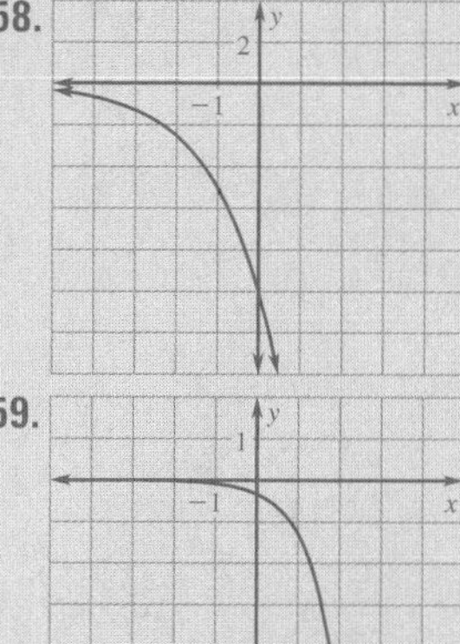

58.

59.

60.
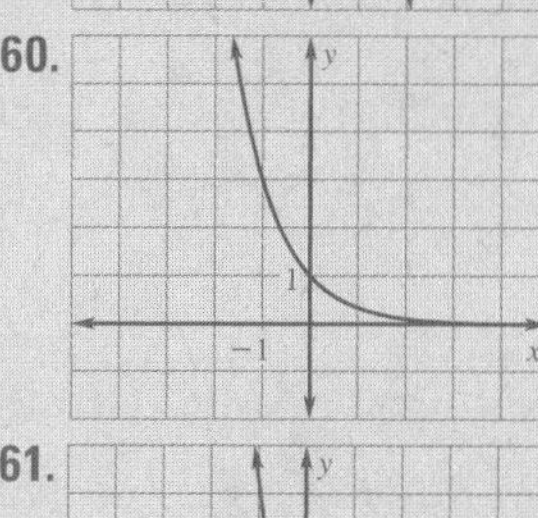

61.
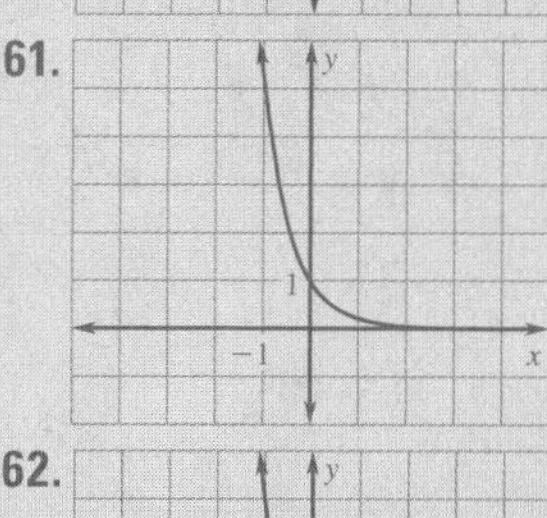

62.
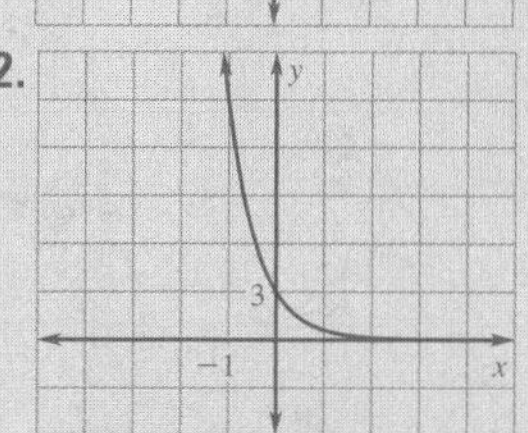

63–67. See Additional Answers beginning on p. AA1.

Chapter 9

Find the sum or difference.

9.1

1. $(6x^2 + 7) + (x^2 - 9)$ $7x^2 - 2$
2. $(8y^2 - 3y - 10) + (-11y^2 + 2y - 7)$ $-3y^2 - y - 17$
3. $(10m^2 - 7m + 2) - (3m^2 - 2m + 5)$ $7m^2 - 5m - 3$
4. $(2t^3 - 3t^2 + 5t) - (6t^3 + 3t^2 - 5t)$ $-4t^3 - 6t^2 + 10t$
5. $(6b^3 + 12b^2 - b) - (15b^2 + 7b - 8)$ $6b^3 - 3b^2 - 8b + 8$
6. $(r^2 - 8 + 4r^3 + 5r) - (7r^3 - 3r^2 + 5)$ $-3r^3 + 4r^2 + 5r - 13$

Find the product.

9.2

7. $5x^4(2x^3 - 3x^2 + 5x - 1)$ $10x^7 - 15x^6 + 25x^5 - 5x^4$
8. $(x^2 + 4x + 2)(x + 7)$ $x^3 + 11x^2 + 30x + 14$
9. $(2x + 3)(4x + 2)$ $8x^2 + 16x + 6$
10. $(2x^2 - 5x + 6)(3x - 2)$ $6x^3 - 19x^2 + 28x - 12$
11. $(3x - 7)(x + 5)$ $3x^2 + 8x - 35$
12. $(9t - 2)(2t - 3)$ $18t^2 - 31t + 6$

9.3

13. $(x + 10)^2$ $x^2 + 20x + 100$
14. $(m + 8)(m - 8)$ $m^2 - 64$
15. $(4x - 2)(4x + 2)$ $16x^2 - 4$
16. $(3x - 4y)(3x + 4y)$ $9x^2 - 16y^2$
17. $(6 - 3t)(6 + 3t)$ $36 - 9t^2$
18. $(-11x - 4y)^2$ $121x^2 + 88xy + 16y^2$

9.4 Solve the equation.

19. $(m + 8)(m - 2) = 0$ $-8, 2$
20. $(2y - 6)(y + 3) = 0$ ± 3
21. $(5y - 3)(2y - 4) = 0$ $\frac{3}{5}, 2$
22. $3b^2 + 9b = 0$ $-3, 0$
23. $-12m^2 - 3m = 0$ $-\frac{1}{4}, 0$
24. $14k^2 = 28k$ $0, 2$

9.5 Factor the trinomial.

25. $y^2 + 7y + 12$ $(y + 3)(y + 4)$
26. $x^2 - 12x + 35$ $(x - 7)(x - 5)$
27. $x^2 + 5x - 36$ $(x - 4)(x + 9)$
28. $q^2 + 3q - 40$ $(q - 5)(q + 8)$
29. $m^2 - 29m + 100$ $(m - 25)(m - 4)$
30. $y^2 + 14y - 72$ $(y - 4)(y + 18)$

9.5 Solve the equation.

31. $m^2 - 7m + 10 = 0$ $2, 5$
32. $p^2 - 7p = 18$ $-2, 9$
33. $z^2 - 13z + 24 = -12$ $4, 9$
34. $n^2 + 8 = 6n$ $2, 4$
35. $r^2 - 15r = -8r - 10$ $2, 5$
36. $c^2 - 8 = -13c + 6$ $-14, 1$

9.6 Factor the trinomial.

37. $-x^2 + 5x - 6$ $-(x - 3)(x - 2)$
38. $3k^2 - 10k + 8$ $(3k - 4)(k - 2)$
39. $4k^2 - 12k + 5$ $(2k - 1)(2k - 5)$
40. $6t^2 - 5t - 6$ $(2t - 3)(3t + 2)$
41. $-3s^2 - 7s - 2$ $-(3s + 1)(s + 2)$
42. $2v^2 - 5v + 3$ $(2v - 3)(v - 1)$

9.6 Solve the equation.

43. $-3x^2 + 14x - 8 = 0$ $\frac{2}{3}, 4$
44. $8t^2 + 6t = 9$ $-\frac{3}{2}, \frac{3}{4}$
45. $2x^2 + 3x - 2 = 0$ $-2, \frac{1}{2}$
46. $3p^2 - 28 = 17p$ $-\frac{4}{3}, 7$
47. $16m^2 - 1 = -15m$ $-1, \frac{1}{16}$
48. $t(6t - 7) = 3$ $-\frac{1}{3}, \frac{3}{2}$

9.7 Factor the polynomial.

49. $y^2 - 36$ $(y + 6)(y - 6)$
50. $9y^2 - 49$ $(3y - 7)(3y + 7)$
51. $12y^2 - 27$ $3(2y - 3)(2y + 3)$
52. $x^2 - 8x + 16$ $(x - 4)^2$
53. $4x^2 - 12x + 9$ $(2x - 3)^2$
54. $27x^2 - 36x + 12$ $3(3x - 2)^2$
55. $g^2 + 10g + 25$ $(g + 5)^2$
56. $9b^2 + 24b + 16$ $(3b + 4)^2$
57. $4w^2 + 28w + 49$ $(2w + 7)^2$

9.8 Factor the polynomial completely.

58. $2x^2 + 8x + 6$ $2(x + 1)(x + 3)$
59. $3z^2 - 16z + 5$ $(3z - 1)(z - 5)$
60. $5m^2 - 23m + 12$ $(5m - 3)(m - 4)$
61. $3y^3 + 15y^2 + 2y + 10$ $(3y^2 + 2)(y + 5)$
62. $30z^3 - 14z^2 - 8z$ $2z(5z - 4)(3z + 1)$
63. $98m^3 - 18m$ $2m(7m - 3)(7m + 3)$
64. $8h^2k - 32k$ $8k(h - 2)(h + 2)$
65. $2h^3 - 3h^2 - 18h + 27$ $(h + 3)(h - 3)(2h - 3)$
66. $-12z^3 + 12z^2 - 3z$ $-3z(2z - 1)^2$

EXTRA PRACTICE

Chapter 10, p. 947

1. 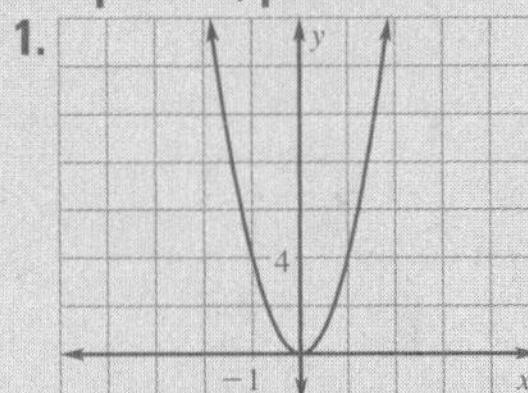

The graph is a vertical stretch by a factor of 4 of the graph of $y = x^2$.

2. 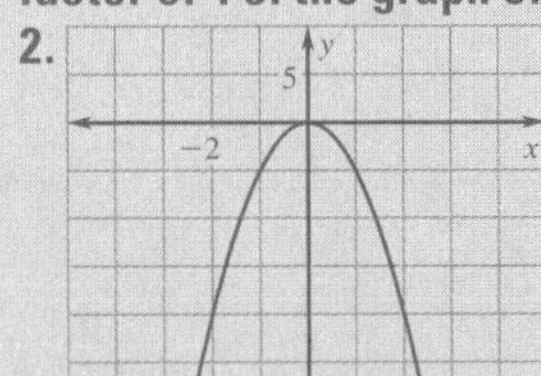

The graph is a vertical stretch by a factor of 5 and a reflection in the x-axis of the graph of $y = x^2$.

3. 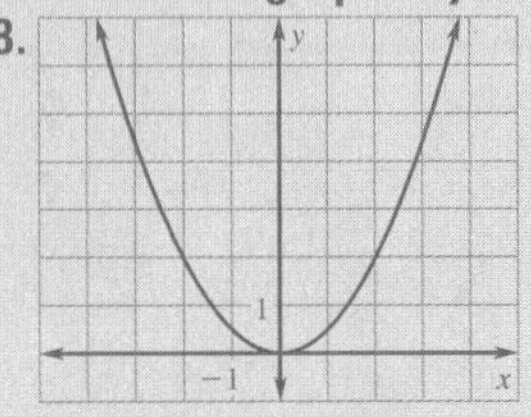

The graph is a vertical shrink by a factor of $\frac{1}{2}$ of the graph of $y = x^2$.

4. 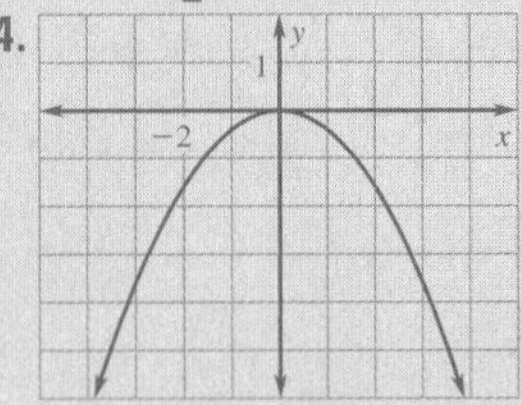

The graph is a vertical shrink by a factor of $\frac{2}{5}$ and a reflection in the x-axis of the graph of $y = x^2$.

5. 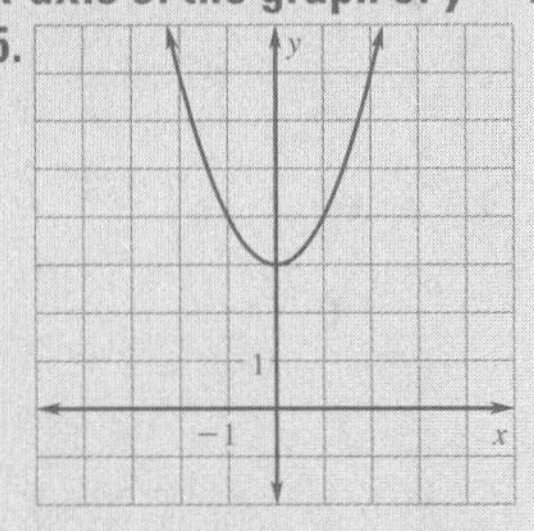

The graph is a vertical translation 3 units up of the graph of $y = x^2$.

6. 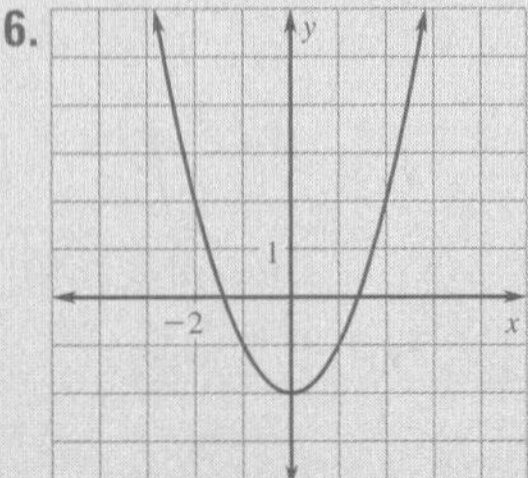

The graph is a vertical translation 2 units down of the graph of $y = x^2$.

7. 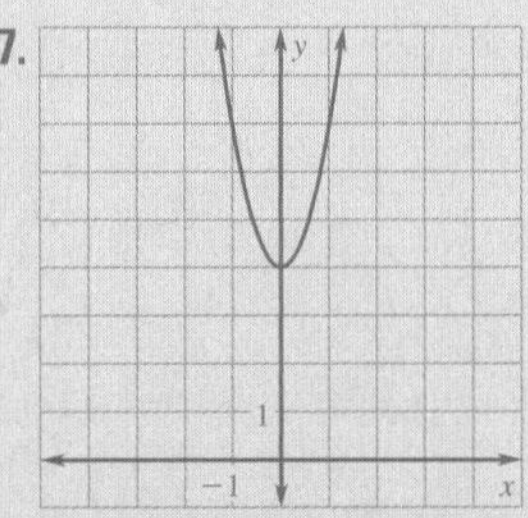

The graph is a vertical stretch by a factor of 3 and a vertical translation 4 units up of the graph of $y = x^2$.

Chapter 10

10.1 Graph the function. Compare the graph with the graph of $y = x^2$. 1–8. See margin.

1. $y = 4x^2$
2. $y = -5x^2$
3. $y = \frac{1}{2}x^2$
4. $y = -\frac{2}{5}x^2$
5. $y = x^2 + 3$
6. $y = x^2 - 2$
7. $y = 3x^2 + 4$
8. $y = -4x^2 - 3$

10.2 Graph the function. Label the vertex and axis of symmetry. 9–14. See margin.

9. $y = x^2 + 4x + 4$
10. $y = -x^2 - 2x + 3$
11. $y = 2x^2 - 6x + 5$
12. $y = 3x^2 + 12x + 8$
13. $y = -2x^2 + 6$
14. $y = \frac{3}{4}x^2 - 3x$

10.3 Solve the equation by graphing.

15. $x^2 + 3x - 10 = 0$ $-5, 2$
16. $x^2 + 14 = 9x$ $2, 7$
17. $-x^2 + 3x = -18$ $-3, 6$
18. $2x^2 + 3x - 20 = 0$ $-4, \frac{5}{2}$
19. $2x^2 + x = 6$ $-2, \frac{3}{2}$
20. $\frac{1}{2}x^2 - x = 12$ $-4, 6$

10.4 Solve the equation. Round the solutions to the nearest hundredth, if necessary.

21. $2x^2 - 20 = 78$ ± 7
22. $3y^2 + 16 = 4$ no solution
23. $16y^2 - 6 = 3$ ± 0.75
24. $48 - x^2 = -52$ ± 10
25. $5m^2 - 5 = 10$ ± 1.73
26. $2 - 5t^2 = 4$ no solution

10.5 Solve the equation by completing the square. Round the solutions to the nearest hundredth, if necessary.

27. $x^2 + 4x - 21 = 0$ $-7, 3$
28. $g^2 - 10g = 24$ $-2, 12$
29. $w^2 - 7w + 6 = 0$ $1, 6$
30. $y^2 - \frac{3}{4}y = \frac{1}{4}$ $-0.25, 1$
31. $x^2 - 6x + 3 = 0$ $0.55, 5.45$
32. $4m^2 + 8m - 7 = 0$ $-2.66, 0.66$

10.6 Use the quadratic formula to solve the equation. Round the solutions to the nearest hundredth, if necessary.

33. $h^2 + 6h - 72 = 0$ $-12, 6$
34. $3x^2 - 7x + 2 = 0$ $0.33, 2$
35. $2k^2 - 5k + 2 = 0$ $0.5, 2$
36. $n^2 + 1 = 5n$ $0.21, 4.79$
37. $2z + 4 = 3z^2$ $-0.87, 1.54$
38. $5x^2 - 4x = 2$ $-0.35, 1.15$

10.7 Tell whether the equation has *two solutions*, *one solution*, or *no solution*.

39. $m^2 - 2m + 1 = 0$ one solution
40. $3x^2 + 6x + 2 = 0$ two solutions
41. $2q^2 + 3q + 5 = 0$ no solution
42. $\frac{3}{4}x^2 - x + 2 = 0$ no solution
43. $2w^2 - 5w + 6 = 8$ two solutions
44. $2y^2 + 10y - 5 = 3y^2 - 30$ two solutions

10.8 Tell whether the table of values represents a *linear function*, an *exponential function*, or a *quadratic function*. Then write an equation for the function. 45–48. See margin.

45.

x	−1	0	1	2	3
y	3	0	3	12	27

46.

x	0	1	2	3	4
y	−5	−2	1	4	7

47.

x	1	2	3	4	5
y	1	2	4	8	16

48.

x	−2	−1	0	1	2
y	18	14	10	6	2

EXTRA PRACTICE

9. 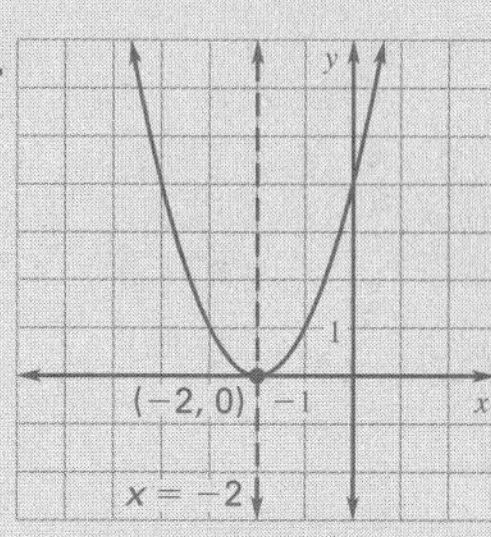

10. 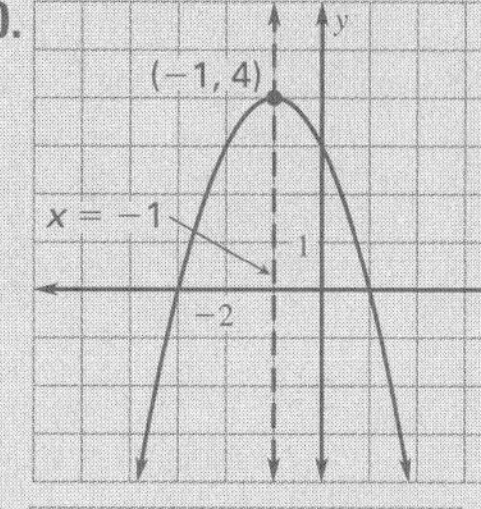

11. 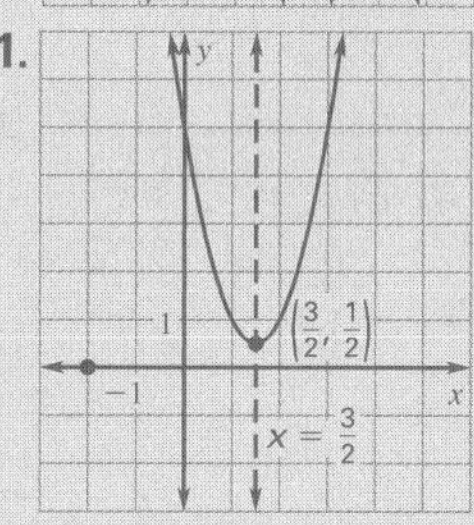

12. 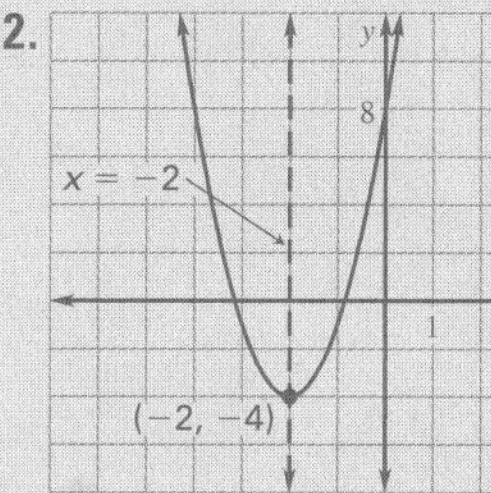

13. 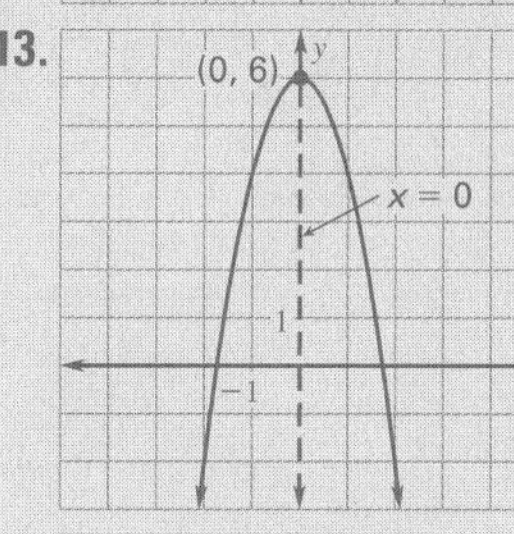

14. 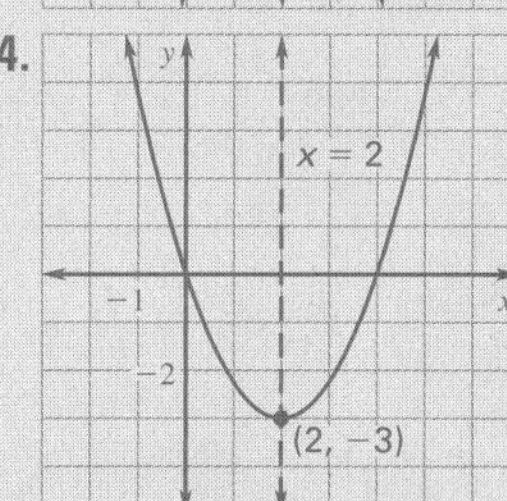

8. 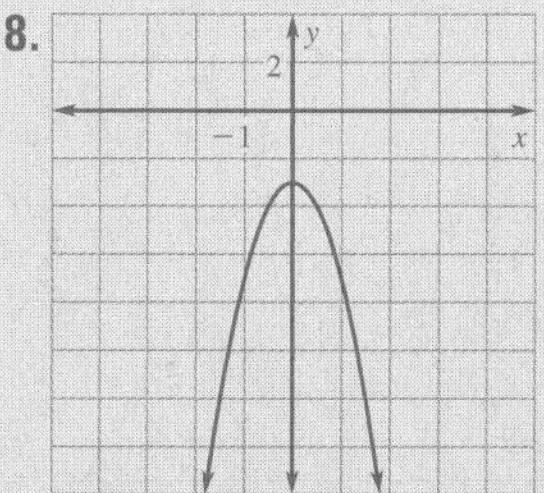

The graph is a vertical stretch by a factor of 4, a reflection in the x-axis, and a vertical translation of 3 units down of $y = x^2$.

45. quadratic function; $y = 3x^2$
46. linear function; $y = 3x - 5$
47. exponential function; $y = 0.5 \cdot 2^x$
48. linear function; $y = -4x + 10$

Chapter 11

11.1 Graph the function and identify its domain and range. Compare the graph with the graph of $y = \sqrt{x}$. 1–9. See margin.

1. $y = 6\sqrt{x}$ **2.** $y = \frac{1}{5}\sqrt{x}$ **3.** $y = -8\sqrt{x}$

4. $y = -\frac{2}{5}\sqrt{x}$ **5.** $y = \sqrt{x} + 3$ **6.** $y = \sqrt{x} - 5$

7. $y = \sqrt{x - 2}$ **8.** $y = \sqrt{x + 5}$ **9.** $y = \sqrt{x - 4} + 2$

EXTRA PRACTICE

11.2 Simplify the expression.

10. $\sqrt{98}$ $7\sqrt{2}$ **11.** $\sqrt{300}$ $10\sqrt{3}$ **12.** $\sqrt{128x^3}$ $8x\sqrt{2x}$ **13.** $\sqrt{17} \cdot \sqrt{17}$ 17

14. $\sqrt{112} \cdot \sqrt{63}$ 84 **15.** $\sqrt{11g} \cdot 5\sqrt{g}$ $5g\sqrt{11}$ **16.** $4m\sqrt{m} \cdot \sqrt{5m}$ $4m^2\sqrt{5}$ **17.** $\sqrt{27x^5} \cdot \sqrt{48x}$ $36x^3$

18. $\sqrt{\frac{19}{49}}$ $\frac{\sqrt{19}}{7}$ **19.** $\sqrt{\frac{1}{6x^2}}$ $\frac{\sqrt{6}}{6x}$ **20.** $\frac{3}{\sqrt{5}}$ $\frac{3\sqrt{5}}{5}$ **21.** $\frac{\sqrt{7}}{\sqrt{8k}}$ $\frac{\sqrt{14k}}{4k}$

22. $\sqrt{\frac{5}{27}}$ $\frac{\sqrt{15}}{9}$ **23.** $2\sqrt{3} + \sqrt{7} + \sqrt{3}$ $3\sqrt{3} + \sqrt{7}$ **24.** $2\sqrt{11} + \sqrt{99}$ $5\sqrt{11}$ **25.** $\sqrt{45} + 3\sqrt{20}$ $9\sqrt{5}$

26. $\sqrt{3}(12 - \sqrt{15})$ $12\sqrt{3} - 3\sqrt{5}$ **27.** $3\sqrt{6}(4\sqrt{6} - \sqrt{600})$ -108 **28.** $(6 - \sqrt{7})(6 - \sqrt{7})$ $43 - 12\sqrt{7}$ **29.** $(4 - \sqrt{13})(10 + \sqrt{13})$ $27 - 6\sqrt{13}$

11.3 Solve the equation. Check for extraneous solutions.

30. $6\sqrt{x} - 30 = 0$ 25 **31.** $\sqrt{8x} + 5 = 13$ 8 **32.** $\sqrt{x + 3} + 5 = 16$ 118

33. $3\sqrt{4x + 1} - 2 = 25$ 20 **34.** $\sqrt{3x - 12} = \sqrt{5x - 26}$ 7 **35.** $\sqrt{2x + 10} - \sqrt{x + 7} = 0$ -3

36. $\sqrt{\frac{1}{2}x + 10} - \sqrt{2x - 8} = 0$ 12 **37.** $x = \sqrt{11x - 10}$ 1, 10 **38.** $x = \sqrt{20 - x}$ 4

39. $5x = \sqrt{20x - 3}$ $\frac{1}{5}, \frac{3}{5}$ **40.** $\sqrt{-4x + 5} = 3x$ $\frac{5}{9}$ **41.** $x + 1 = \sqrt{6 - 2x}$ 1

11.4 Let *a* and *b* represent the lengths of the legs of a right triangle, and let *c* represent the length of the hypotenuse. Find the unknown length.

42. $a = 6, b = 8$ $c = 10$ **43.** $a = 10, c = 26$ $b = 24$ **44.** $b = 40, c = 41$ $a = 9$

45. $a = 2, c = 5$ $b = \sqrt{21}$ **46.** $a = 4, b = 7$ $c = \sqrt{65}$ **47.** $b = 8, c = 11$ $a = \sqrt{57}$

11.4 Tell whether the triangle with the given side lengths is a right triangle.

48. $a = 10, b = 24, c = 26$ right triangle **49.** $a = 2, b = 4, c = 6$ not a right triangle **50.** $a = 14, b = 15, c = 21$ not a right triangle

51. $a = 16, b = 30, c = 34$ right triangle **52.** $a = 1.4, b = 4.8, c = 5$ right triangle **53.** $a = 13, b = 84, c = 95$ not a right triangle

11.5 Find the distance between the two points.

54. $(5, 10), (2, 6)$ 5 **55.** $(2, 8), (7, -4)$ 13 **56.** $(3, -3), (4, 1)$ $\sqrt{17}$

57. $(6, 1.5), (2.5, -4)$ $\sqrt{42.5}$ **58.** $\left(1, \frac{2}{5}\right), \left(\frac{1}{2}, -\frac{4}{5}\right)$ 1.3 **59.** $\left(-\frac{3}{8}, 1\right), \left(\frac{5}{8}, \frac{1}{2}\right)$ $\frac{\sqrt{5}}{2}$

11.5 Find the midpoint of the line segment with the given endpoints.

60. $(6, -2), (8, -6)$ $(7, -4)$ **61.** $(0, -5), (-4, 8)$ $(-2, 1.5)$ **62.** $(0, -6), (0, 2)$ $(0, -2)$

63. $(10, 0), (-8, 0)$ $(1, 0)$ **64.** $(-5, -3), (-8, -7)$ $(-6.5, -5)$ **65.** $\left(5, -\frac{1}{2}\right), \left(8, -\frac{5}{2}\right)$ $\left(6\frac{1}{2}, -1\frac{1}{2}\right)$

6–9. See Additional Answers beginning on p. AA1.

1.

Domain: $x \geq 0$, range: $y \geq 0$; the graph is a vertical stretch by a factor of 6 of the graph of $y = \sqrt{x}$.

2.

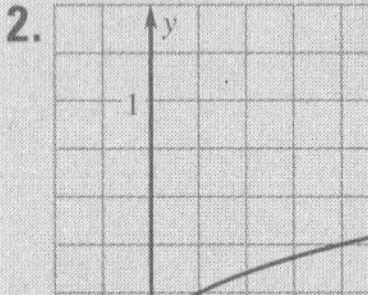

Domain: $x \geq 0$, range: $y \geq 0$; the graph is a vertical shrink by a factor of $\frac{1}{5}$ of the graph of $y = \sqrt{x}$.

3.

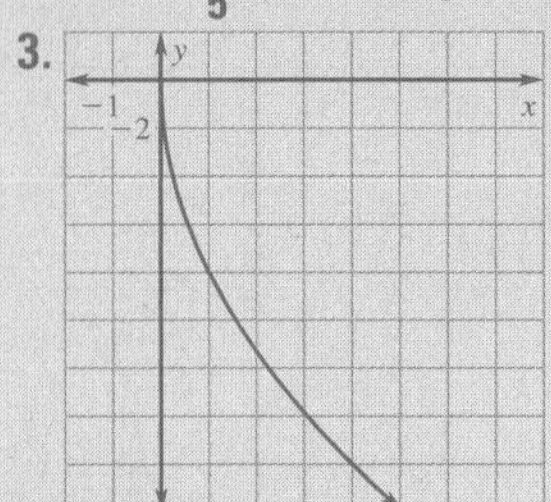

Domain: $x \geq 0$, range: $y \leq 0$; the graph is a vertical stretch by a factor of 8 and a reflection in the x-axis of the graph of $y = \sqrt{x}$.

4.

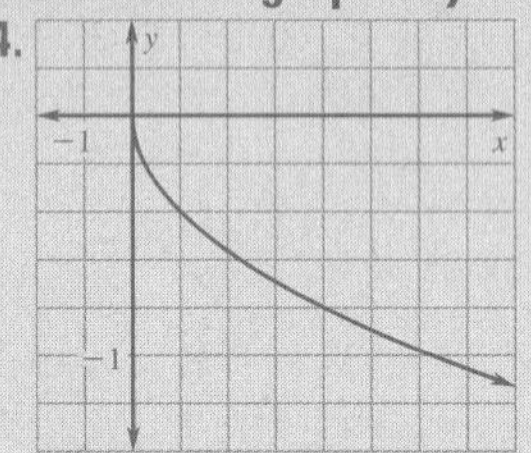

Domain: $x \geq 0$, range: $y \leq 0$; the graph is a vertical shrink by a factor of $\frac{2}{5}$ and a reflection in the x-axis of the graph of $y = \sqrt{x}$.

5.

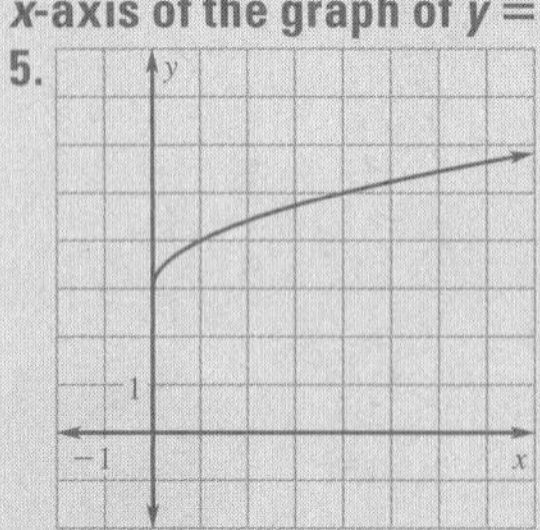

Domain: $x \geq 0$, range: $y \geq 3$; the graph is a vertical translation 3 units up of the graph of $y = \sqrt{x}$.

Chapter 12

12.1 Graph the inverse variation equation. 1–4. See margin.

1. $y = \frac{-1}{x}$ 2. $y = \frac{8}{x}$ 3. $y = \frac{12}{x}$ 4. $y = \frac{-14}{x}$

12.1 Given that y varies inversely with x, use the specified values to write an inverse variation equation that relates x and y. Then find the value of y when $x = 2$.

5. $x = 3, y = 4$ $y = \frac{12}{x}$; 6
6. $x = -2, y = 5$ $y = -\frac{10}{x}$; -5
7. $x = -4, y = -15$ $y = \frac{60}{x}$; 30
8. $x = 8, y = -6$ $y = \frac{-48}{x}$; -24
9. $x = -7, y = -7$ $y = \frac{49}{x}$; 24.5
10. $x = -11, y = 11$ $y = \frac{-121}{x}$; -60.5

12.2 Graph the function. 11–18. See margin.

11. $y = \frac{6}{x}$ 12. $y = \frac{-6}{x}$ 13. $y = \frac{1}{5x}$ 14. $y = \frac{1}{x} + 6$

15. $y = \frac{1}{x - 4}$ 16. $y = \frac{1}{x - 5} + 3$ 17. $y = \frac{4}{x + 2} - 3$ 18. $y = \frac{-2}{x + 1} - 3$

12.3 Divide.

19. $(30x^4 - 12x^3 + 6x^2) \div (-6x)$ $-5x^3 + 2x^2 - x$
20. $(9y^2 + 3y - 6) \div (3y - 2)$ $3y + 3$
21. $(3v^2 + 2v + 12) \div (v + 2)$ $3v - 4 + \frac{20}{v + 2}$
22. $(-24w - 11 + 8w^2) \div (2 + 4w)$ $2w - 7 + \frac{3}{4w + 2}$
23. $(9m^2 - 6) \div (3m - 4)$ $3m + 4 + \frac{10}{3m - 4}$
24. $(-2 + 25n^2) \div (2 + 5n)$ $5n - 2 + \frac{2}{5n + 2}$

12.4 Simplify the rational expression, if possible. State the excluded values. 25–32. See margin.

25. $\frac{44x^3}{24x}$ 26. $\frac{3y + 6}{y + 2}$ 27. $\frac{3a - 15}{4a - 20}$ 28. $\frac{2b - 8}{4 - b}$

29. $\frac{r^2 - 2r - 15}{r^2 + r - 6}$ 30. $\frac{s + 3}{2s^2 + 3s - 9}$ 31. $\frac{2m^2 + 8m - 24}{3m^3 + 24m^2 + 36m}$ 32. $\frac{6n^3 - 18n^2}{3n^3 - 27n}$

Find the sum, difference, product, or quotient.

12.5

33. $\frac{x^2 + 3x - 10}{2x - 4} \cdot \frac{5x}{x^2 + 2x - 15}$ $\frac{5x}{2x - 6}$
34. $\frac{2y^6}{6y^3 + 8y^2} \cdot (3y + 4)$ y^4
35. $\frac{3r^2 - 12}{r - 2} \div \frac{2r^2 + 7r + 6}{2r^2 - r - 6}$ $3r - 6$
36. $\frac{3s^2 + 11s + 10}{s + 2} \div (-3s^2 + s + 10)$ $-\frac{1}{s - 2}$

12.6

37. $\frac{8}{5t} + \frac{3}{2t^2}$ $\frac{16t + 15}{10t^2}$
38. $\frac{3}{u + 2} + \frac{4}{2u + 1}$ $\frac{10u + 11}{(u + 2)(2u + 1)}$
39. $\frac{3}{c^2 - 9} - \frac{2}{2c^2 - 3c - 9}$ $\frac{4c + 3}{(c + 3)(c - 3)(2c + 3)}$
40. $\frac{k + 4}{k^2 + 4k + 4} - \frac{k - 4}{k^2 - k - 6}$ $\frac{3k - 4}{(k + 2)^2(k - 3)}$

12.7 Solve the equation. Check your solution.

41. $\frac{2}{x + 2} = \frac{x - 5}{9}$ $-4, 7$
42. $\frac{y}{y - 1} + \frac{1}{4} = \frac{6}{y - 1}$ 5
43. $\frac{z}{z + 3} + 2 = \frac{5}{z - 1}$ $-\frac{7}{3}, 3$
44. $\frac{1}{w + 5} - \frac{2}{w + 3} = \frac{6}{w^2 + 5w + 6}$ $-11, -4$
45. $\frac{3}{h + 4} - 4 = \frac{6}{h^2 + h - 12}$ $-3, \frac{11}{4}$
46. $\frac{2}{a + 2} - \frac{5}{a + 2} = \frac{4}{a^2 + 4a + 4}$ $-\frac{10}{3}$

EXTRA PRACTICE

1.

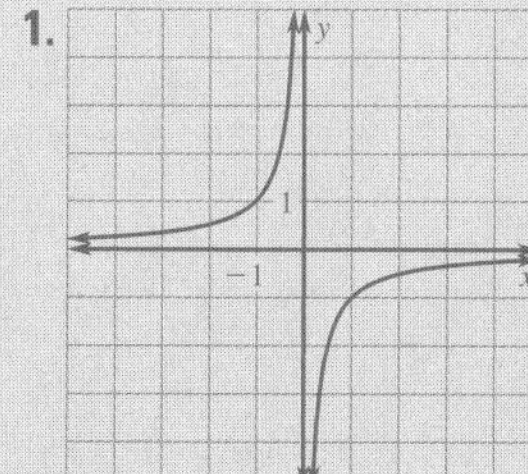

2.

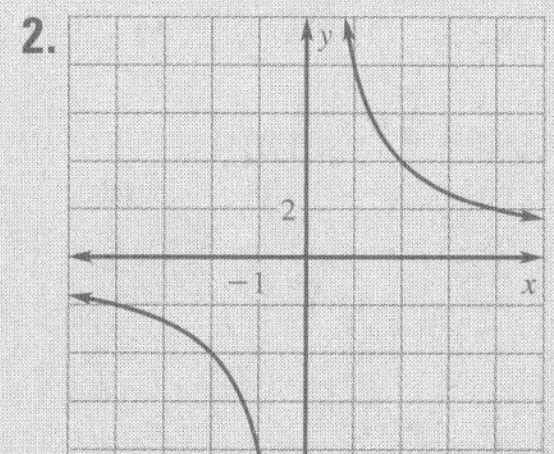

3.

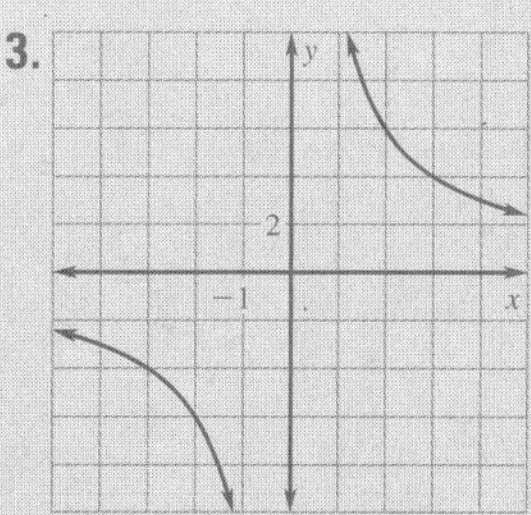

4.

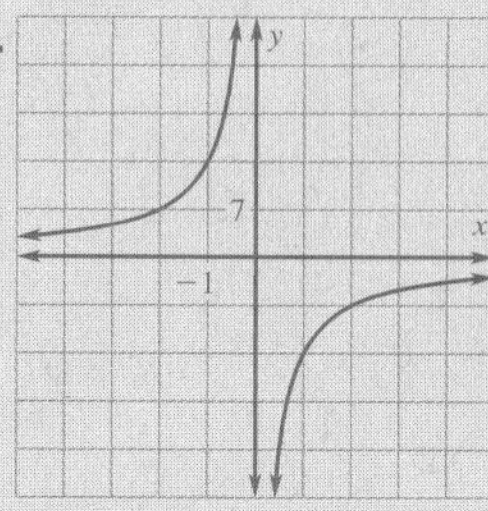

11.

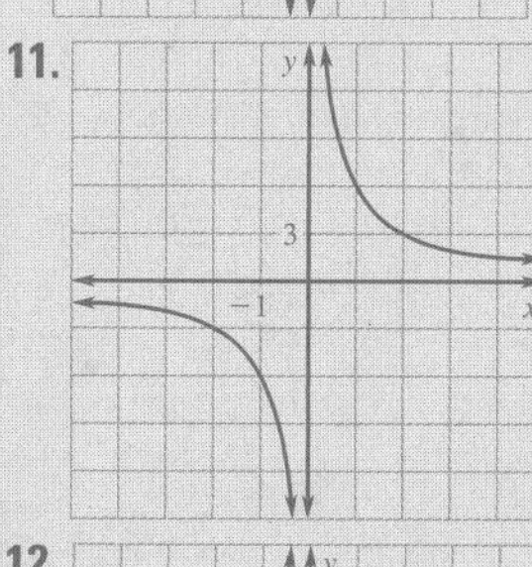

12.

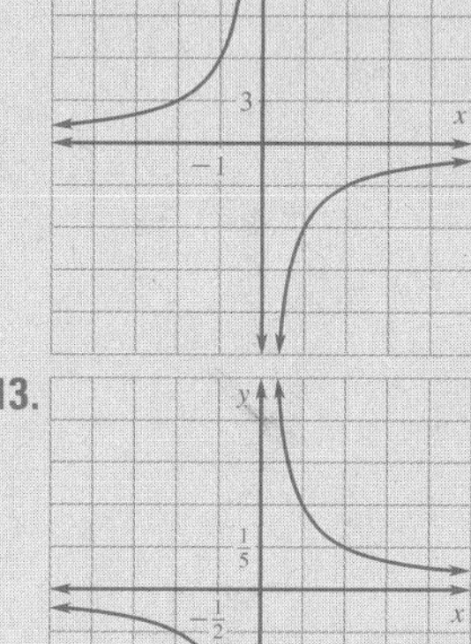

13.

14–18. See Additional Answers beginning on p. AA1.

25. $\frac{11x^2}{6}$, excluded value is 0.

26. 3, excluded value is -2.

27. $\frac{3}{4}$, excluded value is 5.

28. -2, excluded value is 4.

29. $\frac{r - 5}{r - 2}$, excluded values are 2 and -3.

30. $\frac{1}{2s - 3}$, excluded values are -3 and $\frac{3}{2}$.

31. $\frac{2m - 4}{3m^2 + 6m}$, excluded values are -6, -2, and 0.

32. $\frac{2n}{n + 3}$, excluded values are -3, 0, and 3.

18. population: parents or guardians of high school students, sampling method: systematic sample

19. Yes. *Sample answer:* The sampling method might be biased because only the parents or guardians of students are called and not other spectators.

20. Potentially biased. *Sample answer:* The question encourages the listener to agree with the researcher.

22. 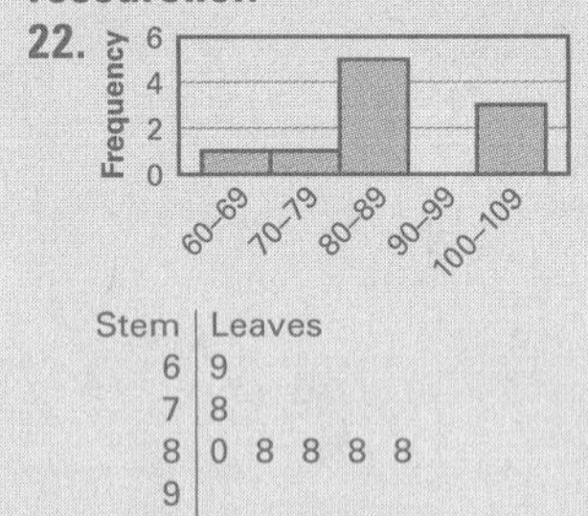

Stem	Leaves
6	9
7	8
8	0 8 8 8 8
9	
10	1 2 8

Key: 6 | 9 = 69

23. 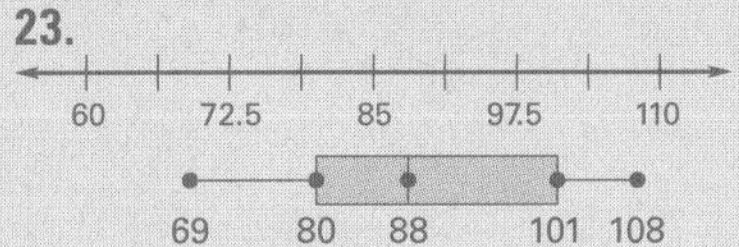

Chapter 13

13.1 In Exercises 1 and 2, use the following information. A bag contains 3 red, 3 blue, and 3 yellow marbles. You toss a coin and then draw a marble out of the bag at random.

1. Find the number of possible outcomes in the sample space. Then list the possible outcomes. 6 possible outcomes; heads, yellow; heads, red; heads, blue; tails, yellow; tails, red; tails, blue
2. What is the probability that the coin shows tails and the marble is blue? $\frac{1}{6}$

13.1 3. You toss a coin 3 times. What are the odds against the coin's showing heads twice and tails once? 5 : 3

13.2 4. In how many ways can you arrange the letters in the word SPRING? 720 ways

5. In how many ways can you arrange 3 of the letters in the word TULIP? 60 ways

13.2 Evaluate the expression.

6. 7! 5040
7. ${}_8P_3$ 336
8. ${}_{10}P_3$ 720
9. ${}_5P_5$ 120

13.3 10. You can choose 3 books from a list of 5 books to read for English class. How many combinations of 3 books are possible? 10 combinations

13.3 Evaluate the expression.

11. ${}_6C_2$ 15
12. ${}_7C_3$ 35
13. ${}_{10}C_4$ 210
14. ${}_{20}C_{15}$ 15,504

13.4 In Exercises 15 and 16, you roll a number cube. Tell whether the events *A* and *B* are *mutually exclusive* or *overlapping*. Then find *P*(*A* or *B*).

15. **Event *A*:** Roll a 5. overlapping; $\frac{1}{2}$
Event *B*: Roll a prime number.

16. **Event *A*:** Roll a 4. mutually exclusive; $\frac{1}{2}$
Event *B*: Roll a multiple of 3.

13.4 17. A bag contains 3 red, 4 blue, and 5 yellow marbles. You randomly draw two marbles, one at a time. Find the probability that both are blue if **(a)** you replace the first marble and **(b)** you do not replace the first marble. a. $\frac{1}{9}$ b. $\frac{1}{11}$

13.5 In Exercises 18–20, use the following information. 18–20. See margin.

Some parents want to gather information about updating the sound system in the high school auditorium. They obtain a list of high school students and call the parents or guardians of every 20th student on the list. The question they ask is "Don't you think the sound system in the high school auditorium needs updating?"

18. Identify the population and classify the sampling method.
19. Is the sampling method used likely to result in a biased sample? *Explain.*
20. Tell whether the question is potentially biased. *Explain* your answer.

In Exercises 21–23, use the following numbers of stories in the world's ten tallest buildings: 101, 88, 88, 108, 88, 88, 80, 69, 102, 78.

13.6 21. Find the mean, median, mode(s), range, and mean absolute deviation of the data. Round to the nearest hundredth, if necessary. mean: 89, median: 88, mode: 88, range: 39, mean absolute deviation: 8.8

13.7 22. Make a histogram and a stem-and-leaf plot of the data. See margin.

13.8 23. Make a box-and-whisker plot of the data. Identify any outliers. See margin for art; no outliers.

EXTRA PRACTICE

Symbols

Symbol	Meaning	Page
$3 \cdot x$ $3x$ $3(x)$	3 times x	2
$\frac{a}{b}$	a divided by b, $b \neq 0$	2
a^4	the fourth power of a, or $a \cdot a \cdot a \cdot a$	3
( )	parentheses—a grouping symbol	9
[ ]	brackets—a grouping symbol	9
$=$	is equal to	21
$<$	is less than	21
$>$	is greater than	21
$\leq$	is less than or equal to	21
$\geq$	is greater than or equal to	21
$\stackrel{?}{=}$	is equal to?	22
(x, y)	ordered pair	43
...	continues on	64
$-a$	the opposite of a	66
$\lvert a \rvert$	the absolute value of a	66
$\begin{bmatrix} 1 & 0 \\ 0 & 1 \end{bmatrix}$	matrix	94
$\frac{1}{a}$	the reciprocal of a, $a \neq 0$	103
$\sqrt{a}$	the nonnegative square root of a, $a \geq 0$	110
$\pm$	plus or minus	110
$\approx$	is approximately equal to	112
$a:b$	the ratio of a to b	162

Symbol	Meaning	Page
$\cong$	is congruent to	174
$\sim$	is similar to	174
A'	the image of point A	213
m	slope	235
b	y-intercept	244
a	constant of variation	253
$f(x)$	the value of the function f at x	262
a^{-n}	$\frac{1}{a^n}$, $a \neq 0$	503
$\sqrt[3]{a}$	the cube root of a	510
$c \times 10^n$	scientific notation, $1 \leq c < 10$ and n is an integer	512
$P(A)$	the probability of an event A	844
$n!$	n factorial, or $n \cdot (n-1) \cdot \ldots \cdot 2 \cdot 1$, n is a nonnegative integer	852
$_nP_r$	the number of permutations of n objects taken r at a time, $r \leq n$	852
$_nC_r$	the number of combinations of n objects taken r at a time, $r \leq n$	856
$\overline{x}$	x bar, the mean of numerical data	875
σ^2	variance, the square of standard deviation	879
σ	standard deviation, the nonnegative square root of variance	879

Geometric Formulas

Pythagorean Theorem (p. 737)

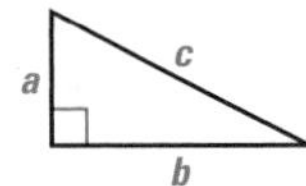

In a right triangle, $a^2 + b^2 = c^2$ where a and b are the lengths of the legs and c is the length of the hypotenuse.

Square (p. 924)

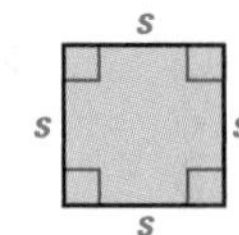
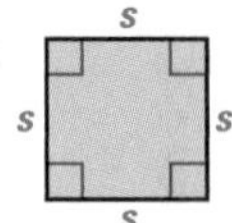

Area
$A = s^2$

Perimeter
$P = 4s$

Rectangle (p. 924)

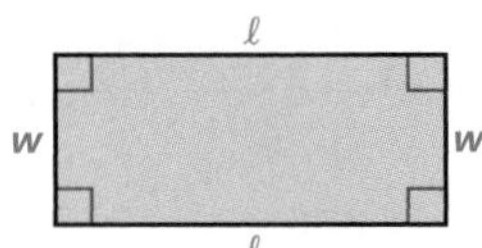

Area
$A = \ell w$

Perimeter
$P = 2\ell + 2w$

Parallelogram (p. 924)

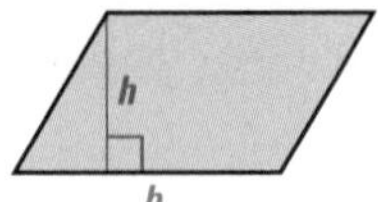

Area
$A = bh$

Triangle (p. 924)

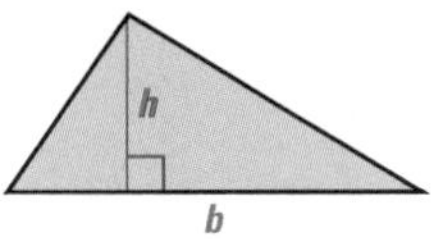

Area
$A = \frac{1}{2}bh$

Trapezoid (p. 924)

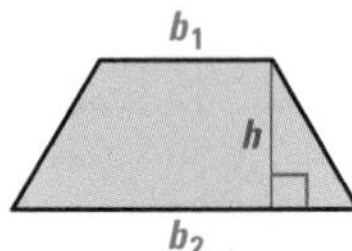

Area
$A = \frac{1}{2}(b_1 + b_2)h$

Circle (p. 926)

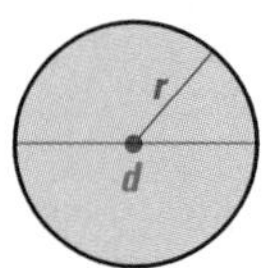

Circumference
$C = \pi d$ or
$C = 2\pi r$

Area
$A = \pi r^2$

Prism (p. 927)

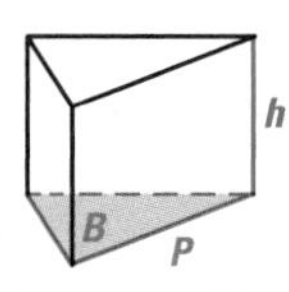

Surface Area
$S = 2B + Ph$

Volume
$V = Bh$

Cylinder (p. 927)

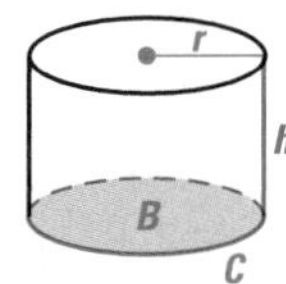

Surface Area
$S = 2B + Ch$
$= 2\pi r^2 + 2\pi rh$

Volume
$V = Bh$
$= \pi r^2 h$

Pyramid (p. 927)

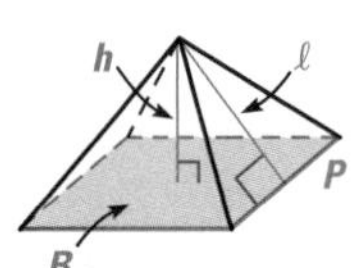

Surface Area
$S = B + \frac{1}{2}P\ell$

Volume
$V = \frac{1}{3}Bh$

Cone (p. 927)

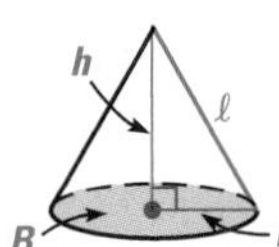

Surface Area
$S = B + \pi r\ell$
$= \pi r^2 + \pi r\ell$

Volume
$V = \frac{1}{3}Bh$
$= \frac{1}{3}\pi r^2 h$

Sphere (p. 927)

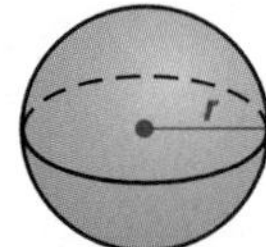

Surface Area
$S = 4\pi r^2$

Volume
$V = \frac{4}{3}\pi r^3$

Other Formulas

Slope (p. 235)	The slope m of a nonvertical line passing through the two points (x_1, y_1) and (x_2, y_2) is $m = \frac{y_2 - y_1}{x_2 - x_1}$.
Compound interest (p. 523)	$y = a(1 + r)^t$ where y is the account balance, a is the initial investment, r is the annual interest rate (in decimal form), and t is the time in years.
Quadratic formula (p. 671)	The real-number solutions of the quadratic equation $ax^2 + bx + c = 0$ are $x = \frac{-b \pm \sqrt{b^2 - 4ac}}{2a}$ where $a \neq 0$ and $b^2 - 4ac \geq 0$.
Distance formula (p. 744)	The distance d between any two points (x_1, y_1) and (x_2, y_2) is $d = \sqrt{(x_2 - x_1)^2 + (y_2 - y_1)^2}$.
Midpoint formula (p. 745)	The midpoint M of the line segment with endpoints $A(x_1, y_1)$ and $B(x_2, y_2)$ is $M\left(\frac{x_1 + x_2}{2}, \frac{y_1 + y_2}{2}\right)$.
Theoretical probability (p. 844)	The probability of an event when all the outcomes are equally likely is $P(\text{event}) = \frac{\text{Number of favorable outcomes}}{\text{Total number of outcomes}}$.
Experimental probability (p. 844)	For repeated trials of an experiment, the probability of an event is $P(\text{event}) = \frac{\text{Number of successes}}{\text{Number of trials}}$.
Permutations (p. 852)	The number of permutations of n objects taken r at a time, where $r \leq n$, is given by ${}_nP_r = \frac{n!}{(n - r)!}$.
Combinations (p. 856)	The number of combinations of n objects taken r at a time, where $r \leq n$, is given by ${}_nC_r = \frac{n!}{(n - r)! \cdot r!}$.
Probability of mutually exclusive or overlapping events (p. 861)	If A and B are mutually exclusive events, then $P(A \text{ or } B) = P(A) + P(B)$. If A and B are overlapping events, then $P(A \text{ or } B) = P(A) + P(B) - P(A \text{ and } B)$.
Probability of independent or dependent events (p. 862)	If A and B are independent events, then $P(A \text{ and } B) = P(A) \cdot P(B)$. If A and B are dependent events, then $P(A \text{ and } B) = P(A) \cdot P(B \text{ given } A)$.

TABLES

953

Properties

Properties of Addition and Multiplication

Commutative Properties (pp. 75, 89)	
The order in which you add two numbers does not change the sum.	$a + b = b + a$
The order in which you multiply two numbers does not change the product.	$a \cdot b = b \cdot a$
Associative Properties (pp. 75, 89)	
The way you group three numbers in a sum does not change the sum.	$(a + b) + c = a + (b + c)$
The way you group three numbers in a product does not change the product.	$(a \cdot b) \cdot c = a \cdot (b \cdot c)$
Identity Properties (pp. 75, 89)	
The sum of a number and the additive identity, 0, is the number.	$a + 0 = 0 + a = a$
The product of a number and the multiplicative identity, 1, is the number.	$a \cdot 1 = 1 \cdot a = a$
Inverse Properties (pp. 75, 103)	
The sum of a number and its additive inverse, or opposite, is 0.	$a + (-a) = -a + a = 0$
The product of a nonzero number and its multiplicative inverse, or reciprocal, is 1.	$a \cdot \frac{1}{a} = \frac{1}{a} \cdot a = 1\ (a \neq 0)$
Distributive Property (p. 96) You can multiply a number and a sum by multiplying each term of the sum by the number and then adding these products. The same property applies to the product of a number and a difference.	$a(b + c) = ab + ac$ $(b + c)a = ba + ca$ $a(b - c) = ab - ac$ $(b - c)a = ba - ca$

Properties of Equality

Addition Property of Equality (p. 134) Adding the same number to each side of an equation produces an equivalent equation.	If $x - a = b$, then $x - a + a = b + a$, or $x = b + a$.
Subtraction Property of Equality (p. 134) Subtracting the same number from each side of an equation produces an equivalent equation.	If $x + a = b$, then $x + a - a = b - a$, or $x = b - a$.
Multiplication Property of Equality (p. 135) Multiplying each side of an equation by the same nonzero number produces an equivalent equation.	If $\frac{x}{a} = b$ and $a \neq 0$, then $a \cdot \frac{x}{a} = a \cdot b$, or $x = ab$.
Division Property of Equality (p. 135) Dividing each side of an equation by the same nonzero number produces an equivalent equation.	If $ax = b$ and $a \neq 0$, then $\frac{ax}{a} = \frac{b}{a}$, or $x = \frac{b}{a}$.

Properties of Inequality

Addition and Subtraction Properties of Inequality (pp. 357, 358) Adding or subtracting the same number on each side of an inequality produces an equivalent inequality.	If $a < b$, then $a + c < b + c$ and $a - c < b - c$. If $a > b$, then $a + c > b + c$ and $a - c > b - c$.
Multiplication and Division Properties of Inequality (pp. 363, 364) Multiplying or dividing each side of an inequality by a *positive* number produces an equivalent inequality. Multiplying or dividing each side of an inequality by a *negative* number and *reversing the direction of the inequality symbol* produces an equivalent inequality.	If $a < b$ and $c > 0$, then $ac < bc$ and $\frac{a}{c} < \frac{b}{c}$. If $a < b$ and $c < 0$, then $ac > bc$ and $\frac{a}{c} > \frac{b}{c}$.

Properties of Exponents

Product of Powers Property (p. 489) To multiply powers having the same base, add the exponents.	$a^m \cdot a^n = a^{m+n}$
Power of a Power Property (p. 490) To find a power of a power, multiply exponents.	$(a^m)^n = a^{mn}$
Power of a Product Property (p. 490) To find a power of a product, find the power of each factor and multiply.	$(ab)^m = a^m b^m$
Quotient of Powers Property (p. 495) To divide powers having the same nonzero base, subtract exponents.	$\frac{a^m}{a^n} = a^{m-n}, a \neq 0$
Power of a Quotient Property (p. 496) To find a power of a quotient, find the power of the numerator and the power of the denominator and divide.	$\left(\frac{a}{b}\right)^m = \frac{a^m}{b^m}, b \neq 0$

Other Properties

Cross Products Property (p. 168) The cross products of a proportion are equal.	If $\frac{a}{b} = \frac{c}{d}$ $(b, d \neq 0)$, then $ad = bc$.
Product Property of Radicals (p. 719) The square root of a product equals the product of the square roots of the factors.	$\sqrt{ab} = \sqrt{a} \cdot \sqrt{b}$, $a \geq 0$ and $b \geq 0$
Quotient Properties of Radicals (p. 720) The square root of a quotient equals the quotient of the square roots of the numerator and denominator.	$\sqrt{\frac{a}{b}} = \frac{\sqrt{a}}{\sqrt{b}}$, $a \geq 0$ and $b > 0$

TABLES

955

Measures

Time	
60 seconds (sec) = 1 minute (min) 60 minutes = 1 hour (h) 24 hours = 1 day 7 days = 1 week 4 weeks (approx.) = 1 month	365 days, 52 weeks (approx.), 12 months = 1 year 10 years = 1 decade 100 years = 1 century

Metric	United States Customary
Length 10 millimeters (mm) = 1 centimeter (cm) 100 cm, 1000 mm = 1 meter (m) 1000 m = 1 kilometer (km)	**Length** 12 inches (in.) = 1 foot (ft) 36 in., 3 ft = 1 yard (yd) 5280 ft, 1760 yd = 1 mile (mi)
Area 100 square millimeters (mm^2) = 1 square centimeter (cm^2) 10,000 cm^2 = 1 square meter (m^2) 10,000 m^2 = 1 hectare (ha)	**Area** 144 square inches ($in.^2$) = 1 square foot (ft^2) 9 ft^2 = 1 square yard (yd^2) 43,560 ft^2, 4840 yd^2 = 1 acre (A)
Volume 1000 cubic millimeters (mm^3) = 1 cubic centimeter (cm^3) 1,000,000 cm^3 = 1 cubic meter (m^3)	**Volume** 1728 cubic inches ($in.^3$) = 1 cubic foot (ft^3) 27 ft^3 = 1 cubic yard (yd^3)
Liquid Capacity 1000 milliliters (mL), 1000 cubic centimeters (cm^3) = 1 liter (L) 1000 L = 1 kiloliter (kL)	**Liquid Capacity** 8 fluid ounces (fl oz) = 1 cup (c) 2 c = 1 pint (pt) 2 pt = 1 quart (qt) 4 qt = 1 gallon (gal)
Mass 1000 milligrams (mg) = 1 gram (g) 1000 g = 1 kilogram (kg) 1000 kg = 1 metric ton (t)	**Weight** 16 ounces (oz) = 1 pound (lb) 2000 lb = 1 ton
Temperature Degrees Celsius (°C) 0°C = freezing point of water 37°C = normal body temperature 100°C = boiling point of water	**Temperature Degrees Fahrenheit (°F)** 32°F = freezing point of water 98.6°F = normal body temperature 212°F = boiling point of water

TABLES

Squares and Square Roots

No.	Square	Sq. Root	No.	Square	Sq. Root	No.	Square	Sq. Root
1	1	1.000	**51**	2601	7.141	**101**	10,201	10.050
2	4	1.414	**52**	2704	7.211	**102**	10,404	10.100
3	9	1.732	**53**	2809	7.280	**103**	10,609	10.149
4	16	2.000	**54**	2916	7.348	**104**	10,816	10.198
5	25	2.236	**55**	3025	7.416	**105**	11,025	10.247
6	36	2.449	**56**	3136	7.483	**106**	11,236	10.296
7	49	2.646	**57**	3249	7.550	**107**	11,449	10.344
8	64	2.828	**58**	3364	7.616	**108**	11,664	10.392
9	81	3.000	**59**	3481	7.681	**109**	11,881	10.440
10	100	3.162	**60**	3600	7.746	**110**	12,100	10.488
11	121	3.317	**61**	3721	7.810	**111**	12,321	10.536
12	144	3.464	**62**	3844	7.874	**112**	12,544	10.583
13	169	3.606	**63**	3969	7.937	**113**	12,769	10.630
14	196	3.742	**64**	4096	8.000	**114**	12,996	10.677
15	225	3.873	**65**	4225	8.062	**115**	13,225	10.724
16	256	4.000	**66**	4356	8.124	**116**	13,456	10.770
17	289	4.123	**67**	4489	8.185	**117**	13,689	10.817
18	324	4.243	**68**	4624	8.246	**118**	13,924	10.863
19	361	4.359	**69**	4761	8.307	**119**	14,161	10.909
20	400	4.472	**70**	4900	8.367	**120**	14,400	10.954
21	441	4.583	**71**	5041	8.426	**121**	14,641	11.000
22	484	4.690	**72**	5184	8.485	**122**	14,884	11.045
23	529	4.796	**73**	5329	8.544	**123**	15,129	11.091
24	576	4.899	**74**	5476	8.602	**124**	15,376	11.136
25	625	5.000	**75**	5625	8.660	**125**	15,625	11.180
26	676	5.099	**76**	5776	8.718	**126**	15,876	11.225
27	729	5.196	**77**	5929	8.775	**127**	16,129	11.269
28	784	5.292	**78**	6084	8.832	**128**	16,384	11.314
29	841	5.385	**79**	6241	8.888	**129**	16,641	11.358
30	900	5.477	**80**	6400	8.944	**130**	16,900	11.402
31	961	5.568	**81**	6561	9.000	**131**	17,161	11.446
32	1024	5.657	**82**	6724	9.055	**132**	17,424	11.489
33	1089	5.745	**83**	6889	9.110	**133**	17,689	11.533
34	1156	5.831	**84**	7056	9.165	**134**	17,956	11.576
35	1225	5.916	**85**	7225	9.220	**135**	18,225	11.619
36	1296	6.000	**86**	7396	9.274	**136**	18,496	11.662
37	1369	6.083	**87**	7569	9.327	**137**	18,769	11.705
38	1444	6.164	**88**	7744	9.381	**138**	19,044	11.747
39	1521	6.245	**89**	7921	9.434	**139**	19,321	11.790
40	1600	6.325	**90**	8100	9.487	**140**	19,600	11.832
41	1681	6.403	**91**	8281	9.539	**141**	19,881	11.874
42	1764	6.481	**92**	8464	9.592	**142**	20,164	11.916
43	1849	6.557	**93**	8649	9.644	**143**	20,449	11.958
44	1936	6.633	**94**	8836	9.695	**144**	20,736	12.000
45	2025	6.708	**95**	9025	9.747	**145**	21,025	12.042
46	2116	6.782	**96**	9216	9.798	**146**	21,316	12.083
47	2209	6.856	**97**	9409	9.849	**147**	21,609	12.124
48	2304	6.928	**98**	9604	9.899	**148**	21,904	12.166
49	2401	7.000	**99**	9801	9.950	**149**	22,201	12.207
50	2500	7.071	**100**	10,000	10.000	**150**	22,500	12.247

957

English–Spanish Glossary

A

absolute deviation (p. 392) The absolute deviation of a number x from a given value is the absolute value of the difference of x and the given value: absolute deviation $= \lvert x - \text{given value} \rvert$ **desviación absoluta** (pág. 392) La desviación absoluta de un número x con respecto a un valor dado es el valor absoluto de la diferencia entre x y el valor dado: desviación absoluta $= \lvert x - \text{valor dado} \rvert$	If the absolute deviation of x from 2 is 3, then $\lvert x - 2 \rvert = 3$. Si la desviación absoluta de x con respecto a 2 es 3, entonces $\lvert x - 2 \rvert = 3$.
absolute value (p. 66) The absolute value of a number a is the distance between a and 0 on a number line. The symbol $\lvert a \rvert$ represents the absolute value of a. **valor absoluto** (pág. 66) El valor absoluto de un número a es la distancia entre a y 0 en una recta numérica. El símbolo $\lvert a \rvert$ representa el valor absoluto de a.	$\lvert 2 \rvert = 2$, $\lvert -5 \rvert = 5$, and $\lvert 0 \rvert = 0$ $\lvert 2 \rvert = 2$, $\lvert -5 \rvert = 5$, y $\lvert 0 \rvert = 0$
absolute value equation (p. 390) An equation that contains an absolute value expression. **ecuación de valor absoluto** (pág. 390) Ecuación que contiene una expresión de valor absoluto.	$\lvert x + 2 \rvert = 3$ is an absolute value equation. $\lvert x + 2 \rvert = 3$ es una ecuación de valor absoluto.
additive identity (p. 76) The number 0 is the additive identity, because the sum of any number and 0 is the number: $a + 0 = 0 + a = a$. **identidad aditiva** (pág. 76) El número 0 es la identidad aditiva ya que la suma de cualquier número y 0 es ese número: $a + 0 = 0 + a = a$.	$-2 + 0 = -2$, $0 + \frac{3}{4} = \frac{3}{4}$
additive inverse (p. 76) The additive inverse of a number a is its opposite, $-a$. The sum of a number and its additive inverse is 0: $a + (-a) = -a + a = 0$. **inverso aditivo** (pág. 76) El inverso aditivo de un número a es su opuesto, $-a$. La suma de un número y su inverso aditivo es 0: $a + (-a) = -a + a = 0$.	The additive inverse of -5 is 5, and $-5 + 5 = 0$. El inverso aditivo de -5 es 5, y $-5 + 5 = 0$.
algebraic expression (p. 2) An expression that includes at least one variable. Also called *variable expression*. **expresión algebraica** (pág. 2) Expresión que incluye por lo menos una variable.	$5n$, $\frac{14}{y}$, $6 + c$, and $8 - x$ are algebraic expressions. $5n$, $\frac{14}{y}$, $6 + c$ y $8 - x$ son expresiones algebraicas.

arithmetic sequence (p. 309) A sequence in which the difference between consecutive terms is constant.

2, 8, 14, 20, 26, . . . is an arithmetic sequence in which the difference between consecutive terms is 6.

progresión aritmética (pág. 309) Progresión en la que la diferencia entre los términos consecutivos es constante.

2, 8, 14, 20, 26, . . . es una progresión aritmética en la que la diferencia entre los términos consecutivos es 6.

---

asymptotes of a hyperbola (p. 767) Lines that a hyperbola approaches but does not intersect.

See hyperbola.

asíntotas de una hipérbola (pág. 767) Rectas a las que la hipérbola se acerca pero sin cortarlas.

***Ver* hipérbola.**

---

axis of symmetry (p. 628) The line that passes through the vertex and divides the parabola into two symmetric parts.

eje de simetría (pág. 628) La recta que pasa por el vértice y divide a la parábola en dos partes simétricas.

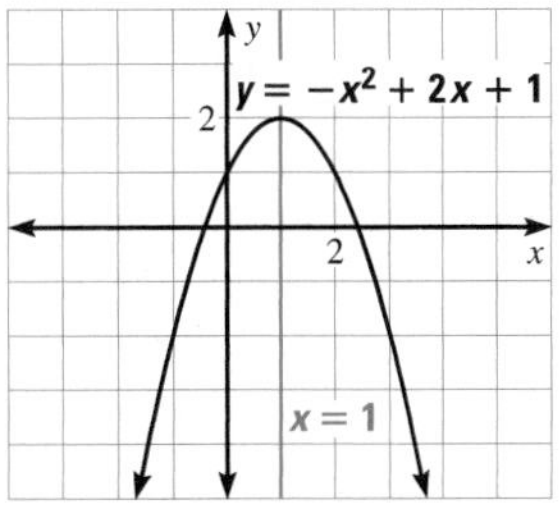

The axis of symmetry of the graph of $y = -x^2 + 2x + 1$ is the line $x = 1$.

El eje de simetría de la gráfica de $y = -x^2 + 2x + 1$ es la recta $x = 1$.

B

base of a power (p. 3) The number or expression that is used as a factor in a repeated multiplication.

In the power 3^4, the base is 3.

base de una potencia (pág. 3) El número o la expresión que se usa como factor en la multiplicación repetida.

En la potencia 3^4, la base es 3.

---

best-fitting line (p. 335) The line that most closely follows a trend in data, found using technology.

mejor recta de regresión (pág. 335) La recta que se ajusta más a la tendencia de los datos y que se encuentra mediante tecnología.

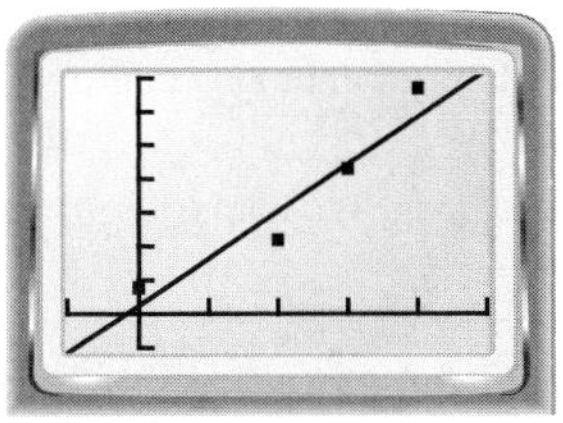

The graph shows the best-fitting line for the data in the scatter plot.

La gráfica muestra la mejor recta de regresión para los datos del diagrama de dispersión.

959

biased question (p. 872) A question that encourages a particular response. **pregunta capciosa** (pág. 872) Pregunta que impulsa a dar una respuesta determinada.	"Don't you agree that the voting age should be lowered to 16 because many 16-year-olds are responsible and informed?" is a biased question. "¿No estás de acuerdo en que se debe bajar la edad para votar a los 16 años ya que muchos jóvenes de 16 años son responsables y están bien informados?" es una pregunta capciosa.
biased sample (p. 872) A sample that is not representative of the population. **muestra sesgada** (pág. 872) Muestra que no es representativa de la población.	The members of a school's basketball team would form a biased sample for a survey about whether to build a new gym. Los miembros del equipo de baloncesto de una escuela formarían una muestra sesgada si participaran en una encuesta sobre si quieren que se construya un nuevo gimnasio.
binomial (p. 555) A polynomial with two terms. **binomio** (pág. 555) Polinomio con dos términos.	$t^3 - 4t$ and $2x + 5$ are binomials. $t^3 - 4t$ y $2x + 5$ son binomios.
box-and-whisker plot (p. 887) A data display that organizes data values into four groups using the minimum value, lower quartile, median, upper quartile, and maximum value. **gráfica de frecuencias acumuladas** (pág. 887) Presentación de datos que organiza los valores de los datos en cuatro grupos usando el valor mínimo, el cuartil inferior, la mediana, el cuartil superior y el valor máximo.	0 10 20 30 40 50 8 19 26 37 45
branches of a hyperbola (p. 767) The two symmetrical parts of a hyperbola. **ramas de una hipérbola** (pág. 767) Las dos partes simétricas de la hipérbola.	*See* hyperbola. *Ver* hipérbola.

C

coefficient (p. 97) The number part of a term with a variable part. **coeficiente** (pág. 97) La parte numérica de un término que tiene una variable.	The coefficient of $-6x$ is -6. El coeficiente de $-6x$ es -6.
combination (p. 856) A selection of objects in which order is *not* important. **combinación** (pág. 856) Selección de objetos en la que el orden *no* es importante.	There are 6 combinations of two of the letters from the list A, B, C, D: AB, AC, AD, BC, BD, and CD. Hay 6 combinaciones de dos de las letras de la lista A, B, C, D: AB, AC, AD, BC, BD y CD.

ENGLISH-SPANISH GLOSSARY

common difference (p. 309) The constant difference between consecutive terms of an arithmetic sequence. **diferencia común** (pág. 309) La diferencia constante entre los términos consecutivos de una progresión aritmética.	2, 8, 14, 20, 26, . . . is an arithmetic sequence with a common difference of 6. **2, 8, 14, 20, 26, . . . es una progresión aritmética con una diferencia común de 6.**
common ratio (p. 539) The ratio of any term of a geometric sequence to the previous term of the sequence. **razón común** (pág. 539) La razón entre cualquier término de una progresión geométrica y el término anterior de la progresión.	The sequence 5, 10, 20, 40, . . . is a geometric sequence with common ratio 2. **La progresión 5, 10, 20, 40, . . . es una progresión geométrica con una razón común de 2.**
completing the square (p. 663) The process of rewriting a quadratic expression so that it is a perfect square trinomial. **completar el cuadrado** (pág. 663) El proceso de escribir una expresión cuadrática de manera que sea un trinomio cuadrado perfecto.	To write $x^2 - 16x$ as a perfect square trinomial, add $\left(\frac{-16}{2}\right)^2$, or $(-8)^2$. This gives $x^2 - 16x + (-8)^2 = (x - 8)^2$. **Para escribir $x^2 - 16x$ como trinomio cuadrado perfecto, suma $\left(\frac{-16}{2}\right)^2$, o $(-8)^2$. Así resulta $x^2 - 16x + (-8)^2 = (x - 8)^2$.**
complex fraction (p. 810) A fraction that contains a fraction in its numerator, denominator, or both. **fracción compleja** (pág. 810) Fracción que contiene una fracción en su numerador, en su denominador o en ambos.	$\frac{\frac{3x}{2}}{-6x^3}$ and $\frac{x^2-1}{\frac{x+1}{x-1}}$ are complex fractions. **$\frac{\frac{3x}{2}}{-6x^3}$ y $\frac{x^2-1}{\frac{x+1}{x-1}}$ son fracciones complejas.**
compound event (p. 861) An event that combines two or more events, using the word *and* or the word *or*. **suceso compuesto** (pág. 861) Suceso que combina dos o más sucesos usando la palabra *y* o la palabra *o*.	When you roll a number cube, the event "roll a 2 or an odd number" is a compound event. **Cuando lanzas un cubo numerado, el suceso "salir el 2 ó número impar" es un suceso compuesto.**
compound inequality (p. 380) Two inequalities joined by *and* or *or*. **desigualdad compuesta** (pág. 380) Dos desigualdades unidas por *y* u *o*.	$-2 < x$ *and* $x < 1$, which can be written as $-2 < x < 1$, is a compound inequality, as is $x < -1$ *or* $x > 0$. **$-2 < x$ *y* $x < 1$, que puede escribirse $-2 < x < 1$, es una desigualdad compuesta, al igual que $x < -1$ *ó* $x > 0$.**
compound interest (p. 523) Interest that is earned on both an initial investment and on previously earned interest. **interés compuesto** (pág. 523) Interés obtenido tanto sobre la inversión inicial como sobre el interés conseguido anteriormente.	You deposit \$250 in an account that earns 4% interest compounded yearly. After 5 years, your account balance is $y = 250(1 + 0.04)^5 \approx$ \$304.16. **Depositas \$250 en una cuenta al 4% anual de interés compuesto. Después de 5 años, el balance de la cuenta es $y = 250(1 + 0.04)^5 \approx$ \$304.16.**

ENGLISH-SPANISH GLOSSARY

conditional statement (p. 66) A statement with a hypothesis and a conclusion.

enunciado condicional (pág. 66) Enunciado que tiene una hipótesis y una conclusión.

conditional statement
enunciado condicional

If $a > 0$, then $|a| = a$.

hypothesis / **hipótesis** — conclusion / **conclusión**

congruent figures (p. 174) Figures that have the same size and shape. The symbol ≅ indicates congruence.

figuras congruentes (pág. 174) Figuras que tienen igual tamaño y forma. El símbolo ≅ indica la congruencia.

$\triangle ABC \cong \triangle DEF$

conjecture (p. 117) A statement that is believed to be true but not yet shown to be true.

conjetura (pág. 117) Enunciado que se considera verdadero sin que haya sido demostrado todavía.

A conclusion reached using inductive reasoning is a conjecture.

Una conclusión que se saca mediante el razonamiento inductivo es una conjetura.

consistent dependent system (p. 459) A linear system with infinitely many solutions. The graphs of the equations of a consistent dependent system coincide.

sistema dependiente compatible (pág. 459) Sistema lineal con infinitas soluciones. Las gráficas de las ecuaciones de un sistema dependiente compatible coinciden.

The linear system $x - 2y = -4$ and $y = \frac{1}{2}x + 2$ is a consistent dependent system because the graphs of the equations coincide.

El sistema lineal $x - 2y = -4$ e $y = \frac{1}{2}x + 2$ es un sistema dependiente compatible ya que las gráficas de las ecuaciones coinciden.

consistent independent system (p. 427) A linear system with exactly one solution. The graphs of the equations of a consistent independent system intersect.

sistema independiente compatible (pág. 427) Sistema lineal con una sola solución. Las gráficas de las ecuaciones de un sistema independiente compatible se cortan.

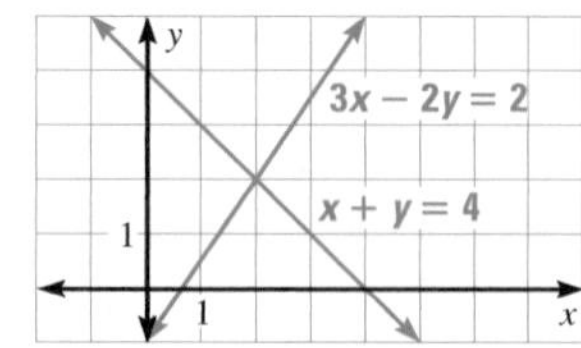

The linear system $3x - 2y = 2$ and $x + y = 4$ is a consistent independent system because the graphs of the equations intersect.

El sistema lineal $3x - 2y = 2$ y $x + y = 4$ es un sistema independiente compatible ya que las gráficas de las ecuaciones se cortan.

constant of variation (pp. 253, 765) The nonzero constant a in a direct variation equation $y = ax$ or in an inverse variation equation $y = \frac{a}{x}$. **constante de variación** (págs. 253, 765) La constante a distinta de cero de una ecuación de variación directa $y = ax$ o de una ecuación de variación inversa $y = \frac{a}{x}$.	The constant of variation in the direct variation equation $y = \frac{2}{3}x$ is $\frac{2}{3}$, and the constant of variation in the inverse variation equation $y = \frac{-1}{x}$ is -1. **La constante de variación de la ecuación de variación directa $y = \frac{2}{3}x$ es $\frac{2}{3}$, y la constante de variación de la ecuación de variación inversa $y = \frac{-1}{x}$ es -1.**
constant term (p. 97) A term with a number part but no variable part. **término constante** (pág. 97) Término que tiene una parte numérica sin variable.	In the expression $3x + (-4) + (-6x) + 2$, the constant terms are -4 and 2. **En la expresión $3x + (-4) + (-6x) + 2$, los términos constantes son -4 y 2.**
continuous function (p. 223) A function with a graph that is unbroken. **función continua** (pág. 223) Función con una gráfica no interrumpida.	y x
convenience sample (p. 871) A sample in which only members of a population who are easily accessible are selected. **muestra de conveniencia** (pág. 871) Muestra en la que se selecciona sólo a los miembros de una población fácilmente accesibles.	You can select a convenience sample of a school's student population by choosing only students who are in your classes. **Para seleccionar una muestra de conveniencia de la población de estudiantes de una escuela, puedes escoger sólo a los estudiantes que están en tus clases.**
converse of a conditional (p. 319) A statement formed by interchanging the hypothesis and the conclusion of the conditional. The converse of a true statement is not necessarily true. **recíproco de un condicional** (pág. 319) Enunciado formado al intercambiar la hipótesis y la conclusión del condicional. El recíproco de un enunciado verdadero no es necesariamente verdadero.	The converse of the statement "If $x = 5$, then $\lvert x \rvert = 5$" is "If $\lvert x \rvert = 5$, then $x = 5$." The original statement is true, but the converse is false. **El recíproco del enunciado "Si $x = 5$, entonces $\lvert x \rvert = 5$" es "Si $\lvert x \rvert = 5$, entonces $x = 5$". El enunciado original es verdadero, pero el recíproco es falso.**

ENGLISH-SPANISH GLOSSARY

correlation (p. 325) The relationship between paired data. The paired data have *positive correlation* if y tends to increase as x increases, *negative correlation* if y tends to decrease as x increases, and *relatively no correlation* if x and y have no apparent relationship. **correlación** (pág. 325) La relación entre los pares de datos. Los pares de datos presentan una *correlación positiva* si y tiende a aumentar al aumentar x, una *correlación negativa* si y tiende a disminuir al aumentar x y una *correlación nula* si x e y no tienen ninguna relación aparente.	Positive correlation **Correlación positiva** Negative correlation **Correlación negativa** Relatively no correlation **Correlación nula**
corresponding parts (p. 174) A pair of sides or angles that have the same relative position in two figures. **partes correspondientes** (pág. 174) Par de lados o ángulos que tienen la misma posición relativa en dos figuras.	A B C J K L $\angle A$ and $\angle J$ are corresponding angles. $\overline{AB}$ and $\overline{JK}$ are corresponding sides. **$\angle A$ y $\angle J$ son ángulos correspondientes. $\overline{AB}$ y $\overline{JK}$ son lados correspondientes.**
counterexample (p. 66) An example used to show that an if-then statement is false. **contraejemplo** (pág. 66) Ejemplo utilizado para demostrar que un enunciado de "si…, entonces…" es falso.	The statement "If a number is a whole number, then the number is positive" is false because 0 is a whole number that is not a positive number. **El enunciado "Si un número es un número natural, entonces es positivo" es falso ya que 0 es un número natural que no es positivo.**
cross product (p. 168) In a proportion, a cross product is the product of the numerator of one ratio and the denominator of the other ratio. The cross products of a proportion are equal. **producto cruzado** (pág. 168) En una proporción, un producto cruzado es el producto del numerador de una de las razones y el denominador de la otra razón. Los productos cruzados de una proporción son iguales.	The cross products of the proportion $\frac{3}{4} = \frac{6}{8}$ are $3 \cdot 8 = 24$ and $4 \cdot 6 = 24$. **Los productos cruzados de la proporción $\frac{3}{4} = \frac{6}{8}$ son $3 \cdot 8 = 24$ y $4 \cdot 6 = 24$.**
cube root (p. 510) If $b^3 = a$, then b is the cube root of a. **raíz cúbica** (pág. 510) Si $b^3 = a$, entonces b es la raíz cúbica de a.	2 is the cube root of 8 because $2^3 = 8$. **2 es la raíz cúbica de 8 ya que $2^3 = 8$.**

D

decay factor (p. 534) The expression $1 - r$ in the exponential decay model $y = a(1 - r)^t$. **factor de decrecimiento** (pág. 534) La expresión $1 - r$ del modelo de decrecimiento exponencial $y = a(1 - r)^t$.	In the exponential decay model $P = 41(0.995)^t$, the decay factor is 0.995. En el modelo de decrecimiento exponencial $P = 41(0.995)^t$, el factor de decrecimiento es 0.995.
decay rate (p. 534) The variable r in the exponential decay model $y = a(1 - r)^t$. **tasa de decrecimiento** (pág. 534) La variable r del modelo de decrecimiento exponencial $y = a(1 - r)^t$.	In the exponential decay model $P = 41(0.995)^t$, the decay rate is 0.005, because $0.995 = 1 - 0.005$. En el modelo de decrecimiento exponencial $P = 41(0.995)^t$, la tasa de decrecimiento es 0.005 ya que $0.995 = 1 - 0.005$.
deductive reasoning (p. 118) A form of reasoning in which a conclusion is based on statements that are assumed or shown to be true. **razonamiento deductivo** (pág. 118) Tipo de razonamiento en el que una conclusión se basa en enunciados que se suponen o se demuestran verdaderos.	$(x + 2) + (-2)$ $= x + [2 + (-2)]$ Associative property of addition $= x + 0$ Inverse property of addition $= x$ Identity property of addition $(x + 2) + (-2)$ $= x + [2 + (-2)]$ Propiedad asociativa de la suma $= x + 0$ Propiedad del elemento inverso de la suma $= x$ Propiedad de identidad de la suma
degree of a monomial (p. 554) The sum of the exponents of the variables in the monomial. The degree of a nonzero constant term is 0. **grado de un monomio** (pág. 554) La suma de los exponentes de las variables del monomio. El grado de un término constante distinto de cero es 0.	The degree of $\frac{1}{2}ab^2$ is $1 + 2$, or 3. El grado de $\frac{1}{2}ab^2$ es $1 + 2$, ó 3.
degree of a polynomial (p. 554) The greatest degree of the terms of the polynomial. **grado de un polinomio** (pág. 554) El mayor grado de los términos del polinomio.	The polynomial $2x^2 + x - 5$ has a degree of 2. El polinomio $2x^2 + x - 5$ tiene un grado de 2.
dependent events (p. 862) Two events such that the occurrence of one event affects the occurrence of the other event. **sucesos dependientes** (pág. 862) Dos sucesos tales que la ocurrencia de uno de ellos afecta a la ocurrencia del otro.	A bag contains 3 red marbles and 5 white marbles. You randomly draw one marble, do not replace it, then randomly draw another marble. The events "draw a red marble first" and "draw a white marble second" are dependent events. Una bolsa contiene 3 canicas rojas y 5 blancas. Sacas al azar una canica sin reemplazarla y luego sacas al azar otra canica. Los sucesos "sacar primero una canica roja" y "sacar después una canica blanca" son sucesos dependientes.

ENGLISH-SPANISH GLOSSARY

965

dependent variable (p. 36) The output variable of a function. **variable dependiente** (pág. 36) La variable de salida de una función.	In the function equation $y = x + 3$, y is the dependent variable. En la ecuación de función $y = x + 3$, y es la variable dependiente.
dimensions of a matrix (p. 94) If a matrix has m rows and n columns, the dimensions of the matrix are written as $m \times n$. **dimensiones de una matriz** (pág. 94) Si una matriz tiene m filas y n columnas, las dimensiones de la matriz se escriben $m \times n$.	The dimensions of a matrix with 2 rows and 3 columns are 2×3 ("2 by 3"). Las dimensiones de una matriz con 2 filas y 3 columnas son 2×3 ("2 por 3").
direct variation (p. 253) The relationship of two variables x and y if there is a nonzero number a such that $y = ax$. If $y = ax$, then y is said to vary directly with x. **variación directa** (pág. 253) La relación entre dos variables x e y si hay un número a distinto de cero tal que $y = ax$. Si $y = ax$, entonces se dice que y varía directamente con x.	The equation $2x - 3y = 0$ represents direct variation because it is equivalent to the equation $y = \frac{2}{3}x$. The equation $y = x + 5$ does *not* represent direct variation. La ecuación $2x - 3y = 0$ representa una variación directa ya que es equivalente a la ecuación $y = \frac{2}{3}x$. La ecuación $y = x + 5$ *no* representa una variación directa.
discrete function (p. 223) A function with a graph that consists of isolated points. **función discreta** (pág. 223) Función cuya gráfica consta de puntos aislados.	y x
discriminant (p. 678) The expression $b^2 - 4ac$ of the assciated equation $ax^2 + bx + c = 0$; also the expression under the radical sign in the quadratic formula. **discriminante** (pág. 678) La expresión $b^2 - 4ac$ de la ecuación asociada $ax^2 + bx + c = 0$; también es la expresión colocada bajo el signo radical de la fórmula cuadrática.	The value of the discriminant of the equation $3x^2 - 2x - 7 = 0$ is: $b^2 - 4ac = (-2)^2 - 4(3)(-7) = 88$ El valor del discriminante de la ecuación $3x^2 - 2x - 7 = 0$ es: $b^2 - 4ac = (-2)^2 - 4(3)(-7) = 88$
distance formula (p. 744) The distance d between any two points (x_1, y_1) and (x_2, y_2) is $d = \sqrt{(x_2 - x_1)^2 + (y_2 - y_1)^2}$. **fórmula de la distancia** (pág. 744) La distancia d entre dos puntos cualesquiera (x_1, y_1) y (x_2, y_2) es $d = \sqrt{(x_2 - x_1)^2 + (y_2 - y_1)^2}$.	The distance d between $(-1, 3)$ and $(5, 2)$ is: $d = \sqrt{(5 - (-1))^2 + (2 - 3)^2} = \sqrt{37}$ La distancia d entre $(-1, 3)$ y $(5, 2)$ es: $d = \sqrt{(5 - (-1))^2 + (2 - 3)^2} = \sqrt{37}$

ENGLISH-SPANISH GLOSSARY

distributive property (p. 96) A property that can be used to find the product of a number and a sum or difference: $a(b + c) = ab + ac$ $(b + c)a = ba + ca$ $a(b - c) = ab - ac$ $(b - c)a = ba - ca$ **propiedad distributiva** (pág. 96) Propiedad que sirve para hallar el producto de un número y una suma o una diferencia: $a(b + c) = ab + ac$ $(b + c)a = ba + ca$ $a(b - c) = ab - ac$ $(b - c)a = ba - ca$	$3(4 + 2) = 3(4) + 3(2)$, $(8 - 6)4 = (8)4 - (6)4$
domain of a function (p. 35) The set of all inputs of a function. **dominio de una función** (pág. 35) El conjunto de todas las entradas de una función.	*See* function. *Ver* función.

E

element of a matrix (p. 94) Each number in a matrix. **elemento de una matriz** (pág. 94) Cada número de la matriz.	*See* matrix. *Ver* matriz.
element of a set (p. 71) Each object in a set. Also called a *member* of a set. **elemento de un conjunto** (pág. 71) Cada objeto de un conjunto; llamado también *miembro* de un conjunto.	5 is an element of the set of whole numbers, $W = \{0, 1, 2, 3, \ldots\}$. 5 es un elemento del conjunto de los números naturales, $W = \{0, 1, 2, 3, \ldots\}$.
empty set (p. 71) The set with no elements, written as $\emptyset$. **conjunto vacío** (pág. 71) El conjunto que no tiene ningún elemento, escrito $\emptyset$.	The set of negative whole numbers $= \emptyset$. El conjunto de los números naturales negativos $= \emptyset$.
equation (p. 21) A mathematical sentence formed by placing the symbol = between two expressions. **ecuación** (pág. 21) Enunciado matemático formado al colocar el símbolo = entre dos expresiones.	$2k - 8 = 12$ is an equation. $2k - 8 = 12$ es una ecuación.
equivalent equations (p. 134) Equations that have the same solution(s). **ecuaciones equivalentes** (pág. 134) Ecuaciones que tienen la misma solución o soluciones.	$x + 7 = 4$ and $x = -3$ are equivalent equations. $x + 7 = 4$ y $x = -3$ son ecuaciones equivalentes.

ENGLISH-SPANISH GLOSSARY

equivalent expressions (p. 96) Two expressions that have the same value for all values of the variable. **expresiones equivalentes** (pág. 96) Dos expresiones que tienen el mismo valor para todos los valores de la variable.	$3(x + 2) + x$ and $4x + 6$ are equivalent expressions. $3(x + 2) + x$ y $4x + 6$ son expresiones equivalentes.
equivalent inequalities (p. 357) Inequalities that have the same solutions. **desigualdades equivalentes** (pág. 357) Desigualdades con las mismas soluciones.	$2t < 4$ and $t < 2$ are equivalent inequalities, because the solutions of both inequalities are all real numbers less than 2. $2t < 4$ y $t < 2$ son desigualdades equivalentes ya que las soluciones de ambas son todos los números reales menores que 2.
evaluate an algebraic expression (p. 2) To find the value of an algebraic expression by substituting a number for each variable and performing the operation(s). **evaluar una expresión algebraica** (pág. 2) Hallar el valor de una expresión algebraica sustituyendo cada variable por un número y realizando la operación o operaciones.	The value of $n - 1$ when $n = 3$ is $3 - 1 = 2$. El valor de $n - 1$ cuando $n = 3$ es $3 - 1 = 2$.
event (p. 843) An outcome or a collection of outcomes. **suceso** (pág. 843) Caso o colección de casos.	When you roll a number cube, "roll an odd number" is an event. Cuando lanzas un cubo numerado, "salir número impar" es un suceso.
excluded value (p. 794) A number that makes a rational expression undefined. **valor excluido** (pág. 794) Número que hace que una expresión racional sea indefinida.	3 is an excluded value of the expression $\frac{2}{x - 3}$ because 3 makes the value of the denominator 0. 3 es un valor excluido de la expresión $\frac{2}{x - 3}$ ya que 3 hace que el valor del denominador sea 0.
experimental probability (p. 844) A probability based on repeated trials of an experiment. The experimental probability of an event is the ratio of the number of successes (trials in which a favorable outcome occurs) to the number of trials. **probabilidad experimental** (pág. 844) Probabilidad basada en la realización repetida de las pruebas de un experimento. La probabilidad experimental de un suceso es la razón entre el número de resultados deseados (pruebas en las que se produce un caso favorable) y el número de pruebas.	You spin a spinner 20 times and it stops on yellow 3 times. The experimental probability that the spinner stops on yellow is $\frac{3}{20}$, 15%, or 0.15. Giras una ruleta 20 veces y ésta se detiene en el amarillo 3 veces. La probabilidad experimental de que la ruleta se detenga en el amarillo es $\frac{3}{20}$, 15% ó 0.15.
exponent (p. 3) The number or variable that represents the number of times the base of a power is used as a factor. **exponente** (pág. 3) El número o la variable que representa la cantidad de veces que se usa la base de una potencia como factor.	In the power 3^4, the exponent is 4. En la potencia 3^4, el exponente es 4.

exponential decay (p. 533) When $a > 0$ and $0 < b < 1$, the function $y = ab^x$ represents exponential decay. When a quantity decays exponentially, it decreases by the same percent over equal time periods. The exponential decay model is $y = a(1 - r)^t$.

decrecimiento exponencial (pág. 533) Cuando $a > 0$ y $0 < b < 1$, la función $y = ab^x$ representa el decrecimiento exponencial. Cuando una cantidad decrece de forma exponencial, disminuye en el mismo porcentaje durante períodos de tiempo iguales. El modelo de decrecimiento exponencial es $y = a(1 - r)^t$.

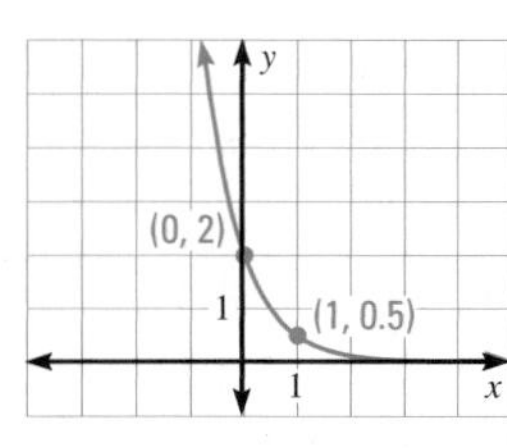

The function $y = 2(0.25)^x$ represents exponential decay. *See also* decay rate *and* decay factor.

La función $y = 2(0.25)^x$ representa el decrecimiento exponencial. *Ver también* tasa de decrecimiento *y* factor de decrecimiento.

---

exponential function (p. 520) A function of the form $y = ab^x$ where $a \neq 0$, $b > 0$, and $b \neq 1$.

función exponencial (pág. 520) Función de la forma $y = ab^x$, donde $a \neq 0$, $b > 0$ y $b \neq 1$.

The functions $y = 2 \cdot 3^x$ and $y = -2 \cdot \left(\frac{1}{2}\right)^x$ are exponential functions.

See also exponential growth *and* exponential decay.

Las funciones $y = 2 \cdot 3^x$ e $y = -2 \cdot \left(\frac{1}{2}\right)^x$ son funciones exponenciales.

***Ver también* crecimiento exponencial *y* decrecimiento exponencial.**

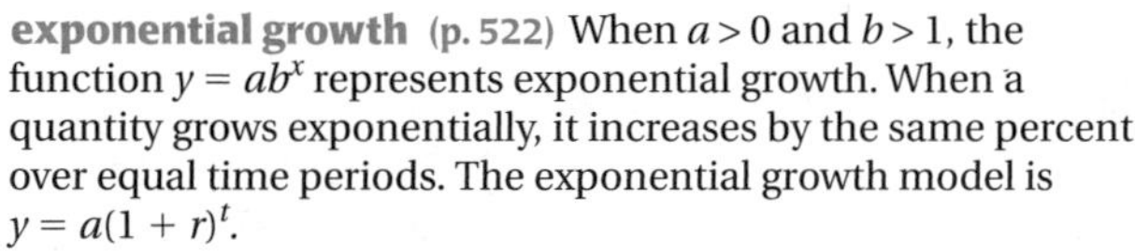

exponential growth (p. 522) When $a > 0$ and $b > 1$, the function $y = ab^x$ represents exponential growth. When a quantity grows exponentially, it increases by the same percent over equal time periods. The exponential growth model is $y = a(1 + r)^t$.

crecimiento exponencial (pág. 522) Cuando $a > 0$ y $b > 1$, la función $y = ab^x$ representa el crecimiento exponencial. Cuando una cantidad crece de forma exponencial, aumenta en el mismo porcentaje durante períodos de tiempo iguales. El modelo de crecimiento exponencial es $y = a(1 + r)^t$.

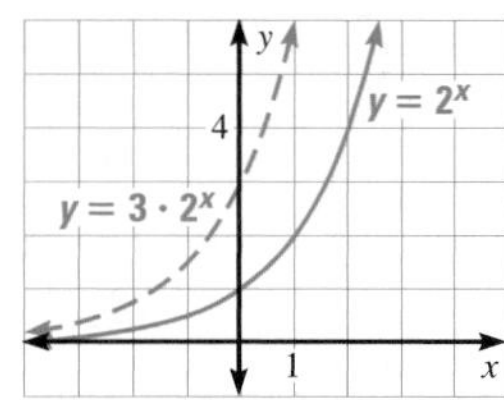

The functions $y = 3 \cdot 2^x$ and $y = 2^x$ represent exponential growth. *See also* growth rate *and* growth factor.

Las funciones $y = 3 \cdot 2^x$ e $y = 2^x$ representan el crecimiento exponencial. *Ver también* tasa de crecimiento *y* factor de crecimiento.

---

extraneous solution (p. 730) A solution of a transformed equation that is not a solution of the original equation.

solución extraña (pág. 730) Solución de una ecuación transformada que no es solución de la ecuación original.

When you square both sides of the radical equation $\sqrt{6 - x} = x$, the resulting equation has two solutions, 2 and -3, but -3 is an extraneous solution because it does not satisfy the original equation $\sqrt{6 - x} = x$.

Al elevar al cuadrado ambos miembros de la ecuación radical $\sqrt{6 - x} = x$, la ecuación resultante tiene dos soluciones, 2 y -3, pero -3 es una solución extraña ya que no satisface la ecuación original $\sqrt{6 - x} = x$.

969

factor by grouping (p. 606) To factor a polynomial with four terms by grouping, factor a common monomial from pairs of terms, and then look for a common binomial factor. **factorizar por grupos** (pág. 606) Para factorizar por grupos un polinomio con cuatro términos, factoriza un monomio común a partir de los pares de términos y luego busca un factor binómico común.	$x^3 + 3x^2 + 5x + 15 = (x^3 + 3x^2) + (5x + 15)$ $= x^2(x + 3) + 5(x + 3)$ $= (x + 3)(x^2 + 5)$
factor completely (p. 607) A factorable polynomial with integer coefficients is factored completely if it is written as a product of unfactorable polynomials with integer coefficients. **factorizar completamente** (pág. 607) Un polinomio que puede descomponerse en factores y que tiene coeficientes enteros está completamente factorizado si está escrito como producto de polinomios que no pueden descomponerse en factores y que tienen coeficientes enteros.	The polynomial $x^3 - x$ is *not* factored completely when written as $x(x^2 - 1)$ but is factored completely when written as $x(x + 1)(x - 1)$. El polinomio $x^3 - x$ *no* está completamente factorizado cuando se escribe $x(x^2 - 1)$, pero sí está completamente factorizado cuando se escribe $x(x + 1)(x - 1)$.
family of functions (p. 263) A group of functions with similar characteristics. **familia de funciones** (pág. 263) Grupo de funciones con características similares.	Functions that have the form $f(x) = mx + b$ constitute the family of linear functions. Las funciones que tienen la forma $f(x) = mx + b$ constituyen la familia de las funciones lineales.
formula (p. 30) An equation that relates two or more quantities. **fórmula** (pág. 30) Ecuación que relaciona dos o más cantidades.	The formula $d = rt$ relates the distance traveled to the rate of speed and travel time. La fórmula $d = rt$ relaciona la distancia recorrida con la velocidad y el tiempo transcurrido.
frequency (p. 882) The frequency of an interval is the number of data values in that interval. **frecuencia** (pág. 882) La frecuencia de un intervalo es el número de datos de valores que hay en ese intervalo.	*See* frequency table *and* histogram. *Ver* tabla de frecuencias *e* histograma.
frequency table (p. 882) A data display that groups data into equal intervals with no gaps between intervals and no intervals overlapping. **tabla de frecuencias** (pág. 882) Presentación de datos en la que se agrupan los datos en intervalos iguales sin que haya interrupciones entre los intervalos y sin intervalos superpuestos.	See table below.

Prices Precios	Sandwiches Sándwiches
\$4.00–4.49	||||
\$4.50–4.99	||
\$5.00–5.49	
\$5.50–5.99	||||

ENGLISH-SPANISH GLOSSARY

function (p. 35) A function consists of:

- A set called the domain containing numbers called inputs, and a set called the range containing numbers called outputs.
- A pairing of inputs with outputs such that each input is paired with exactly one output.

función (pág. 35) Una función consta de:

- Un conjunto llamado dominio que contiene los números conocidos como entradas, y otro conjunto llamado rango que contiene los números conocidos como salidas.
- Una correspondencia entre las entradas y las salidas tal que a cada entrada le corresponde una sola salida.

The pairing in the table below is a function, because each input is paired with exactly one output.

La correspondencia que aparece en la tabla de abajo es una función ya que a cada entrada le corresponde una sola salida.

Input, x / Entrada, x	0	1	2	3	4
Output, y / Salida, y	3	4	5	6	7

The domain is the set of inputs: 0, 1, 2, 3, and 4. The range is the set of outputs: 3, 4, 5, 6, and 7.

El dominio es el conjunto de entradas: 0, 1, 2, 3 y 4. El rango es el conjunto de salidas: 3, 4, 5, 6 y 7.

function notation (p. 262) A way to name a function using the symbol $f(x)$ instead of y. The symbol $f(x)$ is read as "the value of f at x" or as "f of x."

notación de función (pág. 262) Forma de nombrar una función usando el símbolo $f(x)$ en lugar de y. El símbolo $f(x)$ se lee "el valor de f en x" o "f de x".

The function $y = 2x - 9$ can be written in function notation as $f(x) = 2x - 9$.

La función $y = 2x - 9$ escrita en notación de función es $f(x) = 2x - 9$.

G

geometric sequence (p. 539) A sequence in which the ratio of any term to the previous term is constant. The constant ratio is called the common ratio.

progresión geométrica (pág. 539) Progresión en la que la razón entre cualquier término y el término anterior es constante. La razón constante se llama razón común.

The sequence 5, 10, 20, 40, ... is a geometric sequence with common ratio 2.

La progresión 5, 10, 20, 40, ... es una progresión geométrica cuya razón común es 2.

graph of an equation in two variables (p. 215) The set of points in a coordinate plane that represent all solutions of the equation.

gráfica de una ecuación con dos variables (pág. 215) El conjunto de puntos de un plano de coordenadas que representa todas las soluciones de la ecuación.

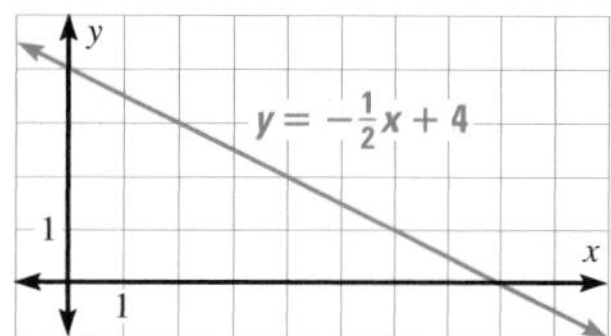

The line is the graph of the equation $y = -\frac{1}{2}x + 4$.

La recta es la gráfica de la ecuación $y = -\frac{1}{2}x + 4$.

ENGLISH-SPANISH GLOSSARY

graph of an inequality in one variable (p. 356) On a number line, the set of points that represent all solutions of the inequality.

gráfica de una desigualdad con una variable (pág. 356) En una recta numérica, el conjunto de puntos que representa todas las soluciones de la desigualdad.

−1 0 1 2 3 4

Graph of $x < 3$

Gráfica de $x < 3$

graph of an inequality in two variables (p. 405) In a coordinate plane, the set of points that represent all solutions of the inequality.

gráfica de una desigualdad con dos variables (pág. 405) En un plano de coordenadas, el conjunto de puntos que representa todas las soluciones de la desigualdad.

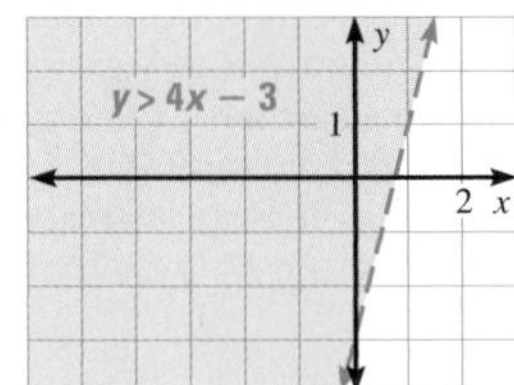

The graph of $y > 4x - 3$ is the shaded half-plane.

La gráfica de $y > 4x - 3$ es el semiplano sombreado.

graph of a system of linear inequalities (p. 466) The graph of all solutions of the system.

gráfica de un sistema de desigualdades lineales (pág. 466) La gráfica de todas las soluciones del sistema.

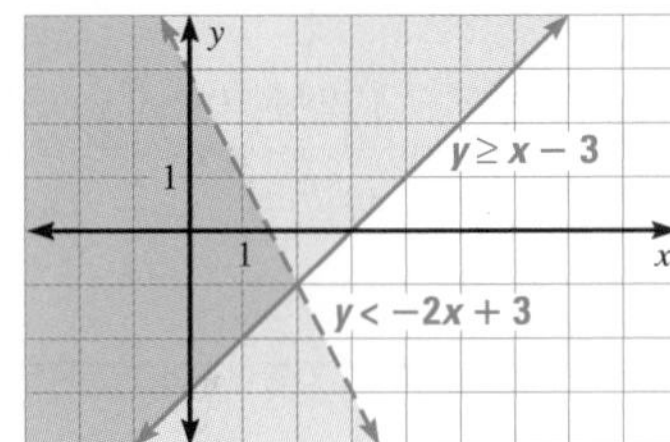

The graph of the system $y < -2x + 3$ and $y \geq x - 3$ is the intersection of the half-planes.

La gráfica del sistema $y < -2x + 3$ e $y \geq x - 3$ es la intersección de los semiplanos.

growth factor (p. 522) The expression $1 + r$ in the exponential growth model $y = a(1 + r)^t$.

factor de crecimiento (pág. 522) La expresión $1 + r$ del modelo de crecimiento exponencial $y = a(1 + r)^t$.

In the exponential growth model $C = 11{,}000(1.069)^t$, the growth factor is 1.069.

En el modelo de crecimiento exponencial $C = 11{,}000(1.069)^t$, el factor de crecimiento es 1.069.

growth rate (p. 522) The variable r in the exponential growth model $y = a(1 + r)^t$.

tasa de crecimiento (pág. 522) La variable r del modelo de crecimiento exponencial $y = a(1 + r)^t$.

In the exponential growth model $C = 11{,}000(1.069)^t$, the growth rate is 0.069.

En el modelo de crecimiento exponencial $C = 11{,}000(1.069)^t$, la tasa de crecimiento es 0.069.

H

half-plane (p. 405) In a coordinate plane, the region on either side of a boundary line.

semiplano (pág. 405) En un plano de coordenadas, la región situada a cada lado de una recta límite.

See graph of an inequality in two variables.

Ver gráfica de una desigualdad con dos variables.

histogram (p. 882) A bar graph that displays data from a frequency table. Each bar represents an interval, and the length of each bar indicates the frequency.

histograma (pág. 882) Gráfica de barras que presenta los datos de una tabla de frecuencias. Cada barra representa un intervalo, y la longitud de cada barra indica la frecuencia.

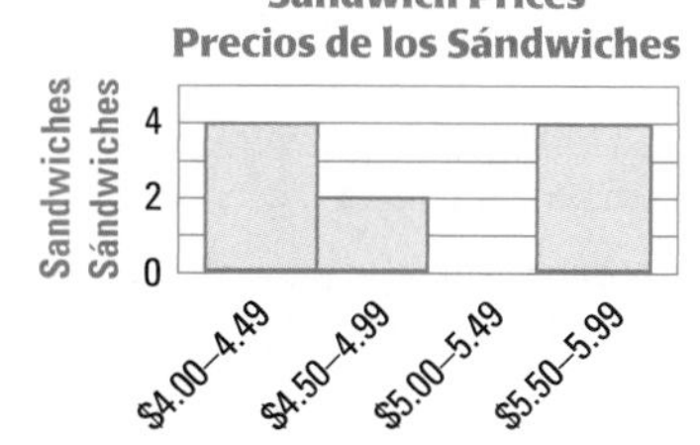

hyperbola (p. 767) The graph of the inverse variation equation $y = \frac{a}{x}$ $(a \neq 0)$ or the graph of a rational function of the form $y = \frac{a}{x - h} + k$ $(a \neq 0)$. A hyperbola has two symmetrical parts called branches. A hyperbola approaches but doesn't intersect lines called asymptotes.

hipérbola (pág. 767) La gráfica de la ecuación de variación inversa $y = \frac{a}{x}$ $(a \neq 0)$ o la gráfica de una función racional de la forma $y = \frac{a}{x - h} + k$ $(a \neq 0)$. La hipérbola tiene dos partes simétricas llamadas ramas. La hipérbola se acerca a las rectas llamadas asíntotas pero sin cortarlas.

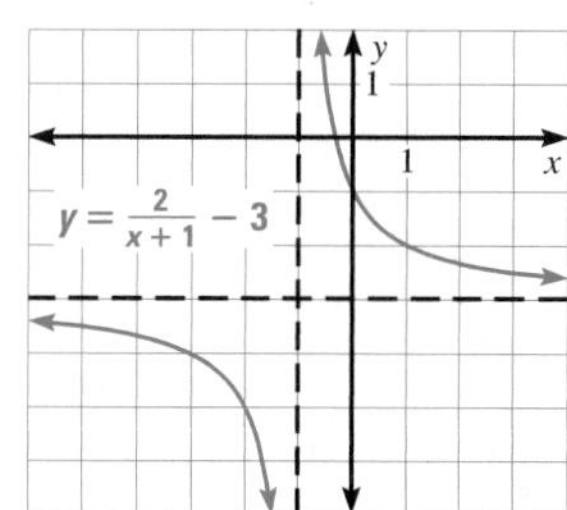

The graph of $y = \frac{2}{x + 1} - 3$ is a hyperbola. The asymptotes of the hyperbola are the lines $x = -1$ and $y = -3$.

La gráfica de $y = \frac{2}{x + 1} - 3$ es una hipérbola. Las asíntotas de la hipérbola son las rectas $x = -1$ e $y = -3$.

hypotenuse (p. 737) The hypotenuse of a right triangle is the side opposite the right angle.

hipotenusa (pág. 737) La hipotenusa de un triángulo rectángulo es el lado opuesto al ángulo recto.

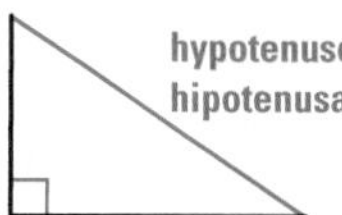

I

identity (p. 156) An equation that is true for all values of the variable.

identidad (pág. 156) Ecuación que es verdadera para todos los valores de la variable.

The equation $2x + 10 = 2(x + 5)$ is an identity.

La ecuación $2x + 10 = 2(x + 5)$ es una identidad.

if-then statement (p. 66) A conditional statement with an *if* part and a *then* part. The *if* part contains the hypothesis, and the *then* part contains the conclusion. **enunciado de "si..., entonces..."** (pág. 66) Enunciado condicional con una parte de *si* y otra de *entonces*. La parte de *si* contiene la hipótesis, y la parte de *entonces* contiene la conclusión.	If $a = -1$, then $\lvert a \rvert = 1$. The hypothesis is $a = -1$. The conclusion is $\lvert a \rvert = 1$. Si $a = -1$, entonces $\lvert a \rvert = 1$. La hipótesis es $a = -1$. La conclusión es $\lvert a \rvert = 1$.
inconsistent system (p. 459) A linear system with no solution. The graphs of the equations of an inconsistent system are parallel lines. **sistema incompatible** (pág. 459) Sistema lineal sin solución. Las gráficas de las ecuaciones de un sistema incompatible son rectas paralelas.	y 2 2 x $y = 2x + 1$ $y = 2x - 3$ The linear system $y = 2x + 1$ and $y = 2x - 3$ is inconsistent because the graphs of the equations are parallel lines. El sistema lineal $y = 2x + 1$ e $y = 2x - 3$ es incompatible ya que las gráficas de las ecuaciones son rectas paralelas.
independent events (p. 862) Two events such that the occurrence of one event has no effect on the occurrence of the other event. **sucesos independientes** (pág. 862) Dos sucesos tales que la ocurrencia de uno de ellos no afecta a la ocurrencia del otro.	You roll a number cube twice. The events "roll a 3 first" and "roll a 6 second" are independent events. Lanzas un cubo numerado dos veces. Los sucesos "salir primero el 3" y "salir después el 6" son sucesos independientes.
independent variable (p. 36) The input variable of a function. **variable independiente** (pág. 36) La variable de entrada de una función.	In the function equation $y = x + 3$, x is the independent variable. En la ecuación de función $y = x + 3$, x es la variable independiente.
inductive reasoning (p. 117) A form of reasoning in which a conclusion is based on several examples. **razonamiento inductivo** (pág. 117) Tipo de razonamiento en el que la conclusión se basa en varios ejemplos.	You add several pairs of odd numbers and notice that the sum is even. You conclude that the sum of any two odd numbers is even. Sumas varias parejas de números impares y observas que la suma es par. Sacas la conclusión de que la suma de dos números impares cualesquiera es par.
inequality (p. 21) A mathematical sentence formed by placing one of the symbols $<, \leq, >,$ or $\geq$ between two expressions. **desigualdad** (pág. 21) Enunciado matemático formado al colocar uno de les siguentes símbolos entre dos expresiones: $<, \leq, >$ o $\geq$.	$6n \geq 24$ and $x - 2 < 7$ are inequalities. $6n \geq 24$ y $x - 2 < 7$ son desigualdades.

input (p. 35) A number in the domain of a function. **entrada** (pág. 35) Número del dominio de una función.	*See* function. *Ver* función.
integers (p. 64) The numbers . . . , −3, −2, −1, 0, 1, 2, 3, . . . , consisting of the negative integers, zero, and the positive integers. **números enteros** (pág. 64) Los números . . . , −3, −2, −1, 0, 1, 2, 3, . . . , que constan de los números enteros negativos, cero y los números enteros positivos.	−8 and 46 are integers. $-8\frac{1}{2}$ and 46.2 are *not* integers. −8 y 46 son números enteros. $-8\frac{1}{2}$ y 46.2 *no* son números enteros.
intercept form of a quadratic function (p. 641) A quadratic function in the form $y = a(x - p)(x - q)$ where $a \neq 0$. The x-intercepts of the graph of the function are p and q. **forma de intercepto de una función cuadrática** (pág. 641) Función cuadrática de la forma $y = a(x - p)(x - q)$, donde $a \neq 0$. Los interceptos en x de la gráfica de la función son p y q.	The quadratic function $y = -(x + 1)(x - 5)$ is in intercept form. The intercepts of the graph of the function are −1 and 5. La función cuadrática $y = -(x + 1)(x - 5)$ está en la forma de intercepto. Los interceptos de la gráfica de la función son −1 y 5.
interquartile range (p. 888) The difference of the upper and the lower quartiles of a data set. **rango intercuartílico** (pág. 888) La diferencia entre el cuartil superior y el cuartil inferior de un conjunto de datos.	The interquartile range of the data set below is 23 − 10 = 13. lower quartile ↓ upper quartile ↓ 8 **10** 14 17 20 **23** 50 El rango intercuartílico del siguiente conjunto de datos es 23 − 10 = 13. cuartil inferior ↓ cuartil superior ↓ 8 **10** 14 17 20 **23** 50
intersection (p. 71) The intersection of two sets A and B is the set of all elements in *both* A and B. The intersection of A and B is written as $A \cap B$. **intersección** (pág. 71) La intersección de dos conjuntos A y B es el conjunto de todos los elementos *tanto* de A *como* de B. La intersección de A y B se escribe $A \cap B$.	U A B 4 6 8 2 3 5 7 1 9 $A \cap B = \{2\}$
inverse operations (p. 134) Two operations that undo each other. **operaciones inversas** (pág. 134) Dos operaciones que se anulan entre sí.	Addition and subtraction are inverse operations. Multiplication and division are also inverse operations. La suma y la resta son operaciones inversas. La multiplicación y la división también son operaciones inversas.

ENGLISH-SPANISH GLOSSARY

inverse variation (p. 765) The relationship of two variables x and y if there is a nonzero number a such that $y = \frac{a}{x}$. If $y = \frac{a}{x}$, then y is said to vary inversely with x.

variación inversa (pág. 765) La relación entre dos variables x e y si hay un número a distinto de cero tal que $y = \frac{a}{x}$. Si $y = \frac{a}{x}$, entonces se dice que y varía inversamente con x.

The equations $xy = 4$ and $y = \frac{-1}{x}$ represent inverse variation.

Las ecuaciones $xy = 4$ e $y = \frac{-1}{x}$ representan una variación inversa.

irrational number (p. 111) A number that cannot be written as the quotient of two integers. The decimal form of an irrational number neither terminates nor repeats.

número irracional (pág. 111) Número que no puede escribirse como cociente de dos números enteros. La forma decimal de un número irracional no termina ni se repite.

$\sqrt{945} = 30.74085...$ is an irrational number. $1.666...$ is *not* an irrational number.

$\sqrt{945} = 30.74085...$ es un número irracional. $1.666...$ *no* es un número irracional.

L

leading coefficient (p. 554) When a polynomial is written so that the exponents of a variable decrease from left to right, the coefficient of the first term is the leading coefficient.

coeficiente inicial (pág. 554) Cuando un polinomio se escribe de tal manera que los exponentes de una variable disminuyen de izquierda a derecha, el coeficiente del primer término es el coeficiente inicial.

The leading coefficient of the polynomial $2x^3 + x^2 - 5x + 12$ is 2.

El coeficiente inicial del polinomio $2x^3 + x^2 - 5x + 12$ es 2.

least common denominator (LCD) of rational expressions (p. 813) The product of the factors of the denominators of the rational expressions with each common factor used only once.

mínimo común denominador (m.c.d.) de las expresiones racionales (pág. 813) El producto de los factores de los denominadores de las expresiones racionales usando cada factor común una sola vez.

The LCD of $\frac{5}{(x-3)^2}$ and $\frac{3x+4}{(x-3)(x+2)}$ is $(x-3)^2(x+2)$.

El m.c.d. de $\frac{5}{(x-3)^2}$ y $\frac{3x+4}{(x-3)(x+2)}$ es $(x-3)^2(x+2)$.

legs of a right triangle (p. 737) The two sides that form the right angle.

catetos de un triángulo rectángulo (pág. 737) Los dos lados que forman el ángulo recto.

leg
cateto
leg
cateto

like terms (p. 97) Terms that have the same variable parts. Constant terms are also like terms.

términos semejantes (pág. 97) Términos que tienen las mismas variables. Los términos constantes también son términos semejantes.

In the expression $3x + (-4) + (-6x) + 2$, $3x$ and $-6x$ are like terms, and -4 and 2 are like terms.

En la expresión $3x + (-4) + (-6x) + 2$, $3x$ y $-6x$ son términos semejantes, y -4 y 2 también son términos semejantes.

line of fit (p. 326) A line used to model the trend in data having a positive or negative correlation.

recta de regresión (pág. 326) Recta utilizada para representar la tendencia de los datos que presentan una correlación positiva o negativa.

The graph shows a line of fit for the data in the scatter plot.

La gráfica muestra una recta de regresión para los datos del diagrama de dispersión.

linear equation (p. 216) An equation whose graph is a line.

ecuación lineal (pág. 216) Ecuación cuya gráfica es una recta.

See standard form of a linear equation.

Ver forma general de una ecuación lineal.

linear extrapolation (p. 336) Using a line or its equation to approximate a value outside the range of known values.

extrapolación lineal (pág. 336) El uso de una recta o su ecuación para hallar por aproximación un valor situado fuera del rango de los valores conocidos.

The best-fitting line can be used to estimate that when $y = 1200$, $x \approx 11.75$.

La mejor recta de regresión puede utilizarse para estimar que cuando $y = 1200$, $x \approx 11.75$.

linear function (p. 217) The equation $Ax + By = C$ represents a linear function provided $B \neq 0$.

función lineal (pág. 217) La ecuación $Ax + By = C$ representa una función lineal siempre que $B \neq 0$.

The equation $2x - y = 3$ represents a linear function. The equation $x = 3$ does *not* represent a function.

La ecuación $2x - y = 3$ representa una función lineal. La ecuación $x = 3$ *no* representa una función.

linear inequality in two variables (p. 405) An inequality that is the result of replacing the = sign in a linear equation with <, ≤, >, or ≥.

desigualdad lineal con dos variables (pág. 405) Desigualdad que se obtiene al reemplazar el símbolo = de la ecuación lineal por <, ≤, > o ≥.

$x - 3y < 6$ is a linear inequality in two variables, x and y.

$x - 3y < 6$ es una desigualdad lineal con dos variables, x e y.

linear interpolation (p. 335) Using a line or its equation to approximate a value between two known values.

interpolación lineal (pág. 335) El uso de una recta o su ecuación para hallar por aproximación un valor situado entre dos valores conocidos.

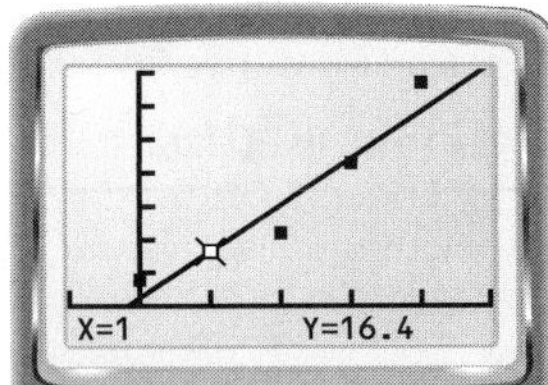

The best-fitting line can be used to estimate that when $x = 1$, $y \approx 16.4$.

La mejor recta de regresión puede utilizarse para estimar que cuando $x = 1$, $y \approx 16.4$.

---

linear regression (p. 335) The process of finding the best-fitting line to model a set of data.

regresión lineal (pág. 335) El proceso de hallar la mejor recta de regresión para representar un conjunto de datos.

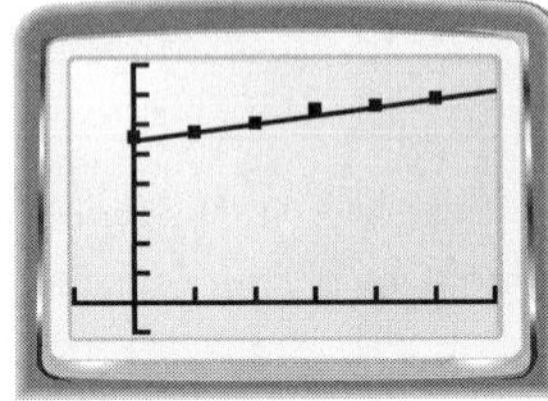

You can use a graphing calculator to perform linear regression on a data set.

Puedes usar una calculadora de gráficas para realizar una regresión lineal a un conjunto de datos.

---

literal equation (p. 184) An equation in which letters are used to replace the coefficients and constants of another equation.

ecuación literal (pág. 184) Ecuación en la que se usan letras para reemplazar los coeficientes y las constantes de otra ecuación.

The equation $5(x + 3) = 20$ can be written as the literal equation $a(x + b) = c$.

La ecuación $5(x + 3) = 20$ puede escribirse como la ecuación literal $a(x + b) = c$.

---

lower quartile (p. 887) The median of the lower half of an ordered data set.

cuartil inferior (pág. 887) La mediana de la mitad inferior de un conjunto de datos ordenados.

The lower quartile of the data set below is 10.

lower quartile ↓ median ↓

8 **10** 14 17 20 23 50

El cuartil inferior del siguiente conjunto de datos es 10.

cuartil inferior ↓ mediana ↓

8 10 14 17 20 23 50

ENGLISH-SPANISH GLOSSARY

M

matrix, matrices (p. 94) A rectangular arrangement of numbers in rows and columns. Each number in a matrix is an element, or *entry*.

matriz, matrices (pág. 94) Disposición rectangular de números colocados en filas y columnas. Cada número de la matriz es un elemento, o *entrada*.

$$A = \begin{bmatrix} 0 & 4 & -1 \\ -3 & 2 & 5 \end{bmatrix}$$ 2 rows / 2 filas

3 columns / 3 columnas

Matrix *A* has 2 rows and 3 columns. The element in the first row and second column is 4.

La matriz *A* tiene 2 filas y 3 columnas. El elemento de la primera fila y la segunda columna es 4.

maximum value (p. 636) For $y = ax^2 + bx + c$ where $a < 0$, the y-coordinate of the vertex is the maximum value of the function.

valor máximo (pág. 636) Para $y = ax^2 + bx + c$ donde $a < 0$, la coordenada y del vértice es el valor máximo de la función.

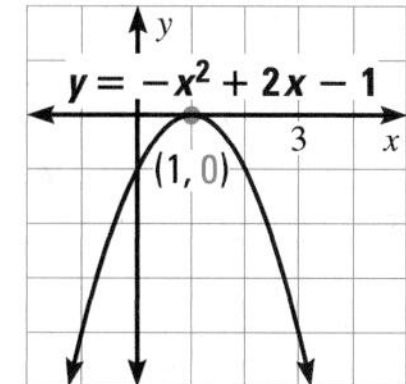

The maximum value of the function $y = -x^2 + 2x - 1$ is 0.

El valor máximo de la función $y = -x^2 + 2x - 1$ es 0.

mean (p. 875) For the numerical data set $x_1, x_2, \ldots, x_n$, the mean, or average, is:

$$\overline{x} = \frac{x_1 + x_2 + \ldots + x_n}{n}$$

media (pág. 875) Para el conjunto de datos numéricos $x_1, x_2, \ldots, x_n$, la media, o el promedio, es:

$$\overline{x} = \frac{x_1 + x_2 + \ldots + x_n}{n}$$

The mean of 5, 9, 14, 23 is $\frac{5 + 9 + 14 + 23}{4} = \frac{51}{4} = 12.75$.

La media de 5, 9, 14, 23 es $\frac{5 + 9 + 14 + 23}{4} = \frac{51}{4} = 12.75$.

mean absolute deviation (p. 876) The mean absolute deviation of the data set $x_1, x_2, \ldots, x_n$ is a measure of dispersion given by:

$$\frac{|x_1 - \overline{x}| + |x_2 - \overline{x}| + \ldots + |x_n - \overline{x}|}{n}$$

desviación absoluta media (pág. 876) La desviación absoluta media del conjunto de datos $x_1, x_2, \ldots, x_n$ es una medida de dispersión dada por:

$$\frac{|x_1 - \overline{x}| + |x_2 - \overline{x}| + \ldots + |x_n - \overline{x}|}{n}$$

The mean absolute deviation of the data set 3, 9, 13, 23 (with mean = 12) is:

$$\frac{|3 - 12| + |9 - 12| + |13 - 12| + |23 - 12|}{4} = 6$$

La desviación absoluta media del conjunto de datos 3, 9, 13, 23 (con media = 12)es:

$$\frac{|3 - 12| + |9 - 12| + |13 - 12| + |23 - 12|}{4} = 6$$

measure of dispersion (p. 876) A measure that describes the dispersion, or spread, of data.

medida de dispersión (pág. 876) Medida que describe la dispersión, o extensión, de los datos.

See range *and* mean absolute deviation.

Ver rango _y_ desviación absoluta media.

median (p. 875) The median of a numerical data set is the middle number when the values are written in numerical order. If the data set has an even number of values, the median is the mean of the two middle values.

mediana (pág. 875) La mediana de un conjunto de datos numéricos es el número central cuando los valores se escriben en orden numérico. Si el conjunto de datos tiene un número par de valores, la mediana es la media de los dos valores centrales.

The median of 5, 9, 14, 23 is the mean of 9 and 14, or $\frac{9 + 14}{2} = 11.5$.

La mediana de 5, 9, 14, 23 es la media de 9 y 14, ó $\frac{9 + 14}{2} = 11.5$.

midpoint (p. 745) The midpoint of a line segment is the point on the segment that is equidistant from the endpoints.

punto medio (pág. 745) El punto medio de un segmento de recta es el punto del segmento que es equidistante de los extremos.

A M B

M is the midpoint of $\overline{AB}$.

M en el punto medio de $\overline{AB}$.

midpoint formula (p. 745) The midpoint *M* of the line segment with endpoints $A(x_1, y_1)$ and $B(x_2, y_2)$ is $M\left(\frac{x_1 + x_2}{2}, \frac{y_1 + y_2}{2}\right)$.

fórmula del punto medio (pág. 745) El punto medio *M* del segmento de recta cuyos extremos son $A(x_1, y_1)$ y $B(x_2, y_2)$ es $M\left(\frac{x_1 + x_2}{2}, \frac{y_1 + y_2}{2}\right)$.

The midpoint *M* of the line segment with endpoints $(-1, -2)$ and $(3, -4)$ is:

$$\left(\frac{-1 + 3}{2}, \frac{-2 + (-4)}{2}\right) = (1, -3)$$

El punto medio *M* del segmento de recta cuyos extremos son $(-1, -2)$ y $(3, -4)$ es:

$$\left(\frac{-1 + 3}{2}, \frac{-2 + (-4)}{2}\right) = (1, -3)$$

minimum value (p. 636) For $y = ax^2 + bx + c$ where $a > 0$, the *y*-coordinate of the vertex is the minimum value of the function.

valor mínimo (pág. 636) Para $y = ax^2 + bx + c$ donde $a > 0$, la coordenada *y* del vértice es el valor mínimo de la función.

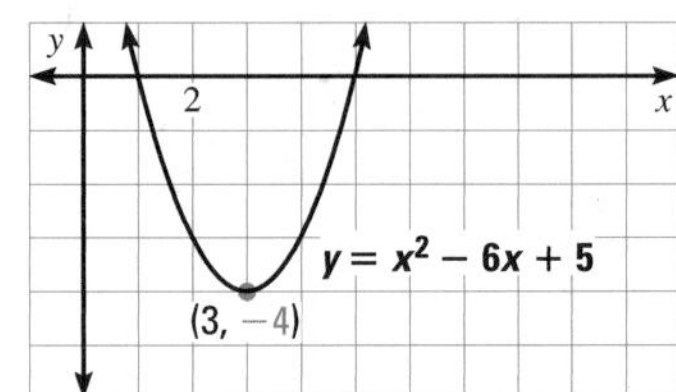

The minimum value of the function $y = x^2 - 6x + 5$ is -4.

El valor mínimo de la función $y = x^2 - 6x + 5$ es -4.

mode (p. 875) The mode of a data set is the value that occurs most frequently. There may be one mode, no mode, or more than one mode.

moda (pág. 875) La moda de un conjunto de datos es el valor que ocurre más veces. Puede haber una moda, más de una moda o ninguna moda.

The mode of the data set 4, 7, 9, 11, 11, 12, 18 is 11.

La moda del conjunto de datos 4, 7, 9, 11, 11, 12, 18 es 11.

980

monomial (p. 554) A number, variable, or the product of a number and one or more variables with whole number exponents. **monomio** (pág. 554) Un número, una variable o el producto de un número y una o más variables que tienen exponentes expresados por números naturales.	$10, 3x, \frac{1}{2}ab^2$, and $-1.8m^5$ are monomials. $10, 3x, \frac{1}{2}ab^2$ y $-1.8m^5$ son monomios.
multiplicative identity (p. 89) The number 1 is the multiplicative identity, because the product of any number and 1 is the number: $a \cdot 1 = 1 \cdot a = a$. **identidad multiplicativa** (pág. 89) El número 1 es la identidad multiplicativa ya que el producto de cualquier número y 1 es ese número: $a \cdot 1 = 1 \cdot a = a$.	$3.6(1) = 3.6, 1(-7) = -7$
multiplicative inverse (p. 103) The multiplicative inverse of a nonzero number a is its reciprocal, $\frac{1}{a}$. The product of a nonzero number and its multiplicative inverse is 1: $a \cdot \frac{1}{a} = \frac{1}{a} \cdot a = 1, a \neq 0$. **inverso multiplicativo** (pág. 103) El inverso multiplicativo de un número a distinto de cero es su recíproco, $\frac{1}{a}$. El producto de un número distinto de cero y su inverso multiplicativo es 1: $a \cdot \frac{1}{a} = \frac{1}{a} \cdot a = 1, a \neq 0$.	The multiplicative inverse of $-\frac{1}{5}$ is -5 because $-\frac{1}{5} \cdot (-5) = 1$. El inverso multiplicativo de $-\frac{1}{5}$ es -5 ya que $-\frac{1}{5} \cdot (-5) = 1$.
mutually exclusive events (p. 861) Events that have no common outcome. **sucesos mutuamente excluyentes** (pág. 861) Sucesos que no tienen ningún caso en común.	When you roll a number cube, "roll a 3" and "roll an even number" are mutually exclusive events. Cuando lanzas un cubo numerado, "salir el 3" y "salir número par" son sucesos mutuamente excluyentes.

N

n* factorial** (p. 852) For any positive integer n, n factorial, written $n!$, is the product of the integers from 1 to n; $0! = 1$. **factorial de *n (pág. 852) Para cualquier número entero positivo n, el factorial de n, escrito $n!$, es el producto de los números enteros de 1 a n; $0! = 1$.	$5! = 5 \cdot 4 \cdot 3 \cdot 2 \cdot 1 = 120$
negative exponent (p. 503) If $a \neq 0$, then a^{-n} is the reciprocal of a^n; $a^{-n} = \frac{1}{a^n}$. **exponente negativo** (pág. 503) Si $a \neq 0$, entonces a^{-n} es el recíproco de a^n; $a^{-n} = \frac{1}{a^n}$.	$3^{-2} = \frac{1}{3^2} = \frac{1}{9}$

ENGLISH-SPANISH GLOSSARY

negative integers (p. 64) The integers that are less than 0. **números enteros negativos** (pág. 64) Los números enteros menores que 0.	$-1, -2, -3, -4, \dots$

O

odds against (p. 845) When all outcomes are equally likely, the odds against an event is the ratio of the number of unfavorable outcomes to the number of favorable outcomes. **probabilidad en contra** (pág. 845) Cuando todos los casos son igualmente posibles, la probabilidad en contra de que ocurra un suceso es la razón entre el número de casos desfavorables y el número de casos favorables.	When you roll a number cube, the odds against rolling a number less than 5 is $\frac{2}{4} = \frac{1}{2}$, or 1 : 2. Cuando lanzas un cubo numerado, la probabilidad en contra de que salga un número menor que 5 es $\frac{2}{4} = \frac{1}{2}$, ó 1 : 2.
odds in favor (p. 845) When all outcomes are equally likely, the odds in favor of an event is the ratio of the number of favorable outcomes to the number of unfavorable outcomes. **probabilidad a favor** (pág. 845) Cuando todos los casos son igualmente posibles, la probabilidad a favor de que ocurra un suceso es la razón entre el número de casos favorables y el número de casos desfavorables.	When you roll a number cube, the odds in favor of rolling a number less than 5 is $\frac{4}{2} = \frac{2}{1}$, or 2 : 1. Cuando lanzas un cubo numerado, la probabilidad a favor de que salga un número menor que 5 es $\frac{4}{2} = \frac{2}{1}$, ó 2 : 1.
open sentence (p. 21) An equation or an equality that contains an algebraic expression. **enunciado con variables** (pág. 21) Ecuación o desigualdad que contiene una expresión algebraica.	$2k - 8 = 12$ and $6n \geq 24$ are open sentences. $2k - 8 = 12$ y $6n \geq 24$ son enunciados con variables.
opposites (p. 66) Two numbers that are the same distance from 0 on a number line but are on opposite sides of 0. **opuestos** (pág. 66) En una recta numérica, dos números que están a la misma distancia de 0 pero en lados opuestos de 0.	4 units 4 units 4 unidades 4 unidades −6 −4 −2 0 2 4 6 4 and −4 are opposites. 4 y −4 son opuestos.
order of magnitude of a quantity (p. 491) The power of 10 nearest the quantity. **orden de magnitud de una cantidad** (pág. 491) La potencia de 10 más próxima a la cantidad.	The order of magnitude of 91,000 is 10^5, or 100,000. El orden de magnitud de 91,000 es 10^5, ó 100,000.

ENGLISH-SPANISH GLOSSARY

order of operations (p. 8) Rules for evaluating an expression involving more than one operation. **orden de operaciones** (pág. 8) Reglas para evaluar una expresión relacionada con más de una operación.	To evaluate $24 - (3^2 + 1)$, evaluate the power, then add within the parentheses, and then subtract: $24 - (3^2 + 1) = 24 - (9 + 1) = 24 - 10 = 14$ **Para evaluar $24 - (3^2 + 1)$, evalúa la potencia, suma las cantidades entre paréntesis y después resta:** $24 - (3^2 + 1) = 24 - (9 + 1) = 24 - 10 = 14$
outcome (p. 843) A possible result of an experiment. **caso** (pág. 843) Resultado posible de un experimento.	When you roll a number cube, there are 6 possible outcomes: a 1, 2, 3, 4, 5, or 6. **Cuando lanzas un cubo numerado, hay 6 casos posibles: 1, 2, 3, 4, 5 ó 6.**
outlier (p. 889) A value that is widely separated from the rest of the data in a data set. Typically, a value that is greater than the upper quartile by more than 1.5 times the interquartile range or is less than the lower quartile by more than 1.5 times the interquartile range. **valor extremo** (pág. 889) En un conjunto de datos, valor muy alejado del resto de los datos. Generalmente, un valor mayor que el cuartil superior en más de 1.5 veces el rango intercuartílico o menor que el cuartil inferior en más de 1.5 veces el rango intercuartílico.	The interquartile range of the data set below is $23 - 10 = 13$. lower quartile ↓ upper quartile ↓ 8 **10** 14 17 20 **23** 50 The data value 50 is greater than $23 + 1.5(13) = 42.5$, so it is an outlier. **El rango intercuartílico del siguiente conjunto de datos es $23 - 10 = 13$.** **cuartil inferior ↓ cuartil superior ↓** **8 10 14 17 20 23 50** **El valor 50 es mayor que $23 + 1.5(13) = 42.5$, por lo que es un valor extremo.**
output (p. 35) A number in the range of a function. **salida** (pág. 35) Número que pertenece al rango de una función.	*See* function. ***Ver* función.**
overlapping events (p. 861) Events that have at least one common outcome. **sucesos de intersección** (pág. 861) Sucesos que tienen al menos un caso en común.	When you roll a number cube, "roll a 3" and "roll an odd number" are overlapping events. **Cuando lanzas un cubo numerado, "salir el 3" y "salir número impar" son sucesos de intersección.**

P

parabola (p. 628) The U-shaped graph of a quadratic function.

parábola (pág. 628) La gráfica en forma de U de una función cuadrática.

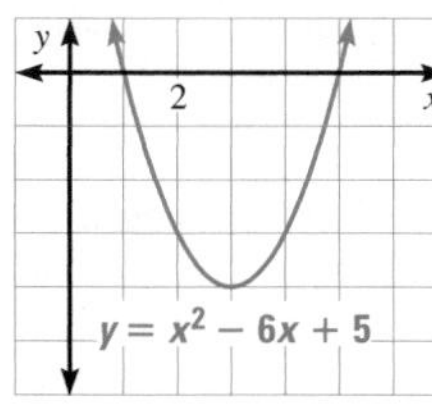

The graph of $y = x^2 - 6x + 5$ is a parabola.

La gráfica de $y = x^2 - 6x + 5$ es una parábola.

parallel lines (p. 246) Two lines in the same plane that do not intersect.

rectas paralelas (pág. 246) Dos rectas del mismo plano que no se cortan.

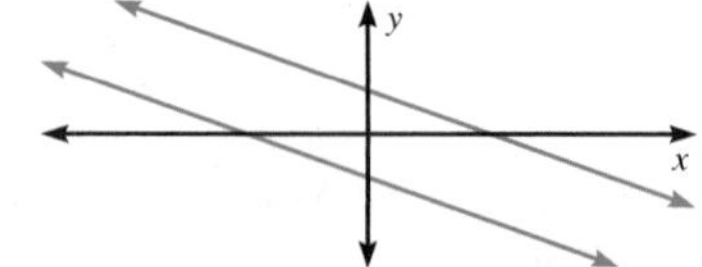

parent linear function (p. 263) The function $f(x) = x$, which is the most basic function in the family of linear functions.

función lineal básica (pág. 263) La función $f(x) = x$, que es la más básica de la familia de las funciones lineales.

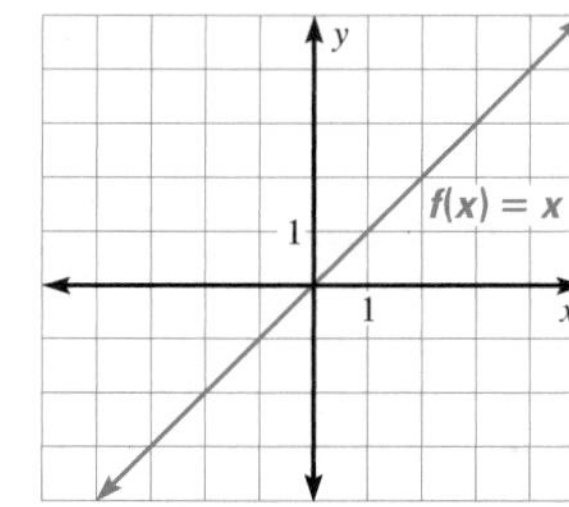

parent quadratic function (p. 628) The function $y = x^2$, which is the most basic function in the family of quadratic functions.

función cuadrática básica (pág. 628) La función $y = x^2$, que es la más básica de la familia de las funciones cuadráticas.

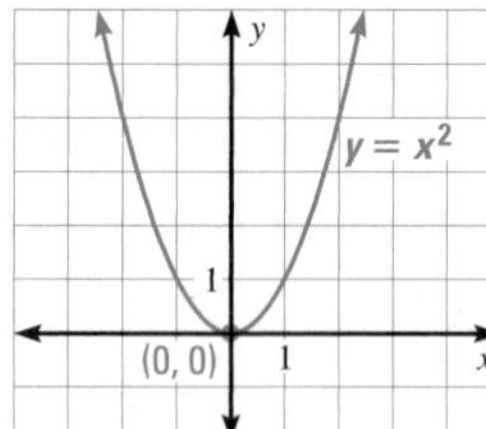

parent square root function (p. 710) The function $y = \sqrt{x}$, which is the most basic function in the family of square root functions.

función con raíz cuadrada básica (pág. 710) La función $y = \sqrt{x}$, que es la más básica de la familia de las funciones con raíz cuadrada.

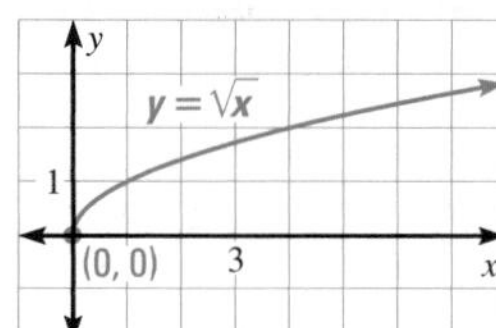

ENGLISH-SPANISH GLOSSARY

percent of change (p. 182) A percent that indicates how much a quantity increases or decreases with respect to the original amount. Percent of change, $p\% = \frac{\text{Amount of increase or decrease}}{\text{Original amount}}$ **porcentaje de cambio** (pág. 182) Porcentaje que indica cuánto aumenta o disminuye una cantidad con respecto a la cantidad original. Porcentaje de cambio, $p\% = \frac{\text{Cantidad de aumento o disminución}}{\text{Cantidad original}}$	The percent of change, $p\%$, from 140 to 189 is: $p\% = \frac{189 - 140}{140} = \frac{49}{140} = 0.35 = 35\%$ El porcentaje de cambio, $p\%$, de 140 a 189 es: $p\% = \frac{189 - 140}{140} = \frac{49}{140} = 0.35 = 35\%$
percent of decrease (p. 182) The percent of change in a quantity when the new amount of the quantity is less than the original amount. **porcentaje de disminución** (pág. 182) El porcentaje de cambio de una cantidad cuando la nueva cantidad es menor que la cantidad original.	*See* percent of change. *Ver* porcentaje de cambio.
percent of increase (p. 182) The percent of change in a quantity when the new amount of the quantity is greater than the original amount. **porcentaje de aumento** (pág. 182) El porcentaje de cambio de una cantidad cuando la nueva cantidad es mayor que la cantidad original.	*See* percent of change. *Ver* porcentaje de cambio.
perfect square (p. 111) A number that is the square of an integer. **cuadrado perfecto** (pág. 111) Número que es el cuadrado de un número entero.	49 is a perfect square, because $49 = 7^2$. 49 es un cuadrado perfecto ya que $49 = 7^2$.
perfect square trinomials (p. 601) Trinomials of the form $a^2 + 2ab + b^2$ and $a^2 - 2ab + b^2$. **trinomios cuadrados perfectos** (pág. 601) Trinomios de la forma $a^2 + 2ab + b^2$ y $a^2 - 2ab + b^2$.	$x^2 + 6x + 9$ and $x^2 - 10x + 25$ are perfect square trinomials. $x^2 + 6x + 9$ y $x^2 - 10x + 25$ son trinomios cuadrados perfectos.
permutation (p. 851) An arrangement of objects in which order is important. **permutación** (pág. 851) Disposición de objetos en la que el orden es importante.	There are 6 permutations of the numbers 1, 2, and 3: 123, 132, 213, 231, 312, and 321. Existen 6 permutaciones de los números 1, 2 y 3: 123, 132, 213, 231, 312 y 321.
perpendicular lines (p. 320) Two lines in the same plane that intersect to form a right angle. **rectas perpendiculares** (pág. 320) Dos rectas del mismo plano que al cortarse forman un ángulo recto.	Horizontal and vertical lines are perpendicular to each other. Las rectas horizontales y verticales son perpendiculares entre sí.

985

point-slope form (p. 302) An equation of a nonvertical line written in the form $y - y_1 = m(x - x_1)$ where the line passes through a given point (x_1, y_1) and has a slope of m. **forma punto-pendiente** (pág. 302) Ecuación de una recta no vertical escrita en la forma $y - y_1 = m(x - x_1)$, donde la recta pasa por un punto dado (x_1, y_1) y tiene pendiente m.	The equation $y + 3 = 2(x - 4)$ is in point-slope form. The graph of the equation is a line that passes through the point $(4, -3)$ and has a slope of 2. La ecuación $y + 3 = 2(x - 4)$ está en la forma punto-pendiente. La gráfica de la ecuación es una recta que pasa por el punto $(4, -3)$ y tiene pendiente 2.
polynomial (p. 554) A monomial or a sum of monomials, each called a term of the polynomial. **polinomio** (pág. 554) Monomio o suma de monomios; cada uno se llama término del polinomio.	9, $2x^2 + x - 5$, and $7bc^3 + 4b^4c$ are polynomials. 9, $2x^2 + x - 5$ y $7bc^3 + 4b^4c$ son polinomios.
population (p. 871) The entire group that you want information about. **población** (pág. 871) El grupo entero sobre el que se desea información.	A magazine invites its readers to mail in answers to a questionnaire rating the magazine. The population consists of all the magazine's readers. Una revista invita a sus lectores a enviar por correo las respuestas a un cuestionario sobre la calidad de la revista. La población está formada por todos los lectores de la revista.
positive integers (p. 64) The integers that are greater than 0. **números enteros positivos** (pág. 64) Los números enteros mayores que 0.	1, 2, 3, 4, . . .
power (p. 3) An expression that represents repeated multiplication of the same factor. **potencia** (pág. 3) Expresión que representa la multiplicación repetida del mismo factor.	81 is a power of 3, because $81 = 3 \cdot 3 \cdot 3 \cdot 3 = 3^4$. 81 es una potencia de 3 ya que $81 = 3 \cdot 3 \cdot 3 \cdot 3 = 3^4$.
probability of an event (p. 843) A number from 0 to 1 that measures the likelihood, or chance, that the event will occur. **probabilidad de un suceso** (pág. 843) Número de 0 a 1 que mide la posibilidad de que ocurra un suceso.	*See* experimental probability *and* theoretical probability. *Ver* probabilidad experimental *y* probabilidad teórica.
proportion (p. 163) An equation that states that two ratios are equivalent: $\frac{a}{b} = \frac{c}{d}$ where $b \neq 0$ and $d \neq 0$. **proporción** (pág. 163) Ecuación que establece que dos razones son equivalentes: $\frac{a}{b} = \frac{c}{d}$ donde $b \neq 0$ y $d \neq 0$.	$\frac{3}{4} = \frac{6}{8}$ and $\frac{11}{6} = \frac{x}{30}$ are proportions. $\frac{3}{4} = \frac{6}{8}$ y $\frac{11}{6} = \frac{x}{30}$ son proporciones.

ENGLISH-SPANISH GLOSSARY

986

Pythagorean theorem (p. 737) If a triangle is a right triangle, then the sum of the squares of the lengths a and b of the legs equals the square of the length c of the hypotenuse: $a^2 + b^2 = c^2$.

teorema de Pitágoras (pág. 737) Si un triángulo es rectángulo, entonces la suma de los cuadrados de las longitudes a y b de los catetos es igual al cuadrado de la longitud c de la hipotenusa: $a^2 + b^2 = c^2$.

$a = 5$, $b = 12$, $c = 13$

$5^2 + 12^2 = 13^2$

Q

quadrants (p. 206) The four regions into which the coordinate plane is divided by the x-axis and the y-axis.

cuadrantes (pág. 206) Las cuatro regiones en las que el eje de x y el eje de y dividen al plano de coordenadas.

y-axis
eje de y
Quadrant II
Cuadrante II
$(-, +)$
Quadrant I
Cuadrante I
$(+, +)$
x-axis
eje de x
$(-, -)$
Cuadrante III
Quadrant III
$(+, -)$
Cuadrante IV
Quadrant IV

quadratic equation (p. 643) An equation that can be written in the standard form $ax^2 + bx + c = 0$ where $a \neq 0$.

ecuación cuadrática (pág. 643) Ecuación que puede escribirse en la forma general $ax^2 + bx + c = 0$, donde $a \neq 0$.

The equations $x^2 - 2x = 3$ and $0.1x^2 = 40$ are quadratic equations.

$x^2 - 2x = 3$ y $0.1x^2 = 40$ son ecuaciones cuadráticas.

quadratic formula (p. 671) The formula below that can be used to find the solutions of the quadratic equation $ax^2 + bx + c = 0$ where $a \neq 0$ and $b^2 - 4ac \geq 0$:

$$x = \frac{-b \pm \sqrt{b^2 - 4ac}}{2a}$$

fórmula cuadrática (pág. 671) La fórmula de abajo puede utilizarse para hallar las soluciones de la ecuación cuadrática $ax^2 + bx + c = 0$ donde $a \neq 0$ y $b^2 - 4ac \geq 0$:

$$x = \frac{-b \pm \sqrt{b^2 - 4ac}}{2a}$$

To solve $3x^2 + 5x - 8 = 0$, substitute 3 for a, 5 for b, and -8 for c in the quadratic formula:

$$x = \frac{-5 \pm \sqrt{5^2 - 4(3)(-8)}}{2(3)}$$

$x = 1$ or $x = -\frac{8}{3}$

Para resolver $3x^2 + 5x - 8 = 0$, sustituye a por 3, b por 5 y c por -8 en la fórmula cuadrática:

$$x = \frac{-5 \pm \sqrt{5^2 - 4(3)(-8)}}{2(3)}$$

$x = 1$ ó $x = -\frac{8}{3}$

quadratic function (p. 628) A nonlinear function that can be written in the standard form $y = ax^2 + bx + c$ where $a \neq 0$.

función cuadrática (pág. 628) Función no lineal que puede escribirse en la forma general $y = ax^2 + bx + c$, donde $a \neq 0$.

$y = 2x^2 + 5x - 3$ is a quadratic function.

$y = 2x^2 + 5x - 3$ es una función cuadrática.

987

R

radical equation (p. 729) An equation that contains a radical expression with a variable in the radicand. **ecuación radical** (pág. 729) Ecuación que contiene una expresión radical en cuyo radicando aparece una variable.	$2\sqrt{x} - 8 = 0$ and $\sqrt{3x - 17} = \sqrt{x + 21}$ are radical equations. $2\sqrt{x} - 8 = 0$ y $\sqrt{3x - 17} = \sqrt{x + 21}$ son ecuaciones radicales.
radical expression (p. 710) An expression that contains a radical, such as a square root, cube root, or other root. **expresión radical** (pág. 710) Expresión que contiene un radical, como una raíz cuadrada, una raíz cúbica u otra raíz.	$3\sqrt{2x}$ and $\sqrt[3]{x - 1}$ are radical expressions. $3\sqrt{2x}$ y $\sqrt[3]{x - 1}$ son expresiones radicales.
radical function (p. 710) A function that contains a radical expression with the independent variable in the radicand. **función radical** (pág. 710) Función que contiene una expresión radical y en cuyo radicando aparece la variable independiente.	$y = \sqrt[3]{2x}$ and $y = \sqrt{x + 2}$ are radical functions. $y = \sqrt[3]{2x}$ e $y = \sqrt{x + 2}$ son funciones radicales.
radicand (p. 110) The number or expression inside a radical symbol. **radicando** (pág. 110) El número o la expresión que aparece bajo el signo radical.	The radicand of $\sqrt{9}$ and $-\sqrt{9}$ is 9. El radicando de $\sqrt{9}$ y $-\sqrt{9}$ es 9.
random sample (p. 871) A sample in which every member of the population has an equal chance of being selected. **muestra aleatoria** (pág. 871) Muestra en la que cada miembro de la población tiene igual probabilidad de ser seleccionado.	You can select a random sample of a school's student population by having a computer randomly choose 100 student identification numbers. Para seleccionar una muestra aleatoria de la población de estudiantes de una escuela, puedes usar la computadora para elegir al azar 100 números de identificación estudiantil.
range of a data set (p. 876) The range of a numerical data set is a measure of dispersion. It is the difference of the greatest value and the least value. **rango de un conjunto de datos** (pág. 876) El rango de un conjunto de datos numéricos es una medida de dispersión. Es la diferencia entre los valores mayor y menor.	The range of the data set 4, 7, 9, 11, 11, 12, 18 is $18 - 4 = 14$. El rango del conjunto de datos 4, 7, 9, 11, 11, 12, 18 es $18 - 4 = 14$.
range of a function (p. 35) The set of all outputs of a function. **rango de una función** (pág. 35) El conjunto de todas las salidas de una función.	*See* function. *Ver* función.

ENGLISH-SPANISH GLOSSARY

rate (p. 17) A fraction that compares two quantities measured in different units. **relación** (pág. 17) Fracción que compara dos cantidades medidas en unidades diferentes.	$\frac{110 \text{ miles}}{2 \text{ hours}}$ and $\frac{55 \text{ miles}}{1 \text{ hour}}$ are rates. $\frac{110 \text{ millas}}{2 \text{ horas}}$ y $\frac{55 \text{ millas}}{1 \text{ hora}}$ son relaciones.
rate of change (p. 237) A comparison of a change in one quantity with a change in another quantity. In real-world situations, you can interpret the slope of a line as a rate of change. **relación de cambio** (pág. 237) Comparación entre el cambio producido en una cantidad y el cambio producido en otra cantidad. En situaciones de la vida real, se puede interpretar la pendiente de una recta como una relación de cambio.	You pay \$7 for 2 hours of computer use and \$14 for 4 hours of computer use. The rate of change is $\frac{\text{change in cost}}{\text{change in time}} = \frac{14 - 7}{4 - 2} = 3.5$, or \$3.50 per hour. Pagas \$7 por usar la computadora 2 horas y \$14 por usarla 4 horas. La relación de cambio es $\frac{\text{cambio en el costo}}{\text{cambio en el tiempo}} = \frac{14 - 7}{4 - 2} = 3.5$, o \$3.50 por hora.
ratio (p. 162) A comparison of two numbers using division. The ratio of a and b, where $b \neq 0$, can be written as a to b, as $a : b$, or as $\frac{a}{b}$. **razón** (pág. 162) Comparacion de dos números mediante la división. La razón entre a y b, donde $b \neq 0$, puede escribirse a a b, $a : b$ o $\frac{a}{b}$.	The ratio of 5 wins to 2 losses can be written as 5 to 2, as 5 : 2, or as $\frac{5}{2}$. La razón de 5 victorias a 2 derrotas puede escribirse 5 a 2, 5 : 2 ó $\frac{5}{2}$.
rational equation (p. 820) An equation that contains one or more rational expressions. **ecuación racional** (pág. 820) Ecuación que contiene una o más expresiones racionales.	The equations $\frac{6}{x + 4} = \frac{x}{2}$ and $\frac{x}{x - 2} + \frac{1}{5} = \frac{2}{x - 2}$ are rational equations. $\frac{6}{x + 4} = \frac{x}{2}$ y $\frac{x}{x - 2} + \frac{1}{5} = \frac{2}{x - 2}$ son ecuaciones racionales.
rational expression (p. 794) An expression that can be written as a ratio of two polynomials where the denominator is not 0. **expresión racional** (pág. 794) Expresión que puede escribirse como razón de dos polinomios, donde el denominador no es 0.	$\frac{x + 8}{10x}$ and $\frac{5}{x^2 - 1}$ are rational expressions. $\frac{x + 8}{10x}$ y $\frac{5}{x^2 - 1}$ son expresiones racionales.
rational function (p. 775) A function whose rule is given by a fraction whose numerator and denominator are polynomials and whose denominator is not 0. **función racional** (pág. 775) Función cuya regla viene dada por una fracción cuyo numerador y denominador son polinomios y cuyo denominador no es 0.	The equations $y = \frac{-1}{x}$ and $y = \frac{2x - 1}{x - 2}$ are rational functions. Las ecuaciones $y = \frac{-1}{x}$ e $y = \frac{2x - 1}{x - 2}$ son funciones racionales.

ENGLISH-SPANISH GLOSSARY

rational number (p. 64) A number that can be written as $\frac{a}{b}$ where a and b are integers and $b \neq 0$. **número racional** (pág. 64) Número que puede escribirse $\frac{a}{b}$, donde a y b son números enteros y $b \neq 0$.	$4 = \frac{4}{1}, 0 = \frac{0}{1}, 2\frac{1}{3} = \frac{7}{3}, -\frac{3}{4} = \frac{-3}{4}$, and $0.6 = \frac{3}{5}$ are all rational numbers. $4 = \frac{4}{1}, 0 = \frac{0}{1}, 2\frac{1}{3} = \frac{7}{3}, -\frac{3}{4} = \frac{-3}{4}$ y $0.6 = \frac{3}{5}$ son todos números racionales.
rationalizing the denominator (p. 721) The process of eliminating a radical from an expression's denominator by multiplying the expression by an appropriate form of 1. **racionalizar el denominador** (pág. 721) El proceso de eliminar el radical del denominador de una expresión multiplicando la expresión por la forma apropiada de 1.	To rationalize the denominator of $\frac{5}{\sqrt{7}}$, multiply the expression by $\frac{\sqrt{7}}{\sqrt{7}}$: $\frac{5}{\sqrt{7}} = \frac{5}{\sqrt{7}} \cdot \frac{\sqrt{7}}{\sqrt{7}} = \frac{5\sqrt{7}}{\sqrt{49}} = \frac{5\sqrt{7}}{7}$ Para racionalizar el denominador de $\frac{5}{\sqrt{7}}$, multiplica la expresión por $\frac{\sqrt{7}}{\sqrt{7}}$: $\frac{5}{\sqrt{7}} = \frac{5}{\sqrt{7}} \cdot \frac{\sqrt{7}}{\sqrt{7}} = \frac{5\sqrt{7}}{\sqrt{49}} = \frac{5\sqrt{7}}{7}$
real numbers (p. 112) The set of all rational and irrational numbers. **números reales** (pág. 112) El conjunto de todos los números racionales e irracionales.	$8, -6.2, \frac{6}{7}, \pi$, and $\sqrt{2}$ are real numbers. $8, -6.2, \frac{6}{7}, \pi$ y $\sqrt{2}$ son números reales.
reflection (p. 213) A reflection flips a figure in a line. **reflexión** (pág. 213) Una reflexión vuelca una figura en una recta.	y x line of reflection recta de reflexión
relation (p. 49) Any pairing of a set of inputs with a set of outputs. **relación** (pág. 49) Cualquier correspondencia establecida entre un conjunto de entradas y un conjunto de salidas.	The pairing in the table below is a relation, but it is *not* a function. La correspondencia en la tabla de abajo es una relación, pero *no* es una función. **Input / Entrada**: 4, 4, 5, 6, 7 **Output / Salida**: 0, 1, 2, 3, 4
roots (p. 575) The solutions of an equation in which one side is zero and other side is a product of polynomial factors. **raíces** (pág. 575) Las soluciones de una ecuación en la que un lado es cero y el otro lado es el producto de factores polinómicos.	The roots of the equation $(x - 4)(x + 2) = 0$ are 4 and -2. Las raíces de la ecuación $(x - 4)(x + 2) = 0$ son 4 y -2.

ENGLISH-SPANISH GLOSSARY

S

sample (p. 871) A part of a population. **muestra** (pág. 871) Parte de una población.	To predict the results of an election, a survey is given to a sample of voters. Para predecir los resultados de una elección, se realiza una encuesta entre una muestra de votantes.
sample space (p. 843) The set of all possible outcomes. **espacio muestral** (pág. 843) El conjunto de todos los casos posibles.	When you toss two coins, the sample space is heads, heads; heads, tails; tails, heads; and tails, tails. Cuando lanzas al aire dos monedas, el espacio muestral es cara, cara; cara, cruz; cruz, cara; y cruz, cruz.
scalar (p. 95) A real number by which you multiply a matrix. **escalar** (pág. 95) Número real por el que se multiplica una matriz.	*See* scalar multiplication. *Ver* multiplicación escalar.
scalar multiplication (p. 95) Multiplication of each element in a matrix by a real number, called a scalar. **multiplicación escalar** (pág. 95) Multiplicación de cada elemento de una matriz por un número real llamado escalar.	The matrix is multiplied by the scalar 3. $3\begin{bmatrix} 1 & 2 \\ 0 & -1 \end{bmatrix} = \begin{bmatrix} 3 & 6 \\ 0 & -3 \end{bmatrix}$ La matriz se multiplica por el escalar 3. $3\begin{bmatrix} 1 & 2 \\ 0 & -1 \end{bmatrix} = \begin{bmatrix} 3 & 6 \\ 0 & -3 \end{bmatrix}$
scale (p. 170) A ratio that relates the dimensions of a scale drawing or scale model and the actual dimensions. **escala** (pág. 170) Razón que relaciona las dimensiones de un dibujo a escala o un modelo a escala con las dimensiones reales.	The scale 1 in. : 12 ft on a floor plan means that 1 inch in the floor plan represents an actual distance of 12 feet. La escala 1 pulg : 12 pies en un diagrama de planta significa que 1 pulgada en el diagrama de planta representa una distancia real de 12 pies.
scale drawing (p. 170) A two-dimensional drawing of an object in which the dimensions of the drawing are in proportion to the dimensions of the object. **dibujo a escala** (pág. 170) Dibujo bidimensional de un objeto en el que las dimensiones del dibujo guardan proporción con las dimensiones del objeto.	A floor plan of a house is a scale drawing. El diagrama de planta de una casa es un dibujo a escala.
scale model (p. 170) A three-dimensional model of an object in which the dimensions of the model are in proportion to the dimensions of the object. **modelo a escala** (pág. 170) Modelo tridimensional de un objeto en el que las dimensiones del modelo guardan proporción con las dimensiones del objeto.	A globe is a scale model of Earth. El globo terráqueo es un modelo a escala de la Tierra.

scatter plot (p. 325) A graph used to determine whether there is a relationship or trend between paired data.

diagrama de dispersión (pág. 325) Gráfica utilizada para determinar si hay una relación o tendencia entre los pares de datos.

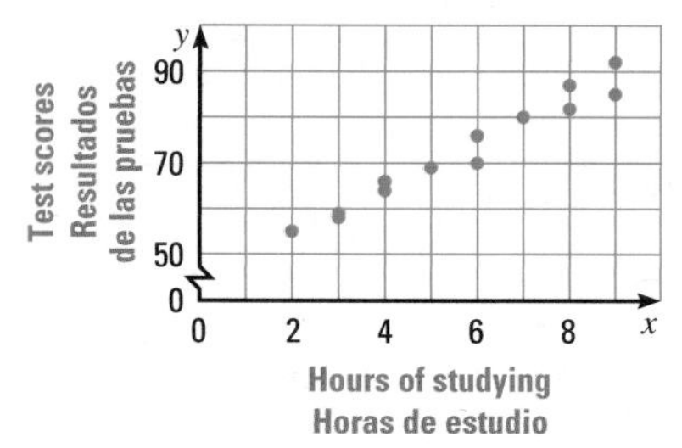

scientific notation (p. 512) A number is written in scientific notation when it is of the form $c \times 10^n$ where $1 \le c < 10$ and n is an integer.

notación científica (pág. 512) Un número está escrito en notación científica cuando es de la forma $c \times 10^n$, donde $1 \le c < 10$ y n es un número entero.

Two million is written in scientific notation as 2×10^6, and 0.547 is written in scientific notation as 5.47×10^{-1}.

El número dos millones escrito en notación científica es 2×10^6, y 0.547 escrito en notación científica es 5.47×10^{-1}.

self-selected sample (p. 871) A sample in which members of the population select themselves by volunteering.

muestra autoseleccionada (pág. 871) Muestra en la que los miembros de la población se seleccionan a sí mismos ofreciéndose a participar.

You can obtain a self-selected sample of a school's student population by asking students to return surveys to a collection box.

Para obtener una muestra autoseleccionada de la población de estudiantes de una escuela, puedes pedir a los estudiantes que hagan la encuesta que la depositen en un recipiente de recogida.

sequence (p. 309) An ordered list of numbers.

progresión (pág. 309) Lista ordenada de números.

$-4, 1, 6, 11, 16, \ldots$ is a sequence.

$-4, 1, 6, 11, 16, \ldots$ es una progresión.

set (p. 71) A collection of distinct objects.

conjunto (pág. 71) Colección de objetos diferenciados.

The set of whole numbers is $W = \{0, 1, 2, 3, \ldots\}$.

El conjunto de los números naturales es $W = \{0, 1, 2, 3, \ldots\}$.

similar figures (p. 174) Figures that have the same shape but not necessarily the same size. Corresponding angles of similar figures are congruent, and the ratios of the lengths of corresponding sides are equal. The symbol ~ indicates that two figures are similar.

figuras semejantes (pág. 174) Figuras que tienen la misma forma pero no necesariamente el mismo tamaño. Los ángulos correspondientes de las figuras semejantes son congruentes, y las razones de las longitudes de los lados correspondientes son iguales. El símbolo ~ indica que dos figuras son semejantes.

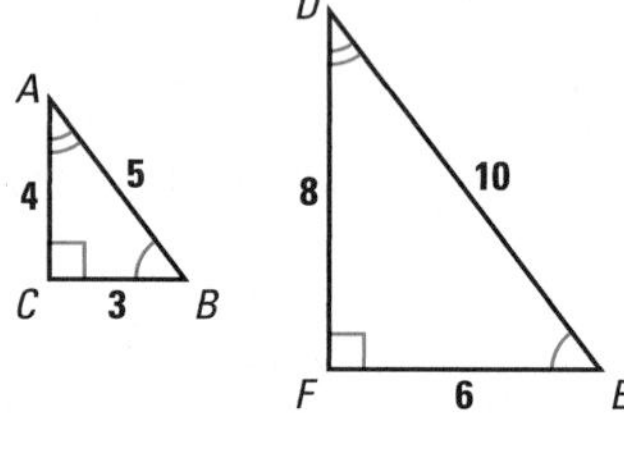

$\triangle ABC \sim \triangle DEF$

ENGLISH-SPANISH GLOSSARY

simplest form of a radical expression (p. 719) A radical expression that has no perfect square factors other than 1 in the radicand, no fractions in the radicand, and no radicals appearing in the denominator of a fraction.

In simplest form, $\sqrt{32}$ is written as $4\sqrt{2}$, and $\frac{5}{\sqrt{7}}$ is written as $\frac{5\sqrt{7}}{7}$.

forma más simple de una expresión radical (pág. 719) Expresión radical que no tiene en el radicando fracciones ni factores cuadrados perfectos distintos de 1 y que no tiene radicales en el denominador de las fracciones.

En la forma más simple, $\sqrt{32}$ se escribe $4\sqrt{2}$, y $\frac{5}{\sqrt{7}}$ se escribe $\frac{5\sqrt{7}}{7}$.

simplest form of a rational expression (p. 795) A rational expression whose numerator and denominator have no factors in common other than 1.

The simplest form of $\frac{2x}{x(x-3)}$ is $\frac{2}{x-3}$.

forma más simple de una expresión racional (pág. 795) Expresión racional cuyo numerador y denominador no tienen más factores en común que el 1.

La forma más simple de $\frac{2x}{x(x-3)}$ es $\frac{2}{x-3}$.

simulation (p. 849) An experiment that you can perform to make predictions about real-world situations.

Each box of Oaties contains 1 of 6 prizes. The probability of getting each prize is $\frac{1}{6}$. To predict the number of boxes of cereal you must buy to win all 6 prizes, you can roll a number cube 1 time for each box of cereal you buy. Keep rolling until you have rolled all 6 numbers.

simulación (pág. 849) Experimento que se puede realizar para hacer predicciones sobre situaciones de la vida real.

Cada paquete de Oaties contiene 1 de un total de 6 premios. La probabilidad de obtener cada premio es $\frac{1}{6}$. Para predecir el número de paquetes de cereales que debes comprar para poder conseguir los 6 premios, puedes lanzar un cubo numerado 1 vez por cada paquete de cereales que compres. Sigue lanzando el cubo hasta obtener los 6 números.

slope (p. 235) The slope m of a nonvertical line is the ratio of the vertical change (the *rise*) to the horizontal change (the *run*) between any two points (x_1, y_1) and (x_2, y_2) on the line: $m = \frac{y_2 - y_1}{x_2 - x_1}$.

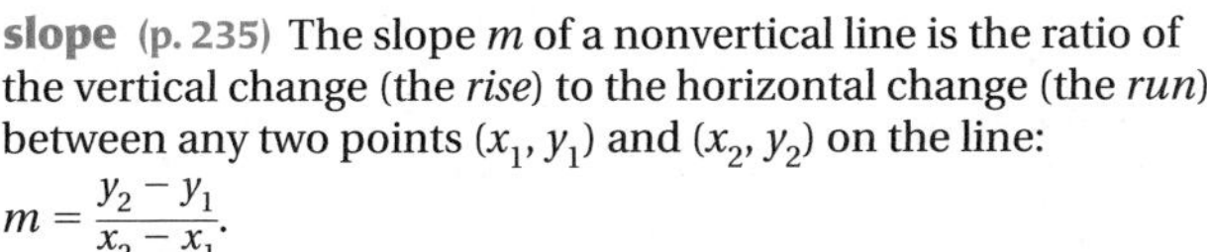

pendiente (pág. 235) La pendiente m de una recta no vertical es la razón del cambio vertical (*distancia vertical*) al cambio horizontal (*distancia horizontal*) entre dos puntos cualesquiera (x_1, y_1) y (x_2, y_2) de la recta: $m = \frac{y_2 - y_1}{x_2 - x_1}$.

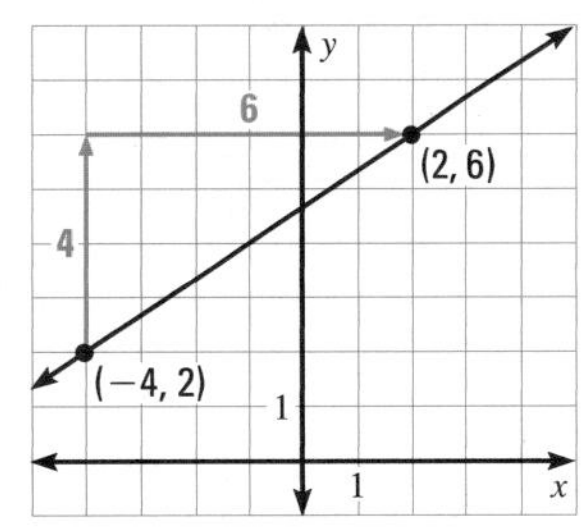

The slope of the line shown is $\frac{4}{6}$, or $\frac{2}{3}$.

La pendiente de la recta indicada es $\frac{4}{6}$, ó $\frac{2}{3}$.

ENGLISH-SPANISH GLOSSARY

slope-intercept form (p. 244) A linear equation written in the form $y = mx + b$ where m is the slope and b is the y-intercept of the equation's graph.	$y = 3x + 4$ is in slope-intercept form. The slope of the line is 3, and the y-intercept is 4.
forma pendiente-intercepto (pág. 244) Ecuación lineal escrita en la forma $y = mx + b$, donde m es la pendiente y b es el intercepto en y de la gráfica de la ecuación.	$y = 3x + 4$ está en la forma pendiente-intercepto. La pendiente de la recta es 3, y el intercepto en y es 4.
solution of an equation in one variable (p. 22) A number that produces a true statement when substituted for the variable in an equation.	The number 3 is a solution of the equation $8 - 2x = 2$, because $8 - 2(3) = 2$.
solución de una ecuación con una variable (pág. 22) Número que, al sustituirse por la variable de la ecuación, produce un enunciado verdadero.	El número 3 es una solución de la ecuación $8 - 2x = 2$ ya que $8 - 2(3) = 2$.
solution of an equation in two variables (p. 215) An ordered pair that produces a true statement when the coordinates of the ordered pair are substituted for the variables in the equation.	$(1, -4)$ is a solution of $3x - y = 7$, because $3(1) - (-4) = 7$.
solución de una ecuación con dos variables (pág. 215) Par ordenado que, al ser sustituidas sus coordenadas por las variables de la ecuación, produce un enunciado verdadero.	$(1, -4)$ es una solución de $3x - y = 7$ ya que $3(1) - (-4) = 7$.
solution of an inequality in one variable (p. 22) A number that produces a true statement when substituted for the variable in an inequality.	The number 3 is a solution of the inequality $5 + 3n \le 20$, because $5 + 3(3) = 14$ and $14 \le 20$.
solución de una desigualdad con una variable (pág. 22) Número que, al sustituirse por la variable de la desigualdad, produce un enunciado verdadero.	El número 3 es una solución de la desigualdad $5 + 3n \le 20$ ya que $5 + 3(3) = 14$ y $14 \le 20$.
solution of an inequality in two variables x and y (p. 405) An ordered pair (x, y) that produces a true statement when the values of x and y are substituted into the inequality.	$(-1, 2)$ is a solution of the inequality $x - 3y < 6$ because $-1 - 3(2) = -7$ and $-7 < 6$.
solución de una desigualdad con las dos variables x e y (pág. 405) Par ordenado (x, y) que, al sustitutirse los valores de x e y en la desigualdad, produce un enunciado verdadero.	$(-1, 2)$ es una solución de la desigualdad $x - 3y < 6$ ya que $-1 - 3(2) = -7$ y $-7 < 6$.
solution of a system of linear equations (p. 427) An ordered pair that is a solution of each equation in the system.	$(3, 2)$ is a solution of the system of linear equations $x + 2y = 7$ $3x - 2y = 5$ because each equation is a true statement when 3 is substituted for x and 2 is substituted for y.
solución de un sistema de ecuaciones lineales (pág. 427) Par ordenado que es una solución de cada ecuación del sistema.	$(3, 2)$ es una solución del sistema de ecuaciones lineales $x + 2y = 7$ $3x - 2y = 5$ ya que cada ecuación es un enunciado verdadero cuando x se sustituye por 3 e y se sustituye por 2.

solution of a system of linear inequalities (p. 466) An ordered pair that is a solution of each inequality in the system.	(6, −5) is a solution of the system of inequalities $x - y > 7$ $2x + y < 8$ because each inequality is a true statement when 6 is substituted for x and −5 is substituted for y.
solución de un sistema de desigualdades lineales (pág. 466) Par ordenado que es una solución de cada desigualdad del sistema.	(6, −5) es una solución del sistema de desigualdades $x - y > 7$ $2x + y < 8$ ya que cada desigualdad es un enunciado verdadero cuando x se sustituye por 6 e y se sustituye por −5.
square root (p. 110) If $b^2 = a$, then b is a square root of a. The radical symbol $\sqrt{\ }$ represents a nonnegative square root.	The square roots of 9 are 3 and −3, because $3^2 = 9$ and $(-3)^2 = 9$. So, $\sqrt{9} = 3$ and $-\sqrt{9} = -3$.
raíz cuadrada (pág. 110) Si $b^2 = a$, entonces b es una raíz cuadrada de a. El signo radical $\sqrt{\ }$ representa una raíz cuadrada no negativa.	Las raíces cuadradas de 9 son 3 y −3 ya que $3^2 = 9$ y $(-3)^2 = 9$. Así pues, $\sqrt{9} = 3$ y $-\sqrt{9} = -3$.
square root function (p. 710) A radical function whose equation contains a square root with the independent variable in the radicand.	$y = 2\sqrt{x+2}$ and $y = \sqrt{x} + 3$ are square root functions.
función con raíz cuadrada (pág. 710) Función radical representada por una ecuación con una raíz cuadrada en cuyo radicando aparece la variable independiente.	$y = 2\sqrt{x+2}$ e $y = \sqrt{x} + 3$ son funciones con raíz cuadrada.
standard deviation (p. 879) The standard deviation of a numerical data set $x_1, x_2, \ldots, x_n$ is a measure of dispersion denoted by σ and computed as the square root of the variance. $\sigma = \sqrt{\frac{(x_1 - \bar{x})^2 + (x_2 - \bar{x})^2 + \ldots + (x_n - \bar{x})^2}{n}}$	The standard deviation of the data set 3, 9, 13, 23 (with mean = 12) is: $\sigma = \sqrt{\frac{(3-12)^2 + (9-12)^2 + (13-12)^2 + (23-12)^2}{4}}$ $= \sqrt{53} \approx 7.3$
desviación típica (pág. 879) La desviación típica de un conjunto de datos numéricos $x_1, x_2, \ldots, x_n$ es una medida de dispersión designada por σ y calculada como raíz cuadrada de la varianza. $\sigma = \sqrt{\frac{(x_1 - \bar{x})^2 + (x_2 - \bar{x})^2 + \ldots + (x_n - \bar{x})^2}{n}}$	La desviación típica del conjunto de datos 3, 9, 13, 23 (con media = 12) es: $\sigma = \sqrt{\frac{(3-12)^2 + (9-12)^2 + (13-12)^2 + (23-12)^2}{4}}$ $= \sqrt{53} \approx 7.3$
standard form of a linear equation (p. 216) $Ax + By = C$, where A, B, and C are real numbers and A and B are not both zero.	The linear equation $y = 2x - 3$ can be written in standard form as $2x - y = 3$.
forma general de una ecuación lineal (pág. 216) $Ax + By = C$, donde A, B y C son números reales, y A y B no son ambos cero.	La ecuación lineal $y = 2x - 3$ puede escribirse en la forma general como $2x - y = 3$.

standard form of a quadratic equation (p. 643) A quadratic equation in the form $ax^2 + bx + c = 0$ where $a \neq 0$. **forma general de una ecuación cuadrática** (pág. 643) Ecuación cuadrática de la forma $ax^2 + bx + c = 0$, donde $a \neq 0$.	The quadratic equation $x^2 - 2x - 3 = 0$ is in standard form. La ecuación cuadrática $x^2 - 2x - 3 = 0$ está en la forma general.
standard form of a quadratic function (p. 628) A quadratic function in the form $y = ax^2 + bx + c$ where $a \neq 0$. **forma general de una función cuadrática** (pág. 628) Función cuadrática de la forma $y = ax^2 + bx + c$, donde $a \neq 0$.	The quadratic function $y = 2x^2 + 5x - 3$ is in standard form. La función cuadrática $y = 2x^2 + 5x - 3$ está en la forma general.
stem-and-leaf plot (p. 881) A data display that organizes data based on their digits. **tabla arborescente** (pág. 881) Presentación de datos que organiza los datos basándose en sus dígitos.	Stem / Raíces | Leaves / Hojas 0 | 8 9 1 | 0 2 3 4 5 5 5 9 2 | 1 1 5 9 Key: / Clave: 1 | 9 = $19
stratified random sample (p. 871) A sample in which a population is divided into distinct groups, and members are selected at random from each group. **muestra aleatoria estratificada** (pág. 871) Muestra en la que la población está dividida en grupos diferenciados, y los miembros de cada grupo se seleccionan al azar.	You can select a stratified random sample of a school's student population by having a computer randomly choose 25 students from each grade level. Para seleccionar una muestra aleatoria estratificada de la población de estudiantes de una escuela, puedes usar la computadora para elegir al azar a 25 estudiantes de cada grado.
survey (p. 871) A study of one or more characteristics of a group. **encuesta** (pág. 871) Estudio de una o más características de un grupo.	A magazine invites its readers to mail in answers to a questionnaire rating the magazine. Una revista invita a sus lectores a enviar por correo las respuestas a un cuestionario sobre la calidad de la revista.
system of linear equations (p. 427) Two or more linear equations in the same variables; also called a *linear system.* **sistema de ecuaciones lineales** (pág. 427) Dos o más ecuaciones lineales con las mismas variables; llamado también *sistema lineal.*	The equations below form a system of linear equations: $x + 2y = 7$ $3x - 2y = 5$ Las siguientes ecuaciones forman un sistema de ecuaciones lineales: $x + 2y = 7$ $3x - 2y = 5$

system of linear inequalities in two variables (p. 466) Two or more linear inequalities in the same variables; also called a *system of inequalities.* **sistema de desigualdades lineales con dos variables** (pág. 466) Dos o más desigualdades lineales con las mismas variables; llamado también *sistema de desigualdades.*	The inequalities below form a system of linear inequalities in two variables: $x - y > 7$ $2x + y < 8$ Las siguientes desigualdades forman un sistema de desigualdades lineales con dos variables: $x - y > 7$ $2x + y < 8$
systematic sample (p. 871) A sample in which a rule is used to select members of the population. **muestra sistemática** (pág. 871) Muestra en la que se usa una regla para seleccionar a los miembros de la población.	You can select a systematic sample of a school's student population by choosing every tenth student on an alphabetical list of all students at the school. Para seleccionar una muestra sistemática de la población de estudiantes de una escuela, puedes elegir a cada décimo estudiante de una lista ordenada alfabéticamente de todos los estudiantes de la escuela.

T

terms of an expression (p. 97) The parts of an expression that are added together. **términos de una expresión** (pág. 97) Las partes de una expresión que se suman.	The terms of the expression $3x + (-4) + (-6x) + 2$ are $3x$, -4, $-6x$, and 2. Los términos de la expresión $3x + (-4) + (-6x) + 2$ son $3x$, -4, $-6x$ y 2.
theoretical probability (p. 844) When all outcomes are equally likely, the theoretical probability of an event is the ratio of the number of favorable outcomes to the total number of possible outcomes. The probability of event *A* is written as $P(A)$. **probabilidad teórica** (pág. 844) Cuando todos los casos son igualmente posibles, la probabilidad teórica de un suceso es la razón entre el número de casos favorables y el número total de casos posibles. La probabilidad del suceso *A* se escribe $P(A)$.	A bag of 20 marbles contains 8 red marbles. The theoretical probability of randomly choosing a red marble from the bag is $\frac{8}{20} = \frac{2}{5}$, 40%, or 0.4. Una bolsa de 20 canicas contiene 8 canicas rojas. La probabilidad teórica de sacar al azar una canica roja de la bolsa es $\frac{8}{20} = \frac{2}{5}$, 40% ó 0.4.
transformation (p. 213) For a given set of points, a transformation produces an image by applying a rule to the coordinates of the points. **transformación** (pág. 213) Para un conjunto dado de puntos, una transformación produce una imagen al aplicar una regla a las coordenadas de los puntos.	Translations, vertical stretches, vertical shrinks, and reflections are transformations. Las traslaciones, las expansiones verticales, las contracciones verticales y las reflexiones son transformaciones.

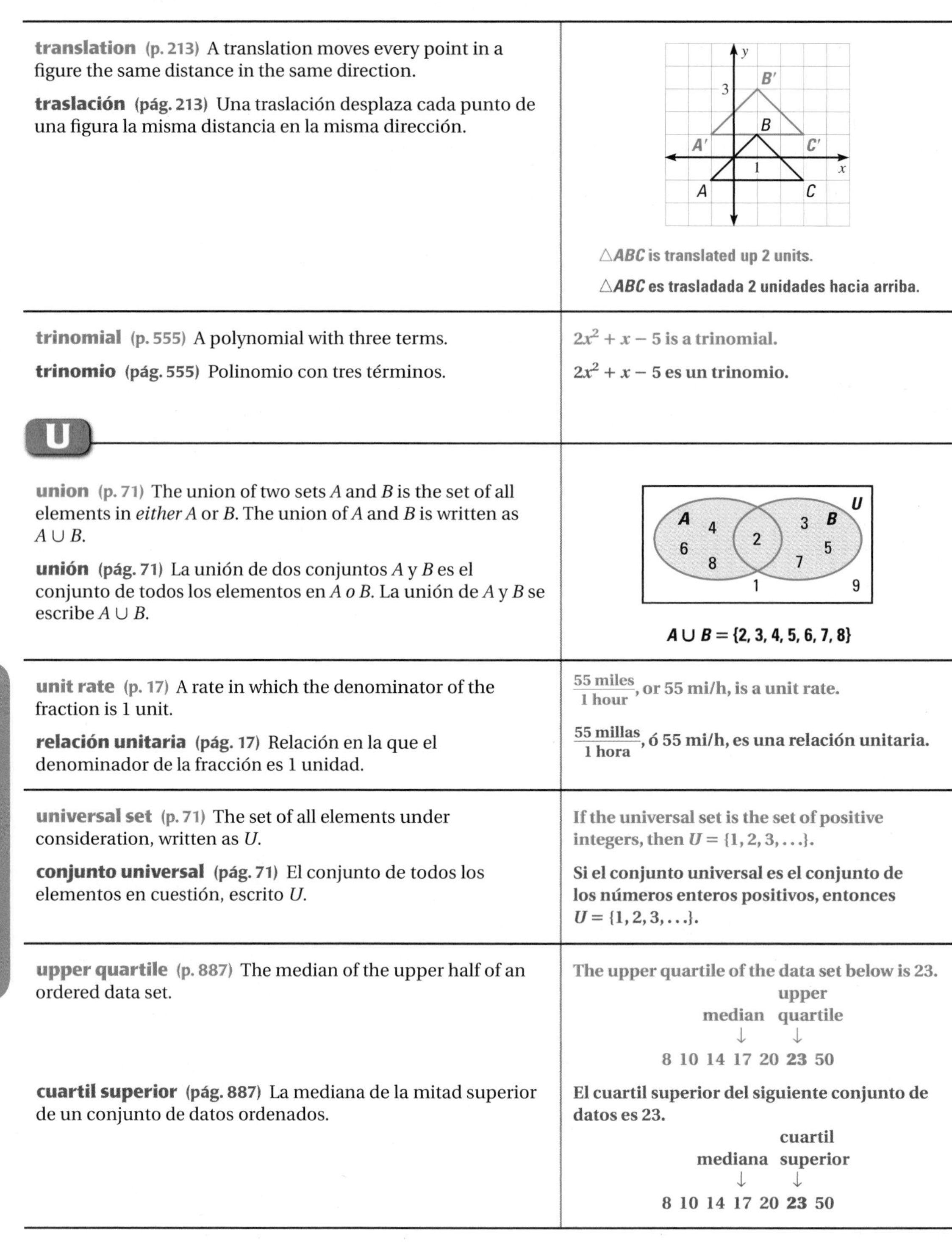

translation (p. 213) A translation moves every point in a figure the same distance in the same direction. **traslación** (pág. 213) Una traslación desplaza cada punto de una figura la misma distancia en la misma dirección.	$\triangle ABC$ is translated up 2 units. $\triangle ABC$ es trasladada 2 unidades hacia arriba.
trinomial (p. 555) A polynomial with three terms. **trinomio** (pág. 555) Polinomio con tres términos.	$2x^2 + x - 5$ is a trinomial. $2x^2 + x - 5$ es un trinomio.

U

union (p. 71) The union of two sets A and B is the set of all elements in *either* A or B. The union of A and B is written as $A \cup B$. **unión** (pág. 71) La unión de dos conjuntos A y B es el conjunto de todos los elementos en *A o B*. La unión de A y B se escribe $A \cup B$.	$A \cup B = \{2, 3, 4, 5, 6, 7, 8\}$
unit rate (p. 17) A rate in which the denominator of the fraction is 1 unit. **relación unitaria** (pág. 17) Relación en la que el denominador de la fracción es 1 unidad.	$\frac{55 \text{ miles}}{1 \text{ hour}}$, or 55 mi/h, is a unit rate. $\frac{55 \text{ millas}}{1 \text{ hora}}$, ó 55 mi/h, es una relación unitaria.
universal set (p. 71) The set of all elements under consideration, written as U. **conjunto universal** (pág. 71) El conjunto de todos los elementos en cuestión, escrito U.	If the universal set is the set of positive integers, then $U = \{1, 2, 3, \ldots\}$. Si el conjunto universal es el conjunto de los números enteros positivos, entonces $U = \{1, 2, 3, \ldots\}$.
upper quartile (p. 887) The median of the upper half of an ordered data set. **cuartil superior** (pág. 887) La mediana de la mitad superior de un conjunto de datos ordenados.	The upper quartile of the data set below is 23. median ↓ upper quartile ↓ 8 10 14 17 20 **23** 50 El cuartil superior del siguiente conjunto de datos es 23. mediana ↓ cuartil superior ↓ 8 10 14 17 20 **23** 50

V

variable (p. 2) A letter that is used to represent one or more numbers.

variable (pág. 2) Letra que sirve para representar uno o más números.

In the expressions $5n$, $n + 1$, and $8 - n$, the letter n is the variable.

En las expresiones $5n$, $n + 1$ y $8 - n$, la letra n es la variable.

variance (p. 879) The variance of a numerical data set $x_1, x_2, \ldots, x_n$ is a measure of dispersion denoted by σ^2 and given by:

$$\sigma^2 = \frac{(x_1 - \bar{x})^2 + (x_2 - \bar{x})^2 + \ldots + (x_n - \bar{x})^2}{n}$$

varianza (pág. 879) La varianza de un conjunto de datos numéricos $x_1, x_2, \ldots, x_n$ es una medida de dispersión designada por σ^2 y dada por:

$$\sigma^2 = \frac{(x_1 - \bar{x})^2 + (x_2 - \bar{x})^2 + \ldots + (x_n - \bar{x})^2}{n}$$

The variance of the data set 3, 9, 13, 23 (with mean = 12) is:

$$\sigma^2 = \frac{(3 - 12)^2 + (9 - 12)^2 + (13 - 12)^2 + (23 - 12)^2}{4}$$
$$= 53$$

La varianza del conjunto de datos 3, 9, 13, 23 (con media = 12) es:

$$\sigma^2 = \frac{(3 - 12)^2 + (9 - 12)^2 + (13 - 12)^2 + (23 - 12)^2}{4}$$
$$= 53$$

verbal model (p. 16) A verbal model describes a real-world situation using words as labels and using math symbols to relate the words.

modelo verbal (pág. 16) Un modelo verbal describe una situación de la vida real mediante palabras que la exponen y símbolos matemáticos que relacionan esas palabras.

A verbal model and algebraic expression for dividing a dollars in a tip jar among 6 people:

Un modelo verbal y una expresión algebraica utilizados para dividir entre 6 personas a dólares del recipiente de las propinas:

Amount in jar / Cantidad del recipiente ÷ Number of people / Número de personas

$a \div 6$

vertex form of a quadratic function (p. 669) A quadratic function in the form $y = a(x - h)^2 + k$ where $a \neq 0$. The vertex of the graph of the function is (h, k).

forma de vértice de una función cuadrática (pág. 669) Función cuadrática de la forma $y = a(x - h)^2 + k$, donde $a \neq 0$. El vértice de la gráfica de la función es (h, k).

The quadratic function $y = -2(x + 1)^2 - 5$ is in vertex form. The vertex of the graph of the function is $(-1, -5)$.

La función cuadrática $y = -2(x + 1)^2 - 5$ está en la forma de vértice. El vértice de la gráfica de la función es $(-1, -5)$.

999

vertex of a parabola (p. 628) The lowest or highest point on a parabola. **vértice de una parábola** (pág. 628) El punto más bajo o más alto de la parábola.	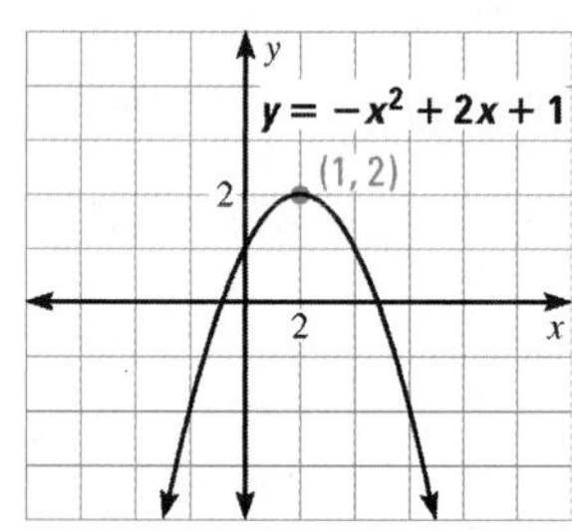 The vertex of the graph of $y = -x^2 + 2x + 1$ is the point (1, 2). El vértice de la gráfica de $y = -x^2 + 2x + 1$ es el punto (1, 2).
vertical motion model (p. 577) A model for the height of an object that is propelled into the air but has no power to keep itself in the air. **modelo de movimiento vertical** (pág. 577) Modelo para representar la altura de un objeto que es lanzado hacia arriba pero que no tiene potencia para mantenerse en el aire.	The vertical motion model for an object thrown upward with an initial vertical velocity of 20 feet per second from an initial height of 8 feet is $h = -16t^2 + 20t + 8$ where h is the height (in feet) of the object t seconds after it is thrown. El modelo de movimiento vertical de un objeto lanzado hacia arriba con una velocidad vertical inicial de 20 pies por segundo desde una altura inicial de 8 pies es $h = -16t^2 + 20t + 8$, donde h es la altura (en pies) del objeto t segundos después del lanzamiento.
vertical shrink (p. 213) A vertical shrink moves every point in a figure toward the x-axis, while points on the x-axis remain fixed. **contracción vertical** (pág. 213) La contracción vertical desplaza cada punto de una figura en dirección del eje de x, mientras los puntos del eje de x permanecen fijos.	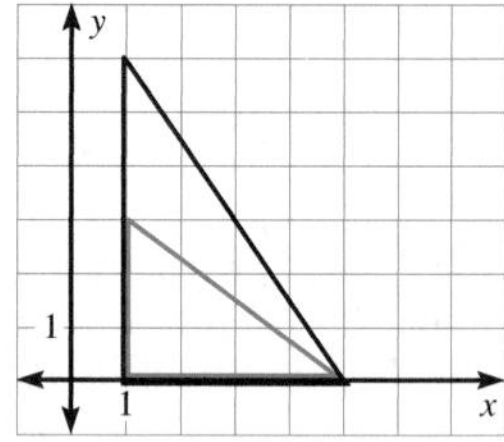 The black triangle is shrunk vertically to the green triangle. El triángulo negro se contrae verticalmente hacia el triángulo verde.

vertical stretch (p. 213) A vertical stretch moves every point in a figure away from the x-axis, while points on the x-axis remain fixed.

expansión vertical (pág. 213) La expansión vertical desplaza cada punto de una figura alejándose del eje de x, mientras los puntos del eje de x permanecen fijos.

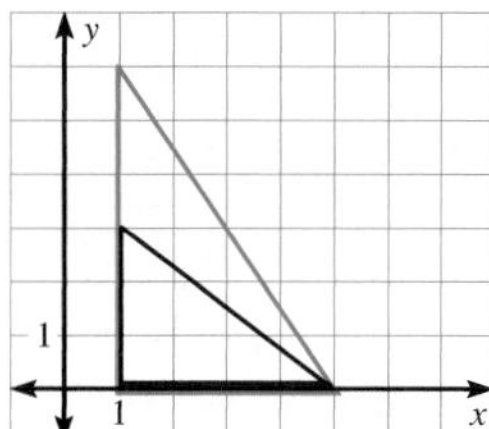

The black triangle is stretched vertically to the green triangle.

El triángulo negro se expande verticalmente hacia el triángulo verde.

W

whole numbers (p. 64) The numbers 0, 1, 2, 3, ...

números naturales (pág. 64) Los números 0, 1, 2, 3, ...

0, 8, and 106 are whole numbers.
−1 and 0.6 are *not* whole numbers.

0, 8 y 106 son números naturales.
−1 y 0.6 *no* son números naturales.

X

x-intercept (p. 225) The x-coordinate of a point where a graph crosses the x-axis.

intercepto en x (pág. 225) La coordenada x de un punto donde la gráfica corta al eje de x.

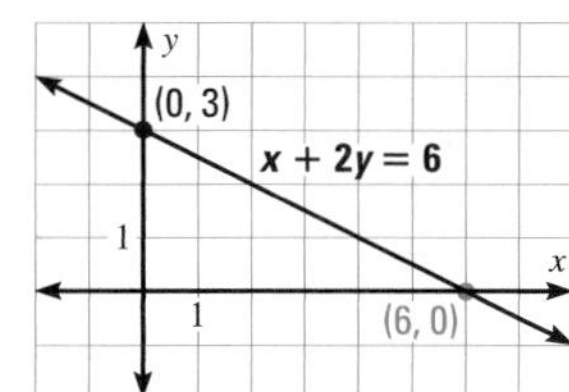

The x-intercept is 6.

El intercepto en x es 6.

Y

y-intercept (p. 225) The y-coordinate of a point where a graph crosses the y-axis.

intercepto en y (pág. 225) La coordenada y de un punto donde la gráfica corta al eje de y.

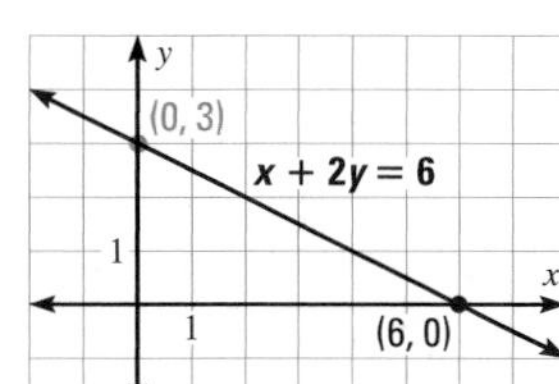

The y-intercept is 3.

El intercepto en y es 3.

ENGLISH-SPANISH GLOSSARY

Z

zero exponent (p. 503) If $a \neq 0$, then $a^0 = 1$. **exponente cero** (pág. 503) Si $a \neq 0$, entonces $a^0 = 1$.	$(-7)^0 = 1$
zero of a function (p. 337) An x-value for which $f(x) = 0$ (or $y = 0$). **cero de una función** (pág. 337) Un valor x para el que $f(x) = 0$ (o $y = 0$).	The zero of $f(x) = 2x - 4$ is 2 because $f(2) = 0$. El cero de $f(x) = 2x - 4$ es 2 ya que $f(2) = 0$.

ENGLISH-SPANISH GLOSSARY

Credits

Photography

Cover © Amy and Chuck Wiley/Wales/Index Stock Imagery; **v** *top* Meridian Creative Group; *top center* Robert C. Jenks, Jenks Studio; *bottom center* McDougal Littell; *bottom* Jerry Head Jr.; **viii** © J.D. Dallet/A.G.E. Fotostock; **ix** © Art Wolfe/Getty Images; **x** © A. Witte/C. Mahaney/Getty Images; **xi** © Rick Havner/AP/Wide World Photos; **xii** © Joseph Sohm/Pan America/PictureQuest; **xiii** © Liz Hymans/Panoramic Images; **xiv** © Kerrick James/Getty Images; **xv** JPL/NASA; **xvi** © Tom Bean/Corbis; **xvii** © Donald Miralle/Getty Images; **xviii** © Hisham F. Ibrahim/Getty Images; **xix** © Joseph Sohm, ChromoSohm Media Inc.; **xx** © Tom Carter/PhotoEdit; **xxii–1** © Geoffrey Clifford/Getty Images; **2** © John C. Russell/Photonica/Getty Images; **4** McDougal Littell; **6** © Scott S. Warren/Aurora Photos; **8** © Royalty-Free/Comstock Images; **10** © David Young-Wolff/PhotoEdit; **12** © Sue Ogrocki/AP/ Wide World Photos; **15** *printer* © PhotoDisc/Getty Images; **15** *photo* © Royalty-Free/Stockbyte; **17** © Steve Dunwell/Index Stock Imagery; **19** © Patrick Ward/Corbis; **21** © Tommy Baynard; **23** © Seb Rogers/Alamy; **24** © Chris Collins/Corbis; **25** © Tommy Baynard; **27** © Tony Avelar/Animals Animals; **28** © Michael Stevens/Fog Stock; **32** © Scott Warren/Aurora Photos; **35** © Michael Newman/PhotoEdit; **37** © Aneal Vohra/Index Stock Imagery; **42** McDougal Littell; **43** Lawrence Migdale/PIX/ McDougal Littell; **47** © Marc Serota/Reuters/Corbis; **51** © Derek Payne/Alamy; **62–63** © Altrendo/Getty Images; **64** © Evan Vucci/ AP/Wide World Photos; **70** © John Chumack/Photo Researchers, Inc.; **74** © Brian Spurlock/SportsChrome; **76** © Bob Krist/Corbis; **78** *center right* © LLC, FogStock/Index Stock Imagery; **80** © Stephen Alvarez/Aurora Photos; **83** © Myrleen Ferguson Cate/ PhotoEdit; **85** © Ron Chapple/Getty Images; **86** © Gregory Bull/ AP/Wide World Photos; **88** © Natphoto/Getty Images; **90** © Peter Essick/Aurora Photos; **92** © Philip Coblentz/Getty Images; **96** © Patrik Giardino/Corbis; **98** © Bob Daemmrich/Image Works, Inc.; **103** © Jonathan Ferrey/Getty Images; **104** © Duncan Adams/AP/ Wide World Photos; **107** Photo courtesy of Mehgan Heaney-Grier, Freedive Champion & Jim Edds, photographer; **108** *both* USGS; **110** © Sylvain Grandadam/Getty Images; **115** Photo from the New York Hall of Science/www.minotaurmazes.com; **130** *top* © Gary Bell/Oceanwide Images; **131** *center right* © Gary Bell/Getty Images; **134** © Barros & Barros/Getty Images; **137** © Anja Niedringhaus/AP/Wide World Photos; **139** *top right* Jay Penni Photography/McDougal Littell; **139** *bottom right* © Gary Bell/ Oceanwide Images ; **141** © Stephen Frink/Corbis; **143** © Royalty-Free/Corbis; **145** © M. Spencer Green/AP/Wide World Photos; **148** © Michael Newman/PhotoEdit; **150** © Jeff Foott/ PictureQuest; **154** © Mark Lennihan/AP/Wide World Photos; **161** © Johner/Photonica/Getty Images; **162** © Reuters/Corbis; **164** © Lowell Georgia/Corbis; **166** © Marc Muench/Getty Images; **168** © Michael S. Yamashita/Corbis; **176** © Reuters/Corbis; **178** © FoodCollection/Index Stock Imagery; **180** © Mark Gibson/Index Stock Imagery; **184** © Tony Garcia/SuperStock; **189** © Royalty-Free/Corbis; **204–205** © Rommel/Masterfile; **206** © Window Observational Research Facility/NASA; **208** © David J. & Janice L. Frent Collection/Corbis; **215** U.S. Navy photo; **220** © Bill Greene Globe Staff/The Boston Globe/Merlin-Net, Inc.; **225** © Alexis Rosenfeld/Photo Researchers, Inc.; **228** © Alexis Rosenfeld/ Photo Researchers, Inc.; **233** © Jim Cooper/AP/Wide World Photos; **234** *all* McDougal Littell; **235** © Kevin Fleming/Corbis; **237** *café* © Paul Edmondson/Getty Images; **237** *soup* © Judd Pilossof/Getty Images; **241** © Kevin Fleming/Corbis; **244** © Peter Williams/AP/Wide World Photos; **245** © Kevin P. Casey/Corbis; **248** © Robert Laberge/Getty Images; **253** © Lionel Cironneau/ AP/ Wide World Photos; **255** © The North Platte Telegraph, Kristina Jergensen/AP/Wide World Photos; **259** © Don Emmert/ Staff/Getty Images; **262** © William Campbell/AP/Wide World Photos; **263** © Robert Winslow/Animals Animals; **267** © Scott Markewitz/Getty Images; **269** © Jeff Greenberg/Image Works, Inc.; **280–281** © Will & Deni McIntyre/Corbis; **282** Jay Penni Photography/McDougal Littell; **283** © Jim Cummins/Getty Images; **285** © Comstock Images/Alamy; **288** © Yann Arthus-Bertrand/Corbis; **292** © Tony Ashby/AFP/Getty Images; **295** © Lester Lefkowitz/Corbis; **302** © Ken Biggs/Getty Images; **307** © Robert W. Ginn/PhotoEdit; **311** © The Photo Library Wales/ Alamy; **313** © BananaStock/Alamy; **317** © Tom Stewart/Corbis; **319** © Phillip Colla/www.OceanLight.com; **325** © Bob & Suzanne Clemenz; **327** © Tim Thompson/Corbis; **335** *both* © Nick Ut/AP/ Wide World Photos; **337** © Cathrine Wessel/Corbis; **339** *bottom right* © Kevin Gilbert/Getty Images; **341** © Erich Kuchling/ Alamy; **343** © David Middleton/Photo Researchers, Inc.; **354–355** © Ryan McVay/PhotoDisc/Getty Images; **356** © Royalty-Free/Corbis; **358** © Ralf-Finn Hestoft/Corbis; **360** © David Madison/Getty Images; **363** © Alan Becker/Getty Images; **365** © John Powell Photographer/Alamy; **368** © William Albert Allard/ National Geographic Image Collection; **369** © Roy Toft/Getty Images ; **371** © Eric Risberg/AP/Wide World Photos; **373** © Melanie Acevedo/Botanica/Getty Images; **375** © Eric Risberg/ AP/Wide World Photos; **380** Courtesy of www.apcamcar.com; **383** DLR/NASA; **386** Courtesy of and Copyright, Peabody Essex Museum, Salem, Massachusetts; **389** © Neil Gilchrist/Panoramic Images; **390** © AP/Wide World Photos; **392** © Darren Sweet/ PictureChasers.com; **394** © Patrik Giardino/Corbis; **398** © Jacqueline Malonson/Jax Photography; **402** © Michael Newman/ PhotoEdit; **403** © D. Robert & Lorri Franz/Corbis; **405** © Greig Cranna/Index Stock Imagery; **408** © Keith Woods/Getty Images; **410** © Paul J. Sutton/Duomo/Corbis; **413** © Thomas Hallstein/ Outsight Photography; **424–425** © Thomas Brownold/Animals Animals; **427** © CB/Cai Daizheng/Photocome/Kyodonews; **429** © Jose Carillo/PhotoEdit; **432** McDougal Littell; **433** *top left* © Royalty-Free/Corbis; **433** *top center* Elliptical Trainer photo courtesy of NordicTrack.com; **433** *top right* © Royalty-Free/ Corbis; **435** © Gary Pearl/StockShot/Alamy; **437** The iOptiJr mouse with color jackets courtesy of macally.com and Mace Group Inc.; **444** © David Young-Wolff/PhotoEdit; **449** © Michael Schmitt/Animals Animals; **450** © Nick Rowe/PhotoDisc/Getty Images; **451** © Amos Schliack/StockFood; **456** © Kob-StockFood Munich/StockFood; **458** © Dennis MacDonald/PhotoEdit; **459** © Bobby Model/Getty Images; **466** © Dennis MacDonald/ PhotoEdit; **471** © Comstock Images; **473** © Jeff Greenberg/A.G.E. Fotostock; **486–487** © Ron Kimball/Ron Kimball Stock; **489** © Scott Camazine/Photo Researchers, Inc.; **491** © Michael Busselle/Corbis; **493** © Royalty-Free/Getty Images; **495** © Roger Ressmeyer/Corbis; **498** © Paul J. Mayo - Australia; **500** Akira Fujii/ESA; **503** © Robin Tinay Sallie/Akron Beacon Journal/AP/ Wide World Photos; **505** *both* © Ted Kinsman/Photo Researchers, Inc.; **507** *center left* © Carlyn Iverson/Photo Researchers, Inc.; **507** *center right* © mediacolor's/Alamy; **512** © Brand X Pictures/ Getty Images; **516** © Mark & Audrey Gibson/Stock Connection; **518** SOHO/NASA; **520** © Ron Kimball/Ron Kimball Stock; **522** © Michael Kelley/Getty Images; **530** McDougal Littell; **531** © Cathrine Wessel/Corbis; **534** © Darrell Gulin/Corbis; **537** *top* Scott Johnson/Indiana DNR/USFWS; **537** *bottom* © PhotoDisc/ Getty Images; **538** © Jon Riley/Getty Images; **541** © PhotoDisc/ Getty Images; **552–553** © Martin Harvey/Alamy; **554** © Tom Bean/Corbis; **556** © Rick Friedman/Corbis; **558** © Digital Vision/ Corbis; **559** © Robert Galbraith/Reuters/Corbis; **562** © Neale Haynes/ImageState/Alamy; **567** *photo* © PhotoDisc/Getty Images; **567** *frame* © PhotoSpin; **568** © Thinkstock/Getty

CREDITS

Images; **569** © Alan Carey/Photo Researchers, Inc.; **571** *top left* © Ulrike Schanz/Animals Animals; **571** *top* © Fritz Prenzel/Animals Animals; **573** *top* © Royalty-Free/Corbis; **573** *football* © PhotoDisc/Getty Images; **573** *grass* © PowerPhotos/PhotoSpin; **574** © Royalty-Free/Corbis; **575** © Aase Bjerner; **577** © George Holton/Photo Researchers, Inc.; **579** © James H. Robinson/Photo Researchers, Inc.; **583** © Richard Berenholtz/Corbis; **588** © Richard Berenholtz/Corbis; **593** © Picture Finders LTD/eStock Photo; **595** © Mike Powell/Getty Images; **598** *bottom right* © Martin Harvey/Natural History Photographic Agency; **598** *top left* © Richard Hutchings/Photo Researchers, Inc.; **598** *top center* © Kevin Peterson/Getty Images; **598** *top right* © Rubberball Productions/Getty Images; **600** © Scott Camazine/Alamy; **602** © HIRB/Index Stock Imagery; **606** © Lawrence M. Sawyer/Getty Images; **614** © Brian Drake/SportsChrome; **626–627** © Bill Stevenson/Alamy; **628** © Digital Vision/Getty Images; **631** © Roger Ressmeyer/Corbis; **635** *top right* © Ric Ergenbright; **637** © Dwight Cendrowski; **639** Courtesy of Dallas Convention Center; **643** *top right* © Jeff Greenberg/PhotoEdit; **648** © Rhoda Peacher/R Photographs; **652** *top right* © Rhoda Peacher/R Photographs; **658** © Kim Karpeles; **661** © Amwell/Getty Images; **663** *center* © Jonathan Nourok/PhotoEdit; **671** © Adam Woolfitt/Corbis; **678** © Jeff Gross/Getty Images; **682** © Davis Barber/PhotoEdit; **684** © David A. Northcott/Corbis ; **687** © John Kelly/Getty Images; **689** © David A. Northcott/Corbis; **690** © Davies & Starr/Getty Images; **708–709** © Robert Holland/Getty Images; **710** © Michael Newman/PhotoEdit; **715** © Vince Streano/Corbis; **716** *top right* © Tim Zurowski/Corbis; **716** *top left* © Darrell Gulin/Corbis; **719** © John Elk/Elk Photography; **726** © Tony Freeman/PhotoEdit; **729** © Robert Winslow/Animals Animals; **731** © Iconica/Photonica/Getty Images; **733** Jacques Descloitres/MODIS Rapid Response Team, NASA/GSFC; **735** *right* © Galen Rowell/Corbis; **735** *left* © Philip Gould/Corbis; **737** © Joseph Pobereskin/Getty Images; **744** © Scott Goodwin/Boston MedFlight; **762–763** © Roland Birke/Phototake; **765** *top right* © Dwight Cendrowski; **768** © Tony Freeman/PhotoEdit; **770** © Rhoda Peacher/R Photographs; **771** *both* © GK Hart/Vikki Hart/Getty Images; **772** *top right* © Lee Snider/Corbis; **775** © Matt York, Staff/AP/Wide World Photos; **778** © Richard Cummins/Corbis; **781** © Phillip Colla/www.OceanLight.com; **784** © Ace Stock Limited/Alamy; **787** © Michael Newman/PhotoEdit; **790** © Rubberball Productions/Getty Images; **791** © Carolina Biological Supply Company/Phototake; **794** © Allana Wesley White/Corbis; **797** © 2005, Motorola, Inc./ Reproduced with Permission from Motorola, Inc. ; **799** © Zigy Kaluzny/Getty Images; **800** © Tom Stewart/Corbis; **802** © Adrees A. Latif/Reuters/Corbis; **807** © David Butow/Corbis; **808** © Ron Kuntz/Bettmann/Corbis; **809** © Bob Daemmrich/PhotoEdit; **812** © Michael Mahovlich/Masterfile; **820** © David Stoecklein/Corbis; **824** © Paul J. Sutton/Duomo/Corbis; **825** © Jim West/Jim West Photography; **840–841** © Comstock Production Department/Alamy; **840** *ball* © PhotoDisc/Getty Images; **843** © Michelle D. Bridwell/PhotoEdit; **847** © Royalty-Free/Corbis; **848** © Matt Brown/NewSport/Corbis; **851** © Mary Kate Denny/PhotoEdit; **856** © Don Smetzer/Getty Images; **857** *both* © Stockbyte/Royalty-Free; **861** © Tim Davis/Corbis; **870** © Dante Fenolio/Photo Researchers, Inc.; **871** © New Moon/Panoramic Images; **872** © Tom Carter/PhotoEdit; **874** © David Young-Wolff/PhotoEdit; **875** © PictureChasers.com 2005; **876** © Alan Thornton/Getty Images; **878** © Leslie Parr/Getty Images; **881** © Paul Conklin/PhotoEdit; **882** © 2003 Robyn Beck/Staff/AFP/Getty; **885** © Bettmann/Corbis; **887** DLR/NASA; **894** © Mark Dadswell/Staff/Getty Images.

Illustration and Map

Argosy **1, 63, 131, 205, 281, 355, 425, 487, 553, 627, 631, 633, 709, 763, 841**; Steve Cowden **32, 40** *center*, **240, 258, 308, 323** *center right*, **440** *bottom center*, **446, 465, 615, 646, 654, 668, 675, 715, 733, 750, 752** *bottom left*, **781, 855**; Stephen Durke **634, 648** *center*, **658, 741** *both*, **741**; John Francis **815**; Patrick Gnan/Deborah Wolfe, Ltd. **228, 249, 323** *bottom right*, **468, 526, 567, 588** *both*, **588, 591, 742, 865**; Sharon and Joel Harris **514**; Mark Heine/Deborah Wolfe **28**; Steve McEntee **640, 683, 702**; Karen Minot **890**; Laurie O'Keefe **866**; Tony Randazzo **508, 604, 819**; Mark Schroeder **690**; Dan Stuckenschneider **20, 116, 145, 146, 152** *center*, **221, 231** *center*, **315, 361, 373, 381, 385, 411, 471, 494, 525, 564, 609, 612** *top right*, **612** *bottom right*, **612, 648** *bottom*, **667, 680, 725, 772** *both*, **772, 829, 862**; Matt Zang/American Artists **511, 657, 722, 749, 771, 891.**

Worked-Out Solutions

This section of the book provides step-by-step solutions to exercises with circled exercise numbers. These solutions provide models that can help guide your work with the homework exercises.

The separate **Selected Answers** section follows this section. It provides numerous answers that you can use to check your own answers.

Chapter 1

Lesson 1.1 (pp. 5–7)

19. three tenths to the fourth power; $(0.3)^4 = 0.3 \cdot 0.3 \cdot 0.3 \cdot 0.3$

35. $\left(\frac{3}{5}\right)^3 = \frac{3}{5} \cdot \frac{3}{5} \cdot \frac{3}{5} = \frac{27}{125}$

51. a. Total length $= 3.5 + 5.5 + 3 = 12$

The total length is 12 inches.

b. Evaluate $12f$ for $f = 12$: $12(12) = 144$

The area of water surface needed is 144 square inches.

Lesson 1.2 (pp. 10–12)

16.
$$\frac{1}{6}(6 + 18) - 2^2 = \frac{1}{6}(6 + 18) - 4$$
$$= \frac{1}{6}(24) - 4$$
$$= 4 - 4 = 0$$

35. a. Total cost $= 3 \cdot 0.99 + 2 \cdot 9.95$

$= 2.97 + 19.90 = 22.87$

The total cost is \$22.87.

b. Amount of money left $= 25 - 22.87 = 2.13$

The amount you have left is \$2.13.

Lesson 1.3 (pp. 18–20)

11. 7 less than twice a number k

Less than is subtraction after the next term, and twice a number is two times a number. The expression is $2k - 7$.

21. [Number of months in y years] = [Number of months in one year] • [Number of years]

$= 12y$

The number of months is $12y$.

33. a. 48 ounce container:

$$\frac{\$2.64}{48 \text{ ounces}} = \frac{\$2.64 \div 48}{48 \text{ ounces} \div 48} = \frac{\$.055}{1 \text{ ounce}}$$

The unit rate is \$.055 per ounce.

64 ounce container:

$$\frac{\$3.84}{64 \text{ ounces}} = \frac{\$3.84 \div 64}{64 \text{ ounces} \div 64} = \frac{\$.06}{1 \text{ ounce}}$$

The unit rate is \$.06 per ounce.

b. Since \$.055 is less than \$.06, the 48 ounce container costs less per ounce.

c. Write a verbal model and an expression. Let n be the number of ounces.

[Savings] = [Unit rate for 64 ounce container] • [Number of ounces] − [Unit rate for 48 ounce container] • [Number of ounces]

$= 0.06n - 0.055n$

Evaluate the expression when $n = 192$.

$0.06(192) - 0.055(192) = 0.96$

The amount of money you save is \$.96.

Lesson 1.4 (pp. 24–26)

7. 5 more than a number t is written as $t + 5$.

The product of 9 and the quantity 5 more than a number t is written as $9(t + 5)$.

The product of 9 and the quantity 5 more than a number t is less than 6 is written as $9(t + 5) < 6$.

WORKED-OUT SOLUTIONS

41. Write a verbal model. Then write an equation. Let w be the winning team's time.

U.S. team's time	$-$	Winning team's time	$=$	Difference in time

$173 - w = 6$

Use mental math to solve the equation. Think: 173 less what number is 6?

Because $173 - 167 = 6$, the solution is 167 hours.

Lesson 1.5 (pp. 31–33)

5. You know that the temperature in Rome, Italy, is 30°C, and the temperature in Dallas, Texas, is 83°F.

You want to find out which temperature is higher.

17. Step 1: You know the total weight of your backpack and its contents is $13\frac{3}{8}$ pounds. The total weight you want to carry is no more than 15 pounds. The weight of each bottle of water is $\frac{3}{4}$ pound. You want to find out how many extra bottles of water you can add to your backpack.

Step 2: Write a verbal model that represents what you want to find out. Then write an equation and solve it.

Step 3: Let n be the number of extra bottles of water.

Weight of backpack	$+$	Weight of each bottle of water	$\cdot$	Number of extra bottles of water	$=$	Total weight

$$13\frac{3}{8} + \frac{3}{4}n = 15$$

$$13\frac{3}{8} - 13\frac{3}{8} + \frac{3}{4}n = 15 - 13\frac{3}{8}$$

$$\frac{3}{4}n = 1\frac{5}{8}$$

$$\frac{4}{3} \cdot \frac{3}{4}n = \frac{4}{3} \cdot \frac{13}{8}$$

$$n = \frac{13}{6}, \text{ or } n = 2\frac{1}{6}$$

Since you cannot carry a fraction of a bottle, round down to 2 bottles.

Step 4: You know that 2 is a solution; check to see if 3 could be a solution. The additional bottle of water weighs $\frac{3}{4}$ pound. Since $14\frac{7}{8}$ pounds is only $\frac{1}{8}$ pound less than the maximum of 15 pounds, and $\frac{3}{4} > \frac{1}{8}$, adding another bottle weighing $\frac{3}{4}$ pound would make the total weight more than 15 pounds. Therefore, the number of extra bottles of water you can add to your backpack is 2 bottles.

Lesson 1.6 (pp. 38–40)

7. The pairing is not a function because the input $\frac{3}{4}$ is paired with two outputs, 3 and 5.

23. You have 10 quarters that you can use for a parking meter.

a. Each time you put 1 quarter in the meter, you have 1 less quarter, so the number of quarters left is a function of the number of quarters used.

b. Let y represent the number of quarters you have left.

Number of quarters you have left	$=$	Total number of quarters	$-$	Number of quarters you have used so far

$y = 10 - x$

The domain of the function is: 0, 1, 2, 3, 4, 5, 6, 7, 8, 9, and 10.

c. Make a table of inputs, x, and use $y = 10 - x$ to find the corresponding outputs.

Input, x	0	1	2	3	4	5
Output, y	10	9	8	7	6	5

Input, x	6	7	8	9	10
Output, y	4	3	2	1	0

The range of the function is: 0, 1, 2, 3, 4, 5, 6, 7, 8, 9, and 10.

Lesson 1.7 (pp. 46–48)

3. Make an input-output table using the given domain values.

x	0	1	2	3	4	5
y	3	4	5	6	7	8

Plot a point for each ordered pair (x, y).

17. Number of voters v as a function of time t in years since 1984.

Years since 1984	Voters	Voters (millions)
0	92,652,680	93
4	91,594,693	92
8	104,405,155	104
12	96,456,345	96
16	105,586,274	106

The t-values range from 0 to 16, so label the t-axis from 0 to 20 in increments of 2 units. The v-values (in millions) range from 93 to 106, so label the v-axis from 90 to 110 in increments of 2 units.

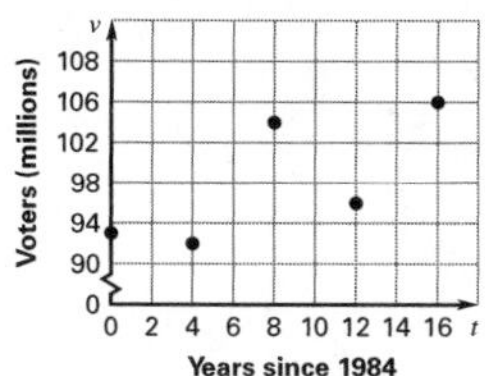

Chapter 2

Lesson 2.1 (pp. 67–70)

7. Graph −5 and −6 on a number line.

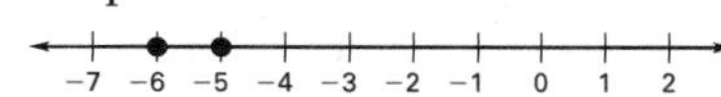

On the number line, −5 is to the right of −6, so −5 > −6. The number −5 is greater.

29. If $a = -6.1$, then $-a = -(-6.1) = 6.1$.

If $a = -6.1$, then $|a| = |-6.1| = 6.1$.

53. Graph the numbers on a number line.

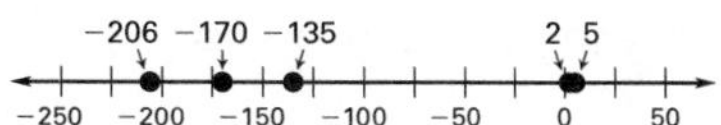

Read the numbers from left to right: −206, −170, −135, 2, 5.

From lowest elevation to highest elevation, the locations are Fondo, Frink, Alamorio, Calexico, and Date City.

Lesson 2.2 (pp. 77–79)

13. $-8.7 + 4.2 = -(|8.7| - |4.2|)$

$= -(8.7 - 4.2) = -4.5$

35. $-2.6 + (-3.4) + 7.6 = [-2.6 + (-3.4)] + 7.6$

$= -6 + 7.6 = 1.6$

55. a. You know the first lens has a strength of −4.75 diopters and the second lens has a strength of 6.25 diopters.

You want to know the strength of the new lens.

Calculate the sum of −4.75 and 6.25:

$-4.75 + 6.25 = 1.5$

The strength of the new lens is 1.5 diopters.

b. You know the first lens has a strength of −2.5 diopters and the second lens has a strength of −1.25 diopters.

You want to know the strength of the new lens.

Calculate the sum of −2.5 and −1.25:

$-2.5 + (-1.25) = -3.75$

The strength of the new lens is −3.75 diopters.

c. You know the first lens has a strength of 1.5 diopters and the second lens has a strength of −3.75 diopters. The greater the absolute value of the strength of a lens, the stronger the lens.

You want to know which new lens is stronger.

Find the absolute value of each lens in part (a) and part (b) and choose the greater.

$|1.5| = 1.5$ $|-3.75| = 3.75$

The new lens in part (b) has a greater absolute value, and is therefore stronger.

WS3

Lesson 2.3 (pp. 82–84)

3. $13 - (-5) = 13 + 5 = 18$

21. When $x = 7.1$ and $y = -2.5$,

$$-y - (1.9 - x) = -(-2.5) - (1.9 - 7.1)$$
$$= 2.5 - [1.9 + (-7.1)]$$
$$= 2.5 - (-5.2)$$
$$= 2.5 + 5.2 = 7.7$$

43. Write a verbal model. Then write an equation.

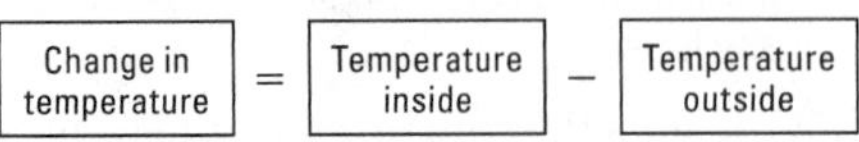

$C = i - t$

Substitute 12.2 for i and −2.4 for t.

$C = 12.2 - (-2.4)$

$C = 12.2 + 2.4 = 14.6$

The change in temperature is 14.6°C.

Lesson 2.4 (pp. 91–93)

11. $-1.9(3.3)(7) = (-6.27)(7) = -43.89$

31. $-2(-6)(-7z) = [-2(-6)](-7z)$

$$= 12(-7z)$$
$$= [12 \cdot (-7)]z$$
$$= -84z$$

51. Write a verbal model.

Total value = Original price per share • Number of shares + Change in price per share • Number of shares

Calculate the original price.
Original price = ($3.50)(50) = $175

Calculate the change in price.

Change in price = (−$.25)(50) = −$12.50

Calculate the total value.

Total value = (3.50)(50) + (−0.25)(50)

= 175 + (−12.50) = 162.50

The total value is $162.50.

Lesson 2.5 (pp. 99–101)

9. $(p - 3)(-8) = p(-8) - 3(-8) = -8p + 24$

23. Write the expression as a sum:
$7x^2 + (-10) + (-2x^2) + 5$

Terms: $7x^2$, -10, $-2x^2$, 5

Like terms: $7x^2$ and $-2x^2$; −10 and 5

Coefficients: 7, −2

Constant terms: −10, 5

51. Write a verbal model. Then write an equation.

Total cost = Number of movies rented • (Regular cost of a rental − Discount per movie)

$C = 3(r - 2)$ or $C = 3r - 6$

Find the value of C when $r = 3.99$.

$$C = 3(3.99 - 2)$$
$$= 3(3.99) - 3(2)$$
$$= 11.97 - 6 = 5.97$$

The total cost is $5.97.

Lesson 2.6 (pp. 106–108)

13. $-1 \div \left(-\frac{7}{2}\right) = -1 \cdot \left(-\frac{2}{7}\right) = \frac{2}{7}$

35. $\frac{9z - 6}{-3} = (9z - 6) \div (-3)$

$$= (9z - 6) \cdot \left(-\frac{1}{3}\right)$$
$$= 9z \cdot \left(-\frac{1}{3}\right) - 6 \cdot \left(-\frac{1}{3}\right)$$
$$= -3z + 2$$

53. To find the daily mean temperature for a day, find the sum of the high and low temperatures for that day and then divide the sum by 2.

$$\text{Mean} = \frac{-10.6 + (-18.9)}{2} = \frac{-29.5}{2} = -14.75$$

The daily mean temperature was −14.75°C.

WS4

Lesson 2.7 (pp. 113–116)

9. Since $50^2 = 2500$, $\pm\sqrt{2500} = \pm 50$.

19. Write a compound inequality that compares $-\sqrt{86}$ with both $-\sqrt{100}$ and $-\sqrt{81}$.

$-\sqrt{100} < -\sqrt{86} < -\sqrt{81}$

Take the square root of each number.

$-10 < -\sqrt{86} < -9$

Because 86 is closer to 81 than to 100, $-\sqrt{86}$ is closer to -9 than to -10. So $-\sqrt{86}$ is about -9.

49. You need to find the side length s of the mazes such that s^2 is the given area in square feet, so s is the positive square root of the area. Then identify the side length as rational or irrational.

Dallas: $s^2 = 1225$, $s = 35$; rational

San Francisco: $s^2 = 576$, $s = 24$; rational

Corona: $s^2 = 2304$, $s = 48$; rational

Waterville: $s^2 = 900$, $s = 30$; rational

The side lengths are 35 feet, 24 feet, 48 feet, and 30 feet. All the lengths are rational numbers.

Chapter 3

Lesson 3.1 (pp. 137–140)

13. $-2 = n - 6$

$-2 + 6 = n - 6 + 6$

$4 = n$

55. Let w represent the width of the trampoline.

$A = \ell \cdot w$

$187 = 17 \cdot w$

$\frac{187}{17} = \frac{17w}{17}$

$11 = w$

The width of the trampoline is 11 feet.

Lesson 3.2 (pp. 144–146)

13. $7 = \frac{5}{6}c - 8$

$7 + 8 = \frac{5}{6}c - 8 + 8$

$15 = \frac{5}{6}c$

$\frac{6}{5} \cdot 15 = \frac{6}{5} \cdot \frac{5}{6}c$

$18 = c$

19. $-32 = -5k + 13k$

$-32 = 8k$

$\frac{-32}{8} = \frac{8k}{8}$

$-4 = k$

39. Write a verbal model. Then write an equation. Let h be the number of half-side advertisements.

Total budget = Cost per month • Number of full bus wrap advertisements + Cost per month • Number of half-side advertisements

$6000 = 2000(1) + 800h$

$6000 = 2000 + 800h$

Solve the equation.

$6000 = 2000 + 800h$

$6000 - 2000 = 2000 - 2000 + 800h$

$4000 = 800h$

$\frac{4000}{800} = \frac{800h}{800}$

$5 = h$

The museum can have 5 half-side advertisements.

WORKED-OUT SOLUTIONS

WS5

Lesson 3.3 (pp. 150–153)

17.

$$-3 = 12y - 5(2y - 7)$$
$$-3 = 12y - 10y + 35$$
$$-3 = 2y + 35$$
$$-3 - 35 = 2y + 35 - 35$$
$$-38 = 2y$$
$$\frac{-32}{8} = \frac{2y}{2}$$
$$-19 = y$$

39. Let x be the amount of space you should leave between posters (in feet).

[Total wall space] = [Width of poster] • [Number of posters] + 2 • [Space at end of wall] + [Amount of space between posters] • [Number of spaces between posters]

$$13.5 = 2(3) + 2(3) + x(2)$$
$$13.5 = 6 + 6 + 2x$$
$$13.5 = 12 + 2x$$
$$13.5 - 12 = 12 - 12 + 2x$$
$$1.5 = 2x$$
$$0.75 = x$$

You should leave 0.75 foot between each poster.

Lesson 3.4 (pp. 157–159)

13.

$$40 + 14j = 2(-4j - 13)$$
$$40 + 14j = -8j - 26$$
$$40 + 14j + 8j = -8j + 8j - 26$$
$$40 + 22j = -26$$
$$40 - 40 + 22j = -26 - 40$$
$$22j = -66$$
$$j = -3$$

51. Let x represent the number of years. So $33x$ represents the increase in the number of students taking Spanish, and $2x$ represents the decreased number of students who are taking French.

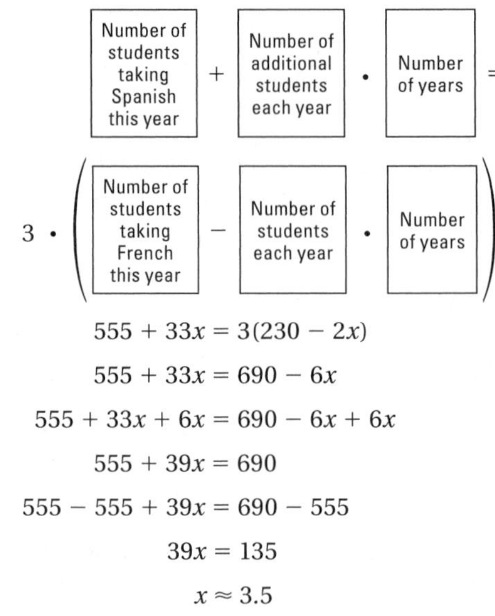

$$555 + 33x = 3(230 - 2x)$$
$$555 + 33x = 690 - 6x$$
$$555 + 33x + 6x = 690 - 6x + 6x$$
$$555 + 39x = 690$$
$$555 - 555 + 39x = 690 - 555$$
$$39x = 135$$
$$x \approx 3.5$$

So it will be after 3 more school years, or in about 4 years, when the number of students taking Spanish will be 3 times the number of students taking French.

Lesson 3.5 (pp. 165–167)

17.

$$\frac{16}{48} = \frac{n}{36}$$
$$36 \cdot \frac{16}{48} \doteq 36 \cdot \frac{n}{36}$$
$$\frac{576}{48} = n$$
$$12 = n$$

49. Find the total number of pizzas: $96 + 144 + 240 = 480$.

The ratio of large pizzas to all pizzas is

$$\frac{\text{number of large pizzas}}{\text{total number of pizzas}} = \frac{240}{480} = \frac{1}{2}.$$

Lesson 3.6 (pp. 171–173)

13. $\frac{11}{w} = \frac{33}{w + 24}$

$11(w + 24) = 33w$

$11w + 264 = 33w$

$11w - 11w + 264 = 33w - 11w$

$264 = 22w$

$12 = w$

39. The ratio of model to height is $\frac{\text{height of model}}{\text{actual height}}$. Write and solve a proportion.

$\frac{1}{25} = \frac{x}{443.2}$

$443.2 = 25x$

$17.728 = x$

The height of the model is 17.728 meters.

Lesson 3.7 (pp. 179–181)

13. $a = p\% \cdot b$

$= 115\% \cdot 60$

$= 1.15 \cdot 60$

$= 69$ 69 is 115% of 60.

35. a. The survey shows that 36% of the 250 listeners who participated in the survey are "tired of" the song.

$a = p\% \cdot b$

$= 36\% \cdot 250$

$= 0.36 \cdot 250$

$= 90$

90 listeners are "tired of" the song.

b. The survey shows that 14% of the 250 listeners who participated in the survey "love" the song.

$a = p\% \cdot b$

$= 14\% \cdot 250$

$= 0.14 \cdot 250$

$= 35$

35 listeners "love" the song.

Lesson 3.8 (pp. 187–189)

17. $30 = 9x - 5y$

$30 + 5y = 9x - 5y + 5y$

$30 + 5y = 9x$

$30 - 30 + 5y = 9x - 30$

$5y = 9x - 30$

$y = \frac{9}{5}x - 6$

33. a. $C = 12x + 25$

$C - 25 = 12x + 25 - 25$

$C - 25 = 12x$

$\frac{C - 25}{12} = x$

b. \$145: $\frac{C - 25}{12} = x$

$\frac{145 - 25}{12} = x$

$10 = x$

For \$145, you bowled 10 league nights.

\$181: $\frac{C - 25}{12} = x$

$\frac{181 - 25}{12} = x$

$13 = x$

For \$181, you bowled 13 league nights.

\$205: $\frac{C - 25}{12} = x$

$\frac{205 - 25}{12} = x$

$15 = x$

For \$205, you bowled 15 league nights.

Chapter 4

Lesson 4.1 (pp. 209–212)

15. To plot $Q(-1, 5)$, begin at the origin. First move 1 unit to the left, then 5 units up. Point Q is in Quadrant II.

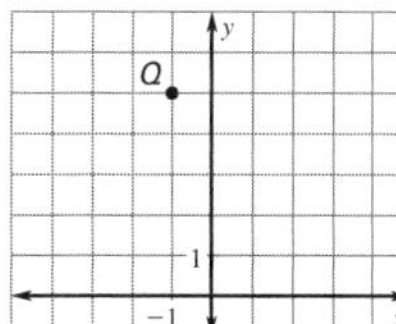

WS7

25. First create a table of values by substituting the domain values into the function.

x	$y = 2x - 5$
−2	$y = 2(-2) - 5 = -9$
−1	$y = 2(-1) - 5 = -7$
0	$y = 2(0) - 5 = -5$
1	$y = 2(1) - 5 = -3$
2	$y = 2(2) - 5 = -1$

The table gives the ordered pairs (−2, −9), (−1, −7), (0, −5), (1, −3), and (2, −1).

Graph the function by plotting these points. The range of the function is the y-values from the table: −9, −7, −5, −3, −1.

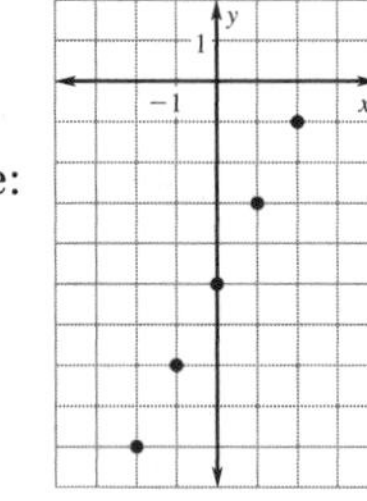

37. The table represents a function because there is exactly one low temperature for each day in the first week of February.

To graph the data, plot the ordered pairs (day, record low).

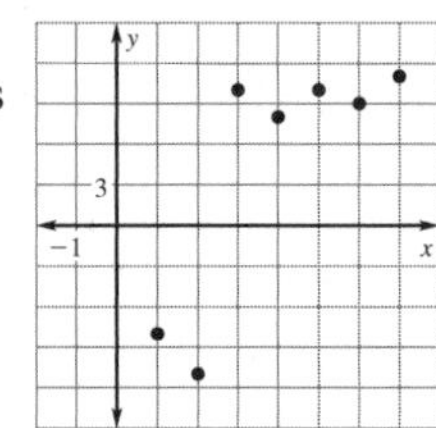

Lesson 4.2 (pp. 219–221)

3. Test (−2, 3):

$2y + x = 4$

$2(3) + (-2) \stackrel{?}{=} 4$ Substitute −2 for x and 3 for y.

$6 + (-2) \stackrel{?}{=} 4$

$4 = 4$ ✓

So, (−2, 3) is a solution of $2y + x = 4$.

11. First, solve the equation for y.

$y + x = 2$

$y + x - x = 2 - x$

$y = 2 - x$

Use this equation to create a table of values.

x	−2	−1	0	1	2
y	4	3	2	1	0

Plot at least three of the points whose ordered pairs (x, y) are indicated by the table. Draw a line through the plotted points.

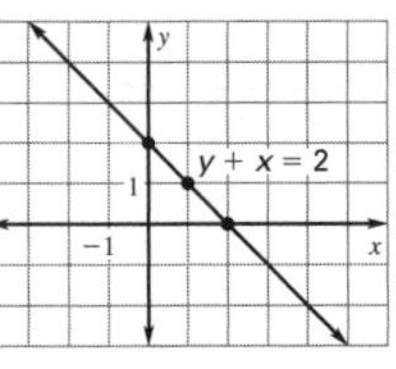

37. a.

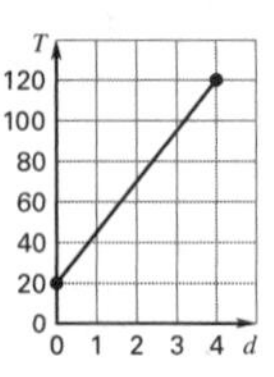

Since the scientist is studying the organisms in the first 4 kilometers of Earth's crust, the domain of the function is $0 \le d \le 4$. The range of the function is $20 \le T \le 120$. The temperature 4 kilometers from the surface is 120°C.

b. Notice in the table for part (a) that the temperatures between 20°C and 95°C occur when the distance from the surface is between 0 kilometers and 3 kilometers.

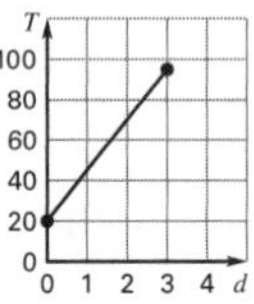

The domain of the function is now $0 \le d \le 3$ and the range is $20 \le T \le 95$. So this section of crust is 3 kilometers deep.

Lesson 4.3 (pp. 229–232)

21. Substitute 0 for y in $y = -4x + 3$ and solve for x.

$0 = -4x + 3$

$-3 = -4x$

$\frac{3}{4} = x$

The x-intercept is $\frac{3}{4}$.

Substitute 0 for x in $y = -4x + 3$ and solve for y.

$y = -4(0) + 3 = 0 + 3 = 3$

The y-intercept is 3.

Plot the two points that correspond to the intercepts and draw a line through them.

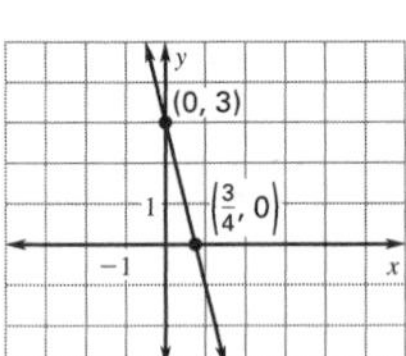

47. a. If $v = 0$ in the function $f = 180 - 1.5v$, then $f = 180 - 1.5(0)$, and $f = 180$. This is the intercept on the vertical axis, and it represents the area (in square feet) available for flowers when no vegetables are planted.

Letting $f = 0$ gives $0 = 180 - 1.5v$, $1.5v = 180$, and $v = 120$. This is the intercept on the horizontal axis, and it represents the area (in square feet) available for vegetables when no flowers are planted.

b. 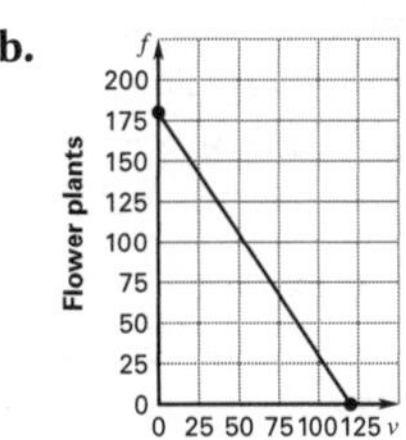

The domain is $0 \le v \le 120$. The range is $0 \le f \le 180$.

c. $f = 180 - 1.5(80)$ Substitute 80 for v.

$= 180 - 120 = 60$

There are 60 square feet left to plant flowers.

Lesson 4.4 (pp. 239–242)

11. Let $(x_1, y_1) = (1, 3)$ and $(x_2, y_2) = (3, -2)$.

$$m = \frac{y_2 - y_1}{x_2 - x_1} = \frac{-2 - 3}{3 - 1} = \frac{-5}{2} \text{ or } -\frac{5}{2}$$

37. a. rate of change $= \dfrac{\text{change in temperature}}{\text{change in time}}$

0–1.5 hours:
$\dfrac{1000 - 250}{1.5 - 0} = \dfrac{750}{1.5} = 500$ degrees per hour

1.5–2.5 hours:
$\dfrac{1300 - 1000}{2.5 - 1.5} = \dfrac{300}{1} = 300$ degrees per hour

2.5–4.65 hours:
$\dfrac{1680 - 1300}{4.65 - 2.5} = \dfrac{380}{2.15} \approx 177$ degrees per hour

4.65–8.95 hours:
$\dfrac{1920 - 1680}{8.95 - 4.65} = \dfrac{240}{4.3} \approx 56$ degrees per hour

The time interval with the greatest rate of change was from 0 hours to 1.5 hours.

b. The time interval that showed the least rate of change was from 4.65 hours to 8.95 hours.

Lesson 4.5 (pp. 247–250)

11.

$$4x + y = 1$$
$$4x - 4x + y = 1 - 4x$$
$$y = -4x + 1$$

The slope is -4 and the y-intercept is 1.

21. The equation $y = -6x + 1$ is in slope-intercept form. The slope is -6 and the y-intercept is 1. Locate the point (0, 1), which corresponds to the intercept. Use the slope to find a second point, (1, -5). Draw a line through the points.

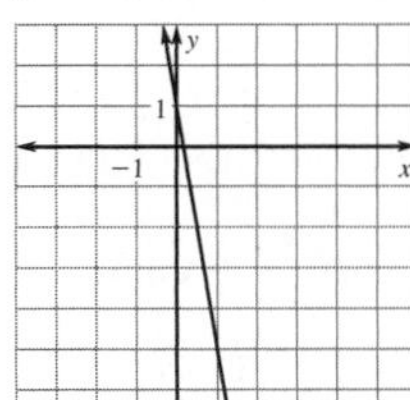

41. a.

b. On the graph, the vertical distance between the lines is about 30 when $t = 3$. To verify this estimate, substitute 3 in $d = 55t$: $d = 55(3) = 165$. Now substitute 3 in $d = 65t$: $d = 65(3) = 195$. Subtract: $195 - 165 = 30$. Driving at the maximum speed limit, a driver could travel 30 miles farther after 1995 than before 1995.

Lesson 4.6 (pp. 256–259)

7. Solve the equation for y: $8x + 2y = 0$

$$2y = -8x$$
$$y = -4x$$

Because $8x + 2y = 0$ can be written in the form $y = ax$, it does represent direct variation. The constant of variation is -4.

WS9

21. When solved for y, the equation is $y = -4x$. The slope of the line is the constant of variation, -4. The graph of a direct variation equation always passes through (0, 0). The slope can be used to locate a second point from the origin, like (1, −4). Draw a line through the points.

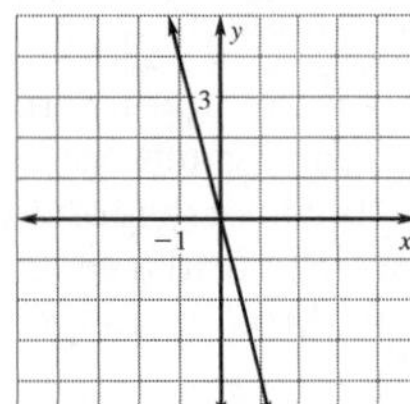

43. a. Compare the ratio $\frac{f}{w}$ or all three data pairs:

$$\frac{2.50}{10} = 0.25, \frac{3.75}{15} = 0.25, \frac{7.50}{30} = 0.25$$

Because the ratios are all equal, f varies directly with w.

b. Since $\frac{f}{w} = 0.25$, multiply both sides by w to obtain the direct variation equation $f = 0.25w$.

The computer weighs 18 pounds, so substitute 18 for w.

$f = 0.25(18) = 4.50$

The printer weighs 10 pounds, so substitute 10 for w.

$f = 0.25(10) = 2.50$

The total recycling fee for the computer and printer is \$4.50 + \$2.50 = \$7.00.

Lesson 4.7 (pp. 265–268)

3. Substitute −2, 0, and 3 for x.

$f(-2) = 12(-2) + 1 = -24 + 1 = -23$

$f(0) = 12(0) + 1 = 0 + 1 = 1$

$f(3) = 12(3) + 1 = 36 + 1 = 37$

17. Substitute −13 for $j(x)$.

$$-13 = 4x + 11$$
$$-13 - 11 = 4x + 11 - 11$$
$$-24 = 4x$$
$$\frac{-24}{4} = \frac{4x}{4}$$
$$-6 = x$$

39. a. Create a table of values for the function.

x	$f(x)$
0	$0.10(0) + 2.75 = 2.75$
5	$0.10(5) + 2.75 = 3.25$
10	$0.10(10) + 2.75 = 3.75$
15	$0.10(15) + 2.75 = 4.25$
20	$0.10(20) + 2.75 = 4.75$

Use the ordered pairs given by the table to graph the function.

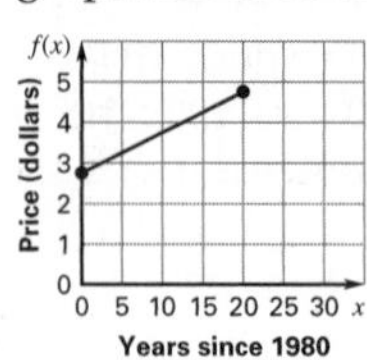

The domain of the function is $0 \le x \le 20$ and the range is $2.75 \le f(x) \le 4.75$.

b. Substitute 4.55 for $f(x)$.

$$4.55 = 0.10x + 2.75$$
$$4.55 - 2.75 = 0.10x + 2.75 - 2.75$$
$$1.8 = 0.10x$$
$$\frac{1.8}{0.10} = \frac{0.10x}{0.10}$$
$$18 = x$$

When $x = 18$, $f(x) = 4.55$. In 1998, 18 years after 1980, the average price of a movie ticket was \$4.55.

Chapter 5

Lesson 5.1 (pp. 286–289)

11. Determine the slope: $m = \frac{\text{rise}}{\text{run}} = \frac{-1}{2} = \text{or } -\frac{1}{2}$.

The line crosses the y-axis at (0, 0), so the y-intercept is 0.

Substitute $-\frac{1}{2}$ for m and 0 for b in the slope-intercept form $y = mx + b$: $y = -\frac{1}{2}x$.

19. Calculate the slope:

$$m = \frac{y_2 - y_1}{x_2 - x_1} = \frac{4 - 0}{0 - (-1)} = \frac{4}{1} = 4.$$

The line crosses the y-axis at (0, 4), so the y-intercept is 4.

Substitute 4 for m and 4 for b in the slope-intercept form $y = mx + b$: $y = 4x + 4$.

47. Let C be the cost of a visit to the aquarium and t be the time parked there. The total cost C is given by the function $C = 3h + 30$, where h is the number of hours parked at the aquarium.

Evaluate the function for $h = 4$:
$C = 3(4) + 30 = 12 + 30 = 42$

The total cost is $42.

Lesson 5.2 (pp. 296–299)

5. The slope is given. To find the y-intercept, substitute the slope, -5, and the coordinates of the given point $(-4, 7)$ into the equation $y = mx + b$, and solve for b.

$y = mx + b$

$7 = -5(-4) + b$

$7 = 20 + b$

$-13 = b$

The equation of the line is $y = -5x - 13$.

11. Calculate the slope:
$m = \frac{y_2 - y_1}{x_2 - x_1} = \frac{7 - 4}{2 - 1} = \frac{3}{1} = 3.$

To find the y-intercept, substitute the slope, 3, and the coordinates of either given point into the equation $y = mx + b$, and solve for b. Using $(1, 4)$,

$y = mx + b$

$4 = 3(1) + b$

$4 = 3 + b$

$1 = b$

The equation of the line is $y = 3x + 1$.

49. Let T be the total time (in minutes) for cooking a roast that weighs p pounds and t be the extra time needed (in minutes). The equation $T = 30p + t$ models the situation.

For a 2 pound roast, the total time was 1 hour 25 minutes, or 85 minutes. Find the extra time t needed by substituting 85 for T and 2 for p, and solving for t.

$85 = 30(2) + t$

$85 = 60 + t$

$25 = t$

Find the value of T for a 3 pound roast by substituting 3 for p.

$T = 30(3) + 25 = 90 + 25 = 115$

You need 115 minutes, or 1 hour 55 minutes, to cook a 3 pound roast.

Lesson 5.3 (pp. 305–308)

3. Substitute 2 for x_1, 1 for y_1, and 2 for m in the point-slope form $y - y_1 = m(x - x_1)$: $y - 1 = 2(x - 2)$.

39. The rate of change is given as $10,000 per year. Let y be the annual sales (in dollars) and x be the number of years since 1994. From the given information about 1997, one data pair is (3, 97000). Use the point-slope form of an equation.

$y - y_1 = m(x - x_1)$

$y - 97000 = 10000(x - 3)$

$y - 97000 = 10000x - 30000$

$y = 10000x + 67000$

To find the sales in 2000, use the equation above with $x = 2000 - 1994$, or 6.

$y = 10000(6) + 67000$

$= 60000 + 67000 = 127000$

The annual sales in 2000 were $127,000.

Lesson 5.4 (pp. 314–316)

17. Calculate the slope:
$m = \frac{y_2 - y_1}{x_2 - x_1} = \frac{-4 - 4}{4 - (-8)} = \frac{-8}{12}$ or $-\frac{2}{3}$.

Use either point to write an equation in point-slope form. Using $(-8, 4)$:

$y - y_1 = m(x - x_1)$

$y - 4 = -\frac{2}{3}[x - (-8)]$

$y - 4 = -\frac{2}{3}(x + 8)$

Rewrite the equation in standard form.

$y - 4 = -\frac{2}{3}x - \frac{16}{3}$

$\frac{2}{3}x + y - 4 = -\frac{16}{3}$

$\frac{2}{3}x + y = -\frac{4}{3}$ (or $2x + 3y = -4$)

WORKED-OUT SOLUTIONS

39. a. Let n be the number of ounces in a box of wheat cereal.

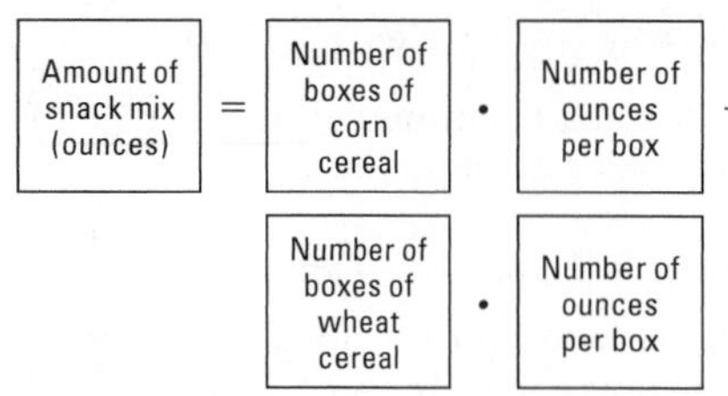

$120 = 5 \cdot 12 + 4 \cdot n$

$120 = 60 + 4n$

$60 = 4n$

$15 = n$

There are 15 ounces in a box of wheat cereal.

b. Let c be the number of boxes of corn cereal and let w be the number of boxes of wheat cereal you use. Use the verbal model from part (a).

$120 = c \cdot 12 + w \cdot 15$

$120 = 12c + 15w$ or $12c + 15w = 120$

c. Substitute different values for c and w in the equation for part (b).

If $c = 0$, then $12(0) + 15w = 120$, and $w = 8$; you can use 0 boxes of corn cereal and 8 boxes of wheat cereal.

If $c = 5$, then $12(5) + 15w = 120$, and $w = 4$; you can use 5 boxes of corn cereal and 4 boxes of wheat cereal.

If $c = 10$, then $12(10) + 15w = 120$, and $w = 0$; you can use 10 boxes of corn cereal and 0 boxes of wheat cereal.

Lesson 5.5 (pp. 322–324)

19. The slope of the line $y = 3x - 12$ is 3, so the slope of the perpendicular line is $-\frac{1}{3}$.

Use the slope $-\frac{1}{3}$ and the point $(-9, 2)$ to find the y-intercept of the line.

$y = mx + b$

$2 = -\frac{1}{3}(-9) + b$

$2 = 3 + b$

$-1 = b$

The equation of the line through $(-9, 2)$ that is perpendicular to the line $y = 3x - 12$ is $y = -\frac{1}{3}x - 1$.

33. a. Let w represent the weight of the blue whale calves and let d represent the number of days since birth.

The rate of change is 200 pounds per day. Use this value and the birth weights to write an equation for each calf.

First calf: $w_1 = 200d + 6000$
Second calf: $w_2 = 200d + 6250$

b. Substitute 30 for d in each equation from part (a).

$w_1 = 200(30) + 6000 = 12{,}000$

After 30 days, the first calf weighs 12,000 pounds.

$w_2 = 200(30) + 6250 = 12{,}250$

After 30 days, the second calf weighs 12,250 pounds.

c. The graphs of the equations in part (a) are parallel, since the two equations have the same slope, 200. The w-intercept of the second line is 250 greater than the w-intercept of the first line.

Lesson 5.6 (pp. 328–331)

7. The ordered pairs from the table are (1.2, 10), (1.8, 7), (2.3, 5), (3.0, −1), (4.4, −4), and (5.2, −8).

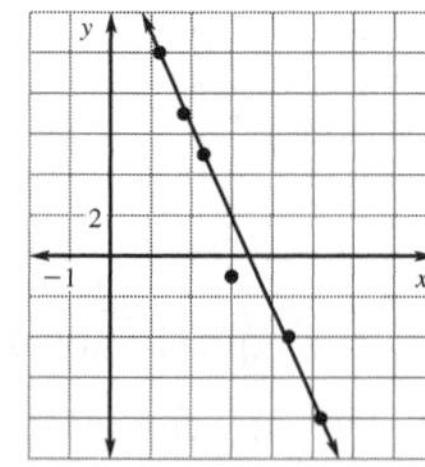

Use the points (1.2, 10) and (5.2, −8) to find the slope of the line of fit.

$m = \frac{y_2 - y_1}{x_2 - x_1} = \frac{-8 - 10}{5.2 - 1.2} = \frac{-18}{4} = -4.4.$

Use the slope −4.4 and the point (5.2, −8) to find the y-intercept of the line.

$y = mx + b$

$-8 = -4.4(5.2) + b$

$-8 = -22.88 + b$

$14.88 = b$

A line of fit is $y = -4.4x + 14.88$.

17. a. The ordered pairs from the diagram are (86, −86), (80, −65), (75, −54), (70, −40), (65, −26), (60, −21), and (52, −4).

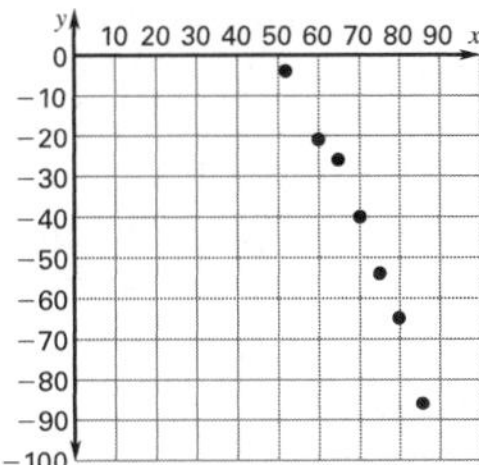

b. Draw a line that appears to fit the points.
Sample:

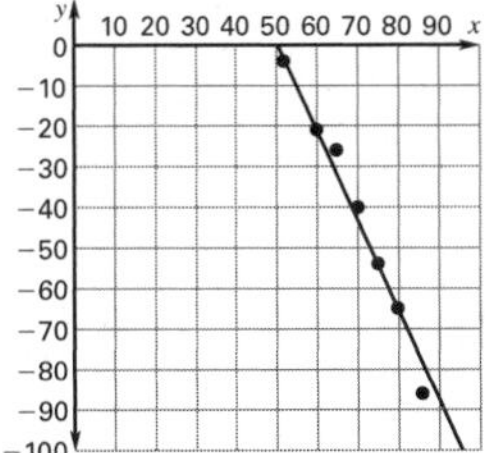

Use the points (60, −21) and (80, −65) to find the slope of the line of fit.

$$m = \frac{y_2 - y_1}{x_2 - x_1} = \frac{-21 - (-65)}{60 - 80} = \frac{44}{-20} = -2.2$$

Use the slope −2.2 and the point (80, −65) to find the y-intercept of the line.

$$y = mx + b$$

$$-65 = -2.2(80) + b$$

$$-65 = -176 + b$$

$$111 = b$$

A line of fit is $y = -2.2x + 111$.

c. The slope of the line of fit models the rate of change. So the temperature changes at an approximate rate of −2.2°C per kilometer of increasing altitude.

Lesson 5.7 (pp. 338–341)

3. Enter the data list on a graphing calculator. Create a scatter plot.

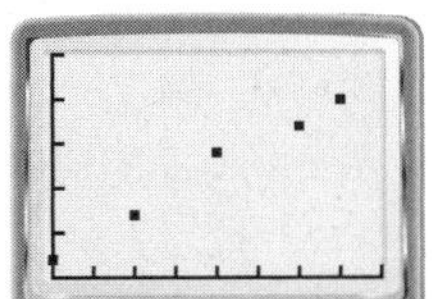

Perform a linear regression using the paired data. An equation of the best-fitting line is approximately $y = 2.6x + 2.5$.

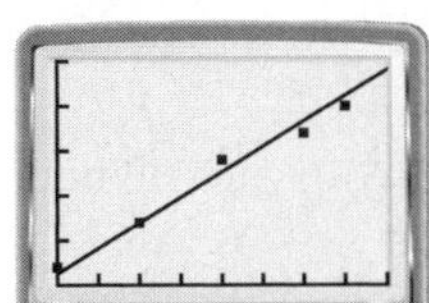

Graph the best-fitting line. Use the trace feature and arrow keys to find the value of y when $x = 5$. For $x = 5$, $y = 15.5$.

19. a. Enter the data list on a graphing calculator. Make a scatter plot.

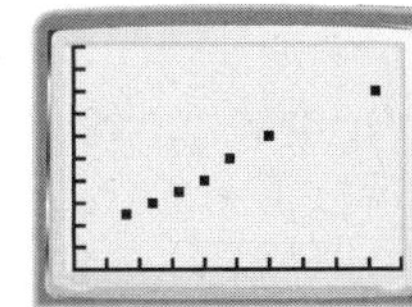

b. Perform a linear regression using the paired data. An equation of the best-fitting line is approximately $y = 0.03x + 1.23$ where y is the recommended space (in square feet) and x is a pig's weight (in pounds).

c. Evaluate $y = 0.03x + 1.23$ for $x = 250$.

$y = 0.03(250) + 1.23 = 7.5 + 1.23 = 8.73$

The model predicts that about 8.73 square feet of space is needed for a pig weighing 250 pounds.

Chapter 6

Lesson 6.1 (pp. 359–361)

7. The open circle means that 10 is not a solution of the inequality. Because the arrow points to the left, all numbers less than 10 are solutions. An inequality represented by the graph is $x < 10$.

15.

$$w + 14.9 > -2.7$$

$$w + 14.9 - 14.9 > -2.7 - 14.9$$

$$w > -17.6$$

33. a. Let s represent score you can earn.

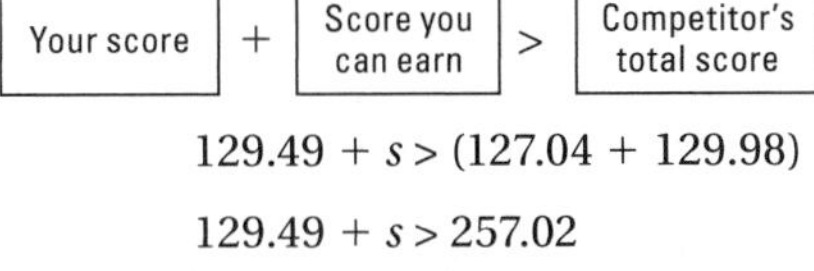

$$129.49 + s > (127.04 + 129.98)$$

$$129.49 + s > 257.02$$

$$129.49 + s - 129.49 > 257.02 - 129.49$$

$$s > 127.53$$

The score you can earn must be greater than 127.53.

WS13

b. Yes; since 128.13 > 127.53, you will beat your competitor.

No; since 126.78 < 127.53, you will not beat your competitor.

No; when your score is 127.53, you and your competitor will tie.

Lesson 6.2 (pp. 366–368)

5. $-6y < -36$

$\frac{-6y}{-6} > \frac{-36}{-6}$ Reverse the inequality symbol when dividing by -6.

$y > 6$

9. $\frac{g}{6} > -20$

$6 \cdot \frac{g}{6} > 6 \cdot (-20)$

$g > -120$

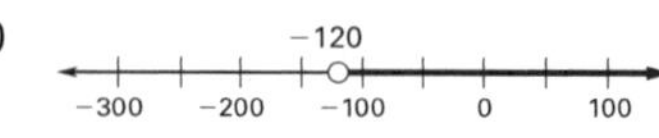

39. $48 \le 15 \cdot w$

$\frac{48}{15} \le \frac{15w}{15}$

$3.2 \le w$

The minimum width of the molding must be greater than or equal to 3.2 inches, or the width must be at least 3.2 inches.

Lesson 6.3 (pp. 372–374)

5. $8v - 3 \ge -11$

$8v \ge -8$

$v \ge -1$

19. $3(s - 4) \ge 2(s - 6)$

$3s - 12 \ge 2s - 12$

$3s \ge 2s$

$3s - 2s \ge 2s - 2s$

$s \ge 0$

39. a. The area of the habitat is (20 feet)(50 feet) = 1000 square feet. Since 500 square feet are needed for the first two swans, 1000 − 500 = 500 square feet are left for the other swans. 500 square feet can hold up to 500 ÷ 125 = 4 more swans; so, the maximum number of swans is 2 + 4 = 6 swans.

b. The area of the new habitat is [(20 + 20) feet][(50 + 20) feet] = (40 feet)(70 feet) = 2800 square feet. Since 2800 − 1000 = 1800, the additional area is 1800 square feet. 1800 square feet can hold up to 1800 ÷ 125 = 14.4 more swans; so the possible number of additional swans is at most 14 swans. The habitat can hold at most 14 more swans.

Lesson 6.4 (pp. 384–387)

7. Let s be the speed of a vehicle that is traveling within the posted speed limits.

$40 \le s \le 60$

11. Separate the compound inequality $-1 \le -4m \le 16$ into two inequalities.

$-1 \le -4m$ *and* $-4m \le 16$

$\frac{-1}{-4} \ge \frac{-4m}{-4}$ *and* $\frac{-4m}{-4} \ge \frac{16}{-4}$

$\frac{1}{4} \ge m$ *and* $m \ge -4$

The inequality can be written as $-4 \le m \le \frac{1}{4}$.

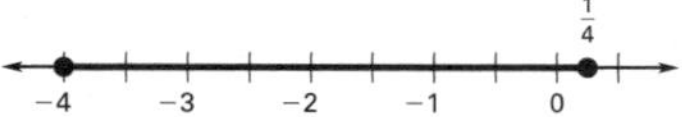

41. An inequality representing values for p is $0.02 \le p \le 0.04$.

$0.02 \le \frac{f}{d} \le 0.04$ Substitute $\frac{f}{d}$ for p.

$0.02 \le \frac{f}{160} \le 0.04$ Substitute 160 for w.

$3.2 \le f \le 6.4$

The possible amounts of food f eaten per day by a deer is greater or equal to 3.2 pounds and less than or equal to 6.4 pounds.

Lesson 6.5 (pp. 393–395)

11. Rewrite the absolute value equation $|3p + 7| = 4$ as two equations.

$3p + 7 = 4$ *or* $3p + 7 = -4$

$3p = -3$ *or* $3p = -11$

$p = -1$ *or* $p = -3\frac{2}{3}$

The solutions are -1 and $-3\frac{2}{3}$.

WORKED-OUT SOLUTIONS

WS14

23. $|x - 1| + 5 = 2$

$|x - 1| = -3$

The absolute value of a number is never negative. So, there are no solutions.

45. a. Let s represent your friend's scores last year.

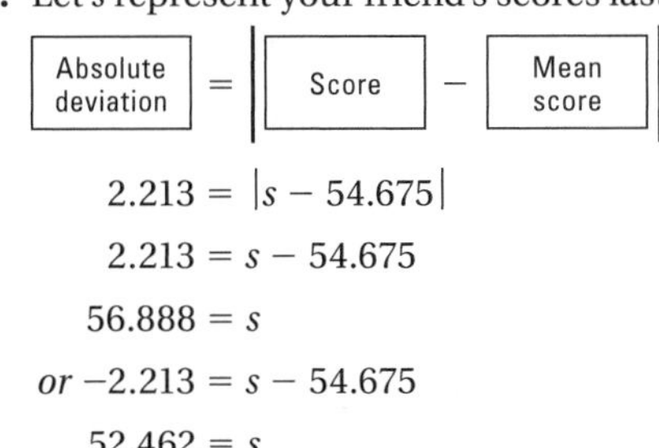

$2.213 = |s - 54.675|$

$2.213 = s - 54.675$

$56.888 = s$

or $-2.213 = s - 54.675$

$52.462 = s$

His least score earned was 52.462, and his greatest score was 56.888 points.

b. Let t represent your friend's scores this year. Find his greatest score for this year. Then find the difference between this year's greatest score and last year's greatest score.

$0.45 = |t - 56.738|$

$0.45 = t - 56.738$

$57.188 = t$

or $-0.45 = t - 56.738$

$56.288 = t$

His greatest score was 57.188 points. This score is 57.188 − 56.888, or 0.3 point more than his greatest score last year.

Lesson 6.6 (pp. 401–403)

9. Rewrite $|d + 4| \geq 3$ as a compound inequality.

$d + 4 \leq -3$ *or* $d + 4 \geq 3$

$d \leq -7$ *or* $d \geq -1$

15. $5\left|\frac{1}{2}r + 3\right| > 5$

$\left|\frac{1}{2}r + 3\right| > 1$

$\frac{1}{2}r + 3 < -1$ *or* $\frac{1}{2}r + 3 > 1$

$\frac{1}{2}r < -4$ *or* $\frac{1}{2}r > -2$

$r < -8$ *or* $r > -4$

37. Let t represent the oven temperature.

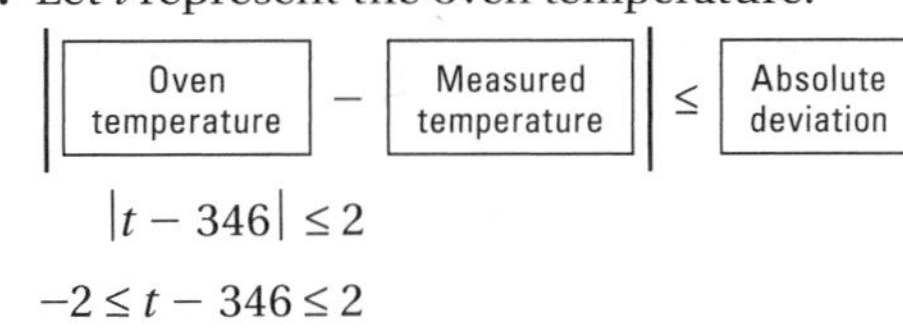

$|t - 346| \leq 2$

$-2 \leq t - 346 \leq 2$

$344 \leq t \leq 348$

The temperature is at least 344°F and at most 348°F. You should continue to preheat; the temperature is still below 350°F.

Lesson 6.7 (pp. 409–412)

5. Substitute −1 for x and −4 for y in the inequality $y - x > -2$.

$-4 - (-1) > -2$

$-3 > -2$ ✗

Since −3 is not greater than −2, the ordered pair (−1, −4) is not a solution.

19. Graph the equation $y = 3x + 5$. The symbol of the given inequality is <, so use a dashed line. Since the line does not pass through the origin, test the ordered pair (0, 0) in $y < 3x + 5$.

$0 < 3(0) + 5$

$0 < 5$ ✓

Shade the half-plane that contains (0, 0) because (0, 0) is a solution of the inequality.

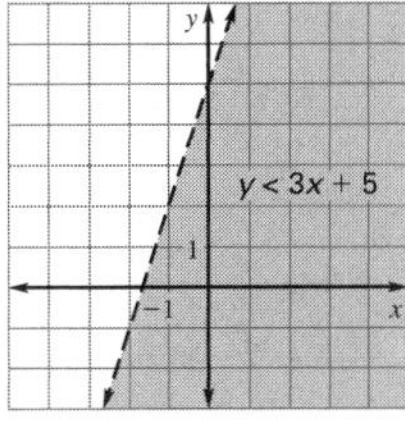

57. a. Let m be the number of muffins and let ℓ be the number of loaves of bread. An inequality modeling this situation is $\frac{1}{6}m + \frac{1}{2}\ell \leq 12$.

To graph $\frac{1}{6}m + \frac{1}{2}\ell \leq 12$, first graph the equation $\frac{1}{6}m + \frac{1}{2}\ell = 12$ in Quadrant I; the inequality symbol is ≤, so use a solid line.

Next, test (12, 12) in $\frac{1}{6}m + \frac{1}{2}\ell \leq 12$.

$\frac{1}{6}(12) + \frac{1}{2}(12) \leq 12$

$2 + 6 \leq 12$ ✓

WS15

Finally, shade the part of Quadrant I that contains (12, 12), because (12, 12) is a solution of the inequality.

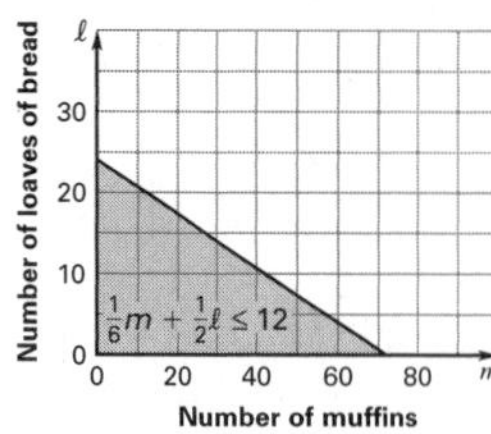

b. $\frac{1}{6}m + \frac{1}{2}(4) \le 12$ Substitute 4 for ℓ.

$\frac{1}{6}m + 2 \le 12$

$\frac{1}{6}m \le 10$

$m \le 60$

You can make up to 60 muffins.

Chapter 7

Lesson 7.1 (pp. 430–433)

15. Graph both equations.

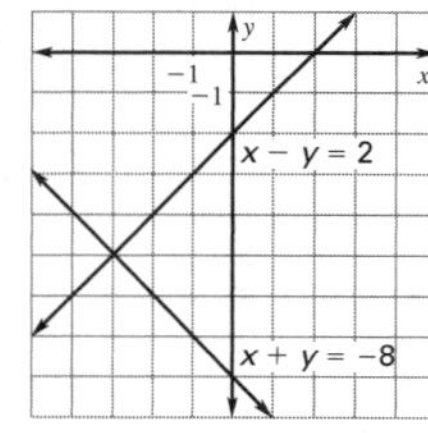

The lines appear to intersect at (−3, −5).

Check: Substitute −3 for x and −5 for y in each equation.

$x - y = 2$ $x + y = -8$

$-3 - (-5) = 2$ $-3 + (-5) = -8$

$2 = 2$ ✓ $-8 = -8$ ✓

So, (−3, −5) is the solution of the system.

31. The two lines appear to intersect at (50, 50). If the value of t is 50, then the year is 1990 + 50, or 2040. So, the percent of eighth graders who watch 1 hour or less of television will equal the percent of eighth graders who watch 1 hour or more of television in the year 2040.

Lesson 7.2 (pp. 439–441)

13. Solve $x + y = -3$ for x: $x = -y - 3$.

Substitute $-y - 3$ for x in the other equation and solve for y.

$5(-y - 3) + 2y = 9$

$-5y - 15 + 2y = 9$

$-3y - 15 = 9$

$-3y = 24$

$y = -8$

Substitute −8 for y in the equation $x = -y - 3$.

$x = -(-8) - 3 = 5$

The solution of the linear system is (5, −8).

33. a. Write a system of two linear equations.

Use the given verbal model to write the first equation: $x \cdot 1.5 = y \cdot 1.2$, or $1.5x = 1.2y$.

Since the length of the dowel is 9 inches, the second equation is $x + y = 9$.

Solve $x + y = 9$ for x: $x = -y + 9$.

Substitute $-y + 9$ for x in the equation $1.5x = 1.2y$ and solve for y.

$1.5x = 1.2y$

$1.5(-y + 9) = 1.2y$

$-1.5y + 13.5 = 1.2y$

$13.5 = 2.7y$

$5 = y$

Substitute 5 for y in the equation $x = -y + 9$.

$x = -5 + 9 = 4$

The solution is (4, 5). So the string should be placed 4 inches from point A.

Lesson 7.3 (pp. 447–450)

17. Rewrite the first equation so that the x-term is first. Subtract the equations to eliminate the variable x, then solve for y.

$6x - 8y = 36$

$\underline{6x - y = 15}$

$-7y = 21$

$y = -3$

Substitute −3 for y in either equation.

$6x - (-3) = 15$

$6x + 3 = 15$

$6x = 12$

$x = 2$

The solution of the linear system is (2, −3).

41. Write a system of equations. Let x be the cost of a monophonic ring tone and let y be the cost of a polyphonic ring tone.

$3 \cdot x + 2 \cdot y = 12.85$ ← Julie's total cost

$1 \cdot x + 2 \cdot y = 8.95$ ← Tate's total cost

Subtract the equations to eliminate y.

$3x + 2y = 12.85$

$x + 2y = 8.95$

$2x = 3.90$

$x = 1.95$

Substitute 1.95 for x in either equation.

$1.95 + 2y = 8.95$

$2y = 7.00$

$y = 3.50$

The solution of the linear system is (1.95, 3.50). The cost of a monophonic ring tone is \$1.95 and the cost of a polyphonic ring tone is \$3.50.

Lesson 7.4 (pp. 454–457)

15. Begin by multiplying $9x + 2y = 39$ by 2 and $6x + 13y = -9$ by 3 so that the coefficient of x is the same in both equations. Then subtract the equations to eliminate x. Solve for y.

$9x + 2y = 39$ [× 2] $18x + 4y = 78$

$6x + 13y = -9$ [× 3] $18x + 39y = -27$

$-35y = 105$

$y = -3$

Substitute −3 for y in either original equations.

$9x + 2(-3) = 39$ Use the equation $9x + 2y = 39$.

$9x - 6 = 39$

$9x = 45$

$x = 5$ The solution is (5, −3).

39. Let x be the number of pies and y be the number of batches of applesauce.

$5x + 4y = 169$ ← Granny Smith apples

$3x + 2y = 95$ ← Golden Delicious apples

Now begin to solve the system by multiplying $5x + 4y = 169$ by 3 and $3x + 2y = 95$ by 5 so that the coefficient of x is the same in both equations. Then subtract the equations to eliminate x. Solve for y.

$5x + 4y = 169$ [× 3] $15x + 12y = 507$

$3x + 2y = 95$ [× 5] $15x + 10y = 475$

$2y = 32$

$y = 16$

Substitute 16 for y in either original equations.

$3x + 2(16) = 95$

$3x + 32 = 95$

$3x = 63$

$x = 21$

The solution is (21, 16). The apples can be used to make 21 pies and 16 batches of applesauce.

Lesson 7.5 (pp. 462–465)

11.

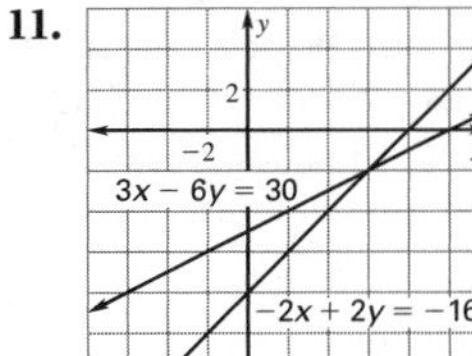

The lines intersect, so the linear system has one solution.

37. Write a system of equations. Let x be the cost of a coach ticket and let y be the cost of a business class ticket.

$150x + 80y = 22{,}860$ ← Washington, D.C.

$170x + 100y = 27{,}280$ ← New York City

Solve the linear system using elimination. Multiply the Washington, D.C. equation by 5 and the New York City equation by 4.

$750x + 400y = 114{,}300$

$680x + 400y = 109{,}120$

$70x = 5180$

$x = 74$

WS17

Substitute 74 for x in either original equations.

$$170(74) + 100y = 27{,}280$$
$$12{,}580 + 100y = 27{,}280$$
$$100y = 14{,}700$$
$$y = 147$$

The solution is (74, 147). Since there is one solution to the system, there is enough information to determine the cost of one coach ticket.

Lesson 7.6 (pp. 469–472)

13. The graph of the system is the intersection of the two half-planes when both inequalities are graphed in the same coordinate plane.

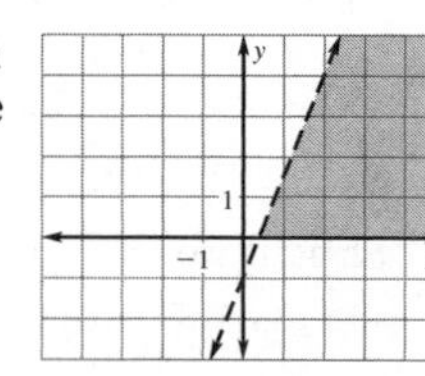

39. a. Let x be the person's age in years and let y be the target heart rate (in beats per minute). A person's maximum heart rate is given by $220 - x$, so 70% of this value is $0.7(220 - x)$ and 85% of this value is $0.85(220 - x)$. So the range for the target heart rate is given by the compound inequality $0.7(220 - x) \le y \le 0.85(220 - x)$, or $154 - 0.70x \le y \le 187 - 0.85x$. This compound inequality can be rewritten as the two inequalities $y \ge 154 - 0.70x$ and $y \le 187 - 0.85x$. The age range for which the heart rate calculations is valid is given as $20 \le x \le 65$.

The system of inequalities is:

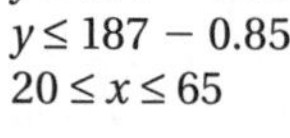

$y \ge 154 - 0.70x$
$y \le 187 - 0.85x$
$20 \le x \le 65$

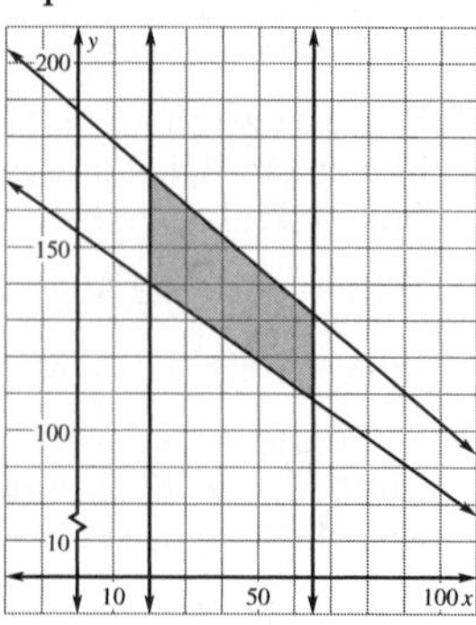

b. No; substituting 40 for x in the inequality $0.70(220 - x) \le y \le 0.85(220 - x)$ gives a range of $126 \le y \le 153$. Since 104 and 120 are both less than 126, his heart rate stays below 70% of the maximum heart rate and is not in the target range for his age.

Chapter 8

Lesson 8.1 (pp. 492–494)

31. $(-10x^6)^2 \cdot x^2 = (-10 \cdot x^6)^2 \cdot x^2$

$= (-10)^2 \cdot (x^6)^2 \cdot x^2$

$= 100 \cdot x^{6 \cdot 2} \cdot x^2$

$= 100 \cdot x^{12} \cdot x^2$

$= 100 \cdot x^{12 + 2}$

$= 100x^{14}$

55. a. For 10 ounces of gold, there are $10^1 \cdot 10^{23} = 10^{1 + 23}$, or 10^{24} atoms of gold; for 100 ounces of gold, there are $10^2 \cdot 10^{23} = 10^{25}$ atoms of gold; for 1000 ounces of gold, there are $10^3 \cdot 10^{23} = 10^{26}$ atoms of gold; for 10,000 ounces of gold, there are $10^4 \cdot 10^{23} = 10^{27}$ atoms of gold; and for 100,000 ounces of gold, there are $10^5 \cdot 10^{23} = 10^{28}$ atoms of gold.

b. The power of 10 closest to 96,000 is 10^5, or 100,000. So there were about $10^5 \cdot 10^{23} = 10^{5 + 23}$, or 10^{28} atoms of gold extracted from the mine.

Lesson 8.2 (pp. 498–501)

33. $\left(\dfrac{3x^3}{2y}\right)^2 \cdot \dfrac{1}{x^2} = \dfrac{(3x^3)^2}{(2y)^2} \cdot \dfrac{1}{x^2}$

$= \dfrac{3^2 \cdot (x^3)^2}{2^2 \cdot y^2} \cdot \dfrac{1}{x^2}$

$= \dfrac{9x^6}{4y^2} \cdot \dfrac{1}{x^2}$

$= \dfrac{9x^6}{4x^2y^2}$

$= \dfrac{9x^4}{4y^2}$

51. Convert the speed of the spacecraft to kilometers per second.

$$\frac{10^4 \text{ m}}{1 \text{ sec}} \cdot \frac{1 \text{ km}}{10^3 \text{ m}} = \frac{10^{4-3} \text{ km}}{1 \text{ sec}} = \frac{10^1 \text{ km}}{1 \text{ sec}}$$

So the speed of the spacecraft is 10 kilometers per second.

WS18

Use the quotient of powers property to calculate the number of seconds it would take to make the trip.

$$\frac{10^{13}\text{ km}}{10^{1}\text{ km/sec}} = 10^{13-1}\text{ sec} = 10^{12}\text{ sec}$$

Calculate the number of seconds in a year (using 365 days = 1 year).

$$\frac{60\text{ sec}}{1\text{ min}} \cdot \frac{60\text{ min}}{1\text{ h}} \cdot \frac{24\text{ h}}{1\text{ day}} \cdot \frac{365\text{ day}}{1\text{ yr}} = \frac{31{,}356{,}000\text{ sec}}{1\text{ yr}}$$

Now convert the trip time, 10^{12} seconds, to years.

$$10^{12}\text{ sec} \div \frac{31{,}536{,}000\text{ sec}}{1\text{ yr}} \approx 31{,}710\text{ yr}$$

It would take about 31,710 years for the spacecraft to reach Alpha Centauri.

Lesson 8.3 (pp. 506–508)

11. $\left(\frac{2}{7}\right)^{-2} = \frac{1}{\left(\frac{2}{7}\right)^2} = \frac{1}{\frac{4}{49}} = \frac{49}{4}$

53. To find the number of red blood cells in the entire sample, multiply the sample size, 10^{-2} liter, by the ratio 10^7 red blood cells per 10^{-6} liter.

$$10^{-2}\text{ L} \cdot \frac{10^7\text{ red blood cells}}{10^{-6}\text{ L}}$$

$$= \frac{10^{-2} \cdot 10^{7}}{10^{-6}}\text{ red blood cells}$$

$$= 10^{-2+7-(-6)}\text{ red blood cells}$$

$$= 10^{11}\text{ red blood cells}$$

The entire sample would contain about 10^{11} red blood cells.

Lesson 8.4 (pp. 515–518)

3. Since 8.5 is already between 1 and 10, you move the decimal point 0 places and the exponent is 0: $8.5 = 8.5 \times 10^0$.

17. Since the exponent is 7, move the decimal point 7 places to the right: $7.5 \times 10^7 = 75{,}000{,}000$.

53. Divide the number of pounds of cotton by the number of acres.

$$\frac{9.7 \times 10^8}{6.9 \times 10^5} = \frac{9.7}{6.9} \times \frac{10^8}{10^5}$$

$$\approx 1.4058 \times 10^3 \approx 1405.8$$

The average number of pounds produced per acre was about 1406 pounds per acre.

Lesson 8.5 (pp. 523–527)

13. Make a table of values by choosing values for x and finding the corresponding values for y. The domain of the function is all real numbers.

x	−2	−1	0	1	2	3
y	$0.\overline{4}$	$0.\overline{6}$	1	1.5	2.25	3.375

Plot the points from the table and draw a smooth curve through them.

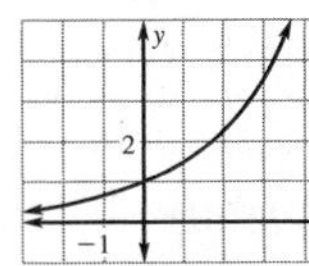

The table and the graph show that the range of the function is all positive real numbers.

41. a. Use the exponential growth model, $y = a(1 + r)^t$.

For tree 1 (with 6% = 0.06), substitute A for y, 154 for a, and 0.06 for r.

$A = 154(1 + 0.06)^t = 154(1.06)^t$

For tree 2 (with 10% = 0.1), substitute A for y, 113 for a, and 0.1 for r.

$A = 113(1 + 0.1)^t = 113(1.1)^t$

The functions are $A = 154(1.06)^t$ for tree 1 and $A = 113(1.1)^t$ for tree 2.

b. 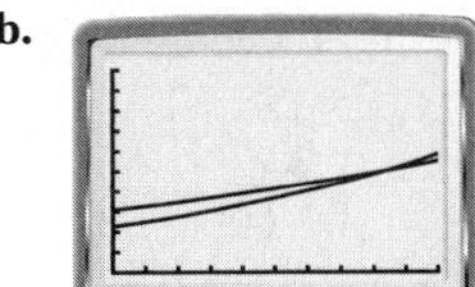

Using the *intersect* feature of the graphing calculator, the graphs intersect at about the point (8.4, 250.6). So, the trees will be the same height in about 8.4 years.

Lesson 8.6 (pp. 535–538)

7. Make a table of values by choosing values for x and finding the corresponding values for y. The domain of the function is all real numbers.

x	−2	−1	0	1	2
y	25	5	1	$\frac{1}{5}$	$\frac{1}{25}$

Plot the points from the table and draw a smooth curve through them.

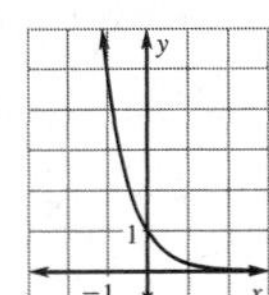

The table and the graph show that the range of the function is all positive real numbers.

WORKED-OUT SOLUTIONS

49. Let V be the value of the boat (in dollars) and let t be the time (in years since 2003).

Use the exponential decay model, $y = a(1 - r)^t$, to write a function for the value of the boat over time. Substitute V for y, 4000 for a, and 0.07 for r.

$V = 4000(1 - 0.07)^t$

$= 4000(0.93)^t$

In 2006, the value of t is 2006 − 2003, or 3.

$V = 4000(0.93)^3 \approx \$3217.43$

The value of the boat in 2006 is about \$3217. The family should not sell the boat, since the \$3000 offer is less than the value of the boat.

Chapter 9

Lesson 9.1 (pp. 557–559)

21. $(6c^2 + 3c + 9) - (3c - 5)$

$= 6c^2 + 3c + 9 - 3c + 5$

$= 6c^2 + (3c - 3c) + (9 + 5)$

$= 6c^2 + 14$

39. a. Add the models for the number of books of each type sold to find a model T for the total number (in millions) of books sold.

$T = A + J$

$= (9.5t^3 - 58t^2 + 66t + 500) + (-15t^2 + 64t + 360)$

$= 9.5t^3 + (-58t^2 - 15t^2) + (66t + 64t) + (500 + 360)$

$= 9.5t^3 - 73t^2 + 130t + 860$

b. To find the total number (in millions) of books sold in the years 1998 and 2002, substitute the number of years since 1998 for t in the model. Then compare the results.

For 1998, $t = 1998 - 1998 = 0$:

$M = 9.5(0)^3 - 73(0)^2 + 130(0) + 860 = 860$

There were 860 million books sold in 1998.

For 2002, $t = 2002 - 1998 = 4$:

$M = 9.5(4)^3 - 73(4)^2 + 130(4) + 860$

$= 9.5(64) - 73(16) + 130(4) + 860$

$= 608 - 1168 + 520 + 860$

$= 820$

There were 820 million books sold in 2002.

More books were sold in 1998 than in 2002.

Lesson 9.2 (pp. 565–568)

23. $(5x + 2)(-3x^2 + 4x - 1)$

$= 5x(-3x^2 + 4x - 1) + 2(-3x^2 + 4x - 1)$

$= -15x^3 + 20x^2 - 5x - 6x^2 + 8x - 2$

$= -15x^3 + (20x^2 - 6x^2) + (-5x + 8x) - 2$

$= -15x^3 + 14x^2 + 3x - 2$

51. a. Substitute 0 for t in each function:

$R = -336(0)^2 + 1730(0) + 12{,}300 = 12{,}300$

$P = 0.00351(0)^2 - 0.0249(0) + 0.171 = 0.171$

Since t is the number of years since 1997, the product $R \cdot P$ when $t = 0$ represents the amount (in million of dollars) spent in 1997 on sound recordings in the U.S. by people between 15 and 19 years old.

b. $R \cdot P = (-336t^2 + 1730t + 12{,}300) \cdot (0.00351t^2 - 0.0249t + 0.171)$

$= -336t^2(0.00351t^2 - 0.0249t + 0.171) + 1730t(0.00351t^2 - 0.0249t + 0.171) + 12{,}300(0.00351t^2 - 0.0249t + 0.171)$

$= -1.17936t^4 + 8.3664t^3 - 57.456t^2 + 6.0723t^3 - 43.077t^2 + 295.83t + 43.173t^2 - 306.27t + 2103.3$

$= -1.17936t^4 + (8.3664t^3 + 6.0723t^3) + (-57.456t^2 - 43.077t^2 + 43.173t^2) + (295.83t - 306.27t) + 2103.3$

$= -1.17936t^4 + 14.4387t^3 - 57.36t^2 - 10.44t + 2103.3$

So, $R \cdot P \approx -1.18t^4 + 14.4t^3 - 57.4t^2 - 10.4t + 2100$.

WS20

c. For 2002, $t = 2002 - 1997 = 5$. Substitute 5 for t in the equation for part (b).

$$R \cdot P \approx -1.18(5)^4 + 14.4(5)^3 - 57.4(5)^2 - 10.4(5) + 2100$$

$$\approx -1.18(625) + 14.4(125) - 57.4(25) - 10.4(5) + 2100$$

$$\approx -737.50 + 1800 - 1435 - 52 + 2100$$

$$\approx 1675.5$$

In 2002, people between the ages of 15 and 19 years old spent about 1680 million dollars (or $1,680,000,000) on sound recordings.

Lesson 9.3 (pp. 572–574)

11. $(t + 4)(t - 4) = t^2 - 4^2 = t^2 - 16$

41. a.

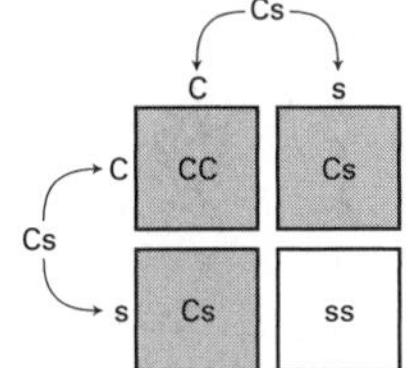

b. Model the gene from each parent with $0.5C + 0.5s$. There is an equal chance that the child inherits a straight thumb gene or a curved thumb gene from each parent. The possible gene combinations of the child can be modeled by $(0.5C + 0.5s)^2$, or

$$(0.5C)^2 + 2(0.5C)(0.5s) + (0.5s)^2$$

$$= 0.25C^2 + 0.5Cs + 0.25s^2$$

c. Consider the coefficients in the polynomial found in part (b). The coefficients show that 25% + 50% = 75% of the possible gene combinations will contain a C, and thus result in a child with a curved thumb.

Lesson 9.4 (pp. 578–580)

3. $(x - 5)(x + 3) = 0$

$x - 5 = 0$ *or* $x + 3 = 0$

$x = 5$ *or* $x = -3$

The solutions of the equation are 5 and −3.

55. a. The initial vertical velocity is given as 4.9 meters per second and the rabbit starts from the ground, so $v = 4.9$ and $s = 0$ in the vertical motion model.

$$h = -4.9t^2 + vt + s$$

$$= -4.9t^2 + 4.9t + 0$$

$$= -4.9t^2 + 4.9t$$

b. When the rabbit lands, its height above the ground is 0 meters. A reasonable domain for t can be found by substituting 0 for h and solving for t.

$$0 = -4.9t^2 + 4.9t$$

$$0 = 4.9t(-t + 1)$$

$4.9t = 0$ *or* $-t + 1 = 0$

$t = 0$ *or* $t = 1$

Since a height of 0 represents when the rabbit is on the ground, $t = 1$ second represents how long it takes for the rabbit to land back on the ground after jumping at $t = 0$ seconds. So, a reasonable domain is all real numbers greater than or equal to 0 and less than or equal to 1, or $0 \le t \le 1$.

Lesson 9.5 (pp. 586–589)

7. In $z^2 + 8z - 48$, $c = -48$. Since c is negative, p and q must have different signs.

Factors of −48	Sum of factors	
−48, 1	−48 + 1 = −47	✗
48, −1	48 + (−1) = 47	✗
−24, 2	−24 + 2 = −22	✗
24, −2	24 + (−2) = 22	✗
−16, 3	−16 + 3 = −13	✗
16, −3	16 + (−3) = 13	✗
−12, 4	−12 + 4 = −8	✗
12, −4	12 + (−4) = 8	← Correct

So, $z^2 + 8z - 48 = (z + 12)(z - 4)$.

WS21

WORKED-OUT SOLUTIONS

61. Let x be the original length of the sides of the square photo. Then the length of the trimmed photo is $(x - 6)$ inches and its width is $(x - 5)$ inches. The formula $A = \ell \cdot w$ models the area of the trimmed photo which is 20 square inches.

$A = \ell \cdot w$

$20 = (x - 6)(x - 5)$

$20 = x^2 - 11x + 30$

$0 = x^2 - 11x + 10$

$0 = (x - 10)(x - 1)$

$x - 10 = 0$ *or* $x - 1 = 0$

$x = 10$ *or* $x = 1$

So, the original square photo had a side length of 10 inches or 1 inch. But an original length of 1 inch does not make sense in this situation, so the side length of the original square photo was 10 inches. Therefore, the perimeter of the original square photo was 4(10), or 40 inches.

Lesson 9.6 (pp. 596–599)

5. Factor −1 from each term of the trinomial: $-y^2 + 2y + 8 = -(y^2 - 2y - 8)$.

In $y^2 - 2y - 8$, $c = -8$. Since c is negative, the factors of c must have different signs.

Factors of −8	Possible factorization	Middle term when multiplied	
−8, 1	$(y - 8)(y + 1)$	$y - 8y = -7y$	✗
8, −1	$(y + 8)(y - 1)$	$-y + 8y = 7y$	✗
−4, 2	$(y - 4)(y + 2)$	$2y - 4y = -2y$	← Correct
4, −2	$(y + 4)(y - 2)$	$-2y + 4y = 2y$	✗

So, $y^2 - 2y - 8 = (y - 4)(y + 2)$. Therefore,

$-y^2 + 2y + 8 = -(y^2 - 2y - 8)$

$= -(y - 4)(y + 2)$

25. $4s^2 + 11s - 3 = 0$

$(4s - 1)(s + 3) = 0$

$4s - 1 = 0$ *or* $s + 3 = 0$

$s = \frac{1}{4}$ *or* $s = -3$

61. Let w be the width of the Parthenon's base. Then $2w + 8$ is the length of the base. The formula $A = \ell \cdot w$ models the area of the rectangular base which is 2170 square meters.

$A = \ell \cdot w$

$2170 = (2w + 8) \cdot w$

$2170 = 2w^2 + 8w$

$0 = 2w^2 + 8w - 2170$

$0 = 2(w^2 + 4w - 1085)$

$0 = 2(w + 35)(w - 31)$

$w + 35 = 0$ *or* $w - 31 = 0$

$w = -35$ *or* $w = 31$

The solutions are −35 and 31.

Since the width cannot be negative, reject −35 as a solution. So, the width is 31 meters and the length is 2(31) + 8, or 70 meters. Therefore, the base of the Parthenon has length 70 meters and width 31 meters.

Lesson 9.7 (pp. 603–605)

11. $49a^2 + 14a + 1 = (7a)^2 + 2(7a \cdot 1) + 1^2$

$= (7a + 1)^2$

49. Use the vertical motion model with $h = 54$, $v = 56$, and $s = 5$.

$h = -16t^2 + vt + s$

$54 = -16t^2 + 56t + 5$

$0 = -16t^2 + 56t - 49$

$0 = -(16t^2 - 56t + 49)$

$0 = -[(4t)^2 - 2(4t \cdot 7) + 7^2]$

$0 = -(4t - 7)^2$

$0 = (4t - 7)^2$

$4t - 7 = 0$

$t = 1.75$

The ball reaches a height of 54 feet in 1.75 seconds. Since there is one solution for t, the ball reaches a height of 54 feet just once.

WS22

Lesson 9.8 (pp. 610–613)

13. $x^3 + x^2 + 2x + 2 = (x^3 + x^2) + (2x + 2)$

$= x^2(x + 1) + 2(x + 1)$

$= (x + 1)(x^2 + 2)$

23. $x^4 - x^2 = x^2(x^2 - 1) = x^2(x - 1)(x + 1)$

71. a. Substitute 0 for h in $h = -4.9t^2 + 3.9t + 1$.

$0 = -4.9t^2 + 3.9t + 1$

$0 = -(4.9t^2 - 3.9t - 1)$

$0 = -(4.9t + 1)(t - 1)$

$4.9t + 1 = 0$ *or* $t - 1 = 0$

$t \approx -0.20$ *or* $t = 1$

The zeros are 1 and about −0.2.

b. The zero $t \approx -0.2$ has no meaning in this situation because t represents time which cannot be negative. The zero $t = 1$ means that the pallino hits the ground (where $h = 0$) 1 second after it is thrown.

Chapter 10

Lesson 10.1 (pp. 632–634)

7. Make a table of values for $y = -2x^2$.

x	−2	−1	0	1	2
y	−8	−2	0	−2	−8

Plot the points from the table. Draw a smooth curve through the points.

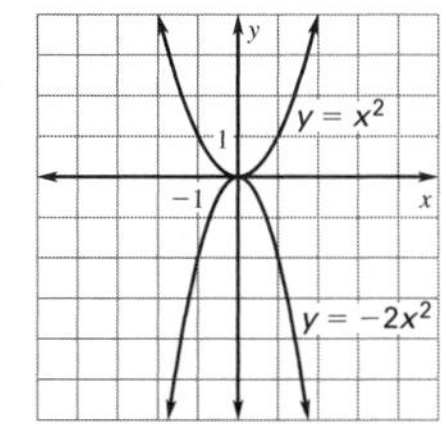

The graphs of $y = -2x^2$ and $y = x^2$ have the same vertex, (0, 0), and the same axis of symmetry, $x = 0$. However, the graph of $-2x^2$ is narrower than the graph of $y = x^2$, and it opens down. This is because the graph of $y = -2x^2$ is a vertical stretch (by a factor of 2) with a reflection in the x-axis of the graph of $y = x^2$.

41. a.

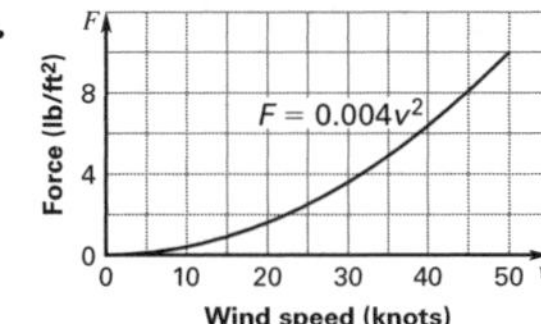

b. From the graph, the wind speed that will produce a force of 1 pound per square foot on a sail is about 16 knots. Using the function to check: $F = 0.004(16)^2 = 1.024$.

c. From the graph, the wind speed that will produce a force of 5 pounds per square foot on a sail is about 35 knots. Using the function to check: $F = 0.004(35)^2 = 4.9$.

Lesson 10.2 (pp. 638–640)

9. For $y = -\frac{2}{3}x^2 - 1$, $a = -\frac{2}{3}$ and $b = 0$.

$$x = -\frac{b}{2a} = \frac{0}{2\left(-\frac{2}{3}\right)} = 0$$

The axis of symmetry is $x = 0$.

The x-coordinate of the vertex, $-\frac{b}{2a}$, is 0. To find the y-coordinate, substitute 0 for x in the function and find y: $y = -\frac{2}{3}(0)^2 - 1 = -1$. The vertex is (0, −1).

41. The highest point of each parabolic arch is at the vertex of the parabola. The height h is the y-coordinate of the vertex.

To find the x-coordinate of the vertex, use $x = -\frac{b}{2a}$ with $a = -0.0019$ and $b = 0.71$.

$$x = -\frac{b}{2a} = -\frac{0.71}{2(-0.0019)} \approx 187$$

Substitute 187 for x in the given equation to find the y-coordinate of the vertex.

$y = -0.0019(187)^2 + 0.71(187) \approx 66.3$

The height h at the highest point of the arch is about 66 feet.

Lesson 10.3 (pp. 647–649)

5. Write the equation $x^2 + 6x = -8$ in standard form: $x^2 + 6x + 8 = 0$.

Graph the function $y = x^2 + 6x + 8$.

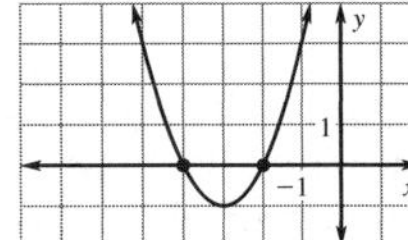

The x-intercepts are -4 and -2.

So, the solutions of $x^2 + 6x = -8$ are -4 and -2.

51. The width of the road can be found by finding the distance between the x-intercepts of the graph $y = -0.0017x^2 + 0.041x$.

Graph the function $y = -0.0017x^2 + 0.041x$ on a graphing calculator.

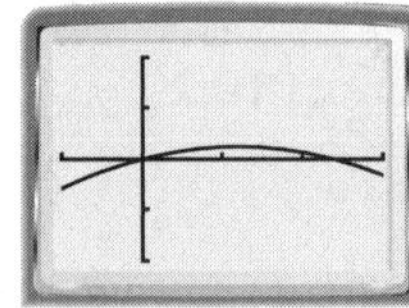

Use the *trace* feature of the graphing calculator to find the x-intercepts. There are two x-intercepts, one at 0 and one at approximately 24.12.

To the nearest tenth of a foot, the width of the road is 24.1 feet.

Lesson 10.4 (pp. 655–658)

25. $7c^2 = 100$

$$c^2 = \frac{100}{7}$$

$$c = \pm\sqrt{\frac{100}{7}}$$

$c \approx \pm 3.78$ Use a calculator.

59. First, solve the formula for D: $D = \pm\sqrt{\frac{w}{0.0018ds}}$.

Since D cannot be negative in this situation, use the positive square root only.

a. For amethyst, substitute 1 for w, 4.5 for d, and 2.65 for s.

$$D = \sqrt{\frac{1}{0.0018(4.5)(2.65)}} \approx 6.83$$

The diameter is about 6.8 millimeters.

b. For diamond, substitute 1 for w, 4.5 for d, and 3.52 for s.

$$D = \sqrt{\frac{1}{0.0018(4.5)(3.52)}} \approx 5.92$$

The diameter is about 5.9 millimeters.

c. For ruby, substitute 1 for w, 4.5 for d, and 4.00 for s.

$$D = \sqrt{\frac{1}{0.0018(4.5)(4.00)}} \approx 5.55$$

The diameter is about 5.6 millimeters.

Lesson 10.5 (pp. 666–668)

19.

$$z^2 + 11z = -\frac{21}{4}$$

$$z^2 + 11z + \left(\frac{11}{2}\right)^2 = -\frac{21}{4} + \left(\frac{11}{2}\right)^2$$

$$\left(z + \frac{11}{2}\right)^2 = -\frac{21}{4} + \frac{121}{4}$$

$$\left(z + \frac{11}{2}\right)^2 = 25$$

$$z + \frac{11}{2} = \pm 5$$

$$z = -\frac{11}{2} \pm 5$$

The solutions of the equation are $-\frac{11}{2} + 5 = -0.5$ and $-\frac{11}{2} - 5 = -10.5$.

47. a. Convert $1,904,000 to thousands of dollars: $1,904,000 \div 1000 = 1904$.

Substitute 1904 for y in $y = 7x^2 - 4x + 392$: $1904 = 7x^2 - 4x + 392$.

$$7x^2 - 4x + 392 = 1904$$

$$7x^2 - 4x = 1512$$

$$x^2 - \frac{4}{7}x = 216$$

$$x^2 - \frac{4}{7}x + \left(\frac{2}{7}\right)^2 = 216 + \left(\frac{2}{7}\right)^2$$

$$\left(x - \frac{2}{7}\right)^2 = 216\frac{4}{49}$$

$$x - \frac{2}{7} = \pm\sqrt{216\frac{4}{49}}$$

$$x = \frac{2}{7} \pm \sqrt{216\frac{4}{49}}$$

Using a calculator, the solutions are about 14.99 and about -14.41.

The negative value does not make sense in this situation because the function does not model the years prior to 1985. So, the year when the average salary was $1,904,000 was 1985 + 15, or 2000.

b. First, graph the function $y = 7x^2 - 4x + 392$ for $x \geq 0$. Then draw a dashed line at about $y = 1904$ until it intersects the curve. Draw a dashed line from this point down to the x-axis. The x-value here is about 15. So, the year when the average salary was \$1,904,000 is about 1985 + 15, or 2000.

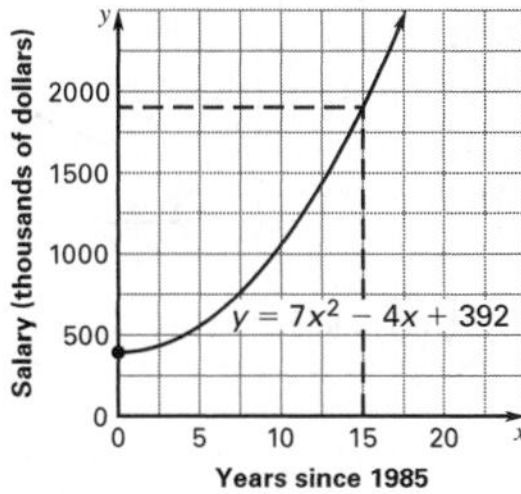

Lesson 10.6 (pp. 674–676)

19. Write $6z^2 = 2z^2 + 7z + 5$ in standard form: $4z^2 - 7z - 5 = 0$.

Use the quadratic formula, with $a = 4$, $b = -7$, and $c = -5$.

$$z = \frac{-(-7) \pm \sqrt{(-7)^2 - 4(4)(-5)}}{2(4)} = \frac{7 \pm \sqrt{129}}{8}$$

Using a calculator, the solutions are about 2.29 and about −0.54.

47. For 16,000,000 subscribers, $y = 16$ in the function.

$$16 = 0.7x^2 - 4.3x + 5.5$$

$$0 = 0.7x^2 - 4.3x - 10.5$$

Use the quadratic formula, with $a = 0.7$, $b = -4.3$, and $c = -10.5$.

$$x = \frac{-(-4.3) \pm \sqrt{(-4.3)^2 - 4(0.7)(-10.5)}}{2(0.7)}$$

$$= \frac{4.3 \pm \sqrt{47.89}}{1.4} \quad \text{Use a calculator.}$$

The solutions are about 8.01 and about −1.87.

The negative value does not make sense in this situation because the function does not model the years prior to 1985. So, the year when the number of subscribers was 16,000,000 was 1985 + 8, or 1993.

Lesson 10.7 (pp. 681–683)

9. Find the value of the discriminant. Substitute 25 for a, −16 for b, and 0 for c.

$$b^2 - 4ac = (-16)^2 - 4(25)(0) = 256$$

Since $256 > 0$, the equation has two solutions.

47. In order for the child not to have to bend over, the height y of the arch must be at least 4 feet. Use the given quadratic equation with 4 substituted for y.

$$4 = -0.18x^2 + 1.6x$$

$$0 = -0.18x^2 + 1.6x - 4$$

Find the value of the discriminant. Substitute −0.18 for a, 1.6 for b, and −4 for c.

$$b^2 - 4ac = (1.6)^2 - 4(-0.18)(-4) = -0.32$$

Because the discriminant is negative, there are no solutions of the equation $0 = -0.18x^2 + 1.6x - 4$, meaning that the height of an arch is less than 4 feet. So, a child who is 4 feet tall would not be able to walk under one of the arches without having to bend over.

Lesson 10.8 (pp. 688–691)

7. 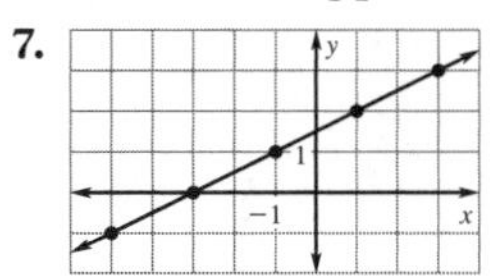
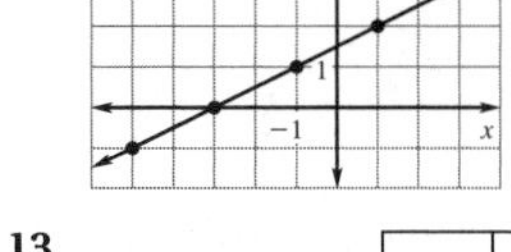
linear function

13.

x	−2	−1	0	1	2
y	−4	−1	0	−1	−4

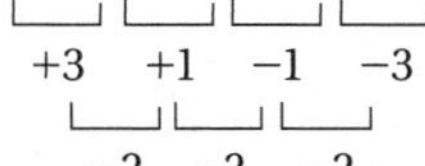

First differences: +3 +1 −1 −3

Second differences: −2 −2 −2

The second differences are equal, so the table of values represents a quadratic function.

The equation has the form $y = ax^2$. Find the value of a by using the coordinates of a point (other than the origin) that lies on the graph, such as $(-1, -1)$.

$$y = ax^2$$

$$-1 = a(-1)^2$$

$$-1 = a$$

An equation for the function is $y = -x^2$.

25. a.

Folds	1	2	3	4	5
Sections	2	4	8	16	32

b. 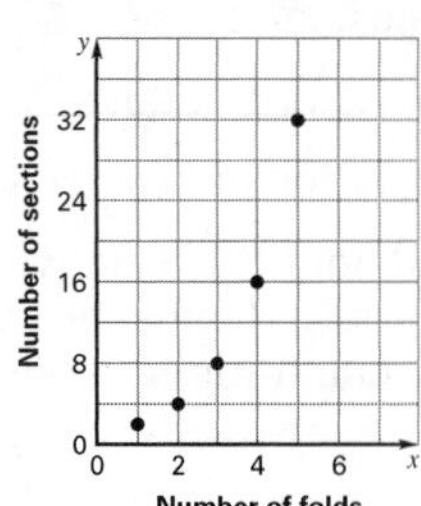

Both the graph and the table show that the data can be modeled by an exponential function.

c. Write an exponential equation of the form $y = ab^x$. From the table, the number of sections increases by a factor of 2, so $b = 2$. Find the value of a using one of the data pairs, such as (3, 8).

$y = ab^x$

$8 = a(2)^3$

$1 = a$

The exponential equation is $y = 2^x$.

To find the number of sections created by 7 folds, substitute 7 for x in $y = 2^x$: $y = 2^7 = 128$.

Chapter 11

Lesson 11.1 (pp. 713–716)

7. Make a table. Because the square root of a negative number is undefined, x must be nonnegative. So the domain of the function is $x \geq 0$.

x	0	1	2	3	4
y	0	1.5	2.1	2.6	3

Plot the ordered pairs from the table and then draw a smooth curve through the points. From the graph, it can seen that the range of the function is $y \geq 0$.

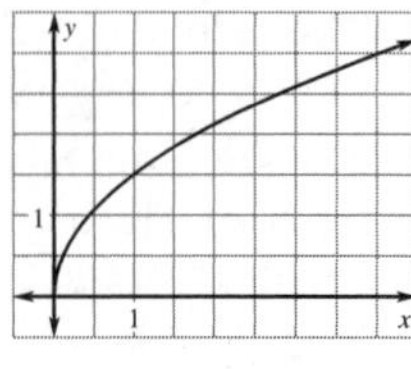

The graph of $y = \frac{3}{2}\sqrt{x}$ is a vertical stretch $\left(\text{by a factor of } \frac{3}{2}\right)$ of the graph of $y = \sqrt{x}$.

23. Make a table. Because the square root of a negative number is undefined, the value of $x - 1$ must be nonnegative: $x - 1 \geq 0$. So the domain of the function is $x \geq 1$.

x	1	2	3	4	5
y	0	1	1.4	1.7	2

Plot the ordered pairs from the table and then draw a smooth curve through the points.

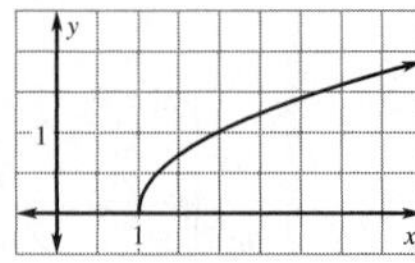

From the graph, it can seen that the range of the function is $y \geq 0$.

The graph of $y = \sqrt{x - 1}$ is a horizontal translation (of 1 unit to the right) of the graph of $y = \sqrt{x}$.

45. Because the square root of a negative number is undefined, h must be nonnegative. So the domain of the function is $h \geq 0$.

h	0	0.25	0.5	0.75	1
s	0	5.45	7.7	9.4	10.9

Plot the ordered pairs from the table and then draw a smooth curve through the points. From the graph, it can seen that the range of the function is $y \geq 0$.

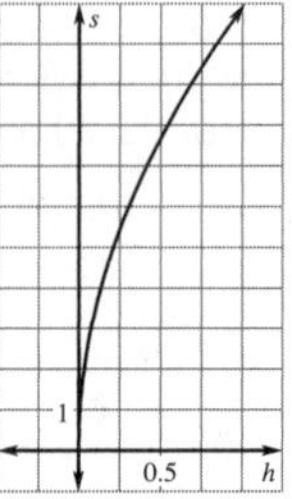

The maximum height reached is about 0.9 meter when the long jumper's speed before jumping is 10.25 meters per second.

Lesson 11.2 (pp. 723–726)

9. $\sqrt{81m^3} = \sqrt{81 \cdot m^2 \cdot m}$

$= \sqrt{81} \cdot \sqrt{m^2} \cdot \sqrt{m}$

$= 9m\sqrt{m}$

37. $9\sqrt{32} + \sqrt{2} = 9\sqrt{16 \cdot 2} + \sqrt{2}$

$= 9\sqrt{16} \cdot \sqrt{2} + \sqrt{2}$

$= 9 \cdot 4 \cdot \sqrt{2} + \sqrt{2}$

$= 36\sqrt{2} + \sqrt{2}$

$= (36 + 1)\sqrt{2}$

$= 37\sqrt{2}$

WORKED-OUT SOLUTIONS

69. a. \$30 ÷ \$6 per square yard = 5 square yards

b. $s \text{ yd} = \sqrt{\frac{S \text{ yd}^2}{6}} = \sqrt{\frac{S}{6} \cdot \frac{\text{yd}^2}{1}}$

$= \sqrt{\frac{S}{6}} \cdot \sqrt{\frac{\text{yd}^2}{1}} = \sqrt{\frac{S}{6}} \text{ yd}$

Therefore s yd$= \sqrt{\frac{S}{6}}$ yd, and the units check.

c. Substitute 5 for S in the formula $s = \sqrt{\frac{S}{6}}$:

$s = \sqrt{\frac{5}{6}} \approx 0.9.$

To the nearest tenth of a yard, the edge length of the largest footrest you can cover with 5 square yards of fabric is 0.9 yard.

Lesson 11.3 (pp. 732–734)

11. $\sqrt{6 - 2x} + 12 = 21$

$\sqrt{6 - 2x} = 9$

$6 - 2x = 81$

$-2x = 75$

$x = -\frac{75}{2}$, or $-37\frac{1}{2}$

37. Substitute 20 for y in the given function.

$\sqrt{18x + 272} = 20$

$18x + 272 = 400$

$18x = 128$

$x = \frac{128}{18}$, or about 7.1

So, the annual banana consumption in the United States reached 20 pounds per person in the year 1970 + 7, or 1977.

Lesson 11.4 (pp. 740–742)

9. $a^2 + b^2 = c^2$

$8^2 + 12^2 = c^2$ Substitute 8 for a and 12 for b.

$208 = c^2$

$\sqrt{208} = c$ Positive square root only.

$4\sqrt{13} = c$

23. Check to see if $a^2 + b^2 = c^2$ when $a = 2$, $b = 3$, and $c = 4$.

$2^2 + 3^2 \stackrel{?}{=} 4^2$

$4 + 9 \stackrel{?}{=} 16$

$13 \neq 16$ Not a right triangle

35. Check to see if $a^2 + b^2 = c^2$ when $a = 87$, $b = 173$, and $c = 190$.

$87^2 + 173^2 \stackrel{?}{=} 190^2$

$7569 + 29{,}929 \stackrel{?}{=} 36{,}100$

$37498 \neq 36100$

So, the triangle is not a right triangle. The sum of the squares of the lengths of the two shorter sides is not equal to the square of the length of the longest side.

Lesson 11.5 (pp. 747–750)

7. Let $(x_1, y_1) = (-4, 1)$ and $(x_2, y_2) = (3, -1)$.

$d = \sqrt{(x_2 - x_1)^2 + (y_2 - y_1)^2}$

$= \sqrt{(3 - (-4))^2 + (-1 - 1)^2}$

$= \sqrt{7^2 + (-2)^2} = \sqrt{53}$

23. Let $(x_1, y_1) = (6, -3)$ and $(x_2, y_2) = (4, -7)$.

$\left(\frac{x_1 + x_2}{2}, \frac{y_1 + y_2}{2}\right) = \left(\frac{6 + 4}{2}, \frac{-3 + (-7)}{2}\right) = (5, -5)$

49. a. The coordinates of the anchor are (2, 3), the coordinates of the sword are (9, 2), and the coordinates of the cup are (8, 5).

Distance between the anchor and sword: Let $(x_1, y_1) = (2, 3)$ and $(x_2, y_2) = (9, 2)$.

$d = \sqrt{(9 - 2)^2 + (2 - 3)^2}$

$= \sqrt{7^2 + (-1)^2} = \sqrt{50}$

Distance between the anchor and cup: Let $(x_1, y_1) = (2, 3)$ and $(x_2, y_2) = (8, 5)$.

$d = \sqrt{(8 - 2)^2 + (5 - 3)^2}$

$= \sqrt{6^2 + (2)^2} = \sqrt{40}$

Since $\sqrt{40} < \sqrt{50}$, the anchor and the cup are closer together.

b. By examining the survey grid, the belt buckle and the sword are closest together; they are 3 units, or 150 feet, apart.

Again, by examining the survey grid, the two objects farthest apart are either the anchor and cup or the anchor and sword. The result in part (a) shows that the anchor and the sword are farthest apart; they are $\sqrt{50}$ units, or $50\sqrt{50} \approx 354$ feet, apart.

WORKED-OUT SOLUTIONS

WS27

Chapter 12

Lesson 12.1 (pp. 769–772)

17. Make a table by choosing several integer values of x and finding the values of y. Notice that x cannot be 0, and that y will never be 0.

x	−7	−5	−2	−1	0	1	2	5	7
y	1	1.4	3.5	7	—	−7	−3.5	−1.4	−1

Plot the points (x, y) from the table.

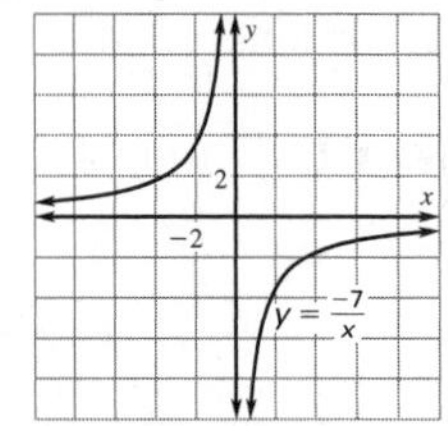

Connect the points in Quadrant II by drawing a smooth curve through them. Draw a separate curve though the points in Quadrant IV.

33. Because y varies inversely with x, the equation has the form $y = \frac{a}{x}$. Use the fact that $x = -22$ when $y = -6$ to find the value of a.

$-6 = \frac{a}{-22}$, so $a = -6(-22)$, or 132

An equation that relates x and y is $y = \frac{132}{x}$.

When $x = 2$, $y = \frac{132}{2}$, or 66.

57. a. An inverse variation equation can be used to model the data if each pair of points (ℓ, f) fits the same equation. Use $f = \frac{a}{\ell}$ to test the data.

For (42.1, 523): $523 = \frac{a}{42.1}$, so $a \approx 22{,}000$

For (37.5, 587): $587 = \frac{a}{37.5}$, so $a \approx 22{,}000$

For (33.4, 659): $659 = \frac{a}{33.4}$, so $a \approx 22{,}000$

For (31.5, 698): $698 = \frac{a}{31.5}$, so $a \approx 22{,}000$

Since the value of a is about the same for each pairing, the inverse equation $f = \frac{22{,}000}{\ell}$ can be used to model the data.

To graph $f = \frac{22{,}000}{\ell}$, make a table of values, plot the points (ℓ, f), and then draw a smooth curve through them. Use only positive values for ℓ since the length of a string cannot be negative.

ℓ	25	50	75	100
f	880	440	293.3	220

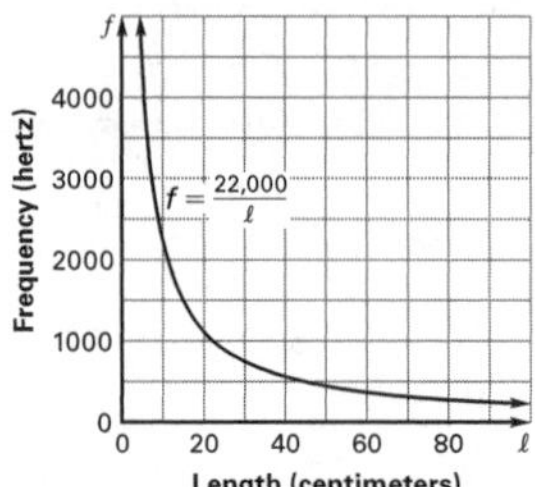

b. Use the equation found in part (a) with $\ell = 29.4$.

$f = \frac{22{,}000}{29.4} \approx 748.3$

The frequency is about 748 hertz.

c. The frequency increases as the length of the string decreases. Yes, the length in part (b), 29.4 centimeters, is shorter than those in the table, but it has the greatest frequency.

Lesson 12.2 (pp. 779–782)

7. Make a table of values for x and y.

x	$-\frac{1}{4}$	$-\frac{1}{2}$	0	$\frac{1}{4}$	$\frac{1}{2}$
y	1	$\frac{1}{2}$	—	−1	$-\frac{1}{2}$

Plot the points (x, y) from the table. Connect the points in Quadrant II by drawing a smooth curve through them. Draw a separate curve though the points in Quadrant IV.

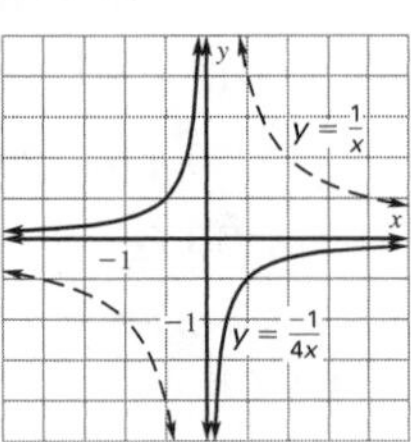

The graph of $y = \frac{-1}{4x}$ is a vertical shrink with a reflection in the x-axis of the graph of $y = \frac{1}{x}$.

WS28

21. The vertical asymptote of the graph is $x = -7$ and the horizontal asymptote is $y = 5$. Plot several points on each side of the vertical asymptote, such as $(-9, 3)$, $(-8, 1)$, $(-5, 7)$, and $(-3, 6)$. Draw the two branches of the graph that pass through the plotted points and approach the asymptotes.

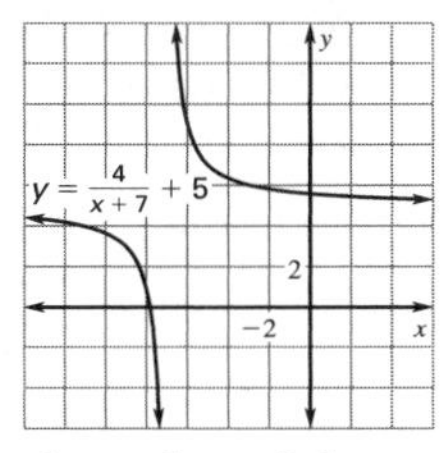

41. a. Use a verbal model to write an equation.

Average cost (dollars) = Total cost (dollars) ÷ (Number of additional rentals + 2)

$C = 22 \div (r + 2)$, or $C = \dfrac{22}{r + 2}$

b.

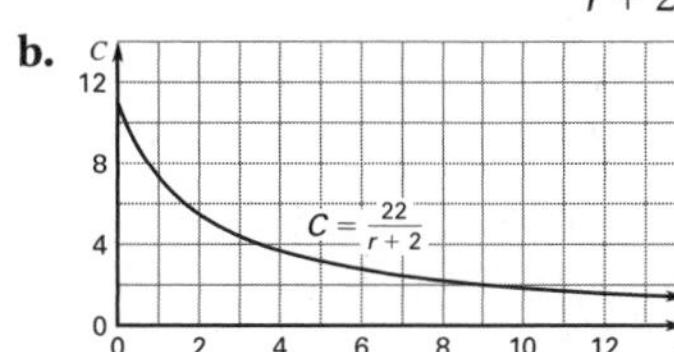

The graph shows that as the number of rentals increases, the average cost per rental decreases.

From the graph, the number of additional rentals needed per month so that the average cost is \$1.50 per rental is 13 additional rentals.

Lesson 12.3 (pp. 788–791)

7.

$$\begin{array}{r} 3v + 5 \\ v - 2\overline{)3v^2 - v - 10} \\ \underline{3v^2 - 6v} \\ 5v - 10 \\ \underline{5v - 10} \\ 0 \end{array}$$

25. Rewrite the function in the form $y = \dfrac{a}{x - h} + k$.

$$\begin{array}{r} 2 \\ x - 1\overline{)2x - 4} \\ \underline{2x - 2} \\ -2 \end{array}$$

So, $y = \dfrac{-2}{x - 1} + 2$.

The asymptotes of the graph can be identified from the equation. The vertical asymptote is $x = 1$ and the horizontal asymptote is $y = 2$. Plot several points on each side of the vertical asymptote, such as $(-1, 3)$, $(0, 4)$, $(2, 0)$, and $(3, 1)$. Draw the two branches of the graph.

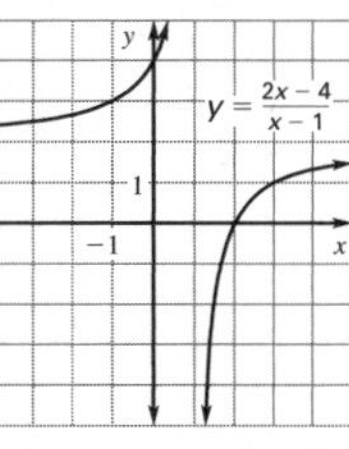

45. a. Since t is defined as the time for 1000 minutes or more, the domain of the function is $t \geq 1000$. The average cost C is found by adding the monthly fee to the product of the number of minutes over 1000 and the per-minute charge for those minutes, and then dividing that sum by the total number of minutes of use. The equation is $C = \dfrac{40 + 0.40(t - 1000)}{t}$, or $C = \dfrac{0.4t - 360}{t}$, where $t \geq 1000$.

b. Choose values of $t \geq 1000$.

t	1000	1100	1200	1300	1400	1500
C	0.04	0.073	0.10	0.123	0.143	0.16

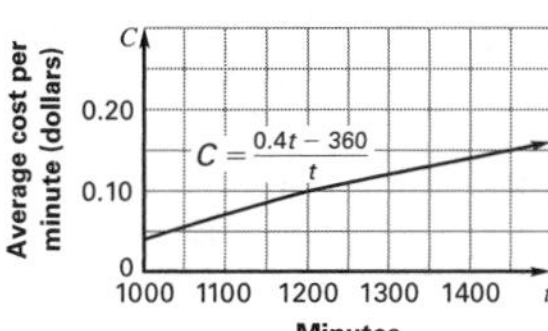

The average cost per minute increases as the number of minutes over 1000 increases.

c. From the graph you can see that the number of minutes used is about 1030 minutes if the average cost is \$.05 per minute.

Lesson 12.4 (pp. 797–800)

9. The expression $\dfrac{-3}{2p^2 - p}$ is undefined when $2p^2 - p = 0$.

$2p^2 - p = 0$

$p(2p - 1) = 0$

$p = 0 \quad \text{or} \quad 2p - 1 = 0$

$p = \dfrac{1}{2}$

The excluded values are 0 and $\dfrac{1}{2}$.

23. $\dfrac{h+3}{h^2-h-12} = \dfrac{h+3}{(h-4)(h+3)}$

$= \dfrac{\cancel{h+3}}{(h-4)\cancel{(h+3)}}$

$= \dfrac{1}{h-4}$

The excluded values are 4 and −3.

43. The percent of wood houses can be found by using the formula $p = \frac{W}{H}$.

$p = \dfrac{-20{,}200x + 366{,}000}{34{,}500x + 913{,}000} = \dfrac{-202x + 3660}{345x + 9130}$

To determine how the percent changed during the period 1990–2002, evaluate the function for several values of x.

For 1990, $x = 0$: $\dfrac{-202(0) + 3660}{345(0) + 9130} = \dfrac{3660}{9130} \approx 0.40$

In 1990, about 40% of new single-family houses were wood houses.

For 1994, $x = 4$: $\dfrac{-202(4) + 3660}{345(4) + 9130} = \dfrac{2852}{10{,}510} \approx 0.27$

In 1994, about 27% of new single-family houses were wood houses.

For 1998, $x = 8$: $\dfrac{-202(8) + 3660}{345(8) + 9130} = \dfrac{2044}{11{,}890} \approx 0.17$

In 1998, about 17% of new single-family houses were wood houses.

For 2002, $x = 12$:
$\dfrac{-202(12) + 3660}{345(12) + 9130} = \dfrac{1236}{13{,}270} \approx 0.09$

In 2002, about 9% of new single-family houses were wood houses.

The percent of wood houses decreased steadily from 1990 to 2002.

Lesson 12.5 (pp. 806–809)

5. $\dfrac{v^2 + v - 12}{5v + 10} \cdot \dfrac{-v - 2}{v^2 + 5v + 4}$

$= \dfrac{(v^2 + v - 12)(-v - 2)}{(5v + 10)(v^2 + 5v + 4)}$

$= \dfrac{\cancel{(v+4)}(v-3)(-1)\cancel{(v+2)}}{5\cancel{(v+2)}\cancel{(v+4)}(v+1)}$

$= \dfrac{-(v-3)}{5(v+1)}$

15. $\dfrac{2w^2 + 5w}{w^2 - 81} \div \dfrac{w^2}{w + 9} = \dfrac{2w^2 + 5w}{w^2 - 81} \cdot \dfrac{w + 9}{w^2}$

$= \dfrac{(2w^2 + 5w)(w + 9)}{(w^2 - 81)(w^2)}$

$= \dfrac{\cancel{(w)}(2w + 5)\cancel{(w+9)}}{\cancel{(w+9)}(w - 9)\cancel{(w)}(w)}$

$= \dfrac{2w + 5}{w(w - 9)}$

35. a. Use the formula $R = Y \div A$.

$R = \dfrac{860 + 1800x}{1 + 0.024x} \div \dfrac{230 + 380x}{1 + 0.014x}$

$= \dfrac{860 + 1800x}{1 + 0.024x} \cdot \dfrac{1 + 0.014x}{230 + 380x}$

$= \dfrac{(860 + 1800x)(1 + 0.014x)}{(1 + 0.024x)(230 + 380x)}$

$= \dfrac{\cancel{(10)}(86 + 180x)(1 + 0.014x)}{(1 + 0.024x)\cancel{(10)}(23 + 38x)}$

$= \dfrac{(86 + 180x)(1 + 0.014x)}{(1 + 0.024x)(23 + 38x)}$

b.

x	0	1	2	3	4	5	6
R	3.74	4.32	4.42	4.44	4.44	4.42	4.40

x	7	8	9	10	11	12
R	4.38	4.35	4.33	4.30	4.28	4.25

Smith's career rushing average increased for the first several years, and then began to decrease.

Lesson 12.6 (pp. 816–819)

7. $\dfrac{b}{b-3} + \dfrac{b+1}{b-3} = \dfrac{b+b+1}{b-3} = \dfrac{2b+1}{b-3}$

29. $\dfrac{2j}{j^2 - 1} + \dfrac{j - 1}{j^2 - 7j + 6}$

$= \dfrac{2j}{(j-1)(j+1)} + \dfrac{j-1}{(j-1)(j-6)}$

$= \dfrac{2j(j-6)}{(j-1)(j+1)(j-6)} + \dfrac{(j-1(j+1)}{(j-1)(j-6)(j+1)}$

$= \dfrac{2j(j-6) + (j-1)(j+1)}{(j-1)(j+1)(j-6)}$

$= \dfrac{2j^2 - 12j + j^2 - 1}{(j-1)(j+1)(j-6)}$

$= \dfrac{3j^2 - 12j - 1}{(j-1)(j+1)(j-6)}$

WORKED-OUT SOLUTIONS

45. a. For $A \le 50$: $\frac{2A^2}{3} + \frac{200A}{3} = \frac{2A^2 + 200A}{3}$

For $A > 50$, $\frac{7A^2}{150} + (125A - 1367)$

$$= \frac{7A^2}{150} + \frac{150(125A - 1367)}{150}$$

$$= \frac{7A^2 + 150(125A - 1367)}{150}$$

$$= \frac{7A^2 + 18{,}750A - 205{,}050}{150}$$

b. For $A = 30$ ft^2, use the formula for $A \le 50$:

$$W = \frac{2(30)^2 + 200(30)}{3} = \frac{7800}{3} = 2600$$

The minimum weight this elevator must hold is 2600 pounds.

For $A = 60$ ft^2, use the formula for $A > 50$:

$$W = \frac{7(60)^2 + 18{,}750(60) - 205{,}050}{150}$$

$$= \frac{945{,}150}{150} = 6301$$

The minimum weight this elevator must hold is 6301 pounds.

Lesson 12.7 (pp. 823–826)

7.

$$\frac{2m}{m+4} = \frac{3}{m-1}$$

$$2m^2 - 2m = 3m + 12$$

$$2m^2 - 5m - 12 = 0$$

$$(2m + 3)(m - 4) = 0$$

$2m + 3 = 0$ *or* $m - 4 = 0$

$m = -1\frac{1}{2}$ *or* $m = 4$

15.

$$\frac{z}{z+7} - 3 = \frac{-1}{z+7}$$

$$\frac{z}{z+7} \cdot (z+7) - 3(z+7) = \frac{-1}{z+7} \cdot (z+7)$$

$$\frac{z(z+7)}{z+7} - 3(z+7) = \frac{-1(z+7)}{z+7}$$

$$z - 3z - 21 = -1$$

$$-2z = 20$$

$$z = -10$$

33. Let w be the number of cups of water needed.

$$\frac{\text{Cups of water in cleaning solution} + \text{Cups of water needed}}{\text{Cups of cleaning solution} + \text{Cups of water needed}} = \text{Desired fraction of water in mixture}$$

$$\frac{7 + w}{9 + w} = \frac{5}{6}$$

$$(7 + w)6 = (9 + w)5$$

$$42 + 6w = 45 + 5w$$

$$w = 3$$

You need to add 3 cups of water to the cleaning solution.

Chapter 13

Lesson 13.1 (pp. 846–848)

3. Use a tree diagram to find the possible outcomes in the sample space.

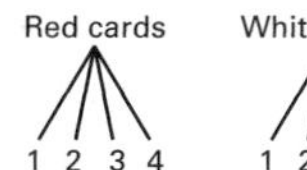

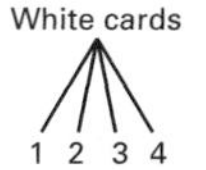

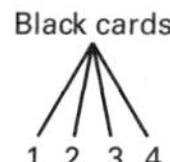

The sample space has 12 possible outcomes. The outcomes are: Red 1, Red 2, Red 3, Red 4, White 1, White 2, White 3, White 4, Black 1, Black 2, Black 3, Black 4.

21. Since there are 15 girls and 12 boys, there are a total of 27 students. So there are 27 possible outcomes.

$$P(\text{boy}) = \frac{\text{Number of boys}}{\text{Total number of students}} = \frac{12}{27} = \frac{4}{9}$$

Odds in favor of choosing a boy

$$= \frac{\text{Number of boys}}{\text{Number of girls}} = \frac{12}{15} = \frac{4}{5}$$

Sample answer: The probability and odds of choosing a boy are related because they each compare the number of favorable outcomes to another number. The probability of choosing a boy compares the number of boys to the total number of outcomes possible, while the odds of choosing a boy compare the number of boys to the total number of outcomes less the number of boys.

WORKED-OUT SOLUTIONS

Lesson 13.2 (pp. 853–855)

21. $_7P_3 = \frac{7!}{(7-3)!} = \frac{7!}{4!} = \frac{7 \cdot 6 \cdot 5 \cdot \cancel{4!}}{\cancel{4!}} = 210$

35. a. The total number of possible outcomes for the order on the first day is the number of permutations of the 4 student presenters on that day: $_4P_4 = 4!$.

The number of favorable outcomes (being chosen to be the first or second presenter) is the number of permutations of the 3 other presenters, given that you are chosen to be the first or second presenter. This is $_3P_3 = 3!$ if you are the first presenter and also $_3P_3 = 3!$ if you are the second presenter.

P(1st or 2nd presenter)
$= P$(1st presenter) $+ P$(2nd presenter)

$= \frac{3!}{4!} + \frac{3!}{4!} = \frac{1}{4} + \frac{1}{4}$, or $\frac{1}{2}$

The probability that you are the first or the second presenter is $\frac{1}{2}$.

b. The number of possible outcomes is still 4!. The number of favorable outcomes is again $_3P_3 = 3!$ for you being the second presenter and $_3P_3 = 3!$ for you being the third presenter.

P(2nd or 3rd presenter)
$= P$(2nd presenter) $+ P$(3rd presenter)

$= \frac{3!}{4!} + \frac{3!}{4!} = \frac{1}{4} + \frac{1}{4}$, or $\frac{1}{2}$

The probability that you are the second or the third presenter is $\frac{1}{2}$.

This answer is the same as the answer in part (a).

Lesson 13.3 (pp. 858–859)

7. $_8C_5 = \frac{8!}{(8-5)!5!} = \frac{8!}{3!5!} = \frac{8 \cdot 7 \cdot 6 \cdot \cancel{5!}}{3! \cdot \cancel{5!}} = 56$

25. a. The number of possible outcomes is the number of combinations of the 9 contestants taken 6 at a time, or $_9C_6$, because the order in which the contestants are chosen is not important.

$_9C_6 = \frac{9!}{(9-6)!6!} = \frac{9!}{3!6!} = \frac{9 \cdot 8 \cdot 7 \cdot \cancel{6!}}{3! \cdot \cancel{6!}} = 84$

There are 84 possible combinations of 6 players from the group of eligible contestants.

b. Find the number of favorable outcomes, those where you and your two friends are 3 of the 6 contestants selected to play. The order of the selections is not important. The favorable outcomes are those where only 3 of the other 6 eligible contestants are chosen. So the number of favorable combinations is $_6C_3 = 20$. Therefore, the probability that you and your friends are chosen is $\frac{20}{84}$, or $\frac{5}{21}$.

Lesson 13.4 (pp. 864–867)

5. Rolling an odd number on a number cube and rolling a number less than 5 are overlapping events as shown in the diagram. There are two numbers less than 5 that are odd, 1 and 3.

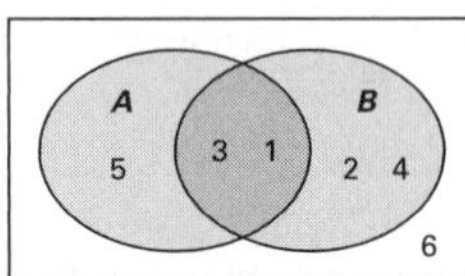

The probability of rolling an odd number is $\frac{3}{6} = \frac{1}{2}$, the probability of rolling a number less than 5 is $\frac{4}{6} = \frac{2}{3}$, and the probability of rolling a number that is both odd and less than 5 is $\frac{2}{6} = \frac{1}{3}$.

Using the formula for finding the probability of overlapping events,

$P(A \text{ or } B) = P(A) + P(B) - P(A \text{ and } B)$
$= \frac{3}{6} + \frac{4}{6} - \frac{2}{6} = \frac{5}{6}$

23. Let Event A be using a flipper to forage for food and let Event B be using the right flipper if the flipper wave technique is used. These two events are dependent.

$P(A) = 70\% = 0.7$ and
$P(B \text{ given } A) = 89\% = 0.89$

Using the formula for finding the probability of dependent events,

$P(A \text{ and } B) = P(A) \cdot P(B \text{ given } A)$
$= 0.7 \cdot 0.89 = 0.623$, or 62.3%

The probability that a walrus foraging for food uses a flipper and that it is the right flipper is 62.3%.

WS32

Lesson 13.5 (pp. 873–874)

3. The population is all persons who dine at the restaurant. Because the diners ultimately decide whether or not to take part in the survey by mailing their comment cards, this is a self-selected sample.

15. Ballots collected at Wrigley Field are not necessarily representative of the opinions of all Chicago Cubs fans. *Sample answer:* Only some of the Chicago Cubs' fans are able to attend games, and those who attend games may have different player preferences than those who do not attend games.

Lesson 13.6 (pp. 877–878)

7. Mean:

$$\bar{x} = \frac{5.52 + 5.44 + 3.60 + 5.76 + 3.80 + 7.22}{6}$$

$$= \frac{31.34}{6} = 5.2233...$$

So, the mean of the data is $5.22\overline{3}$.

Median: The ordered list of numbers is: 3.60, 3.80, 5.44, 5.52, 5.76, 7.22. There are two middle values, 5.44 and 5.52. Therefore, the median is $\frac{5.44 + 5.52}{2} = 5.48$.

Each data value appears just once, so there is no mode.

19. a. The range of the pumpkin weights is the difference of the greatest value and the least value; $24 - 5 = 19$ pounds.

b. Mean: $\bar{x} =$

$$\frac{22 + 21 + 24 + 24 + 5 + 24 + 5 + 23 + 24 + 24}{10}$$

$$= \frac{196}{10} = 19.6$$

The mean of the pumpkin weights is 19.6 pounds.

Median: The ordered list of weights is: 5, 5, 21, 22, 23, 24, 24, 24, 24, 24. There are two middle values, 23 and 24. So, the median is 23.5 pounds.

Mode: The weight that occurs most frequently is 24 pounds.

c. The median best represents the data. *Sample answer:* The mode is the greatest data value and the mean is less than 8 of the 10 data values.

Lesson 13.7 (pp. 883–885)

3. First, separate the data into stems and leaves.

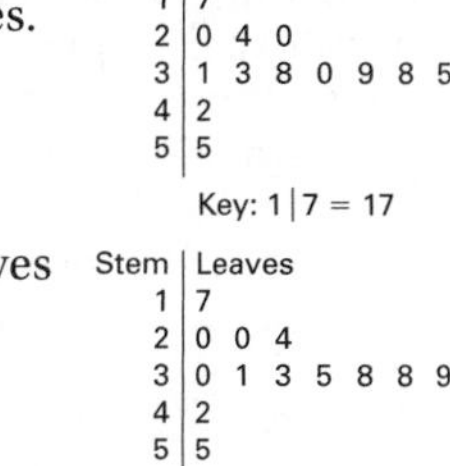

Stem	Leaves
1	7
2	0 4 0
3	1 3 8 0 9 8 5
4	2
5	5

Key: 1 | 7 = 17

Now rewrite the leaves in increasing order.

Stem	Leaves
1	7
2	0 0 4
3	0 1 3 5 8 8 9
4	2
5	5

Key: 1 | 7 = 17

19. a. Draw the bars of the histogram using the intervals from the frequency table.

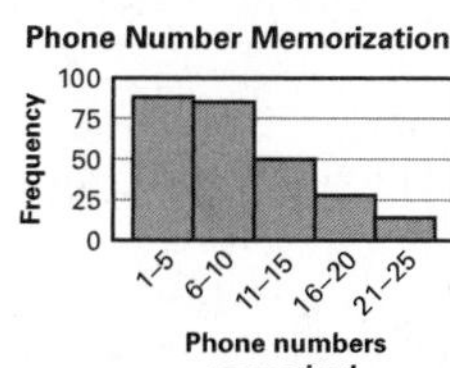

b. Use the table to determine the total number of people surveyed: $88 + 85 + 50 + 28 + 14 = 265$.

Determine the number of favorable outcomes. This number is the sum of the number of people in the 11–15 range, the 16–20 range, and the 21–25 range.

$$P(11\text{–}25) = \frac{\text{Number of favorable outcomes}}{\text{Total number of outcomes}}$$

$$= \frac{50 + 28 + 14}{265} = \frac{92}{265}$$

Lesson 13.8 (pp. 889–892)

3. Write the data in order from least to greatest. Find the median and the quartiles.

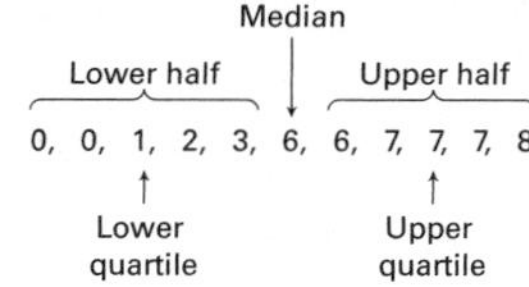

WORKED-OUT SOLUTIONS

Plot the median, the quartiles, the maximum value, and the minimum value below a number line. Draw a box from the lower quartile to the upper quartile. Draw a vertical line through the median. Draw a line segment from the side of the box to the maximum value and another from the other side of the box to the minimum value.

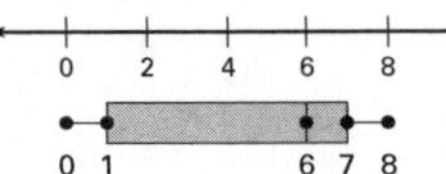

17. a. Order the data, and then find the median and the quartiles.

lower quartile: $\frac{\$38.4 + \$49.9}{2} = \$44.15$

median: $52.4

upper quartile: $\frac{\$107.0 + \$118.2}{2} = \$112.60$

Use the median, the quartiles, the maximum value, and the minimum value to draw the box-and-whisker plot.

30 60 90 120 150 180

35.8 44.15 52.4 112.6 153.1

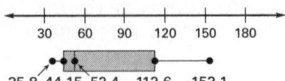

b. To check if any of the data are outliers, find the inner quartile range: $112.6 - 44.15 = 68.45$. An outlier would be any value greater than $1.5(68.45) + 112.6 = 215.275$ or less than $44.15 - 1.5(68.45) = -58.525$. Since all the data values are within these two values, there are no outliers. So, none of the states had retail sales that can be considered outliers.

Selected Answers

Chapter 1

1.1 Skill Practice (pp. 5–6) **1.** exponent: 12, base: 6 **3.** 60 **5.** 12 **7.** 12 **9.** 3 **11.** 10 **13.** $\frac{1}{3}$ **17.** seven to the third power, $7 \cdot 7 \cdot 7$ **19.** three tenths to the fourth power, $0.3 \cdot 0.3 \cdot 0.3 \cdot 0.3$ **21.** n to the seventh power, $n \cdot n \cdot n \cdot n \cdot n \cdot n \cdot n$ **23.** t to the fourth power, $t \cdot t \cdot t \cdot t$ **25.** The base was used as the exponent and the exponent was used as the base; $5^4 = 5 \cdot 5 \cdot 5 \cdot 5 = 625$. **27.** 100 **29.** 1331 **31.** 243 **33.** 1296 **35.** $\frac{27}{125}$ **37.** $\frac{1}{216}$ **39.** 1.21 **41.** 40.5 **43.** 9.6

1.1 Problem Solving (pp. 6–7) **49.** 162.5 cm **51. a.** 12 in. **b.** 144 in.^{2} **53.** New England Patriots

1.2 Skill Practice (pp. 10–11) **1.** Square 4. **3.** 8 **5.** 14 **7.** $3\frac{3}{5}$ **9.** $63\frac{3}{4}$ **11.** 21 **13.** 73.5 **15.** $12\frac{1}{2}$ **17.** 48 **21.** $\frac{1}{2}$ was multiplied by 6 before squaring 6; $20 - \frac{1}{2} \cdot 6^2 = 20 - \frac{1}{2} \cdot 36 = 20 - 18 = 2$. **23.** 29 **25.** 126 **27.** 0.75 **29.** 3 **33.** $(2 \times 2 + 3)^2 - (4 + 3) \times 5$

1.2 Problem Solving (pp. 11–12) **35. a.** \$22.87 **b.** \$2.13 **37.** *Sample answer:* $(3 \times 4) + 5$ **39. a.** \$380, \$237.99; \$142.01 **b.** *Sample answer:* You could write an expression showing the difference of your income and expenses as $P = 10s - (4.50m + 12.99)$.

1.2 Graphing Calculator Activity (p. 13) **1.** 5 **3.** 0.429 **5.** 0.188 **7.** 40.9 BMI units

1.3 Skill Practice (pp. 18–19) **1.** rate **3.** $x + 8$ **5.** $\frac{1}{2}m$ **7.** $7 - n$ **9.** $\frac{2t}{12}$ **11.** $2k - 7$ **15.** $4v$ **17.** $\frac{16}{p}$ **19.** $7 - d$ **21.** $12y$ **23.** 1.5 pints per serving **25.** \$6.80 per share **27.** Feet should cancel out; \$54. **29.** \$19.50 for 1 h

1.3 Problem Solving (pp. 19–20) **31.** $19.95t + 3$; \$102.75 **33. a.** \$.055, \$.06 **b.** 48 oz container **c.** \$.96 **35.** \$500 **37. a.** $12g + h + \frac{1}{4}c$ **b.** 247; 376.75; 242

1.4 Skill Practice (pp. 24–25) **1.** *Sample answer:* $3x + 5 = 20$ **3.** $42 + n = 51$ **5.** $9 - \frac{t}{6} = 5$ **7.** $9(t + 5) < 6$ **9.** $8 < b + 3 < 12$ **11.** $10 < t - 7 < 20$ **13.** $p \geq 12.99$ **15.** The wrong inequality symbol is used; $\frac{t}{4.2} \leq 15$. **17.** solution **19.** not a solution **21.** not a solution **23.** solution **25.** solution **27.** not a solution **29.** 5 **31.** 12 **33.** 9 **35.** $3x - 2 = x + 5$; solution

1.4 Problem Solving (pp. 25–26) **39.** 7.5 mi **41.** 167 h **43.** \$100 **45. a.** $6r + 5(10 - r) \geq 55$ **b.** Yes; you will earn \$30 running errands and \$25 walking dogs; $30 + 25 = 55$. **c.** Yes; if you work 10 hours running errands, you will earn \$60. You will not meet your goal if you work all 10 hours walking dogs.

1.5 Skill Practice (p. 31) **1.** *Sample answer:* $d = rt$ **3.** You know how many collars you've made, how much you have spent to make them, and how much money you want to make. You need to find what to charge for each collar so you make \$90. **5.** You know the temperature in Rome and the temperature in Dallas. You know the formula to convert Fahrenheit temperatures to Celsius temperatures. You need to find the higher temperature. **7.** The formula for perimeter should be used, not area; $P = 2\ell + 2w$; $P = 2(200) + 2(150) = 700$; \$10(700) = \$7000. **9.** $P = I - E$

1.5 Problem Solving (pp. 32–33) **15.** 46.25 in.^{2} **17.** 2 water bottles **19. a.** 960 ft **b.** 480 ft **21. a.**

Room size (feet)	1 by 1	2 by 2	3 by 3	4 by 4	5 by 5
Remaining area (square feet)	431	428	423	416	407

b. $1 \leq s \leq 5$; 5 ft

1.5 Problem Solving Workshop (p. 34)

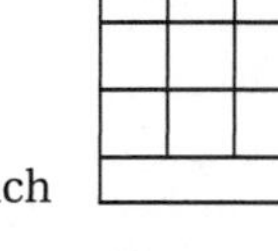

1. 9 pieces of cake; Equation: Let c be the number of pieces of cake; $9c = 99$, $c = 11$. Diagram: Draw a diagram of a 9 inch by 11 inch pan and cut the cake into 3 inch by 3 inch pieces. From the diagram you see that you can cut 9 such pieces. The diagram shows that you cannot actually cut 11 square pieces because of the shape of the pan. **3.** The equation should be $3x + 6 = 12$ because there are only 3 spaces between the 4 floats; $3(2) + 6 = 12$.

1.6 Skill Practice (pp. 38–39) **1.** input; output **3.** domain: 0, 1, 2, and 3, range: 5, 7, 15, and 44 **5.** domain: 6, 12, 21, and 42, range: 5, 7, 10, and 17 **7.** not a function **9.** The pairing is a function. Each input is paired with only one output.

SELECTED ANSWERS

11. *Sample:* Input 0, 1, 2, 3, 4, 5 → Output 5, 6, 7, 9, 10

Input	Output
0	5
1	6
2	7
3	7
4	9
5	10

15.

Input	4	5	7	8	12
Output	7.5	8.5	10.5	11.5	15.5

range: 7.5, 8.5, 10.5, 11.5, and 15.5

17.

Input	4	6	9	11
Output	5	6	7.5	8.5

range: 5, 6, 7.5, and 8.5

19.

Input	0	2	4	6
Output	$\frac{1}{2}$	1	$1\frac{1}{2}$	2

range: $\frac{1}{2}$, 1, $1\frac{1}{2}$, and 2

21. $y = x - 8$

1.6 Problem Solving (pp. 39–40) **23. a.** the number of quarters left; the number of quarters used **b.** $y = 10 - x$; domain: 0, 1, 2, 3, 4, 5, 6, 7, 8, 9, and 10

c.

Input	0	1	2	3	4	5	6	7	8	9	10
Output	10	9	8	7	6	5	4	3	2	1	0

range: 0, 1, 2, 3, 4, 5, 6, 7, 8, 9, and 10

25. $y = 100 + 20m$; independent variable: m, the number of months; dependent variable: y, the amount of money saved; domain: $m > 0$, range: $y \geq 100$; $340

27. a.

2	3	4	5
A, B, C	D, E, F	G, H, I	J, K, L

6	7	8	9
M, N, O	P, Q, R, S	T, U, V	W, X, Y, Z

No; because there is more than one output for each input.

b.

A	B	C	D	E	F	G	H	I	J	K	L
2	2	2	3	3	3	4	4	4	5	5	5

M	N	O	P	Q	R	S	T	U	V	W	X	Y	Z
6	6	6	7	7	7	7	8	8	8	9	9	9	9

Yes; because there is only one output for each input.

1.6 Graphing Calculator Activity (p. 41) **1.** 50°F; scroll down until you see the output 10, look to see that the input is 50.

3.

Input	0	1	2	3
Output	5	5.75	6.5	7.25

5.

Input	1	2	3	4
Output	7	14.5	22	29.5

1.7 Skill Practice (pp. 46–47) **1.** domain; range

3.

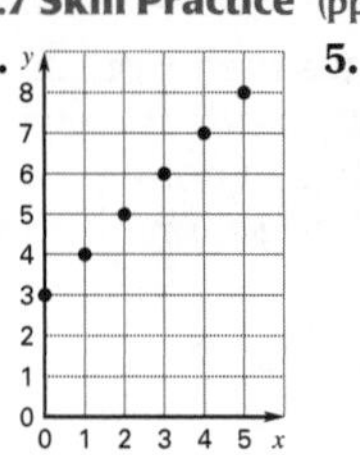

5.

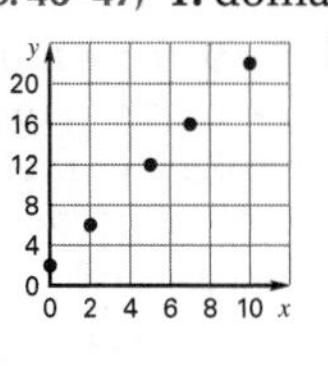

7.

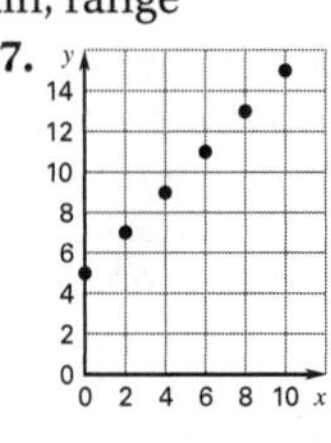

9. The domain and range are graphed backwards.

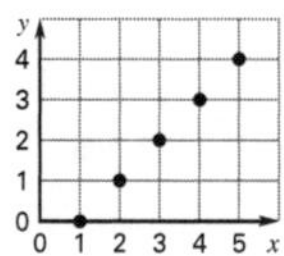

11. $y = 2x - 2$; domain: 1, 2, 3, and 4, range: 0, 2, 4, and 6

1.7 Problem Solving (pp. 47–48)

15.

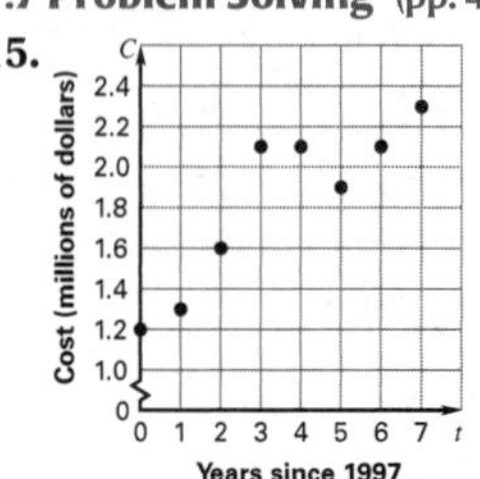

17.

Years since 1984	Voters	Voters (millions)
0	92,652,680	93
4	91,594,693	92
8	104,405,155	104
12	96,456,345	96
16	105,586,274	106

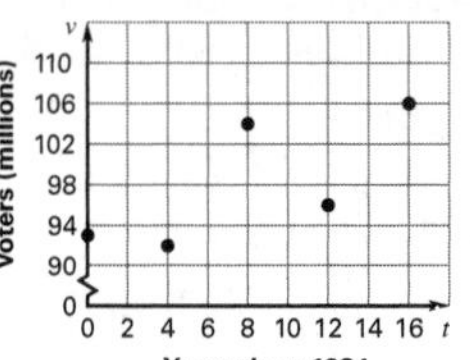

19. a. increases **b.** Yes; 27.5 grams is between the mass of an egg that is just under 38 millimeters long and an egg that is just over 38 millimeters long.

SELECTED ANSWERS

Extension (p. 50) **1.** function **3.** not a function **5.** function **7.** Not a function. *Sample answer:* There could be many students whose first names have 4 letters, for instance, but their last names could all have a different number of letters. **9.** Function; for each of your birthdays, you have only one height.

Chapter Review (pp. 53–56) **1.** 7, 12 **3.** algebraic expression **5.** 16 **7.** 10 **9.** 400 **11.** 25 in.^{2} **13.** 9 **15.** 8 **17.** $\frac{1}{3}$ **19.** 52 **21.** 18 **23.** $z - 5$ **25.** $3x^2$ **27.** $2.95n + 2.19$ **29.** $13 + t \geq 24$ **31.** solution **33.** 240 ft^2

35.

Input	10	12	15	20	21
Output	5	7	10	15	16

range: 5, 7, 10, 15, and 16

37. $y = x + 4$ **39.**

Chapter 2

2.1 Skill Practice (pp. 67–68) **1.** rational number **3.** Zero is in the set of whole numbers, but not in the set of positive integers. **5–13.** Check students' graphs. **5.** 7 **7.** −5 **9.** 5 **11.** −1 **13.** −2 **15.** 1.6: rational number, 1: whole number, integer, rational number, −4: integer, rational number, 0: whole number, integer, rational number; −4, 0, 1, 1.6 **17.** $-\frac{2}{3}$: rational number, −0.6: rational number, −1: integer, rational number, $\frac{1}{3}$: rational number; −1, $-\frac{2}{3}$, −0.6, $\frac{1}{3}$ **19.** 16: whole number, integer, rational number, −1.66: rational number, $\frac{5}{3}$: rational number, −1.6: rational number; −1.66, −1.6, $\frac{5}{3}$, 16 **21.** −4.99: rational number, 5: whole number, integer, rational number, $\frac{16}{3}$: rational number, −5.1: rational number; −5.1, −4.99, 5, $\frac{16}{3}$ **23.** −6, 6 **25.** 18, 18 **27.** −13.4, 13.4 **29.** 6.1, 6.1 **31.** $1\frac{1}{9}$, $1\frac{1}{9}$ **33.** $-\frac{3}{4}$, $\frac{3}{4}$ **35.** Hypothesis: a number is a positive integer, conclusion: the number is a whole number; true. **37.** Hypothesis: a number is positive, conclusion: its opposite is positive; false. *Sample answer:* The opposite of 2 is −2, a negative number. **41.** $-|-0.2|$ is a negative number. *Sample answer:* In the number $-|-0.2|$, remove both negative signs. **43.** 1 **45.** 1.75 **47.** 2.25 **49.** 1.5

2.1 Problem Solving (pp. 69–70) **53.** Fondo, Frink, Alamorio, Calexico, Date City **55.** −3.4; the absolute value of −3.4 is less than the absolute value of −3.8, so it is closer to 0, the exact pitch. **57. a.** 500 Hz **b.** The intensity decreases until 1000 Hz and then increases. **59. a.** Sun, Sirius, Canopus, Arcturus, Capella, Achernar; Canopus, Achernar, Arcturus, Capella, Sirius, Sun **b.** Rigel's apparent magnitude is greater than the Sun's apparent magnitude, so it is dimmer than the Sun; Rigel's absolute magnitude is less than the Sun's absolute magnitude, so it is brighter than the Sun. **c.** No. *Sample answer:* The apparent magnitude of Arcturus is less than the apparent magnitude of Achernar, but the absolute magnitude of Arcturus is greater than the absolute magnitude of Achernar.

Extension (p. 72) **1.** {1, 3, 5, 6, 7, 9}, {3, 9} **3.** {0, 1, 2, 3, 4, 5, 6, 7, 8, 9, 10}, ∅ **5.** R = {2, 4, 6, 8, 10}, f = {(1, 2), (2, 4), (3, 6), (4, 8), (5, 10)} **7.** R = {4, 8, 12, 16, 20}, f = {(1, 4), (5, 8), (9, 12), (13, 16), (17, 20)} **9.** the set of integers, ∅

2.2 Skill Practice (pp. 77–78) **1.** 0 **3.** −8 **5.** 6 **7.** −13 **9.** −6 **11.** −20 **13.** −4.5 **15.** 6.6 **17.** −15.2 **19.** $7\frac{1}{15}$ **21.** $1\frac{16}{45}$ **23.** $-20\frac{23}{24}$ **25.** The numbers have different signs, so their absolute values should have been subtracted, 17 + (−31) = −14. **27.** Associate property of addition **29.** Identity property of addition **31.** Commutative property of addition **33.** −49 **35.** 1.6 **37.** $5\frac{19}{60}$ **39.** −3 **41.** −9.5 **43.** $7\frac{23}{60}$ **45.** 0 **47.** 7.4 **49.** −(−18) + (−18); 0

2.2 Problem Solving (pp. 78–79) **53.** 7°F **55. a.** 1.5 diopters **b.** −3.75 diopters **c.** part (b) **57. a.** your friend **b.** No, if you score 2 double eagles, you will have the same score.

2.3 Skill Practice (pp. 82–83) **1.** −3 + (−6) **3.** 18 **5.** −8 **7.** 14.1 **9.** −25.8 **11.** $-\frac{1}{3}$ **13.** $\frac{3}{4}$ **15.** 8 was substituted for y instead of −8; 3 − (−8) + 2 = 3 + 8 + 2 = 13. **17.** 4.6 **19.** 10.6 **21.** 7.7 **23.** 7.6 **25.** 1.8 **27.** 107°F **29.** −1280 m **31.** 127.1 mi **33.** 8 **35.** −4.2 **37.** 16.4 **39.** *Sample answer:* You are overdrawn on your checking account by \$23. You write two more checks for \$14 and \$8. What is your balance?; −\$45

SELECTED ANSWERS

SELECTED ANSWERS

2.3 Problem Solving (pp. 83–84)
43. 14.6°C **45. a.** $d = t - 342$
b.

t	d
341.7	−0.3
343.8	1.8
340.9	−1.1
342.7	0.7

341.7 and 340.9; you can tell if $t - 342$ is negative.
47. a. 6°; 19° **b.** −4°

2.3 Spreadsheet Activity (p. 85) **1.** 6 hand grips **3.** 4.902; the difference in the lengths has the smallest absolute value.

2.4 Skill Practice (pp. 91–92) **1.** 1 **3.** −28 **5.** 90 **7.** −36 **9.** 7 **11.** −43.89 **13.** −40 **15.** −80 **17.** $2\frac{2}{5}$ **19.** Multiplicative property of zero **21.** Identity property of multiplication **23.** Associative property of multiplication **25.** Identity property of multiplication **27.** Multiplicative property of −1 **29.** $18x$; $18x$, same signs, product is positive. **31.** $-84z$; $12(-7z)$, product of −2 and −6 is 12; $[12 \cdot (-7)]z$, associative property of multiplication; $-84(z)$, product of 12 and −7 is −84; $-84z$, multiply. **33.** $-40c$; $2(4)(-5c)$, product of $-\frac{1}{5}$ and −10 is 2; $8(-5c)$, product of 2 and 4 is 8; $[8 \cdot (-5)]c$, associative property of multiplication; $-40(c)$, product of 8 and −5 is −40; $-40c$, multiply. **35.** $16.8r^2$; $[-6r \cdot (-2.8)]r$, associative property of multiplication; $[-6 \cdot (-2.8) \cdot r]r$, commutative property of multiplication; $(16.8r)r$, product of −6 and −2.8 is 16.8; $16.8(r \cdot r)$, associative property of multiplication; $16.8r^2$, multiply **37.** −0.4 **39.** −12.6 **41.** −6.6 **43.** $-1(7) = -7$, not 7; $-1(7)(-3)(-2x) = -7(-3)(-2x) = 21(-2x) = -42x$ **45.** true **47.** true

2.4 Problem Solving (pp. 92–93) **51.** \$162.50 **55. a.** $f = 11{,}250 + (-30t)$, $f = 135{,}000 + (-240t)$ **b.** 11,160 gal, 134,280 gal **c.** Rhododendron; 45,000 gal; the Rhododendron takes 375 hours to burn all of its fuel; the Spokane takes 562.5 hours to burn all of its fuel; to find the number of hours the Rhododendron will take to burn all its fuel, use the equations in part (a) and find the additive inverse of 11,250, then divide it by −30; to find the number of hours the Spokane will take to burn all its fuel, use the equations in part (a) and find the additive inverse of 135,000, then divide it by −240.

Extension (p. 95) **1.** $\begin{bmatrix} 16 & 4 \\ 8 & 12 \end{bmatrix}$ **3.** $\begin{bmatrix} -15 & -4 & -9 \\ -2 & 2 & -5 \end{bmatrix}$ **5.** Cannot be performed. **7.** $\begin{bmatrix} -28 & -49 \\ 3\frac{1}{2} & 3\frac{1}{9} \end{bmatrix}$ **9.** $\begin{bmatrix} -72 \\ 20.4 \\ 4.2 \end{bmatrix}$

11.

Calcium (mg)	Potassium (mg)
263.52	290.36
270.84	341.6
246.44	324.52

13. $\begin{bmatrix} -41 & -99 \\ 78 & 91 \end{bmatrix}$

2.5 Skill Practice (pp. 99–100) **1.** 4, −9 **3.** The negative was not distributed to the −8; $5y - (2y - 8) = 5y - 2y + 8 = 3y + 8$. **5.** $4x + 12$ **7.** $5m + 25$ **9.** $-8p + 24$ **11.** $4r - 6$ **13.** $6v^2 + 6v$ **15.** $2x^2 - 6x$ **17.** $\frac{1}{4}m - 2$ **19.** $4n - 6$ **21.** terms: $-7, 13x, 2x, 8$; like terms: −7 and 8, $13x$ and $2x$; coefficients: 13, 2; constant terms: −7, 8 **23.** terms: $7x^2, -10, -2x^2, 5$; like terms: $7x^2$ and $-2x^2$, −10 and 5; coefficients: 7, −2; constant terms: −10, 5 **25.** terms: $2, 3xy, -4xy, 6$; like terms: 2 and 6, $3xy$ and $-4xy$; coefficients: 3, −4; constant terms: 2, 6 **29.** $5y$ **31.** $9a - 2$ **33.** $8r + 8$ **35.** $3m + 5$ **37.** $10w - 35$ **39.** $15s + 6$ **41.** $34 - 24w$; $72 - 108w$ **43.** \$38.97 **45.** \$11.88 **47.** $2(6 + x) + (x - 5)$; $3x + 7$

2.5 Problem Solving (pp. 100–101)
51. $C = 3r - 6$; \$5.97 **53.** $s = d(x + y + z)$

2.5 Problem Solving Workshop (p. 102)
1. \$330 **3.** \$287.50

2.6 Skill Practice (pp. 106–107) **1.** multiplicative inverse **3.** $-\frac{1}{18}$ **5.** −1 **7.** $-1\frac{1}{3}$ **9.** $-\frac{3}{13}$ **11.** −7 **13.** $\frac{2}{7}$ **15.** −3 **17.** $-2\frac{1}{2}$ **19.** $\frac{2}{7}$ **21.** −22 **25.** $-1\frac{2}{3}$ **27.** $2\frac{1}{4}$ **29.** $-2\frac{1}{5}$ **31.** 0.1 **33.** $3x - 7$ **35.** $-3z + 2$ **37.** $\frac{1}{2} - \frac{5}{2}q$ **39.** $3a + 1\frac{1}{4}$ **41.** $4 - 3c$ **43.** −2 was added instead of subtracted; $\frac{-15x - 10}{-5} = (-15x - 10) \cdot \left(-\frac{1}{5}\right) = -15x\left(-\frac{1}{5}\right) - 10\left(-\frac{1}{5}\right) = 3x + 2$ **45.** $-1\frac{1}{3}$ **47.** $\frac{1}{3}$

2.6 Problem Solving (pp. 107–108) **53.** −14.75°C **57. a.** −0.034 **b.** Yes; it will improve to −0.012. **c.** If the player had the same number of aces as service errors, then $a = e$, so $f = \frac{a - a}{s} = 0$; if all the serves were aces, a would be equal to s and e would be 0, so $f = \frac{s - 0}{s} = \frac{s}{s} = 1$; if all the serves were errors, then $e = s$ and $a = 0$, so $f = \frac{0 - s}{s} = \frac{-s}{s} = -1$.

2.7 Skill Practice (pp. 113–114) **1.** real numbers **3.** 2 **5.** −3 **7.** 14 **9.** ±50 **11.** −15 **13.** ±13 **15.** 3 **17.** −2 **19.** −9 **21.** 14 **25.** $-\sqrt{12}$: real number, irrational number, −3.7: real number, rational number, $\sqrt{9}$: real number, rational number, integer, whole number, 2.9: real number, rational number; $-3.7, -\sqrt{12}, 2.9, \sqrt{9}$

27. $\sqrt{8}$: real number, irrational number, $-\frac{2}{5}$: real number, rational number, -1: real number, rational number, integer, 0.6: real number, rational number, $\sqrt{6}$: real number, irrational number; -1, $-\frac{2}{5}$, 0.6, $\sqrt{6}$, $\sqrt{8}$ **29.** -8.3: real number, rational number, $-\sqrt{80}$: real number, irrational number, $-\frac{17}{2}$: real number, rational number, -8.25: real number, rational number, $-\sqrt{100}$: real number, rational number, integer; $-\sqrt{100}$, $-\sqrt{80}$, $-\frac{17}{2}$, -8.3, -8.25 **31.** If a number is a real number, then it is an irrational number; false. *Sample answer:* 3 is a real number and a rational number. **33.** If a number is an irrational number, then it is not a whole number; true. **35.** 2 **37.** -42 **39.** 63 **41.** -16

2.7 Problem Solving (pp. 115–116) **47.** 60 in. **49.** 35 ft; 24 ft; 48 ft; 30 ft; they are all rational numbers. **51.** 3; square each fraction, $\left(\frac{265}{153}\right)^2 < 3$, $\left(\frac{1351}{780}\right)^2 > 3$ so the value of x is 3. **53. a.** 144 tiles **b.** 16 ft. *Sample answer:* If the homeowner can buy 144 tiles that are each 256 square inches, then the total area is (144 tiles)(256 square inches per tile) = 36,864 square inches. Divide 36,864 square inches by 144 square inches to find the number of square feet, 256 square feet. If the area of the square is 256 square feet, take the square root of 256 to find the side length, 16 feet.

Extension (p. 118) **1.** *Sample answer:* $3 - 5 = -2$, $-2(6) = -12$, $-12 \div 3 = -4$, $-4 + 10 = 6$; $-2 - 5 = -7$, $-7(6) = -42$, $-42 \div 3 = -14$, $-14 + 10 = -4$; $10 - 5 = 5$, $5(6) = 30$, $30 \div 3 = 10$, $10 + 10 = 20$; double the number; $\frac{(x-5)6}{3} + 10 = (x-5)2 + 10 = 2x - 10 + 10 = 2x$ **3.** Distributive property; Subtraction rule; Associative property of addition; Inverse property of addition; Identity property of addition; Divide

Chapter Review (pp. 121–124) **1.** terms: $-3x$, -5, $-7x$, -9; coefficients: -3, -7; constant terms: -5, -9; like terms: $-3x$ and $-7x$, -5 and -9 **3.** real number, rational number **5.** real number, rational number, integer **7.** -6, -5.2, $-\frac{3}{8}$, $-\frac{1}{4}$, 0.3 **9.** 0.2, 0.2 **11.** $-\frac{7}{8}$, $\frac{7}{8}$ **13.** 3 **15.** -3.5 **17.** $-1\frac{3}{14}$ **19.** $-\$.23$ million **21.** -10 **23.** -6.1 **25.** $-\frac{31}{36}$ **27.** $2\frac{1}{2}$ **29.** -60 **31.** -18 **33.** $6x$; $x \cdot (-18) = -\frac{1}{3}(-18)(x)$, commutative property of multiplication; $6(x)$, product of $-\frac{1}{3}$ and -18; $6x$, multiply **35.** 2.74 ft **37.** $-3y - 27$ **39.** $3x + 8$

41. $9n - 3\frac{1}{2}$ **43.** -14 **45.** $\frac{2}{3}$ **47.** $3x - 5$ **49.** $2n + 1$ **51.** -6 **53.** ± 15 **55.** -7 **57.** 17 **59.** $-\sqrt{4}$, -0.3, 0, 1.25, $\sqrt{11}$

Chapter 3

3.1 Skill Practice (pp. 137–138) **1.** inverse operations **3.** 3 **5.** 5 **7.** -3 **9.** 7 **11.** 17 **13.** 4 **17.** 4 **19.** 6 **21.** -15 **23.** 15 **25.** 48 **27.** 22 **29.** 3.8 should have been subtracted from *both* sides; $x + 3.8 - 3.8 = 2.3 - 3.8$, $x = -1.5$. **31.** 3.5 **33.** -1.1 **35.** -2.05 **37.** $\frac{5}{8}$ **39.** 0.06 **41.** 96 **43.** 12 **45.** -56 **47.** $\frac{3}{5}$ **49.** $54 = 12x$; 4.5 in.

3.1 Problem Solving (pp. 139–140) **53.** 1046.6 ft **55.** 11 ft **57. a.** $\frac{4}{7}x = 200$ **b.** Plants; if you solve the equation in part (a) you find that there are 350 species of birds.

59. a.

t	d
1	6.5
2	13
3	19.5
4	26
5	32.5

b. 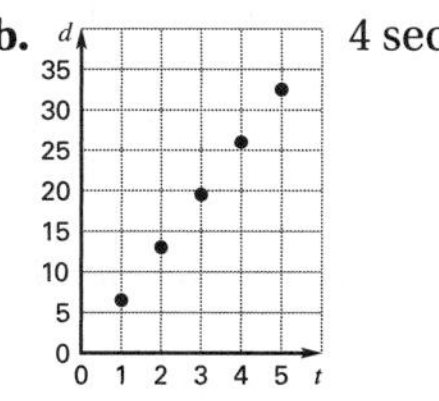

4 sec

c. $26 = 6.5t$; 4 sec **61. a.** 171 hits **b.** 215 hits **c.** No; if Mueller had fewer hits than Wells but had a higher batting average, he must have had fewer at bats than Wells.

3.2 Skill Practice (pp. 144–145) **1.** like terms **3.** 4 **5.** 2 **7.** -3 **9.** 6 **11.** 40 **13.** 18 **15.** 4 **17.** 9 **19.** -4 **23.** The division of $-2x + x$ by -2 is done incorrectly. *Sample answer:* If like terms are combined as the first step, the second line would be $-x = 10$ and the final result would be $x = -10$. **25.** $y = 2x + 4$; -7 **27.** 4 **29.** 5 **31.** 0.5 **33.** 15.9 **35.** 6.9

3.2 Problem Solving (pp. 145–146) **37.** 28 classes **39.** 5 half-side advertisements **41.** Yes; the equation $\$542 = \$50 + 6x$ gives the monthly cost of a guitar that costs \$542. Solving the equation gives $x = \$82$ per month, so you can afford the guitar. **43. a.** $y = 12x$

b.

x (hours)	Marissa	Ryan	Total
1	5	7	12
2	10	14	24
3	15	21	36
4	20	28	48
5	25	35	60

SA5

c. 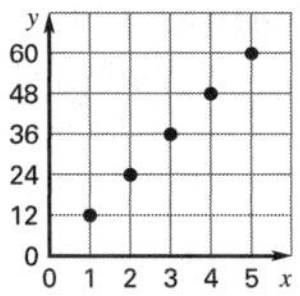 about 4.5 h

3.2 Problem Solving Workshop (p. 147)
1. 7 players **3.** 4 chairs

3.3 Skill Practice (pp. 150–151) **1.** $\frac{5}{3}$ **3.** 3 **5.** 6 **7.** −2 **9.** −8 **11.** −8 **13.** 4 **15.** −9 **17.** −19 **19.** 12 **21.** −2 **23.** −9 **25.** −3 times −6 is 18, not −18; $5x - 3x + 18 = 2$, $2x + 18 = 2$, $2x = -16$, $x = -8$. **27.** 2 **29.** 3 **31.** −5 **33.** 2 **35.** 9.5 in., 6 in.; if you use the perimeter formula $P = 2\ell + 2w$ and substitute $3.5 + w$ for ℓ, the solution is $w = 6$.

3.3 Problem Solving (pp. 152–153) **39.** 0.75 ft **41. a.** 34 mo **b.** 307 ft per mo **c.** After the work crews merged; before the work crews merged they were working at a rate of 117 + 137 = 254 feet per month, and after merging at a rate of 307 feet per month.

3.4 Skill Practice (pp. 157–158) **1.** identity **3.** −2 **5.** −4 **7.** −7 **9.** 8 **11.** −4 **13.** −3 **17.** *Sample answer:* Distribute the 3 to get $6z - 15 = 2z + 13$, then subtract $2z$ from each side to get $4z - 15 = 13$, next add 15 to each side to get $4z = 28$, finally divide each side by 4 to get $z = 7$. **19.** 2 **21.** −7 **23.** no solution **25.** no solution **27.** The 3 was not distributed to both terms; $3x + 15 = 3x + 15$, $15 = 15$, so the equation is an identity. **29.** *Sample answer:* $5x + 4 = 5x$; the number $5x$ cannot be equal to 4 more than itself. **31.** 2 **33.** −4 **35.** 6 **37.** identity **39.** 2 **41.** 10 **43.** identity **45.** $16x + 12$

3.4 Problem Solving (pp. 158–159) **49.** 9 nights **51.** about 4 yr **53. a.** $23.4t = 24(t - 0.3)$; 12 sec **b.** about 4.4 sec **c.** No; it would take 12 seconds for the sheepdog to catch up to the collie and it only takes 4.4 seconds for the collie to complete the last leg.

3.4 Spreadsheet Activity (p. 160) **1.** 2 **3.** 4

3.5 Skill Practice (pp. 165–166) **1.** ratios **3.** no; 7 to 9 **5.** yes **7.** $\frac{6}{5}$ **9.** 22 **11.** 48 **13.** 15 **15.** 40 **17.** 12 **21.** Multiply each side by 6, not $\frac{1}{6}$; $6 \cdot \frac{3}{4} = 6 \cdot \frac{x}{6}$, $4\frac{1}{2} = x$. **23.** $\frac{3}{8} = \frac{x}{32}$; 12 **25.** $\frac{x}{4} = \frac{8}{16}$; 2 **27.** $\frac{b}{10} = \frac{7}{2}$; 35 **29.** $\frac{12}{18} = \frac{d}{27}$; 18 **31.** 1.8 **33.** 2.4 **35.** 4 **37.** 4 **39.** 2 **41.** 3.5 **43.** Yes. *Sample answer:* $\frac{3}{6} = \frac{4}{8}$

3.5 Problem Solving (pp. 166–167) **45.** $\frac{2}{145}$ **47.** $\frac{2}{5}$ **49.** $\frac{1}{2}$ **51.** 45 goals **53. a.** $\frac{10}{23}$ **b.** 110 lift tickets **c.** 40 snowboarders

3.6 Skill Practice (pp. 171–172) **1.** cross product **3.** 6 **5.** 24 **7.** 1 **9.** −49 **11.** 2 **13.** 12 **17.** Use the cross products property to multiply 4 by x and 16 by 3; $4 \cdot x = 3 \cdot 16$, $4x = 48$, $x = 12$. **19.** 15 **21.** 10 **23.** 5.5 **25.** −3.4 **27.** 4.2 **29.** −5.9 **31. a.** Multiplication property of equality **b.** Multiply **c.** Simplify

3.6 Problem Solving (pp. 172–173) **33.** 5 c **35.** 90 km **37.** 7.5 km **39.** 17.728 m **41.** 80 yd; find the actual length of the field by using the ratio 1 in. : 20 yd, then use that number to find the width of the soccer field by using the ratio 3 : 2.

Extension (p. 175) **1.** 24 in. **3.** 16 m **5.** 37.5 ft

3.7 Skill Practice (pp. 179–180) **1.** percent: 15, base: 360, part: 54 **3.** 36% **5.** 28 **7.** 150 **9.** 70% **11.** 6% **13.** 69 **15.** 25 **17.** 95 **21.** 76.5% needs to be changed to 0.765; $153 = 0.765 \cdot b$, $b = 200$. **23.** 96% **25.** 150 **27.** 6% **29.** 30% **31.** No. *Sample answer:* The area of the smaller square would be 16% of the area of the larger square because the percent needs to be squared.

3.7 Problem Solving (pp. 180–181) **33.** 8% **35. a.** 90 listeners **b.** 35 listeners **37.** 59.3%; 16.5%; 13.2%; 11.0% **39. a.** \$48 **b.** \$66.25 **c.** The bicycle in part (a); it will cost \$192, the bicycle in part (b) will cost \$198.75.

Extension (p. 183) **1.** increase; 25% **3.** decrease; 45% **5.** decrease; 33% **7.** 20.3 **9.** 35.2 **11.** 20% increase **13.** 48.0 people per square mile

3.8 Skill Practice (pp. 187–188) **1.** literal equation **3.** $x = \frac{c}{b - a}$; −2 **5.** $x = bc - a$; 9 **7.** $x = a(c - b)$; 28 **9.** b should have been subtracted from both sides, not added; $ax = -b$, $x = -\frac{b}{a}$. **11.** $y = 7 - 2x$ **13.** $4 - 3x = y$ **15.** $2 + \frac{6}{7}x = y$ **17.** $\frac{9}{5}x - 6 = y$ **19.** $y = \frac{1}{2}x + \frac{1}{3}$ **21.** $h = \frac{S - 2B}{P}$ **25.** $y = 18 - 5x$ **27.** $\ell = \frac{S}{\pi r} - r$; 13.03 cm **29.** *Sample answer:* You want to find how long it will take to drive 150 miles if you drive at an average rate of 55 miles per hour.

3.8 Problem Solving (pp. 188–189) **33. a.** $x = \frac{C - 25}{12}$ **b.** 10 nights; 13 nights; 15 nights **35.** Divide each side by the total bill, b, to get $\frac{a}{b} = p\%$.

Chapter Review (pp. 192–196) **1.** scale drawing **3.** If you collect like terms you get $10x = 10x$, so any value of x will make it true. **5.** Subtract $6x$ from each side, then divide each side by -2. **7.** 13 **9.** -15 **11.** -36 **13.** 2 **15.** 18 **17.** 5 **19.** 2 **21.** -6 **23.** 14 **25.** 1 **27.** -4 **29.** no solution **31.** 7 **33.** identity **35.** 3 **37. a.** 4 **b.** 116 **39.** 15 **41.** 10.5 **43.** 70 **45.** 28 **47.** 1 **49.** 10 **51.** 650 words **53.** 16.5 **55.** 37.5% **57.** 1500 general admission tickets **59.** $y = \frac{3}{2}x + 9$ **61. a.** $h = \frac{V}{\ell w}$ **b.** 15 in.

Cumulative Review (pp. 202–203) **1.** 27 **3.** 11 **5.** 42 **7.** solution **9.** not a solution **11.** not a solution **13.** $-6\frac{5}{6}$ **15.** -19.1 **17.** -21 **19.** 6 **21.** 3 **23.** 13.9 **25.** 58.8 **27.** -11 **29.** 6 **31.** $4\frac{2}{3}$ **33.** 3 **35.** 8.5 **37.** 15 **39.** 23 **41.** 1.2 **43.** 18 pieces **45.** $-\$.34$; $-\$.45$; $-\$.25$; \$1.02; \$.08 **47.** 140 people **49. a.** 2 players **b.** 7 players **c.** 11 players

Chapter 4

4.1 Skill Practice (pp. 209–210) **1.** 5; -3 **3.** $(3, -2)$ **5.** $(4, 4)$ **7.** $(4, -1)$ **9.** $(-5, 4)$ **11.** $(-4, -1)$

15–21.

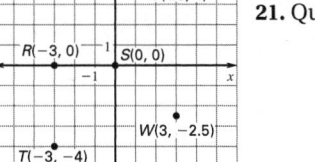

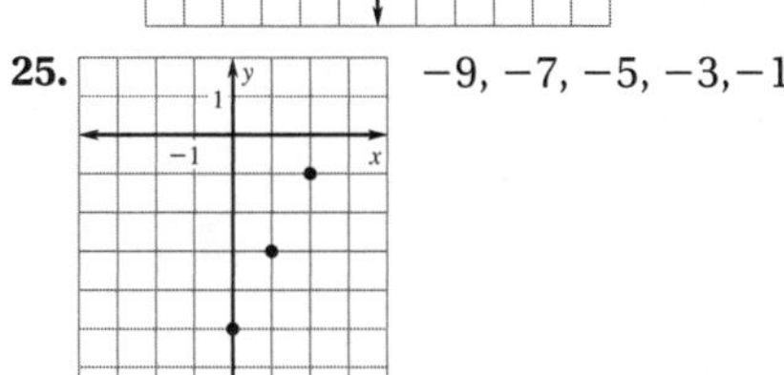

15. Quadrant II **17.** origin **19.** y-axis **21.** Quadrant IV

25.

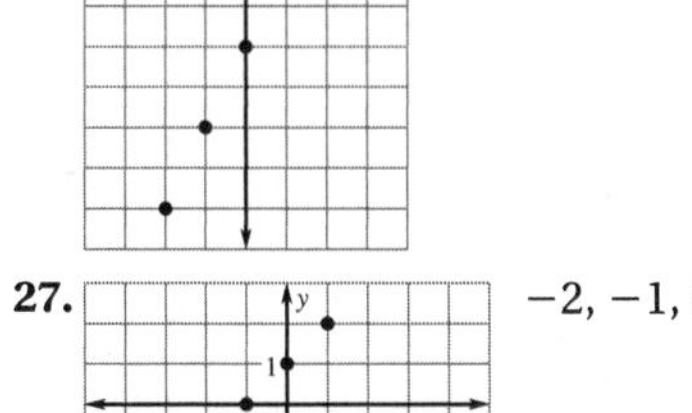

$-9, -7, -5, -3, -1$

27. $-2, -1, 0, 1, 2$

29. Quadrant IV; the x-coordinate is positive and the y-coordinate is negative so the point is in Quadrant IV. **31.** Quadrant II; the x-coordinate is negative and the y-coordinate is positive so the point is in Quadrant II. **33.** If the x-coordinate is 0, then the point is on the y-axis. If the y-coordinate is 0, then the point is on the x-axis.

4.1 Problem Solving (pp. 210–212)

37. There is exactly one low temperature for each day in February.

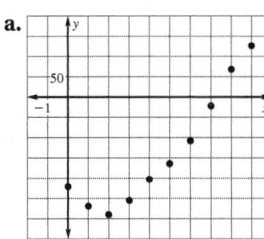

39. a.

b. *Sample answer:* From 1992 to 1999 the federal deficit was decreasing.

41. a.

Height (in.)		
Reported	Measured	Difference
70	68	2
70	67.5	2.5
78.5	77.5	1
68	69	−1
71	72	−1
70	70	0

Weight (lb)		
Reported	Measured	Difference
154	146	8
141	143	−2
165	168	−3
146	143	3
220	223	−3
176	176	0

b. $(2, 8)$, $(2.5, -2)$, $(1, -3)$, $(-1, 3)$, $(-1, -3)$, $(0, 0)$

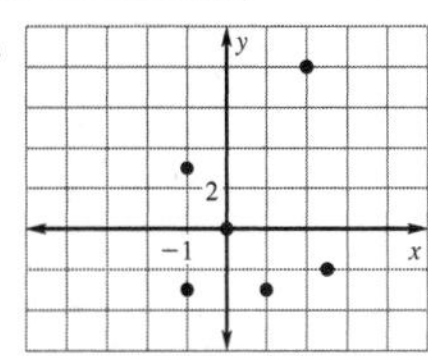

SELECTED ANSWERS

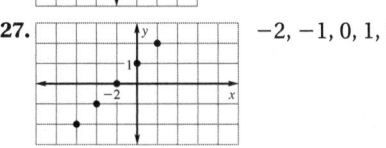

Extension (p. 214) **1.** Translation; a translation moves every point the same distance in the same direction so it will have the same shape and size as the original figure. **3.** Subtract 4 from each y-coordinate. **5.** Add 2 to each y-coordinate. **7.** (0, 1), (0, 3), (2, 3), (2, 1) **9.** (0, 0), (0, −2), (2, −2), (2, 0) **11.** (0, 0), (0, −1), (2, −1), (2, 0) **13.** (−1, 4), (−1, 6), (1, 6), (1, 4) **15.** Use the transformation $(x, y) \to (x, -y)$.

4.2 Skill Practice (pp. 219–220) **1.** linear function **3.** solution **5.** solution **7.** not a solution **9.** The 8 should be substituted for x and 11 for y, $11 - 8 \neq -3$, so (8, 11) is not a solution.

11.

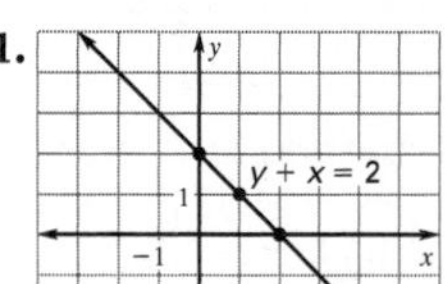

13.

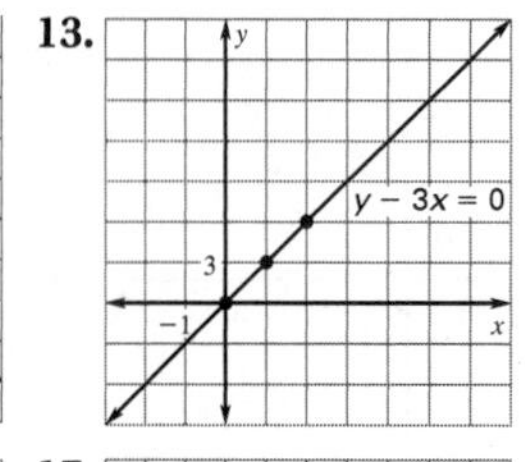

15.

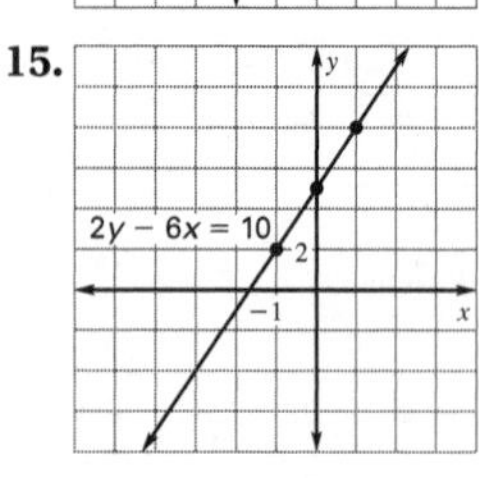

17.

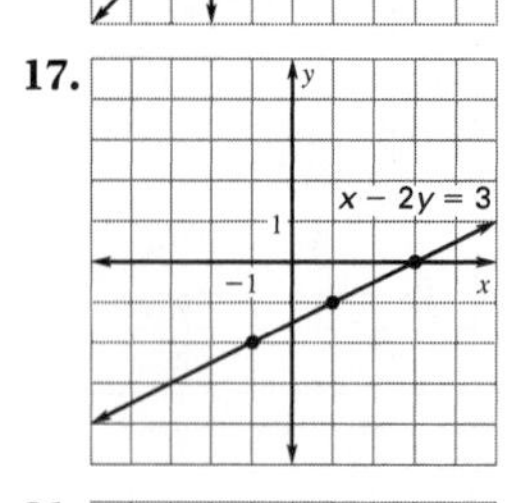

19.

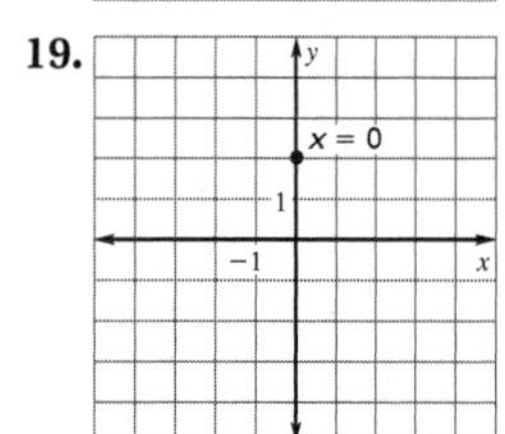

21.

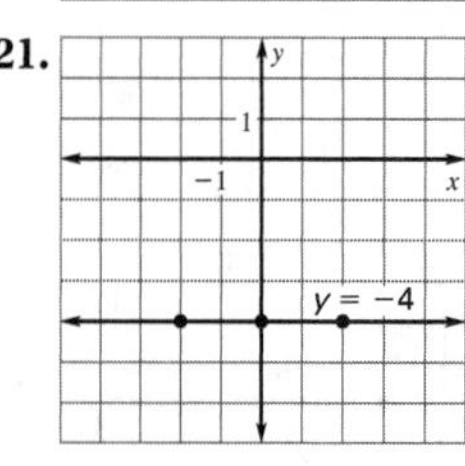

23. C **25.** B

27.

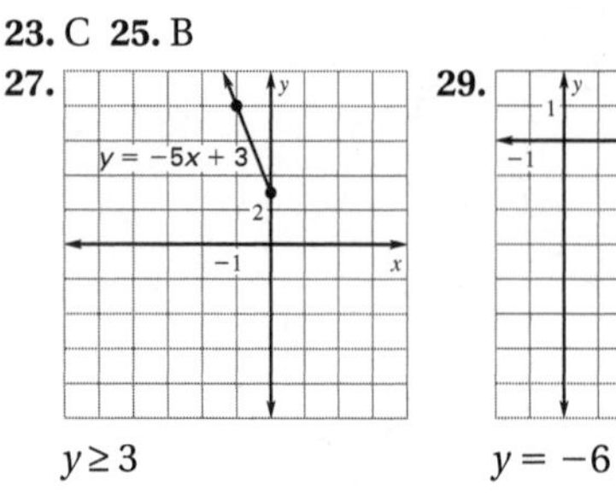

$y \geq 3$

29.

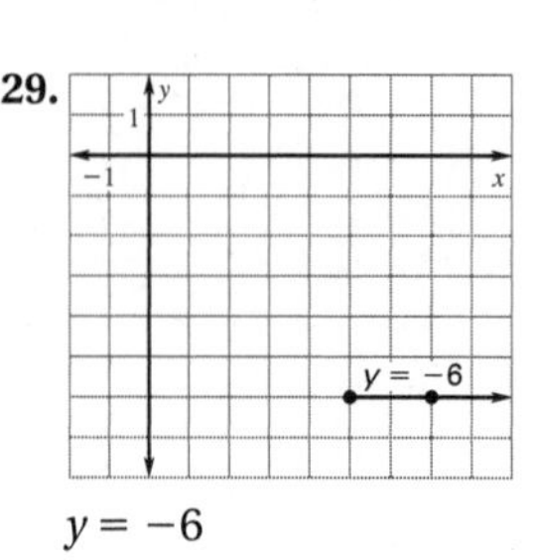

$y = -6$

31.

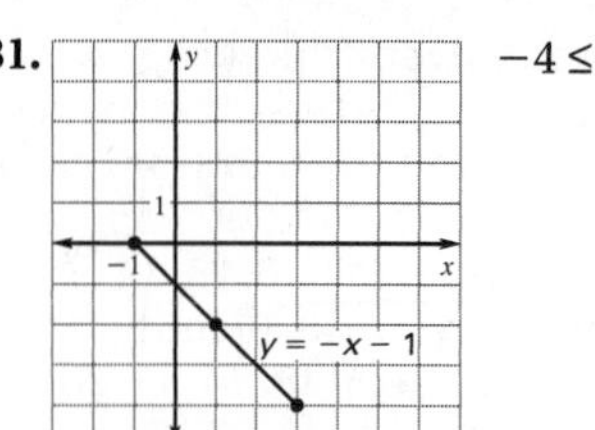

$-4 \leq y \leq 0$

4.2 Problem Solving (pp. 220–221)

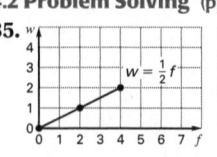

35. domain: $0 \leq f \leq 4$, range: $0 \leq w \leq 2$; 2 lb

37. a.

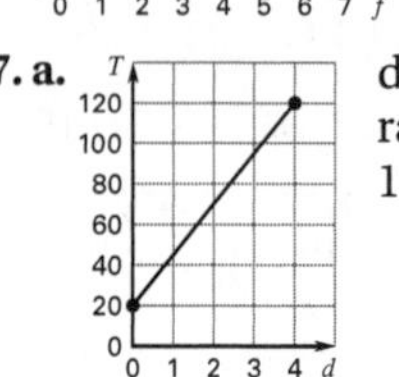

domain: $0 \leq d \leq 4$, range: $20 \leq T \leq 120$; 120°C

b.

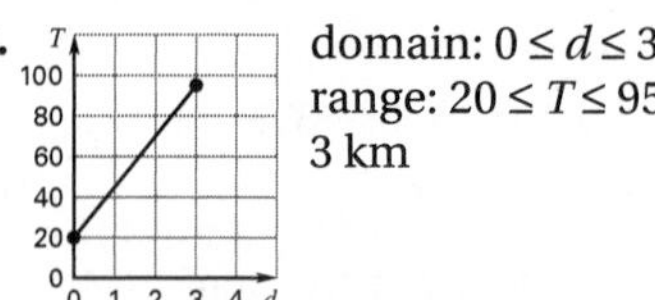

domain: $0 \leq d \leq 3$, range: $20 \leq T \leq 95$; 3 km

39. a.

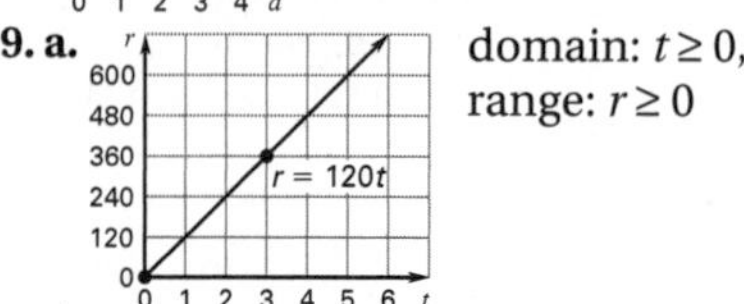

domain: $t \geq 0$, range: $r \geq 0$

b. Domain: $0 \leq t \leq 4$, range: $0 \leq r \leq 480$; the graph was a ray, but is now a segment.

41. a.

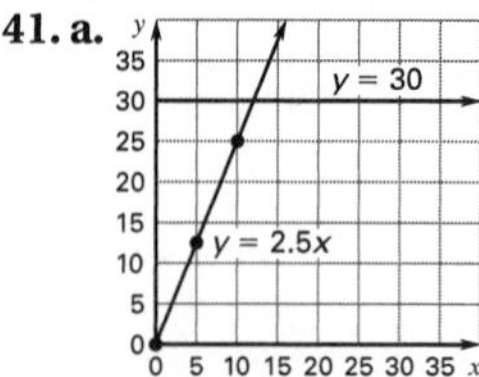

4.2 Graphing Calculator Activity (p. 222) **1.** 5.6 **3.** −5.3

Extension (p. 224)

1.

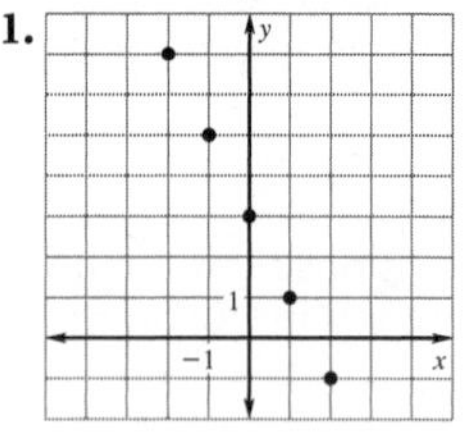

discrete

3. 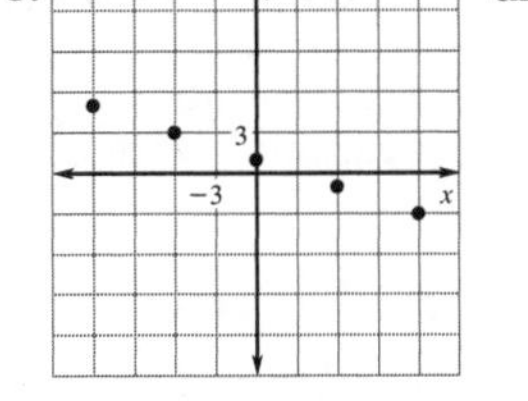

discrete

5. 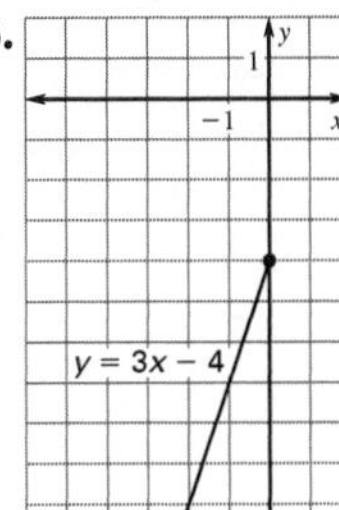

continuous

7. Discrete; you can only rent a whole number of DVDs.

9. Continuous; it makes sense to talk about the weight of water for any volume of water.

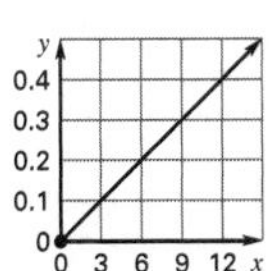

about 0.12

4.3 Skill Practice (pp. 229–230) **1.** x-intercept **3.** The intercepts are switched around; the x-intercept is -2, and the y-intercept is 1. **5.** 3, -3 **7.** 1, 4 **9.** 12, -3 **11.** 64, 4 **13.** $\frac{1}{2}$, 7 **15.** 20, -12

17. 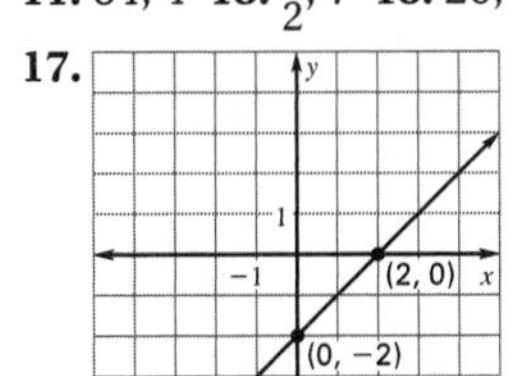

19. 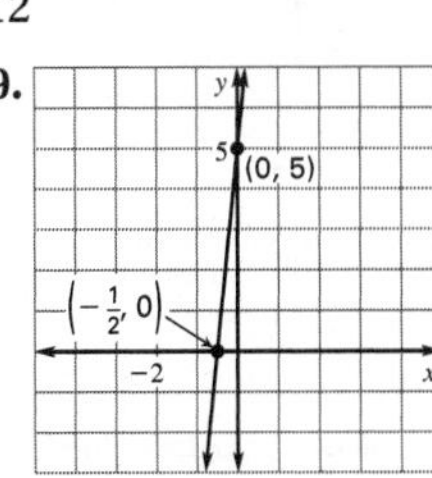

21. 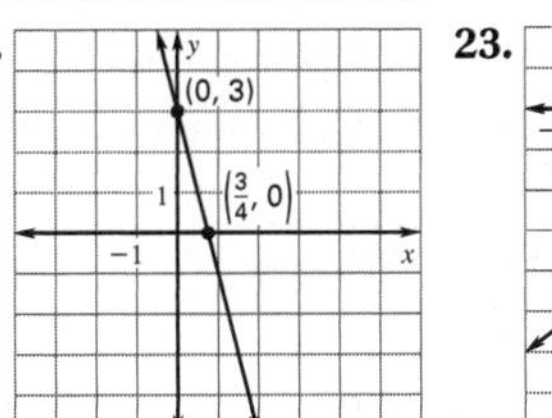

23. 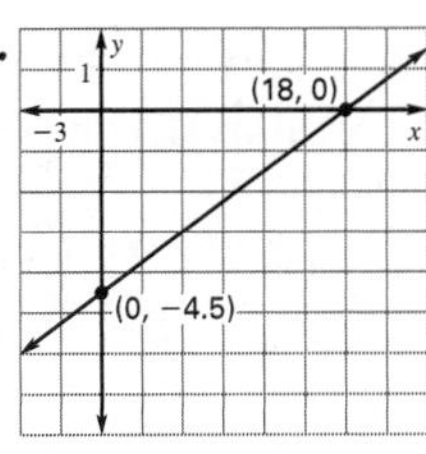

25. 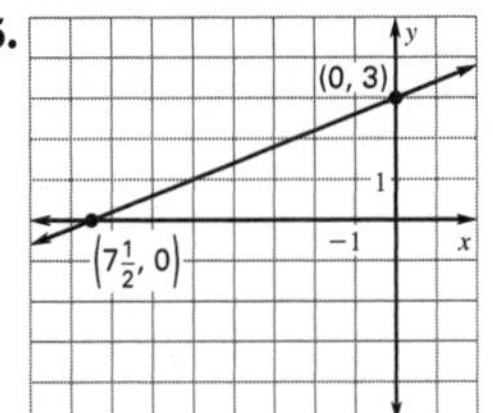

27. 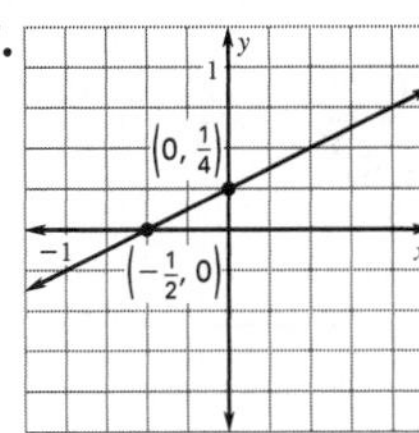

29. 3, -2

31. 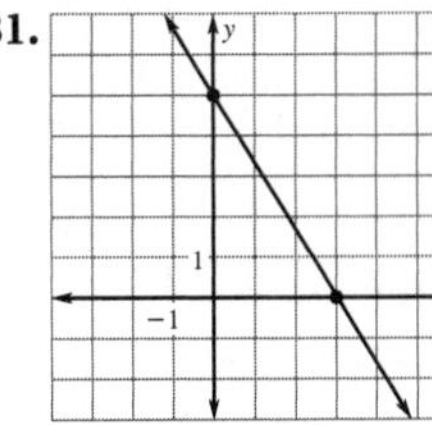

33. 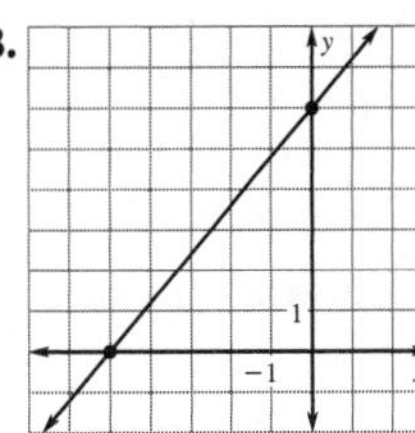

35. 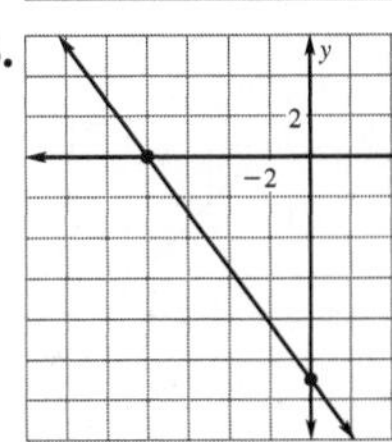

39. B **41.** Yes; yes; a horizontal line does not have an x-intercept if $y \neq 0$, a vertical line does not have a y-intercept if $x \neq 0$.

4.3 Problem Solving (pp. 230–232)

45. a. $x = 14$, $y = 7$

b. *Sample answer:* 2 and 6, 4 and 5, 6 and 4

47. a. v-intercept: 120, f-intercept: 180; the v-intercept means there are no flowers planted, the f-intercept means there are no vegetables planted.

b. 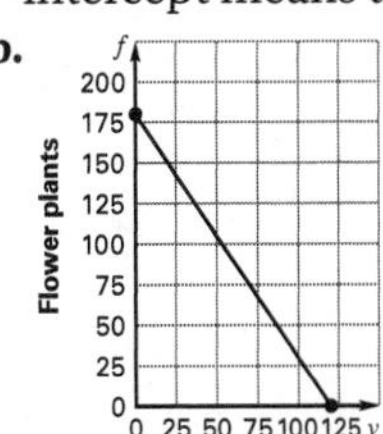

domain: $0 \leq v \leq 120$, range: $0 \leq f \leq 180$

c. 60 ft^2 **49.** 12.5 h. *Sample answer:* Since the tank will be empty when it needs to be refilled, replace w in the function with 0 and then solve the resulting equation for t.

4.4 Skill Practice (pp. 239–241) **1.** slope **3.** The denominator should be $2 - 5$, not $5 - 2$; $m = \frac{6-3}{2-5} = \frac{3}{-3} = -1$. **5.** undefined **7.** The slope was calculated using $\frac{\text{run}}{\text{rise}}$, not $\frac{\text{rise}}{\text{run}}$; $m = \frac{0-3}{12-6} = \frac{-3}{6} = -\frac{1}{2}$. **9.** undefined **11.** $-\frac{5}{2}$ **13.** 1 **15.** 0 **19.** $2.25 per day; it costs $2.25 per day to rent a movie. **21.** 0.3 **23.** 0.1 **25.** -15 **27.** -2 **29.** -3 **31.** -15 **33.** Yes; the slope of the line containing both points is -3.

4.4 Problem Solving (pp. 241–242) **37. a.** 0 h to 1.5 h **b.** 4.65 h to 8.95 h **39.** *Sample answer:* The elevation of the hiker increases for about 60 minutes, then stays the same for about 30 minutes, then decreases for the last 60 minutes.

4.5 Skill Practice (pp. 247–248) **1.** parallel **3.** 2, 1 **5.** −3, 6 **7.** $\frac{2}{3}$, −1 **11.** $y = -4x + 1$; −4, 1 **13.** $y = 2x + 3$; 2, 3 **15.** $y = -\frac{2}{5}x - 2$; $-\frac{2}{5}$, −2 **17.** B **19.** C

21.

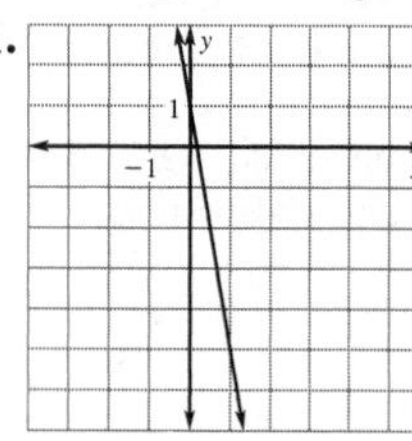

23.

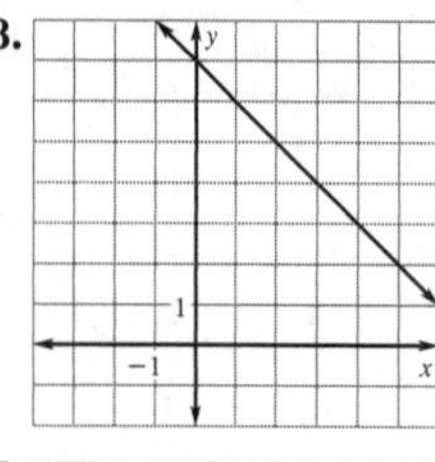

25.

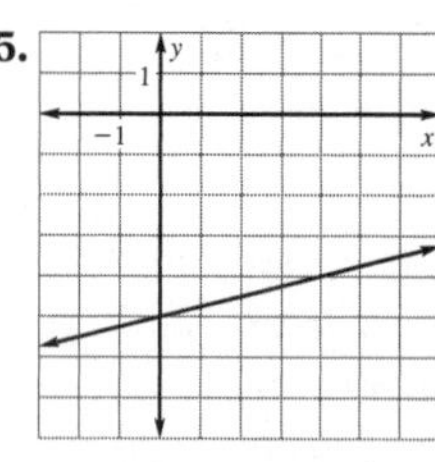

27.

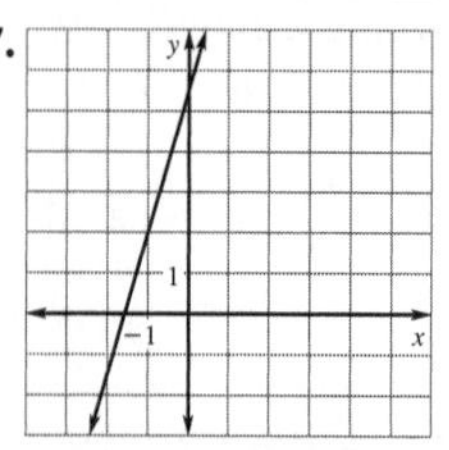

29.

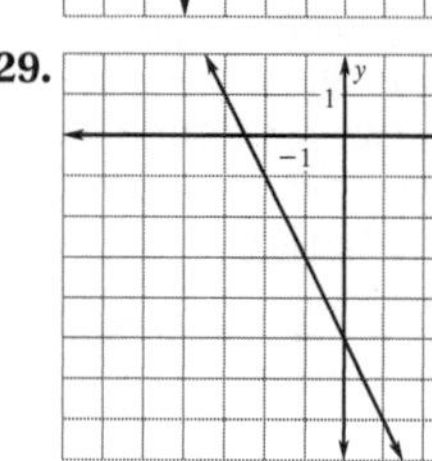

31. red, blue, and green **33.** Parallel; the slopes are both 3. **35.** Not parallel; the slopes are −4 and $-\frac{1}{4}$. **37.** −2

4.5 Problem Solving (pp. 248–250)

41. a.

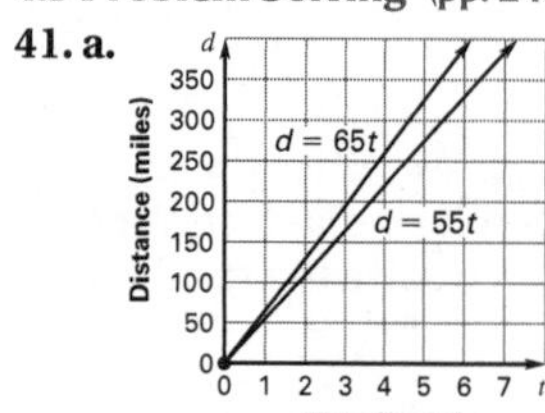

b. 30 mi

43. a.

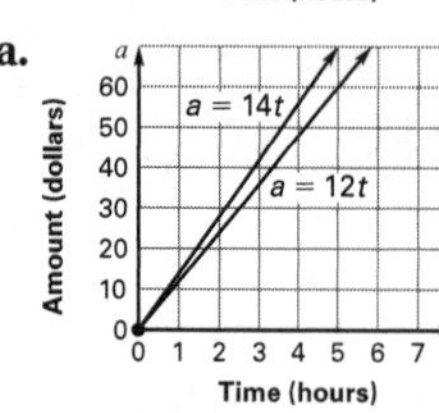

The slopes are the amount of money earned per hour, the *a*-intercepts show the amount of money made at 0 hours. **b.** $80

Extension (p. 252) **1.** −2 **3.** −4 **5.** $\frac{1}{2}$ **7.** 2000 **9.** 2000

4.6 Skill Practice (pp. 256–257) **1.** direct variation **3.** direct variation; 1 **5.** not direct variation **7.** direct variation; −4

11.

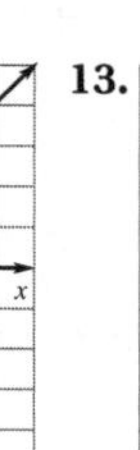

13.

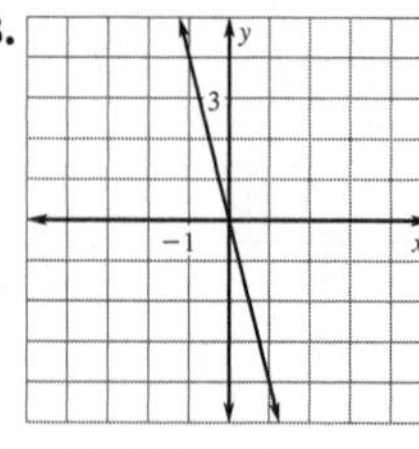

15.

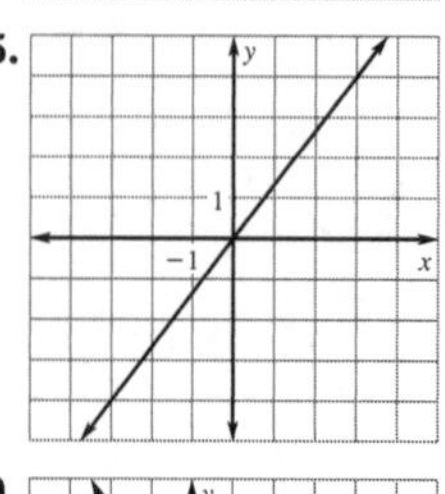

17.

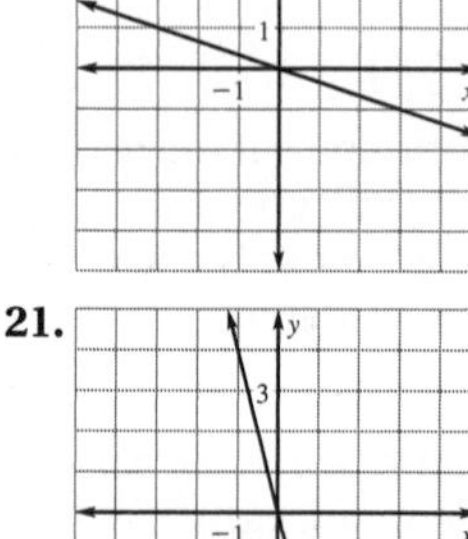

19.

21.

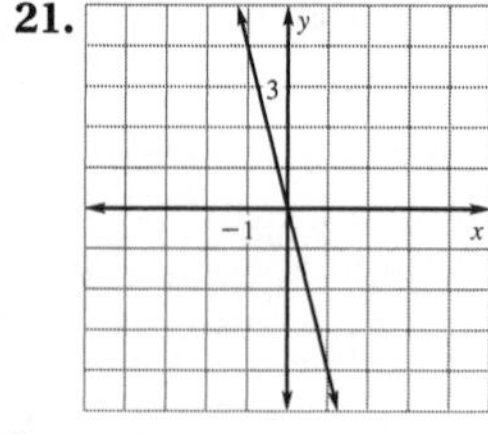

23. $y = -x$; −8 **25.** $y = -\frac{3}{4}x$; −6 **27.** not direct variation **29.** $y = 3x$ **31.** $y = \frac{1}{2}x$ **33.** $y = x$ **35.** $y = 4x$ **37.** $y = -\frac{7}{26}x$

4.6 Problem Solving (pp. 258–259) **41. a.** $v = \frac{3}{2}t$ **b.** 12 h **43. a.** Compare the ratios, $\frac{f}{w}$, for all data pairs (w, f). Since the ratios all equal 0.25, f varies directly with w. **b.** $f = 0.25w$; $7 **45. a.** *Sample answer:*

d	C (dollars)
1	1.5
2	3
3	4.5

b.

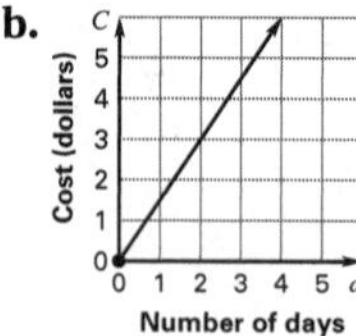

c. $C = 1.5d$; yes; it is in the form $y = ax$; $33.

4.6 Problem Solving Workshop (p. 261) **1.** 110 tbsp. *Sample answer:* Use the proportion $\frac{20}{100} = \frac{22}{x}$. **3.** Because 7 is half of 14, you can take half of 5.88 to find 7 words cost \$2.94. Because 21 is 3 times 7, multiply \$2.94 by 3 to get \$8.82. **5.** The proportion should be $\frac{6}{96} = \frac{10}{x}$; $\frac{6}{96} = \frac{10}{x}$, $960 = 6x$, $x = 160$.

4.7 Skill Practice (pp. 265–266) **1.** function notation **3.** −23, 1, 37 **5.** 14, −2, −26 **7.** 13, 0, −19.5 **9.** $2\frac{1}{5}$, 3, $4\frac{1}{5}$ **11.** $-7\frac{1}{2}$, −6, $-3\frac{3}{4}$ **15.** 3 **17.** −6 **19.** −7.5 **21.** 3.5

23.

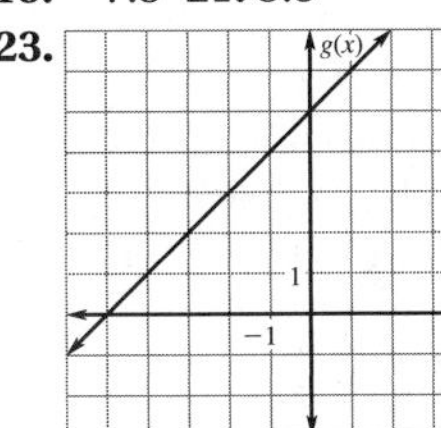

Because the graphs of g and f have the same slope, $m = 1$, the lines are parallel. The y-intercept of the graph of g is 5 more than the y-intercept of the graph of f.

25.

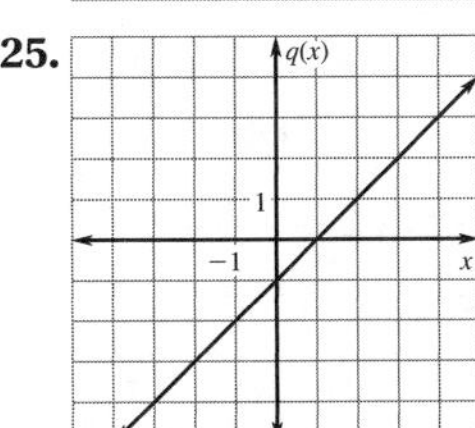

Because the graphs of q and f have the same slope, $m = 1$, the lines are parallel. The y-intercept of the graph of q is 1 less than the y-intercept of the graph of f.

27.

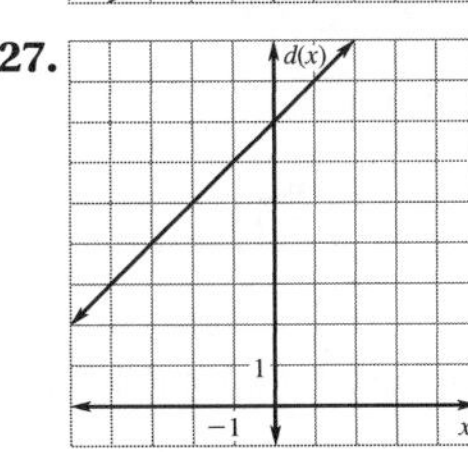

Because the graphs of d and f have the same slope, $m = 1$, the lines are parallel. The y-intercept of the graph of d is 7 more than the y-intercept of the graph of f.

29.

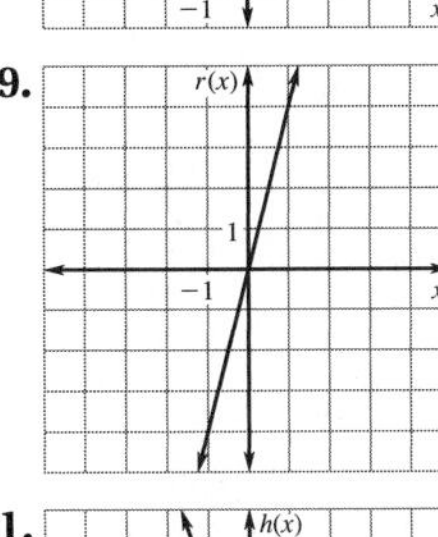

Because the slope of the graph of r is greater than the slope of the graph of f, the graph of r rises faster from left to right. The y-intercept for both graphs is 0, so both lines pass through the origin.

31.

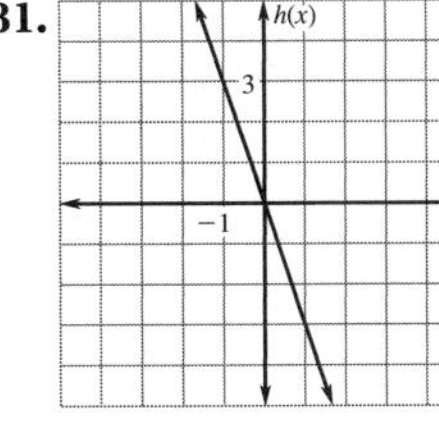

Because the slope of the graph of h is negative, the graph of h falls from left to right. The y-intercept for both graphs is 0, so both lines pass through the origin.

33.

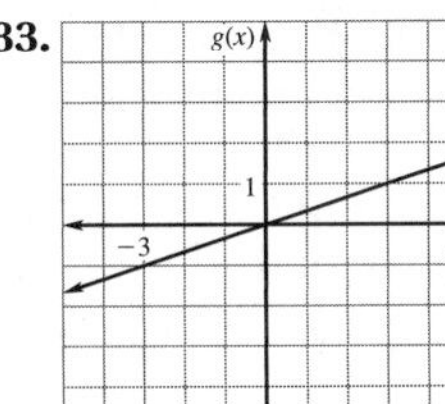

Because the slope of the graph of g is less than the slope of the graph of f, the graph of g rises slower from left to right. The y-intercept for both graphs is 0, so both lines pass through the origin.

37. Since the graphs of g and h have the same slope, $m = 0$, the lines are parallel. The y-intercept of the graph of h is 2 less than the y-intercept of the graph of g.

4.7 Problem Solving (pp. 267–268)

39. a.

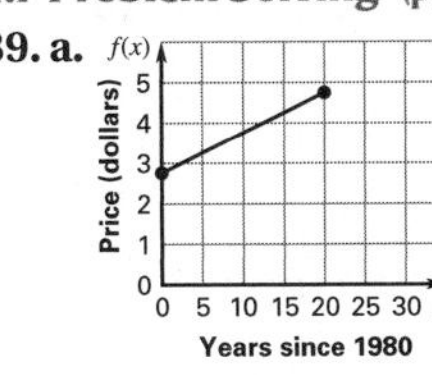

domain: $0 \le x \le 20$, range: $2.75 \le f(x) \le 4.75$ **b.** 18; in 1998, 18 years after 1980, the price of a movie ticket was \$4.55.

41.

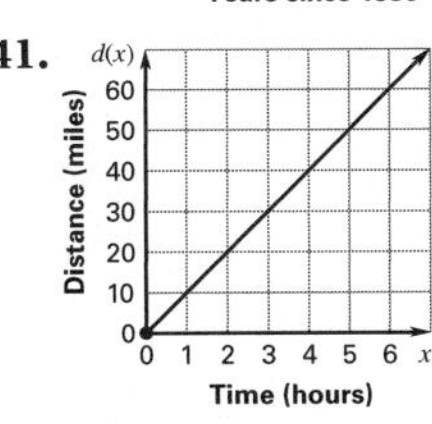

Domain: $x \ge 0$, range: $d(x) \ge 0$; 1.5 h; substitute 15 for $d(x)$ to get the equation $15 = 10x$, solve for x.

43.

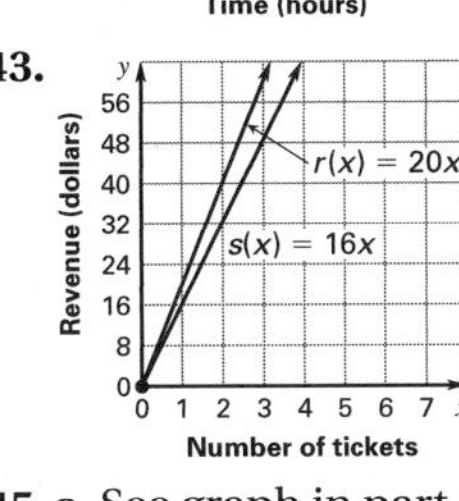

Because the slope of the graph of r is greater than the slope of the graph of s, the graph of r rises faster from left to right. The y-intercept for both graphs is 0, so both lines pass through the origin.

45. a. See graph in part (b); domain: $1 \le x \le 31$, range: $11.53 \le \ell(x) \le 12.43$.

b.

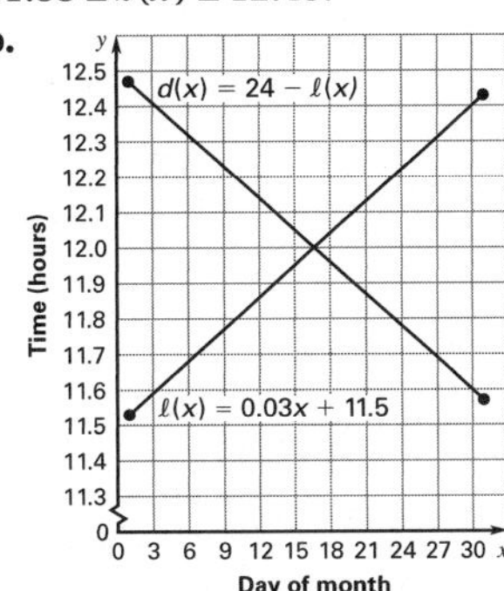

domain: $11.53 \le \ell(x) \le 12.43$, range: $11.57 \le d(x) \le 12.47$

SELECTED ANSWERS

Chapter Review (pp. 271–273) **1.** slope **3.** *Sample answer:* Make a table, use intercepts, and use the slope and y-intercept.

5–7.

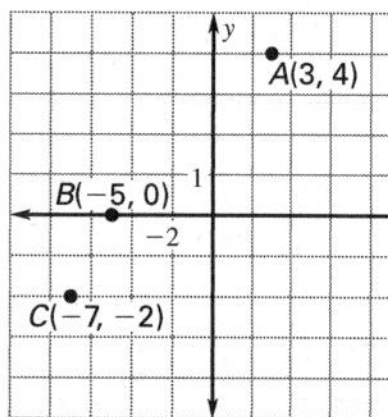

5. Quadrant I **7.** Quadrant III

9.

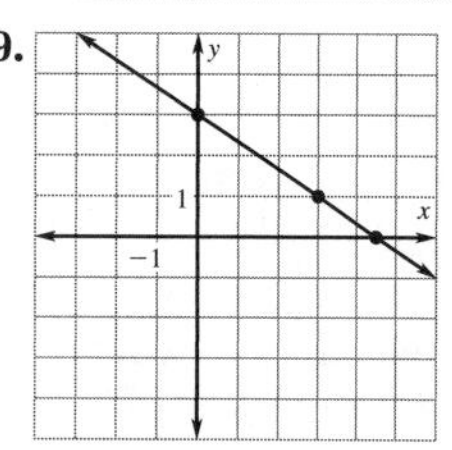

11.

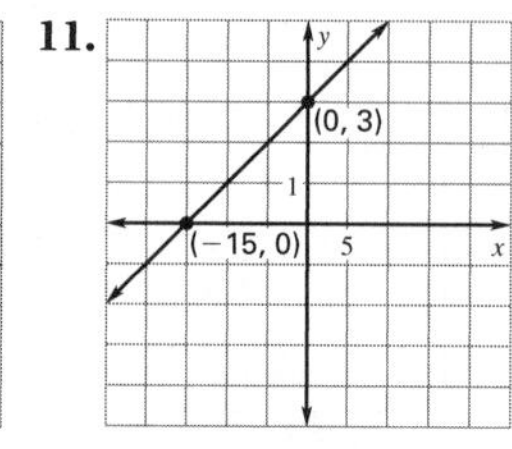

13.

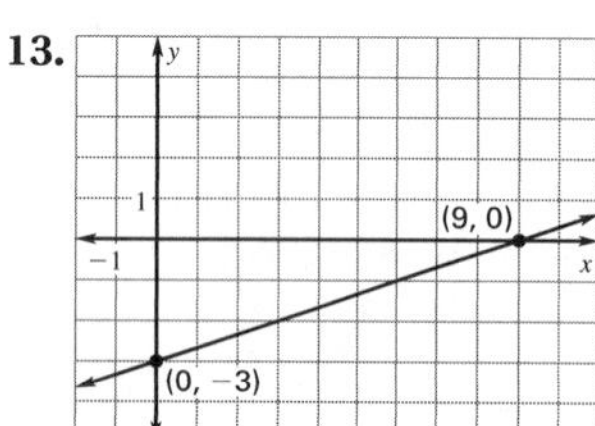

15. $-\frac{1}{3}$ **17.** -2

19.

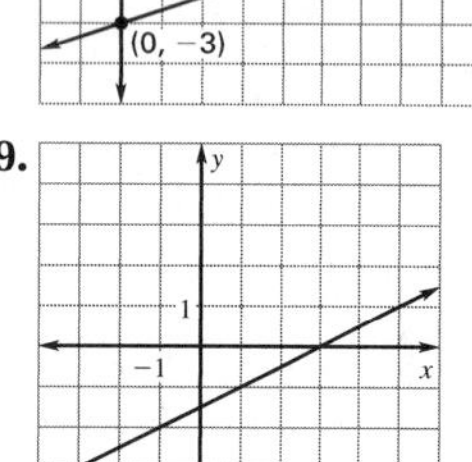

21.

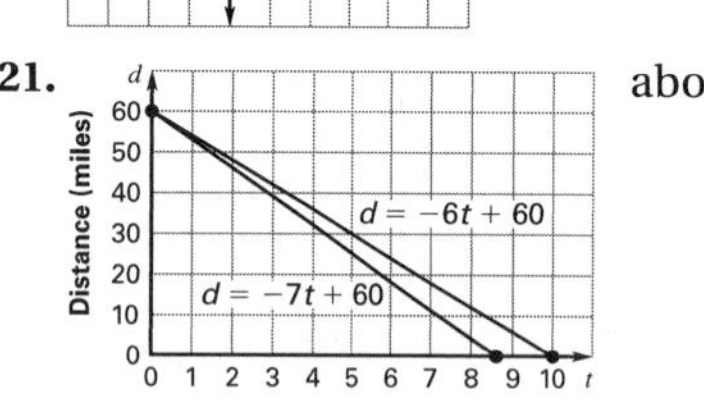

about 1.4 sec

23. direct variation; $-\frac{1}{2}$

25.

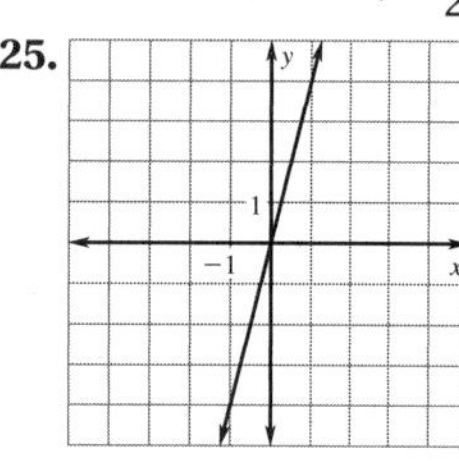

27.

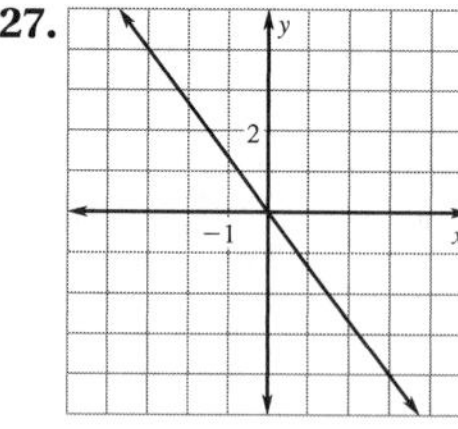

29. 11

31.

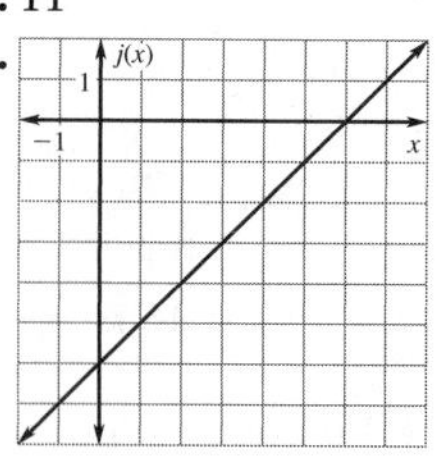

Because the graphs of j and f have the same slope, $m = 1$, the lines are parallel. The y-intercept of the graph of j is 6 less than the y-intercept of the graph of f.

33.

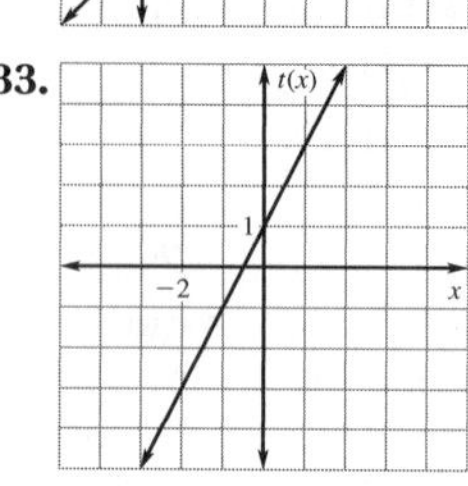

Because the slope of the graph of t is greater than the slope of the graph of f, the graph of t rises faster from left to right. The y-intercept of the graph of t is 1 more than the y-intercept of the graph of f.

Chapter 5

5.1 Skill Practice (pp. 286–287) **1.** slope **3.** $y = 2x + 9$ **5.** $y = -3x$ **7.** $y = \frac{2}{3}x - 9$ **11.** $y = -\frac{1}{2}x$ **13.** $y = \frac{2}{3}x - 8$ **15.** $y = -2x - 2$ **17.** The slope should be $\frac{0-4}{5-0}$, $y = -\frac{4}{5}x + 4$. **19.** $y = 4x + 4$ **21.** $y = -\frac{4}{3}x$ **23.** $y = 2x - 2$ **25.** $y = -x - 5$ **27.** $y = -0.0625x + 4$ **29.** $y = -4x - 24$ **31.** $y = -2x + 7$ **33.** $y = -\frac{4}{5}x - 1$ **35.** $y = \frac{2}{3}x + 3$ **37.** $y = -3x + 9$ **39.** $y = x - 3$ **41.** $y = -2x + 1$ **43.** No; the slope of the line is undefined, the equation is $x = 3$, which is not in slope-intercept form.

5.1 Problem Solving (pp. 288–289) **45. a.** $C = 44m + 48$ **b.** \$312 **47.** $C = 3h + 30$; \$42

49. a.

x (years since 1970)	y (km²)
0	5.2
10	4.1
20	3.0
30	1.9

b.

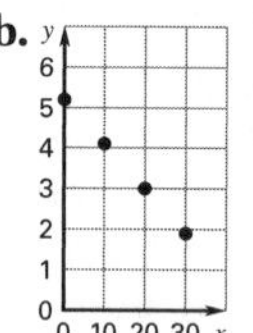

The area of the glaciers changed −1.1 square kilometers between every 10 year interval. **c.** $y = -0.11x + 5.2$; -0.11 km^2

51. a. $t = 0.7d + 2$ **b.** 16 min

SA12

5.1 Graphing Calculator Activity (pp. 290–291)
1. $y = -2x + 5$ **3.** $y = 2x + 1.5$ **5.** $y = 1.5x + 2$ **7.** $y = 4x - 3$ **9.** $y = 0.5x + 1$; substitute 2 for x, 2 for y, and solve for b.

5.2 Skill Practice (pp. 296–297) **1.** y-intercept **3.** $y = 3x - 2$ **5.** $y = -5x - 13$ **7.** $y = -\frac{3}{4}x + 2$ **9.** -3 was substituted for x instead of y and 6 was substituted for y instead of x, $-3 = -2(6) + b$, $-3 = -12 + b$, $9 = b$. **11.** $y = 3x + 1$ **13.** $y = -\frac{2}{5}x - 1$ **15.** $y = -\frac{3}{4}x + \frac{35}{8}$ **17.** $y = 4x - 15$ **19.** $y = -\frac{1}{2}x + \frac{1}{2}$ **21.** $y = \frac{1}{3}x - \frac{4}{3}$ **23.** $y = -2x + 11$ **25.** $y = -\frac{1}{2}x + 8$ **27.** $y = x - 2$ **31.** $y = -\frac{2}{3}x + 6$ **33.** $y = 6x - 4$ **35.** Yes; you can substitute m and the coordinates of the point in $y = mx + b$, solve for b, and write the equation. **37.** Yes; you can find the slope of the line, then substitute the y-intercept for b, and write the equation. **39.** $y = \frac{9}{2}x - \frac{1}{2}$ **41.** The lines $y = \frac{3}{2}x - \frac{1}{2}$ and $y = \frac{9}{2}x - \frac{1}{2}$ and the lines $y = \frac{9}{2}x - \frac{1}{2}$ and $y = \frac{3}{2}x + \frac{11}{2}$ intersect because they have different slopes; the lines $y = \frac{3}{2}x - \frac{1}{2}$ and $y = \frac{3}{2}x + \frac{11}{2}$ will not intersect because they have the same slope, so they are parallel. **43.** The three points do not lie on the same line. If you find the equation of the line between two of the points and then check to see that the third point is a solution, you can see they do not lie on the same line. **45.** The three points do not lie on the same line. If you find the equation of the line between two of the points and then check to see that the third point is a solution, you can see they do not lie on the same line.

5.2 Problem Solving (pp. 298–299) **47.** $\frac{3}{4}$ ft/yr; 6 ft **49.** 115 min or 1 h 55 min; substitute 30 for m, 2 for x, and 85 for y into the equation $y = mx + b$ to find $b = 25$. Then substitute 3 for x into the equation $y = 30x + 25$ to solve for y. **51. a.** about 584 newspapers **b.** $y = 11.8x + 584$ **c.** about 938 newspapers **53. a.** $d = -18t + 234$

b.

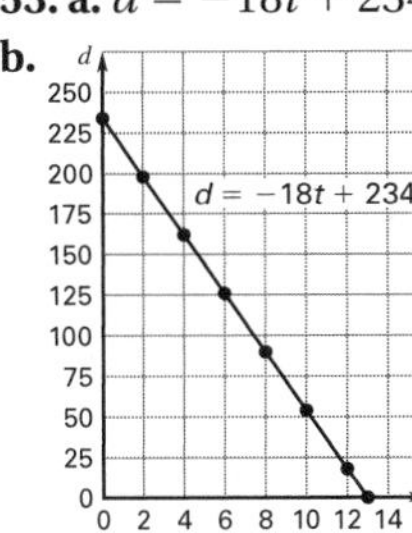

The slope is the rate that the hurricane is traveling, the y-intercept represents the distance from the town at 12 P.M.

c. 1 A.M.; find the t-intercept to find the value of t when the distance to the town is 0; substitute 0 for d and solve for t; $t = 13$, so you need to add 13 hours to 12 P.M. to get 1 A.M.

5.2 Problem Solving Workshop (p. 301) **1.** \$5; \$19 **3.** No; if the cost of the 60 inch bookshelf changes, the cost no longer increases at a constant rate. **5.** The student assumes that there is no fixed fee by using a proportion; $93 - 57 = 36$, $36 \div 2 = 18$, $57 + 18 = 75$.

5.3 Skill Practice (pp. 305–306) **1.** -2; $(-5, 5)$ **3.** $y - 1 = 2(x - 2)$ **5.** $y + 1 = -6(x - 7)$ **7.** $y - 2 = 5(x + 8)$ **9.** $y + 3 = -9(x + 11)$ **11.** $y + 12 = -\frac{2}{5}(x - 5)$ **13.** The form is $y - y_1$, so the left side should be $y - (-5)$ or $y + 5$; $y + 5 = -2(x - 1)$.

15.

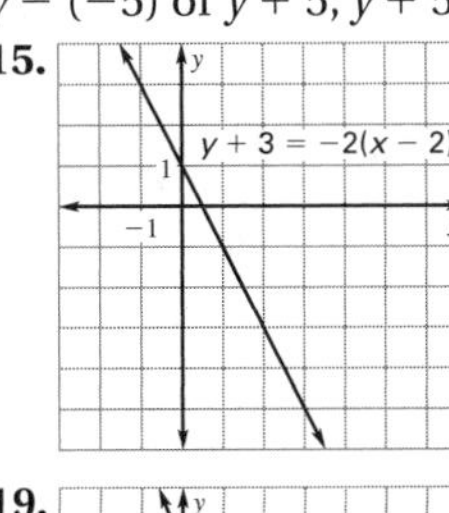

17.

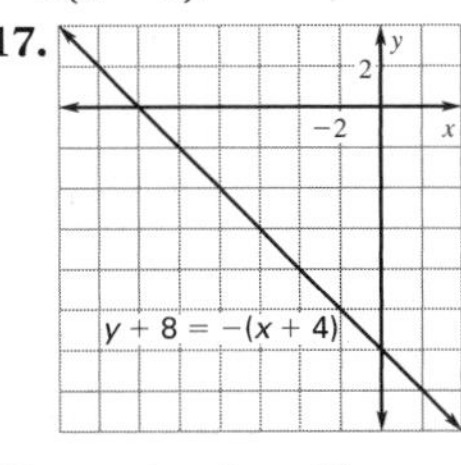

19.

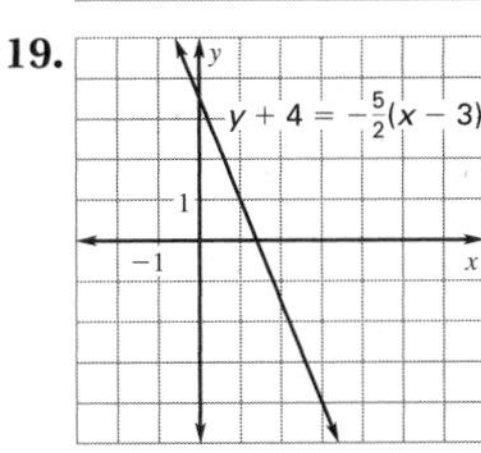

21. $y - 4 = (x - 1)$ or $y - 1 = (x + 2)$ **23.** $y - 2 = -2(x - 7)$ or $y - 12 = -2(x - 2)$ **25.** $y + 1 = -\frac{3}{5}(x + 4)$ or $y + 7 = -\frac{3}{5}(x - 6)$ **27.** $y + 20 = 8(x + 3)$ or $y - 36 = 8(x - 4)$ **29.** A point was not substituted into the equation, the y-coordinates of the two points were substituted; $y - 2 = \frac{2}{3}(x - 1)$. **31.** No; because the increase is not at a constant rate, the situation cannot be modeled by a linear equation. **33.** No; because the increase is not at a constant rate, the situation cannot be modeled by a linear equation.

5.3 Problem Solving (pp. 307–308) **37. a.** $y = 130x + 530$ **b.** \$1570 **39.** $y = 10000x + 67000$; \$127,000 **41. a.** Since the cost increases at a constant rate of \$.49 per print, the situation can be modeled by a linear equation. **b.** *Sample answer:* $y - 1.98 = 0.49(x - 1)$ **c.** \$1.49 **d.** \$1.79 **43. a.** $y - 17.6 = -0.06(x - 60)$ **b.** 16.4 ft/sec

SELECTED ANSWERS

Extension (p. 310) **1.** yes; 2, -1 **3.** yes; -43, -50

5. **7.**

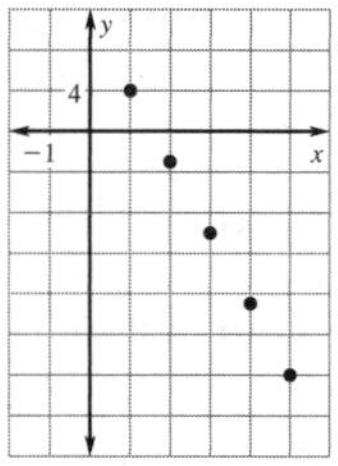

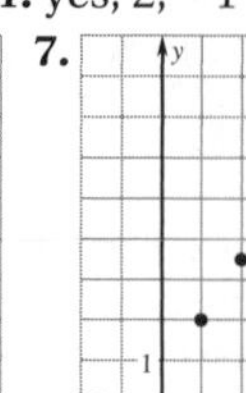

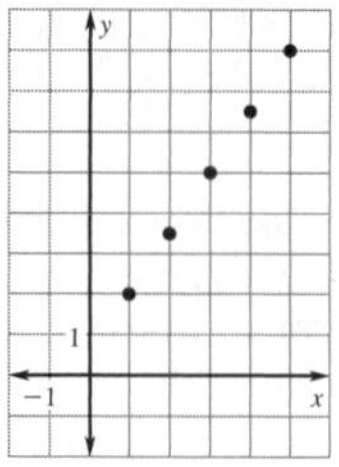

9.

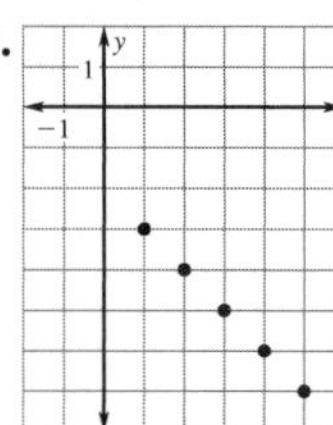

11. $a_n = 51 + (n - 1)21$; 2130 **13.** $a_n = \frac{1}{4} + (n - 1)\frac{1}{8}$; $12\frac{5}{8}$ **15.** $a_n = 1 + (n - 1)\frac{1}{3}$; 34

5.4 Skill Practice (p. 314) **1.** standard form **3.** point-slope form **5–9.** Sample answers are given. **5.** $2x + 2y = -20$, $3x + 3y = -30$ **7.** $x - 2y = -9$, $-2x + 4y = 18$ **9.** $3x - y = -4$, $6x - 2y = -8$ **11.** $-x + y = 5$ **13.** $2x + y = 5$ **15.** $\frac{3}{2}x + y = -10$ **17.** $\frac{2}{3}x + y = -\frac{4}{3}$ **19.** $-\frac{4}{3}x + y = -1$ **21.** $-\frac{1}{2}x + y = 1$ **23.** $y = 2$, $x = 3$ **25.** $y = 3$, $x = -1$ **27.** $y = 4$, $x = -1$ **29.** $(1, -4)$ was substituted incorrectly, 1 should be substituted for x and -4 substituted for y, $A(1) - 3(-4) = 5$, $A + 12 = 5$, $A = -7$. **31.** 4; $4x + 3y = 5$ **33.** -4; $-x - 4y = 10$ **35.** -5; $-5x - 3y = -5$

5.4 Problem Solving (pp. 315–316) **39. a.** 15 oz **b.** $12c + 15w = 120$ **c.** 10 corn, 0 wheat; 5 corn, 4 wheat; 0 corn, 8 wheat **41. a.** $100\ell + 40s = 1600$

b.

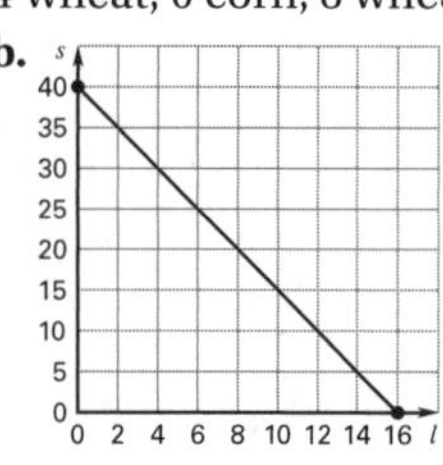

c.

Large rafts	Small rafts
16	0
14	5
12	10
10	15
8	20
6	25
4	30
2	35
0	40

43. $2\ell + 2w = 60$. *Sample answer:*

Length (ft)	Width (ft)
5	25
10	20
15	15
20	10
25	5

5.5 Skill Practice (pp. 322–323) **1.** perpendicular **3.** $y = 2x + 5$ **5.** $y = -\frac{3}{5}x + 2$ **7.** $y = 6x + 1$ **9.** $y = 2x + 9$ **11.** $y = 3x + 30$ **13.** parallel: a and b; perpendicular: none **15.** parallel: none; perpendicular: a and b **17.** The line through points (6, 4) and (4, 1) is perpendicular to the line through points (1, 3) and (4, 1); the slope of the line through the points (6, 4) and (4, 1) is $\frac{3}{2}$, the slope of the line through the points (1, 3) and (4, 1) is $-\frac{2}{3}$. The slopes are negative reciprocals, so the lines are perpendicular. **19.** $y = -\frac{1}{3}x - 1$ **21.** $y = -2x + 24$ **23.** $y = -\frac{3}{4}x - 4$ **25.** $y = -\frac{1}{2}x - \frac{1}{2}$ **27.** (2, 1) was substituted incorrectly, 2 should be substituted for x, and 1 should be substituted for y; $1 = 2(2) + b$, $1 = 4 + b$, $-3 = b$. **29.** Yes; the slope of the line through (4, 3) and (3, -1) is 4 and the slope of the line through (-3, 3) and (1, 2) is $-\frac{1}{4}$. The slopes are negative reciprocals, so the lines are perpendicular.

5.5 Problem Solving (pp. 323–324) **33. a.** $w = 200d + 6000$; $w = 200d + 6250$ **b.** 12,000 lb; 12,250 lb **c.** The graphs of the lines are parallel because they have the same slope, 200. The w-intercept of the second line is 250 more than the w-intercept of the first line. **35.** Different registration fees; because the lines are parallel, the rate of change, the monthly fee, for each must be equal. Therefore, the students paid different registration fees.

5.6 Skill Practice (pp. 328–329) **1.** increase **3.** positive correlation **5.** negative correlation

7.

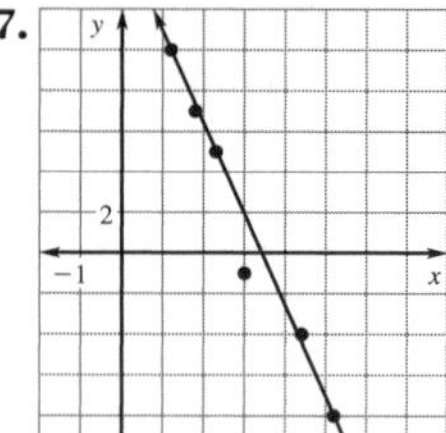

Sample answer: $y = -4.4x + 14.88$

9. The line does not have approximately half the data above it and half below it.

11. *Sample answer:* The amount of time driving a car and the amount of gas left in the gas tank

13.

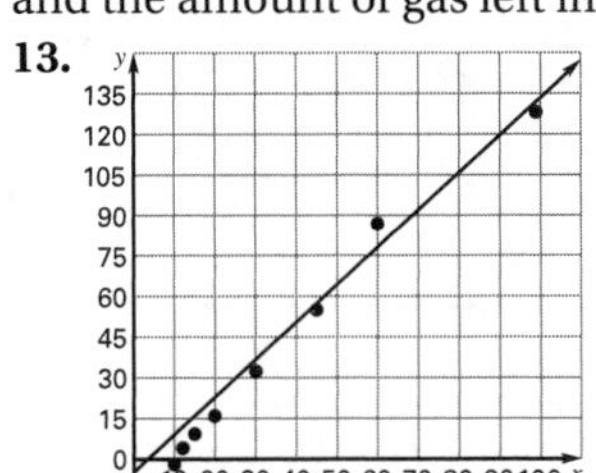

Positive correlation. *Sample answer:* $y = 1.49x - 13$

5.6 Problem Solving (pp. 330–331)

17. a.

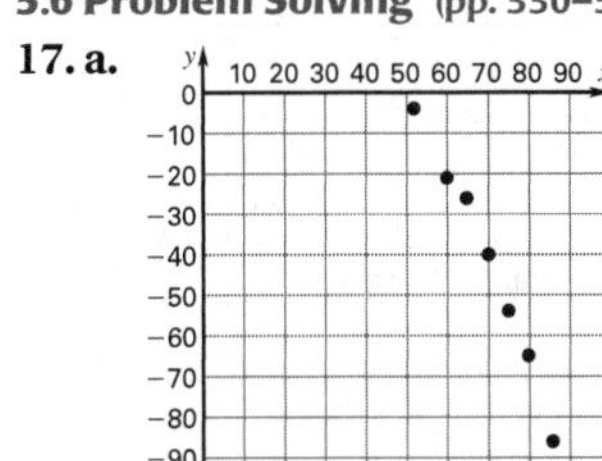

b. *Sample answer:* $y = -2.2x + 111$ **c.** *Sample answer:* -2.2 degrees per kilometer

19. *Sample answer:* $y = 12.6x + 32$

5.6 Graphing Calculator Activity (p. 333) **1.** See art in Exercise 3; negative correlation.

3.

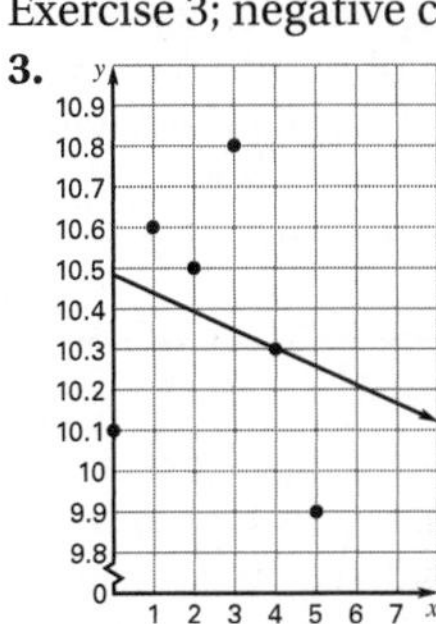

5. *Sample answer:* You cannot use the best-fitting line to predict future sales because the data do not show a strong correlation.

5.7 Skill Practice (pp. 338–339) **1.** linear interpolation

3.

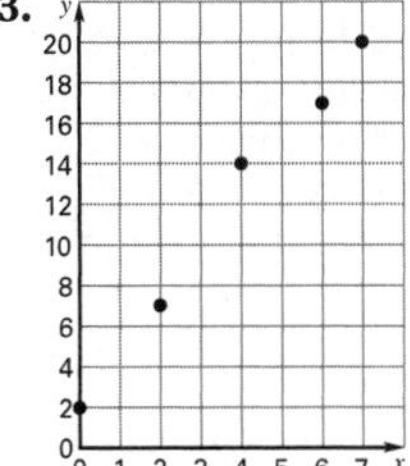

$y = 2.6x + 2.3$; 15.3

5. $y = 10.7x + 20$; 127

7. $2\frac{2}{3}$ **9.** -16 **11.** 1.5 **13.** To find the zero of a function, substitute 0 for y, not x; $0 = 2.3x - 2$, $2 = 2.3x$, $x = \frac{20}{23}$. **15.** a and b were not substituted correctly; $y = 4.47x + 23.1$.

5.7 Problem Solving (pp. 339–341)

19. a.

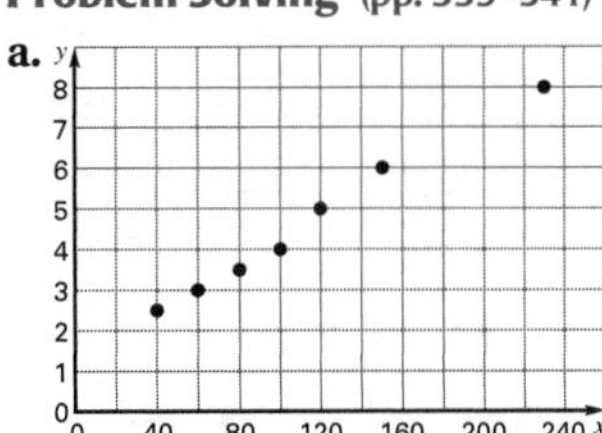

b. $y = 0.03x + 1.23$ **c.** about 8.73 ft^2

21. a. $y = -197.6x + 3542$ **b.** about 17.9; 17.9 years from 1985, or 2002, the number of people living in high noise areas will be 0; no.

5.7 Internet Activity (p. 342)

1. Answers may vary. **3.** Answers may vary.

Chapter Review (pp. 345–348) **1.** negative **3.** The zero of a function is the x-value of the function when $y = 0$; it is the x-intercept of the graph. **5.** $y = \frac{4}{9}x + 5$ **7.** $y = -1.25x + 25$; \$22.50 **9.** $y = x + 3$ **11.** $y - 7 = -6(x - 4)$ or $y - 1 = -6(x - 5)$ **13.** $y + 2 = -\frac{6}{11}(x + 3)$ or $y + 8 = -\frac{6}{11}(x - 8)$ **15.** $4x + y = -1$ **17.** $0.07r + 0.04s = 5$. *Sample answer:* 4 organza, 118 satin; 8 organza, 111 satin; 12 organza, 104 satin

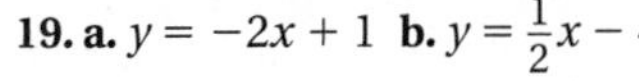

19. a. $y = -2x + 1$ **b.** $y = \frac{1}{2}x - 4$

21.

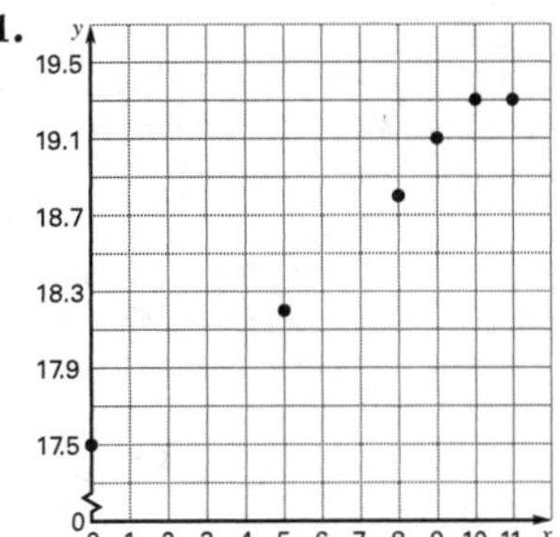

positive correlation

SELECTED ANSWERS

Chapter 6

6.1 Skill Practice (pp. 359–360) **1.** open, left of −8

3. $s \le 60$

5. $h > 48$

7. $x < 10$ **9.** $x \ge -2$

11. $y \ge -16$

13. $n \le -\frac{1}{5}$

15. $w > -17.6$

17. $s \ge 9$

19. $q > -1\frac{1}{6}$

21. $d > -6.84$

23. The number line should be shaded to the right of −3, not the left.

25. $n - 15 \le 37$; $n \le 52$

27. $x < 21.6$ **29.** No; no; there are infinitely many solutions of an inequality, so it is not possible to check them all. One solution might check in the inequality while another does not. For example, if you incorrectly solve $x + 7 > 10$ as $x > 2$, the solution $x = 4$ checks in the original inequality.

6.1 Problem Solving (pp. 360–361) **31.** more than 8350 points **33. a.** $s > 127.53$ **b.** Yes; no; no; $128.13 > 127.53$; $126.78 < 127.53$; when your score is 127.53, you and your competitor will tie.
35. *Sample answer:* You want to improve on your personal best of 16 points scored in a basketball game. In the first three quarters of the game, you scored 14 points. Write and solve an inequality to find the possible numbers of points that you can score in the fourth quarter to give yourself a new personal best; $x \ge 3$, if you score at least 3 points in the fourth quarter, you will have a new personal best.

37. a.

Original price, x ($)	19,459	19,989	20,549	22,679	23,999
Final price, y ($)	16,459	16,989	17,549	19,679	20,999

b. $x - 3000 \le 17{,}000$, $x \le 20{,}000$

6.2 Skill Practice (pp. 366–367)
1. Division property of inequality

3. $p \ge 7$

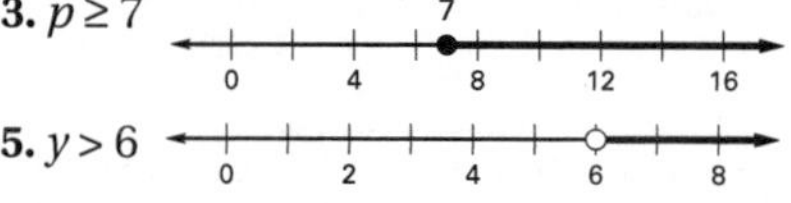

5. $y > 6$

7. $q < 28$

9. $g > -120$

11. $t \le -22.5$

13. $s \le -5$

15. $f < -0.25$

17. $c < -0.6$

19. $z \le -0.25$

21. $j < -0.34$

23. $r > -54$

25. $m > -24$

27. In both cases, you divide both sides of the inequality by a; when $a > 0$, you do not reverse the inequality symbol, but when $a < 0$, you do. **29.** Both sides of the inequality were multiplied by a positive number, so the inequality symbol should not have been reversed; $x \le -63$.

31. $-15y \le 90$; $y \ge -6$

33. $\frac{w}{24} \ge -\frac{1}{6}$; $w \ge -4$

6.2 Problem Solving (pp. 367–368) **37.** at least 200 words **39.** at least 3.2 **41. a.** $400h \le 6560$, $h \le 16.4$, no more than 16 horses **b.** No; the area added by increasing both the length and the width by 20 feet can be divided into 2 rectangles (80 feet by 20 feet and 82 feet by 20 feet) and 1 square (20 feet by 20 feet). The 400 square feet of the square is large enough to hold one horse, and the rectangular areas will be able to hold additional horses. **c.** no more than 23 horses; the area of the new corral is $(80 + 15)(82 + 15) = 9215$ square feet. Find the possible numbers of horses h the corral can hold by solving the inequality $9215 \ge 400h$; $h \le 23.04$.

6.3 Skill Practice (pp. 372–373)
1. equivalent inequalities
3. $x > 5$ 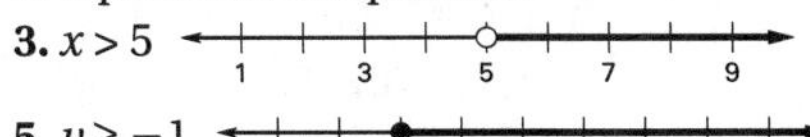
5. $v \ge -1$
7. $r \ge 1\frac{1}{7}$
9. $m > 3$
11. $p < \frac{1}{2}$
13. $d > -10$
15. The inequality symbol was not reversed when dividing both sides by -3; $x \le -13$. **17.** all real numbers **19.** $s \ge 0$ **21.** all real numbers **23.** no solution **25.** no solution **27.** no solution
29. $3x + 4 < 40$; $x < 12$
31. $5x + 2x > 9x - 4$; $x < 2$
35. $\frac{1}{2} \cdot 8(x + 1) \le 44$; $x \le 10$

6.3 Problem Solving (pp. 373–374) **37.** at most 11 songs **39. a.** Up to 6 swans; the area of the habitat is (20 feet)(50 feet) = 1000 square feet. 500 square feet are needed for the first two swans and the remaining 1000 − 500 = 500 square feet can hold up to 500 ÷ 125 = 4 more swans; so, the maximum number of swans is 2 + 4 = 6 swans. **b.** at most 14 more swans

41. a.

Pitches per inning, p	15	16	17	18	19
Total number of pitches, t	98	101	104	107	110

b. $53 + 3p \le 105$, $p \le 17\frac{1}{3}$, at most 17 pitches

6.3 Problem Solving Workshop (p. 376) **1.** at least 9 batches **3.** at most 6 games **5.** less than 7.9 min/mi

Extension (p. 378) **1.** $x > 3$ **3.** $x < 213.75$

6.4 Skill Practice (pp. 384–385)
1. compound inequality
3. $2 < x < 6$
5. $-1.5 \le x < 9.2$
7. $40 \le s \le 60$
9. $1 < x \le 6$
11. $-4 \le m \le \frac{1}{4}$
13. $-\frac{1}{3} \le p < 2$
15. $r < 2$ or $r \ge 7$
17. $v < -5$ or $v > 5$
19. $g < -2\frac{1}{3}$ or $g > 10$
21. 3 was subtracted from only two of the three expressions of the inequality; $1 < -2x < 6$, $-\frac{1}{2} > x > -3$.
23. $x + 5 < 8$ or $x - 3 > 5$; $x < 3$ or $x > 8$
25. $-8 \le 3(x - 4) \le 10$; $1\frac{1}{3} \le x \le 7\frac{1}{3}$
29. true **31.** False. *Sample answer:* $a = -4$ is a solution of $x > 5$ or $x \le -4$, but it is not a solution of $x > 5$.

6.4 Problem Solving (pp. 385–387)
37. $-2600 \le e \le -100$
41. 3.2 lb $\le f \le$ 6.4 lb **43. a.** $\frac{5}{9}(F - 32) < 0$ or $\frac{5}{9}(F - 32) > 100$, $F <$ 32°F or $F >$ 212°F
b.

°F	23	86	140	194	239
°C	−5	30	60	90	115

23°F, 239°F

45. a. $8 \le \frac{w}{300} \le 10$, $2400 \le w \le 3000$; 2400 watts to 3000 watts **b.** Yes; no; the amplification per person for 350 people is $\frac{2900}{350} \approx 8.3$ watts, which is between 8 watts and 10 watts, the amplification per person for 400 people is $\frac{2900}{400} = 7.25$ watts, which is not between 8 watts and 10 watts. **c.** 4800 watts; because each person requires at least 8 watts of amplification, and you want to be sure to provide enough amplification for 600 people, you need at least 8(600) = 4800 watts of amplification.

6.4 Graphing Calculator Activity (p. 388) **1.** $4 < x < 7$; the graphs are the same. **3–7.** Displays should show the graphs of the following inequalities. **3.** $3 \le x \le 7$ **5.** $8 \le x \le 48$ **7.** $x \le 4\frac{1}{2}$ or $x \ge 5$

6.5 Skill Practice (pp. 393–394) **1.** absolute value equation **3.** 5, −5 **5.** 0.7, −0.7 **7.** $\frac{1}{2}, -\frac{1}{2}$ **9.** 4, −10 **11.** $-1, -3\frac{2}{3}$ **13.** 2, −9 **15.** 4, 9 **17.** $8\frac{1}{2}, -3\frac{1}{2}$ **19.** $-\frac{1}{2}, -2\frac{1}{2}$ **21.** The absolute value symbol was removed without writing the second equation, $x + 4 = -13$; $x = 9$ or $x = -17$. **23.** no solution **25.** −4.5, −5.5 **27.** −3, 6 **29.** $13\frac{1}{2}, 14\frac{1}{2}$ **31.** $\frac{1}{4}, -1\frac{1}{4}$ **33.** 13, −3 **35.** −7.5, −10.7 **37.** The distance between x and 3 is 7, 10, −4; $x - 3 = 7$ *or* $x - 3 = -7$, 10, −4; the solutions are the same. **39.** $5|2x + 9| = 15$; −3, −6

6.5 Problem Solving (pp. 394–395) **43.** 235 sec, 245 sec **45. a.** 52.462 points, 56.888 points **b.** 0.3 point **47. a.** $p = |s - 450|$ **b.** 300 points, 600 points **49. a.** June 2005; November 2005 **b.** Yes; make a table of values for (m, p) using integer values of m from 0 to 8. Look for the lowest value of p in the table.

Extension (p. 397)

1.

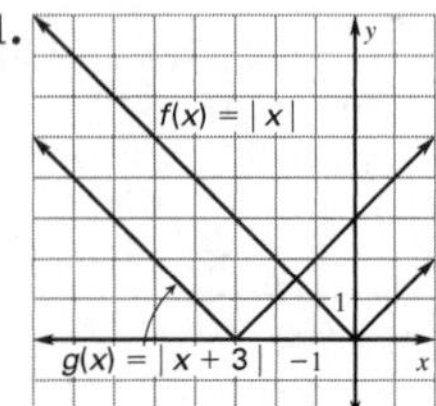

The graph of g is 3 units to the left of the graph of f.

3.

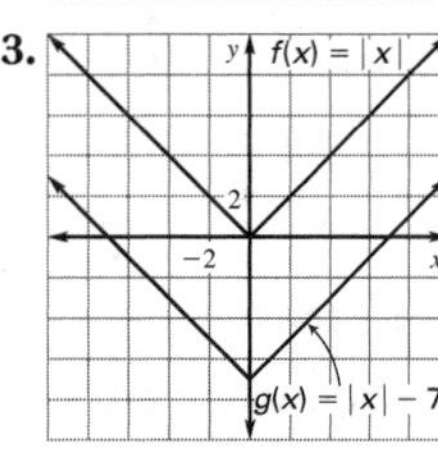

The graph of g is 7 units below the graph of f.

5.

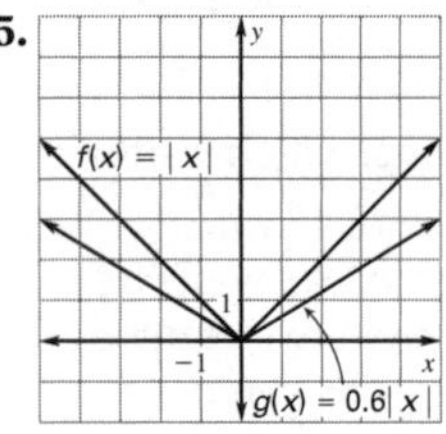

The graph of g opens up and is wider than the graph of f.

7.

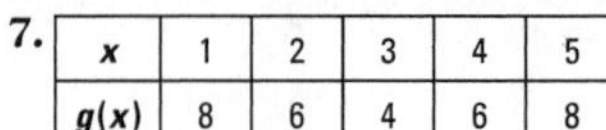

x	1	2	3	4	5
$g(x)$	8	6	4	6	8

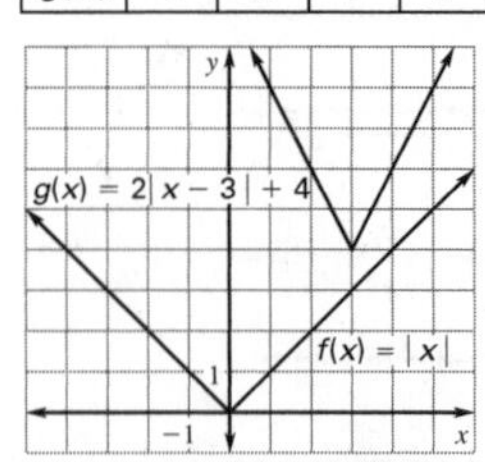

The graph of g is 3 units to the right of the graph of f and 4 units above it. The graph of g is narrower than the graph of f.

6.6 Skill Practice (pp. 401–402) **1.** equivalent inequalities **3.** $-4 < x < 4$ **5.** $h < -4.5$ or $h > 4.5$ **7.** $-\frac{3}{5} \le t \le \frac{3}{5}$

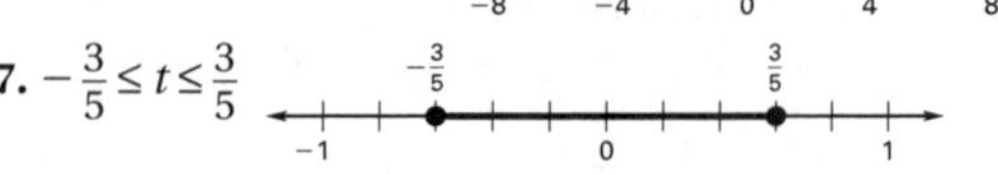

9. $d \le -7$ or $d \ge -1$ **11.** $m < 8$ or $m > 20$

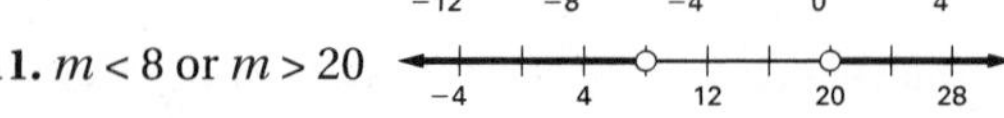

13. $c \le -3$ or $c \ge \frac{1}{2}$ **15.** $r < -8$ or $r > -4$ **17.** $u \le -3\frac{1}{5}$ or $u \ge 6\frac{2}{5}$ **19.** $v < 6$ or $v > 34$ **23.** The compound inequality should use *or*: $x + 4 > 13$ *or* $x + 4 < -13$; $x > 9$ *or* $x < -17$. **25.** $|x - 6| \le 4$; $2 \le x \le 10$ **27.** $|-4x - 7| + 3 > 10$; $x < -3.5$ *or* $x > 0$ **29.** true **31.** False. *Sample answer:* 20

6.6 Problem Solving (pp. 402–403) **35.** at least 470 words and at most 530 words **37.** $|t - 346| \le 2$, at least 344°F and at most 348°F; continue to preheat; the temperature is still below 350°F. **39. a.** 10.02 m/sec^2 **b.** 0.88 m/sec^2

6.7 Skill Practice (pp. 409–410) **1.** solution **3.** not a solution **5.** not a solution **7.** not a solution **9.** solution **11.** not a solution **13.** solution

SELECTED ANSWERS

SA18

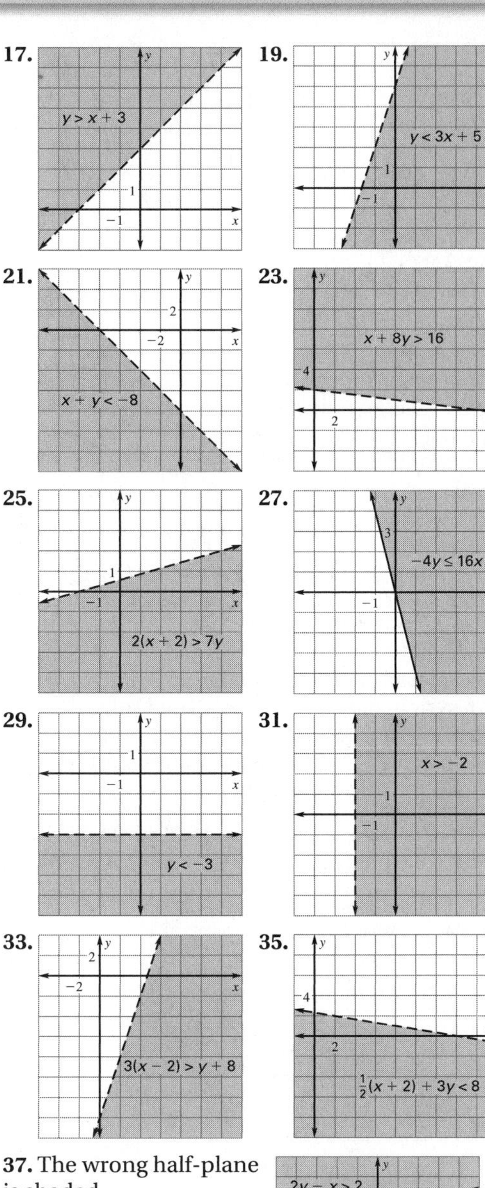

37. The wrong half-plane is shaded.

39. No; (0, 0) is a point on the boundary line $2x = -5y$.

41. $-2y \leq x + 6$ **43.** $x + 4y < -3$

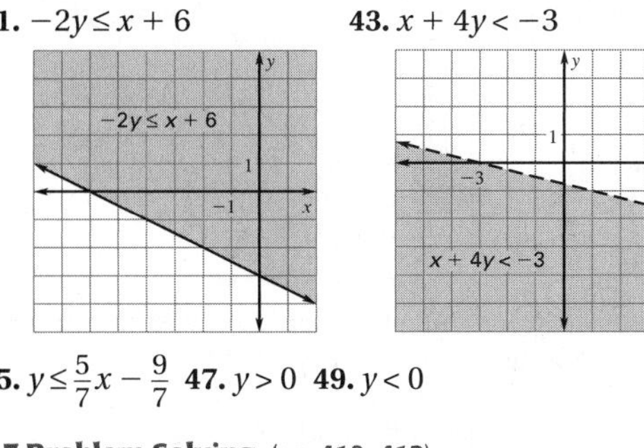

45. $y \leq \frac{5}{7}x - \frac{9}{7}$ **47.** $y > 0$ **49.** $y < 0$

6.7 Problem Solving (pp. 410–412)

53.

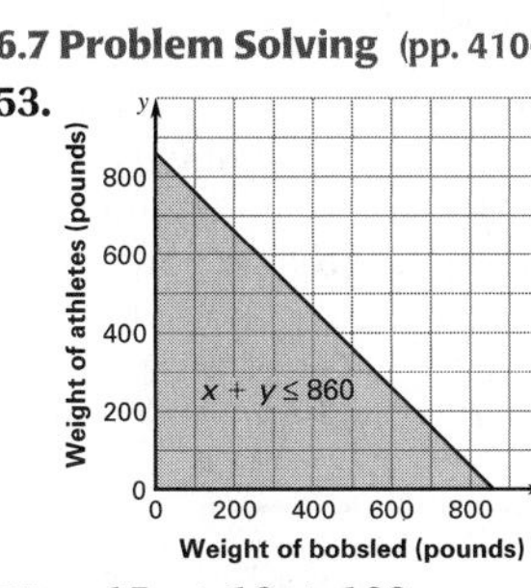

Sample answer: The solution (450, 400) means that the bobsled can weigh 450 pounds when the combined weight of the athletes is 400 pounds.

55. a. $15x + 10y \geq 100$

b.

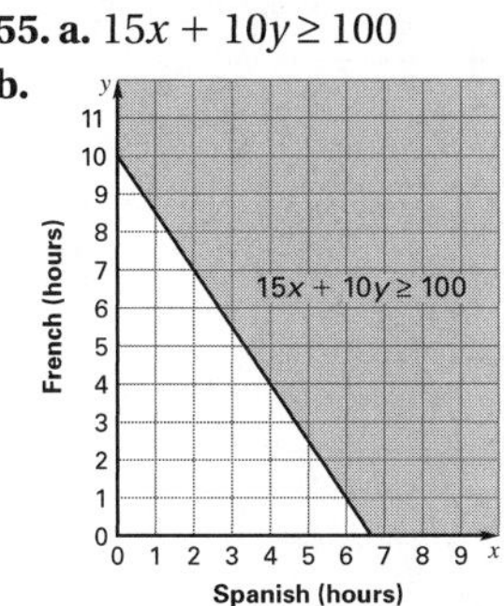

Sample answer: (4, 8), (5, 3), (6, 1)

c. *Sample answer:*

Spanish time (hours)	4	5	6
French time (hours)	8	3	1
Total earnings (dollars)	140	105	100

57. a. $\frac{1}{6}m + \frac{1}{2}\ell \leq 12$
b. $m \leq 60$

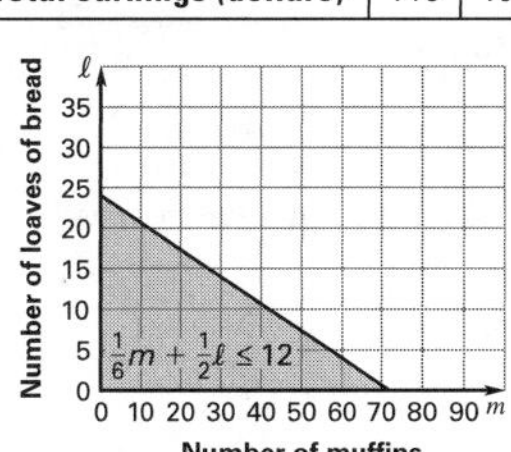

SELECTED ANSWERS

SA19

59. a. $x + y \leq 30$

Bedroll weight (pounds)
Duffel weight (pounds)
$x + y \leq 30$

Sample answer: (20, 4), (25, 5), (26, 2)

b. Yes; no; (0, 30) means that you do not take a duffel and have a 30 pound bedroll, while (30, 0) means you take a 30 pound duffel and do not take a bedroll. You need to bring both a duffel and a bedroll.

Chapter Review (pp. 415–418) **1.** $|x - 19| = 8$ **3.** The boundary line is solid if the inequality symbol is $\leq$ or $\geq$, the boundary line is dashed if the inequality symbol is < or >; choose a test point that is not on the boundary line. If the ordered pair is a solution to the inequality, shade the half-plane that contains the test point; if it not a solution, shade the other half-plane.

5. $x > -18$

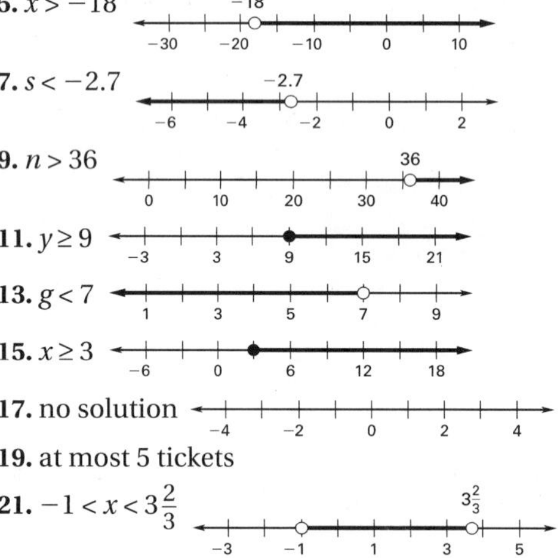

7. $s < -2.7$

9. $n > 36$

11. $y \geq 9$

13. $g < 7$

15. $x \geq 3$

17. no solution

19. at most 5 tickets

21. $-1 < x < 3\frac{2}{3}$

23. $w \leq \frac{1}{2}$ or $w > 2$

25. $-4, -8$ **27.** 5, 1 **29.** $1\frac{1}{6}, \frac{1}{6}$

31. $m \leq -8$ or $m \geq 8$

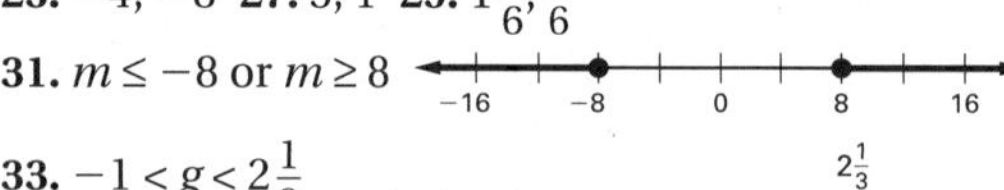

33. $-1 < g < 2\frac{1}{3}$

35. $j < -1\frac{1}{2}$ or $j > 10\frac{1}{2}$

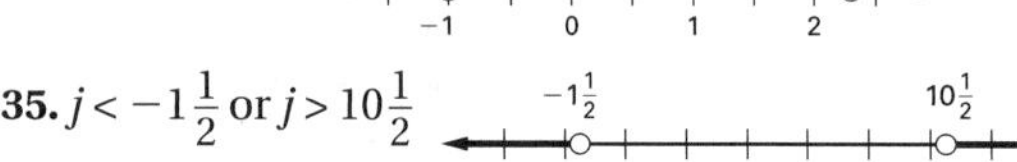

37. solution **39.** solution

41.

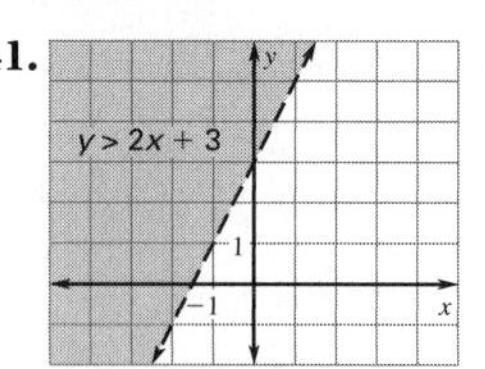

43.

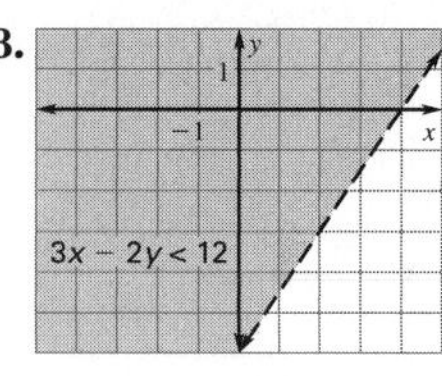

Chapter 7

7.1 Skill Practice (pp. 430–432) **1.** solution **3.** solution **5.** not a solution **9.** (4, 2)

11. The solution $(3, -1)$ does not satisfy Equation 2. The graph of Equation 2 is incorrect; if properly graphed, the lines would intersect at $(-3, -3)$.

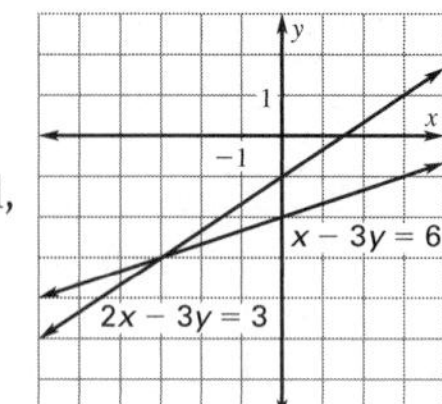

13. (4, 0) **15.** $(-3, -5)$ **17.** $(10, -15)$ **19.** $(7, -5)$ **21.** $(-5, 2)$ **23.** (3, 6) **25.** (4, 6) **27.** *Sample answer:* $m = 0$ and $b = 2$ **29. a.** 4 **b.** (4, 5) **c.** *Sample answer:* Each side of the equation is set equal to y. **d.** *Sample answer:* Set each side of the equation equal to y to create a system of two equations. Then solve the system using the graph-and-check method. The x-coordinate of the system's solution is the solution of the original equation.

7.1 Problem Solving (pp. 432–433) **31.** 2040 **33.** 15 small cards and 10 large cards **35. a.** $y = 5x + 15$, $y = 8x$

b.

Tickets	Cost for members	Cost for nonmembers
1	\$20	\$8
2	\$25	\$16
3	\$30	\$24
4	\$35	\$32
5	\$40	\$40
6	\$45	\$48

c.

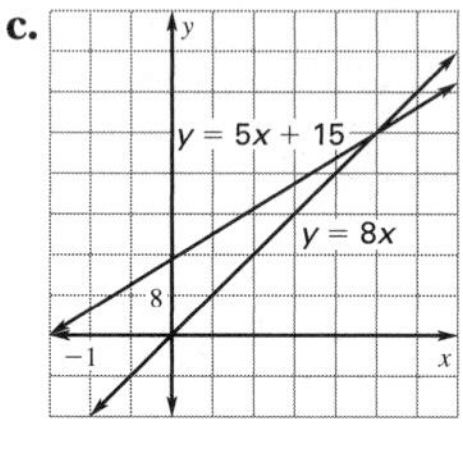

When you view 6 or more movies. *Sample answer:* The graph for a nonmember is below the graph for a member up through 4 movies. For 5 movies, the cost is the same. The graph for members is lower than the graph for nonmembers for 6 or more movies.

7.1 Graphing Calculator Activity (p. 434) **1.** $(-1.5, 2.5)$ **3.** $(0.2, -1.44)$

7.2 Skill Practice (pp. 439–440) **1.** *Sample answer:* $y = x + 1$, $y = 2x + 1$ **3.** (5, 3) **5.** (2, −1) **7.** (−4, 5) **9.** (6, 7) **11.** (2, −2) **13.** (5, −8) **15.** (0, 2) **17.** (1.4, −4.4) **19.** *Sample answer:* In Step 3, 6 is substituted for y instead of x; $y = 9 - 3(6)$, $y = -9$, the solution is (6, −9). **21.** (4, −120) **23.** (3, 7) **25.** (6, −3) **27.** (0, −6) **29.** *Sample answer:* The graphs of the equations should intersect at the solution you found using the substitution method.

7.2 Problem Solving (pp. 440–441) **31.** 96 bags of popcorn; 48 pretzels **33.** 4 in. *Sample answer:* (4, 5) is the solution to the appropriate linear system, so x should equal 4. **35.** 50 milliliters of 1% hydrochloric acid solution and 50 milliliters of 5% hydrochloric acid solution **37.** Yes. *Sample answer:* The cheetah would have to run at 88 feet per second for 23.3 seconds to catch the gazelle.

7.2 Problem Solving Workshop (p. 442) **1.** 5 mi

7.3 Skill Practice (pp. 447–448) **1.** *Sample answer:* $x + y = 10$, $x - y = 5$ **3.** (1, 6) **5.** (−1, −5) **7.** (5, 7) **9.** (−1, 2) **11.** (5, 3) **13.** (4, 5) **17.** (2, −3) **19.** (−18, 4) **21.** (4, −3) **23.** *Sample answer:* The two equations should be subtracted rather than added; $6x = 8$, $x = \frac{4}{3}$. **25.** (26, 14) **27.** (−4, 12) **29.** (−2, 5) **31.** (5, 25) **33.** (−2, 8) **35.** $\ell = 4.5$ ft, $w = 2.5$ ft

7.3 Problem Solving (pp. 449–450) **39.** speed in still water: 4.6 m/sec, speed of current: 0.3 m/sec **41.** monophonic ring tone: \$1.95, polyphonic ring tone: \$3.50 **43. a.** flight to Phoenix: 400 mi/h, flight to Charlotte: 450 mi/h **b.** $s + w = 450$, $s - w = 400$; plane: 425 mi/h, wind: 25 mi/h

7.4 Skill Practice (pp. 454–455) **1.** 36 **3.** (1, 1) **5.** (5, −4) **7.** (2, 1) **9.** (−7, −12) **11.** (5, 6) **13.** (4, 4) **15.** (5, −3) **17.** $\left(4\frac{2}{7}, 5\right)$ **19.** *Sample answer:* The two equations should be subtracted rather than added; $-x = -9$, $x = 9$. **21.** (2, −1) **23.** $\left(-4\frac{5}{22}, -2\frac{1}{11}\right)$ **25.** (5, 4) **27.** (10, 2) **29.** (2, −1) **31.** $\left(\frac{1}{3}, -\frac{2}{3}\right)$ **33. a.** $2\ell + 2w = 18$, $6\ell + 4w = 46$; length: 5 in., width: 4 in. **b.** length: 15 in., width: 8 in.

7.4 Problem Solving (pp. 456–457) **37.** 5 hardcover books **39.** 21 pies, 16 batches of applesauce **41.** \$16.50; a small costs \$2.90, and a large costs \$3.90; 3(2.90) + 2(3.90) = 16.50. **43.** \$800; \$1200

7.5 Skill Practice (pp. 462–464) **1.** inconsistent **3.** *Sample answer:* The lines have the same slope but different y-intercepts. **5.** B; one solution **7.** A; infinitely many solutions

9.

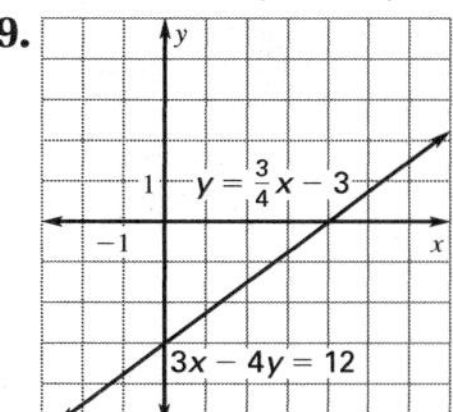
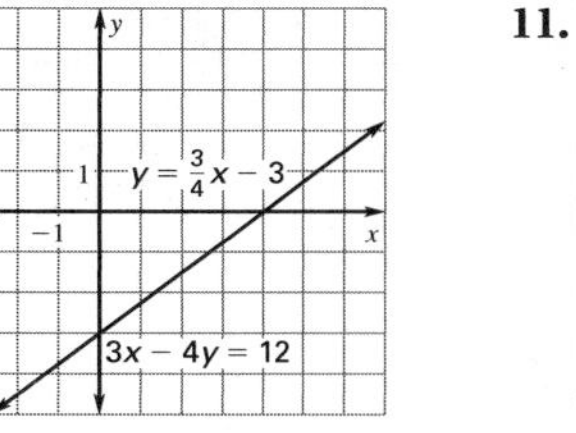

infinitely many solutions

11.

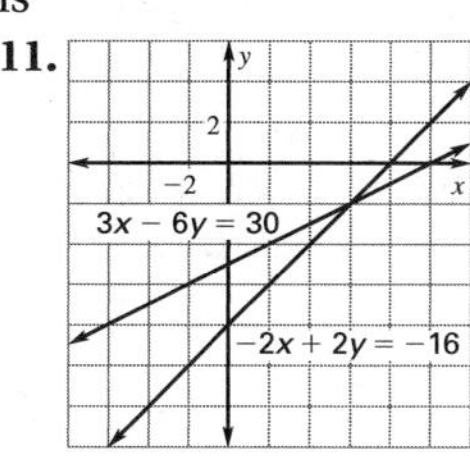

one solution

13.

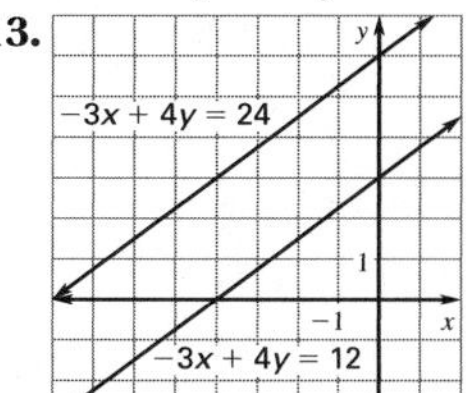

no solution

15. (−3, 4) **17.** (3, 7) **19.** (2, 2) **21.** no solution **23.** (0, 3) **27.** infinitely many solutions **29.** infinitely many solutions **31.** infinitely many solutions **33.** *Sample answer:* $7x - 8y = -9$, $7x - 8y = 4$

7.5 Problem Solving (pp. 464–465) **37.** Yes. *Sample answer:* There is one solution to the resulting linear system. **39. a.** $d = \frac{t}{3}$, $d = \frac{t}{3} - 5$

b.

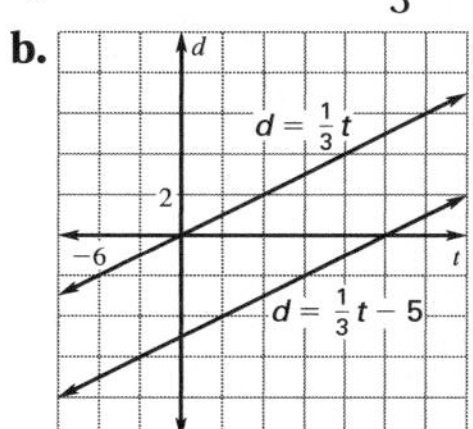

Sample answer: No, since the lines are parallel, the two climbers will never be at the same distance at the same time.

7.6 Skill Practice (pp. 469–470) **1.** solution **3.** not a solution **5.** not a solution **7.** A

9.

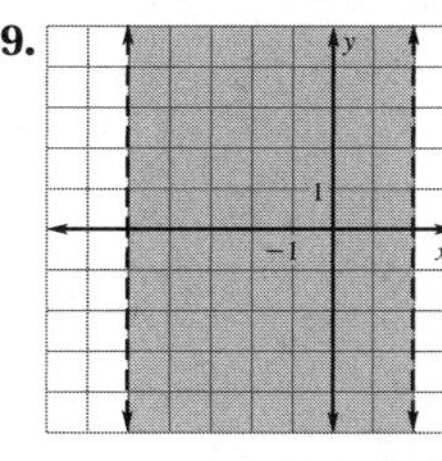

11.

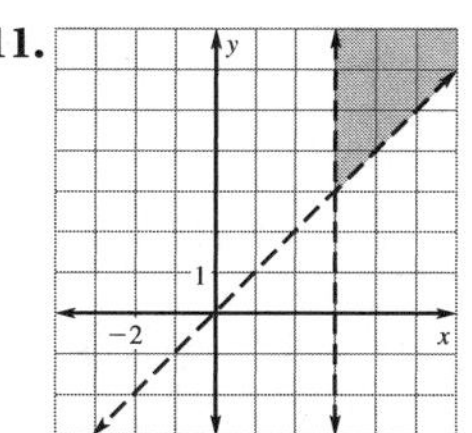

13.

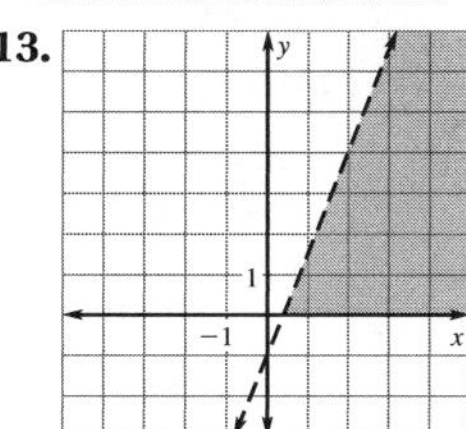

15.

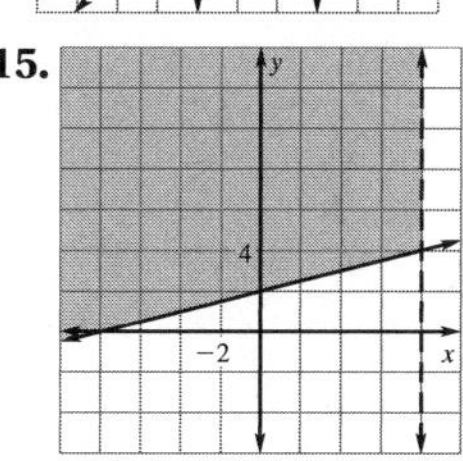

SELECTED ANSWERS

17.

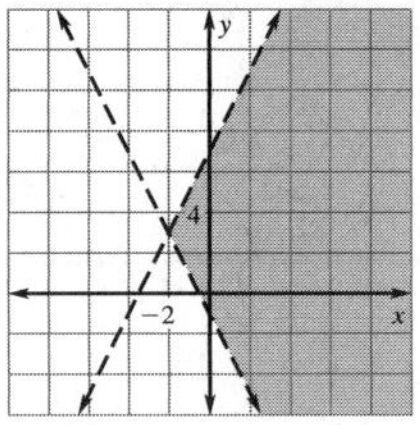

19. 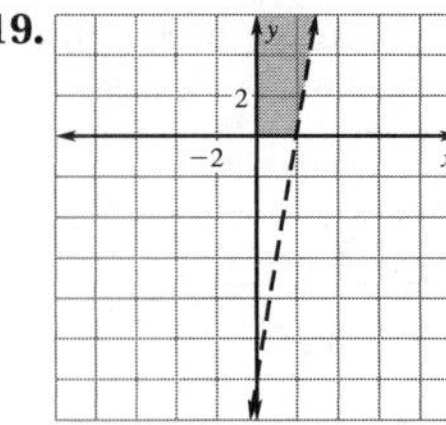

23. The graph is shaded to include $x + y > 3$, not $x + y < 3$.

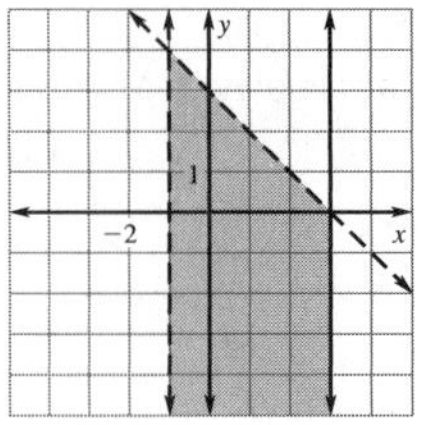

25. $y > -1, y < 4$ **27.** $y \leq 5x + 1, y > x - 2$ **29.** $y \leq x - 3, y > -2x - 1, y > -6$

31. 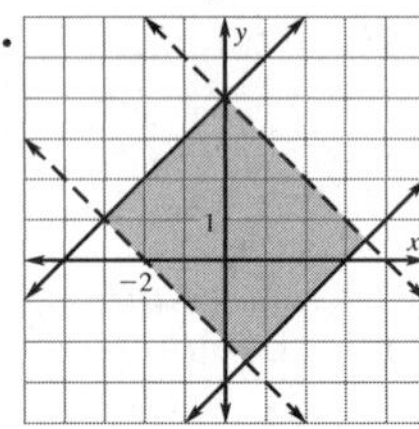

33. No; there are no possible values for x and y that satisfy both equations.

7.6 Problem Solving (pp. 471–472)

37. $14x + 7y < 70, x + y < 8, x \geq 0, y \geq 0$

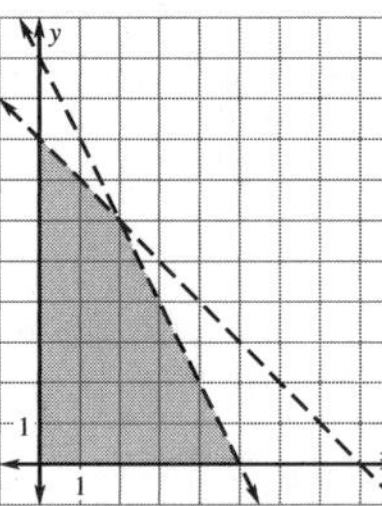

39. a. $20 \leq x \leq 65$, $154 - 0.7x \leq y \leq 187 - 0.85x$

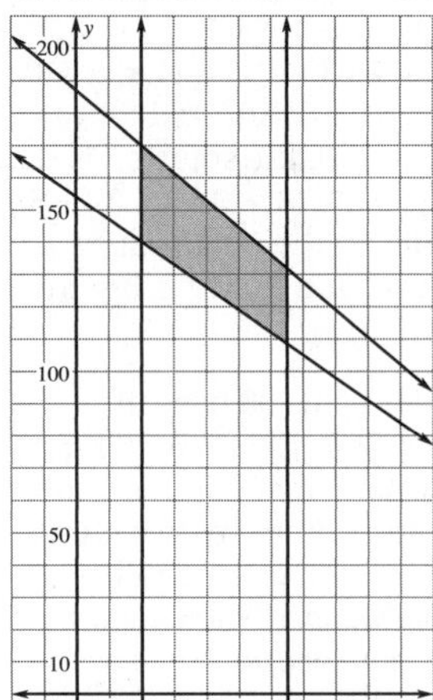

b. No. *Sample answer:* The heart rate is below 70% of the maximum heart rate.

Chapter Review (pp. 475–478) **1.** system of linear inequalities **3.** *Sample answer:* Graph each inequality then shade the region that is the intersection of the solutions to each inequality. Then check the solution with a test point. **5.** (2, −5) **7.** (4, −1) **9.** (5, 1) **11.** 4 tubes of paint, 8 brushes **13.** (1, −2) **15.** (6, 10) **17.** (−7, 8) **19.** (−2, 5) **21.** (4, 5) **23.** (1, 6) **25.** No solution. *Sample answer:* When the variables are eliminated, a false statement remains, which means there is no solution. **27.** One solution. *Sample answer:* The lines have different slopes, so there is only one solution.

29. 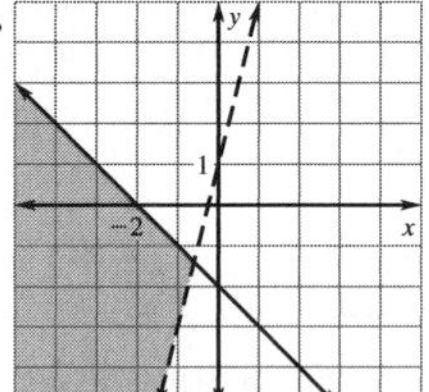

31. Let m represent the number of matinee movies and n represent the number of evening movies; $5m + 8n \leq 40, m \geq 0, n \geq 0$.

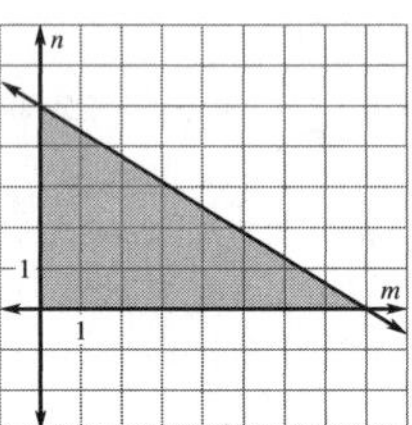

Cumulative Review (pp. 484–485) **1.** 62 **3.** 55 **5.** −50 **7.** solution **9.** not a solution **11.** solution **13.** $5y - 1$ **15.** $-g + 4$ **17.** $-3 + \frac{4}{7}x$ **19.** 29 **21.** −7 **23.** −3 **25.** −3 **27.** $4\frac{4}{9}$

29. 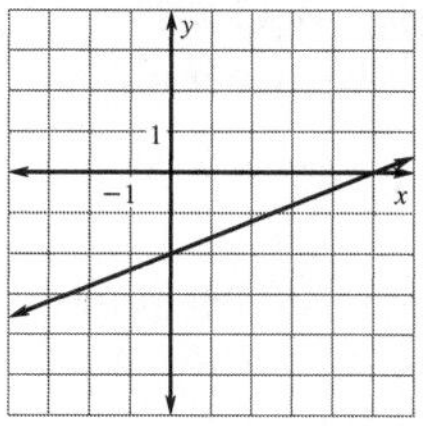 **31.** 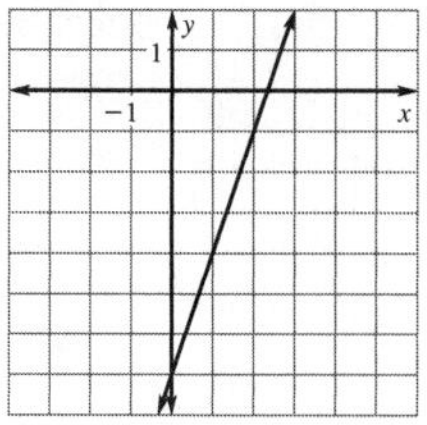

33. 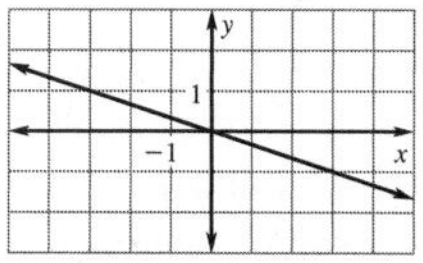

35. $y = -x + 3$ **37.** $y + 10 = -2(x - 1)$ or $y - 2 = -2(x + 5)$ **39.** $y + 2 = \frac{10}{3}(x + 9)$ or $y - 8 = \frac{10}{3}(x + 6)$
41. $y - 4 = -\frac{1}{3}(x - 2)$ or $y - 2 = -\frac{1}{3}(x - 8)$
43. $x < -4$ 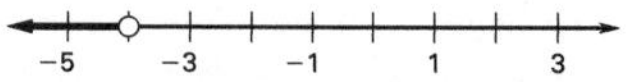
45. $x \geq 7$ 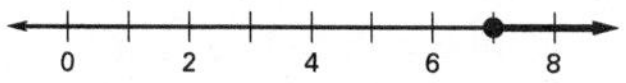
47. $x > -5$ 
49. $x \geq -6$ 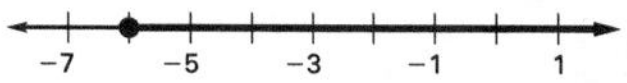
51. $-1 < x < 2$ 
53. $-5 < x < 5$

55. (1, 4) **57.** (2, −3) **59.** \$.02 **61. a.** The ratio $\frac{p}{\ell}$ is always the same, so p varies directly with ℓ. **b.** $p = 2.5\ell$ **63.** $-4 < F < 113$

Chapter 8

8.1 Skill Practice (pp. 492–493) **1.** order of magnitude **3.** 4^8 **5.** 3^4 **7.** $(-7)^9$ **9.** 2^{14} **11.** 3^{10} **13.** $(-5)^{12}$ **15.** $15^3 \cdot 29^3$ **17.** $132^6 \cdot 9^6$ **19.** x^6 **21.** z^6 **23.** x^{10} **25.** $(b - 2)^{12}$ **27.** $25x^2$ **29.** $49x^2y^2$ **31.** $100x^{14}$ **33.** $96d^{22}$ **35.** $12p^{19}$ **37.** $108x^{29}$ **39.** *Sample answer:* The exponents should be added, not multiplied; $c^1 \cdot c^4 \cdot c^5 = c^{1+4+5} = c^{10}$. **43.** 2 **45.** 2 **47.** $-3267x^{12}y^{13}$ **49.** $1000r^{17}s^6t^{17}$

8.1 Problem Solving (pp. 493–494) **53.** 10^{26} m
55. a.

Ounces of gold	10	100	1000	10,000	100,000
Number of atoms	10^{24}	10^{25}	10^{26}	10^{27}	10^{28}

b. $10^5 \cdot 10^{23}$; 10^{28} atoms **57.** 10^{27}

8.2 Skill Practice (pp. 498–499) **1.** base, exponent **3.** 5^4 **5.** 3^4 **7.** $(-4)^3$ **9.** 10^6 **11.** $\frac{1}{3^5}$ **13.** $\frac{5^4}{4^4}$ **15.** 7^7 **17.** 3^8 **21.** y^7 **23.** $\frac{a^9}{y^9}$ **25.** $\frac{p^4}{q^4}$ **27.** $-\frac{64}{x^3}$ **29.** $\frac{64c^3}{d^6}$ **31.** $\frac{x^4}{9y^6}$ **33.** $\frac{9x^4}{4y^2}$ **35.** $\frac{3m^7}{8n^6}$ **39.** 8 **41.** 4 **43.** $54s^3t^3$ **45.** $\frac{27x^{11}y^5}{25}$
47. Identity property of multiplication; Multiply fractions; Quotient of powers property

8.2 Problem Solving (pp. 500–501)
49. a.

Step	Number of new squares	Side length of new square
1	$4 = 4^1$	$\frac{1}{2} = \left(\frac{1}{2}\right)^1$
2	$16 = 4^2$	$\frac{1}{4} = \left(\frac{1}{2}\right)^2$
3	$64 = 4^3$	$\frac{1}{8} = \left(\frac{1}{2}\right)^3$
4	$256 = 4^4$	$\frac{1}{16} = \left(\frac{1}{2}\right)^4$

b. $\frac{4^4}{4^2}$; 16 times

51. about 31,710 yr **53.** 31^3 times greater

8.3 Skill Practice (pp. 506–507) **1.** Product of powers property and definition of zero exponent; the expression simplifies using the product of powers property to 3^0, which by definition equals 1. **3.** $\frac{1}{64}$ **5.** $-\frac{1}{3}$ **7.** 1 **9.** 1 **11.** $\frac{49}{4}$ **13.** undefined **15.** $\frac{1}{32}$ **17.** $\frac{1}{32}$ **19.** 27 **21.** $\frac{1}{243}$ **23.** $\frac{8}{3}$ **25.** 16 **27.** 3^0 is not equivalent to 0, but to 1; $-6 \cdot 3^0 = -6 \cdot 1 = -6$. **29.** $\frac{2}{y^3}$ **31.** $\frac{1}{121h^2}$ **33.** $\frac{5}{m^3n^4}$ **35.** 1 **37.** $\frac{1}{x^5y^2}$ **39.** $\frac{y^8}{15x^{10}}$ **41.** $243d^3$ **43.** $\frac{3x^{12}y^5}{4}$ **49.** *Sample answer:* It approaches 0.

8.3 Problem Solving (pp. 507–508) **51.** about 10^5 grains of rice **53.** about 10^{11} red blood cells
55. a.

Number of folds	0	1	2	3
Fraction of original area	1	$\frac{1}{2}$	$\frac{1}{4}$	$\frac{1}{8}$

b. $\left(\frac{1}{2}\right)^x$ where x is the number of folds **57. a.** 112.5 watts **b.** $I = 9d^{-2}$ **c.** The intensity is divided by 4.

Extension (p. 510) **1.** 1000 **3.** $\frac{1}{729}$ **5.** $\frac{1}{3}$ **7.** 81 **9.** $\frac{1}{216}$ **11.** $-\frac{1}{4}$ **13.** *Sample answer:* $b^3 = a$, substitute a^k for b to create $(a^k)^3 = a$; $a^{3k} = a^1$ by the power of a power property. Solving for k, $3k = 1$ so $k = \frac{1}{3}$.

8.4 Skill Practice (pp. 515–516) **1.** No; 0.5 is not a number greater than or equal to 1.0 and less than 10. **3.** 8.5×10^0 **5.** 8.24×10^1 **7.** 7.2×10^7

SELECTED ANSWERS

9. 1.06525×10^6 **11.** 1.06×10^9 **13.** 9×10^{14} **17.** 75,000,000 **19.** 30,300 **21.** 15,440,000,000 **23.** 0.00000000044 **25.** 0.0000000852 **27.** 0.0000012034 **29.** 6.7×10^3; 12,439; 2×10^4; 45,000 **31.** 9.8×10^{-6}; 0.00008; 0.0005; 5×10^{-3}; 8.2×10^{-3}; 0.04065 **33.** $<$ **35.** $=$ **37.** $>$ **39.** 6.6×10^{-4} **41.** 7.29×10^{-9} **43.** 3×10^{-3} **45.** 1.25×10^{-22} **47.** 1.96×10^6 **49.** *Sample answer:* 2.8×10^1 and 1×10^3; 11.2×10^5 and 4.0×10^1

8.4 Problem Solving (pp. 516–518) **51. a.** 1.4×10^{-4}; 2.5×10^{-1}; 1.67×10^2; 555 **b.** the elephant beetle and the walking stick **53.** 1406 pounds per acre **55. a.** About 3.67; the radius of Earth is about 3.67 times greater than the radius of the moon. **b.** About 49.30; the volume of Earth is about 49.30 times greater than the volume of the moon. **c.** The ratio of the volumes is the cube of the ratio of the radii. **57.** 4 in. by 6 in. **59. a.** 4.9 L **b.** about 2.58×10^6 L, about 2.58×10^7 L, about 2.06×10^8 L **c.** Underestimates. *Sample answer:* They are calculated when a person is at rest. When a person is not resting, the rate will go up.

8.4 Graphing Calculator Activity (p. 519) **1.** 2.7×10^{13} **3.** 2.5×10^{19} **5. a.** about 6.10×10^{18} g **b.** about 3.05×10^{41} atoms

8.5 Skill Practice (pp. 523–524) **1.** growth factor **3.** The graph would be a vertical stretch. *Sample answer:* Since the y-values of $y = 2 \cdot 5^x$ are double those of $y = 5^x$. **5.** $y = 125 \cdot 5^x$ **7.** $y = \frac{1}{9} \cdot 3^x$

9. 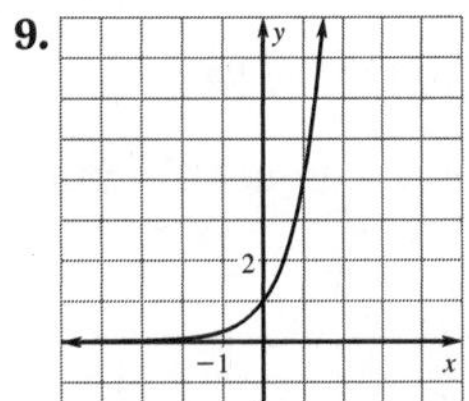 domain: all real numbers, range: all positive real numbers

11. 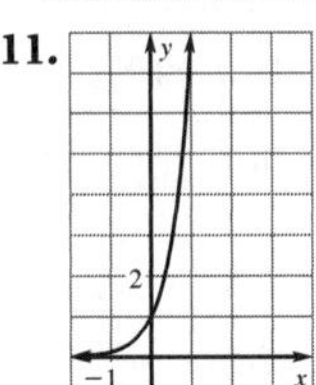 domain: all real numbers, range: all positive real numbers

13. 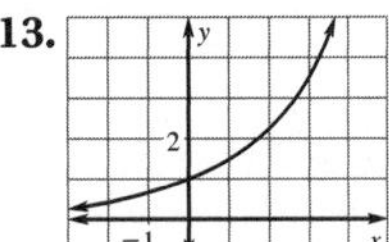 domain: all real numbers, range: all positive real numbers

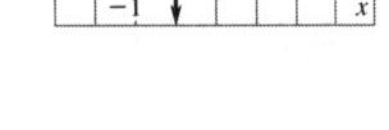

15. 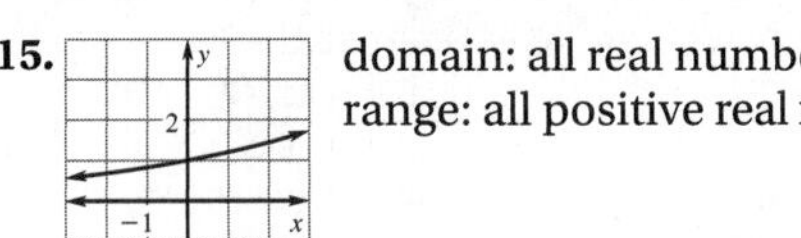 domain: all real numbers, range: all positive real numbers

17. 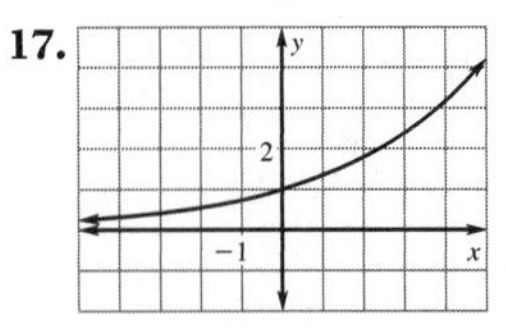 domain: all real numbers, range: all positive real numbers

19. 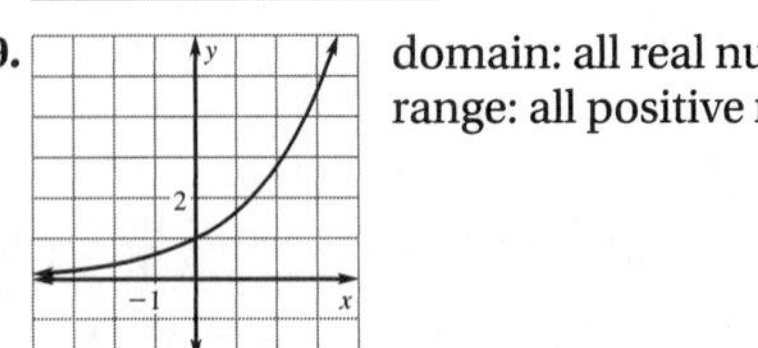 domain: all real numbers, range: all positive real numbers

21. The percent increase was not written as a decimal; $0.27(1 + 0.02)^3 = 0.27(1.02)^3 \approx \$.29$.

23. 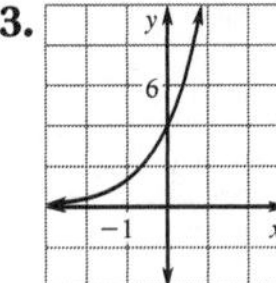 The graph is a vertical stretch.

25. 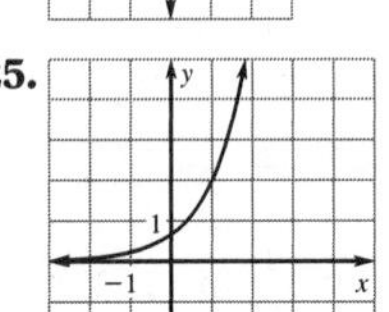 The graph is a vertical shrink.

27. 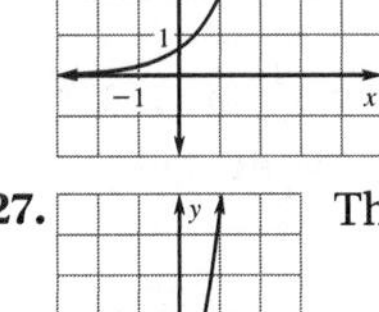 The graph is a vertical stretch.

29. 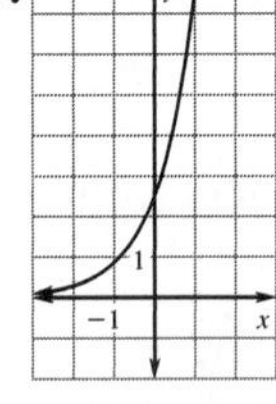 The graph is a vertical stretch with a reflection in the x-axis.

31. 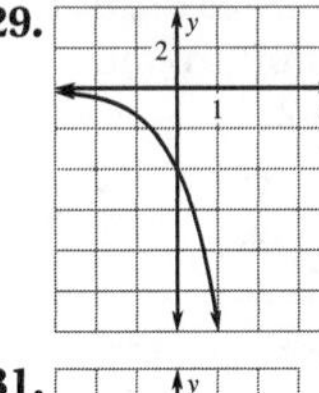 The graph is a vertical shrink with a reflection in the x-axis.

33. 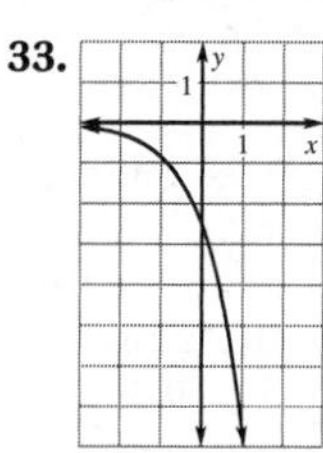 The graph is a vertical stretch with a reflection in the x-axis.

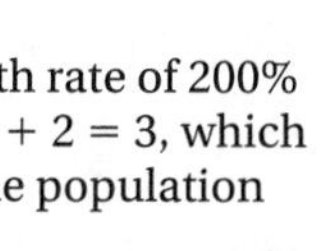

35. 200%. *Sample answer:* A growth rate of 200% would create a growth factor of $1 + 2 = 3$, which would represent the tripling of the population every year.

8.5 Problem Solving (pp. 525–527) **39. a.** Let x represent the number of years since 2001 and $f(x)$ represent the number of computers (in hundreds of millions); $f(x) = 6 \cdot (1.1)^x$. **b.** about 1,286,153,286 computers **41. a.** tree 1: $A = 154 \cdot (1.06)^t$, tree 2: $A = 113 \cdot (1.1)^t$
b. 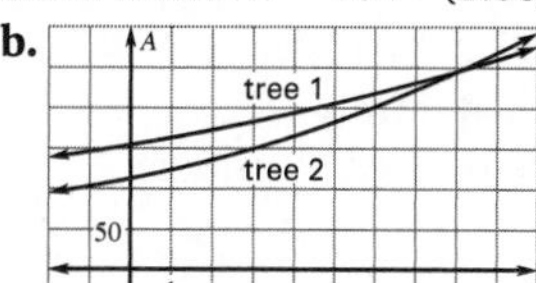

about 8.4 yr

45. $y = 25.96(1.059)^x$; about 145 Hz **47.** \$1266.77 **49.** \$1271.24

8.5 Problem Solving Workshop (pp. 528–529)
1. a. Let t represent the number of years since 1997 and F represent the bus fare; $F = 20(1.12)^t$. **b.** \$22.40 **c.** 2000. *Sample answer:* Make a table of values.
3. a. $T = 7.5(1.039)^t$ **b.** about 37.4 million

8.6 Skill Practice (pp. 535–536) **1.** $1 - r$ **3.** exponential function; $y = 8 \cdot 4^x$ **5.** exponential function; $y = 2\left(\frac{1}{3}\right)^x$

7. 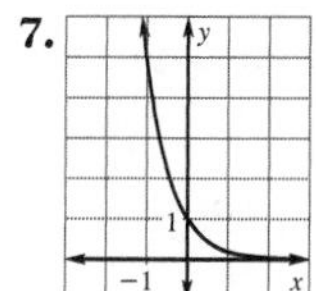 domain: all real numbers, range: all positive real numbers

9. 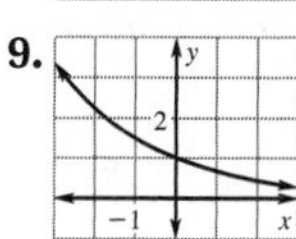 domain: all real numbers, range: all positive real numbers

11. 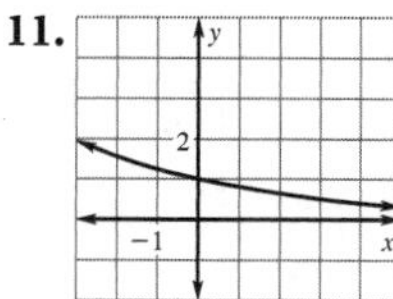 domain: all real numbers, range: all positive real numbers

13. 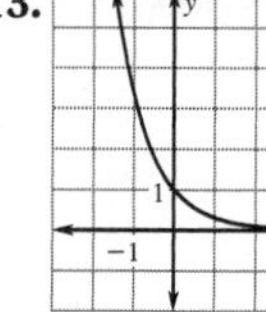 domain: all real numbers, range: all positive real numbers

15. 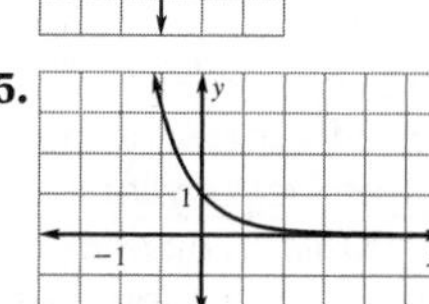 domain: all real numbers, range: all positive real numbers

17. 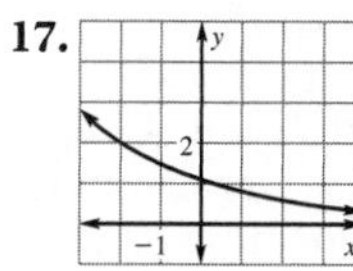 domain: all real numbers, range: all positive real numbers

21. 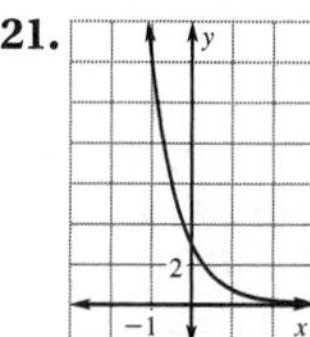 The graph is a vertical stretch.

23. 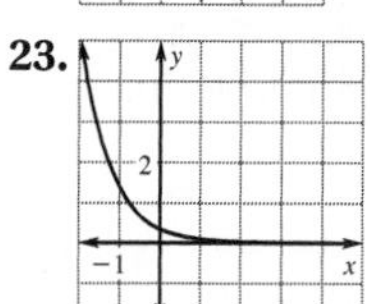 The graph is a vertical shrink.

25. 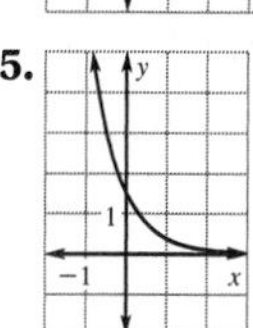 The graph is a vertical stretch.

27. 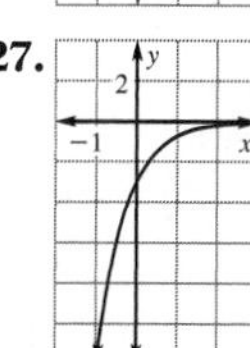 The graph is a vertical stretch with a reflection in the x-axis.

29. 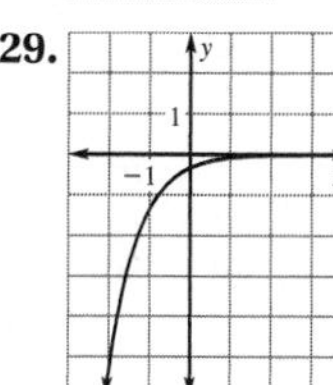 The graph is a vertical shrink with a reflection in the x-axis.

31. The graph is a vertical stretch with a reflection in the x-axis.

33. C **35.** initial amount: 90,000 people, decay factor: 0.975, decay rate: 2.5%; Let P represent the population and t represent the number of years; $P = 90{,}000(0.975)^t$. **37.** *Sample answer:* The decay rate, r, is 0.14. So the decay factor $(1 - r)$ should be 0.86, not 0.14; $y = 25{,}000(0.86)^t$. **39.** exponential decay; $y = 8 \cdot 0.6^x$ **41. a.** The graph is a vertical shrink. **b.** The graph is a vertical stretch with a reflection in the x-axis. **c.** The graph is a vertical shift up 1 unit. **45.** *Sample answer:* After one time period, the new amount is the initial amount minus the amount of decrease: $a - ra = a(1 - r)$.

8.6 Problem Solving (pp. 537–538) **47.** Let V represent the value of the cell phone and t represent the number of years since purchase, $V = 125(0.8)^t$; \$64. **49.** No. *Sample answer:* The boat's value is about \$3217. **51. a.** decay factor: 0.9439, decay rate: 5.61% **b.** about 1.431 in. **c.** about 0.716 in. **53. a.** $y = 4(0.995)^x$, $y = 3.5(0.995)^x$

b. $y = 4(0.995)^x$, $y = 3.5(0.995)^x$ **c.** about 52 yr

Extension (p. 540)

1. geometric **3.** arithmetic

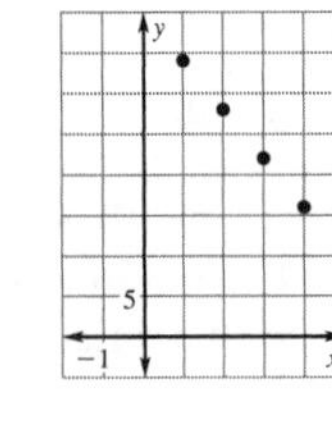

5. geometric

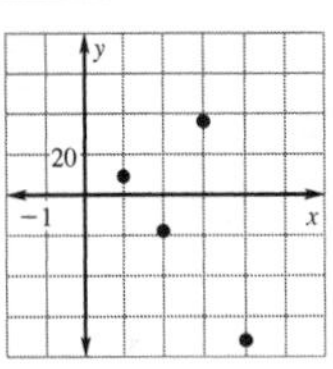

7. $a_n = (-5)^{n-1}$; 15,625 **9.** $a_n = 432\left(\frac{1}{6}\right)^{n-1}$; $\frac{1}{108}$

Chapter Review (pp. 543–546) **1.** decay, decay factor **3.** Exponential decay; $b = 0.85$ which is between 0 and 1, therefore it's exponential decay. **5.** Exponential growth; $b = 2.1$ which is greater than 1, therefore it's exponential growth. **7.** $(-3)^8$ **9.** y^{20} **11.** $(b + 2)^{24}$ **13.** $-64x^2y^2$ **15.** 10^{21} **17.** 5^3 **19.** 17^4 **21.** $\frac{49x^{10}}{y^4}$ **23.** $\frac{6r^{15}}{7s^5}$ **25.** 1 **27.** $\frac{27}{8}$ **29.** 10^6 **31.** 0.000075 **33.** 4.0625×10^{13}

35.

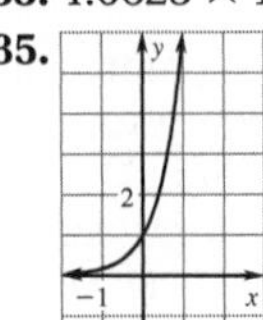

domain: all real numbers, range: all positive real numbers

37.

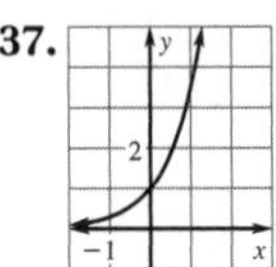

domain: all real numbers, range: all positive real numbers

39.

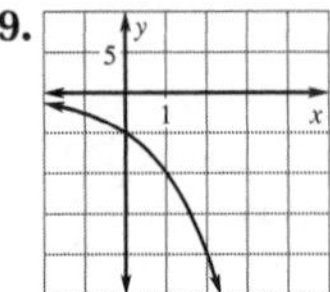

The graph is a vertical stretch with a reflection in the x-axis.

41. exponential decay; $y = 3 \cdot \left(\frac{1}{3}\right)^x$

Chapter 9

9.1 Skill Practice (pp. 557–558) **1.** monomial **3.** $9m^5$; 5, 9 **5.** $2x^2y^2 - 8xy$; 4, 2 **7.** $3z^4 + 2z^3 - z^2 + 5z$; 4, 3 **11.** not a polynomial; variable exponent **13.** polynomial; 1, binomial **15.** polynomial; 3, trinomial **17.** $13a^2 - 4$ **19.** $m^2 + 9m + 9$ **21.** $6c^2 + 14$ **23.** $-2n^3 + n - 12$ **25.** $-15d^3 + 3d^2 - 3d + 2$ **27.** Two unlike terms, $-4x^2$ and $8x$, were combined; $-2x^3 - 4x^2 + 8x + 1$. **29.** $2x^2 + 6x - 9$, $4x^2 - 4x - 5$ **31.** $12x - 3$ **33.** $-x^2 + 10xy + y^2$ **35.** $6a^2b - 6a + 4b - 19$

SA26

9.1 Problem Solving (pp. 558–559) **37.** about 39,800,000 people **39. a.** $T = 9.5t^3 - 73t^2 + 130t + 860$ **b.** 1998; substitute $t = 0$ into the equation for T to find the number of books sold in 1998 to get 860 million books. Substitute 4 into the equation for T to find the number of books sold in 2002 to get 820 million books. More books were sold in 1998. **41. a.** $D = -0.44t^2 + 49t + 19.7$ **b.** about 855 decisions **c.** about 61%; Cy Young's career lasted $1911 - 1890 = 21$ years. To find the number of wins in his career, find the value of W when $t = 21$; about 525 wins. From part (b), we know that the total number of decisions in his career is about 855, so to find the percent of the decisions that were wins, find $525 \div 855 \approx 0.614$, or about 61%.

9.1 Graphing Calculator Activity (p. 560) **1.** $7x^2 + 2x + 1$ **3.** correct

9.2 Skill Practice (pp. 565–566) **1.** binomials **3.** $2x^3 - 3x^2 + 9x$ **5.** $4z^6 + z^5 - 11z^4 - 6z^2$ **7.** $9a^7 - 5a^6 - 13a^5$ **9.** $x^2 - x - 6$ **11.** $4b^2 - 31b + 21$ **13.** $12k^2 + 23k - 9$ **15.** The second term of the first binomial is -5, not 5, so the entries in the second row of the diagram should be $-15x$ and -5; $3x^2 - 14x - 5$. **17.** $y^2 + y - 30$ **19.** $77w^2 + 34w - 15$ **21.** $s^3 + 10s^2 + 19s - 20$ **23.** $-15x^3 + 14x^2 + 3x - 2$ **25.** $54z^3 - 21z^2 - 14z + 5$ **27.** $10r^2 + r - 3$ **29.** $8m^2 + 46m + 63$ **31.** $48x^2 - 88x + 35$ **33.** $3p^2 - 3p - 9$ **35.** $-3c^3 - 45c^2 + 23c - 10$ **37.** $2x^2 + x - 45$ **39.** $x^2 + 8x + 15$ **41.** $80 - 6x^2$ **43.** $2x^2 - 10x - 132$ **45.** $2x^4 - 11x^3 - 20x^2 - 7x$; graph $Y_1 = (x^2 - 7x)(2x^2 + 3x + 1)$ and $Y_2 = 2x^4 - 11x^3 - 20x^2 - 7x$ in the same viewing window. Because the graphs coincide, the expressions for Y_1 and Y_2 must be equivalent.

9.2 Problem Solving (pp. 567–568) **49. a.** $4x^2 + 84x + 440$ **b.** 840 in.^{2} **51. a.** \$12,300 million, 0.171; for $t = 0$, the amount of money (in millions of dollars) people between 15 and 19 years old spent on sound recordings in the U.S. in 1997 **b.** $R \cdot P \approx -1.18t^4 + 14.4t^3 - 57.4t^2 - 10.4t + 2100$ **c.** about \$1680 million **53. a.** *Sample answer:* $T = t + 90$; use the data points from 1995–1999: (5, 95), (6, 96), (7, 97), (8, 98), (9, 99). All these points lie on a line with slope $m = 1$; use any one of the points to find the y-intercept $b = 90$. The other data points, (0, 92), (10, 101), and (11, 102), lie close to the line $T = t + 90$. **b.** $V = -0.0015t^3 - 0.103t^2 + 2.949t + 6.21$ **c.** about 24.2 million households, about 22.2 million households

9.3 Skill Practice (p. 572) **1.** *Sample answer:* $x - 5$, $x + 5$ **3.** $x^2 + 16x + 64$ **5.** $4y^2 + 20y + 25$ **7.** $n^2 - 22n + 121$ **9.** The middle term of the product, $2(s)(-3) = -6s$, was left out; $s^2 - 6s + 9$. **11.** $t^2 - 16$ **13.** $4x^2 - 1$ **15.** $49 - w^2$ **19.** Use the sum and difference pattern to find the product $(20 - 4)(20 + 4)$. **21.** Use the square of a binomial pattern to find the product $(20 - 3)^2$. **23.** $r^2 + 18rs + 81s^2$ **25.** $9m^2 - 121n^2$ **27.** $9m^2 - 42mn + 49n^2$ **29.** $9f^2 - 81$ **31.** $9x^2 + 48xy + 64y^2$ **33.** $4a^2 - 25b^2$ **35.** $9x^2 - 0.25$ **37.** $9x^2 - 3x + 0.25$

9.3 Problem Solving (pp. 573–574)
41. a.

Cs

	C	s
C	CC	Cs
s	Cs	ss

Cs

b. $0.25C^2 + 0.5Cs + 0.25s^2$ **c.** 75%

43. a. 88.1%; the areas of the four regions are: 2 complete passes: $0.655^2 \approx 0.429$ square units; 1 complete pass, 1 incomplete pass: $0.655(0.345) \approx 0.226$ square units; 1 incomplete pass, 1 complete pass: $0.345(0.655) \approx 0.226$ square units; and 2 incomplete passes: $0.345^2 \approx 0.119$ square units. The regions that involve at least one complete pass cover $0.429 + 0.226 + 0.226 = 0.881$ square units, or 88.1% of the whole square region. **b.** The outcome of each attempted pass is modeled by $0.655C + 0.345I$, so the possible outcomes of two attempted passes is modeled by $(0.655C + 0.345I)^2 = 0.429C^2 + 0.452CI + 0.119I^2$. Because any combination of outcomes with a C results in at least one completed pass, the coefficients of the first two terms show that $42.9\% + 45.2\% = 88.1\%$ of the outcomes will have at least one completed pass, and the coefficient of the last term shows that 11.9% of the outcomes will have two incomplete passes.

9.4 Skill Practice (pp. 578–579) **1.** The vertical motion model is the equation $h = -16t^2 + vt + s$, where h is the height (in feet) of a projectile after t seconds in the air, given an initial velocity of v feet per second and an initial height of s feet. **3.** 5, -3 **5.** 13, 14 **7.** 7, $-\frac{4}{3}$ **9.** ± 3 **11.** $-\frac{11}{3}$, -1 **13.** $-\frac{5}{2}, \frac{5}{7}$ **17.** $2(x + y)$ **19.** $s(3s^3 + 16)$ **21.** $7w^2(w^3 - 5)$ **23.** $5n(3n^2 + 5)$ **25.** $\frac{1}{2}x^4(5x^2 - 1)$ **27.** 0, -6 **29.** 0, $\frac{7}{2}$ **31.** 0, $-\frac{1}{3}$ **33.** 0, 2 **35.** 0, $\frac{5}{2}$ **37.** 0, $-\frac{2}{7}$ **41.** $2ab(4a - 3b)$ **43.** $v(v^2 - 5v + 9)$ **45.** $3q^2(2q^3 - 7q^2 - 5)$ **47.** 0, $\frac{1}{2}$

SELECTED ANSWERS

9.4 Problem Solving (pp. 579–580) **51.** about 0.69 sec **53.** 0, about 0.28; the zero $t = 0$ seconds means that the penguin begins at a height of 0 feet in the air as it leaves the water; the zero $t \approx 0.28$ second means that the penguin lands back in the water (at a height of 0 feet in the air) after about 0.28 second. **55. a.** $h = -4.9t^2 + 4.9t$ **b.** $0 \le t \le 1$; a reasonable domain for the function will cover the time from when the rabbit leaves the ground until the rabbit lands back on the ground; these times t are the zeros of the function, 0 seconds and 1 second. **57. a.** $w(w + 2) = w(10 - w)$ **b.** 4 ft **c.** 48 ft^2

9.5 Skill Practice (pp. 586–587) **1.** factors **3.** $(x + 3)(x + 1)$ **5.** $(b - 9)(b - 8)$ **7.** $(z + 12)(z - 4)$ **9.** $(y - 9)(y + 2)$ **11.** $(x + 10)(x - 7)$ **13.** $(m - 15)(m + 8)$ **15.** $(p + 16)(p + 4)$ **17.** $(c + 11)(c + 4)$ **19.** In order to have a product of +24, p and q must have the same sign; $(m - 6)(m - 4)$. **21.** 10, −3 **23.** −10, 5 **25.** −5, −4 **27.** −22, −1 **31.** −3, −2 **33.** 9, 5 **35.** 17, −3 **37.** 14, 2 **39.** −9, 8 **41.** −17, −2 **43.** 20 in., 5 in. **45.** 26 yd, 6 yd **47.** $(x - 2y)^2$ **49.** $(c + 9d)(c + 4d)$ **51.** $(a + 5b)(a - 3b)$ **53.** $(m - 7n)(m + 6n)$ **55.** $(g + 10h)(g - 6h)$

9.5 Problem Solving (pp. 588–589) **59.** 10 cm^2 **61.** 40 in.; the side lengths of the rectangular picture can be represented by $x - 5$ and $x - 6$; the area of the picture is 20 square inches, so to find the side length x of the original square picture, solve the equation $(x - 5)(x - 6) = 20$. The equation has two solutions, 10 and 1, but when $x = 1$ inch, both $x - 5$ and $x - 6$ are negative, which does not make sense in this situation. So, $x = 10$ inches, and the perimeter of the original picture was $4(10) = 40$ inches.

9.5 Problem Solving Workshop (p. 591) **1.** 2 ft **3.** 9 ft

9.6 Skill Practice (pp. 596–597) **1.** roots **3.** To factor the polynomial that has a leading coefficient of 1, $x^2 - x - 2$, you only need to find factors of the constant term, −2, that add to the coefficient of the middle term, −1. To factor the polynomial that has a leading coefficient that is not 1, $6x^2 - x - 2$, you must also take into account how the factors of the leading coefficient, 6, affect the coefficient of the middle term. **5.** $-(y - 4)(y + 2)$ **7.** $(5w - 1)(w - 1)$ **9.** $(6s + 5)(s - 1)$ **11.** $(2c - 1)(c - 3)$ **13.** $-(2h + 1)(h - 3)$ **15.** $(2x + 3)(5x - 9)$ **17.** $(3z + 7)(z - 2)$ **19.** $(2n + 3)(2n + 5)$ **21.** $(3y - 4)(2y + 1)$ **23.** $-\frac{7}{2}, 5$ **25.** $\frac{1}{4}, -3$ **27.** $\frac{3}{4}, -\frac{1}{2}$ **29.** $-\frac{1}{4}, \frac{2}{5}$ **31.** $\frac{1}{3}, -5$ **33.** $\frac{2}{5}, 1$ **35.** $\frac{11}{2}, -3$ **37.** $-\frac{4}{3}, \frac{1}{2}$ **39.** The factorization of the polynomial should be $(3x + 2)(4x - 1)$ instead of $(3x - 1)(4x + 2)$; $-\frac{2}{3}, \frac{1}{4}$. **41.** $9\frac{1}{2}$ in.; to find the width, solve the equation $w(4w + 1) = 3$ to get $w = \frac{3}{4}$ or $w = -1$. The width cannot be negative, so the width is $\frac{3}{4}$ inch. Then the length is $4\left(\frac{3}{4}\right) + 1 = 4$ inches, and the perimeter is $2\left(\frac{3}{4}\right) + 2(4) = 9\frac{1}{2}$ inches. **43.** 5, 7 **45.** $-\frac{7}{3}, 2$ **47.** $\frac{7}{2}, -\frac{3}{2}$ **49.** $-\frac{1}{4}, \frac{5}{2}$ **53.** $2x^2 - 9x - 5 = 0$; any root $x = \frac{r}{s}$ of $ax^2 + bx + c = 0$ comes from setting the factor $sx - r$ equal to 0 after $ax^2 + bx + c$ is written in factored form; so, the roots $-\frac{1}{2}$ and 5 come from the factors $2x - (-1)$, or $2x + 1$, and $x - 5$. The product of these factors is $(2x + 1)(x - 5) = 2x^2 - 10x + x - 5 = 2x^2 - 9x - 5$.

9.6 Problem Solving (pp. 598–599) **59. a.** $24x^2 + 48x + 24$ **b.** 4 cm, 2 cm **61.** 70 m, 31 m

9.7 Skill Practice (pp. 603–604) **1.** perfect square **3.** $(x + 5)(x - 5)$ **5.** $(9c + 2)(9c - 2)$ **7.** $-3(m + 4n)(m - 4n)$ **9.** $(x - 2)^2$ **11.** $(7a + 1)^2$ **13.** $\left(m + \frac{1}{2}\right)^2$ **15.** $4(c + 10)(c - 10)$ **17.** $(2s + 3r)(2s - 3r)$ **19.** $8(3 + 2y)(3 - 2y)$ **21.** $(2x)^2 - 3^2$ is in the form $a^2 - b^2$, so it must be factored using the difference of two squares pattern, not the perfect square trinomial pattern; $9(2x + 3)(2x - 3)$. **25.** −4 **27.** ±3 **29.** −2 **31.** ±12 **33.** $\pm\frac{7}{2}$ **35.** $\frac{5}{6}$ **37.** $\pm\frac{4}{3}$ **39.** 0, 1

9.7 Problem Solving (pp. 604–605) **47.** 2.5 sec **49.** Once; the ball's height (in feet) is modeled by the equation $h = -16t^2 + 56t + 5$, where t is the time (in seconds) since it was thrown. To find when the height is 54 feet, substitute 54 for h and solve the equation $54 = -16t^2 + 56t + 5$, or $16t^2 - 56t + 49 = 0$. Because the left side of the equation factors as a perfect square trinomial, $(4t - 7)^2$, the equation has only one solution, 1.75; so, the ball reaches a height of 54 feet only once, after 1.75 seconds. **51. a.** $4d^2 - 9$ **b.** 10 in.

9.8 Skill Practice (pp. 610–611) **1.** The polynomial is written as a monomial or as a product of a monomial and one or more prime polynomials. **3.** $(x-8)(x+1)$ **5.** $(z-4)(6z-7)$ **7.** $(b+5)(b^2-3)$ **9.** $(x+13)(x-1)$ **11.** $(z-1)(12+5z^2)$ **13.** $(x+1)(x^2+2)$ **15.** $(z-4)(z^2+3)$ **17.** $(a+13)(a^2-5)$ **19.** $(5n-4)(n^2+5)$ **21.** $(y+1)(y+5x)$ **23.** $x^2(x-1)(x+1)$ **25.** $3n^3(n-4)(n+4)$ **27.** $3c^7(5c-1)(5c+1)$ **29.** $8s^2(2s-1)(2s+1)$ **31.** cannot be factored **33.** $3w^2(w+4)^2$ **35.** $(b-5)(b-2)(b+2)$ **37.** $(9t-1)(t^2+2)$ **39.** $7ab^3(a-3)(a+3)$ **43.** $-1, \pm 2$ **45.** $\frac{7}{4}, \pm 2$ **47.** $0, -5, -3$ **49.** $0, \pm 9$ **51.** $0, \pm 2$ **53.** $-\frac{1}{3}, \pm 1$ **55.** No; when the polynomial is factored completely, the equation becomes $(x+2)(x^2+3)=0$. When the factor x^2+3 is set equal to 0, the resulting equation, $x^2+3=0$, or $x^2=-3$, has no real number solutions because x^2 cannot be negative. **57.** 12 ft, 4 ft, 2 ft **59.** $(2b-a)(2b-3)(2b+3)$ **61.** $(3x+4)(2x-1)$ **63.** $(4n-3)(3n-1)$ **65.** $(3w+2)(7w-2)$

9.8 Problem Solving (pp. 612–613) **69. a.** $4w^2+16w$ **b.** 4 in. long by 4 in. wide by 8 in. high **71. a.** 1, about -0.2 **b.** The zero $t \approx -0.2$ has no meaning because t, which represents time in seconds, cannot be negative in this situation. The zero $t=1$ means that the ball lands on the ground 1 second after you throw it. **73. a.** $-h^3+5h^2+36h$ **b.** 4 in. long by 9 in. wide by 5 in. high, 3 in. long by 10 in. wide by 6 in. high **c.** 4 in. long by 9 in. wide by 5 in. high; the 4-inch long box has a surface area of 202 square inches and the 3-inch long box has a surface area of 216 square inches.

Chapter Review (pp. 616–620) **1.** degree of the polynomial **3.** A factorable polynomial with integer coefficients is factored completely if it is written as a product of unfactorable polynomials with integer coefficients. *Sample answer:* $3x(x-4)(2x+1)$ **5.** A **7.** x^3-8x^2+15x **9.** $11y^5+4y^2-y-3$ **11.** $5s^3-7s+13$ **13.** x^3-5x^2+7x-3 **15.** x^2-2x-8 **17.** $z^2-3z-88$ **19.** $18n^2+27n+7$ **21.** $3x^2+10x-8$ **23.** $36y^2+12y+1$ **25.** $16a^2-24a+9$ **27.** $9s^2-25$ **29.** 0, 11 **31.** 0, 9 **33.** $0, \frac{1}{3}$ **35.** $(s+11)(s-1)$ **37.** $(a+12)(a-7)$ **39.** $(x+8)(x-4)$ **41.** $(c+5)(c+3)$ **43.** $\frac{1}{7}, 1$ **45.** $\frac{2}{3}, -2$ **47.** $-\frac{3}{2}, -3$ **49.** 3 sec **51.** $(z-15)(z+15)$ **53.** $12(1-2n)(1+2n)$ **55.** $(4p-1)^2$ **57.** 1 sec **59.** $(y+3)(y+x)$ **61.** $5s^2(s-5)(s+5)$ **63.** $2z(z+6)(z-5)$ **65.** $(2b+3)(b-2)(b+2)$

Chapter 10

10.1 Skill Practice (pp. 632–633) **1.** parabola **3.** C **5.** B

7.

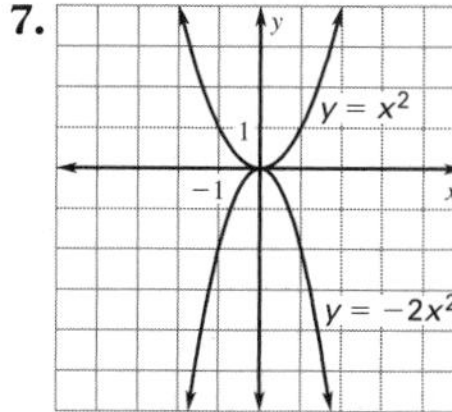

The graph is a vertical stretch (by a factor of 2) with a reflection in the x-axis of the graph of $y=x^2$.

9.

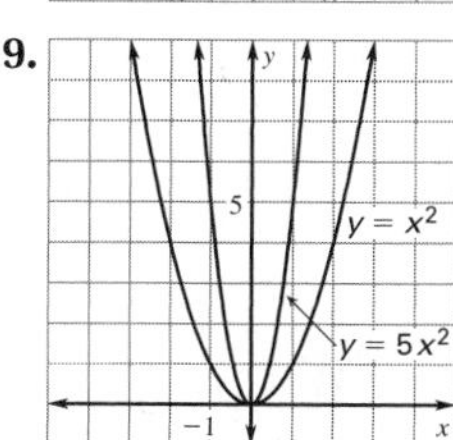

The graph is a vertical stretch (by a factor of 5) of the graph of $y=x^2$.

11.

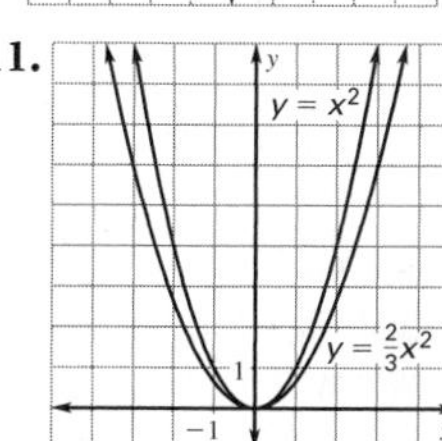

The graph is a vertical shrink $\left(\text{by a factor of } \frac{2}{3}\right)$ of the graph of $y=x^2$.

13.

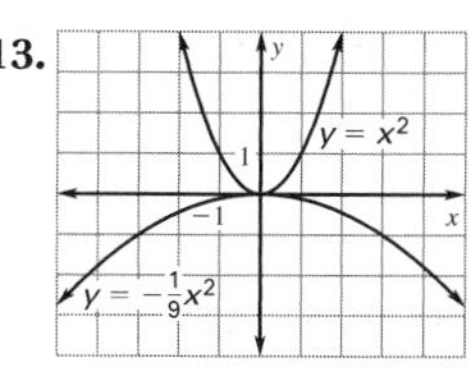

The graph is a vertical shrink $\left(\text{by a factor of } \frac{1}{9}\right)$ with a reflection in the x-axis of the graph of $y=x^2$.

15.

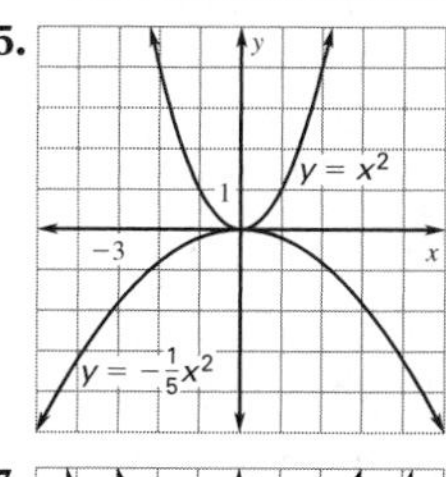

The graph is a vertical shrink $\left(\text{by a factor of } \frac{1}{5}\right)$ with a reflection in the x-axis of the graph of $y=x^2$.

17.

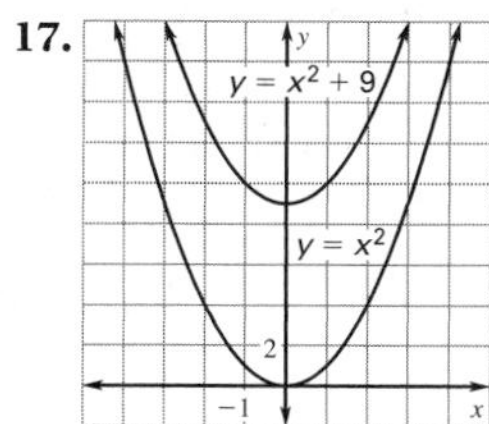

The graph is a vertical translation (of 9 units up) of the graph of $y=x^2$.

SA29

19. 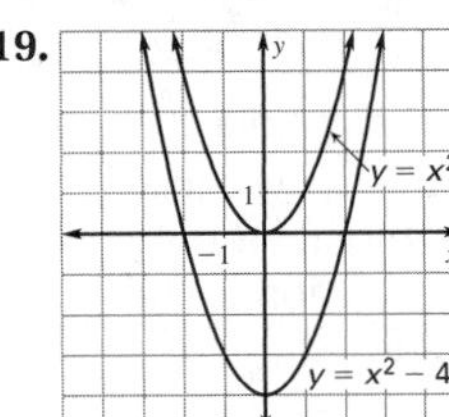

The graph is a vertical translation (of 4 units down) of the graph of $y = x^2$.

21. 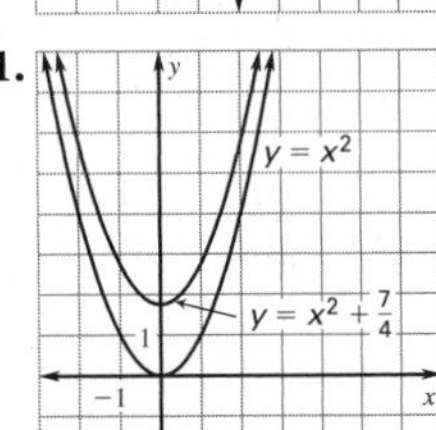

The graph is a vertical translation $\left(\text{of } \frac{7}{4} \text{ units up}\right)$ of the graph of $y = x^2$.

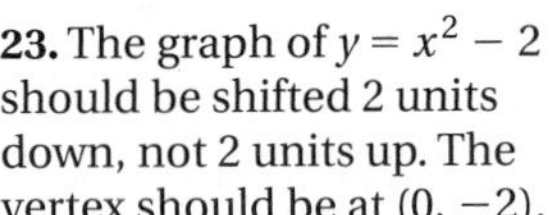

23. The graph of $y = x^2 - 2$ should be shifted 2 units down, not 2 units up. The vertex should be at $(0, -2)$.

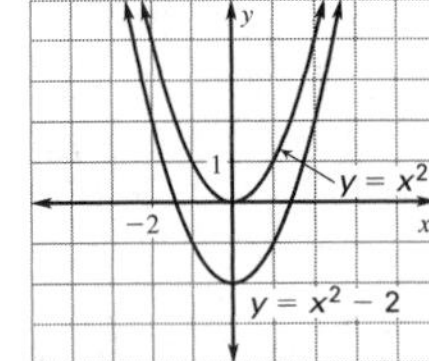

25. 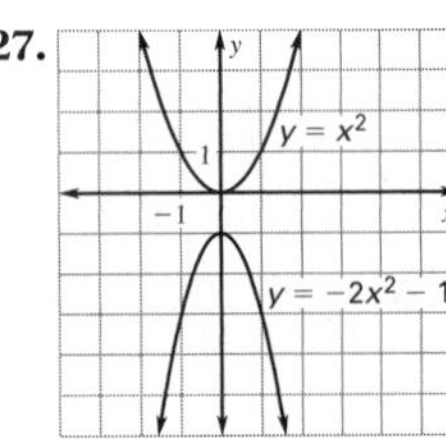

The graph is a reflection in the x-axis with a vertical translation (of 5 units up) of the graph of $y = x^2$.

27. 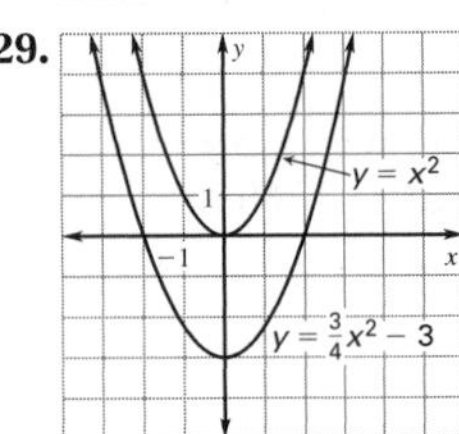

The graph is a vertical stretch (by a factor of 2) with a vertical translation (of 1 unit down) and a reflection in the x-axis of the graph of $y = x^2$.

29. The graph is a vertical shrink $\left(\text{by a factor of } \frac{3}{4}\right)$ with a vertical translation (of 3 units down) of the graph of $y = x^2$.

31. 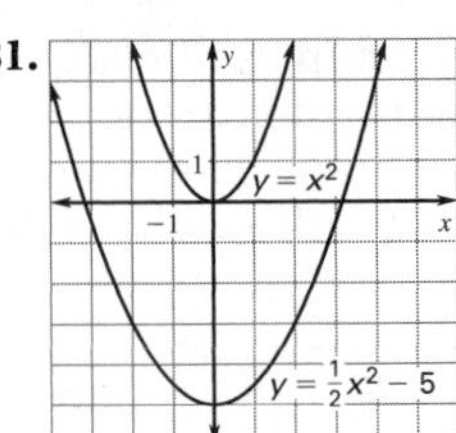

The graph is a vertical shrink $\left(\text{by a factor of } \frac{1}{2}\right)$ with a vertical translation (of 5 units down) of the graph of $y = x^2$.

35. Translate the graph of f 5 units down.

10.1 Problem Solving (pp. 633–634)

41. a. 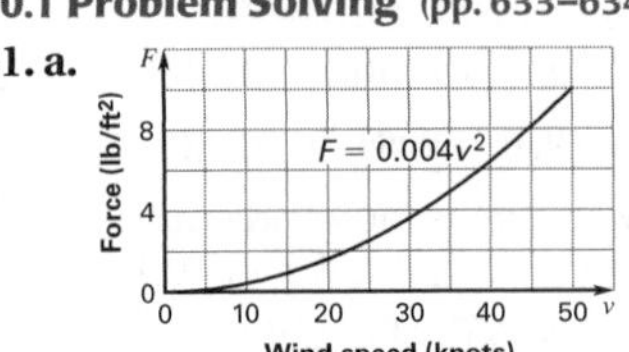

b. about 16 knots **c.** about 35 knots

43. a. 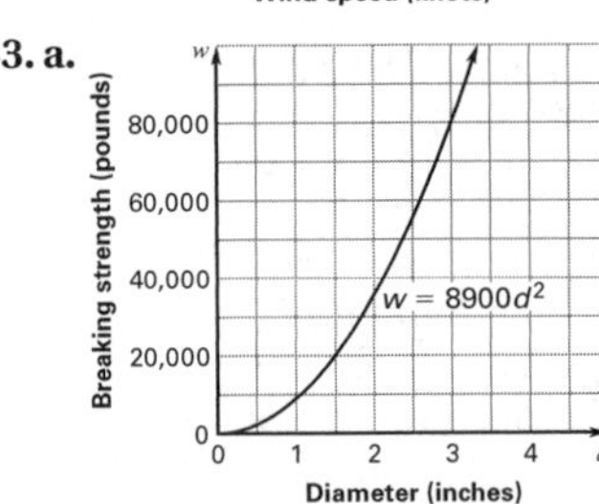

b. No. *Sample answer:* Let D be the diameter of a rope with 4 times the breaking strength of a rope with diameter d. Then $8900D^2 = 4(8900d^2)$; $D^2 = 4d^2$; $D = \sqrt{4d^2}$; $D = 2d$. Thus, the diameter of the rope with 4 times the breaking strength is only two times the diameter of the other rope.

10.2 Skill Practice (pp. 638–639) **1.** When the function is in standard form, $y = ax^2 + bx + c$, it will have a minimum value if $a > 0$ and a maximum value if $a < 0$. **3.** $x = 2$, $(2, -2)$ **5.** $x = 4$, $(4, 26)$ **7.** $x = -\frac{1}{2}$, $\left(-\frac{1}{2}, -\frac{3}{2}\right)$ **9.** $x = 0$, $(0, -1)$ **11.** $x = 6$, $(6, 7)$ **13.** The equation of the axis of symmetry is $x = \frac{-b}{2a}$, not $x = \frac{b}{2a}$; $x = \frac{-b}{2a} = \frac{-16}{2(2)}$, $x = -4$.

15. 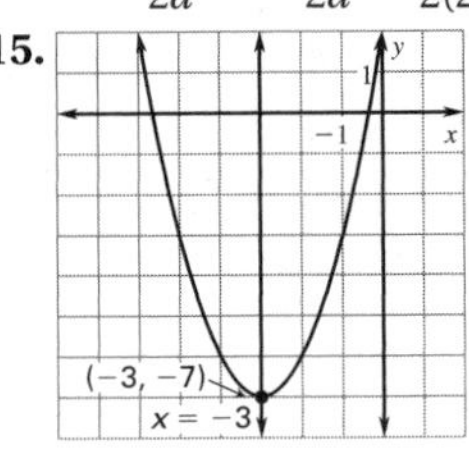

17. 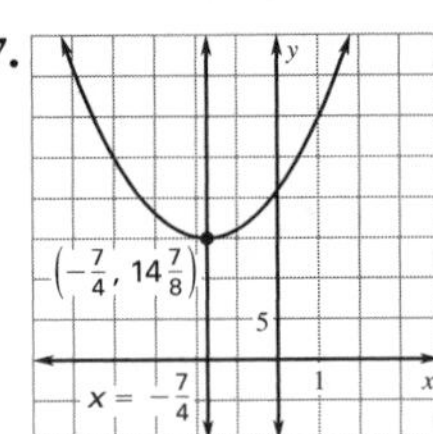

SA30

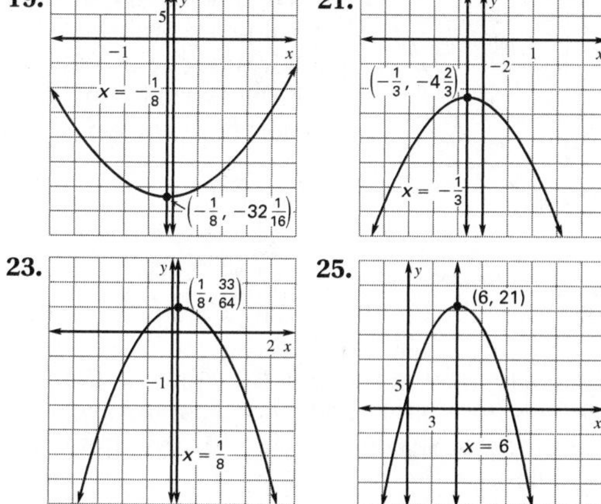

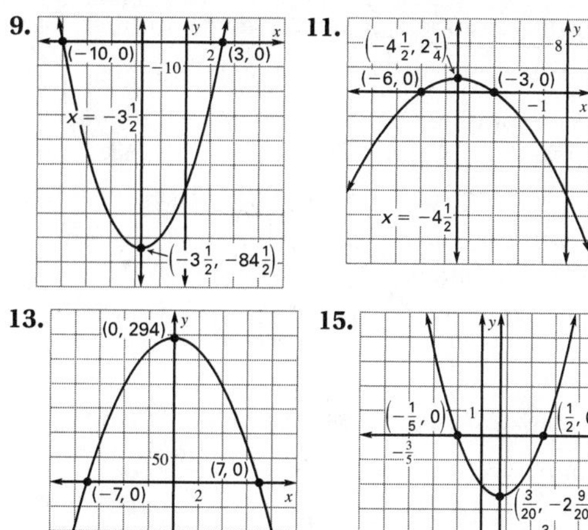

29. maximum value; 7 **31.** maximum value; −8 **33.** maximum value; $\frac{81}{8}$ **35.** maximum value; 54 **37.** The graph of $y = x^2 + 4x + 1$ is a horizontal translation (of 4 units left) of the graph of $y = x^2 - 4x + 1$.

10.2 Problem Solving (pp. 639–640) **41.** about 66 ft **43.** about 243 ft

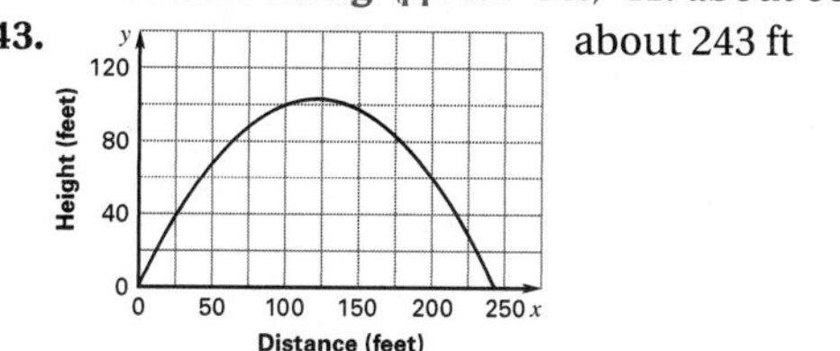

Extension (p. 642)

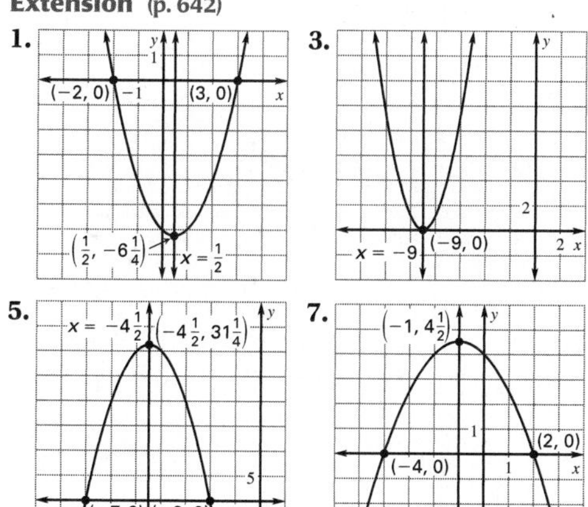

10.3 Skill Practice (pp. 647–648) **1.** $2x^2 - 9x + 11 = 0$ **3.** 4, 1 **5.** −4, −2 **7.** 8, −2 **9.** 3 **11.** −5 **13.** −7 **15.** no solution **17.** no solution **19.** −6, 2 **21.** Any solution of a quadratic equation is an x-intercept of the graph of the related quadratic function. The x-intercept of the function shown in the graph is 2, not 4; the only solution of the equation is 2. **23.** −3, 4 **25.** −5, 2 **27.** −5, 4 **29.** 1, 11 **31.** $-1\frac{1}{2}$, 1 **33.** $\frac{1}{2}$ **35.** no solution **37.** −3.4, −0.6 **39.** −1.4, 3.4 **41.** 0.8, 6.2 **43.** −1.3, 0.8 **45.** −4.7, −1.3

10.3 Problem Solving (pp. 648–649) **51.** 24.1 ft **53.** 16 ft; the distance from the nozzle to the circle is the distance between the x-intercepts of $y = -0.75x^2 + 6x$. Substitute 0 for y and solve for x: $0 = -0.75x^2 + 6x$ has solutions 0 and 8. The radius of the display circle is 8 feet, so the diameter is 16 feet.

10.3 Graphing Calculator Activity (pp. 650–651) **1.** $1\frac{2}{3}$ **3.** −3.75 **5.** about −3.5 **7.** −1.11, 3.61 **9.** −1.61, 5.61 **11.** 0.90, 2.18 **13.** −7.03, 2.15 **15.** 0; the maximum or minimum value of a quadratic function occurs at the vertex of the parabola that is the graph of the function. When a quadratic function has only one zero, its graph has only one x-intercept, which must also be the x-coordinate of the vertex of the parabola. Then the y-coordinate of the vertex is 0, so the maximum or minimum value of the function is 0.

10.4 Skill Practice (pp. 655–656) **1.** square root **3.** ±1 **5.** ±10 **7.** 0 **9.** $\pm\frac{1}{2}$ **11.** $\pm\frac{7}{3}$ **13.** 0 **17.** ±2.65 **19.** no solution **21.** 0 **23.** ±2.24 **25.** ±3.78 **27.** ±1.32

SA31

31. Negative numbers do not have real number square roots, so $\pm\sqrt{-\frac{11}{7}}$ are not real numbers; there is no solution. **33.** 0.76, 5.24 **35.** −8.16, −1.84 **37.** −16.65, −11.35 **39.** −5.69, 3.69 **41.** ±4 **43.** ±1.41 **45.** 0.37, 13.63 **47.** 12 in. **49.** 11.66 ft **51.** $\pm\frac{6}{5}$, or ±1.2. *Sample answer:* Rewrite the decimal as a fraction and then take square roots of each side of the equation: $x^2 = \frac{144}{100}$, so $x = \pm\sqrt{\frac{144}{100}} = \pm\frac{12}{10} = \pm\frac{6}{5}$ or ±1.2.

10.4 Problem Solving (pp. 657–658) **59. a.** 6.8 mm **b.** 5.9 mm **c.** 5.6 mm **61. a.** $D = 4 \pm \sqrt{\frac{16V}{L}}$ **b.** 11.1 ft, 10.7 ft, 10.3 ft, 10.0 ft

10.4 Problem Solving Workshop (p. 660) **1.** about 1.5 sec **3. a.** $V = 25x^2$ **b.** length: about 9 in., width: 5 in., height: about 1.8 in.

c.

Height, *x* (inches)	1.7	1.8	1.9
Width (inches)	5	5	5
Length, 5*x* (inches)	8.5	9	9.5
Volume, *V* (cubic inches)	72.25	81	90.25

The volume in the table closest to 83 cubic inches is 81 cubic inches. To the nearest tenth of an inch, the height of the box is about 1.8 inches. The length of the box is $5x \approx 9$ inches, and the width is 5 inches. **5.** To rewrite the equation $6 = -16t^2 + 54$ so that one side is 0, you must subtract 6 from each side; $0 = -16t^2 + 48$, replace 48 with the closest perfect square, 49. $0 = -16t^2 + 49 = -(16t^2 - 49) = -(4t + 7)(4t - 7)$, so the approximate solutions of this equation are $\pm\frac{7}{4}$. Disregard the negative solution because time cannot be negative; so, it takes about $\frac{7}{4}$, or 1.75, seconds for the shoe to hit the net.

10.5 Skill Practice (pp. 666–667) **1.** completing the square **3.** 9; $(x + 3)^2$ **5.** 4; $(x - 2)^2$ **7.** $\frac{9}{4}$; $\left(x - \frac{3}{2}\right)^2$ **9.** 1.44; $(x + 1.2)^2$ **11.** $\frac{4}{9}$; $\left(x - \frac{2}{3}\right)^2$ **13.** −12, 2 **15.** −6, 12 **17.** −7, 3 **19.** −10.5, −0.5 **21.** −0.80, 8.80 **23.** −2.5, −0.5 **27.** The perfect square trinomial $x^2 - 2x + 1$ factors as $(x - 1)^2$ not $(x + 1)^2$, $(x - 1)^2 = 5$, $x - 1 = \pm\sqrt{5}$, $x = 1 \pm \sqrt{5}$. **29.** −11.57, −0.43 **31.** −1.91, 0.91 **33.** −0.96, 6.96 **35.** 0.79, 2.21 **37.** −3.68, −0.32 **39.** −0.25, 0.75 **41.** 4.87

10.5 Problem Solving (pp. 667–668) **45.** 3 ft **47. a.** $1904 = 7x^2 - 4x + 392$, 2000

b.

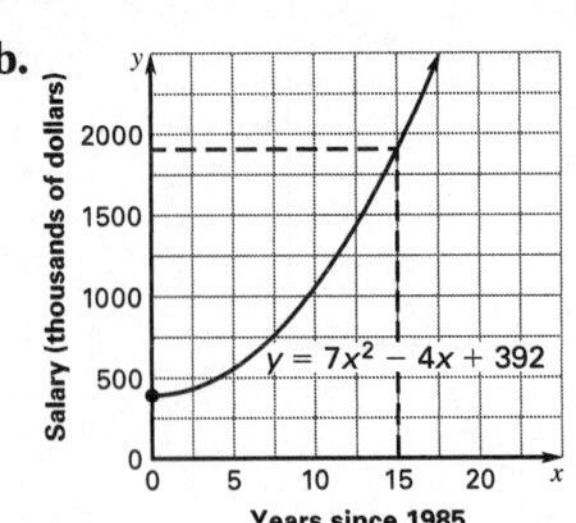

When $y \approx 1904$, the value of x is about 15. So the year 2000 (1985 + 15) found in part (a) is correct.

49. Yes; to find the number of days x after which the stock price was \$23.50 per share, substitute 23.5 for y and solve for x by completing the square to find that the solutions are 10 and 30. You could have sold the stock for \$23.50 per share 10 days after you purchased it.

Extension (p. 670)

1.

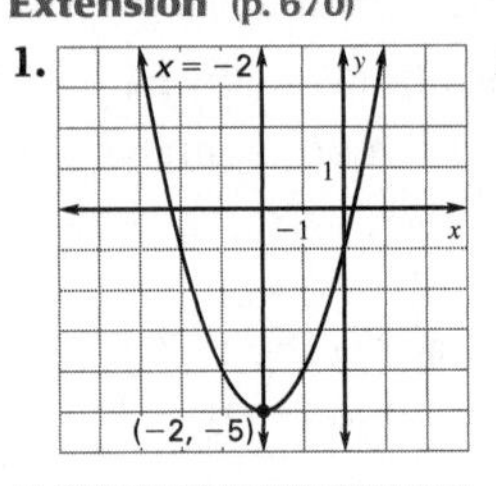

3.

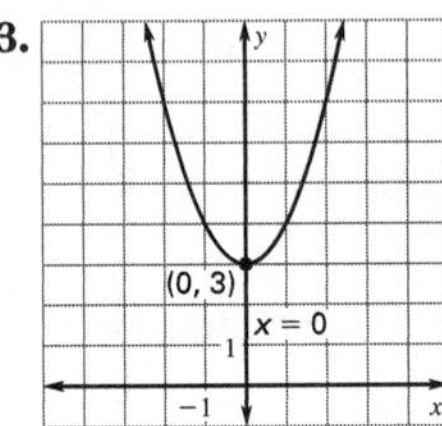

5.

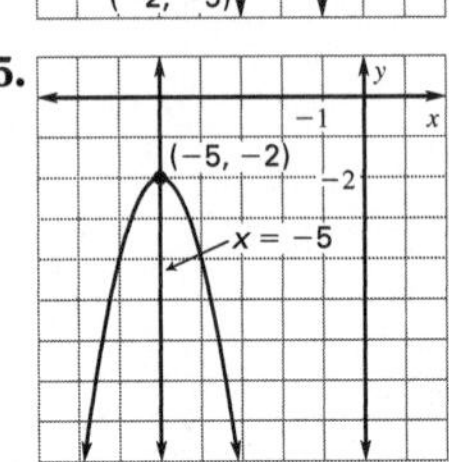

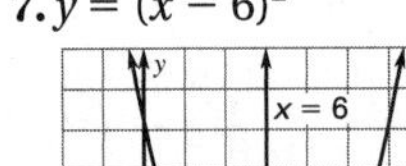

7. $y = (x - 6)^2$

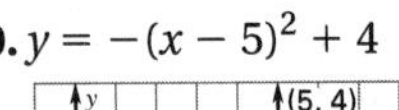

9. $y = -(x - 5)^2 + 4$

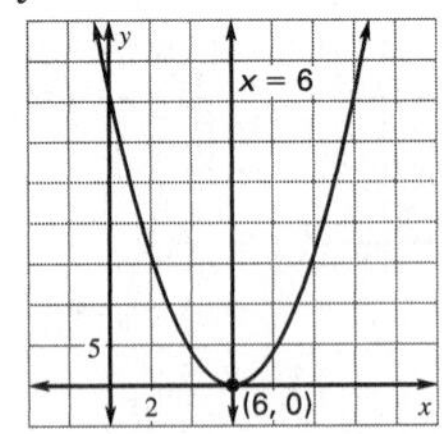

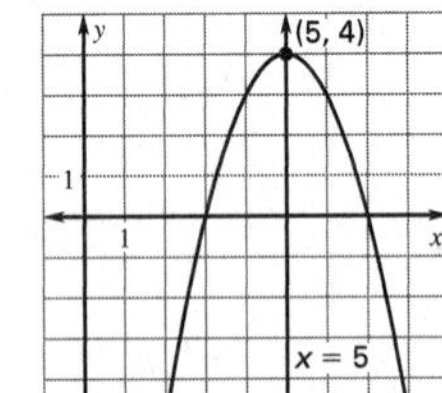

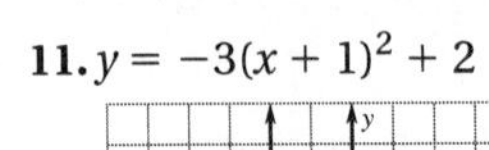

11. $y = -3(x + 1)^2 + 2$

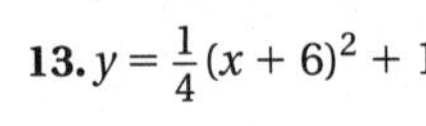

13. $y = \frac{1}{4}(x + 6)^2 + 1$

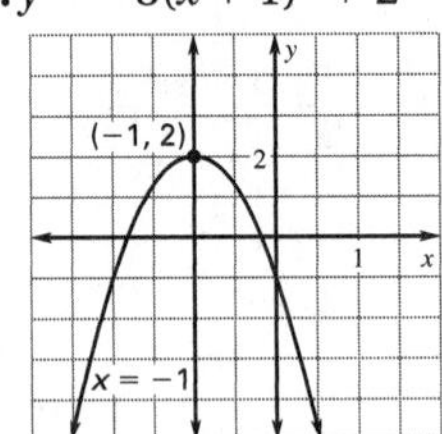

SELECTED ANSWERS

10.6 Skill Practice (pp. 674–675) **1.** quadratic formula **3.** $-13, 8$ **5.** $-2, 2.33$ **7.** $-3.27, 4.27$ **9.** -2.5 **11.** $-0.63, 2.13$ **13.** $-2, 7$ **15.** $-1, 1.29$ **17.** $3.27, 6.73$ **19.** $-0.54, 2.29$ **21.** $-0.66, 1.09$ **23.** $-1.77, -0.57$ **27.** Before identifying the values of a, b, and c, the equation must be written in standard form $ax^2 + bx + c = 0$; $-2x^2 + 3x - 1 = 0$, so $c = -1$, not 1; $x = \frac{-3 \pm \sqrt{3^2 - 4(-2)(-1)}}{2(-2)}$, $x = \frac{-3 \pm \sqrt{1}}{-4}$, $x = \frac{1}{2}$ and $x = 1$. **29–33.** Sample answers are given. **29.** Using square roots, the equation can be written in the form $x^2 = d$. **31.** Factoring, the expression $m^2 + 5m + 6$ factors easily. **33.** Quadratic formula, the equation does not factor easily. **35.** 4 **37.** 6 **39.** $-1.94, 2.19$ **41.** $-0.41, 2.41$ **43.** 5; 13 m by 7 m

10.6 Problem Solving (pp. 675–676)

47. 1993 **49. a.** 2001 **b.**

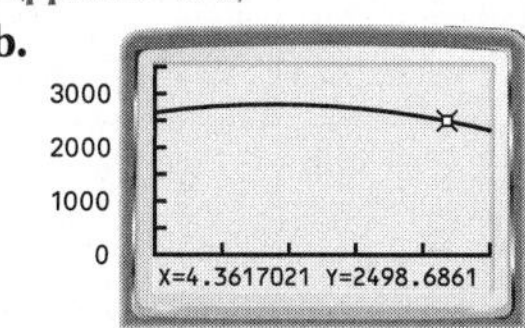

10.7 Skill Practice (pp. 681–682) **1.** $x = \frac{-b \pm \sqrt{b^2 - 4ac}}{2a}$, $b^2 - 4ac$ should be circled. **3.** no solution **5.** two solutions **7.** one solution **9.** two solutions **11.** two solutions **13.** one solution **15.** two solutions **17.** no solution **21.** Before calculating the discriminant, the equation must be written in standard form: $3x^2 - 7x + 5 = 0$. Thus, c is 5, not -4, so $b^2 - 4ac = (-7)^2 - 4(3)(5) = 49 - 60 = -11$; the equation has no solution. **23.** 2 **25.** 0 **27.** 0 **29.** 1 **31–33.** Sample answers are given for parts (a) and (c). **31. a.** 0 **b.** 1 **c.** 2 **33. a.** 8 **b.** 9 **c.** 10 **35.** On; the value of the discriminant is $(-6)^2 - 4(3)(3) = 0$, so the graph has exactly one x-intercept. A parabola that has exactly one x-intercept must have its vertex on the x-axis. **37.** Below; $a < 0$, so the graph opens down. The value of the discriminant is $(10)^2 - 4(-15)(-25) = -1400 < 0$, so the graph has no x-intercepts; a parabola that opens down and has no x-intercepts must have its vertex below the x-axis. **39.** On; the value of the discriminant is $(-24)^2 - 4(9)(16) = 0$, so the graph has exactly one x-intercept; a parabola that has exactly one x-intercept must have its vertex on the x-axis. **41. a.** $314 = 2w^2 + 40w + 64$ **b.** 2 **c.** $-25, 5$; the width w cannot be negative, so the solution -25 meters does not make sense in the context of the problem. The solution 5 meters does makes sense in the context of the problem.

10.7 Problem Solving (pp. 682–683) **45. a.** Substitute 25 for y in the equation and then write the resulting quadratic equation in standard form: $25 = 0.06x^2 - 4x + 87$, or $0 = 0.06x^2 - 4x + 62$. Evaluate the discriminant: $b^2 - 4ac = (-4)^2 - 4(0.06)(62) = 1.12$. Since the discriminant is positive, we know that the equation $25 = 0.06x^2 - 4x + 87$ does have solutions, so it is possible for a parakeet to consume 25 milliliters of oxygen per gram of body mass per hour. **b.** 24.5 km/h and 42.2 km/h **47.** No; to determine if there is any point of the arch at a height of 4 feet, substitute 4 for y in the equation and then determine if the equation has any positive solutions. The equation is $4 = -0.18x^2 + 1.6x$, or $0 = -0.18x^2 + 1.6x - 4$. Evaluate the discriminant: $b^2 - 4ac = (1.6)^2 - 4(-0.18)(-4) = -0.32$. Since the discriminant is negative, we know the equation has no solution; thus, a child who is 4 feet tall cannot walk under one of the arches without having to bend over. **49. a.** $h = -16t^2 + 32t + 6$ **b.** no **c.** yes; about 0.8 sec and about 1.4 sec

10.8 Skill Practice (pp. 688–689) **1.** exponential function **3.** B **5.** A **7.** linear function **9.** exponential function **11.** quadratic function **13.** quadratic function; $y = -x^2$ **15.** linear function; $y = 3x + 1$ **17.** exponential function; $y = 4\left(\frac{1}{4}\right)^x$ **19.** The x- and y-values were reversed when substituting the coordinates of the ordered pair (2, 10) into the equation $y = ax^2$. Substituting 2 for x and 10 for y gives $10 = a(2)^2$, $a = 2.5$; so, the equation is $y = 2.5x^2$. **21.** $A = \left(\frac{\sqrt{3}}{4}\right)s^2$; $25\sqrt{3}$ cm^2

10.8 Problem Solving (pp. 689–691)
23. linear function; $y = 0.34x + 24.6$

25. a.

Folds	1	2	3	4	5
Sections	2	4	8	16	32

b.

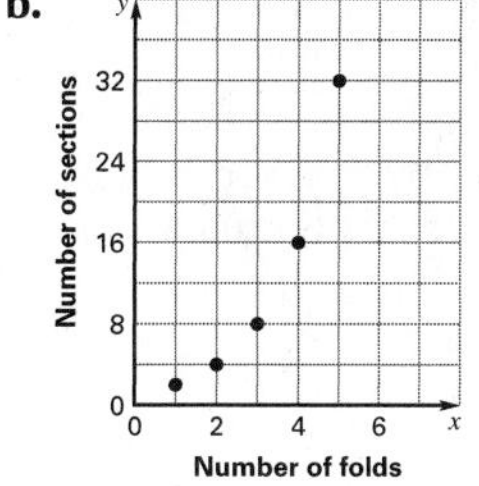

exponential function **c.** $y = 2^x$; 128 sections

SA33

27. a. quadratic function; $\ell = 0.82t^2$ **b.** 0.205 ft **c.** The period decreases by about 71%. For example, consider $t = 4$ for $\ell = 13.12$. To find t for 50% of ℓ, solve $0.5(13.12) = 0.82t^2$; $t \approx 2.83$, and $\frac{2.83}{4} = 0.708$, so the period decreased by about 71%. Consider $t = 2$ for $\ell = 3.28$. To find t for 50% of ℓ, solve $0.5(3.28) = 0.82t^2$; $t \approx 1.41$, and $\frac{1.41}{2} = 0.705$, so the period decreased by about 71%. Consider $t = 1$ for $\ell = 0.82$. To find t for 50% of ℓ, solve $0.5(0.82) = 0.82t^2$; $t \approx 0.707$, and $\frac{0.707}{1} = 0.707$, so the period decreased by about 71%.

10.8 Graphing Calculator Activity (pp. 692–693)
1. $y = 15{,}600(0.866)^x$
3. $y = 179(0.987)^x$, $y = 0.040x^2 - 4.13x + 197$

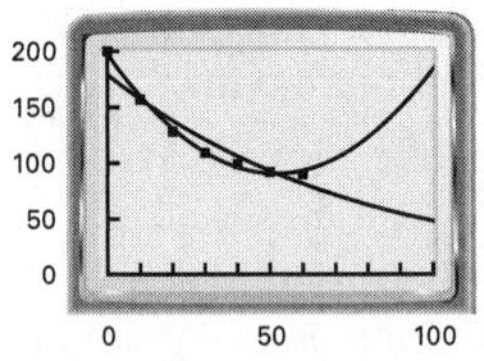

The exponential model; although the quadratic model appears to fit the given data points more closely than the exponential model does, the graph shows that after the last data point, (60, 90), the quadratic model implies increasing temperatures as time goes on, while the exponential model shows gradually decreasing temperatures as time goes on; the exponential model is a more accurate model of what will happen as the hot chocolate continues to cool.

Chapter Review (pp. 696–700)
1. axis of symmetry **3.** maximum
5.

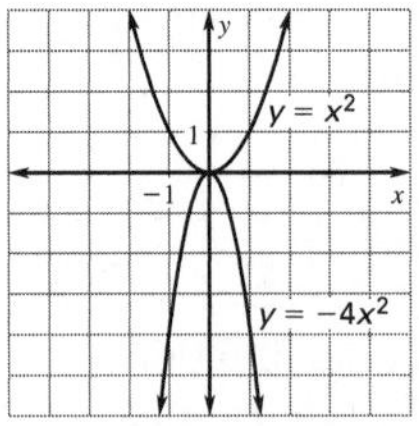

The graph is a vertical stretch (by a factor of 4) with a reflection in the x-axis of the graph of $y = x^2$.

7.

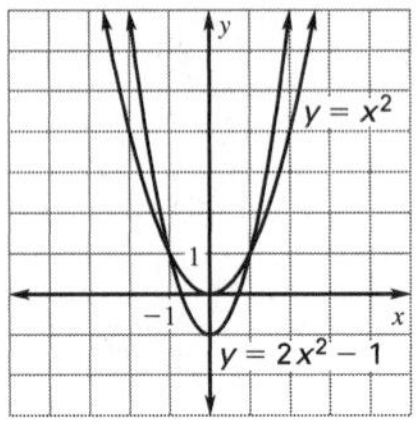

The graph is a vertical stretch (by a factor of 2) with a vertical translation (of 1 unit down) of the graph of $y = x^2$.

9.

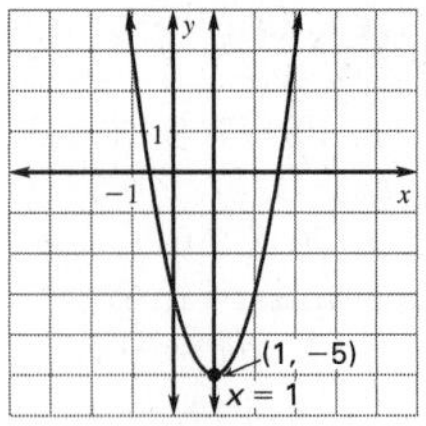

11. no solution **13.** −8, 1 **15.** no solution **17.** ±0.76 **19.** 2.71, 5.29 **21.** 0.32, −6.32 **23.** −0.62, 1.62 **25.** −3.89, 0.39 **27.** 0.16, 1.24 **29.** −1.22, 1 **31.** no solution **33.** two solutions **35.** two solutions **37.** exponential function

Cumulative Review (pp. 706–707) **1.** 3 **3.** 0.2 **5.** −1
7.

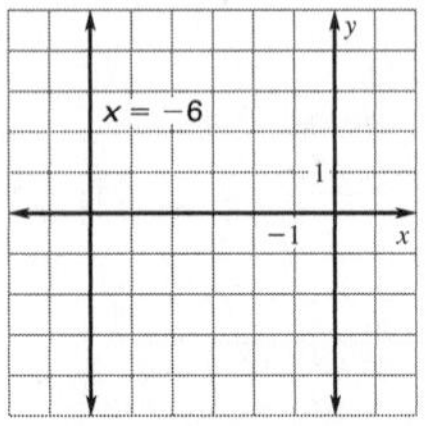

9.

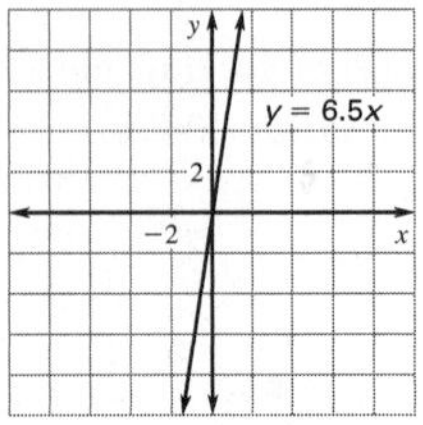

11.

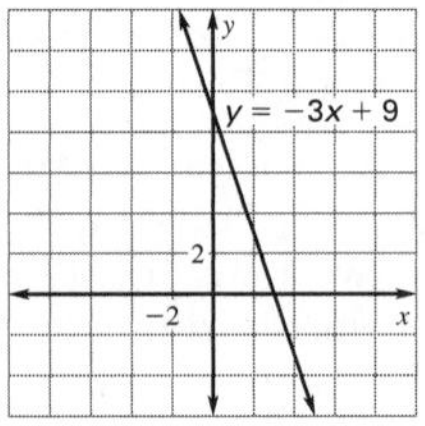

13.

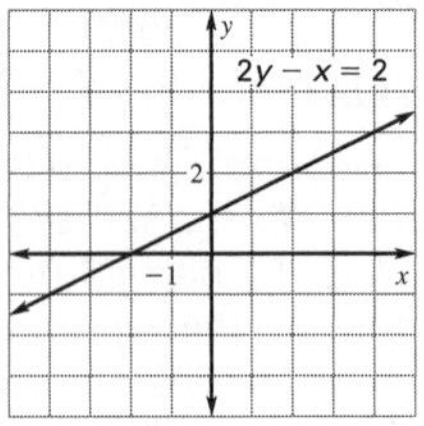

15. $y = \frac{1}{5}x + 3$ **17.** $y = -2x + 19$
19. $x < -36$

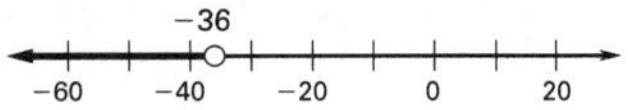

21. $b \geq -1$

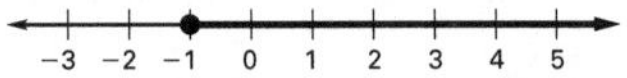

23. $-\frac{3}{2} \leq c \leq 7$

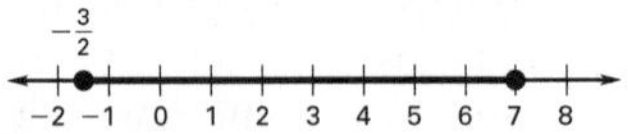

25. all real numbers **27.** $-729r^3$ **29.** $\frac{81x^3}{y^2}$
31.

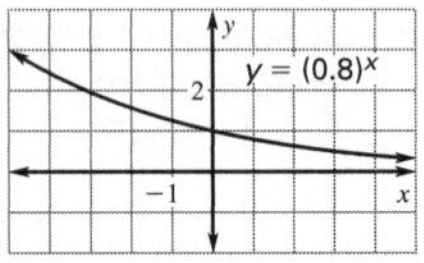

33. $-x^2 + 12x + 12$ **35.** $2z^2 + 11z - 63$ **37.** $-3q^3 + 11q - 2$ **39.** $4k^2 - 44k + 121$ **41.** $(x + 12)(x - 6)$ **43.** $(5d + 6)^2$ **45.** $(z - 6)(z + 2)(z - 2)$

47.

49.

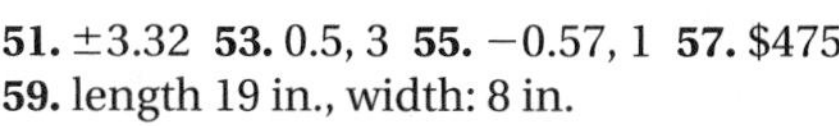

51. ± 3.32 **53.** 0.5, 3 **55.** -0.57, 1 **57.** \$475
59. length 19 in., width: 8 in.

61. a.

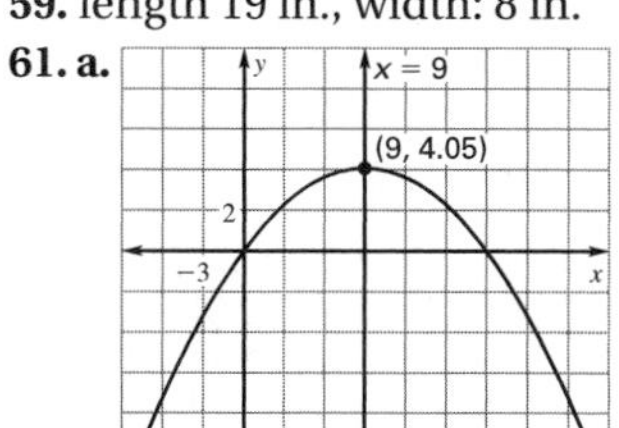

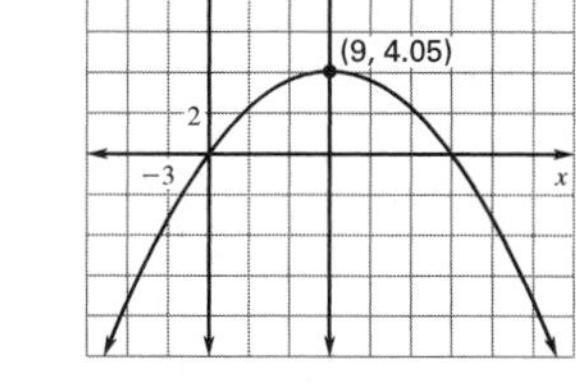

b. 18 ft

Chapter 11

11.1 Skill Practice (pp. 713–714) **1.** radical function

3. 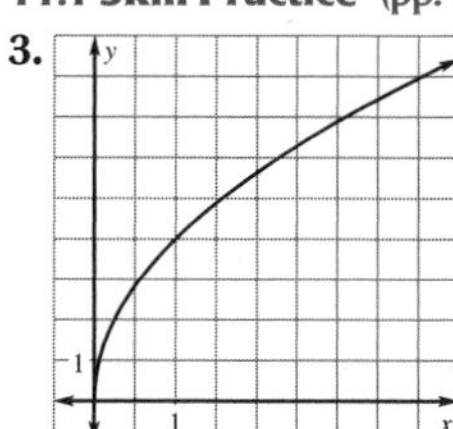

domain: $x \geq 0$, range: $y \geq 0$; vertical stretch by a factor of 4

5. 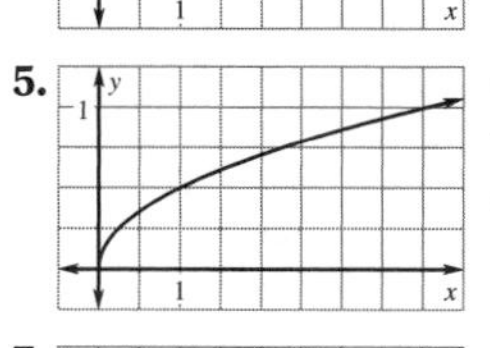

domain: $x \geq 0$, range: $y \geq 0$; vertical shrink by a factor of 0.5

7. 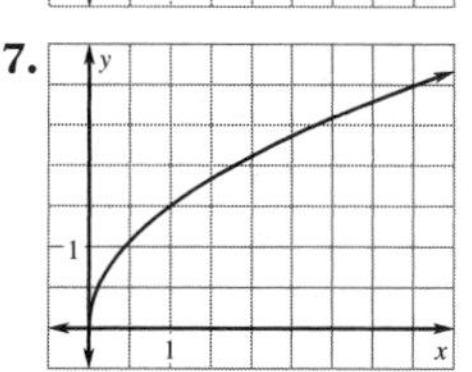

domain: $x \geq 0$, range: $y \geq 0$; vertical stretch by a factor of $\frac{3}{2}$

9. 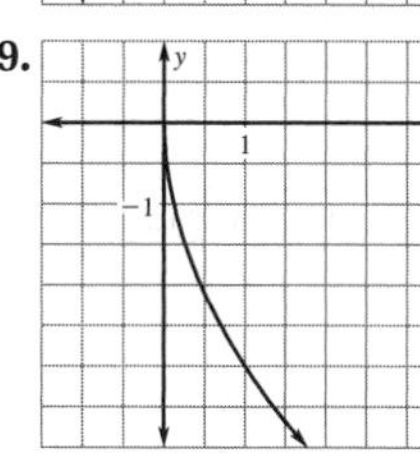

domain: $x \geq 0$, range: $y \leq 0$; vertical stretch by a factor of 3 with a reflection in the x-axis

11. domain: $x \geq 0$, range: $y \leq 0$; vertical shrink by a factor of 0.8 with a reflection in the x-axis

13. 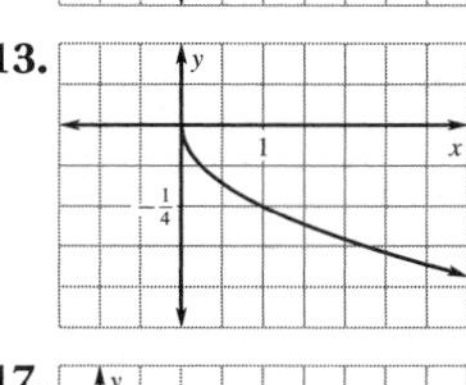

domain: $x \geq 0$, range: $y \leq 0$; vertical shrink by a factor of $\frac{1}{4}$ with a reflection in the x-axis

17. 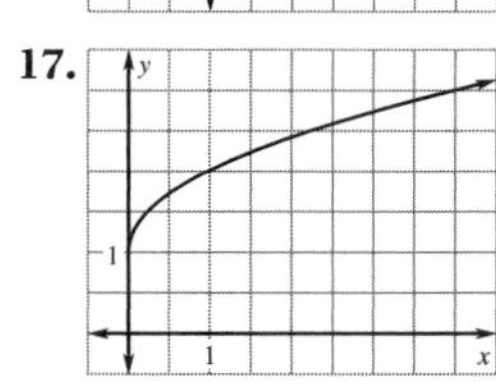

domain: $x \geq 0$, range: $y \geq 1$; vertical translation 1 unit up

19. 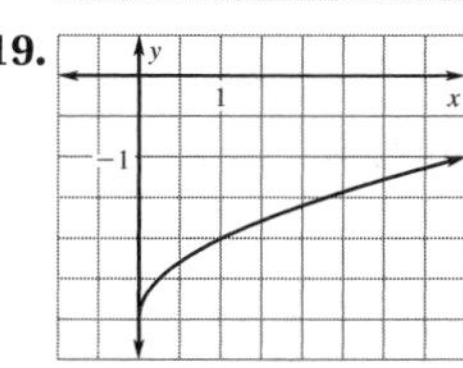

domain: $x \geq 0$, range: $y \geq -3$; vertical translation 3 units down

21. 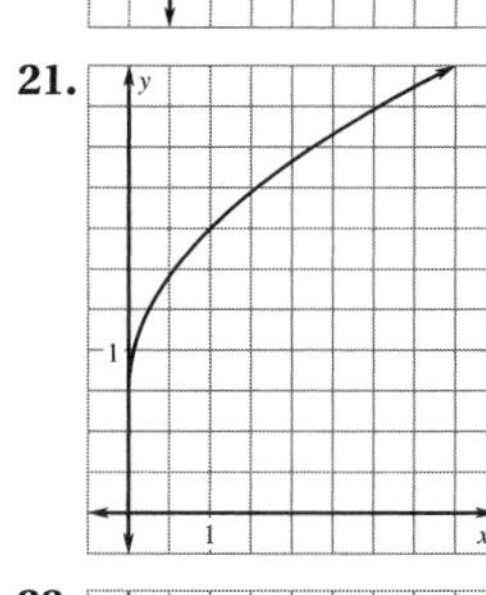

domain: $x \geq 0$, range: $y \geq \frac{3}{4}$; vertical translation $\frac{3}{4}$ unit up

23. 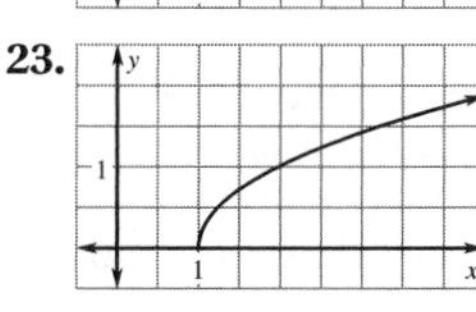

domain: $x \geq 1$, range: $y \geq 0$; horizontal translation 1 unit right

25. 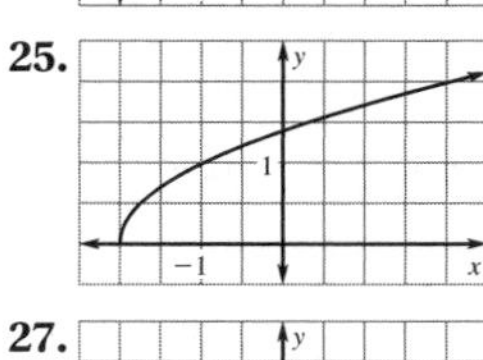

domain: $x \geq -2$, range: $y \geq 0$; horizontal translation 2 units left

27. 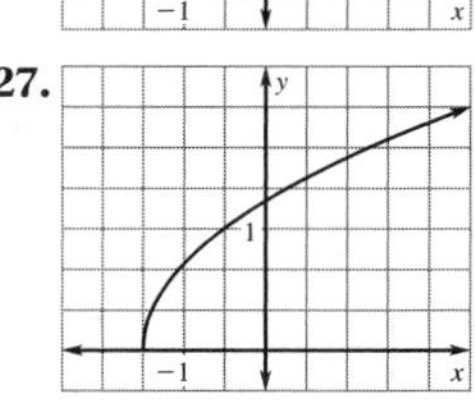

domain: $x \geq -1.5$, range: $y \geq 0$; horizontal translation 1.5 units left

SA35

31. 33. 35. 37.

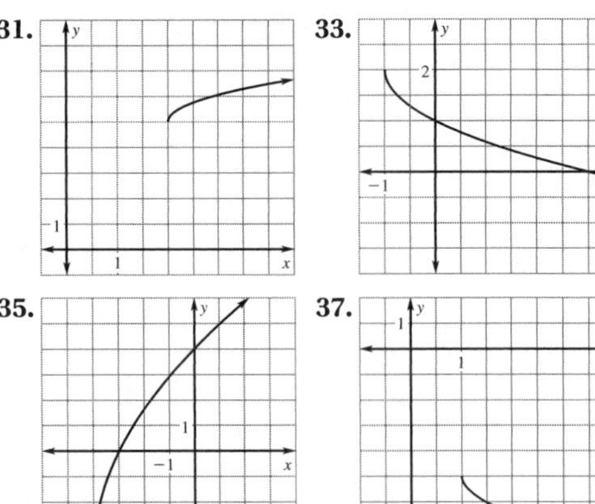

11.1 Problem Solving (pp. 715–716)

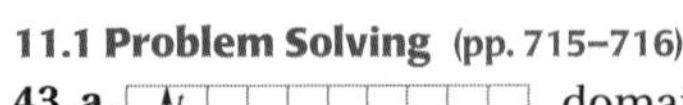

43. a.

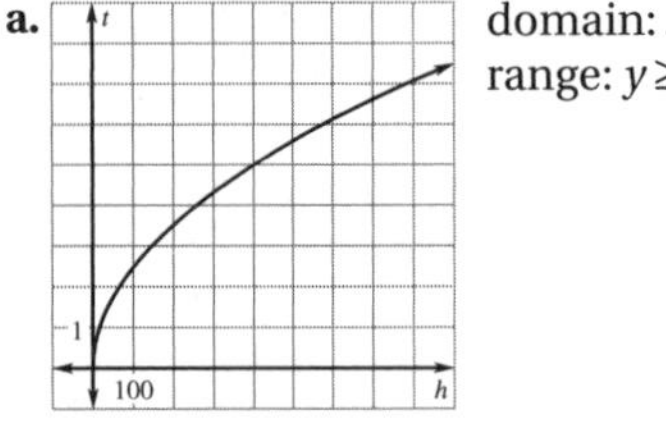

domain: $x \geq 0$, range: $y \geq 0$

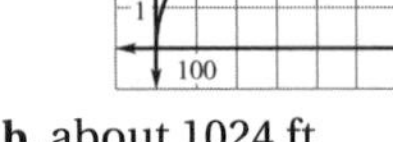

b. about 1024 ft

45.

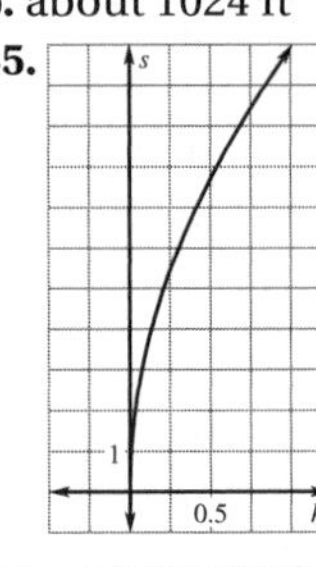

domain: $x \geq 0$, range: $y \geq 0$; about 0.9 m

47. a.

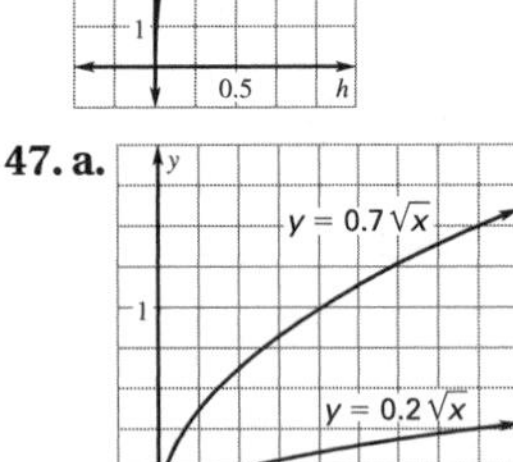

blue-winged teal's domain: $x \geq 0$, range: $y \geq 0$, northern pintail's domain: $x \geq 0$, range: $y \geq 0$

b. blue-winged teal: about 2 hectares, northern pintail: 25 hectares

11.1 Graphing Calculator Activity (p. 717)

1.

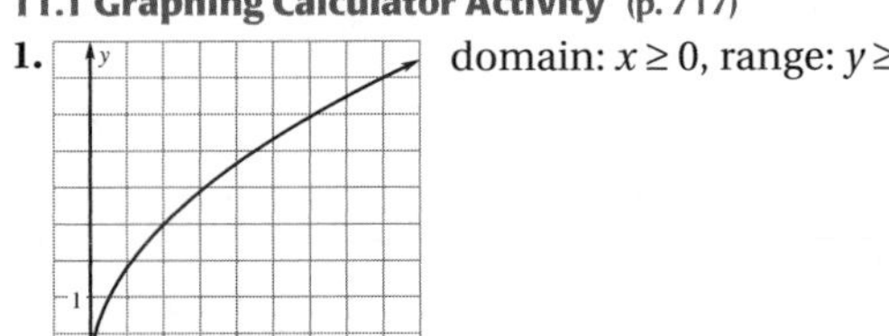

domain: $x \geq 0$, range: $y \geq 0$

3.

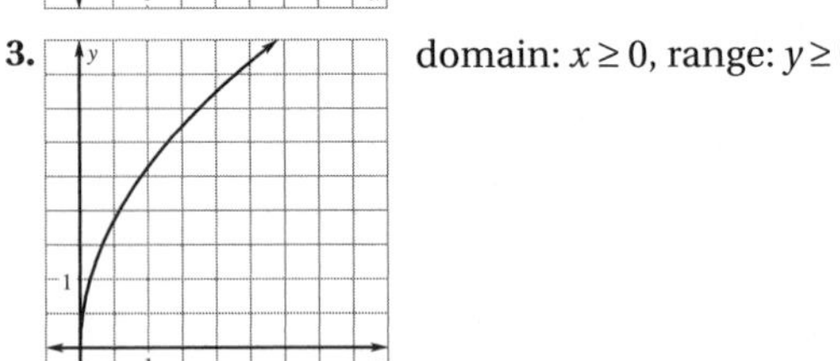

domain: $x \geq 0$, range: $y \geq 0$

5.

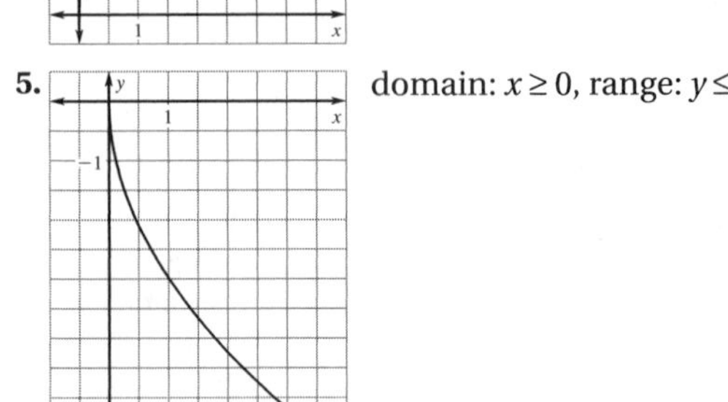

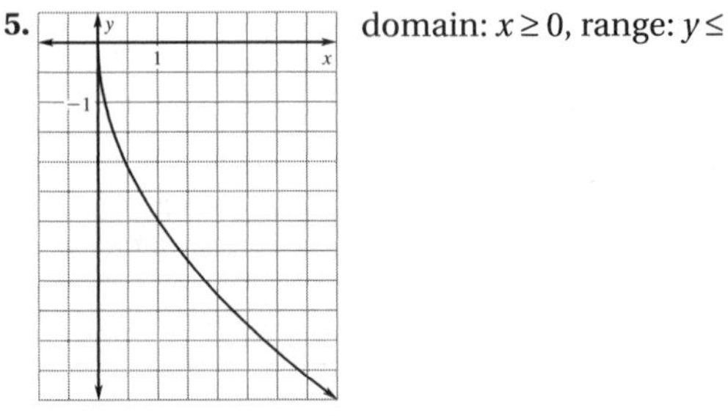

domain: $x \geq 0$, range: $y \leq 0$

7.

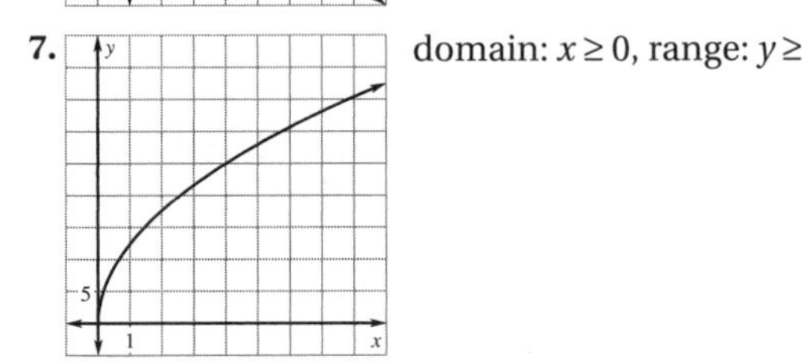

domain: $x \geq 0$, range: $y \geq 0$

9.

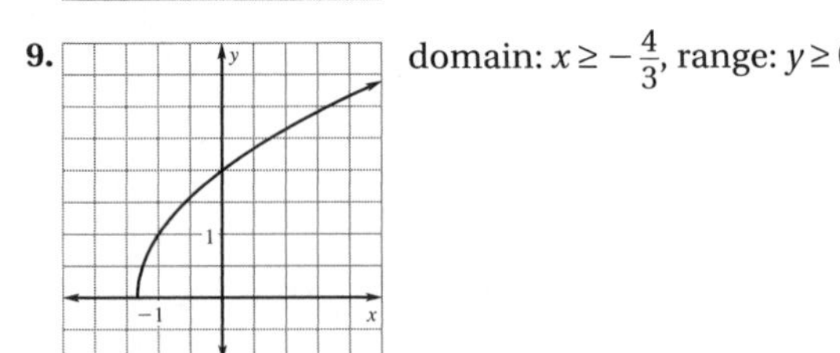

domain: $x \geq -\frac{4}{3}$, range: $y \geq 0$

11.

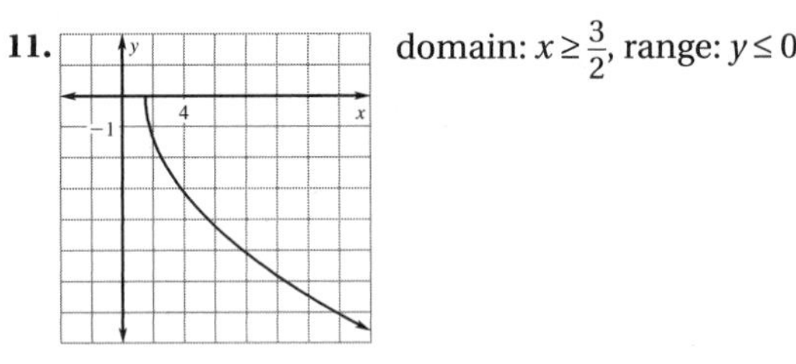

domain: $x \geq \frac{3}{2}$, range: $y \leq 0$

SELECTED ANSWERS

13. a. 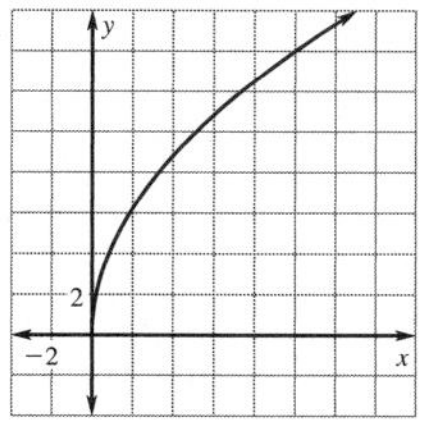 domain: $x \geq 0$, range: $y \geq 0$

b. about 154.3 m

11.2 Skill Practice (pp. 723–724) **1.** rationalizing the denominator **3.** $2\sqrt{5}$ **5.** $4\sqrt{6}$ **7.** $5\sqrt{5b}$ **9.** $9m\sqrt{m}$ **11.** $5\sqrt{6}$ **13.** $2x\sqrt{7}$ **15.** $2a^2b^2\sqrt{b}$ **17.** mn **19.** $\frac{2}{7}$ **21.** $\frac{a\sqrt{a}}{11}$ **25.** *Sample answer:* Simplify $\sqrt{45}$ to $\sqrt{9} \cdot \sqrt{5} = 3\sqrt{5}$. Then multiply $3\sqrt{5} \cdot \sqrt{5} = 3 \cdot 5 = 15$. Or, combine the expressions to create $\sqrt{45 \cdot 5} = \sqrt{225} = 15$. **27.** $\frac{4\sqrt{3}}{3}$ **29.** $\frac{\sqrt{13}}{13}$ **31.** $\frac{\sqrt{2x}}{2x}$ **33.** $\frac{2\sqrt{6n}}{3n^2}$ **35.** $-5\sqrt{5}$ **37.** $37\sqrt{2}$ **39.** $7\sqrt{7} - 5\sqrt{14}$ **41.** $21\sqrt{2} + 6\sqrt{6}$ **43.** $18 - \sqrt{2}$ **45.** $6\sqrt{7} + 6\sqrt{3} + 2\sqrt{14} + 2\sqrt{6}$ **47.** $16s^3t\sqrt{2rt}$ **49.** $\frac{h\sqrt{10gf}}{5f^2}$ **51.** $\frac{\sqrt{5}}{10}$ **53.** $\frac{3\sqrt{x} + 4x\sqrt{x}}{x^2}$ **55.** $\frac{\sqrt{7} - 1}{6}$ **57.** $\frac{7\sqrt{10} + 2\sqrt{5}}{47}$ **59.** $3\sqrt{7} - 3\sqrt{6}$ **61.** $-2\sqrt{3} - 3\sqrt{2}$ **63.** $(a\sqrt{b} + c\sqrt{d})(a\sqrt{b} - c\sqrt{d}) = a^2b - ac\sqrt{bd} + ac\sqrt{bd} - c^2d = a^2b - c^2d$ **65.** $-x$

11.2 Problem Solving (pp. 725–726) **67.** about 9.54% **69. a.** 5 yd^2 **b.** The side length s is in yd, and $\sqrt{\frac{S}{6}}$ is $\sqrt{\text{yd}^2} = \text{yd}$. **c.** 0.9 yd **71. a.** $S = \frac{\sqrt{hw}}{60}$ **b.** Yes. *Sample answer:* If the mass stays the same, then the greater the height the greater the body surface area will be.

Extension (pp. 727–728) **1.** $-2 - \sqrt{2}, -2 + \sqrt{2}$ **3.** $-4 - 2\sqrt{2}, -4 + 2\sqrt{2}$ **5.** $-1 - \frac{2\sqrt{3}}{3}, -1 + \frac{2\sqrt{3}}{3}$ **7.** $\frac{1}{5} - \frac{\sqrt{11}}{5}, \frac{1}{5} + \frac{\sqrt{11}}{5}$ **9.** $\frac{1}{2} - \frac{\sqrt{13}}{2}, \frac{1}{2} + \frac{\sqrt{13}}{2}$ **11.** $\frac{7}{2} - \frac{\sqrt{61}}{2}, \frac{7}{2} + \frac{\sqrt{61}}{2}$ **13.** $2 - \sqrt{2}, 2 + \sqrt{2}$ **15.** $-\frac{\sqrt{6}}{3}, \frac{\sqrt{6}}{3}$ **17.** $-\frac{1}{6} - \frac{\sqrt{73}}{6}, -\frac{1}{6} + \frac{\sqrt{73}}{6}$ **21.** Sum: $-\frac{b}{a}$, product: $\frac{c}{a}$. *Sample answer:* $y = 2x^2 - 4x + 1$

11.3 Skill Practice (pp. 732–733) **1.** extraneous solution **3.** 4 **5.** 48 **7.** 29 **9.** 8 **11.** $-\frac{75}{2}$ **13.** 47 **15.** -2 **17.** 7 **19.** no real solutions **23.** 1 **25.** $\frac{3}{8}, \frac{1}{2}$ **27.** -2 **29.** *Sample answer:* The solution $x = -9$ does not check in the original equation, so it is an extraneous solution. The only real solution is $x = 2$. **31.** no real solutions **33.** $\frac{16}{5}$

11.3 Problem Solving (pp. 733–734) **37.** 1977 **39.** 2.1 m

11.4 Skill Practice (pp. 740–741) **1.** hypotenuse **3.** $b = 4$ **5.** $c = \sqrt{61}$ **7.** $c = 8\sqrt{2}$ **9.** $c = 4\sqrt{13}$ **11.** $a = 8$ **13.** $a = 1.6$ **17.** 2, 4 **19.** 3, 4, 5, or 7, 24, 25 **21.** 2 in., 6 in. **23.** not a right triangle **25.** not a right triangle **27.** right triangle **31.** *Sample answer:* Let $m = 3$ and $n = 6$. Then $a = 6^2 - 3^2 = 27$, $b = 2(3)(6) = 36$, $c = 6^2 + 3^2 = 45$; substitute the values from the equation for a, b, and c in the Pythagorean theorem: $(n^2 - m^2)^2 + (2mn)^2 = (n^2 + m^2)^2$. Simplify to $n^4 - 2m^2n^2 + m^4 + 4m^2n^2 = n^4 + 2m^2n^2 + m^4$; $-2m^2n^2 + 4m^2n^2 = 2m^2n^2$; $2 = 2$. The equations are equal, so by the converse of the Pythagorean theorem, the lengths a, b, and c are a Pythagorean triple.

11.4 Problem Solving (pp. 741–742) **33.** 16 ft **35.** No; the sum of the squares of the two shorter sides is not equal to the square of the longer side. **37. a.** $\sqrt{6}$ **b.** $\sqrt{8}$ **c.** $\sqrt{n+1}$. *Sample answer:* A list of the hypotenuse lengths for the first few triangles is $\sqrt{2}, \sqrt{3}, \sqrt{4}, \sqrt{5}, \ldots$. A general formula for this series is $c_n = \sqrt{n+1}$.

11.5 Skill Practice (pp. 747–748) **1.** midpoint **3.** 1 **5.** 5 **7.** $\sqrt{53}$ **9.** $2\sqrt{17}$ **11.** $\sqrt{397}$ **13.** $\sqrt{73}$ **17.** 1, 25 **19.** -11, 1 **21.** -7, 15 **23.** $(5, -5)$ **25.** $(1, -4)$ **27.** $(-11, -6)$ **29.** $(-2, 0)$ **31.** $(-8, -4.5)$ **33.** $(-21, -33)$ **35.** *Sample answer:* The square of the difference in the x values and the square of the difference in the y values should be added, not subtracted; $d = \sqrt{(3 - (-17))^2 + (8 - (-2))^2} = \sqrt{400 + 100} = \sqrt{500} = 10\sqrt{5}$. **39.** $(8, -2)$ **41.** right triangle **43.** not a right triangle **45.** *Sample answer:* Use the distance formula to find the distance between the midpoint and each of the endpoints. If they are equal, the midpoint is equidistant from each endpoint.

11.5 Problem Solving (pp. 748–750) **47. a.** 10 mi **b.** $\sqrt{2}$ times greater **49. a.** the anchor and the cup **b.** the belt buckle and the sword; the anchor and the sword **51.** Yes; yes; all of them; the quadrilateral is a square.

11.5 Problem Solving Workshop (p. 751) **1. a.** Natural History Museum **b.** 0.24 mi

Chapter Review (pp. 754–756) **1.** It is a vertical stretch by a factor of 3 of the graph of $y = \sqrt{x}$. **3.** converse of the Pythagorean theorem

5.

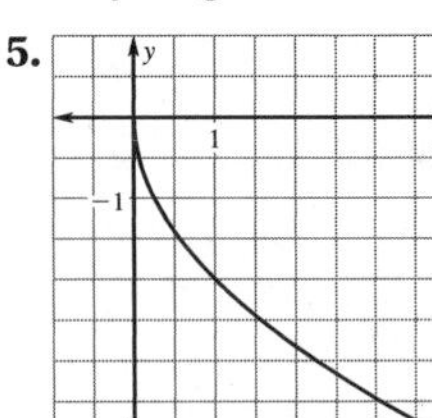

domain: $x \geq 0$, range: $y \leq 0$; vertical stretch by a factor of 2 with a reflection in the x-axis

7.

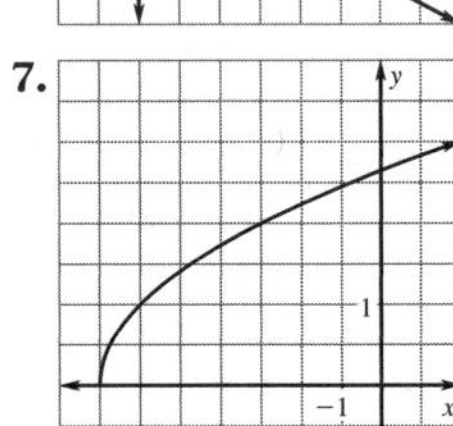

domain: $x \geq -7$, range: $y \geq 0$; horizontal translation of 7 units to the left

9. $11x\sqrt{x}$ **11.** $7x\sqrt{7}$ **13.** $\frac{2\sqrt{5}}{5}$ **15.** $7\sqrt{2} - 2\sqrt{3}$ **17.** 784 **19.** 5 **21.** no real solutions **23.** $c = \sqrt{218}$ **25.** $b = \sqrt{57}$ **27.** $a = \sqrt{209}$ **29.** 2036 ft **31.** 10 **33.** (3.5, −4) **35.** (5, −2)

Chapter 12

12.1 Skill Practice (pp. 769–770) **1.** −3 **3.** direct variation **5.** neither **7.** inverse variation **9.** direct variation **11.** inverse variation **13.** direct variation

15.

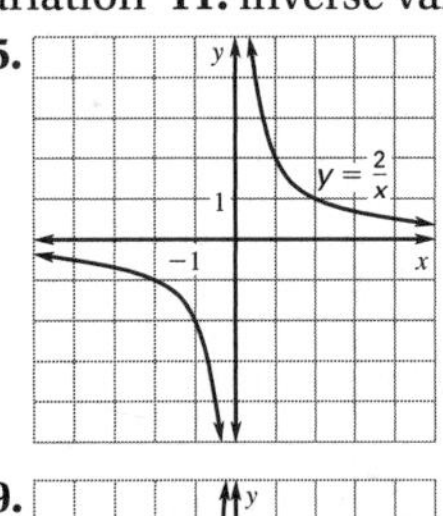

17.

19.

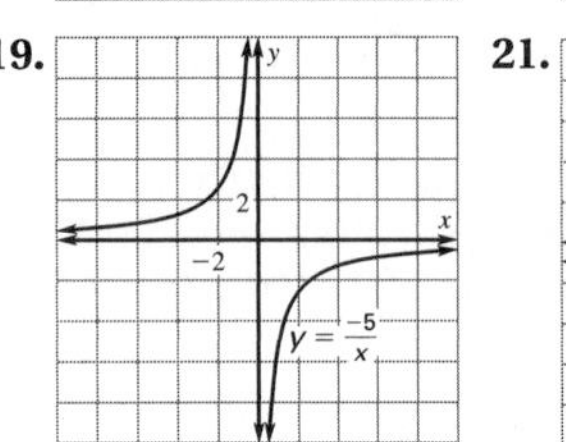

21.

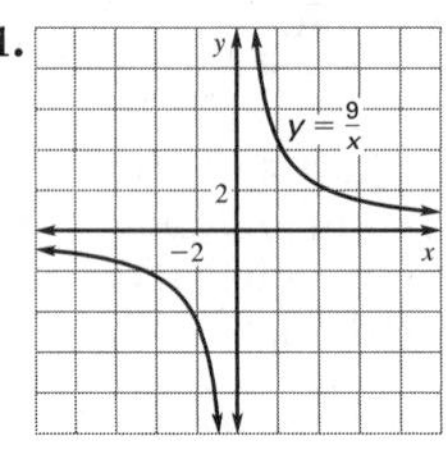

23.

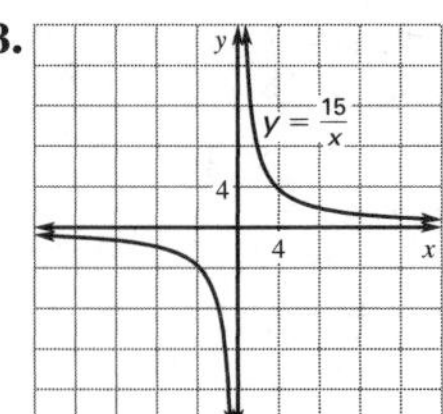

25.

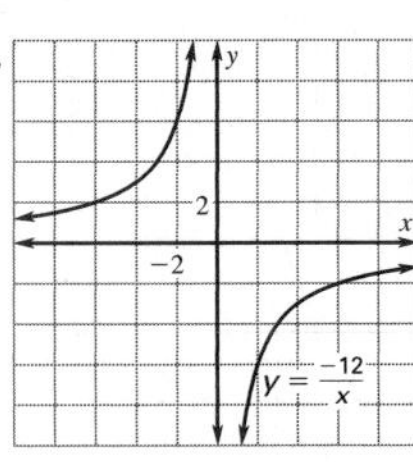

27. An inverse variation equation is in the form $y = \frac{a}{x}$, not $y = ax$; $8 = \frac{a}{2}$, $16 = a$. The correct inverse variation equation is $y = \frac{16}{x}$. **29.** $y = \frac{21}{x}$; 10.5 **31.** $y = \frac{-13}{x}$; −6.5 **33.** $y = \frac{132}{x}$; 66 **35.** $y = \frac{-18}{x}$; −9 **37.** $y = \frac{20}{x}$; 10 **39.** $y = \frac{70}{x}$; 35 **41.** $y = \frac{66}{x}$; 33 **45.** not inverse variation **47.** inverse variation; $y = \frac{-24}{x}$ **49.** $2\pi r = C$; direct variation **51.** $Bh = 400$; inverse variation

12.1 Problem Solving (pp. 770–772)

55. $d = \frac{175{,}000}{p}$; 350 units

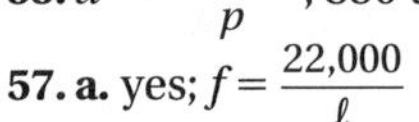

57. a. yes; $f = \frac{22{,}000}{\ell}$

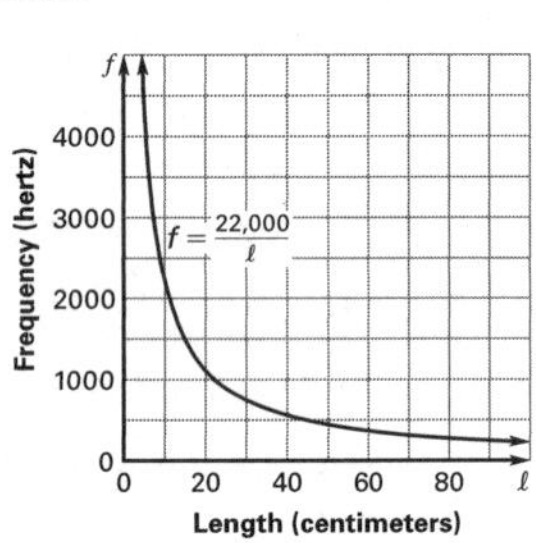

b. about 748 Hz **c.** The frequency increases; yes.

59. a. $s = \frac{35}{a}$

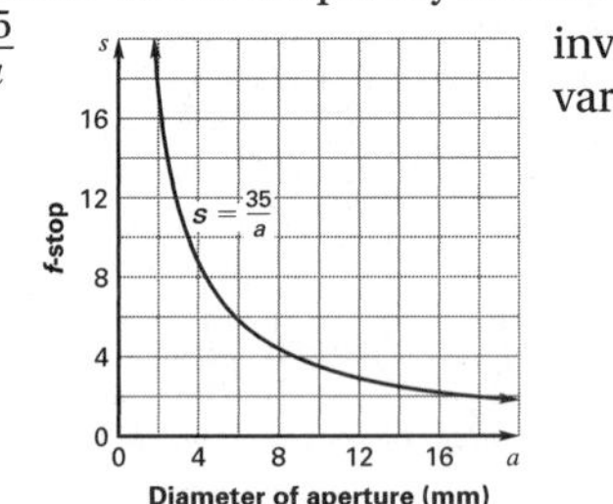

inverse variation

b. 4; when $s = 4$, the diameter of the aperture is $a = \frac{35}{4} = 8.75$ millimeters, and when $s = 8$, the diameter of the aperture is $a = \frac{35}{8} = 4.375$ millimeters.

12.2 Skill Practice (pp. 779–780) **1.** $x = 3, y = -6$

3. 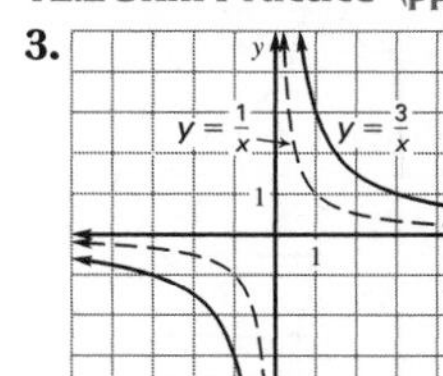

Domain: all real numbers except 0, range: all real numbers except 0; the graph is a vertical stretch of the graph of $y = \frac{1}{x}$.

5. 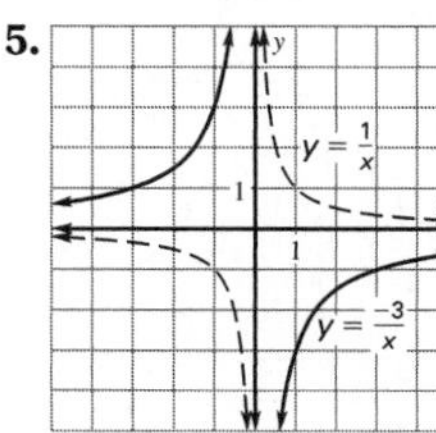

Domain: all real numbers except 0, range: all real numbers except 0; the graph is a vertical stretch of the graph of $y = \frac{1}{x}$ that is then reflected in the x-axis.

7. 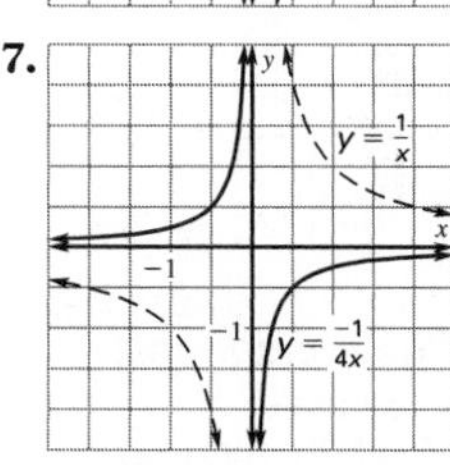

Domain: all real numbers except 0, range: all real numbers except 0; the graph is a vertical shrink of the graph of $y = \frac{1}{x}$ that is then reflected in the x-axis.

9. 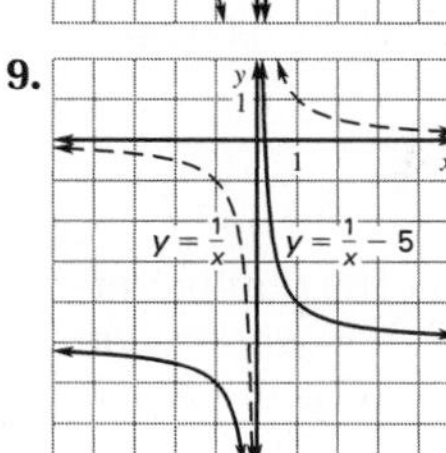

Domain: all real numbers except 0, range: all real numbers except -5; the graph is a vertical translation (of 5 units down) of the graph of $y = \frac{1}{x}$.

11. 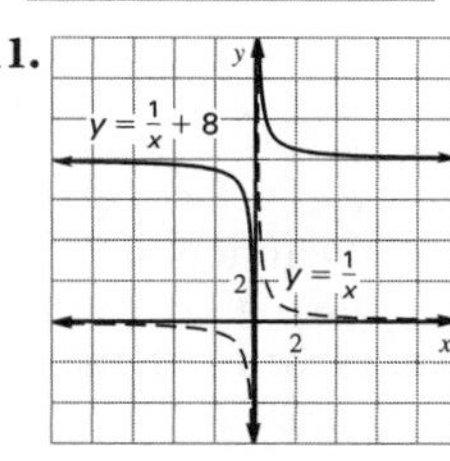

Domain: all real numbers except 0, range: all real numbers except 8; the graph is a vertical translation (of 8 units up) of the graph of $y = \frac{1}{x}$.

13. 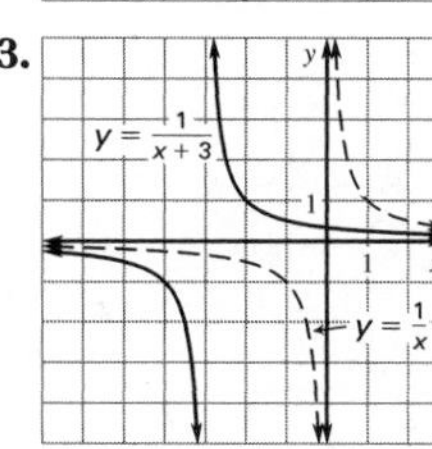

Domain: all real numbers except -3, range: all real numbers except 0; the graph is a horizontal translation (of 3 units left) of the graph of $y = \frac{1}{x}$.

15. Domain: all real numbers except -8, range: all real numbers except 0; the graph is a horizontal translation (of 8 units left) of the graph of $y = \frac{1}{x}$.

17. 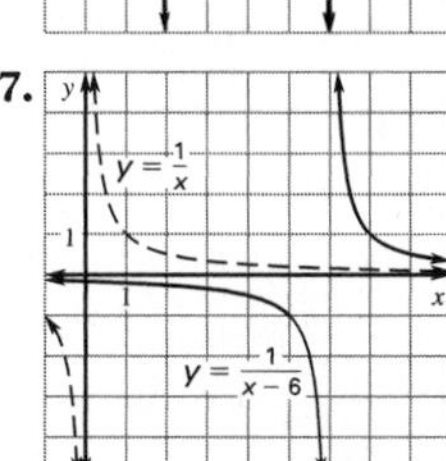

Domain: all real numbers except 6, range: all real numbers except 0; the graph is a horizontal translation (of 6 units right) of the graph of $y = \frac{1}{x}$.

19. 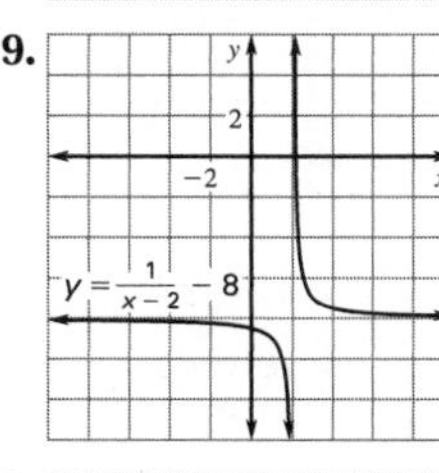

21. 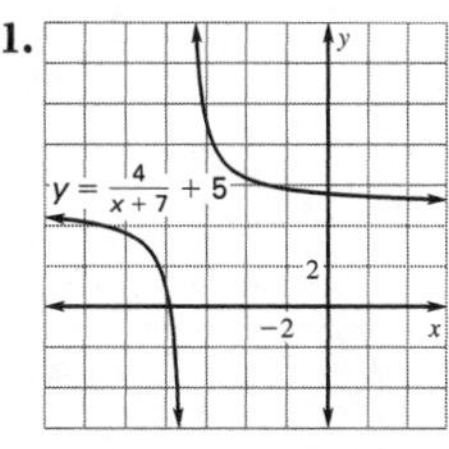

23. 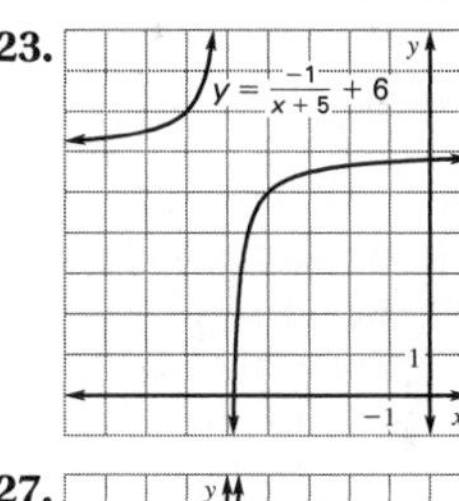

25. 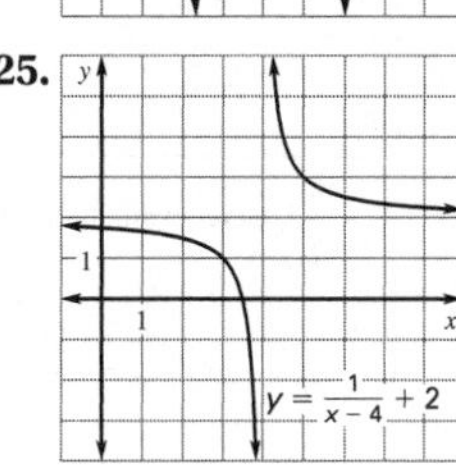

27. 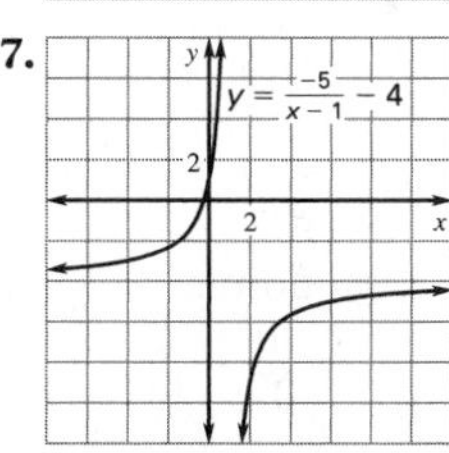

29. *Sample answer:* $y = \frac{1}{x + 1} + 2$ **31.** To identify the asymptotes of the hyperbola, write its equation in the form $y = \frac{a}{x - h} + k$: $y = \frac{-2}{x - 6} + 7$; thus the horizontal asymptote is $y = 7$, not $y = -7$. **33.** $y = \frac{-28}{x + 2} + 5$ **35.** $y = \frac{-28}{x + 4} - 4$

37. a. $h = \dfrac{100}{b_2 + 4}$

domain: $b_2 > 0$, range: $0 < h < 25$ **b.** about 13

12.2 Problem Solving (pp. 780–782)

39. $C = \dfrac{900}{p} + 400$

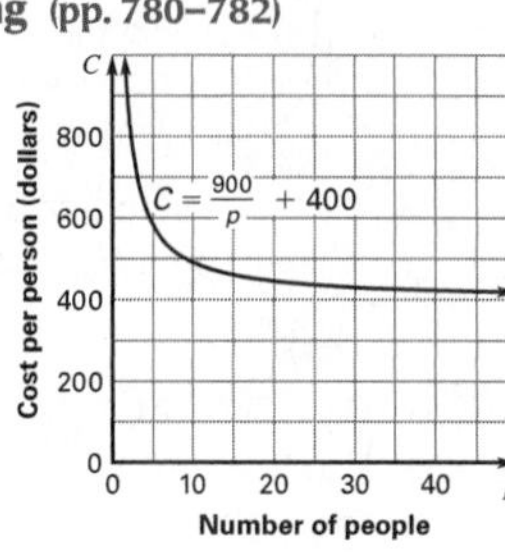

41. a. $C = \dfrac{22}{r + 2}$

b.

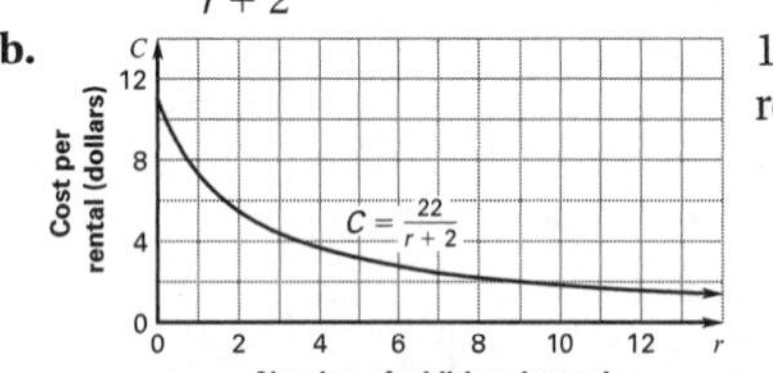

13 additional rentals

43.

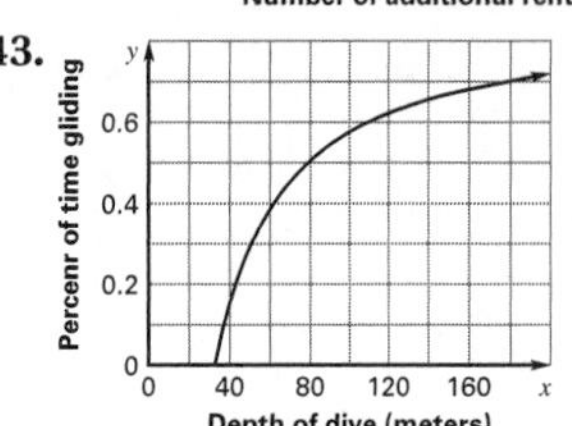

Domain: $d \geq 32.8$, range: $0 \leq p < 0.859$; the percent of time gliding increases.

12.3 Skill Practice (pp. 788–789) **1.** monomial **3.** $2x^2 - 3x + 4$ **5.** $-2r^3 + 5r + 12$ **7.** $3v + 5$ **9.** $m - 4$ **11.** $a - 4 + \dfrac{-1}{a - 1}$ **13.** $3p - 13 + \dfrac{18}{3 + p}$ **15.** $x + 3 + \dfrac{-12}{6 + x}$ **17.** $-t - 3 + \dfrac{-4}{t - 3}$ **21.** When subtracting $8x - 24$ from $8x - 9$, the result is $-9 - (-24) = -9 + 24 = 15$; $(8x - 9) \div (x - 3) = 8 + \dfrac{15}{x - 3}$.

23.

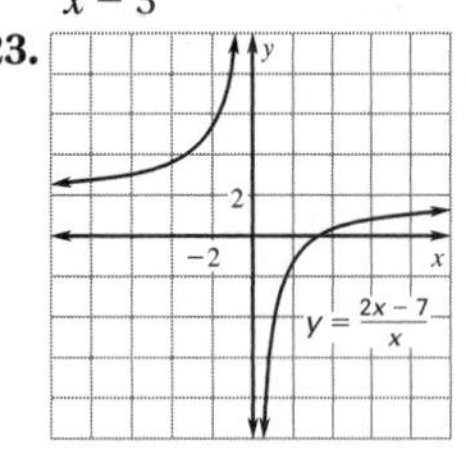

25.

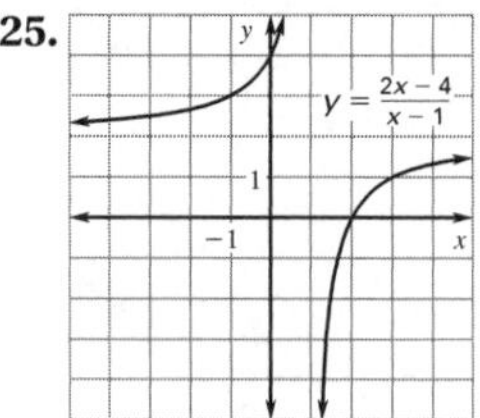

27.

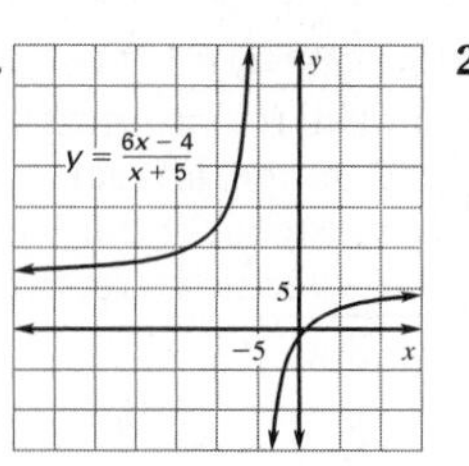

29.

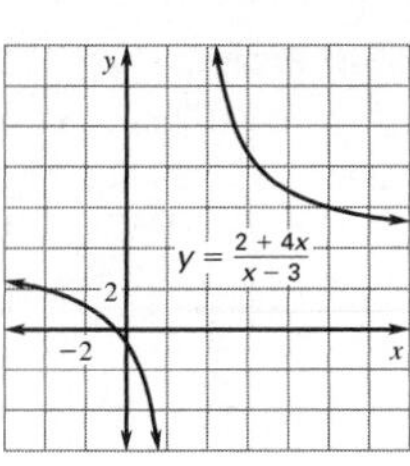

31. $\dfrac{7}{6} + \dfrac{2}{\ell}$ **35.** 10 **37.** -5

12.3 Problem Solving (pp. 789–791)

43. $C = \dfrac{80 + 3d}{d}$

45. a. $C = \dfrac{0.4t - 360}{t}$

b.

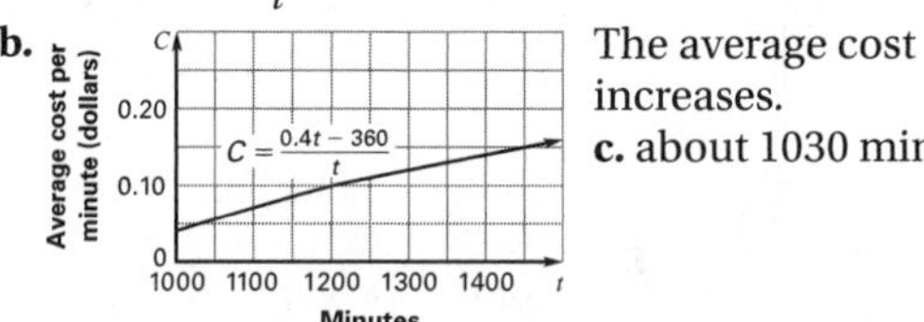

The average cost increases. **c.** about 1030 min

47. a. The number of households with VCRs increased.

b. No; as x increases, the graph of the function approaches its horizontal asymptote $y = 120$ from below, so the value of y will never exceed 120 million if this model applies to years beyond 2000.

49. a. $y = \dfrac{2r + 2\ell}{r\ell}$

b. More efficient; the graph in part (a) shows that as the length increases, the ratio decreases, implying that the microorganism becomes more efficient at performing metabolic tasks. **c.** The microorganism's efficiency would increase. *Sample answer:* Suppose the length is fixed at 50 micrometers. Then $y = \frac{2r + 100}{50r}$, or $y = \frac{2}{r} + 0.04$. This equation has the same graph as the graph shown in part (a); from the graph we see that as the radius increases, the ratio decreases, implying that the microorganism's efficiency increases.

12.3 Graphing Calculator Activity (pp. 792–793)

1. 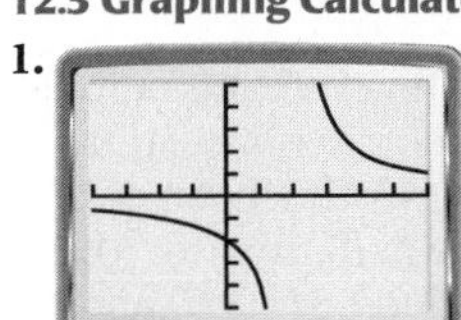 vertical: $x = 2$, horizontal: $y = 0$

3. 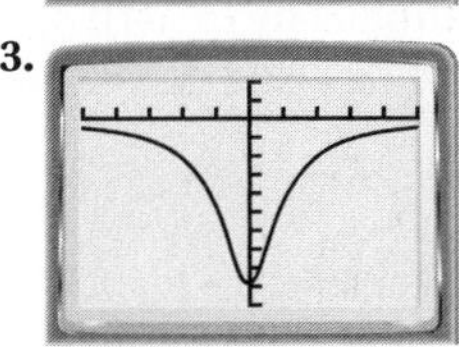 vertical: none, horizontal: $y = 0$

5. 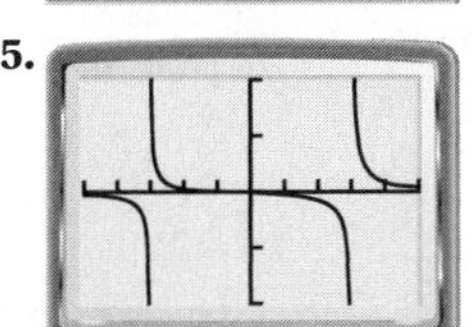 vertical: $x = -3$, $x = 3$, horizontal: $y = 0$

9. 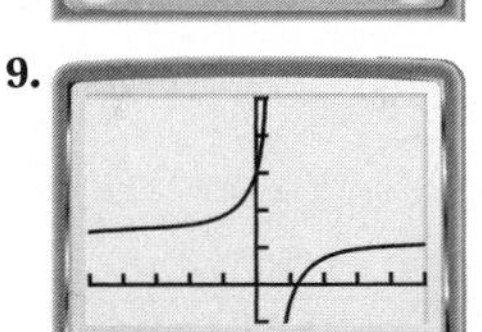 vertical: $x = 1$, horizontal: $y = 5$

11. 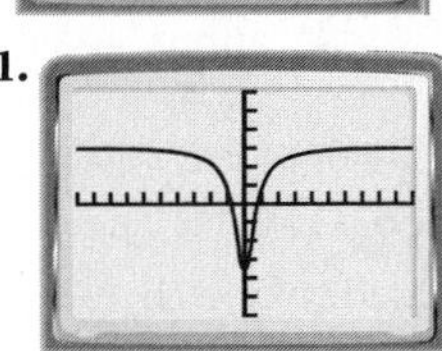 vertical: none, horizontal: $y = 3$

13. 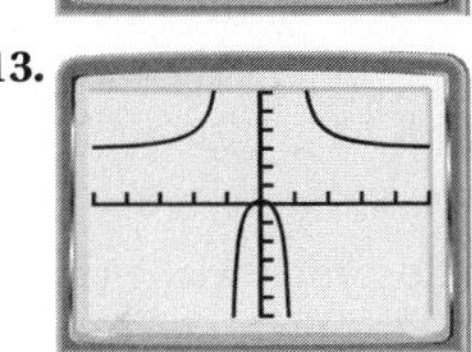 vertical: $x = -1$, $x = 1$, horizontal: $y = 3$

15. Vertical lines $x = a$, where a is an x-value that makes the denominator of the rational function equal to 0. **17.** $y = a$, where a is the quotient of the leading coefficient of the numerator and the leading coefficient of the denominator.

12.4 Skill Practice (pp. 797–798) **1.** excluded value **3.** none **5.** -1 **7.** none **9.** $0, \frac{1}{2}$ **11.** When finding the excluded values you must find the values for which the denominator of the original expression, $2x^2 - 11x + 12$, is 0; the excluded values are $\frac{3}{2}$ and 4. **13.** $\frac{2x}{5}$; none **15.** $-3a$; 0 **17.** 3; -11 **19.** -2; 3 **21.** $\frac{2}{f^2 - 9}$; ± 3 **23.** $\frac{1}{h - 4}$; $-3, 4$ **25.** $\frac{-6}{2w - 5}$; $0, \frac{5}{2}$ **27.** 3; 0, 4 **29.** $\frac{s + 8}{s - 1}$; $-8, 1$ **31.** $\frac{1}{m^2 + 5m}$; $0, -5$ **33.** No; the two expressions do not have the same excluded values; the excluded values for $\frac{x^2 + x}{x^2 - 1}$ are ± 1, while the excluded values for $\frac{x^2}{x^2 - x}$ are 0 and 1. The expressions are not equivalent for $x = 0$ and for $x = -1$. **37.** $\frac{3(x + 2)}{x(x + 6)}$

12.4 Problem Solving (pp. 799–800)

41. $p = \frac{3x^2 - 12}{22x^2 + 2500}$; about 11% **43.** $p = \frac{-202x + 3660}{345x + 9130}$; the percent of wood houses decreased. **45. a.** $R = \frac{37{,}500 + 2500x}{125 + x}$; about \$522 million

b. 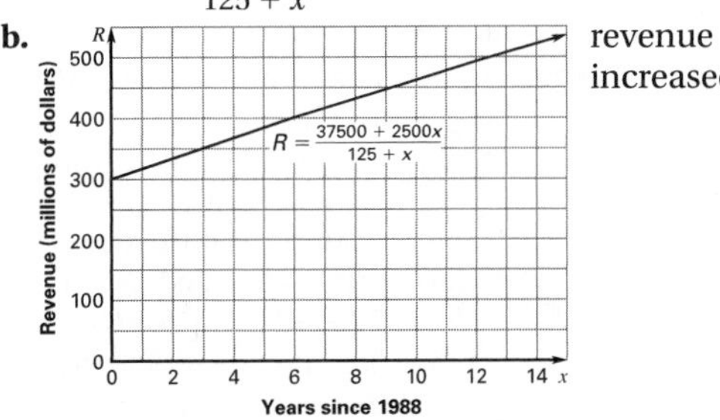

revenue increased

c. No; if the price per copy of printed music went up during the period 1988–2002, then the revenue may have increased without the number of copies sold increasing.

SELECTED ANSWERS

12.5 Skill Practice (pp. 806–807) **1.** multiplicative inverse **3.** $\frac{15}{14p^2}$ **5.** $\frac{-(v-3)}{5(v+1)}$ **7.** $\frac{x+4}{2x+1}$ **9.** $\frac{-3m}{m-2}$

11. To divide by the rational expression $\frac{15x^3}{2}$, you must multiply by its multiplicative inverse, $\frac{2}{15x^3}$; $\frac{x^3}{5} \cdot \frac{2}{15x^3} = \frac{2x^3}{75x^3} = \frac{2}{75}$. **13.** $\frac{20r^3}{9}$ **15.** $\frac{2w+5}{w(w-9)}$ **17.** $\frac{a+5}{3a^2}$

19. 1 **23.** $8x^2 \cdot \frac{1}{2x^3}$; $\frac{4}{x}$ **25.** $\frac{1}{x^2-3x-4} \div \frac{2}{x^2-1}$; $\frac{x-1}{2(x-4)}$

27. *Sample answer:* $\frac{x^2-2x-3}{x^2-2x-8}$, $\frac{x^2-9x+20}{x^2-4x-5}$

29. $(x-1)(x-3)$. *Sample answer:* 0

12.5 Problem Solving (pp. 807–809)

33. $p = \frac{100+2.2x}{(1-0.014x)(1500+63x)}$; about 7%

35. a. $R = \frac{(86+180x)(1+0.014x)}{(1+0.024x)(23+38x)}$

b.

Year	1990	1991	1992	1993	1994	1995	1996
Rushing average, *R* (yards per attempt)	3.74	4.32	4.42	4.44	4.44	4.42	4.40

Year	1997	1998	1999	2000	2001	2002
Rushing average, *R* (yards per attempt)	4.38	4.35	4.33	4.30	4.28	4.25

Smith's career rushing average increased for the first several years and then began to decrease.

37. a. $T = \frac{4700-74x}{(1-0.053x)(0.015x^2+4.1)}$

b.

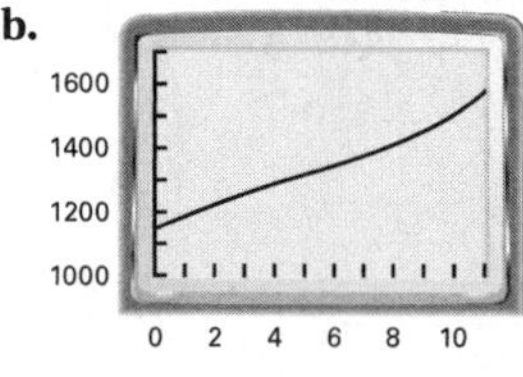

The number of tickets increased. No; the graph only shows how the *ratio* of the gross revenue and the ticket prices changed. *R* and *P* could go up and/or down while their ratio increases.

c.

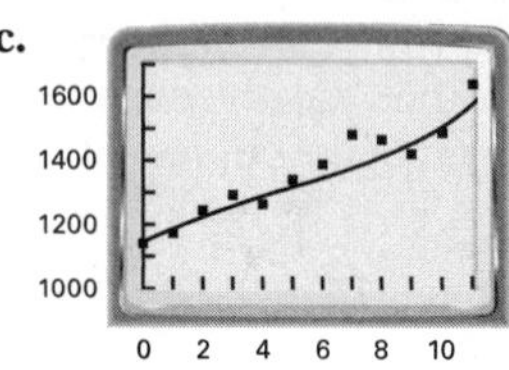

The points of the scatter plot are very close to the graph of the model for all years except 1998, 1999, and 2002.

Extension (p. 811) **1.** $\frac{3x^3}{28}$ **3.** $\frac{x}{2(x-3)(x-7)}$ **5.** $x^2(x-1)$

7. $\frac{5(x+4)}{2}$ **9.** $\frac{2(x+3)(x-1)}{5(3x+1)}$ **11.** $\frac{3(r+\ell)}{rh}$

13. No; $\frac{\frac{a}{b}}{c} = \frac{a}{b} \div c = \frac{a}{b} \cdot \frac{1}{c} = \frac{a}{bc}$ and $\frac{a}{\frac{b}{c}} = a \div \frac{b}{c} = \frac{a}{1} \cdot \frac{c}{b} = \frac{ac}{b}$. Thus, $\frac{\frac{a}{b}}{c} \neq \frac{a}{\frac{b}{c}}$.

12.6 Skill Practice (pp. 816–817) **1.** least common denominator **3.** $\frac{1}{x}$ **5.** $\frac{4}{z}$ **7.** $\frac{2b+1}{b-3}$ **9.** $\frac{-1}{m^2+1}$

11. $\frac{3r+1}{r^2+r-7}$ **13.** $60v^3$ **15.** $(s+2)(s-1)$

17. $(u+7)(u+1)(u-3)$ **19.** To rewrite each rational expression using the least common denominator, you must multiply its numerator by the factor of the LCD that is missing from the denominator: the numerator $5x$ should be multiplied by $(x+3)$ and the numerator 2 should be multiplied by $(x-4)$; $\frac{5x}{x-4} + \frac{2}{x+3} = \frac{5x(x+3)}{(x-4)(x+3)} + \frac{2(x-4)}{(x-4)(x+3)} = \frac{5x^2+15x+2x-8}{(x-4)(x+3)} = \frac{5x^2+17x-8}{(x-4)(x+3)}$.

21. $\frac{149}{33y}$ **23.** $\frac{5r^2-17r}{(r-2)(r-3)}$ **25.** $\frac{4c^2+13c+30}{(c-6)(3c+10)}$

27. $\frac{-20f^2+7f+12}{7f(f+4)}$ **29.** $\frac{3j^2-12j-1}{(j+1)(j-1)(j-6)}$

31. $\frac{-v^2+6v+20}{(2v+5)(v-3)(v+5)}$ **33.** $\frac{S-2\ell w}{2(\ell+w)}$

35. $\frac{15x^2+120x+20}{(x-2)(x+8)}$ **37.** $\frac{-3x^2+29x-4}{x-9}$

39. $y = \frac{-4x-16}{x+2}$

12.6 Problem Solving (pp. 817–819) **43.** $t = \frac{400r-1000}{r(r-5)}$; about 8.4 h **45. a.** $\frac{2A^2+200A}{3}$; $\frac{7A^2+18{,}750A-205{,}050}{150}$

b. 2600 lb; 6301 lb **47.** $f = \frac{2.5+0.215x}{5.3+0.30x}$; about 58%

12.7 Skill Practice (pp. 823–824) **1.** rational equation **3.** ± 10 **5.** $-1\frac{1}{2}$ **7.** $-1\frac{1}{2}$, 4 **9.** -6, 5 **11.** 6 **13.** The distributive property must be used to find the product of 5 and $(4x+1)$; $5(4x+1) = 3(8x-1)$, $20x+5 = 24x-3$, $8 = 4x$, $2 = x$. The solution is 2. **15.** -10 **17.** -22 **19.** $2 \pm 2\sqrt{3}$ **21.** no solution

23. $-\frac{1}{5}$, -1 **25.** All real numbers except 2; 2; two fractions with equal denominators must also have equal numerators, so $x = 2$, and the denominator of both fractions is $2 - a$. The equation has this one solution as long as the denominator $2 - a$ is not 0; so, the equation has no solution when $a = 2$.

SELECTED ANSWERS

27. a. $\left(\frac{8}{3}, 9\right)$, $(-2, -5)$ **b.**

29. No; suppose that $\frac{x+a}{x+1+a} = \frac{x}{x+1}$. Then, using the cross products property, $(x+1)(x+a) = x(x+1+a)$; $x^2 + xa + x + a = x^2 + x + xa$; $x^2 + x(a+1) + a = x^2 + x(1+a)$. Then, subtracting $x^2 + x(1+a)$ from both sides gives the result $a = 0$; so, the only value of a for which the equation is true is 0.

12.7 Problem Solving (pp. 824–826) **31.** 50 consecutive shots **33.** 3 c **35. a.** $\frac{30}{t} + \frac{30}{1.5t} = 1$; 50 min **b.** Change each 30 to 20, and change 1.5 to 1; 40 min. **c.** Because you now both rake at the same rate, whenever you work together, the time it takes to rake a portion of the lawn will be half the time it takes either of you to rake that portion alone. Suppose you rake together for m minutes. Then you each rake $\frac{m}{40}$ of the lawn, and together you rake $\frac{m}{40} + \frac{m}{40} = \frac{2m}{40} = \frac{m}{20}$ of the lawn. To rake $\frac{m}{20}$ of the lawn alone would take you $2m$ minutes. **37.** From 8 psi to 7 psi; substitute the given psi values for p in the given equation and then solve for a: for $p = 10$, $a \approx 10{,}722$; for $p = 9$, $a \approx 13{,}536$; for $p = 8$, $a \approx 16{,}600$; for $p = 7$, $a \approx 19{,}948$. The change in altitude when the atmospheric pressure changes from 10 psi to 9 psi is about $13{,}536 - 10{,}722 = 2814$, and the change in altitude when the atmospheric pressure changes from 8 psi to 7 psi is about $19{,}948 - 16{,}600 = 3348$.

12.7 Problem Solving Workshop (p. 828) **1.** \$1250 **3.** 6 free throws **5.** 75 min

Chapter Review (pp. 831–834) **1.** asymptote **3.** $x = -2$, $y = -4$ **5.** $y = \frac{63}{x}$, 12.6 **7.** inverse variation; $y = \frac{-8}{x}$

9.

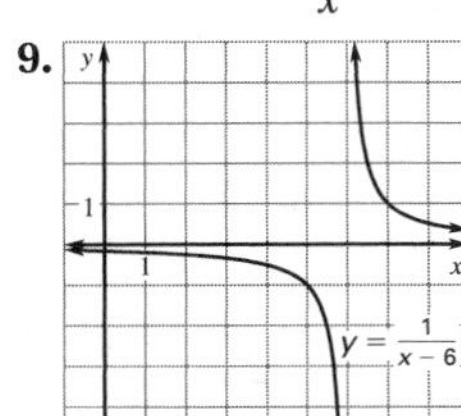

11. $x + 5$ **13.** $z - 1 + \frac{4}{z+5}$

15. $a = \frac{500 + 2d}{d}$

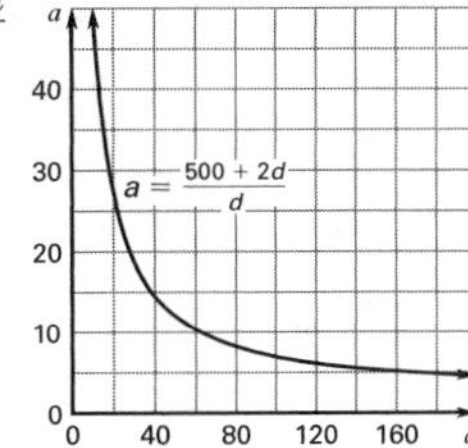

17. $-2, 6$ **19.** $\frac{m-3}{4}$; 0 **21.** $\frac{-(r+2)}{r+1}$; $-1, 2$ **23.** $\frac{21v^7}{4}$ **25.** $\frac{-8x+33}{5x-3}$ **27.** $\frac{5c^2 - 13c - 48}{(c+1)(c-4)(c+2)}$ **29.** $-6, 9$ **31.** $\frac{-21}{5}$

Chapter 13

13.1 Skill Practice (pp. 846–847) **1.** probability **3.** 12 outcomes; R1, R2, R3, R4, W1, W2, W3, W4, B1, B2, B3, B4 **5.** 48; HHH1, HHH2, HHH3, HHH4, HHH5, HHH6, HHT1, HHT2, HHT3, HHT4, HHT5, HHT6, HTH1, HTH2, HTH3, HTH4, HTH5, HTH6, HTT1, HTT2, HTT3, HTT4, HTT5, HTT6, THH1, THH2, THH3, THH4, THH5, THH6, THT1, THT2, THT3, THT4, THT5, THT6, TTH1, TTH2, TTH3, TTH4, TTH5, TTH6, TTT1, TTT2, TTT3, TTT4, TTT5, TTT6 **7.** $\frac{9}{10}$ **9.** $\frac{1}{10}$ **11.** $\frac{3}{7}$ or 3 : 7 **13.** *Sample answer:* Odds in favor is the number of favorable outcomes divided by the number of unfavorable outcomes; odds in favor of a multiple of 3 $= \frac{\text{Number of favorable outcomes}}{\text{Number of unfavorable outcomes}} = \frac{9}{1}$ or 9 : 1. **15.** *Sample answer:* Rolling a standard number cube and getting a 0, flipping a coin and getting heads or tails.

17.

	1	2	3	4	5	6
1	2	3	4	5	6	7
2	3	4	5	6	7	8
3	4	5	6	7	8	9
4	5	6	7	8	9	10
5	6	7	8	9	10	11
6	7	8	9	10	11	12

$P(2) = \frac{1}{36}$; $P(3) = \frac{1}{18}$; $P(4) = \frac{1}{12}$; $P(5) = \frac{1}{9}$; $P(6) = \frac{5}{36}$; $P(7) = \frac{1}{6}$; $P(8) = \frac{5}{36}$; $P(9) = \frac{1}{9}$; $P(10) = \frac{1}{12}$; $P(11) = \frac{1}{18}$; $P(12) = \frac{1}{36}$

13.1 Problem Solving (pp. 847–848) **19.** $\frac{1}{7}$ **21.** $\frac{4}{9}$; $\frac{4}{5}$. *Sample answer:* The probability and odds of choosing a boy are related because both compare the number of boys to another number. The probability of choosing a boy compares the number of boys to the total number of outcomes, while the odds of choosing a boy compare the number of boys to the total number of outcomes minus the number of boys.

SA43

Extension (p. 850) **1.** Answers will vary. **3.** *Sample answer:* There are 3 prizes to win, but since the prizes do not have an equal likelihood of being won, generating a list of random integers from 1 to 3 would not represent the situation. The probability of winning a CD is $\frac{1}{6}$, so if there were only 3 possible outcomes in the simulation you could not represent winning a CD properly.

13.2 Skill Practice (pp. 853–854) **1.** permutation **3. a.** 2 ways **b.** 2 ways **5. a.** 24 ways **b.** 12 ways **7. a.** 120 ways **b.** 20 ways **9. a.** 120 ways **b.** 20 ways **11.** *Sample answer:* 5 people are running in a race. How many different results can there be for first and second place? **13.** 6 **15.** 120 **17.** 3,628,800 **19.** 6,227,020,800 **21.** 210 **23.** 720 **25.** 1 **27.** 6,375,600 **29.** The denominator should be $(5 - 3)! = 2!$, not $3!$; ${}_5P_3 = \frac{5!}{(5-3)!} = \frac{5!}{2!} = 60$.

13.2 Problem Solving (pp. 854–855) **35. a.** $\frac{1}{2}$. *Sample answer:* Make a list of possible permutations, count the number in which you are first or second, and divide it by the total number of outcomes. **b.** $\frac{1}{2}$; the answers are the same. **37.** $\frac{1}{720}$

13.3 Skill Practice (p. 858) **1.** combination **3.** 20 combinations **5.** *Sample answer:* The answer given is for ${}_9P_4$, not ${}_9C_4$; ${}_9C_4 = \frac{9!}{(9-4)! \cdot 4!} = \frac{9!}{5! \cdot 4!} = 126$. **7.** 56 **9.** 28 **11.** 330 **13.** 15,504 **17.** Permutations; since the roles are different, the order in which students are selected for the roles matters; 720 ways. **19.** Permutations; the arrangement of people in the car matters; 120 ways. **21.** ${}_nC_r = {}_nP_r \cdot \frac{1}{r!}$. *Sample answer:* To find the number of combinations, you find the number of permutations and then divide by the number of ways the items being chosen can be arranged, or $r!$.

13.3 Problem Solving (p. 859) **23.** 840 burritos **25. a.** 84 combinations **b.** $\frac{5}{21}$. *Sample answer:* There are 84 possible outcomes of the choice. Find the number of combinations that include you and your 2 friends. After you and your friends are chosen, 3 other contestants from a pool of 6 can be chosen in any combination, so the number of favorable combinations is ${}_6C_3 = 20$. The probability that you and your friends are chosen is $\frac{20}{84} = \frac{5}{21}$.

13.3 Graphing Calculator Activity (p. 860) **1.** 35 **3.** 120 **5.** 15,120 **7.** 6,652,800 **9. a.** 3276 groups **b.** 6 ways

13.4 Skill Practice (pp. 864–865) **1.** dependent **3.** mutually exclusive; $\frac{2}{3}$ **5.** overlapping; $\frac{5}{6}$ **7.** To find the probability that you draw a yellow *or* a blue marble, the individual probabilities should be added, not multiplied; $\frac{7}{16} + \frac{5}{16} = \frac{12}{16} = \frac{3}{4}$. **9.** independent; $\frac{1}{36}$ **11.** independent; $\frac{1}{12}$ **15.** $\frac{1}{64}$ **17.** If you first draw a pawn and then do not replace it, the probability of drawing a second pawn is not $\frac{16}{32}$, but $\frac{15}{31}$. $\frac{16}{32} \cdot \frac{15}{31} = \frac{15}{62}$. **19.** 69%

13.4 Problem Solving (pp. 866–867) **23.** 62.3%

25. a.

Mon	Tues	Wed	Thurs	Fri	Sat	Sun
st. gov.		st. gov.				
tutor			tutor	tutor	tutor	

b.

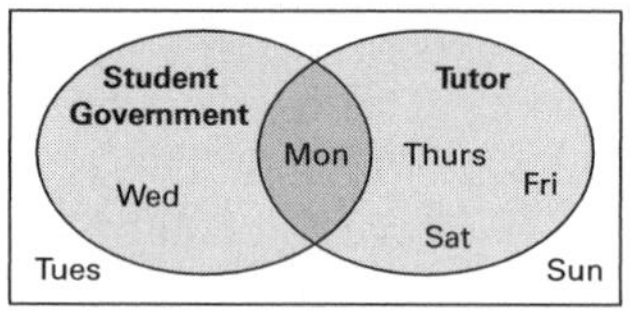

c. $\frac{5}{7}$

13.4 Problem Solving Workshop (pp. 868–869) **1.** $\frac{4}{15}$ **3.** $\frac{1}{16}$. *Sample answer:* The third friend can arrive any time in a 20 minute span, and I will be away from the house for 15 of those minutes. The probability is $\frac{1}{4}$ that I will be home when the third friend arrives. Since the three friends arrive independently of each other, you can multiply the probability that you are home when the other two friends arrive by $\frac{1}{4}$ to calculate the probability that you are home when all three friends arrive; $\frac{1}{4} \cdot \frac{1}{4} = \frac{1}{16}$. **5.** *Sample answer:* The times at which the raffles are announced are independent, so the two probabilities should be calculated separately and then multiplied; $\frac{10}{30} \cdot \frac{25}{30} = \frac{1}{3} \cdot \frac{5}{6} = \frac{5}{18}$.

13.5 Skill Practice (p. 873) **1.** systematic **3.** people who have eaten at the restaurant, self-selected **5.** passengers of the airline, random **7.** Not likely. *Sample answer:* The sample should represent the neighborhood. **9.** Not potentially biased. *Sample answer:* This question simply presents the two choices.

SA44

11. *Sample answer:* The new question presumes that the driving age should be changed, and does not present the option that it should remain the same; "What do you think about the current driving age?"

13.5 Problem Solving (p. 874) **13.** *Sample answer:* This question is phrased to prompt people into agreeing that the athletic field is more important than the science lab; "Which do you think the school needs more: a new athletic field or a new science lab?" **15.** No. *Sample answer:* Only some of the fans are able to attend games, and those who attend games may have different player preferences than those who do not attend games. **17. a.** *Sample answer:* Obtain a list of everyone at the school and select names randomly using a random number generator. **b.** *Sample answer:* "How many hours per night do you study?"; This question is unbiased because it does not prompt respondents to give any particular answer.

13.6 Skill Practice (p. 877) **1.** mode **3.** 3, 3, 1 **5.** 22, 21, no mode **7.** 5.223, 5.48, no mode **11.** 65, 21.2 **13.** 70, 12.56 **15.** 0.85, 0.23 **17.** *Sample answer:* The range only considers the two extreme values, while the mean absolute deviation is affected by all of the values.

13.6 Problem Solving (pp. 877–878) **19. a.** 19 **b.** 19.6 lb, 23.5 lb, 24 lb **c.** Median. *Sample answer:* The mode is the greatest data value and the mean is less than 8 of the 10 data values. **21. a.** The range for Team 2 is 56 and the range for Team 1 is 52, so the scores for Team 2 cover a slightly wider range. **b.** The mean absolute deviation for Team 1 is 15.75 and the mean absolute deviation for Team 2 is 22.5, so the scores for Team 2 are more dispersed.

Extension (pp. 879–880) **1.** 6.3, 2.5 **3.** 76,656.6; 276.9 **5.** 29.1 **7. a.** 5.6 **b.** *Sample answer:* Since 136 is much greater than the mean, the standard deviation will increase. **c.** 17.7. *Sample answer:* The standard deviation more than tripled, so the prediction was correct.

13.7 Skill Practice (pp. 883–884) **1.** frequency

3.

Stem	Leaves
1	7
2	0 0 4
3	0 1 3 5 8 8 9
4	2
5	5

Key: 1 | 7 = 17

5.

Stem	Leaves
10	5 9
11	1
12	1 4 7
13	3
14	2
15	6
16	
17	9
18	2

Key: 10 | 5 = 105

7. There is no key given for the stem-and-leaf plot; Key: 1 | 8 = 18.

11. **13.**

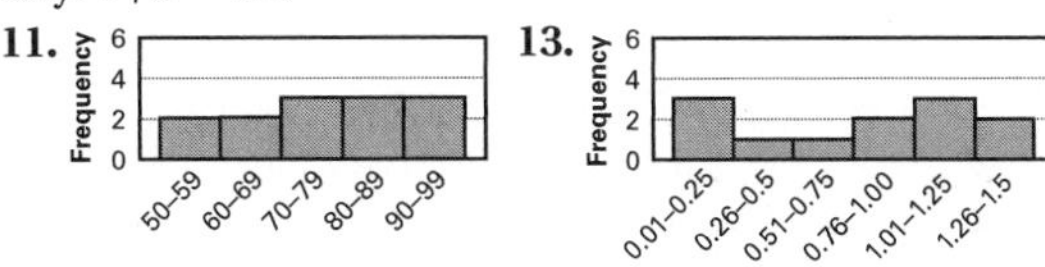

15. *Sample answer:* The given data range from 10 to 21, so a stem-and-leaf plot would place all the data into only two intervals, making it difficult to see the distribution of the data. The histogram could use more than two intervals.

13.7 Problem Solving (pp. 884–885)

17.

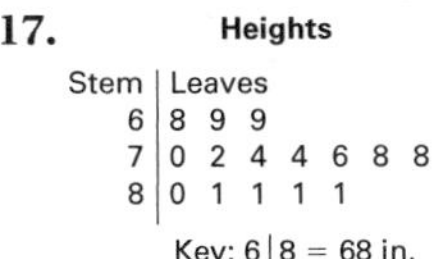

Heights

Stem	Leaves
6	8 9 9
7	0 2 4 4 6 8 8
8	0 1 1 1 1

Key: 6 | 8 = 68 in.

19. a.

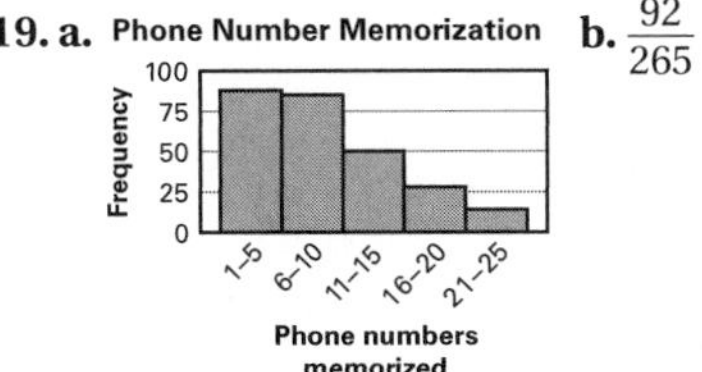

b. $\frac{92}{265}$

21. a.

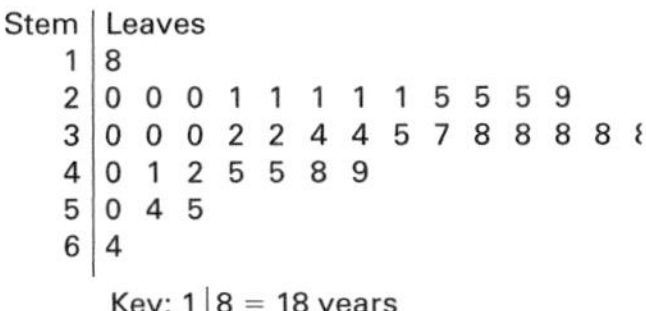

Ages of *Mayflower* Passengers

Stem	Leaves
1	8
2	0 0 0 1 1 1 1 1 5 5 5 9
3	0 0 0 2 2 4 4 5 7 8 8 8 8 8
4	0 1 2 5 5 8 9
5	0 4 5
6	4

Key: 1 | 8 = 18 years

b. median: 34 yr, range: 46 yr **c.** $\frac{1}{3}$. *Sample answer:* Since 13 of the 39 passengers or $\frac{1}{3}$ of them were ages 18–29, we can predict that another passenger about whom we have no information has a $\frac{1}{3}$ probability of being in that age group.

13.7 Graphing Calculator Activity (p. 886) **1.** *Sample answer:* The majority of the data are at the lower end of the scale, between 3000 and 12,000, with the highest frequency between 3000 and 6000.

13.8 Skill Practice (pp. 889–890) **1.** the difference of the upper quartile and the lower quartile

3.

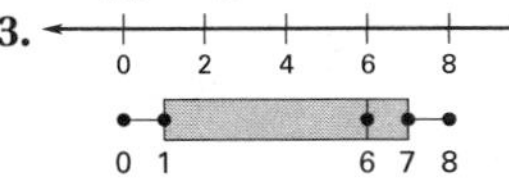

SELECTED ANSWERS

SA45

5. 20 30 40 50 60 70

20 24 37 45 64

7. *Sample answer:* The upper quartile is incorrect. The upper quartile should be the median of 8 and 10, or 9.

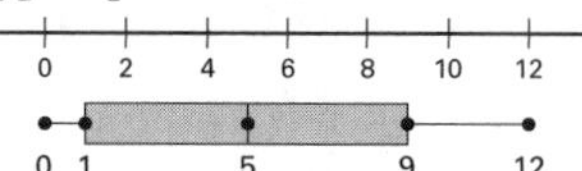

11. 5 10 15 20 25 There are no outliers.

8 10 14 18 22

13. There are no outliers.

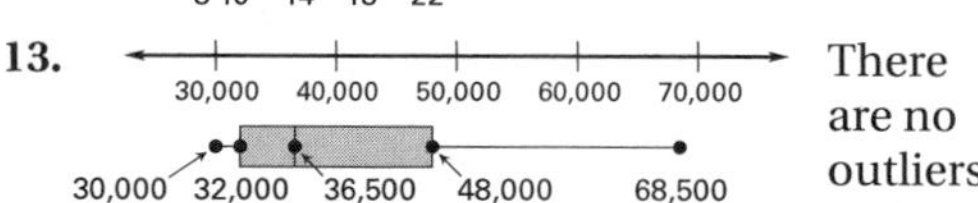

13.8 Problem Solving (pp. 890–892)

15.

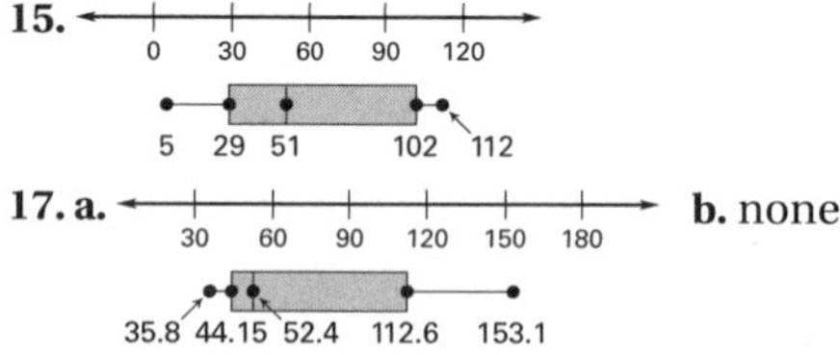

17. a. (see graph) **b.** none

19. a. *Sample answer:* The craters on Ganymede are generally smaller than the craters on Callisto. The lower extreme, lower quartile, median, upper quartile, and upper extreme values are all lower for Ganymede than for Callisto. **b.** *Sample answer:* Chesapeake Bay is larger than between 50% and 75% of the craters on both Callisto and Ganymede. **c.** *Sample answer:* Vredefort is larger than at least 75% of the craters on both Callisto and Ganymede.

Chapter Review (pp. 896–900) **1.** compound event **3.** *Sample answer:* Theoretical probability is based on knowing the likelihood of all possible outcomes of an event. Experimental probability is based on the results of an experiment. **5.** $\frac{2}{9}$ **7.** 30 **9.** 1,037,836,800 **11.** 7 **13.** 56 **15.** 126 ways **17.** $\frac{3}{8}$ **19.** $\frac{5}{8}$ **21.** $\frac{1}{120}$ **23. a.** about 5.045, 4.5, 1 **b.** Median. *Sample answer:* The mode is much lower than many of the values, and the mean is affected by the two extreme values (17 and 19) that are much greater than the rest of the data. So, the median best represents the data.

25.

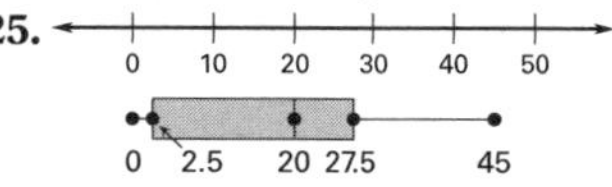

Cumulative Review (pp. 906–907) **1.** 44 **3.** ± 45 **5.** 2

7.

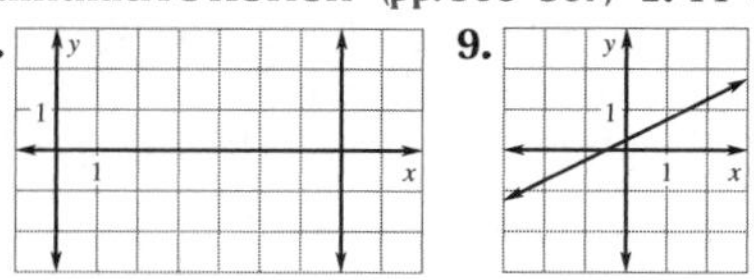

9.

11. $y = -8x + 3$

13. $4 \le x < 24$

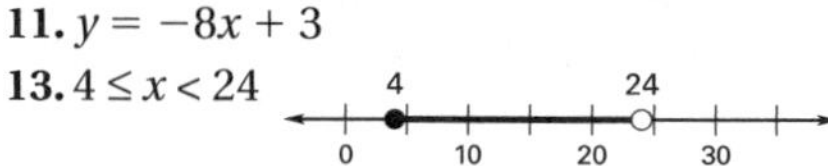

15. $\left(4, \frac{1}{4}\right)$ **17.** no solution **19.** $\frac{-81x^{12}}{4}$ **21.** $(a - 18)(a + 3)$ **23.** $(2f + g)^2$ **25.** $-7, 3$ **27.** $\frac{1}{2}, 4$ **29.** $2\sqrt{37}$ **31.** 15 **33.** $\frac{x + 4}{x + 3}$ **35.** -3 **37.** $\frac{9 - 3x}{x^2 - 3x}$ **39.** 336 **41.** 210 **43.** $\frac{1}{2}$ **45.** $\frac{3}{20}$ **47.** *Sample answer:* 120 min after the first runner starts **49.** 42.4 ft **51. a.** $45

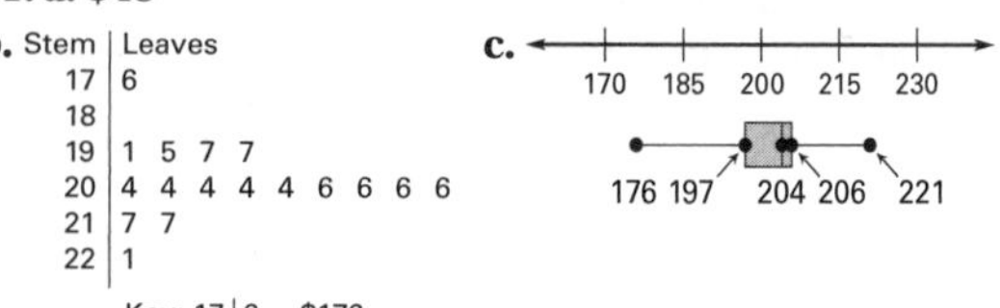

b.

Stem	Leaves
17	6
18	
19	1 5 7 7
20	4 4 4 4 4 6 6 6 6
21	7 7
22	1

Key: 17 | 6 = $176

c.

d. Yes. *Sample answer:* The interquartile range is 9, so any data value more than 13.5 less than the lower quartile of 197 or greater than the upper quartile of 206 can be considered outliers. 176 and 221 are both outliers.

Skills Review Handbook

Comparing and Ordering Decimals (p. 909) **1.** > **3.** > **5.** > **7.** < **9.** > **11.** 7.01, 7.03, 7.13, 7.3 **13.** 0.15, 0.3, 0.47, 0.9 **15.** 10.9, 11, 11.9, 12.6 **17.** 0.3, 1.33, 3.1, 3.3

Factors and Multiples (pp. 910–911) **1.** $2^2 \cdot 7$ **3.** prime **5.** 3^4 **7.** $2^2 \cdot 3 \cdot 5$ **9.** $2^2 \cdot 3^2 \cdot 5$ **11.** $3 \cdot 17$ **13.** 4 **15.** 6 **17.** 9 **19.** 4 **21.** 8 **23.** 4 **25.** 18 **27.** 45 **29.** 130 **31.** 90 **33.** 14 **35.** 49

Finding Equivalent Fractions and Simplifying Fractions (p. 912) **1–5.** Sample answers are given. **1.** $\frac{3}{4}$ and $\frac{18}{24}$ **3.** $\frac{2}{4}$ and $\frac{3}{6}$ **5.** $\frac{5}{7}$ and $\frac{20}{28}$ **7.** $\frac{1}{4}$ **9.** $\frac{1}{8}$ **11.** $\frac{1}{4}$ **13.** $\frac{7}{20}$ **15.** $\frac{4}{5}$ **17.** $\frac{3}{7}$ **19.** $\frac{4}{13}$

Mixed Numbers and Improper Fractions (p. 913) **1.** $\frac{5}{3}$ **3.** $\frac{103}{10}$ **5.** $\frac{9}{2}$ **7.** $\frac{23}{12}$ **9.** $\frac{53}{8}$ **11.** $\frac{65}{8}$ **13.** $\frac{65}{9}$ **15.** $\frac{38}{3}$ **17.** $2\frac{2}{5}$ **19.** $6\frac{1}{4}$ **21.** $1\frac{3}{4}$ **23.** $2\frac{9}{10}$ **25.** $10\frac{4}{5}$ **27.** $4\frac{2}{5}$ **29.** $4\frac{7}{9}$

Adding and Subtracting Fractions (p. 914) **1.** $\frac{1}{4}$ **3.** $\frac{1}{6}$ **5.** 1 **7.** $\frac{1}{2}$ **9.** $1\frac{1}{5}$ **11.** $\frac{3}{16}$ **13.** $\frac{25}{48}$ **15.** $1\frac{17}{24}$ **17.** $\frac{11}{20}$ **19.** $\frac{4}{5}$ **21.** $6\frac{3}{4}$ **23.** 5 **25.** $1\frac{1}{16}$

Multiplying and Dividing Fractions (p. 915) **1.** $\frac{1}{2}$ **3.** $\frac{1}{2}$ **5.** $1\frac{1}{8}$ **7.** $\frac{3}{64}$ **9.** $\frac{1}{8}$ **11.** $1\frac{1}{2}$ **13.** $\frac{1}{2}$ **15.** $\frac{2}{7}$ **17.** $\frac{1}{50}$ **19.** $\frac{3}{5}$ **21.** $3\frac{3}{32}$ **23.** $4\frac{3}{8}$ **25.** $1\frac{1}{3}$

Fractions, Decimals, and Percents (pp. 916–917) **1.** 0.7, $\frac{7}{10}$ **3.** 0.03, $\frac{3}{100}$ **5.** 0.35, $\frac{7}{20}$ **7.** 1.1, $1\frac{1}{10}$ **9.** 0.003, $\frac{3}{1000}$ **11.** $\frac{7}{25}$, 28% **13.** $\frac{1}{20}$, 5% **15.** $\frac{13}{25}$, 52% **17.** $\frac{1}{40}$, 2.5% **19.** $\frac{3}{2}$, 150% **21.** 0.188, 18.8% **23.** 0.61, 61% **25.** 0.19, 19% **27.** 0.36, 36% **29.** 0.571, 57.1%

Mean, Median, and Mode (p. 918) **1.** 92.4; 93; 94 **3.** 41 yr; 41 yr; 52 yr **5.** \$7; \$7; \$6.75 **7.** 2.25; 2; 2

Classifying Triangles and Quadrilaterals (pp. 919–920) **1.** isosceles right triangle **3.** pentagon **5.** hexagon **7.** parallelogram, rhombus **9.** quadrilateral, parallelogram

The Coordinate Plane (p. 921) **1.** (5, 4) **3.** (10, 8) **5.** (9, 2) **7.** (2, 6) **9.** (10, 0) **11.** (0, 5)

13–23.

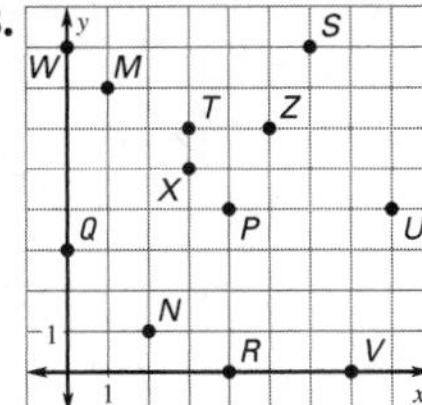

Transformations (pp. 922–923)

1.

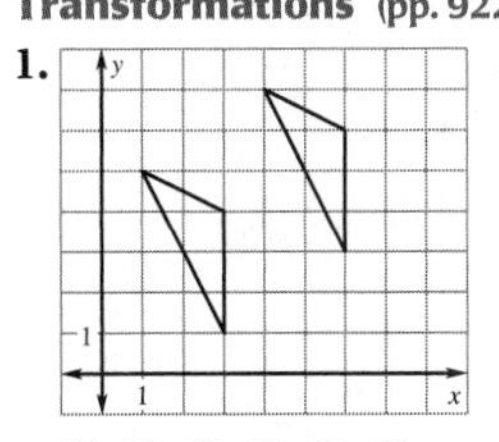

(4, 7), (6, 6), (6, 3)

3.

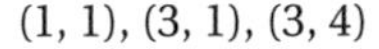

(1, 1), (3, 1), (3, 4)

5.

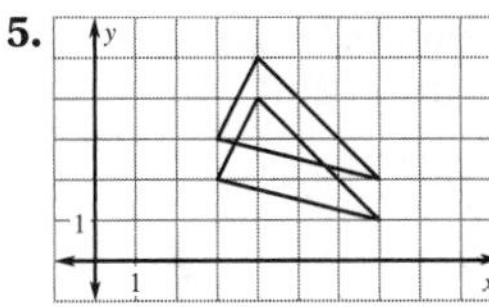

(4, 4), (7, 1), (3, 2)

7. (2, 0), (5, 0), (5, 2), (2, 2)

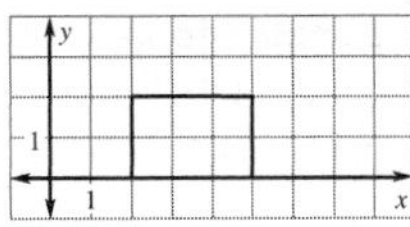

9.

(2, 4), (4, 8), (10, 6)

11.

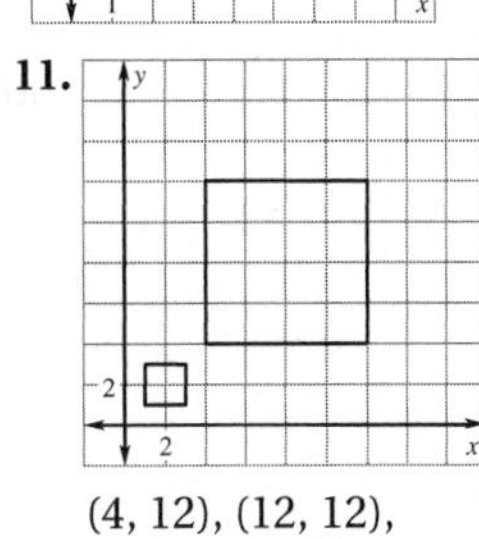

(4, 12), (12, 12), (12, 4), (4, 4)

13.

(0, 3), (6, 6), (9, 0)

Perimeter and Area (pp. 924–925) **1.** 36 ft **3.** 20 ft **5.** 66 yd^2 **7.** 110 $in.^2$ **9.** 21 ft^2 **11.** 70 yd^2

Circumference and Area of a Circle (p. 926) **1.** 12π in. or 37.7 in., 36π $in.^2$ or 113.0 $in.^2$ **3.** 16π in. or 50.2 in., 64π $in.^2$ or 201.0 $in.^2$ **5.** 4π ft or 12.6 ft, 4π ft^2 or 12.6 ft^2 **7.** 18π m or 56.5 m, 81π m^2 or 254.3 m^2

Surface Area and Volume (pp. 927–928) **1.** 320 cm^2, 336 cm^3 **3.** 900π m^2 or 2826 m^2, 4500π m^3 or 14,130 m^3 **5.** 200π $in.^2$ or 628 $in.^2$, 320π $in.^3$ or 1004.8 $in.^3$ **7.** 96 $in.^2$, 48 $in.^3$ **9.** 1888π $in.^2$ or 5928.3 $in.^2$, $11{,}008\pi$ $in.^3$ or 34,565.1 $in.^3$ **11.** 96π m^2 or 301.4 m^2, 96π m^3 or 301.4 m^3

Converting Units of Measurement (p. 929) **1.** 5 **3.** 4 **5.** 6 **7.** 14 **9.** 300 **11.** 70,000 **13.** 3000 **15.** 15 **17.** 2.5 **19.** 1,000,000 **21.** 28,800

Venn Diagrams and Logical Reasoning (p. 930)

1.

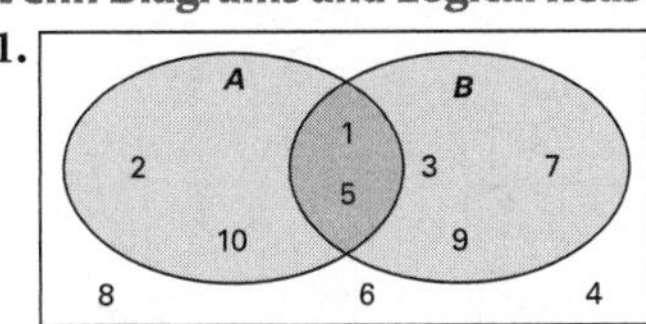

3. a. False; there are whole numbers less than 10 that are odd but are not factors of 10, such as 3, 7, and 9. **b.** False; there is a whole number less than 10 that is a factor of 10 but is not odd, 2.

SELECTED ANSWERS

Counting Methods (pp. 931–932) **1.** 6 ways **3.** 17,576 3-letter monograms **5.** 1,679,616 computer passwords **7.** 72 dinners

Bar Graphs (p. 933) **1.** bronze **3.** 103 medals **5.** 25 medals **7.** Switzerland **9.** United States **11.** 96 medals

Line Graphs (p. 934) **1.** about 24 lb **3.** between ages 4 and 5 **5.** about 15 lb **7.** about 2 years old **9.** between ages 3 and 4 **11.** between ages 1 and 2 **13.** about 4 yr

Circle Graphs (p. 935) **1.** 9% **3.** 24.5% **5.** 37% **7.** woodwinds **9.** brass

Problem Solving Strategies (pp. 936–937) **1.** Pam owes \$4 that she can pay to Bonnie who is owed a total of \$5. Holly should pay both Barb and Bonnie \$1. **3.** 25 years old **5.** 10 ways **7.** 1:45 P.M. **9.** 3 soccer games per week **11.** Quinn

SELECTED ANSWERS

Extra Practice

Chapter 1 (p. 938) **1.** 16 **3.** 4.4 **5.** 2.4 **7.** $\frac{8}{27}$ **9.** 26 **11.** 28 **13.** 10 **15.** 111 **17.** $\frac{3}{4}m$ **19.** $y - 3$ **21.** $45 - m$ **23.** $12 \cdot (r - 4) = 72$ **25.** 38 **27.** 16 **29.** *Sample answer:* You know the temperature in Quito in degrees Celsius and the temperature in Miami in degrees Fahrenheit. You need to find out which one is greater. **31.** domain: 3, 4, 5, 6; range: 9, 11, 13, 15

33.

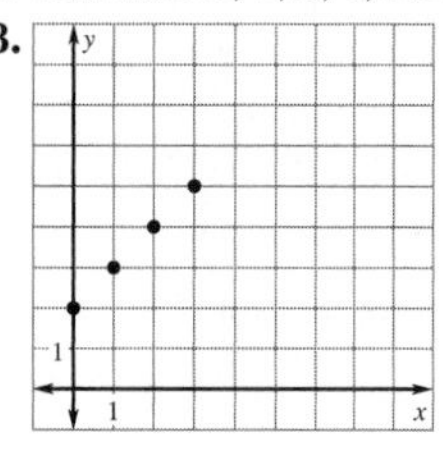

35.

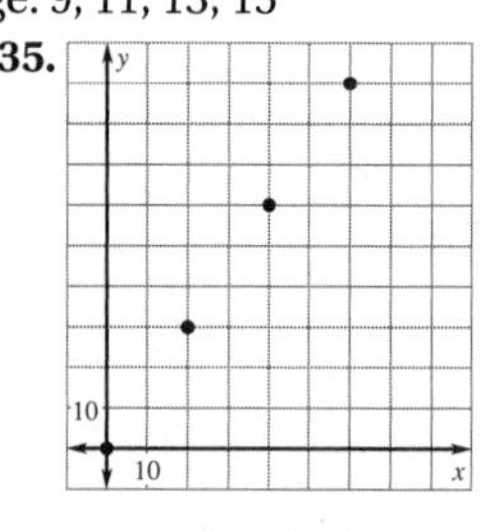

Chapter 2 (p. 939)

1. 0 **3.** −3

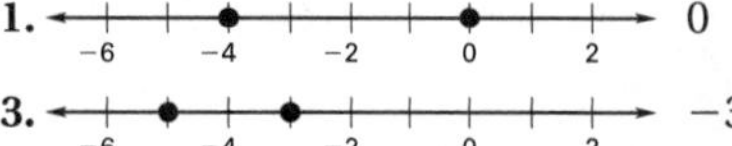

5. Each number is a rational number; $-\frac{1}{5}, -\frac{1}{8}, -\frac{1}{10}$, 0.25. **7.** 3 and 0 are whole numbers, −4 and −5 are integers; −5, −4, 0, 3. **9.** −61 **11.** 0 **13.** −19.7 **15.** $-4\frac{13}{30}$ **17.** 66 **19.** $\frac{3}{10}$ **21.** $\frac{5}{12}$ **23.** −7.2 **25.** 5.5 **27.** −12.5 **29.** −40 **31.** 2.2 **33.** Associative property of multiplication **35.** Property of zero **37.** Property of −1 **39.** $30 - 5y$ **41.** $-3k + 42$ **43.** $14s + 7$ **45.** $5w + 25$ **47.** 23 **49.** 64 **51.** $-\frac{5}{6}$ **53.** $\frac{25}{36}$ **55.** ±20 **57.** ±12 **59.** −9 **61.** 16

Chapter 3 (p. 940) **1.** 16 **3.** −12 **5.** 9 **7.** 52 **9.** 6 **11.** 8 **13.** −35 **15.** 3 **17.** −6 **19.** −1 **21.** 2 **23.** 3 **25.** $-\frac{1}{2}$ **27.** 56 **29.** 16 **31.** $\frac{5}{7} = \frac{15}{x}$; 21 **33.** $\frac{g}{9} = \frac{16}{12}$; 12 **35.** 14 **37.** 8 **39.** 4 **41.** −2 **43.** 12.5% **45.** 35 **47.** 45 **49.** 86 **51.** $x = \frac{c + b}{a}$; 5 **53.** $y = -5x + 10$ **55.** $y = -4x + 2$

Chapter 4 (p. 941)

1.

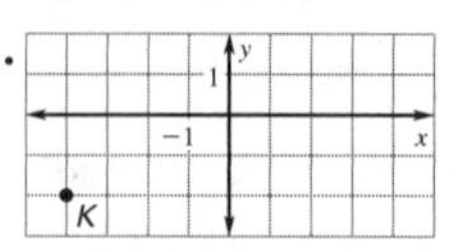

Quadrant III

3.

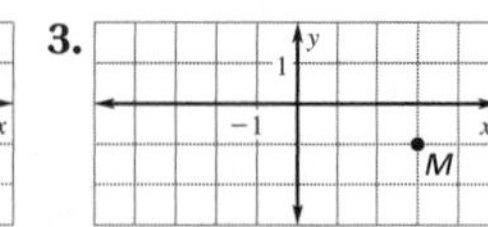

Quadrant IV

5. on the y-axis

7.

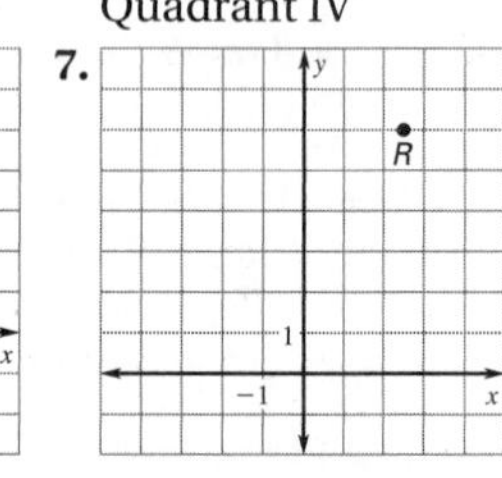

Quadrant I

9. range: −2, 0, 2, 4, 6

11.

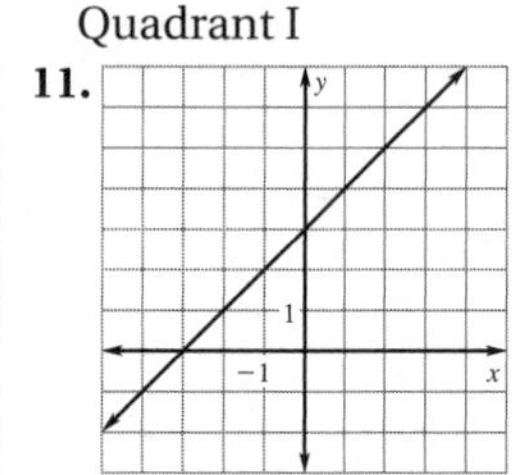

13.

15.

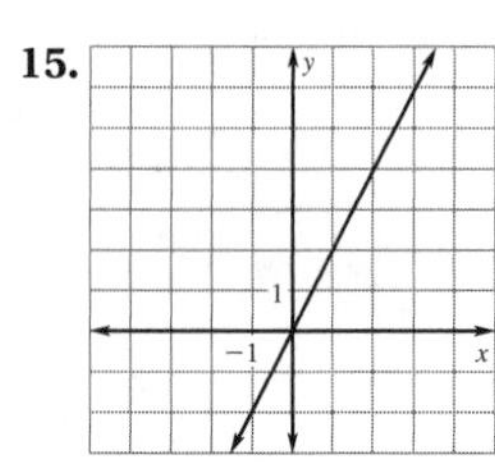

17.

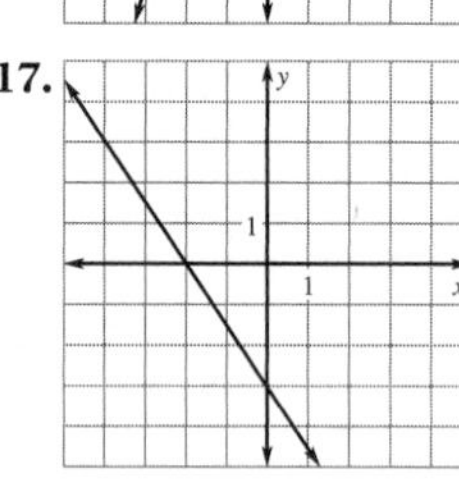

19. x-intercept: 6, y-intercept: −12 **21.** x-intercept: −1, y-intercept: $\frac{8}{3}$

SA48

23.

25. 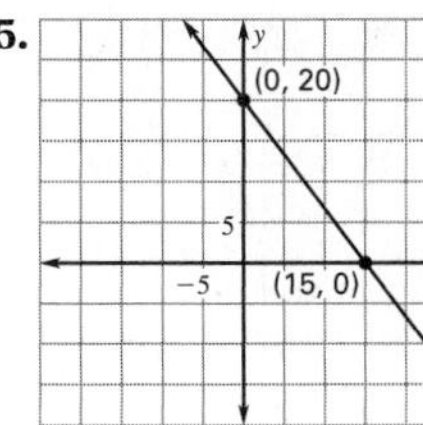

27. 3 **29.** $-\frac{7}{3}$ **31.** no slope **33.** slope: 7, y-intercept: 8 **35.** slope: -4, y-intercept: 3 **37.** $y = -2x + 8$; slope: -2, y-intercept: 8 **39.** $y = -\frac{5}{2}x + 5$; slope: $-\frac{5}{2}$, y-intercept: 5

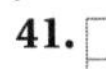

41. 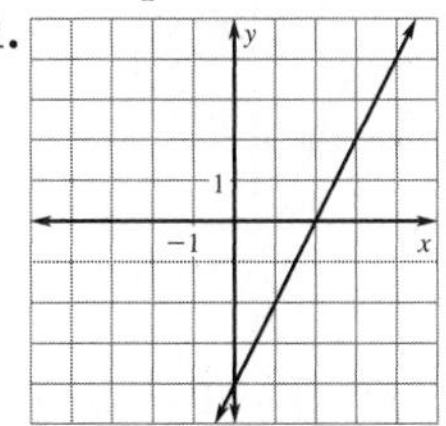

43. 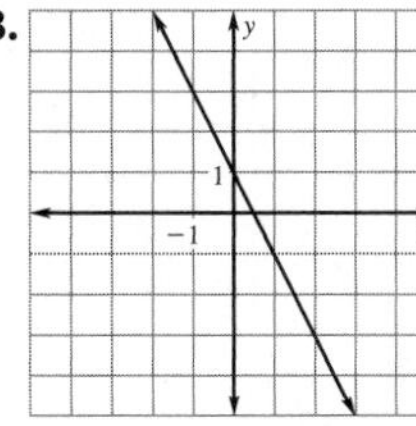

45. 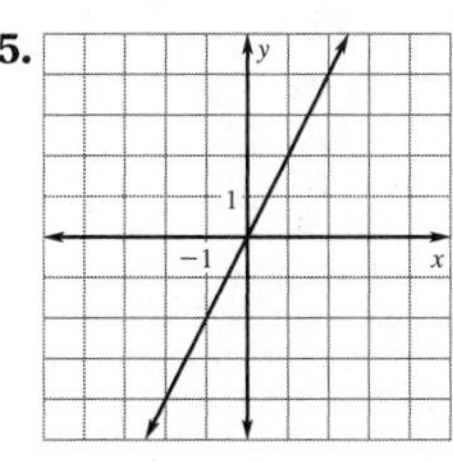

47. 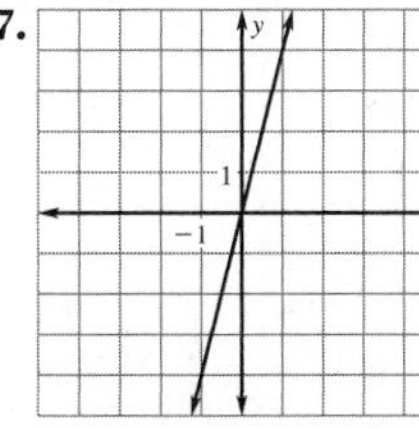

49. 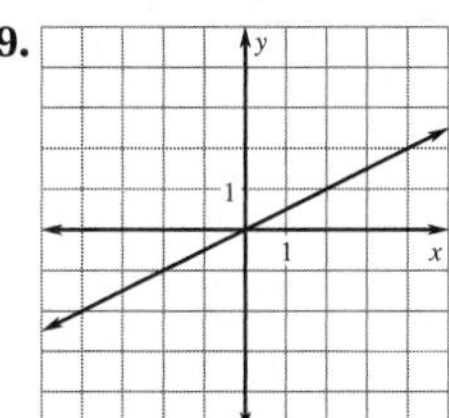

51. 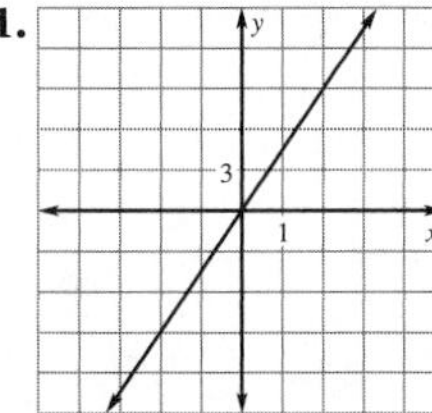

53. 2 **55.** -4

57. 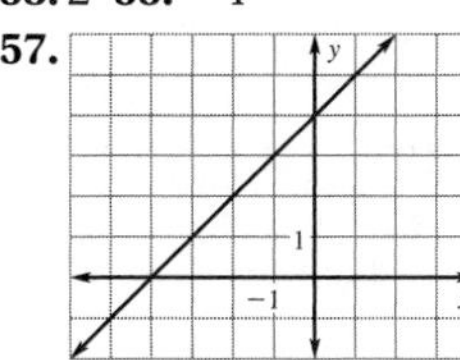

The graph is a vertical translation 4 units up of $f(x) = x$.

59. 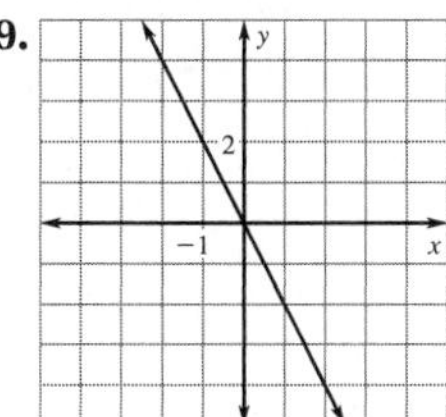

The graph is a vertical stretch by a factor of 2 with a reflection in the x-axis of $f(x) = x$.

Chapter 5 (p. 942)

1. $y = 3x + 6$ **3.** $y = 5x - 1$ **5.** $y = \frac{1}{2}x - 5$ **7.** $y = 2x + 2$ **9.** $y = \frac{2}{3}x + 7$ **11.** $y = -5x + 3$

13. 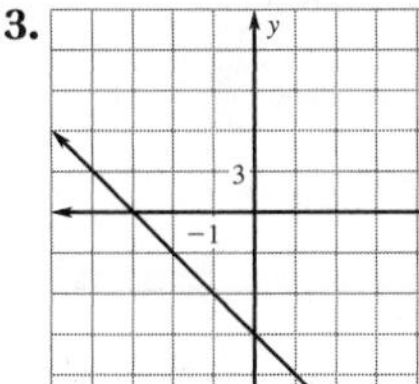

15. 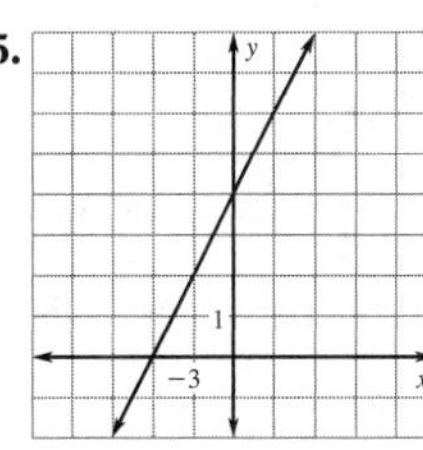

17. *Sample answer:* $y - 9 = \frac{1}{2}(x - 3)$ **19.** $4x + y = 15$ **21.** $2x + y = 0$ **23.** $y = -5x - 22$ **25.** $y = -\frac{1}{3}x - 6$ **27.** $y = \frac{3}{2}x - \frac{33}{2}$

29. 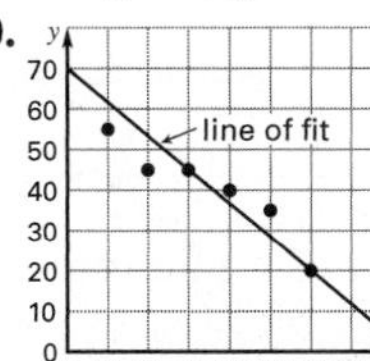

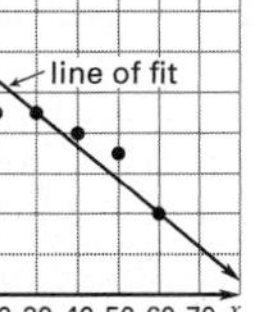

Sample answer: $y = -0.6x + 61$

31. 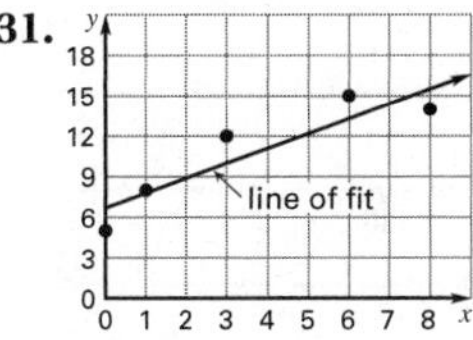

$y = 1.1x + 6.7$; 14.4

Chapter 6 (p. 943)

1. $y > 5$

3. $x \le 7$

5. $n \le 2\frac{1}{2}$

7. $z < -4\frac{7}{8}$

9. $t \ge 1.5$

11. $y < -5.5$

13. $p \le 9$

15. $x \ge 6$

17. $m \le \frac{3}{2}$

19. $z \le 8$

SELECTED ANSWERS

SA49

21. $z \le \frac{2}{3}$

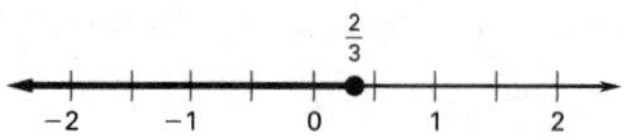

23. $y > -4.5$

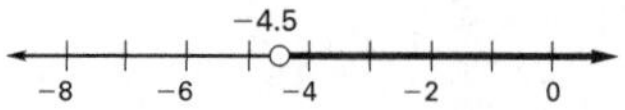

25. $x \ge 5$

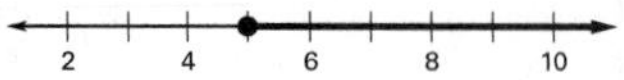

27. $t > -5$

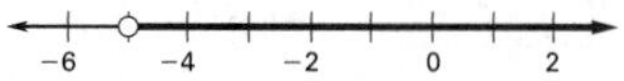

29. all real numbers

31. $y < 6$

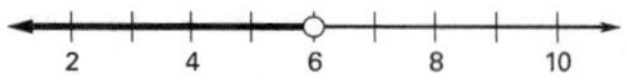

33. no solution

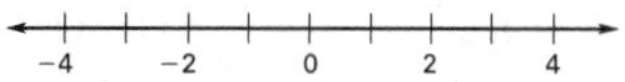

35. $-3 < x < 3$

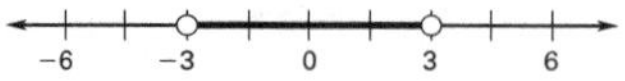

37. $2 < a \le 3.5$

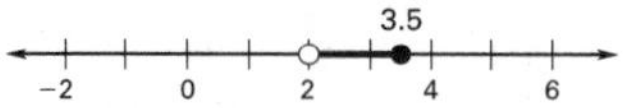

39. $r < -4$ or $r \ge -2$

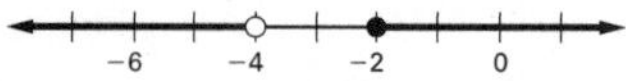

41. $t \ge 4$ or $t < -8$

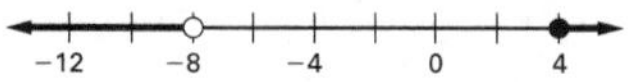

43. ± 8 **45.** $-11, -1$ **47.** $-14, 28$ **49.** no solution
51. $-1, 1$ **53.** no solution

55. $-3 \le x \le 3$

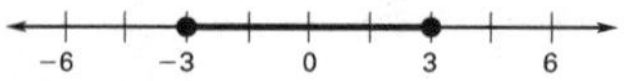

57. $s < -1.2$ or $s > 1.2$

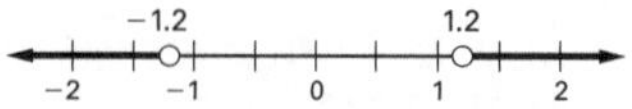

59. $x < -8$ or $x > 4$

61. $5 < m < 11$

63. $-1 \le p \le 7$

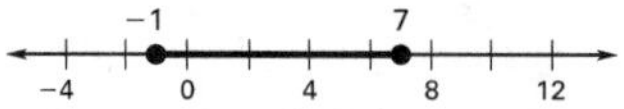

65. $-\frac{3}{5} \le a \le 1$

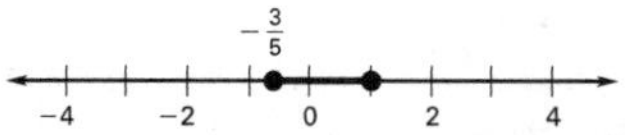

67. $y \ge x + 5$ **69.** $y > -4x + 3$

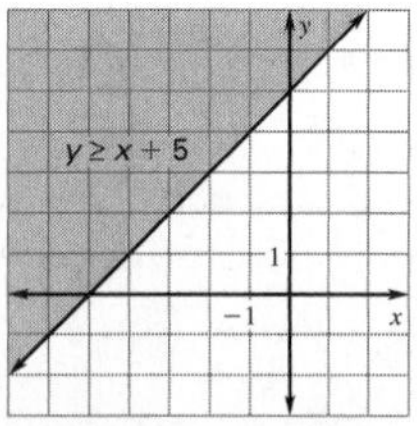

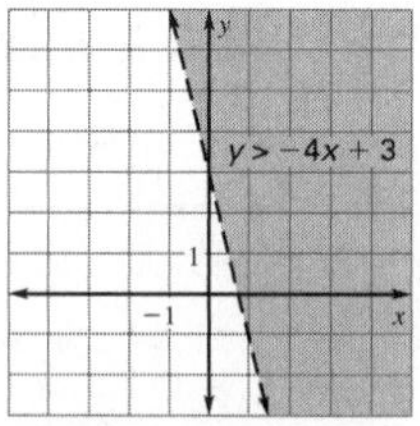

71. $y \ge \frac{1}{2}x - 4$ **73.** $y > 8$

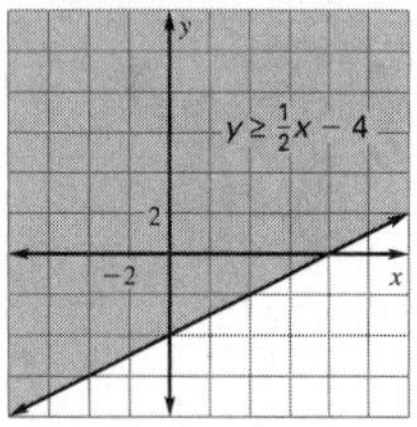

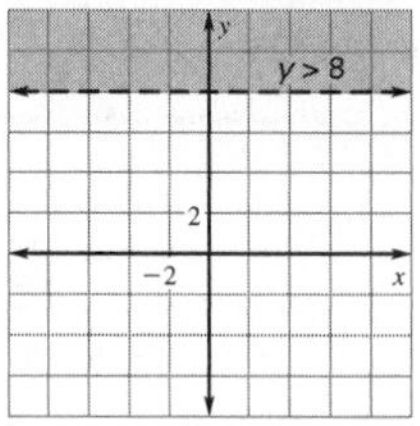

75.

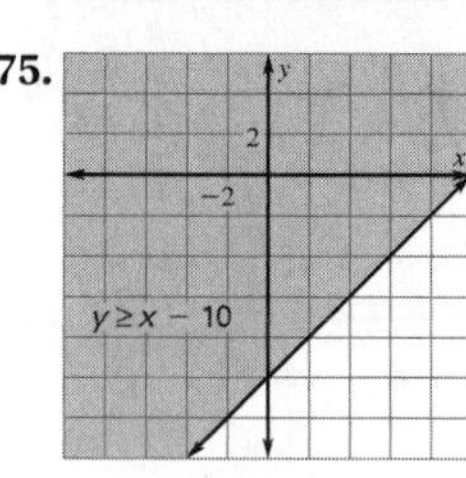

77.

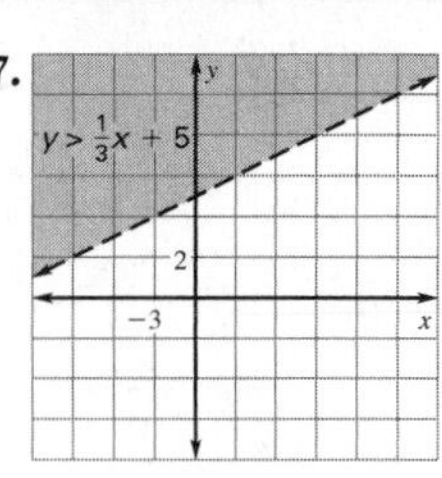

Chapter 7 (p. 944) **1.** (3, 2) **3.** (1, −3) **5.** (−3, −2) **7.** (−3, 0) **9.** (9, 7) **11.** (3, −7) **13.** (−4, 3) **15.** (−9, −2) **17.** (−3, −5) **19.** (−6, 3) **21.** (11, 9) **23.** $\left(10, -\frac{3}{2}\right)$

25.

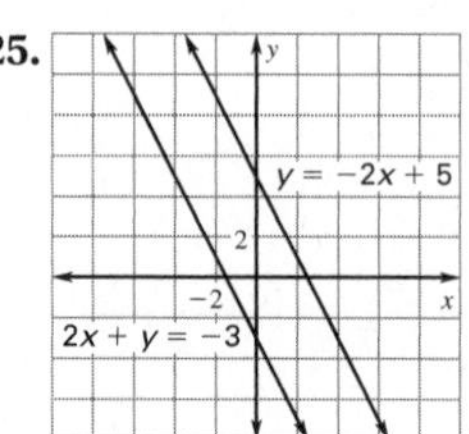

no solution

27.

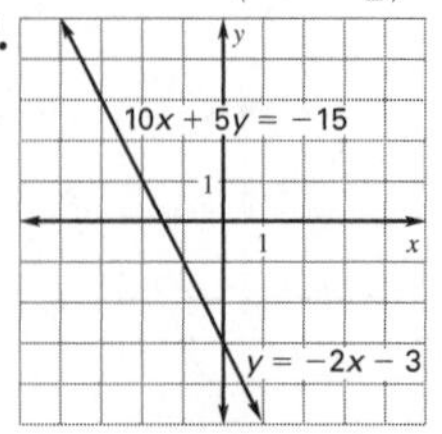

infinitely many solutions

29. (20, 48) **31.** no solution **33.** (−30, 0)

35.

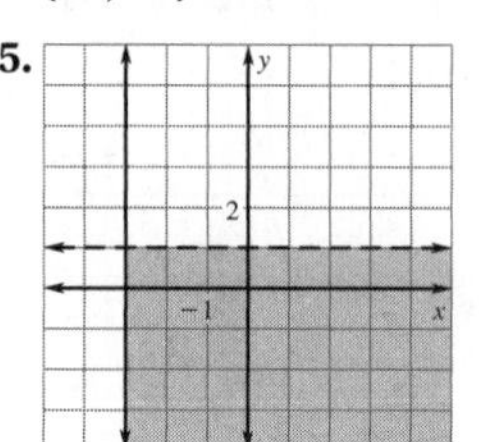

37.

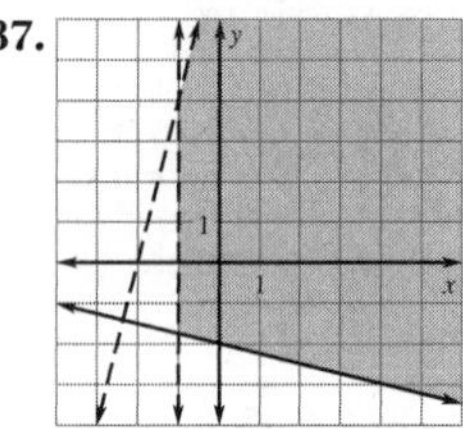

39.

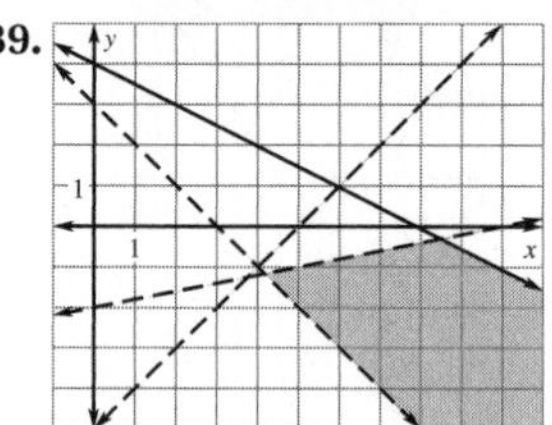

Chapter 8 (p. 945) **1.** 5^7 **3.** $(-2)^9$ **5.** $(-4)^6$ **7.** m^7 **9.** y^{15} **11.** $54d^8$ **13.** 8^5 **15.** $-\frac{2^5}{3^5}$ **17.** 7^5 **19.** $\frac{p^7}{q^7}$ **21.** $\frac{64y^9}{27}$ **23.** $\frac{25x^2y^6}{4}$ **25.** $\frac{1}{81}$ **27.** 1 **29.** 8 **31.** 32 **33.** $\frac{1}{y^{10}}$ **35.** $\frac{10c^5}{b^3}$ **37.** $\frac{y^5}{x^4}$ **39.** $-96z^5$ **41.** 8.7×10^{-1} **43.** 3.59×10^{-4}

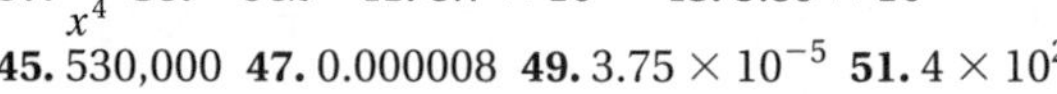

45. 530,000 **47.** 0.000008 **49.** 3.75×10^{-5} **51.** 4×10^2

SA50

53.

55. 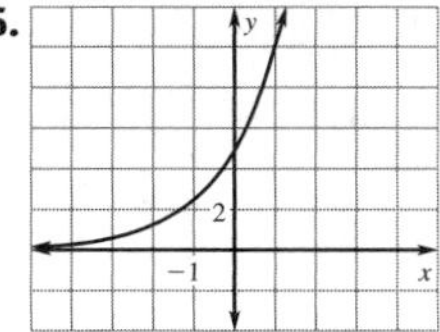

57. 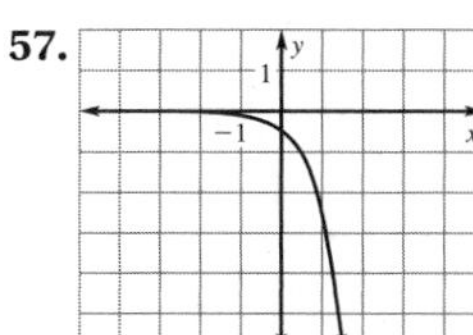

59. 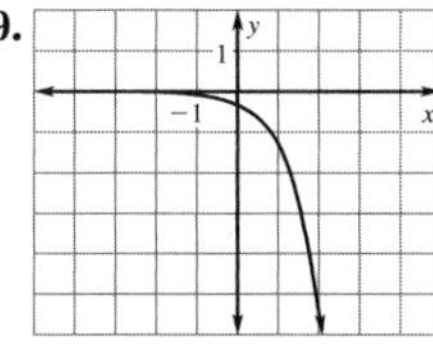

61. 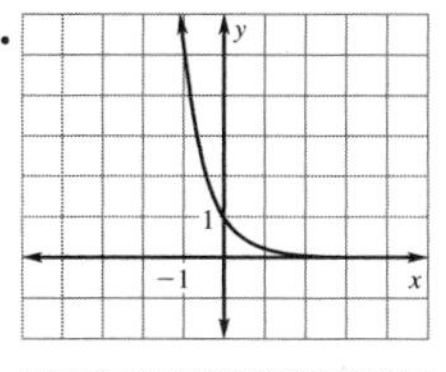

63. 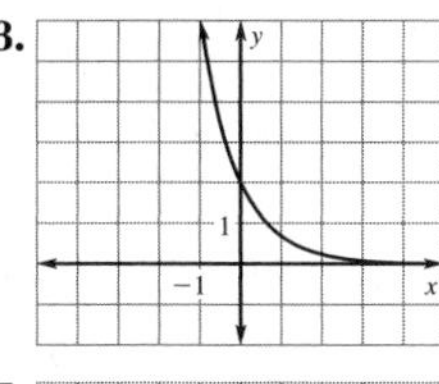

65. 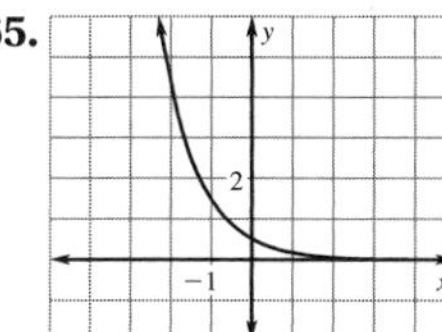

67. 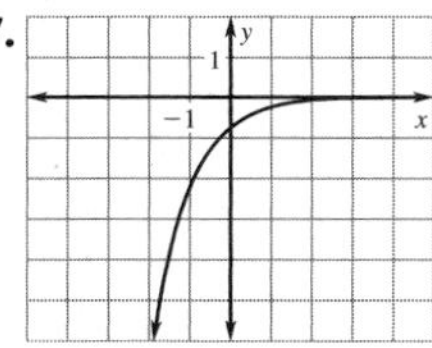

Chapter 9 (p. 946) **1.** $7x^2 - 2$ **3.** $7m^2 - 5m - 3$ **5.** $6b^3 - 3b^2 - 8b + 8$ **7.** $10x^7 - 15x^6 + 25x^5 - 5x^4$ **9.** $8x^2 + 16x + 6$ **11.** $3x^2 + 8x - 35$ **13.** $x^2 + 20x + 100$ **15.** $16x^2 - 4$ **17.** $36 - 9t^2$ **19.** $-8, 2$ **21.** $\frac{3}{5}, 2$ **23.** $-\frac{1}{4}, 0$ **25.** $(y + 3)(y + 4)$ **27.** $(x - 4)(x + 9)$ **29.** $(m - 25)(m - 4)$ **31.** 2, 5 **33.** 4, 9 **35.** 2, 5 **37.** $-(x - 3)(x - 2)$ **39.** $(2k - 1)(2k - 5)$ **41.** $-(3s + 1)(s + 2)$ **43.** $\frac{2}{3}, 4$ **45.** $-2, \frac{1}{2}$ **47.** $-1, \frac{1}{16}$ **49.** $(y + 6)(y - 6)$ **51.** $3(2y - 3)(2y + 3)$ **53.** $(2x - 3)^2$ **55.** $(g + 5)^2$ **57.** $(2w + 7)^2$ **59.** $(3z - 1)(z - 5)$ **61.** $(3y^2 + 2)(y + 5)$ **63.** $2m(7m - 3)(7m + 3)$ **65.** $(h + 3)(h - 3)(2h - 3)$

Chapter 10 (p. 947)

1. 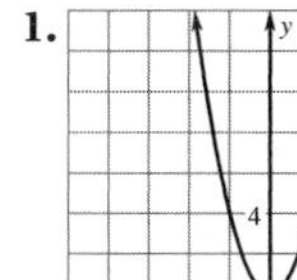

The graph is a vertical stretch by a factor of 4 of $y = x^2$.

3. 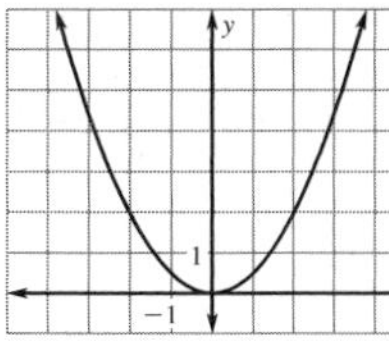

The graph is a vertical shrink by a factor of $\frac{1}{2}$ of $y = x^2$.

5. 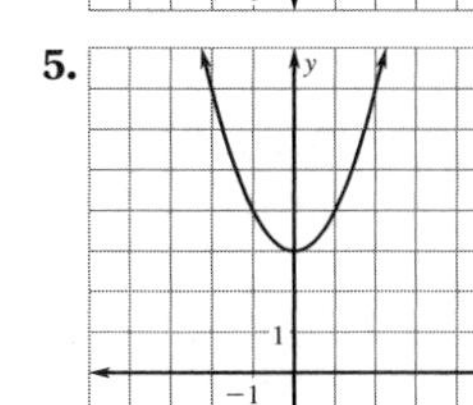

The graph is a vertical translation 3 units up of $y = x^2$.

7. 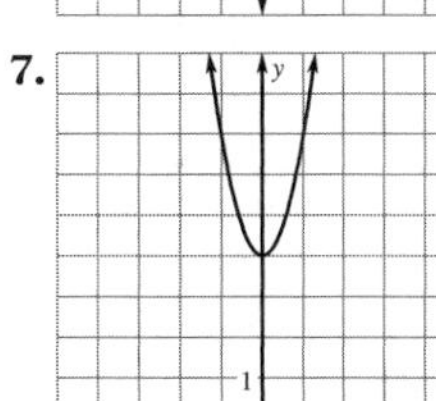

The graph is a vertical stretch by a factor of 3 with a vertical translation 4 units up of $y = x^2$.

9. 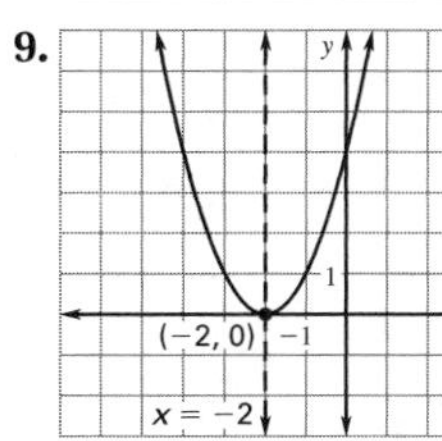

11.

13. 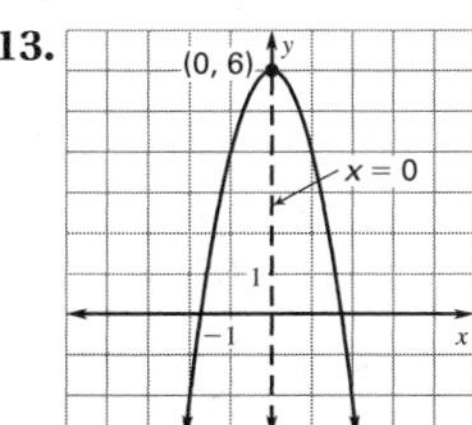

15. $-5, 2$ **17.** $-3, 6$ **19.** $-2, \frac{3}{2}$ **21.** ± 7 **23.** ± 0.75 **25.** ± 1.73 **27.** $-7, 3$ **29.** 1, 6 **31.** 0.55, 5.45 **33.** $-12, 6$ **35.** 0.5, 2 **37.** $-0.87, 1.54$

39. one solution **41.** no solution **43.** two solutions **45.** quadratic function; $y = 3x^2$ **47.** exponential function; $y = 0.5 \cdot 2^x$

Chapter 11 (p. 948)

1. 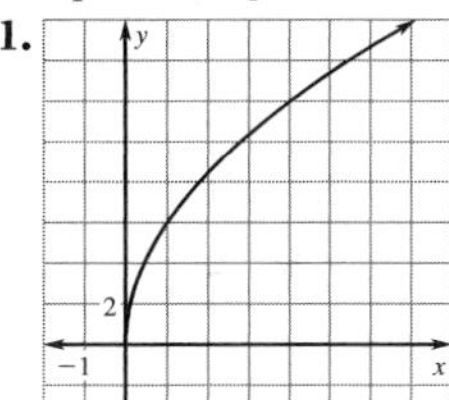

Domain: $x \geq 0$, range: $y \geq 0$; the graph is a vertical stretch by a factor of 6 of the graph of $y = \sqrt{x}$.

SELECTED ANSWERS

SA51

3. Domain: $x \geq 0$, range: $y \leq 0$; the graph is a vertical stretch by a factor of 8 with a reflection in the x-axis of the graph of $y = \sqrt{x}$.

5. 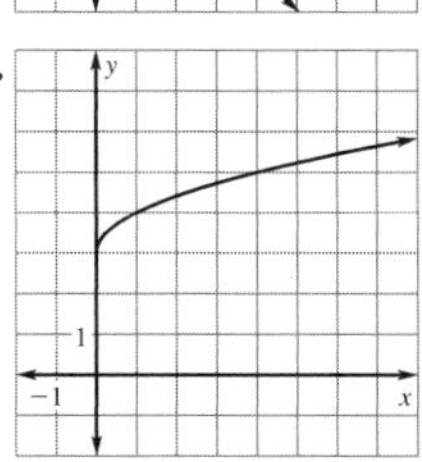 Domain: $x \geq 0$, range: $y \geq 3$; the graph is a vertical translation 3 units up of the graph of $y = \sqrt{x}$.

7. 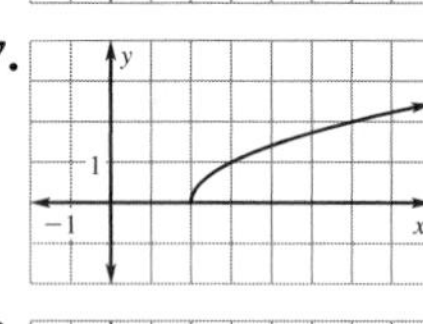 Domain: $x \geq 2$, range: $y \geq 0$; the graph is a horizontal translation 2 units right of the graph of $y = \sqrt{x}$.

9. 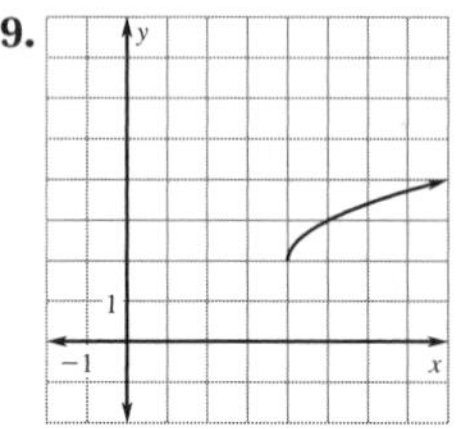 Domain: $x \geq 4$, range: $y \geq 2$; the graph is a vertical translation 2 units up and a horizontal translation 4 units right of the graph of $y = \sqrt{x}$.

11. $10\sqrt{3}$ **13.** 17 **15.** $5g\sqrt{11}$ **17.** $36x^3$ **19.** $\frac{\sqrt{6}}{6x}$ **21.** $\frac{\sqrt{14k}}{4k}$ **23.** $3\sqrt{3} + \sqrt{7}$ **25.** $9\sqrt{5}$ **27.** -108 **29.** $27 - 6\sqrt{13}$ **31.** 8 **33.** 20 **35.** -3 **37.** 1, 10 **39.** $\frac{1}{5}, \frac{3}{5}$ **41.** 1 **43.** $b = 24$ **45.** $b = \sqrt{21}$ **47.** $a = \sqrt{57}$ **49.** not a right triangle **51.** right triangle **53.** not a right triangle **55.** 13 **57.** $\sqrt{42.5}$ **59.** $\frac{\sqrt{5}}{2}$ **61.** $(-2, 1.5)$ **63.** $(1, 0)$ **65.** $\left(6\frac{1}{2}, -1\frac{1}{2}\right)$

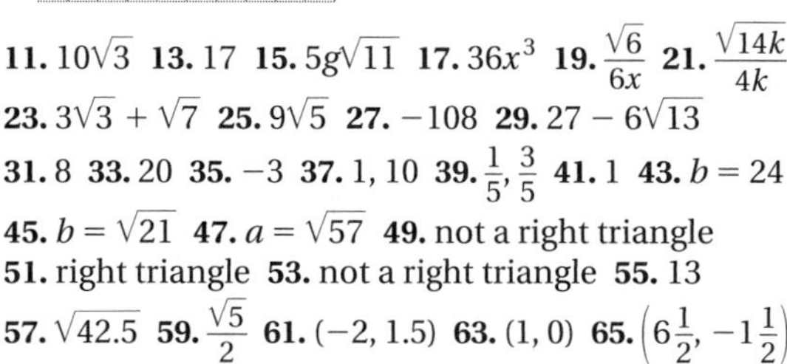

Chapter 12 (p. 949)

1. 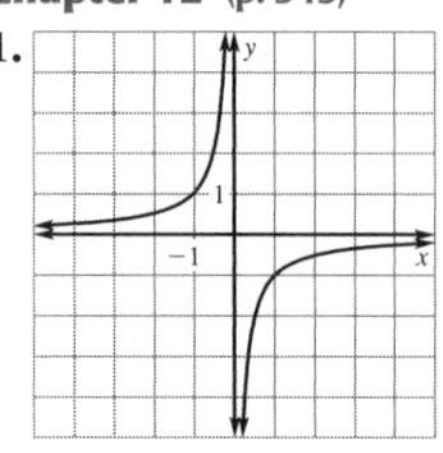 **3.**

5. $y = \frac{12}{x}$; 6 **7.** $y = \frac{60}{x}$; 30 **9.** $y = \frac{49}{x}$; 24.5

11. 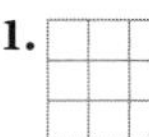 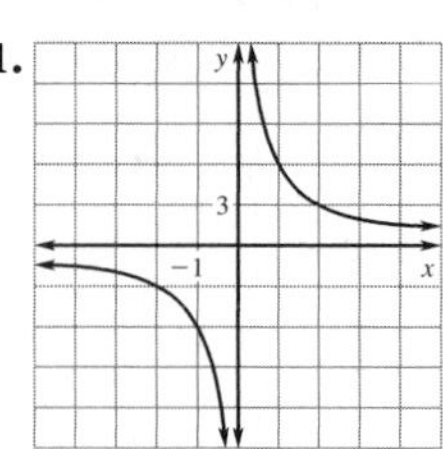 **13.**

15. 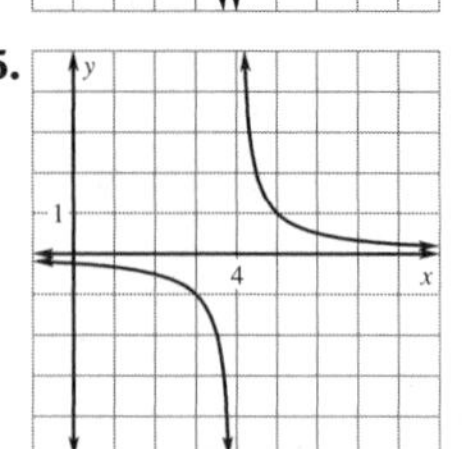 **17.**

19. $-5x^3 + 2x^2 - x$ **21.** $3v - 4 + \frac{20}{v + 2}$ **23.** $3m + 4 + \frac{10}{3m - 4}$ **25.** $\frac{11x^2}{6}$, excluded value is 0. **27.** $\frac{3}{4}$, excluded value is 5. **29.** $\frac{r - 5}{r - 2}$, excluded values are 2 and -3. **31.** $\frac{2m - 4}{3m^2 + 6m}$, excluded values are -6, -2, and 0. **33.** $\frac{5x}{2x - 6}$ **35.** $3r - 6$ **37.** $\frac{16t + 15}{10t^2}$ **39.** $\frac{4c + 3}{(c + 3)(c - 3)(2c + 3)}$ **41.** -4, 7 **43.** $-\frac{7}{3}$, 3 **45.** -3, $\frac{11}{4}$

Chapter 13 (p. 950) **1.** 6 possible outcomes; heads, yellow; heads, red; heads, blue; tails, yellow; tails, red; tails, blue **3.** 5 : 3 **5.** 60 ways **7.** 336 **9.** 120 **11.** 15 **13.** 210 **15.** overlapping; $\frac{1}{2}$ **17. a.** $\frac{1}{9}$ **b.** $\frac{1}{11}$ **19.** No. *Sample answer:* The systematic sample should produce an unbiased sample of parents or guardians of high school students. **21.** mean: 89, median: 88, mode: 88, range: 39, mean absolute deviation: 8.8

23. 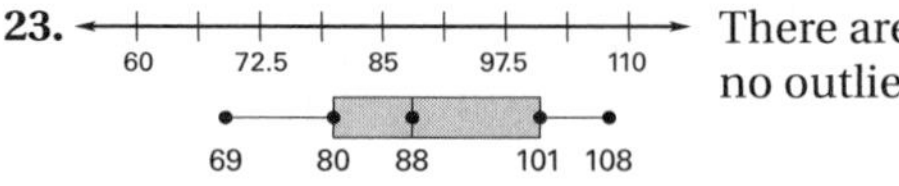

There are no outliers.

Teacher's Edition Index

Pupil's Edition in black
Teacher's Edition in blue

INDEX

D

E

INDEX

INDEX

N

INDEX

R

INDEX

S

T

INDEX

Additional Answers

Chapter 1

1.5 Skill Practice (p. 31) **5.** You know the temperature in Rome and the temperature in Dallas. You know the formula to convert Fahrenheit temperatures to Celsius temperatures. You need to find the higher temperature. **6.** The formula for perimeter is wrong; $P = 2\ell + 2w$; $P = 2(200) + 2(150) = 700$; $\$10(700) = \$7000$. **7.** The formula for perimeter should be used, not area; $P = 2\ell + 2w$; $P = 2(200) + 2(150) = 700$; $\$10(700) = \$7000$.

1.6 Problem Solving (pp. 39–40)

27. a.

2	3	4	5
A, B, C	D, E, F	G, H, I	J, K, L

6	7	8	9
M, N, O	P, Q, R, S	T, U, V	W, X, Y, Z

No; because there is more than one output for each input.

b.

A	B	C	D	E	F	G	H	I	J	K	L
2	2	2	3	3	3	4	4	4	5	5	5

M	N	O	P	Q	R	S	T	U	V	W	X	Y	Z
6	6	6	7	7	7	7	8	8	8	9	9	9	9

Yes; because there is only one output for each input.

1.7 Skill Practice (pp. 46–47)

3.
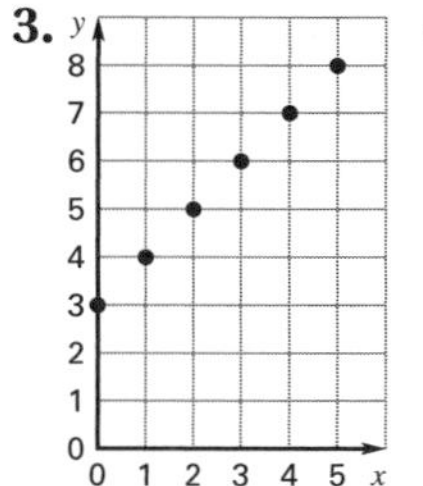

4.
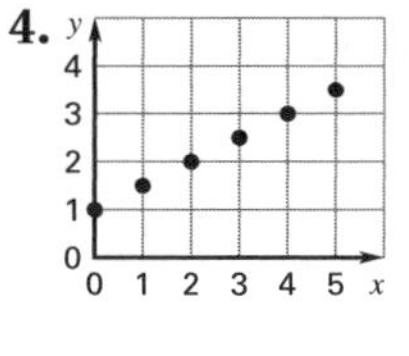

5.
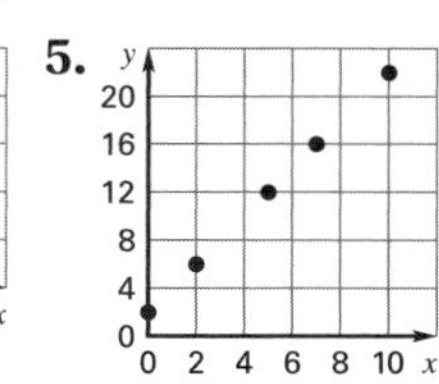

6.
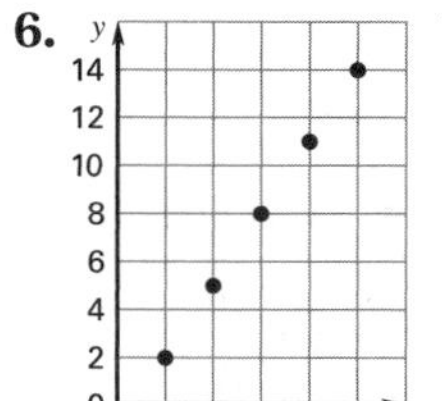

7.
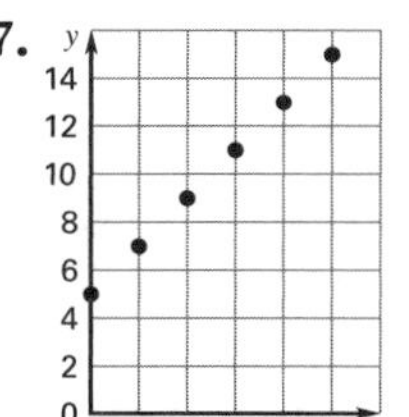

8.
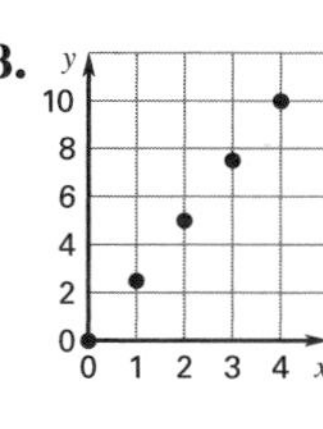

1.7 Problem Solving (pp. 47–48) **20. a.** *Sample answer:* Count the number of blocks between the men's and women's times. Each block represents 10 minutes.

Quiz for Lessons 1.6–1.7 (p. 48)

1.

Input	0	2	3	4	5
Output	12	8	6	4	2

4.
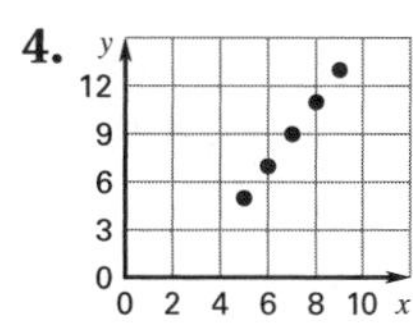

5.
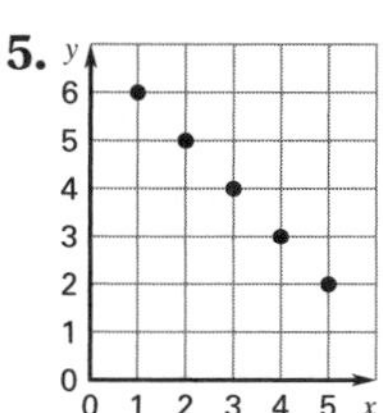

Chapter 2

2.1 Skill Practice (pp. 67–68) **52.** $a < 0$; $a > 0$; $a = 0$. *Sample answer:* When a number a is negative, its opposite will be positive, which is greater than a. When a number a is positive, its opposite will be negative, which is less than a. When a is 0, its opposite is 0, which is equal to a.

2.3 Spreadsheet Activity (p. 85)

Step 2.

	A	B	C
1	Grip	Length (in.)	Difference
2	1	4.878	−0.122
3	2	4.902	−0.098
4	3	5.115	0.115
5	4	5.13	0.13
6	5	4.877	−0.123
7	6	4.874	−0.126
8	7	4.799	−0.201
9	8	4.819	−0.181
10	9	4.879	−0.121
11	10	5.124	0.124

4.

	A	B	C
1	Grip	Length (in.)	Difference
2	1	4.871	−0.129
3	2	5.019	0.019
4	3	5.112	0.112
5	4	4.987	−0.013
6	5	5.067	0.067
7	6	4.899	−0.101
8	7	4.859	−0.141
9	8	5.132	0.132
10	9	5.126	0.126
11	10	5.093	0.093

2.4 Skill Practice (pp. 91–92) **28.** $16y$; $y(16)$, product of -2 and -8; $16y$, commutative property of multiplication **29.** $18x$; $18x$, same signs, product is positive. **30.** $-3q$; $\left[\frac{3}{5}(-5)\right]q$, associative property of multiplication; $-3(q)$, product of $\frac{3}{5}$ and -5 is -3; $-3q$, multiply. **31.** $-84z$; $12(-7z)$, product of -2 and -6 is 12; $[12 \cdot (-7)]z$, associative property of multiplication; $-84(z)$, product of 12 and -7 is -84; $-84z$, multiply. **32.** $42z$; $20(-2.1)(-z)$, product of -5 and -4 is 20; $-42(-z)$, product of 20 and -2.1 is -42; $42z$, multiply. **33.** $-40c$; $2(4)(-5c)$, product of $-\frac{1}{5}$ and -10 is 2; $8(-5c)$, product of 2 and 4 is 8; $[8 \cdot (-5)]c$, associative property of multiplication; $-40(c)$, product of 8 and -5 is -40; $-40c$, multiply. **34.** $5t^2$; $(t)(-t)(-5)$, commutative property of multiplication; $-t^2(-5)$, product of t and $-t$ is $-t^2$; $(-5)(-t^2)$, commutative property of multiplication; $5t^2$, multiply. **35.** $16.8r^2$; $[-6r \cdot (-2.8)]r$, associative property of multiplication; $[-6 \cdot (-2.8) \cdot r]r$, commutative property of multiplication; $(16.8r)r$, product of -6 and -2.8 is 16.8; $16.8(r \cdot r)$, associative property of multiplication; $16.8r^2$, multiply. **36.** $-\frac{3}{10}m^2$; $-\frac{3}{10}(-m)(-m)$, product of $\frac{1}{3}$ and $-\frac{9}{10}$ is $-\frac{3}{10}$; $-\frac{3}{10}m^2$, multiply.

2.5 Problem Solving Workshop (p. 102) **3.** \$287.50; Method 1: Write an equation for a, the total amount earned as a function of d, the number of hours spent making deliveries; $a = 9.50d + 8(35 - d)$ or $a = 1.5d + 280$. Substitute 5 for d, giving you $a =$ \$287.50; Method 2: Break the problem into parts. Find the amount earned working 5 hours making deliveries: \$9.50 per hour • 5 hours = \$47.50. Find the number of hours spent working at the register: 35 hours − 5 hours = 30 hours. Find the amount earned working at the register for 30 hours: \$8 per hour • 30 hours = \$240. Add the amount earned making deliveries to the amount earned working at the register: \$47.50 + \$240 = \$287.50.

2.7 Skill Practice (pp. 113–114) **24.** $\sqrt{49}$: real number, rational number, integer, whole number, 8: real number, rational number, integer, whole number, $-\sqrt{4}$: real number, rational number, integer, -3: real number, rational number, integer; $-3, -\sqrt{4}, \sqrt{49}, 8$ **25.** $-\sqrt{12}$: real number, irrational number, -3.7: real number, rational number, $\sqrt{9}$: real number, rational number, integer, whole number, 2.9: real number, rational number; $-3.7, -\sqrt{12}, 2.9, \sqrt{9}$ **26.** -11.5: real number, rational number, $-\sqrt{121}$: real number, rational number, integer, -10: real number, rational number, integer, $\frac{25}{2}$: real number, rational number, $\sqrt{144}$: real number, rational number, integer, whole number; $-11.5, -\sqrt{121}, -10, \sqrt{144}, \frac{25}{2}$

27. $\sqrt{8}$: real number, irrational number, $-\frac{2}{5}$: real number, rational number, -1: real number, rational number, integer, 0.6: real number, rational number, $\sqrt{6}$: real number, irrational number; $-1, -\frac{2}{5}, 0.6, \sqrt{6}, \sqrt{8}$

28. $-\frac{8}{3}$: real number, rational number, $-\sqrt{5}$: real number, irrational number, 2.6: real number, rational number, -1.5: real number, rational number, $\sqrt{5}$: real number, irrational number; $-\frac{8}{3}, -\sqrt{5}, -1.5, \sqrt{5}, 2.6$ **29.** -8.3: real number, rational number, $-\sqrt{80}$: real number, irrational number, $-\frac{17}{2}$: real number, rational number, -8.25: real number, rational number, $-\sqrt{100}$: real number, rational number, integer; $-\sqrt{100}, -\sqrt{80}, -\frac{17}{2}, -8.3, -8.25$

2.7 Problem Solving (pp. 115–116)

54. a.

Quotient of pyramids	Quotient of area of bases	Quotient of side length of bases
Khafre / Menafaure	3.9	2.0
Khufu / Menafaure	4.6	2.1
Khufu / Khafre	1.2	1.1

The quotient of the areas is the square of the quotient of the side lengths.

Chapter 3

3.2 Problem Solving (pp. 145–146)

43. b.

x (h)	Marissa	Ryan	Total
1	5	7	12
2	10	14	24
3	15	21	36
4	20	28	48
5	25	35	60

3.2 Problem Solving Workshop (p. 147)

1. 7 players; Method 1: Use the equation $600 + 25x = 775$ to get $x = 7$; Method 2: Make a table that lists the number of non-members and the amount the team would pay. The team has 7 members who are not club members.

Non-members	Total fee (dollars)
0	600
1	625
2	650
3	675
4	700
5	725
6	750
7	775

3. 4 chairs; Method 1: Use the equation $220 + 35x = 370$ to get $x \approx 4.3$; Method 2: Make a table that lists the number of chairs and the total cost of the table and chairs; because you cannot afford \$395 for 5 chairs, you can afford to buy 4 chairs.

Chairs	Total cost (dollars)
1	255
2	290
3	325
4	360
5	395

3.4 Problem Solving (pp. 158–159)

52. b.

Visits	Members' cost (dollars)	Non-members' cost (dollars)
5	380	80
10	400	160
15	420	240
20	440	320
25	460	400
30	480	480
35	500	560

3.4 Spreadsheet Activity (p. 160)

4. a–b.

	A	B	C	D
1	Possible solutions	Left side	Right side	Difference
2	0	38.5	0	38.5
3	1	33.7	6.2	27.5
4	2	28.9	12.4	16.5
5	3	24.1	18.6	5.5
6	4	19.3	24.8	−5.5
7	5	14.5	31	−16.5
8	6	9.7	37.2	−27.5
9	7	4.9	43.4	−38.5
10	8	0.1	49.6	−49.5
11	9	−4.7	55.8	−60.5
12	10	−9.5	62	−71.5

Chapter 4

4.1 Guided Practice (pp. 206–208)

3–6.

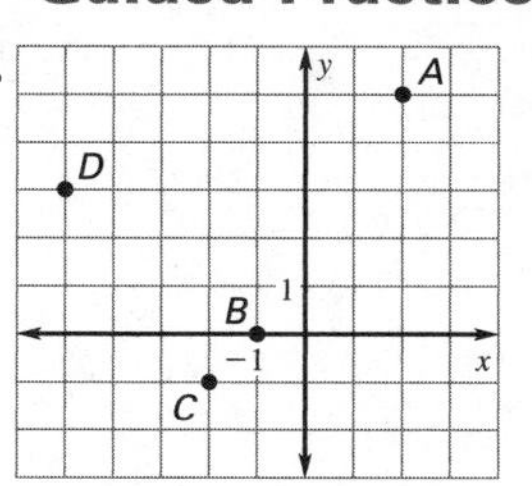

7.

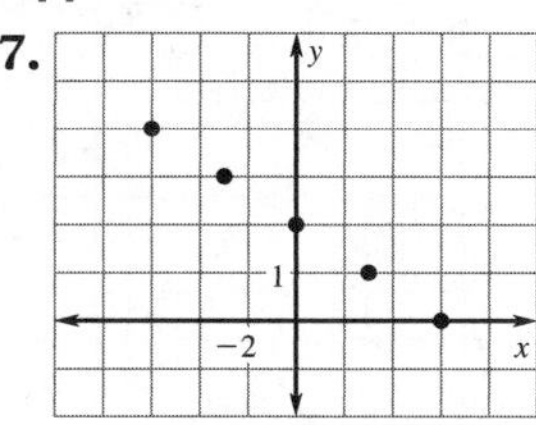

4.1 Skill Practice (pp. 209–210)

29. Quadrant IV; the x-coordinate is positive and the y-coordinate is negative so the point is in Quadrant IV. **30.** Quadrant IV; the x-coordinate is positive and the y-coordinate is negative so the point is in Quadrant IV. **31.** Quadrant II; the x-coordinate is negative and the y-coordinate is positive so the point is in Quadrant II. **32.** Quadrant III; the x-coordinate is negative and the y-coordinate is negative so the point is in Quadrant III.

4.2 Guided Practice (pp. 215–218)

2.

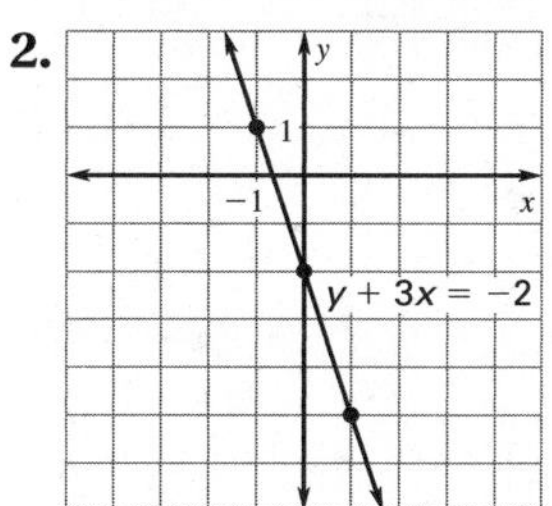

3.

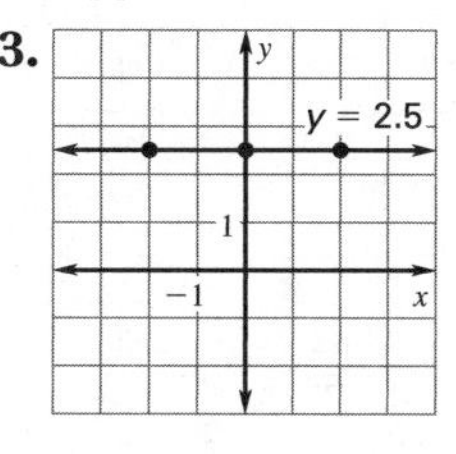

4.

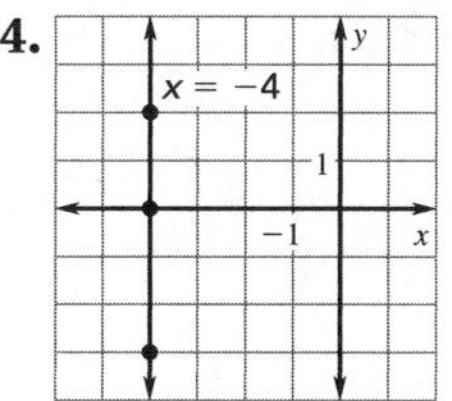

4.2 Skill Practice (pp. 219–220)

11.

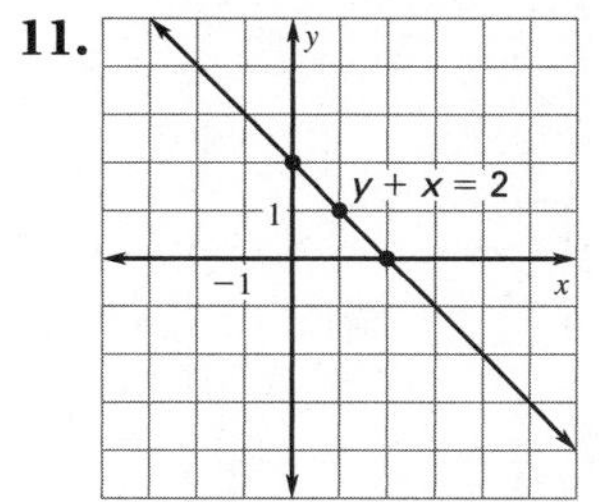

12.

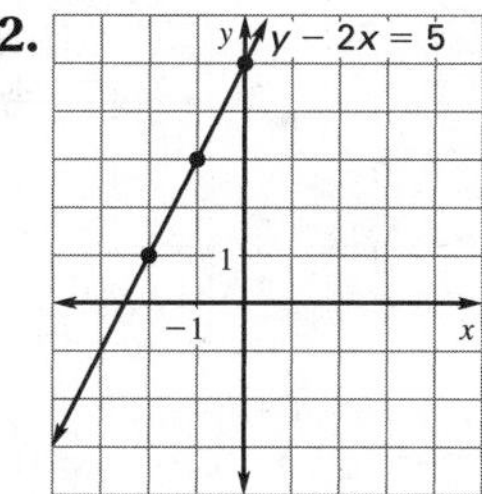

13.

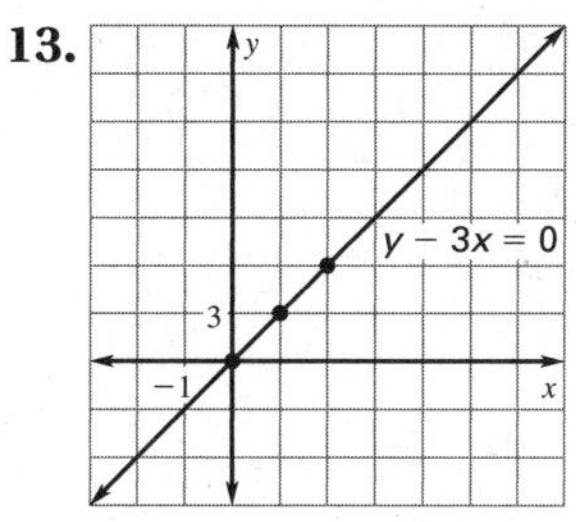

14.

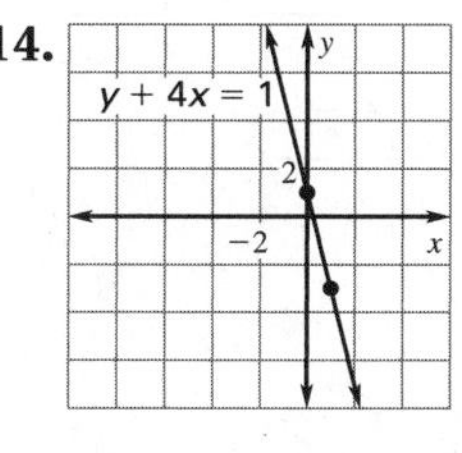

15.

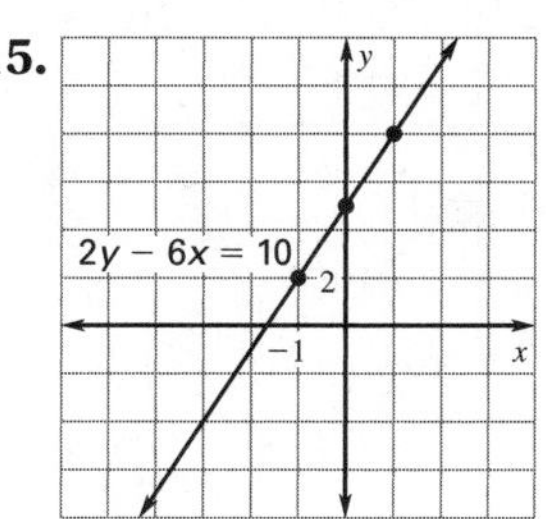

16.

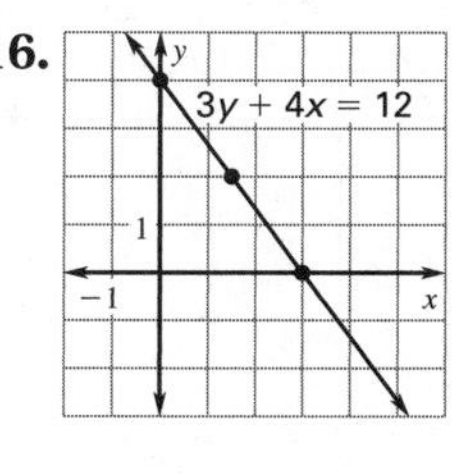

17.

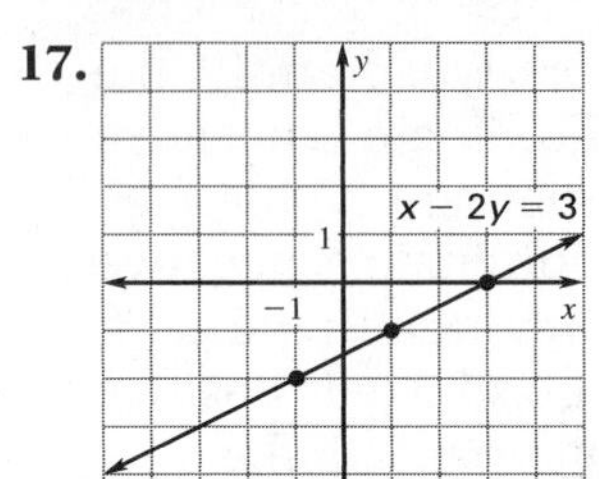

18.

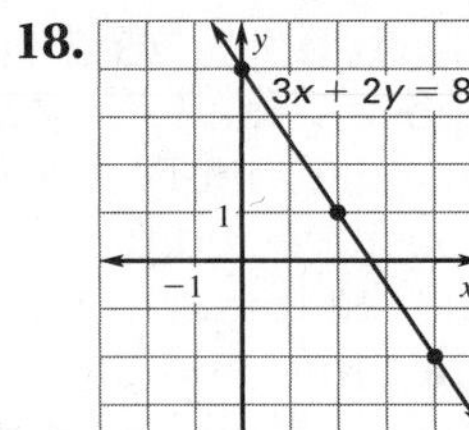

19.

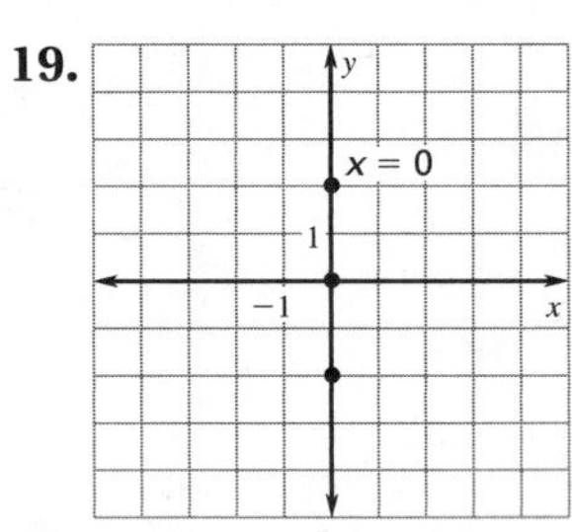

20.

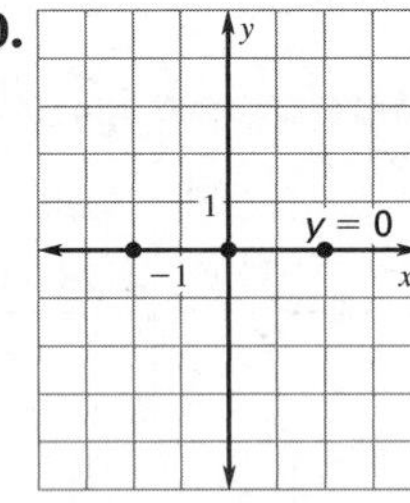

21.

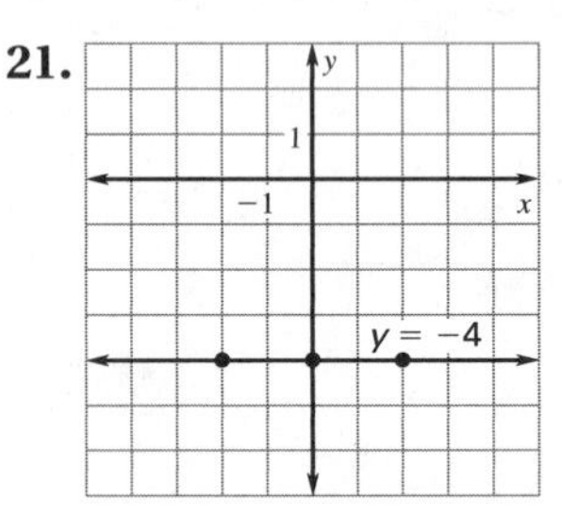

22.

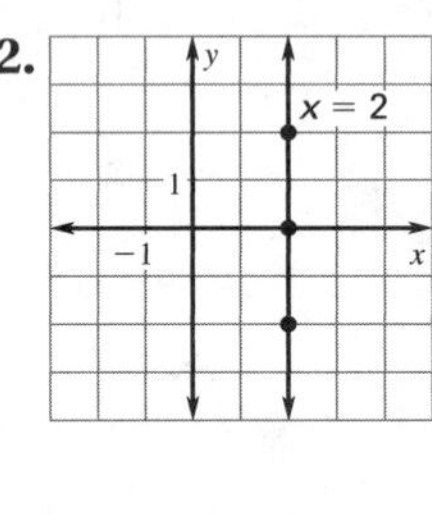

26.

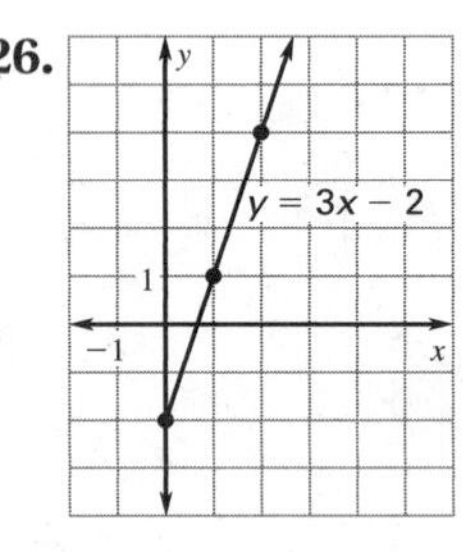

27.

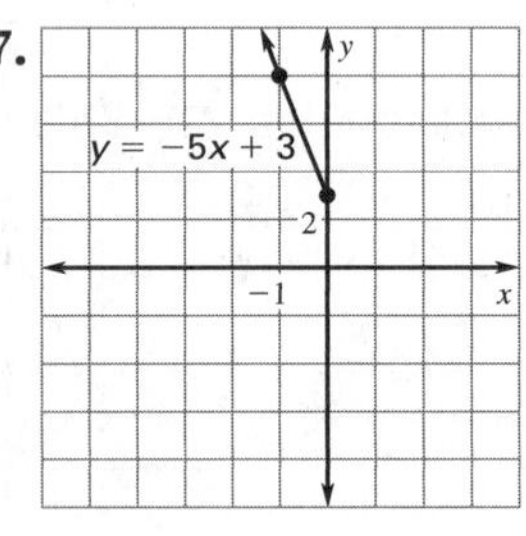

28.

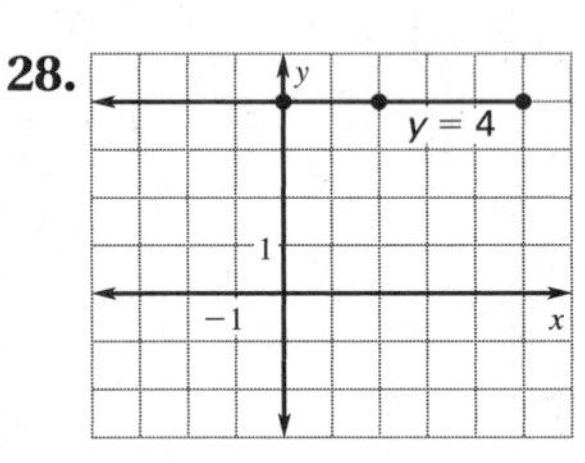

29.

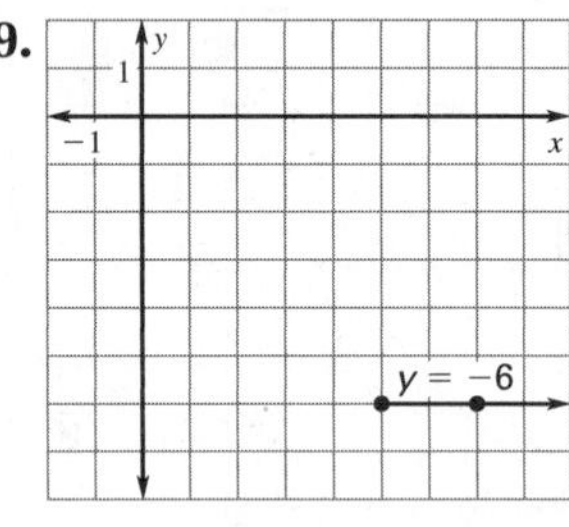

30.

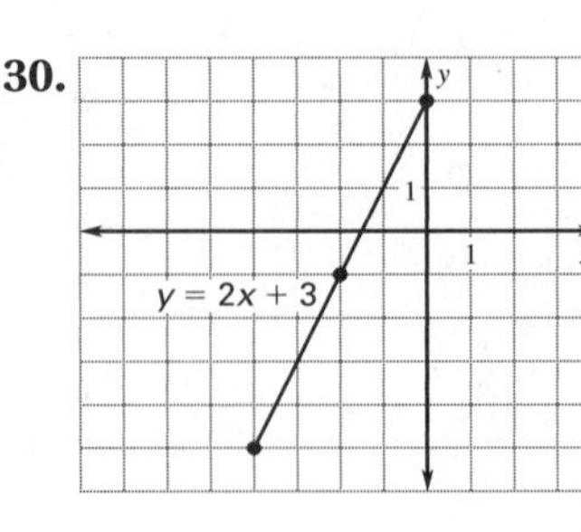

31.

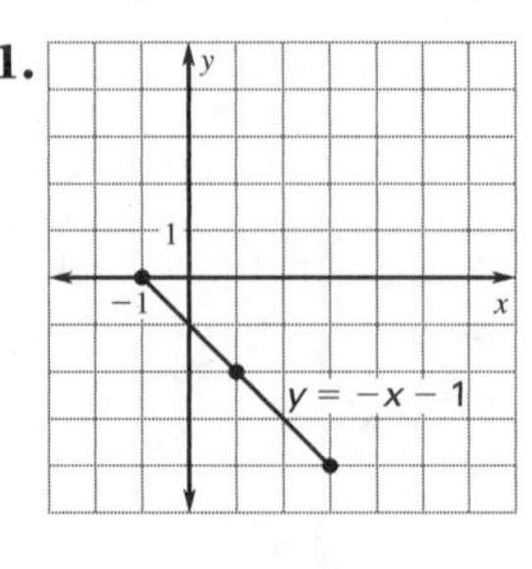

4.2 Problem Solving (pp. 220–221)

40. a.

t (seconds)	h (feet)
0	5
1	19
2	33
3	47
4	61
5	75
6	89
7	103
8	117
9	131
10	145

b.

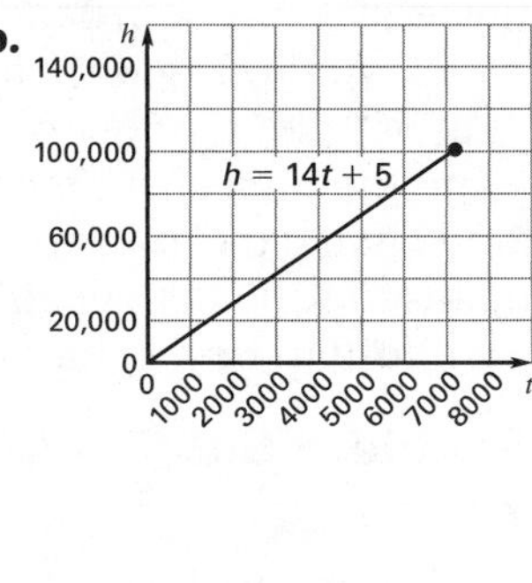

41. a.

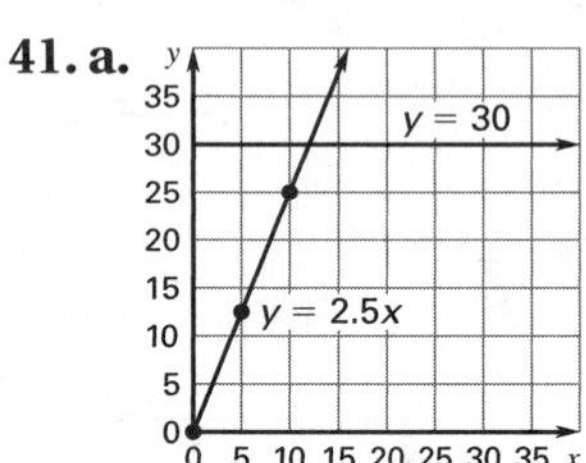

Extension (p. 224)

1.

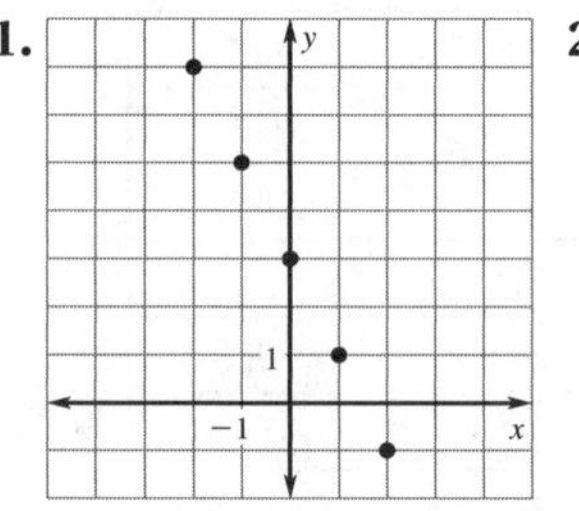

2.

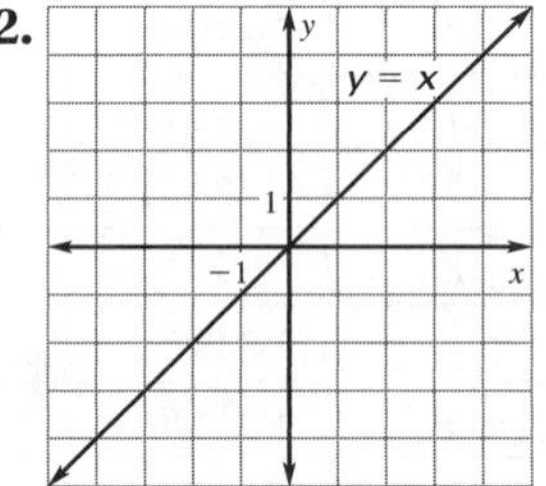

3.

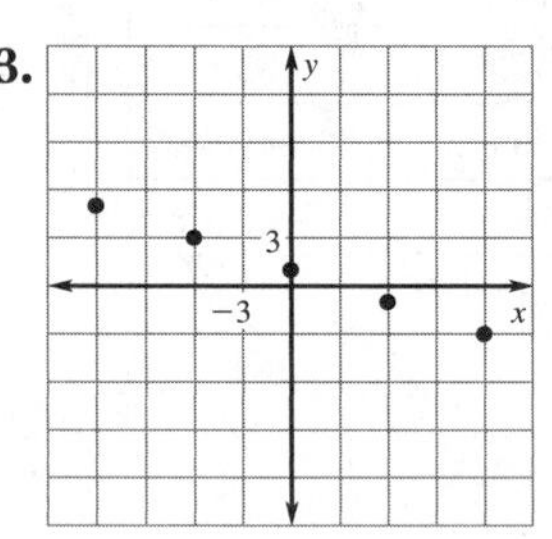

4.

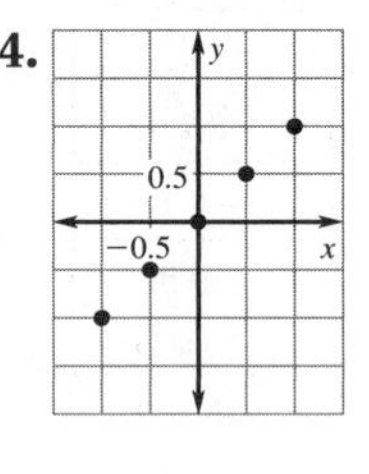

5.

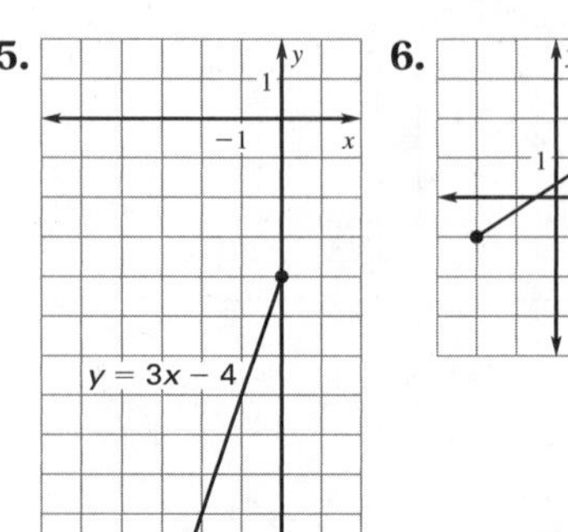

6.

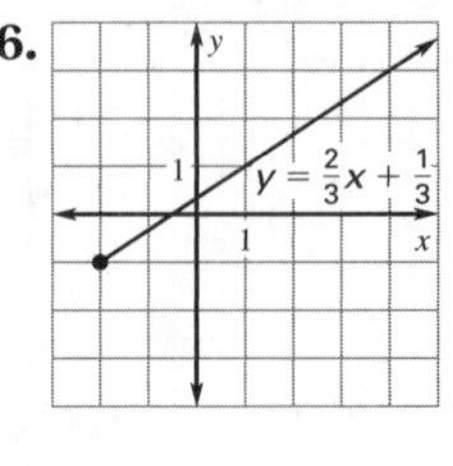

ADDITIONAL ANSWERS

4.3 Skill Practice (pp. 229–230)

16.
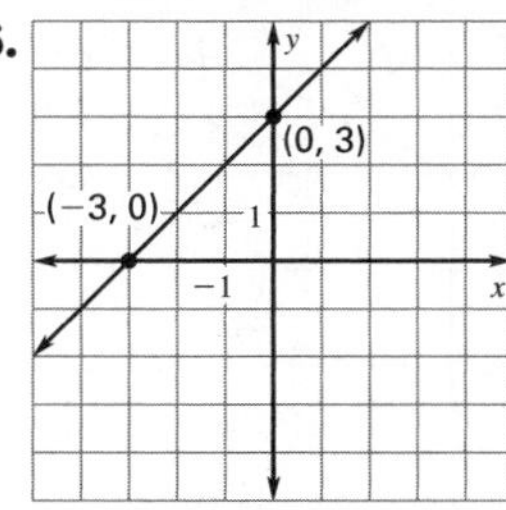

17.
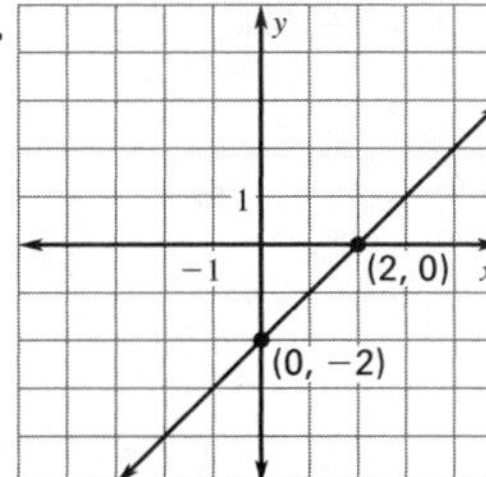

18.
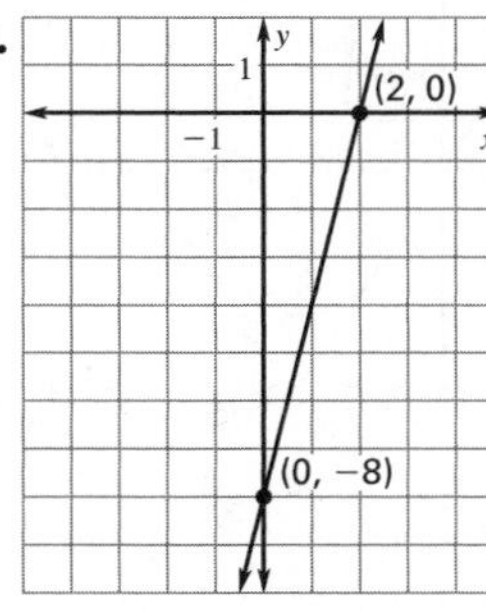

19.
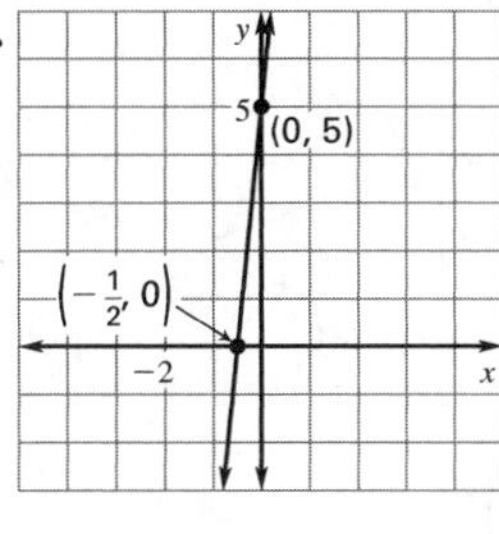

20.
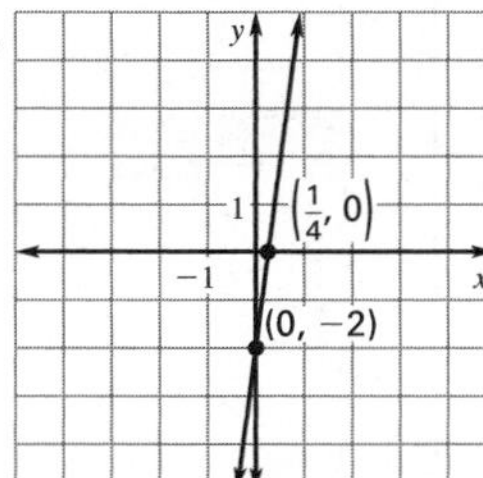

21.
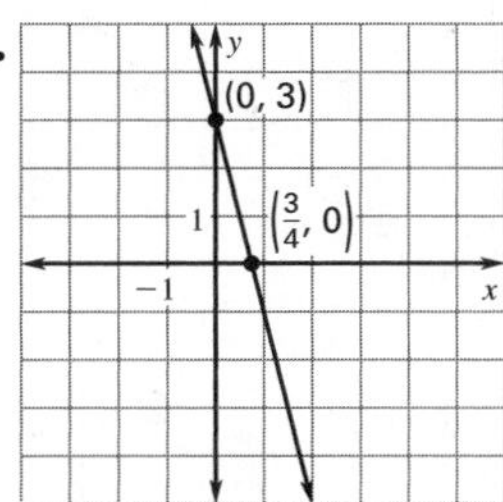

22.
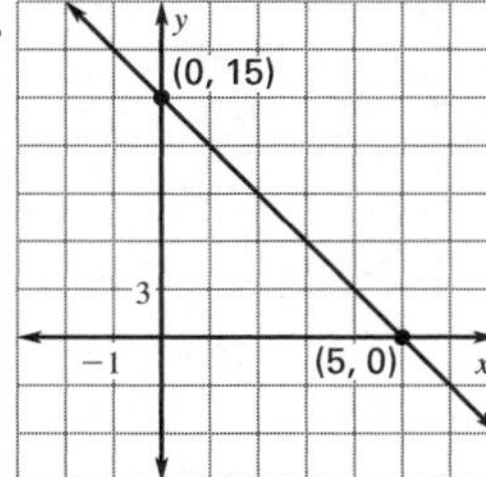

23.
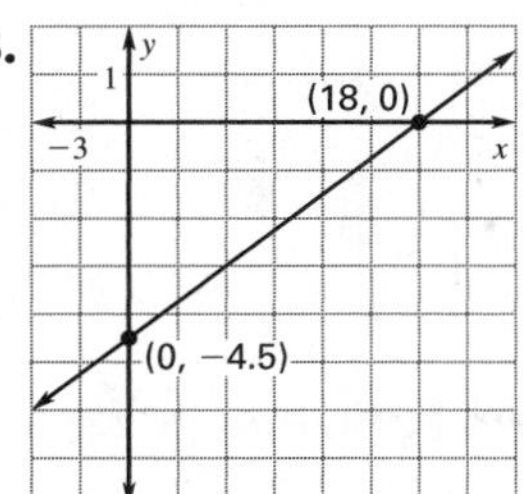

24.
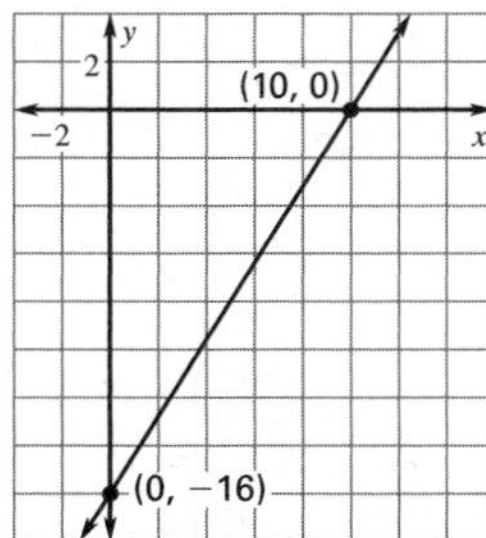

25.
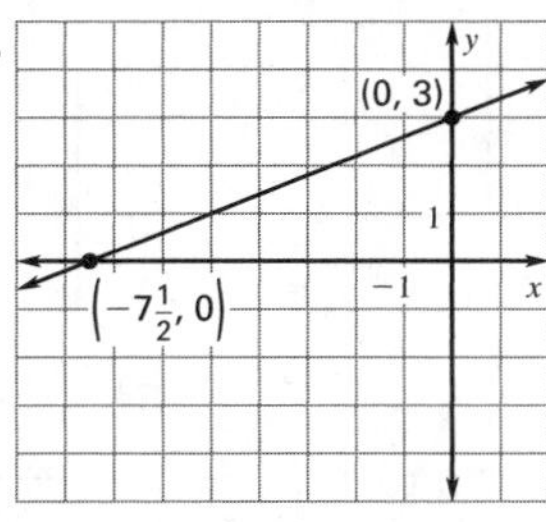

26.
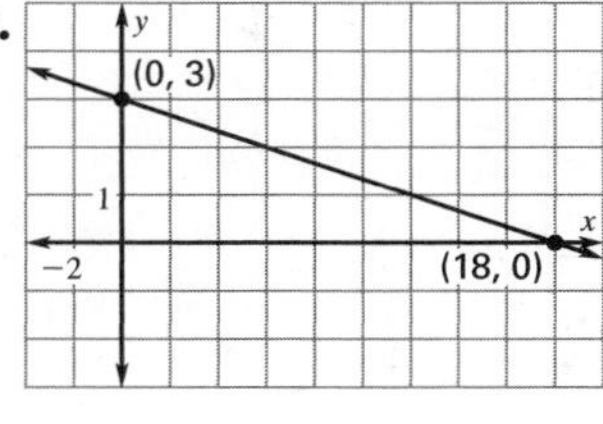

27.
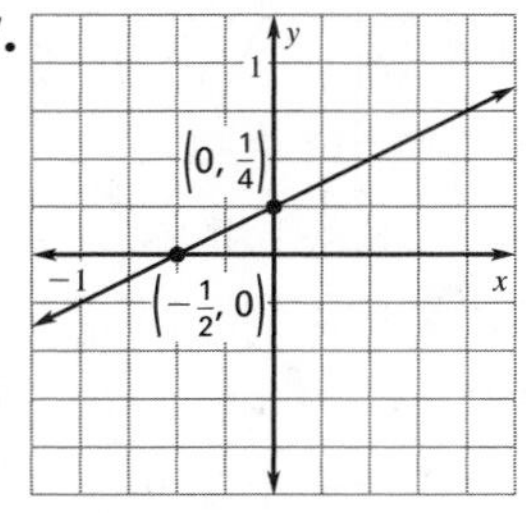

4.3 Problem Solving (pp. 230–232)

50. b.
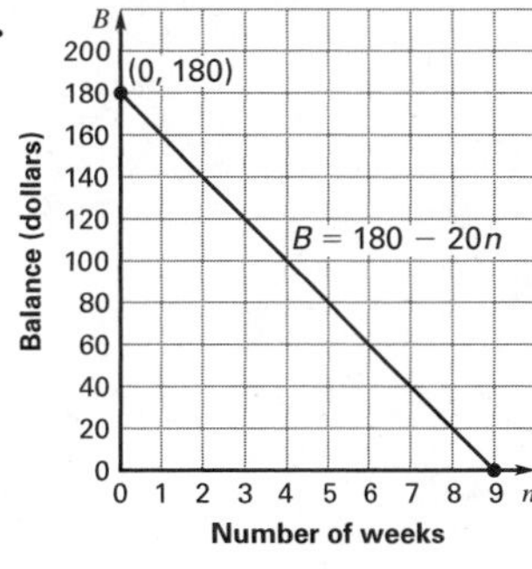

Quiz for Lessons 4.1–4.3 (p. 232)

1–3.
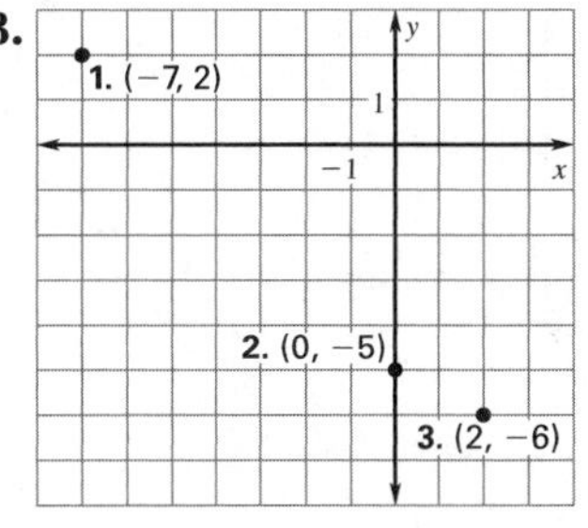

4.
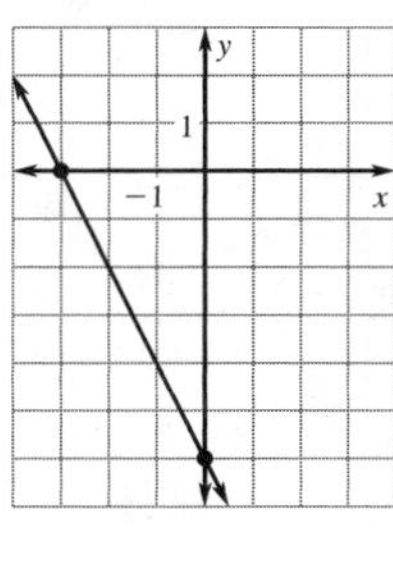

5.
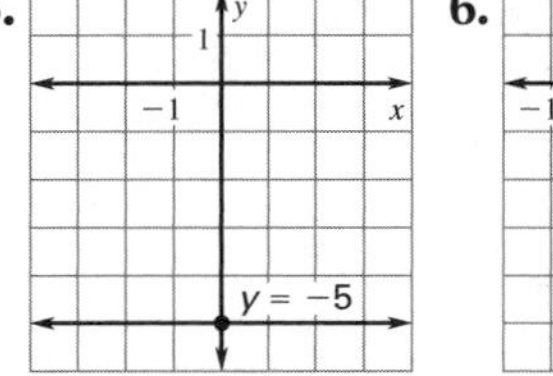

6.
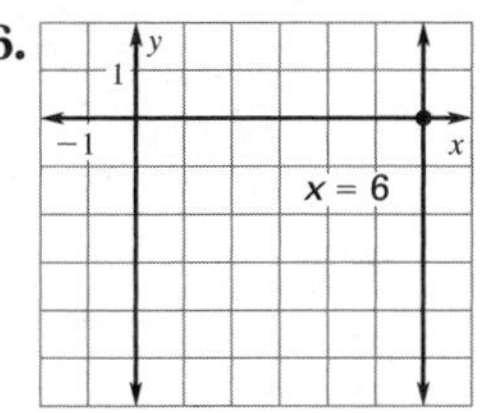

13.
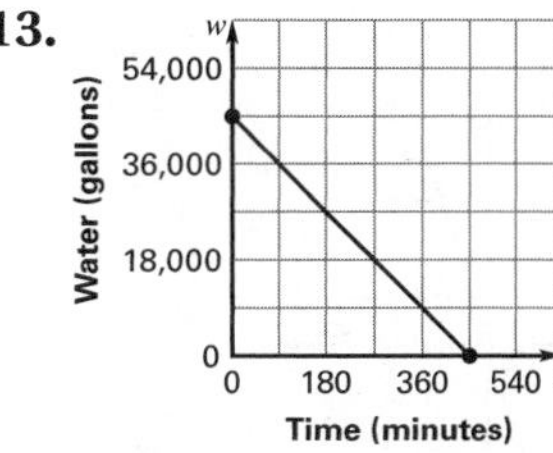

4.4 Problem Solving (pp. 241–242)

41. a.
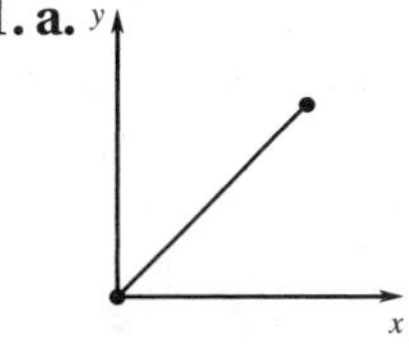

b. **c.**
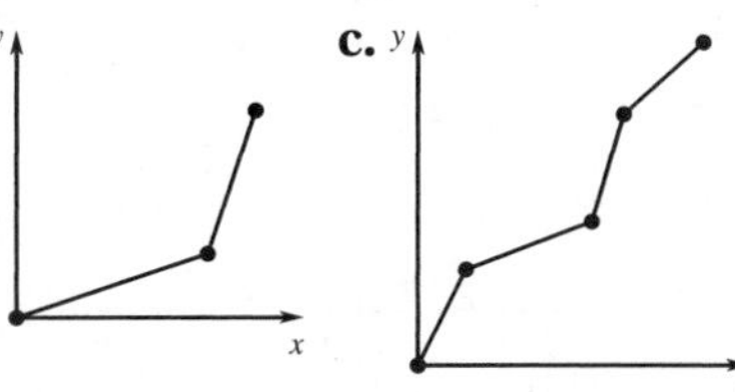

4.5 Guided Practice (pp. 244–246)

4.
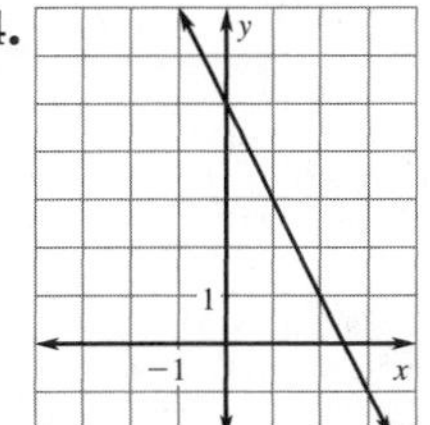

ADDITIONAL ANSWERS

4.5 Problem Solving (pp. 248–250)

45. a.

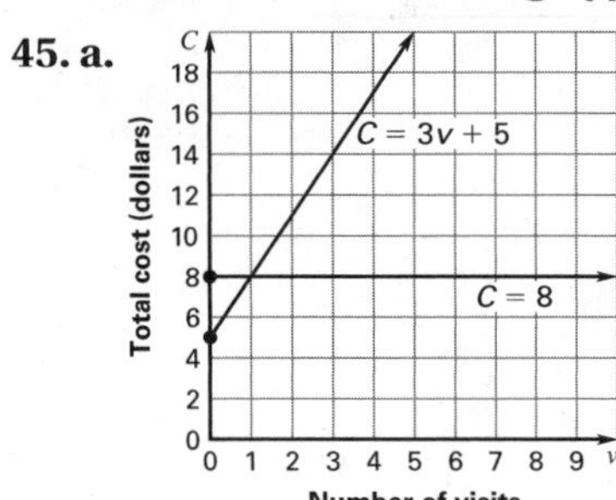

Quiz for Lessons 4.4–4.5 (p. 250)

7.

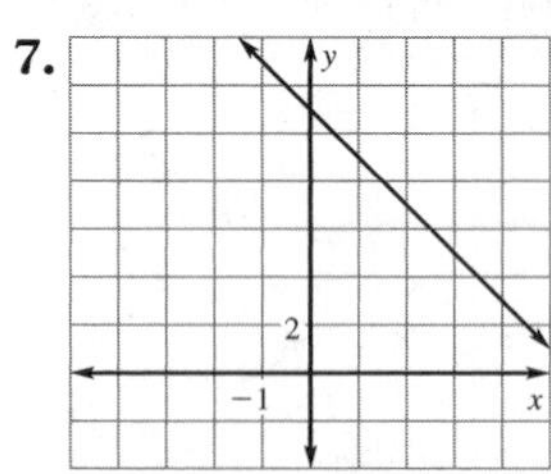

8.

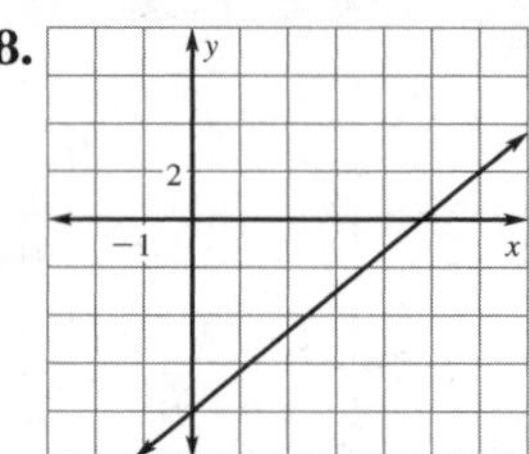

9.

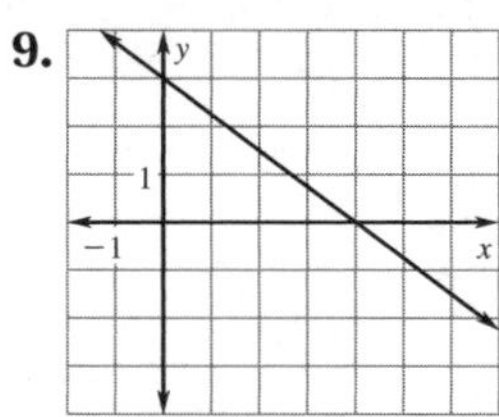

10. a.

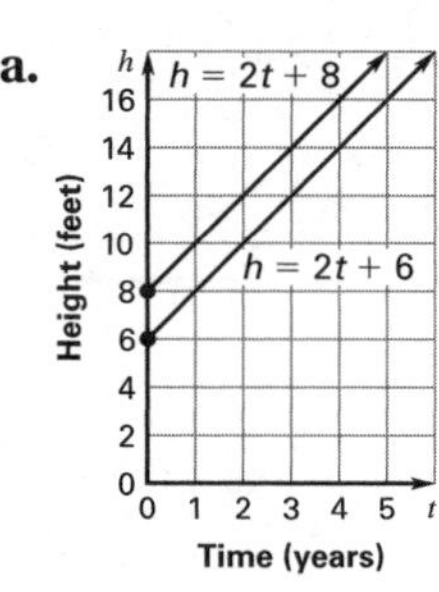

4.6 Skill Practice (pp. 256–257)

11.

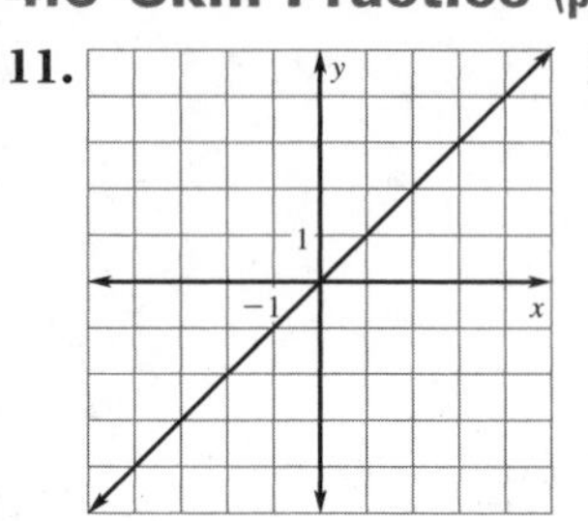

12.

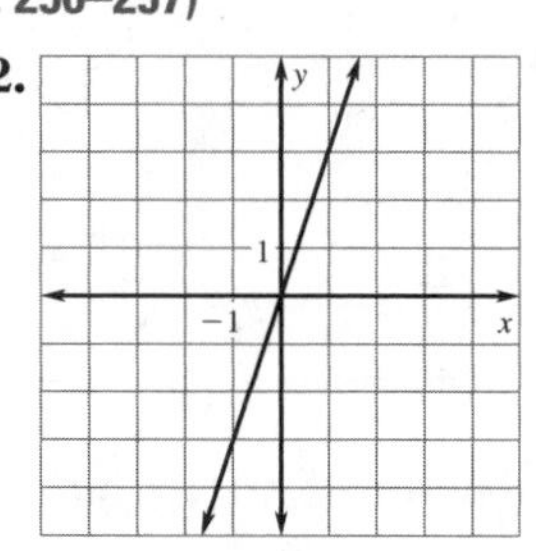

13.

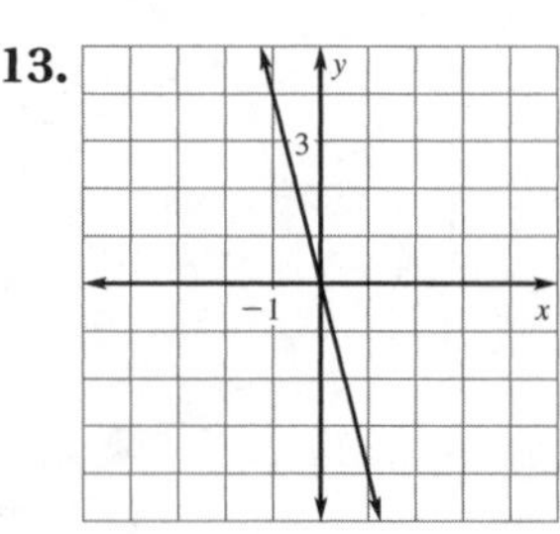

14.

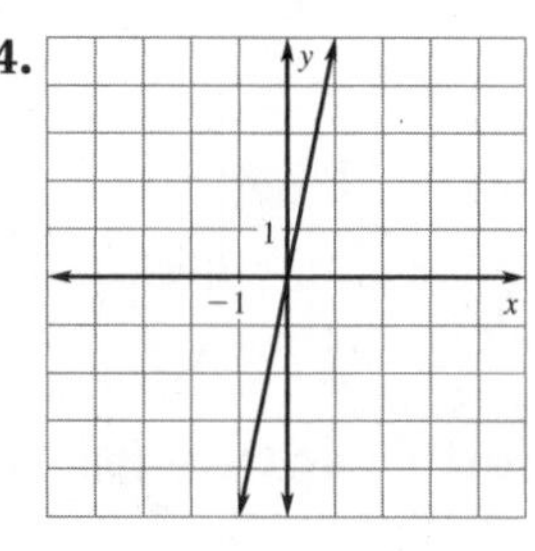

15.

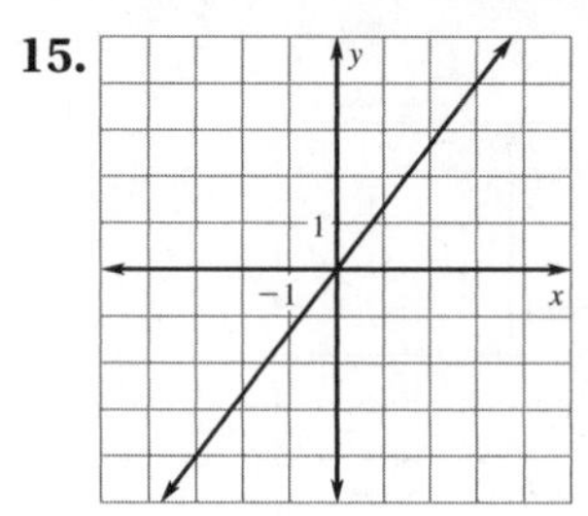

16.

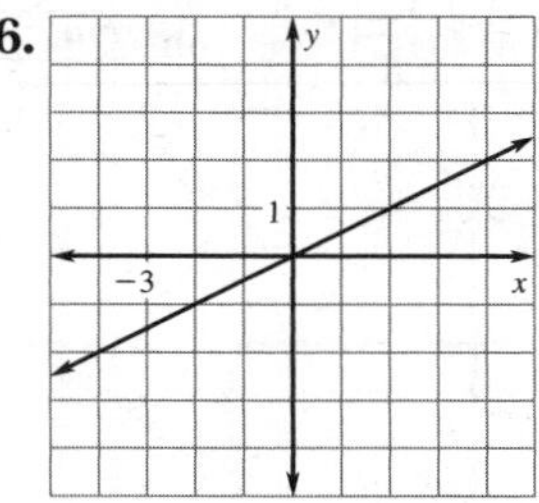

17.

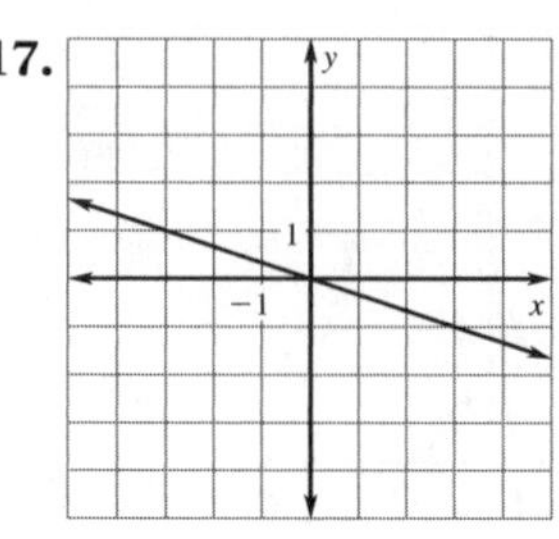

18.

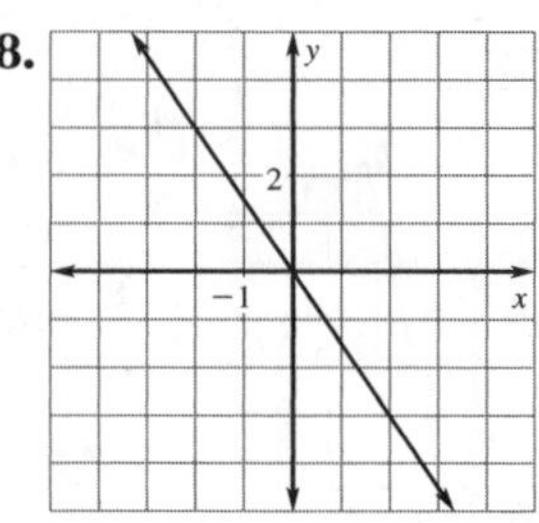

19.

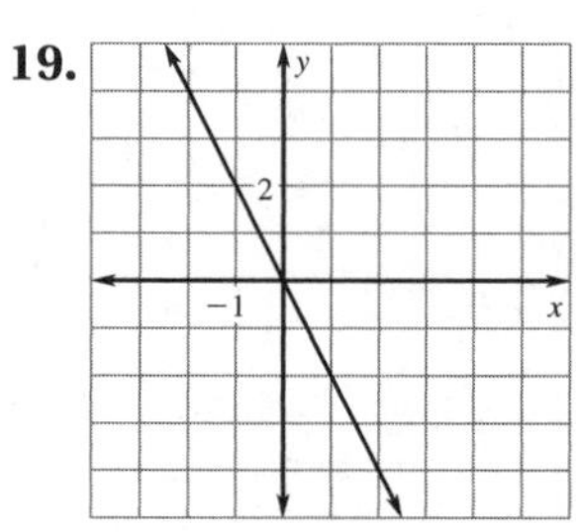

20.

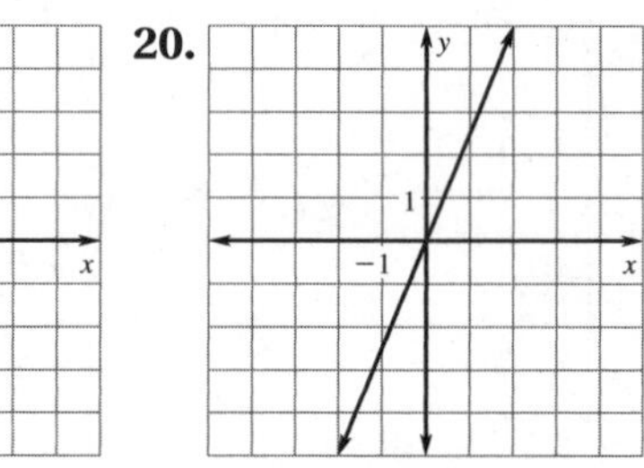

21.

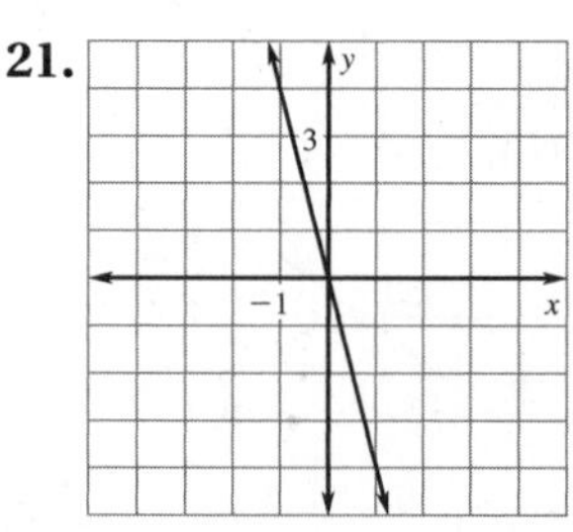

22.

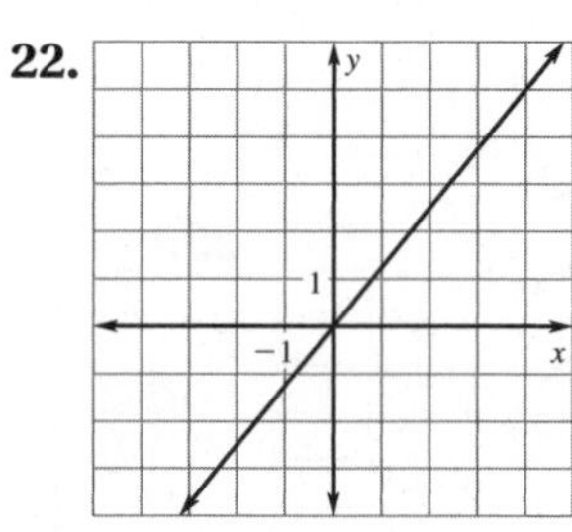

4.6 Mixed Review (p. 259)

48.

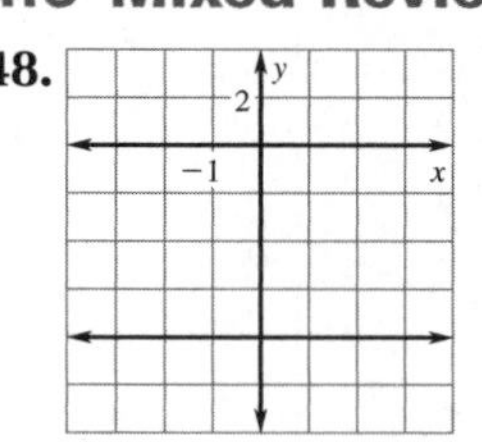

49.

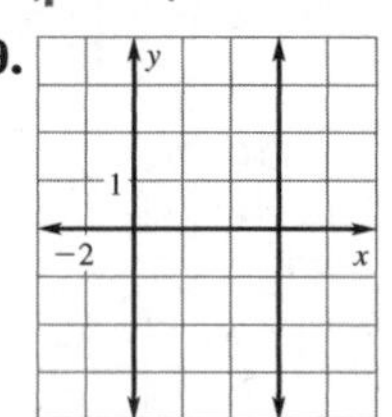

50.

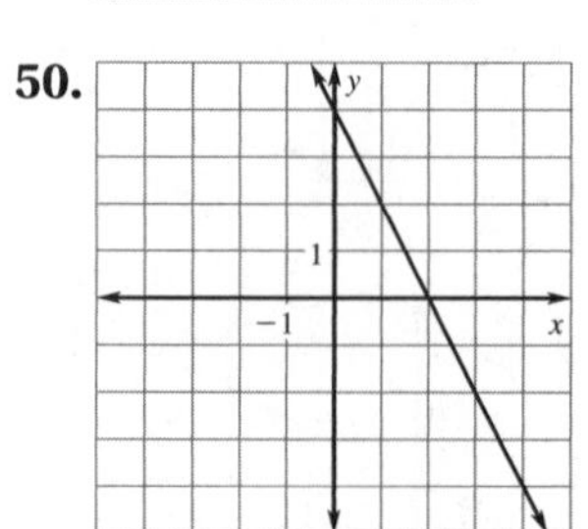

51.

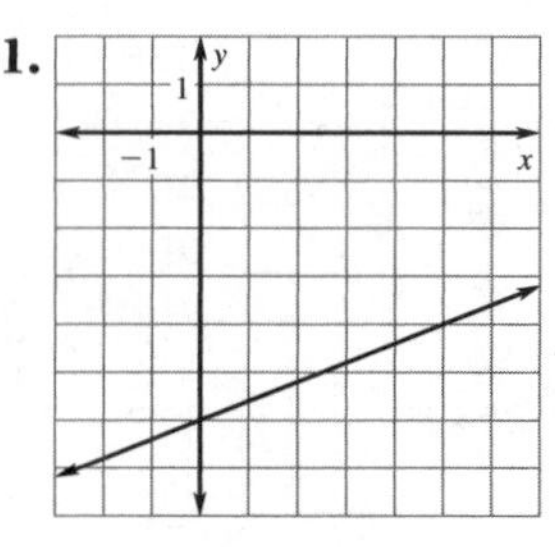

ADDITIONAL ANSWERS

52. 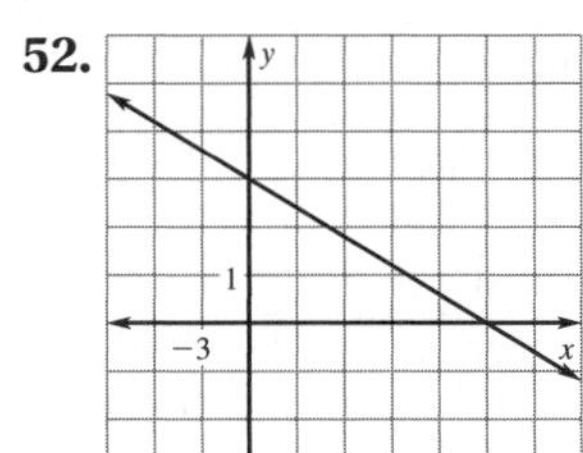

53. 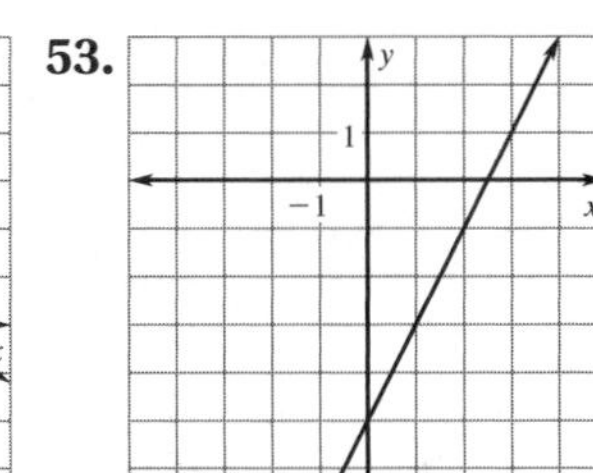

54. 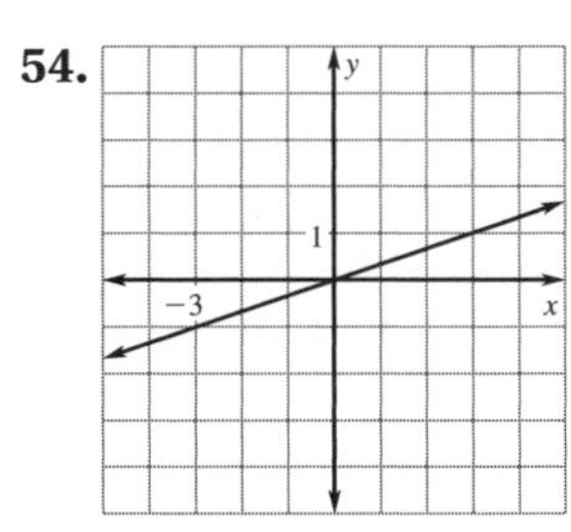

55. 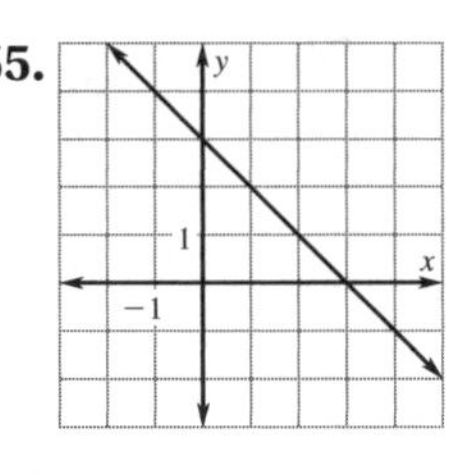

56. 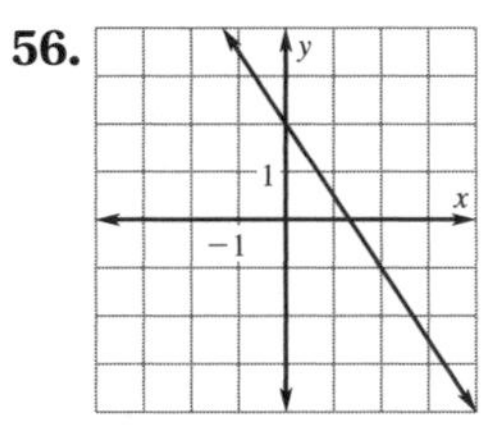

4.7 Skill Practice (pp. 265–266)

23. 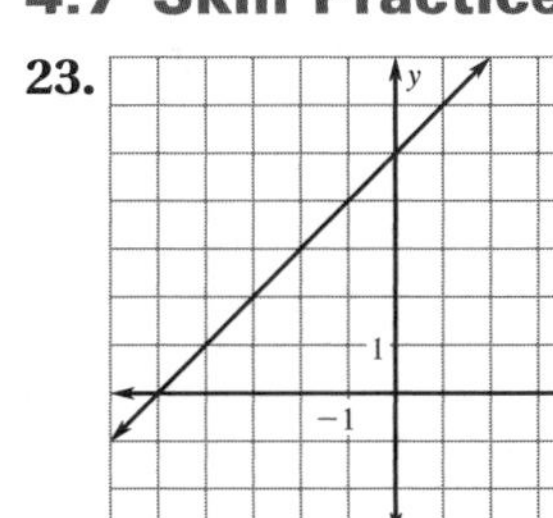

Because the graphs of g and f have the same slope, $m = 1$, the lines are parallel. The y-intercept of the graph of g is 5 more than the y-intercept of the graph of f.

24. 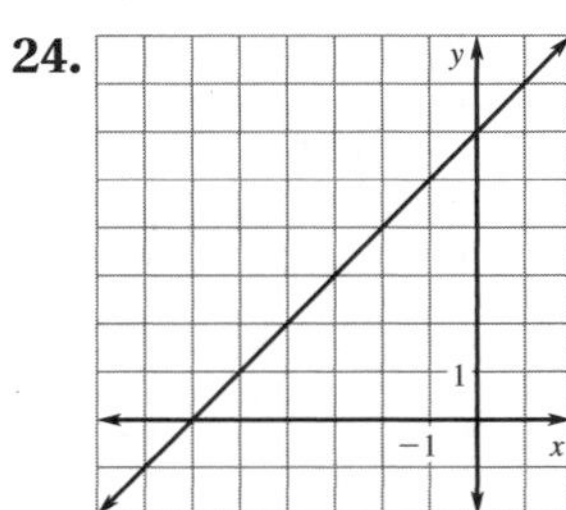

Because the graphs of h and f have the same slope, $m = 1$, the lines are parallel. The y-intercept of the graph of h is 6 more than the y-intercept of the graph of f.

25. 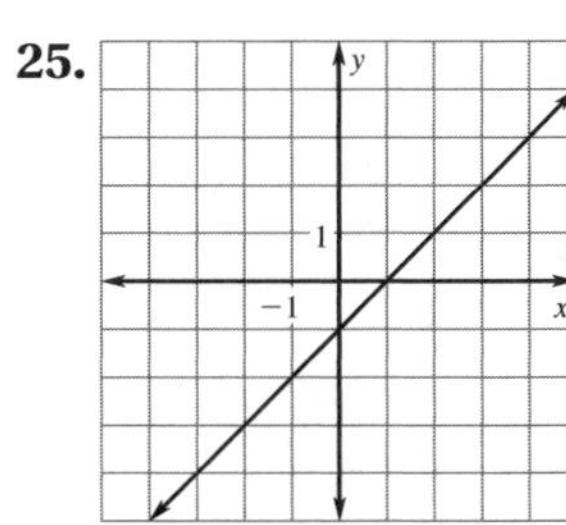

Because the graphs of q and f have the same slope, $m = 1$, the lines are parallel. The y-intercept of the graph of q is 1 less than the y-intercept of the graph of f.

26. 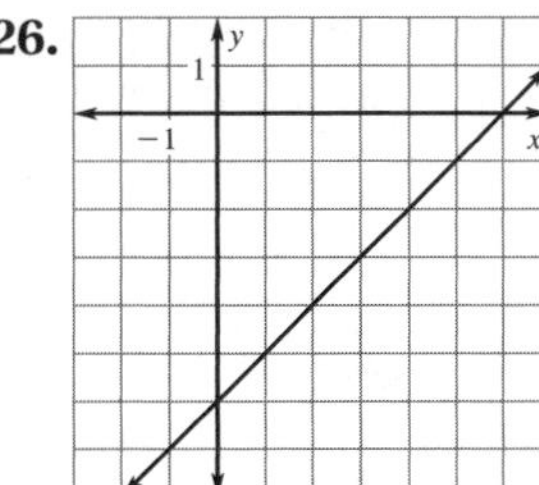

Because the graphs of m and f have the same slope, $m = 1$, the lines are parallel. The y-intercept of the graph of m is 6 less than the y-intercept of the graph of f.

27. 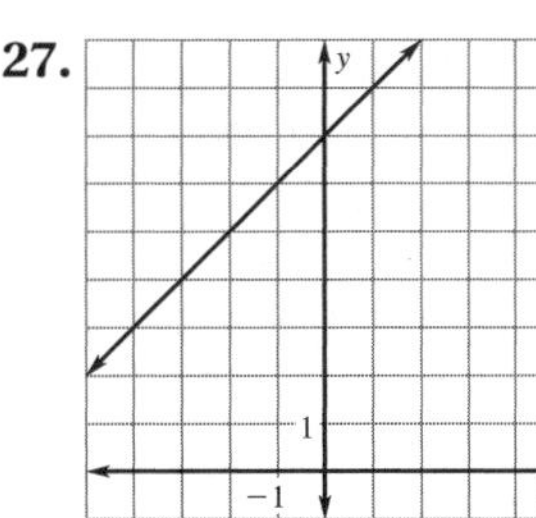

Because the graphs of d and f have the same slope, $m = 1$, the lines are parallel. The y-intercept of the graph of d is 7 more than the y-intercept of the graph of f.

28. 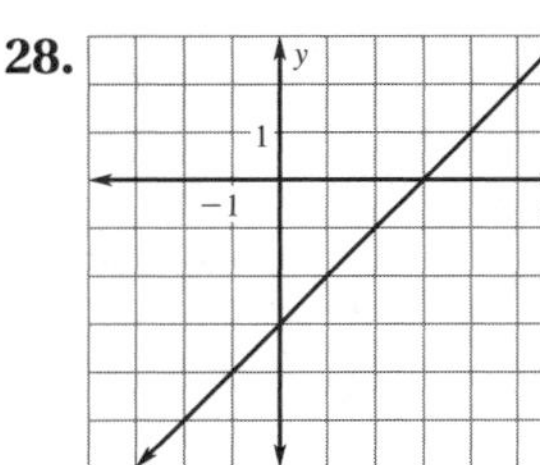

Because the graphs of t and f have the same slope, $m = 1$, the lines are parallel. The y-intercept of the graph of t is 3 less than the y-intercept of the graph of f.

29. 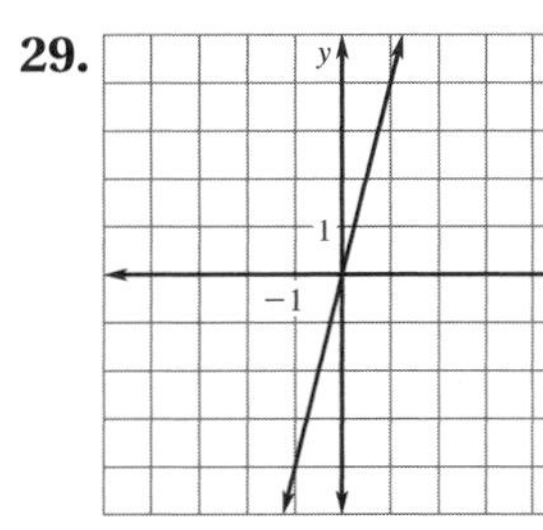

Because the slope of the graph of r is greater than the slope of the graph of f, the graph of r rises faster from left to right. The y-intercept for both graphs is 0, so both lines pass through the origin.

30. 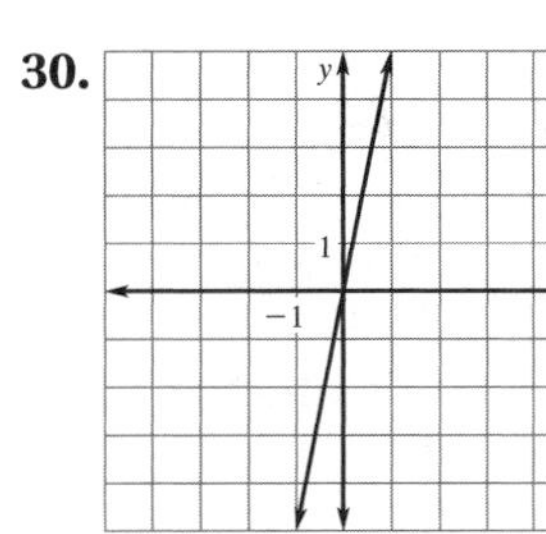

Because the slope of the graph of w is greater than the slope of the graph of f, the graph of w rises faster from left to right. The y-intercept for both graphs is 0, so both lines pass through the origin.

31. 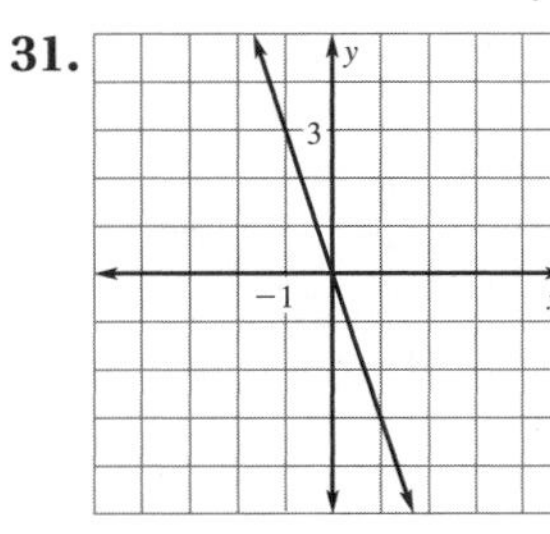

Because the slope of the graph of h is negative, the graph of h falls from left to right. The y-intercept for both graphs is 0, so both lines pass through the origin.

32. 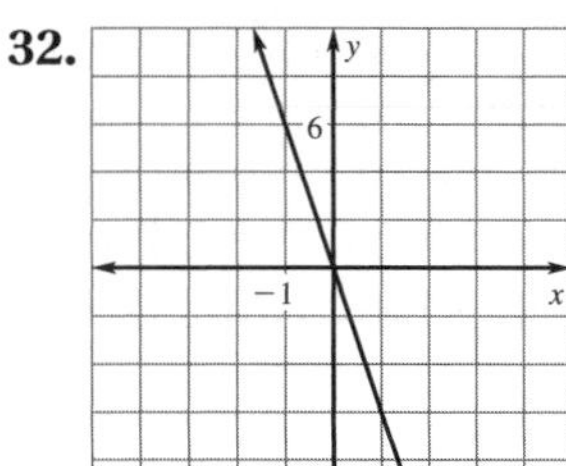

Because the slope of the graph of k is negative, the graph of k falls from left to right. The y-intercept for both graphs is 0, so both lines pass through the origin.

33. 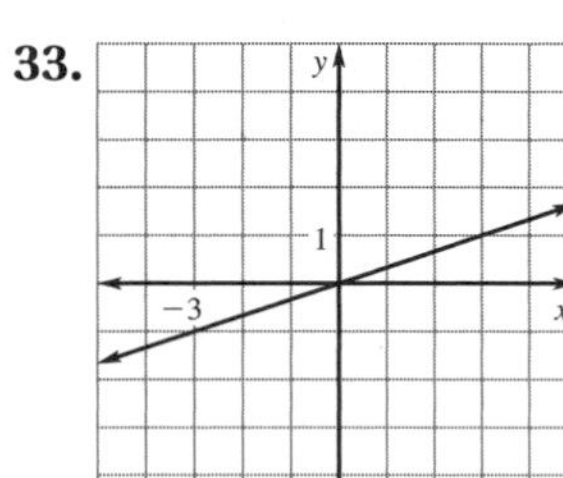

Because the slope of the graph of g is less than the slope of the graph of f, the graph of g rises slower from left to right. The y-intercept for both graphs is 0, so both lines pass through the origin.

34. 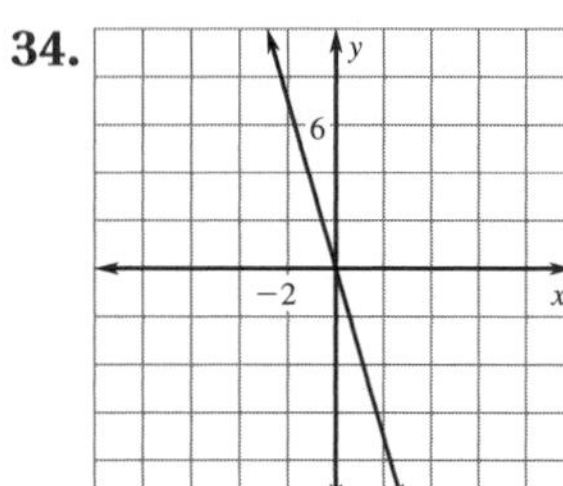

Because the slope of the graph of m is negative, the graph of m falls from left to right. The y-intercept for both graphs is 0, so both lines pass through the origin.

36. a. 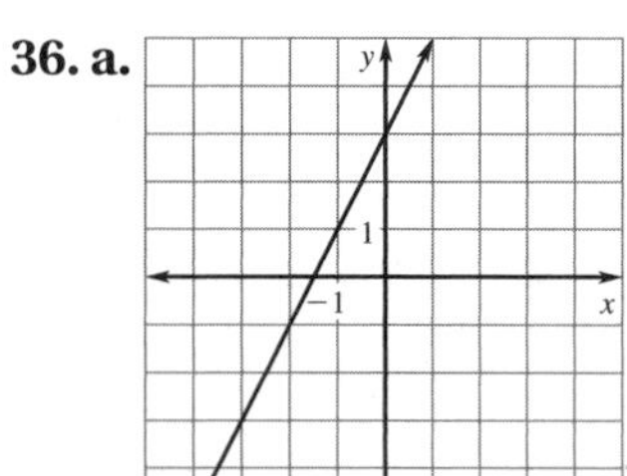

b. Because the slope of the graph of g is greater than the slope of the graph of f, the graph of g rises faster from left to right. The y-intercept for both graphs is the same, so both lines pass through the point (0, 3).

c. 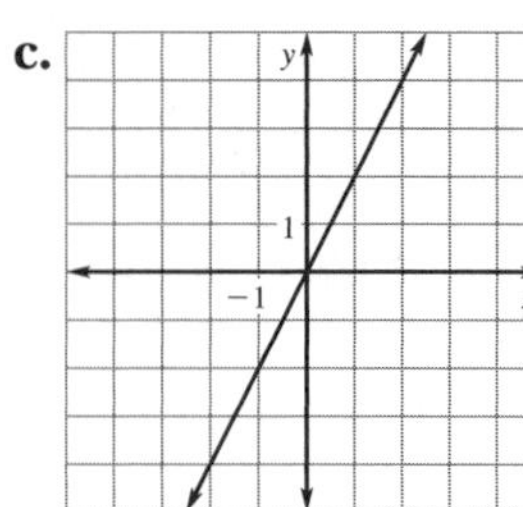

Because the graphs of h and f have the same slope, $m = 2$, the lines are parallel. The y-intercept of the graph of h is 3 less than the y-intercept of the graph of f.

4.7 Problem Solving (pp. 267–268)

42. Because the graphs of g and f have the same slope, $m = 40$, the lines are parallel. The y-intercept of the graph of g is 80 less than the y-intercept of the graph of f.

43. 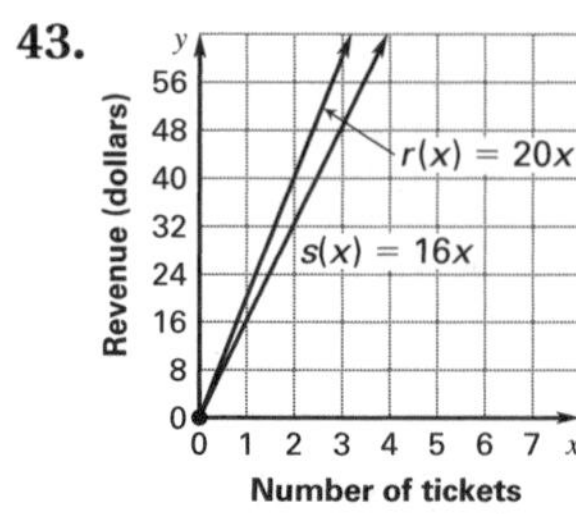

Because the slope of the graph of r is greater than the slope of the graph of s, the graph of r rises faster from left to right. The y-intercept for both graphs is 0, so both lines pass through the origin.

45. b. 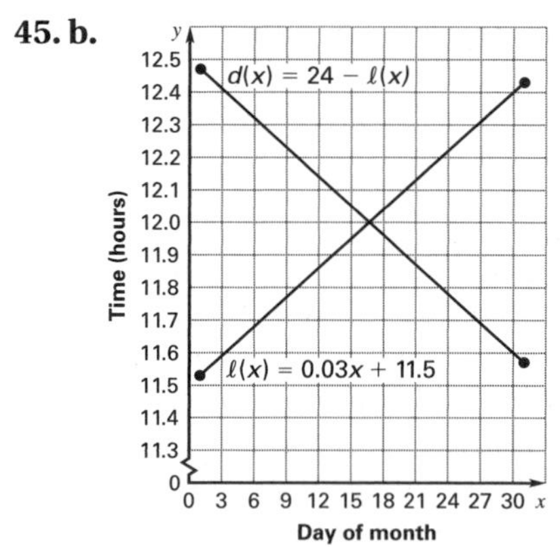

4.7 Mixed Review (p. 268)

55. 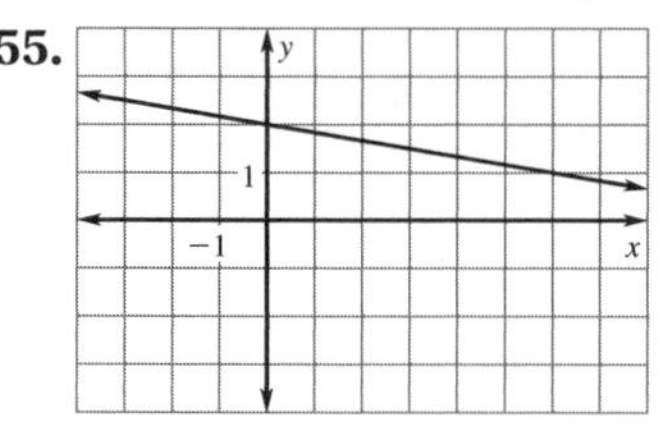

56. 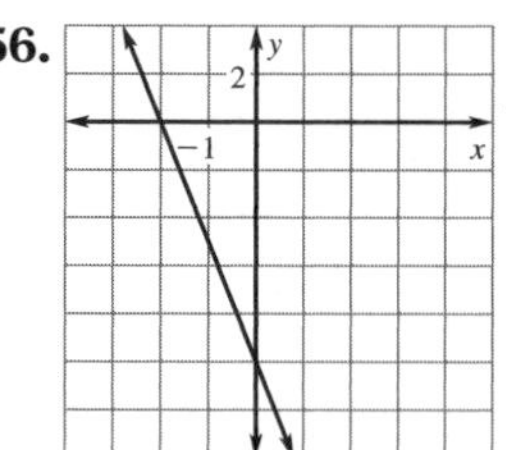

57. 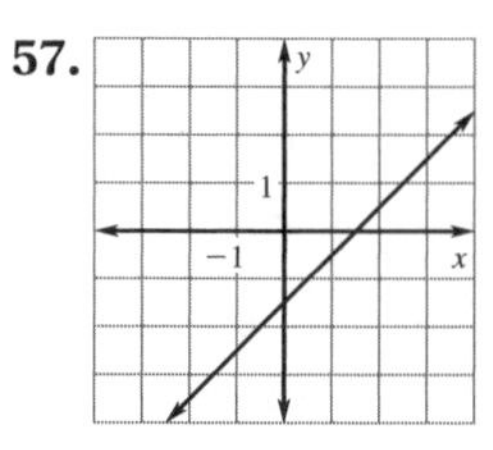

58. 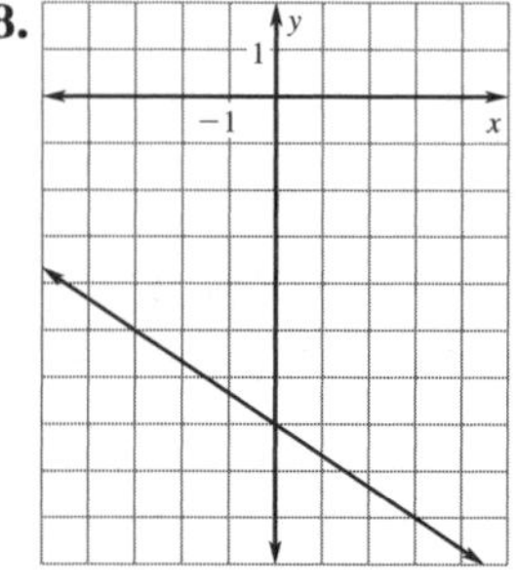

59.

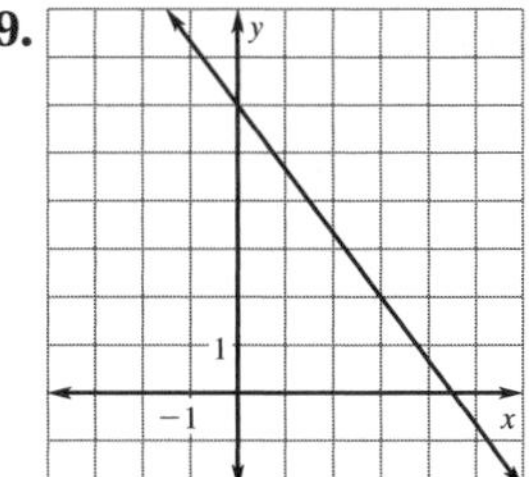

60.

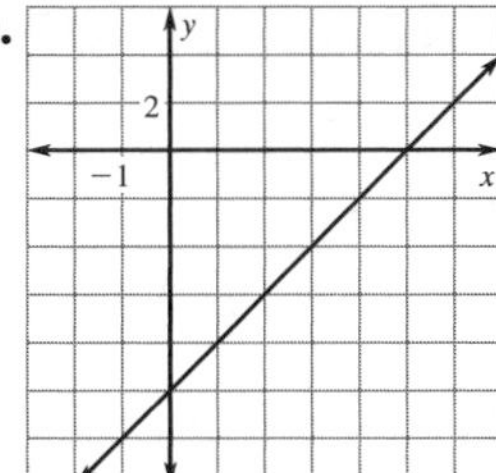

Quiz for Lessons 4.6–4.7 (p. 268)

8.

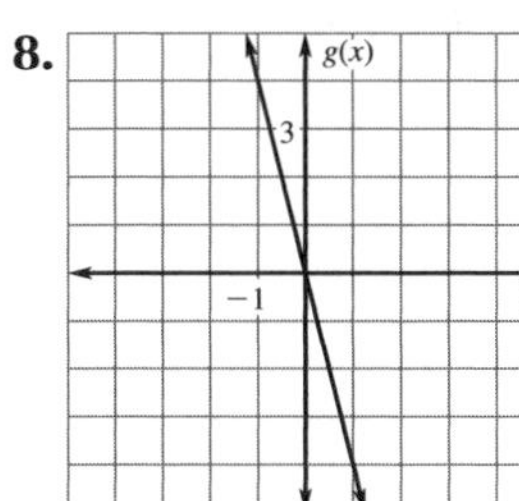

Because the slope of the graph of g is negative, the graph of g falls from left to right. The y-intercept for both graphs is 0, so both lines pass through the origin.

9.

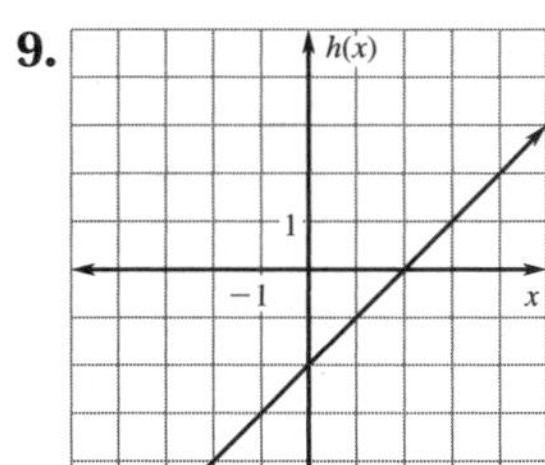

Because the graphs of h and f have the same slope, $m = 1$, the lines are parallel. The y-intercept of the graph of h is 2 less than the y-intercept of the graph of f.

Chapter Review (pp. 271–274)

31.

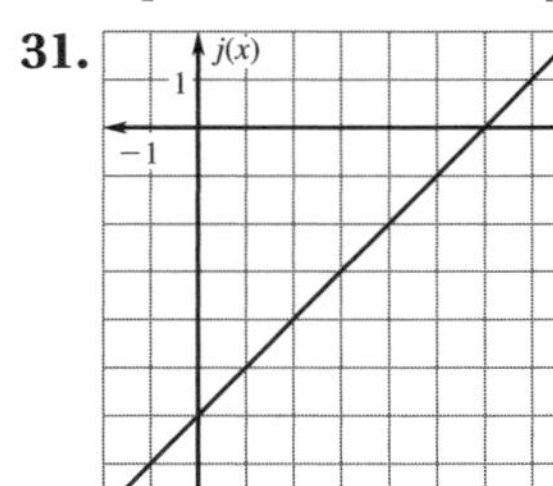

Because the graphs of j and f have the same slope, $m = 1$, the lines are parallel. The y-intercept of the graph of j is 6 less than the y-intercept of the graph of f.

32.

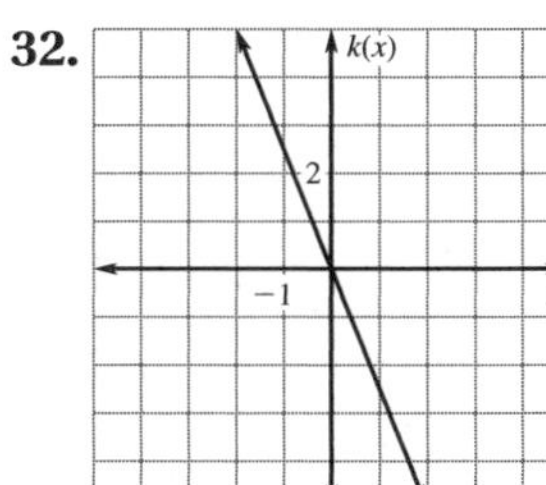

Because the slope of the graph of k is negative, the graph of k falls from left to right. The y-intercept for both graphs is 0, so both lines pass through the origin.

33.

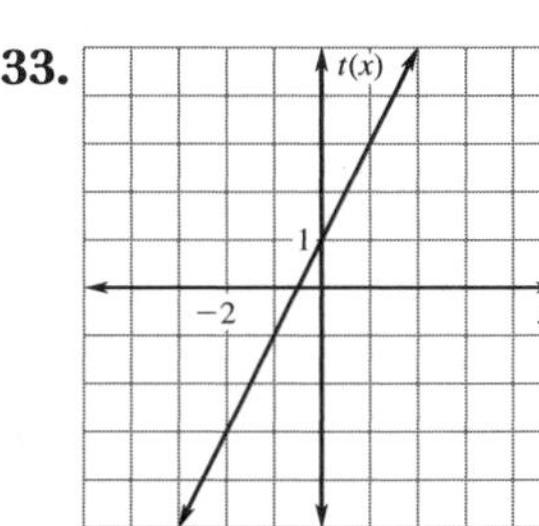

Because the slope of the graph of t is greater than the slope of the graph of f, the graph of t rises faster from left to right. The y-intercept of the graph of t is 1 more than the y-intercept of the graph of f.

Chapter Test (p. 275)

16.

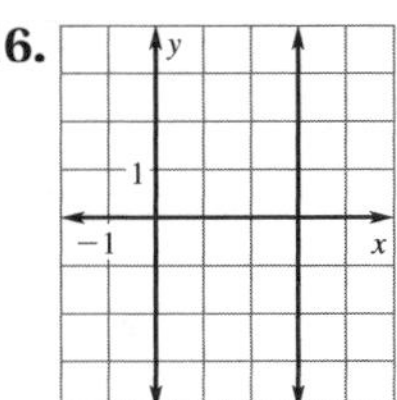

17.

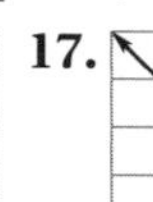

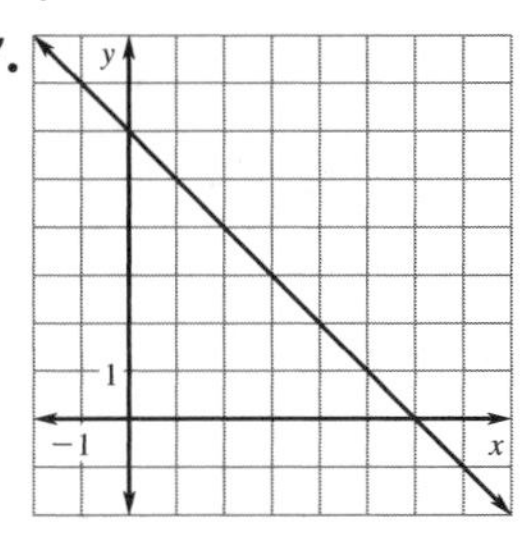

18.

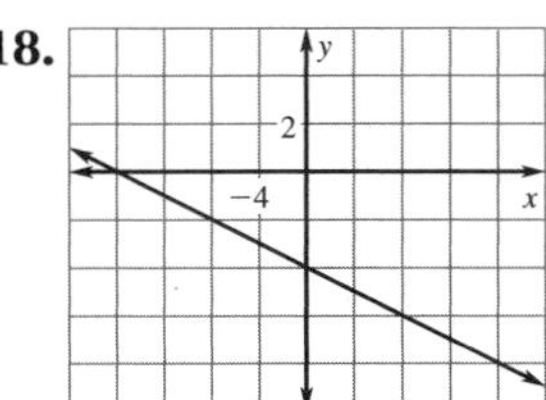

Chapter 5

5.3 Guided Practice (pp. 302–305)

2.

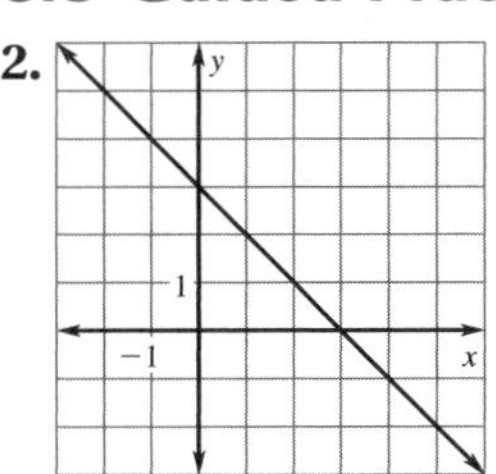

5.3 Skill Practice (pp. 305–306) **31.** No; because the increase is not at a constant rate, the situation cannot be modeled by a linear equation. **32.** Yes; because the rate is increasing at a constant rate, the situation can be modeled by a linear equation. *Sample answer:* $y - 1.2 = \frac{1}{5}(x - 1)$. **33.** No; because the increase is not at a constant rate, the situation cannot be modeled by a linear equation. **34.** Yes; because the rate is decreasing at a constant rate, the situation can be modeled by a linear equation. *Sample answer:* $y - 16 = -3(x + 3)$.

5.3 Mixed Review (p. 308)

48.

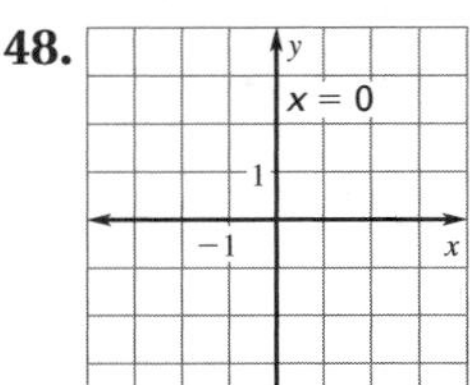

49.

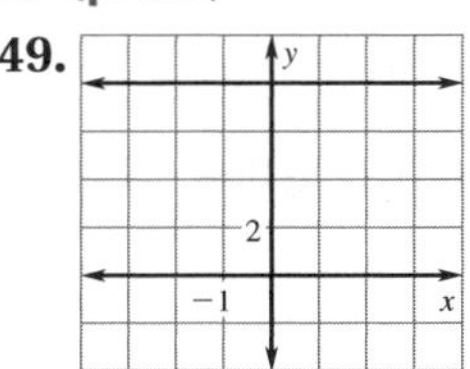

50. 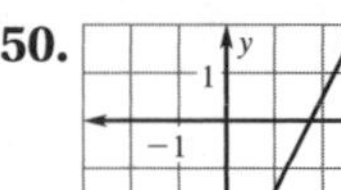 **51.** 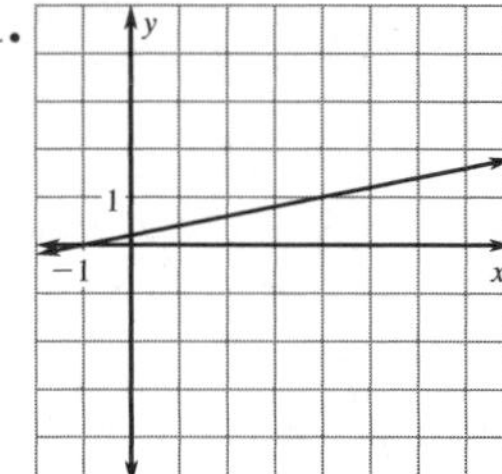

52. 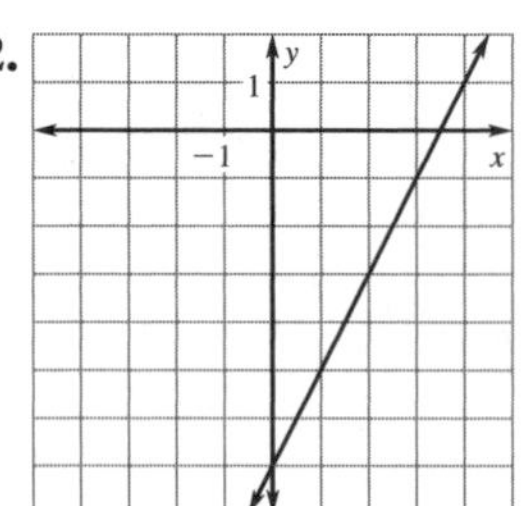 **53.** 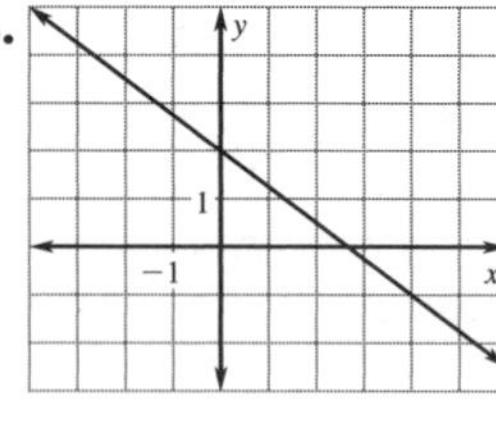

Extension (p. 310)

4. **5.** **6.**

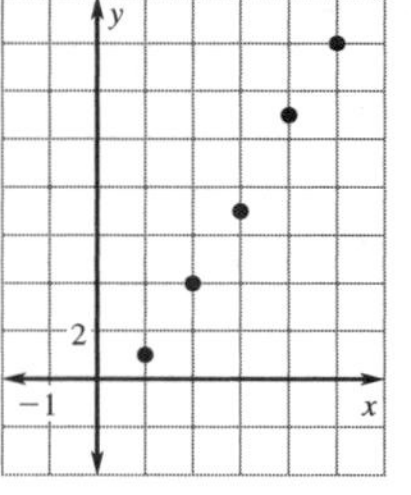
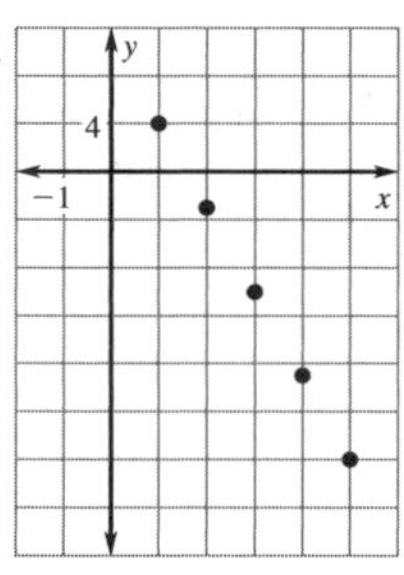
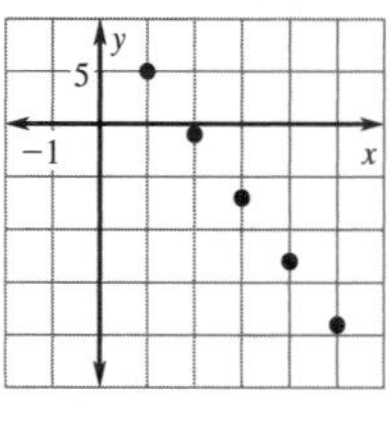

7. **8.** **9.**

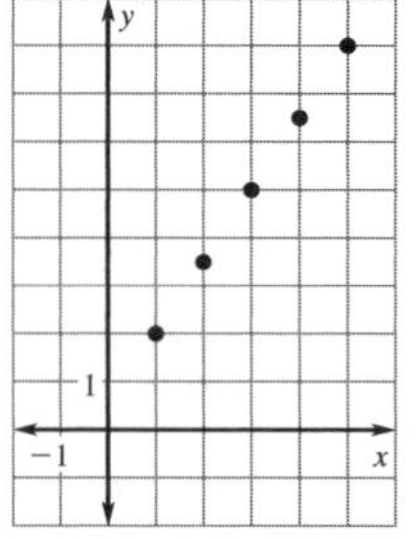
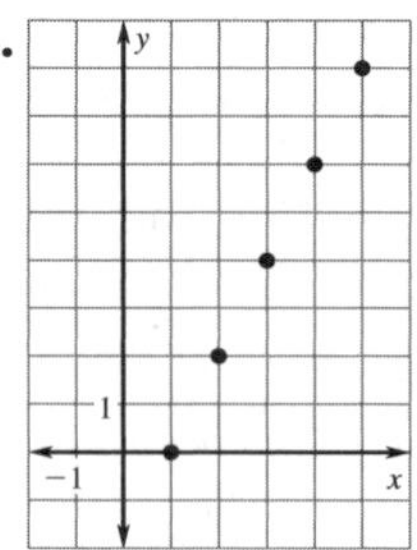
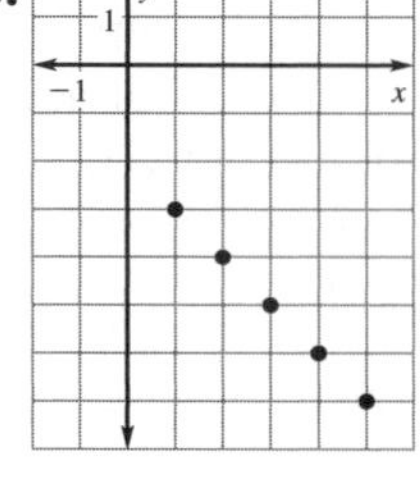

5.4 Skill Practice (p. 314)

5–10. Sample answers are given. **5.** $2x + 2y = -20$, $3x + 3y = -30$ **6.** $x + 2y = 3$, $10x + 20y = 30$ **7.** $x - 2y = -9$, $-2x + 4y = 18$ **8.** $-3x - 4y = 2$, $-6x - 8y = 4$ **9.** $3x - y = -4$, $6x - 2y = -8$ **10.** $2x - 4y = 5$, $-4x + 8y = -10$

5.4 Problem Solving (pp. 315–316)

43. *Sample answer:*

Length (ft)	Width (ft)
5	25
10	20
15	15
20	10
25	5

Quiz for Lessons 5.1–5.4 (p. 316)

7. a. $y - 2 = x + 5$ or $y - 3 = x + 4$ **b.** $-x + y = 7$ **8. a.** $y + 9 = \frac{4}{3}(x + 6)$ or $y + 1 = \frac{4}{3}x$ **b.** $-\frac{4}{3}x + y = -1$ **9. a.** $y - 1 = 4(x - 1)$ or $y - 9 = 4(x - 3)$ **b.** $-4x + y = -3$

Chapter 6

6.1 Guided Practice (pp. 357–358)

1. 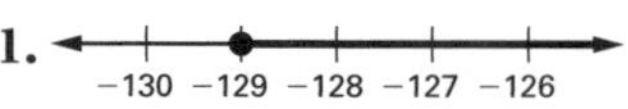 **4.** 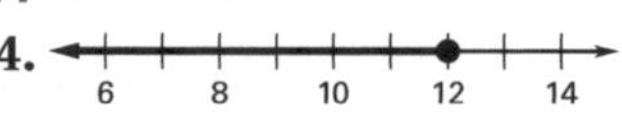

5. 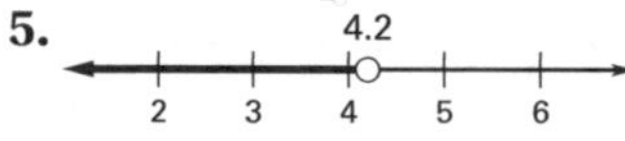 **6.** 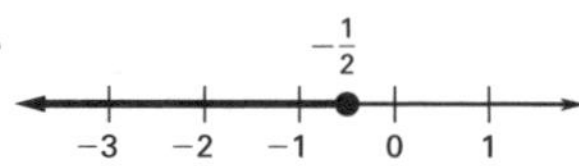

6.1 Skill Practice (pp. 359–360)

10.

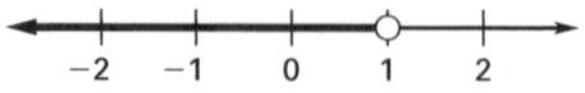

11.

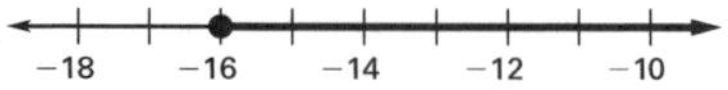

12. 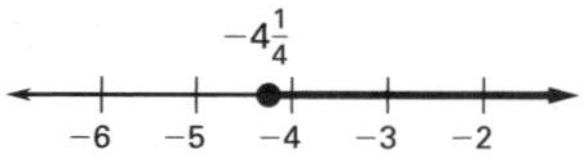 $-4\frac{1}{4}$

13. 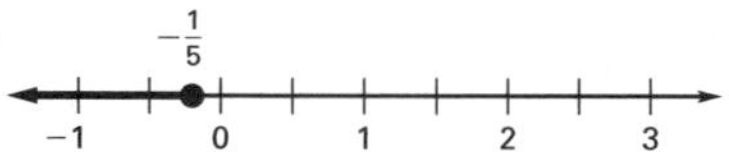 $-\frac{1}{5}$

14. 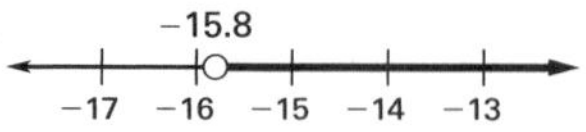 -15.8

15. -17.6

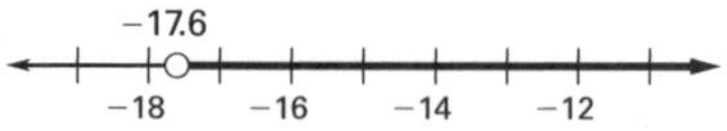

16.

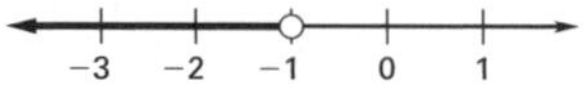

17.

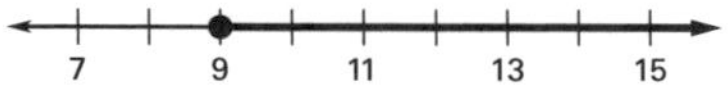

18.

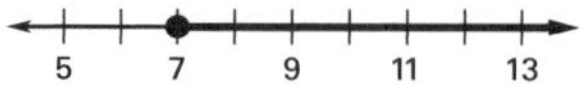

19. 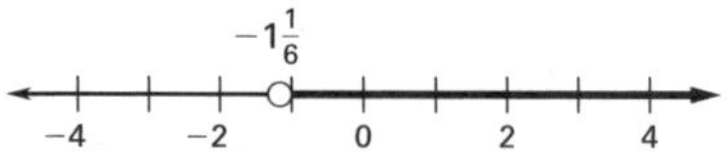 $-1\frac{1}{6}$

20. 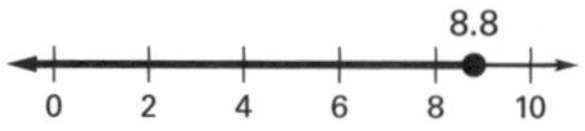 8.8

21. 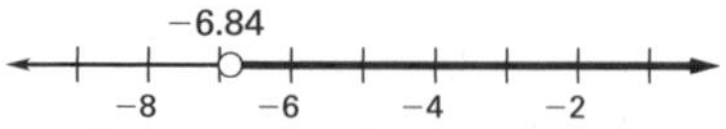 -6.84

22.

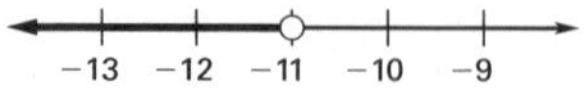

23.

6.1 Problem Solving (pp. 360–361)

36. 2 axles: $w \le 19{,}800$ lb, 3 axles: $w \le 39{,}800$ lb, 4 axles: $w \le 54{,}800$ lb, 5 axles: $w \le 65{,}800$ lb; no; the total weight, 34,200 pounds, would exceed the maximum weight allowed, 34,000 pounds.

37. a.

Original price, x ($)	19,459	19,989	20,549	22,679	23,999
Final price, y ($)	16,459	16,989	17,549	19,679	20,999

6.2 Skill Practice (pp. 366–367)

3.

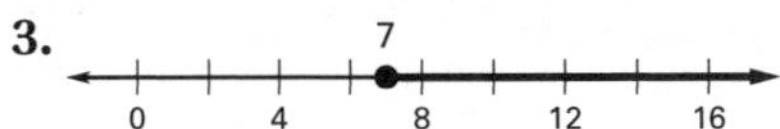

4.

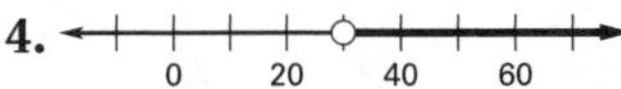

5. 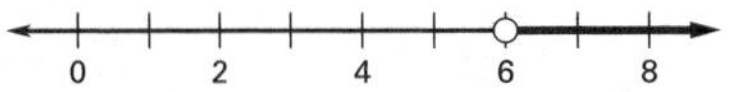 0 2 4 6 8

6.  −400 −200 0 200 400

7. 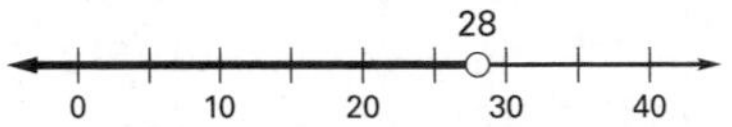 28; 0 10 20 30 40

8.  0 4 8 12 16

9. 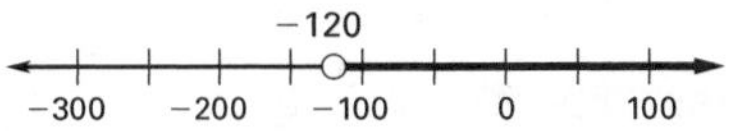 −120; −300 −200 −100 0 100

10.  −2 0 2 4 6

11. 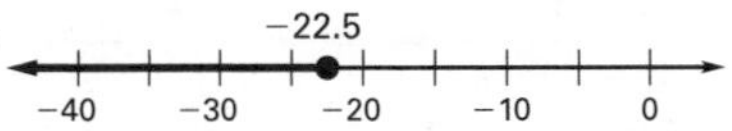 −22.5; −40 −30 −20 −10 0

12. 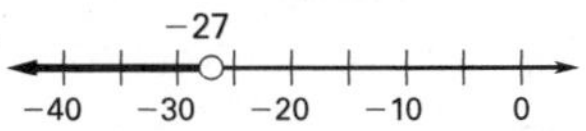 −27; −40 −30 −20 −10 0

13. 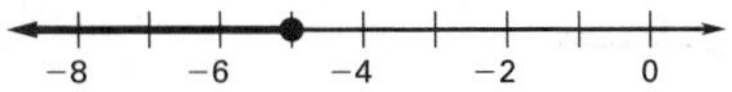 −8 −6 −4 −2 0

14.  32; −40 −20 0 20 40

15. 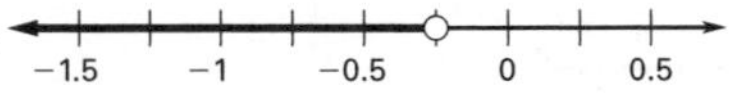 −1.5 −1 −0.5 0 0.5

16. 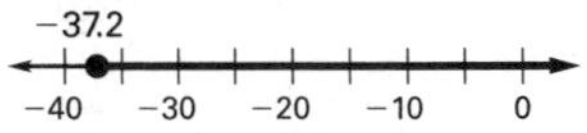 −37.2; −40 −30 −20 −10 0

17. 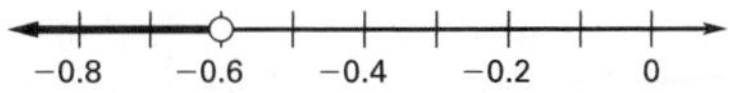 −0.8 −0.6 −0.4 −0.2 0

18. 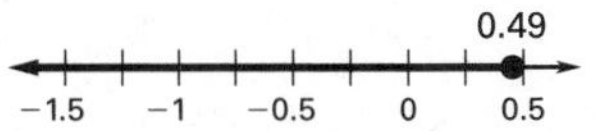 0.49; −1.5 −1 −0.5 0 0.5

19. 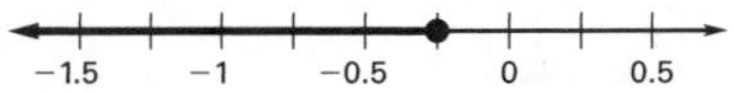 −1.5 −1 −0.5 0 0.5

20. 37.5; 0 20 40 60 80

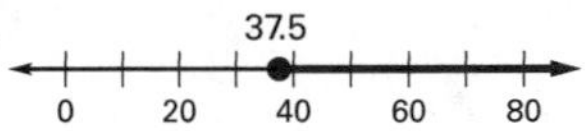

21.

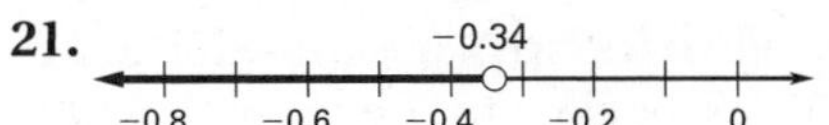

22. 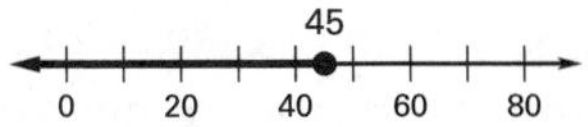 45; 0 20 40 60 80

23. 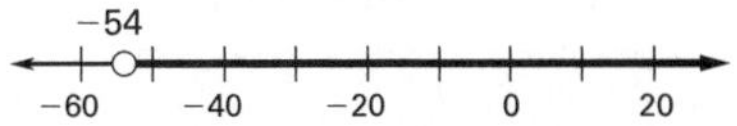 −54; −60 −40 −20 0 20

24. 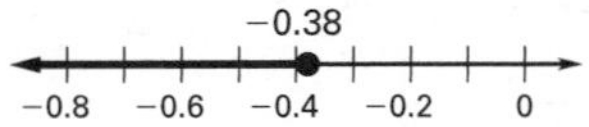 −0.38; −0.8 −0.6 −0.4 −0.2 0

25. 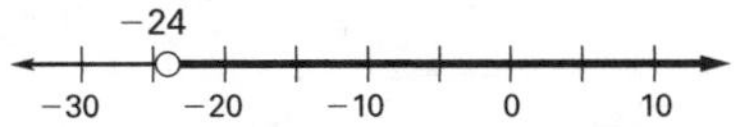 −24; −30 −20 −10 0 10

26. 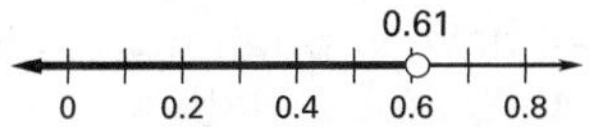 0.61; 0 0.2 0.4 0.6 0.8

6.2 Problem Solving (pp. 367–368)

41. b. No; the area added by increasing both the length and the width by 20 feet can be divided into 2 rectangles (80 feet by 20 feet and 82 feet by 20 feet) and 1 square (20 feet by 20 feet). The 400 square feet of the square is large enough to hold one horse, and the rectangular areas will be able to hold additional horses.

Quiz for Lessons 6.1–6.2 (p. 368)

1. **2.**

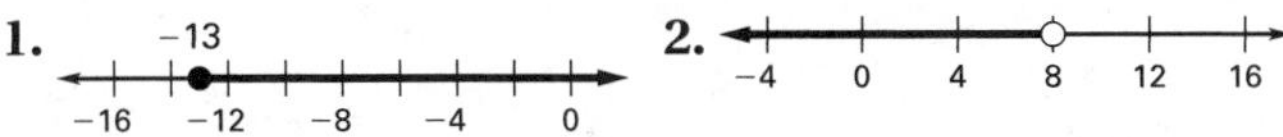

3. 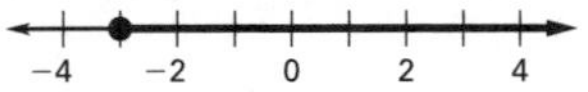 −4  −2 0 2 4

4. 13; 0 4 8 12 16

5. **6.**

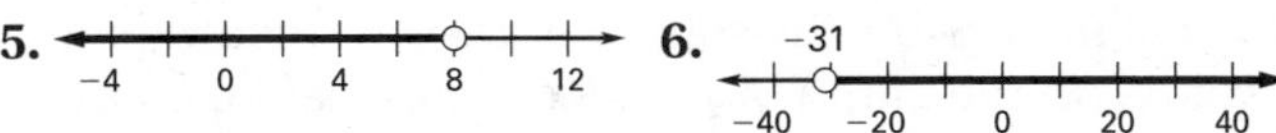

7. 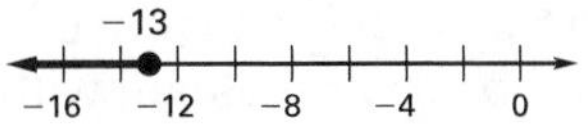 −13; −16 −12 −8 −4 0

8. 28; −40 −20 0 20 40

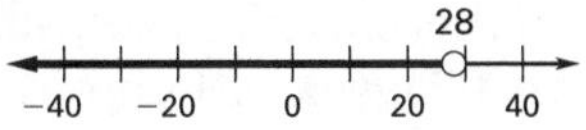

9. 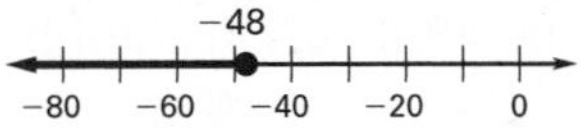 −48; −80 −60 −40 −20 0

6.3 Problem Solving (pp. 373–374)

41. a.

Pitches per inning, p	15	16	17	18	19
Total number of pitches, t	98	101	104	107	110

42. c. More than \$875; for price $p > 400$, the tax paid in the 4% sales tax state is $0.04p$, and the tax paid in the other state is $0.05(p - 175)$, or $0.05p - 8.75$. To find the values of p for which the first expression is less than the second, solve the inequality $0.04p < 0.05p - 8.75$ to get $p > \frac{8.75}{0.01}$, or $p > 875$. Check $p = \$900$: The tax paid in the 4% sales tax state is $0.04(\$900) = \$36$ and the tax paid in the other state is $0.05(\$900 - \$175) = \$36.25$.

ADDITIONAL ANSWERS

6.3 Problem Solving Workshop (pp. 375–376) **2.** At most 4 games; Method 1: Work backward. Begin with \$400 and subtract the cost of the console to find out how much money you have to spend on games: \$400 − \$259 = \$141. Make a table of values showing the amount of money you have left after buying various numbers of games.

Number of games bought	Amount of money left
0	\$141
1	\$112
2	\$83
3	\$54
4	\$25

After buying 4 games, you will not have enough money left to buy a fifth. You can buy at most 4 games. Method 2: Use a graph. Write and graph an equation that gives the total amount of money y you spend as a function of the number of games x that you buy: $y = 29x + 259$. Graph $y = 400$ on the same coordinate plane.

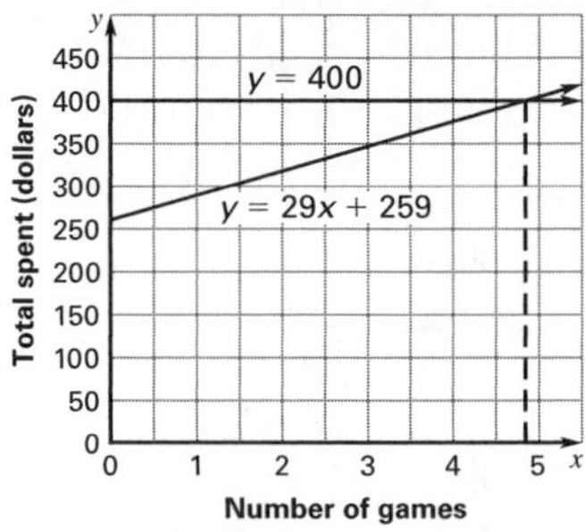

The graphs intersect between $x = 4$ and $x = 5$. Because you can spend at most \$400, the solutions are the x-coordinates of the points on the graph of $y = 29x + 259$ that lie on or below the graph of $y = 400$. Only integer values of x make sense in this situation, so you can buy at most 4 games.
4. At most 7 weeks; Method 1: Work backward. Begin with \$247 and make a table of values showing the amount of money you have left in your account after various numbers of \$20 withdrawals.

Number of \$20 withdrawals	Amount of money left in account
0	\$247
1	\$227
2	\$207
3	\$187
4	\$167
5	\$147
6	\$127
7	\$107
8	\$87

If you make \$20 withdrawals for 8 weeks your account balance will fall below the required \$100, so you can make \$20 withdrawals for at most 7 weeks. Method 2: Use a graph. Write and graph an equation that gives the total amount of money y in your account as a function of the number x of \$20 withdrawals that you make: $y = -20x + 247$. Graph $y = 100$ on the same coordinate plane.

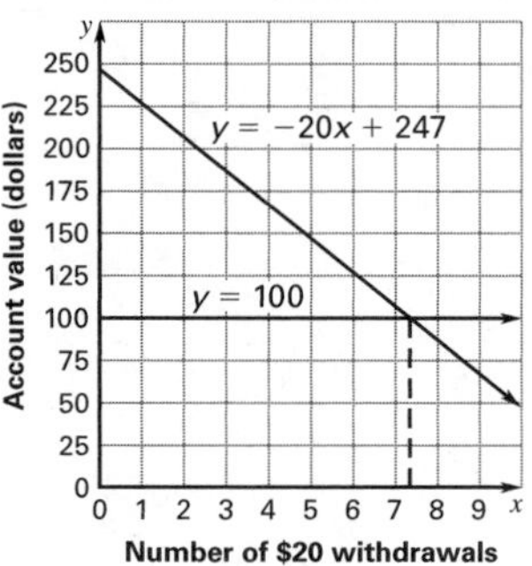

The graphs intersect between $x = 7$ and $x = 8$. Because your account must have at least \$100, the solutions are the x-coordinates of the points on the graph of $y = -20x + 247$ that lie on or above the graph of $y = 100$. Only integer values of x make sense in this situation, so you can make \$20 withdrawals for at most 7 weeks.

6.4 Guided Practice (pp. 380–383)

1. **2.**

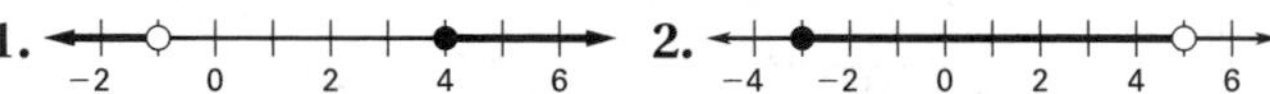

3. 4.5 **4.** 9

5. **6.**

6.4 Skill Practice (pp. 384–385)

9.

10.

11. $\frac{1}{4}$

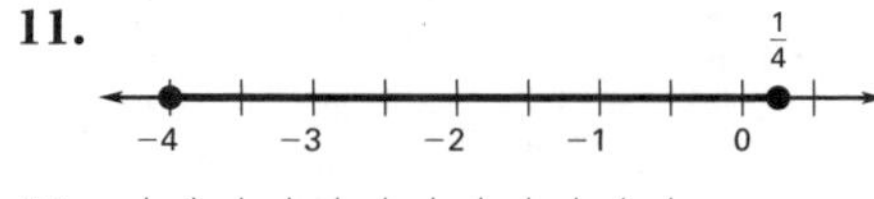

12.

13. $-\frac{1}{3}$

14. $-5\frac{1}{4}$ $-1\frac{1}{4}$

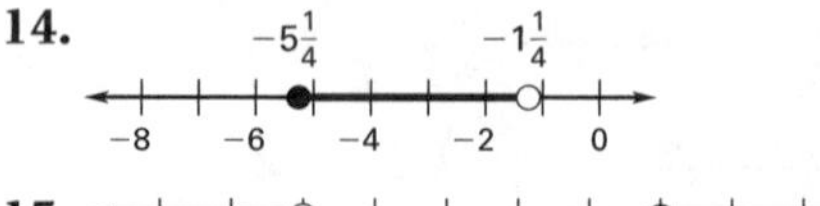

15.

16. −22 3

17. 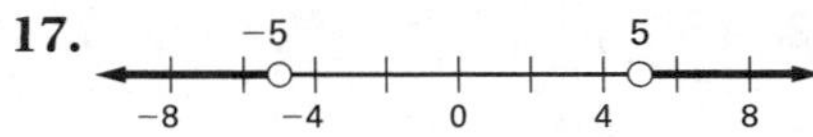

18.
−17
−30 −20 −10 0 10

19.
$-2\frac{1}{3}$
−4 0 4 8 12

20. 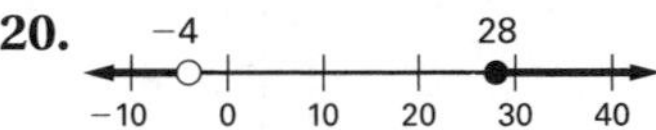

Extension (pp. 396–397)

1. 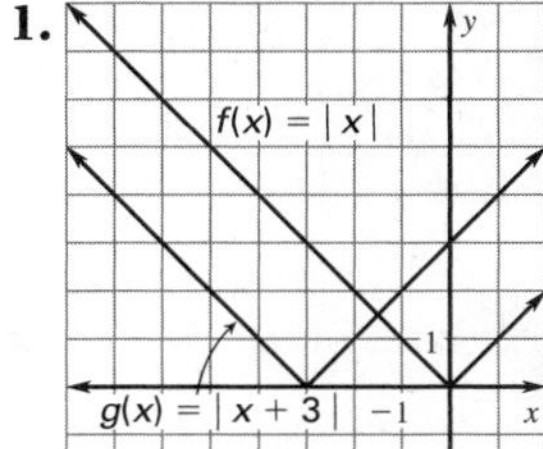

The graph of g is 3 units to the left of the graph of f.

2. 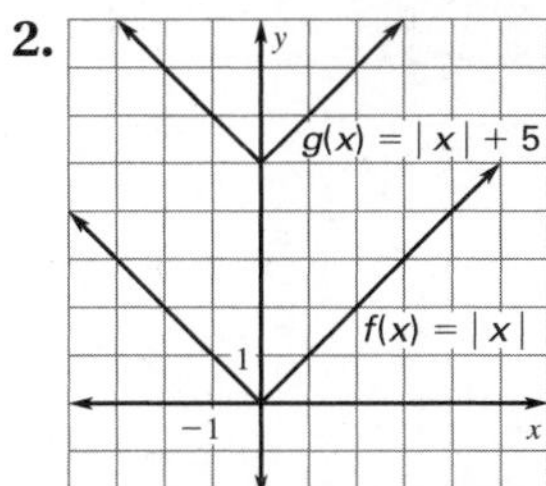

The graph of g is 5 units above the graph of f.

3. 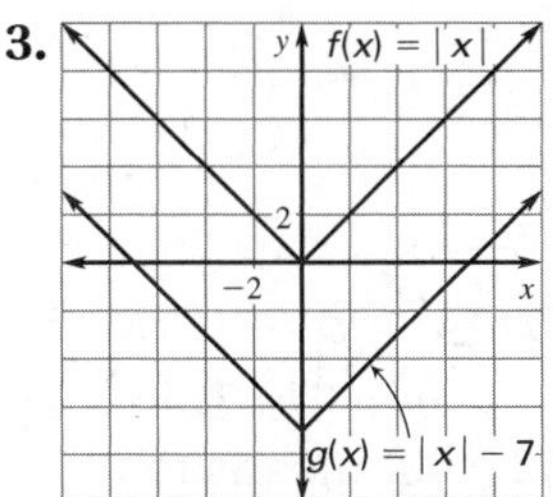

The graph of g is 7 units below the graph of f.

4. 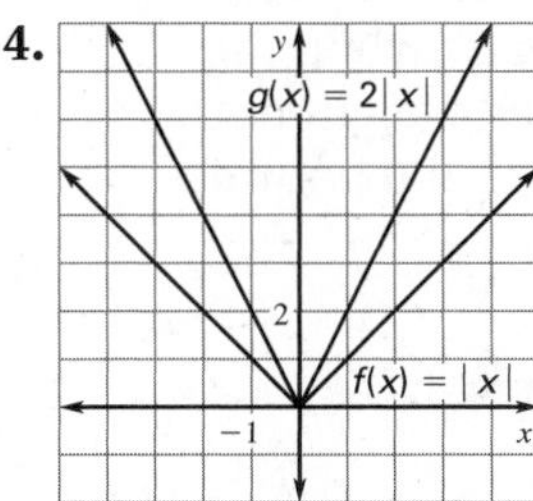

The graph of g opens up and is narrower than the graph of f.

5. 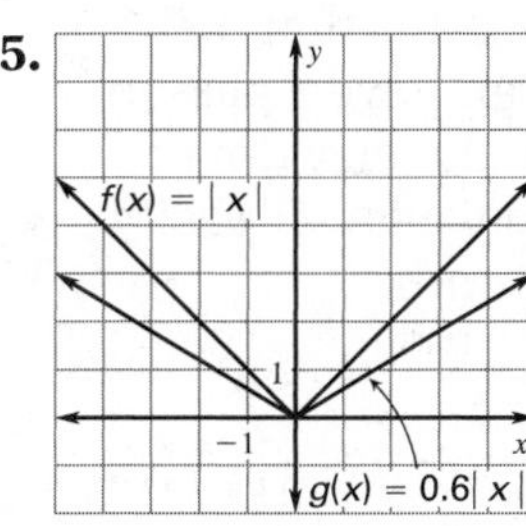

The graph of g opens up and is wider than the graph of f.

6. 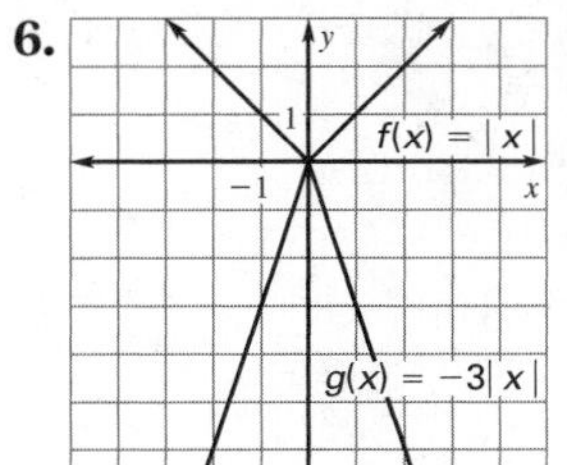

The graph of g opens down and is narrower than the graph of f.

6.6 Problem Solving (pp. 402–403)

38. a.

Measured compression, p (lb)	275	325	375	425	475
Absolute deviation from 350 (lb)	75	25	25	75	125

6.6 Mixed Review (p. 403)

42. 43. 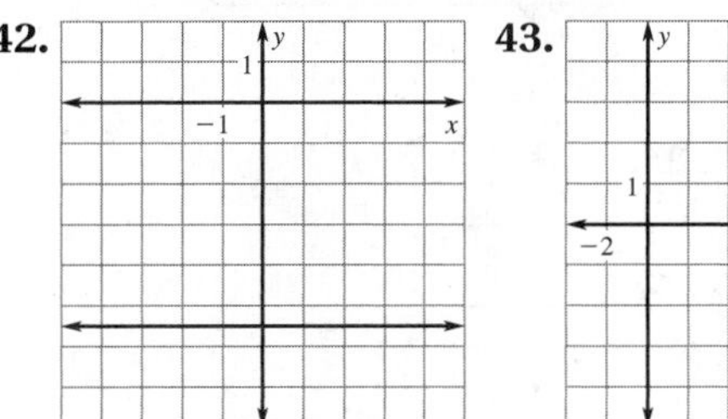

44. 45. 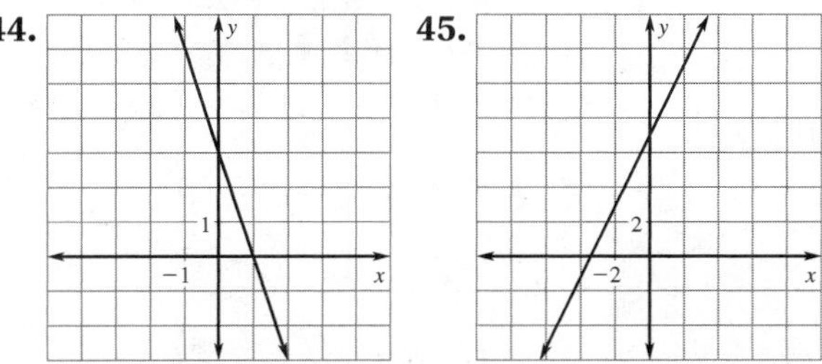

46. 47. 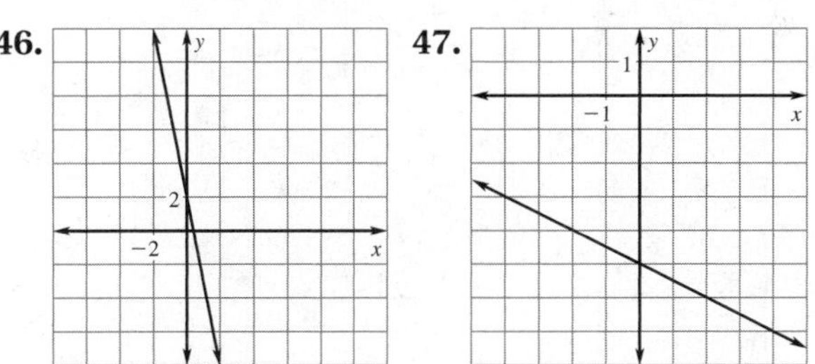

6.7 Skill Practice (pp. 409–410)

17. 18. 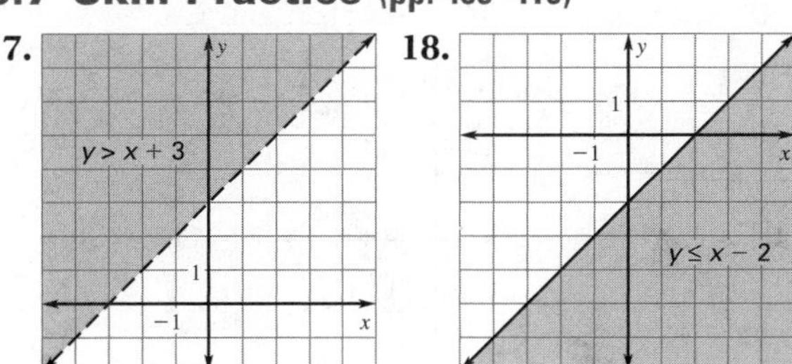

ADDITIONAL ANSWERS

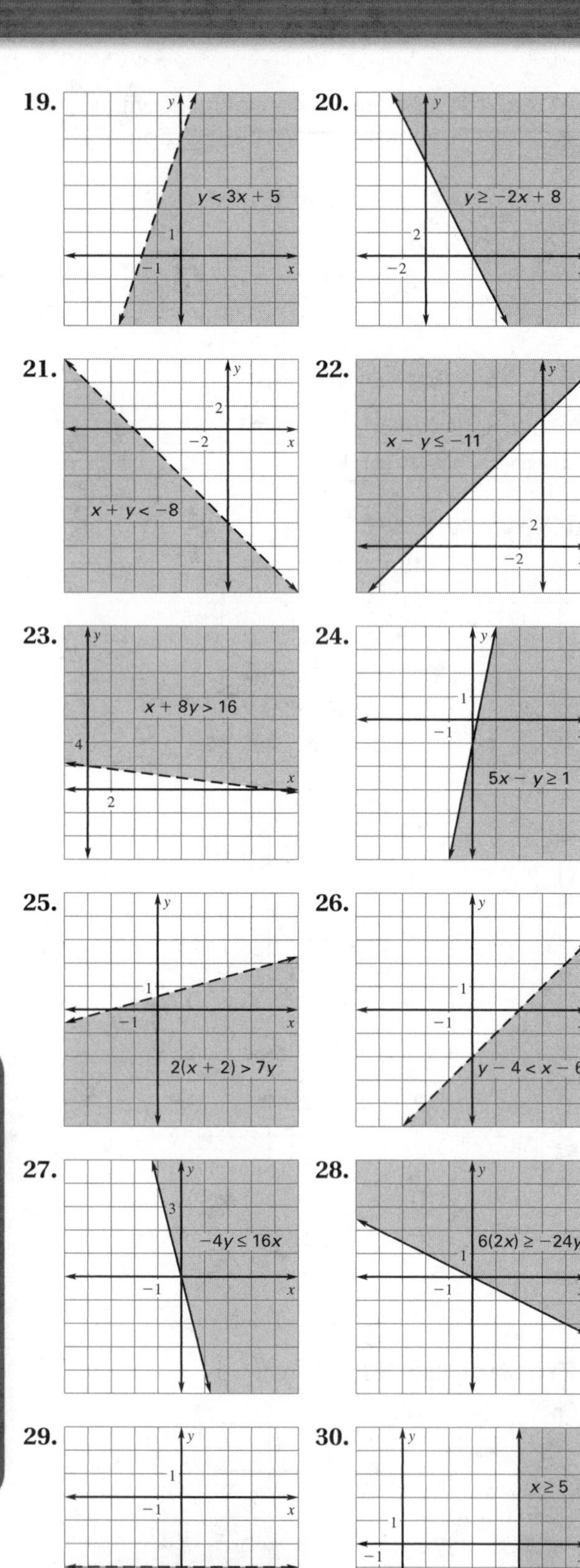

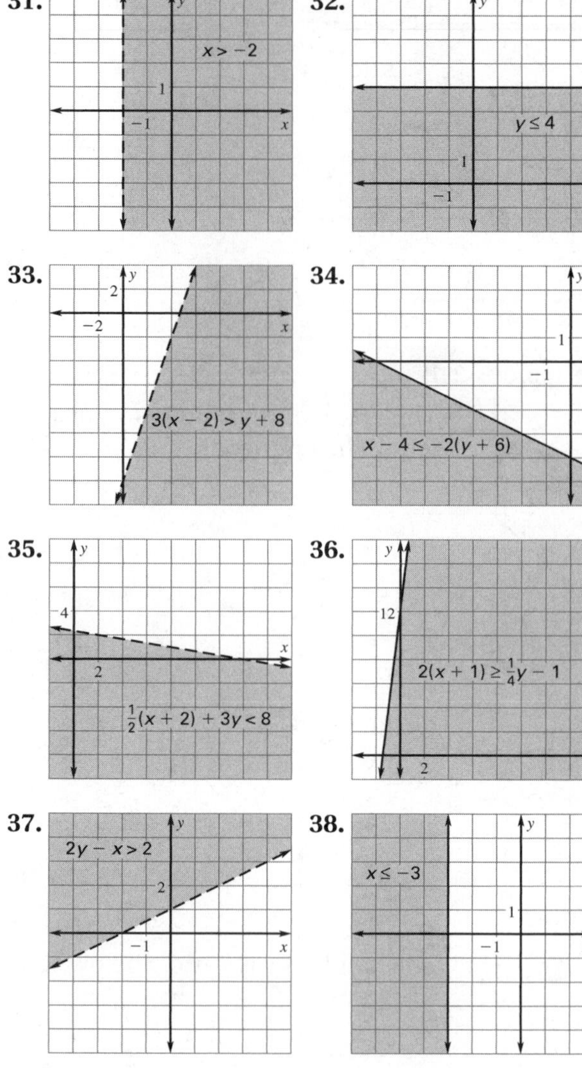

6.7 Problem Solving (pp. 410–412)

53.

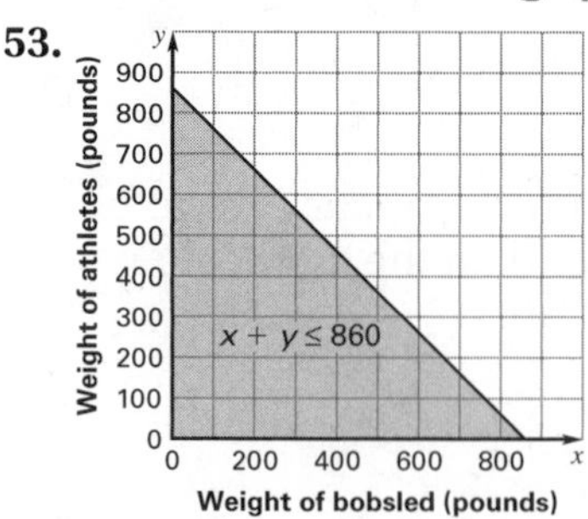

Sample answer: The solution (450, 400) means that the bobsled can weigh 450 pounds when the combined weight of the athletes is 400 pounds.

54.

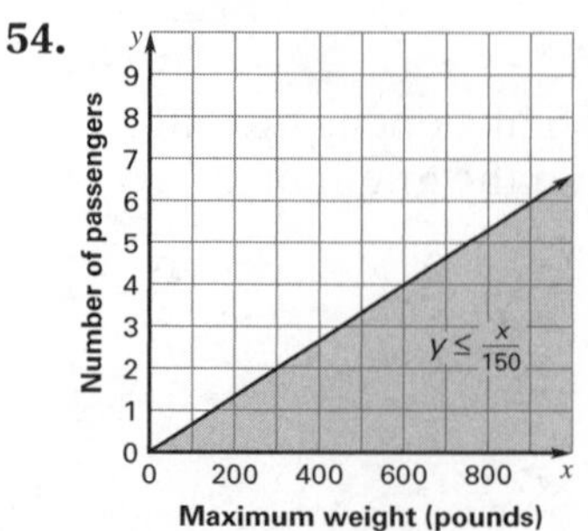

Sample answer: The solution (1200, 8) means that the elevator can have 8 passengers when the elevator's maximum weight capacity is 1200 pounds.

ADDITIONAL ANSWERS

60. a.

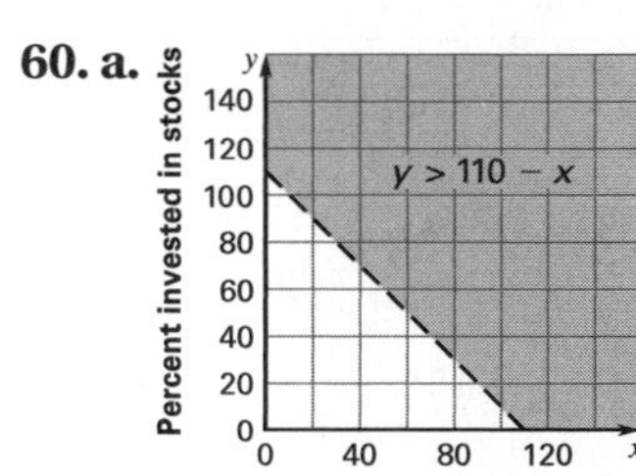

b. Greater than 80% and up to 100%; substitute $x = 30$ into the inequality to get $y > 110 - 30$, so the investor should invest more than 80% of the money in stocks. The investor cannot invest more than 100% of the money in stocks.

61. a. sinks:

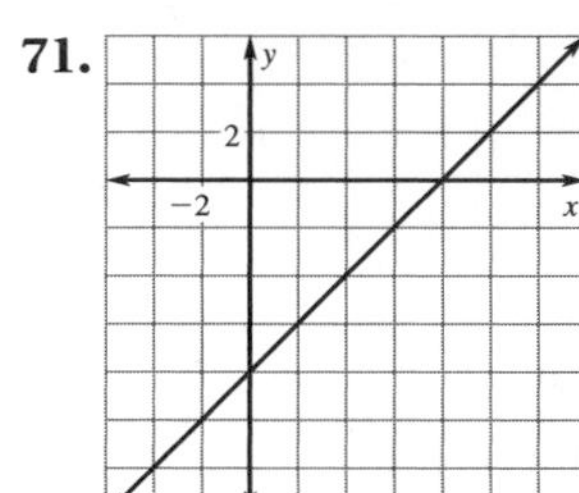

floats:

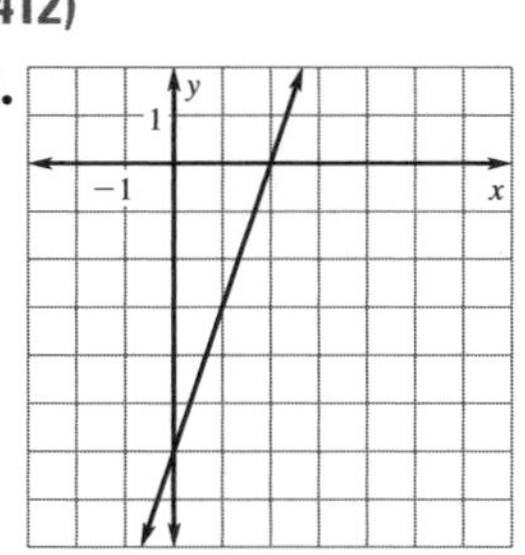

6.7 Mixed Review (p. 412)

71.

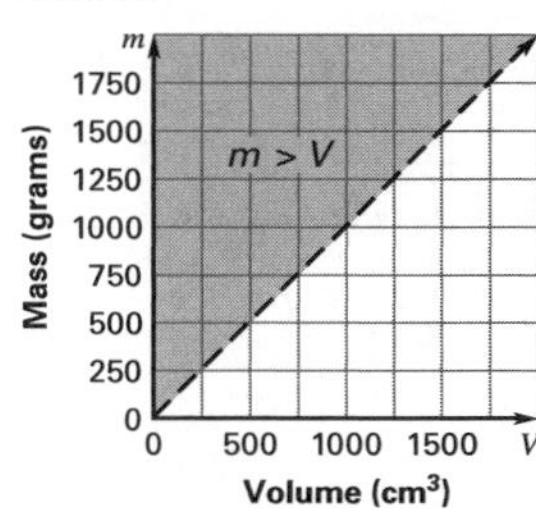

72.

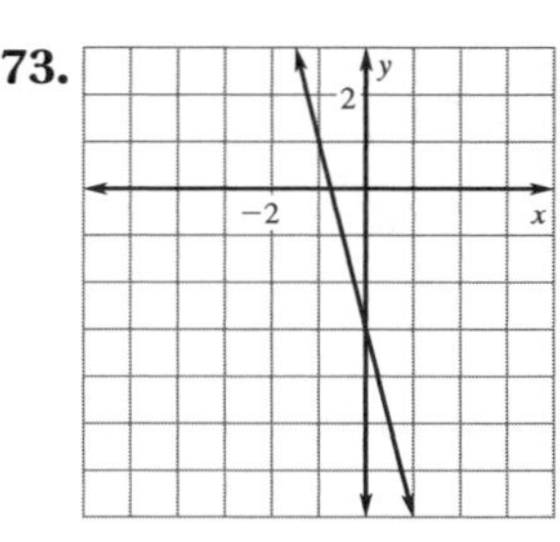

73.

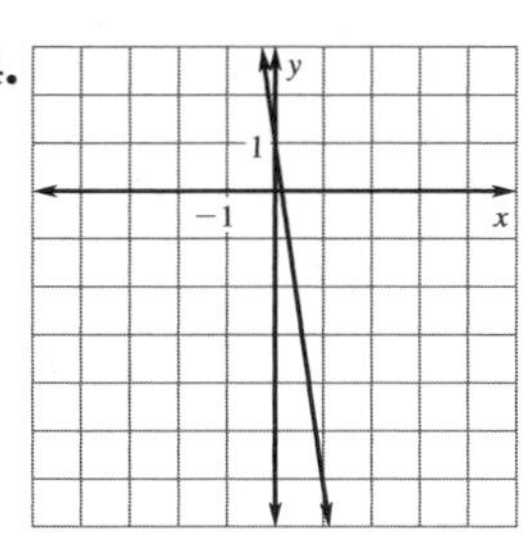

74.

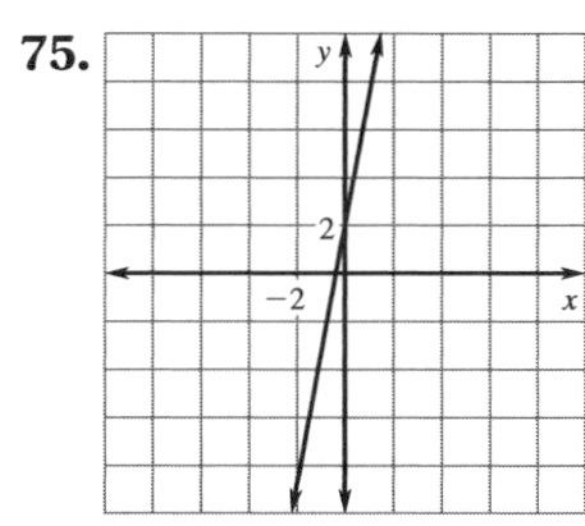

75.

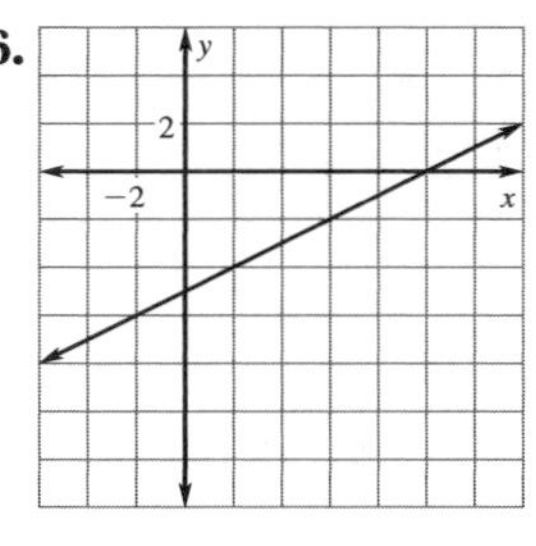

76.

Quiz for Lessons 6.5–6.7 (p. 412)

4.

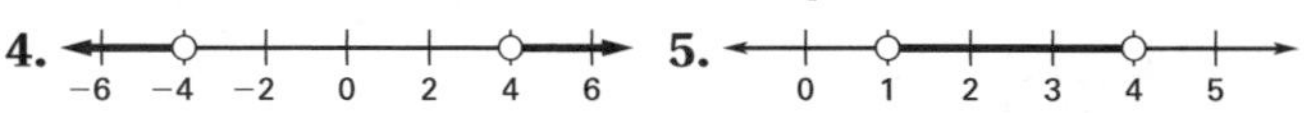

5.

6.

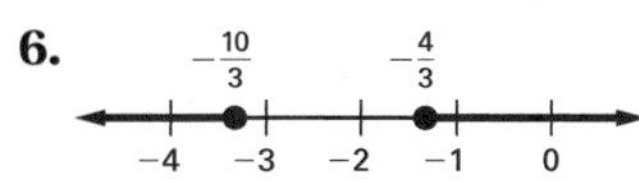

7.

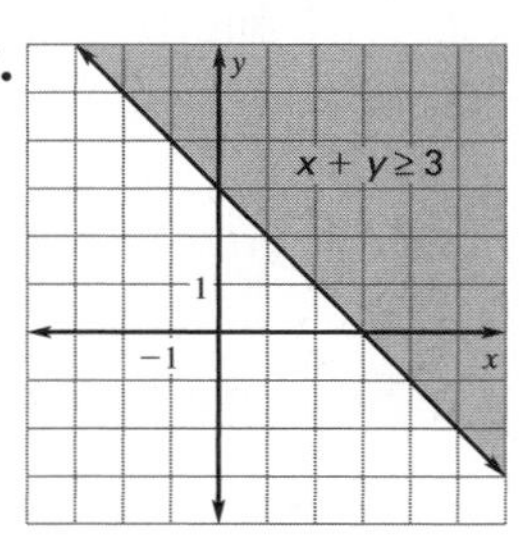

8.

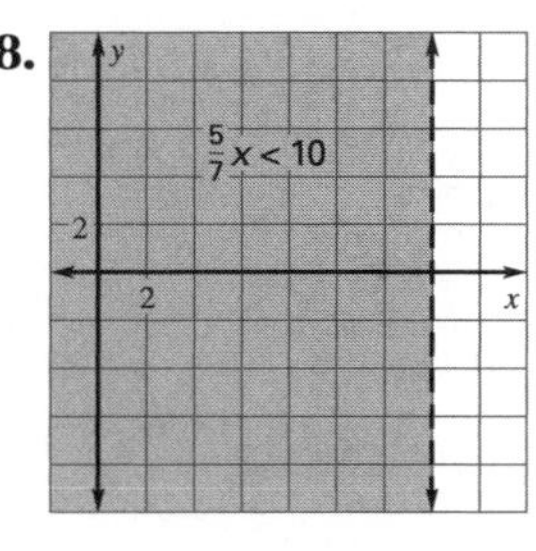

9.

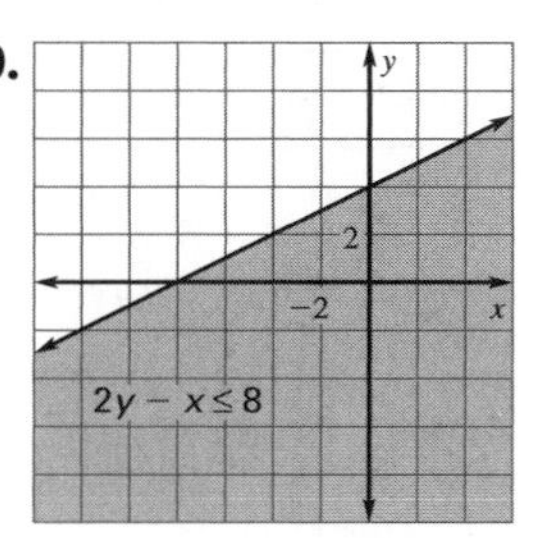

Chapter Test (p. 419)

29.

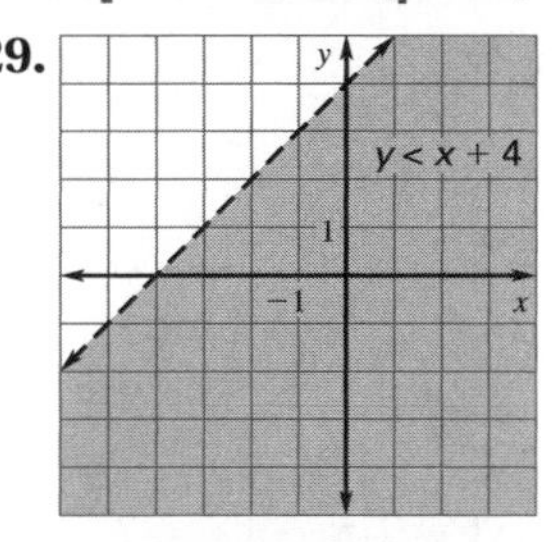

30.

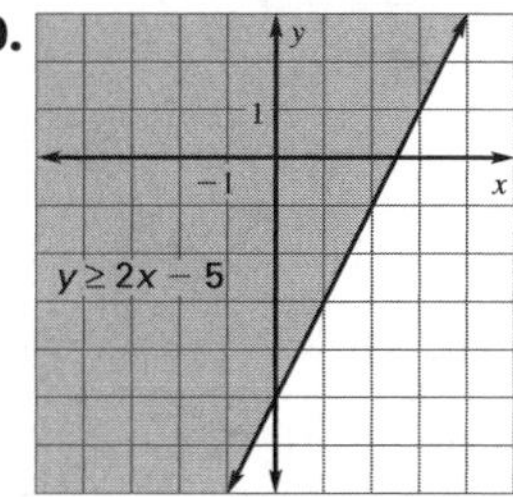

31.

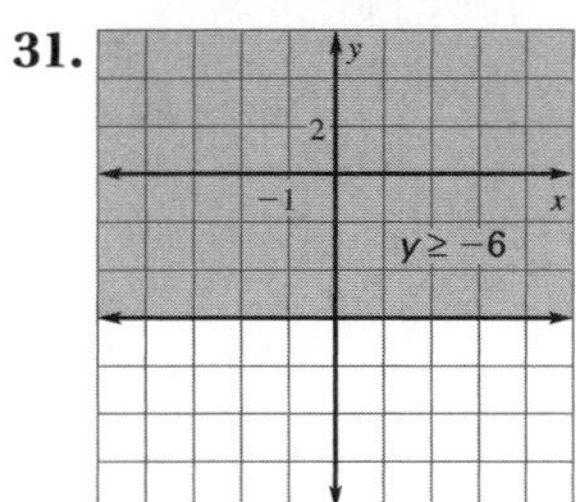

Chapter 7

7.3 Mixed Review (p. 450)

46.

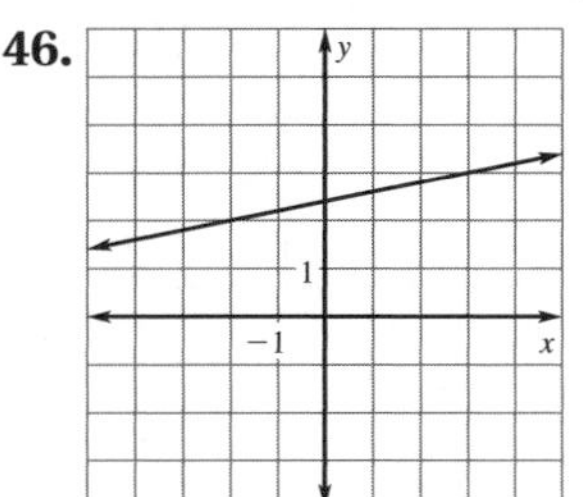

47.

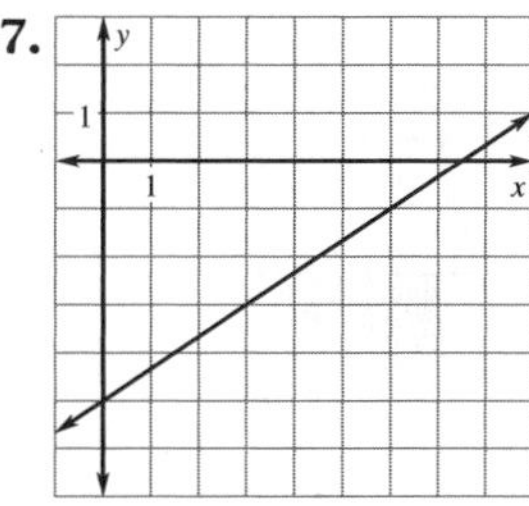

48. 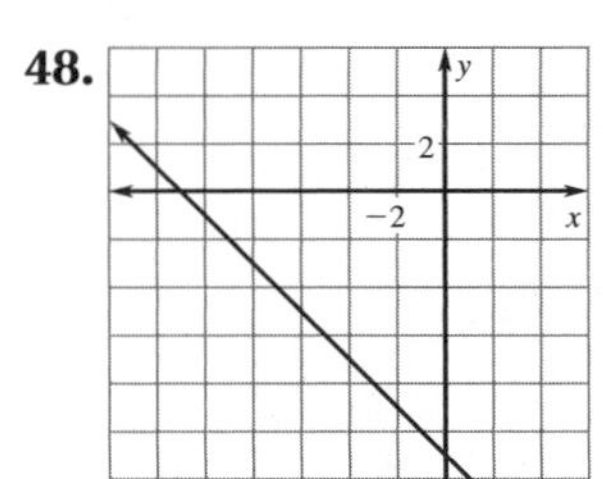

49. 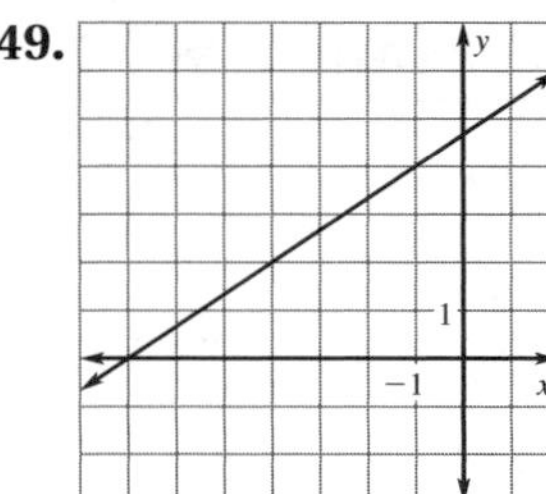

7.4 Mixed Review (p. 457)

45. 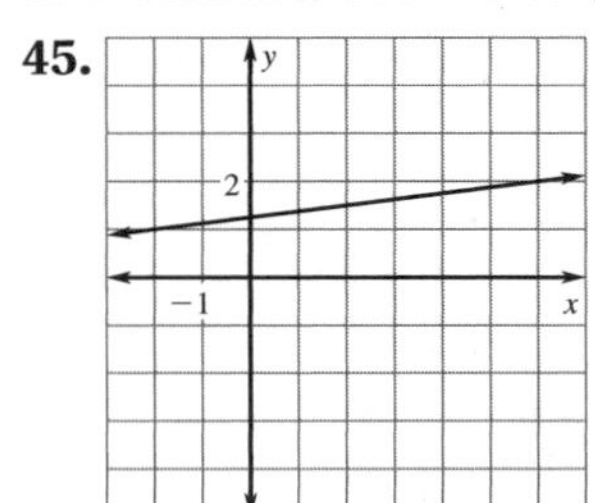

46. 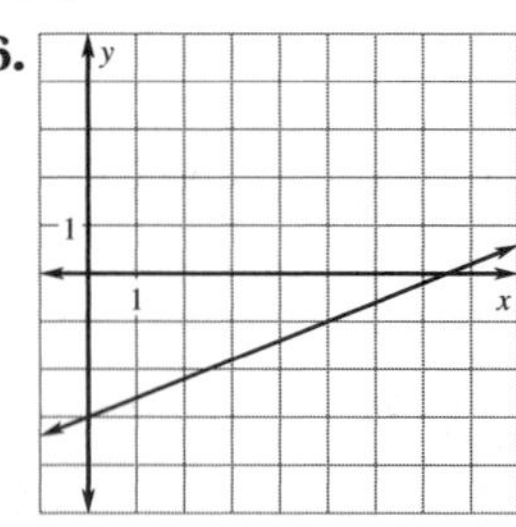

47. 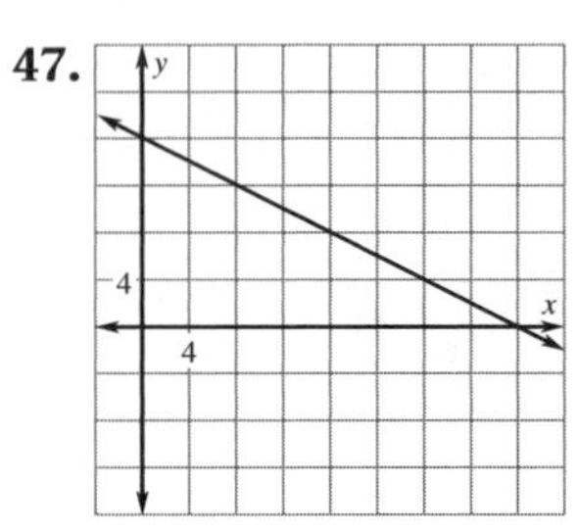

48. 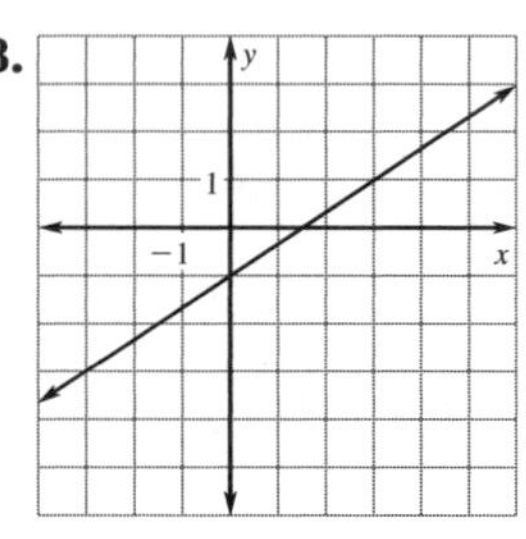

49. 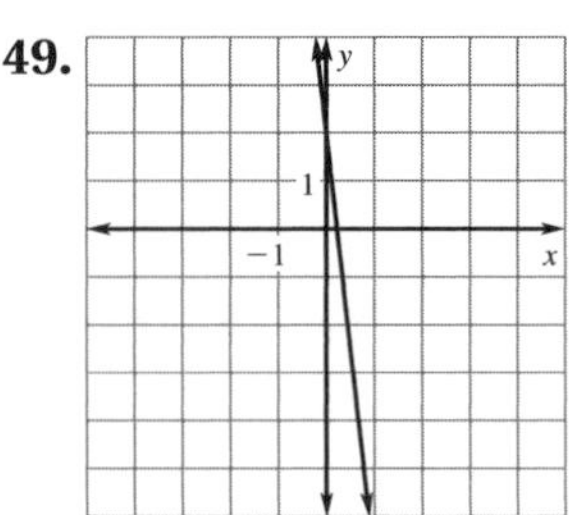

50. 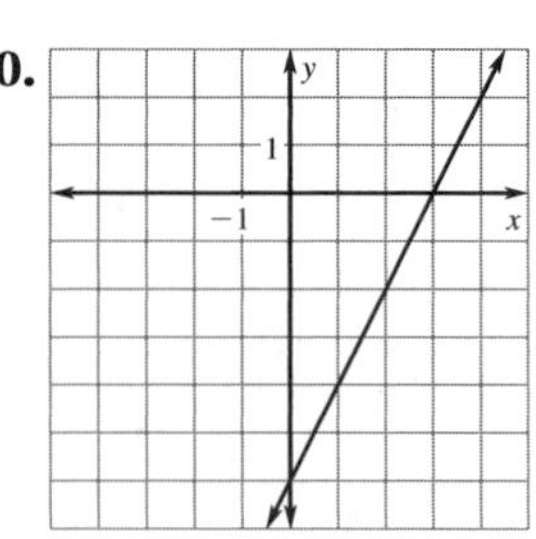

7.5 Mixed Review (p. 465)

46. 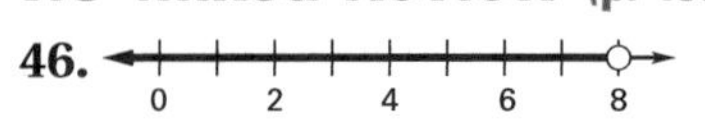

47. 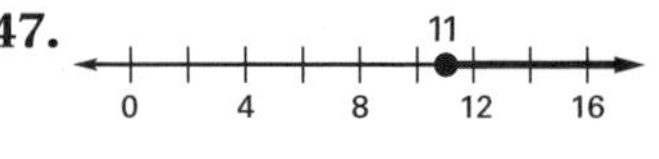

48. 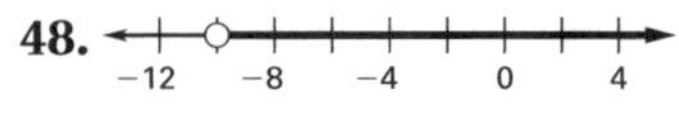

49. 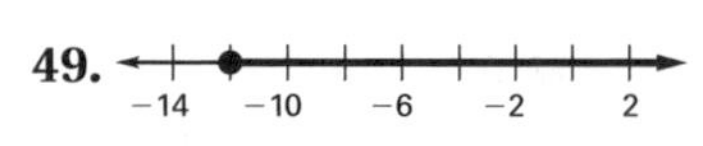

50. 

51. 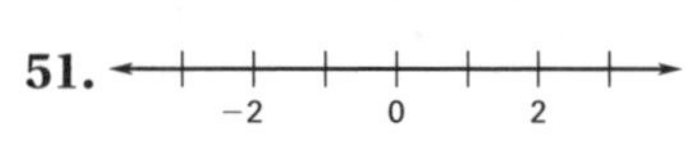

52. 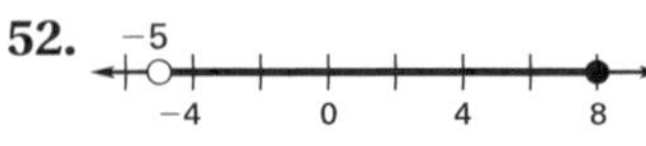

53. 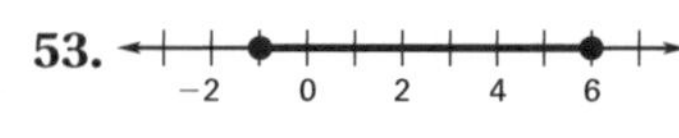

54. 55. 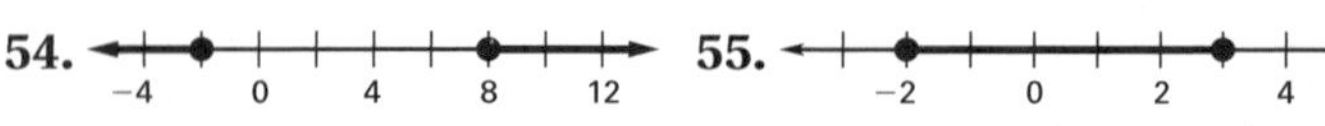

56. 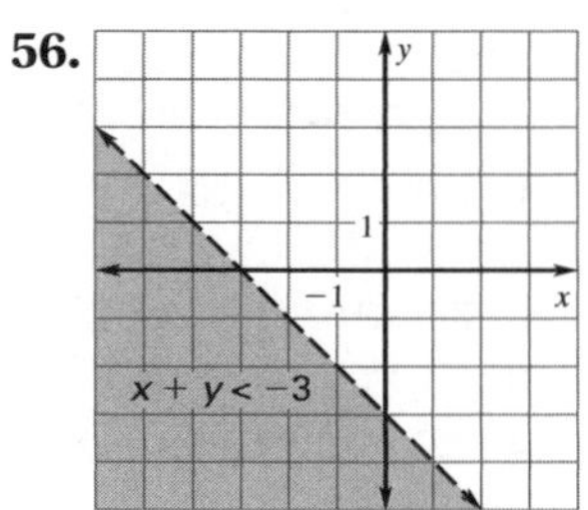

57. 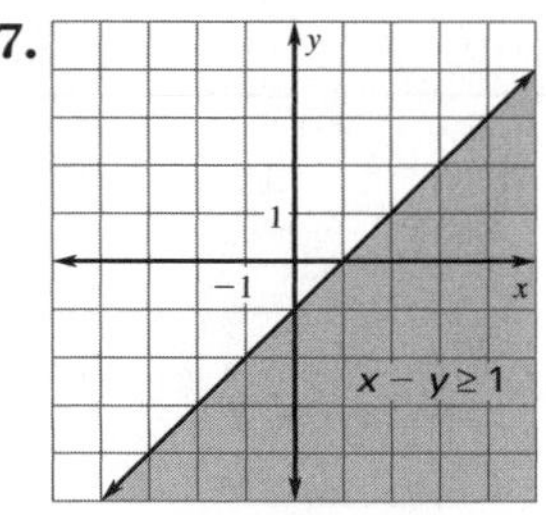

58. 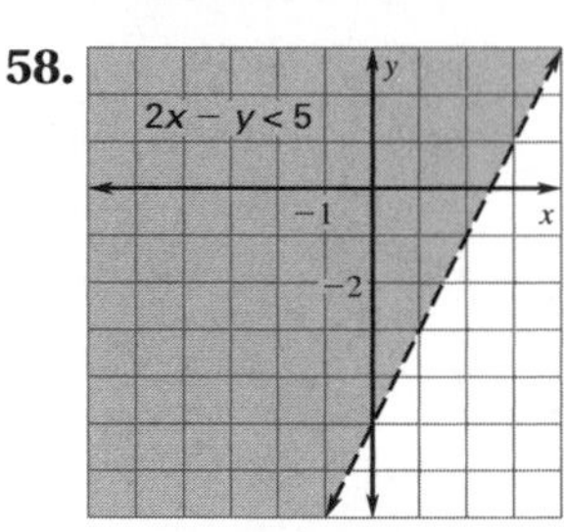

59. 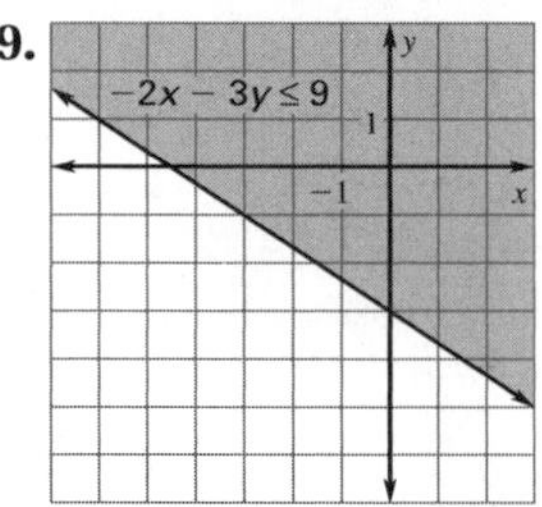

60. 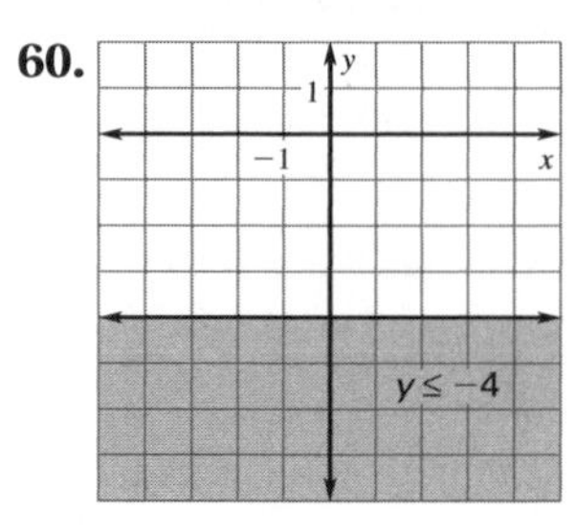

61. 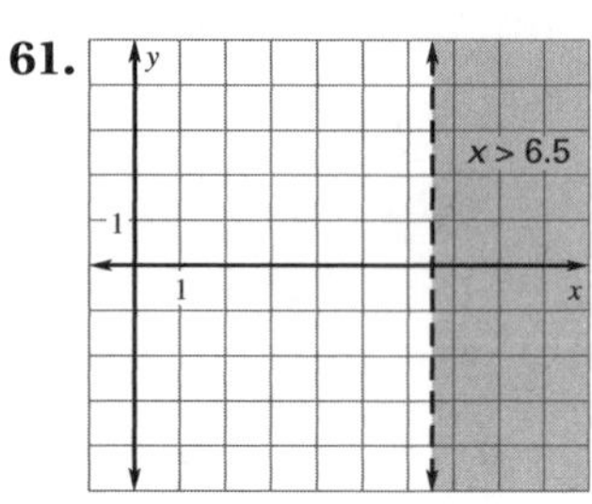

7.6 Guided Practice (pp. 467–468)

1. 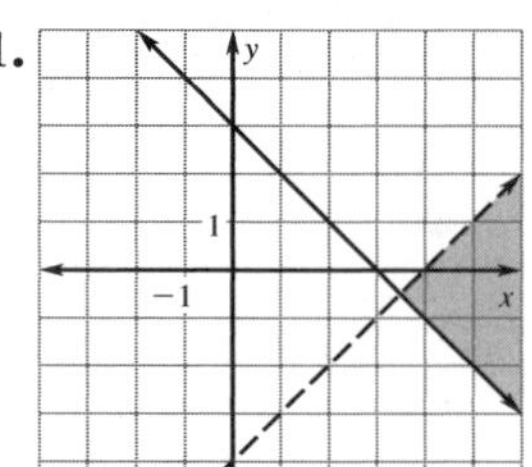

2. 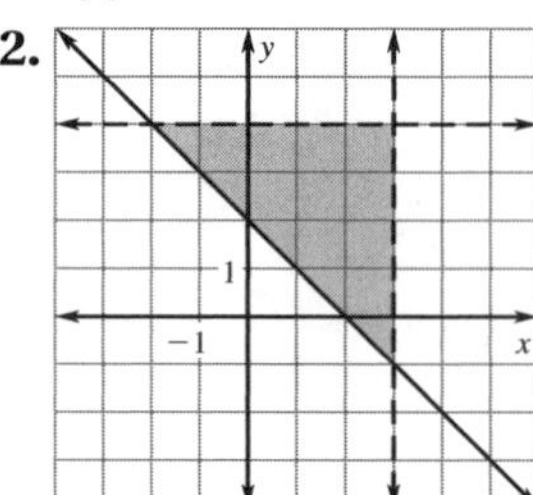

3. 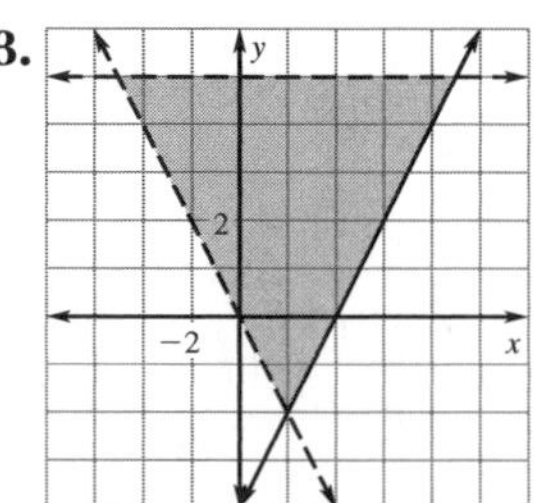

7.6 Skill Practice (pp. 469–470)

9. 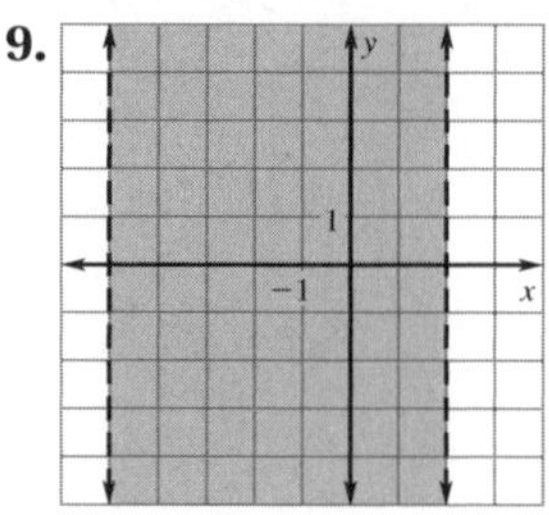

10. 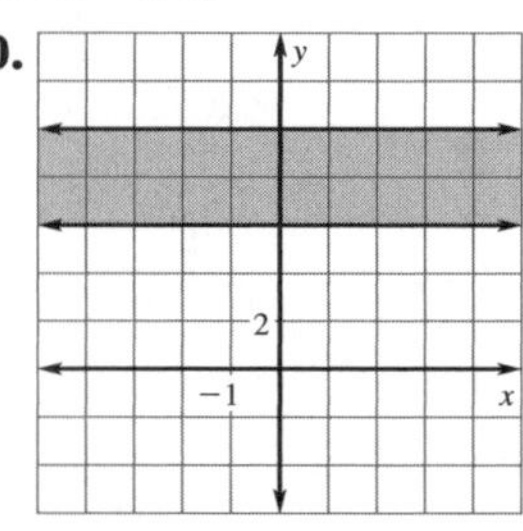

ADDITIONAL ANSWERS

11. 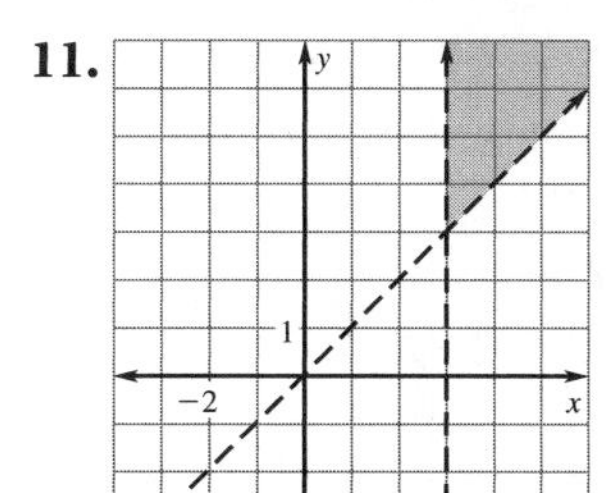

12. 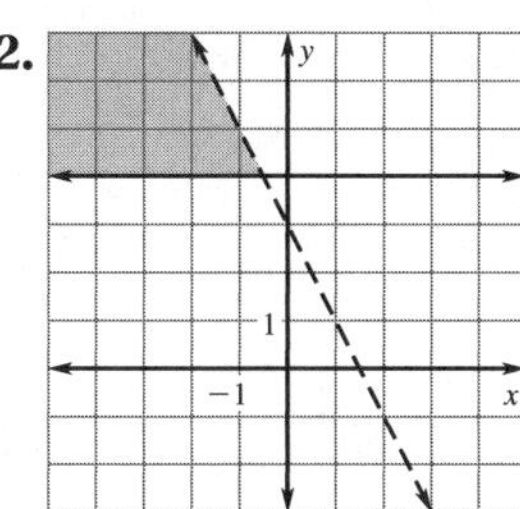

13. 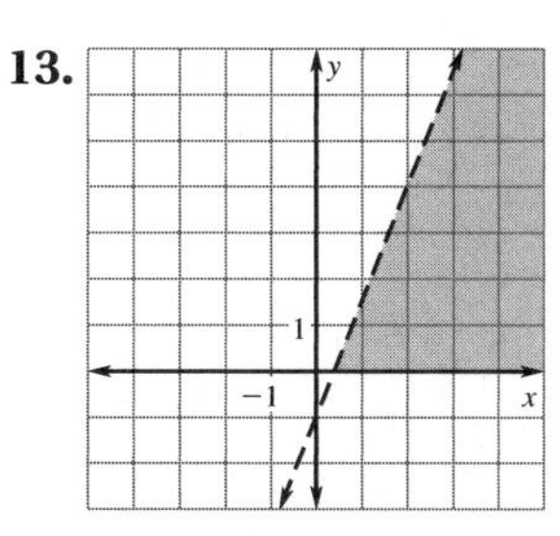

14. 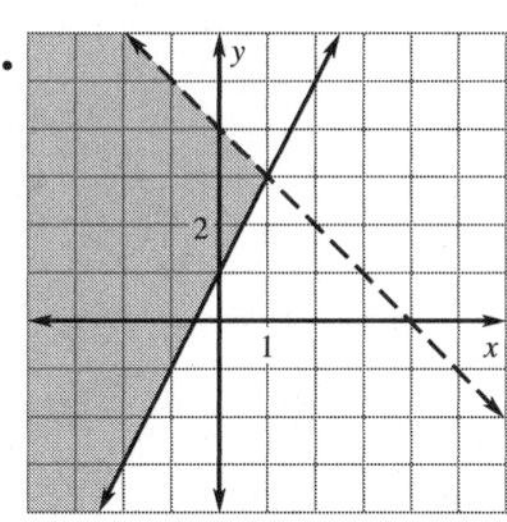

15. 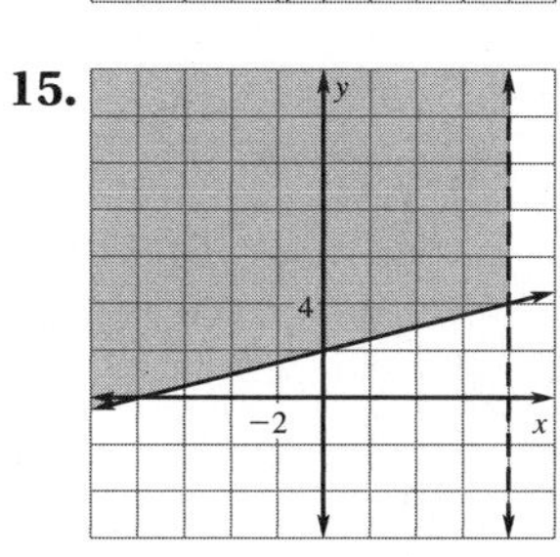

16. 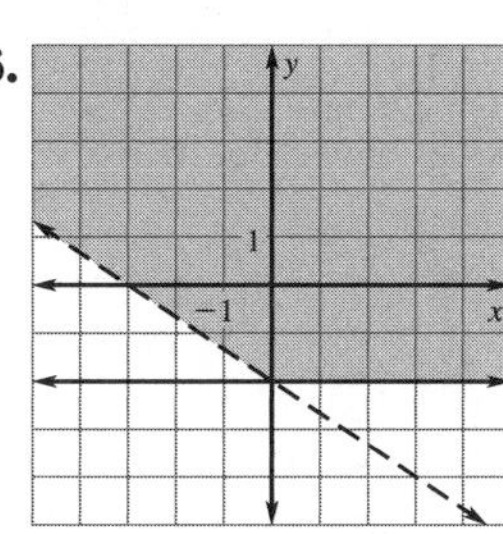

17. 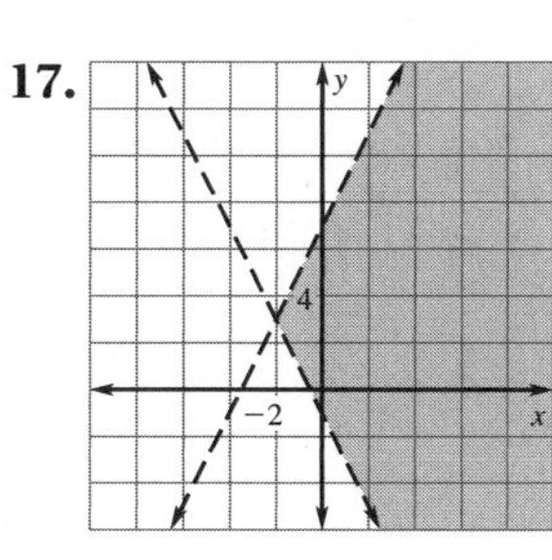

18. 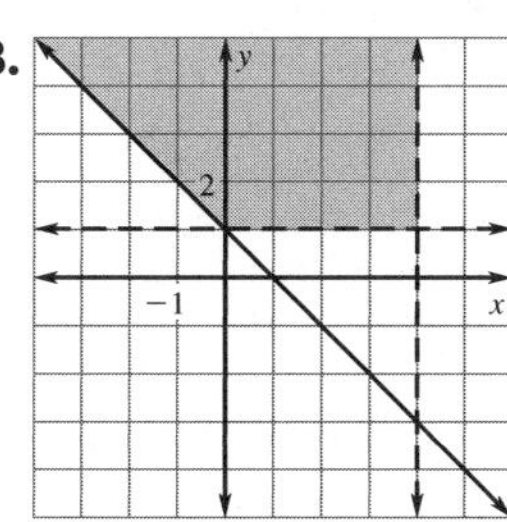

19. 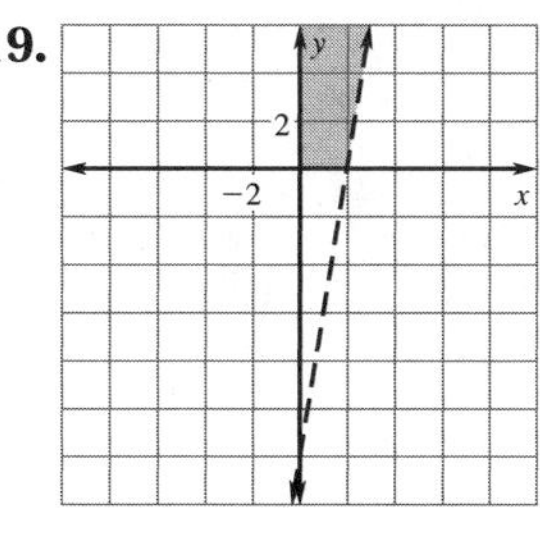

20. 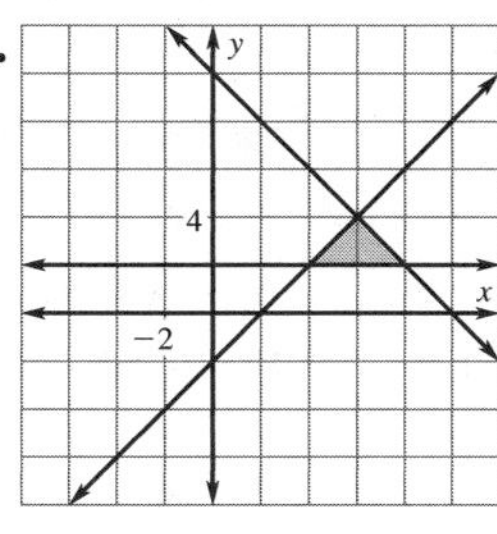

7.6 Problem Solving (pp. 471–472)

41. a. 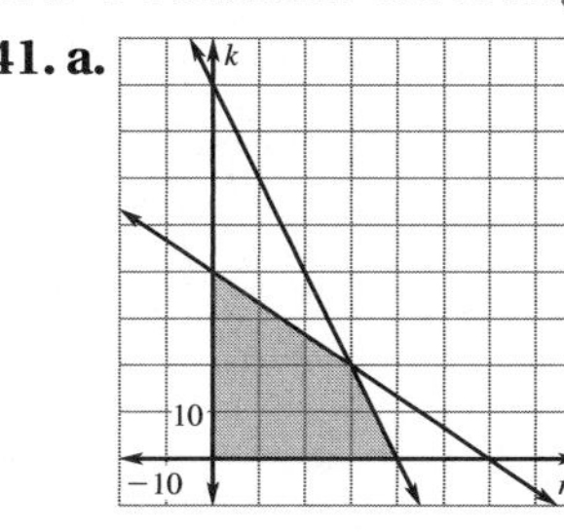

Quiz for Lessons 7.5–7.6 (p. 472)

1. 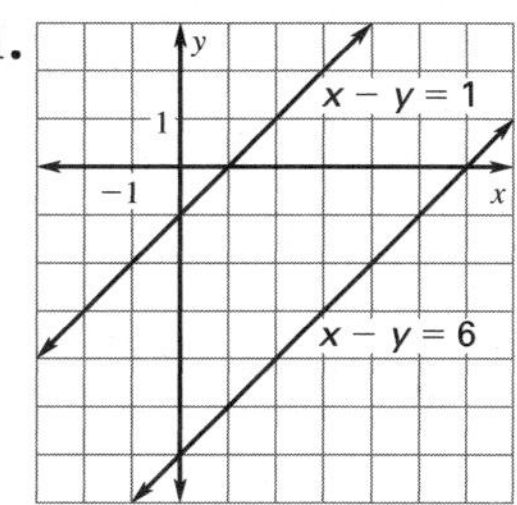

2. 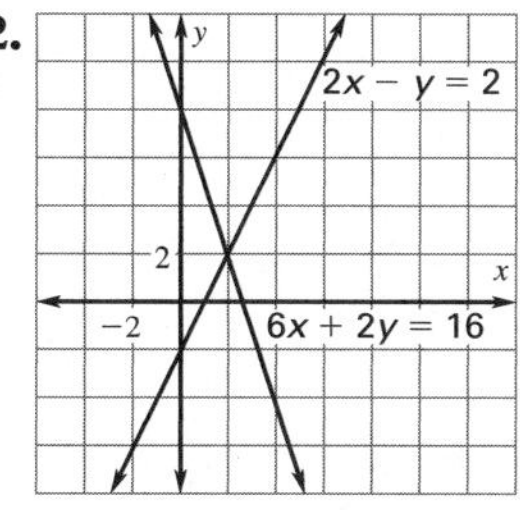

3. 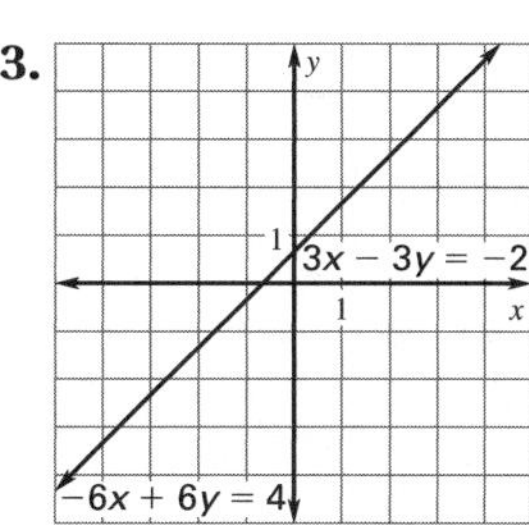

4. 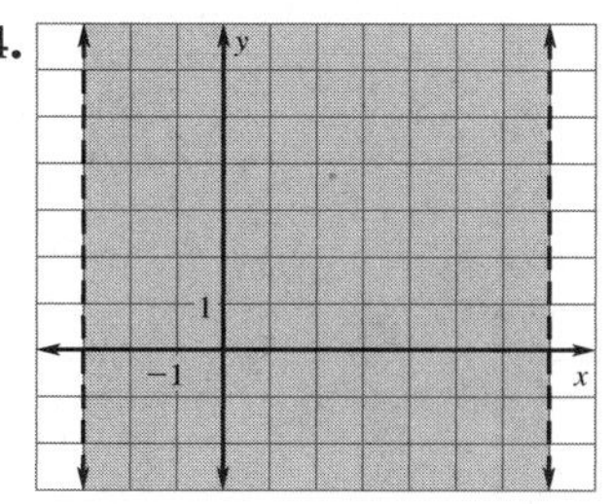

5. 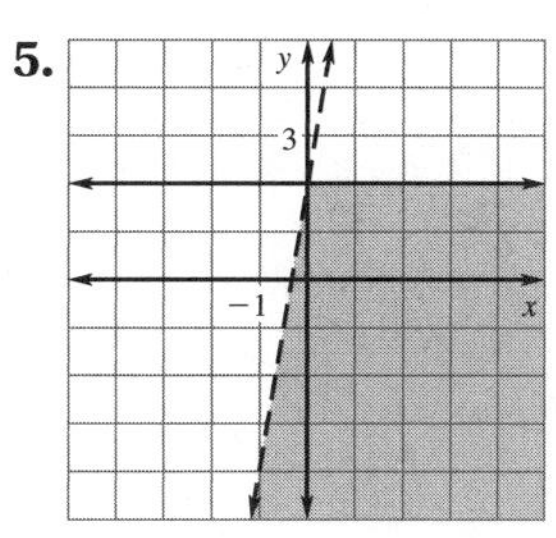

6. 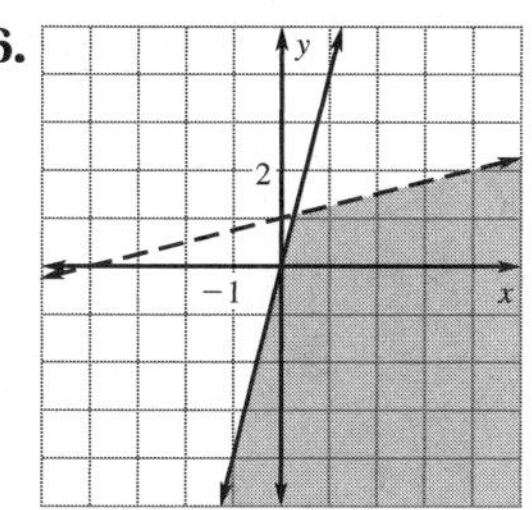

7. 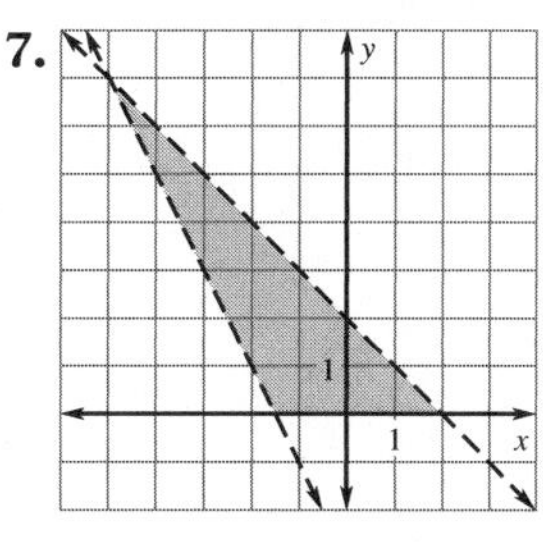

8. 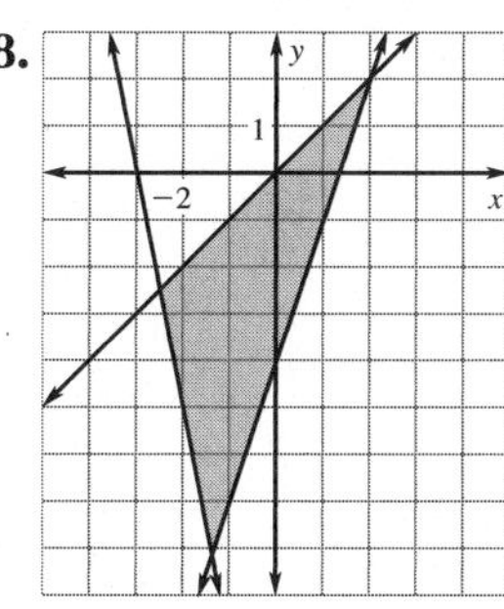

9. 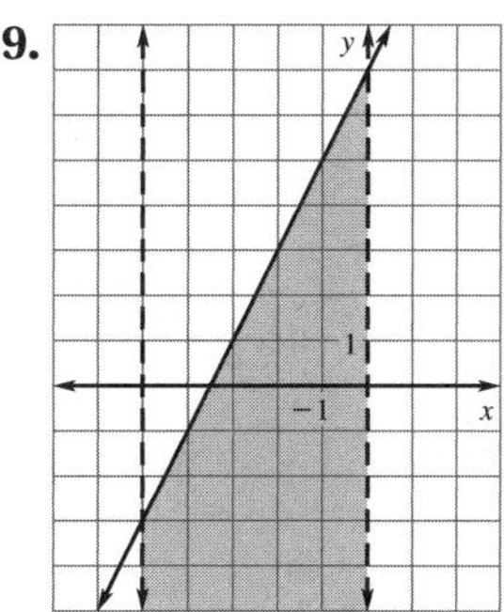

ADDITIONAL ANSWERS

Chapter 8

8.1 Mixed Review (p. 494)

66. 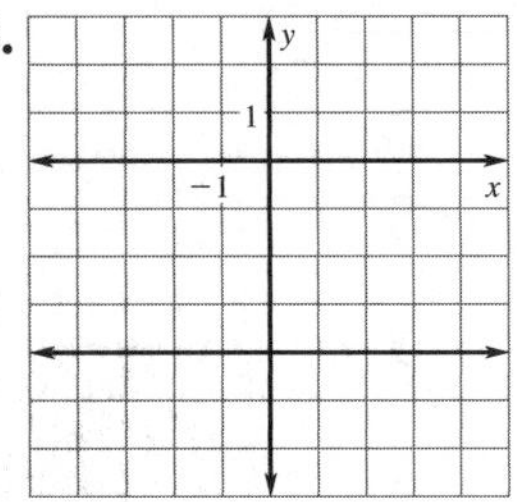

67. 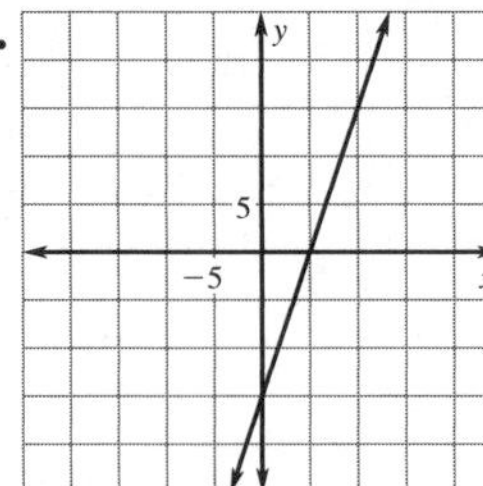

68. 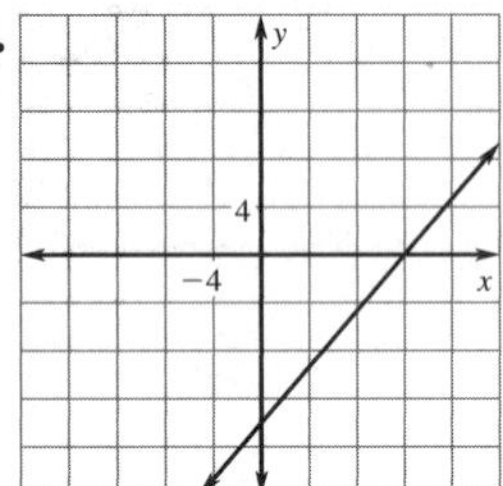

69. 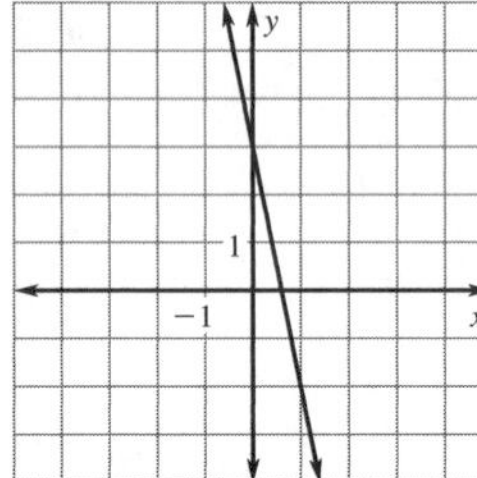

70. 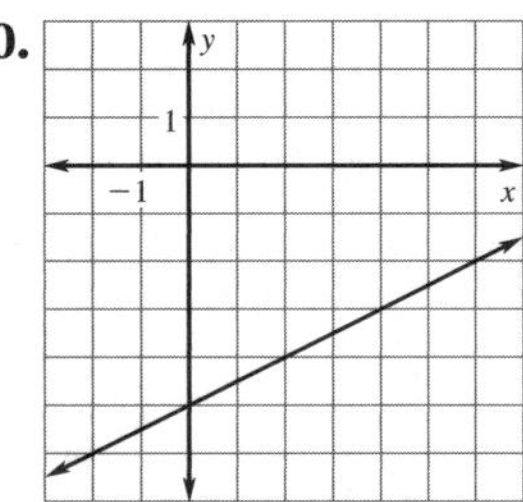

71. 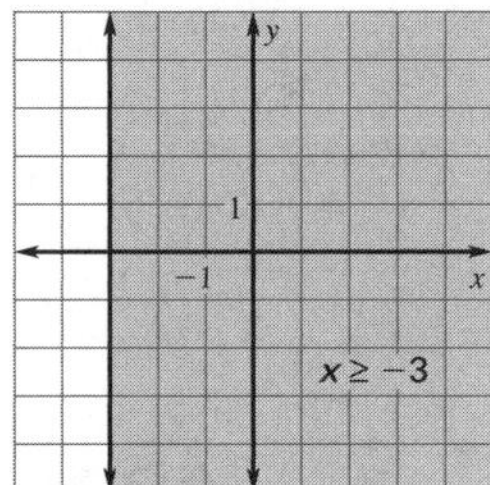

72. 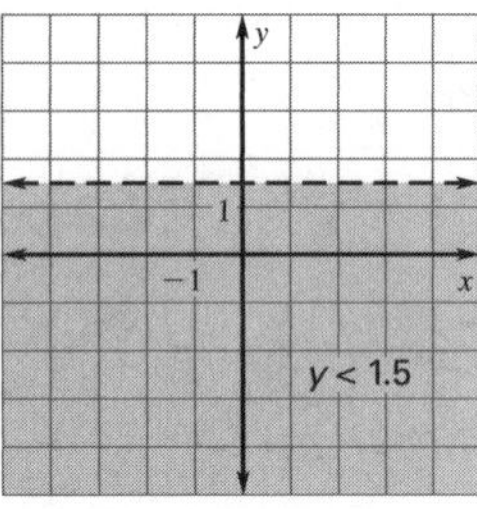

73. 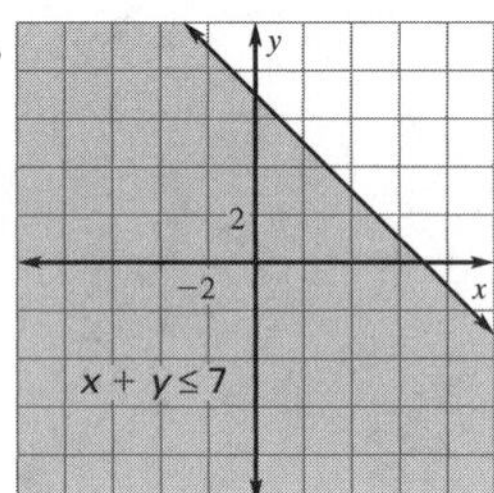

74. 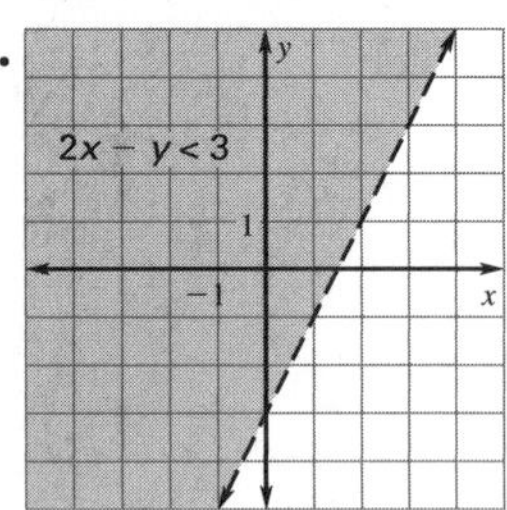

8.4 Mixed Review (p. 518)

69. 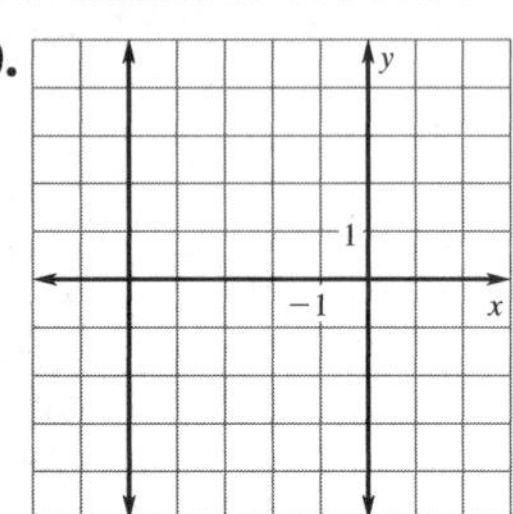

70. 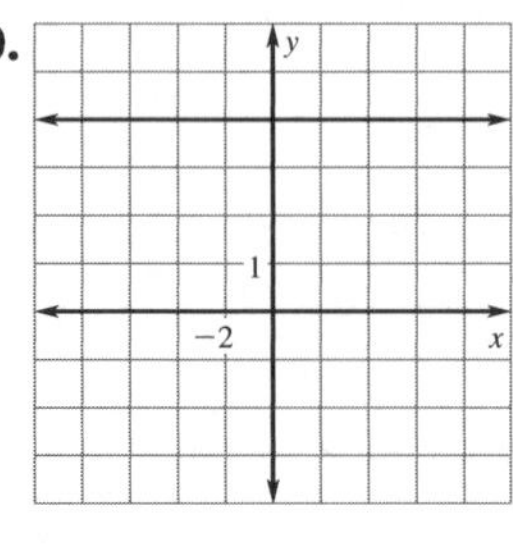

71. 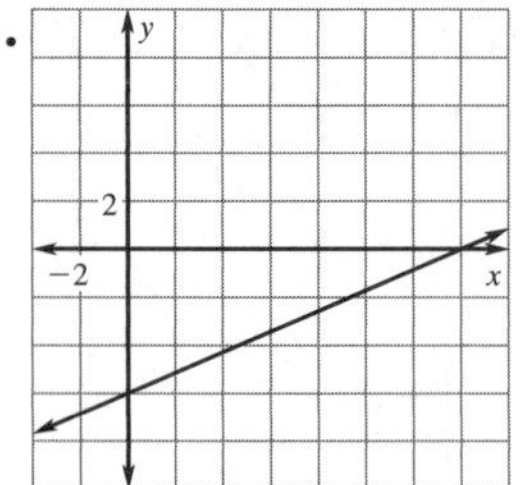

72. 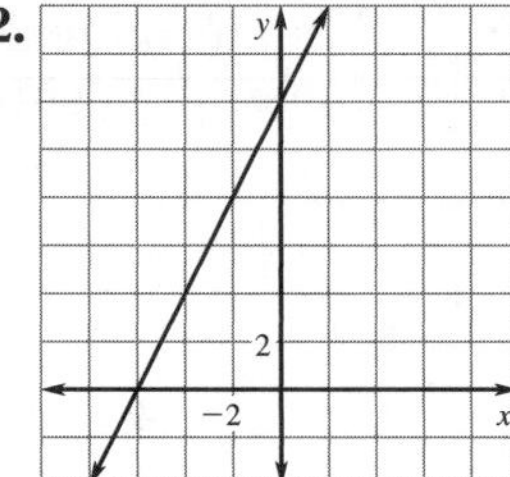

73. 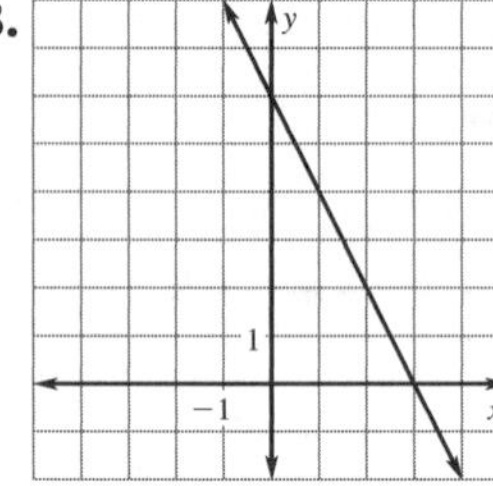

74. 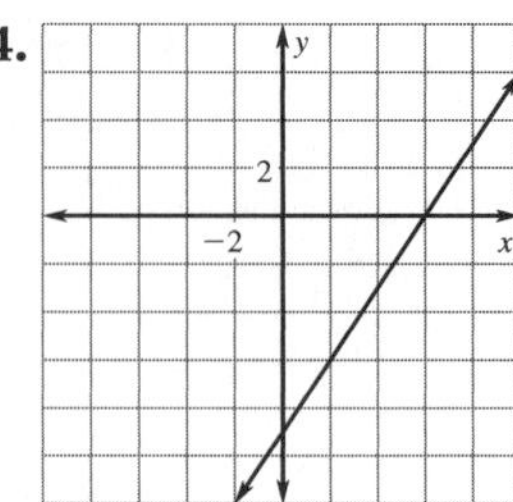

8.5 Guided Practice (pp. 520–523)

2. 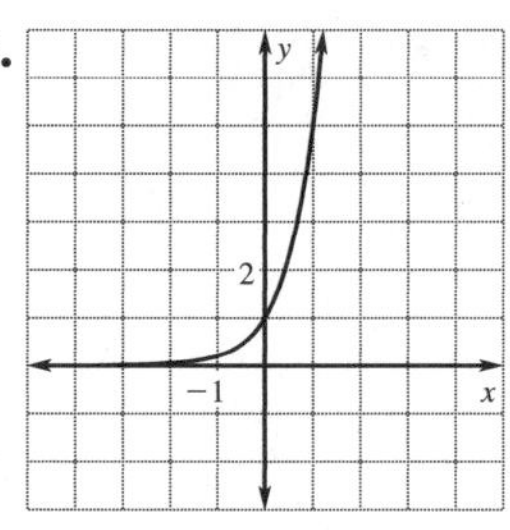

3. 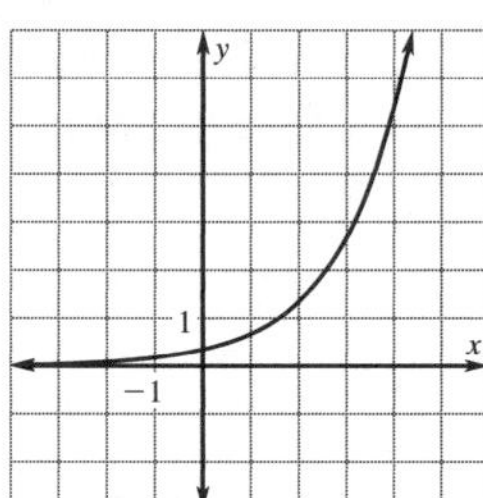

4. 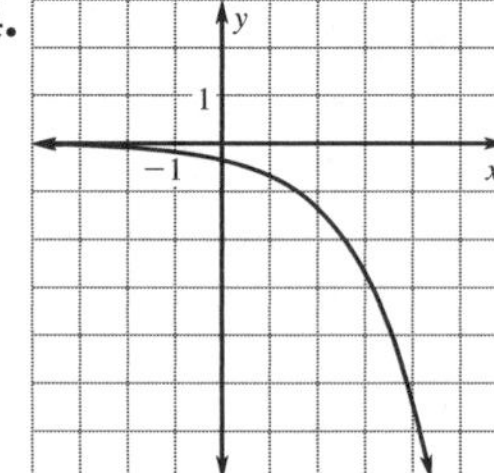

8.5 Skill Practice (pp. 523–524)

9. 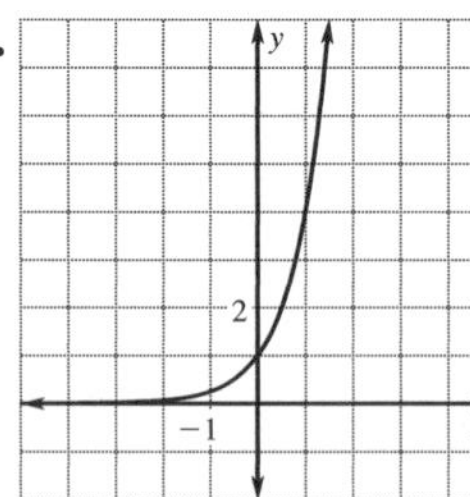

domain: all real numbers,
range: all positive real numbers

10. 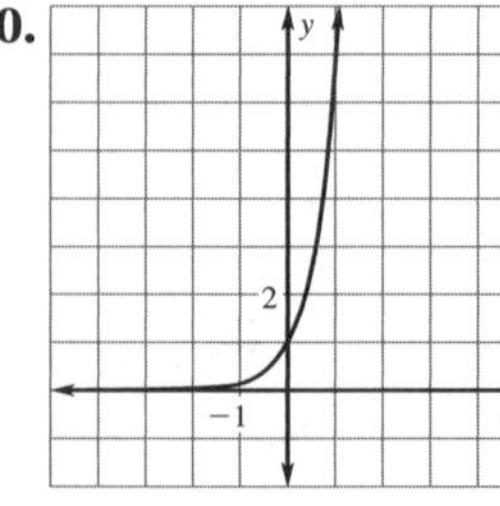

domain: all real numbers,
range: all positive real numbers

11. 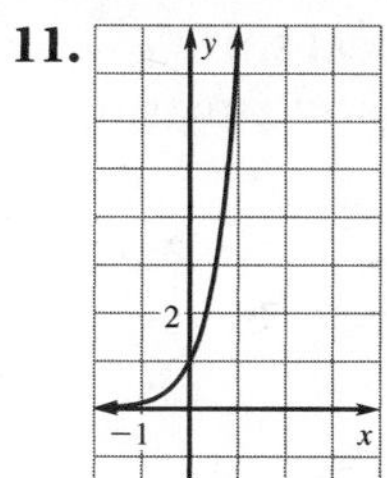
domain: all real numbers, range: all positive real numbers

12. 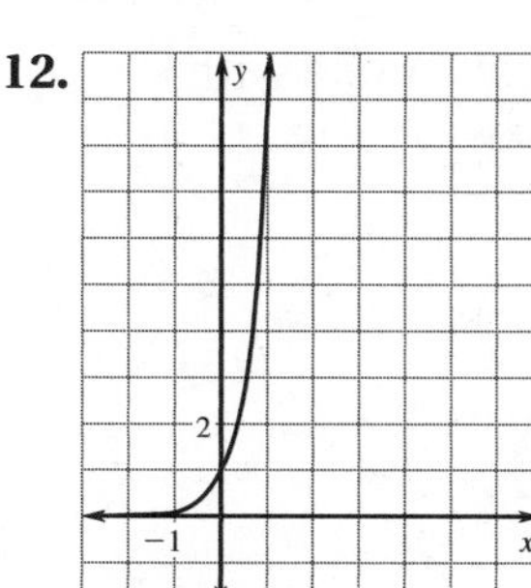
domain: all real numbers, range: all positive real numbers

13. 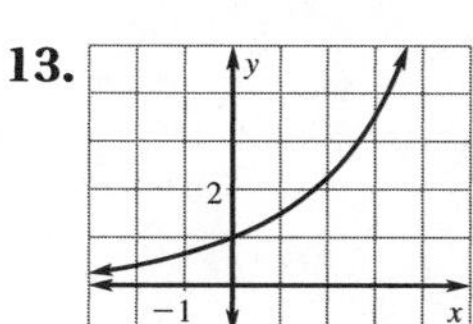
domain: all real numbers, range: all positive real numbers

14. 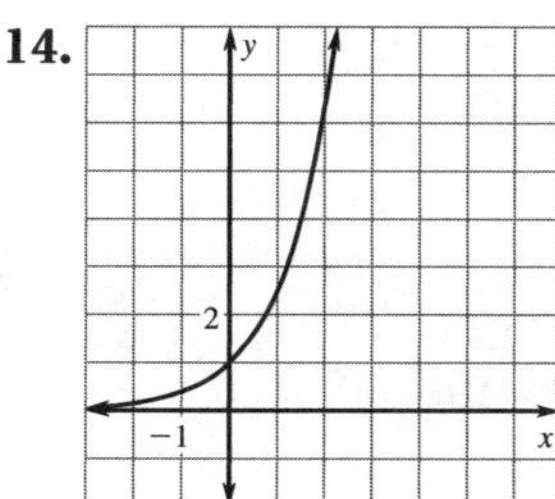
domain: all real numbers, range: all positive real numbers

15. 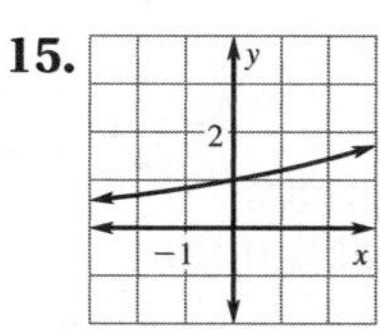
domain: all real numbers, range: all positive real numbers

16. 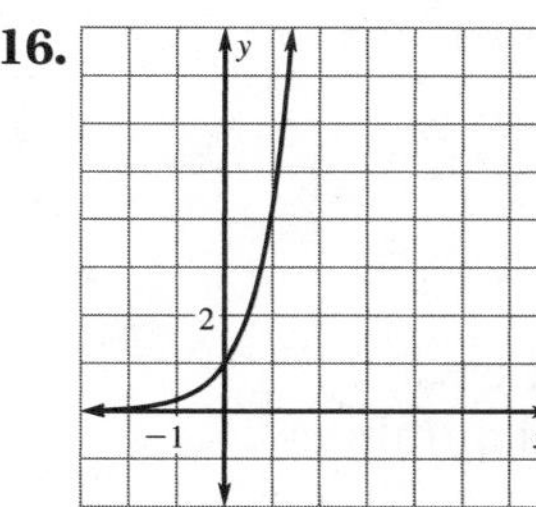
domain: all real numbers, range: all positive real numbers

17. 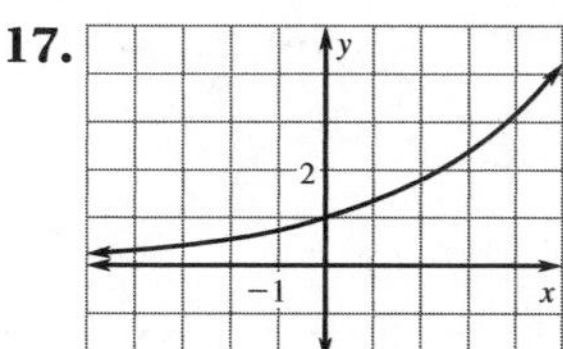
domain: all real numbers, range: all positive real numbers

18. 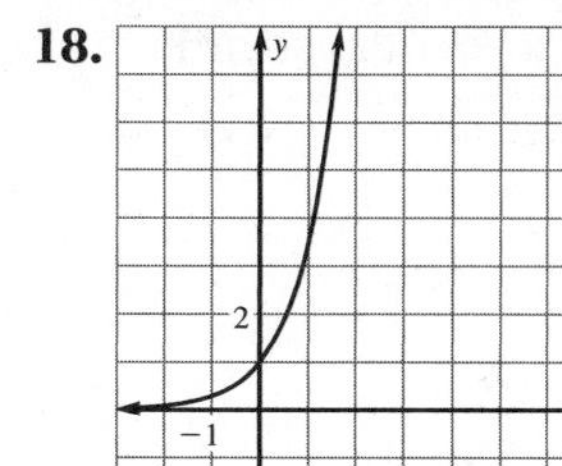
domain: all real numbers, range: all positive real numbers

19. 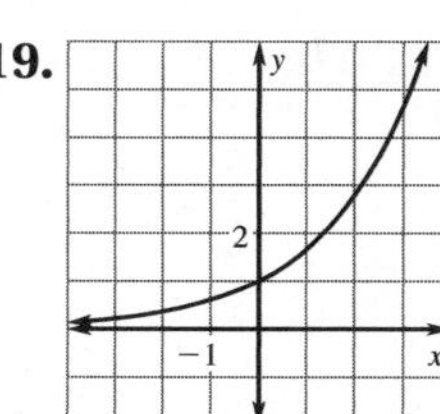
domain: all real numbers, range: all positive real numbers

20. 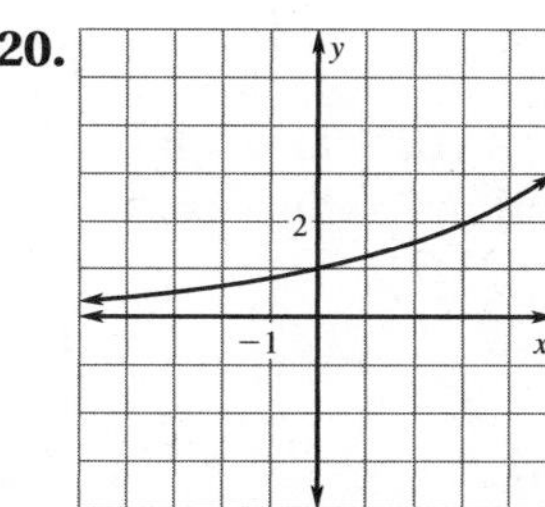
domain: all real numbers, range: all positive real numbers

22. 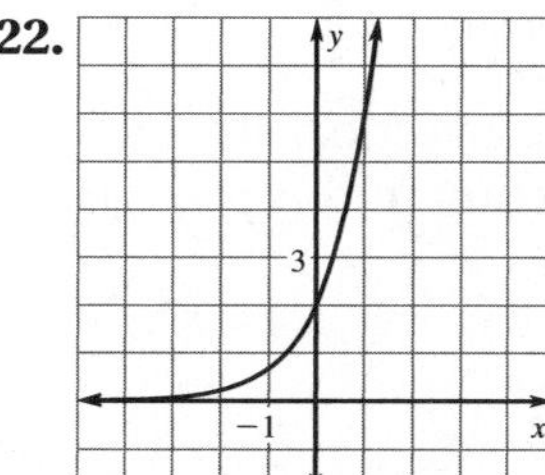
The graph is a vertical stretch.

23. 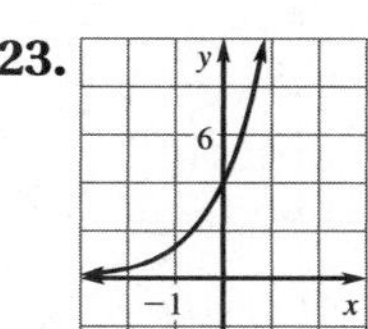
The graph is a vertical stretch.

24. 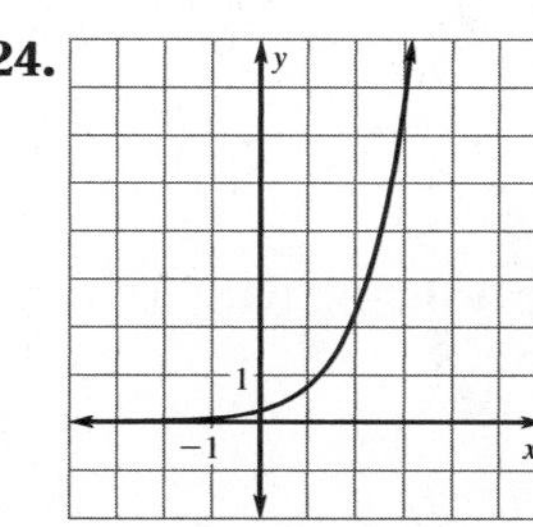
The graph is a vertical shrink.

25. 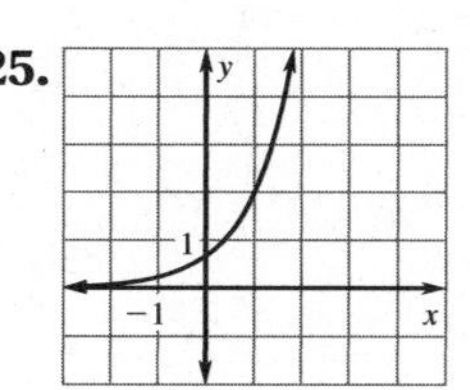
The graph is a vertical shrink.

26. 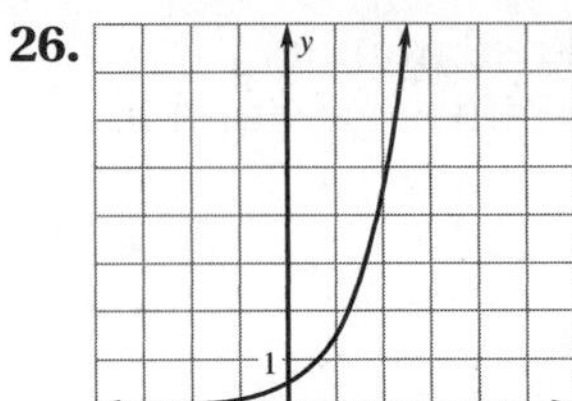
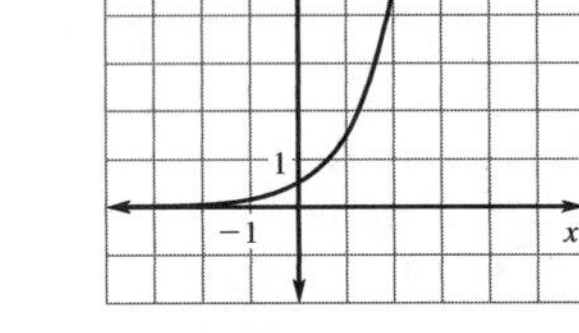
The graph is a vertical shrink.

27. 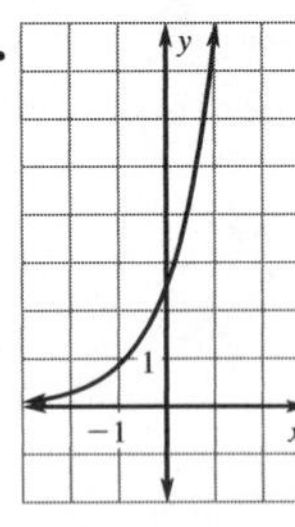
The graph is a vertical stretch.

28. 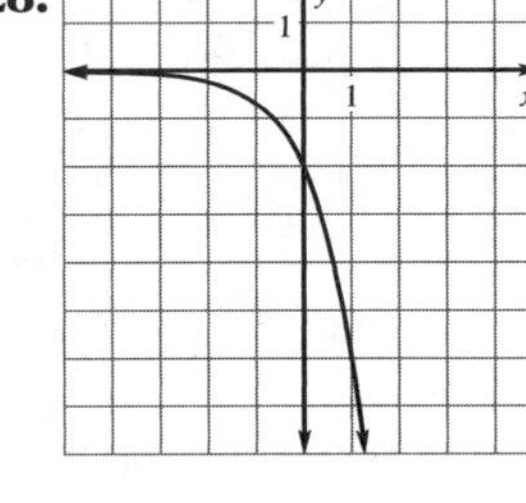
The graph is a vertical stretch with a reflection in the x-axis.

29. 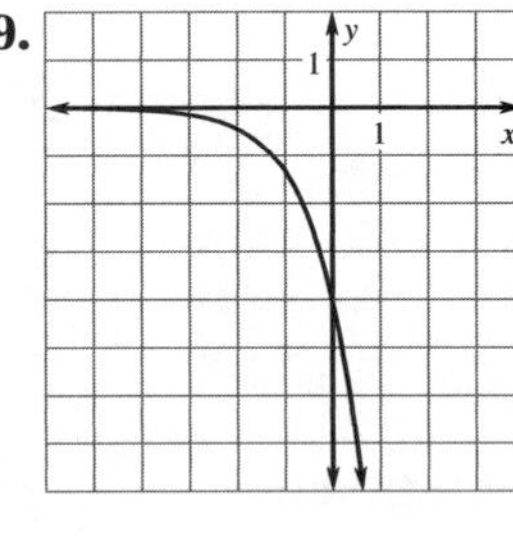
The graph is a vertical stretch with a reflection in the x-axis.

30. 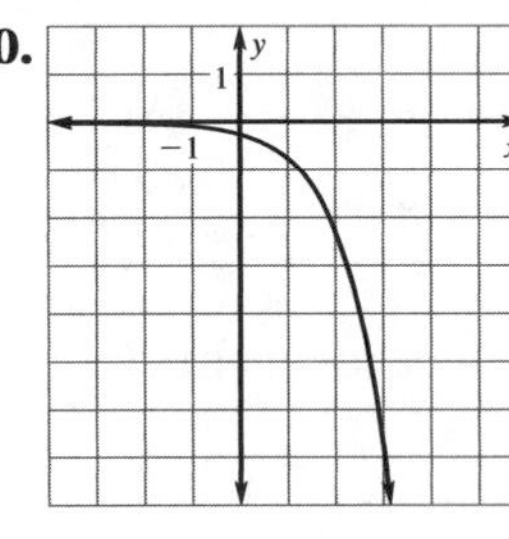
The graph is a vertical shrink with a reflection in the x-axis.

31. The graph is a vertical shrink with a reflection in the x-axis.

32. 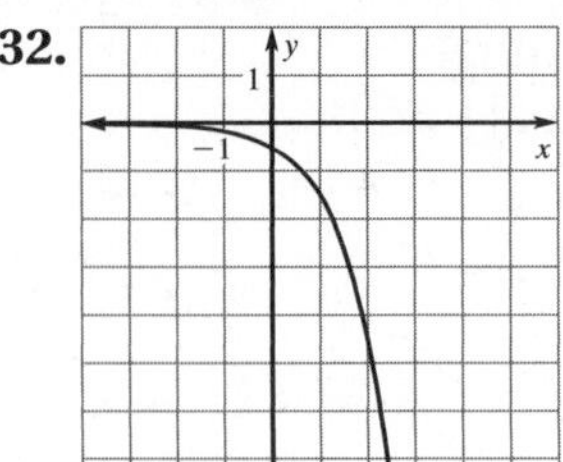
The graph is a vertical shrink with a reflection in the x-axis.

33. 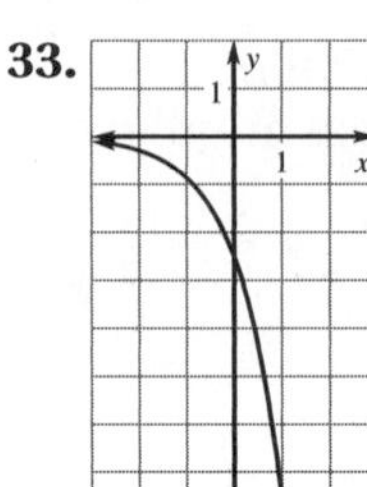
The graph is a vertical stretch with a reflection in the x-axis.

8.6 Guided Practice (pp. 531–534)

2. 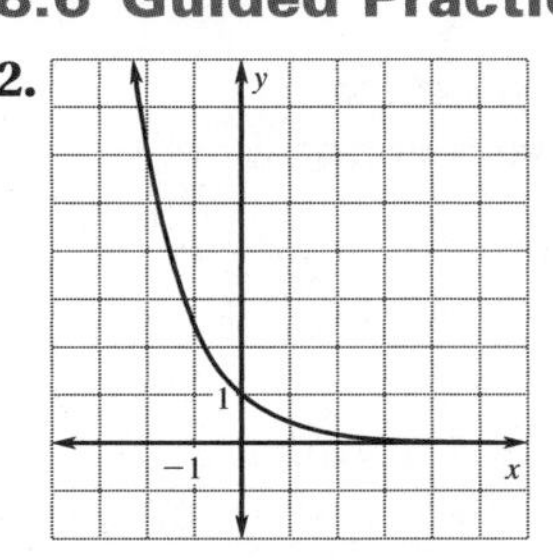

3.

8.6 Skill Practice (pp. 535–536)

7. 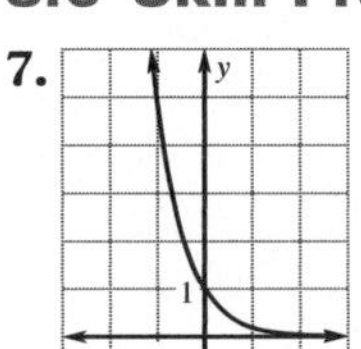
domain: all real numbers, range: all positive real numbers

8. 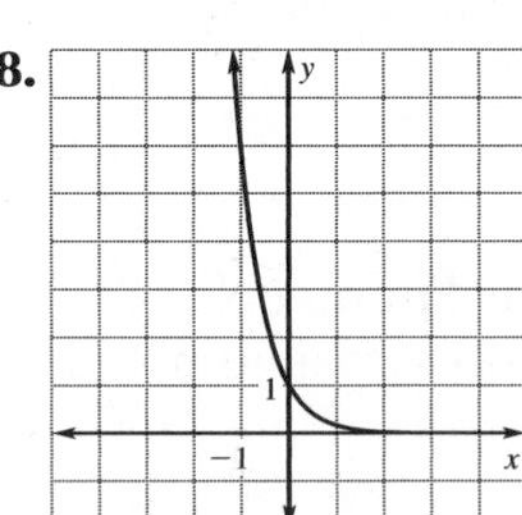
domain: all real numbers, range: all positive real numbers

9. 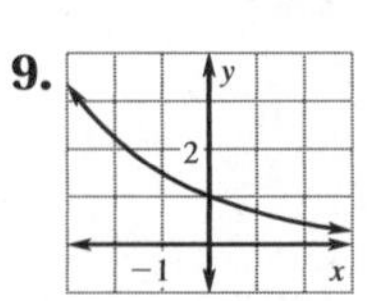
domain: all real numbers, range: all positive real numbers

10. 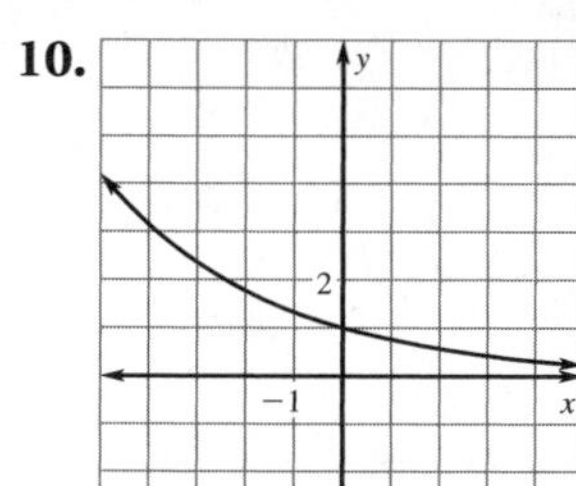

domain: all real numbers, range: all positive real numbers

11. 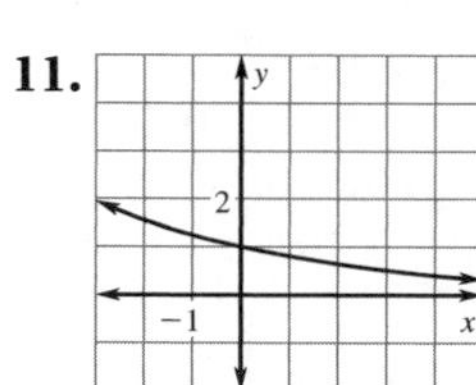

domain: all real numbers, range: all positive real numbers

12. 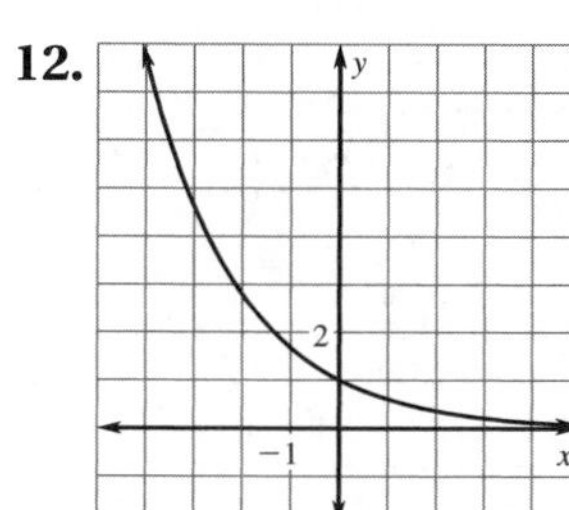

domain: all real numbers, range: all positive real numbers

13. 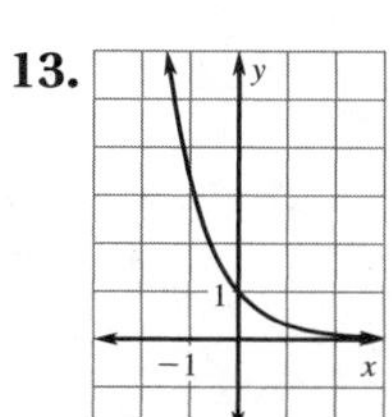

domain: all real numbers, range: all positive real numbers

14. 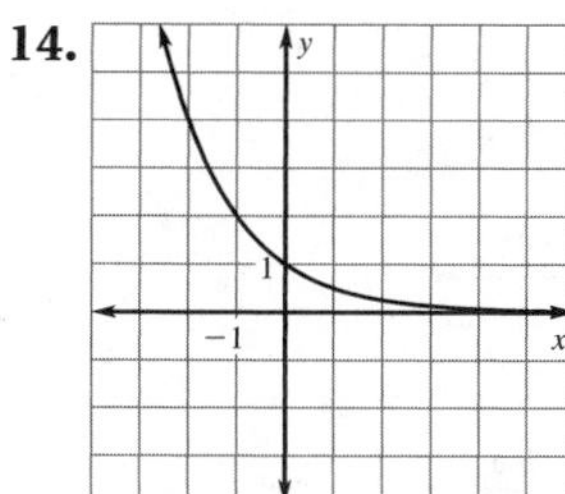

domain: all real numbers, range: all positive real numbers

15. 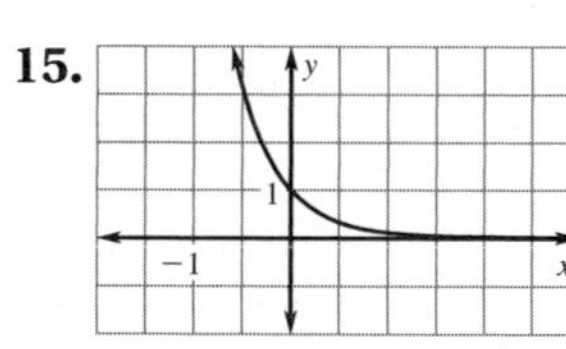

domain: all real numbers, range: all positive real numbers

16. 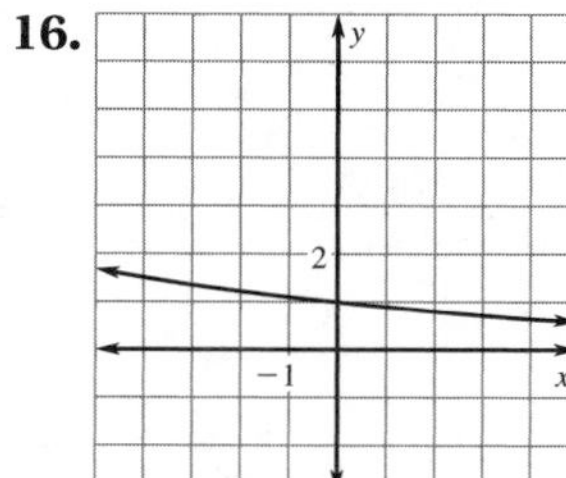

domain: all real numbers, range: all positive real numbers

17. 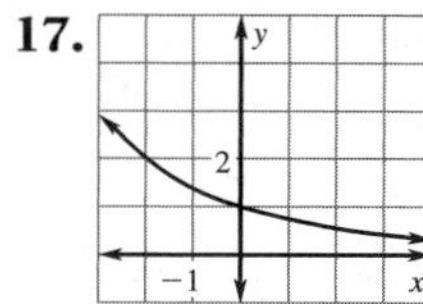

domain: all real numbers, range: all positive real numbers

18. 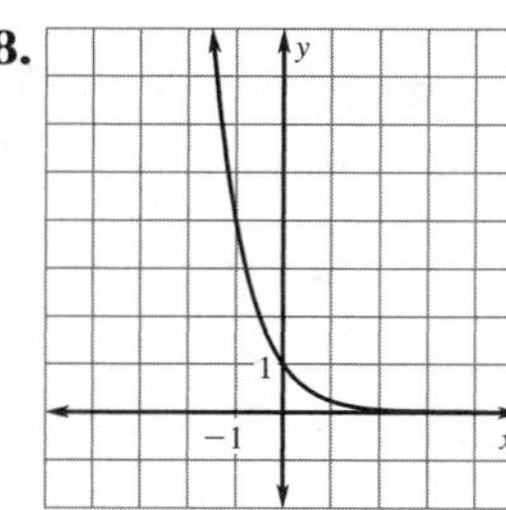

domain: all real numbers, range: all positive real numbers

20. 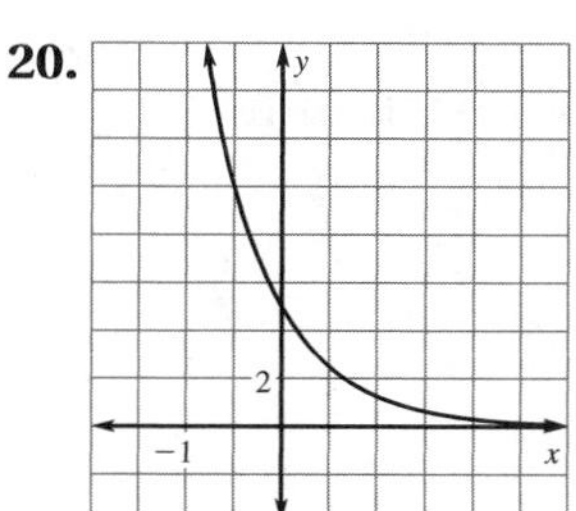

The graph is a vertical stretch.

21. 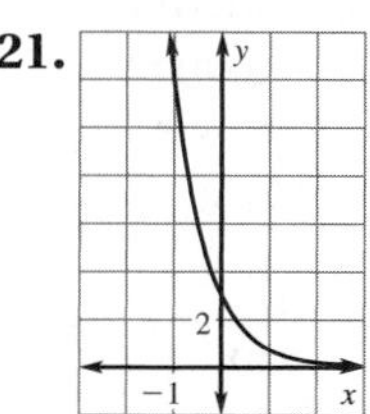

The graph is a vertical stretch.

22. 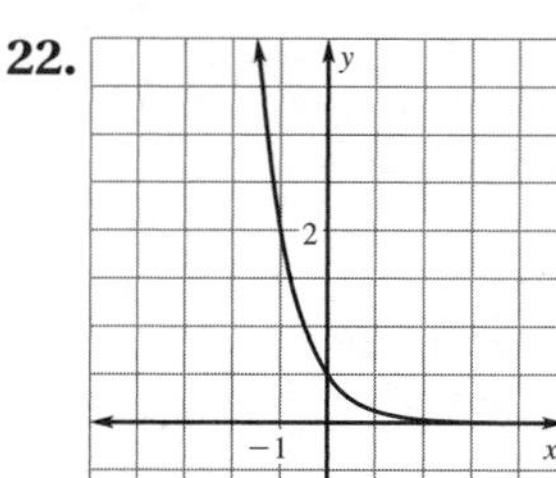

The graph is a vertical shrink.

23. 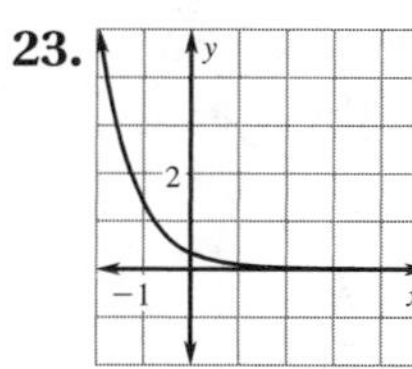

The graph is a vertical shrink.

24. 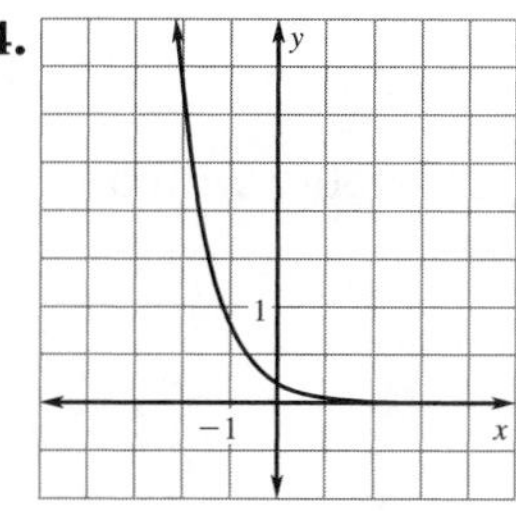

The graph is a vertical shrink.

25. 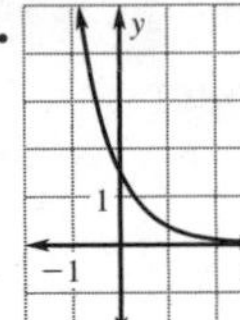 The graph is a vertical stretch.

26. 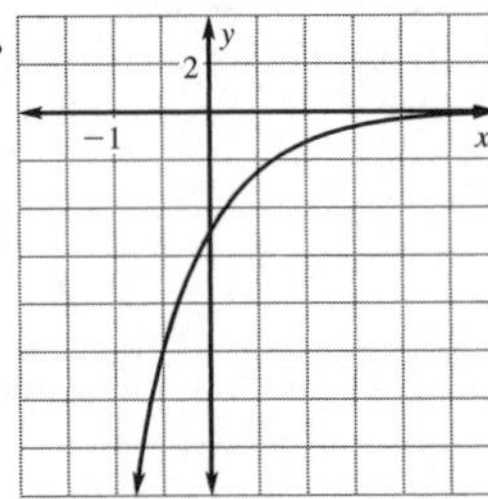 The graph is a vertical stretch with a reflection in the x-axis.

27. 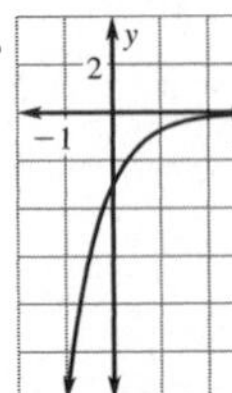 The graph is a vertical stretch with a reflection in the x-axis.

28. 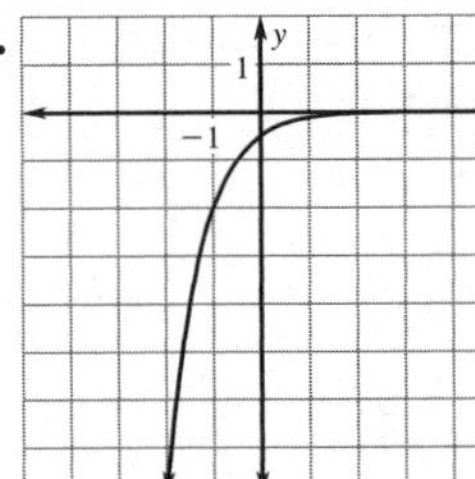 The graph is a vertical shrink with a reflection in the x-axis.

29. 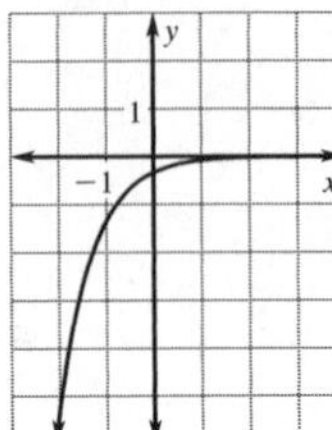 The graph is a vertical shrink with a reflection in the x-axis.

30. 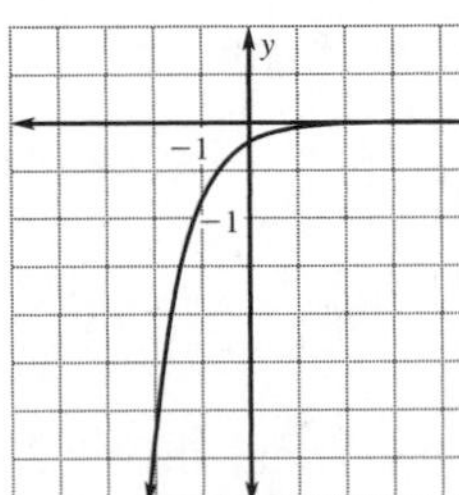 The graph is a vertical shrink with a reflection in the x-axis.

31. 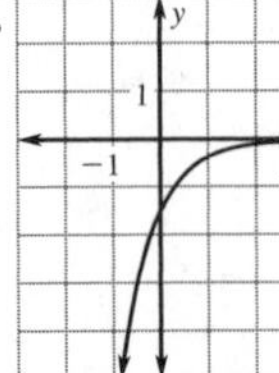 The graph is a vertical stretch with a reflection in the x-axis.

Quiz for Lessons 8.5–8.6 (p. 538)

1. 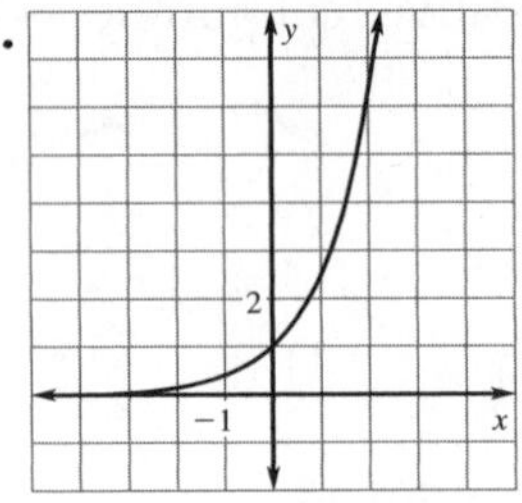

2. 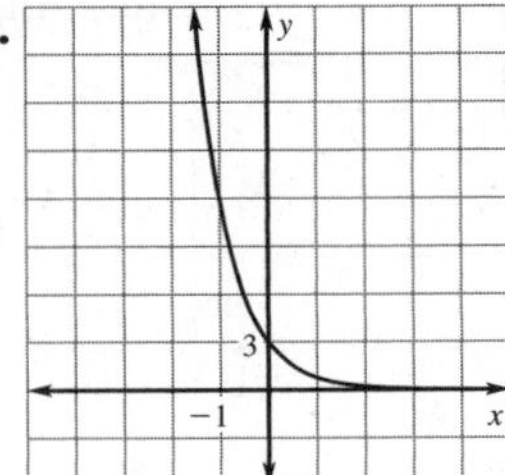

3. 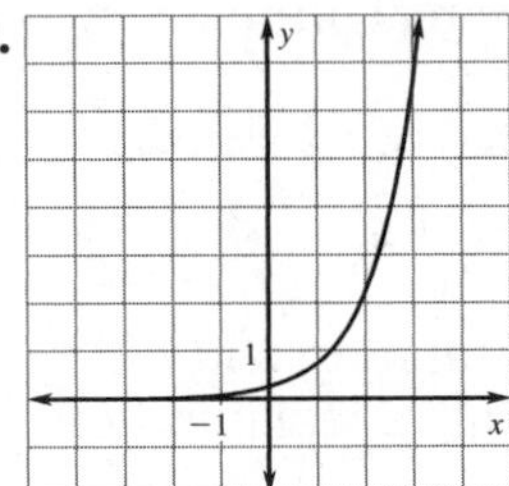

4. 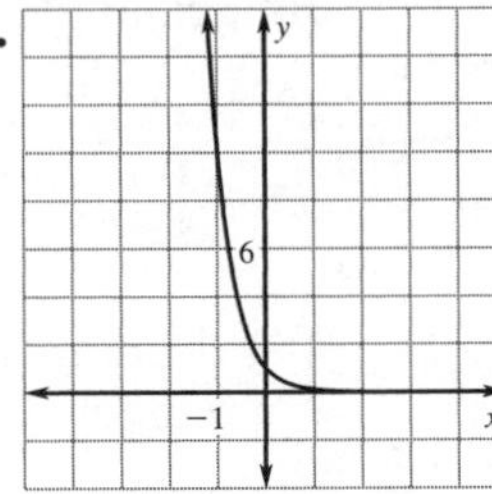

5. 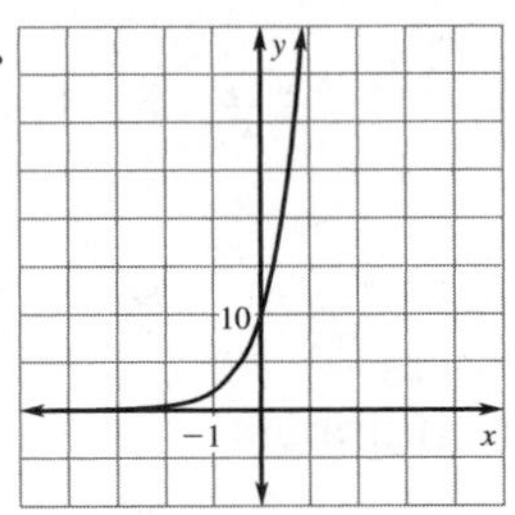

6. 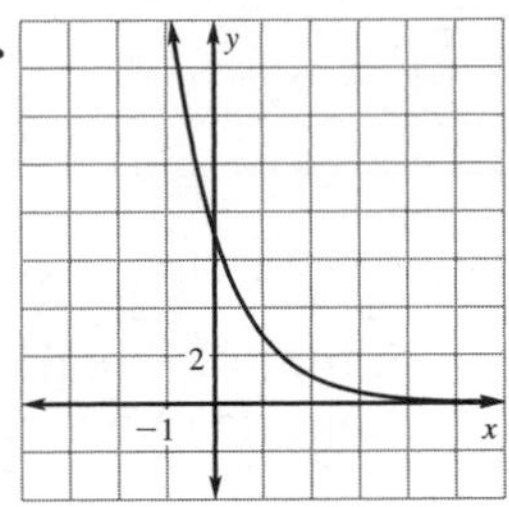

Extension (p. 540)

1. 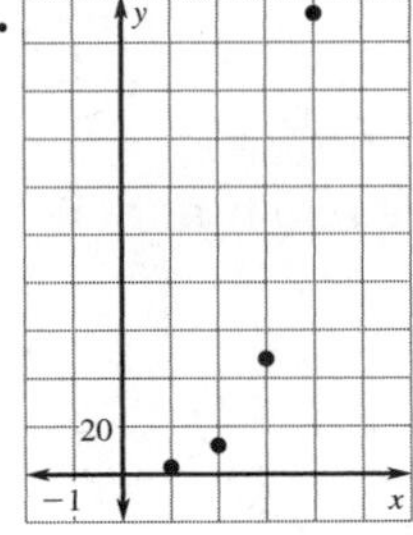

2. 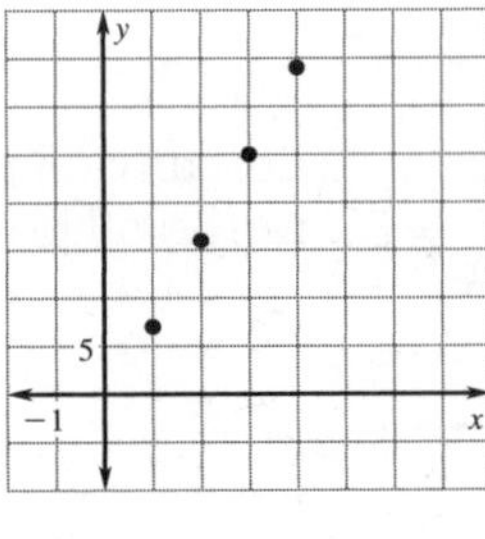

3. 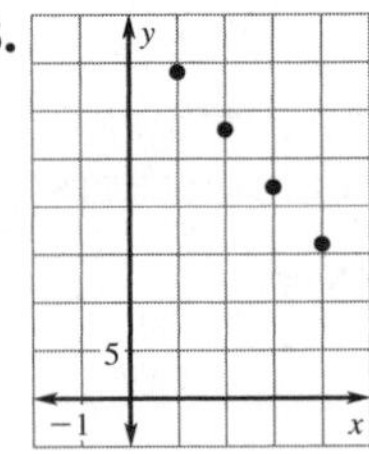

4. 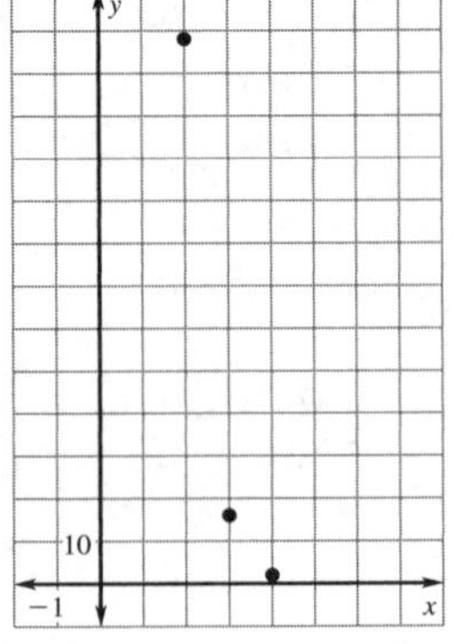

5. 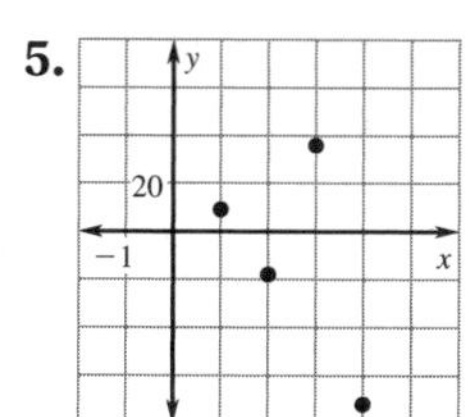

6. 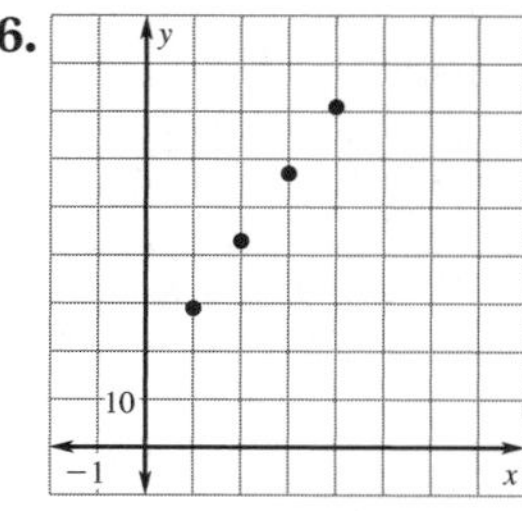

Chapter 9

9.1 Mixed Review (p. 559)

49. 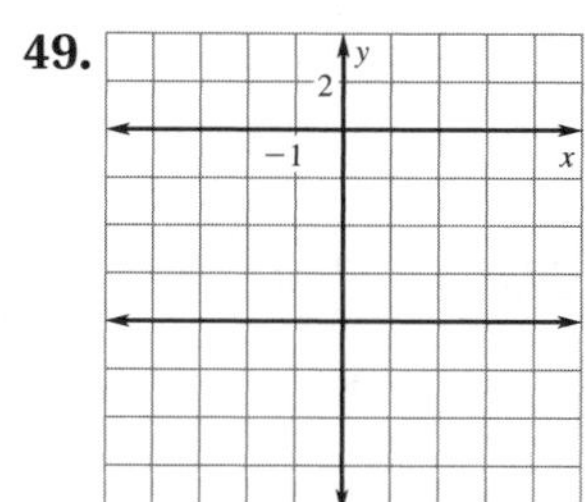

50. 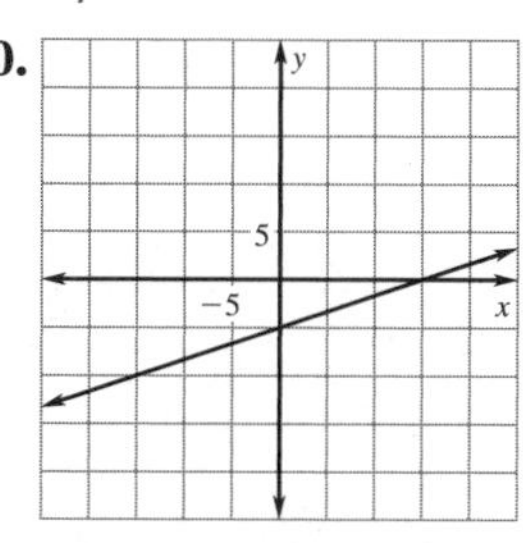

51. 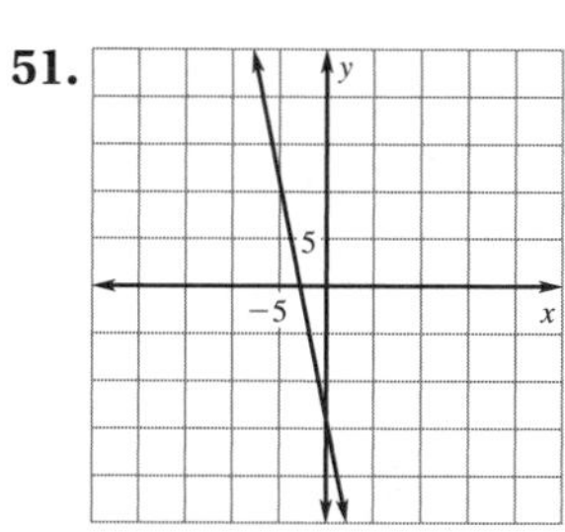

52. 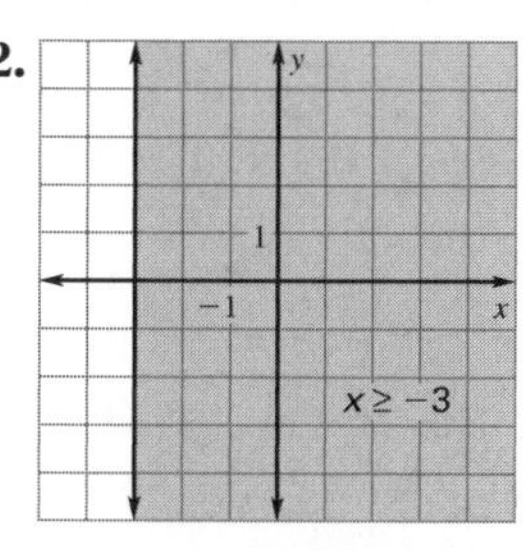

53. 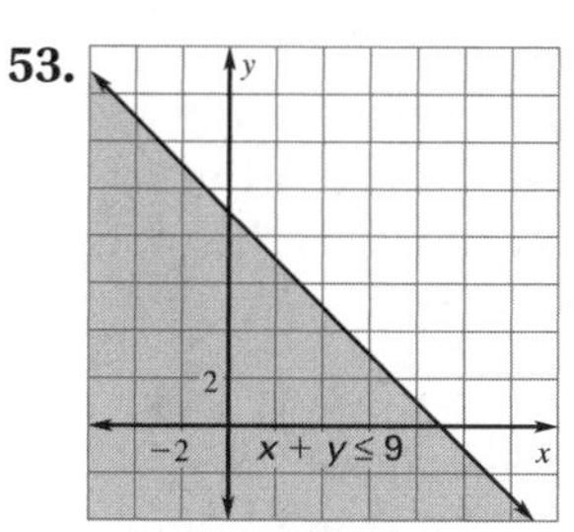

54. 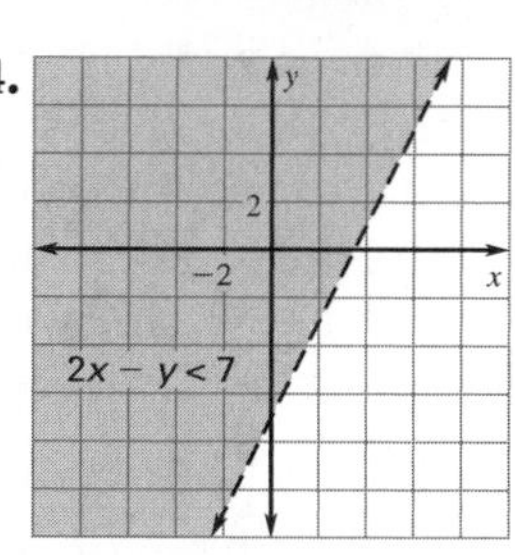

9.2 Investigating Algebra Activity (p. 561)

1. 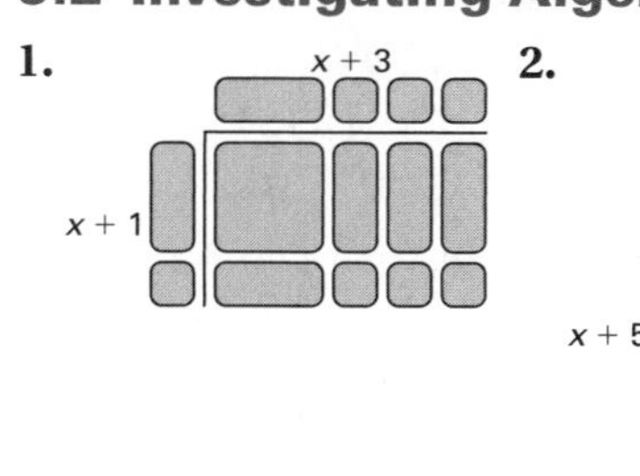

2. 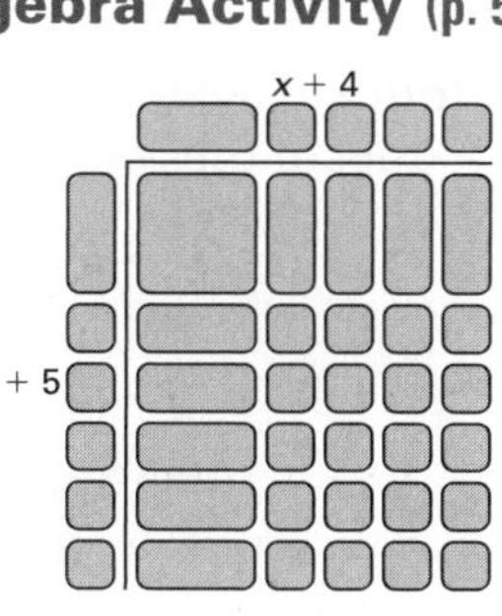

3. **4.** 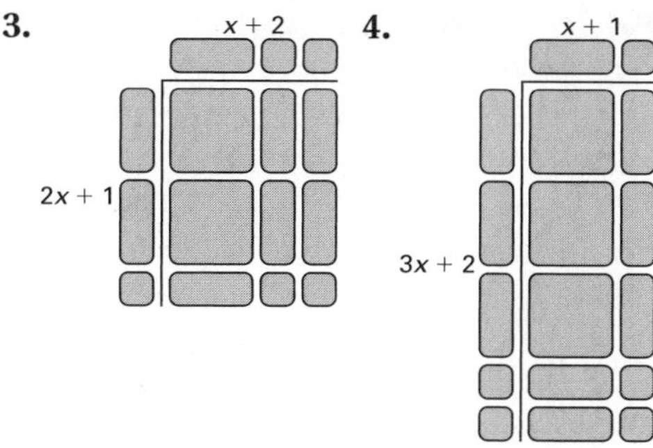

5. **6.** 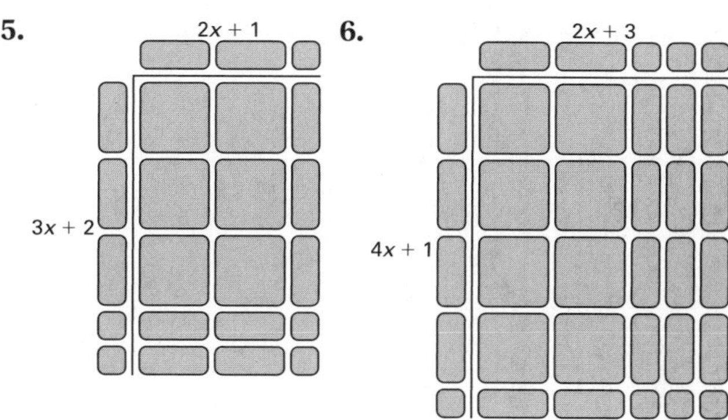

9.3 Skill Practice (p. 572) **2.** The square of a binomial is a trinomial. To find the first term of the trinomial, square the first term of the binomial. To find the second term of the trinomial, find twice the product of the terms of the binomial, using the sign of the second term. To find the third term of the trinomial, square the second term of the binomial.

9.3 Problem Solving (pp. 573–574) **43. a.** 88.1%; the areas of the four regions are: 2 complete passes: $0.655^2 \approx 0.429$ square units; 1 complete pass, 1 incomplete pass: $0.655(0.345) \approx 0.226$ square units; 1 incomplete pass, 1 complete pass: $0.345(0.655) \approx 0.226$ square units; and 2 incomplete passes: $0.345^2 \approx 0.119$ square units. The regions that involve at least one complete pass cover $0.429 + 0.226 + 0.226 = 0.881$ square units, or 88.1% of the whole square region. **b.** The outcome of each attempted pass is modeled by $0.655C + 0.345I$, so the possible outcomes of two attempted passes is modeled by $(0.655C + 0.345I)^2 = 0.429C^2 + 0.452CI + 0.119I^2$. Because any combination of outcomes with a C results in at least one completed pass, the coefficients of the first two terms show that $42.9\% + 45.2\% = 88.1\%$ of the outcomes will have at least one completed pass, and the coefficient of the last term shows that 11.9% of the outcomes will have two incomplete passes.

9.4 Problem Solving (pp. 579–580) **59. a.** 8 ft; the zeros of the function, 0 and 8, are the x-intercepts of the graph, which represent the edges of the base of the doorway. The distance between 0 and 8 on the x-axis is 8 units, so the width of the doorway at its base is 8 feet. **b.** 8 ft; the center of the base is the midpoint of the segment joining the x-intercepts 0 and 8, so at the center of the base $x = 4$. The doorway's highest point will be the point $(4, y)$ on the graph of $y = -0.5x(x - 8)$. Substitute $x = 4$ into the equation for y to find the height: $y = -0.5(4)(4 - 8) = 8$ feet.

9.5 Investigating Algebra Activity (p. 582)

2. **3.**

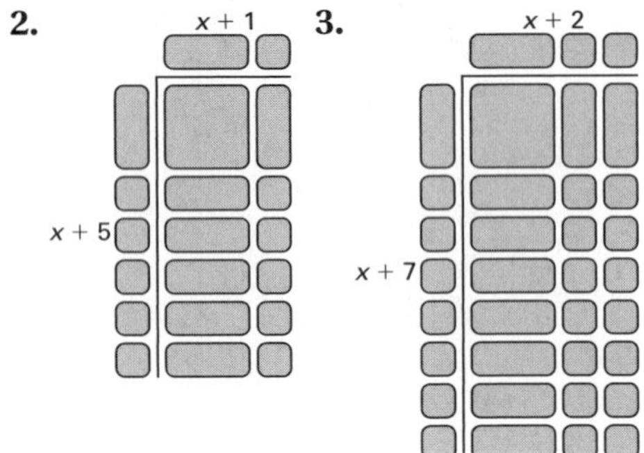

4. **5.**

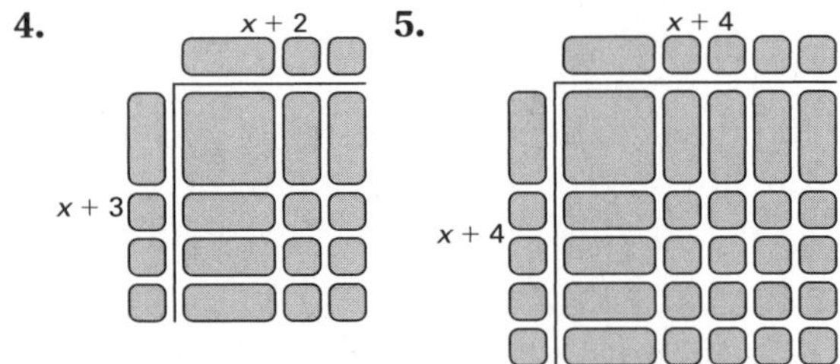

6. **7.**

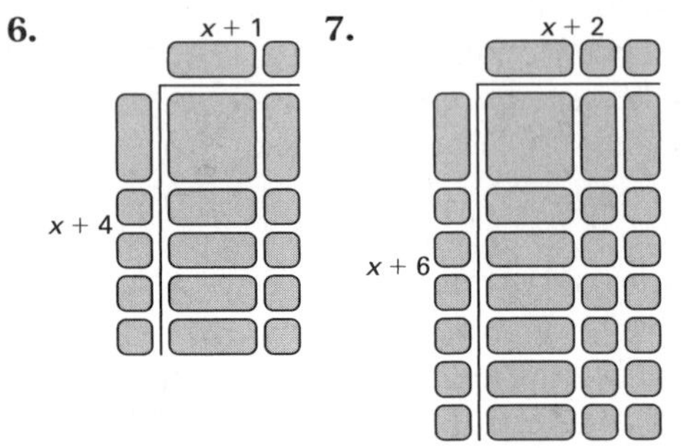

9.6 Investigating Algebra Activity (p. 592)

2. **3.**

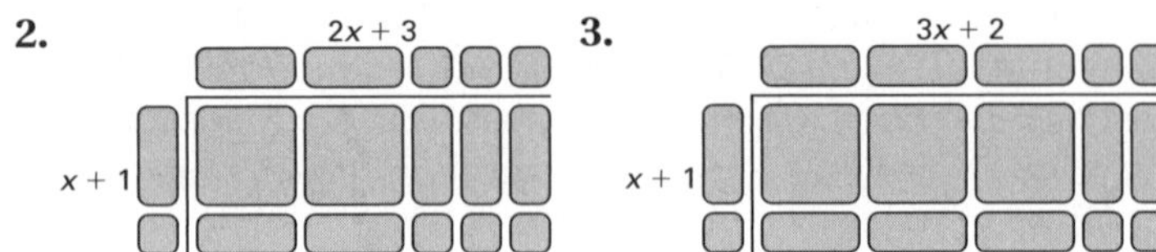

4.

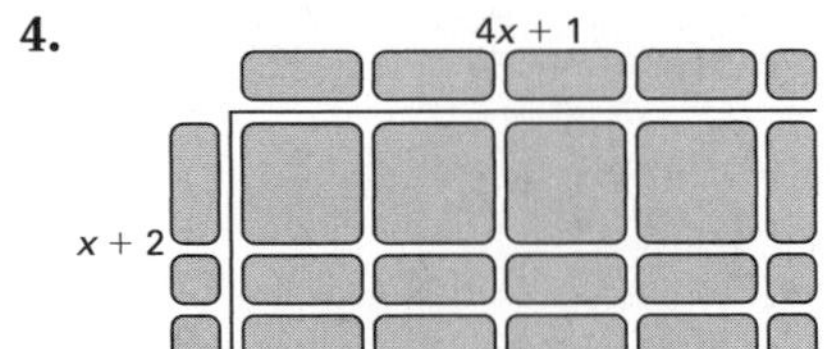

5.

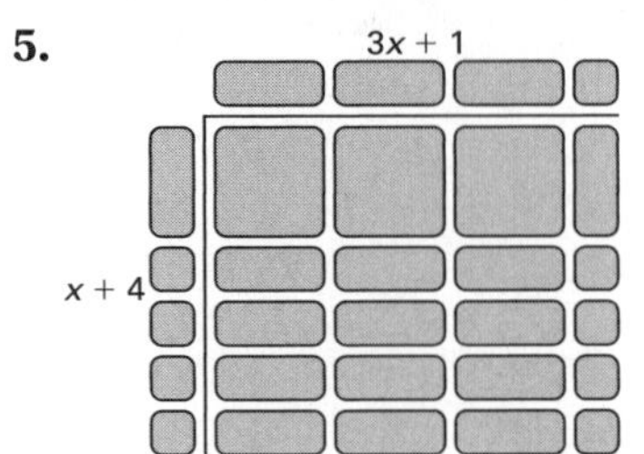

6.

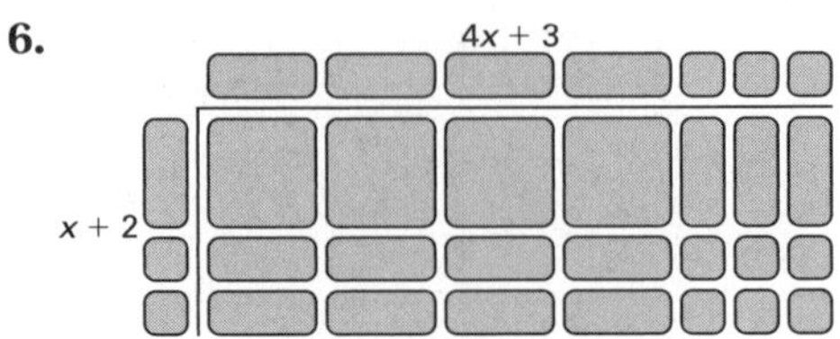

7.

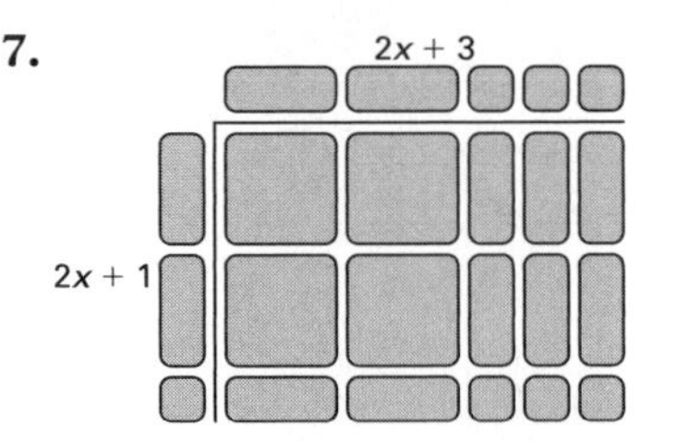

9.6 Skill Practice (pp. 596–597) **52.** $x^2 + x - 6 = 0$; any root $x = r$ of $x^2 + bx + c = 0$ comes from setting the factor $x - r$ equal to zero after $x^2 + bx + c$ is written in factored form; so, the roots -3 and 2 come from the factors $x - (-3)$, or $x + 3$, and $x - 2$. The product of these factors is $(x + 3)(x - 2) = x^2 - 2x + 3x - 6 = x^2 + x - 6$.

53. $2x^2 - 9x - 5 = 0$; any root $x = \frac{r}{s}$ of $ax^2 + bx + c = 0$ comes from setting the factor $sx - r$ equal to zero after $ax^2 + bx + c$ is written in factored form; so, the roots $-\frac{1}{2}$ and 5 come from the factors $2x - (-1)$, or $2x + 1$, and $x - 5$. The product of these factors is $(2x + 1)(x - 5) = 2x^2 - 10x + x - 5 = 2x^2 - 9x - 5$. **54.** $12x^2 + 13x + 3 = 0$; any root $x = \frac{r}{s}$ of $ax^2 + bx + c = 0$ comes from setting the factor $sx - r$ equal to zero after $ax^2 + bx + c$ is written in factored form; so, the roots $-\frac{3}{4}$ and $-\frac{1}{3}$ come from the factors $4x - (-3)$, or $4x + 3$, and $3x - (-1)$, or $3x + 1$. The product of these factors is $(4x + 3)(3x + 1) = 12x^2 + 4x + 9x + 3 = 12x^2 + 13x + 3$.

9.7 Problem Solving (pp. 604–605) **52. d.** 6 rows; let $x =$ the number of chairs in the last row, so that the sum of the odd integers from 15 to x is 120. x can be written in the form $2n - 1$. 15 is the eighth odd integer and x is the nth odd integer, so the sum of the odd integers from 15 to x can be found as described in part (c): the sum of the first n odd integers minus the sum of the first 7 odd integers, $n^2 - 7^2$, or $n^2 - 49$. The total number of chairs is to be 120, so this leads to the equation $n^2 - 49 = 120$, or $n^2 - 169 = 0$. This equation has two solutions, 13 and -13. Disregard the solution -13 because n cannot be negative in this situation. So, x is the thirteenth odd integer. The numbers of chairs in the rows go from the eighth odd integer (15) to the thirteenth odd integer (25). There are $13 - 8 + 1 =$ 6 rows of chairs.

9.7 Mixed Review (p. 605)

62. 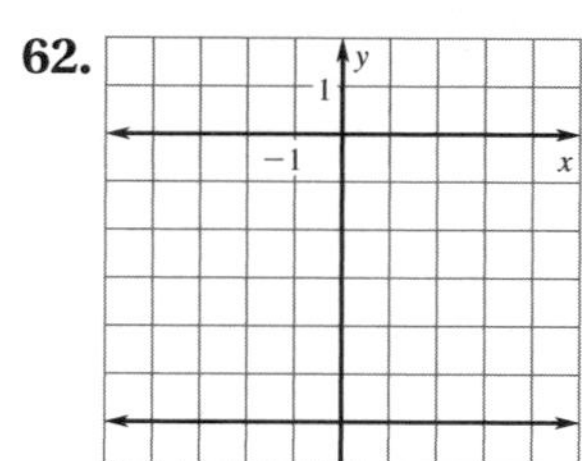

63. 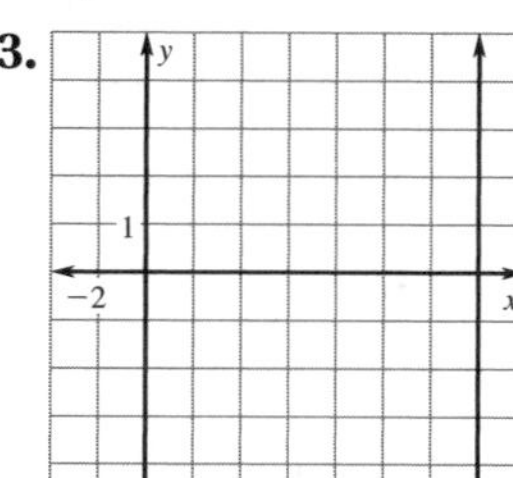

64. 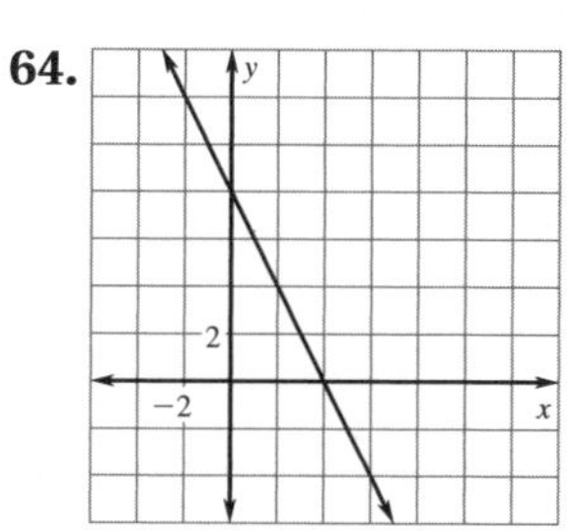

65. 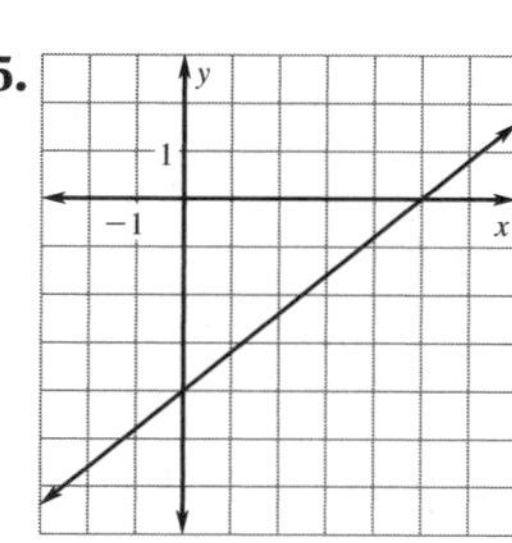

66. 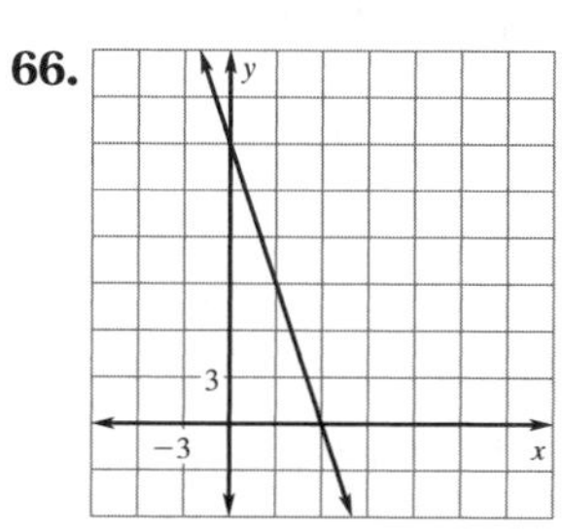

67. 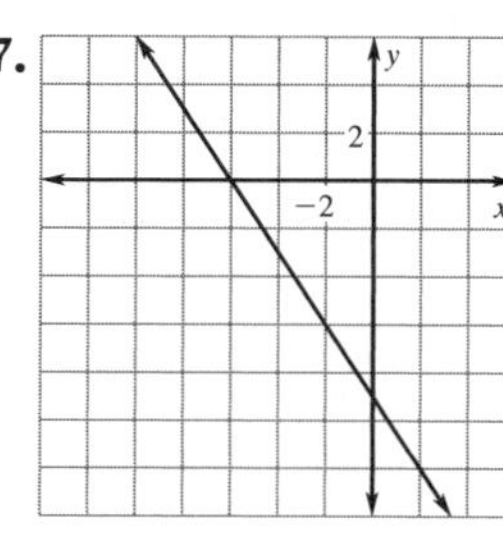

68. 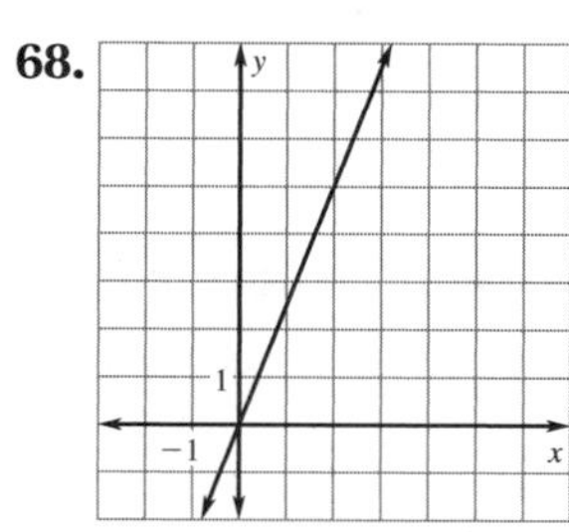

69. 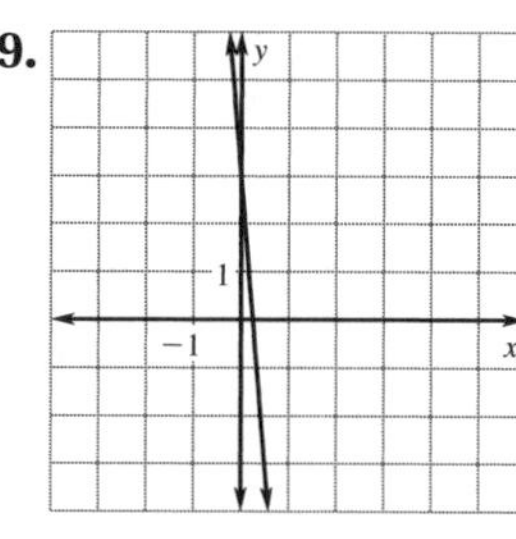

70. 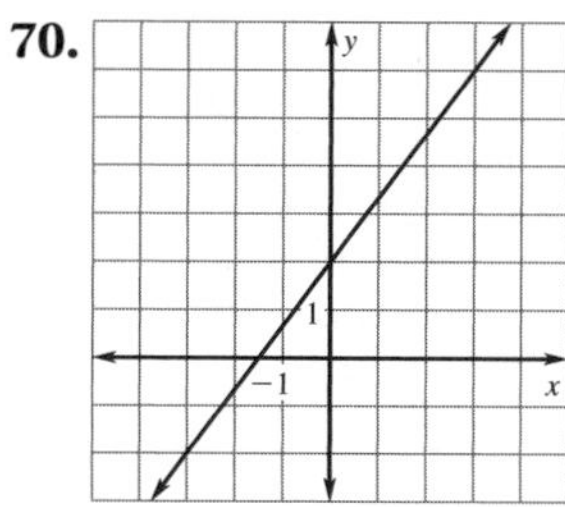

9.8 Mixed Review (p. 613)

75. 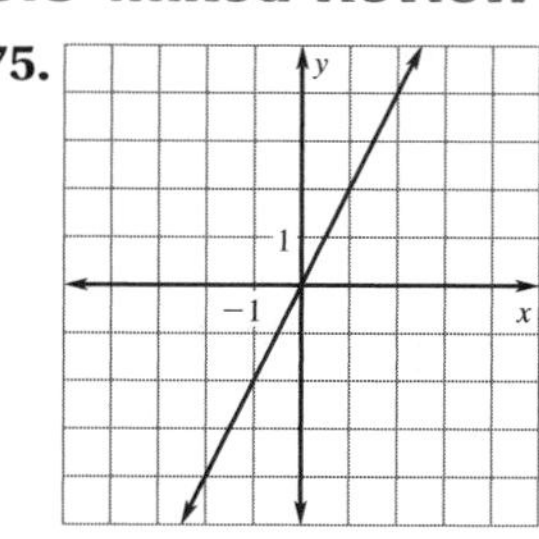

76. 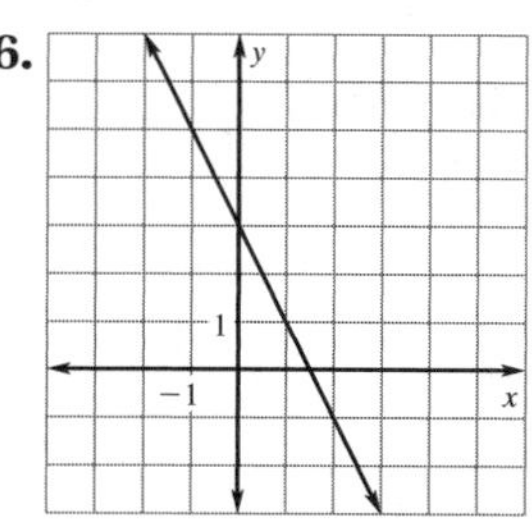

77. 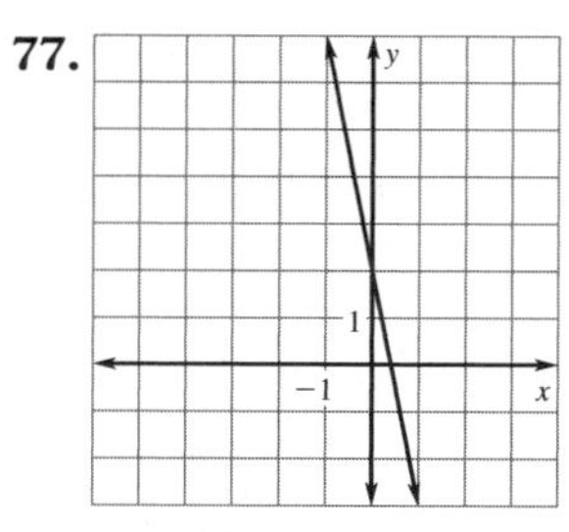

78. 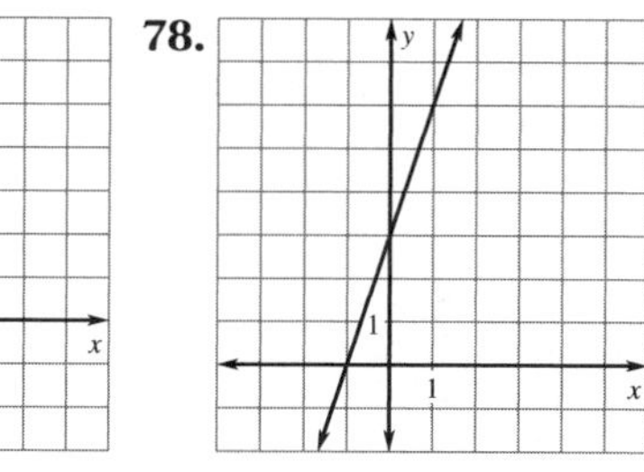

79. 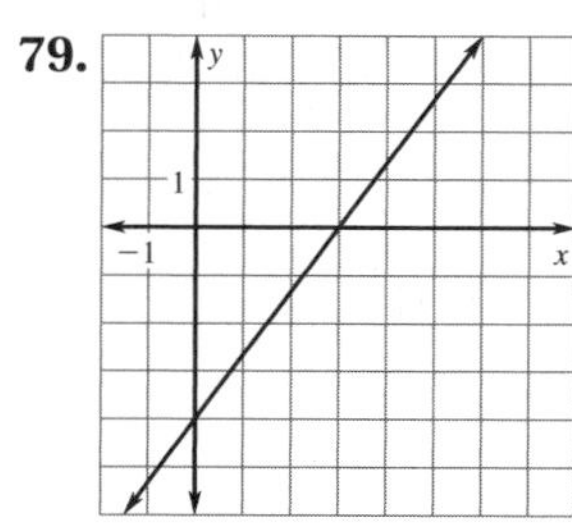

80. 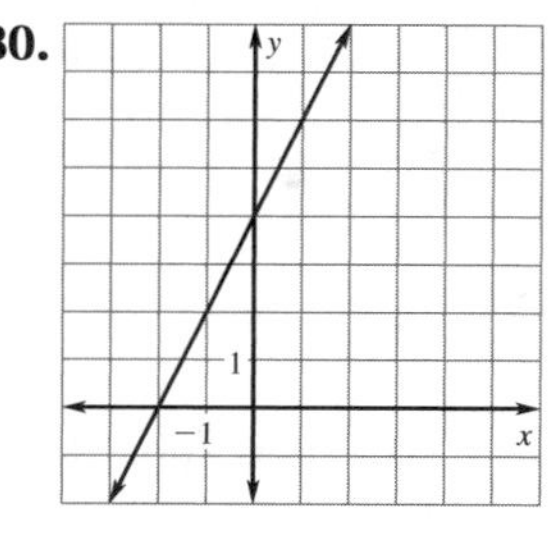

81. 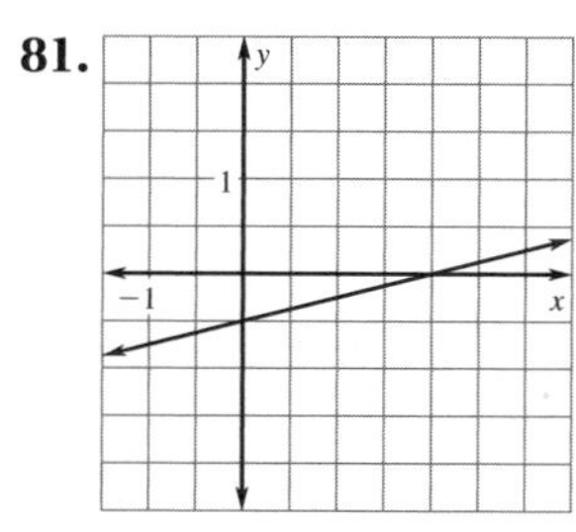

82. 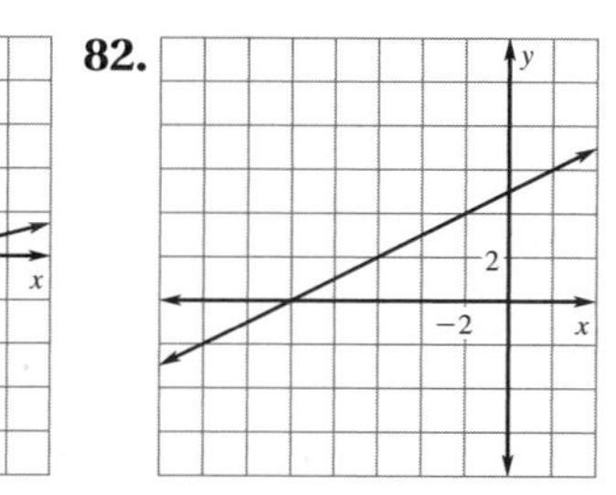

83. 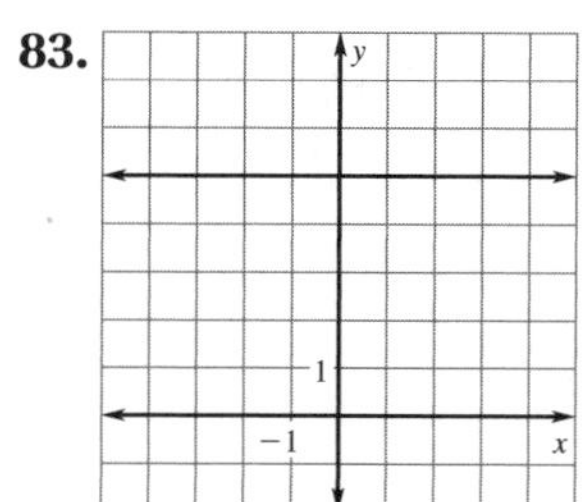

84. 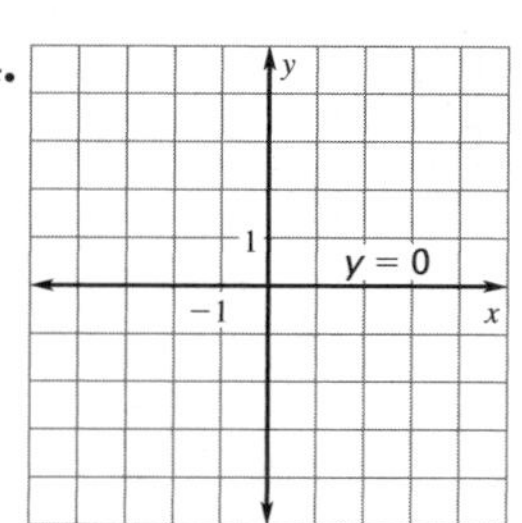

85. 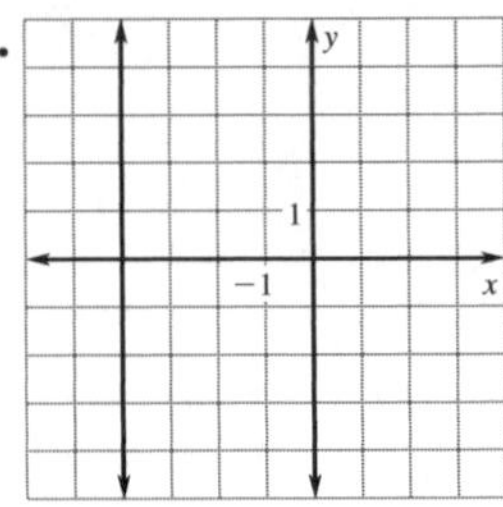

86. 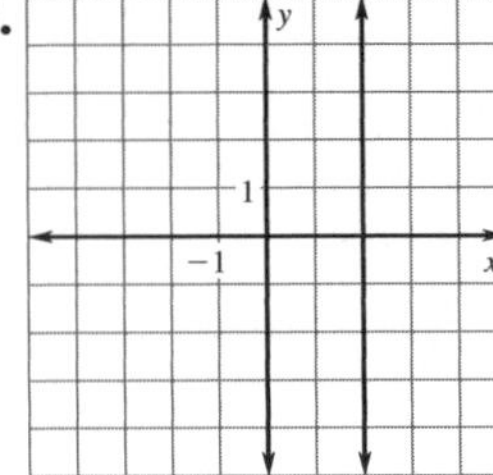

Chapter 10

10.1 Guided Practice (pp. 629–631)

1. 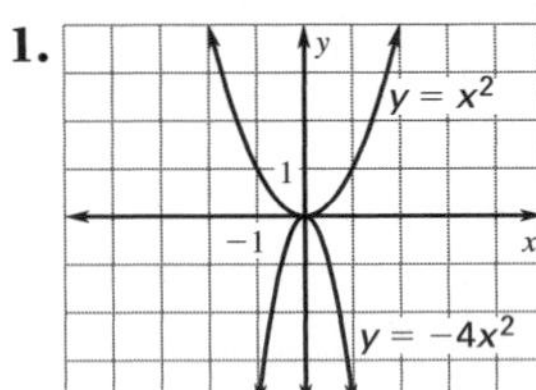

The graph is a vertical stretch (by a factor of 4) with a reflection in the x-axis of the graph of $y = x^2$.

2. 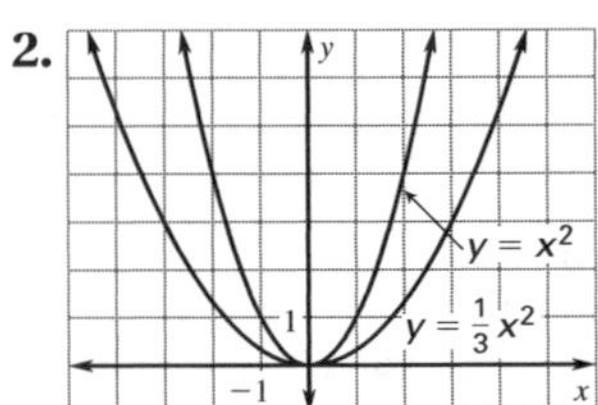

The graph is a vertical shrink $\left(\text{by a factor of } \frac{1}{3}\right)$ of the graph of $y = x^2$.

3. 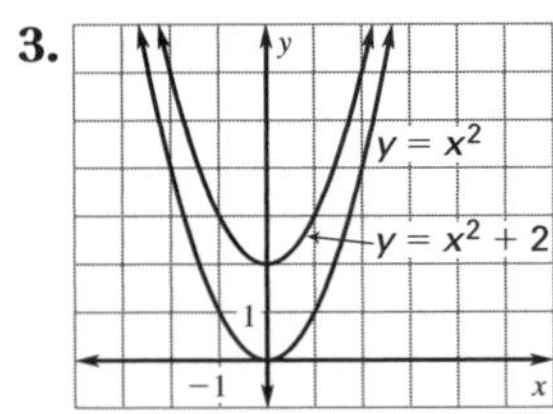

The graph is a vertical translation (of 2 units up) of the graph of $y = x^2$.

10.1 Skill Practice (pp. 632–633)

6. 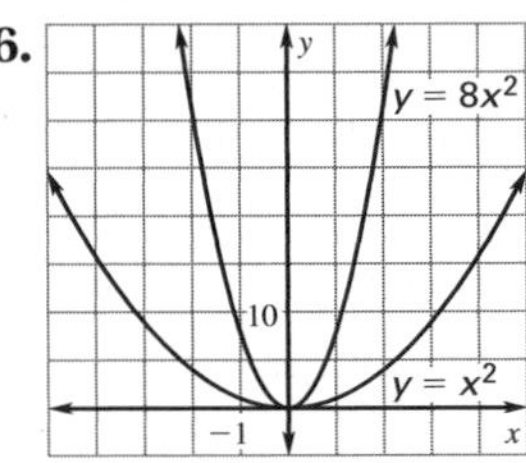

The graph is a vertical stretch (by a factor of 8) of the graph of $y = x^2$.

7. 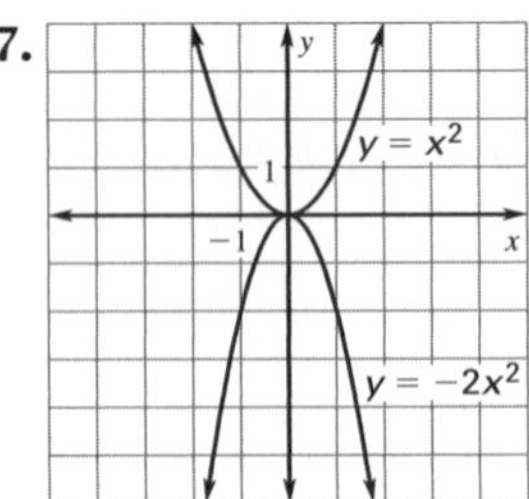

The graph is a vertical stretch (by a factor of 2) with a reflection in the x-axis of the graph of $y = x^2$.

8. 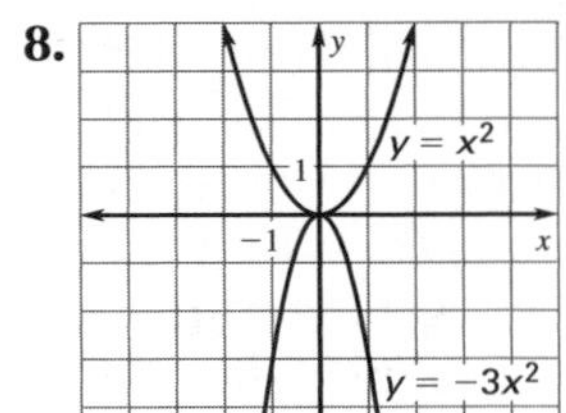

The graph is a vertical stretch (by a factor of 3) with a reflection in the x-axis of the graph of $y = x^2$.

9. 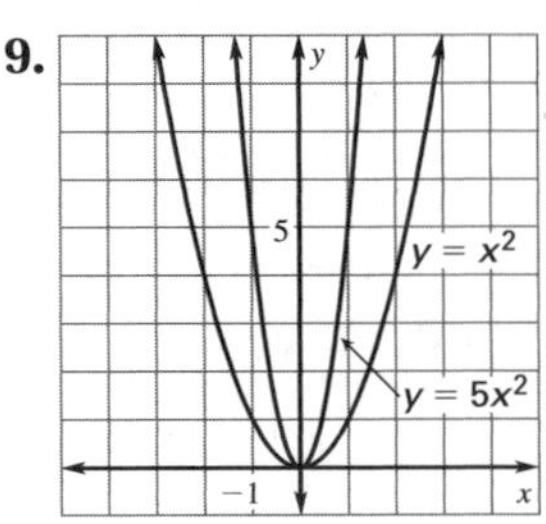

The graph is a vertical stretch (by a factor of 5) of the graph of $y = x^2$.

10. 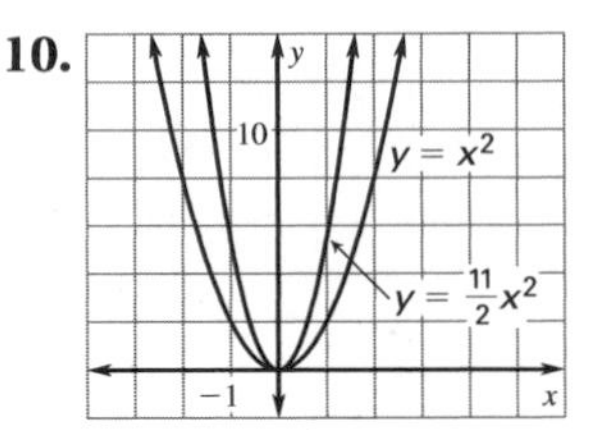

The graph is a vertical stretch $\left(\text{by a factor of } \frac{11}{2}\right)$ of the graph of $y = x^2$.

11. 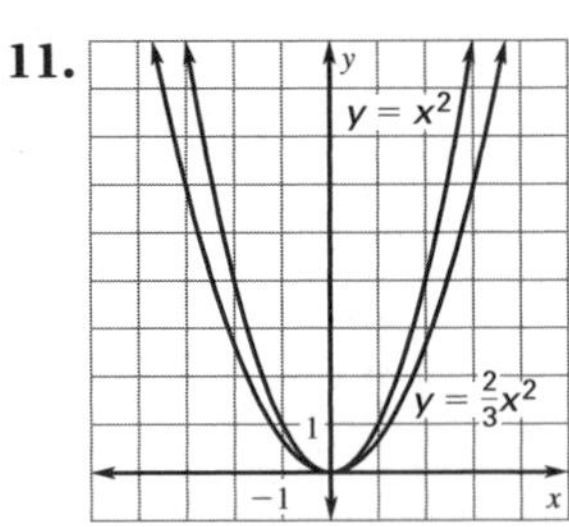

The graph is a vertical shrink $\left(\text{by a factor of } \frac{2}{3}\right)$ of the graph of $y = x^2$.

12. 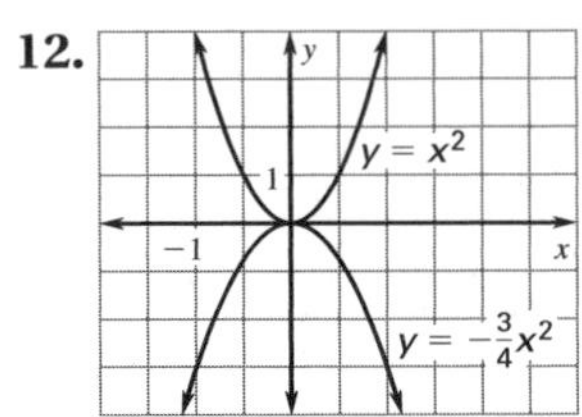

The graph is a vertical shrink $\left(\text{by a factor of } \frac{3}{4}\right)$ with a reflection in the x-axis of the graph of $y = x^2$.

13. 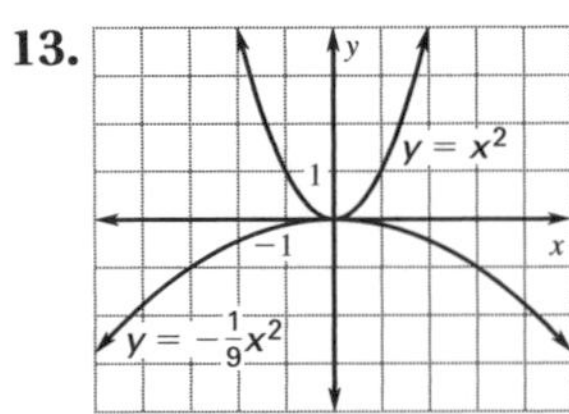

The graph is a vertical shrink $\left(\text{by a factor of } \frac{1}{9}\right)$ with a reflection in the x-axis of the graph of $y = x^2$.

14. 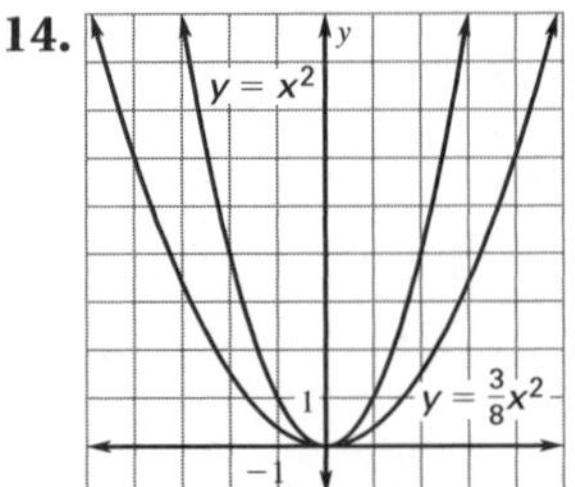

The graph is a vertical shrink $\left(\text{by a factor of } \frac{3}{8}\right)$ of the graph of $y = x^2$.

15. 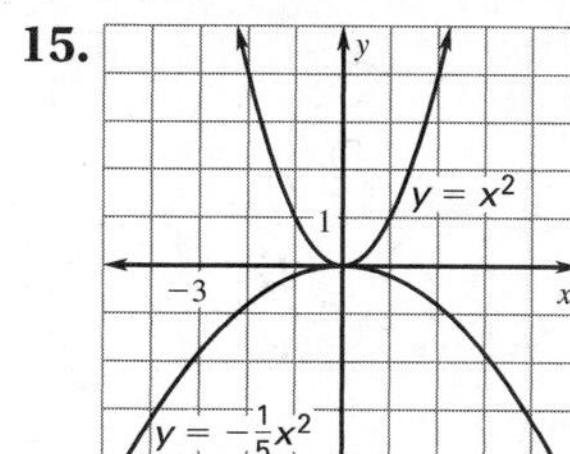

The graph is a vertical shrink $\left(\text{by a factor of } \frac{1}{5}\right)$ with a reflection in the x-axis of the graph of $y = x^2$.

16. 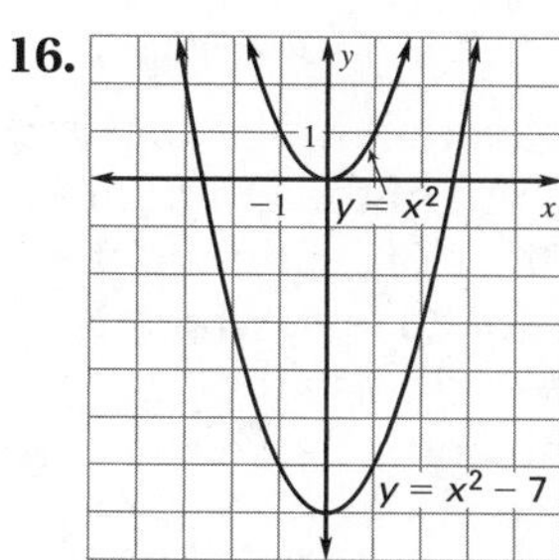

The graph is a vertical translation (of 7 units down) of the graph of $y = x^2$.

17. 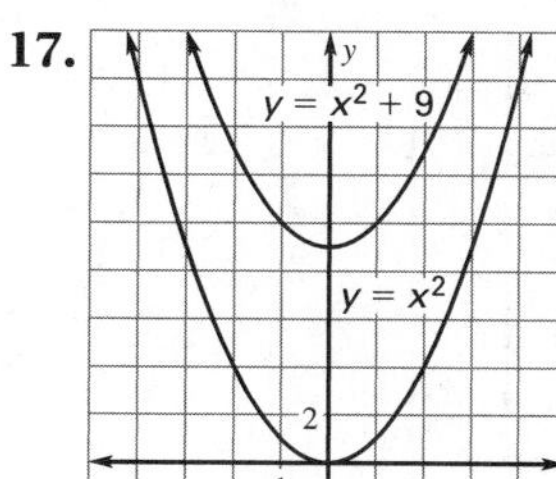

The graph is a vertical translation (of 9 units up) of the graph of $y = x^2$.

18. 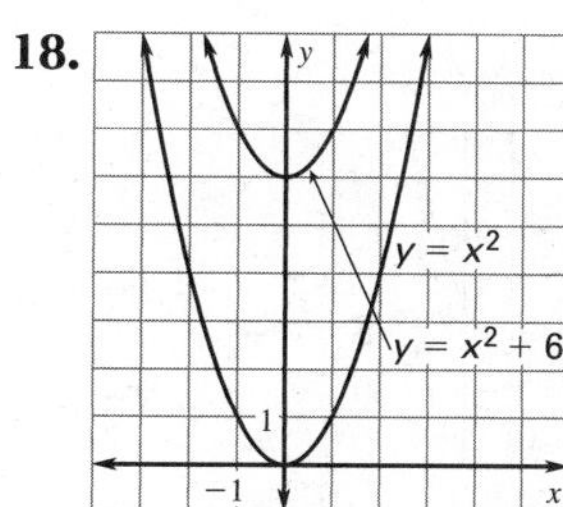

The graph is a vertical translation (of 6 units up) of the graph of $y = x^2$.

19. 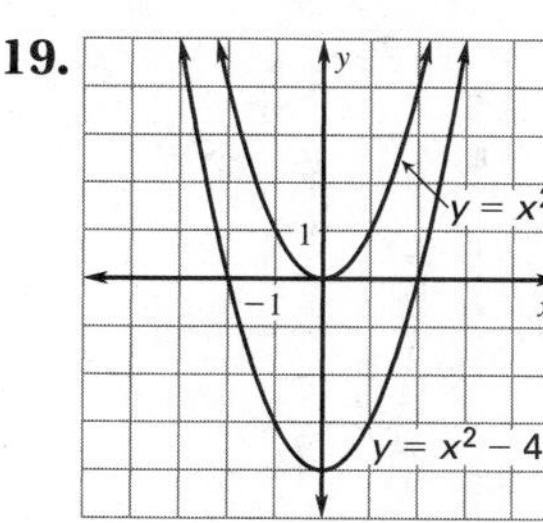

The graph is a vertical translation (of 4 units down) of the graph of $y = x^2$.

20. 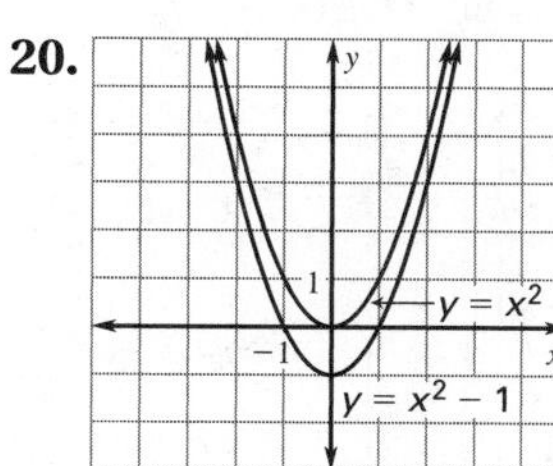

The graph is a vertical translation (of 1 unit down) of the graph of $y = x^2$.

21. 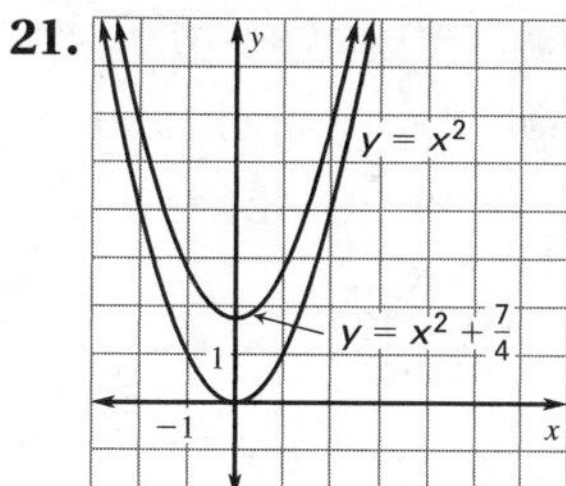

The graph is a vertical translation $\left(\text{of } \frac{7}{4} \text{ units up}\right)$ of the graph of $y = x^2$.

24. 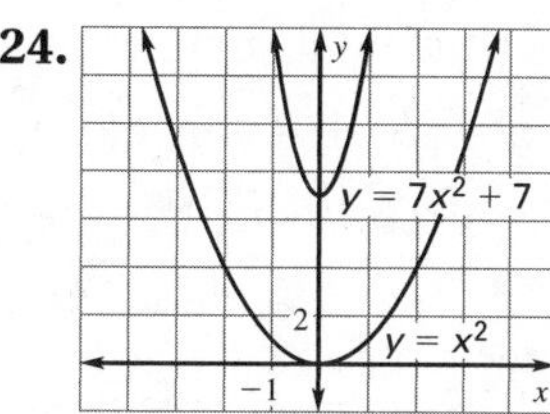

The graph is a vertical stretch (by a factor of 7) with a vertical translation (of 7 units up) of the graph of $y = x^2$.

25. 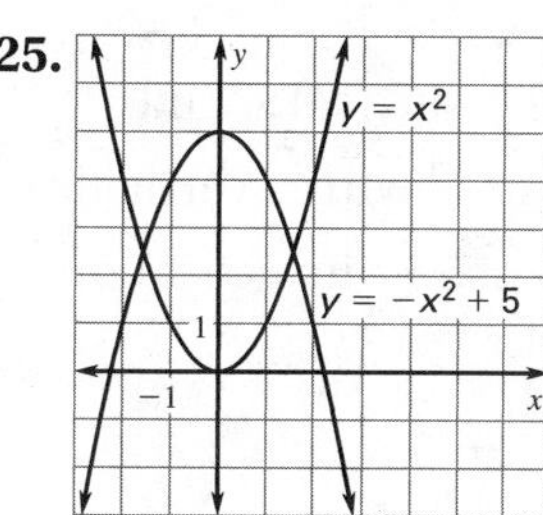

The graph is a reflection in the x-axis with a vertical translation (of 5 units up) of the graph of $y = x^2$.

26. 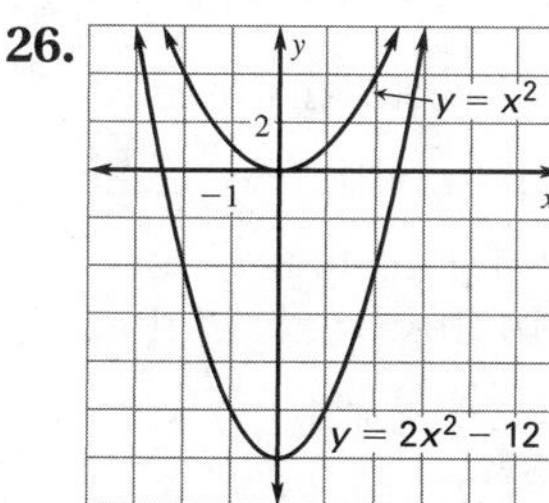

The graph is a vertical stretch (by a factor of 2) with a vertical translation (of 12 units down) of the graph of $y = x^2$.

27. 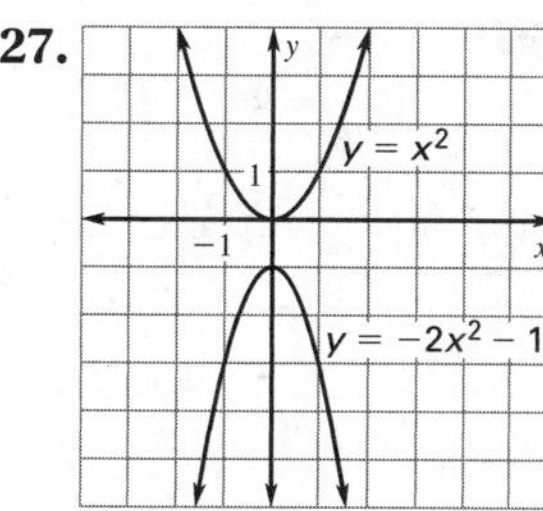

The graph is a vertical stretch (by a factor of 2) with a vertical translation (of 1 unit down) and a reflection in the x-axis of the graph of $y = x^2$.

28. 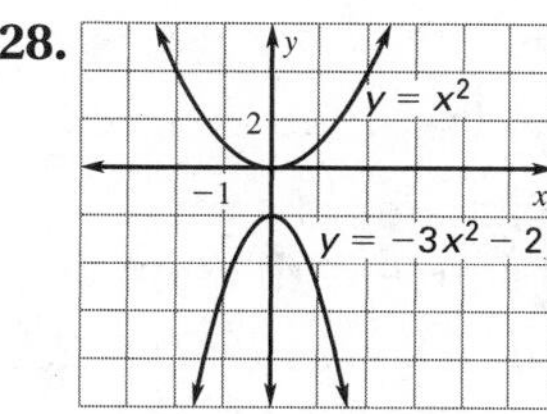

The graph is a vertical stretch (by a factor of 3) with a vertical translation (of 2 units down) and a reflection in the x-axis of the graph of $y = x^2$.

29.
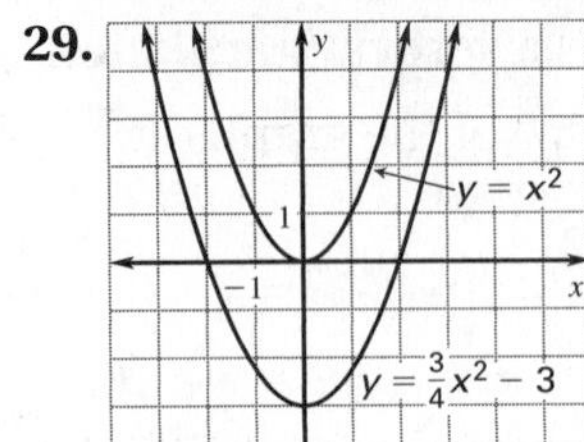

The graph is a vertical shrink $\left(\text{by a factor of } \frac{3}{4}\right)$ with a vertical translation (of 3 units down) of the graph of $y = x^2$.

30.
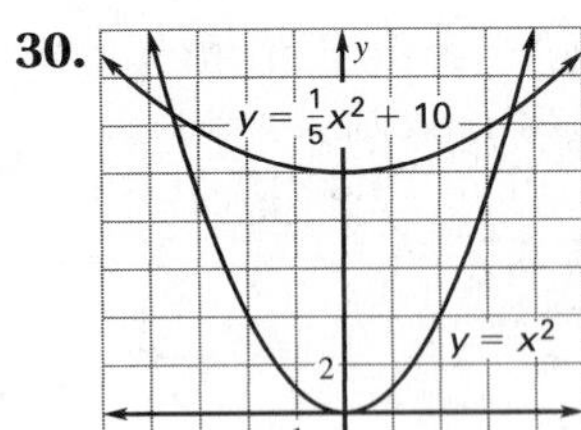

The graph is a vertical shrink $\left(\text{by a factor of } \frac{1}{5}\right)$ with a vertical translation (of 10 units up) of the graph of $y = x^2$.

31.
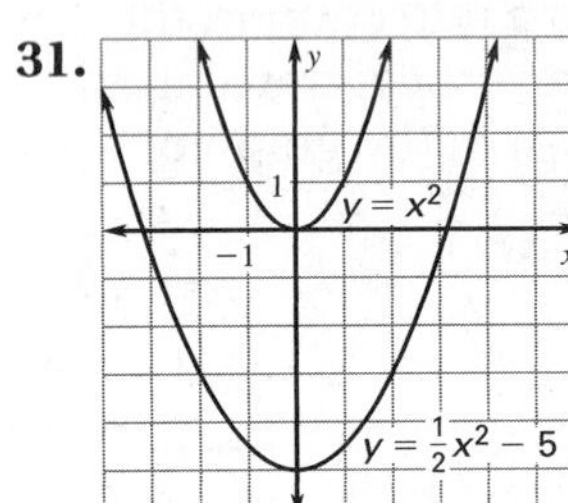

The graph is a vertical shrink $\left(\text{by a factor of } \frac{1}{2}\right)$ with a vertical translation (of 5 units down) of the graph of $y = x^2$.

32.
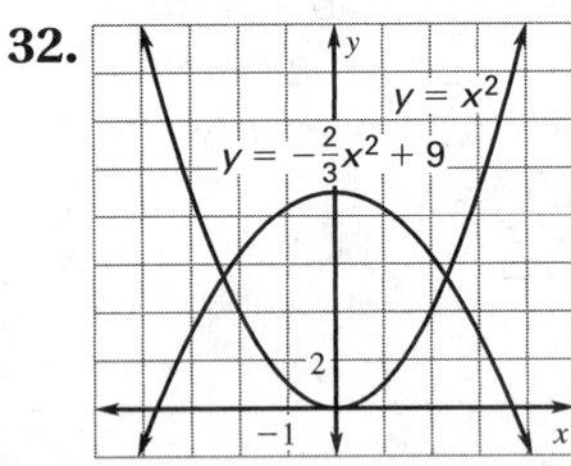

The graph is a vertical shrink $\left(\text{by a factor of } \frac{2}{3}\right)$ with a vertical translation (of 9 units up) and a reflection in the x-axis of the graph of $y = x^2$.

10.1 Problem Solving (pp. 633–634)

43. a.
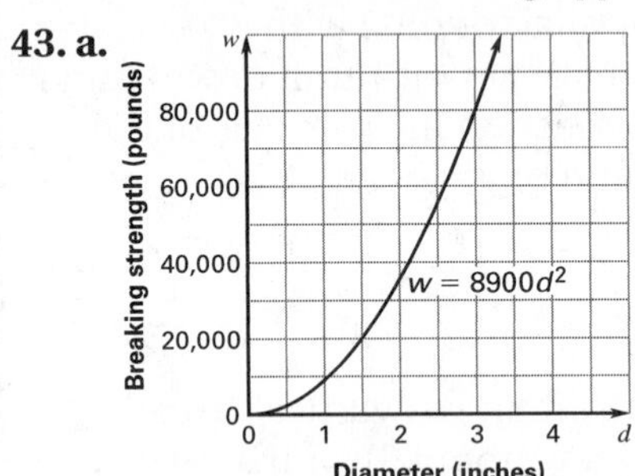

b. No. *Sample answer:* Let D be the diameter of a rope with 4 times the breaking strength of a rope with diameter d. Then $8900D^2 = 4(8900d^2)$; $D^2 = 4d^2$; $D = \sqrt{4d^2}$; $D = 2d$. Thus, the diameter of the rope with 4 times the breaking weight is only two times the diameter of the other rope.

44. a.
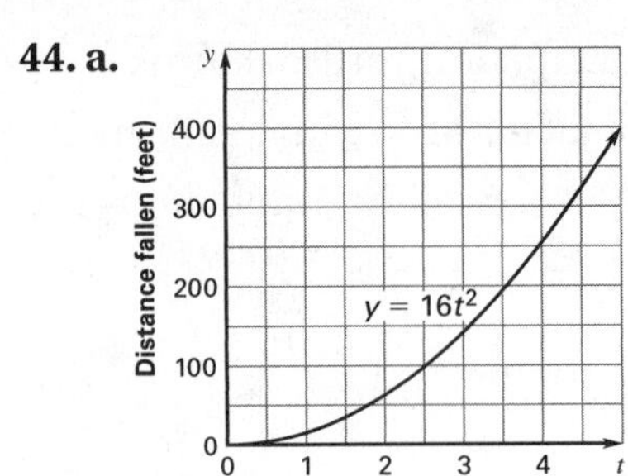

b.
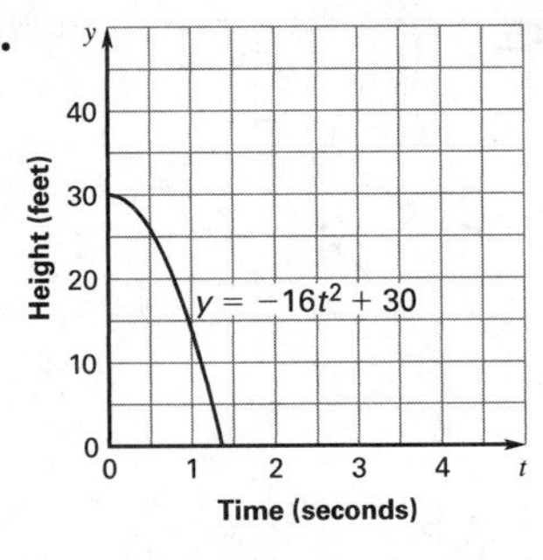

c. The graph of $y = -16t^2 + 30$ is a reflection in the x-axis and a vertical translation (of 30 units up) of the graph of $y = 16t^2$. To use the graph of $y = -16t^2 + 30$, estimate the t-value of the point that has a y-value of 20 feet, which is the height of the egg after it falls 10 feet. To use the graph of $y = 16t^2$, estimate the t-value of the point that has a y-value of 10 feet.

10.2 Skill Practice (pp. 638–639)

15.
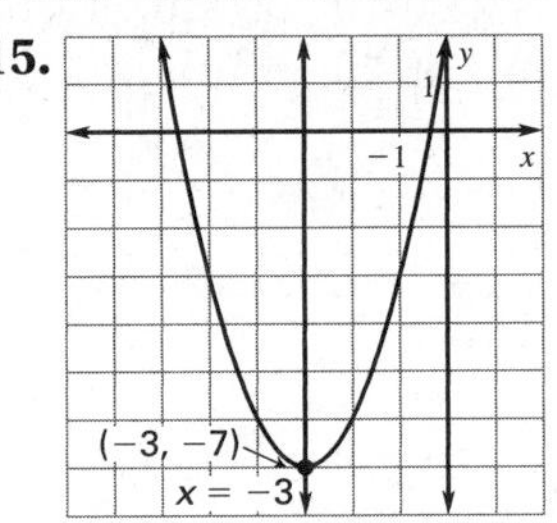

16.
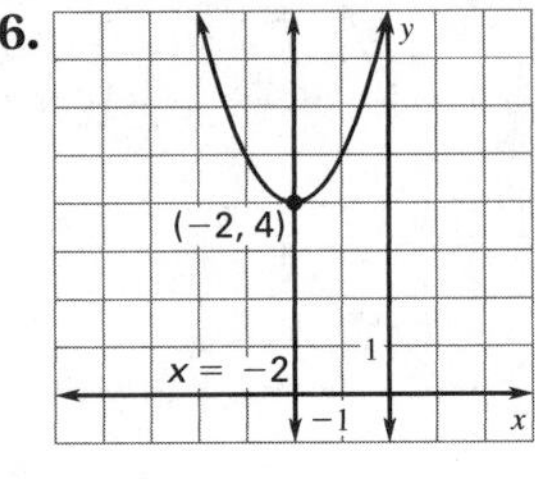

17.
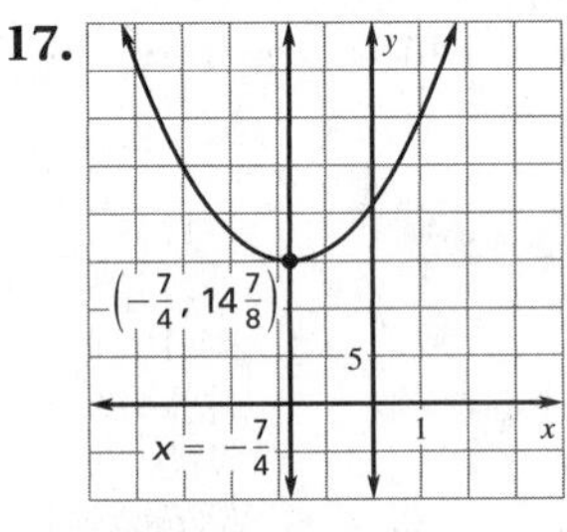

18.
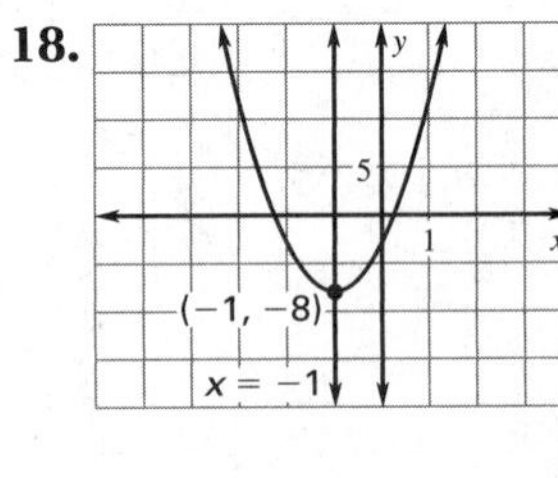

19.
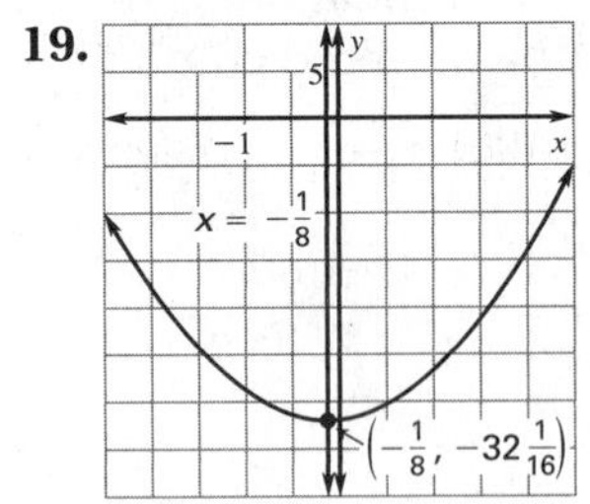

20.
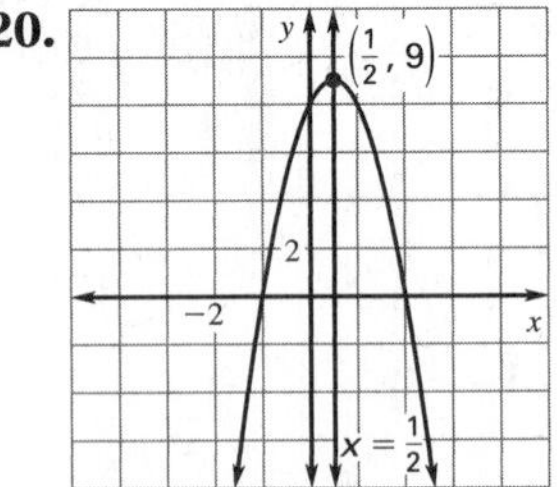

21.
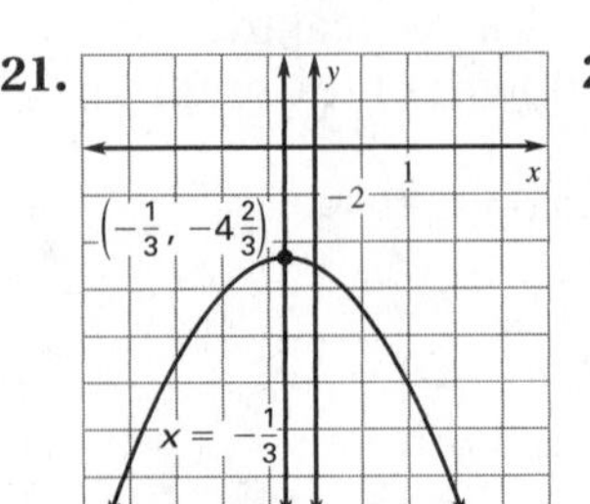

22.
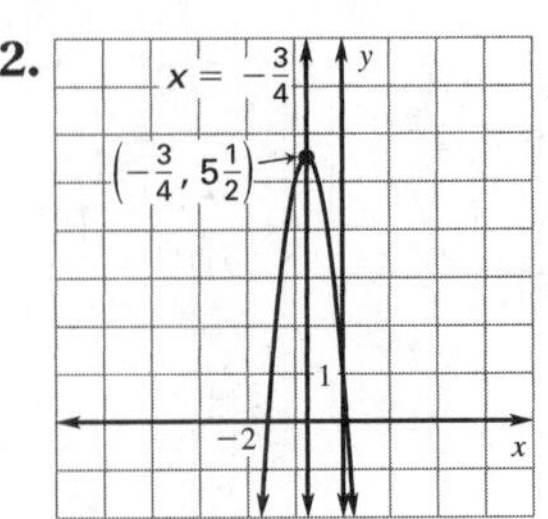

23.

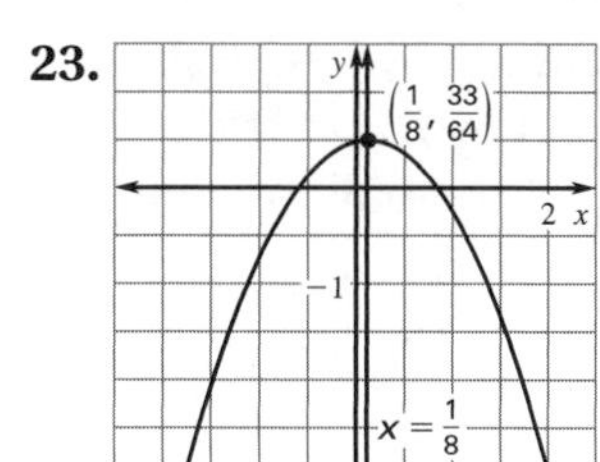

24.

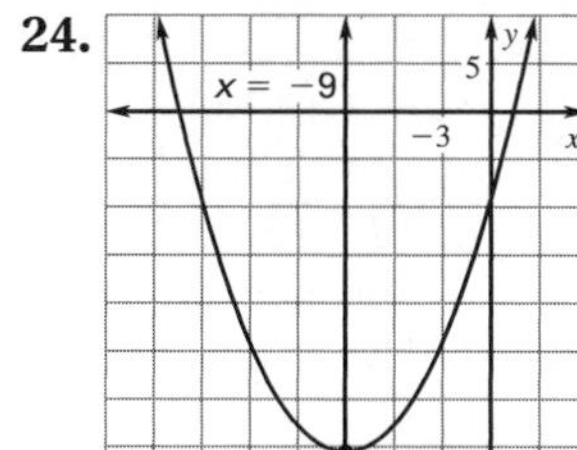

25.

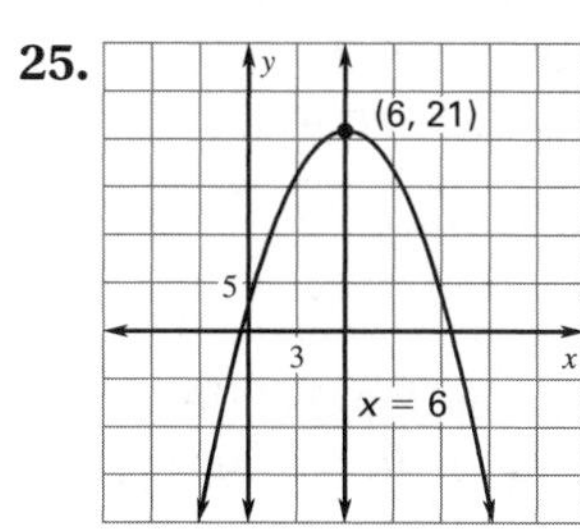

26.

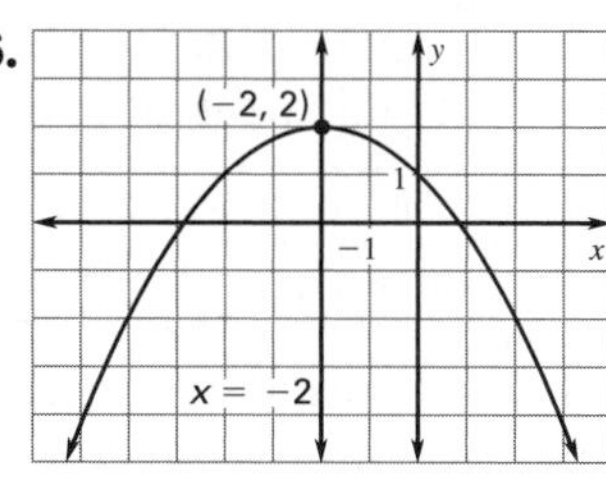

10.2 Problem Solving (pp. 639–640)

43.

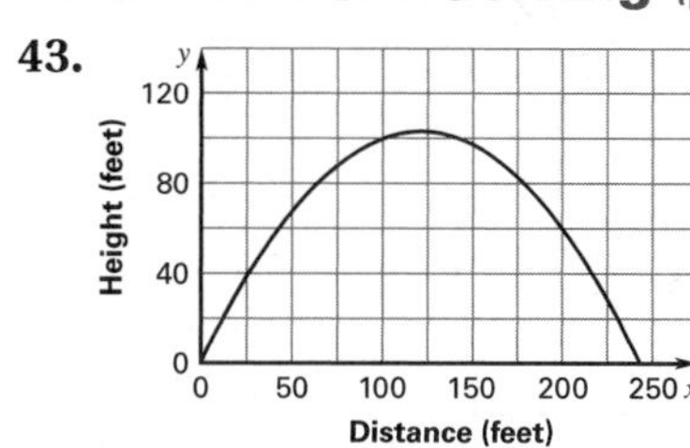

Extension (p. 642)

1.

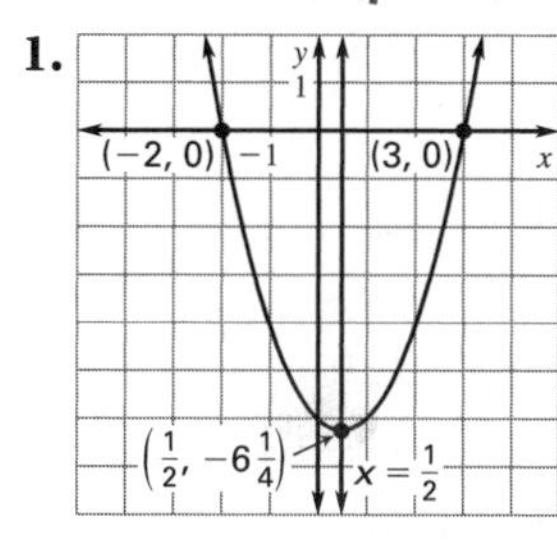

2.

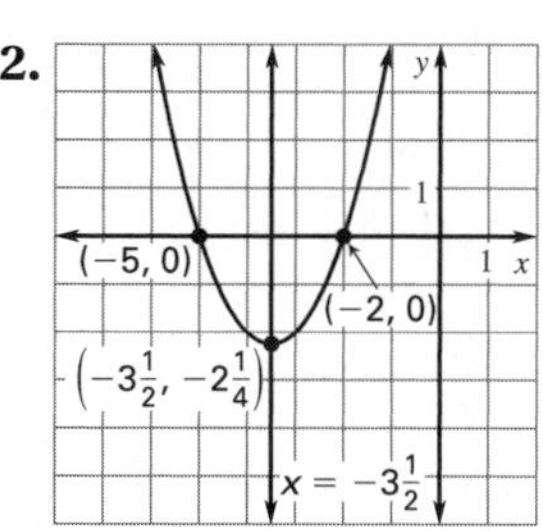

3.

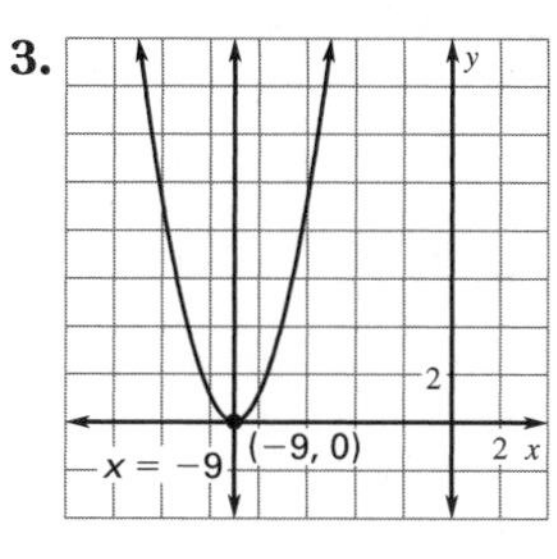

4.

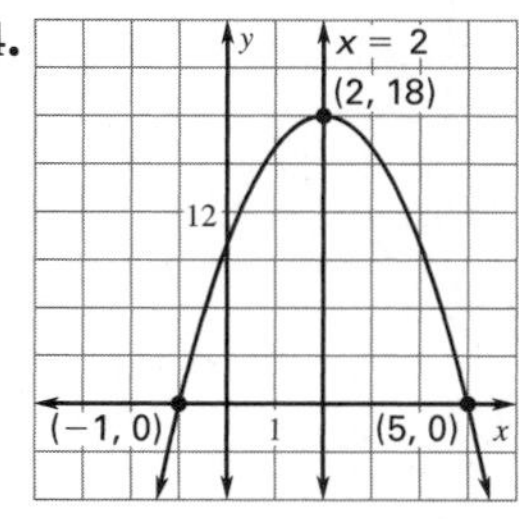

5.

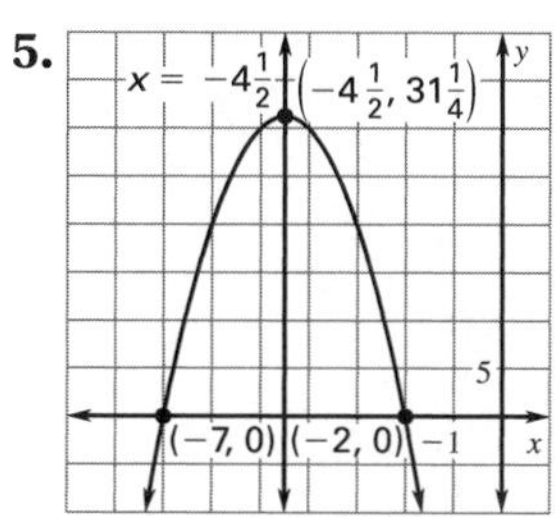

6.

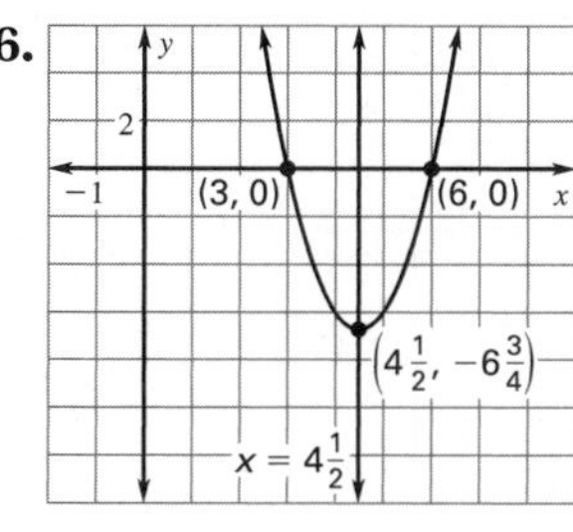

7.

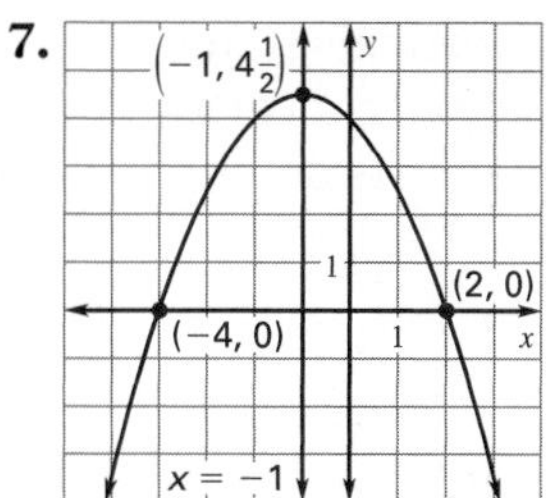

8.

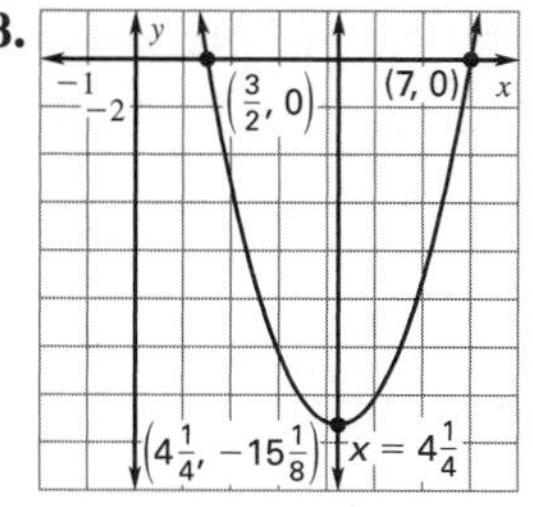

9.

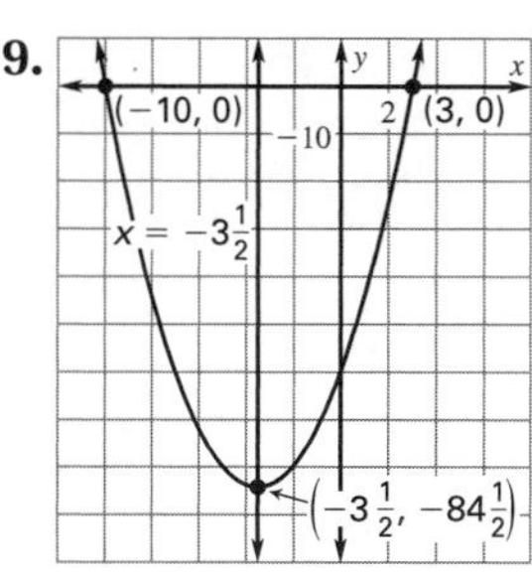

10.

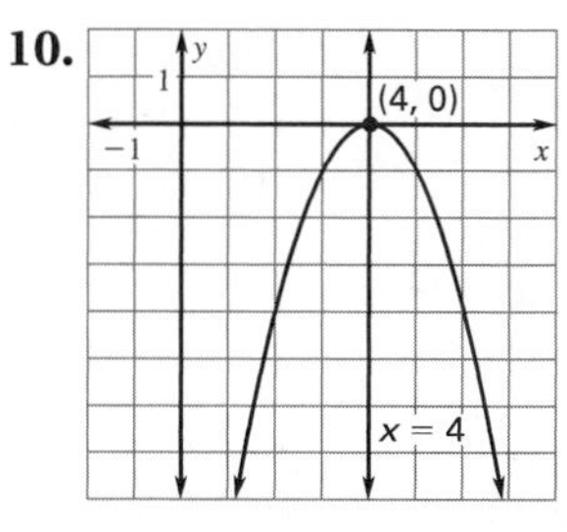

11.

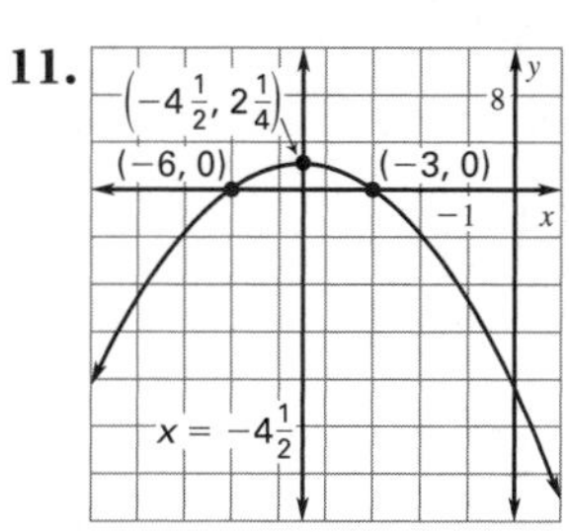

12.

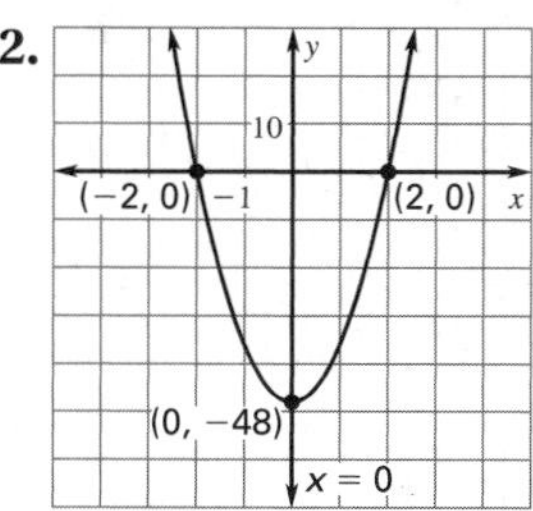

13.

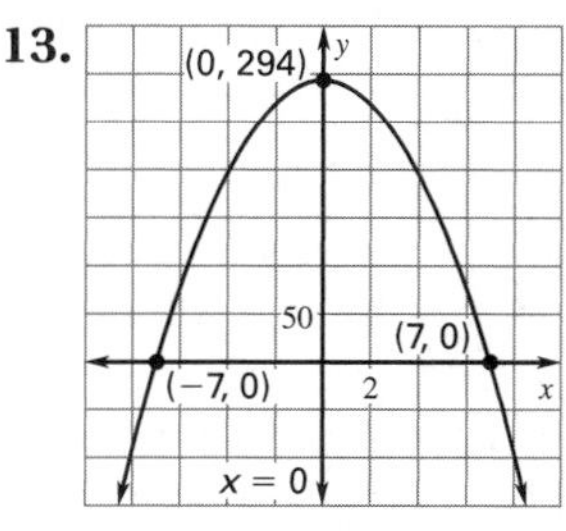

14.

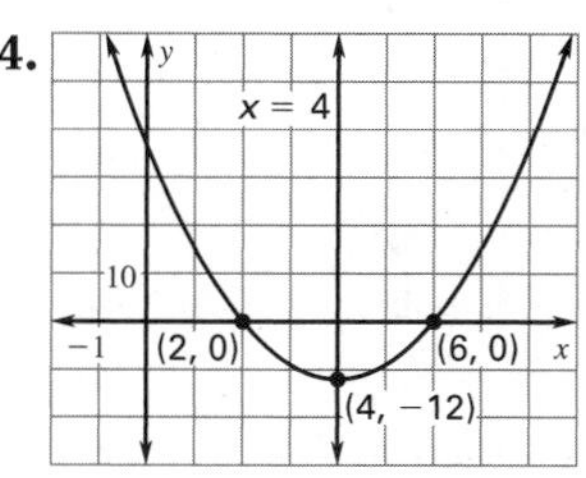

15.

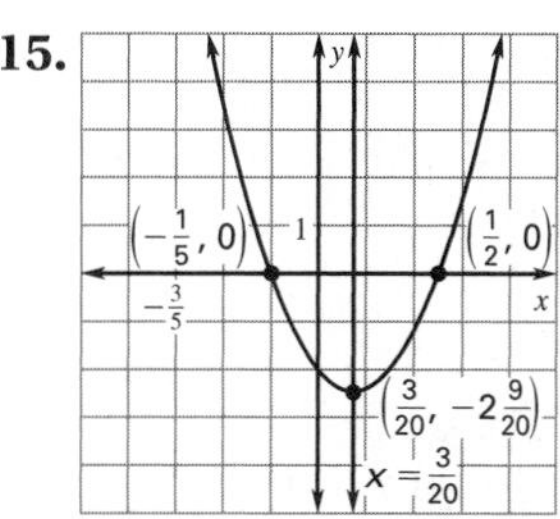

Quiz for Lessons 10.1–10.3 (p. 649)

1.

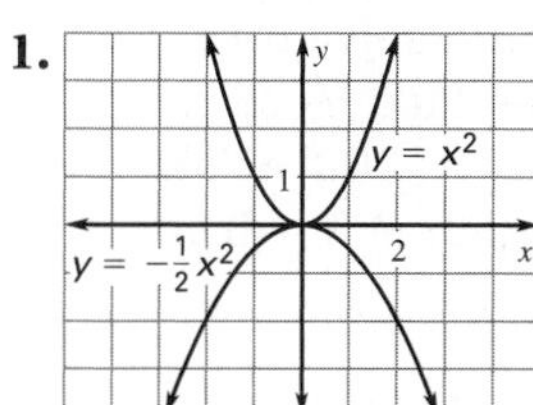

The graph is a vertical shrink $\left(\text{by a factor of } \frac{1}{2}\right)$ with a reflection in the x-axis of the graph of $y = x^2$.

ADDITIONAL ANSWERS

2. 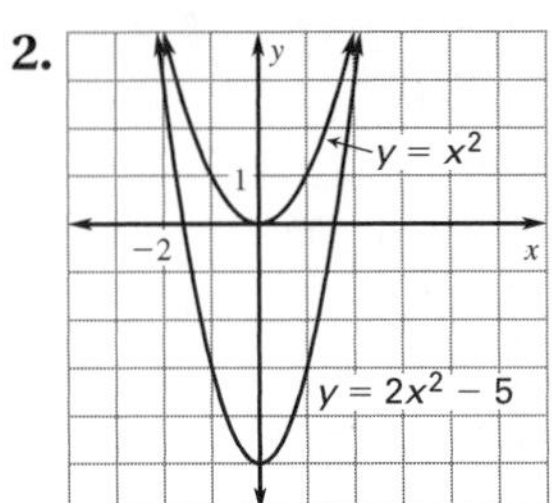

The graph is a vertical stretch (by a factor of 2) with a vertical translation (of 5 units down) of the graph of $y = x^2$.

3. 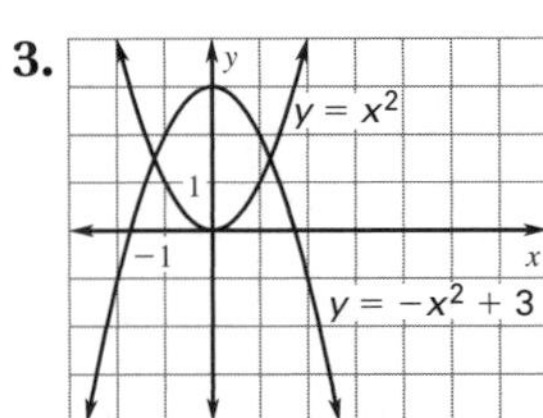

The graph is a vertical translation (of 3 units up) with a reflection in the x-axis of the graph of $y = x^2$.

4. 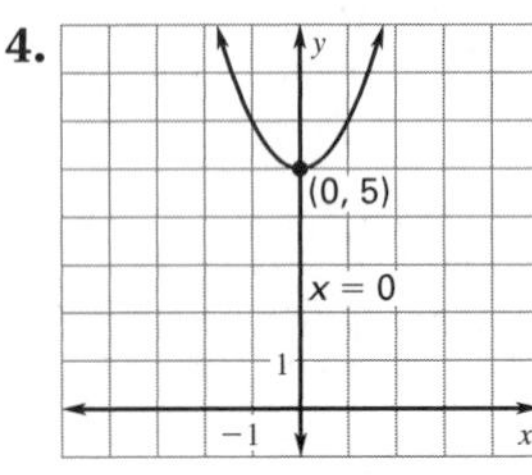

5. 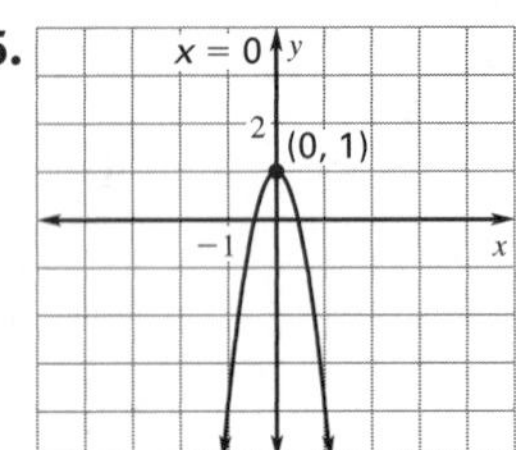

6. 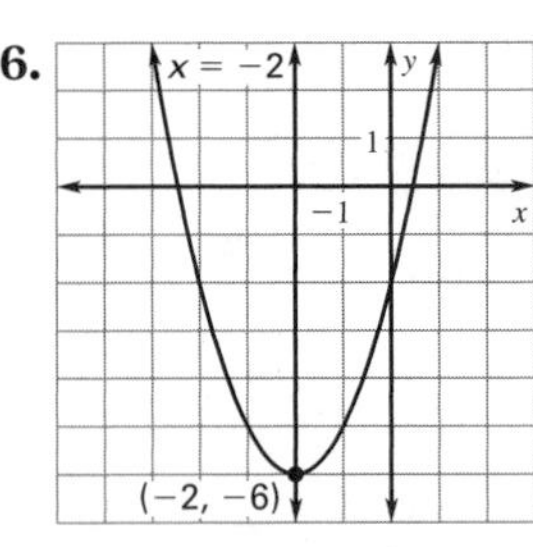

7. 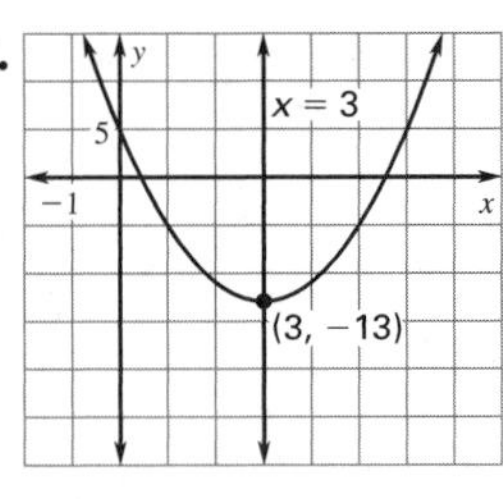

8. 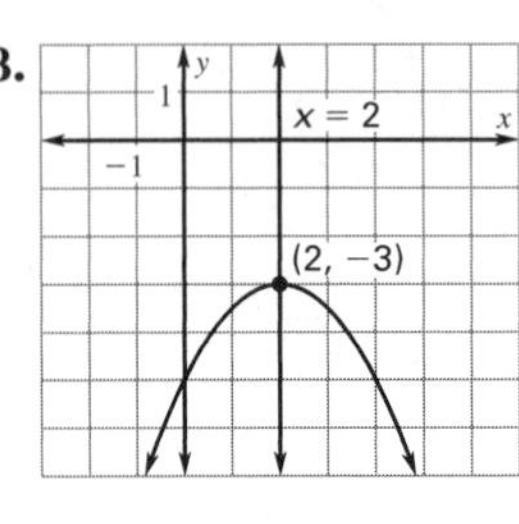

9. 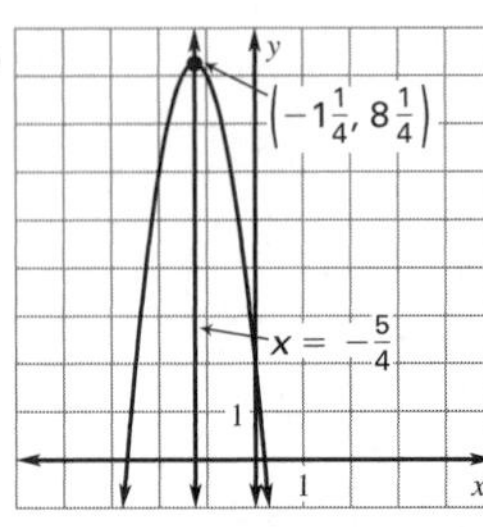

10.4 Problem Solving Workshop (p. 660) **1.** About 1.5 sec; Method 1: Use factoring. The height h (in feet) of the ball t seconds after it is dropped is modeled by $h = -16t^2 + 45$. To find the time it takes the ball to reach a height of 10 feet, substitute 10 for h and solve for t: $10 = -16t^2 + 45$, or $0 = -16t^2 + 35$. Replace 35 with the closest perfect square and factor: $0 = -16t^2 + 36$; $0 = -4(4t^2 - 9)$; $0 = -4(2t + 3)(2t - 3)$; $2t + 3 = 0$ *or* $2t - 3 = 0$; $t = -\frac{3}{2}$ or $t = \frac{3}{2}$. The time cannot be negative, so disregard the negative solution; the ball is in the air about 1.5 seconds.

Method 2: Use a table. The height h (in feet) of the ball t seconds after it is dropped is modeled by $h = -16t^2 + 45$. Make a table that shows the height h of the ball for values of t in increments of 1 second:

Time, t (sec)	0	1	2
Height, h (ft)	45	29	−19

Look in the table for the time interval in which the ball reaches a height of 10 feet; this happens between 1 and 2 seconds. Make a second table using increments of 0.1 second:

Time, t (sec)	1.0	1.1	1.2	1.3	1.4	1.5
Height, h (ft)	29.00	25.64	21.96	17.96	13.64	9

The height in the table that is closest to 10 feet is 9 feet. To the nearest tenth of a second, the ball is in the air for about 1.5 seconds.

3. b. length: about 9 in., width: 5 in., height: about 1.8 in.

c.

Height, x (in.)	1.7	1.8	1.9
Width (in.)	5	5	5
Length, $5x$ (in.)	8.5	9	9.5
Volume, V (in.^{3})	72.25	81	90.25

The volume in the table closest to 83 cubic inches is 81 cubic inches. To the nearest tenth of an inch, the height of the box is about 1.8 inches. The length of the box is $5x \approx 9$ inches, and the width is 5 inches.

Extension (p. 670)

1. 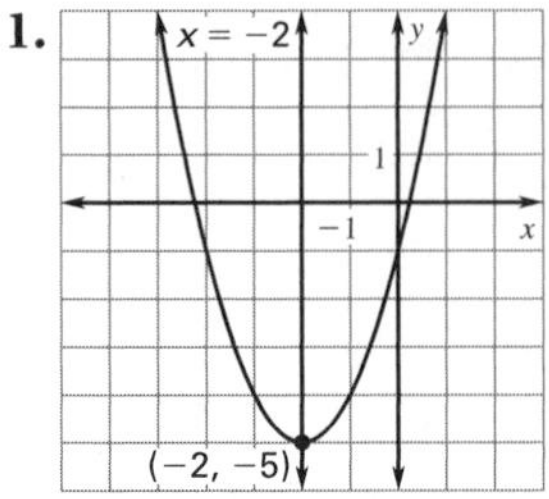

2. 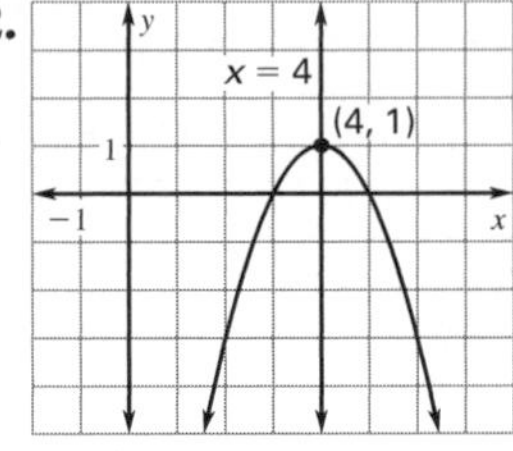

3. 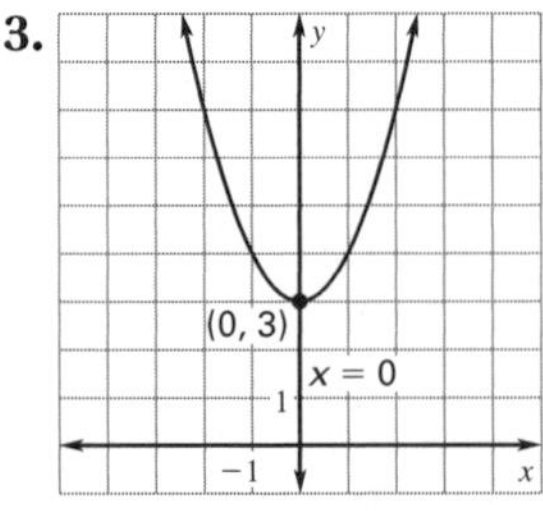

4. 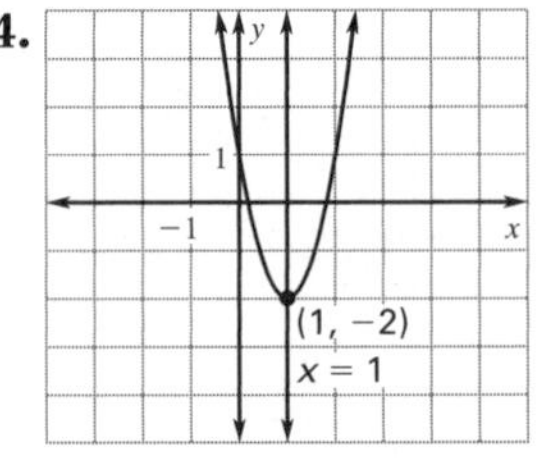

5. 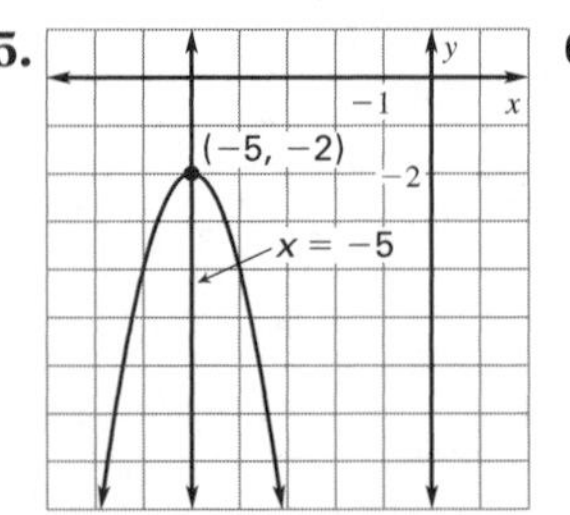

6. 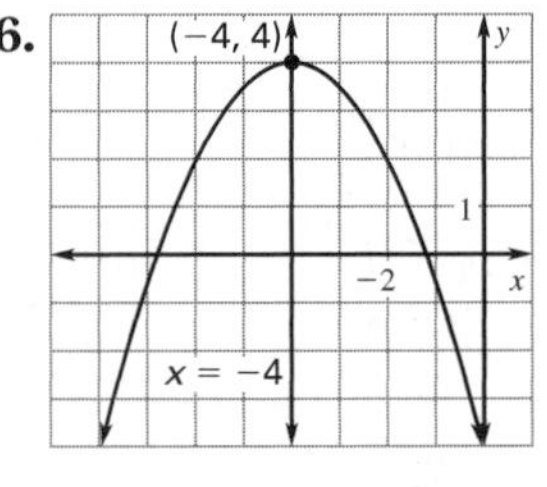

7. $y = (x - 6)^2$

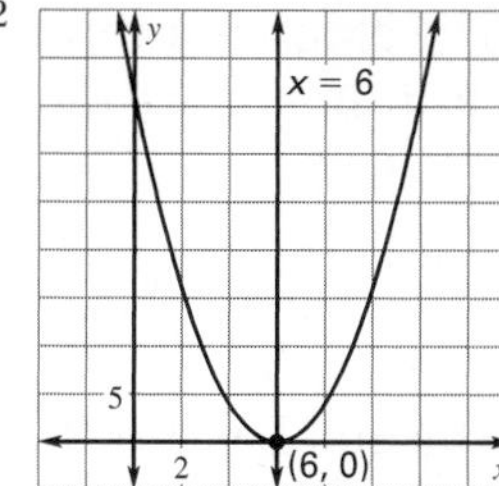

8. $y = (x + 4)^2 - 1$

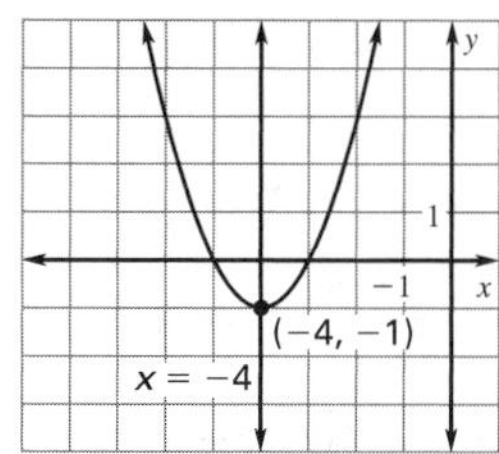

9. $y = -(x - 5)^2 + 4$

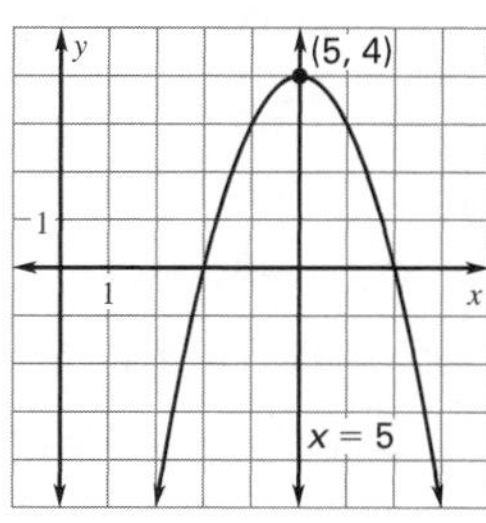

10. $y = 2(x - 3)^2 + 1$

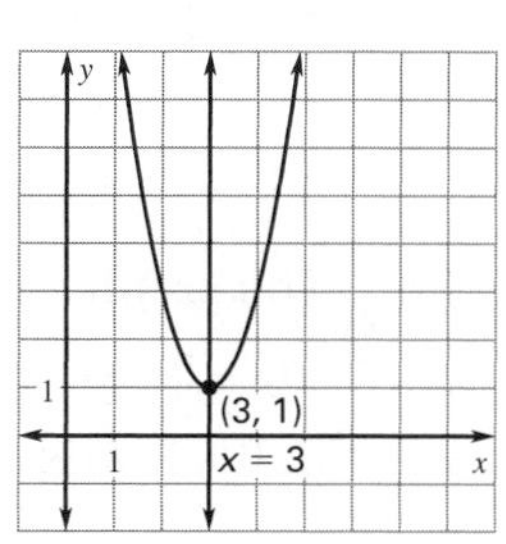

11. $y = -3(x + 1)^2 + 2$

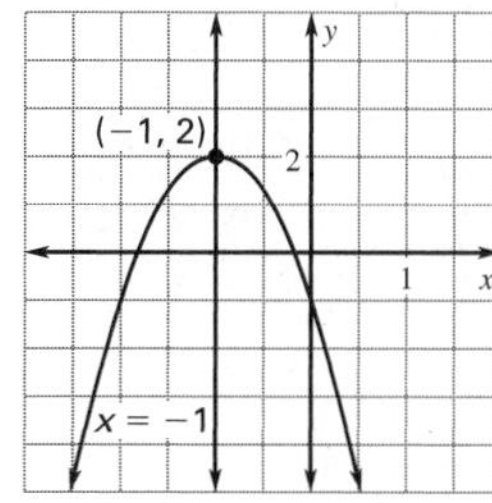

12. $y = -\frac{1}{2}(x + 6)^2 - 3$

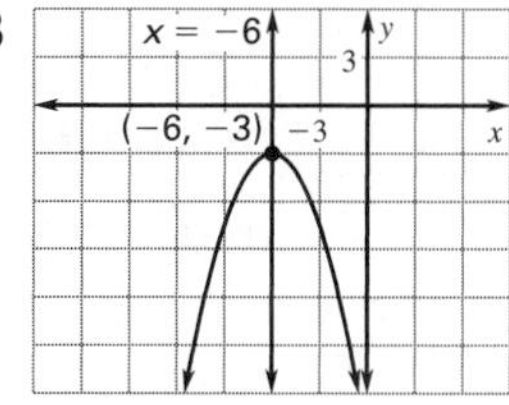

10.6 Mixed Review (p. 676)

56.

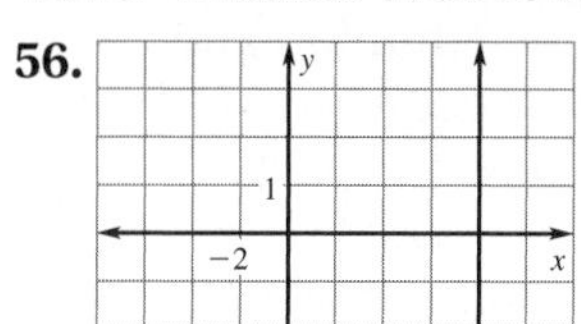

57.

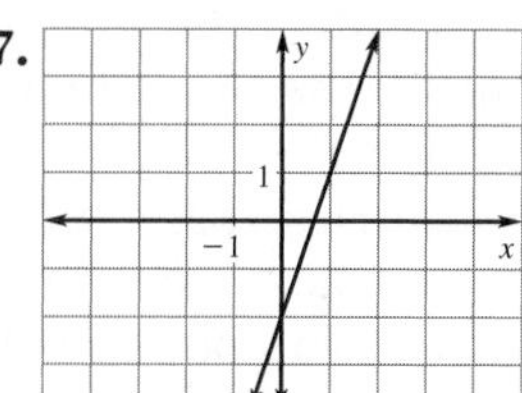

58.

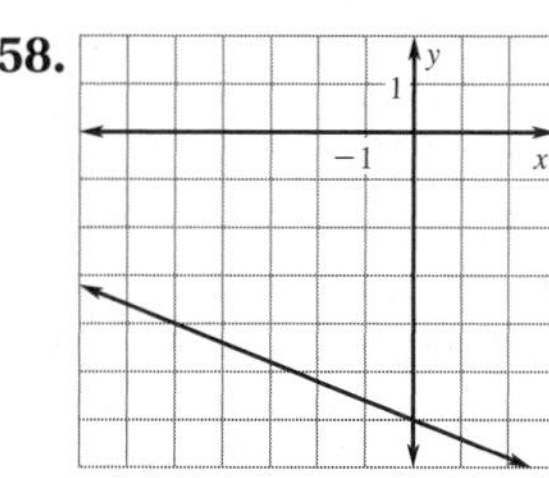

59.

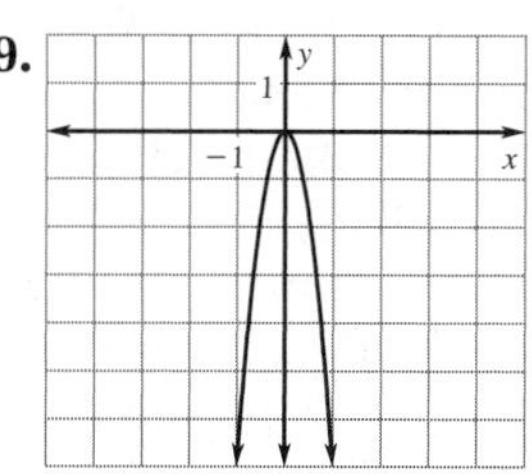

60.

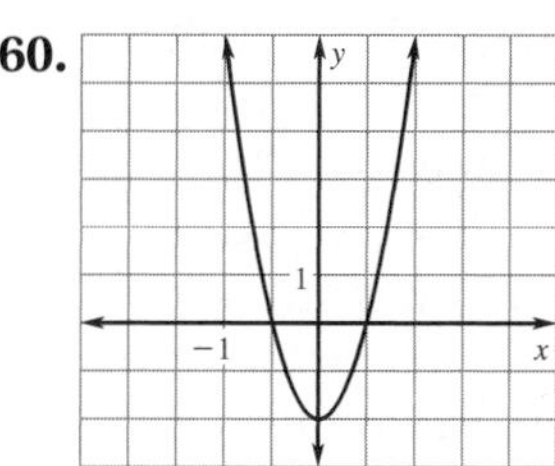

61.

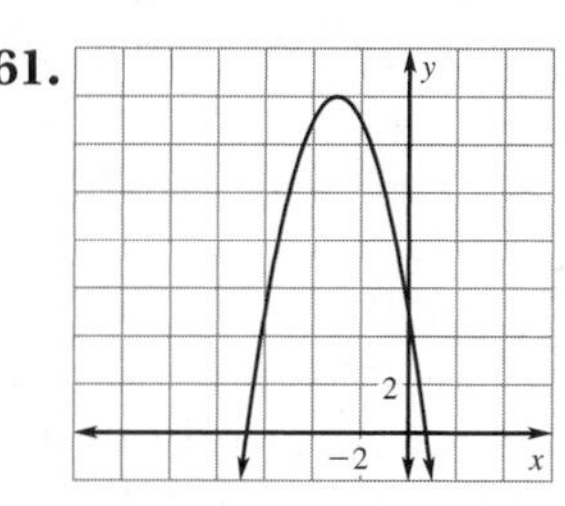

10.7 Investigating Algebra Activity (p. 677)

2. When $b^2 - 4ac$ is positive, $b^2 - 4ac$ has two square roots, one positive and one negative, so there are two different solutions to the quadratic equation $ax^2 + bx + c = 0$: $\frac{-b + \sqrt{b^2 - 4ac}}{2a}$ and $\frac{-b - \sqrt{b^2 - 4ac}}{2a}$. When $b^2 - 4ac$ is zero, $\sqrt{b^2 - 4ac} = 0$, so there is only one solution to the quadratic equation $ax^2 + bx + c = 0$: $\frac{-b \pm 0}{2a} = -\frac{b}{2a}$. When $b^2 - 4ac$ is negative, there is a negative number under the radical in the quadratic formula. Because negative numbers do not have real-number square roots, the quadratic formula cannot be evaluated and the quadratic equation $ax^2 + bx + c = 0$ has no real solution.

10.7 Skill Practice (pp. 681–682)

41. c. $-25, 5$; the width w cannot be negative, so the solution -25 meters does not make sense in the context of the problem. The solution 5 meters does makes sense in the context of the problem. **42. a.** $k < \frac{1}{24}$ **b.** $\frac{1}{24}$ **c.** $k > \frac{1}{24}$ **43. a.** $k < -3$ *or* $k > 3$ **b.** ± 3 **c.** $-3 < k < 3$ **44. a.** $k > -\frac{25}{64}$ **b.** $-\frac{25}{64}$ **c.** $k < -\frac{25}{64}$

10.7 Problem Solving (pp. 682–683)

45. a. Substitute 25 for y in the equation and then write the resulting quadratic equation in standard form: $25 = 0.06x^2 - 4x + 87$, or $0 = 0.06x^2 - 4x + 62$. Evaluate the discriminant: $b^2 - 4ac = (-4)^2 - 4(0.06)(62) = 1.12$. Since the discriminant is positive, we know that the equation $25 = 0.06x^2 - 4x + 87$ does have solutions, so it is possible for a parakeet to consume 25 milliliters of oxygen per gram of body mass per hour.

47. No; to determine if there is any point of the arch at a height of 4 feet, substitute 4 for y in the equation and then determine if the equation has any positive solutions. The equation is $4 = -0.18x^2 + 1.6x$, or $0 = -0.18x^2 + 1.6x - 4$. Evaluate the discriminant: $b^2 - 4ac = (1.6)^2 - 4(-0.18)(-4) = -0.32$. Since the discriminant is negative, we know the equation has no solution; thus, a child who is 4 feet tall cannot walk under one of the arches without having to bend over. **50. b.** Yes; no; \$28,900; to decide if a weekly revenue of \$28,000 is possible, check the discriminant of the equation $28{,}000 = -100x^2 + 1400x + 24{,}000$, or $0 = -100x^2 + 1400x - 4000$. The discriminant is 360,000. Since the discriminant is positive, it may be possible to receive a weekly revenue of \$28,000. To decide if a weekly revenue of \$30,000 is possible, check the discriminant of the equation $30{,}000 = -100x^2 + 1400x + 24{,}000$, or $0 = -100x^2 + 1400x - 6000$. The discriminant is $-440{,}000$. Since the discriminant is negative, it is not possible to receive a weekly revenue of \$30,000. Since $r = -100x^2 + 1400x + 24{,}000$ is equivalent to the quadratic equation $0 = -100x^2 + 1400x + (24{,}000 - r)$, the maximum revenue r will occur when this equation has exactly one solution, or when its discriminant is 0. Solve $1400^2 - 4(-100)(24{,}000 - r) = 0$ for r; $r = \$28{,}900$.

10.7 Mixed Review (p. 683)

51.

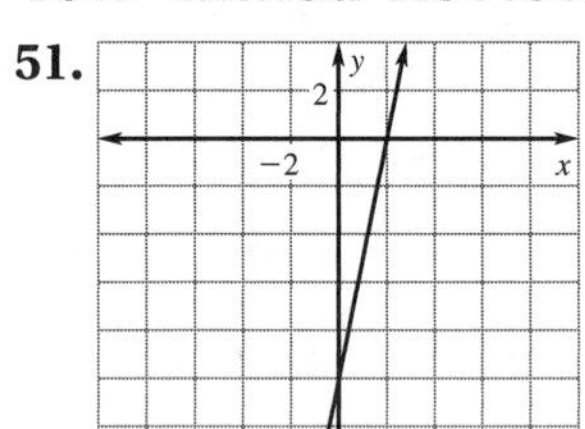

52.

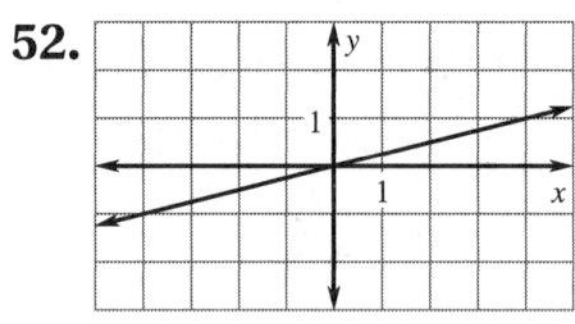

53.

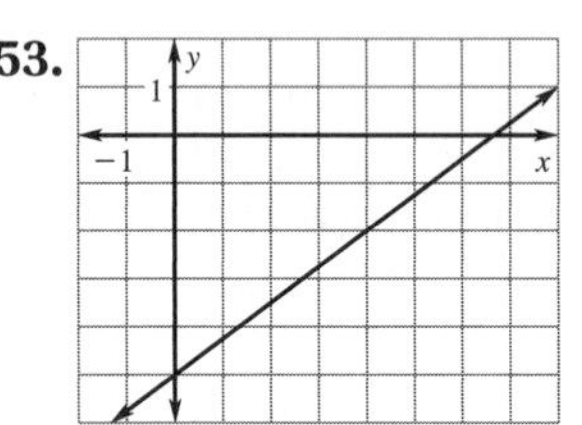

54.

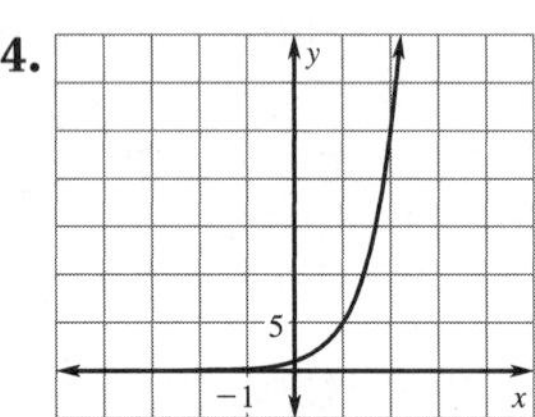

55.

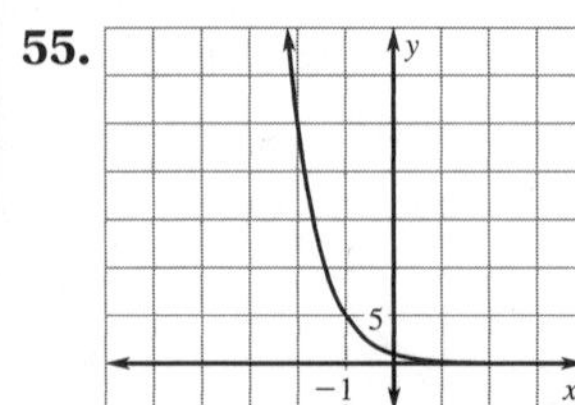

56.

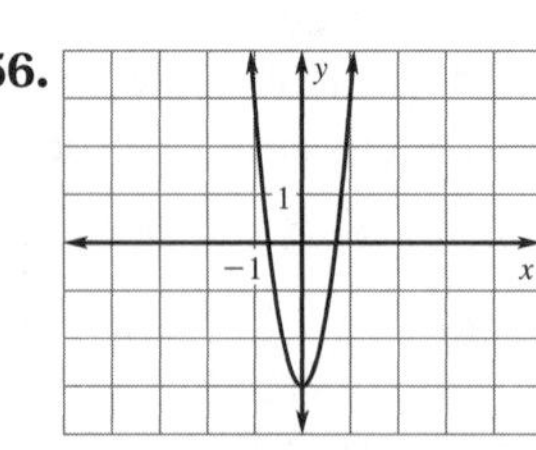

10.8 Mixed Review (p. 691)

35.

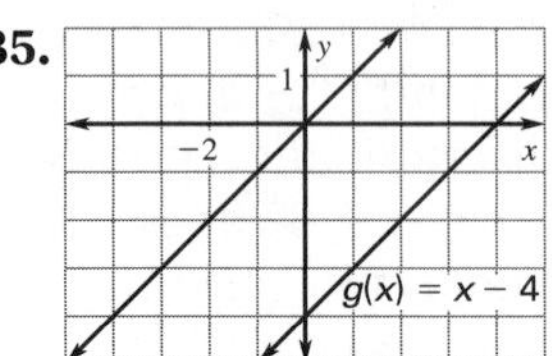

The graph is a vertical translation (of 4 units down) of the graph of $y = x$.

36.

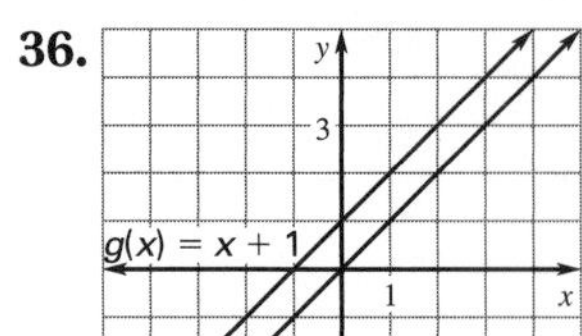

The graph is a vertical translation (of 1 unit up) of the graph of $y = x$.

37.

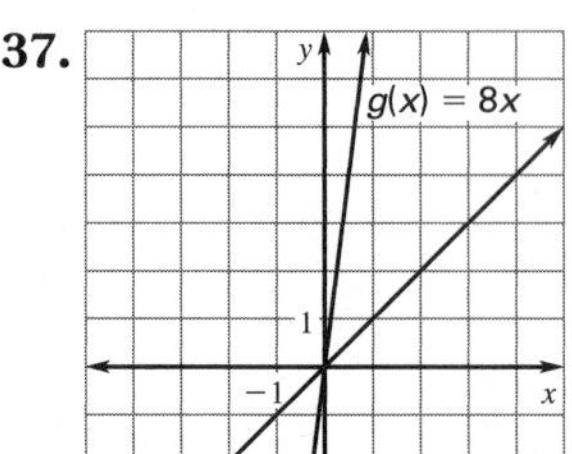

The graph is a vertical stretch (by a factor of 8) of the graph of $y = x$.

38.

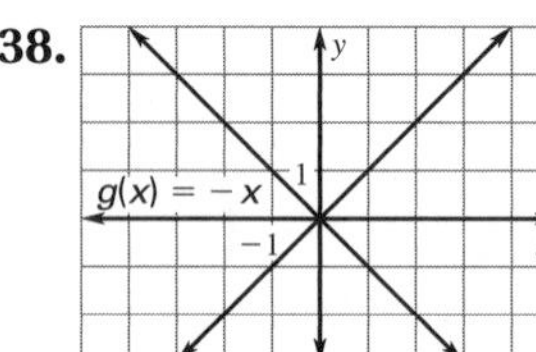

The graph is a reflection in the x-axis of the graph of $y = x$.

39.

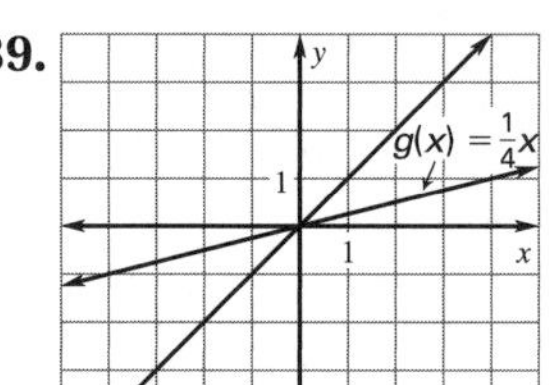

The graph is a vertical shrink $\left(\text{by a factor of } \frac{1}{4}\right)$ of the graph of $y = x$.

40.

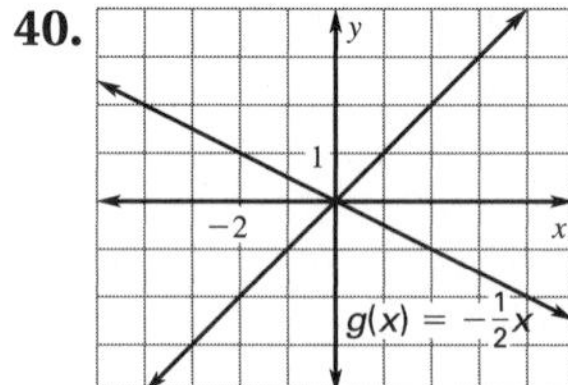

The graph is a vertical shrink $\left(\text{by a factor of } \frac{1}{2}\right)$ with a reflection in the x-axis of the graph of $y = x$.

41.

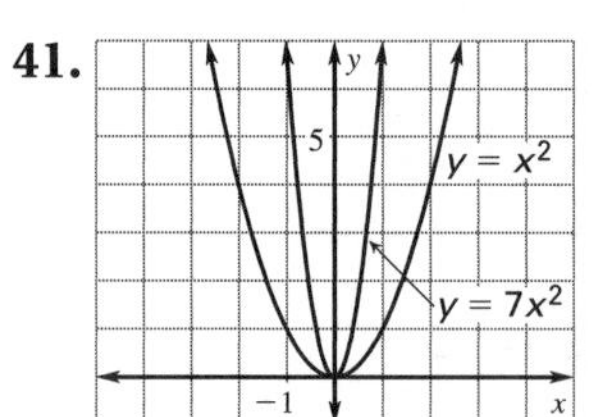

The graph is a vertical stretch (by a factor of 7) of the graph of $y = x^2$.

42.

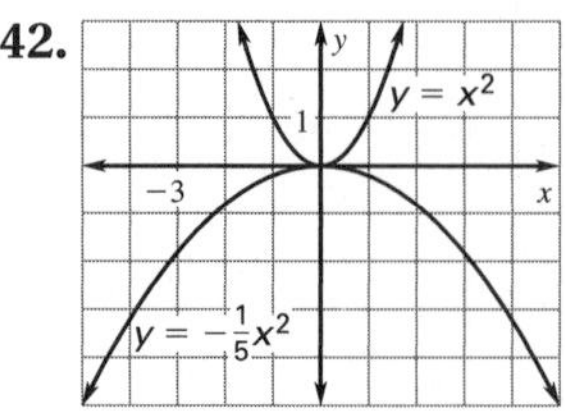

The graph is a vertical shrink $\left(\text{by a factor of } \frac{1}{5}\right)$ with a reflection in the x-axis of the graph of $y = x^2$.

ADDITIONAL ANSWERS

43. 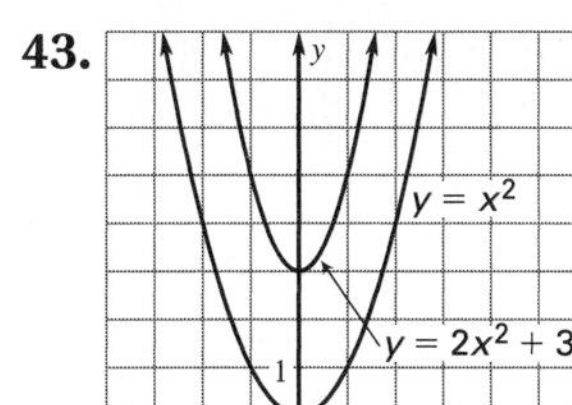

The graph is a vertical stretch (by a factor of 2) with a vertical translation (of 3 units up) of the graph of $y = x^2$.

Cumulative Review (pp. 706–707)

18. 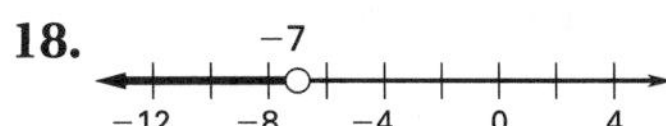

19. −36

−60 −40 −20 0 20

20. −2 0 2 4 6

21. −3 −2 −1 0 1 2 3 4 5

22. 0 2 4 6 8

23. $-\frac{3}{2}$

−2 −1 0 1 2 3 4 5 6 7 8

Chapter 11

11.1 Guided Practice (pp. 711–713)

1. 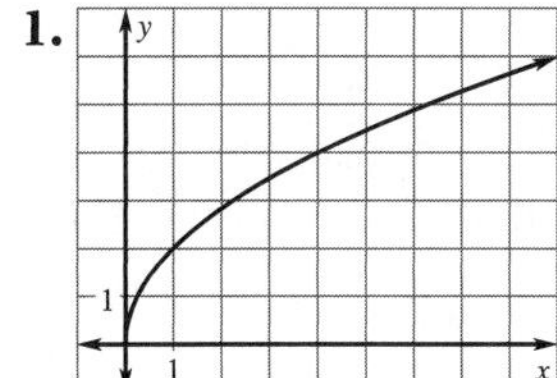
domain: $x \geq 0$, range: $y \geq 0$; vertical stretch by a factor of 2

2. 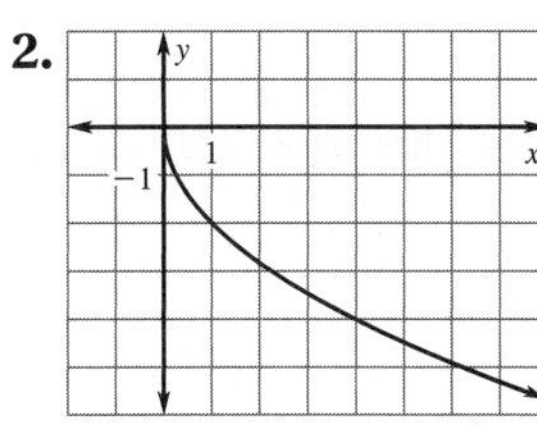
domain: $x \geq 0$, range: $y \leq 0$; vertical stretch by a factor of 2 and a reflection in the x-axis

3. 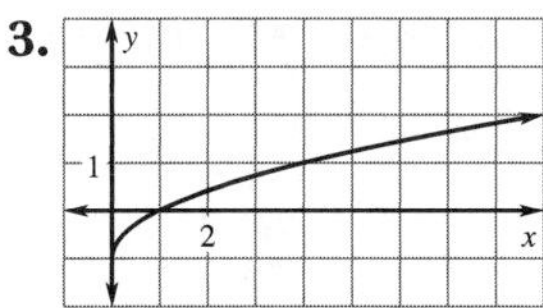
domain: $x \geq 0$, range: $y \geq -1$; vertical translation of 1 unit down

4. 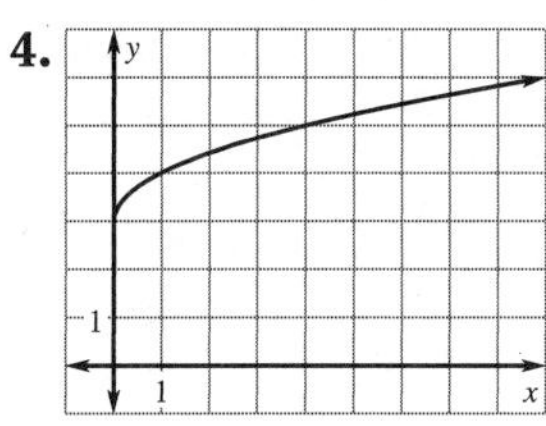
domain: $x \geq 0$, range: $y \geq 3$; vertical translation of 3 units up

11.1 Skill Practice (pp. 713–714)

3. 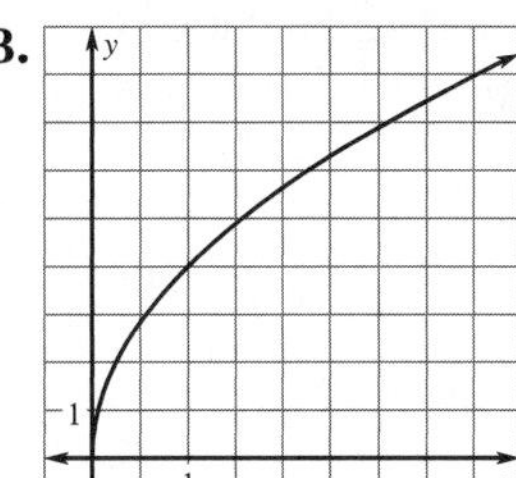
domain: $x \geq 0$, range: $y \geq 0$; vertical stretch by a factor of 4

4. 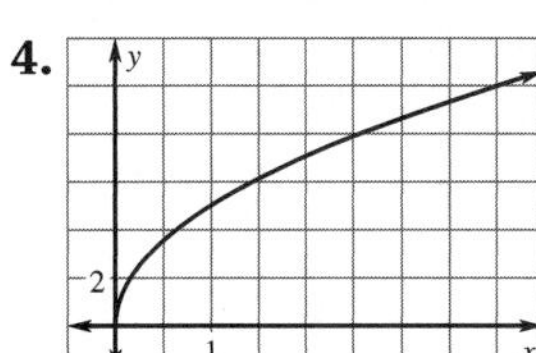
domain: $x \geq 0$, range: $y \geq 0$; vertical stretch by a factor of 5

5. 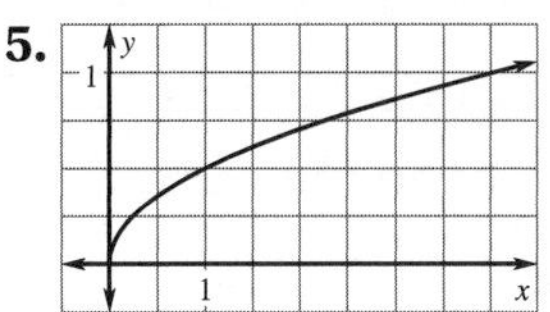
domain: $x \geq 0$, range: $y \geq 0$; vertical shrink by a factor of 0.5

6. 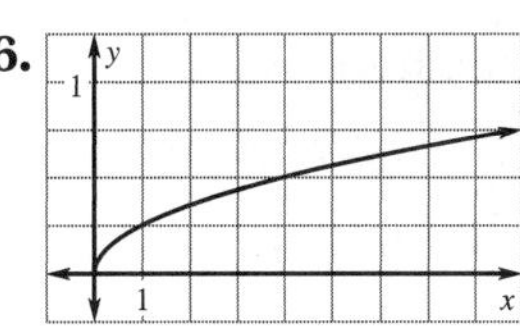
domain: $x \geq 0$, range: $y \geq 0$; vertical shrink by a factor of 0.25

7. 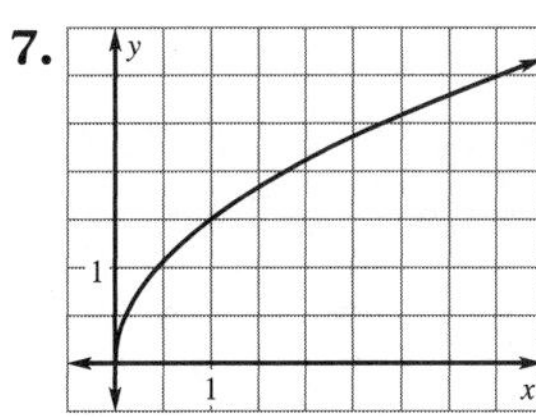
domain: $x \geq 0$, range: $y \geq 0$; vertical stretch by a factor of $\frac{3}{2}$

8. 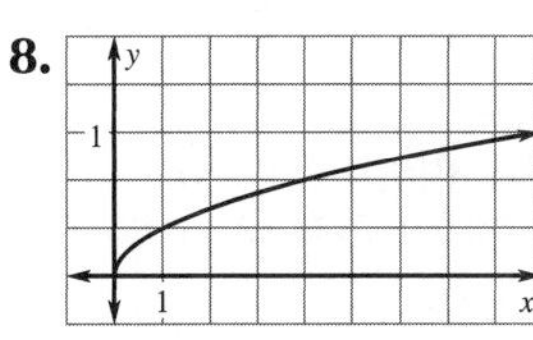
domain: $x \geq 0$, range: $y \geq 0$; vertical shrink by a factor of $\frac{1}{3}$

9. 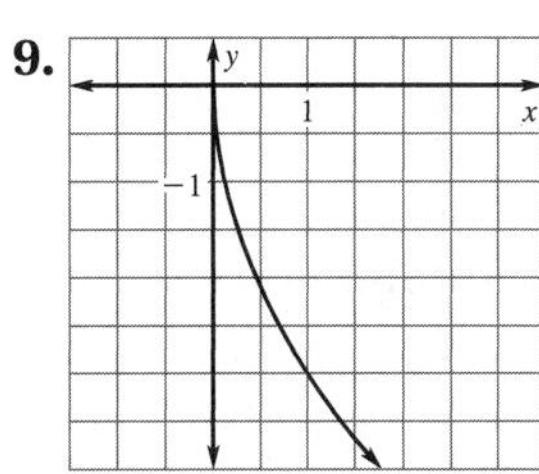
domain: $x \geq 0$, range: $y \leq 0$; vertical stretch by a factor of 3 with a reflection in the x-axis

10. 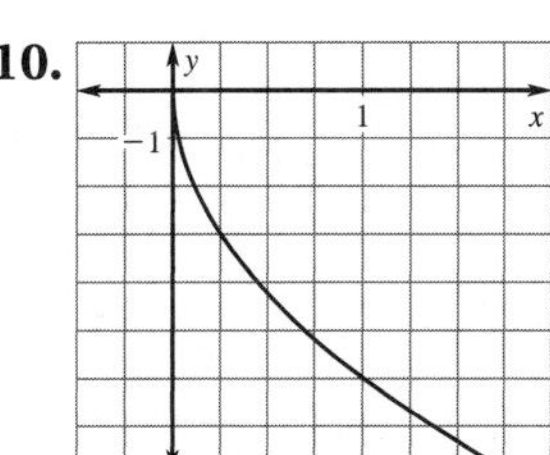
domain: $x \geq 0$, range: $y \leq 0$; vertical stretch by a factor of 6 with a reflection in the x-axis

11. 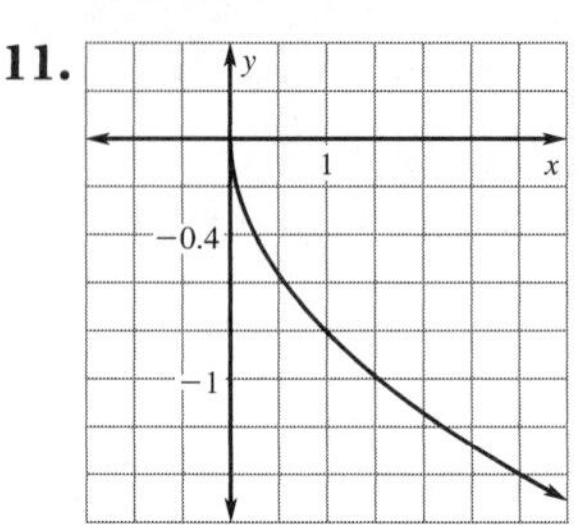

domain: $x \geq 0$, range: $y \leq 0$; vertical shrink by a factor of 0.8 with a reflection in the x-axis

12. 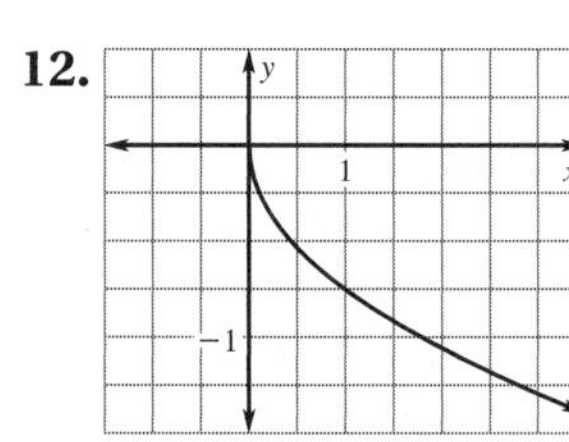

domain: $x \geq 0$, range: $y \leq 0$; vertical shrink by a factor of 0.75 with a reflection in the x-axis

13. 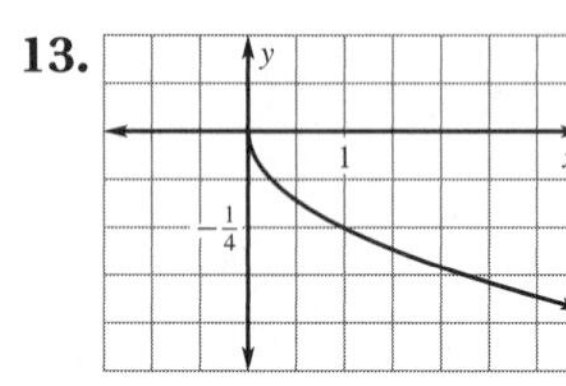

domain: $x \geq 0$, range: $y \leq 0$; vertical shrink by a factor of $\frac{1}{4}$ with a reflection in the x-axis

14. 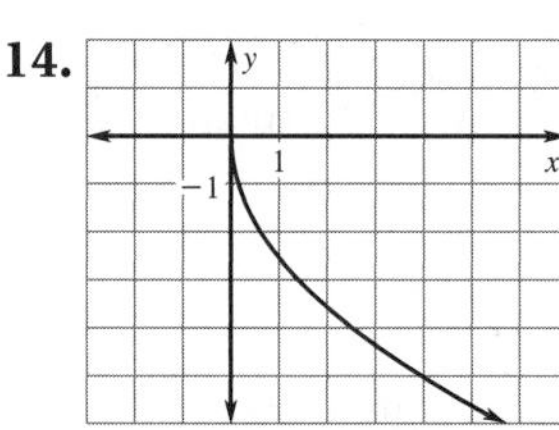

domain: $x \geq 0$, range: $y \leq 0$; vertical stretch by a factor of $\frac{5}{2}$ with a reflection in the x-axis

17. 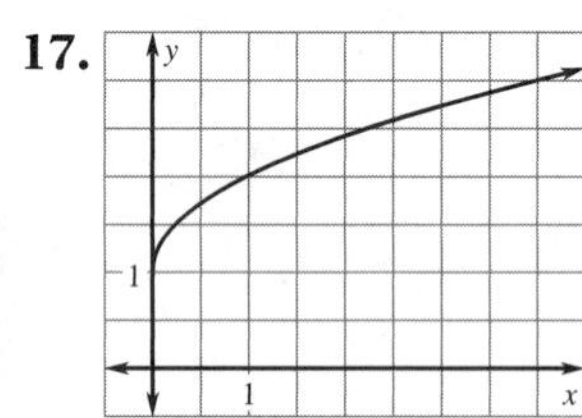

domain: $x \geq 0$, range: $y \geq 1$; vertical translation 1 unit up

18. 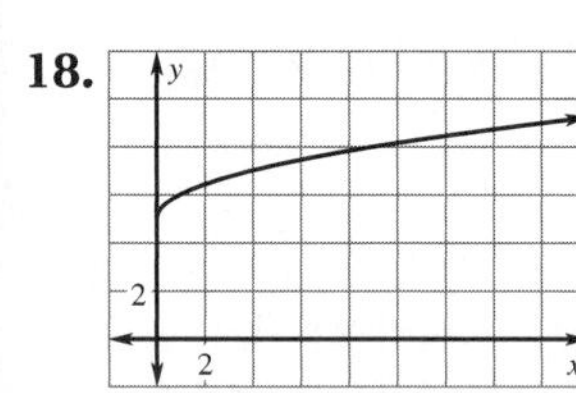

domain: $x \geq 0$, range: $y \geq 5$; vertical translation 5 units up

19. 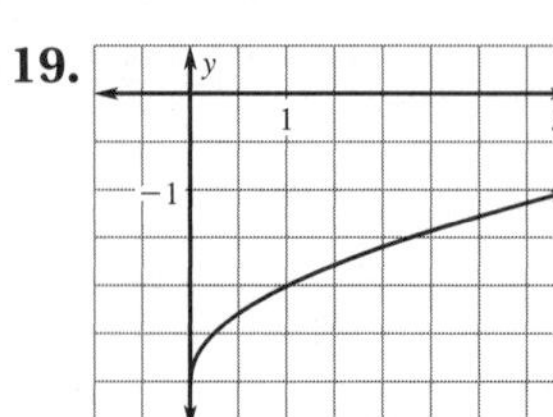

domain: $x \geq 0$, range: $y \geq -3$; vertical translation 3 units down

20. 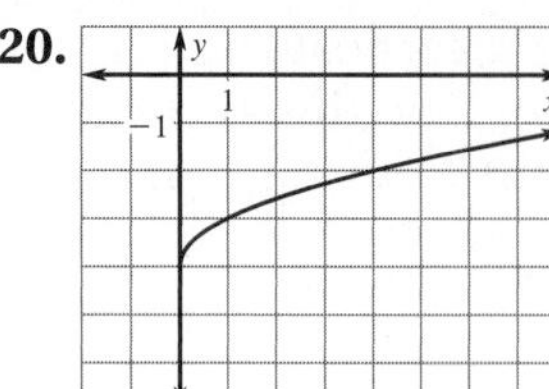

domain: $x \geq 0$, range: $y \geq -4$; vertical translation 4 units down

21. 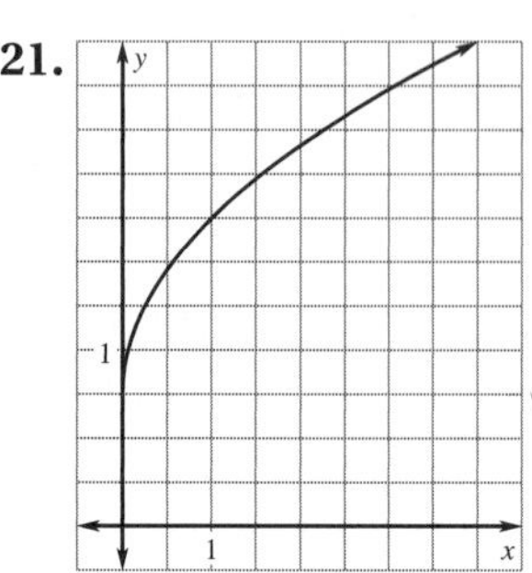

domain: $x \geq 0$, range: $y \geq \frac{3}{4}$; vertical translation $\frac{3}{4}$ unit up

22. 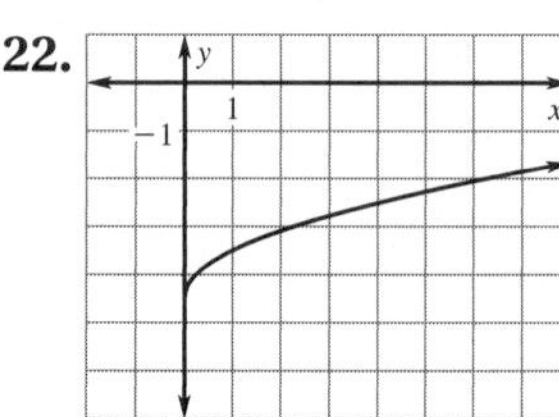

domain: $x \geq 0$, range: $y \geq -4.5$; vertical translation 4.5 units down

23. 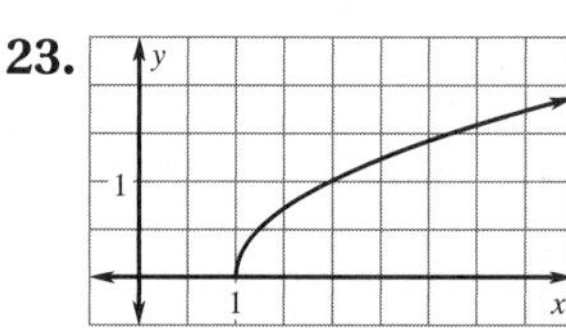

domain: $x \geq 1$, range: $y \geq 0$; horizontal translation 1 unit right

24. 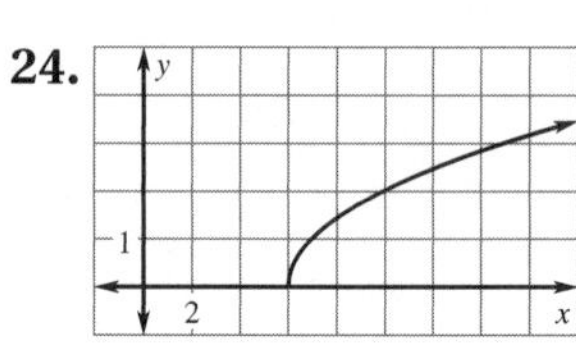

domain: $x \geq 6$, range: $y \geq 0$; horizontal translation 6 units right

25. 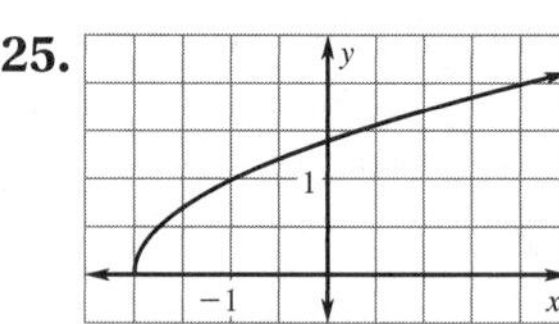

domain: $x \geq -2$, range: $y \geq 0$; horizontal translation 2 units left

26. 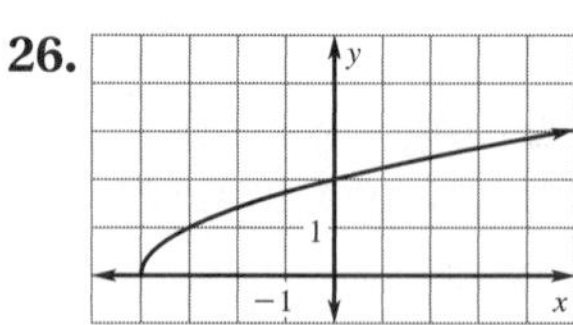

domain: $x \geq -4$, range: $y \geq 0$; horizontal translation 4 units left

27. 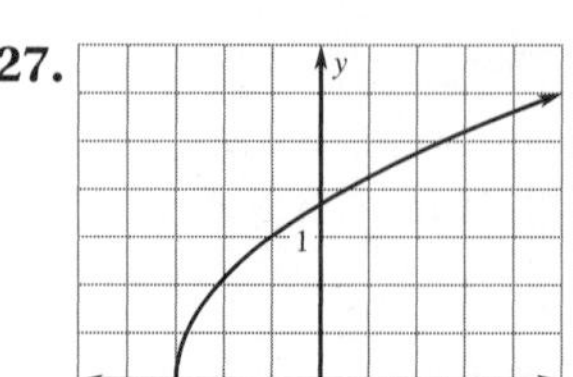

domain: $x \geq -1.5$, range: $y \geq 0$; horizontal translation 1.5 units left

ADDITIONAL ANSWERS

28. 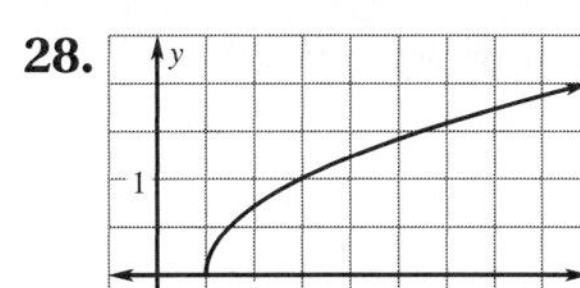 domain: $x \geq \frac{1}{2}$, range: $y \geq 0$; horizontal translation $\frac{1}{2}$ unit right

30. 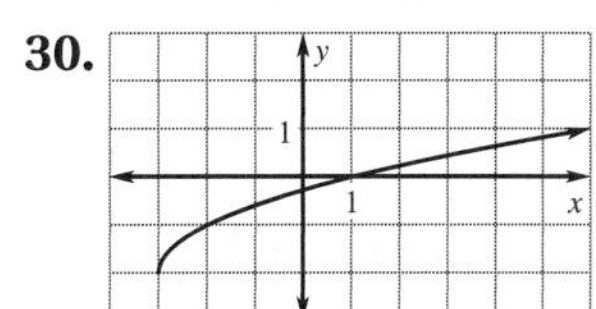

31. 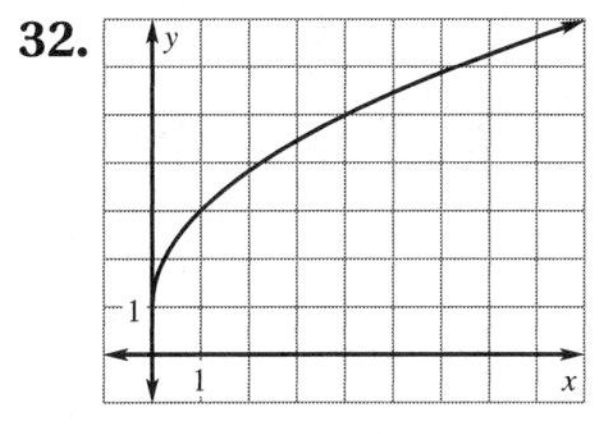

32. 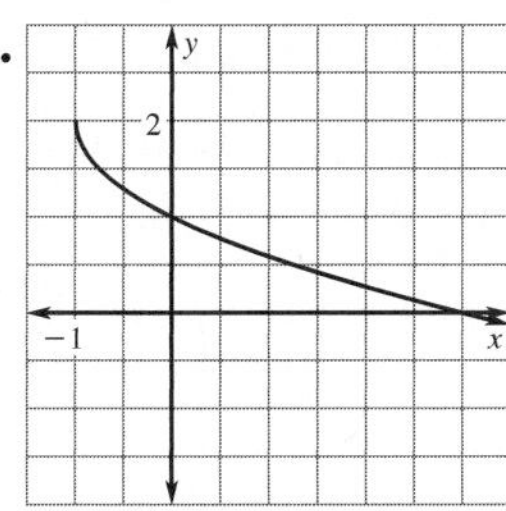

33. 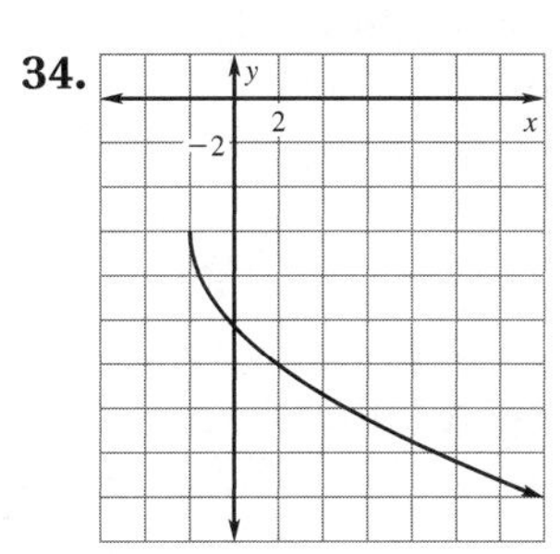

34. 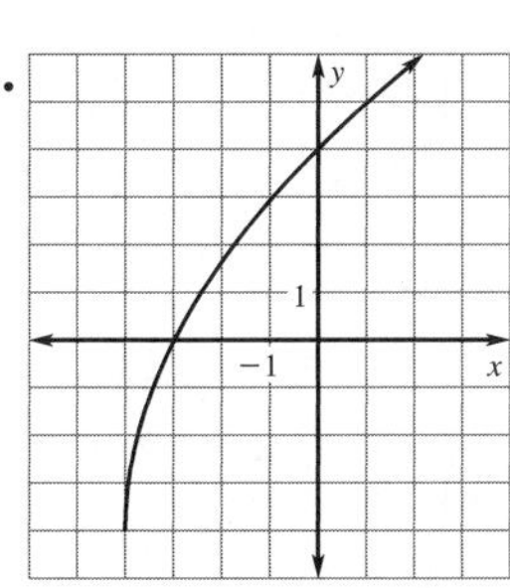

35. 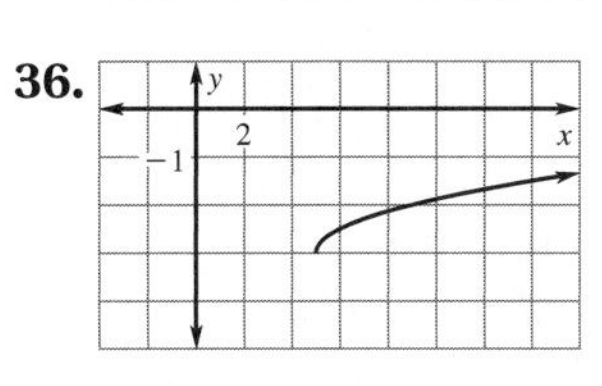

36. 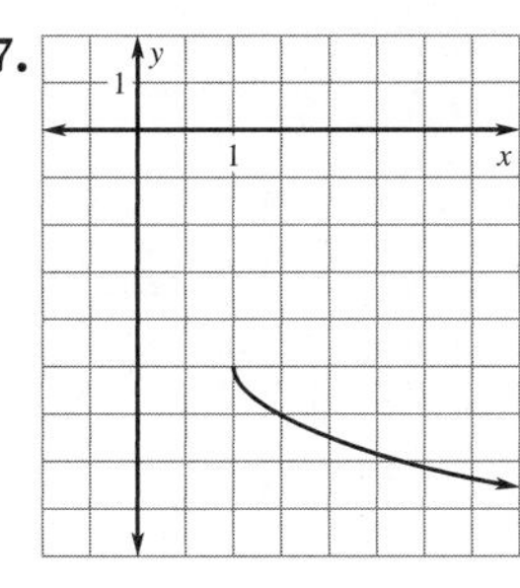

37. 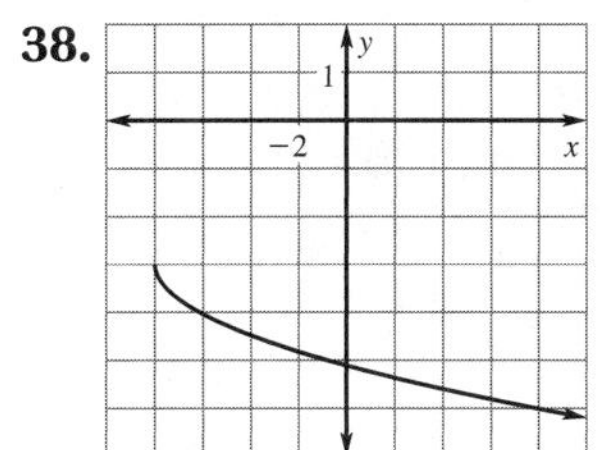

38.

11.1 Problem Solving (pp. 715–716)

47. a. 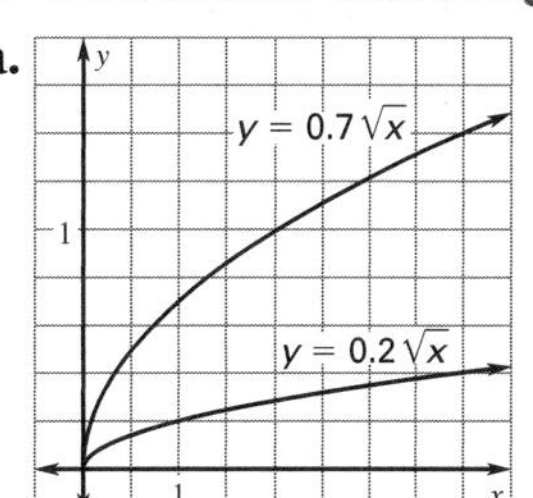

blue-winged teal's domain: $x \geq 0$, range: $y \geq 0$, northern pintail's domain: $x \geq 0$, range: $y \geq 0$

48. a. 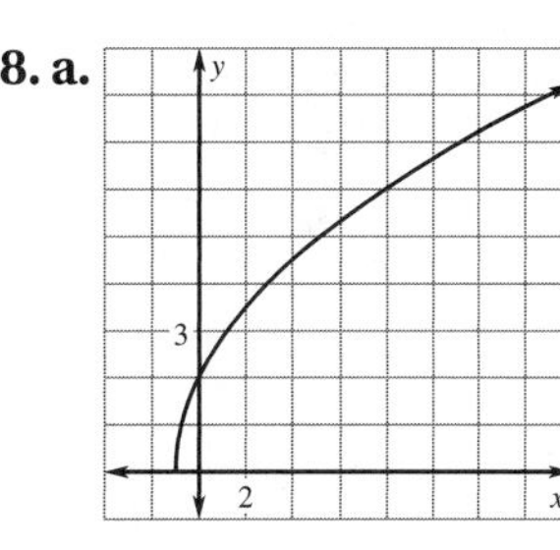

c. 1983; to find the year when the amount consumed doubled the amount consumed in 1980, solve the equation for $y = 4$; find $x = 3$, so 3 years after 1980, or 1983.

11.1 Graphing Calculator Activity (p. 717)

1. 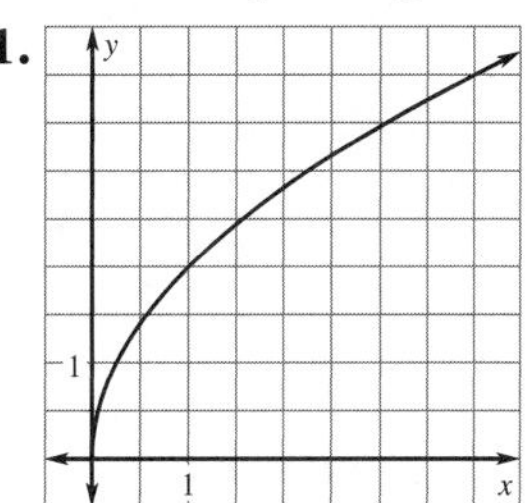 domain: $x \geq 0$, range: $y \geq 0$

2. 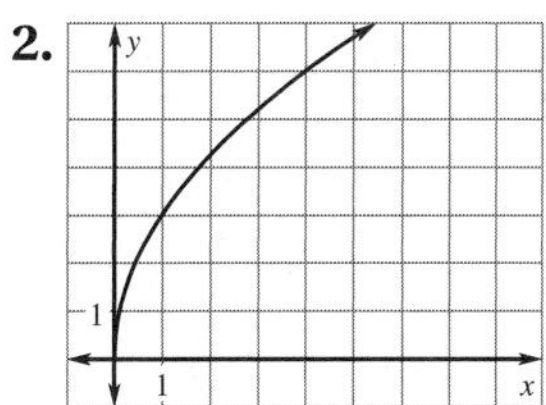 domain: $x \geq 0$, range: $y \geq 0$

3. 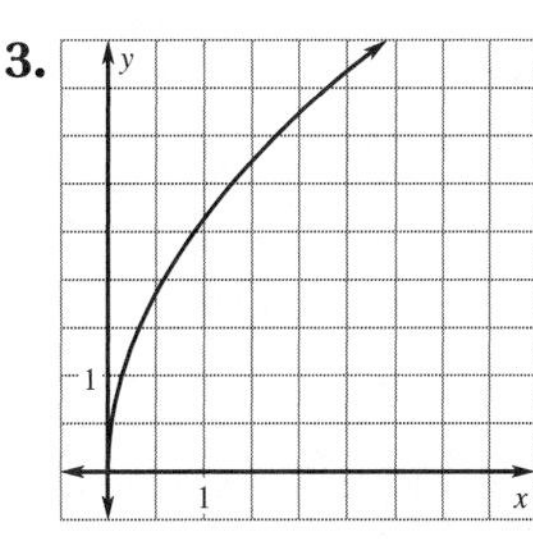 domain: $x \geq 0$, range: $y \geq 0$

4. 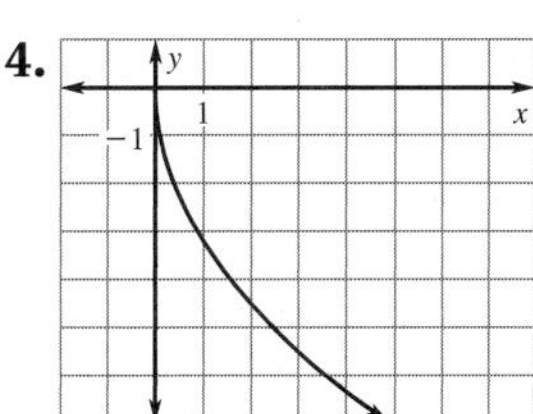 domain: $x \geq 0$, range: $y \leq 0$

5. 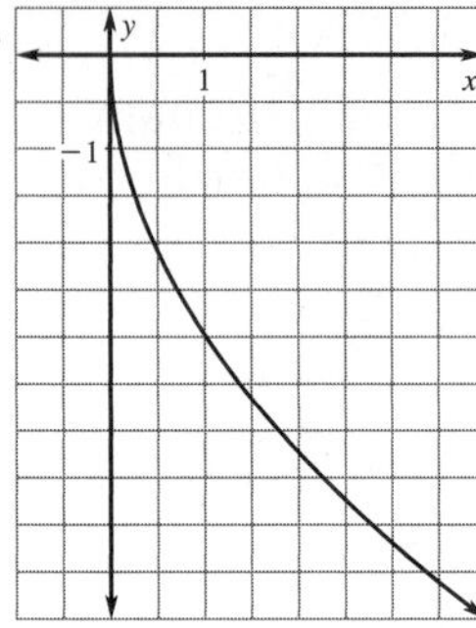
domain: $x \geq 0$, range: $y \leq 0$

6. 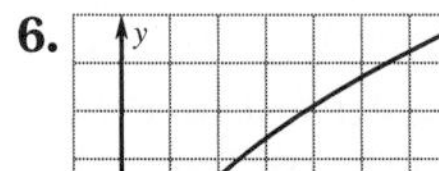
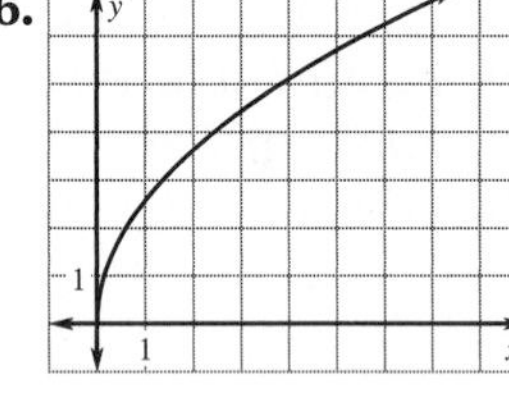
domain: $x \geq 0$, range: $y \geq 0$

7. 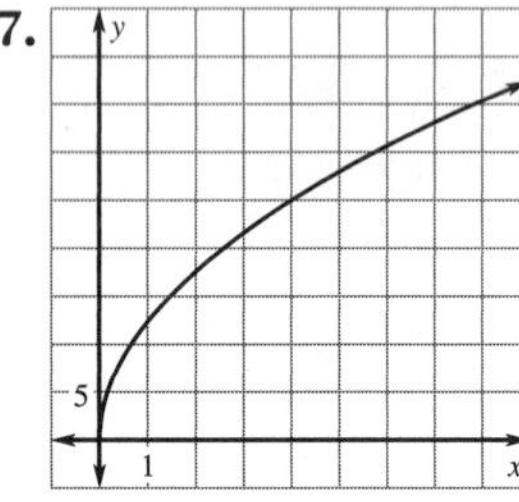
domain: $x \geq 0$, range: $y \geq 0$

8. 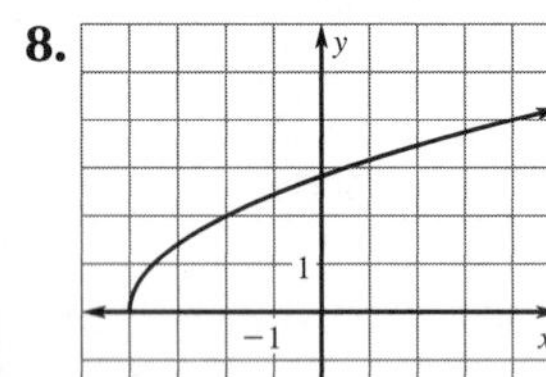
domain: $x \geq -4$, range: $y \geq 0$

9. 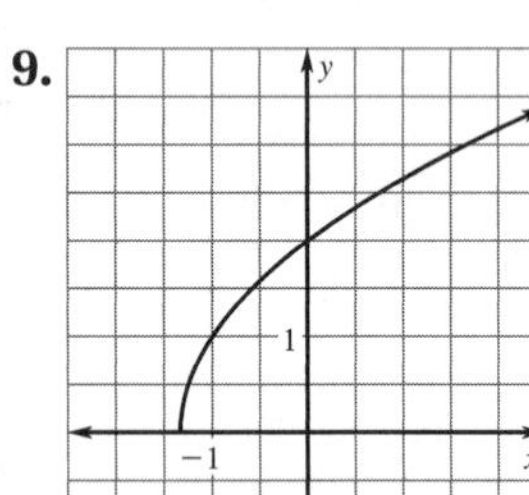
domain: $x \geq -\frac{4}{3}$, range: $y \geq 0$

10. 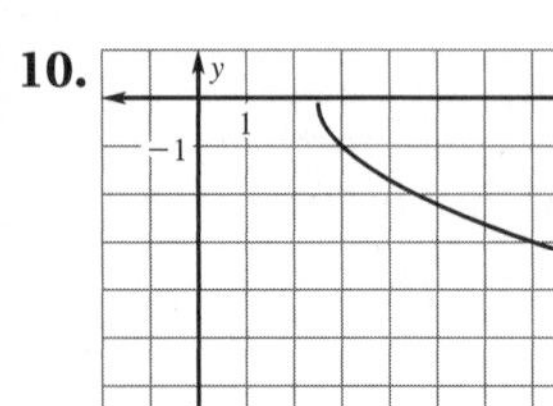
domain: $x \geq \frac{5}{2}$, range: $y \leq 0$

11. 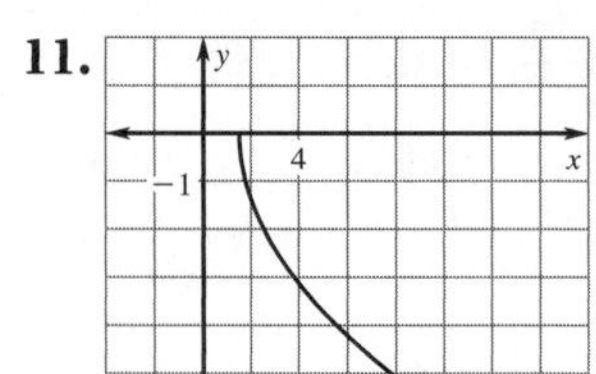
domain: $x \geq \frac{3}{2}$, range: $y \leq 0$

12. 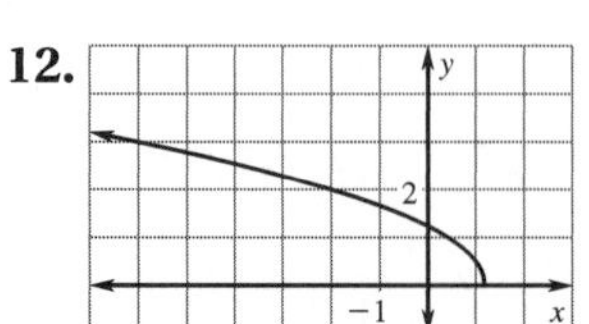
domain: $x \leq \frac{6}{5}$, range: $y \geq 0$

11.2 Mixed Review (p. 726)

73. 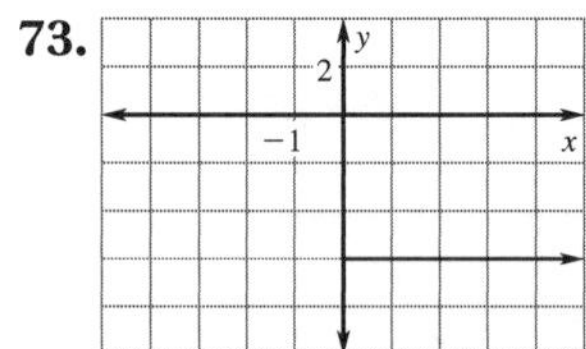
domain: $x \geq 0$, range: $y = -6$

74. 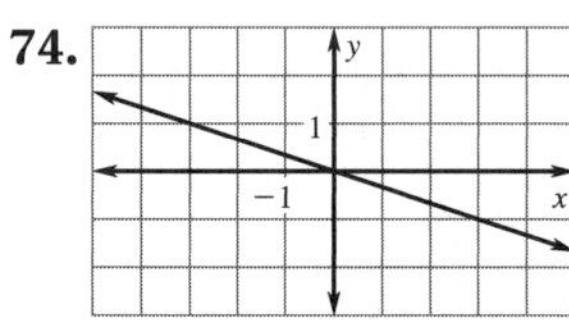
domain: all real numbers, range: all real numbers

75. 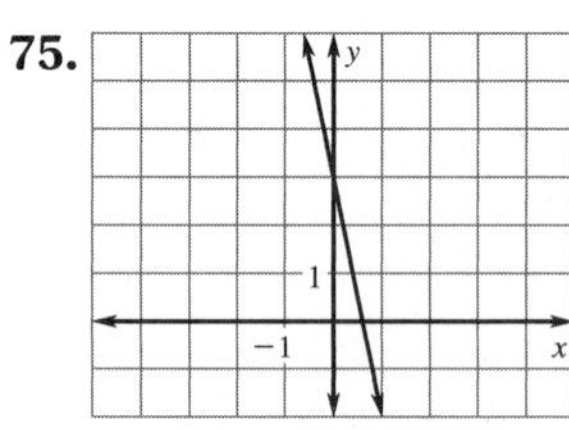
domain: all real numbers, range: all real numbers

76. 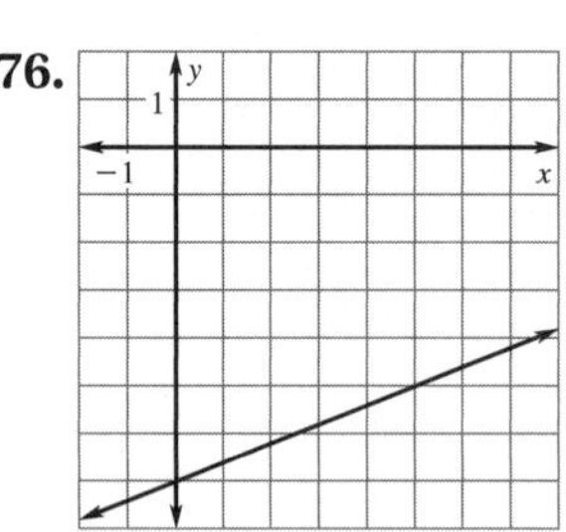
domain: all real numbers, range: all real numbers

77. 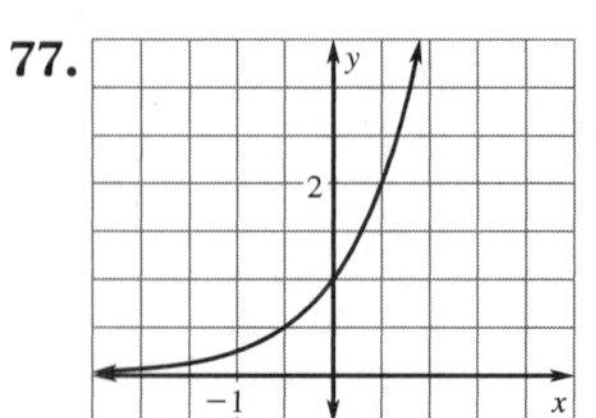
domain: all real numbers, range: $y > 0$

78. 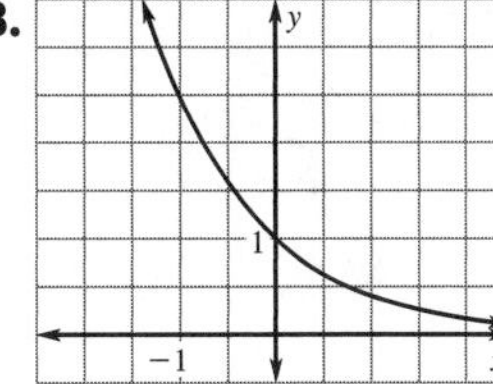
domain: all real numbers, range: $y > 0$

79. 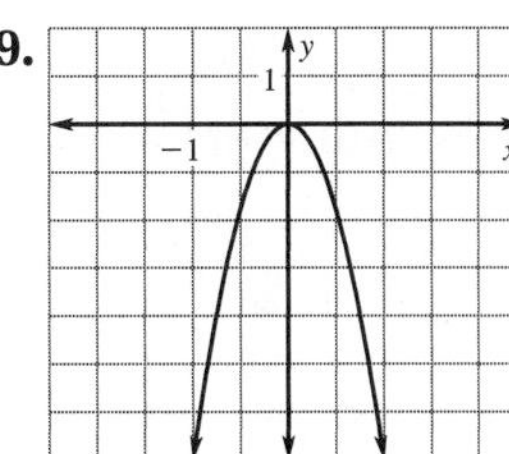
domain: all real numbers, range: $y \leq 0$

80. 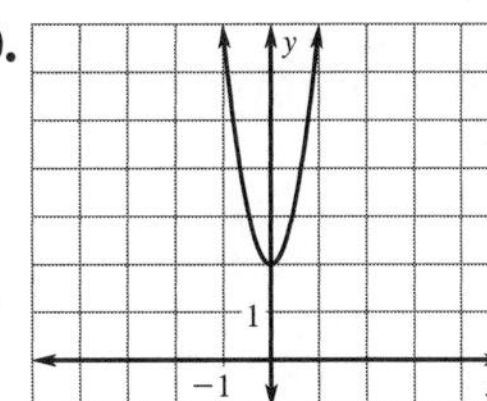
domain: all real numbers, range: $y \geq 2$

81. 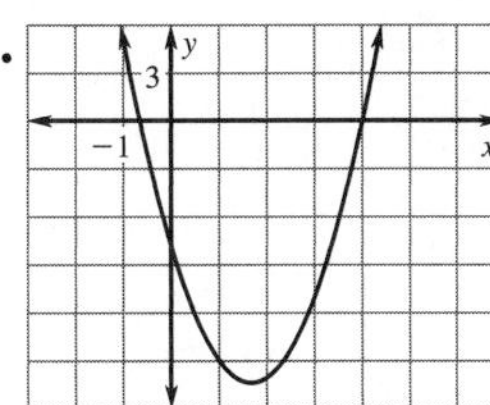
domain: all real numbers, range: $y \geq -\frac{49}{3}$

Extension (pp. 727–728)

19. Substitute $\frac{-b + \sqrt{b^2 - 4ac}}{2a}$ for x:

$$a\left(\frac{-b + \sqrt{b^2 - 4ac}}{2a}\right)^2 + b\left(\frac{-b + \sqrt{b^2 - 4ac}}{2a}\right) + c = 0$$

$$a\left(\frac{b^2 - 2b\sqrt{b^2 - 4ac} + b^2 - 4ac}{4a^2}\right) + \frac{-b^2 + b\sqrt{b^2 - 4ac}}{2a} + c = 0$$

$$\frac{b^2}{4a} - \frac{b\sqrt{b^2 - 4ac}}{2a} + \frac{b^2}{4a} - c - \frac{b^2}{2a} + \frac{b\sqrt{b^2 - 4ac}}{2a} + c = 0$$

$$0 = 0$$

Substitute $\frac{-b - \sqrt{b^2 - 4ac}}{2a}$ for x:

$$a\left(\frac{-b - \sqrt{b^2 - 4ac}}{2a}\right)^2 + b\left(\frac{-b - \sqrt{b^2 - 4ac}}{2a}\right) + c = 0$$

$$a\left(\frac{b^2 + 2b\sqrt{b^2 - 4ac} + b^2 - 4ac}{4a^2}\right) + \frac{-b^2 - b\sqrt{b^2 - 4ac}}{2a} + c = 0$$

$$\frac{b^2}{4a} + \frac{b\sqrt{b^2 - 4ac}}{2a} + \frac{b^2}{4a} - c - \frac{b^2}{2a} - \frac{b\sqrt{b^2 - 4ac}}{2a} + c = 0$$

$$0 = 0$$

22. $a \leq 12$. *Sample answer:* For a quadratic equation to have one or two real solutions, the value of $b^2 - 4ac$ must be greater than or equal to 0. Substituting values and solving: $12^2 - 4 \cdot a \cdot 3 \geq 0$, $a \leq 12$.

11.4 Mixed Review (p. 742)

39. 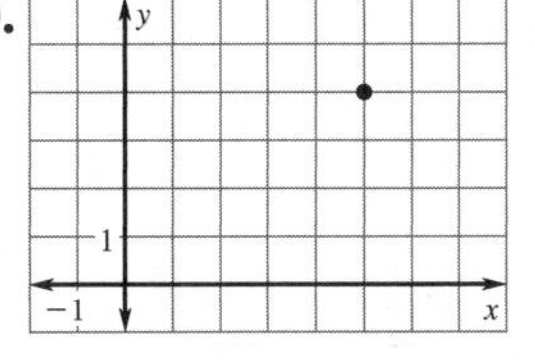

40. 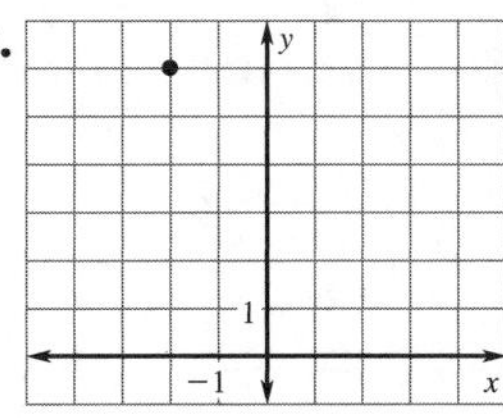

41. 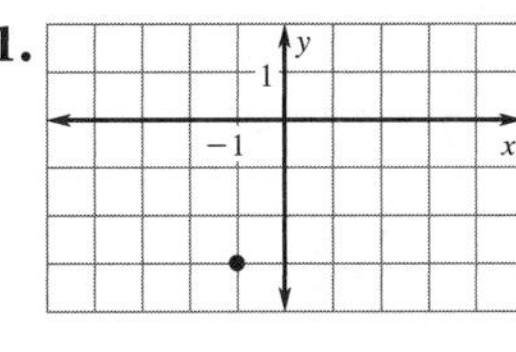

42. 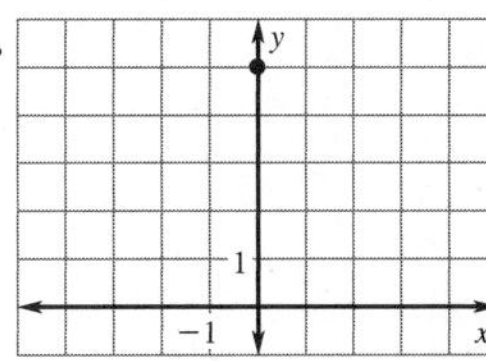

43. 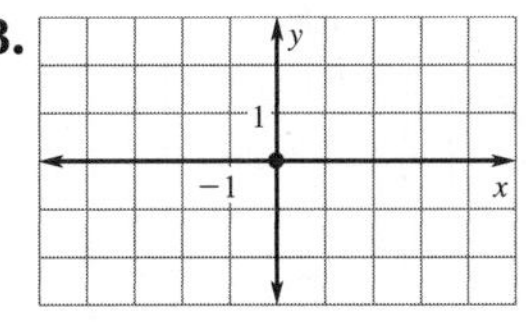

44. 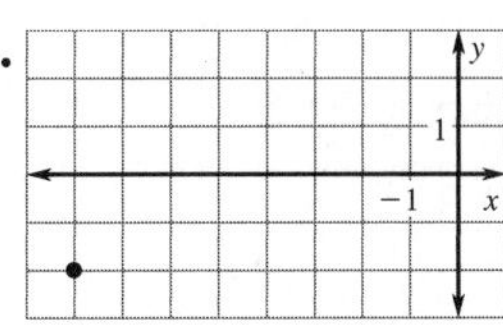

45. 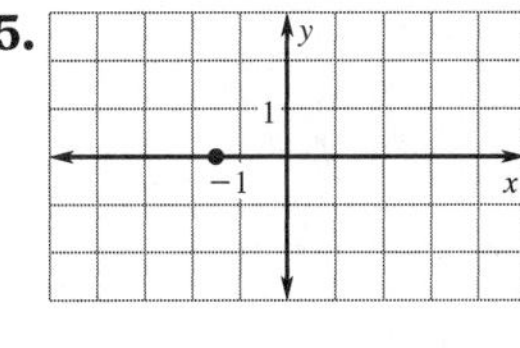

46. 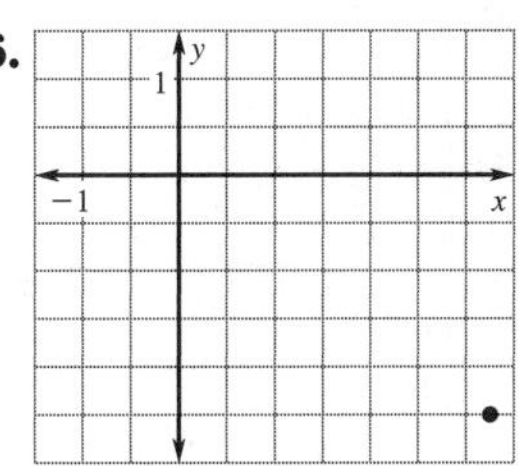

11.5 Mixed Review (p. 750)

59. 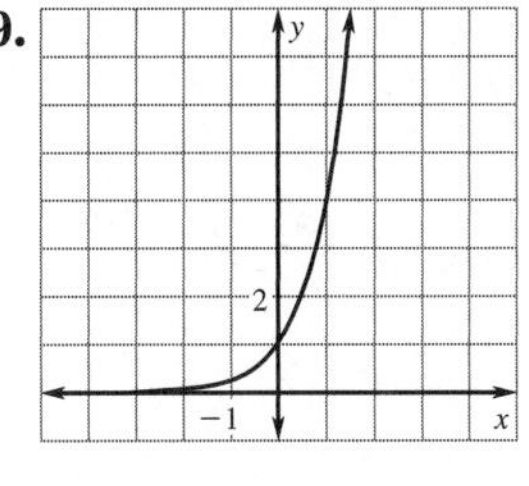

60. 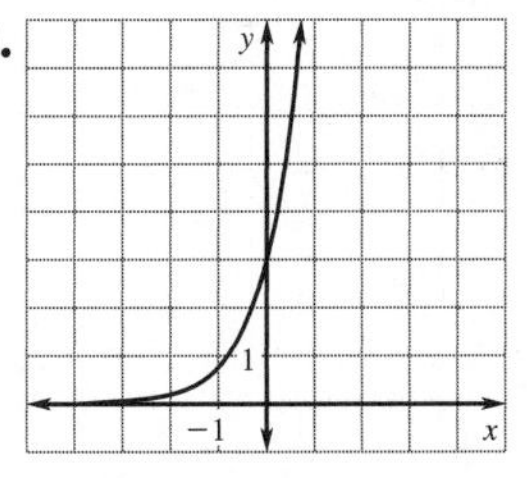

61. 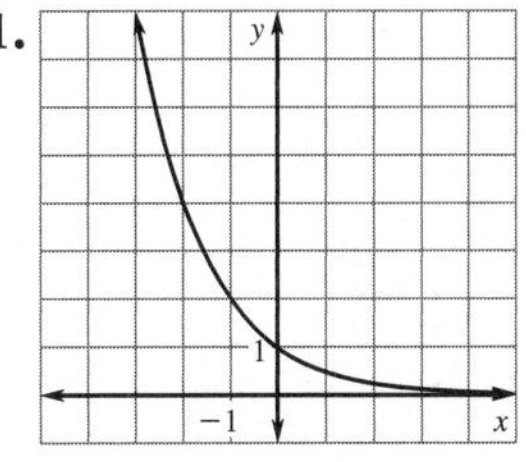

62. 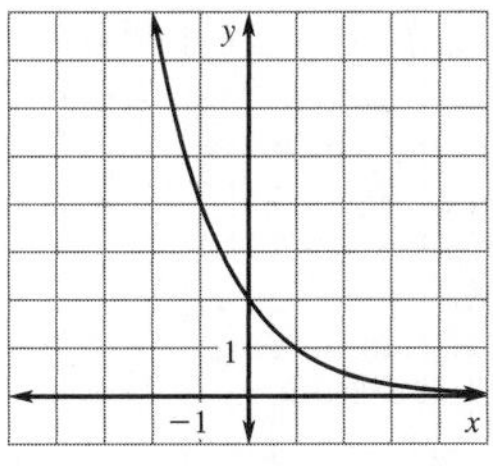

63. 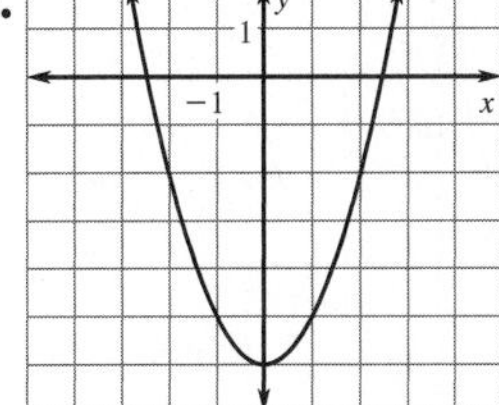

64. 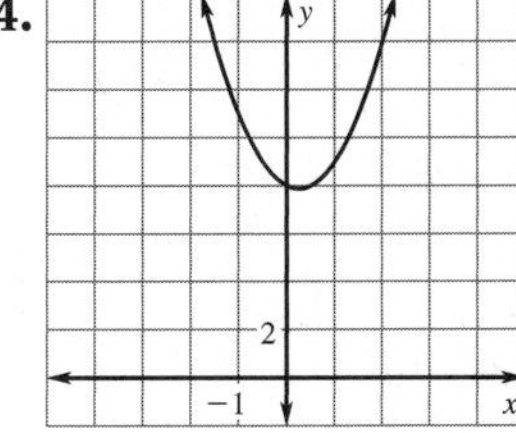

Chapter 12

12.1 Skill Practice (pp. 769–770)

15. 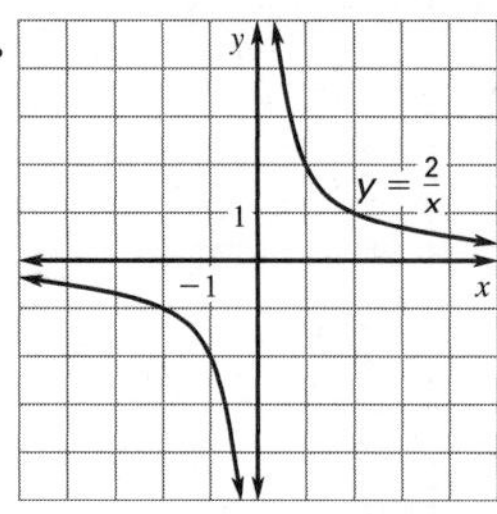

16. 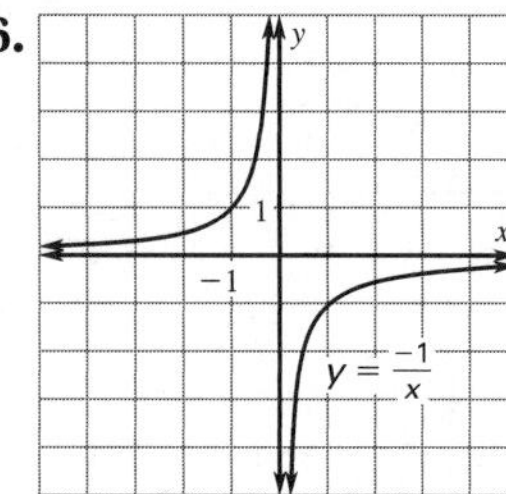

17. 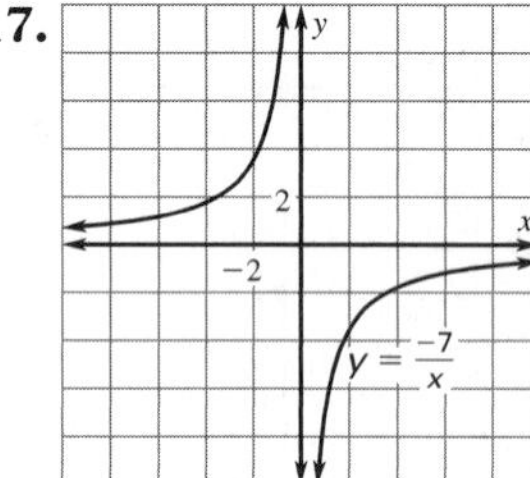

18. 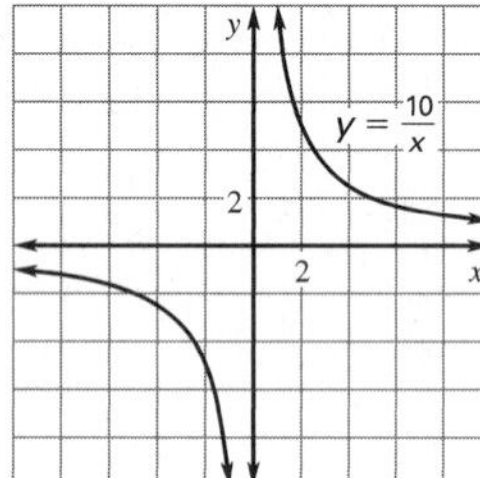

19. 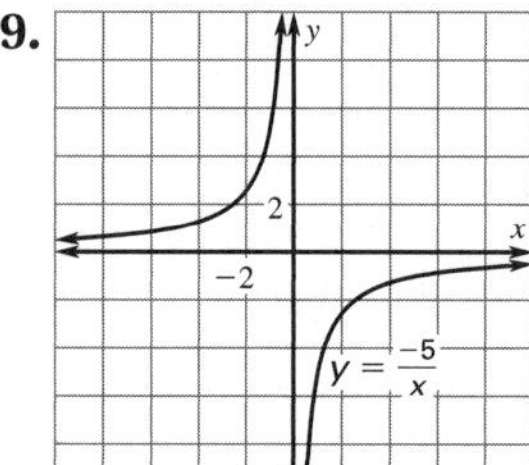

20. 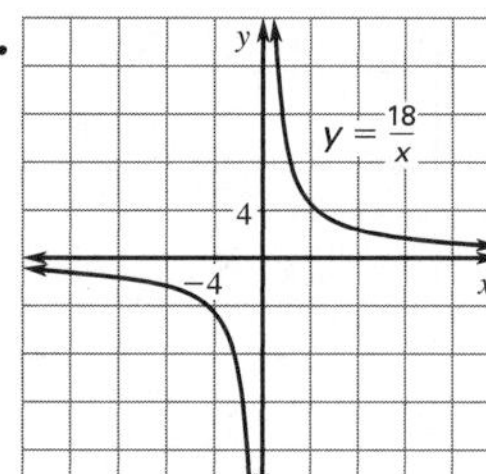

21. 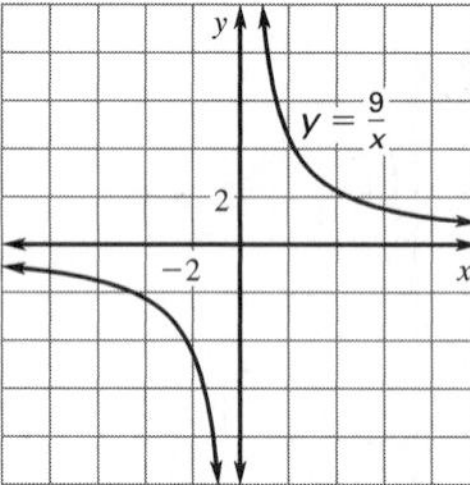

22. 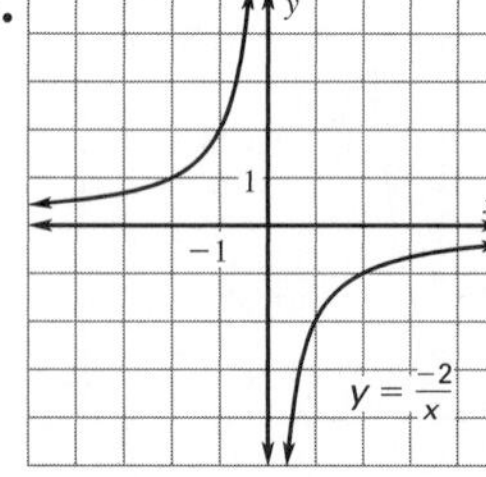

23. 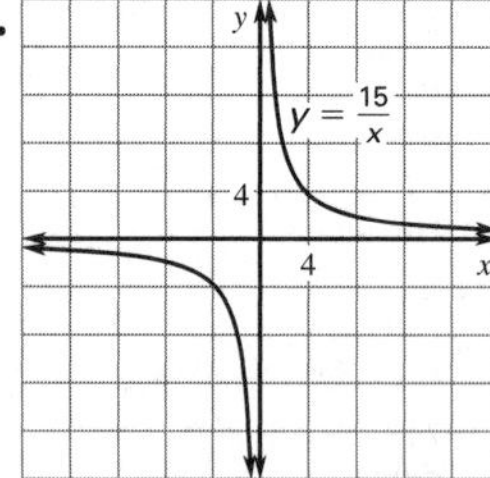

24. 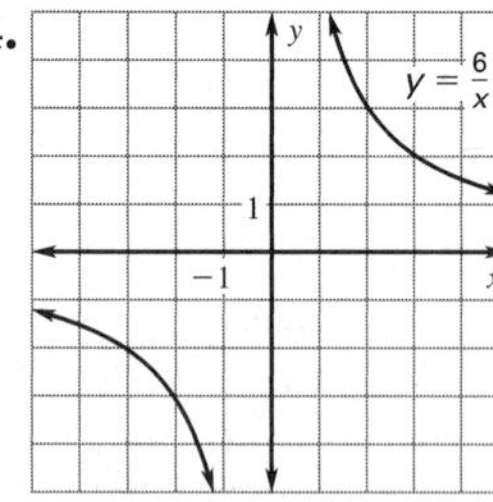

25. 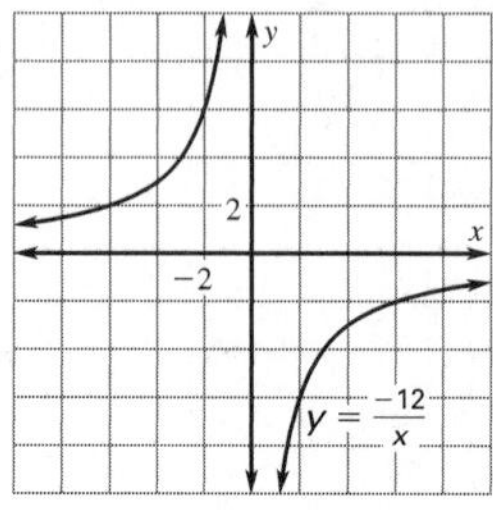

26. 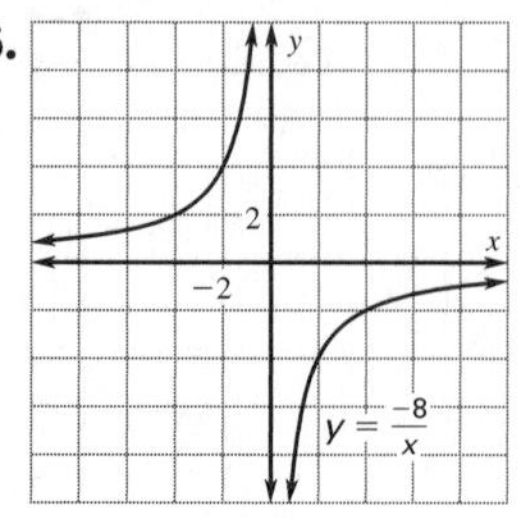

12.1 Mixed Review (p. 772)

63. 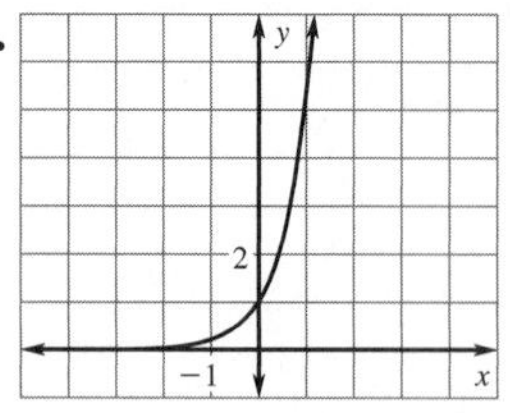
domain: all real numbers, range: $y > 0$

64. 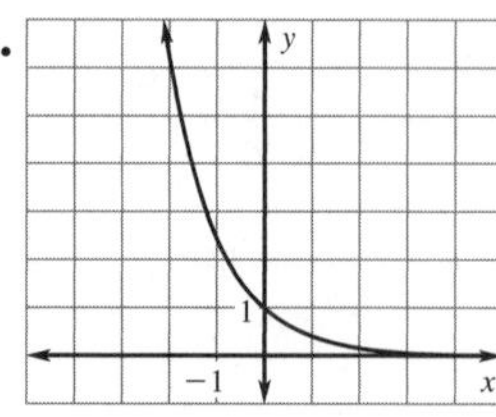
domain: all real numbers, range: $y > 0$

65. 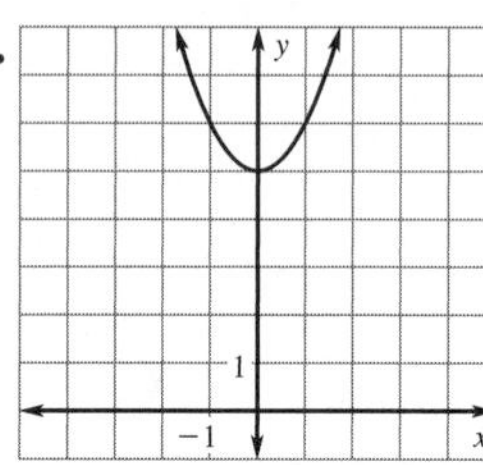
domain: all real numbers, range: $y \geq 5$

66. 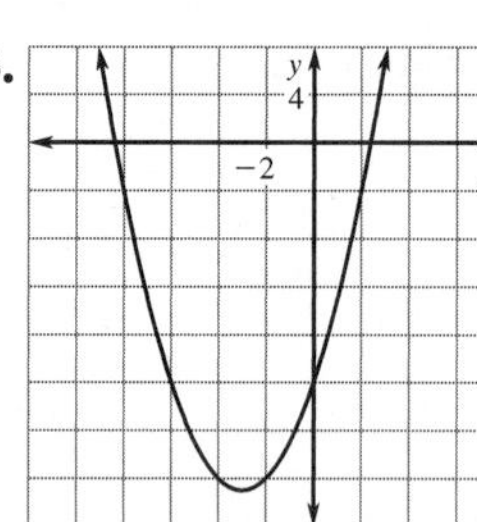
domain: all real numbers, range: $y \geq -29$

67. 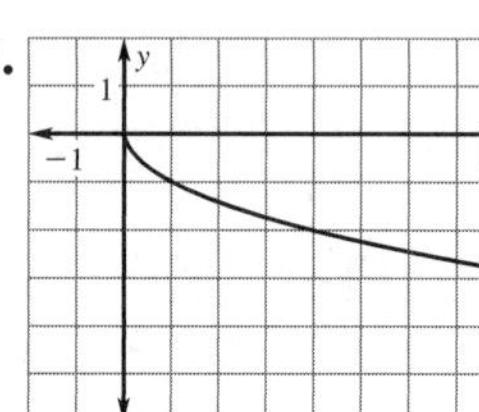
domain: $x \geq 0$, range: $y \leq 0$

68. 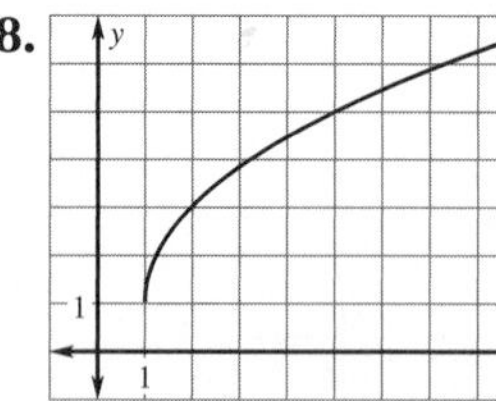
domain: $x \geq 1$, range: $y \geq 1$

12.2 Guided Practice (pp. 776–778)

1. Domain: all real numbers except 0, range: all real numbers except 0; the graph is a vertical stretch of the graph of $y = \frac{1}{x}$ that is then reflected in the x-axis.

2. 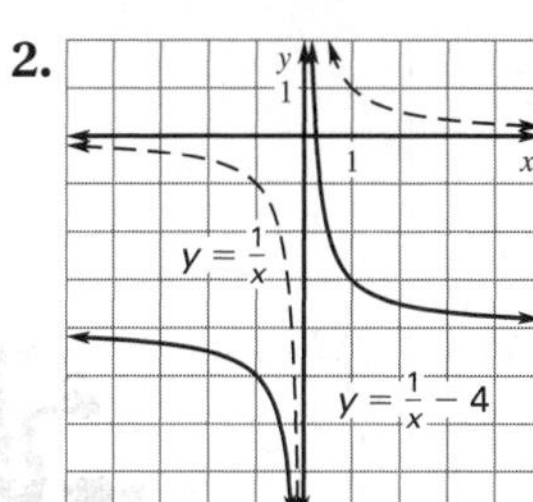

Domain: all real numbers except 0, range: all real numbers except -4; the graph is a vertical translation (of 4 units down) of the graph of $y = \frac{1}{x}$.

3. 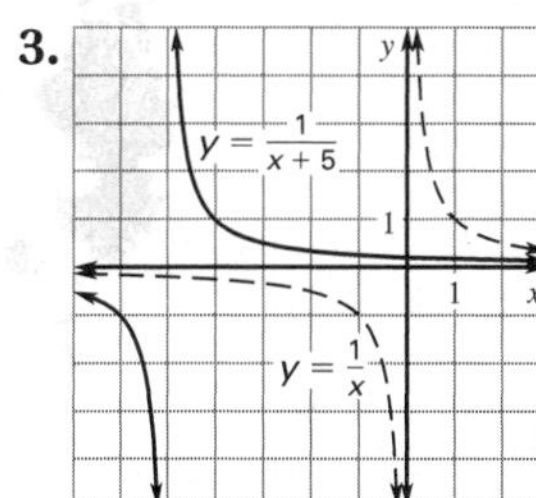

Domain: all real numbers except -5, range: all real numbers except 0; the graph is a horizontal translation (of 5 units left) of the graph of $y = \frac{1}{x}$.

4. The graph of $y = \frac{1}{x+3}$ is a horizontal translation (of 3 units left) of the graph of $y = \frac{1}{x}$.

12.2 Skill Practice (pp. 779–780)

3. 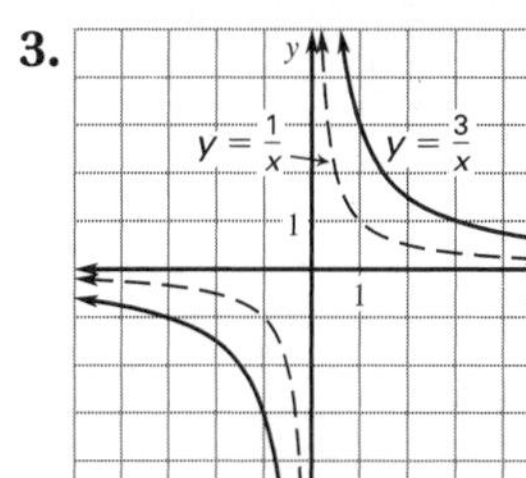

Domain: all real numbers except 0, range: all real numbers except 0; the graph is a vertical stretch of the graph of $y = \frac{1}{x}$.

4. 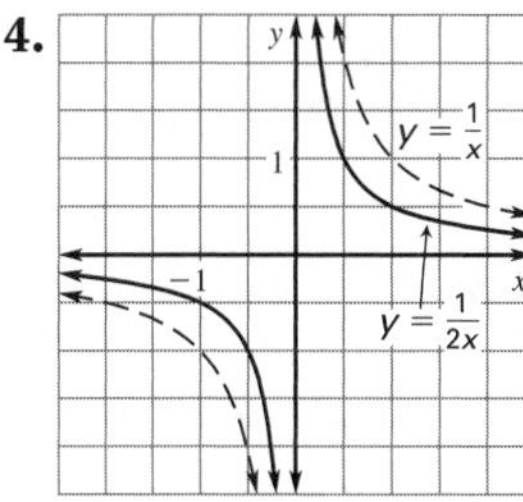

Domain: all real numbers except 0, range: all real numbers except 0; the graph is a vertical shrink of the graph of $y = \frac{1}{x}$.

5. 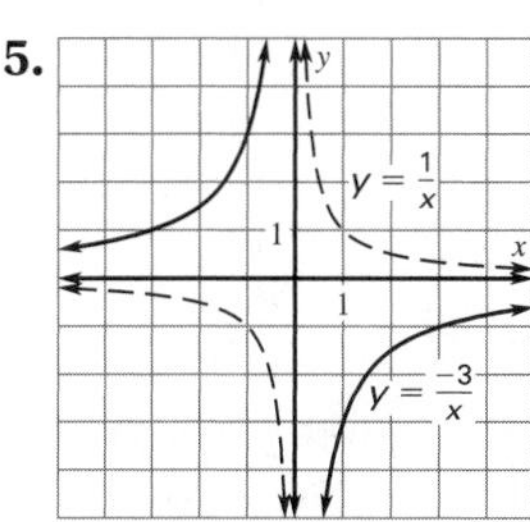

Domain: all real numbers except 0, range: all real numbers except 0; the graph is a vertical stretch of the graph of $y = \frac{1}{x}$ that is then reflected in the x-axis.

6. 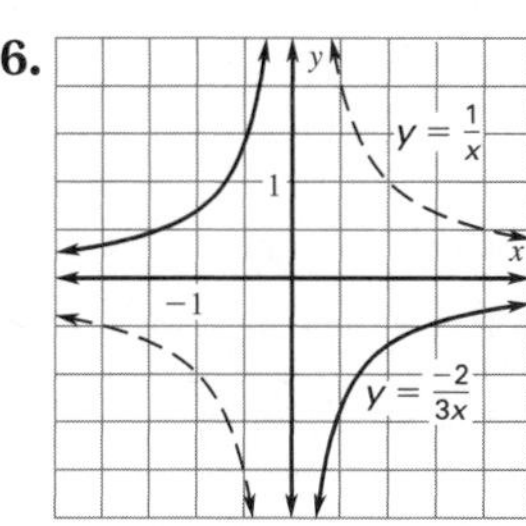

Domain: all real numbers except 0, range: all real numbers except 0; the graph is a vertical shrink of the graph of $y = \frac{1}{x}$ that is then reflected in the x-axis.

7. 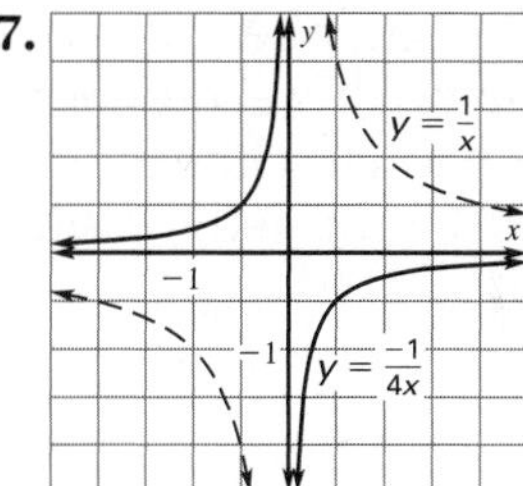

Domain: all real numbers except 0, range: all real numbers except 0; the graph is a vertical shrink of the graph of $y = \frac{1}{x}$ that is then reflected in the x-axis.

8. 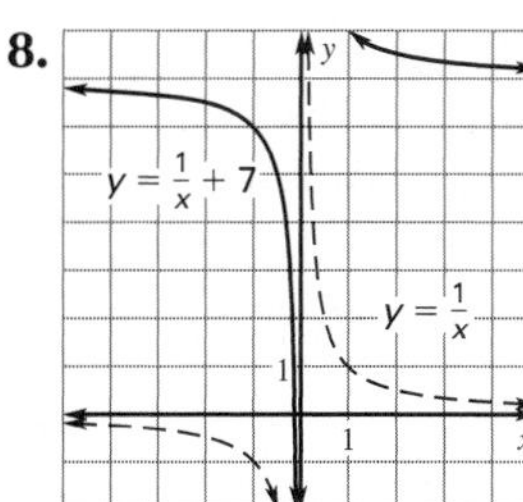

Domain: all real numbers except 0, range: all real numbers except 7; the graph is a vertical translation (of 7 units up) of the graph of $y = \frac{1}{x}$.

9. 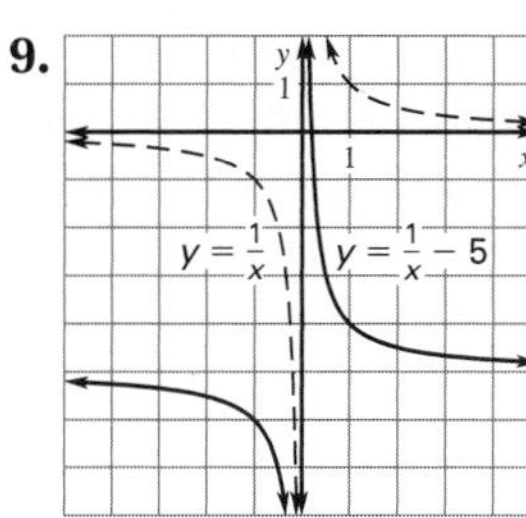

Domain: all real numbers except 0, range: all real numbers except -5; the graph is a vertical translation (of 5 units down) of the graph of $y = \frac{1}{x}$.

10. 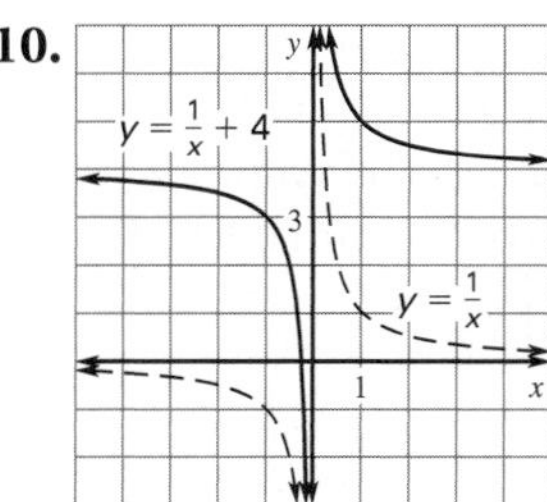

Domain: all real numbers except 0, range: all real numbers except 4; the graph is a vertical translation (of 4 units up) of the graph of $y = \frac{1}{x}$.

11. 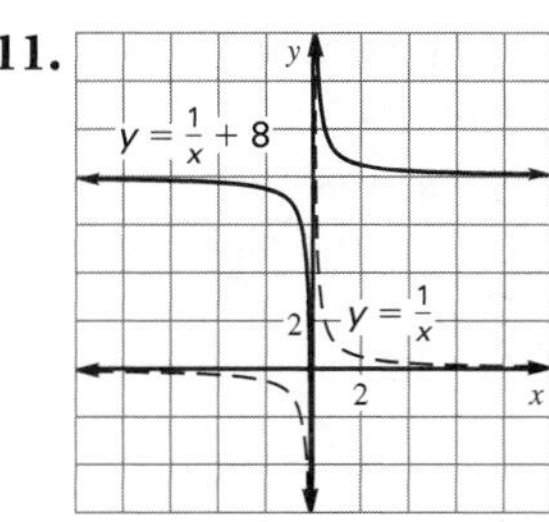

Domain: all real numbers except 0, range: all real numbers except 8; the graph is a vertical translation (of 8 units up) of the graph of $y = \frac{1}{x}$.

12. 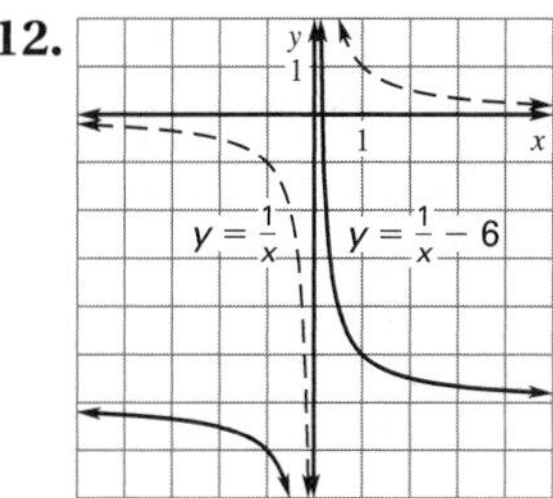

Domain: all real numbers except 0, range: all real numbers except -6; the graph is a vertical translation (of 6 units down) of the graph of $y = \frac{1}{x}$.

13. 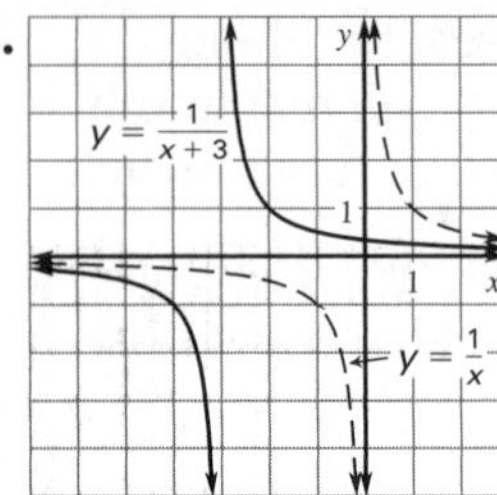

Domain: all real numbers except −3, range: all real numbers except 0; the graph is a horizontal translation (of 3 units left) of the graph of $y = \frac{1}{x}$.

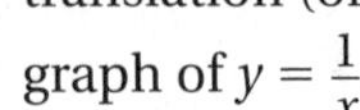

14. 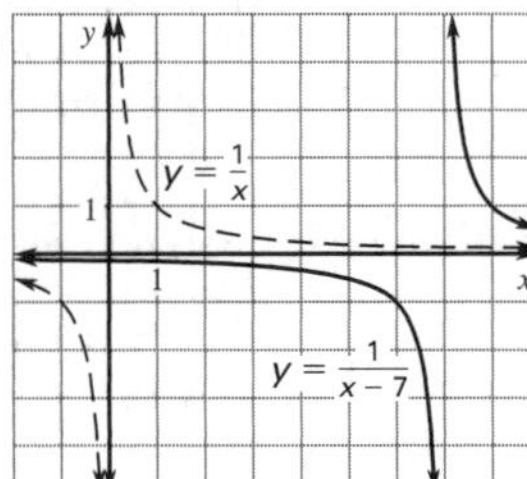

Domain: all real numbers except 7, range: all real numbers except 0; the graph is a horizontal translation (of 7 units right) of the graph of $y = \frac{1}{x}$.

15. 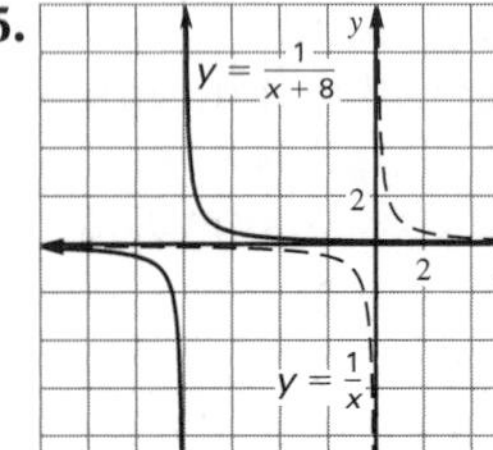

Domain: all real numbers except −8, range: all real numbers except 0; the graph is a horizontal translation (of 8 units left) of the graph of $y = \frac{1}{x}$.

16. 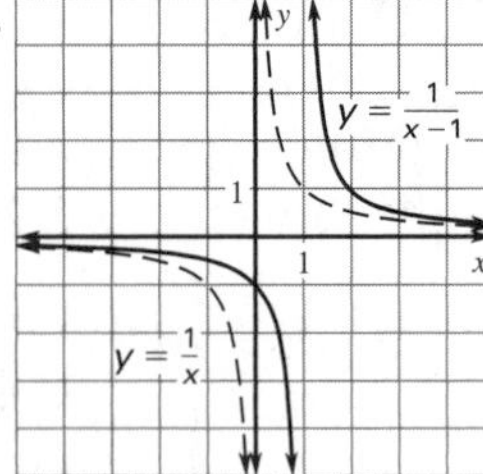

Domain: all real numbers except 1, range: all real numbers except 0; the graph is a horizontal translation (of 1 unit right) of the graph of $y = \frac{1}{x}$.

17. 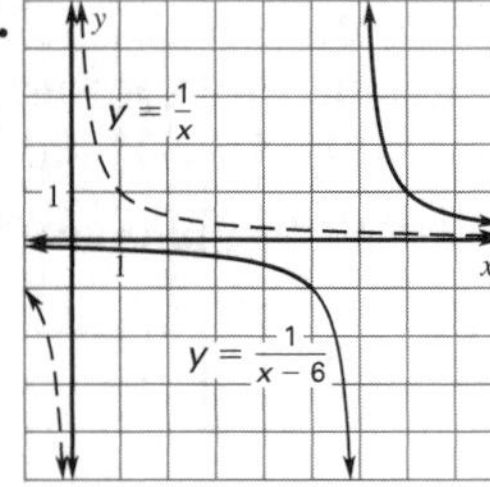

Domain: all real numbers except 6, range: all real numbers except 0; the graph is a horizontal translation (of 6 units right) of the graph of $y = \frac{1}{x}$.

19. 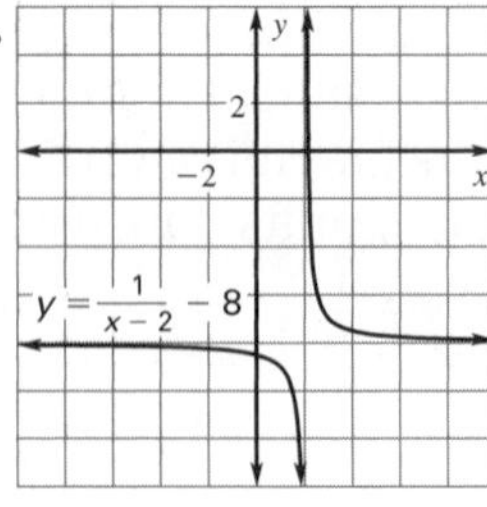

20. 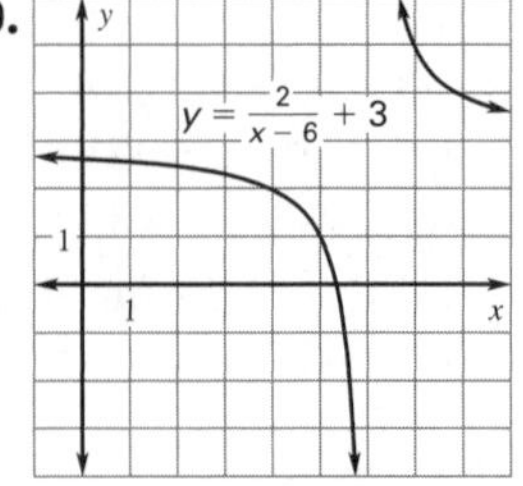

21. 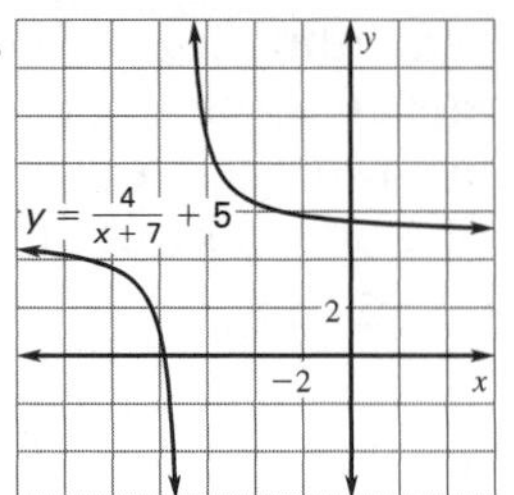

22. 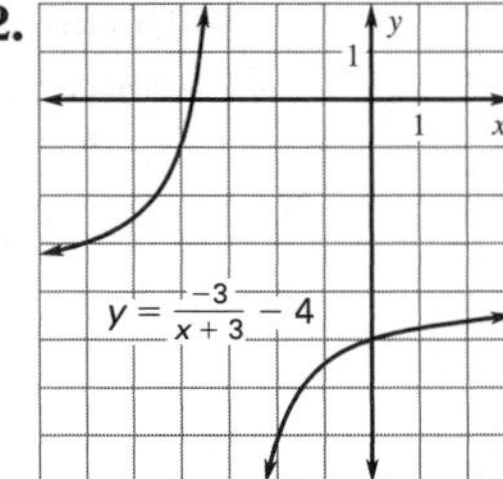

23. 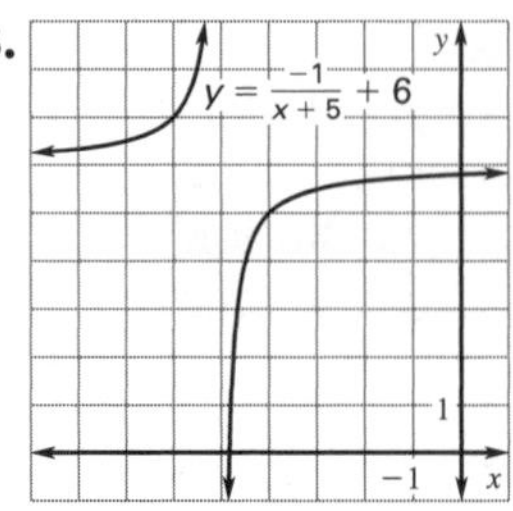

24. 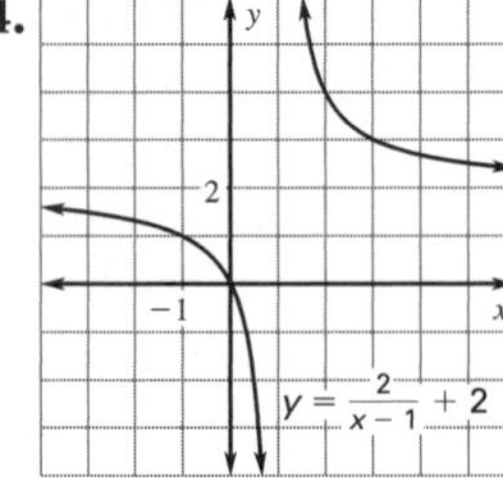

25. 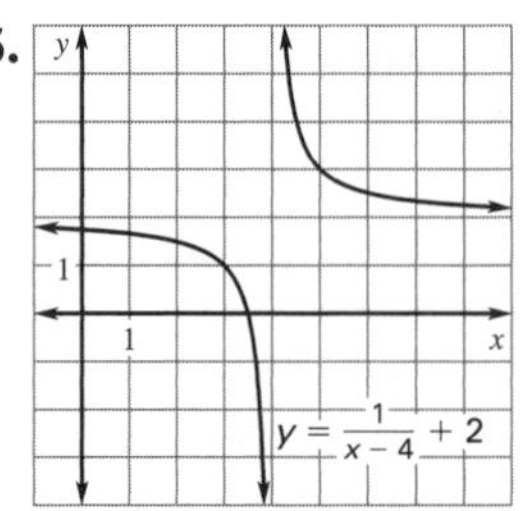

26. 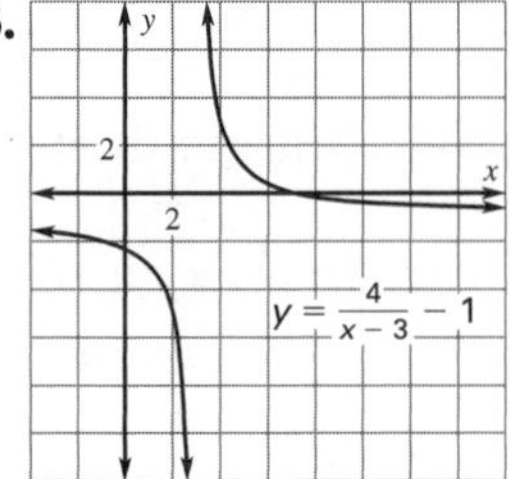

27. 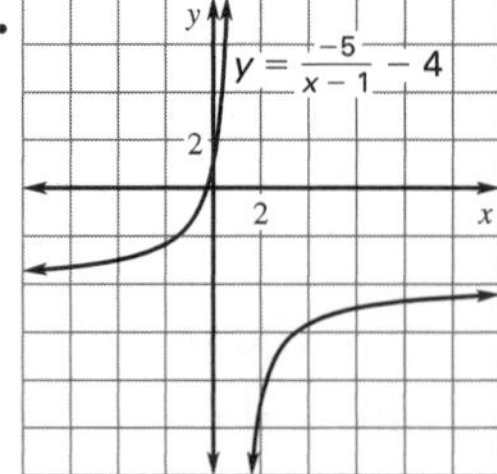

12.2 Problem Solving (pp. 780–782)

45. a. 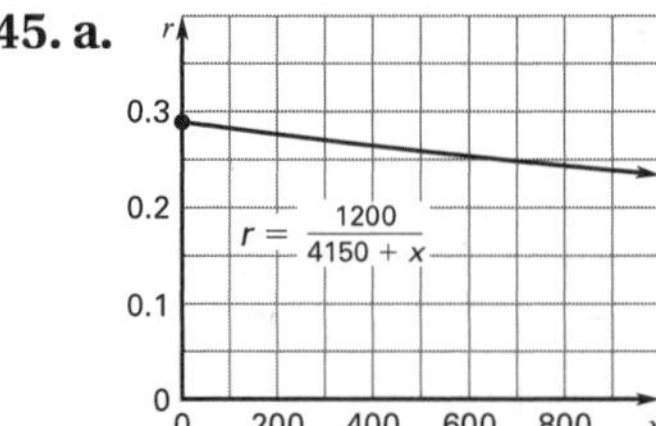

Quiz for Lessons 12.1–12.2 (p. 782)

7. 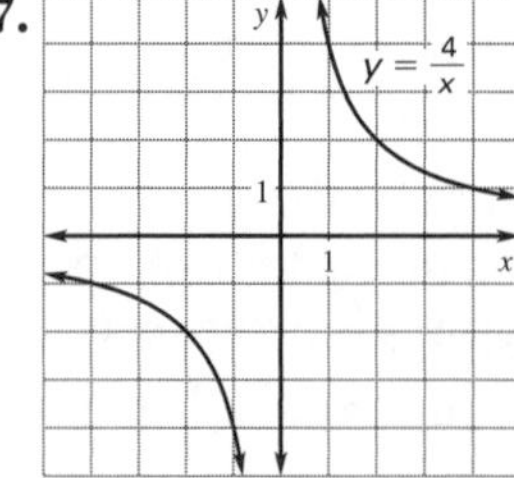

domain: all real numbers except 0, range: all real numbers except 0

8. 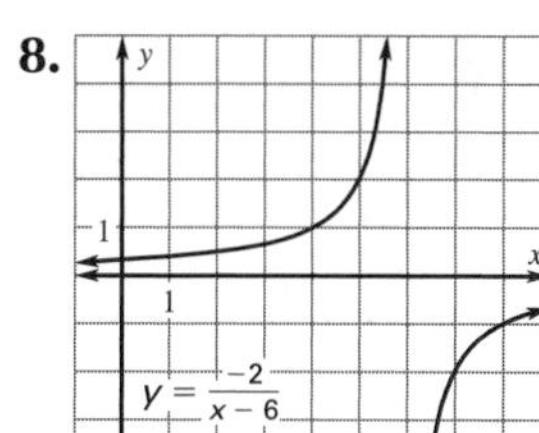

domain: all real numbers except 6, range: all real numbers except 0

9. 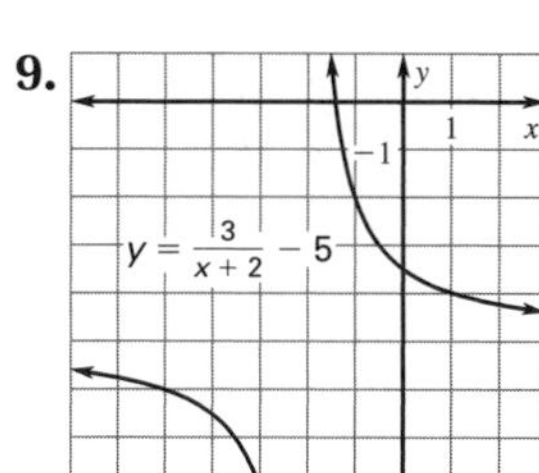

domain: all real numbers except −2, range: all real numbers except −5

12.3 Investigating Algebra Activity (p. 783)

2. $2x + 3$

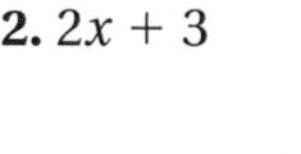
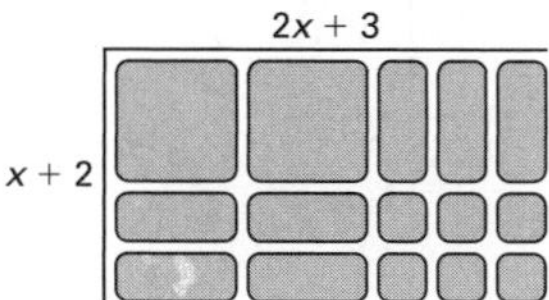

3. $2x + 3 + \frac{1}{x+3}$

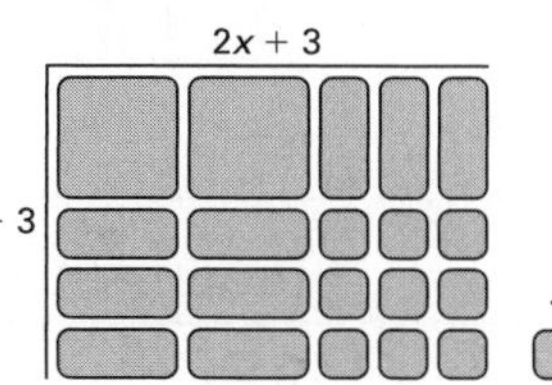

4. $2x + 1 + \frac{4}{2x+1}$

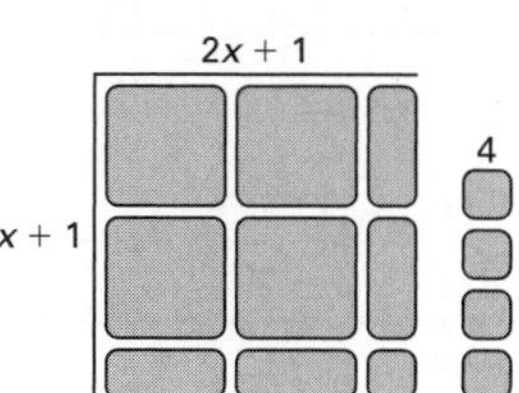

5. $x + 1 + \frac{4}{2x+3}$

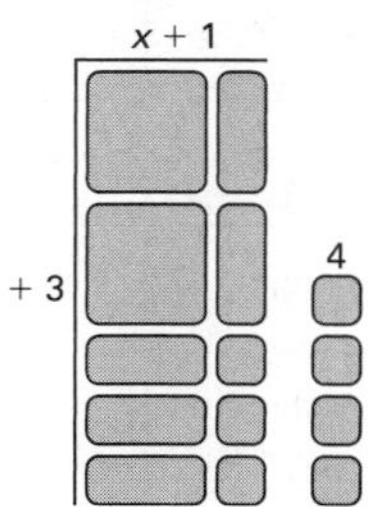

6. $3x + 1 + \frac{1}{x+2}$

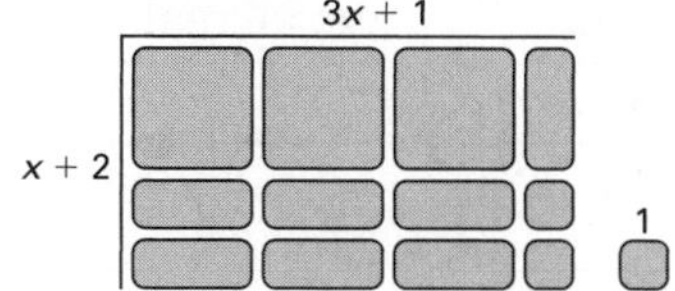

7. $4x + 2 + \frac{3}{x+1}$

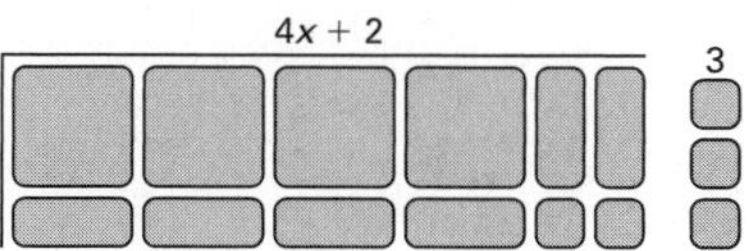

12.3 Skill Practice (pp. 788–789)

22. 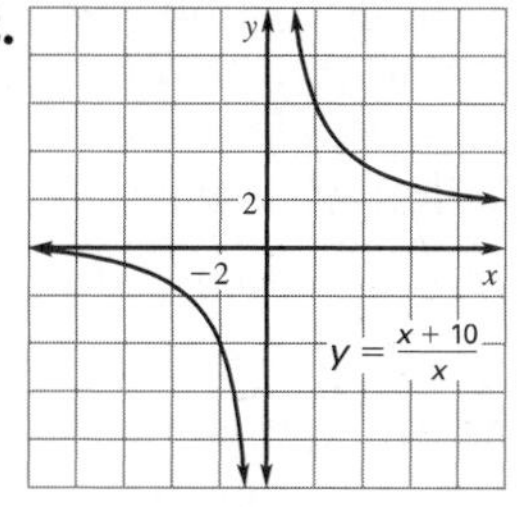

23. 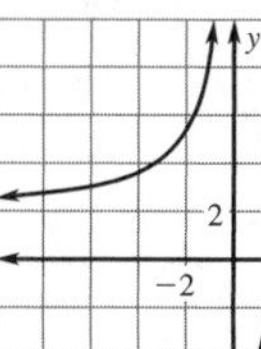

24. 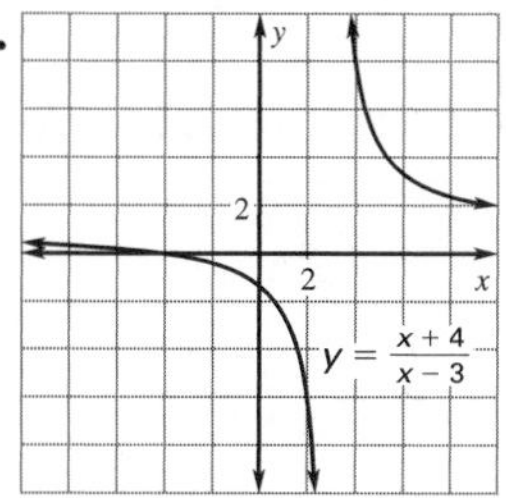

25. 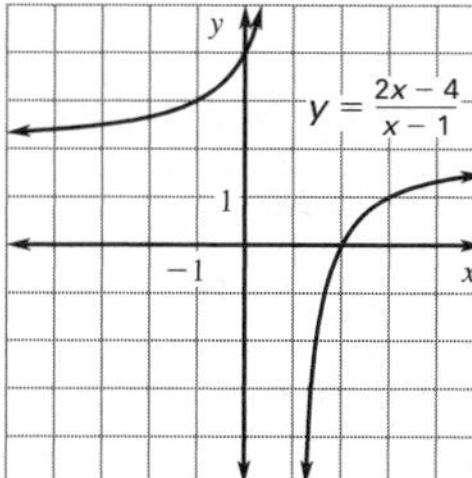

26. 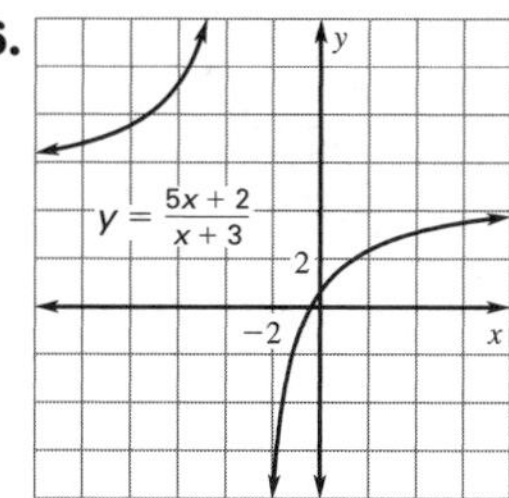

27. 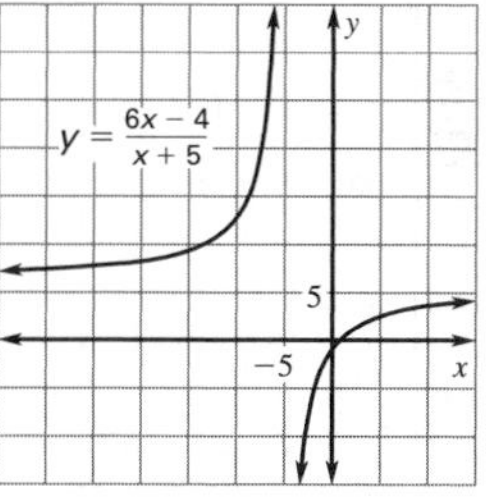

28. 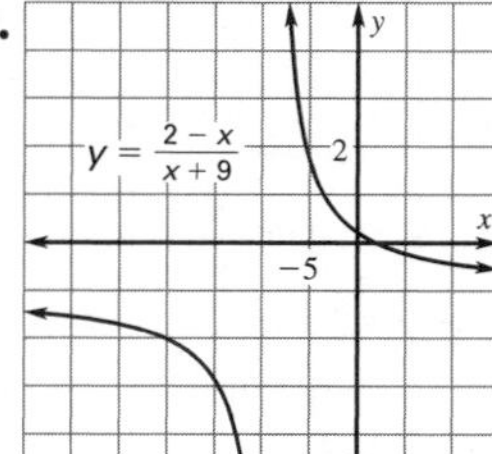

29. 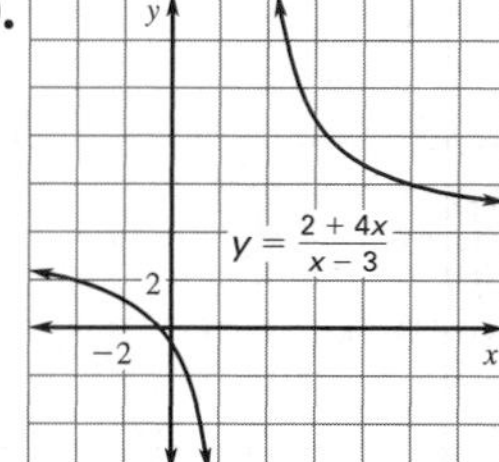

30. 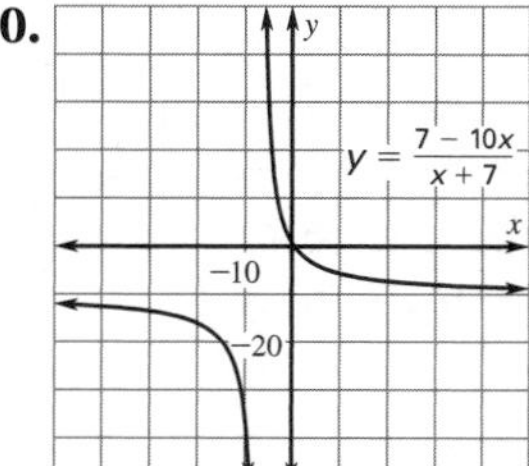

12.3 Problem Solving (pp. 789–791)

49. a. $y = \frac{2r + 2\ell}{r\ell}$;

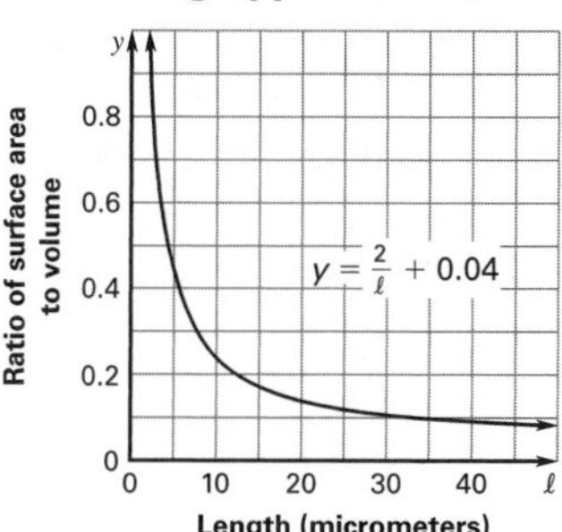

ADDITIONAL ANSWERS

b. More efficient; the graph in part (a) shows that as the length increases, the ratio decreases, implying that the microorganism becomes more efficient at performing metabolic tasks. **c.** The microorganism's efficiency would increase. *Sample answer:* Suppose the length is fixed at 50 micrometers. Then $y = \frac{2r + 100}{50r}$, or $y = \frac{2}{r} + 0.04$. This equation has the same graph as the graph shown in part (a); from the graph we see that as the radius increases, the ratio decreases, implying that the microorganism's efficiency increases.

12.3 Graphing Calculator Activity (pp. 792–793)

7.

	$y=\frac{8}{x-2}$	$y=\frac{4}{6x-7}$	$y=\frac{x-9}{x^2+1}$
Vertical asymptotes	$x=2$	$x=\frac{7}{6}$	none
x-values for which y is undefined	2	$\frac{7}{6}$	none
Horizontal asymptotes	$y=0$	$y=0$	$y=0$
Degree of numerator	0	0	1
Degree of denominator	1	1	2

	$y=\frac{x+5}{x^2+4x+4}$	$y=\frac{x+1}{4x^2-36}$	$y=\frac{5}{10x^2+9}$
Vertical asymptotes	$x=-2$	$x=-3$, $x=3$	none
x-values for which y is undefined	−2	−3, 3	none
Horizontal asymptotes	$y=0$	$y=0$	$y=0$
Degree of numerator	1	1	0
Degree of denominator	2	2	2

8. 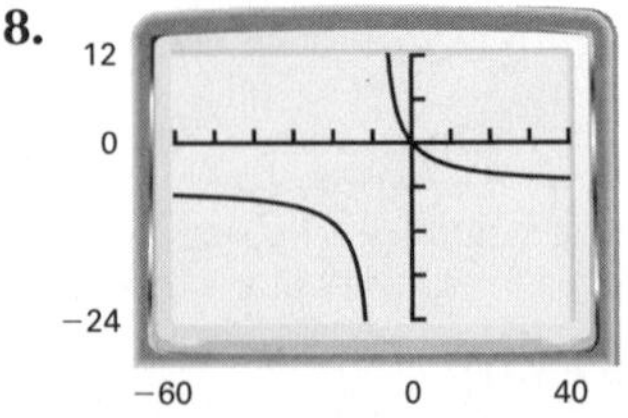

vertical: $x = -9$, horizontal: $y = -6$

9. 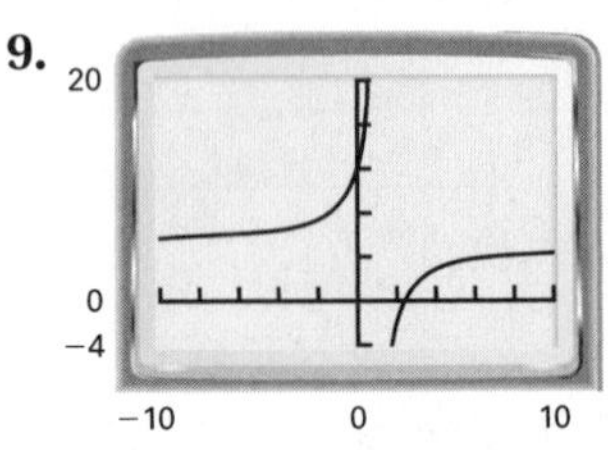

vertical: $x = 1$, horizontal: $y = 5$

10. 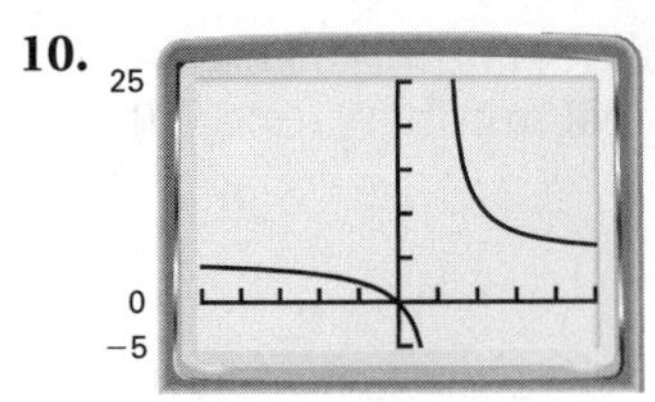

vertical: $x = \frac{9}{2}$, horizontal: $y = 5$

11. 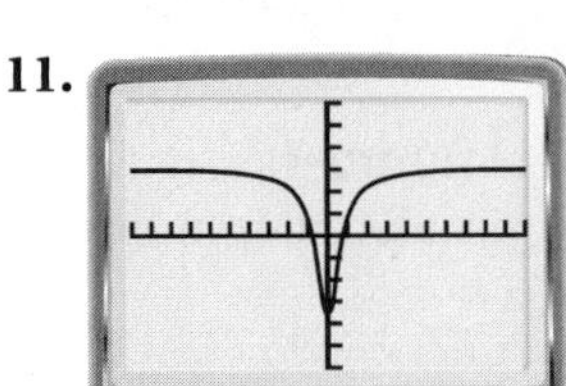

vertical: none, horizontal: $y = 3$

12. 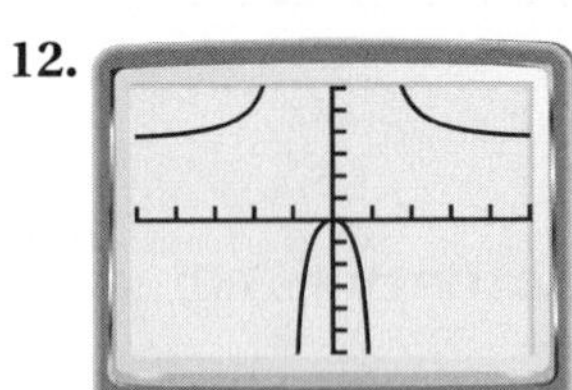

vertical: $x = \frac{-4}{3}$, $x = \frac{4}{3}$, horizontal: $y = 3$

13. 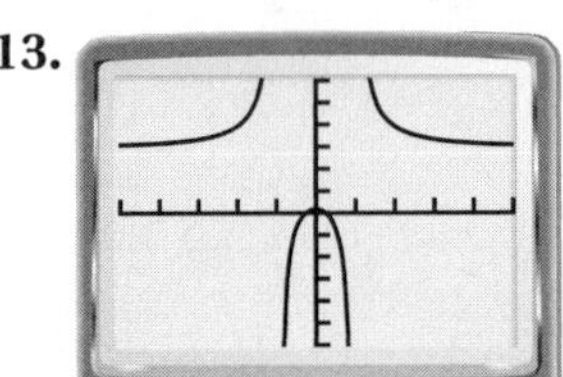

vertical: $x = -1$, $x = 1$, horizontal: $y = 3$

14.

	$y=\frac{-6x}{x+9}$	$y=\frac{5x-12}{x-1}$	$y=\frac{10x}{2x-9}$
Vertical asymptotes	$x=-9$	$x=1$	$x=\frac{9}{2}$
x-values for which y is undefined	−9	1	$\frac{9}{2}$
Horizontal asymptotes	$y=-6$	$y=5$	$y=5$
Degree of numerator	1	1	1
Degree of denominator	1	1	1
Quotient of leading coefficients	−6	5	5

	$y=\frac{12x^2-7}{4x^2+2}$	$y=\frac{27x^2-x}{9x^2-16}$	$y=\frac{18x^2-1}{6x^2-6}$
Vertical asymptotes	none	$x=\frac{-4}{3}$, $x=\frac{4}{3}$	$x=-1$, $x=1$
x-values for which y is undefined	none	$\frac{-4}{3}$, $\frac{4}{3}$	−1, 1
Horizontal asymptotes	$y=3$	$y=3$	$y=3$
Degree of numerator	2	2	2
Degree of denominator	2	2	2
Quotient of leading coefficients	3	3	3

12.4 Problem Solving (pp. 799–800)

45. b.

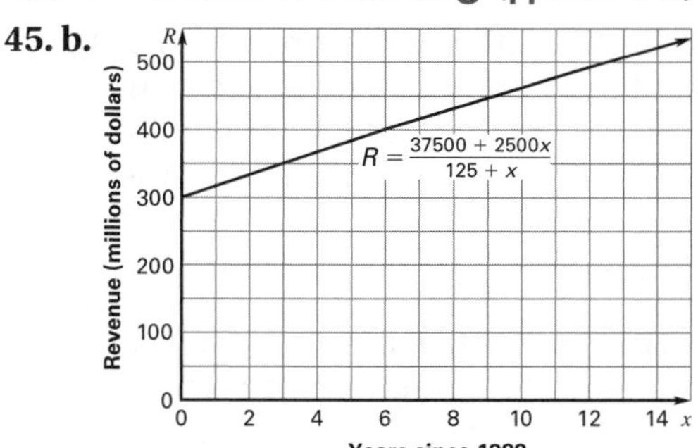

Quiz for Lessons 12.3–12.4 (p. 800)

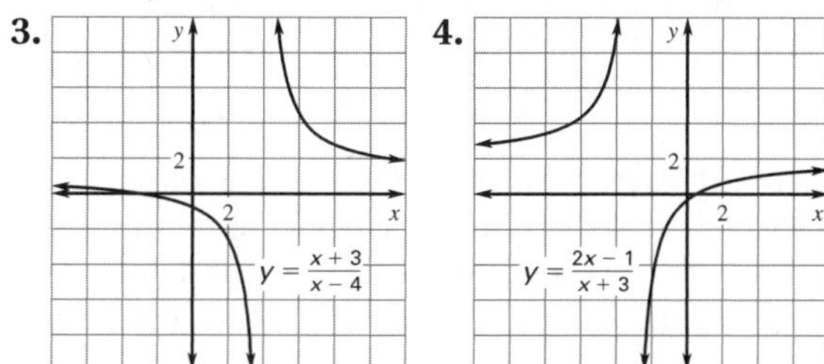

12.6 Skill Practice (pp. 816–817) **19.** To rewrite each rational expression using the least common denominator, you must multiply its numerator by the factor of the LCD that is missing from the denominator: the numerator $5x$ should be multiplied by $(x + 3)$ and the numerator 2 should be multiplied by $(x - 4)$; $\frac{5x}{x - 4} + \frac{2}{x + 3} = \frac{5x(x + 3)}{(x - 4)(x + 3)} + \frac{2(x - 4)}{(x - 4)(x + 3)} = \frac{5x^2 + 15x + 2x - 8}{(x - 4)(x + 3)} = \frac{5x^2 + 17x - 8}{(x - 4)(x + 3)}$.

12.7 Problem Solving Workshop (p. 828) **1.** \$1250; Method 1: Use a table. Make a table that shows the percent of Jill's investment money that is in the mutual fund after various amounts are added to the mutual fund.

Amount in mutual fund (\$)	Amount in all investments (\$)	Percent in mutual fund (%)
1000	10,000	10
1200	10,200	about 11.8
1400	10,400	about 13.5
1600	10,600	about 15
1800	10,800	about 16.7
2000	11,000	about 18.1
2050	11,050	about 18.6
2100	11,100	about 18.9
2150	11,150	about 19.3
2200	11,200	about 19.6
2250	11,250	20

Method 2: Reinterpret the problem. When 20% of Jill's investment money is in the mutual fund, $\frac{1}{5}$ of her money will be in the mutual fund and $\frac{4}{5}$ of her money will be in other accounts. The ratio of money in the mutual fund to money in other accounts (which is \$10,000 − \$1000 = \$9000) needs to be 1 : 4. Let a = amount of money (in dollars) added to the mutual fund and write a proportion: $\frac{1000 + a}{9000} = \frac{1}{4}$. Solving for a gives $a = 1250$, so Jill needs to add \$1250 to the mutual fund. **3.** 6 free throws; Method 1: Use a table. Make a table that shows the percent of free throw attempts made after various numbers of consecutive successful free throw attempts.

Number of consecutive successful free throw attempts	Total number of free throw attempts	Percent of free throw attempts made
12	30	40%
13	31	about 42%
14	32	about 44%
15	33	about 45%
16	34	about 47%
17	35	about 49%
18	36	50%

Method 2: Reinterpret the problem. When 50% of the free throw attempts have been successful, the number of attempts made will equal the number of attempts not made. After the first 30 attempts, the number of attempts made is $0.40(30) = 12$, and the number of attempts not made is $0.60(30) = 18$. Let n = number of consecutive successful free throw attempts and write an equation that shows that the number of attempts made and the number of attempts not made are equal: $12 + n = 18$. Solving for n gives $n = 6$, so the basketball player needs to make 6 consecutive free throws. **5.** 75 minutes; Method 1: Use a table. Make a table that shows the total time it takes you and your friend to shovel the driveway together for various amounts of time that it takes your friend to shovel the driveway alone.

Time m for your friend to shovel the driveway alone (min)	Time for you to shovel the driveway alone (min)	Time it takes to shovel the driveway together (min)
50	50	25
55	50	about 26
60	50	about 27
65	50	about 28
70	50	about 29
75	50	30

Method 2: Reinterpret the problem. Because you can shovel the driveway alone in 50 minutes, during each of the 30 minutes that you and your friend work together you shovel $\frac{1}{50}$ of the driveway. So, in 30 minutes you have shoveled $\frac{30}{50}$, or $\frac{3}{5}$ of the driveway. Your friend shovels $\frac{2}{5}$ of the driveway in 30 minutes, so 30 minutes is $\frac{2}{5}$ of the time that it will take your friend to shovel the whole driveway. Let m be the number of minutes it takes your friend to shovel the whole driveway and write an equation: $30 = \frac{2}{5}m$. Solving for m gives $m = 75$ minutes, so it takes your friend 75 minutes to shovel the driveway alone.

Chapter 13

13.1 Skill Practice (pp. 846–847) **13.** *Sample answer:* Odds in favor is the number of favorable outcomes divided by the number of unfavorable outcomes; odds in favor of a multiple of 3 $= \frac{\text{Number of favorable outcomes}}{\text{Number of unfavorable outcomes}} = \frac{9}{1}$ or 9 : 1. **21.** $\frac{4}{9}$; $\frac{4}{5}$. *Sample answer:* The probability and odds of choosing a boy are related because both compare the number of boys to another number. The probability of choosing a boy compares the number of boys to the total number of outcomes, while the odds of choosing a boy compare the number of boys to the total number of outcomes minus the number of boys.

13.2 Skill Practice (pp. 853–854) **31. b.** There are the same number of permutations. *Sample answer:* The formula for n objects taken n at a time is $\frac{n!}{(n-n)!} = n!$, while the formula for n objects taken $n - 1$ at a time is $\frac{n!}{(n-(n-1))!} = \frac{n!}{1!} = n!$. Thus, both formulas are equal.

13.3 Skill Practice (p. 858) **20.** ${}_6P_r \geq {}_6C_r$. *Sample answer:* The formula for ${}_6C_r$ is the same as ${}_6P_r$ multiplied by $\frac{1}{r!}$. For any value of $r > 1$, this will result in ${}_6C_r$ being less than ${}_6P_r$. If $r = 1$ or $r = 0$ then the values will be the same. **21.** ${}_nC_r = {}_nP_r \bullet \frac{1}{r!}$. *Sample answer:* To find the number of combinations, you find the number of permutations and then divide by the number of ways the items being chosen can be arranged, or $r!$. **22.** ${}_nC_{n-r} = \frac{n!}{[n-(n-r)]! \bullet (n-r)!} = \frac{n!}{r! \bullet (n-r)!} = \frac{n!}{(n-r)! \bullet r!} = {}_nC_r$. *Sample answer:* When you select a combination of r items from a group of n, you divide the group into 2 sections: a group of r selected items and a group of $n - r$ items that were not selected. Since each combination you select results in a unique combination of items not selected, the number of combinations of r items you can select from a group of n is the same as the number of combinations of $(n - r)$ items you cannot select in the group of n.

13.3 Problem Solving (p. 859) **27.** $\frac{351}{142,506} \approx 0.25\%$. *Sample answer:* The number of possible groups chosen is ${}_{30}C_5 = 142,506$. To find the number of groups that include me and my 2 best friends, find the number of combinations of students to fill the remaining group once me and my 2 best friends have been chosen, or ${}_{27}C_2 = 351$. There are 351 favorable groups out of 142,506 possible groups.

13.5 Guided Practice (pp. 871–872) **2. a.** Yes. *Sample answer:* All the people sampled were visiting a soccer game, so they may be more likely than the American population to be interested in soccer. **b.** Yes. *Sample answer:* The question suggests that soccer is popular and may encourage respondents to say they are interested in soccer. *Sample answer:* "How interested or disinterested are you in soccer?"

13.5 Problem Solving (p. 874) **16.** Yes. *Sample answer:* The sample is not likely to be truly representative of the world's fresh water since it was such a small sample of the population. **17. b.** *Sample answer:* "How many hours per night do you study?" This question is unbiased because it does not prompt respondents to give any particular answer. **18.** *Sample answer:* If the rule used to select the systematic survey is not representative then the results will be biased; if a survey designed to determine the favorite clothes shops of students at a school selected all the students who were over 6 feet tall, this might bias the results towards shops that sold clothes for tall people.

13.6 Problem Solving (pp. 877–878) **22. c.** Range: 219, mean absolute deviation: 50.7. *Sample answer:* The range is much higher than the mean which indicates that the data covers a wide spread of values. The mean absolute deviation tells you that the data points are not very close to the mean. **23. b.** No. *Sample answer:* If your median is 86, it means the final test score was greater than or equal to 88. You may or may not have scored greater than 94.

13.7 Guided Practice (pp. 881–883)

4. *Sample:*

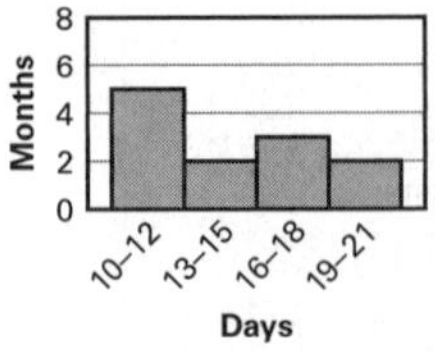

13.7 Skill Practice (pp. 883–884)

10. *Sample answer:* The range 20–29 even though it has a frequency of 0 needs to be included on the axis. Without it the histogram gives a distorted view of the spread of data.

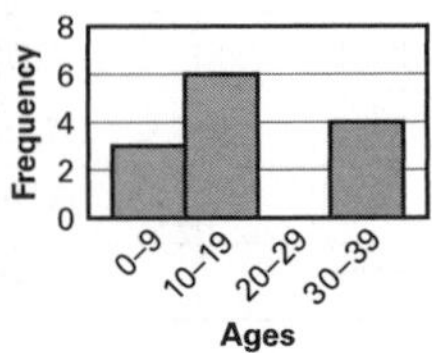

11. **12.** **13.** **14.**

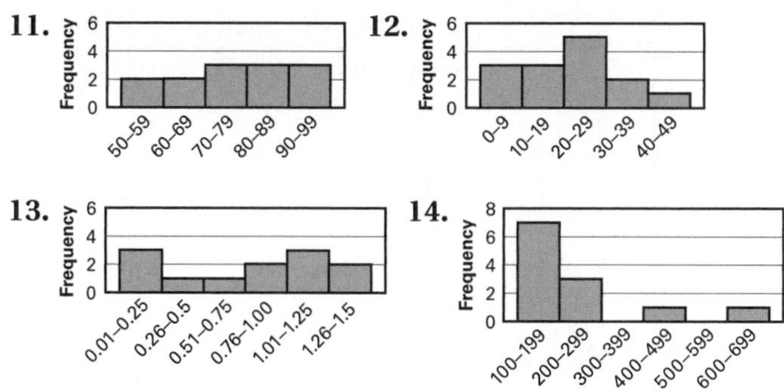

13.7 Problem Solving (pp. 884–885)

17. Heights **18.** Water Intake

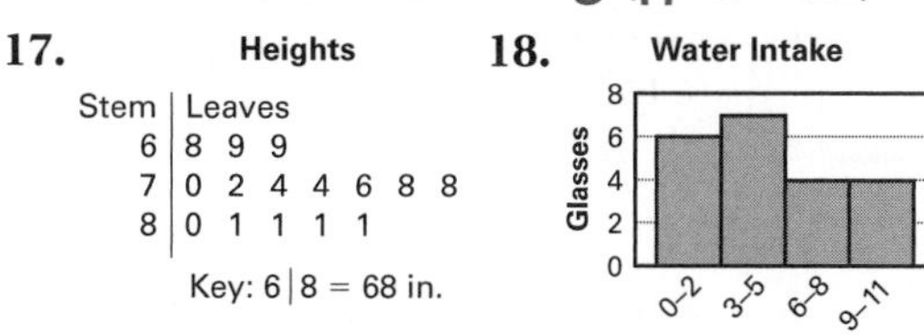

Stem	Leaves
6	8 9 9
7	0 2 4 4 6 8 8
8	0 1 1 1 1

Key: 6 | 8 = 68 in.

19. a. Phone Number Memorization

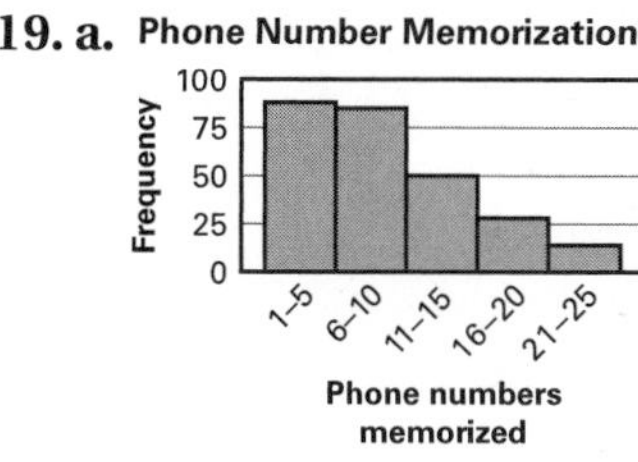

21. a. Ages of *Mayflower* Passengers

Stem	Leaves
1	8
2	0 0 0 1 1 1 1 1 5 5 5 9
3	0 0 0 2 2 4 4 5 7 8 8 8 8 8 9
4	0 1 2 5 5 8 9
5	0 4 5
6	4

Key: 1 | 8 = 18 years

22. a. 29.5, 39.5, 49.5, 59.5, 69.5; 4100.5, 6833.5, 7573.5, 5950, 4865; 29,322.5; 46.177 **b.** The mean. *Sample answer:* By estimating likely average values for each interval, a sum was found for all the data values that created the histogram. This sum was divided by the total number of data values, to create an estimate of the mean.

13.8 Skill Practice (pp. 889–890) **2.** *Sample answer:* Find the interquartile range and multiply it by 1.5. Add the result to the upper quartile, and subtract it from the lower quartile. Any data values outside these values are outliers.

13.8 Problem Solving (pp. 890–892) **20.** *Sample answer:* Generally, the lower the voice part the taller the singer in the chorus. 50% of the bass parts are between 68 and 72 inches, while 50% of the tenors are between 66.5 and 71.5 inches, 50% of the altos are between 63 and 67 inches, and sopranos are the shortest with 50% between 62.5 and 66 inches. Around 75% of all bass singers are taller than all sopranos and around 50% of tenors are taller than all sopranos.

13.8 Mixed Review (p. 892)

23. **24.**

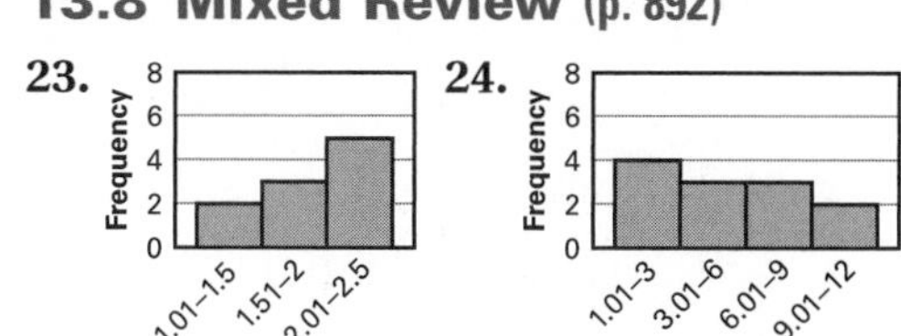

Quiz for Lessons 13.5–13.8 (p. 892)

4.

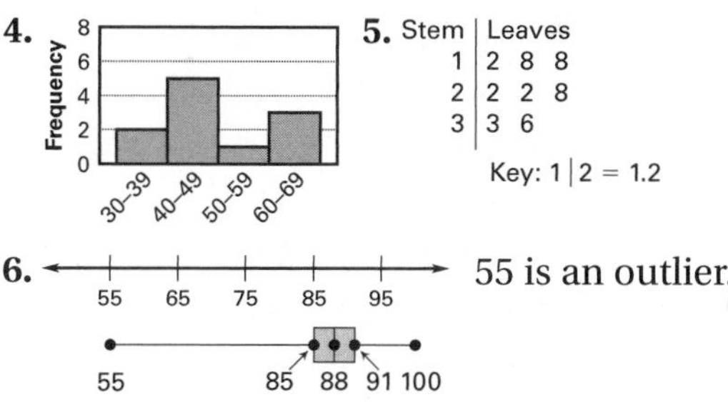

5.

Stem	Leaves
1	2 8 8
2	2 2 8
3	3 6

Key: 1 | 2 = 1.2

6. 55 is an outlier.

Extra Practice

Chapter 4 (p. 941)

23. **24.**

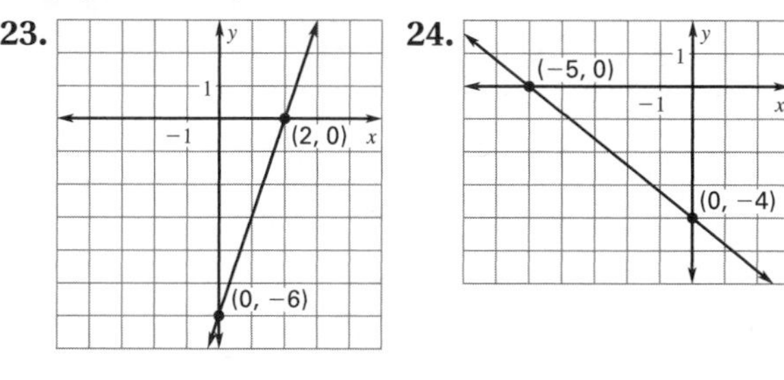

25. **26.**

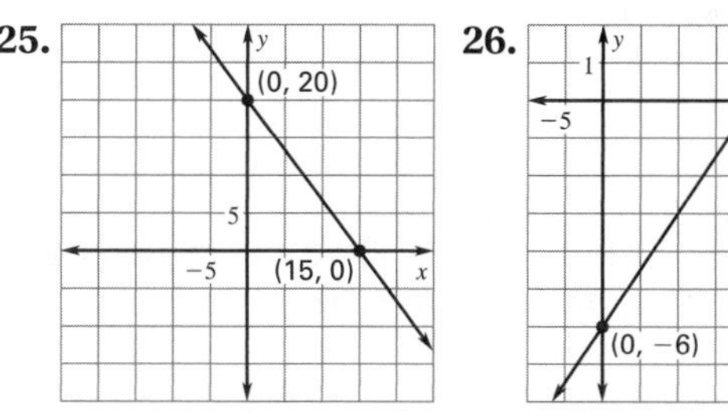

41. **42.**

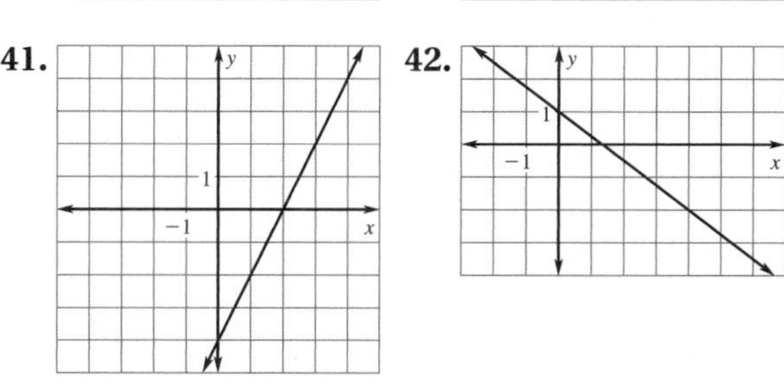

43. **44.**

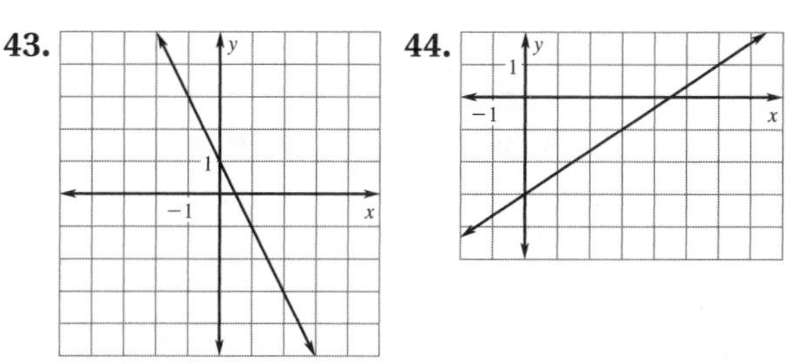

ADDITIONAL ANSWERS

45.
y
1
−1
x

46.
y
1
−1
x

47.
y
1
−1
x

48.
y
5
−1
x

49.
y
1
1
x

50.
y
3
−1
x

51.
y
3
1
x

52.
y
1
−1
x

56.
y
1
−1
x

The graph is a vertical translation 2 units down of $f(x) = x$.

57.
y
1
−1
x

The graph is a vertical translation 4 units up of $f(x) = x$.

58.
y
2
−1
x

The graph is a vertical stretch by a factor of 6 of $f(x) = x$.

59.
y
2
−1
x

The graph is a vertical stretch by a factor of 2 and a reflection in the x-axis of $f(x) = x$.

Chapter 6 (p. 943)

34.
6
8
10
12

35.
−6
−3
0
3
6

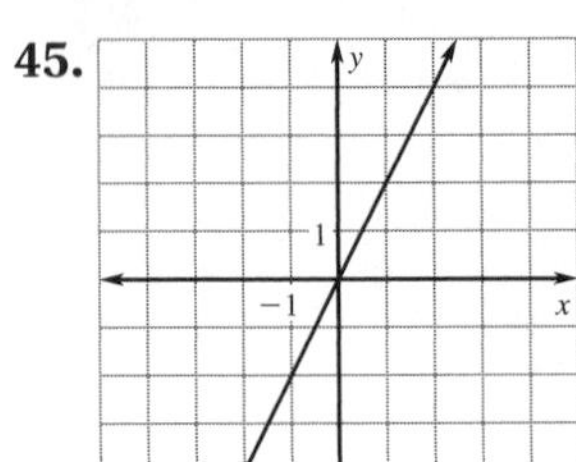

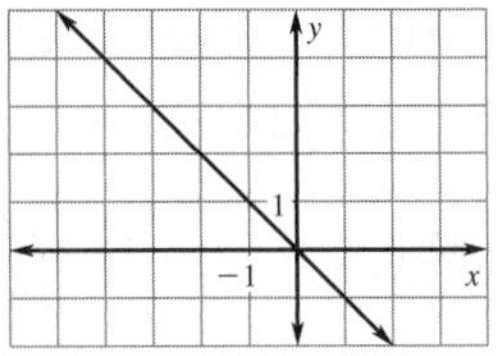

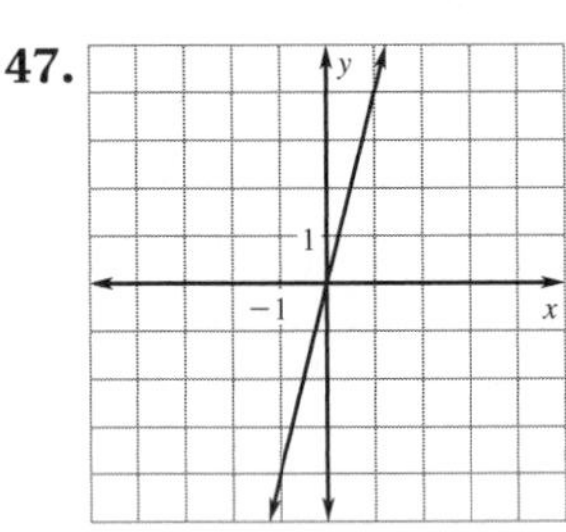

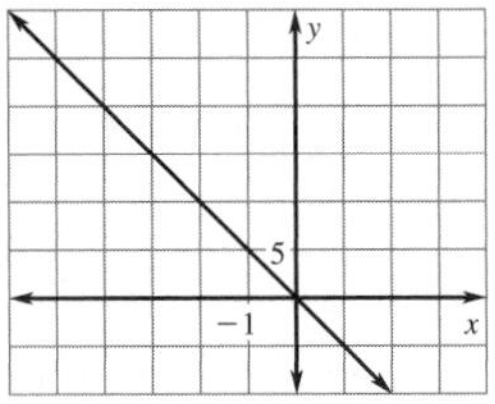

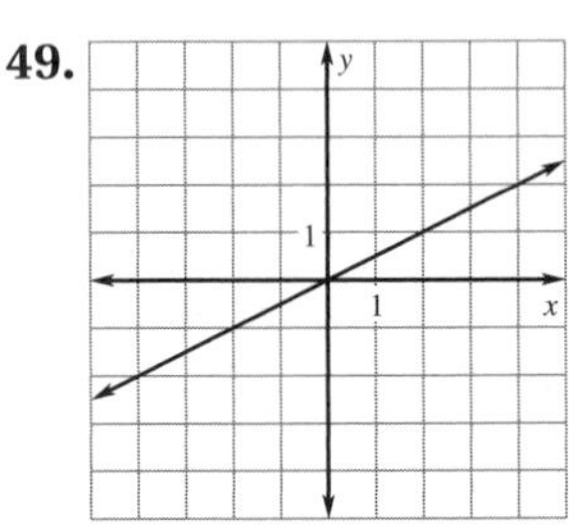

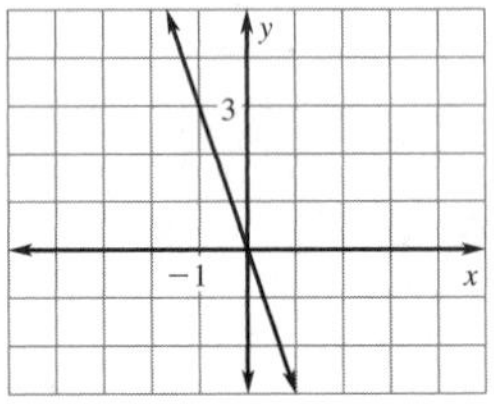

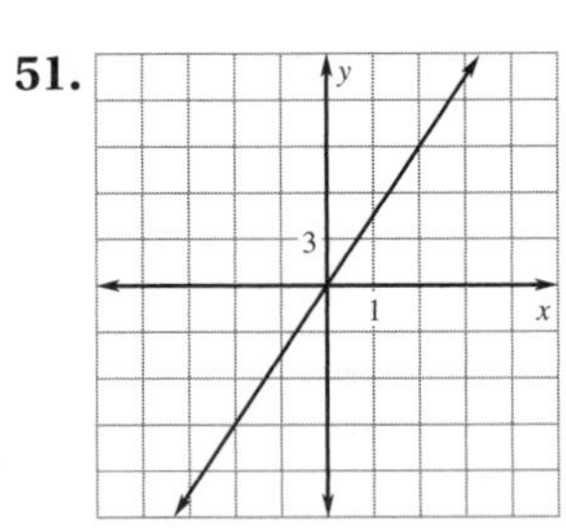

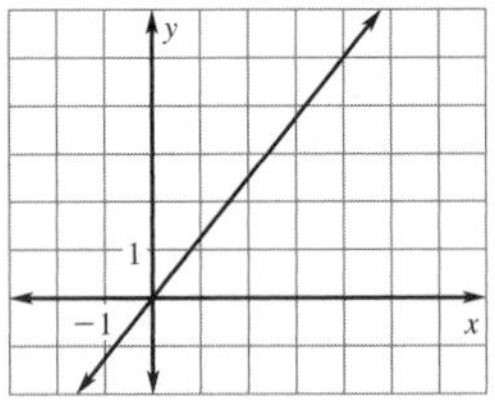

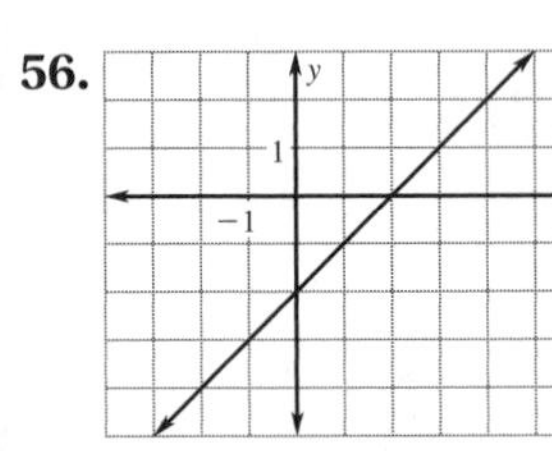

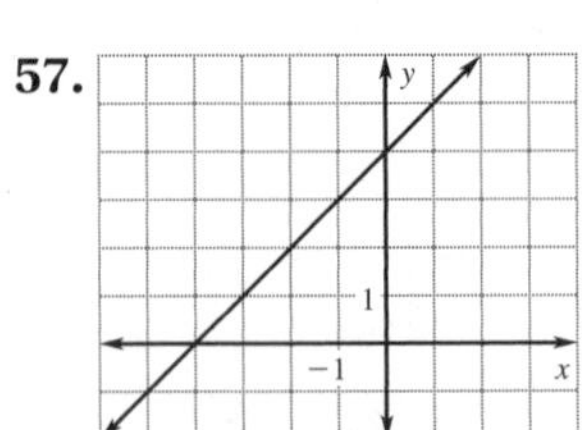

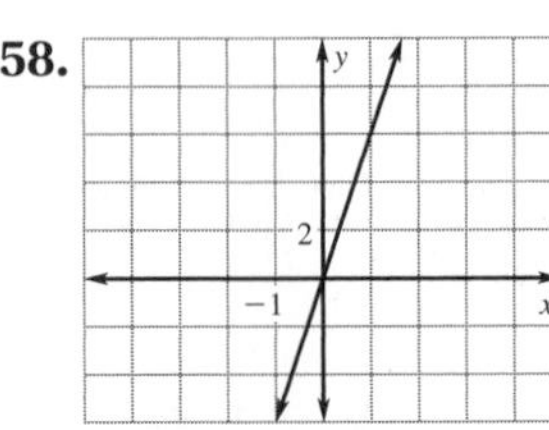

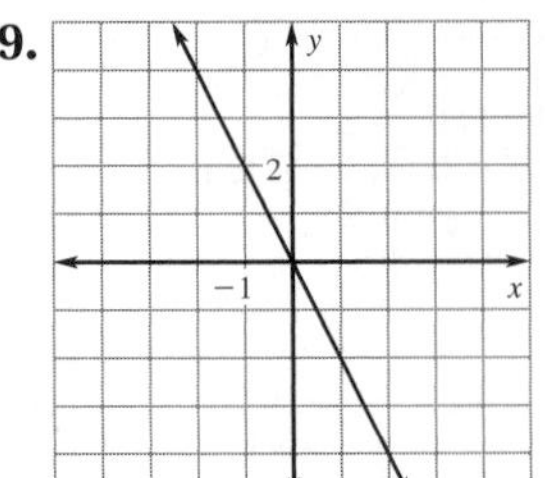

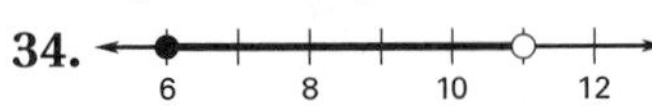

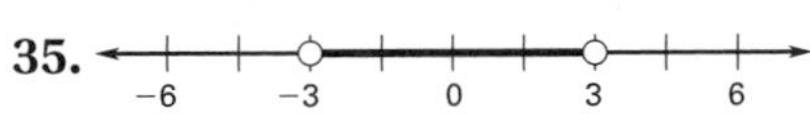

36.
0
2
4
6

37.
3.5
−2
0
2
4
6

38.
2
4
6
8

39.
−6
−4
−2
0

40.
−6
−4
−2
0

41.
−12
−8
−4
0
4

42.
−4
−2
0
2

55.
−6
−3
0
3
6

56.
−6
−4
−2
0
2
4
6

57.
−1.2
1.2
−2
−1
0
1
2

58.
−2/5
2/5
−2
−1
0
1
2

59.
−8
−4
0
4
8

60.
−8
−4
0
4

61.
5
7
9
11

62.
−3/2
−2
0
2
4

63.
−1
7
−4
0
4
8
12

64.
−4 1/3
−4
−2
0
2
4

ADDITIONAL ANSWERS

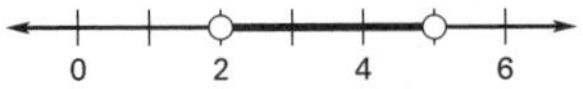

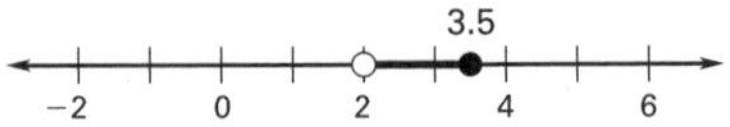

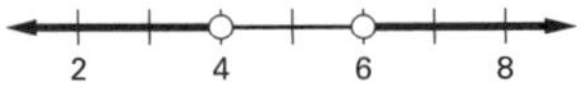

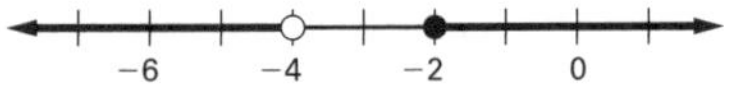

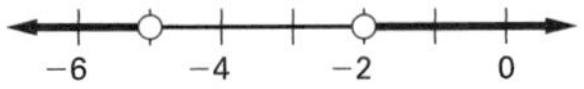

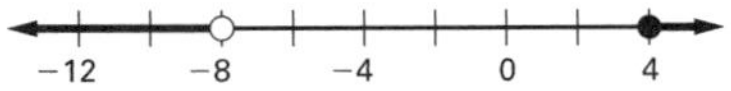

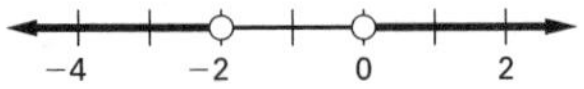

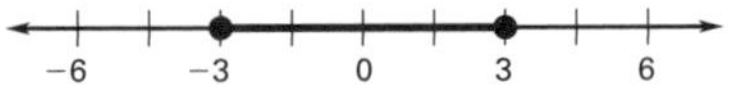

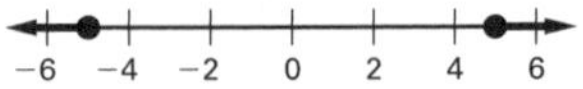

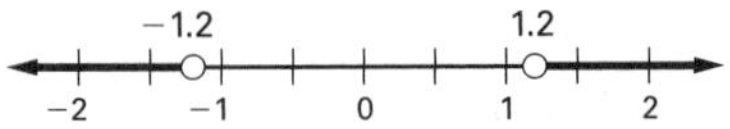

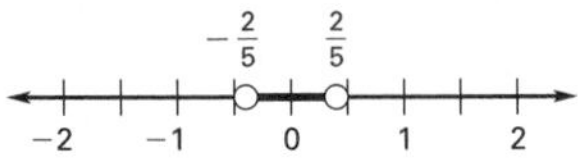

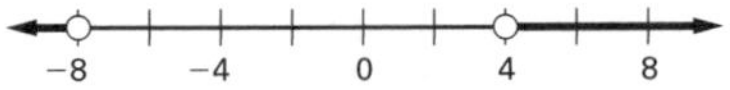

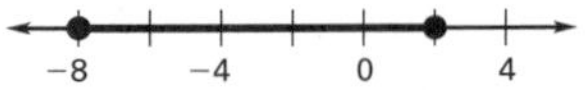

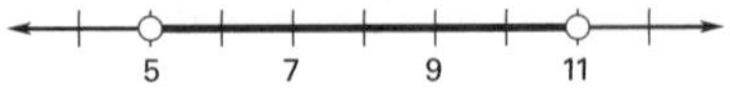

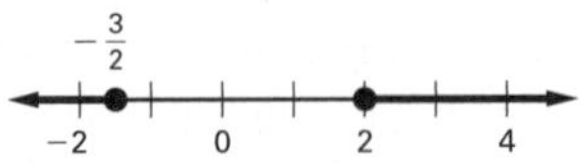

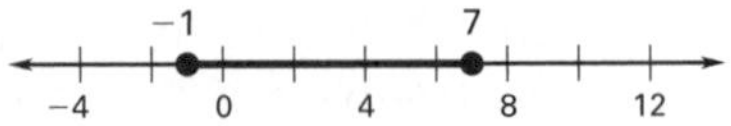

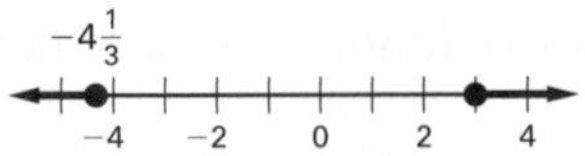

65. 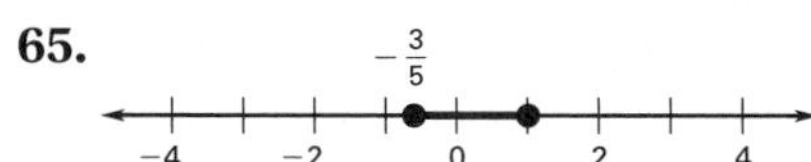

66. 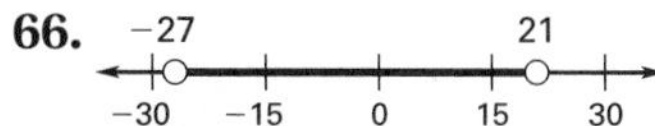

67. 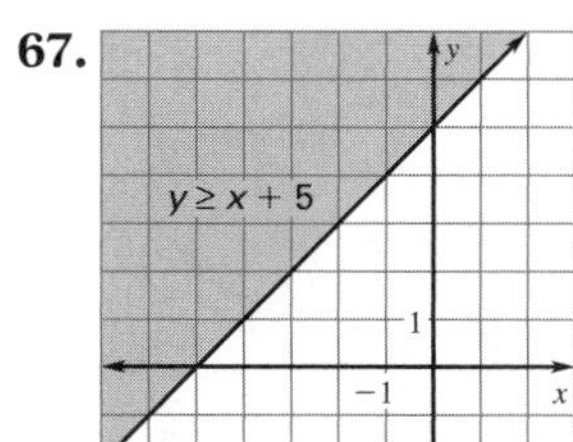

68. 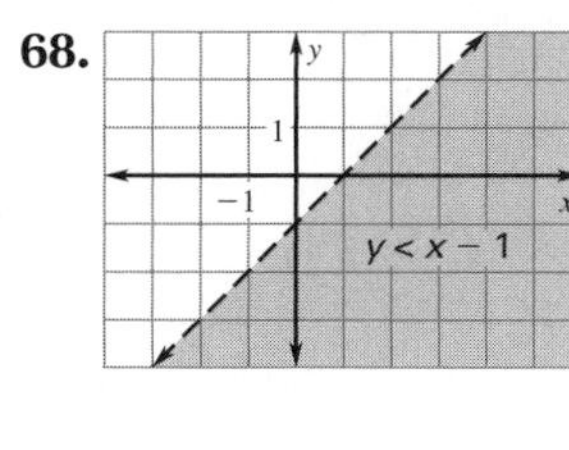

69. 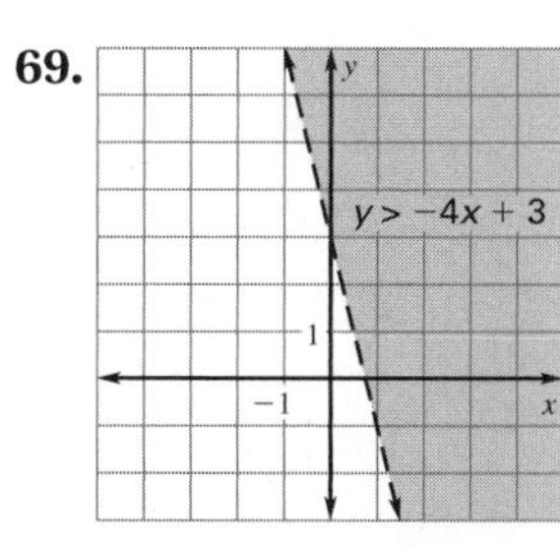

70. 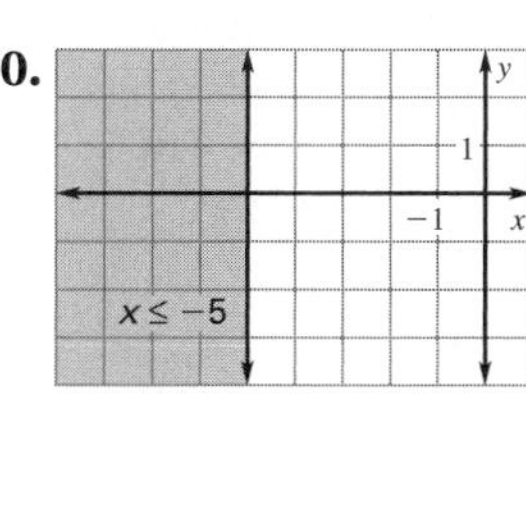

71. 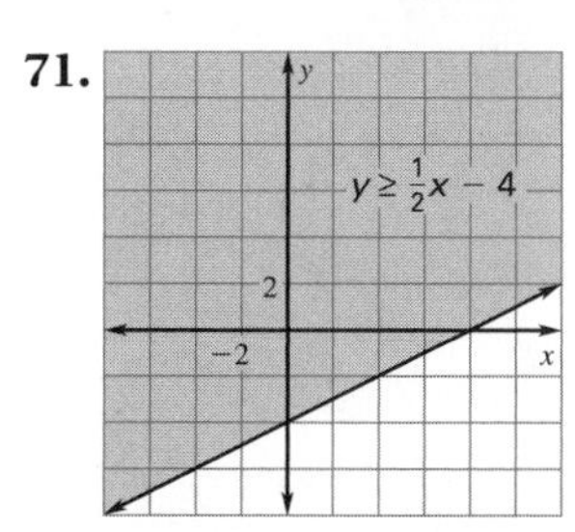

72. 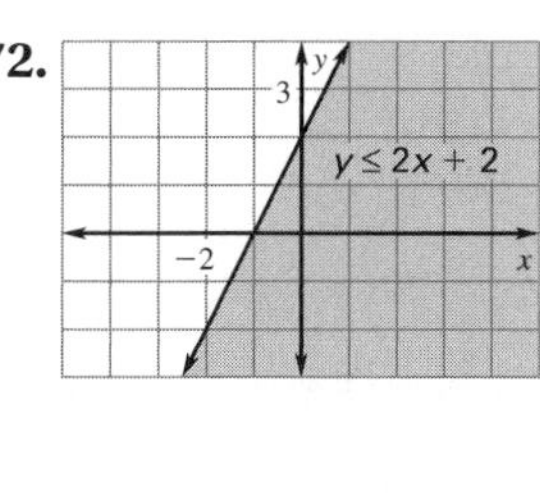

73. 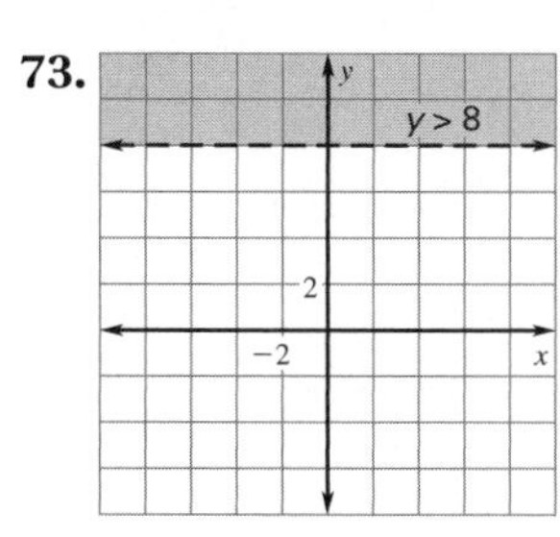

74. 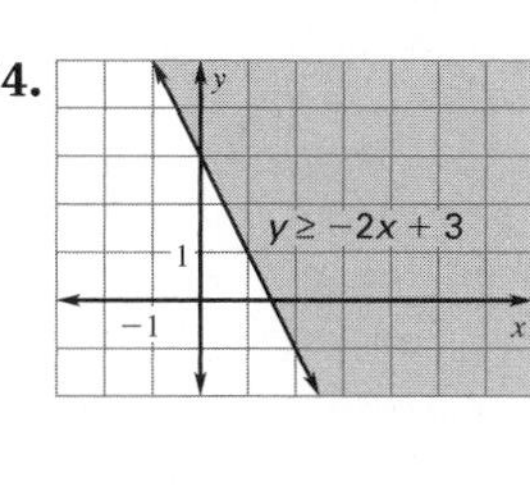

75. 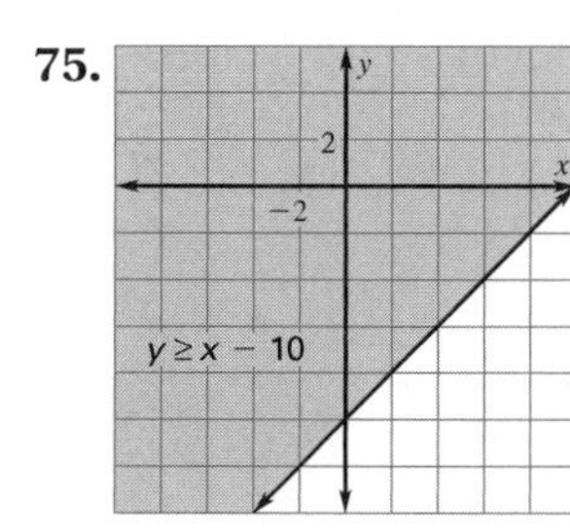

76. 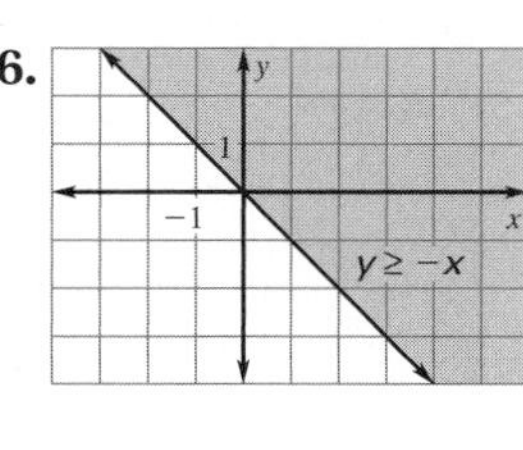

77. 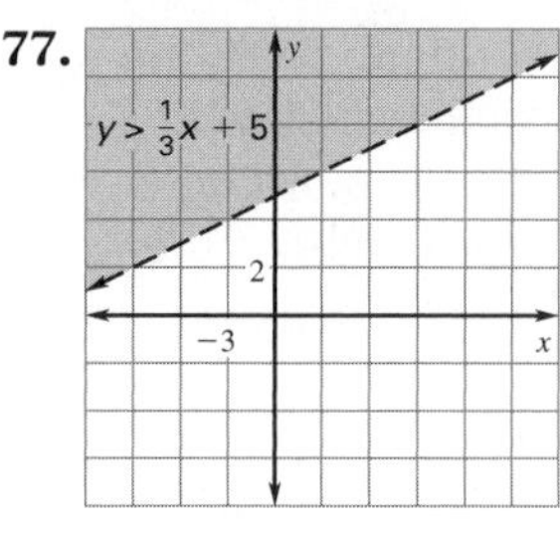

78. 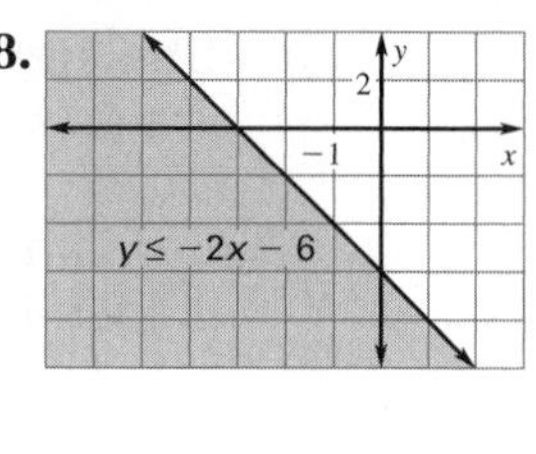

Chapter 8 (p. 945)

63. 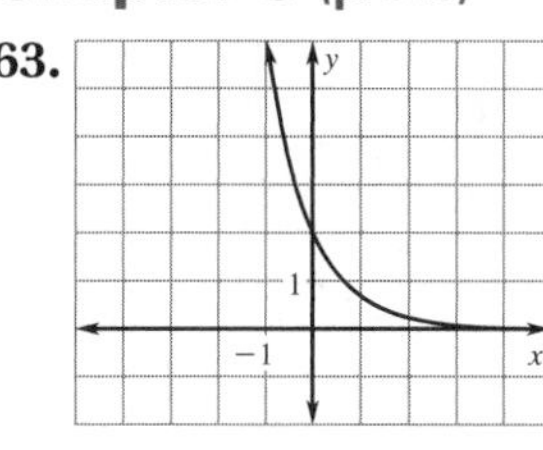

64. 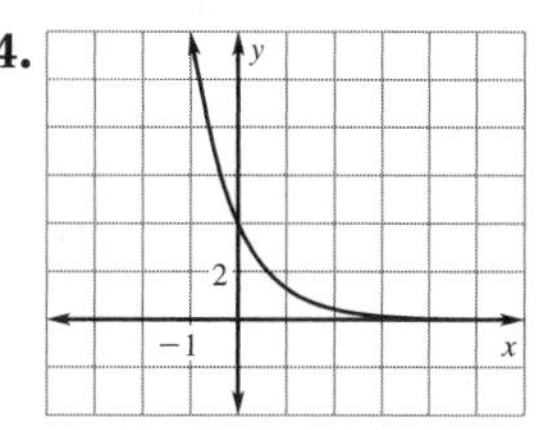

65. 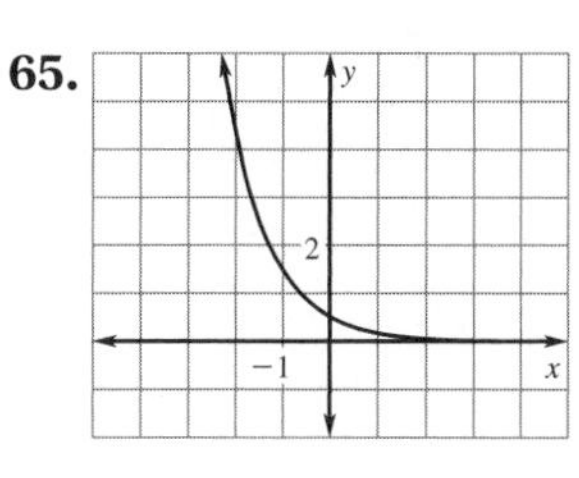

66. 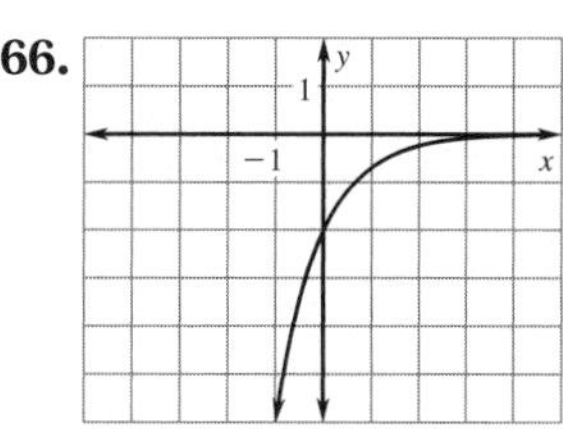

67. 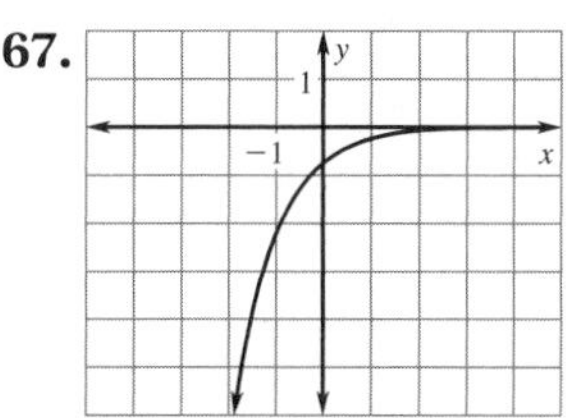

Chapter 11 (p. 948)

6. 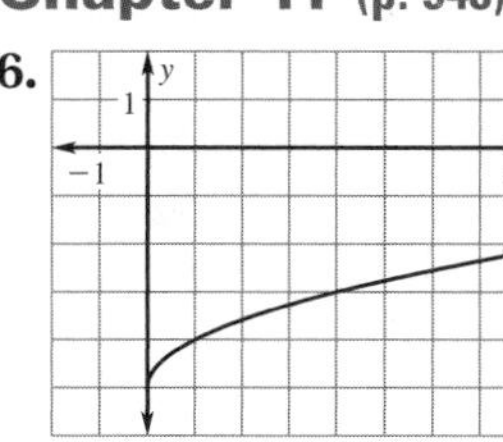

Domain: $x \geq 0$, range: $y \geq -5$; the graph is a vertical translation 5 units down of the graph of $y = \sqrt{x}$.

7. 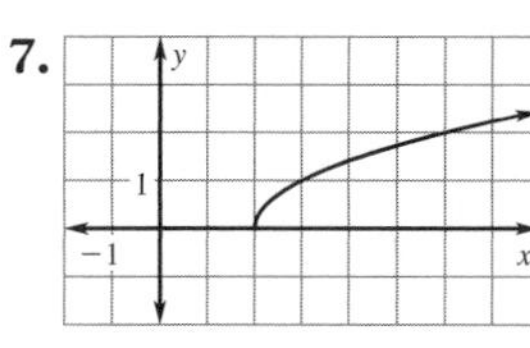

Domain: $x \geq 2$, range: $y \geq 0$; the graph is a horizontal translation 2 units right of the graph of $y = \sqrt{x}$.

8. 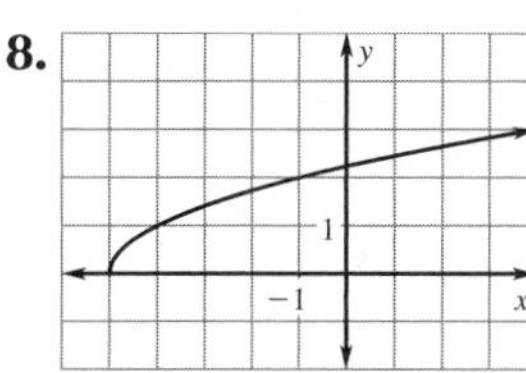

Domain: $x \geq -5$, range: $y \geq 0$; the graph is a horizontal translation 5 units left of the graph of $y = \sqrt{x}$.

9. 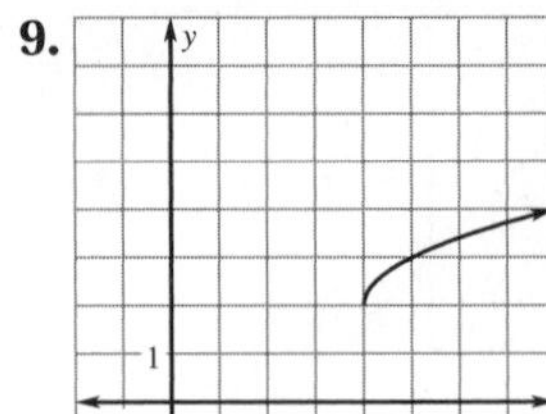

Domain: $x \geq 4$, range: $y \geq 2$; the graph is a vertical translation 2 units up and a horizontal translation 4 units right of the graph of $y = \sqrt{x}$.

Chapter 12 (p. 949)

14. 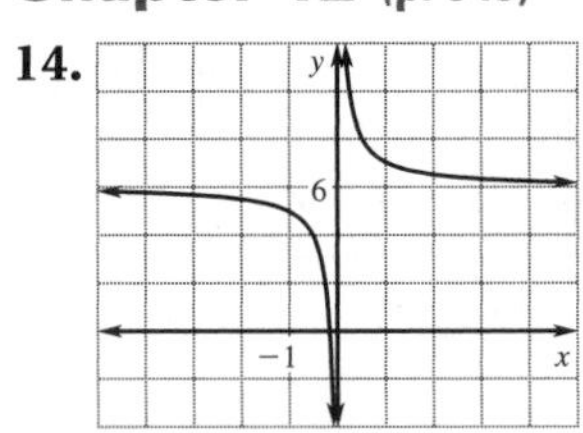

15. 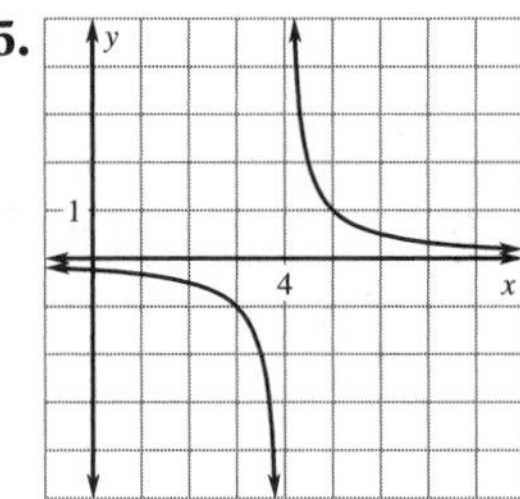

16. 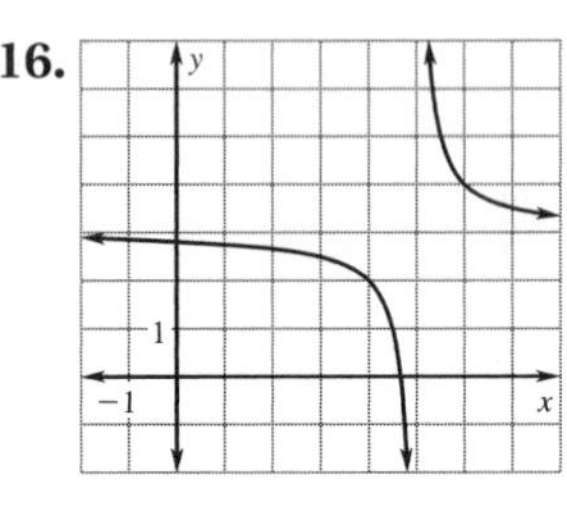

17. 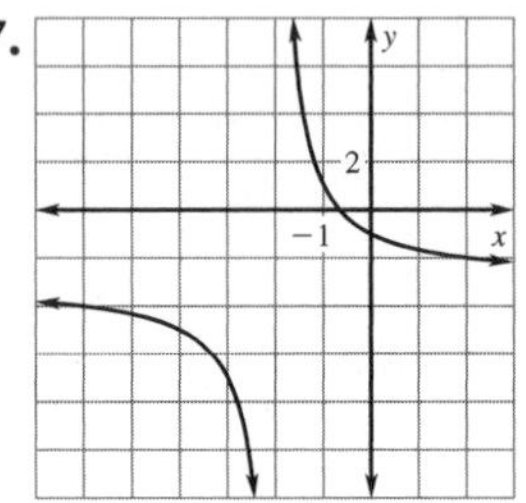

18. 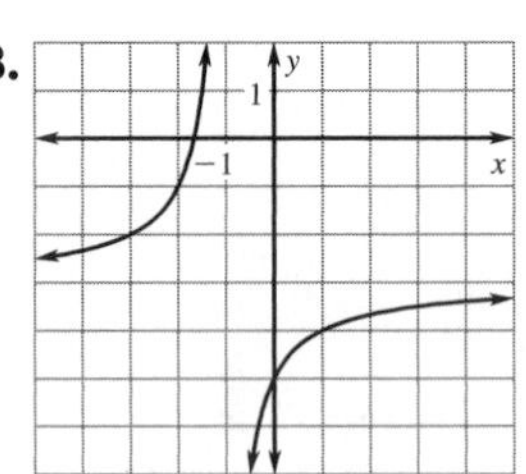

MCDOUGAL LITTELL ALGEBRA 1
CORRELATED TO THE
ILLINOIS MATHEMATICS ASSESSMENT FRAMEWORK

Mathematics–State Goal 6: Number Sense

Demonstrate and apply a knowledge and sense of numbers, including numeration and operations (addition, subtraction, multiplication, division), patterns, ratios and proportions.

STANDARD 6A – Demonstrate knowledge and use of numbers and their representations in a broad range of theoretical and practical settings. (Calculators Allowed)

6.11.01 Recognize, represent, order, compare real numbers, and locate real numbers on a number line (e.g., π, $\sqrt{2}$, $\sqrt{5}$, 2/3, −1.6).
64–70, 110–116, 120, 121–124, 125, 513, 515 (#29–38), 876, 909

6.11.02 Represent numbers in equivalent forms (e.g., fraction/decimal/percent, exponential/logarithmic, radical/rational exponents, absolute value, scientific notation).
110–118, 124, 512–518, 912, 913, 916–917

6.11.03 Use matrices to organize data.
94–95

STANDARD 6B, 6C – Investigate, represent and solve problems using number facts, operations (addition, subtraction, multiplication, division) and their properties, algorithms and relationships./ Compute and estimate using mental mathematics, paper-and-pencil methods, calculators and computers.

6.11.04 Apply the rules of order of operations to real-number expressions.
8–12, 13, 54, 57 (#1–3)

6.11.05 Simplify or test expressions by applying field properties (commutative, associative, distributive), order properties (transitive, reflexive, symmetric), and properties of equality for the set of real numbers.
2–7, 75–79, 84 (#53–56), 89–93, 96–101, 120, 123, 135, 137 (#2), 153 (#1–12), 191, 193, 357–358, 363–364, 954–955

6.11.06 Apply number theory concepts to the solution of problems (e.g., prime and composite numbers, prime factorization, greatest common factor, least common multiple, divisibility rules).
450 (#53–55), 574 (#46–53), 910–911, 914

CORRELATIONS

STANDARD 6B, 6C – Investigate, represent and solve problems using number facts, operations (addition, subtraction, multiplication, division) and their properties, algorithms and relationships./ Compute and estimate using mental mathematics, paper-and-pencil methods, calculators and computers. *(continued)*

6.11.07 Determine the effects of operations on the magnitudes of quantities (e.g., multiplication, division, powers, roots).
3–7, 88–95, 103–108, 110–116, 124, 491, 509–510, 716

6.11.08 Determine the appropriate solution, including rounding, from a context (e.g., rounding up, down, to the nearest integer).
110–116, 124, 805

6.11.09 Solve problems involving estimates or data (e.g., use averages to estimate the cost of a job that includes labor and materials).
110–116, 124, 805

6.11.10 Perform numerical computations with real numbers.
73, 74–79, 80–84, 85, 87, 88–93, 103–108, 914, 915

6.11.11 Perform numerical computations with non-real complex numbers.
See correlation for *McDougal Littell Algebra* 2.

6.11.12 Solve problems using simple matrix operations (addition, subtraction, multiplication, scalar multiplication).
94–95
See also, correlation for *McDougal Littell Algebra* 2.

6.11.13 Set up, evaluate, or solve single- and multi-step number sentences and word problems with rational numbers using the four basic operations.
28–33, 34, 78–79, 83–84, 92–93, 100–101, 102, 260, 375–376, 931, 932, 936–937

6.11.14 Determine the most cost effective option using single- and multi-step calculations and then comparing results.
11 (#34), 12 (#38), 31 (#3), 32 (#14, 20), 51 (#2), 57 (#18), 60 (#2–3), 100 (#52), 123 (#42)

6.11.15 Judge the reasonableness of solutions, and find mistakes in calculation, logic, and formula application.
Found throughout the text. See, for example: 5 (#24–25), 11 (#20–21), 18 (#26–27), 24 (#14–15), 31 (#6–7), 38 (#9–10), 68 (#40–41), 77 (#24–25), 82 (#15–16), 91 (#43–44), 99 (#3–4), 106 (#42–43), 138 (#29–30), 144 (#22–23), 151 (#25–26), 157 (#27–28), 165 (#21–22)

6.11.16 Simplify numerical problems involving absolute value.
66–69, 202 (#23), 308 (#45), 387 (#49), 390–395, 395 (#49), 396–397, 398–403, 412 (#1–6, 70), 599 (#69–72)

STANDARD 6D – Solve problems using comparison of quantities, ratios, proportions and percents.

6.11.17 Set up, evaluate, or solve number sentences or word problems involving ratios and proportions with rational numbers (e.g., scale drawing, unit rate, scale factor, rate of change).
17–19, 162–167, 168–173, 174–175, 176–181, 182–183, 194–195, 197 (#36), 203 (#48), 232 (#54–56), 235–242, 273, 304, 539–540, 922–923

6.11.18 Set up, evaluate, or solve common problems involving percent (e.g., sales tax, tip, interest, discount, markup, commission, compound interest).
30, 176–183, 189 (#44–45), 189 (#1–4), 196, 197 (#25–30), 197 (#37), 523, 527, 537 (#47–49), 538 (#7), 547 (#40), 916–917

6.11.19 Set up, evaluate, or solve problems stated in terms of direct and inverse variation of simple quantities.
253–259, 260–261, 268 (#1–3), 269 (#2), 274, 275, 276–279, 324 (#41), 764, 765–772, 782 (#1–6), 831

Mathematics–State Goal 7: Measurement

Estimate, make and use measurements of objects, quantities and relationships and determine acceptable levels of accuracy.

STANDARDS 7A, 7B, 7C – Measure and compare quantities using appropriate units, instruments and methods./ Estimate measurements and determine acceptable levels of accuracy./ Select and use appropriate technology, instruments and formulas to solve problems, interpret results and communicate findings.

7.11.01 Change from one unit to another within the same system of measurement, including calculations with mixed units (e.g., $3\frac{1}{2}$ hours plus 4 hours and 20 minutes; $2\frac{1}{2}$ feet minus 16 inches).
12 (#41–44), 929

7.11.02 Change from one unit in one system of measurement to a unit in another system of measurement, given a conversion factor.
Opportunities to address this standard can be found on the following pages: 929, A4–A5

7.11.03 Determine and calculate to an indicated precision the length, width, height, perimeter/circumference, area, volume, surface area, angle measures, or sums of angle measures of common geometric figures or combinations of common geometric figures.
4, 6 (#48), 7 (#54, 64–65), 26 (#52–54), 30, 33 (#28), 53 (#11–12), 181 (#41–42), 185, 188, 190 (#4, 7, 8), 194 (#37), 203 (#46), 282, 494, 574 (#9), 613 (#19), 782 (#52–54), 811 (#10–12), 924–925, 926, 927–928, 956. See also, correlation for *McDougal Littell Geometry*.

7.11.04 Describe the general trends of how the change in one measure affects other measures in the same figure (e.g., length, area, volume).
Opportunities to address this standard can be found on the following pages: 4, 7 (#64–65), 26 (#52–54), 30, 41, 53 (#11–12), 181 (#41–42), 184–189, 190 (#4, 7, 8), 203 (#46), 211 (#38), 282, 494, 574 (#9), 613 (#19), 782 (#52–54), 811, 924–925, 926, 927–928, 956. See also, correlation for *McDougal Littell Geometry*.

7.11.05 Determine the linear measure, perimeter, area, surface area, and volume of similar figures.
7, 174–175, 282, 956. See also, correlation for *McDougal Littell Geometry*.

7.11.06 Determine the ratio of perimeters, areas, and volumes of figures.
Opportunities to address this standard can be found on the following pages: 162–167, 168–175 (#16), 203 (#48). See also, correlation for *McDougal Littell Geometry*.

7.11.07 Use measures expressed as rates (e.g., speed, density), measures expressed as products (e.g., person-days), and dimensional analysis (e.g., converting ft/sec to yards/min) to solve problems.
17–19, 150, 162, 173 (#16), 203 (#48), 235–242, 255, 273, 285, 289, 304, 365, 522

Mathematics–State Goal 8: Algebra

Use algebraic and analytical methods to identify and describe patterns and relationships in data, solve problems and predict results.

STANDARD 8A – Describe numerical relationships using variables and patterns.

8.11.01 Simplify or identify equivalent algebraic expressions (e.g., exponential, rational, logarithmic, factored, polynomial).
96–101, 123 (#32–42), 125 (#23–26), 140 (#70–75), 189 (#40–43), 212 (#46–48), 488, 575–580, 583–589, 592, 593–599, 600–605, 606–613, 615, 616, 617, 618–620, 621, 719–726, 794–800, 833–834

8.11.02 Represent mathematical relationships using symbolic algebra.
20 (#7–9), 33 (#29–32), 140 (#64–67), 242, 380–388, 429–430, 432–433, 437–438, 440–441, 446, 448–450, 461, 464–465, 467–468, 470–472, 512–518, 519, 520–529, 530, 531–540, 542, 545, 546, 547, 595–599, 615, 619, 686, 768, 770, 844–848

8.11.03 Identify essential quantitative relationships in a situation, and determine the class or classes of functions (e.g., linear, quadratic, exponential) that model the relationships.
215–221, 222, 223–224, 262–268, 270, 274, 520–527, 528–529, 530, 531–538, 539–540, 628–634, 635–640, 641–642, 643–649, 669–670, 684–691, 695–697

8.11.04 Determine a specific term, a finite sum, or a rule that generates terms of a pattern.
35–40, 56, 61 (#9, 18), 203 (#44), 208–212, 212 (#53–54), 309–310, 317 (#3), 502, 520, 524, 531, 535, 539–540, 554

8.11.05 Model and describe slope as a constant rate of change.
235–242, 255, 269 (#5), 273, 299 (#54), 304, 317 (#1), 330 (#17), 331 (#20)

8.11.06 Evaluate variable expressions and functions.
2–7, 8–12, 13, 17, 20, 35–40, 53–54, 57 (#4–9), 98, 122 (#26–28), 125 (#19–22), 215–221, 262–268

STANDARD 8B – Interpret and describe numerical relationships using tables, graphs and symbols.

8.11.07 Identify an equation of a line or an equation of a line of best fit from given information (e.g., from a set of ordered pairs, graphs, tables).
216, 253–259, 266 (#35), 283–289, 290–291, 292–299, 302–308, 311–316, 319–324, 325–331, 332–333, 334, 335–341, 342, 343, 344, 345–348, 349, 352 (#5, 8), 353 (#17–18)

8.11.08 Recognize and describe the general shape and properties of functions from graphs, tables, or equations (e.g., linear, absolute value, quadratic, exponential, logarithmic).
217–221, 274, 284, 287–289, 396–397, 520–527, 530, 531–538, 628–634, 635–640, 641–642, 643–649, 650–651, 669–670, 684–691, 695, 696–697, 700

8.11.09 Identify slope from an equation, table of values, or graph.
234–242, 243, 244–250, 256 (#2), 257 (#39), 259 (#57–62), 270–273, 283–289, 290–291, 292–299, 300–301, 302–308, 311–316, 319–324, 325–331, 332–333, 334, 335–341, 342, 344, 345–348, 349

8.11.10 Interpret the role of the coefficients and constants on the graphs of linear and quadratic functions, given a set of equations.
242, 243, 244–250, 253–261, 270–273, 283–289, 290–291, 292–299, 302–308, 311–316, 319–324, 325–331, 332–333, 334, 335–341, 342, 344, 345–348, 349, 396–397, 628–634, 635–640, 641–642, 643–649, 650–651, 669–670, 684–691, 695, 696–697, 700

8.11.11 Analyze functions by investigating domain, range, rates of change, intercepts, and zeros.
35–37, 43, 44, 72, 207, 217–224, 225–232, 235–242, 262–268, 270–274, 284, 287–289, 304, 328, 337–342, 520–527, 531–539, 541 (#2), 545 (#35–39), 547 (#37), 628–634, 635–640, 641–642, 643–649, 669, 684–691, 695, 697, 710–717, 775–782

8.11.12 Create and connect representations that are tabular, graphic, numeric, and symbolic from a set of data.
35–37, 43, 44, 72, 207, 215–221, 225–232, 234–242, 243, 244–250, 251–252, 253–259, 260–261, 262–268, 270–274, 283–289, 290–291, 292–299, 300–301, 302–308, 309–310, 311–316, 319–324, 325–331, 332–333, 334, 335–341, 342, 344, 345–348, 349, 396–397, 520–527, 530, 531–539, 628–634, 635–640, 641–642, 643–649, 650–651, 669–670, 684–691, 695, 696–697, 700, 710–717, 775–782

8.11.13 Represent quantitative relationships graphically, and interpret the meaning of the graph or a specific part of the graph as it relates to the situation represented by the graph.
35–37, 43, 44, 72, 207, 215–221, 225–232, 232 (#4–6, 7–13), 234–242, 242 (#57–62), 243, 244–250, 251–252, 253–259, 260–261, 262–268, 270–274, 283–289, 290–291, 292–299, 300–301, 302–308, 309–310, 311–316, 319–324, 325–331, 332–333, 334, 335–341, 342, 344, 345–348, 349, 396–397, 520–527, 530, 531–539, 628–634, 635–640, 641–642, 643–649, 650–651, 669–670, 684–691, 695, 696–697, 700, 710–717, 775–782

STANDARDS 8C, 8D – Solve problems using systems of numbers and their properties./ Use algebraic concepts and procedures to represent and solve problems.

8.11.14 Model problems using mathematical functions and relations (e.g., linear, non-linear).
49–50, 189 (#38–39), 203 (#44), 215–221, 222, 223–224, 225–232, 232 (#7–13), 242 (#57–62), 262–268, 270–274, 284, 287–289, 396–397, 520–527, 528–529, 530, 531–538, 539–540, 541, 545 (#35–39), 546, 547 (#37–38), 628–634, 635–640, 641–642, 643–649, 650–651, 669–670, 676 (#59–61), 684–691, 695, 696–697, 700, 701 (#1–6)

8.11.15 Interpret the graph of a system of equations and inequalities, including cases where there are no solutions.
427–433, 434, 457 (#51–52), 459–465, 466–472

8.11.16 Solve linear equations and inequalities, including selecting and evaluating formulas.
4, 30, 41, 185, 186, 187, 190, 251–252, 262–268, 270, 274, 275, 283–289, 292–299, 300–301, 302–308, 311–316, 319–324, 331 (#22–24), 345 (#7), 346 (#14), 356–361, 362, 363–368, 369–374, 377–378, 380–387, 388, 389, 395 (#54–59), 405–412, 413, 414, 415, 416, 417, 418, 419, 420–421, 924–925, 926

8.11.17 Solve systems of equations and inequalities.
426, 427–433, 434, 435–441, 443, 444–450, 451–457, 459–465, 466–472 (#48–53), 472 (#1–9), 508 (#63–68), 568 (#61–66), 580 (#72–74), 634 (#52–54), 906 (#15–17)

8.11.18 Solve quadratic equations over the complex number system, including selecting and evaluating formulas.
Opportunities to address this standard can be found on the following pages: 628–634, 635–642, 643–649, 650, 652–658, 662, 663–670, 671–676, 677, 678–683, 684–691, 692, 810–811

8.11.19 Solve problems that include nonlinear functions, including selecting and evaluating formulas (i.e., absolute value, trigonometric, logarithmic, exponential).
4, 30, 41, 185, 186, 187, 190, 396–397, 520–527, 528–529, 530, 531–538, 539–540, 650–651, 652–658, 628–634, 635–640, 641–642, 643–649, 659–660, 663–668, 669–676, 677, 678–683, 684–691, 696–697, 701, 924–925, 926, 927–928

8.11.20 Identify, interpret, and write equations for circles and other conic sections.
See correlation for *McDougal Littell Geometry.*

8.11.21 Recognize and apply mathematical and algebraic axioms, theorems of algebra, and deductive reasoning.
118

8.11.22 Identify equivalent forms of equations, inequalities, and systems of equations.
4, 30, 41, 140 (#68–69), 189 (#5–7), 212 (#50–52), 216, 234–242, 243, 244–250, 251–252, 253–261, 262–268, 270–273, 283–289, 290–291, 292–299, 300–301, 302–308, 309–310, 311–316, 319–324, 325–331, 332–333, 334, 335–341, 342, 344, 345–348, 349 356–361, 368 (#51–53), 426, 427–433, 434, 435–441, 443, 444–450, 451–457, 459–465, 466–472

CORRELATIONS

Mathematics–State Goal 9: Geometry

Use geometric methods to analyze, categorize and draw conclusions about points, lines, planes and space.

STANDARD 9A – Demonstrate and apply geometric concepts involving points, lines, planes and space.

9.11.01 Apply the Pythagorean theorem.
736, 737–742, 748 (#41–44, 47), 750 (#1–6), 751–752, 753 756, 757, 759, 761, 907 (#49), 948 (#42–47), 952

9.11.02 Identify and represent transformations (rotations, reflections, translations, dilations) of an object in the plane, and describe the effects of transformations on points in words or coordinates.
213–214, 396, 397, 922–923

9.11.03 Determine how changing the scale factor affects the size and position of a figure in the plane.
170–172, 922–923. See also, correlation for *McDougal Littell Geometry.*

9.11.04 Classify plane figures according to their properties.
Opportunities to address this standard can be found on the following pages: 4, 30, 185, 186, 187, 190, 919–920, 924–925, 926. See also, correlation for *McDougal Littell Geometry*.

9.11.05 Identify, apply, or solve problems that require knowledge of geometric properties of plane figures (e.g., triangles, quadrilaterals, parallel lines cut by a transversal, angles, diagonals, triangle inequality).
4, 7 (#64–65), 26 (#52–54), 30, 53 (#11–12), 70 (#64–66), 79 (#65),174–175, 181 (#41–42), 185–189, 190 (#4, 7, 8), 203 (#46), 282, 494 (#58), 574 (#9), 613 (#19), 782 (#52–54), 811 (#10–12), 919–920, 924–925, 926, 927–928, 956

9.11.06 Identify a three-dimensional object from different perspectives.
Opportunities to address this standard can be found on the following pages: 927–928. See also, correlation for *McDougal Littell Geometry.*

9.11.07 Identify the relationship between two-dimensional patterns (e.g., nets) and related three-dimensional objects (e.g., cylinders, prisms, cones).
Opportunities to address this standard can be found on the following pages: 4, 7 (#64–65), 26 (#52–54), 30, 41, 53 (#11–12), 174–175, 181 (#41–42), 184–189, 190 (#4, 7, 8), 203 (#46), 246, 282, 319, 320–324, 347, 494, 574 (#9), 613 (#19), 782 (#52–54), 811, 919–920, 924–925, 926, 927–928, 956. See also, correlation for *McDougal Littell Geometry.*

9.11.08. Identify two- and three-dimensional figures that would match a set of given conditions.
Opportunities to address this standard can be found on the following pages: 4, 7 (#64–65), 26 (#52–54), 30, 41, 53 (#11–12), 174–175, 181 (#41–42), 184–189, 190 (#4, 7, 8), 203 (#46), 246, 282, 319, 320–324, 347, 494, 574 (#9), 613 (#19), 782 (#52–54), 811, 919–920, 924–925, 926, 927–928, 956. See also, correlation for *McDougal Littell Geometry.*

STANDARD 9A – Demonstrate and apply geometric concepts involving points, lines, planes and space. *(continued)*

9.11.09 Solve problems that involve calculating distance, midpoint, and slope using coordinate geometry.
206, 235–242, 244–250, 269 (#4), 271, 273, 317 (#2, 5)743, 744–750, 753, 756, 757 (#22–25), 906 (#29–31), 921, 922–923

9.11.10 Identify, apply, and solve problems that require knowledge of geometric relationships of circles (e.g. arcs, chords, tangents, secants, central angles, inscribed angles).
Opportunities to address this standard can be found on the following pages: 188 (#34), 613 (#19), 782 (#52–53), 811 (#10), 926, 927–928, 956. See also, correlation for *McDougal Littell Geometry.*

9.11.11 Graph, locate, and identify points on a coordinate system.
40 (#30–33), 211 (#40), 212 (#41), 221 (#48–55), 232 (#1–3), 268 (#45), 921

STANDARD 9B – Identify, describe, classify and compare relationships using points, lines, planes and solids.

9.11.12 Solve problems involving similar figures.
174–175. See also, correlation for *McDougal Littell Geometry.*

9.11.13 Solve problems using triangle congruence.
See correlation for *McDougal Littell Geometry.*

9.11.14 Describe how two or more objects are related in space (e.g., skew lines, the possible ways three planes might intersect).
See correlation for *McDougal Littell Geometry.*

9.11.15 Identify relationships between circles and other objects in the plane (e.g., inscribed circles, concentric circles, internal/external tangency).
See correlation for *McDougal Littell Geometry.*

STANDARD 9C – Construct convincing arguments and proofs to solve problems.

9.11.16 Recognize and apply the conditions that assure congruence and similarity.
174–175

9.11.17 Recognize and apply mathematical and geometric axioms, fundamental theorems of geometry, and deductive reasoning.
See correlation for *McDougal Littell Geometry.*

9.11.18 Identify a counter-example to disprove a conjecture.
66–68, 108 (#63–64), 109, 113, 114, 116 (#7) 117–118, 318, 464 (#34), 793

STANDARD 9D – Use trigonometric ratios and circular functions to solve problems.

9.11.19 Determine distances and angle measures using indirect measurement (e.g., properties of right triangles, Law of Sines, Law of Cosines).
174–175. See also, correlation for *McDougal Littell Geometry.*

9.11.20. Solve problems using 45°-45°-90° and 30°-60°-90° triangles.
A6–A7. See also, correlation for *McDougal Littell Geometry.*

9.11.21 Identify graphs of a given trigonometric function (sin x, cos x) using its characteristics (e.g., period, amplitude).
See correlation for *McDougal Littell Geometry.*

9.11.22. Define, identify, and evaluate trigonometric ratios.
A10–A11, A12–A13. See correlation for *McDougal Littell Geometry.*

9.11.23. Use trigonometric identities (e.g., $\sin^2 x + \cos^2 x = 1$)
See correlation for *McDougal Littell Geometry.*

Mathematics–State Goal 10: Data Analysis, Statistics, and Probability

Collect, organize and analyze data using statistical methods; predict results; and interpret uncertainty using concepts of probability.

STANDARDS 10A, 10B – Organize, describe and make predictions from existing data./ Formulate questions, design data collection methods, gather and analyze data and communicate findings.

10.11.01 **Read, interpret, predict, interpolate, extrapolate, and use information from a variety of graphs, charts, and tables.**
35–40, 41, 42, 43–50, 215–221, 222, 225–232, 234, 235–242, 243, 244–252, 253–259, 262–268, 282, 283–289, 290, 292, 302–310, 311–316, 319–324, 335–342, 520–527, 530, 531–540, 628–634, 635–642, 643–649, 650, 652–657, 663–670, 671–676, 677, 678–683, 684–691, 692, 765–776, 775–782

10.11.02 **Translate from one representation of data to another (e.g., a bar graph to a circle graph).**
Opportunities to address this standard can be found on the following pages: 35–40, 41, 42, 43–50, 215–221, 222, 225–232, 234, 235–242, 243, 244–252, 253–259, 262–268, 282, 283–289, 290, 292, 302–310, 311–316, 319–324, 520–527, 530, 531–540, 628–634, 635–642, 643–649, 650, 652–657, 663–670, 671–676, 677, 678–683, 684–691, 692, 765–776, 775–782. See also, correlation for *McDougal Littell Geometry.*

10.11.03 **Solve problems involving Venn diagrams.**
374 (#44), 861, 930. See also, correlation for *McDougal Littell Algebra 2.*

10.11.04 **Find an unknown value in a dataset given information about descriptive statistics.**
Opportunities to address this standard can be found on the following pages: 35–40, 41, 42, 43–50, 215–221, 222, 225–232, 234, 235–242, 243, 244–252, 253–259, 262–268, 282, 283–289, 290, 292, 302–310, 311–316, 319–324, 520–527, 530, 531–540, 628–634, 635–642, 643–649, 650, 652–657, 663–670, 671–676, 677, 678–683, 684–691, 692, 765–776, 775–782, 875–878, 879–880, 881–885, 887–892, 893, 894, 895, 899

10.11.05 **Calculate, interpret, and use measures of central tendency and dispersion.**
875–878, 879–880, 881–885, 887–892, 893, 894 (#3–5), 895, 899, 905 (#14), 907 (#51), 918

10.11.06 **Compare two or more data sets on measures of central tendency and dispersion.**
Opportunities to address this standard can be found on the following pages: 875–878, 879–880, 881–885, 887–892, 893, 894 (#3–5), 895, 899, 905 (#14), 907 (#51), 918

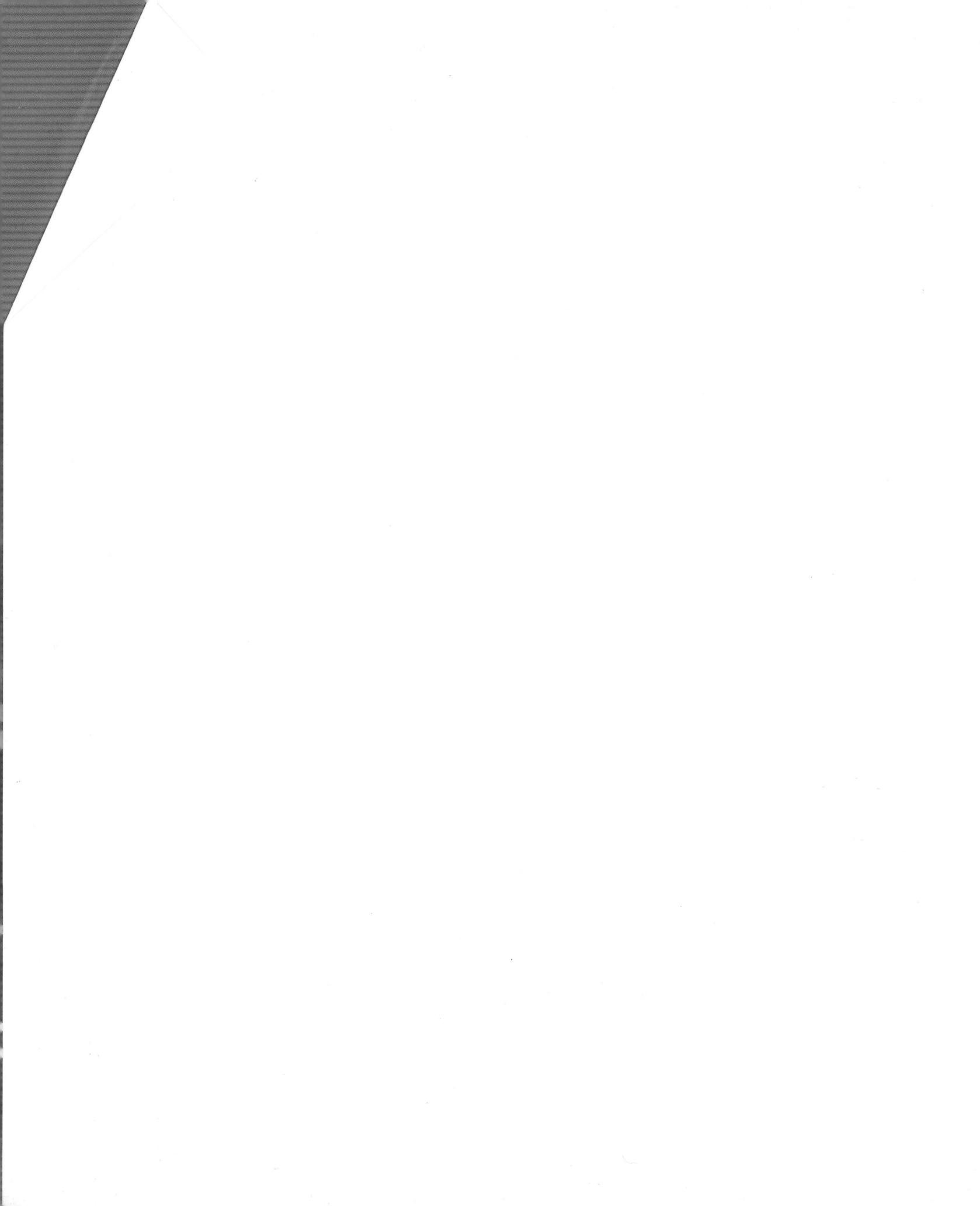